Heilongjiang
黑龍江
Jilin
吉林
Liaoning
遼寧
Beijing 北京
Tianjin 天津
Hebei
河北
Shanxi
山西
Shandong
山東
Xinjiang
新疆維吾爾自治區
Gansu
甘肅
Inner Mongolia
內蒙古自治區
Ningxia
寧夏回族
自治區
Qinghai
青海
Tibet
西藏自治區
Shaanxi
陝西
Henan
河南
Jiangsu
江蘇
Anhui
安徽
Shanghai
上海
Hubei
湖北
Sichuan
四川
Chongqing 重慶
Zhejiang
浙江
Jiangxi
江西
Hunan
湖南
Guizhou
貴州
Fujian
福建
Yunnan
雲南
Guangxi
廣西壯族
自治區
Guangdong
廣東
Taiwan
台灣
Macau
澳門
Hong Kong
香港
Hainan
海南

MAP OF CHINA

China Markets Yearbook 1999

中國市場年鑑 1999

China Markets Yearbook 1999

(Reports on 563 Markets)

香 港 城 市 大 學 出 版 社
City University of Hong Kong Press

ISBN: 962-937-041-7

Editors: Shaomin Li and David K. Tse

Editorial Committee: Yuxian Gao, Shaomin Li, David K. Tse, Saiwei Yuan

Technical Support: Leida Du, Yanzhao Qiao

Published by: City University of Hong Kong Press
City University of Hong Kong
Tat Chee Avenue, Kowloon, Hong Kong
Phone: (852) 2788-9162
Fax: (852) 2779-3071
Email: upress@cityu.edu.hk
Internet: http://www.cityu.edu.hk/upress/

All data are exclusively provided by the State Statistical Bureau of China based on the 1997 Industrial Census of China.

This Yearbook is joinly produced by All China Marketing Research Company (ACMR), Beijing, and MarketInfo Limited, Hong Kong.

Printed in Hong Kong

Contents

Section 1 Description

Section 2 Summary Report by Industry

(Complete list on page xxxiii)

Mining and Forestry

Manufacturing

About the Editors

Shaomin Li is Associate Professor of Marketing at the Department of Marketing, City University of Hong Kong. He went to Peking University for his undergraduate studies, obtained his PhD from Princeton University, and was a post-doctoral fellow at Harvard University. Before joining the City University, he served as the Director of AT&T EastGate Services in New Jersey, USA.

Professor Li is also Adjunct Professor at Peking University and a senior advisor to Tianjin Statistical Bureau. He has served as a United Nation advisor to China on business applications of demographic data.

His research interests are in the areas of strategic management, international business, and political economy. He has published over twenty research articles and eight books. His most recent book is *China's Reform, Industrial Markets and Business Management* (in Chinese, with Xiaofeng He and Oliver H. M. Yau) which is also published by the City University of Hong Kong Press.

David K. Tse is Chair Professor of International Marketing at the Business School of The University of Hong Kong (HKU). He taught for ten years at the the University of British Columbia after he received his MBA (1978) and PhD (1984) from University of California at Berkeley. In 1993 he returned to Hong Kong and later joined the University of Hong Kong in 1998.

He is known for his research in international marketing, marketing in Chinese economies, and satisfaction research. On these subjects he has published over fifty top international journal papers, book chapters, and conference papers. For his joint research projects on Mainland China and Chinese economies, he has received competitive government grants that total more than two million Hong Kong dollars. He has established and now directs the Chinese Management Centre at HKU.

Professor Tse is the founding vice president of the Asia Academy of Management. He is listed on *Who's Who in International Business Education and Research*, and on *Who's Who in the World*. In recent surveys, he is rated as the world's most productive scholar in marketing in China and among the world's top five scholars in Chinese management research. He consults for many companies including China Vest, Hong Kong Bank, Swire Properties, and Elec and Eltec. He also conducts executive programmes for companies such as Elec and Eltec, Hong Kong Bank, Acer Computer, Tetra-Pak, AT&T, and for some departments of the Hong Kong Government.

Editors' Note

We are happy to edit the 1999 issue of this *China Markets Yearbook* which is based on the most comprehensive database on the world's largest market. The database is painstakingly developed from the 1997 census of all state-owned, collectively-owned, privately-owned, joint-venture, and foreign-owned enterprises in China. We want to help international business executives conducting sucessful businesses in China. Also, we believe that this tool would help China effectively allocating its vast resources.

This is a sequel to our previous publication *China's Industrial Markets Yearbook 1997* which was published by the City University of Hong Kong Press in December 1997. We are of the opinion that the present title better reflects the nature of our exclusive data set. The reason is that our data set covers not only industrial goods but also vast numbers of consumer goods. The present volume is designated 1999 instead of 1998 because it contains the most authoritative and the latest data that are available as of early 1999.

In compiling this *Yearbook*, we apply three principles: quality, relevance, and focus. We want to ensure that the *Yearbook* would be helpful to business executives in their decision-making. We have pre-tested the *Yearbook* concept by collecting information on their data needs in different business situations. We have also evaluated various presentation approaches until we come up with the present two-page-per-industry format.

This *Yearbook* is a joint effort by three organizations: All China Marketing Research Co. in Beijing, MarketInfo of City University of Hong Kong, and the City University of Hong Kong Press.

We would like to express our sincere thanks to all the technical staff in Beijing and Hong Kong who laboured hard to produce the database and the *Yearbook*. Our special thanks go to Mr. Yuxian Gao, President of the All China Market Research Co. Limited. Without his enthusiastic support and trust, the project would not have been started.

Shaomin Li, David K. Tse

March 1999

Introduction

China's market has been growing fast and is poised to become the largest one in the world. How to succeed in this market remains a formidable challenge. One of the major difficulties is the absence of comprehensive and reliable data about China's markets and individual firms. The key question business executives often ask is: how and where to invest. To effectively address the question, detailed and decision-oriented data are needed. Until now, however, only general socioeconomic statistics and scattered industrial estimates are available. We publish the *China Markets Yearbook* to fill the data gap and we intend it to become a fundamental reference for all those who do business in China.

What the *Yearbook* offers

China Markets Yearbook is targeted at the manufacturing and consumer markets in China. It contains the latest and the most comprehensive market data and firm-level information available on China. The coverage of the book includes the entire industrial and consumer goods sector (563 industries) of China's economy—more than 500,000 firms including foreign-owned operations, state enterprises, town and village enterprises, and different types of joint ventures that are operating in China. For each industry, we provide data on past sales, production volume, productivity, number of employees, firm size, key products, changes in assets, loans, geographic locations, top 10 firms, and the key distributors.

The information in this *Yearbook* is not a simple compilation of the census data. They are extracted from our own extensive studies of China's market structure and firm performance. The indicators contained in the book are "value-added" items that have been produced on the basis of our knowledge about those key factors that influence the profitability and productivity of an industry. We seek answers to the following investment and operation decisions:

- Forecasting trends in sales, production, and productivity;
- Estimating market shares for each region and firm type;
- Gauging the technology level of firms and their equipment need;
- Assessing capital structures and financial health of firms;
- Evaluating competitiveness of firms by different characteristics;
- Understanding the structure of the market;
- Establishing contacts with top firms in both production and distribution; and
- Benchmarking firms against market norms.

The *Yearbook* helps users in making such business decisions as:

- Choosing the geographic market(s) to enter;
- Selecting distributor(s) for products and services;
- Selecting OEM producers; and
- Assessing joint venture partners in operations.

Most comprehensive and reliable information available

We are committed to ensure the highest quality because anything less would be unethical and unacceptable. In developing the *Yearbook*, we have installed quality control systems to assure the accuracy of the information published.

Data source

Every year tens of thousands of interviewers from over 2,500 local branches of the State Statistical Bureau of China (SSB) interview all firms registered at the *xiang* (village) government or above. All 563 industries and thousands of consumer products are covered. Firms are asked questions on their operations and other firm characteristics. In short, this is an annual census of the industries. Each firm is required by law to report accurate information to the State Statistical Bureau. As each firm also regularly files reports to the particular industry that the firm belongs to, we have obtained data originating from two parallel reporting "tracks".

For the State Statistical Bureau "track", the SSB has developed a rigorous logic test system to detect errors. For example, the SSB specifies more than 120 logic tests for major project surveys and more than 30 logic tests for industrial surveys. The data obtained are then checked and compared to past years' performance at each of the municipal and provincial levels. Additional interviews are conducted to resolve doubts or inconsistencies throughout the system. The data are then compiled and compared to the report by the second track, which is the "industries track". Data from the second track have also gone through similar municipal, provincial and national checks.

Data quality

First, we obtained the final data from the State Statistic Bureau of China. The data went through our pre-designed quality control system which consists of sequences of logical checks. A point worth mentioning is the continuous improvement of the reported data. For example, the 1994 and earlier surveys data had less than 0.5% inconsistent entries. By 1995 data have been substantially improved, since then there are less than 0.1% inconsistent entries.

Still, we were not satisfied with this 0.1% error rate. We have since then made extra effort to further reduce the errors. We have designed a two-track system and now we assign two separate teams to independently derive our indicators for each of the 563 tables and compare the figures at the end. Inconsistencies are resolved through further investigations.

Information on firms

For each of the 563 industries, we selected top ten companies for listing in the *Yearbook*: a total of more than 5,000 largest companies in China. For all these 5,000-plus companies, we went through a rigorous verification round to assure each firm's contact information are most up-to-date.

Who should use the *Yearbook*

The *Yearbook* is catered to market researchers, market analysts, industrial analysts, strategic planners and consultants who need to compile comprehensive industrial and market profiles for executives who make business decisions. The information will also be useful to business students who need to address issues presented by management cases in China.

In selecting the information to report in the *Yearbook*, we have pretested the information among business managers whose jobs relate to China. Their responses to the project have been encouraging; over 50% of them look forward to the publication of this book.

An Indispensable reference for libraries

The *Yearbook* offers such a comprehensive coverage on China's industrial and consumer goods markets that it is a "must" reference for academic, public, as well as corporate libraries.

Beyond the *Yearbook*

The original electronic database contains information beyond the tables printed in the *Yearbook*. For readers who need to have more specific information for their business decisions, we have designed special industrial reports with more details. These reports can be tailor-made to meet the need of a user. We encourage readers seeking more information on China's markets to contact us. (Contact information available at the bottom of the main tables.)

Explanation of Terms

Industry Overall	All the relevant "Industry Overall" figures are calculated using the unit of the measurement for the indicator. For example, "Return on assets" is calculated by dividing "the total profits" of the industry by "the total assets" of the industry. (Note: firms with large assets will have a larger weight.)
No. of Employees	Number of employees
Revenue	Revenues in units of 1,000 Renminbi (RMB). In 1997 one RMB was about US$ 0.12.
Profit	Profit in units of 1,000 RMB.
Return on Assets	Profit divided by total assets: (profit) / (total assets).
Return on Equity	Profit divided by equity, which is total assets less total debts: (profit) / [(total assets) – (total debts)].
Labour Productivity	Revenue per employee, which is revenue divided by the number of employees: (revenue) / (number of employees).
Debts / Assets	Debts to assets ratio.
Total Assets	The sum of fixed assets and current assets (including all debts).
Rate of Change	from year t to year $t+1$: {[(year $t+1$ figure) – (year t figure)] / (year t figure)} $\times$ 100%
Major Wholesalers	To facilitate the reader to contact wholesalers which carry the products of an industry. Please note that wholesalers listed here may carry not only the specific products of an industry, but also products of other industries.
Market Share	(A region's revenue in an industry) / (Total revenue of the industry)
Ownership	***State-Owned***. Firms owned by different level of governments such as the central government, the provincial government, or the local government.

Collectively-Owned. Firms owned by a collective body, such as a village, a township [town and village enterprises (TVEs)], all workers of a firm, or individuals who give up their private ownership. Collective-ownership is considered "public-ownership."

Privately-Owned. Firms owned by individuals.

Domestic Joint Ventures (JVs). This category includes firms that are joint ventures (JVs) between domestic firms with different ownership types. For example, JVs between state- and collectively-owned, or JVs between state- and privately-owned.

Joint Stock. This category refers to all companies with limited liabilities, including (1) companies that explicitly issue stock certificates which may be traded publicly and (2) companies that have two or more shareholders with limited liabilities.

Foreign-Funded. "Foreign" is defined as foreign investors excluding Chinese outside China (overseas Chinese and Chinese from Taiwan, Hong Kong, and Macao). This category includes three types of "foreign-funded" firms: (1) Foreign-invested equity JVs; (2) foreign-involved contractual JVs; (3) foreign wholly-owned firms.

Overseas Chinese-Funded. "Overseas Chinese" includes all Chinese outside China, including Chinese from Taiwan, Hong Kong, Macao, and other countries. This category includes three types of firms: (1) equity JVs by Overseas Chinese, (2) contractual JVs by Overseas Chinese, and (3) firms wholly owned by Overseas Chinese.

Size

This is based on a government classification, which classifies the firms into "large," "medium," or "small".

Selected Socioeconomic Statistics by Province, 1996

Province or Municipality	Capital	(1) Year-end Population (million)	(2) Urban Population (%)	(3) Literacy rate of population aged 15+ (%)	(4) Annual GDP growth 1992–1996 (%)	(5) Per capita income (RMB)		(6) Color TV sets per 100 families		(7) Telephones per 100 people
						Urban	Rural	Urban	Rural	
Beijing	Beijing	12.40	68.5	92.36	11.4	7,813	3,662	123.8	83.3	23.6
Tianjin	Tianjin	9.53	66.0	90.16	13.2	6,608	3,244	110.6	68.0	23.1
Hebei	Shijiazhuang	65.25	33.9	85.70	14.7	4,959	2,286	100.1	39.2	5.0
Shanxi	Taiyuan	31.41	37.6	90.13	11.3	3,990	1,738	99.5	34.8	4.8
Inner Mongolia	Huhhot	23.26	33.6	83.22	10.5	3,945	1,780	93.3	29.0	4.5
Liaoning	Shenyang	41.38	70.3	91.79	10.4	4,518	2,301	98.2	48.9	13.4
Jilin	Changchun	26.28	65.1	91.87	12.0	4,191	2,186	92.5	33.1	8.8
Heilongjiang	Harbin	37.51	57.9	90.82	8.9	4,091	2,308	91.2	31.6	7.4
Shanghai	Shanghai	14.57	78.0	89.83	14.0	8,439	5,277	118.6	61.8	38.8
Jiangsu	Nanjing	71.48	59.2	80.72	17.0	5,765	3,270	101.1	34.4	12.6
Zhejiang	Hangzhou	44.35	61.8	81.62	16.8	7,359	3,684	111.0	47.3	15.6
Anhui	Hefei	61.27	30.4	79.83	16.6	4,599	1,809	90.9	17.5	3.9
Fujian	Fuzhou	32.82	43.7	82.55	18.6	6,144	2,786	109.4	43.8	10.4
Jiangxi	Nanchang	41.50	33.6	87.53	14.1	4,071	2,107	91.5	13.3	4.0
Shandong	Jinan	87.85	55.8	77.36	14.8	5,191	2,292	100.7	31.4	4.7
Henan	Zhengzhou	92.43	30.5	85.12	13.7	4,094	1,734	95.8	23.0	3.8
Hubei	Wuhan	58.73	58.8	84.95	14.1	4,673	2,102	94.0	14.2	6.6
Hunan	Changsha	64.65	32.7	88.73	11.8	5,210	2,037	95.1	11.2	4.5
Guangdong	Guangzhou	70.51	65.1	90.39	16.5	8,562	3,468	119.1	46.1	14.3
Guangxi	Nanning	46.33	29.3	84.88	14.9	5,110	1,875	98.6	9.9	3.6
Hainan	Haikou	7.43	55.2	85.89	14.2	4,850	1,917	101.4	24.6	6.4
Chongqing	Chongqing	30.42	51.8	83.18	13.2	5,323	1,643	107.0	11.2	4.2
Sichuan	Chengdu	84.30	32.7	82.00	11.4	4,763	1,681	104.9	14.6	2.5
Guizhou	Guiyang	66.06	27.1	74.12	8.6	4,442	1,299	100.9	7.0	2.0
Yunnan	Kunming	40.94	22.3	74.78	10.7	5,558	1,376	101.3	20.5	3.9
Tibet	Lhasa	2.48	9.3	45.92	12.2	NA	1,195	NA	7.5	2.9
Shaanxi	Xi'an	35.70	27.5	82.66	9.9	4,001	1,273	102.0	26.9	4.6
Gansu	Lanzhou	24.94	27.0	73.23	10.3	3,592	1,185	99.5	22.5	2.9
Qinghai	Xining	4.96	18.1	56.38	8.5	3,999	1,321	100.9	17.3	4.4
Ningxia	Yinchuan	5.30	31.7	74.17	9.0	3,837	1,513	101.8	43.8	6.7
Xinjiang	Urumqi	17.18	35.1	88.48	10.1	4,845	1,504	97.7	23.4	7.1

Note: "NA" means not available

Sources of data by column:

(1) Data for year-end population, per capita income, and color TV sets per 100 families are from the 1998 edition of the *China Statistical Yearbook*

(2) Urban population as percentage of total population is calculated from the 1998 edition of the *China Demographic Yearbook* which uses the total and urban population figures that are compiled by the Ministry of Public Security on the basis of registration of households

(3) Literacy rate of population aged 15-plus is calculated from figures in the 1998 edition of the *China Statistical Yearbook*, based on the data for proportions of illiterate population, semi-illiterate population and the 15-plus population

(4) Annual GDP growth is based on the 1997 and 1998 editions of the *China Statistical Yearbook*; GDP of the previous year is used as the base

(5) Same source as (1); urban per capita income refers to disposable income; rural per capita income refers to net income

(6) Same source as (1)

(7) Data for telephones per 100 people are from various provincial statistical yearbooks

中國市場年鑑 1999
(563 個行業報告)

香 港 城 市 大 學 出 版 社
City University of Hong Kong Press

國際標準書號：962-937-041-7

編輯：　李少民、謝貴枝

編輯委員會：　高余先、李少民、謝貴枝、袁賽薇

技術負責：　杜雷達、喬燕昭

出版：　香港城市大學出版社
香港城市大學
香港九龍達之路
電話：(852) 2788 9162
電傳：(852) 2779 3071
電郵：upress@cityu.edu.hk
網址：http://www.cityu.edu.hk/upress/

本書中的獨家數據由中國國家統計局根據1997年工業普查提供，並由北京華通人市場信息有限責任公司和香港城市大學MarketInfo公司共同編纂。

目錄

第一部份

第二部份

563 個行業總覽

（詳細行業分類表載於第 *li* 頁）

採掘業

製造業

索引

編者

李少民為香港城市大學市場營銷系副教授。曾任美國AT&T東方資訊部主任。畢業於北京大學，獲普林斯頓大學博士學位，並為哈佛大學博士後研究員。研究興趣包括企業戰略，國際投資，以及政治經濟學。李教授為北京大學特約教授，天津統計局高級顧問，以及聯合國派中國顧問（人口統計的商業應用）。著有八本書和二十多篇研究論文，近著為《中國的改革與工商經營》（與何小鋒、游漢明合著，香港城市大學出版社出版）。

謝貴枝為香港大學商學院講座教授及華人管理中心創辦人和中心主任，亞洲管理學院創院副院長。獲加州大學柏克萊分校工商碩士及博士學位之後，在加拿大卑詩大學任教十年。一九九三年回港，九八年加入香港大學。以研究國際市場營銷學、華人經濟體系的市場、顧客的滿意問題等方面著稱。著作五十多種，載於國際上頂級學術期刊、論文集、會議文集等。近年研究成果卓越，屢次評審均名列前茅，此外亦曾在多間香港及國際企業以及香港政府擔當顧問和主持培訓項目。

序

本書是一九九七年十二月出版的《中國工業市場年鑑 1997》的下一年版本，但書名改為《中國市場年鑑 1999》。我們考慮到本書的數據除了反映工業產品的市場情況以外，還反映了中國龐大的消費品市場的情況，因此作出修改書名的決定。書名用“1999”，表示內容方面是截至本年初為止的最新資料。

編纂本書，我們一直遵循三個原則：高質量、用戶取向、內容明確。可以說，這部書是歷史給我們一個好機會。作為工商研究的學者，有機會把世上最大市場的資料整理為決策依據的訊息，實在是我們夢寐以求的一個目標。

面對重任，我們不敢絲毫疏忽。我們本着以上三個原則，向各界經理人員作調查，開座談會，以便確定各行業人士對本書的要求，然後設計本書。每一個統計指標的設計和用途説明，也都經過詳細考慮。總之，本書要達到的目的，就是輔助業內同寅作出正確的決策。

本書是北京華通人市場信息有限責任公司、香港城市大學 MarketInfo 公司、和香港城市大學出版社三方面合作的成果。

在此我們要特別感謝北京華通人市場信息有限責任公司總經理高余先先生，沒有高先生的熱情支持和誠摯的合作，本書是不可能完成的。

李少民、謝貴枝
一九九九年三月

前言

縱橫中國市場的指南

改革開放以來，中國工業發展迅速，為我們提供了許多的機會。競爭愈激烈，市場訊息愈重要。沒有掌握市場訊息之前就盲目地進入一個行業競爭，後果不堪設想。中國工業有五、六百個行業，產品（包括消費品）數以萬計，可是能幫助我們決策的行業訊息或企業資料，書市中卻幾乎沒有。可以說，這是業界目前面臨的最大困擾。我們出版這部《中國市場年鑑 1999》，目的就是填補這一個空白。

《年鑑》為公司經理、廠長、以及有關的業界人士提供一些能夠縱橫中國工業和消費市場中各個行業的數據。本書為中國所有的行業逐一提供一份詳細的報告，其中包括整個行業的概況，各種企業（國有，集體，外資等等）的經營狀況、地區分佈、生產率、資產、負債產值、利潤、產品產量，及最大的生產和經銷廠家的詳細情況等等。根據這些，我們可以對這 563 個行業進行以下的分析及運作。

- 預測產品產量、生產率、以及銷售量;
- 估算各類企業、各個地區的市場份額;
- 分析各行業及企業的技術水平及設備需求;
- 了解各行業及企業資本結構、負債、以及經營狀況;
- 找出各行業及企業的競爭優勢;
- 掌握各行業的市場結構及規律;
- 聯系本行業最大的生產和經銷廠家;
- 用本年鑑提供的行業水平來衡量某一個企業的經營情況。

根據以上的分析，我們可以作出以下的決策:

- 選擇市場（包括地區、行業等等);
- 決定進入市場的方式（合資、獨資、進出口、技術轉讓等等);
- 考核和選擇合作對象;
- 選擇產品的經銷方式、渠道、以及經銷的伙伴。

我們放在第一位的工作，就是為了提供以上的服務，怎樣準確性和全面性地掌握和保證數據資料的質量。本書所有訊息都是根據中國國家統計局的全國工業普查的數據獨家整理出來的，是目前世上最全面、最新和最準確的。數據由統計局遍佈全國的分支機構搜集，並經過嚴格核定，以及多條的邏輯檢驗。工業普查所得到不一致的數據，誤差僅為千分之一。

但我們並沒有停留在這千分之一水平上，我們進一步對書中五千多公司當中最大的企業，逐一複查，以保證用戶取得最準確和最新的企業情況。我們還與北京華通市場信息有限責任公司組織了兩個項目組，獨立地同時根據原始數據編製各個行業的報告，並對比結果，以保證獲得最正確無誤的信息。

我們將每年出版最新的中國市場（所有行業）的報告，為用戶提供決策的指南。我們的目的，是將《年鑑》成為一本助人了解中國工商業改革的字典，更成為每一間圖書館必備的參考書。

除了本書出版之外，我們還開發了一系列關於中國行業研究的專題服務。如行業報告，企業資訊調查，市場研究等等，有興趣的用戶，請與我們聯繫。（我們在香港和北京的詳細聯絡電郵和傳真號碼，載於本書每一個表的底部）

我们做[illegible]的工作，就是为了提供以上的服务，这样准确并且全面[illegible]和[illegible]
[illegible]的方案。本书所有的信息都是来源于中国国家统计局的全国工业普查[illegible]的数据[illegible]
[illegible]是目前世上最全面、最新和最准确的。数据由统计局[illegible]全国的分支机构[illegible]
集，[illegible]格式，以及文字的逻辑校验。工业普查[illegible]不同的数据，[illegible]
[illegible]之一。

[illegible]在这个百分之[illegible]水平上，我们进一步将书中[illegible]了[illegible]中[illegible]最大的企业[illegible]，以保证[illegible]得到最准确和最新的企业情况。我们[illegible]的信息[illegible]公司组织了两个[illegible]，独立地[illegible]根据原始数据[illegible]，[illegible]，以保证获得最正确无误的信息。

我们[illegible]出版最新的中国[illegible]（所有行业）的[illegible]，为用户提供决策的指南。我们的目的[illegible]成为一本[illegible]了解中国[illegible]的[illegible]。[illegible]

[illegible]

指標解釋

行業總體	此欄的平均值是根據行業總體、全行業總人數、總資本數、和總利潤數計算的，並沒為用「企業數」作加權計算。如甲行業有10,000人員，30,000元銷售收入，則人均銷售收入為30,000 / 10,000 = 30。
職工數	職工人數
銷售收入	以人民幣為單位。1997年每一人民幣可兑換大約0.12美元
利潤	以人民幣為單位的利潤
資產利潤率	（利潤）／（總資產）
權益利潤率	（利潤）／（淨資產）。即（利潤）／〔（總資產）－（總負債）〕
勞動生產率	（銷售收入）／（職工數）
資產負債率	總負債／總資產
總資產	淨資產＋總負債
每年變化	｛（今年比去年的增長）／（去年總值）｝ × 100%
主要批發商	為方便用戶，我們列出經銷本行業（但不限於本行業）的最大的批發商
地區的市場份額	（甲行業在本地區的產值）／（甲行業的總產值）
產業所有權	**國有**：生產資料歸國家所有的企業 **集體**：生產資料歸公民集體所有的企業，包括城鄉使用集體投資舉辦的企業 **私有**：包括各種生產資料歸公民私人所有的企業 **聯營**：國內不同所有制（國有、集體、私有）的企業的各種形式的聯營的企業 **股份制**：指由股東出資，以股份形式投資舉辦的企業，包括各種有限責任公司和發行股票的公司

外資: 中外合資、合作、以及外國獨資的三資企業，但不含由海外華人和港、澳、台投資的企業

港澳台資: 由港、澳、台和海外華人投資的三資企業

規模 政府按企業的大小把所有企業劃分為大、中、小

1996年各省市社會經濟狀況

省／市	省會	(1) 年底總人口 (萬人)	(2) 城市人口所佔比率 (%)	(3) 15^{+}歲人口識字率 (%)	(4) 1992–1996年 GDP增長率 (%)	(5) 人均收入 (元)		(6) 每百戶彩電擁有量(台)		(7) 每百人電話擁有數 (部)
						城鎮	農村	城鎮	農村	
北京	北京	1,240	68.5	92.36	11.4	7,813	3,662	123.8	83.3	23.6
天津	天津	953	66.0	90.16	13.2	6,608	3,244	110.6	68.0	23.1
河北	石家莊	6,525	33.9	85.70	14.7	4,959	2,286	100.1	39.2	5.0
山西	太原	3,141	37.6	90.13	11.3	3,990	1,738	99.5	34.8	4.8
內蒙古	呼和浩特	2,326	33.6	83.22	10.5	3,945	1,780	93.3	29.0	4.5
遼寧	沈陽	4,138	70.3	91.79	10.4	4,518	2,301	98.2	48.9	13.4
吉林	長春	2,628	65.1	91.87	12.0	4,191	2,186	92.5	33.1	8.8
黑龍江	哈爾濱	3,751	57.9	90.82	8.9	4,091	2,308	91.2	31.6	7.4
上海	上海	1,457	78.0	89.83	14.0	8,439	5,277	118.6	61.8	38.8
江蘇	南京	7,148	59.2	80.72	17.0	5,765	3,270	101.1	34.4	12.6
浙江	杭州	4,435	61.8	81.62	16.8	7,359	3,684	111.0	47.3	15.6
安徽	合肥	6,127	30.4	79.83	16.6	4,599	1,809	90.9	17.5	3.9
福建	福州	3,282	43.7	82.55	18.6	6,144	2,786	109.4	43.8	10.4
江西	南昌	4,150	33.6	87.53	14.1	4,071	2,107	91.5	13.3	4.0
山東	濟南	8,785	55.8	77.36	14.8	5,191	2,292	100.7	31.4	4.7
河南	鄭州	9,243	30.5	85.12	13.7	4,094	1,734	95.8	23.0	3.8
湖北	武漢	5,873	58.8	84.95	14.1	4,673	2,102	94.0	14.2	6.6
湖南	長沙	6,465	32.7	88.73	11.8	5,210	2,037	95.1	11.2	4.5
廣東	廣州	7,051	65.1	90.39	16.5	8,562	3,468	119.1	46.1	14.3
廣西	南寧	4,633	29.3	84.88	14.9	5,110	1,875	98.6	9.9	3.6
海南	海口	743	55.2	85.89	14.2	4,850	1,917	101.4	24.6	6.4
重慶	重慶	3,042	51.8	83.18	13.2	5,323	1,643	107.0	11.2	4.2
四川	成都	8,430	32.7	82.00	11.4	4,763	1,681	104.9	14.6	2.5
貴州	貴陽	3,606	27.1	74.12	8.6	4,442	1,299	100.9	7.0	2.0
雲南	昆明	4,094	22.3	74.78	10.7	5,558	1,376	101.3	20.5	3.9
西藏	拉薩	248	9.3	45.92	12.2	NA	1,195	NA	7.5	2.9
陝西	西安	3,570	27.5	82.66	9.9	4,001	1,273	102.0	26.9	4.6
甘肅	蘭州	2,494	27.0	73.23	10.3	3,592	1,185	99.5	22.5	2.9
青海	西寧	496	18.1	56.38	8.5	3,999	1,321	100.9	17.3	4.4
寧夏	銀川	530	31.7	74.17	9.0	3,837	1,513	101.8	43.8	6.7
新疆	烏魯木齊	1,718	35.1	88.48	10.1	4,845	1,504	97.7	23.4	7.1

"NA" 即欠缺資料

各欄資料來源説明：

(1) 年底總人口數、城鄉人均收入、每百戶彩電擁有量都是源自1998年《中國統計年鑑》。

(2) 城市人口所佔比重是根據1998年《中國人口統計年鑑》中公安部戶籍統計的總人口和城市人口數計算的。

(3) 15歲及以上人口的識字率是根據1998年《中國人口統計年鑑》中的文盲、半文盲佔15歲及以上人口比例倒減出來的。（是一項人口變動情況抽樣調查的資料，抽樣比為1.016%）

(4) GDP平均增長速度是根據1997、1998《中國統計年鑑》中環比指數計算的。

(5) 同(1)來源。城鎮人均收入是支配收入，農村人均收入是指純收入。

(6) 同(1)來源。

(7) 每百人電話機擁有量是根據各省市1998年統計年鑑的數據計算的。

Chinese Industrial Classification Code

國民經濟行業分類代碼

Chinese Industrial Classification Code	Industry	Page

Mining and Forestry

Chinese Industrial Classification Code	Industry	Page

Chinese Industrial Classification Code	Industry	Page

Oil Processing and Coking

Chemical Raw Material and Chemical Products

Chinese Industrial Classification Code	Industry	Page

General Machinery Manufacturing

採掘業

煤炭採選業

石油和天然氣開採業

黑色金屬礦採選業

有色金屬礦採選業

非金屬礦採選業

塑料製品業

非金屬礦物製品業

國民經濟行業分類代碼	工業名稱	頁碼

自來水的生產和供應業

Reports on 563 Markets
563 行業報告

0610: Coal Mining 煤炭開採業

The industry accounts for 2.211% of the total revenue of China's industrial sector in 1996. The revenue growth rate of the industry is 18.6% from 1995, as compared to the growth rate of China's industrial sector, 9.51%. The rate of return on asset is 1.34%. 74.62% of all firms in the industry made a profit while 18.27% had negative returns. The top province in terms of the industry's revenue is Shanxi, accounting for 19.26% of the total revenue.
本行業在1996年佔全行業總產值2.211%，行業年增長率為18.6%（全國工業年增長率9.51%）。行業的資產回報率1.34%，74.62%的企業盈利，18.27%的企業虧損。銷售收入最高的省份為山西省，佔本行業的19.26%。

	Total number of firms 企業總數	Total number of employees 職工總數	Total revenue (mil. RMB) 總銷售收入（百萬元）	Total profit (mil. RMB) 總利潤（百萬元）	Return on assets 資產利潤率 (%)	Return on equity 權益利潤率 (%)	Labour productivity ('000 RMB / worker) 勞動生產率（千元/人）	Debts / assets 資產負債率 (%)	Total assets (mil. RMB) 總資產（百萬元）
Industry Overall 行業總體	11,608	5,628,453	128,178	3,852	1.34	3.50	22.77	61.75	287,880

	Number of firms 企業個數	Average number of employees 平均職工人數	Average revenue ('000 RMB) 平均銷售收入（千元）	Average profit ('000 RMB) 平均利潤（千元）	Return on assets 資產利潤率 (%)	Return on equity 權益利潤率 (%)	Labour productivity ('000 RMB / worker) 勞動生產率（千元/人）	Average debts / assets 平均資產負債率(%)	Average Total assets ('000 RMB) 平均總資產（千元）
By ownership 產業所有權									
State-owned 國有	1,957	2,206	51,397	1,179	0.89	2.32	23.30	61.57	132,345
Collectively-owned 集體	9,501	136	2,872	160	5.34	14.61	21.05	63.42	2,999
Privately-owned 私有	34	88	1,208	42	2.16	5.69	13.74	62.12	1,937
Domestic JVs 聯營	71	74	2,047	124	7.00	14.56	27.48	51.91	1,773
Joint stock 股份制	30	211	4,904	309	5.49	12.52	23.26	56.19	5,631
Foreign-funded 外資	3	30	560	-561	-13.46	-37.94	18.66	64.52	4,167
Overseas Chinese-funded 港澳台資	3	72	3,421	-63	-1.74	-4.36	47.29	60.04	3,629
By size 規模									
Large 大型	117	27,090	705,410	21,693	1.21	3.21	26.04	62.30	1,792,401
Medium 中型	163	2,865	59,243	1,121	0.79	2.00	20.68	60.61	142,005
Small 小型	11,073	179	3,315	102	2.06	5.16	18.55	60.14	4,969
By regional distribution 地區分布									
Central-North 華北	2,927	472	12,802	550	1.82	4.58	27.10	60.19	30,177
Beijing 北京	98	415	9,393	199	0.92	2.63	22.63	64.94	21,632
Tianjin 天津									
Hebei 河北	383	788	19,659	740	1.72	3.96	24.96	56.55	42,989
Shanxi 山西	1,992	413	12,394	641	2.24	5.76	30.00	61.06	28,609
Inner Mongolia 內蒙	454	479	9,542	64	0.23	0.57	19.93	60.21	28,097
Northeast 東北	1,094	896	14,820	-425	-0.88	-2.80	16.53	68.61	48,390
Liaoning 遼寧	320	977	19,786	-268	-0.48	-1.45	20.26	66.81	55,667
Jilin 吉林	219	822	9,372	-894	-2.59	-6.87	11.41	62.23	34,497
Heilongjiang 黑龍江	555	880	14,108	-331	-0.67	-2.34	16.04	71.53	49,676
Central East 華東	1,251	967	29,558	1,452	2.77	7.05	30.58	60.68	52,366
Shanghai 上海									
Jiangsu 江蘇	57	3,108	91,219	328	0.24	0.55	29.35	56.21	135,418
Zhejiang 浙江	38	442	17,515	-243	-0.93	-2.59	39.61	64.21	26,266
Anhui 安徽	181	1,813	49,825	2,017	1.81	5.23	27.48	65.50	111,725
Fujian 福建	177	264	6,243	163	1.83	3.42	23.65	46.55	8,915
Jiangxi 江西	458	331	5,020	9	0.09	0.26	15.15	65.58	10,695
Shandong 山東	340	1,437	54,968	4,144	4.68	11.26	38.26	58.42	88,515
Central-South 中南	2,160	447	9,642	376	2.20	5.83	21.59	62.30	17,133
Henan 河南	545	954	24,901	1,615	3.63	9.70	26.09	62.52	44,421
Hubei 湖北	434	148	2,786	41	1.11	2.34	18.83	52.44	3,677
Hunan 湖南	962	275	4,339	21	0.29	0.73	15.78	60.42	7,316
Guangdong 廣東	125	414	6,470	-782	-4.37	-25.31	15.64	82.72	17,884
Guangxi 廣西	93	681	11,325	-70	-0.35	-0.72	16.62	51.60	20,160
Hainan 海南	1	589	9,870	-740	-1.39	-1.92	16.76	27.69	53,240
Southwest 西南	2,933	233	3,402	28	0.35	0.86	14.59	59.09	7,969
Chongqing 重慶	737	243	3,306	-8	-0.10	-0.25	13.56	59.12	7,641
Sichuan 四川	1,147	272	3,844	-15	-0.18	-0.47	14.13	61.10	8,007
Guizhou 貴州	796	153	2,433	94	1.49	2.86	15.95	48.06	6,350
Yunnan 雲南	250	281	4,771	122	0.87	2.89	16.99	69.80	13,952
Tibet 西藏	2	39	100	-170	-5.69	-6.20	2.56	8.36	2,990
Northwest 西北	1,243	328	5,400	-3	-0.02	-0.04	16.47	56.23	16,673
Shaanxi 陝西	435	380	5,074	-283	-1.62	-3.63	13.36	55.26	17,404
Gansu 甘肅	305	286	4,483	95	0.70	1.73	15.65	59.79	13,612
Qinghai 青海	39	406	3,346	-813	-6.03	-13.16	8.24	54.19	13,486
Ningxia 寧夏	74	935	20,662	404	0.67	1.41	22.10	52.75	60,747
Xinjiang 新疆	390	180	3,789	236	2.31	5.57	21.10	58.55	10,207

Year 年份	Number of firms 企業個數	Rate of change 每年變化 (%)	Number of employees 職工人數 (人)	Rate of change 每年變化 (%)	Total revenue (mil. RMB) 總銷售收入 (百萬元)	Rate of change 每年變化 (%)	Total profit (mil. RMB) 總利潤 (百萬元)	Rate of change 每年變化 (%)
1993	9,448		4,713,024		83,132		-743	
1994	10,246	8.45%	5,282,958	12.09%	91,144	9.64%	2,355	417.25%
1995	11,443	11.68%	6,005,977	13.69%	108,066	18.57%	3,360	42.68%
1996	11,608	1.44%	5,628,453	-6.29%	128,178	18.61%	3,852	14.64%

3 Major products* 3 種主要產品 *	Output 產量	Sales volume 銷售量	Unit 單位
a) Coking Coal Dressing 篩選塊煤	55,225,512	55,225,512	ton 噸
b) Raw Coal 原煤	1,353,331,884	1,177,398,739	ton 噸
c) Bituminous Coal 一般煙煤	273,689,502	270,952,607	ton 噸

Top 10 firms by revenue (year founded) 收入排名前 10 家企業 (創辦年份)	City 城市	Province 省	Telephone / fax 電話 / 傳真	Number of employees 職工人數	Ownership 產業所有權	Revenue ('000 RMB) 銷售收入 (千元)	Profit ('000 RMB) (rank) 利潤 (千元) (排名)	Total assets ('000 RMB) 總資產 (千元)	Major products 主要產品
Yanzhou Mining (Group) General Co. 兗州礦業(集團)總公司(1978)	Jining 濟寧市	Shandong 山東省	(0537)5213701	61,170	State-owned 國有	4,974,900	364180(2)	8,229,910	b,c
Shanxi Datong Mining Administration 山西省大同礦務局(1925)	Datong 大同市	Shanxi 山西省	(0352)7013315	121,265	State-owned 國有	4,680,130	220000(3)	12,353,570	a,b,c
Huaibei Mining Administration 淮北礦務局(1959)	Huaibei 淮北市	Anhui 安徽省	(0561)3021112 (0561)3024421	108,456	State-owned 國有	3,070,710	1560(376)	6,701,880	b
Kai Luan Coal Mining Administration 開灤礦務局(1878)	Tangshan 唐山市	Hebei 河北省	(0315)2823811 (0315)2827307	116,371	State-owned 國有	2,951,900	73500(5)	7,503,770	a,b
Huainan Mining Administration 淮南礦務局(1911)	Huainan 淮南市	Anhui 安徽省	(0554)6644334 (0554)6644356	116,614	State-owned 國有	2,718,150	67860(6)	6,352,510	a,b
Xuzhou Mine Administrative Bureau 徐州礦務局(1934)	Xuzhou 徐州市	Jiangsu 江蘇省	(0516)5753940 (0516)5768590	99,185	State-owned 國有	2,606,600	-33927(4157)	4,264,838	a,b
Xinwen Mining Administration 新汶礦務局(1956)	Tai'an 泰安市	Shandong 山東省	(0538)7872147	67,923	State-owned 國有	2,480,380	1020(547)	3,625,430	a,b
Xi Shan Mining Administration 西山礦務局(1956)	Taiyuan 太原市	Shanxi 山西省	(0351)6125941 (0351)6123129	65,500	State-owned 國有	2,315,270	13940(48)	6,397,520	b,c
Yangquan Mining Administration 陽泉市礦務局(1950)	Yangquan 陽泉市	Shanxi 山西省	(0353)7073112 (0353)7073525	59,992	State-owned 國有	2,034,400	25880(28)	5,151,610	a,b
Fushun Mine Administrative Bureau 撫順礦務局(1907)	Fushun 撫順市	Liaoning 遼寧省	(0413)2533889 (0413)2621823	65,799	State-owned 國有	1,825,540	10180(57)	4,374,790	b

Top 10 Cities by Production Output 產出排名前 10 位城市	Province 省	Market share 市場份額	Number of firms 企業個數
Datong 大同市	Shanxi 山西省	5.17%	352
Xuzhou 徐州市	Jiangsu 江蘇省	4.97%	71
Pingdingshan 平頂山市	Henan 河南省	4.22%	129
Tai'an 泰安市	Shandong 山東省	4.11%	47
Huaibei 淮北市	Anhui 安徽省	3.62%	26
Zaozhuang 棗莊市	Shandong 山東省	3.00%	117
Taiyuan 太原市	Shanxi 山西省	2.96%	153
Zhengzhou 鄭州市	Henan 河南省	2.92%	144
Tangshan 唐山市	Hebei 河北省	2.86%	33
Yangquan 陽泉市	Shanxi 山西省	2.65%	69

10 Major Wholesalers 10 家主要批發商	City 城市	Province 省	Telephone / Fax 電話 / 傳真
Qinhuangdao Fuel General Company 秦皇島市燃料總公司	Qinhuangdao 秦皇島市	Hebei 河北省	(0335)3414850 (0335)3412260
Shanxi Coal Import & Export Group Corp. 山西煤炭進出口集團公司	Taiyuan 太原市	Shanxi 山西省	(0351)4061543 (0351)4049310
Jiangsu Electric Power Fuel Co. Ltd. 江蘇電力燃料有限公司	Nanjing 南京市	Jiangsu 江蘇省	(025)3609203 (025)3300300
Shanxi Yuci Coal Transport & Marketing Company 山西省榆次市煤炭運銷公司	Yuci 榆次市	Shanxi 山西省	(0354)3024290 (0354)3025581
China Coal Industry Import & Export General Co. 中國煤炭工業進出口總公司	Beijing 北京市	Beijing 北京市	(010)64678866 (010)64664863
Changshu Electric Power Generating Factory Su Yu Electric Power Industrial General Company 常熟市發電廠蘇虞電力實業總公司	Suzhou 蘇州市	Jiangsu 江蘇省	(0512)2657357 (0512)2657357
Singbo Da Xie Development Zone Zhejiang Electric Power Fuel Company 寧波大榭開發區浙江電力燃料公司	Ningbo 寧波市	Zhejiang 浙江省	(0574)7216200 (0574)7216200
Shandong Commerce Goods & Materials Supply Company 山東省商業物資供應公司	Ji'nan 濟南市	Shandong 山東省	(0531)6955062 (0531)6942124
Yulin Area Fine Coal Company 榆林地區精煤公司	Yulin 榆林市	Shaanxi 陝西省	(0912)8312285 (0912)8314457
Beijing Shi Dian Fuel Company 北京市石電燃料公司	Beijing 北京市	Beijing 北京市	(010)68861155

*Also include sales by firms outside this industry.包括本行業以外廠家的銷售。"o" stands for "others". "o" 代表"其他產品"。

0620: Coal Dressing 煤炭洗選業

The industry accounts for 0.112% of the total revenue of China's industrial sector in 1996. The revenue growth rate of the industry is 71.7% from 1995, as compared to the growth rate of China's industrial sector, 9.51%. The rate of return on asset is 1.32%. 75.03% of all firms in the industry made a profit while 17.56% had negative returns. The top province in terms of the industry's revenue is Hebei, accounting for 34.11% of the total revenue.
本行業在1996年佔全行業總產值0.112%，行業年增長率為71.7%（全國工業年增長率9.51%）。行業的資產回報率1.32%，75.03%的企業盈利，17.56%的企業虧損。銷售收入最高的省份為河北省，佔本行業的34.11%。

	Total number of firms 企業總數	Total number of employees 職工總數	Total revenue (mil. RMB) 總銷售收入（百萬元）	Total profit (mil. RMB) 總利潤（百萬元）	Return on assets 資產利潤率 (%)	Return on equity 權益利潤率 (%)	Labour productivity ('000 RMB / worker) 勞動生產率（千元/人）	Debts / assets 資產負債率 (%)	Total assets (mil. RMB) 總資產（百萬元）
Industry Overall 行業總體	598	169,236	6,473	112	1.32	4.12	38.25	68.04	8,523

	Number of firms 企業個數	Average number of employees 平均職工人數	Average revenue ('000 RMB) 平均銷售收入（千元）	Average profit ('000 RMB) 平均利潤（千元）	Return on assets 資產利潤率 (%)	Return on equity 權益利潤率 (%)	Labour productivity ('000 RMB / worker) 勞動生產率（千元/人）	Average debts / assets 平均資產負債率(%)	Average Total assets ('000 RMB) 平均總資產（千元）
By ownership 產業所有權									
State-owned 國有	54	1,495	47,352	-259	-0.28	-0.86	31.67	67.66	93,056
Collectively-owned 集體	496	170	7,025	235	3.92	12.12	41.42	67.66	6,004
Privately-owned 私有	1	23	2,626				114.19	111.55	610
Domestic JVs 聯營	8	85	9,514	1,115	9.23	47.77	111.93	80.69	12,081
Joint stock 股份制	13	158	9,292	-92	-1.32	-6.52	58.90	79.77	6,942
Foreign-funded 外資	11	81	6,656	468	2.54	8.18	82.08	68.97	18,434
Overseas Chinese-funded 港澳台資	13	77	12,228	-282	-2.83	-10.18	158.17	72.22	9,960
By size 規模									
Large 大型	4	2,263	198,040	9,135	2.68	5.96	87.50	54.99	340,787
Medium 中型	7	1,029	71,250	385	0.26	0.82	69.23	67.65	146,048
Small 小型	576	265	8,997	126	1.19	4.09	33.95	71.00	10,656
By regional distribution 地區分布									
Central-North 華北	193	473	18,099	288	0.94	2.74	38.25	65.72	30,662
Beijing 北京	5	4	642	-106	-17.43	-45.69	160.50	61.84	608
Tianjin 天津	3	4		-103	-6.54	-15.50		57.59	1,580
Hebei 河北	20	3,680	110,413	553	0.27	0.78	30.00	64.95	202,856
Shanxi 山西	140	108	8,486	344	2.81	8.02	78.92	64.89	12,206
Inner Mongolia 內蒙	25	106	3,742	-111	-1.92	-79.83	35.43	97.59	5,757
Northeast 東北	135	374	6,307	17	0.23	0.84	16.87	73.00	7,633
Liaoning 遼寧	107	410	5,019	76	1.46	4.15	12.24	64.89	5,193
Jilin 吉林	4	106	9,423	980	7.15	10.93	89.31	34.54	13,700
Heilongjiang 黑龍江	24	257	11,531	-403	-2.30	-20.45	44.84	88.74	17,501
Central East 華東	70	145	10,286	351	6.29	23.10	70.86	72.74	5,580
Shanghai 上海									
Jiangsu 江蘇	5	60	9,240	354	10.58	86.34	154.52	87.75	3,346
Zhejiang 浙江									
Anhui 安徽	3	1,533	18,767	-33	-0.24	-0.64	12.24	63.29	14,147
Fujian 福建	2	16	460	15	1.73	15.79	28.75	89.02	865
Jiangxi 江西	14	54	3,150	58	1.86	16.95	58.41	89.03	3,112
Shandong 山東	46	97	12,445	480	7.72	26.33	127.87	70.69	6,221
Central-South 中南	61	102	13,183	340	2.83	10.39	128.79	72.78	12,012
Henan 河南	36	95	13,792	318	2.56	12.38	145.26	79.35	12,415
Hubei 湖北									
Hunan 湖南	19	136	15,605	463	3.20	8.68	114.47	63.18	14,487
Guangdong 廣東	4	33	338	8	1.73	3.16	10.31	45.66	433
Guangxi 廣西	2	53	4,910	230	5.22	9.48	93.52	44.95	4,405
Hainan 海南									
Southwest 西南	119	80	4,408	48	1.63	7.84	55.15	79.23	2,957
Chongqing 重慶	19	181	4,049	-345	-11.88	-50.22	22.36	76.34	2,900
Sichuan 四川	67	73	5,930	180	5.31	35.65	81.09	85.10	3,389
Guizhou 貴州	26	27	1,023	9	0.71	1.30	38.18	45.33	1,302
Yunnan 雲南	6	69	3,033	-15	-0.28	-1.26	43.86	78.04	5,420
Tibet 西藏									
Northwest 西北	20	76	3,996	164	3.28	8.53	52.79	61.53	4,998
Shaanxi 陝西	5	71	2,150	132	12.97	28.82	30.28	55.01	1,018
Gansu 甘肅									
Qinghai 青海									
Ningxia 寧夏	14	83	4,941	187	2.76	7.25	59.68	61.88	6,776
Xinjiang 新疆	1								

Year 年份	Number of firms 企業個數	Rate of change 每年變化 (%)	Number of employees 職工人數 (人)	Rate of change 每年變化 (%)	Total revenue (mil. RMB) 總銷售收入 (百萬元)	Rate of change 每年變化 (%)	Total profit (mil. RMB) 總利潤 (百萬元)	Rate of change 每年變化 (%)
1993	337		69,325		2,270		140	
1994	418	24.04%	90,703	30.84%	2,463	8.51%	108	-22.59%
1995	510	22.01%	93,095	2.64%	3,769	53.02%	91	-16.11%
1996	598	17.25%	169,236	81.79%	6,473	71.74%	112	23.57%

3 Major products* 3 種主要產品 *	Output 產量	Sales volume 銷售量	Unit 單位
a) Washed Middlings 洗中煤	1,888,278	1,850,512	ton 噸
b) Fine Coal Washing 洗精煤	21,551,910	21,120,871	ton 噸
c) Slime 煤泥	309,023	296,662	ton 噸

Top 10 firms by revenue (year founded) 收入排名前 10 家企業 (創辦年份)	City 城市	Province 省	Telephone / fax 電話 / 傳真	Number of employees 職工人數	Ownership 產業所有權	Revenue ('000 RMB) 銷售收入 (千元)	Profit ('000 RMB) (rank) 利潤 (千元) (排名)	Total assets ('000 RMB) 總資產 (千元)	Major products 主要產品
Feng Feng Mine Administrative Bureau 峯峯礦務局(1922)	Handan 邯鄲市	Hebei 河北省	(0310)5012323 (0310)5012752	71,793	State-owned 國有	1,899,840	1090(35)	3,855,250	a,b,c
Shuozhou Mining Co. 朔州市礦業公司(1974)	Shuozhou 朔州市	Shanxi 山西省	(0349)3022572	2,167	Collectively-owned 集體	304,965	21056(1)	576,888	o
Hunan Zhuzhou Coal Washing Plant 湖南省株洲洗煤廠(1959)	Zhuzhou 株洲市	Hunan 湖南省	(0733)8350448 (0733)8331339	1,814	State-owned 國有	190,320	1120(33)	219,820	b,c
Yangyuan Hua Nan Coal Marketing Transportation Company Yangyuan Branch 陽原縣華南煤炭銷售運輸公司陽原分公司(1995)	Zhangjiakou 張家口市	Hebei 河北省	(0313)7513266	85	Collectively-owned 集體	112,230	1011(44)	89,421	o
Huozhou Xin Zhi Zhen Coal Washing Factory 霍州市辛置鎮洗煤廠(1987)	Linfen 臨汾市	Shanxi 山西省	(0357)5662048	510	Collectively-owned 集體	70,010	70(184)	46,048	a,b
Fuxin Mine Administrative Bureau Haizhou Open Air Coal Mine Collective Enterprise Company 阜新礦務局海州露天煤礦集體企業公司(1982)	Fuxin 阜新市	Liaoning 遼寧省	(0418)2482010	7,166	Collectively-owned 集體	68,934	1(251)	90,147	o
Panzhihua Renhe Qianjin Coal Washing Factory 攀枝花市仁和區前進洗煤廠	Panzhihua 攀枝花市	Sichuan 四川省			Collectively-owned 集體	65,437	1206(31)	15,564	b
Qitaihe Fuel Company Coal Dressing Factory 七台河市燃料公司選煤廠(1994)	Qitaihe 七臺河市	Heilongjiang 黑龍江省	(0453)8263415	478	State-owned 國有	62,582	3985(6)	59,239	b
Loudi Gao Xi Coal Washing & Coking Co. Ltd. 婁底市高溪洗煤焦化有限公司(1995)	Loudi 婁底市	Hunan 湖南省	(0738)8617294	155	Foreign-funded 外資	59,108	6330(3)	32,812	a,b,c
Cheng'an Dao Dong Bao Xiang Washed Coal Factory 成安縣道東堡鄉洗選廠(1991)	Handan 邯鄲市	Hebei 河北省		90	Collectively-owned 集體	54,008	2520(14)	13,421	o

Top 10 Cities by Production Output 產出排名前 10 位城市	Province 省	Market share 市場份額	Number of firms 企業個數
Handan 邯鄲市	Hebei 河北省	35.16%	10
Pingdingshan 平頂山市	Henan 河南省	9.11%	30
Huainan 淮南市	Anhui 安徽省	5.00%	1
Shuozhou 朔州市	Shanxi 山西省	4.94%	1
Zaozhuang 棗莊市	Shandong 山東省	4.92%	24
Taiyuan 太原市	Shanxi 山西省	4.17%	52
Linfen 臨汾市	Shanxi 山西省	3.91%	48
Zhuzhou 株洲市	Hunan 湖南省	3.40%	3
Panzhihua 攀枝花市	Sichuan 四川省	3.09%	42
Yuci 榆次市	Shanxi 山西省	2.03%	25

10 Major Wholesalers 10 家主要批發商	City 城市	Province 省	Telephone / Fax 電話 / 傳真
Qinhuangdao Fuel General Company 秦皇島市燃料總公司	Qinhuangdao 秦皇島市	Hebei 河北省	(0335)3414850 (0335)3412260
Shanxi Coal Import & Export Group Corp. 山西煤炭進出口集團公司	Taiyuan 太原市	Shanxi 山西省	(0351)4061543 (0351)4049310
Jiangsu Electric Power Fuel Co. Ltd. 江蘇電力燃料有限公司	Nanjing 南京市	Jiangsu 江蘇省	(025)3609203 (025)3300300
Shanxi Yuci Coal Transport & Marketing Company 山西省榆次市煤炭運銷公司	Yuci 榆次市	Shanxi 山西省	(0354)3024290 (0354)3025581
China Coal Industry Import & Export General Co. 中國煤炭工業進出口總公司	Beijing 北京市	Beijing 北京市	(010)64678866 (010)64664863
Changshu Electric Power Generating Factory Su Yu Electric Power Industrial General Company 常熟市發電廠蘇虞電力實業總公司	Suzhou 蘇州市	Jiangsu 江蘇省	(0512)2657357 (0512)2657357
Ningbo Da Xie Development Zone Zhejiang Electric Power Fuel Company 寧波大榭開發區浙江電力燃料公司	Ningbo 寧波市	Zhejiang 浙江省	(0574)7216200 (0574)7216200
Shandong Commerce Goods & Materials Supply Company 山東省商業物資供應公司	Ji'nan 濟南市	Shandong 山東省	(0531)6955062 (0531)6942124
Yulin Area Fine Coal Company 榆林地區精煤公司	Yulin 榆林市	Shaanxi 陝西省	(0912)8312285 (0912)8314457
Beijing Shi Dian Fuel Company 北京市石電燃料公司	Beijing 北京市	Beijing 北京市	(010)68861155

*Also include sales by firms outside this industry.包括本行業以外廠家的銷售。"o" stands for "others". "o" 代表"其他產品"。

0710: Crude Petroleum Extraction 天然原油開採業

The industry accounts for 2.530% of the total revenue of China's industrial sector in 1996. The revenue growth rate of the industry is 10.7% from 1995, as compared to the growth rate of China's industrial sector, 9.51%. The rate of return on asset is 5.96%. 77.50% of all firms in the industry made a profit while 10.96% had negative returns. The top province in terms of the industry's revenue is Helongjiang, accounting for 29.84% of the total revenue.
本行業在1996年佔全行業總產值2.530%，行業年增長率為10.7%（全國工業年增長率9.51%）。行業的資產回報率5.96%，77.50%的企業盈利，10.96%的企業虧損。銷售收入最高的省份為黑龍江省，佔本行業的29.84%。

	Total number of firms 企業總數	Total number of employees 職工總數	Total revenue (mil. RMB) 總銷售收入（百萬元）	Total profit (mil. RMB) 總利潤（百萬元）	Return on assets 資產利潤率 (%)	Return on equity 權益利潤率 (%)	Labour productivity ('000 RMB / worker) 勞動生產率（千元/人）	Debts / assets 資產負債率 (%)	Total assets (mil. RMB) 總資產（百萬元）
Industry Overall 行業總體	119	1,092,764	146,675	15,950	5.96	13.81	134.22	56.89	267,821

	Number of firms 企業個數	Average number of employees 平均職工人數	Average revenue ('000 RMB) 平均銷售收入（千元）	Average profit ('000 RMB) 平均利潤（千元）	Return on assets 資產利潤率 (%)	Return on equity 權益利潤率 (%)	Labour productivity ('000 RMB / worker) 勞動生產率（千元/人）	Average debts / assets 平均資產負債率(%)	Average Total assets ('000 RMB) 平均總資產（千元）
By ownership 產業所有權									
State-owned 國有	66	16,381	2,120,894	197,697	5.02	12.05	129.47	58.34	3,938,955
Collectively-owned 集體	11	489	13,178	1,480	6.57	31.20	26.92	78.94	22,525
Privately-owned 私有									
Domestic JVs 聯營	35	51	5,413	-40	-0.53	-1.18	105.55	54.70	7,583
Joint stock 股份制	5	180	236,817	31,747	16.96	25.37	1314.19	33.15	187,192
Foreign-funded 外資	2	1,710	2,589,428	1,364,453	42.63	42.88	1514.73	0.58	3,200,445
Overseas Chinese-funded 港澳台資									
By size 規模									
Large 大型	21	51,401	6,786,565	704,427	5.77	13.95	132.03	58.60	12,200,478
Medium 中型	1	225	18,403	3,604	8.68	19.83	81.79	56.21	41,512
Small 小型	95	137	43,573	12,143	9.97	12.32	317.00	19.06	121,784
By regional distribution 地區分布									
Central-North 華北	9	14,269	1,539,888	7,184	0.22	0.49	107.92	55.16	3,240,850
Beijing 北京	2								
Tianjin 天津	4	17,985	1,500,448	14,090	0.50	1.51	83.43	66.74	2,800,758
Hebei 河北	2	26,189	3,461,090	4,150	0.06	0.12	132.16	54.88	7,427,405
Shanxi 山西									
Inner Mongolia 內蒙	1	4,102	935,020				227.94	14.78	3,109,810
Northeast 東北	9	32,039	6,756,141	1,389,873	16.06	30.57	210.87	47.45	8,652,564
Liaoning 遼寧	1	127,667	13,298,430	588,150	2.66	6.32	104.16	58.01	22,146,780
Jilin 吉林	5	7,818	747,038	9,956	0.44	1.27	95.55	65.49	2,280,652
Heilongjiang 黑龍江	3	40,531	14,590,550	3,956,977	26.78	42.88	359.99	37.54	14,774,347
Central East 華東	3	70,572	7,723,867	58,677	0.44	1.38	109.45	67.91	13,250,300
Shanghai 上海									
Jiangsu 江蘇	1	20,718	1,138,890	12,850	0.41	0.96	54.97	56.78	3,097,900
Zhejiang 浙江									
Anhui 安徽									
Fujian 福建									
Jiangxi 江西									
Shandong 山東	2	95,500	11,016,355	81,590	0.45	1.43	115.36	68.85	18,326,500
Central-South 中南	13	12,634	1,512,554	247,461	7.81	14.42	119.72	45.87	3,169,656
Henan 河南	8	14,916	1,035,585	-11,606	-0.48	-1.31	69.43	63.48	2,424,011
Hubei 湖北	1	36,507	2,697,390	-30,590	-0.51	-0.92	73.89	44.33	5,957,180
Hunan 湖南	1								
Guangdong 廣東	2	4,190	4,340,305	1,670,190	21.07	28.06	1035.87	24.91	7,927,490
Guangxi 廣西									
Hainan 海南	1	24	520	50	3.91	4.35	21.67	10.16	1,280
Southwest 西南	1	13,118	852,160	-18,520	-1.04	-2.98	64.96	65.00	1,776,310
Chongqing 重慶									
Sichuan 四川									
Guizhou 貴州									
Yunnan 雲南	1	13,118	852,160	-18,520	-1.04	-2.98	64.96	65.00	1,776,310
Tibet 西藏									
Northwest 西北	84	3,416	337,186	25		0.01	98.72	66.96	929,142
Shaanxi 陝西	65	267	17,784	2,175	4.88	11.55	66.62	57.78	44,594
Gansu 甘肅	10	8,225	635,558	-4,943	-0.35	-0.93	77.27	62.51	1,421,366
Qinghai 青海	2	12,704	781,810	-74,840	-2.83	-9.14	61.54	69.05	2,644,405
Ningxia 寧夏	1	5,275	543,700				103.07	33.49	601,370
Xinjiang 新疆	6	26,107	3,117,462	9,965	0.11	0.35	119.41	68.76	9,174,247

0710: Crude Petroleum Extraction 天然原油開採業

Year 年份	Number of firms 企業個數	Rate of change 每年變化 (%)	Number of employees 職工人數 (人)	Rate of change 每年變化 (%)	Total revenue (mil. RMB) 總銷售收入 (百萬元)	Rate of change 每年變化 (%)	Total profit (mil. RMB) 總利潤 (百萬元)	Rate of change 每年變化 (%)
1993	55		882,197		84,934		-2,300	
1994	74	34.55%	1,187,611	34.62%	109,682	29.14%	9,449	510.81%
1995	123	66.22%	1,376,996	15.95%	132,446	20.75%	12,293	30.09%
1996	119	-3.25%	1,092,764	-20.64%	146,675	10.74%	15,950	29.75%

3 Major products* 3種主要產品*	Output 產量	Sales volume 銷售量	Unit 單位
a) Crude Petroleum 天然原油	156,618,031	150,353,310	ton 噸
b) Associated Gas 伴生氣	736,756	221,027	10,000 cubic metre 萬立方米
c) Natural Gas 天然氣	1,030,983	814,477	10,000 cubic metre 萬立方米

Top 10 firms by revenue (year founded) 收入排名前10家企業 (創辦年份)	City 城市	Province 省	Telephone / fax 電話 / 傳真	Number of employees 職工人數	Ownership 產業所有權	Revenue ('000 RMB) 銷售收入 (千元)	Profit ('000 RMB) (rank) 利潤 (千元) (排名)	Total assets ('000 RMB) 總資產 (千元)	Major products 主要產品
Daqing Petroleum Management Bureau 大慶石油管理局(1960)	Daqing 大慶市	Heilongjiang 黑龍江省	(0459)5995126 (0459)5996162	256,581	State-owned 國有	43,737,970	11871900(1)	44,209,330	a,b,c
Sheng Li Petroleum Management Bureau 勝利石油管理局(1962)	Dongying 東營市	Shandong 山東省	(0546)8552754	190,951	State-owned 國有	21,952,710	163180(6)	36,653,000	a,b,c
Liao He Petroleum Prospecting Bureau 遼河石油勘探局(1970)	Panjin 盤錦市	Liaoning 遼寧省	(0427)7801151 (0427)7801151	149,764	State-owned 國有	13,298,430	588150(3)	22,146,780	o
Xinjiang Uygur Autonomous Region Petroleum Management Bureau 新疆維吾爾自治區石油管理局(1942)	Karamay 克拉瑪依市	Xinjiang 新疆	(0990)884412 (0990)883607	125,294	State-owned 國有	13,199,860	-191570(51)	31,301,510	a,b,c
Hua Bei Petroleum Management Bureau 華北石油管理局(1975)	Cangzhou 滄州市	Hebei 河北省	(0317)2725215 (0317)2725215	47,428	State-owned 國有	6,320,400	2960(23)	12,877,460	a,b,c
China Ocean Petroleum Nanhai Dong Bu Company 中國海洋石油南海東部公司(1983)	Guangzhou 廣州市	Guangdong 廣東省	(020)84429072 (020)84420984	1,502	Foreign-funded 外資	6,129,454	2894935(2)	7,134,966	a
Dagang Oilfield Group Co. Ltd. 大港油田集團有限責任公司(1964)	Tianjin 天津市	Tianjin 天津市	(022)25922402 (022)25924939	72,137	State-owned 國有	6,001,790	56360(10)	11,203,030	a,b,c
Jilin Oilfield Management Bureau 吉林省油田管理局(1960)	Songyuan 松原市	Jilin 吉林省	(0438)6224653	68,434	State-owned 國有	3,678,210	48720(11)	11,145,180	a,b,c
Chang Qing Petroleum Prospecting Bureau 長慶石油勘探局(1970)	Xifeng 西峯市	Gansu 甘肅省	(0934)3593236 (0934)3593236	63,118	State-owned 國有	3,640,920	197570(5)	11,427,670	a,b,c
Tarim Petroleum Exploration & Development Bureau 新疆塔里木石油勘探開發局(1989)	Korla 庫爾勒市	Xinjiang 新疆	(0996)2171393 (0996)2171210	4,650	State-owned 國有	3,167,380	133750(7)	14,039,490	a,b,c

Top 10 Cities by Production Output 產出排名前10位城市	Province 省	Market share 市場份額	Number of firms 企業個數
Tianjin 天津市	Tianjin 天津市	11.81%	2
Puyang 濮陽市	Henan 河南省	11.06%	1
Cangzhou 滄州市	Hebei 河北省	10.46%	1
Guangzhou 廣州市	Guangdong 廣東省	8.40%	1
Songyuan 松原市	Jilin 吉林省	5.95%	3
Xifeng 西峯市	Gansu 甘肅省	5.69%	8
Panjin 盤錦市	Liaoning 遼寧省	5.42%	1
Korla 庫爾勒市	Xinjiang 新疆	5.23%	1
Karamay 克拉瑪依市	Xinjiang 新疆	5.14%	2
Suizhou 隨州市	Hubei 湖北省	4.89%	1

10 Major Wholesalers 10家主要批發商	City 城市	Province 省	Telephone / Fax 電話 / 傳真
Zhong Hua Liaoning Import & Export Company 中化遼寧進出口公司	Dalian 大連市	Liaoning 遼寧省	(0411)2821888 (0411)2639378
Huzhou Petrochemical Marketing General Company 湖州市石化銷售總公司	Huzhou 湖州市	Zhejiang 浙江省	(0572)2067002
Xinjiang Uygur Autonomous Region Petroleum General Company Urumqi Branch 新疆維吾爾自治區石油總公司烏魯木齊分公司	Urumqi 烏魯木齊市	Xinjiang 新疆	(0991)6897333
Shanghai Petroleum (Group) Co. Ltd. 上海石油(集團)有限公司	Shanghai 上海市	Shanghai 上海市	(021)63219490
Guangzhou Development Zone Zhong Sui Petrochemical Products Supply & Marketing Company 廣州開發區中穗石油化工產品供銷公司	Guangzhou 廣州市	Guangdong 廣東省	(020)82393431 (020)82398354
China Petrochemical Marketing Maoming Company 中國石化銷售茂名公司	Maoming 茂名市	Guangdong 廣東省	(0668)2245836 (0668)2269297
Zhejiang Petroleum General Co. 浙江省石油總公司	Hangzhou 杭州市	Zhejiang 浙江省	(0571)7805026 (0571)7805201
Guangdong Petroleum Enterprise Group Co. 廣東省石油企業集團公司	Guangzhou 廣州市	Guangdong 廣東省	(020)81850888 (020)81856088
China Shipping Fuel Supply Shanghai Company 中國船舶燃料供應上海公司	Shanghai 上海市	Shanghai 上海市	(021)63290555
Zhejiang Petroleum General Company Singbo Branch 浙江省石油總公司寧波分公司	Ningbo 寧波市	Zhejiang 浙江省	(0574)7267937 (0574)7268027

*Also include sales by firms outside this industry.包括本行業以外廠家的銷售。"o" stands for "others". "o" 代表"其他產品"。

0720: Natural Gas Extraction 天然氣開採業

The industry accounts for 0.084% of the total revenue of China's industrial sector in 1996. The revenue growth rate of the industry is 13.7% from 1995, as compared to the growth rate of China's industrial sector, 9.51%. The rate of return on asset is 0.53%. 85.71% of all firms in the industry made a profit while 14.29% had negative returns. The top province in terms of the industry's revenue is Sichuan, accounting for 99.56% of the total revenue.
本行業在1996年佔全行業總產值0.084%，行業年增長率為13.7%（全國工業年增長率9.51%）。行業的資產回報率0.53%，85.71%的企業盈利，14.29%的企業虧損。銷售收入最高的省份為四川省，佔本行業的99.56%。

	Total number of firms 企業總數	Total number of employees 職工總數	Total revenue (mil. RMB) 總銷售收入（百萬元）	Total profit (mil. RMB) 總利潤（百萬元）	Return on assets 資產利潤率 (%)	Return on equity 權益利潤率 (%)	Labour productivity ('000 RMB / worker) 勞動生產率（千元/人）	Debts / assets 資產負債率 (%)	Total assets (mil. RMB) 總資產（百萬元）
Industry Overall 行業總體	10	109,038	4,849	63	0.53	1.01	44.47	48.11	12,040

	Number of firms 企業個數	Average number of employees 平均職工人數	Average revenue ('000 RMB) 平均銷售收入（千元）	Average profit ('000 RMB) 平均利潤（千元）	Return on assets 資產利潤率 (%)	Return on equity 權益利潤率 (%)	Labour productivity ('000 RMB / worker) 勞動生產率（千元/人）	Average debts / assets 平均資產負債率(%)	Average Total assets ('000 RMB) 平均總資產（千元）
By ownership 產業所有權									
State-owned 國有	5	21,713	964,400	10,400	0.43	0.84	44.42	48.23	2,392,000
Collectively-owned 集體	2	42	863	95	18.23	26.47	20.78	31.14	521
Privately-owned 私有									
Domestic JVs 聯營									
Joint stock 股份制	2	148	9,124	5,442	15.10	21.66	61.65	30.28	36,031
Foreign-funded 外資	2	48	3,562	-37	-1.04	-1.44	74.21	27.75	3,576
Overseas Chinese-funded 港澳台資									
By size 規模									
Large 大型	1	108,296	4,739,528	-126,241	-1.08	-2.10	43.76	48.75	11,740,919
Medium 中型									
Small 小型	8	88	13,726	23,651	63.12	81.72	155.32	22.76	37,471
By regional distribution 地區分布									
Central-North 華北	1	97	5,520	110	0.95	1.80	56.91	47.32	11,580
Beijing 北京	1	97	5,520	110	0.95	1.80	56.91	47.32	11,580
Tianjin 天津									
Hebei 河北									
Shanxi 山西									
Inner Mongolia 內蒙									
Northeast 東北									
Liaoning 遼寧									
Jilin 吉林									
Heilongjiang 黑龍江									
Central East 華東									
Shanghai 上海									
Jiangsu 江蘇									
Zhejiang 浙江									
Anhui 安徽									
Fujian 福建									
Jiangxi 江西									
Shandong 山東									
Central-South 中南									
Henan 河南									
Hubei 湖北									
Hunan 湖南									
Guangdong 廣東									
Guangxi 廣西									
Hainan 海南									
Southwest 西南	7	15,551	691,523	9,131	0.53	1.03	44.47	48.13	1,716,597
Chongqing 重慶	1	243	11,163	46,489	102.23	176.18	45.86	41.97	45,474
Sichuan 四川	5	18,612	827,600	1,659	0.08	0.16	44.46	48.16	2,050,833
Guizhou 貴州									
Yunnan 雲南									
Tibet 西藏									
Northwest 西北	2	42	1,280	-380	-6.00	-8.24	30.48	27.09	6,330
Shaanxi 陝西									
Gansu 甘肅									
Qinghai 青海									
Ningxia 寧夏									
Xinjiang 新疆	2	42	1,280	-380	-6.00	-8.24	30.48	27.09	6,330

0720: Natural Gas Extraction 天然氣開採業

Year 年份	Number of firms 企業個數	Rate of change 每年變化 (%)	Number of employees 職工人數 (人)	Rate of change 每年變化 (%)	Total revenue (mil. RMB) 總銷售收入 (百萬元)	Rate of change 每年變化 (%)	Total profit (mil. RMB) 總利潤 (百萬元)	Rate of change 每年變化 (%)
1993	10		674		65		2	
1994	11	10.00%	109,842	16197.03%	3,583	5444.34%	-98	-4547.57%
1995	9	-18.18%	109,505	-0.31%	4,266	19.06%	10	110.15%
1996	10	11.11%	109,038	-0.43%	4,849	13.67%	63	534.06%

3 Major products* 3 種主要產品 *	Output 產量	Sales volume 銷售量	Unit 單位
a) Gas From Gas Stratum 氣層氣	822,123	756,353	10,000 cubic metre 萬立方米
b) Natural Gas 天然氣	897,426	708,967	10,000 cubic metre 萬立方米
c) Liquefied Petroleum Gas 液化石油氣	7,517	7,066	ton 噸

Top 10 firms by revenue (year founded) 收入排名前10家企業 (創辦年份)	City 城市	Province 省	Telephone / fax 電話 / 傳真	Number of employees 職工人數	Ownership 產業所有權	Revenue ('000 RMB) 銷售收入 (千元)	Profit ('000 RMB) (rank) 利潤 (千元) (排名)	Total assets ('000 RMB) 總資產 (千元)	Major products 主要產品
Sichuan Petroleum Management Bureau 四川石油管理局(1953)	Chengdu 成都市	Sichuan 四川省	(028)3324911	106,662	State-owned 國有	4,815,330	53260(1)	11,933,280	a,b,c
Dianjiang Qian Ceng Natural Gas Mine 墊江縣淺層天然氣礦(1983)	Chongqing 重慶市	Chongqing 重慶市	(023)512449	300	Joint stock 股份制	17,396	10519(2)	66,656	a,b
Changchun Shuangyang Qu Natural Gas General Company 長春市雙陽區天然氣總公司(1990)	Changchun 長春市	Jilin 吉林省	(0431)4222471	117	State-owned 國有	6,533	95(5)	26,606	o
Chuanxinan Huayou Group Co. Zigong Oil Gas Sales Co. 川西南華油集團自貢油氣銷售公司(1992)	Zigong 自貢市	Sichuan 四川省	(0813)225211	73	Collectively-owned 集體	4,248	225(4)	2,568	b
Sichuan Cangxi Natural Gas Company 四川省蒼溪縣天然氣公司(1989)	Guangyuan 廣元市	Sichuan 四川省	(0839)5224263	68	State-owned 國有	3,556	269(3)	9,584	o
Aksu Kuqa Ministry of Geology & Mineral Resource Xi Bei Liquefied Petroleum Gas Factory 阿克蘇庫車縣地質礦產部西北石油液化氣廠(1990)	Aksu 阿克蘇市	Xinjiang 新疆	(0997)7123541	75	State-owned 國有	2,560	-758(6)	12,659	c

Top 10 Cities by Production Output 產出排名前10位城市	Province 省	Market share 市場份額	Number of firms 企業個數
Zigong 自貢市	Sichuan 四川省	80.38%	1
Changchun 長春市	Jilin 吉林省	9.57%	2
Neijiang 內江市	Sichuan 四川省	3.57%	2
Chongqing 重慶市	Chongqing 重慶市	3.09%	1
Guangyuan 廣元市	Sichuan 四川省	1.10%	1
Beijing 北京市	Beijing 北京市	1.03%	1
Changzhou 常州市	Jiangsu 江蘇省	0.45%	1
Aksu 阿克蘇市	Xinjiang 新疆	0.36%	1
Dongying 東營市	Shandong 山東省	0.26%	1
Suining 遂寧市	Sichuan 四川省	0.11%	1

10 Major Wholesalers 10家主要批發商	City 城市	Province 省	Telephone / Fax 電話 / 傳真
Zhong Hua Liaoning Import & Export Company 中化遼寧進出口公司	Dalian 大連市	Liaoning 遼寧省	(0411)2821888 (0411)2639378
Huzhou Petrochemical Marketing General Company 湖州市石化銷售總公司	Huzhou 湖州市	Zhejiang 浙江省	(0572)2067002
Xinjiang Uygur Autonomous Region Petroleum General Company Urumqi Branch 新疆維吾爾自治區石油總公司烏魯木齊分公司	Urumqi 烏魯木齊市	Xinjiang 新疆	(0991)6897333
Shanghai Petroleum (Group) Co. Ltd. 上海石油(集團)有限公司	Shanghai 上海市	Shanghai 上海市	(021)63219490
Guangzhou Development Zone Zhong Sui Petrochemical Products Supply & Marketing Company 廣州開發區中穗石油化工產品供銷公司	Guangzhou 廣州市	Guangdong 廣東省	(020)82393431 (020)82398354
China Petrochemical Marketing Maoming Company 中國石化銷售茂名公司	Maoming 茂名市	Guangdong 廣東省	(0668)2245836 (0668)2269297
Zhejiang Petroleum General Co. 浙江省石油總公司	Hangzhou 杭州市	Zhejiang 浙江省	(0571)7805026 (0571)7805201
Guangdong Petroleum Enterprise Group Co. 廣東省石油企業集團公司	Guangzhou 廣州市	Guangdong 廣東省	(020)81850888 (020)81856088
China Shipping Fuel Supply Shanghai Company 中國船舶燃料供應上海公司	Shanghai 上海市	Shanghai 上海市	(021)63290555
Zhejiang Petroleum General Company Singbo Branch 浙江省石油總公司寧波分公司	Ningbo 寧波市	Zhejiang 浙江省	(0574)7267937 (0574)7268027

*Also include sales by firms outside this industry.包括本行業以外廠家的銷售。"o" stands for "others". "o" 代表 "其他產品"。

0730: Oil Shale Mining and Dressing 油頁巖開採業

The industry accounts for 0.000% of the total revenue of China's industrial sector in 1996. The revenue growth rate of the industry is 295.3% from 1995, as compared to the growth rate of China's industrial sector, 9.51%. The rate of return on asset is 49.10%. 100.00% of all firms in the industry made a profit while 0.00% had negative returns. The top province in terms of the industry's revenue is Guangdong, accounting for 40.89% of the total revenue.
本行業在1996年佔全行業總產值0.000% ，行業年增長率為295.3%（全國工業年增長率9.51%）。行業的資產回報率49.10% ，100.00%的企業盈利，0.00%的企業虧損。銷售收入最高的省份為廣東省，佔本行業的40.89% 。

	Total number of firms 企業總數	Total number of employees 職工總數	Total revenue (mil. RMB) 總銷售收入（百萬元）	Total profit (mil. RMB) 總利潤（百萬元）	Return on assets 資產利潤率 (%)	Return on equity 權益利潤率 (%)	Labour productivity ('000 RMB / worker) 勞動生產率（千元/人）	Debts / assets 資產負債率 (%)	Total assets (mil. RMB) 總資產（百萬元）
Industry Overall 行業總體	4	178	9	1	49.10	167.35	50.56	70.66	2

	Number of firms 企業個數	Average number of employees 平均職工人數	Average revenue ('000 RMB) 平均銷售收入（千元）	Average profit ('000 RMB) 平均利潤（千元）	Return on assets 資產利潤率 (%)	Return on equity 權益利潤率 (%)	Labour productivity ('000 RMB / worker) 勞動生產率（千元/人）	Average debts / assets 平均資產負債率(%)	Average Total assets ('000 RMB) 平均總資產（千元）
By ownership 產業所有權									
State-owned 國有									
Collectively-owned 集體	4	45	2,249	250	50.00	100.00	50.54	50.00	500
Privately-owned 私有									
Domestic JVs 聯營									
Joint stock 股份制									
Foreign-funded 外資									
Overseas Chinese-funded 港澳台資									
By size 規模									
Large 大型									
Medium 中型									
Small 小型	4	45	2,249	250	50.00	100.00	50.54	50.00	500
By regional distribution 地區分布									
Central-North 華北									
Beijing 北京									
Tianjin 天津									
Hebei 河北									
Shanxi 山西									
Inner Mongolia 內蒙									
Northeast 東北	2	40	2,420	305	51.69	1525.00	60.50	96.61	590
Liaoning 遼寧	1		1,840	160	27.59	48.48		43.10	580
Jilin 吉林	1	80	3,000	450	75.00	-155.17	37.50	148.33	600
Heilongjiang 黑龍江									
Central East 華東									
Shanghai 上海									
Jiangsu 江蘇									
Zhejiang 浙江									
Anhui 安徽									
Fujian 福建									
Jiangxi 江西									
Shandong 山東									
Central-South 中南	1	68	3,680	210	44.68	46.67	54.12	4.26	470
Henan 河南									
Hubei 湖北									
Hunan 湖南									
Guangdong 廣東	1	68	3,680	210	44.68	46.67	54.12	4.26	470
Guangxi 廣西									
Hainan 海南									
Southwest 西南	1	30	130				4.33	100.00	20
Chongqing 重慶									
Sichuan 四川	1	30	130			-42.86	4.33	100.00	20
Guizhou 貴州									
Yunnan 雲南									
Tibet 西藏									
Northwest 西北									
Shaanxi 陝西									
Gansu 甘肅									
Qinghai 青海									
Ningxia 寧夏									
Xinjiang 新疆									

0730: Oil Shale Mining and Dressing 油頁巖開採業

Year 年份	Number of firms 企業個數	Rate of change 每年變化 (%)	Number of employees 職工人數 (人)	Rate of change 每年變化 (%)	Total revenue (mil. RMB) 總銷售收入 (百萬元)	Rate of change 每年變化 (%)	Total profit (mil. RMB) 總利潤 (百萬元)	Rate of change 每年變化 (%)
1993	3		145		4		1	
1994	12	300.00%	337	132.41%	1	-68.05%	0	-78.70%
1995	2	-83.33%	90	-73.29%	2	65.60%	0	166.41%
1996	4	100.00%	178	97.78%	9	295.26%	1	193.26%

3 Major products* 3種主要產品 *	Output 產量	Sales volume 銷售量	Unit 單位
a) Oil Shale 油母頁岩	52,666	52,139	ton 噸

Top 10 firms by revenue (year founded) 收入排名前10家企業 (創辦年份)	City 城市	Province 省	Telephone / fax 電話 / 傳真	Number of employees 職工人數	Ownership 產業所有權	Revenue ('000 RMB) 銷售收入 (千元)	Profit ('000 RMB) (rank) 利潤 (千元) (排名)	Total assets ('000 RMB) 總資產 (千元)	Major products 主要產品
Dianbai Yang Jiao Zhen Small Coal Mine 電白縣羊角鎮小煤礦(1976)	Maoming 茂名市	Guangdong 廣東省	(0668)5270766	68	Collectively-owned 集體	3,680	210(1)	470	a

Top 10 Cities by Production Output 產出排名前10位城市	Province 省	Market share 市場份額	Number of firms 企業個數
Maoming 茂名市	Guangdong 廣東省	55.20%	1
Jilin 吉林市	Jilin 吉林省	30.47%	3
Shenyang 瀋陽市	Liaoning 遼寧省	10.75%	1
Chengdu 成都市	Sichuan 四川省	3.58%	1

10 Major Wholesalers 10家主要批發商	City 城市	Province 省	Telephone / Fax 電話 / 傳真
Zhong Hua Liaoning Import & Export Company 中化遼寧進出口公司	Dalian 大連市	Liaoning 遼寧省	(0411)2821888 (0411)2639378
Huzhou Petrochemical Marketing General Company 湖州市石化銷售總公司	Huzhou 湖州市	Zhejiang 浙江省	(0572)2067002
Xinjiang Uygur Autonomous Region Petroleum General Company Urumqi Branch 新疆維吾爾自治區石油總公司烏魯木齊分公司	Urumqi 烏魯木齊市	Xinjiang 新疆	(0991)6897333
Shanghai Petroleum (Group) Co. Ltd. 上海石油(集團)有限公司	Shanghai 上海市	Shanghai 上海市	(021)63219490
Guangzhou Development Zone Zhong Sui Petrochemical Products Supply & Marketing Company 廣州開發區中穗石油化工產品供銷公司	Guangzhou 廣州市	Guangdong 廣東省	(020)82393431 (020)82398354
China Petrochemical Marketing Maoming Company 中國石化銷售茂名公司	Maoming 茂名市	Guangdong 廣東省	(0668)2245836 (0668)2269297
Zhejiang Petroleum General Co. 浙江省石油總公司	Hangzhou 杭州市	Zhejiang 浙江省	(0571)7805026 (0571)7805201
Guangdong Petroleum Enterprise Group Co. 廣東省石油企業集團公司	Guangzhou 廣州市	Guangdong 廣東省	(020)81850888 (020)81856088
China Shipping Fuel Supply Shanghai Company 中國船舶燃料供應上海公司	Shanghai 上海市	Shanghai 上海市	(021)63290555
Zhejiang Petroleum General Company Singbo Branch 浙江省石油總公司寧波分公司	Ningbo 寧波市	Zhejiang 浙江省	(0574)7267937 (0574)7268027

*Also include sales by firms outside this industry.包括本行業以外廠家的銷售。"o" stands for "others". "o" 代表"其他產品"。

0810: Iron Ores Mining and Dressing 鐵礦採選業

The industry accounts for 0.185% of the total revenue of China's industrial sector in 1996. The revenue growth rate of the industry is 22.7% from 1995, as compared to the growth rate of China's industrial sector, 9.51%. The rate of return on asset is 0.76%. 77.04% of all firms in the industry made a profit while 14.82% had negative returns. The top province in terms of the industry's revenue is Hebei, accounting for 30.46% of the total revenue.
本行業在1996年佔全行業總產值0.185%，行業年增長率為22.7%（全國工業年增長率9.51%）。行業的資產回報率0.76%，77.04%的企業盈利，14.82%的企業虧損。銷售收入最高的省份為河北省，佔本行業的30.46%。

	Total number of firms 企業總數	Total number of employees 職工總數	Total revenue (mil. RMB) 總銷售收入（百萬元）	Total profit (mil. RMB) 總利潤（百萬元）	Return on assets 資產利潤率 (%)	Return on equity 權益利潤率 (%)	Labour productivity ('000 RMB / worker) 勞動生產率（千元/人）	Debts / assets 資產負債率 (%)	Total assets (mil. RMB) 總資產（百萬元）
Industry Overall 行業總體	1,632	292,658	10,702	213	0.76	1.48	36.57	48.72	28,049

	Number of firms 企業個數	Average number of employees 平均職工人數	Average revenue ('000 RMB) 平均銷售收入（千元）	Average profit ('000 RMB) 平均利潤（千元）	Return on assets 資產利潤率 (%)	Return on equity 權益利潤率 (%)	Labour productivity ('000 RMB / worker) 勞動生產率（千元/人）	Average debts / assets 平均資產負債率(%)	Average Total assets ('000 RMB) 平均總資產（千元）
By ownership 產業所有權									
State-owned 國有	191	752	21,764	-476	-0.44	-0.75	28.95	41.94	109,351
Collectively-owned 集體	1,355	106	4,623	197	4.19	14.69	43.69	71.46	4,706
Privately-owned 私有	38	48	3,969	624	4.55	7.65	81.88	40.59	13,739
Domestic JVs 聯營	26	57	2,989	203	9.04	20.66	52.75	56.22	2,247
Joint stock 股份制	14	112	2,520	380	3.68	8.98	22.46	59.05	10,345
Foreign-funded 外資	5	180	2,969	459	3.85	5.41	16.51	28.81	11,924
Overseas Chinese-funded 港澳台資	3	27	1,017				38.14	41.46	176
By size 規模									
Large 大型	6	13,210	439,877	-23,440	-0.91	-1.34	33.30	32.35	2,577,963
Medium 中型	14	1,932	58,324	-290	-0.22	-0.51	30.19	57.54	134,175
Small 小型	1,584	117	4,575	226	3.34	11.46	39.09	70.83	6,756
By regional distribution 地區分布									
Central-North 華北	622	148	6,614	255	2.78	10.84	44.63	74.33	9,170
Beijing 北京	15	187	11,972	643	2.24	8.96	64.09	75.03	28,741
Tianjin 天津	1	109	3,250	360	10.03	19.05	29.82	47.35	3,590
Hebei 河北	425	168	7,669	283	2.86	11.69	45.67	75.52	9,876
Shanxi 山西	107	101	3,520	55	0.94	3.70	34.97	74.68	5,818
Inner Mongolia 內蒙	74	96	3,986	306	5.04	13.38	41.41	62.29	6,073
Northeast 東北	266	177	5,131	73	0.77	2.65	28.98	70.96	9,440
Liaoning 遼寧	235	184	5,485	145	1.55	5.16	29.83	69.85	9,307
Jilin 吉林	22	118	3,184	-477	-4.02	-26.93	27.07	85.07	11,867
Heilongjiang 黑龍江	9	144	641	-462	-6.61	-13.49	4.47	51.04	6,997
Central East 華東	211	393	12,640	437	0.63	0.87	32.19	28.04	69,442
Shanghai 上海									
Jiangsu 江蘇	8	1,088	35,680	233	0.45	1.49	32.78	69.95	51,804
Zhejiang 浙江	3	1,370	74,440	1,663	1.46	2.22	54.32	34.46	114,113
Anhui 安徽	66	634	18,503	996	0.57	0.72	29.16	21.65	175,557
Fujian 福建	49	74	3,805	67	1.07	2.49	51.59	56.79	6,250
Jiangxi 江西	26	50	1,659	-240	-5.50	-13.90	33.31	60.47	4,367
Shandong 山東	59	394	11,992	382	1.19	2.40	30.44	50.30	32,016
Central-South 中南	341	135	5,199	-220	-2.05	-6.63	38.43	69.01	10,727
Henan 河南	74	73	3,287	111	3.21	9.28	44.80	65.46	3,460
Hubei 湖北	93	122	6,176	145	3.97	8.93	50.63	55.53	3,639
Hunan 湖南	36	136	2,327	-335	-8.77	-30.54	17.08	71.29	3,818
Guangdong 廣東	85	131	5,846	-176	-1.21	-4.74	44.61	74.42	14,517
Guangxi 廣西	52	35	1,329	14	0.55	2.00	38.07	72.39	2,504
Hainan 海南	1	11,492	305,380	-70,480	-4.51	-13.99	26.57	67.75	1,561,960
Southwest 西南	108	163	5,073	124	1.23	3.97	31.13	68.90	10,080
Chongqing 重慶	5	139	1,503	-3	-0.18	-0.61	10.74	71.13	1,621
Sichuan 四川	49	212	4,634	8	0.06	0.19	21.80	69.31	13,847
Guizhou 貴州	27	46	590	63	10.43	23.33	12.83	55.30	607
Yunnan 雲南	25	202	11,763	453	2.97	9.51	58.23	68.70	15,220
Tibet 西藏	1	39	890	40	133.33	133.33	22.82		30
Northwest 西北	84	81	2,800	51	0.99	2.47	34.48	59.87	5,180
Shaanxi 陝西	32	88	1,775	-28	-0.74	-2.72	20.22	72.64	3,699
Gansu 甘肅	28	65	2,842	87	2.34	6.64	43.46	64.70	3,704
Qinghai 青海	4	25	18	-10	-4.76	-9.09	0.71	47.62	210
Ningxia 寧夏	2	65	400	15	0.63	100.00	6.15	99.58	2,365
Xinjiang 新疆	18	108	5,441	154	1.34	2.64	50.17	49.31	11,529

0810: Iron Ores Mining and Dressing 鐵礦採選業

Year 年份	Number of firms 企業個數	Rate of change 每年變化 (%)	Number of employees 職工人數 (人)	Rate of change 每年變化 (%)	Total revenue (mil. RMB) 總銷售收入 (百萬元)	Rate of change 每年變化 (%)	Total profit (mil. RMB) 總利潤 (百萬元)	Rate of change 每年變化 (%)
1993	1,482		211,247		5,916		545	
1994	1,578	6.48%	286,693	35.71%	7,544	27.50%	241	-55.79%
1995	1,692	7.22%	290,235	1.24%	8,721	15.61%	127	-47.40%
1996	1,632	-3.55%	292,658	0.83%	10,702	22.72%	213	68.15%

3 Major products* 3 種主要產品 *	Output 產量	Sales volume 銷售量	Unit 單位
a) Iron Ore 鐵礦石	93,622,110	78,642,572	ton 噸
b) Finished Iron Ore 鐵礦石成品礦	37,670,415	31,266,445	ton 噸

Top 10 firms by revenue (year founded) 收入排名前 10 家企業 (創辦年份)	City 城市	Province 省	Telephone / fax 電話 / 傳真	Number of employees 職工人數	Ownership 產業所有權	Revenue ('000 RMB) 銷售收入 (千元)	Profit ('000 RMB) (rank) 利潤 (千元) (排名)	Total assets ('000 RMB) 總資產 (千元)	Major products 主要產品
Ma'anshan Iron & Steel Corporation General Co. 馬鞍山馬鋼總公司(1993)	Ma'anshan 馬鞍山市	Anhui 安徽省	(0555)2882148 (0555)2888133	30,031	State-owned 國有	830,026	51267(1)	11,283,351	a,b
Zhejiang Li Tie Group Co. 浙江漓鐵集團公司(1959)	Shaoxing 紹興市	Zhejiang 浙江省	(0575)5058761 (0575)5150280	3,383	State-owned 國有	204,778	3697(20)	298,289	a,b
Yunnan Xin Ping Lu Kui Shan Mining and Smelting (Group) Co. Ltd. 雲南省新平魯奎山礦冶(集團)有限責任公司(1987)	Yuxi 玉溪市	Yunnan 雲南省	(0877)7080048 (0877)7080016	1,257	Joint stock 股份制	183,701	8056(3)	240,202	a,b
Guangdong Da Bao Shan Mining Co. Ltd. 廣東省大寶山礦(1970)	Shaoguan 韶關市	Guangdong 廣東省	(0751)6618321 (0751)6618216	4,909	State-owned 國有	149,919	40(516)	470,297	a,b
Shandong Jin Ling Iron Mine 山東金嶺鐵礦(1949)	Zibo 淄博市	Shandong 山東省	(0533)3081201 (0533)3081263	4,379	State-owned 國有	131,402	80(489)	397,295	a,b
Xuzhou Li Guo Iron Mine 徐州利國鐵礦(1950)	Xuzhou 徐州市	Jiangsu 江蘇省	(0516)6710173 (0516)6710173	4,858	State-owned 國有	112,824	-2924(732)	152,414	a,b
Miyun Metallurgy Mine Company 密雲縣冶金礦山公司(1985)	Beijing 北京市	Beijing 北京市	(010)69944227	447	State-owned 國有	102,221	8780(2)	283,299	a,b
Huangshi Lu Feng Mining Co. Ltd. 黃石市鹿峯礦業有限公司(1993)	Huangshi 黃石市	Hubei 湖北省	(0714)5418908	160	Collectively-owned 集體	99,475	1084(98)	39,789	a,b
Jiangsu Dong Li Group 江蘇東利集團(1984)	Xuzhou 徐州市	Jiangsu 江蘇省	(0516)6711487	1,516	Collectively-owned 集體	98,235	7763(4)	61,080	a
Liaoyang Gongchangling Industrial Company 遼陽市弓長嶺區工業公司(1995)	Liaoyang 遼陽市	Liaoning 遼寧省		450	Collectively-owned 集體	88,510	6270(9)	8,097	o

Top 10 Cities by Production Output 產出排名前 10 位城市	Province 省	Market share 市場份額	Number of firms 企業個數
Tangshan 唐山市	Hebei 河北省	10.89%	100
Ma'anshan 馬鞍山市	Anhui 安徽省	10.50%	13
Xinzhou 忻州市	Shanxi 山西省	4.54%	13
Handan 邯鄲市	Hebei 河北省	4.37%	69
Chengde 承德市	Hebei 河北省	4.22%	87
Tongshi 通什市	Hainan 海南省	3.78%	1
Liaoyang 遼陽市	Liaoning 遼寧省	2.92%	51
Ezhou 鄂州市	Hubei 湖北省	2.90%	19
Chaoyang 朝陽市	Liaoning 遼寧省	2.82%	50
Benxi 本溪市	Liaoning 遼寧省	2.64%	51

10 Major Wholesalers 10 家主要批發商	City 城市	Province 省	Telephone / Fax 電話 / 傳真
China Metallurgy Import & Export Liaoning Company 中國冶金進出口遼寧公司	Shenyang 瀋陽市	Liaoning 遼寧省	(024)23867070 (024)23875451
Liaoning Foreign Trade General Company 遼寧省對外貿易總公司	Dalian 大連市	Liaoning 遼寧省	(0411)3632157 (0411)3638243
Zhong Xin Trade Company 中信貿易公司	Beijing 北京市	Beijing 北京市	(010)64662170 (010)64662161
China Metallurgy Import & Export Shandong Company 中國冶金進出口山東公司	Qingdao 青島市	Shandong 山東省	(0532)2801118 (0532)2801331
Yongzhou Ferromanganese Mine Company 永州市錳鐵礦公司	Yongzhou 永州市	Hunan 湖南省	(0746)8464135
Zhengzhou Advanced Technology Industrial Development Zone Development General Company 鄭州高新技術產業開發區發展總公司	Zhengzhou 鄭州市	Henan 河南省	(0371)7981924 (0371)7981422
Guangdong Hardware Import & Export Group Company 廣東省五金進出口集團公司	Guangzhou 廣州市	Guangdong 廣東省	(020)87752204 (020)87752205
Xi Shan Shi Wu Kuang Trade Company 錫山市五礦貿易公司	Wuxi 無錫市	Jiangsu 江蘇省	(0510)7760988
Xiamen Ocean Petroleum Company 廈門海洋石油公司	Xiamen 廈門市	Fujian 福建省	(0592)2095495 (0592)2087292
Hainan Shen Hai Import & Export Co. Ltd. 海南深海進出口有限公司	Haikou 海口市	Hainan 海南省	(0898)6717646 (0898)6717639

*Also include sales by firms outside this industry.包括本行業以外廠家的銷售。"o" stands for "others". "o" 代表 "其他產品"。

0821: Manganese Ores Mining and Dressing 錳礦採選業

The industry accounts for 0.026% of the total revenue of China's industrial sector in 1996. The revenue growth rate of the industry is 13.3% from 1995, as compared to the growth rate of China's industrial sector, 9.51%. The rate of return on asset is -0.01%. 69.02% of all firms in the industry made a profit while 20.53% had negative returns. The top province in terms of the industry's revenue is Hunan, accounting for 42.28% of the total revenue.
本行業在1996年佔全行業總產值0.026%，行業年增長率為13.3%（全國工業年增長率9.51%）。行業的資產回報率-0.01%，69.02%的企業盈利，20.53%的企業虧損。銷售收入最高的省份為湖南省，佔本行業的42.28%。

	Total number of firms 企業總數	Total number of employees 職工總數	Total revenue (mil. RMB) 總銷售收入（百萬元）	Total profit (mil. RMB) 總利潤（百萬元）	Return on assets 資產利潤率 (%)	Return on equity 權益利潤率 (%)	Labour productivity ('000 RMB / worker) 勞動生產率（千元/人）	Debts / assets 資產負債率 (%)	Total assets (mil. RMB) 總資產（百萬元）
Industry Overall 行業總體	426	59,843	1,506		-0.01	-0.02	25.17	74.06	2,584

	Number of firms 企業個數	Average number of employees 平均職工人數	Average revenue ('000 RMB) 平均銷售收入（千元）	Average profit ('000 RMB) 平均利潤（千元）	Return on assets 資產利潤率 (%)	Return on equity 權益利潤率 (%)	Labour productivity ('000 RMB / worker) 勞動生產率（千元/人）	Average debts / assets 平均資產負債率(%)	Average Total assets ('000 RMB) 平均總資產（千元）
By ownership 產業所有權									
State-owned 國有	78	354	9,256	-551	-2.09	-8.63	26.14	75.78	26,359
Collectively-owned 集體	338	93	2,256	123	8.20	25.62	24.28	67.97	1,501
Privately-owned 私有	1	26	1,868	79	16.95	27.39	71.84	38.10	464
Domestic JVs 聯營	5	134	1,514	76	3.60	7.11	11.31	49.42	2,116
Joint stock 股份制	3	27	2,871	94	3.36	8.15	105.05	58.77	2,804
Foreign-funded 外資	1	9	205	-5	-0.78	-1.60	22.76	50.92	647
Overseas Chinese-funded 港澳台資	1	26	3,864	634	49.83	260.50	148.63	80.87	1,273
By size 規模									
Large 大型	1	8,147	250,867				30.79	95.63	617,206
Medium 中型	11	1,098	32,632				29.72	64.44	76,713
Small 小型	405	96	2,214				23.11	69.46	2,775
By regional distribution 地區分布									
Central-North 華北	12	54	1,428	141	5.36	203.61	26.57	97.40	2,628
Beijing 北京	1	88	2,200	500	20.75	-555.56	25.00	103.73	2,410
Tianjin 天津									
Hebei 河北	7	30	994	106	14.04	40.22	32.83	65.28	753
Shanxi 山西	3	110	2,660	150	1.90	-41.28	24.18	104.60	7,893
Inner Mongolia 內蒙	1	15							170
Northeast 東北	40	180	1,053	104	5.36	25.05	5.86	78.60	1,930
Liaoning 遼寧	40	180	1,053	104	5.36	25.05	5.86	78.60	1,930
Jilin 吉林									
Heilongjiang 黑龍江									
Central East 華東	25	60	2,168	-28	-1.20	-2.99	36.05	59.79	2,296
Shanghai 上海									
Jiangsu 江蘇									
Zhejiang 浙江	1	35	50				1.43	98.95	1,910
Anhui 安徽	5	51	968	-20	-1.98	-18.18	19.13	89.13	1,012
Fujian 福建	16	75	2,971	-39	-1.25	-2.77	39.61	54.78	3,099
Jiangxi 江西	3	5	590	10	3.53	33.33	118.00	89.41	283
Shandong 山東									
Central-South 中南	219	163	4,933	-68	-0.83	-3.11	30.35	73.26	8,178
Henan 河南	9	44	1,899	77	4.65	12.41	42.73	62.53	1,649
Hubei 湖北	3	63	9,970	1,497	27.55	45.54	157.42	39.51	5,433
Hunan 湖南	117	211	5,442	-94	-1.11	-6.74	25.74	83.52	8,505
Guangdong 廣東	12	79	4,263	163	2.67	6.82	54.19	60.83	6,080
Guangxi 廣西	78	120	4,429	-141	-1.59	-4.06	37.02	60.83	8,871
Hainan 海南									
Southwest 西南	98	135	2,842	95	1.69	6.86	21.00	75.38	5,648
Chongqing 重慶	37	68	1,030	-45	-2.16	-13.12	15.02	83.55	2,105
Sichuan 四川	13	82	2,837	457	4.54	14.32	34.59	68.30	10,056
Guizhou 貴州	39	149	1,300	28	1.02	4.74	8.71	78.36	2,727
Yunnan 雲南	8	470	18,959	505	1.71	6.90	40.32	75.21	29,514
Tibet 西藏									
Northwest 西北	32	52	1,043	8	0.33	1.67	20.12	80.25	2,278
Shaanxi 陝西	18	77	1,308	-31	-0.87	-6.27	16.91	86.08	3,559
Gansu 甘肅	11	19	873	72	10.81	16.95	45.07	35.98	665
Qinghai 青海									
Ningxia 寧夏									
Xinjiang 新疆	3	18	77	3	0.66	1.27	4.34	47.37	507

0821: Manganese Ores Mining and Dressing 錳礦採選業

Year 年份	Number of firms 企業個數	Rate of change 每年變化 (%)	Number of employees 職工人數 (人)	Rate of change 每年變化 (%)	Total revenue (mil. RMB) 總銷售收入 (百萬元)	Rate of change 每年變化 (%)	Total profit (mil. RMB) 總利潤 (百萬元)	Rate of change 每年變化 (%)
1993	419		43,595		1,356		47	
1994	424	1.19%	44,612	2.33%	1,315	-3.05%	-3	-105.81%
1995	433	2.12%	55,157	23.64%	1,329	1.11%	-40	-1385.88%
1996	426	-1.62%	59,843	8.50%	1,506	13.32%		

3 Major products* 3 種主要產品 *	Output 產量	Sales volume 銷售量	Unit 單位
a) Manganese Ore 錳礦石	6,797,117	6,661,175	ton 噸
b) Finished Manganese Ore 錳礦石成品礦	3,618,741	3,401,616	ton 噸
c) Carbon Ferromanganese 碳素錳鐵	87,778	83,9	ton 噸

Top 10 firms by revenue (year founded) 收入排名前 10 家企業 (創辦年份)	City 城市	Province 省	Telephone / fax 電話 / 傳真	Number of employees 職工人數	Ownership 產業所有權	Revenue ('000 RMB) 銷售收入 (千元)	Profit ('000 RMB) (rank) 利潤 (千元) (排名)	Total assets ('000 RMB) 總資產 (千元)	Major products 主要產品
Xiangtan Manganese Mine 湘潭錳礦(1914)	Xiangtan 湘潭市	Hunan 湖南省	(0732)8271538 (0732)8271238	7,057	State-owned 國有	155,888	-29921(134)	633,287	a,b,c
Yunnan Jianshui Manganese Mine 雲南建水錳礦(1958)	Gejiu 個舊市	Yunnan 雲南省	(0873)7652721 (0873)7653838	1,560	State-owned 國有	88,784	2805(4)	100,487	a,b,c
Yongzhou Zhi Shan Qu Zhushan Zhen Manganese Mine Company 永州市芝山區珠山鎮錳礦公司(1995)	Yongzhou 永州市	Hunan 湖南省	(0746)6222007	3,574	Collectively-owned 集體	82,860	12590(1)	7,620	a,b
Guangxi Daxin Manganese Mine 廣西大新錳礦(1963)	Pingxiang 憑祥市	Guangxi 廣西	(0771)3783189 (0771)3783899	1,553	State-owned 國有	55,186	864(13)	111,857	o
Hunan Yongzhou Shi Yan Tou Zhen Manganese Mine 永州市芝山區石岩頭鎮錳礦(1969)	Yongzhou 永州市	Hunan 湖南省	(0746)6551021	1,500	Collectively-owned 集體	49,720	4722(2)	3,560	a,b
Hunan Taojiang Manganese Mine 湖南省桃江錳礦(1964)	Yiyang 益陽市	Hunan 湖南省	(0737)8865080 (0737)8865353	1,998	State-owned 國有	37,916	-7118(133)	110,388	a,b,c
Guangxi Zhuangzu Autonomous Region Xia Tian Manganese Mine 廣西壯族自治區下田錳礦(1958)	Heshan 合山市	Guangxi 廣西	(0772)4362310	953	State-owned 國有	36,770	1159(11)	93,648	o
Yongzhou Zhi Shan Qu Shui Kou Shan Zhen Manganese Mine 永州市芝山區水口山鎮錳礦(1963)	Yongzhou 永州市	Hunan 湖南省	(0746)6591213	1,302	Collectively-owned 集體	31,400	3200(3)	10,490	a,b
Qinzhou Qinnan Huangwutun Zhen Kuang Hu Development Center 欽州市欽南區黃屋屯鎮礦戶開發中心(1996)	Qinzhou 欽州市	Guangxi 廣西	(0777)3525228	392	Collectively-owned 集體	30,960	2470(6)	3,740	o
Yunnan Wenshan Dou Nan Manganese Industry Co. Ltd. 雲南文山斗南錳業有限責任公司(1973)	Wenshan 文山縣	Yunnan 雲南省	(0876)3882337	732	State-owned 國有	30,824	220(45)	72,219	a,b,c

Top 10 Cities by Production Output 產出排名前 10 位城市	Province 省	Market share 市場份額	Number of firms 企業個數
Qinzhou 欽州市	Guangxi 廣西	16.79%	10
Yongzhou 永州市	Hunan 湖南省	13.55%	35
Xiangtan 湘潭市	Hunan 湖南省	10.97%	10
Pingxiang 憑祥市	Guangxi 廣西	9.57%	18
Gejiu 個舊市	Yunnan 雲南省	5.27%	7
Heshan 合山市	Guangxi 廣西	4.36%	12
Chenzhou 郴州市	Hunan 湖南省	3.80%	12
Lingchuan 靈川縣	Guangxi 廣西	3.80%	30
Tongren 銅仁市	Guizhou 貴州省	3.21%	18
Wenshan 文山縣	Yunnan 雲南省	3.09%	4

10 Major Wholesalers 10 家主要批發商	City 城市	Province 省	Telephone / Fax 電話 / 傳真
China Metallurgy Import & Export Liaoning Company 中國冶金進出口遼寧公司	Shenyang 瀋陽市	Liaoning 遼寧省	(024)23867070 (024)23875451
Liaoning Foreign Trade General Company 遼寧省對外貿易總公司	Dalian 大連市	Liaoning 遼寧省	(0411)3632157 (0411)3638243
Zhong Xin Trade Company 中信貿易公司	Beijing 北京市	Beijing 北京市	(010)64662170 (010)64662161
China Metallurgy Import & Export Shandong Company 中國冶金進出口山東公司	Qingdao 青島市	Shandong 山東省	(0532)2801118 (0532)2801331
Yongzhou Ferromanganese Mine Company 永州市錳鐵礦公司	Yongzhou 永州市	Hunan 湖南省	(0746)8464135
Zhengzhou Advanced Technology Industrial Development Zone Development General Company 鄭州高新技術產業開發區發展總公司	Zhengzhou 鄭州市	Henan 河南省	(0371)7981924 (0371)7981422
Guangdong Hardware Import & Export Group Company 廣東省五金進出口集團公司	Guangzhou 廣州市	Guangdong 廣東省	(020)87752204 (020)87752205
Xi Shan Shi Wu Kuang Trade Company 錫山市五礦貿易公司	Wuxi 無錫市	Jiangsu 江蘇省	(0510)7760988
Xiamen Ocean Petroleum Company 廈門海洋石油公司	Xiamen 廈門市	Fujian 福建省	(0592)2095495 (0592)2087292
Hainan Shen Hai Import & Export Co. Ltd. 海南深海進出口有限公司	Haikou 海口市	Hainan 海南省	(0898)6717646 (0898)6717639

*Also include sales by firms outside this industry.包括本行業以外廠家的銷售。"o" stands for "others". "o" 代表"其他產品"。

0822: Chrome Ores Mining and Dressing 鉻礦採選業

The industry accounts for 0.003% of the total revenue of China's industrial sector in 1996. The revenue growth rate of the industry is 70.0% from 1995, as compared to the growth rate of China's industrial sector, 9.51%. The rate of return on asset is 7.14%. 85.71% of all firms in the industry made a profit while 14.29% had negative returns. The top province in terms of the industry's revenue is Tibet, accounting for 80.40% of the total revenue.
本行業在1996年佔全行業總產值0.003%，行業年增長率為70.0%（全國工業年增長率9.51%）。行業的資產回報率7.14%，85.71%的企業盈利，14.29%的企業虧損。銷售收入最高的省份為西藏，佔本行業的80.40%。

	Total number of firms 企業總數	Total number of employees 職工總數	Total revenue (mil. RMB) 總銷售收入（百萬元）	Total profit (mil. RMB) 總利潤（百萬元）	Return on assets 資產利潤率 (%)	Return on equity 權益利潤率 (%)	Labour productivity ('000 RMB / worker) 勞動生產率（千元/人）	Debts / assets 資產負債率 (%)	Total assets (mil. RMB) 總資產（百萬元）
Industry Overall 行業總體	19	1,144	185	27	7.14	12.99	161.71	45.02	380

	Number of firms 企業個數	Average number of employees 平均職工人數	Average revenue ('000 RMB) 平均銷售收入（千元）	Average profit ('000 RMB) 平均利潤（千元）	Return on assets 資產利潤率 (%)	Return on equity 權益利潤率 (%)	Labour productivity ('000 RMB / worker) 勞動生產率（千元/人）	Average debts / assets 平均資產負債率(%)	Average Total assets ('000 RMB) 平均總資產（千元）
By ownership 產業所有權									
State-owned 國有	7	111	20,286	3,571	8.28	15.06	182.75	45.03	43,143
Collectively-owned 集體	12	31	3,583	167	2.56	4.65	117.15	44.87	6,500
Privately-owned 私有									
Domestic JVs 聯營									
Joint stock 股份制									
Foreign-funded 外資									
Overseas Chinese-funded 港澳台資									
By size 規模									
Large 大型									
Medium 中型	1	271	73,450	1,717	0.95	1.42	271.03	33.07	180,412
Small 小型	18	49	6,197	1,404	12.66	28.63	127.77	55.78	11,087
By regional distribution 地區分布									
Central-North 華北	2	13	140				11.20	54.32	1,215
Beijing 北京									
Tianjin 天津									
Hebei 河北									
Shanxi 山西									
Inner Mongolia 內蒙	2	13	140				11.20	54.32	1,215
Northeast 東北									
Liaoning 遼寧									
Jilin 吉林									
Heilongjiang 黑龍江									
Central East 華東									
Shanghai 上海									
Jiangsu 江蘇									
Zhejiang 浙江									
Anhui 安徽									
Fujian 福建									
Jiangxi 江西									
Shandong 山東									
Central-South 中南	2	33	1,755	-45	-2.11	-5.36	54.00	60.80	2,130
Henan 河南	1	5	1,020	-100	-3.91	-11.63	204.00	66.41	2,560
Hubei 湖北									
Hunan 湖南	1	60	2,490	10	0.59	1.22	41.50	52.35	1,700
Guangdong 廣東									
Guangxi 廣西									
Hainan 海南									
Southwest 西南	7	63	21,249	3,271	6.85	11.88	336.52	42.35	47,743
Chongqing 重慶									
Sichuan 四川									
Guizhou 貴州									
Yunnan 雲南									
Tibet 西藏	7	63	21,249	3,271	6.85	11.88	336.52	42.35	47,743
Northwest 西北	8	77	4,054	545	11.07	32.08	52.99	65.46	4,921
Shaanxi 陝西	3	103	4,447	37	0.86	3.00	43.17	71.17	4,243
Gansu 甘肅	2	103	6,080	940	11.24	40.96	59.03	72.55	8,360
Qinghai 青海	2	23	2,665	1,005	26.55	63.21	115.87	57.86	3,785
Ningxia 寧夏									
Xinjiang 新疆	1	51	1,600	360	15.32	16.74	31.37	8.51	2,350

0822: Chrome Ores Mining and Dressing 鉻礦採選業

Year 年份	Number of firms 企業個數	Rate of change 每年變化 (%)	Number of employees 職工人數 (人)	Rate of change 每年變化 (%)	Total revenue (mil. RMB) 總銷售收入 (百萬元)	Rate of change 每年變化 (%)	Total profit (mil. RMB) 總利潤 (百萬元)	Rate of change 每年變化 (%)
1993	12		2,153		44		8	
1994	16	33.33%	2,149	-0.19%	42	-4.70%	1	-88.57%
1995	16	0	2,319	7.91%	109	157.96%	14	1493.01%
1996	19	18.75%	1,144	-50.67%	185	70.02%	27	97.54%

3 Major products* 3 種主要產品 *	Output 產量	Sales volume 銷售量	Unit 單位
a) Chrome Ore 鉻礦石	130,200	123,690	ton 噸
b) Finished Chrome Ore 鉻礦石成品礦	64,486	67,711	ton 噸

Top 10 firms by revenue (year founded) 收入排名前 10 家企業 (創辦年份)	City 城市	Province 省	Telephone / fax 電話 / 傳真	Number of employees 職工人數	Ownership 產業所有權	Revenue ('000 RMB) 銷售收入 (千元)	Profit ('000 RMB) (rank) 利潤 (千元) (排名)	Total assets ('000 RMB) 總資產 (千元)	Major products 主要產品
Liuba Chengguanzhen Mining Factory 留壩縣城關鎮採礦廠(1979)	Hanzhong 漢中市	Shaanxi 陝西省	(0916)3921353	160	Collectively-owned 集體	12,510	620(3)	8,870	o
Subei Mongol Autonomous County Chrome Development Co. 肅北蒙古族自治縣鉻業開發公司(1993)	Yumen 玉門市	Gansu 甘肅省	(0937)8122505	86	State-owned 國有	10,550	1800(2)	15,270	a,b
Qinghai Qi Lianxian Mining and Smelting General Company 青海省祁連縣礦冶總公司(1987)	Menyuan 門源縣	Qinghai 青海省	(0978)672525	46	State-owned 國有	5,327	2005(1)	7,567	a

Top 10 Cities by Production Output 產出排名前 10 位城市	Province 省	Market share 市場份額	Number of firms 企業個數
Nedong 乃東縣	Tibet 西藏	57.44%	4
Yumen 玉門市	Gansu 甘肅省	11.96%	1
Nagqu 那曲縣	Tibet 西藏	9.68%	2
Menyuan 門源縣	Qinghai 青海省	7.09%	1
Shangzhou 商州市	Shaanxi 陝西省	4.95%	2
Tacheng 塔城市	Xinjiang 新疆	3.57%	3
Changsha 長沙市	Hunan 湖南省	3.12%	1
Sanmenxia 三門峽市	Henan 河南省	1.04%	1
Lhasa 拉薩市	Tibet 西藏	0.71%	2
Erenhot 二連浩特市	Inner Mong 內蒙	0.29%	1

10 Major Wholesalers 10 家主要批發商	City 城市	Province 省	Telephone / Fax 電話 / 傳真
China Metallurgy Import & Export Liaoning Company 中國冶金進出口遼寧公司	Shenyang 瀋陽市	Liaoning 遼寧省	(024)23867070 (024)23875451
Liaoning Foreign Trade General Company 遼寧省對外貿易總公司	Dalian 大連市	Liaoning 遼寧省	(0411)3632157 (0411)3638243
Zhong Xin Trade Company 中信貿易公司	Beijing 北京市	Beijing 北京市	(010)64662170 (010)64662161
China Metallurgy Import & Export Shandong Company 中國冶金進出口山東公司	Qingdao 青島市	Shandong 山東省	(0532)2801118 (0532)2801331
Yongzhou Ferromanganese Mine Company 永州市錳鐵礦公司	Yongzhou 永州市	Hunan 湖南省	(0746)8464135
Zhengzhou Advanced Technology Industrial Development Zone Development General Company 鄭州高新技術產業開發區發展總公司	Zhengzhou 鄭州市	Henan 河南省	(0371)7981924 (0371)7981422
Guangdong Hardware Import & Export Group Company 廣東省五金進出口集團公司	Guangzhou 廣州市	Guangdong 廣東省	(020)87752204 (020)87752205
Xi Shan Shi Wu Kuang Trade Company 錫山市五礦貿易公司	Wuxi 無錫市	Jiangsu 江蘇省	(0510)7760988
Xiamen Ocean Petroleum Company 廈門海洋石油公司	Xiamen 廈門市	Fujian 福建省	(0592)2095495 (0592)2087292
Hainan Shen Hai Import & Export Co. Ltd. 海南深海進出口有限公司	Haikou 海口市	Hainan 海南省	(0898)6717646 (0898)6717639

*Also include sales by firms outside this industry.包括本行業以外廠家的銷售。"o" stands for "others". "o" 代表 "其他產品"。

0911: Copper Ores Mining and Dressing 銅礦採選業

The industry accounts for 0.105% of the total revenue of China's industrial sector in 1996. The revenue growth rate of the industry is 5.5% from 1995, as compared to the growth rate of China's industrial sector, 9.51%. The rate of return on asset is -1.07%. 76.24% of all firms in the industry made a profit while 17.01% had negative returns. The top province in terms of the industry's revenue is Jiangxi, accounting for 36.50% of the total revenue.
本行業在1996年佔全行業總產值0.105%，行業年增長率為5.5%（全國工業年增長率9.51%）。行業的資產回報率-1.07%，76.24%的企業盈利，17.01%的企業虧損。銷售收入最高的省份為江西省，佔本行業的36.50%。

	Total number of firms 企業總數	Total number of employees 職工總數	Total revenue (mil. RMB) 總銷售收入（百萬元）	Total profit (mil. RMB) 總利潤（百萬元）	Return on assets 資產利潤率 (%)	Return on equity 權益利潤率 (%)	Labour productivity ('000 RMB / worker) 勞動生產率（千元/人）	Debts / assets 資產負債率 (%)	Total assets (mil. RMB) 總資產（百萬元）
Industry Overall 行業總體	478	148,052	6,076	-125	-1.07	-4.22	41.04	74.54	11,616

	Number of firms 企業個數	Average number of employees 平均職工人數	Average revenue ('000 RMB) 平均銷售收入（千元）	Average profit ('000 RMB) 平均利潤（千元）	Return on assets 資產利潤率 (%)	Return on equity 權益利潤率 (%)	Labour productivity ('000 RMB / worker) 勞動生產率（千元/人）	Average debts / assets 平均資產負債率(%)	Average Total assets ('000 RMB) 平均總資產（千元）
By ownership 產業所有權									
State-owned 國有	99	1,210	50,343	-1,808	-1.68	-6.97	41.60	75.92	107,747
Collectively-owned 集體	353	76	2,880	167	7.12	19.42	38.00	63.37	2,347
Privately-owned 私有	1	27	1,127	100	6.65	12.23	41.75	45.63	1,501
Domestic JVs 聯營	10	74	3,501	247	8.02	15.42	47.11	47.98	3,074
Joint stock 股份制	8	124	2,908	26	0.46	0.61	23.50	24.33	5,654
Foreign-funded 外資	2	65	1,419				22.00	42.05	282
Overseas Chinese-funded 港澳台資	4	200	3,035	-1,985	-19.62	-24.68	15.16	20.48	10,116
By size 規模									
Large 大型	8	7,112	384,453	-6,590	-0.85	-5.28	54.06	83.86	773,786
Medium 中型	25	1,641	60,298	2,571	2.22	6.80	36.75	67.35	115,835
Small 小型	418	117	3,571	-326	-5.39	-13.50	30.40	60.09	6,044
By regional distribution 地區分布									
Central-North 華北	52	290	8,038	92	0.51	3.01	27.72	82.98	18,000
Beijing 北京	1	50	1,190	20	3.33	4.76	23.80	30.00	600
Tianjin 天津									
Hebei 河北	9	687	22,500	212	0.67	3.03	32.76	77.91	31,747
Shanxi 山西	19	75	1,936	51	1.17	2.06	25.78	43.03	4,359
Inner Mongolia 內蒙	23	323	7,717	82	0.33	3.89	23.93	91.42	24,647
Northeast 東北	19	789	23,935	-214	-0.65	-1.74	30.33	62.62	32,857
Liaoning 遼寧	15	653	23,780	-181	-0.62	-1.75	36.40	64.53	29,183
Jilin 吉林	1	1,482							
Heilongjiang 黑龍江	3	1,237	32,690	-453	-0.73	-1.74	26.42	58.14	62,177
Central East 華東	109	423	27,626	-979	-1.76	-11.36	65.31	84.47	55,479
Shanghai 上海									
Jiangsu 江蘇	2	869	15,360	110	0.25	1.26	17.69	79.86	43,405
Zhejiang 浙江	2	1,169	85,625	3,875	3.08	5.64	73.28	45.37	125,685
Anhui 安徽	60	210	7,463	394	4.57	11.60	35.53	60.64	8,620
Fujian 福建	5	79	3,554	638	22.21	54.25	45.10	59.05	2,872
Jiangxi 江西	35	713	63,370	-3,661	-2.67	-24.09	88.93	88.93	137,257
Shandong 山東	5	819	25,166	-2,660	-3.56	-31.09	30.72	88.55	74,698
Central-South 中南	119	174	6,551	151	1.89	4.08	37.74	53.63	7,963
Henan 河南	12	129	3,632	34	0.45	0.94	28.06	51.78	7,579
Hubei 湖北	55	187	6,019	197	2.86	8.61	32.23	66.74	6,882
Hunan 湖南	23	207	5,087	-441	-4.54	-7.89	24.53	42.44	9,720
Guangdong 廣東	8	258	19,870	1,206	5.73	11.94	76.90	51.99	21,044
Guangxi 廣西	21	95	6,145	343	8.35	11.96	64.59	30.23	4,108
Hainan 海南									
Southwest 西南	83	499	13,607	-482	-1.56	-3.82	27.28	59.13	30,834
Chongqing 重慶		34							
Sichuan 四川	23	246	7,863	415	1.77	3.02	31.85	41.34	23,374
Guizhou 貴州	3	95	2,127	57	1.25	2.21	22.39	43.45	4,527
Yunnan 雲南	55	643	17,072	-905	-2.50	-7.03	26.57	64.40	36,192
Tibet 西藏	1		600	-30	-0.31	-0.31			9,680
Northwest 西北	96	102	2,946	34	0.66	2.34	28.81	71.92	5,225
Shaanxi 陝西	38	106	3,144	73	1.40	5.43	29.66	74.28	5,241
Gansu 甘肅	42	88	3,034	155	2.79	11.80	34.39	76.36	5,566
Qinghai 青海	6	270	5,257	-980	-11.20	-23.70	19.51	52.77	8,752
Ningxia 寧夏	2	23	150	5	20.00	25.00	6.52		25
Xinjiang 新疆	8	53	513	-18	-0.87	-1.47	9.76	40.86	2,016

0911: Copper Ores Mining and Dressing 銅礦採選業

Year 年份	Number of firms 企業個數	Rate of change 每年變化 (%)	Number of employees 職工人數 (人)	Rate of change 每年變化 (%)	Total revenue (mil. RMB) 總銷售收入 (百萬元)	Rate of change 每年變化 (%)	Total profit (mil. RMB) 總利潤 (百萬元)	Rate of change 每年變化 (%)
1993	363		127,402		3,751		-102	
1994	385	6.06%	138,508	8.72%	4,367	16.41%	-15	85.20%
1995	512	32.99%	155,130	12.00%	5,757	31.84%	59	491.26%
1996	478	-6.64%	148,052	-4.56%	6,076	5.54%	-125	-310.80%

3 Major products* 3 種主要產品 *	Output 產量	Sales volume 銷售量	Unit 單位

Top 10 firms by revenue (year founded) 收入排名前10家企業 (創辦年份)	City 城市	Province 省	Telephone / fax 電話 / 傳真	Number of employees 職工人數	Ownership 產業所有權	Revenue ('000 RMB) 銷售收入 (千元)	Profit ('000 RMB) (rank) 利潤 (千元) (排名)	Total assets ('000 RMB) 總資產 (千元)	Major products 主要產品
Jiangxi Copper Industry Co. Ltd. Dexing Copper Mine 江西省銅業公司德興市銅礦	Shangrao 上饒市	Jiangxi 江西省	(0793)7520279 (0793)3850001	10,997	State-owned 國有	1,516,564	-123737(163)	3,549,720	o
Yong Ping Copper Mine 永平銅礦(1985)	Shangrao 上饒市	Jiangxi 江西省	(0793)3755113	4,078	State-owned 國有	364,537	72143(1)	426,743	o
Yimen Mining Administration 易門礦務局(1960)	Yuxi 玉溪市	Yunnan 雲南省	(0877)4981142 (0877)4981414	7,843	State-owned 國有	281,395	63(98)	737,903	o
Dongchuan Mining Administration 東川礦務局(1960)	Dongchuan 東川市	Yunnan 雲南省	(0881)2528973 (0881)2528020	14,838	State-owned 國有	250,460	-33000(161)	507,410	o
Fushun Hong Tou Shan Copper Mine 撫順紅透山銅礦(1948)	Fushun 撫順市	Liaoning 遼寧省	(0413)3265313 (0413)3265924	5,507	State-owned 國有	215,373	1199(27)	248,871	o
Meizhou Jin Yan Copper Industry Company 梅州市金雁銅業公司(1996)	Meizhou 梅州市	Guangdong 廣東省	(0752)2352718 (0752)2352718	1,447	State-owned 國有	145,696	9808(3)	141,518	o
Huanren Copper & Zinc Mine 桓仁銅鋅礦(1951)	Benxi 本溪市	Liaoning 遼寧省	(0414)8172372	3,788	State-owned 國有	127,478	-4959(154)	180,497	o
Yunnan Dayao Copper Mine 雲南大姚銅礦(1976)	Chuxiong 楚雄市	Yunnan 雲南省	(0878)6386329	3,717	State-owned 國有	126,030	100(91)	225,120	o
Jiangxi Da Mao Shan Copper Mine 大茅山銅礦	Shangrao 上饒市	Jiangxi 江西省	(0793)7560046 (0793)7560039	1,791	State-owned 國有	120,406	-2168(149)	233,370	o
Laiyuan Copper Mine 淶源銅礦(1972)	Baoding 保定市	Hebei 河北省	(0312)7391588	1,422	State-owned 國有	114,018	368(47)	53,100	o

Top 10 Cities by Production Output 產出排名前10位城市	Province 省	Market share 市場份額	Number of firms 企業個數
Yuxi 玉溪市	Yunnan 雲南省	20.03%	4
Dongchuan 東川市	Yunnan 雲南省	18.26%	2
Meizhou 梅州市	Guangdong 廣東省	8.63%	1
Hangzhou 杭州市	Zhejiang 浙江省	7.38%	1
Tongling 銅陵市	Anhui 安徽省	5.50%	8
Gejiu 個舊市	Yunnan 雲南省	5.07%	11
Xuanzhou 宣州市	Anhui 安徽省	4.07%	2
Chuzhou 滁州市	Anhui 安徽省	3.65%	1
Nanning 南寧市	Guangxi 廣西	2.73%	15
Menyuan 門源縣	Qinghai 青海省	2.25%	2

10 Major Wholesalers 10家主要批發商	City 城市	Province 省	Telephone / Fax 電話 / 傳真
China Metallurgy Import & Export Liaoning Company 中國冶金進出口遼寧公司	Shenyang 瀋陽市	Liaoning 遼寧省	(024)23867070 (024)23875451
Liaoning Foreign Trade General Company 遼寧省對外貿易總公司	Dalian 大連市	Liaoning 遼寧省	(0411)3632157 (0411)3638243
Zhong Xin Trade Company 中信貿易公司	Beijing 北京市	Beijing 北京市	(010)64662170 (010)64662161
China Metallurgy Import & Export Shandong Company 中國冶金進出口山東公司	Qingdao 青島市	Shandong 山東省	(0532)2801118 (0532)2801331
Yongzhou Ferromanganese Mine Company 永州市錳鐵礦公司	Yongzhou 永州市	Hunan 湖南省	(0746)8464135
Zhengzhou Advanced Technology Industrial Development Zone Development General Company 鄭州高新技術產業開發區發展總公司	Zhengzhou 鄭州市	Henan 河南省	(0371)7981924 (0371)7981422
Guangdong Hardware Import & Export Group Company 廣東省五金進出口集團公司	Guangzhou 廣州市	Guangdong 廣東省	(020)87752204 (020)87752205
Xi Shan Shi Wu Kuang Trade Company 錫山市五礦貿易公司	Wuxi 無錫市	Jiangsu 江蘇省	(0510)7760988
Xiamen Ocean Petroleum Company 廈門海洋石油公司	Xiamen 廈門市	Fujian 福建省	(0592)2095495 (0592)2087292
Hainan Shen Hai Import & Export Co. Ltd. 海南深海進出口有限公司	Haikou 海口市	Hainan 海南省	(0898)6717646 (0898)6717639

*Also include sales by firms outside this industry.包括本行業以外廠家的銷售。"o" stands for "others". "o" 代表 "其他產品"。

0912: Lead and Zinc Ores Mining and Dressing 鉛鋅礦採選業

The industry accounts for 0.090% of the total revenue of China's industrial sector in 1996. The revenue growth rate of the industry is 0.1% from 1995, as compared to the growth rate of China's industrial sector, 9.51%. The rate of return on asset is 2.13%. 78.37% of all firms in the industry made a profit while 14.89% had negative returns. The top province in terms of the industry's revenue is Guangxi, accounting for 20.24% of the total revenue.
本行業在1996年佔全行業總產值0.090%，行業年增長率為0.1%（全國工業年增長率9.51%）。行業的資產回報率2.13%，78.37%的企業盈利，14.89%的企業虧損。銷售收入最高的省份為廣西省，佔本行業的20.24%。

	Total number of firms 企業總數	Total number of employees 職工總數	Total revenue (mil. RMB) 總銷售收入（百萬元）	Total profit (mil. RMB) 總利潤（百萬元）	Return on assets 資產利潤率 (%)	Return on equity 權益利潤率 (%)	Labour productivity ('000 RMB / worker) 勞動生產率（千元/人）	Debts / assets 資產負債率 (%)	Total assets (mil. RMB) 總資產（百萬元）
Industry Overall 行業總體	807	131,645	5,200	151	2.13	5.49	39.50	61.09	7,054

	Number of firms 企業個數	Average number of employees 平均職工人數	Average revenue ('000 RMB) 平均銷售收入（千元）	Average profit ('000 RMB) 平均利潤（千元）	Return on assets 資產利潤率 (%)	Return on equity 權益利潤率 (%)	Labour productivity ('000 RMB / worker) 勞動生產率（千元/人）	Average debts / assets 平均資產負債率(%)	Average Total assets ('000 RMB) 平均總資產（千元）
By ownership 產業所有權									
State-owned 國有	133	613	17,662	-233	-0.64	-1.61	28.82	60.19	36,316
Collectively-owned 集體	624	73	4,003	266	9.30	25.31	54.84	63.25	2,861
Privately-owned 私有	1	50	546	-1,170	-57.82	3412.71	10.91	101.69	2,024
Domestic JVs 聯營	22	64	3,979	-111	-2.11	-7.31	61.95	71.10	5,250
Joint stock 股份制	13	189	13,534	550	3.50	8.25	71.67	57.51	15,706
Foreign-funded 外資	8	34	2,804	123	3.33	4.70	81.58	29.15	3,686
Overseas Chinese-funded 港澳台資	7	58	9,695	1,608	12.77	44.77	166.34	71.47	12,587
By size 規模									
Large 大型	5	3,439	230,488	13,754	4.29	7.71	67.02	44.30	320,405
Medium 中型	31	1,340	39,707	-251	-0.35	-1.12	29.63	68.38	71,066
Small 小型	739	97	3,812	122	2.77	7.78	39.16	64.42	4,397
By regional distribution 地區分布									
Central-North 華北	62	205	6,590	136	1.26	3.43	32.20	63.27	10,762
Beijing 北京	1								
Tianjin 天津									
Hebei 河北	16	42	2,531	234	11.53	42.66	60.52	72.94	2,033
Shanxi 山西	2	46	1,325	10	0.38	0.52	29.12	26.29	2,625
Inner Mongolia 內蒙	43	277	8,499	108	0.74	2.00	30.63	63.07	14,639
Northeast 東北	62	204	6,162	-70	-0.92	-3.57	30.26	74.32	7,643
Liaoning 遼寧	54	177	6,363	-87	-1.26	-6.29	35.85	80.04	6,964
Jilin 吉林	7	363	4,834	50	0.42	0.82	13.31	48.54	11,850
Heilongjiang 黑龍江	1	499	4,620	20	0.13	0.51	9.26	73.38	14,840
Central East 華東	78	163	7,272	-293	-2.23	-5.80	44.72	61.62	13,146
Shanghai 上海									
Jiangsu 江蘇	5	541	29,226	1,544	2.05	5.73	54.06	64.26	75,404
Zhejiang 浙江	18	125	5,216	316	2.78	4.35	41.87	35.98	11,359
Anhui 安徽	9	109	7,783	339	4.36	51.43	71.41	91.53	7,781
Fujian 福建	20	69	2,666	-104	-3.21	-7.95	38.44	59.69	3,229
Jiangxi 江西	24	217	8,144	-1,582	-12.62	-39.48	37.45	68.02	12,529
Shandong 山東	2	76	4,215	370	8.63	-296.00	55.46	102.92	4,285
Central-South 中南	295	162	7,751	199	2.29	5.12	47.89	55.29	8,697
Henan 河南	38	59	3,527	475	9.26	32.95	59.88	71.90	5,133
Hubei 湖北	2	19	835	85	10.83	29.31	45.14	62.42	785
Hunan 湖南	103	268	9,167	51	0.43	0.90	34.25	52.21	11,829
Guangdong 廣東	36	83	4,278	-94	-1.55	-5.15	51.29	69.90	6,091
Guangxi 廣西	116	128	9,073	333	4.14	8.71	70.63	52.41	8,029
Hainan 海南									
Southwest 西南	134	177	5,368	431	4.65	10.15	30.32	54.16	9,252
Chongqing 重慶	1	225	10,237	50	19.42	22.14	45.32	12.29	257
Sichuan 四川	27	151	5,137	230	2.45	4.60	33.85	46.78	9,415
Guizhou 貴州	60	92	2,254	59	1.90	3.41	24.42	44.18	3,071
Yunnan 雲南	42	310	9,929	1,129	6.87	18.13	32.06	62.08	16,419
Tibet 西藏	3	222	3,243	133	0.37	0.60	14.61	38.35	36,023
Northwest 西北	176	126	4,754	301	4.90	19.70	37.73	75.11	6,148
Shaanxi 陝西	97	94	3,614	104	2.03	9.86	38.48	79.41	5,096
Gansu 甘肅	64	141	7,380	688	8.06	26.71	52.47	69.83	8,542
Qinghai 青海	12	337	1,151	-85	-2.53	-44.54	3.42	94.32	3,358
Ningxia 寧夏									
Xinjiang 新疆	3	8	10	-3	-1.25	-3.33	1.20	62.50	267

0912: Lead and Zinc Ores Mining and Dressing 鉛鋅礦採選業

Year 年份	Number of firms 企業個數	Rate of change 每年變化 (%)	Number of employees 職工人數 (人)	Rate of change 每年變化 (%)	Total revenue (mil. RMB) 總銷售收入 (百萬元)	Rate of change 每年變化 (%)	Total profit (mil. RMB) 總利潤 (百萬元)	Rate of change 每年變化 (%)
1993	603		105,793		2,861		56	
1994	587	-2.65%	121,854	15.18%	3,829	33.81%	90	60.23%
1995	762	29.81%	147,031	20.66%	5,193	35.64%	264	193.37%
1996	807	5.91%	131,645	-10.46%	5,200	0.13%	151	-42.70%

3 Major products* 3 種主要產品 *	Output 產量	Sales volume 銷售量	Unit 單位

Top 10 firms by revenue (year founded) 收入排名前10家企業 (創辦年份)	City 城市	Province 省	Telephone / fax 電話 / 傳真	Number of employees 職工人數	Ownership 產業所有權	Revenue ('000 RMB) 銷售收入 (千元)	Profit ('000 RMB) (rank) 利潤 (千元) (排名)	Total assets ('000 RMB) 總資產 (千元)	Major products 主要產品
Xitie Shan Mine Administrative Bureau 錫鐵山礦務局(1983)	Golmud 格爾木市	Qinghai 青海省	(0979)222844 (0979)221491	3,362	State-owned 國有	320,521	4515(17)	530,393	o
Hunan Huang Shaping Lead-zinc Mine 湖南黃沙坪鉛鋅礦(1967)	Chenzhou 郴州市	Hunan 湖南省	(0735)4421160 (0735)4421175	3,737	State-owned 國有	157,127	16206(1)	182,164	o
Qing Cheng Zi Lead Mine 青城子鉛礦(1949)	Dandong 丹東市	Liaoning 遼寧省	(0415)8551180 (0415)8551405	3,314	State-owned 國有	113,160	-10060(369)	96,100	o
Tao Lin Lead & Zinc Mine 桃林鉛鋅礦(1959)	Yueyang 岳陽市	Hunan 湖南省	(0730)3689403 (0730)3688778	3,828	State-owned 國有	101,923	-11002(370)	153,827	o
Lanping Baizu Primi Autonomous County Lead-zinc Mine 蘭坪白族普米族自治縣鉛鋅礦(1973)	Lushui 瀘水縣	Yunnan 雲南省	(0886)3211672	1,182	State-owned 國有	89,702	8414(5)	147,882	o
Heilongjiang Xilin Lead & Zinc Mine 黑龍江西林鉛鋅礦(1969)	Yichun 伊春市	Heilongjiang 黑龍江省	(0458)3714720	3,038	State-owned 國有	76,861	-246(329)	153,329	o
Nanjing Xixia Shan Xin Yang Mining Co. Ltd. 南京栖霞山鋅陽礦業有限公司(1995)	Nanjing 南京市	Jiangsu 江蘇省	(025)5761651 (025)5761981	766	State-owned 國有	72,766	1014(68)	127,276	o
Huludao Ba Jia Zi Lead & Zinc Mine 葫蘆島八家子鉛鋅礦(1969)	Huludao 葫蘆島市	Liaoning 遼寧省	(0429)7530195	2,399	State-owned 國有	65,323	-2032(358)	112,283	o
Huili Zinc Mine 會理鋅礦(1952)	Xichang 西昌市	Sichuan 四川省	(0834)22140 (0834)22078	2,175	State-owned 國有	64,779	1091(64)	162,789	o
Yunnan Lancang Lead Mine 雲南瀾滄鉛礦(1955)	Simao 思茅市	Yunnan 雲南省	(0879)7222021 (0879)7222717	2,254	State-owned 國有	62,660	656(101)	135,472	o

Top 10 Cities by Production Output 產出排名前10位城市	Province 省	Market share 市場份額	Number of firms 企業個數
Wudu 武都縣	Gansu 甘肅省	36.54%	37
Hechi 河池市	Guangxi 廣西	14.51%	50
Golmud 格爾木市	Qinghai 青海省	9.31%	5
Xichang 西昌市	Sichuan 四川省	6.15%	79
Chenzhou 郴州市	Hunan 湖南省	2.73%	22
Nanjing 南京市	Jiangsu 江蘇省	2.20%	1
Baoji 寶雞市	Shaanxi 陝西省	2.05%	26
Anshan 鞍山市	Liaoning 遼寧省	1.99%	4
Sanmenxia 三門峽市	Henan 河南省	1.78%	8
Lingchuan 靈川縣	Guangxi 廣西	1.77%	8

10 Major Wholesalers 10家主要批發商	City 城市	Province 省	Telephone / Fax 電話 / 傳真
China Metallurgy Import & Export Liaoning Company 中國冶金進出口遼寧公司	Shenyang 瀋陽市	Liaoning 遼寧省	(024)23867070 (024)23875451
Liaoning Foreign Trade General Company 遼寧省對外貿易總公司	Dalian 大連市	Liaoning 遼寧省	(0411)3632157 (0411)3638243
Zhong Xin Trade Company 中信貿易公司	Beijing 北京市	Beijing 北京市	(010)64662170 (010)64662161
China Metallurgy Import & Export Shandong Company 中國冶金進出口山東公司	Qingdao 青島市	Shandong 山東省	(0532)2801118 (0532)2801331
Yongzhou Ferromanganese Mine Company 永州市錳鐵礦公司	Yongzhou 永州市	Hunan 湖南省	(0746)8464135
Zhengzhou Advanced Technology Industrial Development Zone Development General Company 鄭州高新技術產業開發區發展總公司	Zhengzhou 鄭州市	Henan 河南省	(0371)7981924 (0371)7981422
Guangdong Hardware Import & Export Group Company 廣東省五金進出口集團公司	Guangzhou 廣州市	Guangdong 廣東省	(020)87752204 (020)87752205
Xi Shan Shi Wu Kuang Trade Company 錫山市五礦貿易公司	Wuxi 無錫市	Jiangsu 江蘇省	(0510)7760988
Xiamen Ocean Petroleum Company 廈門海洋石油公司	Xiamen 廈門市	Fujian 福建省	(0592)2095495 (0592)2087292
Hainan Shen Hai Import & Export Co. Ltd. 海南深海進出口有限公司	Haikou 海口市	Hainan 海南省	(0898)6717646 (0898)6717639

*Also include sales by firms outside this industry.包括本行業以外廠家的銷售。"o" stands for "others". "o" 代表"其他產品"。

0914: Nickel and Cobalt Ores Mining and Dressing 鎳鈷礦採選業

The industry accounts for 0.002% of the total revenue of China's industrial sector in 1996. The revenue growth rate of the industry is -7.5% from 1995, as compared to the growth rate of China's industrial sector, 9.51%. The rate of return on asset is -0.65%. 80.00% of all firms in the industry made a profit while 20.00% had negative returns. The top province in terms of the industry's revenue is Yunnan, accounting for 35.26% of the total revenue.
本行業在1996年佔全行業總產值0.002%，行業年增長率為-7.5%（全國工業年增長率9.51%）。行業的資產回報率-0.65%，80.00%的企業盈利，20.00%的企業虧損。銷售收入最高的省份為雲南省，佔本行業的35.26%。

	Total number of firms 企業總數	Total number of employees 職工總數	Total revenue (mil. RMB) 總銷售收入（百萬元）	Total profit (mil. RMB) 總利潤（百萬元）	Return on assets 資產利潤率 (%)	Return on equity 權益利潤率 (%)	Labour productivity ('000 RMB / worker) 勞動生產率（千元/人）	Debts / assets 資產負債率 (%)	Total assets (mil. RMB) 總資產（百萬元）
Industry Overall 行業總體	10	4,446	107	-2	-0.65	-1.53	24.07	57.87	251

	Number of firms 企業個數	Average number of employees 平均職工人數	Average revenue ('000 RMB) 平均銷售收入（千元）	Average profit ('000 RMB) 平均利潤（千元）	Return on assets 資產利潤率 (%)	Return on equity 權益利潤率 (%)	Labour productivity ('000 RMB / worker) 勞動生產率（千元/人）	Average debts / assets 平均資產負債率(%)	Average Total assets ('000 RMB) 平均總資產（千元）
By ownership 產業所有權									
State-owned 國有	4	1,040	22,000	-500	-0.89	-2.00	21.16	55.56	56,250
Collectively-owned 集體	6	48	3,167				65.97	76.91	4,332
Privately-owned 私有									
Domestic JVs 聯營									
Joint stock 股份制									
Foreign-funded 外資									
Overseas Chinese-funded 港澳台資									
By size 規模									
Large 大型									
Medium 中型	2	1,748	28,605	-264	-0.45	-1.05	16.36	57.55	59,242
Small 小型	7	132	7,112	-210	-1.11	-2.64	53.76	57.96	18,931
By regional distribution 地區分布									
Central-North 華北									
Beijing 北京									
Tianjin 天津									
Hebei 河北									
Shanxi 山西									
Inner Mongolia 內蒙									
Northeast 東北	3	266	7,690	67	0.61	0.85	28.87	28.83	10,983
Liaoning 遼寧									
Jilin 吉林	3	266	7,690	67	0.61	0.85	28.87	28.83	10,983
Heilongjiang 黑龍江									
Central East 華東									
Shanghai 上海									
Jiangsu 江蘇									
Zhejiang 浙江									
Anhui 安徽									
Fujian 福建									
Jiangxi 江西									
Shandong 山東									
Central-South 中南	2	110	8,520	375	3.17	20.78	77.45	84.75	11,835
Henan 河南									
Hubei 湖北									
Hunan 湖南	1	80	920	50	55.56	125.00	11.50	55.56	90
Guangdong 廣東	1	140	16,120	700	2.97	19.61	115.14	84.86	23,580
Guangxi 廣西									
Hainan 海南									
Southwest 西南	2	1,596	32,750	-595	-0.67	-1.71	20.53	60.90	88,915
Chongqing 重慶									
Sichuan 四川	1	2,770	27,770	-2,250	-2.38	-6.40	10.03	62.71	94,350
Guizhou 貴州									
Yunnan 雲南	1	421	37,730	1,060	1.27	3.09	89.62	58.85	83,480
Tibet 西藏									
Northwest 西北	3	79	357	-463	-8.44	-15.21	4.53	44.57	5,490
Shaanxi 陝西	1	20							890
Gansu 甘肅									
Qinghai 青海	1	216	1,070	-1,390	-9.10	-17.48	4.95	48.04	15,280
Ningxia 寧夏									
Xinjiang 新疆	1								300

0914: Nickel and Cobalt Ores Mining and Dressing 鎳鈷礦採選業

Year 年份	Number of firms 企業個數	Rate of change 每年變化 (%)	Number of employees 職工人數 (人)	Rate of change 每年變化 (%)	Total revenue (mil. RMB) 總銷售收入 (百萬元)	Rate of change 每年變化 (%)	Total profit (mil. RMB) 總利潤 (百萬元)	Rate of change 每年變化 (%)
1993	4		3,842		15		2	
1994	3	-25.00%	3,685	-4.09%	56	285.33%	-4	-294.00%
1995	9	200.00%	4,626	25.54%	116	106.15%	6	247.40%
1996	10	11.11%	4,446	-3.89%	107	-7.52%	-2	-131.07%

3 Major products* 3 種主要產品 *	Output 產量	Sales volume 銷售量	Unit 單位

Top 10 firms by revenue (year founded) 收入排名前 10 家企業 (創辦年份)	City 城市	Province 省	Telephone / fax 電話 / 傳真	Number of employees 職工人數	Ownership 產業所有權	Revenue ('000 RMB) 銷售收入 (千元)	Profit ('000 RMB) (rank) 利潤 (千元) (排名)	Total assets ('000 RMB) 總資產 (千元)	Major products 主要產品
Huili Nickel Mine 會理鎳礦(1958)	Xichang 西昌市	Sichuan 四川省	(0834)68098 (0834)68018	2,676	State-owned 國有	27,774	-2250(4)	94,349	o
Jilin Tonghua Chi Bai Song Copper-nickel Mine 吉林省通化縣赤柏松銅鎳礦(1994)	Tonghua 通化市	Jilin 吉林省	(0435)5224715 (0435)5224961	754	State-owned 國有	21,476	161(3)	31,848	o
Longmen Lead & Zinc Mine Co. Ltd. 龍門鉛鋅礦有限公司(1991)	Huizhou 惠州市	Guangdong 廣東省	(0751)7782718	140	Foreign-funded 外資	16,116	699(2)	23,580	o

Top 10 Cities by Production Output 產出排名前 10 位城市	Province 省	Market share 市場份額	Number of firms 企業個數
ZhangJiaJie 張家界市	Hunan 湖南省	63.24%	1
Dali 大理市	Yunnan 雲南省	18.97%	1
Ankang 安康市	Shaanxi 陝西省	8.93%	1
Wuhu 蕪湖市	Anhui 安徽省	8.85%	1

10 Major Wholesalers 10 家主要批發商	City 城市	Province 省	Telephone / Fax 電話 / 傳真
China Metallurgy Import & Export Liaoning Company 中國冶金進出口遼寧公司	Shenyang 瀋陽市	Liaoning 遼寧省	(024)23867070 (024)23875451
Liaoning Foreign Trade General Company 遼寧省對外貿易總公司	Dalian 大連市	Liaoning 遼寧省	(0411)3632157 (0411)3638243
Zhong Xin Trade Company 中信貿易公司	Beijing 北京市	Beijing 北京市	(010)64662170 (010)64662161
China Metallurgy Import & Export Shandong Company 中國冶金進出口山東公司	Qingdao 青島市	Shandong 山東省	(0532)2801118 (0532)2801331
Yongzhou Ferromanganese Mine Company 永州市錳鐵礦公司	Yongzhou 永州市	Hunan 湖南省	(0746)8464135
Zhengzhou Advanced Technology Industrial Development Zone Development General Company 鄭州高新技術產業開發區發展總公司	Zhengzhou 鄭州市	Henan 河南省	(0371)7981924 (0371)7981422
Guangdong Hardware Import & Export Group Company 廣東省五金進出口集團公司	Guangzhou 廣州市	Guangdong 廣東省	(020)87752204 (020)87752205
Xi Shan Shi Wu Kuang Trade Company 錫山市五礦貿易公司	Wuxi 無錫市	Jiangsu 江蘇省	(0510)7760988
Xiamen Ocean Petroleum Company 廈門海洋石油公司	Xiamen 廈門市	Fujian 福建省	(0592)2095495 (0592)2087292
Hainan Shen Hai Import & Export Co. Ltd. 海南深海進出口有限公司	Haikou 海口市	Hainan 海南省	(0898)6717646 (0898)6717639

*Also include sales by firms outside this industry.包括本行業以外廠家的銷售。"o" stands for "others". "o" 代表"其他產品"。

0915: Tin Ores Mining and Dressing 錫礦採選業

The industry accounts for 0.028% of the total revenue of China's industrial sector in 1996. The revenue growth rate of the industry is -14.2% from 1995, as compared to the growth rate of China's industrial sector, 9.51%. The rate of return on asset is 1.03%. 77.71% of all firms in the industry made a profit while 19.12% had negative returns. The top province in terms of the industry's revenue is Guangxi, accounting for 51.63% of the total revenue.
本行業在1996年佔全行業總產值0.028%，行業年增長率為-14.2%（全國工業年增長率9.51%）。行業的資產回報率1.03%，77.71%的企業盈利，19.12%的企業虧損。銷售收入最高的省份為廣西省，佔本行業的51.63%。

	Total number of firms 企業總數	Total number of employees 職工總數	Total revenue (mil. RMB) 總銷售收入（百萬元）	Total profit (mil. RMB) 總利潤（百萬元）	Return on assets 資產利潤率 (%)	Return on equity 權益利潤率 (%)	Labour productivity ('000 RMB / worker) 勞動生產率（千元/人）	Debts / assets 資產負債率 (%)	Total assets (mil. RMB) 總資產（百萬元）
Industry Overall 行業總體	147	42,198	1,622	34	1.03	3.57	38.44	71.22	3,286

	Number of firms 企業個數	Average number of employees 平均職工人數	Average revenue ('000 RMB) 平均銷售收入（千元）	Average profit ('000 RMB) 平均利潤（千元）	Return on assets 資產利潤率 (%)	Return on equity 權益利潤率 (%)	Labour productivity ('000 RMB / worker) 勞動生產率（千元/人）	Average debts / assets 平均資產負債率(%)	Average Total assets ('000 RMB) 平均總資產（千元）
By ownership 產業所有權									
State-owned 國有	43	446	17,465	465	0.81	3.16	39.16	74.49	57,698
Collectively-owned 集體	98	225	8,789	747	9.49	25.27	39.08	62.45	7,873
Privately-owned 私有	2	232	1,030	-355	-22.14	-658.18	4.45	96.64	1,605
Domestic JVs 聯營	2	186	3,573	-26,676	-218.80	-258.15	19.26	15.24	12,192
Joint stock 股份制									
Foreign-funded 外資	1	52							
Overseas Chinese-funded 港澳台資	1	94	388	-5,135	-86.64	-203.08	4.13	57.34	5,926
By size 規模									
Large 大型	2	7,828	369,164	8,339	0.86	4.18	47.16	79.45	970,288
Medium 中型	4	919	18,955	338	0.88	1.78	20.63	50.95	38,568
Small 小型	140	163	5,770	114	1.34	3.39	35.38	60.41	8,509
By regional distribution 地區分布									
Central-North 華北	4	93	1,398	163	4.43	11.55	15.03	61.53	3,665
Beijing 北京									
Tianjin 天津									
Hebei 河北									
Shanxi 山西									
Inner Mongolia 內蒙	4	93	1,398	163	4.43	11.55	15.03	61.53	3,665
Northeast 東北									
Liaoning 遼寧									
Jilin 吉林									
Heilongjiang 黑龍江									
Central East 華東	8	80	2,163	135	4.00	15.86	27.12	74.82	3,376
Shanghai 上海									
Jiangsu 江蘇									
Zhejiang 浙江	1	15	510	20	25.00	33.33	34.00	25.00	80
Anhui 安徽									
Fujian 福建									
Jiangxi 江西	7	89	2,399	151	3.94	15.70	26.95	74.97	3,847
Shandong 山東									
Central-South 中南	88	177	11,194	447	1.77	5.93	63.12	70.17	25,288
Henan 河南									
Hubei 湖北									
Hunan 湖南	41	115	3,242	-34	-1.18	-2.34	28.09	49.56	2,867
Guangdong 廣東	15	26	979	-54	-2.41	-10.42	37.84	76.91	2,243
Guangxi 廣西	32	328	26,169	1,299	2.00	6.97	79.87	71.23	64,818
Hainan 海南									
Southwest 西南	46	535	12,282	-330	-1.72	-5.95	22.94	71.18	19,245
Chongqing 重慶									
Sichuan 四川	1	12	50				4.17	39.88	1,730
Guizhou 貴州									
Yunnan 雲南	44	559	12,840	-345	-1.72	-5.98	22.95	71.24	20,080
Tibet 西藏	1								
Northwest 西北	1	958	49,300	7,850	5.88	54.40	51.46	89.19	133,510
Shaanxi 陝西	1	958	49,300	7,850	5.88	54.40	51.46	89.19	133,510
Gansu 甘肅									
Qinghai 青海									
Ningxia 寧夏									
Xinjiang 新疆									

0915: Tin Ores Mining and Dressing 錫礦採選業

Year 年份	Number of firms 企業個數	Rate of change 每年變化 (%)	Number of employees 職工人數 (人)	Rate of change 每年變化 (%)	Total revenue (mil. RMB) 總銷售收入 (百萬元)	Rate of change 每年變化 (%)	Total profit (mil. RMB) 總利潤 (百萬元)	Rate of change 每年變化 (%)
1993	168		47,558		1,545		-20	
1994	153	-8.93%	59,177	24.43%	1,547	0.11%	41	302.85%
1995	140	-8.50%	62,412	5.47%	1,890	22.15%	30	-28.45%
1996	147	5.00%	42,198	-32.39%	1,622	-14.18%	34	15.19%

3 Major products* 3 種主要產品 *	Output 產量	Sales volume 銷售量	Unit 單位

Top 10 firms by revenue (year founded) 收入排名前 10 家企業 (創辦年份)	City 城市	Province 省	Telephone / fax 電話 / 傳真	Number of employees 職工人數	Ownership 產業所有權	Revenue ('000 RMB) 銷售收入 (千元)	Profit ('000 RMB) (rank) 利潤 (千元) (排名)	Total assets ('000 RMB) 總資產 (千元)	Major products 主要產品
Gejiu Xi Du Industrial General Co. 個舊錫都實業總公司(1979)	Gejiu 個舊市	Yunnan 雲南省	(0873)2125200 (0873)2125200	14,675	Collectively-owned 集體	350,687	-3870(60)	383,973	o
Liuzhou Hua Xi Group Co. Ltd. 柳州華錫集團有限公司(1953)	Liuzhou 柳州市	Guangxi 廣西	(0772)2610111 (0772)2612186	6,359	State-owned 國有	348,176	-8936(63)	1,595,347	o
Dachang Hua Xi Group Gao Feng Tin Ore 大廠華錫集團高峯錫礦(1985)	Hechi 河池市	Guangxi 廣西	(0778)7577054	1,068	State-owned 國有	133,492	29320(1)	193,598	o
Nandan Hua Xi Dressing Mine Co. Ltd. 南丹縣華錫選礦有限公司(1995)	Hechi 河池市	Guangxi 廣西	(0778)7577447	598	Foreign-funded 外資	82,790	7766(3)	49,019	o
Nandan Che He Zhen Hui Le Tin Mine 南丹縣車河鎮灰樂錫礦(1988)	Hechi 河池市	Guangxi 廣西		535	Collectively-owned 集體	61,128	4821(4)	37,586	o
Nan Dan Xian Che He Zhen Keng Ma Mine 南丹縣車河鎮坑馬礦(1980)	Hechi 河池市	Guangxi 廣西		590	Collectively-owned 集體	57,100	4080(5)	36,968	o
Dachang Hua Xi Labour Service Co. Ltd. 大廠華錫勞動服務有限公司(1995)	Hechi 河池市	Guangxi 廣西	(0778)7577236	200	Collectively-owned 集體	54,399	549(15)	61,240	o
Xiang Hua Ling Tin Mine 香花嶺錫礦(1951)	Chenzhou 郴州市	Hunan 湖南省	(0735)6395001 (0735)6395005	2,504	State-owned 國有	35,389	-4499(61)	67,519	o
Gejiu Xinjian Mine 個舊市新建礦(1951)	Gejiu 個舊市	Yunnan 雲南省	(0873)2752479	1,139	State-owned 國有	27,841	2500(6)	21,612	o
Gejiu Ke La Industry & Trade Co. Ltd. 個舊市克拉工貿有限責任公司(1994)	Gejiu 個舊市	Yunnan 雲南省	(0873)2131134 (0873)2131381	27	Collectively-owned 集體	23,538	253(27)	27,328	o

Top 10 Cities by Production Output 產出排名前 10 位城市	Province 省	Market share 市場份額	Number of firms 企業個數
Liuzhou 柳州市	Guangxi 廣西	46.68%	2
Hechi 河池市	Guangxi 廣西	28.53%	9
Gejiu 個舊市	Yunnan 雲南省	13.68%	28
Lingchuan 靈川縣	Guangxi 廣西	4.98%	7
Wenshan 文山縣	Yunnan 雲南省	1.96%	4
Chenzhou 郴州市	Hunan 湖南省	1.54%	14
Lincang 臨滄縣	Yunnan 雲南省	0.79%	2
Hengyang 衡陽市	Hunan 湖南省	0.47%	4
Heshan 合山市	Guangxi 廣西	0.45%	2
Yunfu 雲浮市	Guangdong 廣東省	0.26%	1

10 Major Wholesalers 10 家主要批發商	City 城市	Province 省	Telephone / Fax 電話 / 傳真
China Metallurgy Import & Export Liaoning Company 中國冶金進出口遼寧公司	Shenyang 瀋陽市	Liaoning 遼寧省	(024)23867070 (024)23875451
Liaoning Foreign Trade General Company 遼寧省對外貿易總公司	Dalian 大連市	Liaoning 遼寧省	(0411)3632157 (0411)3638243
Zhong Xin Trade Company 中信貿易公司	Beijing 北京市	Beijing 北京市	(010)64662170 (010)64662161
China Metallurgy Import & Export Shandong Company 中國冶金進出口山東公司	Qingdao 青島市	Shandong 山東省	(0532)2801118 (0532)2801331
Yongzhou Ferromanganese Mine Company 永州市錳鐵礦公司	Yongzhou 永州市	Hunan 湖南省	(0746)8464135
Zhengzhou Advanced Technology Industrial Development Zone Development General Company 鄭州高新技術產業開發區發展總公司	Zhengzhou 鄭州市	Henan 河南省	(0371)7981924 (0371)7981422
Guangdong Hardware Import & Export Group Company 廣東省五金進出口集團公司	Guangzhou 廣州市	Guangdong 廣東省	(020)87752204 (020)87752205
Xi Shan Shi Wu Kuang Trade Company 錫山市五礦貿易公司	Wuxi 無錫市	Jiangsu 江蘇省	(0510)7760988
Xiamen Ocean Petroleum Company 廈門海洋石油公司	Xiamen 廈門市	Fujian 福建省	(0592)2095495 (0592)2087292
Hainan Shen Hai Import & Export Co. Ltd. 海南深海進出口有限公司	Haikou 海口市	Hainan 海南省	(0898)6717646 (0898)6717639

*Also include sales by firms outside this industry.包括本行業以外廠家的銷售。"o" stands for "others". "o" 代表 "其他產品"。

0916: Antimony Ores Mining and Dressing 銻礦採選業

The industry accounts for 0.007% of the total revenue of China's industrial sector in 1996. The revenue growth rate of the industry is -6.9% from 1995, as compared to the growth rate of China's industrial sector, 9.51%. The rate of return on asset is 5.36%. 72.85% of all firms in the industry made a profit while 14.65% had negative returns. The top province in terms of the industry's revenue is Guangxi, accounting for 40.23% of the total revenue.
本行業在1996年佔全行業總產值0.007%，行業年增長率為-6.9%（全國工業年增長率9.51%）。行業的資產回報率5.36%，72.85%的企業盈利，14.65%的企業虧損。銷售收入最高的省份為廣西省，佔本行業的40.23%。

	Total number of firms 企業總數	Total number of employees 職工總數	Total revenue (mil. RMB) 總銷售收入（百萬元）	Total profit (mil. RMB) 總利潤（百萬元）	Return on assets 資產利潤率 (%)	Return on equity 權益利潤率 (%)	Labour productivity ('000 RMB / worker) 勞動生產率（千元/人）	Debts / assets 資產負債率 (%)	Total assets (mil. RMB) 總資產（百萬元）
Industry Overall 行業總體	167	11,310	424	14	5.36	14.62	37.49	63.33	267

	Number of firms 企業個數	Average number of employees 平均職工人數	Average revenue ('000 RMB) 平均銷售收入（千元）	Average profit ('000 RMB) 平均利潤（千元）	Return on assets 資產利潤率 (%)	Return on equity 權益利潤率 (%)	Labour productivity ('000 RMB / worker) 勞動生產率（千元/人）	Average debts / assets 平均資產負債率(%)	Average Total assets ('000 RMB) 平均總資產（千元）
By ownership 產業所有權									
State-owned 國有	18	147	2,611	-222	-4.17	-12.12	17.74	65.63	5,333
Collectively-owned 集體	140	60	2,630	125	11.08	28.54	43.87	61.17	1,130
Privately-owned 私有									
Domestic JVs 聯營	7	33	960	58	4.95	13.78	28.85	64.06	1,174
Joint stock 股份制	2	17	1,043	23	0.99	7.39	61.35	86.65	2,282
Foreign-funded 外資									
Overseas Chinese-funded 港澳台資									
By size 規模									
Large 大型									
Medium 中型	1	562	43,012	4,921	9.09	13.84	76.53	34.29	54,122
Small 小型	163	66	2,337	56	4.26	14.54	35.55	70.67	1,306
By regional distribution 地區分布									
Central-North 華北									
Beijing 北京									
Tianjin 天津									
Hebei 河北									
Shanxi 山西									
Inner Mongolia 內蒙									
Northeast 東北	1	95	1,450	130	68.42	144.44	15.26	52.63	190
Liaoning 遼寧									
Jilin 吉林	1	95	1,450	130	68.42	144.44	15.26	52.63	190
Heilongjiang 黑龍江									
Central East 華東	17	55	1,709	106	5.97	16.56	30.87	63.97	1,785
Shanghai 上海									
Jiangsu 江蘇	1	50	3,250	400	9.03	18.02	65.00	49.89	4,430
Zhejiang 浙江	3	26	840				32.31	41.72	543
Anhui 安徽	3	27	1,533	147	30.56	34.92	56.10	12.50	480
Fujian 福建									
Jiangxi 江西	10	73	1,868	97	4.25	14.92	25.55	71.54	2,284
Shandong 山東									
Central-South 中南	111	71	3,142	138	9.09	22.74	44.52	60.04	1,522
Henan 河南	15	23	859	-87	-4.00	-11.85	37.47	66.25	2,167
Hubei 湖北	8	30	1,578	101	14.24	52.60	53.47	72.93	711
Hunan 湖南	59	96	2,169	77	8.49	24.53	22.57	65.40	913
Guangdong 廣東	5	95	4,932	222	6.15	19.54	52.14	68.51	3,608
Guangxi 廣西	24	46	7,107	423	17.27	33.12	153.53	47.87	2,451
Hainan 海南									
Southwest 西南	13	124	2,318	-270	-8.67	-38.36	18.63	77.37	3,113
Chongqing 重慶									
Sichuan 四川	1	5	990	30	8.33	21.43	198.00	61.11	360
Guizhou 貴州	8	149	1,953	-519	-13.09	-48.88	13.15	73.19	3,963
Yunnan 雲南	2	153	5,445	350	12.37	368.42	35.70	96.64	2,830
Tibet 西藏	2	60	1,315	-45	-3.27	-27.27	22.10	88.00	1,375
Northwest 西北	25	33	594	23	2.11	5.60	18.06	62.31	1,100
Shaanxi 陝西	16	39	809	25	2.40	6.91	20.99	65.27	1,042
Gansu 甘肅	7	24	273	26	1.66	3.94	11.24	57.76	1,546
Qinghai 青海	2	18							
Ningxia 寧夏									
Xinjiang 新疆									

0916: Antimony Ores Mining and Dressing 銻礦採選業

Year 年份	Number of firms 企業個數	Rate of change 每年變化 (%)	Number of employees 職工人數 (人)	Rate of change 每年變化 (%)	Total revenue (mil. RMB) 總銷售收入 (百萬元)	Rate of change 每年變化 (%)	Total profit (mil. RMB) 總利潤 (百萬元)	Rate of change 每年變化 (%)
1993	116		7,444		161		7	
1994	125	7.76%	9,071	21.86%	284	76.48%	34	414.98%
1995	182	45.60%	15,082	66.27%	455	60.29%	58	68.83%
1996	167	-8.24%	11,310	-25.01%	424	-6.85%	14	-75.82%

3 Major products* 3 種主要產品 *	Output 產量	Sales volume 銷售量	Unit 單位

Top 10 firms by revenue (year founded) 收入排名前 10 家企業 (創辦年份)	City 城市	Province 省	Telephone / fax 電話 / 傳真	Number of employees 職工人數	Ownership 產業所有權	Revenue ('000 RMB) 銷售收入 (千元)	Profit ('000 RMB) (rank) 利潤 (千元) (排名)	Total assets ('000 RMB) 總資產 (千元)	Major products 主要產品
Guanyang Guan Hong Company 灌陽縣灌宏公司(1993)	Lingchuan 靈川縣	Guangxi 廣西	(0773)4212231		Collectively-owned 集體	48,750	1920(3)	660	o
Nandan Che He Zhen San Cha He Antimony Mine 南丹縣車河鎮三岔河銻礦(1988)	Hechi 河池市	Guangxi 廣西		329	Collectively-owned 集體	19,960	2430(1)	10,861	o
Guanyang Antimony Products Co. Ltd. 灌陽縣銻品責任有限公司(1995)	Lingchuan 靈川縣	Guangxi 廣西	(0773)4218798		Collectively-owned 集體	18,920	738(9)	1,370	o
Zhongshan Hui Long Antimony Products Factory 鐘山縣回龍銻品廠(1987)	Cenxi 岑溪縣	Guangxi 廣西		114	Collectively-owned 集體	18,120	1440(5)	6,680	o
Guanyang Yin He Smelting Factory 灌陽縣銀河冶煉廠(1995)	Lingchuan 靈川縣	Guangxi 廣西	(0773)4218049		Collectively-owned 集體	15,250	500(11)	2,130	o
Guizhou Qinglong Antimony Mine 貴州省晴隆銻礦(1952)	Xingyi 興義市	Guizhou 貴州省	(0859)7610244 (0859)20000000	1,242	State-owned 國有	13,911	-3788(64)	24,705	o
Dong'an Lu Ma Qiao Antimony Mine 東安縣鹿馬橋銻礦(1986)	Yongzhou 永州市	Hunan 湖南省	(0746)4526126	210	Collectively-owned 集體	13,500	481(12)	947	o
Xinshao Dai Shui Qiao You Gui Antimony Mine 新邵縣岱水橋筱圭銻礦(1993)	Shaoyang 邵陽市	Hunan 湖南省	(0739)3310907	480	Collectively-owned 集體	13,000	0(48)	1,310	o
Xing'an Cui Jia Xiang Antimony Mine Factory 興安縣崔家鄉銻礦廠(1981)	Lingchuan 靈川縣	Guangxi 廣西	(0773)6162128		Joint stock 股份制	12,030	960(7)	3,166	o
Xinning Longkou Antimony Mine 新寧縣龍口銻礦(1992)	Shaoyang 邵陽市	Hunan 湖南省	(0739)4782621	500	Collectively-owned 集體	10,619	2124(2)	9,400	o

Top 10 Cities by Production Output 產出排名前 10 位城市	Province 省	Market share 市場份額	Number of firms 企業個數
Lingchuan 靈川縣	Guangxi 廣西	59.79%	5
Baise 百色市	Guangxi 廣西	8.28%	7
Wudu 武都縣	Gansu 甘肅省	6.84%	6
Sanmenxia 三門峽市	Henan 河南省	3.82%	11
Nanning 南寧市	Guangxi 廣西	3.77%	1
Cenxi 岑溪縣	Guangxi 廣西	2.58%	1
Yongzhou 永州市	Hunan 湖南省	1.69%	2
Wuxi 無錫市	Jiangsu 江蘇省	1.66%	1
Yiyang 益陽市	Hunan 湖南省	1.59%	2
Shaoyang 邵陽市	Hunan 湖南省	1.48%	2

10 Major Wholesalers 10 家主要批發商	City 城市	Province 省	Telephone / Fax 電話 / 傳真
China Metallurgy Import & Export Liaoning Company 中國冶金進出口遼寧公司	Shenyang 瀋陽市	Liaoning 遼寧省	(024)23867070 (024)23875451
Liaoning Foreign Trade General Company 遼寧省對外貿易總公司	Dalian 大連市	Liaoning 遼寧省	(0411)3632157 (0411)3638243
Zhong Xin Trade Company 中信貿易公司	Beijing 北京市	Beijing 北京市	(010)64662170 (010)64662161
China Metallurgy Import & Export Shandong Company 中國冶金進出口山東公司	Qingdao 青島市	Shandong 山東省	(0532)2801118 (0532)2801331
Yongzhou Ferromanganese Mine Company 永州市錳鐵礦公司	Yongzhou 永州市	Hunan 湖南省	(0746)8464135
Zhengzhou Advanced Technology Industrial Development Zone Development General Company 鄭州高新技術產業開發區發展總公司	Zhengzhou 鄭州市	Henan 河南省	(0371)7981924 (0371)7981422
Guangdong Hardware Import & Export Group Company 廣東省五金進出口集團公司	Guangzhou 廣州市	Guangdong 廣東省	(020)87752204 (020)87752205
Xi Shan Shi Wu Kuang Trade Company 錫山市五礦貿易公司	Wuxi 無錫市	Jiangsu 江蘇省	(0510)7760988
Xiamen Ocean Petroleum Company 廈門海洋石油公司	Xiamen 廈門市	Fujian 福建省	(0592)2095495 (0592)2087292
Hainan Shen Hai Import & Export Co. Ltd. 海南深海進出口有限公司	Haikou 海口市	Hainan 海南省	(0898)6717646 (0898)6717639

*Also include sales by firms outside this industry.包括本行業以外廠家的銷售。"o" stands for "others". "o" 代表 "其他產品"。

0917: Mercury Ores Mining and Dressing 汞礦採選業

The industry accounts for 0.000% of the total revenue of China's industrial sector in 1996. The revenue growth rate of the industry is 236.0% from 1995, as compared to the growth rate of China's industrial sector, 9.51%. The rate of return on asset is -7.74%. 62.50% of all firms in the industry made a profit while 37.50% had negative returns. The top province in terms of the industry's revenue is Hunan, accounting for 81.53% of the total revenue.
本行業在 1996 年佔全行業總產值 0.000% ，行業年增長率為 236.0%（全國工業年增長率 9.51%）。行業的資產回報率 -7.74% ， 62.50% 的企業盈利， 37.50% 的企業虧損。銷售收入最高的省份為湖南省，佔本行業的 81.53% 。

	Total number of firms 企業總數	Total number of employees 職工總數	Total revenue (mil. RMB) 總銷售收入（百萬元）	Total profit (mil. RMB) 總利潤（百萬元）	Return on assets 資產利潤率 (%)	Return on equity 權益利潤率 (%)	Labour productivity ('000 RMB / worker) 勞動生產率（千元／人）	Debts / assets 資產負債率 (%)	Total assets (mil. RMB) 總資產（百萬元）
Industry Overall 行業總體	9	2,398	17	-4	-7.74	-38.38	7.09	79.81	51

	Number of firms 企業個數	Average number of employees 平均職工人數	Average revenue ('000 RMB) 平均銷售收入（千元）	Average profit ('000 RMB) 平均利潤（千元）	Return on assets 資產利潤率 (%)	Return on equity 權益利潤率 (%)	Labour productivity ('000 RMB / worker) 勞動生產率（千元／人）	Average debts / assets 平均資產負債率(%)	Average Total assets ('000 RMB) 平均總資產（千元）
By ownership 產業所有權									
State-owned 國有	5	437	3,200	-800	-7.84	-40.00	7.33	80.39	10,200
Collectively-owned 集體	4	54	250		-15.60	3.25	4.65	68.49	
Privately-owned 私有									
Domestic JVs 聯營									
Joint stock 股份制									
Foreign-funded 外資									
Overseas Chinese-funded 港澳台資									
By size 規模									
Large 大型									
Medium 中型									
Small 小型	9	266	1,889	-444	-7.84	-40.00	7.09	80.39	5,667
By regional distribution 地區分布									
Central-North 華北									
Beijing 北京									
Tianjin 天津									
Hebei 河北									
Shanxi 山西									
Inner Mongolia 內蒙									
Northeast 東北									
Liaoning 遼寧									
Jilin 吉林									
Heilongjiang 黑龍江									
Central East 華東									
Shanghai 上海									
Jiangsu 江蘇									
Zhejiang 浙江									
Anhui 安徽									
Fujian 福建									
Jiangxi 江西									
Shandong 山東									
Central-South 中南	1	1,088	13,860	-2,980	-8.37	-21.85	12.74	61.71	35,620
Henan 河南									
Hubei 湖北									
Hunan 湖南	1	1,088	13,860	-2,980	-8.37	-21.85	12.74	61.71	35,620
Guangdong 廣東									
Guangxi 廣西									
Hainan 海南									
Southwest 西南	5	248	514	-242	-8.01	32.70	2.07	124.49	3,022
Chongqing 重慶	2	258	945	-600	-14.56	151.86	3.66	109.59	4,120
Sichuan 四川									
Guizhou 貴州	3	242	227	-3	-0.15	0.34	0.94	142.36	2,290
Yunnan 雲南									
Tibet 西藏									
Northwest 西北	3	23	320	70	31.34	48.84	13.71	35.82	223
Shaanxi 陝西	3	23	320	70	31.34	48.84	13.71	35.82	223
Gansu 甘肅									
Qinghai 青海									
Ningxia 寧夏									
Xinjiang 新疆									

0917: Mercury Ores Mining and Dressing 汞礦採選業

Year 年份	Number of firms 企業個數	Rate of change 每年變化 (%)	Number of employees 職工人數 (人)	Rate of change 每年變化 (%)	Total revenue (mil. RMB) 總銷售收入 (百萬元)	Rate of change 每年變化 (%)	Total profit (mil. RMB) 總利潤 (百萬元)	Rate of change 每年變化 (%)
1993	10		2,362		39		3	
1994	6	-40.00%	1,807	-23.50%	27	-29.23%	-3	-226.98%
1995	8	33.33%	830	-54.07%	5	-81.50%	-3	1.68%
1996	9	12.50%	2,398	188.92%	17	235.97%	-4	-24.38%

3 Major products* 3 種主要產品 *	Output 產量	Sales volume 銷售量	Unit 單位

Top 10 firms by revenue (year founded) 收入排名前 10 家企業 (創辦年份)	City 城市	Province 省	Telephone / fax 電話 / 傳真	Number of employees 職工人數	Ownership 產業所有權	Revenue ('000 RMB) 銷售收入 (千元)	Profit ('000 RMB) (rank) 利潤 (千元) (排名)	Total assets ('000 RMB) 總資產 (千元)	Major products 主要產品
Xinhuang Dong Zu Autonomous County Zhong Xing General Company 新晃侗族自治縣中興總公司(1953)	Huaihua 懷化市	Hunan 湖南省	(0745)6321288 (0745)6321288	994	State-owned 國有	13,862	-2983(1)	35,618	o

Top 10 Cities by Production Output 產出排名前 10 位城市	Province 省	Market share 市場份額	Number of firms 企業個數
Huaihua 懷化市	Hunan 湖南省	89.61%	1
Ankang 安康市	Shaanxi 陝西省	10.34%	2
Wudu 武都縣	Gansu 甘肅省	0.05%	1

10 Major Wholesalers 10 家主要批發商	City 城市	Province 省	Telephone / Fax 電話 / 傳真
China Metallurgy Import & Export Liaoning Company 中國冶金進出口遼寧公司	Shenyang 瀋陽市	Liaoning 遼寧省	(024)23867070 (024)23875451
Liaoning Foreign Trade General Company 遼寧省對外貿易總公司	Dalian 大連市	Liaoning 遼寧省	(0411)3632157 (0411)3638243
Zhong Xin Trade Company 中信貿易公司	Beijing 北京市	Beijing 北京市	(010)64662170 (010)64662161
China Metallurgy Import & Export Shandong Company 中國冶金進出口山東公司	Qingdao 青島市	Shandong 山東省	(0532)2801118 (0532)2801331
Yongzhou Ferromanganese Mine Company 永州市錳鐵礦公司	Yongzhou 永州市	Hunan 湖南省	(0746)8464135
Zhengzhou Advanced Technology Industrial Development Zone Development General Company 鄭州高新技術產業開發區發展總公司	Zhengzhou 鄭州市	Henan 河南省	(0371)7981924 (0371)7981422
Guangdong Hardware Import & Export Group Company 廣東省五金進出口集團公司	Guangzhou 廣州市	Guangdong 廣東省	(020)87752204 (020)87752205
Xi Shan Shi Wu Kuang Trade Company 錫山市五礦貿易公司	Wuxi 無錫市	Jiangsu 江蘇省	(0510)7760988
Xiamen Ocean Petroleum Company 廈門海洋石油公司	Xiamen 廈門市	Fujian 福建省	(0592)2095495 (0592)2087292
Hainan Shen Hai Import & Export Co. Ltd. 海南深海進出口有限公司	Haikou 海口市	Hainan 海南省	(0898)6717646 (0898)6717639

*Also include sales by firms outside this industry.包括本行業以外廠家的銷售。"o" stands for "others". "o" 代表 "其他產品"。

0919: Other Heavy Non-ferrous Metal Ores Mining and Dressing
其他重有色金屬礦採選業

The industry accounts for 0.002% of the total revenue of China's industrial sector in 1996. The revenue growth rate of the industry is -8.7% from 1995, as compared to the growth rate of China's industrial sector, 9.51%. The rate of return on asset is 12.68%. 84.85% of all firms in the industry made a profit while 6.06% had negative returns. The top province in terms of the industry's revenue is Hunan, accounting for 36.58% of the total revenue.
本行業在 1996 年佔全行業總產值 0.002% ，行業年增長率為 -8.7%（全國工業年增長率 9.51%）。行業的資產回報率 12.68% ，84.85% 的企業盈利，6.06% 的企業虧損。銷售收入最高的省份為湖南省，佔本行業的 36.58% 。

	Total number of firms 企業總數	Total number of employees 職工總數	Total revenue (mil. RMB) 總銷售收入（百萬元）	Total profit (mil. RMB) 總利潤（百萬元）	Return on assets 資產利潤率 (%)	Return on equity 權益利潤率 (%)	Labour productivity ('000 RMB / worker) 勞動生產率（千元/人）	Debts / assets 資產負債率 (%)	Total assets (mil. RMB) 總資產（百萬元）
Industry Overall 行業總體	43	2,914	94	7	12.68	22.06	32.26	42.45	54

	Number of firms 企業個數	Average number of employees 平均職工人數	Average revenue ('000 RMB) 平均銷售收入（千元）	Average profit ('000 RMB) 平均利潤（千元）	Return on assets 資產利潤率 (%)	Return on equity 權益利潤率 (%)	Labour productivity ('000 RMB / worker) 勞動生產率（千元/人）	Average debts / assets 平均資產負債率(%)	Average Total assets ('000 RMB) 平均總資產（千元）
By ownership 產業所有權									
State-owned 國有	5	29	600				20.98	50.00	1,200
Collectively-owned 集體	35	69	2,402	247	25.22	51.05	34.95	50.60	981
Privately-owned 私有									
Domestic JVs 聯營	3	122	2,313	-554	-12.17	-15.06	18.96	19.17	4,549
Joint stock 股份制									
Foreign-funded 外資									
Overseas Chinese-funded 港澳台資									
By size 規模									
Large 大型									
Medium 中型									
Small 小型	43	68	2,186	163	12.96	22.58	32.25	42.59	1,256
By regional distribution 地區分布									
Central-North 華北									
Beijing 北京									
Tianjin 天津									
Hebei 河北									
Shanxi 山西									
Inner Mongolia 內蒙									
Northeast 東北	4	77	1,650	-233	-28.88	273.53	21.57	110.56	805
Liaoning 遼寧	4	77	1,650	-233	-28.88	273.53	21.57	110.56	805
Jilin 吉林									
Heilongjiang 黑龍江									
Central East 華東	10	25	1,843	387	47.48	123.64	72.56	61.60	815
Shanghai 上海									
Jiangsu 江蘇									
Zhejiang 浙江									
Anhui 安徽									
Fujian 福建	4	28	1,180	78	7.09	12.02	42.14	40.96	1,093
Jiangxi 江西	6	24	2,285	593	94.18	647.27	96.55	85.45	630
Shandong 山東									
Central-South 中南	21	86	2,253	116	8.74	12.36	26.27	29.36	1,330
Henan 河南									
Hubei 湖北	4	134	2,478	65	5.53	17.57	18.49	68.51	1,175
Hunan 湖南	9	118	3,821	233	11.97	13.90	32.26	13.85	1,949
Guangdong 廣東	5	32	310	30	4.87	8.43	9.81	42.21	616
Guangxi 廣西	3	14	487	-23	-2.68	-5.11	35.61	47.89	870
Hainan 海南									
Southwest 西南	2	120	180	5	0.09	0.15	1.50	41.47	5,775
Chongqing 重慶					6.70	7.04	83.39	4.82	
Sichuan 四川					9.68	18.75	7.38	48.39	
Guizhou 貴州									
Yunnan 雲南	2	120	180	5	0.09	0.15	1.50	41.47	5,775
Tibet 西藏									
Northwest 西北	6	52	3,627	242	49.49	87.88	69.52	43.69	488
Shaanxi 陝西	1	6						63.64	110
Gansu 甘肅	4	73	5,415	440	78.22	114.29	74.69	31.56	563
Qinghai 青海									
Ningxia 寧夏									
Xinjiang 新疆	1	17	100	-310	-54.39	-442.86	5.88	87.72	570

0919: Other Heavy Non-ferrous Metal Ores Mining and Dressing
其他重有色金屬礦採選業

Year 年份	Number of firms 企業個數	Rate of change 每年變化 (%)	Number of employees 職工人數 (人)	Rate of change 每年變化 (%)	Total revenue (mil. RMB) 總銷售收入 (百萬元)	Rate of change 每年變化 (%)	Total profit (mil. RMB) 總利潤 (百萬元)	Rate of change 每年變化 (%)
1993	34		3,109		105		1	
1994	40	17.65%	9,589	208.43%	302	187.04%	-11	-906.81%
1995	34	-15.00%	2,699	-71.85%	103	-65.86%	4	136.51%
1996	43	26.47%	2,914	7.97%	94	-8.72%	7	74.09%

3 Major products* 3 種主要產品 *	Output 產量	Sales volume 銷售量	Unit 單位

Top 10 firms by revenue (year founded) 收入排名前 10 家企業 (創辦年份)	City 城市	Province 省	Telephone / fax 電話 / 傳真	Number of employees 職工人數	Ownership 產業所有權	Revenue ('000 RMB) 銷售收入 (千元)	Profit ('000 RMB) (rank) 利潤 (千元) (排名)	Total assets ('000 RMB) 總資產 (千元)	Major products 主要產品
Su Xian Qu Bai Lu Tang Zhao Jia Long Iron & Bismuth Mine 蘇仙區白露塘趙家壠鐵鉍礦(1987)	Chenzhou 郴州市	Hunan 湖南省	(0735)2652508	117	Collectively-owned 集體	10,555	916(2)	3,970	o
Tianshui Qin Yang Ore Dressing Factory 天水秦楊選礦廠(1990)	Tianshui 天水市	Gansu 甘肅省	(0938)214867	86	Collectively-owned 集體	8,700	700(3)	800	o
Tianshui Qin Jing Ore Dressing Factory 天水秦京選礦廠(1990)	Tianshui 天水市	Gansu 甘肅省	(0938)214867	80	Collectively-owned 集體	7,300	650(4)	900	o
Guiyang Bao Ling Iron Bismuth Mine 桂陽縣寶嶺鐵礦(1995)	Chenzhou 郴州市	Hunan 湖南省	(0735)4571428	204	Collectively-owned 集體	6,810	114(8)	1,270	o
Ganzhou Shahe Ore Dressing Factory 贛州市沙河選礦廠(1996)	Ganzhou 贛州市	Jiangxi 江西省	(0797)8248067		Collectively-owned 集體	5,670	425(5)	1,707	o
Qinchengqu Lizi Welfare Multiple Processing Factory 秦城區李子福利綜合加工廠(1994)	Tianshui 天水市	Gansu 甘肅省		51	Collectively-owned 集體	5,660	405(6)	550	o
Jing'an Guan Zhuang Tungsten Mine 靖安縣官裝鎢礦(1979)	Yichun 宜春市	Jiangxi 江西省	(0795)4786113		Collectively-owned 集體	5,399	3219(1)	807	o
Fujian Shaowu Min Yue Gan Mineral Products Development Co. Ltd. 福建省邵武市閩粵贛礦產品開發有限公司(1994)	Nangping 南平市	Fujian 福建省	(0599)6321968	39	Collectively-owned 集體	2,880	270(7)	1,898	o
Dong'an Ziyun Tungsten Mine 東安縣紫雲鎢礦(1980)	Yongzhou 永州市	Hunan 湖南省	(0746)4210393	32	Collectively-owned 集體	2,600	50(9)	208	o
Shi Jing Xiang Tungsten Mine 石境鄉鎢礦(1977)	Yichun 宜春市	Jiangxi 江西省			Collectively-owned 集體	2,360	0(10)	705	o

Top 10 Cities by Production Output 產出排名前 10 位城市	Province 省	Market share 市場份額	Number of firms 企業個數
Chenzhou 郴州市	Hunan 湖南省	61.32%	8
Hengyang 衡陽市	Hunan 湖南省	16.78%	1
Tongling 銅陵市	Anhui 安徽省	9.11%	1
Shangrao 上饒市	Jiangxi 江西省	4.06%	1
Shangzhou 商州市	Shaanxi 陜西省	2.03%	1
Shaoguan 韶關市	Guangdong 廣東省	1.82%	2
Ezhou 鄂州市	Hubei 湖北省	1.35%	1
Yumen 玉門市	Gansu 甘肅省	1.12%	1
Huludao 葫蘆島市	Liaoning 遼寧省	0.68%	1
Huizhou 惠州市	Guangdong 廣東省	0.54%	1

10 Major Wholesalers 10 家主要批發商	City 城市	Province 省	Telephone / Fax 電話 / 傳真
China Metallurgy Import & Export Liaoning Company 中國冶金進出口遼寧公司	Shenyang 瀋陽市	Liaoning 遼寧省	(024)23867070 (024)23875451
Liaoning Foreign Trade General Company 遼寧省對外貿易總公司	Dalian 大連市	Liaoning 遼寧省	(0411)3632157 (0411)3638243
Zhong Xin Trade Company 中信貿易公司	Beijing 北京市	Beijing 北京市	(010)64662170 (010)64662161
China Metallurgy Import & Export Shandong Company 中國冶金進出口山東公司	Qingdao 青島市	Shandong 山東省	(0532)2801118 (0532)2801331
Yongzhou Ferromanganese Mine Company 永州市錳鐵礦公司	Yongzhou 永州市	Hunan 湖南省	(0746)8464135
Zhengzhou Advanced Technology Industrial Development Zone Development General Company 鄭州高新技術產業開發區發展總公司	Zhengzhou 鄭州市	Henan 河南省	(0371)7981924 (0371)7981422
Guangdong Hardware Import & Export Group Company 廣東省五金進出口集團公司	Guangzhou 廣州市	Guangdong 廣東省	(020)87752204 (020)87752205
Xi Shan Shi Wu Kuang Trade Company 錫山市五礦貿易公司	Wuxi 無錫市	Jiangsu 江蘇省	(0510)7760988
Xiamen Ocean Petroleum Company 廈門海洋石油公司	Xiamen 廈門市	Fujian 福建省	(0592)2095495 (0592)2087292
Hainan Shen Hai Import & Export Co. Ltd. 海南深海進出口有限公司	Haikou 海口市	Hainan 海南省	(0898)6717646 (0898)6717639

*Also include sales by firms outside this industry.包括本行業以外廠家的銷售。"o" stands for "others". "o" 代表"其他產品"。

0931: Aluminium Ores Mining and Dressing 鋁礦採選業

The industry accounts for 0.004% of the total revenue of China's industrial sector in 1996. The revenue growth rate of the industry is 56.3% from 1995, as compared to the growth rate of China's industrial sector, 9.51%. The rate of return on asset is 2.71%. 70.79% of all firms in the industry made a profit while 9.21% had negative returns. The top province in terms of the industry's revenue is Henan, accounting for 55.79% of the total revenue.
本行業在1996年佔全行業總產值0.004%，行業年增長率為56.3%（全國工業年增長率9.51%）。行業的資產回報率2.71%，70.79%的企業盈利，9.21%的企業虧損。銷售收入最高的省份為河南省，佔本行業的55.79%。

	Total number of firms 企業總數	Total number of employees 職工總數	Total revenue (mil. RMB) 總銷售收入（百萬元）	Total profit (mil. RMB) 總利潤（百萬元）	Return on assets 資產利潤率 (%)	Return on equity 權益利潤率 (%)	Labour productivity ('000 RMB / worker) 勞動生產率（千元/人）	Debts / assets 資產負債率 (%)	Total assets (mil. RMB) 總資產（百萬元）
Industry Overall 行業總體	101	6,221	254	8	2.71	7.71	40.83	64.87	288

	Number of firms 企業個數	Average number of employees 平均職工人數	Average revenue ('000 RMB) 平均銷售收入（千元）	Average profit ('000 RMB) 平均利潤（千元）	Return on assets 資產利潤率 (%)	Return on equity 權益利潤率 (%)	Labour productivity ('000 RMB / worker) 勞動生產率（千元/人）	Average debts / assets 平均資產負債率(%)	Average Total assets ('000 RMB) 平均總資產（千元）
By ownership 產業所有權									
State-owned 國有	5	132	6,200	600	3.00	10.71	47.04	72.00	20,000
Collectively-owned 集體	86	59	2,150	44	2.37	5.75	36.22	58.77	1,844
Privately-owned 私有									
Domestic JVs 聯營	5	58	1,619	-7	-0.19	-0.69	27.72	71.64	3,812
Joint stock 股份制	1	37	681	16	2.65	-13.39	18.42	119.82	608
Foreign-funded 外資									
Overseas Chinese-funded 港澳台資									
By size 規模									
Large 大型									
Medium 中型									
Small 小型	100	60	2,540	80	2.78	7.92	42.22	64.93	2,879
By regional distribution 地區分布									
Central-North 華北	22	53	2,065	100	9.58	19.26	38.69	50.28	1,040
Beijing 北京									
Tianjin 天津									
Hebei 河北									
Shanxi 山西	22	53	2,065	100	9.58	19.26	38.69	50.28	1,040
Inner Mongolia 內蒙									
Northeast 東北	1								
Liaoning 遼寧	1								
Jilin 吉林									
Heilongjiang 黑龍江									
Central East 華東	5	80	1,900	36	1.08	2.40	23.81	54.79	3,322
Shanghai 上海									
Jiangsu 江蘇									
Zhejiang 浙江									
Anhui 安徽									
Fujian 福建	2	32	595	-5	-0.11	-0.15	18.89	27.91	4,515
Jiangxi 江西	1	25	650	40	40.00	80.00	26.00	40.00	100
Shandong 山東	2	156	3,830	75	2.01	15.96	24.63	87.43	3,740
Central-South 中南	34	81	4,361	98	1.45	4.45	53.95	67.38	6,773
Henan 河南	26	101	5,450	113	1.36	4.50	53.78	69.91	8,372
Hubei 湖北	2	26	1,760	95	13.38	-316.67	67.69	104.23	710
Hunan 湖南	3	19	943	60	7.83	15.65	50.54	49.57	767
Guangdong 廣東	1		70	-10	-0.11	-0.12		4.09	8,800
Guangxi 廣西	2	3	70	15	37.50	50.00	28.00	25.00	40
Hainan 海南									
Southwest 西南	38	49	1,316	54	11.42	29.11	26.68	60.78	477
Chongqing 重慶	4	100	2,959	45	1.73	9.24	29.42	81.30	2,596
Sichuan 四川	1	86	610	13	4.70	13.83	7.08	66.03	284
Guizhou 貴州	32	40	1,118	58	30.73	38.70	27.66	20.60	188
Yunnan 雲南									
Tibet 西藏									
Northwest 西北	1	26	370	20	10.00	20.00	14.23	50.00	200
Shaanxi 陝西	1	26	370	20	10.00	20.00	14.23	50.00	200
Gansu 甘肅									
Qinghai 青海									
Ningxia 寧夏									
Xinjiang 新疆									

0931: Aluminium Ores Mining and Dressing 鋁礦採選業

Year 年份	Number of firms 企業個數	Rate of change 每年變化(%)	Number of employees 職工人數(人)	Rate of change 每年變化(%)	Total revenue (mil. RMB) 總銷售收入(百萬元)	Rate of change 每年變化(%)	Total profit (mil. RMB) 總利潤(百萬元)	Rate of change 每年變化(%)
1993	52		17,459		759		16	
1994	62	19.23%	18,118	3.77%	744	-1.95%	-54	-438.30%
1995	88	41.94%	5,293	-70.79%	163	-78.15%	13	123.48%
1996	101	14.77%	6,221	17.53%	254	56.31%	8	-37.02%

3 Major products* 3 種主要產品*	Output 產量	Sales volume 銷售量	Unit 單位
a) Aluminium Raw Ore 鋁原礦含鋁量	1,362,375	1,362,375	ton 噸

Top 10 firms by revenue (year founded) 收入排名前10家企業(創辦年份)	City 城市	Province 省	Telephone / fax 電話 / 傳真	Number of employees 職工人數	Ownership 產業所有權	Revenue ('000 RMB) 銷售收入(千元)	Profit ('000 RMB) (rank) 利潤(千元)(排名)	Total assets ('000 RMB) 總資產(千元)	Major products 主要產品
Yuzhou Fangshan Zhen Zhong Zhou Industrial Development Company 禹州市方山鎮中州實業開發公司(1973)	Xuchang 許昌市	Henan 河南省	(0374)8641288	1,200	Collectively-owned 集體	55,580	1800(2)	20,800	o
Jiaozuo Cryolite Factory 焦作市冰晶石廠(1992)	Jiaozuo 焦作市	Henan 河南省	(0391)2947615	600	State-owned 國有	28,353	2988(1)	89,508	o
Henan Yanshi Fu Dian Zhen Joint Operation Aluminium Mine 河南省偃師市府店鎮聯辦鋁礦(1989)	Luoyang 洛陽市	Henan 河南省	(0379)7408043	40	Domestic JVs 聯營	17,040	1065(3)	15,000	o
Guiyang Baiyun Mai Jia Xiang Village & Township Enterprise Company 貴陽市白雲區麥架鄉鄉鎮企業公司(1984)	Guiyang 貴陽市	Guizhou 貴州省	(0851)4831007	24	Collectively-owned 集體	16,436	-347(33)	2,124	a
Wenquan Aluminium Mine Transport Marketing Company 温泉鋁礦運銷公司(1992)	Xiaoyi 孝義市	Shanxi 山西省	(0358)5484149	20	Collectively-owned 集體	13,910	500(7)	2,750	a
Nanchuan Aluminium Mine Factory 南川市鋁礦廠	Chongqing 重慶市	Chongqing 重慶市	(023)71490012	190	Collectively-owned 集體	8,654	96(18)	5,806	a
Mianchi Chen Cun Xiang No.2 Bauxite Calcination Factory 澠池縣陳村鄉第二鋁礬土煅燒廠(1989)	Sanmenxia 三門峽市	Henan 河南省	(0398)4813370	30	Collectively-owned 集體	7,300	770(5)	420	o
Yuanping Duan Jia Bao Xiang Jiang Jun Mu Alumina Factory 原平市段家堡鄉將軍墓鋁礬土廠(1988)	Xinzhou 忻州市	Shanxi 山西省		127	Collectively-owned 集體	5,730	387(8)	2,686	a
Mianchi Zhang Cun Zhen Yu Mei Di Aluminium Mine 澠池縣張村鎮豫美迪鋁礦(1993)	Sanmenxia 三門峽市	Henan 河南省		74	Collectively-owned 集體	4,970	620(6)	490	a
Zichuan Longquan Bauxite 淄川龍泉鋁土礦(1980)	Zibo 淄博市	Shandong 山東省	(0533)5880316	260	Collectively-owned 集體	4,474	101(16)	5,236	o

Top 10 Cities by Production Output 產出排名前10位城市	Province 省	Market share 市場份額	Number of firms 企業個數
Xuchang 許昌市	Henan 河南省	23.74%	1
Jiaozuo 焦作市	Henan 河南省	13.42%	3
Xinzhou 忻州市	Shanxi 山西省	9.96%	21
Yangquan 陽泉市	Shanxi 山西省	8.47%	1
Sanmenxia 三門峽市	Henan 河南省	7.62%	5
Luoyang 洛陽市	Henan 河南省	7.56%	2
Guiyang 貴陽市	Guizhou 貴州省	7.27%	26
Zhengzhou 鄭州市	Henan 河南省	5.45%	8
Ji'nan 濟南市	Shandong 山東省	4.05%	1
Zibo 淄博市	Shandong 山東省	2.79%	2

10 Major Wholesalers 10家主要批發商	City 城市	Province 省	Telephone / Fax 電話 / 傳真
China Metallurgy Import & Export Liaoning Company 中國冶金進出口遼寧公司	Shenyang 瀋陽市	Liaoning 遼寧省	(024)23867070 (024)23875451
Liaoning Foreign Trade General Company 遼寧省對外貿易總公司	Dalian 大連市	Liaoning 遼寧省	(0411)3632157 (0411)3638243
Zhong Xin Trade Company 中信貿易公司	Beijing 北京市	Beijing 北京市	(010)64662170 (010)64662161
China Metallurgy Import & Export Shandong Company 中國冶金進出口山東公司	Qingdao 青島市	Shandong 山東省	(0532)2801118 (0532)2801331
Yongzhou Ferromanganese Mine Company 永州市錳鐵礦公司	Yongzhou 永州市	Hunan 湖南省	(0746)8464135
Zhengzhou Advanced Technology Industrial Development Zone Development General Company 鄭州高新技術產業開發區發展總公司	Zhengzhou 鄭州市	Henan 河南省	(0371)7981924 (0371)7981422
Guangdong Hardware Import & Export Group Company 廣東省五金進出口集團公司	Guangzhou 廣州市	Guangdong 廣東省	(020)87752204 (020)87752205
Xi Shan Shi Wu Kuang Trade Company 錫山市五礦貿易公司	Wuxi 無錫市	Jiangsu 江蘇省	(0510)7760988
Xiamen Ocean Petroleum Company 廈門海洋石油公司	Xiamen 廈門市	Fujian 福建省	(0592)2095495 (0592)2087292
Hainan Shen Hai Import & Export Co. Ltd. 海南深海進出口有限公司	Haikou 海口市	Hainan 海南省	(0898)6717646 (0898)6717639

*Also include sales by firms outside this industry.包括本行業以外廠家的銷售。"o" stands for "others". "o" 代表"其他產品"。

0932: Magnesium Ores Mining and Dressing 鎂礦採選業

The industry accounts for 0.002% of the total revenue of China's industrial sector in 1996. The revenue growth rate of the industry is 17.8% from 1995, as compared to the growth rate of China's industrial sector, 9.51%. The rate of return on asset is 4.28%. 67.30% of all firms in the industry made a profit while 12.70% had negative returns. The top province in terms of the industry's revenue is Liaoning, accounting for 65.47% of the total revenue.
本行業在1996年佔全行業總產值0.002%，行業年增長率為17.8%（全國工業年增長率9.51%）。行業的資產回報率4.28%，67.30%的企業盈利，12.70%的企業虧損。銷售收入最高的省份為遼寧省，佔本行業的65.47%。

	Total number of firms 企業總數	Total number of employees 職工總數	Total revenue (mil. RMB) 總銷售收入（百萬元）	Total profit (mil. RMB) 總利潤（百萬元）	Return on assets 資產利潤率 (%)	Return on equity 權益利潤率 (%)	Labour productivity ('000 RMB / worker) 勞動生產率（千元/人）	Debts / assets 資產負債率 (%)	Total assets (mil. RMB) 總資產（百萬元）
Industry Overall 行業總體	50	2,549	100	4	4.28	19.71	39.23	78.26	96

	Number of firms 企業個數	Average number of employees 平均職工人數	Average revenue ('000 RMB) 平均銷售收入（千元）	Average profit ('000 RMB) 平均利潤（千元）	Return on assets 資產利潤率 (%)	Return on equity 權益利潤率 (%)	Labour productivity ('000 RMB / worker) 勞動生產率（千元/人）	Average debts / assets 平均資產負債率(%)	Average Total assets ('000 RMB) 平均總資產（千元）
By ownership 產業所有權									
State-owned 國有	7	24	429				17.96	81.82	1,571
Collectively-owned 集體	38	54	2,409	100	5.29	38.55	44.28	86.28	1,899
Privately-owned 私有									
Domestic JVs 聯營									
Joint stock 股份制									
Foreign-funded 外資	2	7							
Overseas Chinese-funded 港澳台資	3	101	1,817	61	1.43	2.02	18.05	29.03	4,273
By size 規模									
Large 大型	2	325	23,893	1,185	3.29	20.78	73.52	84.15	35,959
Medium 中型									
Small 小型	48	40	1,087	34	6.77	17.00	27.48	60.15	502
By regional distribution 地區分布									
Central-North 華北	6	23	1,347	73	9.17	23.16	59.85	60.21	800
Beijing 北京									
Tianjin 天津									
Hebei 河北	2								
Shanxi 山西	2	30	105				3.50	100.00	1,205
Inner Mongolia 內蒙	2	38	3,935	220	18.41	23.16	104.93	20.08	1,195
Northeast 東北	28	59	2,684	108	5.50	35.37	45.32	84.46	1,956
Liaoning 遼寧	26	60	2,518	64	3.15	23.59	41.76	86.66	2,041
Jilin 吉林	1	70	9,660	1,340	78.82	93.71	138.00	15.88	1,700
Heilongjiang 黑龍江	1	20							
Central East 華東	2	97	1,475	100	2.22	37.74	15.28	94.11	4,500
Shanghai 上海									
Jiangsu 江蘇									
Zhejiang 浙江									
Anhui 安徽									
Fujian 福建									
Jiangxi 江西									
Shandong 山東	2	97	1,475	100	2.22	37.74	15.28	94.11	4,500
Central-South 中南	8	47	1,290	43	2.12	4.33	27.45	50.90	2,004
Henan 河南	5	65	1,302	32	1.54	5.05	20.03	69.45	2,082
Hubei 湖北	2	20	1,810	85	3.06	3.63	90.50	15.68	2,775
Hunan 湖南									
Guangdong 廣東									
Guangxi 廣西	1	11	190	10	14.29	100.00	17.27	85.71	70
Hainan 海南									
Southwest 西南	3	21	593	3	0.15	1.23	27.81	87.52	2,163
Chongqing 重慶									
Sichuan 四川									
Guizhou 貴州	3	21	593	3	0.15	1.23	27.81	87.52	2,163
Yunnan 雲南									
Tibet 西藏									
Northwest 西北	3	41	733	37	2.22	8.80	17.89	74.75	1,650
Shaanxi 陝西	2	22	805	45	3.05	50.00	37.44	93.90	1,475
Gansu 甘肅	1	80	590	20	1.00	1.87	7.38	46.50	2,000
Qinghai 青海									
Ningxia 寧夏									
Xinjiang 新疆									

0932: Magnesium Ores Mining and Dressing 鎂礦採選業

Year 年份	Number of firms 企業個數	Rate of change 每年變化 (%)	Number of employees 職工人數 (人)	Rate of change 每年變化 (%)	Total revenue (mil. RMB) 總銷售收入 (百萬元)	Rate of change 每年變化 (%)	Total profit (mil. RMB) 總利潤 (百萬元)	Rate of change 每年變化 (%)
1993	27		1,912		23		1	
1994	26	-3.70%	4,442	132.32%	75	218.05%	5	510.55%
1995	31	19.23%	2,743	-38.25%	85	13.74%	7	50.33%
1996	50	61.29%	2,549	-7.07%	100	17.81%	4	-45.25%

3 Major products* 3 種主要產品 *	Output 產量	Sales volume 銷售量	Unit 單位
a) Magnesium 鎂	39,039	38,258	ton 噸

Top 10 firms by revenue (year founded) 收入排名前10家企業 (創辦年份)	City 城市	Province 省	Telephone / fax 電話 / 傳真	Number of employees 職工人數	Ownership 產業所有權	Revenue ('000 RMB) 銷售收入 (千元)	Profit ('000 RMB) (rank) 利潤 (千元) (排名)	Total assets ('000 RMB) 總資產 (千元)	Major products 主要產品
Xiuyan Magnesium Mine 岫岩縣鎂礦(1966)	Anshan 鞍山市	Liaoning 遼寧省	(0412)7892029	600	Collectively-owned 集體	21,630	410(4)	19,850	o
Nuclear Industry General Company No.712 Mine 核工業總公司712礦(1965)	Hengyang 衡陽市	Hunan 湖南省	(0734)5375081	2,696	State-owned 國有	16,744	-6949(20)	148,377	a
Siping Shiling Electric Smelting Magnesium Factory 四平市電熔鎂廠(1992)	Siping 四平市	Jilin 吉林省		70	Collectively-owned 集體	9,660	1340(1)	1,695	a
Fengcheng Jiguan Shan Zhen Magnesite Mine 鳳城市雞冠山鎮菱鎂礦(1994)	Dandong 丹東市	Liaoning 遼寧省	(0415)8190113	18	Collectively-owned 集體	6,806	310(6)	312	a
Kuandian Man Zu Autonomous County Gun Zi Gou Primary School Magnesium Mine 寬甸滿族自治縣磙子溝小學鎂礦(1993)	Dandong 丹東市	Liaoning 遼寧省		81	Collectively-owned 集體	6,025	-193(19)	4,353	a
Bei Ning Shi Gao Li Ban Xiang Magnesite Factory 北寧市高力板鄉鎂砂廠(1988)	Jinzhou 錦州市	Liaoning 遼寧省		19	Collectively-owned 集體	4,600	470(3)	390	a
Hebi Shang Yu Xiang Dolomite Development Co. Ltd. 鶴壁市上峪鄉白雲岩開發有限總公司(1995)	Hebi 鶴壁市	Henan 河南省	(0392)2641266	185	Collectively-owned 集體	4,520	614(2)	1,365	o
Huanren Man Zu Autonomous County Magnesium Mine 桓仁滿族自治縣鎂礦(1994)	Benxi 本溪市	Liaoning 遼寧省	(0414)8132233	25	Collectively-owned 集體	3,860	300(7)	310	a
Fengcheng City Jiguan Shan Zhen Magnesium Mine 鳳城市雞冠山鎮水鎂石礦(1995)	Dandong 丹東市	Liaoning 遼寧省	(0415)8190286	26	Collectively-owned 集體	3,490	390(5)	1,562	a
Xiuyan Hua Jian Mining Joint Company Mining Factory 岫岩縣華建礦業聯合公司採礦廠(1988)	Anshan 鞍山市	Liaoning 遼寧省	(0412)7732004	140	Collectively-owned 集體	3,300	0(16)	4,810	a

Top 10 Cities by Production Output 產出排名前10位城市	Province 省	Market share 市場份額	Number of firms 企業個數
Anshan 鞍山市	Liaoning 遼寧省	38.12%	6
Siping 四平市	Jilin 吉林省	14.20%	1
Jixi 雞西市	Heilongjiang 黑龍江省	14.20%	1
Hebi 鶴壁市	Henan 河南省	6.54%	3
Yingkou 營口市	Liaoning 遼寧省	5.68%	4
Dandong 丹東市	Liaoning 遼寧省	4.67%	10
Yantai 煙台市	Shandong 山東省	2.34%	1
Benxi 本溪市	Liaoning 遼寧省	2.24%	4
Nanyang 南陽市	Henan 河南省	2.24%	3
Xichang 西昌市	Sichuan 四川省	2.13%	1

10 Major Wholesalers 10家主要批發商	City 城市	Province 省	Telephone / Fax 電話 / 傳真
China Metallurgy Import & Export Liaoning Company 中國冶金進出口遼寧公司	Shenyang 瀋陽市	Liaoning 遼寧省	(024)23867070 (024)23875451
Liaoning Foreign Trade General Company 遼寧省對外貿易總公司	Dalian 大連市	Liaoning 遼寧省	(0411)3632157 (0411)3638243
Zhong Xin Trade Company 中信貿易公司	Beijing 北京市	Beijing 北京市	(010)64662170 (010)64662161
China Metallurgy Import & Export Shandong Company 中國冶金進出口山東公司	Qingdao 青島市	Shandong 山東省	(0532)2801118 (0532)2801331
Yongzhou Ferromanganese Mine Company 永州市錳鐵礦公司	Yongzhou 永州市	Hunan 湖南省	(0746)8464135
Zhengzhou Advanced Technology Industrial Development Zone Development General Company 鄭州高新技術產業開發區發展總公司	Zhengzhou 鄭州市	Henan 河南省	(0371)7981924 (0371)7981422
Guangdong Hardware Import & Export Group Company 廣東省五金進出口集團公司	Guangzhou 廣州市	Guangdong 廣東省	(020)87752204 (020)87752205
Xi Shan Shi Wu Kuang Trade Company 錫山市五礦貿易公司	Wuxi 無錫市	Jiangsu 江蘇省	(0510)7760988
Xiamen Ocean Petroleum Company 廈門海洋石油公司	Xiamen 廈門市	Fujian 福建省	(0592)2095495 (0592)2087292
Hainan Shen Hai Import & Export Co. Ltd. 海南深海進出口有限公司	Haikou 海口市	Hainan 海南省	(0898)6717646 (0898)6717639

*Also include sales by firms outside this industry.包括本行業以外廠家的銷售。"o" stands for "others". "o" 代表 "其他產品"。

0933: Titanium Ores Mining and Dressing 鈦礦採選業

The industry accounts for 0.003% of the total revenue of China's industrial sector in 1996. The revenue growth rate of the industry is 10.1% from 1995, as compared to the growth rate of China's industrial sector, 9.51%. The rate of return on asset is -3.96%. 61.44% of all firms in the industry made a profit while 32.31% had negative returns. The top province in terms of the industry's revenue is Guangdong, accounting for 42.26% of the total revenue.
本行業在1996年佔全行業總產值0.003%，行業年增長率為10.1%（全國工業年增長率9.51%）。行業的資產回報率-3.96%，61.44%的企業盈利，32.31%的企業虧損。銷售收入最高的省份為廣東省，佔本行業的42.26%。

	Total number of firms 企業總數	Total number of employees 職工總數	Total revenue (mil. RMB) 總銷售收入（百萬元）	Total profit (mil. RMB) 總利潤（百萬元）	Return on assets 資產利潤率 (%)	Return on equity 權益利潤率 (%)	Labour productivity ('000 RMB / worker) 勞動生產率（千元/人）	Debts / assets 資產負債率 (%)	Total assets (mil. RMB) 總資產（百萬元）
Industry Overall 行業總體	80	4,630	188	-11	-3.96	-28.72	40.60	86.22	287

	Number of firms 企業個數	Average number of employees 平均職工人數	Average revenue ('000 RMB) 平均銷售收入（千元）	Average profit ('000 RMB) 平均利潤（千元）	Return on assets 資產利潤率 (%)	Return on equity 權益利潤率 (%)	Labour productivity ('000 RMB / worker) 勞動生產率（千元/人）	Average debts / assets 平均資產負債率(%)	Average Total assets ('000 RMB) 平均總資產（千元）
By ownership 產業所有權									
State-owned 國有	19	102	1,263	-842	-10.26	533.33	12.40	101.92	8,211
Collectively-owned 集體	57	42	2,571	-449	-27.98	-97.25	61.71	71.23	1,606
Privately-owned 私有									
Domestic JVs 聯營	1	128	10,982	2,491	13.10	41.37	85.80	68.34	19,020
Joint stock 股份制	1	154	1,640	-18	-0.98	2.63	10.65	137.23	1,839
Foreign-funded 外資	1	24	4,748	28,129	174.15	300.08	197.82	41.97	16,153
Overseas Chinese-funded 港澳台資	1	14						19.23	2,418
By size 規模									
Large 大型									
Medium 中型									
Small 小型	79	58	2,379	-139	-3.83	-27.50	40.73	86.06	3,633
By regional distribution 地區分布									
Central-North 華北	2	178	10,455	415	3.37	58.87	58.90	94.27	12,300
Beijing 北京									
Tianjin 天津									
Hebei 河北									
Shanxi 山西	2	178	10,455	415	3.37	58.87	58.90	94.27	12,300
Inner Mongolia 內蒙									
Northeast 東北									
Liaoning 遼寧									
Jilin 吉林									
Heilongjiang 黑龍江									
Central East 華東	2	106	750	25	0.74	500.00	7.11	99.85	3,390
Shanghai 上海									
Jiangsu 江蘇	1	40	1,050	50	3.25	500.00	26.25	99.35	1,540
Zhejiang 浙江									
Anhui 安徽									
Fujian 福建									
Jiangxi 江西									
Shandong 山東	1	171	450				2.63	100.00	5,240
Central-South 中南	59	54	2,523	-197	-5.47	-63.06	46.31	91.32	3,604
Henan 河南	3	34	1,157	53	4.00	13.22	34.02	69.75	1,333
Hubei 湖北									
Hunan 湖南									
Guangdong 廣東	14	62	5,675	150	5.65	19.91	91.96	71.59	2,653
Guangxi 廣西	29	37	1,240	-161	-6.02	-112.50	33.42	94.65	2,683
Hainan 海南	13	90	2,308	-709	-9.84	-362.99	25.58	97.29	7,208
Southwest 西南	16	53	1,059	-37	-1.38	-3.00	20.09	54.20	2,681
Chongqing 重慶									
Sichuan 四川	1	22							
Guizhou 貴州									
Yunnan 雲南	15	55	1,048	-48	-1.72	-3.75	19.15	54.13	2,789
Tibet 西藏									
Northwest 西北	1	6							
Shaanxi 陝西	1	6							
Gansu 甘肅									
Qinghai 青海									
Ningxia 寧夏									
Xinjiang 新疆									

0933: Titanium Ores Mining and Dressing 鈦礦採選業

Year 年份	Number of firms 企業個數	Rate of change 每年變化 (%)	Number of employees 職工人數 (人)	Rate of change 每年變化 (%)	Total revenue (mil. RMB) 總銷售收入 (百萬元)	Rate of change 每年變化 (%)	Total profit (mil. RMB) 總利潤 (百萬元)	Rate of change 每年變化 (%)
1993	60		2,567		191		-2	
1994	85	41.67%	4,948	92.75%	218	14.33%	-1	15.05%
1995	76	-10.59%	4,780	-3.40%	171	-21.71%	-15	-907.65%
1996	80	5.26%	4,630	-3.14%	188	10.09%	-11	26.74%

3 Major products* 3 種主要產品 *	Output 產量	Sales volume 銷售量	Unit 單位
a) Titanium Concentrate 鈦精礦折合量	86,820	85,083	ton 噸

Top 10 firms by revenue (year founded) 收入排名前 10 家企業 (創辦年份)	City 城市	Province 省	Telephone / fax 電話 / 傳真	Number of employees 職工人數	Ownership 產業所有權	Revenue ('000 RMB) 銷售收入 (千元)	Profit ('000 RMB) (rank) 利潤 (千元) (排名)	Total assets ('000 RMB) 總資產 (千元)	Major products 主要產品
Huazhou Pingding Zhen Luo Jiang Titanium Mine Company 化州市平定鎮羅江鈦礦公司(1992)	Maoming 茂名市	Guangdong 廣東省	(0668)7530388	300	Collectively-owned 集體	48,000	2960(1)	10,400	a
Pinglu Ferro Alloy Co. Ltd. 平陸縣鐵合金有限公司(1989)	Yuncheng 運城市	Shanxi 山西省	(0359)3522810	180	Joint stock 股份制	18,151	829(2)	11,641	o
Fang Cheng Qu Mao Ling Xiang Ore Dressing Factory 防城區茅嶺鄉選礦廠(1988)	Fangchenggang 防城港市	Guangxi 廣西		24	Collectively-owned 集體	9,420	100(7)	1,025	o
Fengkai Ping Feng Zhen Titanium Mine Joint Operation Ore Dressing Factory 封開縣平鳳鎮鈦礦聯辦選礦廠(1989)	Zhaoqing 肇慶市	Guangdong 廣東省		84	Collectively-owned 集體	7,350	550(3)	6,940	a
Ping Feng Zhen Mine 平鳳鎮礦山(1994)	Zhaoqing 肇慶市	Guangdong 廣東省	(0757)6552209	62	Collectively-owned 集體	7,100	500(4)	500	a
Bama Titanium Industry Development Co. 巴馬瑤族自治縣鈦業開發公司(1988)	Hechi 河池市	Guangxi 廣西	(0778)6212187	21	State-owned 國有	6,859	-256(14)	4,988	a
Kunming Xishan Xin Fa Building Materials Decoration Company Bai Zi Tian Titanium Dressing Factory 昆明市西山新發建材裝飾公司稗子田鈦選廠(1995)	Kunming 昆明市	Yunnan 雲南省	(0871)8400536	150	Collectively-owned 集體	4,177	48(8)	5,166	o
Leizhou Baisha Zhen Copper Powder Factory 雷州市白沙鎮金粉末廠(1995)	Zhanjiang 湛江市	Guangdong 廣東省		65	Collectively-owned 集體	3,939	100(6)	3,226	o
Yunnan Lu Da Chang Kou Titanium Dressing Factory 雲南路達廠口鈦選廠(1988)	Kunming 昆明市	Yunnan 雲南省	(0871)8400515 (0871)4149765	240	Collectively-owned 集體	3,903	-59(13)	20,606	a
Jiang Urban He Fa Mineral Products Concentration Factory 江城區和發礦產精選廠(1991)	Yangjiang 陽江市	Guangdong 廣東省	(0662)3810048	30	Collectively-owned 集體	3,550	267(5)	1,180	a

Top 10 Cities by Production Output 產出排名前 10 位城市	Province 省	Market share 市場份額	Number of firms 企業個數
Maoming 茂名市	Guangdong 廣東省	28.64%	3
Tongshi 通什市	Hainan 海南省	22.57%	49
Kunming 昆明市	Yunnan 雲南省	14.54%	16
Zhaoqing 肇慶市	Guangdong 廣東省	8.76%	2
Fangchenggang 防城港市	Guangxi 廣西	7.37%	2
Zhanjiang 湛江市	Guangdong 廣東省	5.92%	7
Hechi 河池市	Guangxi 廣西	4.29%	5
Xinzhou 忻州市	Shanxi 山西省	2.03%	1
Yangjiang 陽江市	Guangdong 廣東省	1.87%	1
Xinyang 信陽市	Henan 河南省	0.70%	2

10 Major Wholesalers 10 家主要批發商	City 城市	Province 省	Telephone / Fax 電話 / 傳真
China Metallurgy Import & Export Liaoning Company 中國冶金進出口遼寧公司	Shenyang 瀋陽市	Liaoning 遼寧省	(024)23867070 (024)23875451
Liaoning Foreign Trade General Company 遼寧省對外貿易總公司	Dalian 大連市	Liaoning 遼寧省	(0411)3632157 (0411)3638243
Zhong Xin Trade Company 中信貿易公司	Beijing 北京市	Beijing 北京市	(010)64662170 (010)64662161
China Metallurgy Import & Export Shandong Company 中國冶金進出口山東公司	Qingdao 青島市	Shandong 山東省	(0532)2801118 (0532)2801331
Yongzhou Ferromanganese Mine Company 永州市錳鐵礦公司	Yongzhou 永州市	Hunan 湖南省	(0746)8464135
Zhengzhou Advanced Technology Industrial Development Zone Development General Company 鄭州高新技術產業開發區發展總公司	Zhengzhou 鄭州市	Henan 河南省	(0371)7981924 (0371)7981422
Guangdong Hardware Import & Export Group Company 廣東省五金進出口集團公司	Guangzhou 廣州市	Guangdong 廣東省	(020)87752204 (020)87752205
Xi Shan Shi Wu Kuang Trade Company 錫山市五礦貿易公司	Wuxi 無錫市	Jiangsu 江蘇省	(0510)7760988
Xiamen Ocean Petroleum Company 廈門海洋石油公司	Xiamen 廈門市	Fujian 福建省	(0592)2095495 (0592)2087292
Hainan Shen Hai Import & Export Co. Ltd. 海南深海進出口有限公司	Haikou 海口市	Hainan 海南省	(0898)6717646 (0898)6717639

*Also include sales by firms outside this industry.包括本行業以外廠家的銷售。"o" stands for "others". "o" 代表 "其他產品"。

0939: Other Light Non-ferrous Metal Ores Mining and Dressing
其他輕有色金屬礦採選業

The industry accounts for 0.002% of the total revenue of China's industrial sector in 1996. The revenue growth rate of the industry is 298.1% from 1995, as compared to the growth rate of China's industrial sector, 9.51%. The rate of return on asset is -6.52%. 93.75% of all firms in the industry made a profit while 6.25% had negative returns. The top province in terms of the industry's revenue is Guangdong, accounting for 86.26% of the total revenue.
本行業在1996年佔全行業總產值0.002%，行業年增長率為298.1%（全國工業年增長率9.51%）。行業的資產回報率-6.52%，93.75%的企業盈利，6.25%的企業虧損。銷售收入最高的省份為廣東省，佔本行業的86.26%。

	Total number of firms 企業總數	Total number of employees 職工總數	Total revenue (mil. RMB) 總銷售收入（百萬元）	Total profit (mil. RMB) 總利潤（百萬元）	Return on assets 資產利潤率 (%)	Return on equity 權益利潤率 (%)	Labour productivity ('000 RMB / worker) 勞動生產率（千元/人）	Debts / assets 資產負債率 (%)	Total assets (mil. RMB) 總資產（百萬元）
Industry Overall 行業總體	13	498	88	-2	-6.52	-24.97	176.71	73.91	36

	Number of firms 企業個數	Average number of employees 平均職工人數	Average revenue ('000 RMB) 平均銷售收入（千元）	Average profit ('000 RMB) 平均利潤（千元）	Return on assets 資產利潤率 (%)	Return on equity 權益利潤率 (%)	Labour productivity ('000 RMB / worker) 勞動生產率（千元/人）	Average debts / assets 平均資產負債率(%)	Average Total assets ('000 RMB) 平均總資產（千元）
By ownership 產業所有權									
State-owned 國有	2	106	3,000	-1,500	-20.00	75.00	28.44	126.67	7,500
Collectively-owned 集體	10	27	8,180	97	4.76	7.57	304.11	37.03	2,046
Privately-owned 私有									
Domestic JVs 聯營	1	18	171	25	4.66	21.47	9.49	78.29	540
Joint stock 股份制									
Foreign-funded 外資									
Overseas Chinese-funded 港澳台資									
By size 規模									
Large 大型									
Medium 中型									
Small 小型	12	41	7,331	-167	-5.56	-22.23	180.27	75.00	2,999
By regional distribution 地區分布									
Central-North 華北									
Beijing 北京									
Tianjin 天津									
Hebei 河北									
Shanxi 山西									
Inner Mongolia 內蒙									
Northeast 東北	3	25	2,487	173	29.05	226.09	100.81	87.15	597
Liaoning 遼寧	3	25	2,487	173	29.05	226.09	100.81	87.15	597
Jilin 吉林									
Heilongjiang 黑龍江									
Central East 華東	1	20	1,970	20	3.23	5.26	98.50	38.71	620
Shanghai 上海									
Jiangsu 江蘇									
Zhejiang 浙江	1	20	1,970	20	3.23	5.26	98.50	38.71	620
Anhui 安徽									
Fujian 福建									
Jiangxi 江西									
Shandong 山東									
Central-South 中南	8	49	9,828	-358	-8.58	-32.76	202.11	73.85	4,169
Henan 河南	1	10	760	40	11.43	17.39	76.00	34.29	350
Hubei 湖北									
Hunan 湖南	1	15	1,300	100	26.32	26.32	86.67		380
Guangdong 廣東	5	73	15,182	-614	-9.47	-38.38	208.54	75.36	6,486
Guangxi 廣西	1		650	70	36.84	58.33		36.84	190
Hainan 海南									
Southwest 西南									
Chongqing 重慶									
Sichuan 四川									
Guizhou 貴州									
Yunnan 雲南									
Tibet 西藏									
Northwest 西北	1	15							
Shaanxi 陝西									
Gansu 甘肅	1	15							
Qinghai 青海									
Ningxia 寧夏									
Xinjiang 新疆									

0939: Other Light Non-ferrous Metal Ores Mining and Dressing
其他輕有色金屬礦採選業

Year 年份	Number of firms 企業個數	Rate of change 每年變化 (%)	Number of employees 職工人數 (人)	Rate of change 每年變化 (%)	Total revenue (mil. RMB) 總銷售收入 (百萬元)	Rate of change 每年變化 (%)	Total profit (mil. RMB) 總利潤 (百萬元)	Rate of change 每年變化 (%)
1993	18		504		15		0	
1994	17	-5.56%	824	63.49%	31	113.28%	16	6675.30%
1995	12	-29.41%	436	-47.09%	22	-29.28%	0	-101.10%
1996	13	8.33%	498	14.22%	88	298.08%	-2	-1023.60%

3 Major products* 3 種主要產品 *	Output 產量	Sales volume 銷售量	Unit 單位

Top 10 firms by revenue (year founded) 收入排名前 10 家企業 (創辦年份)	City 城市	Province 省	Telephone / fax 電話 / 傳真	Number of employees 職工人數	Ownership 產業所有權	Revenue ('000 RMB) 銷售收入 (千元)	Profit ('000 RMB) (rank) 利潤 (千元) (排名)	Total assets ('000 RMB) 總資產 (千元)	Major products 主要產品
Chao'an Kai Da Mineral Products Processing Factory 潮安縣開達礦產品加工廠(1987)	Chaozhou 潮州市	Guangdong 廣東省	(0768)6721388	120	Collectively-owned 集體	65,900	136(3)	13,444	o
Zhanjiang Ore Dressing Factory 湛江選礦廠(1952)	Zhanjiang 湛江市	Guangdong 廣東省	(0758)2220474	211	State-owned 國有	6,385	-3232(6)	14,557	o
Liaoyang Ta Zi Ling Xiang Albite No.2 Mine 遼陽縣塔子嶺鄉鈉長石二礦(1991)	Liaoyang 遼陽市	Liaoning 遼寧省	(0419)6130043	20	Collectively-owned 集體	3,500	170(2)	900	o
Liaoyang Taziling Albite Mine 遼陽縣塔子嶺鄉鈉長石礦(1991)	Liaoyang 遼陽市	Liaoning 遼寧省	(0419)6130043	20	Collectively-owned 集體	2,890	257(1)	556	o
Zhanjiang Xiashan Hai Tou Ore Dressing Factory 湛江市霞山海頭選礦廠(1992)	Zhanjiang 湛江市	Guangdong 廣東省	(0758)2231480	15	Collectively-owned 集體	2,300	24(5)	624	o

Top 10 Cities by Production Output 產出排名前 10 位城市	Province 省	Market share 市場份額	Number of firms 企業個數
Chaozhou 潮州市	Guangdong 廣東省	74.71%	1
Zhanjiang 湛江市	Guangdong 廣東省	7.68%	2
Chuxiong 楚雄市	Yunnan 雲南省	7.65%	1
Wuhu 蕪湖市	Anhui 安徽省	2.51%	1
Chenzhou 郴州市	Hunan 湖南省	2.22%	1
Guangzhou 廣州市	Guangdong 廣東省	1.73%	1
Nangping 南平市	Fujian 福建省	1.24%	1
Shangzhou 商州市	Shaanxi 陝西省	1.17%	1
Liaoyang 遼陽市	Liaoning 遼寧省	0.49%	3
Zhumadian 駐馬店市	Henan 河南省	0.43%	1

10 Major Wholesalers 10 家主要批發商	City 城市	Province 省	Telephone / Fax 電話 / 傳真
China Metallurgy Import & Export Liaoning Company 中國冶金進出口遼寧公司	Shenyang 瀋陽市	Liaoning 遼寧省	(024)23867070 (024)23875451
Liaoning Foreign Trade General Company 遼寧省對外貿易總公司	Dalian 大連市	Liaoning 遼寧省	(0411)3632157 (0411)3638243
Zhong Xin Trade Company 中信貿易公司	Beijing 北京市	Beijing 北京市	(010)64662170 (010)64662161
China Metallurgy Import & Export Shandong Company 中國冶金進出口山東公司	Qingdao 青島市	Shandong 山東省	(0532)2801118 (0532)2801331
Yongzhou Ferromanganese Mine Company 永州市錳鐵礦公司	Yongzhou 永州市	Hunan 湖南省	(0746)8464135
Zhengzhou Advanced Technology Industrial Development Zone Development General Company 鄭州高新技術產業開發區發展總公司	Zhengzhou 鄭州市	Henan 河南省	(0371)7981924 (0371)7981422
Guangdong Hardware Import & Export Group Company 廣東省五金進出口集團公司	Guangzhou 廣州市	Guangdong 廣東省	(020)87752204 (020)87752205
Xi Shan Shi Wu Kuang Trade Company 錫山市五礦貿易公司	Wuxi 無錫市	Jiangsu 江蘇省	(0510)7760988
Xiamen Ocean Petroleum Company 廈門海洋石油公司	Xiamen 廈門市	Fujian 福建省	(0592)2095495 (0592)2087292
Hainan Shen Hai Import & Export Co. Ltd. 海南深海進出口有限公司	Haikou 海口市	Hainan 海南省	(0898)6717646 (0898)6717639

*Also include sales by firms outside this industry.包括本行業以外廠家的銷售。"o" stands for "others". "o" 代表 "其他產品"。

1011: Limestone Quarrying 石灰石開採業

The industry accounts for 0.074% of the total revenue of China's industrial sector in 1996. The revenue growth rate of the industry is 17.7% from 1995, as compared to the growth rate of China's industrial sector, 9.51%. The rate of return on asset is 5.32%. 82.48% of all firms in the industry made a profit while 10.56% had negative returns. The top province in terms of the industry's revenue is Anhui, accounting for 14.07% of the total revenue.
本行業在1996年佔全行業總產值0.074%，行業年增長率為17.7%（全國工業年增長率9.51%）。行業的資產回報率5.32%，82.48%的企業盈利，10.56%的企業虧損。銷售收入最高的省份為安徽省，佔本行業的14.07%。

	Total number of firms 企業總數	Total number of employees 職工總數	Total revenue (mil. RMB) 總銷售收入（百萬元）	Total profit (mil. RMB) 總利潤（百萬元）	Return on assets 資產利潤率 (%)	Return on equity 權益利潤率 (%)	Labour productivity ('000 RMB / worker) 勞動生產率（千元/人）	Debts / assets 資產負債率 (%)	Total assets (mil. RMB) 總資產（百萬元）
Industry Overall 行業總體	1,678	139,498	4,297	201	5.32	12.45	30.80	57.30	3,774

	Number of firms 企業個數	Average number of employees 平均職工人數	Average revenue ('000 RMB) 平均銷售收入（千元）	Average profit ('000 RMB) 平均利潤（千元）	Return on assets 資產利潤率 (%)	Return on equity 權益利潤率 (%)	Labour productivity ('000 RMB / worker) 勞動生產率（千元/人）	Average debts / assets 平均資產負債率(%)	Average Total assets ('000 RMB) 平均總資產（千元）
By ownership 產業所有權									
State-owned 國有	111	221	5,856	-108	-0.77	-1.46	26.45	47.04	14,018
Collectively-owned 集體	1,539	74	2,306	137	9.84	27.98	31.36	64.84	1,393
Privately-owned 私有	6	43	785	211	28.59	38.87	18.18	26.46	739
Domestic JVs 聯營	9	107	7,357	211	5.28	10.02	68.75	47.27	3,998
Joint stock 股份制	5	43	1,600	96	5.82	9.96	37.56	41.58	1,656
Foreign-funded 外資	2	30							
Overseas Chinese-funded 港澳台資	5	107	3,822	-331	-6.92	-29.83	35.85	76.82	4,787
By size 規模									
Large 大型	2	2,277	134,359	2,297	0.69	1.20	59.02	42.23	332,607
Medium 中型	11	908	31,859	1,361	2.41	5.27	35.09	54.23	56,428
Small 小型	1,654	75	2,223	110	7.29	19.25	29.52	62.11	1,504
By regional distribution 地區分布									
Central-North 華北	186	99	1,702	108	6.81	17.39	17.19	60.82	1,579
Beijing 北京	22	6	70	-5	-1.92	-15.28	10.85	87.46	261
Tianjin 天津	1	8,201	1,960				0.24	71.68	3,460
Hebei 河北	91	70	2,716	187	7.85	17.97	38.69	56.29	2,381
Shanxi 山西	28	44	1,196	20	1.73	7.47	27.16	76.82	1,176
Inner Mongolia 內蒙	44	56	738	57	7.24	22.95	13.21	68.46	791
Northeast 東北	203	55	1,287	51	3.83	15.87	23.31	75.85	1,341
Liaoning 遼寧	96	45	1,239	50	3.76	10.81	27.24	65.21	1,338
Jilin 吉林	49	69	1,208	17	0.86	9.96	17.62	91.41	2,023
Heilongjiang 黑龍江	58	60	1,432	82	10.65	37.97	23.88	71.92	769
Central East 華東	484	107	4,029	218	5.84	11.43	37.62	48.92	3,738
Shanghai 上海	2	116	2,405	-350	-6.84	-12.92	20.82	47.02	5,115
Jiangsu 江蘇	62	200	8,790	390	3.62	5.62	44.04	35.55	10,778
Zhejiang 浙江	58	125	4,432	134	1.86	3.75	35.43	50.50	7,211
Anhui 安徽	154	98	3,925	335	16.75	41.06	39.90	59.20	2,000
Fujian 福建	73	60	2,105	49	2.90	11.79	34.95	75.42	1,693
Jiangxi 江西	98	59	1,266	75	9.66	34.38	21.56	71.90	779
Shandong 山東	37	180	7,050	319	5.76	11.38	39.06	49.35	5,534
Central-South 中南	511	74	3,017	118	5.08	13.22	40.52	61.62	2,322
Henan 河南	44	115	4,834	255	8.41	21.79	41.87	61.41	3,028
Hubei 湖北	90	79	2,934	93	5.37	8.84	37.24	39.32	1,724
Hunan 湖南	139	69	2,091	64	9.74	25.81	30.50	62.24	655
Guangdong 廣東	172	60	3,278	144	3.46	10.80	54.90	67.97	4,152
Guangxi 廣西	58	103	3,625	123	7.66	15.24	35.26	49.72	1,602
Hainan 海南	8	14							
Southwest 西南	170	67	847	5	0.95	4.20	12.69	77.38	575
Chongqing 重慶	33	64	843	0	0.08	0.26	13.05	69.65	564
Sichuan 四川	110	75	948	1	0.18	0.89	12.56	80.22	665
Guizhou 貴州	15	33	296	31	26.14	50.00	9.10	47.73	117
Yunnan 雲南	11	36	585	33	10.29	39.13	16.45	73.71	318
Tibet 西藏									
Northwest 西北	124	70	675	29	3.11	12.27	9.68	74.67	927
Shaanxi 陝西	51	99	663	25	1.80	7.23	6.72	75.06	1,359
Gansu 甘肅	38	47	585	32	5.85	31.68	12.54	81.43	544
Qinghai 青海	10	32	198	4	1.96	33.33	6.21	93.63	204
Ningxia 寧夏	5	72	840	66	19.41	28.95	11.60	32.94	340
Xinjiang 新疆	20	58	1,073	37	3.49	11.00	18.42	68.30	1,060

1011: Limestone Quarrying 石灰石開採業

Year 年份	Number of firms 企業個數	Rate of change 每年變化 (%)	Number of employees 職工人數 (人)	Rate of change 每年變化 (%)	Total revenue (mil. RMB) 總銷售收入 (百萬元)	Rate of change 每年變化 (%)	Total profit (mil. RMB) 總利潤 (百萬元)	Rate of change 每年變化 (%)
1993	1,047		63,041		1,464		115	
1994	1,306	24.74%	107,516	70.55%	2,235	52.57%	135	17.41%
1995	1,693	29.63%	137,011	27.43%	3,652	63.41%	175	29.90%
1996	1,678	-0.89%	139,498	1.82%	4,297	17.66%	201	14.97%

3 Major products* 3種主要產品*	Output 產量	Sales volume 銷售量	Unit 單位
a) Limestone 石灰石	115,478	94,692	10,000 ton 萬噸
b) Building Lime 建築用石灰	8,719,110	8,719,110	ton 噸
c) Light Calcium Carbonate 輕質碳酸鈣	130,792	124,253	ton 噸

Top 10 firms by revenue (year founded) 收入排名前10家企業 (創辦年份)	City 城市	Province 省	Telephone / fax 電話 / 傳真	Number of employees 職工人數	Ownership 產業所有權	Revenue ('000 RMB) 銷售收入 (千元)	Profit ('000 RMB) (rank) 利潤 (千元) (排名)	Total assets ('000 RMB) 總資產 (千元)	Major products 主要產品
Zhenjiang Chuan Shan Group Co. Ltd. 鎮江船山集團有限責任公司(1973)	Zhenjiang 鎮江市	Jiangsu 江蘇省	(0511)5626944 (0511)5681894	2,941	State-owned 國有	196,911	3826(8)	444,435	a
Yulin Mao Lin Quarry Company 玉林市茂林石料公司	Yulin 玉林市	Guangxi 廣西		3,670	Collectively-owned 集體	86,000	892(53)	39,100	a
Yu Lao Zhen Quarry Development Co. Ltd. 漁澇鎮石料開發有限公司(1980)	Zhaoqing 肇慶市	Guangdong 廣東省		726	Collectively-owned 集體	71,739	9650(1)	13,225	a
Jilin Chemical Industrial Group Ming Cheng Limestone Mine 吉林化學工業公司明城石灰石礦(1950)	Jilin 吉林市	Jilin 吉林省	(0432)5714141 (0432)5712467	2,132	State-owned 國有	65,069	1770(21)	395,846	o
Huazhou Baishi Industry General Company 化州市白石工業總公司(1992)	Maoming 茂名市	Guangdong 廣東省	(0668)7550068	560	Collectively-owned 集體	60,232	5104(6)	26,476	c
Zhejiang Jin He Group Company 浙江金鶴集團公司(1994)	Huzhou 湖州市	Zhejiang 浙江省	(0572)6061125	486	Collectively-owned 集體	51,341	1841(19)	94,410	a
Huazhou Wen Lou Zhen Huan Yu Shuang Fei Fen Co. Ltd. 化州市文樓鎮環宇雙飛粉有限公司(1993)	Maoming 茂名市	Guangdong 廣東省	(0668)7550208	250	Collectively-owned 集體	45,174	3828(7)	17,550	c
Nanyang Wolongqu Pu Shan Min Cai Co. 南陽市卧龍區蒲山民採公司(1992)	Nanyang 南陽市	Henan 河南省	(0377)9811245	1,500	Collectively-owned 集體	42,100	3231(10)	2,224	b
Lai Binxian Chengxiang Xiang Quarry 來賓縣城廂鄉採石場(1987)	Heshan 合山市	Guangxi 廣西	(0772)4212284	397	Collectively-owned 集體	38,120	2750(14)	490	a
Tongshan Da Miao Zhen Xishan Quarrying Factory 銅山縣大廟鎮西山採石廠(1973)	Xuzhou 徐州市	Jiangsu 江蘇省	(0516)6730240	150	Collectively-owned 集體	38,101	3200(11)	28,186	a

Top 10 Cities by Production Output 產出排名前10位城市	Province 省	Market share 市場份額	Number of firms 企業個數
Zhenjiang 鎮江市	Jiangsu 江蘇省	9.64%	22
Chuzhou 滁州市	Anhui 安徽省	5.98%	25
Huzhou 湖州市	Zhejiang 浙江省	4.48%	44
Zhaoqing 肇慶市	Guangdong 廣東省	4.12%	17
Chongqing 重慶市	Chongqing 重慶市	3.36%	30
Yulin 玉林市	Guangxi 廣西	3.26%	23
Jilin 吉林市	Jilin 吉林省	2.18%	20
Guangzhou 廣州市	Guangdong 廣東省	2.15%	28
Tangshan 唐山市	Hebei 河北省	2.15%	27
Nanjing 南京市	Jiangsu 江蘇省	2.07%	22

10 Major Wholesalers 10家主要批發商	City 城市	Province 省	Telephone / Fax 電話 / 傳真
China Metallurgy Import & Export Liaoning Company 中國冶金進出口遼寧公司	Shenyang 瀋陽市	Liaoning 遼寧省	(024)23867070 (024)23875451
Liaoning Foreign Trade General Company 遼寧省對外貿易總公司	Dalian 大連市	Liaoning 遼寧省	(0411)3632157 (0411)3638243
Zhong Xin Trade Company 中信貿易公司	Beijing 北京市	Beijing 北京市	(010)64662170 (010)64662161
China Metallurgy Import & Export Shandong Company 中國冶金進出口山東公司	Qingdao 青島市	Shandong 山東省	(0532)2801118 (0532)2801331
Yongzhou Ferromanganese Mine Company 永州市錳鐵礦公司	Yongzhou 永州市	Hunan 湖南省	(0746)8464135
Zhengzhou Advanced Technology Industrial Development Zone Development General Company 鄭州高新技術產業開發區發展總公司	Zhengzhou 鄭州市	Henan 河南省	(0371)7981924 (0371)7981422
Guangdong Hardware Import & Export Group Company 廣東省五金進出口集團公司	Guangzhou 廣州市	Guangdong 廣東省	(020)87752204 (020)87752205
Xi Shan Shi Wu Kuang Trade Company 錫山市五礦貿易公司	Wuxi 無錫市	Jiangsu 江蘇省	(0510)7760988
Xiamen Ocean Petroleum Company 廈門海洋石油公司	Xiamen 廈門市	Fujian 福建省	(0592)2095495 (0592)2087292
Hainan Shen Hai Import & Export Co. Ltd. 海南深海進出口有限公司	Haikou 海口市	Hainan 海南省	(0898)6717646 (0898)6717639

*Also include sales by firms outside this industry.包括本行業以外廠家的銷售。"o" stands for "others". "o" 代表"其他產品"。

1012: Constructing Stone Quarrying 建築用石開採業

The industry accounts for 0.119% of the total revenue of China's industrial sector in 1996. The revenue growth rate of the industry is 5.7% from 1995, as compared to the growth rate of China's industrial sector, 9.51%. The rate of return on asset is 5.50%. 84.88% of all firms in the industry made a profit while 10.03% had negative returns. The top province in terms of the industry's revenue is Guangdong, accounting for 15.22% of the total revenue.
本行業在1996年佔全行業總產值0.119%，行業年增長率為5.7%（全國工業年增長率9.51%）。行業的資產回報率5.50%，84.88%的企業盈利，10.03%的企業虧損。銷售收入最高的省份為廣東省，佔本行業的15.22%。

	Total number of firms 企業總數	Total number of employees 職工總數	Total revenue (mil. RMB) 總銷售收入（百萬元）	Total profit (mil. RMB) 總利潤（百萬元）	Return on assets 資產利潤率 (%)	Return on equity 權益利潤率 (%)	Labour productivity ('000 RMB / worker) 勞動生產率（千元／人）	Debts / assets 資產負債率 (%)	Total assets (mil. RMB) 總資產（百萬元）
Industry Overall 行業總體	2,488	153,907	6,909	294	5.50	12.48	44.89	55.89	5,350

	Number of firms 企業個數	Average number of employees 平均職工人數	Average revenue ('000 RMB) 平均銷售收入（千元）	Average profit ('000 RMB) 平均利潤（千元）	Return on assets 資產利潤率 (%)	Return on equity 權益利潤率 (%)	Labour productivity ('000 RMB / worker) 勞動生產率（千元／人）	Average debts / assets 平均資產負債率(%)	Average Total assets ('000 RMB) 平均總資產（千元）
By ownership 產業所有權									
State-owned 國有	171	108	2,333	-47	-0.73	-2.04	21.66	64.23	6,409
Collectively-owned 集體	2,148	59	2,764	141	9.46	22.36	46.60	57.71	1,489
Privately-owned 私有	7	12	1,378	127	12.13	20.96	110.85	42.12	1,049
Domestic JVs 聯營	26	46	3,043	-185	-3.71	-7.93	65.71	53.20	4,988
Joint stock 股份制	16	96	2,128	89	3.44	7.19	22.12	52.15	2,587
Foreign-funded 外資	41	45	3,031	3	0.04	0.06	67.69	32.79	7,229
Overseas Chinese-funded 港澳台資	78	46	4,160	25	0.34	0.60	89.48	42.93	7,446
By size 規模									
Large 大型	2	485	31,235	249	0.40	2.27	64.47	82.40	62,256
Medium 中型	6	212	10,748	886	1.80	2.79	50.74	35.60	49,335
Small 小型	2,445	62	2,774	118	5.85	13.42	44.84	56.44	2,016
By regional distribution 地區分布									
Central-North 華北	284	43	1,721	152	8.15	19.33	40.40	57.82	1,864
Beijing 北京	24	18	1,401	47	1.96	3.11	79.29	37.16	2,406
Tianjin 天津	15	30	797	68	21.03	56.67	26.32	62.89	323
Hebei 河北	112	48	1,765	118	10.58	29.97	36.83	64.69	1,110
Shanxi 山西	61	39	2,763	405	10.11	24.45	70.72	58.65	4,007
Inner Mongolia 內蒙	72	48	1,069	44	3.21	7.82	22.19	58.97	1,360
Northeast 東北	442	53	1,610	119	10.09	28.25	30.24	64.29	1,175
Liaoning 遼寧	155	49	1,448	149	11.56	33.71	29.47	65.71	1,285
Jilin 吉林	137	44	888	38	4.71	13.01	20.12	63.76	816
Heilongjiang 黑龍江	150	66	2,435	161	11.57	31.46	37.04	63.22	1,389
Central East 華東	838	84	3,534	174	6.77	14.49	42.18	53.30	2,574
Shanghai 上海	3	128	3,743	-303	-7.12	-21.02	29.32	66.12	4,260
Jiangsu 江蘇	155	139	4,175	72	2.02	4.33	30.11	53.28	3,544
Zhejiang 浙江	189	98	3,144	70	1.87	4.06	31.99	53.83	3,748
Anhui 安徽	148	96	4,108	363	30.79	61.34	42.65	49.82	1,179
Fujian 福建	155	36	2,365	108	7.45	14.22	66.34	47.63	1,453
Jiangxi 江西	108	30	1,054	42	7.51	21.87	34.76	65.68	557
Shandong 山東	80	84	7,753	594	11.13	24.58	92.49	54.72	5,335
Central-South 中南	641	55	3,701	61	2.19	5.06	67.87	56.74	2,765
Henan 河南	94	78	2,888	149	7.23	20.10	36.82	64.01	2,053
Hubei 湖北	142	55	2,958	38	2.20	10.56	53.44	79.12	1,718
Hunan 湖南	79	62	1,811	74	7.80	16.03	29.21	51.35	954
Guangdong 廣東	250	51	4,207	23	0.59	1.40	82.92	58.03	3,946
Guangxi 廣西	66	29	7,004	152	4.15	5.67	238.90	26.89	3,669
Hainan 海南	10	21	2,389	-223	-7.11	-12.03	114.31	40.90	3,137
Southwest 西南	176	49	1,718	64	4.88	10.71	35.03	54.45	1,310
Chongqing 重慶	22	24	327	0	0.13	0.83	13.37	84.27	221
Sichuan 四川	86	54	2,001	51	3.15	9.19	37.02	65.73	1,633
Guizhou 貴州	51	28	728	33	3.22	3.64	26.07	11.51	1,012
Yunnan 雲南	11	167	7,015	486	21.55	75.25	41.92	71.41	2,257
Tibet 西藏	5	19	1,448	-36	-2.39	-6.16	76.21	61.17	1,504
Northwest 西北	107	42	681	27	2.03	4.01	16.23	49.22	1,318
Shaanxi 陝西	56	40	604	31	4.89	8.38	15.12	41.66	639
Gansu 甘肅	24	28	870	78	7.54	20.48	31.48	63.25	1,028
Qinghai 青海	3	5	70	-37	-12.79	-16.92	15.00	23.26	287
Ningxia 寧夏	14	44	411	40	13.43	21.88	9.26	38.61	298
Xinjiang 新疆	10	95	1,220	-119	-1.58	-3.10	12.82	49.10	7,552

1012: Constructing Stone Quarrying 建築用石開採業

Year 年份	Number of firms 企業個數	Rate of change 每年變化 (%)	Number of employees 職工人數 (人)	Rate of change 每年變化 (%)	Total revenue (mil. RMB) 總銷售收入 (百萬元)	Rate of change 每年變化 (%)	Total profit (mil. RMB) 總利潤 (百萬元)	Rate of change 每年變化 (%)
1993	3,062		140,728		4,324		398	
1994	3,679	20.15%	219,650	56.08%	5,789	33.87%	348	-12.51%
1995	2,631	-28.49%	177,015	-19.41%	6,537	12.92%	327	-6.16%
1996	2,488	-5.44%	153,907	-13.05%	6,909	5.69%	294	-9.98%

3 Major products* 3 種主要產品 *	Output 產量	Sales volume 銷售量	Unit 單位
a) Rough Granite Material 花崗石荒料	17,744,466	17,567,022	cubic metre 立方米
b) Marble Slab 大理石板材	3,132,952	2,882,316	square metre 平方米
c) Granite Slab 花崗石板材	1,666,115	1,666,115	square metre 平方米

Top 10 firms by revenue (year founded) 收入排名前 10 家企業 (創辦年份)	City 城市	Province 省	Telephone / fax 電話 / 傳真	Number of employees 職工人數	Ownership 產業所有權	Revenue ('000 RMB) 銷售收入 (千元)	Profit ('000 RMB) (rank) 利潤 (千元) (排名)	Total assets ('000 RMB) 總資產 (千元)	Major products 主要產品
Gongcheng Lianhua Zhen Stone Material General Company 恭城縣蓮花鎮石材總公司(1993)	Lingchuan 靈川縣	Guangxi 廣西	(0773)8112123		Collectively-owned 集體	331,090	6752(7)	153,170	a,c
Anhui Guoyang Longshan Zhen Building Materials Enterprise Group 安徽省渦陽縣龍山鎮建材企業集團(1992)	Fuyang 阜陽市	Anhui 安徽省		1,454	Collectively-owned 集體	158,550	26690(1)	26,810	o
Ji'nan Liu Bu Hong Granite Mill Processing Factory 濟南柳埠紅花崗石加工廠(1989)	Ji'nan 濟南市	Shandong 山東省	(0531)2993032	435	Collectively-owned 集體	93,350	9980(3)	13,540	a,c
Henan Nanzhao Ban Shan Ping Zhen Mine Products Resources Manage Office 河南省南召縣板山坪鎮礦產資源管理辦公室(1989)	Nanyang 南陽市	Henan 河南省		510	Collectively-owned 集體	85,190	600(115)	1,550	b
Kunming Xishan Hei Lin Pu Pian Di Fang Building Materials Management Station 昆明市西山區黑林鋪片地方建築材料管理站(1979)	Kunming 昆明市	Yunnan 雲南省	(0871)8183432	1,135	Collectively-owned 集體	72,164	5284(11)	3,170	o
Zhangjiagang Water Conservancy Mining Plant 張家港市水利採礦廠(1968)	Suzhou 蘇州市	Jiangsu 江蘇省	(0512)8392435	397	Collectively-owned 集體	69,717	4435(14)	15,539	o
Longhai Long Jia Quarry Co. Ltd. 龍海市龍佳石料有限公司(1988)	Zhangzhou 漳州市	Fujian 福建省	(0596)6777029 (0596)6777008	118	Overseas Chinese-funded 港澳台資	68,200	261(246)	15,471	a
Guangdong Yunan Suinan Industry & Trade Co. 廣東省郁南縣穗南工業貿易公司(1986)	Yunfu 雲浮市	Guangdong 廣東省	(0766)7593793	310	Collectively-owned 集體	60,853	20(525)	13,665	c
Shenzhen Da Peng Hong Li Quarry 深圳大鵬鴻利石場(1987)	Shenzhen 深圳市	Guangdong 廣東省	(0755)9197548	80	Foreign-funded 外資	57,950	-4230(683)	11,631	a
Qingdao Lei Xin Industrial General Company 青島磊鑫實業總公司(1994)	Qingdao 青島市	Shandong 山東省	(0532)7871288 (0532)7871288	65	Collectively-owned 集體	56,859	5783(10)	25,082	a

Top 10 Cities by Production Output 產出排名前 10 位城市	Province 省	Market share 市場份額	Number of firms 企業個數
Lingchuan 靈川縣	Guangxi 廣西	7.01%	9
Maoming 茂名市	Guangdong 廣東省	4.83%	39
Huzhou 湖州市	Zhejiang 浙江省	4.39%	78
Fuyang 阜陽市	Anhui 安徽省	3.73%	3
Wuxi 無錫市	Jiangsu 江蘇省	3.02%	26
Guangzhou 廣州市	Guangdong 廣東省	2.85%	51
Jiaxing 嘉興市	Zhejiang 浙江省	2.72%	25
Zhangjiakou 張家口市	Hebei 河北省	2.70%	19
Hangzhou 杭州市	Zhejiang 浙江省	2.42%	50
Changzhou 常州市	Jiangsu 江蘇省	2.07%	26

10 Major Wholesalers 10 家主要批發商	City 城市	Province 省	Telephone / Fax 電話 / 傳真
China Metallurgy Import & Export Liaoning Company 中國冶金進出口遼寧公司	Shenyang 瀋陽市	Liaoning 遼寧省	(024)23867070 (024)23875451
Liaoning Foreign Trade General Company 遼寧省對外貿易總公司	Dalian 大連市	Liaoning 遼寧省	(0411)3632157 (0411)3638243
Zhong Xin Trade Company 中信貿易公司	Beijing 北京市	Beijing 北京市	(010)64662170 (010)64662161
China Metallurgy Import & Export Shandong Company 中國冶金進出口山東公司	Qingdao 青島市	Shandong 山東省	(0532)2801118 (0532)2801331
Yongzhou Ferromanganese Mine Company 永州市錳鐵礦公司	Yongzhou 永州市	Hunan 湖南省	(0746)8464135
Zhengzhou Advanced Technology Industrial Development Zone Development General Company 鄭州高新技術產業開發區發展總公司	Zhengzhou 鄭州市	Henan 河南省	(0371)7981924 (0371)7981422
Guangdong Hardware Import & Export Group Company 廣東省五金進出口集團公司	Guangzhou 廣州市	Guangdong 廣東省	(020)87752204 (020)87752205
Xi Shan Shi Wu Kuang Trade Company 錫山市五礦貿易公司	Wuxi 無錫市	Jiangsu 江蘇省	(0510)7760988
Xiamen Ocean Petroleum Company 廈門海洋石油公司	Xiamen 廈門市	Fujian 福建省	(0592)2095495 (0592)2087292
Hainan Shen Hai Import & Export Co. Ltd. 海南深海進出口有限公司	Haikou 海口市	Hainan 海南省	(0898)6717646 (0898)6717639

*Also include sales by firms outside this industry.包括本行業以外廠家的銷售。"o" stands for "others". "o" 代表 "其他產品"。

1013: Refractory Clay and Stone Mining 耐火土石開採業

The industry accounts for 0.021% of the total revenue of China's industrial sector in 1996. The revenue growth rate of the industry is 18.5% from 1995, as compared to the growth rate of China's industrial sector, 9.51%. The rate of return on asset is 4.04%. 73.82% of all firms in the industry made a profit while 16.09% had negative returns. The top province in terms of the industry's revenue is Henan, accounting for 19.52% of the total revenue.
本行業在1996年佔全行業總產值0.021%，行業年增長率為18.5%（全國工業年增長率9.51%）。行業的資產回報率4.04%，73.82%的企業盈利，16.09%的企業虧損。銷售收入最高的省份為河南省，佔本行業的19.52%。

	Total number of firms 企業總數	Total number of employees 職工總數	Total revenue (mil. RMB) 總銷售收入（百萬元）	Total profit (mil. RMB) 總利潤（百萬元）	Return on assets 資產利潤率 (%)	Return on equity 權益利潤率 (%)	Labour productivity ('000 RMB / worker) 勞動生產率（千元/人）	Debts / assets 資產負債率 (%)	Total assets (mil. RMB) 總資產（百萬元）
Industry Overall 行業總體	419	36,475	1,197	65	4.04	11.93	32.82	66.12	1,607

	Number of firms 企業個數	Average number of employees 平均職工人數	Average revenue ('000 RMB) 平均銷售收入（千元）	Average profit ('000 RMB) 平均利潤（千元）	Return on assets 資產利潤率 (%)	Return on equity 權益利潤率 (%)	Labour productivity ('000 RMB / worker) 勞動生產率（千元/人）	Average debts / assets 平均資產負債率(%)	Average Total assets ('000 RMB) 平均總資產（千元）
By ownership 產業所有權									
State-owned 國有	38	357	5,763	-53	-0.19	-0.57	16.15	66.67	27,474
Collectively-owned 集體	372	59	2,304	154	11.27	32.93	39.32	65.78	1,365
Privately-owned 私有	1	8	275	149	144.44	189.48	34.40	23.77	103
Domestic JVs 聯營	1	8	826	33	15.94	323.62	103.20	95.07	206
Joint stock 股份制	1	50	2,653	-216	-5.53	-9.64	53.06	42.66	3,908
Foreign-funded 外資	3	292	30,428	3,585	43.86	69.78	104.32	37.14	8,173
Overseas Chinese-funded 港澳台資	4	45	6,604	-240	-3.63	-21.65	145.94	83.22	6,597
By size 規模									
Large 大型	3	2,711	71,698	132,497	47.22	161.63	26.44	70.78	280,586
Medium 中型	5	652	13,577	-1,087	-3.65	-8.08	20.82	54.81	29,765
Small 小型	408	61	2,242	-802	-53.04	-141.66	36.58	62.56	1,511
By regional distribution 地區分布									
Central-North 華北	65	101	1,365	55	0.89	4.16	13.46	78.54	6,189
Beijing 北京	1	25	270	-140	-8.97	56.00	10.80	116.03	1,560
Tianjin 天津									
Hebei 河北	16	177	1,678	123	1.08	6.21	9.47	82.56	11,306
Shanxi 山西	20	143	1,837	1	0.01	0.04	12.83	75.87	9,767
Inner Mongolia 內蒙	28	31	888	63	7.14	22.18	28.60	67.78	876
Northeast 東北	49	97	1,805	-30	-0.82	-2.71	18.53	69.56	3,638
Liaoning 遼寧	27	74	2,073	-28	-0.93	-3.68	27.99	74.71	2,986
Jilin 吉林	14	141	983	12	0.28	0.54	6.99	48.47	4,331
Heilongjiang 黑龍江	8	101	2,336	-111	-2.40	-33.84	23.25	92.90	4,629
Central East 華東	101	116	5,627	390	5.75	13.28	48.71	56.70	6,776
Shanghai 上海									
Jiangsu 江蘇	12	344	12,088	138	0.37	0.78	35.14	52.20	37,266
Zhejiang 浙江	8	61	868	-3	-0.25	-0.51	14.22	51.49	1,010
Anhui 安徽	31	94	6,630	453	12.49	41.52	70.44	69.91	3,628
Fujian 福建	11	15	762	35	19.79	36.19	52.05	45.31	175
Jiangxi 江西	11	44	540	21	4.61	15.75	12.27	70.74	454
Shandong 山東	28	125	7,016	823	21.00	54.48	56.32	61.45	3,919
Central-South 中南	123	87	3,200	169	8.99	31.22	36.97	71.19	1,879
Henan 河南	36	135	6,491	448	10.40	33.49	48.12	68.95	4,312
Hubei 湖北	12	80	3,703	78	3.45	34.94	46.47	90.16	2,270
Hunan 湖南	59	72	1,370	36	5.85	25.67	18.97	77.20	611
Guangdong 廣東	9	37	1,918	102	12.25	18.81	51.99	34.75	834
Guangxi 廣西	7	35	2,496	97	13.20	26.05	71.60	49.51	736
Hainan 海南									
Southwest 西南	51	32	738	31	1.84	5.12	22.90	64.13	1,667
Chongqing 重慶	20	31	324	-23	-1.94	-6.04	10.39	67.83	1,182
Sichuan 四川	20	30	1,138	69	2.61	7.57	36.89	65.48	2,637
Guizhou 貴州	9	34	811	73	20.06	50.00	23.93	59.88	366
Yunnan 雲南	1	87	760	10	0.25	0.34	8.74	27.23	4,040
Tibet 西藏									
Northwest 西北	30	38	663	38	4.38	10.88	17.24	59.85	875
Shaanxi 陝西	11	48	731	-3	-0.28	-1.44	15.31	80.30	960
Gansu 甘肅	15	28	623	65	7.10	13.40	21.92	47.14	911
Qinghai 青海	3	31	277	7	1.34	2.86	9.02	53.02	497
Ningxia 寧夏	1	110	1,670	190	35.19	35.19	15.18		540
Xinjiang 新疆									

1013: Refractory Clay and Stone Mining 耐火土石開採業

Year 年份	Number of firms 企業個數	Rate of change 每年變化 (%)	Number of employees 職工人數 (人)	Rate of change 每年變化 (%)	Total revenue (mil. RMB) 總銷售收入 (百萬元)	Rate of change 每年變化 (%)	Total profit (mil. RMB) 總利潤 (百萬元)	Rate of change 每年變化 (%)
1993	420		34,543		674		5	
1994	437	4.05%	29,930	-13.36%	703	4.30%	8	38.07%
1995	458	4.81%	42,283	41.27%	1,010	43.81%	-7	-186.90%
1996	419	-8.52%	36,475	-13.74%	1,197	18.51%	65	1093.43%

3 Major products* 3 種主要產品 *	Output 產量	Sales volume 銷售量	Unit 單位
a) Aluminium Raw Ore 鋁原礦	592,739	598,667	ton 噸
b) Finished Dolomite Ore 白雲石成品礦	3,066,222	2,820,924	ton 噸
c) Finished Refractory Clay Ore 耐火粘土成品礦	4,684,174	4,215,757	ton 噸

Top 10 firms by revenue (year founded) 收入排名前 10 家企業 (創辦年份)	City 城市	Province 省	Telephone / fax 電話 / 傳真	Number of employees 職工人數	Ownership 產業所有權	Revenue ('000 RMB) 銷售收入 (千元)	Profit ('000 RMB) (rank) 利潤 (千元) (排名)	Total assets ('000 RMB) 總資產 (千元)	Major products 主要產品
Suzhou Wan Bei Dolomite Mine 宿州市皖北白雲石礦(1992)	Suzhou 宿州市	Anhui 安徽省	(0557)3027517	151	Collectively-owned 集體	80,100	11151(1)	13,149	o
Nanjing Dolomite Mine 南京白雲石礦(1950)	Nanjing 南京市	Jiangsu 江蘇省	(025)5504711 (025)5502113	2,111	State-owned 國有	73,944	1002(9)	367,209	b
Dengfeng Aluminium Industry Group Company 登封市鋁業集團公司(1985)	Zhengzhou 鄭州市	Henan 河南省		800	Collectively-owned 集體	59,940	6000(3)	28,620	o
Jinan Huier Bauxiticlay Co. Ltd. 濟南惠爾頓硬質粘土有限公司(1993)	Ji'nan 濟南市	Shandong 山東省	(0531)3471494	573	Foreign-funded 外資	50,087	11003(2)	25,722	a
Yicheng Zuo Zhuang Xiang Dolomite Mine 嶧城區左裝鄉白雲石礦(1991)	Zaozhuang 棗莊市	Shandong 山東省	(0632)7011098 (0632)7011098	180	Collectively-owned 集體	37,360	950(11)	500	b
Nanyang Yin Shan Cyanite Mine 南陽隱山藍晶石礦(1987)	Nanyang 南陽市	Henan 河南省	(0377)3722236	299	Collectively-owned 集體	36,570	2150(7)	10,023	o
Yuzhou Chang Zhuang Xiang Alumina Mine 禹州市萇裝鄉鋁礬土礦(1972)	Xuchang 許昌市	Henan 河南省	(0374)8761118	818	Collectively-owned 集體	24,100	3020(4)	3,200	c
Henan Gongyi Kaolin Ore Dressing Factory 河南省鞏義市高嶺土選礦廠(1990)	Zhengzhou 鄭州市	Henan 河南省	(0371)4056132	212	Collectively-owned 集體	23,859	127(61)	11,365	o
Dantu Jian Bi Baiyun General Factory 丹徒縣諫壁白雲總廠(1952)	Zhenjiang 鎮江市	Jiangsu 江蘇省	(0511)3361259	380	State-owned 國有	21,673	5(87)	9,630	b
Dantu Qing Long Shan Dolomite Mine 丹徒縣青龍山白雲石礦(1959)	Zhenjiang 鎮江市	Jiangsu 江蘇省	(0511)3361571 (0511)3372570	950	State-owned 國有	20,836	260(47)	55,194	b

Top 10 Cities by Production Output 產出排名前 10 位城市	Province 省	Market share 市場份額	Number of firms 企業個數
Zhengzhou 鄭州市	Henan 河南省	12.42%	4
Ji'nan 濟南市	Shandong 山東省	10.42%	7
Nanjing 南京市	Jiangsu 江蘇省	8.02%	4
Yueyang 岳陽市	Hunan 湖南省	5.85%	31
Nanyang 南陽市	Henan 河南省	5.32%	12
Xuchang 許昌市	Henan 河南省	3.83%	6
Zaozhuang 棗莊市	Shandong 山東省	3.51%	3
Chuzhou 滁州市	Anhui 安徽省	3.45%	6
Yangquan 陽泉市	Shanxi 山西省	3.40%	11
Zhenjiang 鎮江市	Jiangsu 江蘇省	2.68%	3

10 Major Wholesalers 10 家主要批發商	City 城市	Province 省	Telephone / Fax 電話 / 傳真
China Metallurgy Import & Export Liaoning Company 中國冶金進出口遼寧公司	Shenyang 瀋陽市	Liaoning 遼寧省	(024)23867070 (024)23875451
Liaoning Foreign Trade General Company 遼寧省對外貿易總公司	Dalian 大連市	Liaoning 遼寧省	(0411)3632157 (0411)3638243
Zhong Xin Trade Company 中信貿易公司	Beijing 北京市	Beijing 北京市	(010)64662170 (010)64662161
China Metallurgy Import & Export Shandong Company 中國冶金進出口山東公司	Qingdao 青島市	Shandong 山東省	(0532)2801118 (0532)2801331
Yongzhou Ferromanganese Mine Company 永州市錳鐵礦公司	Yongzhou 永州市	Hunan 湖南省	(0746)8464135
Zhengzhou Advanced Technology Industrial Development Zone Development General Company 鄭州高新技術產業開發區發展總公司	Zhengzhou 鄭州市	Henan 河南省	(0371)7981924 (0371)7981422
Guangdong Hardware Import & Export Group Company 廣東省五金進出口集團公司	Guangzhou 廣州市	Guangdong 廣東省	(020)87752204 (020)87752205
Xi Shan Shi Wu Kuang Trade Company 錫山市五礦貿易公司	Wuxi 無錫市	Jiangsu 江蘇省	(0510)7760988
Xiamen Ocean Petroleum Company 廈門海洋石油公司	Xiamen 廈門市	Fujian 福建省	(0592)2095495 (0592)2087292
Hainan Shen Hai Import & Export Co. Ltd. 海南深海進出口有限公司	Haikou 海口市	Hainan 海南省	(0898)6717646 (0898)6717639

*Also include sales by firms outside this industry.包括本行業以外廠家的銷售。"o" stands for "others". "o" 代表 "其他產品"。

1019: Other Clay, Sand and Stone Mining 其他土砂石開採業

The industry accounts for 0.139% of the total revenue of China's industrial sector in 1996. The revenue growth rate of the industry is 22.4% from 1995, as compared to the growth rate of China's industrial sector, 9.51%. The rate of return on asset is 8.38%. 85.81% of all firms in the industry made a profit while 9.69% had negative returns. The top province in terms of the industry's revenue is Anhui, accounting for 27.41% of the total revenue.
本行業在1996年佔全行業總產值0.139%，行業年增長率為22.4%（全國工業年增長率9.51%）。行業的資產回報率8.38%，85.81%的企業盈利，9.69%的企業虧損。銷售收入最高的省份為安徽省，佔本行業的27.41%。

	Total number of firms 企業總數	Total number of employees 職工總數	Total revenue (mil. RMB) 總銷售收入（百萬元）	Total profit (mil. RMB) 總利潤（百萬元）	Return on assets 資產利潤率 (%)	Return on equity 權益利潤率 (%)	Labour productivity ('000 RMB / worker) 勞動生產率（千元/人）	Debts / assets 資產負債率 (%)	Total assets (mil. RMB) 總資產（百萬元）
Industry Overall 行業總體	3,383	219,472	8,065	444	8.38	20.87	36.75	59.84	5,297

	Number of firms 企業個數	Average number of employees 平均職工人數	Average revenue ('000 RMB) 平均銷售收入（千元）	Average profit ('000 RMB) 平均利潤（千元）	Return on assets 資產利潤率 (%)	Return on equity 權益利潤率 (%)	Labour productivity ('000 RMB / worker) 勞動生產率（千元/人）	Average debts / assets 平均資產負債率(%)	Average Total assets ('000 RMB) 平均總資產（千元）
By ownership 產業所有權									
State-owned 國有	222	108	2,986	72	0.98	2.60	27.66	62.28	7,356
Collectively-owned 集體	3,097	61	2,311	136	13.49	33.19	37.69	59.36	1,005
Privately-owned 私有	7	21	1,391	160	12.28	35.57	67.15	65.47	1,301
Domestic JVs 聯營	13	62	1,379	16	0.83	1.78	22.22	53.23	1,961
Joint stock 股份制	19	184	5,310	739	5.20	14.19	28.92	63.37	14,219
Foreign-funded 外資	10	61	6,282	129	2.06	4.24	103.15	51.54	6,295
Overseas Chinese-funded 港澳台資	15	52	3,611	-581	-4.75	-8.60	69.62	44.75	12,216
By size 規模									
Large 大型	1	941	21,021	11,191	6.12	16.72	22.34	63.40	182,888
Medium 中型	9	593	13,828	443	0.96	1.72	23.32	44.22	46,094
Small 小型	3,355	63	2,360	128	9.13	23.46	37.22	61.09	1,400
By regional distribution 地區分布									
Central-North 華北	404	43	1,307	101	4.73	10.52	30.08	55.06	2,145
Beijing 北京	77	35	1,103	8	0.24	0.40	31.75	39.39	3,128
Tianjin 天津	5	101	914	-428	-4.96	-5.57	9.05	10.91	8,632
Hebei 河北	129	50	1,964	209	7.97	21.31	39.35	62.62	2,628
Shanxi 山西	65	44	1,016	61	5.37	17.11	22.86	68.59	1,131
Inner Mongolia 內蒙	128	39	929	90	6.79	20.92	23.61	67.53	1,330
Northeast 東北	529	38	1,148	58	5.07	16.61	30.26	69.46	1,139
Liaoning 遼寧	191	41	1,046	59	6.17	20.71	25.57	70.21	964
Jilin 吉林	110	33	1,111	66	6.70	24.43	34.15	72.59	991
Heilongjiang 黑龍江	228	38	1,251	52	3.85	11.99	32.89	67.92	1,358
Central East 華東	1,164	98	3,632	226	12.17	29.32	37.10	58.48	1,855
Shanghai 上海									
Jiangsu 江蘇	194	88	4,052	145	7.38	18.88	46.17	60.93	1,972
Zhejiang 浙江	99	65	2,643	139	5.85	16.25	40.85	63.96	2,377
Anhui 安徽	445	154	4,968	357	25.21	55.02	32.30	54.19	1,415
Fujian 福建	114	43	1,594	117	5.40	8.40	37.06	35.70	2,164
Jiangxi 江西	206	45	844	13	1.05	5.23	18.79	80.02	1,235
Shandong 山東	106	75	5,791	434	11.23	28.07	77.47	60.01	3,868
Central-South 中南	781	59	2,761	116	7.12	17.73	47.05	59.87	1,631
Henan 河南	101	54	1,665	59	3.56	9.93	30.60	64.10	1,642
Hubei 湖北	174	98	5,415	257	10.79	32.62	55.36	66.92	2,384
Hunan 湖南	252	58	1,899	87	8.81	22.34	32.54	60.54	982
Guangdong 廣東	154	28	1,905	55	2.59	5.60	67.27	53.83	2,123
Guangxi 廣西	95	44	2,860	101	9.28	16.55	65.45	43.94	1,086
Hainan 海南	5	20	522	32	1.00	1.95	26.10	49.07	3,216
Southwest 西南	294	43	1,268	30	4.81	14.02	29.16	65.70	634
Chongqing 重慶	42	41	540	5	1.06	6.43	13.06	83.55	457
Sichuan 四川	178	49	1,810	30	3.62	10.60	36.50	65.87	825
Guizhou 貴州	52	23	211	23	17.29	31.68	9.01	45.57	135
Yunnan 雲南	19	46	823	111	17.46	32.66	18.04	46.55	633
Tibet 西藏	2	46	220	95	26.76	67.86	4.78	60.56	355
Northwest 西北	211	44	817	48	4.85	12.29	18.55	60.54	988
Shaanxi 陝西	61	32	815	29	4.79	10.15	25.60	52.80	605
Gansu 甘肅	68	68	1,219	88	5.99	17.60	17.92	66.01	1,474
Qinghai 青海	25	22	189	22	4.89	8.96	8.44	45.37	450
Ningxia 寧夏	20	48	561	61	12.47	26.81	11.72	53.48	489
Xinjiang 新疆	37	33	646	15	1.13	2.84	19.70	60.09	1,359

1019: Other Clay, Sand and Stone Mining 其他土砂石開採業

Year 年份	Number of firms 企業個數	Rate of change 每年變化 (%)	Number of employees 職工人數（人）	Rate of change 每年變化 (%)	Total revenue (mil. RMB) 總銷售收入（百萬元）	Rate of change 每年變化 (%)	Total profit (mil. RMB) 總利潤（百萬元）	Rate of change 每年變化 (%)
1993	3,135		111,572		3,693		257	
1994	3,720	18.66%	183,763	64.70%	5,047	36.68%	312	21.24%
1995	3,356	-9.79%	194,186	5.67%	6,591	30.58%	399	28.12%
1996	3,383	0.80%	219,472	13.02%	8,065	22.36%	444	11.21%

3 Major products* 3 種主要產品*	Output 產量	Sales volume 銷售量	Unit 單位
a) Silica 硅石	27,559,182	26,181,223	ton 噸
b) Fluorite 螢石	413,733	376,497	ton 噸

Top 10 firms by revenue (year founded) 收入排名前10家企業（創辦年份）	City 城市	Province 省	Telephone / fax 電話／傳真	Number of employees 職工人數	Ownership 產業所有權	Revenue ('000 RMB) 銷售收入（千元）	Profit ('000 RMB) (rank) 利潤（千元）（排名）	Total assets ('000 RMB) 總資產（千元）	Major products 主要產品
Tang Chi Sandstone Company 湯池砂石公司(1992)	Liu'an 六安市	Anhui 安徽省		65	Collectively-owned 集體	88,850	1600(41)	18,200	a
Pizhou Gang Shang Mine Products Resources Management Office 邳州市港上礦產資源管理所(1987)	Xuzhou 徐州市	Jiangsu 江蘇省	(0516)6451174	150	Collectively-owned 集體	70,008	340(268)	408	o
Dianbai Po Xin Zhen River Sand Company 電白縣坡心鎮河沙公司(1992)	Maoming 茂名市	Guangdong 廣東省	(0668)5210043	307	Collectively-owned 集體	62,500	1310(54)	7,860	o
Rongcheng Xu Kou Silicon Sand Mine 榮成市旭口硅砂礦(1976)	Weihai 威海市	Shandong 山東省	(0896)7861083	110	Collectively-owned 集體	58,500	2800(16)	10,330	a
Zhangwan Sandstone Development Company 張灣砂石開發公司	Yichang 宜昌市	Hubei 湖北省		78	Collectively-owned 集體	57,060	3400(11)	813	o
Suqian Shiling Yellow Sand Purchasing & Marketing Management Co. 宿遷市侍嶺鄉黃砂採銷管理公司(1980)	Suqian 宿遷市	Jiangsu 江蘇省	(0527)4880066	500	Collectively-owned 集體	48,840	-70(737)	2,994	o
Shuangliu Huang Shui Zhen River Management Station 雙流縣黃水鎮江河管理站	Chengdu 成都市	Sichuan 四川省		516	Collectively-owned 集體	48,642	256(340)	435	o
Funan Gao Tai Yellow Sand Development Company 阜南縣郜台黃砂開發公司(1992)	Fuyang 阜陽市	Anhui 安徽省		250	Collectively-owned 集體	46,000	15950(1)	1,880	o
Laizhou Hong Xing Group General Company 萊州市宏興集團總公司(1979)	Yantai 煙台市	Shandong 山東省	(0535)2571126 (0535)2571126	410	Collectively-owned 集體	45,690	3460(10)	42,863	b
Mingguan Daxing Building Materials Company 明光大興建材公司(1972)	Chuzhou 滁州市	Anhui 安徽省	(0550)8024312	821	Collectively-owned 集體	44,000	80(540)	2,810	o

Top 10 Cities by Production Output 產出排名前10位城市	Province 省	Market share 市場份額	Number of firms 企業個數
Chuzhou 滁州市	Anhui 安徽省	13.85%	128
Liu'an 六安市	Anhui 安徽省	5.88%	57
Beijing 北京市	Beijing 北京市	4.35%	75
Suqian 宿遷市	Jiangsu 江蘇省	3.33%	34
Wuhu 蕪湖市	Anhui 安徽省	2.01%	38
Chaohu 巢湖市	Anhui 安徽省	1.90%	29
Xuanzhou 宣州市	Anhui 安徽省	1.80%	42
Shaoxing 紹興市	Zhejiang 浙江省	1.79%	21
Huludao 葫蘆島市	Liaoning 遼寧省	1.69%	32
Chengde 承德市	Hebei 河北省	1.48%	61

10 Major Wholesalers 10家主要批發商	City 城市	Province 省	Telephone / Fax 電話／傳真
China Metallurgy Import & Export Liaoning Company 中國冶金進出口遼寧公司	Shenyang 瀋陽市	Liaoning 遼寧省	(024)23867070 (024)23875451
Liaoning Foreign Trade General Company 遼寧省對外貿易總公司	Dalian 大連市	Liaoning 遼寧省	(0411)3632157 (0411)3638243
Zhong Xin Trade Company 中信貿易公司	Beijing 北京市	Beijing 北京市	(010)64662170 (010)64662161
China Metallurgy Import & Export Shandong Company 中國冶金進出口山東公司	Qingdao 青島市	Shandong 山東省	(0532)2801118 (0532)2801331
Yongzhou Ferromanganese Mine Company 永州市錳鐵礦公司	Yongzhou 永州市	Hunan 湖南省	(0746)8464135
Zhengzhou Advanced Technology Industrial Development Zone Development General Company 鄭州高新技術產業開發區發展總公司	Zhengzhou 鄭州市	Henan 河南省	(0371)7981924 (0371)7981422
Guangdong Hardware Import & Export Group Company 廣東省五金進出口集團公司	Guangzhou 廣州市	Guangdong 廣東省	(020)87752204 (020)87752205
Xi Shan Shi Wu Kuang Trade Company 錫山市五礦貿易公司	Wuxi 無錫市	Jiangsu 江蘇省	(0510)7760988
Xiamen Ocean Petroleum Company 廈門海洋石油公司	Xiamen 廈門市	Fujian 福建省	(0592)2095495 (0592)2087292
Hainan Shen Hai Import & Export Co. Ltd. 海南深海進出口有限公司	Haikou 海口市	Hainan 海南省	(0898)6717646 (0898)6717639

*Also include sales by firms outside this industry.包括本行業以外廠家的銷售。"o" stands for "others". "o" 代表"其他產品"。

1021: Sulfur Ores Mining and Dressing 硫礦採選業

The industry accounts for 0.024% of the total revenue of China's industrial sector in 1996. The revenue growth rate of the industry is 19.8% from 1995, as compared to the growth rate of China's industrial sector, 9.51%. The rate of return on asset is 1.09%. 71.55% of all firms in the industry made a profit while 17.83% had negative returns. The top province in terms of the industry's revenue is Guangdong, accounting for 25.83% of the total revenue.
本行業在1996年佔全行業總產值0.024%，行業年增長率為19.8%（全國工業年增長率9.51%）。行業的資產回報率1.09%，71.55%的企業盈利，17.83%的企業虧損。銷售收入最高的省份為廣東省，佔本行業的25.83%。

	Total number of firms 企業總數	Total number of employees 職工總數	Total revenue (mil. RMB) 總銷售收入（百萬元）	Total profit (mil. RMB) 總利潤（百萬元）	Return on assets 資產利潤率 (%)	Return on equity 權益利潤率 (%)	Labour productivity ('000 RMB / worker) 勞動生產率（千元/人）	Debts / assets 資產負債率 (%)	Total assets (mil. RMB) 總資產（百萬元）
Industry Overall 行業總體	362	67,849	1,369	34	1.09	2.91	20.18	62.62	3,155

	Number of firms 企業個數	Average number of employees 平均職工人數	Average revenue ('000 RMB) 平均銷售收入（千元）	Average profit ('000 RMB) 平均利潤（千元）	Return on assets 資產利潤率 (%)	Return on equity 權益利潤率 (%)	Labour productivity ('000 RMB / worker) 勞動生產率（千元/人）	Average debts / assets 平均資產負債率(%)	Average Total assets ('000 RMB) 平均總資產（千元）
By ownership 產業所有權									
State-owned 國有	72	571	10,208	-125	-0.35	-0.89	17.89	60.58	35,583
Collectively-owned 集體	284	96	2,204	168	8.51	28.91	22.97	70.57	1,973
Privately-owned 私有									
Domestic JVs 聯營	1	21						5.20	897
Joint stock 股份制	2	56	2,847	944	26.36	136.91	51.29	80.75	3,581
Foreign-funded 外資	1	34	1,945	-944	-5.69	159.95	57.20	103.56	16,586
Overseas Chinese-funded 港澳台資	1	79	937	-5,618	-74.02	-374.23	11.86	80.22	7,590
By size 規模									
Large 大型	1	5,817	255,831	21,333	2.12	4.27	43.98	50.34	1,005,514
Medium 中型	11	1,391	24,848	-3,111	-5.51	-19.12	17.86	71.16	56,416
Small 小型	346	135	2,428	136	3.07	9.36	17.92	67.25	4,421
By regional distribution 地區分布									
Central-North 華北	50	244	3,734	183	1.86	5.38	15.29	65.39	9,821
Beijing 北京									
Tianjin 天津									
Hebei 河北	6	337	6,148	1,117	7.91	26.01	18.26	69.60	14,123
Shanxi 山西	36	138	2,347	9	0.17	0.56	17.05	69.91	5,093
Inner Mongolia 內蒙	8	655	8,166	266	0.96	2.39	12.48	60.07	27,866
Northeast 東北	31	344	3,514	91	1.12	8.65	10.22	87.06	8,162
Liaoning 遼寧	26	368	3,726	66	0.75	5.69	10.12	86.83	8,828
Jilin 吉林	3	45	1,997	213	46.72	256.00	44.37	81.75	457
Heilongjiang 黑龍江	2	473	3,025	235	2.13	20.80	6.40	89.73	11,055
Central East 華東	54	164	6,347	403	4.54	10.63	38.59	57.35	8,892
Shanghai 上海									
Jiangsu 江蘇	6	490	11,890	215	0.69	1.27	24.25	45.40	31,063
Zhejiang 浙江	2	8	230				30.67	86.27	255
Anhui 安徽	25	171	9,176	756	10.11	28.96	53.56	65.10	7,477
Fujian 福建	12	80	2,758	79	1.24	2.66	34.58	53.28	6,373
Jiangxi 江西	7	76	751	64	1.83	15.20	9.87	87.94	3,507
Shandong 山東	2	76	1,590	100	3.74	-21.05	20.92	117.94	2,675
Central-South 中南	85	206	6,317	26	0.15	0.35	30.70	56.44	16,709
Henan 河南	17	63	2,261	194	3.41	29.95	35.85	88.61	5,687
Hubei 湖北	28	75	1,364	16	1.43	5.09	18.07	71.91	1,148
Hunan 湖南	12	410	7,107	-418	-2.13	-10.80	17.33	80.27	19,595
Guangdong 廣東	17	498	20,804	168	0.28	0.53	41.76	47.55	60,474
Guangxi 廣西	11	83	1,945	53	2.05	4.45	23.41	53.89	2,569
Hainan 海南									
Southwest 西南	119	139	1,406	-14	-0.39	-1.25	10.08	69.10	3,714
Chongqing 重慶	12	221	917	-6	-0.18	1.07	4.15	116.68	3,130
Sichuan 四川	45	234	2,768	-1	-0.01	-0.04	11.78	63.46	7,898
Guizhou 貴州	55	51	399	-40	-7.02	-26.56	7.83	73.56	575
Yunnan 雲南	5	69	1,456	106	4.87	20.31	21.10	76.03	2,178
Tibet 西藏	1	20	440	90	25.71	25.71	22.00		350
Northwest 西北	23	87	1,160	6	0.20	0.83	13.27	75.60	2,988
Shaanxi 陝西	20	89	1,144	36	1.23	4.12	12.81	70.20	2,895
Gansu 甘肅									
Qinghai 青海	1	190	2,160	-610	-7.79	40.13	11.37	119.41	7,830
Ningxia 寧夏									
Xinjiang 新疆	2	18	825	20	1.33	3.85	47.14	65.45	1,505

1021: Sulfur Ores Mining and Dressing 硫礦採選業

Year 年份	Number of firms 企業個數	Rate of change 每年變化 (%)	Number of employees 職工人數 (人)	Rate of change 每年變化 (%)	Total revenue (mil. RMB) 總銷售收入 (百萬元)	Rate of change 每年變化 (%)	Total profit (mil. RMB) 總利潤 (百萬元)	Rate of change 每年變化 (%)
1993	338		59,198		727		1	
1994	345	2.07%	65,699	10.98%	851	17.04%	-7	-808.44%
1995	354	2.61%	72,568	10.46%	1,143	34.31%	11	262.27%
1996	362	2.26%	67,849	-6.50%	1,369	19.77%	34	211.98%

3 Major products* 3 種主要產品 *	Output 產量	Sales volume 銷售量	Unit 單位
a) Ferric Sulfide Ore 硫鐵礦	16,327,586	14,694,828	ton 噸
b) Sulfuric Acid 硫酸	403,272	217,767	ton 噸

Top 10 firms by revenue (year founded) 收入排名前 10 家企業 (創辦年份)	City 城市	Province 省	Telephone / fax 電話 / 傳真	Number of employees 職工人數	Ownership 產業所有權	Revenue ('000 RMB) 銷售收入 (千元)	Profit ('000 RMB) (rank) 利潤 (千元) (排名)	Total assets ('000 RMB) 總資產 (千元)	Major products 主要產品
Yunfu Sulfurous Iron Ore Enterprise Group Corp. 雲浮硫鐵礦企業集團公司(1988)	Yunfu 雲浮市	Guangdong 廣東省	(0766)8825123 (0766)8828120	6,257	State-owned 國有	277,983	2832(7)	863,894	a,b
Tongling Tian Xiang Industrial General Co. 銅陵市天翔實業總公司(1969)	Tongling 銅陵市	Anhui 安徽省	(0562)2850350	680	Collectively-owned 集體	47,980	1634(12)	32,292	o
Nanjing Yuntai Shan Sulfuration Iron Mine 南京雲台山硫鐵礦(1958)	Nanjing 南京市	Jiangsu 江蘇省	(025)6161993 (025)6161992	1,479	State-owned 國有	45,807	654(20)	81,992	a,b
Anhui Tongling Zhong Ming Sulfuration Iron Mine 安徽省銅陵縣鐘鳴硫鐵礦(1986)	Tongling 銅陵市	Anhui 安徽省		444	Collectively-owned 集體	42,000	6720(2)	17,000	a
Tianquan Chang He Multiple Development Company 天全長河綜合開發公司(1978)	Ya'an 雅安市	Sichuan 四川省	(0835)382216	750	State-owned 國有	38,429	7896(1)	113,651	a,b
Hunan Qi Baoshan Sulfurous Iron Ore 湖南省七寶山硫鐵礦(1973)	Changsha 長沙市	Hunan 湖南省	(0731)3539287	1,671	State-owned 國有	36,778	6(78)	110,558	a
Fushun Hong Tou Shan Copper Mine Service Co. 撫順紅透山銅礦服務公司(1978)	Fushun 撫順市	Liaoning 遼寧省	(0413)3265524	3,593	Collectively-owned 集體	32,727	35(68)	24,244	a
Lujiang Jing Xiang Mining Company 廬江縣井巷開採公司(1996)	Chaohu 巢湖市	Anhui 安徽省		46	Collectively-owned 集體	24,480	500(27)	1,068	o
Guangdong Yingde Hongyan Sulfurous Iron Ore 廣東省英德市紅岩硫鐵礦(1977)	Qingyuan 清遠市	Guangdong 廣東省	(0763)2821322	253	Collectively-owned 集體	23,478	3300(5)	20,579	a
Anhui Tongling Xin Qiao Sulfurous Iron Ore 安徽省銅陵縣新橋硫鐵礦(1989)	Tongling 銅陵市	Anhui 安徽省	(0562)8701441	374	Collectively-owned 集體	18,065	2891(6)	11,868	a

Top 10 Cities by Production Output 產出排名前 10 位城市	Province 省	Market share 市場份額	Number of firms 企業個數
Yunfu 雲浮市	Guangdong 廣東省	23.87%	1
Tongling 銅陵市	Anhui 安徽省	7.80%	8
Ma'anshan 馬鞍山市	Anhui 安徽省	6.07%	3
Nanjing 南京市	Jiangsu 江蘇省	4.69%	1
Xiaoyi 孝義市	Shanxi 山西省	3.93%	4
Ya'an 雅安市	Sichuan 四川省	3.25%	13
Linhe 臨河市	Inner Mong 內蒙	3.24%	3
Yangquan 陽泉市	Shanxi 山西省	3.03%	12
Changsha 長沙市	Hunan 湖南省	2.84%	1
Huludao 葫蘆島市	Liaoning 遼寧省	2.72%	7

10 Major Wholesalers 10 家主要批發商	City 城市	Province 省	Telephone / Fax 電話 / 傳真
China Metallurgy Import & Export Liaoning Company 中國冶金進出口遼寧公司	Shenyang 瀋陽市	Liaoning 遼寧省	(024)23867070 (024)23875451
Liaoning Foreign Trade General Company 遼寧省對外貿易總公司	Dalian 大連市	Liaoning 遼寧省	(0411)3632157 (0411)3638243
Zhong Xin Trade Company 中信貿易公司	Beijing 北京市	Beijing 北京市	(010)64662170 (010)64662161
China Metallurgy Import & Export Shandong Company 中國冶金進出口山東公司	Qingdao 青島市	Shandong 山東省	(0532)2801118 (0532)2801331
Yongzhou Ferromanganese Mine Company 永州市錳鐵礦公司	Yongzhou 永州市	Hunan 湖南省	(0746)8464135
Zhengzhou Advanced Technology Industrial Development Zone Development General Company 鄭州高新技術產業開發區發展總公司	Zhengzhou 鄭州市	Henan 河南省	(0371)7981924 (0371)7981422
Guangdong Hardware Import & Export Group Company 廣東省五金進出口集團公司	Guangzhou 廣州市	Guangdong 廣東省	(020)87752204 (020)87752205
Xi Shan Shi Wu Kuang Trade Company 錫山市五礦貿易公司	Wuxi 無錫市	Jiangsu 江蘇省	(0510)7760988
Xiamen Ocean Petroleum Company 廈門海洋石油公司	Xiamen 廈門市	Fujian 福建省	(0592)2095495 (0592)2087292
Hainan Shen Hai Import & Export Co. Ltd. 海南深海進出口有限公司	Haikou 海口市	Hainan 海南省	(0898)6717646 (0898)6717639

*Also include sales by firms outside this industry.包括本行業以外廠家的銷售。"o" stands for "others". "o" 代表"其他產品"。

1022: Phosphorus Ores Mining and Dressing 磷礦採選業

The industry accounts for 0.039% of the total revenue of China's industrial sector in 1996. The revenue growth rate of the industry is 16.4% from 1995, as compared to the growth rate of China's industrial sector, 9.51%. The rate of return on asset is 0.27%. 67.24% of all firms in the industry made a profit while 18.60% had negative returns. The top province in terms of the industry's revenue is Hubei, accounting for 49.20% of the total revenue.
本行業在1996年佔全行業總產值0.039%，行業年增長率為16.4%（全國工業年增長率9.51%）。行業的資產回報率0.27%，67.24%的企業盈利，18.60%的企業虧損。銷售收入最高的省份為湖北省，佔本行業的49.20%。

	Total number of firms 企業總數	Total number of employees 職工總數	Total revenue (mil. RMB) 總銷售收入（百萬元）	Total profit (mil. RMB) 總利潤（百萬元）	Return on assets 資產利潤率 (%)	Return on equity 權益利潤率 (%)	Labour productivity ('000 RMB / worker) 勞動生產率（千元/人）	Debts / assets 資產負債率 (%)	Total assets (mil. RMB) 總資產（百萬元）
Industry Overall 行業總體	300	79,715	2,270	13	0.27	0.76	28.48	63.96	4,810

	Number of firms 企業個數	Average number of employees 平均職工人數	Average revenue ('000 RMB) 平均銷售收入（千元）	Average profit ('000 RMB) 平均利潤（千元）	Return on assets 資產利潤率 (%)	Return on equity 權益利潤率 (%)	Labour productivity ('000 RMB / worker) 勞動生產率（千元/人）	Average debts / assets 平均資產負債率(%)	Average Total assets ('000 RMB) 平均總資產（千元）
By ownership 產業所有權									
State-owned 國有	48	1,208	26,896	-646	-0.78	-2.20	22.26	64.39	82,604
Collectively-owned 集體	248	87	3,892	171	5.05	13.31	44.85	62.06	3,385
Privately-owned 私有									
Domestic JVs 聯營	3	51	4,734	541	25.15	41.99	93.44	40.10	2,150
Joint stock 股份制									
Foreign-funded 外資									
Overseas Chinese-funded 港澳台資									
By size 規模									
Large 大型	7	6,001	116,524	-7,164	-1.73	-5.58	19.42	69.07	414,953
Medium 中型	10	655	23,421	614	1.28	2.42	35.78	46.90	47,816
Small 小型	281	103	4,344	203	3.99	9.80	42.11	59.25	5,082
By regional distribution 地區分布									
Central-North 華北	1	16	1,500	60	3.31	6.67	93.75	49.72	1,810
Beijing 北京									
Tianjin 天津									
Hebei 河北									
Shanxi 山西	1	16	1,500	60	3.31	6.67	93.75	49.72	1,810
Inner Mongolia 內蒙									
Northeast 東北	2	28	60				2.18	97.71	655
Liaoning 遼寧	2	28	60				2.18	97.71	655
Jilin 吉林									
Heilongjiang 黑龍江									
Central East 華東	16	414	4,229	-754	-4.27	-8.50	10.21	49.77	17,668
Shanghai 上海									
Jiangsu 江蘇	4	1,038	10,163	-2,718	-5.23	-8.32	9.80	37.09	51,940
Zhejiang 浙江									
Anhui 安徽	4	212	1,040	-350	-3.87	-49.65	4.92	92.21	9,053
Fujian 福建									
Jiangxi 江西	6	231	3,757	37	0.78	1.99	16.26	60.79	4,688
Shandong 山東	2	122	160	-10	-0.19	0.78	1.32	124.10	5,290
Central-South 中南	144	252	8,535	-58	-0.38	-1.14	33.86	66.65	15,219
Henan 河南	1	4							
Hubei 湖北	112	276	9,971	-95	-0.55	-1.79	36.18	69.17	17,208
Hunan 湖南	30	180	3,640	147	1.71	3.38	20.20	49.35	8,616
Guangdong 廣東									
Guangxi 廣西	1	30	3,140	-2,090	-36.10	-36.10	104.67		5,790
Hainan 海南									
Southwest 西南	118	298	8,048	287	1.49	4.06	27.02	63.21	19,191
Chongqing 重慶									
Sichuan 四川	30	284	5,017	219	1.22	4.75	17.67	74.26	17,900
Guizhou 貴州	50	319	9,975	293	1.30	3.09	31.24	57.87	22,508
Yunnan 雲南	38	280	7,906	333	2.10	5.72	28.23	63.31	15,847
Tibet 西藏									
Northwest 西北	19	83	1,179	-20	-0.56	-1.43	14.23	60.86	3,571
Shaanxi 陝西	18	64	983	12	0.70	4.22	15.38	83.29	1,656
Gansu 甘肅									
Qinghai 青海									
Ningxia 寧夏	1	424	4,710	-590	-1.55	-2.73	11.11	43.30	38,040
Xinjiang 新疆									

1022: Phosphorus Ores Mining and Dressing 磷礦採選業

Year 年份	Number of firms 企業個數	Rate of change 每年變化 (%)	Number of employees 職工人數 (人)	Rate of change 每年變化 (%)	Total revenue (mil. RMB) 總銷售收入 (百萬元)	Rate of change 每年變化 (%)	Total profit (mil. RMB) 總利潤 (百萬元)	Rate of change 每年變化 (%)
1993	247		77,081		1,341		21	
1994	245	-0.81%	66,305	-13.98%	1,402	4.53%	2	-89.36%
1995	283	15.51%	83,049	25.25%	1,951	39.16%	8	268.01%
1996	300	6.01%	79,715	-4.01%	2,270	16.35%	13	54.80%

3 Major products* 3種主要產品*	Output 產量	Sales volume 銷售量	Unit 單位
a) Rock Phosphate 磷礦石	24,546,590	23,564,727	ton 噸
b) Phosphate Fertilize 磷肥	200,886	188,833	ton 噸

Top 10 firms by revenue (year founded) 收入排名前10家企業 (創辦年份)	City 城市	Province 省	Telephone / fax 電話 / 傳真	Number of employees 職工人數	Ownership 產業所有權	Revenue ('000 RMB) 銷售收入 (千元)	Profit ('000 RMB) (rank) 利潤 (千元) (排名)	Total assets ('000 RMB) 總資產 (千元)	Major products 主要產品
Guizhou Kai Lin (Group) Co. Ltd. 貴州開磷(集團)有限責任公司(1958)	Guiyang 貴陽市	Guizhou 貴州省	(0851)7588751 (0851)7588218	6,597	State-owned 國有	263,487	0(85)	922,690	a,b
Yunnan Phospham Chemistry Industry (Group) Co. 雲南磷化學工業(集團)公司(1966)	Kunming 昆明市	Yunnan 雲南省	(0871)7896013 (0871)7896019	6,203	State-owned 國有	125,802	1913(10)	415,980	a,b
Hubei Huang Mai Ling Phosphor Chemical Group Company 湖北省黃麥嶺磷化工集團公司(1973)	Xiaogan 孝感市	Hubei 湖北省	(0712)7422014	3,727	State-owned 國有	120,678	5413(3)	151,696	a,b
Yuan'an Feng Yuan Mining General Co. 遠安縣豐源礦業總公司(1993)	Yichang 宜昌市	Hubei 湖北省	(0717)771080	942	Collectively-owned 集體	78,639	283(44)	62,586	a
Hubei Zhongxiang Mineralization Co. 湖北省鐘祥市礦化公司	Jingsha 荊沙市	Hubei 湖北省	(0724)4949185	380	Collectively-owned 集體	74,070	3500(4)	26,103	a
Hunan Phosphor Chemical General Factory 湖南磷化工總廠(1964)	Changsha 長沙市	Hunan 湖南省	(0731)3500138 (0731)3500165	2,718	State-owned 國有	70,903	5761(2)	159,466	a,b
Sichuan Jin He Phosphoreted Mine 四川省金河磷礦(1961)	Deyang 德陽市	Sichuan 四川省	(0838)8901165 (0838)8901481	4,067	State-owned 國有	60,308	304(41)	209,343	a,b
Sichuan Qing Ping Phosphoreted Mine 四川省清平磷礦(1966)	Deyang 德陽市	Sichuan 四川省	(0838)6373098 (0838)6373098	2,407	State-owned 國有	41,989	204(50)	226,401	a,b
Hubei Jingsha Fang Ma Shan Phosphoreted Mine Mine Administration 湖北省荊沙市放馬山磷礦礦務局(1971)	Jingsha 荊沙市	Hubei 湖北省	(0716)4858460 (0716)4858461	1,427	State-owned 國有	41,660	24(77)	85,988	a,b
Cattle Farm Shuang Xing Chemical Fertilizer Factory 牛場雙星化肥廠(1992)	Duyun 都勻市	Guizhou 貴州省	(0854)666188	500	Collectively-owned 集體	34,278	-2495(111)	4,650	a

Top 10 Cities by Production Output 產出排名前10位城市	Province 省	Market share 市場份額	Number of firms 企業個數
Jingmen 荊門市	Hubei 湖北省	18.18%	40
Kunming 昆明市	Yunnan 雲南省	17.63%	49
Guiyang 貴陽市	Guizhou 貴州省	14.26%	23
Deyang 德陽市	Sichuan 四川省	9.75%	15
Xiaogan 孝感市	Hubei 湖北省	8.49%	3
Duyun 都勻市	Guizhou 貴州省	7.17%	10
Yichang 宜昌市	Hubei 湖北省	6.08%	49
Changsha 長沙市	Hunan 湖南省	4.56%	2
Lianyungang 連雲港市	Jiangsu 江蘇省	3.29%	4
Xiangfan 襄樊市	Hubei 湖北省	2.93%	27

10 Major Wholesalers 10家主要批發商	City 城市	Province 省	Telephone / Fax 電話 / 傳真
China Metallurgy Import & Export Liaoning Company 中國冶金進出口遼寧公司	Shenyang 瀋陽市	Liaoning 遼寧省	(024)23867070 (024)23875451
Liaoning Foreign Trade General Company 遼寧省對外貿易總公司	Dalian 大連市	Liaoning 遼寧省	(0411)3632157 (0411)3638243
Zhong Xin Trade Company 中信貿易公司	Beijing 北京市	Beijing 北京市	(010)64662170 (010)64662161
China Metallurgy Import & Export Shandong Company 中國冶金進出口山東公司	Qingdao 青島市	Shandong 山東省	(0532)2801118 (0532)2801331
Yongzhou Ferromanganese Mine Company 永州市錳鐵礦公司	Yongzhou 永州市	Hunan 湖南省	(0746)8464135
Zhengzhou Advanced Technology Industrial Development Zone Development General Company 鄭州高新技術產業開發區發展總公司	Zhengzhou 鄭州市	Henan 河南省	(0371)7981924 (0371)7981422
Guangdong Hardware Import & Export Group Company 廣東省五金進出口集團公司	Guangzhou 廣州市	Guangdong 廣東省	(020)87752204 (020)87752205
Xi Shan Shi Wu Kuang Trade Company 錫山市五礦貿易公司	Wuxi 無錫市	Jiangsu 江蘇省	(0510)7760988
Xiamen Ocean Petroleum Company 廈門海洋石油公司	Xiamen 廈門市	Fujian 福建省	(0592)2095495 (0592)2087292
Hainan Shen Hai Import & Export Co. Ltd. 海南深海進出口有限公司	Haikou 海口市	Hainan 海南省	(0898)6717646 (0898)6717639

*Also include sales by firms outside this industry.包括本行業以外廠家的銷售。"o" stands for "others". "o" 代表"其他產品"。

1023: Potash Mining and Dressing 天然鉀鹽採選業

The industry accounts for 0.000% of the total revenue of China's industrial sector in 1996. The revenue growth rate of the industry is 3.0% from 1995, as compared to the growth rate of China's industrial sector, 9.51%. The rate of return on asset is -1.48%. 100.00% of all firms in the industry made a profit while 0.00% had negative returns. The top province in terms of the industry's revenue is Jiangsu, accounting for 44.06% of the total revenue.
本行業在 1996 年佔全行業總產值 0.000% ，行業年增長率為 3.0%（全國工業年增長率 9.51%）。行業的資產回報率 -1.48% ， 100.00% 的企業盈利， 0.00% 的企業虧損。銷售收入最高的省份為江蘇省，佔本行業的 44.06% 。

	Total number of firms 企業總數	Total number of employees 職工總數	Total revenue (mil. RMB) 總銷售收入（百萬元）	Total profit (mil. RMB) 總利潤（百萬元）	Return on assets 資產利潤率 (%)	Return on equity 權益利潤率 (%)	Labour productivity ('000 RMB / worker) 勞動生產率（千元/人）	Debts / assets 資產負債率 (%)	Total assets (mil. RMB) 總資產（百萬元）
Industry Overall 行業總體	7	699	16	-1	-1.48	-4.35	22.89	65.87	36

	Number of firms 企業個數	Average number of employees 平均職工人數	Average revenue ('000 RMB) 平均銷售收入（千元）	Average profit ('000 RMB) 平均利潤（千元）	Return on assets 資產利潤率 (%)	Return on equity 權益利潤率 (%)	Labour productivity ('000 RMB / worker) 勞動生產率（千元/人）	Average debts / assets 平均資產負債率(%)	Average Total assets ('000 RMB) 平均總資產（千元）
By ownership 產業所有權									
State-owned 國有	1	443	7,000	-1,000	-3.45	-11.11	15.80	68.97	29,000
Collectively-owned 集體	6	43	1,499				35.13	57.14	1,167
Privately-owned 私有									
Domestic JVs 聯營									
Joint stock 股份制									
Foreign-funded 外資									
Overseas Chinese-funded 港澳台資									
By size 規模									
Large 大型									
Medium 中型									
Small 小型	7	100	2,285	-143	-2.78	-8.33	22.88	66.67	5,142
By regional distribution 地區分布									
Central-North 華北									
Beijing 北京									
Tianjin 天津									
Hebei 河北									
Shanxi 山西									
Inner Mongolia 內蒙									
Northeast 東北									
Liaoning 遼寧									
Jilin 吉林									
Heilongjiang 黑龍江									
Central East 華東	4	58	2,025	78	8.09	19.50	34.76	58.49	958
Shanghai 上海									
Jiangsu 江蘇	2	45	3,525	95	10.73	70.37	78.33	84.75	885
Zhejiang 浙江									
Anhui 安徽									
Fujian 福建									
Jiangxi 江西									
Shandong 山東	2	72	525	60	5.83	9.09	7.34	35.92	1,030
Central-South 中南	2	12	595	-30	-2.30	-6.98	51.74	66.67	1,305
Henan 河南	1	23	1,180	-60	-2.36	-7.59	51.30	68.50	2,540
Hubei 湖北									
Hunan 湖南									
Guangdong 廣東									
Guangxi 廣西	1		10						70
Hainan 海南									
Southwest 西南	1	443	6,850	-790	-2.69	-8.10	15.46	66.79	29,360
Chongqing 重慶									
Sichuan 四川									
Guizhou 貴州									
Yunnan 雲南	1	443	6,850	-790	-2.69	-8.10	15.46	66.79	29,360
Tibet 西藏									
Northwest 西北									
Shaanxi 陝西									
Gansu 甘肅									
Qinghai 青海									
Ningxia 寧夏									
Xinjiang 新疆									

1023: Potash Mining and Dressing 天然鉀鹽採選業

Year 年份	Number of firms 企業個數	Rate of change 每年變化 (%)	Number of employees 職工人數 (人)	Rate of change 每年變化 (%)	Total revenue (mil. RMB) 總銷售收入 (百萬元)	Rate of change 每年變化 (%)	Total profit (mil. RMB) 總利潤 (百萬元)	Rate of change 每年變化 (%)
1993	5		420		9		-1	
1994	11	120.00%	1,057	151.67%	36	311.98%	1	190.12%
1995	8	-27.27%	805	-23.84%	16	-56.43%	0	-60.49%
1996	7	-12.50%	699	-13.17%	16	3.05%	-1	-442.47%

3 Major products* 3種主要產品 *	Output 產量	Sales volume 銷售量	Unit 單位
a) Potassium Chlorate 氯酸鉀	171	154	ton 噸

Top 10 firms by revenue (year founded) 收入排名前10家企業 (創辦年份)	City 城市	Province 省	Telephone / fax 電話 / 傳真	Number of employees 職工人數	Ownership 產業所有權	Revenue ('000 RMB) 銷售收入 (千元)	Profit ('000 RMB) (rank) 利潤 (千元) (排名)	Total assets ('000 RMB) 總資產 (千元)	Major products 主要產品
Yunnan Simao Potast Mine 雲南省思茅地區鉀鹽礦(1975)	Simao 思茅市	Yunnan 雲南省	(0879)3831117	493	State-owned 國有	6,846	-786(3)	29,356	a
Fengxian Huashan Potast Mine 豐縣華山鉀礦(1995)	Xuzhou 徐州市	Jiangsu 江蘇省		40	Collectively-owned 集體	3,692	163(1)	1,558	o
Cheng Gang Xiang Mining Factory 城崗鄉採礦廠(1984)	Xuzhou 徐州市	Jiangsu 江蘇省		50	Collectively-owned 集體	3,360	30(2)	210	o

Top 10 Cities by Production Output 產出排名前10位城市	Province 省	Market share 市場份額	Number of firms 企業個數
Zhengzhou 鄭州市	Henan 河南省	42.06%	1
Dongying 東營市	Shandong 山東省	39.71%	1
Binzhou 濱州市	Shandong 山東省	18.23%	1
Jingmen 荊門市	Hubei 湖北省		1

10 Major Wholesalers 10家主要批發商	City 城市	Province 省	Telephone / Fax 電話 / 傳真
China Metallurgy Import & Export Liaoning Company 中國冶金進出口遼寧公司	Shenyang 瀋陽市	Liaoning 遼寧省	(024)23867070 (024)23875451
Liaoning Foreign Trade General Company 遼寧省對外貿易總公司	Dalian 大連市	Liaoning 遼寧省	(0411)3632157 (0411)3638243
Zhong Xin Trade Company 中信貿易公司	Beijing 北京市	Beijing 北京市	(010)64662170 (010)64662161
China Metallurgy Import & Export Shandong Company 中國冶金進出口山東公司	Qingdao 青島市	Shandong 山東省	(0532)2801118 (0532)2801331
Yongzhou Ferromanganese Mine Company 永州市錳鐵礦公司	Yongzhou 永州市	Hunan 湖南省	(0746)8464135
Zhengzhou Advanced Technology Industrial Development Zone Development General Company 鄭州高新技術產業開發區發展總公司	Zhengzhou 鄭州市	Henan 河南省	(0371)7981924 (0371)7981422
Guangdong Hardware Import & Export Group Company 廣東省五金進出口集團公司	Guangzhou 廣州市	Guangdong 廣東省	(020)87752204 (020)87752205
Xi Shan Shi Wu Kuang Trade Company 錫山市五礦貿易公司	Wuxi 無錫市	Jiangsu 江蘇省	(0510)7760988
Xiamen Ocean Petroleum Company 廈門海洋石油公司	Xiamen 廈門市	Fujian 福建省	(0592)2095495 (0592)2087292
Hainan Shen Hai Import & Export Co. Ltd. 海南深海進出口有限公司	Haikou 海口市	Hainan 海南省	(0898)6717646 (0898)6717639

*Also include sales by firms outside this industry.包括本行業以外廠家的銷售。"o" stands for "others". "o" 代表 "其他產品"。

1024: Boron Ores Mining and Dressing 硼礦採選業

The industry accounts for 0.005% of the total revenue of China's industrial sector in 1996. The revenue growth rate of the industry is 1.0% from 1995, as compared to the growth rate of China's industrial sector, 9.51%. The rate of return on asset is 1.19%. 54.10% of all firms in the industry made a profit while 23.68% had negative returns. The top province in terms of the industry's revenue is Liaoning, accounting for 74.18% of the total revenue.
本行業在1996年佔全行業總產值0.005%，行業年增長率為1.0%（全國工業年增長率9.51%）。行業的資產回報率1.19%，54.10%的企業盈利，23.68%的企業虧損。銷售收入最高的省份為遼寧省，佔本行業的74.18%。

	Total number of firms 企業總數	Total number of employees 職工總數	Total revenue (mil. RMB) 總銷售收入（百萬元）	Total profit (mil. RMB) 總利潤（百萬元）	Return on assets 資產利潤率 (%)	Return on equity 權益利潤率 (%)	Labour productivity ('000 RMB / worker) 勞動生產率（千元/人）	Debts / assets 資產負債率 (%)	Total assets (mil. RMB) 總資產（百萬元）
Industry Overall 行業總體	40	8,951	278	6	1.19	4.74	31.06	74.82	509

	Number of firms 企業個數	Average number of employees 平均職工人數	Average revenue ('000 RMB) 平均銷售收入（千元）	Average profit ('000 RMB) 平均利潤（千元）	Return on assets 資產利潤率 (%)	Return on equity 權益利潤率 (%)	Labour productivity ('000 RMB / worker) 勞動生產率（千元/人）	Average debts / assets 平均資產負債率(%)	Average Total assets ('000 RMB) 平均總資產（千元）
By ownership 產業所有權									
State-owned 國有	11	553	14,182	-91	-0.30	-1.14	25.64	73.65	30,364
Collectively-owned 集體	29	99	4,206	241	4.00	17.50	42.56	77.14	6,034
Privately-owned 私有									
Domestic JVs 聯營									
Joint stock 股份制									
Foreign-funded 外資									
Overseas Chinese-funded 港澳台資									
By size 規模									
Large 大型	1	2,741	72,327	-274	-0.18	-0.57	26.39	68.73	154,036
Medium 中型	1	1,076	32,645	98	0.10	0.43	30.34	77.02	100,062
Small 小型	38	135	4,553	163	2.42	10.87	33.70	77.70	6,708
By regional distribution 地區分布									
Central-North 華北									
Beijing 北京									
Tianjin 天津									
Hebei 河北									
Shanxi 山西									
Inner Mongolia 內蒙									
Northeast 東北	30	261	7,655	-184	-1.26	-5.29	29.31	76.11	14,561
Liaoning 遼寧	25	268	8,249	-302	-1.88	-7.84	30.76	76.07	16,111
Jilin 吉林	5	226	4,682	408	5.99	25.60	20.72	76.59	6,810
Heilongjiang 黑龍江									
Central East 華東	1	60	1,240	400	7.89	26.49	20.67	70.22	5,070
Shanghai 上海									
Jiangsu 江蘇									
Zhejiang 浙江									
Anhui 安徽									
Fujian 福建									
Jiangxi 江西									
Shandong 山東	1	60	1,240	400	7.89	26.49	20.67	70.22	5,070
Central-South 中南	3	122	663				5.42	37.25	823
Henan 河南									
Hubei 湖北	1	42	1,110				26.43	61.54	910
Hunan 湖南	2	163	440				2.71	23.08	780
Guangdong 廣東									
Guangxi 廣西									
Hainan 海南									
Southwest 西南	5	48	9,018	2,240	17.28	53.85	188.66	67.93	12,964
Chongqing 重慶									
Sichuan 四川									
Guizhou 貴州									
Yunnan 雲南									
Tibet 西藏	5	48	9,018	2,240	17.28	53.85	188.66	67.93	12,964
Northwest 西北	1	450							
Shaanxi 陝西									
Gansu 甘肅									
Qinghai 青海	1	450							
Ningxia 寧夏									
Xinjiang 新疆									

1024: Boron Ores Mining and Dressing 硼礦採選業

Year 年份	Number of firms 企業個數	Rate of change 每年變化 (%)	Number of employees 職工人數 (人)	Rate of change 每年變化 (%)	Total revenue (mil. RMB) 總銷售收入 (百萬元)	Rate of change 每年變化 (%)	Total profit (mil. RMB) 總利潤 (百萬元)	Rate of change 每年變化 (%)
1993	42		4,879		156		12	
1994	31	-26.19%	8,896	82.33%	188	20.78%	9	-24.65%
1995	39	25.81%	8,787	-1.23%	275	46.27%	28	203.16%
1996	40	2.56%	8,951	1.87%	278	0.97%	6	-78.23%

3 Major products* 3 種主要產品 *	Output 產量	Sales volume 銷售量	Unit 單位
a) Boron Rack 硼礦	1,465,262	908,462	ton 噸
b) Boric Acid 硼酸	11,395	7,179	ton 噸
c) Borax (Sodium Tetraborate) 硼砂	65,470	15,058	ton 噸

Top 10 firms by revenue (year founded) 收入排名前 10 家企業 (創辦年份)	City 城市	Province 省	Telephone / fax 電話 / 傳真	Number of employees 職工人數	Ownership 產業所有權	Revenue ('000 RMB) 銷售收入 (千元)	Profit ('000 RMB) (rank) 利潤 (千元) (排名)	Total assets ('000 RMB) 總資產 (千元)	Major products 主要產品
Dandong Peng Yuan Chemical Group Co. Ltd. 丹東硼源化工集團有限公司(1996)	Dandong 丹東市	Liaoning 遼寧省	(0415)5177198	1,258	Collectively-owned 集體	88,050	4060(1)	129,740	a,b,c
Dandong Kuandian Boron Mine 丹東寬甸硼礦(1958)	Dandong 丹東市	Liaoning 遼寧省	(0415)5100148 (0415)5100148	2,782	State-owned 國有	56,761	-13977(9)	135,131	a,b,c
Yingkou No.501 Mine 營口五 0 一礦(1961)	Yingkou 營口市	Liaoning 遼寧省	(0417)5859321 (0417)5859604	1,100	State-owned 國有	25,363	670(3)	73,353	o
Liaoning Dashiqiao Lv Wang Xiang Boron Stone Mine 大石橋市呂王鄉硼廠礦(1971)	Yingkou 營口市	Liaoning 遼寧省	(0417)5863127	345	Collectively-owned 集體	8,503	0(6)	12,761	o
Dashiqiao Jian Yi Boron Stone Mine 大石橋市建一硼石礦(1979)	Yingkou 營口市	Liaoning 遼寧省	(0417)5862238	193	Collectively-owned 集體	6,312	2470(2)	5,982	o
Dandong Eryingou Boron Mine 丹東二人溝硼礦(1973)	Dandong 丹東市	Liaoning 遼寧省		350	State-owned 國有	6,090	-1270(8)	28,757	o
Fengcheng Si Men Zi Zhen No.1 Boron Mine 鳳城市四門子鎮第一硼礦(1993)	Dandong 丹東市	Liaoning 遼寧省	(0415)8571004	67	Collectively-owned 集體	2,850	141(4)	434	o
Kuandian Man Zu Autonomous County Hong Shi Zhen Boron Mine 寬甸滿族自治縣紅石鎮硼礦(1971)	Dandong 丹東市	Liaoning 遼寧省	(0415)5763351	80	Collectively-owned 集體	2,685	26(5)	4,100	a
Hai Xi Autonomous Prefecture Dachaidan Chemical Factory 海西自治州大柴旦化工廠(1958)	Golmud 格爾木市	Qinghai 青海省	(0979)81291	450	State-owned 國有	2,295	0(7)	22,412	b,c

Top 10 Cities by Production Output 產出排名前 10 位城市	Province 省	Market share 市場份額	Number of firms 企業個數
Dandong 丹東市	Liaoning 遼寧省	50.96%	18
Yingkou 營口市	Liaoning 遼寧省	19.59%	3
Lhasa 拉薩市	Tibet 西藏	8.97%	2
Burang 普蘭縣	Tibet 西藏	7.35%	2
Xigaze 日喀則市	Tibet 西藏	6.61%	1
Zibo 淄博市	Shandong 山東省	3.30%	1
Dalian 大連市	Liaoning 遼寧省	0.85%	1
Liaoyang 遼陽市	Liaoning 遼寧省	0.85%	1
Golmud 格爾木市	Qinghai 青海省	0.52%	1
Hengyang 衡陽市	Hunan 湖南省	0.42%	1

10 Major Wholesalers 10 家主要批發商	City 城市	Province 省	Telephone / Fax 電話 / 傳真
China Metallurgy Import & Export Liaoning Company 中國冶金進出口遼寧公司	Shenyang 瀋陽市	Liaoning 遼寧省	(024)23867070 (024)23875451
Liaoning Foreign Trade General Company 遼寧省對外貿易總公司	Dalian 大連市	Liaoning 遼寧省	(0411)3632157 (0411)3638243
Zhong Xin Trade Company 中信貿易公司	Beijing 北京市	Beijing 北京市	(010)64662170 (010)64662161
China Metallurgy Import & Export Shandong Company 中國冶金進出口山東公司	Qingdao 青島市	Shandong 山東省	(0532)2801118 (0532)2801331
Yongzhou Ferromanganese Mine Company 永州市錳鐵礦公司	Yongzhou 永州市	Hunan 湖南省	(0746)8464135
Zhengzhou Advanced Technology Industrial Development Zone Development General Company 鄭州高新技術產業開發區發展總公司	Zhengzhou 鄭州市	Henan 河南省	(0371)7981924 (0371)7981422
Guangdong Hardware Import & Export Group Company 廣東省五金進出口集團公司	Guangzhou 廣州市	Guangdong 廣東省	(020)87752204 (020)87752205
Xi Shan Shi Wu Kuang Trade Company 錫山市五礦貿易公司	Wuxi 無錫市	Jiangsu 江蘇省	(0510)7760988
Xiamen Ocean Petroleum Company 廈門海洋石油公司	Xiamen 廈門市	Fujian 福建省	(0592)2095495 (0592)2087292
Hainan Shen Hai Import & Export Co. Ltd. 海南深海進出口有限公司	Haikou 海口市	Hainan 海南省	(0898)6717646 (0898)6717639

*Also include sales by firms outside this industry.包括本行業以外廠家的銷售。"o" stands for "others". "o" 代表"其他產品"。

1029: Other Chemical Ores Mining and Dressing 其他化學礦採選業

The industry accounts for 0.010% of the total revenue of China's industrial sector in 1996. The revenue growth rate of the industry is 18.8% from 1995, as compared to the growth rate of China's industrial sector, 9.51%. The rate of return on asset is 2.30%. 77.80% of all firms in the industry made a profit while 15.95% had negative returns. The top province in terms of the industry's revenue is Zhejiang, accounting for 13.58% of the total revenue.
本行業在1996年佔全行業總產值0.010%，行業年增長率為18.8%（全國工業年增長率9.51%）。行業的資產回報率2.30%，77.80%的企業盈利，15.95%的企業虧損。銷售收入最高的省份為浙江省，佔本行業的13.58%。

	Total number of firms 企業總數	Total number of employees 職工總數	Total revenue (mil. RMB) 總銷售收入（百萬元）	Total profit (mil. RMB) 總利潤（百萬元）	Return on assets 資產利潤率 (%)	Return on equity 權益利潤率 (%)	Labour productivity ('000 RMB / worker) 勞動生產率（千元/人）	Debts / assets 資產負債率 (%)	Total assets (mil. RMB) 總資產（百萬元）
Industry Overall 行業總體	248	21,262	592	27	2.30	5.21	27.84	55.86	1,193

	Number of firms 企業個數	Average number of employees 平均職工人數	Average revenue ('000 RMB) 平均銷售收入（千元）	Average profit ('000 RMB) 平均利潤（千元）	Return on assets 資產利潤率 (%)	Return on equity 權益利潤率 (%)	Labour productivity ('000 RMB / worker) 勞動生產率（千元/人）	Average debts / assets 平均資產負債率(%)	Average Total assets ('000 RMB) 平均總資產（千元）
By ownership 產業所有權									
State-owned 國有	35	363	7,743	114	0.43	0.91	21.31	52.94	26,714
Collectively-owned 集體	205	40	1,424	111	11.69	35.32	35.42	66.91	948
Privately-owned 私有									
Domestic JVs 聯營	3	52	1,621	62	2.68	6.08	31.37	55.90	2,328
Joint stock 股份制									
Foreign-funded 外資	2	23	3,884	376	7.75	14.78	168.88	47.58	4,850
Overseas Chinese-funded 港澳台資	2	52	8,238	-326	-1.39	-4.50	158.41	69.06	23,451
By size 規模									
Large 大型									
Medium 中型	6	1,066	20,332	4,436	8.60	18.09	19.07	52.49	51,609
Small 小型	239	62	1,966	2	0.04	0.10	31.81	56.99	3,695
By regional distribution 地區分布									
Central-North 華北	43	37	1,426	61	3.07	22.89	38.51	86.59	1,978
Beijing 北京									
Tianjin 天津									
Hebei 河北	1	46	310	70	1.38	17.95	6.74	92.29	5,060
Shanxi 山西									
Inner Mongolia 內蒙	42	37	1,452	60	3.18	23.07	39.46	86.23	1,904
Northeast 東北	8	295	8,776	245	0.49	0.73	29.78	33.26	50,285
Liaoning 遼寧	2	64	475	10	0.46	0.99	7.48	53.46	2,170
Jilin 吉林	6	372	11,543	323	0.49	0.73	31.04	33.04	66,323
Heilongjiang 黑龍江									
Central East 華東	50	156	3,141	72	1.30	4.18	20.15	68.97	5,518
Shanghai 上海									
Jiangsu 江蘇	3	329	8,337	257	1.39	10.20	25.31	86.34	18,423
Zhejiang 浙江	27	173	2,977	76	1.29	3.29	17.18	60.59	5,892
Anhui 安徽	4	102	1,043	143	19.52	54.29	10.22	64.04	730
Fujian 福建	6	34	3,437	270	4.91	15.25	101.08	67.80	5,497
Jiangxi 江西	7	178	2,400	-296	-12.05	-183.19	13.52	93.42	2,454
Shandong 山東	3	91	3,350	210	7.43	24.61	36.95	69.81	2,827
Central-South 中南	46	96	4,109	146	2.72	5.81	42.71	53.18	5,369
Henan 河南	9	167	5,803	320	2.41	13.57	34.84	82.22	13,261
Hubei 湖北	10	33	451	60	20.07	428.57	13.54	95.32	299
Hunan 湖南	9	231	4,962	68	0.86	1.14	21.48	24.64	7,859
Guangdong 廣東	9	42	5,754	154	4.63	6.13	136.65	24.49	3,339
Guangxi 廣西	9	15	3,982	138	5.20	6.78	263.53	23.39	2,651
Hainan 海南									
Southwest 西南	31	80	2,315	278	7.05	25.29	29.00	72.13	3,949
Chongqing 重慶	2	350	18,679	4,447	23.31	78.02	53.36	70.12	19,075
Sichuan 四川	17	62	1,306	-28	-0.75	-2.94	20.81	74.52	3,746
Guizhou 貴州	8	55	530	36	11.37	27.62	9.64	58.82	319
Yunnan 雲南	3	62	1,613	-170	-4.03	-12.78	26.16	68.51	4,223
Tibet 西藏									
Northwest 西北	70	37	616	57	6.59	34.66	16.47	81.04	869
Shaanxi 陝西	7	24	716	16	2.61	7.24	29.30	63.90	601
Gansu 甘肅	39	43	487	63	9.69	165.54	11.30	94.27	648
Qinghai 青海	13	34	295	-33	-2.93	-33.86	8.70	91.35	1,129
Ningxia 寧夏									
Xinjiang 新疆	11	29	1,387	171	11.27	25.75	47.10	56.24	1,516

1029: Other Chemical Ores Mining and Dressing 其他化學礦採選業

Year 年份	Number of firms 企業個數	Rate of change 每年變化 (%)	Number of employees 職工人數 (人)	Rate of change 每年變化 (%)	Total revenue (mil. RMB) 總銷售收入 (百萬元)	Rate of change 每年變化 (%)	Total profit (mil. RMB) 總利潤 (百萬元)	Rate of change 每年變化 (%)
1993	285		24,736		451		12	
1994	277	-2.81%	29,704	20.08%	537	19.03%	-28	-336.03%
1995	216	-22.02%	21,923	-26.20%	498	-7.14%	-3	87.75%
1996	248	14.81%	21,262	-3.02%	592	18.80%	27	900.71%

3 Major products* 3 種主要產品 *	Output 產量	Sales volume 銷售量	Unit 單位
a) China Clay 瓷土	695,386	667,571	ton 噸
b) Anhydrous Sodium Sulfate 無水硫酸鈉	61,314	60,087	ton 噸
c) Sulfuric Acid 硫酸	46,147	24,920	ton 噸

Top 10 firms by revenue (year founded) 收入排名前 10 家企業 (創辦年份)	City 城市	Province 省	Telephone / fax 電話 / 傳真	Number of employees 職工人數	Ownership 產業所有權	Revenue ('000 RMB) 銷售收入 (千元)	Profit ('000 RMB) (rank) 利潤 (千元) (排名)	Total assets ('000 RMB) 總資產 (千元)	Major products 主要產品
Zhejiang Pingyang Alumina Mine 浙江省平陽礬礦(1956)	Wenzhou 溫州市	Zhejiang 浙江省	(0577)4652241 (0577)4651050	3,279	State-owned 國有	37,410	2090(2)	103,780	o
Hunan Realgar Mine 湖南雄磺礦(1950)	Changde 常德市	Hunan 湖南省	(0736)5473422 (0736)5473422	1,089	State-owned 國有	35,301	400(9)	68,632	c
Chongqing Dazu Lazurite Mine Co. 重慶市大足縣天青石礦業公司	Chongqing 重慶市	Chongqing 重慶市	(023)43451527	578	Collectively-owned 集體	29,990	12857(1)	27,544	o
Yongfu County Barite Mine 永福縣重晶石礦(1982)	Lingchuan 靈川縣	Guangxi 廣西	(0773)8511528	177	Collectively-owned 集體	27,640	701(6)	17,741	o
Enping Na Ji Saponite Factory 恩平市那吉石粉廠(1987)	Jiangmen 江門市	Guangdong 廣東省	(0750)7281241	40	Collectively-owned 集體	24,310	274(16)	531	a
Jiangsu Donghai Serpentine Mine 東海縣蛇紋石礦(1965)	Lianyungang 連雲港市	Jiangsu 江蘇省	(0518)222300	658	State-owned 國有	18,958	521(8)	52,608	c
Yong'an Qi Sheng Mineral Products Co. Ltd. 永安市啟勝礦產有限公司(1994)	Sanming 三明市	Fujian 福建省	(0598)3632967 (0598)3621188	50	Foreign-funded 外資	18,306	1592(3)	27,236	o
Tongliang Chemical Industry Co. 銅梁縣化學工業公司	Chongqing 重慶市	Chongqing 重慶市	(023)45632930	118	State-owned 國有	16,877	1313(5)	33,629	o
Guangzhou Economic Technical Development District Express Metal Co. Ltd. 廣州經濟技術開發區運通礦產品有限公司(1992)	Guangzhou 廣州市	Guangdong 廣東省	(020)83832008 (020)83810218	69	Overseas Chinese-funded 港澳台資	11,592	244(20)	18,582	o
Barkol Kazak Ha Sa Ke Autonomous County Mirabilite Mine 巴里坤哈薩克自治縣芒硝礦(1989)	Hami 哈密市	Xinjiang 新疆	(0902)4622558	120	State-owned 國有	11,126	1381(4)	13,829	o

Top 10 Cities by Production Output 產出排名前 10 位城市	Province 省	Market share 市場份額	Number of firms 企業個數
Chongqing 重慶市	Chongqing 重慶市	11.45%	3
Wenzhou 溫州市	Zhejiang 浙江省	10.31%	15
Nanyang 南陽市	Henan 河南省	7.69%	5
Changde 常德市	Hunan 湖南省	7.51%	1
Xuanzhou 宣州市	Anhui 安徽省	7.29%	5
Lingchuan 靈川縣	Guangxi 廣西	5.95%	2
Jiangmen 江門市	Guangdong 廣東省	5.18%	1
Sanming 三明市	Fujian 福建省	3.76%	2
Chaohu 巢湖市	Anhui 安徽省	3.61%	2
Dongsheng 東勝市	Inner Mong 內蒙	3.07%	17

10 Major Wholesalers 10 家主要批發商	City 城市	Province 省	Telephone / Fax 電話 / 傳真
China Metallurgy Import & Export Liaoning Company 中國冶金進出口遼寧公司	Shenyang 瀋陽市	Liaoning 遼寧省	(024)23867070 (024)23875451
Liaoning Foreign Trade General Company 遼寧省對外貿易總公司	Dalian 大連市	Liaoning 遼寧省	(0411)3632157 (0411)3638243
Zhong Xin Trade Company 中信貿易公司	Beijing 北京市	Beijing 北京市	(010)64662170 (010)64662161
China Metallurgy Import & Export Shandong Company 中國冶金進出口山東公司	Qingdao 青島市	Shandong 山東省	(0532)2801118 (0532)2801331
Yongzhou Ferromanganese Mine Company 永州市錳鐵礦公司	Yongzhou 永州市	Hunan 湖南省	(0746)8464135
Zhengzhou Advanced Technology Industrial Development Zone Development General Company 鄭州高新技術產業開發區發展總公司	Zhengzhou 鄭州市	Henan 河南省	(0371)7981924 (0371)7981422
Guangdong Hardware Import & Export Group Company 廣東省五金進出口集團公司	Guangzhou 廣州市	Guangdong 廣東省	(020)87752204 (020)87752205
Xi Shan Shi Wu Kuang Trade Company 錫山市五礦貿易公司	Wuxi 無錫市	Jiangsu 江蘇省	(0510)7760988
Xiamen Ocean Petroleum Company 廈門海洋石油公司	Xiamen 廈門市	Fujian 福建省	(0592)2095495 (0592)2087292
Hainan Shen Hai Import & Export Co. Ltd. 海南深海進出口有限公司	Haikou 海口市	Hainan 海南省	(0898)6717646 (0898)6717639

*Also include sales by firms outside this industry.包括本行業以外廠家的銷售。"o" stands for "others". "o" 代表 "其他產品"。

1031: Sea Salt Mining 海鹽業

The industry accounts for 0.057% of the total revenue of China's industrial sector in 1996. The revenue growth rate of the industry is 2.5% from 1995, as compared to the growth rate of China's industrial sector, 9.51%. The rate of return on asset is 0.67%. 72.56% of all firms in the industry made a profit while 25.20% had negative returns. The top province in terms of the industry's revenue is Shandong, accounting for 27.04% of the total revenue.
本行業在1996年佔全行業總產值0.057%，行業年增長率為2.5%（全國工業年增長率9.51%）。行業的資產回報率0.67%，72.56%的企業盈利，25.20%的企業虧損。銷售收入最高的省份為山東省，佔本行業的27.04%。

	Total number of firms 企業總數	Total number of employees 職工總數	Total revenue (mil. RMB) 總銷售收入（百萬元）	Total profit (mil. RMB) 總利潤（百萬元）	Return on assets 資產利潤率 (%)	Return on equity 權益利潤率 (%)	Labour productivity ('000 RMB / worker) 勞動生產率（千元/人）	Debts / assets 資產負債率 (%)	Total assets (mil. RMB) 總資產（百萬元）
Industry Overall 行業總體	398	155,253	3,285	68	0.67	1.60	21.16	57.99	10,179

	Number of firms 企業個數	Average number of employees 平均職工人數	Average revenue ('000 RMB) 平均銷售收入（千元）	Average profit ('000 RMB) 平均利潤（千元）	Return on assets 資產利潤率 (%)	Return on equity 權益利潤率 (%)	Labour productivity ('000 RMB / worker) 勞動生產率（千元/人）	Average debts / assets 平均資產負債率(%)	Average Total assets ('000 RMB) 平均總資產（千元）
By ownership 產業所有權									
State-owned 國有	90	1,309	26,900	-11	-0.01	-0.03	20.55	58.39	94,900
Collectively-owned 集體	307	119	2,815	225	4.21	9.55	23.66	55.92	5,338
Privately-owned 私有									
Domestic JVs 聯營									
Joint stock 股份制									
Foreign-funded 外資									
Overseas Chinese-funded 港澳台資	1	844							
By size 規模									
Large 大型	16	4,882	126,135	2,913	0.73	1.60	25.84	54.39	399,825
Medium 中型	24	696	14,548	-14	-0.02	-0.06	20.91	67.14	65,299
Small 小型	357	167	2,571	61	0.98	2.57	15.42	61.91	6,205
By regional distribution 地區分布									
Central-North 華北	24	1,518	43,140	2,045	1.45	3.09	28.41	53.00	140,796
Beijing 北京									
Tianjin 天津	6	2,574	74,753	152	0.05	0.10	29.05	46.45	281,875
Hebei 河北	18	1,166	32,603	2,676	2.85	7.06	27.95	59.56	93,770
Shanxi 山西									
Inner Mongolia 內蒙									
Northeast 東北	35	516	10,848	54	0.14	0.49	21.03	72.30	39,605
Liaoning 遼寧	35	516	10,848	54	0.14	0.49	21.03	72.30	39,605
Jilin 吉林									
Heilongjiang 黑龍江									
Central East 華東	278	300	6,183	89	0.54	1.33	20.58	59.28	16,556
Shanghai 上海									
Jiangsu 江蘇	40	768	15,149	-737	-1.51	-3.65	19.73	58.57	48,775
Zhejiang 浙江	45	154	1,886	245	3.76	5.22	12.23	27.96	6,500
Anhui 安徽									
Fujian 福建	82	192	1,705	89	2.65	5.36	8.88	50.60	3,370
Jiangxi 江西									
Shandong 山東	111	271	8,002	325	1.73	5.01	29.48	65.50	18,763
Central-South 中南	61	283	2,483	-120	-0.91	-1.71	8.79	46.94	13,304
Henan 河南									
Hubei 湖北									
Hunan 湖南	1	10	1,420	20	4.17	4.17	142.00		480
Guangdong 廣東	38	245	2,242	-51	-0.65	-1.68	9.15	61.60	7,817
Guangxi 廣西	12	331	2,406	-378	-2.37	-3.56	7.26	33.49	15,941
Hainan 海南	10	394	3,600	-92	-0.29	-0.49	9.14	41.48	32,270
Southwest 西南									
Chongqing 重慶									
Sichuan 四川									
Guizhou 貴州									
Yunnan 雲南									
Tibet 西藏									
Northwest 西北									
Shaanxi 陝西									
Gansu 甘肅									
Qinghai 青海									
Ningxia 寧夏									
Xinjiang 新疆									

Year 年份	Number of firms 企業個數	Rate of change 每年變化 (%)	Number of employees 職工人數（人）	Rate of change 每年變化 (%)	Total revenue (mil. RMB) 總銷售收入（百萬元）	Rate of change 每年變化 (%)	Total profit (mil. RMB) 總利潤（百萬元）	Rate of change 每年變化 (%)
1993	431		172,509		2,711		162	
1994	465	7.89%	167,182	-3.09%	2,592	-4.39%	71	-56.33%
1995	425	-8.60%	177,765	6.33%	3,204	23.59%	66	-7.59%
1996	398	-6.35%	155,253	-12.66%	3,285	2.53%	68	3.72%

3 Major products* 3 種主要產品 *	Output 產量	Sales volume 銷售量	Unit 單位
a) Baysalt 海鹽	12,805,168	12,036,858	ton 噸
b) Processed Salt 加工鹽	1,025,195	902,172	ton 噸

Top 10 firms by revenue (year founded) 收入排名前 10 家企業 (創辦年份)	City 城市	Province 省	Telephone / fax 電話 / 傳真	Number of employees 職工人數	Ownership 產業所有權	Revenue ('000 RMB) 銷售收入（千元）	Profit ('000 RMB) (rank) 利潤（千元）（排名）	Total assets ('000 RMB) 總資產（千元）	Major products 主要產品
Jiangsu Provincial Salt Industry Corp. 江蘇省鹽業公司(1800)	Lianyungang 連雲港市	Jiangsu 江蘇省	(0518)5412111 (0518)5414973	25,032	State-owned 國有	426,736	-38040(134)	1,628,822	a,b
Hebei Tangshan Nan Pu Saltworks 河北省唐山南堡鹽場(1956)	Tangshan 唐山市	Hebei 河北省	(0315)8515105 (0315)8515154	7,526	State-owned 國有	272,776	48321(1)	540,313	a
Tianjin Chang Lu Hai Jing Group Co. Ltd 天津長蘆海晶集團有限公司(1942)	Tianjin 天津市	Tianjin 天津市	(022)25874445 (022)25895796	7,441	State-owned 國有	266,012	108(85)	1,192,666	a
Yingkou Salt Industry (Group) Co. 營口鹽業(集團)公司(1730)	Yingkou 營口市	Liaoning 遼寧省	(0417)3840701 (0417)3840709	6,425	State-owned 國有	190,320	1275(20)	477,351	o
Tianjin Changlu Hangu Saltworks Co. Ltd. 天津長蘆漢沽鹽場有限責任公司(1948)	Tianjin 天津市	Tianjin 天津市	(022)25694997 (022)25694997	7,734	State-owned 國有	179,828	25(104)	495,311	a,b
Shan Dong Chang Yi Salinization (Group) Co. Ltd. 山東昌邑鹽化(集團)有限公司(1958)	Weifang 濰坊市	Shandong 山東省	(0536)7211854 (0536)7211453	1,507	State-owned 國有	112,860	3300(5)	183,586	a
Changlu Daqinghe Saltworks 長蘆大清河鹽廠(1942)	Tangshan 唐山市	Hebei 河北省	(0315)4055101 (0315)4055365	4,196	State-owned 國有	102,900	1802(14)	241,154	a,b
Hai Hua No.2 Salt Refining Company 海化第二製鹽公司	Weifang 濰坊市	Shandong 山東省	(0536)5327216 (0536)5327239	2,250	Collectively-owned 集體	93,233	16959(2)	91,082	o
Weifang Hanting Salt Industry Chemical Group Company 濰坊寒亭鹽業化工集團公司(1958)	Weifang 濰坊市	Shandong 山東省	(0536)7251035 (0536)251618	2,235	Collectively-owned 集體	67,441	769(32)	83,251	a,b
Chang Lu Huanghua Saltworks 長蘆黃驊鹽場(1958)	Cangzhou 滄州市	Hebei 河北省	(0317)5222251	3,320	State-owned 國有	62,383	-15336(133)	295,519	a,b

Top 10 Cities by Production Output 產出排名前 10 位城市	Province 省	Market share 市場份額	Number of firms 企業個數
Lianyungang 連雲港市	Jiangsu 江蘇省	18.53%	32
Tianjin 天津市	Tianjin 天津市	14.94%	7
Weifang 濰坊市	Shandong 山東省	13.56%	74
Tangshan 唐山市	Hebei 河北省	12.17%	11
Dalian 大連市	Liaoning 遼寧省	8.33%	17
Yingkou 營口市	Liaoning 遼寧省	4.31%	2
Yancheng 鹽城市	Jiangsu 江蘇省	3.70%	9
Cangzhou 滄州市	Hebei 河北省	3.58%	5
Qingdao 青島市	Shandong 山東省	2.74%	10
Yantai 煙台市	Shandong 山東省	1.89%	11

10 Major Wholesalers 10 家主要批發商	City 城市	Province 省	Telephone / Fax 電話 / 傳真
Guangdong Meizhou Salt Industry General Company 廣東省梅州鹽業總公司	Meizhou 梅州市	Guangdong 廣東省	(0752)2234242 (0752)2234720
Shannxi Import & Export Company 陝西省進出口公司	Xi'an 西安市	Shaanxi 陝西省	(029)7424946 (029)7420131
Fujian Salt Industry Company 福建省鹽業公司	Fuzhou 福州市	Fujian 福建省	(0591)7535047 (0591)7535047
Sichuan Salt Industry Company Zigong Branch 四川省鹽業公司自貢分公司	Zigong 自貢市	Sichuan 四川省	(0813)2203215 (0813)2203215
Shanghai Shi Liu Pu Non-staple Food Trade Company 上海市十六鋪副食品貿易公司	Shanghai 上海市	Shanghai 上海市	(021)63736787
Shandong Salt Industry General Company Shandong Salt Administration Bureau 山東省鹽業總公司山東省鹽務局	Ji'nan 濟南市	Shandong 山東省	(0531)6925633 (0531)6925021
Yunnan Salt Industry General Company 雲南省鹽業總公司	Kunming 昆明市	Yunnan 雲南省	(0871)3166719
Shanghai Jia Le Condiment Mill Marketing Company 上海家樂調味食品銷售公司	Shanghai 上海市	Shanghai 上海市	(021)59139194
Zhong Yan Shanghai Salt Company 中鹽上海鹽業公司	Shanghai 上海市	Shanghai 上海市	(021)62180345 (021)62187068
Zhejiang Salt Industry Company 浙江省鹽業公司	Hangzhou 杭州市	Zhejiang 浙江省	(0571)7800292 (0571)7800292

*Also include sales by firms outside this industry.包括本行業以外廠家的銷售。"o" stands for "others". "o" 代表 "其他產品"。

1032: Lake Salt Mining 湖鹽業

The industry accounts for 0.007% of the total revenue of China's industrial sector in 1996. The revenue growth rate of the industry is -2.2% from 1995, as compared to the growth rate of China's industrial sector, 9.51%. The rate of return on asset is 3.25%. 69.36% of all firms in the industry made a profit while 22.95% had negative returns. The top province in terms of the industry's revenue is Inner Mongolia, accounting for 59.81% of the total revenue.
本行業在1996年佔全行業總產值0.007%，行業年增長率為-2.2%（全國工業年增長率9.51%）。行業的資產回報率3.25%，69.36%的企業盈利，22.95%的企業虧損。銷售收入最高的省份為內蒙省，佔本行業的59.81%。

	Total number of firms 企業總數	Total number of employees 職工總數	Total revenue (mil. RMB) 總銷售收入（百萬元）	Total profit (mil. RMB) 總利潤（百萬元）	Return on assets 資產利潤率 (%)	Return on equity 權益利潤率 (%)	Labour productivity ('000 RMB / worker) 勞動生產率（千元/人）	Debts / assets 資產負債率 (%)	Total assets (mil. RMB) 總資產（百萬元）
Industry Overall 行業總體	57	11,330	380	39	3.25	11.26	33.54	71.12	1,204

	Number of firms 企業個數	Average number of employees 平均職工人數	Average revenue ('000 RMB) 平均銷售收入（千元）	Average profit ('000 RMB) 平均利潤（千元）	Return on assets 資產利潤率 (%)	Return on equity 權益利潤率 (%)	Labour productivity ('000 RMB / worker) 勞動生產率（千元/人）	Average debts / assets 平均資產負債率(%)	Average Total assets ('000 RMB) 平均總資產（千元）
By ownership 產業所有權									
State-owned 國有	34	308	10,824	1,147	3.31	11.64	35.14	71.61	34,706
Collectively-owned 集體	23	37	521				13.96	46.00	1,063
Privately-owned 私有									
Domestic JVs 聯營									
Joint stock 股份制									
Foreign-funded 外資									
Overseas Chinese-funded 港澳台資									
By size 規模									
Large 大型	3	1,526	65,929	12,601	6.62	18.59	43.20	64.41	190,443
Medium 中型	4	807	24,381	-977	-1.00	-4.78	30.20	79.14	98,004
Small 小型	50	70	1,693	102	2.12	8.09	24.04	73.86	4,823
By regional distribution 地區分布									
Central-North 華北	16	343	14,206	2,364	6.03	19.20	41.44	68.60	39,208
Beijing 北京									
Tianjin 天津									
Hebei 河北									
Shanxi 山西									
Inner Mongolia 內蒙	16	343	14,206	2,364	6.03	19.20	41.44	68.60	39,208
Northeast 東北									
Liaoning 遼寧									
Jilin 吉林									
Heilongjiang 黑龍江									
Central East 華東									
Shanghai 上海									
Jiangsu 江蘇									
Zhejiang 浙江									
Anhui 安徽									
Fujian 福建									
Jiangxi 江西									
Shandong 山東									
Central-South 中南	1	142	1,070	-30	-0.87	-1.42	7.54	39.02	3,460
Henan 河南									
Hubei 湖北									
Hunan 湖南									
Guangdong 廣東	1	142	1,070	-30	-0.87	-1.42	7.54	39.02	3,460
Guangxi 廣西									
Hainan 海南									
Southwest 西南	1	52	810	10	0.84	1.67	15.58	49.58	1,190
Chongqing 重慶									
Sichuan 四川	1	52	810	10	0.84	1.67	15.58	49.58	1,190
Guizhou 貴州									
Yunnan 雲南									
Tibet 西藏									
Northwest 西北	39	145	3,869	36	0.24	0.94	26.71	74.12	14,679
Shaanxi 陝西	7	100	2,220	-239	-4.40	-19.79	22.23	77.76	5,421
Gansu 甘肅	6	52	1,012	85	3.88	11.62	19.52	66.69	2,192
Qinghai 青海	5	341	8,066	622	1.29	4.80	23.68	73.01	48,032
Ningxia 寧夏	3	12	17	3	0.32	0.59	1.43	45.69	1,043
Xinjiang 新疆	18	161	4,940	-32	-0.20	-0.83	30.63	75.25	15,451

1032: Lake Salt Mining 湖鹽業

Year 年份	Number of firms 企業個數	Rate of change 每年變化(%)	Number of employees 職工人數(人)	Rate of change 每年變化(%)	Total revenue (mil. RMB) 總銷售收入(百萬元)	Rate of change 每年變化(%)	Total profit (mil. RMB) 總利潤(百萬元)	Rate of change 每年變化(%)
1993	46		12,948		296		12	
1994	60	30.43%	16,525	27.63%	552	86.31%	41	245.70%
1995	65	8.33%	13,883	-15.99%	388	-29.63%	24	-42.22%
1996	57	-12.31%	11,330	-18.39%	380	-2.17%	39	63.84%

3 Major products* 3 種主要產品 *	Output 產量	Sales volume 銷售量	Unit 單位
a) Lake Salt 湖鹽	1,264,182	998,704	ton 噸
b) Anhydrous Sodium Sulfate 無水硫酸鈉	254,364	249,277	ton 噸
c) Processed Salt 加工鹽	119,799	105,423	ton 噸

Top 10 firms by revenue (year founded) 收入排名前 10 家企業 (創辦年份)	City 城市	Province 省	Telephone / fax 電話 / 傳真	Number of employees 職工人數	Ownership 產業所有權	Revenue ('000 RMB) 銷售收入(千元)	Profit ('000 RMB) (rank) 利潤(千元)(排名)	Total assets ('000 RMB) 總資產(千元)	Major products 主要產品
Xinjiang Yan Hu Chemical Plant 新疆鹽湖化工廠(1958)	Urumqi 烏魯木齊市	Xinjiang 新疆	(0991)5940131	1989	State-owned 國有	60,152	-338(10)	203,313	a,b,c
Qinghai Ke Ke Saltworks 青海省柯柯鹽廠(1979)	Golmud 格爾木市	Qinghai 青海省	(0979)21501	793	State-owned 國有	18,294	1951(1)	117,730	a,c
Qinghai Cha Ka Saltworks 青海省茶卡鹽廠(1950)	Golmud 格爾木市	Qinghai 青海省		75	State-owned 國有	17,372	1176(2)	86,852	a,b,c
Shannxi Dingbian Salinization Factory 陝西省定邊縣鹽化廠(1960)	Yulin 榆林市	Shaanxi 陝西省	(0912)4221931	532	State-owned 國有	12,919	-1784(13)	37,727	o
Hoboksar Inner Mongolia Autonomous County Saltern 和布克賽爾蒙古自治縣鹽場(1958)	Tacheng 塔城市	Xinjiang 新疆	(0990)720005	231	State-owned 國有	10,428	-825(12)	22,251	a,c
Jinghe Salinization General Factory 精河縣鹽化總廠(1902)	Bole 博樂市	Xinjiang 新疆	(0909)5332228	210	State-owned 國有	5,201	803(3)	17,958	a,b,c
Lenghu Salt Industry Company 冷湖鹽業公司(1958)	Golmud 格爾木市	Qinghai 青海省	(0979)71269	100	State-owned 國有	2,911	0(9)	23,326	a,b
Hami Saltpetre Industrial General Company 哈密市鹽硝實業有限責任總公司(1995)	Hami 哈密市	Xinjiang 新疆	(0902)2233965	79	State-owned 國有	2,833	134(5)	2,331	a,c
Hoboksar Inner Mongolia Autonomous County Xia Zi Gai Saltern 和布克賽爾蒙古自治縣夏孜蓋鹽場(1988)	Tacheng 塔城市	Xinjiang 新疆	(0990)720119	70	State-owned 國有	2,694	84(8)	7,605	c
Gaotai Salt Pond Saltern 高台縣鹽池鹽廠(1989)	Zhangye 張掖市	Gansu 甘肅省	(0936)21480	150	Collectively-owned 集體	2,335	120(6)	1,863	o

Top 10 Cities by Production Output 產出排名前 10 位城市	Province 省	Market share 市場份額	Number of firms 企業個數
Alxa Zuo 阿拉善左旗	Inner Mong 內蒙	51.14%	5
Urumqi 烏魯木齊市	Xinjiang 新疆	17.74%	1
Dongsheng 東勝市	Inner Mong 內蒙	8.88%	4
Golmud 格爾木市	Qinghai 青海省	8.16%	4
Yulin 榆林市	Shaanxi 陝西省	3.69%	7
Erenhot 二連浩特市	Inner Mong 內蒙	1.56%	2
Korla 庫爾勒市	Xinjiang 新疆	1.24%	4
Bole 博樂市	Xinjiang 新疆	1.23%	1
Hami 哈密市	Xinjiang 新疆	1.09%	2
Tacheng 塔城市	Xinjiang 新疆	0.95%	2

10 Major Wholesalers 10 家主要批發商	City 城市	Province 省	Telephone / Fax 電話 / 傳真
Guangdong Meizhou Salt Industry General Company 廣東省梅州鹽業總公司	Meizhou 梅州市	Guangdong 廣東省	(0752)2234242 (0752)2234720
Shannxi Import & Export Company 陝西省進出口公司	Xi'an 西安市	Shaanxi 陝西省	(029)7424946 (029)7420131
Fujian Salt Industry Company 福建省鹽業公司	Fuzhou 福州市	Fujian 福建省	(0591)7535047 (0591)7535047
Sichuan Salt Industry Company Zigong Branch 四川省鹽業公司自貢分公司	Zigong 自貢市	Sichuan 四川省	(0813)2203215 (0813)2203215
Shanghai Shi Liu Pu Non-staple Food Trade Company 上海市十六鋪副食品貿易公司	Shanghai 上海市	Shanghai 上海市	(021)63736787
Shandong Salt Industry General Company Shandong Salt Administration Bureau 山東省鹽業總公司山東省鹽務局	Ji'nan 濟南市	Shandong 山東省	(0531)6925633 (0531)6925021
Yunnan Salt Industry General Company 雲南省鹽業總公司	Kunming 昆明市	Yunnan 雲南省	(0871)3166719
Shanghai Jia Le Condiment Mill Marketing Company 上海家樂調味食品銷售公司	Shanghai 上海市	Shanghai 上海市	(021)59139194
Zhong Yan Shanghai Salt Company 中鹽上海鹽業公司	Shanghai 上海市	Shanghai 上海市	(021)62180345 (021)62187068
Zhejiang Salt Industry Company 浙江省鹽業公司	Hangzhou 杭州市	Zhejiang 浙江省	(0571)7800292 (0571)7800292

*Also include sales by firms outside this industry.包括本行業以外廠家的銷售。"o" stands for "others". "o" 代表 "其他產品" 。

1033: Well Salt Mining 井鹽業

The industry accounts for 0.024% of the total revenue of China's industrial sector in 1996. The revenue growth rate of the industry is 14.7% from 1995, as compared to the growth rate of China's industrial sector, 9.51%. The rate of return on asset is -4.99%. 70.99% of all firms in the industry made a profit while 26.97% had negative returns. The top province in terms of the industry's revenue is Sichuan, accounting for 70.71% of the total revenue.
本行業在1996年佔全行業總產值0.024%，行業年增長率為14.7%（全國工業年增長率9.51%）。行業的資產回報率-4.99%，70.99%的企業盈利，26.97%的企業虧損。銷售收入最高的省份為四川省，佔本行業的70.71%。

	Total number of firms 企業總數	Total number of employees 職工總數	Total revenue (mil. RMB) 總銷售收入（百萬元）	Total profit (mil. RMB) 總利潤（百萬元）	Return on assets 資產利潤率 (%)	Return on equity 權益利潤率 (%)	Labour productivity ('000 RMB / worker) 勞動生產率（千元/人）	Debts / assets 資產負債率 (%)	Total assets (mil. RMB) 總資產（百萬元）
Industry Overall 行業總體	98	52,380	1,388	-204	-4.99	-16.84	26.50	70.38	4,088

	Number of firms 企業個數	Average number of employees 平均職工人數	Average revenue ('000 RMB) 平均銷售收入（千元）	Average profit ('000 RMB) 平均利潤（千元）	Return on assets 資產利潤率 (%)	Return on equity 權益利潤率 (%)	Labour productivity ('000 RMB / worker) 勞動生產率（千元/人）	Average debts / assets 平均資產負債率(%)	Average Total assets ('000 RMB) 平均總資產（千元）
By ownership 產業所有權									
State-owned 國有	37	1,026	21,946	-1,432	-2.18	-7.09	21.39	69.17	65,568
Collectively-owned 集體	59	120	4,568	-108	-1.46	-19.55	38.19	92.54	7,397
Privately-owned 私有									
Domestic JVs 聯營	1	157	16,107	4,433	6.53	16.31	102.59	59.96	67,869
Joint stock 股份制	2	3,593	145,433	-74,536	-12.88	-36.96	40.48	65.16	578,875
Foreign-funded 外資									
Overseas Chinese-funded 港澳台資									
By size 規模									
Large 大型	4	5,108	153,045	-44,620	-7.52	-20.81	29.96	63.88	593,652
Medium 中型	6	2,875	55,834	-2,126	-1.55	-5.96	19.42	74.07	137,623
Small 小型	88	167	5,014	-145	-1.44	-9.16	30.03	84.31	10,087
By regional distribution 地區分布									
Central-North 華北									
Beijing 北京									
Tianjin 天津									
Hebei 河北									
Shanxi 山西									
Inner Mongolia 內蒙									
Northeast 東北	2	145	2,950	255	20.99	82.26	20.34	74.49	1,215
Liaoning 遼寧	2	145	2,950	255	20.99	82.26	20.34	74.49	1,215
Jilin 吉林									
Heilongjiang 黑龍江									
Central East 華東	28	203	12,589	594	3.16	18.74	62.05	83.15	18,809
Shanghai 上海									
Jiangsu 江蘇	9	28	3,820	368	4.71	8.73	134.82	46.14	7,817
Zhejiang 浙江									
Anhui 安徽	3	712	75,503	4,143	7.99	38.04	106.09	79.00	51,883
Fujian 福建									
Jiangxi 江西	4	366	9,728	38	0.23	0.99	26.61	76.68	16,200
Shandong 山東	12	152	4,391	62	0.31	24.18	28.81	98.70	19,653
Central-South 中南	9	108	1,986	-62	-1.59	-5.91	18.35	73.17	3,922
Henan 河南	6	75	390	-18	-2.02	-18.03	5.19	88.81	908
Hubei 湖北	3	174	5,177	-150	-1.51	-5.08	29.69	70.32	9,950
Hunan 湖南									
Guangdong 廣東									
Guangxi 廣西									
Hainan 海南									
Southwest 西南	57	791	17,645	-3,849	-6.28	-19.66	22.30	68.08	61,306
Chongqing 重慶	6	408	4,578	-1,842	-7.90	-29.93	11.20	73.60	23,316
Sichuan 四川	50	837	19,245	-4,095	-6.21	-19.30	22.97	67.84	65,958
Guizhou 貴州									
Yunnan 雲南									
Tibet 西藏									
Northwest 西北	2	164	2,815	-570	-3.88	32.66	17.16	111.89	14,675
Shaanxi 陝西									
Gansu 甘肅	1	310	4,960	-1,170	-4.11	26.65	16.00	115.43	28,450
Qinghai 青海	1	18	670	30	3.33	3.33	37.22		900
Ningxia 寧夏									
Xinjiang 新疆									

1033: Well Salt Mining 井鹽業

Year 年份	Number of firms 企業個數	Rate of change 每年變化 (%)	Number of employees 職工人數 (人)	Rate of change 每年變化 (%)	Total revenue (mil. RMB) 總銷售收入 (百萬元)	Rate of change 每年變化 (%)	Total profit (mil. RMB) 總利潤 (百萬元)	Rate of change 每年變化 (%)
1993	98		49,275		1,032		68	
1994	92	-6.12%	50,327	2.13%	1,002	-2.94%	42	-37.87%
1995	109	18.48%	55,115	9.51%	1,210	20.80%	-87	-307.61%
1996	98	-10.09%	52,380	-4.96%	1,388	14.71%	-204	-133.24%

3 Major products* 3 種主要產品 *	Output 產量	Sales volume 銷售量	Unit 單位
a) Well Salt 井鹽	3,333,100	3,466,424	ton 噸
b) Refined Salt 精製鹽	1,720,251	1,599,834	ton 噸

Top 10 firms by revenue (year founded) 收入排名前 10 家企業 (創辦年份)	City 城市	Province 省	Telephone / fax 電話 / 傳真	Number of employees 職工人數	Ownership 產業所有權	Revenue ('000 RMB) 銷售收入 (千元)	Profit ('000 RMB) (rank) 利潤 (千元) (排名)	Total assets ('000 RMB) 總資產 (千元)	Major products 主要產品
Sichuan Jiu Da Salt Industry (Group) Co. 四川久大鹽業(集團)公司(1951)	Zigong 自貢市	Sichuan 四川省	(0813)8105828 (0813)8105472	10,342	State-owned 國有	227,908	-23236(48)	982,120	a
Salinization (Group) Co. Ltd. 鹽化集團股份有限公司(1955)	Leshan 樂山市	Sichuan 四川省	(0833)3352270	7,904	Joint stock 股份制	209,642	-143339(49)	831,286	a
Anhui Dingyuan Salt Mine 安徽省定遠鹽礦(1990)	Chuzhou 滁州市	Anhui 安徽省	(0550)4480012 (0550)4480023	1,767	State-owned 國有	100,809	4836(1)	144,748	a,b
Zigongshi Zigong Well Salt Works 自貢市貢井鹽廠(1938)	Zigong 自貢市	Sichuan 四川省	(0813)3301114	5,066	State-owned 國有	71,703	-7964(45)	150,866	a
Sichuan Sote (Group) Co. Ltd. 四川索特(集團)股份有限公司	Chongqing 重慶市	Chongqing 重慶市	(023)8260318 (023)8260313	1,215	Joint stock 股份制	68,395	-12967(47)	405,988	a,b
Dingyuan Dongxing Salinization Industrial Company 定遠縣東興鹽化工業公司(1994)	Chuzhou 滁州市	Anhui 安徽省	(0550)4490458	500	Collectively-owned 集體	63,100	3320(3)	5,000	a
Dingyuan Dongxing Refined Salt Factory 定遠縣東興精製鹽廠(1987)	Chuzhou 滁州市	Anhui 安徽省	(0550)4040413	220	Collectively-owned 集體	62,600	4270(2)	5,900	a
Zigong Ziliujing Well Salt Works 自貢市自流井鹽廠(1951)	Zigong 自貢市	Sichuan 四川省	(0813)2601641 (0813)262800	3,408	State-owned 國有	59,542	-4997(42)	129,064	a
Zigong Deng Guan Well Salt Works 自貢市鄧關鹽廠(1959)	Zigong 自貢市	Sichuan 四川省	(0813)3901029	3,477	State-owned 國有	45,527	4(26)	138,775	a
The Salt Chemical Plant of Peng Lai, Sui Ning 遂寧市蓬萊製鹽化工廠(1960)	Suining 遂寧市	Sichuan 四川省	(0825)5541421	1,737	State-owned 國有	44,386	-945(36)	85,613	a,b

Top 10 Cities by Production Output 產出排名前 10 位城市	Province 省	Market share 市場份額	Number of firms 企業個數
Zigong 自貢市	Sichuan 四川省	34.47%	17
Leshan 樂山市	Sichuan 四川省	25.50%	11
Chongqing 重慶市	Chongqing 重慶市	8.78%	7
Chuzhou 滁州市	Anhui 安徽省	6.45%	2
Yichun 宜春市	Jiangxi 江西省	4.20%	3
Suining 遂寧市	Sichuan 四川省	3.69%	4
Dongying 東營市	Shandong 山東省	2.39%	10
Nanchong 南充市	Sichuan 四川省	2.19%	1
Dachuan 達川市	Sichuan 四川省	2.13%	2
Weifang 濰坊市	Shandong 山東省	2.00%	12

10 Major Wholesalers 10 家主要批發商	City 城市	Province 省	Telephone / Fax 電話 / 傳真
Guangdong Meizhou Salt Industry General Company 廣東省梅州鹽業總公司	Meizhou 梅州市	Guangdong 廣東省	(0752)2234242 (0752)2234720
Shannxi Import & Export Company 陝西省進出口公司	Xi'an 西安市	Shaanxi 陝西省	(029)7424946 (029)7420131
Fujian Salt Industry Company 福建省鹽業公司	Fuzhou 福州市	Fujian 福建省	(0591)7535047 (0591)7535047
Sichuan Salt Industry Company Zigong Branch 四川省鹽業公司自貢分公司	Zigong 自貢市	Sichuan 四川省	(0813)2203215 (0813)2203215
Shanghai Shi Liu Pu Non-staple Food Trade Company 上海市十六鋪副食品貿易公司	Shanghai 上海市	Shanghai 上海市	(021)63736787
Shandong Salt Industry General Company Shandong Salt Administration Bureau 山東省鹽業總公司山東省鹽務局	Ji'nan 濟南市	Shandong 山東省	(0531)6925633 (0531)6925021
Yunnan Salt Industry General Company 雲南省鹽業總公司	Kunming 昆明市	Yunnan 雲南省	(0871)3166719
Shanghai Jia Le Condiment Mill Marketing Company 上海家樂調味食品銷售公司	Shanghai 上海市	Shanghai 上海市	(021)59139194
Zhong Yan Shanghai Salt Company 中鹽上海鹽業公司	Shanghai 上海市	Shanghai 上海市	(021)62180345 (021)62187068
Zhejiang Salt Industry Company 浙江省鹽業公司	Hangzhou 杭州市	Zhejiang 浙江省	(0571)7800292 (0571)7800292

*Also include sales by firms outside this industry.包括本行業以外廠家的銷售。"o" stands for "others". "o" 代表 "其他產品" 。

1034: Underground Salt Mining 礦鹽業

The industry accounts for 0.012% of the total revenue of China's industrial sector in 1996. The revenue growth rate of the industry is 9.1% from 1995, as compared to the growth rate of China's industrial sector, 9.51%. The rate of return on asset is -0.79%. 65.41% of all firms in the industry made a profit while 29.03% had negative returns. The top province in terms of the industry's revenue is Hubei, accounting for 39.30% of the total revenue.
本行業在 1996 年佔全行業總產值 0.012%，行業年增長率為 9.1%（全國工業年增長率 9.51%）。行業的資產回報率 -0.79%，65.41% 的企業盈利，29.03% 的企業虧損。銷售收入最高的省份為湖北省，佔本行業的 39.30%。

	Total number of firms 企業總數	Total number of employees 職工總數	Total revenue (mil. RMB) 總銷售收入（百萬元）	Total profit (mil. RMB) 總利潤（百萬元）	Return on assets 資產利潤率 (%)	Return on equity 權益利潤率 (%)	Labour productivity ('000 RMB / worker) 勞動生產率（千元/人）	Debts / assets 資產負債率 (%)	Total assets (mil. RMB) 總資產（百萬元）
Industry Overall 行業總體	36	19,526	696	-14	-0.79	-2.02	35.64	61.09	1,831

	Number of firms 企業個數	Average number of employees 平均職工人數	Average revenue ('000 RMB) 平均銷售收入（千元）	Average profit ('000 RMB) 平均利潤（千元）	Return on assets 資產利潤率 (%)	Return on equity 權益利潤率 (%)	Labour productivity ('000 RMB / worker) 勞動生產率（千元/人）	Average debts / assets 平均資產負債率(%)	Average Total assets ('000 RMB) 平均總資產（千元）
By ownership 產業所有權									
State-owned 國有	26	712	25,731	-731	-1.07	-2.73	36.12	60.81	68,308
Collectively-owned 集體	10	100	2,698	500	8.94	30.63	26.87	70.80	5,591
Privately-owned 私有									
Domestic JVs 聯營									
Joint stock 股份制									
Foreign-funded 外資									
Overseas Chinese-funded 港澳台資									
By size 規模									
Large 大型	4	1,836	83,614	-1,128	-0.55	-1.49	45.54	62.85	203,386
Medium 中型	7	949	35,454	-1,407	-1.42	-3.67	37.35	61.20	98,875
Small 小型	25	221	4,534	15	0.11	0.26	20.47	56.60	13,045
By regional distribution 地區分布									
Central-North 華北	2	27	205	30	11.32	11.76	7.74	1.89	265
Beijing 北京									
Tianjin 天津									
Hebei 河北									
Shanxi 山西									
Inner Mongolia 內蒙	2	27	205	30	11.32	11.76	7.74	1.89	265
Northeast 東北									
Liaoning 遼寧									
Jilin 吉林									
Heilongjiang 黑龍江									
Central East 華東	6	173	5,185	783	7.43	58.02	29.91	87.20	10,548
Shanghai 上海									
Jiangsu 江蘇	3	45	7,387	1,423	13.64	347.15	165.37	96.04	10,433
Zhejiang 浙江									
Anhui 安徽									
Fujian 福建									
Jiangxi 江西	3	302	2,983	143	1.34	6.26	9.88	78.56	10,663
Shandong 山東									
Central-South 中南	9	1,290	52,371	-2,146	-1.51	-3.71	40.59	59.34	142,141
Henan 河南									
Hubei 湖北	7	1,138	39,076	-2,860	-2.44	-7.43	34.33	67.18	117,217
Hunan 湖南	2	1,822	98,905	355	0.15	0.28	54.30	45.32	229,375
Guangdong 廣東									
Guangxi 廣西									
Hainan 海南									
Southwest 西南	14	452	13,126	-29	-0.09	-0.24	29.04	61.70	32,434
Chongqing 重慶		58	751	-255	-3.24	-9.59	12.82	66.24	7,873
Sichuan 四川	1	215	5,032	52	3.22	10.78	23.38	70.16	1,629
Guizhou 貴州									
Yunnan 雲南	12	500	14,713	-43	-0.11	-0.30	29.42	61.60	37,222
Tibet 西藏									
Northwest 西北	5	99	1,834	108	1.59	5.49	18.53	71.03	6,794
Shaanxi 陝西									
Gansu 甘肅	1	2	60	10	25.00	50.00	30.00	25.00	40
Qinghai 青海									
Ningxia 寧夏									
Xinjiang 新疆	4	123	2,278	133	1.56	5.40	18.48	71.09	8,483

1034: Underground Salt Mining 礦鹽業

Year 年份	Number of firms 企業個數	Rate of change 每年變化 (%)	Number of employees 職工人數 (人)	Rate of change 每年變化 (%)	Total revenue (mil. RMB) 總銷售收入 (百萬元)	Rate of change 每年變化 (%)	Total profit (mil. RMB) 總利潤 (百萬元)	Rate of change 每年變化 (%)
1993	27		16,399		456		-50	
1994	43	59.26%	20,507	25.05%	464	1.55%	-57	-13.73%
1995	39	-9.30%	20,495	-0.06%	638	37.56%	-43	24.01%
1996	36	-7.69%	19,526	-4.73%	696	9.15%	-14	67.46%

3 Major products* 3 種主要產品 *	Output 產量	Sales volume 銷售量	Unit 單位
a) Mine Salt 礦鹽	1,067,981	1,035,942	ton 噸
b) Refined Salt 精製鹽	1,558,046	1,448,983	ton 噸
c) Anhydrous Sodium Sulfate 無水硫酸鈉	99,748	97,753	ton 噸

Top 10 firms by revenue (year founded) 收入排名前 10 家企業 (創辦年份)	City 城市	Province 省	Telephone / fax 電話 / 傳真	Number of employees 職工人數	Ownership 產業所有權	Revenue ('000 RMB) 銷售收入 (千元)	Profit ('000 RMB) (rank) 利潤 (千元) (排名)	Total assets ('000 RMB) 總資產 (千元)	Major products 主要產品
Hunan Xiang Li Salt Mine 湖南省湘澧鹽礦(1972)	Changde 常德市	Hunan 湖南省	(0736)4223188 (0736)4223106	2,457	State-owned 國有	120,687	354(7)	276,411	a,c
Hunan Xiang Heng Salt Mine 湖南省湘衡鹽礦(1969)	Hengyang 衡陽市	Hunan 湖南省	(0734)8301060 (0734)8301210	1,244	State-owned 國有	77,124	360(6)	182,340	a
Yunnan Yi Ping Lang Salt Mine 雲南一平浪鹽礦(1938)	Chuxiong 楚雄市	Yunnan 雲南省	(0878)4821446 (0878)4821105	2,409	State-owned 國有	70,499	4565(1)	129,322	a,b,c
Ying City No.1 Zhi Saltern 應城市第一製鹽廠(1988)	Xiaogan 孝感市	Hubei 湖北省	(0712)3223732 (0712)3223389	1,729	State-owned 國有	64,980	1007(3)	232,658	b
Kunming Salt Mine 昆明鹽礦(1993)	Kunming 昆明市	Yunnan 雲南省	(0871)8697052 (0871)8699927	553	State-owned 國有	54,435	154(11)	172,672	a,b,c
Yunnan Simao Area Mohei Salt Mine 思茅地區磨黑鹽礦(1725)	Simao 思茅市	Yunnan 雲南省	(0879)3311083	619	State-owned 國有	15,589	-1631(18)	41,699	a,b
Zaoyang Nitrate Factory 棗陽市鹽硝廠(1988)	Xiangfan 襄樊市	Hubei 湖北省	(0710)6653146	239	State-owned 國有	15,349	0(14)	28,560	b
Yunnan Simao Area Fenggang Salt Mine 雲南省思茅地區鳳崗鹽礦(1929)	Simao 思茅市	Yunnan 雲南省	(0879)5223030	671	State-owned 國有	11,004	-568(15)	18,215	a,b
Dali Bai Zu Autonomous Prefecture Qiao Hou Salt Mine 大理白族自治州喬后鹽礦(1857)	Dali 大理市	Yunnan 雲南省	(0872)5360708	840	State-owned 國有	10,634	-1501(17)	26,170	a,b
Jiangsu Hongze Mirabilite Mine 江蘇省洪澤縣芒硝礦(1994)	Huaiyin 淮陰市	Jiangsu 江蘇省	(0517)7223099	60	State-owned 國有	9,842	509(5)	16,349	a

Top 10 Cities by Production Output 產出排名前 10 位城市	Province 省	Market share 市場份額	Number of firms 企業個數
Xiaogan 孝感市	Hubei 湖北省	24.55%	4
Changde 常德市	Hunan 湖南省	21.54%	1
Hengyang 衡陽市	Hunan 湖南省	13.79%	1
Chuxiong 楚雄市	Yunnan 雲南省	11.61%	1
Kunming 昆明市	Yunnan 雲南省	9.81%	2
Changzhou 常州市	Jiangsu 江蘇省	3.58%	2
Simao 思茅市	Yunnan 雲南省	2.54%	3
Xiangfan 襄樊市	Hubei 湖北省	2.21%	1
Dali 大理市	Yunnan 雲南省	2.03%	1
Huaiyin 淮陰市	Jiangsu 江蘇省	1.72%	1

10 Major Wholesalers 10 家主要批發商	City 城市	Province 省	Telephone / Fax 電話 / 傳真
Guangdong Meizhou Salt Industry General Company 廣東省梅州鹽業總公司	Meizhou 梅州市	Guangdong 廣東省	(0752)2234242 (0752)2234720
Shannxi Import & Export Company 陝西省進出口公司	Xi'an 西安市	Shaanxi 陝西省	(029)7424946 (029)7420131
Fujian Salt Industry Company 福建省鹽業公司	Fuzhou 福州市	Fujian 福建省	(0591)7535047 (0591)7535047
Sichuan Salt Industry Company Zigong Branch 四川省鹽業公司自貢分公司	Zigong 自貢市	Sichuan 四川省	(0813)2203215 (0813)2203215
Shanghai Shi Liu Pu Non-staple Food Trade Company 上海市十六鋪副食品貿易公司	Shanghai 上海市	Shanghai 上海市	(021)63736787
Shandong Salt Industry General Company Shandong Salt Administration Bureau 山東省鹽業總公司山東省鹽務局	Ji'nan 濟南市	Shandong 山東省	(0531)6925633 (0531)6925021
Yunnan Salt Industry General Company 雲南省鹽業總公司	Kunming 昆明市	Yunnan 雲南省	(0871)3166719
Shanghai Jia Le Condiment Mill Marketing Company 上海家樂調味食品銷售公司	Shanghai 上海市	Shanghai 上海市	(021)59139194
Zhong Yan Shanghai Salt Company 中鹽上海鹽業公司	Shanghai 上海市	Shanghai 上海市	(021)62180345 (021)62187068
Zhejiang Salt Industry Company 浙江省鹽業公司	Hangzhou 杭州市	Zhejiang 浙江省	(0571)7800292 (0571)7800292

*Also include sales by firms outside this industry.包括本行業以外廠家的銷售。"o" stands for "others". "o" 代表 "其他產品"。

1091: Asbestos Mining 石棉採選業

The industry accounts for 0.009% of the total revenue of China's industrial sector in 1996. The revenue growth rate of the industry is 21.1% from 1995, as compared to the growth rate of China's industrial sector, 9.51%. The rate of return on asset is 0.65%. 81.91% of all firms in the industry made a profit while 15.53% had negative returns. The top province in terms of the industry's revenue is Gansu, accounting for 33.28% of the total revenue.
本行業在1996年佔全行業總產值0.009%，行業年增長率為21.1%（全國工業年增長率9.51%）。行業的資產回報率0.65%，81.91%的企業盈利，15.53%的企業虧損。銷售收入最高的省份為甘肅省，佔本行業的33.28%。

	Total number of firms 企業總數	Total number of employees 職工總數	Total revenue (mil. RMB) 總銷售收入（百萬元）	Total profit (mil. RMB) 總利潤（百萬元）	Return on assets 資產利潤率 (%)	Return on equity 權益利潤率 (%)	Labour productivity ('000 RMB / worker) 勞動生產率（千元/人）	Debts / assets 資產負債率 (%)	Total assets (mil. RMB) 總資產（百萬元）
Industry Overall 行業總體	120	23,441	525	8	0.65	1.58	22.40	58.87	1,164

	Number of firms 企業個數	Average number of employees 平均職工人數	Average revenue ('000 RMB) 平均銷售收入（千元）	Average profit ('000 RMB) 平均利潤（千元）	Return on assets 資產利潤率 (%)	Return on equity 權益利潤率 (%)	Labour productivity ('000 RMB / worker) 勞動生產率（千元/人）	Average debts / assets 平均資產負債率(%)	Average Total assets ('000 RMB) 平均總資產（千元）
By ownership 產業所有權									
State-owned 國有	17	939	16,765	-529	-1.07	-2.54	17.84	57.79	49,471
Collectively-owned 集體	102	73	2,350	167	5.27	13.72	32.18	61.62	3,169
Privately-owned 私有									
Domestic JVs 聯營	1	21	160	-23	-4.82	-8.69	7.60	44.51	482
Joint stock 股份制									
Foreign-funded 外資									
Overseas Chinese-funded 港澳台資									
By size 規模									
Large 大型	5	2,650	50,046	3,433	2.29	5.14	18.89	55.54	150,229
Medium 中型	7	425	7,357	386	2.19	6.05	17.30	63.84	17,674
Small 小型	107	67	2,086	-111	-4.09	-11.79	30.97	65.28	2,710
By regional distribution 地區分布									
Central-North 華北	8	138	255	-29	-1.68	-8.16	1.85	79.47	1,711
Beijing 北京									
Tianjin 天津									
Hebei 河北	7	148	279	-33	-1.75	-8.07	1.88	78.34	1,880
Shanxi 山西									
Inner Mongolia 內蒙	1	65	90				1.38	107.55	530
Northeast 東北	9	73	554	-24	-0.88	-3.99	7.61	77.95	2,781
Liaoning 遼寧	9	73	554	-24	-0.88	-3.99	7.61	77.95	2,781
Jilin 吉林									
Heilongjiang 黑龍江									
Central East 華東	5	126	4,180	118	1.28	4.55	33.28	71.86	9,218
Shanghai 上海									
Jiangsu 江蘇	1	35	8,570	310	96.88	182.35	244.86	50.00	320
Zhejiang 浙江									
Anhui 安徽	2	40	890	40	1.98	6.96	22.53	71.53	2,020
Fujian 福建									
Jiangxi 江西									
Shandong 山東	2	257	5,275	100	0.48	1.72	20.53	72.06	20,865
Central-South 中南	1	50	690	110	11.70	39.29	13.80	70.21	940
Henan 河南									
Hubei 湖北	1	50	690	110	11.70	39.29	13.80	70.21	940
Hunan 湖南									
Guangdong 廣東									
Guangxi 廣西									
Hainan 海南									
Southwest 西南	10	838	10,240	-1,026	-2.97	-6.64	12.22	55.28	34,551
Chongqing 重慶									
Sichuan 四川	7	1,186	14,583	-1,467	-2.99	-6.70	12.30	55.43	49,090
Guizhou 貴州	2	16	80	5	1.59	2.27	5.00	30.16	315
Yunnan 雲南	1	48	160				3.33	28.00	1,250
Tibet 西藏									
Northwest 西北	87	145	4,528	202	2.40	5.81	31.20	58.70	8,420
Shaanxi 陝西	8	110	778	-238	-8.42	-35.85	7.07	76.51	2,820
Gansu 甘肅	65	81	2,688	230	7.57	24.68	32.99	69.34	3,046
Qinghai 青海	4	1,076	29,635	-1,625	-2.15	-3.99	27.54	46.16	75,575
Ningxia 寧夏									
Xinjiang 新疆	10	214	9,443	1,099	5.24	14.89	44.06	64.82	20,973

1091: Asbestos Mining 石棉採選業

Year 年份	Number of firms 企業個數	Rate of change 每年變化 (%)	Number of employees 職工人數 (人)	Rate of change 每年變化 (%)	Total revenue (mil. RMB) 總銷售收入 (百萬元)	Rate of change 每年變化 (%)	Total profit (mil. RMB) 總利潤 (百萬元)	Rate of change 每年變化 (%)
1993	123		20,697		386		27	
1994	141	14.63%	23,582	13.94%	446	15.47%	19	-30.03%
1995	123	-12.77%	26,537	12.53%	433	-2.78%	-7	-137.10%
1996	120	-2.44%	23,441	-11.67%	525	21.12%	8	214.30%

3 Major products* 3 種主要產品 *	Output 產量	Sales volume 銷售量	Unit 單位
a) Asbestos 石棉	417,845	447,094	ton 噸

Top 10 firms by revenue (year founded) 收入排名前 10 家企業 (創辦年份)	City 城市	Province 省	Telephone / fax 電話 / 傳真	Number of employees 職工人數	Ownership 產業所有權	Revenue ('000 RMB) 銷售收入 (千元)	Profit ('000 RMB) (rank) 利潤 (千元) (排名)	Total assets ('000 RMB) 總資產 (千元)	Major products 主要產品
Mangya Asbestos Mine, Sabmi. 國家建築材料工業局茫崖石棉礦(1958)	Golmud 格爾木市	Qinghai 青海省	(0979)51433	3,347	State-owned 國有	75,638	-9843(39)	216,363	a
Xinjiang Corps Nong Er Shi 36 Tuan Asbestos Mine 新疆兵團農二師三十六團石棉礦(1966)	Korla 庫爾勒市	Xinjiang 新疆	(0996)7561166	951	State-owned 國有	54,392	10172(1)	96,773	a
Sichuan Asbestos Mine 四川省石棉礦(1950)	Ya'an 雅安市	Sichuan 四川省	(0835)862129	5,695	State-owned 國有	52,240	-7089(38)	191,352	a
Sichuan Xin Kang Asbestos Mine 四川新康石棉礦(1952)	Ya'an 雅安市	Sichuan 四川省	(0835)862414	2,412	State-owned 國有	40,250	-3692(37)	149,538	a
Xinjiang Ruoqiang Asbestos Mine 新疆若羌縣石棉礦(1960)	Korla 庫爾勒市	Xinjiang 新疆	(0996)7561188	900	Collectively-owned 集體	35,668	1285(6)	99,310	a
Qilian Asbestos Industry General Co. 祁連縣石棉工業總公司(1969)	Menyuan 門源縣	Qinghai 青海省	(0978)672384	489	State-owned 國有	23,359	3217(2)	45,723	a
Mang Ya Asbestos Mine Labour Service Co. 國家建材局茫崖石棉礦勞動服務公司(1982)	Golmud 格爾木市	Qinghai 青海省	(0979)51433 (0979)51213	418	Collectively-owned 集體	18,167	-274(34)	28,406	a
Dunhuang Xin Mian Industrial Co. 敦煌市鑫棉實業公司(1979)	Yumen 玉門市	Gansu 甘肅省	(0937)8825381	190	Collectively-owned 集體	16,500	1460(4)	12,714	a
Jiuquan Sealing Material Industrial Co. 酒泉密封材料實業公司(1973)	Yumen 玉門市	Gansu 甘肅省	(0937)2611205	300	Collectively-owned 集體	15,000	1790(3)	14,680	o
Changchun Blue Sky Advanced Technology Sealing Material Co. Ltd. 長春藍天高新技術密封材料有限責任公司(1992)	Changchun 長春市	Jilin 吉林省	(0431)4719924 (0431)4719924	228	Joint stock 股份制	14,616	351(15)	36,314	o

Top 10 Cities by Production Output 產出排名前 10 位城市	Province 省	Market share 市場份額	Number of firms 企業個數
Yumen 玉門市	Gansu 甘肅省	31.02%	51
Korla 庫爾勒市	Xinjiang 新疆	20.72%	6
Golmud 格爾木市	Qinghai 青海省	19.08%	2
Ya'an 雅安市	Sichuan 四川省	11.75%	6
Menyuan 門源縣	Qinghai 青海省	7.36%	8
Ma'anshan 馬鞍山市	Anhui 安徽省	2.97%	1
Hanzhong 漢中市	Shaanxi 陝西省	1.89%	3
Chaoyang 朝陽市	Liaoning 遼寧省	1.04%	6
Weihai 威海市	Shandong 山東省	1.03%	1
Rizhao 日照市	Shandong 山東省	0.93%	2

10 Major Wholesalers 10 家主要批發商	City 城市	Province 省	Telephone / Fax 電話 / 傳真
Chengdu Sheng Xing Trade Company 成都盛興商貿公司	Chengdu 成都市	Sichuan 四川省	(028)7762591
Shanghai Municipal Administration Engineering Material Company 上海市市政工程材料公司	Shanghai 上海市	Shanghai 上海市	(021)64372632
Shanghai Construction Engineering Material Co. 上海市建築工程材料公司	Shanghai 上海市	Shanghai 上海市	(021)63298630
Yixing Jin San Jiao Zhao Bazaar 宜興市金三角招商城	Wuxi 無錫市	Jiangsu 江蘇省	(0510)7935138 (0510)7935138
Fujian Hua Fu Import & Export Company 福建省華福進出口公司	Fuzhou 福州市	Fujian 福建省	(0591)7810477 (0591)7810485
China Building Goods & Materials Company 中國建築物資公司	Beijing 北京市	Beijing 北京市	(010)68586253
Dalian Jinzhou Xin Gang Industry & Trade Company 大連金州新港工貿公司	Dalian 大連市	Liaoning 遼寧省	(0411)7624747
Shanghai Zhan Dong Industrial Co. Ltd. 上海展東實業有限公司	Shanghai 上海市	Shanghai 上海市	(021)58201778 (021)58200874
China Building Materials and Equipment Import & Export Company 中國建築材料及設備進出口公司	Beijing 北京市	Beijing 北京市	(010)68393420
Dandong Chemical Light Industry Material Company Chemical Construction Material Marketing Station 丹東市化工輕工材料公司化工建材經銷站	Dandong 丹東市	Liaoning 遼寧省	(0415)2146396

*Also include sales by firms outside this industry.包括本行業以外廠家的銷售。"o" stands for "others". "o" 代表 "其他產品"。

1092: Mica Mining and Dressing 雲母採選業

The industry accounts for 0.001% of the total revenue of China's industrial sector in 1996. The revenue growth rate of the industry is 38.7% from 1995, as compared to the growth rate of China's industrial sector, 9.51%. The rate of return on asset is -28.29%. 78.95% of all firms in the industry made a profit while 21.05% had negative returns. The top province in terms of the industry's revenue is Xinjiang, accounting for 42.41% of the total revenue.
本行業在1996年佔全行業總產值0.001%，行業年增長率為38.7%（全國工業年增長率9.51%）。行業的資產回報率-28.29%，78.95%的企業盈利，21.05%的企業虧損。銷售收入最高的省份為新疆，佔本行業的42.41%。

	Total number of firms 企業總數	Total number of employees 職工總數	Total revenue (mil. RMB) 總銷售收入（百萬元）	Total profit (mil. RMB) 總利潤（百萬元）	Return on assets 資產利潤率 (%)	Return on equity 權益利潤率 (%)	Labour productivity ('000 RMB / worker) 勞動生產率（千元／人）	Debts / assets 資產負債率 (%)	Total assets (mil. RMB) 總資產（百萬元）
Industry Overall 行業總體	19	1,956	39	-10	-28.29	650.00	19.94	104.33	37

	Number of firms 企業個數	Average number of employees 平均職工人數	Average revenue ('000 RMB) 平均銷售收入（千元）	Average profit ('000 RMB) 平均利潤（千元）	Return on assets 資產利潤率 (%)	Return on equity 權益利潤率 (%)	Labour productivity ('000 RMB / worker) 勞動生產率（千元／人）	Average debts / assets 平均資產負債率(%)	Average Total assets ('000 RMB) 平均總資產（千元）
By ownership 產業所有權									
State-owned 國有	6	201	500	-2,000	-70.59	171.43	2.48	141.18	2,833
Collectively-owned 集體	13	58	2,769	154	10.00	40.01	48.12	75.00	1,538
Privately-owned 私有									
Domestic JVs 聯營									
Joint stock 股份制									
Foreign-funded 外資									
Overseas Chinese-funded 港澳台資									
By size 規模									
Large 大型									
Medium 中型									
Small 小型	19	103	2,052	-526	-27.03	500.05	19.93	105.41	1,947
By regional distribution 地區分布									
Central-North 華北	4	67	1,320	75	5.61	17.96	19.85	68.79	1,338
Beijing 北京									
Tianjin 天津									
Hebei 河北	3	57	1,647	110	7.27	19.53	29.06	62.78	1,513
Shanxi 山西									
Inner Mongolia 內蒙	1	96	340	-30	-3.70	150.00	3.54	102.47	810
Northeast 東北									
Liaoning 遼寧									
Jilin 吉林									
Heilongjiang 黑龍江									
Central East 華東	2	48	6,595	205	14.29	48.81	138.84	70.73	1,435
Shanghai 上海									
Jiangsu 江蘇									
Zhejiang 浙江									
Anhui 安徽	2	48	6,595	205	14.29	48.81	138.84	70.73	1,435
Fujian 福建									
Jiangxi 江西									
Shandong 山東									
Central-South 中南	1	8	1,140	30	11.54	25.00	142.50	53.85	260
Henan 河南									
Hubei 湖北									
Hunan 湖南									
Guangdong 廣東	1	8	1,140	30	11.54	25.00	142.50	53.85	260
Guangxi 廣西									
Hainan 海南									
Southwest 西南	2	20	355				17.75	75.63	800
Chongqing 重慶									
Sichuan 四川	2	20	355				17.75		800
Guizhou 貴州									
Yunnan 雲南									
Tibet 西藏									
Northwest 西北	10	155	1,853	-1,113	-41.70	240.91	11.98	117.31	2,669
Shaanxi 陝西	2	45	995	-50	-2.64	-31.25	22.11	91.56	1,895
Gansu 甘肅	1								
Qinghai 青海									
Ningxia 寧夏									
Xinjiang 新疆	7	208	2,363	-1,576	-48.17	223.28	11.35	121.57	3,271

1092: Mica Mining and Dressing 雲母採選業

Year 年份	Number of firms 企業個數	Rate of change 每年變化(%)	Number of employees 職工人數(人)	Rate of change 每年變化(%)	Total revenue (mil. RMB) 總銷售收入(百萬元)	Rate of change 每年變化(%)	Total profit (mil. RMB) 總利潤(百萬元)	Rate of change 每年變化(%)
1993	17		829		12		0	
1994	29	70.59%	2,524	204.46%	28	140.22%	-7	-6783.81%
1995	22	-24.14%	1,904	-24.57%	28	1.37%	-9	-22.77%
1996	19	-13.64%	1,956	2.73%	39	38.73%	-10	-16.06%

3 Major products* 3種主要產品*	Output 產量	Sales volume 銷售量	Unit 單位
a) Industrial Raw Material Mica 工業原料雲母	135,336	129,923	ton 噸

Top 10 firms by revenue (year founded) 收入排名前10家企業(創辦年份)	City 城市	Province 省	Telephone / fax 電話 / 傳真	Number of employees 職工人數	Ownership 產業所有權	Revenue ('000 RMB) 銷售收入(千元)	Profit ('000 RMB) (rank) 利潤(千元)(排名)	Total assets ('000 RMB) 總資產(千元)	Major products 主要產品
Chuzhou Nanqiao Spun Mica Development Co. 滁州市南譙絹雲母開發公司(1993)	Chuzhou 滁州市	Anhui 安徽省	(0550)3095262	45	Collectively-owned 集體	11,800	250(3)	1,820	a
Fuyun Tu Er Hong Xiang Resource Development Company 富蘊縣吐爾洪鄉資源開發公司(1975)	Altay 阿勒泰市	Xinjiang 新疆		121	Collectively-owned 集體	5,965	779(1)	2,746	a
Fuyun Ku Er Te Xiang Natural Mineral Products Development Company 富蘊縣庫爾特鄉自然礦產開發公司(1994)	Altay 阿勒泰市	Xinjiang 新疆		120	Collectively-owned 集體	5,230	456(2)	3,587	a
Hebei Luanping Deng Chang Xiang Mining Company Mica Mine 河北省灤平縣鄧廠鄉礦業公司雲母礦(1894)	Chengde 承德市	Hebei 河北省	(0314)8818152	70	Collectively-owned 集體	2,618	91(5)	2,610	o
Tie Mai Ke Xiang Farm, Industry & Commerce Joint Enterprise General Co. 鐵買克鄉牧工商聯合公司(1965)	Altay 阿勒泰市	Xinjiang 新疆		40	Collectively-owned 集體	2,290	60(6)	561	a
Shahe Bai Cuo Porcelain Clay Mine 沙河市白錯瓷土礦(1989)	Xingtai 邢臺市	Hebei 河北省		20	Private-owned 私營	2,200	223(4)	590	o

Top 10 Cities by Production Output 產出排名前10位城市	Province 省	Market share 市場份額	Number of firms 企業個數
Altay 阿勒泰市	Xinjiang 新疆	62.74%	7
Chengde 承德市	Hebei 河北省	10.88%	1
Quanzhou 泉州市	Fujian 福建省	5.87%	2
Maoming 茂名市	Guangdong 廣東省	5.59%	1
Tianshui 天水市	Gansu 甘肅省	3.87%	1
Hanzhong 漢中市	Shaanxi 陝西省	3.10%	2
Weifang 濰坊市	Shandong 山東省	2.83%	1
Ankang 安康市	Shaanxi 陝西省	2.18%	1
Jining 集寧市	Inner Mong 內蒙	1.50%	1
Xiamen 廈門市	Fujian 福建省	0.70%	1

10 Major Wholesalers 10家主要批發商	City 城市	Province 省	Telephone / Fax 電話 / 傳真
Chengdu Sheng Xing Trade Company 成都盛興商貿公司	Chengdu 成都市	Sichuan 四川省	(028)7762591
Shanghai Municipal Administration Engineering Material Company 上海市市政工程材料公司	Shanghai 上海市	Shanghai 上海市	(021)64372632
Shanghai Construction Engineering Material Co. 上海市建築工程材料公司	Shanghai 上海市	Shanghai 上海市	(021)63298630
Yixing Jin San Jiao Zhao Bazaar 宜興市金三角招商城	Wuxi 無錫市	Jiangsu 江蘇省	(0510)7935138 (0510)7935138
Fujian Hua Fu Import & Export Company 福建省華福進出口公司	Fuzhou 福州市	Fujian 福建省	(0591)7810477 (0591)7810485
China Building Goods & Materials Company 中國建築物資公司	Beijing 北京市	Beijing 北京市	(010)68586253
Dalian Jinzhou Xin Gang Industry & Trade Company 大連金州新港工貿公司	Dalian 大連市	Liaoning 遼寧省	(0411)7624747
Shanghai Zhan Dong Industrial Co. Ltd. 上海展東實業有限公司	Shanghai 上海市	Shanghai 上海市	(021)58201778 (021)58200874
China Building Materials and Equipment Import & Export Company 中國建築材料及設備進出口公司	Beijing 北京市	Beijing 北京市	(010)68393420
Dandong Chemical Light Industry Material Company Chemical Construction Material Marketing Station 丹東市化工輕工材料公司化工建材經銷站	Dandong 丹東市	Liaoning 遼寧省	(0415)2146396

*Also include sales by firms outside this industry.包括本行業以外廠家的銷售。"o" stands for "others". "o" 代表"其他產品"。

1093: Graphite Mining and Dressing 石墨採選業

The industry accounts for 0.012% of the total revenue of China's industrial sector in 1996. The revenue growth rate of the industry is -16.4% from 1995, as compared to the growth rate of China's industrial sector, 9.51%. The rate of return on asset is -0.40%. 72.01% of all firms in the industry made a profit while 14.95% had negative returns. The top province in terms of the industry's revenue is Shandong, accounting for 52.45% of the total revenue.
本行業在1996年佔全行業總產值0.012%，行業年增長率為-16.4%（全國工業年增長率9.51%）。行業的資產回報率-0.40%，72.01%的企業盈利，14.95%的企業虧損。銷售收入最高的省份為山東省，佔本行業的52.45%。

	Total number of firms 企業總數	Total number of employees 職工總數	Total revenue (mil. RMB) 總銷售收入（百萬元）	Total profit (mil. RMB) 總利潤（百萬元）	Return on assets 資產利潤率 (%)	Return on equity 權益利潤率 (%)	Labour productivity ('000 RMB / worker) 勞動生產率（千元/人）	Debts / assets 資產負債率 (%)	Total assets (mil. RMB) 總資產（百萬元）
Industry Overall 行業總體	128	22,510	699	-6	-0.40	-1.35	31.05	70.05	1,475

	Number of firms 企業個數	Average number of employees 平均職工人數	Average revenue ('000 RMB) 平均銷售收入（千元）	Average profit ('000 RMB) 平均利潤（千元）	Return on assets 資產利潤率 (%)	Return on equity 權益利潤率 (%)	Labour productivity ('000 RMB / worker) 勞動生產率（千元/人）	Average debts / assets 平均資產負債率(%)	Average Total assets ('000 RMB) 平均總資產（千元）
By ownership 產業所有權									
State-owned 國有	24	518	8,917	-1,000	-2.87	-10.26	17.22	71.98	34,792
Collectively-owned 集體	94	99	4,944	189	3.12	9.51	49.91	67.18	6,043
Privately-owned 私有	1	9							
Domestic JVs 聯營	1	201	443				2.20		1,265
Joint stock 股份制									
Foreign-funded 外資	4	84	1,447	6	0.07	0.21	17.22	68.07	8,167
Overseas Chinese-funded 港澳台資	3	72	4,635	82	0.63	2.43	64.08	73.86	12,877
By size 規模									
Large 大型	5	1,783	57,366	-779	-0.56	-1.61	32.17	65.42	140,345
Medium 中型	13	403	7,472	506	1.80	7.49	18.54	75.91	28,046
Small 小型	108	77	2,917	-80	-2.12	-7.78	37.82	72.72	3,787
By regional distribution 地區分布									
Central-North 華北	26	124	1,958	75	1.11	3.77	15.78	70.45	6,773
Beijing 北京	2								
Tianjin 天津									
Hebei 河北	9	57	972	19	0.73	-15.18	16.96	104.79	2,600
Shanxi 山西	1	128	1,740	220	5.93	23.40	13.59	74.39	3,710
Inner Mongolia 內蒙	14	184	2,886	112	1.05	3.01	15.65	64.96	10,642
Northeast 東北	24	358	5,468	-418	-1.90	-7.86	15.29	75.78	21,984
Liaoning 遼寧	2	89	3,460	165	2.72	80.49	38.88	96.62	6,070
Jilin 吉林	3	393	4,390	-453	-2.27	-7.09	11.17	68.04	20,013
Heilongjiang 黑龍江	19	380	5,849	-474	-1.98	-8.33	15.39	76.24	23,971
Central East 華東	42	186	9,280	88	0.60	1.97	49.88	69.46	14,644
Shanghai 上海									
Jiangsu 江蘇	1	33	3,720	-70	-4.70	-233.33	112.73	98.66	1,490
Zhejiang 浙江									
Anhui 安徽	3	61	2,233	387	14.74	64.09	36.41	77.00	2,623
Fujian 福建	3	46	4,207	210	21.58	29.30	91.45	26.37	973
Jiangxi 江西	1	3	40	-70	-9.46	-175.00	13.33	94.59	740
Shandong 山東	34	219	10,784	61	0.34	1.12	49.18	69.47	17,707
Central-South 中南	28	83	4,272	-60	-1.35	-2.94	51.78	53.96	4,413
Henan 河南	8	73	1,903	20	0.61	2.28	26.20	73.21	3,280
Hubei 湖北	1	28	1,000	-30	-1.88	-60.00	35.71	96.88	1,600
Hunan 湖南	18	95	5,744	-100	-1.88	-3.61	60.79	47.97	5,318
Guangdong 廣東									
Guangxi 廣西									
Hainan 海南	1								
Southwest 西南	5	86	808	-12	-0.22	-0.41	9.44	45.24	5,394
Chongqing 重慶									
Sichuan 四川	5	86	808	-12	-0.22	-0.41	9.40	45.24	5,394
Guizhou 貴州									
Yunnan 雲南									
Tibet 西藏									
Northwest 西北	3	51	1,300	40	2.15	4.92	25.66	56.19	1,857
Shaanxi 陝西	3	51	1,300	40	2.15	4.92	25.66	56.19	1,857
Gansu 甘肅									
Qinghai 青海									
Ningxia 寧夏									
Xinjiang 新疆									

1093: Graphite Mining and Dressing 石墨採選業

Year 年份	Number of firms 企業個數	Rate of change 每年變化 (%)	Number of employees 職工人數 (人)	Rate of change 每年變化 (%)	Total revenue (mil. RMB) 總銷售收入 (百萬元)	Rate of change 每年變化 (%)	Total profit (mil. RMB) 總利潤 (百萬元)	Rate of change 每年變化 (%)
1993	95		11,114		425		9	
1994	99	4.21%	20,059	80.48%	433	1.83%	-5	-157.25%
1995	136	37.37%	26,897	34.09%	836	93.18%	7	229.38%
1996	128	-5.88%	22,510	-16.31%	699	-16.43%	-6	-186.52%

3 Major products* 3 種主要產品 *	Output 產量	Sales volume 銷售量	Unit 單位
a) Graphite 石墨	1,562,652	1,515,772	ton 噸

Top 10 firms by revenue (year founded) 收入排名前 10 家企業 (創辦年份)	City 城市	Province 省	Telephone / fax 電話 / 傳真	Number of employees 職工人數	Ownership 產業所有權	Revenue ('000 RMB) 銷售收入 (千元)	Profit ('000 RMB) (rank) 利潤 (千元) (排名)	Total assets ('000 RMB) 總資產 (千元)	Major products 主要產品
Qingdao Graphite Co. Ltd. 青島石墨股份有限公司(1948)	Qingdao 青島市	Shandong 山東省	(0532)3431085 (0532)3431082	2,443	Joint stock 股份制	80,605	0(31)	165,980	a
Shandong Bei Shu Sheng Jian Graphite Mine 山東北墅生建石墨礦(1954)	Qingdao 青島市	Shandong 山東省	(0532)3431039 (0532)3431107	1,115	State-owned 國有	70,598	-4750(45)	174,835	a
Heilong Jiang Jixi Liu Mao Graphite Mine 黑龍江省雞西市柳毛鄉石墨礦(1936)	Jixi 雞西市	Heilongjiang 黑龍江省	(0453)2352864 (0453)2352876	3,448	State-owned 國有	62,570	-16230(46)	205,960	a
Shandong Tianxiang Co. 山東天象集團公司(1996)	Qingdao 青島市	Shandong 山東省	(0532)7388078 (0532)7388127	1,157	Collectively-owned 集體	54,400	310(10)	136,526	o
Qingdao Pingdu Jin Lin Graphite Industrial Company 青島市平度金鱗石墨工業公司(1996)	Qingdao 青島市	Shandong 山東省	(0532)6371336 (0532)6371336	450	Collectively-owned 集體	38,500	1600(2)	26,467	o
Chenzhou Bei Hu Qu Changsha Ling Graphite Mine 郴州市北湖區長沙嶺石墨礦(1990)	Chenzhou 郴州市	Hunan 湖南省	(0735)2672562	120	Collectively-owned 集體	20,750	5(28)	4,252	a
Qingdao Yan Xin Industry General Co. 青島閻鑫實業總公司(1992)	Qingdao 青島市	Shandong 山東省	(0532)6339008 (0532)6331097	200	Collectively-owned 集體	19,180	1220(3)	20,949	o
Hunan Lu Tang Graphite Mine 湖南魯塘石墨礦(1950)	Chenzhou 郴州市	Hunan 湖南省	(0735)2672835	961	State-owned 國有	18,216	-3170(44)	40,155	a
Zhaoyuan Industrial Co. Ltd. 五礦招遠實業有限公司(1989)	Yantai 煙台市	Shandong 山東省	(0535)8443027 (0535)8443027	190	Collectively-owned 集體	17,300	900(5)	5,520	a
Jixi Non-metal Mine Industrial Co. 雞西非金屬礦工業公司(1975)	Jixi 雞西市	Heilongjiang 黑龍江省	(0453)2352865 (0453)2483131	2,360	State-owned 國有	11,712	6568(1)	177,880	a

Top 10 Cities by Production Output 產出排名前 10 位城市	Province 省	Market share 市場份額	Number of firms 企業個數
Qingdao 青島市	Shandong 山東省	50.42%	40
Jixi 雞西市	Heilongjiang 黑龍江省	21.16%	12
Chenzhou 郴州市	Hunan 湖南省	12.49%	16
Jining 集寧市	Inner Mong 內蒙	3.72%	10
Yantai 煙台市	Shandong 山東省	2.18%	3
Jilin 吉林市	Jilin 吉林省	1.85%	2
Yichang 宜昌市	Hubei 湖北省	0.97%	1
Nanyang 南陽市	Henan 河南省	0.85%	5
Hegang 鶴崗市	Heilongjiang 黑龍江省	0.83%	5
Panzhihua 攀枝花市	Sichuan 四川省	0.74%	2

10 Major Wholesalers 10 家主要批發商	City 城市	Province 省	Telephone / Fax 電話 / 傳真
Chengdu Sheng Xing Trade Company 成都盛興商貿公司	Chengdu 成都市	Sichuan 四川省	(028)7762591
Shanghai Municipal Administration Engineering Material Company 上海市市政工程材料公司	Shanghai 上海市	Shanghai 上海市	(021)64372632
Shanghai Construction Engineering Material Co. 上海市建築工程材料公司	Shanghai 上海市	Shanghai 上海市	(021)63298630
Yixing Jin San Jiao Zhao Bazaar 宜興市金三角招商城	Wuxi 無錫市	Jiangsu 江蘇省	(0510)7935138 (0510)7935138
Fujian Hua Fu Import & Export Company 福建省華福進出口公司	Fuzhou 福州市	Fujian 福建省	(0591)7810477 (0591)7810485
China Building Goods & Materials Company 中國建築物資公司	Beijing 北京市	Beijing 北京市	(010)68586253
Dalian Jinzhou Xin Gang Industry & Trade Company 大連金州新港工貿公司	Dalian 大連市	Liaoning 遼寧省	(0411)7624747
Shanghai Zhan Dong Industrial Co. Ltd. 上海展東實業有限公司	Shanghai 上海市	Shanghai 上海市	(021)58201778 (021)58200874
China Building Materials and Equipment Import & Export Company 中國建築材料及設備進出口公司	Beijing 北京市	Beijing 北京市	(010)68393420
Dandong Chemical Light Industry Material Company Chemical Construction Material Marketing Station 丹東市化工輕工材料公司化工建材經銷站	Dandong 丹東市	Liaoning 遼寧省	(0415)2146396

*Also include sales by firms outside this industry.包括本行業以外廠家的銷售。"o" stands for "others". "o" 代表 "其他產品"。

1094: Gypsum Mining and Dressing 石膏採選業

The industry accounts for 0.024% of the total revenue of China's industrial sector in 1996. The revenue growth rate of the industry is 13.4% from 1995, as compared to the growth rate of China's industrial sector, 9.51%. The rate of return on asset is 4.51%. 81.78% of all firms in the industry made a profit while 14.58% had negative returns. The top province in terms of the industry's revenue is Shandong, accounting for 33.56% of the total revenue.
本行業在1996年佔全行業總產值0.024%，行業年增長率為13.4%（全國工業年增長率9.51%）。行業的資產回報率4.51%，81.78%的企業盈利，14.58%的企業虧損。銷售收入最高的省份為山東省，佔本行業的33.56%。

	Total number of firms 企業總數	Total number of employees 職工總數	Total revenue (mil. RMB) 總銷售收入（百萬元）	Total profit (mil. RMB) 總利潤（百萬元）	Return on assets 資產利潤率 (%)	Return on equity 權益利潤率 (%)	Labour productivity ('000 RMB / worker) 勞動生產率（千元/人）	Debts / assets 資產負債率 (%)	Total assets (mil. RMB) 總資產（百萬元）
Industry Overall 行業總體	299	51,783	1,420	100	4.51	9.28	27.42	51.39	2,216

	Number of firms 企業個數	Average number of employees 平均職工人數	Average revenue ('000 RMB) 平均銷售收入（千元）	Average profit ('000 RMB) 平均利潤（千元）	Return on assets 資產利潤率 (%)	Return on equity 權益利潤率 (%)	Labour productivity ('000 RMB / worker) 勞動生產率（千元/人）	Average debts / assets 平均資產負債率(%)	Average Total assets ('000 RMB) 平均總資產（千元）
By ownership 產業所有權									
State-owned 國有	39	490	9,487	231	0.73	1.43	19.37	48.86	31,538
Collectively-owned 集體	249	117	3,199	334	10.15	24.91	27.36	59.27	3,296
Privately-owned 私有									
Domestic JVs 聯營	3	238	16,848	963	4.66	5.53	70.79	15.63	20,664
Joint stock 股份制	5	457	9,965	356	2.76	4.55	21.82	39.30	12,881
Foreign-funded 外資	2	152	9,408	579	6.19	7.44	62.10	16.81	9,348
Overseas Chinese-funded 港澳台資	2	289	67,403	951	9.22	27.11	233.23	65.99	10,311
By size 規模									
Large 大型	4	1,445	21,900	-315	-0.36	-0.82	15.15	56.17	87,922
Medium 中型	18	733	21,452	2,594	5.56	9.47	29.25	41.32	46,691
Small 小型	270	118	3,507	202	5.33	12.69	29.76	58.03	3,794
By regional distribution 地區分布									
Central-North 華北	53	65	2,053	105	3.25	8.04	31.50	59.51	3,241
Beijing 北京									
Tianjin 天津									
Hebei 河北	8	72	6,520	353	17.27	37.06	90.24	53.40	2,041
Shanxi 山西	34	77	1,454	52	1.23	3.11	19.00	60.44	4,208
Inner Mongolia 內蒙	11	25	654	92	8.18	18.91	26.24	56.76	1,123
Northeast 東北	6	63	1,870	60	1.18	4.17	29.84	71.81	5,102
Liaoning 遼寧									
Jilin 吉林	6	63	1,870	60	1.18	4.17	29.84	71.81	5,102
Heilongjiang 黑龍江									
Central East 華東	49	460	12,403	1,147	6.03	11.59	26.98	47.95	19,018
Shanghai 上海									
Jiangsu 江蘇	9	523	11,893	306	1.17	1.78	22.72	34.52	26,156
Zhejiang 浙江									
Anhui 安徽	4	832	5,653	-275	-2.13	-3.66	6.79	41.93	12,925
Fujian 福建									
Jiangxi 江西	2	27	755	10	1.22	1.69	27.96	28.05	820
Shandong 山東	34	425	14,017	1,604	8.48	18.20	33.02	53.40	18,916
Central-South 中南	76	247	7,541	506	4.33	8.66	30.59	49.94	11,679
Henan 河南	3	57	1,817	90	3.08	12.44	31.69	75.37	2,923
Hubei 湖北	19	398	9,243	94	0.63	1.69	23.25	62.57	14,767
Hunan 湖南	42	147	2,533	1	0.02	0.07	17.20	73.09	3,566
Guangdong 廣東	9	393	18,071	3,092	6.43	9.57	45.98	32.85	48,109
Guangxi 廣西	3	430	41,017	2,853	55.01	139.41	95.39	60.54	5,187
Hainan 海南									
Southwest 西南	38	91	1,490	53	2.86	7.47	16.34	61.70	1,841
Chongqing 重慶	10	64	1,440	137	8.56	16.46	22.18	48.01	1,603
Sichuan 四川	20	114	1,791	-21	-0.87	-2.65	15.64	67.24	2,377
Guizhou 貴州									
Yunnan 雲南	7	59	727	121	14.55	36.02	12.41	59.59	834
Tibet 西藏	1	120	1,320	190	36.54	36.54	11.00		520
Northwest 西北	77	42	816	-34	-2.08	-6.03	19.49	65.49	1,611
Shaanxi 陝西	18	27	832	42	7.04	15.80	31.38	55.42	599
Gansu 甘肅	36	46	967	21	1.52	4.11	20.99	63.10	1,409
Qinghai 青海	8	32	244	-315	-29.68	136.22	7.68	121.67	1,061
Ningxia 寧夏	10	67	796	-101	-2.62	-8.14	11.85	67.87	3,862
Xinjiang 新疆	5	32	624	-116	-3.77	-6.67	19.38	43.51	3,080

1094: Gypsum Mining and Dressing 石膏採選業

Year 年份	Number of firms 企業個數	Rate of change 每年變化 (%)	Number of employees 職工人數 (人)	Rate of change 每年變化 (%)	Total revenue (mil. RMB) 總銷售收入 (百萬元)	Rate of change 每年變化 (%)	Total profit (mil. RMB) 總利潤 (百萬元)	Rate of change 每年變化 (%)
1993	249		34,913		898		166	
1994	273	9.64%	44,454	27.33%	973	8.41%	119	-28.55%
1995	321	17.58%	51,131	15.02%	1,252	28.73%	111	-6.76%
1996	299	-6.85%	51,783	1.28%	1,420	13.42%	100	-9.73%

3 Major products* 3 種主要產品 *	Output 產量	Sales volume 銷售量	Unit 單位
a) Gypsum 石膏	25,914,171	25,395,888	ton 噸
b) Gypsum Board 石膏板	6,844,081	6,228,114	square metre 平方米

Top 10 firms by revenue (year founded) 收入排名前 10 家企業 (創辦年份)	City 城市	Province 省	Telephone / fax 電話 / 傳真	Number of employees 職工人數	Ownership 產業所有權	Revenue ('000 RMB) 銷售收入 (千元)	Profit ('000 RMB) (rank) 利潤 (千元) (排名)	Total assets ('000 RMB) 總資產 (千元)	Major products 主要產品
Pingyi Gypsum Mine 平邑縣石膏礦(1978)	Linyi 臨沂市	Shandong 山東省	(0539)4331150 (0539)4331150	1,650	State-owned 國有	61,131	14(82)	132,751	a,b
Lai Bin Chengxiang Xiang Putian Gypsum Mine 來賓縣城廂鄉莆田石膏礦(1991)	Heshan 合山市	Guangxi 廣西	(0772)4212788	498	Collectively-owned 集體	46,120	3170(7)	6,190	a
Guangdong Sihui Gypsum Mine 廣東省四會石膏礦(1977)	Zhaoqing 肇慶市	Guangdong 廣東省	(0757)3866268	956	State-owned 國有	45,948	11322(2)	123,351	a
Guangdong Sanshui Gypsum Mine 廣東省三水市石膏礦(1987)	Foshan 佛山市	Guangdong 廣東省	(0757)7673203 (0757)7673483	1,028	State-owned 國有	43,381	-698(105)	145,607	a
Lai Bin Pu Tian Longfeng Gypsum Mine 來賓縣蒲田龍鳳石膏礦(1994)	Heshan 合山市	Guangxi 廣西	(0772)4214968	416	Collectively-owned 集體	40,060	2754(10)	5,010	a
Guangdong Sanshui Qing Qi Gypsum Mine 廣東省三水市青岐石膏礦(1981)	Foshan 佛山市	Guangdong 廣東省	(0757)7613388	455	Collectively-owned 集體	40,012	16563(1)	65,387	a
Lai Bin Chengxiang Xiang Ji Xiang Gypsum Mine 來賓縣城廂鄉吉祥石膏礦(1995)	Heshan 合山市	Guangxi 廣西	(0772)4212962	376	Collectively-owned 集體	36,870	2633(12)	4,358	a
Nanjing Gypsum Mine 南京石膏礦(1985)	Nanjing 南京市	Jiangsu 江蘇省	(025)4435554	1,136	State-owned 國有	33,720	346(44)	101,472	a
Zaozhuang Jointly-operated Gypsum Mine 棗裝市聯營石膏礦(1980)	Zaozhuang 棗莊市	Shandong 山東省	(0632)7761030 (0632)7761030	806	Domestic JVs 聯營	30,120	6690(3)	18,190	a
Cangshan Tian Peng Jointly-operated Gypsum Mine 蒼山縣田彭聯營石膏礦(1988)	Linyi 臨沂市	Shandong 山東省	(0539)8900231 (0539)8900231	200	Collectively-owned 集體	26,910	2699(11)	14,723	a

Top 10 Cities by Production Output 產出排名前 10 位城市	Province 省	Market share 市場份額	Number of firms 企業個數
Zaozhuang 棗莊市	Shandong 山東省	25.86%	24
Linyi 臨沂市	Shandong 山東省	11.07%	12
Foshan 佛山市	Guangdong 廣東省	8.73%	3
Heshan 合山市	Guangxi 廣西	8.21%	3
Xuzhou 徐州市	Jiangsu 江蘇省	5.41%	8
Xingtai 邢臺市	Hebei 河北省	5.07%	8
Zhaoqing 肇慶市	Guangdong 廣東省	4.21%	2
Nanjing 南京市	Jiangsu 江蘇省	3.46%	1
Taiyuan 太原市	Shanxi 山西省	2.79%	10
Hengyang 衡陽市	Hunan 湖南省	2.63%	13

10 Major Wholesalers 10 家主要批發商	City 城市	Province 省	Telephone / Fax 電話 / 傳真
Chengdu Sheng Xing Trade Company 成都盛興商貿公司	Chengdu 成都市	Sichuan 四川省	(028)7762591
Shanghai Municipal Administration Engineering Material Company 上海市市政工程材料公司	Shanghai 上海市	Shanghai 上海市	(021)64372632
Shanghai Construction Engineering Material Co. 上海市建築工程材料公司	Shanghai 上海市	Shanghai 上海市	(021)63298630
Yixing Jin San Jiao Zhao Bazaar 宜興市金三角招商城	Wuxi 無錫市	Jiangsu 江蘇省	(0510)7935138 (0510)7935138
Fujian Hua Fu Import & Export Company 福建省華福進出口公司	Fuzhou 福州市	Fujian 福建省	(0591)7810477 (0591)7810485
China Building Goods & Materials Company 中國建築物資公司	Beijing 北京市	Beijing 北京市	(010)68586253
Dalian Jinzhou Xin Gang Industry & Trade Company 大連金州新港工貿公司	Dalian 大連市	Liaoning 遼寧省	(0411)7624747
Shanghai Zhan Dong Industrial Co. Ltd. 上海展東實業有限公司	Shanghai 上海市	Shanghai 上海市	(021)58201778 (021)58200874
China Building Materials and Equipment Import & Export Company 中國建築材料及設備進出口公司	Beijing 北京市	Beijing 北京市	(010)68393420
Dandong Chemical Light Industry Material Company Chemical Construction Material Marketing Station 丹東市化工輕工材料公司化工建材經銷站	Dandong 丹東市	Liaoning 遼寧省	(0415)2146396

*Also include sales by firms outside this industry.包括本行業以外廠家的銷售。"o" stands for "others". "o" 代表"其他產品"。

1095: Gem and Jade Mining and Dressing 寶石、玉石採選業

The industry accounts for 0.001% of the total revenue of China's industrial sector in 1996. The revenue growth rate of the industry is 35.0% from 1995, as compared to the growth rate of China's industrial sector, 9.51%. The rate of return on asset is 0.05%. 78.41% of all firms in the industry made a profit while 9.09% had negative returns. The top province in terms of the industry's revenue is Liaoning, accounting for 40.69% of the total revenue.
本行業在1996年佔全行業總產值0.001%，行業年增長率為35.0%（全國工業年增長率9.51%）。行業的資產回報率0.05%，78.41%的企業盈利，9.09%的企業虧損。銷售收入最高的省份為遼寧省，佔本行業的40.69%。

	Total number of firms 企業總數	Total number of employees 職工總數	Total revenue (mil. RMB) 總銷售收入（百萬元）	Total profit (mil. RMB) 總利潤（百萬元）	Return on assets 資產利潤率 (%)	Return on equity 權益利潤率 (%)	Labour productivity ('000 RMB / worker) 勞動生產率（千元/人）	Debts / assets 資產負債率 (%)	Total assets (mil. RMB) 總資產（百萬元）
Industry Overall 行業總體	35	2,648	61		0.05	0.13	23.04	64.89	87

	Number of firms 企業個數	Average number of employees 平均職工人數	Average revenue ('000 RMB) 平均銷售收入（千元）	Average profit ('000 RMB) 平均利潤（千元）	Return on assets 資產利潤率 (%)	Return on equity 權益利潤率 (%)	Labour productivity ('000 RMB / worker) 勞動生產率（千元/人）	Average debts / assets 平均資產負債率(%)	Average Total assets ('000 RMB) 平均總資產（千元）
By ownership 產業所有權									
State-owned 國有	7	103	857	-857	-18.18	-85.71	8.29	78.79	4,714
Collectively-owned 集體	28	69	1,963	214	11.12	25.01	28.56	55.55	1,927
Privately-owned 私有									
Domestic JVs 聯營									
Joint stock 股份制									
Foreign-funded 外資									
Overseas Chinese-funded 港澳台資									
By size 規模									
Large 大型									
Medium 中型									
Small 小型	34	78	1,793				23.12	64.37	2,558
By regional distribution 地區分布									
Central-North 華北	4	17	2,658	223	37.55	85.58	154.06	55.27	593
Beijing 北京	1	12	60	-10	-0.75	-1.14	5.00	33.58	1,340
Tianjin 天津									
Hebei 河北	1	1	8,950	790			8950.00		
Shanxi 山西									
Inner Mongolia 內蒙	2	28	810	55	10.68	68.75	28.93	83.50	515
Northeast 東北	7	160	3,546	530	12.67	24.95	22.22	49.23	4,184
Liaoning 遼寧	7	160	3,546	530	12.67	24.95	22.22	49.23	4,184
Jilin 吉林									
Heilongjiang 黑龍江									
Central East 華東	4	14	1,128	115	9.27	52.27	79.12	82.26	1,240
Shanghai 上海									
Jiangsu 江蘇									
Zhejiang 浙江									
Anhui 安徽	3	6	223	17	13.89	27.78	35.26	50.00	120
Fujian 福建									
Jiangxi 江西									
Shandong 山東	1	38	3,840	410	8.91	58.57	101.05	84.78	4,600
Central-South 中南	11	99	1,551	-454	-12.55	-55.69	15.68	77.46	3,615
Henan 河南	5	88	2,038	114	4.57	14.69	23.21	68.86	2,492
Hubei 湖北	1	472	3,320	-5,830	-26.17	-239.92	7.03	89.09	22,280
Hunan 湖南	1	32	430	60	100.00	100.00	13.44		60
Guangdong 廣東	2	58	1,275	80	3.54	6.72	22.17	47.35	2,260
Guangxi 廣西	2	15	285	25	11.36	23.81	19.00	52.27	220
Hainan 海南									
Southwest 西南	1	78	1,320	30	1.80	2.61	16.92	31.14	1,670
Chongqing 重慶									
Sichuan 四川									
Guizhou 貴州	1	78	1,320	30	1.80	2.61	16.92	31.14	1,670
Yunnan 雲南									
Tibet 西藏									
Northwest 西北	8	30	338	-6	-0.59	-1.45	11.30	59.17	1,056
Shaanxi 陝西									
Gansu 甘肅	1	7							
Qinghai 青海	1	115							
Ningxia 寧夏									
Xinjiang 新疆	6	20	450	-8	-0.59	-1.45	23.08	59.17	1,408

1095: Gem and Jade Mining and Dressing 寶石、玉石採選業

Year 年份	Number of firms 企業個數	Rate of change 每年變化 (%)	Number of employees 職工人數 (人)	Rate of change 每年變化 (%)	Total revenue (mil. RMB) 總銷售收入 (百萬元)	Rate of change 每年變化 (%)	Total profit (mil. RMB) 總利潤 (百萬元)	Rate of change 每年變化 (%)
1993	17		1,245		14		1	
1994	31	82.35%	1,777	42.73%	27	94.85%	3	191.74%
1995	28	-9.68%	2,119	19.25%	45	67.93%	6	142.38%
1996	35	25.00%	2,648	24.96%	61	34.96%	0	-100.00%

3 Major products* 3種主要產品 *	Output 產量	Sales volume 銷售量	Unit 單位
a) Hardstone Ore 玉石類礦	10,800	8,964	ton 噸
b) Jewellery 首飾	6,446	6,253	1,000 yuan 千元

Top 10 firms by revenue (year founded) 收入排名前10家企業 (創辦年份)	City 城市	Province 省	Telephone / fax 電話 / 傳真	Number of employees 職工人數	Ownership 產業所有權	Revenue ('000 RMB) 銷售收入 (千元)	Profit ('000 RMB) (rank) 利潤 (千元) (排名)	Total assets ('000 RMB) 總資產 (千元)	Major products 主要產品
Xiuyan Jade Mine 岫岩滿族自治縣玉石礦(1957)	Anshan 鞍山市	Liaoning 遼寧省		687	Collectively-owned 集體	12,800	2890(2)	20,230	a
Xiuyan Ha Da Bei Zhen Jade Mine 岫岩縣哈達碑鎮玉石礦(1970)	Anshan 鞍山市	Liaoning 遼寧省		170	Collectively-owned 集體	9,480	380(5)	3,030	a
Wanquan Olive Stone Mine 萬全縣橄欖石礦(1989)	Zhangjiakou 張家口市	Hebei 河北省	(0313)4812763	1	Collectively-owned 集體	8,950	790(3)		a
Qinghai Golmud Kun Lun Jade Co. 格爾木市昆侖寶玉石公司(1994)	Golmud 格爾木市	Qinghai 青海省	(0979)418298	115	State-owned 國有	6,000	3152(1)	5,930	a
Changle Wu Tu Zhen Orchid Gem Factory Company 昌樂縣五圖鎮蘭寶石公司(1992)	Weifang 濰坊市	Shandong 山東省	(0536)6751144 (0536)6751144	38	Collectively-owned 集體	3,840	410(4)	4,600	a
Yunxian Turquoise Development General Company 鄖縣綠松石開發總公司(1971)	Shiyan 十堰市	Hubei 湖北省		310	State-owned 國有	3,318	-5834(8)	22,280	b

Top 10 Cities by Production Output 產出排名前10位城市	Province 省	Market share 市場份額	Number of firms 企業個數
Anshan 鞍山市	Liaoning 遼寧省	34.58%	5
Zhangjiakou 張家口市	Hebei 河北省	17.48%	1
Shiyan 十堰市	Hubei 湖北省	13.47%	2
Nanyang 南陽市	Henan 河南省	12.88%	4
Golmud 格爾木市	Qinghai 青海省	9.40%	1
Maoming 茂名市	Guangdong 廣東省	5.10%	2
Weifang 濰坊市	Shandong 山東省	2.02%	1
Tongren 銅仁市	Guizhou 貴州省	1.85%	1
Korla 庫爾勒市	Xinjiang 新疆	1.01%	3
Beijing 北京市	Beijing 北京市	0.73%	1

10 Major Wholesalers 10家主要批發商	City 城市	Province 省	Telephone / Fax 電話 / 傳真
China Metallurgy Import & Export Liaoning Company 中國冶金進出口遼寧公司	Shenyang 瀋陽市	Liaoning 遼寧省	(024)23867070 (024)23875451
Liaoning Foreign Trade General Company 遼寧省對外貿易總公司	Dalian 大連市	Liaoning 遼寧省	(0411)3632157 (0411)3638243
Zhong Xin Trade Company 中信貿易公司	Beijing 北京市	Beijing 北京市	(010)64662170 (010)64662161
China Metallurgy Import & Export Shandong Company 中國冶金進出口山東公司	Qingdao 青島市	Shandong 山東省	(0532)2801118 (0532)2801331
Yongzhou Ferromanganese Mine Company 永州市錳鐵礦公司	Yongzhou 永州市	Hunan 湖南省	(0746)8464135
Zhengzhou Advanced Technology Industrial Development Zone Development General Company 鄭州高新技術產業開發區發展總公司	Zhengzhou 鄭州市	Henan 河南省	(0371)7981924 (0371)7981422
Guangdong Hardware Import & Export Group Company 廣東省五金進出口集團公司	Guangzhou 廣州市	Guangdong 廣東省	(020)87752204 (020)87752205
Xi Shan Shi Wu Kuang Trade Company 錫山市五礦貿易公司	Wuxi 無錫市	Jiangsu 江蘇省	(0510)7760988
Xiamen Ocean Petroleum Company 廈門海洋石油公司	Xiamen 廈門市	Fujian 福建省	(0592)2095495 (0592)2087292
Hainan Shen Hai Import & Export Co. Ltd. 海南深海進出口有限公司	Haikou 海口市	Hainan 海南省	(0898)6717646 (0898)6717639

*Also include sales by firms outside this industry.包括本行業以外廠家的銷售。"o" stands for "others". "o" 代表"其他產品"。

1096: Crystal Mining and Dressing 水晶採選業

The industry accounts for 0.000% of the total revenue of China's industrial sector in 1996. The revenue growth rate of the industry is -59.0% from 1995, as compared to the growth rate of China's industrial sector, 9.51%. The rate of return on asset is 5.41%. 72.73% of all firms in the industry made a profit while 27.27% had negative returns. The top province in terms of the industry's revenue is Jiangxi, accounting for 72.69% of the total revenue.
本行業在1996年佔全行業總產值0.000%，行業年增長率為-59.0%（全國工業年增長率9.51%）。行業的資產回報率5.41%，72.73%的企業盈利，27.27%的企業虧損。銷售收入最高的省份為江西省，佔本行業的72.69%。

	Total number of firms 企業總數	Total number of employees 職工總數	Total revenue (mil. RMB) 總銷售收入（百萬元）	Total profit (mil. RMB) 總利潤（百萬元）	Return on assets 資產利潤率 (%)	Return on equity 權益利潤率 (%)	Labour productivity ('000 RMB / worker) 勞動生產率（千元/人）	Debts / assets 資產負債率 (%)	Total assets (mil. RMB) 總資產（百萬元）
Industry Overall 行業總體	7	952	26	1	5.41	-539.13	27.31	100.96	23

	Number of firms 企業個數	Average number of employees 平均職工人數	Average revenue ('000 RMB) 平均銷售收入（千元）	Average profit ('000 RMB) 平均利潤（千元）	Return on assets 資產利潤率 (%)	Return on equity 權益利潤率 (%)	Labour productivity ('000 RMB / worker) 勞動生產率（千元/人）	Average debts / assets 平均資產負債率(%)	Average Total assets ('000 RMB) 平均總資產（千元）
By ownership 產業所有權									
State-owned 國有					-3.13	-12.22	9.19	74.36	
Collectively-owned 集體	6	153	4,333	167	4.35	3134796.24	28.41	100.00	3,833
Privately-owned 私有									
Domestic JVs 聯營									
Joint stock 股份制									
Foreign-funded 外資	1	37							
Overseas Chinese-funded 港澳台資									
By size 規模									
Large 大型									
Medium 中型									
Small 小型	7	136	3,714	143	4.35	11.07	27.31	100.00	3,286
By regional distribution 地區分布									
Central-North 華北	1	769	770	20	1.04		1.00	100.00	1,930
Beijing 北京									
Tianjin 天津									
Hebei 河北	1	769	770	20	1.04		1.00	100.00	1,930
Shanxi 山西									
Inner Mongolia 內蒙									
Northeast 東北	1	49	4,670	460	306.67	1533.33	95.31	80.00	150
Liaoning 遼寧									
Jilin 吉林									
Heilongjiang 黑龍江	1	49	4,670	460	306.67	1533.33	95.31	80.00	150
Central East 華東	2	40	9,450	285	3.17	-67.06	239.24	104.72	8,995
Shanghai 上海									
Jiangsu 江蘇									
Zhejiang 浙江									
Anhui 安徽									
Fujian 福建									
Jiangxi 江西	2	40	9,450	285	3.17	-67.06	239.24	104.72	8,995
Shandong 山東									
Central-South 中南	1	50	1,220	-170	-21.25	106.25	24.40	118.75	800
Henan 河南									
Hubei 湖北	1	50	1,220	-170	-21.25	106.25	24.40	118.75	800
Hunan 湖南									
Guangdong 廣東									
Guangxi 廣西									
Hainan 海南									
Southwest 西南	2	3	390	180	17.73	48.00	156.00	63.05	1,015
Chongqing 重慶									
Sichuan 四川									
Guizhou 貴州	1	5	30	-10	-0.79	50.00	6.00	101.59	1,260
Yunnan 雲南									
Tibet 西藏	1		750	370	48.05	48.05			770
Northwest 西北									
Shaanxi 陝西									
Gansu 甘肅									
Qinghai 青海									
Ningxia 寧夏									
Xinjiang 新疆									

1096: Crystal Mining and Dressing 水晶採選業

Year 年份	Number of firms 企業個數	Rate of change 每年變化 (%)	Number of employees 職工人數 (人)	Rate of change 每年變化 (%)	Total revenue (mil. RMB) 總銷售收入 (百萬元)	Rate of change 每年變化 (%)	Total profit (mil. RMB) 總利潤 (百萬元)	Rate of change 每年變化 (%)
1993	16		744		11		0	
1994	11	-31.25%	683	-8.20%	7	-34.17%	-1	-395.88%
1995	13	18.18%	984	44.07%	63	763.21%	2	510.14%
1996	7	-46.15%	952	-3.25%	26	-59.05%	1	-51.53%

3 Major products* 3種主要產品 *	Output 產量	Sales volume 銷售量	Unit 單位

Top 10 firms by revenue (year founded) 收入排名前10家企業 (創辦年份)	City 城市	Province 省	Telephone / fax 電話 / 傳真	Number of employees 職工人數	Ownership 產業所有權	Revenue ('000 RMB) 銷售收入 (千元)	Profit ('000 RMB) (rank) 利潤 (千元) (排名)	Total assets ('000 RMB) 總資產 (千元)	Major products 主要產品
Jiangxi Shangrao Quartz Crystal General Factory 江西省上饒石英晶體總廠(1987)	Shangrao 上饒市	Jiangxi 江西省	(0793)8442993 (0793)8442557	34	Collectively-owned 集體	16,500	450(1)	15,900	o
Yongxiu Industry & Trade Co. 永修縣工貿公司(1994)	Jiujiang 九江市	Jiangxi 江西省	(0792)3220946	21	Collectively-owned 集體	2,400	120(2)	2,090	o

Top 10 Cities by Production Output 產出排名前10位城市	Province 省	Market share 市場份額	Number of firms 企業個數
Shangrao 上饒市	Jiangxi 江西省	34.28%	1
Jiujiang 九江市	Jiangxi 江西省	32.89%	1
Shijiazhuang 石家莊市	Hebei 河北省	10.57%	1
Nedong 乃東縣	Tibet 西藏	6.99%	1
Xichang 西昌市	Sichuan 四川省	4.11%	1
Zunyi 遵義市	Guizhou 貴州省	4.11%	1
Weifang 濰坊市	Shandong 山東省	3.43%	1
Tianshui 天水市	Gansu 甘肅省	2.06%	1
Pingxiang 憑祥市	Guangxi 廣西	1.03%	1
Linyi 臨沂市	Shandong 山東省	0.55%	1

10 Major Wholesalers 10家主要批發商	City 城市	Province 省	Telephone / Fax 電話 / 傳真
China Metallurgy Import & Export Liaoning Company 中國冶金進出口遼寧公司	Shenyang 瀋陽市	Liaoning 遼寧省	(024)23867070 (024)23875451
Liaoning Foreign Trade General Company 遼寧省對外貿易總公司	Dalian 大連市	Liaoning 遼寧省	(0411)3632157 (0411)3638243
Zhong Xin Trade Company 中信貿易公司	Beijing 北京市	Beijing 北京市	(010)64662170 (010)64662161
China Metallurgy Import & Export Shandong Company 中國冶金進出口山東公司	Qingdao 青島市	Shandong 山東省	(0532)2801118 (0532)2801331
Yongzhou Ferromanganese Mine Company 永州市錳鐵礦公司	Yongzhou 永州市	Hunan 湖南省	(0746)8464135
Zhengzhou Advanced Technology Industrial Development Zone Development General Company 鄭州高新技術產業開發區發展總公司	Zhengzhou 鄭州市	Henan 河南省	(0371)7981924 (0371)7981422
Guangdong Hardware Import & Export Group Company 廣東省五金進出口集團公司	Guangzhou 廣州市	Guangdong 廣東省	(020)87752204 (020)87752205
Xi Shan Shi Wu Kuang Trade Company 錫山市五礦貿易公司	Wuxi 無錫市	Jiangsu 江蘇省	(0510)7760988
Xiamen Ocean Petroleum Company 廈門海洋石油公司	Xiamen 廈門市	Fujian 福建省	(0592)2095495 (0592)2087292
Hainan Shen Hai Import & Export Co. Ltd. 海南深海進出口有限公司	Haikou 海口市	Hainan 海南省	(0898)6717646 (0898)6717639

*Also include sales by firms outside this industry.包括本行業以外廠家的銷售。"o" stands for "others". "o" 代表 "其他產品"。

1097: Talcum Mining and Dressing 滑石採選業

The industry accounts for 0.014% of the total revenue of China's industrial sector in 1996. The revenue growth rate of the industry is 30.5% from 1995, as compared to the growth rate of China's industrial sector, 9.51%. The rate of return on asset is 3.51%. 85.74% of all firms in the industry made a profit while 8.70% had negative returns. The top province in terms of the industry's revenue is Liaoning, accounting for 39.66% of the total revenue.
本行業在 1996 年佔全行業總產值 0.014%，行業年增長率為 30.5%（全國工業年增長率 9.51%）。行業的資產回報率 3.51%，85.74% 的企業盈利，8.70% 的企業虧損。銷售收入最高的省份為遼寧省，佔本行業的 39.66%。

	Total number of firms 企業總數	Total number of employees 職工總數	Total revenue (mil. RMB) 總銷售收入（百萬元）	Total profit (mil. RMB) 總利潤（百萬元）	Return on assets 資產利潤率 (%)	Return on equity 權益利潤率 (%)	Labour productivity ('000 RMB / worker) 勞動生產率（千元／人）	Debts / assets 資產負債率 (%)	Total assets (mil. RMB) 總資產（百萬元）
Industry Overall 行業總體	135	14,330	823	39	3.51	8.19	57.43	57.14	1,115

	Number of firms 企業個數	Average number of employees 平均職工人數	Average revenue ('000 RMB) 平均銷售收入（千元）	Average profit ('000 RMB) 平均利潤（千元）	Return on assets 資產利潤率 (%)	Return on equity 權益利潤率 (%)	Labour productivity ('000 RMB / worker) 勞動生產率（千元／人）	Average debts / assets 平均資產負債率(%)	Average Total assets ('000 RMB) 平均總資產（千元）
By ownership 產業所有權									
State-owned 國有	19	362	9,316	316	1.11	2.21	25.73	49.91	28,579
Collectively-owned 集體	103	63	4,895	253	5.58	16.99	77.12	67.17	4,543
Privately-owned 私有	6	28	872	34	5.42	6.26	30.96	13.31	625
Domestic JVs 聯營	1	65	3,541	107	12.72	22.40	54.47	43.23	840
Joint stock 股份制	1	15							
Foreign-funded 外資	3	205	42,044	2,099	6.73	14.30	205.09	52.90	31,184
Overseas Chinese-funded 港澳台資	2	25	3,405	144	4.99	6.36	136.21	21.67	2,880
By size 規模									
Large 大型	3	1,236	74,292	4,846	3.97	7.58	60.11	47.67	122,212
Medium 中型	4	694	61,103	2,698	3.06	8.76	88.04	65.04	88,063
Small 小型	125	62	2,845	109	3.45	8.39	45.62	58.85	3,169
By regional distribution 地區分布									
Central-North 華北	3	20	860	77	10.65	14.20	43.00	25.46	720
Beijing 北京									
Tianjin 天津									
Hebei 河北	3	20	860	77	10.65	14.20	43.00	25.46	720
Shanxi 山西									
Inner Mongolia 內蒙									
Northeast 東北	24	262	13,640	624	2.63	6.11	52.11	56.96	23,702
Liaoning 遼寧	23	261	14,193	662	2.73	6.24	54.39	56.20	24,224
Jilin 吉林	1	280	920	-260	-2.22	-31.71	3.29	93.07	11,690
Heilongjiang 黑龍江									
Central East 華東	27	145	8,501	370	3.92	10.93	58.55	64.10	9,419
Shanghai 上海		128	18,900	1,530	12.66	51.52	147.66	75.52	12,090
Jiangsu 江蘇	4	57	5,140	288	10.57	22.86	90.57	53.77	2,720
Zhejiang 浙江									
Anhui 安徽	2	225	4,475	35	1.46	9.21	19.89	83.99	2,405
Fujian 福建									
Jiangxi 江西	6	31	3,378	177	100.00	203.85	110.16	50.94	177
Shandong 山東	15	195	10,723	411	2.74	7.52	54.88	63.62	15,031
Central-South 中南	58	51	4,294	235	5.27	10.35	84.63	49.09	4,463
Henan 河南	10	55	2,325	66	4.53	14.67	42.20	69.02	1,456
Hubei 湖北	15	44	2,725	73	4.60	13.38	62.03	65.62	1,594
Hunan 湖南	6	36	2,900	202	31.68	57.08	81.69	44.50	637
Guangdong 廣東	10	22	1,762	22	3.03	8.91	81.95	65.98	726
Guangxi 廣西	17	77	8,818	615	4.99	9.13	114.87	45.31	12,312
Hainan 海南									
Southwest 西南	2	166	3,220	-105	-2.04	-5.00	19.46	59.26	5,155
Chongqing 重慶									
Sichuan 四川	1	303	3,440	-260	-2.76	-6.90	11.35	59.94	9,410
Guizhou 貴州	1	28	3,000	50	5.56	11.63	107.14	52.22	900
Yunnan 雲南									
Tibet 西藏									
Northwest 西北	21	38	375	24	2.48	12.66	9.92	80.41	960
Shaanxi 陝西	12	49	407	32	3.87	38.78	8.33	90.02	818
Gansu 甘肅	3	17	170	17	31.25	125.00	10.20	75.00	53
Qinghai 青海	1	10							
Ningxia 寧夏									
Xinjiang 新疆	5	30	498	14	0.69	2.39	16.82	71.22	2,036

1097: Talcum Mining and Dressing 滑石採選業

Year 年份	Number of firms 企業個數	Rate of change 每年變化 (%)	Number of employees 職工人數 (人)	Rate of change 每年變化 (%)	Total revenue (mil. RMB) 總銷售收入 (百萬元)	Rate of change 每年變化 (%)	Total profit (mil. RMB) 總利潤 (百萬元)	Rate of change 每年變化 (%)
1993	93		9,450		292		20	
1994	115	23.66%	12,924	36.76%	443	51.89%	28	38.30%
1995	136	18.26%	15,327	18.59%	631	42.44%	41	46.56%
1996	135	-0.74%	14,330	-6.50%	823	30.48%	39	-5.58%

3 Major products* 3 種主要產品 *	Output 產量	Sales volume 銷售量	Unit 單位
a) Soap Stone for Industrial Raw Material 工業原料滑石	5,297,243	6,621,554	ton 噸

Top 10 firms by revenue (year founded) 收入排名前 10 家企業 (創辦年份)	City 城市	Province 省	Telephone / fax 電話 / 傳真	Number of employees 職工人數	Ownership 產業所有權	Revenue ('000 RMB) 銷售收入 (千元)	Profit ('000 RMB) (rank) 利潤 (千元) (排名)	Total assets ('000 RMB) 總資產 (千元)	Major products 主要產品
Haicheng Pai Lou Talcum Mine 海城市牌樓滑石礦(1971)	Anshan 鞍山市	Liaoning 遼寧省	(0412)3772137 (0412)3772288	1,243	Collectively-owned 集體	232,130	11730(1)	278,330	o
Xixia Talcum Powder General Factory 栖霞市滑石粉總廠(1972)	Yantai 煙台市	Shandong 山東省	(0535)5541018 (0535)5541018	150	Collectively-owned 集體	81,200	1870(5)	11,890	o
Guangxi Talcum Development Co. Ltd. 廣西滑石工業公司(1970)	Guilin 桂林市	Guangxi 廣西	(0773)5592275 (0773)5592420	959	State-owned 國有	77,591	6020(2)	140,313	a
Longsheng Ge Zu Autonomous County Hua Mei Talcum Development Co. Ltd. 龍勝各族自治縣華美滑石開發有限公司(1985)	Lingchuan 靈川縣	Guangxi 廣西	(0773)7432224 (0773)7432229	436	Foreign-funded 外資	59,816	4073(3)	49,529	a
Haicheng Talcum Mine 海城滑石礦(1949)	Anshan 鞍山市	Liaoning 遼寧省	(0412)3335951 (0412)3333365	2,200	State-owned 國有	30,460	260(18)	167,890	a
Haicheng Jin Xin Mining Co. Ltd. 海城金新礦業有限公司(1988)	Anshan 鞍山市	Liaoning 遼寧省	(0412)3230764	238	Foreign-funded 外資	26,080	510(15)	20,670	o
Laizhou Talcum Mine 萊州市滑石礦(1949)	Yantai 煙台市	Shandong 山東省	(0535)2321036 (0535)2321035	452	State-owned 國有	19,620	1090(9)	26,602	a
Shanghai Xian Feng Saponite Factory 上海先鋒石粉廠(1958)	Shanghai 上海市	Shanghai 上海市	(021)56683406 (021)56684265	131	Collectively-owned 集體	18,904	1529(7)	12,093	o
Shandong Pingdu Talcum Mine 山東省平度滑石礦(1971)	Qingdao 青島市	Shandong 山東省	(0532)3351137 (0532)3351198	695	State-owned 國有	18,902	1126(8)	25,641	o
Fangcheng Du Shu Talcum Mining Factory 方城縣獨樹滑石採礦廠(1985)	Nanyang 南陽市	Henan 河南省		150	Collectively-owned 集體	12,770	110(24)	160	a

Top 10 Cities by Production Output 產出排名前 10 位城市	Province 省	Market share 市場份額	Number of firms 企業個數
Anshan 鞍山市	Liaoning 遼寧省	40.38%	12
Lingchuan 靈川縣	Guangxi 廣西	14.08%	7
Guilin 桂林市	Guangxi 廣西	11.47%	2
Yantai 煙台市	Shandong 山東省	8.63%	10
Qingdao 青島市	Shandong 山東省	4.06%	2
Nanyang 南陽市	Henan 河南省	3.45%	7
Lianyungang 連雲港市	Jiangsu 江蘇省	1.99%	3
Shangrao 上饒市	Jiangxi 江西省	1.77%	1
Zhaoqing 肇慶市	Guangdong 廣東省	1.77%	4
Xichang 西昌市	Sichuan 四川省	1.57%	16

10 Major Wholesalers 10 家主要批發商	City 城市	Province 省	Telephone / Fax 電話 / 傳真
China Metallurgy Import & Export Liaoning Company 中國冶金進出口遼寧公司	Shenyang 瀋陽市	Liaoning 遼寧省	(024)23867070 (024)23875451
Liaoning Foreign Trade General Company 遼寧省對外貿易總公司	Dalian 大連市	Liaoning 遼寧省	(0411)3632157 (0411)3638243
Zhong Xin Trade Company 中信貿易公司	Beijing 北京市	Beijing 北京市	(010)64662170 (010)64662161
China Metallurgy Import & Export Shandong Company 中國冶金進出口山東公司	Qingdao 青島市	Shandong 山東省	(0532)2801118 (0532)2801331
Yongzhou Ferromanganese Mine Company 永州市錳鐵礦公司	Yongzhou 永州市	Hunan 湖南省	(0746)8464135
Zhengzhou Advanced Technology Industrial Development Zone Development General Company 鄭州高新技術產業開發區發展總公司	Zhengzhou 鄭州市	Henan 河南省	(0371)7981924 (0371)7981422
Guangdong Hardware Import & Export Group Company 廣東省五金進出口集團公司	Guangzhou 廣州市	Guangdong 廣東省	(020)87752204 (020)87752205
Xi Shan Shi Wu Kuang Trade Company 錫山市五礦貿易公司	Wuxi 無錫市	Jiangsu 江蘇省	(0510)7760988
Xiamen Ocean Petroleum Company 廈門海洋石油公司	Xiamen 廈門市	Fujian 福建省	(0592)2095495 (0592)2087292
Hainan Shen Hai Import & Export Co. Ltd. 海南深海進出口有限公司	Haikou 海口市	Hainan 海南省	(0898)6717646 (0898)6717639

*Also include sales by firms outside this industry.包括本行業以外廠家的銷售。"o" stands for "others". "o" 代表 "其他產品"。

1099: Other Non-metal Ores Mining and Dressing
其他類未包括的非金屬礦採選業

The industry accounts for 0.065% of the total revenue of China's industrial sector in 1996. The revenue growth rate of the industry is 31.7% from 1995, as compared to the growth rate of China's industrial sector, 9.51%. The rate of return on asset is 2.96%. 79.70% of all firms in the industry made a profit while 14.57% had negative returns. The top province in terms of the industry's revenue is Zhejiang, accounting for 15.05% of the total revenue.
本行業在1996年佔全行業總產值0.065%，行業年增長率為31.7%（全國工業年增長率9.51%）。行業的資產回報率2.96%，79.70%的企業盈利，14.57%的企業虧損。銷售收入最高的省份為浙江省，佔本行業的15.05%。

	Total number of firms 企業總數	Total number of employees 職工總數	Total revenue (mil. RMB) 總銷售收入（百萬元）	Total profit (mil. RMB) 總利潤（百萬元）	Return on assets 資產利潤率 (%)	Return on equity 權益利潤率 (%)	Labour productivity ('000 RMB / worker) 勞動生產率（千元/人）	Debts / assets 資產負債率 (%)	Total assets (mil. RMB) 總資產（百萬元）
Industry Overall 行業總體	1,400	113,851	3,756	123	2.96	8.73	32.99	66.05	4,143

	Number of firms 企業個數	Average number of employees 平均職工人數	Average revenue ('000 RMB) 平均銷售收入（千元）	Average profit ('000 RMB) 平均利潤（千元）	Return on assets 資產利潤率 (%)	Return on equity 權益利潤率 (%)	Labour productivity ('000 RMB / worker) 勞動生產率（千元/人）	Average debts / assets 平均資產負債率(%)	Average Total assets ('000 RMB) 平均總資產（千元）
By ownership 產業所有權									
State-owned 國有	139	267	5,993	-22	-0.15	-0.46	22.46	67.67	14,576
Collectively-owned 集體	1,170	60	2,146	102	7.37	23.26	35.51	68.32	1,385
Privately-owned 私有	4	49	6,722	158	15.59	20.90	137.89	25.42	1,017
Domestic JVs 聯營	19	42	4,088	107	2.97	5.88	98.32	49.44	3,595
Joint stock 股份制	19	92	5,497	282	7.65	16.38	59.93	53.28	3,684
Foreign-funded 外資	16	85	3,796	-10	-0.15	-0.37	44.92	59.50	6,545
Overseas Chinese-funded 港澳台資	33	64	4,133	-62	-0.83	-1.64	64.94	49.49	7,515
By size 規模									
Large 大型	3	1,527	51,031	1,227	1.22	2.24	33.41	45.43	100,340
Medium 中型	6	1,386	64,032	-9	-0.01	-0.03	46.19	60.49	81,345
Small 小型	1,375	73	2,340	87	3.56	11.37	32.08	68.70	2,439
By regional distribution 地區分布									
Central-North 華北	130	39	1,080	45	3.25	11.54	27.73	71.81	1,393
Beijing 北京	9	19	634	7	1.11	2.48	34.19	55.35	602
Tianjin 天津									
Hebei 河北	55	39	1,268	88	8.91	29.54	32.70	69.81	991
Shanxi 山西	18	33	461	9	1.03	2.16	14.07	52.16	862
Inner Mongolia 內蒙	48	45	1,182	17	0.77	3.28	26.06	76.58	2,200
Northeast 東北	269	71	2,698	165	5.36	18.32	38.11	70.73	3,068
Liaoning 遼寧	181	65	2,916	194	7.20	20.86	44.88	65.49	2,693
Jilin 吉林	65	63	1,809	118	3.89	18.51	28.57	78.97	3,022
Heilongjiang 黑龍江	23	138	3,492	67	1.08	4.77	25.35	77.32	6,154
Central East 華東	460	106	3,391	92	2.28	6.43	32.01	64.48	4,024
Shanghai 上海									
Jiangsu 江蘇	19	243	8,998	476	4.66	12.18	36.96	61.75	10,209
Zhejiang 浙江	134	103	4,218	4	0.07	0.20	40.97	63.37	5,342
Anhui 安徽	38	80	3,542	95	3.97	13.08	44.41	69.66	2,387
Fujian 福建	95	59	2,205	57	2.43	6.46	37.60	62.32	2,332
Jiangxi 江西	130	132	1,475	40	1.70	9.67	11.19	82.43	2,380
Shandong 山東	44	104	6,548	420	5.78	11.87	62.95	51.28	7,256
Central-South 中南	382	84	3,122	88	3.76	10.91	37.13	65.52	2,327
Henan 河南	54	59	2,238	73	2.64	9.21	38.21	71.31	2,755
Hubei 湖北	56	240	2,288	56	2.95	13.43	9.52	78.07	1,896
Hunan 湖南	120	72	2,872	125	7.41	18.62	40.13	60.20	1,681
Guangdong 廣東	102	42	4,875	108	3.47	10.90	117.40	68.13	3,118
Guangxi 廣西	48	55	2,090	-3	-0.14	-0.27	37.79	48.23	2,349
Hainan 海南	2	14	700	275	36.67	110.00	51.85	66.67	750
Southwest 西南	71	61	896	-15	-0.75	-3.26	14.73	77.08	2,076
Chongqing 重慶	4	34	349	-11	-1.88	-12.74	10.24	85.21	572
Sichuan 四川	28	91	1,443	-56	-1.40	-7.41	15.83	81.12	3,974
Guizhou 貴州	28	32	453	37	7.03	12.50	14.09	43.79	524
Yunnan 雲南	10	66	787	-48	-3.07	-13.60	11.94	77.42	1,563
Tibet 西藏									
Northwest 西北	88	52	836	-23	-0.82	-1.76	16.10	53.43	2,830
Shaanxi 陝西	41	41	536	1	0.15	2.38	13.10	93.67	970
Gansu 甘肅	37	63	1,049	-51	-1.02	-1.70	16.55	40.27	5,030
Qinghai 青海									
Ningxia 寧夏									
Xinjiang 新疆	10	55	1,285	-21	-0.91	-9.09	23.36	90.03	2,316

1099: Other Non-metal Ores Mining and Dressing
其他類未包括的非金屬礦採選業

Year 年份	Number of firms 企業個數	Rate of change 每年變化 (%)	Number of employees 職工人數 (人)	Rate of change 每年變化 (%)	Total revenue (mil. RMB) 總銷售收入 (百萬元)	Rate of change 每年變化 (%)	Total profit (mil. RMB) 總利潤 (百萬元)	Rate of change 每年變化 (%)
1993	1,058		68,662		1,539		104	
1994	1,162	9.83%	87,387	27.27%	1,896	23.19%	73	-29.44%
1995	1,363	17.30%	93,470	6.96%	2,852	50.40%	92	25.87%
1996	1,400	2.71%	113,851	21.80%	3,756	31.70%	123	33.55%

3 Major products* 3 種主要產品 *	Output 產量	Sales volume 銷售量	Unit 單位
a) China Clay 瓷土	15,514,579	14,893,996	ton 噸
b) Fluorite 螢石	595,391	541,806	ton 噸
c) Anhydrous Hydrogen Fluoride 無水氟化氫	1,675	1,507	ton 噸

Top 10 firms by revenue (year founded) 收入排名前 10 家企業 (創辦年份)	City 城市	Province 省	Telephone / fax 電話 / 傳真	Number of employees 職工人數	Ownership 產業所有權	Revenue ('000 RMB) 銷售收入 (千元)	Profit ('000 RMB) (rank) 利潤 (千元) (排名)	Total assets ('000 RMB) 總資產 (千元)	Major products 主要產品
Zhejiang Dongfeng Fluorspar (Group) Co. Ltd 浙江東風螢石集團有限公司(1950)	Jinhua 金華市	Zhejiang 浙江省	(0579)7661923 (0579)7661997	2,142	State-owned 國有	191,346	2191(11)	227,231	o
Shenyang Bei Fang Industrial General Company 瀋陽市北方實業總公司(1992)	Shenyang 瀋陽市	Liaoning 遼寧省	(024)24824482 (024)24823472	274	Collectively-owned 集體	147,954	20000(1)	71,732	o
Sihui Di Dou Zhen Mud & Sand Field 四會市地豆鎮泥沙場(1980)	Zhaoqing 肇慶市	Guangdong 廣東省	(0757)3756482	90	Collectively-owned 集體	134,550	1900(15)	1,200	o
Weifang Bao Lin Chemical Construction Group Co. Ltd. 濰坊市寶林化建集團有限公司(1981)	Weifang 濰坊市	Shandong 山東省	(0536)4222526 (0536)4222303	350	Collectively-owned 集體	83,778	4560(4)	72,160	o
China Kaolin Co. 中國高嶺土公司(1955)	Suzhou 蘇州市	Jiangsu 江蘇省	(0512)5391621 (0512)5391459	2,153	State-owned 國有	61,781	312(106)	101,082	a
Wafangdian Diamond General Co. 瓦房店金剛石股份有限公司(1989)	Dalian 大連市	Liaoning 遼寧省	(0411)5613014 (0411)5611621	922	State-owned 國有	55,476	4762(2)	134,162	o
Zhejiang Lin'an Bentonite Mine 浙江省臨安膨潤土礦(1955)	Hangzhou 杭州市	Zhejiang 浙江省	(0571)3724951 (0571)3724950	1,028	State-owned 國有	31,930	-2402(343)	82,051	o
Ningguo Zhuangcun Mining Co. Ltd. 寧國縣裝村礦業有限責任公司(1979)	Xuanzhou 宣州市	Anhui 安徽省	(0563)4090856 (0563)4090818	576	Collectively-owned 集體	31,019	1811(17)	20,860	b
De'an Fluorite Company 德安縣螢石公司(1958)	Jiujiang 九江市	Jiangxi 江西省	(0792)4680002 (0792)4680001	1,104	State-owned 國有	30,115	1606(20)	46,077	b,c
Panshi Calcite Group Company 磐石市方解石集團公司(1994)	Jilin 吉林市	Jilin 吉林省	(0432)5912423	117	Collectively-owned 集體	28,091	782(35)	47,407	o

Top 10 Cities by Production Output 產出排名前 10 位城市	Province 省	Market share 市場份額	Number of firms 企業個數
Jinhua 金華市	Zhejiang 浙江省	7.51%	60
Zhaoqing 肇慶市	Guangdong 廣東省	4.98%	9
Hangzhou 杭州市	Zhejiang 浙江省	3.72%	31
Weifang 濰坊市	Shandong 山東省	3.51%	25
Maoming 茂名市	Guangdong 廣東省	3.47%	23
Suzhou 蘇州市	Jiangsu 江蘇省	3.38%	14
Guangzhou 廣州市	Guangdong 廣東省	3.01%	17
Lishui 麗水市	Zhejiang 浙江省	2.82%	34
Shenyang 瀋陽市	Liaoning 遼寧省	2.57%	28
Hengyang 衡陽市	Hunan 湖南省	2.46%	36

10 Major Wholesalers 10 家主要批發商	City 城市	Province 省	Telephone / Fax 電話 / 傳真
China Metallurgy Import & Export Liaoning Company 中國冶金進出口遼寧公司	Shenyang 瀋陽市	Liaoning 遼寧省	(024)23867070 (024)23875451
Liaoning Foreign Trade General Company 遼寧省對外貿易總公司	Dalian 大連市	Liaoning 遼寧省	(0411)3632157 (0411)3638243
Zhong Xin Trade Company 中信貿易公司	Beijing 北京市	Beijing 北京市	(010)64662170 (010)64662161
China Metallurgy Import & Export Shandong Company 中國冶金進出口山東公司	Qingdao 青島市	Shandong 山東省	(0532)2801118 (0532)2801331
Yongzhou Ferromanganese Mine Company 永州市錳鐵礦公司	Yongzhou 永州市	Hunan 湖南省	(0746)8464135
Zhengzhou Advanced Technology Industrial Development Zone Development General Company 鄭州高新技術產業開發區發展總公司	Zhengzhou 鄭州市	Henan 河南省	(0371)7981924 (0371)7981422
Guangdong Hardware Import & Export Group Company 廣東省五金進出口集團公司	Guangzhou 廣州市	Guangdong 廣東省	(020)87752204 (020)87752205
Xi Shan Shi Wu Kuang Trade Company 錫山市五礦貿易公司	Wuxi 無錫市	Jiangsu 江蘇省	(0510)7760988
Xiamen Ocean Petroleum Company 廈門海洋石油公司	Xiamen 廈門市	Fujian 福建省	(0592)2095495 (0592)2087292
Hainan Shen Hai Import & Export Co. Ltd. 海南深海進出口有限公司	Haikou 海口市	Hainan 海南省	(0898)6717646 (0898)6717639

*Also include sales by firms outside this industry.包括本行業以外廠家的銷售。"o" stands for "others". "o" 代表 "其他產品"。

1100: Other Ores Mining and Dressing 其他礦採選業

The industry accounts for 0.007% of the total revenue of China's industrial sector in 1996. The revenue growth rate of the industry is 19.0% from 1995, as compared to the growth rate of China's industrial sector, 9.51%. The rate of return on asset is 4.00%. 81.32% of all firms in the industry made a profit while 15.45% had negative returns. The top province in terms of the industry's revenue is Guangxi, accounting for 24.38% of the total revenue.
本行業在1996年佔全行業總產值0.007%，行業年增長率為19.0%（全國工業年增長率9.51%）。行業的資產回報率4.00%，81.32%的企業盈利，15.45%的企業虧損。銷售收入最高的省份為廣西省，佔本行業的24.38%。

	Total number of firms 企業總數	Total number of employees 職工總數	Total revenue (mil. RMB) 總銷售收入（百萬元）	Total profit (mil. RMB) 總利潤（百萬元）	Return on assets 資產利潤率 (%)	Return on equity 權益利潤率 (%)	Labour productivity ('000 RMB / worker) 勞動生產率（千元/人）	Debts / assets 資產負債率 (%)	Total assets (mil. RMB) 總資產（百萬元）
Industry Overall 行業總體	154	13,114	411	17	4.00	10.06	31.34	60.20	426

	Number of firms 企業個數	Average number of employees 平均職工人數	Average revenue ('000 RMB) 平均銷售收入（千元）	Average profit ('000 RMB) 平均利潤（千元）	Return on assets 資產利潤率 (%)	Return on equity 權益利潤率 (%)	Labour productivity ('000 RMB / worker) 勞動生產率（千元/人）	Average debts / assets 平均資產負債率(%)	Average Total assets ('000 RMB) 平均總資產（千元）
By ownership 產業所有權									
State-owned 國有	24	165	4,750	42	0.49	1.20	28.84	59.51	8,542
Collectively-owned 集體	120	70	2,119	118	7.06	17.38	30.34	59.37	1,669
Privately-owned 私有	1	47	1,157	29	2.79	3.42	24.63	18.43	1,049
Domestic JVs 聯營	4	70	1,075	11	0.90	1.65	15.30	45.40	1,217
Joint stock 股份制	2	169	14,652	1,124	24.08	200.13	86.70	87.97	4,668
Foreign-funded 外資	1	34							
Overseas Chinese-funded 港澳台資	1	54	7,058	-210	-5.85	-44.28	130.70	86.80	3,596
By size 規模									
Large 大型									
Medium 中型	2	714	14,444	-41	-0.10	-0.34	20.24	70.99	41,821
Small 小型	150	78	2,546	114	4.99	11.72	32.83	57.43	2,282
By regional distribution 地區分布									
Central-North 華北	12	37	446	10	3.05	8.45	12.16	63.87	328
Beijing 北京	4	60	793	-18	-2.17	-6.73	13.15	67.70	805
Tianjin 天津									
Hebei 河北	7	27	286	26	58.06	150.00	10.75	61.29	44
Shanxi 山西	1	13	180	10	2.50	3.85	13.85	35.00	400
Inner Mongolia 內蒙									
Northeast 東北	15	89	1,693	23	0.55	3.06	18.93	82.17	4,157
Liaoning 遼寧	9	99	1,887	57	1.84	6.38	18.97	71.19	3,086
Jilin 吉林	4	102	2,035	-48	-0.55	-6.11	20.00	91.02	8,633
Heilongjiang 黑龍江	2	20	140	10	33.33	100.00	7.00	66.67	30
Central East 華東	33	72	3,831	160	4.66	10.43	53.26	55.29	3,432
Shanghai 上海									
Jiangsu 江蘇									
Zhejiang 浙江	10	66	3,450	62	1.72	4.93	51.96	65.09	3,606
Anhui 安徽	3	76	7,123	347	10.51	29.97	93.73	64.95	3,300
Fujian 福建	3								
Jiangxi 江西	10	52	1,046	16	1.04	2.47	19.96	58.04	1,542
Shandong 山東	7	137	8,586	494	6.67	12.31	62.73	45.83	7,413
Central-South 中南	74	107	3,319	154	4.92	11.41	31.14	56.88	3,135
Henan 河南	15	88	2,180	58	1.15	3.51	24.90	67.37	5,061
Hubei 湖北	19	41	2,167	43	4.27	9.96	52.51	57.17	999
Hunan 湖南	13	56	1,915	55	4.58	15.54	33.91	70.54	1,193
Guangdong 廣東	5	209	9,334	78	0.96	1.67	44.70	42.93	8,162
Guangxi 廣西	21	191	4,771	411	10.69	21.99	24.96	51.39	3,845
Hainan 海南	1								
Southwest 西南	15	21	345	-9	-1.23	-2.55	16.14	51.76	702
Chongqing 重慶	4	22	603	16	2.08	18.07	27.00	88.51	773
Sichuan 四川	4	11	99	0	-0.09	0.18	8.47	152.38	65
Guizhou 貴州	7	27	339	-10	-0.97	-1.44	12.54	32.31	1,026
Yunnan 雲南									
Tibet 西藏									
Northwest 西北	5	150	516	12	1.55	4.80	3.45	67.70	774
Shaanxi 陝西	3	240	813	13	1.05	3.28	3.38	68.06	1,273
Gansu 甘肅									
Qinghai 青海									
Ningxia 寧夏	2	14	70	10	40.00	66.67	5.19	40.00	25
Xinjiang 新疆									

1100: Other Ores Mining and Dressing 其他礦採選業

Year 年份	Number of firms 企業個數	Rate of change 每年變化 (%)	Number of employees 職工人數 (人)	Rate of change 每年變化 (%)	Total revenue (mil. RMB) 總銷售收入 (百萬元)	Rate of change 每年變化 (%)	Total profit (mil. RMB) 總利潤 (百萬元)	Rate of change 每年變化 (%)
1993	94		7,247		208		6	
1994	111	18.09%	6,467	-10.76%	231	11.12%	7	8.74%
1995	149	34.23%	13,441	107.84%	345	49.50%	19	173.37%
1996	154	3.36%	13,114	-2.43%	411	18.99%	17	-11.06%

3 Major products* 3種主要產品*	Output 產量	Sales volume 銷售量	Unit 單位
a) Barium Carbonate 碳酸鋇	45,533	42,801	ton 噸
b) China Clay 瓷土	482,034	462,753	ton 噸

Top 10 firms by revenue (year founded) 收入排名前10家企業 (創辦年份)	City 城市	Province 省	Telephone / fax 電話 / 傳真	Number of employees 職工人數	Ownership 產業所有權	Revenue ('000 RMB) 銷售收入 (千元)	Profit ('000 RMB) (rank) 利潤 (千元) (排名)	Total assets ('000 RMB) 總資產 (千元)	Major products 主要產品
Xiangzhou Sicun Town Mineral Products Co. 象州縣寺村鎮礦管站(1975)	Heshan 合山市	Guangxi 廣西	(0772)4371335	2,850	Collectively-owned 集體	43,113	4190(1)	12,951	o
Guangdong Huizhou Powder Metallurgy Factory 廣東省惠州市粉末冶金製品廠(1967)	Huizhou 惠州市	Guangdong 廣東省	(0751)2264050	451	State-owned 國有	35,394	517(7)	29,347	o
Yin Ma Quartz Mine 飲馬石英礦(1982)	Weifang 濰坊市	Shandong 山東省	(0536)8900231 (0536)8900231	500	Collectively-owned 集體	22,060	1640(2)	32,740	o
Fanchang Lu Nan Xiang Kaolin Development Company 繁昌縣蘆南鄉高嶺土開發公司(1994)	Wuhu 蕪湖市	Anhui 安徽省	(0553)7892292	25	Collectively-owned 集體	19,121	910(4)	8,988	b
Feicheng Hong Da Chemical General Factory 肥城市宏達化工總廠(1978)	Tai'an 泰安市	Shandong 山東省	(0538)3461083 (0538)3461083	80	Collectively-owned 集體	17,717	427(11)	2,455	o
Ju Hua Group Quzhou Ore Dressing Factory 巨化集團衢州選礦廠(1991)	Quzhou 衢州市	Zhejiang 浙江省	(0570)3021081	65	State-owned 國有	13,436	443(10)	8,699	o
Gaomi Tu Zhuang Xiang Barite Mine 高密市土裝鄉重晶石礦(1980)	Weifang 濰坊市	Shandong 山東省	(0536)2672178	60	Collectively-owned 集體	12,800	900(5)	4,808	o
Panzhihua Dongxian Yin Jiang Zhen Xu Jia Gou Iron Mine 攀枝花市東區銀江鎮徐家溝鐵礦(1989)	Panzhihua 攀枝花市	Sichuan 四川省	(0812)6664327	110	Collectively-owned 集體	11,430	238(14)	512	o
Xiangzhou Breeze Factory 象州縣礦粉廠(1978)	Heshan 合山市	Guangxi 廣西	(0772)4362145	67	State-owned 國有	10,769	472(9)	13,180	o
Resource Xian Zhong Feng Xiang Breeze Factory 資源縣中峯鄉礦粉廠(1992)	Lingchuan 靈川縣	Guangxi 廣西	(0773)4391026	14	Collectively-owned 集體	9,500	520(6)	750	o

Top 10 Cities by Production Output 產出排名前10位城市	Province 省	Market share 市場份額	Number of firms 企業個數
Heshan 合山市	Guangxi 廣西	34.21%	8
Huizhou 惠州市	Guangdong 廣東省	15.17%	1
Yulin 玉林市	Guangxi 廣西	6.86%	3
Huaihua 懷化市	Hunan 湖南省	6.77%	6
Quzhou 衢州市	Zhejiang 浙江省	5.80%	4
Ankang 安康市	Shaanxi 陝西省	4.92%	2
Lingchuan 靈川縣	Guangxi 廣西	4.49%	8
Foshan 佛山市	Guangdong 廣東省	2.00%	1
Beijing 北京市	Beijing 北京市	1.51%	4
Heyuan 河源市	Guangdong 廣東省	1.39%	3

10 Major Wholesalers 10家主要批發商	City 城市	Province 省	Telephone / Fax 電話 / 傳真
China Metallurgy Import & Export Liaoning Company 中國冶金進出口遼寧公司	Shenyang 瀋陽市	Liaoning 遼寧省	(024)23867070 (024)23875451
Liaoning Foreign Trade General Company 遼寧省對外貿易總公司	Dalian 大連市	Liaoning 遼寧省	(0411)3632157 (0411)3638243
Zhong Xin Trade Company 中信貿易公司	Beijing 北京市	Beijing 北京市	(010)64662170 (010)64662161
China Metallurgy Import & Export Shandong Company 中國冶金進出口山東公司	Qingdao 青島市	Shandong 山東省	(0532)2801118 (0532)2801331
Yongzhou Ferromanganese Mine Company 永州市錳鐵礦公司	Yongzhou 永州市	Hunan 湖南省	(0746)8464135
Zhengzhou Advanced Technology Industrial Development Zone Development General Company 鄭州高新技術產業開發區發展總公司	Zhengzhou 鄭州市	Henan 河南省	(0371)7981924 (0371)7981422
Guangdong Hardware Import & Export Group Company 廣東省五金進出口集團公司	Guangzhou 廣州市	Guangdong 廣東省	(020)87752204 (020)87752205
Xi Shan Shi Wu Kuang Trade Company 錫山市五礦貿易公司	Wuxi 無錫市	Jiangsu 江蘇省	(0510)7760988
Xiamen Ocean Petroleum Company 廈門海洋石油公司	Xiamen 廈門市	Fujian 福建省	(0592)2095495 (0592)2087292
Hainan Shen Hai Import & Export Co. Ltd. 海南深海進出口有限公司	Haikou 海口市	Hainan 海南省	(0898)6717646 (0898)6717639

*Also include sales by firms outside this industry.包括本行業以外廠家的銷售。"o" stands for "others". "o" 代表 "其他產品"。

1210: Logging and Transport of Timber 木材採運業

The industry accounts for 0.292% of the total revenue of China's industrial sector in 1996. The revenue growth rate of the industry is 2.8% from 1995, as compared to the growth rate of China's industrial sector, 9.51%. The rate of return on asset is 0.62%. 67.49% of all firms in the industry made a profit while 28.52% had negative returns. The top province in terms of the industry's revenue is Helongjiang, accounting for 33.84% of the total revenue.
本行業在1996年佔全行業總產值0.292%，行業年增長率為2.8%（全國工業年增長率9.51%）。行業的資產回報率0.62%，67.49%的企業盈利，28.52%的企業虧損。銷售收入最高的省份為黑龍江省，佔本行業的33.84%。

	Total number of firms 企業總數	Total number of employees 職工總數	Total revenue (mil. RMB) 總銷售收入（百萬元）	Total profit (mil. RMB) 總利潤（百萬元）	Return on assets 資產利潤率 (%)	Return on equity 權益利潤率 (%)	Labour productivity ('000 RMB / worker) 勞動生產率（千元/人）	Debts / assets 資產負債率 (%)	Total assets (mil. RMB) 總資產（百萬元）
Industry Overall 行業總體	1,323	1,082,661	16,913	251	0.62	1.72	15.62	63.98	40,426

	Number of firms 企業個數	Average number of employees 平均職工人數	Average revenue ('000 RMB) 平均銷售收入（千元）	Average profit ('000 RMB) 平均利潤（千元）	Return on assets 資產利潤率 (%)	Return on equity 權益利潤率 (%)	Labour productivity ('000 RMB / worker) 勞動生產率（千元/人）	Average debts / assets 平均資產負債率(%)	Average Total assets ('000 RMB) 平均總資產（千元）
By ownership 產業所有權									
State-owned 國有	867	1,226	18,623	234	0.52	1.46	15.19	64.42	45,142
Collectively-owned 集體	447	36	1,164	57	3.96	7.88	32.33	49.68	1,448
Privately-owned 私有	1	5	353	29	33.41	55.14	70.59	39.41	87
Domestic JVs 聯營	2	13	746	14	1.46	1.59	57.35	8.23	991
Joint stock 股份制	3	868	81,265	7,498	3.64	7.71	93.62	52.77	206,005
Foreign-funded 外資	1	84	737	-70	-1.40	-1.96	8.77	28.27	5,011
Overseas Chinese-funded 港澳台資	2	23	524	-73	-0.92	-1.04	22.79	10.93	7,876
By size 規模									
Large 大型	87	9,552	125,242	1,813	0.58	1.68	13.11	65.58	314,281
Medium 中型	33	2,635	50,758	-174	-0.14	-0.35	19.26	61.12	126,072
Small 小型	1,200	137	3,618	82	1.11	2.80	26.47	60.40	7,435
By regional distribution 地區分布									
Central-North 華北	35	3,954	58,163	302	0.18	0.44	14.71	59.86	170,893
Beijing 北京									
Tianjin 天津									
Hebei 河北	1	53	2,270	40	0.41	0.46	42.83	12.46	9,870
Shanxi 山西	3	519	11,177	240	1.36	4.29	21.52	68.34	17,680
Inner Mongolia 內蒙	31	4,413	64,513	316	0.17	0.41	14.62	59.87	190,914
Northeast 東北	127	5,751	73,364	1,187	0.68	2.02	12.76	66.13	173,750
Liaoning 遼寧	19	9	179	3	2.09	5.88	19.94	64.81	151
Jilin 吉林	30	6,807	119,658	1,980	0.89	2.15	17.58	58.67	222,560
Heilongjiang 黑龍江	78	6,743	73,387	1,171	0.59	1.94	10.88	69.36	197,264
Central East 華東	503	159	4,736	66	0.68	1.82	29.70	62.83	9,702
Shanghai 上海									
Jiangsu 江蘇									
Zhejiang 浙江	5	26	970	86	14.14	22.16	37.31	36.18	608
Anhui 安徽	17	119	5,061	98	1.18	2.20	42.53	46.30	8,316
Fujian 福建	185	210	9,298	123	0.59	1.58	44.21	62.52	20,671
Jiangxi 江西	296	132	1,930	28	0.90	2.70	14.59	66.77	3,079
Shandong 山東									
Central-South 中南	288	100	2,528	-61	-1.15	-2.44	25.20	52.79	5,330
Henan 河南	1	4	150	10	5.56	16.67	37.50	66.67	180
Hubei 湖北	15	242	5,413	-37	-0.40	-0.96	22.34	57.98	9,082
Hunan 湖南	127	92	2,423	-20	-0.47	-1.48	26.28	68.23	4,227
Guangdong 廣東	102	89	2,222	-43	-0.85	-1.58	25.03	46.10	5,091
Guangxi 廣西	30	88	3,538	-237	-2.36	-3.57	40.33	33.80	10,054
Hainan 海南	13	142	475	-237	-7.51	-17.81	3.33	57.88	3,156
Southwest 西南	315	237	6,226	170	1.16	3.67	26.23	68.47	14,710
Chongqing 重慶	5	135	1,062	-540	-24.04	-32.51	7.83	26.04	2,248
Sichuan 四川	156	274	7,419	72	0.39	1.34	27.04	71.07	18,577
Guizhou 貴州	58	102	2,971	97	1.80	3.58	29.02	49.54	5,389
Yunnan 雲南	85	283	7,039	655	4.17	13.37	24.91	68.78	15,702
Tibet 西藏	10	107	2,116	82	1.36	2.36	19.76	42.19	6,011
Northwest 西北	55	546	8,878	375	1.55	3.01	16.25	48.34	24,171
Shaanxi 陝西	28	425	5,959	365	2.37	3.94	14.02	39.81	15,359
Gansu 甘肅	8	1,586	27,424	509	0.79	1.55	17.29	48.87	64,203
Qinghai 青海	4	116	1,893	68	1.08	1.55	16.39	30.32	6,250
Ningxia 寧夏									
Xinjiang 新疆	15	333	6,301	406	1.69	4.12	18.91	59.01	24,049

1210: Logging and Transport of Timber 木材採運業

Year 年份	Number of firms 企業個數	Rate of change 每年變化 (%)	Number of employees 職工人數 (人)	Rate of change 每年變化 (%)	Total revenue (mil. RMB) 總銷售收入 (百萬元)	Rate of change 每年變化 (%)	Total profit (mil. RMB) 總利潤 (百萬元)	Rate of change 每年變化 (%)
1993	1,051		535,892		14,206		945	
1994	1,087	3.43%	1,088,473	103.11%	16,484	16.04%	922	-2.39%
1995	1,200	10.40%	1,175,438	7.99%	16,448	-0.22%	653	-29.15%
1996	1,323	10.25%	1,082,661	-7.89%	16,913	2.83%	251	-61.58%

3 Major products* 3 種主要產品 *	Output 產量	Sales volume 銷售量	Unit 單位
a) Timber 木材	64,638,689	63,345,915	cubic metre 立方米
b) Fire Wood 薪材	488,479	473,825	cubic metre 立方米
c) Sawmilling 鋸材	7,362,555	6,773,550	cubic metre 立方米

Top 10 firms by revenue (year founded) 收入排名前 10 家企業 (創辦年份)	City 城市	Province 省	Telephone / fax 電話 / 傳真	Number of employees 職工人數	Ownership 產業所有權	Revenue ('000 RMB) 銷售收入 (千元)	Profit ('000 RMB) (rank) 利潤 (千元) (排名)	Total assets ('000 RMB) 總資產 (千元)	Major products 主要產品
Da Xing'an Ling Xinlin Forestry Bureau 大興安嶺新林林業局(1965)	Jagdaqi,Daxinganling 大興安嶺加	Heilongjiang 黑龍江省	(0457)2725141 (0457)2725030	30,570	State-owned 國有	330,317	13600(5)	989,044	a,c
Baihe Forestry Bureau of Jilin Province 吉林省白河林業局(1971)	Yanji 延吉市	Jilin 吉林省	(0433)5718216	11,237	State-owned 國有	317,830	4580(37)	632,690	a,b,c
Jilin Sanchazi Forestry Bureau 吉林省三岔子林業局(1967)	Baishan 白山市	Jilin 吉林省	(0439)3748380 (0439)3749379	13,783	State-owned 國有	310,677	11487(10)	413,868	a,b,c
Jilin Dunhua Forestry Bureau 吉林省敦化林業局(1957)	Yanji 延吉市	Jilin 吉林省	(0433)6209781 (0433)6208020	16,015	State-owned 國有	301,610	9810(14)	440,290	a,b,c
Jilin Lu Shui He Forestry Bureau 吉林省露水河林業局(1970)	Baishan 白山市	Jilin 吉林省	(0439)6369104 (0439)6369104	14,729	State-owned 國有	265,480	6050(26)	589,820	a,b,c
Jilin Provincial Song Jiang He Forestry Bureau 吉林省松江河林業局(1957)	Baishan 白山市	Jilin 吉林省	(0439)6312519 (0439)6312519	16,836	State-owned 國有	264,906	3490(45)	381,435	a,b,c
Jilin Baishan Linjiang Forestry Bureau 吉林省臨江林業局(1953)	Baishan 白山市	Jilin 吉林省	(0439)5224377	17,988	State-owned 國有	263,860	3467(46)	516,763	a,b,c
Jilin Hong Shi Forestry Bureau 吉林省紅石林業局(1974)	Jilin 吉林市	Jilin 吉林省	(0432)6887902 (0432)6887902	6,302	State-owned 國有	263,525	12059(8)	565,506	a,b,c
Fujian Yong'an Forestry (Group) Co. Ltd. 福建省永安林業(集團)股份有限公司(1994)	Sanming 三明市	Fujian 福建省	(0598)3614866 (0598)3633415	2,428	Joint stock 股份制	248,548	14980(4)	845,587	b
Da Xing'an Ling Tahe Forestry Bureau 大興安嶺塔河林業局(1965)	Jagdaqi,Daxinganling 大興安嶺加	Heilongjiang 黑龍江省	(0457)2729754	28,115	State-owned 國有	227,104	-26943(475)	839,922	a

Top 10 Cities by Production Output 產出排名前 10 位城市	Province 省	Market share 市場份額	Number of firms 企業個數
Hailar 海拉爾市	Inner Mong 內蒙	13.03%	29
Jagdaqi,Daxinganling 大興安嶺加	Heilongjiang 黑龍江省	10.58%	10
Yichun 伊春市	Heilongjiang 黑龍江省	9.42%	17
Baishan 白山市	Jilin 吉林省	8.55%	13
Yanji 延吉市	Jilin 吉林省	8.40%	12
Mudanjiang 牡丹江市	Heilongjiang 黑龍江省	3.75%	8
Sanming 三明市	Fujian 福建省	3.45%	101
Shuangcheng 雙城市	Heilongjiang 黑龍江省	3.09%	26
Nangping 南平市	Fujian 福建省	2.84%	61
Jilin 吉林市	Jilin 吉林省	2.63%	4

10 Major Wholesalers 10 家主要批發商	City 城市	Province 省	Telephone / Fax 電話 / 傳真
Jilin Forestry Import & Export Company 吉林省林業進出口公司	Changchun 長春市	Jilin 吉林省	(0431)5629740 (0431)5638250
Shanghai Local Products Goods & Materials General Co. 上海市土產物資總公司	Shanghai 上海市	Shanghai 上海市	(021)63200857 (021)63200857
Kunming Import & Export Company 昆明市進出口公司	Kunming 昆明市	Yunnan 雲南省	(0871)5155192 (0871)5155193
Wujin Supply & Marketing Cooperative Means of Production General Company 武進市供銷社生產資料總公司	Changzhou 常州市	Jiangsu 江蘇省	(0519)6609079 (0519)6609079
China Timber Import & Export Company 中國木材進出口公司	Beijing 北京市	Beijing 北京市	(010)65132383 (010)65124788
Jinchen Urban Goods & Materials General Company Timber Company 晉城市城區物資總公司木材公司	Jincheng 晉城市	Shanxi 山西省	
Zhangjiagang Timber General Company 張家港市木材總公司	Suzhou 蘇州市	Jiangsu 江蘇省	(0512)8223241
Wujiang Timber General Company 吳江市木材總公司	Suzhou 蘇州市	Jiangsu 江蘇省	(0512)3422179
China Forest Products Marketing Company 中國林產品經銷公司	Beijing 北京市	Beijing 北京市	(010)64228370 (010)64216443
Yangzhou Timber General Company 揚州市木材總公司	Yangzhou 揚州市	Jiangsu 江蘇省	(0514)7246917 (0514)7247383

*Also include sales by firms outside this industry.包括本行業以外廠家的銷售。"o" stands for "others". "o" 代表"其他產品"。

1220: Logging and Transport of Bamboo 竹材採運業

The industry accounts for 0.001% of the total revenue of China's industrial sector in 1996. The revenue growth rate of the industry is -18.9% from 1995, as compared to the growth rate of China's industrial sector, 9.51%. The rate of return on asset is 9.59%. 64.85% of all firms in the industry made a profit while 15.15% had negative returns. The top province in terms of the industry's revenue is Anhui, accounting for 31.79% of the total revenue.
本行業在1996年佔全行業總產值0.001%，行業年增長率為-18.9%（全國工業年增長率9.51%）。行業的資產回報率9.59%，64.85%的企業盈利，15.15%的企業虧損。銷售收入最高的省份為安徽省，佔本行業的31.79%。

	Total number of firms 企業總數	Total number of employees 職工總數	Total revenue (mil. RMB) 總銷售收入（百萬元）	Total profit (mil. RMB) 總利潤（百萬元）	Return on assets 資產利潤率 (%)	Return on equity 權益利潤率 (%)	Labour productivity ('000 RMB / worker) 勞動生產率（千元/人）	Debts / assets 資產負債率 (%)	Total assets (mil. RMB) 總資產（百萬元）
Industry Overall 行業總體	31	1,227	43	3	9.59	33.25	35.04	71.17	29

	Number of firms 企業個數	Average number of employees 平均職工人數	Average revenue ('000 RMB) 平均銷售收入（千元）	Average profit ('000 RMB) 平均利潤（千元）	Return on assets 資產利潤率 (%)	Return on equity 權益利潤率 (%)	Labour productivity ('000 RMB / worker) 勞動生產率（千元/人）	Average debts / assets 平均資產負債率(%)	Average Total assets ('000 RMB) 平均總資產（千元）
By ownership 產業所有權									
State-owned 國有	10	65	1,800	100	6.25	50.00	27.78	87.50	1,600
Collectively-owned 集體	19	29	1,298	102	18.13	36.46	45.07	50.26	563
Privately-owned 私有									
Domestic JVs 聯營	2	16	167	30	2.63	8.89	10.41	70.48	1,152
Joint stock 股份制									
Foreign-funded 外資									
Overseas Chinese-funded 港澳台資									
By size 規模									
Large 大型									
Medium 中型									
Small 小型	31	40	1,387	97	10.35	37.51	35.04	72.41	935
By regional distribution 地區分布									
Central-North 華北									
Beijing 北京									
Tianjin 天津									
Hebei 河北									
Shanxi 山西									
Inner Mongolia 內蒙									
Northeast 東北									
Liaoning 遼寧									
Jilin 吉林									
Heilongjiang 黑龍江									
Central East 華東	24	45	1,122	57	5.67	24.64	24.98	77.03	1,007
Shanghai 上海									
Jiangsu 江蘇									
Zhejiang 浙江									
Anhui 安徽	1	221	13,670	30	0.39	2.48	61.86	84.24	7,680
Fujian 福建	13	34	613	45	8.69	15.73	18.24	44.92	522
Jiangxi 江西	10	42	529	75	7.74	125.00	12.60	93.81	969
Shandong 山東									
Central-South 中南	4	7	2,943	310	35.84	50.61	420.36	29.19	865
Henan 河南									
Hubei 湖北									
Hunan 湖南	3	8	257	10	6.38	18.75	30.80	65.96	157
Guangdong 廣東	1	3	11,000	1,210	40.47	52.84	3666.67	23.41	2,990
Guangxi 廣西									
Hainan 海南									
Southwest 西南	3	40	1,430	53	12.50	48.48	35.45	74.22	427
Chongqing 重慶									
Sichuan 四川	1	47	750	20	4.00	18.18	15.96	78.00	500
Guizhou 貴州	2	37	1,770	90	23.08	81.82	47.84	71.79	390
Yunnan 雲南									
Tibet 西藏									
Northwest 西北									
Shaanxi 陝西									
Gansu 甘肅									
Qinghai 青海									
Ningxia 寧夏									
Xinjiang 新疆									

1220: Logging and Transport of Bamboo 竹材採運業

Year 年份	Number of firms 企業個數	Rate of change 每年變化 (%)	Number of employees 職工人數 (人)	Rate of change 每年變化 (%)	Total revenue (mil. RMB) 總銷售收入 (百萬元)	Rate of change 每年變化 (%)	Total profit (mil. RMB) 總利潤 (百萬元)	Rate of change 每年變化 (%)
1993	23		1,406		29		1	
1994	36	56.52%	2,690	91.32%	61	115.32%	5	238.62%
1995	37	2.78%	2,674	-0.60%	53	-13.64%	1	-77.64%
1996	31	-16.22%	1,227	-54.11%	43	-18.87%	3	188.18%

3 Major products* 3 種主要產品 *	Output 產量	Sales volume 銷售量	Unit 單位
a) Bamboo 竹材	78,288,580	75,939,923	piece 根

Top 10 firms by revenue (year founded) 收入排名前10家企業 (創辦年份)	City 城市	Province 省	Telephone / fax 電話 / 傳真	Number of employees 職工人數	Ownership 產業所有權	Revenue ('000 RMB) 銷售收入 (千元)	Profit ('000 RMB) (rank) 利潤 (千元) (排名)	Total assets ('000 RMB) 總資產 (千元)	Major products 主要產品
Guangde Wood & Bamboo Co. 廣德縣木竹公司(1972)	Xuanzhou 宣州市	Anhui 安徽省	(0563)6022561	228	State-owned 國有	13,666	30(4)	7,675	a
Nanxiong Lan He Zhen Forestry Development Company 南雄市瀾河鎮林業開發公司(1988)	Shaoguan 韶關市	Guangdong 廣東省	(0751)3532096	3	Collectively-owned 集體	11,000	1210(1)	2,987	o
Shaowu Na Kou Lumbering & Breeding Factory 邵武市拿口採育場(1958)	Nangping 南平市	Fujian 福建省		120	Collectively-owned 集體	3,680	320(2)	940	o
Chishui Hu Shi Zhen Joint Forest Farm 赤水市葫市鎮聯合林場(1995)	Zunyi 遵義市	Guizhou 貴州省	(0852)731012	50	Domestic JVs 聯營	3,150	160(3)	758	a

Top 10 Cities by Production Output 產出排名前10位城市	Province 省	Market share 市場份額	Number of firms 企業個數
Xuanzhou 宣州市	Anhui 安徽省	32.89%	1
Zunyi 遵義市	Guizhou 貴州省	20.51%	3
Longyan 龍巖市	Fujian 福建省	12.88%	1
Shaoguan 韶關市	Guangdong 廣東省	11.19%	1
Shangrao 上饒市	Jiangxi 江西省	8.02%	3
Nangping 南平市	Fujian 福建省	7.06%	7
Jiujiang 九江市	Jiangxi 江西省	1.99%	2
Fuzhou 撫州市	Jiangxi 江西省	1.47%	1
Changsha 長沙市	Hunan 湖南省	0.85%	1
Chenzhou 郴州市	Hunan 湖南省	0.74%	1

10 Major Wholesalers 10家主要批發商	City 城市	Province 省	Telephone / Fax 電話 / 傳真
Jilin Forestry Import & Export Company 吉林省林業進出口公司	Changchun 長春市	Jilin 吉林省	(0431)5629740 (0431)5638250
Shanghai Local Products Goods & Materials General Co. 上海市土產物資總公司	Shanghai 上海市	Shanghai 上海市	(021)63200857 (021)63200857
Kunming Import & Export Company 昆明市進出口公司	Kunming 昆明市	Yunnan 雲南省	(0871)5155192 (0871)5155193
Wujin Supply & Marketing Cooperative Means of Production General Company 武進市供銷社生產資料總公司	Changzhou 常州市	Jiangsu 江蘇省	(0519)6609079 (0519)6609079
China Timber Import & Export Company 中國木材進出口公司	Beijing 北京市	Beijing 北京市	(010)65132383 (010)65124788
Jinchen Urban Goods & Materials General Company Timber Company 晉城市城區物資總公司木材公司	Jincheng 晉城市	Shanxi 山西省	
Zhangjiagang Timber General Company 張家港市木材總公司	Suzhou 蘇州市	Jiangsu 江蘇省	(0512)8223241
Wujiang Timber General Company 吳江市木材總公司	Suzhou 蘇州市	Jiangsu 江蘇省	(0512)3422179
China Forest Products Marketing Company 中國林產品經銷公司	Beijing 北京市	Beijing 北京市	(010)64228370 (010)64216443
Yangzhou Timber General Company 揚州市木材總公司	Yangzhou 揚州市	Jiangsu 江蘇省	(0514)7246917 (0514)7247383

*Also include sales by firms outside this industry.包括本行業以外廠家的銷售。"o" stands for "others". "o" 代表 "其他產品"。

1311: Rice Milling 碾米業

The industry accounts for 0.371% of the total revenue of China's industrial sector in 1996. The revenue growth rate of the industry is 4.5% from 1995, as compared to the growth rate of China's industrial sector, 9.51%. The rate of return on asset is 0.40%. 74.74% of all firms in the industry made a profit while 18.79% had negative returns. The top province in terms of the industry's revenue is Anhui, accounting for 22.85% of the total revenue.
本行業在1996年佔全行業總產值0.371%，行業年增長率為4.5%（全國工業年增長率9.51%）。行業的資產回報率0.40%，74.74%的企業盈利，18.79%的企業虧損。銷售收入最高的省份為安徽省，佔本行業的22.85%。

	Total number of firms 企業總數	Total number of employees 職工總數	Total revenue (mil. RMB) 總銷售收入（百萬元）	Total profit (mil. RMB) 總利潤（百萬元）	Return on assets 資產利潤率 (%)	Return on equity 權益利潤率 (%)	Labour productivity ('000 RMB / worker) 勞動生產率（千元/人）	Debts / assets 資產負債率 (%)	Total assets (mil. RMB) 總資產（百萬元）
Industry Overall 行業總體	4,102	196,257	21,507	65	0.40	1.53	109.59	73.60	16,037

	Number of firms 企業個數	Average number of employees 平均職工人數	Average revenue ('000 RMB) 平均銷售收入（千元）	Average profit ('000 RMB) 平均利潤（千元）	Return on assets 資產利潤率 (%)	Return on equity 權益利潤率 (%)	Labour productivity ('000 RMB / worker) 勞動生產率（千元/人）	Average debts / assets 平均資產負債率(%)	Average Total assets ('000 RMB) 平均總資產（千元）
By ownership 產業所有權									
State-owned 國有	1,523	89	7,309	-240	-2.84	-12.41	82.55	77.13	8,445
Collectively-owned 集體	2,508	23	3,874	185	19.90	51.10	169.22	61.06	930
Privately-owned 私有	17	41	6,667	158	10.59	30.36	163.54	65.11	1,490
Domestic JVs 聯營	10	74	7,150	600	10.69	15.42	96.10	30.68	5,612
Joint stock 股份制	10	58	11,075	645	14.33	48.48	190.62	70.45	4,501
Foreign-funded 外資	18	54	3,216	-1,171	-8.34	-20.70	59.56	59.70	14,031
Overseas Chinese-funded 港澳台資	16	78	18,949	-1,756	-6.04	-12.65	244.50	52.27	29,090
By size 規模									
Large 大型	5	906	171,853	-321	-0.13	-0.51	189.64	75.01	252,035
Medium 中型	21	508	62,744	350	0.48	1.76	123.40	72.59	72,633
Small 小型	4,059	45	4,762	15	0.45	1.69	107.00	73.58	3,264
By regional distribution 地區分布									
Central-North 華北	71	33	5,126	709	25.68	65.81	154.94	60.96	2,759
Beijing 北京	8	8	2,366	-10	-0.19	-0.50	282.54	61.73	5,206
Tianjin 天津	8	53	5,105	-70	-1.24	-2.04	96.55	38.96	5,634
Hebei 河北	22	51	12,500	2,380	84.54	223.15	243.80	62.10	2,815
Shanxi 山西	8	21	1,298	45	6.58	10.84	63.29	39.12	684
Inner Mongolia 內蒙	25	23	752	-70	-4.19	-28.09	33.14	85.08	1,672
Northeast 東北	316	106	8,431	-739	-4.66	-21.28	79.85	78.11	15,865
Liaoning 遼寧	84	160	12,218	-2,147	-6.26	-32.60	76.18	80.79	34,277
Jilin 吉林	91	110	6,498	-262	-2.43	-5.65	59.30	56.96	10,766
Heilongjiang 黑龍江	141	70	7,423	-208	-2.54	-23.93	105.49	89.37	8,187
Central East 華東	1,928	46	5,661	115	3.83	13.51	123.96	71.55	3,005
Shanghai 上海	6	35	2,207	-572	-8.93	-132.43	63.35	93.26	6,405
Jiangsu 江蘇	344	96	9,599	-41	-0.67	-2.57	100.51	73.97	6,168
Zhejiang 浙江	100	48	8,043	-84	-1.85	-5.01	168.05	63.15	4,527
Anhui 安徽	821	36	5,987	286	13.18	43.80	165.79	69.91	2,171
Fujian 福建	164	26	2,719	-49	-3.91	-7.55	104.14	48.21	1,262
Jiangxi 江西	480	32	2,867	37	1.54	6.74	90.42	76.51	2,427
Shandong 山東	13	80	4,381	228	10.87	30.83	54.45	64.74	2,095
Central-South 中南	1,287	48	5,254	42	1.27	4.56	110.48	72.03	3,263
Henan 河南	75	44	3,968	59	1.81	7.34	90.34	75.39	3,256
Hubei 湖北	487	73	8,257	175	4.08	15.84	113.48	74.25	4,283
Hunan 湖南	487	30	2,743	-38	-2.00	-6.55	91.24	69.45	1,904
Guangdong 廣東	169	25	2,728		0.01	0.03	108.55	66.28	2,109
Guangxi 廣西	58	52	10,869	-280	-3.05	-10.13	209.43	69.93	9,201
Hainan 海南	11	53	1,541	-107	-2.26	-8.75	28.88	74.21	4,755
Southwest 西南	441	22	1,631	-49	-3.13	-11.03	74.86	71.64	1,579
Chongqing 重慶	87	15	865	-9	-2.00	20.82	54.23	109.61	437
Sichuan 四川	267	17	1,230	-40	-4.12	-20.41	70.93	79.83	963
Guizhou 貴州	38	33	1,014	-33	-1.39	-3.33	30.48	58.09	2,377
Yunnan 雲南	48	51	5,753	-190	-2.94	-8.18	112.12	64.10	6,460
Tibet 西藏									
Northwest 西北	59	29	1,404	-91	-3.90	-13.47	49.21	71.06	2,343
Shaanxi 陝西	48	29	1,593	-95	-3.81	-13.57	54.32	71.93	2,499
Gansu 甘肅	5	9	50				5.32	54.47	246
Qinghai 青海									
Ningxia 寧夏	3	60	1,803	-330	-6.25	-20.63	29.89	69.70	5,280
Xinjiang 新疆	3	16	227	57	13.60	17.35	14.47	21.60	417

Year 年份	Number of firms 企業個數	Rate of change 每年變化 (%)	Number of employees 職工人數 (人)	Rate of change 每年變化 (%)	Total revenue (mil. RMB) 總銷售收入 (百萬元)	Rate of change 每年變化 (%)	Total profit (mil. RMB) 總利潤 (百萬元)	Rate of change 每年變化 (%)
1993	3,913		147,243		12,236		226	
1994	5,599	43.09%	201,444	36.81%	14,627	19.54%	333	47.26%
1995	4,252	-24.06%	181,409	-9.95%	20,574	40.65%	363	9.17%
1996	4,102	-3.53%	196,257	8.18%	21,507	4.53%	65	-82.10%

3 Major products* 3 種主要產品 *	Output 產量	Sales volume 銷售量	Unit 單位
a) Rice 大米	81,934,262	72,102,151	ton 噸
b) Wheat Flour 小麥粉	1,450,222	1,247,191	10,000 ton 萬噸
c) Mingled Feedstuff 配合飼料	1,292,436	1,253,663	ton 噸

Top 10 firms by revenue (year founded) 收入排名前 10 家企業 (創辦年份)	City 城市	Province 省	Telephone / fax 電話 / 傳真	Number of employees 職工人數	Ownership 產業所有權	Revenue ('000 RMB) 銷售收入 (千元)	Profit ('000 RMB) (rank) 利潤 (千元) (排名)	Total assets ('000 RMB) 總資產 (千元)	Major products 主要產品
Shenyang Jia Yu Cereals Food General Company 瀋陽佳玉糧食食品總公司(1939)	Shenyang 瀋陽市	Liaoning 遼寧省	(024)25872708 (024)25850596	2,986	State-owned 國有	274,967	-49638(1653)	1,063,515	a,b
Zhangshu Grain & Oil Processing Company 樟樹糧油公司(1957)	Yichun 宜春市	Jiangxi 江西省	(0795)7340821	1,493	State-owned 國有	259,657	468(239)	399,338	b,c
Huo Pai Industry & Commerce Industrial General Co. 伙牌農工商實業公司	Yichang 宜昌市	Hubei 湖北省		308	Collectively-owned 集體	238,130	20160(1)	121,270	o
Guilin Rice Factory 桂林市大米廠(1953)	Guilin 桂林市	Guangxi 廣西	(0773)2603237 (0773)2603237	363	State-owned 國有	233,974	6882(5)	86,985	a,c
Chuzhou Chang Da Group Company 滁州市昌達集團公司(1992)	Chuzhou 滁州市	Anhui 安徽省	(0550)3911511	117	Collectively-owned 集體	191,802	4045(18)	41,853	a
Suining Grain & Oil Industrial Co. 睢寧縣糧食局糧油工業公司(1994)	Xuzhou 徐州市	Jiangsu 江蘇省	(0516)8333871 (0516)8332370	1,786	State-owned 國有	139,570	4600(16)	81,384	a,b,c
Suqian Nan Cai Xiang Grain Processing Factory 宿遷市南蔡鄉糧食加工廠(1995)	Suqian 宿遷市	Jiangsu 江蘇省		300	Collectively-owned 集體	123,710	0(1352)	267	a
Jilin City Central Grain Depot 吉林市中心糧庫(1969)	Jilin 吉林市	Jilin 吉林省	(0432)3516500 (0432)3516508	2,108	State-owned 國有	118,056	7163(4)	99,921	a,b,c
Jilin Grain & Oil Processing Factory 吉林省吉林市糧油加工廠(1977)	Jilin 吉林市	Jilin 吉林省	(0432)4841331 (0432)4844176	2,111	State-owned 國有	115,925	6355(8)	159,587	a,b,c
Xuzhou Food Bureau Huan Cheng Grain Depot 徐州市糧食局環城糧庫(1966)	Xuzhou 徐州市	Jiangsu 江蘇省	(0516)3575486	315	State-owned 國有	111,818	512(214)	21,201	c

Top 10 Cities by Production Output 產出排名前 10 位城市	Province 省	Market share 市場份額	Number of firms 企業個數
Chuzhou 滁州市	Anhui 安徽省	8.50%	173
Liu'an 六安市	Anhui 安徽省	5.97%	204
Yancheng 鹽城市	Jiangsu 江蘇省	2.93%	44
Chaohu 巢湖市	Anhui 安徽省	2.76%	103
Jiaxing 嘉興市	Zhejiang 浙江省	2.71%	23
Shenyang 瀋陽市	Liaoning 遼寧省	2.50%	15
Yueyang 岳陽市	Hunan 湖南省	2.38%	78
Suzhou 蘇州市	Jiangsu 江蘇省	2.35%	29
Huaiyin 淮陰市	Jiangsu 江蘇省	2.17%	75
Yichun 宜春市	Jiangxi 江西省	2.14%	42

10 Major Wholesalers 10 家主要批發商	City 城市	Province 省	Telephone / Fax 電話 / 傳真
Zhejiang Cereal & Oils Food Import & Export Co. Ltd. 浙江省糧油食品進出口股份有限公司	Hangzhou 杭州市	Zhejiang 浙江省	(0571)5152515 (0571)5152514
Henan Cereal & Oils Food Import & Export Company 河南省糧油食品進出口公司	Zhengzhou 鄭州市	Henan 河南省	(0371)3942915 (0371)3942790
Shanghai Land Reclamation & Cultivation Cooking Oil Mill Marketing Company 上海市農墾糧油食品經營公司	Shanghai 上海市	Shanghai 上海市	(021)64714931
Changtu Da Chang Cooking Oil Mill Trade Jointly-operated Company 昌圖縣大昌糧油貿易聯營公司	Tieling 鐵嶺市	Liaoning 遼寧省	(0410)5824099
China Vegetable Oil Company 中國植物油公司	Beijing 北京市	Beijing 北京市	(010)66038248
Zhong Liang Shandong Cooking Oil Mill Import & Export Company 中糧山東糧油進出口公司	Qingdao 青島市	Shandong 山東省	(0532)2972342 (0532)2972379
Zhejiang Cooking Oil Mill Storage & Transport Trade Company 浙江省糧油儲運貿易公司	Hangzhou 杭州市	Zhejiang 浙江省	(0571)5161408 (0571)5161411
Anhui Cereal & Oils Food Import & Export (Group) Company 安徽省糧油食品進出口(集團)公司	Hefei 合肥市	Anhui 安徽省	(0551)2653731 (0551)2652831
Shanghai Farm, Industry & Commerce Group Cooking Oil Mill General Company 上海農工商集團糧油總公司	Shanghai 上海市	Shanghai 上海市	(021)62593423 (021)62748578
Sichuan Chang Jiang Enterprise Co. Ltd. 四川省長江企業股份有限公司	Chengdu 成都市	Sichuan 四川省	(028)3339888 (028)3333896

*Also include sales by firms outside this industry.包括本行業以外廠家的銷售。"o" stands for "others". "o" 代表 "其他產品" 。

1312: Flour Milling 磨粉業

The industry accounts for 0.847% of the total revenue of China's industrial sector in 1996. The revenue growth rate of the industry is 5.6% from 1995, as compared to the growth rate of China's industrial sector, 9.51%. The rate of return on asset is 0.11%. 75.81% of all firms in the industry made a profit while 18.70% had negative returns. The top province in terms of the industry's revenue is Shandong, accounting for 14.55% of the total revenue.
本行業在1996年佔全行業總產值0.847%，行業年增長率為5.6%（全國工業年增長率9.51%）。行業的資產回報率0.11%，75.81%的企業盈利，18.70%的企業虧損。銷售收入最高的省份為山東省，佔本行業的14.55%。

	Total number of firms 企業總數	Total number of employees 職工總數	Total revenue (mil. RMB) 總銷售收入（百萬元）	Total profit (mil. RMB) 總利潤（百萬元）	Return on assets 資產利潤率 (%)	Return on equity 權益利潤率 (%)	Labour productivity ('000 RMB / worker) 勞動生產率（千元/人）	Debts / assets 資產負債率 (%)	Total assets (mil. RMB) 總資產（百萬元）
Industry Overall 行業總體	5,806	384,725	49,119	52	0.11	0.44	127.67	74.90	46,970

	Number of firms 企業個數	Average number of employees 平均職工人數	Average revenue ('000 RMB) 平均銷售收入（千元）	Average profit ('000 RMB) 平均利潤（千元）	Return on assets 資產利潤率 (%)	Return on equity 權益利潤率 (%)	Labour productivity ('000 RMB / worker) 勞動生產率（千元/人）	Average debts / assets 平均資產負債率(%)	Average Total assets ('000 RMB) 平均總資產（千元）
By ownership 產業所有權									
State-owned 國有	1,703	157	17,937	-322	-1.57	-7.73	113.98	79.72	20,570
Collectively-owned 集體	3,919	23	2,845	125	12.42	29.41	123.18	57.77	1,010
Privately-owned 私有	18	18	6,770	214	13.03	16.51	379.62	21.09	1,639
Domestic JVs 聯營	19	30	2,997	129	4.95	13.62	99.74	63.67	2,604
Joint stock 股份制	50	200	46,697	846	1.85	6.58	233.23	71.94	45,767
Foreign-funded 外資	29	170	50,571	637	0.85	2.07	298.26	59.03	75,083
Overseas Chinese-funded 港澳台資	52	203	62,640	492	0.75	1.80	308.75	58.30	65,591
By size 規模									
Large 大型	58	729	138,065	62	0.04	0.15	189.42	76.09	175,434
Medium 中型	149	386	60,871	48	0.07	0.29	157.62	75.20	67,065
Small 小型	5,567	51	5,755	7	0.15	0.60	112.79	74.34	4,814
By regional distribution 地區分布									
Central-North 華北	1,062	52	6,708	89	1.26	3.68	130.15	65.70	7,040
Beijing 北京	54	134	42,563	536	2.05	5.55	317.06	62.97	26,087
Tianjin 天津	45	106	12,856	-298	-1.63	-4.22	120.73	61.48	18,306
Hebei 河北	561	36	4,551	135	3.07	7.23	125.66	57.54	4,393
Shanxi 山西	150	51	3,077	-24	-0.45	-1.32	59.80	66.05	5,343
Inner Mongolia 內蒙	252	58	4,889	27	0.35	1.69	84.05	79.42	7,848
Northeast 東北	491	133	11,952	-469	-2.61	-15.19	89.71	82.78	17,917
Liaoning 遼寧	59	403	48,140	-2,204	-3.09	-18.21	119.49	83.02	71,270
Jilin 吉林	58	138	12,063	105	0.53	1.36	87.62	61.33	19,934
Heilongjiang 黑龍江	374	90	6,226	-284	-3.09	-30.01	69.18	89.71	9,187
Central East 華東	1,814	70	11,295	199	2.36	9.13	160.86	74.20	8,465
Shanghai 上海	19	253	73,959	743	1.47	5.55	292.70	73.49	50,457
Jiangsu 江蘇	336	103	14,300	119	1.28	5.57	138.37	77.11	9,362
Zhejiang 浙江	47	112	24,218	-257	-1.08	-3.54	215.58	69.42	23,748
Anhui 安徽	693	43	6,603	361	10.66	38.06	155.14	71.98	3,383
Fujian 福建	55	47	14,214	-895	-8.18	-20.11	304.78	59.35	10,942
Jiangxi 江西	66	76	9,632	-203	-2.15	-12.06	126.69	82.15	9,442
Shandong 山東	598	76	11,952	221	2.01	8.09	157.13	75.13	10,980
Central-South 中南	1,255	60	8,005	17	0.23	0.96	132.54	75.65	7,297
Henan 河南	922	46	4,691	56	1.20	5.13	102.24	76.53	4,696
Hubei 湖北	203	106	10,198	135	1.70	7.94	96.44	78.59	7,950
Hunan 湖南	43	44	5,485	-98	-1.51	-6.28	124.00	75.89	6,451
Guangdong 廣東	60	102	37,216	-449	-1.51	-5.87	365.51	74.29	29,716
Guangxi 廣西	25	150	45,923	-936	-2.21	-7.06	306.65	68.75	42,406
Hainan 海南	2	137	17,220	-1,790	-3.82	-31.49	126.15	87.88	46,895
Southwest 西南	378	63	6,509	-215	-3.43	-15.21	102.61	77.43	6,255
Chongqing 重慶	51	66	7,351	-505	-6.78	-31.48	110.74	78.45	7,440
Sichuan 四川	222	65	6,522	-177	-3.06	-19.82	98.95	84.54	5,785
Guizhou 貴州	43	50	4,708	-76	-1.45	-3.62	93.38	59.88	5,207
Yunnan 雲南	54	63	7,635	-193	-2.54	-8.00	120.79	68.22	7,606
Tibet 西藏	7	45	2,276	-301	-3.57	-6.69	51.06	46.67	8,451
Northwest 西北	806	46	3,884	-141	-2.98	-11.54	83.64	74.15	4,738
Shaanxi 陝西	285	48	4,529	-409	-7.80	-44.37	94.34	82.41	5,235
Gansu 甘肅	262	36	2,231	11	0.48	1.16	61.67	58.29	2,333
Qinghai 青海	34	45	5,076	-63	-1.23	-3.13	112.64	60.68	5,138
Ningxia 寧夏	46	37	3,336	-10	-0.21	-0.69	89.80	70.24	4,865
Xinjiang 新疆	179	62	5,192	12	0.16	0.64	84.27	74.62	7,356

1312: Flour Milling 磨粉業

Year 年份	Number of firms 企業個數	Rate of change 每年變化 (%)	Number of employees 職工人數 (人)	Rate of change 每年變化 (%)	Total revenue (mil. RMB) 總銷售收入 (百萬元)	Rate of change 每年變化 (%)	Total profit (mil. RMB) 總利潤 (百萬元)	Rate of change 每年變化 (%)
1993	4,834		293,547		24,155		560	
1994	5,831	20.62%	310,862	5.90%	30,995	28.32%	603	7.64%
1995	5,882	0.87%	383,359	23.32%	46,535	50.13%	803	33.15%
1996	5,806	-1.29%	384,725	0.36%	49,119	5.55%	52	-93.52%

3 Major products* 3種主要產品 *	Output 產量	Sales volume 銷售量	Unit 單位
a) Wheat Flour 小麥粉	16,056,625	13,808,697	10,000 ton 萬噸
b) Wheat Flour Product 小麥粉製品	559,053	525,510	ton 噸

Top 10 firms by revenue (year founded) 收入排名前10家企業 (創辦年份)	City 城市	Province 省	Telephone / fax 電話 / 傳真	Number of employees 職工人數	Ownership 產業所有權	Revenue ('000 RMB) 銷售收入 (千元)	Profit ('000 RMB) (rank) 利潤 (千元) (排名)	Total assets ('000 RMB) 總資產 (千元)	Major products 主要產品
Shanghai Flour Co. 上海市麵粉公司(1900)	Shanghai 上海市	Shanghai 上海市	(021)62663000 (021)62661967	2,443	State-owned 國有	862,870	20652(3)	635,241	a,b
Dalian No.3 Cereals Storing & Transporting Industrial Co. 大連市第三糧食儲運工業公司(1992)	Dalian 大連市	Liaoning 遼寧省	(0411)6601015 (0411)6601209	353	State-owned 國有	522,216	21924(2)	490,980	a
Dalian Cereals Industry General Factory 大連糧食工業總廠(1907)	Dalian 大連市	Liaoning 遼寧省	(0411)2713841 (0411)2708936	2,011	State-owned 國有	422,132	-3528(2600)	267,099	a,b
Beijing Lu He Flour Milling Co. 北京市潞河麵粉公司(1991)	Beijing 北京市	Beijing 北京市	(010)69547045 (010)69542183	751	State-owned 國有	375,425	-14234(2648)	283,674	a
Beijing Heng Tong Foods Co. Ltd. 北京恒通食品有限公司(1993)	Beijing 北京市	Beijing 北京市	(010)65063377 (010)65061257	1,214	Foreign-funded 外資	358,553	22658(1)	251,122	a
Guangzhou Nan Fang Flour Co. Ltd. 廣州市南方麵粉股份有限公司(1949)	Guangzhou 廣州市	Guangdong 廣東省	(020)85524901 (020)85525172	851	Joint stock 股份制	346,004	-7782(2638)	251,973	a
Jiangsu Wei Sang Industrial Group 維桑實業集團(1971)	Xuzhou 徐州市	Jiangsu 江蘇省	(0516)3811864 (0516)3811864	769	State-owned 國有	339,810	8050(10)	146,400	a
Ji'nan Center Flour Factory 濟南中心麵粉廠(1990)	Ji'nan 濟南市	Shandong 山東省	(0531)7964094 (0531)7964094	499	State-owned 國有	330,570	3236(33)	194,531	a
Pacific Flour & Foods (Fujian) Co. Ltd. 元洪麵粉食品(福建)有限公司(1992)	Fuzhou 福州市	Fujian 福建省	(0591)5576868 (0591)5576422	297	Overseas Chinese-funded 港澳台資	306,841	-35690(2658)	263,283	a
Harbin Grain & Oil Multiple Processing Factory 哈爾濱糧油綜合加工廠(1979)	Harbin 哈爾濱市	Heilongjiang 黑龍江省	(0451)6661065 (0451)6674341	682	State-owned 國有	294,530	-53115(2659)	718,659	b

Top 10 Cities by Production Output 產出排名前10位城市	Province 省	Market share 市場份額	Number of firms 企業個數
Beijing 北京市	Beijing 北京市	5.32%	54
Shanghai 上海市	Shanghai 上海市	2.94%	26
Fuyang 阜陽市	Anhui 安徽省	2.71%	259
Jining 濟寧市	Shandong 山東省	2.44%	84
Ji'nan 濟南市	Shandong 山東省	1.91%	42
Shenyang 瀋陽市	Liaoning 遼寧省	1.78%	5
Xuzhou 徐州市	Jiangsu 江蘇省	1.54%	60
Tianjin 天津市	Tianjin 天津市	1.50%	57
Jiangmen 江門市	Guangdong 廣東省	1.45%	9
Dalian 大連市	Liaoning 遼寧省	1.39%	7

10 Major Wholesalers 10家主要批發商	City 城市	Province 省	Telephone / Fax 電話 / 傳真
Zhejiang Cereal & Oils Food Import & Export Co. Ltd. 浙江省糧油食品進出口股份有限公司	Hangzhou 杭州市	Zhejiang 浙江省	(0571)5152515 (0571)5152514
Henan Cereal & Oils Food Import & Export Company 河南省糧油食品進出口公司	Zhengzhou 鄭州市	Henan 河南省	(0371)3942915 (0371)3942790
Shanghai Land Reclamation & Cultivation Cooking Oil Mill Marketing Company 上海市農墾糧油食品經營公司	Shanghai 上海市	Shanghai 上海市	(021)64714931
Changtu Da Chang Cooking Oil Mill Trade Jointly-operated Company 昌圖縣大昌糧油貿易聯營公司	Tieling 鐵嶺市	Liaoning 遼寧省	(0410)5824099
China Vegetable Oil Company 中國植物油公司	Beijing 北京市	Beijing 北京市	(010)66038248
Zhong Liang Shandong Cooking Oil Mill Import & Export Company 中糧山東糧油進出口公司	Qingdao 青島市	Shandong 山東省	(0532)2972342 (0532)2972379
Zhejiang Cooking Oil Mill Storage & Transport Trade Company 浙江省糧油儲運貿易公司	Hangzhou 杭州市	Zhejiang 浙江省	(0571)5161408 (0571)5161411
Anhui Cereal & Oils Food Import & Export (Group) Company 安徽省糧油食品進出口(集團)公司	Hefei 合肥市	Anhui 安徽省	(0551)2653731 (0551)2652831
Shanghai Farm, Industry & Commerce Group Cooking Oil Mill General Company 上海農工商集團糧油總公司	Shanghai 上海市	Shanghai 上海市	(021)62593423 (021)62748578
Sichuan Chang Jiang Enterprise Co. Ltd. 四川省長江企業股份有限公司	Chengdu 成都市	Sichuan 四川省	(028)3339888 (028)3333896

*Also include sales by firms outside this industry.包括本行業以外廠家的銷售。"o" stands for "others". "o" 代表"其他產品"。

1313: Rice and Flour Products 麵米製品業

The industry accounts for 0.093% of the total revenue of China's industrial sector in 1996. The revenue growth rate of the industry is 5.7% from 1995, as compared to the growth rate of China's industrial sector, 9.51%. The rate of return on asset is -2.62%. 64.92% of all firms in the industry made a profit while 28.76% had negative returns. The top province in terms of the industry's revenue is Guangdong, accounting for 26.98% of the total revenue.
本行業在1996年佔全行業總產值0.093%，行業年增長率為5.7%（全國工業年增長率9.51%）。行業的資產回報率-2.62%，64.92%的企業盈利，28.76%的企業虧損。銷售收入最高的省份為廣東省，佔本行業的26.98%。

	Total number of firms 企業總數	Total number of employees 職工總數	Total revenue (mil. RMB) 總銷售收入（百萬元）	Total profit (mil. RMB) 總利潤（百萬元）	Return on assets 資產利潤率 (%)	Return on equity 權益利潤率 (%)	Labour productivity ('000 RMB / worker) 勞動生產率（千元/人）	Debts / assets 資產負債率 (%)	Total assets (mil. RMB) 總資產（百萬元）
Industry Overall 行業總體	1,648	83,251	5,377	-157	-2.62	-10.84	64.59	75.79	5,993

	Number of firms 企業個數	Average number of employees 平均職工人數	Average revenue ('000 RMB) 平均銷售收入（千元）	Average profit ('000 RMB) 平均利潤（千元）	Return on assets 資產利潤率 (%)	Return on equity 權益利潤率 (%)	Labour productivity ('000 RMB / worker) 勞動生產率（千元/人）	Average debts / assets 平均資產負債率(%)	Average Total assets ('000 RMB) 平均總資產（千元）
By ownership 產業所有權									
State-owned 國有	516	92	5,519	-248	-3.53	-17.02	59.98	79.28	7,033
Collectively-owned 集體	1,064	29	1,368	-4	-0.46	-1.33	47.90	65.38	789
Privately-owned 私有	7	26	456	-1	-0.12	-0.19	17.36	39.80	1,157
Domestic JVs 聯營	6	137	11,885	-1	-0.02	-0.07	86.65	69.53	7,197
Joint stock 股份制	7	98	3,821	84	0.79	14.26	39.04	94.47	10,699
Foreign-funded 外資	20	58	3,676	0	0.00	0.01	63.71	65.76	5,961
Overseas Chinese-funded 港澳台資	28	104	32,100	-918	-2.01	-7.44	308.02	73.00	45,682
By size 規模									
Large 大型	1	544	19,624	380	0.95	1.14	36.07	16.24	39,806
Medium 中型	11	531	30,800	748	1.70	5.90	57.96	71.26	44,124
Small 小型	1,620	47	3,098	-102	-3.03	-12.96	65.34	76.62	3,375
By regional distribution 地區分布									
Central-North 華北	132	40	1,423	-79	-3.19	-15.42	35.29	79.34	2,494
Beijing 北京	26	15	600	-124	-9.61	-52.61	40.10	81.73	1,288
Tianjin 天津	8	94	2,006	-323	-7.02	-14.21	21.46	50.56	4,591
Hebei 河北	38	36	1,761	-4	-0.14	-0.67	49.30	79.23	2,659
Shanxi 山西	29	63	2,191	-93	-2.47	-15.18	34.75	83.73	3,771
Inner Mongolia 內蒙	31	32	831	-60	-3.81	-37.30	25.75	89.77	1,568
Northeast 東北	132	66	2,441	-4	-0.12	-0.43	37.00	71.50	3,461
Liaoning 遼寧	25	81	2,631	-181	-4.80	-10.10	32.42	52.42	3,772
Jilin 吉林	34	73	3,637	37	0.78	2.50	49.71	68.77	4,715
Heilongjiang 黑龍江	73	57	1,818	37	1.35	7.71	31.67	82.56	2,770
Central East 華東	441	57	4,002	-63	-1.76	-7.81	69.63	77.43	3,572
Shanghai 上海	11	73	3,707	-346	-7.57	-48.91	50.85	84.53	4,577
Jiangsu 江蘇	57	81	5,185	-88	-1.98	-15.35	64.29	87.11	4,468
Zhejiang 浙江	43	60	8,680	-320	-5.08	-19.17	143.84	73.50	6,291
Anhui 安徽	80	72	5,037	132	3.32	14.13	70.09	76.53	3,981
Fujian 福建	103	36	1,643	-55	-3.35	-8.66	45.66	61.28	1,642
Jiangxi 江西	96	30	1,375	-31	-2.36	-9.47	45.38	75.12	1,313
Shandong 山東	51	98	6,884	-139	-1.84	-9.91	70.40	81.47	7,569
Central-South 中南	359	64	6,448	-211	-2.78	-12.70	100.77	78.09	7,599
Henan 河南	66	64	3,561	74	2.16	6.05	55.45	64.33	3,417
Hubei 湖北	61	68	4,800	-26	-0.74	-3.37	71.03	78.16	3,559
Hunan 湖南	71	28	1,702	-92	-4.84	-22.02	60.72	78.00	1,900
Guangdong 廣東	104	93	13,950	-548	-3.26	-16.78	149.99	80.57	16,819
Guangxi 廣西	48	50	3,105	-288	-9.90	-45.02	62.51	78.01	2,913
Hainan 海南	9	63	7,391	-196	-0.67	-2.53	117.73	73.41	29,087
Southwest 西南	503	34	1,321	-69	-4.66	-13.87	39.14	66.40	1,474
Chongqing 重慶	159	37	1,267	-103	-6.07	-18.72	33.98	67.55	1,690
Sichuan 四川	261	25	1,282	-50	-5.00	-18.33	50.16	72.71	1,000
Guizhou 貴州	41	56	902	9	0.80	1.62	16.08	50.50	1,155
Yunnan 雲南	37	48	2,422	-152	-3.75	-9.98	50.59	62.47	4,055
Tibet 西藏	4	30	233	-13	-0.40	-0.49	7.88	16.68	3,088
Northwest 西北	81	48	1,514	-99	-4.94	-15.92	31.27	69.01	2,000
Shaanxi 陝西	39	44	1,364	-105	-5.70	-29.50	30.82	80.69	1,850
Gansu 甘肅	11	71	827	-129	-3.92	-9.16	11.68	57.26	3,293
Qinghai 青海	6	50	3,850	-217	-9.14	-16.67	77.52	45.15	2,370
Ningxia 寧夏	3	70	1,703	17	0.85	1.38	24.33	38.71	1,963
Xinjiang 新疆	22	41	1,462	-55	-3.64	-12.99	35.34	72.01	1,525

1313: Rice and Flour Products 麵米製品業

Year 年份	Number of firms 企業個數	Rate of change 每年變化 (%)	Number of employees 職工人數 (人)	Rate of change 每年變化 (%)	Total revenue (mil. RMB) 總銷售收入 (百萬元)	Rate of change 每年變化 (%)	Total profit (mil. RMB) 總利潤 (百萬元)	Rate of change 每年變化 (%)
1993	1,824		95,659		4,344		-1	
1994	2,017	10.58%	103,078	7.76%	5,895	35.70%	476	56351.59%
1995	1,676	-16.91%	94,862	-7.97%	5,086	-13.72%	213	-55.27%
1996	1,648	-1.67%	83,251	-12.24%	5,377	5.72%	-157	-173.66%

3 Major products* 3 種主要產品 *	Output 產量	Sales volume 銷售量	Unit 單位
a) Rice Made Products 米製品	59,220	58,627	ton 噸
b) Wheat Flour Product 小麥粉製品	277,699	261,037	ton 噸

Top 10 firms by revenue (year founded) 收入排名前 10 家企業 (創辦年份)	City 城市	Province 省	Telephone / fax 電話 / 傳真	Number of employees 職工人數	Ownership 產業所有權	Revenue ('000 RMB) 銷售收入 (千元)	Profit ('000 RMB) (rank) 利潤（千元）(排名)	Total assets ('000 RMB) 總資產 (千元)	Major products 主要產品
She Kou Lamsoon Flour Co. Ltd. 蛇口南順麵粉有限公司(1990)	Shenzhen 深圳市	Guangdong 廣東省	(0755)6681092 (0755)6682801	133	Overseas Chinese-funded 港澳台資	353,444	-10400(442)	650,088	o
Bai Yan Grain & Oil Processing Industrial Company 白燕糧油實業公司(1995)	Foshan 佛山市	Guangdong 廣東省	(0757)8886065 (0757)8886057	217	State-owned 國有	215,204	1861(5)	101,022	o
Zhaodong Gang Qiao Food Company 肇東市港橋食品公司(1990)	Suihua 綏化市	Heilongjiang 黑龍江省	(0455)7710428	368	State-owned 國有	164,043	3024(3)	25,265	o
Da Cheng Foods (She Kou) Co. Ltd. 大成食品(蛇口)有限公司(1991)	Shenzhen 深圳市	Guangdong 廣東省	(0755)6691298 (0755)6696285	279	Overseas Chinese-funded 港澳台資	125,739	-5161(438)	191,033	o
Shaoguan Flour Factory 韶關市麵粉廠(1950)	Shaoguan 韶關市	Guangdong 廣東省	(0751)8777994 (0751)8777520	285	State-owned 國有	77,331	5(224)	72,482	b
Zhejiang Qian Wang Industrial Co. 浙江錢王實業公司(1994)	Hangzhou 杭州市	Zhejiang 浙江省	(0571)3721628 (0571)3715718	301	State-owned 國有	69,074	-1198(395)	35,376	o
Jiaxing Flour Factory 嘉興麵粉廠(1972)	Jiaxing 嘉興市	Zhejiang 浙江省	(0573)2085889	67	State-owned 國有	65,235	303(56)	34,422	o
Anhui Shuang Dun Food Development General Company 安徽省雙墩食品發展總公司(1985)	Hefei 合肥市	Anhui 安徽省	(0551)6694215	450	Collectively-owned 集體	50,070	3100(2)	20,115	o
Nanyang Kang Yuan Grain & Oil Food Processing Co. Ltd. 南陽康元糧油食品加工有限公司(1988)	Nanyang 南陽市	Henan 河南省	(0377)3552045 (0377)3551536	154	Foreign-funded 外資	49,230	-1961(420)	43,397	b
Ji'nan Licheng No.2 Flour Factory 濟南市歷城區第二麵粉廠(1984)	Ji'nan 濟南市	Shandong 山東省	(0531)8991591	167	State-owned 國有	48,220	330(52)	28,829	o

Top 10 Cities by Production Output 產出排名前 10 位城市	Province 省	Market share 市場份額	Number of firms 企業個數
Shanghai 上海市	Shanghai 上海市	5.37%	51
Huaiyin 淮陰市	Jiangsu 江蘇省	4.14%	23
Pingxiang 憑祥市	Guangxi 廣西	3.12%	2
Guangzhou 廣州市	Guangdong 廣東省	3.09%	22
Jiangmen 江門市	Guangdong 廣東省	2.58%	8
Zhaoqing 肇慶市	Guangdong 廣東省	2.36%	14
Shenzhen 深圳市	Guangdong 廣東省	2.18%	2
Nanyang 南陽市	Henan 河南省	2.09%	15
Dongguan 東莞市	Guangdong 廣東省	1.79%	6
Weifang 濰坊市	Shandong 山東省	1.70%	5

10 Major Wholesalers 10 家主要批發商	City 城市	Province 省	Telephone / Fax 電話 / 傳真
Zhejiang Cereal & Oils Food Import & Export Co. Ltd. 浙江省糧油食品進出口股份有限公司	Hangzhou 杭州市	Zhejiang 浙江省	(0571)5152515 (0571)5152514
Henan Cereal & Oils Food Import & Export Company 河南省糧油食品進出口公司	Zhengzhou 鄭州市	Henan 河南省	(0371)3942915 (0371)3942790
Shanghai Land Reclamation & Cultivation Cooking Oil Mill Marketing Company 上海市農墾糧油食品經營公司	Shanghai 上海市	Shanghai 上海市	(021)64714931
Changtu Da Chang Cooking Oil Mill Trade Jointly-operated Company 昌圖縣大昌糧油貿易聯營公司	Tieling 鐵嶺市	Liaoning 遼寧省	(0410)5824099
China Vegetable Oil Company 中國植物油公司	Beijing 北京市	Beijing 北京市	(010)66038248
Zhong Liang Shandong Cooking Oil Mill Import & Export Company 中糧山東糧油進出口公司	Qingdao 青島市	Shandong 山東省	(0532)2972342 (0532)2972379
Zhejiang Cooking Oil Mill Storage & Transport Trade Company 浙江省糧油儲運貿易公司	Hangzhou 杭州市	Zhejiang 浙江省	(0571)5161408 (0571)5161411
Anhui Cereal & Oils Food Import & Export (Group) Company 安徽省糧油食品進出口(集團)公司	Hefei 合肥市	Anhui 安徽省	(0551)2653731 (0551)2652831
Shanghai Farm, Industry & Commerce Group Cooking Oil Mill General Company 上海農工商集團糧油總公司	Shanghai 上海市	Shanghai 上海市	(021)62593423 (021)62748578
Sichuan Chang Jiang Enterprise Co. Ltd. 四川省長江企業股份有限公司	Chengdu 成都市	Sichuan 四川省	(028)3339888 (028)3333896

*Also include sales by firms outside this industry.包括本行業以外廠家的銷售。"o" stands for "others". "o" 代表 "其他產品"。

1314: Mixed Feed 配合及混合飼料製造業

The industry accounts for 0.940% of the total revenue of China's industrial sector in 1996. The revenue growth rate of the industry is 1.3% from 1995, as compared to the growth rate of China's industrial sector, 9.51%. The rate of return on asset is 1.44%. 61.69% of all firms in the industry made a profit while 31.79% had negative returns. The top province in terms of the industry's revenue is Guangdong, accounting for 20.91% of the total revenue.
本行業在1996年佔全行業總產值0.940%，行業年增長率為1.3%（全國工業年增長率9.51%）。行業的資產回報率1.44%，61.69%的企業盈利，31.79%的企業虧損。銷售收入最高的省份為廣東省，佔本行業的20.91%。

	Total number of firms 企業總數	Total number of employees 職工總數	Total revenue (mil. RMB) 總銷售收入（百萬元）	Total profit (mil. RMB) 總利潤（百萬元）	Return on assets 資產利潤率 (%)	Return on equity 權益利潤率 (%)	Labour productivity ('000 RMB / worker) 勞動生產率（千元/人）	Debts / assets 資產負債率 (%)	Total assets (mil. RMB) 總資產（百萬元）
Industry Overall 行業總體	4,215	226,550	54,485	523	1.44	4.72	240.50	69.43	36,244

	Number of firms 企業個數	Average number of employees 平均職工人數	Average revenue ('000 RMB) 平均銷售收入（千元）	Average profit ('000 RMB) 平均利潤（千元）	Return on assets 資產利潤率 (%)	Return on equity 權益利潤率 (%)	Labour productivity ('000 RMB / worker) 勞動生產率（千元/人）	Average debts / assets 平均資產負債率(%)	Average Total assets ('000 RMB) 平均總資產（千元）
By ownership 產業所有權									
State-owned 國有	1,964	62	9,460	-186	-2.24	-10.24	151.72	78.08	8,302
Collectively-owned 集體	1,824	32	5,376	94	3.68	10.53	170.38	65.08	2,552
Privately-owned 私有	43	117	44,454	1,129	8.32	19.45	380.33	57.24	13,569
Domestic JVs 聯營	71	83	36,487	642	4.64	9.92	437.68	53.19	13,834
Joint stock 股份制	56	92	40,310	762	3.59	8.32	440.12	56.87	21,235
Foreign-funded 外資	140	156	102,671	3,643	5.29	14.30	658.30	63.00	68,866
Overseas Chinese-funded 港澳台資	110	81	44,776	648	2.51	6.70	551.43	62.61	25,859
By size 規模									
Large 大型	8	503	347,815	13,895	5.34	13.32	692.00	59.92	260,216
Medium 中型	62	241	122,762	1,600	2.10	6.39	508.74	67.08	76,049
Small 小型	4,100	50	10,753	76	1.06	3.60	213.12	70.48	7,182
By regional distribution 地區分布									
Central-North 華北	672	41	7,245	35	0.55	2.31	176.25	76.01	6,279
Beijing 北京	141	39	10,484	48	0.53	2.36	268.13	77.66	9,192
Tianjin 天津	44	52	18,833	192	1.07	3.79	362.01	71.80	17,971
Hebei 河北	246	39	8,022	186	3.84	15.20	203.88	74.70	4,832
Shanxi 山西	110	33	2,728	-58	-1.57	-6.00	81.88	73.88	3,674
Inner Mongolia 內蒙	131	49	2,203	-239	-5.80	-33.50	44.54	82.68	4,120
Northeast 東北	520	54	7,708	-35	-0.46	-2.11	141.77	78.16	7,557
Liaoning 遼寧	175	52	9,657	61	0.69	2.72	184.59	74.52	8,728
Jilin 吉林	142	56	7,581	-27	-0.44	-2.64	135.04	83.38	6,118
Heilongjiang 黑龍江	203	55	6,117	-123	-1.62	-7.66	111.41	78.82	7,554
Central East 華東	1,192	65	13,484	216	2.36	6.36	208.38	62.91	9,158
Shanghai 上海	50	78	26,103	248	1.70	4.30	334.73	60.45	14,593
Jiangsu 江蘇	195	80	18,636	306	2.79	8.21	233.00	66.04	10,987
Zhejiang 浙江	185	51	17,380	133	1.55	3.99	337.91	61.18	8,613
Anhui 安徽	198	54	8,777	176	2.29	7.72	162.93	70.28	7,668
Fujian 福建	167	31	8,930	257	4.27	8.77	285.00	51.31	6,027
Jiangxi 江西	210	54	8,840	132	1.81	6.24	165.18	70.93	7,276
Shandong 山東	187	112	15,150	296	2.31	5.39	134.99	57.10	12,821
Central-South 中南	1,026	58	22,700	265	2.17	6.93	389.28	68.68	12,221
Henan 河南	196	67	12,504	205	2.40	7.40	187.25	67.65	8,564
Hubei 湖北	167	68	11,065	19	0.22	0.82	162.13	73.09	8,520
Hunan 湖南	336	45	11,147	68	0.88	2.77	248.77	68.39	7,741
Guangdong 廣東	166	73	68,641	1,174	3.88	12.27	945.04	68.37	30,260
Guangxi 廣西	152	50	22,967	206	2.01	5.70	456.34	64.74	10,236
Hainan 海南	9	65	40,102	-2,247	-7.85	-47.82	621.20	83.58	28,603
Southwest 西南	545	46	9,669	25	0.38	1.38	212.00	72.78	6,632
Chongqing 重慶	87	41	7,441	1	0.01	0.05	178.43	76.28	5,574
Sichuan 四川	309	51	11,154	18	0.25	0.88	218.41	72.00	7,193
Guizhou 貴州	99	30	2,343	-53	-2.00	-5.99	77.10	66.63	2,633
Yunnan 雲南	49	51	19,078	268	2.05	8.31	372.74	75.31	13,055
Tibet 西藏									
Northwest 西北	260	34	3,752	-100	-2.53	-10.43	110.45	75.73	3,948
Shaanxi 陝西	95	39	4,075	-254	-5.70	-30.59	105.78	81.37	4,449
Gansu 甘肅	72	29	1,568	-84	-3.57	-10.53	53.55	66.09	2,353
Qinghai 青海	15	32	2,331	-167	-6.28	-15.03	71.93	58.24	2,655
Ningxia 寧夏	20	29	2,880	-145	-3.99	-17.82	101.05	77.61	3,624
Xinjiang 新疆	58	35	6,604	165	2.96	11.92	190.66	75.13	5,554

1314: Mixed Feed 配合及混合飼料製造業

Year 年份	Number of firms 企業個數	Rate of change 每年變化 (%)	Number of employees 職工人數 (人)	Rate of change 每年變化 (%)	Total revenue (mil. RMB) 總銷售收入 (百萬元)	Rate of change 每年變化 (%)	Total profit (mil. RMB) 總利潤 (百萬元)	Rate of change 每年變化 (%)
1993	3,406		166,456		22,633		158	
1994	3,739	9.78%	193,131	16.03%	33,111	46.30%	718	355.04%
1995	4,220	12.86%	225,159	16.58%	53,788	62.44%	1,042	45.21%
1996	4,215	-0.12%	226,550	0.62%	54,485	1.30%	523	-49.81%

3 Major products* 3 種主要產品 *	Output 產量	Sales volume 銷售量	Unit 單位
a) Mingled Feedstuff 配合飼料	26,112,590	25,329,213	ton 噸
b) Concentrated Feedstuff 濃縮飼料	1,220,954	1,184,325	ton 噸
c) Mixed Feedstuff 混合飼料	12,807,279	12,935,352	ton 噸

Top 10 firms by revenue (year founded) 收入排名前 10 家企業 (創辦年份)	City 城市	Province 省	Telephone / fax 電話 / 傳真	Number of employees 職工人數	Ownership 產業所有權	Revenue ('000 RMB) 銷售收入 (千元)	Profit ('000 RMB) (rank) 利潤 (千元) (排名)	Total assets ('000 RMB) 總資產 (千元)	Major products 主要產品
Guangdong Chia Tai Conti Co. Ltd. 廣東正大康地有限公司(1985)	Guangzhou 廣州市	Guangdong 廣東省	(020)82300823 (020)82309166	250	Foreign-funded 外資	763,731	41860(1)	435,027	o
Chia Tai Conti (She Kou) Co. Ltd. 正大康地(蛇口)有限公司(1991)	Shenzhen 深圳市	Guangdong 廣東省	(0755)6851238 (0755)6688564	127	Foreign-funded 外資	754,545	2915(90)	355,486	a,b
Chia Tai Conti (Shenzhen) Co. Ltd. 正大康地(深圳)有限公司(1983)	Shenzhen 深圳市	Guangdong 廣東省	(0755)6630422 (0755)6630528	535	Foreign-funded 外資	718,504	27272(8)	519,932	a,b,c
Guangdong Heng Chang Industrial Ltd. Jiu Jiang Feed Factory 廣東恒昌股份九江飼料廠(1984)	Foshan 佛山市	Guangdong 廣東省	(0757)6556688 (0757)6558164	197	State-owned 國有	608,467	19066(16)	111,833	a,b
Nantong Chia Tai Co. Ltd. 南通正大有限公司(1990)	Nantong 南通市	Jiangsu 江蘇省	(0513)4588888 (0513)4589898	584	Overseas Chinese-funded 港澳台資	579,998	34171(4)	284,225	a
Chengdu Xi Wang Feed No.1 Factory 新津希望飼料一廠(1988)	Chengdu 成都市	Sichuan 四川省		465	Collectively-owned 集體	566,724	37594(3)	129,520	a
Tianjin Chia Tai Feed Science & Technology Co. Ltd. 天津正大飼料科技有限公司(1992)	Tianjin 天津市	Tianjin 天津市	(022)5324550 (022)5328454	265	Foreign-funded 外資	545,169	38148(2)	389,114	c
Qingdao Chia Tai Co. Ltd. 青島市正大有限公司(1992)	Qingdao 青島市	Shandong 山東省	(0532)4844989 (0532)4844695	1,942	Foreign-funded 外資	537,760	29340(7)	588,070	a
Guiping Xin Gui Feed Company 桂平市新桂飼料公司(1993)	Guiping 桂平市	Guangxi 廣西	(0775)3383047	54	Foreign-funded 外資	512,655	231(481)	135,425	a
Guangdong Guan Hua Feed Industrial Company 廣東冠華飼料實業公司(1988)	Foshan 佛山市	Guangdong 廣東省	(0757)6624569 (0757)6625179	375	Collectively-owned 集體	500,908	20793(14)	190,412	a

Top 10 Cities by Production Output 產出排名前 10 位城市	Province 省	Market share 市場份額	Number of firms 企業個數
Shanghai 上海市	Shanghai 上海市	5.55%	100
Beijing 北京市	Beijing 北京市	4.18%	128
Yueyang 岳陽市	Hunan 湖南省	3.51%	56
Jiangmen 江門市	Guangdong 廣東省	3.05%	17
Foshan 佛山市	Guangdong 廣東省	3.00%	20
Shenzhen 深圳市	Guangdong 廣東省	2.99%	7
Guangzhou 廣州市	Guangdong 廣東省	2.92%	22
Nanchang 南昌市	Jiangxi 江西省	2.32%	27
Jiaxing 嘉興市	Zhejiang 浙江省	2.21%	30
Huaiyin 淮陰市	Jiangsu 江蘇省	2.00%	26

10 Major Wholesalers 10 家主要批發商	City 城市	Province 省	Telephone / Fax 電話 / 傳真
China Agricultural Machinery Hua Bei Company 中國農業機械華北公司	Tianjin 天津市	Tianjin 天津市	(022)23394240 (022)23304247
Shandong Agriculture Means of Production Company 山東省農業生產資料公司	Ji'nan 濟南市	Shandong 山東省	(0531)8957052 (0531)8957142
Yantai Agriculture Means of Production General Company 煙台市農業生產資料總公司	Yantai 煙台市	Shandong 山東省	(0535)6216668 (0535)6211348
Sichuan Agriculture Means of Production General Company 四川省農業生產資料總公司	Chengdu 成都市	Sichuan 四川省	(028)6751135 (028)6751646
Heilongjiang Agriculture Means of Production Company 黑龍江省農業生產資料公司	Harbin 哈爾濱市	Heilongjiang 黑龍江省	(0451)8989948 (0451)8382367
Shannxi Agriculture Means of Production General Company 陝西省農業生產資料總公司	Xi'an 西安市	Shaanxi 陝西省	(029)7422104 (029)7411799
Gansu Agriculture Means of Production General Company 甘肅省農業生產資料總公司	Lanzhou 蘭州市	Gansu 甘肅省	(0931)8822971
Yitong Man Zu Autonomous County Agricultural Goods & Materials Co. Ltd. 伊通滿族自治縣農用物資有限責任公司	Siping 四平市	Jilin 吉林省	(0434)4223146
Langfang Agriculture Means of Production Company 廊坊市農業生產資料公司	Langfang 廊坊市	Hebei 河北省	(0316)2013148
Anhui Agriculture Means of Production Company 安徽省農業生產資料公司	Hefei 合肥市	Anhui 安徽省	(0551)2656541 (0551)2655720

*Also include sales by firms outside this industry.包括本行業以外廠家的銷售。"o" stands for "others". "o" 代表 "其他產品" 。

1315: Protein Feed 蛋白飼料製造業

The industry accounts for 0.020% of the total revenue of China's industrial sector in 1996. The revenue growth rate of the industry is -7.4% from 1995, as compared to the growth rate of China's industrial sector, 9.51%. The rate of return on asset is -2.97%. 69.55% of all firms in the industry made a profit while 17.55% had negative returns. The top province in terms of the industry's revenue is Liaoning, accounting for 31.90% of the total revenue.
本行業在1996年佔全行業總產值0.020%，行業年增長率為-7.4%（全國工業年增長率9.51%）。行業的資產回報率-2.97%，69.55%的企業盈利，17.55%的企業虧損。銷售收入最高的省份為遼寧省，佔本行業的31.90%。

	Total number of firms 企業總數	Total number of employees 職工總數	Total revenue (mil. RMB) 總銷售收入（百萬元）	Total profit (mil. RMB) 總利潤（百萬元）	Return on assets 資產利潤率 (%)	Return on equity 權益利潤率 (%)	Labour productivity ('000 RMB / worker) 勞動生產率（千元/人）	Debts / assets 資產負債率 (%)	Total assets (mil. RMB) 總資產（百萬元）
Industry Overall 行業總體	262	8,666	1,168	-32	-2.97	-14.73	134.78	79.81	1,066

	Number of firms 企業個數	Average number of employees 平均職工人數	Average revenue ('000 RMB) 平均銷售收入（千元）	Average profit ('000 RMB) 平均利潤（千元）	Return on assets 資產利潤率 (%)	Return on equity 權益利潤率 (%)	Labour productivity ('000 RMB / worker) 勞動生產率（千元/人）	Average debts / assets 平均資產負債率(%)	Average Total assets ('000 RMB) 平均總資產（千元）
By ownership 產業所有權									
State-owned 國有	39	40	1,513	-51	-2.17	-15.38	37.87	85.87	2,359
Collectively-owned 集體	196	30	3,347	257	11.62	55.71	112.24	79.14	2,213
Privately-owned 私有	2	11	1,153	-90	-58.58	-172.41	109.86	66.02	154
Domestic JVs 聯營	6	44	7,032	-171	-1.85	-4.95	159.81	62.52	9,222
Joint stock 股份制	2	60	5,093	-3	-0.07	-0.12	84.88	40.07	4,341
Foreign-funded 外資	9	74	41,728	-8,868	-17.88	-109.34	566.45	83.65	49,592
Overseas Chinese-funded 港澳台資	9	29	2,567	69	2.09	4.95	89.55	57.81	3,294
By size 規模									
Large 大型	1	169	261,688	-77,950	-20.92	-169.49	1548.45	87.65	372,542
Medium 中型									
Small 小型	250	33	3,627	184	6.62	27.18	108.95	75.63	2,775
By regional distribution 地區分布									
Central-North 華北	50	35	2,879	143	5.06	14.98	81.82	66.23	2,836
Beijing 北京	5	18	954	8	0.34	2.52	51.85	86.57	2,368
Tianjin 天津	1	10	1,860				186.00	90.99	2,220
Hebei 河北	29	38	3,962	101	3.48	10.58	102.96	67.13	2,907
Shanxi 山西	5	43	3,542	834	15.86	25.82	81.61	38.59	5,260
Inner Mongolia 內蒙	10	32	469	3	0.18	1.35	14.48	86.97	1,712
Northeast 東北	40	38	12,823	-1,504	-10.09	-96.47	341.93	89.54	14,911
Liaoning 遼寧	17	37	21,915	-3,934	-13.32	-303.86	594.18	95.62	29,538
Jilin 吉林	9	30	1,772	239	6.13	12.91	59.51	52.54	3,900
Heilongjiang 黑龍江	14	43	8,886	326	7.70	19.23	205.62	59.95	4,229
Central East 華東	59	44	5,319	280	10.38	25.93	119.68	59.97	2,699
Shanghai 上海	4	76	8,405	508	10.35	15.30	110.59	32.33	4,903
Jiangsu 江蘇	12	31	3,192	-18	-0.85	-8.91	101.59	90.47	2,159
Zhejiang 浙江	8	97	7,609	125	3.94	17.15	78.85	76.98	3,171
Anhui 安徽	7	28	3,763	384	34.27	84.86	136.48	59.62	1,121
Fujian 福建	1	25	4,180	150	12.82	20.55	167.20	38.46	1,170
Jiangxi 江西	5	62	4,534	24	1.30	2.36	72.66	44.84	1,842
Shandong 山東	22	29	5,810	489	15.34	32.41	200.05	52.66	3,188
Central-South 中南	52	21	2,738	140	7.71	26.04	128.71	70.39	1,811
Henan 河南	27	23	1,579	79	5.26	13.46	67.97	60.93	1,493
Hubei 湖北	6	28	2,610	103	6.78	21.75	94.91	68.85	1,525
Hunan 湖南	10	15	2,095	117	8.11	29.40	143.49	72.42	1,443
Guangdong 廣東	7	20	3,250	-36	-0.99	-5.81	164.86	82.90	3,591
Guangxi 廣西	2	15	20,185	1,800	70.31	360.00	1345.67	80.47	2,560
Hainan 海南									
Southwest 西南	51	29	988	-53	-4.23	-23.01	33.83	81.60	1,262
Chongqing 重慶	3	16	133	-93	-39.97	1275.78	8.20	103.13	232
Sichuan 四川	32	36	1,318	-66	-4.18	-48.89	36.59	91.46	1,588
Guizhou 貴州	12	16	488	-18	-2.22	-3.67	31.17	39.42	827
Yunnan 雲南	3	23	477				20.72	34.08	743
Tibet 西藏									
Northwest 西北	10	19	502	21	2.17	15.00	26.42	85.42	967
Shaanxi 陝西	2	16	115	65	6.22	162.50	7.42	96.17	1,045
Gansu 甘肅	3	13	273	20	3.61	16.67	21.58	78.31	553
Qinghai 青海									
Ningxia 寧夏	1	20	160	10	14.29	25.00	8.00	42.86	70
Xinjiang 新疆	4	25	953	3	0.17	1.09	37.72	84.10	1,463

1315: Protein Feed 蛋白飼料製造業

Year 年份	Number of firms 企業個數	Rate of change 每年變化 (%)	Number of employees 職工人數 (人)	Rate of change 每年變化 (%)	Total revenue (mil. RMB) 總銷售收入 (百萬元)	Rate of change 每年變化 (%)	Total profit (mil. RMB) 總利潤 (百萬元)	Rate of change 每年變化 (%)
1993	185		4,978		356		5	
1994	217	17.30%	7,292	46.48%	562	57.85%	9	90.87%
1995	295	35.94%	12,219	67.57%	1,262	124.73%	-17	-290.54%
1996	262	-11.19%	8,666	-29.08%	1,168	-7.45%	-32	-83.89%

3 Major products* 3 種主要產品 *	Output 產量	Sales volume 銷售量	Unit 單位
a) Protein Feedstuff 蛋白質飼料	637,377	427,043	ton 噸
b) Mingled Feedstuff 配合飼料	149,546	145,060	ton 噸
c) Mixed Feedstuff 混合飼料	65,277	65,930	ton 噸

Top 10 firms by revenue (year founded) 收入排名前 10 家企業 (創辦年份)	City 城市	Province 省	Telephone / fax 電話 / 傳真	Number of employees 職工人數	Ownership 產業所有權	Revenue ('000 RMB) 銷售收入 (千元)	Profit ('000 RMB) (rank) 利潤 (千元) (排名)	Total assets ('000 RMB) 總資產 (千元)	Major products 主要產品
Dalian Nisshin Oil Mills Ltd. 大連日清製油有限公司(1990)	Dalian 大連市	Liaoning 遼寧省	(0411)7611515 (0411)7612327	228	Foreign-funded 外資	335,007	-69311(93)	460,294	a
Guanghan Chia Tai Feed Science & Technology Co. Ltd. 廣漢市正大飼料科技有限公司(1995)	Deyang 德陽市	Sichuan 四川省	(0838)5400247	165	Foreign-funded 外資	135,979	26544(1)	128,245	o
Yulin Hui Feng Feed Company 玉林市惠豐飼料公司(1994)	Yulin 玉林市	Guangxi 廣西	(0775)2082780	30	Collectively-owned 集體	40,370	3595(3)	5,115	c
Shuangcheng Lin Jiang Xiang High Protein Feed Factory 雙城市臨江鄉高蛋白飼料廠(1993)	Shuangcheng 雙城市	Heilongjiang 黑龍江省		89	Collectively-owned 集體	36,183	750(17)	2,360	a,c
Zheng Xing Feed Factory 正興飼料廠(1992)	Chengdu 成都市	Sichuan 四川省		150	Collectively-owned 集體	34,457	396(27)	10,295	b
Rongcheng Ming Dong Aquatic Products Co. Ltd. 榮成明東水產有限公司(1994)	Weihai 威海市	Shandong 山東省	(0896)7831087	100	Collectively-owned 集體	29,780	2860(4)	21,150	a
Shanghai Kai Quan Industrial Company 上海開泉實業公司(1993)	Shanghai 上海市	Shanghai 上海市	(021)59556443	156	Collectively-owned 集體	25,890	1910(6)	8,541	o
Shandong Rongcheng Flour Group Company 山東榮成市麵粉集團公司(1992)	Weihai 威海市	Shandong 山東省		70	Collectively-owned 集體	25,130	1880(7)	11,920	a,b
Shuangcheng San Long Feed Co. Ltd. 雙城市三龍飼料有限公司(1995)	Shuangcheng 雙城市	Heilongjiang 黑龍江省	(0451)3176945	58	Collectively-owned 集體	21,600	2100(5)	16,000	o
Yancheng Aquatic Products Freezing Factory 鹽城市水產冷凍廠(1980)	Yancheng 鹽城市	Jiangsu 江蘇省	(0515)8281354	100	Collectively-owned 集體	16,240	0(75)	2,390	o

Top 10 Cities by Production Output 產出排名前 10 位城市	Province 省	Market share 市場份額	Number of firms 企業個數
Dalian 大連市	Liaoning 遼寧省	28.03%	4
Binzhou 濱州市	Shandong 山東省	7.06%	13
Weifang 濰坊市	Shandong 山東省	4.67%	4
Shaoxing 紹興市	Zhejiang 浙江省	3.45%	1
Shanghai 上海市	Shanghai 上海市	3.10%	4
Wenzhou 溫州市	Zhejiang 浙江省	3.03%	6
Dachuan 達川市	Sichuan 四川省	2.96%	3
Shijiazhuang 石家莊市	Hebei 河北省	2.71%	5
Jixi 雞西市	Heilongjiang 黑龍江省	2.59%	3
Shuangcheng 雙城市	Heilongjiang 黑龍江省	2.27%	1

10 Major Wholesalers 10 家主要批發商	City 城市	Province 省	Telephone / Fax 電話 / 傳真
China Agricultural Machinery Hua Bei Company 中國農業機械華北公司	Tianjin 天津市	Tianjin 天津市	(022)23394240 (022)23304247
Shandong Agriculture Means of Production Company 山東省農業生產資料公司	Ji'nan 濟南市	Shandong 山東省	(0531)8957052 (0531)8957142
Yantai Agriculture Means of Production General Company 煙台市農業生產資料總公司	Yantai 煙台市	Shandong 山東省	(0535)6216668 (0535)6211348
Sichuan Agriculture Means of Production General Company 四川省農業生產資料總公司	Chengdu 成都市	Sichuan 四川省	(028)6751135 (028)6751646
Heilongjiang Agriculture Means of Production Company 黑龍江省農業生產資料公司	Harbin 哈爾濱市	Heilongjiang 黑龍江省	(0451)8989948 (0451)8382367
Shannxi Agriculture Means of Production General Company 陝西省農業生產資料總公司	Xi'an 西安市	Shaanxi 陝西省	(029)7422104 (029)7411799
Gansu Agriculture Means of Production General Company 甘肅省農業生產資料總公司	Lanzhou 蘭州市	Gansu 甘肅省	(0931)8822971
Yitong Man Zu Autonomous County Agricultural Goods & Materials Co. Ltd. 伊通滿族自治縣農用物資有限責任公司	Siping 四平市	Jilin 吉林省	(0434)4223146
Langfang Agriculture Means of Production Company 廊坊市農業生產資料公司	Langfang 廊坊市	Hebei 河北省	(0316)2013148
Anhui Agriculture Means of Production Company 安徽省農業生產資料公司	Hefei 合肥市	Anhui 安徽省	(0551)2656541 (0551)2655720

*Also include sales by firms outside this industry.包括本行業以外廠家的銷售。"o" stands for "others". "o" 代表"其他產品"。

1317: Aquatic Feed 水產飼料製造業

The industry accounts for 0.089% of the total revenue of China's industrial sector in 1996. The revenue growth rate of the industry is 91.5% from 1995, as compared to the growth rate of China's industrial sector, 9.51%. The rate of return on asset is 6.58%. 74.21% of all firms in the industry made a profit while 19.91% had negative returns. The top province in terms of the industry's revenue is Jiangsu, accounting for 39.60% of the total revenue.
本行業在1996年佔全行業總產值0.089%，行業年增長率為91.5%（全國工業年增長率9.51%）。行業的資產回報率6.58%，74.21%的企業盈利，19.91%的企業虧損。銷售收入最高的省份為江蘇省，佔本行業的39.60%。

	Total number of firms 企業總數	Total number of employees 職工總數	Total revenue (mil. RMB) 總銷售收入（百萬元）	Total profit (mil. RMB) 總利潤（百萬元）	Return on assets 資產利潤率 (%)	Return on equity 權益利潤率 (%)	Labour productivity ('000 RMB / worker) 勞動生產率（千元/人）	Debts / assets 資產負債率 (%)	Total assets (mil. RMB) 總資產（百萬元）
Industry Overall 行業總體	222	14,798	5,132	323	6.58	22.50	346.80	70.78	4,911

	Number of firms 企業個數	Average number of employees 平均職工人數	Average revenue ('000 RMB) 平均銷售收入（千元）	Average profit ('000 RMB) 平均利潤（千元）	Return on assets 資產利潤率 (%)	Return on equity 權益利潤率 (%)	Labour productivity ('000 RMB / worker) 勞動生產率（千元/人）	Average debts / assets 平均資產負債率(%)	Average Total assets ('000 RMB) 平均總資產（千元）
By ownership 產業所有權									
State-owned 國有	48	37	4,479	-146	-2.09	-9.72	122.09	78.51	6,979
Collectively-owned 集體	134	78	15,435	1,216	8.66	119.73	197.63	92.77	14,037
Privately-owned 私有	2	38	1,490	-129	-0.74	31.92	39.73	102.31	17,520
Domestic JVs 聯營	1	23	1,526	194	7.27	-123.75	66.36	105.88	2,672
Joint stock 股份制	3	29	1,636	82	3.01	38.31	56.42	92.15	2,742
Foreign-funded 外資	16	54	101,974	6,084	6.70	8.43	1877.54	20.48	90,806
Overseas Chinese-funded 港澳台資	18	108	67,193	3,861	5.80	96.07	624.40	93.96	66,551
By size 規模									
Large 大型	1	2,983	1,223,733	138,761	11.35	79.94	410.24	85.80	1,222,589
Medium 中型	3	254	142,896	16,030	12.73	57.93	563.32	78.03	125,920
Small 小型	213	53	16,343	639	4.11	11.55	309.21	64.41	15,550
By regional distribution 地區分布									
Central-North 華北	37	44	35,828	2,634	5.85	16.81	821.84	65.21	45,031
Beijing 北京	7	70	178,401	14,259	6.58	18.38	2548.59	64.22	216,809
Tianjin 天津	7	23	3,486	306	4.83	28.88	153.46	83.29	6,336
Hebei 河北	18	45	2,111	-102	-3.07	-27.06	47.02	88.65	3,327
Shanxi 山西	3	49	4,807	-887	-6.09	-12.10	98.77	49.62	14,550
Inner Mongolia 內蒙	2	5						25.86	290
Northeast 東北	18	25	4,247	-64	-1.22	-3.22	168.02	61.93	5,263
Liaoning 遼寧	11	34	5,890	-87	-1.14	-2.81	174.17	59.54	7,667
Jilin 吉林	2	19	1,050	-480	-24.12	143.28	55.26	116.83	1,990
Heilongjiang 黑龍江	5	9	1,912	152	11.84	29.01	212.44	59.19	1,284
Central East 華東	120	88	27,903	1,958	8.69	33.37	316.33	73.96	22,525
Shanghai 上海	3	44	9,737	-2,157	-5.08	-8.15	222.98	37.74	42,480
Jiangsu 江蘇	19	349	106,975	6,959	9.07	52.38	306.52	82.68	76,726
Zhejiang 浙江	28	38	7,269	484	17.51	42.92	188.98	59.20	2,765
Anhui 安徽	3	153	4,497	477	14.05	23.29	29.33	39.69	3,393
Fujian 福建	44	29	19,660	1,808	9.04	25.74	669.55	64.89	20,000
Jiangxi 江西	3	14	3,153	63	2.91	4.91	230.73	40.74	2,177
Shandong 山東	20	48	9,756	724	10.08	66.88	204.74	84.93	7,184
Central-South 中南	34	45	10,669	-154	-1.30	-5.13	235.70	74.68	11,899
Henan 河南	3	14	6,320	250	15.34	32.33	451.43	52.56	1,630
Hubei 湖北	3	21	1,333	7	0.28	4.17	64.52	93.16	2,340
Hunan 湖南	7	34	2,299	81	5.32	-228.00	68.18	102.33	1,531
Guangdong 廣東	17	66	18,240	-294	-1.36	-5.16	278.35	73.65	21,598
Guangxi 廣西	2	20	3,890	-805	-20.88	-76.67	194.50	72.76	3,855
Hainan 海南	2	23	2,915	5	0.14	0.98	129.56	85.41	3,530
Southwest 西南	7	71	1,496	-429	-10.29	-28.06	21.15	63.33	4,164
Chongqing 重慶	1	78	3,747	-595	-49.22	-173.21	47.50	71.58	1,209
Sichuan 四川	5	69	933	-388	-7.90	-21.26	13.52	62.82	4,903
Guizhou 貴州									
Yunnan 雲南									
Tibet 西藏									
Northwest 西北	6	19	1,320	-5	-0.23	-1.27	71.35	82.03	2,198
Shaanxi 陝西	2	13	205	30	12.77	60.00	16.40	78.72	235
Gansu 甘肅	1	8	500	40	6.67	8.00	62.50	16.67	600
Qinghai 青海	1	15	390	-180	-10.98	-32.14	26.00	65.85	1,640
Ningxia 寧夏	1	50	6,280	50	0.52	5.56	125.60	90.64	9,620
Xinjiang 新疆	1	13	340				26.15	63.95	860

Year 年份	Number of firms 企業個數	Rate of change 每年變化 (%)	Number of employees 職工人數 (人)	Rate of change 每年變化 (%)	Total revenue (mil. RMB) 總銷售收入 (百萬元)	Rate of change 每年變化 (%)	Total profit (mil. RMB) 總利潤 (百萬元)	Rate of change 每年變化 (%)
1993	165		6,328		1,043		49	
1994	179	8.48%	8,473	33.90%	1,474	41.30%	137	178.69%
1995	202	12.85%	8,930	5.39%	2,680	81.87%	245	78.19%
1996	222	9.90%	14,798	65.71%	5,132	91.49%	323	31.91%

3 Major products* 3 種主要產品 *	Output 產量	Sales volume 銷售量	Unit 單位
a) Protein Feedstuff 蛋白質飼料	169,252	113,399	ton 噸
b) Mixed Feedstuff 混合飼料	637,430	643,804	ton 噸
c) Mingled Feedstuff 配合飼料	449,278	435,800	ton 噸

Top 10 firms by revenue (year founded) 收入排名前 10 家企業 (創辦年份)	City 城市	Province 省	Telephone / fax 電話 / 傳真	Number of employees 職工人數	Ownership 產業所有權	Revenue ('000 RMB) 銷售收入 (千元)	Profit ('000 RMB) (rank) 利潤 (千元) (排名)	Total assets ('000 RMB) 總資產 (千元)	Major products 主要產品
Dantu Long Shan Eel Industry Joint Co. 丹徒縣龍山鰻業聯合公司(1987)	Zhenjiang 鎮江市	Jiangsu 江蘇省	(0511)3321901 (0511)3321557	3,095	Collectively-owned 集體	1,958,290	132090(1)	1,393,419	a
Beijing Hede (Group) Co. Ltd. 和德集團有限公司(1993)	Beijing 北京市	Beijing 北京市	(010)68329222 (010)68320042	102	Foreign-funded 外資	1,200,257	100418(2)	1,467,481	b
Fujian Mawei Allied Aquatic Feed Co. Ltd. 福建馬尾聯合水產飼料有限公司(1985)	Fuzhou 福州市	Fujian 福建省	(0591)3682578 (0591)3681422	259	Overseas Chinese-funded 港澳台資	281,989	45757(3)	125,654	c
Fuzhou Da Chang Sheng Feed Co. Ltd. 福州大昌盛飼料有限公司(1992)	Fuzhou 福州市	Fujian 福建省	(0591)3681692 (0591)3681244	185	Overseas Chinese-funded 港澳台資	148,639	12775(4)	144,612	c
Xiamen Fu Shou Industrial Co. Ltd. 廈門福壽實業有限公司(1992)	Xiamen 廈門市	Fujian 福建省	(0592)7023739 (0592)7021199	107	Foreign-funded 外資	69,983	1031(24)	98,380	c
Shunde Jin Guan Eel Feed Factory Co. Ltd. 順德金冠鰻魚飼料廠有限公司(1993)	Foshan 佛山市	Guangdong 廣東省	(0757)5566527 (0757)5564198	61	Overseas Chinese-funded 港澳台資	67,734	-738(106)	35,709	c
Fuqing Jin Sheng Feed Co. Ltd. 福清金盛飼料有限公司(1995)	Fuzhou 福州市	Fujian 福建省	(0591)5381177	36	Overseas Chinese-funded 港澳台資	58,764	-471(102)	97,775	o
Tong Da Feed Factory 通達飼料廠(1988)	Zhuhai 珠海市	Guangdong 廣東省	(0756)5524195	143	Foreign-funded 外資	53,262	-147(99)	34,385	c
Fuzhou Jia Lian Feed Co. Ltd. 福州佳聯飼料有限公司(1996)	Fuzhou 福州市	Fujian 福建省	(0591)3680576	20	Overseas Chinese-funded 港澳台資	53,032	10057(5)	17,686	o
Shunde Jin Guan Feed Factory 順德市金冠飼料廠(1981)	Foshan 佛山市	Guangdong 廣東省	(0757)5566527 (0757)5564198	130	Collectively-owned 集體	48,961	-2041(114)	94,259	c

Top 10 Cities by Production Output 產出排名前 10 位城市	Province 省	Market share 市場份額	Number of firms 企業個數
Fuzhou 福州市	Fujian 福建省	27.32%	18
Foshan 佛山市	Guangdong 廣東省	17.87%	7
Wenzhou 溫州市	Zhejiang 浙江省	7.23%	25
Mianyang 綿陽市	Sichuan 四川省	6.11%	1
Zhanjiang 湛江市	Guangdong 廣東省	4.87%	4
Jiangmen 江門市	Guangdong 廣東省	2.75%	5
Beijing 北京市	Beijing 北京市	2.08%	6
Putian 莆田市	Fujian 福建省	2.03%	4
Changzhou 常州市	Jiangsu 江蘇省	1.90%	2
Weihai 威海市	Shandong 山東省	1.84%	8

10 Major Wholesalers 10 家主要批發商	City 城市	Province 省	Telephone / Fax 電話 / 傳真
China Agricultural Machinery Hua Bei Company 中國農業機械華北公司	Tianjin 天津市	Tianjin 天津市	(022)23394240 (022)23304247
Shandong Agriculture Means of Production Company 山東省農業生產資料公司	Ji'nan 濟南市	Shandong 山東省	(0531)8957052 (0531)8957142
Yantai Agriculture Means of Production General Company 煙台市農業生產資料總公司	Yantai 煙台市	Shandong 山東省	(0535)6216668 (0535)6211348
Sichuan Agriculture Means of Production General Company 四川省農業生產資料總公司	Chengdu 成都市	Sichuan 四川省	(028)6751135 (028)6751646
Heilongjiang Agriculture Means of Production Company 黑龍江省農業生產資料公司	Harbin 哈爾濱市	Heilongjiang 黑龍江省	(0451)8989948 (0451)8382367
Shannxi Agriculture Means of Production General Company 陝西省農業生產資料總公司	Xi'an 西安市	Shaanxi 陝西省	(029)7422104 (029)7411799
Gansu Agriculture Means of Production General Company 甘肅省農業生產資料總公司	Lanzhou 蘭州市	Gansu 甘肅省	(0931)8822971
Yitong Man Zu Autonomous County Agricultural Goods & Materials Co. Ltd. 伊通滿族自治縣農用物資有限責任公司	Siping 四平市	Jilin 吉林省	(0434)4223146
Langfang Agriculture Means of Production Company 廊坊市農業生產資料公司	Langfang 廊坊市	Hebei 河北省	(0316)2013148
Anhui Agriculture Means of Production Company 安徽省農業生產資料公司	Hefei 合肥市	Anhui 安徽省	(0551)2656541 (0551)2655720

*Also include sales by firms outside this industry.包括本行業以外廠家的銷售。"o" stands for "others". "o" 代表 "其他產品"。

1319: Other Animal Feed 其他飼料製造業

The industry accounts for 0.029% of the total revenue of China's industrial sector in 1996. The revenue growth rate of the industry is 118.7% from 1995, as compared to the growth rate of China's industrial sector, 9.51%. The rate of return on asset is 1.97%. 72.51% of all firms in the industry made a profit while 19.54% had negative returns. The top province in terms of the industry's revenue is Guangdong, accounting for 42.17% of the total revenue.
本行業在1996年佔全行業總產值0.029%，行業年增長率為118.7%（全國工業年增長率9.51%）。行業的資產回報率1.97%，72.51%的企業盈利，19.54%的企業虧損。銷售收入最高的省份為廣東省，佔本行業的42.17%。

	Total number of firms 企業總數	Total number of employees 職工總數	Total revenue (mil. RMB) 總銷售收入（百萬元）	Total profit (mil. RMB) 總利潤（百萬元）	Return on assets 資產利潤率 (%)	Return on equity 權益利潤率 (%)	Labour productivity ('000 RMB / worker) 勞動生產率（千元/人）	Debts / assets 資產負債率 (%)	Total assets (mil. RMB) 總資產（百萬元）
Industry Overall 行業總體	318	11,610	1,660	25	1.97	6.36	142.98	68.97	1,274

	Number of firms 企業個數	Average number of employees 平均職工人數	Average revenue ('000 RMB) 平均銷售收入（千元）	Average profit ('000 RMB) 平均利潤（千元）	Return on assets 資產利潤率 (%)	Return on equity 權益利潤率 (%)	Labour productivity ('000 RMB / worker) 勞動生產率（千元/人）	Average debts / assets 平均資產負債率(%)	Average Total assets ('000 RMB) 平均總資產（千元）
By ownership 產業所有權									
State-owned 國有	56	43	4,554	-89	-1.51	-4.07	105.85	62.95	5,929
Collectively-owned 集體	215	34	4,634	151	5.57	19.44	135.79	71.37	2,707
Privately-owned 私有	4	15	6,081	141	26.49	35.44	398.73	25.26	533
Domestic JVs 聯營	6	34	8,267	-326	-5.45	-16.84	241.97	67.66	5,977
Joint stock 股份制	5	33	9,958	169	4.77	13.57	303.61	64.89	3,557
Foreign-funded 外資	15	38	6,484	-382	-3.68	-18.66	172.74	80.30	10,396
Overseas Chinese-funded 港澳台資	15	53	12,402	257	2.64	7.07	235.77	62.67	9,748
By size 規模									
Large 大型									
Medium 中型	1	48							
Small 小型	310	37	5,350	85	2.07	6.64	145.09	68.85	4,094
By regional distribution 地區分布									
Central-North 華北	38	29	3,639	116	3.75	40.57	123.80	90.75	3,078
Beijing 北京	6	28	11,420	335	3.17	-49.51	415.27	106.40	10,575
Tianjin 天津	10	46	3,522	257	10.73	24.81	76.07	56.76	2,396
Hebei 河北	8	15	2,480	81	9.26	127.45	165.33	92.74	878
Shanxi 山西	3	20	730	-50	-1.98	-36.59	36.50	94.72	2,527
Inner Mongolia 內蒙	11	28	1,137	-63	-4.61	-19.17	40.49	75.89	1,361
Northeast 東北	84	39	1,579	50	3.16	14.98	40.35	78.91	1,580
Liaoning 遼寧	26	28	1,145	28	2.55	9.52	40.38	73.17	1,101
Jilin 吉林	15	27	642	48	7.02	18.37	24.01	61.79	684
Heilongjiang 黑龍江	43	50	2,168	64	2.92	16.73	43.39	82.54	2,182
Central East 華東	83	37	5,376	42	0.93	3.06	144.44	69.60	4,488
Shanghai 上海	1	7	290	40	6.25	-200.00	41.43	101.56	640
Jiangsu 江蘇	11	34	3,174	-46	-2.20	-6.16	92.85	64.38	2,111
Zhejiang 浙江	7	62	14,313	394	2.84	7.41	230.32	61.70	13,891
Anhui 安徽	11	72	12,550	173	1.98	15.36	174.97	87.14	8,744
Fujian 福建	13	12	1,588	-44	-1.31	-3.41	129.81	61.64	3,353
Jiangxi 江西	19	20	2,135	-15	-1.59	-6.29	107.90	74.79	929
Shandong 山東	21	45	5,310	6	0.14	0.38	117.76	63.59	4,477
Central-South 中南	66	36	13,409	200	2.25	5.91	370.92	61.98	8,905
Henan 河南	19	21	2,672	17	0.62	2.02	128.51	69.40	2,723
Hubei 湖北	7	63	624	3	1.05	-5.00	9.98	120.94	273
Hunan 湖南	13	18	1,637	-49	-2.54	-7.79	92.12	67.36	1,937
Guangdong 廣東	17	64	41,182	682	3.23	9.69	645.85	66.61	21,077
Guangxi 廣西	9	25	12,056	212	1.27	2.38	490.95	46.76	16,737
Hainan 海南	1	17							
Southwest 西南	30	48	1,470	-19	-1.18	-4.22	30.82	72.14	1,616
Chongqing 重慶	2	22	1,104	-181	-9.14	-81.65	49.19	88.81	1,984
Sichuan 四川	16	74	2,391	76	3.04	10.49	32.12	70.98	2,487
Guizhou 貴州	10	16	206	13	5.70	15.66	12.88	63.60	228
Yunnan 雲南									
Tibet 西藏	1	5	120	50	15.63	15.63	24.00		320
Northwest 西北	17	18	800	31	3.29	8.23	45.18	60.05	931
Shaanxi 陝西	5	24	594	-22	-2.08	-4.64	25.17	54.92	1,056
Gansu 甘肅	4	18	423	25	2.77	8.20	24.14	66.48	903
Qinghai 青海									
Ningxia 寧夏	2								
Xinjiang 新疆	6	19	1,490	88	7.65	19.41	79.12	60.61	1,155

1319: Other Animal Feed 其他飼料製造業

Year 年份	Number of firms 企業個數	Rate of change 每年變化 (%)	Number of employees 職工人數（人）	Rate of change 每年變化 (%)	Total revenue (mil. RMB) 總銷售收入（百萬元）	Rate of change 每年變化 (%)	Total profit (mil. RMB) 總利潤（百萬元）	Rate of change 每年變化 (%)
1993	200		4,170		265		2	
1994	274	37.00%	9,128	118.90%	506	90.45%	4	95.33%
1995	283	3.28%	10,733	17.58%	759	50.10%	17	334.00%
1996	318	12.37%	11,610	8.17%	1,660	118.72%	25	49.62%

3 Major products* 3 種主要產品 *	Output 產量	Sales volume 銷售量	Unit 單位
a) Feedstuff Additive 飼料添加劑	12,954	12,695	ton 噸
b) Mingled Feedstuff 配合飼料	1,088,452	1,055,798	ton 噸

Top 10 firms by revenue (year founded) 收入排名前 10 家企業 (創辦年份)	City 城市	Province 省	Telephone / fax 電話 / 傳真	Number of employees 職工人數	Ownership 產業所有權	Revenue ('000 RMB) 銷售收入（千元）	Profit ('000 RMB) (rank) 利潤（千元）(排名)	Total assets ('000 RMB) 總資產（千元）	Major products 主要產品
Shunde Hua Xing Feed Factory 順德市華星飼料廠(1983)	Foshan 佛山市	Guangdong 廣東省	(0757)6656817 (0757)6657277	380	Joint stock 股份制	526,660	8165(2)	230,764	b
Chengdu Chia Tai Co. Ltd. 成都正大有限公司(1985)	Chengdu 成都市	Sichuan 四川省	(028)3113991 (028)3116691	400	Foreign-funded 外資	306,260	4827(4)	258,357	b
Shanghai Zhan Wang Animal Husbandry Development Co. Ltd. 上海展望牧業發展有限公司(1995)	Shanghai 上海市	Shanghai 上海市	(021)59507883 (021)59155478	6	其他經濟	182,976	7096(3)	67,441	b
Shanghai Min Fa Industry & Trade Development Company 上海民發工貿發展公司(1995)	Shanghai 上海市	Shanghai 上海市		1,520	其他經濟	135,800	11144(1)	31,904	o
Anqiu Feed Company 安丘市飼料公司(1984)	Weifang 濰坊市	Shandong 山東省	(0536)4224139 (0536)4223215	467	State-owned 國有	66,255	278(24)	56,704	a,b
Bozhou Cotton & Linen Company Oil Pressing Factory 亳州市棉麻公司榨油加工廠(1987)	Fuyang 阜陽市	Anhui 安徽省	(0558)5522469	96	Collectively-owned 集體	53,880	525(13)	60,020	o
Nanning Jin Long Feed Factory 南寧市金龍飼料廠(1995)	Nanning 南寧市	Guangxi 廣西	(0771)3828086	10	Collectively-owned 集體	49,617	1157(7)	96,372	o
Mingguang Ao Tu Bang Feedstuffs Factory 明光市凹凸棒飼料廠(1989)	Chuzhou 滁州市	Anhui 安徽省	(0550)8031960 (0550)8022089	93	Collectively-owned 集體	46,000	170(33)	15,060	a
Guangdong Nanhai Zhong Hong Feed Factory 廣東南海中宏飼料廠(1996)	Foshan 佛山市	Guangdong 廣東省	(0757)6660368 (0757)6660368	100	State-owned 國有	31,960	-55(78)	17,862	b
Guangdong Yan Tang Feed Industrial Company 廣東省燕塘飼料工業公司(1991)	Guangzhou 廣州市	Guangdong 廣東省	(020)87705560 (020)87703302	90	State-owned 國有	29,576	166(35)	35,605	b

Top 10 Cities by Production Output 產出排名前 10 位城市	Province 省	Market share 市場份額	Number of firms 企業個數
Foshan 佛山市	Guangdong 廣東省	36.64%	4
Langfang 廊坊市	Hebei 河北省	12.82%	1
Harbin 哈爾濱市	Heilongjiang 黑龍江省	10.85%	9
Chengdu 成都市	Sichuan 四川省	8.54%	4
Nanning 南寧市	Guangxi 廣西	3.36%	7
Weifang 濰坊市	Shandong 山東省	2.92%	5
Guangzhou 廣州市	Guangdong 廣東省	1.85%	5
Yichang 宜昌市	Hubei 湖北省	1.60%	1
Suihua 綏化市	Heilongjiang 黑龍江省	1.25%	10
Changzhou 常州市	Jiangsu 江蘇省	0.95%	3

10 Major Wholesalers 10 家主要批發商	City 城市	Province 省	Telephone / Fax 電話 / 傳真
China Agricultural Machinery Hua Bei Company 中國農業機械華北公司	Tianjin 天津市	Tianjin 天津市	(022)23394240 (022)23304247
Shandong Agriculture Means of Production Company 山東省農業生產資料公司	Ji'nan 濟南市	Shandong 山東省	(0531)8957052 (0531)8957142
Yantai Agriculture Means of Production General Company 煙台市農業生產資料總公司	Yantai 煙台市	Shandong 山東省	(0535)6216668 (0535)6211348
Sichuan Agriculture Means of Production General Company 四川省農業生產資料總公司	Chengdu 成都市	Sichuan 四川省	(028)6751135 (028)6751646
Heilongjiang Agriculture Means of Production Company 黑龍江省農業生產資料公司	Harbin 哈爾濱市	Heilongjiang 黑龍江省	(0451)8989948 (0451)8382367
Shannxi Agriculture Means of Production General Company 陝西省農業生產資料總公司	Xi'an 西安市	Shaanxi 陝西省	(029)7422104 (029)7411799
Gansu Agriculture Means of Production General Company 甘肅省農業生產資料總公司	Lanzhou 蘭州市	Gansu 甘肅省	(0931)8822971
Yitong Man Zu Autonomous County Agricultural Goods & Materials Co. Ltd. 伊通滿族自治縣農用物資有限責任公司	Siping 四平市	Jilin 吉林省	(0434)4223146
Langfang Agriculture Means of Production Company 廊坊市農業生產資料公司	Langfang 廊坊市	Hebei 河北省	(0316)2013148
Anhui Agriculture Means of Production Company 安徽省農業生產資料公司	Hefei 合肥市	Anhui 安徽省	(0551)2656541 (0551)2655720

*Also include sales by firms outside this industry.包括本行業以外廠家的銷售。"o" stands for "others". "o" 代表"其他產品"。

1321: Edible Vegetable Oil 食用植物油加工業

The industry accounts for 0.946% of the total revenue of China's industrial sector in 1996. The revenue growth rate of the industry is 7.7% from 1995, as compared to the growth rate of China's industrial sector, 9.51%. The rate of return on asset is -0.96%. 73.54% of all firms in the industry made a profit while 18.39% had negative returns. The top province in terms of the industry's revenue is Helongjiang, accounting for 14.29% of the total revenue.
本行業在 1996 年佔全行業總產值 0.946%，行業年增長率為 7.7%（全國工業年增長率 9.51%）。行業的資產回報率 -0.96%，73.54% 的企業盈利，18.39% 的企業虧損。銷售收入最高的省份為黑龍江省，佔本行業的 14.29%。

	Total number of firms 企業總數	Total number of employees 職工總數	Total revenue (mil. RMB) 總銷售收入（百萬元）	Total profit (mil. RMB) 總利潤（百萬元）	Return on assets 資產利潤率 (%)	Return on equity 權益利潤率 (%)	Labour productivity ('000 RMB / worker) 勞動生產率（千元／人）	Debts / assets 資產負債率 (%)	Total assets (mil. RMB) 總資產（百萬元）
Industry Overall 行業總體	5,260	349,412	54,863	-531	-0.96	-6.12	157.02	84.31	55,349

	Number of firms 企業個數	Average number of employees 平均職工人數	Average revenue ('000 RMB) 平均銷售收入（千元）	Average profit ('000 RMB) 平均利潤（千元）	Return on assets 資產利潤率 (%)	Return on equity 權益利潤率 (%)	Labour productivity ('000 RMB / worker) 勞動生產率（千元／人）	Average debts / assets 平均資產負債率(%)	Average Total assets ('000 RMB) 平均總資產（千元）
By ownership 產業所有權									
State-owned 國有	1,164	173	20,740	-690	-2.70	-22.42	120.01	87.98	25,594
Collectively-owned 集體	3,896	31	3,742	76	3.06	14.49	119.23	78.91	2,486
Privately-owned 私有	16	48	6,940	227	6.68	25.46	144.02	73.77	3,401
Domestic JVs 聯營	22	85	11,443	-34	-0.26	-1.46	134.48	82.38	13,360
Joint stock 股份制	32	173	31,138	279	1.16	4.84	180.31	76.04	24,112
Foreign-funded 外資	74	138	64,251	-658	-0.96	-3.68	467.23	74.04	68,876
Overseas Chinese-funded 港澳台資	55	156	182,283	232	0.13	0.86	1171.49	84.61	175,478
By size 規模									
Large 大型	22	760	472,060	15,203	2.94	24.33	620.76	87.91	516,833
Medium 中型	147	354	75,751	-2,293	-3.22	-20.02	214.20	83.90	71,124
Small 小型	5,028	55	6,631	-105	-1.58	-9.39	119.93	83.22	6,667
By regional distribution 地區分布									
Central-North 華北	478	67	16,261	-168	-1.26	-6.89	244.42	81.74	13,327
Beijing 北京	20	85	37,842	-2,315	-7.27	-21.96	444.93	66.87	31,822
Tianjin 天津	22	165	173,680	-2,332	-2.53	-22.73	1055.80	88.89	92,317
Hebei 河北	236	61	7,635	177	2.09	10.44	125.18	79.97	8,454
Shanxi 山西	59	49	3,014	69	1.16	5.52	61.87	78.94	5,915
Inner Mongolia 內蒙	141	65	8,620	-201	-2.09	-11.20	131.93	81.36	9,637
Northeast 東北	800	106	16,117	-561	-2.87	-32.15	151.88	91.07	19,539
Liaoning 遼寧	165	119	21,134	-1,712	-6.55	-57.77	178.11	88.65	26,120
Jilin 吉林	129	170	12,157	-1,345	-4.93	-57.91	71.68	91.48	27,252
Heilongjiang 黑龍江	506	86	15,491	14	0.09	1.19	180.44	92.22	15,426
Central East 華東	1,807	64	11,097	38	0.42	1.76	173.67	75.87	9,056
Shanghai 上海	33	168	70,992	-555	-1.51	-5.86	423.34	74.30	36,868
Jiangsu 江蘇	275	115	18,959	38	0.23	0.74	164.59	69.18	16,623
Zhejiang 浙江	124	77	23,292	-223	-1.43	-6.24	304.31	77.04	15,554
Anhui 安徽	840	37	3,900	90	2.88	16.20	105.18	82.24	3,118
Fujian 福建	36	50	33,722	-960	-4.62	-17.67	674.81	73.85	20,779
Jiangxi 江西	217	42	2,652	-76	-1.71	-8.68	63.75	80.34	4,452
Shandong 山東	282	95	16,109	286	1.87	8.63	169.59	78.35	15,299
Central-South 中南	1,106	61	9,734	61	0.53	5.21	158.56	89.82	11,443
Henan 河南	276	88	7,973	211	2.45	18.08	90.82	86.46	8,606
Hubei 湖北	344	86	10,619	89	1.03	6.28	123.12	83.55	8,573
Hunan 湖南	311	31	2,861	-63	-2.61	289.23	93.21	100.90	2,417
Guangdong 廣東	126	26	31,371	45	0.09	1.21	1194.53	92.77	51,423
Guangxi 廣西	39	28	1,776	-177	-7.16	-34.01	63.01	78.95	2,475
Hainan 海南	10	4	43	-59	-13.82	1475.00	9.77	100.94	427
Southwest 西南	693	40	2,779	-151	-4.63	-24.32	69.64	80.96	3,255
Chongqing 重慶	101	26	1,701	-83	-4.42	-26.63	64.31	83.42	1,888
Sichuan 四川	511	37	2,448	-113	-4.30	-21.66	64.59	80.15	2,626
Guizhou 貴州	58	75	7,179	-554	-5.35	-30.21	96.05	82.30	10,362
Yunnan 雲南	14	63	5,764	-455	-6.15	-34.92	91.90	82.39	7,396
Tibet 西藏	8	9	559	9	0.44	1.07	62.08	59.39	2,010
Northwest 西北	376	58	3,861	-92	-1.67	-7.52	66.90	77.82	5,508
Shaanxi 陝西	143	51	3,817	-112	-3.01	-10.10	74.14	70.19	3,729
Gansu 甘肅	100	42	1,588	-109	-3.07	-13.82	37.92	77.82	3,544
Qinghai 青海	20	50	2,066	-32	-0.83	-2.34	41.43	64.71	3,873
Ningxia 寧夏	17	25	719	-132	-5.67	155.17	29.16	103.65	2,335
Xinjiang 新疆	96	91	7,225	-49	-0.44	-2.41	79.42	81.63	11,105

1321: Edible Vegetable Oil 食用植物油加工業

Year 年份	Number of firms 企業個數	Rate of change 每年變化 (%)	Number of employees 職工人數（人）	Rate of change 每年變化 (%)	Total revenue (mil. RMB) 總銷售收入（百萬元）	Rate of change 每年變化 (%)	Total profit (mil. RMB) 總利潤（百萬元）	Rate of change 每年變化 (%)
1993	5,208		266,144		27,161		413	
1994	5,386	3.42%	305,946	14.96%	37,914	39.59%	825	99.48%
1995	5,623	4.40%	355,595	16.23%	50,922	34.31%	171	-79.25%
1996	5,260	-6.46%	349,412	-1.74%	54,863	7.74%	-531	-410.28%

3 Major products* 3 種主要產品 *	Output 產量	Sales volume 銷售量	Unit 單位
a) Salad Oil 色拉油	821,212	780,152	ton 噸
b) Refined & Edible Vegetable Oil 精煉食用植物油	2,813,351	2,700,817	ton 噸
c) Soyabean Oil 大豆油	2,020,295	1,535,425	ton 噸

Top 10 firms by revenue (year founded) 收入排名前 10 家企業 (創辦年份)	City 城市	Province 省	Telephone / fax 電話 / 傳真	Number of employees 職工人數	Ownership 產業所有權	Revenue ('000 RMB) 銷售收入（千元）	Profit ('000 RMB) (rank) 利潤（千元）（排名）	Total assets ('000 RMB) 總資產（千元）	Major products 主要產品
Southseas Oil & Fats Industry (Chi Wan) Co. Ltd. 南海油脂工業(赤灣)有限公司(1988)	Shenzhen 深圳市	Guangdong 廣東省	(0755)6694322 (0755)6694326	484	Overseas Chinese-funded 港澳台資	3,015,947	23668(2)	5,572,004	a,b
Northsea Grains & Oils Industries (Tianjin) Co. Ltd. 北海糧油工業(天津)有限公司(1992)	Tianjin 天津市	Tianjin 天津市	(022)25306834 (022)25306314	871	Overseas Chinese-funded 港澳台資	2,255,863	-54019(1896)	886,107	o
Thia Tai Group (Tianjin) Oils & Fats Co. Ltd. 正大集團(天津)油脂有限公司(1989)	Tianjin 天津市	Tianjin 天津市	(022)5322724 (022)5327583	294	Foreign-funded 外資	1,120,069	874(201)	728,949	o
Yingkou Bo Hai Oils & Fats Industrial Ltd. 營口渤海油脂工業有限公司(1995)	Yingkou 營口市	Liaoning 遼寧省	(0417)6268388 (0417)6269727	280	Foreign-funded 外資	1,094,887	2500(72)	473,355	o
Xiamen Zhong Lu Vegetable Oil Co. Ltd. 廈門中鷺植物油有限公司(1991)	Xiamen 廈門市	Fujian 福建省	(0592)6011041 (0592)6011062	303	Foreign-funded 外資	932,081	-36996(1893)	352,148	a,c
Shanghai Kerry Grains & Oils Industrial Ltd. 上海嘉里糧油工業有限公司(1993)	Shanghai 上海市	Shanghai 上海市	(021)58712277 (021)58467008	312	Overseas Chinese-funded 港澳台資	771,276	-49776(1894)	353,294	a,b
Donghai Grain & Oil Processing Industry Co. Ltd. 東海糧油工業(保税區)有限公司(1995)	Suzhou 蘇州市	Jiangsu 江蘇省	(0512)8381018	372	Foreign-funded 外資	759,312	-7765(1865)	903,234	a
Shenzhen Nan Shun Fat Co. Ltd. 深圳南順油脂有限公司(1992)	Shenzhen 深圳市	Guangdong 廣東省	(0755)6681092 (0755)6676695	185	Overseas Chinese-funded 港澳台資	484,045	-9277(1875)	542,058	b
Ningbo Donghai Fat Co. Ltd. 寧波東海油脂有限公司(1993)	Ningbo 寧波市	Zhejiang 浙江省	(0574)8483787 (0574)8483219	129	Foreign-funded 外資	433,962	-5949(1852)	219,235	o
Shenyang Zhong Fa Cereal & Oils Food General Company 瀋陽中發糧油食品總公司(1952)	Shenyang 瀋陽市	Liaoning 遼寧省	(024)88420137 (024)88420137	1,968	State-owned 國有	400,446	-49888(1895)	785,412	c

Top 10 Cities by Production Output 產出排名前 10 位城市	Province 省	Market share 市場份額	Number of firms 企業個數
Tianjin 天津市	Tianjin 天津市	8.79%	27
Shenzhen 深圳市	Guangdong 廣東省	6.35%	6
Shanghai 上海市	Shanghai 上海市	3.88%	44
Suzhou 蘇州市	Jiangsu 江蘇省	3.88%	20
Jiamusi 佳木斯市	Heilongjiang 黑龍江省	2.31%	41
Dalian 大連市	Liaoning 遼寧省	1.93%	17
Huzhou 湖州市	Zhejiang 浙江省	1.88%	19
Suihua 綏化市	Heilongjiang 黑龍江省	1.75%	104
Qiqiha'er 齊齊哈爾市	Heilongjiang 黑龍江省	1.61%	77
Harbin 哈爾濱市	Heilongjiang 黑龍江省	1.60%	56

10 Major Wholesalers 10 家主要批發商	City 城市	Province 省	Telephone / Fax 電話 / 傳真
Zhejiang Cereal & Oils Food Import & Export Co. Ltd. 浙江省糧油食品進出口股份有限公司	Hangzhou 杭州市	Zhejiang 浙江省	(0571)5152515 (0571)5152514
Henan Cereal & Oils Food Import & Export Company 河南省糧油食品進出口公司	Zhengzhou 鄭州市	Henan 河南省	(0371)3942915 (0371)3942790
Shanghai Land Reclamation & Cultivation Cooking Oil Mill Marketing Company 上海市農墾糧油食品經營公司	Shanghai 上海市	Shanghai 上海市	(021)64714931
Changtu Da Chang Cooking Oil Mill Trade Jointly-operated Company 昌圖縣大昌糧油貿易聯營公司	Tieling 鐵嶺市	Liaoning 遼寧省	(0410)5824099
China Vegetable Oil Company 中國植物油公司	Beijing 北京市	Beijing 北京市	(010)66038248
Zhong Liang Shandong Cooking Oil Mill Import & Export Company 中糧山東糧油進出口公司	Qingdao 青島市	Shandong 山東省	(0532)2972342 (0532)2972379
Zhejiang Cooking Oil Mill Storage & Transport Trade Company 浙江省糧油儲運貿易公司	Hangzhou 杭州市	Zhejiang 浙江省	(0571)5161408 (0571)5161411
Anhui Cereal & Oils Food Import & Export (Group) Company 安徽省糧油食品進出口(集團)公司	Hefei 合肥市	Anhui 安徽省	(0551)2653731 (0551)2652831
Shanghai Farm, Industry & Commerce Group Cooking Oil Mill General Company 上海農工商集團糧油總公司	Shanghai 上海市	Shanghai 上海市	(021)62593423 (021)62748578
Sichuan Chang Jiang Enterprise Co. Ltd. 四川省長江企業股份有限公司	Chengdu 成都市	Sichuan 四川省	(028)3339888 (028)3333896

*Also include sales by firms outside this industry.包括本行業以外廠家的銷售。"o" stands for "others"."o" 代表"其他產品"。

1322: Inedible Vegetable Oil 非食用植物油加工業

The industry accounts for 0.011% of the total revenue of China's industrial sector in 1996. The revenue growth rate of the industry is 33.6% from 1995, as compared to the growth rate of China's industrial sector, 9.51%. The rate of return on asset is -3.63%. 70.40% of all firms in the industry made a profit while 15.71% had negative returns. The top province in terms of the industry's revenue is Guangdong, accounting for 24.00% of the total revenue.
本行業在1996年佔全行業總產值0.011%，行業年增長率為33.6%（全國工業年增長率9.51%）。行業的資產回報率-3.63%，70.40%的企業盈利，15.71%的企業虧損。銷售收入最高的省份為廣東省，佔本行業的24.00%。

	Total number of firms 企業總數	Total number of employees 職工總數	Total revenue (mil. RMB) 總銷售收入（百萬元）	Total profit (mil. RMB) 總利潤（百萬元）	Return on assets 資產利潤率 (%)	Return on equity 權益利潤率 (%)	Labour productivity ('000 RMB / worker) 勞動生產率（千元/人）	Debts / assets 資產負債率 (%)	Total assets (mil. RMB) 總資產（百萬元）
Industry Overall 行業總體	337	8,561	664	-42	-3.63	-61.88	77.56	94.14	1,152

	Number of firms 企業個數	Average number of employees 平均職工人數	Average revenue ('000 RMB) 平均銷售收入（千元）	Average profit ('000 RMB) 平均利潤（千元）	Return on assets 資產利潤率 (%)	Return on equity 權益利潤率 (%)	Labour productivity ('000 RMB / worker) 勞動生產率（千元/人）	Average debts / assets 平均資產負債率(%)	Average Total assets ('000 RMB) 平均總資產（千元）
By ownership 產業所有權									
State-owned 國有	47	56	2,532	-489	-5.10	109.52	45.42	104.66	9,596
Collectively-owned 集體	272	19	1,494	15	1.12	8.44	77.61	86.71	1,325
Privately-owned 私有	4	22	1,474	-8	-1.05	-1.88	67.01	44.23	742
Domestic JVs 聯營	4	48	5,749	-153	-1.85	-7.28	119.15	74.54	8,245
Joint stock 股份制	2	49	5,541	-359	-7.09	-53.91	113.08	86.86	5,069
Foreign-funded 外資	3	51	14,991	-4,506	-8.15	354.62	295.88	102.30	55,285
Overseas Chinese-funded 港澳台資	6	29	8,936	-1,361	-6.37	-24.40	308.15	73.90	21,366
By size 規模									
Large 大型	1	134	16,337	-14,956	-11.97	71.87	121.91	116.65	124,985
Medium 中型									
Small 小型	331	25	1,957	-82	-2.63	-30.46	78.12	91.35	3,102
By regional distribution 地區分布									
Central-North 華北	16	42	2,117	-983	-7.18	-1893.98	50.33	99.63	13,681
Beijing 北京	1	15	4,840	-5,470	-16.01	-300.55	322.67	94.70	34,160
Tianjin 天津	3	16	2,437	-7	-0.05	-0.18	155.53	71.52	13,133
Hebei 河北	4	26	1,713	130	25.49	33.33	67.16	23.53	510
Shanxi 山西	2	31	1,365	-415	-5.88	-26.02	44.75	77.41	7,060
Inner Mongolia 內蒙	6	75	2,023	-1,653	-7.68	58.49	27.10	113.13	21,530
Northeast 東北	27	46	2,112	-194	-3.33	13.76	45.76	124.18	5,833
Liaoning 遼寧	9	42	1,858	62	3.66	16.33	44.71	77.61	1,702
Jilin 吉林	12	57	2,904	-454	-4.03	12.65	51.17	131.86	11,275
Heilongjiang 黑龍江	6	32	908	-58	-5.10	-22.01	28.53	76.82	1,143
Central East 華東	28	39	3,082	108	3.67	25.66	79.24	85.73	2,950
Shanghai 上海	3	59	2,780	-110	-2.07	17.28	46.85	111.97	5,320
Jiangsu 江蘇	7	65	5,326	191	3.73	17.31	82.11	78.47	5,136
Zhejiang 浙江	3	38	3,020	-110	-3.41	-26.19	80.18	87.00	3,230
Anhui 安徽	4	35	3,985	513	47.24	73.74	113.05	36.18	1,085
Fujian 福建	1	15	700	10	4.35	8.33	46.67	47.83	230
Jiangxi 江西	6	8	910	17	2.06	27.78	113.75	92.59	810
Shandong 山東	4	35	2,378	48	1.64	13.01	67.93	87.48	2,895
Central-South 中南	82	27	3,740	-235	-4.44	-60.81	138.63	92.70	5,302
Henan 河南	15	22	2,964	63	1.95	10.22	135.96	80.89	3,209
Hubei 湖北	14	31	2,119	18	1.31	-1.87	67.89	170.01	1,367
Hunan 湖南	16	18	1,704	91	6.63	27.97	95.65	76.31	1,377
Guangdong 廣東	5	37	31,866	-116	-0.30	-0.86	861.24	65.10	38,776
Guangxi 廣西	32	31	1,435	-668	-14.09	57.79	46.96	124.38	4,738
Hainan 海南									
Southwest 西南	142	18	1,004	-37	-2.55	-10.45	56.43	75.63	1,451
Chongqing 重慶	29	11	1,017	5	0.34	1.29	86.36	73.43	1,321
Sichuan 四川	29	14	623	5	1.10	4.23	43.78	74.08	499
Guizhou 貴州	71	21	1,099	-49	-2.67	-9.92	53.58	73.06	1,839
Yunnan 雲南	13	24	1,310	-159	-9.12	-184.82	53.55	95.11	1,746
Tibet 西藏									
Northwest 西北	42	19	891	15	1.18	5.60	45.97	78.85	1,248
Shaanxi 陝西	38	19	848	13	1.03	6.32	43.76	83.71	1,226
Gansu 甘肅	4	20	1,303	35	2.41	4.01	66.79	39.93	1,453
Qinghai 青海									
Ningxia 寧夏									
Xinjiang 新疆									

1322: Inedible Vegetable Oil 非食用植物油加工業

Year 年份	Number of firms 企業個數	Rate of change 每年變化 (%)	Number of employees 職工人數 (人)	Rate of change 每年變化 (%)	Total revenue (mil. RMB) 總銷售收入 (百萬元)	Rate of change 每年變化 (%)	Total profit (mil. RMB) 總利潤 (百萬元)	Rate of change 每年變化 (%)
1993	306		9,349		546		-15	
1994	271	-11.44%	12,046	28.85%	798	46.28%	-1	94.25%
1995	345	27.31%	10,055	-16.53%	497	-37.77%	-55	-6238.88%
1996	337	-2.32%	8,561	-14.86%	664	33.64%	-42	24.02%

3 Major products* 3 種主要產品 *	Output 產量	Sales volume 銷售量	Unit 單位
a) Inedible Vegetable Oil 非食用植物油	93,897	92,958	ton 噸
b) Animal Fat 動物油脂	15,270	13,285	ton 噸

Top 10 firms by revenue (year founded) 收入排名前 10 家企業 (創辦年份)	City 城市	Province 省	Telephone / fax 電話 / 傳真	Number of employees 職工人數	Ownership 產業所有權	Revenue ('000 RMB) 銷售收入 (千元)	Profit ('000 RMB) (rank) 利潤 (千元) (排名)	Total assets ('000 RMB) 總資產 (千元)	Major products 主要產品
Dong Zhou Fat Industrial Co. Ltd. 東洲油脂工業有限公司	Guangzhou 廣州市	Guangdong 廣東省	(020)82773716 (020)82773713	130	Overseas Chinese-funded 港澳台資	142,046	-1334(70)	190,375	a
Shanghai Chang Qiao Fat Factory 上海長橋油脂廠(1993)	Shanghai 上海市	Shanghai 上海市	(021)64763668	185	Collectively-owned 集體	93,366	24(35)	52,299	b
Sichuan Wanteng Oils & Fats Co. Ltd. 四川萬藤油脂有限公司	Chongqing 重慶市	Chongqing 重慶市	(023)8260038 (023)8260018	29	Foreign-funded 外資	21,412	563(5)	31,846	a
Yancheng Nan Yang Cotton Ginning Mill 鹽城市南洋軋花油脂廠(1985)	Yancheng 鹽城市	Jiangsu 江蘇省	(0515)8892163	225	Collectively-owned 集體	20,100	1010(2)	20,360	a
Xixia Oil Pressing Mill 西峽縣榨油廠(1983)	Nanyang 南陽市	Henan 河南省	(0377)4663611	85	State-owned 國有	19,940	-298(59)	19,455	a
Yancheng Qing Dun Cotton Ginning Mill 鹽城市青墩軋花油脂廠(1982)	Yancheng 鹽城市	Jiangsu 江蘇省	(0515)8540176	131	Collectively-owned 集體	10,360	200(15)	9,220	a
Anhui Guoyang Sugar Industry Cigarette & Wine Company Food No.1 Factory 安徽省渦陽縣糖業煙酒公司食品一廠(1992)	Fuyang 阜陽市	Anhui 安徽省		120	Collectively-owned 集體	10,000	1450(1)	2,250	o
Hunan Hongjiang Vegetable Oil Refiner Co. 湖南省洪江植物油製煉公司(1951)	Huaihua 懷化市	Hunan 湖南省	(0745)7622068	125	State-owned 國有	9,754	21(36)	16,990	a
Wubu Fat Factory 吳堡縣油脂工廠(1985)	Yulin 榆林市	Shaanxi 陝西省	(0912)6521438	40	Collectively-owned 集體	9,060	20(38)	6,000	a
Dechengqu Song Guan Tun Oil & Cotton Processing Mill 德城區宋官屯鎮油棉加工廠(1985)	Dezhou 德州市	Shandong 山東省	(0534)2753025 (0534)2753025	97	Collectively-owned 集體	8,394	21(37)	8,420	a

Top 10 Cities by Production Output 產出排名前 10 位城市	Province 省	Market share 市場份額	Number of firms 企業個數
Yancheng 鹽城市	Jiangsu 江蘇省	9.32%	6
Weifang 濰坊市	Shandong 山東省	6.02%	1
Nanyang 南陽市	Henan 河南省	5.54%	7
Chongqing 重慶市	Chongqing 重慶市	4.77%	7
Suzhou 蘇州市	Jiangsu 江蘇省	4.58%	4
Hechi 河池市	Guangxi 廣西	4.02%	16
Beijing 北京市	Beijing 北京市	3.77%	1
Taizhou 泰州市	Jiangsu 江蘇省	3.52%	1
Duyun 都勻市	Guizhou 貴州省	3.11%	21
Suzhou 宿州市	Anhui 安徽省	3.02%	4

10 Major Wholesalers 10 家主要批發商	City 城市	Province 省	Telephone / Fax 電話 / 傳真
Zhejiang Cereal & Oils Food Import & Export Co. Ltd. 浙江省糧油食品進出口股份有限公司	Hangzhou 杭州市	Zhejiang 浙江省	(0571)5152515 (0571)5152514
Henan Cereal & Oils Food Import & Export Company 河南省糧油食品進出口公司	Zhengzhou 鄭州市	Henan 河南省	(0371)3942915 (0371)3942790
Shanghai Land Reclamation & Cultivation Cooking Oil Mill Marketing Company 上海市農墾糧油食品經營公司	Shanghai 上海市	Shanghai 上海市	(021)64714931
Changtu Da Chang Cooking Oil Mill Trade Jointly-operated Company 昌圖縣大昌糧油貿易聯營公司	Tieling 鐵嶺市	Liaoning 遼寧省	(0410)5824099
China Vegetable Oil Company 中國植物油公司	Beijing 北京市	Beijing 北京市	(010)66038248
Zhong Liang Shandong Cooking Oil Mill Import & Export Company 中糧山東糧油進出口公司	Qingdao 青島市	Shandong 山東省	(0532)2972342 (0532)2972379
Zhejiang Cooking Oil Mill Storage & Transport Trade Company 浙江省糧油儲運貿易公司	Hangzhou 杭州市	Zhejiang 浙江省	(0571)5161408 (0571)5161411
Anhui Cereal & Oils Food Import & Export (Group) Company 安徽省糧油食品進出口(集團)公司	Hefei 合肥市	Anhui 安徽省	(0551)2653731 (0551)2652831
Shanghai Farm, Industry & Commerce Group Cooking Oil Mill General Company 上海農工商集團糧油總公司	Shanghai 上海市	Shanghai 上海市	(021)62593423 (021)62748578
Sichuan Chang Jiang Enterprise Co. Ltd. 四川省長江企業股份有限公司	Chengdu 成都市	Sichuan 四川省	(028)3339888 (028)3333896

*Also include sales by firms outside this industry.包括本行業以外廠家的銷售。"o" stands for "others". "o" 代表 "其他產品" 。

1331: Cane Sugar 甘蔗糖業

The industry accounts for 0.366% of the total revenue of China's industrial sector in 1996. The revenue growth rate of the industry is -2.2% from 1995, as compared to the growth rate of China's industrial sector, 9.51%. The rate of return on asset is -3.41%. 36.89% of all firms in the industry made a profit while 60.15% had negative returns. The top province in terms of the industry's revenue is Guangxi, accounting for 41.35% of the total revenue.
本行業在1996年佔全行業總產值0.366%，行業年增長率為-2.2%（全國工業年增長率9.51%）。行業的資產回報率-3.41%，36.89%的企業盈利，60.15%的企業虧損。銷售收入最高的省份為廣西省，佔本行業的41.35%。

	Total number of firms 企業總數	Total number of employees 職工總數	Total revenue (mil. RMB) 總銷售收入（百萬元）	Total profit (mil. RMB) 總利潤（百萬元）	Return on assets 資產利潤率 (%)	Return on equity 權益利潤率 (%)	Labour productivity ('000 RMB / worker) 勞動生產率（千元/人）	Debts / assets 資產負債率 (%)	Total assets (mil. RMB) 總資產（百萬元）
Industry Overall 行業總體	440	261,151	21,214	-1,260	-3.41	-12.94	81.23	73.61	36,895

	Number of firms 企業個數	Average number of employees 平均職工人數	Average revenue ('000 RMB) 平均銷售收入（千元）	Average profit ('000 RMB) 平均利潤（千元）	Return on assets 資產利潤率 (%)	Return on equity 權益利潤率 (%)	Labour productivity ('000 RMB / worker) 勞動生產率（千元/人）	Average debts / assets 平均資產負債率(%)	Average Total assets ('000 RMB) 平均總資產（千元）
By ownership 產業所有權									
State-owned 國有	349	641	49,192	-3,968	-4.51	-19.70	76.80	77.11	88,017
Collectively-owned 集體	72	155	15,280	515	2.70	11.77	98.41	77.10	19,100
Privately-owned 私有									
Domestic JVs 聯營	1	224	29,511	736	12.78	13.06	131.75	2.17	5,763
Joint stock 股份制	8	1,973	205,500	5,942	2.00	5.08	104.14	60.60	297,086
Foreign-funded 外資	9	1,113	134,604	4,370	1.66	2.73	120.89	39.36	264,062
Overseas Chinese-funded 港澳台資	2	268	30,593	214	0.98	5.38	114.37	81.80	21,823
By size 規模									
Large 大型	32	1,987	268,192	-11,220	-3.29	-9.12	134.96	63.98	341,524
Medium 中型	211	728	49,140	-3,611	-3.59	-15.82	67.53	77.28	100,478
Small 小型	186	232	12,170	-750	-2.93	-14.18	52.50	79.34	25,625
By regional distribution 地區分布									
Central-North 華北	1	10	210	10	1.01	2.13	21.00	52.53	990
Beijing 北京									
Tianjin 天津	1	10	210	10	1.01	2.13	21.00	52.53	990
Hebei 河北									
Shanxi 山西									
Inner Mongolia 內蒙									
Northeast 東北									
Liaoning 遼寧									
Jilin 吉林									
Heilongjiang 黑龍江									
Central East 華東	46	612	25,000	-1,052	-1.83	-7.19	40.84	74.48	57,366
Shanghai 上海	1	138	1,980	-810	-34.47	180.00	14.35	119.15	2,350
Jiangsu 江蘇	2	41	4,350	-15	-0.56	-1.91	106.10	70.49	2,660
Zhejiang 浙江									
Anhui 安徽									
Fujian 福建	30	492	22,969	-926	-2.01	-5.87	46.69	65.76	46,079
Jiangxi 江西	13	1,014	34,635	-1,521	-1.58	-9.94	34.16	84.07	96,062
Shandong 山東									
Central-South 中南	255	697	64,481	-4,743	-4.30	-16.98	92.54	74.69	110,360
Henan 河南	1	20	2,270	-120	-2.45	-7.84	113.50	68.71	4,890
Hubei 湖北	2	413	28,220	-1,420	-3.08	-15.00	68.41	79.47	46,075
Hunan 湖南	16	586	15,789	-3,527	-12.24	510.22	26.94	102.40	28,813
Guangdong 廣東	99	721	66,118	-7,673	-6.12	-32.23	91.67	81.03	125,470
Guangxi 廣西	105	773	83,536	-2,787	-2.12	-6.60	108.03	67.87	131,520
Hainan 海南	32	464	25,446	-3,059	-7.24	-30.67	54.82	76.41	42,274
Southwest 西南	138	401	26,240	-12	-0.03	-0.08	65.47	68.26	44,298
Chongqing 重慶	2	507	6,458	-15,559	-43.73	-264.81	12.72	83.49	35,584
Sichuan 四川	36	407	16,069	437	2.13	10.45	39.43	79.58	20,491
Guizhou 貴州	4	118	3,003	-278	-3.07	-22.33	25.50	86.29	9,043
Yunnan 雲南	95	407	31,652	244	0.44	1.31	77.74	66.26	55,152
Tibet 西藏									
Northwest 西北									
Shaanxi 陝西									
Gansu 甘肅									
Qinghai 青海									
Ningxia 寧夏									
Xinjiang 新疆									

Year 年份	Number of firms 企業個數	Rate of change 每年變化 (%)	Number of employees 職工人數（人）	Rate of change 每年變化 (%)	Total revenue (mil. RMB) 總銷售收入（百萬元）	Rate of change 每年變化 (%)	Total profit (mil. RMB) 總利潤（百萬元）	Rate of change 每年變化 (%)
1993	456		244,111		17,720		685	
1994	454	-0.44%	260,717	6.80%	16,581	-6.43%	1,469	114.51%
1995	464	2.20%	325,211	24.74%	21,694	30.83%	1,456	-0.91%
1996	440	-5.17%	261,151	-19.70%	21,214	-2.21%	-1,260	-186.54%

3 Major products* 3 種主要產品 *	Output 產量	Sales volume 銷售量	Unit 單位
a) Machine-made Cane Sugar 機製甘蔗糖	4,851,367	4,657,312	ton 噸
b) Sugar 糖	5,250,216	5,197,714	ton 噸

Top 10 firms by revenue (year founded) 收入排名前 10 家企業 (創辦年份)	City 城市	Province 省	Telephone / fax 電話 / 傳真	Number of employees 職工人數	Ownership 產業所有權	Revenue ('000 RMB) 銷售收入（千元）	Profit ('000 RMB) (rank) 利潤（千元）（排名）	Total assets ('000 RMB) 總資產（千元）	Major products 主要產品
Guangdong Mei Shan Sugar Industry General Co. 廣東梅山糖業總公司(1983)	Guangzhou 廣州市	Guangdong 廣東省	(020)84971385 (020)84971308	2,455	State-owned 國有	636,638	-66927(338)	1,442,229	a,b
Guangxi Guitang (Group) Co. Ltd. 廣西貴糖(集團)股份有限公司(1956)	Guiping 桂平市	Guangxi 廣西	(0775)4214012 (0775)4214835	4,725	Joint stock 股份制	448,356	753(86)	611,355	a,b
Jiangmen Sugarcane Chemical Plant (Group) Co. Ltd. 江門甘蔗化工廠(集團)股份有限公司(1959)	Jiangmen 江門市	Guangdong 廣東省	(0750)3361611 (0750)3361973	4,675	Joint stock 股份制	415,370	83216(1)	1,081,013	a,b
Chongzuo Dong Ya Sugar Industry Co. Ltd. 崇左東亞糖業有限公司(1993)	Pingxiang 憑祥市	Guangxi 廣西	(0771)7828188	1,481	Foreign-funded 外資	356,416	29543(4)	296,034	a,b
Zhuhai Doumen Bai Jiao Sugar Refinery 廣東省斗門縣白蕉糖廠(1965)	Zhuhai 珠海市	Guangdong 廣東省	(0756)5501452 (0756)5501428	1,454	State-owned 國有	341,877	1609(65)	456,717	a,b
Guangxi Tuo Lu Dong Ya Sugar Industry Co. Ltd. 廣西馱盧東亞糖業有限公司(1993)	Pingxiang 憑祥市	Guangxi 廣西	(0771)7950371	1,306	Foreign-funded 外資	332,063	33184(3)	322,373	a,b
Fusui Dong Ya Sugar Industry Co. Ltd. 扶綏縣東亞糖業有限公司(1993)	Pingxiang 憑祥市	Guangxi 廣西	(0771)7538089 (0771)7531062	1,275	Foreign-funded 外資	321,284	21325(7)	359,562	a,b
Guangxi Nanning Shi Sugar Refining Paper Mill 廣西南寧市製糖造紙廠(1960)	Nanning 南寧市	Guangxi 廣西	(0771)4832302 (0771)4832302	3,092	State-owned 國有	299,527	18164(8)	308,736	a,b
Dongguan Dong Tang Industrial Group Co. 東莞市東糖實業集團公司(1935)	Dongguan 東莞市	Guangdong 廣東省	(0769)8812123 (0769)8812817	2,518	State-owned 國有	285,882	-718(157)	371,432	a,b
Ping Sha Sugar Refinery 平沙糖廠(1963)	Zhuhai 珠海市	Guangdong 廣東省	(0756)7752391 (0756)7751332	1,221	State-owned 國有	284,180	25263(6)	267,160	a,b

Top 10 Cities by Production Output 產出排名前 10 位城市	Province 省	Market share 市場份額	Number of firms 企業個數
Zhanjiang 湛江市	Guangdong 廣東省	15.92%	36
Pingxiang 憑祥市	Guangxi 廣西	8.77%	23
Nanning 南寧市	Guangxi 廣西	6.60%	10
Guangzhou 廣州市	Guangdong 廣東省	5.15%	9
Heshan 合山市	Guangxi 廣西	4.59%	13
Liuzhou 柳州市	Guangxi 廣西	4.08%	7
Guigang 貴港市	Guangxi 廣西	4.05%	6
Zhuhai 珠海市	Guangdong 廣東省	3.97%	5
Tongshi 通什市	Hainan 海南省	3.53%	30
Lincang 臨滄縣	Yunnan 雲南省	2.76%	18

10 Major Wholesalers 10 家主要批發商	City 城市	Province 省	Telephone / Fax 電話 / 傳真
Zhong Liang Sugar Industry Groceries Import & Export Company 中糧糖業雜品進出口公司	Beijing 北京市	Beijing 北京市	(010)65268888 (010)65276023
China National Sugar & Alcohol Group Corp. 中國糖業酒類集團公司	Beijing 北京市	Beijing 北京市	(010)68360994
Shanxi Sugar & Wine Non-staple Food Company 山西省糖酒副食公司	Taiyuan 太原市	Shanxi 山西省	(0351)2027938 (0351)2027931
Putian Xue Jin Beer Marketing Agency Co. Ltd. 莆田縣雪津啤酒營銷代理有限公司	Putian 莆田市	Fujian 福建省	
Suzhou Sugar, Cigarette & Wine General Company 蘇州糖煙酒總公司	Suzhou 蘇州市	Jiangsu 江蘇省	(0512)7276392 (0512)7276406
Yuhang Sugar Industry Tobacco & Wine Company 余杭市糖業煙酒公司	Hangzhou 杭州市	Zhejiang 浙江省	(0571)6225788 (0571)6225407
Wuxi Sugar Industry Cigarette & Wine General Company 無錫市糖業煙酒總公司	Wuxi 無錫市	Jiangsu 江蘇省	(0510)2720023 (0510)2707693
Wuxi Chaoyang Co. Ltd. 無錫朝陽股份有限公司	Wuxi 無錫市	Jiangsu 江蘇省	(0510)2767704
Yinchuan Shen Da Non-staple Food Co. Ltd. 銀川申達副食有限公司	Yinchuan 銀川市	Ningxia 寧夏	(0951)5031694
Shanghai Sugar Industry Cigarette & Wine (Group) Co. Ltd. 上海市糖業煙酒(集團)有限公司	Shanghai 上海市	Shanghai 上海市	(021)63224190 (021)63223169

*Also include sales by firms outside this industry.包括本行業以外廠家的銷售。"o" stands for "others". "o" 代表"其他產品"。

1332: Beet Sugar 甜菜糖業

The industry accounts for 0.098% of the total revenue of China's industrial sector in 1996. The revenue growth rate of the industry is 36.0% from 1995, as compared to the growth rate of China's industrial sector, 9.51%. The rate of return on asset is -8.51%. 38.54% of all firms in the industry made a profit while 50.52% had negative returns. The top province in terms of the industry's revenue is Helongjiang, accounting for 30.12% of the total revenue.
本行業在1996年佔全行業總產值0.098%，行業年增長率為36.0%（全國工業年增長率9.51%）。行業的資產回報率-8.51%，38.54%的企業盈利，50.52%的企業虧損。銷售收入最高的省份為黑龍江省，佔本行業的30.12%。

	Total number of firms 企業總數	Total number of employees 職工總數	Total revenue (mil. RMB) 總銷售收入（百萬元）	Total profit (mil. RMB) 總利潤（百萬元）	Return on assets 資產利潤率 (%)	Return on equity 權益利潤率 (%)	Labour productivity ('000 RMB / worker) 勞動生產率（千元/人）	Debts / assets 資產負債率 (%)	Total assets (mil. RMB) 總資產（百萬元）
Industry Overall 行業總體	101	108,925	5,683	-1,203	-8.51	3005.02	52.17	100.28	14,138

	Number of firms 企業個數	Average number of employees 平均職工人數	Average revenue ('000 RMB) 平均銷售收入（千元）	Average profit ('000 RMB) 平均利潤（千元）	Return on assets 資產利潤率 (%)	Return on equity 權益利潤率 (%)	Labour productivity ('000 RMB / worker) 勞動生產率（千元/人）	Average debts / assets 平均資產負債率(%)	Average Total assets ('000 RMB) 平均總資產（千元）
By ownership 產業所有權									
State-owned 國有	92	1,178	61,685	-13,076	-8.52	3251.35	52.37	100.26	153,489
Collectively-owned 集體	8	42	776				18.70	111.00	1,392
Privately-owned 私有									
Domestic JVs 聯營									
Joint stock 股份制	1	213	1,816				8.53	130.27	5,863
Foreign-funded 外資									
Overseas Chinese-funded 港澳台資									
By size 規模									
Large 大型	18	2,172	120,507	-51,628	-17.33	570.71	55.49	103.04	297,967
Medium 中型	47	1,141	62,246	-5,254	-3.58	-1965.96	54.56	99.82	146,688
Small 小型	34	448	17,310	-787	-1.42	-24.26	38.62	94.14	55,303
By regional distribution 地區分布									
Central-North 華北	26	909	59,039	-5,354	-4.52	-36.56	64.99	87.65	118,567
Beijing 北京									
Tianjin 天津	1	12	1,800	190	23.46	105.56	150.00	77.78	810
Hebei 河北	1	480	24,800	20	0.06	0.19	51.67	65.67	30,990
Shanxi 山西	6	652	24,887	-3,902	-5.05	-24.63	38.19	79.52	77,317
Inner Mongolia 內蒙	18	1,068	75,506	-6,445	-4.48	-42.19	70.72	89.37	143,724
Northeast 東北	40	1,384	55,309	-16,580	-10.84	76.76	39.96	114.12	152,943
Liaoning 遼寧	7	728	25,439	-3,449	-6.06	34.09	34.96	117.78	56,913
Jilin 吉林	5	1,483	64,508	-32,792	-13.87	873.99	43.51	101.59	236,400
Heilongjiang 黑龍江	28	1,531	61,134	-16,967	-10.47	61.34	39.94	117.07	162,048
Central East 華東	3	291	19,573	423	0.85	2.43	67.26	64.88	49,597
Shanghai 上海									
Jiangsu 江蘇									
Zhejiang 浙江									
Anhui 安徽									
Fujian 福建									
Jiangxi 江西									
Shandong 山東	3	291	19,573	423	0.85	2.43	67.26	64.88	49,597
Central-South 中南	5	55	1,204	42	3.49	11.67	21.73	69.88	1,202
Henan 河南	3	80	1,600	70	3.87	12.88	20.08	69.93	1,807
Hubei 湖北	1	12	800				66.67	58.82	340
Hunan 湖南	1	26	420				16.15	84.00	250
Guangdong 廣東									
Guangxi 廣西									
Hainan 海南									
Southwest 西南									
Chongqing 重慶									
Sichuan 四川									
Guizhou 貴州									
Yunnan 雲南									
Tibet 西藏									
Northwest 西北	27	1,066	69,286	-14,900	-8.41	-103.39	64.97	91.86	177,125
Shaanxi 陝西	3	114	490	10	0.17	0.36	4.30	51.67	5,773
Gansu 甘肅	5	1,117	70,958	-9,436	-5.04	-28.40	63.55	82.27	187,372
Qinghai 青海									
Ningxia 寧夏	3	1,559	67,593	-23,737	-10.16	-1435.69	43.37	99.29	233,607
Xinjiang 新疆	16	1,137	81,979	-17,747	-9.08	-135.43	72.10	93.30	195,461

1332: Beet Sugar 甜菜糖業

Year 年份	Number of firms 企業個數	Rate of change 每年變化 (%)	Number of employees 職工人數 (人)	Rate of change 每年變化 (%)	Total revenue (mil. RMB) 總銷售收入 (百萬元)	Rate of change 每年變化 (%)	Total profit (mil. RMB) 總利潤 (百萬元)	Rate of change 每年變化 (%)
1993	104		71,480		5,387		-197	
1994	103	-0.96%	110,399	54.45%	4,097	-23.95%	-213	-8.31%
1995	103		128,603	16.49%	4,179	2.00%	-390	-82.91%
1996	101	-1.94%	108,925	-15.30%	5,683	35.99%	-1,203	-208.14%

3 Major products* 3 種主要產品 *	Output 產量	Sales volume 銷售量	Unit 單位
a) Machine-made Beet Sugar 機製甜菜糖	886,283	1,010,363	ton 噸
b) Sugar 糖	1,100,120	1,089,118	ton 噸

Top 10 firms by revenue (year founded) 收入排名前 10 家企業 (創辦年份)	City 城市	Province 省	Telephone / fax 電話 / 傳真	Number of employees 職工人數	Ownership 產業所有權	Revenue ('000 RMB) 銷售收入 (千元)	Profit ('000 RMB) (rank) 利潤 (千元) (排名)	Total assets ('000 RMB) 總資產 (千元)	Major products 主要產品
Shihezi Ba Yi Sugar Refinery 石河子八一製糖廠(1959)	Shihezi 石河子市	Xinjiang 新疆	(0993)2012756 (0993)2012756	3,553	State-owned 國有	227,493	-34020(54)	408,055	a,b
Heilongjiang Friendship Sugar Refinery 黑龍江省友誼糖廠(1955)	Jiamusi 佳木斯市	Heilongjiang 黑龍江省	(0454)8582712 (0454)8582915	3,596	State-owned 國有	158,110	-81572(64)	274,461	a,b
Jilin Xin Zhong Guo Sugar Refinery 吉林新中國糖廠(1955)	Jilin 吉林市	Jilin 吉林省	(0432)3058291 (0432)3059702	3,300	State-owned 國有	153,137	-74816(62)	613,453	a,b
Heilong Jiang Hong Guang Sugar Refinery 黑龍江省紅光糖廠(1954)	Qiqiha'er 齊齊哈爾市	Heilongjiang 黑龍江省	(0452)3712541 (0452)3712163	4,769	State-owned 國有	143,429	-59014(60)	362,784	a,b
Xinjiang Corps Nong Si Shi Huo Er Guo Si Sugar Refinery 新疆兵團農四師霍爾果斯糖廠(1991)	Yining 伊寧市	Xinjiang 新疆	(0999)3022249	1,073	State-owned 國有	141,879	-31506(52)	187,802	a,b
Yi Li Sugar Refinery 伊犁糖廠(1984)	Yining 伊寧市	Xinjiang 新疆	(0999)8611126 (0999)8611461	1,678	State-owned 國有	141,341	-35578(55)	268,056	a,b
Gansu Jiuquan Sugar Refinery 甘肅省酒泉糖廠(1985)	Yumen 玉門市	Gansu 甘肅省	(0937)2614363 (0937)2614393	2,039	State-owned 國有	138,005	-9540(31)	269,580	a,b
Qiqiha'er Sugar Refinery 齊齊哈爾糖廠(1957)	Qiqiha'er 齊齊哈爾市	Heilongjiang 黑龍江省	(0452)2347951	2,894	State-owned 國有	134,855	-58477(59)	265,096	a,b
Heilongjiang Ning'an Sugar Refinery 黑龍江省寧安糖廠(1961)	Mudanjiang 牡丹江市	Heilongjiang 黑龍江省	(0453)7621151 (0453)7621156	1,783	State-owned 國有	128,133	-8976(28)	190,375	a,b
Ningxia Yinchuan Sugar Refinery 寧夏銀川糖廠(1970)	Yinchuan 銀川市	Ningxia 寧夏	(0951)3067190	2,917	State-owned 國有	123,911	91(8)	285,249	a,b

Top 10 Cities by Production Output 產出排名前 10 位城市	Province 省	Market share 市場份額	Number of firms 企業個數
Qiqiha'er 齊齊哈爾市	Heilongjiang 黑龍江省	9.61%	6
Chifeng 赤峯市	Inner Mong 內蒙	8.29%	4
Yining 伊寧市	Xinjiang 新疆	7.13%	4
Heihe 黑河市	Heilongjiang 黑龍江省	5.99%	3
Linhe 臨河市	Inner Mong 內蒙	4.81%	5
Suihua 綏化市	Heilongjiang 黑龍江省	4.68%	4
Changji 昌吉市	Xinjiang 新疆	4.12%	3
Baotou 包頭市	Inner Mong 內蒙	3.77%	1
Yumen 玉門市	Gansu 甘肅省	3.61%	2
Shihezi 石河子市	Xinjiang 新疆	3.49%	1

10 Major Wholesalers 10 家主要批發商	City 城市	Province 省	Telephone / Fax 電話 / 傳真
Zhong Liang Sugar Industry Groceries Import & Export Company 中糧糖業雜品進出口公司	Beijing 北京市	Beijing 北京市	(010)65268888 (010)65276023
China National Sugar & Alcohol Group Corp. 中國糖業酒類集團公司	Beijing 北京市	Beijing 北京市	(010)68360994
Shanxi Sugar & Wine Non-staple Food Company 山西省糖酒副食公司	Taiyuan 太原市	Shanxi 山西省	(0351)2027938 (0351)2027931
Putian Xue Jin Beer Marketing Agency Co. Ltd. 莆田縣雪津啤酒營銷代理有限公司	Putian 莆田市	Fujian 福建省	
Suzhou Sugar, Cigarette & Wine General Company 蘇州糖煙酒總公司	Suzhou 蘇州市	Jiangsu 江蘇省	(0512)7276392 (0512)7276406
Yuhang Sugar Industry Tobacco & Wine Company 余杭市糖業煙酒公司	Hangzhou 杭州市	Zhejiang 浙江省	(0571)6225788 (0571)6225407
Wuxi Sugar Industry Cigarette & Wine General Company 無錫市糖業煙酒總公司	Wuxi 無錫市	Jiangsu 江蘇省	(0510)2720023 (0510)2707693
Wuxi Chaoyang Co. Ltd. 無錫朝陽股份有限公司	Wuxi 無錫市	Jiangsu 江蘇省	(0510)2767704
Yinchuan Shen Da Non-staple Food Co. Ltd. 銀川申達副食有限公司	Yinchuan 銀川市	Ningxia 寧夏	(0951)5031694
Shanghai Sugar Industry Cigarette & Wine (Group) Co. Ltd. 上海市糖業煙酒(集團)有限公司	Shanghai 上海市	Shanghai 上海市	(021)63224190 (021)63223169

*Also include sales by firms outside this industry.包括本行業以外廠家的銷售。"o" stands for "others". "o" 代表"其他產品"。

1334: Sugar 加工糖業

The industry accounts for 0.027% of the total revenue of China's industrial sector in 1996. The revenue growth rate of the industry is 0.7% from 1995, as compared to the growth rate of China's industrial sector, 9.51%. The rate of return on asset is -1.36%. 63.85% of all firms in the industry made a profit while 21.52% had negative returns. The top province in terms of the industry's revenue is Guangdong, accounting for 65.11% of the total revenue.
本行業在1996年佔全行業總產值0.027%，行業年增長率為0.7%（全國工業年增長率9.51%）。行業的資產回報率-1.36%，63.85%的企業盈利，21.52%的企業虧損。銷售收入最高的省份為廣東省，佔本行業的65.11%。

	Total number of firms 企業總數	Total number of employees 職工總數	Total revenue (mil. RMB) 總銷售收入（百萬元）	Total profit (mil. RMB) 總利潤（百萬元）	Return on assets 資產利潤率 (%)	Return on equity 權益利潤率 (%)	Labour productivity ('000 RMB / worker) 勞動生產率（千元/人）	Debts / assets 資產負債率 (%)	Total assets (mil. RMB) 總資產（百萬元）
Industry Overall 行業總體	75	12,907	1,557	-37	-1.36	-4.24	120.63	67.93	2,756

	Number of firms 企業個數	Average number of employees 平均職工人數	Average revenue ('000 RMB) 平均銷售收入（千元）	Average profit ('000 RMB) 平均利潤（千元）	Return on assets 資產利潤率 (%)	Return on equity 權益利潤率 (%)	Labour productivity ('000 RMB / worker) 勞動生產率（千元/人）	Average debts / assets 平均資產負債率(%)	Average Total assets ('000 RMB) 平均總資產（千元）
By ownership 產業所有權									
State-owned 國有	27	362	42,037	-1,259	-1.42	-4.34	116.07	67.31	88,815
Collectively-owned 集體	39	77	8,838	-100	-2.16	-8.56	114.62	74.72	4,624
Privately-owned 私有	2	40	2,989	-9	-0.50	-0.70	74.73	28.71	1,724
Domestic JVs 聯營	1	75	3,550	1,012	2.92	6.91	47.34	57.77	34,697
Joint stock 股份制	2	107	261	-5	-0.95	-1.36	2.44	30.61	518
Foreign-funded 外資	1	123	33,411				271.63	73.98	110,771
Overseas Chinese-funded 港澳台資	4	49	8,998	-21	-0.29	-1.01	185.53	71.78	7,190
By size 規模									
Large 大型	2	2,960	582,541	-2,004	-0.19	-0.53	196.84	64.42	1,061,145
Medium 中型	2	308	14,733	531	0.89	3.87	47.91	77.02	59,720
Small 小型	69	91	5,263	-494	-6.61	-33.50	58.13	80.26	7,464
By regional distribution 地區分布									
Central-North 華北	20	118	12,027	613	5.61	22.55	101.53	75.11	10,921
Beijing 北京	3	53	6,660	120	1.01	3.43	125.66	70.64	11,910
Tianjin 天津	4	117	2,628	100	2.32	181.82	22.51	98.73	4,318
Hebei 河北	12	86	14,134	1,066	15.76	41.20	164.67	61.76	6,762
Shanxi 山西									
Inner Mongolia 內蒙	1	713	40,430	-1,290	-1.53	-10.21	56.70	85.01	84,280
Northeast 東北	8	34	8,353	253	1.76	8.77	245.66	79.94	14,350
Liaoning 遼寧	1	35	100	20	1.60	1.63	2.86	1.60	1,250
Jilin 吉林	1	12	1,560	120	12.77	20.34	130.00	37.23	940
Heilongjiang 黑龍江	6	38	10,860	313	1.67	8.86	289.60	81.17	18,768
Central East 華東	19	103	9,424	-1,405	-14.28	-39.46	91.63	63.82	9,842
Shanghai 上海	1	35	2,950	110	4.93	13.41	84.29	63.68	2,230
Jiangsu 江蘇	6	230	23,250	-4,335	-18.57	-52.43	101.31	64.57	23,342
Zhejiang 浙江	1	22	2,090				95.00	59.44	1,800
Anhui 安徽	1	104	8,600				82.69	91.08	3,250
Fujian 福建	4	42	2,820	-318	-5.00	-12.07	67.54	58.62	6,355
Jiangxi 江西	4	30	2,233	68	6.54	11.34	75.68	42.62	1,033
Shandong 山東	2	66	2,850	100	1.98	6.04	43.51	67.26	5,055
Central-South 中南	20	378	52,386	-759	-0.69	-2.03	138.51	65.85	109,197
Henan 河南	4	54	4,265	108	4.10	20.38	78.98	79.89	2,623
Hubei 湖北	4	93	3,425	-458	-13.83	-29.00	36.93	52.31	3,308
Hunan 湖南	3	113	420	-203	-2.38	-14.73	3.73	83.85	8,543
Guangdong 廣東	6	1,092	168,972	-2,198	-0.62	-1.81	154.76	65.72	354,933
Guangxi 廣西	2	40	735	10	0.96	3.64	18.61	73.68	1,045
Hainan 海南	1	9	400	10	0.34	0.35	44.44	2.76	2,900
Southwest 西南	5	106	3,094	-2,006	-22.84	91.60	29.24	124.94	8,782
Chongqing 重慶	1	35	458	-97	-38.52	-65.01	12.87	40.75	252
Sichuan 四川	1	161	5,928	-4,452	-23.72	104.89	36.76	122.62	18,765
Guizhou 貴州									
Yunnan 雲南	2	99	2,125	-950	-19.33	54.44	21.57	135.50	4,915
Tibet 西藏									
Northwest 西北	3	73	2,410	47	1.66	3.41	33.01	51.25	2,803
Shaanxi 陝西									
Gansu 甘肅	3	73	2,410	47	1.66	3.41	33.01	51.25	2,803
Qinghai 青海									
Ningxia 寧夏									
Xinjiang 新疆									

Year 年份	Number of firms 企業個數	Rate of change 每年變化 (%)	Number of employees 職工人數（人）	Rate of change 每年變化 (%)	Total revenue (mil. RMB) 總銷售收入（百萬元）	Rate of change 每年變化 (%)	Total profit (mil. RMB) 總利潤（百萬元）	Rate of change 每年變化 (%)
1993	66		5,373		376		-45	
1994	80	21.21%	12,441	131.55%	1,129	200.16%	-16	64.42%
1995	88	10.00%	12,779	2.72%	1,546	36.92%	-8	47.98%
1996	75	-14.77%	12,907	1.00%	1,557	0.71%	-37	-340.42%

3 Major products* 3 種主要產品 *	Output 產量	Sales volume 銷售量	Unit 單位
a) Processed Sugar 加工糖	279,029	231,594	ton 噸
b) Candy 糖果	6,506	6,376	ton 噸

Top 10 firms by revenue (year founded) 收入排名前 10 家企業 (創辦年份)	City 城市	Province 省	Telephone / fax 電話 / 傳真	Number of employees 職工人數	Ownership 產業所有權	Revenue ('000 RMB) 銷售收入（千元）	Profit ('000 RMB) (rank) 利潤（千元）（排名）	Total assets ('000 RMB) 總資產（千元）	Major products 主要產品
Nanhai Electric Power Industrial Group Corp. 南海電力實業集團公司(1957)	Foshan 佛山市	Guangdong 廣東省	(0757)6822168 (0757)6822909	3,859	State-owned 國有	811,889	20161(1)	1,643,631	a,b
Zhongshan Zhong Tang Group Co. Ltd. 中山市中糖集團有限公司(1957)	Zhongshan 中山市	Guangdong 廣東省	(0760)3226412 (0760)3229090	1,840	State-owned 國有	146,103	-16946(40)	356,177	a
Zhaoxian Xing Bai Starch Factory 趙縣興柏澱粉廠(1987)	Shijiazhuang 石家莊市	Hebei 河北省	(0311)4701057	650	Collectively-owned 集體	104,598	10410(2)	23,519	o
Wuxi Leaf Confectionery Co. Ltd. 無錫市利夫糖果有限公司(1988)	Wuxi 無錫市	Jiangsu 江蘇省	(0510)5111284 (0510)5100253	284	Foreign-funded 外資	67,210	-20300(41)	69,518	o
State-owned Rugao Sugar Refinery 國營如皋市糖廠(1976)	Nantong 南通市	Jiangsu 江蘇省	(0513)8591067 (0513)8591066	348	State-owned 國有	48,224	46(18)	21,474	a
Shanghai Hua Er Candy Packing Factory 上海華二糖果包裝廠(1986)	Shanghai 上海市	Shanghai 上海市	(021)64102415	100	Collectively-owned 集體	39,803	604(6)	3,138	o
Nanhai Glucose Refinery 南海市葡萄糖廠(1958)	Foshan 佛山市	Guangdong 廣東省	(0757)5887445 (0757)5887445	92	Collectively-owned 集體	26,860	150(15)	12,610	o
Guangdong Yingde Sugar Refinery 廣東省英德市糖廠(1978)	Qingyuan 清遠市	Guangdong 廣東省	(0763)2851330	404	State-owned 國有	21,076	-14141(39)	75,259	o
Jiangsu Hai'an Sugar Refinery 江蘇海安糖廠(1979)	Nantong 南通市	Jiangsu 江蘇省	(0513)8711140	262	State-owned 國有	15,992	-3157(37)	12,734	a
Hua Wei Nutritive Food Company 華威營養食品公司(1985)	Beijing 北京市	Beijing 北京市	(010)65070809 (010)65019021	100	Overseas Chinese-funded 港澳台資	14,692	561(7)	23,700	b

Top 10 Cities by Production Output 產出排名前 10 位城市	Province 省	Market share 市場份額	Number of firms 企業個數
Foshan 佛山市	Guangdong 廣東省	24.57%	3
Wuxi 無錫市	Jiangsu 江蘇省	13.12%	1
Nantong 南通市	Jiangsu 江蘇省	11.59%	3
Shijiazhuang 石家莊市	Hebei 河北省	10.42%	2
Zhongshan 中山市	Guangdong 廣東省	9.78%	1
Huaiyin 淮陰市	Jiangsu 江蘇省	9.20%	1
Beijing 北京市	Beijing 北京市	3.82%	3
Shuangcheng 雙城市	Heilongjiang 黑龍江省	1.97%	1
Xingtai 邢臺市	Hebei 河北省	1.84%	5
Dongguan 東莞市	Guangdong 廣東省	1.32%	2

10 Major Wholesalers 10 家主要批發商	City 城市	Province 省	Telephone / Fax 電話 / 傳真
Zhong Liang Sugar Industry Groceries Import & Export Company 中糧糖業雜品進出口公司	Beijing 北京市	Beijing 北京市	(010)65268888 (010)65276023
China National Sugar & Alcohol Group Corp. 中國糖業酒類集團公司	Beijing 北京市	Beijing 北京市	(010)68360994
Shanxi Sugar & Wine Non-staple Food Company 山西省糖酒副食公司	Taiyuan 太原市	Shanxi 山西省	(0351)2027938 (0351)2027931
Putian Xue Jin Beer Marketing Agency Co. Ltd. 莆田縣雪津啤酒營銷代理有限公司	Putian 莆田市	Fujian 福建省	
Suzhou Sugar, Cigarette & Wine General Company 蘇州糖煙酒總公司	Suzhou 蘇州市	Jiangsu 江蘇省	(0512)7276392 (0512)7276406
Yuhang Sugar Industry Tobacco & Wine Company 余杭市糖業煙酒公司	Hangzhou 杭州市	Zhejiang 浙江省	(0571)6225788 (0571)6225407
Wuxi Sugar Industry Cigarette & Wine General Company 無錫市糖業煙酒總公司	Wuxi 無錫市	Jiangsu 江蘇省	(0510)2720023 (0510)2707693
Wuxi Chaoyang Co. Ltd. 無錫朝陽股份有限公司	Wuxi 無錫市	Jiangsu 江蘇省	(0510)2767704
Yinchuan Shen Da Non-staple Food Co. Ltd. 銀川申達副食有限公司	Yinchuan 銀川市	Ningxia 寧夏	(0951)5031694
Shanghai Sugar Industry Cigarette & Wine (Group) Co. Ltd. 上海市糖業煙酒(集團)有限公司	Shanghai 上海市	Shanghai 上海市	(021)63224190 (021)63223169

*Also include sales by firms outside this industry.包括本行業以外廠家的銷售。"o" stands for "others". "o" 代表"其他產品"。

1341: Slaughtering 屠宰業

The industry accounts for 0.221% of the total revenue of China's industrial sector in 1996. The revenue growth rate of the industry is -16.1% from 1995, as compared to the growth rate of China's industrial sector, 9.51%. The rate of return on asset is -3.61%. 59.59% of all firms in the industry made a profit while 29.79% had negative returns. The top province in terms of the industry's revenue is Shandong, accounting for 17.13% of the total revenue.
本行業在1996年佔全行業總產值0.221%，行業年增長率為-16.1%（全國工業年增長率9.51%）。行業的資產回報率-3.61%，59.59%的企業盈利，29.79%的企業虧損。銷售收入最高的省份為山東省，佔本行業的17.13%。

	Total number of firms 企業總數	Total number of employees 職工總數	Total revenue (mil. RMB) 總銷售收入（百萬元）	Total profit (mil. RMB) 總利潤（百萬元）	Return on assets 資產利潤率 (%)	Return on equity 權益利潤率 (%)	Labour productivity ('000 RMB / worker) 勞動生產率（千元/人）	Debts / assets 資產負債率 (%)	Total assets (mil. RMB) 總資產（百萬元）
Industry Overall 行業總體	922	161,903	12,840	-492	-3.61	-16.89	79.31	78.63	13,627

	Number of firms 企業個數	Average number of employees 平均職工人數	Average revenue ('000 RMB) 平均銷售收入（千元）	Average profit ('000 RMB) 平均利潤（千元）	Return on assets 資產利潤率 (%)	Return on equity 權益利潤率 (%)	Labour productivity ('000 RMB / worker) 勞動生產率（千元/人）	Average debts / assets 平均資產負債率(%)	Average Total assets ('000 RMB) 平均總資產（千元）
By ownership 產業所有權									
State-owned 國有	573	240	18,045	-934	-4.48	-21.37	75.22	79.05	20,859
Collectively-owned 集體	315	50	6,174	59	1.56	11.56	124.20	86.53	3,816
Privately-owned 私有	6	70	28,918	2,071	14.56	17.86	411.15	18.44	14,221
Domestic JVs 聯營	11	598	14,477	802	4.20	7.43	24.23	43.44	19,066
Joint stock 股份制	8	64	4,563	-94	-2.93	-25.51	71.29	88.50	3,213
Foreign-funded 外資	8	174	20,648	344	2.04	5.29	118.49	61.43	16,864
Overseas Chinese-funded 港澳台資	2	51	10,631	512	5.76	35.17	208.45	83.64	8,893
By size 規模									
Large 大型	32	1,298	146,610	-3,172	-2.03	-8.11	112.92	74.98	156,234
Medium 中型	77	537	36,962	-3,367	-7.53	-38.52	68.88	80.45	44,712
Small 小型	802	98	6,612	-164	-2.53	-13.29	67.18	80.95	6,461
By regional distribution 地區分布									
Central-North 華北	179	135	13,519	-618	-4.56	-21.04	100.01	78.33	13,548
Beijing 北京	60	106	26,307	-779	-4.91	-21.84	247.05	77.52	15,873
Tianjin 天津	4	690	44,340	-5,418	-8.65	-34.97	64.24	75.27	62,650
Hebei 河北	48	112	7,323	-317	-3.42	-17.85	65.33	80.85	9,280
Shanxi 山西	14	171	5,339	-222	-1.32	-2.23	31.18	40.89	16,836
Inner Mongolia 內蒙	53	137	4,488	-450	-4.41	-95.78	32.72	95.39	10,206
Northeast 東北	157	125	6,969	-450	-4.68	-17.82	55.79	73.75	9,614
Liaoning 遼寧	72	117	10,615	-128	-1.54	-6.35	90.63	75.69	8,292
Jilin 吉林	34	165	4,827	-1,473	-9.39	-46.15	29.24	79.64	15,675
Heilongjiang 黑龍江	51	109	3,248	-222	-2.98	-7.94	29.76	62.43	7,440
Central East 華東	223	293	23,052	-487	-2.02	-10.28	78.67	80.33	24,115
Shanghai 上海	12	893	80,944	1,175	1.89	4.53	90.67	58.16	62,052
Jiangsu 江蘇	38	442	27,405	-1,346	-4.14	-26.38	61.94	84.32	32,536
Zhejiang 浙江	7	94	8,057	-313	-3.42	-8.75	86.11	60.89	9,139
Anhui 安徽	38	238	19,397	-1,004	-6.03	-60.52	81.62	90.03	16,647
Fujian 福建	14	33	3,982	110	10.29	15.40	120.93	33.20	1,069
Jiangxi 江西	15	221	5,267	-251	-1.68	-5.54	23.83	69.70	14,973
Shandong 山東	99	246	22,219	-294	-1.18	-7.53	90.30	84.30	24,854
Central-South 中南	158	141	11,036	-214	-1.98	-8.93	78.09	77.79	10,802
Henan 河南	47	151	20,214	157	1.02	8.25	133.64	87.58	15,371
Hubei 湖北	34	255	9,513	-975	-5.97	-26.51	37.24	77.47	16,323
Hunan 湖南	25	190	9,243	-538	-4.53	-14.58	48.72	68.92	11,881
Guangdong 廣東	40	18	3,351	127	21.55	50.85	188.24	57.62	589
Guangxi 廣西	12	90	8,757	24	0.27	0.47	97.39	43.01	9,060
Hainan 海南									
Southwest 西南	132	149	13,154	-941	-8.15	-63.71	88.51	87.20	11,538
Chongqing 重慶	14	238	16,157	-1,800	-8.99	-98.18	67.75	90.85	20,029
Sichuan 四川	97	132	13,504	-833	-8.58	-253.85	101.84	96.62	9,700
Guizhou 貴州	10	187	4,447	-1,044	-9.12	-17.77	23.84	48.67	11,447
Yunnan 雲南	10	135	14,179	-674	-3.83	-8.64	105.03	55.60	17,578
Tibet 西藏									
Northwest 西北	73	148	9,661	-604	-4.06	-12.28	65.29	66.92	14,868
Shaanxi 陝西	23	247	22,290	-320	-1.35	-4.71	90.27	71.42	23,781
Gansu 甘肅	18	166	3,430	-1,776	-12.50	-43.55	20.70	71.30	14,201
Qinghai 青海	22	61	4,810	-125	-1.49	-3.33	79.27	55.31	8,420
Ningxia 寧夏	3	129	3,610	-403	-1.67	-3.44	27.91	51.35	24,130
Xinjiang 新疆	7	60	2,026	-113	-3.14	-6.98	33.92	55.03	3,593

1341: Slaughtering 屠宰業

Year 年份	Number of firms 企業個數	Rate of change 每年變化 (%)	Number of employees 職工人數 (人)	Rate of change 每年變化 (%)	Total revenue (mil. RMB) 總銷售收入 (百萬元)	Rate of change 每年變化 (%)	Total profit (mil. RMB) 總利潤 (百萬元)	Rate of change 每年變化 (%)
1993	599		160,516		9,322		-130	
1994	697	16.36%	152,223	-5.17%	11,124	19.33%	17	113.21%
1995	838	20.23%	169,067	11.07%	15,305	37.59%	-249	-1547.59%
1996	922	10.02%	161,903	-4.24%	12,840	-16.11%	-492	-97.21%

3 Major products* 3種主要產品 *	Output 產量	Sales volume 銷售量	Unit 單位
a) Fresh & Frozen Animal Meat 鮮、凍畜肉	398,638	263,101	ton 噸
b) Animal Fat 動物油脂	3,987	3,468	ton 噸
c) Meat Products 畜肉製品	163,113	158,220	ton 噸

Top 10 firms by revenue (year founded) 收入排名前10家企業 (創辦年份)	City 城市	Province 省	Telephone / fax 電話 / 傳真	Number of employees 職工人數	Ownership 產業所有權	Revenue ('000 RMB) 銷售收入 (千元)	Profit ('000 RMB) (rank) 利潤 (千元) (排名)	Total assets ('000 RMB) 總資產 (千元)	Major products 主要產品
Beijing Shunyi Meat Combined Processing Factory 順義縣肉類聯合加工廠(1984)	Beijing 北京市	Beijing 北京市	(010)69441744	1,035	State-owned 國有	568,960	31891(1)	177,719	a
Beijing Meat Combined Processing Factory 北京市肉類聯合加工廠(1957)	Beijing 北京市	Beijing 北京市	(010)67212381	820	State-owned 國有	490,339	-58768(452)	224,575	a,b
Shannxi Yan You Si Group Company 陝西宴友思集團公司(1964)	Xianyang 咸陽市	Shaanxi 陝西省	(0910)2283953	1,600	State-owned 國有	370,606	13095(2)	143,934	o
Shanghai Long Hua Foods Co. 上海龍華食品公司(1953)	Shanghai 上海市	Shanghai 上海市	(021)64365407 (021)64704851	1,674	State-owned 國有	347,684	0(263)	188,946	a,b,c
Shanghai Da Chang Meat Combined Processing Factory 上海大場肉類聯合加工廠(1954)	Shanghai 上海市	Shanghai 上海市	(021)56682219 (021)56684008	1,635	State-owned 國有	287,761	0(265)	177,308	a,b,c
Tianchang Meat Combined Processing Factory 天長市肉類加工廠(1976)	Chuzhou 滁州市	Anhui 安徽省	(0550)7021705	560	State-owned 國有	205,345	603(49)	53,791	a,b
Nanjing Tian Huan Food (Group) Co. Ltd. 南京天環食品(集團)有限公司(1958)	Nanjing 南京市	Jiangsu 江蘇省	(025)8805191 (025)8802979	2,652	State-owned 國有	177,983	212(97)	287,931	a,b,c
Sichuan Liangping Food Company 四川省梁平縣食品公司	Chongqing 重慶市	Chongqing 重慶市	(023)222128 (023)227116	830	State-owned 國有	163,538	158(104)	19,747	a,b,c
Sichuan Zigong Food Company 四川自貢食品公司(1954)	Zigong 自貢市	Sichuan 四川省	(0813)2202577	1,134	State-owned 國有	154,639	-15184(446)	148,803	b,c
Jiangsu Foods Co. Rugao Joint Meat Combined Processing Factory 江蘇省食品公司如皋市肉聯廠(1951)	Nantong 南通市	Jiangsu 江蘇省	(0513)7532111 (0513)7533216	2,040	State-owned 國有	144,495	-475(321)	132,581	a,b,c

Top 10 Cities by Production Output 產出排名前10位城市	Province 省	Market share 市場份額	Number of firms 企業個數
Beijing 北京市	Beijing 北京市	15.05%	59
Shanghai 上海市	Shanghai 上海市	6.49%	47
Ji'nan 濟南市	Shandong 山東省	5.08%	22
Xinyang 信陽市	Henan 河南省	3.85%	4
Weifang 濰坊市	Shandong 山東省	3.11%	37
Leshan 樂山市	Sichuan 四川省	2.89%	13
Linyi 臨沂市	Shandong 山東省	2.38%	26
Nantong 南通市	Jiangsu 江蘇省	2.25%	13
Shenzhen 深圳市	Guangdong 廣東省	2.08%	6
Zhanjiang 湛江市	Guangdong 廣東省	1.97%	1

10 Major Wholesalers 10家主要批發商	City 城市	Province 省	Telephone / Fax 電話 / 傳真
Fujian Fuzhou Food Company 福建省福州市食品公司	Fuzhou 福州市	Fujian 福建省	(0591)3367954
Lingshan Food Company Tan Xu Zhen Purchasing & Marketing Station 靈山縣食品公司檀圩鎮購銷站	Qinzhou 欽州市	Guangxi 廣西	(0777)6581121
Shanghai Foods (Group) Co. 上海市食品(集團)公司	Shanghai 上海市	Shanghai 上海市	(021)58323730 (021)58304115
Guangzhou Food Enterprise Group Co. Ltd. 廣州食品企業集團有限公司	Guangzhou 廣州市	Guangdong 廣東省	(020)81816454 (020)81815255
Qingdao Cereal & Oils Food Import & Export Company 青島市糧油食品進出口公司	Qingdao 青島市	Shandong 山東省	(0532)3887020 (0532)3887001
China Food Company 中國食品公司	Beijing 北京市	Beijing 北京市	(010)66060831
Guangxi Bobai Food Co. Ltd. 廣西博白食品股份有限公司	Yulin 玉林市	Guangxi 廣西	(0775)8227058 (0775)8222737
Foshan Food Enterprise Group 佛山市食品企業集團	Foshan 佛山市	Guangdong 廣東省	(0757)3350559 (0757)3323329
Zhong Liang International Goods in Storehouse Transportation Company 中糧國際倉儲運輸公司	Beijing 北京市	Beijing 北京市	(010)65268888 (010)65278667
Shandong Meat Eggs Import & Export Company 山東省肉食蛋品進出口公司	Qingdao 青島市	Shandong 山東省	(0532)5879667 (0532)5879154

*Also include sales by firms outside this industry.包括本行業以外廠家的銷售。"o" stands for "others". "o" 代表"其他產品"。

1342: Meat Products 肉製品加工業

The industry accounts for 0.565% of the total revenue of China's industrial sector in 1996. The revenue growth rate of the industry is 19.0% from 1995, as compared to the growth rate of China's industrial sector, 9.51%. The rate of return on asset is 1.02%. 63.91% of all firms in the industry made a profit while 27.89% had negative returns. The top province in terms of the industry's revenue is Shandong, accounting for 33.30% of the total revenue.
本行業在1996年佔全行業總產值0.565%，行業年增長率為19.0%（全國工業年增長率9.51%）。行業的資產回報率1.02%，63.91%的企業盈利，27.89%的企業虧損。銷售收入最高的省份為山東省，佔本行業的33.30%。

	Total number of firms 企業總數	Total number of employees 職工總數	Total revenue (mil. RMB) 總銷售收入（百萬元）	Total profit (mil. RMB) 總利潤（百萬元）	Return on assets 資產利潤率 (%)	Return on equity 權益利潤率 (%)	Labour productivity ('000 RMB / worker) 勞動生產率（千元/人）	Debts / assets 資產負債率 (%)	Total assets (mil. RMB) 總資產（百萬元）
Industry Overall 行業總體	2,372	283,601	32,731	281	1.02	3.82	115.41	73.27	27,460

	Number of firms 企業個數	Average number of employees 平均職工人數	Average revenue ('000 RMB) 平均銷售收入（千元）	Average profit ('000 RMB) 平均利潤（千元）	Return on assets 資產利潤率 (%)	Return on equity 權益利潤率 (%)	Labour productivity ('000 RMB / worker) 勞動生產率（千元/人）	Average debts / assets 平均資產負債率(%)	Average Total assets ('000 RMB) 平均總資產（千元）
By ownership 產業所有權									
State-owned 國有	782	197	17,224	-515	-2.63	-12.56	87.26	79.03	19,570
Collectively-owned 集體	1,300	64	8,280	319	7.60	27.37	128.88	72.24	4,203
Privately-owned 私有	14	59	5,097	167	5.65	21.91	86.92	74.21	2,960
Domestic JVs 聯營	24	135	12,480	1,322	11.94	29.99	92.36	60.18	11,077
Joint stock 股份制	32	261	63,372	5,432	9.09	17.75	243.16	48.76	59,743
Foreign-funded 外資	81	171	24,042	-438	-2.05	-6.64	141.00	69.20	21,403
Overseas Chinese-funded 港澳台資	136	152	30,293	681	3.38	9.43	199.82	64.11	20,120
By size 規模									
Large 大型	31	1,669	273,509	26,552	10.94	31.49	163.90	65.26	242,735
Medium 中型	77	590	49,579	-8,077	-14.38	-62.90	84.06	77.14	56,179
Small 小型	2,218	84	9,213	36	0.52	2.16	109.93	76.07	7,036
By regional distribution 地區分布									
Central-North 華北	350	102	10,304	38	0.35	1.17	101.11	70.32	10,936
Beijing 北京	99	40	4,898	-11	-0.20	-0.44	123.58	54.02	5,266
Tianjin 天津	32	155	12,140	-826	-5.18	-9.27	78.24	44.15	15,955
Hebei 河北	129	119	13,891	183	1.34	7.02	116.99	80.84	13,617
Shanxi 山西	35	157	13,724	55	0.38	1.31	87.43	71.16	14,561
Inner Mongolia 內蒙	55	109	8,375	278	2.89	11.98	77.18	75.91	9,629
Northeast 東北	223	89	7,803	55	0.82	3.16	87.84	73.93	6,643
Liaoning 遼寧	93	116	13,817	274	3.02	8.99	119.08	66.43	9,062
Jilin 吉林	32	67	3,210	-229	-3.49	-33.26	48.02	89.50	6,568
Heilongjiang 黑龍江	98	70	3,596	-60	-1.37	-7.24	51.22	81.03	4,372
Central East 華東	862	155	20,378	517	3.27	10.88	131.17	69.96	15,809
Shanghai 上海	35	172	18,975	827	3.94	8.37	110.63	52.86	20,965
Jiangsu 江蘇	110	181	17,736	-222	-1.61	-6.54	98.09	75.31	13,719
Zhejiang 浙江	96	56	6,046	52	0.82	2.15	108.47	61.56	6,250
Anhui 安徽	250	116	12,097	542	8.12	29.06	104.16	72.07	6,681
Fujian 福建	44	27	2,425	15	0.56	0.89	90.19	37.50	2,725
Jiangxi 江西	72	60	4,697	96	3.12	14.37	78.45	78.28	3,088
Shandong 山東	255	267	42,749	1,147	3.34	11.45	159.98	70.87	34,401
Central-South 中南	410	112	13,951	214	1.89	6.97	124.75	72.85	11,301
Henan 河南	218	119	19,204	448	3.54	15.07	161.25	76.54	12,683
Hubei 湖北	46	131	11,402	253	3.30	12.15	87.21	72.81	7,663
Hunan 湖南	76	112	5,734	-296	-3.44	-10.38	51.32	66.85	8,599
Guangdong 廣東	54	63	8,650	311	2.64	8.29	137.34	68.15	11,774
Guangxi 廣西	14	140	7,553	-1,097	-6.95	-16.38	53.95	57.55	15,780
Hainan 海南	2	12	230	-315	-11.17	-110.53	19.17	89.72	2,820
Southwest 西南	446	93	8,512	-549	-7.40	-65.45	91.90	88.70	7,422
Chongqing 重慶	56	128	9,355	-1,214	-13.74	-165.40	72.86	91.69	8,835
Sichuan 四川	318	92	9,661	-520	-6.61	-73.24	104.34	90.98	7,875
Guizhou 貴州	54	63	2,366	-210	-6.01	-18.72	37.85	67.91	3,489
Yunnan 雲南	15	61	3,677	56	0.82	2.01	60.42	59.31	6,854
Tibet 西藏	2	60	3,920	20	0.35	0.97	65.88	63.81	5,665
Northwest 西北	81	87	3,741	-410	-5.73	-36.44	43.01	84.27	7,154
Shaanxi 陝西	28	117	5,652	-719	-8.21	-52.62	48.13	84.39	8,750
Gansu 甘肅	22	72	3,959	-75	-1.24	-6.71	55.02	81.50	6,002
Qinghai 青海	9	45	1,660	-733	-11.31	262.95	37.07	104.28	6,483
Ningxia 寧夏	7	106	1,800	-217	-4.32	475.00	16.98	100.91	5,029
Xinjiang 新疆	15	69	2,009	-221	-3.05	-10.61	29.26	71.27	7,259

1342: Meat Products 肉製品加工業

Year 年份	Number of firms 企業個數	Rate of change 每年變化 (%)	Number of employees 職工人數（人）	Rate of change 每年變化 (%)	Total revenue (mil. RMB) 總銷售收入（百萬元）	Rate of change 每年變化 (%)	Total profit (mil. RMB) 總利潤（百萬元）	Rate of change 每年變化 (%)
1993	1,960		228,868		16,552		-57	
1994	2,204	12.45%	230,057	0.52%	21,311	28.75%	200	449.79%
1995	2,441	10.75%	282,084	22.61%	27,497	29.03%	39	-80.52%
1996	2,372	-2.83%	283,601	0.54%	32,731	19.03%	281	622.12%

3 Major products* 3 種主要產品 *	Output 產量	Sales volume 銷售量	Unit 單位
a) Meat Products 畜肉製品	1,380,160	1,338,755	ton 噸
b) Fresh & Frozen Poultry Meat 鮮、凍禽肉	884,120	848,755	ton 噸
c) Meat Products 禽肉製品	815,223	611,418	ton 噸

Top 10 firms by revenue (year founded) 收入排名前 10 家企業 (創辦年份)	City 城市	Province 省	Telephone / fax 電話 / 傳真	Number of employees 職工人數	Ownership 產業所有權	Revenue ('000 RMB) 銷售收入（千元）	Profit ('000 RMB) (rank) 利潤（千元）（排名）	Total assets ('000 RMB) 總資產（千元）	Major products 主要產品
Zhucheng Foreign Trade Group Company 諸城市對外貿易集團公司(1975)	Weifang 濰坊市	Shandong 山東省	(0536)6213672 (0536)6213672	5,138	State-owned 國有	2,458,111	82367(1)	1,913,641	a,b,c
Linyi Jin Luo Enterprise Group General Company 臨沂市金鑼企業集團總公司(1985)	Linyi 臨沂市	Shandong 山東省	(0539)8641049	3,500	Collectively-owned 集體	672,657	35061(2)	242,676	a,b
Liaocheng Jiaming Group General Corp. 聊城嘉明實業有限公司(1993)	Liaocheng 聊城市	Shandong 山東省	(0635)8721031 (0635)8721031	4,919	Foreign-funded 外資	629,784	26666(4)	449,276	b
China De Li Si Group Company 中國得利斯集團公司(1986)	Weifang 濰坊市	Shandong 山東省	(0536)6401234 (0536)6401236	1,880	Collectively-owned 集體	601,046	31068(3)	352,822	a
Liaoning Da Cheng Agriculture & Animal Husbandry Industrial Co. Ltd. 遼寧大成農牧實業有限公司(1990)	Shenyang 瀋陽市	Liaoning 遼寧省	(024)25833083 (024)25832257	1,040	Overseas Chinese-funded 港澳台資	547,557	16000(11)	143,527	c
Zhoukou Area Food General Company 周口地區食品總公司(1964)	Zhoukou 周口市	Henan 河南省	(0394)82235422 (0394)8222887	930	State-owned 國有	516,832	6171(28)	126,496	o
Linyi Hua Meng Food Group Company 臨沂華蒙食品集團公司(1989)	Linyi 臨沂市	Shandong 山東省	(0539)8568352 (0539)8568236	2,100	Collectively-owned 集體	431,028	21767(7)	236,614	b
Shandong Feng Xiang General Co. 山東鳳祥總公司(1991)	Liaocheng 聊城市	Shandong 山東省	(0635)6775276 (0635)6775261	2,640	Collectively-owned 集體	402,082	26655(5)	276,038	b
Datong Tong Feng Meat Products Factory 大同市同風肉製品廠(1987)	Datong 大同市	Shanxi 山西省	(0352)6025442 (0352)6022585	1,371	State-owned 國有	325,693	16434(10)	185,580	a
Weifang Yongchang Food Industrial Co. Ltd. 濰坊永昌食品工業有限公司(1994)	Weifang 濰坊市	Shandong 山東省	(0536)6228022 (0536)6228022	1,170	Foreign-funded 外資	306,475	4407(40)	181,835	b

Top 10 Cities by Production Output 產出排名前 10 位城市	Province 省	Market share 市場份額	Number of firms 企業個數
Wuxi 無錫市	Jiangsu 江蘇省	16.43%	8
Weifang 濰坊市	Shandong 山東省	11.50%	90
Luohe 漯河市	Henan 河南省	6.20%	17
Linyi 臨沂市	Shandong 山東省	5.99%	53
Fuyang 阜陽市	Anhui 安徽省	5.65%	181
Luoyang 洛陽市	Henan 河南省	4.23%	4
Liaocheng 聊城市	Shandong 山東省	2.11%	23
Zhoukou 周口市	Henan 河南省	1.84%	24
Shanghai 上海市	Shanghai 上海市	1.73%	82
Nanyang 南陽市	Henan 河南省	1.69%	48

10 Major Wholesalers 10 家主要批發商	City 城市	Province 省	Telephone / Fax 電話 / 傳真
Fujian Fuzhou Food Company 福建省福州市食品公司	Fuzhou 福州市	Fujian 福建省	(0591)3367954
Lingshan Food Company Tan Xu Zhen Purchasing & Marketing Station 靈山縣食品公司檀圩鎮購銷站	Qinzhou 欽州市	Guangxi 廣西	(0777)6581121
Shanghai Foods (Group) Co. 上海市食品(集團)公司	Shanghai 上海市	Shanghai 上海市	(021)58323730 (021)58304115
Guangzhou Food Enterprise Group Co. Ltd. 廣州食品企業集團有限公司	Guangzhou 廣州市	Guangdong 廣東省	(020)81816454 (020)81815255
Qingdao Cereal & Oils Food Import & Export Company 青島市糧油食品進出口公司	Qingdao 青島市	Shandong 山東省	(0532)3887020 (0532)3887001
China Food Company 中國食品公司	Beijing 北京市	Beijing 北京市	(010)66060831
Guangxi Bobai Food Co. Ltd. 廣西博白食品股份有限公司	Yulin 玉林市	Guangxi 廣西	(0775)8227058 (0775)8222737
Foshan Food Enterprise Group 佛山市食品企業集團	Foshan 佛山市	Guangdong 廣東省	(0757)3350559 (0757)3323329
Zhong Liang International Goods in Storehouse Transportation Company 中糧國際倉儲運輸公司	Beijing 北京市	Beijing 北京市	(010)65268888 (010)65278667
Shandong Meat Eggs Import & Export Company 山東省肉食蛋品進出口公司	Qingdao 青島市	Shandong 山東省	(0532)5879667 (0532)5879154

*Also include sales by firms outside this industry.包括本行業以外廠家的銷售。"o" stands for "others". "o" 代表"其他產品"。

1343: Meat By-products 肉類副產品加工業

The industry accounts for 0.040% of the total revenue of China's industrial sector in 1996. The revenue growth rate of the industry is 17.9% from 1995, as compared to the growth rate of China's industrial sector, 9.51%. The rate of return on asset is -0.02%. 66.57% of all firms in the industry made a profit while 24.05% had negative returns. The top province in terms of the industry's revenue is Jiangsu, accounting for 20.44% of the total revenue.
本行業在1996年佔全行業總產值0.040%，行業年增長率為17.9%（全國工業年增長率9.51%）。行業的資產回報率-0.02%，66.57%的企業盈利，24.05%的企業虧損。銷售收入最高的省份為江蘇省，佔本行業的20.44%。

	Total number of firms 企業總數	Total number of employees 職工總數	Total revenue (mil. RMB) 總銷售收入（百萬元）	Total profit (mil. RMB) 總利潤（百萬元）	Return on assets 資產利潤率 (%)	Return on equity 權益利潤率 (%)	Labour productivity ('000 RMB / worker) 勞動生產率（千元/人）	Debts / assets 資產負債率 (%)	Total assets (mil. RMB) 總資產（百萬元）
Industry Overall 行業總體	252	17,510	2,302		-0.02	-0.07	131.47	74.24	1,750

	Number of firms 企業個數	Average number of employees 平均職工人數	Average revenue ('000 RMB) 平均銷售收入（千元）	Average profit ('000 RMB) 平均利潤（千元）	Return on assets 資產利潤率 (%)	Return on equity 權益利潤率 (%)	Labour productivity ('000 RMB / worker) 勞動生產率（千元/人）	Average debts / assets 平均資產負債率(%)	Average Total assets ('000 RMB) 平均總資產（千元）
By ownership 產業所有權									
State-owned 國有	51	123	10,588	-824	-6.23	-37.50	85.93	83.38	13,216
Collectively-owned 集體	154	49	6,092	275	8.15	25.94	125.07	68.57	3,378
Privately-owned 私有	8	27	9,200	484	11.58	32.02	339.16	63.85	4,180
Domestic JVs 聯營	1	52	10,620	-5,577	-77.42	215.83	204.24	135.87	7,203
Joint stock 股份制	2	36	4,031	-136	-4.39	-10.75	113.54	59.21	3,090
Foreign-funded 外資	16	66	15,495	4	0.03	0.09	235.89	69.07	12,274
Overseas Chinese-funded 港澳台資	20	117	24,207	76	0.49	1.48	207.34	67.13	15,630
By size 規模									
Large 大型	2	507	83,648				165.15	69.80	112,110
Medium 中型	2	342	49,164				143.96	45.73	36,703
Small 小型	238	65	8,557				130.77	76.35	6,103
By regional distribution 地區分布									
Central-North 華北	57	46	8,789	244	4.21	14.95	191.14	71.84	5,794
Beijing 北京	6	23	11,080	1,600	35.57	53.87	481.74	33.98	4,498
Tianjin 天津	1	340	15,670	-6,750	-15.57	-937.50	46.09	98.34	43,350
Hebei 河北	42	44	9,558	281	5.20	16.76	218.04	68.96	5,410
Shanxi 山西	2	10							
Inner Mongolia 內蒙	6	47	2,903	-128	-2.36	-19.64	61.55	88.00	5,445
Northeast 東北	16	25	1,609	28	2.08	3.51	63.56	40.84	1,354
Liaoning 遼寧	6	33	3,025	40	1.82	2.69	91.21	32.40	2,202
Jilin 吉林	4	15	338	28	3.94	4.37	22.13	9.68	698
Heilongjiang 黑龍江	6	24	1,040	17	1.76	7.30	43.03	75.84	945
Central East 華東	70	88	13,051	53	0.56	2.36	149.09	76.35	9,533
Shanghai 上海	4	177	19,008	-75	-0.16	-0.88	107.54	81.43	45,943
Jiangsu 江蘇	24	110	19,610	204	2.60	11.27	179.09	76.91	7,841
Zhejiang 浙江	8	38	4,290	20	0.44	1.93	112.52	77.07	4,525
Anhui 安徽	11	60	9,262	71	2.70	14.63	153.20	81.54	2,625
Fujian 福建	2	36	20,715	5	0.02	0.03	583.52	34.70	26,020
Jiangxi 江西	5	20	5,894	-640	-8.57	-30.80	291.78	72.16	7,464
Shandong 山東	16	103	9,989	86	0.98	6.20	96.80	84.21	8,808
Central-South 中南	58	81	8,684	41	0.56	2.41	107.05	76.62	7,258
Henan 河南	37	89	10,013	97	1.14	5.53	112.13	79.37	8,523
Hubei 湖北	5	100	11,678	724	7.51	15.24	117.01	50.72	9,638
Hunan 湖南	13	57	4,354	-191	-6.54	-55.61	75.87	88.24	2,918
Guangdong 廣東	1								
Guangxi 廣西	1	99	2,950	-2,410	-13.84	-47.44	29.80	70.82	17,410
Hainan 海南	1	57	15,250	40	1.96	57.14	267.54	96.57	2,040
Southwest 西南	34	71	8,337	-233	-3.93	-12.20	117.76	67.80	5,930
Chongqing 重慶	6	95	7,276	-538	-5.41	-19.36	76.31	72.04	9,936
Sichuan 四川	26	64	8,705	-131	-2.67	-7.63	134.76	65.01	4,921
Guizhou 貴州									
Yunnan 雲南	1	49	6,030	-790	-16.74	-96.34	123.06	82.63	4,720
Tibet 西藏									
Northwest 西北	17	73	4,390	-755	-11.84	-53.57	59.99	77.90	6,380
Shaanxi 陝西	1	15	450	20	5.41	10.53	30.00	48.65	370
Gansu 甘肅	5	122	2,404	-1,264	-13.38	-121.54	19.74	88.99	9,448
Qinghai 青海	1	11							
Ningxia 寧夏									
Xinjiang 新疆	10	61	6,216	-654	-10.75	-35.20	102.07	69.47	6,085

1343: Meat By-products 肉類副產品加工業

Year 年份	Number of firms 企業個數	Rate of change 每年變化 (%)	Number of employees 職工人數 (人)	Rate of change 每年變化 (%)	Total revenue (mil. RMB) 總銷售收入 (百萬元)	Rate of change 每年變化 (%)	Total profit (mil. RMB) 總利潤 (百萬元)	Rate of change 每年變化 (%)
1993	200		14,960		1,009		1	
1994	236	18.00%	17,373	16.13%	1,266	25.50%	-19	-1486.10%
1995	272	15.25%	17,395	0.13%	1,952	54.10%	-19	-1.29%
1996	252	-7.35%	17,510	0.66%	2,302	17.93%	0	100.00%

3 Major products* 3 種主要產品 *	Output 產量	Sales volume 銷售量	Unit 單位
a) Animal Fat 動物油脂	2,628	2,286	ton 噸
b) Meat Products 畜肉製品	35,267	34,209	ton 噸

Top 10 firms by revenue (year founded) 收入排名前 10 家企業 (創辦年份)	City 城市	Province 省	Telephone / fax 電話 / 傳真	Number of employees 職工人數	Ownership 產業所有權	Revenue ('000 RMB) 銷售收入 (千元)	Profit ('000 RMB) (rank) 利潤 (千元) (排名)	Total assets ('000 RMB) 總資產 (千元)	Major products 主要產品
Nanyang Meat Enterprise Group Co. Ltd. 南陽肉食企業集團有限公司(1994)	Nanyang 南陽市	Henan 河南省	(0377)3223392	600	Joint stock 股份制	119,887	3308(4)	106,705	o
Rugao Xin Min Bei Jiao School-run Factory 如皋市新民北郊校辦廠(1989)	Nantong 南通市	Jiangsu 江蘇省	(0513)7542004	82	Collectively-owned 集體	119,430	612(16)	21,820	o
Baoding Huali Casing for Sausages Factory 保定華立腸衣廠(1993)	Baoding 保定市	Hebei 河北省	(0312)7625095	550	Overseas Chinese-funded 港澳台資	110,020	250(37)	51,000	o
Shanghai Xing Xing Casing for Sausages Co. Ltd. 上海星星腸衣有限公司(1989)	Shanghai 上海市	Shanghai 上海市	(021)64090992 (021)64090424	685	Foreign-funded 外資	91,926	15202(1)	89,570	o
Nanjing Yu Run Food Company 南京市雨潤食品公司(1993)	Nanjing 南京市	Jiangsu 江蘇省	(025)2417454	680	Collectively-owned 集體	80,950	930(12)	59,467	o
Anhui Fanchang Animal Products General Factory 安徽省繁昌縣畜產品總廠(1979)	Wuhu 蕪湖市	Anhui 安徽省	(0553)7811626 (0553)7811608	450	Collectively-owned 集體	74,759	-553(111)	16,028	o
Feixian Livestock Raising Development Company 費縣畜牧開發公司(1992)	Linyi 臨沂市	Shandong 山東省	(0539)5222935 (0539)5222935	582	State-owned 國有	70,556	10(81)	64,454	o
Henan Wan Xin Casing for Sausages Co. Ltd. 河南省萬新腸衣有限公司(1993)	Shangqiu 商丘市	Henan 河南省	(0370)4112526	278	Overseas Chinese-funded 港澳台資	69,649	1917(7)	49,311	o
Fangshan Xi Wang Feed Company 房山區希望飼料公司(1994)	Beijing 北京市	Beijing 北京市	(010)69311343	178	Domestic JVs 聯營	66,475	9595(2)	26,993	o
Pizhou Li Fu Animal Products Co. Ltd. (No.1 Casing for Sausages Factory) 邳州市利富畜產品有限公司(第一腸衣廠)(1984)	Xuzhou 徐州市	Jiangsu 江蘇省	(0516)6222129	700	Collectively-owned 集體	46,330	3008(5)	20,590	b

Top 10 Cities by Production Output 產出排名前 10 位城市	Province 省	Market share 市場份額	Number of firms 企業個數
Shanghai 上海市	Shanghai 上海市	12.25%	21
Nantong 南通市	Jiangsu 江蘇省	9.01%	19
Wuhu 蕪湖市	Anhui 安徽省	6.29%	2
Nanyang 南陽市	Henan 河南省	5.63%	2
Chengdu 成都市	Sichuan 四川省	5.14%	13
Baoding 保定市	Hebei 河北省	4.46%	23
Weifang 濰坊市	Shandong 山東省	3.98%	2
Shangqiu 商丘市	Henan 河南省	3.92%	14
Linyi 臨沂市	Shandong 山東省	3.74%	3
Chongqing 重慶市	Chongqing 重慶市	3.53%	8

10 Major Wholesalers 10 家主要批發商	City 城市	Province 省	Telephone / Fax 電話 / 傳真
Fujian Fuzhou Food Company 福建省福州市食品公司	Fuzhou 福州市	Fujian 福建省	(0591)3367954
Lingshan Food Company Tan Xu Zhen Purchasing & Marketing Station 靈山縣食品公司檀圩鎮購銷站	Qinzhou 欽州市	Guangxi 廣西	(0777)6581121
Shanghai Foods (Group) Co. 上海市食品(集團)公司	Shanghai 上海市	Shanghai 上海市	(021)58323730 (021)58304115
Guangzhou Food Enterprise Group Co. Ltd. 廣州食品企業集團有限公司	Guangzhou 廣州市	Guangdong 廣東省	(020)81816454 (020)81815255
Qingdao Cereal & Oils Food Import & Export Company 青島市糧油食品進出口公司	Qingdao 青島市	Shandong 山東省	(0532)3887020 (0532)3887001
China Food Company 中國食品公司	Beijing 北京市	Beijing 北京市	(010)66060831
Guangxi Bobai Food Co. Ltd. 廣西博白食品股份有限公司	Yulin 玉林市	Guangxi 廣西	(0775)8227058 (0775)8222737
Foshan Food Enterprise Group 佛山市食品企業集團	Foshan 佛山市	Guangdong 廣東省	(0757)3350559 (0757)3323329
Zhong Liang International Goods in Storehouse Transportation Company 中糧國際倉儲運輸公司	Beijing 北京市	Beijing 北京市	(010)65268888 (010)65278667
Shandong Meat Eggs Import & Export Company 山東省肉食蛋品進出口公司	Qingdao 青島市	Shandong 山東省	(0532)5879667 (0532)5879154

*Also include sales by firms outside this industry.包括本行業以外廠家的銷售。"o" stands for "others". "o" 代表 "其他產品" 。

1344: Egg Products 蛋品加工業

The industry accounts for 0.042% of the total revenue of China's industrial sector in 1996. The revenue growth rate of the industry is 345.7% from 1995, as compared to the growth rate of China's industrial sector, 9.51%. The rate of return on asset is 4.04%. 80.08% of all firms in the industry made a profit while 10.24% had negative returns. The top province in terms of the industry's revenue is Henan, accounting for 81.26% of the total revenue.
本行業在1996年佔全行業總產值0.042%，行業年增長率為345.7%（全國工業年增長率9.51%）。行業的資產回報率4.04%，80.08%的企業盈利，10.24%的企業虧損。銷售收入最高的省份為河南省，佔本行業的81.26%。

	Total number of firms 企業總數	Total number of employees 職工總數	Total revenue (mil. RMB) 總銷售收入（百萬元）	Total profit (mil. RMB) 總利潤（百萬元）	Return on assets 資產利潤率 (%)	Return on equity 權益利潤率 (%)	Labour productivity ('000 RMB / worker) 勞動生產率（千元/人）	Debts / assets 資產負債率 (%)	Total assets (mil. RMB) 總資產（百萬元）
Industry Overall 行業總體	182	11,571	2,462	100	4.04	10.30	212.77	60.74	2,481

	Number of firms 企業個數	Average number of employees 平均職工人數	Average revenue ('000 RMB) 平均銷售收入（千元）	Average profit ('000 RMB) 平均利潤（千元）	Return on assets 資產利潤率 (%)	Return on equity 權益利潤率 (%)	Labour productivity ('000 RMB / worker) 勞動生產率（千元/人）	Average debts / assets 平均資產負債率(%)	Average Total assets ('000 RMB) 平均總資產（千元）
By ownership 產業所有權									
State-owned 國有	47	61	3,043	-149	-3.11	-15.22	49.74	79.56	4,787
Collectively-owned 集體	124	60	16,208	2,440	27.73	230.75	270.32	87.98	8,799
Privately-owned 私有									
Domestic JVs 聯營	2	48	22,487	-24,655	-8.90	-10.41	468.48	14.50	276,898
Joint stock 股份制	2	224	16,898	12,108	56.09	159.05	75.44	64.73	21,585
Foreign-funded 外資	4	108	40,803	-35,350	-30.78	-48.88	379.57	37.03	114,844
Overseas Chinese-funded 港澳台資	4	72	16,633	-7,269	-27.04	-155.16	232.62	82.57	26,881
By size 規模									
Large 大型	1	468	47,272	63,592	12.06	30.88	101.01	60.94	527,270
Medium 中型	1	327							
Small 小型	178	58	13,563	205	1.86	4.74	232.06	60.69	10,974
By regional distribution 地區分布									
Central-North 華北	11	84	4,287	-243	-1.54	-4.60	51.04	66.52	15,772
Beijing 北京	3	9	3,360	-13	-0.16	-0.27	373.33	41.27	8,473
Tianjin 天津									
Hebei 河北	8	112	4,635	-329	-1.78	-6.09	41.34	70.85	18,509
Shanxi 山西									
Inner Mongolia 內蒙									
Northeast 東北	2	31	4,700	20	11.11	100.00	151.61	88.89	180
Liaoning 遼寧	1	28	9,400	40	12.50	100.00	335.71	87.50	320
Jilin 吉林	1	34						100.00	40
Heilongjiang 黑龍江									
Central East 華東	78	29	2,661	79	4.06	19.66	91.85	79.36	1,939
Shanghai 上海	4	22	4,290	130	11.09	42.98	192.81	74.20	1,173
Jiangsu 江蘇	17	38	3,744	1	0.02	0.20	98.99	89.50	2,824
Zhejiang 浙江	7	16	3,187	60	5.49	14.38	202.82	61.83	1,093
Anhui 安徽	12	35	3,539	208	7.08	24.18	102.34	70.75	2,943
Fujian 福建	14	25	1,481	106	12.40	23.80	60.26	47.92	859
Jiangxi 江西	10	16	254	6	1.08	-6.00	15.49	118.02	555
Shandong 山東	14	35	2,765	81	3.00	17.65	78.20	83.02	2,718
Central-South 中南	72	111	30,414	1,357	4.56	11.01	275.03	58.63	29,787
Henan 河南	5	981	400,146	19,494	4.92	11.64	407.73	57.71	395,908
Hubei 湖北	37	59	3,415	2	0.08	0.24	57.62	66.50	3,086
Hunan 湖南	25	32	2,096	4	0.23	1.04	65.84	77.61	1,885
Guangdong 廣東	4	17	2,570	5	0.53	1.55	155.76	66.05	950
Guangxi 廣西	1								
Hainan 海南									
Southwest 西南	13	12	446	8	2.18	-10.64	37.91	120.70	353
Chongqing 重慶									
Sichuan 四川	7	14	751	11	2.07	-4.94	53.64	141.94	531
Guizhou 貴州	6	10	90	3	2.30	3.23	9.47	29.89	145
Yunnan 雲南									
Tibet 西藏									
Northwest 西北	6	35	465	-158	-14.82	53.98	13.29	127.46	1,068
Shaanxi 陝西	1	40	1,300	-1,070	-28.53	48.42	32.50	158.93	3,750
Gansu 甘肅	4	43	373	30	4.51	26.67	8.76	83.08	665
Qinghai 青海									
Ningxia 寧夏									
Xinjiang 新疆	1								

1344: Egg Products 蛋品加工業

Year 年份	Number of firms 企業個數	Rate of change 每年變化 (%)	Number of employees 職工人數（人）	Rate of change 每年變化 (%)	Total revenue (mil. RMB) 總銷售收入（百萬元）	Rate of change 每年變化 (%)	Total profit (mil. RMB) 總利潤（百萬元）	Rate of change 每年變化 (%)
1993	217		12,326		443		-5	
1994	223	2.76%	14,057	14.04%	659	48.67%	-1	77.99%
1995	214	-4.04%	11,196	-20.35%	552	-16.13%	-8	-695.25%
1996	182	-14.95%	11,571	3.35%	2,462	345.71%	100	1318.47%

3 Major products* 3 種主要產品 *	Output 產量	Sales volume 銷售量	Unit 單位
a) Reconstituted Egg 再製蛋	123,705	106,386	ton 噸
b) Dried Egg 乾蛋品	5,125	4,869	ton 噸

Top 10 firms by revenue (year founded) 收入排名前 10 家企業 (創辦年份)	City 城市	Province 省	Telephone / fax 電話 / 傳真	Number of employees 職工人數	Ownership 產業所有權	Revenue ('000 RMB) 銷售收入（千元）	Profit ('000 RMB) (rank) 利潤（千元）（排名）	Total assets ('000 RMB) 總資產（千元）	Major products 主要產品
Hebei Wuqiao Honey Products Co. 河北省吳橋縣蜂產品公司(1994)	Cangzhou 滄州市	Hebei 河北省	(0317)7341227 (0317)7340694	257	State-owned 國有	21,879	0(43)	21,806	o
Jieshou Heng Run Food Co. Ltd. 界首市恒潤食品有限公司(1995)	Fuyang 阜陽市	Anhui 安徽省		104	Collectively-owned 集體	15,160	1970(1)	5,890	o
Yiyang Qing Song Foods General Factory 益陽市青松食品總廠(1976)	Yiyang 益陽市	Hunan 湖南省	(0737)4425386	167	State-owned 國有	13,660	60(25)	9,488	a
Bozhou Eggs Factory 亳州市蛋廠(1958)	Fuyang 阜陽市	Anhui 安徽省	(0558)5522323 (0558)5520377	214	State-owned 國有	13,556	92(23)	19,756	b
Jiangsu Hongze Reproduced Egg Processing Factory 江蘇省洪澤縣再製蛋加工廠(1980)	Huaiyin 淮陰市	Jiangsu 江蘇省	(0517)7222163	42	State-owned 國有	13,021	101(22)	1,350	a
Ningbo Jiangbei Eggs Processing Factory 寧波市江北區蛋品加工廠(1989)	Ningbo 寧波市	Zhejiang 浙江省	(0574)7586465	30	Collectively-owned 集體	12,977	6(42)	2,521	o
Funing Xin Gou Poultry & Eggs Processing Factory 阜寧縣新溝禽蛋加工廠(1973)	Yancheng 鹽城市	Jiangsu 江蘇省	(0515)7221882	62	Collectively-owned 集體	11,830	290(10)	4,650	a
Hunan Baojing Eggs Meat Processing General Factory 湖南省保靖蛋品肉類加工總廠(1957)	Jishou 吉首市	Hunan 湖南省	(0743)7723495 (0743)7721298	156	State-owned 國有	10,437	-298(57)	16,991	a
Longhai Jiao Mei Eggs Processing Factory 龍海市角美鴨場蛋品加工廠(1958)	Zhangzhou 漳州市	Fujian 福建省	(0596)6777064	12	Collectively-owned 集體	10,000	1080(2)	5,160	o
Shouguang Gu Cheng Industrial General Co. 壽光市古城鄉實業總公司(1990)	Weifang 濰坊市	Shandong 山東省	(0536)5431566	118	Collectively-owned 集體	9,709	913(3)	6,203	o

Top 10 Cities by Production Output 產出排名前 10 位城市	Province 省	Market share 市場份額	Number of firms 企業個數
Luoyang 洛陽市	Henan 河南省	47.02%	1
Yangzhou 揚州市	Jiangsu 江蘇省	4.02%	5
Beijing 北京市	Beijing 北京市	3.54%	4
Shanghai 上海市	Shanghai 上海市	3.28%	10
Ningbo 寧波市	Zhejiang 浙江省	3.28%	5
Cangzhou 滄州市	Hebei 河北省	2.59%	1
Wuhan 武漢市	Hubei 湖北省	2.50%	4
Yiyang 益陽市	Hunan 湖南省	2.41%	10
Yancheng 鹽城市	Jiangsu 江蘇省	2.25%	6
Foshan 佛山市	Guangdong 廣東省	2.10%	1

10 Major Wholesalers 10 家主要批發商	City 城市	Province 省	Telephone / Fax 電話 / 傳真
Fujian Fuzhou Food Company 福建省福州市食品公司	Fuzhou 福州市	Fujian 福建省	(0591)3367954
Lingshan Food Company Tan Xu Zhen Purchasing & Marketing Station 靈山縣食品公司檀圩鎮購銷站	Qinzhou 欽州市	Guangxi 廣西	(0777)6581121
Shanghai Foods (Group) Co. 上海市食品(集團)公司	Shanghai 上海市	Shanghai 上海市	(021)58323730 (021)58304115
Guangzhou Food Enterprise Group Co. Ltd. 廣州食品企業集團有限公司	Guangzhou 廣州市	Guangdong 廣東省	(020)81816454 (020)81815255
Qingdao Cereal & Oils Food Import & Export Company 青島市糧油食品進出口公司	Qingdao 青島市	Shandong 山東省	(0532)3887020 (0532)3887001
China Food Company 中國食品公司	Beijing 北京市	Beijing 北京市	(010)66060831
Guangxi Bobai Food Co. Ltd. 廣西博白食品股份有限公司	Yulin 玉林市	Guangxi 廣西	(0775)8227058 (0775)8222737
Foshan Food Enterprise Group 佛山市食品企業集團	Foshan 佛山市	Guangdong 廣東省	(0757)3350559 (0757)3323329
Zhong Liang International Goods in Storehouse Transportation Company 中糧國際倉儲運輸公司	Beijing 北京市	Beijing 北京市	(010)65268888 (010)65278667
Shandong Meat Eggs Import & Export Company 山東省肉食蛋品進出口公司	Qingdao 青島市	Shandong 山東省	(0532)5879667 (0532)5879154

*Also include sales by firms outside this industry.包括本行業以外廠家的銷售。"o" stands for "others". "o" 代表"其他產品"。

1351: Frozen Aquatic Products 冷凍水產品加工業

The industry accounts for 0.308% of the total revenue of China's industrial sector in 1996. The revenue growth rate of the industry is 14.3% from 1995, as compared to the growth rate of China's industrial sector, 9.51%. The rate of return on asset is 3.48%. 69.80% of all firms in the industry made a profit while 24.83% had negative returns. The top province in terms of the industry's revenue is Shandong, accounting for 42.75% of the total revenue.
本行業在1996年佔全行業總產值0.308%，行業年增長率為14.3%（全國工業年增長率9.51%）。行業的資產回報率3.48%，69.80%的企業盈利，24.83%的企業虧損。銷售收入最高的省份為山東省，佔本行業的42.75%。

	Total number of firms 企業總數	Total number of employees 職工總數	Total revenue (mil. RMB) 總銷售收入（百萬元）	Total profit (mil. RMB) 總利潤（百萬元）	Return on assets 資產利潤率 (%)	Return on equity 權益利潤率 (%)	Labour productivity ('000 RMB / worker) 勞動生產率（千元/人）	Debts / assets 資產負債率 (%)	Total assets (mil. RMB) 總資產（百萬元）
Industry Overall 行業總體	1,241	134,701	17,869	594	3.48	10.17	132.66	65.76	17,039

	Number of firms 企業個數	Average number of employees 平均職工人數	Average revenue ('000 RMB) 平均銷售收入（千元）	Average profit ('000 RMB) 平均利潤（千元）	Return on assets 資產利潤率 (%)	Return on equity 權益利潤率 (%)	Labour productivity ('000 RMB / worker) 勞動生產率（千元/人）	Average debts / assets 平均資產負債率(%)	Average Total assets ('000 RMB) 平均總資產（千元）
By ownership 產業所有權									
State-owned 國有	310	177	12,865	-129	-0.67	-2.30	72.70	71.03	19,397
Collectively-owned 集體	662	81	12,924	746	9.31	28.67	159.97	67.52	8,012
Privately-owned 私有	6	47	4,592	86	3.20	14.24	98.05	77.52	2,678
Domestic JVs 聯營	12	32	4,626	-98	-2.25	-5.57	144.19	59.55	4,363
Joint stock 股份制	9	354	135,118	12,859	6.22	12.46	381.45	50.10	206,760
Foreign-funded 外資	130	101	15,690	217	1.36	3.33	154.66	59.16	15,951
Overseas Chinese-funded 港澳台資	111	86	17,603	-67	-0.44	-1.34	205.01	67.23	15,328
By size 規模									
Large 大型	15	984	176,708	10,461	4.72	10.18	179.64	53.66	221,758
Medium 中型	55	674	64,100	2,396	3.42	8.81	95.05	61.12	69,986
Small 小型	1,145	72	10,212	267	3.10	10.94	141.71	71.68	8,606
By regional distribution 地區分布									
Central-North 華北	91	42	2,841	-17	-0.28	-0.83	68.40	65.65	5,872
Beijing 北京	4	10	2,715	18	0.42	0.99	271.50	57.24	4,145
Tianjin 天津	22	60	4,412	274	2.48	5.63	73.26	55.97	11,046
Hebei 河北	65	37	2,318	-117	-2.77	-10.96	62.38	74.72	4,226
Shanxi 山西									
Inner Mongolia 內蒙									
Northeast 東北	156	96	7,031	-251	-2.15	-9.00	73.31	76.12	11,676
Liaoning 遼寧	148	99	7,363	-265	-2.17	-9.15	74.50	76.33	12,220
Jilin 吉林	1	28	920	-10	-0.30	-0.33	32.86	8.98	3,340
Heilongjiang 黑龍江	7	44	881	1	0.11	0.26	20.10	59.62	1,359
Central East 華東	844	118	15,530	598	4.47	13.96	131.26	67.99	13,390
Shanghai 上海	6	95	7,742	23	0.31	0.63	81.49	50.72	7,505
Jiangsu 江蘇	115	76	12,219	115	1.31	6.18	160.74	78.80	8,769
Zhejiang 浙江	177	156	18,410	233	1.21	3.84	117.84	68.46	19,230
Anhui 安徽	11	88	7,422	249	3.73	14.58	84.60	74.45	6,685
Fujian 福建	146	61	4,631	-61	-1.29	-2.58	75.91	50.23	4,771
Jiangxi 江西	8	2	98	3	1.12		43.33	100.00	223
Shandong 山東	381	139	20,049	1,198	7.52	23.50	144.11	68.00	15,938
Central-South 中南	142	112	23,906	914	3.85	8.15	214.04	52.72	23,723
Henan 河南	3	19	1,530	53	2.62	8.47	81.96	69.07	2,037
Hubei 湖北	10	79	6,349	-450	-5.79	98.25	79.96	105.89	7,771
Hunan 湖南	8	33	1,144	-94	-5.26	-19.43	34.66	72.86	1,783
Guangdong 廣東	82	140	35,420	1,725	5.18	10.57	253.88	51.00	33,304
Guangxi 廣西	19	110	9,447	-241	-1.45	-3.96	85.59	63.40	16,577
Hainan 海南	20	60	11,672	-101	-0.89	-1.46	193.09	38.59	11,234
Southwest 西南	8	30	1,478	-69	-4.32	-9.91	49.66	56.32	1,591
Chongqing 重慶									
Sichuan 四川									
Guizhou 貴州	1	43	1,040	-520	-39.10	92.86	24.19	141.35	1,330
Yunnan 雲南	7	28	1,540	-4	-0.26	-0.49	55.28	46.40	1,629
Tibet 西藏									
Northwest 西北									
Shaanxi 陜西									
Gansu 甘肅									
Qinghai 青海									
Ningxia 寧夏									
Xinjiang 新疆									

1351: Frozen Aquatic Products 冷凍水產品加工業

Year 年份	Number of firms 企業個數	Rate of change 每年變化 (%)	Number of employees 職工人數 (人)	Rate of change 每年變化 (%)	Total revenue (mil. RMB) 總銷售收入 (百萬元)	Rate of change 每年變化 (%)	Total profit (mil. RMB) 總利潤 (百萬元)	Rate of change 每年變化 (%)
1993	1,012		108,973		9,609		395	
1994	1,231	21.64%	136,819	25.55%	12,742	32.61%	443	12.34%
1995	1,192	-3.17%	141,743	3.60%	15,631	22.67%	527	18.83%
1996	1,241	4.11%	134,701	-4.97%	17,869	14.32%	594	12.72%

3 Major products* 3 種主要產品 *	Output 產量	Sales volume 銷售量	Unit 單位
a) Aquatic Animal Frozen Products 水生動物冷凍品	2,674,706	2,514,224	ton 噸
b) Artical of Aquatic Products Industry 水產加工品	2,605,822	2,423,414	ton 噸
c) Aquatic Animal Dried Products 水生動物乾製品	69,327	67,941	ton 噸

Top 10 firms by revenue (year founded) 收入排名前 10 家企業 (創辦年份)	City 城市	Province 省	Telephone / fax 電話 / 傳真	Number of employees 職工人數	Ownership 產業所有權	Revenue ('000 RMB) 銷售收入 (千元)	Profit ('000 RMB) (rank) 利潤 (千元) (排名)	Total assets ('000 RMB) 總資產 (千元)	Major products 主要產品
Guangdong Kingman Group Co. Ltd. 廣東金曼集團股份有限公司(1984)	Chaozhou 潮州市	Guangdong 廣東省	(0768)2268898 (0768)2263934	2,978	Joint stock 股份制	1,207,086	122428(1)	1,844,297	a,b
Wendeng Ze Ku Zhen Aquatic Products General Co. 文登市澤庫水產總公司(1985)	Weihai 威海市	Shandong 山東省	(0896)8900231 (0896)8900231	1,158	Collectively-owned 集體	646,900	53800(2)	103,330	b
Guangzhou Lushi Aquatic Enterprises Co. Ltd. 廣州陸仕水產企業有限公司(1993)	Guangzhou 廣州市	Guangdong 廣東省	(020)86742606 (020)86843747	400	Overseas Chinese-funded 港澳台資	432,762	22682(5)	194,633	a,b
Zhongshan Zhong Long Aquatic Products Co. Ltd. 中山中龍水產有限公司(1995)	Zhongshan 中山市	Guangdong 廣東省	(0760)5700664 (0760)5700664	316	Foreign-funded 外資	396,439	3457(46)	77,202	b,c
Zhoushan Aquatic Products Joint Co. 舟山市水產聯合公司(1985)	Zhoushan 舟山市	Zhejiang 浙江省	(0580)3011931 (0580)3011949	427	State-owned 國有	384,954	3515(41)	186,579	a,b,c
Shandong Shi Dao Aquatic Products Supply & Marketing Group General Co. 山東石島水產供銷集團總公司(1956)	Weihai 威海市	Shandong 山東省	(0896)7382260 (0896)7381605	1,454	State-owned 國有	347,329	18058(7)	153,838	a,b
Weihai Gu Shan Aquatic Products General Company Cold Storage Factory 威海市崮山水產總公司冷藏廠(1990)	Weihai 威海市	Shandong 山東省	(0896)5382190 (0896)5382190	850	Collectively-owned 集體	339,740	23580(4)	54,420	a,b
Qingdao Hai Feng Group Co. 青島海豐集團公司(1956)	Qingdao 青島市	Shandong 山東省	(0532)2875058 (0532)2874821	998	State-owned 國有	293,521	4157(36)	262,347	a,b
China Qingdao Canned Food Co. Ltd. 中國青島罐頭食品有限公司(1993)	Qingdao 青島市	Shandong 山東省	(0532)301001 (0532)2825180	1,446	Overseas Chinese-funded 港澳台資	242,999	39532(3)	316,914	a,b
Shandou Shengping Wu Xing Industry General Company 汕頭市升平區五星工業總公司(1964)	Shantou 汕頭市	Guangdong 廣東省	(0754)8274080	2,200	Collectively-owned 集體	231,870	1850(80)	79,500	b

Top 10 Cities by Production Output 產出排名前 10 位城市	Province 省	Market share 市場份額	Number of firms 企業個數
Weihai 威海市	Shandong 山東省	21.40%	194
Zhoushan 舟山市	Zhejiang 浙江省	10.14%	67
Chaozhou 潮州市	Guangdong 廣東省	8.43%	2
Dalian 大連市	Liaoning 遼寧省	6.77%	124
Nantong 南通市	Jiangsu 江蘇省	6.64%	71
Qingdao 青島市	Shandong 山東省	6.17%	96
Yantai 煙台市	Shandong 山東省	4.57%	112
Ningbo 寧波市	Zhejiang 浙江省	3.58%	68
Taizhou 臺州市	Zhejiang 浙江省	3.39%	64
Fuzhou 福州市	Fujian 福建省	2.60%	48

10 Major Wholesalers 10 家主要批發商	City 城市	Province 省	Telephone / Fax 電話 / 傳真
China National Fisheries Corp. 中國水產總公司	Beijing 北京市	Beijing 北京市	(010)66024101
Beijing He De Industrial Company 北京和德實業公司	Beijing 北京市	Beijing 北京市	(010)68329222 (010)68320042
Shanghai Food Import & Export Company 上海市食品進出口公司	Shanghai 上海市	Shanghai 上海市	(021)63216233 (021)63291730
Zhongshan Food & Aquatic Products Import & Export Group Company 中山市食品水產進出口集團公司	Zhongshan 中山市	Guangdong 廣東省	(0760)8310882 (0760)8311207
Liaoning Food Import & Export Company 遼寧省食品進出口公司	Dalian 大連市	Liaoning 遼寧省	(0411)2717149 (0411)2705713
Guangzhou Aquatic Products Trade Co. 廣州市水產貿易公司	Guangzhou 廣州市	Guangdong 廣東省	(020)81861065
Xiamen Temao Corp. 廈門特貿有限公司	Xiamen 廈門市	Fujian 福建省	(0592)5059188 (0592)5061435
Shandong Aquatic Products Enterprise Group General Company 山東省水產企業集團總公司	Ji'nan 濟南市	Shandong 山東省	(0531)6957468 (0531)6955357
Dalian Aquatic Products Joint Co. 大連水產集團公司	Dalian 大連市	Liaoning 遼寧省	(0411)2820447 (0411)2820503
Shanghai Aquatic Product Supply & Marketing Development Company 上海水產供銷發展公司	Shanghai 上海市	Shanghai 上海市	(021)65357222 (021)65356999

*Also include sales by firms outside this industry.包括本行業以外廠家的銷售。"o" stands for "others". "o" 代表 "其他產品"。

1352: Dried Aquatic Products 乾製水產品加工業

The industry accounts for 0.079% of the total revenue of China's industrial sector in 1996. The revenue growth rate of the industry is 20.7% from 1995, as compared to the growth rate of China's industrial sector, 9.51%. The rate of return on asset is 4.03%. 75.78% of all firms in the industry made a profit while 19.67% had negative returns. The top province in terms of the industry's revenue is Fujian, accounting for 62.74% of the total revenue.
本行業在1996年佔全行業總產值0.079%，行業年增長率為20.7%（全國工業年增長率9.51%）。行業的資產回報率4.03%，75.78%的企業盈利，19.67%的企業虧損。銷售收入最高的省份為福建省，佔本行業的62.74%。

	Total number of firms 企業總數	Total number of employees 職工總數	Total revenue (mil. RMB) 總銷售收入（百萬元）	Total profit (mil. RMB) 總利潤（百萬元）	Return on assets 資產利潤率 (%)	Return on equity 權益利潤率 (%)	Labour productivity ('000 RMB / worker) 勞動生產率（千元/人）	Debts / assets 資產負債率 (%)	Total assets (mil. RMB) 總資產（百萬元）
Industry Overall 行業總體	181	14,100	4,565	130	4.03	11.70	323.76	65.56	3,225

	Number of firms 企業個數	Average number of employees 平均職工人數	Average revenue ('000 RMB) 平均銷售收入（千元）	Average profit ('000 RMB) 平均利潤（千元）	Return on assets 資產利潤率 (%)	Return on equity 權益利潤率 (%)	Labour productivity ('000 RMB / worker) 勞動生產率（千元/人）	Average debts / assets 平均資產負債率(%)	Average Total assets ('000 RMB) 平均總資產（千元）
By ownership 產業所有權									
State-owned 國有	9	69	10,333	222	2.86	7.41	150.73	61.43	7,778
Collectively-owned 集體	80	69	4,971	1,146	28.88	86.78	71.56	66.72	3,969
Privately-owned 私有									
Domestic JVs 聯營	3	59	13,528	11,344	129.51	259.33	228.00	50.06	8,759
Joint stock 股份制	4	137	63,650	28,439	109.12	966.48	465.45	88.71	26,063
Foreign-funded 外資	35	76	19,567	-1,058	-6.64	-14.86	257.85	55.31	15,939
Overseas Chinese-funded 港澳台資	50	91	61,901	-1,489	-3.46	-10.57	681.28	67.24	43,003
By size 規模									
Large 大型	1	2,636	136,515	325	0.32	1.15	51.79	72.13	101,566
Medium 中型	1	230	159,919	11,403	32.93	71.70	695.30	54.07	34,625
Small 小型	172	64	24,821	688	3.83	11.08	388.08	65.46	17,964
By regional distribution 地區分布									
Central-North 華北	2	150	14,540	655	6.05	24.26	96.93	75.06	10,825
Beijing 北京									
Tianjin 天津									
Hebei 河北	2	150	14,540	655	6.05	24.26	96.93	75.06	10,825
Shanxi 山西									
Inner Mongolia 內蒙									
Northeast 東北	13	56	3,943	-165	-2.12	-5.67	69.84	62.55	7,792
Liaoning 遼寧	7	68	6,799	-229	-1.94	-4.68	99.98	58.46	11,756
Jilin 吉林	3	52	857	33	0.87	3.25	16.37	73.33	3,837
Heilongjiang 黑龍江	3	34	367	-217	-8.67	-94.20	10.89	90.80	2,500
Central East 華東	140	78	24,398	820	4.57	15.83	314.03	71.15	17,947
Shanghai 上海	2	23	400				17.78	27.03	2,220
Jiangsu 江蘇	37	58	9,689	944	10.31	21.08	166.73	51.11	9,156
Zhejiang 浙江	20	40	5,439	-75	-1.85	-6.39	137.68	71.07	4,027
Anhui 安徽	1	20	4,900	250	64.10	500.00	245.00	87.18	390
Fujian 福建	56	109	51,145	1,399	3.88	15.28	468.07	74.61	36,080
Jiangxi 江西	2	5	60	5	11.11	25.00	12.00	55.56	45
Shandong 山東	22	79	3,571	123	4.00	13.85	45.07	71.16	3,083
Central-South 中南	26	84	41,102	619	2.73	4.70	488.19	41.93	22,692
Henan 河南									
Hubei 湖北	2	37	4,305	275	5.72	29.41	116.35	80.67	4,810
Hunan 湖南	1	13	320				24.62	66.67	120
Guangdong 廣東	19	104	55,638	845	2.83	4.80	537.15	41.03	29,850
Guangxi 廣西	4	34	648	-125	-3.82	-7.96	19.33	52.02	3,273
Hainan 海南									
Southwest 西南									
Chongqing 重慶									
Sichuan 四川									
Guizhou 貴州									
Yunnan 雲南									
Tibet 西藏									
Northwest 西北									
Shaanxi 陝西									
Gansu 甘肅									
Qinghai 青海									
Ningxia 寧夏									
Xinjiang 新疆									

1352: Dried Aquatic Products 乾製水產品加工業

Year 年份	Number of firms 企業個數	Rate of change 每年變化 (%)	Number of employees 職工人數 (人)	Rate of change 每年變化 (%)	Total revenue (mil. RMB) 總銷售收入 (百萬元)	Rate of change 每年變化 (%)	Total profit (mil. RMB) 總利潤 (百萬元)	Rate of change 每年變化 (%)
1993	84		8,869		903		73	
1994	95	13.10%	13,596	53.30%	2,420	168.06%	114	55.63%
1995	146	53.68%	15,512	14.09%	3,781	56.21%	23	-79.69%
1996	181	23.97%	14,100	-9.10%	4,565	20.74%	130	460.06%

3 Major products* 3 種主要產品 *	Output 產量	Sales volume 銷售量	Unit 單位
a) Aquatic Animal Dried Products 水生動物乾製品	33,169	32,506	ton 噸
b) Artical of Aquatic Products Industry 水產加工品	118,462	110,170	ton 噸
c) Aquatic Animal Frozen Products 水生動物冷凍品	50,488	47,459	ton 噸

Top 10 firms by revenue (year founded) 收入排名前 10 家企業 (創辦年份)	City 城市	Province 省	Telephone / fax 電話 / 傳真	Number of employees 職工人數	Ownership 產業所有權	Revenue ('000 RMB) 銷售收入 (千元)	Profit ('000 RMB) (rank) 利潤 (千元) (排名)	Total assets ('000 RMB) 總資產 (千元)	Major products 主要產品
Zhoushan Xing Ye Co. Ltd. 舟山興業有限公司(1995)	Zhoushan 舟山市	Zhejiang 浙江省	(0580)3013812 (0580)3012196	3,632	Foreign-funded 外資	487,187	20377(2)	472,725	a,b,c
Shunde Long Chang Roast Eel Co. Ltd. 順德市龍昌烤鰻有限公司(1994)	Foshan 佛山市	Guangdong 廣東省	(0757)7776260 (0757)7776210	202	Overseas Chinese-funded 港澳台資	402,100	1476(19)	52,728	a,b
Fujian Xinfang Frozen Foods Co. Ltd. 福建信芳冷凍食品有限公司(1993)	Fuzhou 福州市	Fujian 福建省	(0591)5311083 (0591)5311166	268	Overseas Chinese-funded 港澳台資	334,192	5230(7)	163,364	b
Fuqing Fu Rong Foods Co. Ltd. 福清市福榮食品有限公司(1995)	Fuzhou 福州市	Fujian 福建省	(0591)5621678 (0591)5621518	317	Overseas Chinese-funded 港澳台資	288,979	-1283(104)	149,033	b
Fuqing Hua Wan Aquatic Products Foods Co. Ltd. 福清市華萬水產食品有限公司(1993)	Fuzhou 福州市	Fujian 福建省	(0591)5222105 (0591)5222104	124	Overseas Chinese-funded 港澳台資	265,290	1635(16)	59,196	b
Min Dong Fu Ning Food Co. Ltd. 閩東福寧食品有限公司(1995)	Ningde 寧德市	Fujian 福建省	(0593)8890868 (0593)8899986	250	Foreign-funded 外資	221,827	-2954(106)	57,734	b,c
Fuqing Qi Xiang Foods Co. Ltd. 福清市齊翔食品有限公司(1993)	Fuzhou 福州市	Fujian 福建省	(0591)5381618 (0591)5380167	296	Overseas Chinese-funded 港澳台資	221,791	-8087(110)	104,992	b,c
Fujian Allied Frozen Foods Stuff Co. Ltd. 福建聯合冷凍食品有限公司(1991)	Fuzhou 福州市	Fujian 福建省	(0591)3682855	280	Foreign-funded 外資	196,947	4966(9)	85,696	b,c
Shunde Ping Rong Food Development Co. Ltd. 順德屏榮食品發展有限公司(1994)	Foshan 佛山市	Guangdong 廣東省	(0757)5565205 (0757)5568698	224	Overseas Chinese-funded 港澳台資	189,965	1444(20)	52,353	b,c
Fujian Yi Feng Eel Industry Foods Co. Ltd. 福建益豐鰻業食品有限公司(1993)	Fuzhou 福州市	Fujian 福建省	(0591)5381651 (0591)5381728	296	Overseas Chinese-funded 港澳台資	183,245	11289(5)	103,927	b

Top 10 Cities by Production Output 產出排名前 10 位城市	Province 省	Market share 市場份額	Number of firms 企業個數
Fuzhou 福州市	Fujian 福建省	25.57%	19
Foshan 佛山市	Guangdong 廣東省	17.94%	6
Zhoushan 舟山市	Zhejiang 浙江省	11.27%	4
Guangzhou 廣州市	Guangdong 廣東省	11.23%	5
Putian 莆田市	Fujian 福建省	6.54%	2
Ningde 寧德市	Fujian 福建省	5.10%	4
Qingdao 青島市	Shandong 山東省	3.58%	6
Ningbo 寧波市	Zhejiang 浙江省	2.98%	8
Nantong 南通市	Jiangsu 江蘇省	2.95%	17
Lianyungang 連雲港市	Jiangsu 江蘇省	2.33%	23

10 Major Wholesalers 10 家主要批發商	City 城市	Province 省	Telephone / Fax 電話 / 傳真
China National Fisheries Corp. 中國水產總公司	Beijing 北京市	Beijing 北京市	(010)66024101
Beijing He De Industrial Company 北京和德實業公司	Beijing 北京市	Beijing 北京市	(010)68329222 (010)68320042
Shanghai Food Import & Export Company 上海市食品進出口公司	Shanghai 上海市	Shanghai 上海市	(021)63216233 (021)63291730
Zhongshan Food & Aquatic Products Import & Export Group Company 中山市食品水產進出口集團公司	Zhongshan 中山市	Guangdong 廣東省	(0760)8310882 (0760)8311207
Liaoning Food Import & Export Company 遼寧省食品進出口公司	Dalian 大連市	Liaoning 遼寧省	(0411)2717149 (0411)2705713
Guangzhou Aquatic Products Trade Co. 廣州市水產貿易公司	Guangzhou 廣州市	Guangdong 廣東省	(020)81861065
Xiamen Temao Corp. 廈門特貿有限公司	Xiamen 廈門市	Fujian 福建省	(0592)5059188 (0592)5061435
Shandong Aquatic Products Enterprise Group General Company 山東省水產企業集團總公司	Ji'nan 濟南市	Shandong 山東省	(0531)6957468 (0531)6955357
Dalian Aquatic Products Joint Co. 大連水產集團公司	Dalian 大連市	Liaoning 遼寧省	(0411)2820447 (0411)2820503
Shanghai Aquatic Product Supply & Marketing Development Company 上海水產供銷發展公司	Shanghai 上海市	Shanghai 上海市	(021)65357222 (021)65356999

*Also include sales by firms outside this industry.包括本行業以外廠家的銷售。"o" stands for "others". "o" 代表"其他產品"。

1353: Preserved Aquatic Products 腌製水產品加工業

The industry accounts for 0.004% of the total revenue of China's industrial sector in 1996. The revenue growth rate of the industry is 6.6% from 1995, as compared to the growth rate of China's industrial sector, 9.51%. The rate of return on asset is 0.51%. 69.45% of all firms in the industry made a profit while 26.00% had negative returns. The top province in terms of the industry's revenue is Jiangsu, accounting for 17.45% of the total revenue.
本行業在1996年佔全行業總產值0.004%，行業年增長率為6.6%（全國工業年增長率9.51%）。行業的資產回報率0.51%，69.45%的企業盈利，26.00%的企業虧損。銷售收入最高的省份為江蘇省，佔本行業的17.45%。

	Total number of firms 企業總數	Total number of employees 職工總數	Total revenue (mil. RMB) 總銷售收入（百萬元）	Total profit (mil. RMB) 總利潤（百萬元）	Return on assets 資產利潤率 (%)	Return on equity 權益利潤率 (%)	Labour productivity ('000 RMB / worker) 勞動生產率（千元/人）	Debts / assets 資產負債率 (%)	Total assets (mil. RMB) 總資產（百萬元）
Industry Overall 行業總體	44	2,074	214	1	0.51	1.26	103.18	59.19	234

	Number of firms 企業個數	Average number of employees 平均職工人數	Average revenue ('000 RMB) 平均銷售收入（千元）	Average profit ('000 RMB) 平均利潤（千元）	Return on assets 資產利潤率 (%)	Return on equity 權益利潤率 (%)	Labour productivity ('000 RMB / worker) 勞動生產率（千元/人）	Average debts / assets 平均資產負債率(%)	Average Total assets ('000 RMB) 平均總資產（千元）
By ownership 產業所有權									
State-owned 國有	2	61	500				8.20	100.00	4,000
Collectively-owned 集體	31	41	4,713	31	0.96	2.51	116.31	61.80	3,278
Privately-owned 私有									
Domestic JVs 聯營									
Joint stock 股份制									
Foreign-funded 外資	2	35	546	-88	-1.55	-3.53	15.82	56.01	5,691
Overseas Chinese-funded 港澳台資	9	70	7,312	23	0.18	0.40	104.96	54.72	12,554
By size 規模									
Large 大型									
Medium 中型									
Small 小型	43	48	4,976	23	0.43	1.05	103.52	59.40	5,441
By regional distribution 地區分布									
Central-North 華北	5	18	1,036	66	1.50	4.71	58.86	68.11	4,390
Beijing 北京	2								
Tianjin 天津	1			-40	-2.65	-4.82		45.03	1,510
Hebei 河北	2	44	2,590	185	1.81	6.00	58.86	69.81	10,220
Shanxi 山西									
Inner Mongolia 內蒙									
Northeast 東北	5	47	5,672	-338	-4.50	-34.70	120.68	87.04	7,516
Liaoning 遼寧	5	47	5,672	-338	-4.50	-34.70	120.68	87.04	7,516
Jilin 吉林									
Heilongjiang 黑龍江									
Central East 華東	19	33	4,868	21	0.30	0.54	147.29	45.37	7,125
Shanghai 上海	1	36	7,680	350	5.48	25.36	213.33	78.40	6,390
Jiangsu 江蘇	5	39	7,468	220	8.74	19.75	191.49	55.76	2,518
Zhejiang 浙江	4	11	730	-155	-8.62	-20.26	67.91	57.44	1,798
Anhui 安徽	1	54	20,000	140	25.93	77.78	370.37	66.67	540
Fujian 福建	6	31	3,870	-67	-0.40	-0.63	125.51	36.90	16,735
Jiangxi 江西	1	99	1,080	-190	-2.43	-57.58	10.91	95.79	7,830
Shandong 山東	1	16	260	20	4.65	25.00	16.25	81.40	430
Central-South 中南	10	44	4,975	236	11.67	36.59	114.37	68.17	2,023
Henan 河南									
Hubei 湖北	2	84	6,235	450	23.62	40.72	74.23	42.26	1,905
Hunan 湖南	2	18	1,410	160	11.94	15.76	80.57	24.25	1,340
Guangdong 廣東	4	53	7,548	268	8.64	56.61	143.76	84.75	3,098
Guangxi 廣西	2	11	2,135	35	5.19	21.88	194.09	76.30	675
Hainan 海南									
Southwest 西南	4	150	8,163	-50	-1.37	-8.97	54.51	84.78	3,663
Chongqing 重慶									
Sichuan 四川	4	150	8,163	-50	-1.37	-8.97	54.42	84.78	3,663
Guizhou 貴州									
Yunnan 雲南									
Tibet 西藏									
Northwest 西北	1	89	5,200	10	0.26	1.15	58.43	77.69	3,900
Shaanxi 陝西	1	89	5,200	10	0.26	1.15	58.43	77.69	3,900
Gansu 甘肅									
Qinghai 青海									
Ningxia 寧夏									
Xinjiang 新疆									

1353: Preserved Aquatic Products 腌製水產品加工業

Year 年份	Number of firms 企業個數	Rate of change 每年變化 (%)	Number of employees 職工人數 (人)	Rate of change 每年變化 (%)	Total revenue (mil. RMB) 總銷售收入 (百萬元)	Rate of change 每年變化 (%)	Total profit (mil. RMB) 總利潤 (百萬元)	Rate of change 每年變化 (%)
1993	25		1,102		38		2	
1994	25	0	1,441	30.76%	110	189.32%	3	78.11%
1995	44	76.00%	1,949	35.25%	201	82.69%	7	114.30%
1996	44	0	2,074	6.41%	214	6.56%	1	-86.41%

3 Major products* 3 種主要產品 *	Output 產量	Sales volume 銷售量	Unit 單位
a) Aquatic Animal Pickled Products 水生動物腌製品	171	168	ton 噸
b) Aquatic Animal Dried Products 水生動物乾製品	1,449	1,420	ton 噸
c) Artical of Aquatic Products Industry 水產加工品	6,619	6,156	ton 噸

Top 10 firms by revenue (year founded) 收入排名前 10 家企業 (創辦年份)	City 城市	Province 省	Telephone / fax 電話 / 傳真	Number of employees 職工人數	Ownership 產業所有權	Revenue ('000 RMB) 銷售收入 (千元)	Profit ('000 RMB) (rank) 利潤 (千元) (排名)	Total assets ('000 RMB) 總資產 (千元)	Major products 主要產品
Sihong Lin Huai Liquor-saturated Crab Factory 泗洪臨淮醉蟹廠(1993)	Suqian 宿遷市	Jiangsu 江蘇省	(0527)6402014	132	Collectively-owned 集體	29,376	1028(1)	2,617	a,c
Dalian Chun Qiu Food Co. Ltd. 大連春秋食品有限公司(1993)	Dalian 大連市	Liaoning 遼寧省	(0411)2649045 (0411)2820487	60	Foreign-funded 外資	22,648	-590(20)	7,306	o
Anhui Wuhe Tuo Hu Food General Factory 安徽省五河縣沱湖食品總廠(1991)	Bengbu 蚌埠市	Anhui 安徽省		55	Collectively-owned 集體	20,000	140(11)	540	a,c
Xiamen Jin Xin Wang Food Co. Ltd. 廈門金鑫旺食品有限公司(1996)	Xiamen 廈門市	Fujian 福建省	(0592)7011670	80	Overseas Chinese-funded 港澳台資	17,834	-177(19)	96,262	o
Hua Guang Casing for Sausages Factory 華光腸衣廠	Chengdu 成都市	Sichuan 四川省		35	Collectively-owned 集體	14,000	443(5)	4,536	o
Maoming Zhu Zhou High Science & Technology Soy Material Co. Ltd. 茂名市竹洲高科技醬料有限公司(1995)	Maoming 茂名市	Guangdong 廣東省	(0668)5490173	90	Collectively-owned 集體	12,100	600(3)	1,960	a,c
Sichuan Tea Import & Export Co. Wild Source Processing Factory 四川茶葉進出口公司野生資源加工廠	Chengdu 成都市	Sichuan 四川省	(028)5190356	30	Collectively-owned 集體	11,866	-37(18)	1,307	o
Xinhui Tai Feng Marine Products Co. Ltd. 新會泰豐海產有限公司(1994)	Jiangmen 江門市	Guangdong 廣東省	(0750)6523402 (0750)6524718	27	Overseas Chinese-funded 港澳台資	9,254	0(17)	9,137	c
Maoming Dianbai Jue Shan Zhen Fishery Products Factory 茂名市電白縣爵山鎮漁業製品廠(1991)	Maoming 茂名市	Guangdong 廣東省		80	Collectively-owned 集體	8,600	480(4)	836	a,b,c
Shanghai Xin Xing Natural Food Co. Ltd. 上海新星天然食品有限公司(1991)	Shanghai 上海市	Shanghai 上海市	(021)58811961 (021)63029398	36	Overseas Chinese-funded 港澳台資	7,681	350(8)	6,388	a,c

Top 10 Cities by Production Output 產出排名前 10 位城市	Province 省	Market share 市場份額	Number of firms 企業個數
Dalian 大連市	Liaoning 遼寧省	14.75%	5
Weihai 威海市	Shandong 山東省	14.46%	3
Taizhou 泰州市	Jiangsu 江蘇省	13.28%	2
Maoming 茂名市	Guangdong 廣東省	12.62%	2
Tianjin 天津市	Tianjin 天津市	6.85%	1
Shantou 汕頭市	Guangdong 廣東省	5.39%	3
Liaoyuan 遼源市	Jilin 吉林省	4.76%	1
Suqian 宿遷市	Jiangsu 江蘇省	3.71%	1
Huangshan 黃山市	Anhui 安徽省	3.30%	2
Langfang 廊坊市	Hebei 河北省	3.19%	1

10 Major Wholesalers 10 家主要批發商	City 城市	Province 省	Telephone / Fax 電話 / 傳真
China National Fisheries Corp. 中國水產總公司	Beijing 北京市	Beijing 北京市	(010)66024101
Beijing He De Industrial Company 北京和德實業公司	Beijing 北京市	Beijing 北京市	(010)68329222 (010)68320042
Shanghai Food Import & Export Company 上海市食品進出口公司	Shanghai 上海市	Shanghai 上海市	(021)63216233 (021)63291730
Zhongshan Food & Aquatic Products Import & Export Group Company 中山市食品水產進出口集團公司	Zhongshan 中山市	Guangdong 廣東省	(0760)8310882 (0760)8311207
Liaoning Food Import & Export Company 遼寧省食品進出口公司	Dalian 大連市	Liaoning 遼寧省	(0411)2717149 (0411)2705713
Guangzhou Aquatic Products Trade Co. 廣州市水產貿易公司	Guangzhou 廣州市	Guangdong 廣東省	(020)81861065
Xiamen Temao Corp. 廈門特貿有限公司	Xiamen 廈門市	Fujian 福建省	(0592)5059188 (0592)5061435
Shandong Aquatic Products Enterprise Group General Company 山東省水產企業集團總公司	Ji'nan 濟南市	Shandong 山東省	(0531)6957468 (0531)6955357
Dalian Aquatic Products Joint Co. 大連水產集團公司	Dalian 大連市	Liaoning 遼寧省	(0411)2820447 (0411)2820503
Shanghai Aquatic Product Supply & Marketing Development Company 上海水產供銷發展公司	Shanghai 上海市	Shanghai 上海市	(021)65357222 (021)65356999

*Also include sales by firms outside this industry.包括本行業以外廠家的銷售。"o" stands for "others". "o" 代表"其他產品"。

1354: Fish Meat and Fish Meat Products 魚糜及魚糜製品加工業

The industry accounts for 0.005% of the total revenue of China's industrial sector in 1996. The revenue growth rate of the industry is -57.9% from 1995, as compared to the growth rate of China's industrial sector, 9.51%. The rate of return on asset is 4.72%. 81.08% of all firms in the industry made a profit while 18.92% had negative returns. The top province in terms of the industry's revenue is Shandong, accounting for 39.41% of the total revenue.
本行業在1996年佔全行業總產值0.005%，行業年增長率為-57.9%（全國工業年增長率9.51%）。行業的資產回報率4.72%，81.08%的企業盈利，18.92%的企業虧損。銷售收入最高的省份為山東省，佔本行業的39.41%。

	Total number of firms 企業總數	Total number of employees 職工總數	Total revenue (mil. RMB) 總銷售收入（百萬元）	Total profit (mil. RMB) 總利潤（百萬元）	Return on assets 資產利潤率 (%)	Return on equity 權益利潤率 (%)	Labour productivity ('000 RMB / worker) 勞動生產率（千元/人）	Debts / assets 資產負債率 (%)	Total assets (mil. RMB) 總資產（百萬元）
Industry Overall 行業總體	35	2,344	278	14	4.72	9.97	118.60	52.63	294

	Number of firms 企業個數	Average number of employees 平均職工人數	Average revenue ('000 RMB) 平均銷售收入（千元）	Average profit ('000 RMB) 平均利潤（千元）	Return on assets 資產利潤率 (%)	Return on equity 權益利潤率 (%)	Labour productivity ('000 RMB / worker) 勞動生產率（千元/人）	Average debts / assets 平均資產負債率(%)	Average Total assets ('000 RMB) 平均總資產（千元）
By ownership 產業所有權									
State-owned 國有	1	85	1,000				11.76	20.00	5,000
Collectively-owned 集體	15	39	941	8	0.32	0.67	24.14	52.81	2,399
Privately-owned 私有									
Domestic JVs 聯營									
Joint stock 股份制									
Foreign-funded 外資	12	71	5,907	806	9.44	15.80	82.80	40.26	8,536
Overseas Chinese-funded 港澳台資	8	102	23,999	527	2.80	7.42	234.71	62.27	18,822
By size 規模									
Large 大型	1	393	16,931	15	0.04	0.11	43.08	60.59	34,645
Medium 中型	3	117	9,638	2,892	12.69	26.05	82.61	51.30	22,792
Small 小型	30	53	7,738	177	2.78	5.77	145.73	51.80	6,366
By regional distribution 地區分布									
Central-North 華北	2	27	2,220	-135	-3.04	-15.52	82.22	80.43	4,445
Beijing 北京	1	29	520	-390	-5.15	-58.21	17.93	91.16	7,580
Tianjin 天津									
Hebei 河北	1	25	3,920	120	9.16	11.21	156.80	18.32	1,310
Shanxi 山西									
Inner Mongolia 內蒙									
Northeast 東北	3	137	22,333	3,440	12.26	29.17	163.41	57.96	28,050
Liaoning 遼寧	2	163	32,500	5,095	12.19	29.11	199.39	58.12	41,785
Jilin 吉林	1	84	2,000	130	22.41	34.21	23.81	34.48	580
Heilongjiang 黑龍江									
Central East 華東	22	62	6,971	297	5.05	10.11	113.36	50.10	5,889
Shanghai 上海									
Jiangsu 江蘇	6	63	3,698	252	16.18	35.36	59.17	54.23	1,555
Zhejiang 浙江	3	68	7,090	1,300	19.56	42.25	104.78	53.76	6,647
Anhui 安徽									
Fujian 福建	3	3	100	3	1.00	2.00	37.50	50.00	333
Jiangxi 江西	1	6	60				10.00	28.57	70
Shandong 山東	9	85	12,172	124	1.13	2.21	143.96	48.99	11,023
Central-South 中南	6	83	8,760	-450	-3.87	-7.32	105.97	47.07	11,623
Henan 河南									
Hubei 湖北	1	76	4,400	-680	-6.25	-33.17	57.89	81.16	10,880
Hunan 湖南									
Guangdong 廣東	5	84	9,632	-404	-3.43	-5.79	114.67	40.77	11,772
Guangxi 廣西									
Hainan 海南									
Southwest 西南	2	16	515	5	0.48	1.33	33.23	63.77	1,035
Chongqing 重慶	1	6	790	10	16.67	20.00	131.67	16.67	60
Sichuan 四川									
Guizhou 貴州									
Yunnan 雲南	1	25	240				9.60	65.17	2,010
Tibet 西藏									
Northwest 西北									
Shaanxi 陝西									
Gansu 甘肅									
Qinghai 青海									
Ningxia 寧夏									
Xinjiang 新疆									

1354: Fish Meat and Fish Meat Products 魚糜及魚糜製品加工業

Year 年份	Number of firms 企業個數	Rate of change 每年變化 (%)	Number of employees 職工人數 (人)	Rate of change 每年變化 (%)	Total revenue (mil. RMB) 總銷售收入 (百萬元)	Rate of change 每年變化 (%)	Total profit (mil. RMB) 總利潤 (百萬元)	Rate of change 每年變化 (%)
1993	19		899		101		12	
1994	32	68.42%	4,582	409.68%	316	213.19%	36	191.69%
1995	39	21.88%	4,800	4.76%	661	109.15%	25	-30.68%
1996	35	-10.26%	2,344	-51.17%	278	-57.92%	14	-43.29%

3 Major products* 3 種主要產品 *	Output 產量	Sales volume 銷售量	Unit 單位
a) Aquatic Products 水產加工品	23,167	21,545	ton 噸
b) Aquatic Animal Dried Products 水生動物乾製品	564	553	ton 噸
c) Aquatic Plant Dried Products 水生植物乾製品	0	0	ton 噸

Top 10 firms by revenue (year founded) 收入排名前 10 家企業 (創辦年份)	City 城市	Province 省	Telephone / fax 電話 / 傳真	Number of employees 職工人數	Ownership 產業所有權	Revenue ('000 RMB) 銷售收入 (千元)	Profit ('000 RMB) (rank) 利潤 (千元) (排名)	Total assets ('000 RMB) 總資產 (千元)	Major products 主要產品
Dalian Fa Ri Sea Foods Co. Ltd. 大連發日海產食品有限公司(1988)	Dalian 大連市	Liaoning 遼寧省	(0411)7613197 (0411)7613463	194	Foreign-funded 外資	57,628	11564(1)	44,611	o
Qingdao Hua Yang International Aquatic Products Foods Co. Ltd. 青島華洋國際水產食品有限公司(1994)	Qingdao 青島市	Shandong 山東省	(0532)2814584 (0532)2827914	170	Foreign-funded 外資	48,298	4555(2)	40,890	a
Qingdao Dong Yuan Food Co. Ltd. 青島東遠食品有限公司(1995)	Qingdao 青島市	Shandong 山東省	(0532)4820136 (0532)4820135	108	Foreign-funded 外資	23,810	-20(12)	27,210	o
Yuhuan Long Sheng Aquatic Products Co. Ltd. 玉環龍生水產製品有限公司(1993)	Taizhou 臺州市	Zhejiang 浙江省	(0576)7552206	138	Foreign-funded 外資	19,483	3918(3)	17,236	o
Guangzhou Yong Xing Sea Aquatic Products Foods Co. Ltd. 廣州永興海洋水產食品公司(1987)	Guangzhou 廣州市	Guangdong 廣東省	(020)84431451 (020)84416272	50	Foreign-funded 外資	19,394	-82(13)	12,914	a
Yi Shun Food Co. Ltd. 億順食品有限公司(1992)	Maoming 茂名市	Guangdong 廣東省	(0668)5602299	93	Overseas Chinese-funded 港澳台資	18,000	991(5)	15,326	a
Qingdao Kohyo Foods Products Corp. 青島交洋食品有限公司(1989)	Qingdao 青島市	Shandong 山東省	(0532)2813352 (0532)2820538	75	Foreign-funded 外資	17,067	1067(4)	13,651	a
Qingdao Da Shui Food Co. Ltd. 青島大水食品有限公司(1995)	Qingdao 青島市	Shandong 山東省	(0532)4812182 (0532)4812184	290	Foreign-funded 外資	14,590	-4529(19)		o
Yancheng Yunyang Food Co. Ltd. 鹽城雲陽食品有限公司(1995)	Yancheng 鹽城市	Jiangsu 江蘇省	(0515)9602014	250	Foreign-funded 外資	12,130	420(7)	2,820	c
Dalian You Lian Seafood Products Co. Ltd. 大連市友聯海味品有限公司(1993)	Dalian 大連市	Liaoning 遼寧省	(0411)7803979	120	Overseas Chinese-funded 港澳台資	7,375	-1370(17)	38,954	a

Top 10 Cities by Production Output 產出排名前 10 位城市	Province 省	Market share 市場份額	Number of firms 企業個數
Dalian 大連市	Liaoning 遼寧省	21.31%	2
Qingdao 青島市	Shandong 山東省	13.11%	3
Shenzhen 深圳市	Guangdong 廣東省	12.98%	1
Maoming 茂名市	Guangdong 廣東省	10.82%	2
Weihai 威海市	Shandong 山東省	7.77%	4
Taizhou 臺州市	Zhejiang 浙江省	7.10%	2
Guangzhou 廣州市	Guangdong 廣東省	6.54%	1
Yancheng 鹽城市	Jiangsu 江蘇省	3.41%	2
Yangjiang 陽江市	Guangdong 廣東省	3.27%	2
Xiamen 廈門市	Fujian 福建省	3.16%	3

10 Major Wholesalers 10 家主要批發商	City 城市	Province 省	Telephone / Fax 電話 / 傳真
China National Fisheries Corp. 中國水產總公司	Beijing 北京市	Beijing 北京市	(010)66024101
Beijing He De Industrial Company 北京和德實業公司	Beijing 北京市	Beijing 北京市	(010)68329222 (010)68320042
Shanghai Food Import & Export Company 上海市食品進出口公司	Shanghai 上海市	Shanghai 上海市	(021)63216233 (021)63291730
Zhongshan Food & Aquatic Products Import & Export Group Company 中山市食品水產進出口集團公司	Zhongshan 中山市	Guangdong 廣東省	(0760)8310882 (0760)8311207
Liaoning Food Import & Export Company 遼寧省食品進出口公司	Dalian 大連市	Liaoning 遼寧省	(0411)2717149 (0411)2705713
Guangzhou Aquatic Products Trade Co. 廣州市水產貿易公司	Guangzhou 廣州市	Guangdong 廣東省	(020)81861065
Xiamen Temao Corp. 廈門特貿有限公司	Xiamen 廈門市	Fujian 福建省	(0592)5059188 (0592)5061435
Shandong Aquatic Products Enterprise Group General Company 山東省水產企業集團總公司	Ji'nan 濟南市	Shandong 山東省	(0531)6957468 (0531)6955357
Dalian Aquatic Products Joint Co. 大連水產集團公司	Dalian 大連市	Liaoning 遼寧省	(0411)2820447 (0411)2820503
Shanghai Aquatic Product Supply & Marketing Development Company 上海水產供銷發展公司	Shanghai 上海市	Shanghai 上海市	(021)65357222 (021)65356999

*Also include sales by firms outside this industry.包括本行業以外廠家的銷售。"o" stands for "others". "o" 代表 "其他產品"。

1359: Other Aquatic Products 其他水產品加工業

The industry accounts for 0.026% of the total revenue of China's industrial sector in 1996. The revenue growth rate of the industry is -30.5% from 1995, as compared to the growth rate of China's industrial sector, 9.51%. The rate of return on asset is 1.39%. 76.06% of all firms in the industry made a profit while 19.71% had negative returns. The top province in terms of the industry's revenue is Jiangsu, accounting for 31.43% of the total revenue.
本行業在1996年佔全行業總產值0.026%，行業年增長率為-30.5%（全國工業年增長率9.51%）。行業的資產回報率1.39%，76.06%的企業盈利，19.71%的企業虧損。銷售收入最高的省份為江蘇省，佔本行業的31.43%。

	Total number of firms 企業總數	Total number of employees 職工總數	Total revenue (mil. RMB) 總銷售收入（百萬元）	Total profit (mil. RMB) 總利潤（百萬元）	Return on assets 資產利潤率 (%)	Return on equity 權益利潤率 (%)	Labour productivity ('000 RMB / worker) 勞動生產率（千元/人）	Debts / assets 資產負債率 (%)	Total assets (mil. RMB) 總資產（百萬元）
Industry Overall 行業總體	159	12,116	1,486	24	1.39	3.59	122.65	61.32	1,714

	Number of firms 企業個數	Average number of employees 平均職工人數	Average revenue ('000 RMB) 平均銷售收入（千元）	Average profit ('000 RMB) 平均利潤（千元）	Return on assets 資產利潤率 (%)	Return on equity 權益利潤率 (%)	Labour productivity ('000 RMB / worker) 勞動生產率（千元/人）	Average debts / assets 平均資產負債率(%)	Average Total assets ('000 RMB) 平均總資產（千元）
By ownership 產業所有權									
State-owned 國有	29	172	9,759	-172	-1.11	-3.70	56.65	69.93	15,483
Collectively-owned 集體	78	52	5,059	208	3.39	6.43	97.11	47.17	6,127
Privately-owned 私有									
Domestic JVs 聯營	6	27	3,478	6	0.11	0.26	128.04	58.44	5,259
Joint stock 股份制									
Foreign-funded 外資	19	32	8,465	-2	-0.02	-0.04	266.28	49.66	8,689
Overseas Chinese-funded 港澳台資	27	85	23,224	473	2.16	7.12	273.82	69.63	21,873
By size 規模									
Large 大型	3	690	59,250	102	0.07	0.26	85.91	71.34	136,675
Medium 中型	3	886	42,712	2,210	4.19	10.29	48.19	59.23	52,693
Small 小型	144	51	8,197	119	1.49	3.55	161.33	58.02	7,958
By regional distribution 地區分布									
Central-North 華北	7	14	5,323	103	5.35	10.03	380.20	46.62	1,921
Beijing 北京	3	15	1,543	-110	-17.10	-62.26	102.89	72.54	643
Tianjin 天津	2	22	145	5	0.87	-2.94	6.59	129.57	575
Hebei 河北	2	5	16,170	520	10.03	14.88	3593.33	32.59	5,185
Shanxi 山西									
Inner Mongolia 內蒙									
Northeast 東北	12	44	1,937	-271	-8.53	-25.21	43.60	66.15	3,173
Liaoning 遼寧	9	43	2,571	-151	-4.58	-10.57	60.10	56.64	3,298
Jilin 吉林	1	93	70	10	0.70	1.19	0.75	41.26	1,430
Heilongjiang 黑龍江	2	28	15	-950	-27.26	231.71	0.55	111.76	3,485
Central East 華東	99	95	11,586	288	2.13	5.68	121.90	62.43	13,480
Shanghai 上海	2	685	43,360	45	0.09	0.32	63.35	71.66	49,960
Jiangsu 江蘇	21	97	22,241	950	3.76	7.36	229.97	48.86	25,222
Zhejiang 浙江	16	65	5,863	564	8.68	18.28	89.93	52.53	6,504
Anhui 安徽	4	35	2,470	-185	-4.03	-38.95	70.57	89.64	4,585
Fujian 福建	29	54	9,532	-206	-1.97	-8.22	176.41	76.03	10,463
Jiangxi 江西	4	57	1,960	98	3.50	8.61	34.24	59.37	2,788
Shandong 山東	23	132	8,927	250	2.15	7.81	67.74	72.53	11,650
Central-South 中南	41	51	6,797	-52	-0.65	-1.51	134.29	56.84	8,005
Henan 河南									
Hubei 湖北	4	104	29,990	15	0.09	0.20	289.06	52.96	16,238
Hunan 湖南	1								
Guangdong 廣東	20	40	5,916	134	2.60	7.98	148.27	67.46	5,160
Guangxi 廣西	7	38	790	-384	-4.68	-10.73	20.71	56.39	8,213
Hainan 海南	9	66	3,872	-243	-2.14	-4.17	58.57	48.86	11,396
Southwest 西南									
Chongqing 重慶									
Sichuan 四川									
Guizhou 貴州									
Yunnan 雲南									
Tibet 西藏									
Northwest 西北									
Shaanxi 陝西									
Gansu 甘肅									
Qinghai 青海									
Ningxia 寧夏									
Xinjiang 新疆									

1359: Other Aquatic Products 其他水產品加工業

Year 年份	Number of firms 企業個數	Rate of change 每年變化 (%)	Number of employees 職工人數 (人)	Rate of change 每年變化 (%)	Total revenue (mil. RMB) 總銷售收入 (百萬元)	Rate of change 每年變化 (%)	Total profit (mil. RMB) 總利潤 (百萬元)	Rate of change 每年變化 (%)
1993	111		19,275		822		34	
1994	140	26.13%	13,829	-28.26%	1,484	80.59%	44	27.65%
1995	160	14.29%	18,919	36.81%	2,138	44.02%	84	90.61%
1996	159	-0.63%	12,116	-35.96%	1,486	-30.50%	24	-71.36%

3 Major products* 3種主要產品*	Output 產量	Sales volume 銷售量	Unit 單位
a) Capsule 膠囊	623	511	ton 噸
b) Aquatic Animal Dried Products 水生動物乾製品	1,870	1,833	ton 噸

Top 10 firms by revenue (year founded) 收入排名前10家企業 (創辦年份)	City 城市	Province 省	Telephone / fax 電話/傳真	Number of employees 職工人數	Ownership 產業所有權	Revenue ('000 RMB) 銷售收入 (千元)	Profit ('000 RMB) (rank) 利潤(千元) (排名)	Total assets ('000 RMB) 總資產 (千元)	Major products 主要產品
Shanghai Qi Feng Food Co. Ltd. 上海旗豐食品有限公司(1993)	Shanghai 上海市	Shanghai 上海市	(021)64193777 (021)64193894	800	Foreign-funded 外資	276,474	9732(2)	73,358	o
Jiangsu Hua Xin Group Co. 江蘇華鑫集團公司(1990)	Suzhou 蘇州市	Jiangsu 江蘇省	(0512)3870824	930	Collectively-owned 集體	220,569	15522(1)	267,909	a
Xiamen Xing Cun Eel Industry Co. Ltd. 廈門杏村鰻業有限公司(1994)	Xiamen 廈門市	Fujian 福建省	(0592)6070692 (0592)6072688	123	Overseas Chinese-funded 港澳台資	213,721	795(17)	91,335	b
Hubei Honghu Lantian Aquatic Products Development Co. Ltd. 湖北省洪湖市藍田水產品開發有限公司(1994)	Jingsha 荊沙市	Hubei 湖北省	(0716)742218 (0716)742275	380	Collectively-owned 集體	114,517	501(22)	61,738	o
Changshu Chang You Eel Industry Co. Ltd. 常熟市常友鰻業有限公司(1992)	Suzhou 蘇州市	Jiangsu 江蘇省	(0512)2703788 (0512)2787188	170	Foreign-funded 外資	106,010	-190(66)	90,150	o
Shanghe Food Group General Company 商河縣食品集團總公司(1978)	Ji'nan 濟南市	Shandong 山東省	(0531)4880424	810	State-owned 國有	103,947	1524(5)	127,056	o
Shanghai Fish Products Factory 上海魚品廠(1951)	Shanghai 上海市	Shanghai 上海市	(021)65430810 (021)65431379	1,303	State-owned 國有	85,497	15(53)	95,387	o
Xiamen Xing Feng Aquatic Industrial Co. Ltd. 廈門特貿杏豐水產實業有限公司(1995)	Xiamen 廈門市	Fujian 福建省	(0592)6251878 (0592)6251879	297	Overseas Chinese-funded 港澳台資	41,987	-5003(71)	178,351	o
Zhejiang Zhuji Body Building Bao Nutrition Tonic General Factory 浙江省諸暨市健美寶營養補品總廠(1992)	Shaoxing 紹興市	Zhejiang 浙江省	(0575)7681836	56	Collectively-owned 集體	41,473	5340(3)	50,430	o
Long Tai Aquatic Products Co. Ltd. 隆泰水產有限公司(1994)	Qinhuangdao 秦皇島市	Hebei 河北省	(0335)2024294 (0335)2024294	9	Foreign-funded 外資	32,333	1039(8)	10,309	o

Top 10 Cities by Production Output 產出排名前10位城市	Province 省	Market share 市場份額	Number of firms 企業個數
Xiamen 廈門市	Fujian 福建省	18.59%	8
Shantou 汕頭市	Guangdong 廣東省	18.47%	7
Suzhou 蘇州市	Jiangsu 江蘇省	10.91%	7
Zhongshan 中山市	Guangdong 廣東省	9.95%	1
Shanghai 上海市	Shanghai 上海市	4.86%	6
Weihai 威海市	Shandong 山東省	3.50%	9
Shaoxing 紹興市	Zhejiang 浙江省	2.86%	6
Dalian 大連市	Liaoning 遼寧省	2.68%	20
Nantong 南通市	Jiangsu 江蘇省	2.54%	6
Maoming 茂名市	Guangdong 廣東省	2.52%	3

10 Major Wholesalers 10家主要批發商	City 城市	Province 省	Telephone / Fax 電話/傳真
China National Fisheries Corp. 中國水產總公司	Beijing 北京市	Beijing 北京市	(010)66024101
Beijing He De Industrial Company 北京和德實業公司	Beijing 北京市	Beijing 北京市	(010)68329222 (010)68320042
Shanghai Food Import & Export Company 上海市食品進出口公司	Shanghai 上海市	Shanghai 上海市	(021)63216233 (021)63291730
Zhongshan Food & Aquatic Products Import & Export Group Company 中山市食品水產進出口集團公司	Zhongshan 中山市	Guangdong 廣東省	(0760)8310882 (0760)8311207
Liaoning Food Import & Export Company 遼寧省食品進出口公司	Dalian 大連市	Liaoning 遼寧省	(0411)2717149 (0411)2705713
Guangzhou Aquatic Products Trade Co. 廣州市水產貿易公司	Guangzhou 廣州市	Guangdong 廣東省	(020)81861065
Xiamen Temao Corp. 廈門特貿有限公司	Xiamen 廈門市	Fujian 福建省	(0592)5059188 (0592)5061435
Shandong Aquatic Products Enterprise Group General Company 山東省水產企業集團總公司	Ji'nan 濟南市	Shandong 山東省	(0531)6957468 (0531)6955357
Dalian Aquatic Products Joint Co. 大連水產集團公司	Dalian 大連市	Liaoning 遼寧省	(0411)2820447 (0411)2820503
Shanghai Aquatic Product Supply & Marketing Development Company 上海水產供銷發展公司	Shanghai 上海市	Shanghai 上海市	(021)65357222 (021)65356999

*Also include sales by firms outside this industry.包括本行業以外廠家的銷售。"o" stands for "others". "o" 代表"其他產品"。

1360: Salt 食用鹽加工業

The industry accounts for 0.010% of the total revenue of China's industrial sector in 1996. The revenue growth rate of the industry is 7.3% from 1995, as compared to the growth rate of China's industrial sector, 9.51%. The rate of return on asset is -3.07%. 62.74% of all firms in the industry made a profit while 32.00% had negative returns. The top province in terms of the industry's revenue is Jiangsu, accounting for 25.17% of the total revenue.
本行業在1996年佔全行業總產值0.010%，行業年增長率為7.3%（全國工業年增長率9.51%）。行業的資產回報率-3.07%，62.74%的企業盈利，32.00%的企業虧損。銷售收入最高的省份為江蘇省，佔本行業的25.17%。

	Total number of firms 企業總數	Total number of employees 職工總數	Total revenue (mil. RMB) 總銷售收入（百萬元）	Total profit (mil. RMB) 總利潤（百萬元）	Return on assets 資產利潤率 (%)	Return on equity 權益利潤率 (%)	Labour productivity ('000 RMB / worker) 勞動生產率（千元/人）	Debts / assets 資產負債率 (%)	Total assets (mil. RMB) 總資產（百萬元）
Industry Overall 行業總體	86	12,313	590	-33	-3.07	-12.85	47.92	76.11	1,080

	Number of firms 企業個數	Average number of employees 平均職工人數	Average revenue ('000 RMB) 平均銷售收入（千元）	Average profit ('000 RMB) 平均利潤（千元）	Return on assets 資產利潤率 (%)	Return on equity 權益利潤率 (%)	Labour productivity ('000 RMB / worker) 勞動生產率（千元/人）	Average debts / assets 平均資產負債率(%)	Average Total assets ('000 RMB) 平均總資產（千元）
By ownership 產業所有權									
State-owned 國有	33	263	12,788	-1,030	-3.98	-16.50	48.68	75.91	25,909
Collectively-owned 集體	47	58	1,881	5	0.43	2.22	32.63	80.81	1,234
Privately-owned 私有									
Domestic JVs 聯營	1	14	570	-16	-1.98	-9.31	40.70	78.76	808
Joint stock 股份制	1	850	68,607	805	0.51	2.16	80.71	76.54	158,924
Foreign-funded 外資	1	18	8,638	1	0.03	0.10	479.86	70.14	2,876
Overseas Chinese-funded 港澳台資	2	50	874	-19	-0.80	-1.44	17.49	44.48	2,330
By size 規模									
Large 大型									
Medium 中型	5	538	22,674	8,814	20.28	58.22	42.11	65.16	43,453
Small 小型	79	120	6,032	-976	-8.93	-42.25	50.21	78.87	10,926
By regional distribution 地區分布									
Central-North 華北	5	12	1,372	212	13.50	40.00	114.33	66.24	1,570
Beijing 北京									
Tianjin 天津	2	16	1,525	390	13.31	104.00	95.31	87.20	2,930
Hebei 河北	1	20	2,300	280	16.77	17.07	115.00	1.80	1,670
Shanxi 山西	1	8	1,510				188.75	18.75	320
Inner Mongolia 內蒙	1								
Northeast 東北	8	81	893	-188	-4.12	-8.78	10.98	53.05	4,548
Liaoning 遼寧	4	68	783	-185	-4.81	-11.99	11.51	59.86	3,843
Jilin 吉林	4	95	1,003	-190	-3.62	-6.97	10.61	48.07	5,253
Heilongjiang 黑龍江									
Central East 華東	38	117	6,022	-29	-0.24	-1.48	51.38	83.86	11,985
Shanghai 上海	1	20	840	410	29.29	87.23	42.00	66.43	1,400
Jiangsu 江蘇	11	222	13,500	-460	-1.65	-22.31	60.86	92.58	27,797
Zhejiang 浙江	5	59	1,092	-52	-1.30	-1.91	18.57	32.05	4,006
Anhui 安徽	4	48	2,310	35	4.13	8.75	48.63	52.80	848
Fujian 福建	10	20	207	9	0.95	1.19	10.51	20.27	947
Jiangxi 江西	1	464	22,120	800	1.80	7.46	47.67	75.93	44,500
Shandong 山東	6	142	6,767	465	3.94	16.53	47.82	76.19	11,810
Central-South 中南	21	277	15,403	-1,565	-6.32	-21.66	55.54	70.83	24,760
Henan 河南	5	574	22,104	-4,446	-12.33	-479.09	38.48	97.43	36,054
Hubei 湖北	2	925	64,775	-3,170	-2.38	-5.03	70.03	52.61	133,095
Hunan 湖南	3	91	4,143	-790	-10.33	-80.07	45.70	87.10	7,647
Guangdong 廣東	6	74	4,605	-307	-5.27	-18.42	62.51	71.37	5,815
Guangxi 廣西	5	78	8,666	-16	-0.51	-1.01	111.68	49.23	3,136
Hainan 海南									
Southwest 西南	5	83	1,364	4	0.15	1.53	16.43	90.26	2,690
Chongqing 重慶	1	187	3,852	100	1.05	-8.03	20.51	113.13	9,526
Sichuan 四川	2	44	133	-5	-2.20	110.21	3.03	102.00	237
Guizhou 貴州	1	64	990	60	11.76	19.35	15.47	39.22	510
Yunnan 雲南	1	76	1,710	50	1.70	2.21	22.50	23.13	2,940
Tibet 西藏									
Northwest 西北	9	101	1,926	128	2.43	9.66	19.04	74.89	5,261
Shaanxi 陝西									
Gansu 甘肅	1	379	10,080	680	1.90	12.83	26.60	85.17	35,750
Qinghai 青海	2	149	220	70	16.87	66.67	1.48	75.90	415
Ningxia 寧夏									
Xinjiang 新疆	6	39	1,135	55	3.06	5.16	29.23	40.67	1,795

Year 年份	Number of firms 企業個數	Rate of change 每年變化 (%)	Number of employees 職工人數 (人)	Rate of change 每年變化 (%)	Total revenue (mil. RMB) 總銷售收入 (百萬元)	Rate of change 每年變化 (%)	Total profit (mil. RMB) 總利潤 (百萬元)	Rate of change 每年變化 (%)
1993	66		8,632		156		-12	
1994	65	-1.52%	9,137	5.85%	201	28.50%	-7	40.85%
1995	90	38.46%	15,439	68.97%	550	174.03%	6	177.20%
1996	86	-4.44%	12,313	-20.25%	590	7.32%	-33	-697.07%

3 Major products* 3 種主要產品 *	Output 產量	Sales volume 銷售量	Unit 單位
a) Processed Salt 加工鹽	2,139,895	1,883,108	ton 噸
b) Well Salt 井鹽	297,179	309,066	ton 噸
c) Lake Salt 湖鹽	115,798	91,480	ton 噸

Top 10 firms by revenue (year founded) 收入排名前 10 家企業 (創辦年份)	City 城市	Province 省	Telephone / fax 電話 / 傳真	Number of employees 職工人數	Ownership 產業所有權	Revenue ('000 RMB) 銷售收入 (千元)	Profit ('000 RMB) (rank) 利潤 (千元) (排名)	Total assets ('000 RMB) 總資產 (千元)	Major products 主要產品
Yunmeng Salt Nitre Factory 雲夢鹽硝廠(1989)	Xiaogan 孝感市	Hubei 湖北省	(0712)4325263 (0712)4325510	1,217	State-owned 國有	101,827	2021(2)	201,460	a,b
Henan Pingdingshan Saltworks 河南省平頂山鹽廠(1994)	Pingdingshan 平頂山市	Henan 河南省	(0375)3924949	1,452	State-owned 國有	57,354	-20890(38)	47,754	a
Jiangsu Huai Hai Salinization Factory 江蘇省淮陰市淮海鹽化廠(1991)	Huaiyin 淮陰市	Jiangsu 江蘇省	(0517)5986333 (0517)5986165	1,067	State-owned 國有	48,860	660(11)	113,990	a,b
Guangxi Nanning Health Care Salt Industrial Co. Ltd. 廣西南寧保健鹽產業有限公司(1993)	Nanning 南寧市	Guangxi 廣西	(0771)5628020 (0771)5628020	300	其他經濟	43,000	-100(28)	11,000	o
Huai'an Salinization General Factory 淮安鹽化總廠(1989)	Huaiyin 淮陰市	Jiangsu 江蘇省	(0517)5912911	400	State-owned 國有	39,385	-4403(36)	95,758	a
Xingan Refine Saltworks 新乾縣精製鹽廠(1991)	Ji'an 吉安市	Jiangxi 江西省	(0796)2781260	465	State-owned 國有	22,117	801(8)	44,501	a
Yexian Yu Kun Refine Saltworks 葉縣豫昆精製鹽廠(1992)	Pingdingshan 平頂山市	Henan 河南省	(0375)8051099 (0375)8053729	421	State-owned 國有	21,274	1227(5)	36,069	a
Yexian Tian He Refine Saltworks 葉縣天河精製鹽廠(1993)	Pingdingshan 平頂山市	Henan 河南省	(0375)8051569	425	State-owned 國有	21,050	70(21)	55,727	a
Qinghai Golmud Salinization General Factory 青海省格爾木市鹽化總廠(1965)	Golmud 格爾木市	Qinghai 青海省	(0979)413157 (0979)413042	283	State-owned 國有	17,097	810(7)	42,785	c
Guangdong Various Kinds Salt Co. 廣東省多品種鹽公司(1993)	Guangzhou 廣州市	Guangdong 廣東省	(020)81587964 (020)81897864	222	State-owned 國有	16,913	-2011(31)	22,736	a

Top 10 Cities by Production Output 產出排名前 10 位城市	Province 省	Market share 市場份額	Number of firms 企業個數
Xiaogan 孝感市	Hubei 湖北省	23.01%	1
Pingdingshan 平頂山市	Henan 河南省	21.33%	5
Huaiyin 淮陰市	Jiangsu 江蘇省	8.80%	2
Binzhou 濱州市	Shandong 山東省	7.44%	1
Ji'an 吉安市	Jiangxi 江西省	4.67%	1
Yancheng 鹽城市	Jiangsu 江蘇省	3.66%	5
Guangzhou 廣州市	Guangdong 廣東省	3.57%	1
Golmud 格爾木市	Qinghai 青海省	3.31%	2
Weifang 濰坊市	Shandong 山東省	3.13%	3
Simao 思茅市	Yunnan 雲南省	2.13%	1

10 Major Wholesalers 10 家主要批發商	City 城市	Province 省	Telephone / Fax 電話 / 傳真
Guangdong Meizhou Salt Industry General Company 廣東省梅州鹽業總公司	Meizhou 梅州市	Guangdong 廣東省	(0752)2234242 (0752)2234720
Shannxi Import & Export Company 陝西省進出口公司	Xi'an 西安市	Shaanxi 陝西省	(029)7424946 (029)7420131
Fujian Salt Industry Company 福建省鹽業公司	Fuzhou 福州市	Fujian 福建省	(0591)7535047 (0591)7535047
Sichuan Salt Industry Company Zigong Branch 四川省鹽業公司自貢分公司	Zigong 自貢市	Sichuan 四川省	(0813)2203215 (0813)2203215
Shanghai Shi Liu Pu Non-staple Food Trade Company 上海市十六鋪副食品貿易公司	Shanghai 上海市	Shanghai 上海市	(021)63736787
Shandong Salt Industry General Company Shandong Salt Administration Bureau 山東省鹽業總公司山東省鹽務局	Ji'nan 濟南市	Shandong 山東省	(0531)6925633 (0531)6925021
Yunnan Salt Industry General Company 雲南省鹽業總公司	Kunming 昆明市	Yunnan 雲南省	(0871)3166719
Shanghai Jia Le Condiment Mill Marketing Company 上海家樂調味食品銷售公司	Shanghai 上海市	Shanghai 上海市	(021)59139194
Zhong Yan Shanghai Salt Company 中鹽上海鹽業公司	Shanghai 上海市	Shanghai 上海市	(021)62180345 (021)62187068
Zhejiang Salt Industry Company 浙江省鹽業公司	Hangzhou 杭州市	Zhejiang 浙江省	(0571)7800292 (0571)7800292

*Also include sales by firms outside this industry.包括本行業以外廠家的銷售。"o" stands for "others". "o" 代表"其他產品"。

1390: Other Food Processing 其他食品加工業

The industry accounts for 0.210% of the total revenue of China's industrial sector in 1996. The revenue growth rate of the industry is 32.2% from 1995, as compared to the growth rate of China's industrial sector, 9.51%. The rate of return on asset is 2.41%. 74.10% of all firms in the industry made a profit while 18.85% had negative returns. The top province in terms of the industry's revenue is Shandong, accounting for 32.10% of the total revenue.
本行業在1996年佔全行業總產值0.210%，行業年增長率為32.2%（全國工業年增長率9.51%）。行業的資產回報率2.41%，74.10%的企業盈利，18.85%的企業虧損。銷售收入最高的省份為山東省，佔本行業的32.10%。

	Total number of firms 企業總數	Total number of employees 職工總數	Total revenue (mil. RMB) 總銷售收入（百萬元）	Total profit (mil. RMB) 總利潤（百萬元）	Return on assets 資產利潤率 (%)	Return on equity 權益利潤率 (%)	Labour productivity ('000 RMB / worker) 勞動生產率（千元/人）	Debts / assets 資產負債率 (%)	Total assets (mil. RMB) 總資產（百萬元）
Industry Overall 行業總體	1,953	138,401	12,158	315	2.41	7.34	87.85	67.17	13,074

	Number of firms 企業個數	Average number of employees 平均職工人數	Average revenue ('000 RMB) 平均銷售收入（千元）	Average profit ('000 RMB) 平均利潤（千元）	Return on assets 資產利潤率 (%)	Return on equity 權益利潤率 (%)	Labour productivity ('000 RMB / worker) 勞動生產率（千元/人）	Average debts / assets 平均資產負債率(%)	Average Total assets ('000 RMB) 平均總資產（千元）
By ownership 產業所有權									
State-owned 國有	221	106	6,507	-149	-1.27	-4.89	61.26	74.05	11,769
Collectively-owned 集體	1,262	57	4,760	228	6.38	23.45	82.88	72.79	3,577
Privately-owned 私有	13	59	2,999	-20	-0.68	-16.09	51.23	95.76	2,865
Domestic JVs 聯營	26	51	3,801	15	0.47	1.24	74.41	62.01	3,111
Joint stock 股份制	25	109	6,568	346	6.92	47.08	60.46	85.31	5,002
Foreign-funded 外資	233	91	10,687	452	3.25	7.59	117.44	57.21	13,898
Overseas Chinese-funded 港澳台資	167	94	10,880	-336	-2.36	-6.21	115.50	62.03	14,259
By size 規模									
Large 大型	3	313	82,013	8,936	12.10	17.04	261.74	28.95	73,825
Medium 中型	25	548	60,857	1,733	2.22	6.96	111.13	68.17	78,200
Small 小型	1,853	65	5,607	132	2.25	6.97	85.74	67.77	5,881
By regional distribution 地區分布									
Central-North 華北	231	67	4,749	243	4.17	11.03	71.19	62.24	5,845
Beijing 北京	41	76	5,369	609	8.13	17.18	70.69	52.68	7,492
Tianjin 天津	70	48	4,543	225	5.45	16.91	95.41	67.76	4,127
Hebei 河北	66	72	7,033	343	4.60	15.34	97.12	69.99	7,454
Shanxi 山西	32	92	1,999	-186	-3.59	-8.64	21.77	58.42	5,186
Inner Mongolia 內蒙	22	57	1,397	-53	-1.22	-2.14	24.69	43.18	4,376
Northeast 東北	229	41	3,804	85	3.06	9.25	91.87	66.93	2,773
Liaoning 遼寧	106	48	4,424	11	0.30	0.94	91.28	68.10	3,819
Jilin 吉林	47	37	1,908		-0.02	-0.06	51.10	67.48	2,119
Heilongjiang 黑龍江	76	34	4,114	240	13.96	37.62	120.66	62.89	1,718
Central East 華東	911	92	9,182	276	2.72	7.97	100.28	65.93	10,147
Shanghai 上海	28	76	9,238	561	6.21	12.45	120.98	50.11	9,029
Jiangsu 江蘇	80	106	9,649	215	1.82	4.88	91.14	62.63	11,812
Zhejiang 浙江	136	66	7,594	152	2.06	5.11	115.56	59.69	7,379
Anhui 安徽	81	68	7,362	724	19.27	65.02	108.78	70.36	3,758
Fujian 福建	268	63	6,642	-63	-1.07	-2.16	106.01	50.53	5,912
Jiangxi 江西	40	33	566	11	0.94	3.52	17.39	73.29	1,143
Shandong 山東	278	145	14,040	559	3.04	11.25	96.84	72.99	18,376
Central-South 中南	330	48	3,917	34	1.04	3.86	81.57	73.09	3,292
Henan 河南	91	53	4,081	177	6.05	23.07	76.63	73.78	2,923
Hubei 湖北	52	40	4,471	231	10.29	24.11	111.14	57.33	2,244
Hunan 湖南	51	75	3,698	158	6.99	30.02	49.58	76.73	2,256
Guangdong 廣東	114	37	4,103	-213	-4.78	-24.89	112.41	80.80	4,451
Guangxi 廣西	17	37	1,708	52	3.72	10.62	45.57	64.97	1,409
Hainan 海南	5	62	694	-296	-2.59	-3.69	11.27	29.79	11,440
Southwest 西南	149	54	2,223	-133	-4.33	-33.75	41.10	87.17	3,063
Chongqing 重慶	69	56	2,545	-121	-3.77	-16.54	45.17	77.23	3,220
Sichuan 四川	59	53	2,439	-210	-5.82	-973.47	45.65	99.40	3,608
Guizhou 貴州	10	11	72	-3	-0.60	18.75	6.55	103.21	499
Yunnan 雲南	10	92	859	115	8.79	18.31	9.38	51.99	1,308
Tibet 西藏									
Northwest 西北	103	60	1,947	-31	-1.05	-4.40	32.47	76.19	2,928
Shaanxi 陝西	25	61	3,471	252	11.76	34.03	56.72	65.44	2,146
Gansu 甘肅	53	60	1,542	-150	-5.22	-41.64	25.73	87.48	2,880
Qinghai 青海									
Ningxia 寧夏	15	72	1,001	-59	-3.39	-83.96	13.88	95.96	1,749
Xinjiang 新疆	10	39	1,709	-61	-0.88	-1.84	43.71	52.04	6,901

1390: Other Food Processing 其他食品加工業

Year 年份	Number of firms 企業個數	Rate of change 每年變化 (%)	Number of employees 職工人數 (人)	Rate of change 每年變化 (%)	Total revenue (mil. RMB) 總銷售收入 (百萬元)	Rate of change 每年變化 (%)	Total profit (mil. RMB) 總利潤 (百萬元)	Rate of change 每年變化 (%)
1993	1,203		70,253		3,714		209	
1994	1,582	31.50%	150,870	114.75%	5,725	54.17%	136	-35.21%
1995	1,848	16.81%	126,299	-16.29%	9,197	60.63%	251	85.24%
1996	1,953	5.68%	138,401	9.58%	12,158	32.20%	315	25.40%

3 Major products* 3 種主要產品 *	Output 產量	Sales volume 銷售量	Unit 單位
a) Quickly-frozen Vegetable 速凍蔬菜	196,019	178,377	ton 噸
b) Dried Vegetable Products 蔬菜乾製品	81,400	77,330	ton 噸
c) Vegetable Pickled in Soy Sauce 醬腌菜	164,809	161,513	ton 噸

Top 10 firms by revenue (year founded) 收入排名前 10 家企業 (創辦年份)	City 城市	Province 省	Telephone / fax 電話 / 傳真	Number of employees 職工人數	Ownership 產業所有權	Revenue ('000 RMB) 銷售收入 (千元)	Profit ('000 RMB) (rank) 利潤 (千元) (排名)	Total assets ('000 RMB) 總資產 (千元)	Major products 主要產品
Yantai Long Da Enterprise Group Co. 煙台龍大企業集團(1986)	Yantai 煙台市	Shandong 山東省	(0535)7710314 (0535)7710314	2,956	Collectively-owned 集體	404,999	11405(8)	419,401	a
Longkou Fu Fa Zhong Ji Cold Storage Co. Ltd. 龍口復發中記冷藏有限公司(1993)	Yantai 煙台市	Shandong 山東省	(0535)8857288 (0535)8857035	255	Foreign-funded 外資	250,285	3683(33)	615,846	o
Shouguang Grain & Oil General Company 壽光市糧油總公司	Weifang 濰坊市	Shandong 山東省		1,067	State-owned 國有	224,147	3887(31)	280,675	o
Anhui Da Yu Industrial General Co. 安徽省達裕實業總公司(1986)	Fuyang 阜陽市	Anhui 安徽省	(0558)6512727	536	Collectively-owned 集體	214,900	33355(1)	51,724	b
Gaoming Cang Jiang Local Products Multiple Processing Factory 高明市滄江土產綜合加工廠(1986)	Foshan 佛山市	Guangdong 廣東省	(0757)8822389	32	Collectively-owned 集體	158,820	29(548)	34,467	o
Longhai Dong Hai Frozen Foods Co. Ltd. 龍海市東海冷凍食品有限公司(1992)	Zhangzhou 漳州市	Fujian 福建省	(0596)6777307 (0596)6777309	753	Overseas Chinese-funded 港澳台資	148,600	-6051(833)	92,383	a
Qingdao Wan Fu Food Co. Ltd. 青島萬福食品有限公司(1991)	Qingdao 青島市	Shandong 山東省	(0532)8484723 (0532)8486666	456	Foreign-funded 外資	138,051	13392(5)	48,752	a,c
Lianyungang Ru Yi Food Co. Ltd. 連雲港如意食品有限公司(1991)	Lianyungang 連雲港市	Jiangsu 江蘇省	(0518)5456326 (0518)5456248	728	Foreign-funded 外資	125,550	14650(4)	261,250	a
Shanghai Xiao Long Ren Foods General Factory 上海小龍人食品總廠(1985)	Shanghai 上海市	Shanghai 上海市	(021)58637846 (021)58631720	775	Collectively-owned 集體	125,338	15186(2)	95,813	o
Cixi General Cold Starage Co. Zhejiang 浙江省慈溪冷凍總公司(1985)	Ningbo 寧波市	Zhejiang 浙江省	(0574)3813938 (0574)3813225	1,105	Collectively-owned 集體	119,653	1304(90)	106,470	o

Top 10 Cities by Production Output 產出排名前 10 位城市	Province 省	Market share 市場份額	Number of firms 企業個數
Yantai 煙台市	Shandong 山東省	9.11%	69
Linyi 臨沂市	Shandong 山東省	6.07%	77
Yancheng 鹽城市	Jiangsu 江蘇省	5.39%	23
Qingdao 青島市	Shandong 山東省	4.37%	43
Weihai 威海市	Shandong 山東省	3.97%	23
Tangshan 唐山市	Hebei 河北省	3.72%	23
Ningbo 寧波市	Zhejiang 浙江省	2.92%	19
Beijing 北京市	Beijing 北京市	2.78%	36
Hangzhou 杭州市	Zhejiang 浙江省	2.61%	56
Fuzhou 福州市	Fujian 福建省	2.60%	38

10 Major Wholesalers 10 家主要批發商	City 城市	Province 省	Telephone / Fax 電話 / 傳真
Shanghai Jiu Zhou Group Co. Ltd. 上海九州集團有限公司	Shanghai 上海市	Shanghai 上海市	(021)62401515 (021)62123848
Shanghai Tobacco (Group) Co. Trade Center 上海煙草集團上海煙草貿易中心	Shanghai 上海市	Shanghai 上海市	(021)58781921 (021)58786584
China Tax-free Company 中國免稅公司	Beijing 北京市	Beijing 北京市	(010)64668397 (010)64635846
Liaoning Cigarette Marketing Company 遼寧省卷煙銷售公司	Shenyang 瀋陽市	Liaoning 遼寧省	(024)22834388 (024)22837853
Hunan Import & Export General Company Shenzhen Company 湖南省進出口總公司深圳公司	Shenzhen 深圳市	Guangdong 廣東省	(0755)2339793 (0755)2339793
Anhui Tobacco Company Wuhu Branch 安徽省煙草公司蕪湖分公司	Wuhu 蕪湖市	Anhui 安徽省	(0553)4812288 (0553)4812467
Luoyang Jianxi Fountain Sugar & Wine Company 洛陽市澗西噴泉糖酒公司	Luoyang 洛陽市	Henan 河南省	(0379)4321729 (0379)4324531
Shanghai Putuo Supply & Marketing Co-operative 上海市普陀區供銷合作社	Shanghai 上海市	Shanghai 上海市	(021)62576900 (021)62577469
Zhejiang Native and Non-staple Food General Co. 浙江省土產副食品總公司	Hangzhou 杭州市	Zhejiang 浙江省	(0571)7912957 (0571)7911808
Hebei Tobacco Company Zhangjiakou Branch 河北省煙草公司張家口分公司	Zhangjiakou 張家口市	Hebei 河北省	(0313)2015537 (0313)2017607

*Also include sales by firms outside this industry.包括本行業以外廠家的銷售。"o" stands for "others". "o" 代表 "其他產品"。

1411: Candy 糖果業

The industry accounts for 0.105% of the total revenue of China's industrial sector in 1996. The revenue growth rate of the industry is 6.2% from 1995, as compared to the growth rate of China's industrial sector, 9.51%. The rate of return on asset is 0.94%. 60.98% of all firms in the industry made a profit while 31.33% had negative returns. The top province in terms of the industry's revenue is Guangdong, accounting for 25.23% of the total revenue.
本行業在1996年佔全行業總產值0.105%，行業年增長率為6.2%（全國工業年增長率9.51%）。行業的資產回報率0.94%，60.98%的企業盈利，31.33%的企業虧損。銷售收入最高的省份為廣東省，佔本行業的25.23%。

	Total number of firms 企業總數	Total number of employees 職工總數	Total revenue (mil. RMB) 總銷售收入（百萬元）	Total profit (mil. RMB) 總利潤（百萬元）	Return on assets 資產利潤率 (%)	Return on equity 權益利潤率 (%)	Labour productivity ('000 RMB / worker) 勞動生產率（千元/人）	Debts / assets 資產負債率 (%)	Total assets (mil. RMB) 總資產（百萬元）
Industry Overall 行業總體	893	90,102	6,078	93	0.94	3.15	67.46	70.20	9,943

	Number of firms 企業個數	Average number of employees 平均職工人數	Average revenue ('000 RMB) 平均銷售收入（千元）	Average profit ('000 RMB) 平均利潤（千元）	Return on assets 資產利潤率 (%)	Return on equity 權益利潤率 (%)	Labour productivity ('000 RMB / worker) 勞動生產率（千元/人）	Average debts / assets 平均資產負債率(%)	Average Total assets ('000 RMB) 平均總資產（千元）
By ownership 產業所有權									
State-owned 國有	273	181	6,685	-168	-0.98	-4.76	36.99	79.40	17,194
Collectively-owned 集體	463	57	4,037	113	2.90	9.75	71.05	70.29	3,884
Privately-owned 私有	7	22	2,977	80	4.61	9.00	132.74	48.78	1,735
Domestic JVs 聯營	9	108	3,445	9	0.12	0.56	31.93	78.85	7,598
Joint stock 股份制	11	208	13,800	57	0.24	0.80	66.32	70.05	23,562
Foreign-funded 外資	56	82	25,344	1,332	3.76	8.89	309.54	57.70	35,443
Overseas Chinese-funded 港澳台資	74	97	10,272	148	0.98	2.10	105.59	53.49	15,208
By size 規模									
Large 大型	14	922	144,507	1,859	0.80	2.80	156.78	71.33	231,873
Medium 中型	32	544	44,755	2,691	3.72	13.31	82.23	72.01	72,274
Small 小型	831	72	3,156	-23	-0.44	-1.38	43.71	68.41	5,275
By regional distribution 地區分布									
Central-North 華北	94	116	5,838	-1,261	-6.36	-19.86	50.30	67.98	19,829
Beijing 北京	28	135	6,815	-2,930	-8.38	-41.04	50.39	79.59	34,981
Tianjin 天津	38	120	7,922	-974	-4.71	-9.96	65.81	52.68	20,652
Hebei 河北	12	56	2,263	73	2.03	7.31	40.52	72.21	3,610
Shanxi 山西	5	42	480	-20	-0.62	-1.73	11.43	64.05	3,210
Inner Mongolia 內蒙	11	152	2,489	-27	-0.74	-3.88	16.41	80.81	3,667
Northeast 東北	87	114	1,915	-281	-4.02	15.78	16.79	125.48	6,994
Liaoning 遼寧	33	39	2,203	80	2.47	9.54	56.19	74.11	3,251
Jilin 吉林	16	244	3,217	-1,472	-9.42	12.86	13.16	173.23	15,626
Heilongjiang 黑龍江	38	124	1,117	-94	-1.42	-1369.23	9.00	99.90	6,610
Central East 華東	287	114	10,005	347	2.53	7.37	87.75	65.70	13,732
Shanghai 上海	36	264	38,339	1,757	2.91	8.71	145.07	66.62	60,411
Jiangsu 江蘇	51	158	10,259	-198	-1.44	-4.46	64.88	67.60	13,701
Zhejiang 浙江	34	100	6,043	71	0.73	1.76	60.49	58.39	9,648
Anhui 安徽	56	81	5,635	511	12.16	34.70	69.78	64.97	4,205
Fujian 福建	51	54	3,367	170	3.61	8.02	62.28	55.07	4,709
Jiangxi 江西	24	42	1,038	15	0.41	6.96	24.50	94.14	3,579
Shandong 山東	35	99	7,153	184	3.62	9.50	72.54	61.95	5,081
Central-South 中南	242	92	8,987	786	6.94	18.66	97.62	62.81	11,325
Henan 河南	29	132	9,868	769	6.37	23.21	74.77	72.54	12,064
Hubei 湖北	24	72	1,038	-118	-4.59	147.64	14.33	103.11	2,561
Hunan 湖南	43	51	1,113	-142	-7.90	-28.46	21.65	72.23	1,798
Guangdong 廣東	103	88	14,890	1,799	10.83	24.65	168.49	56.04	16,603
Guangxi 廣西	35	132	7,506	-178	-1.34	-4.50	56.99	70.13	13,217
Hainan 海南	8	99	2,448	-281	-2.83	-16.32	24.72	82.63	9,926
Southwest 西南	130	79	1,861	-237	-5.51	-22.41	23.45	75.40	4,304
Chongqing 重慶	28	109	1,422	-544	-11.94	-210.66	13.03	94.33	4,558
Sichuan 四川	63	71	2,335	-129	-2.55	-8.12	32.84	68.65	5,081
Guizhou 貴州	11	42	204	-8	-0.51	-1.29	4.89	60.10	1,593
Yunnan 雲南	27	81	1,890	-256	-7.71	-30.77	23.43	74.94	3,319
Tibet 西藏									
Northwest 西北	53	75	1,399	-427	-9.89	-187.81	18.74	94.74	4,322
Shaanxi 陝西	17	44	508	-155	-8.58	-37.25	11.45	76.96	1,802
Gansu 甘肅	15	27	447	2	0.21	0.67	16.26	68.77	952
Qinghai 青海									
Ningxia 寧夏	3	158	4,797	-330	-3.96	-14.75	30.29	73.19	8,343
Xinjiang 新疆	18	129	2,467	-1,059	-11.98	308.91	19.18	103.88	8,840

Year 年份	Number of firms 企業個數	Rate of change 每年變化 (%)	Number of employees 職工人數 (人)	Rate of change 每年變化 (%)	Total revenue (mil. RMB) 總銷售收入 (百萬元)	Rate of change 每年變化 (%)	Total profit (mil. RMB) 總利潤 (百萬元)	Rate of change 每年變化 (%)
1993	912		138,895		4,516		23	
1994	944	3.51%	122,411	-11.87%	5,031	11.40%	13	-43.66%
1995	883	-6.46%	117,798	-3.77%	5,725	13.80%	88	574.51%
1996	893	1.13%	90,102	-23.51%	6,078	6.17%	93	5.11%

3 Major products* 3 種主要產品 *	Output 產量	Sales volume 銷售量	Unit 單位
a) Candy 糖果	4,969	4,870	ton 噸
b) Frozen Food 冷凍飲品	39,492	36,727	ton 噸

Top 10 firms by revenue (year founded) 收入排名前 10 家企業 (創辦年份)	City 城市	Province 省	Telephone / fax 電話 / 傳真	Number of employees 職工人數	Ownership 產業所有權	Revenue ('000 RMB) 銷售收入 (千元)	Profit ('000 RMB) (rank) 利潤 (千元) (排名)	Total assets ('000 RMB) 總資產 (千元)	Major products 主要產品
Guan Sheng Yuan (Group) General Co. 冠生園(集團)總公司(1919)	Shanghai 上海市	Shanghai 上海市	(021)62101090 (021)62102524	2,561	State-owned 國有	572,571	22491(5)	748,788	a,b
Guangzhou Panyu Confectionery Co. Ltd. 廣州番禺糖果有限公司(1987)	Guangzhou 廣州市	Guangdong 廣東省	(020)84732801 (020)84732623	638	Foreign-funded 外資	552,853	195885(1)	370,420	a
Jian Pai Chewing Gum Co. Ltd. 箭牌口香糖有限公司(1989)	Guangzhou 廣州市	Guangdong 廣東省	(020)82218816 (020)82215107	713	Foreign-funded 外資	455,679	47827(4)	324,371	o
Shanghai Jia Feng Foods Products Mill 上海佳豐食品廠(1991)	Shanghai 上海市	Shanghai 上海市	(021)58972888 (021)58973020	1,409	Collectively-owned 集體	425,965	95733(2)	433,487	a
Henan Yu Heng Foods Co. Ltd. 河南裕恒食品有限公司(1992)	Zhoukou 周口市	Henan 河南省	(0394)53224465 (0394)5322451	2,126	Overseas Chinese-funded 港澳台資	148,264	16176(6)	97,606	a
Shanghai Da Chang Children Foods Co. Ltd. 上海大昌兒童食品有限公司(1993)	Shanghai 上海市	Shanghai 上海市	(021)64042478 (021)64039463	1,093	Overseas Chinese-funded 港澳台資	140,235	8793(7)	124,580	a
Liuzhou Candy No.2 Factory 柳州市糖果二廠(1956)	Liuzhou 柳州市	Guangxi 廣西	(0772)2827391	898	State-owned 國有	105,753	3223(15)	133,150	a
Shanghai Shen Feng Food Co. Ltd. 上海申豐食品有限公司(1990)	Shanghai 上海市	Shanghai 上海市	(021)64308888 (021)64300642	218	Overseas Chinese-funded 港澳台資	98,486	5524(10)	164,527	a
Shanghai Min Fu Food Factory 上海市民福食品廠(1985)	Shanghai 上海市	Shanghai 上海市	(021)57401308	426	Collectively-owned 集體	92,000	960(54)	23,374	a
Yangzhou Wu Yi Food Group Company 揚州五一食品集團公司(1958)	Yangzhou 揚州市	Jiangsu 江蘇省	(0514)7231954 (0514)7232466	1,431	State-owned 國有	91,392	32(177)	242,806	a,b

Top 10 Cities by Production Output 產出排名前 10 位城市	Province 省	Market share 市場份額	Number of firms 企業個數
Shanghai 上海市	Shanghai 上海市	29.05%	71
Guangzhou 廣州市	Guangdong 廣東省	9.31%	14
Beijing 北京市	Beijing 北京市	8.11%	28
Suzhou 蘇州市	Jiangsu 江蘇省	6.89%	26
Tianjin 天津市	Tianjin 天津市	4.83%	43
Fuyang 阜陽市	Anhui 安徽省	4.32%	34
Xuzhou 徐州市	Jiangsu 江蘇省	2.24%	8
Liuzhou 柳州市	Guangxi 廣西	2.17%	13
Shenzhen 深圳市	Guangdong 廣東省	1.87%	5
Zhenjiang 鎮江市	Jiangsu 江蘇省	1.63%	11

10 Major Wholesalers 10 家主要批發商	City 城市	Province 省	Telephone / Fax 電話 / 傳真
Zhong Liang Sugar Industry Groceries Import & Export Company 中糧糖業雜品進出口公司	Beijing 北京市	Beijing 北京市	(010)65268888 (010)65276023
China National Sugar & Alcohol Group Corp. 中國糖業酒類集團公司	Beijing 北京市	Beijing 北京市	(010)68360994
Shanxi Sugar & Wine Non-staple Food Company 山西省糖酒副食公司	Taiyuan 太原市	Shanxi 山西省	(0351)2027938 (0351)2027931
Putian Xue Jin Beer Marketing Agency Co. Ltd. 莆田縣雪津啤酒營銷代理有限公司	Putian 莆田市	Fujian 福建省	
Suzhou Sugar, Cigarette & Wine General Company 蘇州糖煙酒總公司	Suzhou 蘇州市	Jiangsu 江蘇省	(0512)7276392 (0512)7276406
Yuhang Sugar Industry Tobacco & Wine Company 余杭市糖業煙酒公司	Hangzhou 杭州市	Zhejiang 浙江省	(0571)6225788 (0571)6225407
Wuxi Sugar Industry Cigarette & Wine General Company 無錫市糖業煙酒總公司	Wuxi 無錫市	Jiangsu 江蘇省	(0510)2720023 (0510)2707693
Wuxi Chaoyang Co. Ltd. 無錫朝陽股份有限公司	Wuxi 無錫市	Jiangsu 江蘇省	(0510)2767704
Yinchuan Shen Da Non-staple Food Co. Ltd. 銀川申達副食有限公司	Yinchuan 銀川市	Ningxia 寧夏	(0951)5031694
Shanghai Sugar Industry Cigarette & Wine (Group) Co. Ltd. 上海市糖業煙酒(集團)有限公司	Shanghai 上海市	Shanghai 上海市	(021)63224190 (021)63223169

*Also include sales by firms outside this industry.包括本行業以外廠家的銷售。"o" stands for "others". "o" 代表 "其他產品"。

1412: Pastry 糕點業

The industry accounts for 0.074% of the total revenue of China's industrial sector in 1996. The revenue growth rate of the industry is 10.0% from 1995, as compared to the growth rate of China's industrial sector, 9.51%. The rate of return on asset is -1.16%. 62.48% of all firms in the industry made a profit while 26.74% had negative returns. The top province in terms of the industry's revenue is Shanghai, accounting for 10.93% of the total revenue.
本行業在1996年佔全行業總產值0.074%，行業年增長率為10.0%（全國工業年增長率9.51%）。行業的資產回報率-1.16%，62.48%的企業盈利，26.74%的企業虧損。銷售收入最高的省份為上海市，佔本行業的10.93%。

	Total number of firms 企業總數	Total number of employees 職工總數	Total revenue (mil. RMB) 總銷售收入（百萬元）	Total profit (mil. RMB) 總利潤（百萬元）	Return on assets 資產利潤率 (%)	Return on equity 權益利潤率 (%)	Labour productivity ('000 RMB / worker) 勞動生產率（千元／人）	Debts / assets 資產負債率 (%)	Total assets (mil. RMB) 總資產（百萬元）
Industry Overall 行業總體	2,527	131,728	4,312	-80	-1.16	-3.45	32.73	66.47	6,937

	Number of firms 企業個數	Average number of employees 平均職工人數	Average revenue ('000 RMB) 平均銷售收入（千元）	Average profit ('000 RMB) 平均利潤（千元）	Return on assets 資產利潤率 (%)	Return on equity 權益利潤率 (%)	Labour productivity ('000 RMB / worker) 勞動生產率（千元／人）	Average debts / assets 平均資產負債率(%)	Average Total assets ('000 RMB) 平均總資產（千元）
By ownership 產業所有權									
State-owned 國有	1,121	72	1,633	-59	-1.78	-6.50	22.58	72.53	3,299
Collectively-owned 集體	1,198	33	1,286	-118	-9.26	-28.54	39.37	67.54	1,278
Privately-owned 私有	4	35	2,067	-205	-9.21	-17.16	59.90	46.29	2,222
Domestic JVs 聯營	8	118	1,792	-306	-3.48	-33.57	15.19	89.63	8,794
Joint stock 股份制	9	89	8,191	15,984	65.51	1586.19	91.58	95.87	24,400
Foreign-funded 外資	89	60	4,707	-293	-3.57	-5.11	78.39	30.24	8,215
Overseas Chinese-funded 港澳台資	97	56	4,367	137	1.97	4.74	77.50	58.42	6,982
By size 規模									
Large 大型	2	400	8,027	-5,908	-4.85	-7.27	20.09	33.23	121,762
Medium 中型	16	428	19,089	57	0.12	0.46	44.58	74.20	47,363
Small 小型	2,496	50	1,598	-28	-1.16	-3.51	31.99	66.85	2,378
By regional distribution 地區分布									
Central-North 華北	510	45	1,294	-94	-3.32	-9.62	28.57	65.51	2,822
Beijing 北京	143	41	2,015	-275	-5.53	-12.48	48.93	55.65	4,978
Tianjin 天津	65	53	1,272	29	1.24	3.49	24.21	64.53	2,339
Hebei 河北	110	50	1,436		-0.01	-0.07	28.99	83.63	2,364
Shanxi 山西	101	49	928	-68	-3.27	-11.48	19.01	71.52	2,092
Inner Mongolia 內蒙	91	38	414	-36	-3.15	-13.67	11.00	76.95	1,143
Northeast 東北	362	52	757	-21	-1.15	-4.15	14.41	72.34	1,815
Liaoning 遼寧	157	57	771	-9	-0.45	-1.32	13.54	66.13	1,907
Jilin 吉林	77	57	713	-48	-2.14	-9.08	12.47	76.37	2,222
Heilongjiang 黑龍江	128	44	765	-20	-1.36	-6.35	17.30	78.62	1,457
Central East 華東	772	52	2,213	1	0.04	0.10	42.17	64.14	2,985
Shanghai 上海	125	56	3,772	-40	-0.80	-1.56	67.87	48.78	5,001
Jiangsu 江蘇	120	63	2,769	2	0.08	0.26	43.94	69.07	2,768
Zhejiang 浙江	103	39	1,614	7	0.28	0.65	41.40	56.94	2,353
Anhui 安徽	145	42	1,294	-25	-1.71	-6.12	30.58	72.13	1,455
Fujian 福建	52	43	3,768	223	8.35	18.52	88.42	54.90	2,676
Jiangxi 江西	84	33	806	12	1.36	5.90	24.52	76.88	908
Shandong 山東	143	76	2,011	-29	-0.61	-2.59	26.42	76.42	4,746
Central-South 中南	403	60	2,375	-26	-0.75	-2.47	39.91	69.78	3,437
Henan 河南	142	47	1,161	30	2.18	8.56	24.49	74.51	1,356
Hubei 湖北	95	73	2,553	14	0.53	2.23	35.04	76.08	2,629
Hunan 湖南	77	47	875	-65	-5.56	-24.73	18.51	77.53	1,173
Guangdong 廣東	41	94	9,080	-219	-1.14	-3.45	96.72	67.00	19,203
Guangxi 廣西	46	54	2,330	-40	-3.26	-7.24	43.54	54.99	1,220
Hainan 海南	2	190	1,490	-35	-0.79	-1.62	7.86	51.46	4,450
Southwest 西南	231	55	1,819	-20	-0.88	-2.54	32.82	65.37	2,314
Chongqing 重慶	22	66	4,074	6,714	200.74	620.17	61.10	67.63	3,345
Sichuan 四川	63	54	962	-2,362	-111.41	-669.71	17.54	83.36	2,121
Guizhou 貴州	36	45	1,010	8	0.44	1.22	22.55	64.06	1,709
Yunnan 雲南	106	57	2,149	3	0.11	0.27	37.81	58.34	2,281
Tibet 西藏	3	49	627	-90	-1.30	-1.78	12.70	27.06	6,947
Northwest 西北	249	49	1,171	-44	-1.77	-5.01	23.68	64.72	2,476
Shaanxi 陝西	101	53	1,307	-47	-1.94	-8.17	24.85	76.24	2,437
Gansu 甘肅	63	39	600	-27	-1.41	-2.97	15.27	52.42	1,910
Qinghai 青海	14	48	501	-131	-9.02	-25.92	10.35	65.26	1,458
Ningxia 寧夏	19	59	1,825	75	2.42	4.60	30.98	47.36	3,111
Xinjiang 新疆	52	53	1,541	-77	-2.35	-6.31	29.32	62.71	3,278

Year 年份	Number of firms 企業個數	Rate of change 每年變化 (%)	Number of employees 職工人數 (人)	Rate of change 每年變化 (%)	Total revenue (mil. RMB) 總銷售收入 (百萬元)	Rate of change 每年變化 (%)	Total profit (mil. RMB) 總利潤 (百萬元)	Rate of change 每年變化 (%)
1993	2,982		215,020		4,147		-56	
1994	2,796	-6.24%	191,084	-11.13%	4,390	5.86%	-21	63.38%
1995	2,605	-6.83%	156,637	-18.03%	3,921	-10.69%	-36	-75.40%
1996	2,527	-2.99%	131,728	-15.90%	4,312	9.97%	-80	-120.45%

3 Major products* 3種主要產品*	Output 產量	Sales volume 銷售量	Unit 單位
a) Cake 糕點	95,728	91,899	ton 噸
b) Biscuit 餅乾	4,086	4,086	ton 噸
c) Candy 糖果	103	101	ton 噸

Top 10 firms by revenue (year founded) 收入排名前10家企業 (創辦年份)	City 城市	Province 省	Telephone / fax 電話 / 傳真	Number of employees 職工人數	Ownership 產業所有權	Revenue ('000 RMB) 銷售收入 (千元)	Profit ('000 RMB) (rank) 利潤 (千元) (排名)	Total assets ('000 RMB) 總資產 (千元)	Major products 主要產品
Xiapu Songcheng Enterprise Food Processing Company 霞浦縣松城企業食品加工公司(1995)	Ningde 寧德市	Fujian 福建省	(0593)8892218	500	Collectively-owned 集體	135,010	12820(2)	17,383	o
Guangzhou Qu Xiang Cakes Maker 廣州市趣香餅家(1934)	Guangzhou 廣州市	Guangdong 廣東省	(020)84484921 (020)84417533	485	State-owned 國有	85,609	2104(13)	38,829	a,c
Guangzhou Guo Qiang Foods Products Mill 廣州市國強食品廠(1956)	Guangzhou 廣州市	Guangdong 廣東省	(020)86300377 (020)86644461	512	State-owned 國有	53,100	1446(21)	69,150	a,b,c
Shanghai Yuan Zu Foods Co. Ltd. 上海元祖食品有限公司(1993)	Shanghai 上海市	Shanghai 上海市	(021)65372828 (021)65372828	388	Foreign-funded 外資	48,239	9675(3)	22,767	a
Wuxi Yuan Zu Food Co. Ltd. 無錫市元祖食品有限公司(1995)	Wuxi 無錫市	Jiangsu 江蘇省	(0510)2105278 (0510)2105768	80	Foreign-funded 外資	44,543	4115(8)	11,198	a
Shanghai Fu Wang Food Co. Ltd. 上海福旺食品有限公司(1993)	Shanghai 上海市	Shanghai 上海市	(021)64061257 (021)64061254	143	Foreign-funded 外資	44,466	16693(1)	66,005	o
Kunming Ji Qing Xiang Pastry Factory 昆明吉慶祥糕點廠(1907)	Kunming 昆明市	Yunnan 雲南省	(0871)5173202 (0871)5173202	316	State-owned 國有	42,109	1911(14)	29,285	a,b
State-owned Chongqing Jiangjin Confectionery Plant 國營重慶江津糖果廠(1957)	Chongqing 重慶市	Chongqing 重慶市	(023)47522316	358	State-owned 國有	36,950	1126(28)	21,143	a,c
Dongguan Hou Jie Food Factory 東莞厚街食品廠(1983)	Dongguan 東莞市	Guangdong 廣東省	(0769)5581088	232	Collectively-owned 集體	36,525	47(233)	28,981	b
Shanghai Lian Quan Food Co. Ltd. 上海聯全食品有限公司(1993)	Shanghai 上海市	Shanghai 上海市	(021)58747278 (021)58800750	388	Foreign-funded 外資	34,008	5522(5)	20,301	a

Top 10 Cities by Production Output 產出排名前10位城市	Province 省	Market share 市場份額	Number of firms 企業個數
Shanghai 上海市	Shanghai 上海市	18.17%	215
Guangzhou 廣州市	Guangdong 廣東省	5.62%	49
Beijing 北京市	Beijing 北京市	5.14%	119
Kunming 昆明市	Yunnan 雲南省	2.57%	25
Tianjin 天津市	Tianjin 天津市	2.34%	79
Chongqing 重慶市	Chongqing 重慶市	2.15%	30
Hangzhou 杭州市	Zhejiang 浙江省	1.92%	40
Qingdao 青島市	Shandong 山東省	1.85%	24
Dalian 大連市	Liaoning 遼寧省	1.47%	32
Zhongshan 中山市	Guangdong 廣東省	1.36%	4

10 Major Wholesalers 10家主要批發商	City 城市	Province 省	Telephone / Fax 電話 / 傳真
Zhong Liang Sugar Industry Groceries Import & Export Company 中糧糖業雜品進出口公司	Beijing 北京市	Beijing 北京市	(010)65268888 (010)65276023
China National Sugar & Alcohol Group Corp. 中國糖業酒類集團公司	Beijing 北京市	Beijing 北京市	(010)68360994
Shanxi Sugar & Wine Non-staple Food Company 山西省糖酒副食公司	Taiyuan 太原市	Shanxi 山西省	(0351)2027938 (0351)2027931
Putian Xue Jin Beer Marketing Agency Co. Ltd. 莆田縣雪津啤酒營銷代理有限公司	Putian 莆田市	Fujian 福建省	
Suzhou Sugar, Cigarette & Wine General Company 蘇州糖煙酒總公司	Suzhou 蘇州市	Jiangsu 江蘇省	(0512)7276392 (0512)7276406
Yuhang Sugar Industry Tobacco & Wine Company 余杭市糖業煙酒公司	Hangzhou 杭州市	Zhejiang 浙江省	(0571)6225788 (0571)6225407
Wuxi Sugar Industry Cigarette & Wine General Company 無錫市糖業煙酒總公司	Wuxi 無錫市	Jiangsu 江蘇省	(0510)2720023 (0510)2707693
Wuxi Chaoyang Co. Ltd. 無錫朝陽股份有限公司	Wuxi 無錫市	Jiangsu 江蘇省	(0510)2767704
Yinchuan Shen Da Non-staple Food Co. Ltd. 銀川申達副食有限公司	Yinchuan 銀川市	Ningxia 寧夏	(0951)5031694
Shanghai Sugar Industry Cigarette & Wine (Group) Co. Ltd. 上海市糖業煙酒(集團)有限公司	Shanghai 上海市	Shanghai 上海市	(021)63224190 (021)63223169

*Also include sales by firms outside this industry.包括本行業以外廠家的銷售。"o" stands for "others". "o" 代表 "其他產品"。

1413: Biscuits 餅乾業

The industry accounts for 0.118% of the total revenue of China's industrial sector in 1996. The revenue growth rate of the industry is 29.4% from 1995, as compared to the growth rate of China's industrial sector, 9.51%. The rate of return on asset is 3.78%. 66.01% of all firms in the industry made a profit while 26.90% had negative returns. The top province in terms of the industry's revenue is Guangdong, accounting for 30.36% of the total revenue.
本行業在1996年佔全行業總產值0.118%，行業年增長率為29.4%（全國工業年增長率9.51%）。行業的資產回報率3.78%，66.01%的企業盈利，26.90%的企業虧損。銷售收入最高的省份為廣東省，佔本行業的30.36%。

	Total number of firms 企業總數	Total number of employees 職工總數	Total revenue (mil. RMB) 總銷售收入（百萬元）	Total profit (mil. RMB) 總利潤（百萬元）	Return on assets 資產利潤率 (%)	Return on equity 權益利潤率 (%)	Labour productivity ('000 RMB / worker) 勞動生產率（千元/人）	Debts / assets 資產負債率 (%)	Total assets (mil. RMB) 總資產（百萬元）
Industry Overall 行業總體	621	74,376	6,851	308	3.78	10.96	92.11	65.46	8,145

	Number of firms 企業個數	Average number of employees 平均職工人數	Average revenue ('000 RMB) 平均銷售收入（千元）	Average profit ('000 RMB) 平均利潤（千元）	Return on assets 資產利潤率 (%)	Return on equity 權益利潤率 (%)	Labour productivity ('000 RMB / worker) 勞動生產率（千元/人）	Average debts / assets 平均資產負債率(%)	Average Total assets ('000 RMB) 平均總資產（千元）
By ownership 產業所有權									
State-owned 國有	177	142	5,350	-362	-3.67	-34.78	37.73	89.44	9,847
Collectively-owned 集體	322	72	5,534	223	6.47	19.73	77.27	67.19	3,445
Privately-owned 私有	6	99	6,818	264	5.14	10.16	68.64	49.41	5,145
Domestic JVs 聯營	8	184	16,559	-978	-7.67	-11560.70	89.93	99.93	12,750
Joint stock 股份制	19	465	57,664	2,335	2.46	6.47	123.99	62.01	94,995
Foreign-funded 外資	37	200	43,481	3,456	6.35	12.99	217.08	51.14	54,435
Overseas Chinese-funded 港澳台資	50	155	24,638	2,668	10.06	23.46	159.22	57.11	26,516
By size 規模									
Large 大型	9	947	142,748	11,217	4.86	13.59	150.77	64.22	230,747
Medium 中型	26	590	74,949	-1,098	-1.40	-3.15	126.93	55.46	78,139
Small 小型	575	87	6,293	410	5.84	20.22	72.00	71.13	7,020
By regional distribution 地區分布									
Central-North 華北	78	114	6,336	-158	-1.69	-5.37	55.51	68.43	9,332
Beijing 北京	13	91	12,383	530	5.34	12.83	135.85	58.39	9,931
Tianjin 天津	13	124	10,785	-1,483	-7.21	-26.12	87.09	72.41	20,577
Hebei 河北	31	103	4,402	68	1.02	3.30	42.92	69.20	6,730
Shanxi 山西	15	169	3,413	-133	-1.90	-5.74	20.14	66.98	7,000
Inner Mongolia 內蒙	6	65	897	-12	-0.40	-2.10	13.90	81.13	2,950
Northeast 東北	62	103	3,836	-465	-7.44	85.28	37.27	108.72	6,247
Liaoning 遼寧	21	80	4,026	102	2.76	12.93	50.05	78.66	3,693
Jilin 吉林	13	70	839	-121	-3.66	-54.51	12.00	93.29	3,304
Heilongjiang 黑龍江	28	135	5,086	-1,049	-11.01	55.21	37.63	119.94	9,529
Central East 華東	190	127	14,750	1,009	8.00	19.12	115.71	58.16	12,612
Shanghai 上海	14	223	38,705	2,049	4.40	9.48	173.79	53.63	46,599
Jiangsu 江蘇	22	155	12,948	962	6.01	17.85	83.32	66.32	15,995
Zhejiang 浙江	16	113	34,921	9,244	36.10	56.66	309.37	36.29	25,604
Anhui 安徽	23	42	2,936	167	8.24	32.49	69.61	74.65	2,027
Fujian 福建	44	67	7,999	-569	-9.55	-17.32	119.84	44.84	5,951
Jiangxi 江西	24	38	566	-22	-1.99	-12.68	15.06	84.30	1,088
Shandong 山東	47	236	20,936	333	2.41	9.76	88.90	75.26	13,783
Central-South 中南	235	135	13,832	691	3.60	10.28	102.68	65.03	19,220
Henan 河南	62	67	3,988	58	1.86	8.18	59.79	77.28	3,109
Hubei 湖北	19	217	4,239	-286	-4.52	-25.48	19.56	82.26	6,326
Hunan 湖南	24	65	26,977	6,982	31.79	93.83	412.91	66.13	21,966
Guangdong 廣東	94	207	22,128	-41	-0.11	-0.30	106.84	62.53	36,943
Guangxi 廣西	32	51	5,298	86	1.72	8.54	104.45	79.89	4,989
Hainan 海南	4	186	6,440	-545	-4.93	-87.55	34.58	94.37	11,048
Southwest 西南	34	59	1,244	-64	-3.39	-13.52	21.15	74.95	1,885
Chongqing 重慶	2	78	522	-754	-41.30	104.91	6.69	139.37	1,826
Sichuan 四川	13	76	1,687	345	13.27	83.09	21.97	84.02	2,597
Guizhou 貴州	10	28	487	37	6.86	10.69	17.39	35.81	539
Yunnan 雲南	8	60	1,728	-28	-1.13	-2.38	28.73	52.27	2,425
Tibet 西藏									
Northwest 西北	22	55	1,078	-114	-4.72	-13.22	19.57	64.30	2,408
Shaanxi 陝西	11	89	1,618	-231	-6.25	-22.36	18.16	72.03	3,693
Gansu 甘肅	2	34	1,790	80	6.64	14.81	52.65	55.19	1,205
Qinghai 青海	1	33	240	10	0.83	1.89	7.27	56.20	1,210
Ningxia 寧夏	2	25	145	-35	-1.41	-1.59	5.80	11.27	2,485
Xinjiang 新疆	6	14	302	-10	-1.60	-3.92	22.35	59.31	627

1413: Biscuits 餅乾業

Year 年份	Number of firms 企業個數	Rate of change 每年變化 (%)	Number of employees 職工人數 (人)	Rate of change 每年變化 (%)	Total revenue (mil. RMB) 總銷售收入 (百萬元)	Rate of change 每年變化 (%)	Total profit (mil. RMB) 總利潤 (百萬元)	Rate of change 每年變化 (%)
1993	437		65,969		3,500		93	
1994	515	17.85%	69,720	5.69%	4,593	31.23%	214	129.96%
1995	619	20.19%	79,818	14.48%	5,294	15.26%	149	-30.50%
1996	621	0.32%	74,376	-6.82%	6,851	29.41%	308	107.21%

3 Major products* 3 種主要產品 *	Output 產量	Sales volume 銷售量	Unit 單位
a) Biscuit 餅乾	78,148	78,148	ton 噸
b) Cake 糕點	24,391	23,415	ton 噸
c) Candy 糖果	426	418	ton 噸

Top 10 firms by revenue (year founded) 收入排名前 10 家企業 (創辦年份)	City 城市	Province 省	Telephone / fax 電話 / 傳真	Number of employees 職工人數	Ownership 產業所有權	Revenue ('000 RMB) 銷售收入 (千元)	Profit ('000 RMB) (rank) 利潤 (千元) (排名)	Total assets ('000 RMB) 總資產 (千元)	Major products 主要產品
Hunan Want Want Foods Co. Ltd. 湖南旺旺食品有限公司(1992)	Changsha 長沙市	Hunan 湖南省	(0731)8063111 (0731)8063116	1,301	Overseas Chinese-funded 港澳台資	615,520	165847(1)	503,612	a
Yishui Qing Yuan Food Factory 沂水縣青援食品廠(1986)	Linyi 臨沂市	Shandong 山東省	(0539)2252837 (0539)2252837	3,318	Collectively-owned 集體	462,895	9046(7)	113,961	a,c
Hangzhou Want Want Foods Ltd. 杭州旺旺食品有限公司(1993)	Hangzhou 杭州市	Zhejiang 浙江省	(0571)6228915 (0571)6223981	1,076	Foreign-funded 外資	408,155	136870(2)	325,583	o
United Biscuit (China) Co. Ltd. 聯合餅乾(中國)有限公司(1989)	Shenzhen 深圳市	Guangdong 廣東省	(0755)6696573 (0755)6695455	1,022	Foreign-funded 外資	278,593	-27206(254)	313,582	a
Dongguan Hua Jia Foods Co. Ltd. 東莞市華嘉食品有限公司(1987)	Dongguan 東莞市	Guangdong 廣東省	(0769)2467239 (0769)2467239	706	Overseas Chinese-funded 港澳台資	258,911	53399(3)	250,212	a,b
Jiangmen Da Neng Biscuit Co. Ltd. 江門達能餅乾有限公司(1995)	Jiangmen 江門市	Guangdong 廣東省	(0750)3333726 (0750)3351204	1,531	Foreign-funded 外資	219,941	-23589(252)	354,400	a,b
Shanghai Da Neng Biscuit Foods Co. Ltd. 上海達能餅乾食品有限公司(1992)	Shanghai 上海市	Shanghai 上海市	(021)64823280 (021)64364600	449	Foreign-funded 外資	201,332	17373(6)	226,362	a
Taishan Entally Enterprise Bloc 台山市英達利企業集團股份有限公司(1993)	Jiangmen 江門市	Guangdong 廣東省	(0750)5619220 (0750)5612035	1,177	Joint stock 股份制	173,866	6536(11)	593,713	a
Eastern Asia Foods Products Co. Ltd. 東亞食品有限公司(1991)	Shanghai 上海市	Shanghai 上海市	(021)64307766 (021)64300756	775	Foreign-funded 外資	156,402	21652(4)	186,647	a
Qingdao Foods Co. Ltd. 青島食品股份有限公司(1950)	Qingdao 青島市	Shandong 山東省	(0532)2827900 (0532)2822146	1,379	Joint stock 股份制	151,245	3003(15)	136,954	b,c

Top 10 Cities by Production Output 產出排名前 10 位城市	Province 省	Market share 市場份額	Number of firms 企業個數
Jiangmen 江門市	Guangdong 廣東省	11.04%	8
Linyi 臨沂市	Shandong 山東省	9.10%	14
Shanghai 上海市	Shanghai 上海市	7.71%	20
Hangzhou 杭州市	Zhejiang 浙江省	7.19%	11
Dongguan 東莞市	Guangdong 廣東省	5.00%	4
Guangzhou 廣州市	Guangdong 廣東省	4.32%	17
Qingdao 青島市	Shandong 山東省	4.27%	3
Zhangzhou 漳州市	Fujian 福建省	3.65%	16
Jining 濟寧市	Shandong 山東省	3.09%	8
Zaozhuang 棗莊市	Shandong 山東省	2.76%	4

10 Major Wholesalers 10 家主要批發商	City 城市	Province 省	Telephone / Fax 電話 / 傳真
Zhong Liang Sugar Industry Groceries Import & Export Company 中糧糖業雜品進出口公司	Beijing 北京市	Beijing 北京市	(010)65268888 (010)65276023
China National Sugar & Alcohol Group Corp. 中國糖業酒類集團公司	Beijing 北京市	Beijing 北京市	(010)68360994
Shanxi Sugar & Wine Non-staple Food Company 山西省糖酒副食公司	Taiyuan 太原市	Shanxi 山西省	(0351)2027938 (0351)2027931
Putian Xue Jin Beer Marketing Agency Co. Ltd. 莆田縣雪津啤酒營銷代理有限公司	Putian 莆田市	Fujian 福建省	
Suzhou Sugar, Cigarette & Wine General Company 蘇州糖煙酒總公司	Suzhou 蘇州市	Jiangsu 江蘇省	(0512)7276392 (0512)7276406
Yuhang Sugar Industry Tobacco & Wine Company 余杭市糖業煙酒公司	Hangzhou 杭州市	Zhejiang 浙江省	(0571)6225788 (0571)6225407
Wuxi Sugar Industry Cigarette & Wine General Company 無錫市糖業煙酒總公司	Wuxi 無錫市	Jiangsu 江蘇省	(0510)2720023 (0510)2707693
Wuxi Chaoyang Co. Ltd. 無錫朝陽股份有限公司	Wuxi 無錫市	Jiangsu 江蘇省	(0510)2767704
Yinchuan Shen Da Non-staple Food Co. Ltd. 銀川申達副食有限公司	Yinchuan 銀川市	Ningxia 寧夏	(0951)5031694
Shanghai Sugar Industry Cigarette & Wine (Group) Co. Ltd. 上海市糖業煙酒(集團)有限公司	Shanghai 上海市	Shanghai 上海市	(021)63224190 (021)63223169

*Also include sales by firms outside this industry.包括本行業以外廠家的銷售。"o" stands for "others". "o" 代表"其他產品"。

1414: Convenient Principal Food 方便主食品業

The industry accounts for 0.260% of the total revenue of China's industrial sector in 1996. The revenue growth rate of the industry is 32.4% from 1995, as compared to the growth rate of China's industrial sector, 9.51%. The rate of return on asset is 5.35%. 59.65% of all firms in the industry made a profit while 31.32% had negative returns. The top province in terms of the industry's revenue is Henan, accounting for 15.69% of the total revenue.
本行業在1996年佔全行業總產值0.260%，行業年增長率為32.4%（全國工業年增長率9.51%）。行業的資產回報率5.35%，59.65%的企業盈利，31.32%的企業虧損。銷售收入最高的省份為河南省，佔本行業的15.69%。

	Total number of firms 企業總數	Total number of employees 職工總數	Total revenue (mil. RMB) 總銷售收入（百萬元）	Total profit (mil. RMB) 總利潤（百萬元）	Return on assets 資產利潤率 (%)	Return on equity 權益利潤率 (%)	Labour productivity ('000 RMB / worker) 勞動生產率（千元/人）	Debts / assets 資產負債率 (%)	Total assets (mil. RMB) 總資產（百萬元）
Industry Overall 行業總體	823	100,242	15,073	924	5.35	11.87	150.37	54.88	17,261

	Number of firms 企業個數	Average number of employees 平均職工人數	Average revenue ('000 RMB) 平均銷售收入（千元）	Average profit ('000 RMB) 平均利潤（千元）	Return on assets 資產利潤率 (%)	Return on equity 權益利潤率 (%)	Labour productivity ('000 RMB / worker) 勞動生產率（千元/人）	Average debts / assets 平均資產負債率(%)	Average Total assets ('000 RMB) 平均總資產（千元）
By ownership 產業所有權									
State-owned 國有	233	117	8,815				75.58	74.58	9,777
Collectively-owned 集體	322	93	9,432	308	4.02	12.75	101.18	68.51	7,657
Privately-owned 私有	5	86	25,094	1,033	6.51	16.90	291.79	61.48	15,857
Domestic JVs 聯營	8	103	6,928	-22	-0.13	-0.46	67.35	70.56	16,114
Joint stock 股份制	10	60	6,142	29	1.01	5.45	102.19	81.53	2,887
Foreign-funded 外資	96	155	28,037	751	1.83	3.23	180.65	43.49	41,103
Overseas Chinese-funded 港澳台資	147	185	47,245	5,076	9.00	18.17	255.90	50.43	56,372
By size 規模									
Large 大型	8	2,745	926,936	155,945	17.85	34.10	337.71	47.64	873,542
Medium 中型	21	416	58,340	-297	-0.36	-0.87	140.22	58.64	82,963
Small 小型	762	86	9,658	-212	-1.89	-4.73	111.77	60.04	11,195
By regional distribution 地區分布									
Central-North 華北	229	120	17,977	2,072	10.54	18.49	149.64	42.99	19,647
Beijing 北京	98	66	8,123	39	0.54	1.22	122.62	55.33	7,214
Tianjin 天津	31	248	75,653	14,423	15.05	22.69	304.73	33.64	95,801
Hebei 河北	46	163	13,293	448	4.45	10.42	81.50	57.31	10,083
Shanxi 山西	25	159	10,894	188	1.77	8.44	68.64	79.08	10,674
Inner Mongolia 內蒙	29	64	3,160	-64	-2.04	-7.53	49.45	72.92	3,164
Northeast 東北	144	75	7,801	-155	-1.87	-4.54	103.40	58.84	8,298
Liaoning 遼寧	61	95	11,175	-677	-4.65	-10.32	117.75	54.88	14,552
Jilin 吉林	27	58	4,147	16	0.29	0.87	70.91	66.82	5,410
Heilongjiang 黑龍江	56	62	5,889	332	11.52	43.23	94.33	73.36	2,879
Central East 華東	196	141	20,700	1,063	4.39	12.34	146.62	64.40	24,210
Shanghai 上海	35	136	18,071	-1,205	-3.85	-11.30	132.43	65.93	31,283
Jiangsu 江蘇	27	199	37,690	1,866	5.12	9.93	189.01	48.45	36,456
Zhejiang 浙江	13	286	69,694	13,762	16.55	48.16	244.08	65.64	83,152
Anhui 安徽	11	47	4,811	246	7.25	22.93	101.57	68.36	3,396
Fujian 福建	42	49	4,645	-416	-6.36	-11.83	94.65	46.20	6,537
Jiangxi 江西	7	184	4,994	-7	-0.11	-0.45	27.16	76.23	6,696
Shandong 山東	61	163	19,967	591	2.94	13.53	122.66	78.26	20,101
Central-South 中南	190	141	25,841	1,419	4.97	10.74	182.92	53.72	28,559
Henan 河南	86	115	27,502	932	5.49	17.24	238.44	68.18	16,995
Hubei 湖北	26	244	22,939	309	1.00	2.07	94.19	51.73	30,968
Hunan 湖南	7	44	990	-33	-2.19	-6.48	22.72	66.22	1,497
Guangdong 廣東	50	177	36,487	3,845	6.41	12.14	205.63	47.19	59,970
Guangxi 廣西	19	69	5,732	-565	-7.49	-15.68	83.51	52.23	7,539
Hainan 海南	2	55	4,000	75	2.09	6.85	73.39	69.41	3,580
Southwest 西南	31	135	17,755	41	0.12	0.29	131.17	60.42	35,553
Chongqing 重慶	3	688	52,459	-189	-0.29	0.64	76.16	146.02	64,378
Sichuan 四川	18	88	20,080	-26	-0.06	-0.09	227.68	41.00	46,490
Guizhou 貴州	4	46	1,068	23	0.55	1.18	23.21	53.43	4,085
Yunnan 雲南	5	37	518	24	1.76	2.63	14.15	33.04	1,362
Tibet 西藏									
Northwest 西北	33	96	9,578	-216	-2.43	-7.57	100.09	67.89	8,903
Shaanxi 陜西	16	81	16,156	130	1.76	5.71	199.14	69.16	7,376
Gansu 甘肅	6	122	3,157	-413	-3.66	-10.65	25.80	65.65	11,292
Qinghai 青海	2	37	340	-90	-2.88	-60.00	9.19	95.37	3,130
Ningxia 寧夏	1	6	90	10	20.00	20.00	15.00		50
Xinjiang 新疆	8	131	4,736	-821	-6.46	-19.14	36.22	66.27	12,718

1414: Convenient Principal Food 方便主食品業

Year 年份	Number of firms 企業個數	Rate of change 每年變化 (%)	Number of employees 職工人數（人）	Rate of change 每年變化 (%)	Total revenue (mil. RMB) 總銷售收入（百萬元）	Rate of change 每年變化 (%)	Total profit (mil. RMB) 總利潤（百萬元）	Rate of change 每年變化 (%)
1993	558		61,801		2,895		132	
1994	610	9.32%	58,655	-5.09%	4,368	50.86%	237	80.00%
1995	840	37.70%	111,790	90.59%	11,383	160.59%	651	174.10%
1996	823	-2.02%	100,242	-10.33%	15,073	32.42%	924	41.94%

3 Major products* 3 種主要產品 *	Output 產量	Sales volume 銷售量	Unit 單位
a) Instant Noodle 方便麵	1,273,731	1,235,520	ton 噸
b) Convenient Staple Food 方便主食品	1,651,013	1,617,993	ton 噸

Top 10 firms by revenue (year founded) 收入排名前 10 家企業 (創辦年份)	City 城市	Province 省	Telephone / fax 電話 / 傳真	Number of employees 職工人數	Ownership 產業所有權	Revenue ('000 RMB) 銷售收入（千元）	Profit ('000 RMB) (rank) 利潤（千元）(排名)	Total assets ('000 RMB) 總資產（千元）	Major products 主要產品
Tianjin Ding Yi International Foods Co. Ltd. 天津頂益國際食品有限公司(1991)	Tianjin 天津市	Tianjin 天津市	(022)5325954 (022)5325964	6,695	Overseas Chinese-funded 港澳台資	2,221,675	463842(1)	2,776,243	a,b
Hangzhou Ding Yi International Food Co. Ltd. 杭州頂益國際食品有限公司(1994)	Hangzhou 杭州市	Zhejiang 浙江省	(0571)6910122 (0571)6910119	2,583	Foreign-funded 外資	790,696	192438(2)	934,410	o
Guangzhou Ding Yi International Foods Co. Ltd. 廣州頂益國際食品有限公司(1994)	Guangzhou 廣州市	Guangdong 廣東省	(020)82230331 (020)82234113	1,150	Overseas Chinese-funded 港澳台資	719,874	129876(3)	741,435	a,b
Shandong Long Feng Group Co. 山東龍豐集團公司(1950)	Yantai 煙台市	Shandong 山東省	(0535)8526306 (0535)8526306	1,094	State-owned 國有	407,957	32724(6)	263,402	a,b
Zhuhai Hua Feng Foods Industry (Group) Co. Ltd. 珠海華豐食品工業股份有限公司(1994)	Zhuhai 珠海市	Guangdong 廣東省	(0756)7751333	2,405	Foreign-funded 外資	334,385	81910(4)	1,007,918	a,b
Chongqing Ding Yi International Food Co. Ltd. 重慶頂益國際食品有限公司(1995)	Chongqing 重慶市	Chongqing 重慶市	(023)62826999 (023)62827147	1,692	Overseas Chinese-funded 港澳台資	271,748	22062(9)	651,536	a,b
Zhuhai Hua Feng Foods Industry (Group) Co. Ltd. Fuxin Branch 珠海華豐食品工業股份有限公司阜新分公司(1994)	Fuxin 阜新市	Liaoning 遼寧省	(0418)2821828 (0418)2828983	1,084	Foreign-funded 外資	255,766	-672(4)	39,101	a,b
Beijing President Foods Co. Ltd. 北京統一食品有限公司(1985)	Beijing 北京市	Beijing 北京市	(010)69746442 (010)69741589	748	Overseas Chinese-funded 港澳台資	245,541	29750(8)	123,866	a,b
Chinese-foreign Joint Venture Zhenjiang Tai Xinglong Fast Food Co. Ltd. 中外合資鎮江泰興隆快餐食品有限公司(1993)	Zhenjiang 鎮江市	Jiangsu 江蘇省	(0511)5625397 (0511)5625397	295	Foreign-funded 外資	233,754	32323(7)	147,190	a
Unification Enterprise Food Co. Ltd. 統一企業食品有限公司(1994)	Suzhou 蘇州市	Jiangsu 江蘇省	(0512)2305877	608	Overseas Chinese-funded 港澳台資	218,521	0(204)	306,237	a,b

Top 10 Cities by Production Output 產出排名前 10 位城市	Province 省	Market share 市場份額	Number of firms 企業個數
Tianjin 天津市	Tianjin 天津市	23.71%	43
Beijing 北京市	Beijing 北京市	10.84%	90
Guangzhou 廣州市	Guangdong 廣東省	8.25%	15
Shanghai 上海市	Shanghai 上海市	5.08%	54
Yantai 煙台市	Shandong 山東省	4.64%	7
Xinxiang 新鄉市	Henan 河南省	3.22%	10
Dongguan 東莞市	Guangdong 廣東省	2.58%	6
Shantou 汕頭市	Guangdong 廣東省	2.41%	9
Yangzhou 揚州市	Jiangsu 江蘇省	2.25%	7
Jiaozuo 焦作市	Henan 河南省	2.24%	11

10 Major Wholesalers 10 家主要批發商	City 城市	Province 省	Telephone / Fax 電話 / 傳真
Zhong Liang Sugar Industry Groceries Import & Export Company 中糧糖業雜品進出口公司	Beijing 北京市	Beijing 北京市	(010)65268888 (010)65276023
China National Sugar & Alcohol Group Corp. 中國糖業酒類集團公司	Beijing 北京市	Beijing 北京市	(010)68360994
Shanxi Sugar & Wine Non-staple Food Company 山西省糖酒副食公司	Taiyuan 太原市	Shanxi 山西省	(0351)2027938 (0351)2027931
Putian Xue Jin Beer Marketing Agency Co. Ltd. 莆田縣雪津啤酒營銷代理有限公司	Putian 莆田市	Fujian 福建省	
Suzhou Sugar, Cigarette & Wine General Company 蘇州糖煙酒總公司	Suzhou 蘇州市	Jiangsu 江蘇省	(0512)7276392 (0512)7276406
Yuhang Sugar Industry Tobacco & Wine Company 余杭市糖業煙酒公司	Hangzhou 杭州市	Zhejiang 浙江省	(0571)6225788 (0571)6225407
Wuxi Sugar Industry Cigarette & Wine General Company 無錫市糖業煙酒總公司	Wuxi 無錫市	Jiangsu 江蘇省	(0510)2720023 (0510)2707693
Wuxi Chaoyang Co. Ltd. 無錫朝陽股份有限公司	Wuxi 無錫市	Jiangsu 江蘇省	(0510)2767704
Yinchuan Shen Da Non-staple Food Co. Ltd. 銀川申達副食有限公司	Yinchuan 銀川市	Ningxia 寧夏	(0951)5031694
Shanghai Sugar Industry Cigarette & Wine (Group) Co. Ltd. 上海市糖業煙酒(集團)有限公司	Shanghai 上海市	Shanghai 上海市	(021)63224190 (021)63223169

*Also include sales by firms outside this industry.包括本行業以外廠家的銷售。"o" stands for "others". "o" 代表 "其他產品"。

1415: Preserved Fruits 蜜餞業

The industry accounts for 0.031% of the total revenue of China's industrial sector in 1996. The revenue growth rate of the industry is 7.7% from 1995, as compared to the growth rate of China's industrial sector, 9.51%. The rate of return on asset is 0.90%. 75.45% of all firms in the industry made a profit while 19.96% had negative returns. The top province in terms of the industry's revenue is Guangdong, accounting for 44.98% of the total revenue.
本行業在1996年佔全行業總產值0.031%，行業年增長率為7.7%（全國工業年增長率9.51%）。行業的資產回報率0.90%，75.45%的企業盈利，19.96%的企業虧損。銷售收入最高的省份為廣東省，佔本行業的44.98%。

	Total number of firms 企業總數	Total number of employees 職工總數	Total revenue (mil. RMB) 總銷售收入（百萬元）	Total profit (mil. RMB) 總利潤（百萬元）	Return on assets 資產利潤率 (%)	Return on equity 權益利潤率 (%)	Labour productivity ('000 RMB / worker) 勞動生產率（千元/人）	Debts / assets 資產負債率 (%)	Total assets (mil. RMB) 總資產（百萬元）
Industry Overall 行業總體	628	27,711	1,777	17	0.90	2.87	64.13	68.72	1,922

	Number of firms 企業個數	Average number of employees 平均職工人數	Average revenue ('000 RMB) 平均銷售收入（千元）	Average profit ('000 RMB) 平均利潤（千元）	Return on assets 資產利潤率 (%)	Return on equity 權益利潤率 (%)	Labour productivity ('000 RMB / worker) 勞動生產率（千元/人）	Average debts / assets 平均資產負債率(%)	Average Total assets ('000 RMB) 平均總資產（千元）
By ownership 產業所有權									
State-owned 國有	86	65	2,047	-151	-3.71	-23.21	31.58	84.00	4,070
Collectively-owned 集體	453	38	1,898	41	1.91	6.95	50.13	72.56	2,144
Privately-owned 私有	7	28	5,335	339	23.18	47.13	192.49	50.83	1,463
Domestic JVs 聯營	3	98	24,497	822	14.75	30.25	249.12	51.23	5,572
Joint stock 股份制	6	70	4,834	648	10.47	38.11	69.38	72.52	6,188
Foreign-funded 外資	21	78	13,015	318	3.82	8.05	166.76	52.50	8,303
Overseas Chinese-funded 港澳台資	53	47	6,195	-74	-1.09	-2.28	132.45	52.45	6,833
By size 規模									
Large 大型									
Medium 中型	1	336	50,381	91	0.14	0.34	149.94	59.79	67,242
Small 小型	621	44	2,781	27	0.91	2.95	63.28	69.05	2,987
By regional distribution 地區分布									
Central-North 華北	79	52	1,856	96	4.05	15.38	35.41	73.67	2,376
Beijing 北京	15	72	4,430	350	7.55	27.39	61.93	72.42	4,633
Tianjin 天津	6	33	893	-28	-1.64	-8.67	26.93	81.20	1,728
Hebei 河北	34	49	1,631	91	5.18	16.49	33.64	68.58	1,749
Shanxi 山西	21	54	866	-27	-1.42	-6.36	16.15	77.73	1,882
Inner Mongolia 內蒙	3	32	393				12.42	90.74	2,953
Northeast 東北	6	26	1,517	3	0.17		57.96	100.00	1,980
Liaoning 遼寧	3	3	90	-60	-2.74	138.46	33.75	101.98	2,193
Jilin 吉林									
Heilongjiang 黑龍江	3	50	2,943	67	3.77	153.85	59.26	97.55	1,767
Central East 華東	223	42	2,883	19	0.61	2.14	69.07	71.34	3,092
Shanghai 上海	2	99	2,075	-885	-16.00	1966.67	20.96	100.81	5,530
Jiangsu 江蘇	18	76	8,726	121	2.01	7.82	114.31	74.23	6,012
Zhejiang 浙江	29	49	4,084	-30	-0.64	-2.82	83.77	77.23	4,676
Anhui 安徽	15	42	2,347	194	13.14	34.60	55.80	62.06	1,476
Fujian 福建	73	29	2,293	-50	-1.72	-4.07	79.85	57.66	2,880
Jiangxi 江西	55	18	598		0.02	0.08	33.90	74.13	929
Shandong 山東	31	85	4,120	174	3.56	18.99	48.68	81.25	4,876
Central-South 中南	235	44	3,888	41	1.11	2.97	88.04	62.64	3,707
Henan 河南	10	71	2,030	-293	-10.74	-181.99	28.51	94.10	2,728
Hubei 湖北	10	38	2,669	74	5.28	27.11	69.51	80.51	1,401
Hunan 湖南	15	32	745	-23	-2.07	-7.85	23.44	73.58	1,125
Guangdong 廣東	150	51	5,329	117	2.50	6.07	104.87	58.81	4,673
Guangxi 廣西	50	24	1,121	-107	-4.77	-19.13	47.45	75.06	2,239
Hainan 海南									
Southwest 西南	24	50	642	-53	-2.28	-8.23	12.82	72.29	2,318
Chongqing 重慶	1	11	103	-14	-4.49	-22.27	8.84	79.85	321
Sichuan 四川	7	80	1,033	-174	-4.89	-29.69	12.84	83.53	3,548
Guizhou 貴州	5	46	210	-42	-1.61	-3.78	4.61	57.57	2,616
Yunnan 雲南	10	35	645	26	1.68	4.82	18.43	65.16	1,547
Tibet 西藏									
Northwest 西北	61	41	810	-49	-2.78	-22.12	19.55	87.48	1,748
Shaanxi 陝西	15	36	415	-97	-6.48	-122.69	11.39	94.76	1,503
Gansu 甘肅	33	37	800	34	2.34	12.25	21.72	80.91	1,448
Qinghai 青海									
Ningxia 寧夏	1								
Xinjiang 新疆	12	64	1,398	-218	-7.22	-85.90	21.93	91.59	3,023

1415: Preserved Fruits 蜜餞業

Year 年份	Number of firms 企業個數	Rate of change 每年變化 (%)	Number of employees 職工人數 (人)	Rate of change 每年變化 (%)	Total revenue (mil. RMB) 總銷售收入 (百萬元)	Rate of change 每年變化 (%)	Total profit (mil. RMB) 總利潤 (百萬元)	Rate of change 每年變化 (%)
1993	539		29,796		1,044		9	
1994	551	2.23%	28,675	-3.76%	1,295	24.06%	2	-77.26%
1995	665	20.69%	32,189	12.25%	1,650	27.37%	18	767.97%
1996	628	-5.56%	27,711	-13.91%	1,777	7.70%	17	-6.78%

3 Major products* 3種主要產品*	Output 產量	Sales volume 銷售量	Unit 單位
a) Preserved Fruit 蜜餞果脯	91,344	73,989	ton 噸

Top 10 firms by revenue (year founded) 收入排名前10家企業 (創辦年份)	City 城市	Province 省	Telephone / fax 電話 / 傳真	Number of employees 職工人數	Ownership 產業所有權	Revenue ('000 RMB) 銷售收入 (千元)	Profit ('000 RMB) (rank) 利潤 (千元) (排名)	Total assets ('000 RMB) 總資產 (千元)	Major products 主要產品
Xin Xingxian Dongbao Food Industrial Co. Ltd. 新興縣東寶食品工業有限公司(1991)	Yunfu 雲浮市	Guangdong 廣東省	(0766)2711002 (0766)2889001	250	Foreign-funded 外資	128,328	3270(2)	33,130	a
Haifeng Fengcheng Foods Co. Ltd. 海豐縣豐城食品有限公司(1994)	Shanwei 汕尾市	Guangdong 廣東省	(0660)6685607	80	Overseas Chinese-funded 港澳台資	41,000	300(61)	9,160	a
Wuxian Xishan Flower & Fruit Food Factory 吳縣市西山花果食品廠(1993)	Suzhou 蘇州市	Jiangsu 江蘇省	(0512)6271733	71	Collectively-owned 集體	37,940	450(41)	6,166	a
Wuxian Ye Da Chang Food Co. Ltd. 吳縣市葉大昌食品有限責任公司(1993)	Suzhou 蘇州市	Jiangsu 江蘇省	(0512)6271469	65	Collectively-owned 集體	31,650	470(39)	2,082	a
Guangzhou Fruit Food Factory 廣州果子食品廠(1952)	Guangzhou 廣州市	Guangdong 廣東省	(020)81891992 (020)81563351	799	Collectively-owned 集體	31,644	654(27)	77,223	a
Guangdong Jiexi Mian Hu Fruit Candy Factory 廣東省揭西縣棉湖果子糖廠(1956)	Jieyang 揭陽市	Guangdong 廣東省	(0663)5255916	489	State-owned 國有	31,600	-320(178)	5,385	o
Chaozhou Yuan Yun Tong Food Co. Ltd. 潮州市園運通食品有限公司(1992)	Chaozhou 潮州市	Guangdong 廣東省	(0768)6838868 (0768)6838389	120	Foreign-funded 外資	30,000	1550(4)	24,253	a
Heshan Dongxing Kernel Food Co. Ltd. 鶴山東興果仁食品有限公司(1992)	Jiangmen 江門市	Guangdong 廣東省	(0750)8820607 (0750)8821217	37	Overseas Chinese-funded 港澳台資	29,680	-3930(195)	54,235	a
Xinxing Jicheng Zhen Longshan Fruit Factory 新興縣集成鎮龍山果品廠(1987)	Yunfu 雲浮市	Guangdong 廣東省	(0766)2682168	40	Collectively-owned 集體	24,000	1220(11)	1,440	a
Xin Xingxian Integrated Zhen Food Factory 新興縣集成鎮食品廠(1987)	Yunfu 雲浮市	Guangdong 廣東省	(0766)2682009	50	Collectively-owned 集體	24,000	1250(7)	2,320	a

Top 10 Cities by Production Output 產出排名前10位城市	Province 省	Market share 市場份額	Number of firms 企業個數
Yunfu 雲浮市	Guangdong 廣東省	16.51%	19
Shantou 汕頭市	Guangdong 廣東省	7.83%	21
Chaozhou 潮州市	Guangdong 廣東省	7.26%	42
Jieyang 揭陽市	Guangdong 廣東省	6.95%	28
Beijing 北京市	Beijing 北京市	4.15%	14
Shanghai 上海市	Shanghai 上海市	3.17%	10
Guangzhou 廣州市	Guangdong 廣東省	3.09%	7
Chaoyang 朝陽市	Liaoning 遼寧省	3.09%	2
Zhangzhou 漳州市	Fujian 福建省	2.73%	28
Hangzhou 杭州市	Zhejiang 浙江省	2.35%	15

10 Major Wholesalers 10家主要批發商	City 城市	Province 省	Telephone / Fax 電話 / 傳真
Zhong Liang Sugar Industry Groceries Import & Export Company 中糧糖業雜品進出口公司	Beijing 北京市	Beijing 北京市	(010)65268888 (010)65276023
China National Sugar & Alcohol Group Corp. 中國糖業酒類集團公司	Beijing 北京市	Beijing 北京市	(010)68360994
Shanxi Sugar & Wine Non-staple Food Company 山西省糖酒副食公司	Taiyuan 太原市	Shanxi 山西省	(0351)2027938 (0351)2027931
Putian Xue Jin Beer Marketing Agency Co. Ltd. 莆田縣雪津啤酒營銷代理有限公司	Putian 莆田市	Fujian 福建省	
Suzhou Sugar, Cigarette & Wine General Company 蘇州糖煙酒總公司	Suzhou 蘇州市	Jiangsu 江蘇省	(0512)7276392 (0512)7276406
Yuhang Sugar Industry Tobacco & Wine Company 余杭市糖業煙酒公司	Hangzhou 杭州市	Zhejiang 浙江省	(0571)6225788 (0571)6225407
Wuxi Sugar Industry Cigarette & Wine General Company 無錫市糖業煙酒總公司	Wuxi 無錫市	Jiangsu 江蘇省	(0510)2720023 (0510)2707693
Wuxi Chaoyang Co. Ltd. 無錫朝陽股份有限公司	Wuxi 無錫市	Jiangsu 江蘇省	(0510)2767704
Yinchuan Shen Da Non-staple Food Co. Ltd. 銀川申達副食有限公司	Yinchuan 銀川市	Ningxia 寧夏	(0951)5031694
Shanghai Sugar Industry Cigarette & Wine (Group) Co. Ltd. 上海市糖業煙酒(集團)有限公司	Shanghai 上海市	Shanghai 上海市	(021)63224190 (021)63223169

*Also include sales by firms outside this industry.包括本行業以外廠家的銷售。"o" stands for "others". "o" 代表 "其他產品"。

1419: Other Pastry and Confectionery Manufacturing
其他糕點、糖果製造業

The industry accounts for 0.017% of the total revenue of China's industrial sector in 1996. The revenue growth rate of the industry is -12.1% from 1995, as compared to the growth rate of China's industrial sector, 9.51%. The rate of return on asset is 4.51%. 65.12% of all firms in the industry made a profit while 27.53% had negative returns. The top province in terms of the industry's revenue is Jiangsu, accounting for 21.79% of the total revenue.
本行業在1996年佔全行業總產值0.017%，行業年增長率為-12.1%（全國工業年增長率9.51%）。行業的資產回報率4.51%，65.12%的企業盈利，27.53%的企業虧損。銷售收入最高的省份為江蘇省，佔本行業的21.79%。

	Total number of firms 企業總數	Total number of employees 職工總數	Total revenue (mil. RMB) 總銷售收入（百萬元）	Total profit (mil. RMB) 總利潤（百萬元）	Return on assets 資產利潤率 (%)	Return on equity 權益利潤率 (%)	Labour productivity ('000 RMB / worker) 勞動生產率（千元/人）	Debts / assets 資產負債率 (%)	Total assets (mil. RMB) 總資產（百萬元）
Industry Overall 行業總體	255	14,768	1,014	59	4.51	11.74	68.66	61.58	1,315

	Number of firms 企業個數	Average number of employees 平均職工人數	Average revenue ('000 RMB) 平均銷售收入（千元）	Average profit ('000 RMB) 平均利潤（千元）	Return on assets 資產利潤率 (%)	Return on equity 權益利潤率 (%)	Labour productivity ('000 RMB / worker) 勞動生產率（千元/人）	Average debts / assets 平均資產負債率(%)	Average Total assets ('000 RMB) 平均總資產（千元）
By ownership 產業所有權									
State-owned 國有	76	83	2,447	-13	-0.29	-0.97	29.67	69.88	4,500
Collectively-owned 集體	135	34	1,684	131	13.37	48.43	49.00	72.39	976
Privately-owned 私有	1	8							
Domestic JVs 聯營									
Joint stock 股份制	2	116	10,536	-2,647	-12.87	-38.44	91.22	66.52	20,571
Foreign-funded 外資	17	113	19,871	3,376	13.22	28.11	176.40	52.97	25,540
Overseas Chinese-funded 港澳台資	23	75	10,536	-423	-2.66	-6.58	139.59	59.64	15,922
By size 規模									
Large 大型									
Medium 中型	5	371	45,787	3,678	5.90	24.59	123.28	76.00	62,330
Small 小型	244	53	3,219	166	4.05	9.44	60.85	57.12	4,113
By regional distribution 地區分布									
Central-North 華北	38	58	3,041	433	8.74	26.08	52.47	66.49	4,960
Beijing 北京	20	54	2,989	482	6.34	20.08	55.34	68.44	7,598
Tianjin 天津	2	388	23,085	3,325	36.84	55.60	59.57	33.74	9,025
Hebei 河北	2	35	2,820	85	5.48	51.52	80.57	89.35	1,550
Shanxi 山西	11	22	339	2	0.14	0.79	15.67	81.81	1,265
Inner Mongolia 內蒙	3	13	77				5.90	74.48	483
Northeast 東北	29	33	1,238	-35	-1.80	-4.45	37.25	59.50	1,950
Liaoning 遼寧	12	20	2,054	120	5.02	8.23	101.86	38.97	2,388
Jilin 吉林	6	29	1,610	-315	-9.94	-35.53	55.52	72.01	3,168
Heilongjiang 黑龍江	11	50	145	-52	-6.43	-570.00	2.92	98.99	806
Central East 華東	74	72	7,257	803	10.27	22.39	100.15	54.15	7,824
Shanghai 上海	4	155	34,853	8,583	16.98	25.05	225.22	32.20	50,530
Jiangsu 江蘇	24	78	9,205	692	10.90	29.36	117.39	62.89	6,348
Zhejiang 浙江	7	35	1,399	-61	-2.06	-5.08	39.48	59.38	2,979
Anhui 安徽	9	69	5,667	594	16.17	50.57	82.66	68.03	3,677
Fujian 福建	9	18	333	-9	-0.68	-1.20	18.63	43.51	1,310
Jiangxi 江西	12	65	3,270	204	4.28	10.62	50.44	59.65	4,767
Shandong 山東	9	117	8,183	136	1.20	5.28	69.68	77.24	11,289
Central-South 中南	71	57	4,055	-173	-2.99	-10.09	70.74	70.42	5,788
Henan 河南	14	39	1,084	6	0.41	1.35	28.01	69.62	1,566
Hubei 湖北	6	153	8,383	290	3.69	18.13	54.85	79.65	7,855
Hunan 湖南	14	33	834	24	1.77	9.48	25.54	81.35	1,333
Guangdong 廣東	23	64	8,356	-506	-3.99	-13.09	130.92	69.48	12,659
Guangxi 廣西	12	34	1,270	-136	-8.14	-15.66	36.90	48.00	1,668
Hainan 海南	2	137	1,675	-585	-9.70	-45.88	12.27	78.94	6,030
Southwest 西南	27	51	942	-85	-4.11	-12.33	18.43	66.71	2,066
Chongqing 重慶	1	31	39	-56	-7.03	30.31	1.25	123.18	794
Sichuan 四川	17	64	1,163	147	6.48	20.38	17.99	68.19	2,271
Guizhou 貴州	3	23	650				27.86	63.19	1,277
Yunnan 雲南	4	19	750	15	1.71	4.65	39.47	63.53	878
Tibet 西藏	1	55	100	140	1.86	3.98	1.82	53.12	7,530
Northwest 西北	16	49	771	-63	-4.11	-7.33	15.62	44.01	1,523
Shaanxi 陝西	6	55	530	23	3.26	7.29	9.58	55.35	717
Gansu 甘肅	3	94	2,343	37	0.78	1.17	24.84	33.50	4,727
Qinghai 青海	1								
Ningxia 寧夏									
Xinjiang 新疆	6	29	355	-208	-21.26	-54.59	12.17	61.05	980

1419: Other Pastry and Confectionery Manufacturing
其他糕點、糖果製造業

Year 年份	Number of firms 企業個數	Rate of change 每年變化 (%)	Number of employees 職工人數（人）	Rate of change 每年變化 (%)	Total revenue (mil. RMB) 總銷售收入（百萬元）	Rate of change 每年變化 (%)	Total profit (mil. RMB) 總利潤（百萬元）	Rate of change 每年變化 (%)
1993	410		31,504		978		-1	
1994	404	-1.46%	27,974	-11.21%	1,082	10.75%	23	2780.23%
1995	256	-36.63%	18,315	-34.53%	1,154	6.63%	34	47.78%
1996	255	-0.39%	14,768	-19.37%	1,014	-12.13%	59	72.20%

3 Major products* 3 種主要產品 *	Output 產量	Sales volume 銷售量	Unit 單位
a) Cake 糕點	5,636	5,410	ton 噸
b) Candy 糖果	173	169	ton 噸

Top 10 firms by revenue (year founded) 收入排名前 10 家企業 (創辦年份)	City 城市	Province 省	Telephone / fax 電話 / 傳真	Number of employees 職工人數	Ownership 產業所有權	Revenue ('000 RMB) 銷售收入（千元）	Profit ('000 RMB) (rank) 利潤（千元）（排名）	Total assets ('000 RMB) 總資產（千元）	Major products 主要產品
Henze Joint Co. Ltd. 亨氏聯合有限公司(1984)	Guangzhou 廣州市	Guangdong 廣東省	(020)87706218 (020)87705808	334	Foreign-funded 外資	106,680	-12494(68)	155,252	o
Jiangsu Jia Li Jia Foods Co. Ltd. 江蘇加力加食品有限公司(1992)	Zhenjiang 鎮江市	Jiangsu 江蘇省	(0511)6882677	480	Foreign-funded 外資	103,860	8433(3)	44,019	o
Shanghai Pepsi Food Co. Ltd. 上海百事食品有限公司(1995)	Shanghai 上海市	Shanghai 上海市	(021)59155177 (021)59155077	230	Foreign-funded 外資	94,174	2876(7)	70,203	o
Jiangsu Hali Hali Foods Co. Ltd. 江蘇省哈里哈里食品有限公司(1992)	Zhenjiang 鎮江市	Jiangsu 江蘇省	(0511)6886717 (0511)6881798	289	Overseas Chinese-funded 港澳台資	57,850	9896(2)	20,620	o
Tianjin Shi You Food Factory 天津市食友食品廠(1989)	Tianjin 天津市	Tianjin 天津市	(022)29411817	680	Collectively-owned 集體	42,920	7100(4)	15,320	o
Rongcheng Cereal & Oils Foods Import & Export Co. 榮成市糧油食品進出口公司(1958)	Weihai 威海市	Shandong 山東省	(0896)7381602 (0896)7381602	378	State-owned 國有	36,830	110(33)	51,340	o
Dayu Foods Products Mill 大余縣食品廠(1958)	Ganzhou 贛州市	Jiangxi 江西省	(0797)8722195	262	State-owned 國有	25,347	4000(5)	24,740	a
Shanghai Liwayway Foods Ind. Ltd. 上海晨光食品工業有限公司(1993)	Shanghai 上海市	Shanghai 上海市	(021)62735630 (021)62735630	137	Foreign-funded 外資	20,657	31446(1)	98,754	o
Rongcheng Zhong Rong Peanut Products Co. Ltd. 榮成市中榮花生製品有限公司(1989)	Weihai 威海市	Shandong 山東省	(0896)7563271	155	State-owned 國有	18,365	500(16)	30,453	o
Guanyun Candy Food Factory 灌雲縣糖果食品廠(1953)	Lianyungang 連雲港市	Jiangsu 江蘇省	(0518)8812220	200	State-owned 國有	16,999	83(37)	14,542	a,b

Top 10 Cities by Production Output 產出排名前 10 位城市	Province 省	Market share 市場份額	Number of firms 企業個數
Shanghai 上海市	Shanghai 上海市	53.53%	26
Shantou 汕頭市	Guangdong 廣東省	9.51%	4
Beijing 北京市	Beijing 北京市	6.39%	17
Guangzhou 廣州市	Guangdong 廣東省	3.10%	6
Ganzhou 贛州市	Jiangxi 江西省	2.29%	4
Dongguan 東莞市	Guangdong 廣東省	1.60%	2
Xiaogan 孝感市	Hubei 湖北省	1.52%	3
Dalian 大連市	Liaoning 遼寧省	1.43%	3
Fuyang 阜陽市	Anhui 安徽省	1.11%	3
Zhenjiang 鎮江市	Jiangsu 江蘇省	1.03%	1

10 Major Wholesalers 10 家主要批發商	City 城市	Province 省	Telephone / Fax 電話 / 傳真
Zhong Liang Sugar Industry Groceries Import & Export Company 中糧糖業雜品進出口公司	Beijing 北京市	Beijing 北京市	(010)65268888 (010)65276023
China National Sugar & Alcohol Group Corp. 中國糖業酒類集團公司	Beijing 北京市	Beijing 北京市	(010)68360994
Shanxi Sugar & Wine Non-staple Food Company 山西省糖酒副食公司	Taiyuan 太原市	Shanxi 山西省	(0351)2027938 (0351)2027931
Putian Xue Jin Beer Marketing Agency Co. Ltd. 莆田縣雪津啤酒營銷代理有限公司	Putian 莆田市	Fujian 福建省	
Suzhou Sugar, Cigarette & Wine General Company 蘇州糖煙酒總公司	Suzhou 蘇州市	Jiangsu 江蘇省	(0512)7276392 (0512)7276406
Yuhang Sugar Industry Tobacco & Wine Company 余杭市糖業煙酒公司	Hangzhou 杭州市	Zhejiang 浙江省	(0571)6225788 (0571)6225407
Wuxi Sugar Industry Cigarette & Wine General Company 無錫市糖業煙酒總公司	Wuxi 無錫市	Jiangsu 江蘇省	(0510)2720023 (0510)2707693
Wuxi Chaoyang Co. Ltd. 無錫朝陽股份有限公司	Wuxi 無錫市	Jiangsu 江蘇省	(0510)2767704
Yinchuan Shen Da Non-staple Food Co. Ltd. 銀川申達副食有限公司	Yinchuan 銀川市	Ningxia 寧夏	(0951)5031694
Shanghai Sugar Industry Cigarette & Wine (Group) Co. Ltd. 上海市糖業煙酒(集團)有限公司	Shanghai 上海市	Shanghai 上海市	(021)63224190 (021)63223169

*Also include sales by firms outside this industry.包括本行業以外廠家的銷售。"o" stands for "others". "o" 代表"其他產品"。

1420: Dairy Products 乳製品製造業

The industry accounts for 0.152% of the total revenue of China's industrial sector in 1996. The revenue growth rate of the industry is 19.5% from 1995, as compared to the growth rate of China's industrial sector, 9.51%. The rate of return on asset is -2.17%. 63.99% of all firms in the industry made a profit while 29.32% had negative returns. The top province in terms of the industry's revenue is Helongjiang, accounting for 18.33% of the total revenue.
本行業在1996年佔全行業總產值0.152%，行業年增長率為19.5%（全國工業年增長率9.51%）。行業的資產回報率-2.17%，63.99%的企業盈利，29.32%的企業虧損。銷售收入最高的省份為黑龍江省，佔本行業的18.33%。

	Total number of firms 企業總數	Total number of employees 職工總數	Total revenue (mil. RMB) 總銷售收入（百萬元）	Total profit (mil. RMB) 總利潤（百萬元）	Return on assets 資產利潤率 (%)	Return on equity 權益利潤率 (%)	Labour productivity ('000 RMB / worker) 勞動生產率（千元/人）	Debts / assets 資產負債率 (%)	Total assets (mil. RMB) 總資產（百萬元）
Industry Overall 行業總體	610	87,784	8,799	-260	-2.17	-7.01	100.23	69.03	11,956

	Number of firms 企業個數	Average number of employees 平均職工人數	Average revenue ('000 RMB) 平均銷售收入（千元）	Average profit ('000 RMB) 平均利潤（千元）	Return on assets 資產利潤率 (%)	Return on equity 權益利潤率 (%)	Labour productivity ('000 RMB / worker) 勞動生產率（千元/人）	Average debts / assets 平均資產負債率(%)	Average Total assets ('000 RMB) 平均總資產（千元）
By ownership 產業所有權									
State-owned 國有	300	201	15,663	183	0.93	3.13	78.09	70.41	19,807
Collectively-owned 集體	230	71	9,786	1,199	12.88	75.54	136.89	82.95	9,308
Privately-owned 私有	1	11	681	459	24.53	100.24	61.87	75.53	1,870
Domestic JVs 聯營	1	57	9,952	1,624	31.03	55.01	174.59	43.60	5,235
Joint stock 股份制	17	312	34,168	10,835	36.82	130.31	109.62	71.74	29,426
Foreign-funded 外資	37	110	25,637	-20,037	-27.12	-58.72	232.66	53.82	73,896
Overseas Chinese-funded 港澳台資	22	104	13,483	-2,024	-7.47	-28.01	129.53	73.34	27,100
By size 規模									
Large 大型	15	536	110,319	-3,847	-2.37	-5.03	205.79	52.75	162,015
Medium 中型	42	498	54,129	-7,051	-10.58	-37.55	108.77	71.83	66,668
Small 小型	533	108	9,140	176	1.40	5.32	84.30	73.74	12,619
By regional distribution 地區分布									
Central-North 華北	151	148	13,432	-847	-4.18	-14.37	91.00	70.90	20,260
Beijing 北京	22	171	21,812	-1,792	-4.71	-10.43	127.25	54.91	38,091
Tianjin 天津	14	216	23,846	-8,180	-12.88	-40.65	110.66	68.31	63,508
Hebei 河北	30	136	23,220	796	5.35	23.46	170.49	77.18	14,859
Shanxi 山西	20	104	8,359	196	1.78	9.52	80.34	81.28	10,973
Inner Mongolia 內蒙	65	144	5,397	-26	-0.26	-1.96	37.58	86.83	10,259
Northeast 東北	102	191	17,441	-310	-1.21	-3.73	91.09	67.46	25,521
Liaoning 遼寧	15	156	8,361	-207	-1.97	-9.03	53.64	78.14	10,468
Jilin 吉林	13	132	3,095	-712	-5.53	-38.83	23.53	85.76	12,874
Heilongjiang 黑龍江	74	209	21,801	-260	-0.84	-2.43	104.21	65.38	30,794
Central East 華東	154	147	19,638	-82	-0.34	-1.00	133.94	65.88	24,249
Shanghai 上海	23	196	40,539	-1,192	-2.11	-6.04	207.29	65.14	56,635
Jiangsu 江蘇	32	156	19,932	603	4.78	11.66	127.67	59.05	12,634
Zhejiang 浙江	32	140	16,446	-252	-1.67	-5.78	117.26	71.13	15,106
Anhui 安徽	10	194	9,173	-678	-5.82	-32.52	47.36	82.11	11,656
Fujian 福建	15	73	3,028	45	0.64	1.45	41.52	55.87	6,969
Jiangxi 江西	13	114	10,935	282	3.28	11.85	96.31	72.34	8,589
Shandong 山東	29	141	22,362	204	0.49	1.42	158.56	65.56	41,767
Central-South 中南	57	148	16,053	-1,344	-6.78	-27.64	108.11	75.45	19,810
Henan 河南	18	121	4,979	-151	-1.71	-3.95	41.32	56.78	8,857
Hubei 湖北	15	148	13,728	303	2.87	12.92	92.59	77.75	10,557
Hunan 湖南	5	190	14,252	380	2.50	5.56	74.85	54.94	15,170
Guangdong 廣東	16	171	32,247	-5,094	-11.76	-71.02	188.72	83.44	43,311
Guangxi 廣西	3	128	10,757	390	2.75	4.86	83.82	43.41	14,190
Hainan 海南									
Southwest 西南	21	149	11,776	100	0.73	1.84	78.91	60.57	13,710
Chongqing 重慶	3	255	36,052	1,646	4.89	17.03	140.92	71.30	33,677
Sichuan 四川	12	121	2,621	13	0.21	0.49	21.64	57.25	6,214
Guizhou 貴州	1	296	10,900	60	0.49	1.09	36.82	54.98	12,240
Yunnan 雲南	3	139	26,487	2,580	9.74	19.90	190.10	51.06	26,490
Tibet 西藏	1	16	380	100	3.85	3.85	23.75		2,600
Northwest 西北	125	94	6,445	-104	-1.13	-4.31	68.34	73.72	9,143
Shaanxi 陝西	51	116	8,465	53	0.59	1.63	73.06	64.08	9,042
Gansu 甘肅	17	84	4,455	84	1.25	2.83	53.26	55.76	6,718
Qinghai 青海	6	136	3,653	-1,758	-10.00	267.77	26.86	103.73	17,583
Ningxia 寧夏	15	111	12,142	-399	-1.92	-10.59	109.32	81.90	20,829
Xinjiang 新疆	36	55	2,615	-15	-0.36	-1.71	47.64	78.91	4,155

1420: Dairy Products 乳製品製造業

Year 年份	Number of firms 企業個數	Rate of change 每年變化 (%)	Number of employees 職工人數（人）	Rate of change 每年變化 (%)	Total revenue (mil. RMB) 總銷售收入（百萬元）	Rate of change 每年變化 (%)	Total profit (mil. RMB) 總利潤（百萬元）	Rate of change 每年變化 (%)
1993	521		78,214		4,229		59	
1994	566	8.64%	90,750	16.03%	5,916	39.89%	143	142.09%
1995	607	7.24%	99,521	9.67%	7,361	24.44%	50	-64.72%
1996	610	0.49%	87,784	-11.79%	8,799	19.54%	-260	-616.28%

3 Major products* 3 種主要產品 *	Output 產量	Sales volume 銷售量	Unit 單位
a) Dried Milk 奶粉	343,882	299,178	ton 噸
b) Dairy Products 乳製品	479,949	451,152	ton 噸
c) Liquid Milk 液體乳	480,645	418,161	ton 噸

Top 10 firms by revenue (year founded) 收入排名前 10 家企業（創辦年份）	City 城市	Province 省	Telephone / fax 電話 / 傳真	Number of employees 職工人數	Ownership 產業所有權	Revenue ('000 RMB) 銷售收入（千元）	Profit ('000 RMB) (rank) 利潤（千元）（排名）	Total assets ('000 RMB) 總資產（千元）	Major products 主要產品
Shuangcheng Nestle Co. Ltd. 雙城雀巢有限公司(1987)	Shuangcheng 雙城市	Heilongjiang 黑龍江省	(0451)3123734 (0451)3123712	402	Foreign-funded 外資	537,710	15800(5)	690,349	a,b
Shijiazhuang Milk Industry Group Co. Ltd. 石家莊市乳業集團公司(1956)	Shijiazhuang 石家莊市	Hebei 河北省	(0311)7044184 (0311)7055423	1,129	Collectively-owned 集體	364,455	10600(7)	97,635	a,b,c
Changzhou Super Food Co. Ltd. 常州超級食品有限公司(1994)	Changzhou 常州市	Jiangsu 江蘇省	(0519)8400277 (0519)8400582	300	Foreign-funded 外資	309,890	24610(3)	80,269	o
Shanghai No.2 Milk Products Factory 上海乳品二廠(1949)	Shanghai 上海市	Shanghai 上海市	(021)62427340 (021)62428026	663	State-owned 國有	303,027	38065(1)	300,486	a,b,c
Shenzhen Guang Ming Hua Qiao Livestock Farm Chen Guang Beverage Co. 深圳市光明華僑畜牧場晨光飲料公司(1980)	Shenzhen 深圳市	Guangdong 廣東省	(0755)7402788 (0755)7400241	338	State-owned 國有	233,484	25338(2)	83,917	c
Shanghai No.8 Milk Products Factory 上海乳品八廠(1988)	Shanghai 上海市	Shanghai 上海市	(021)58800064 (021)58834060	452	State-owned 國有	148,352	11293(6)	102,968	a,b,c
Wendeng Jin Yang Dairy Products Co. Ltd. 文登市金洋乳品有限公司(1995)	Weihai 威海市	Shandong 山東省	(0896)8681188 (0896)8681188	198	Collectively-owned 集體	129,570	18140(4)	32,100	a,b
Harbin Song Hua Jiang No.2 Milk Products Factory 哈爾濱松花江第二乳品廠(1982)	Harbin 哈爾濱市	Heilongjiang 黑龍江省	(0451)7322754	610	State-owned 國有	128,933	4674(15)	63,332	a,b
Jiangxi Dairy Products Factory 江西乳品廠(1966)	Nanchang 南昌市	Jiangxi 江西省	(0791)3800746 (0791)3804264	394	State-owned 國有	100,910	3667(18)	39,928	a,b
Xi'an Yin Qiao Dairy Products Industrial Co. Ltd. 西安銀橋乳製品實業有限公司(1979)	Xi'an 西安市	Shaanxi 陝西省	(029)3961148 (029)3961188	305	Overseas Chinese-funded 港澳台資	100,501	5780(12)	40,458	o

Top 10 Cities by Production Output 產出排名前 10 位城市	Province 省	Market share 市場份額	Number of firms 企業個數
Shanghai 上海市	Shanghai 上海市	30.93%	33
Xuzhou 徐州市	Jiangsu 江蘇省	27.96%	8
Beijing 北京市	Beijing 北京市	2.53%	19
Tianjin 天津市	Tianjin 天津市	2.49%	18
Shijiazhuang 石家莊市	Hebei 河北省	2.28%	9
Hangzhou 杭州市	Zhejiang 浙江省	1.99%	18
Suihua 綏化市	Heilongjiang 黑龍江省	1.58%	16
Guangzhou 廣州市	Guangdong 廣東省	1.40%	10
Tangshan 唐山市	Hebei 河北省	1.29%	8
Xi'an 西安市	Shaanxi 陝西省	1.27%	20

10 Major Wholesalers 10 家主要批發商	City 城市	Province 省	Telephone / Fax 電話 / 傳真
Zhong Liang Sugar Industry Groceries Import & Export Company 中糧糖業雜品進出口公司	Beijing 北京市	Beijing 北京市	(010)65268888 (010)65276023
China National Sugar & Alcohol Group Corp. 中國糖業酒類集團公司	Beijing 北京市	Beijing 北京市	(010)68360994
Shanxi Sugar & Wine Non-staple Food Company 山西省糖酒副食公司	Taiyuan 太原市	Shanxi 山西省	(0351)2027938 (0351)2027931
Putian Xue Jin Beer Marketing Agency Co. Ltd. 莆田縣雪津啤酒營銷代理有限公司	Putian 莆田市	Fujian 福建省	
Suzhou Sugar, Cigarette & Wine General Company 蘇州糖煙酒總公司	Suzhou 蘇州市	Jiangsu 江蘇省	(0512)7276392 (0512)7276406
Yuhang Sugar Industry Tobacco & Wine Company 余杭市糖業煙酒公司	Hangzhou 杭州市	Zhejiang 浙江省	(0571)6225788 (0571)6225407
Wuxi Sugar Industry Cigarette & Wine General Company 無錫市糖業煙酒總公司	Wuxi 無錫市	Jiangsu 江蘇省	(0510)2720023 (0510)2707693
Wuxi Chaoyang Co. Ltd. 無錫朝陽股份有限公司	Wuxi 無錫市	Jiangsu 江蘇省	(0510)2767704
Yinchuan Shen Da Non-staple Food Co. Ltd. 銀川申達副食有限公司	Yinchuan 銀川市	Ningxia 寧夏	(0951)5031694
Shanghai Sugar Industry Cigarette & Wine (Group) Co. Ltd. 上海市糖業煙酒(集團)有限公司	Shanghai 上海市	Shanghai 上海市	(021)63224190 (021)63223169

*Also include sales by firms outside this industry.包括本行業以外廠家的銷售。"o" stands for "others". "o" 代表 "其他產品"。

1431: Canned Meat 肉類罐頭製造業

The industry accounts for 0.038% of the total revenue of China's industrial sector in 1996. The revenue growth rate of the industry is -19.3% from 1995, as compared to the growth rate of China's industrial sector, 9.51%. The rate of return on asset is -4.00%. 58.56% of all firms in the industry made a profit while 33.63% had negative returns. The top province in terms of the industry's revenue is Henan, accounting for 23.27% of the total revenue.
本行業在1996年佔全行業總產值0.038%，行業年增長率為-19.3%（全國工業年增長率9.51%）。行業的資產回報率-4.00%，58.56%的企業盈利，33.63%的企業虧損。銷售收入最高的省份為河南省，佔本行業的23.27%。

	Total number of firms 企業總數	Total number of employees 職工總數	Total revenue (mil. RMB) 總銷售收入（百萬元）	Total profit (mil. RMB) 總利潤（百萬元）	Return on assets 資產利潤率 (%)	Return on equity 權益利潤率 (%)	Labour productivity ('000 RMB / worker) 勞動生產率（千元/人）	Debts / assets 資產負債率 (%)	Total assets (mil. RMB) 總資產（百萬元）
Industry Overall 行業總體	121	42,212	2,214	-145	-4.00	-56.82	52.45	92.96	3,623

	Number of firms 企業個數	Average number of employees 平均職工人數	Average revenue ('000 RMB) 平均銷售收入（千元）	Average profit ('000 RMB) 平均利潤（千元）	Return on assets 資產利潤率 (%)	Return on equity 權益利潤率 (%)	Labour productivity ('000 RMB / worker) 勞動生產率（千元/人）	Average debts / assets 平均資產負債率(%)	Average Total assets ('000 RMB) 平均總資產（千元）
By ownership 產業所有權									
State-owned 國有	51	632	24,725	-2,745	-5.09	-254.55	39.15	98.00	53,961
Collectively-owned 集體	47	102	5,502	-87	-1.65	-20.09	53.71	91.77	5,272
Privately-owned 私有	1	25							
Domestic JVs 聯營	1	130	8,372	129	0.83	1.37	64.40	39.58	15,626
Joint stock 股份制	4	748	106,921	1,110	1.56	6.30	142.89	75.16	70,922
Foreign-funded 外資	10	39	3,866	-577	-7.38	-18.52	99.37	60.18	7,829
Overseas Chinese-funded 港澳台資	7	241	31,501	44	0.12	0.44	130.55	72.16	35,212
By size 規模									
Large 大型	11	1,350	98,087	-2,781	-1.74	-23.45	72.68	92.57	159,676
Medium 中型	24	762	25,405	-3,979	-7.58	-1760.68	33.35	99.57	52,492
Small 小型	84	107	6,262	-225	-3.11	-15.87	58.27	80.38	7,233
By regional distribution 地區分布									
Central-North 華北	10	558	8,141	-2,583	-3.88	-42.96	14.59	90.96	66,501
Beijing 北京	4	363	203	-6,000	-16.18	-41.52	0.56	61.04	37,085
Tianjin 天津	1	907	25,100	-100	-0.05	-1.69	27.67	96.79	183,810
Hebei 河北	1	1,867	30,870				16.53	100.46	282,530
Shanxi 山西	2	162	11,180	-875	-4.55	23.94	69.23	119.00	19,235
Inner Mongolia 內蒙	2	515	1,135	10	0.17	0.40	2.21	57.42	5,930
Northeast 東北	16	220	12,214	781	2.45	18.32	55.57	86.60	31,840
Liaoning 遼寧	6	422	4,342	-1,928	-4.41	-21.57	10.30	79.56	43,735
Jilin 吉林	4	13	203	-3	-0.19	-0.82	15.28	76.66	1,318
Heilongjiang 黑龍江	6	156	28,095	4,013	9.96	179.97	180.48	94.46	40,293
Central East 華東	25	393	27,586	-986	-2.86	-20.35	70.19	85.94	34,468
Shanghai 上海	5	410	88,064	86	0.14	0.35	214.69	58.93	60,042
Jiangsu 江蘇	7	732	25,810	-2,916	-4.51	155.33	35.24	102.91	64,589
Zhejiang 浙江	1	652							
Anhui 安徽									
Fujian 福建	2	188	18,665	-2,680	-31.11	425.40	99.55	107.37	8,615
Jiangxi 江西	2	163	1,420	-95	-0.62	-20.00	8.74	96.92	15,430
Shandong 山東	8	162	3,563	109	1.42	7.71	22.01	81.56	7,659
Central-South 中南	29	343	29,768	354	1.43	14.40	86.85	90.10	24,855
Henan 河南	24	309	21,470	380	1.78	20.74	69.48	91.41	21,323
Hubei 湖北	2	1,181	84,435	680	0.91	14.59	71.52	93.78	74,975
Hunan 湖南									
Guangdong 廣東	3	54	59,703	-67	-0.34	-1.11	1098.83	69.40	19,697
Guangxi 廣西									
Hainan 海南									
Southwest 西南	33	387	11,017	-3,488	-14.21	135.91	28.46	110.45	24,547
Chongqing 重慶	11	426	14,027	-5,071	-16.62	87.20	32.86	119.06	30,514
Sichuan 四川	16	437	9,312	-3,541	-13.79	161.49	21.30	108.54	25,674
Guizhou 貴州	2	43						91.98	1,310
Yunnan 雲南	3	192	16,673	400	3.50	7.01	86.84	50.16	11,443
Tibet 西藏									
Northwest 西北	8	72	2,533	-269	-3.82	-11.39	35.23	66.41	7,026
Shaanxi 陝西	1	1							
Gansu 甘肅	6	49	1,450	-262	-5.63	-25.32	29.90	77.75	4,645
Qinghai 青海	1	283	11,560	-580	-2.05	-4.57	40.85	55.26	28,340
Ningxia 寧夏									
Xinjiang 新疆									

1431: Canned Meat 肉類罐頭製造業

Year 年份	Number of firms 企業個數	Rate of change 每年變化 (%)	Number of employees 職工人數 (人)	Rate of change 每年變化 (%)	Total revenue (mil. RMB) 總銷售收入 (百萬元)	Rate of change 每年變化 (%)	Total profit (mil. RMB) 總利潤 (百萬元)	Rate of change 每年變化 (%)
1993	145		68,730		2,770		-125	
1994	134	-7.59%	60,567	-11.88%	2,258	-18.48%	-155	-24.26%
1995	128	-4.48%	61,588	1.69%	2,743	21.49%	-161	-3.96%
1996	121	-5.47%	42,212	-31.46%	2,214	-19.29%	-145	9.92%

3 Major products* 3種主要產品*	Output 產量	Sales volume 銷售量	Unit 單位
a) Canned Meat 肉類罐頭	163,765	168,678	ton 噸
b) Can 罐頭	359,904	334,711	ton 噸

Top 10 firms by revenue (year founded) 收入排名前10家企業 (創辦年份)	City 城市	Province 省	Telephone / fax 電話 / 傳真	Number of employees 職工人數	Ownership 產業所有權	Revenue ('000 RMB) 銷售收入 (千元)	Profit ('000 RMB) (rank) 利潤 (千元) (排名)	Total assets ('000 RMB) 總資產 (千元)	Major products 主要產品
Shanghai Mei Lin Foods Co. Ltd. 上海梅林食品有限公司(1992)	Shanghai 上海市	Shanghai 上海市	(021)65430188 (021)65431797	1,495	Overseas Chinese-funded 港澳台資	256,995	472(10)	181,974	a,b
Shenzhen Nanshan Meat Packing Factory 深圳南山肉聯廠(1992)	Shenzhen 深圳市	Guangdong 廣東省	(0755)6611066 (0755)6646686	130	State-owned 國有	167,550	-200(41)	56,444	o
Shanghai Meilin Canned Food Factory 上海梅林罐頭食品廠(1930)	Shanghai 上海市	Shanghai 上海市	(021)65430188 (021)65202234	238	State-owned 國有	155,368	18(27)	62,185	o
Hubei State-owned Wu San Canned Factory 湖北省國營五三罐頭廠(1983)	Jingmen 荊門市	Hubei 湖北省	(0724)7413845	1,737	State-owned 國有	143,371	1355(4)	119,308	a,b
Harbin Song Jiang Canned Factory 哈爾濱松江罐頭廠(1935)	Harbin 哈爾濱市	Heilongjiang 黑龍江省	(0451)7682430	1,570	State-owned 國有	134,392	25189(1)	197,347	a,b
Yangzhou Foods Making General Factory 揚州食品製造總廠(1917)	Yangzhou 揚州市	Jiangsu 江蘇省	(0514)7245361 (0514)7245881	1,195	State-owned 國有	116,890	1029(6)	216,401	a,b
Chongqing Yong Sheng Canned Food Factory 重慶市永生食品罐頭廠(1984)	Chongqing 重慶市	Chongqing 重慶市	(023)42823728	834	Collectively-owned 集體	66,087	658(8)	28,153	a,b
Kunming De He Can Factory 昆明德和罐頭廠(1948)	Kunming 昆明市	Yunnan 雲南省	(0871)5812708 (0871)5814800	544	State-owned 國有	50,022	1201(5)	34,331	a,b
Sichuan Suining Canned Food Factory 四川遂寧罐頭食品廠(1977)	Suining 遂寧市	Sichuan 四川省	(0825)2224393 (0825)2225700	794	State-owned 國有	41,326	28(24)	60,897	a,b
Sichuan Bazhong Canned Food Factory 四川省巴中罐頭食品廠(1958)	Bazhong 巴中市	Sichuan 四川省	(08279)223961 (08279)221728	2,081	State-owned 國有	41,074	-59510(64)	105,080	a,b

Top 10 Cities by Production Output 產出排名前10位城市	Province 省	Market share 市場份額	Number of firms 企業個數
Luohe 漯河市	Henan 河南省	18.82%	3
Shanghai 上海市	Shanghai 上海市	12.86%	5
Chongqing 重慶市	Chongqing 重慶市	9.93%	11
Jingmen 荊門市	Hubei 湖北省	8.26%	2
Yangzhou 揚州市	Jiangsu 江蘇省	7.85%	3
Zhoukou 周口市	Henan 河南省	6.84%	4
Kunming 昆明市	Yunnan 雲南省	2.57%	2
Nantong 南通市	Jiangsu 江蘇省	2.53%	2
Lianyungang 連雲港市	Jiangsu 江蘇省	2.36%	1
Bazhong 巴中市	Sichuan 四川省	2.08%	2

10 Major Wholesalers 10家主要批發商	City 城市	Province 省	Telephone / Fax 電話 / 傳真
Zhong Liang Sugar Industry Groceries Import & Export Company 中糧糖業雜品進出口公司	Beijing 北京市	Beijing 北京市	(010)65268888 (010)65276023
China National Sugar & Alcohol Group Corp. 中國糖業酒類集團公司	Beijing 北京市	Beijing 北京市	(010)68360994
Shanxi Sugar & Wine Non-staple Food Company 山西省糖酒副食公司	Taiyuan 太原市	Shanxi 山西省	(0351)2027938 (0351)2027931
Putian Xue Jin Beer Marketing Agency Co. Ltd. 莆田縣雪津啤酒營銷代理有限公司	Putian 莆田市	Fujian 福建省	
Suzhou Sugar, Cigarette & Wine General Company 蘇州糖煙酒總公司	Suzhou 蘇州市	Jiangsu 江蘇省	(0512)7276392 (0512)7276406
Yuhang Sugar Industry Tobacco & Wine Company 余杭市糖業煙酒公司	Hangzhou 杭州市	Zhejiang 浙江省	(0571)6225788 (0571)6225407
Wuxi Sugar Industry Cigarette & Wine General Company 無錫市糖業煙酒總公司	Wuxi 無錫市	Jiangsu 江蘇省	(0510)2720023 (0510)2707693
Wuxi Chaoyang Co. Ltd. 無錫朝陽股份有限公司	Wuxi 無錫市	Jiangsu 江蘇省	(0510)2767704
Yinchuan Shen Da Non-staple Food Co. Ltd. 銀川申達副食有限公司	Yinchuan 銀川市	Ningxia 寧夏	(0951)5031694
Shanghai Sugar Industry Cigarette & Wine (Group) Co. Ltd. 上海市糖業煙酒(集團)有限公司	Shanghai 上海市	Shanghai 上海市	(021)63224190 (021)63223169

*Also include sales by firms outside this industry.包括本行業以外廠家的銷售。"o" stands for "others". "o" 代表"其他產品"。

1432: Canned Fowl Meat 禽類罐頭製造業

The industry accounts for 0.005% of the total revenue of China's industrial sector in 1996. The revenue growth rate of the industry is 107.6% from 1995, as compared to the growth rate of China's industrial sector, 9.51%. The rate of return on asset is 22.14%. 44.57% of all firms in the industry made a profit while 30.43% had negative returns. The top province in terms of the industry's revenue is Anhui, accounting for 59.78% of the total revenue.
本行業在 1996 年佔全行業總產值 0.005% ，行業年增長率為 107.6%（全國工業年增長率 9.51%）。行業的資產回報率 22.14% ，44.57% 的企業盈利，30.43% 的企業虧損。銷售收入最高的省份為安徽省，佔本行業的 59.78% 。

	Total number of firms 企業總數	Total number of employees 職工總數	Total revenue (mil. RMB) 總銷售收入（百萬元）	Total profit (mil. RMB) 總利潤（百萬元）	Return on assets 資產利潤率 (%)	Return on equity 權益利潤率 (%)	Labour productivity ('000 RMB / worker) 勞動生產率（千元/人）	Debts / assets 資產負債率 (%)	Total assets (mil. RMB) 總資產（百萬元）
Industry Overall 行業總體	25	1,817	267	17	22.14	80.14	146.95	72.39	77

	Number of firms 企業個數	Average number of employees 平均職工人數	Average revenue ('000 RMB) 平均銷售收入（千元）	Average profit ('000 RMB) 平均利潤（千元）	Return on assets 資產利潤率 (%)	Return on equity 權益利潤率 (%)	Labour productivity ('000 RMB / worker) 勞動生產率（千元/人）	Average debts / assets 平均資產負債率(%)	Average Total assets ('000 RMB) 平均總資產（千元）
By ownership 產業所有權									
State-owned 國有	4	81	500				6.19	80.00	1,250
Collectively-owned 集體	20	73	13,112	837	24.03	89.38	180.36	73.11	3,484
Privately-owned 私有									
Domestic JVs 聯營									
Joint stock 股份制									
Foreign-funded 外資									
Overseas Chinese-funded 港澳台資	1	40	2,710	253	10.97	20.06	67.75	45.35	2,305
By size 規模									
Large 大型	1	551	34,939	7,749	25.55	139.61	63.41	81.70	30,330
Medium 中型									
Small 小型	24	53	9,668	385	19.82	59.88	183.29	66.90	1,944
By regional distribution 地區分布									
Central-North 華北	3	42	4,530	373	12.08	29.95	107.86	59.65	3,090
Beijing 北京									
Tianjin 天津									
Hebei 河北	3	42	4,530	373	12.08	29.95	107.86	59.65	3,090
Shanxi 山西									
Inner Mongolia 內蒙									
Northeast 東北	3	32	283	-213	-33.16	-1280.00	8.95	97.41	643
Liaoning 遼寧	1	20	710	-650	-35.14	-1625.00	35.50	97.84	1,850
Jilin 吉林	1	5							
Heilongjiang 黑龍江	1	70	140	10	12.50	100.00	2.00	87.50	80
Central East 華東	5	122	34,112	3,564	58.87	123.32	280.07	52.33	6,054
Shanghai 上海									
Jiangsu 江蘇									
Zhejiang 浙江	2	57	4,270	75	1.94	7.81	75.58	75.19	3,870
Anhui 安徽	1	377	159,600	17,560	82.40	147.69	423.34	44.20	21,310
Fujian 福建									
Jiangxi 江西	1	15	620	30	6.52	9.68	41.33	34.78	460
Shandong 山東	1	104	1,800	80	10.53	24.24	17.31	57.89	760
Central-South 中南	6	72	828	-23	-1.40	-4.39	11.56	68.26	1,670
Henan 河南	6	72	828	-23	-1.40	-4.39	11.56	68.26	1,670
Hubei 湖北									
Hunan 湖南									
Guangdong 廣東									
Guangxi 廣西									
Hainan 海南									
Southwest 西南	5	104	15,176	-224	-4.45	746.67	146.49	100.56	5,034
Chongqing 重慶									
Sichuan 四川	2	141	33,270				235.96	115.17	5,305
Guizhou 貴州									
Yunnan 雲南	3	79	3,113	-373	-7.69	-76.19	39.58	89.90	4,853
Tibet 西藏									
Northwest 西北	3	13	250	23	10.61	77.78	19.23	86.36	220
Shaanxi 陝西	3	13	250	23	10.61	77.78	19.23	86.36	220
Gansu 甘肅									
Qinghai 青海									
Ningxia 寧夏									
Xinjiang 新疆									

1432: Canned Fowl Meat 禽類罐頭製造業

Year 年份	Number of firms 企業個數	Rate of change 每年變化 (%)	Number of employees 職工人數 (人)	Rate of change 每年變化 (%)	Total revenue (mil. RMB) 總銷售收入 (百萬元)	Rate of change 每年變化 (%)	Total profit (mil. RMB) 總利潤 (百萬元)	Rate of change 每年變化 (%)
1993	29		2,005		103		0	
1994	27	-6.90%	1,711	-14.66%	184	77.83%	5	1763.96%
1995	20	-25.93%	2,960	73.00%	129	-30.04%	-4	-175.26%
1996	25	25.00%	1,817	-38.61%	267	107.59%	17	540.76%

3 Major products* 3 種主要產品 *	Output 產量	Sales volume 銷售量	Unit 單位
a) Canned Poultry Meat 禽類罐頭	338	338	ton 噸
b) Can 罐頭	3,561	3,312	ton 噸

Top 10 firms by revenue (year founded) 收入排名前 10 家企業 (創辦年份)	City 城市	Province 省	Telephone / fax 電話 / 傳真	Number of employees 職工人數	Ownership 產業所有權	Revenue ('000 RMB) 銷售收入 (千元)	Profit ('000 RMB) (rank) 利潤 (千元) (排名)	Total assets ('000 RMB) 總資產 (千元)	Major products 主要產品
Anhui Fu Li Ji Roast Chicken Group Co. 安徽省符離集燒雞集團公司(1985)	Suzhou 宿州市	Anhui 安徽省	(0557)4081888	377	Collectively-owned 集體	159,600	17560(1)	21,310	o
Jinzhou He Tou Broiler Processing Factory 晉州市河頭肉雞加工廠(1994)	Shijiazhuang 石家莊市	Hebei 河北省		80	Collectively-owned 集體	8,963	817(2)	7,240	o
Zhoushan Dinghai Foreign Trade Freezing Factory 舟山市定海外貿冷凍廠(1980)	Zhoushan 舟山市	Zhejiang 浙江省	(0580)8070075 (0580)8070760	70	Collectively-owned 集體	7,643	58(4)	5,810	o
Yunnan Tonghai Li Min Canned Foods Factory 雲南省通海縣利民罐頭食品廠(1986)	Yuxi 玉溪市	Yunnan 雲南省	(0877)3011566	134	Collectively-owned 集體	4,486	-671(12)	8,355	a,b
Shijiazhuang Yu Dong Food Factory 石家莊市宇東食品廠(1991)	Shijiazhuang 石家莊市	Hebei 河北省	(0311)4628005	35	Collectively-owned 集體	4,250	220(3)	1,430	o
Kunming Yiliang Soft Packing Foods Products Factory 昆明市宜良軟包裝食品廠(1987)	Kunming 昆明市	Yunnan 雲南省	(0871)7524623	69	Collectively-owned 集體	4,134	-10(10)	5,147	o
Huaxian Road Junction Zhen Roast Chicken Canned Factory 滑縣道口鎮燒雞罐頭廠(1984)	Anyang 安陽市	Henan 河南省	(0372)812536	60	Collectively-owned 集體	3,600	7(5)	1,729	b
Huaxian Daokou Can General Factory 滑縣道口罐頭總廠(1995)	Anyang 安陽市	Henan 河南省	(0372)8111512	134	State-owned 國有	2,558	3(6)	4,625	b

Top 10 Cities by Production Output 產出排名前 10 位城市	Province 省	Market share 市場份額	Number of firms 企業個數
Shanghai 上海市	Shanghai 上海市	24.11%	2
Kunming 昆明市	Yunnan 雲南省	11.67%	2
Yangzhou 揚州市	Jiangsu 江蘇省	10.85%	1
Shijiazhuang 石家莊市	Hebei 河北省	9.34%	2
Anyang 安陽市	Henan 河南省	8.01%	5
Yancheng 鹽城市	Jiangsu 江蘇省	7.47%	1
Suzhou 蘇州市	Jiangsu 江蘇省	6.89%	2
Suzhou 宿州市	Anhui 安徽省	6.79%	3
Zhoushan 舟山市	Zhejiang 浙江省	5.36%	1
Suihua 綏化市	Heilongjiang 黑龍江省	2.65%	1

10 Major Wholesalers 10 家主要批發商	City 城市	Province 省	Telephone / Fax 電話 / 傳真
Zhong Liang Sugar Industry Groceries Import & Export Company 中糧糖業雜品進出口公司	Beijing 北京市	Beijing 北京市	(010)65268888 (010)65276023
China National Sugar & Alcohol Group Corp. 中國糖業酒類集團公司	Beijing 北京市	Beijing 北京市	(010)68360994
Shanxi Sugar & Wine Non-staple Food Company 山西省糖酒副食公司	Taiyuan 太原市	Shanxi 山西省	(0351)2027938 (0351)2027931
Putian Xue Jin Beer Marketing Agency Co. Ltd. 莆田縣雪津啤酒營銷代理有限公司	Putian 莆田市	Fujian 福建省	
Suzhou Sugar, Cigarette & Wine General Company 蘇州糖煙酒總公司	Suzhou 蘇州市	Jiangsu 江蘇省	(0512)7276392 (0512)7276406
Yuhang Sugar Industry Tobacco & Wine Company 余杭市糖業煙酒公司	Hangzhou 杭州市	Zhejiang 浙江省	(0571)6225788 (0571)6225407
Wuxi Sugar Industry Cigarette & Wine General Company 無錫市糖業煙酒總公司	Wuxi 無錫市	Jiangsu 江蘇省	(0510)2720023 (0510)2707693
Wuxi Chaoyang Co. Ltd. 無錫朝陽股份有限公司	Wuxi 無錫市	Jiangsu 江蘇省	(0510)2767704
Yinchuan Shen Da Non-staple Food Co. Ltd. 銀川申達副食有限公司	Yinchuan 銀川市	Ningxia 寧夏	(0951)5031694
Shanghai Sugar Industry Cigarette & Wine (Group) Co. Ltd. 上海市糖業煙酒(集團)有限公司	Shanghai 上海市	Shanghai 上海市	(021)63224190 (021)63223169

*Also include sales by firms outside this industry.包括本行業以外廠家的銷售。"o" stands for "others". "o" 代表"其他產品"。

1433: Canned Seafood 水產罐頭製造業

The industry accounts for 0.015% of the total revenue of China's industrial sector in 1996. The revenue growth rate of the industry is 59.6% from 1995, as compared to the growth rate of China's industrial sector, 9.51%. The rate of return on asset is -3.84%. 72.50% of all firms in the industry made a profit while 27.50% had negative returns. The top province in terms of the industry's revenue is Guangdong, accounting for 59.55% of the total revenue.
本行業在1996年佔全行業總產值0.015%，行業年增長率為59.6%（全國工業年增長率9.51%）。行業的資產回報率-3.84%，72.50%的企業盈利，27.50%的企業虧損。銷售收入最高的省份為廣東省，佔本行業的59.55%。

	Total number of firms 企業總數	Total number of employees 職工總數	Total revenue (mil. RMB) 總銷售收入（百萬元）	Total profit (mil. RMB) 總利潤（百萬元）	Return on assets 資產利潤率 (%)	Return on equity 權益利潤率 (%)	Labour productivity ('000 RMB / worker) 勞動生產率（千元/人）	Debts / assets 資產負債率 (%)	Total assets (mil. RMB) 總資產（百萬元）
Industry Overall 行業總體	51	10,356	895	-44	-3.84	-24.38	86.42	84.26	1,142

	Number of firms 企業個數	Average number of employees 平均職工人數	Average revenue ('000 RMB) 平均銷售收入（千元）	Average profit ('000 RMB) 平均利潤（千元）	Return on assets 資產利潤率 (%)	Return on equity 權益利潤率 (%)	Labour productivity ('000 RMB / worker) 勞動生產率（千元/人）	Average debts / assets 平均資產負債率(%)	Average Total assets ('000 RMB) 平均總資產（千元）
By ownership 產業所有權									
State-owned 國有	18	366	25,944	-2,000	-4.74	-21.82	70.86	78.29	42,222
Collectively-owned 集體	27	111	12,577	-339	-3.37	102.10	113.42	103.30	10,071
Privately-owned 私有									
Domestic JVs 聯營	1	68	133	1,316	71.41	596.68	1.96	88.03	1,843
Joint stock 股份制									
Foreign-funded 外資	2	47	5,016	671	6.58	14.40	107.87	54.27	10,191
Overseas Chinese-funded 港澳台資	4	153	19,560	-377	-1.72	-10.46	128.05	83.59	21,963
By size 規模									
Large 大型	2	1,991	254,841	-47,581	-14.79	-68.78	128.00	78.50	321,743
Medium 中型	1	347	51,066	-333	-0.31	3.43	147.16	108.89	109,273
Small 小型	48	126	6,962	1,073	13.23	100.28	55.44	86.80	8,108
By regional distribution 地區分布									
Central-North 華北	5	401	13,126	-310	-0.98	-6.48	32.72	84.89	31,666
Beijing 北京									
Tianjin 天津									
Hebei 河北	4	396	14,093	228	0.65	3.89	35.59	83.34	35,130
Shanxi 山西									
Inner Mongolia 內蒙	1	422	9,260	-2,460	-13.81	-492.00	21.94	97.14	17,810
Northeast 東北	6	47	2,610	-472	-13.68	-49.91	56.13	72.58	3,447
Liaoning 遼寧	3	67	5,033	-970	-15.65	-71.15	75.12	78.01	6,200
Jilin 吉林	1	12						47.37	190
Heilongjiang 黑龍江	2	33	280	40	4.23	5.41	8.48	21.69	945
Central East 華東	17	114	12,948	698	5.48	15.26	113.35	64.09	12,734
Shanghai 上海	1	8	500	-10	-1.03	-1.27	62.50	18.56	970
Jiangsu 江蘇	3	33	847	-20	-0.58	-2.79	25.92	79.46	3,473
Zhejiang 浙江	6	228	25,875	1,997	8.00	18.99	113.49	57.86	24,948
Anhui 安徽									
Fujian 福建	1								
Jiangxi 江西	3	66	140	-103	-2.63	-6.53	2.11	59.80	3,930
Shandong 山東	3	90	20,470	87	0.60	3.72	228.29	83.97	14,533
Central-South 中南	18	318	32,834	-2,541	-6.37	-59.97	103.20	89.37	39,853
Henan 河南									
Hubei 湖北	2	514	535	-1,010	-5.47	-88.60	1.04	93.83	18,465
Hunan 湖南									
Guangdong 廣東	14	298	38,068	-3,208	-6.78	-63.23	127.78	89.28	47,335
Guangxi 廣西	2	265	28,500	600	6.76	40.68	107.75	83.37	8,870
Hainan 海南									
Southwest 西南	1	32	280	-320	-10.06	-25.81	8.75	61.01	3,180
Chongqing 重慶									
Sichuan 四川									
Guizhou 貴州									
Yunnan 雲南	1	32	280	-320	-10.06	-25.81	8.75	61.01	3,180
Tibet 西藏									
Northwest 西北	4	93	683	-1,313	-20.52	103.14	7.38	119.89	6,398
Shaanxi 陝西	1	123							
Gansu 甘肅									
Qinghai 青海									
Ningxia 寧夏									
Xinjiang 新疆	3	82	910	-1,750	-20.52	103.14	11.05	119.89	8,530

1433: Canned Seafood 水產罐頭製造業

Year 年份	Number of firms 企業個數	Rate of change 每年變化 (%)	Number of employees 職工人數 (人)	Rate of change 每年變化 (%)	Total revenue (mil. RMB) 總銷售收入 (百萬元)	Rate of change 每年變化 (%)	Total profit (mil. RMB) 總利潤 (百萬元)	Rate of change 每年變化 (%)
1993	85		9,479		828		18	
1994	73	-14.12%	12,555	32.45%	694	-16.10%	23	22.36%
1995	53	-27.40%	9,712	-22.65%	561	-19.23%	8	-63.78%
1996	51	-3.77%	10,356	6.63%	895	59.56%	-44	-637.70%

3 Major products* 3 種主要產品 *	Output 產量	Sales volume 銷售量	Unit 單位
a) Canned Aquatic Products 水產罐頭	60,658	62,478	ton 噸
b) Other Cans 其他罐頭	19,441	17,497	ton 噸
c) Canned Fruit 水果罐頭	53,908	53,369	ton 噸

Top 10 firms by revenue (year founded) 收入排名前 10 家企業 (創辦年份)	City 城市	Province 省	Telephone / fax 電話 / 傳真	Number of employees 職工人數	Ownership 產業所有權	Revenue ('000 RMB) 銷售收入 (千元)	Profit ('000 RMB) (rank) 利潤 (千元) (排名)	Total assets ('000 RMB) 總資產 (千元)	Major products 主要產品
Shun Dexing Shun Food Development Co. Ltd. 順德興順食品發展有限公司(1990)	Foshan 佛山市	Guangdong 廣東省	(0757)6656799 (0757)6654798	866	Overseas Chinese-funded 港澳台資	191,350	500(6)	162,391	o
Guangzhou Ying Jin Qian Enterprise Group Co. 廣州鷹金錢企業集團公司(1958)	Guangzhou 廣州市	Guangdong 廣東省	(020)85525785 (020)85525388	1,730	State-owned 國有	179,541	-37335(18)	326,499	a,b
Zhoushan Hai Li Sheng Group Co. Ltd. 舟山海力生(集團)公司(1954)	Zhoushan 舟山市	Zhejiang 浙江省	(0580)3012812 (0580)3012170	1,233	State-owned 國有	152,584	11769(1)	147,397	a,b,c
Shunde Yue Hua Canned Food Co. Ltd. 順德市粵花罐頭食品有限公司(1987)	Foshan 佛山市	Guangdong 廣東省	(0757)8883801 (0757)8886460	627	Collectively-owned 集體	80,175	-188(12)	53,111	a
Bobai Xicheng Canned Food Factory 博白縣西城罐頭食品廠(1994)	Yulin 玉林市	Guangxi 廣西	(0775)8225646	401	Collectively-owned 集體	51,650	1680(2)	4,600	c
Shandong Food Import & Export Company Juxian Canned Food Factory 山東省食品進出口公司莒縣罐頭食品廠(1990)	Rizhao 日照市	Shandong 山東省	(0633)6223741 (0633)6223741	164	State-owned 國有	48,235	298(7)	33,383	a
Baoding Canned Factory 保定罐頭廠(1956)	Baoding 保定市	Hebei 河北省	(0312)5062985 (0312)5064046	1,023	State-owned 國有	47,277	197(8)	135,038	c
Zhongshan Guang Li Industry Group Co. 中山市廣利工業集團公司(1988)	Zhongshan 中山市	Guangdong 廣東省	(0760)3115505 (0760)3116676	300	Collectively-owned 集體	31,869	-6004(17)	53,002	a
Zhongshan Bao Li Foods Co. Ltd. 中山寶利食品有限公司(1988)	Zhongshan 中山市	Guangdong 廣東省	(0760)2601899 (0760)2601928	256	Overseas Chinese-funded 港澳台資	25,085	833(3)	30,727	a
Qingdao Fu Ji Gao Food Co. Ltd. 青島富吉高食品有限公司(1995)	Qingdao 青島市	Shandong 山東省	(0532)6907551 (0532)6907554	40	Foreign-funded 外資	11,935	-37(11)	7,438	a

Top 10 Cities by Production Output 產出排名前 10 位城市	Province 省	Market share 市場份額	Number of firms 企業個數
Foshan 佛山市	Guangdong 廣東省	36.90%	3
Guangzhou 廣州市	Guangdong 廣東省	26.73%	3
Zhongshan 中山市	Guangdong 廣東省	8.26%	4
Baoding 保定市	Hebei 河北省	6.80%	1
Weihai 威海市	Shandong 山東省	5.35%	2
Shantou 汕頭市	Guangdong 廣東省	1.85%	1
Zhangzhou 漳州市	Fujian 福建省	1.70%	1
Zhuhai 珠海市	Guangdong 廣東省	1.54%	2
Dalian 大連市	Liaoning 遼寧省	1.36%	1
Zhaoqing 肇慶市	Guangdong 廣東省	1.08%	1

10 Major Wholesalers 10 家主要批發商	City 城市	Province 省	Telephone / Fax 電話 / 傳真
Zhong Liang Sugar Industry Groceries Import & Export Company 中糧糖業雜品進出口公司	Beijing 北京市	Beijing 北京市	(010)65268888 (010)65276023
China National Sugar & Alcohol Group Corp. 中國糖業酒類集團公司	Beijing 北京市	Beijing 北京市	(010)68360994
Shanxi Sugar & Wine Non-staple Food Company 山西省糖酒副食公司	Taiyuan 太原市	Shanxi 山西省	(0351)2027938 (0351)2027931
Putian Xue Jin Beer Marketing Agency Co. Ltd. 莆田縣雪津啤酒營銷代理有限公司	Putian 莆田市	Fujian 福建省	
Suzhou Sugar, Cigarette & Wine General Company 蘇州糖煙酒總公司	Suzhou 蘇州市	Jiangsu 江蘇省	(0512)7276392 (0512)7276406
Yuhang Sugar Industry Tobacco & Wine Company 余杭市糖業煙酒公司	Hangzhou 杭州市	Zhejiang 浙江省	(0571)6225788 (0571)6225407
Wuxi Sugar Industry Cigarette & Wine General Company 無錫市糖業煙酒總公司	Wuxi 無錫市	Jiangsu 江蘇省	(0510)2720023 (0510)2707693
Wuxi Chaoyang Co. Ltd. 無錫朝陽股份有限公司	Wuxi 無錫市	Jiangsu 江蘇省	(0510)2767704
Yinchuan Shen Da Non-staple Food Co. Ltd. 銀川申達副食有限公司	Yinchuan 銀川市	Ningxia 寧夏	(0951)5031694
Shanghai Sugar Industry Cigarette & Wine (Group) Co. Ltd. 上海市糖業煙酒(集團)有限公司	Shanghai 上海市	Shanghai 上海市	(021)63224190 (021)63223169

*Also include sales by firms outside this industry.包括本行業以外廠家的銷售。"o" stands for "others". "o" 代表 "其他產品" 。

1434: Canned Fruits 水果罐頭製造業

The industry accounts for 0.068% of the total revenue of China's industrial sector in 1996. The revenue growth rate of the industry is 26.9% from 1995, as compared to the growth rate of China's industrial sector, 9.51%. The rate of return on asset is -2.09%. 65.75% of all firms in the industry made a profit while 26.86% had negative returns. The top province in terms of the industry's revenue is Hainan, accounting for 28.93% of the total revenue.
本行業在1996年佔全行業總產值0.068%，行業年增長率為26.9%（全國工業年增長率9.51%）。行業的資產回報率-2.09%，65.75%的企業盈利，26.86%的企業虧損。銷售收入最高的省份為海南省，佔本行業的28.93%。

	Total number of firms 企業總數	Total number of employees 職工總數	Total revenue (mil. RMB) 總銷售收入（百萬元）	Total profit (mil. RMB) 總利潤（百萬元）	Return on assets 資產利潤率 (%)	Return on equity 權益利潤率 (%)	Labour productivity ('000 RMB / worker) 勞動生產率（千元/人）	Debts / assets 資產負債率 (%)	Total assets (mil. RMB) 總資產（百萬元）
Industry Overall 行業總體	565	63,725	3,941	-112	-2.09	-18.33	61.84	88.60	5,351

	Number of firms 企業個數	Average number of employees 平均職工人數	Average revenue ('000 RMB) 平均銷售收入（千元）	Average profit ('000 RMB) 平均利潤（千元）	Return on assets 資產利潤率 (%)	Return on equity 權益利潤率 (%)	Labour productivity ('000 RMB / worker) 勞動生產率（千元/人）	Average debts / assets 平均資產負債率(%)	Average Total assets ('000 RMB) 平均總資產（千元）
By ownership 產業所有權									
State-owned 國有	126	236	16,262	-1,071	-4.11	-69.95	68.97	94.13	26,087
Collectively-owned 集體	402	68	3,163	22	0.66	4.63	46.40	85.66	3,358
Privately-owned 私有	3	61	6,522	232	10.77	34.27	106.92	68.57	2,156
Domestic JVs 聯營	3	129	4,332	-243	-3.01	-13.95	33.58	78.43	8,074
Joint stock 股份制	2	142	8,250	-23	-0.05	-0.29	58.10	83.77	49,935
Foreign-funded 外資	13	295	27,161	1,295	6.81	19.30	92.14	64.73	19,018
Overseas Chinese-funded 港澳台資	15	136	14,600	-182	-0.81	-2.42	107.41	66.51	22,431
By size 規模									
Large 大型	4	2,407	97,992	-19,893	-11.97	131.65	40.71	109.09	166,236
Medium 中型	17	650	41,197	-2,999	-3.87	-85.80	63.38	95.49	77,438
Small 小型	538	80	5,297	34	0.55	3.04	66.02	81.87	6,264
By regional distribution 地區分布									
Central-North 華北	80	56	1,832	24	0.46	3.82	32.83	87.87	5,071
Beijing 北京	5	62	4,492	-174	-1.48	-24.37	72.22	93.94	11,782
Tianjin 天津	6	130	678	32	0.17	1.80	5.23	90.38	18,322
Hebei 河北	48	51	2,286	46	1.18	7.96	44.95	85.23	3,916
Shanxi 山西	17	54	552	16	0.56	3.84	10.32	85.46	2,849
Inner Mongolia 內蒙	4	6	228	20	20.00	32.00	37.92	37.50	100
Northeast 東北	56	67	3,660	39	1.18	9.70	54.58	87.89	3,294
Liaoning 遼寧	32	96	5,573	31	0.64	5.29	57.96	87.92	4,893
Jilin 吉林	10	29	1,108	84	12.21	-763.64	38.08	101.60	688
Heilongjiang 黑龍江	14	28	1,109	24	1.57	9.30	40.13	83.17	1,503
Central East 華東	177	161	8,403	-34	-0.29	-2.66	52.05	88.92	11,633
Shanghai 上海									
Jiangsu 江蘇	10	169	14,401	-10	-0.10	0.91	85.26	111.06	9,978
Zhejiang 浙江	64	219	10,891	-150	-0.95	-5.71	49.73	83.40	15,765
Anhui 安徽	33	168	8,109	162	2.52	14.44	48.35	82.55	6,422
Fujian 福建	17	10	1,723	28	2.61	4.86	172.29	46.16	1,058
Jiangxi 江西	17	32	662	-101	-5.26	-11.33	20.74	53.57	1,911
Shandong 山東	36	184	9,396	-14	-0.07	-4.90	51.08	98.55	19,108
Central-South 中南	139	136	14,024	-385	-2.48	-19.88	103.31	87.52	15,504
Henan 河南	26	45	1,742	23	0.85	4.64	38.94	81.65	2,708
Hubei 湖北	28	149	4,422	48	1.02	9.66	29.70	89.44	4,728
Hunan 湖南	21	143	2,019	-957	-11.28	64.34	14.10	117.53	8,489
Guangdong 廣東	12	87	5,701	346	8.50	21.36	65.46	60.21	4,069
Guangxi 廣西	50	105	10,581	-779	-6.36	-81.36	100.83	92.19	12,251
Hainan 海南	2	2,119	570,160	-265	-0.05	-0.26	269.07	81.49	556,350
Southwest 西南	59	93	1,786	-943	-17.18	248.64	19.27	106.91	5,487
Chongqing 重慶	13	202	2,343	-1,420	-13.20	111.71	11.57	111.82	10,754
Sichuan 四川	36	67	1,844	-120	-2.83	121.41	27.53	102.33	4,225
Guizhou 貴州	4	4	305	-8	-1.28	-1.69	71.76	23.93	585
Yunnan 雲南	5	65	1,068	-6,470	-138.13	888.74	16.33	115.54	4,684
Tibet 西藏									
Northwest 西北	54	48	884	-14	-0.34	-1.18	18.41	71.54	4,139
Shaanxi 陝西	20	35	284	-9	-1.25	10.24	8.15	112.16	683
Gansu 甘肅	23	47	887	33	2.81	12.46	18.80	77.40	1,160
Qinghai 青海									
Ningxia 寧夏	2	15	425	80	10.32	57.14	29.31	81.29	775
Xinjiang 新疆	9	87	2,312	-166	-0.82	-2.53	26.58	67.54	20,183

1434: Canned Fruits 水果罐頭製造業

Year 年份	Number of firms 企業個數	Rate of change 每年變化 (%)	Number of employees 職工人數 (人)	Rate of change 每年變化 (%)	Total revenue (mil. RMB) 總銷售收入 (百萬元)	Rate of change 每年變化 (%)	Total profit (mil. RMB) 總利潤 (百萬元)	Rate of change 每年變化 (%)
1993	854		74,525		2,794		-84	
1994	806	-5.62%	90,127	20.94%	2,879	3.02%	-120	-41.66%
1995	654	-18.86%	97,956	8.69%	3,106	7.91%	-86	27.91%
1996	565	-13.61%	63,725	-34.95%	3,941	26.88%	-112	-29.87%

3 Major products* 3 種主要產品 *	Output 產量	Sales volume 銷售量	Unit 單位
a) Canned Poultry Meat 禽類罐頭	9,817	9,817	ton 噸
b) Canned Fruit 水果罐頭	860,804	852,196	ton 噸
c) Can 罐頭	906,613	843,150	ton 噸

Top 10 firms by revenue (year founded) 收入排名前 10 家企業 (創辦年份)	City 城市	Province 省	Telephone / fax 電話 / 傳真	Number of employees 職工人數	Ownership 產業所有權	Revenue ('000 RMB) 銷售收入 (千元)	Profit ('000 RMB) (rank) 利潤 (千元) (排名)	Total assets ('000 RMB) 總資產 (千元)	Major products 主要產品
Guangxi Tian Tian Ke Food Co. Ltd. 廣西天天可食品有限公司(1989)	Yulin 玉林市	Guangxi 廣西		1,250	Collectively-owned 集體	228,000	7660(1)	68,900	b,c
Zhejiang Huangyan Canned Foods Factory 浙江黃岩罐頭食品廠(1958)	Taizhou 臺州市	Zhejiang 浙江省	(0576)4222641 (0576)4111951	2,881	State-owned 國有	109,087	417(48)	147,776	o
Lipu Canned Foods Factory 荔浦縣罐頭食品廠(1981)	Lingchuan 靈川縣	Guangxi 廣西	(0773)7212467	796	State-owned 國有	95,196	30(108)	114,481	b,c
Ningbo Bao Ding Industrial Co. Ltd. 寧波市寶鼎實業有限公司(1996)	Ningbo 寧波市	Zhejiang 浙江省	(0574)7111714 (0574)7293064	1,392	Joint stock 股份制	95,121	76(91)	131,423	b,c
Huoshan Foreign Trade Products Joint Processing Factory 霍山縣外貿產品聯合加工廠(1981)	Liu'an 六安市	Anhui 安徽省	(0564)5022825 (0564)5023583	613	Collectively-owned 集體	81,521	2130(7)	33,495	b
Chengdu Chu Chu Chun Group Co. Ltd. 成都處處春集團有限公司(1994)	Chengdu 成都市	Sichuan 四川省	(028)2524217 (028)2524259	600	Private-owned 私營	66,134	0(139)	8,415	a,c
Linhai Can Factory 臨海罐頭廠(1982)	Taizhou 臺州市	Zhejiang 浙江省	(0576)5112170	1,338	State-owned 國有	65,222	-1167(182)	97,682	o
Zhejiang Cereal & Oils Food Import & Export Products Company 浙江省糧油食品進出品公司(1992)	Ningbo 寧波市	Zhejiang 浙江省	(0574)8436827 (0574)8436810	170	Collectively-owned 集體	61,088	3826(3)	45,978	o
Bobai Jin Bao Canned Drink Food Industrial Co. Ltd. 博白縣津寶罐頭飲料食品實業有限公司(1989)	Yulin 玉林市	Guangxi 廣西	(0775)8222373	620	Foreign-funded 外資	56,750	1500(11)	43,760	b,c
Suizhou Hongshan Zhen Food Industry Group Company 隨州市洪山鎮食品工業集團公司(1978)	Suizhou 隨州市	Hubei 湖北省		1,950	Collectively-owned 集體	47,400	900(17)	6,180	o

Top 10 Cities by Production Output 產出排名前 10 位城市	Province 省	Market share 市場份額	Number of firms 企業個數
Ningbo 寧波市	Zhejiang 浙江省	15.83%	16
Taizhou 臺州市	Zhejiang 浙江省	13.73%	54
Lingchuan 靈川縣	Guangxi 廣西	7.78%	13
Yulin 玉林市	Guangxi 廣西	6.40%	20
Suzhou 宿州市	Anhui 安徽省	5.33%	21
Liu'an 六安市	Anhui 安徽省	4.50%	6
Yantai 煙台市	Shandong 山東省	3.17%	9
Chengdu 成都市	Sichuan 四川省	2.65%	13
Shijiazhuang 石家莊市	Hebei 河北省	2.02%	9
Wenzhou 温州市	Zhejiang 浙江省	1.90%	7

10 Major Wholesalers 10 家主要批發商	City 城市	Province 省	Telephone / Fax 電話 / 傳真
Zhong Liang Sugar Industry Groceries Import & Export Company 中糧糖業雜品進出口公司	Beijing 北京市	Beijing 北京市	(010)65268888 (010)65276023
China National Sugar & Alcohol Group Corp. 中國糖業酒類集團公司	Beijing 北京市	Beijing 北京市	(010)68360994
Shanxi Sugar & Wine Non-staple Food Company 山西省糖酒副食公司	Taiyuan 太原市	Shanxi 山西省	(0351)2027938 (0351)2027931
Putian Xue Jin Beer Marketing Agency Co. Ltd. 莆田縣雪津啤酒營銷代理有限公司	Putian 莆田市	Fujian 福建省	
Suzhou Sugar, Cigarette & Wine General Company 蘇州糖煙酒總公司	Suzhou 蘇州市	Jiangsu 江蘇省	(0512)7276392 (0512)7276406
Yuhang Sugar Industry Tobacco & Wine Company 余杭市糖業煙酒公司	Hangzhou 杭州市	Zhejiang 浙江省	(0571)6225788 (0571)6225407
Wuxi Sugar Industry Cigarette & Wine General Company 無錫市糖業煙酒總公司	Wuxi 無錫市	Jiangsu 江蘇省	(0510)2720023 (0510)2707693
Wuxi Chaoyang Co. Ltd. 無錫朝陽股份有限公司	Wuxi 無錫市	Jiangsu 江蘇省	(0510)2767704
Yinchuan Shen Da Non-staple Food Co. Ltd. 銀川申達副食有限公司	Yinchuan 銀川市	Ningxia 寧夏	(0951)5031694
Shanghai Sugar Industry Cigarette & Wine (Group) Co. Ltd. 上海市糖業煙酒(集團)有限公司	Shanghai 上海市	Shanghai 上海市	(021)63224190 (021)63223169

*Also include sales by firms outside this industry.包括本行業以外廠家的銷售。"o" stands for "others". "o" 代表"其他產品"。

1435: Canned Vegetable 蔬菜罐頭製造業

The industry accounts for 0.073% of the total revenue of China's industrial sector in 1996. The revenue growth rate of the industry is -9.9% from 1995, as compared to the growth rate of China's industrial sector, 9.51%. The rate of return on asset is -2.77%. 61.83% of all firms in the industry made a profit while 30.63% had negative returns. The top province in terms of the industry's revenue is Fujian, accounting for 54.50% of the total revenue.
本行業在1996年佔全行業總產值0.073%，行業年增長率為-9.9%（全國工業年增長率9.51%）。行業的資產回報率-2.77%，61.83%的企業盈利，30.63%的企業虧損。銷售收入最高的省份為福建省，佔本行業的54.50%。

	Total number of firms 企業總數	Total number of employees 職工總數	Total revenue (mil. RMB) 總銷售收入（百萬元）	Total profit (mil. RMB) 總利潤（百萬元）	Return on assets 資產利潤率 (%)	Return on equity 權益利潤率 (%)	Labour productivity ('000 RMB / worker) 勞動生產率（千元/人）	Debts / assets 資產負債率 (%)	Total assets (mil. RMB) 總資產（百萬元）
Industry Overall 行業總體	654	69,097	4,251	-158	-2.77	-16.01	61.52	82.61	5,711

	Number of firms 企業個數	Average number of employees 平均職工人數	Average revenue ('000 RMB) 平均銷售收入（千元）	Average profit ('000 RMB) 平均利潤（千元）	Return on assets 資產利潤率 (%)	Return on equity 權益利潤率 (%)	Labour productivity ('000 RMB / worker) 勞動生產率（千元/人）	Average debts / assets 平均資產負債率(%)	Average Total assets ('000 RMB) 平均總資產（千元）
By ownership 產業所有權									
State-owned 國有	122	282	10,123	-1,287	-4.93	-40.46	35.85	87.81	26,090
Collectively-owned 集體	417	57	4,854	-6	-0.20	-0.97	85.29	78.95	3,173
Privately-owned 私有	7	33	3,880	2	0.04	0.31	119.12	86.26	3,880
Domestic JVs 聯營	17	97	8,334	18	0.18	0.56	86.34	67.97	9,913
Joint stock 股份制	8	187	24,026	5	0.03	0.21	128.57	87.84	21,136
Foreign-funded 外資	45	78	6,314	14	0.19	1.60	81.20	88.36	7,586
Overseas Chinese-funded 港澳台資	39	109	8,885	18	0.14	0.34	81.73	58.24	12,799
By size 規模									
Large 大型	5	2,853	221,196	30,046	11.94	33.92	77.53	64.80	251,638
Medium 中型	26	563	21,714	-6,343	-12.32	208.98	38.56	105.89	51,488
Small 小型	614	65	4,203	-233	-4.60	-22.78	64.65	79.80	5,073
By regional distribution 地區分布									
Central-North 華北	28	59	1,094	-240	-4.52	-1066.67	18.61	99.58	5,304
Beijing 北京	6	55	143	-83	-11.06	27.93	2.63	139.60	753
Tianjin 天津	1	120	2,500	230	5.28	104.55	20.83	94.95	4,360
Hebei 河北	7	36	749	31	1.51	9.48	20.79	84.08	2,081
Shanxi 山西	7	52	2,150	216	10.46	75.50	41.57	86.15	2,063
Inner Mongolia 內蒙	7	84	997	-1,169	-7.39	385.85	11.93	101.93	15,803
Northeast 東北	30	69	1,618	-800	-12.99	-41.69	23.39	68.83	6,156
Liaoning 遼寧	4	73	5,195	-2,973	-24.95	-82.00	70.92	69.58	11,915
Jilin 吉林	15	56	1,069	-81	-2.44	-20.13	19.22	87.87	3,330
Heilongjiang 黑龍江	11	86	1,067	-990	-12.51	-29.42	12.37	57.50	7,916
Central East 華東	446	105	7,710	-139	-1.69	-8.53	73.76	80.01	8,197
Shanghai 上海	3	632	16,847	-3,233	-4.53	-73.15	26.67	93.80	71,303
Jiangsu 江蘇	14	162	12,749	96	0.63	3.18	78.73	80.29	15,268
Zhejiang 浙江	115	46	4,811	-33	-0.64	-5.43	105.21	88.13	5,179
Anhui 安徽	25	92	5,141	30	0.52	8.27	55.76	93.71	5,695
Fujian 福建	201	141	11,526	-234	-2.15	-8.08	81.57	73.38	10,865
Jiangxi 江西	78	56	1,285	-73	-2.58	93.43	22.81	99.88	2,822
Shandong 山東	10	210	11,111	228	2.65	16.10	52.86	83.55	8,603
Central-South 中南	94	136	4,971	-465	-5.49	-26.67	36.45	79.43	8,485
Henan 河南	10	57	2,641	-97	-4.91	-17.26	46.58	71.48	1,974
Hubei 湖北	10	68	3,714	134	8.00	29.71	54.46	73.12	1,674
Hunan 湖南	48	111	3,638	-272	-8.38	-56.60	32.84	85.19	3,242
Guangdong 廣東	17	101	5,101	64	0.59	2.71	50.27	78.08	10,785
Guangxi 廣西	8	561	17,253	-3,853	-7.48	-35.47	30.78	78.91	51,486
Hainan 海南	1	45	4,390	-1,350	-13.12	-35.34	97.56	62.88	10,290
Southwest 西南	31	55	2,689	-77	-2.06	-15.30	49.30	86.55	3,732
Chongqing 重慶	1	19	1,525	-30	-3.28	-29.65	76.46	88.93	925
Sichuan 四川	17	70	4,068	-48	-1.03	-15.09	58.09	93.19	4,680
Guizhou 貴州	8	49	1,075	-74	-2.81	-19.22	21.99	85.43	2,625
Yunnan 雲南	4	7	98	-225	-8.89	-13.45	13.45	33.79	2,530
Tibet 西藏									
Northwest 西北	25	170	7,287	-773	-2.39	-78.60	42.96	96.96	32,360
Shaanxi 陝西	3	235	2,723	-1,350	-19.75	39.67	11.59	149.73	6,837
Gansu 甘肅	2	112	265	5	0.02	0.10	2.38	79.77	24,420
Qinghai 青海									
Ningxia 寧夏	4	204	3,228	-2,225	-8.90	341.00	15.82	102.61	25,013
Xinjiang 新疆	16	156	10,036	-399	-1.00	-23.18	64.31	95.70	39,974

1435: Canned Vegetable 蔬菜罐頭製造業

Year 年份	Number of firms 企業個數	Rate of change 每年變化 (%)	Number of employees 職工人數 (人)	Rate of change 每年變化 (%)	Total revenue (mil. RMB) 總銷售收入 (百萬元)	Rate of change 每年變化 (%)	Total profit (mil. RMB) 總利潤 (百萬元)	Rate of change 每年變化 (%)
1993	515		86,874		3,209		-118	
1994	571	10.87%	84,694	-2.51%	3,604	12.33%	-109	7.58%
1995	682	19.44%	90,383	6.72%	4,717	30.87%	-67	38.67%
1996	654	-4.11%	69,097	-23.55%	4,251	-9.88%	-158	-136.92%

3 Major products* 3 種主要產品 *	Output 產量	Sales volume 銷售量	Unit 單位
a) Canned Vegetable 蔬菜罐頭	707,631	679,325	ton 噸
b) Canned Fruit 水果罐頭	76,167	75,405	ton 噸
c) Other Cans 其他罐頭	11,895	10,705	ton 噸

Top 10 firms by revenue (year founded) 收入排名前 10 家企業 (創辦年份)	City 城市	Province 省	Telephone / fax 電話 / 傳真	Number of employees 職工人數	Ownership 產業所有權	Revenue ('000 RMB) 銷售收入 (千元)	Profit ('000 RMB) (rank) 利潤 (千元) (排名)	Total assets ('000 RMB) 總資產 (千元)	Major products 主要產品
Xiamen Canned Factory 廈門罐頭廠(1954)	Xiamen 廈門市	Fujian 福建省	(0592)2024750 (0592)2025943	4,850	State-owned 國有	285,969	421(45)	304,567	a,b
Longhai Xing De Food Industrial Co. Ltd. 龍海市興德食品工業有限公司(1995)	Zhangzhou 漳州市	Fujian 福建省	(0596)6775370 (0596)6766371	303	Overseas Chinese-funded 港澳台資	135,340	553(35)	45,273	a
Longhai Zhong Liang Foods Co. Ltd. 龍海市中糧食品有限公司(1994)	Zhangzhou 漳州市	Fujian 福建省	(0596)6882288 (0596)6882289	600	Joint stock 股份制	121,920	530(37)	60,580	a
Fujian Zishan Foods & Beverage General Co. 福建紫山食品飲料總公司(1985)	Zhangzhou 漳州市	Fujian 福建省	(0596)6658522	878	Collectively-owned 集體	106,598	425(44)	55,001	a
Ningbo Luye Fa Zhan Co. Ltd. Yuyao Branch 寧波綠野發展有限公司余姚分公司(1993)	Ningbo 寧波市	Zhejiang 浙江省	(0574)2153127 (0574)2151404	40	Foreign-funded 外資	103,099	8019(2)	17,375	o
Fujian Zhangzhou Canned Foods General Factory 福建省漳州罐頭食品總廠(1958)	Zhangzhou 漳州市	Fujian 福建省	(0596)2927944 (0596)2928321	3,264	State-owned 國有	92,589	0(194)	205,109	a,b,c
Yunxiao Tian Di Food & Beverage Co. Ltd. 雲霄縣天第食品飲料有限公司(1993)	Zhangzhou 漳州市	Fujian 福建省	(0596)8628119 (0596)8628121	446	Overseas Chinese-funded 港澳台資	88,520	-1326(270)	68,325	a
Zhejiang Bei Hu Group 浙江北湖集團(1992)	Huzhou 湖州市	Zhejiang 浙江省	(0572)8015089	117	Foreign-funded 外資	86,882	1996(10)	203,399	o
Ji'nan Duan Hong Food Co. Ltd. 濟南端宏食品有限公司(1995)	Ji'nan 濟南市	Shandong 山東省	(0531)8994075	1,150	Foreign-funded 外資	85,100	8260(1)	18,720	a
Fujian Putian Canned Factory 福建省莆田縣罐頭廠(1956)	Putian 莆田市	Fujian 福建省	(0594)3597174 (0594)3597174	3,998	State-owned 國有	83,768	9(176)	162,136	a,b,c

Top 10 Cities by Production Output 產出排名前 10 位城市	Province 省	Market share 市場份額	Number of firms 企業個數
Zhangzhou 漳州市	Fujian 福建省	31.09%	68
Xiamen 廈門市	Fujian 福建省	7.79%	1
Heze 菏澤市	Shandong 山東省	5.31%	3
Huzhou 湖州市	Zhejiang 浙江省	5.27%	22
Ningbo 寧波市	Zhejiang 浙江省	4.64%	29
Quzhou 衢州市	Zhejiang 浙江省	3.40%	30
Shanghai 上海市	Shanghai 上海市	2.63%	7
Chaozhou 潮州市	Guangdong 廣東省	2.52%	6
Nangping 南平市	Fujian 福建省	2.16%	51
Shaoyang 邵陽市	Hunan 湖南省	1.98%	18

10 Major Wholesalers 10 家主要批發商	City 城市	Province 省	Telephone / Fax 電話 / 傳真
Zhong Liang Sugar Industry Groceries Import & Export Company 中糧糖業雜品進出口公司	Beijing 北京市	Beijing 北京市	(010)65268888 (010)65276023
China National Sugar & Alcohol Group Corp. 中國糖業酒類集團公司	Beijing 北京市	Beijing 北京市	(010)68360994
Shanxi Sugar & Wine Non-staple Food Company 山西省糖酒副食公司	Taiyuan 太原市	Shanxi 山西省	(0351)2027938 (0351)2027931
Putian Xue Jin Beer Marketing Agency Co. Ltd. 莆田縣雪津啤酒營銷代理有限公司	Putian 莆田市	Fujian 福建省	
Suzhou Sugar, Cigarette & Wine General Company 蘇州糖煙酒總公司	Suzhou 蘇州市	Jiangsu 江蘇省	(0512)7276392 (0512)7276406
Yuhang Sugar Industry Tobacco & Wine Company 余杭市糖業煙酒公司	Hangzhou 杭州市	Zhejiang 浙江省	(0571)6225788 (0571)6225407
Wuxi Sugar Industry Cigarette & Wine General Company 無錫市糖業煙酒總公司	Wuxi 無錫市	Jiangsu 江蘇省	(0510)2720023 (0510)2707693
Wuxi Chaoyang Co. Ltd. 無錫朝陽股份有限公司	Wuxi 無錫市	Jiangsu 江蘇省	(0510)2767704
Yinchuan Shen Da Non-staple Food Co. Ltd. 銀川申達副食有限公司	Yinchuan 銀川市	Ningxia 寧夏	(0951)5031694
Shanghai Sugar Industry Cigarette & Wine (Group) Co. Ltd. 上海市糖業煙酒(集團)有限公司	Shanghai 上海市	Shanghai 上海市	(021)63224190 (021)63223169

*Also include sales by firms outside this industry.包括本行業以外廠家的銷售。"o" stands for "others". "o" 代表 "其他產品"。

1439: Other Canned Food 其他罐頭食品製造業

The industry accounts for 0.035% of the total revenue of China's industrial sector in 1996. The revenue growth rate of the industry is -11.1% from 1995, as compared to the growth rate of China's industrial sector, 9.51%. The rate of return on asset is -1.49%. 65.68% of all firms in the industry made a profit while 28.37% had negative returns. The top province in terms of the industry's revenue is Guangdong, accounting for 29.38% of the total revenue.
本行業在1996年佔全行業總產值0.035%，行業年增長率為-11.1%（全國工業年增長率9.51%）。行業的資產回報率-1.49%，65.68%的企業盈利，28.37%的企業虧損。銷售收入最高的省份為廣東省，佔本行業的29.38%。

	Total number of firms 企業總數	Total number of employees 職工總數	Total revenue (mil. RMB) 總銷售收入（百萬元）	Total profit (mil. RMB) 總利潤（百萬元）	Return on assets 資產利潤率 (%)	Return on equity 權益利潤率 (%)	Labour productivity ('000 RMB / worker) 勞動生產率（千元/人）	Debts / assets 資產負債率 (%)	Total assets (mil. RMB) 總資產（百萬元）
Industry Overall 行業總體	239	22,251	2,051	-31	-1.49	-5.95	92.18	74.96	2,099

	Number of firms 企業個數	Average number of employees 平均職工人數	Average revenue ('000 RMB) 平均銷售收入（千元）	Average profit ('000 RMB) 平均利潤（千元）	Return on assets 資產利潤率 (%)	Return on equity 權益利潤率 (%)	Labour productivity ('000 RMB / worker) 勞動生產率（千元/人）	Average debts / assets 平均資產負債率(%)	Average Total assets ('000 RMB) 平均總資產（千元）
By ownership 產業所有權									
State-owned 國有	40	274	20,625	-1,150	-5.17	-31.29	75.41	83.48	22,250
Collectively-owned 集體	147	50	4,003	-28	-1.01	-3.72	80.28	72.86	2,800
Privately-owned 私有	3	18	587	-25	-3.81	-8.48	33.21	55.06	654
Domestic JVs 聯營	8	68	3,565	46	0.60	1.15	52.43	47.76	7,637
Joint stock 股份制	2	67	6,639	-11	-0.32	9.60	99.08	103.35	3,320
Foreign-funded 外資	14	101	19,275	1,220	5.71	26.08	190.30	78.12	21,376
Overseas Chinese-funded 港澳台資	24	79	13,528	75	0.42	1.07	170.79	60.50	17,855
By size 規模									
Large 大型	4	1,151	238,320	-3,688	-1.67	-7.35	207.06	77.30	221,124
Medium 中型	5	798	45,219	-2,342	-4.64	-15.56	56.64	70.18	50,462
Small 小型	224	61	3,892	-20	-0.47	-1.82	64.28	74.02	4,296
By regional distribution 地區分布									
Central-North 華北	25	46	2,277	12	0.25	0.51	49.58	51.60	4,886
Beijing 北京	6	33	2,605	3	0.11	0.61	78.54	82.35	3,117
Tianjin 天津	3	4	3	-10	-2.86	-3.06	0.83	6.67	350
Hebei 河北	8	43	1,641	85	3.48	12.50	38.39	72.16	2,443
Shanxi 山西	4	101	6,673	-15	-0.08	-0.12	66.23	36.35	19,148
Inner Mongolia 內蒙	4	48	365	-78	-4.95	-47.69	7.60	89.62	1,565
Northeast 東北	22	207	7,546	-770	-5.86	406.97	36.46	101.44	13,136
Liaoning 遼寧	9	77	8,039	33	0.17	1.49	104.25	88.78	19,947
Jilin 吉林	6	338	1,825	-1,917	-14.04	36.57	5.39	138.38	13,653
Heilongjiang 黑龍江	7	261	11,816	-819	-20.79	-80.25	45.22	74.09	3,937
Central East 華東	130	67	7,248	132	1.78	6.20	107.43	71.34	7,441
Shanghai 上海	6	86	11,333	12	0.12	0.36	131.27	67.04	9,882
Jiangsu 江蘇	9	60	12,477	141	3.41	-158.75	207.56	102.15	4,137
Zhejiang 浙江	17	66	10,853	214	1.31	3.46	165.32	62.03	16,249
Anhui 安徽	13	43	7,038	748	17.76	47.16	162.79	62.33	4,211
Fujian 福建	53	60	5,503	-13	-0.40	-1.26	91.92	68.57	3,381
Jiangxi 江西	24	38	1,098	-52	-2.29	-24.32	29.21	90.58	2,274
Shandong 山東	8	245	20,995	556	1.45	6.23	85.74	76.64	38,254
Central-South 中南	41	140	17,529	-786	-5.96	-18.03	125.49	66.94	13,189
Henan 河南	6	93	1,398	32	1.92	7.17	15.12	73.23	1,650
Hubei 湖北	5	109	15,370	30	0.51	1.18	141.53	56.65	5,854
Hunan 湖南	8	36	2,756	-8	-0.75	-2.49	76.83	69.85	995
Guangdong 廣東	19	222	31,716	-1,623	-6.46	-20.00	143.03	67.72	25,139
Guangxi 廣西	3	43	2,937	-557	-10.45	-24.45	68.29	57.26	5,327
Hainan 海南									
Southwest 西南	13	30	1,134	-28	-1.55	-76.60	37.70	98.06	1,785
Chongqing 重慶	1	51	951	1	0.08	-0.19	18.61	140.24	937
Sichuan 四川	5	41	1,690	-84	-3.07	-32.18	40.85	90.47	2,743
Guizhou 貴州	2	7							35
Yunnan 雲南	5	24	1,068	12	0.71	-11.11	44.13	106.49	1,696
Tibet 西藏									
Northwest 西北	8	208	19,060	94	0.48	5.33	91.80	91.00	19,529
Shaanxi 陝西	7	235	21,516	97	0.44	4.85	91.61	90.95	22,129
Gansu 甘肅									
Qinghai 青海									
Ningxia 寧夏									
Xinjiang 新疆	1	17	1,870	70	5.26	175.00	110.00	96.99	1,330

1439: Other Canned Food 其他罐頭食品製造業

Year 年份	Number of firms 企業個數	Rate of change 每年變化 (%)	Number of employees 職工人數 (人)	Rate of change 每年變化 (%)	Total revenue (mil. RMB) 總銷售收入 (百萬元)	Rate of change 每年變化 (%)	Total profit (mil. RMB) 總利潤 (百萬元)	Rate of change 每年變化 (%)
1993	243		18,062		715		-23	
1994	231	-4.94%	20,418	13.04%	1,185	65.73%	0	100.76%
1995	238	3.03%	29,734	45.63%	2,308	94.68%	-61	-35047.13%
1996	239	0.42%	22,251	-25.17%	2,051	-11.14%	-31	49.02%

3 Major products* 3 種主要產品 *	Output 產量	Sales volume 銷售量	Unit 單位
a) Other Cans 其他罐頭	97,899	88,109	ton 噸
b) Canned Fruit 水果罐頭	42,311	41,888	ton 噸
c) Canned Vegetable 蔬菜罐頭	32,712	31,404	ton 噸

Top 10 firms by revenue (year founded) 收入排名前 10 家企業 (創辦年份)	City 城市	Province 省	Telephone / fax 電話 / 傳真	Number of employees 職工人數	Ownership 產業所有權	Revenue ('000 RMB) 銷售收入 (千元)	Profit ('000 RMB) (rank) 利潤 (千元) (排名)	Total assets ('000 RMB) 總資產 (千元)	Major products 主要產品
Shantou Sincerity Group Co. 汕頭中孚集團公司(1952)	Shantou 汕頭市	Guangdong 廣東省	(0754)8106396 (0754)8106396	1,556	State-owned 國有	416,141	-655(71)	143,272	o
Xiamen Tongmao Canning Factory Co. Ltd. 廈門同茂食品罐頭有限公司(1990)	Xiamen 廈門市	Fujian 福建省	(0592)7070017	480	Foreign-funded 外資	183,728	1271(6)	58,887	a,b,c
Xi'an Tourism Foods Products Mill 西安旅遊食品廠(1971)	Xi'an 西安市	Shaanxi 陝西省	(029)5253220 (029)5251989	1,400	State-owned 國有	147,976	1038(8)	137,664	o
Linyi Yuli Kernel Foods Co. Ltd. 臨沂裕利果仁食品有限公司(1990)	Linyi 臨沂市	Shandong 山東省	(0539)8316061 (0539)8315232	450	Overseas Chinese-funded 港澳台資	75,895	2221(3)	72,978	a
Suzhou Qing Qing Food Co. Ltd. 宿州市青青食品有限公司(1994)	Suzhou 宿州市	Anhui 安徽省	(0557)3021759	120	Collectively-owned 集體	59,621	8754(1)	36,352	o
Dalian San Dao Foods Co. Ltd. 大連三島食品有限公司(1992)	Dalian 大連市	Liaoning 遼寧省	(0411)7611161 (0411)7612034	283	Foreign-funded 外資	58,170	1219(7)	162,314	a
Shantou Sez Meiwei Foods Industrial Co. Ltd. 汕特美味食品工業有限公司(1988)	Shantou 汕頭市	Guangdong 廣東省	(0754)8224184 (0754)8224409	140	Foreign-funded 外資	47,511	-677(72)	16,857	a
Zhuhai Western Tian Yuan Food Co. Ltd. 珠海市西部天元食品有限公司(1992)	Zhuhai 珠海市	Guangdong 廣東省	(0756)7761702	102	State-owned 國有	45,568	120(31)	52,381	a
Shanghai Tai Kang Canned Food Factory 上海泰康罐頭食品廠(1981)	Shanghai 上海市	Shanghai 上海市	(021)57575324	305	Domestic JVs 聯營	45,344	1365(5)	28,768	a,b,c
Weifang Faint Scent Food Co. Ltd. 濰坊清香食品有限公司(1993)	Weifang 濰坊市	Shandong 山東省	(0536)7618291	378	Overseas Chinese-funded 港澳台資	45,180	3682(2)	21,120	o

Top 10 Cities by Production Output 產出排名前 10 位城市	Province 省	Market share 市場份額	Number of firms 企業個數
Haikou 海口市	Hainan 海南省	49.72%	1
Xi'an 西安市	Shaanxi 陝西省	6.31%	1
Wuxi 無錫市	Jiangsu 江蘇省	4.45%	10
Wuzhou 梧州市	Guangxi 廣西	3.47%	2
Beijing 北京市	Beijing 北京市	3.32%	7
Putian 莆田市	Fujian 福建省	2.85%	2
Dalian 大連市	Liaoning 遼寧省	2.45%	2
Linyi 臨沂市	Shandong 山東省	2.19%	5
Weifang 濰坊市	Shandong 山東省	1.88%	5
Zhuhai 珠海市	Guangdong 廣東省	1.52%	1

10 Major Wholesalers 10 家主要批發商	City 城市	Province 省	Telephone / Fax 電話 / 傳真
Zhong Liang Sugar Industry Groceries Import & Export Company 中糧糖業雜品進出口公司	Beijing 北京市	Beijing 北京市	(010)65268888 (010)65276023
China National Sugar & Alcohol Group Corp. 中國糖業酒類集團公司	Beijing 北京市	Beijing 北京市	(010)68360994
Shanxi Sugar & Wine Non-staple Food Company 山西省糖酒副食公司	Taiyuan 太原市	Shanxi 山西省	(0351)2027938 (0351)2027931
Putian Xue Jin Beer Marketing Agency Co. Ltd. 莆田縣雪津啤酒營銷代理有限公司	Putian 莆田市	Fujian 福建省	
Suzhou Sugar, Cigarette & Wine General Company 蘇州糖煙酒總公司	Suzhou 蘇州市	Jiangsu 江蘇省	(0512)7276392 (0512)7276406
Yuhang Sugar Industry Tobacco & Wine Company 余杭市糖業煙酒公司	Hangzhou 杭州市	Zhejiang 浙江省	(0571)6225788 (0571)6225407
Wuxi Sugar Industry Cigarette & Wine General Company 無錫市糖業煙酒總公司	Wuxi 無錫市	Jiangsu 江蘇省	(0510)2720023 (0510)2707693
Wuxi Chaoyang Co. Ltd. 無錫朝陽股份有限公司	Wuxi 無錫市	Jiangsu 江蘇省	(0510)2767704
Yinchuan Shen Da Non-staple Food Co. Ltd. 銀川申達副食有限公司	Yinchuan 銀川市	Ningxia 寧夏	(0951)5031694
Shanghai Sugar Industry Cigarette & Wine (Group) Co. Ltd. 上海市糖業煙酒(集團)有限公司	Shanghai 上海市	Shanghai 上海市	(021)63224190 (021)63223169

*Also include sales by firms outside this industry.包括本行業以外廠家的銷售。"o" stands for "others". "o" 代表 "其他產品" 。

1441: Amino Acid 氨基酸製造業

The industry accounts for 0.007% of the total revenue of China's industrial sector in 1996. The revenue growth rate of the industry is 32.4% from 1995, as compared to the growth rate of China's industrial sector, 9.51%. The rate of return on asset is 5.88%. 62.50% of all firms in the industry made a profit while 37.50% had negative returns. The top province in terms of the industry's revenue is Zhejiang, accounting for 52.29% of the total revenue.
本行業在1996年佔全行業總產值0.007%，行業年增長率為32.4%（全國工業年增長率9.51%）。行業的資產回報率5.88%，62.50%的企業盈利，37.50%的企業虧損。銷售收入最高的省份為浙江省，佔本行業的52.29%。

	Total number of firms 企業總數	Total number of employees 職工總數	Total revenue (mil. RMB) 總銷售收入（百萬元）	Total profit (mil. RMB) 總利潤（百萬元）	Return on assets 資產利潤率 (%)	Return on equity 權益利潤率 (%)	Labour productivity ('000 RMB / worker) 勞動生產率（千元/人）	Debts / assets 資產負債率 (%)	Total assets (mil. RMB) 總資產（百萬元）
Industry Overall 行業總體	42	3,018	415	23	5.88	16.66	137.51	64.70	388

	Number of firms 企業個數	Average number of employees 平均職工人數	Average revenue ('000 RMB) 平均銷售收入（千元）	Average profit ('000 RMB) 平均利潤（千元）	Return on assets 資產利潤率 (%)	Return on equity 權益利潤率 (%)	Labour productivity ('000 RMB / worker) 勞動生產率（千元/人）	Average debts / assets 平均資產負債率(%)	Average Total assets ('000 RMB) 平均總資產（千元）
By ownership 產業所有權									
State-owned 國有	8	95	5,750	-625	-7.35	-38.46	60.29	80.88	8,500
Collectively-owned 集體	24	64	8,220	714	15.03	50.69	128.61	70.34	4,750
Privately-owned 私有	1	17	3,337	590	60.24	112.83	196.27	46.61	979
Domestic JVs 聯營	2	63	24,652	2,143	14.75	47.11	394.44	68.68	14,524
Joint stock 股份制	1	76	66	-1,400	-28.13	-34.19	0.87	17.74	4,977
Foreign-funded 外資	3	92	13,917	312	0.64	1.35	150.72	52.95	49,011
Overseas Chinese-funded 港澳台資	3	75	25,736	2,148	26.91	88.43	341.63	69.57	7,984
By size 規模									
Large 大型									
Medium 中型	1	103	32,924	-8,041	-6.62	-13.26	319.66	50.10	121,530
Small 小型	38	73	10,054	817	11.65	40.66	137.29	71.34	7,012
By regional distribution 地區分布									
Central-North 華北	5	38	1,022	-24	-0.76	23.08	27.18	103.37	3,144
Beijing 北京	1								
Tianjin 天津									
Hebei 河北	3	63	1,703	-40	-0.76	23.08	27.18	103.37	5,240
Shanxi 山西	1								
Inner Mongolia 內蒙									
Northeast 東北	2	76	29,035	10,010	16.98	25.18	384.57	32.57	58,950
Liaoning 遼寧	1	20	50	-70	-5.30	17.50	2.50	130.30	1,320
Jilin 吉林									
Heilongjiang 黑龍江	1	131	58,020	20,090	17.23	25.14	442.90	31.46	116,580
Central East 華東	9	50	26,290	993	11.93	32.81	530.52	63.62	8,327
Shanghai 上海	1	35	4,250	20	0.27	0.67	121.43	59.26	7,340
Jiangsu 江蘇	2	24	2,615	-315	-9.91	-53.85	111.28	81.60	3,180
Zhejiang 浙江	4	57	54,248	2,363	16.41	40.79	955.90	59.77	14,400
Anhui 安徽	1	40	10,000	100	3.40		250.00	100.00	2,940
Fujian 福建									
Jiangxi 江西	1	97	140				1.44	110.00	700
Shandong 山東									
Central-South 中南	13	103	5,467	-71	-1.26	-6.19	53.28	79.70	5,630
Henan 河南	5	151	9,882	92	1.16	17.76	65.62	93.44	7,902
Hubei 湖北	3	32	2,623	-120	-2.73	-4.40	81.98	37.91	4,397
Hunan 湖南	4	101	3,250	-170	-4.10	-29.96	32.10	86.30	4,143
Guangdong 廣東									
Guangxi 廣西	1	80	790	-340	-8.67	-18.78	9.88	53.83	3,920
Hainan 海南									
Southwest 西南	11	63	3,536	7	0.10	1.76	56.46	94.03	6,927
Chongqing 重慶	5	72	4,483	-12	-0.13	3.44	62.19	103.67	9,781
Sichuan 四川	5	39	3,203	42	0.82	3.73	80.23	77.92	5,151
Guizhou 貴州	1	128	470	-70	-4.55	-10.61	3.67	57.14	1,540
Yunnan 雲南									
Tibet 西藏									
Northwest 西北	2	105	2,495	-2,575	-17.06	-45.41	23.76	62.43	15,090
Shaanxi 陝西									
Gansu 甘肅	1	20	990	30	2.97	4.76	49.50	37.62	1,010
Qinghai 青海									
Ningxia 寧夏	1	190	4,000	-5,180	-17.76	-48.37	21.05	63.28	29,170
Xinjiang 新疆									

1441: Amino Acid 氨基酸製造業

Year 年份	Number of firms 企業個數	Rate of change 每年變化 (%)	Number of employees 職工人數 (人)	Rate of change 每年變化 (%)	Total revenue (mil. RMB) 總銷售收入 (百萬元)	Rate of change 每年變化 (%)	Total profit (mil. RMB) 總利潤 (百萬元)	Rate of change 每年變化 (%)
1993	26		1,636		212		9	
1994	34	30.77%	2,973	81.72%	283	33.70%	11	14.76%
1995	44	29.41%	3,545	19.24%	313	10.54%	-3	-125.44%
1996	42	-4.55%	3,018	-14.87%	415	32.43%	23	958.21%

3 Major products* 3 種主要產品 *	Output 產量	Sales volume 銷售量	Unit 單位
a) Fermentum 酵母	8,685	8,772	ton 噸
b) Ferment Pretaration 製劑	4,378	3,940	ton 噸

Top 10 firms by revenue (year founded) 收入排名前 10 家企業 (創辦年份)	City 城市	Province 省	Telephone / fax 電話 / 傳真	Number of employees 職工人數	Ownership 產業所有權	Revenue ('000 RMB) 銷售收入 (千元)	Profit ('000 RMB) (rank) 利潤 (千元) (排名)	Total assets ('000 RMB) 總資產 (千元)	Major products 主要產品
Ningbo Hai De Amino-acids Industrial Co. Ltd. 寧波海德氨基酸工業有限公司(1994)	Ningbo 寧波市	Zhejiang 浙江省	(0574)6251666 (0574)6251777	100	Overseas Chinese-funded 港澳台資	154,760	7866(2)	41,118	o
Ningbo Natural Biological Products Co. Ltd. 寧波天然生物製品有限公司(1981)	Ningbo 寧波市	Zhejiang 浙江省	(0574)8420027 (0574)7839097	50	Private-owned 私營	60,705	2547(3)	9,571	o
Ningbo Zhenhai Amino-acids Plant 寧波市鎮海氨基酸廠(1993)	Ningbo 寧波市	Zhejiang 浙江省	(0574)6261149 (0574)6261281	85	Collectively-owned 集體	60,314	1540(4)	12,142	o
Harbin Mavri Yeast Co. Ltd. 哈爾濱馬利酵母有限公司(1992)	Harbin 哈爾濱市	Heilongjiang 黑龍江省	(0451)3721555 (0451)3723106	121	Foreign-funded 外資	58,021	20090(1)	116,584	a
Hebei Zhoukou Monosodium Glutamate Plant – Fugou Branch 河南省周口地區味精廠扶溝分廠(1981)	Zhoukou 周口市	Henan 河南省	(0394)6221278	435	State-owned 國有	36,308	405(10)	24,003	b
Yongchuan Ju Long Amino-acids Plant 永川市巨龍氨基酸廠	Chongqing 重慶市	Chongqing 重慶市	(023)49401024	90	Collectively-owned 集體	12,539	556(7)	11,199	o
Chongzhou Shu Zhou Biochemistry Factory 崇州市蜀州生化廠	Chengdu 成都市	Sichuan 四川省	(028)272594	57	Collectively-owned 集體	11,879	424(9)	3,665	o
Wangjiang Amino Acid Factory 望江縣氨基酸廠(1992)	Anqing 安慶市	Anhui 安徽省	(0556)7173006	35	Collectively-owned 集體	10,000	100(15)	2,940	o
Huaxian Ci Zhou Zhai Amino Acid Factory 滑縣慈周寨氨基酸廠(1991)	Anyang 安陽市	Henan 河南省		70	Collectively-owned 集體	8,180	490(8)	3,620	o
Sanmenxia Yan Yuan Amino Acid Co. Ltd. 三門峽延源氨基酸有限責任公司(1994)	Sanmenxia 三門峽市	Henan 河南省	(0398)2826821 (0398)2826009	120	Joint stock 股份制	5,090	191(13)	6,152	o

Top 10 Cities by Production Output 產出排名前 10 位城市	Province 省	Market share 市場份額	Number of firms 企業個數
Ningbo 寧波市	Zhejiang 浙江省	55.93%	4
Anqing 安慶市	Anhui 安徽省	10.02%	3
Zhoukou 周口市	Henan 河南省	7.37%	1
Shanghai 上海市	Shanghai 上海市	5.83%	6
Sanmenxia 三門峽市	Henan 河南省	4.91%	2
Huaihua 懷化市	Hunan 湖南省	2.50%	2
Dongguan 東莞市	Guangdong 廣東省	2.46%	2
Chongqing 重慶市	Chongqing 重慶市	2.32%	3
Shaoyang 邵陽市	Hunan 湖南省	1.72%	2
Anyang 安陽市	Henan 河南省	1.66%	1

10 Major Wholesalers 10 家主要批發商	City 城市	Province 省	Telephone / Fax 電話 / 傳真
Guangdong Meizhou Salt Industry General Company 廣東省梅州鹽業總公司	Meizhou 梅州市	Guangdong 廣東省	(0752)2234242 (0752)2234720
Shannxi Import & Export Company 陝西省進出口公司	Xi'an 西安市	Shaanxi 陝西省	(029)7424946 (029)7420131
Fujian Salt Industry Company 福建省鹽業公司	Fuzhou 福州市	Fujian 福建省	(0591)7535047 (0591)7535047
Sichuan Salt Industry Company Zigong Branch 四川省鹽業公司自貢分公司	Zigong 自貢市	Sichuan 四川省	(0813)2203215 (0813)2203215
Shanghai Shi Liu Pu Non-staple Food Trade Company 上海市十六鋪副食品貿易公司	Shanghai 上海市	Shanghai 上海市	(021)63736787
Shandong Salt Industry General Company Shandong Salt Administration Bureau 山東省鹽業總公司山東省鹽務局	Ji'nan 濟南市	Shandong 山東省	(0531)6925633 (0531)6925021
Yunnan Salt Industry General Company 雲南省鹽業總公司	Kunming 昆明市	Yunnan 雲南省	(0871)3166719
Shanghai Jia Le Condiment Mill Marketing Company 上海家樂調味食品銷售公司	Shanghai 上海市	Shanghai 上海市	(021)59139194
Zhong Yan Shanghai Salt Company 中鹽上海鹽業公司	Shanghai 上海市	Shanghai 上海市	(021)62180345 (021)62187068
Zhejiang Salt Industry Company 浙江省鹽業公司	Hangzhou 杭州市	Zhejiang 浙江省	(0571)7800292 (0571)7800292

*Also include sales by firms outside this industry.包括本行業以外廠家的銷售。"o" stands for "others". "o" 代表 "其他產品"。

1442: Gourmet Powder 味精製造業

The industry accounts for 0.138% of the total revenue of China's industrial sector in 1996. The revenue growth rate of the industry is 4.4% from 1995, as compared to the growth rate of China's industrial sector, 9.51%. The rate of return on asset is 2.05%. 58.79% of all firms in the industry made a profit while 33.98% had negative returns. The top province in terms of the industry's revenue is Henan, accounting for 27.97% of the total revenue.
本行業在1996年佔全行業總產值0.138%，行業年增長率為4.4%（全國工業年增長率9.51%）。行業的資產回報率2.05%，58.79%的企業盈利，33.98%的企業虧損。銷售收入最高的省份為河南省，佔本行業的27.97%。

	Total number of firms 企業總數	Total number of employees 職工總數	Total revenue (mil. RMB) 總銷售收入（百萬元）	Total profit (mil. RMB) 總利潤（百萬元）	Return on assets 資產利潤率 (%)	Return on equity 權益利潤率 (%)	Labour productivity ('000 RMB / worker) 勞動生產率（千元/人）	Debts / assets 資產負債率 (%)	Total assets (mil. RMB) 總資產（百萬元）
Industry Overall 行業總體	110	78,291	7,994	224	2.05	4.85	102.11	57.69	10,928

	Number of firms 企業個數	Average number of employees 平均職工人數	Average revenue ('000 RMB) 平均銷售收入（千元）	Average profit ('000 RMB) 平均利潤（千元）	Return on assets 資產利潤率 (%)	Return on equity 權益利潤率 (%)	Labour productivity ('000 RMB / worker) 勞動生產率（千元/人）	Average debts / assets 平均資產負債率(%)	Average Total assets ('000 RMB) 平均總資產（千元）
By ownership 產業所有權									
State-owned 國有	59	753	79,814	1,661	1.68	7.80	105.96	78.41	98,695
Collectively-owned 集體	32	417	50,624	2,620	5.31	9.25	121.34	42.66	49,384
Privately-owned 私有									
Domestic JVs 聯營									
Joint stock 股份制	4	862	121,542	7,051	3.32	5.41	141.08	38.69	212,655
Foreign-funded 外資	7	1,995	103,506	1,934	0.67	0.87	51.89	23.45	290,417
Overseas Chinese-funded 港澳台資	8	386	56,903	44	0.06	0.09	147.51	40.24	80,154
By size 規模									
Large 大型	18	2,543	302,298	13,252	3.22	7.16	118.89	54.96	411,146
Medium 中型	23	728	69,523	-383	-0.40	-1.11	95.48	64.39	96,587
Small 小型	68	232	14,037	-85	-0.44	-1.15	60.57	61.73	19,206
By regional distribution 地區分布									
Central-North 華北	4	336	31,233	-113	-0.25	-0.56	93.02	54.87	44,135
Beijing 北京	1	182	8,230	-720	-6.19	-42.35	45.22	85.40	11,640
Tianjin 天津	3	387	38,900	90	0.16	0.35	100.52	52.72	54,967
Hebei 河北									
Shanxi 山西									
Inner Mongolia 內蒙									
Northeast 東北	12	476	27,913	-815	-1.40	-10.99	58.63	87.23	58,098
Liaoning 遼寧	7	507	44,597	-234	-0.29	-1.60	87.89	81.63	79,749
Jilin 吉林	2	784	5,825	-3,515	-6.23	54.67	7.43	111.40	56,390
Heilongjiang 黑龍江	3	198	3,707	-370	-4.24	156.34	18.72	102.71	8,720
Central East 華東	52	728	66,260	2,411	2.34	4.12	90.99	43.04	102,855
Shanghai 上海	4	297	82,845	628	1.36	11.90	278.70	88.52	45,973
Jiangsu 江蘇	13	524	52,558	122	0.20	0.90	100.24	77.89	61,200
Zhejiang 浙江	9	476	75,194	3,944	6.68	19.54	157.82	65.83	59,061
Anhui 安徽	1	142	7,710	-1,900	-17.40	36.05	54.30	148.26	10,920
Fujian 福建	13	1,057	41,095	998	1.43	2.72	38.86	47.40	69,695
Jiangxi 江西	5	182	2,128	-788	-8.90	68.28	11.72	113.04	8,852
Shandong 山東	7	1,540	171,651	11,237	2.73	3.57	111.46	23.43	410,887
Central-South 中南	27	1,050	140,877	4,724	2.90	9.48	134.22	69.38	162,836
Henan 河南	7	2,630	319,386	17,367	4.48	19.13	121.45	76.60	387,987
Hubei 湖北	3	357	81,440	-4,353	-5.37	-16.18	227.91	66.80	81,060
Hunan 湖南	1	591	47,920	1,330	4.87	72.68	81.08	93.30	27,330
Guangdong 廣東	12	522	78,178	2,214	2.56	5.12	149.65	50.07	86,628
Guangxi 廣西	4	500	84,405	-2,213	-2.39	-8.12	168.81	70.60	92,658
Hainan 海南									
Southwest 西南	12	310	22,824	-1,368	-5.92	-27.52	73.59	78.48	23,092
Chongqing 重慶	4	590	47,433	-636	-1.33	-6.35	80.31	79.01	47,672
Sichuan 四川	6	124	8,953	2,603	31.29	142.03	71.69	77.97	8,318
Guizhou 貴州									
Yunnan 雲南	1	377	12,610	-1,480	-7.74	-30.39	33.45	74.52	19,110
Tibet 西藏									
Northwest 西北	3	435	3,817	-700	-6.57	-75.81	8.78	91.34	10,660
Shaanxi 陝西	2	81	1,610	-200	-3.80	-114.29	20.00	96.68	5,270
Gansu 甘肅	1	1,143	8,230	-1,700	-7.93	-70.25	7.20	88.71	21,440
Qinghai 青海									
Ningxia 寧夏									
Xinjiang 新疆									

1442: Gourmet Powder 味精製造業

Year 年份	Number of firms 企業個數	Rate of change 每年變化 (%)	Number of employees 職工人數 (人)	Rate of change 每年變化 (%)	Total revenue (mil. RMB) 總銷售收入 (百萬元)	Rate of change 每年變化 (%)	Total profit (mil. RMB) 總利潤 (百萬元)	Rate of change 每年變化 (%)
1993	124		70,152		4,407		24	
1994	115	-7.26%	52,362	-25.36%	5,125	16.29%	109	356.53%
1995	127	10.43%	77,523	48.05%	7,659	49.43%	494	352.59%
1996	110	-13.39%	78,291	0.99%	7,994	4.37%	224	-54.67%

3 Major products* 3 種主要產品 *	Output 產量	Sales volume 銷售量	Unit 單位
a) Flavor Essence 味精	461,315	461,315	ton 噸

Top 10 firms by revenue (year founded) 收入排名前 10 家企業 (創辦年份)	City 城市	Province 省	Telephone / fax 電話 / 傳真	Number of employees 職工人數	Ownership 產業所有權	Revenue ('000 RMB) 銷售收入 (千元)	Profit ('000 RMB) (rank) 利潤 (千元) (排名)	Total assets ('000 RMB) 總資產 (千元)	Major products 主要產品
Ling Hua Group Co. 菱花集團公司(1979)	Jining 濟寧市	Shandong 山東省	(0537)2080655 (0537)2080657	6,200	Collectively-owned 集體	805,494	59998(1)	2,301,215	a
Guangzhou Ao Sang Monosodium Glutamate Food Co. Ltd. 廣州奧桑味精食品有限公司(1995)	Guangzhou 廣州市	Guangdong 廣東省	(020)84318368 (020)84300974	795	Foreign-funded 外資	322,591	16381(5)	313,403	a
Jiangsu Chrysanthemum Monosodium Glutamate Group Co. 江蘇菊花味精集團公司(1978)	Suzhou 蘇州市	Jiangsu 江蘇省	(0512)8480406 (0512)8480585	2,071	Collectively-owned 集體	312,340	12689(6)	238,376	a
Shanghai Tianchu Monosodium Glutamate Plant 上海天廚味精廠(1923)	Shanghai 上海市	Shanghai 上海市	(021)62411080 (021)62747347	911	State-owned 國有	301,401	2405(14)	166,294	a
Q.f.g.c.(limited) 泉州中僑(集團)股份有限公司(1992)	Quanzhou 泉州市	Fujian 福建省	(0595)2183914 (0595)2184258	9,088	Foreign-funded 外資	278,715	9524(7)	652,609	a
Shenyang Monosodium Glutamate Plant 瀋陽味精廠(1939)	Shenyang 瀋陽市	Liaoning 遼寧省	(024)25820297 (024)25820297	2,269	State-owned 國有	274,368	4504(12)	464,636	o
Xing Hu Monosodium Glutamate Co. Ltd. 肇慶星湖味精股份有限公司(1992)	Zhaoqing 肇慶市	Guangdong 廣東省	(0757)2227048 (0757)2239449	1,823	Joint stock 股份制	207,570	30870(2)	288,160	a
Hangzhou Feng Hui Fermentation Co. Ltd. 杭州豐匯發酵有限公司(1992)	Hangzhou 杭州市	Zhejiang 浙江省	(0571)6064795 (0571)6064336	821	Overseas Chinese-funded 港澳台資	203,612	20683(4)	126,321	a
Wuhan Wei Quan Food Co. Ltd. 武漢味全食品有限公司(1995)	Wuhan 武漢市	Hubei 湖北省	(027)84847929 (027)84846233	644	Foreign-funded 外資	177,354	-16918(81)	195,310	a
Chiping San Jiu Monosodium Glutamate Co. Ltd. 茌平縣三九味精有限公司(1978)	Liaocheng 聊城市	Shandong 山東省	(0635)4271455 (0635)4271650	853	State-owned 國有	162,946	25393(3)	132,823	a

Top 10 Cities by Production Output 產出排名前 10 位城市	Province 省	Market share 市場份額	Number of firms 企業個數
Zhoukou 周口市	Henan 河南省	36.27%	4
Jining 濟寧市	Shandong 山東省	8.69%	1
Suzhou 蘇州市	Jiangsu 江蘇省	4.89%	4
Zhaoqing 肇慶市	Guangdong 廣東省	4.80%	2
Hangzhou 杭州市	Zhejiang 浙江省	4.58%	5
Guangzhou 廣州市	Guangdong 廣東省	4.12%	1
Shenyang 瀋陽市	Liaoning 遼寧省	3.49%	2
Wuhan 武漢市	Hubei 湖北省	3.13%	2
Chongqing 重慶市	Chongqing 重慶市	1.93%	4
Wenzhou 溫州市	Zhejiang 浙江省	1.85%	3

10 Major Wholesalers 10 家主要批發商	City 城市	Province 省	Telephone / Fax 電話 / 傳真
Guangdong Meizhou Salt Industry General Company 廣東省梅州鹽業總公司	Meizhou 梅州市	Guangdong 廣東省	(0752)2234242 (0752)2234720
Shannxi Import & Export Company 陝西省進出口公司	Xi'an 西安市	Shaanxi 陝西省	(029)7424946 (029)7420131
Fujian Salt Industry Company 福建省鹽業公司	Fuzhou 福州市	Fujian 福建省	(0591)7535047 (0591)7535047
Sichuan Salt Industry Company Zigong Branch 四川省鹽業公司自貢分公司	Zigong 自貢市	Sichuan 四川省	(0813)2203215 (0813)2203215
Shanghai Shi Liu Pu Non-staple Food Trade Company 上海市十六鋪副食品貿易公司	Shanghai 上海市	Shanghai 上海市	(021)63736787
Shandong Salt Industry General Company Shandong Salt Administration Bureau 山東省鹽業總公司山東省鹽務局	Ji'nan 濟南市	Shandong 山東省	(0531)6925633 (0531)6925021
Yunnan Salt Industry General Company 雲南省鹽業總公司	Kunming 昆明市	Yunnan 雲南省	(0871)3166719
Shanghai Jia Le Condiment Mill Marketing Company 上海家樂調味食品銷售公司	Shanghai 上海市	Shanghai 上海市	(021)59139194
Zhong Yan Shanghai Salt Company 中鹽上海鹽業公司	Shanghai 上海市	Shanghai 上海市	(021)62180345 (021)62187068
Zhejiang Salt Industry Company 浙江省鹽業公司	Hangzhou 杭州市	Zhejiang 浙江省	(0571)7800292 (0571)7800292

*Also include sales by firms outside this industry.包括本行業以外廠家的銷售。"o" stands for "others". "o" 代表 "其他產品"。

1443: Citric Acid 檸檬酸製造業

The industry accounts for 0.018% of the total revenue of China's industrial sector in 1996. The revenue growth rate of the industry is -3.3% from 1995, as compared to the growth rate of China's industrial sector, 9.51%. The rate of return on asset is -3.07%. 53.51% of all firms in the industry made a profit while 40.43% had negative returns. The top province in terms of the industry's revenue is Jiangsu, accounting for 31.15% of the total revenue.
本行業在1996年佔全行業總產值0.018%，行業年增長率為-3.3%（全國工業年增長率9.51%）。行業的資產回報率-3.07%，53.51%的企業盈利，40.43%的企業虧損。銷售收入最高的省份為江蘇省，佔本行業的31.15%。

	Total number of firms 企業總數	Total number of employees 職工總數	Total revenue (mil. RMB) 總銷售收入（百萬元）	Total profit (mil. RMB) 總利潤（百萬元）	Return on assets 資產利潤率 (%)	Return on equity 權益利潤率 (%)	Labour productivity ('000 RMB / worker) 勞動生產率（千元/人）	Debts / assets 資產負債率 (%)	Total assets (mil. RMB) 總資產（百萬元）
Industry Overall 行業總體	51	16,086	1,068	-79	-3.07	-15.12	66.39	79.70	2,561

	Number of firms 企業個數	Average number of employees 平均職工人數	Average revenue ('000 RMB) 平均銷售收入（千元）	Average profit ('000 RMB) 平均利潤（千元）	Return on assets 資產利潤率 (%)	Return on equity 權益利潤率 (%)	Labour productivity ('000 RMB / worker) 勞動生產率（千元/人）	Average debts / assets 平均資產負債率(%)	Average Total assets ('000 RMB) 平均總資產（千元）
By ownership 產業所有權									
State-owned 國有	24	357	16,875	-2,208	-4.83	-81.54	47.26	94.08	45,750
Collectively-owned 集體	15	338	25,099	-1,561	-3.64	-13.63	74.26	73.26	42,822
Privately-owned 私有									
Domestic JVs 聯營	3	58	1,783	1,155	34.27	111.80	30.75	69.35	3,371
Joint stock 股份制	1	428	17,131				40.03	87.82	61,289
Foreign-funded 外資	4	124	1,605	1,035	8.25	21.19	12.97	61.06	12,550
Overseas Chinese-funded 港澳台資	5	341	51,526	-2,036	-1.46	-4.02	151.19	63.80	139,841
By size 規模									
Large 大型	4	919	65,745	-7,313	-5.01	-34.90	71.52	85.65	145,971
Medium 中型	16	417	34,253	-471	-0.69	-4.44	82.17	84.51	68,450
Small 小型	28	208	9,178	-1,508	-4.79	-15.84	44.03	69.78	31,501
By regional distribution 地區分布									
Central-North 華北	10	215	16,735	1,409	5.74	13.14	77.95	56.30	24,536
Beijing 北京									
Tianjin 天津									
Hebei 河北	7	264	22,121	1,971	6.15	13.92	83.88	55.82	32,054
Shanxi 山西	3	100	4,167	97	1.38	3.58	41.53	61.44	6,993
Inner Mongolia 內蒙									
Northeast 東北	2	119	4,390	-100	-0.31	-0.94	37.05	66.81	32,120
Liaoning 遼寧									
Jilin 吉林									
Heilongjiang 黑龍江	2	119	4,390	-100	-0.31	-0.94	37.05	66.81	32,120
Central East 華東	17	401	34,925	-1,228	-1.68	-6.53	87.13	74.27	73,046
Shanghai 上海	1	614	43,970	-9,580	-12.39	-28.70	71.61	56.81	77,290
Jiangsu 江蘇	8	384	41,591	-1,208	-1.75	-7.42	108.28	76.45	69,070
Zhejiang 浙江	1	335	31,120	610	3.10	5.38	92.90	42.41	19,690
Anhui 安徽	3	426	38,793	480	0.46	1.57	91.06	70.70	104,560
Fujian 福建									
Jiangxi 江西									
Shandong 山東	4	379	17,380	-920	-1.32	-6.99	45.92	81.09	69,643
Central-South 中南	16	352	16,006	-2,886	-5.89	-73.02	45.49	91.94	49,022
Henan 河南	3	458	17,243	-5,853	-8.46	-376.02	37.62	97.75	69,180
Hubei 湖北	5	257	9,270	-252	-0.43	-2.50	36.13	82.99	59,252
Hunan 湖南	3	694	33,853	-6,413	-13.62	92.01	48.80	114.81	47,100
Guangdong 廣東	2								
Guangxi 廣西	2	320	28,225	-4,055	-5.82	-27.88	88.20	79.11	69,625
Hainan 海南	1	250							
Southwest 西南	2	248	6,275	-6,365	-18.06	-71.48	25.30	74.73	35,245
Chongqing 重慶					-12.40		10.76	112.40	
Sichuan 四川									
Guizhou 貴州									
Yunnan 雲南	2	248	6,275	-6,365	-18.06	-71.48	25.30	74.73	35,245
Tibet 西藏									
Northwest 西北	4	191	7,295	-3,190	-8.24	139.61	38.24	105.90	38,715
Shaanxi 陝西	2	103		-220	-8.15	13.02		162.59	2,700
Gansu 甘肅									
Qinghai 青海									
Ningxia 寧夏	2	279	14,590	-6,160	-8.24	213.89	52.39	103.85	74,730
Xinjiang 新疆									

1443: Citric Acid 檸檬酸製造業

Year 年份	Number of firms 企業個數	Rate of change 每年變化 (%)	Number of employees 職工人數 (人)	Rate of change 每年變化 (%)	Total revenue (mil. RMB) 總銷售收入 (百萬元)	Rate of change 每年變化 (%)	Total profit (mil. RMB) 總利潤 (百萬元)	Rate of change 每年變化 (%)
1993	56		20,004		947		40	
1994	61	8.93%	21,397	6.96%	1,242	31.24%	-27	-167.73%
1995	62	1.64%	22,314	4.29%	1,104	-11.16%	-54	-100.36%
1996	51	-17.74%	16,086	-27.91%	1,068	-3.26%	-79	-46.07%

3 Major products* 3 種主要產品 *	Output 產量	Sales volume 銷售量	Unit 單位
a) Citric Acid 檸檬酸	116,037	103,273	ton 噸

Top 10 firms by revenue (year founded) 收入排名前 10 家企業 (創辦年份)	City 城市	Province 省	Telephone / fax 電話 / 傳真	Number of employees 職工人數	Ownership 產業所有權	Revenue ('000 RMB) 銷售收入 (千元)	Profit ('000 RMB) (rank) 利潤 (千元) (排名)	Total assets ('000 RMB) 總資產 (千元)	Major products 主要產品
Wuxi Zhong Ya Chemical Co. Ltd. 無錫市中亞化學有限公司(1993)	Wuxi 無錫市	Jiangsu 江蘇省	(0510)5408888 (0510)5409300	564	Overseas Chinese-funded 港澳台資	136,671	2646(4)	344,610	a
Baoding Citric Acid Plant 保定市檸檬酸廠(1990)	Baoding 保定市	Hebei 河北省	(0312)7031609	430	Overseas Chinese-funded 港澳台資	108,000	16100(1)	129,540	o
Ningxiang Petrochemical General Factory 寧鄉縣石油化工總廠(1955)	Changsha 長沙市	Hunan 湖南省	(0731)7882919 (0731)7882731	1,879	Collectively-owned 集體	100,479	-19137(33)	127,774	a
Bbci 安徽省蚌埠檸檬酸廠(1970)	Bengbu 蚌埠市	Anhui 安徽省	(0552)4096486 (0552)4072216	646	State-owned 國有	88,354	4053(3)	233,776	a
Nantong Citric Acid Factory 南通檸檬酸廠(1984)	Nantong 南通市	Jiangsu 江蘇省	(0513)5531069 (0513)5537829	610	State-owned 國有	68,623	-1220(21)	74,589	a
Industry & Trade Joint Venture Lianyungang Citric Acid Plant 工貿合營連雲港市檸檬酸廠(1966)	Lianyungang 連雲港市	Jiangsu 江蘇省	(0518)5430692 (0518)5430016	668	Collectively-owned 集體	55,657	-3466(25)	62,809	a
Nanning Citric Acid Co. Ltd. 南寧檸檬酸有限公司(1988)	Nanning 南寧市	Guangxi 廣西	(0771)3133658 (0771)3134332	317	Overseas Chinese-funded 港澳台資	52,115	207(11)	63,108	a
Shanghai Jin Yi Food Co. Ltd. 上海金益食品有限公司(1958)	Shanghai 上海市	Shanghai 上海市	(021)59529938 (021)59155152	550	Foreign-funded 外資	43,967	-9577(30)	77,289	a
Linyi Citric Acid Plant 臨沂檸檬酸廠(1988)	Linyi 臨沂市	Shandong 山東省	(0539)8891140 (0539)8891140	248	Collectively-owned 集體	38,214	8500(2)	118,112	a
Hangzhou Fang Da Biochemistry Co. Ltd. 杭州方大生化有限公司(1993)	Hangzhou 杭州市	Zhejiang 浙江省	(0571)8541856	353	Overseas Chinese-funded 港澳台資	31,117	612(6)	19,688	a

Top 10 Cities by Production Output 產出排名前 10 位城市	Province 省	Market share 市場份額	Number of firms 企業個數
Wuxi 無錫市	Jiangsu 江蘇省	11.79%	1
Baoding 保定市	Hebei 河北省	11.73%	2
Bengbu 蚌埠市	Anhui 安徽省	11.62%	3
Changsha 長沙市	Hunan 湖南省	9.15%	1
Nantong 南通市	Jiangsu 江蘇省	8.04%	3
Lianyungang 連雲港市	Jiangsu 江蘇省	7.64%	2
Shanghai 上海市	Shanghai 上海市	6.43%	4
Xuchang 許昌市	Henan 河南省	5.28%	3
Linyi 臨沂市	Shandong 山東省	3.81%	1
Hangzhou 杭州市	Zhejiang 浙江省	3.15%	1

10 Major Wholesalers 10 家主要批發商	City 城市	Province 省	Telephone / Fax 電話 / 傳真
Guangdong Meizhou Salt Industry General Company 廣東省梅州鹽業總公司	Meizhou 梅州市	Guangdong 廣東省	(0752)2234242 (0752)2234720
Shannxi Import & Export Company 陝西省進出口公司	Xi'an 西安市	Shaanxi 陝西省	(029)7424946 (029)7420131
Fujian Salt Industry Company 福建省鹽業公司	Fuzhou 福州市	Fujian 福建省	(0591)7535047 (0591)7535047
Sichuan Salt Industry Company Zigong Branch 四川省鹽業公司自貢分公司	Zigong 自貢市	Sichuan 四川省	(0813)2203215 (0813)2203215
Shanghai Shi Liu Pu Non-staple Food Trade Company 上海市十六鋪副食品貿易公司	Shanghai 上海市	Shanghai 上海市	(021)63736787
Shandong Salt Industry General Company Shandong Salt Administration Bureau 山東省鹽業總公司山東省鹽務局	Ji'nan 濟南市	Shandong 山東省	(0531)6925633 (0531)6925021
Yunnan Salt Industry General Company 雲南省鹽業總公司	Kunming 昆明市	Yunnan 雲南省	(0871)3166719
Shanghai Jia Le Condiment Mill Marketing Company 上海家樂調味食品銷售公司	Shanghai 上海市	Shanghai 上海市	(021)59139194
Zhong Yan Shanghai Salt Company 中鹽上海鹽業公司	Shanghai 上海市	Shanghai 上海市	(021)62180345 (021)62187068
Zhejiang Salt Industry Company 浙江省鹽業公司	Hangzhou 杭州市	Zhejiang 浙江省	(0571)7800292 (0571)7800292

*Also include sales by firms outside this industry.包括本行業以外廠家的銷售。"o" stands for "others". "o" 代表 "其他產品"。

1444: Yeast Products 酵母製造業

The industry accounts for 0.011% of the total revenue of China's industrial sector in 1996. The revenue growth rate of the industry is 80.5% from 1995, as compared to the growth rate of China's industrial sector, 9.51%. The rate of return on asset is 2.18%. 77.22% of all firms in the industry made a profit while 19.75% had negative returns. The top province in terms of the industry's revenue is Shandong, accounting for 23.02% of the total revenue.
本行業在1996年佔全行業總產值0.011%，行業年增長率為80.5%（全國工業年增長率9.51%）。行業的資產回報率2.18%，77.22%的企業盈利，19.75%的企業虧損。銷售收入最高的省份為山東省，佔本行業的23.02%。

	Total number of firms 企業總數	Total number of employees 職工總數	Total revenue (mil. RMB) 總銷售收入（百萬元）	Total profit (mil. RMB) 總利潤（百萬元）	Return on assets 資產利潤率 (%)	Return on equity 權益利潤率 (%)	Labour productivity ('000 RMB / worker) 勞動生產率（千元/人）	Debts / assets 資產負債率 (%)	Total assets (mil. RMB) 總資產（百萬元）
Industry Overall 行業總體	92	7,229	628	20	2.18	5.50	86.87	60.36	896

	Number of firms 企業個數	Average number of employees 平均職工人數	Average revenue ('000 RMB) 平均銷售收入（千元）	Average profit ('000 RMB) 平均利潤（千元）	Return on assets 資產利潤率 (%)	Return on equity 權益利潤率 (%)	Labour productivity ('000 RMB / worker) 勞動生產率（千元/人）	Average debts / assets 平均資產負債率(%)	Average Total assets ('000 RMB) 平均總資產（千元）
By ownership 產業所有權									
State-owned 國有	16	148	9,438	250	0.88	2.92	63.79	69.89	28,438
Collectively-owned 集體	64	62	4,492	-4,651	-183.79	-644.57	72.89	71.49	2,531
Privately-owned 私有	1	58	17,321	-14,154	-385.43	-1318.66	298.63	70.77	3,672
Domestic JVs 聯營	3	69	4,169	2,930	54.33	156.54	60.42	65.29	5,394
Joint stock 股份制	1	84	21,669	-440	-1.71	-5.63	257.96	69.63	25,724
Foreign-funded 外資	3	173	24,398	106,901	252.36	264.83	141.30	4.71	42,361
Overseas Chinese-funded 港澳台資	4	81	16,196	-308	-1.16	-3.40	199.95	65.95	26,576
By size 規模									
Large 大型	1	485	108,785	4,545	2.43	8.06	224.30	69.82	186,902
Medium 中型	3	365	10,782	-405,960	-1548.28	-2489.85	29.51	37.82	26,220
Small 小型	87	64	5,596	14,176	195.64	493.98	87.80	60.40	7,246
By regional distribution 地區分布									
Central-North 華北	19	34	3,932	247	5.27	8.62	116.73	38.86	4,686
Beijing 北京	2	27	2,825	65	1.62	14.61	106.60	88.90	4,010
Tianjin 天津	1	40	1,880	180	4.01	5.16	47.00	22.27	4,490
Hebei 河北	14	35	4,619	251	4.76	7.08	131.69	32.75	5,264
Shanxi 山西	2	28	1,260	435	30.85	177.55	45.00	82.62	1,410
Inner Mongolia 內蒙									
Northeast 東北	11	83	2,403	-116	-1.41	-3.83	29.04	63.02	8,226
Liaoning 遼寧	4	36	748	-730	-13.18	-77.25	20.76	82.89	5,538
Jilin 吉林	5	108	1,982	-22	-0.23	-1.03	18.42	78.15	9,730
Heilongjiang 黑龍江	2	114	6,765	875	8.89	9.19	59.34	3.30	9,845
Central East 華東	26	134	12,247	300	2.93	6.88	91.16	57.45	10,256
Shanghai 上海	4	242	9,210	-825	-3.82	-8.51	38.06	55.07	21,588
Jiangsu 江蘇	2	122	8,220	185	2.39	14.29	67.38	83.30	7,725
Zhejiang 浙江	5	40	9,814	114	5.35	23.65	246.58	77.39	2,132
Anhui 安徽	4	78	16,375	315	7.15	8.14	209.94	12.20	4,408
Fujian 福建	4	63	1,505	20	0.74	2.08	23.89	64.48	2,710
Jiangxi 江西									
Shandong 山東	7	217	20,649	1,261	7.02	17.54	95.22	59.95	17,961
Central-South 中南	21	81	8,509	404	2.06	6.13	105.23	66.31	19,580
Henan 河南	8	69	3,116	180	3.33	10.23	44.92	67.45	5,404
Hubei 湖北	3	187	32,640	2,233	3.64	13.31	174.55	72.64	61,323
Hunan 湖南	1	9							
Guangdong 廣東	5	88	10,624	20	0.06	0.14	120.73	60.12	35,914
Guangxi 廣西	3	37	463	40	3.77	6.03	12.64	37.74	1,060
Hainan 海南	1	23	1,320	130	10.66	25.00	57.39	57.38	1,220
Southwest 西南	11	30	2,168	17	2.34	6.71	72.94	65.10	737
Chongqing 重慶	1	43	1,432	63	6.11	19.68	32.76	68.94	1,034
Sichuan 四川	4	16	588	-43	-18.41	-81.71	35.50	77.47	235
Guizhou 貴州	1	12							
Yunnan 雲南	4	46	4,828	15	1.05	2.74	106.10	61.85	1,435
Tibet 西藏									
Northwest 西北	4	40	1,500	-83	-1.07	-2.62	37.27	59.14	7,698
Shaanxi 陝西	1	20	870	20	3.39	15.38	43.50	77.97	590
Gansu 甘肅	3	47	1,710	-117	-1.16	-2.81	36.38	58.77	10,067
Qinghai 青海									
Ningxia 寧夏									
Xinjiang 新疆									

1444: Yeast Products 酵母製造業

Year 年份	Number of firms 企業個數	Rate of change 每年變化 (%)	Number of employees 職工人數（人）	Rate of change 每年變化 (%)	Total revenue (mil. RMB) 總銷售收入（百萬元）	Rate of change 每年變化 (%)	Total profit (mil. RMB) 總利潤（百萬元）	Rate of change 每年變化 (%)
1993	81		9,548		454		25	
1994	107	32.10%	8,397	-12.06%	517	13.88%	5	-81.44%
1995	95	-11.22%	7,131	-15.08%	348	-32.67%	0	-98.58%
1996	92	-3.16%	7,229	1.37%	628	80.51%	20	30203.03%

3 Major products* 3 種主要產品 *	Output 產量	Sales volume 銷售量	Unit 單位
a) Fermentum 酵母	7,014	7,084	ton 噸
b) Ferment Pretaration 製劑	10,008	9,007	ton 噸

Top 10 firms by revenue (year founded) 收入排名前 10 家企業（創辦年份）	City 城市	Province 省	Telephone / fax 電話 / 傳真	Number of employees 職工人數	Ownership 產業所有權	Revenue ('000 RMB) 銷售收入（千元）	Profit ('000 RMB) (rank) 利潤（千元）（排名）	Total assets ('000 RMB) 總資產（千元）	Major products 主要產品
Shandong Shouguang Hua Bao Foods Group Co. 山東壽光華寶實業有限公司(1993)	Weifang 濰坊市	Shandong 山東省	(0536)5411069 (0536)5411069	1,198	Collectively-owned 集體	120,527	7518(1)	100,272	o
Mengcheng Hubin Dehydration Vegetables Food Company San Yi Branch 蒙城縣湖濱脫水蔬菜食品公司三義分公司(1995)	Fuyang 阜陽市	Anhui 安徽省	(0558)7791091	154	Overseas Chinese-funded 港澳台資	63,120	1080(6)	14,040	o
Jiangmen Center for Biotech Development 江門生物技術開發中心(1988)	Jiangmen 江門市	Guangdong 廣東省	(0750)3793525 (0750)3793404	376	State-owned 國有	47,569	99(18)	170,420	b
Shangyu Malt Factory 上虞市麥芽廠(1988)	Shaoxing 紹興市	Zhejiang 浙江省	(0575)2051485	18	Collectively-owned 集體	39,001	600(11)	2,200	o
Hebei Malt Co. Ltd. 河北麥芽有限責任公司(1996)	Tangshan 唐山市	Hebei 河北省	(0315)2012347	114	Collectively-owned 集體	21,000	1400(5)	13,468	o
Shanghai Zhang Ze Ferment Products Factory 上海張澤酵母製品廠(1989)	Shanghai 上海市	Shanghai 上海市	(021)57881289	124	Collectively-owned 集體	20,725	3147(2)	10,626	o
Zhejiang Deqing Jiang Lin Feed Ferment Protein Co. Ltd. 浙江省德清縣江林飼料酵母蛋白有限公司(1983)	Huzhou 湖州市	Zhejiang 浙江省	(0572)8444392	45	Joint stock 股份制	20,269	82(19)	4,145	o
Lingbao San Bao Group Co. Ltd. 靈寶市三寶集團股份有限公司(1974)	Sanmenxia 三門峽市	Henan 河南省	(0398)8667084 (0398)8663197	379	Joint stock 股份制	18,818	1481(4)	30,006	o
Jiangchuan Yeast & Drink General Factory 江川縣酵曲飲料總廠(1979)	Yuxi 玉溪市	Yunnan 雲南省	(0877)8091238	215	Collectively-owned 集體	18,340	11(25)	5,051	a
Shanghai Mauri Foods Co. Ltd. 上海馬利食品有限公司(1993)	Shanghai 上海市	Shanghai 上海市	(021)62593760 (021)62744895	206	Foreign-funded 外資	16,116	-6447(33)	43,806	a

Top 10 Cities by Production Output 產出排名前 10 位城市	Province 省	Market share 市場份額	Number of firms 企業個數
Guangzhou 廣州市	Guangdong 廣東省	14.05%	2
Yichang 宜昌市	Hubei 湖北省	12.36%	2
Harbin 哈爾濱市	Heilongjiang 黑龍江省	9.25%	2
Jiangmen 江門市	Guangdong 廣東省	8.69%	2
Weifang 濰坊市	Shandong 山東省	7.76%	2
Lanzhou 蘭州市	Gansu 甘肅省	7.09%	2
Huzhou 湖州市	Zhejiang 浙江省	4.31%	2
Shanghai 上海市	Shanghai 上海市	4.17%	4
Sanmenxia 三門峽市	Henan 河南省	3.34%	1
Yuxi 玉溪市	Yunnan 雲南省	3.26%	1

10 Major Wholesalers 10 家主要批發商	City 城市	Province 省	Telephone / Fax 電話 / 傳真
Guangdong Meizhou Salt Industry General Company 廣東省梅州鹽業總公司	Meizhou 梅州市	Guangdong 廣東省	(0752)2234242 (0752)2234720
Shannxi Import & Export Company 陝西省進出口公司	Xi'an 西安市	Shaanxi 陝西省	(029)7424946 (029)7420131
Fujian Salt Industry Company 福建省鹽業公司	Fuzhou 福州市	Fujian 福建省	(0591)7535047 (0591)7535047
Sichuan Salt Industry Company Zigong Branch 四川省鹽業公司自貢分公司	Zigong 自貢市	Sichuan 四川省	(0813)2203215 (0813)2203215
Shanghai Shi Liu Pu Non-staple Food Trade Company 上海市十六鋪副食品貿易公司	Shanghai 上海市	Shanghai 上海市	(021)63736787
Shandong Salt Industry General Company Shandong Salt Administration Bureau 山東省鹽業總公司山東省鹽務局	Ji'nan 濟南市	Shandong 山東省	(0531)6925633 (0531)6925021
Yunnan Salt Industry General Company 雲南省鹽業總公司	Kunming 昆明市	Yunnan 雲南省	(0871)3166719
Shanghai Jia Le Condiment Mill Marketing Company 上海家樂調味食品銷售公司	Shanghai 上海市	Shanghai 上海市	(021)59139194
Zhong Yan Shanghai Salt Company 中鹽上海鹽業公司	Shanghai 上海市	Shanghai 上海市	(021)62180345 (021)62187068
Zhejiang Salt Industry Company 浙江省鹽業公司	Hangzhou 杭州市	Zhejiang 浙江省	(0571)7800292 (0571)7800292

*Also include sales by firms outside this industry.包括本行業以外廠家的銷售。"o" stands for "others". "o" 代表"其他產品"。

1445: Enzyme Preparations 酶製劑製造業

The industry accounts for 0.009% of the total revenue of China's industrial sector in 1996. The revenue growth rate of the industry is -1.9% from 1995, as compared to the growth rate of China's industrial sector, 9.51%. The rate of return on asset is -2.89%. 60.52% of all firms in the industry made a profit while 25.97% had negative returns. The top province in terms of the industry's revenue is Jiangsu, accounting for 35.72% of the total revenue.
本行業在1996年佔全行業總產值0.009%，行業年增長率為-1.9%（全國工業年增長率9.51%）。行業的資產回報率-2.89%，60.52%的企業盈利，25.97%的企業虧損。銷售收入最高的省份為江蘇省，佔本行業的35.72%。

	Total number of firms 企業總數	Total number of employees 職工總數	Total revenue (mil. RMB) 總銷售收入（百萬元）	Total profit (mil. RMB) 總利潤（百萬元）	Return on assets 資產利潤率 (%)	Return on equity 權益利潤率 (%)	Labour productivity ('000 RMB / worker) 勞動生產率（千元／人）	Debts / assets 資產負債率 (%)	Total assets (mil. RMB) 總資產（百萬元）
Industry Overall 行業總體	85	9,623	499	-26	-2.89	-16.90	51.85	82.88	900

	Number of firms 企業個數	Average number of employees 平均職工人數	Average revenue ('000 RMB) 平均銷售收入（千元）	Average profit ('000 RMB) 平均利潤（千元）	Return on assets 資產利潤率 (%)	Return on equity 權益利潤率 (%)	Labour productivity ('000 RMB / worker) 勞動生產率（千元／人）	Average debts / assets 平均資產負債率(%)	Average Total assets ('000 RMB) 平均總資產（千元）
By ownership 產業所有權									
State-owned 國有	29	151	4,276	-828	-10.81	342.86	28.30	103.15	7,655
Collectively-owned 集體	43	80	4,375	-28	-0.37	-3.90	54.94	90.45	7,502
Privately-owned 私有									
Domestic JVs 聯營	1								
Joint stock 股份制	1	58	1,293	1	0.07	0.23	22.29	67.34	1,325
Foreign-funded 外資	10	163	18,503	-82	-0.23	-0.64	113.72	63.41	35,111
Overseas Chinese-funded 港澳台資	1	132	513	22	0.76	1.69	3.89	55.10	2,911
By size 規模									
Large 大型	1	435	102,349	-1,386	-0.90	-2.69	235.28	66.44	153,437
Medium 中型	3	285	11,100	150	0.81	9.94	38.95	91.80	18,417
Small 小型	80	105	4,542	-313	-3.63	-25.59	43.19	85.83	8,641
By regional distribution 地區分布									
Central-North 華北	14	138	4,920	76	0.92	3.33	35.65	72.33	8,299
Beijing 北京	4	52	4,980	140	2.67	11.52	95.31	76.85	5,248
Tianjin 天津	3	36							
Hebei 河北	3	301	11,330				37.68	76.63	20,327
Shanxi 山西	1	202	2,600				12.87	70.49	13,760
Inner Mongolia 內蒙	3	170	4,123	170	2.49	5.68	24.25	56.11	6,820
Northeast 東北	10	116	3,315	-253	-3.62	30.74	28.58	111.77	6,994
Liaoning 遼寧	1	92	10				0.11	251.11	3,600
Jilin 吉林	5	161	4,990	-296	-3.02	-56.49	30.96	94.65	9,800
Heilongjiang 黑龍江	4	66	2,048	-263	-6.06	19.41	31.26	131.20	4,335
Central East 華東	21	166	13,116	-1,141	-4.48	-19.47	78.95	76.97	25,447
Shanghai 上海	1	18	1,250	70	10.45	43.75	69.44	76.12	670
Jiangsu 江蘇	6	230	29,703	-470	-0.83	-2.70	129.33	69.18	56,468
Zhejiang 浙江	5	59	2,424	-414	-6.92	-87.34	40.95	92.04	5,980
Anhui 安徽	2	323	5,000	-9,855	-64.90	80.22	15.50	180.90	15,185
Fujian 福建	2	31						4.08	2,085
Jiangxi 江西									
Shandong 山東	5	218	14,770	114	0.44	1.55	67.69	71.86	26,092
Central-South 中南	26	81	3,598	51	0.93	32.60	44.36	97.15	5,511
Henan 河南	9	88	2,563	33	0.88	7.32	29.17	87.97	3,787
Hubei 湖北	4	150	9,815	138	0.87	-10.07	65.32	108.66	15,770
Hunan 湖南	4	154	5,155	15	0.20	2.26	33.53	91.17	7,530
Guangdong 廣東	5	15	1,722	68	2.17	12.27	111.82	82.30	3,130
Guangxi 廣西	4	6	500	20	22.86	800.00	80.00	97.14	88
Hainan 海南									
Southwest 西南	13	65	1,583	-173	-7.75	-113.07	24.41	93.18	2,234
Chongqing 重慶		63	817	4	0.42	1.72	12.92	75.46	1,063
Sichuan 四川	9	68	1,828	-248	-11.82	-9687.49	26.69	99.88	2,097
Guizhou 貴州									
Yunnan 雲南	3	56	1,073				19.28	80.91	3,003
Tibet 西藏									
Northwest 西北	1	90	7,100	280	4.07	28.57	78.89	85.76	6,880
Shaanxi 陝西	1	90	7,100	280	4.07	28.57	78.89	85.76	6,880
Gansu 甘肅									
Qinghai 青海									
Ningxia 寧夏									
Xinjiang 新疆									

1445: Enzyme Preparations 酶製劑製造業

Year 年份	Number of firms 企業個數	Rate of change 每年變化 (%)	Number of employees 職工人數 (人)	Rate of change 每年變化 (%)	Total revenue (mil. RMB) 總銷售收入 (百萬元)	Rate of change 每年變化 (%)	Total profit (mil. RMB) 總利潤 (百萬元)	Rate of change 每年變化 (%)
1993	75		11,301		276		-7	
1994	78	4.00%	10,865	-3.86%	369	33.79%	-17	-133.42%
1995	95	21.79%	12,534	15.36%	508	37.79%	-11	36.01%
1996	85	-10.53%	9,623	-23.22%	499	-1.86%	-26	-133.29%

3 Major products* 3種主要產品*	Output 產量	Sales volume 銷售量	Unit 單位
a) Ferment Pretaration 酶製劑	153,251	137,926	ton 噸
b) Biochemical 生化藥	1,643	1,577	ton 噸
c) Fermentum 酵母	4,726	4,774	ton 噸

Top 10 firms by revenue (year founded) 收入排名前10家企業 (創辦年份)	City 城市	Province 省	Telephone / fax 電話 / 傳真	Number of employees 職工人數	Ownership 產業所有權	Revenue ('000 RMB) 銷售收入 (千元)	Profit ('000 RMB) (rank) 利潤 (千元) (排名)	Total assets ('000 RMB) 總資產 (千元)	Major products 主要產品
Wuxi Synder Bio-products Co. Ltd. 無錫星達生物工程有限公司(1993)	Wuxi 無錫市	Jiangsu 江蘇省	(0510)3709751 (0510)3709726	553	Foreign-funded 外資	106,843	311(6)	163,889	a
Li Shi Malt Factory 李市麥芽廠	Jingmen 荊門市	Hubei 湖北省		200	Collectively-owned 集體	34,992	360(4)	50,361	o
Shandong Yishui Fermented Preparation Factory 山東省沂水縣酶製劑廠(1976)	Linyi 臨沂市	Shandong 山東省	(0539)2251063 (0539)2251063	524	Collectively-owned 集體	28,450	5(21)	55,427	a
Jiang Yin Synder Bio-products Co. Ltd. 江陰市星達生物工程有限公司(1992)	Wuxi 無錫市	Jiangsu 江蘇省	(0510)6521706 (0510)6521265	196	Foreign-funded 外資	24,201	2561(1)	55,133	o
Hebei Xingtai Fermented Preparation Works 河北省邢台市酶製劑廠(1953)	Xingtai 邢臺市	Hebei 河北省	(0319)3037466	467	State-owned 國有	22,266	26(18)	34,667	o
Anqiu Fermented Preparation Factory 安丘市酶製劑廠(1990)	Weifang 濰坊市	Shandong 山東省	(0536)4611134 (0536)4611134	110	Collectively-owned 集體	18,720	500(2)	6,869	a
Jiangsu Suzhou Hong Da Zhi Mei Co. Ltd. 江蘇蘇州宏達製酶有限公司(1995)	Suzhou 蘇州市	Jiangsu 江蘇省	(0512)3211506 (0512)3211506	131	Foreign-funded 外資	17,540	-2570(36)	51,980	a
Jilin Ji Fa Agriculture Development Group Co. Ltd. 吉林省吉發農業開發集團股份有限公司(1991)	Siping 四平市	Jilin 吉林省	(0434)6812288	160	Joint stock 股份制	17,206	115(13)	32,177	o
Yantai Fermentation Factory 煙台發酵廠(1985)	Yantai 煙台市	Shandong 山東省	(0535)6362614 (0535)6362614	232	Collectively-owned 集體	16,623	9(20)	55,675	a,c
Yixing Bioengineering Co. 宜興市生物工程公司(1993)	Wuxi 無錫市	Jiangsu 江蘇省	(0510)7281625 (0510)7281625	160	Collectively-owned 集體	14,778	-2200(35)	34,352	a

Top 10 Cities by Production Output 產出排名前10位城市	Province 省	Market share 市場份額	Number of firms 企業個數
Wuxi 無錫市	Jiangsu 江蘇省	35.32%	7
Weifang 濰坊市	Shandong 山東省	5.58%	1
Linyi 臨沂市	Shandong 山東省	5.37%	1
Yantai 煙台市	Shandong 山東省	4.81%	2
Changde 常德市	Hunan 湖南省	4.18%	3
Xingtai 邢臺市	Hebei 河北省	4.06%	1
Siping 四平市	Jilin 吉林省	3.56%	1
Beijing 北京市	Beijing 北京市	3.19%	4
Zhuhai 珠海市	Guangdong 廣東省	2.85%	1
Zhangye 張掖市	Gansu 甘肅省	2.75%	1

10 Major Wholesalers 10家主要批發商	City 城市	Province 省	Telephone / Fax 電話 / 傳真
Guangdong Meizhou Salt Industry General Company 廣東省梅州鹽業總公司	Meizhou 梅州市	Guangdong 廣東省	(0752)2234242 (0752)2234720
Shannxi Import & Export Company 陝西省進出口公司	Xi'an 西安市	Shaanxi 陝西省	(029)7424946 (029)7420131
Fujian Salt Industry Company 福建省鹽業公司	Fuzhou 福州市	Fujian 福建省	(0591)7535047 (0591)7535047
Sichuan Salt Industry Company Zigong Branch 四川省鹽業公司自貢分公司	Zigong 自貢市	Sichuan 四川省	(0813)2203215 (0813)2203215
Shanghai Shi Liu Pu Non-staple Food Trade Company 上海市十六鋪副食品貿易公司	Shanghai 上海市	Shanghai 上海市	(021)63736787
Shandong Salt Industry General Company Shandong Salt Administration Bureau 山東省鹽業總公司山東省鹽務局	Ji'nan 濟南市	Shandong 山東省	(0531)6925633 (0531)6925021
Yunnan Salt Industry General Company 雲南省鹽業總公司	Kunming 昆明市	Yunnan 雲南省	(0871)3166719
Shanghai Jia Le Condiment Mill Marketing Company 上海家樂調味食品銷售公司	Shanghai 上海市	Shanghai 上海市	(021)59139194
Zhong Yan Shanghai Salt Company 中鹽上海鹽業公司	Shanghai 上海市	Shanghai 上海市	(021)62180345 (021)62187068
Zhejiang Salt Industry Company 浙江省鹽業公司	Hangzhou 杭州市	Zhejiang 浙江省	(0571)7800292 (0571)7800292

*Also include sales by firms outside this industry.包括本行業以外廠家的銷售。"o" stands for "others". "o" 代表 "其他產品"。

1449: Other Fermented Products 其他發酵製品業

The industry accounts for 0.008% of the total revenue of China's industrial sector in 1996. The revenue growth rate of the industry is -32.8% from 1995, as compared to the growth rate of China's industrial sector, 9.51%. The rate of return on asset is 0.61%. 82.32% of all firms in the industry made a profit while 15.05% had negative returns. The top province in terms of the industry's revenue is Henan, accounting for 22.19% of the total revenue.
本行業在1996年佔全行業總產值0.008%，行業年增長率為-32.8%（全國工業年增長率9.51%）。行業的資產回報率0.61%，82.32%的企業盈利，15.05%的企業虧損。銷售收入最高的省份為河南省，佔本行業的22.19%。

	Total number of firms 企業總數	Total number of employees 職工總數	Total revenue (mil. RMB) 總銷售收入（百萬元）	Total profit (mil. RMB) 總利潤（百萬元）	Return on assets 資產利潤率 (%)	Return on equity 權益利潤率 (%)	Labour productivity ('000 RMB / worker) 勞動生產率（千元/人）	Debts / assets 資產負債率 (%)	Total assets (mil. RMB) 總資產（百萬元）
Industry Overall 行業總體	85	5,876	438	5	0.61	2.64	74.54	76.70	760

	Number of firms 企業個數	Average number of employees 平均職工人數	Average revenue ('000 RMB) 平均銷售收入（千元）	Average profit ('000 RMB) 平均利潤（千元）	Return on assets 資產利潤率 (%)	Return on equity 權益利潤率 (%)	Labour productivity ('000 RMB / worker) 勞動生產率（千元/人）	Average debts / assets 平均資產負債率(%)	Average Total assets ('000 RMB) 平均總資產（千元）
By ownership 產業所有權									
State-owned 國有	13	163	8,308	154	0.78	2.63	50.92	70.54	19,846
Collectively-owned 集體	62	49	3,971	15	0.25	2.16	80.91	88.30	5,946
Privately-owned 私有	1	26	1,644	2	0.09	1.97	63.23	95.46	1,787
Domestic JVs 聯營	1	364	56,046	1,915	2.79	5.60	153.97	50.18	68,572
Joint stock 股份制	2	32	1,012	-3	-0.03	-0.08	32.12	65.39	11,334
Foreign-funded 外資	3	33	2,942	13	0.25	0.30	90.05	17.26	5,464
Overseas Chinese-funded 港澳台資	3	54	5,083	40	0.50	5.39	94.71	90.70	7,966
By size 規模									
Large 大型									
Medium 中型	4	246	19,727	9	0.02	0.27	80.19	91.22	40,051
Small 小型	77	63	4,663	64	0.83	3.05	74.59	72.84	7,789
By regional distribution 地區分布									
Central-North 華北	20	68	3,714	-292	-6.40	150.52	54.73	104.23	4,561
Beijing 北京	3		560	17	1.50	20.00		92.19	1,110
Tianjin 天津	2	8	330	185	22.42	115.63	41.25	80.00	825
Hebei 河北	14	77	4,664	-447	-8.40	191.44	60.40	104.39	5,324
Shanxi 山西	1	260	6,640				25.54	110.09	11,700
Inner Mongolia 內蒙									
Northeast 東北	4	36	290	-15	-0.35	-2.58	8.11	86.57	4,338
Liaoning 遼寧	1								
Jilin 吉林	1	30	60	-60	-6.98	100.00	2.00	106.98	860
Heilongjiang 黑龍江	2	57	550				9.73	85.51	8,245
Central East 華東	19	84	11,032	435	3.42	8.52	130.92	59.91	12,745
Shanghai 上海	5	96	15,880	776	3.38	5.89	166.11	42.54	22,948
Jiangsu 江蘇	3	115	27,500	197	1.07	5.71	239.13	81.28	18,397
Zhejiang 浙江									
Anhui 安徽	5	82	8,116	640	9.38	45.07	99.46	79.19	6,824
Fujian 福建	1								
Jiangxi 江西	1	70	2,200	40	4.17	7.69	31.43	45.83	960
Shandong 山東	4	75	1,233	140	1.51	4.24	16.43	64.46	9,285
Central-South 中南	21	101	6,283	188	1.53	5.79	62.27	73.51	12,263
Henan 河南	10	166	9,719	77	0.46	6.15	58.73	92.53	16,765
Hubei 湖北	2	116	3,860	975	2.69	3.79	33.28	29.11	36,255
Hunan 湖南	1	16	2,230	340	680.00	850.00	139.38	20.00	50
Guangdong 廣東	5	27	3,632	142	8.82	30.21	133.53	70.81	1,610
Guangxi 廣西	3	27	2,213	60	1.94	9.52	83.00	79.59	3,087
Hainan 海南									
Southwest 西南	6	11	350	-127	-25.50	-271.43	33.33	90.60	497
Chongqing 重慶	4	12	453	190	26.03	281.38	37.75	90.75	730
Sichuan 四川									
Guizhou 貴州	1								
Yunnan 雲南	1	15	290				19.33	83.33	60
Tibet 西藏									
Northwest 西北	15	40	1,276	-59	-0.59	-6.78	32.28	91.26	9,890
Shaanxi 陝西	2	49	965	70	2.44	6.17	19.69	60.45	2,870
Gansu 甘肅	9	10	677	23	1.18	5.59	64.79	78.91	1,981
Qinghai 青海									
Ningxia 寧夏	1	54	6,820	-660	-5.50	-23.91	126.30	77.02	12,010
Xinjiang 新疆	3	116	1,433	-190	-0.51	-13.60	12.39	96.29	37,590

1449: Other Fermented Products 其他發酵製品業

Year 年份	Number of firms 企業個數	Rate of change 每年變化 (%)	Number of employees 職工人數（人）	Rate of change 每年變化 (%)	Total revenue (mil. RMB) 總銷售收入（百萬元）	Rate of change 每年變化 (%)	Total profit (mil. RMB) 總利潤（百萬元）	Rate of change 每年變化 (%)
1993	41		1,880		117		0	
1994	68	65.85%	5,702	203.30%	348	198.07%	0	-47.43%
1995	87	27.94%	8,918	56.40%	652	87.50%	51	23646.98%
1996	85	-2.30%	5,876	-34.11%	438	-32.83%	5	-90.21%

3 Major products* 3 種主要產品 *	Output 產量	Sales volume 銷售量	Unit 單位
a) Food Additive 食品添加劑	128,250	123,120	ton 噸
b) Fermentum 酵母	2,341	2,365	ton 噸

Top 10 firms by revenue (year founded) 收入排名前 10 家企業（創辦年份）	City 城市	Province 省	Telephone / fax 電話 / 傳真	Number of employees 職工人數	Ownership 產業所有權	Revenue ('000 RMB) 銷售收入（千元）	Profit ('000 RMB) (rank) 利潤（千元）（排名）	Total assets ('000 RMB) 總資產（千元）	Major products 主要產品
Dongtai Hua Long Industrial Company 東台市華龍實業公司(1992)	Yancheng 鹽城市	Jiangsu 江蘇省	(0515)5630441	235	Collectively-owned 集體	60,250	380(11)	29,800	o
Dancheng Jin Dan Lactic Acid Industrial Co. Ltd. 鄲城縣金丹乳酸實業有限公司(1984)	Zhoukou 周口市	Henan 河南省	(0394)3222255	885	State-owned 國有	40,311	49(24)	63,744	a
Shanghai Jtu Only Biological Products Co. Ltd. 上海交大昂立生物製品有限公司(1990)	Shanghai 上海市	Shanghai 上海市	(021)57833414 (021)64685582	345	Domestic JVs 聯營	31,832	493(8)	70,493	o
Shanghai Shen Guang Edible Chemical Products Factory 上海申光食用化學品廠(1994)	Shanghai 上海市	Shanghai 上海市	(021)57586363	53	Collectively-owned 集體	25,420	2301(2)	25,532	a
Jiaozuo Zhongyuan Malt Factory 焦作市中原麥芽廠(1993)	Jiaozuo 焦作市	Henan 河南省	(0391)2622755	94	State-owned 國有	22,964	2(32)	28,805	o
Cheng'an Hui Huang Malt Factory 成安縣輝煌麥芽廠(1994)	Handan 邯鄲市	Hebei 河北省	(0310)7216215	58	Collectively-owned 集體	21,021	1348(5)	8,430	o
Henan Zhumadian Malt Factory 河南省駐馬店市麥芽廠(1987)	Zhumadian 駐馬店市	Henan 河南省	(0396)2812258 (0396)2817855	160	Collectively-owned 集體	14,920	192(20)	51,236	o
Changli Great Wall Malt Factory 昌黎縣長城麥芽廠(1994)	Qinhuangdao 秦皇島市	Hebei 河北省	(0335)2046354	70	Collectively-owned 集體	14,220	404(9)	8,378	o
Shanghai Shen Wan Brewing Co. Ltd. 上海申萬釀造有限公司(1991)	Shanghai 上海市	Shanghai 上海市	(021)56601263 (021)56601075	56	Foreign-funded 外資	14,029	1006(6)	15,867	o
Yancheng Bian Cang Malt Factory 鹽城市便倉麥芽廠(1986)	Yancheng 鹽城市	Jiangsu 江蘇省	(0515)8830306	70	Collectively-owned 集體	12,150	10(30)	13,350	o

Top 10 Cities by Production Output 產出排名前 10 位城市	Province 省	Market share 市場份額	Number of firms 企業個數
Guangzhou 廣州市	Guangdong 廣東省	16.22%	2
Shanghai 上海市	Shanghai 上海市	13.68%	7
Zhoukou 周口市	Henan 河南省	7.65%	1
Jiaozuo 焦作市	Henan 河南省	6.04%	2
Yancheng 鹽城市	Jiangsu 江蘇省	5.78%	2
Shuangcheng 雙城市	Heilongjiang 黑龍江省	5.69%	1
Qinhuangdao 秦皇島市	Hebei 河北省	5.23%	6
Handan 邯鄲市	Hebei 河北省	4.90%	2
Shenzhen 深圳市	Guangdong 廣東省	4.72%	1
Beijing 北京市	Beijing 北京市	3.81%	4

10 Major Wholesalers 10 家主要批發商	City 城市	Province 省	Telephone / Fax 電話 / 傳真
Guangdong Meizhou Salt Industry General Company 廣東省梅州鹽業總公司	Meizhou 梅州市	Guangdong 廣東省	(0752)2234242 (0752)2234720
Shannxi Import & Export Company 陝西省進出口公司	Xi 惊 n 西安市	Shaanxi 陝西省	(029)7424946 (029)7420131
Fujian Salt Industry Company 福建省鹽業公司	Fuzhou 福州市	Fujian 福建省	(0591)7535047 (0591)7535047
Sichuan Salt Industry Company Zigong Branch 四川省鹽業公司自貢分公司	Zigong 自貢市	Sichuan 四川省	(0813)2203215 (0813)2203215
Shanghai Shi Liu Pu Non-staple Food Trade Company 上海市十六鋪副食品貿易公司	Shanghai 上海市	Shanghai 上海市	(021)63736787
Shandong Salt Industry General Company Shandong Salt Administration Bureau 山東省鹽業總公司山東省鹽務局	Ji 減 an 濟南市	Shandong 山東省	(0531)6925633 (0531)6925021
Yunnan Salt Industry General Company 雲南省鹽業總公司	Kunming 昆明市	Yunnan 雲南省	(0871)3166719
Shanghai Jia Le Condiment Mill Marketing Company 上海家樂調味食品銷售公司	Shanghai 上海市	Shanghai 上海市	(021)59139194
Zhong Yan Shanghai Salt Company 中鹽上海鹽業公司	Shanghai 上海市	Shanghai 上海市	(021)62180345 (021)62187068
Zhejiang Salt Industry Company 浙江省鹽業公司	Hangzhou 杭州市	Zhejiang 浙江省	(0571)7800292 (0571)7800292

*Also include sales by firms outside this industry.包括本行業以外廠家的銷售。"o" stands for "others". "o" 代表 "其他產品"。

1451: Soy-sauce and Sauce 醬油、醬類製造業

The industry accounts for 0.113% of the total revenue of China's industrial sector in 1996. The revenue growth rate of the industry is 31.6% from 1995, as compared to the growth rate of China's industrial sector, 9.51%. The rate of return on asset is 0.70%. 60.94% of all firms in the industry made a profit while 29.12% had negative returns. The top province in terms of the industry's revenue is Guangdong, accounting for 21.62% of the total revenue.
本行業在1996年佔全行業總產值0.113%，行業年增長率為31.6%（全國工業年增長率9.51%）。行業的資產回報率0.70%，60.94%的企業盈利，29.12%的企業虧損。銷售收入最高的省份為廣東省，佔本行業的21.62%。

	Total number of firms 企業總數	Total number of employees 職工總數	Total revenue (mil. RMB) 總銷售收入（百萬元）	Total profit (mil. RMB) 總利潤（百萬元）	Return on assets 資產利潤率 (%)	Return on equity 權益利潤率 (%)	Labour productivity ('000 RMB / worker) 勞動生產率（千元/人）	Debts / assets 資產負債率 (%)	Total assets (mil. RMB) 總資產（百萬元）
Industry Overall 行業總體	2,047	159,061	6,540	64	0.70	1.81	41.12	61.20	9,100

	Number of firms 企業個數	Average number of employees 平均職工人數	Average revenue ('000 RMB) 平均銷售收入（千元）	Average profit ('000 RMB) 平均利潤（千元）	Return on assets 資產利潤率 (%)	Return on equity 權益利潤率 (%)	Labour productivity ('000 RMB / worker) 勞動生產率（千元/人）	Average debts / assets 平均資產負債率(%)	Average Total assets ('000 RMB) 平均總資產（千元）
By ownership 產業所有權									
State-owned 國有	952	118	3,499	-34	-0.53	-1.36	29.70	60.60	6,289
Collectively-owned 集體	1,012	40	2,328	-291	-14.23	-42.45	57.86	66.47	2,044
Privately-owned 私有	5	32	1,727	3,696	216.55	254.76	53.29	15.00	1,707
Domestic JVs 聯營	9	32	1,062	837	91.12	189.08	33.67	51.81	919
Joint stock 股份制	10	105	4,040	1,841	48.82	151.02	38.41	67.67	3,771
Foreign-funded 外資	37	79	9,027	12,503	75.29	184.30	114.19	59.15	16,608
Overseas Chinese-funded 港澳台資	22	103	20,554	-5,084	-29.98	-55.16	199.90	45.65	16,957
By size 規模									
Large 大型	4	1,313	141,302	-2,603	-1.39	-3.60	107.66	61.37	187,382
Medium 中型	28	565	38,221	-438	-0.96	-2.44	67.67	60.62	45,662
Small 小型	2,000	69	2,452	43	1.23	3.17	35.52	61.28	3,536
By regional distribution 地區分布									
Central-North 華北	223	88	2,605	-2	-0.04	-0.11	29.47	58.64	4,353
Beijing 北京	32	128	5,987	62	0.87	2.25	46.84	61.32	7,114
Tianjin 天津	20	165	5,137	81	0.97	2.02	31.12	51.93	8,312
Hebei 河北	90	85	2,187	6	0.13	0.32	25.87	58.11	4,171
Shanxi 山西	19	70	2,088	22	0.69	1.51	29.99	54.66	3,222
Inner Mongolia 內蒙	62	55	808	-80	-3.52	-10.17	14.77	65.38	2,263
Northeast 東北	308	80	1,830	-25	-0.83	-1.80	22.76	53.93	2,974
Liaoning 遼寧	95	110	2,629	-40	-0.75	-1.57	23.88	51.80	5,285
Jilin 吉林	67	89	1,983	-36	-1.35	-3.53	22.15	61.83	2,672
Heilongjiang 黑龍江	146	57	1,241	-10	-0.60	-1.25	21.78	52.47	1,610
Central East 華東	640	85	4,175	92	1.66	3.94	49.25	57.83	5,541
Shanghai 上海	17	199	21,855	744	2.51	5.08	109.73	50.66	29,664
Jiangsu 江蘇	171	83	2,873	-40	-0.85	-2.19	34.49	61.01	4,727
Zhejiang 浙江	54	95	4,855	72	1.11	2.33	50.85	52.38	6,489
Anhui 安徽	117	48	1,678	41	2.17	7.67	34.96	71.73	1,889
Fujian 福建	69	32	1,329	-4	-0.18	-0.34	40.91	45.70	2,272
Jiangxi 江西	96	38	656	-8	-0.65	-3.19	17.07	79.55	1,231
Shandong 山東	116	172	10,309	393	3.29	7.69	60.03	57.26	11,958
Central-South 中南	400	84	5,151	100	1.77	6.15	61.16	71.30	5,637
Henan 河南	96	72	1,922	-67	-2.14	-7.54	26.88	71.58	3,114
Hubei 湖北	76	137	2,961	54	1.51	4.96	21.57	69.57	3,602
Hunan 湖南	79	42	1,434	16	0.69	1.74	34.44	60.35	2,252
Guangdong 廣東	96	105	14,731	527	4.05	16.37	140.31	75.26	13,012
Guangxi 廣西	48	55	2,537	-157	-3.16	-8.01	46.33	60.54	4,971
Hainan 海南	5	79	314	-432	-13.23	-42.86	3.96	69.08	3,266
Southwest 西南	369	56	1,430	-51	-1.89	-5.23	25.72	63.85	2,681
Chongqing 重慶	55	75	1,860	-59	-1.66	-4.31	24.53	61.62	3,555
Sichuan 四川	198	59	1,553	-55	-1.98	-6.35	26.14	68.85	2,792
Guizhou 貴州	63	30	698	-7	-0.40	-0.87	22.99	54.48	1,683
Yunnan 雲南	51	53	1,413	-78	-3.01	-6.50	26.54	53.69	2,579
Tibet 西藏	1								
Northwest 西北	107	57	1,263	-77	-1.96	-4.00	22.06	51.13	3,957
Shaanxi 陝西	55	55	1,195	-51	-1.50	-2.62	21.83	42.81	3,385
Gansu 甘肅	23	40	965	-70	-2.58	-5.81	24.07	55.48	2,708
Qinghai 青海	9	48	1,084	-14	-0.77	-1.68	22.70	53.96	1,868
Ningxia 寧夏	4	105	2,903	-70	-1.16	-1.96	27.78	40.67	6,013
Xinjiang 新疆	16	84	1,614	-217	-2.59	-6.85	19.23	62.18	8,378

1451: Soy-sauce and Sauce 醬油、醬類製造業

Year 年份	Number of firms 企業個數	Rate of change 每年變化 (%)	Number of employees 職工人數 (人)	Rate of change 每年變化 (%)	Total revenue (mil. RMB) 總銷售收入 (百萬元)	Rate of change 每年變化 (%)	Total profit (mil. RMB) 總利潤 (百萬元)	Rate of change 每年變化 (%)
1993	2,026		146,677		3,786		-2	
1994	2,083	2.81%	151,970	3.61%	4,003	5.71%	-24	-907.23%
1995	2,179	4.61%	162,746	7.09%	4,968	24.10%	-77	-221.75%
1996	2,047	-6.06%	159,061	-2.26%	6,540	31.64%	64	183.01%

3 Major products* 3 種主要產品 *	Output 產量	Sales volume 銷售量	Unit 單位
a) Soy Sauce 醬油	2,634,764	2,318,592	ton 噸
b) Paste 醬	129,121	99,423	ton 噸
c) Table Vinegar 食醋	780,502	725,867	ton 噸

Top 10 firms by revenue (year founded) 收入排名前 10 家企業 (創辦年份)	City 城市	Province 省	Telephone / fax 電話 / 傳真	Number of employees 職工人數	Ownership 產業所有權	Revenue ('000 RMB) 銷售收入 (千元)	Profit ('000 RMB) (rank) 利潤 (千元) (排名)	Total assets ('000 RMB) 總資產 (千元)	Major products 主要產品
Heze Sand Brewing Factory 菏澤市沙土釀造廠(1980)	Heze 菏澤市	Shandong 山東省	(0530)5770034 (0530)5770558	4,126	Foreign-funded 外資	669,227	41488(1)	450,323	a,c
Shi Hai Tian Condiment Mill Co. Ltd. 市海天調味食品有限公司(1955)	Foshan 佛山市	Guangdong 廣東省	(0757)2831099 (0757)2831099	1,013	Joint stock 股份制	466,557	35235(2)	292,958	a,b,c
Kaiping Wei Shi Da Condiment Co. Ltd. 開平市味事達調味品有限公司(1996)	Jiangmen 江門市	Guangdong 廣東省	(0750)2287751 (0750)2299038	942	Foreign-funded 外資	176,602	617(45)	173,318	a
Jammy Chai (Guangzhou) Foods Co. Ltd. 廣州致美齋食品有限公司(1992)	Guangzhou 廣州市	Guangdong 廣東省	(020)86624314 (020)86625141	577	Overseas Chinese-funded 港澳台資	155,393	17032(4)	105,391	a,b,c
Shanghai Seaguall Fermentation Co. 上海海鷗釀造公司(1861)	Shanghai 上海市	Shanghai 上海市	(021)62661417 (021)62661417	1,699	State-owned 國有	142,328	34145(3)	223,095	a,b,c
Zhongshan Delicious Food Fresh Food General Factory 中山市美味鮮食品總廠(1956)	Zhongshan 中山市	Guangdong 廣東省	(0760)8620393 (0760)8637834	478	State-owned 國有	79,015	1306(13)	34,574	a,b,c
Shanghai Ding Feng Foods Brewing General Factory 上海鼎豐釀造食品總廠(1864)	Shanghai 上海市	Shanghai 上海市	(021)57420320 (021)57420320	440	Collectively-owned 集體	77,931	481(54)	73,576	a,b,c
Shanghai Hua Nan Lao Cai Food Industrial Co. Ltd. 上海華南老蔡食品工業有限公司(1994)	Shanghai 上海市	Shanghai 上海市	(021)57241777 (021)57241406	310	Overseas Chinese-funded 港澳台資	77,479	-4495(489)	62,852	o
Nanjing Brewing (Group) Company 南京市釀造(集團)公司(1996)	Nanjing 南京市	Jiangsu 江蘇省	(025)3728991 (025)3738895	1,851	State-owned 國有	76,299	7(305)	175,347	a,b,c
Guangzhou Meiweiyuan Foods Products Factory 廣州市美味源食品廠(1987)	Guangzhou 廣州市	Guangdong 廣東省	(020)84768321 (020)84769012	263	State-owned 國有	74,769	4409(5)	78,444	a,b

Top 10 Cities by Production Output 產出排名前 10 位城市	Province 省	Market share 市場份額	Number of firms 企業個數
Shanghai 上海市	Shanghai 上海市	9.01%	34
Foshan 佛山市	Guangdong 廣東省	8.90%	5
Guangzhou 廣州市	Guangdong 廣東省	7.65%	21
Jiangmen 江門市	Guangdong 廣東省	3.76%	4
Beijing 北京市	Beijing 北京市	3.31%	30
Tianjin 天津市	Tianjin 天津市	2.17%	25
Zhongshan 中山市	Guangdong 廣東省	1.97%	3
Heze 菏澤市	Shandong 山東省	1.95%	9
Chengdu 成都市	Sichuan 四川省	1.60%	37
Hangzhou 杭州市	Zhejiang 浙江省	1.46%	11

10 Major Wholesalers 10 家主要批發商	City 城市	Province 省	Telephone / Fax 電話 / 傳真
Guangdong Meizhou Salt Industry General Company 廣東省梅州鹽業總公司	Meizhou 梅州市	Guangdong 廣東省	(0752)2234242 (0752)2234720
Shannxi Import & Export Company 陝西省進出口公司	Xi'an 西安市	Shaanxi 陝西省	(029)7424946 (029)7420131
Fujian Salt Industry Company 福建省鹽業公司	Fuzhou 福州市	Fujian 福建省	(0591)7535047 (0591)7535047
Sichuan Salt Industry Company Zigong Branch 四川省鹽業公司自貢分公司	Zigong 自貢市	Sichuan 四川省	(0813)2203215 (0813)2203215
Shanghai Shi Liu Pu Non-staple Food Trade Company 上海市十六鋪副食品貿易公司	Shanghai 上海市	Shanghai 上海市	(021)63736787
Shandong Salt Industry General Company Shandong Salt Administration Bureau 山東省鹽業總公司山東省鹽務局	Ji'nan 濟南市	Shandong 山東省	(0531)6925633 (0531)6925021
Yunnan Salt Industry General Company 雲南省鹽業總公司	Kunming 昆明市	Yunnan 雲南省	(0871)3166719
Shanghai Jia Le Condiment Mill Marketing Company 上海家樂調味食品銷售公司	Shanghai 上海市	Shanghai 上海市	(021)59139194
Zhong Yan Shanghai Salt Company 中鹽上海鹽業公司	Shanghai 上海市	Shanghai 上海市	(021)62180345 (021)62187068
Zhejiang Salt Industry Company 浙江省鹽業公司	Hangzhou 杭州市	Zhejiang 浙江省	(0571)7800292 (0571)7800292

*Also include sales by firms outside this industry.包括本行業以外廠家的銷售。"o" stands for "others". "o" 代表"其他產品"。

1452: Vinegar 食醋製造業

The industry accounts for 0.009% of the total revenue of China's industrial sector in 1996. The revenue growth rate of the industry is 9.2% from 1995, as compared to the growth rate of China's industrial sector, 9.51%. The rate of return on asset is 3.33%. 60.71% of all firms in the industry made a profit while 28.42% had negative returns. The top province in terms of the industry's revenue is Jiangsu, accounting for 28.57% of the total revenue.
本行業在1996年佔全行業總產值0.009%，行業年增長率為9.2%（全國工業年增長率9.51%）。行業的資產回報率3.33%，60.71%的企業盈利，28.42%的企業虧損。銷售收入最高的省份為江蘇省，佔本行業的28.57%。

	Total number of firms 企業總數	Total number of employees 職工總數	Total revenue (mil. RMB) 總銷售收入（百萬元）	Total profit (mil. RMB) 總利潤（百萬元）	Return on assets 資產利潤率 (%)	Return on equity 權益利潤率 (%)	Labour productivity ('000 RMB / worker) 勞動生產率（千元/人）	Debts / assets 資產負債率 (%)	Total assets (mil. RMB) 總資產（百萬元）
Industry Overall 行業總體	310	14,564	532	25	3.33	8.90	36.53	62.55	749

	Number of firms 企業個數	Average number of employees 平均職工人數	Average revenue ('000 RMB) 平均銷售收入（千元）	Average profit ('000 RMB) 平均利潤（千元）	Return on assets 資產利潤率 (%)	Return on equity 權益利潤率 (%)	Labour productivity ('000 RMB / worker) 勞動生產率（千元/人）	Average debts / assets 平均資產負債率(%)	Average Total assets ('000 RMB) 平均總資產（千元）
By ownership 產業所有權									
State-owned 國有	113	78	2,434	168	4.33	10.50	31.12	58.77	3,885
Collectively-owned 集體	186	28	1,176	30	2.24	9.49	41.51	76.37	1,360
Privately-owned 私有	1	11	120	-72	-13.61	-37.97	10.92	64.16	526
Domestic JVs 聯營	2	29	1,701	149	13.00	15.74	59.69	17.40	1,148
Joint stock 股份制	2	10	784	90	10.34	12.72	78.36	18.72	866
Foreign-funded 外資	3	76	4,079	-43	-0.30	-0.38	53.44	21.29	14,239
Overseas Chinese-funded 港澳台資	3	46	6,889	17	0.54	1.69	148.67	68.16	3,232
By size 規模									
Large 大型									
Medium 中型	1	623	85,754	26,894	40.19	49.20	137.65	18.31	66,912
Small 小型	307	45	1,453	-6	-0.28	-0.84	32.06	66.82	2,221
By regional distribution 地區分布									
Central-North 華北	82	53	1,619	53	2.11	5.44	30.71	61.11	2,526
Beijing 北京	6	86	3,773	42	2.18	4.59	44.05	52.53	1,913
Tianjin 天津	5	122	5,864	742	6.08	8.82	47.99	31.03	12,202
Hebei 河北	17	33	745	32	2.93	7.24	22.27	59.59	1,086
Shanxi 山西	48	53	1,383	-5	-0.19	-0.93	26.15	79.15	2,371
Inner Mongolia 內蒙	6	15	300	17	4.27	5.49	19.57	22.22	390
Northeast 東北	30	56	1,026	-66	-3.53	-355.36	18.25	98.99	1,881
Liaoning 遼寧	19	47	966	-73	-3.82	-63.18	20.66	93.92	1,913
Jilin 吉林	4	125	1,178	-123	-5.06	9.23	9.42	154.86	2,420
Heilongjiang 黑龍江	7	43	1,101	-16	-1.06	-3.00	25.87	64.71	1,486
Central East 華東	37	83	5,945	678	9.40	19.10	71.58	50.79	7,218
Shanghai 上海									
Jiangsu 江蘇	14	122	10,857	1,668	13.31	23.86	89.25	44.19	12,529
Zhejiang 浙江	2	18	1,490	30	2.06	17.65	85.14	88.32	1,455
Anhui 安徽	10	35	1,225	83	6.68	17.58	35.20	62.00	1,242
Fujian 福建	2	74	7,250	120	1.75	5.16	97.97	66.13	6,865
Jiangxi 江西	5	103	608	-22	-1.41	-4.31	5.89	67.22	1,556
Shandong 山東	4	81	8,800	183	1.33	3.44	108.98	61.20	13,700
Central-South 中南	37	25	1,421	13	0.81	3.84	56.24	78.93	1,637
Henan 河南	17	28	1,138	36	2.17	8.01	40.23	72.88	1,679
Hubei 湖北	4	68	6,415	215	4.74	27.56	94.69	82.79	4,533
Hunan 湖南	5	17	420	-36	-5.77	-24.00	24.71	75.96	624
Guangdong 廣東	8	12	654	-96	-7.83	-57.46	53.37	86.38	1,230
Guangxi 廣西	3		80	-13	-4.30	21.05		120.43	310
Hainan 海南									
Southwest 西南	32	49	1,489	1	0.04	0.17	30.54	76.06	1,514
Chongqing 重慶	3	39	249	1	0.24	1.20	6.27	79.98	380
Sichuan 四川	20	64	2,161	-4	-0.18	-0.78	33.32	76.92	2,063
Guizhou 貴州	6	9	292	8	3.31	9.26	32.41	64.24	252
Yunnan 雲南	2	23	545	25	1.37	4.50	23.70	69.59	1,825
Tibet 西藏									
Northwest 西北	92	32	520	-32	-2.70	-6.77	16.02	60.10	1,194
Shaanxi 陝西	28	27	251	-4	-0.64	-1.46	9.14	55.82	610
Gansu 甘肅	38	39	804	-6	-0.38	-0.88	20.87	57.29	1,465
Qinghai 青海	7	44	703	-107	-6.82	-27.08	15.97	74.80	1,570
Ningxia 寧夏	5	21	150	-86	-8.46	-14.38	7.08	41.14	1,016
Xinjiang 新疆	14	24	326	-105	-7.00	-21.81	13.48	67.90	1,500

1452: Vinegar 食醋製造業

Year 年份	Number of firms 企業個數	Rate of change 每年變化 (%)	Number of employees 職工人數（人）	Rate of change 每年變化 (%)	Total revenue (mil. RMB) 總銷售收入（百萬元）	Rate of change 每年變化 (%)	Total profit (mil. RMB) 總利潤（百萬元）	Rate of change 每年變化 (%)
1993	236		11,961		307		9	
1994	283	19.92%	14,265	19.26%	335	9.15%	10	1.77%
1995	334	18.02%	17,437	22.24%	487	45.38%	10	1.35%
1996	310	-7.19%	14,564	-16.48%	532	9.16%	25	155.99%

3 Major products* 3 種主要產品 *	Output 產量	Sales volume 銷售量	Unit 單位
a) Table Vinegar 食醋	318,469	296,177	ton 噸
b) Soy Sauce 醬油	60,378	53,133	ton 噸
c) Paste 醬	2,528	1,947	ton 噸

Top 10 firms by revenue (year founded) 收入排名前 10 家企業 (創辦年份)	City 城市	Province 省	Telephone / fax 電話 / 傳真	Number of employees 職工人數	Ownership 產業所有權	Revenue ('000 RMB) 銷售收入（千元）	Profit ('000 RMB) (rank) 利潤（千元）(排名)	Total assets ('000 RMB) 總資產（千元）	Major products 主要產品
Zhenjiang Heng Shun Soy Sauce & Vinegar Factory 鎮江恒順醬醋廠(1840)	Zhenjiang 鎮江市	Jiangsu 江蘇省	(0511)5233758 (0511)5230209	743	State-owned 國有	109,675	21953(1)	136,199	a,b,c
Sichuan Bao Ning Vinegar Co. Ltd. 四川保寧醋有限公司(1954)	Nanchong 南充市	Sichuan 四川省	(0817)623209	504	Collectively-owned 集體	22,069	452(9)	19,932	a,b
Tianjin Du Liu Old Vinegar Factory 天津市天立獨流老醋有限責任公司(1984)	Tianjin 天津市	Tianjin 天津市	(022)8815122 (022)8816107	334	Collectively-owned 集體	20,935	2752(2)	46,528	a,b
Beijing Longmen Vinegar Factory 北京市龍門醋廠(1820)	Beijing 北京市	Beijing 北京市	(010)63521184	158	State-owned 國有	15,460	95(22)	8,994	a,c
Shanxi Yuci Huairen Industrial Company 山西省榆次市懷仁工業公司(1991)	Yuci 榆次市	Shanxi 山西省	(0354)2773017	295	Collectively-owned 集體	12,694	-458(46)	15,313	a,b
Yongchun Shunde Tang Condiment Factory 永春縣順德堂調味品廠(1992)	Quanzhou 泉州市	Fujian 福建省	(0595)3883374 (0595)3883374	30	Collectively-owned 集體	12,000	230(15)	8,250	o
Shandong Wang Cun Brewing Co. Ltd. 山東王村釀造股份有限公司(1977)	Zibo 淄博市	Shandong 山東省	(0533)6680061 (0533)6680061	90	Joint stock 股份制	11,144	135(19)	12,769	a
Jiangsu Land Reclamation & Cultivation Heng He Brewing General Factory 江蘇省農墾恒河釀造總廠(1986)	Huaiyin 淮陰市	Jiangsu 江蘇省	(0517)8511135 (0517)8511475	370	State-owned 國有	11,040	2043(3)	15,586	a,b
Ji'nan Lu Xing Vinegar Factory 濟南市魯興醋廠(1979)	Ji'nan 濟南市	Shandong 山東省	(0531)5954985	44	Collectively-owned 集體	10,223	523(6)	7,440	a
Guanyun Ban Pu Zhen Wang Shu You Di Vinegar Company 灌雲縣板浦鎮汪恕有滴醋公司(1956)	Lianyungang 連雲港市	Jiangsu 江蘇省	(0518)8362141	98	Collectively-owned 集體	9,568	310(12)	2,807	a

Top 10 Cities by Production Output 產出排名前 10 位城市	Province 省	Market share 市場份額	Number of firms 企業個數
Zhenjiang 鎮江市	Jiangsu 江蘇省	38.41%	16
Beijing 北京市	Beijing 北京市	5.49%	6
Tianjin 天津市	Tianjin 天津市	4.93%	5
Nanchong 南充市	Sichuan 四川省	4.61%	6
Chaozhou 潮州市	Guangdong 廣東省	3.44%	2
Taiyuan 太原市	Shanxi 山西省	3.07%	8
Zibo 淄博市	Shandong 山東省	2.73%	2
Foshan 佛山市	Guangdong 廣東省	2.46%	1
Ji'nan 濟南市	Shandong 山東省	2.42%	2
Huaiyin 淮陰市	Jiangsu 江蘇省	2.25%	2

10 Major Wholesalers 10 家主要批發商	City 城市	Province 省	Telephone / Fax 電話 / 傳真
Guangdong Meizhou Salt Industry General Company 廣東省梅州鹽業總公司	Meizhou 梅州市	Guangdong 廣東省	(0752)2234242 (0752)2234720
Shannxi Import & Export Company 陝西省進出口公司	Xi'an 西安市	Shaanxi 陝西省	(029)7424946 (029)7420131
Fujian Salt Industry Company 福建省鹽業公司	Fuzhou 福州市	Fujian 福建省	(0591)7535047 (0591)7535047
Sichuan Salt Industry Company Zigong Branch 四川省鹽業公司自貢分公司	Zigong 自貢市	Sichuan 四川省	(0813)2203215 (0813)2203215
Shanghai Shi Liu Pu Non-staple Food Trade Company 上海市十六鋪副食品貿易公司	Shanghai 上海市	Shanghai 上海市	(021)63736787
Shandong Salt Industry General Company Shandong Salt Administration Bureau 山東省鹽業總公司山東省鹽務局	Ji'nan 濟南市	Shandong 山東省	(0531)6925633 (0531)6925021
Yunnan Salt Industry General Company 雲南省鹽業總公司	Kunming 昆明市	Yunnan 雲南省	(0871)3166719
Shanghai Jia Le Condiment Mill Marketing Company 上海家樂調味食品銷售公司	Shanghai 上海市	Shanghai 上海市	(021)59139194
Zhong Yan Shanghai Salt Company 中鹽上海鹽業公司	Shanghai 上海市	Shanghai 上海市	(021)62180345 (021)62187068
Zhejiang Salt Industry Company 浙江省鹽業公司	Hangzhou 杭州市	Zhejiang 浙江省	(0571)7800292 (0571)7800292

*Also include sales by firms outside this industry.包括本行業以外廠家的銷售。"o" stands for "others". "o" 代表"其他產品"。

1453: Condiment 調味料製造業

The industry accounts for 0.025% of the total revenue of China's industrial sector in 1996. The revenue growth rate of the industry is 40.6% from 1995, as compared to the growth rate of China's industrial sector, 9.51%. The rate of return on asset is 1.81%. 71.44% of all firms in the industry made a profit while 26.34% had negative returns. The top province in terms of the industry's revenue is Guangdong, accounting for 17.42% of the total revenue.
本行業在 1996 年佔全行業總產值 0.025%，行業年增長率為 40.6%（全國工業年增長率 9.51%）。行業的資產回報率 1.81%，71.44% 的企業盈利，26.34% 的企業虧損。銷售收入最高的省份為廣東省，佔本行業的 17.42%。

	Total number of firms 企業總數	Total number of employees 職工總數	Total revenue (mil. RMB) 總銷售收入（百萬元）	Total profit (mil. RMB) 總利潤（百萬元）	Return on assets 資產利潤率 (%)	Return on equity 權益利潤率 (%)	Labour productivity ('000 RMB / worker) 勞動生產率（千元/人）	Debts / assets 資產負債率 (%)	Total assets (mil. RMB) 總資產（百萬元）
Industry Overall 行業總體	251	12,843	1,434	35	1.81	3.86	111.66	53.24	1,928

	Number of firms 企業個數	Average number of employees 平均職工人數	Average revenue ('000 RMB) 平均銷售收入（千元）	Average profit ('000 RMB) 平均利潤（千元）	Return on assets 資產利潤率 (%)	Return on equity 權益利潤率 (%)	Labour productivity ('000 RMB / worker) 勞動生產率（千元/人）	Average debts / assets 平均資產負債率(%)	Average Total assets ('000 RMB) 平均總資產（千元）
By ownership 產業所有權									
State-owned 國有	40	68	5,325	100	1.18	2.82	78.02	58.11	8,475
Collectively-owned 集體	155	45	4,391	178	4.75	13.22	96.84	64.10	3,744
Privately-owned 私有	1	181	12,889	153	1.13	1.41	71.21	20.11	13,510
Domestic JVs 聯營	2	342	30,949	1,191	2.29	2.70	90.49	15.17	51,994
Joint stock 股份制	1	40	4,667	35	0.81	3.11	116.67	74.11	4,300
Foreign-funded 外資	35	52	9,343	-207	-1.14	-2.44	179.96	53.41	18,183
Overseas Chinese-funded 港澳台資	18	32	7,503	451	3.24	5.23	236.93	38.11	13,925
By size 規模									
Large 大型	1	1,408	37,896	225	0.24	1.20	26.91	79.60	91,769
Medium 中型	6	307	67,686	7,704	9.85	16.67	220.24	40.90	78,207
Small 小型	234	40	4,235	-49	-0.84	-1.89	104.64	55.67	5,843
By regional distribution 地區分布									
Central-North 華北	51	35	3,962	99	2.11	3.85	114.04	45.05	4,667
Beijing 北京	19	12	1,285	16	1.17	3.65	107.06	68.04	1,355
Tianjin 天津	10	113	10,923	396	5.12	7.72	96.92	33.74	7,739
Hebei 河北	20	20	3,416	39	0.57	1.08	168.69	47.17	6,737
Shanxi 山西	1	5	90				18.00	25.00	40
Inner Mongolia 內蒙	1	7	30				4.29	25.00	80
Northeast 東北	15	25	1,381	177	4.86	9.56	55.08	49.16	3,632
Liaoning 遼寧	7	19	857	84	2.23	2.85	45.45	21.54	3,774
Jilin 吉林	2	51	4,170	705	8.09	63.23	82.57	87.21	8,715
Heilongjiang 黑龍江	6	24	1,062	108	6.11	13.68	44.55	55.41	1,772
Central East 華東	76	65	8,859	91	0.85	1.65	135.31	48.62	10,704
Shanghai 上海	11	114	20,618	1,305	6.17	11.06	181.59	44.22	21,170
Jiangsu 江蘇	6	62	4,283	65	1.20	5.03	69.46	76.12	5,408
Zhejiang 浙江	9	200	22,879	-570	-1.79	-3.73	114.27	52.09	31,898
Anhui 安徽	2	23	7,695	1,035	35.88	113.11	334.57	68.11	2,885
Fujian 福建	19	24	1,280	121	11.79	20.43	54.29	42.29	1,027
Jiangxi 江西	3	4	533				145.45	81.60	2,247
Shandong 山東	26	40	6,677	-273	-3.10	-5.53	165.32	43.93	8,811
Central-South 中南	66	49	6,217	240	2.37	5.72	127.23	58.57	10,133
Henan 河南	14	36	2,467	23	1.02	2.69	68.80	61.86	2,231
Hubei 湖北	15	60	6,169	229	7.97	33.96	102.59	76.53	2,869
Hunan 湖南	5	22	228	-172	-5.88	-2150.00	10.36	99.73	2,926
Guangdong 廣東	21	59	11,894	588	2.48	6.02	201.11	58.79	23,709
Guangxi 廣西	9	27	3,518	136	4.12	5.70	129.75	27.82	3,291
Hainan 海南	2	113	325	-300	-1.15	-2.11	2.89	45.63	26,190
Southwest 西南	33	55	3,171	102	3.01	8.89	58.17	66.19	3,377
Chongqing 重慶	4	52	1,449	-178	-4.92	-26.03	27.49	81.08	3,619
Sichuan 四川	24	61	3,965	168	4.40	12.05	64.65	63.49	3,827
Guizhou 貴州	4	15	223	5	1.45	6.06	14.83	76.09	345
Yunnan 雲南									
Tibet 西藏									
Northwest 西北	10	70	2,330	107	2.58	10.50	33.53	75.48	4,151
Shaanxi 陝西	4	62	2,508	133	3.28	12.30	40.77	73.42	4,045
Gansu 甘肅	3	29	110	-47	-3.44	-93.33	3.84	96.31	1,357
Qinghai 青海	1	11	490	20	1.47	2.90	44.55	49.26	1,360
Ningxia 寧夏	2	176	6,225	330	3.32	13.10	35.37	74.67	9,950
Xinjiang 新疆									

1453: Condiment 調味料製造業

Year 年份	Number of firms 企業個數	Rate of change 每年變化 (%)	Number of employees 職工人數 (人)	Rate of change 每年變化 (%)	Total revenue (mil. RMB) 總銷售收入 (百萬元)	Rate of change 每年變化 (%)	Total profit (mil. RMB) 總利潤 (百萬元)	Rate of change 每年變化 (%)
1993	183		9,045		402		15	
1994	222	21.31%	12,417	37.28%	579	44.23%	11	-25.99%
1995	243	9.46%	14,878	19.82%	1,020	76.24%	23	106.07%
1996	251	3.29%	12,843	-13.68%	1,434	40.59%	35	50.86%

3 Major products* 3種主要產品 *	Output 產量	Sales volume 銷售量	Unit 單位
a) Compound Condiment 複合調味品	22,368	21,697	ton 噸
b) Paste 醬	12,378	9,531	ton 噸
c) Flavor Essence 味精	10,097	10,097	ton 噸

Top 10 firms by revenue (year founded) 收入排名前10家企業 (創辦年份)	City 城市	Province 省	Telephone / fax 電話 / 傳真	Number of employees 職工人數	Ownership 產業所有權	Revenue ('000 RMB) 銷售收入 (千元)	Profit ('000 RMB) (rank) 利潤 (千元) (排名)	Total assets ('000 RMB) 總資產 (千元)	Major products 主要產品
Jia Le Condiment Co. Ltd. 家樂調味食品有限公司(1989)	Shanghai 上海市	Shanghai 上海市	(021)59139490	203	Foreign-funded 外資	228,733	15133(2)	235,083	c
Zhejiang Wei Yuan Food Co. Ltd. 浙江味元食品有限公司(1995)	Jinhua 金華市	Zhejiang 浙江省	(0579)8823113 (0579)8824513	942	Foreign-funded 外資	112,028	-3396(87)	129,500	o
Shanghai Mccormick Foods Co. Ltd. 上海邁考美調味食品有限公司(1990)	Shanghai 上海市	Shanghai 上海市	(021)64760859 (021)64761620	110	Foreign-funded 外資	97,136	4404(4)	67,770	o
Lee Kum Kee (Guangzhou) Foods Co. Ltd. 李錦記(廣州)食品有限公司(1994)	Guangzhou 廣州市	Guangdong 廣東省	(020)82216198 (020)82216194	140	Overseas Chinese-funded 港澳台資	88,410	33812(1)	60,249	b
Cpc (Guangzhou) Foods Ltd. 廣州越興家樂食品有限公司(1993)	Guangzhou 廣州市	Guangdong 廣東省	(020)87573413 (020)87573422	231	Foreign-funded 外資	86,231	-6391(88)	157,612	o
Tianjin No.1 Condiment Brewage Factory 天津市第一調料釀造廠(1956)	Tianjin 天津市	Tianjin 天津市	(022)26321052 (022)26364746	631	State-owned 國有	83,096	4381(5)	55,309	a,b
Shanghai Chuan Qi Foods Co. 上海川崎食品公司(1991)	Shanghai 上海市	Shanghai 上海市	(021)58480164 (021)64345178	463	Collectively-owned 集體	60,200	9011(3)	97,886	a
Xiangyang Lu Chi Wine Make Condiment Mill 襄陽鹿池釀造調味品廠	Xiangfan 襄樊市	Hubei 湖北省			Collectively-owned 集體	50,257	2010(7)	7,632	o
Xi Jie (Qingdao) Food Co. Ltd. 希傑(青島)食品有限公司(1995)	Qingdao 青島市	Shandong 山東省	(0532)8461141 (0532)8461141	101	Foreign-funded 外資	40,711	1099(11)	74,582	o
Shanghai Condiment Factory 上海調味食品廠(1936)	Shanghai 上海市	Shanghai 上海市	(021)56625122	224	Collectively-owned 集體	39,234	1013(14)	32,273	o

Top 10 Cities by Production Output 產出排名前10位城市	Province 省	Market share 市場份額	Number of firms 企業個數
Shanghai 上海市	Shanghai 上海市	33.86%	17
Guangzhou 廣州市	Guangdong 廣東省	11.90%	10
Tianjin 天津市	Tianjin 天津市	9.26%	14
Jinhua 金華市	Zhejiang 浙江省	8.17%	3
Fuyang 阜陽市	Anhui 安徽省	5.07%	5
Beijing 北京市	Beijing 北京市	2.30%	18
Chengdu 成都市	Sichuan 四川省	2.20%	11
Shenzhen 深圳市	Guangdong 廣東省	2.16%	1
Wuxi 無錫市	Jiangsu 江蘇省	2.00%	8
Baoding 保定市	Hebei 河北省	1.66%	4

10 Major Wholesalers 10家主要批發商	City 城市	Province 省	Telephone / Fax 電話 / 傳真
Guangdong Meizhou Salt Industry General Company 廣東省梅州鹽業總公司	Meizhou 梅州市	Guangdong 廣東省	(0752)2234242 (0752)2234720
Shannxi Import & Export Company 陝西省進出口公司	Xi'an 西安市	Shaanxi 陝西省	(029)7424946 (029)7420131
Fujian Salt Industry Company 福建省鹽業公司	Fuzhou 福州市	Fujian 福建省	(0591)7535047 (0591)7535047
Sichuan Salt Industry Company Zigong Branch 四川省鹽業公司自貢分公司	Zigong 自貢市	Sichuan 四川省	(0813)2203215 (0813)2203215
Shanghai Shi Liu Pu Non-staple Food Trade Company 上海市十六鋪副食品貿易公司	Shanghai 上海市	Shanghai 上海市	(021)63736787
Shandong Salt Industry General Company Shandong Salt Administration Bureau 山東省鹽業總公司山東省鹽務局	Ji'nan 濟南市	Shandong 山東省	(0531)6925633 (0531)6925021
Yunnan Salt Industry General Company 雲南省鹽業總公司	Kunming 昆明市	Yunnan 雲南省	(0871)3166719
Shanghai Jia Le Condiment Mill Marketing Company 上海家樂調味食品銷售公司	Shanghai 上海市	Shanghai 上海市	(021)59139194
Zhong Yan Shanghai Salt Company 中鹽上海鹽業公司	Shanghai 上海市	Shanghai 上海市	(021)62180345 (021)62187068
Zhejiang Salt Industry Company 浙江省鹽業公司	Hangzhou 杭州市	Zhejiang 浙江省	(0571)7800292 (0571)7800292

*Also include sales by firms outside this industry.包括本行業以外廠家的銷售。"o" stands for "others". "o" 代表"其他產品"。

1454: Seasoning Oil 調味油製造業

The industry accounts for 0.013% of the total revenue of China's industrial sector in 1996. The revenue growth rate of the industry is -4.2% from 1995, as compared to the growth rate of China's industrial sector, 9.51%. The rate of return on asset is -2.24%. 72.05% of all firms in the industry made a profit while 21.05% had negative returns. The top province in terms of the industry's revenue is Guangxi, accounting for 64.63% of the total revenue.
本行業在1996年佔全行業總產值0.013%，行業年增長率為-4.2%（全國工業年增長率9.51%）。行業的資產回報率-2.24%，72.05%的企業盈利，21.05%的企業虧損。銷售收入最高的省份為廣西省，佔本行業的64.63%。

	Total number of firms 企業總數	Total number of employees 職工總數	Total revenue (mil. RMB) 總銷售收入（百萬元）	Total profit (mil. RMB) 總利潤（百萬元）	Return on assets 資產利潤率 (%)	Return on equity 權益利潤率 (%)	Labour productivity ('000 RMB / worker) 勞動生產率（千元/人）	Debts / assets 資產負債率 (%)	Total assets (mil. RMB) 總資產（百萬元）
Industry Overall 行業總體	85	6,250	764	-16	-2.24	-6.93	122.24	67.60	698

	Number of firms 企業個數	Average number of employees 平均職工人數	Average revenue ('000 RMB) 平均銷售收入（千元）	Average profit ('000 RMB) 平均利潤（千元）	Return on assets 資產利潤率 (%)	Return on equity 權益利潤率 (%)	Labour productivity ('000 RMB / worker) 勞動生產率（千元/人）	Average debts / assets 平均資產負債率(%)	Average Total assets ('000 RMB) 平均總資產（千元）
By ownership 產業所有權									
State-owned 國有	22	160	5,409	-455	-4.57	-17.86	33.80	74.43	9,955
Collectively-owned 集體	53	35	841	4	0.27	1.49	24.17	82.14	1,595
Privately-owned 私有	1	18							
Domestic JVs 聯營									
Joint stock 股份制									
Foreign-funded 外資	4	167	148,938	-1,577	-1.65	-4.20	891.84	60.75	95,585
Overseas Chinese-funded 港澳台資	4	50	1,168	21	0.68	1.71	23.36	60.31	3,031
By size 規模									
Large 大型	2	310	327,551	-8,667	-3.78	-13.11	1058.32	71.17	229,355
Medium 中型									
Small 小型	82	68	1,328	16	0.56	1.42	19.56	60.81	2,918
By regional distribution 地區分布									
Central-North 華北	17	135	2,731	-12	-0.26	-1.34	20.24	80.53	4,529
Beijing 北京	2	86	1,120	-360	-9.64	-28.92	13.02	66.67	3,735
Tianjin 天津	5	25	1,506	62	4.19	8.40	61.22	49.93	1,478
Hebei 河北	3	56	593	10	0.86	2.86	10.66	69.45	1,157
Shanxi 山西	7	262	4,981	26	0.31	2.33	19.04	86.81	8,380
Inner Mongolia 內蒙									
Northeast 東北	5	103	2,376	-628	-3.75	-8.54	23.16	56.04	16,728
Liaoning 遼寧	4	47	275	5	0.32	0.80	5.91	59.94	1,573
Jilin 吉林	1	327	10,780	-3,160	-4.09	-9.23	32.97	55.72	77,350
Heilongjiang 黑龍江									
Central East 華東	21	42	3,208	84	2.53	4.57	76.03	44.60	3,309
Shanghai 上海									
Jiangsu 江蘇	2	9	220	-25	-3.85	125.00	25.88	103.08	650
Zhejiang 浙江	2	5	610	15	7.50	7.50	122.00		200
Anhui 安徽	4	62	3,623	353	24.65	44.48	58.19	44.58	1,430
Fujian 福建	7	59	6,787	107	1.35	2.07	114.21	34.87	7,931
Jiangxi 江西	5	14	260	18	2.94	90.00	18.84	97.06	612
Shandong 山東	1	125	2,400	-470	-13.47	36.43	19.20	136.68	3,490
Central-South 中南	24	83	25,043	-609	-3.48	-11.95	303.39	70.90	17,507
Henan 河南	4	34	2,800	220	17.25	43.56	82.96	60.39	1,275
Hubei 湖北	1	38	370	-240	-8.60	-300.00	9.74	97.13	2,790
Hunan 湖南	10	125	6,184	-808	-12.66	-384.76	49.43	96.71	6,384
Guangdong 廣東	5	52	6,766	324	5.02	14.73	130.62	65.94	6,460
Guangxi 廣西	4	75	123,445	-2,198	-2.78	-8.21	1656.98	66.14	79,035
Hainan 海南									
Southwest 西南	12	24	2,638	17	0.80	2.55	111.09	68.80	2,094
Chongqing 重慶	1	3	27	3	9.72	10.51	8.38	7.56	35
Sichuan 四川	4	34	6,696	102	2.15	10.73	195.76	79.99	4,734
Guizhou 貴州	7	20	693	-30	-3.41	-5.22	33.92	34.74	880
Yunnan 雲南									
Tibet 西藏									
Northwest 西北	6	49	1,015	48	1.27	4.92	20.86	74.15	3,792
Shaanxi 陝西	5	54	1,216	58	1.63	5.26	22.35	69.01	3,556
Gansu 甘肅									
Qinghai 青海									
Ningxia 寧夏									
Xinjiang 新疆	1	20	10				0.50	92.56	4,970

1454: Seasoning Oil 調味油製造業

Year 年份	Number of firms 企業個數	Rate of change 每年變化 (%)	Number of employees 職工人數 (人)	Rate of change 每年變化 (%)	Total revenue (mil. RMB) 總銷售收入 (百萬元)	Rate of change 每年變化 (%)	Total profit (mil. RMB) 總利潤 (百萬元)	Rate of change 每年變化 (%)
1993	46		3,334		213		9	
1994	52	13.04%	1,840	-44.81%	74	-65.13%	1	-88.82%
1995	50	-3.85%	2,222	20.76%	797	975.53%	-24	-2544.27%
1996	85	70.00%	6,250	181.28%	764	-4.19%	-16	32.45%

3 Major products* 3 種主要產品 *	Output 產量	Sales volume 銷售量	Unit 單位
a) Table Vinegar 食醋	81,489	75,785	ton 噸
b) Edible Vegetable Oil 食用植物油	415,531	386,444	ton 噸
c) Compound Condiment 複合調味品	1,487	1,442	ton 噸

Top 10 firms by revenue (year founded) 收入排名前 10 家企業 (創辦年份)	City 城市	Province 省	Telephone / fax 電話 / 傳真	Number of employees 職工人數	Ownership 產業所有權	Revenue ('000 RMB) 銷售收入 (千元)	Profit ('000 RMB) (rank) 利潤 (千元) (排名)	Total assets ('000 RMB) 總資產 (千元)	Major products 主要產品
Fangcheng Port New Ocean Oils & Fats Industrial Co. Ltd. 防城港新海油脂工業有限公司(1992)	Fangchenggang 防城港市	Guangxi 廣西	(0770)2823788 (0770)2826018	250	Foreign-funded 外資	489,041	-8981(29)	311,317	b
Hunan State-owned Qian Liang Hu Fat Chemical Industry Factory 湖南省國營錢糧湖油脂化工廠(1958)	Yueyang 岳陽市	Hunan 湖南省	(0730)4727314	693	State-owned 國有	32,945	-6915(28)	24,065	b
Wu Hua Rice & Oil Foods (Fujian) Co. Ltd. 物華粟米油食品(福建)有限公司(1994)	Quanzhou 泉州市	Fujian 福建省	(0595)8681985 (0595)8681885	120	Foreign-funded 外資	32,000	930(2)	30,940	o
Shenzhen Nanshan Can Factory 深圳市南山罐頭廠(1958)	Shenzhen 深圳市	Guangdong 廣東省	(0755)6661203	149	State-owned 國有	28,145	1653(1)	22,914	c
Shanghai Hua Yuan Food Factory 上海華源食品廠(1990)	Shanghai 上海市	Shanghai 上海市	(021)64766138 (021)64766138	67	Collectively-owned 集體	26,092	74(14)	17,151	o
Sichuan Hanyuan Chinese Prickly Ash Oil Factory 四川省漢源縣花椒油廠(1987)	Ya'an 雅安市	Sichuan 四川省	(0835)382292	77	Collectively-owned 集體	25,328	305(8)	16,950	c
Xiang Xi Autonomous Prefecture Vegetable Oil Factory 湘西自治州植物油廠(1993)	Jishou 吉首市	Hunan 湖南省	(0743)8551898	156	Collectively-owned 集體	24,714	3(19)	25,038	b
Shanxi Qingxu No.2 Vinegar Factory 山西省清徐第二醋廠(1976)	Taiyuan 太原市	Shanxi 山西省	(0351)5722226	655	Collectively-owned 集體	17,112	479(5)	13,902	a
Shanxi Mei He Ju Lao Mature Vinegar Co. Ltd. 山西省美和店老陳醋有限公司(1956)	Taiyuan 太原市	Shanxi 山西省	(0351)5722373	1,000	State-owned 國有	16,366	0(21)	33,075	a
Fujian Jianyang Monosodium Glutamate Factory 福建省建陽市味精廠(1984)	Nangping 南平市	Fujian 福建省	(0599)5622862	282	State-owned 國有	15,507	10(17)	21,793	o

Top 10 Cities by Production Output 產出排名前 10 位城市	Province 省	Market share 市場份額	Number of firms 企業個數
Shanghai 上海市	Shanghai 上海市	70.15%	2
Wuxi 無錫市	Jiangsu 江蘇省	6.76%	1
Yueyang 岳陽市	Hunan 湖南省	3.32%	1
Jishou 吉首市	Hunan 湖南省	2.72%	1
Shenzhen 深圳市	Guangdong 廣東省	2.71%	2
Nangping 南平市	Fujian 福建省	2.37%	1
Ya'an 雅安市	Sichuan 四川省	1.94%	2
Taiyuan 太原市	Shanxi 山西省	1.77%	4
Zhumadian 駐馬店市	Henan 河南省	0.95%	1
Weifang 濰坊市	Shandong 山東省	0.78%	1

10 Major Wholesalers 10 家主要批發商	City 城市	Province 省	Telephone / Fax 電話 / 傳真
Guangdong Meizhou Salt Industry General Company 廣東省梅州鹽業總公司	Meizhou 梅州市	Guangdong 廣東省	(0752)2234242 (0752)2234720
Shannxi Import & Export Company 陝西省進出口公司	Xi'an 西安市	Shaanxi 陝西省	(029)7424946 (029)7420131
Fujian Salt Industry Company 福建省鹽業公司	Fuzhou 福州市	Fujian 福建省	(0591)7535047 (0591)7535047
Sichuan Salt Industry Company Zigong Branch 四川省鹽業公司自貢分公司	Zigong 自貢市	Sichuan 四川省	(0813)2203215 (0813)2203215
Shanghai Shi Liu Pu Non-staple Food Trade Company 上海市十六鋪副食品貿易公司	Shanghai 上海市	Shanghai 上海市	(021)63736787
Shandong Salt Industry General Company Shandong Salt Administration Bureau 山東省鹽業總公司山東省鹽務局	Ji'nan 濟南市	Shandong 山東省	(0531)6925633 (0531)6925021
Yunnan Salt Industry General Company 雲南省鹽業總公司	Kunming 昆明市	Yunnan 雲南省	(0871)3166719
Shanghai Jia Le Condiment Mill Marketing Company 上海家樂調味食品銷售公司	Shanghai 上海市	Shanghai 上海市	(021)59139194
Zhong Yan Shanghai Salt Company 中鹽上海鹽業公司	Shanghai 上海市	Shanghai 上海市	(021)62180345 (021)62187068
Zhejiang Salt Industry Company 浙江省鹽業公司	Hangzhou 杭州市	Zhejiang 浙江省	(0571)7800292 (0571)7800292

*Also include sales by firms outside this industry.包括本行業以外廠家的銷售。"o" stands for "others". "o" 代表"其他產品"。

1459: Other Spices 其他調味品製造業

The industry accounts for 0.010% of the total revenue of China's industrial sector in 1996. The revenue growth rate of the industry is 1.1% from 1995, as compared to the growth rate of China's industrial sector, 9.51%. The rate of return on asset is 0.04%. 67.05% of all firms in the industry made a profit while 23.72% had negative returns. The top province in terms of the industry's revenue is Shandong, accounting for 16.64% of the total revenue.
本行業在1996年佔全行業總產值0.010%，行業年增長率為1.1%（全國工業年增長率9.51%）。行業的資產回報率0.04%，67.05%的企業盈利，23.72%的企業虧損。銷售收入最高的省份為山東省，佔本行業的16.64%。

	Total number of firms 企業總數	Total number of employees 職工總數	Total revenue (mil. RMB) 總銷售收入（百萬元）	Total profit (mil. RMB) 總利潤（百萬元）	Return on assets 資產利潤率 (%)	Return on equity 權益利潤率 (%)	Labour productivity ('000 RMB / worker) 勞動生產率（千元/人）	Debts / assets 資產負債率 (%)	Total assets (mil. RMB) 總資產（百萬元）
Industry Overall 行業總體	152	9,493	564		0.04	0.10	59.41	60.33	702

	Number of firms 企業個數	Average number of employees 平均職工人數	Average revenue ('000 RMB) 平均銷售收入（千元）	Average profit ('000 RMB) 平均利潤（千元）	Return on assets 資產利潤率 (%)	Return on equity 權益利潤率 (%)	Labour productivity ('000 RMB / worker) 勞動生產率（千元/人）	Average debts / assets 平均資產負債率(%)	Average Total assets ('000 RMB) 平均總資產（千元）
By ownership 產業所有權									
State-owned 國有	30	94	2,600	-233	-3.85	-10.00	27.76	61.54	6,067
Collectively-owned 集體	97	48	2,806	57	2.09	8.34	58.69	74.90	2,728
Privately-owned 私有									
Domestic JVs 聯營	1	222	30,714	1,225	5.80	12.08	138.35	52.00	21,130
Joint stock 股份制	3	148	10,146	460	3.20	8.68	68.71	63.15	14,374
Foreign-funded 外資	10	117	13,538	114	0.84	1.45	115.71	41.82	13,582
Overseas Chinese-funded 港澳台資	11	29	1,565	-208	-4.13	-6.25	53.29	33.96	5,027
By size 規模									
Large 大型									
Medium 中型									
Small 小型	151	63	3,735				58.82	60.40	4,649
By regional distribution 地區分布									
Central-North 華北	21	25	3,000	-125	-1.83	-2.70	120.71	32.32	6,847
Beijing 北京	6	21	3,170	-290	-3.49	-3.74	152.16	6.62	8,305
Tianjin 天津	10	23	3,730	-102	-1.21	-1.97	164.32	38.48	8,408
Hebei 河北	4	41	1,673	33	1.32	-13.68	41.04	109.62	2,470
Shanxi 山西	1	7							
Inner Mongolia 內蒙									
Northeast 東北	12	37	1,194	52	2.11	8.41	32.64	74.97	2,450
Liaoning 遼寧	5	23	634	-34	-1.08	-5.31	27.33	79.66	3,136
Jilin 吉林	3	32	1,427	207	6.96	35.03	44.12	80.13	2,970
Heilongjiang 黑龍江	4	57	1,720	43	3.53	7.08	30.44	50.10	1,203
Central East 華東	60	85	5,330	73	1.29	3.30	62.63	60.85	5,607
Shanghai 上海	5	89	7,834	-760	-7.23	-18.42	88.02	60.74	10,510
Jiangsu 江蘇	14	109	6,335	134	2.72	14.59	58.16	81.39	4,919
Zhejiang 浙江									
Anhui 安徽	8	42	5,039	573	37.33	53.26	121.05	29.83	1,534
Fujian 福建	20	49	2,890	2	0.05	0.09	59.45	42.14	2,893
Jiangxi 江西	2	29							
Shandong 山東	11	161	8,531	152	1.15	2.97	52.90	61.22	13,172
Central-South 中南	37	55	3,366	58	2.09	6.75	61.23	69.09	2,786
Henan 河南	7	56	1,270	33	1.79	7.80	22.85	77.02	1,834
Hubei 湖北	5	48	1,416	-8	-0.62	-1.12	29.38	44.65	1,290
Hunan 湖南	6	45	4,115	-140	-3.14	-28.00	91.78	88.77	4,453
Guangdong 廣東	14	68	5,804	217	6.68	17.51	84.82	61.83	3,249
Guangxi 廣西	5	35	524	-48	-2.07	-4.82	14.80	57.03	2,318
Hainan 海南									
Southwest 西南	16	66	2,208	-184	-4.11	106.14	33.71	103.89	4,468
Chongqing 重慶	1	285	5,938	-1,438	-7.35	179.43	20.80	104.10	19,551
Sichuan 四川	11	38	2,079	-23	-0.84	10.72	53.63	107.83	2,729
Guizhou 貴州	1								360
Yunnan 雲南	2	40	570	-10	-0.45	-2.74	14.25	83.45	2,205
Tibet 西藏									
Northwest 西北	6	57	1,115	-208	-7.04	-9.65	19.45	26.99	2,958
Shaanxi 陝西	3	24	573	20	3.41	4.62	23.89	26.14	587
Gansu 甘肅	2	136	2,485	-655	-8.19	-11.23	18.27	27.08	7,995
Qinghai 青海									
Ningxia 寧夏									
Xinjiang 新疆	1								

1459: Other Spices 其他調味品製造業

Year 年份	Number of firms 企業個數	Rate of change 每年變化 (%)	Number of employees 職工人數（人）	Rate of change 每年變化 (%)	Total revenue (mil. RMB) 總銷售收入（百萬元）	Rate of change 每年變化 (%)	Total profit (mil. RMB) 總利潤（百萬元）	Rate of change 每年變化 (%)
1993	277		25,485		758		20	
1994	275	-0.72%	19,487	-23.54%	807	6.51%	17	-12.69%
1995	175	-36.36%	10,377	-46.75%	558	-30.83%	3	-83.90%
1996	152	-13.14%	9,493	-8.52%	564	1.06%		-100.00%

3 Major products* 3 種主要產品 *	Output 產量	Sales volume 銷售量	Unit 單位
a) Compound Condiment 複合調味品	7,686	7,455	ton 噸
b) Dried Vegetable Products 蔬菜乾製品	15,234	14,472	ton 噸
c) Milk Product Substitute 代乳品	389	350	ton 噸

Top 10 firms by revenue (year founded) 收入排名前 10 家企業 (創辦年份)	City 城市	Province 省	Telephone / fax 電話 / 傳真	Number of employees 職工人數	Ownership 產業所有權	Revenue ('000 RMB) 銷售收入（千元）	Profit ('000 RMB) (rank) 利潤（千元）（排名）	Total assets ('000 RMB) 總資產（千元）	Major products 主要產品
Yanzhou Jin Hai Food Co. Ltd. 兖州市金海食品有限公司(1994)	Jining 濟寧市	Shandong 山東省	(0537)3772237 (0537)3772237	821	Collectively-owned 集體	54,524	2475(1)	53,401	a
Pizhou Sihu Dehydrate Vegatable Factory 邳州市四戶脱水菜廠(1993)	Xuzhou 徐州市	Jiangsu 江蘇省	(0516)6491188	650	Overseas Chinese-funded 港澳台資	42,640	2300(3)	8,080	b
Shanghai No.6 Pharmaceutical Factory Wang Xin Branch 上海第六製藥廠望新分廠(1992)	Shanghai 上海市	Shanghai 上海市	(021)59588717 (021)59580581	252	Domestic JVs 聯營	28,668	-712(57)	29,887	o
Panyu Xin Zao Zhen Foods Products Mill 番禺市新造鎮食品廠(1993)	Guangzhou 廣州市	Guangdong 廣東省	(020)84726839 (020)84728088	201	Collectively-owned 集體	25,811	238(14)	10,794	o
Shenzhen Triwell Foods Factory 深圳市三井食品廠(1983)	Shenzhen 深圳市	Guangdong 廣東省	(0755)5534743 (0755)5534743	99	Joint stock 股份制	25,317	2388(2)	13,658	a
Xiapu Sha Jiang Zhen Shrimp Sauce Factory 霞浦縣沙江鎮蝦油廠(1976)	Ningde 寧德市	Fujian 福建省		69	Collectively-owned 集體	23,739	53(35)	8,341	o
Tianjin Shi Zhong Foods Co. Ltd. 天津世鐘食品有限公司(1993)	Tianjin 天津市	Tianjin 天津市	(022)5320757 (022)5320561	17	Foreign-funded 外資	20,887	237(15)	7,921	o
Sichuan Pixian Soy Material Factory 四川省郫縣豆辦廠(1955)	Chengdu 成都市	Sichuan 四川省	(028)7862774	176	State-owned 國有	18,544	627(8)	25,211	a
Beijing Qiu Bi Food Co. Ltd. 北京丘比食品有限公司(1993)	Beijing 北京市	Beijing 北京市	(010)62980274	70	Foreign-funded 外資	16,126	-1833(63)	45,279	a
Xuzhou Jiawang Brewing Factory 徐州市賈汪區釀造廠(1958)	Xuzhou 徐州市	Jiangsu 江蘇省	(0516)7715287	163	Collectively-owned 集體	16,000	423(12)	13,940	c

Top 10 Cities by Production Output 產出排名前 10 位城市	Province 省	Market share 市場份額	Number of firms 企業個數
Quanzhou 泉州市	Fujian 福建省	91.33%	3
Shanghai 上海市	Shanghai 上海市	2.50%	7
Shenzhen 深圳市	Guangdong 廣東省	0.70%	2
Chengdu 成都市	Sichuan 四川省	0.67%	10
Qingdao 青島市	Shandong 山東省	0.57%	4
Guangzhou 廣州市	Guangdong 廣東省	0.56%	3
Harbin 哈爾濱市	Heilongjiang 黑龍江省	0.33%	4
Jiangmen 江門市	Guangdong 廣東省	0.21%	2
Beijing 北京市	Beijing 北京市	0.21%	4
Tianjin 天津市	Tianjin 天津市	0.20%	6

10 Major Wholesalers 10 家主要批發商	City 城市	Province 省	Telephone / Fax 電話 / 傳真
Guangdong Meizhou Salt Industry General Company 廣東省梅州鹽業總公司	Meizhou 梅州市	Guangdong 廣東省	(0752)2234242 (0752)2234720
Shannxi Import & Export Company 陝西省進出口公司	Xi'an 西安市	Shaanxi 陝西省	(029)7424946 (029)7420131
Fujian Salt Industry Company 福建省鹽業公司	Fuzhou 福州市	Fujian 福建省	(0591)7535047 (0591)7535047
Sichuan Salt Industry Company Zigong Branch 四川省鹽業公司自貢分公司	Zigong 自貢市	Sichuan 四川省	(0813)2203215 (0813)2203215
Shanghai Shi Liu Pu Non-staple Food Trade Company 上海市十六鋪副食品貿易公司	Shanghai 上海市	Shanghai 上海市	(021)63736787
Shandong Salt Industry General Company Shandong Salt Administration Bureau 山東省鹽業總公司山東省鹽務局	Ji'nan 濟南市	Shandong 山東省	(0531)6925633 (0531)6925021
Yunnan Salt Industry General Company 雲南省鹽業總公司	Kunming 昆明市	Yunnan 雲南省	(0871)3166719
Shanghai Jia Le Condiment Mill Marketing Company 上海家樂調味食品銷售公司	Shanghai 上海市	Shanghai 上海市	(021)59139194
Zhong Yan Shanghai Salt Company 中鹽上海鹽業公司	Shanghai 上海市	Shanghai 上海市	(021)62180345 (021)62187068
Zhejiang Salt Industry Company 浙江省鹽業公司	Hangzhou 杭州市	Zhejiang 浙江省	(0571)7800292 (0571)7800292

*Also include sales by firms outside this industry.包括本行業以外廠家的銷售。"o" stands for "others". "o" 代表"其他產品"。

1491: Bean Products 豆製品製造業

The industry accounts for 0.070% of the total revenue of China's industrial sector in 1996. The revenue growth rate of the industry is 42.4% from 1995, as compared to the growth rate of China's industrial sector, 9.51%. The rate of return on asset is 7.63%. 67.91% of all firms in the industry made a profit while 25.46% had negative returns. The top province in terms of the industry's revenue is Jiangsu, accounting for 61.35% of the total revenue.
本行業在1996年佔全行業總產值0.070%，行業年增長率為42.4%（全國工業年增長率9.51%）。行業的資產回報率7.63%，67.91%的企業盈利，25.46%的企業虧損。銷售收入最高的省份為江蘇省，佔本行業的61.35%。

	Total number of firms 企業總數	Total number of employees 職工總數	Total revenue (mil. RMB) 總銷售收入（百萬元）	Total profit (mil. RMB) 總利潤（百萬元）	Return on assets 資產利潤率 (%)	Return on equity 權益利潤率 (%)	Labour productivity ('000 RMB / worker) 勞動生產率（千元/人）	Debts / assets 資產負債率 (%)	Total assets (mil. RMB) 總資產（百萬元）
Industry Overall 行業總體	678	50,536	4,038	251	7.63	16.88	79.90	54.79	3,283

	Number of firms 企業個數	Average number of employees 平均職工人數	Average revenue ('000 RMB) 平均銷售收入（千元）	Average profit ('000 RMB) 平均利潤（千元）	Return on assets 資產利潤率 (%)	Return on equity 權益利潤率 (%)	Labour productivity ('000 RMB / worker) 勞動生產率（千元/人）	Average debts / assets 平均資產負債率(%)	Average Total assets ('000 RMB) 平均總資產（千元）
By ownership 產業所有權									
State-owned 國有	180	151	16,417	1,339	10.70	21.69	108.88	50.69	12,517
Collectively-owned 集體	431	45	1,656	19	2.00	6.28	36.94	68.17	927
Privately-owned 私有	3	18	1,315	29	2.63	2.69	74.43	2.32	1,086
Domestic JVs 聯營	5	157	2,747	18	2.14	3.64	17.50	41.13	845
Joint stock 股份制	6	193	29,134	412	0.69	2.41	150.69	71.42	59,934
Foreign-funded 外資	26	49	4,547	132	2.09	3.90	92.58	46.44	6,317
Overseas Chinese-funded 港澳台資	28	41	2,097	-147	-4.15	-8.32	50.61	50.14	3,541
By size 規模									
Large 大型	2	876	176,522	7,164	2.04	5.76	201.51	64.63	351,532
Medium 中型	6	865	245,804	37,592	33.67	57.81	284.28	41.76	111,650
Small 小型	655	67	3,374	17	0.58	1.32	50.47	55.75	2,916
By regional distribution 地區分布									
Central-North 華北	80	58	3,082	149	4.12	10.72	52.71	61.58	3,604
Beijing 北京	22	89	7,379	376	6.35	17.07	83.25	62.82	5,929
Tianjin 天津	12	31	2,037	239	8.80	16.47	66.05	46.55	2,718
Hebei 河北	23	59	1,492	63	2.74	12.20	25.40	77.56	2,286
Shanxi 山西	12	51	1,403	55	1.24	2.54	27.46	51.09	4,423
Inner Mongolia 內蒙	11	36	782	-125	-6.99	-19.35	21.88	63.90	1,783
Northeast 東北	152	68	1,436	-96	-2.94	-7.75	21.18	62.12	3,260
Liaoning 遼寧	45	58	1,297	-165	-5.70	-19.26	22.33	70.41	2,900
Jilin 吉林	27	69	779	-202	-4.62	-10.10	11.20	54.26	4,375
Heilongjiang 黑龍江	80	73	1,735	-21	-0.67	-1.74	23.89	61.50	3,087
Central East 華東	209	102	14,246	1,300	15.20	27.67	139.66	45.09	8,556
Shanghai 上海	19	136	5,963	-123	-2.13	-4.04	43.88	47.25	5,779
Jiangsu 江蘇	54	203	45,878	5,013	20.70	35.22	226.56	41.21	24,214
Zhejiang 浙江	25	102	4,622	-36	-0.86	-1.62	45.37	47.36	4,209
Anhui 安徽	29	59	2,836	106	4.68	9.18	48.27	49.05	2,263
Fujian 福建	39	13	333	-3	-0.62	-1.05	25.47	40.90	411
Jiangxi 江西	26	75	1,242	7	0.27	1.14	16.46	76.08	2,677
Shandong 山東	17	64	8,448	66	0.98	2.78	132.97	64.69	6,722
Central-South 中南	146	71	3,355	-79	-2.21	-7.43	47.00	70.27	3,598
Henan 河南	30	42	955	21	2.01	8.05	22.87	75.06	1,063
Hubei 湖北	26	62	5,127	180	4.18	16.77	83.10	75.06	4,303
Hunan 湖南	31	23	617	-5	-0.57	-2.01	27.08	71.83	970
Guangdong 廣東	38	131	6,017	-382	-5.18	-15.52	45.97	66.62	7,367
Guangxi 廣西	21	90	3,811	-107	-3.14	-12.20	42.51	74.23	3,409
Hainan 海南									
Southwest 西南	62	44	911	-45	-2.80	-9.10	20.65	69.18	1,617
Chongqing 重慶	13	47	775	-44	-3.68	-18.13	16.38	79.72	1,193
Sichuan 四川	23	31	680	-50	-3.61	-9.83	21.77	63.30	1,394
Guizhou 貴州	5	59	2,148	52	1.78	7.81	36.53	77.12	2,920
Yunnan 雲南	20	54	967	-64	-3.48	-10.49	18.07	66.78	1,838
Tibet 西藏									
Northwest 西北	29	37	1,698	-141	-4.79	-24.35	45.47	80.33	2,942
Shaanxi 陝西	15	40	2,585	-61	-1.55	-7.85	64.51	80.27	3,960
Gansu 甘肅	9	20	336	-322	-37.42	150.26	16.78	125.16	861
Qinghai 青海									
Ningxia 寧夏	2	93	2,640	-115	-1.66	-4.41	28.39	62.49	6,945
Xinjiang 新疆	3	39	723	-13	-0.94	-2.22	18.71	57.85	1,423

1491: Bean Products 豆製品製造業

Year 年份	Number of firms 企業個數	Rate of change 每年變化 (%)	Number of employees 職工人數（人）	Rate of change 每年變化 (%)	Total revenue (mil. RMB) 總銷售收入（百萬元）	Rate of change 每年變化 (%)	Total profit (mil. RMB) 總利潤（百萬元）	Rate of change 每年變化 (%)
1993	703		48,938		1,424		28	
1994	691	-1.71%	55,367	13.14%	1,873	31.58%	55	94.99%
1995	708	2.46%	62,187	12.32%	2,836	51.38%	200	260.92%
1996	678	-4.24%	50,536	-18.74%	4,038	42.38%	251	25.69%

3 Major products* 3 種主要產品 *	Output 產量	Sales volume 銷售量	Unit 單位
a) Bean Products 豆製品	302,100	697,851	ton 噸
b) Solid Drink 固體飲料	72,880	71,422	ton 噸
c) Milk Product Substitute 代乳品	4,078	3,670	ton 噸

Top 10 firms by revenue (year founded) 收入排名前 10 家企業（創辦年份）	City 城市	Province 省	Telephone / fax 電話 / 傳真	Number of employees 職工人數	Ownership 產業所有權	Revenue ('000 RMB) 銷售收入（千元）	Profit ('000 RMB) (rank) 利潤（千元）（排名）	Total assets ('000 RMB) 總資產（千元）	Major products 主要產品
Wei Wei Group 維維集團(1975)	Xuzhou 徐州市	Jiangsu 江蘇省	(0516)2704086 (0516)2704303	4,876	State-owned 國有	2,191,223	270091(1)	1,049,584	b
Kaiping Guang He Fermented Bean Curd Co. Ltd. 開平廣合腐乳有限公司(1996)	Jiangmen 江門市	Guangdong 廣東省	(0750)2713995 (0750)2713995	902	Foreign-funded 外資	75,820	2632(6)	96,217	a
Beijing Wang Zhi He Fermented Bean Curd Mill 北京市王致和腐乳廠(1669)	Beijing 北京市	Beijing 北京市	(010)68213336 (010)68211798	588	State-owned 國有	66,520	3506(4)	48,736	a
Hangzhou Bean Products General Factory 杭州市豆製品總廠(1993)	Hangzhou 杭州市	Zhejiang 浙江省	(0571)5235882	947	State-owned 國有	62,338	23(82)	44,084	o
Longjiang Soybean Foodsstuffs General Corp. of Heilong Jiang 黑龍江省龍江大豆食品總公司(1983)	Jiamusi 佳木斯市	Heilongjiang 黑龍江省	(0454)8582806 (0454)8581852	747	State-owned 國有	53,068	0(113)	126,290	a
Rongcheng Jun Le Food Co. Ltd. 榮成市君樂食品有限公司(1982)	Weihai 威海市	Shandong 山東省	(0896)7481076	53	Collectively-owned 集體	50,900	900(15)	5,880	o
Shandong Li Yuan Group Company 山東力源集團公司(1978)	Yantai 煙台市	Shandong 山東省	(0535)8475028 (0535)8220988	328	State-owned 國有	41,096	515(22)	43,819	o
Xuzhou Jiawang Food Processing Factory 徐州市賈汪區副食品加工廠(1964)	Xuzhou 徐州市	Jiangsu 江蘇省	(0516)7715427	120	Collectively-owned 集體	40,690	381(24)	23,611	a,c
Yunmeng Plant Protein Factory 雲夢植物蛋白質廠(1987)	Xiaogan 孝感市	Hubei 湖北省	(0712)4325042	220	State-owned 國有	36,250	1250(11)	78,842	o
Shunde State-owned Rong Ji Food Factory 順德市國營容奇食品廠(1956)	Foshan 佛山市	Guangdong 廣東省	(0757)6682810 (0757)6687103	475	State-owned 國有	35,249	30(78)	23,111	a

Top 10 Cities by Production Output 產出排名前 10 位城市	Province 省	Market share 市場份額	Number of firms 企業個數
Jiangmen 江門市	Guangdong 廣東省	10.42%	6
Beijing 北京市	Beijing 北京市	7.34%	21
Shanghai 上海市	Shanghai 上海市	7.20%	46
Xuzhou 徐州市	Jiangsu 江蘇省	6.10%	8
Wuxi 無錫市	Jiangsu 江蘇省	4.44%	7
Hangzhou 杭州市	Zhejiang 浙江省	3.53%	5
Nantong 南通市	Jiangsu 江蘇省	3.47%	13
Xiaogan 孝感市	Hubei 湖北省	3.12%	4
Jiamusi 佳木斯市	Heilongjiang 黑龍江省	3.11%	5
Yantai 煙台市	Shandong 山東省	2.55%	3

10 Major Wholesalers 10 家主要批發商	City 城市	Province 省	Telephone / Fax 電話 / 傳真
Shanghai Jiu Zhou Group Co. Ltd. 上海九州集團有限公司	Shanghai 上海市	Shanghai 上海市	(021)62401515 (021)62123848
Shanghai Tobacco (Group) Co. Trade Center 上海煙草集團上海煙草貿易中心	Shanghai 上海市	Shanghai 上海市	(021)58781921 (021)58786584
China Tax – Free Company 中國免稅公司	Beijing 北京市	Beijing 北京市	(010)64668397 (010)64635846
Liaoning Cigarette Marketing Company 遼寧省卷煙銷售公司	Shenyang 瀋陽市	Liaoning 遼寧省	(024)22834388 (024)22837853
Hunan Import & Export General Company Shenzhen Company 湖南省進出口總公司深圳公司	Shenzhen 深圳市	Guangdong 廣東省	(0755)2339793 (0755)2339793
Anhui Tobacco Company Wuhu Branch 安徽省煙草公司蕪湖分公司	Wuhu 蕪湖市	Anhui 安徽省	(0553)4812288 (0553)4812467
Luoyang Jianxi Fountain Sugar & Wine Company 洛陽市澗西噴泉糖酒公司	Luoyang 洛陽市	Henan 河南省	(0379)4321729 (0379)4324531
Shanghai Putuo Supply & Marketing Co-operative 上海市普陀區供銷合作社	Shanghai 上海市	Shanghai 上海市	(021)62576900 (021)62577469
Zhejiang Native and Non-staple Food General Co. 浙江省土產副食品總公司	Hangzhou 杭州市	Zhejiang 浙江省	(0571)7912957 (0571)7911808
Hebei Tobacco Company Zhangjiakou Branch 河北省煙草公司張家口分公司	Zhangjiakou 張家口市	Hebei 河北省	(0313)2015537 (0313)2017607

*Also include sales by firms outside this industry.包括本行業以外廠家的銷售。"o" stands for "others". "o" 代表"其他產品"。

1492: Starch and Starch Products 澱粉及澱粉製品業

The industry accounts for 0.133% of the total revenue of China's industrial sector in 1996. The revenue growth rate of the industry is 9.1% from 1995, as compared to the growth rate of China's industrial sector, 9.51%. The rate of return on asset is 0.54%. 69.32% of all firms in the industry made a profit while 22.38% had negative returns. The top province in terms of the industry's revenue is Shandong, accounting for 23.45% of the total revenue.
本行業在1996年佔全行業總產值0.133%，行業年增長率為9.1%（全國工業年增長率9.51%）。行業的資產回報率0.54%，69.32%的企業盈利，22.38%的企業虧損。銷售收入最高的省份為山東省，佔本行業的23.45%。

	Total number of firms 企業總數	Total number of employees 職工總數	Total revenue (mil. RMB) 總銷售收入（百萬元）	Total profit (mil. RMB) 總利潤（百萬元）	Return on assets 資產利潤率 (%)	Return on equity 權益利潤率 (%)	Labour productivity ('000 RMB / worker) 勞動生產率（千元/人）	Debts / assets 資產負債率 (%)	Total assets (mil. RMB) 總資產（百萬元）
Industry Overall 行業總體	1,170	107,372	7,709	56	0.54	3.22	71.80	83.30	10,330

	Number of firms 企業個數	Average number of employees 平均職工人數	Average revenue ('000 RMB) 平均銷售收入（千元）	Average profit ('000 RMB) 平均利潤（千元）	Return on assets 資產利潤率 (%)	Return on equity 權益利潤率 (%)	Labour productivity ('000 RMB / worker) 勞動生產率（千元/人）	Average debts / assets 平均資產負債率(%)	Average Total assets ('000 RMB) 平均總資產（千元）
By ownership 產業所有權									
State-owned 國有	239	164	8,728	-268	-1.66	-17.11	53.16	90.29	16,121
Collectively-owned 集體	830	68	4,710	101	2.21	9.08	69.61	75.65	4,553
Privately-owned 私有	5	36	1,673	49	4.90	13.01	45.96	62.35	999
Domestic JVs 聯營	8	60	4,207	-17	-0.43	-0.86	70.12	49.77	3,929
Joint stock 股份制	15	156	15,632	360	2.64	12.05	100.33	78.08	13,648
Foreign-funded 外資	37	80	6,849	26	0.25	0.61	85.67	59.55	10,556
Overseas Chinese-funded 港澳台資	34	186	34,803	880	1.45	14.26	187.53	89.85	60,772
By size 規模									
Large 大型	7	909	166,625	4,049	1.32	13.33	183.39	90.12	307,414
Medium 中型	30	470	51,829	428	0.67	5.62	110.16	88.02	63,624
Small 小型	1,093	78	4,563	14	0.24	1.15	58.65	79.54	5,735
By regional distribution 地區分布									
Central-North 華北	203	101	6,622	253	3.85	14.52	65.61	73.51	6,577
Beijing 北京	10	59	6,133	14	0.22	0.70	104.48	67.97	6,238
Tianjin 天津	10	187	13,523	1,041	9.25	19.84	72.47	53.38	11,255
Hebei 河北	94	137	10,145	289	3.47	18.27	74.23	81.00	8,322
Shanxi 山西	39	60	1,778	1	0.02	0.06	29.39	67.97	4,061
Inner Mongolia 內蒙	50	57	2,494	272	6.20	16.63	44.11	62.72	4,393
Northeast 東北	142	137	9,244	-300	-1.36	-12.15	67.30	88.84	22,125
Liaoning 遼寧	30	138	2,579	-1,082	-5.50	-17.87	18.65	69.21	19,673
Jilin 吉林	34	278	28,128	-247	-0.38	-6.50	101.36	94.09	64,338
Heilongjiang 黑龍江	78	76	3,576	-22	-0.48	-4.41	47.11	89.09	4,667
Central East 華東	242	113	11,381	484	4.92	19.18	100.42	74.36	9,848
Shanghai 上海	13	55	3,319	-80	-2.02	-4.85	60.35	58.32	3,962
Jiangsu 江蘇	44	94	9,177	2	0.02	0.08	97.79	71.80	8,880
Zhejiang 浙江	11	71	7,108	-82	-0.75	-3.30	99.86	77.42	10,975
Anhui 安徽	51	65	5,743	366	11.36	75.17	88.41	84.90	3,220
Fujian 福建	9	43	1,571	-253	-6.59	-32.02	36.16	79.41	3,842
Jiangxi 江西	29	85	3,949	28	0.57	800.00	46.66	99.92	4,868
Shandong 山東	85	184	21,265	1,199	6.88	24.25	115.55	71.62	17,415
Central-South 中南	338	77	5,324	-113	-1.58	-14.39	68.71	89.05	7,184
Henan 河南	102	95	6,812	255	3.16	19.05	71.62	83.40	8,054
Hubei 湖北	49	52	3,286	28	0.95	7.30	62.95	86.93	2,975
Hunan 湖南	35	26	1,846	-53	-2.96	-14.58	70.53	79.72	1,778
Guangdong 廣東	37	80	7,844	-518	-3.79	121.16	97.63	103.12	13,694
Guangxi 廣西	108	89	5,392	-399	-5.06	-40.73	60.26	87.56	7,879
Hainan 海南	7	54	936	-216	-3.67	-19.04	17.33	80.72	5,876
Southwest 西南	82	39	2,361	-65	-2.09	-12.64	60.85	83.45	3,112
Chongqing 重慶	10	42	1,592	201	6.43	-70.32	37.34	109.14	3,123
Sichuan 四川	40	51	3,660	-168	-3.79	-17.23	70.46	78.01	4,435
Guizhou 貴州	19	14	434	-55	-7.68	-51.98	31.33	85.22	719
Yunnan 雲南	11	35	1,886	31	1.16	8.67	53.21	86.64	2,667
Tibet 西藏	1								
Northwest 西北	163	65	1,870	-165	-3.41	-26.34	28.80	87.05	4,825
Shaanxi 陝西	41	53	2,024	-69	-1.76	-51.45	38.49	96.57	3,912
Gansu 甘肅	70	75	1,850	-298	-6.63	-41.51	24.58	84.05	4,504
Qinghai 青海	5	19	376	20	2.54	71.43	19.38	96.45	788
Ningxia 寧夏	33	54	1,561	-32	-0.53	-2.20	29.09	75.80	5,924
Xinjiang 新疆	14	92	2,781	-156	-1.96	159.12	30.20	101.23	7,956

1492: Starch and Starch Products 澱粉及澱粉製品業

Year 年份	Number of firms 企業個數	Rate of change 每年變化 (%)	Number of employees 職工人數 (人)	Rate of change 每年變化 (%)	Total revenue (mil. RMB) 總銷售收入 (百萬元)	Rate of change 每年變化 (%)	Total profit (mil. RMB) 總利潤 (百萬元)	Rate of change 每年變化 (%)
1993	948		86,513		3,498		42	
1994	976	2.95%	79,513	-8.09%	4,383	25.27%	25	-41.79%
1995	1,172	20.08%	111,383	40.08%	7,067	61.24%	115	364.34%
1996	1,170	-0.17%	107,372	-3.60%	7,709	9.08%	56	-51.23%

3 Major products* 3種主要產品*	Output 產量	Sales volume 銷售量	Unit 單位
a) Bean Vermicelli 粉絲、粉條	124,707	119,719	ton 噸
b) Starch 澱粉	2,319,316	2,226,543	ton 噸

Top 10 firms by revenue (year founded) 收入排名前10家企業 (創辦年份)	City 城市	Province 省	Telephone / fax 電話 / 傳真	Number of employees 職工人數	Ownership 產業所有權	Revenue ('000 RMB) 銷售收入 (千元)	Profit ('000 RMB) (rank) 利潤 (千元) (排名)	Total assets ('000 RMB) 總資產 (千元)	Major products 主要產品
Yellow Dragon Foods Industrial Co. Ltd. 黃龍食品工業有限公司(1991)	Siping 四平市	Jilin 吉林省	(0434)6213632	1,110	Foreign-funded 外資	404,500	33900(1)	535,300	b
Jilin Novel Source Corn Development Ltd. 吉林新源玉米開發有限公司(1989)	Jilin 吉林市	Jilin 吉林省	(0432)3522966 (0432)3521799	1,450	Overseas Chinese-funded 港澳台資	200,429	-28973(494)	831,473	b
Qingdao Qing Fu Food Co. Ltd. 青島清福食品有限公司(1991)	Qingdao 青島市	Shandong 山東省	(0532)2210447 (0532)2210448	132	Foreign-funded 外資	191,881	39(249)	28,393	a,b
Shandong Da Yang Foods Group Co. Ltd 山東大洋食品集團有限公司	Qingdao 青島市	Shandong 山東省	(0532)8900231 (0532)8900231	2,200	Private-owned 私營	191,145	14760(2)	167,369	o
Qinhuangdao Funing Starch Glucose Refinery 秦皇島市撫寧縣澱粉葡萄糖廠(1989)	Qinhuangdao 秦皇島市	Hebei 河北省	(0335)6012550 (0335)6017779	930	State-owned 國有	158,389	5583(14)	134,514	b
Shandong Liu Xu Group Co. Ltd. 山東柳絮集團有限公司(1984)	Jining 濟寧市	Shandong 山東省	(0537)4211125 (0537)4211127	1,640	Collectively-owned 集體	148,809	11799(3)	133,041	a,b
Zibo Qi Bao Group Co. Ltd. 淄博齊寶集團股份有限公司(1992)	Zibo 淄博市	Shandong 山東省	(0533)8681666 (0533)8681666	1,000	Joint stock 股份制	138,672	7311(7)	91,617	b
Jining Antibiotics Factory Yanzhou Starch Factory 濟寧抗生素廠兗州澱粉廠(1989)	Jining 濟寧市	Shandong 山東省	(0537)3862556 (0537)3862556	664	Collectively-owned 集體	133,680	7050(8)	131,960	b
Zhucheng Starch Co. Ltd. 諸城市澱粉股份有限公司(1993)	Weifang 濰坊市	Shandong 山東省	(0536)6521283 (0536)6521283	579	Joint stock 股份制	118,683	10063(4)	102,668	b
Guangxi Ming Yang Starch Chemical General Factory 廣西明陽澱粉化工總廠(1959)	Nanning 南寧市	Guangxi 廣西	(0771)2802389 (0771)2821119	591	State-owned 國有	103,688	5627(13)	162,566	b

Top 10 Cities by Production Output 產出排名前10位城市	Province 省	Market share 市場份額	Number of firms 企業個數
Siping 四平市	Jilin 吉林省	8.15%	10
Weifang 濰坊市	Shandong 山東省	7.85%	12
Nanning 南寧市	Guangxi 廣西	4.61%	36
Qinhuangdao 秦皇島市	Hebei 河北省	4.29%	13
Jining 濟寧市	Shandong 山東省	3.52%	22
Jilin 吉林市	Jilin 吉林省	3.28%	4
Tieling 鐵嶺市	Liaoning 遼寧省	2.49%	3
Jiaozuo 焦作市	Henan 河南省	2.31%	13
Shijiazhuang 石家莊市	Hebei 河北省	2.25%	25
Yantai 煙台市	Shandong 山東省	2.02%	9

10 Major Wholesalers 10家主要批發商	City 城市	Province 省	Telephone / Fax 電話 / 傳真
Shanghai Jiu Zhou Group Co. Ltd. 上海九州集團有限公司	Shanghai 上海市	Shanghai 上海市	(021)62401515 (021)62123848
Shanghai Tobacco (Group) Co. Trade Center 上海煙草集團上海煙草貿易中心	Shanghai 上海市	Shanghai 上海市	(021)58781921 (021)58786584
China Tax - Free Company 中國免稅公司	Beijing 北京市	Beijing 北京市	(010)64668397 (010)64635846
Liaoning Cigarette Marketing Company 遼寧省卷煙銷售公司	Shenyang 瀋陽市	Liaoning 遼寧省	(024)22834388 (024)22837853
Hunan Import & Export General Company Shenzhen Company 湖南省進出口總公司深圳公司	Shenzhen 深圳市	Guangdong 廣東省	(0755)2339793 (0755)2339793
Anhui Tobacco Company Wuhu Branch 安徽省煙草公司蕪湖分公司	Wuhu 蕪湖市	Anhui 安徽省	(0553)4812288 (0553)4812467
Luoyang Jianxi Fountain Sugar & Wine Company 洛陽市澗西噴泉糖酒公司	Luoyang 洛陽市	Henan 河南省	(0379)4321729 (0379)4324531
Shanghai Putuo Supply & Marketing Co-operative 上海市普陀區供銷合作社	Shanghai 上海市	Shanghai 上海市	(021)62576900 (021)62577469
Zhejiang Native and Non-staple Food General Co. 浙江省土產副食品總公司	Hangzhou 杭州市	Zhejiang 浙江省	(0571)7912957 (0571)7911808
Hebei Tobacco Company Zhangjiakou Branch 河北省煙草公司張家口分公司	Zhangjiakou 張家口市	Hebei 河北省	(0313)2015537 (0313)2017607

*Also include sales by firms outside this industry.包括本行業以外廠家的銷售。"o" stands for "others". "o" 代表"其他產品"。

1493: Dairy Substitute 代乳品製造業

The industry accounts for 0.001% of the total revenue of China's industrial sector in 1996. The revenue growth rate of the industry is -55.1% from 1995, as compared to the growth rate of China's industrial sector, 9.51%. The rate of return on asset is -5.13%. 58.93% of all firms in the industry made a profit while 28.57% had negative returns. The top province in terms of the industry's revenue is Zhejiang, accounting for 30.13% of the total revenue.
本行業在1996年佔全行業總產值0.001%，行業年增長率為-55.1%（全國工業年增長率9.51%）。行業的資產回報率-5.13%，58.93%的企業盈利，28.57%的企業虧損。銷售收入最高的省份為浙江省，佔本行業的30.13%。

	Total number of firms 企業總數	Total number of employees 職工總數	Total revenue (mil. RMB) 總銷售收入（百萬元）	Total profit (mil. RMB) 總利潤（百萬元）	Return on assets 資產利潤率 (%)	Return on equity 權益利潤率 (%)	Labour productivity ('000 RMB / worker) 勞動生產率（千元/人）	Debts / assets 資產負債率 (%)	Total assets (mil. RMB) 總資產（百萬元）
Industry Overall 行業總體	30	1,884	46	-11	-5.13	-31.30	24.42	83.62	209

	Number of firms 企業個數	Average number of employees 平均職工人數	Average revenue ('000 RMB) 平均銷售收入（千元）	Average profit ('000 RMB) 平均利潤（千元）	Return on assets 資產利潤率 (%)	Return on equity 權益利潤率 (%)	Labour productivity ('000 RMB / worker) 勞動生產率（千元/人）	Average debts / assets 平均資產負債率(%)	Average Total assets ('000 RMB) 平均總資產（千元）
By ownership 產業所有權									
State-owned 國有	12	100	2,083	-417	-6.02	-100.00	20.89	93.98	6,917
Collectively-owned 集體	14	42	1,273	-335	-7.60	-101.47	30.53	92.51	4,408
Privately-owned 私有									
Domestic JVs 聯營									
Joint stock 股份制									
Foreign-funded 外資	1	15	313	1,129	30.83	32.15	20.86	4.11	3,662
Overseas Chinese-funded 港澳台資	2	44	1,428	-1,220	-4.03	-11.69	32.45	65.57	30,308
By size 規模									
Large 大型									
Medium 中型									
Small 小型	29	64	1,586	-379	-5.26	-32.36	24.81	83.73	7,206
By regional distribution 地區分布									
Central-North 華北	7	77	1,300	-196	-6.58	-122.32	16.79	94.67	2,976
Beijing 北京	2								
Tianjin 天津									
Hebei 河北	3	144	2,887	-457	-20.21	360.53	20.09	105.60	2,260
Shanxi 山西	1	70	120				1.71	94.10	11,520
Inner Mongolia 內蒙	1	41	320				7.80	67.98	2,530
Northeast 東北	3	76	1,583	37	0.37	6.18	20.83	94.06	9,933
Liaoning 遼寧									
Jilin 吉林	2	65						98.61	13,695
Heilongjiang 黑龍江	1	98	4,750	110	4.56	7.86	48.47	42.32	2,410
Central East 華東	9	65	2,643	-592	-7.85	-50.52	40.88	84.45	7,540
Shanghai 上海									
Jiangsu 江蘇									
Zhejiang 浙江	4	44	3,465	-1,280	-27.28	1462.86	78.75	101.86	4,693
Anhui 安徽	1	32	1,800	260	15.95	15.95	56.25		1,630
Fujian 福建									
Jiangxi 江西	1	129	200	-190	-3.44	126.67	1.55	102.72	5,520
Shandong 山東	3	82	2,643	-93	-0.67	-2.97	32.37	77.54	13,980
Central-South 中南	7	29	351	-390	-3.76	-15.66	12.24	75.97	10,360
Henan 河南	3	52	373	7	0.89	3.23	7.23	72.44	750
Hubei 湖北									
Hunan 湖南	1	10	100	10	0.47	1.00	10.00	52.61	2,110
Guangdong 廣東	2	18	620	-1,380	-4.05	-17.46	34.44	76.80	34,080
Guangxi 廣西	1								
Hainan 海南									
Southwest 西南	1	130	1,310	-850	-23.68	326.92	10.08	107.24	3,590
Chongqing 重慶									
Sichuan 四川	1	130	1,310	-850	-23.68	327.03	10.08	107.24	3,590
Guizhou 貴州									
Yunnan 雲南									
Tibet 西藏									
Northwest 西北	3	67	1,487	-180	-3.82	-15.04	22.19	74.56	4,717
Shaanxi 陝西	2	72	2,025	-160	-4.06	-39.51	28.32	89.73	3,945
Gansu 甘肅									
Qinghai 青海									
Ningxia 寧夏									
Xinjiang 新疆	1	58	410	-220	-3.51	-7.91	7.07	55.43	6,260

1493: Dairy Substitute 代乳品製造業

Year 年份	Number of firms 企業個數	Rate of change 每年變化 (%)	Number of employees 職工人數 (人)	Rate of change 每年變化 (%)	Total revenue (mil. RMB) 總銷售收入 (百萬元)	Rate of change 每年變化 (%)	Total profit (mil. RMB) 總利潤 (百萬元)	Rate of change 每年變化 (%)
1993	33		2,974		105		-4	
1994	24	-27.27%	1,895	-36.28%	45	-57.16%	0	95.64%
1995	25	4.17%	1,994	5.22%	102	127.70%	1	809.68%
1996	30	20.00%	1,884	-5.52%	46	-55.05%	-11	-933.33%

3 Major products* 3種主要產品*	Output 產量	Sales volume 銷售量	Unit 單位
a) Bean Products 豆製品	5,059	11,685	ton 噸

Top 10 firms by revenue (year founded) 收入排名前10家企業 (創辦年份)	City 城市	Province 省	Telephone / fax 電話/傳真	Number of employees 職工人數	Ownership 產業所有權	Revenue ('000 RMB) 銷售收入 (千元)	Profit ('000 RMB) (rank) 利潤(千元)(排名)	Total assets ('000 RMB) 總資產 (千元)	Major products 主要產品
Shanghai Hua Fu Beverage Food Factory 上海華福飲料食品廠(1992)	Shanghai 上海市	Shanghai 上海市	(021)56990158	82	Collectively-owned 集體	5,787	14(3)	4,879	o
Yantai Kang Sheng Food General Factory 煙台康盛食品總廠(1957)	Yantai 煙台市	Shandong 山東省	(0535)4212838	164	State-owned 國有	5,505	58(2)	14,051	o
Bayan Wan Fa Dairy Products Factory 巴彥縣萬發乳品廠(1982)	Shuangcheng 雙城市	Heilongjiang 黑龍江省	(0451)7565119	36	Collectively-owned 集體	4,750	110(1)	2,413	a
Zhangjiakou Milk Company 張家口市牛奶公司(1956)	Zhangjiakou 張家口市	Hebei 河北省	(0313)4061011	386	State-owned 國有	4,425	-1389(7)	5,882	o
Qinhuangdao Lulong Sheet Jelly Factory 秦皇島市盧龍粉皮廠(1992)	Qinhuangdao 秦皇島市	Hebei 河北省	(0335)7021403	25	Collectively-owned 集體	4,050	0(4)	640	o
Longkou Chang Sheng Bao Group Company 龍口市長生寶集團公司(1993)	Yantai 煙台市	Shandong 山東省	(0535)8526288	81	Overseas Chinese-funded 港澳台資	2,424	-342(6)	27,888	o
Shannxi Sanyuan Dairy Products Factory 陝西省三原縣乳品廠(1979)	Xianyang 咸陽市	Shaanxi 陝西省	(0910)2282653	107	State-owned 國有	2,085	-324(5)	5,026	o
Leqing Dairy Products Factory 樂清市乳製品廠(1979)	Wenzhou 温州市	Zhejiang 浙江省	(0577)2522685	38	Collectively-owned 集體	2,056	-2186(8)	8,409	o

Top 10 Cities by Production Output 產出排名前10位城市	Province 省	Market share 市場份額	Number of firms 企業個數
Suzhou 蘇州市	Jiangsu 江蘇省	66.48%	1
Harbin 哈爾濱市	Heilongjiang 黑龍江省	22.33%	5
Jiaozuo 焦作市	Henan 河南省	2.89%	1
Guangzhou 廣州市	Guangdong 廣東省	2.28%	1
Wenzhou 温州市	Zhejiang 浙江省	0.85%	3
Shanghai 上海市	Shanghai 上海市	0.77%	1
Zhangjiakou 張家口市	Hebei 河北省	0.62%	1
Ji'nan 濟南市	Shandong 山東省	0.61%	1
Yantai 煙台市	Shandong 山東省	0.60%	2
Qinhuangdao 秦皇島市	Hebei 河北省	0.59%	1

10 Major Wholesalers 10家主要批發商	City 城市	Province 省	Telephone / Fax 電話/傳真
Shanghai Jiu Zhou Group Co. Ltd. 上海九州集團有限公司	Shanghai 上海市	Shanghai 上海市	(021)62401515 (021)62123848
Shanghai Tobacco (Group) Co. Trade Center 上海煙草集團上海煙草貿易中心	Shanghai 上海市	Shanghai 上海市	(021)58781921 (021)58786584
China Tax – Free Company 中國免稅公司	Beijing 北京市	Beijing 北京市	(010)64668397 (010)64635846
Liaoning Cigarette Marketing Company 遼寧省卷煙銷售公司	Shenyang 瀋陽市	Liaoning 遼寧省	(024)22834388 (024)22837853
Hunan Import & Export General Company Shenzhen Company 湖南省進出口總公司深圳公司	Shenzhen 深圳市	Guangdong 廣東省	(0755)2339793 (0755)2339793
Anhui Tobacco Company Wuhu Branch 安徽省煙草公司蕪湖分公司	Wuhu 蕪湖市	Anhui 安徽省	(0553)4812288 (0553)4812467
Luoyang Jianxi Fountain Sugar & Wine Company 洛陽市澗西噴泉糖酒公司	Luoyang 洛陽市	Henan 河南省	(0379)4321729 (0379)4324531
Shanghai Putuo Supply & Marketing Co-operative 上海市普陀區供銷合作社	Shanghai 上海市	Shanghai 上海市	(021)62576900 (021)62577469
Zhejiang Native and Non-staple Food General Co. 浙江省土產副食品總公司	Hangzhou 杭州市	Zhejiang 浙江省	(0571)7912957 (0571)7911808
Hebei Tobacco Company Zhangjiakou Branch 河北省煙草公司張家口分公司	Zhangjiakou 張家口市	Hebei 河北省	(0313)2015537 (0313)2017607

*Also include sales by firms outside this industry.包括本行業以外廠家的銷售。"o" stands for "others". "o" 代表"其他產品"。

1495: Ice 製冰業

The industry accounts for 0.006% of the total revenue of China's industrial sector in 1996. The revenue growth rate of the industry is 12.5% from 1995, as compared to the growth rate of China's industrial sector, 9.51%. The rate of return on asset is 1.10%. 70.00% of all firms in the industry made a profit while 30.00% had negative returns. The top province in terms of the industry's revenue is Guangdong, accounting for 39.89% of the total revenue.
本行業在1996年佔全行業總產值0.006%，行業年增長率為12.5%（全國工業年增長率9.51%）。行業的資產回報率1.10%，70.00%的企業盈利，30.00%的企業虧損。銷售收入最高的省份為廣東省，佔本行業的39.89%。

	Total number of firms 企業總數	Total number of employees 職工總數	Total revenue (mil. RMB) 總銷售收入（百萬元）	Total profit (mil. RMB) 總利潤（百萬元）	Return on assets 資產利潤率 (%)	Return on equity 權益利潤率 (%)	Labour productivity ('000 RMB / worker) 勞動生產率（千元／人）	Debts / assets 資產負債率 (%)	Total assets (mil. RMB) 總資產（百萬元）
Industry Overall 行業總體	161	6,377	325	7	1.10	2.28	50.96	51.57	635

	Number of firms 企業個數	Average number of employees 平均職工人數	Average revenue ('000 RMB) 平均銷售收入（千元）	Average profit ('000 RMB) 平均利潤（千元）	Return on assets 資產利潤率 (%)	Return on equity 權益利潤率 (%)	Labour productivity ('000 RMB / worker) 勞動生產率（千元／人）	Average debts / assets 平均資產負債率(%)	Average Total assets ('000 RMB) 平均總資產（千元）
By ownership 產業所有權									
State-owned 國有	53	68	2,491				36.47	58.06	7,019
Collectively-owned 集體	90	27	1,750	90	4.34	8.23	65.11	47.26	2,083
Privately-owned 私有	3	14	797	755	59.75	248.05	55.57	75.91	1,264
Domestic JVs 聯營	5	30	4,222	-44	-0.69	-1.38	138.87	50.35	6,438
Joint stock 股份制									
Foreign-funded 外資	5	19	371	-1,135	-35.63	-41.55	19.93	14.24	3,185
Overseas Chinese-funded 港澳台資	3	12	3,161	827	10.80	11.27	270.93	4.18	7,654
By size 規模									
Large 大型									
Medium 中型	2	52	9,572	3,904	14.08	22.38	184.07	37.07	27,724
Small 小型	158	40	1,935	-5	-0.14	-0.30	48.91	52.88	3,668
By regional distribution 地區分布									
Central-North 華北	1	29	200	-10	-6.25	7.69	6.90	181.25	160
Beijing 北京									
Tianjin 天津	1	29	200	-10	-6.25	7.69	6.90	181.25	160
Hebei 河北									
Shanxi 山西									
Inner Mongolia 內蒙									
Northeast 東北	3	57	60	103	5.36	8.93	1.05	39.97	1,927
Liaoning 遼寧	2	8	90	15	4.92	6.52	12.00	24.59	305
Jilin 吉林	1	156		280	5.42	9.30		41.78	5,170
Heilongjiang 黑龍江									
Central East 華東	70	39	2,244	31	0.89	1.70	58.19	47.33	3,418
Shanghai 上海	7	45	1,267	77	2.56	4.50	28.07	43.07	3,009
Jiangsu 江蘇	8	85	5,356	-233	-2.92	-6.31	63.20	53.68	7,961
Zhejiang 浙江	29	34	2,028	39	1.12	2.54	59.95	55.81	3,446
Anhui 安徽									
Fujian 福建	18	22	1,032	18	0.90	1.02	47.98	11.98	1,971
Jiangxi 江西	2	7	575				82.14	29.03	310
Shandong 山東	6	54	4,467	337	10.95	23.27	82.97	52.93	3,073
Central-South 中南	77	42	1,993	45	0.95	2.16	47.96	55.82	4,739
Henan 河南	1	8							
Hubei 湖北									
Hunan 湖南	3	15	580	20	16.67	27.27	39.55	41.67	120
Guangdong 廣東	51	49	2,542	23	0.45	0.96	52.37	53.13	5,119
Guangxi 廣西	5	14	426				30.43	36.51	882
Hainan 海南	17	35	1,175	132	2.26	6.24	33.13	63.80	5,829
Southwest 西南	8	22	1,569	110	7.65	21.46	71.31	64.43	1,438
Chongqing 重慶									
Sichuan 四川	5	20	1,766	90	7.55	44.13	88.30	82.89	1,192
Guizhou 貴州									
Yunnan 雲南	3	26	1,240	143	7.76	14.01	47.69	44.58	1,847
Tibet 西藏									
Northwest 西北	2	51	795	105	1.51	1.60	15.59	5.76	6,940
Shaanxi 陝西	2	51	795	105	1.51	1.60	15.59	5.76	6,940
Gansu 甘肅									
Qinghai 青海									
Ningxia 寧夏									
Xinjiang 新疆									

Year 年份	Number of firms 企業個數	Rate of change 每年變化 (%)	Number of employees 職工人數 (人)	Rate of change 每年變化 (%)	Total revenue (mil. RMB) 總銷售收入 (百萬元)	Rate of change 每年變化 (%)	Total profit (mil. RMB) 總利潤 (百萬元)	Rate of change 每年變化 (%)
1993	121		6,138		276		7	
1994	128	5.79%	10,993	79.10%	218	-21.17%	9	39.09%
1995	154	20.31%	8,579	-21.96%	289	32.69%	4	-59.18%
1996	161	4.55%	6,377	-25.67%	325	12.48%	7	84.94%

3 Major products* 3 種主要產品 *	Output 產量	Sales volume 銷售量	Unit 單位
a) Artical of Aquatic Products Industry 水產加工品	25,610	23,817	ton 噸
b) Meat Products 禽肉製品	10,632	7,974	ton 噸
c) Aquatic Animal Frozen Products 水生動物冷凍品	10,080	9,475	ton 噸

Top 10 firms by revenue (year founded) 收入排名前 10 家企業 (創辦年份)	City 城市	Province 省	Telephone / fax 電話 / 傳真	Number of employees 職工人數	Ownership 產業所有權	Revenue ('000 RMB) 銷售收入 (千元)	Profit ('000 RMB) (rank) 利潤 (千元) (排名)	Total assets ('000 RMB) 總資產 (千元)	Major products 主要產品
Zhangjiagang Meat Joint Processing Factory 張家港市肉類聯合加工廠(1980)	Suzhou 蘇州市	Jiangsu 江蘇省	(0512)8223459	165	State-owned 國有	27,830	950(5)	28,179	b
Qingdao Huangdao Xue Jia Dao Chang Sheng Industrial Company 青島市黃島區薛家島昌盛工業公司(1981)	Qingdao 青島市	Shandong 山東省	(0532)6878187 (0532)6878187	226	Collectively-owned 集體	21,012	1540(2)	10,830	o
Shantou Freezing Factory 汕頭市冷凍廠(1960)	Shantou 汕頭市	Guangdong 廣東省	(0754)8551858 (0754)8532889	238	State-owned 國有	19,962	1265(3)	50,293	o
Dongguan Xinwan Freezing Factory 東莞新灣冷凍廠(1991)	Dongguan 東莞市	Guangdong 廣東省	(0769)5516054	50	Collectively-owned 集體	19,924	1(30)	8,711	a
Sheng Shan Aquatic Products Food Freezing Factory 嵊山水產食品冷凍廠(1983)	Zhoushan 舟山市	Zhejiang 浙江省	(0580)5021971	76	State-owned 國有	13,478	8(27)	7,752	o
Rui'an Yu Du Ice-making General Factory 瑞安市漁都製冰總廠(1993)	Wenzhou 溫州市	Zhejiang 浙江省	(0577)5602424	166	Collectively-owned 集體	10,500	1137(4)	20,870	o
Guangdong Huazhou Jian Lian Freezing Factory 廣東省化州市鑒聯冰凍廠(1989)	Maoming 茂名市	Guangdong 廣東省	(0668)7310883	98	Collectively-owned 集體	10,300	560(8)	4,700	o
Zhuhai Aquatic Products Freezing Factory 珠海市水產冷凍廠(1976)	Zhuhai 珠海市	Guangdong 廣東省	(0756)2222363	125	State-owned 國有	10,293	1668(1)	4,774	o
Dianbai Hai Yu Ice-making Co. Ltd. 電白縣海裕製冰有限公司(1994)	Maoming 茂名市	Guangdong 廣東省	(0668)5601731	30	Foreign-funded 外資	9,650	660(6)	11,600	o
Dianbai Dan Chang Xing Da Ice-making Factory 電白縣旦場興達冰廠(1996)	Maoming 茂名市	Guangdong 廣東省	(0668)5821622	32	Collectively-owned 集體	9,400	410(9)	1,850	a,c

Top 10 Cities by Production Output 產出排名前 10 位城市	Province 省	Market share 市場份額	Number of firms 企業個數
Suzhou 蘇州市	Jiangsu 江蘇省	14.78%	1
Foshan 佛山市	Guangdong 廣東省	12.60%	2
Wenzhou 溫州市	Zhejiang 浙江省	9.68%	18
Zhanjiang 湛江市	Guangdong 廣東省	7.49%	19
Dongguan 東莞市	Guangdong 廣東省	6.48%	1
Maoming 茂名市	Guangdong 廣東省	5.36%	11
Zhoushan 舟山市	Zhejiang 浙江省	3.67%	6
Fuzhou 福州市	Fujian 福建省	3.56%	8
Ningbo 寧波市	Zhejiang 浙江省	3.28%	9
Yangjiang 陽江市	Guangdong 廣東省	3.26%	7

10 Major Wholesalers 10 家主要批發商	City 城市	Province 省	Telephone / Fax 電話 / 傳真
Shanghai Jiu Zhou Group Co. Ltd. 上海九州集團有限公司	Shanghai 上海市	Shanghai 上海市	(021)62401515 (021)62123848
Shanghai Tobacco (Group) Co. Trade Center 上海煙草集團上海煙草貿易中心	Shanghai 上海市	Shanghai 上海市	(021)58781921 (021)58786584
China Tax - Free Company 中國免税公司	Beijing 北京市	Beijing 北京市	(010)64668397 (010)64635846
Liaoning Cigarette Marketing Company 遼寧省卷煙銷售公司	Shenyang 瀋陽市	Liaoning 遼寧省	(024)22834388 (024)22837853
Hunan Import & Export General Company Shenzhen Company 湖南省進出口總公司深圳公司	Shenzhen 深圳市	Guangdong 廣東省	(0755)2339793 (0755)2339793
Anhui Tobacco Company Wuhu Branch 安徽省煙草公司蕪湖分公司	Wuhu 蕪湖市	Anhui 安徽省	(0553)4812288 (0553)4812467
Luoyang Jianxi Fountain Sugar & Wine Company 洛陽市澗西噴泉糖酒公司	Luoyang 洛陽市	Henan 河南省	(0379)4321729 (0379)4324531
Shanghai Putuo Supply & Marketing Co-operative 上海市普陀區供銷合作社	Shanghai 上海市	Shanghai 上海市	(021)62576900 (021)62577469
Zhejiang Native and Non-staple Food General Co. 浙江省土產副食品總公司	Hangzhou 杭州市	Zhejiang 浙江省	(0571)7912957 (0571)7911808
Hebei Tobacco Company Zhangjiakou Branch 河北省煙草公司張家口分公司	Zhangjiakou 張家口市	Hebei 河北省	(0313)2015537 (0313)2017607

*Also include sales by firms outside this industry.包括本行業以外廠家的銷售。"o" stands for "others". "o" 代表 "其他產品"。

1497: Starch Sugar 澱粉糖業

The industry accounts for 0.017% of the total revenue of China's industrial sector in 1996. The revenue growth rate of the industry is 2.0% from 1995, as compared to the growth rate of China's industrial sector, 9.51%. The rate of return on asset is -0.27%. 62.84% of all firms in the industry made a profit while 31.36% had negative returns. The top province in terms of the industry's revenue is Guangdong, accounting for 20.23% of the total revenue.
本行業在1996年佔全行業總產值0.017%，行業年增長率為2.0%（全國工業年增長率9.51%）。行業的資產回報率-0.27%，62.84%的企業盈利，31.36%的企業虧損。銷售收入最高的省份為廣東省，佔本行業的20.23%。

	Total number of firms 企業總數	Total number of employees 職工總數	Total revenue (mil. RMB) 總銷售收入（百萬元）	Total profit (mil. RMB) 總利潤（百萬元）	Return on assets 資產利潤率 (%)	Return on equity 權益利潤率 (%)	Labour productivity ('000 RMB / worker) 勞動生產率（千元/人）	Debts / assets 資產負債率 (%)	Total assets (mil. RMB) 總資產（百萬元）
Industry Overall 行業總體	119	13,963	964	-5	-0.27	-1.24	69.04	77.86	1,857

	Number of firms 企業個數	Average number of employees 平均職工人數	Average revenue ('000 RMB) 平均銷售收入（千元）	Average profit ('000 RMB) 平均利潤（千元）	Return on assets 資產利潤率 (%)	Return on equity 權益利潤率 (%)	Labour productivity ('000 RMB / worker) 勞動生產率（千元/人）	Average debts / assets 平均資產負債率(%)	Average Total assets ('000 RMB) 平均總資產（千元）
By ownership 產業所有權									
State-owned 國有	44	180	10,886	-250	-0.89	-5.14	60.47	82.77	28,227
Collectively-owned 集體	65	79	6,137	106	1.37	5.43	77.39	74.72	7,731
Privately-owned 私有									
Domestic JVs 聯營	3	84	24,422	963	5.79	14.20	291.90	59.21	16,627
Joint stock 股份制									
Foreign-funded 外資	3	49	1,538	-1,523	-18.40	-22.21	31.38	17.16	8,277
Overseas Chinese-funded 港澳台資	4	123	2,051	194	2.03	2.66	16.75	23.88	9,585
By size 規模									
Large 大型	2	372	46,295	175	0.21	0.75	124.62	71.64	82,480
Medium 中型	5	426	32,497	-355	-0.44	-2.24	76.36	80.41	80,804
Small 小型	112	99	6,329	-32	-0.28	-1.25	63.91	77.87	11,507
By regional distribution 地區分布									
Central-North 華北	10	120	12,561	65	0.17	3.28	104.50	94.92	38,943
Beijing 北京	2	78	3,960	130	1.82	3.71	51.10	50.98	7,150
Tianjin 天津	3	48	1,713	-110	-3.93	-23.91	35.94	83.55	2,797
Hebei 河北	5	181	22,510	144	0.20	6.32	124.50	96.89	73,348
Shanxi 山西									
Inner Mongolia 內蒙									
Northeast 東北	9	74	4,271	-150	-1.78	-5.18	57.54	65.53	8,407
Liaoning 遼寧	2	64	4,210	315	6.96	17.21	66.30	59.45	4,525
Jilin 吉林									
Heilongjiang 黑龍江	7	77	4,289	-283	-2.97	-8.84	55.49	66.36	9,516
Central East 華東	50	115	8,249	56	0.46	1.79	71.66	74.35	12,265
Shanghai 上海	3	261	30,070	-430	-0.91	-2.95	115.21	69.08	47,217
Jiangsu 江蘇	5	192	10,980	-330	-1.62	-8.95	57.25	81.84	20,308
Zhejiang 浙江	11	76	7,759	196	2.58	6.99	101.61	63.11	7,612
Anhui 安徽	11	67	3,250	-216	-3.31	-643.24	48.44	99.50	6,543
Fujian 福建	6	60	2,938	-330	-3.71	-6.30	48.70	41.18	8,900
Jiangxi 江西	5	69	2,810	-534	-11.13	-50.66	40.72	78.08	4,800
Shandong 山東	9	192	12,729	1,181	7.76	39.20	66.26	80.19	15,220
Central-South 中南	39	125	8,550	4	0.02	0.08	68.50	71.80	16,473
Henan 河南	12	185	7,981	178	0.88	3.19	43.08	72.51	20,229
Hubei 湖北	6	89	3,643	-242	-5.98	70.39	40.78	108.50	4,038
Hunan 湖南	3	172	3,370	-720	-3.89	-11.73	19.63	66.84	18,527
Guangdong 廣東	10	134	19,506	176	0.56	1.84	145.57	69.55	31,347
Guangxi 廣西	8	32	1,331	-16	-2.03	-4.96	41.93	58.97	801
Hainan 海南									
Southwest 西南	4	106	5,083	-800	-17.31	-117.22	47.95	85.24	4,623
Chongqing 重慶	1	157	9,494	-2,637	-39.90	49.18	60.46	181.12	6,608
Sichuan 四川	1	10	316	-33	-1.30	-1.75	28.83	25.70	2,572
Guizhou 貴州	1	8	50	20	66.67	66.67	6.25		30
Yunnan 雲南	1	249	10,470	-550	-5.93	-8.94	42.05	33.73	9,280
Tibet 西藏									
Northwest 西北	7	149	4,747	-601	-3.58	-17.53	31.80	79.62	16,823
Shaanxi 陝西	4	131	5,560	-930	-6.01	-22.12	42.61	72.83	15,475
Gansu 甘肅	1	414	7,620	20	0.04	0.49	18.41	90.78	44,590
Qinghai 青海									
Ningxia 寧夏	1	78	1,160	-390	-5.50	-43.82	14.87	87.59	7,090
Xinjiang 新疆	1	31	2,210	-120	-2.87	-5.48	71.29	47.61	4,180

Year 年份	Number of firms 企業個數	Rate of change 每年變化 (%)	Number of employees 職工人數（人）	Rate of change 每年變化 (%)	Total revenue (mil. RMB) 總銷售收入（百萬元）	Rate of change 每年變化 (%)	Total profit (mil. RMB) 總利潤（百萬元）	Rate of change 每年變化 (%)
1993	102		11,153		458		-6	
1994	112	9.80%	11,986	7.47%	585	27.63%	-4	42.37%
1995	137	22.32%	19,002	58.53%	945	61.58%	-10	-196.16%
1996	119	-13.14%	13,963	-26.52%	964	2.03%	-5	52.00%

3 Major products* 3 種主要產品 *	Output 產量	Sales volume 銷售量	Unit 單位
a) Starch Sugar 澱粉糖	118,834	110,516	ton 噸
b) Other Chemical Raw Material Medicine 其他化學原料藥	12,056	11,574	ton 噸

Top 10 firms by revenue (year founded) 收入排名前 10 家企業（創辦年份）	City 城市	Province 省	Telephone / fax 電話 / 傳真	Number of employees 職工人數	Ownership 產業所有權	Revenue ('000 RMB) 銷售收入（千元）	Profit ('000 RMB) (rank) 利潤（千元）（排名）	Total assets ('000 RMB) 總資產（千元）	Major products 主要產品
Hebei Glucose Factory 河北葡萄糖廠(1994)	Shijiazhuang 石家莊市	Hebei 河北省	(0311)8031577 (0311)8032474	706	State-owned 國有	87,648	986(6)	354,447	o
Guangdong Guangning Glucose Factory 廣東省廣寧縣葡萄糖廠(1956)	Zhaoqing 肇慶市	Guangdong 廣東省	(0757)8711598 (0757)8711739	493	State-owned 國有	86,303	1413(3)	171,596	o
Shanghai Golden Spring Enterprise Co. Ltd. 上海金泉葡萄糖企業有限公司(1987)	Shanghai 上海市	Shanghai 上海市	(021)57271000 (021)57271002	542	Collectively-owned 集體	64,530	1216(4)	104,106	a
Guangzhou Zhu Jiang Foods Products Factory 廣州市珠江食品廠(1954)	Guangzhou 廣州市	Guangdong 廣東省	(020)81984441 (020)81984441	368	Collectively-owned 集體	51,540	514(12)	51,203	a
State-owned Jiangsu Baoying Glucose Factory 國營江蘇寶應葡萄糖廠(1954)	Yangzhou 揚州市	Jiangsu 江蘇省	(0514)8223872 (0514)8221045	728	State-owned 國有	42,628	-1862(63)	84,629	o
Weifang No.5 Pharmaceutical Factory 濰坊第五製藥廠(1977)	Weifang 濰坊市	Shandong 山東省	(0536)6223123 (0536)6223123	470	Collectively-owned 集體	40,417	350(17)	39,747	b
Shandong Duqing Group Co. 山東都慶集團公司(1988)	Heze 菏澤市	Shandong 山東省	(0530)2791146 (0530)2791202	830	Collectively-owned 集體	39,716	8229(1)	68,315	a
Haining Feng Yuan Foods Co. Ltd. 海寧豐園食品有限公司(1993)	Jiaxing 嘉興市	Zhejiang 浙江省	(0573)7777195 (0573)7777261	175	Collectively-owned 集體	26,197	2455(2)	18,288	o
Shanghai Zheng Guang He Glucose Refinery 上海正廣和葡萄糖廠(1994)	Shanghai 上海市	Shanghai 上海市	(021)59266214 (021)59266396	122	Domestic JVs 聯營	24,028	-1255(60)	32,039	a
Hangzhou Grain & Oil Chemical Factory 杭州糧油化工廠(1946)	Hangzhou 杭州市	Zhejiang 浙江省	(0571)6051456 (0571)6052938	262	State-owned 國有	22,182	0(47)	35,902	a

Top 10 Cities by Production Output 產出排名前 10 位城市	Province 省	Market share 市場份額	Number of firms 企業個數
Shanghai 上海市	Shanghai 上海市	11.68%	5
Fuyang 阜陽市	Anhui 安徽省	8.70%	5
Shijiazhuang 石家莊市	Hebei 河北省	7.75%	2
Heze 菏澤市	Shandong 山東省	6.56%	2
Jiaxing 嘉興市	Zhejiang 浙江省	6.03%	6
Guangzhou 廣州市	Guangdong 廣東省	5.68%	2
Jiamusi 佳木斯市	Heilongjiang 黑龍江省	5.17%	2
Zhaoqing 肇慶市	Guangdong 廣東省	4.33%	1
Hangzhou 杭州市	Zhejiang 浙江省	4.28%	2
Weifang 濰坊市	Shandong 山東省	3.76%	4

10 Major Wholesalers 10 家主要批發商	City 城市	Province 省	Telephone / Fax 電話 / 傳真
Zhong Liang Sugar Industry Groceries Import & Export Company 中糧糖業雜品進出口公司	Beijing 北京市	Beijing 北京市	(010)65268888 (010)65276023
China National Sugar & Alcohol Group Corp. 中國糖業酒類集團公司	Beijing 北京市	Beijing 北京市	(010)68360994
Shanxi Sugar & Wine Non-staple Food Company 山西省糖酒副食公司	Taiyuan 太原市	Shanxi 山西省	(0351)2027938 (0351)2027931
Putian Xue Jin Beer Marketing Agency Co. Ltd. 莆田縣雪津啤酒營銷代理有限公司	Putian 莆田市	Fujian 福建省	
Suzhou Sugar, Cigarette & Wine General Company 蘇州糖煙酒總公司	Suzhou 蘇州市	Jiangsu 江蘇省	(0512)7276392 (0512)7276406
Yuhang Sugar Industry Tobacco & Wine Company 余杭市糖業煙酒公司	Hangzhou 杭州市	Zhejiang 浙江省	(0571)6225788 (0571)6225407
Wuxi Sugar Industry Cigarette & Wine General Company 無錫市糖業煙酒總公司	Wuxi 無錫市	Jiangsu 江蘇省	(0510)2720023 (0510)2707693
Wuxi Chaoyang Co. Ltd. 無錫朝陽股份有限公司	Wuxi 無錫市	Jiangsu 江蘇省	(0510)2767704
Yinchuan Shen Da Non-staple Food Co. Ltd. 銀川申達副食有限公司	Yinchuan 銀川市	Ningxia 寧夏	(0951)5031694
Shanghai Sugar Industry Cigarette & Wine (Group) Co. Ltd. 上海市糖業煙酒(集團)有限公司	Shanghai 上海市	Shanghai 上海市	(021)63224190 (021)63223169

*Also include sales by firms outside this industry.包括本行業以外廠家的銷售。"o" stands for "others". "o" 代表"其他產品"。

1498: Ice Cream and Frozen Desserts 冷飲品製造業

The industry accounts for 0.089% of the total revenue of China's industrial sector in 1996. The revenue growth rate of the industry is 17.7% from 1995, as compared to the growth rate of China's industrial sector, 9.51%. The rate of return on asset is -2.44%. 60.41% of all firms in the industry made a profit while 29.10% had negative returns. The top province in terms of the industry's revenue is Zhejiang, accounting for 14.38% of the total revenue.
本行業在1996年佔全行業總產值0.089%，行業年增長率為17.7%（全國工業年增長率9.51%）。行業的資產回報率-2.44%，60.41%的企業盈利，29.10%的企業虧損。銷售收入最高的省份為浙江省，佔本行業的14.38%。

	Total number of firms 企業總數	Total number of employees 職工總數	Total revenue (mil. RMB) 總銷售收入（百萬元）	Total profit (mil. RMB) 總利潤（百萬元）	Return on assets 資產利潤率 (%)	Return on equity 權益利潤率 (%)	Labour productivity ('000 RMB / worker) 勞動生產率（千元/人）	Debts / assets 資產負債率 (%)	Total assets (mil. RMB) 總資產（百萬元）
Industry Overall 行業總體	1,139	89,542	5,176	-236	-2.44	-6.29	57.81	61.23	9,682

	Number of firms 企業個數	Average number of employees 平均職工人數	Average revenue ('000 RMB) 平均銷售收入（千元）	Average profit ('000 RMB) 平均利潤（千元）	Return on assets 資產利潤率 (%)	Return on equity 權益利潤率 (%)	Labour productivity ('000 RMB / worker) 勞動生產率（千元/人）	Average debts / assets 平均資產負債率(%)	Average Total assets ('000 RMB) 平均總資產（千元）
By ownership 產業所有權									
State-owned 國有	339	132	5,322	-327	-3.27	-13.60	40.16	75.95	10,009
Collectively-owned 集體	644	41	1,690	20	0.94	2.71	41.58	65.37	2,174
Privately-owned 私有	2	95	7,458	509	3.17	6.20	78.92	48.86	16,056
Domestic JVs 聯營	11	83	3,080	-409	-7.03	-14.25	37.27	50.66	5,818
Joint stock 股份制	14	100	10,499	1,169	12.19	32.28	105.44	62.24	9,591
Foreign-funded 外資	73	115	14,777	-1,122	-2.63	-4.74	128.90	44.63	42,735
Overseas Chinese-funded 港澳台資	56	144	18,025	-1,234	-4.49	-11.02	125.31	59.25	27,488
By size 規模									
Large 大型	7	1,135	139,893	-3,735	-2.00	-5.77	123.30	65.26	186,397
Medium 中型	35	451	30,162	1,547	3.18	7.72	66.85	58.80	48,620
Small 小型	1,079	61	2,911	-245	-3.95	-10.15	47.86	61.06	6,188
By regional distribution 地區分布									
Central-North 華北	174	106	7,051	-387	-2.59	-4.67	66.65	44.61	14,955
Beijing 北京	40	81	9,630	-3,148	-7.94	-12.80	118.30	37.97	39,651
Tianjin 天津	53	92	6,001	337	4.79	11.18	65.26	57.14	7,038
Hebei 河北	40	42	2,308	47	1.39	3.92	55.12	64.48	3,336
Shanxi 山西	15	174	2,609	29	0.29	0.86	15.00	66.29	10,084
Inner Mongolia 內蒙	26	231	15,087	1,477	10.71	19.28	65.41	44.44	13,789
Northeast 東北	379	28	1,166	53	4.70	11.56	41.91	59.36	1,137
Liaoning 遼寧	164	33	1,924	108	6.04	14.47	57.78	58.28	1,783
Jilin 吉林	82	28	411	-19	-2.88	-8.94	14.60	67.76	656
Heilongjiang 黑龍江	133	21	698	31	4.89	11.57	33.40	57.77	635
Central East 華東	293	119	7,563	-439	-2.99	-9.62	63.59	68.95	14,690
Shanghai 上海	35	218	14,669	-2,336	-8.67	-32.83	67.36	73.59	26,939
Jiangsu 江蘇	67	132	6,901	-483	-2.97	-7.51	52.35	60.49	16,281
Zhejiang 浙江	54	143	13,781	328	1.86	5.85	96.56	68.10	17,606
Anhui 安徽	31	112	3,818	-110	-1.74	-6.02	34.14	71.06	6,308
Fujian 福建	25	53	811	-140	-3.86	-13.80	15.21	72.04	3,640
Jiangxi 江西	29	88	2,640	-28	-0.57	-2.44	30.17	76.50	4,921
Shandong 山東	52	64	5,402	-470	-2.75	-10.30	83.85	73.33	17,126
Central-South 中南	182	98	5,694	-214	-2.23	-5.92	58.19	62.26	9,588
Henan 河南	49	62	1,835	-43	-1.21	-6.52	29.58	81.48	3,602
Hubei 湖北	22	46	5,336	-32	-0.43	-1.42	117.05	69.72	7,505
Hunan 湖南	65	124	2,566	-384	-4.71	-13.27	20.63	64.53	8,149
Guangdong 廣東	33	144	18,362	-293	-1.21	-2.71	127.81	55.29	24,154
Guangxi 廣西	13	73	4,333	-118	-2.01	-4.86	59.73	58.70	5,902
Hainan 海南									
Southwest 西南	60	97	2,552	-335	-4.41	-19.76	26.28	77.70	7,613
Chongqing 重慶	15	101	496	-818	-36.95	-434.36	4.89	91.49	2,214
Sichuan 四川	34	97	3,495	-166	-1.51	-7.24	35.67	79.09	10,999
Guizhou 貴州	4	88	2,930	113	2.73	6.11	33.39	55.31	4,123
Yunnan 雲南	7	89	2,160	-377	-7.98	-19.64	24.19	59.37	4,726
Tibet 西藏									
Northwest 西北	51	41	1,999	-24	-0.87	-3.04	48.51	71.35	2,796
Shaanxi 陝西	24	36	1,450	13	0.46	2.47	40.32	81.47	2,913
Gansu 甘肅	10	41	4,444	-93	-3.15	-9.70	108.92	67.44	2,948
Qinghai 青海									
Ningxia 寧夏	1	10	30				3.00	13.33	300
Xinjiang 新疆	16	51	1,419	-39	-1.47	-3.49	27.65	57.95	2,681

1498: Ice Cream and Frozen Desserts 冷飲品製造業

Year 年份	Number of firms 企業個數	Rate of change 每年變化 (%)	Number of employees 職工人數（人）	Rate of change 每年變化 (%)	Total revenue (mil. RMB) 總銷售收入（百萬元）	Rate of change 每年變化 (%)	Total profit (mil. RMB) 總利潤（百萬元）	Rate of change 每年變化 (%)
1993	786		58,349		2,180		76	
1994	873	11.07%	59,459	1.90%	2,673	22.59%	64	-15.90%
1995	1,135	30.01%	91,468	53.83%	4,398	64.53%	-121	-290.11%
1996	1,139	0.35%	89,542	-2.11%	5,176	17.69%	-236	-95.29%

3 Major products* 3 種主要產品 *	Output 產量	Sales volume 銷售量	Unit 單位
a) Frozen Food 冷凍飲品	784,222	729,327	ton 噸
b) Liquid Milk 液體乳	40,702	35,411	ton 噸

Top 10 firms by revenue (year founded) 收入排名前 10 家企業 (創辦年份)	City 城市	Province 省	Telephone / fax 電話 / 傳真	Number of employees 職工人數	Ownership 產業所有權	Revenue ('000 RMB) 銷售收入（千元）	Profit ('000 RMB) (rank) 利潤（千元）（排名）	Total assets ('000 RMB) 總資產（千元）	Major products 主要產品
Zhongshan Mei Yi Le Foods General Factory 中山市美怡樂食品總廠(1958)	Zhongshan 中山市	Guangdong 廣東省	(0760)8891838 (0760)8891339	1,218	State-owned 國有	288,029	10352(2)	235,501	a
Shanghai A.s. Watson Yi Min Foods Co. Ltd. 上海屈臣氏益民食品有限公司(1993)	Shanghai 上海市	Shanghai 上海市	(021)65084949 (021)65080534	1,821	Overseas Chinese-funded 港澳台資	188,883	-33255(324)	248,780	a
Hangzhou-n.f. Refrigerated Foods Co. Ltd. 杭州五豐冷食有限公司(1993)	Hangzhou 杭州市	Zhejiang 浙江省	(0571)6064691 (0571)6064020	791	Overseas Chinese-funded 港澳台資	172,644	22606(1)	118,329	a
Guangzhou Refrigerated Foods Ltd. 廣州冷凍食品有限公司(1986)	Guangzhou 廣州市	Guangdong 廣東省	(020)83839883 (020)83804223	673	Foreign-funded 外資	139,956	10234(3)	138,179	a
Shanghai Fuller Icecream Foods Co. Ltd. 上海福樂冰淇淋食品有限公司(1993)	Shanghai 上海市	Shanghai 上海市	(021)58995352 (021)58992707	409	Overseas Chinese-funded 港澳台資	106,082	0(192)	205,935	a,b
Zhejiang Jinhua Meat Joint Processing Factory 浙江金華肉類聯合加工廠(1959)	Jinhua 金華市	Zhejiang 浙江省	(0579)2342600 (0579)2344427	1,120	State-owned 國有	102,044	841(34)	113,471	o
Zhejiang De Xuan Foods Co. Ltd. 浙江德軒食品有限公司(1994)	Huzhou 湖州市	Zhejiang 浙江省	(0572)2037905 (0572)2023767	358	Overseas Chinese-funded 港澳台資	95,984	3140(13)	75,808	a
Walls (China) Co. Ltd. Taicang Branch 和路雪(中國)有限公司太倉分公司(1996)	Suzhou 蘇州市	Jiangsu 江蘇省	(0512)3534455	288	Foreign-funded 外資	84,970	0(176)	461,210	o
Liyang Food Company Meat Joint Processing Factory 溧陽市食品公司肉類聯合加工廠(1974)	Changzhou 常州市	Jiangsu 江蘇省	(0519)7220364 (0519)7222368	132	State-owned 國有	82,206	-589(255)	22,780	a
Wendeng Peng Cheng Foods Co. Ltd. 文登市鵬程食品有限公司(1986)	Weihai 威海市	Shandong 山東省	(0896)8571018 (0896)8571035	625	Joint stock 股份制	81,730	10182(4)	80,040	a,b

Top 10 Cities by Production Output 產出排名前 10 位城市	Province 省	Market share 市場份額	Number of firms 企業個數
Shanghai 上海市	Shanghai 上海市	14.03%	60
Tianjin 天津市	Tianjin 天津市	8.41%	65
Zhongshan 中山市	Guangdong 廣東省	6.69%	2
Beijing 北京市	Beijing 北京市	4.20%	40
Guangzhou 廣州市	Guangdong 廣東省	3.91%	10
Hangzhou 杭州市	Zhejiang 浙江省	3.50%	20
Weihai 威海市	Shandong 山東省	3.33%	5
Shenyang 瀋陽市	Liaoning 遼寧省	3.12%	39
Huzhou 湖州市	Zhejiang 浙江省	2.69%	5
Nanjing 南京市	Jiangsu 江蘇省	2.57%	18

10 Major Wholesalers 10 家主要批發商	City 城市	Province 省	Telephone / Fax 電話 / 傳真
Shanghai Jiu Zhou Group Co. Ltd. 上海九州集團有限公司	Shanghai 上海市	Shanghai 上海市	(021)62401515 (021)62123848
Shanghai Tobacco (Group) Co. Trade Center 上海煙草集團上海煙草貿易中心	Shanghai 上海市	Shanghai 上海市	(021)58781921 (021)58786584
China Tax - Free Company 中國免税公司	Beijing 北京市	Beijing 北京市	(010)64668397 (010)64635846
Liaoning Cigarette Marketing Company 遼寧省卷煙銷售公司	Shenyang 瀋陽市	Liaoning 遼寧省	(024)22834388 (024)22837853
Hunan Import & Export General Company Shenzhen Company 湖南省進出口總公司深圳公司	Shenzhen 深圳市	Guangdong 廣東省	(0755)2339793 (0755)2339793
Anhui Tobacco Company Wuhu Branch 安徽省煙草公司蕪湖分公司	Wuhu 蕪湖市	Anhui 安徽省	(0553)4812288 (0553)4812467
Luoyang Jianxi Fountain Sugar & Wine Company 洛陽市澗西噴泉糖酒公司	Luoyang 洛陽市	Henan 河南省	(0379)4321729 (0379)4324531
Shanghai Putuo Supply & Marketing Co-operative 上海市普陀區供銷合作社	Shanghai 上海市	Shanghai 上海市	(021)62576900 (021)62577469
Zhejiang Native and Non-staple Food General Co. 浙江省土產副食品總公司	Hangzhou 杭州市	Zhejiang 浙江省	(0571)7912957 (0571)7911808
Hebei Tobacco Company Zhangjiakou Branch 河北省煙草公司張家口分公司	Zhangjiakou 張家口市	Hebei 河北省	(0313)2015537 (0313)2017607

*Also include sales by firms outside this industry.包括本行業以外廠家的銷售。"o" stands for "others". "o" 代表 "其他產品"。

1499: Other Food 其他類未包括的食品製造業

The industry accounts for 0.172% of the total revenue of China's industrial sector in 1996. The revenue growth rate of the industry is 18.9% from 1995, as compared to the growth rate of China's industrial sector, 9.51%. The rate of return on asset is 7.07%. 67.38% of all firms in the industry made a profit while 25.51% had negative returns. The top province in terms of the industry's revenue is Guangdong, accounting for 23.32% of the total revenue.
本行業在1996年佔全行業總產值0.172%，行業年增長率為18.9%（全國工業年增長率9.51%）。行業的資產回報率7.07%，67.38%的企業盈利，25.51%的企業虧損。銷售收入最高的省份為廣東省，佔本行業的23.32%。

	Total number of firms 企業總數	Total number of employees 職工總數	Total revenue (mil. RMB) 總銷售收入（百萬元）	Total profit (mil. RMB) 總利潤（百萬元）	Return on assets 資產利潤率 (%)	Return on equity 權益利潤率 (%)	Labour productivity ('000 RMB / worker) 勞動生產率（千元/人）	Debts / assets 資產負債率 (%)	Total assets (mil. RMB) 總資產（百萬元）
Industry Overall 行業總體	1,028	77,365	9,946	733	7.07	18.08	128.56	60.91	10,375

	Number of firms 企業個數	Average number of employees 平均職工人數	Average revenue ('000 RMB) 平均銷售收入（千元）	Average profit ('000 RMB) 平均利潤（千元）	Return on assets 資產利潤率 (%)	Return on equity 權益利潤率 (%)	Labour productivity ('000 RMB / worker) 勞動生產率（千元/人）	Average debts / assets 平均資產負債率(%)	Average Total assets ('000 RMB) 平均總資產（千元）
By ownership 產業所有權									
State-owned 國有	134	129	10,000	209	1.26	3.78	77.49	66.74	16,604
Collectively-owned 集體	578	55	5,683	360	8.88	36.26	103.97	75.50	4,048
Privately-owned 私有	6	40	1,973	578	47.82	271.04	49.33	82.36	1,210
Domestic JVs 聯營	11	110	5,137	-313	-2.15	-3.33	46.63	35.55	14,599
Joint stock 股份制	15	93	4,771	-743	-10.60	-32.16	51.34	67.02	7,003
Foreign-funded 外資	146	97	19,553	2,491	12.16	26.14	201.25	53.46	20,475
Overseas Chinese-funded 港澳台資	137	93	16,975	1,052	5.66	11.90	182.10	52.43	18,593
By size 規模									
Large 大型	9	945	268,579	30,175	10.81	19.67	284.34	45.06	279,230
Medium 中型	16	398	55,011	3,963	6.16	15.15	138.13	59.30	64,291
Small 小型	949	65	7,006	419	5.82	17.64	108.26	66.98	7,200
By regional distribution 地區分布									
Central-North 華北	188	68	6,575	533	6.00	12.01	96.48	50.09	8,882
Beijing 北京	52	87	13,820	1,843	10.64	19.04	158.26	44.13	17,322
Tianjin 天津	33	111	4,387	-261	-2.31	-3.59	39.68	35.53	11,287
Hebei 河北	55	52	5,800	209	3.80	22.49	110.60	83.11	5,507
Shanxi 山西	20	54	1,416	16	0.71	1.59	26.01	54.99	2,239
Inner Mongolia 內蒙	28	23	909	38	2.19	5.72	39.15	61.74	1,749
Northeast 東北	144	77	5,952	250	3.67	12.79	77.34	71.33	6,822
Liaoning 遼寧	51	97	8,756	587	8.51	22.26	90.69	61.76	6,893
Jilin 吉林	43	62	4,266	-69	-1.28	-5.27	68.78	75.67	5,408
Heilongjiang 黑龍江	50	70	4,540	181	2.28	10.01	65.05	77.25	7,966
Central East 華東	361	86	10,452	471	4.50	14.01	121.86	67.88	10,456
Shanghai 上海	32	75	8,102	145	0.98	1.97	108.16	50.55	14,880
Jiangsu 江蘇	81	143	20,975	614	2.88	12.08	146.51	76.13	21,283
Zhejiang 浙江	37	37	5,203	-59	-1.10	-5.39	139.81	79.64	5,421
Anhui 安徽	38	35	4,954	303	13.52	82.11	142.93	83.52	2,242
Fujian 福建	60	36	4,233	410	8.42	12.28	118.68	31.43	4,862
Jiangxi 江西	35	26	929	17	0.86	4.23	35.58	79.76	1,934
Shandong 山東	78	144	14,714	1,039	8.72	27.29	102.26	68.06	11,917
Central-South 中南	229	64	15,319	1,883	12.85	26.76	239.01	52.00	14,656
Henan 河南	49	50	3,840	124	2.48	6.96	76.96	64.43	5,008
Hubei 湖北	40	41	4,215	104	3.58	17.96	101.92	80.06	2,891
Hunan 湖南	33	32	2,307	70	4.83	15.53	71.15	68.91	1,456
Guangdong 廣東	76	76	30,522	4,643	15.06	27.65	402.86	45.55	30,842
Guangxi 廣西	29	123	26,028	2,284	11.43	32.09	212.03	64.39	19,992
Hainan 海南	2	96	400	-250	-2.15	-17.36	4.19	87.63	11,645
Southwest 西南	49	42	3,689	40	1.12	3.57	88.34	68.65	3,534
Chongqing 重慶	6	26	865	-63	-2.51	-7.04	32.86	64.30	2,492
Sichuan 四川	20	42	3,015	-69	-2.11	-9.79	71.75	78.44	3,245
Guizhou 貴州	6	12	468	-128	-13.46	-36.49	39.58	63.11	953
Yunnan 雲南	16	60	6,964	283	5.32	14.14	117.04	62.40	5,314
Tibet 西藏									
Northwest 西北	57	101	6,857	-104	-1.41	-9.41	67.59	85.00	7,343
Shaanxi 陝西	17	119	1,714	-4	-0.14	-0.83	14.44	83.73	2,599
Gansu 甘肅	28	109	9,802	-64	-0.65	-2.44	89.66	73.22	9,713
Qinghai 青海	4	71	16,628	-665	-4.31	87.79	234.19	104.91	15,425
Ningxia 寧夏	2	29	3,465	120	4.20	29.27	119.48	85.64	2,855
Xinjiang 新疆	6	60	2,305	-275	-4.72	10.98	38.20	142.99	5,827

1499: Other Food 其他類未包括的食品製造業

Year 年份	Number of firms 企業個數	Rate of change 每年變化 (%)	Number of employees 職工人數 (人)	Rate of change 每年變化 (%)	Total revenue (mil. RMB) 總銷售收入 (百萬元)	Rate of change 每年變化 (%)	Total profit (mil. RMB) 總利潤 (百萬元)	Rate of change 每年變化 (%)
1993	947		62,897		4,377		200	
1994	1,080	14.04%	78,870	25.40%	6,076	38.79%	195	-2.41%
1995	1,055	-2.32%	85,348	8.21%	8,367	37.71%	504	157.96%
1996	1,028	-2.56%	77,365	-9.35%	9,946	18.87%	733	45.43%

3 Major products* 3 種主要產品 *	Output 產量	Sales volume 銷售量	Unit 單位
a) Dried Egg 乾蛋品	984	935	ton 噸
b) Solid Drink 固體飲料	15,432	15,123	ton 噸
c) Convenient Staple Food 方便主食品	86,091	84,370	ton 噸

Top 10 firms by revenue (year founded) 收入排名前 10 家企業 (創辦年份)	City 城市	Province 省	Telephone / fax 電話 / 傳真	Number of employees 職工人數	Ownership 產業所有權	Revenue ('000 RMB) 銷售收入 (千元)	Profit ('000 RMB) (rank) 利潤 (千元) (排名)	Total assets ('000 RMB) 總資產 (千元)	Major products 主要產品
Xian Ni Lei De (Guangzhou) Co. Ltd. 仙妮蕾德(廣州)有限公司(1993)	Guangzhou 廣州市	Guangdong 廣東省	(020)87571088 (020)87542637	272	Foreign-funded 外資	933,353	343239(1)	423,375	o
Guangxi Hei Wu Lei Food Group Company 廣西黑五類食品集團公司(1994)	Yulin 玉林市	Guangxi 廣西	(0775)5321628 (0775)5322443	1,900	Collectively-owned 集體	558,000	41042(2)	382,456	c
Landy Group Co. 大地集團公司(1971)	Xuzhou 徐州市	Jiangsu 江蘇省	(0516)3821015 (0516)3805672	1,839	State-owned 國有	497,089	10224(11)	362,370	b
Guangzhou Malting Co. Ltd. 廣州麥芽有限公司(1987)	Guangzhou 廣州市	Guangdong 廣東省	(020)82224341 (020)82212988	208	Overseas Chinese-funded 港澳台資	371,431	36410(3)	425,122	o
Xuzhou Dongfang Soya-bean Milk Powder Factory 徐州東方豆奶粉廠	Xuzhou 徐州市	Jiangsu 江蘇省	(0516)7711304	700	Collectively-owned 集體	217,400	8720(14)	43,830	o
Jiangsu Zhen Feng Group Co. 江蘇省珍豐集團公司(1985)	Yancheng 鹽城市	Jiangsu 江蘇省	(0515)3512974 (0515)3510583	1,180	Collectively-owned 集體	183,050	10180(12)	254,970	o
Gaoming Shinan Fang Health Care Products Factory 高明市南方保健品廠(1995)	Foshan 佛山市	Guangdong 廣東省	(0757)8881918 (0757)8881642	50	Collectively-owned 集體	159,429	-58(310)	10,121	o
Shandong Ganoderma Lucidum Group Company 山東靈芝集團公司(1993)	Ji'nan 濟南市	Shandong 山東省	(0531)7463069 (0531)7463216	1,068	Collectively-owned 集體	144,521	23393(5)	184,257	o
Rongcheng Rong Dong Foods Co. Ltd. 榮成市榮東食品有限公司(1992)	Weihai 威海市	Shandong 山東省	(0896)7431075	620	Collectively-owned 集體	137,860	16400(7)	30,670	o
Shanghai Guo Fu Longfeng Food Co. Ltd. 上海國福龍鳳食品有限公司(1992)	Shanghai 上海市	Shanghai 上海市	(021)64063433 (021)64063417	768	Overseas Chinese-funded 港澳台資	133,782	17805(6)	172,905	o

Top 10 Cities by Production Output 產出排名前 10 位城市	Province 省	Market share 市場份額	Number of firms 企業個數
Guangzhou 廣州市	Guangdong 廣東省	27.99%	32
Yulin 玉林市	Guangxi 廣西	11.16%	9
Putian 莆田市	Fujian 福建省	4.06%	5
Shanghai 上海市	Shanghai 上海市	3.54%	51
Dalian 大連市	Liaoning 遼寧省	3.47%	31
Zhuhai 珠海市	Guangdong 廣東省	2.47%	7
Weihai 威海市	Shandong 山東省	2.36%	17
Suzhou 蘇州市	Jiangsu 江蘇省	2.26%	18
Tianjin 天津市	Tianjin 天津市	2.22%	58
Taizhou 泰州市	Jiangsu 江蘇省	2.19%	8

10 Major Wholesalers 10 家主要批發商	City 城市	Province 省	Telephone / Fax 電話 / 傳真
Shanghai Jiu Zhou Group Co. Ltd. 上海九州集團有限公司	Shanghai 上海市	Shanghai 上海市	(021)62401515 (021)62123848
Shanghai Tobacco (Group) Co. Trade Center 上海煙草集團上海煙草貿易中心	Shanghai 上海市	Shanghai 上海市	(021)58781921 (021)58786584
China Tax – Free Company 中國免稅公司	Beijing 北京市	Beijing 北京市	(010)64668397 (010)64635846
Liaoning Cigarette Marketing Company 遼寧省卷煙銷售公司	Shenyang 瀋陽市	Liaoning 遼寧省	(024)22834388 (024)22837853
Hunan Import & Export General Company Shenzhen Company 湖南省進出口總公司深圳公司	Shenzhen 深圳市	Guangdong 廣東省	(0755)2339793 (0755)2339793
Anhui Tobacco Company Wuhu Branch 安徽省煙草公司蕪湖分公司	Wuhu 蕪湖市	Anhui 安徽省	(0553)4812288 (0553)4812467
Luoyang Jianxi Fountain Sugar & Wine Company 洛陽市澗西噴泉糖酒公司	Luoyang 洛陽市	Henan 河南省	(0379)4321729 (0379)4324531
Shanghai Putuo Supply & Marketing Co-operative 上海市普陀區供銷合作社	Shanghai 上海市	Shanghai 上海市	(021)62576900 (021)62577469
Zhejiang Native and Non-staple Food General Co. 浙江省土產副食品總公司	Hangzhou 杭州市	Zhejiang 浙江省	(0571)7912957 (0571)7911808
Hebei Tobacco Company Zhangjiakou Branch 河北省煙草公司張家口分公司	Zhangjiakou 張家口市	Hebei 河北省	(0313)2015537 (0313)2017607

*Also include sales by firms outside this industry.包括本行業以外廠家的銷售。"o" stands for "others". "o" 代表 "其他產品" 。

1511: Alcohol 酒精製造業

The industry accounts for 0.133% of the total revenue of China's industrial sector in 1996. The revenue growth rate of the industry is -1.0% from 1995, as compared to the growth rate of China's industrial sector, 9.51%. The rate of return on asset is -1.23%. 57.82% of all firms in the industry made a profit while 34.93% had negative returns. The top province in terms of the industry's revenue is Jiangsu, accounting for 14.32% of the total revenue.
本行業在1996年佔全行業總產值0.133%，行業年增長率為-1.0%（全國工業年增長率9.51%）。行業的資產回報率-1.23%，57.82%的企業盈利，34.93%的企業虧損。銷售收入最高的省份為江蘇省，佔本行業的14.32%。

	Total number of firms 企業總數	Total number of employees 職工總數	Total revenue (mil. RMB) 總銷售收入（百萬元）	Total profit (mil. RMB) 總利潤（百萬元）	Return on assets 資產利潤率 (%)	Return on equity 權益利潤率 (%)	Labour productivity ('000 RMB / worker) 勞動生產率（千元/人）	Debts / assets 資產負債率 (%)	Total assets (mil. RMB) 總資產（百萬元）
Industry Overall 行業總體	304	82,682	7,686	-144	-1.23	-8.00	92.96	84.66	11,740

	Number of firms 企業個數	Average number of employees 平均職工人數	Average revenue ('000 RMB) 平均銷售收入（千元）	Average profit ('000 RMB) 平均利潤（千元）	Return on assets 資產利潤率 (%)	Return on equity 權益利潤率 (%)	Labour productivity ('000 RMB / worker) 勞動生產率（千元/人）	Average debts / assets 平均資產負債率(%)	Average Total assets ('000 RMB) 平均總資產（千元）
By ownership 產業所有權									
State-owned 國有	172	371	28,151	-1,308	-2.87	-20.29	75.93	85.86	45,605
Collectively-owned 集體	108	117	16,445	474	2.49	17.88	140.69	86.08	19,049
Privately-owned 私有									
Domestic JVs 聯營	1	280	60,033	39	0.08	0.11	214.40	26.01	48,638
Joint stock 股份制	8	254	38,225	270	0.65	1.59	150.49	59.36	41,690
Foreign-funded 外資	6	325	46,552	525	0.52	2.15	143.16	75.98	101,685
Overseas Chinese-funded 港澳台資	8	254	58,626	3,054	2.88	27.87	231.15	89.66	105,957
By size 規模									
Large 大型	25	1,003	116,061	10,040	4.62	34.67	115.68	86.69	217,528
Medium 中型	40	489	50,481	-2,226	-3.25	-16.41	103.25	80.20	68,488
Small 小型	230	160	12,548	-1,330	-8.59	-57.22	78.20	84.99	15,492
By regional distribution 地區分布									
Central-North 華北	24	353	49,886	-187	-0.27	-1.31	141.27	78.99	68,197
Beijing 北京	2	1,122	271,190	5,065	2.27	11.29	241.70	79.94	223,575
Tianjin 天津	4	716	95,533	-2,403	-1.87	-7.63	133.47	75.48	128,323
Hebei 河北	15	217	17,837	-347	-0.78	-4.07	82.30	80.84	44,408
Shanxi 山西	2	53	2,550	95	1.92	41.30	48.11	95.36	4,960
Inner Mongolia 內蒙	1	11	100				9.09	16.67	240
Northeast 東北	40	294	24,901	-153	-0.23	-2.86	84.57	91.98	66,767
Liaoning 遼寧	10	182	9,827	-642	-8.86	25.56	54.08	134.66	7,248
Jilin 吉林	16	311	34,579	-775	-0.95	-7.78	111.32	87.76	81,349
Heilongjiang 黑龍江	14	357	24,606	907	0.98	15.90	69.02	93.84	92,615
Central East 華東	96	314	30,454	-275	-0.69	-3.93	96.87	82.55	40,191
Shanghai 上海	1	834	5,830	-1,360	-12.04	16.00	6.99	175.22	11,300
Jiangsu 江蘇	23	417	47,868	-253	-0.51	-3.26	114.89	84.42	49,812
Zhejiang 浙江	19	213	24,846	-549	-1.77	-8.86	116.45	80.02	31,046
Anhui 安徽	17	371	23,181	-683	-1.68	-43.43	62.46	96.13	40,594
Fujian 福建	5	45	510	306	2.08	5.61	11.28	62.93	14,712
Jiangxi 江西	9	93	4,244	-217	-3.75	-28.22	45.58	86.70	5,774
Shandong 山東	22	379	41,360	146	0.25	0.99	109.14	74.95	58,901
Central-South 中南	91	204	15,257	-46	-0.20	-1.13	74.67	82.16	23,001
Henan 河南	33	354	30,997	788	1.88	8.63	87.68	78.25	41,997
Hubei 湖北	19	154	9,084	-566	-4.04	-38.92	58.91	89.62	14,014
Hunan 湖南	12	161	5,238	-991	-7.64	59450.00	32.55	100.01	12,967
Guangdong 廣東	7	31	1,494	-327	-5.47	-12.84	48.43	57.42	5,981
Guangxi 廣西	20	92	5,977	-265	-2.17	-19.88	64.65	89.06	12,171
Hainan 海南									
Southwest 西南	42	266	22,569	-2,319	-8.93	-68.78	84.82	87.01	25,960
Chongqing 重慶	8	231	12,669	-397	-2.50	-13.14	54.64	80.96	15,881
Sichuan 四川	26	275	30,508	-334	-1.36	-6.05	110.83	77.46	24,507
Guizhou 貴州	6	314	4,667	-14,197	-28.01	274.95	14.85	110.18	50,682
Yunnan 雲南	1	7							
Tibet 西藏									
Northwest 西北	11	225	21,153	-485	-1.36	-9.85	93.82	86.15	35,572
Shaanxi 陝西	5	187	9,306	-130	-0.81	-21.31	49.87	96.19	16,026
Gansu 甘肅	3	392	45,397	-987	-1.40	-12.43	115.71	88.72	70,373
Qinghai 青海									
Ningxia 寧夏									
Xinjiang 新疆	3	123	16,653	-577	-1.73	-6.33	135.03	72.68	33,347

1511: Alcohol 酒精製造業

Year 年份	Number of firms 企業個數	Rate of change 每年變化 (%)	Number of employees 職工人數（人）	Rate of change 每年變化 (%)	Total revenue (mil. RMB) 總銷售收入（百萬元）	Rate of change 每年變化 (%)	Total profit (mil. RMB) 總利潤（百萬元）	Rate of change 每年變化 (%)
1993	200		54,514		3,487		-32	
1994	201	0.50%	53,445	-1.96%	4,725	35.51%	-17	49.09%
1995	291	44.78%	85,996	60.91%	7,760	64.21%	9	154.63%
1996	304	4.47%	82,682	-3.85%	7,686	-0.95%	-144	-1693.98%

3 Major products* 3 種主要產品 *	Output 產量	Sales volume 銷售量	Unit 單位
a) Ferment Alcohol 發酵酒精	1,006,808	926,263	ton 噸
b) Spirit 白酒	286,235	274,786	ton 噸

Top 10 firms by revenue (year founded) 收入排名前 10 家企業 (創辦年份)	City 城市	Province 省	Telephone / fax 電話 / 傳真	Number of employees 職工人數	Ownership 產業所有權	Revenue ('000 RMB) 銷售收入（千元）	Profit ('000 RMB) (rank) 利潤（千元）（排名）	Total assets ('000 RMB) 總資產（千元）	Major products 主要產品
Beijing Red Star Brewing Group Company 北京紅星釀酒集團公司(1949)	Beijing 北京市	Beijing 北京市	(010)65022454 (010)65025488	2,157	State-owned 國有	541,893	10124(4)	445,222	a,b
Meng Zhou Shi Alcohol General Factory 孟州市酒精總廠(1991)	Jiaozuo 焦作市	Henan 河南省	(0391)8571389	500	Collectively-owned 集體	281,914	32930(1)	39,984	a
Heilong Jiang Zhaodong Jinyu Industry Co. Ltd. 黑龍江省肇東金玉有限責任公司(1993)	Suihua 綏化市	Heilongjiang 黑龍江省	(0455)7714809	1,004	Collectively-owned 集體	239,499	32298(2)	961,397	a
Tengzhou Winery General Factory 滕州市釀酒總廠(1948)	Zaozhuang 棗莊市	Shandong 山東省	(0632)5583322	2,030	State-owned 國有	201,813	2823(11)	160,689	a,b
Jilin Tianhe Industry Co. Ltd. 吉林天河實業有限公司(1990)	Jilin 吉林市	Jilin 吉林省	(0432)3057200 (0432)3058110	864	Overseas Chinese-funded 港澳台資	198,330	8999(5)	486,694	a,b
Peixian Han Gong Wine-making Industry Co. Ltd. 沛縣漢宮酒業有限公司(1978)	Xuzhou 徐州市	Jiangsu 江蘇省	(0516)4860189	350	Overseas Chinese-funded 港澳台資	175,360	7920(6)	111,290	a,b
Mianzhu Alcohol Factory 綿竹酒精廠(1984)	Deyang 德陽市	Sichuan 四川省	(0838)6590250	457	Collectively-owned 集體	166,153	1818(15)	107,606	a
Xu Zhou Fang Ting Distillery 徐州房亭酒廠(1959)	Xuzhou 徐州市	Jiangsu 江蘇省	(0516)6739453 (0516)6739968	434	State-owned 國有	165,770	3030(8)	100,912	a,b
Shandong Alcohol General Factory 山東酒精總廠(1920)	Ji'nan 濟南市	Shandong 山東省	(0531)8962185 (0531)8962729	1,490	State-owned 國有	146,835	46(79)	570,042	a
Yancheng San Ai Group Co. 鹽城三愛集團公司(1969)	Yancheng 鹽城市	Jiangsu 江蘇省	(0515)4223002	455	State-owned 國有	131,130	2770(12)	91,510	o

Top 10 Cities by Production Output 產出排名前 10 位城市	Province 省	Market share 市場份額	Number of firms 企業個數
Zaozhuang 棗莊市	Shandong 山東省	6.74%	3
Suihua 綏化市	Heilongjiang 黑龍江省	6.16%	5
Tianjin 天津市	Tianjin 天津市	5.49%	4
Beijing 北京市	Beijing 北京市	5.32%	2
Nanyang 南陽市	Henan 河南省	5.08%	4
Jiaozuo 焦作市	Henan 河南省	4.65%	3
Linyi 臨沂市	Shandong 山東省	4.18%	7
Jilin 吉林市	Jilin 吉林省	3.44%	7
Xuzhou 徐州市	Jiangsu 江蘇省	3.36%	5
Huzhou 湖州市	Zhejiang 浙江省	2.63%	6

10 Major Wholesalers 10 家主要批發商	City 城市	Province 省	Telephone / Fax 電話 / 傳真
Changzhou Hardware Alternating-current Appliance and Chemical Wholesale General Company 常州五金交電化工批發總公司	Changzhou 常州市	Jiangsu 江蘇省	(0519)6609929 (0519)6609925
Suzhou Hardware & Alternating Electricity Co. Ltd. 蘇州五金交電股份有限公司	Suzhou 蘇州市	Jiangsu 江蘇省	(0512)5239572 (0512)5213248
Tianjin Foreign Trade General Company 天津市對外貿易總公司	Tianjin 天津市	Tianjin 天津市	(022)23310922
Chongqing International Trade Center 重慶國際貿易中心	Chongqing 重慶市	Chongqing 重慶市	(023)67853232 (023)67850402
China Chemical Plastics Co. Ltd. 中化塑料有限公司	Beijing 北京市	Beijing 北京市	(010)68569863 (010)68569041
Ningbo Hualian Group Co. Ltd. 寧波華聯集團股份有限公司	Ningbo 寧波市	Zhejiang 浙江省	(0574)7367626 (0574)7367652
Kaiyuan Wei Wei Electromechanical Building Materials Marketing Dept. 廈門市開元區威威機電建材經營部	Xiamen 廈門市	Fujian 福建省	(0592)2071044
Rudong Industry Product General Company 如東縣工業品總公司	Nantong 南通市	Jiangsu 江蘇省	(0513)4516110 (0513)4516110
Fujian Fu Ri Group Company 福建福日集團公司	Fuzhou 福州市	Fujian 福建省	(0591)3269325 (0591)3270426
Guangdong Hardware & Alternating Electrical Co. 廣東省五金交電公司	Guangzhou 廣州市	Guangdong 廣東省	(020)81884078 (020)81861287

*Also include sales by firms outside this industry.包括本行業以外廠家的銷售。"o" stands for "others". "o" 代表 "其他產品"。

1512: Liquor 白酒製造業

The industry accounts for 0.799% of the total revenue of China's industrial sector in 1996. The revenue growth rate of the industry is 17.2% from 1995, as compared to the growth rate of China's industrial sector, 9.51%. The rate of return on asset is 3.88%. 73.28% of all firms in the industry made a profit while 18.97% had negative returns. The top province in terms of the industry's revenue is Shandong, accounting for 20.99% of the total revenue.
本行業在1996年佔全行業總產值0.799%，行業年增長率為17.2%（全國工業年增長率9.51%）。行業的資產回報率3.88%，73.28%的企業盈利，18.97%的企業虧損。銷售收入最高的省份為山東省，佔本行業的20.99%。

	Total number of firms 企業總數	Total number of employees 職工總數	Total revenue (mil. RMB) 總銷售收入（百萬元）	Total profit (mil. RMB) 總利潤（百萬元）	Return on assets 資產利潤率 (%)	Return on equity 權益利潤率 (%)	Labour productivity ('000 RMB / worker) 勞動生產率（千元/人）	Debts / assets 資產負債率 (%)	Total assets (mil. RMB) 總資產（百萬元）
Industry Overall 行業總體	5,424	624,315	46,343	2,420	3.88	13.56	74.23	71.41	62,441

	Number of firms 企業個數	Average number of employees 平均職工人數	Average revenue ('000 RMB) 平均銷售收入（千元）	Average profit ('000 RMB) 平均利潤（千元）	Return on assets 資產利潤率 (%)	Return on equity 權益利潤率 (%)	Labour productivity ('000 RMB / worker) 勞動生產率（千元/人）	Average debts / assets 平均資產負債率(%)	Average Total assets ('000 RMB) 平均總資產（千元）
By ownership 產業所有權									
State-owned 國有	1,537	310	22,848	1,079	3.20	11.51	73.71	72.21	33,749
Collectively-owned 集體	3,753	32	1,940	73	4.57	19.70	61.07	76.78	1,599
Privately-owned 私有	23	41	2,454	154	9.55	25.03	59.73	61.84	1,609
Domestic JVs 聯營	20	62	3,004	-100	-3.18	-29.96	48.46	89.38	3,136
Joint stock 股份制	46	486	72,491	9,863	11.94	25.56	149.01	53.28	82,612
Foreign-funded 外資	26	97	11,598	739	6.30	14.79	120.09	57.37	11,719
Overseas Chinese-funded 港澳台資	17	134	11,057	715	3.36	10.42	82.51	67.72	21,268
By size 規模									
Large 大型	92	2,001	245,718	26,208	7.76	19.96	122.82	61.14	337,925
Medium 中型	198	653	47,976	338	0.51	2.39	73.43	78.73	66,555
Small 小型	5,115	61	2,783	-11	-0.31	-1.93	45.94	83.67	3,553
By regional distribution 地區分布									
Central-North 華北	375	200	13,392	670	3.14	9.02	66.89	65.24	21,373
Beijing 北京	24	252	23,063	3,329	12.46	39.57	91.69	68.52	26,723
Tianjin 天津	11	193	20,548	125	0.66	1.67	106.67	60.50	18,856
Hebei 河北	130	215	15,064	531	2.15	8.44	69.97	74.50	24,668
Shanxi 山西	60	268	19,057	1,181	3.08	5.39	71.16	42.84	38,362
Inner Mongolia 內蒙	150	152	7,604	202	1.82	8.19	49.88	77.72	11,052
Northeast 東北	756	97	3,821	-105	-1.89	-12.32	39.21	84.65	5,557
Liaoning 遼寧	182	136	5,147	-127	-1.43	-8.92	37.76	83.93	8,892
Jilin 吉林	241	87	2,096	-370	-7.44	-219.84	24.07	96.62	4,974
Heilongjiang 黑龍江	333	84	4,345	99	2.38	9.58	51.91	75.13	4,156
Central East 華東	882	236	22,454	1,130	4.39	13.95	95.31	68.53	25,721
Shanghai 上海	5	159	24,366	138	0.55	2.13	153.63	74.20	25,096
Jiangsu 江蘇	158	277	23,251	314	1.18	3.81	84.06	69.12	26,678
Zhejiang 浙江	57	32	2,329	5	0.20	0.69	73.87	71.47	2,316
Anhui 安徽	185	279	29,222	3,288	10.32	27.04	104.84	61.83	31,864
Fujian 福建	38	64	2,922	17	0.35	0.82	45.89	56.96	4,782
Jiangxi 江西	190	99	3,335	-22	-0.34	-2.10	33.63	83.92	6,592
Shandong 山東	249	356	39,058	1,370	3.13	10.53	109.68	70.25	43,712
Central-South 中南	1,123	101	6,586	158	1.60	7.10	65.48	77.50	9,879
Henan 河南	200	261	18,813	580	2.29	9.77	72.05	76.55	25,333
Hubei 湖北	389	69	3,675	65	1.33	7.98	53.49	83.35	4,913
Hunan 湖南	196	82	3,974	185	1.98	8.19	48.66	75.87	9,353
Guangdong 廣東	215	58	4,870	48	0.67	2.98	83.76	77.56	7,216
Guangxi 廣西	116	44	3,175	-89	-1.51	-5.26	71.60	71.40	5,909
Hainan 海南	7	51	1,451	-86	-1.31	-20.07	28.70	93.48	6,551
Southwest 西南	2,101	59	4,596	539	9.06	27.82	77.96	67.43	5,947
Chongqing 重慶	473	25	929	-45	-4.14	-45.28	36.47	90.85	1,091
Sichuan 四川	1,229	67	6,801	966	13.13	37.43	100.37	64.92	7,359
Guizhou 貴州	265	89	2,331	-103	-1.08	-3.73	26.18	71.01	9,521
Yunnan 雲南	133	43	1,781	-55	-1.78	-6.20	41.81	71.31	3,073
Tibet 西藏									
Northwest 西北	187	166	8,427	-308	-1.46	-8.06	50.88	81.92	21,124
Shaanxi 陝西	62	158	7,049	-589	-3.21	-23.43	44.48	86.32	18,375
Gansu 甘肅	61	166	7,309	326	1.56	6.74	44.06	76.83	20,906
Qinghai 青海	15	170	14,069	-117	-0.41	-3.44	82.53	88.00	28,218
Ningxia 寧夏	5	323	26,910	2,310	5.99	19.55	83.31	69.35	38,562
Xinjiang 新疆	44	156	7,895	-1,154	-5.52	-33.16	50.68	83.35	20,899

1512: Liquor 白酒製造業

Year 年份	Number of firms 企業個數	Rate of change 每年變化 (%)	Number of employees 職工人數 (人)	Rate of change 每年變化 (%)	Total revenue (mil. RMB) 總銷售收入 (百萬元)	Rate of change 每年變化 (%)	Total profit (mil. RMB) 總利潤 (百萬元)	Rate of change 每年變化 (%)
1993	4,952		514,465		30,388		1,638	
1994	5,232	5.65%	537,132	4.41%	29,435	-3.14%	1,371	-16.30%
1995	5,714	9.21%	646,164	20.30%	39,544	34.35%	2,106	53.59%
1996	5,424	-5.08%	624,315	-3.38%	46,343	17.19%	2,420	14.91%

3 Major products* 3 種主要產品 *	Output 產量	Sales volume 銷售量	Unit 單位
a) Spirit 白酒	7,316,704	7,024,036	ton 噸
b) Alcoholic Drink 料酒	5,922,264	5,448,483	ton 噸

Top 10 firms by revenue (year founded) 收入排名前 10 家企業 (創辦年份)	City 城市	Province 省	Telephone / fax 電話 / 傳真	Number of employees 職工人數	Ownership 產業所有權	Revenue ('000 RMB) 銷售收入 (千元)	Profit ('000 RMB) (rank) 利潤 (千元) (排名)	Total assets ('000 RMB) 總資產 (千元)	Major products 主要產品
Sichuan Yibin Wu Liang Ye Distillery 四川省宜賓市五糧液酒廠(1952)	Yibin 宜賓市	Sichuan 四川省	(0831)3553988 (0831)3552852	10,327	State-owned 國有	2,361,080	451230(1)	1,977,664	a,b
Luzhou Old-cellar Co. Ltd. 瀘州市老窖股份有限公司(1650)	Luzhou 瀘州市	Sichuan 四川省	(0830)2390660	2,698	Joint stock 股份制	964,353	300874(2)	728,024	a,b
Shandong Qin Chi Liquor Factory 山東秦池酒廠(1963)	Weifang 濰坊市	Shandong 山東省	(0536)3218252 (0536)3212118	1,862	State-owned 國有	950,279	56720(13)	375,845	a,b
Anhui Gujinggong Distillery Co. Ltd. 安徽亳州古井貢酒股份有限公司(1959)	Fuyang 阜陽市	Anhui 安徽省	(0558)5571018 (0558)5571006	4,914	State-owned 國有	948,248	252973(3)	1,403,118	a,b
Shandong Lan Ling Enterprise Group General Co. 山東省蘭陵企業集團總公司(1948)	Linyi 臨沂市	Shandong 山東省	(0539)5581308 (0539)5581298	5,675	State-owned 國有	833,379	68171(10)	639,020	a,b
Anhui Seeds Liquor General Factory 安徽種子酒總廠(1949)	Fuyang 阜陽市	Anhui 安徽省	(0558)2262001 (0558)2268475	3,256	State-owned 國有	782,172	124060(7)	417,429	a,b
Sichuan Tuo Pai Group Co. Ltd. 四川沱牌集團有限公司(1952)	Suining 遂寧市	Sichuan 四川省	(0825)6766352 (0825)6766868	12,039	State-owned 國有	755,225	125292(6)	1,073,779	a,b
Anhui Shuang Lun Group High Furnace Liquor Factory 安徽雙輪集團高爐酒廠(1949)	Fuyang 阜陽市	Anhui 安徽省	(0558)7471181 (0558)7471188	3,347	State-owned 國有	747,692	130448(5)	502,946	a,b
Shandong Jing Zhi Wine-making Industry Co. Ltd. 山東景芝酒業股份有限公司(1948)	Weifang 濰坊市	Shandong 山東省	(0536)4611195 (0536)4611423	4,560	Joint stock 股份制	694,174	8831(39)	330,089	a,b
Shandong Qufu Kong Fu Jia Group General Co. 曲阜孔府家集團總公司(1958)	Jining 濟寧市	Shandong 山東省	(0537)4411612 (0537)4412819	2,298	State-owned 國有	675,991	65206(12)	649,679	a,b

Top 10 Cities by Production Output 產出排名前 10 位城市	Province 省	Market share 市場份額	Number of firms 企業個數
Fuyang 阜陽市	Anhui 安徽省	9.31%	100
Weifang 濰坊市	Shandong 山東省	6.81%	25
Yibin 宜賓市	Sichuan 四川省	5.59%	96
Jining 濟寧市	Shandong 山東省	4.77%	44
Suqian 宿遷市	Jiangsu 江蘇省	4.36%	56
Linyi 臨沂市	Shandong 山東省	3.76%	22
Shangqiu 商丘市	Henan 河南省	3.08%	44
Suining 遂寧市	Sichuan 四川省	2.02%	27
Chengdu 成都市	Sichuan 四川省	1.99%	151
Zunyi 遵義市	Guizhou 貴州省	1.55%	100

10 Major Wholesalers 10 家主要批發商	City 城市	Province 省	Telephone / Fax 電話 / 傳真
Zhong Liang Sugar Industry Groceries Import & Export Company 中糧糖業雜品進出口公司	Beijing 北京市	Beijing 北京市	(010)65268888 (010)65276023
China National Sugar & Alcohol Group Corp. 中國糖業酒類集團公司	Beijing 北京市	Beijing 北京市	(010)68360994
Shanxi Sugar & Wine Non-staple Food Company 山西省糖酒副食公司	Taiyuan 太原市	Shanxi 山西省	(0351)2027938 (0351)2027931
Putian Xue Jin Beer Marketing Agency Co. Ltd. 莆田縣雪津啤酒營銷代理有限公司	Putian 莆田市	Fujian 福建省	
Suzhou Sugar, Cigarette & Wine General Company 蘇州糖煙酒總公司	Suzhou 蘇州市	Jiangsu 江蘇省	(0512)7276392 (0512)7276406
Yuhang Sugar Industry Tobacco & Wine Company 余杭市糖業煙酒公司	Hangzhou 杭州市	Zhejiang 浙江省	(0571)6225788 (0571)6225407
Wuxi Sugar Industry Cigarette & Wine General Company 無錫市糖業煙酒總公司	Wuxi 無錫市	Jiangsu 江蘇省	(0510)2720023 (0510)2707693
Wuxi Chaoyang Co. Ltd. 無錫朝陽股份有限公司	Wuxi 無錫市	Jiangsu 江蘇省	(0510)2767704
Yinchuan Shen Da Non-staple Food Co. Ltd. 銀川申達副食有限公司	Yinchuan 銀川市	Ningxia 寧夏	(0951)5031694
Shanghai Sugar Industry Cigarette & Wine (Group) Co. Ltd. 上海市糖業煙酒(集團)有限公司	Shanghai 上海市	Shanghai 上海市	(021)63224190 (021)63223169

*Also include sales by firms outside this industry.包括本行業以外廠家的銷售。"o" stands for "others". "o" 代表"其他產品"。

1513: Beer 啤酒製造業

The industry accounts for 0.586% of the total revenue of China's industrial sector in 1996. The revenue growth rate of the industry is 12.7% from 1995, as compared to the growth rate of China's industrial sector, 9.51%. The rate of return on asset is 1.35%. 56.38% of all firms in the industry made a profit while 37.07% had negative returns. The top province in terms of the industry's revenue is Shandong, accounting for 16.06% of the total revenue.
本行業在1996年佔全行業總產值0.586%，行業年增長率為12.7%（全國工業年增長率9.51%）。行業的資產回報率1.35%，56.38%的企業盈利，37.07%的企業虧損。銷售收入最高的省份為山東省，佔本行業的16.06%。

	Total number of firms 企業總數	Total number of employees 職工總數	Total revenue (mil. RMB) 總銷售收入（百萬元）	Total profit (mil. RMB) 總利潤（百萬元）	Return on assets 資產利潤率 (%)	Return on equity 權益利潤率 (%)	Labour productivity ('000 RMB / worker) 勞動生產率（千元/人）	Debts / assets 資產負債率 (%)	Total assets (mil. RMB) 總資產（百萬元）
Industry Overall 行業總體	741	340,103	33,991	897	1.35	3.51	99.94	61.60	66,617

	Number of firms 企業個數	Average number of employees 平均職工人數	Average revenue ('000 RMB) 平均銷售收入（千元）	Average profit ('000 RMB) 平均利潤（千元）	Return on assets 資產利潤率 (%)	Return on equity 權益利潤率 (%)	Labour productivity ('000 RMB / worker) 勞動生產率（千元/人）	Average debts / assets 平均資產負債率(%)	Average Total assets ('000 RMB) 平均總資產（千元）
By ownership 產業所有權									
State-owned 國有	384	516	40,865	549	0.66	2.54	79.20	73.97	83,044
Collectively-owned 集體	192	290	20,747	287	0.86	4.52	71.45	80.97	33,326
Privately-owned 私有	1	30	1,165	-55	-0.56	96.57	38.84	100.58	9,870
Domestic JVs 聯營	9	159	23,913	442	1.56	5.92	150.18	73.73	28,384
Joint stock 股份制	30	756	72,414	3,862	2.81	6.56	95.73	57.20	137,465
Foreign-funded 外資	70	445	75,506	-1,709	-1.16	-2.20	169.75	47.36	147,728
Overseas Chinese-funded 港澳台資	54	561	122,775	11,821	4.71	7.26	218.88	35.07	250,791
By size 規模									
Large 大型	68	1,409	220,600	12,768	2.94	6.30	156.54	53.31	434,071
Medium 中型	192	641	65,662	411	0.33	0.92	102.49	63.46	122,771
Small 小型	468	256	13,638	-106	-0.37	-1.57	53.33	76.63	28,753
By regional distribution 地區分布									
Central-North 華北	95	562	40,248	-884	-0.93	-2.18	71.62	57.43	95,314
Beijing 北京	13	837	128,759	1,640	0.59	1.12	153.83	47.67	279,711
Tianjin 天津	3	386	20,760	-13,973	-12.71	-22.57	53.78	43.69	109,963
Hebei 河北	38	638	34,551	-1,882	-1.92	-4.93	54.18	61.11	98,221
Shanxi 山西	12	261	14,144	-384	-1.29	-4.50	54.19	71.22	29,698
Inner Mongolia 內蒙	29	482	20,852	440	1.28	6.02	43.26	78.83	34,479
Northeast 東北	154	436	32,311	436	0.67	1.79	74.04	62.58	64,999
Liaoning 遼寧	44	553	45,145	1,697	2.11	5.03	81.61	57.98	80,270
Jilin 吉林	40	481	32,540	-978	-1.13	-2.93	67.69	61.46	86,596
Heilongjiang 黑龍江	70	338	24,112	452	1.05	3.41	71.42	69.27	43,059
Central East 華東	281	426	51,300	1,858	2.16	5.32	120.35	59.50	86,222
Shanghai 上海	9	360	67,098	-1,692	-1.07	-1.87	186.56	42.87	158,718
Jiangsu 江蘇	36	444	45,156	1,615	2.01	4.90	101.75	58.91	80,178
Zhejiang 浙江	82	298	31,645	1,045	1.96	4.47	106.06	56.12	53,283
Anhui 安徽	26	545	43,379	-345	-0.45	-3.39	79.59	86.79	77,212
Fujian 福建	50	320	46,009	2,558	3.41	8.84	143.79	61.49	75,123
Jiangxi 江西	28	407	25,090	384	0.77	4.09	61.69	81.28	50,160
Shandong 山東	50	691	109,202	5,278	3.15	6.73	158.10	53.22	167,521
Central-South 中南	118	469	62,400	2,483	1.76	4.52	132.93	60.99	140,791
Henan 河南	37	495	30,654	680	1.43	5.95	61.91	76.00	47,622
Hubei 湖北	31	547	46,690	670	0.57	1.30	85.41	56.10	117,015
Hunan 湖南	15	349	29,995	280	0.43	1.32	85.96	67.72	65,555
Guangdong 廣東	25	399	151,546	10,755	3.06	8.11	379.81	62.27	351,629
Guangxi 廣西	6	788	85,205	-4,035	-1.85	-3.12	108.13	40.61	217,718
Hainan 海南	4	48	7,943	-458	-1.28	-3.27	167.21	60.96	35,878
Southwest 西南	54	452	36,026	1,808	2.71	10.66	79.78	74.59	66,753
Chongqing 重慶	11	469	50,737	6,068	6.87	26.49	107.98	74.08	88,375
Sichuan 四川	21	599	46,336	1,985	2.48	11.88	77.30	79.12	80,033
Guizhou 貴州	8	326	18,206	-4,275	-8.45	-23.87	55.89	64.58	50,564
Yunnan 雲南	12	268	17,053	342	1.19	5.54	63.61	78.56	28,759
Tibet 西藏	1	237	16,250	16,040	13.41	20.77	68.57	35.43	119,570
Northwest 西北	39	512	37,631	19	0.02	0.10	73.51	75.17	79,650
Shaanxi 陝西	11	598	49,592	-2,595	-2.89	-14.51	82.87	80.11	89,922
Gansu 甘肅	10	760	60,969	5,122	5.74	18.13	80.19	68.35	89,229
Qinghai 青海	1	354	14,290	-3,420	-7.94	-40.47	40.37	80.38	43,060
Ningxia 寧夏	2	500	5,340	175	1.33	19.23	10.68	93.06	13,110
Xinjiang 新疆	15	295	19,161	-1,256	-1.63	-6.68	64.95	75.61	77,043

1513: Beer 啤酒製造業

Year 年份	Number of firms 企業個數	Rate of change 每年變化 (%)	Number of employees 職工人數（人）	Rate of change 每年變化 (%)	Total revenue (mil. RMB) 總銷售收入（百萬元）	Rate of change 每年變化 (%)	Total profit (mil. RMB) 總利潤（百萬元）	Rate of change 每年變化 (%)
1993	676		284,900		19,277		918	
1994	705	4.29%	307,191	7.82%	22,663	17.56%	675	-26.40%
1995	738	4.68%	335,713	9.28%	30,148	33.03%	1,010	49.68%
1996	741	0.41%	340,103	1.31%	33,991	12.75%	897	-11.19%

3 Major products* 3 種主要產品 *	Output 產量	Sales volume 銷售量	Unit 單位
a) Beer 啤酒	16,226,899	14,766,479	ton 噸
b) Alcoholic Drink 飲料酒	18,825,807	17,319,742	ton 噸

Top 10 firms by revenue (year founded) 收入排名前 10 家企業 (創辦年份)	City 城市	Province 省	Telephone / fax 電話 / 傳真	Number of employees 職工人數	Ownership 產業所有權	Revenue ('000 RMB) 銷售收入（千元）	Profit ('000 RMB) (rank) 利潤（千元）（排名）	Total assets ('000 RMB) 總資產（千元）	Major products 主要產品
Qingdao Brewery Co. Ltd. 青島啤酒股份有限公司(1995)	Qingdao 青島市	Shandong 山東省	(0532)2817110 (0532)3834533	4,857	Foreign-funded 外資	1,503,596	130000(1)	3,063,560	a,b
Beijing Yan Jing Brewery Group Co. 北京燕京啤酒集團公司(1980)	Beijing 北京市	Beijing 北京市	(010)69444645 (010)69441273	3,298	State-owned 國有	725,489	118805(2)	1,127,983	a,b
Zhaoqing Blue Ribbor Brewery Noble Ltd. 肇慶藍帶啤酒盧堡有限公司(1990)	Zhaoqing 肇慶市	Guangdong 廣東省	(0757)2822688 (0757)2827440	778	Overseas Chinese-funded 港澳台資	694,909	108629(3)	779,118	a,b
Guangzhou Zhu Jiang Brewery Group Co. 廣州市珠江啤酒集團公司(1985)	Guangzhou 廣州市	Guangdong 廣東省	(020)84206636 (020)84202502	1,846	State-owned 國有	680,480	75076(6)	2,100,326	a,b
China Resources (Shenyang) Snowflake Brewery Co. Ltd. 瀋陽華潤雪花啤酒有限公司(1993)	Shenyang 瀋陽市	Liaoning 遼寧省	(024)25872059 (024)25872059	4,013	Overseas Chinese-funded 港澳台資	568,741	50168(12)	919,846	a,b
Zhejiang Qian Pi Group Co. Ltd. 浙江錢啤集團股份有限公司(1996)	Hangzhou 杭州市	Zhejiang 浙江省	(0571)2614888 (0571)2610008	1,716	Joint stock 股份制	533,058	32523(18)	509,012	a,b
Shenzhen Brewery Co. Ltd. 深圳啤酒有限公司(1990)	Shenzhen 深圳市	Guangdong 廣東省	(0755)5565998 (0755)5560994	971	Overseas Chinese-funded 港澳台資	484,216	101317(4)	961,944	a,b
Lanzhou Yellow River Beer Co. Ltd. 蘭州黃河啤酒有限公司(1992)	Lanzhou 蘭州市	Gansu 甘肅省	(0931)2335811	1,607	Overseas Chinese-funded 港澳台資	461,482	48138(13)	554,261	a,b
Guangzhou San Miguel Brewery Co. Ltd. 廣州生力啤酒有限公司(1991)	Guangzhou 廣州市	Guangdong 廣東省	(020)86509983 (020)86505322	899	Overseas Chinese-funded 港澳台資	447,179	57447(8)	402,066	a,b
Shannxi Baoji Beer Factory Shannxi Baoji Alcohol Factory 陜西寶雞啤酒廠陜西寶雞酒精廠(1959)	Baoji 寶雞市	Shaanxi 陜西省	(0917)6212072 (0917)6213414	3,065	State-owned 國有	440,598	2008(96)	471,067	o

Top 10 Cities by Production Output 產出排名前 10 位城市	Province 省	Market share 市場份額	Number of firms 企業個數
Xi'an 西安市	Shaanxi 陜西省	11.18%	6
Qingdao 青島市	Shandong 山東省	5.96%	9
Guangzhou 廣州市	Guangdong 廣東省	3.71%	7
Beijing 北京市	Beijing 北京市	3.26%	14
Zhaoqing 肇慶市	Guangdong 廣東省	3.07%	3
Hangzhou 杭州市	Zhejiang 浙江省	2.62%	13
Wuhan 武漢市	Hubei 湖北省	2.10%	3
Putian 莆田市	Fujian 福建省	1.90%	2
Shenyang 瀋陽市	Liaoning 遼寧省	1.86%	7
Shanghai 上海市	Shanghai 上海市	1.75%	14

10 Major Wholesalers 10 家主要批發商	City 城市	Province 省	Telephone / Fax 電話 / 傳真
Zhong Liang Sugar Industry Groceries Import & Export Company 中糧糖業雜品進出口公司	Beijing 北京市	Beijing 北京市	(010)65268888 (010)65276023
China National Sugar & Alcohol Group Corp. 中國糖業酒類集團公司	Beijing 北京市	Beijing 北京市	(010)68360994
Shanxi Sugar & Wine Non-staple Food Company 山西省糖酒副食公司	Taiyuan 太原市	Shanxi 山西省	(0351)2027938 (0351)2027931
Putian Xue Jin Beer Marketing Agency Co. Ltd. 莆田縣雪津啤酒營銷代理有限公司	Putian 莆田市	Fujian 福建省	
Suzhou Sugar, Cigarette & Wine General Company 蘇州糖煙酒總公司	Suzhou 蘇州市	Jiangsu 江蘇省	(0512)7276392 (0512)7276406
Yuhang Sugar Industry Tobacco & Wine Company 余杭市糖業煙酒公司	Hangzhou 杭州市	Zhejiang 浙江省	(0571)6225788 (0571)6225407
Wuxi Sugar Industry Cigarette & Wine General Company 無錫市糖業煙酒總公司	Wuxi 無錫市	Jiangsu 江蘇省	(0510)2720023 (0510)2707693
Wuxi Chaoyang Co. Ltd. 無錫朝陽股份有限公司	Wuxi 無錫市	Jiangsu 江蘇省	(0510)2767704
Yinchuan Shen Da Non-staple Food Co. Ltd. 銀川申達副食有限公司	Yinchuan 銀川市	Ningxia 寧夏	(0951)5031694
Shanghai Sugar Industry Cigarette & Wine (Group) Co. Ltd. 上海市糖業煙酒(集團)有限公司	Shanghai 上海市	Shanghai 上海市	(021)63224190 (021)63223169

*Also include sales by firms outside this industry.包括本行業以外廠家的銷售。"o" stands for "others". "o" 代表"其他產品"。

1514: Cooking Wine 黃酒製造業

The industry accounts for 0.044% of the total revenue of China's industrial sector in 1996. The revenue growth rate of the industry is 26.2% from 1995, as compared to the growth rate of China's industrial sector, 9.51%. The rate of return on asset is 1.79%. 67.12% of all firms in the industry made a profit while 26.59% had negative returns. The top province in terms of the industry's revenue is Zhejiang, accounting for 60.11% of the total revenue.
本行業在 1996 年占全行業總產值 0.044%，行業年增長率為 26.2%（全國工業年增長率 9.51%）。行業的資產回報率 1.79%，67.12% 的企業盈利，26.59% 的企業虧損。銷售收入最高的省份為浙江省，占本行業的 60.11%。

	Total number of firms 企業總數	Total number of employees 職工總數	Total revenue (mil. RMB) 總銷售收入（百萬元）	Total profit (mil. RMB) 總利潤（百萬元）	Return on assets 資產利潤率 (%)	Return on equity 權益利潤率 (%)	Labour productivity ('000 RMB / worker) 勞動生產率（千元/人）	Debts / assets 資產負債率 (%)	Total assets (mil. RMB) 總資產（百萬元）
Industry Overall 行業總體	410	34,612	2,568	92	1.79	5.11	74.19	65.01	5,128

	Number of firms 企業個數	Average number of employees 平均職工人數	Average revenue ('000 RMB) 平均銷售收入（千元）	Average profit ('000 RMB) 平均利潤（千元）	Return on assets 資產利潤率 (%)	Return on equity 權益利潤率 (%)	Labour productivity ('000 RMB / worker) 勞動生產率（千元/人）	Average debts / assets 平均資產負債率(%)	Average Total assets ('000 RMB) 平均總資產（千元）
By ownership 產業所有權									
State-owned 國有	129	187	13,868	465	1.62	4.80	74.16	66.35	28,775
Collectively-owned 集體	264	33	2,147	62	1.68	5.32	64.81	68.44	3,706
Privately-owned 私有	2	48	3,706	-11	-0.33	-2.07	77.21	84.10	3,290
Domestic JVs 聯營	7	105	7,986	200	1.71	6.78	76.27	74.76	11,709
Joint stock 股份制	3	156	29,959	3,123	3.45	5.84	191.63	40.91	90,471
Foreign-funded 外資	5	85	11,533	951	6.18	8.91	135.68	30.61	15,382
Overseas Chinese-funded 港澳台資	1	20	1,978	75	7.40	8.82	98.92	16.10	1,020
By size 規模									
Large 大型	2	1,447	247,958	33,520	5.31	12.42	171.42	57.28	631,550
Medium 中型	12	571	55,330	1,453	1.38	3.54	96.86	60.99	105,189
Small 小型	390	63	3,612	19	0.29	0.99	57.59	70.72	6,674
By regional distribution 地區分布									
Central-North 華北	8	32	756	-4	-0.38	-0.57	23.91	34.09	998
Beijing 北京	2								
Tianjin 天津	3	42	1,460	7	0.32	0.43	34.76	25.36	2,063
Hebei 河北	1	27	530	30	5.36	25.00	19.63	80.36	560
Shanxi 山西	2	50	570	-40	-6.50	-14.81	11.40	56.91	615
Inner Mongolia 內蒙									
Northeast 東北	2	46	315	-60	-2.27	6.63	6.85	134.40	2,645
Liaoning 遼寧									
Jilin 吉林	1	60	460	-120	-3.08	5.06	7.67	160.93	3,890
Heilongjiang 黑龍江	1	32	170				5.31	60.71	1,400
Central East 華東	316	88	6,881	287	2.10	6.00	78.61	64.96	13,629
Shanghai 上海	10	179	16,665	371	1.77	11.73	92.94	84.92	20,979
Jiangsu 江蘇	21	151	11,541	-174	-1.40	-5.91	76.26	76.29	12,408
Zhejiang 浙江	190	96	8,124	512	2.76	7.21	84.62	61.67	18,511
Anhui 安徽	10	96	12,135	-42	-0.38	-1.84	126.01	79.10	10,910
Fujian 福建	37	36	959	-153	-8.67	-19.91	26.83	56.46	1,761
Jiangxi 江西	46	31	635	-23	-1.12	-92.11	20.40	98.77	2,038
Shandong 山東	2	367	17,955	220	0.86	2.95	48.99	70.88	25,615
Central-South 中南	38	88	6,064	471	3.34	7.29	69.06	54.15	14,072
Henan 河南	13	85	3,115	-10	-0.10	-0.22	36.51	54.78	10,141
Hubei 湖北	7	82	1,580	76	1.91	20.62	19.37	90.73	3,960
Hunan 湖南	10	26	972	-43	-3.46	-12.43	36.82	72.12	1,241
Guangdong 廣東	4	96	3,345	-60	-0.73	-3.86	34.93	80.98	8,178
Guangxi 廣西	3	169	6,423	-420	-2.13	-6.68	37.93	68.17	19,730
Hainan 海南	1	502	136,520	19,410	7.17	12.57	271.95	42.98	270,860
Southwest 西南	14	68	1,427	-266	-4.44	-25.99	20.86	82.92	6,006
Chongqing 重慶	2	26	1,586	9	0.16	0.21	60.35	19.99	5,534
Sichuan 四川	5	121	1,755	-600	-7.66	-191.80	14.50	96.01	7,834
Guizhou 貴州	5	48	952	-10	-0.26	-2.76	19.67	90.46	3,816
Yunnan 雲南	2	29	1,635	-350	-4.74	-33.02	56.38	85.65	7,385
Tibet 西藏									
Northwest 西北	32	72	4,276	-401	-6.79	-57.18	59.24	88.13	5,903
Shaanxi 陝西	11	118	8,375	-63	-0.53	-5.56	70.87	90.42	11,772
Gansu 甘肅	19	51	2,321	-606	-21.22	-114.07	45.70	81.38	2,855
Qinghai 青海									
Ningxia 寧夏									
Xinjiang 新疆	2	23	305	-310	-11.97	775.00	13.56	101.54	2,590

1514: Cooking Wine 黄酒製造業

Year 年份	Number of firms 企業個數	Rate of change 每年變化 (%)	Number of employees 職工人數 (人)	Rate of change 每年變化 (%)	Total revenue (mil. RMB) 總銷售收入 (百萬元)	Rate of change 每年變化 (%)	Total profit (mil. RMB) 總利潤 (百萬元)	Rate of change 每年變化 (%)
1993	450		36,902		1,540		13	
1994	435	-3.33%	35,262	-4.45%	1,658	7.67%	63	392.48%
1995	439	0.92%	38,100	8.05%	2,035	22.72%	91	45.64%
1996	410	-6.61%	34,612	-9.15%	2,568	26.19%	92	0.94%

3 Major products* 3 種主要產品 *	Output 產量	Sales volume 銷售量	Unit 單位
a) Rice Wine 黃酒	966,330	860,034	ton 噸
b) Alcoholic Drink Mixed with Fruit Juice 露酒	11,970	11,850	ton 噸

Top 10 firms by revenue (year founded) 收入排名前 10 家企業 (創辦年份)	City 城市	Province 省	Telephone / fax 電話 / 傳真	Number of employees 職工人數	Ownership 產業所有權	Revenue ('000 RMB) 銷售收入 (千元)	Profit ('000 RMB) (rank) 利潤 (千元) (排名)	Total assets ('000 RMB) 總資產 (千元)	Major products 主要產品
China Shaoxing Yellow Rice Brewery Group Corp. 中國紹興黃酒集團公司(1951)	Shaoxing 紹興市	Zhejiang 浙江省	(0575)5157501 (0575)5156989	2,085	State-owned 國有	314,368	52316(1)	875,093	a
Shaoxing Dong Feng Distillery 紹興東風酒廠(1952)	Shaoxing 紹興市	Zhejiang 浙江省	(0575)4072779 (0575)4093974	1,030	State-owned 國有	202,530	41130(2)	522,100	a
Jiashan Distillery 加善縣酒廠(1952)	Jiaxing 嘉興市	Zhejiang 浙江省	(0573)4564577 (0573)4444197	1,242	State-owned 國有	130,755	5599(3)	192,074	a,b
Shangyu Shaoxing Nu Er Hong Brewing General Company 上虞市紹興女兒紅釀酒總公司(1919)	Shaoxing 紹興市	Zhejiang 浙江省	(0575)2051558 (0575)2053871	510	State-owned 國有	73,836	4360(4)	102,859	a
Shanghai Jin Feng Brewery Co. 上海金楓釀酒公司(1939)	Shanghai 上海市	Shanghai 上海市	(021)57353990 (021)57353990	316	State-owned 國有	68,059	4239(5)	72,408	a
Shannxi Qin Yang Foods & Beverage Co. Ltd. 陝西省秦洋食品飲料有限公司(1984)	Hanzhong 漢中市	Shaanxi 陝西省	(0916)8212884 (0916)8212899	522	State-owned 國有	67,404	-874(126)	84,494	a
Huzhou Shuanglin Liquor Factory 湖州市雙林酒廠(1951)	Huzhou 湖州市	Zhejiang 浙江省	(0572)3974279 (0572)3975679	227	State-owned 國有	63,982	313(31)	58,557	a
Huzhou Huan Zhong Brewing Group Co. Ltd. 湖州歡眾釀酒集團有限公司(1953)	Huzhou 湖州市	Zhejiang 浙江省	(0572)6022115	749	State-owned 國有	58,216	29(61)	83,783	a,b
State-owned Rugao Distillery 國營如皋市酒廠(1956)	Nantong 南通市	Jiangsu 江蘇省	(0513)7512683	595	State-owned 國有	56,177	813(16)	35,565	a
Jiangsu Dangyang Hua Liquor Group Co. Ltd. 江蘇省丹陽華酒集團有限公司(1958)	Zhenjiang 鎮江市	Jiangsu 江蘇省	(0511)6523211	501	State-owned 國有	46,179	121(43)	70,829	a

Top 10 Cities by Production Output 產出排名前 10 位城市	Province 省	Market share 市場份額	Number of firms 企業個數
Shaoxing 紹興市	Zhejiang 浙江省	33.08%	56
Shanghai 上海市	Shanghai 上海市	6.92%	15
Suzhou 蘇州市	Jiangsu 江蘇省	6.70%	33
Jiaxing 嘉興市	Zhejiang 浙江省	6.24%	6
Nantong 南通市	Jiangsu 江蘇省	5.94%	29
Huzhou 湖州市	Zhejiang 浙江省	5.58%	9
Ningbo 寧波市	Zhejiang 浙江省	4.93%	30
Hangzhou 杭州市	Zhejiang 浙江省	3.42%	19
Hanzhong 漢中市	Shaanxi 陝西省	3.16%	8
Taizhou 臺州市	Zhejiang 浙江省	2.96%	31

10 Major Wholesalers 10 家主要批發商	City 城市	Province 省	Telephone / Fax 電話 / 傳真
Zhong Liang Sugar Industry Groceries Import & Export Company 中糧糖業雜品進出口公司	Beijing 北京市	Beijing 北京市	(010)65268888 (010)65276023
China National Sugar & Alcohol Group Corp. 中國糖業酒類集團公司	Beijing 北京市	Beijing 北京市	(010)68360994
Shanxi Sugar & Wine Non-staple Food Company 山西省糖酒副食公司	Taiyuan 太原市	Shanxi 山西省	(0351)2027938 (0351)2027931
Putian Xue Jin Beer Marketing Agency Co. Ltd. 莆田縣雪津啤酒營銷代理有限公司	Putian 莆田市	Fujian 福建省	
Suzhou Sugar, Cigarette & Wine General Company 蘇州糖煙酒總公司	Suzhou 蘇州市	Jiangsu 江蘇省	(0512)7276392 (0512)7276406
Yuhang Sugar Industry Tobacco & Wine Company 余杭市糖業煙酒公司	Hangzhou 杭州市	Zhejiang 浙江省	(0571)6225788 (0571)6225407
Wuxi Sugar Industry Cigarette & Wine General Company 無錫市糖業煙酒總公司	Wuxi 無錫市	Jiangsu 江蘇省	(0510)2720023 (0510)2707693
Wuxi Chaoyang Co. Ltd. 無錫朝陽股份有限公司	Wuxi 無錫市	Jiangsu 江蘇省	(0510)2767704
Yinchuan Shen Da Non-staple Food Co. Ltd. 銀川申達副食有限公司	Yinchuan 銀川市	Ningxia 寧夏	(0951)5031694
Shanghai Sugar Industry Cigarette & Wine (Group) Co. Ltd. 上海市糖業煙酒(集團)有限公司	Shanghai 上海市	Shanghai 上海市	(021)63224190 (021)63223169

*Also include sales by firms outside this industry.包括本行業以外廠家的銷售。"o" stands for "others". "o" 代表"其他產品"。

1515: Wine 葡萄酒製造業

The industry accounts for 0.032% of the total revenue of China's industrial sector in 1996. The revenue growth rate of the industry is 34.0% from 1995, as compared to the growth rate of China's industrial sector, 9.51%. The rate of return on asset is 8.36%. 64.31% of all firms in the industry made a profit while 25.69% had negative returns. The top province in terms of the industry's revenue is Shandong, accounting for 31.72% of the total revenue.
本行業在1996年佔全行業總產值0.032%，行業年增長率為34.0%（全國工業年增長率9.51%）。行業的資產回報率8.36%，64.31%的企業盈利，25.69%的企業虧損。銷售收入最高的省份為山東省，佔本行業的31.72%。

	Total number of firms 企業總數	Total number of employees 職工總數	Total revenue (mil. RMB) 總銷售收入（百萬元）	Total profit (mil. RMB) 總利潤（百萬元）	Return on assets 資產利潤率 (%)	Return on equity 權益利潤率 (%)	Labour productivity ('000 RMB / worker) 勞動生產率（千元/人）	Debts / assets 資產負債率 (%)	Total assets (mil. RMB) 總資產（百萬元）
Industry Overall 行業總體	158	18,969	1,859	322	8.36	21.90	98.00	61.81	3,844

	Number of firms 企業個數	Average number of employees 平均職工人數	Average revenue ('000 RMB) 平均銷售收入（千元）	Average profit ('000 RMB) 平均利潤（千元）	Return on assets 資產利潤率 (%)	Return on equity 權益利潤率 (%)	Labour productivity ('000 RMB / worker) 勞動生產率（千元/人）	Average debts / assets 平均資產負債率(%)	Average Total assets ('000 RMB) 平均總資產（千元）
By ownership 產業所有權									
State-owned 國有	61	232	14,787	2,426	6.84	17.13	63.60	60.07	35,475
Collectively-owned 集體	67	35	2,157	33	1.39	13.56	61.50	89.72	2,396
Privately-owned 私有									
Domestic JVs 聯營	1	37	533	205	1.13	4.77	14.41	76.26	18,128
Joint stock 股份制	2	141	17,134	290	1.38	10.18	121.95	86.46	21,028
Foreign-funded 外資	20	64	26,100	6,406	11.86	28.54	409.09	58.43	54,005
Overseas Chinese-funded 港澳台資	6	141	42,635	7,141	11.28	33.28	303.45	66.11	63,308
By size 規模									
Large 大型	6	980	211,695	54,508	17.06	40.88	216.13	58.27	319,468
Medium 中型	7	396	15,477	-1,533	-1.58	-3.10	39.06	49.15	97,153
Small 小型	140	73	3,433	40	0.45	1.76	46.92	74.15	8,912
By regional distribution 地區分布									
Central-North 華北	24	110	29,093	10,121	17.31	39.41	263.98	56.08	58,473
Beijing 北京	6	116	20,017	-2,167	-3.75	-9.53	172.81	60.67	57,777
Tianjin 天津	8	102	45,056	28,205	36.88	65.93	441.73	44.07	76,483
Hebei 河北	6	129	34,903	5,218	7.69	22.13	269.87	65.25	67,868
Shanxi 山西	3	53	2,497	-247	-3.39	15.38	46.81	122.02	7,280
Inner Mongolia 內蒙	1	198	770	-300	-1.90	-29.13	3.89	93.41	15,770
Northeast 東北	20	154	4,078	96	0.44	1.61	26.40	72.90	22,041
Liaoning 遼寧	3	308	4,320	17	0.02	0.07	14.01	67.02	67,537
Jilin 吉林	11	174	3,965	-24	-0.12	-0.52	22.73	77.88	20,482
Heilongjiang 黑龍江	6	41	4,163	355	16.50	75.53	101.96	78.16	2,152
Central East 華東	49	125	15,316	1,170	5.07	15.21	122.77	66.64	23,052
Shanghai 上海	2	63	26,040	-1,050	-1.53	-5.28	416.64	71.09	68,720
Jiangsu 江蘇	8	73	7,188	66	0.85	44.17	98.46	98.08	7,803
Zhejiang 浙江	1	25	120				4.80	52.33	860
Anhui 安徽	8	167	3,688	-138	-0.89	-2.39	22.10	62.73	15,463
Fujian 福建	5	12	4,062	260	2.62	4.55	344.24	42.45	9,922
Jiangxi 江西	4	93	348	-298	-6.27	26.68	3.73	123.43	4,748
Shandong 山東	21	172	28,076	2,851	8.13	22.57	163.23	63.98	35,073
Central-South 中南	40	84	2,094	-196	-2.99	-20.11	24.81	85.14	6,548
Henan 河南	26	98	2,038	-276	-3.79	-34.52	20.86	89.03	7,283
Hubei 湖北	6	29	1,418	25	1.51	6.61	49.48	77.14	1,655
Hunan 湖南	1	206	1,030	-230	-1.52	-2.78	5.00	45.38	15,160
Guangdong 廣東	2	30	2,070	220	2.11	6.34	69.00	66.67	10,410
Guangxi 廣西	5	79	3,416	-204	-3.83	-152.24	43.02	97.52	5,326
Hainan 海南									
Southwest 西南	5	24	232	-30	-2.19	-6.25	9.51	65.01	1,372
Chongqing 重慶									
Sichuan 四川	5	24	232	30	2.19	6.25	9.67	65.01	1,372
Guizhou 貴州									
Yunnan 雲南									
Tibet 西藏									
Northwest 西北	20	181	12,215	1,369	4.55	8.71	67.39	47.82	30,096
Shaanxi 陝西	10	92	940	-76	-1.61	-4.76	10.20	66.12	4,716
Gansu 甘肅	4	83	1,868	35	1.46	4.46	22.50	67.29	2,400
Qinghai 青海									
Ningxia 寧夏									
Xinjiang 新疆	6	395	37,905	4,665	5.13	9.49	95.92	45.90	90,860

1515: Wine 葡萄酒製造業

Year 年份	Number of firms 企業個數	Rate of change 每年變化 (%)	Number of employees 職工人數 (人)	Rate of change 每年變化 (%)	Total revenue (mil. RMB) 總銷售收入 (百萬元)	Rate of change 每年變化 (%)	Total profit (mil. RMB) 總利潤 (百萬元)	Rate of change 每年變化 (%)
1993	128		20,742		921		2	
1994	145	13.28%	17,110	-17.51%	1,102	19.80%	100	4392.61%
1995	155	6.90%	19,598	14.54%	1,387	25.79%	119	19.02%
1996	158	1.94%	18,969	-3.21%	1,859	34.03%	322	171.25%

3 Major products* 3 種主要產品 *	Output 產量	Sales volume 銷售量	Unit 單位
a) Grape Wine 葡萄酒	161,881	145,693	ton 噸
b) Fruit Wine 果酒	10,191	9,783	ton 噸
c) Alcoholic Drink Mixed with Fruit Juice 露酒	10,575	10,469	ton 噸

Top 10 firms by revenue (year founded) 收入排名前 10 家企業 (創辦年份)	City 城市	Province 省	Telephone / fax 電話 / 傳真	Number of employees 職工人數	Ownership 產業所有權	Revenue ('000 RMB) 銷售收入 (千元)	Profit ('000 RMB) (rank) 利潤 (千元) (排名)	Total assets ('000 RMB) 總資產 (千元)	Major products 主要產品
Yantai Zhang Yu Group Co. Ltd. 煙台張裕葡萄釀酒公司(1914)	Yantai 煙台市	Shandong 山東省	(0535)6242258 (0535)6244616	2,105	State-owned 國有	469,020	50020(3)	510,480	a,b,c
Sino French Joint Venture Dynasty Winery Ltd. 中法合營王朝葡萄釀酒有限公司(1980)	Tianjin 天津市	Tianjin 天津市	(022)26998888 (022)26990996	136	Foreign-funded 外資	307,517	136300(1)	310,093	a
Xinjiang Corps Si Shi Yi Li Brewing General Factory 新疆兵團四師伊犁釀酒總廠(1988)	Yining 伊寧市	Xinjiang 新疆	(0999)5266017 (0999)5266014	1,817	State-owned 國有	205,951	33397(4)	476,481	o
China Great Wall Grape Wine Co. Ltd. 中國長城葡萄酒有限公司(1985)	Zhangjiakou 張家口市	Hebei 河北省	(0313)6221421 (0313)6223795	646	Overseas Chinese-funded 港澳台資	177,670	29345(5)	280,711	a
Beijing Pernod Ricard Winery Co. Ltd. 北京保樂力加釀酒有限公司(1994)	Beijing 北京市	Beijing 北京市	(010)68216611 (010)68279742	439	Foreign-funded 外資	54,664	-23821(60)	199,309	a,c
Lianyungang Grape Wine Factory 連雲港市葡萄酒廠(1958)	Lianyungang 連雲港市	Jiangsu 江蘇省	(0518)5413322 (0518)5414950	378	State-owned 國有	45,920	1250(13)	48,307	a,b
Yantai Wei Long Grape Wine Co. Ltd. 煙台威龍葡萄酒股份公司(1982)	Yantai 煙台市	Shandong 山東省	(0535)8526425 (0535)8526425	272	Joint stock 股份制	41,271	4301(8)	45,424	a
Beijing Shun Xing Sing Winery Co. Ltd. 北京順興葡萄酒有限公司(1980)	Beijing 北京市	Beijing 北京市	(010)67643377	150	Foreign-funded 外資	40,709	10523(7)	37,691	a
Tonghua Grape Wine General Co. 通化葡萄酒總公司(1941)	Tonghua 通化市	Jilin 吉林省	(0435)3516212 (0435)3516127	1,169	State-owned 國有	38,030	821(17)	103,500	a,c
Tianjin Tian Chao Grape Wine Co. Ltd. 天津天朝葡萄釀酒有限公司(1993)	Tianjin 天津市	Tianjin 天津市	(022)26998888	98	Foreign-funded 外資	28,158	12518(6)	50,345	a

Top 10 Cities by Production Output 產出排名前 10 位城市	Province 省	Market share 市場份額	Number of firms 企業個數
Tianjin 天津市	Tianjin 天津市	29.68%	9
Yantai 煙台市	Shandong 山東省	19.80%	12
Yining 伊寧市	Xinjiang 新疆	9.13%	2
Qingdao 青島市	Shandong 山東省	6.91%	6
Beijing 北京市	Beijing 北京市	5.70%	5
Shanghai 上海市	Shanghai 上海市	4.30%	2
Shangqiu 商丘市	Henan 河南省	3.22%	5
Tonghua 通化市	Jilin 吉林省	2.92%	4
Lianyungang 連雲港市	Jiangsu 江蘇省	2.92%	3
Qinhuangdao 秦皇島市	Hebei 河北省	2.37%	1

10 Major Wholesalers 10 家主要批發商	City 城市	Province 省	Telephone / Fax 電話 / 傳真
Zhong Liang Sugar Industry Groceries Import & Export Company 中糧糖業雜品進出口公司	Beijing 北京市	Beijing 北京市	(010)65268888 (010)65276023
China National Sugar & Alcohol Group Corp. 中國糖業酒類集團公司	Beijing 北京市	Beijing 北京市	(010)68360994
Shanxi Sugar & Wine Non-staple Food Company 山西省糖酒副食公司	Taiyuan 太原市	Shanxi 山西省	(0351)2027938 (0351)2027931
Putian Xue Jin Beer Marketing Agency Co. Ltd. 莆田縣雪津啤酒營銷代理有限公司	Putian 莆田市	Fujian 福建省	
Suzhou Sugar, Cigarette & Wine General Company 蘇州糖煙酒總公司	Suzhou 蘇州市	Jiangsu 江蘇省	(0512)7276392 (0512)7276406
Yuhang Sugar Industry Tobacco & Wine Company 余杭市糖業煙酒公司	Hangzhou 杭州市	Zhejiang 浙江省	(0571)6225788 (0571)6225407
Wuxi Sugar Industry Cigarette & Wine General Company 無錫市糖業煙酒總公司	Wuxi 無錫市	Jiangsu 江蘇省	(0510)2720023 (0510)2707693
Wuxi Chaoyang Co. Ltd. 無錫朝陽股份有限公司	Wuxi 無錫市	Jiangsu 江蘇省	(0510)2767704
Yinchuan Shen Da Non-staple Food Co. Ltd. 銀川申達副食有限公司	Yinchuan 銀川市	Ningxia 寧夏	(0951)5031694
Shanghai Sugar Industry Cigarette & Wine (Group) Co. Ltd. 上海市糖業煙酒(集團)有限公司	Shanghai 上海市	Shanghai 上海市	(021)63224190 (021)63223169

*Also include sales by firms outside this industry.包括本行業以外廠家的銷售。"o" stands for "others". "o" 代表"其他產品"。

1516: Fruit Wine 果露酒製造業

The industry accounts for 0.015% of the total revenue of China's industrial sector in 1996. The revenue growth rate of the industry is 22.9% from 1995, as compared to the growth rate of China's industrial sector, 9.51%. The rate of return on asset is 0.71%. 60.36% of all firms in the industry made a profit while 30.89% had negative returns. The top province in terms of the industry's revenue is Guangdong, accounting for 17.14% of the total revenue.
本行業在1996年佔全行業總產值0.015%，行業年增長率為22.9%（全國工業年增長率9.51%）。行業的資產回報率0.71%，60.36%的企業盈利，30.89%的企業虧損。銷售收入最高的省份為廣東省，佔本行業的17.14%。

	Total number of firms 企業總數	Total number of employees 職工總數	Total revenue (mil. RMB) 總銷售收入（百萬元）	Total profit (mil. RMB) 總利潤（百萬元）	Return on assets 資產利潤率 (%)	Return on equity 權益利潤率 (%)	Labour productivity ('000 RMB / worker) 勞動生產率（千元/人）	Debts / assets 資產負債率 (%)	Total assets (mil. RMB) 總資產（百萬元）
Industry Overall 行業總體	285	18,669	893	12	0.71	2.47	47.83	71.09	1,655

	Number of firms・企業個數	Average number of employees 平均職工人數	Average revenue ('000 RMB) 平均銷售收入（千元）	Average profit ('000 RMB) 平均利潤（千元）	Return on assets 資產利潤率 (%)	Return on equity 權益利潤率 (%)	Labour productivity ('000 RMB / worker) 勞動生產率（千元/人）	Average debts / assets 平均資產負債率(%)	Average Total assets ('000 RMB) 平均總資產（千元）
By ownership 產業所有權									
State-owned 國有	75	140	6,600	-213	-1.75	-7.41	46.99	76.32	12,160
Collectively-owned 集體	170	35	1,426	79	3.24	11.97	41.09	72.92	2,447
Privately-owned 私有	1	6							
Domestic JVs 聯營	2	132	10,084	2,645	17.87	25.92	76.40	31.05	14,800
Joint stock 股份制	12	96	5,232	466	4.44	10.47	54.36	57.62	10,489
Foreign-funded 外資	12	23	1,054	517	9.61	15.69	45.51	38.75	5,386
Overseas Chinese-funded 港澳台資	13	45	4,583	-198	-2.46	-7.62	102.02	67.67	8,041
By size 規模									
Large 大型	1	403	49,693	-629	-0.96	-2.01	123.31	52.09	65,419
Medium 中型	6	660	38,463	89	0.10	0.34	58.25	71.15	91,129
Small 小型	262	52	2,338	46	1.16	4.18	45.09	72.29	3,984
By regional distribution 地區分布									
Central-North 華北	19	40	1,964	-46	-0.92	-1.87	48.85	50.89	4,995
Beijing 北京	3	8	903	250	10.87	14.56	117.83	25.36	2,300
Tianjin 天津	3	162	7,767	-530	-2.42	-5.01	47.84	51.64	21,887
Hebei 河北	9	21	603	-44	-2.66	-4.53	28.73	41.29	1,671
Shanxi 山西									
Inner Mongolia 內蒙	4	16	1,470	93	5.06	42.05	90.46	87.96	1,828
Northeast 東北	42	59	976	-107	-3.05	-20.90	16.53	85.39	3,508
Liaoning 遼寧	4	13	908	118	6.89	8.70	68.49	20.82	1,705
Jilin 吉林	29	62	1,127	-136	-3.28	-27.79	18.04	88.19	4,139
Heilongjiang 黑龍江	9	68	520	-114	-5.03	-52.82	7.61	90.47	2,274
Central East 華東	73	57	3,207	246	3.60	11.25	56.47	68.03	6,851
Shanghai 上海	2	168	18,375	400	0.62	1.66	109.38	62.86	64,740
Jiangsu 江蘇	15	40	1,312	12	0.71	2.12	33.08	66.63	1,700
Zhejiang 浙江	9	45	1,601	-164	-1.31	-3.08	35.67	57.50	12,584
Anhui 安徽	14	64	4,185	381	12.78	120.59	65.24	89.40	2,979
Fujian 福建	6	26	243	-25	-0.86	-1.63	9.48	47.16	2,902
Jiangxi 江西	15	45	1,143	43	2.25	13.06	25.47	82.78	1,897
Shandong 山東	12	91	7,176	1,056	8.78	34.59	79.29	74.62	12,028
Central-South 中南	80	93	5,869	-27	-0.36	-1.53	63.24	76.15	7,450
Henan 河南	22	121	5,555	69	1.09	6.87	45.82	84.09	6,320
Hubei 湖北	18	93	7,443	22	0.28	0.95	80.13	70.15	7,658
Hunan 湖南	10	34	1,542	-128	-6.74	-18.44	44.96	63.44	1,898
Guangdong 廣東	18	84	8,501	-5	-0.05	-0.18	101.20	69.35	9,191
Guangxi 廣西	11	106	4,029	-213	-2.07	-10.32	37.88	79.99	10,301
Hainan 海南	1	60	580	-370	-1.73	25.52	9.67	106.79	21,360
Southwest 西南	56	54	1,397	-141	-3.00	-9.24	25.73	67.53	4,715
Chongqing 重慶	4	24	86	-225	-39.77	-4614.35	3.57	99.14	566
Sichuan 四川	15	52	1,315	248	5.53	18.95	25.18	70.79	4,484
Guizhou 貴州	16	70	1,739	-206	-2.53	-6.29	25.02	59.88	8,168
Yunnan 雲南	20	51	1,479	-89	-2.90	-13.69	29.10	78.85	3,055
Tibet 西藏									
Northwest 西北	15	54	2,217	619	17.52	40.94	40.76	57.19	3,532
Shaanxi 陝西	11	63	1,375	44	2.37	5.50	21.72	56.90	1,839
Gansu 甘肅									
Qinghai 青海									
Ningxia 寧夏	1	87	17,950	9,290	31.87	76.40	206.32	58.28	29,150
Xinjiang 新疆	3	11	63	-163	-13.61	-27.37	5.76	50.00	1,200

1516: Fruit Wine 果露酒製造業

Year 年份	Number of firms 企業個數	Rate of change 每年變化 (%)	Number of employees 職工人數（人）	Rate of change 每年變化 (%)	Total revenue (mil. RMB) 總銷售收入（百萬元）	Rate of change 每年變化 (%)	Total profit (mil. RMB) 總利潤（百萬元）	Rate of change 每年變化 (%)
1993	278		18,433		556		-7	
1994	252	-9.35%	20,348	10.39%	647	16.52%	-7	12.68%
1995	276	9.52%	19,885	-2.28%	727	12.24%	-4	34.51%
1996	285	3.26%	18,669	-6.12%	893	22.89%	12	381.89%

3 Major products* 3 種主要產品 *	Output 產量	Sales volume 銷售量	Unit 單位
a) Fruit Wine 果酒	25,749	24,719	ton 噸
b) Alcoholic Drink Mixed with Fruit Juice 露酒	18,333	18,149	ton 噸

Top 10 firms by revenue (year founded) 收入排名前 10 家企業 (創辦年份)	City 城市	Province 省	Telephone / fax 電話 / 傳真	Number of employees 職工人數	Ownership 產業所有權	Revenue ('000 RMB) 銷售收入（千元）	Profit ('000 RMB) (rank) 利潤（千元）（排名）	Total assets ('000 RMB) 總資產（千元）	Major products 主要產品
Yangchun Jia Hua Biochemical Industry Company 陽春市嘉華生物化工公司(1984)	Yangjiang 陽江市	Guangdong 廣東省	(0662)7734606 (0662)7722273	132	State-owned 國有	79,018	93(32)	23,789	b
Jiyuan Hong Yuan Brewery Industrial Co. 濟源市鴻源酒造實業公司(1981)	Jiaozuo 焦作市	Henan 河南省	(0391)6692040	911	State-owned 國有	51,815	1039(6)	47,422	o
Wuzhou Long Shan Animal & Plant Wine General Factory 梧州市龍山動植物酒總廠(1935)	Wuzhou 梧州市	Guangxi 廣西	(0774)3827278 (0774)3823910	716	State-owned 國有	33,278	-1783(77)	76,921	a,b
Tai'an Lu Xin Health Care Products Co. Ltd. 泰安魯新保健品有限公司(1992)	Tai'an 泰安市	Shandong 山東省	(0538)2827591 (0538)2825735	179	Foreign-funded 外資	29,830	11630(1)	46,603	o
Wuli Brewing Factory 無棣縣釀酒廠(1957)	Binzhou 濱州市	Shandong 山東省	(0543)6320546 (0543)6321991	251	State-owned 國有	27,158	194(20)	37,853	a
Nan Hainan Feng Engineering Plastics Co. Ltd. 南海南豐工程塑料有限公司(1991)	Foshan 佛山市	Guangdong 廣東省	(0757)5932263 (0757)5931208	50	Overseas Chinese-funded 港澳台資	23,933	-1079(74)	24,688	o
Fuyang Ying DongQu Shen Qi Health Care Wine Factory 阜陽市穎東區神奇保健酒廠(1996)	Fuyang 阜陽市	Anhui 安徽省	(0558)2327089	160	Collectively-owned 集體	22,600	3470(3)	6,050	o
Tianjin Jin Yi Wine-making Industry Co. Ltd. 天津津意酒業有限公司(1996)	Tianjin 天津市	Tianjin 天津市	(022)29628548	24	Foreign-funded 外資	21,630	1620(4)	27,790	a
Shanghai Hua Guang Medicine Wine Co. Ltd. 上海華光釀酒藥業有限公司(1996)	Shanghai 上海市	Shanghai 上海市	(021)65390272 (021)65433215	461	State-owned 國有	20,352	0(61)	107,229	b
Guizhou Changshou Changle Group 貴州長壽長樂集團(1994)	Zunyi 遵義市	Guizhou 貴州省	(0852)225273	742	Collectively-owned 集體	19,860	-774(73)	80,016	o

Top 10 Cities by Production Output 產出排名前 10 位城市	Province 省	Market share 市場份額	Number of firms 企業個數
Kunming 昆明市	Yunnan 雲南省	17.25%	8
Zunyi 遵義市	Guizhou 貴州省	7.27%	2
Shanghai 上海市	Shanghai 上海市	6.38%	2
Nanyang 南陽市	Henan 河南省	5.76%	2
Jiaozuo 焦作市	Henan 河南省	5.56%	2
Wuzhou 梧州市	Guangxi 廣西	5.18%	6
Binzhou 濱州市	Shandong 山東省	4.43%	4
Suizhou 隨州市	Hubei 湖北省	4.30%	3
Tai'an 泰安市	Shandong 山東省	2.65%	2
Foshan 佛山市	Guangdong 廣東省	2.41%	3

10 Major Wholesalers 10 家主要批發商	City 城市	Province 省	Telephone / Fax 電話 / 傳真
Zhong Liang Sugar Industry Groceries Import & Export Company 中糧糖業雜品進出口公司	Beijing 北京市	Beijing 北京市	(010)65268888 (010)65276023
China National Sugar & Alcohol Group Corp. 中國糖業酒類集團公司	Beijing 北京市	Beijing 北京市	(010)68360994
Shanxi Sugar & Wine Non-staple Food Company 山西省糖酒副食公司	Taiyuan 太原市	Shanxi 山西省	(0351)2027938 (0351)2027931
Putian Xue Jin Beer Marketing Agency Co. Ltd. 莆田縣雪津啤酒營銷代理有限公司	Putian 莆田市	Fujian 福建省	
Suzhou Sugar, Cigarette & Wine General Company 蘇州糖煙酒總公司	Suzhou 蘇州市	Jiangsu 江蘇省	(0512)7276392 (0512)7276406
Yuhang Sugar Industry Tobacco & Wine Company 余杭市糖業煙酒公司	Hangzhou 杭州市	Zhejiang 浙江省	(0571)6225788 (0571)6225407
Wuxi Sugar Industry Cigarette & Wine General Company 無錫市糖業煙酒總公司	Wuxi 無錫市	Jiangsu 江蘇省	(0510)2720023 (0510)2707693
Wuxi Chaoyang Co. Ltd. 無錫朝陽股份有限公司	Wuxi 無錫市	Jiangsu 江蘇省	(0510)2767704
Yinchuan Shen Da Non-staple Food Co. Ltd. 銀川申達副食有限公司	Yinchuan 銀川市	Ningxia 寧夏	(0951)5031694
Shanghai Sugar Industry Cigarette & Wine (Group) Co. Ltd. 上海市糖業煙酒(集團)有限公司	Shanghai 上海市	Shanghai 上海市	(021)63224190 (021)63223169

*Also include sales by firms outside this industry.包括本行業以外廠家的銷售。"o" stands for "others". "o" 代表 "其他產品" 。

1521: Carbonic-acid Beverage 碳酸飲料製造業

The industry accounts for 0.229% of the total revenue of China's industrial sector in 1996. The revenue growth rate of the industry is 31.8% from 1995, as compared to the growth rate of China's industrial sector, 9.51%. The rate of return on asset is 6.85%. 68.83% of all firms in the industry made a profit while 23.63% had negative returns. The top province in terms of the industry's revenue is Shanghai, accounting for 21.39% of the total revenue.
本行業在1996年佔全行業總產值0.229%，行業年增長率為31.8%（全國工業年增長率9.51%）。行業的資產回報率6.85%，68.83%的企業盈利，23.63%的企業虧損。銷售收入最高的省份為上海市，佔本行業的21.39%。

	Total number of firms 企業總數	Total number of employees 職工總數	Total revenue (mil. RMB) 總銷售收入（百萬元）	Total profit (mil. RMB) 總利潤（百萬元）	Return on assets 資產利潤率 (%)	Return on equity 權益利潤率 (%)	Labour productivity ('000 RMB / worker) 勞動生產率（千元/人）	Debts / assets 資產負債率 (%)	Total assets (mil. RMB) 總資產（百萬元）
Industry Overall 行業總體	1,519	86,245	13,251	1,091	6.85	12.69	153.64	46.02	15,926

	Number of firms 企業個數	Average number of employees 平均職工人數	Average revenue ('000 RMB) 平均銷售收入（千元）	Average profit ('000 RMB) 平均利潤（千元）	Return on assets 資產利潤率 (%)	Return on equity 權益利潤率 (%)	Labour productivity ('000 RMB / worker) 勞動生產率（千元/人）	Average debts / assets 平均資產負債率(%)	Average Total assets ('000 RMB) 平均總資產（千元）
By ownership 產業所有權									
State-owned 國有	290	101	6,248	424	3.06	5.99	61.78	48.98	13,876
Collectively-owned 集體	1,095	35	1,413	-18	-0.96	-3.01	39.84	67.96	1,874
Privately-owned 私有	8	157	11,702	-436	-2.25	-8.71	74.66	74.17	19,393
Domestic JVs 聯營	12	49	13,036	729	8.78	12.63	267.41	30.48	8,305
Joint stock 股份制	12	222	10,966	-506	-0.69	-1.21	49.49	43.06	73,517
Foreign-funded 外資	61	160	122,662	14,713	13.87	21.73	767.50	36.18	106,080
Overseas Chinese-funded 港澳台資	37	106	54,552	2,457	4.06	7.94	513.46	48.89	60,534
By size 規模									
Large 大型	16	589	445,595	73,761	18.82	30.60	756.53	38.51	391,989
Medium 中型	31	317	79,766	2,442	2.40	3.94	251.65	39.05	101,693
Small 小型	1,452	46	2,513	-113	-2.53	-5.83	54.87	56.65	4,477
By regional distribution 地區分布									
Central-North 華北	152	51	7,906	436	4.99	13.65	156.12	63.43	8,734
Beijing 北京	31	43	16,749	1,192	9.08	18.98	393.95	52.15	13,124
Tianjin 天津	12	139	47,669	2,620	5.13	12.13	343.97	57.70	51,041
Hebei 河北	51	51	1,372	-55	-1.18	-20.03	27.02	94.10	4,700
Shanxi 山西	21	59	993	-16	-0.75	-2.84	16.74	73.72	2,106
Inner Mongolia 內蒙	37	24	530	28	4.20	17.03	22.25	75.31	657
Northeast 東北	452	40	2,516	59	1.46	3.86	62.75	62.32	4,047
Liaoning 遼寧	164	57	4,749	110	1.59	4.52	83.06	64.97	6,939
Jilin 吉林	110	40	1,509	51	1.26	2.87	37.63	56.26	4,096
Heilongjiang 黑龍江	178	24	1,081	16	1.21	3.12	44.38	61.13	1,352
Central East 華東	306	74	20,761	2,714	12.46	17.79	280.12	29.95	21,776
Shanghai 上海	20	177	141,688	25,641	23.04	28.19	802.53	18.27	111,307
Jiangsu 江蘇	43	65	22,510	1,634	9.08	18.83	348.93	51.78	17,990
Zhejiang 浙江	47	108	34,277	4,156	9.55	12.09	316.32	21.00	43,530
Anhui 安徽	62	79	4,227	95	1.95	8.23	53.76	76.31	4,849
Fujian 福建	47	42	11,006	1,131	5.34	7.11	263.78	24.84	21,177
Jiangxi 江西	50	36	1,306	-128	-5.78	174.46	36.59	103.31	2,221
Shandong 山東	37	72	2,583	-14	-0.25	-1.21	35.91	79.22	5,700
Central-South 中南	415	66	9,547	510	4.34	9.87	143.84	56.04	11,749
Henan 河南	87	61	3,143	12	0.26	0.52	51.80	50.44	4,752
Hubei 湖北	95	78	6,273	135	1.58	5.41	80.63	70.89	8,540
Hunan 湖南	44	28	1,346	1	0.13	0.53	47.81	74.62	1,022
Guangdong 廣東	111	82	19,738	1,582	5.99	12.18	241.34	50.87	26,421
Guangxi 廣西	74	54	6,538	13	0.19	0.56	120.80	65.84	6,844
Hainan 海南	4	139	89,730	5,285	12.67	27.34	647.87	53.67	41,720
Southwest 西南	122	61	3,504	-188	-2.82	-6.50	57.46	56.62	6,676
Chongqing 重慶	22	128	12,882	-834	-3.61	-6.60	99.90	45.32	23,121
Sichuan 四川	61	50	1,652	-65	-1.88	-8.76	32.63	78.58	3,476
Guizhou 貴州	23	26	516	2	0.14	0.41	20.14	66.21	1,244
Yunnan 雲南	15	54	1,306	3	0.09	0.47	24.34	80.40	2,925
Tibet 西藏									
Northwest 西北	72	38	2,357	-296	-5.13	-8.29	61.54	38.14	5,768
Shaanxi 陝西	28	43	4,684	-682	-6.34	-8.63	108.21	26.55	10,761
Gansu 甘肅	22	52	1,165	-89	-2.15	-6.64	22.41	67.66	4,139
Qinghai 青海	2	27	200	-30	-2.27	-8.82	7.55	74.62	1,320
Ningxia 寧夏	3	25	933	43	4.68	13.00	36.84	64.03	927
Xinjiang 新疆	17	16	574	-19	-1.83	-7.13	35.62	74.37	1,031

1521: Carbonic-acid Beverage 碳酸飲料製造業

Year 年份	Number of firms 企業個數	Rate of change 每年變化 (%)	Number of employees 職工人數 (人)	Rate of change 每年變化 (%)	Total revenue (mil. RMB) 總銷售收入 (百萬元)	Rate of change 每年變化 (%)	Total profit (mil. RMB) 總利潤 (百萬元)	Rate of change 每年變化 (%)
1993	1,336		88,875		4,675		176	
1994	1,413	5.76%	91,322	2.75%	6,640	42.05%	499	183.18%
1995	1,605	13.59%	100,310	9.84%	10,052	51.38%	570	14.27%
1996	1,519	-5.36%	86,245	-14.02%	13,251	31.82%	1,091	91.24%

3 Major products* 3種主要產品 *	Output 產量	Sales volume 銷售量	Unit 單位
a) Carbonated Drink 碳酸飲料	3,806,882	3,616,538	ton 噸
b) Soft Drink 軟飲料	3,988,030	3,828,509	ton 噸

Top 10 firms by revenue (year founded) 收入排名前10家企業 (創辦年份)	City 城市	Province 省	Telephone / fax 電話 / 傳真	Number of employees 職工人數	Ownership 產業所有權	Revenue ('000 RMB) 銷售收入 (千元)	Profit ('000 RMB) (rank) 利潤 (千元) (排名)	Total assets ('000 RMB) 總資產 (千元)	Major products 主要產品
Shanghai Shen-mei Beverage & Foods Co. Ltd. 上海申美飲料食品有限公司(1988)	Shanghai 上海市	Shanghai 上海市	(021)64302200 (021)64301250	1,019	Foreign-funded 外資	2,020,490	455974(1)	1,582,222	a,b
Nanjing Zhong Cui Food Co. Ltd. 南京中萃食品有限公司(1987)	Nanjing 南京市	Jiangsu 江蘇省	(025)5410950 (025)5412735	480	Foreign-funded 外資	641,580	53490(4)	324,620	a,b
Shanghai Pepsi Cola Beverage Co. Ltd. 上海百事可樂飲料有限公司(1990)	Shanghai 上海市	Shanghai 上海市	(021)64303279 (021)64301377	682	Foreign-funded 外資	581,733	67001(3)	425,459	a,b
Tianjin Coca-cola Beverage Co. Ltd. 天津可口可樂飲料有限公司(1993)	Tianjin 天津市	Tianjin 天津市	(022)25328404 (022)25328408	698	Overseas Chinese-funded 港澳台資	547,186	27160(10)	482,503	a,b
Hangzhou Bc Foods Co. Ltd. 杭州中萃食品有限公司(1989)	Hangzhou 杭州市	Zhejiang 浙江省	(0571)6042244 (0571)6047899	660	Foreign-funded 外資	469,472	46963(5)	319,527	a,b
Guangzhou Pepsi Cola Beverage Co. Ltd. 廣州百事可樂飲料有限公司(1995)	Guangzhou 廣州市	Guangdong 廣東省	(020)84202108	644	Foreign-funded 外資	398,287	34873(8)	396,525	a,b
Beijing Jian Li Bao Beverage Co. Ltd. 北京健力寶飲料有限公司(1992)	Beijing 北京市	Beijing 北京市	(010)69643485	239	Foreign-funded 外資	381,647	42773(6)	190,165	a,b
Wuhan Coca-cola Beverage Co. Ltd. 武漢可口可樂飲料有限公司(1993)	Wuhan 武漢市	Hubei 湖北省	(027)84892503 (027)84892060	500	Foreign-funded 外資	357,778	12182(17)	425,668	a,b
Swire Guangdong Coca-cola Ltd. 廣東太古可口可樂有限公司(1995)	Guangzhou 廣州市	Guangdong 廣東省	(020)82296288 (020)82275984	403	Overseas Chinese-funded 港澳台資	353,788	25336(12)	565,311	a,b
Dalian Coca-cola Beverage Co. Ltd. 大連可口可樂飲料有限公司(1994)	Dalian 大連市	Liaoning 遼寧省	(0411)6641600 (0411)6651027	411	Overseas Chinese-funded 港澳台資	327,840	26315(11)	252,689	a

Top 10 Cities by Production Output 產出排名前10位城市	Province 省	Market share 市場份額	Number of firms 企業個數
Shanghai 上海市	Shanghai 上海市	19.17%	32
Guangzhou 廣州市	Guangdong 廣東省	11.78%	14
Tongshi 通什市	Hainan 海南省	11.51%	4
Beijing 北京市	Beijing 北京市	6.83%	28
Nanjing 南京市	Jiangsu 江蘇省	5.38%	5
Tianjin 天津市	Tianjin 天津市	4.74%	17
Hangzhou 杭州市	Zhejiang 浙江省	3.87%	12
Wuhan 武漢市	Hubei 湖北省	3.39%	22
Dalian 大連市	Liaoning 遼寧省	2.86%	15
Xiamen 廈門市	Fujian 福建省	2.40%	4

10 Major Wholesalers 10家主要批發商	City 城市	Province 省	Telephone / Fax 電話 / 傳真
Zhong Liang Sugar Industry Groceries Import & Export Company 中糧糖業雜品進出口公司	Beijing 北京市	Beijing 北京市	(010)65268888 (010)65276023
China National Sugar & Alcohol Group Corp. 中國糖業酒類集團公司	Beijing 北京市	Beijing 北京市	(010)68360994
Shanxi Sugar & Wine Non-staple Food Company 山西省糖酒副食公司	Taiyuan 太原市	Shanxi 山西省	(0351)2027938 (0351)2027931
Putian Xue Jin Beer Marketing Agency Co. Ltd. 莆田縣雪津啤酒營銷代理有限公司	Putian 莆田市	Fujian 福建省	
Suzhou Sugar, Cigarette & Wine General Company 蘇州糖煙酒總公司	Suzhou 蘇州市	Jiangsu 江蘇省	(0512)7276392 (0512)7276406
Yuhang Sugar Industry Tobacco & Wine Company 余杭市糖業煙酒公司	Hangzhou 杭州市	Zhejiang 浙江省	(0571)6225788 (0571)6225407
Wuxi Sugar Industry Cigarette & Wine General Company 無錫市糖業煙酒總公司	Wuxi 無錫市	Jiangsu 江蘇省	(0510)2720023 (0510)2707693
Wuxi Chaoyang Co. Ltd. 無錫朝陽股份有限公司	Wuxi 無錫市	Jiangsu 江蘇省	(0510)2767704
Yinchuan Shen Da Non-staple Food Co. Ltd. 銀川申達副食有限公司	Yinchuan 銀川市	Ningxia 寧夏	(0951)5031694
Shanghai Sugar Industry Cigarette & Wine (Group) Co. Ltd. 上海市糖業煙酒(集團)有限公司	Shanghai 上海市	Shanghai 上海市	(021)63224190 (021)63223169

*Also include sales by firms outside this industry.包括本行業以外廠家的銷售。"o" stands for "others". "o" 代表 "其他產品"。

1522: Natural Mineral Water 天然礦泉水製造業

The industry accounts for 0.042% of the total revenue of China's industrial sector in 1996. The revenue growth rate of the industry is 22.2% from 1995, as compared to the growth rate of China's industrial sector, 9.51%. The rate of return on asset is 1.43%. 59.06% of all firms in the industry made a profit while 31.65% had negative returns. The top province in terms of the industry's revenue is Guangdong, accounting for 36.05% of the total revenue.
本行業在1996年佔全行業總產值0.042%，行業年增長率為22.2%（全國工業年增長率9.51%）。行業的資產回報率1.43%，59.06%的企業盈利，31.65%的企業虧損。銷售收入最高的省份為廣東省，佔本行業的36.05%。

	Total number of firms 企業總數	Total number of employees 職工總數	Total revenue (mil. RMB) 總銷售收入（百萬元）	Total profit (mil. RMB) 總利潤（百萬元）	Return on assets 資產利潤率 (%)	Return on equity 權益利潤率 (%)	Labour productivity ('000 RMB / worker) 勞動生產率（千元/人）	Debts / assets 資產負債率 (%)	Total assets (mil. RMB) 總資產（百萬元）
Industry Overall 行業總體	698	30,136	2,424	55	1.43	3.56	80.44	59.78	3,876

	Number of firms 企業個數	Average number of employees 平均職工人數	Average revenue ('000 RMB) 平均銷售收入（千元）	Average profit ('000 RMB) 平均利潤（千元）	Return on assets 資產利潤率 (%)	Return on equity 權益利潤率 (%)	Labour productivity ('000 RMB / worker) 勞動生產率（千元/人）	Average debts / assets 平均資產負債率(%)	Average Total assets ('000 RMB) 平均總資產（千元）
By ownership 產業所有權									
State-owned 國有	113	45	2,920	27	0.45	2.44	65.50	81.75	5,965
Collectively-owned 集體	320	38	2,972	-177	-5.63	-18.63	78.48	69.80	3,144
Privately-owned 私有	3	50	814	132	2.50	5.35	16.28	53.33	5,276
Domestic JVs 聯營	27	69	7,575	-660	-7.53	-17.93	110.49	58.04	8,775
Joint stock 股份制	29	69	9,425	-2,153	-15.70	-24.17	136.39	35.04	13,718
Foreign-funded 外資	98	49	3,780	525	6.64	11.84	77.02	43.89	7,905
Overseas Chinese-funded 港澳台資	105	41	2,730	1,303	17.83	41.28	67.15	56.81	7,310
By size 規模									
Large 大型	4	118	53,841	-7,401	-12.55	-22.84	455.32	45.06	58,978
Medium 中型	5	284	25,970	-452	-0.71	-1.87	91.38	62.08	63,814
Small 小型	657	42	3,165	132	2.62	6.64	75.05	60.57	5,046
By regional distribution 地區分布									
Central-North 華北	73	29	1,765	-68	-2.02	-5.03	61.49	59.80	3,385
Beijing 北京	34	20	1,390	-139	-5.57	-8.75	69.51	36.37	2,493
Tianjin 天津	5	28	2,054	264	15.05	21.64	73.36	30.44	1,754
Hebei 河北	18	43	3,340	-34	-0.83	-5.15	77.28	83.84	4,140
Shanxi 山西	6	18	355	-143	-12.87	-252.94	20.09	94.91	1,113
Inner Mongolia 內蒙	10	39	904	-12	-0.17	-0.45	23.12	62.82	7,237
Northeast 東北	81	51	1,812	-28	-0.71	-2.23	35.73	68.15	3,944
Liaoning 遼寧	20	31	723	29	0.65	2.93	23.10	77.83	4,389
Jilin 吉林	29	63	1,407	-154	-6.18	-51.91	22.20	88.09	2,499
Heilongjiang 黑龍江	32	51	2,860	51	1.03	2.23	55.67	53.74	4,976
Central East 華東	230	38	3,667	120	2.61	6.09	97.45	57.15	4,593
Shanghai 上海	15	32	1,573	-440	-7.86	-14.74	49.45	46.69	5,599
Jiangsu 江蘇	21	35	3,971	-79	-1.72	-2.90	114.88	40.55	4,590
Zhejiang 浙江	21	41	5,047	264	4.11	7.59	121.96	45.80	6,413
Anhui 安徽	19	48	3,776	138	5.14	12.50	78.50	58.85	2,691
Fujian 福建	53	26	2,772	51	1.79	3.67	108.51	51.28	2,828
Jiangxi 江西	36	22	680	3	0.31	0.83	30.44	62.99	1,084
Shandong 山東	65	54	5,959	382	4.96	14.69	110.33	66.27	7,712
Central-South 中南	212	52	5,450	232	2.68	6.50	105.18	58.82	8,685
Henan 河南	25	54	732	28	1.63	5.31	13.66	69.31	1,719
Hubei 湖北	31	50	3,345	11	0.21	0.60	67.04	64.90	5,236
Hunan 湖南	36	40	1,199	-19	-1.08	-2.86	30.08	62.32	1,755
Guangdong 廣東	89	64	9,819	582	4.16	9.68	154.16	56.97	13,986
Guangxi 廣西	22	23	1,775	-217	-7.44	-25.87	75.95	71.24	2,921
Hainan 海南	9	53	8,577	207	0.71	1.69	160.81	58.21	29,289
Southwest 西南	67	47	1,999	-129	-3.00	-8.89	42.81	66.23	4,287
Chongqing 重慶	11	33	3,065	-47	-1.66	-6.19	92.87	73.24	2,854
Sichuan 四川	22	49	2,458	-59	-1.04	-2.56	49.65	59.27	5,640
Guizhou 貴州	20	38	957	-83	-4.88	-11.17	25.09	56.34	1,701
Yunnan 雲南	10	72	2,284	-610	-7.43	-57.28	31.68	87.02	8,206
Tibet 西藏	4	48	1,043	235	5.99	7.48	21.61	19.90	3,920
Northwest 西北	35	33	457	-155	-4.37	-10.90	13.72	59.95	3,559
Shaanxi 陝西	7	34	379	14	1.25	5.75	11.28	78.43	1,146
Gansu 甘肅	8	37	854	-20	-0.34	-0.60	23.00	42.42	5,803
Qinghai 青海	4	32	140	-128	-4.93	-13.67	4.34	63.86	2,588
Ningxia 寧夏	1	52	320	-120	-2.89	4.74	6.15	161.20	4,150
Xinjiang 新疆	15	30	375	-317	-8.54	-23.47	12.43	63.64	3,709

1522: Natural Mineral Water 天然礦泉水製造業

Year 年份	Number of firms 企業個數	Rate of change 每年變化 (%)	Number of employees 職工人數 (人)	Rate of change 每年變化 (%)	Total revenue (mil. RMB) 總銷售收入 (百萬元)	Rate of change 每年變化 (%)	Total profit (mil. RMB) 總利潤 (百萬元)	Rate of change 每年變化 (%)
1993	323		16,873		774		-4	
1994	463	43.34%	22,730	34.71%	1,226	58.39%	-28	-547.26%
1995	674	45.57%	31,110	36.87%	1,984	61.88%	-43	-55.82%
1996	698	3.56%	30,136	-3.13%	2,424	22.18%	55	228.22%

3 Major products* 3 種主要產品 *	Output 產量	Sales volume 銷售量	Unit 單位
a) Natural Mineral Water 天然礦泉水	1,023,063	1,012,833	ton 噸
b) Soft Drink 軟飲料	923,052	886,130	ton 噸

Top 10 firms by revenue (year founded) 收入排名前 10 家企業 (創辦年份)	City 城市	Province 省	Telephone / fax 電話 / 傳真	Number of employees 職工人數	Ownership 產業所有權	Revenue ('000 RMB) 銷售收入 (千元)	Profit ('000 RMB) (rank) 利潤 (千元) (排名)	Total assets ('000 RMB) 總資產 (千元)	Major products 主要產品
Wendeng Hei Bao Mineral Water Co. Ltd. 文登市黑豹礦泉水有限公司(1994)	Weihai 威海市	Shandong 山東省	(0896)8832148 (0896)8832149	86	Domestic JVs 聯營	149,630	17950(2)	32,490	a,b
Shenzhen Yi Bao Foods & Beverage Co. Ltd. 深圳怡寶食品飲料有限公司(1984)	Shenzhen 深圳市	Guangdong 廣東省	(0755)6692266 (0755)6692265	160	State-owned 國有	117,294	10653(4)	83,207	o
Blue Ribbon Mineral Water Co. Ltd. 藍帶礦泉水有限公司(1991)	Zhaoqing 肇慶市	Guangdong 廣東省	(0757)2862088 (0757)2833887	80	Overseas Chinese-funded 港澳台資	112,667	9368(5)	80,758	o
Shenzhen Health Mineral Water Co. Ltd. No.2 Mineral Water Factory 深圳益力礦泉水股份有限公司益力礦泉水二廠(1993)	Shenzhen 深圳市	Guangdong 廣東省	(0755)6622870 (0755)6622738	156	Joint stock 股份制	85,197	35650(1)	105,433	a,b
Guangzhou Le Bai Shi Industrial Co. Ltd. 廣州市樂百氏實業有限公司(1988)	Guangzhou 廣州市	Guangdong 廣東省	(020)87826138 (020)87826069	130	Collectively-owned 集體	65,250	4920(9)	21,030	o
Shenzhen Health Mineral Water Co. Ltd. Yili Mineral Water Factory 深圳市益力礦泉水股份有限公司一廠(1986)	Shenzhen 深圳市	Guangdong 廣東省	(0755)3357782 (0755)3351522	184	Joint stock 股份制	56,525	16295(3)	47,696	a,b
Huaiji Yan Feng Natural Mineral Water Co. Ltd. 懷集縣燕峯天然礦泉水有限公司(1988)	Zhaoqing 肇慶市	Guangdong 廣東省	(0757)5523338	116	State-owned 國有	51,278	3670(12)	18,085	a,b
Hangzhou Wa Ha Ha Mineral Water Drink Pinghu Co. Ltd. 杭州娃哈哈礦泉飲料平湖有限公司(1995)	Jiaxing 嘉興市	Zhejiang 浙江省	(0573)5017954 (0573)5017954	57	Joint stock 股份制	41,875	4246(11)	34,960	o
Yongchun Xiang Ye Mineral Water Co. Ltd. 永春祥業礦泉水有限公司	Quanzhou 泉州市	Fujian 福建省	(0595)3882870	37	Overseas Chinese-funded 港澳台資	36,000	5200(8)	6,597	a
Zhuhai Yong Long Jialinshan Mineral Water Factory 珠海市永隆加林山礦泉水廠(1984)	Zhuhai 珠海市	Guangdong 廣東省	(0756)8821178 (0756)8822178	203	Overseas Chinese-funded 港澳台資	34,597	4852(10)	47,594	a,b

Top 10 Cities by Production Output 產出排名前 10 位城市	Province 省	Market share 市場份額	Number of firms 企業個數
Shanghai 上海市	Shanghai 上海市	13.80%	48
Zhaoqing 肇慶市	Guangdong 廣東省	9.90%	7
Beijing 北京市	Beijing 北京市	9.26%	32
Shenzhen 深圳市	Guangdong 廣東省	3.88%	8
Yulin 玉林市	Guangxi 廣西	3.44%	3
Guangzhou 廣州市	Guangdong 廣東省	3.39%	19
Qingdao 青島市	Shandong 山東省	3.35%	31
Zhoukou 周口市	Henan 河南省	3.25%	2
Chongqing 重慶市	Chongqing 重慶市	2.87%	9
Zhangzhou 漳州市	Fujian 福建省	2.12%	10

10 Major Wholesalers 10 家主要批發商	City 城市	Province 省	Telephone / Fax 電話 / 傳真
Zhong Liang Sugar Industry Groceries Import & Export Company 中糧糖業雜品進出口公司	Beijing 北京市	Beijing 北京市	(010)65268888 (010)65276023
China National Sugar & Alcohol Group Corp. 中國糖業酒類集團公司	Beijing 北京市	Beijing 北京市	(010)68360994
Shanxi Sugar & Wine Non-staple Food Company 山西省糖酒副食公司	Taiyuan 太原市	Shanxi 山西省	(0351)2027938 (0351)2027931
Putian Xue Jin Beer Marketing Agency Co. Ltd. 莆田縣雪津啤酒營銷代理有限公司	Putian 莆田市	Fujian 福建省	
Suzhou Sugar, Cigarette & Wine General Company 蘇州糖煙酒總公司	Suzhou 蘇州市	Jiangsu 江蘇省	(0512)7276392 (0512)7276406
Yuhang Sugar Industry Tobacco & Wine Company 余杭市糖業煙酒公司	Hangzhou 杭州市	Zhejiang 浙江省	(0571)6225788 (0571)6225407
Wuxi Sugar Industry Cigarette & Wine General Company 無錫市糖業煙酒總公司	Wuxi 無錫市	Jiangsu 江蘇省	(0510)2720023 (0510)2707693
Wuxi Chaoyang Co. Ltd. 無錫朝陽股份有限公司	Wuxi 無錫市	Jiangsu 江蘇省	(0510)2767704
Yinchuan Shen Da Non-staple Food Co. Ltd. 銀川申達副食有限公司	Yinchuan 銀川市	Ningxia 寧夏	(0951)5031694
Shanghai Sugar Industry Cigarette & Wine (Group) Co. Ltd. 上海市糖業煙酒(集團)有限公司	Shanghai 上海市	Shanghai 上海市	(021)63224190 (021)63223169

*Also include sales by firms outside this industry.包括本行業以外廠家的銷售。"o" stands for "others". "o" 代表"其他產品"。

1523: Fruit and Vegetable Juice Drinks 果菜汁飲料製造業

The industry accounts for 0.092% of the total revenue of China's industrial sector in 1996. The revenue growth rate of the industry is 27.9% from 1995, as compared to the growth rate of China's industrial sector, 9.51%. The rate of return on asset is -2.25%. 55.81% of all firms in the industry made a profit while 35.65% had negative returns. The top province in terms of the industry's revenue is Guangdong, accounting for 22.34% of the total revenue.
本行業在1996年佔全行業總產值0.092%，行業年增長率為27.9%（全國工業年增長率9.51%）。行業的資產回報率-2.25%，55.81%的企業盈利，35.65%的企業虧損。銷售收入最高的省份為廣東省，佔本行業的22.34%。

	Total number of firms 企業總數	Total number of employees 職工總數	Total revenue (mil. RMB) 總銷售收入（百萬元）	Total profit (mil. RMB) 總利潤（百萬元）	Return on assets 資產利潤率 (%)	Return on equity 權益利潤率 (%)	Labour productivity ('000 RMB / worker) 勞動生產率（千元/人）	Debts / assets 資產負債率 (%)	Total assets (mil. RMB) 總資產（百萬元）
Industry Overall 行業總體	772	53,702	5,342	-237	-2.25	-8.52	99.47	73.55	10,517

	Number of firms 企業個數	Average number of employees 平均職工人數	Average revenue ('000 RMB) 平均銷售收入（千元）	Average profit ('000 RMB) 平均利潤（千元）	Return on assets 資產利潤率 (%)	Return on equity 權益利潤率 (%)	Labour productivity ('000 RMB / worker) 勞動生產率（千元/人）	Average debts / assets 平均資產負債率(%)	Average Total assets ('000 RMB) 平均總資產（千元）
By ownership 產業所有權									
State-owned 國有	154	94	4,727	-565	-4.04	-51.48	50.04	92.15	13,987
Collectively-owned 集體	384	54	3,388	-20	-0.33	-1.36	62.68	75.90	6,008
Privately-owned 私有	4	22	1,811	-60	-4.26	41.75	82.33	110.20	1,408
Domestic JVs 聯營	14	38	1,874	-445	-5.42	-14.13	49.59	61.65	8,219
Joint stock 股份制	18	105	7,897	219	1.29	2.80	75.01	54.02	17,073
Foreign-funded 外資	84	79	8,600	-538	-2.69	-8.77	109.42	69.30	19,967
Overseas Chinese-funded 港澳台資	113	84	21,371	-838	-2.40	-6.98	253.96	65.65	34,961
By size 規模									
Large 大型	7	635	207,141	884	0.25	1.03	326.28	75.55	351,470
Medium 中型	19	268	37,114	-1,389	-2.23	-7.68	138.65	70.89	62,170
Small 小型	714	61	4,463	-304	-3.15	-11.80	73.25	73.29	9,629
By regional distribution 地區分布									
Central-North 華北	169	65	3,961	-103	-0.98	-3.17	60.57	68.95	10,497
Beijing 北京	36	53	5,179	107	0.80	1.57	97.47	48.87	13,274
Tianjin 天津	22	50	5,389	20	0.20	1.00	106.81	80.37	10,231
Hebei 河北	60	97	5,089	-278	-1.89	-8.66	52.22	78.13	14,650
Shanxi 山西	25	55	1,533	-215	-3.58	-9.11	28.12	60.66	5,992
Inner Mongolia 內蒙	26	31	797	11	0.69	2.59	25.34	73.56	1,628
Northeast 東北	77	47	1,986	-130	-2.27	-41.56	41.94	94.54	5,721
Liaoning 遼寧	33	49	2,177	-228	-3.40	-130.50	44.26	97.39	6,704
Jilin 吉林	7	81	-17	-476	-8.54	-64.66	-0.21	86.79	5,570
Heilongjiang 黑龍江	37	39	2,195	23	0.48	6.54	55.71	92.71	4,872
Central East 華東	217	77	6,138	-339	-2.55	-7.51	79.59	66.02	13,271
Shanghai 上海	15	134	6,218	-1,306	-3.52	-9.51	46.40	63.04	37,149
Jiangsu 江蘇	24	71	6,312	31	0.26	0.99	89.42	73.80	12,058
Zhejiang 浙江	30	113	7,584	-1,880	-9.53	-25.51	67.23	62.63	19,717
Anhui 安徽	26	62	2,329	-150	-4.37	-19.36	37.80	77.42	3,420
Fujian 福建	53	57	7,154	-163	-1.32	-2.63	124.85	49.68	12,351
Jiangxi 江西	22	47	2,049	-129	-3.25	-13.95	43.97	76.66	3,968
Shandong 山東	47	85	7,975	364	2.80	16.17	94.11	82.67	12,999
Central-South 中南	166	82	16,382	-281	-1.16	-5.18	199.25	77.55	24,154
Henan 河南	47	86	7,210	-94	-0.76	-11.19	83.86	93.21	12,328
Hubei 湖北	18	59	3,312	-37	-0.69	-2.29	56.56	69.92	5,397
Hunan 湖南	15	56	3,756	148	2.71	32.55	66.83	91.67	5,457
Guangdong 廣東	44	115	27,121	-1,152	-2.34	-11.97	236.02	80.48	49,293
Guangxi 廣西	31	33	981	-911	-18.18	313.67	29.52	105.79	5,010
Hainan 海南	11	148	94,616	3,194	3.79	8.56	640.87	55.74	84,265
Southwest 西南	91	63	3,333	-536	-4.89	-21.02	52.58	76.74	10,956
Chongqing 重慶	9	70	2,281	-20	-0.19	-0.71	32.20	72.86	10,240
Sichuan 四川	40	66	4,456	-134	-1.77	-9.66	67.42	81.66	7,546
Guizhou 貴州	7	10	64				6.34	81.23	533
Yunnan 雲南	34	68	2,964	-1,269	-7.31	-29.00	43.28	74.80	17,362
Tibet 西藏									
Northwest 西北	52	55	3,172	-782	-9.77	-42.01	57.84	76.74	8,005
Shaanxi 陝西	19	71	5,839	73	0.75	2.01	82.61	62.79	9,692
Gansu 甘肅	19	39	393	-443	-29.53	-2004.76	10.19	98.56	1,501
Qinghai 青海	1	36	270	10	0.19	9.09	7.50	97.88	5,190
Ningxia 寧夏	2	51	405	95	3.64	-79.17	7.94	104.41	2,610
Xinjiang 新疆	11	58	4,133	-3,075	-17.51	-120.91	71.14	85.52	17,562

1523: Fruit and Vegetable Juice Drinks 果菜汁飲料製造業

Year 年份	Number of firms 企業個數	Rate of change 每年變化 (%)	Number of employees 職工人數 (人)	Rate of change 每年變化 (%)	Total revenue (mil. RMB) 總銷售收入 (百萬元)	Rate of change 每年變化 (%)	Total profit (mil. RMB) 總利潤 (百萬元)	Rate of change 每年變化 (%)
1993	628		46,301		4,414		137	
1994	775	23.41%	57,791	24.82%	6,183	40.09%	9	-93.27%
1995	890	14.84%	62,999	9.01%	4,178	-32.44%	-220	-2482.42%
1996	772	-13.26%	53,702	-14.76%	5,342	27.86%	-237	-7.88%

3 Major products* 3 種主要產品 *	Output 產量	Sales volume 銷售量	Unit 單位
a) Fruit & Vegetable Juice Drink 果菜汁飲料	688,625	619,762	ton 噸
b) Soft Drink 軟飲料	640,829	615,196	ton 噸

Top 10 firms by revenue (year founded) 收入排名前 10 家企業 (創辦年份)	City 城市	Province 省	Telephone / fax 電話 / 傳真	Number of employees 職工人數	Ownership 產業所有權	Revenue ('000 RMB) 銷售收入 (千元)	Profit ('000 RMB) (rank) 利潤 (千元) (排名)	Total assets ('000 RMB) 總資產 (千元)	Major products 主要產品
Guangdong Jianlibao Natural Beverage Co. Ltd. 廣東省健力寶天然飲品有限公司(1993)	Foshan 佛山市	Guangdong 廣東省	(0757)7821266 (0757)7830222	400	Overseas Chinese-funded 港澳台資	223,911	18220(3)	270,183	a,b
Yeo Hiap Seng (Guangzhou) Co. Ltd. 楊協成(廣州)有限公司(1992)	Guangzhou 廣州市	Guangdong 廣東省	(020)84219833 (020)84293478	320	Foreign-funded 外資	212,773	12706(4)	210,427	a,b
Castlee Beverages & Foods Inc. 華力飲料食品有限公司(1994)	Foshan 佛山市	Guangdong 廣東省	(0757)7820138 (0757)7829622	367	Overseas Chinese-funded 港澳台資	153,253	2556(12)	155,905	a,b
Shenzhen Vitamin (Guang Ming) Foods & Beverage Co. Ltd. 深圳維他(光明)食品飲料有限公司(1991)	Shenzhen 深圳市	Guangdong 廣東省	(0755)7402888 (0755)7401998	281	Overseas Chinese-funded 港澳台資	152,524	-6028(230)	197,815	a,b
Shandong Zhong Lu Fruit-juice Group Co. Ltd. 山東中魯果汁集團公司(1983)	Weihai 威海市	Shandong 山東省	(0896)6621834 (0896)6623574	481	State-owned 國有	141,240	20190(2)	179,140	a,b
Hangzhou Ding Yu Food Co. Ltd. 杭州頂育食品有限公司(1996)	Hangzhou 杭州市	Zhejiang 浙江省	(0571)6910856 (0571)6910847	316	Overseas Chinese-funded 港澳台資	105,109	-36834(246)	232,455	o
Henan Jiaozuo Si Lian Industrial Company 河南省焦作市四聯實業公司(1975)	Jiaozuo 焦作市	Henan 河南省	(0391)8571238	700	Collectively-owned 集體	99,764	25800(1)	54,750	o
Hebei Er Yue Hua Group Company 河北二月花集團公司(1993)	Xingtai 邢臺市	Hebei 河北省	(0319)4225619 (0319)4225620	680	Collectively-owned 集體	94,731	5800(8)	50,221	o
Beijing Shen Zhou Moqi Food & Beverage Co. Ltd. 北京神州摩奇食品飲料有限公司(1994)	Beijing 北京市	Beijing 北京市	(010)62019682	290	Foreign-funded 外資	90,894	6334(7)	83,655	a,b
Du Le Beverage (Huizhou) Co. Ltd. 都樂飲料(惠州)有限公司(1995)	Huizhou 惠州市	Guangdong 廣東省	(0751)2292464 (0751)2292814	109	Overseas Chinese-funded 港澳台資	89,634	1830(16)	119,110	a,b

Top 10 Cities by Production Output 產出排名前 10 位城市	Province 省	Market share 市場份額	Number of firms 企業個數
Foshan 佛山市	Guangdong 廣東省	10.65%	4
Guangzhou 廣州市	Guangdong 廣東省	7.09%	12
Shenzhen 深圳市	Guangdong 廣東省	5.95%	8
Huizhou 惠州市	Guangdong 廣東省	4.26%	8
Tianjin 天津市	Tianjin 天津市	3.99%	30
Weihai 威海市	Shandong 山東省	3.98%	5
Shanghai 上海市	Shanghai 上海市	3.10%	19
Taizhou 臺州市	Zhejiang 浙江省	2.75%	26
Jiaozuo 焦作市	Henan 河南省	2.72%	4
Beijing 北京市	Beijing 北京市	2.46%	34

10 Major Wholesalers 10 家主要批發商	City 城市	Province 省	Telephone / Fax 電話 / 傳真
Zhong Liang Sugar Industry Groceries Import & Export Company 中糧糖業雜品進出口公司	Beijing 北京市	Beijing 北京市	(010)65268888 (010)65276023
China National Sugar & Alcohol Group Corp. 中國糖業酒類集團公司	Beijing 北京市	Beijing 北京市	(010)68360994
Shanxi Sugar & Wine Non-staple Food Company 山西省糖酒副食公司	Taiyuan 太原市	Shanxi 山西省	(0351)2027938 (0351)2027931
Putian Xue Jin Beer Marketing Agency Co. Ltd. 莆田縣雪津啤酒營銷代理有限公司	Putian 莆田市	Fujian 福建省	
Suzhou Sugar, Cigarette & Wine General Company 蘇州糖煙酒總公司	Suzhou 蘇州市	Jiangsu 江蘇省	(0512)7276392 (0512)7276406
Yuhang Sugar Industry Tobacco & Wine Company 余杭市糖業煙酒公司	Hangzhou 杭州市	Zhejiang 浙江省	(0571)6225788 (0571)6225407
Wuxi Sugar Industry Cigarette & Wine General Company 無錫市糖業煙酒總公司	Wuxi 無錫市	Jiangsu 江蘇省	(0510)2720023 (0510)2707693
Wuxi Chaoyang Co. Ltd. 無錫朝陽股份有限公司	Wuxi 無錫市	Jiangsu 江蘇省	(0510)2767704
Yinchuan Shen Da Non-staple Food Co. Ltd. 銀川申達副食有限公司	Yinchuan 銀川市	Ningxia 寧夏	(0951)5031694
Shanghai Sugar Industry Cigarette & Wine (Group) Co. Ltd. 上海市糖業煙酒(集團)有限公司	Shanghai 上海市	Shanghai 上海市	(021)63224190 (021)63223169

*Also include sales by firms outside this industry.包括本行業以外廠家的銷售。"o" stands for "others". "o" 代表"其他產品"。

1524: Instant Drinks 固體飲料製造業

The industry accounts for 0.034% of the total revenue of China's industrial sector in 1996. The revenue growth rate of the industry is 39.5% from 1995, as compared to the growth rate of China's industrial sector, 9.51%. The rate of return on asset is -1.33%. 65.30% of all firms in the industry made a profit while 32.23% had negative returns. The top province in terms of the industry's revenue is Guangdong, accounting for 33.88% of the total revenue.
本行業在1996年佔全行業總產值0.034%，行業年增長率為39.5%（全國工業年增長率9.51%）。行業的資產回報率-1.33%，65.30%的企業盈利，32.23%的企業虧損。銷售收入最高的省份為廣東省，佔本行業的33.88%。

	Total number of firms 企業總數	Total number of employees 職工總數	Total revenue (mil. RMB) 總銷售收入（百萬元）	Total profit (mil. RMB) 總利潤（百萬元）	Return on assets 資產利潤率 (%)	Return on equity 權益利潤率 (%)	Labour productivity ('000 RMB / worker) 勞動生產率（千元/人）	Debts / assets 資產負債率 (%)	Total assets (mil. RMB) 總資產（百萬元）
Industry Overall 行業總體	226	14,806	1,983	-47	-1.33	-4.30	133.93	69.09	3,511

	Number of firms 企業個數	Average number of employees 平均職工人數	Average revenue ('000 RMB) 平均銷售收入（千元）	Average profit ('000 RMB) 平均利潤（千元）	Return on assets 資產利潤率 (%)	Return on equity 權益利潤率 (%)	Labour productivity ('000 RMB / worker) 勞動生產率（千元/人）	Average debts / assets 平均資產負債率(%)	Average Total assets ('000 RMB) 平均總資產（千元）
By ownership 產業所有權									
State-owned 國有	44	98	5,727	-318	-1.57	-4.61	58.35	65.84	20,227
Collectively-owned 集體	123	48	3,317	18	0.54	1.98	69.23	72.69	3,412
Privately-owned 私有	1	191	524	-103	-0.40	-0.54	2.74	26.52	26,009
Domestic JVs 聯營	7	43	3,566	180	1.87	4.86	83.21	61.58	9,661
Joint stock 股份制	5	99	14,406	-181	-0.47	-1.12	146.11	57.91	38,530
Foreign-funded 外資	26	110	41,835	-1,321	-1.97	-7.02	380.59	72.00	67,176
Overseas Chinese-funded 港澳台資	21	53	6,606	-56	-0.70	-2.29	125.78	69.63	8,027
By size 規模									
Large 大型	6	440	165,905	-6,367	-1.81	-5.69	377.20	68.15	351,548
Medium 中型	4	221	74,424	-918	-1.03	-2.79	337.52	63.20	89,338
Small 小型	209	54	3,306	-25	-0.49	-1.82	61.14	73.04	4,997
By regional distribution 地區分布									
Central-North 華北	33	73	11,719	868	6.30	15.44	161.55	59.18	13,768
Beijing 北京	6	22	1,643	-97	-2.93	-9.03	75.85	67.58	3,300
Tianjin 天津	9	81	31,191	2,670	6.61	15.08	385.60	56.18	40,392
Hebei 河北	13	74	6,787	305	6.06	21.34	92.00	71.60	5,027
Shanxi 山西	2	263	2,955	585	24.79	109.35	11.24	77.33	2,360
Inner Mongolia 內蒙	3	17	673	20	6.45	60.00	39.61	88.17	310
Northeast 東北	44	29	802	22	1.47	8.19	27.64	82.03	1,466
Liaoning 遼寧	17	22	324	-5	-0.53	-2.43	14.77	78.15	886
Jilin 吉林	17	46	1,332	48	1.70	10.61	28.88	84.02	2,845
Heilongjiang 黑龍江	10	12	715	21	19.63	36.21	59.58	46.73	107
Central East 華東	45	80	9,635	-1,352	-8.54	-26.12	120.91	67.32	15,832
Shanghai 上海	5	175	41,604	-14,250	-14.58	-45.29	237.74	67.80	97,704
Jiangsu 江蘇	8	113	5,763	-286	-5.70	-53.26	51.05	89.30	5,024
Zhejiang 浙江	11	95	4,862	-113	-1.59	-22.88	50.98	93.06	7,102
Anhui 安徽	4	69	9,765	1,193	41.09	68.73	142.55	40.31	2,903
Fujian 福建	12	31	6,528	782	10.72	16.19	208.35	33.80	7,293
Jiangxi 江西	4	23	683	-73	-9.60		29.67	100.00	755
Shandong 山東	1	17	5,840	90	2.60	9.47	343.53	72.54	3,460
Central-South 中南	80	81	13,236	-179	-0.65	-2.21	163.76	70.74	27,674
Henan 河南	22	38	2,815	58	1.92	5.23	74.72	63.33	3,010
Hubei 湖北	9	66	2,764	-67	-2.37	-9.69	41.96	75.60	2,819
Hunan 湖南	6	75	3,727	-342	-8.21	-40.43	49.58	79.69	4,160
Guangdong 廣東	17	179	39,522	-926	-0.89	-3.19	221.37	72.06	103,976
Guangxi 廣西	24	55	9,642	107	1.22	3.46	174.65	64.72	8,783
Hainan 海南	2	117	23,220	100	0.17	0.45	199.31	62.92	59,475
Southwest 西南	16	40	3,537	-91	-2.92	-36.05	88.28	91.91	3,130
Chongqing 重慶	3	80	2,066	-336	-11.02	92.31	25.63	111.94	3,052
Sichuan 四川	7	22	354	57	9.11	56.87	15.69	83.99	626
Guizhou 貴州	2	38	1,125	55	3.69	39.29	29.61	90.60	1,490
Yunnan 雲南	3	43	14,930	-300	-2.79	-21.43	347.21	86.96	10,737
Tibet 西藏									
Northwest 西北	8	55	1,498	48	2.40	11.69	27.10	79.46	1,978
Shaanxi 陝西	4	29	1,210	70	6.09	22.05	41.72	72.39	1,150
Gansu 甘肅	2	124	3,055	155	3.36	16.94	24.64	80.17	4,615
Qinghai 青海	1	6							
Ningxia 寧夏									
Xinjiang 新疆	1	72	1,030	-210	-10.55	-140.00	14.31	92.46	1,990

1524: Instant Drinks 固體飲料製造業

Year 年份	Number of firms 企業個數	Rate of change 每年變化 (%)	Number of employees 職工人數 (人)	Rate of change 每年變化 (%)	Total revenue (mil. RMB) 總銷售收入 (百萬元)	Rate of change 每年變化 (%)	Total profit (mil. RMB) 總利潤 (百萬元)	Rate of change 每年變化 (%)
1993	252		12,111		1,414		64	
1994	280	11.11%	17,211	42.11%	1,552	9.76%	2	-96.22%
1995	243	-13.22%	16,216	-5.78%	1,422	-8.35%	-104	-4410.70%
1996	226	-7.00%	14,806	-8.70%	1,983	39.45%	-47	54.96%

3 Major products* 3 種主要產品 *	Output 產量	Sales volume 銷售量	Unit 單位
a) Solid Drink 固體飲料	36,421	35,693	ton 噸
b) Soft Drink 軟飲料	163,011	156,491	ton 噸

Top 10 firms by revenue (year founded) 收入排名前 10 家企業 (創辦年份)	City 城市	Province 省	Telephone / fax 電話 / 傳真	Number of employees 職工人數	Ownership 產業所有權	Revenue ('000 RMB) 銷售收入 (千元)	Profit ('000 RMB) (rank) 利潤 (千元) (排名)	Total assets ('000 RMB) 總資產 (千元)	Major products 主要產品
Nestle Dongguan Ltd. 東莞市雀巢有限公司(1988)	Dongguan 東莞市	Guangdong 廣東省	(0769)2404088 (0769)2402804	436	Foreign-funded 外資	422,536	21183(2)	581,022	a,b
Shanghai Wen De Nutritive Foods Co. Ltd. 上海溫德營養食品有限公司(1993)	Shanghai 上海市	Shanghai 上海市	(021)64303038 (021)64309938	275	Foreign-funded 外資	165,614	-41788(81)	262,039	a,b
Bingquan Industrial Ltd. Co. Wuzhou, Guangxi 廣西梧州冰泉實業股份公司(1961)	Wuzhou 梧州市	Guangxi 廣西	(0774)5822476 (0774)5821545	1,036	Joint stock 股份制	150,455	4238(5)	137,935	a,b
Kraft Tianmei Foods (Tianjin) Co. Ltd. 卡夫天美食品(天津)有限公司(1984)	Tianjin 天津市	Tianjin 天津市	(022)25324561 (022)25323450	228	Foreign-funded 外資	135,400	-18112(78)	263,893	a,b
Tianjin Nutrexpa Foods Co. Ltd. 天津努德莱斯巴食品有限公司(1990)	Tianjin 天津市	Tianjin 天津市	(022)27383006 (022)27385941	101	Foreign-funded 外資	133,774	41555(1)	73,409	a,b
Foods Guangtong Co. Ltd. 廣通食品有限公司(1985)	Guangzhou 廣州市	Guangdong 廣東省	(020)82222883 (020)82222976	371	Foreign-funded 外資	95,075	-30863(80)	432,965	a,b
Meiwei Food Industry (Longhai) Co. Ltd. 美味食品工業(龍海)有限公司(1993)	Zhangzhou 漳州市	Fujian 福建省	(0596)6777605 (0596)6778605	120	Foreign-funded 外資	69,560	10661(3)	61,401	a
Hebei Jizhou Xu Ri Health Protection Goods Co. Ltd. 河北省冀州市旭日保健製品有限公司(1995)	Hengshui 衡水市	Hebei 河北省	(0318)8613781	88	Overseas Chinese-funded 港澳台資	57,000	1864(7)	18,890	o
Guangzhou Guangzhou Candy Factory 廣州市廣州糖果廠(1956)	Guangzhou 廣州市	Guangdong 廣東省	(020)87778831 (020)87756747	798	State-owned 國有	53,199	-3579(76)	471,122	a,b
Shenzhen East Enterprise Co. Ltd. 深圳市東方企業有限公司(1956)	Shenzhen 深圳市	Guangdong 廣東省	(0755)2233899 (0755)2224539	569	State-owned 國有	52,720	-954(70)	209,740	b

Top 10 Cities by Production Output 產出排名前 10 位城市	Province 省	Market share 市場份額	Number of firms 企業個數
Tianjin 天津市	Tianjin 天津市	17.11%	9
Dongguan 東莞市	Guangdong 廣東省	14.53%	1
Shanghai 上海市	Shanghai 上海市	13.50%	9
Wuzhou 梧州市	Guangxi 廣西	11.08%	11
Guangzhou 廣州市	Guangdong 廣東省	9.66%	8
Lingchuan 靈川縣	Guangxi 廣西	5.09%	14
Haikou 海口市	Hainan 海南省	2.75%	2
Kunming 昆明市	Yunnan 雲南省	2.69%	3
Hangzhou 杭州市	Zhejiang 浙江省	1.99%	5
Yuncheng 運城市	Shanxi 山西省	1.50%	1

10 Major Wholesalers 10 家主要批發商	City 城市	Province 省	Telephone / Fax 電話 / 傳真
Zhong Liang Sugar Industry Groceries Import & Export Company 中糧糖業雜品進出口公司	Beijing 北京市	Beijing 北京市	(010)65268888 (010)65276023
China National Sugar & Alcohol Group Corp. 中國糖業酒類集團公司	Beijing 北京市	Beijing 北京市	(010)68360994
Shanxi Sugar & Wine Non-staple Food Company 山西省糖酒副食公司	Taiyuan 太原市	Shanxi 山西省	(0351)2027938 (0351)2027931
Putian Xue Jin Beer Marketing Agency Co. Ltd. 莆田縣雪津啤酒營銷代理有限公司	Putian 莆田市	Fujian 福建省	
Suzhou Sugar, Cigarette & Wine General Company 蘇州糖煙酒總公司	Suzhou 蘇州市	Jiangsu 江蘇省	(0512)7276392 (0512)7276406
Yuhang Sugar Industry Tobacco & Wine Company 余杭市糖業煙酒公司	Hangzhou 杭州市	Zhejiang 浙江省	(0571)6225788 (0571)6225407
Wuxi Sugar Industry Cigarette & Wine General Company 無錫市糖業煙酒總公司	Wuxi 無錫市	Jiangsu 江蘇省	(0510)2720023 (0510)2707693
Wuxi Chaoyang Co. Ltd. 無錫朝陽股份有限公司	Wuxi 無錫市	Jiangsu 江蘇省	(0510)2767704
Yinchuan Shen Da Non-staple Food Co. Ltd. 銀川申達副食有限公司	Yinchuan 銀川市	Ningxia 寧夏	(0951)5031694
Shanghai Sugar Industry Cigarette & Wine (Group) Co. Ltd. 上海市糖業煙酒(集團)有限公司	Shanghai 上海市	Shanghai 上海市	(021)63224190 (021)63223169

*Also include sales by firms outside this industry.包括本行業以外廠家的銷售。"o" stands for "others". "o" 代表"其他產品"。

1529: Other Soft Drinks 其他軟飲料製造業

The industry accounts for 0.062% of the total revenue of China's industrial sector in 1996. The revenue growth rate of the industry is 18.0% from 1995, as compared to the growth rate of China's industrial sector, 9.51%. The rate of return on asset is 2.92%. 58.49% of all firms in the industry made a profit while 34.26% had negative returns. The top province in terms of the industry's revenue is Guangdong, accounting for 72.80% of the total revenue.
本行業在1996年佔全行業總產值0.062%，行業年增長率為18.0%（全國工業年增長率9.51%）。行業的資產回報率2.92%，58.49%的企業盈利，34.26%的企業虧損。銷售收入最高的省份為廣東省，佔本行業的72.80%。

	Total number of firms 企業總數	Total number of employees 職工總數	Total revenue (mil. RMB) 總銷售收入（百萬元）	Total profit (mil. RMB) 總利潤（百萬元）	Return on assets 資產利潤率 (%)	Return on equity 權益利潤率 (%)	Labour productivity ('000 RMB / worker) 勞動生產率（千元/人）	Debts / assets 資產負債率 (%)	Total assets (mil. RMB) 總資產（百萬元）
Industry Overall 行業總體	282	18,703	3,610	130	2.92	8.99	193.02	67.48	4,443

	Number of firms 企業個數	Average number of employees 平均職工人數	Average revenue ('000 RMB) 平均銷售收入（千元）	Average profit ('000 RMB) 平均利潤（千元）	Return on assets 資產利潤率 (%)	Return on equity 權益利潤率 (%)	Labour productivity ('000 RMB / worker) 勞動生產率（千元/人）	Average debts / assets 平均資產負債率(%)	Average Total assets ('000 RMB) 平均總資產（千元）
By ownership 產業所有權									
State-owned 國有	51	134	8,824	118	0.47	1.73	66.03	72.83	25,039
Collectively-owned 集體	150	40	2,178	26	0.92	2.89	54.92	68.25	2,848
Privately-owned 私有	2	91	2,686	-20	-1.40	-5.04	29.68	72.23	1,452
Domestic JVs 聯營	10	38	323	-136	-10.41	-17.93	8.46	41.91	1,310
Joint stock 股份制	5	108	5,455	-1,910	-15.80	-47.73	50.42	66.89	12,092
Foreign-funded 外資	34	52	10,080	421	2.68	5.62	195.74	52.31	15,677
Overseas Chinese-funded 港澳台資	29	109	84,526	4,011	5.50	17.43	778.18	68.45	72,933
By size 規模									
Large 大型	4	846	622,302	36,461	6.27	21.50	735.36	70.84	581,498
Medium 中型	6	464	41,387	4,188	4.37	9.64	89.20	54.67	95,844
Small 小型	265	48	3,295	-155	-2.66	-8.10	68.95	67.19	5,819
By regional distribution 地區分布									
Central-North 華北	47	82	8,503	-128	-0.54	-1.36	103.22	59.95	23,577
Beijing 北京	14	46	3,099	-779	-8.16	-19.49	68.12	58.16	9,554
Tianjin 天津	12	26	2,373	-83	-0.84	-1.01	89.84	17.37	9,852
Hebei 河北	11	232	29,358	754	0.99	2.91	126.59	65.78	75,775
Shanxi 山西	5	54	684	-462	-13.60	-366.67	12.62	96.29	3,396
Inner Mongolia 內蒙	5	19	284	-20	-1.77	-2.39	14.79	25.71	1,128
Northeast 東北	26	73	587	-357	-12.12	-70.17	8.04	82.71	2,948
Liaoning 遼寧	9	18	903	-919	-20.15	-38.30	51.13	47.38	4,561
Jilin 吉林	6	260	587	-167	-3.74	7.72	2.25	148.38	4,462
Heilongjiang 黑龍江	11	16	328	-2	-0.23	-0.43	20.28	47.90	803
Central East 華東	76	41	4,666	-98	-1.40	-4.05	112.97	65.60	7,008
Shanghai 上海	11	69	9,564	-2,593	-9.97	-27.86	138.79	64.20	25,993
Jiangsu 江蘇	10	65	9,260	450	5.92	24.21	142.24	75.54	7,596
Zhejiang 浙江	11	48	4,240	331	8.38	28.87	88.00	70.98	3,950
Anhui 安徽	3	24	1,650	37	3.59	6.47	69.72	44.44	1,020
Fujian 福建	20	16	3,029	562	19.04	45.08	186.98	57.79	2,950
Jiangxi 江西	12	25	1,124	-23	-1.51	-11.34	44.67	86.68	1,545
Shandong 山東	9	56	3,460	210	4.05	9.18	61.91	55.88	5,186
Central-South 中南	97	79	28,415	1,509	5.77	19.51	360.90	70.43	26,153
Henan 河南	19	78	3,255	835	18.48	40.78	41.56	54.67	4,519
Hubei 湖北	15	23	2,541	211	7.00	10.78	112.78	35.04	3,008
Hunan 湖南	12	68	1,565	-116	-2.75	-11.46	22.93	75.98	4,208
Guangdong 廣東	39	121	67,389	3,303	5.49	19.30	558.83	71.56	60,183
Guangxi 廣西	10	24	929	-7	-0.86	-3.00	38.87	71.39	818
Hainan 海南	2	25							
Southwest 西南	26	66	3,044	297	4.97	17.69	45.88	71.91	5,967
Chongqing 重慶		146	20,473	2,139	2.08	10.68	139.99	80.52	102,802
Sichuan 四川	15	69	1,182	-248	-7.62	-15.55	16.97	51.02	3,253
Guizhou 貴州	7	50	13	1	10.00	14.29	0.26	40.00	14
Yunnan 雲南	3	72	15,573	3,337	29.69	192.87	215.30	84.61	11,240
Tibet 西藏									
Northwest 西北	10	43	522	-148	-4.35	-13.70	12.11	68.23	3,403
Shaanxi 陝西	2	12	75	-240	-19.35	-33.33	6.25	41.94	1,240
Gansu 甘肅	5	70	840	18	0.48	2.66	12.07	82.05	3,778
Qinghai 青海									
Ningxia 寧夏									
Xinjiang 新疆	3	20	290	-363	-8.61	-18.23	14.75	52.76	4,220

1529: Other Soft Drinks 其他軟飲料製造業

Year 年份	Number of firms 企業個數	Rate of change 每年變化 (%)	Number of employees 職工人數 (人)	Rate of change 每年變化 (%)	Total revenue (mil. RMB) 總銷售收入 (百萬元)	Rate of change 每年變化 (%)	Total profit (mil. RMB) 總利潤 (百萬元)	Rate of change 每年變化 (%)
1993	259		16,342		1,218		52	
1994	300	15.83%	16,344	0.01%	1,237	1.52%	91	73.16%
1995	285	-5.00%	21,390	30.87%	3,059	147.26%	93	2.08%
1996	282	-1.05%	18,703	-12.56%	3,610	18.01%	130	40.54%

3 Major products* 3 種主要產品 *	Output 產量	Sales volume 銷售量	Unit 單位
a) Lactobacillus Drink 乳酸菌飲料	47,965	47,006	ton 噸
b) Soft Drink 軟飲料	1,491,913	1,432,236	ton 噸

Top 10 firms by revenue (year founded) 收入排名前 10 家企業 (創辦年份)	City 城市	Province 省	Telephone / fax 電話 / 傳真	Number of employees 職工人數	Ownership 產業所有權	Revenue ('000 RMB) 銷售收入 (千元)	Profit ('000 RMB) (rank) 利潤 (千元) (排名)	Total assets ('000 RMB) 總資產 (千元)	Major products 主要產品
Guangdong Jian Li Bao Beverage Factory 廣東健力寶飲料廠(1986)	Foshan 佛山市	Guangdong 廣東省	(0757)7721102 (0757)7739168	1,432	Overseas Chinese-funded 港澳台資	2,232,705	120902(2)	1,509,175	b
Hangzhou Wahaha Group Corp. 杭州娃哈哈集團公司(1993)	Hangzhou 杭州市	Zhejiang 浙江省	(0571)7026360 (0571)7816540	3,410	State-owned 國有	1,114,502	154764(1)	1,569,234	b
Hebei Lu Lu Enterprise Group Co. 河北露露企業集團公司(1950)	Chengde 承德市	Hebei 河北省	(0314)2066791 (0314)2062592	1,631	State-owned 國有	281,982	10018(5)	711,662	b
Kunshan Xin Long Foods Co. Ltd. 昆山市鑫隆食品有限公司(1988)	Suzhou 蘇州市	Jiangsu 江蘇省	(0512)7303779 (0512)7302667	85	Foreign-funded 外資	82,820	6250(8)	55,580	o
Guangdong Narcissus Flower Enterprise Co. Ltd. 廣東水仙花企業有限公司(1957)	Zhaoqing 肇慶市	Guangdong 廣東省	(0757)2833851 (0757)2833851	750	State-owned 國有	59,997	2388(12)	146,708	b
Shanghai Yan Zhong Drinking Water Co. Ltd. 上海延中飲用水有限公司(1994)	Shanghai 上海市	Shanghai 上海市	(021)59511214	160	Foreign-funded 外資	51,419	8972(6)	37,935	o
Foshan Foods Products Factory 佛山市食品廠(1956)	Foshan 佛山市	Guangdong 廣東省	(0757)2257215 (0757)2833347	301	Collectively-owned 集體	46,896	1124(18)	41,552	b
Yue Li Industrial Co. Ltd. Le Tian Electric Appliance Industrial Co. 粵力實業有限公司樂天電器工業公司	Yangjiang 陽江市	Guangdong 廣東省	(0662)669538	158	Overseas Chinese-funded 港澳台資	44,717	269(29)	229,677	b
Guangdong Dongguan De Le Duo Industrial Co. 廣東省東莞市得樂多工業公司(1956)	Dongguan 東莞市	Guangdong 廣東省	(0769)6611169 (0769)6622667	176	Collectively-owned 集體	39,280	257(30)	24,507	a
Zhejiang Tonglu Jin Yi Huang Jia Industrial Co. Ltd. 浙江桐廬金義皇家實業有限公司(1996)	Hangzhou 杭州市	Zhejiang 浙江省	(0571)4361153	260	Collectively-owned 集體	39,084	4022(9)	20,818	o

Top 10 Cities by Production Output 產出排名前 10 位城市	Province 省	Market share 市場份額	Number of firms 企業個數
Foshan 佛山市	Guangdong 廣東省	44.12%	3
Hangzhou 杭州市	Zhejiang 浙江省	24.04%	8
Shanghai 上海市	Shanghai 上海市	11.40%	32
Chengde 承德市	Hebei 河北省	4.74%	3
Suzhou 蘇州市	Jiangsu 江蘇省	1.82%	6
Zhaoqing 肇慶市	Guangdong 廣東省	1.57%	4
Dongguan 東莞市	Guangdong 廣東省	1.50%	6
Guangzhou 廣州市	Guangdong 廣東省	1.39%	9
Zhongshan 中山市	Guangdong 廣東省	0.95%	1
Shenzhen 深圳市	Guangdong 廣東省	0.93%	10

10 Major Wholesalers 10 家主要批發商	City 城市	Province 省	Telephone / Fax 電話 / 傳真
Zhong Liang Sugar Industry Groceries Import & Export Company 中糧糖業雜品進出口公司	Beijing 北京市	Beijing 北京市	(010)65268888 (010)65276023
China National Sugar & Alcohol Group Corp. 中國糖業酒類集團公司	Beijing 北京市	Beijing 北京市	(010)68360994
Shanxi Sugar & Wine Non-staple Food Company 山西省糖酒副食公司	Taiyuan 太原市	Shanxi 山西省	(0351)2027938 (0351)2027931
Putian Xue Jin Beer Marketing Agency Co. Ltd. 莆田縣雪津啤酒營銷代理有限公司	Putian 莆田市	Fujian 福建省	
Suzhou Sugar, Cigarette & Wine General Company 蘇州糖煙酒總公司	Suzhou 蘇州市	Jiangsu 江蘇省	(0512)7276392 (0512)7276406
Yuhang Sugar Industry Tobacco & Wine Company 余杭市糖業煙酒公司	Hangzhou 杭州市	Zhejiang 浙江省	(0571)6225788 (0571)6225407
Wuxi Sugar Industry Cigarette & Wine General Company 無錫市糖業煙酒總公司	Wuxi 無錫市	Jiangsu 江蘇省	(0510)2720023 (0510)2707693
Wuxi Chaoyang Co. Ltd. 無錫朝陽股份有限公司	Wuxi 無錫市	Jiangsu 江蘇省	(0510)2767704
Yinchuan Shen Da Non-staple Food Co. Ltd. 銀川申達副食有限公司	Yinchuan 銀川市	Ningxia 寧夏	(0951)5031694
Shanghai Sugar Industry Cigarette & Wine (Group) Co. Ltd. 上海市糖業煙酒(集團)有限公司	Shanghai 上海市	Shanghai 上海市	(021)63224190 (021)63223169

*Also include sales by firms outside this industry.包括本行業以外廠家的銷售。"o" stands for "others". "o" 代表"其他產品"。

1550: Tea 製茶業

The industry accounts for 0.101% of the total revenue of China's industrial sector in 1996. The revenue growth rate of the industry is 13.5% from 1995, as compared to the growth rate of China's industrial sector, 9.51%. The rate of return on asset is -1.99%. 73.24% of all firms in the industry made a profit while 18.90% had negative returns. The top province in terms of the industry's revenue is Zhejiang, accounting for 22.06% of the total revenue.
本行業在1996年佔全行業總產值0.101%，行業年增長率為13.5%（全國工業年增長率9.51%）。行業的資產回報率-1.99%，73.24%的企業盈利，18.90%的企業虧損。銷售收入最高的省份為浙江省，佔本行業的22.06%。

	Total number of firms 企業總數	Total number of employees 職工總數	Total revenue (mil. RMB) 總銷售收入（百萬元）	Total profit (mil. RMB) 總利潤（百萬元）	Return on assets 資產利潤率 (%)	Return on equity 權益利潤率 (%)	Labour productivity ('000 RMB / worker) 勞動生產率（千元/人）	Debts / assets 資產負債率 (%)	Total assets (mil. RMB) 總資產（百萬元）
Industry Overall 行業總體	2,782	117,535	5,878	-144	-1.99	-8.73	50.01	77.18	7,226

	Number of firms 企業個數	Average number of employees 平均職工人數	Average revenue ('000 RMB) 平均銷售收入（千元）	Average profit ('000 RMB) 平均利潤（千元）	Return on assets 資產利潤率 (%)	Return on equity 權益利潤率 (%)	Labour productivity ('000 RMB / worker) 勞動生產率（千元/人）	Average debts / assets 平均資產負債率(%)	Average Total assets ('000 RMB) 平均總資產（千元）
By ownership 產業所有權									
State-owned 國有	265	134	6,796	-426	-3.88	-21.08	50.84	81.58	10,981
Collectively-owned 集體	2,422	32	1,571	-11	-0.67	-3.00	48.88	77.49	1,588
Privately-owned 私有	12	19	1,564	18	2.02	6.20	80.55	67.41	879
Domestic JVs 聯營	14	47	5,448	-135	-2.50	-6.27	115.04	60.10	5,397
Joint stock 股份制	17	95	3,168	-70	-1.41	-3.20	33.24	55.82	4,934
Foreign-funded 外資	24	42	2,813	25	0.37	0.61	66.99	39.34	6,902
Overseas Chinese-funded 港澳台資	29	37	1,930	-97	-2.09	-3.70	52.07	43.49	4,644
By size 規模									
Large 大型	1	1,216	43,912	4,628	4.19	6.01	36.11	30.20	110,392
Medium 中型	22	476	63,675	-1,189	-1.42	-5.13	133.83	72.39	84,014
Small 小型	2,748	38	1,613	-45	-2.33	-11.54	41.90	79.84	1,916
By regional distribution 地區分布									
Central-North 華北	18	44	9,452	134	1.56	6.27	216.45	75.18	8,604
Beijing 北京	8	42	19,120	158	1.03	4.81	452.54	78.70	15,363
Tianjin 天津									
Hebei 河北	7	55	2,324	157	3.72	9.56	42.37	61.09	4,226
Shanxi 山西									
Inner Mongolia 內蒙	3	21	300	17	2.08	6.76	14.06	68.75	800
Northeast 東北	10	632	3,690	264	1.89	6.07	5.83	68.79	13,933
Liaoning 遼寧	4	29	2,735	815	27.56	72.44	95.96	61.88	2,958
Jilin 吉林	3	66	2,317	120	0.83	1.50	35.10	44.71	14,463
Heilongjiang 黑龍江	3	2,004	6,337	-327	-1.17	-6.54	3.16	82.18	28,037
Central East 華東	1,132	43	2,675	-94	-2.90	-14.32	62.33	79.74	3,225
Shanghai 上海	3	263	45,703	-77	-0.30	-1.02	174.00	70.33	25,247
Jiangsu 江蘇	29	62	3,552	109	2.69	7.36	57.51	63.41	4,035
Zhejiang 浙江	219	54	5,921	-184	-2.43	-10.69	110.58	77.27	7,559
Anhui 安徽	275	34	1,367	-191	-11.47	223.95	40.06	105.12	1,667
Fujian 福建	417	41	1,982	-7	-0.33	-0.93	48.90	64.53	2,094
Jiangxi 江西	171	40	1,224	-85	-3.79	79.29	30.25	104.78	2,234
Shandong 山東	18	59	4,396	73	1.49	4.41	74.36	66.23	4,921
Central-South 中南	935	38	1,831	13	0.69	2.17	48.51	68.23	1,926
Henan 河南	21	28	1,513	73	4.18	11.93	53.13	64.95	1,743
Hubei 湖北	342	36	1,425	53	3.87	9.03	39.60	57.08	1,377
Hunan 湖南	380	41	1,788	-8	-0.45	-3.40	44.04	86.62	1,770
Guangdong 廣東	77	51	4,404	14	0.28	0.47	85.76	40.31	4,780
Guangxi 廣西	110	26	1,535	-48	-2.18	-13.23	58.22	83.53	2,197
Hainan 海南	5	22	1,144	-16	-0.71	-1.03	51.53	31.27	2,264
Southwest 西南	585	43	1,538	-94	-3.80	-21.80	35.77	82.58	2,463
Chongqing 重慶	137	25	290	-98	-11.64	-106.83	11.25	89.11	840
Sichuan 四川	271	33	1,454	-73	-3.85	-36.13	43.26	89.33	1,883
Guizhou 貴州	87	50	537	-27	-2.14	-15.75	10.75	86.41	1,267
Yunnan 雲南	89	93	4,696	-218	-2.76	-11.49	50.75	75.99	7,908
Tibet 西藏									
Northwest 西北	102	14	309	-7	-1.91	-17.16	22.59	88.91	391
Shaanxi 陝西	96	14	304	-6	-1.70	-11.73	22.07	85.54	362
Gansu 甘肅	4	4	458				107.65		13
Qinghai 青海									
Ningxia 寧夏	2	28	245	-85	-3.34	26.15	8.91	112.77	2,545
Xinjiang 新疆									

Year 年份	Number of firms 企業個數	Rate of change 每年變化 (%)	Number of employees 職工人數（人）	Rate of change 每年變化 (%)	Total revenue (mil. RMB) 總銷售收入（百萬元）	Rate of change 每年變化 (%)	Total profit (mil. RMB) 總利潤（百萬元）	Rate of change 每年變化 (%)
1993	2,773		109,410		5,638		21	
1994	2,868	3.43%	141,410	29.25%	4,897	-13.14%	-114	-640.23%
1995	2,883	0.52%	124,419	-12.02%	5,181	5.79%	-190	-67.15%
1996	2,782	-3.50%	117,535	-5.53%	5,878	13.45%	-144	24.21%

3 Major products* 3 種主要產品 *	Output 產量	Sales volume 銷售量	Unit 單位
a) Refined Tea 精製茶	678,160	678,160	ton 噸
b) Health Protection Drink 保健飲料	5,040	4,888	ton 噸

Top 10 firms by revenue (year founded) 收入排名前 10 家企業 (創辦年份)	City 城市	Province 省	Telephone / fax 電話 / 傳真	Number of employees 職工人數	Ownership 產業所有權	Revenue ('000 RMB) 銷售收入（千元）	Profit ('000 RMB) (rank) 利潤（千元）（排名）	Total assets ('000 RMB) 總資產（千元）	Major products 主要產品
Zhejiang Tea Import & Export Co. No.2 Tea Refinery 浙江茶葉進出口公司第二茶廠(1950)	Shaoxing 紹興市	Zhejiang 浙江省	(0575)5133333 (0575)5134072	703	State-owned 國有	154,069	24(305)	197,317	a
Beijing Tea Processing Factory 北京市茶葉加工廠(1951)	Beijing 北京市	Beijing 北京市	(010)63267808 (010)63267829	286	State-owned 國有	151,498	1061(15)	122,298	a
Guangdong Tea Import & Export Corp. The No.1 Tea Factory 廣東省茶葉進出口公司第一茶廠(1954)	Guangzhou 廣州市	Guangdong 廣東省	(020)84337536 (020)84367747	473	State-owned 國有	116,085	-1877(523)	54,724	a
Chaoyang Da Yin Xiang (Group) Co. Ltd. 潮陽市大印象(集團)有限公司(1990)	Shantou 汕頭市	Guangdong 廣東省	(0754)2211286	268	Collectively-owned 集體	101,280	1000(16)	108,060	a
Zhejiang No.1 Export Tea Refinery 浙江省第一出口茶廠(1992)	Hangzhou 杭州市	Zhejiang 浙江省	(0571)6041793 (0571)6042095	580	Collectively-owned 集體	96,422	31(289)	194,485	a
Zhejiang Sanjie Tea Refinery 浙江省三界茶廠(1950)	Shaoxing 紹興市	Zhejiang 浙江省	(0575)3081547 (0575)3081545	378	Collectively-owned 集體	83,805	177(123)	73,785	o
Jiangxi Ning Hong Group Co. 江西寧紅集團公司(1950)	Jiujiang 九江市	Jiangxi 江西省	(0792)7221749	579	State-owned 國有	77,131	11797(1)	98,764	a
Yunnan Xia Guan Tea Refinery 雲南省下關茶廠(1941)	Dali 大理市	Yunnan 雲南省	(0872)2121801 (0872)2120001	398	State-owned 國有	66,177	2879(5)	70,972	a
Zhejiang Lin'an Tea Refinery 浙江省臨安茶廠(1969)	Hangzhou 杭州市	Zhejiang 浙江省	(0571)3723503 (0571)3722720	360	Collectively-owned 集體	63,854	44(271)	97,128	a
Zhejiang Huzhou Tea Factory 浙江省湖州市茶廠(1979)	Huzhou 湖州市	Zhejiang 浙江省	(0572)2046017 (0572)2046194	115	Collectively-owned 集體	62,366	164(132)	19,739	o

Top 10 Cities by Production Output 產出排名前 10 位城市	Province 省	Market share 市場份額	Number of firms 企業個數
Shaoxing 紹興市	Zhejiang 浙江省	12.00%	54
Hangzhou 杭州市	Zhejiang 浙江省	7.21%	53
Ningde 寧德市	Fujian 福建省	3.73%	99
Quanzhou 泉州市	Fujian 福建省	3.22%	88
Beijing 北京市	Beijing 北京市	3.12%	8
Changsha 長沙市	Hunan 湖南省	3.03%	25
Huangshan 黃山市	Anhui 安徽省	2.93%	133
Lincang 臨滄縣	Yunnan 雲南省	2.78%	47
Shanghai 上海市	Shanghai 上海市	2.58%	6
Ningbo 寧波市	Zhejiang 浙江省	2.54%	22

10 Major Wholesalers 10 家主要批發商	City 城市	Province 省	Telephone / Fax 電話 / 傳真
China Local Products Animal Products Zhejiang Tea Import & Export Company 中國土產畜產浙江茶葉進出口公司	Hangzhou 杭州市	Zhejiang 浙江省	(0571)7069835 (0571)7075320
Chongqing Tea Local Products Import & Export Company 重慶茶葉土產進出口公司	Chongqing 重慶市	Chongqing 重慶市	(023)67858281 (023)67859096
China Local Products Animal Products Yunnan Tea Import & Export Company 中國土產畜產雲南茶葉進出口公司	Kunming 昆明市	Yunnan 雲南省	(0871)3191045 (0871)3135685
China Local Products Livestock Products Guangdong Tea Import & Export Co. 中國土產畜產廣東茶葉進出口公司	Guangzhou 廣州市	Guangdong 廣東省	(020)87577168 (020)87592270
China Local Products Animal Products Fujian Tea Import & Export Company 中國土產畜產福建茶葉進出口公司	Fuzhou 福州市	Fujian 福建省	(0591)7821777 (0591)7853402
China Local Products Animal Products Jiangxi Tea Import & Export Company 中國土產畜產江西茶葉進出口公司	Nanchang 南昌市	Jiangxi 江西省	(0791)6236153 (0791)6224813
China Local Products Animal Products Hunan Tea Import & Export Company 中國土產畜產湖南茶葉進出口公司	Changsha 長沙市	Hunan 湖南省	(0731)2228128 (0731)4446695
Xiamen Tea Import & Export Co. Ltd., Fujian 福建廈門茶葉進出口公司	Xiamen 廈門市	Fujian 福建省	(0592)5111961 (0592)5077202
China Local Products Animal Products Anhui Tea Import & Export Company 中國土產畜產安徽茶葉進出口公司	Hefei 合肥市	Anhui 安徽省	(0551)2652408 (0551)2654664
Panzhihua Foreign Economy Trade Company 攀枝花市對外經濟貿易公司	Panzhihua 攀枝花市	Sichuan 四川省	(0812)2222882

*Also include sales by firms outside this industry.包括本行業以外廠家的銷售。"o" stands for "others". "o" 代表 "其他產品"。

1590: Other Beverages 其他飲料製造業

The industry accounts for 0.056% of the total revenue of China's industrial sector in 1996. The revenue growth rate of the industry is 46.2% from 1995, as compared to the growth rate of China's industrial sector, 9.51%. The rate of return on asset is 1.27%. 60.50% of all firms in the industry made a profit while 30.54% had negative returns. The top province in terms of the industry's revenue is Guangdong, accounting for 58.32% of the total revenue.
本行業在 1996 年佔全行業總產值 0.056% ，行業年增長率為 46.2%（全國工業年增長率 9.51%）。行業的資產回報率 1.27% ， 60.50% 的企業盈利， 30.54% 的企業虧損。銷售收入最高的省份為廣東省，佔本行業的 58.32% 。

	Total number of firms 企業總數	Total number of employees 職工總數	Total revenue (mil. RMB) 總銷售收入（百萬元）	Total profit (mil. RMB) 總利潤（百萬元）	Return on assets 資產利潤率 (%)	Return on equity 權益利潤率 (%)	Labour productivity ('000 RMB / worker) 勞動生產率（千元/人）	Debts / assets 資產負債率 (%)	Total assets (mil. RMB) 總資產（百萬元）
Industry Overall 行業總體	529	28,832	3,245	72	1.27	4.08	112.55	68.80	5,665

	Number of firms 企業個數	Average number of employees 平均職工人數	Average revenue ('000 RMB) 平均銷售收入（千元）	Average profit ('000 RMB) 平均利潤（千元）	Return on assets 資產利潤率 (%)	Return on equity 權益利潤率 (%)	Labour productivity ('000 RMB / worker) 勞動生產率（千元/人）	Average debts / assets 平均資產負債率(%)	Average Total assets ('000 RMB) 平均總資產（千元）
By ownership 產業所有權									
State-owned 國有	92	56	3,413	-98	-1.29	-8.11	60.50	84.05	7,565
Collectively-owned 集體	247	52	4,535	-6	-0.10	-0.63	86.82	84.20	6,520
Privately-owned 私有	5	31	2,807	-61	-1.46	-4.11	91.13	64.53	4,182
Domestic JVs 聯營	12	63	3,982	-223	-1.44	-5.30	63.63	72.82	15,483
Joint stock 股份制	19	45	2,681	71	1.02	1.89	59.71	46.13	6,983
Foreign-funded 外資	72	46	4,022	-65	-0.92	-3.58	86.76	74.27	7,060
Overseas Chinese-funded 港澳台資	78	78	17,910	1,108	3.49	7.66	228.64	54.45	31,773
By size 規模									
Large 大型	2	1,154	550,682	59,036	8.44	15.06	477.40	43.92	699,299
Medium 中型	5	426	55,855	-1,114	-0.79	-2.07	131.05	62.02	141,587
Small 小型	483	50	3,861	-84	-1.14	-5.66	77.28	79.93	7,369
By regional distribution 地區分布									
Central-North 華北	77	28	2,016	36	1.03	3.77	71.50	72.65	3,477
Beijing 北京	37	20	1,583	116	3.23	9.29	77.69	65.26	3,594
Tianjin 天津	17	26	1,848	-279	-7.58	-564.29	71.41	98.64	3,680
Hebei 河北	12	49	3,633	288	9.78	49.57	74.13	80.27	2,939
Shanxi 山西	4	11							
Inner Mongolia 內蒙	7	49	3,090	-34	-0.65	-1.25	62.51	47.90	5,270
Northeast 東北	51	41	3,641	65	0.48	1.99	88.97	75.86	13,425
Liaoning 遼寧	38	44	4,590	51	0.29	1.19	104.45	75.36	17,335
Jilin 吉林	8	38	618	40	1.33	13.73	16.30	90.34	3,001
Heilongjiang 黑龍江	5	23	1,260	208	54.17	157.58	55.26	65.63	384
Central East 華東	140	43	4,352	72	0.94	2.92	102.27	67.80	7,599
Shanghai 上海	10	83	20,476	521	1.16	3.87	247.59	69.94	44,749
Jiangsu 江蘇	18	72	5,027	14	0.15	0.46	69.82	67.44	9,682
Zhejiang 浙江	19	44	5,039	-96	-1.43	-4.16	115.64	65.59	6,686
Anhui 安徽	11	47	4,658	550	6.70	14.62	98.73	54.16	8,208
Fujian 福建	37	19	1,180	-63	-2.57	-8.08	60.89	68.24	2,444
Jiangxi 江西	28	33	435	-58	-3.83	-12.63	13.01	69.67	1,500
Shandong 山東	17	49	6,544	249	4.60	17.15	133.39	73.20	5,428
Central-South 中南	187	79	11,238	355	2.04	5.92	142.27	65.63	17,433
Henan 河南	29	56	3,412	38	0.68	4.32	61.26	84.27	5,634
Hubei 湖北	15	21	1,259	26	2.07	17.97	59.94	88.48	1,256
Hunan 湖南	18	22	879	-46	-1.84	-5.45	39.38	66.26	2,478
Guangdong 廣東	89	127	21,264	697	2.11	5.81	167.41	63.63	33,002
Guangxi 廣西	36	32	2,090	101	3.78	39.12	66.34	90.34	2,666
Hainan 海南									
Southwest 西南	43	52	3,330	-237	-4.16	-24.94	64.52	83.30	5,702
Chongqing 重慶	5	35	613	-332	-8.60	41.21	17.43	120.86	3,860
Sichuan 四川	13	68	8,849	-1	-0.01	-0.03	128.41	84.40	10,895
Guizhou 貴州	18	41	237	-159	-18.27	-37.88	5.76	51.76	869
Yunnan 雲南	3	86	2,690	-1,117	-8.90	-744.44	31.28	98.80	12,543
Tibet 西藏	3	35	2,910	-713	-8.84	-14.61	83.14	39.42	8,067
Northwest 西北	31	52	1,632	-1	-0.03	-0.16	31.11	82.53	4,638
Shaanxi 陝西	11	46	900	-231	-7.67	33.29	19.57	123.05	3,009
Gansu 甘肅	9	75	957	-293	-3.57	-14.98	12.77	76.16	8,209
Qinghai 青海	1								
Ningxia 寧夏	2	51	1,020	50	2.32	27.78	20.00	91.65	2,155
Xinjiang 新疆	8	43	3,755	630	15.51	34.10	87.33	54.51	4,061

1590: Other Beverages 其他飲料製造業

Year 年份	Number of firms 企業個數	Rate of change 每年變化 (%)	Number of employees 職工人數（人）	Rate of change 每年變化 (%)	Total revenue (mil. RMB) 總銷售收入（百萬元）	Rate of change 每年變化 (%)	Total profit (mil. RMB) 總利潤（百萬元）	Rate of change 每年變化 (%)
1993	281		26,652		2,460		302	
1994	361	28.47%	24,749	-7.14%	1,293	-47.43%	42	-86.07%
1995	524	45.15%	29,888	20.76%	2,219	71.64%	113	169.45%
1996	529	0.95%	28,832	-3.53%	3,245	46.24%	72	-36.52%

3 Major products* 3種主要產品 *	Output 產量	Sales volume 銷售量	Unit 單位
a) Health Protection Drink 保健飲料	154,321	149,692	ton 噸
b) Lactobacillus Drink 乳酸菌飲料	123,531	121,061	ton 噸
c) Biotic Products 生物製品	829,954	780,156	1,000 yuan 千元

Top 10 firms by revenue (year founded) 收入排名前10家企業（創辦年份）	City 城市	Province 省	Telephone / fax 電話 / 傳真	Number of employees 職工人數	Ownership 產業所有權	Revenue ('000 RMB) 銷售收入（千元）	Profit ('000 RMB) (rank) 利潤（千元）（排名）	Total assets ('000 RMB) 總資產（千元）	Major products 主要產品
Zhuhai Ju Ren Organism Development Co. 珠海巨人生物開發公司(1993)	Zhuhai 珠海市	Guangdong 廣東省	(0756)2262299 (0756)2265774	1,200	Collectively-owned 集體	647,818	43498(3)	628,845	o
Wuhan Hong Tao K Group Co. Ltd. 武漢紅桃K集團股份公司(1995)	Wuhan 武漢市	Hubei 湖北省	(027)87396967 (027)87393885	896	Joint stock 股份制	552,327	152281(1)	287,652	c
Guangdong Apollo (Group) Co. Ltd. 廣東省太陽神集團公司(1988)	Dongguan 東莞市	Guangdong 廣東省	(0769)5512188 (0769)7504555	2,163	Overseas Chinese-funded 港澳台資	418,811	72718(2)	873,156	o
Guangdong Jin Ri (Group) Co. Ltd. 廣東今日(集團)有限公司(1989)	Zhongshan 中山市	Guangdong 廣東省	(0760)2101803 (0760)2101802	2,070	Collectively-owned 集體	399,392	6948(4)	377,252	b
Shanghai Lai Fu (Group) Co. Ltd. 上海萊福(集團)股份有限公司(1993)	Shanghai 上海市	Shanghai 上海市	(021)56660605 (021)56660605	292	Collectively-owned 集體	86,000	5141(7)	310,067	a
Red Bulls Vitamin Ming Beverage Co. Ltd. 紅牛維他命飲料有限公司(1995)	Shenzhen 深圳市	Guangdong 廣東省	(0755)3252288 (0755)3217692	45	Foreign-funded 外資	84,564	-10562(132)	180,051	o
Chengdu Milting Factory 成都麥芽廠(1989)	Chengdu 成都市	Sichuan 四川省	(028)8223715 (028)8223755	233	State-owned 國有	61,058	53(71)	97,750	o
Shenyang Fei Long Health Care Products Co. Ltd. 瀋陽飛龍保健品有限公司(1990)	Shenyang 瀋陽市	Liaoning 遼寧省	(024)23843954	715	Overseas Chinese-funded 港澳台資	58,214	-25899(134)	447,365	o
Kaifeng Peanut Group Co. 開封花生集團公司(1993)	Kaifeng 開封市	Henan 河南省	(0378)9261081 (0378)261191	405	State-owned 國有	49,190	348(43)	91,333	o
Shan Donghai Lan Bao Organism Food Co. Ltd. 山東海藍寶生物食品有限公司(1995)	Zibo 淄博市	Shandong 山東省	(0533)7314577 (0533)7314577	76	Collectively-owned 集體	46,923	2652(11)	30,921	a

Top 10 Cities by Production Output 產出排名前10位城市	Province 省	Market share 市場份額	Number of firms 企業個數
Zhuhai 珠海市	Guangdong 廣東省	22.22%	12
Zhongshan 中山市	Guangdong 廣東省	15.47%	9
Shanghai 上海市	Shanghai 上海市	7.36%	27
Shenyang 瀋陽市	Liaoning 遼寧省	5.33%	12
Shenzhen 深圳市	Guangdong 廣東省	4.04%	17
Guangzhou 廣州市	Guangdong 廣東省	2.86%	16
Changzhou 常州市	Jiangsu 江蘇省	2.71%	18
Beijing 北京市	Beijing 北京市	1.99%	34
Jiaxing 嘉興市	Zhejiang 浙江省	1.98%	7
Chengdu 成都市	Sichuan 四川省	1.96%	4

10 Major Wholesalers 10家主要批發商	City 城市	Province 省	Telephone / Fax 電話 / 傳真
Zhong Liang Sugar Industry Groceries Import & Export Company 中糧糖業雜品進出口公司	Beijing 北京市	Beijing 北京市	(010)65268888 (010)65276023
China National Sugar & Alcohol Group Corp. 中國糖業酒類集團公司	Beijing 北京市	Beijing 北京市	(010)68360994
Shanxi Sugar & Wine Non-staple Food Company 山西省糖酒副食公司	Taiyuan 太原市	Shanxi 山西省	(0351)2027938 (0351)2027931
Putian Xue Jin Beer Marketing Agency Co. Ltd. 莆田縣雪津啤酒營銷代理有限公司	Putian 莆田市	Fujian 福建省	
Suzhou Sugar, Cigarette & Wine General Company 蘇州糖煙酒總公司	Suzhou 蘇州市	Jiangsu 江蘇省	(0512)7276392 (0512)7276406
Yuhang Sugar Industry Tobacco & Wine Company 余杭市糖業煙酒公司	Hangzhou 杭州市	Zhejiang 浙江省	(0571)6225788 (0571)6225407
Wuxi Sugar Industry Cigarette & Wine General Company 無錫市糖業煙酒總公司	Wuxi 無錫市	Jiangsu 江蘇省	(0510)2720023 (0510)2707693
Wuxi Chaoyang Co. Ltd. 無錫朝陽股份有限公司	Wuxi 無錫市	Jiangsu 江蘇省	(0510)2767704
Yinchuan Shen Da Non-staple Food Co. Ltd. 銀川申達副食有限公司	Yinchuan 銀川市	Ningxia 寧夏	(0951)5031694
Shanghai Sugar Industry Cigarette & Wine (Group) Co. Ltd. 上海市糖業煙酒(集團)有限公司	Shanghai 上海市	Shanghai 上海市	(021)63224190 (021)63223169

*Also include sales by firms outside this industry.包括本行業以外廠家的銷售。"o" stands for "others". "o" 代表"其他產品"。

1610: Tobacco Stemming and Redrying 煙葉複烤業

The industry accounts for 0.099% of the total revenue of China's industrial sector in 1996. The revenue growth rate of the industry is 51.9% from 1995, as compared to the growth rate of China's industrial sector, 9.51%. The rate of return on asset is 6.49%. 80.80% of all firms in the industry made a profit while 14.85% had negative returns. The top province in terms of the industry's revenue is Yunnan, accounting for 24.52% of the total revenue.
本行業在1996年佔全行業總產值0.099%，行業年增長率為51.9%（全國工業年增長率9.51%）。行業的資產回報率6.49%，80.80%的企業盈利，14.85%的企業虧損。銷售收入最高的省份為雲南省，佔本行業的24.52%。

	Total number of firms 企業總數	Total number of employees 職工總數	Total revenue (mil. RMB) 總銷售收入（百萬元）	Total profit (mil. RMB) 總利潤（百萬元）	Return on assets 資產利潤率 (%)	Return on equity 權益利潤率 (%)	Labour productivity ('000 RMB / worker) 勞動生產率（千元/人）	Debts / assets 資產負債率 (%)	Total assets (mil. RMB) 總資產（百萬元）
Industry Overall 行業總體	100	23,470	5,748	512	6.49	39.39	244.91	83.51	7,889

	Number of firms 企業個數	Average number of employees 平均職工人數	Average revenue ('000 RMB) 平均銷售收入（千元）	Average profit ('000 RMB) 平均利潤（千元）	Return on assets 資產利潤率 (%)	Return on equity 權益利潤率 (%)	Labour productivity ('000 RMB / worker) 勞動生產率（千元/人）	Average debts / assets 平均資產負債率(%)	Average Total assets ('000 RMB) 平均總資產（千元）
By ownership 產業所有權									
State-owned 國有	82	260	63,415	5,537	6.24	38.84	243.64	83.94	88,793
Collectively-owned 集體	14	103	27,679	3,690	28.31	138.38	269.29	79.54	13,032
Privately-owned 私有									
Domestic JVs 聯營	1	57	45,091	9,892	12.17	-356.53	791.07	103.41	81,272
Joint stock 股份制	1	86	56,551	1,323	4.78	14.96	657.57	68.05	27,687
Foreign-funded 外資	2	273	30,695	-2,748	-1.72	-6.18	112.64	72.11	159,528
Overseas Chinese-funded 港澳台資									
By size 規模									
Large 大型	2	1,375	143,096	6,300	2.51	10.20	104.11	75.40	251,182
Medium 中型	7	402	92,209	4,216	2.85	13.56	229.46	78.96	147,729
Small 小型	91	197	52,939	5,162	7.39	48.93	269.01	84.89	69,822
By regional distribution 地區分布									
Central-North 華北	4	42	11,893	1,530	12.64	39.03	286.57	67.60	12,105
Beijing 北京									
Tianjin 天津									
Hebei 河北	2	30	820	-45	-10.47	14.52	27.33	172.09	430
Shanxi 山西	2	53	22,965	3,105	13.06	38.10	433.30	65.71	23,780
Inner Mongolia 內蒙									
Northeast 東北	13	337	94,937	13,417	13.31	94.33	281.58	85.89	100,788
Liaoning 遼寧	1								
Jilin 吉林	3	282	68,447	7,597	11.90	420.48	243.01	97.18	63,860
Heilongjiang 黑龍江	9	393	114,316	16,848	13.55	84.48	290.80	83.96	124,297
Central East 華東	17	144	47,258	2,620	5.86	27.93	329.26	79.00	44,673
Shanghai 上海									
Jiangsu 江蘇									
Zhejiang 浙江									
Anhui 安徽	2	364	88,500	-2,600	-2.21	-12.24	243.13	81.96	117,795
Fujian 福建	8	55	24,568	1,689	12.49	26.04	444.66	52.05	13,525
Jiangxi 江西	3	41	22,493	-1,023	-5.16	-62.40	553.11	91.75	19,827
Shandong 山東	4	287	90,593	9,825	11.03	65.29	315.65	83.10	89,043
Central-South 中南	22	261	37,809	418	0.56	2.53	144.99	77.70	74,038
Henan 河南	11	255	26,359	107	0.18	0.94	103.52	80.75	58,990
Hubei 湖北	3	628	96,980	2,547	1.32	6.62	154.34	80.01	192,373
Hunan 湖南	1	507	54,510	-4,010	-2.33	-9.29	107.51	74.94	172,260
Guangdong 廣東	3	122	46,507	370	0.60	1.97	380.16	69.37	61,420
Guangxi 廣西	4	44	14,218	820	7.08	14.10	321.30	49.74	11,575
Hainan 海南									
Southwest 西南	31	263	78,963	8,679	7.60	64.71	300.76	88.26	114,266
Chongqing 重慶	2	237	46,062	2,249	5.16	15.35	193.94	66.40	43,612
Sichuan 四川	5	117	19,440	3,334	18.31	89.62	165.02	79.57	18,212
Guizhou 貴州	14	285	60,634	8,530	7.69	74.14	212.91	89.62	110,880
Yunnan 雲南	10	309	140,965	12,845	7.09	62.13	456.49	88.59	181,166
Tibet 西藏									
Northwest 西北	13	200	29,452	701	1.52	5.62	146.98	73.00	46,167
Shaanxi 陝西	7	227	48,110	969	1.53	13.55	212.21	88.71	63,274
Gansu 甘肅	4	247	9,733	205	0.62	0.76	39.36	18.85	33,328
Qinghai 青海									
Ningxia 寧夏	1	29	7,170	1,510	6.31	39.53	247.24	84.04	23,940
Xinjiang 新疆	1								

1610: Tobacco Stemming and Redrying 煙葉複烤業

Year 年份	Number of firms 企業個數	Rate of change 每年變化 (%)	Number of employees 職工人數 (人)	Rate of change 每年變化 (%)	Total revenue (mil. RMB) 總銷售收入 (百萬元)	Rate of change 每年變化 (%)	Total profit (mil. RMB) 總利潤 (百萬元)	Rate of change 每年變化 (%)
1993	112		25,724		3,234		136	
1994	105	-6.25%	21,690	-15.68%	2,397	-25.88%	39	-71.08%
1995	98	-6.67%	24,981	15.17%	3,785	57.90%	249	534.62%
1996	100	2.04%	23,470	-6.05%	5,748	51.86%	512	105.76%

3 Major products* 3 種主要產品 *	Output 產量	Sales volume 銷售量	Unit 單位
a) Redried & Stemmed Tobacco Leaf 複烤煙葉	944,566	859,555	ton 噸

Top 10 firms by revenue (year founded) 收入排名前 10 家企業 (創辦年份)	City 城市	Province 省	Telephone / fax 電話 / 傳真	Number of employees 職工人數	Ownership 產業所有權	Revenue ('000 RMB) 銷售收入 (千元)	Profit ('000 RMB) (rank) 利潤 (千元) (排名)	Total assets ('000 RMB) 總資產 (千元)	Major products 主要產品
Dali Prefecture Redried Factory 大理州複烤廠(1986)	Dali 大理市	Yunnan 雲南省	(0872)3121468 (0872)3121468	1,354	State-owned 國有	748,973	54058(3)	459,999	a
China Tobacco General Company Shandong Company Yishui Tobacco Factory 中國煙草總公司山東省公司沂水煙葉複烤廠(1977)	Linyi 臨沂市	Shandong 山東省	(0539)2252131 (0539)2252131	485	State-owned 國有	304,538	16571(13)	256,328	a
Da Long Tobacco Leaf Redried Factory 大龍煙葉複烤廠(1987)	Tongren 銅仁市	Guizhou 貴州省	(0856)321088	1,191	State-owned 國有	279,972	73459(1)	351,085	a
Guiyang Nanming Tobacco Factory 貴陽南明煙葉複烤廠(1984)	Guiyang 貴陽市	Guizhou 貴州省	(0851)3849914 (0851)3849055	959	State-owned 國有	225,501	26616(5)	632,370	a
Heilongjiang Tobacco Company Boli Tobacco Marketing Company 黑龍江省煙草公司勃利煙葉經銷公司(1982)	Qitaihe 七臺河市	Heilongjiang 黑龍江省	(0453)8521809 (0453)8523926	350	State-owned 國有	197,180	25000(6)	187,890	a
Yunnan Tobacco Wenshan Zhou Tobacco Factory 雲南煙草文山州複烤廠(1996)	Wenshan 文山縣	Yunnan 雲南省	(0876)2120356 (0876)2129771	522	State-owned 國有	173,091	59588(2)	403,164	a
Kunming Cigarette Plant Branch Songming Redried Factory 昆明卷煙廠分廠嵩明複烤廠(1991)	Kunming 昆明市	Yunnan 雲南省	(0871)7911351	490	State-owned 國有	170,442	1118(40)	207,850	a
Heilong Jiang Tobacco Co. Suihua Tobacco Leaf Marking Co. 黑龍江省煙草公司綏化煙葉經銷公司(1983)	Suihua 綏化市	Heilongjiang 黑龍江省	(0455)8223782 (0455)8223782	612	State-owned 國有	158,796	33308(4)	150,243	a
E Xi Tobacco Leaf Redried Factory 鄂西煙葉複烤廠(1986)	Enshi 恩施市	Hubei 湖北省	(0718)8224467	639	State-owned 國有	149,141	6611(22)	312,575	o
Heilongjiang Tobacco Company Jixian Tobacco Leaf Marketing Company 黑龍江省煙草公司集賢煙葉經銷公司(1989)	Shuangyashan 雙鴨山市	Heilongjiang 黑龍江省	(0454)4662181 (0454)4665127	166	State-owned 國有	144,439	21105(9)	156,074	a

Top 10 Cities by Production Output 產出排名前 10 位城市	Province 省	Market share 市場份額	Number of firms 企業個數
Kunming 昆明市	Yunnan 雲南省	15.51%	3
Chuxiong 楚雄市	Yunnan 雲南省	13.69%	1
Dali 大理市	Yunnan 雲南省	8.59%	1
Gejiu 個舊市	Yunnan 雲南省	4.81%	2
Tongren 銅仁市	Guizhou 貴州省	4.59%	1
Weifang 濰坊市	Shandong 山東省	4.55%	1
Harbin 哈爾濱市	Heilongjiang 黑龍江省	4.10%	1
Linyi 臨沂市	Shandong 山東省	2.58%	2
Xianyang 咸陽市	Shaanxi 陝西省	2.48%	4
Suihua 綏化市	Heilongjiang 黑龍江省	2.47%	4

10 Major Wholesalers 10 家主要批發商	City 城市	Province 省	Telephone / Fax 電話 / 傳真
China Tobacco General Company Henan Company 中國煙草總公司河南省公司	Zhengzhou 鄭州市	Henan 河南省	(0371)5957503 (0371)5957096
Guiyang Cigarette Marketing Company 貴陽卷煙銷售公司	Guiyang 貴陽市	Guizhou 貴州省	(0851)06857369 (0851)06857521
Jiangsu Tobacco Company Xuzhou Branch 江蘇煙草公司徐州分公司	Xuzhou 徐州市	Jiangsu 江蘇省	(0516)3673208 (0516)3579838
Sichuan Tobacco Company Fuling Tobacco Diao Bo Supply Station 四川省煙草公司涪陵煙草調撥供應站	Chongqing 重慶市	Chongqing 重慶市	(023)2224713
Yunnan Tobacco Co. Goods and form A Complete Set or System Branch Co. 雲南省煙草公司物資配套分公司	Kunming 昆明市	Yunnan 雲南省	(0871)5328136 (0871)5328136
Fujian Tobacco Company 福建省煙草公司	Fuzhou 福州市	Fujian 福建省	(0591)7713388 (0591)7723940
Zhunyi Cigarette Marketing Company 遵義卷煙銷售公司	Zunyi 遵義市	Guizhou 貴州省	(0852)7223545 (0852)7223545
Zhuzhou Tobacco Company 株洲市煙草公司	Zhuzhou 株洲市	Hunan 湖南省	(0733)8223576
Chongqing Tobacco Company 重慶市煙草公司	Chongqing 重慶市	Chongqing 重慶市	(023)63835131 (023)63819214
Sichuan Tobacco Company Chengdu Branch 四川省煙草公司成都分公司	Chengdu 成都市	Sichuan 四川省	(028)5547994 (028)5547994

*Also include sales by firms outside this industry.包括本行業以外廠家的銷售。"o" stands for "others". "o" 代表 "其他產品" 。

1620: Cigarettes 卷煙製造業

The industry accounts for 1.914% of the total revenue of China's industrial sector in 1996. The revenue growth rate of the industry is 16.5% from 1995, as compared to the growth rate of China's industrial sector, 9.51%. The rate of return on asset is 8.29%. 68.56% of all firms in the industry made a profit while 20.49% had negative returns. The top province in terms of the industry's revenue is Yunnan, accounting for 31.03% of the total revenue.

本行業在1996年佔全行業總產值1.914%，行業年增長率為16.5%（全國工業年增長率9.51%）。行業的資產回報率8.29%，68.56%的企業盈利，20.49%的企業虧損。銷售收入最高的省份為雲南省，佔本行業的31.03%。

	Total number of firms 企業總數	Total number of employees 職工總數	Total revenue (mil. RMB) 總銷售收入（百萬元）	Total profit (mil. RMB) 總利潤（百萬元）	Return on assets 資產利潤率 (%)	Return on equity 權益利潤率 (%)	Labour productivity ('000 RMB / worker) 勞動生產率（千元/人）	Debts / assets 資產負債率 (%)	Total assets (mil. RMB) 總資產（百萬元）
Industry Overall 行業總體	258	277,723	110,927	11,427	8.29	20.77	399.42	60.08	137,805

	Number of firms 企業個數	Average number of employees 平均職工人數	Average revenue ('000 RMB) 平均銷售收入（千元）	Average profit ('000 RMB) 平均利潤（千元）	Return on assets 資產利潤率 (%)	Return on equity 權益利潤率 (%)	Labour productivity ('000 RMB / worker) 勞動生產率（千元/人）	Average debts / assets 平均資產負債率(%)	Average Total assets ('000 RMB) 平均總資產（千元）
By ownership 產業所有權									
State-owned 國有	199	1,324	543,889	56,849	8.48	21.09	410.87	59.78	670,332
Collectively-owned 集體	50	261	41,329	270	0.40	1.64	158.26	75.39	66,938
Privately-owned 私有									
Domestic JVs 聯營	1	25	1,869	-7	-0.21	-0.48	74.78	55.73	3,307
Joint stock 股份制	2	169	40,150	3,639	9.65	23.81	238.28	59.49	37,730
Foreign-funded 外資	3	155	161,741	52,081	26.69	47.89	1041.25	44.28	195,153
Overseas Chinese-funded 港澳台資	3	66	8,856	-18,288	-14.88	-35.10	134.87	57.60	122,893
By size 規模									
Large 大型	40	2,886	1,930,615	279,156	12.73	26.19	668.93	51.40	2,193,174
Medium 中型	89	1,301	315,623	3,623	0.79	3.13	242.64	74.71	457,436
Small 小型	129	359	43,502	-478	-0.66	-2.97	121.01	77.83	72,612
By regional distribution 地區分布									
Central-North 華北	14	1,332	271,952	3,599	0.92	3.97	204.15	76.82	390,838
Beijing 北京	4	252	156,793	480	0.28	0.50	622.19	43.36	169,225
Tianjin 天津	1	3,757	316,690				84.29	101.44	783,870
Hebei 河北	3	2,792	647,483	9,607	1.14	5.30	231.88	78.55	844,903
Shanxi 山西	3	969	124,230	6,337	2.89	13.94	128.25	79.25	219,147
Inner Mongolia 內蒙	3	867	182,777	210	0.08	0.29	210.73	73.59	272,937
Northeast 東北	20	1,021	161,967	1,705	0.71	2.11	158.61	66.19	238,868
Liaoning 遼寧	4	1,459	143,690	7,283	1.95	9.99	98.49	80.46	373,193
Jilin 吉林	7	973	133,161	-1,727	-0.95	-2.52	136.82	62.07	181,051
Heilongjiang 黑龍江	9	864	192,493	1,894	0.85	2.02	222.85	58.21	224,137
Central East 華東	53	1,074	451,867	40,579	7.23	15.92	420.83	54.56	560,981
Shanghai 上海	3	2,216	1,677,393	269,737	9.21	13.70	757.06	32.79	2,928,787
Jiangsu 江蘇	7	707	359,751	32,721	9.66	28.15	508.74	65.68	338,734
Zhejiang 浙江	4	1,057	522,763	30,585	4.29	9.19	494.45	53.30	712,710
Anhui 安徽	11	1,348	492,650	11,532	2.15	7.58	365.44	71.66	536,812
Fujian 福建	7	676	340,094	18,573	4.38	11.73	502.89	62.69	424,287
Jiangxi 江西	8	669	121,986	2,753	1.55	11.32	182.27	86.31	177,519
Shandong 山東	13	1,244	425,522	54,708	13.10	28.62	342.19	54.22	417,583
Central-South 中南	101	942	303,851	9,412	2.78	8.10	322.47	65.74	339,062
Henan 河南	27	1,091	264,623	2,471	0.87	4.91	242.58	82.30	284,463
Hubei 湖北	26	821	215,559	6,430	2.47	9.54	262.52	74.09	260,059
Hunan 湖南	20	1,354	542,704	22,103	3.81	7.85	400.90	51.49	580,137
Guangdong 廣東	13	622	356,755	14,991	3.59	8.29	573.56	56.69	417,622
Guangxi 廣西	14	594	153,696	5,441	3.43	15.51	258.96	77.91	158,811
Hainan 海南	1	897	296,000	3,580	0.65	2.36	329.99	72.37	548,090
Southwest 西南	50	1,363	914,126	164,533	13.90	31.73	670.88	56.19	1,183,725
Chongqing 重慶	10	948	206,289	-2,239	-0.94	-7.73	217.59	87.84	238,012
Sichuan 四川	12	906	311,560	12,271	3.51	13.89	343.68	74.71	349,194
Guizhou 貴州	12	1,302	433,117	1,642	0.23	1.83	332.74	87.33	707,214
Yunnan 雲南	15	2,082	2,294,607	538,203	18.43	34.46	1102.08	46.52	2,920,315
Tibet 西藏									
Northwest 西北	20	922	176,829	737	0.34	1.54	191.76	78.22	219,638
Shaanxi 陝西	12	1,136	203,488	1,383	0.56	3.40	179.10	83.62	248,098
Gansu 甘肅	4	699	153,890	2,980	1.41	4.45	220.31	68.26	211,088
Qinghai 青海	1	419	45,740	-8,340	-9.95	-27.43	109.16	63.72	83,800
Ningxia 寧夏	1	610	67,330	-9,840	-6.35	-24.72	110.38	74.31	154,860
Xinjiang 新疆	2	493	183,045	2,200	1.32	3.37	371.29	60.75	166,285

1620: Cigarettes 卷煙製造業

Year 年份	Number of firms 企業個數	Rate of change 每年變化 (%)	Number of employees 職工人數 (人)	Rate of change 每年變化 (%)	Total revenue (mil. RMB) 總銷售收入 (百萬元)	Rate of change 每年變化 (%)	Total profit (mil. RMB) 總利潤 (百萬元)	Rate of change 每年變化 (%)
1993	196		301,689		75,447		3,497	
1994	208	6.12%	229,479	-23.94%	85,166	12.88%	10,944	212.95%
1995	267	28.37%	298,166	29.93%	95,202	11.78%	12,315	12.53%
1996	258	-3.37%	277,723	-6.86%	110,927	16.52%	11,427	-7.21%

3 Major products* 3 種主要產品 *	Output 產量	Sales volume 銷售量	Unit 單位
a) No.1 Cigarette 一類卷煙	1,882,651	1,844,998	box 箱
b) No.2 Cigarette 二類卷煙	14,981,605	14,831,789	box 箱
c) No.3 Cigarette 三類卷煙	12,805,434	12,805,434	box 箱

Top 10 firms by revenue (year founded) 收入排名前 10 家企業 (創辦年份)	City 城市	Province 省	Telephone / fax 電話 / 傳真	Number of employees 職工人數	Ownership 產業所有權	Revenue ('000 RMB) 銷售收入 (千元)	Profit ('000 RMB) (rank) 利潤 (千元) (排名)	Total assets ('000 RMB) 總資產 (千元)	Major products 主要產品
Yuxi Hong Ta Tobacco (Group) Co. Ltd. 玉溪紅塔煙草(集團)有限責任公司(1957)	Yuxi 玉溪市	Yunnan 雲南省	(0877)2968872 (0877)2968872	5,380	State-owned 國有	18,944,702	6074226(1)	22,249,545	a,b,c
Kunming Cigarette Factory 昆明卷煙廠(1942)	Kunming 昆明市	Yunnan 雲南省	(0871)5818118 (0871)5812822	5,485	State-owned 國有	5,638,834	1006412(2)	6,138,398	a,b,c
Shanghai Tobacco (Group) Corp. 上海煙草(集團)公司(1993)	Shanghai 上海市	Shanghai 上海市	(021)65127623 (021)65129500	6,421	State-owned 國有	4,983,020	838685(3)	8,429,940	a,b,c
Changde Cigarette Factory 常德卷煙廠(1951)	Changde 常德市	Hunan 湖南省	(0736)7288888 (0736)7286888	4,692	State-owned 國有	2,711,260	100000(13)	2,220,760	a,b,c
Guiyang Cigarette Factory 貴陽卷煙廠(1940)	Guiyang 貴陽市	Guizhou 貴州省	(0851)5841288 (0851)5822791	6,393	State-owned 國有	2,453,169	16847(39)	4,064,108	a,b,c
Qujing Cigarette Factory 曲靖卷煙廠(1973)	Qujing 曲靖市	Yunnan 雲南省	(0874)3511001 (0874)3511040	3,532	State-owned 國有	2,245,401	511134(4)	2,956,305	a,b,c
Chuxiong Cigarette Factory, Yunnan 雲南楚雄卷煙廠(1976)	Chuxiong 楚雄市	Yunnan 雲南省	(0878)3122929 (0878)3122782	3,186	State-owned 國有	2,175,288	25142(31)	2,792,413	b,c
Ji'nan Cigarette Factory 濟南卷煙廠(1928)	Ji'nan 濟南市	Shandong 山東省	(0531)8960088 (0531)8962427	2,695	State-owned 國有	2,052,420	200324(7)	1,685,983	a,b,c
Bengbu Cigarette Factory 蚌埠卷煙廠(1949)	Bengbu 蚌埠市	Anhui 安徽省	(0552)4082440 (0552)4081534	3,413	State-owned 國有	2,023,627	89305(16)	2,071,621	a,b,c
Yi Zhong Tobacco (Group) Co. Ltd. 頤中煙草(集團)有限公司(1995)	Qingdao 青島市	Shandong 山東省	(0532)3834361 (0532)3834769	3,607	State-owned 國有	1,988,787	319792(5)	1,793,211	a,c

Top 10 Cities by Production Output 產出排名前 10 位城市	Province 省	Market share 市場份額	Number of firms 企業個數
Kunming 昆明市	Yunnan 雲南省	5.96%	3
Shanghai 上海市	Shanghai 上海市	5.13%	3
Changsha 長沙市	Hunan 湖南省	4.65%	1
Foshan 佛山市	Guangdong 廣東省	4.33%	1
Zhengzhou 鄭州市	Henan 河南省	3.37%	5
Guangzhou 廣州市	Guangdong 廣東省	2.84%	2
Yuxi 玉溪市	Yunnan 雲南省	2.81%	1
Changde 常德市	Hunan 湖南省	2.63%	1
Qujing 曲靖市	Yunnan 雲南省	2.61%	2
Nanning 南寧市	Guangxi 廣西省	2.47%	2

10 Major Wholesalers 10 家主要批發商	City 城市	Province 省	Telephone / Fax 電話 / 傳真
China Tobacco General Company Henan Company 中國煙草總公司河南省公司	Zhengzhou 鄭州市	Henan 河南省	(0371)5957503 (0371)5957096
Guiyang Cigarette Marketing Company 貴陽卷煙銷售公司	Guiyang 貴陽市	Guizhou 貴州省	(0851)06857369 (0851)06857521
Jiangsu Tobacco Company Xuzhou Branch 江蘇煙草公司徐州分公司	Xuzhou 徐州市	Jiangsu 江蘇省	(0516)3673208 (0516)3579838
Sichuan Tobacco Company Fuling Tobacco Diao Bo Supply Station 四川省煙草公司涪陵煙草調撥供應站	Chongqing 重慶市	Chongqing 重慶市	(023)2224713
Yunnan Tobacco Co. Goods and Form A Complete Set or System Branch Co. 雲南省煙草公司物資配套分公司	Kunming 昆明市	Yunnan 雲南省	(0871)5328136 (0871)5328136
Fujian Tobacco Company 福建省煙草公司	Fuzhou 福州市	Fujian 福建省	(0591)7713388 (0591)7723940
Zhunyi Cigarette Marketing Company 遵義卷煙銷售公司	Zunyi 遵義市	Guizhou 貴州省	(0852)7223545 (0852)7223545
Zhuzhou Tobacco Company 株洲市煙草公司	Zhuzhou 株洲市	Hunan 湖南省	(0733)8223576
Chongqing Tobacco Company 重慶市煙草公司	Chongqing 重慶市	Chongqing 重慶市	(023)63835131 (023)63819214
Sichuan Tobacco Company Chengdu Branch 四川省煙草公司成都分公司	Chengdu 成都市	Sichuan 四川省	(028)5547994 (028)5547994

*Also include sales by firms outside this industry.包括本行業以外廠家的銷售。"o" stands for "others". "o" 代表 "其他產品"。

1690: Other Tobacco 其他煙草加工業

The industry accounts for 0.023% of the total revenue of China's industrial sector in 1996. The revenue growth rate of the industry is 183.9% from 1995, as compared to the growth rate of China's industrial sector, 9.51%. The rate of return on asset is 1.82%. 61.28% of all firms in the industry made a profit while 33.96% had negative returns. The top province in terms of the industry's revenue is Guangdong, accounting for 67.95% of the total revenue.
本行業在1996年佔全行業總產值0.023%，行業年增長率為183.9%（全國工業年增長率9.51%）。行業的資產回報率1.82%，61.28%的企業盈利，33.96%的企業虧損。銷售收入最高的省份為廣東省，佔本行業的67.95%。

	Total number of firms 企業總數	Total number of employees 職工總數	Total revenue (mil. RMB) 總銷售收入（百萬元）	Total profit (mil. RMB) 總利潤（百萬元）	Return on assets 資產利潤率 (%)	Return on equity 權益利潤率 (%)	Labour productivity ('000 RMB / worker) 勞動生產率（千元/人）	Debts / assets 資產負債率 (%)	Total assets (mil. RMB) 總資產（百萬元）
Industry Overall 行業總體	58	7,544	1,313	32	1.82	4.36	174.05	58.22	1,731

	Number of firms 企業個數	Average number of employees 平均職工人數	Average revenue ('000 RMB) 平均銷售收入（千元）	Average profit ('000 RMB) 平均利潤（千元）	Return on assets 資產利潤率 (%)	Return on equity 權益利潤率 (%)	Labour productivity ('000 RMB / worker) 勞動生產率（千元/人）	Average debts / assets 平均資產負債率(%)	Average Total assets ('000 RMB) 平均總資產（千元）
By ownership 產業所有權									
State-owned 國有	23	180	30,435	174	0.40	1.31	169.41	69.32	43,217
Collectively-owned 集體	32	101	17,374	630	3.45	6.90	172.88	49.99	18,243
Privately-owned 私有									
Domestic JVs 聯營	1	151	21,611	6,620	8.26	10.48	143.12	21.23	80,190
Joint stock 股份制									
Foreign-funded 外資									
Overseas Chinese-funded 港澳台資	2	23	17,659	617	1.69	1.96	784.83	13.84	36,463
By size 規模									
Large 大型									
Medium 中型	2	407	59,858	4,232	3.05	6.69	147.25	54.44	138,947
Small 小型	55	122	21,695	428	1.62	3.95	177.46	58.96	26,420
By regional distribution 地區分布									
Central-North 華北	2								
Beijing 北京	1								
Tianjin 天津									
Hebei 河北									
Shanxi 山西									
Inner Mongolia 內蒙	1								
Northeast 東北	2	167	4,680	200	4.09	6.91	28.11	40.80	4,890
Liaoning 遼寧	2	167	4,680	200	4.09	6.91	28.11	40.80	4,890
Jilin 吉林									
Heilongjiang 黑龍江									
Central East 華東	11	213	25,892	325	1.01	2.83	121.51	64.09	31,986
Shanghai 上海	1	365	56,590	520	0.49	1.84	155.04	73.25	105,850
Jiangsu 江蘇	2	231	74,605	595	0.92	2.04	322.97	54.96	64,690
Zhejiang 浙江	2	75	7,655	1,000	16.45	31.45	102.07	47.70	6,080
Anhui 安徽	2	398	24,865	-325	-1.14	-15.40	62.47	92.56	28,445
Fujian 福建	3	54	1,393	3	0.22	0.45	25.96	50.66	1,507
Jiangxi 江西									
Shandong 山東	1	410	9,790	500	1.16	1.86	23.88	37.44	43,050
Central-South 中南	23	158	43,662	1,222	2.09	4.83	276.87	56.60	58,324
Henan 河南	1	60	1,680				28.00	79.49	4,340
Hubei 湖北	2	69	15,975	-115	-0.72	-18.70	231.52	96.16	16,005
Hunan 湖南	2	182	39,100	1,550	11.99	31.38	214.84	61.74	12,925
Guangdong 廣東	16	191	55,763	1,582	1.98	4.44	292.05	55.41	79,914
Guangxi 廣西	2	5	95	-40	-12.70	-160.00	19.00	92.06	315
Hainan 海南									
Southwest 西南	5	126	1,706	72	5.32	15.13	13.54	64.84	1,354
Chongqing 重慶									
Sichuan 四川	1	28	1,170	40	4.04	57.15	41.79	92.93	990
Guizhou 貴州									
Yunnan 雲南	4	151	1,840	80	5.54	13.85	12.23	60.03	1,445
Tibet 西藏									
Northwest 西北	15	41	435	-60	-4.23	-13.66	10.69	69.00	1,419
Shaanxi 陜西									
Gansu 甘肅	7	69	651	-134	-5.57	-25.20	9.50	77.83	2,410
Qinghai 青海									
Ningxia 寧夏									
Xinjiang 新疆	8	16	245	5	0.90	1.40	15.08	35.29	553

1690: Other Tobacco 其他煙草加工業

Year 年份	Number of firms 企業個數	Rate of change 每年變化 (%)	Number of employees 職工人數（人）	Rate of change 每年變化 (%)	Total revenue (mil. RMB) 總銷售收入（百萬元）	Rate of change 每年變化 (%)	Total profit (mil. RMB) 總利潤（百萬元）	Rate of change 每年變化 (%)
1993	78		11,978		755		40	
1994	72	-7.69%	7,476	-37.59%	664	-12.07%	32	-20.43%
1995	58	-19.45%	5,710	-23.62%	463	-30.30%	20	-38.10%
1996	58	0	7,544	32.12%	1,313	183.89%	32	63.08%

3 Major products* 3種主要產品*	Output 產量	Sales volume 銷售量	Unit 單位
a) Tobacco Tow 用絲束	62,881	58,479	ton 噸
b) No.3 Cigarette 三類卷煙	160,455	160,455	box 箱

Top 10 firms by revenue (year founded) 收入排名前10家企業（創辦年份）	City 城市	Province 省	Telephone / fax 電話 / 傳真	Number of employees 職工人數	Ownership 產業所有權	Revenue ('000 RMB) 銷售收入（千元）	Profit ('000 RMB) (rank) 利潤（千元）（排名）	Total assets ('000 RMB) 總資產（千元）	Major products 主要產品
Guangdong Meizhou Cigarette Factory 廣東梅州卷煙廠(1939)	Meizhou 梅州市	Guangdong 廣東省	(0752)2359066 (0752)2354508	1,267	State-owned 國有	441,642	6342(2)	496,010	b
Zhuhai Acetic Acid Fiber Co. Ltd. 珠海醋酸纖維有限公司(1993)	Zhuhai 珠海市	Guangdong 廣東省	(0756)8619933 (0756)8618654	429	Foreign-funded 外資	354,474	18620(1)	508,979	a
Nantong Filter-tip Experiment Mill 南通煙濾嘴實驗工廠(1981)	Nantong 南通市	Jiangsu 江蘇省	(0513)5517171 (0513)5511096	434	State-owned 國有	148,940	1037(5)	128,522	o
Shanghai Tobacco Material Factory 上海煙草材料廠(1980)	Shanghai 上海市	Shanghai 上海市	(021)65414645 (021)65450913	367	Collectively-owned 集體	56,591	518(6)	105,851	o
Zhuhai Sez Tobacco Processing Dept. 珠海經濟特區煙草加工部(1987)	Zhuhai 珠海市	Guangdong 廣東省	(0756)8611971 (0756)8611974	1	Domestic JVs 聯營	36,195	3090(3)	30,346	o
Bengbu Tobacco Branch Co. No.2 Cigarette Material Factory 蚌埠煙草分公司第二卷煙材料廠(1991)	Bengbu 蚌埠市	Anhui 安徽省	(0552)4011713	653	Collectively-owned 集體	30,650	-653(18)	9,651	o
Heshan Cut Tobacco Factory 鶴山煙絲廠(1956)	Jiangmen 江門市	Guangdong 廣東省	(0750)8888467	187	State-owned 國有	24,440	-1320(21)	27,171	a
E'xi Cigarette Material Factory 恩施州卷煙材料廠(1990)	Enshi 恩施市	Hubei 湖北省	(0718)8224948	125	State-owned 國有	21,683	-760(19)	29,725	o
Anhui Cigarette Filter-tip Tows General Factory 安徽煙用濾嘴絲束總廠(1990)	Bengbu 蚌埠市	Anhui 安徽省	(0552)4021274	173	State-owned 國有	19,083	1(15)	47,234	a
Ningbo Jinye Tobacco Factory 寧波金葉煙絲廠(1993)	Ningbo 寧波市	Zhejiang 浙江省	(0574)7337150	116	Domestic JVs 聯營	14,099	2000(4)	10,958	o

Top 10 Cities by Production Output 產出排名前10位城市	Province 省	Market share 市場份額	Number of firms 企業個數
Meizhou 梅州市	Guangdong 廣東省	40.41%	1
Zhuhai 珠海市	Guangdong 廣東省	35.69%	2
Beijing 北京市	Beijing 北京市	6.01%	1
Shanghai 上海市	Shanghai 上海市	5.18%	3
Jiangmen 江門市	Guangdong 廣東省	2.59%	3
Bengbu 蚌埠市	Anhui 安徽省	1.72%	2
Fuzhou 福州市	Fujian 福建省	1.51%	2
Zhanjiang 湛江市	Guangdong 廣東省	1.38%	4
Enshi 恩施市	Hubei 湖北省	1.17%	1
Yuxi 玉溪市	Yunnan 雲南省	0.66%	2

10 Major Wholesalers 10家主要批發商	City 城市	Province 省	Telephone / Fax 電話 / 傳真
China Tobacco General Company Henan Company 中國煙草總公司河南省公司	Zhengzhou 鄭州市	Henan 河南省	(0371)5957503 (0371)5957096
Guiyang Cigarette Marketing Company 貴陽卷煙銷售公司	Guiyang 貴陽市	Guizhou 貴州省	(0851)06857369 (0851)06857521
Jiangsu Tobacco Company Xuzhou Branch 江蘇煙草公司徐州分公司	Xuzhou 徐州市	Jiangsu 江蘇省	(0516)3673208 (0516)3579838
Sichuan Tobacco Company Fuling Tobacco Diao Bo Supply Station 四川省煙草公司涪陵煙草調撥供應站	Chongqing 重慶市	Chongqing 重慶市	(023)2224713
Yunnan Tobacco Co. Goods and form A Complete Set or System Branch Co. 雲南省煙草公司物資配套分公司	Kunming 昆明市	Yunnan 雲南省	(0871)5328136 (0871)5328136
Fujian Tobacco Company 福建省煙草公司	Fuzhou 福州市	Fujian 福建省	(0591)7713388 (0591)7723940
Zhunyi Cigarette Marketing Company 遵義卷煙銷售公司	Zunyi 遵義市	Guizhou 貴州省	(0852)7223545 (0852)7223545
Zhuzhou Tobacco Company 株洲市煙草公司	Zhuzhou 株洲市	Hunan 湖南省	(0733)8223576
Chongqing Tobacco Company 重慶市煙草公司	Chongqing 重慶市	Chongqing 重慶市	(023)63835131 (023)63819214
Sichuan Tobacco Company Chengdu Branch 四川省煙草公司成都分公司	Chengdu 成都市	Sichuan 四川省	(028)5547994 (028)5547994

*Also include sales by firms outside this industry.包括本行業以外廠家的銷售。"o" stands for "others". "o" 代表 "其他產品"。

1711: Cotton Ginning 軋花業

The industry accounts for 0.363% of the total revenue of China's industrial sector in 1996. The revenue growth rate of the industry is 17.9% from 1995, as compared to the growth rate of China's industrial sector, 9.51%. The rate of return on asset is 0.79%. 63.94% of all firms in the industry made a profit while 19.20% had negative returns. The top province in terms of the industry's revenue is Shandong, accounting for 30.19% of the total revenue.
本行業在1996年佔全行業總產值0.363%，行業年增長率為17.9%（全國工業年增長率9.51%）。行業的資產回報率0.79%，63.94%的企業盈利，19.20%的企業虧損。銷售收入最高的省份為山東省，佔本行業的30.19%。

	Total number of firms 企業總數	Total number of employees 職工總數	Total revenue (mil. RMB) 總銷售收入（百萬元）	Total profit (mil. RMB) 總利潤（百萬元）	Return on assets 資產利潤率 (%)	Return on equity 權益利潤率 (%)	Labour productivity ('000 RMB / worker) 勞動生產率（千元/人）	Debts / assets 資產負債率 (%)	Total assets (mil. RMB) 總資產（百萬元）
Industry Overall 行業總體	1,612	270,401	21,053	256	0.79	5.25	77.86	84.96	32,395

	Number of firms 企業個數	Average number of employees 平均職工人數	Average revenue ('000 RMB) 平均銷售收入（千元）	Average profit ('000 RMB) 平均利潤（千元）	Return on assets 資產利潤率 (%)	Return on equity 權益利潤率 (%)	Labour productivity ('000 RMB / worker) 勞動生產率（千元/人）	Average debts / assets 平均資產負債率(%)	Average Total assets ('000 RMB) 平均總資產（千元）
By ownership 產業所有權									
State-owned 國有	176	135	14,420	267	1.61	8.92	107.01	81.92	16,563
Collectively-owned 集體	1,422	172	12,856	144	0.70	4.80	74.76	85.39	20,514
Privately-owned 私有	1	5	1,140	47	19.56	181.23	227.98	89.20	242
Domestic JVs 聯營	2	120	8,959	-50	-0.18	-4.00	74.66	95.43	27,164
Joint stock 股份制	3	322	26,070	613	1.59	11.33	81.05	85.99	38,636
Foreign-funded 外資	4	357	26,989	615	2.49	4.53	75.55	45.11	24,713
Overseas Chinese-funded 港澳台資	4	56	6,952	27	0.27	0.98	124.70	72.40	10,114
By size 規模									
Large 大型	7	973	82,866	952	0.78	4.73	85.18	83.47	121,660
Medium 中型	81	477	38,290	193	0.31	1.75	80.33	82.12	61,631
Small 小型	1,517	148	11,450	154	0.88	6.09	77.22	85.54	17,503
By regional distribution 地區分布									
Central-North 華北	319	87	7,317	217	1.91	11.99	83.75	84.04	11,341
Beijing 北京	5	42	3,948	126	3.25	32.14	93.11	89.88	3,872
Tianjin 天津	5	24	40,462	2,004	5.27	10.02	1714.49	47.39	38,014
Hebei 河北	258	96	7,704	226	1.79	13.00	80.32	86.24	12,648
Shanxi 山西	49	55	2,513	4	0.12	0.68	45.48	81.64	2,950
Inner Mongolia 內蒙	2	42	570	30	10.53	85.71	13.57	87.72	285
Northeast 東北	6	65	742	7	0.47	11.11	11.35	95.90	1,422
Liaoning 遼寧	2	31	280				9.03	93.13	655
Jilin 吉林	1	112	1,300	20	1.30	100.00	11.61	98.70	1,540
Heilongjiang 黑龍江	3	73	863	7	0.35	8.00	11.88	95.77	1,893
Central East 華東	832	225	17,051	209	0.74	5.05	75.93	85.30	28,157
Shanghai 上海	8	43	3,205	174	2.79	3.93	74.10	29.05	6,230
Jiangsu 江蘇	202	294	18,265	338	1.74	7.11	62.14	75.57	19,431
Zhejiang 浙江	33	88	10,707	98	0.90	4.34	121.72	79.21	10,848
Anhui 安徽	141	168	23,399	419	1.91	15.87	139.43	87.96	21,944
Fujian 福建									
Jiangxi 江西	83	127	5,585	41	0.31	2.73	44.14	88.47	13,026
Shandong 山東	365	247	17,411	105	0.26	2.04	70.57	87.42	40,872
Central-South 中南	326	135	11,259	3	0.03	0.18	83.13	84.03	11,722
Henan 河南	179	163	10,053	-148	-1.17	-8.99	61.79	86.99	12,625
Hubei 湖北	96	96	11,643	276	3.70	20.13	121.56	81.63	7,471
Hunan 湖南	46	106	14,701	-11	-0.07	-0.47	139.08	85.66	16,612
Guangdong 廣東	4	244	19,295	380	1.90	2.03	79.00	6.62	20,003
Guangxi 廣西	1								
Hainan 海南									
Southwest 西南	11	358	11,429	35	0.36	2.04	31.90	82.24	9,767
Chongqing 重慶									
Sichuan 四川	11	358	11,429	35	0.36	2.02	31.92	82.24	9,767
Guizhou 貴州									
Yunnan 雲南									
Tibet 西藏									
Northwest 西北	118	61	6,202	97	0.81	5.19	101.67	84.37	11,976
Shaanxi 陝西	78	58	1,971	-26	-0.32	-1.69	34.27	81.02	7,995
Gansu 甘肅	8	115	42,078	1,041	2.20	24.70	365.49	91.11	47,394
Qinghai 青海	1	15	300	70	12.28	15.56	20.00	21.05	570
Ningxia 寧夏									
Xinjiang 新疆	31	57	7,780	164	1.24	7.42	135.81	83.32	13,218

1711: Cotton Ginning 軋花業

Year 年份	Number of firms 企業個數	Rate of change 每年變化 (%)	Number of employees 職工人數（人）	Rate of change 每年變化 (%)	Total revenue (mil. RMB) 總銷售收入（百萬元）	Rate of change 每年變化 (%)	Total profit (mil. RMB) 總利潤（百萬元）	Rate of change 每年變化 (%)
1993	1,447		215,315		10,848		104	
1994	1,477	2.07%	213,612	-0.79%	10,428	-3.87%	262	152.31%
1995	1,591	7.72%	258,896	21.20%	17,858	71.24%	307	17.47%
1996	1,612	1.32%	270,401	4.44%	21,053	17.89%	256	-16.68%

3 Major products* 3 種主要產品 *	Output 產量	Sales volume 銷售量	Unit 單位
a) Cotton Lint 皮棉	1,304,517	1,174,065	ton 噸
b) Cotton Short-staple 棉短絨	288,002	267,842	ton 噸

Top 10 firms by revenue (year founded) 收入排名前 10 家企業（創辦年份）	City 城市	Province 省	Telephone / fax 電話 / 傳真	Number of employees 職工人數	Ownership 產業所有權	Revenue ('000 RMB) 銷售收入（千元）	Profit ('000 RMB) (rank) 利潤（千元）（排名）	Total assets ('000 RMB) 總資產（千元）	Major products 主要產品
Jiangsu State-owned Dong Xin Farm Cotton Ginning Mill 江蘇省國營東辛農場軋花廠(1983)	Lianyungang 連雲港市	Jiangsu 江蘇省	(0518)5498515 (0518)5498515	290	State-owned 國有	255,010	19016(1)	110,243	a,b
Zhangqiu Cotton & Linen Company 章丘市棉麻公司(1958)	Ji'nan 濟南市	Shandong 山東省	(0531)3651501 (0531)3651743	1,232	Collectively-owned 集體	206,815	996(83)	181,583	a,b
Viction (Tianjin) Industrial & Trade Co. Ltd. 維信(天津)工貿有限公司(1992)	Tianjin 天津市	Tianjin 天津市	(022)25701188 (022)25763011	43	Overseas Chinese-funded 港澳台資	197,000	9723(3)	178,652	o
Jinxiang Cotton Processing No.1 Factory 金鄉縣棉花加工一廠(1966)	Jining 濟寧市	Shandong 山東省	(0537)8722754 (0537)8722109	1,980	Collectively-owned 集體	184,943	5328(6)	228,246	a,b
Zibo Cotton Multiple Processing Factory 淄博棉花綜合加工廠(1989)	Zibo 淄博市	Shandong 山東省	(0533)9662076	1,335	Collectively-owned 集體	167,869	901(87)	259,971	a,b
Dunhuang Cotton Co. 敦煌市棉花公司(1956)	Yumen 玉門市	Gansu 甘肅省	(0937)8822340	878	Collectively-owned 集體	164,306	4000(11)	197,078	a
Shouxian Cotton & Linen Industry & Trade Co. Ltd. 壽縣棉麻工貿有限責任公司(1996)	Liu'an 六安市	Anhui 安徽省	(0564)4029343 (0564)4022283	1,671	Collectively-owned 集體	163,517	-4667(1109)	132,185	a,b
Guannan Xin Jin Hua Company 灌南縣新金花公司(1958)	Lianyungang 連雲港市	Jiangsu 江蘇省	(0518)9629102 (0518)3221414	2,812	Collectively-owned 集體	156,559	-7480(1114)	163,300	b
Guanyun Cotton Improved Variety Farm Cotton Ginning Factory 灌雲縣棉花良種場軋花廠(1988)	Lianyungang 連雲港市	Jiangsu 江蘇省	(0518)8641069	572	State-owned 國有	124,470	1796(41)	132,782	a,b
Anhui Dongzhi Cotton & Linen Company 安徽省東至縣棉麻公司(1953)	Guichi 貴池市	Anhui 安徽省	(0566)7011841	224	Collectively-owned 集體	115,756	2034(32)	199,350	a,b

Top 10 Cities by Production Output 產出排名前 10 位城市	Province 省	Market share 市場份額	Number of firms 企業個數
Binzhou 濱州市	Shandong 山東省	6.58%	37
Yancheng 鹽城市	Jiangsu 江蘇省	6.28%	49
Liaocheng 聊城市	Shandong 山東省	4.51%	80
Nanyang 南陽市	Henan 河南省	4.07%	20
Heze 菏澤市	Shandong 山東省	4.01%	62
Dezhou 德州市	Shandong 山東省	3.92%	84
Chaohu 巢湖市	Anhui 安徽省	3.62%	29
Anqing 安慶市	Anhui 安徽省	3.59%	37
Weifang 濰坊市	Shandong 山東省	3.42%	27
Jining 濟寧市	Shandong 山東省	3.19%	31

10 Major Wholesalers 10 家主要批發商	City 城市	Province 省	Telephone / Fax 電話 / 傳真
Anhui Clothing Import & Export Company 安徽省服裝進出口公司	Hefei 合肥市	Anhui 安徽省	(0551)3632212 (0551)3632002
Qingdao Textile Clothing Industrial Group Company 青島紡織服裝實業集團公司	Qingdao 青島市	Shandong 山東省	(0532)2877853 (0532)2869315
Hebei Textile Import & Export (Group) Company 河北省紡織品進出口(集團)公司	Shijiazhuang 石家莊市	Hebei 河北省	(0311)7028530 (0311)7027781
Zhong Fang Pledget Import & Export Company 中紡紗布進出口公司	Beijing 北京市	Beijing 北京市	(010)65124718 (010)65124713
Shaoxing Import & Export Company 紹興市進出口公司	Shaoxing 紹興市	Zhejiang 浙江省	(0575)5132822 (0575)5141577
Hunan Hua Xiang Import & Export (Group) Company 湖南省華湘進出口(集團)公司	Changsha 長沙市	Hunan 湖南省	(0731)2282440 (0731)2286995
City's Import & Export Company Trade Dept. 市進出口公司貿易部	Yichang 宜昌市	Hubei 湖北省	(0717)6450778 (0717)6441875
Shanghai Pu Dong Xinqu Import & Export Company 上海浦東新區進出口公司	Shanghai 上海市	Shanghai 上海市	(021)58878801 (021)58827444
Ningbo Yinxian Import & Export Company 寧波市鄞縣進出口公司	Ningbo 寧波市	Zhejiang 浙江省	(0574)7875205 (0574)7873168
Zhejiang Silk Import & Export Company 浙江省絲綢進出口公司	Hangzhou 杭州市	Zhejiang 浙江省	(0571)5195588 (0571)5192542

*Also include sales by firms outside this industry.包括本行業以外廠家的銷售。"o" stands for "others". "o" 代表 "其他產品"。

1712: Wool Washing 洗毛業

The industry accounts for 0.013% of the total revenue of China's industrial sector in 1996. The revenue growth rate of the industry is 117.4% from 1995, as compared to the growth rate of China's industrial sector, 9.51%. The rate of return on asset is -3.25%. 76.45% of all firms in the industry made a profit while 19.00% had negative returns. The top province in terms of the industry's revenue is Jiangsu, accounting for 21.70% of the total revenue.
本行業在1996年佔全行業總產值0.013%，行業年增長率為117.4%（全國工業年增長率9.51%）。行業的資產回報率-3.25%，76.45%的企業盈利，19.00%的企業虧損。銷售收入最高的省份為江蘇省，佔本行業的21.70%。

	Total number of firms 企業總數	Total number of employees 職工總數	Total revenue (mil. RMB) 總銷售收入（百萬元）	Total profit (mil. RMB) 總利潤（百萬元）	Return on assets 資產利潤率 (%)	Return on equity 權益利潤率 (%)	Labour productivity ('000 RMB / worker) 勞動生產率（千元/人）	Debts / assets 資產負債率 (%)	Total assets (mil. RMB) 總資產（百萬元）
Industry Overall 行業總體	98	15,216	782	-38	-3.25	-17.53	51.39	81.45	1,182

	Number of firms 企業個數	Average number of employees 平均職工人數	Average revenue ('000 RMB) 平均銷售收入（千元）	Average profit ('000 RMB) 平均利潤（千元）	Return on assets 資產利潤率 (%)	Return on equity 權益利潤率 (%)	Labour productivity ('000 RMB / worker) 勞動生產率（千元/人）	Average debts / assets 平均資產負債率(%)	Average Total assets ('000 RMB) 平均總資產（千元）
By ownership 產業所有權									
State-owned 國有	20	337	12,200	-3,000	-8.81	-68.18	36.20	87.08	34,050
Collectively-owned 集體	66	114	6,533	3,217	54.36	221.56	57.07	75.46	5,918
Privately-owned 私有	3	37	16,692	31,890	670.50	911.50	451.13	26.44	4,756
Domestic JVs 聯營	2	98	249	-55,793	-320.53	-1838.55	2.55	82.57	17,406
Joint stock 股份制	2	80	7,898	1,870	18.52	255.94	98.72	92.77	10,101
Foreign-funded 外資	3	108	8,878	-59,153	-628.60	-1613.91	82.46	61.05	9,410
Overseas Chinese-funded 港澳台資	3	44	4,563	-232	-5.41	-11.37	104.51	52.40	4,294
By size 規模									
Large 大型									
Medium 中型	1	1,131	2,181				1.93	79.70	156,216
Small 小型	95	148	8,207	-400	-3.70	-20.29	55.59	81.74	10,798
By regional distribution 地區分布									
Central-North 華北	38	60	5,522	391	9.58	39.23	92.60	75.59	4,086
Beijing 北京	1	165	2,410	10	0.32	0.51	14.61	37.38	3,130
Tianjin 天津	3	37	4,137	227	11.64	23.29	111.80	50.00	1,947
Hebei 河北	15	72	9,363	810	20.37	52.92	130.76	61.52	3,976
Shanxi 山西	1	12	5,900	270	12.00	23.68	491.67	48.89	2,250
Inner Mongolia 內蒙	18	50	2,704	98	2.09	19.73	53.85	89.43	4,688
Northeast 東北	2	324	105				0.32	78.99	40,790
Liaoning 遼寧	1	643	70				0.11	79.03	81,500
Jilin 吉林									
Heilongjiang 黑龍江	1	5	140				28.00	37.50	80
Central East 華東	26	153	8,186	246	2.70	11.91	53.59	77.36	9,130
Shanghai 上海	1	173						71.56	7,350
Jiangsu 江蘇	13	223	13,055	289	1.95	9.05	58.56	78.48	14,849
Zhejiang 浙江	2	187	6,995	15	0.13	0.72	37.51	81.30	11,125
Anhui 安徽	5	48	4,030	440	25.55	43.05	83.61	40.65	1,722
Fujian 福建									
Jiangxi 江西									
Shandong 山東	5	57	1,796	82	6.68	49.40	31.29	86.48	1,228
Central-South 中南	15	190	10,078	-441	-2.27	-6.04	53.00	62.41	19,427
Henan 河南	2	21	320	10	2.08	15.38	15.24	85.42	480
Hubei 湖北	9	282	14,667	-812	-2.61	-7.01	52.01	62.72	31,068
Hunan 湖南									
Guangdong 廣東	4	68	4,633	168	6.19	12.96	68.13	52.26	2,708
Guangxi 廣西									
Hainan 海南									
Southwest 西南	2	64	12,250	-415	-1.89	-7.58	191.41	75.02	21,920
Chongqing 重慶									
Sichuan 四川									
Guizhou 貴州									
Yunnan 雲南									
Tibet 西藏	2	64	12,250	-415	-1.89	-7.58	191.41	75.02	21,920
Northwest 西北	15	357	12,227	-3,482	-14.03	516.11	34.28	102.72	24,814
Shaanxi 陝西	2	179	10,570	1,025	10.67	37.41	59.05	71.47	9,605
Gansu 甘肅	3	106	2,167	-1,393	-27.81	314.29	20.44	108.85	5,010
Qinghai 青海	5	115	5,218	-3,094	-26.28	96.57	45.22	127.21	11,774
Ningxia 寧夏	1	97	2,600	150	1.36	11.28	26.80	87.99	10,990
Xinjiang 新疆	4	1,000	31,768	-8,695	-12.97	-8280.95	31.77	99.85	67,028

1712: Wool Washing 洗毛業

Year 年份	Number of firms 企業個數	Rate of change 每年變化 (%)	Number of employees 職工人數（人）	Rate of change 每年變化 (%)	Total revenue (mil. RMB) 總銷售收入（百萬元）	Rate of change 每年變化 (%)	Total profit (mil. RMB) 總利潤（百萬元）	Rate of change 每年變化 (%)
1993	135		11,389		979		-31	
1994	136	0.74%	12,192	7.05%	863	-11.88%	-16	48.24%
1995	104	-23.53%	8,582	-29.61%	360	-58.33%	-3	83.29%
1996	98	-5.77%	15,216	77.30%	782	117.42%	-38	-1338.30%

3 Major products* 3 種主要產品 *	Output 產量	Sales volume 銷售量	Unit 單位
a) Cotton Yarn 棉紗	8,400	6,804	ton 噸
b) Thread 線	1,219	1,085	ton 噸

Top 10 firms by revenue (year founded) 收入排名前 10 家企業（創辦年份）	City 城市	Province 省	Telephone / fax 電話 / 傳真	Number of employees 職工人數	Ownership 產業所有權	Revenue ('000 RMB) 銷售收入（千元）	Profit ('000 RMB) (rank) 利潤（千元）（排名）	Total assets ('000 RMB) 總資產（千元）	Major products 主要產品
Xinjiang Hu Guang Textile & Knitting Factory 新疆湖光紡織針織廠(1962)	Korla 庫爾勒市	Xinjiang 新疆	(0996)2022112 (0996)2027690	3,820	State-owned 國有	121,938	-33379(44)	249,444	a,b
Jiangsu Yang Yang Worsted Wearing & Dyeing Group Co. Ltd. 江蘇陽洋毛紡織染集團有限公司(1993)	Xuzhou 徐州市	Jiangsu 江蘇省	(0516)4622159	1,684	Collectively-owned 集體	114,882	3085(3)	117,209	o
Wuhan No.1 Flour Factory 武漢第一麵粉廠(1919)	Wuhan 武漢市	Hubei 湖北省	(027)83852669 (027)83828175	1,005	State-owned 國有	69,673	-3000(39)	130,310	o
Rongcheng Wool Scouring Factory 容城縣洗毛廠(1989)	Baoding 保定市	Hebei 河北省	(0312)5582497	150	Private-owned 私營	40,000	4700(1)	4,500	o
Rongcheng Dong Sheng Wool Scouring Factory 容城縣東升洗毛廠(1992)	Baoding 保定市	Hebei 河北省	(0312)5582283	60	Private-owned 私營	29,000	4150(2)	7,000	o
Hebei Xushui Zhong Xing Wool Scouring Mill 徐水縣中興洗毛廠(1985)	Baoding 保定市	Hebei 河北省	(0312)8961512	280	Collectively-owned 集體	23,060	1870(5)	8,240	o
Xiangfan Wan Li Lai Special Type Industrial Co. Ltd. 襄樊市萬利來特種實業有限公司(1980)	Xiangfan 襄樊市	Hubei 湖北省	(0710)3564238	55	Joint stock 股份制	20,470	200(19)	16,752	o
Taicang Sha Xi Wool Scouring Factory 太倉市沙溪洗毛廠(1985)	Suzhou 蘇州市	Jiangsu 江蘇省	(0512)3213052 (0512)3217582	162	Collectively-owned 集體	17,140	1180(7)	8,270	o
Jingbian Feng Hua Group General Company 靖邊縣風華集團總公司(1985)	Yulin 榆林市	Shaanxi 陕西省	(0912)621392	334	Collectively-owned 集體	16,370	2086(4)	13,458	o
Changshu San Lian Wool Spinning Factory 常熟市三聯毛紡廠(1995)	Suzhou 蘇州市	Jiangsu 江蘇省	(0512)2671809	120	Collectively-owned 集體	15,007	-776(36)	31,291	o

Top 10 Cities by Production Output 產出排名前 10 位城市	Province 省	Market share 市場份額	Number of firms 企業個數
Wuxi 無錫市	Jiangsu 江蘇省	42.42%	8
Korla 庫爾勒市	Xinjiang 新疆	11.74%	1
Lanzhou 蘭州市	Gansu 甘肅省	7.21%	1
Fuzhou 福州市	Fujian 福建省	3.92%	1
Jiaxing 嘉興市	Zhejiang 浙江省	2.70%	2
Zhangjiakou 張家口市	Hebei 河北省	2.16%	4
Ezhou 鄂州市	Hubei 湖北省	2.15%	1
Tianjin 天津市	Tianjin 天津市	1.88%	5
Erenhot 二連浩特市	Inner Mong 內蒙	1.87%	4
Wuhan 武漢市	Hubei 湖北省	1.82%	2

10 Major Wholesalers 10 家主要批發商	City 城市	Province 省	Telephone / Fax 電話 / 傳真
Anhui Clothing Import & Export Company 安徽省服裝進出口公司	Hefei 合肥市	Anhui 安徽省	(0551)3632212 (0551)3632002
Qingdao Textile Clothing Industrial Group Company 青島紡織服裝實業集團公司	Qingdao 青島市	Shandong 山東省	(0532)2877853 (0532)2869315
Hebei Textile Import & Export (Group) Company 河北省紡織品進出口(集團)公司	Shijiazhuang 石家莊市	Hebei 河北省	(0311)7028530 (0311)7027781
Zhong Fang Pledget Import & Export Company 中紡紗布進出口公司	Beijing 北京市	Beijing 北京市	(010)65124718 (010)65124713
Shaoxing Import & Export Company 紹興市進出口公司	Shaoxing 紹興市	Zhejiang 浙江省	(0575)5132822 (0575)5141577
Hunan Hua Xiang Import & Export (Group) Company 湖南省華湘進出口(集團)公司	Changsha 長沙市	Hunan 湖南省	(0731)2282440 (0731)2286995
City's Import & Export Company Trade Dept. 市進出口公司貿易部	Yichang 宜昌市	Hubei 湖北省	(0717)6450778 (0717)6441875
Shanghai Pu Dong Xinqu Import & Export Company 上海浦東新區進出口公司	Shanghai 上海市	Shanghai 上海市	(021)58878801 (021)58827444
Ningbo Yinxian Import & Export Company 寧波市鄞縣進出口公司	Ningbo 寧波市	Zhejiang 浙江省	(0574)7875205 (0574)7873168
Zhejiang Silk Import & Export Company 浙江省絲綢進出口公司	Hangzhou 杭州市	Zhejiang 浙江省	(0571)5195588 (0571)5192542

*Also include sales by firms outside this industry.包括本行業以外廠家的銷售。"o" stands for "others". "o" 代表"其他產品"。

1713: Flax Fibre Primary 亞麻纖維初步加工業

The industry accounts for 0.014% of the total revenue of China's industrial sector in 1996. The revenue growth rate of the industry is 12.4% from 1995, as compared to the growth rate of China's industrial sector, 9.51%. The rate of return on asset is -0.29%. 82.69% of all firms in the industry made a profit while 14.57% had negative returns. The top province in terms of the industry's revenue is Helongjiang, accounting for 69.82% of the total revenue.
本行業在1996年佔全行業總產值0.014%，行業年增長率為12.4%（全國工業年增長率9.51%）。行業的資產回報率-0.29%，82.69%的企業盈利，14.57%的企業虧損。銷售收入最高的省份為黑龍江省，佔本行業的69.82%。

	Total number of firms 企業總數	Total number of employees 職工總數	Total revenue (mil. RMB) 總銷售收入（百萬元）	Total profit (mil. RMB) 總利潤（百萬元）	Return on assets 資產利潤率 (%)	Return on equity 權益利潤率 (%)	Labour productivity ('000 RMB / worker) 勞動生產率（千元/人）	Debts / assets 資產負債率 (%)	Total assets (mil. RMB) 總資產（百萬元）
Industry Overall 行業總體	194	25,804	822	-5	-0.29	-4.62	31.86	93.78	1,666

	Number of firms 企業個數	Average number of employees 平均職工人數	Average revenue ('000 RMB) 平均銷售收入（千元）	Average profit ('000 RMB) 平均利潤（千元）	Return on assets 資產利潤率 (%)	Return on equity 權益利潤率 (%)	Labour productivity ('000 RMB / worker) 勞動生產率（千元/人）	Average debts / assets 平均資產負債率(%)	Average Total assets ('000 RMB) 平均總資產（千元）
By ownership 產業所有權									
State-owned 國有	30	483	7,733	-967	-2.65	-152.63	16.00	98.26	36,433
Collectively-owned 集體	157	64	3,194	143	5.58	65.38	49.90	91.47	2,571
Privately-owned 私有	1	19	1,458	-12	-0.46	-8.60	76.73	94.61	2,605
Domestic JVs 聯營									
Joint stock 股份制	1	910	27,619	1,943	3.15	22.74	30.35	86.14	61,640
Foreign-funded 外資	1	69	1,400	-140	-0.55	-0.55	20.28	0.59	25,543
Overseas Chinese-funded 港澳台資	3	85	19,286	-99	-0.37	-1.81	226.00	79.34	26,630
By size 規模									
Large 大型	1	1,833	33,921	-1,248	-1.03	-62.17	18.51	98.35	121,573
Medium 中型	4	920	27,484	-1,055	-1.40	-32.00	29.88	95.62	75,344
Small 小型	183	110	3,706	3	0.04	0.53	33.59	92.86	6,795
By regional distribution 地區分布									
Central-North 華北	18	38	1,664	83	4.37	16.54	43.55	73.57	1,908
Beijing 北京									
Tianjin 天津									
Hebei 河北	14	26	712	24	3.90	9.60	27.85	59.29	623
Shanxi 山西	2	70	7,045	130	2.18	12.04	100.64	81.89	5,965
Inner Mongolia 內蒙	2	95	2,950	450	6.57	26.71	31.05	75.40	6,850
Northeast 東北	138	135	4,233	103	1.28	11.49	31.42	88.85	8,006
Liaoning 遼寧	4	61	2,450	-293	-9.06	-53.18	40.16	82.97	3,230
Jilin 吉林	3	17	180	-153	-1.38	-21.80	10.80	93.67	11,103
Heilongjiang 黑龍江	131	140	4,381	121	1.49	13.28	31.36	88.77	8,080
Central East 華東	3	709	18,160	227	0.72	-2.77	25.61	125.87	31,643
Shanghai 上海									
Jiangsu 江蘇									
Zhejiang 浙江									
Anhui 安徽	1	10	4,010	100	10.87	10.87	401.00		920
Fujian 福建									
Jiangxi 江西									
Shandong 山東	2	1,059	25,235	290	0.62	-2.28	23.84	127.10	47,005
Central-South 中南	9	143	14,038	-344	-1.85	-11.80	98.24	84.36	18,669
Henan 河南	1	17	710	30	3.75	12.50	41.76	70.00	800
Hubei 湖北	3	153	5,493	177	3.16	-165.63	35.98	101.91	5,590
Hunan 湖南									
Guangdong 廣東	1	98	30,550	520	1.37	5.32	311.73	74.17	37,830
Guangxi 廣西	3	124	23,743	-1,490	-4.64	-26.94	191.48	82.80	32,147
Hainan 海南	1	341	7,370	290	1.79		21.61	100.00	16,180
Southwest 西南									
Chongqing 重慶									
Sichuan 四川									
Guizhou 貴州									
Yunnan 雲南									
Tibet 西藏									
Northwest 西北	26	120	1,028	-693	-6.83	59.13	8.59	111.55	10,143
Shaanxi 陝西	1	60	1,850	-100	-4.93	-17.24	30.83	71.43	2,030
Gansu 甘肅	14	49	635	-3	-0.15	-1.00	12.92	85.11	1,934
Qinghai 青海	1	24							
Ningxia 寧夏	8	80	524	11	0.51	0.97	6.59	47.71	2,214
Xinjiang 新疆	2	852	5,895	-8,980	-8.28	40.51	6.92	120.44	108,455

1713: Flax Fibre Primary 亞麻纖維初步加工業

Year 年份	Number of firms 企業個數	Rate of change 每年變化 (%)	Number of employees 職工人數 (人)	Rate of change 每年變化 (%)	Total revenue (mil. RMB) 總銷售收入 (百萬元)	Rate of change 每年變化 (%)	Total profit (mil. RMB) 總利潤 (百萬元)	Rate of change 每年變化 (%)
1993	157		4,642		397		-9	
1994	149	-5.10%	23,141	398.51%	681	71.56%	46	608.24%
1995	179	20.13%	25,451	9.98%	731	7.31%	10	-77.24%
1996	194	8.38%	25,804	1.39%	822	12.40%	-5	-147.83%

3 Major products* 3 種主要產品 *	Output 產量	Sales volume 銷售量	Unit 單位

Top 10 firms by revenue (year founded) 收入排名前 10 家企業 (創辦年份)	City 城市	Province 省	Telephone / fax 電話 / 傳真	Number of employees 職工人數	Ownership 產業所有權	Revenue ('000 RMB) 銷售收入 (千元)	Profit ('000 RMB) (rank) 利潤 (千元) (排名)	Total assets ('000 RMB) 總資產 (千元)	Major products 主要產品
Liu Jing Flour Co. Ltd. 柳晶麵粉有限公司(1996)	Liuzhou 柳州市	Guangxi 廣西	(0772)2520448	83	Foreign-funded 外資	62,700	-3682(71)	79,574	o
Shandong Hua Da Spinning and Weaving Industrial General Company 山東華達紡織實業總公司(1989)	Heze 菏澤市	Shandong 山東省	(0530)2421415	2,050	State-owned 國有	46,252	115(47)	81,012	o
Wangkui Xianfeng Flax Factory 望奎縣先鋒亞麻廠(1973)	Suihua 綏化市	Heilongjiang 黑龍江省	(0455)6761713	190	Collectively-owned 集體	42,800	2330(2)	21,510	o
Heilong Jiang Suihua Area Lanxi Flax Raw Material General Co. 黑龍江省綏化地區蘭西縣亞麻原料總公司(1937)	Suihua 綏化市	Heilongjiang 黑龍江省	(0455)7623216	1,270	State-owned 國有	35,911	2017(3)	169,649	o
Shenzhen Xinlong Linen Textile Bleaching & Dyeing Co. Ltd. 深圳新龍亞麻紡織漂染有限公司(1993)	Shenzhen 深圳市	Guangdong 廣東省	(0755)6648042 (0755)6404350	98	Overseas Chinese-funded 港澳台資	30,553	516(14)	37,833	o
Local State-owned Keshan Flax Raw Materials Factory 地方國營克山縣亞麻原料廠(1993)	Qiqiha'er 齊齊哈爾市	Heilongjiang 黑龍江省	(0452)4523150 (0452)4523430	1,808	State-owned 國有	26,876	984(6)	84,250	o
Hailun Flax Raw Material Factory 海倫市亞麻原料廠(1934)	Suihua 綏化市	Heilongjiang 黑龍江省	(0455)5723364	633	State-owned 國有	21,170	121(45)	62,141	o
Shuangcheng Chaoyang Xiang Flax Factory 雙城市朝陽鄉亞麻廠(1980)	Shuangcheng 雙城市	Heilongjiang 黑龍江省	(0451)3123729	80	Collectively-owned 集體	18,265	4260(1)	1,000	o
Baiquan Flax Co. Ltd. 拜泉縣亞麻有限公司(1935)	Qiqiha'er 齊齊哈爾市	Heilongjiang 黑龍江省	(0452)7323138 (0452)7323138	786	State-owned 國有	15,698	-1499(69)	64,208	o
Heilongjiang Yi'an Flax Raw Material Factory 黑龍江省依安亞麻原料廠(1987)	Qiqiha'er 齊齊哈爾市	Heilongjiang 黑龍江省	(0452)7022388	644	State-owned 國有	15,087	0(62)	59,607	o

Top 10 Cities by Production Output 產出排名前 10 位城市	Province 省	Market share 市場份額	Number of firms 企業個數
Suihua 綏化市	Heilongjiang 黑龍江省	35.48%	63
Qiqiha'er 齊齊哈爾市	Heilongjiang 黑龍江省	22.64%	17
Shuangcheng 雙城市	Heilongjiang 黑龍江省	11.64%	14
Heze 菏澤市	Shandong 山東省	8.28%	1
Harbin 哈爾濱市	Heilongjiang 黑龍江省	3.46%	8
Qitaihe 七臺河市	Heilongjiang 黑龍江省	3.43%	3
Jiamusi 佳木斯市	Heilongjiang 黑龍江省	2.98%	2
Daqing 大慶市	Heilongjiang 黑龍江省	2.41%	11
Ji'an 吉安市	Jiangxi 江西省	1.58%	1
Shenyang 瀋陽市	Liaoning 遼寧省	1.47%	2

10 Major Wholesalers 10 家主要批發商	City 城市	Province 省	Telephone / Fax 電話 / 傳真
Anhui Clothing Import & Export Company 安徽省服裝進出口公司	Hefei 合肥市	Anhui 安徽省	(0551)3632212 (0551)3632002
Qingdao Textile Clothing Industrial Group Company 青島紡織服裝實業集團公司	Qingdao 青島市	Shandong 山東省	(0532)2877853 (0532)2869315
Hebei Textile Import & Export (Group) Company 河北省紡織品進出口(集團)公司	Shijiazhuang 石家莊市	Hebei 河北省	(0311)7028530 (0311)7027781
Zhong Fang Pledget Import & Export Company 中紡紗布進出口公司	Beijing 北京市	Beijing 北京市	(010)65124718 (010)65124713
Shaoxing Import & Export Company 紹興市進出口公司	Shaoxing 紹興市	Zhejiang 浙江省	(0575)5132822 (0575)5141577
Hunan Hua Xiang Import & Export (Group) Company 湖南省華湘進出口(集團)公司	Changsha 長沙市	Hunan 湖南省	(0731)2282440 (0731)2286995
City's Import & Export Company Trade Dept. 市進出口公司貿易部	Yichang 宜昌市	Hubei 湖北省	(0717)6450778 (0717)6441875
Shanghai Pu Dong Xinqu Import & Export Company 上海浦東新區進出口公司	Shanghai 上海市	Shanghai 上海市	(021)58878801 (021)58827444
Ningbo Yinxian Import & Export Company 寧波市鄞縣進出口公司	Ningbo 寧波市	Zhejiang 浙江省	(0574)7875205 (0574)7873168
Zhejiang Silk Import & Export Company 浙江省絲綢進出口公司	Hangzhou 杭州市	Zhejiang 浙江省	(0571)5195588 (0571)5192542

*Also include sales by firms outside this industry.包括本行業以外廠家的銷售。"o" stands for "others". "o" 代表"其他產品"。

1714: Ramie Fibre Primary 苧麻纖維初步加工業

The industry accounts for 0.012% of the total revenue of China's industrial sector in 1996. The revenue growth rate of the industry is 19.1% from 1995, as compared to the growth rate of China's industrial sector, 9.51%. The rate of return on asset is -2.13%. 82.25% of all firms in the industry made a profit while 15.96% had negative returns. The top province in terms of the industry's revenue is Sichuan, accounting for 28.99% of the total revenue.
本行業在1996年佔全行業總產值0.012%，行業年增長率為19.1%（全國工業年增長率9.51%）。行業的資產回報率-2.13%，82.25%的企業盈利，15.96%的企業虧損。銷售收入最高的省份為四川省，佔本行業的28.99%。

	Total number of firms 企業總數	Total number of employees 職工總數	Total revenue (mil. RMB) 總銷售收入（百萬元）	Total profit (mil. RMB) 總利潤（百萬元）	Return on assets 資產利潤率 (%)	Return on equity 權益利潤率 (%)	Labour productivity ('000 RMB / worker) 勞動生產率（千元/人）	Debts / assets 資產負債率 (%)	Total assets (mil. RMB) 總資產（百萬元）
Industry Overall 行業總體	103	13,142	718	-12	-2.13	-18.92	54.63	88.76	548

	Number of firms 企業個數	Average number of employees 平均職工人數	Average revenue ('000 RMB) 平均銷售收入（千元）	Average profit ('000 RMB) 平均利潤（千元）	Return on assets 資產利潤率 (%)	Return on equity 權益利潤率 (%)	Labour productivity ('000 RMB / worker) 勞動生產率（千元/人）	Average debts / assets 平均資產負債率(%)	Average Total assets ('000 RMB) 平均總資產（千元）
By ownership 產業所有權									
State-owned 國有	6	144	2,667	-1,167	-11.29	50.00	18.58	122.58	10,333
Collectively-owned 集體	94	122	7,139	-192	-3.95	-26.77	58.63	85.25	4,868
Privately-owned 私有									
Domestic JVs 聯營									
Joint stock 股份制	1	78	375	627	24.42	499.63	4.80	95.11	2,569
Foreign-funded 外資	2	436	15,275	6,216	48.11	148.03	35.03	67.50	12,922
Overseas Chinese-funded 港澳台資									
By size 規模									
Large 大型									
Medium 中型	3	334	9,110	5	0.02	-0.11	27.28	119.62	21,991
Small 小型	100	122	6,906	-120	-2.49	-16.03	56.39	84.45	4,819
By regional distribution 地區分布									
Central-North 華北	1	40	1,030	20	2.06	6.90	25.75	70.10	970
Beijing 北京									
Tianjin 天津									
Hebei 河北	1	40	1,030	20	2.06	6.90	25.75	70.10	970
Shanxi 山西									
Inner Mongolia 內蒙									
Northeast 東北	1	20	890				44.50	11.36	2,200
Liaoning 遼寧	1	20	890				44.50	11.36	2,200
Jilin 吉林									
Heilongjiang 黑龍江									
Central East 華東	20	121	10,207	154	2.13	13.77	84.11	84.54	7,230
Shanghai 上海									
Jiangsu 江蘇	4	89	9,450	-18	-0.42	-3.37	106.48	87.62	4,200
Zhejiang 浙江									
Anhui 安徽	8	185	14,583	75	0.77	3.31	79.04	76.65	9,706
Fujian 福建									
Jiangxi 江西	5	22	644	44	2.82	-21.15	29.81	113.35	1,558
Shandong 山東	3	163	15,483	777	5.50	73.04	95.18	92.47	14,120
Central-South 中南	40	81	5,522	65	2.51	8.12	68.17	69.16	2,574
Henan 河南									
Hubei 湖北	10	78	5,893	139	4.12	14.27	75.84	71.15	3,373
Hunan 湖南	29	85	5,584	41	1.72	5.40	65.75	68.19	2,387
Guangdong 廣東									
Guangxi 廣西	1								
Hainan 海南									
Southwest 西南	41	181	7,094	-423	-5.84	-332.63	39.22	98.25	7,242
Chongqing 重慶	6	154	13,243	-1,301	-13.00	163.13	85.60	107.97	10,007
Sichuan 四川	33	190	6,123	-266	-3.84	-86.32	32.08	95.55	6,927
Guizhou 貴州	1								
Yunnan 雲南									
Tibet 西藏									
Northwest 西北									
Shaanxi 陝西									
Gansu 甘肅									
Qinghai 青海									
Ningxia 寧夏									
Xinjiang 新疆									

1714: Ramie Fibre Primary 苧麻纖維初步加工業

Year 年份	Number of firms 企業個數	Rate of change 每年變化 (%)	Number of employees 職工人數 (人)	Rate of change 每年變化 (%)	Total revenue (mil. RMB) 總銷售收入 (百萬元)	Rate of change 每年變化 (%)	Total profit (mil. RMB) 總利潤 (百萬元)	Rate of change 每年變化 (%)
1993	96		11,720		255		3	
1994	102	6.25%	15,794	34.76%	564	121.74%	13	307.66%
1995	118	15.69%	16,759	6.11%	603	6.80%	-2	-113.44%
1996	103	-12.71%	13,142	-21.58%	718	19.11%	-12	-579.50%

3 Major products* 3 種主要產品 *	Output 產量	Sales volume 銷售量	Unit 單位
a) Ramie Yarn 苧麻紗線	5,020	4,718	ton 噸
b) Ramie Cloth 苧麻布	1,651,549	1,552,456	metre 米

Top 10 firms by revenue (year founded) 收入排名前 10 家企業 (創辦年份)	City 城市	Province 省	Telephone / fax 電話 / 傳真	Number of employees 職工人數	Ownership 產業所有權	Revenue ('000 RMB) 銷售收入 (千元)	Profit ('000 RMB) (rank) 利潤 (千元) (排名)	Total assets ('000 RMB) 總資產 (千元)	Major products 主要產品
Jingde Heng Da Textiles Co. Ltd. 旌德恒大有限公司(1987)	Xuanzhou 宣州市	Anhui 安徽省	(0563)8022018	692	Collectively-owned 集體	47,967	-1214(51)	54,546	a
Chongqing Rongchang Xia Bu Co. Ltd. 重慶榮昌夏布有限公司	Chongqing 重慶市	Chongqing 重慶市	(023)46732003 (023)732175	1,500	Collectively-owned 集體	42,000	-3177(55)	22,545	b
Laiyang Hemp Fibre Factory 萊陽市大麻纖維廠(1987)	Yantai 煙台市	Shandong 山東省	(0535)7316856 (0535)7316856	140	Collectively-owned 集體	40,186	2021(1)	25,892	o
Daxian No.1 Spinning Factory 達縣第一麻紡廠	Dachuan 達川市	Sichuan 四川省	(0818)3360176	250	Collectively-owned 集體	32,680	217(10)	2,052	o
Daxian No.2 Spinning Factory 達縣第二麻織廠	Dachuan 達川市	Sichuan 四川省	(0818)3360057	390	Collectively-owned 集體	30,563	361(6)	7,000	o
Hubei Jiayu Ramie Weaving Factory 湖北省嘉魚縣苧麻紡織廠(1979)	Xianning 咸寧市	Hubei 湖北省	(0715)322637	1,284	Collectively-owned 集體	25,932	142(15)	22,960	o
Jintan Ramie Factory 金壇市苧麻製球廠(1986)	Changzhou 常州市	Jiangsu 江蘇省	(0519)2762741	232	Collectively-owned 集體	24,730	-300(40)	9,630	o
Rongchang Panlong Zhen Chun Guang Xia Bu Company 榮昌縣盤龍鎮春光夏布公司	Chongqing 重慶市	Chongqing 重慶市	(023)46732266	1,800	Private-owned 私營	22,601	318(7)	19,404	b
Hunan Changde Anxiang An Chang Xiang Ramie Factory 湖南省常德市安鄉縣安昌鄉苧麻廠(1993)	Changde 常德市	Hunan 湖南省	(0736)4649893	185	Collectively-owned 集體	20,884	1638(2)	4,144	o
Jingde Spinning and Weaving Factory 旌德縣紡織廠(1995)	Xuanzhou 宣州市	Anhui 安徽省	(0563)8022018	121	Collectively-owned 集體	20,180	-610(47)	3,684	a

Top 10 Cities by Production Output 產出排名前 10 位城市	Province 省	Market share 市場份額	Number of firms 企業個數
Yiyang 益陽市	Hunan 湖南省	20.19%	13
Chongqing 重慶市	Chongqing 重慶市	18.80%	32
Changde 常德市	Hunan 湖南省	12.78%	9
Xuanzhou 宣州市	Anhui 安徽省	11.78%	2
Dachuan 達川市	Sichuan 四川省	10.84%	17
Yantai 煙台市	Shandong 山東省	5.48%	1
Linyi 臨沂市	Shandong 山東省	5.08%	4
Wuxi 無錫市	Jiangsu 江蘇省	3.51%	1
Huangshi 黃石市	Hubei 湖北省	3.10%	3
Liu'an 六安市	Anhui 安徽省	2.77%	1

10 Major Wholesalers 10 家主要批發商	City 城市	Province 省	Telephone / Fax 電話 / 傳真
Anhui Clothing Import & Export Company 安徽省服裝進出口公司	Hefei 合肥市	Anhui 安徽省	(0551)3632212 (0551)3632002
Qingdao Textile Clothing Industrial Group Company 青島紡織服裝實業集團公司	Qingdao 青島市	Shandong 山東省	(0532)2877853 (0532)2869315
Hebei Textile Import & Export (Group) Company 河北省紡織品進出口(集團)公司	Shijiazhuang 石家莊市	Hebei 河北省	(0311)7028530 (0311)7027781
Zhong Fang Pledget Import & Export Company 中紡紗布進出口公司	Beijing 北京市	Beijing 北京市	(010)65124718 (010)65124713
Shaoxing Import & Export Company 紹興市進出口公司	Shaoxing 紹興市	Zhejiang 浙江省	(0575)5132822 (0575)5141577
Hunan Hua Xiang Import & Export (Group) Company 湖南省華湘進出口(集團)公司	Changsha 長沙市	Hunan 湖南省	(0731)2282440 (0731)2286995
City's Import & Export Company Trade Dept. 市進出口公司貿易部	Yichang 宜昌市	Hubei 湖北省	(0717)6450778 (0717)6441875
Shanghai Pu Dong Xinqu Import & Export Company 上海浦東新區進出口公司	Shanghai 上海市	Shanghai 上海市	(021)58878801 (021)58827444
Ningbo Yinxian Import & Export Company 寧波市鄞縣進出口公司	Ningbo 寧波市	Zhejiang 浙江省	(0574)7875205 (0574)7873168
Zhejiang Silk Import & Export Company 浙江省絲綢進出口公司	Hangzhou 杭州市	Zhejiang 浙江省	(0571)5195588 (0571)5192542

*Also include sales by firms outside this industry.包括本行業以外廠家的銷售。"o" stands for "others". "o" 代表 "其他產品" 。

1719: Preliminary Processing of Other Raw Fibre Materials
其他纖維原料初步加工業

The industry accounts for 0.078% of the total revenue of China's industrial sector in 1996. The revenue growth rate of the industry is 6.8% from 1995, as compared to the growth rate of China's industrial sector, 9.51%. The rate of return on asset is 3.81%. 79.22% of all firms in the industry made a profit while 15.47% had negative returns. The top province in terms of the industry's revenue is Jiangsu, accounting for 25.98% of the total revenue.
本行業在1996年佔全行業總產值0.078%，行業年增長率為6.8%（全國工業年增長率9.51%）。行業的資產回報率3.81%，79.22%的企業盈利，15.47%的企業虧損。銷售收入最高的省份為江蘇省，佔本行業的25.98%。

	Total number of firms 企業總數	Total number of employees 職工總數	Total revenue (mil. RMB) 總銷售收入（百萬元）	Total profit (mil. RMB) 總利潤（百萬元）	Return on assets 資產利潤率 (%)	Return on equity 權益利潤率 (%)	Labour productivity ('000 RMB / worker) 勞動生產率（千元／人）	Debts / assets 資產負債率 (%)	Total assets (mil. RMB) 總資產（百萬元）
Industry Overall 行業總體	490	38,770	4,519	190	3.81	11.57	116.56	67.09	5,002

	Number of firms 企業個數	Average number of employees 平均職工人數	Average revenue ('000 RMB) 平均銷售收入（千元）	Average profit ('000 RMB) 平均利潤（千元）	Return on assets 資產利潤率 (%)	Return on equity 權益利潤率 (%)	Labour productivity ('000 RMB / worker) 勞動生產率（千元／人）	Average debts / assets 平均資產負債率(%)	Average Total assets ('000 RMB) 平均總資產（千元）
By ownership 產業所有權									
State-owned 國有	26	245	13,269	-692	-1.61	-13.74	54.07	88.28	43,000
Collectively-owned 集體	393	59	7,526	499	10.38	32.57	126.57	68.15	4,805
Privately-owned 私有	2	53	189	18	6.68	15.07	3.61	55.67	268
Domestic JVs 聯營	4	60	14,813	1,953	19.49	23.08	246.88	15.56	10,021
Joint stock 股份制	3	209	3,867	-5	-0.12	-0.39	18.47	68.81	3,941
Foreign-funded 外資	24	183	22,907	-1,738	-4.39	-10.53	125.41	58.32	39,600
Overseas Chinese-funded 港澳台資	38	96	15,642	1,213	4.66	9.62	162.71	51.49	26,000
By size 規模									
Large 大型	2	649	230,909	41,230	15.55	28.37	355.79	45.19	265,154
Medium 中型	7	415	28,651	-693	-1.31	-4.65	69.09	71.96	53,138
Small 小型	477	73	8,086	236	2.74	8.98	111.48	69.48	8,594
By regional distribution 地區分布									
Central-North 華北	96	68	12,987	1,358	17.51	31.07	189.88	43.65	7,757
Beijing 北京	5	11	928	-410	-16.65	-32.33	84.36	48.50	2,462
Tianjin 天津	13	158	9,110	-300	-1.85	-5.29	57.60	64.93	16,174
Hebei 河北	72	48	15,007	1,876	33.89	43.78	312.65	22.60	5,536
Shanxi 山西	1	587	9,770				16.64	70.38	72,900
Inner Mongolia 內蒙	5	82	6,674	248	2.45	13.15	81.00	81.36	10,120
Northeast 東北	26	59	1,584	-44	-1.66	-7.73	26.64	78.56	2,643
Liaoning 遼寧	16	57	1,148	-5	-0.64	-2.01	19.99	68.39	787
Jilin 吉林	3	138	5,797	-350	-3.51	-34.31	42.00	89.78	9,983
Heilongjiang 黑龍江	7	30	776	-1	-0.04	-0.13	25.49	70.62	3,739
Central East 華東	186	104	12,699	318	2.74	7.78	122.45	64.85	11,615
Shanghai 上海	11	97	14,627	-109	-0.36	-0.88	150.94	59.02	30,109
Jiangsu 江蘇	65	127	18,064	701	4.96	15.52	142.30	68.06	14,149
Zhejiang 浙江	42	88	7,828	134	1.36	4.50	89.20	69.81	9,896
Anhui 安徽	27	56	12,717	786	24.65	42.64	225.75	42.19	3,190
Fujian 福建	6	21	1,445				69.36	61.14	905
Jiangxi 江西	8	4	376	41	24.09	41.77	86.00	43.07	171
Shandong 山東	27	171	12,707	-463	-3.11	-8.23	74.51	62.15	14,853
Central-South 中南	83	109	8,960	-10	-0.05	-0.21	82.40	78.64	22,702
Henan 河南	39	38	2,947	193	6.81	31.98	77.40	78.69	2,826
Hubei 湖北	7	239	5,203	-967	-10.15	44.42	21.77	122.85	9,527
Hunan 湖南	10	59	1,951	13	2.23	4.55	33.29	51.03	584
Guangdong 廣東	22	168	19,926	78	0.15	0.54	118.77	72.21	52,108
Guangxi 廣西	5	318	26,890	-690	-0.62	-4.74	84.56	86.88	111,038
Hainan 海南									
Southwest 西南	14	53	2,861	34	0.95	3.21	53.92	70.60	3,551
Chongqing 重慶	5	18	331	637	246.28	2725.84	17.42	90.96	259
Sichuan 四川	6	99	5,859	-611	-8.25	-25.26	58.77	67.35	7,415
Guizhou 貴州	1								
Yunnan 雲南	2	24	1,625	-5	-0.25	50.00	67.71	100.51	1,970
Tibet 西藏									
Northwest 西北	85	19	1,009	30	2.69	7.19	53.59	62.59	1,103
Shaanxi 陝西	75	15	964	32	4.17	8.22	64.97	49.23	757
Gansu 甘肅	4	85	1,420	-140	-3.81	-224.00	16.76	98.30	3,678
Qinghai 青海									
Ningxia 寧夏	3	21	2,160	230	4.77	13.35	104.52	64.27	4,823
Xinjiang 新疆	3	29	440	7	0.26	2.44	15.17	89.46	2,593

1719: Preliminary Processing of Other Raw Fibre Materials
其他纖維原料初步加工業

Year 年份	Number of firms 企業個數	Rate of change 每年變化 (%)	Number of employees 職工人數（人）	Rate of change 每年變化 (%)	Total revenue (mil. RMB) 總銷售收入（百萬元）	Rate of change 每年變化 (%)	Total profit (mil. RMB) 總利潤（百萬元）	Rate of change 每年變化 (%)
1993	399		38,121		2,285		74	
1994	416	4.26%	36,240	-4.94%	3,008	31.61%	134	81.56%
1995	538	29.33%	43,330	19.56%	4,232	40.71%	130	-2.95%
1996	490	-8.92%	38,770	-10.52%	4,519	6.78%	190	46.56%

3 Major products* 3 種主要產品 *	Output 產量	Sales volume 銷售量	Unit 單位
a) Polymide Fibre 錦綸纖維	8,314	7,898	ton 噸
b) Polyester Processing Silk 滌綸加工絲	7,446	6,924	ton 噸

Top 10 firms by revenue (year founded) 收入排名前 10 家企業 (創辦年份)	City 城市	Province 省	Telephone / fax 電話 / 傳真	Number of employees 職工人數	Ownership 產業所有權	Revenue ('000 RMB) 銷售收入（千元）	Profit ('000 RMB) (rank) 利潤（千元）（排名）	Total assets ('000 RMB) 總資產（千元）	Major products 主要產品
Jiangsu Tai Qing Group Co. Ltd. 江蘇泰清集團公司有限公司(1976)	Wuxi 無錫市	Jiangsu 江蘇省	(0510)6201399 (0510)6201412	805	Collectively-owned 集體	386,207	32688(1)	170,439	o
Jiangsu Yang Ba (Group) Co. 江蘇洋霸(集團)公司(1994)	Wuxi 無錫市	Jiangsu 江蘇省	(0510)7591259	350	Collectively-owned 集體	123,000	3029(23)	44,560	a
Yingshang Xie Qiao Zhen Ya Zhong Nap Group 潁上縣謝橋鎮亞中絨毛集團(1996)	Fuyang 阜陽市	Anhui 安徽省	(0558)4281068	210	Collectively-owned 集體	99,300	4890(14)	37,000	o
Xin Xingxian Hong Fa Polyester Processing Co. Ltd. 新興縣宏法滌綸加工有限公司(1992)	Yunfu 雲浮市	Guangdong 廣東省	(0766)2883392	1,167	Overseas Chinese-funded 港澳台資	99,137	1734(40)	12,908	b
Yingshang Run He Zhen Rabbit Hair Processing Factory 潁上縣潤河鎮兔毛加工廠(1992)	Fuyang 阜陽市	Anhui 安徽省	(0558)4146001	212	Collectively-owned 集體	90,000	8100(5)	6,521	o
Shanghai Jin Ling Textile Company 上海金靈紡織品公司(1987)	Shanghai 上海市	Shanghai 上海市	(021)57456953 (021)57456950	400	Collectively-owned 集體	89,611	3247(21)	132,976	o
Guilin Hong Wei Group Co. 桂林宏偉集團公司(1994)	Guilin 桂林市	Guangxi 廣西	(0773)3603893 (0773)3602540	1,081	State-owned 國有	88,707	129(136)	428,480	a
Qingdao Er He Fiber Co. Ltd. 青島二和纖維有限公司(1993)	Qingdao 青島市	Shandong 山東省	(0532)6461150 (0532)6461147	1,020	Foreign-funded 外資	85,520	3590(16)	113,060	o
Qingdao Cotton Fiber Co. Ltd. 青島棉花纖維有限公司(1994)	Qingdao 青島市	Shandong 山東省	(0532)6461156 (0532)6461158	1,100	Foreign-funded 外資	79,600	3430(19)	94,270	o
Hebei Nap Factory 河北絨毛廠(1989)	Shijiazhuang 石家莊市	Hebei 河北省	(0311)2237332	390	Collectively-owned 集體	75,520	9000(4)	12,430	o

Top 10 Cities by Production Output 產出排名前 10 位城市	Province 省	Market share 市場份額	Number of firms 企業個數
Xingtai 邢臺市	Hebei 河北省	19.96%	43
Wuxi 無錫市	Jiangsu 江蘇省	6.96%	7
Tianjin 天津市	Tianjin 天津市	6.31%	19
Suzhou 蘇州市	Jiangsu 江蘇省	4.71%	16
Shanghai 上海市	Shanghai 上海市	4.31%	23
Fuyang 阜陽市	Anhui 安徽省	4.00%	10
Changzhou 常州市	Jiangsu 江蘇省	3.29%	18
Guilin 桂林市	Guangxi 廣西	3.04%	2
Huzhou 湖州市	Zhejiang 浙江省	2.78%	6
Zhongshan 中山市	Guangdong 廣東省	2.37%	3

10 Major Wholesalers 10 家主要批發商	City 城市	Province 省	Telephone / Fax 電話 / 傳真
Anhui Clothing Import & Export Company 安徽省服裝進出口公司	Hefei 合肥市	Anhui 安徽省	(0551)3632212 (0551)3632002
Qingdao Textile Clothing Industrial Group Company 青島紡織服裝實業集團公司	Qingdao 青島市	Shandong 山東省	(0532)2877853 (0532)2869315
Hebei Textile Import & Export (Group) Company 河北省紡織品進出口(集團)公司	Shijiazhuang 石家莊市	Hebei 河北省	(0311)7028530 (0311)7027781
Zhong Fang Pledget Import & Export Company 中紡紗布進出口公司	Beijing 北京市	Beijing 北京市	(010)65124718 (010)65124713
Shaoxing Import & Export Company 紹興市進出口公司	Shaoxing 紹興市	Zhejiang 浙江省	(0575)5132822 (0575)5141577
Hunan Hua Xiang Import & Export (Group) Company 湖南省華湘進出口(集團)公司	Changsha 長沙市	Hunan 湖南省	(0731)2282440 (0731)2286995
City's Import & Export Company Trade Dept. 市進出口公司貿易部	Yichang 宜昌市	Hubei 湖北省	(0717)6450778 (0717)6441875
Shanghai Pu Dong Xinqu Import & Export Company 上海浦東新區進出口公司	Shanghai 上海市	Shanghai 上海市	(021)58878801 (021)58827444
Ningbo Yinxian Import & Export Company 寧波市鄞縣進出口公司	Ningbo 寧波市	Zhejiang 浙江省	(0574)7875205 (0574)7873168
Zhejiang Silk Import & Export Company 浙江省絲綢進出口公司	Hangzhou 杭州市	Zhejiang 浙江省	(0571)5195588 (0571)5192542

*Also include sales by firms outside this industry.包括本行業以外廠家的銷售。“o” stands for “others”. “o” 代表“其他產品”。

1721: Cotton Spinning 棉紡業

The industry accounts for 1.800% of the total revenue of China's industrial sector in 1996. The revenue growth rate of the industry is -11.3% from 1995, as compared to the growth rate of China's industrial sector, 9.51%. The rate of return on asset is -2.86%. 59.19% of all firms in the industry made a profit while 34.10% had negative returns. The top province in terms of the industry's revenue is Jiangsu, accounting for 18.23% of the total revenue.
本行業在1996年佔全行業總產值1.800%，行業年增長率為-11.3%（全國工業年增長率9.51%）。行業的資產回報率-2.86%，59.19%的企業盈利，34.10%的企業虧損。銷售收入最高的省份為江蘇省，佔本行業的18.23%。

	Total number of firms 企業總數	Total number of employees 職工總數	Total revenue (mil. RMB) 總銷售收入（百萬元）	Total profit (mil. RMB) 總利潤（百萬元）	Return on assets 資產利潤率 (%)	Return on equity 權益利潤率 (%)	Labour productivity ('000 RMB / worker) 勞動生產率（千元/人）	Debts / assets 資產負債率 (%)	Total assets (mil. RMB) 總資產（百萬元）
Industry Overall 行業總體	1,876	2,340,278	104,350	-4,299	-2.86	-14.07	44.59	79.70	150,544

	Number of firms 企業個數	Average number of employees 平均職工人數	Average revenue ('000 RMB) 平均銷售收入（千元）	Average profit ('000 RMB) 平均利潤（千元）	Return on assets 資產利潤率 (%)	Return on equity 權益利潤率 (%)	Labour productivity ('000 RMB / worker) 勞動生產率（千元/人）	Average debts / assets 平均資產負債率(%)	Average Total assets ('000 RMB) 平均總資產（千元）
By ownership 產業所有權									
State-owned 國有	622	2,785	110,715	-6,370	-3.70	-19.47	39.75	80.99	172,132
Collectively-owned 集體	1,034	398	20,639	-246	-1.12	-6.29	51.89	82.18	21,920
Privately-owned 私有	6	48	7,738	-295	-7.78	-23.01	160.65	66.22	3,799
Domestic JVs 聯營	36	780	42,060	-328	-0.81	-2.57	53.90	68.58	40,727
Joint stock 股份制	35	3,025	180,641	-3,083	-1.44	-3.94	59.72	63.43	214,000
Foreign-funded 外資	55	465	43,028	-754	-1.06	-3.09	92.50	65.60	70,905
Overseas Chinese-funded 港澳台資	86	508	46,308	932	1.01	4.94	91.19	79.51	92,006
By size 規模									
Large 大型	196	5,442	236,446	-19,677	-5.26	-23.61	43.45	77.70	373,863
Medium 中型	319	2,268	99,786	-994	-0.73	-3.55	43.99	79.35	135,695
Small 小型	1,337	410	19,756	-94	-0.37	-2.37	48.18	84.46	25,415
By regional distribution 地區分布									
Central-North 華北	219	1,424	60,545	-2,055	-2.23	-10.81	42.51	79.42	92,356
Beijing 北京	21	1,337	91,425	-8,427	-6.91	-29.95	68.38	76.93	121,986
Tianjin 天津	28	1,829	84,263	-4,817	-4.25	-19.14	46.07	77.82	113,467
Hebei 河北	132	1,216	56,012	-141	-0.17	-0.90	46.07	81.07	82,731
Shanxi 山西	32	1,853	40,394	-3,723	-4.30	-19.81	21.80	78.30	86,603
Inner Mongolia 內蒙	6	2,141	48,962	-80	-0.06	-0.24	22.87	74.93	132,577
Northeast 東北	115	1,694	38,303	-5,407	-4.89	-60.66	22.60	91.95	110,658
Liaoning 遼寧	65	1,730	45,296	-3,185	-2.92	-21.46	26.18	86.40	109,163
Jilin 吉林	22	1,430	39,832	-3,951	-4.18	-50.16	27.86	91.66	94,460
Heilongjiang 黑龍江	28	1,820	20,866	-11,708	-9.23	289.64	11.47	103.19	126,856
Central East 華東	881	1,089	60,938	-538	-0.74	-2.82	55.95	73.78	72,838
Shanghai 上海	72	1,361	87,361	-1,360	-1.34	-3.76	64.18	64.27	101,311
Jiangsu 江蘇	247	1,081	76,998	-316	-0.43	-1.43	71.22	70.31	74,274
Zhejiang 浙江	134	799	43,067	-103	-0.20	-0.75	53.91	73.53	51,828
Anhui 安徽	90	1,281	60,710	-2,198	-3.38	-17.17	47.38	80.29	64,970
Fujian 福建	30	811	50,495	27	0.05	0.16	62.29	69.78	53,599
Jiangxi 江西	43	1,398	45,939	-1,154	-1.64	-8.21	32.87	79.99	70,219
Shandong 山東	265	1,086	51,520	-141	-0.18	-0.80	47.45	77.76	79,664
Central-South 中南	471	1,189	48,659	-2,245	-3.19	-17.51	40.93	81.77	70,341
Henan 河南	180	994	46,705	-515	-0.84	-4.27	47.00	80.28	61,153
Hubei 湖北	128	1,529	64,361	-3,631	-4.53	-23.09	42.08	80.37	80,109
Hunan 湖南	68	1,944	32,425	-3,478	-6.67	-68.35	16.68	90.24	52,145
Guangdong 廣東	77	452	42,931	-2,417	-2.66	-16.06	94.96	83.47	91,027
Guangxi 廣西	17	1,072	43,766	-4,538	-5.89	-22.05	40.82	73.29	77,044
Hainan 海南	1	98	18,490	-20	-0.45	-1.80	188.67	74.77	4,440
Southwest 西南	79	1,758	49,070	-4,943	-5.32	-36.75	27.91	85.53	92,990
Chongqing 重慶	21	1,704	55,628	-10,579	-11.24	-323.81	32.64	96.53	94,150
Sichuan 四川	36	1,886	47,111	-2,144	-2.35	-13.78	24.98	82.94	91,203
Guizhou 貴州	10	1,380	36,429	-5,570	-6.44	-31.28	26.39	79.43	86,542
Yunnan 雲南	11	1,785	54,053	-2,452	-2.39	-10.81	30.28	77.86	102,449
Tibet 西藏									
Northwest 西北	111	1,577	55,895	-11,766	-10.09	-90.75	35.44	88.88	116,620
Shaanxi 陝西	42	1,886	54,745	-15,649	-12.86	-152.35	29.03	91.56	121,690
Gansu 甘肅	7	1,612	35,771	-10,740	-13.14	-349.51	22.19	96.24	81,739
Qinghai 青海	2	2,630	73,605	-21,540	-11.87	288.74	27.99	104.11	181,500
Ningxia 寧夏	3	825	6,530	-7,077	-24.75	245.72	7.92	110.07	28,593
Xinjiang 新疆	57	1,348	61,190	-8,936	-7.48	-50.44	45.39	85.18	119,524

1721: Cotton Spinning 棉紡業

Year 年份	Number of firms 企業個數	Rate of change 每年變化 (%)	Number of employees 職工人數 (人)	Rate of change 每年變化 (%)	Total revenue (mil. RMB) 總銷售收入 (百萬元)	Rate of change 每年變化 (%)	Total profit (mil. RMB) 總利潤 (百萬元)	Rate of change 每年變化 (%)
1993	2013		2,562,281		77,463		-1,097	
1994	2072	2.93%	2,245,841	-12.35%	104,761	35.24%	1,361	224.15%
1995	1869	-9.80%	2,412,646	7.43%	117,647	12.30%	-816	-159.96%
1996	1876	0.37%	2,340,278	-3.00%	104,350	-11.30%	-4,299	-426.59%

3 Major products* 3 種主要產品 *	Output 產量	Sales volume 銷售量	Unit 單位
a) Combed Yarn 精梳棉紗	488,442	473,789	ton 噸
b) Polyester Blended Yarn 滌綸混紡紗	1,194,122	1,062,768	ton 噸
c) Cotton Yarn 棉紗	2,311,306	1,872,157	ton 噸

Top 10 firms by revenue (year founded) 收入排名前 10 家企業 (創辦年份)	City 城市	Province 省	Telephone / fax 電話 / 傳真	Number of employees 職工人數	Ownership 產業所有權	Revenue ('000 RMB) 銷售收入 (千元)	Profit ('000 RMB) (rank) 利潤 (千元) (排名)	Total assets ('000 RMB) 總資產 (千元)	Major products 主要產品
Shanghai Shen Da Co. Ltd. 上海申達股份有限公司(1914)	Shanghai 上海市	Shanghai 上海市	(021)62156215 (021)62553400	4,102	Joint stock 股份制	1,052,563	5144(47)	965,290	a,b,c
Huafang Industry General Co. 華芳實業總公司(1976)	Suzhou 蘇州市	Jiangsu 江蘇省	(0512)8441711	3,829	Collectively-owned 集體	929,530	55780(2)	462,640	c
Xinjiang Textile Industry (Group) Co. 新疆紡織工業(集團)公司(1952)	Urumqi 烏魯木齊市	Xinjiang 新疆	(0991)4871767	14,891	State-owned 國有	721,364	-167457(1372)	1,404,581	a,b,c
Zouping Wei Qiao Cotton Textile Mill 鄒平縣位橋棉紡織廠(1951)	Binzhou 濱州市	Shandong 山東省	(0543)4731194 (0543)4731194	3,246	Collectively-owned 集體	690,415	73128(1)	668,758	c
Dezhou Cotton Textile Mill 德州棉紡織廠(1958)	Dezhou 德州市	Shandong 山東省	(0534)2421735 (0534)2447402	10,439	State-owned 國有	664,672	-22512(1310)	911,793	c
Wuxi No.1 Cotton Manufacturing Factory 無錫市第一棉紡織廠(1921)	Wuxi 無錫市	Jiangsu 江蘇省	(0510)2723567 (0510)2702374	4,710	State-owned 國有	662,163	163(411)	613,675	a,b,c
Anhui Anqing Textile Mill 安徽省安慶市紡織廠(1958)	Anqing 安慶市	Anhui 安徽省	(0556)5510810 (0556)5510166	8,905	State-owned 國有	594,790	10150(15)	603,090	a,b,c
Jiangsu Zhongxiang Group Co. Ltd. 江蘇眾想集團有限公司(1959)	Yancheng 鹽城市	Jiangsu 江蘇省	(0515)8365352 (0515)8365468	11,342	State-owned 國有	540,010	5050(49)	621,590	c
Zhejiang Jin Wei Group Company 浙江金威集團公司(1969)	Shaoxing 紹興市	Zhejiang 浙江省	(0575)2019145 (0575)2019151	5,049	State-owned 國有	532,353	15035(9)	433,750	o
Hubei Puqi Textile General Factory 湖北蒲圻紡織總廠(1971)	Xianning 咸寧市	Hubei 湖北省	(0715)5513471 (0715)5510947	15,402	State-owned 國有	521,082	-65355(1365)	679,746	o

Top 10 Cities by Production Output 產出排名前 10 位城市	Province 省	Market share 市場份額	Number of firms 企業個數
Shanghai 上海市	Shanghai 上海市	6.82%	97
Nantong 南通市	Jiangsu 江蘇省	4.82%	82
Suzhou 蘇州市	Jiangsu 江蘇省	3.74%	68
Yancheng 鹽城市	Jiangsu 江蘇省	3.19%	31
Shijiazhuang 石家莊市	Hebei 河北省	2.63%	41
Tianjin 天津市	Tianjin 天津市	2.22%	35
Binzhou 濱州市	Shandong 山東省	2.00%	31
Beijing 北京市	Beijing 北京市	1.94%	21
Wuxi 無錫市	Jiangsu 江蘇省	1.93%	31
Zhengzhou 鄭州市	Henan 河南省	1.91%	12

10 Major Wholesalers 10 家主要批發商	City 城市	Province 省	Telephone / Fax 電話 / 傳真
Anhui Clothing Import & Export Company 安徽省服裝進出口公司	Hefei 合肥市	Anhui 安徽省	(0551)3632212 (0551)3632002
Qingdao Textile Clothing Industrial Group Company 青島紡織服裝實業集團公司	Qingdao 青島市	Shandong 山東省	(0532)2877853 (0532)2869315
Hebei Textile Import & Export (Group) Company 河北省紡織品進出口(集團)公司	Shijiazhuang 石家莊市	Hebei 河北省	(0311)7028530 (0311)7027781
Zhong Fang Pledget Import & Export Company 中紡紗布進出口公司	Beijing 北京市	Beijing 北京市	(010)65124718 (010)65124713
Shaoxing Import & Export Company 紹興市進出口公司	Shaoxing 紹興市	Zhejiang 浙江省	(0575)5132822 (0575)5141577
Hunan Hua Xiang Import & Export (Group) Company 湖南省華湘進出口(集團)公司	Changsha 長沙市	Hunan 湖南省	(0731)2282440 (0731)2286995
City's Import & Export Company Trade Dept. 市進出口公司貿易部	Yichang 宜昌市	Hubei 湖北省	(0717)6450778 (0717)6441875
Shanghai Pu Dong Xinqu Import & Export Company 上海浦東新區進出口公司	Shanghai 上海市	Shanghai 上海市	(021)58878801 (021)58827444
Ningbo Yinxian Import & Export Company 寧波市鄞縣進出口公司	Ningbo 寧波市	Zhejiang 浙江省	(0574)7875205 (0574)7873168
Zhejiang Silk Import & Export Company 浙江省絲綢進出口公司	Hangzhou 杭州市	Zhejiang 浙江省	(0571)5195588 (0571)5192542

*Also include sales by firms outside this industry.包括本行業以外廠家的銷售。"o" stands for "others". "o" 代表"其他產品"。

1722: Cotton Weaving 棉織業

The industry accounts for 0.741% of the total revenue of China's industrial sector in 1996. The revenue growth rate of the industry is -11.3% from 1995, as compared to the growth rate of China's industrial sector, 9.51%. The rate of return on asset is -1.20%. 58.18% of all firms in the industry made a profit while 34.33% had negative returns. The top province in terms of the industry's revenue is Jiangsu, accounting for 31.41% of the total revenue.
本行業在1996年佔全行業總產值0.741%，行業年增長率為-11.3%（全國工業年增長率9.51%）。行業的資產回報率-1.20%，58.18%的企業盈利，34.33%的企業虧損。銷售收入最高的省份為江蘇省，佔本行業的31.41%。

	Total number of firms 企業總數	Total number of employees 職工總數	Total revenue (mil. RMB) 總銷售收入（百萬元）	Total profit (mil. RMB) 總利潤（百萬元）	Return on assets 資產利潤率 (%)	Return on equity 權益利潤率 (%)	Labour productivity ('000 RMB / worker) 勞動生產率（千元／人）	Debts / assets 資產負債率 (%)	Total assets (mil. RMB) 總資產（百萬元）
Industry Overall 行業總體	2,847	912,132	42,953	-619	-1.20	-5.63	47.09	78.66	51,530

	Number of firms 企業個數	Average number of employees 平均職工人數	Average revenue ('000 RMB) 平均銷售收入（千元）	Average profit ('000 RMB) 平均利潤（千元）	Return on assets 資產利潤率 (%)	Return on equity 權益利潤率 (%)	Labour productivity ('000 RMB / worker) 勞動生產率（千元／人）	Average debts / assets 平均資產負債率(%)	Average Total assets ('000 RMB) 平均總資產（千元）
By ownership 產業所有權									
State-owned 國有	547	767	22,594	-1,589	-3.83	-29.84	29.47	87.18	41,523
Collectively-owned 集體	1,981	201	11,128	133	1.53	5.76	55.39	73.51	8,699
Privately-owned 私有	20	54	3,726	315	13.29	28.75	68.56	53.75	2,372
Domestic JVs 聯營	57	344	18,022	-311	-1.99	-7.07	52.35	71.80	15,591
Joint stock 股份制	29	1,070	70,961	3,715	4.15	11.11	66.29	62.62	89,460
Foreign-funded 外資	57	331	33,861	526	0.86	3.56	102.41	75.73	60,934
Overseas Chinese-funded 港澳台資	154	202	22,512	-895	-3.03	-9.67	111.60	68.70	29,596
By size 規模									
Large 大型	60	2,356	142,532	1,545	0.73	3.06	60.49	76.05	210,550
Medium 中型	232	1,047	51,004	-1,149	-1.72	-8.77	48.72	80.35	66,675
Small 小型	2,543	208	8,924	-175	-1.90	-9.03	42.86	78.95	9,213
By regional distribution 地區分布									
Central-North 華北	329	289	9,458	-130	-0.93	-5.15	32.75	82.03	14,068
Beijing 北京	21	197	9,257	-30	-0.17	-0.64	46.92	72.88	17,339
Tianjin 天津	55	322	11,491	-677	-3.36	-20.47	35.72	83.60	20,160
Hebei 河北	186	263	9,820	14	0.11	0.56	37.33	80.16	12,511
Shanxi 山西	58	351	6,692	-101	-0.94	-8.55	19.07	88.99	10,749
Inner Mongolia 內蒙	9	434	7,854	-191	-0.84	-8.37	18.12	89.97	22,753
Northeast 東北	213	321	6,242	-744	-4.98	-102.48	19.43	95.14	14,950
Liaoning 遼寧	121	356	8,212	-741	-4.18	-46.20	23.07	90.95	17,722
Jilin 吉林	42	412	5,085	-1,466	-8.15	82.61	12.35	109.87	17,977
Heilongjiang 黑龍江	50	161	2,445	-146	-2.57	-20.80	15.19	87.67	5,700
Central East 華東	1,292	322	19,421	-115	-0.62	-2.44	60.26	74.63	18,570
Shanghai 上海	92	324	16,089	-248	-1.51	-7.49	49.71	79.81	16,399
Jiangsu 江蘇	490	388	27,537	-102	-0.49	-1.80	71.02	72.82	20,845
Zhejiang 浙江	216	202	14,214	-163	-1.06	-4.27	70.33	75.14	15,325
Anhui 安徽	127	311	10,190	-578	-5.57	681.88	32.73	100.82	10,365
Fujian 福建	67	137	8,851	-670	-3.06	-7.40	64.70	58.69	21,944
Jiangxi 江西	62	231	6,300	-420	-2.87	-22.54	27.23	87.26	14,627
Shandong 山東	238	378	20,046	436	1.97	7.05	53.03	72.07	22,127
Central-South 中南	719	321	14,888	61	0.31	1.33	46.41	76.89	19,919
Henan 河南	191	336	11,636	425	3.09	11.56	34.66	73.27	13,755
Hubei 湖北	271	343	13,406	-267	-2.03	-12.56	39.08	83.81	13,111
Hunan 湖南	88	270	5,979	-370	-3.82	-22.12	22.15	82.73	9,673
Guangdong 廣東	143	257	26,953	738	1.68	6.77	104.89	75.15	43,877
Guangxi 廣西	25	523	18,746	-1,517	-3.73	-11.64	35.83	67.93	40,642
Hainan 海南	1								
Southwest 西南	194	283	6,735	-753	-5.98	-47.91	23.81	87.51	12,586
Chongqing 重慶	73	167	3,305	-726	-14.51	234.10	19.75	106.20	5,002
Sichuan 四川	94	338	7,939	-669	-4.15	-36.26	23.49	88.56	16,133
Guizhou 貴州	10	486	14,213	-1,433	-4.63	-11.03	29.26	58.03	30,953
Yunnan 雲南	16	369	10,794	-956	-6.28	-63.10	29.26	90.05	15,218
Tibet 西藏									
Northwest 西北	100	467	14,086	-1,665	-5.62	-53.96	30.15	89.58	29,613
Shaanxi 陝西	71	564	16,392	-1,939	-5.14	-41.05	29.08	87.48	37,722
Gansu 甘肅	6	133	6,162	472	12.81	112.75	46.21	88.64	3,682
Qinghai 青海									
Ningxia 寧夏	2	131	2,035	15	0.31	-0.96	15.59	132.23	4,840
Xinjiang 新疆	21	269	9,699	-1,507	-12.60	120.30	36.10	110.47	11,965

1722: Cotton Weaving 棉織業

Year 年份	Number of firms 企業個數	Rate of change 每年變化 (%)	Number of employees 職工人數 (人)	Rate of change 每年變化 (%)	Total revenue (mil. RMB) 總銷售收入 (百萬元)	Rate of change 每年變化 (%)	Total profit (mil. RMB) 總利潤 (百萬元)	Rate of change 每年變化 (%)
1993	3,219		1,094,730		32,885		-623	
1994	3,356	4.26%	1,079,390	-1.40%	40,838	24.19%	-118	81.01%
1995	3,228	-3.82%	1,075,659	-0.35%	48,439	18.61%	-303	-156.38%
1996	2,847	-11.80%	912,132	-15.20%	42,953	-11.33%	-619	-104.10%

3 Major products* 3種主要產品 *	Output 產量	Sales volume 銷售量	Unit 單位
a) Coloured Woven Cloth 色織布	101,819	107,928	10,000 metre 萬米
b) Cotton Cloth 棉布	463,790	459,152	10,000 metre 萬米

Top 10 firms by revenue (year founded) 收入排名前10家企業 (創辦年份)	City 城市	Province 省	Telephone / fax 電話 / 傳真	Number of employees 職工人數	Ownership 產業所有權	Revenue ('000 RMB) 銷售收入 (千元)	Profit ('000 RMB) (rank) 利潤 (千元) (排名)	Total assets ('000 RMB) 總資產 (千元)	Major products 主要產品
Zhuhai Qian Shan Yu Xin Weaving & Dyeing Co. Ltd. 珠海市前山裕新織染有限公司(1989)	Zhuhai 珠海市	Guangdong 廣東省	(0756)8612042 (0756)8611847	1,868	Overseas Chinese-funded 港澳台資	568,736	49699(3)	936,428	a,b
Hei Peony (Group) Co. Ltd. 黑牡丹(集團)股份有限公司(1940)	Changzhou 常州市	Jiangsu 江蘇省	(0519)8811238 (0519)8828817	1,994	Joint stock 股份制	507,630	16750(11)	416,900	a,b
Baoding No.1 Cotton Textile Co. Ltd. 保定一棉紡織有限責任公司(1960)	Baoding 保定市	Hebei 河北省	(0312)3099043 (0312)3028894	7,284	State-owned 國有	441,848	2(928)	480,537	b
Jiangsu Cheng Gong Group Co. 江蘇成功集團公司(1953)	Suzhou 蘇州市	Jiangsu 江蘇省	(0512)8390281 (0512)8391484	1,534	Collectively-owned 集體	408,788	19139(8)	123,144	b
Jiangyin Cha Mei Corduroy Group Co. Ltd. 江陰市茶梅燈芯絨集團有限責任公司(1980)	Wuxi 無錫市	Jiangsu 江蘇省	(0510)6651052 (0510)6601051	1,990	Collectively-owned 集體	399,500	20897(7)	124,452	b
Shandong Da Xing Hua Industry Group General Co. 山東大興華實業(集團)公司(1985)	Laiwu 萊蕪市	Shandong 山東省	(0634)6213850 (0634)6215203	7,500	Collectively-owned 集體	336,207	1238(125)	406,279	a,b
Wuhan No.2 Cotton Textile Mill 武漢市第二棉紡織廠(1965)	Wuhan 武漢市	Hubei 湖北省	(027)6552491 (027)6553654	7,124	State-owned 國有	323,225	-24756(1742)	308,228	o
Wuxi Jiangsu Yin Yang Group Company 無錫市江蘇銀洋集團公司(1993)	Wuxi 無錫市	Jiangsu 江蘇省	(0510)5014415	754	Collectively-owned 集體	323,177	9839(17)	236,068	b
Shannxi No.9 Cotton Textile Factory 陝西第九棉紡織廠(1941)	Baoji 寶雞市	Shaanxi 陝西省	(0917)8561340 (0917)8562075	7,336	State-owned 國有	313,487	-14543(1730)	1,114,445	o
Northwest No.2 Cotton Ltd. Liability Co. 國營西北第二棉紡織廠(1953)	Xianyang 咸陽市	Shaanxi 陝西省	(0910)3212823 (0910)3216101	7,672	State-owned 國有	299,993	-49082(1748)	544,795	o

Top 10 Cities by Production Output 產出排名前10位城市	Province 省	Market share 市場份額	Number of firms 企業個數
Wuxi 無錫市	Jiangsu 江蘇省	6.96%	131
Changzhou 常州市	Jiangsu 江蘇省	6.08%	69
Nantong 南通市	Jiangsu 江蘇省	5.56%	157
Suzhou 蘇州市	Jiangsu 江蘇省	4.55%	93
Shanghai 上海市	Shanghai 上海市	4.13%	120
Shaoxing 紹興市	Zhejiang 浙江省	4.02%	96
Yancheng 鹽城市	Jiangsu 江蘇省	3.37%	61
Taizhou 泰州市	Jiangsu 江蘇省	2.51%	45
Weifang 濰坊市	Shandong 山東省	2.32%	92
Guangzhou 廣州市	Guangdong 廣東省	1.93%	36

10 Major Wholesalers 10家主要批發商	City 城市	Province 省	Telephone / Fax 電話 / 傳真
Anhui Clothing Import & Export Company 安徽省服裝進出口公司	Hefei 合肥市	Anhui 安徽省	(0551)3632212 (0551)3632002
Qingdao Textile Clothing Industrial Group Company 青島紡織服裝實業集團公司	Qingdao 青島市	Shandong 山東省	(0532)2877853 (0532)2869315
Hebei Textile Import & Export (Group) Company 河北省紡織品進出口(集團)公司	Shijiazhuang 石家莊市	Hebei 河北省	(0311)7028530 (0311)7027781
Zhong Fang Pledget Import & Export Company 中紡紗布進出口公司	Beijing 北京市	Beijing 北京市	(010)65124718 (010)65124713
Shaoxing Import & Export Company 紹興市進出口公司	Shaoxing 紹興市	Zhejiang 浙江省	(0575)5132822 (0575)5141577
Hunan Hua Xiang Import & Export (Group) Company 湖南省華湘進出口(集團)公司	Changsha 長沙市	Hunan 湖南省	(0731)2282440 (0731)2286995
City's Import & Export Company Trade Dept. 市進出口公司貿易部	Yichang 宜昌市	Hubei 湖北省	(0717)6450778 (0717)6441875
Shanghai Pu Dong Xinqu Import & Export Company 上海浦東新區進出口公司	Shanghai 上海市	Shanghai 上海市	(021)58878801 (021)58827444
Ningbo Yinxian Import & Export Company 寧波市鄞縣進出口公司	Ningbo 寧波市	Zhejiang 浙江省	(0574)7875205 (0574)7873168
Zhejiang Silk Import & Export Company 浙江省絲綢進出口公司	Hangzhou 杭州市	Zhejiang 浙江省	(0571)5195588 (0571)5192542

*Also include sales by firms outside this industry.包括本行業以外廠家的銷售。"o" stands for "others". "o" 代表 "其他產品"。

1723: Cotton Printing and Dyeing 印染業

The industry accounts for 0.680% of the total revenue of China's industrial sector in 1996. The revenue growth rate of the industry is -10.1% from 1995, as compared to the growth rate of China's industrial sector, 9.51%. The rate of return on asset is -1.05%. 61.22% of all firms in the industry made a profit while 32.31% had negative returns. The top province in terms of the industry's revenue is Guangdong, accounting for 21.06% of the total revenue.
本行業在1996年佔全行業總產值0.680%，行業年增長率為-10.1%（全國工業年增長率9.51%）。行業的資產回報率-1.05%，61.22%的企業盈利，32.31%的企業虧損。銷售收入最高的省份為廣東省，佔本行業的21.06%。

	Total number of firms 企業總數	Total number of employees 職工總數	Total revenue (mil. RMB) 總銷售收入（百萬元）	Total profit (mil. RMB) 總利潤（百萬元）	Return on assets 資產利潤率 (%)	Return on equity 權益利潤率 (%)	Labour productivity ('000 RMB / worker) 勞動生產率（千元/人）	Debts / assets 資產負債率 (%)	Total assets (mil. RMB) 總資產（百萬元）
Industry Overall 行業總體	1,261	389,277	39,391	-482	-1.05	-4.33	101.19	75.72	45,869

	Number of firms 企業個數	Average number of employees 平均職工人數	Average revenue ('000 RMB) 平均銷售收入（千元）	Average profit ('000 RMB) 平均利潤（千元）	Return on assets 資產利潤率 (%)	Return on equity 權益利潤率 (%)	Labour productivity ('000 RMB / worker) 勞動生產率（千元/人）	Average debts / assets 平均資產負債率(%)	Average Total assets ('000 RMB) 平均總資產（千元）
By ownership 產業所有權									
State-owned 國有	230	909	62,622	-3,326	-3.79	-33.91	68.88	88.82	87,726
Collectively-owned 集體	671	157	16,313	390	2.94	10.28	104.14	71.42	13,257
Privately-owned 私有	9	50	6,319	332	9.98	34.14	126.39	70.77	3,326
Domestic JVs 聯營	25	332	36,901	-931	-2.00	-5.64	111.16	64.44	46,467
Joint stock 股份制	20	454	76,063	2,384	4.58	12.89	167.43	64.51	52,114
Foreign-funded 外資	85	166	22,501	-502	-1.38	-3.42	135.14	59.52	36,249
Overseas Chinese-funded 港澳台資	216	216	44,710	171	0.32	0.86	206.99	62.44	52,971
By size 規模									
Large 大型	64	1,749	179,322	-4,803	-2.07	-11.06	102.52	81.24	231,517
Medium 中型	122	883	94,043	-1,329	-1.32	-6.13	106.53	78.45	100,549
Small 小型	1,051	160	15,801	-12	-0.07	-0.22	98.99	69.58	17,873
By regional distribution 地區分布									
Central-North 華北	155	319	26,401	52	0.13	0.70	82.89	81.19	39,509
Beijing 北京	32	183	9,980	-243	-0.45	-1.80	54.51	75.20	54,568
Tianjin 天津	45	280	20,238	-568	-1.73	-27.25	72.36	93.66	32,902
Hebei 河北	68	375	39,425	702	1.98	7.76	105.09	74.46	35,402
Shanxi 山西	9	588	20,000	-690	-1.28	-79.72	34.03	98.40	53,976
Inner Mongolia 內蒙	1	126	1,250	-90	-2.23	-3.77	9.92	40.59	4,040
Northeast 東北	81	267	10,017	-522	-2.12	-11.84	37.48	82.07	24,582
Liaoning 遼寧	54	328	13,313	-219	-0.72	-3.29	40.55	78.15	30,571
Jilin 吉林	11	212	6,324	-1,978	-10.15	79.53	29.82	112.77	19,483
Heilongjiang 黑龍江	16	99	1,433	-541	-6.88	-36.43	14.42	81.13	7,873
Central East 華東	602	298	33,583	-104	-0.30	-1.10	112.57	72.69	34,493
Shanghai 上海	85	336	32,024	-687	-1.72	-5.68	95.24	69.65	39,843
Jiangsu 江蘇	169	344	48,606	-198	-0.48	-1.72	141.41	72.01	41,111
Zhejiang 浙江	164	193	20,415	409	1.99	7.05	105.83	71.79	20,585
Anhui 安徽	24	574	37,385	-503	-1.03	-12.12	65.17	91.47	48,654
Fujian 福建	55	143	23,926	571	1.57	3.25	167.85	51.78	36,386
Jiangxi 江西	14	655	19,341	-2,583	-4.56	-42.50	29.54	89.26	56,587
Shandong 山東	91	335	37,893	-230	-0.68	-3.51	113.03	80.72	33,990
Central-South 中南	349	308	32,649	-394	-0.99	-3.64	106.17	72.83	39,786
Henan 河南	51	275	17,767	-135	-0.57	-3.57	64.71	84.09	23,866
Hubei 湖北	43	622	33,322	-3,551	-7.67	-85.08	53.54	90.98	46,273
Hunan 湖南	32	569	15,053	-1,834	-7.12	692.92	26.47	101.03	25,767
Guangdong 廣東	204	208	40,671	595	1.32	3.60	195.91	63.26	45,009
Guangxi 廣西	17	339	12,585	-2,245	-6.24	-218.06	37.12	97.14	35,948
Hainan 海南	2	125	31,575	-1,175	-3.86	-14.27	252.60	72.97	30,465
Southwest 西南	49	343	45,407	-2,378	-6.82	-94.46	132.20	92.78	34,877
Chongqing 重慶	9	534	65,423	-3,770	-9.52	107.96	122.51	108.82	39,583
Sichuan 四川	29	325	49,811	-2,165	-5.65	-56.19	152.93	89.94	38,316
Guizhou 貴州	2	23	880	-275	-4.23	-211.54	39.11	98.00	6,500
Yunnan 雲南	8	253	15,601	-1,938	-8.20	-33.67	61.73	75.64	23,626
Tibet 西藏									
Northwest 西北	25	581	26,053	-5,244	-9.40	-213.82	44.88	95.61	55,803
Shaanxi 陝西	23	601	28,214	-5,052	-8.78	-206.93	46.92	95.76	57,544
Gansu 甘肅	1	634	2,150	-14,700	-21.55	-365.67	3.39	94.11	68,220
Qinghai 青海									
Ningxia 寧夏									
Xinjiang 新疆	1	49	250	-200	-6.01	-17.54	5.10	66.07	3,330

1723: Cotton Printing and Dyeing 印染業

Year 年份	Number of firms 企業個數	Rate of change 每年變化 (%)	Number of employees 職工人數 (人)	Rate of change 每年變化 (%)	Total revenue (mil. RMB) 總銷售收入 (百萬元)	Rate of change 每年變化 (%)	Total profit (mil. RMB) 總利潤 (百萬元)	Rate of change 每年變化 (%)
1993	1,084		490,127		30,092		-188	
1994	1,245	14.85%	402,758	-17.83%	39,131	30.04%	-40	78.78%
1995	1,362	9.40%	446,303	10.81%	43,808	11.95%	-545	-1266.52%
1996	1,261	-7.42%	389,277	-12.78%	39,391	-10.08%	-482	11.51%

3 Major products* 3 種主要產品 *	Output 產量	Sales volume 銷售量	Unit 單位
a) Print Cloth 印花布	255,933	253,374	10,000 metre 萬米
b) Dyeing Cloth 染色布	499,253	474,290	10,000 metre 萬米

Top 10 firms by revenue (year founded) 收入排名前 10 家企業 (創辦年份)	City 城市	Province 省	Telephone / fax 電話 / 傳真	Number of employees 職工人數	Ownership 產業所有權	Revenue ('000 RMB) 銷售收入 (千元)	Profit ('000 RMB) (rank) 利潤 (千元) (排名)	Total assets ('000 RMB) 總資產 (千元)	Major products 主要產品
Mianyang Printing & Dyeing Factory 綿陽印染廠(1987)	Mianyang 綿陽市	Sichuan 四川省	(0816)2223963 (0816)2220246	825	State-owned 國有	1,448,442	-1724(727)	113,709	a
Panyu Tan Zhou Zhen Yu Textile Printing & Dyeing Co. Ltd. 番禺譚洲振裕紡織染印有限公司(1993)	Guangzhou 廣州市	Guangdong 廣東省	(020)84931001 (020)84931233	550	Overseas Chinese-funded 港澳台資	572,278	0(521)	334,447	b
Zhejiang Ya Tai Cloth Factory 浙江亞太布廠(1984)	Shaoxing 紹興市	Zhejiang 浙江省	(0575)5184998 (0575)5184274	885	Collectively-owned 集體	572,030	40022(1)	344,020	o
Shandou Sez Jingwei Spinning and Weaving Co. Ltd. 汕頭經濟特區經緯紡織有限公司(1990)	Shantou 汕頭市	Guangdong 廣東省	(0754)8899333 (0754)8898333	550	Overseas Chinese-funded 港澳台資	571,769	14372(14)	454,465	a
Zhangjiagang Sha Zhou Textile Printing & Dyeing Co. 張家港市沙洲紡織印染公司(1976)	Suzhou 蘇州市	Jiangsu 江蘇省	(0512)8500592 (0512)8500591	2,012	Collectively-owned 集體	554,780	9705(25)	268,527	a
Weifang Hua Shi Textile (Group) Company 濰坊華實紡織品(集團)公司(1994)	Weifang 濰坊市	Shandong 山東省	(0536)8232971 (0536)8234465	2,317	State-owned 國有	545,774	301(262)	400,782	o
Dongguan Fuan Textile Printing & Dyeing Ltd. 東莞長安鎮福安紡織印染有限公司(1988)	Dongguan 東莞市	Guangdong 廣東省	(0769)5532318 (0769)5532005	4,113	Overseas Chinese-funded 港澳台資	536,100	19700(4)	545,163	b
Shandong Binzhou Printing & Dyeing Group 山東濱州印染集團股份有限公司(1980)	Binzhou 濱州市	Shandong 山東省	(0543)3311888 (0543)3323513	1,401	Joint stock 股份制	428,622	2818(73)	243,101	a,b
Yixing Le Qi Textile Printing & Dyeing Co. Ltd. 宜興樂祺紡織印染有限公司(1993)	Wuxi 無錫市	Jiangsu 江蘇省	(0510)7733516 (0510)7732400	543	Overseas Chinese-funded 港澳台資	395,175	14784(13)	151,498	b
Yangzhou Printing & Dyeing Mill 揚州印染廠(1956)	Yangzhou 揚州市	Jiangsu 江蘇省	(0514)7246034 (0514)7242764	1,655	State-owned 國有	384,986	915(176)	206,900	a,b

Top 10 Cities by Production Output 產出排名前 10 位城市	Province 省	Market share 市場份額	Number of firms 企業個數
Suzhou 蘇州市	Jiangsu 江蘇省	8.49%	95
Wuxi 無錫市	Jiangsu 江蘇省	7.05%	67
Shanghai 上海市	Shanghai 上海市	6.79%	115
Foshan 佛山市	Guangdong 廣東省	4.97%	33
Guangzhou 廣州市	Guangdong 廣東省	4.71%	70
Shaoxing 紹興市	Zhejiang 浙江省	4.41%	40
Weifang 濰坊市	Shandong 山東省	3.84%	19
Nantong 南通市	Jiangsu 江蘇省	2.94%	54
Shijiazhuang 石家莊市	Hebei 河北省	2.93%	21
Shantou 汕頭市	Guangdong 廣東省	2.60%	16

10 Major Wholesalers 10 家主要批發商	City 城市	Province 省	Telephone / Fax 電話 / 傳真
Anhui Clothing Import & Export Company 安徽省服裝進出口公司	Hefei 合肥市	Anhui 安徽省	(0551)3632212 (0551)3632002
Qingdao Textile Clothing Industrial Group Company 青島紡織服裝實業集團公司	Qingdao 青島市	Shandong 山東省	(0532)2877853 (0532)2869315
Hebei Textile Import & Export (Group) Company 河北省紡織品進出口(集團)公司	Shijiazhuang 石家莊市	Hebei 河北省	(0311)7028530 (0311)7027781
Zhong Fang Pledget Import & Export Company 中紡紗布進出口公司	Beijing 北京市	Beijing 北京市	(010)65124718 (010)65124713
Shaoxing Import & Export Company 紹興市進出口公司	Shaoxing 紹興市	Zhejiang 浙江省	(0575)5132822 (0575)5141577
Hunan Hua Xiang Import & Export (Group) Company 湖南省華湘進出口(集團)公司	Changsha 長沙市	Hunan 湖南省	(0731)2282440 (0731)2286995
City's Import & Export Company Trade Dept. 市進出口公司貿易部	Yichang 宜昌市	Hubei 湖北省	(0717)6450778 (0717)6441875
Shanghai Pu Dong Xinqu Import & Export Company 上海浦東新區進出口公司	Shanghai 上海市	Shanghai 上海市	(021)58878801 (021)58827444
Ningbo Yinxian Import & Export Company 寧波市鄞縣進出口公司	Ningbo 寧波市	Zhejiang 浙江省	(0574)7875205 (0574)7873168
Zhejiang Silk Import & Export Company 浙江省絲綢進出口公司	Hangzhou 杭州市	Zhejiang 浙江省	(0571)5195588 (0571)5192542

*Also include sales by firms outside this industry.包括本行業以外廠家的銷售。"o" stands for "others". "o" 代表"其他產品"。

1724: Cotton Products 棉製品業

The industry accounts for 0.287% of the total revenue of China's industrial sector in 1996. The revenue growth rate of the industry is 6.9% from 1995, as compared to the growth rate of China's industrial sector, 9.51%. The rate of return on asset is -0.33%. 58.54% of all firms in the industry made a profit while 32.00% had negative returns. The top province in terms of the industry's revenue is Jiangsu, accounting for 21.21% of the total revenue.
本行業在1996年佔全行業總產值0.287%，行業年增長率為6.9%（全國工業年增長率9.51%）。行業的資產回報率-0.33%，58.54%的企業盈利，32.00%的企業虧損。銷售收入最高的省份為江蘇省，佔本行業的21.21%。

	Total number of firms 企業總數	Total number of employees 職工總數	Total revenue (mil. RMB) 總銷售收入（百萬元）	Total profit (mil. RMB) 總利潤（百萬元）	Return on assets 資產利潤率 (%)	Return on equity 權益利潤率 (%)	Labour productivity ('000 RMB / worker) 勞動生產率（千元/人）	Debts / assets 資產負債率 (%)	Total assets (mil. RMB) 總資產（百萬元）
Industry Overall 行業總體	1,669	431,051	16,643	-69	-0.33	-1.71	38.61	80.88	21,088

	Number of firms 企業個數	Average number of employees 平均職工人數	Average revenue ('000 RMB) 平均銷售收入（千元）	Average profit ('000 RMB) 平均利潤（千元）	Return on assets 資產利潤率 (%)	Return on equity 權益利潤率 (%)	Labour productivity ('000 RMB / worker) 勞動生產率（千元/人）	Average debts / assets 平均資產負債率(%)	Average Total assets ('000 RMB) 平均總資產（千元）
By ownership 產業所有權									
State-owned 國有	292	662	19,401	-753	-2.35	-18.11	29.32	87.02	32,062
Collectively-owned 集體	1,171	167	6,820	92	1.28	6.47	40.86	80.28	7,219
Privately-owned 私有	13	48	2,326	381	29.19	56.51	48.76	48.35	1,305
Domestic JVs 聯營	28	287	16,615	868	6.93	18.69	57.96	62.92	12,519
Joint stock 股份制	11	351	11,953	-1,735	-13.33	587.91	34.06	102.27	13,019
Foreign-funded 外資	67	222	20,589	297	1.15	2.93	92.77	60.67	25,800
Overseas Chinese-funded 港澳台資	84	214	11,634	155	1.27	3.90	54.32	67.53	12,260
By size 規模									
Large 大型	31	1,356	86,754	-72	-0.05	-0.19	64.00	73.75	148,090
Medium 中型	124	968	34,325	-350	-0.68	-5.18	35.46	86.89	51,508
Small 小型	1,496	181	6,482	-16	-0.23	-1.18	35.89	80.33	6,758
By regional distribution 地區分布									
Central-North 華北	183	245	4,882	-100	-0.92	-7.31	19.90	87.47	10,910
Beijing 北京	36	92	3,658	-213	-2.15	-7.09	39.88	69.66	9,887
Tianjin 天津	47	305	9,429	25	0.13	1.17	30.92	88.80	19,098
Hebei 河北	66	317	4,062	-124	-1.44	-72.27	12.82	98.01	8,630
Shanxi 山西	22	184	1,619	-89	-1.88	-5.92	8.82	68.23	4,717
Inner Mongolia 內蒙	12	191	1,232	-137	-2.36	59.64	6.43	103.95	5,798
Northeast 東北	103	204	5,506	-142	-1.28	-6.61	26.95	80.56	11,032
Liaoning 遼寧	54	293	9,447	-120	-0.65	-2.84	32.26	77.23	18,586
Jilin 吉林	17	171	1,391	-352	-7.93	90.21	8.12	108.78	4,444
Heilongjiang 黑龍江	32	72	1,042	-66	-3.71	192.73	14.38	101.93	1,784
Central East 華東	792	269	13,848	200	1.32	5.83	51.43	77.41	15,163
Shanghai 上海	107	327	19,607	267	1.12	4.85	60.05	77.00	23,930
Jiangsu 江蘇	210	281	16,808	80	0.55	1.92	59.77	71.40	14,513
Zhejiang 浙江	106	142	11,036	648	5.91	16.64	77.57	64.47	10,953
Anhui 安徽	105	228	8,289	39	0.54	3.19	36.28	82.97	7,152
Fujian 福建	47	134	5,190	-12	-0.19	-0.66	38.64	71.18	6,293
Jiangxi 江西	53	194	2,806	-153	-2.20	-41.35	14.48	94.69	6,982
Shandong 山東	164	388	17,729	298	1.28	8.06	45.70	84.14	23,311
Central-South 中南	457	249	7,632	-282	-2.81	-18.37	30.67	84.71	10,041
Henan 河南	159	220	6,355	-60	-0.72	-3.13	28.93	76.86	8,229
Hubei 湖北	100	401	9,467	-315	-2.21	-38.81	23.63	94.30	14,260
Hunan 湖南	74	234	4,425	-263	-4.78	-74.06	18.94	93.55	5,505
Guangdong 廣東	84	142	10,530	-271	-2.50	-12.37	74.26	79.80	10,844
Guangxi 廣西	40	239	7,974	-1,141	-8.51	-42.53	33.37	80.00	13,410
Hainan 海南									
Southwest 西南	79	302	6,025	-455	-3.78	-30.29	19.94	87.53	12,046
Chongqing 重慶	17	273	5,621	-699	-6.35	190.41	20.58	103.34	11,009
Sichuan 四川	38	344	7,432	-370	-2.69	-20.26	21.58	86.72	13,744
Guizhou 貴州	12	224	2,713	-493	-5.03	-45.46	12.14	88.94	9,799
Yunnan 雲南	11	288	5,362	-323	-3.16	-8.48	18.65	62.73	10,215
Tibet 西藏									
Northwest 西北	55	259	4,566	-535	-7.25	-100.93	17.63	92.82	7,375
Shaanxi 陝西	27	417	6,700	-1,089	-9.99	-493.46	16.07	97.98	10,901
Gansu 甘肅	14	133	3,159	24	0.62	2.85	23.80	78.13	3,776
Qinghai 青海									
Ningxia 寧夏	4	116	1,138	25	0.61	1.40	9.81	56.24	4,085
Xinjiang 新疆	10	67	2,143	-44	-1.04	-9.87	32.23	89.41	4,211

1724: Cotton Products 棉製品業

Year 年份	Number of firms 企業個數	Rate of change 每年變化 (%)	Number of employees 職工人數（人）	Rate of change 每年變化 (%)	Total revenue (mil. RMB) 總銷售收入（百萬元）	Rate of change 每年變化 (%)	Total profit (mil. RMB) 總利潤（百萬元）	Rate of change 每年變化 (%)
1993	1,670		565,466		10,716		-167	
1994	1,757	5.21%	475,953	-15.83%	13,900	29.70%	-116	30.20%
1995	1,735	-1.25%	482,187	1.31%	15,565	11.98%	-152	-30.21%
1996	1,669	-3.80%	431,051	-10.61%	16,643	6.93%	-69	54.46%

3 Major products* 3種主要產品*	Output 產量	Sales volume 銷售量	Unit 單位
a) Bed Sheet 床褥單	9,979	9,381	10,000 piece 萬條
b) Towel 毛巾	292,973	386,724	10,000 piece 萬條
c) Converted Yarn Capacite of Cotton Knitgoods 針棉織品折用紗線量	286,865	272,521	ton 噸

Top 10 firms by revenue (year founded) 收入排名前10家企業（創辦年份）	City 城市	Province 省	Telephone / fax 電話 / 傳真	Number of employees 職工人數	Ownership 產業所有權	Revenue ('000 RMB) 銷售收入（千元）	Profit ('000 RMB) (rank) 利潤（千元）（排名）	Total assets ('000 RMB) 總資產（千元）	Major products 主要產品
Jiangsu Hong Liu Sheet Group Co. 江蘇紅柳床單集團公司(1966)	Wuxi 無錫市	Jiangsu 江蘇省	(0510)6282341 (0510)6282341	2,522	Collectively-owned 集體	433,411	23365(1)	229,523	a
Binzhou Knitgoods Group Co. 濱州針棉織品集團公司(1976)	Binzhou 濱州市	Shandong 山東省	(0543)3512878 (0543)3512688	2,118	State-owned 國有	273,199	1350(62)	190,902	b,c
Qingdao Xi Ying Men Group Co. 青島喜盈門集團公司(1992)	Qingdao 青島市	Shandong 山東省	(0532)7869888 (0532)7869922	3,778	Collectively-owned 集體	248,114	3248(28)	245,901	b
Zhejiang Ya Long Light & Textile Industry Group Co. Ltd. 浙江亞龍輕紡集團有限公司(1988)	Shaoxing 紹興市	Zhejiang 浙江省	(0575)2061528 (0575)2061576	1,628	Collectively-owned 集體	230,862	21505(2)	162,183	o
Shanghai Min Guang Sheet Factory 上海民光被單廠(1935)	Shanghai 上海市	Shanghai 上海市	(021)65375118 (021)65454445	1,133	State-owned 國有	203,695	15014(5)	140,567	a,c
Shenxian Cotton Textile Factory 莘縣棉紡織廠(1977)	Liaocheng 聊城市	Shandong 山東省	(0635)7321201 (0635)7321201	3,009	State-owned 國有	200,124	2524(34)	289,698	o
Nanjing Shang Shen Chemical Fibre Products Co. Ltd. 南京上申化纖製品有限公司(1993)	Nanjing 南京市	Jiangsu 江蘇省	(025)2281693	240	Overseas Chinese-funded 港澳台資	180,550	4170(21)	56,130	o
Changzhou Towel & Sheet General Factory 常州市被總廠(1918)	Changzhou 常州市	Jiangsu 江蘇省	(0519)8812087 (0519)8812087	1,530	State-owned 國有	167,210	5660(12)	106,240	a,c
State-owned Changshu Sheet Factory 國營常熟被單廠(1969)	Suzhou 蘇州市	Jiangsu 江蘇省	(0512)2881713 (0512)2880996	1,222	State-owned 國有	166,090	3180(30)	188,650	a
Ningbo Bed Shall Mill 寧波床單廠(1951)	Ningbo 寧波市	Zhejiang 浙江省	(0574)7472236 (0574)7474727	1,202	State-owned 國有	156,631	12116(6)	125,939	a,c

Top 10 Cities by Production Output 產出排名前10位城市	Province 省	Market share 市場份額	Number of firms 企業個數
Shanghai 上海市	Shanghai 上海市	14.67%	148
Nantong 南通市	Jiangsu 江蘇省	6.13%	61
Suzhou 蘇州市	Jiangsu 江蘇省	4.12%	53
Ningbo 寧波市	Zhejiang 浙江省	3.62%	34
Qingdao 青島市	Shandong 山東省	2.64%	24
Tianjin 天津市	Tianjin 天津市	2.48%	49
Zibo 淄博市	Shandong 山東省	2.39%	9
Weifang 濰坊市	Shandong 山東省	2.30%	27
Binzhou 濱州市	Shandong 山東省	1.96%	7
Changzhou 常州市	Jiangsu 江蘇省	1.94%	27

10 Major Wholesalers 10家主要批發商	City 城市	Province 省	Telephone / Fax 電話 / 傳真
Anhui Clothing Import & Export Company 安徽省服裝進出口公司	Hefei 合肥市	Anhui 安徽省	(0551)3632212 (0551)3632002
Qingdao Textile Clothing Industrial Group Company 青島紡織服裝實業集團公司	Qingdao 青島市	Shandong 山東省	(0532)2877853 (0532)2869315
Hebei Textile Import & Export (Group) Company 河北省紡織品進出口(集團)公司	Shijiazhuang 石家莊市	Hebei 河北省	(0311)7028530 (0311)7027781
Zhong Fang Pledget Import & Export Company 中紡紗布進出口公司	Beijing 北京市	Beijing 北京市	(010)65124718 (010)65124713
Shaoxing Import & Export Company 紹興市進出口公司	Shaoxing 紹興市	Zhejiang 浙江省	(0575)5132822 (0575)5141577
Hunan Hua Xiang Import & Export (Group) Company 湖南省華湘進出口(集團)公司	Changsha 長沙市	Hunan 湖南省	(0731)2282440 (0731)2286995
City's Import & Export Company Trade Dept. 市進出口公司貿易部	Yichang 宜昌市	Hubei 湖北省	(0717)6450778 (0717)6441875
Shanghai Pu Dong Xinqu Import & Export Company 上海浦東新區進出口公司	Shanghai 上海市	Shanghai 上海市	(021)58878801 (021)58827444
Ningbo Yinxian Import & Export Company 寧波市鄞縣進出口公司	Ningbo 寧波市	Zhejiang 浙江省	(0574)7875205 (0574)7873168
Zhejiang Silk Import & Export Company 浙江省絲綢進出口公司	Hangzhou 杭州市	Zhejiang 浙江省	(0571)5195588 (0571)5192542

*Also include sales by firms outside this industry.包括本行業以外廠家的銷售。"o" stands for "others". "o" 代表"其他產品"。

1725: Cotton Thread 棉線帶製造業

The industry accounts for 0.055% of the total revenue of China's industrial sector in 1996. The revenue growth rate of the industry is -9.7% from 1995, as compared to the growth rate of China's industrial sector, 9.51%. The rate of return on asset is 0.24%. 61.02% of all firms in the industry made a profit while 32.17% had negative returns. The top province in terms of the industry's revenue is Jiangsu, accounting for 24.54% of the total revenue.
本行業在 1996 年佔全行業總產值 0.055%，行業年增長率為 -9.7%（全國工業年增長率 9.51%）。行業的資產回報率 0.24%，61.02% 的企業盈利，32.17% 的企業虧損。銷售收入最高的省份為江蘇省，佔本行業的 24.54%。

	Total number of firms 企業總數	Total number of employees 職工總數	Total revenue (mil. RMB) 總銷售收入（百萬元）	Total profit (mil. RMB) 總利潤（百萬元）	Return on assets 資產利潤率 (%)	Return on equity 權益利潤率 (%)	Labour productivity ('000 RMB / worker) 勞動生產率（千元/人）	Debts / assets 資產負債率 (%)	Total assets (mil. RMB) 總資產（百萬元）
Industry Overall 行業總體	721	77,808	3,185	9	0.24	0.78	40.93	69.41	3,604

	Number of firms 企業個數	Average number of employees 平均職工人數	Average revenue ('000 RMB) 平均銷售收入（千元）	Average profit ('000 RMB) 平均利潤（千元）	Return on assets 資產利潤率 (%)	Return on equity 權益利潤率 (%)	Labour productivity ('000 RMB / worker) 勞動生產率（千元/人）	Average debts / assets 平均資產負債率(%)	Average Total assets ('000 RMB) 平均總資產（千元）
By ownership 產業所有權									
State-owned 國有	69	298	7,000	-188	-1.19	-5.94	23.53	80.02	15,884
Collectively-owned 集體	553	90	2,989	9	0.35	1.18	33.39	70.42	2,588
Privately-owned 私有	3	56	2,494	8	0.44	2.02	44.27	78.04	1,884
Domestic JVs 聯營	3	171	7,193	50	1.08	3.75	41.98	71.07	4,624
Joint stock 股份制	5	33	1,292	2	0.28	1.50	39.62	81.63	700
Foreign-funded 外資	23	62	12,367	273	2.47	4.75	199.19	48.04	11,058
Overseas Chinese-funded 港澳台資	62	86	11,609	172	1.35	3.34	135.01	59.52	12,696
By size 規模									
Large 大型	4	1,250	93,004	1,772	1.59	3.96	74.43	59.75	111,240
Medium 中型	20	496	23,461	-174	-0.50	-1.74	47.34	71.19	34,734
Small 小型	695	91	3,373	8	0.22	0.75	37.15	70.67	3,545
By regional distribution 地區分布									
Central-North 華北	84	118	2,449	-18	-0.35	-1.07	20.75	67.65	5,115
Beijing 北京	16	158	3,816				24.17	43.53	8,909
Tianjin 天津	17	154	2,406	-80	-0.83	-5.68	15.63	85.42	9,664
Hebei 河北	41	65	2,161	-4	-0.15	-0.53	33.07	71.58	2,571
Shanxi 山西	7	256	969	3	0.20	0.60	3.79	66.60	1,420
Inner Mongolia 內蒙	3	100	2,783	3	0.13	0.80	27.74	83.33	2,500
Northeast 東北	67	87	1,776	-92	-3.01	-15.92	20.36	81.09	3,050
Liaoning 遼寧	38	59	1,836	52	2.26	8.65	31.21	73.88	2,295
Jilin 吉林	9	145	3,383	-369	-8.44	-40.34	23.33	79.09	4,372
Heilongjiang 黑龍江	20	115	940	-240	-6.17	-62.91	8.16	90.19	3,888
Central East 華東	339	95	5,296	56	1.03	3.27	55.64	68.56	5,458
Shanghai 上海	56	170	8,306	168	1.67	5.94	48.86	71.92	10,080
Jiangsu 江蘇	111	96	7,040	-10	-0.18	-0.53	73.33	65.48	5,712
Zhejiang 浙江	36	62	6,681	326	5.42	12.24	107.23	55.73	6,012
Anhui 安徽	24	84	1,952	-96	-5.88	-127.78	23.12	95.43	1,631
Fujian 福建	47	24	1,182	-13	-1.10	-2.59	48.46	57.60	1,179
Jiangxi 江西	19	82	1,420	-34	-1.30	-8.48	17.36	84.61	2,583
Shandong 山東	46	111	3,886	56	0.88	3.39	34.92	74.01	6,341
Central-South 中南	161	140	5,661	31	0.54	1.62	40.35	66.83	5,840
Henan 河南	32	113	2,788	15	0.45	2.06	24.76	78.28	3,347
Hubei 湖北	38	166	4,746	28	0.50	2.92	28.54	82.84	5,574
Hunan 湖南	30	112	3,037	7	0.20	0.55	27.05	64.25	3,370
Guangdong 廣東	49	171	10,663	81	0.81	1.91	62.26	57.58	10,033
Guangxi 廣西	12	76	2,358	-56	-2.35	-8.85	31.23	73.51	2,378
Hainan 海南									
Southwest 西南	48	109	1,711	-147	-5.92	-28.66	15.74	79.37	2,486
Chongqing 重慶	17	128	1,293	-246	-21.20	51.47	10.09	141.19	1,162
Sichuan 四川	17	62	1,447	-77	-2.70	-6.29	23.28	57.07	2,863
Guizhou 貴州	7	91	1,429	-13	-0.88	-2.55	15.65	65.63	1,467
Yunnan 雲南	6	204	4,040	-205	-3.12	-14.11	19.84	77.85	6,562
Tibet 西藏									
Northwest 西北	22	90	3,236	-32	-1.18	-10.76	35.94	88.99	2,724
Shaanxi 陝西	12	108	4,012	-109	-3.17	-46.62	37.29	93.19	3,441
Gansu 甘肅	4	48	1,678	130	21.67	53.61	34.95	59.58	600
Qinghai 青海	1	95	420	-170	-10.97	-283.33	4.42	96.13	1,550
Ningxia 寧夏	2	65	2,290	10	0.26	0.99	35.50	73.39	3,795
Xinjiang 新疆	3	91	3,780	77	3.24	31.08	41.39	89.58	2,367

1725: Cotton Thread 棉線帶製造業

Year 年份	Number of firms 企業個數	Rate of change 每年變化 (%)	Number of employees 職工人數（人）	Rate of change 每年變化 (%)	Total revenue (mil. RMB) 總銷售收入（百萬元）	Rate of change 每年變化 (%)	Total profit (mil. RMB) 總利潤（百萬元）	Rate of change 每年變化 (%)
1993	753		118,529		2,914		4	
1994	766	1.73%	93,930	-20.75%	3,144	7.93%	-1	-123.28%
1995	736	-3.92%	84,881	-9.63%	3,527	12.18%	20	2096.85%
1996	721	-2.04%	77,808	-8.33%	3,185	-9.70%	9	-55.68%

3 Major products* 3種主要產品*	Output 產量	Sales volume 銷售量	Unit 單位
a) Sewing Thread 縫紉線	88,687	88,687	10,000 piece 萬個
b) Converted Chemical Fibre Filament Capacite of Cotton Knitgoods 針棉織品折用化纖長絲量	11,511	10,015	ton 噸

Top 10 firms by revenue (year founded) 收入排名前10家企業（創辦年份）	City 城市	Province 省	Telephone / fax 電話 / 傳真	Number of employees 職工人數	Ownership 產業所有權	Revenue ('000 RMB) 銷售收入（千元）	Profit ('000 RMB) (rank) 利潤（千元）（排名）	Total assets ('000 RMB) 總資產（千元）	Major products 主要產品
Coats Guangzhou Ltd. 廣州高士線業有限公司(1991)	Guangzhou 廣州市	Guangdong 廣東省	(020)84212898 (020)84227702	510	Overseas Chinese-funded 港澳台資	202,798	4079(5)	221,772	a
Jiangyin Ming Tai Thread Making Co. Ltd. 江陰銘泰製線有限公司(1994)	Wuxi 無錫市	Jiangsu 江蘇省	(0510)6381030 (0510)6381030	888	Overseas Chinese-funded 港澳台資	199,736	1648(15)	81,952	a
Ningbo Dunhuang Group Co. Ltd. 寧波敦煌集團股份有限公司(1955)	Ningbo 寧波市	Zhejiang 浙江省	(0574)7311507 (0574)7313272	2,217	Joint stock 股份制	147,166	12822(1)	413,818	a
Taifa Colored Thread Weaving Co. Ltd. 泰發花線織造有限公司(1993)	Suzhou 蘇州市	Jiangsu 江蘇省	(0512)6551338 (0512)6551716	220	Foreign-funded 外資	88,995	2750(6)	36,900	o
Ningbo Qiaotaixing Textile Co. Ltd. 寧波僑泰興紡織有限公司(1993)	Ningbo 寧波市	Zhejiang 浙江省	(0574)6221627 (0574)6222576	300	Overseas Chinese-funded 港澳台資	68,260	7380(2)	48,762	o
Shanghai No.3 Thread-making Factory 上海第三製線廠(1930)	Shanghai 上海市	Shanghai 上海市	(021)63772276 (021)63778215	532	State-owned 國有	67,760	6006(3)	57,111	a
China Feilum Thread-making Factary 中國飛綸製線廠(1929)	Shanghai 上海市	Shanghai 上海市	(021)63035484 (021)63032712	782	State-owned 國有	64,283	1(207)	101,467	a
Guangzhou Yue Hua Thread-making Industry Co. Ltd. 廣州越華線業有限公司(1954)	Guangzhou 廣州市	Guangdong 廣東省	(020)82303738 (020)82277527	476	Overseas Chinese-funded 港澳台資	50,939	-1136(309)	47,998	a,b
Shandong Huan Qiu Thread Making Group General Company 山東環球製線集團總公司(1979)	Weifang 濰坊市	Shandong 山東省	(0536)8235461 (0536)8235461	550	Overseas Chinese-funded 港澳台資	45,039	1680(13)	18,725	a
Shanghai Bi Jia Clothing Auxiliary Mererial Co. Ltd. 上海比加服裝輔料有限公司(1992)	Shanghai 上海市	Shanghai 上海市	(021)64891549	72	Overseas Chinese-funded 港澳台資	41,312	1732(12)	21,096	a

Top 10 Cities by Production Output 產出排名前10位城市	Province 省	Market share 市場份額	Number of firms 企業個數
Shanghai 上海市	Shanghai 上海市	14.00%	83
Guangzhou 廣州市	Guangdong 廣東省	12.18%	30
Suzhou 蘇州市	Jiangsu 江蘇省	7.16%	57
Ningbo 寧波市	Zhejiang 浙江省	6.01%	8
Wuxi 無錫市	Jiangsu 江蘇省	4.36%	26
Huizhou 惠州市	Guangdong 廣東省	3.61%	4
Wenzhou 溫州市	Zhejiang 浙江省	2.96%	16
Beijing 北京市	Beijing 北京市	2.63%	14
Jiangmen 江門市	Guangdong 廣東省	2.11%	3
Suizhou 隨州市	Hubei 湖北省	2.01%	6

10 Major Wholesalers 10家主要批發商	City 城市	Province 省	Telephone / Fax 電話 / 傳真
Anhui Clothing Import & Export Company 安徽省服裝進出口公司	Hefei 合肥市	Anhui 安徽省	(0551)3632212 (0551)3632002
Qingdao Textile Clothing Industrial Group Company 青島紡織服裝實業集團公司	Qingdao 青島市	Shandong 山東省	(0532)2877853 (0532)2869315
Hebei Textile Import & Export (Group) Company 河北省紡織品進出口(集團)公司	Shijiazhuang 石家莊市	Hebei 河北省	(0311)7028530 (0311)7027781
Zhong Fang Pledget Import & Export Company 中紡紗布進出口公司	Beijing 北京市	Beijing 北京市	(010)65124718 (010)65124713
Shaoxing Import & Export Company 紹興市進出口公司	Shaoxing 紹興市	Zhejiang 浙江省	(0575)5132822 (0575)5141577
Hunan Hua Xiang Import & Export (Group) Company 湖南省華湘進出口(集團)公司	Changsha 長沙市	Hunan 湖南省	(0731)2282440 (0731)2286995
City's Import & Export Company Trade Dept. 市進出口公司貿易部	Yichang 宜昌市	Hubei 湖北省	(0717)6450778 (0717)6441875
Shanghai Pu Dong Xinqu Import & Export Company 上海浦東新區進出口公司	Shanghai 上海市	Shanghai 上海市	(021)58878801 (021)58827444
Ningbo Yinxian Import & Export Company 寧波市鄞縣進出口公司	Ningbo 寧波市	Zhejiang 浙江省	(0574)7875205 (0574)7873168
Zhejiang Silk Import & Export Company 浙江省絲綢進出口公司	Hangzhou 杭州市	Zhejiang 浙江省	(0571)5195588 (0571)5192542

*Also include sales by firms outside this industry.包括本行業以外廠家的銷售。"o" stands for "others". "o" 代表"其他產品"。

1726: Cotton Cord Fabric 簾子布製造業

The industry accounts for 0.082% of the total revenue of China's industrial sector in 1996. The revenue growth rate of the industry is 37.2% from 1995, as compared to the growth rate of China's industrial sector, 9.51%. The rate of return on asset is 3.13%. 72.81% of all firms in the industry made a profit while 19.13% had negative returns. The top province in terms of the industry's revenue is Zhejiang, accounting for 43.46% of the total revenue.

本行業在1996年佔全行業總產值0.082%，行業年增長率為37.2%（全國工業年增長率9.51%）。行業的資產回報率3.13%，72.81%的企業盈利，19.13%的企業虧損。銷售收入最高的省份為浙江省，佔本行業的43.46%。

	Total number of firms 企業總數	Total number of employees 職工總數	Total revenue (mil. RMB) 總銷售收入（百萬元）	Total profit (mil. RMB) 總利潤（百萬元）	Return on assets 資產利潤率 (%)	Return on equity 權益利潤率 (%)	Labour productivity ('000 RMB / worker) 勞動生產率（千元/人）	Debts / assets 資產負債率 (%)	Total assets (mil. RMB) 總資產（百萬元）
Industry Overall 行業總體	114	36,068	4,730	172	3.13	9.62	131.14	67.45	5,505

	Number of firms 企業個數	Average number of employees 平均職工人數	Average revenue ('000 RMB) 平均銷售收入（千元）	Average profit ('000 RMB) 平均利潤（千元）	Return on assets 資產利潤率 (%)	Return on equity 權益利潤率 (%)	Labour productivity ('000 RMB / worker) 勞動生產率（千元/人）	Average debts / assets 平均資產負債率(%)	Average Total assets ('000 RMB) 平均總資產（千元）
By ownership 產業所有權									
State-owned 國有	12	834	74,417	1,167	0.89	4.67	89.22	81.00	131,583
Collectively-owned 集體	85	262	41,669	1,866	6.96	17.59	159.11	60.41	26,789
Privately-owned 私有									
Domestic JVs 聯營	6	244	15,910	-206	-0.64	-1.86	65.11	65.63	32,103
Joint stock 股份制	2	325	15,249	1,210	0.20	0.63	46.92	68.98	616,041
Foreign-funded 外資	6	261	15,856	-203	-0.65	-0.97	60.67	32.70	30,940
Overseas Chinese-funded 港澳台資	3	143	24,869	-192	-1.49	-3.34	173.91	55.35	12,895
By size 規模									
Large 大型	7	2,984	401,597	18,961	3.17	9.62	134.60	67.03	597,718
Medium 中型	8	622	69,292	-1,364	-2.96	-12.52	111.45	76.32	46,013
Small 小型	97	102	14,074	517	5.27	15.42	138.16	65.85	9,824
By regional distribution 地區分布									
Central-North 華北	11	44	3,595	124	3.33	11.85	81.86	71.85	3,710
Beijing 北京	3	31	3,047	20	0.80	1.49	99.35	46.26	2,493
Tianjin 天津	5	33	3,132	140	3.37	21.21	93.77	84.09	4,160
Hebei 河北	2	31	3,260	250	17.73	41.67	105.16	57.45	1,410
Shanxi 山西	1	162	8,220	100	1.03	3.38	50.74	69.52	9,710
Inner Mongolia 內蒙									
Northeast 東北	19	48	1,959	39	2.35	37.50	40.87	93.72	1,677
Liaoning 遼寧	12	69	2,957	44	1.73	41.09	43.01	95.80	2,560
Jilin 吉林	2	7	125	100	333.33	500.00	17.86	33.33	30
Heilongjiang 黑龍江	5	14	300	4	1.83	2.99	20.83	38.53	218
Central East 華東	67	493	66,771	2,623	3.38	10.11	135.42	66.57	77,630
Shanghai 上海	7	207	13,617	-557	-2.08	-11.31	65.92	81.64	26,824
Jiangsu 江蘇	24	426	68,911	2,080	3.73	14.72	161.65	74.69	55,833
Zhejiang 浙江	13	1,108	158,118	7,773	4.77	11.27	142.65	57.72	163,122
Anhui 安徽	7	337	31,436	1	0.01	0.19	93.20	96.37	21,197
Fujian 福建	3								
Jiangxi 江西									
Shandong 山東	13	353	34,530	2,202	2.04	6.18	97.86	67.03	108,035
Central-South 中南	15	84	10,959	-111	-0.87	-3.90	129.95	77.76	12,741
Henan 河南	8	66	4,500	-120	-1.05	-3.07	68.70	65.63	11,385
Hubei 湖北	3	210	27,047	130	0.59	4.10	129.00	85.69	22,157
Hunan 湖南									
Guangdong 廣東	4	28	11,813	-273	-3.25	-64.12	421.88	94.94	8,393
Guangxi 廣西									
Hainan 海南									
Southwest 西南	1	331	13,030	-4,000	-10.43	113.31	39.37	109.21	38,340
Chongqing 重慶									
Sichuan 四川									
Guizhou 貴州									
Yunnan 雲南	1	331	13,030	-4,000	-10.43	113.31	39.37	109.21	38,340
Tibet 西藏									
Northwest 西北	1	43	2,300	260	20.47	33.77	53.49	39.37	1,270
Shaanxi 陝西									
Gansu 甘肅	1	43	2,300	260	20.47	33.77	53.49	39.37	1,270
Qinghai 青海									
Ningxia 寧夏									
Xinjiang 新疆									

1726: Cotton Cord Fabric 簾子布製造業

Year 年份	Number of firms 企業個數	Rate of change 每年變化 (%)	Number of employees 職工人數 (人)	Rate of change 每年變化 (%)	Total revenue (mil. RMB) 總銷售收入 (百萬元)	Rate of change 每年變化 (%)	Total profit (mil. RMB) 總利潤 (百萬元)	Rate of change 每年變化 (%)
1993	127		37,597		2,824		152	
1994	121	-4.73%	22,359	-40.53%	2,913	3.15%	180	18.48%
1995	102	-15.70%	33,623	50.38%	3,448	18.38%	110	-38.88%
1996	114	11.76%	36,068	7.27%	4,730	37.18%	172	56.78%

3 Major products* 3 種主要產品 *	Output 產量	Sales volume 銷售量	Unit 單位
a) Cord Fabric 簾子布	165,019	189,772	ton 噸
b) Polymide Fibre 錦綸纖維	99,923	94,927	ton 噸

Top 10 firms by revenue (year founded) 收入排名前 10 家企業 (創辦年份)	City 城市	Province 省	Telephone / fax 電話 / 傳真	Number of employees 職工人數	Ownership 產業所有權	Revenue ('000 RMB) 銷售收入 (千元)	Profit ('000 RMB) (rank) 利潤 (千元) (排名)	Total assets ('000 RMB) 總資產 (千元)	Major products 主要產品
Jin Lun Group Co. 金輪集團公司(1987)	Ningbo 寧波市	Zhejiang 浙江省	(0574)3205611 (0574)3205943	13,453	Collectively-owned 集體	1,954,275	100323(1)	2,017,324	a,b
Jiangsu Jun Ma Group Co. Ltd. 江蘇駿馬集團有限責任公司(1995)	Suzhou 蘇州市	Jiangsu 江蘇省	(0512)8292709	850	Collectively-owned 集體	548,698	35670(2)	362,163	o
Yangzhou Organic Chemical Industry Plant 揚州有機化工廠(1964)	Yangzhou 揚州市	Jiangsu 江蘇省	(0514)7233421 (0514)7232380	2,154	State-owned 國有	292,608	3010(7)	279,048	a
Qingdao No.2 Cotton Textile Mill 青島第二棉紡織廠(1916)	Qingdao 青島市	Shandong 山東省	(0532)3717403 (0532)3710893	2,746	State-owned 國有	228,006	5601(4)	953,632	a,b
Xuzhou Su Shan Cord Fabric Factory 徐州市蘇山簾子布廠(1989)	Xuzhou 徐州市	Jiangsu 江蘇省	(0516)5770331	437	Collectively-owned 集體	162,005	4540(6)	46,090	a
Taizhou Chemical Fibre Co. 泰州化纖公司(1970)	Taizhou 泰州市	Jiangsu 江蘇省	(0523)6559771 (0523)6558656	1,836	Collectively-owned 集體	160,028	0(49)	186,304	a
Anqiu Cord Fabric & Canvas Factory 安丘市簾帆布廠(1995)	Weifang 濰坊市	Shandong 山東省	(0536)4222158 (0536)4222187	460	Foreign-funded 外資	149,541	21799(3)	281,578	a
Xuzhou Cord Fabric Factory 徐州簾子布廠(1964)	Xuzhou 徐州市	Jiangsu 江蘇省	(0516)5757690 (0516)5765754	1,827	State-owned 國有	122,573	5222(5)	136,759	a,b
Bengbu Cord Fabric Factory 蚌埠市簾子布廠(1979)	Bengbu 蚌埠市	Anhui 安徽省	(0552)4081660 (0552)4083411	601	State-owned 國有	106,830	2087(9)	95,585	a,b
Bengbu Industry Cloth Factory 蚌埠工業用布廠(1989)	Bengbu 蚌埠市	Anhui 安徽省	(0552)4081773	208	State-owned 國有	87,211	-2596(59)	39,375	o

Top 10 Cities by Production Output 產出排名前 10 位城市	Province 省	Market share 市場份額	Number of firms 企業個數
Ningbo 寧波市	Zhejiang 浙江省	39.23%	2
Suzhou 蘇州市	Jiangsu 江蘇省	13.92%	11
Shanghai 上海市	Shanghai 上海市	8.08%	16
Weifang 濰坊市	Shandong 山東省	7.06%	6
Qingdao 青島市	Shandong 山東省	5.21%	4
Xuzhou 徐州市	Jiangsu 江蘇省	5.06%	2
Taizhou 泰州市	Jiangsu 江蘇省	3.79%	5
Wuxi 無錫市	Jiangsu 江蘇省	3.75%	14
Bengbu 蚌埠市	Anhui 安徽省	2.72%	2
Nanjing 南京市	Jiangsu 江蘇省	1.78%	2

10 Major Wholesalers 10 家主要批發商	City 城市	Province 省	Telephone / Fax 電話 / 傳真
Anhui Clothing Import & Export Company 安徽省服裝進出口公司	Hefei 合肥市	Anhui 安徽省	(0551)3632212 (0551)3632002
Qingdao Textile Clothing Industrial Group Company 青島紡織服裝實業集團公司	Qingdao 青島市	Shandong 山東省	(0532)2877853 (0532)2869315
Hebei Textile Import & Export (Group) Company 河北省紡織品進出口(集團)公司	Shijiazhuang 石家莊市	Hebei 河北省	(0311)7028530 (0311)7027781
Zhong Fang Pledget Import & Export Company 中紡紗布進出口公司	Beijing 北京市	Beijing 北京市	(010)65124718 (010)65124713
Shaoxing Import & Export Company 紹興市進出口公司	Shaoxing 紹興市	Zhejiang 浙江省	(0575)5132822 (0575)5141577
Hunan Hua Xiang Import & Export (Group) Company 湖南省華湘進出口(集團)公司	Changsha 長沙市	Hunan 湖南省	(0731)2282440 (0731)2286995
City's Import & Export Company Trade Dept. 市進出口公司貿易部	Yichang 宜昌市	Hubei 湖北省	(0717)6450778 (0717)6441875
Shanghai Pu Dong Xinqu Import & Export Company 上海浦東新區進出口公司	Shanghai 上海市	Shanghai 上海市	(021)58878801 (021)58827444
Ningbo Yinxian Import & Export Company 寧波市鄞縣進出口公司	Ningbo 寧波市	Zhejiang 浙江省	(0574)7875205 (0574)7873168
Zhejiang Silk Import & Export Company 浙江省絲綢進出口公司	Hangzhou 杭州市	Zhejiang 浙江省	(0571)5195588 (0571)5192542

*Also include sales by firms outside this industry.包括本行業以外廠家的銷售。"o" stands for "others". "o" 代表 "其他產品"。

1729: Other Cotton Goods 其他棉紡織業

The industry accounts for 0.082% of the total revenue of China's industrial sector in 1996. The revenue growth rate of the industry is -1.9% from 1995, as compared to the growth rate of China's industrial sector, 9.51%. The rate of return on asset is 0.23%. 67.73% of all firms in the industry made a profit while 23.53% had negative returns. The top province in terms of the industry's revenue is Hubei, accounting for 23.97% of the total revenue.
本行業在1996年佔全行業總產值0.082%，行業年增長率為-1.9%（全國工業年增長率9.51%）。行業的資產回報率0.23%，67.73%的企業盈利，23.53%的企業虧損。銷售收入最高的省份為湖北省，佔本行業的23.97%。

	Total number of firms 企業總數	Total number of employees 職工總數	Total revenue (mil. RMB) 總銷售收入（百萬元）	Total profit (mil. RMB) 總利潤（百萬元）	Return on assets 資產利潤率 (%)	Return on equity 權益利潤率 (%)	Labour productivity ('000 RMB / worker) 勞動生產率（千元/人）	Debts / assets 資產負債率 (%)	Total assets (mil. RMB) 總資產（百萬元）
Industry Overall 行業總體	421	80,974	4,728	14	0.23	0.73	58.39	68.40	6,139

	Number of firms 企業個數	Average number of employees 平均職工人數	Average revenue ('000 RMB) 平均銷售收入（千元）	Average profit ('000 RMB) 平均利潤（千元）	Return on assets 資產利潤率 (%)	Return on equity 權益利潤率 (%)	Labour productivity ('000 RMB / worker) 勞動生產率（千元/人）	Average debts / assets 平均資產負債率(%)	Average Total assets ('000 RMB) 平均總資產（千元）
By ownership 產業所有權									
State-owned 國有	47	1,046	50,170				47.96	71.32	75,213
Collectively-owned 集體	306	87	5,000	39	0.81	2.76	57.64	70.64	4,854
Privately-owned 私有									
Domestic JVs 聯營	4	328	17,683	161	1.64	2.97	53.99	44.62	9,814
Joint stock 股份制	4	94	5,882	14	0.78	2.36	62.58	66.95	1,757
Foreign-funded 外資	22	92	15,265	146	0.88	1.80	165.35	51.14	16,654
Overseas Chinese-funded 港澳台資	38	96	10,789	-51	-0.28	-0.68	112.23	59.37	18,587
By size 規模									
Large 大型	8	3,795	230,886	715	0.22	0.61	60.84	64.38	330,526
Medium 中型	14	967	74,001	751	0.80	2.85	76.53	71.89	93,599
Small 小型	395	94	4,671	-6	-0.10	-0.36	49.64	71.20	5,528
By regional distribution 地區分布									
Central-North 華北	59	190	8,193	199	1.18	3.93	43.11	69.60	16,823
Beijing 北京	7	282	7,487	1,377	6.57	11.60	26.56	41.65	20,961
Tianjin 天津	17	31	3,008	-29	-1.01	-2.51	96.29	59.80	2,914
Hebei 河北	26	170	11,049	93	0.38	1.43	64.86	73.67	24,793
Shanxi 山西	5	84	494	4	0.30	1.09	5.85	72.73	1,342
Inner Mongolia 內蒙	4	964	22,525	45	0.12	0.73	23.36	83.01	36,235
Northeast 東北	40	95	2,089	-74	-1.13	-14.00	22.02	91.92	6,559
Liaoning 遼寧	16	123	3,940	-201	-1.57	-22.84	32.03	93.13	12,819
Jilin 吉林	9	71	1,420	12	0.36	4.15	20.06	91.41	3,429
Heilongjiang 黑龍江	15	79	515	9	0.53	3.14	6.50	83.10	1,759
Central East 華東	191	152	11,672	131	1.04	2.80	76.93	62.82	12,596
Shanghai 上海	32	174	11,315	98	1.11	2.62	64.99	57.58	8,853
Jiangsu 江蘇	51	132	15,767	241	1.60	3.90	119.75	59.03	15,083
Zhejiang 浙江	36	159	14,274	99	0.55	1.23	89.76	55.04	18,050
Anhui 安徽	20	158	9,758	56	0.55	2.45	61.62	77.39	10,025
Fujian 福建	12	112	6,386	85	0.78	1.84	57.06	57.92	10,956
Jiangxi 江西	6	15	1,723	2	0.10	0.36	114.89	71.89	1,660
Shandong 山東	34	187	7,855	114	1.08	6.12	41.94	82.42	10,636
Central-South 中南	96	307	16,985	-141	-0.67	-2.12	55.24	68.61	21,211
Henan 河南	24	132	3,829	-10	-0.12	-0.40	28.91	69.17	7,807
Hubei 湖北	22	973	51,507	-145	-0.25	-0.70	52.93	64.51	58,397
Hunan 湖南	9	28	350	-60	-7.28	-27.41	12.70	73.32	824
Guangdong 廣東	37	120	10,644	-256	-1.78	-8.26	88.42	78.45	14,373
Guangxi 廣西	3	56	1,153	-47	-0.85	-2.16	20.47	60.69	5,487
Hainan 海南	1	56	5,030	20	0.24	0.86	89.82	72.64	8,480
Southwest 西南	19	329	12,151	-336	-1.83	-11.93	36.90	84.65	18,380
Chongqing 重慶	3	23	1,351	36	2.38	7.11	57.30	66.50	1,494
Sichuan 四川	6	883	33,431	873	1.74	11.56	37.83	84.92	50,086
Guizhou 貴州	5	14	126				9.00	53.42	292
Yunnan 雲南	4	55	715	-113	-5.07	-50.00	13.12	89.85	2,218
Tibet 西藏									
Northwest 西北	16	76	4,384	18	0.30	0.94	57.63	67.92	5,812
Shaanxi 陝西	7	97	7,229	89	1.02	2.82	74.52	63.79	8,684
Gansu 甘肅	2	57	1,750	25	1.03	4.03	30.70	74.43	2,425
Qinghai 青海									
Ningxia 寧夏	1	30	50	-460	-14.84	93.88	1.67	115.81	3,100
Xinjiang 新疆	6	66	2,665	12	0.29	0.99	40.58	70.85	4,042

1729: Other Cotton Goods 其他棉紡織業

Year 年份	Number of firms 企業個數	Rate of change 每年變化 (%)	Number of employees 職工人數 (人)	Rate of change 每年變化 (%)	Total revenue (mil. RMB) 總銷售收入 (百萬元)	Rate of change 每年變化 (%)	Total profit (mil. RMB) 總利潤 (百萬元)	Rate of change 每年變化 (%)
1993	465		81,812		2,898		36	
1994	480	3.23%	62,688	-23.38%	3,986	37.54%	82	126.51%
1995	444	-7.50%	79,754	27.22%	4,820	20.91%	35	-56.93%
1996	421	-5.18%	80,974	1.53%	4,728	-1.91%	14	-60.24%

3 Major products* 3 種主要產品 *	Output 產量	Sales volume 銷售量	Unit 單位
a) Blended Yarn 混紡紗	42,592	29,814	ton 噸
b) Cotton Cloth 棉布	23,038	22,808	10,000 metre 萬米
c) Pure Chemical Fabric 純化纖布	7,430	7,058	10,000 metre 萬米

Top 10 firms by revenue (year founded) 收入排名前 10 家企業 (創辦年份)	City 城市	Province 省	Telephone / fax 電話 / 傳真	Number of employees 職工人數	Ownership 產業所有權	Revenue ('000 RMB) 銷售收入 (千元)	Profit ('000 RMB) (rank) 利潤 (千元) (排名)	Total assets ('000 RMB) 總資產 (千元)	Major products 主要產品
Hubei Xiangfan Cotton Textile Group Corp. Ltd. 湖北襄棉集團總公司(1969)	Xiangfan 襄樊市	Hubei 湖北省	(0710)3223601 (0710)3223601	9,866	State-owned 國有	460,185	-4982(204)	651,802	a,b
Hubei Yin He Textile Group Co. Ltd. 湖北銀河紡織(集團)股份有限公司(1975)	Xiangfan 襄樊市	Hubei 湖北省	(0710)3223471 (0710)3232466	3,658	State-owned 國有	270,434	-755(187)	275,715	o
Cixi Textiles Group Co. 慈溪紡織集團公司(1982)	Ningbo 寧波市	Zhejiang 浙江省	(0574)3813611 (0574)3811931	2,774	State-owned 國有	186,711	355(41)	241,665	a,b
Sichuan Yinhua Group Co. Ltd. 四川銀華集團有限責任公司(1971)	Suining 遂寧市	Sichuan 四川省	(0825)6624941 (0825)6622663	5,018	State-owned 國有	176,092	-5633(205)	302,387	a,b,c
Suzhou Taicang Knitting General Factory 蘇州市太倉針織總廠(1979)	Suzhou 蘇州市	Jiangsu 江蘇省	(0512)3524332 (0512)3520795	1,173	State-owned 國有	164,380	8870(2)	205,980	o
Shijiazhuang Tourist Decoration Textiles Corp. 石家莊旅遊裝飾公司(1987)	Shijiazhuang 石家莊市	Hebei 河北省	(0311)3834559 (0311)3813112	2,216	State-owned 國有	159,582	1(130)	511,617	a,b
Nantong Hymo Co. Ltd. 南通海盟有限公司(1984)	Nantong 南通市	Jiangsu 江蘇省	(0513)5537344 (0513)5513420	348	Foreign-funded 外資	141,239	2586(6)	124,318	o
Zhongshan Hengfa Dyeing & Weaving Factory Co. Ltd. 中山市恒發染織廠有限公司(1989)	Zhongshan 中山市	Guangdong 廣東省	(0760)8807811 (0760)8829233	804	Overseas Chinese-funded 港澳台資	113,302	-206(170)	166,422	b
Jiangsu Bai Lan Group Co. Ltd. 江蘇白蘭集團有限公司(1977)	Nantong 南通市	Jiangsu 江蘇省	(0513)2591201 (0513)2591201	366	Collectively-owned 集體	97,250	1510(11)	49,880	b
Shanghai Hua Zhong San Shan Printing & Dyeing Knitting Co. Ltd. 上海華鐘三山印染針織有限公司(1993)	Shanghai 上海市	Shanghai 上海市	(021)65190044 (021)65430833	143	Foreign-funded 外資	93,447	867(19)	55,026	o

Top 10 Cities by Production Output 產出排名前 10 位城市	Province 省	Market share 市場份額	Number of firms 企業個數
Xiangfan 襄樊市	Hubei 湖北省	17.14%	5
Wuxi 無錫市	Jiangsu 江蘇省	7.91%	10
Nantong 南通市	Jiangsu 江蘇省	7.03%	24
Chaohu 巢湖市	Anhui 安徽省	5.99%	5
Shanghai 上海市	Shanghai 上海市	5.63%	38
Ningbo 寧波市	Zhejiang 浙江省	5.44%	5
Suining 遂寧市	Sichuan 四川省	4.71%	2
Shijiazhuang 石家莊市	Hebei 河北省	3.59%	5
Fuyang 阜陽市	Anhui 安徽省	3.56%	6
Zhongshan 中山市	Guangdong 廣東省	2.91%	3

10 Major Wholesalers 10 家主要批發商	City 城市	Province 省	Telephone / Fax 電話 / 傳真
Anhui Clothing Import & Export Company 安徽省服裝進出口公司	Hefei 合肥市	Anhui 安徽省	(0551)3632212 (0551)3632002
Qingdao Textile Clothing Industrial Group Company 青島紡織服裝實業集團公司	Qingdao 青島市	Shandong 山東省	(0532)2877853 (0532)2869315
Hebei Textile Import & Export (Group) Company 河北省紡織品進出口(集團)公司	Shijiazhuang 石家莊市	Hebei 河北省	(0311)7028530 (0311)7027781
Zhong Fang Pledget Import & Export Company 中紡紗布進出口公司	Beijing 北京市	Beijing 北京市	(010)65124718 (010)65124713
Shaoxing Import & Export Company 紹興市進出口公司	Shaoxing 紹興市	Zhejiang 浙江省	(0575)5132822 (0575)5141577
Hunan Hua Xiang Import & Export (Group) Company 湖南省華湘進出口(集團)公司	Changsha 長沙市	Hunan 湖南省	(0731)2282440 (0731)2286995
City's Import & Export Company Trade Dept. 市進出口公司貿易部	Yichang 宜昌市	Hubei 湖北省	(0717)6450778 (0717)6441875
Shanghai Pu Dong Xinqu Import & Export Company 上海浦東新區進出口公司	Shanghai 上海市	Shanghai 上海市	(021)58878801 (021)58827444
Ningbo Yinxian Import & Export Company 寧波市鄞縣進出口公司	Ningbo 寧波市	Zhejiang 浙江省	(0574)7875205 (0574)7873168
Zhejiang Silk Import & Export Company 浙江省絲綢進出口公司	Hangzhou 杭州市	Zhejiang 浙江省	(0571)5195588 (0571)5192542

*Also include sales by firms outside this industry.包括本行業以外廠家的銷售。"o" stands for "others". "o" 代表 "其他產品"。

1741: Wool Tops 毛條加工業

The industry accounts for 0.076% of the total revenue of China's industrial sector in 1996. The revenue growth rate of the industry is -24.8% from 1995, as compared to the growth rate of China's industrial sector, 9.51%. The rate of return on asset is -0.42%. 54.60% of all firms in the industry made a profit while 37.36% had negative returns. The top province in terms of the industry's revenue is Jiangsu, accounting for 38.74% of the total revenue.
本行業在1996年佔全行業總產值0.076%，行業年增長率為-24.8%（全國工業年增長率9.51%）。行業的資產回報率-0.42%，54.60%的企業盈利，37.36%的企業虧損。銷售收入最高的省份為江蘇省，佔本行業的38.74%。

	Total number of firms 企業總數	Total number of employees 職工總數	Total revenue (mil. RMB) 總銷售收入（百萬元）	Total profit (mil. RMB) 總利潤（百萬元）	Return on assets 資產利潤率 (%)	Return on equity 權益利潤率 (%)	Labour productivity ('000 RMB / worker) 勞動生產率（千元/人）	Debts / assets 資產負債率 (%)	Total assets (mil. RMB) 總資產（百萬元）
Industry Overall 行業總體	186	40,616	4,420	-22	-0.42	-1.98	108.82	79.05	5,375

	Number of firms 企業個數	Average number of employees 平均職工人數	Average revenue ('000 RMB) 平均銷售收入（千元）	Average profit ('000 RMB) 平均利潤（千元）	Return on assets 資產利潤率 (%)	Return on equity 權益利潤率 (%)	Labour productivity ('000 RMB / worker) 勞動生產率（千元/人）	Average debts / assets 平均資產負債率(%)	Average Total assets ('000 RMB) 平均總資產（千元）
By ownership 產業所有權									
State-owned 國有	25	458	23,720	-1,440	-2.86	-15.19	51.81	81.15	50,280
Collectively-owned 集體	113	179	19,493	36	0.23	1.68	108.83	86.25	15,663
Privately-owned 私有	2	43	1,905	37	1.90	4.93	44.31	61.42	1,941
Domestic JVs 聯營	8	99	8,623	62	0.44	1.18	87.55	62.64	14,076
Joint stock 股份制	4	557	117,730	361	0.18	0.85	211.37	78.83	201,225
Foreign-funded 外資	19	201	32,025	417	0.92	3.46	159.12	73.34	45,206
Overseas Chinese-funded 港澳台資	15	171	31,467	-2	0.00	-0.01	183.66	64.75	37,648
By size 規模									
Large 大型	6	1,109	102,764	644	0.29	1.27	92.65	77.41	225,003
Medium 中型	12	759	55,558	2,930	3.37	30.06	73.21	88.80	87,017
Small 小型	166	150	18,897	-368	-2.05	-8.67	125.64	76.38	17,959
By regional distribution 地區分布									
Central-North 華北	55	184	9,459	-336	-1.79	-9.39	51.48	80.91	18,732
Beijing 北京	12	215	10,520	-1,393	-4.70	-41.80	48.84	88.74	29,608
Tianjin 天津	6	300	9,615	-1,320	-5.05	-33.18	32.03	84.79	26,163
Hebei 河北	7	105	10,903	993	14.22	23.72	103.98	40.06	6,983
Shanxi 山西	9	107	10,166	-299	-1.32	-4.37	95.40	69.89	22,728
Inner Mongolia 內蒙	21	192	8,024	90	0.72	4.53	41.86	84.14	12,598
Northeast 東北	8	144	1,176	-91	-0.73	-11.83	8.20	93.84	12,533
Liaoning 遼寧	6	47	1,357	-133	-3.78	-7.31	28.66	48.18	3,525
Jilin 吉林	2	432	635	35	0.09	-1.46	1.47	106.04	39,555
Heilongjiang 黑龍江									
Central East 華東	92	216	31,319	102	0.34	1.35	144.86	74.58	29,798
Shanghai 上海	8	343	47,176	225	0.61	1.39	137.59	56.09	36,864
Jiangsu 江蘇	60	189	28,537	-39	-0.17	-1.02	151.36	83.57	23,289
Zhejiang 浙江	16	163	34,651	506	1.37	3.36	213.07	59.24	36,978
Anhui 安徽	3	746	51,103	-193	-0.19	-2.66	68.47	92.93	102,720
Fujian 福建									
Jiangxi 江西									
Shandong 山東	5	199	16,798	486	1.63	3.24	84.41	49.80	29,866
Central-South 中南	18	324	44,281	404	0.65	4.58	136.74	85.80	62,117
Henan 河南	3	19	650	37	11.34	18.97	34.82	41.24	323
Hubei 湖北	4	371	3,753	-3,953	-12.26	-118.96	10.12	89.70	32,250
Hunan 湖南	2	730	17,990	4,340	43.18	55.78	24.66	22.64	10,050
Guangdong 廣東	7	397	104,933	2,069	1.64	16.73	264.60	90.21	126,311
Guangxi 廣西									
Hainan 海南	2	28	4,795	-90	-0.21	-0.42	174.36	48.90	41,925
Southwest 西南	3	110	20,260	-4,153	-21.77	62.05	184.74	135.08	19,080
Chongqing 重慶		190	75,251	-10,817	-17.26	54.68	395.72	131.56	62,684
Sichuan 四川	2	83	1,930	-1,932	-42.50	82.88	23.17	151.28	4,545
Guizhou 貴州									
Yunnan 雲南									
Tibet 西藏									
Northwest 西北	10	331	15,144	-738	-2.25	-8.46	45.70	73.35	32,741
Shaanxi 陝西									
Gansu 甘肅	4	361	13,835	-370	-3.08	-14.30	38.32	78.49	12,028
Qinghai 青海									
Ningxia 寧夏									
Xinjiang 新疆	6	312	16,017	-983	-2.11	-7.67	51.39	72.46	46,550

1741: Wool Tops 毛條加工業

Year 年份	Number of firms 企業個數	Rate of change 每年變化 (%)	Number of employees 職工人數 (人)	Rate of change 每年變化 (%)	Total revenue (mil. RMB) 總銷售收入 (百萬元)	Rate of change 每年變化 (%)	Total profit (mil. RMB) 總利潤 (百萬元)	Rate of change 每年變化 (%)
1993	161		48,447		3,027		11	
1994	185	14.91%	48,009	-0.91%	3,974	31.27%	28	145.13%
1995	209	12.97%	54,851	14.25%	5,875	47.80%	30	9.83%
1996	186	-11.00%	40,616	-25.95%	4,420	-24.77%	-22	-172.56%

3 Major products* 3 種主要產品 *	Output 產量	Sales volume 銷售量	Unit 單位
a) Wool Top 毛條	71,428	59,285	ton 噸
b) Wool Yarn 毛紗	5,315	4,890	ton 噸

Top 10 firms by revenue (year founded) 收入排名前 10 家企業 (創辦年份)	City 城市	Province 省	Telephone / fax 電話 / 傳真	Number of employees 職工人數	Ownership 產業所有權	Revenue ('000 RMB) 銷售收入 (千元)	Profit ('000 RMB) (rank) 利潤 (千元) (排名)	Total assets ('000 RMB) 總資產 (千元)	Major products 主要產品
Nanhai Wool Textile Enterprise Corp. 南海毛紡織企業股份有限公司(1956)	Foshan 佛山市	Guangdong 廣東省	(0757)6773599 (0757)6778728	2,094	Joint stock 股份制	559,242	10598(2)	728,882	a
Reward (Ningbo) Wool Industry Co. Ltd. 利華(寧波)羊毛工業股份有限公司(1992)	Ningbo 寧波市	Zhejiang 浙江省	(0574)6177765 (0574)6177551	454	Foreign-funded 外資	382,581	5327(4)	443,766	o
Shanghai No.1 Top Making Mill 上海第一毛條廠(1964)	Shanghai 上海市	Shanghai 上海市	(021)65127093 (021)65128552	1,129	State-owned 國有	261,082	1507(15)	211,997	a
Jiangsu Ren He Group Co. Ltd 江蘇人和集團有限公司(1992)	Suzhou 蘇州市	Jiangsu 江蘇省	(0512)7651707 (0512)7651745	607	Collectively-owned 集體	258,031	2142(10)	123,373	a,b
Changzhou Wool-top Factory 常州市毛條廠(1952)	Changzhou 常州市	Jiangsu 江蘇省	(0519)8819170 (0519)8826136	1,035	Collectively-owned 集體	166,890	150(43)	139,150	a,b
Changshu Cheng Da Wool Top Factory 常熟市澄達毛條廠(1989)	Suzhou 蘇州市	Jiangsu 江蘇省	(0512)2691628	792	Collectively-owned 集體	162,140	3030(8)	169,560	a
Maoming Shuanglin Wool Top Co. Ltd. 茂名雙琳毛條有限公司(1989)	Maoming 茂名市	Guangdong 廣東省	(0668)2272802 (0668)2273713	155	Foreign-funded 外資	149,299	3342(6)	79,434	a
Jiangsu Chang Sheng Group Company 江蘇長盛集團公司(1995)	Wuxi 無錫市	Jiangsu 江蘇省	(0510)3761971	809	Collectively-owned 集體	136,208	440(29)	111,502	o
Bengbu Tian Rabbit Hair Spinning Group Co. Ltd. 蚌埠天兔毛紡集團有限公司(1981)	Bengbu 蚌埠市	Anhui 安徽省	(0552)3017181 (0552)3017362	1,697	State-owned 國有	116,092	5(65)	232,717	a,b
Haimen Shen Hai Industrial General Company 海門市申海實業總公司(1988)	Nantong 南通市	Jiangsu 江蘇省	(0513)2233083	327	Collectively-owned 集體	101,003	1485(17)	55,857	a

Top 10 Cities by Production Output 產出排名前 10 位城市	Province 省	Market share 市場份額	Number of firms 企業個數
Suzhou 蘇州市	Jiangsu 江蘇省	33.80%	60
Wuxi 無錫市	Jiangsu 江蘇省	13.21%	21
Ningbo 寧波市	Zhejiang 浙江省	7.28%	3
Shanghai 上海市	Shanghai 上海市	7.08%	16
Foshan 佛山市	Guangdong 廣東省	5.90%	3
Changzhou 常州市	Jiangsu 江蘇省	3.00%	6
Jiaxing 嘉興市	Zhejiang 浙江省	2.74%	5
Maoming 茂名市	Guangdong 廣東省	2.60%	1
Beijing 北京市	Beijing 北京市	2.32%	11
Huzhou 湖州市	Zhejiang 浙江省	1.99%	2

10 Major Wholesalers 10 家主要批發商	City 城市	Province 省	Telephone / Fax 電話 / 傳真
Anhui Clothing Import & Export Company 安徽省服裝進出口公司	Hefei 合肥市	Anhui 安徽省	(0551)3632212 (0551)3632002
Qingdao Textile Clothing Industrial Group Company 青島紡織服裝實業集團公司	Qingdao 青島市	Shandong 山東省	(0532)2877853 (0532)2869315
Hebei Textile Import & Export (Group) Company 河北省紡織品進出口(集團)公司	Shijiazhuang 石家莊市	Hebei 河北省	(0311)7028530 (0311)7027781
Zhong Fang Pledget Import & Export Company 中紡紗布進出口公司	Beijing 北京市	Beijing 北京市	(010)65124718 (010)65124713
Shaoxing Import & Export Company 紹興市進出口公司	Shaoxing 紹興市	Zhejiang 浙江省	(0575)5132822 (0575)5141577
Hunan Hua Xiang Import & Export (Group) Company 湖南省華湘進出口(集團)公司	Changsha 長沙市	Hunan 湖南省	(0731)2282440 (0731)2286995
City's Import & Export Company Trade Dept. 市進出口公司貿易部	Yichang 宜昌市	Hubei 湖北省	(0717)6450778 (0717)6441875
Shanghai Pu Dong Xinqu Import & Export Company 上海浦東新區進出口公司	Shanghai 上海市	Shanghai 上海市	(021)58878801 (021)58827444
Ningbo Yinxian Import & Export Company 寧波市鄞縣進出口公司	Ningbo 寧波市	Zhejiang 浙江省	(0574)7875205 (0574)7873168
Zhejiang Silk Import & Export Company 浙江省絲綢進出口公司	Hangzhou 杭州市	Zhejiang 浙江省	(0571)5195588 (0571)5192542

*Also include sales by firms outside this industry.包括本行業以外廠家的銷售。"o" stands for "others". "o" 代表"其他產品"。

1742: Wool Spinning 毛紡業

The industry accounts for 0.528% of the total revenue of China's industrial sector in 1996. The revenue growth rate of the industry is 3.1% from 1995, as compared to the growth rate of China's industrial sector, 9.51%. The rate of return on asset is 0.12%. 55.17% of all firms in the industry made a profit while 38.05% had negative returns. The top province in terms of the industry's revenue is Jiangsu, accounting for 33.94% of the total revenue.
本行業在1996年佔全行業總產值0.528%，行業年增長率為3.1%（全國工業年增長率9.51%）。行業的資產回報率0.12%，55.17%的企業盈利，38.05%的企業虧損。銷售收入最高的省份為江蘇省，佔本行業的33.94%。

	Total number of firms 企業總數	Total number of employees 職工總數	Total revenue (mil. RMB) 總銷售收入（百萬元）	Total profit (mil. RMB) 總利潤（百萬元）	Return on assets 資產利潤率 (%)	Return on equity 權益利潤率 (%)	Labour productivity ('000 RMB / worker) 勞動生產率（千元/人）	Debts / assets 資產負債率 (%)	Total assets (mil. RMB) 總資產（百萬元）
Industry Overall 行業總體	1,023	513,785	30,601	60	0.12	0.54	59.56	77.24	48,890

	Number of firms 企業個數	Average number of employees 平均職工人數	Average revenue ('000 RMB) 平均銷售收入（千元）	Average profit ('000 RMB) 平均利潤（千元）	Return on assets 資產利潤率 (%)	Return on equity 權益利潤率 (%)	Labour productivity ('000 RMB / worker) 勞動生產率（千元/人）	Average debts / assets 平均資產負債率(%)	Average Total assets ('000 RMB) 平均總資產（千元）
By ownership 產業所有權									
State-owned 國有	240	1,158	40,667	-2,463	-2.44	-19.35	35.10	87.42	101,125
Collectively-owned 集體	507	305	23,571	633	2.52	9.36	77.21	73.07	25,096
Privately-owned 私有	87	97	7,184	260	5.42	13.95	73.77	61.16	4,802
Domestic JVs 聯營	25	413	26,277	280	0.81	2.59	63.63	68.59	34,460
Joint stock 股份制	12	1,617	206,897	17,096	5.93	11.36	127.96	47.83	288,439
Foreign-funded 外資	49	331	33,674	755	1.63	4.63	101.80	64.70	46,225
Overseas Chinese-funded 港澳台資	103	283	33,680	572	1.21	3.67	118.94	67.11	47,384
By size 規模									
Large 大型	83	2,421	160,830	1,124	0.39	1.57	66.43	75.07	286,613
Medium 中型	167	939	41,517	-342	-0.44	-2.74	44.21	83.90	77,411
Small 小型	764	204	13,507	31	0.20	0.76	66.05	74.42	15,934
By regional distribution 地區分布									
Central-North 華北	264	337	15,029	88	0.34	1.74	44.58	80.57	26,109
Beijing 北京	36	447	21,889	-277	-0.60	-2.04	49.00	70.56	46,062
Tianjin 天津	33	823	28,748	-488	-0.88	-7.47	34.94	88.21	55,415
Hebei 河北	151	179	11,700	360	3.19	15.37	65.32	79.24	11,290
Shanxi 山西	7	365	8,833	-47	-0.25	-1.08	24.18	76.65	18,684
Inner Mongolia 內蒙	37	437	10,873	-127	-0.30	-1.88	24.89	84.03	42,436
Northeast 東北	40	1,179	23,390	-3,990	-4.42	-76.74	19.84	94.25	90,360
Liaoning 遼寧	17	1,181	11,229	-2,921	-3.84	-64.81	9.51	94.08	76,113
Jilin 吉林	12	722	20,650	-1,296	-2.30	-10.50	28.58	78.09	56,305
Heilongjiang 黑龍江	11	1,675	45,174	-8,581	-5.74	564.87	26.97	101.02	149,528
Central East 華東	501	481	39,481	1,198	2.45	8.16	82.09	70.00	48,938
Shanghai 上海	55	729	61,923	2,765	3.04	8.81	84.95	65.54	91,063
Jiangsu 江蘇	186	528	55,831	2,350	4.36	12.64	105.74	65.49	53,882
Zhejiang 浙江	128	300	22,211	151	0.49	1.82	74.12	73.02	30,845
Anhui 安徽	16	430	6,499	-1,899	-7.89	124.15	15.12	106.36	24,053
Fujian 福建	16	342	24,339	135	0.49	1.33	71.24	63.33	27,752
Jiangxi 江西	10	565	10,071	-611	-1.80	-11.56	17.83	84.39	33,851
Shandong 山東	90	515	28,359	290	0.60	2.86	55.11	79.09	48,576
Central-South 中南	118	461	34,242	78	0.12	0.47	74.21	73.44	62,518
Henan 河南	37	600	14,048	-210	-0.59	-3.65	23.40	83.88	35,697
Hubei 湖北	20	415	10,883	-511	-2.11	-14.32	26.23	85.26	24,209
Hunan 湖南	6	775	10,218	-15,742	-41.61	516.68	13.19	108.06	37,832
Guangdong 廣東	52	363	60,319	2,338	2.50	7.33	165.97	65.96	93,703
Guangxi 廣西	2	199	4,975	-550	-3.04	-16.98	25.06	82.07	18,070
Hainan 海南	1	1	95,330	1,100	0.25	3.93	95330.00	93.58	436,420
Southwest 西南	32	491	7,475	-1,957	-5.95	131.61	15.22	104.52	32,887
Chongqing 重慶	6	801	13,176	-6,456	-14.49	46.73	16.44	131.00	44,565
Sichuan 四川	14	500	8,440	-1,157	-3.11	80.65	16.85	103.86	37,227
Guizhou 貴州	2	590	5,275	-1,375	-3.60	28.03	8.94	112.84	38,200
Yunnan 雲南	5	349	3,458	-1,032	-3.87	-25.05	9.91	84.53	26,634
Tibet 西藏	5	194	2,828	44	0.41	0.49	14.61	17.80	10,852
Northwest 西北	68	978	24,095	-5,159	-6.45	-111.54	24.64	94.21	79,932
Shaanxi 陝西	16	1,043	23,869	-7,958	-8.70	-142.51	22.89	93.90	91,491
Gansu 甘肅	23	730	19,357	-317	-0.59	-2.34	26.52	74.90	53,883
Qinghai 青海	6	1,746	36,140	-16,308	-11.30	80.24	20.69	114.08	144,328
Ningxia 寧夏	7	908	15,540	-6,170	-10.96	95.51	17.12	111.48	56,307
Xinjiang 新疆	16	1,012	30,357	-4,699	-5.11	-92.54	30.01	94.48	92,004

1742: Wool Spinning 毛紡業

Year 年份	Number of firms 企業個數	Rate of change 每年變化 (%)	Number of employees 職工人數（人）	Rate of change 每年變化 (%)	Total revenue (mil. RMB) 總銷售收入（百萬元）	Rate of change 每年變化 (%)	Total profit (mil. RMB) 總利潤（百萬元）	Rate of change 每年變化 (%)
1993	986		638,484		19,879		247	
1994	1,022	3.65%	539,900	-15.44%	26,265	32.12%	317	28.24%
1995	1,052	2.94%	553,548	2.53%	29,686	13.03%	196	-38.11%
1996	1,023	-2.76%	513,785	-7.18%	30,601	3.08%	60	-69.38%

3 Major products* 3種主要產品*	Output 產量	Sales volume 銷售量	Unit 單位
a) Pure Woollen Fabric 純毛毛織品	9,826	8,843	10,000 metre 萬米
b) Wool Blended Floss For Embroidery 毛混紡絨線	137,991	132,471	ton 噸
c) Wool Fabric 呢絨	27,510	25,860	10,000 metre 萬米

Top 10 firms by revenue (year founded) 收入排名前10家企業（創辦年份）	City 城市	Province 省	Telephone / fax 電話 / 傳真	Number of employees 職工人數	Ownership 產業所有權	Revenue ('000 RMB) 銷售收入（千元）	Profit ('000 RMB) (rank) 利潤（千元）（排名）	Total assets ('000 RMB) 總資產（千元）	Major products 主要產品
Jiangsu Sunshine Group Co. 江蘇陽光集團公司(1986)	Wuxi 無錫市	Jiangsu 江蘇省	(0510)6121888 (0510)6121893	6,282	Collectively-owned 集體	2,328,686	192365(1)	1,525,503	a,c
Guangdong Mei Ya Group Co. Ltd. 廣東美雅集團股份有限公司(1979)	Jiangmen 江門市	Guangdong 廣東省	(0750)8888888 (0750)8889673	6,884	Joint stock 股份制	1,821,862	182597(2)	2,306,127	o
Jiangsu Hua Fang Group Co. 江蘇華紡(集團)公司(1980)	Suzhou 蘇州市	Jiangsu 江蘇省	(0512)8591800 (0512)8592341	2,750	Collectively-owned 集體	924,963	57650(4)	970,758	b,c
Sanmao Group Corp. 江蘇三毛集團公司(1989)	Wuxi 無錫市	Jiangsu 江蘇省	(0510)6121388 (0510)6121377	2,550	Collectively-owned 集體	586,040	123234(3)	521,570	a,c
Jiangsu Gang Yang Group Company 江蘇港洋集團公司(1985)	Suzhou 蘇州市	Jiangsu 江蘇省	(0512)8581208	1,406	Collectively-owned 集體	460,324	36594(7)	176,837	o
Zhejiang Jiaxing Worsted General Factory 浙江嘉興毛紡織總廠(1958)	Jiaxing 嘉興市	Zhejiang 浙江省	(0573)2089934 (0573)2083856	4,375	State-owned 國有	396,020	10180(27)	408,940	a,b,c
Jiangsu Shen Zhou Worsted Group Co. 江蘇申洲毛紡集團公司(1982)	Suzhou 蘇州市	Jiangsu 江蘇省	(0512)8292477 (0512)8292469	1,350	Collectively-owned 集體	370,180	18120(11)	211,880	b
Shanghai No.2 Worsted Mill 上海第二毛紡織廠(1933)	Shanghai 上海市	Shanghai 上海市	(021)65430518 (021)65431387	2,308	State-owned 國有	331,676	36777(6)	470,473	a,c
Wuxi Xie Xin Worsted Spinning & Dyeing Co. Ltd. 無錫協新毛紡織染有限公司(1993)	Wuxi 無錫市	Jiangsu 江蘇省	(0510)3707890 (0510)3701378	2,790	Overseas Chinese-funded 港澳台資	320,099	39114(5)	536,162	a,c
Shanghai No.1 Wool Textile Factory 上海第一毛紡織廠(1925)	Shanghai 上海市	Shanghai 上海市	(021)62582600 (021)62582600	2,613	State-owned 國有	312,019	16143(14)	319,621	a,b,c

Top 10 Cities by Production Output 產出排名前10位城市	Province 省	Market share 市場份額	Number of firms 企業個數
Suzhou 蘇州市	Jiangsu 江蘇省	15.19%	134
Shanghai 上海市	Shanghai 上海市	10.68%	65
Jiangmen 江門市	Guangdong 廣東省	7.00%	9
Wuxi 無錫市	Jiangsu 江蘇省	6.59%	74
Tianjin 天津市	Tianjin 天津市	3.48%	39
Jiaxing 嘉興市	Zhejiang 浙江省	3.11%	22
Beijing 北京市	Beijing 北京市	3.05%	33
Changzhou 常州市	Jiangsu 江蘇省	2.86%	27
Baoding 保定市	Hebei 河北省	2.81%	57
Huzhou 湖州市	Zhejiang 浙江省	2.47%	22

10 Major Wholesalers 10家主要批發商	City 城市	Province 省	Telephone / Fax 電話 / 傳真
Anhui Clothing Import & Export Company 安徽省服裝進出口公司	Hefei 合肥市	Anhui 安徽省	(0551)3632212 (0551)3632002
Qingdao Textile Clothing Industrial Group Company 青島紡織服裝實業集團公司	Qingdao 青島市	Shandong 山東省	(0532)2877853 (0532)2869315
Hebei Textile Import & Export (Group) Company 河北省紡織品進出口(集團)公司	Shijiazhuang 石家莊市	Hebei 河北省	(0311)7028530 (0311)7027781
Zhong Fang Pledget Import & Export Company 中紡紗布進出口公司	Beijing 北京市	Beijing 北京市	(010)65124718 (010)65124713
Shaoxing Import & Export Company 紹興市進出口公司	Shaoxing 紹興市	Zhejiang 浙江省	(0575)5132822 (0575)5141577
Hunan Hua Xiang Import & Export (Group) Company 湖南省華湘進出口(集團)公司	Changsha 長沙市	Hunan 湖南省	(0731)2282440 (0731)2286995
City's Import & Export Company Trade Dept. 市進出口公司貿易部	Yichang 宜昌市	Hubei 湖北省	(0717)6450778 (0717)6441875
Shanghai Pu Dong Xinqu Import & Export Company 上海浦東新區進出口公司	Shanghai 上海市	Shanghai 上海市	(021)58878801 (021)58827444
Ningbo Yinxian Import & Export Company 寧波市鄞縣進出口公司	Ningbo 寧波市	Zhejiang 浙江省	(0574)7875205 (0574)7873168
Zhejiang Silk Import & Export Company 浙江省絲綢進出口公司	Hangzhou 杭州市	Zhejiang 浙江省	(0571)5195588 (0571)5192542

*Also include sales by firms outside this industry.包括本行業以外廠家的銷售。"o" stands for "others". "o"代表"其他產品"。

1743: Wool Weaving 毛織業

The industry accounts for 0.147% of the total revenue of China's industrial sector in 1996. The revenue growth rate of the industry is 12.4% from 1995, as compared to the growth rate of China's industrial sector, 9.51%. The rate of return on asset is 0.58%. 64.21% of all firms in the industry made a profit while 29.83% had negative returns. The top province in terms of the industry's revenue is Jiangsu, accounting for 39.92% of the total revenue.
本行業在1996年佔全行業總產值0.147%，行業年增長率為12.4%（全國工業年增長率9.51%）。行業的資產回報率0.58%，64.21%的企業盈利，29.83%的企業虧損。銷售收入最高的省份為江蘇省，佔本行業的39.92%。

	Total number of firms 企業總數	Total number of employees 職工總數	Total revenue (mil. RMB) 總銷售收入（百萬元）	Total profit (mil. RMB) 總利潤（百萬元）	Return on assets 資產利潤率 (%)	Return on equity 權益利潤率 (%)	Labour productivity ('000 RMB / worker) 勞動生產率（千元/人）	Debts / assets 資產負債率 (%)	Total assets (mil. RMB) 總資產（百萬元）
Industry Overall 行業總體	600	186,469	8,505	86	0.58	2.33	45.61	75.17	14,785

	Number of firms 企業個數	Average number of employees 平均職工人數	Average revenue ('000 RMB) 平均銷售收入（千元）	Average profit ('000 RMB) 平均利潤（千元）	Return on assets 資產利潤率 (%)	Return on equity 權益利潤率 (%)	Labour productivity ('000 RMB / worker) 勞動生產率（千元/人）	Average debts / assets 平均資產負債率(%)	Average Total assets ('000 RMB) 平均總資產（千元）
By ownership 產業所有權									
State-owned 國有	91	934	21,703	-2,088	-3.04	-27.18	23.25	88.82	68,725
Collectively-owned 集體	384	192	10,696	310	2.38	7.76	55.59	69.37	13,022
Privately-owned 私有	9	107	7,182	768	11.67	68.97	67.40	83.08	6,585
Domestic JVs 聯營	12	306	26,900	1,033	4.82	12.48	88.00	61.41	21,459
Joint stock 股份制	4	396	128,254	25,143	12.26	17.88	324.08	31.43	205,123
Foreign-funded 外資	49	222	18,415	477	1.74	5.00	83.02	65.14	27,408
Overseas Chinese-funded 港澳台資	50	220	12,399	276	1.31	4.60	56.33	71.43	21,010
By size 規模									
Large 大型	24	2,144	98,845	-889	-0.38	-1.69	46.11	77.22	231,054
Medium 中型	42	966	38,182	-3,945	-5.50	-50.51	39.54	89.11	71,700
Small 小型	529	178	8,561	516	4.38	13.13	48.05	66.61	11,774
By regional distribution 地區分布									
Central-North 華北	134	352	8,578	216	0.91	5.40	24.34	83.06	23,672
Beijing 北京	35	282	4,226	-66	-0.73	-3.20	14.97	77.31	9,125
Tianjin 天津	13	121	3,483	151	3.17	9.30	28.75	65.88	4,753
Hebei 河北	46	231	5,784	20	0.12	-1.58	25.00	107.41	17,263
Shanxi 山西	6	969	8,343	-4,182	-5.15	-29.89	8.61	82.77	81,190
Inner Mongolia 內蒙	34	568	18,830	1,574	3.55	12.78	33.16	72.26	44,404
Northeast 東北	42	573	6,499	-2,359	-8.20	100.52	11.35	108.16	28,767
Liaoning 遼寧	19	625	9,904	-2,187	-5.96	125.37	15.85	104.76	36,686
Jilin 吉林	14	707	5,722	-3,926	-15.06	107.15	8.10	114.05	26,074
Heilongjiang 黑龍江	9	254	518	-282	-1.74	18.00	2.03	109.66	16,238
Central East 華東	226	302	25,268	1,040	3.13	9.24	83.71	66.15	33,244
Shanghai 上海	17	330	43,780	6,311	8.11	12.49	132.64	35.07	77,819
Jiangsu 江蘇	89	374	38,151	1,470	4.04	11.69	102.06	65.43	36,378
Zhejiang 浙江	59	175	15,158	-54	-0.19	-0.80	86.60	76.59	28,660
Anhui 安徽	11	368	8,087	-694	-4.08	41.99	21.97	109.72	17,000
Fujian 福建	13	101	11,893	-188	-1.54	-3.21	117.84	52.17	12,274
Jiangxi 江西	7	281	5,757	-96	-0.72	-16.92	20.46	95.76	13,357
Shandong 山東	30	389	13,088	359	1.31	10.04	33.61	86.96	27,388
Central-South 中南	145	150	5,135	-217	-2.69	-9.00	34.33	70.14	8,083
Henan 河南	16	213	2,809	30	0.45	1.96	13.17	76.77	6,599
Hubei 湖北	17	160	8,002	78	0.56	17.57	50.05	96.81	13,953
Hunan 湖南	5	123	392	-92	-3.52	-21.80	3.18	83.86	2,614
Guangdong 廣東	100	124	5,298	-218	-3.28	-7.41	42.84	55.69	6,634
Guangxi 廣西	7	368	4,551	-1,581	-7.24	-50.66	12.37	85.70	21,829
Hainan 海南									
Southwest 西南	12	376	6,829	-280	-2.15	68.99	18.17	103.11	13,003
Chongqing 重慶									
Sichuan 四川	8	440	9,200	-124	-1.25	13.14	20.91	109.48	9,953
Guizhou 貴州	1	945	7,870	-2,430	-3.22	-123.35	8.33	97.38	75,580
Yunnan 雲南									
Tibet 西藏	3	16	160	20	7.23	8.45	9.80	14.46	277
Northwest 西北	41	507	13,300	-1,082	-2.84	-12.91	26.25	78.01	38,124
Shaanxi 陝西	7	133	634	16	2.63	22.92	4.77	88.54	599
Gansu 甘肅	8	871	23,294	-3,876	-6.42	-21.05	26.73	69.50	60,391
Qinghai 青海	12	180	1,308	-765	-12.51	24.41	7.25	151.24	6,115
Ningxia 寧夏	2	43	165	-15	-1.07	-1.59	3.84	32.74	1,405
Xinjiang 新疆	12	885	28,208	-353	-0.42	-1.83	31.88	76.84	83,298

1743: Wool Weaving 毛織業

Year 年份	Number of firms 企業個數	Rate of change 每年變化 (%)	Number of employees 職工人數 (人)	Rate of change 每年變化 (%)	Total revenue (mil. RMB) 總銷售收入 (百萬元)	Rate of change 每年變化 (%)	Total profit (mil. RMB) 總利潤 (百萬元)	Rate of change 每年變化 (%)
1993	732		220,685		7,042		98	
1994	713	-2.60%	220,273	-0.19%	6,492	-7.80%	-62	-163.21%
1995	591	-17.11%	199,801	-9.29%	7,570	16.60%	33	153.20%
1996	600	1.52%	186,469	-6.67%	8,505	12.35%	86	160.57%

3 Major products* 3種主要產品 *	Output 產量	Sales volume 銷售量	Unit 單位
a) Wool Union Goods 毛混紡交織品	5,764	5,302	10,000 metre 萬米
b) Wool Fabric 呢絨	10,105	9,498	10,000 metre 萬米

Top 10 firms by revenue (year founded) 收入排名前10家企業 (創辦年份)	City 城市	Province 省	Telephone / fax 電話 / 傳真	Number of employees 職工人數	Ownership 產業所有權	Revenue ('000 RMB) 銷售收入 (千元)	Profit ('000 RMB) (rank) 利潤 (千元) (排名)	Total assets ('000 RMB) 總資產 (千元)	Major products 主要產品
Jiangyin No.9 Worsted Mill 江陰市第九毛紡織廠(1985)	Wuxi 無錫市	Jiangsu 江蘇省	(0510)6151260 (0510)6751666	1,200	Collectively-owned 集體	708,179	40777(2)	426,448	b
Zhangjiagang Pu Kun Wool Spinning & Dyeing Co. Ltd. 張家港普坤毛紡織染有限公司(1994)	Suzhou 蘇州市	Jiangsu 江蘇省	(0512)8442888 (0512)8440088	1,580	Overseas Chinese-funded 港澳台資	474,110	34020(3)	364,510	o
Jiangsu (Ling Feng) Group Company 江蘇(靈豐)集團公司(1993)	Suzhou 蘇州市	Jiangsu 江蘇省	(0512)2541582 (0512)2541468	2,027	Collectively-owned 集體	327,081	19919(4)	278,329	b
Shanghai Hai Xin Co. Ltd. 上海海欣股份有限公司(1987)	Shanghai 上海市	Shanghai 上海市	(021)57610168 (021)57610180	856	Joint stock 股份制	311,729	88165(1)	674,928	o
Zhejiang Shen Zhou Wool Spinning Group Co. Ltd. 浙江神州毛紡集團有限公司(1983)	Jiaxing 嘉興市	Zhejiang 浙江省	(0573)4023835 (0573)4024008	1,594	Collectively-owned 集體	190,085	7002(8)	113,509	a,b
Jiangsu Zhang Lu Group Co. 江蘇章鹿集團公司(1993)	Suzhou 蘇州市	Jiangsu 江蘇省	(0512)8471806 (0512)8471806	1,755	Collectively-owned 集體	188,950	6563(9)	224,102	a
Zhejiang Guang Hua Textile Group Co. 浙江光華紡織集團公司(1994)	Ningbo 寧波市	Zhejiang 浙江省	(0574)6262520 (0574)6262416	1,189	State-owned 國有	160,588	2057(33)	264,886	a,b
Xinjiang Yi Li Worsted Mill 新疆伊犁毛紡織廠(1961)	Yining 伊寧市	Xinjiang 新疆	(0999)8320055 (0999)8324189	3,581	State-owned 國有	148,049	2105(31)	382,124	b
Nanhai Zhu Jiang Plush Co. Ltd. 南海市珠江長毛絨有限公司(1988)	Shanghai 上海市	Shanghai 上海市	(021)63341430	437	Overseas Chinese-funded 港澳台資	144,816	14847(5)	76,752	o
Yangzhou Guang Da Wool & Velvet Industrial Company 揚州廣大毛絨實業公司(1958)	Yangzhou 揚州市	Jiangsu 江蘇省	(0514)7887541 (0514)7888141	1,548	Collectively-owned 集體	140,780	4555(16)	219,000	a,b

Top 10 Cities by Production Output 產出排名前10位城市	Province 省	Market share 市場份額	Number of firms 企業個數
Suzhou 蘇州市	Jiangsu 江蘇省	21.21%	61
Wuxi 無錫市	Jiangsu 江蘇省	12.26%	30
Shanghai 上海市	Shanghai 上海市	5.99%	18
Shaoxing 紹興市	Zhejiang 浙江省	3.91%	14
Hohhot 呼和浩特市	Inner Mong 內蒙	3.32%	7
Jiaxing 嘉興市	Zhejiang 浙江省	2.77%	8
Beijing 北京市	Beijing 北京市	2.66%	29
Ningbo 寧波市	Zhejiang 浙江省	2.61%	13
Weihai 威海市	Shandong 山東省	2.35%	3
Yangzhou 揚州市	Jiangsu 江蘇省	2.32%	6

10 Major Wholesalers 10家主要批發商	City 城市	Province 省	Telephone / Fax 電話 / 傳真
Anhui Clothing Import & Export Company 安徽省服裝進出口公司	Hefei 合肥市	Anhui 安徽省	(0551)3632212 (0551)3632002
Qingdao Textile Clothing Industrial Group Company 青島紡織服裝實業集團公司	Qingdao 青島市	Shandong 山東省	(0532)2877853 (0532)2869315
Hebei Textile Import & Export (Group) Company 河北省紡織品進出口(集團)公司	Shijiazhuang 石家莊市	Hebei 河北省	(0311)7028530 (0311)7027781
Zhong Fang Pledget Import & Export Company 中紡紗布進出口公司	Beijing 北京市	Beijing 北京市	(010)65124718 (010)65124713
Shaoxing Import & Export Company 紹興市進出口公司	Shaoxing 紹興市	Zhejiang 浙江省	(0575)5132822 (0575)5141577
Hunan Hua Xiang Import & Export (Group) Company 湖南省華湘進出口(集團)公司	Changsha 長沙市	Hunan 湖南省	(0731)2282440 (0731)2286995
City's Import & Export Company Trade Dept. 市進出口公司貿易部	Yichang 宜昌市	Hubei 湖北省	(0717)6450778 (0717)6441875
Shanghai Pu Dong Xinqu Import & Export Company 上海浦東新區進出口公司	Shanghai 上海市	Shanghai 上海市	(021)58878801 (021)58827444
Ningbo Yinxian Import & Export Company 寧波市鄞縣進出口公司	Ningbo 寧波市	Zhejiang 浙江省	(0574)7875205 (0574)7873168
Zhejiang Silk Import & Export Company 浙江省絲綢進出口公司	Hangzhou 杭州市	Zhejiang 浙江省	(0571)5195588 (0571)5192542

*Also include sales by firms outside this industry.包括本行業以外廠家的銷售。"o" stands for "others". "o" 代表 "其他產品"。

1744: Wool Printing and Dyeing 毛染整業

The industry accounts for 0.040% of the total revenue of China's industrial sector in 1996. The revenue growth rate of the industry is 40.7% from 1995, as compared to the growth rate of China's industrial sector, 9.51%. The rate of return on asset is 3.58%. 67.45% of all firms in the industry made a profit while 26.14% had negative returns. The top province in terms of the industry's revenue is Jiangsu, accounting for 38.09% of the total revenue.
本行業在1996年佔全行業總產值0.040%，行業年增長率為40.7%（全國工業年增長率9.51%）。行業的資產回報率3.58%，67.45%的企業盈利，26.14%的企業虧損。銷售收入最高的省份為江蘇省，佔本行業的38.09%。

	Total number of firms 企業總數	Total number of employees 職工總數	Total revenue (mil. RMB) 總銷售收入（百萬元）	Total profit (mil. RMB) 總利潤（百萬元）	Return on assets 資產利潤率 (%)	Return on equity 權益利潤率 (%)	Labour productivity ('000 RMB / worker) 勞動生產率（千元/人）	Debts / assets 資產負債率 (%)	Total assets (mil. RMB) 總資產（百萬元）
Industry Overall 行業總體	156	22,178	2,302	96	3.58	9.28	103.80	61.38	2,688

	Number of firms 企業個數	Average number of employees 平均職工人數	Average revenue ('000 RMB) 平均銷售收入（千元）	Average profit ('000 RMB) 平均利潤（千元）	Return on assets 資產利潤率 (%)	Return on equity 權益利潤率 (%)	Labour productivity ('000 RMB / worker) 勞動生產率（千元/人）	Average debts / assets 平均資產負債率(%)	Average Total assets ('000 RMB) 平均總資產（千元）
By ownership 產業所有權									
State-owned 國有	5	943	48,000	4,200	3.67	17.36	50.90	78.85	114,400
Collectively-owned 集體	96	116	6,450	360	4.41	11.84	55.42	62.80	8,171
Privately-owned 私有	9	91	6,242	364	8.23	13.04	68.76	36.90	4,425
Domestic JVs 聯營	4	79	135	-46	-0.67	-0.76	1.71	11.29	6,790
Joint stock 股份制									
Foreign-funded 外資	7	146	13,719	-2,634	-9.40	-19.08	94.15	50.73	28,024
Overseas Chinese-funded 港澳台資	34	122	36,385	1,589	5.14	11.35	298.02	54.74	30,918
By size 規模									
Large 大型									
Medium 中型	2	1,078	52,943	-7,093	-4.11	-9.84	49.14	58.25	172,725
Small 小型	154	131	14,263	715	4.70	12.32	108.88	61.85	15,216
By regional distribution 地區分布									
Central-North 華北	61	131	10,302	479	2.95	11.25	78.80	73.80	16,238
Beijing 北京	11	451	25,173	1,285	2.38	11.18	55.86	78.75	54,058
Tianjin 天津	7	95	5,949	320	9.12	43.33	62.34	78.94	3,507
Hebei 河北	10	59	3,566	274	14.61	27.21	60.44	46.29	1,875
Shanxi 山西	1	23	7,430	30	1.59	23.08	323.04	93.12	1,890
Inner Mongolia 內蒙	32	54	8,338	314	2.87	8.53	153.60	66.41	10,959
Northeast 東北	1								
Liaoning 遼寧	1								
Jilin 吉林									
Heilongjiang 黑龍江									
Central East 華東	65	109	17,331	922	7.60	14.04	158.73	45.83	12,131
Shanghai 上海	11	90	5,244	735	6.19	9.79	58.09	36.82	11,890
Jiangsu 江蘇	23	139	38,119	2,057	12.02	19.85	275.18	39.45	17,107
Zhejiang 浙江	26	102	6,615	258	3.13	7.65	64.76	59.08	8,255
Anhui 安徽									
Fujian 福建	3	30	140	-57	-3.53	-4.29	4.67	17.63	1,607
Jiangxi 江西									
Shandong 山東	2	86	9,860	-990	-4.42	-13.72	114.65	67.78	22,395
Central-South 中南	25	220	19,602	256	0.85	1.96	89.20	56.72	30,169
Henan 河南	5	66	7,142	10	0.16	0.40	108.54	60.18	6,348
Hubei 湖北	1	2,764	96,300	3,050	1.24	5.66	34.84	78.12	246,140
Hunan 湖南									
Guangdong 廣東	19	126	18,844	173	0.69	1.27	149.12	45.43	25,071
Guangxi 廣西									
Hainan 海南									
Southwest 西南	3	499	18,693	253	0.50	3.14	37.49	83.98	50,423
Chongqing 重慶									
Sichuan 四川	2	97	8,105	-625	-4.32	-3086.27	83.56	99.86	14,465
Guizhou 貴州									
Yunnan 雲南	1	1,302	39,870	2,010	1.64	8.31	30.62	80.23	122,340
Tibet 西藏									
Northwest 西北	1	116	890	10	0.31	1.59	7.67	80.56	3,240
Shaanxi 陝西									
Gansu 甘肅									
Qinghai 青海									
Ningxia 寧夏	1	116	890	10	0.31	1.59	7.67	80.56	3,240
Xinjiang 新疆									

1744: Wool Printing and Dyeing 毛染整業

Year 年份	Number of firms 企業個數	Rate of change 每年變化 (%)	Number of employees 職工人數 (人)	Rate of change 每年變化 (%)	Total revenue (mil. RMB) 總銷售收入 (百萬元)	Rate of change 每年變化 (%)	Total profit (mil. RMB) 總利潤 (百萬元)	Rate of change 每年變化 (%)
1993	96		18,824		793		17	
1994	122	27.08%	13,864	-26.35%	940	18.65%	27	60.63%
1995	135	10.66%	17,761	28.11%	1,636	73.99%	24	-10.76%
1996	156	15.56%	22,178	24.87%	2,302	40.71%	96	297.14%

3 Major products* 3種主要產品 *	Output 產量	Sales volume 銷售量	Unit 單位
a) Pure Jacquard Woollen Blanket 純毛提花毛毯	113,827	126,348	piece 條
b) Wool Blended Floss For Embroidery 毛混紡絨線	10,187	9,779	ton 噸
c) Wool Fabric 呢絨	716	673	10,000 metre 萬米

Top 10 firms by revenue (year founded) 收入排名前10家企業 (創辦年份)	City 城市	Province 省	Telephone / fax 電話 / 傳真	Number of employees 職工人數	Ownership 產業所有權	Revenue ('000 RMB) 銷售收入 (千元)	Profit ('000 RMB) (rank) 利潤 (千元) (排名)	Total assets ('000 RMB) 總資產 (千元)	Major products 主要產品
Suzhou Jin Xiang Weaving & Dyeing & Finishing Co. Ltd. 蘇州錦祥紡織染整有限公司(1990)	Suzhou 蘇州市	Jiangsu 江蘇省	(0512)6291129 (0512)6291129	350	Overseas Chinese-funded 港澳台資	590,720	33200(1)	203,290	b
Beijing No.2 Wool Textile Group 北京二毛紡織集團(1962)	Beijing 北京市	Beijing 北京市	(010)69742131 (010)69743687	3,959	State-owned 國有	193,380	16662(2)	430,008	c
Zhangjigang Qing Nian Wool Textile Factory 張家港市青年毛紡織廠(1982)	Suzhou 蘇州市	Jiangsu 江蘇省	(0512)8581168	195	Collectively-owned 集體	86,139	5782(3)	11,128	o
Zhejiang Heng Chang Industry & Trade Group 浙江恒昌工貿集團(1994)	Jinhua 金華市	Zhejiang 浙江省	(0579)4291363	1,288	Joint stock 股份制	55,399	5034(5)	62,699	o
Zhejiang A Long Weaving Bleaching & Dyeing Co. Ltd. 浙江阿龍織造漂染有限公司(1990)	Shaoxing 紹興市	Zhejiang 浙江省	(0575)2061482 (0575)2061333	60	Overseas Chinese-funded 港澳台資	46,758	413(25)	15,290	o
Dongguan Shatian Jianxin Dyeing Co. Ltd. 東莞沙田建新染有限公司(1990)	Dongguan 東莞市	Guangdong 廣東省	(0769)8861540 (0769)8861441	202	Overseas Chinese-funded 港澳台資	44,607	13(53)	21,738	o
Shunde Hua Cheng Finishing Co. Ltd. 順德華誠染整廠有限公司(1991)	Foshan 佛山市	Guangdong 廣東省	(0757)8886389 (0757)8889628	26	Overseas Chinese-funded 港澳台資	42,150	1019(18)	39,238	o
Yunnan Zhan Yi Wool Textile Mill 雲南省沾益毛紡織廠(1970)	Qujing 曲靖市	Yunnan 雲南省	(0874)3162275 (0874)3163226	1,297	State-owned 國有	39,872	2008(11)	122,344	a,b,c
Guangdong Qiao Xin Dyeing & Finishing Factory 廣東樵新染整廠(1990)	Foshan 佛山市	Guangdong 廣東省	(0757)6832243 (0757)6220000	266	Collectively-owned 集體	37,503	3027(9)	48,924	o
Yixing Wool Fabric Dyeing & Finishing Factory 宜興市毛呢染整廠(1984)	Wuxi 無錫市	Jiangsu 江蘇省	(0510)7541881	110	Collectively-owned 集體	31,850	0(57)	4,990	o

Top 10 Cities by Production Output 產出排名前10位城市	Province 省	Market share 市場份額	Number of firms 企業個數
Changzhou 常州市	Jiangsu 江蘇省	28.18%	5
Wuxi 無錫市	Jiangsu 江蘇省	15.68%	10
Suzhou 蘇州市	Jiangsu 江蘇省	13.65%	24
Beijing 北京市	Beijing 北京市	11.51%	10
Foshan 佛山市	Guangdong 廣東省	5.84%	8
Shanghai 上海市	Shanghai 上海市	3.19%	18
Dongguan 東莞市	Guangdong 廣東省	2.87%	5
Jinhua 金華市	Zhejiang 浙江省	2.64%	1
Zhangzhou 漳州市	Fujian 福建省	2.03%	2
Nantong 南通市	Jiangsu 江蘇省	1.51%	4

10 Major Wholesalers 10家主要批發商	City 城市	Province 省	Telephone / Fax 電話 / 傳真
Anhui Clothing Import & Export Company 安徽省服裝進出口公司	Hefei 合肥市	Anhui 安徽省	(0551)3632212 (0551)3632002
Qingdao Textile Clothing Industrial Group Company 青島紡織服裝實業集團公司	Qingdao 青島市	Shandong 山東省	(0532)2877853 (0532)2869315
Hebei Textile Import & Export (Group) Company 河北省紡織品進出口(集團)公司	Shijiazhuang 石家莊市	Hebei 河北省	(0311)7028530 (0311)7027781
Zhong Fang Pledget Import & Export Company 中紡紗布進出口公司	Beijing 北京市	Beijing 北京市	(010)65124718 (010)65124713
Shaoxing Import & Export Company 紹興市進出口公司	Shaoxing 紹興市	Zhejiang 浙江省	(0575)5132822 (0575)5141577
Hunan Hua Xiang Import & Export (Group) Company 湖南省華湘進出口(集團)公司	Changsha 長沙市	Hunan 湖南省	(0731)2282440 (0731)2286995
City's Import & Export Company Trade Dept. 市進出口公司貿易部	Yichang 宜昌市	Hubei 湖北省	(0717)6450778 (0717)6441875
Shanghai Pu Dong Xinqu Import & Export Company 上海浦東新區進出口公司	Shanghai 上海市	Shanghai 上海市	(021)58878801 (021)58827444
Ningbo Yinxian Import & Export Company 寧波市鄞縣進出口公司	Ningbo 寧波市	Zhejiang 浙江省	(0574)7875205 (0574)7873168
Zhejiang Silk Import & Export Company 浙江省絲綢進出口公司	Hangzhou 杭州市	Zhejiang 浙江省	(0571)5195588 (0571)5192542

*Also include sales by firms outside this industry.包括本行業以外廠家的銷售。"o" stands for "others". "o" 代表 "其他產品"。

1745: Industrial Woollen and Felt Products 工業用呢、工業用氈製造業

The industry accounts for 0.010% of the total revenue of China's industrial sector in 1996. The revenue growth rate of the industry is 2.3% from 1995, as compared to the growth rate of China's industrial sector, 9.51%. The rate of return on asset is -0.17%. 61.57% of all firms in the industry made a profit while 26.57% had negative returns. The top province in terms of the industry's revenue is Shanghai, accounting for 25.02% of the total revenue.
本行業在1996年佔全行業總產值0.010%，行業年增長率為2.3%（全國工業年增長率9.51%）。行業的資產回報率-0.17%，61.57%的企業盈利，26.57%的企業虧損。銷售收入最高的省份為上海市，佔本行業的25.02%。

	Total number of firms 企業總數	Total number of employees 職工總數	Total revenue (mil. RMB) 總銷售收入（百萬元）	Total profit (mil. RMB) 總利潤（百萬元）	Return on assets 資產利潤率 (%)	Return on equity 權益利潤率 (%)	Labour productivity ('000 RMB / worker) 勞動生產率（千元/人）	Debts / assets 資產負債率 (%)	Total assets (mil. RMB) 總資產（百萬元）
Industry Overall 行業總體	137	13,695	598	-2	-0.17	-0.68	43.67	75.48	1,033

	Number of firms 企業個數	Average number of employees 平均職工人數	Average revenue ('000 RMB) 平均銷售收入（千元）	Average profit ('000 RMB) 平均利潤（千元）	Return on assets 資產利潤率 (%)	Return on equity 權益利潤率 (%)	Labour productivity ('000 RMB / worker) 勞動生產率（千元/人）	Average debts / assets 平均資產負債率(%)	Average Total assets ('000 RMB) 平均總資產（千元）
By ownership 產業所有權									
State-owned 國有	16	313	13,563	-563	-1.58	-7.44	43.29	78.73	35,563
Collectively-owned 集體	108	69	2,762	34	0.95	3.68	40.25	74.14	3,564
Privately-owned 私有	3	199	15,885	930	8.18	19.36	79.69	57.75	11,370
Domestic JVs 聯營	4	74	4,051	88	1.70	3.48	54.56	51.08	5,170
Joint stock 股份制	2	104	5,266	67	1.03	2.58	50.64	59.85	6,509
Foreign-funded 外資	2	83	3,556	34	0.67	2.97	43.11	77.45	5,020
Overseas Chinese-funded 港澳台資	1	47	1,150	-9	-0.66	-1.87	24.47	64.69	1,358
By size 規模									
Large 大型	2	1,225	73,507	-28	-0.02	-0.07	60.01	77.29	180,939
Medium 中型	1	175	17,466	-158	-0.48	-1.03	99.81	53.22	32,768
Small 小型	134	83	3,234	-13	-0.28	-1.15	38.94	75.64	4,764
By regional distribution 地區分布									
Central-North 華北	41	93	3,569	99	1.21	6.42	38.31	81.17	8,156
Beijing 北京	5	54	1,760	-98	-3.28	-15.22	32.84	78.46	2,990
Tianjin 天津	5	319	12,368	14	0.04	0.50	38.77	92.19	35,764
Hebei 河北	22	76	3,301	221	4.27	17.34	43.54	75.36	5,172
Shanxi 山西									
Inner Mongolia 內蒙	9	32	338	-44	-1.49	-2.26	10.56	33.94	2,982
Northeast 東北	38	42	1,362	48	2.16	9.56	32.57	77.43	2,242
Liaoning 遼寧	13	55	1,718	71	1.65	8.70	31.14	81.05	4,292
Jilin 吉林	8	52	721	-29	-1.29	-8.55	13.87	84.95	2,234
Heilongjiang 黑龍江	17	27	1,392	68	9.96	19.26	51.89	48.31	679
Central East 華東	32	149	7,648	-43	-0.35	-1.06	51.45	67.08	12,316
Shanghai 上海	8	298	18,701	-158	-0.46	-1.24	62.68	63.12	34,304
Jiangsu 江蘇	13	109	4,240	-66	-1.19	-4.34	38.98	72.51	5,537
Zhejiang 浙江	3	74	3,043	10	0.20	0.90	41.13	78.11	5,070
Anhui 安徽									
Fujian 福建									
Jiangxi 江西	1	123	1,160	-290	-4.20	10.10	9.43	141.59	6,900
Shandong 山東	7	87	4,246	144	3.95	12.21	48.64	67.71	3,654
Central-South 中南	14	144	8,616	178	2.48	8.38	59.83	70.43	7,172
Henan 河南	6	160	5,303	213	2.65	8.48	33.22	68.71	8,037
Hubei 湖北	5	203	17,198	246	2.58	9.06	84.72	71.50	9,524
Hunan 湖南									
Guangdong 廣東	3	14	937	-7	-0.44	-1.92	65.35	77.46	1,523
Guangxi 廣西									
Hainan 海南									
Southwest 西南	3	47	2,690	-440	-7.44	-44.44	57.23	83.26	5,913
Chongqing 重慶		33	685	-12,586	-127.88	-559.82	20.26	77.16	9,842
Sichuan 四川	2	49	3,091	3,045	59.39	412.54	62.27	85.60	5,127
Guizhou 貴州									
Yunnan 雲南									
Tibet 西藏									
Northwest 西北	9	153	2,980	-822	-7.30	-84.57	19.53	91.37	11,267
Shaanxi 陝西	1	60	1,330	-110	-5.29	-29.73	22.17	82.21	2,080
Gansu 甘肅	2	140	3,190	215	2.01	7.88	22.79	74.53	10,720
Qinghai 青海	1	296	4,990	110	0.67	1.63	16.86	58.85	16,380
Ningxia 寧夏	1	244	1,960	-1,460	-8.86	-37.82	8.03	76.56	16,470
Xinjiang 新疆	4	123	3,040	-1,593	-14.15	82.94	24.67	117.06	11,258

1745: Industrial Woollen and Felt Products 工業用呢、工業用氈製造業

Year 年份	Number of firms 企業個數	Rate of change 每年變化 (%)	Number of employees 職工人數（人）	Rate of change 每年變化 (%)	Total revenue (mil. RMB) 總銷售收入（百萬元）	Rate of change 每年變化 (%)	Total profit (mil. RMB) 總利潤（百萬元）	Rate of change 每年變化 (%)
1993	137		25,612		485		5	
1994	150	9.49%	17,248	-32.66%	497	2.67%	4	-31.25%
1995	170	13.33%	17,731	2.80%	585	17.50%	19	406.99%
1996	137	-19.41%	13,695	-22.76%	598	2.31%	-2	-110.52%

3 Major products* 3 種主要產品 *	Output 產量	Sales volume 銷售量	Unit 單位
a) Industrial Felt 工業用氈	5,563	4,895	ton 噸
b) Industrial Suiting 工業用呢	6,859	6,859	ton 噸

Top 10 firms by revenue (year founded) 收入排名前 10 家企業 (創辦年份)	City 城市	Province 省	Telephone / fax 電話 / 傳真	Number of employees 職工人數	Ownership 產業所有權	Revenue ('000 RMB) 銷售收入（千元）	Profit ('000 RMB) (rank) 利潤（千元）（排名）	Total assets ('000 RMB) 總資產（千元）	Major products 主要產品
Shanghai Industry Woollen Cloth Factory 上海工業用呢廠(1937)	Shanghai 上海市	Shanghai 上海市	(021)62416500 (021)62748270	1,296	State-owned 國有	92,057	2010(2)	198,357	b
Tianjin Industry Woollen Cloth Factory 天津市工業用呢廠(1957)	Tianjin 天津市	Tianjin 天津市	(022)27370960 (022)27377168	1,625	State-owned 國有	59,938	0(44)	175,696	b
Hubei Songzi Shou Xin Industry Cloth Factory 湖北省松滋市首鑫工業用布廠(1991)	Jingsha 荊沙市	Hubei 湖北省	(0716)6222635	80	Collectively-owned 集體	21,980	274(18)	4,382	o
Shanghai No.1 Felt Mill 上海第一製氈廠(1980)	Shanghai 上海市	Shanghai 上海市	(021)62538265 (021)62660406	379	Collectively-owned 集體	21,038	300(16)	23,874	a
Shanghai Xinfeng Felt Making Factory 上海新豐製氈廠(1956)	Shanghai 上海市	Shanghai 上海市	(021)64702466 (021)64700555	166	State-owned 國有	19,677	-4299(58)	30,299	o
Taicang Industry Woollen Cloth Factory 太倉市工業用呢廠(1987)	Suzhou 蘇州市	Jiangsu 江蘇省	(0512)3212498	228	Collectively-owned 集體	17,660	1250(3)	33,580	b
Weifang Industry Woollen Cloth Factory 濰坊市工業用呢廠(1993)	Weifang 濰坊市	Shandong 山東省	(0536)8216798 (0536)8216798	130	Collectively-owned 集體	14,946	458(9)	7,059	b
Hebei Lixian Ji Su Li Xian Wan'an Wool Spinning & Dyeing Factory 河北蠡縣冀蘇里縣萬安毛紡織染廠(1991)	Baoding 保定市	Hebei 河北省	(0312)9013521	115	Private-owned 私營	10,495	0(49)	10,516	o
Altay Area Nap Industrial Co. Ltd. 阿勒泰地區絨毛工業有限公司(1970)	Altay 阿勒泰市	Xinjiang 新疆	(0906)2123118	430	State-owned 國有	9,911	-6358(59)	42,073	o
Henan Pingdingshan Industrial Woolen Mill Factory 河南省平頂山市工業用呢廠(1989)	Pingdingshan 平頂山市	Henan 河南省	(0375)3932178 (0375)332238	420	Collectively-owned 集體	9,424	403(12)	12,581	b

Top 10 Cities by Production Output 產出排名前 10 位城市	Province 省	Market share 市場份額	Number of firms 企業個數
Shanghai 上海市	Shanghai 上海市	21.23%	10
Putian 莆田市	Fujian 福建省	13.13%	1
Baoding 保定市	Hebei 河北省	11.20%	11
Tianjin 天津市	Tianjin 天津市	8.75%	6
Suzhou 蘇州市	Jiangsu 江蘇省	7.34%	7
Xuzhou 徐州市	Jiangsu 江蘇省	5.13%	1
Wuhu 蕪湖市	Anhui 安徽省	2.73%	1
Weifang 濰坊市	Shandong 山東省	2.58%	3
Weihai 威海市	Shandong 山東省	1.79%	1
Pingdingshan 平頂山市	Henan 河南省	1.44%	1

10 Major Wholesalers 10 家主要批發商	City 城市	Province 省	Telephone / Fax 電話 / 傳真
Anhui Clothing Import & Export Company 安徽省服裝進出口公司	Hefei 合肥市	Anhui 安徽省	(0551)3632212 (0551)3632002
Qingdao Textile Clothing Industrial Group Company 青島紡織服裝實業集團公司	Qingdao 青島市	Shandong 山東省	(0532)2877853 (0532)2869315
Hebei Textile Import & Export (Group) Company 河北省紡織品進出口(集團)公司	Shijiazhuang 石家莊市	Hebei 河北省	(0311)7028530 (0311)7027781
Zhong Fang Pledget Import & Export Company 中紡紗布進出口公司	Beijing 北京市	Beijing 北京市	(010)65124718 (010)65124713
Shaoxing Import & Export Company 紹興市進出口公司	Shaoxing 紹興市	Zhejiang 浙江省	(0575)5132822 (0575)5141577
Hunan Hua Xiang Import & Export (Group) Company 湖南省華湘進出口(集團)公司	Changsha 長沙市	Hunan 湖南省	(0731)2282440 (0731)2286995
City's Import & Export Company Trade Dept. 市進出口公司貿易部	Yichang 宜昌市	Hubei 湖北省	(0717)6450778 (0717)6441875
Shanghai Pu Dong Xinqu Import & Export Company 上海浦東新區進出口公司	Shanghai 上海市	Shanghai 上海市	(021)58878801 (021)58827444
Ningbo Yinxian Import & Export Company 寧波市鄞縣進出口公司	Ningbo 寧波市	Zhejiang 浙江省	(0574)7875205 (0574)7873168
Zhejiang Silk Import & Export Company 浙江省絲綢進出口公司	Hangzhou 杭州市	Zhejiang 浙江省	(0571)5195588 (0571)5192542

*Also include sales by firms outside this industry.包括本行業以外廠家的銷售。"o" stands for "others". "o" 代表 "其他產品"。

1749: Other Wool Spinning and Weaving 其他毛紡織業

The industry accounts for 0.082% of the total revenue of China's industrial sector in 1996. The revenue growth rate of the industry is 6.2% from 1995, as compared to the growth rate of China's industrial sector, 9.51%. The rate of return on asset is 4.35%. 65.79% of all firms in the industry made a profit while 29.58% had negative returns. The top province in terms of the industry's revenue is Inner Mongolia, accounting for 40.08% of the total revenue.

本行業在1996年佔全行業總產值0.082%，行業年增長率為6.2%（全國工業年增長率9.51%）。行業的資產回報率4.35%，65.79%的企業盈利，29.58%的企業虧損。銷售收入最高的省份為內蒙省，佔本行業的40.08%。

	Total number of firms 企業總數	Total number of employees 職工總數	Total revenue (mil. RMB) 總銷售收入（百萬元）	Total profit (mil. RMB) 總利潤（百萬元）	Return on assets 資產利潤率 (%)	Return on equity 權益利潤率 (%)	Labour productivity ('000 RMB / worker) 勞動生產率（千元/人）	Debts / assets 資產負債率 (%)	Total assets (mil. RMB) 總資產（百萬元）
Industry Overall 行業總體	252	66,909	4,758	352	4.35	12.57	71.11	65.39	8,080

	Number of firms 企業個數	Average number of employees 平均職工人數	Average revenue ('000 RMB) 平均銷售收入（千元）	Average profit ('000 RMB) 平均利潤（千元）	Return on assets 資產利潤率 (%)	Return on equity 權益利潤率 (%)	Labour productivity ('000 RMB / worker) 勞動生產率（千元/人）	Average debts / assets 平均資產負債率(%)	Average Total assets ('000 RMB) 平均總資產（千元）
By ownership 產業所有權									
State-owned 國有	38	482	11,737	-553	-1.31	-6.65	24.35	80.26	42,132
Collectively-owned 集體	160	185	12,255	-173	-1.39	-3.68	66.32	62.19	12,449
Privately-owned 私有	1	46	1,912	587	68.47	89.33	41.58	23.35	857
Domestic JVs 聯營	5	628	55,175	-5,985	-6.41	-20.60	87.91	68.87	93,304
Joint stock 股份制	2	97	3,464	378	7.27	21.42	35.89	66.05	5,203
Foreign-funded 外資	24	370	45,660	2,788	3.56	9.35	123.25	61.99	78,424
Overseas Chinese-funded 港澳台資	21	409	46,115	17,273	17.07	42.08	112.88	59.42	101,173
By size 規模									
Large 大型	4	2,029	381,142	85,549	13.58	27.66	187.89	50.90	629,784
Medium 中型	26	875	43,899	-625	-0.73	-2.70	50.19	72.79	85,176
Small 小型	217	163	9,641	120	0.78	2.72	59.22	71.41	15,425
By regional distribution 地區分布									
Central-North 華北	75	245	29,532	4,379	8.05	19.42	120.66	58.57	54,417
Beijing 北京	10	9	1,222	26	0.79	3.08	131.40	74.31	3,277
Tianjin 天津	12	51	21,487	4,114	10.91	25.74	417.89	57.62	37,711
Hebei 河北	11	76	2,728	371	11.33	50.06	35.81	77.33	3,273
Shanxi 山西	1	741	7,590	-1,430	-1.96	-3.74	10.24	47.53	72,900
Inner Mongolia 內蒙	41	392	46,518	6,735	7.92	19.12	118.70	58.58	85,051
Northeast 東北	21	77	1,449	-196	-2.91	-14.08	18.78	79.34	6,743
Liaoning 遼寧	11	71	1,457	-173	-2.74	-5.70	20.55	52.02	6,315
Jilin 吉林	6	58	1,442	75	3.63	14.52	24.86	74.96	2,063
Heilongjiang 黑龍江	4	123	1,435	-668	-4.47	37.24	11.67	112.00	14,940
Central East 華東	101	290	20,452	498	2.02	6.71	70.56	69.98	24,686
Shanghai 上海	23	297	27,083	802	1.89	6.72	91.23	71.83	42,394
Jiangsu 江蘇	38	353	26,608	921	4.63	13.20	75.30	64.96	19,903
Zhejiang 浙江	17	289	12,596	-300	-1.14	-3.73	43.58	69.44	26,313
Anhui 安徽	2	31	870	40	24.24	32.00	28.52	24.24	165
Fujian 福建	5	188	12,504	-370	-2.16	-60.86	66.65	96.46	17,162
Jiangxi 江西									
Shandong 山東	16	194	9,576	231	1.62	5.37	49.33	69.92	14,280
Central-South 中南	26	379	15,322	252	0.66	2.24	40.45	70.53	38,294
Henan 河南	6	181	1,387	42	2.94	9.23	7.65	68.24	1,417
Hubei 湖北	6	542	26,100	667	1.75	5.68	48.14	69.22	38,120
Hunan 湖南									
Guangdong 廣東	11	308	17,269	399	0.74	2.30	56.00	67.88	53,971
Guangxi 廣西	3	705	14,500	-693	-1.26	-7.03	20.56	82.03	54,917
Hainan 海南									
Southwest 西南	7	205	1,386	-1,354	-20.41	34.69	6.77	158.79	6,636
Chongqing 重慶		688	2,284	-8,464	-39.02	23.17	3.32	268.42	21,692
Sichuan 四川	4	54	360	-17	-1.77	2.31	6.60	176.64	987
Guizhou 貴州									
Yunnan 雲南	1	807	6,630	-4,780	-17.52	74.92	8.22	123.34	27,290
Tibet 西藏	1		200	80	2.94	2.94			2,720
Northwest 西北	22	290	1,768	-912	-6.23	-32.31	6.10	80.72	14,634
Shaanxi 陝西	5	210	646	-2,752	-15.92	-2698.04	3.07	99.41	17,286
Gansu 甘肅	7	726	3,829	-897	-2.79	-10.56	5.27	73.55	32,119
Qinghai 青海	7	27	1,014	20	1.65	7.11	38.17	76.86	1,210
Ningxia 寧夏									
Xinjiang 新疆	3	20	590	-53	-7.24	-114.29	29.50	93.67	737

1749: Other Wool Spinning and Weaving 其他毛紡織業

Year 年份	Number of firms 企業個數	Rate of change 每年變化 (%)	Number of employees 職工人數（人）	Rate of change 每年變化 (%)	Total revenue (mil. RMB) 總銷售收入（百萬元）	Rate of change 每年變化 (%)	Total profit (mil. RMB) 總利潤（百萬元）	Rate of change 每年變化 (%)
1993	241		54,860		1,932		50	
1994	294	21.99%	55,891	1.88%	3,127	61.78%	129	159.09%
1995	275	-6.46%	67,123	20.10%	4,479	43.23%	215	66.29%
1996	252	-8.36%	66,909	-0.32%	4,758	6.23%	352	63.64%

3 Major products* 3種主要產品*	Output 產量	Sales volume 銷售量	Unit 單位
a) Fake Fur 人造毛皮	18,012,109	17,471,746	metre 米
b) Jacquard Woollen Blanket 提花毛毯	2,104,956	2,062,857	piece 條
c) Woolen Blanket 純毛毛毯	604,596	574,366	piece 條

Top 10 firms by revenue (year founded) 收入排名前10家企業（創辦年份）	City 城市	Province 省	Telephone / fax 電話／傳真	Number of employees 職工人數	Ownership 產業所有權	Revenue ('000 RMB) 銷售收入（千元）	Profit ('000 RMB) (rank) 利潤（千元）（排名）	Total assets ('000 RMB) 總資產（千元）	Major products 主要產品
Shanghai Da Shun Artificial Fur Co. Ltd. 上海大順人造毛皮有限公司(1989)	Shanghai 上海市	Shanghai 上海市	(021)62210345 (021)62210333	812	Foreign-funded 外資	260,525	14061(3)	353,435	a
Jiangsu Die Mei Group Co. 江蘇蝶美集團公司(1981)	Wuxi 無錫市	Jiangsu 江蘇省	(0510)6181977 (0510)6181978	1,551	Collectively-owned 集體	245,537	9058(5)	93,367	o
Suqian No.1 Wool Manufacturing Mill 宿遷市第一毛紡織廠(1987)	Suqian 宿遷市	Jiangsu 江蘇省	(0527)4213708 (0527)4213708	1,750	Collectively-owned 集體	206,798	14468(2)	95,739	o
Tianjin Mu Jin Enterprise Co. Ltd. 天津牧津企業有限公司(1991)	Tianjin 天津市	Tianjin 天津市	(022)24320924 (022)24412044	219	Overseas Chinese-funded 港澳台資	145,504	37537(1)	365,624	o
Jiangyin No.4 Cloth Mill 江陰市第四織布廠(1952)	Wuxi 無錫市	Jiangsu 江蘇省	(0510)6151116 (0510)6151116	1,368	Collectively-owned 集體	118,575	5669(9)	99,238	o
Shanghai Woollen Blanket Mill 上海毛毯廠(1922)	Shanghai 上海市	Shanghai 上海市	(021)65414734 (021)65455145	1,366	State-owned 國有	117,939	8066(6)	220,037	b,c
Guangdong Luoding Yin He Textile General Factory 廣東省羅定市銀河紡織總廠(1986)	Yunfu 雲浮市	Guangdong 廣東省	(0766)3823280 (0766)3823780	1,001	State-owned 國有	97,373	6113(8)	304,468	o
Tianjin Wan Xing Wool Spinning (Group) Co. Ltd. 天津萬興毛紡(集團)有限公司(1995)	Tianjin 天津市	Tianjin 天津市	(022)29439168	150	Overseas Chinese-funded 港澳台資	94,810	10650(4)	69,740	o
Shanghai Huisong Worsted Mill 上海惠松毛紡織廠(1981)	Shanghai 上海市	Shanghai 上海市	(021)57820461 (021)57720804	1,037	Domestic JVs 聯營	65,400	1535(17)	96,216	o
Yixing Zhong Xing Group Company 宜興市中興集團公司(1966)	Wuxi 無錫市	Jiangsu 江蘇省	(0510)7601957 (0510)7601957	645	Collectively-owned 集體	55,748	-652(90)	41,262	o

Top 10 Cities by Production Output 產出排名前10位城市	Province 省	Market share 市場份額	Number of firms 企業個數
Dongsheng 東勝市	Inner Mong 內蒙	30.50%	11
Shanghai 上海市	Shanghai 上海市	13.50%	14
Baotou 包頭市	Inner Mong 內蒙	12.97%	11
Yunfu 雲浮市	Guangdong 廣東省	4.87%	3
Tianjin 天津市	Tianjin 天津市	3.99%	11
Shenzhen 深圳市	Guangdong 廣東省	3.73%	5
Nanjing 南京市	Jiangsu 江蘇省	3.14%	2
Wuxi 無錫市	Jiangsu 江蘇省	2.79%	12
Nantong 南通市	Jiangsu 江蘇省	2.56%	7
Ningbo 寧波市	Zhejiang 浙江省	2.08%	6

10 Major Wholesalers 10家主要批發商	City 城市	Province 省	Telephone / Fax 電話／傳真
Anhui Clothing Import & Export Company 安徽省服裝進出口公司	Hefei 合肥市	Anhui 安徽省	(0551)3632212 (0551)3632002
Qingdao Textile Clothing Industrial Group Company 青島紡織服裝實業集團公司	Qingdao 青島市	Shandong 山東省	(0532)2877853 (0532)2869315
Hebei Textile Import & Export (Group) Company 河北省紡織品進出口(集團)公司	Shijiazhuang 石家莊市	Hebei 河北省	(0311)7028530 (0311)7027781
Zhong Fang Pledget Import & Export Company 中紡紗布進出口公司	Beijing 北京市	Beijing 北京市	(010)65124718 (010)65124713
Shaoxing Import & Export Company 紹興市進出口公司	Shaoxing 紹興市	Zhejiang 浙江省	(0575)5132822 (0575)5141577
Hunan Hua Xiang Import & Export (Group) Company 湖南省華湘進出口(集團)公司	Changsha 長沙市	Hunan 湖南省	(0731)2282440 (0731)2286995
City's Import & Export Company Trade Dept. 市進出口公司貿易部	Yichang 宜昌市	Hubei 湖北省	(0717)6450778 (0717)6441875
Shanghai Pu Dong Xinqu Import & Export Company 上海浦東新區進出口公司	Shanghai 上海市	Shanghai 上海市	(021)58878801 (021)58827444
Ningbo Yinxian Import & Export Company 寧波市鄞縣進出口公司	Ningbo 寧波市	Zhejiang 浙江省	(0574)7875205 (0574)7873168
Zhejiang Silk Import & Export Company 浙江省絲綢進出口公司	Hangzhou 杭州市	Zhejiang 浙江省	(0571)5195588 (0571)5192542

*Also include sales by firms outside this industry.包括本行業以外廠家的銷售。"o" stands for "others". "o" 代表"其他產品"。

1761: Ramie Spinning and Weaving 苧麻紡織業

The industry accounts for 0.043% of the total revenue of China's industrial sector in 1996. The revenue growth rate of the industry is -11.0% from 1995, as compared to the growth rate of China's industrial sector, 9.51%. The rate of return on asset is -4.60%. 55.19% of all firms in the industry made a profit while 32.61% had negative returns. The top province in terms of the industry's revenue is Hubei, accounting for 19.73% of the total revenue.
本行業在1996年佔全行業總產值0.043%，行業年增長率為-11.0%（全國工業年增長率9.51%）。行業的資產回報率-4.60%，55.19%的企業盈利，32.61%的企業虧損。銷售收入最高的省份為湖北省，佔本行業的19.73%。

	Total number of firms 企業總數	Total number of employees 職工總數	Total revenue (mil. RMB) 總銷售收入（百萬元）	Total profit (mil. RMB) 總利潤（百萬元）	Return on assets 資產利潤率 (%)	Return on equity 權益利潤率 (%)	Labour productivity ('000 RMB / worker) 勞動生產率（千元/人）	Debts / assets 資產負債率 (%)	Total assets (mil. RMB) 總資產（百萬元）
Industry Overall 行業總體	159	79,318	2,495	-193	-4.60	-2414.66	31.46	99.81	4,191

	Number of firms 企業個數	Average number of employees 平均職工人數	Average revenue ('000 RMB) 平均銷售收入（千元）	Average profit ('000 RMB) 平均利潤（千元）	Return on assets 資產利潤率 (%)	Return on equity 權益利潤率 (%)	Labour productivity ('000 RMB / worker) 勞動生產率（千元/人）	Average debts / assets 平均資產負債率(%)	Average Total assets ('000 RMB) 平均總資產（千元）
By ownership 產業所有權									
State-owned 國有	47	1,168	23,851	-4,255	-7.08	-188.68	20.42	96.25	60,064
Collectively-owned 集體	97	209	11,621	6	0.07	-0.59	55.63	111.14	9,694
Privately-owned 私有									
Domestic JVs 聯營	1	322	24,787	562	2.89	12.59	76.98	77.02	19,402
Joint stock 股份制	1	245	9,103	-11	-0.11	0.49	37.15	122.08	9,901
Foreign-funded 外資	10	297	14,166	706	2.13	38.17	47.65	94.43	33,186
Overseas Chinese-funded 港澳台資	3	203	23,909	-409	-1.83	8.67	117.97	121.08	22,367
By size 規模									
Large 大型	14	2,420	83,606	-3,385	-2.30	-21.51	34.55	89.30	147,016
Medium 中型	23	954	25,288	-5,573	-11.13	49.41	26.52	122.54	50,048
Small 小型	120	194	6,194	-145	-1.78	-36.98	31.92	95.20	8,184
By regional distribution 地區分布									
Central-North 華北	2	30	675	-85	-6.64	17.00	22.50	139.45	1,280
Beijing 北京									
Tianjin 天津									
Hebei 河北	2	30	675	-85	-6.64	17.00	22.50	139.45	1,280
Shanxi 山西									
Inner Mongolia 內蒙									
Northeast 東北	1	385		-60	-0.76	-0.90		16.02	7,930
Liaoning 遼寧									
Jilin 吉林	1	385		-60	-0.76	-0.90		16.02	7,930
Heilongjiang 黑龍江									
Central East 華東	55	415	19,621	-1,381	-5.09	-49.96	47.32	89.81	27,150
Shanghai 上海									
Jiangsu 江蘇	10	255	17,754	-245	-1.13	-3.04	69.71	62.91	21,723
Zhejiang 浙江	8	324	55,488	2,554	6.71	16.72	171.52	59.88	38,074
Anhui 安徽	8	1,118	30,939	-11,533	-22.45	63.03	27.67	135.61	51,376
Fujian 福建	1	402	16,110	250	0.34	0.98	40.07	65.71	74,370
Jiangxi 江西	24	339	7,975	-62	-0.31	-2.16	23.50	85.70	19,926
Shandong 山東	4	44	668	-118	-6.00	-25.68	15.17	76.76	1,958
Central-South 中南	76	554	15,942	-927	-3.20	68.05	28.78	104.70	28,990
Henan 河南	4	59	943	33	1.51	8.90	16.04	82.89	2,148
Hubei 湖北	32	417	15,384	314	2.36	366.79	36.89	99.36	13,289
Hunan 湖南	33	681	13,332	-1,414	-4.50	13.61	19.57	133.07	31,404
Guangdong 廣東	5	1,051	46,136	-6,354	-5.56	-12.00	43.91	53.70	114,348
Guangxi 廣西	2	394	22,475	-1,110	-1.38	7.48	57.04	118.38	80,670
Hainan 海南									
Southwest 西南	25	559	8,133	-1,842	-9.51	99.61	14.56	109.55	19,367
Chongqing 重慶	9	758	12,571	-4,125	-12.58	88.31	16.58	114.25	32,792
Sichuan 四川	12	441	6,258	-569	-4.89	49.13	14.19	109.96	11,624
Guizhou 貴州	2	155	3,060				19.74	57.03	14,430
Yunnan 雲南	1	961							
Tibet 西藏									
Northwest 西北									
Shaanxi 陝西									
Gansu 甘肅									
Qinghai 青海									
Ningxia 寧夏									
Xinjiang 新疆									

1761: Ramie Spinning and Weaving 苧麻紡織業

Year 年份	Number of firms 企業個數	Rate of change 每年變化 (%)	Number of employees 職工人數 (人)	Rate of change 每年變化 (%)	Total revenue (mil. RMB) 總銷售收入 (百萬元)	Rate of change 每年變化 (%)	Total profit (mil. RMB) 總利潤 (百萬元)	Rate of change 每年變化 (%)
1993	210		112,617		1,976		-108	
1994	214	1.90%	125,226	11.20%	3,395	71.79%	-105	3.28%
1995	156	-27.10%	101,058	-19.30%	2,804	-17.41%	-157	-50.07%
1996	159	1.92%	79,318	-21.51%	2,495	-11.02%	-193	-23.07%

3 Major products* 3 種主要產品 *	Output 產量	Sales volume 銷售量	Unit 單位
a) Ramie Cloth 苧麻布	66,095,905	62,130,151	metre 米
b) Ramie Yarn 苧麻紗線	40,043	37,640	ton 噸
c) Ramie Printing & Dyeing Cloth 苧麻印染布	13,626,694	11,718,957	metre 米

Top 10 firms by revenue (year founded) 收入排名前 10 家企業 (創辦年份)	City 城市	Province 省	Telephone / fax 電話 / 傳真	Number of employees 職工人數	Ownership 產業所有權	Revenue ('000 RMB) 銷售收入 (千元)	Profit ('000 RMB) (rank) 利潤 (千元) (排名)	Total assets ('000 RMB) 總資產 (千元)	Major products 主要產品
Zhejiang Yu Le Industry & Trade Group 浙江虞樂工貿集團公司(1984)	Shaoxing 紹興市	Zhejiang 浙江省	(0575)2673628 (0575)2071960	1,202	Collectively-owned 集體	394,464	25820(1)	221,051	o
Tongling Ramie Textiles Printing & Dyeing Joint Co. 銅陵市苧麻紡織印染聯合公司(1982)	Tongling 銅陵市	Anhui 安徽省	(0562)2833838 (0562)237818	3,710	State-owned 國有	170,837	-34866(81)	154,906	a,b,c
Hunan Dong Ting Ramie Textile Printing & Dyeing Factory 湖南洞庭苧麻紡織印染廠(1985)	Yueyang 岳陽市	Hunan 湖南省	(0730)8267411 (0730)8267041	5,579	State-owned 國有	159,045	-14032(77)	291,804	a,b
Guangzhou Spun Linen Textile Mill 廣州絹麻紡織廠(1958)	Guangzhou 廣州市	Guangdong 廣東省	(020)85525512 (020)85525340	2,816	State-owned 國有	115,175	-31953(80)	352,989	a,b,c
Yiyang Ramie Textile Printing & Dyeing Mill 益陽苧麻紡織印染廠(1982)	Yiyang 益陽市	Hunan 湖南省	(0737)4422592 (0737)4425627	4,592	State-owned 國有	85,652	12(26)	216,806	a,b,c
Jiangxi Ramie Textile Printing & Dyeing Co. Ltd. 江西苧麻紡織印染有限責任公司(1986)	Yichun 宜春市	Jiangxi 江西省	(0795)3241901 (0795)3241974	3,139	State-owned 國有	81,996	159(15)	189,215	a,b
Zhuzhou Ramie Textile Printing & Dyeing Mill 株洲苧麻紡織印染廠(1958)	Zhuzhou 株洲市	Hunan 湖南省	(0733)8221551 (0733)8221668	4,561	State-owned 國有	78,616	-12438(76)	238,940	a,b,c
Fuling Jin Di Industry Group Co. Ltd. 涪陵市金帝工業集團有限公司	Chongqing 重慶市	Chongqing 重慶市	(023)2224408	3,103	State-owned 國有	71,377	-16461(78)	96,795	a,b
Kunshan Dong Su Ke Spinning and Weaving Co. Ltd. 昆山東蘇克紡織有限公司(1995)	Suzhou 蘇州市	Jiangsu 江蘇省	(0520)7252095 (0520)7251888	500	Foreign-funded 外資	66,258	968(4)	73,304	o
Xianning Ramie Textile Factory 咸寧地區苧麻紡織廠(1982)	Xianning 咸寧市	Hubei 湖北省	(0715)8256875 (0715)8251525	1,393	State-owned 國有	62,978	308(10)	85,310	b

Top 10 Cities by Production Output 產出排名前 10 位城市	Province 省	Market share 市場份額	Number of firms 企業個數
Shaoxing 紹興市	Zhejiang 浙江省	16.59%	1
Shanghai 上海市	Shanghai 上海市	7.94%	1
Tongling 銅陵市	Anhui 安徽省	7.24%	5
Guangzhou 廣州市	Guangdong 廣東省	6.56%	3
Yueyang 岳陽市	Hunan 湖南省	6.49%	4
Chongqing 重慶市	Chongqing 重慶市	6.07%	13
Yiyang 益陽市	Hunan 湖南省	5.81%	16
Yichun 宜春市	Jiangxi 江西省	4.40%	8
Zhuzhou 株洲市	Hunan 湖南省	3.30%	2
Xianning 咸寧市	Hubei 湖北省	3.19%	9

10 Major Wholesalers 10 家主要批發商	City 城市	Province 省	Telephone / Fax 電話 / 傳真
Anhui Clothing Import & Export Company 安徽省服裝進出口公司	Hefei 合肥市	Anhui 安徽省	(0551)3632212 (0551)3632002
Qingdao Textile Clothing Industrial Group Company 青島紡織服裝實業集團公司	Qingdao 青島市	Shandong 山東省	(0532)2877853 (0532)2869315
Hebei Textile Import & Export (Group) Company 河北省紡織品進出口(集團)公司	Shijiazhuang 石家莊市	Hebei 河北省	(0311)7028530 (0311)7027781
Zhong Fang Pledget Import & Export Company 中紡紗布進出口公司	Beijing 北京市	Beijing 北京市	(010)65124718 (010)65124713
Shaoxing Import & Export Company 紹興市進出口公司	Shaoxing 紹興市	Zhejiang 浙江省	(0575)5132822 (0575)5141577
Hunan Hua Xiang Import & Export (Group) Company 湖南省華湘進出口(集團)公司	Changsha 長沙市	Hunan 湖南省	(0731)2282440 (0731)2286995
City's Import & Export Company Trade Dept. 市進出口公司貿易部	Yichang 宜昌市	Hubei 湖北省	(0717)6450778 (0717)6441875
Shanghai Pu Dong Xinqu Import & Export Company 上海浦東新區進出口公司	Shanghai 上海市	Shanghai 上海市	(021)58878801 (021)58827444
Ningbo Yinxian Import & Export Company 寧波市鄞縣進出口公司	Ningbo 寧波市	Zhejiang 浙江省	(0574)7875205 (0574)7873168
Zhejiang Silk Import & Export Company 浙江省絲綢進出口公司	Hangzhou 杭州市	Zhejiang 浙江省	(0571)5195588 (0571)5192542

*Also include sales by firms outside this industry.包括本行業以外廠家的銷售。"o" stands for "others". "o" 代表 "其他產品"。

1762: Flax Spinning and Weaving 亞麻紡織業

The industry accounts for 0.020% of the total revenue of China's industrial sector in 1996. The revenue growth rate of the industry is -15.8% from 1995, as compared to the growth rate of China's industrial sector, 9.51%. The rate of return on asset is -1.56%. 63.88% of all firms in the industry made a profit while 27.03% had negative returns. The top province in terms of the industry's revenue is Helongjiang, accounting for 69.21% of the total revenue.
本行業在1996年佔全行業總產值0.020%，行業年增長率為-15.8%（全國工業年增長率9.51%）。行業的資產回報率-1.56%，63.88%的企業盈利，27.03%的企業虧損。銷售收入最高的省份為黑龍江省，佔本行業的69.21%。

	Total number of firms 企業總數	Total number of employees 職工總數	Total revenue (mil. RMB) 總銷售收入（百萬元）	Total profit (mil. RMB) 總利潤（百萬元）	Return on assets 資產利潤率 (%)	Return on equity 權益利潤率 (%)	Labour productivity ('000 RMB / worker) 勞動生產率（千元／人）	Debts / assets 資產負債率 (%)	Total assets (mil. RMB) 總資產（百萬元）
Industry Overall 行業總體	75	44,856	1,131	-72	-1.56	-11.58	25.21	86.52	4,583

	Number of firms 企業個數	Average number of employees 平均職工人數	Average revenue ('000 RMB) 平均銷售收入（千元）	Average profit ('000 RMB) 平均利潤（千元）	Return on assets 資產利潤率 (%)	Return on equity 權益利潤率 (%)	Labour productivity ('000 RMB / worker) 勞動生產率（千元／人）	Average debts / assets 平均資產負債率(%)	Average Total assets ('000 RMB) 平均總資產（千元）
By ownership 產業所有權									
State-owned 國有	26	1,147	21,115	-2,154	-1.91	-16.37	18.42	88.31	112,500
Collectively-owned 集體	32	103	3,699	-11	-0.32	10.23	35.87	103.10	3,549
Privately-owned 私有									
Domestic JVs 聯營									
Joint stock 股份制	1	2,409	102,926	-9,247	-5.76	-28.68	42.73	79.92	160,558
Foreign-funded 外資	5	649	10,435	965	1.38	4.18	16.07	67.09	70,141
Overseas Chinese-funded 港澳台資	11	552	28,070	-1,020	-1.08	-8.49	50.82	87.23	94,009
By size 規模									
Large 大型	6	3,124	87,791	-23,163	-5.22	-26.82	28.10	80.52	443,338
Medium 中型	12	1,276	28,007	9,248	9.13	10676.36	21.94	99.91	101,244
Small 小型	56	192	4,793	-785	-6.20	-44.44	24.91	86.05	12,662
By regional distribution 地區分布									
Central-North 華北	4	786	21,328	-1,473	-1.46	-5.33	27.14	72.51	100,570
Beijing 北京									
Tianjin 天津	1	100	16,100	1,610	16.81	22.74	161.00	26.10	9,580
Hebei 河北	1								
Shanxi 山西	1	625	22,770	1,020	1.19	7.12	36.43	83.24	85,400
Inner Mongolia 內蒙	1	2,418	46,440	-8,520	-2.77	-9.55	19.21	70.98	307,300
Northeast 東北	49	778	17,763	-1,234	-1.54	-13.41	22.85	88.51	80,111
Liaoning 遼寧	2	2,008	20,440	-3,640	-3.62	-29.68	10.18	87.80	100,540
Jilin 吉林	7	551	6,681	-1,516	-3.73	-340.06	12.13	98.91	40,673
Heilongjiang 黑龍江	40	756	19,569	-1,064	-1.24	-10.06	25.90	87.69	85,991
Central East 華東	7	151	17,421	689	4.84	8.76	115.16	44.71	14,219
Shanghai 上海									
Jiangsu 江蘇	2	221	32,330	1,270	4.94	10.85	146.62	54.50	25,725
Zhejiang 浙江	2	65	15,490	425	3.07	3.79	238.31	18.97	13,840
Anhui 安徽									
Fujian 福建									
Jiangxi 江西									
Shandong 山東	3	163	8,770	477	7.01	15.54	53.91	54.95	6,800
Central-South 中南	8	122	5,513	-171	-2.36	-106.20	45.37	97.78	7,249
Henan 河南	4	94	1,740	38	1.03	6.44	18.46	83.98	3,635
Hubei 湖北	3	198	12,380	-507	-3.50	146.15	62.42	102.39	14,483
Hunan 湖南									
Guangdong 廣東	1								
Guangxi 廣西									
Hainan 海南									
Southwest 西南	2	128	750	10	2.25	9.09	5.88	76.40	445
Chongqing 重慶									
Sichuan 四川	2	128	750	-10	-2.25	-9.52	5.86	76.40	445
Guizhou 貴州									
Yunnan 雲南									
Tibet 西藏									
Northwest 西北	5	266	1,472	-1,738	-8.94	7900.00	5.54	100.11	19,438
Shaanxi 陝西	1	38	3,150	470	18.80	25.97	82.89	27.60	2,500
Gansu 甘肅	2	15	75				5.00	123.56	955
Qinghai 青海									
Ningxia 寧夏	1	1,245	4,060	-9,160	-11.58	86.17	3.26	113.44	79,120
Xinjiang 新疆	1	16						32.94	13,660

1762: Flax Spinning and Weaving 亞麻紡織業

Year 年份	Number of firms 企業個數	Rate of change 每年變化 (%)	Number of employees 職工人數 (人)	Rate of change 每年變化 (%)	Total revenue (mil. RMB) 總銷售收入 (百萬元)	Rate of change 每年變化 (%)	Total profit (mil. RMB) 總利潤 (百萬元)	Rate of change 每年變化 (%)
1993	66		13,139		915		-16	
1994	85	28.79%	55,391	321.58%	1,695	85.29%	139	995.66%
1995	75	-11.77%	59,011	6.54%	1,344	-20.74%	12	-91.22%
1996	75	0	44,856	-23.99%	1,131	-15.85%	-72	-687.90%

3 Major products* 3 種主要產品 *	Output 產量	Sales volume 銷售量	Unit 單位
a) Linen Plied Yarn 亞麻紗線	16,047	13,480	ton 噸
b) Linen Cloth 亞麻布	36,013,667	41,055,581	metre 米

Top 10 firms by revenue (year founded) 收入排名前 10 家企業 (創辦年份)	City 城市	Province 省	Telephone / fax 電話 / 傳真	Number of employees 職工人數	Ownership 產業所有權	Revenue ('000 RMB) 銷售收入(千元)	Profit ('000 RMB) (rank) 利潤(千元)(排名)	Total assets ('000 RMB) 總資產(千元)	Major products 主要產品
Harbin Flax Spinning and Weaving Mill 哈爾濱亞麻紡織廠(1952)	Harbin 哈爾濱市	Heilongjiang 黑龍江省	(0451)2610568 (0451)2623100	8,173	State-owned 國有	229,045	800(8)	1,193,932	a,b
Heilong Jiang Lanxi Flax Spinning and Weaving Industry Joint General Co. 黑龍江蘭西亞麻紡織工業聯合公司(1984)	Suihua 綏化市	Heilongjiang 黑龍江省	(0455)7623334 (0455)7623366	3,954	State-owned 國有	67,001	0(19)	211,477	b
Heilongjiang Wangkui Flax Textile Mill 黑龍江省望奎縣亞麻紡織廠(1982)	Suihua 綏化市	Heilongjiang 黑龍江省	(0455)6761640	490	Collectively-owned 集體	65,000	3710(1)	127,450	a,b
Jiamusi Linen Corp., Ltd. 佳木斯亞麻有限公司(1986)	Jiamusi 佳木斯市	Heilongjiang 黑龍江省	(0454)8582241 (0454)8582830	3,447	Overseas Chinese-funded 港澳台資	64,839	-8444(30)	757,021	o
Changshu Fan Jia Flax Textile Co. Ltd. 常熟泛佳亞麻紡織有限公司(1993)	Suzhou 蘇州市	Jiangsu 江蘇省	(0512)2381159 (0512)2381497	416	Overseas Chinese-funded 港澳台資	63,241	2535(2)	48,538	o
Qiqihar Flax Textile Mill 齊齊哈爾亞麻紡織廠(1989)	Qiqiha'er 齊齊哈爾市	Heilongjiang 黑龍江省	(0452)2347211 (0452)2347047	2,327	State-owned 國有	52,362	40(17)	197,381	a,b
Zhao Rong Flax Spinning and Weaving Co. Ltd. 肇融亞麻紡織有限公司(1990)	Daqing 大慶市	Heilongjiang 黑龍江省	(0459)8524018 (0459)8522266	1,500	Overseas Chinese-funded 港澳台資	49,542	-9117(31)	134,046	a,b
Harbin Xiangfang Spinning and Weaving Factory 哈爾濱市香坊區紡織廠(1988)	Harbin 哈爾濱市	Heilongjiang 黑龍江省		60	Collectively-owned 集體	45,368	1895(3)	14,062	o
Kaiyuan Flax Spinning and Weaving Mill 開原市亞麻紡織廠(1975)	Tieling 鐵嶺市	Liaoning 遼寧省	(0410)3822849 (0410)3821531	3,964	State-owned 國有	40,879	-7280(29)	201,080	o
Zhuji Tian Long Industry & Trade Industrial Company 諸暨市天龍工貿實業公司(1992)	Shaoxing 紹興市	Zhejiang 浙江省	(0575)7361295	86	Collectively-owned 集體	30,380	851(7)	7,413	o

Top 10 Cities by Production Output 產出排名前 10 位城市	Province 省	Market share 市場份額	Number of firms 企業個數
Harbin 哈爾濱市	Heilongjiang 黑龍江省	26.49%	17
Shuangcheng 雙城市	Heilongjiang 黑龍江省	9.75%	3
Suihua 綏化市	Heilongjiang 黑龍江省	6.74%	7
Daqing 大慶市	Heilongjiang 黑龍江省	5.87%	2
Xinxiang 新鄉市	Henan 河南省	5.80%	2
Qiqiha'er 齊齊哈爾市	Heilongjiang 黑龍江省	5.52%	2
Tieling 鐵嶺市	Liaoning 遼寧省	4.92%	2
Baotou 包頭市	Inner Mong 內蒙	4.66%	1
Jiamusi 佳木斯市	Heilongjiang 黑龍江省	4.51%	1
Suzhou 蘇州市	Jiangsu 江蘇省	4.46%	4

10 Major Wholesalers 10 家主要批發商	City 城市	Province 省	Telephone / Fax 電話 / 傳真
Anhui Clothing Import & Export Company 安徽省服裝進出口公司	Hefei 合肥市	Anhui 安徽省	(0551)3632212 (0551)3632002
Qingdao Textile Clothing Industrial Group Company 青島紡織服裝實業集團公司	Qingdao 青島市	Shandong 山東省	(0532)2877853 (0532)2869315
Hebei Textile Import & Export (Group) Company 河北省紡織品進出口(集團)公司	Shijiazhuang 石家莊市	Hebei 河北省	(0311)7028530 (0311)7027781
Zhong Fang Pledget Import & Export Company 中紡紗布進出口公司	Beijing 北京市	Beijing 北京市	(010)65124718 (010)65124713
Shaoxing Import & Export Company 紹興市進出口公司	Shaoxing 紹興市	Zhejiang 浙江省	(0575)5132822 (0575)5141577
Hunan Hua Xiang Import & Export (Group) Company 湖南省華湘進出口(集團)公司	Changsha 長沙市	Hunan 湖南省	(0731)2282440 (0731)2286995
City's Import & Export Company Trade Dept. 市進出口公司貿易部	Yichang 宜昌市	Hubei 湖北省	(0717)6450778 (0717)6441875
Shanghai Pu Dong Xinqu Import & Export Company 上海浦東新區進出口公司	Shanghai 上海市	Shanghai 上海市	(021)58878801 (021)58827444
Ningbo Yinxian Import & Export Company 寧波市鄞縣進出口公司	Ningbo 寧波市	Zhejiang 浙江省	(0574)7875205 (0574)7873168
Zhejiang Silk Import & Export Company 浙江省絲綢進出口公司	Hangzhou 杭州市	Zhejiang 浙江省	(0571)5195588 (0571)5192542

*Also include sales by firms outside this industry.包括本行業以外廠家的銷售。"o" stands for "others". "o" 代表"其他產品"。

1763: Jute Spinning and Weaving 黄、洋、青麻紡織業

The industry accounts for 0.047% of the total revenue of China's industrial sector in 1996. The revenue growth rate of the industry is -14.2% from 1995, as compared to the growth rate of China's industrial sector, 9.51%. The rate of return on asset is -2.71%. 69.53% of all firms in the industry made a profit while 26.27% had negative returns. The top province in terms of the industry's revenue is Shandong, accounting for 18.00% of the total revenue.

本行業在1996年佔全行業總產值0.047%，行業年增長率為-14.2%（全國工業年增長率9.51%）。行業的資產回報率-2.71%，69.53%的企業盈利，26.27%的企業虧損。銷售收入最高的省份為山東省，佔本行業的18.00%。

	Total number of firms 企業總數	Total number of employees 職工總數	Total revenue (mil. RMB) 總銷售收入（百萬元）	Total profit (mil. RMB) 總利潤（百萬元）	Return on assets 資產利潤率 (%)	Return on equity 權益利潤率 (%)	Labour productivity ('000 RMB / worker) 勞動生產率（千元／人）	Debts / assets 資產負債率 (%)	Total assets (mil. RMB) 總資產（百萬元）
Industry Overall 行業總體	252	121,977	2,719	-142	-2.71	-24.28	22.29	88.83	5,235

	Number of firms 企業個數	Average number of employees 平均職工人數	Average revenue ('000 RMB) 平均銷售收入（千元）	Average profit ('000 RMB) 平均利潤（千元）	Return on assets 資產利潤率 (%)	Return on equity 權益利潤率 (%)	Labour productivity ('000 RMB / worker) 勞動生產率（千元／人）	Average debts / assets 平均資產負債率(%)	Average Total assets ('000 RMB) 平均總資產（千元）
By ownership 產業所有權									
State-owned 國有	95	954	18,863	-1,611	-3.77	-35.42	19.78	89.37	42,768
Collectively-owned 集體	151	204	5,977	66	0.88	7.44	29.25	88.12	7,518
Privately-owned 私有									
Domestic JVs 聯營	2	109	656	304	8.77	83.38	6.05	89.49	3,464
Joint stock 股份制	3	96	4,392	-24	-0.34	-0.65	45.75	48.09	7,076
Foreign-funded 外資									
Overseas Chinese-funded 港澳台資	2	80	4,993	214	4.97	6.66	62.42	25.40	4,303
By size 規模									
Large 大型	6	2,147	74,142	-477	-0.31	-1.16	34.53	73.18	153,766
Medium 中型	36	1,531	35,506	-1,859	-2.52	-20.38	23.19	87.64	73,790
Small 小型	209	259	4,765	-346	-4.36	-784.47	18.38	99.44	7,924
By regional distribution 地區分布									
Central-North 華北	14	326	7,787	-984	-4.45	-11.61	23.90	61.68	22,114
Beijing 北京	1	135	2,630	-850	-14.14	72.03	19.48	119.63	6,010
Tianjin 天津	2	75	835	20	1.57	-12.90	11.13	112.16	1,275
Hebei 河北	6	411	15,635	-570	-1.32	-2.53	38.07	47.69	43,097
Shanxi 山西	3	351	977	-20	-0.32	24.00	2.79	101.32	6,303
Inner Mongolia 內蒙	2	380	3,990	-4,745	-40.31	63.78	10.50	163.25	11,770
Northeast 東北	17	859	13,332	-1,474	-3.05	-28.14	15.51	89.16	48,338
Liaoning 遼寧	7	842	9,149	-3,060	-6.33	-174.15	10.87	96.37	48,351
Jilin 吉林	5	1,256	30,212	34	0.04	0.17	24.05	75.85	82,380
Heilongjiang 黑龍江	5	487	2,308	-762	-5.34	16.75	4.74	131.84	14,278
Central East 華東	98	489	14,207	-187	-0.87	-6.90	29.06	87.37	21,438
Shanghai 上海									
Jiangsu 江蘇	13	444	23,794	-668	-2.27	-13.01	53.65	82.59	29,512
Zhejiang 浙江	12	114	4,739	28	0.49	1.49	41.48	67.07	5,762
Anhui 安徽	36	521	13,289	-121	-0.64	18.73	25.53	103.43	18,898
Fujian 福建	4	396	2,088	-393	-2.42	-27.16	5.27	91.11	16,253
Jiangxi 江西	8	599	6,221	-205	-0.75	-3.80	10.39	80.22	27,265
Shandong 山東	25	626	19,582	-96	-0.35	-1.59	31.27	78.07	27,387
Central-South 中南	89	496	9,662	-605	-3.18	-29.03	19.49	89.04	19,013
Henan 河南	40	450	8,182	59	0.45	3.53	18.18	87.38	13,290
Hubei 湖北	20	641	13,213	-390	-1.72	37.00	20.61	104.65	22,689
Hunan 湖南	12	475	8,007	-2,630	-10.27	-120.27	16.85	91.46	25,615
Guangdong 廣東	9	270	8,563	12	0.09	0.46	31.76	81.45	14,372
Guangxi 廣西	8	646	11,908	-2,118	-6.27	-19.00	18.43	66.98	33,759
Hainan 海南									
Southwest 西南	32	316	3,859	-968	-11.04	41.62	12.23	126.53	8,760
Chongqing 重慶	2	173	2,112	215	11.76	25.37	12.20	53.63	1,825
Sichuan 四川	20	379	3,405	-1,571	-15.87	38.38	8.97	141.35	9,902
Guizhou 貴州	4	217	5,305	3	0.03	0.35	24.48	92.71	9,743
Yunnan 雲南	5	213	5,502	48	0.67	7.23	25.83	90.72	7,174
Tibet 西藏									
Northwest 西北	2	342	4,050				11.86	98.22	14,895
Shaanxi 陝西	2	342	4,050				11.86	98.22	14,895
Gansu 甘肅									
Qinghai 青海									
Ningxia 寧夏									
Xinjiang 新疆									

1763: Jute Spinning and Weaving 黃、洋、青麻紡織業

Year 年份	Number of firms 企業個數	Rate of change 每年變化 (%)	Number of employees 職工人數 (人)	Rate of change 每年變化 (%)	Total revenue (mil. RMB) 總銷售收入 (百萬元)	Rate of change 每年變化 (%)	Total profit (mil. RMB) 總利潤 (百萬元)	Rate of change 每年變化 (%)
1993	293		152,241		2,669		-123	
1994	291	-0.68%	131,047	-13.92%	2,332	-12.61%	-99	19.56%
1995	290	-0.34%	152,581	16.43%	3,168	35.81%	-109	-10.04%
1996	252	-13.10%	121,977	-20.06%	2,719	-14.17%	-142	-30.13%

3 Major products* 3種主要產品*	Output 產量	Sales volume 銷售量	Unit 單位
a) Gunny Bag 麻袋	32,982	33,972	10,000 piece 萬條
b) Jute, Kenaf & Abutilon Wrapper 黃、洋、青麻包布	10,487	10,067	10,000 metre 萬米
c) Jute, Kenaf & Abutilon Yarn 黃、洋、青麻紗線	64,348	57,913	ton 噸

Top 10 firms by revenue (year founded) 收入排名前10家企業 (創辦年份)	City 城市	Province 省	Telephone / fax 電話 / 傳真	Number of employees 職工人數	Ownership 產業所有權	Revenue ('000 RMB) 銷售收入 (千元)	Profit ('000 RMB) (rank) 利潤 (千元) (排名)	Total assets ('000 RMB) 總資產 (千元)	Major products 主要產品
Wuxi Tian Yuan Linen & Cotton Mill 無錫市天元麻棉紡織廠(1947)	Wuxi 無錫市	Jiangsu 江蘇省	(0510)2723071 (0510)2706246	2,314	State-owned 國有	203,072	99(43)	157,529	o
Anhui Shu Cheng Linen Textile Mill 安徽省舒城麻紡織廠(1970)	Liu'an 六安市	Anhui 安徽省	(0564)8621358 (0564)8621815	4,483	State-owned 國有	121,302	-2914(129)	146,577	a,b,c
Qingdao Li Da Group Co. Ltd. 青島立大集團股份有限公司(1970)	Qingdao 青島市	Shandong 山東省	(0532)8411520 (0532)8411574	2,082	Joint stock 股份制	109,327	-410(104)	128,248	a,c
Hebei Chengde Jute & Chemical Fibre Textile General Factory 河北省承德市黃麻纖紡織總廠(1952)	Chengde 承德市	Hebei 河北省	(0314)4044468 (0314)4044331	2,254	State-owned 國有	85,898	-3636(133)	242,051	a,b,c
Jilin City Linen & Cotton Textile General Factory 吉林市麻棉紡織總廠(1951)	Jilin 吉林市	Jilin 吉林省	(0432)2732934 (0432)2738638	4,014	State-owned 國有	75,443	105(41)	259,775	a,b,c
Shanxian Linen Textile Mill 單縣麻紡織廠(1971)	Heze 菏澤市	Shandong 山東省	(0530)4661401	3,100	State-owned 國有	67,903	451(15)	61,114	a
Baicheng Linen Textile Mill 白城市麻紡織廠(1952)	Baicheng 白城市	Jilin 吉林省	(0436)3224512 (0436)3236291	2,083	State-owned 國有	66,907	23(62)	123,320	a,b,c
Shandong Jining Luotuo Textile Group Co. Ltd. 山東濟寧駱駝紡織集團有限責任公司(1952)	Jining 濟寧市	Shandong 山東省	(0537)2212092 (0537)2219385	1,548	State-owned 國有	63,109	606(12)	97,109	a,b
Lianyungang Linen Textile Factory 連雲港麻紡織廠(1958)	Lianyungang 連雲港市	Jiangsu 江蘇省	(0518)5412811 (0518)5412604	1,611	State-owned 國有	53,927	-4013(136)	166,168	a,c
Shouguang Jian Yuan Chun Co. Ltd. 壽光市健元春股份有限公司(1969)	Weifang 濰坊市	Shandong 山東省	(0536)5221118 (0536)5224588	1,090	Collectively-owned 集體	53,599	153(36)	34,909	a,c

Top 10 Cities by Production Output 產出排名前10位城市	Province 省	Market share 市場份額	Number of firms 企業個數
Wuxi 無錫市	Jiangsu 江蘇省	7.28%	1
Xinyang 信陽市	Henan 河南省	6.87%	16
Liu'an 六安市	Anhui 安徽省	6.23%	9
Qingdao 青島市	Shandong 山東省	4.95%	4
Jining 濟寧市	Shandong 山東省	4.25%	5
Jilin 吉林市	Jilin 吉林省	3.96%	1
Bengbu 蚌埠市	Anhui 安徽省	3.75%	3
Weifang 濰坊市	Shandong 山東省	3.64%	3
Chengde 承德市	Hebei 河北省	3.44%	1
Heze 菏澤市	Shandong 山東省	3.25%	2

10 Major Wholesalers 10家主要批發商	City 城市	Province 省	Telephone / Fax 電話 / 傳真
Anhui Clothing Import & Export Company 安徽省服裝進出口公司	Hefei 合肥市	Anhui 安徽省	(0551)3632212 (0551)3632002
Qingdao Textile Clothing Industrial Group Company 青島紡織服裝實業集團公司	Qingdao 青島市	Shandong 山東省	(0532)2877853 (0532)2869315
Hebei Textile Import & Export (Group) Company 河北省紡織品進出口(集團)公司	Shijiazhuang 石家莊市	Hebei 河北省	(0311)7028530 (0311)7027781
Zhong Fang Pledget Import & Export Company 中紡紗布進出口公司	Beijing 北京市	Beijing 北京市	(010)65124718 (010)65124713
Shaoxing Import & Export Company 紹興市進出口公司	Shaoxing 紹興市	Zhejiang 浙江省	(0575)5132822 (0575)5141577
Hunan Hua Xiang Import & Export (Group) Company 湖南省華湘進出口(集團)公司	Changsha 長沙市	Hunan 湖南省	(0731)2282440 (0731)2286995
City's Import & Export Company Trade Dept. 市進出口公司貿易部	Yichang 宜昌市	Hubei 湖北省	(0717)6450778 (0717)6441875
Shanghai Pu Dong Xinqu Import & Export Company 上海浦東新區進出口公司	Shanghai 上海市	Shanghai 上海市	(021)58878801 (021)58827444
Ningbo Yinxian Import & Export Company 寧波市鄞縣進出口公司	Ningbo 寧波市	Zhejiang 浙江省	(0574)7875205 (0574)7873168
Zhejiang Silk Import & Export Company 浙江省絲綢進出口公司	Hangzhou 杭州市	Zhejiang 浙江省	(0571)5195588 (0571)5192542

*Also include sales by firms outside this industry.包括本行業以外廠家的銷售。"o" stands for "others". "o" 代表"其他產品"。

1769: Other Flax, Ramie and Jute Spinning and Weaving 其他麻紡織業

The industry accounts for 0.009% of the total revenue of China's industrial sector in 1996. The revenue growth rate of the industry is 3.8% from 1995, as compared to the growth rate of China's industrial sector, 9.51%. The rate of return on asset is 1.32%. 64.40% of all firms in the industry made a profit while 29.60% had negative returns. The top province in terms of the industry's revenue is Shandong, accounting for 19.93% of the total revenue.
本行業在1996年佔全行業總產值0.009%，行業年增長率為3.8%（全國工業年增長率9.51%）。行業的資產回報率1.32%，64.40%的企業盈利，29.60%的企業虧損。銷售收入最高的省份為山東省，佔本行業的19.93%。

	Total number of firms 企業總數	Total number of employees 職工總數	Total revenue (mil. RMB) 總銷售收入（百萬元）	Total profit (mil. RMB) 總利潤（百萬元）	Return on assets 資產利潤率 (%)	Return on equity 權益利潤率 (%)	Labour productivity ('000 RMB / worker) 勞動生產率（千元/人）	Debts / assets 資產負債率 (%)	Total assets (mil. RMB) 總資產（百萬元）
Industry Overall 行業總體	116	15,601	496	12	1.32	4.93	31.79	73.31	935

	Number of firms 企業個數	Average number of employees 平均職工人數	Average revenue ('000 RMB) 平均銷售收入（千元）	Average profit ('000 RMB) 平均利潤（千元）	Return on assets 資產利潤率 (%)	Return on equity 權益利潤率 (%)	Labour productivity ('000 RMB / worker) 勞動生產率（千元/人）	Average debts / assets 平均資產負債率(%)	Average Total assets ('000 RMB) 平均總資產（千元）
By ownership 產業所有權									
State-owned 國有	14	251	3,500	-71	-0.39	-1.52	13.94	74.02	18,143
Collectively-owned 集體	96	102	3,914	127	3.28	14.97	38.23	78.08	3,877
Privately-owned 私有	1	72	6,264	413	10.04	23.94	87.00	58.07	4,119
Domestic JVs 聯營									
Joint stock 股份制	1	232	12,713	219	8.82	30.81	54.80	71.36	2,485
Foreign-funded 外資	2	915	22,864	474	0.32	0.99	25.00	67.59	147,420
Overseas Chinese-funded 港澳台資	2	25	3,272	-396	-10.90	-17.98	133.56	39.39	3,636
By size 規模									
Large 大型	2	1,057	19,328	23,366	22.97	146.34	18.29	84.31	101,738
Medium 中型	1	1,397	32,209	-13,879	-5.50	-17.95	23.06	69.36	252,323
Small 小型	113	106	3,761	-185	-4.35	-14.82	35.36	70.63	4,240
By regional distribution 地區分布									
Central-North 華北	6	40	2,153	223	20.15	44.67	53.39	54.89	1,108
Beijing 北京	1								
Tianjin 天津									
Hebei 河北	3	75	4,280	453	21.22	47.22	57.32	55.07	2,137
Shanxi 山西	1	10	50	-20	-40.00	-66.67	5.00	60.00	50
Inner Mongolia 內蒙	1	8	30				3.75	47.37	190
Northeast 東北	21	43	1,807	93	7.67	101.56	42.11	92.44	1,210
Liaoning 遼寧	8	20	1,164	68	7.03	17.53	57.47	59.90	960
Jilin 吉林	3	24	660	17	2.63	20.00	27.89	86.84	633
Heilongjiang 黑龍江	10	67	2,665	136	8.59	-96.45	39.90	108.91	1,583
Central East 華東	49	202	6,018	191	1.40	7.22	29.81	80.57	13,641
Shanghai 上海	1	25							
Jiangsu 江蘇	10	221	7,366	45	0.38	2.01	33.30	81.08	11,826
Zhejiang 浙江	3	132	7,610	763	3.19	4.17	57.65	23.47	23,947
Anhui 安徽	16	145	5,868	423	11.92	71.11	40.49	83.24	3,550
Fujian 福建	4	67	605	-360	-9.50	-40.22	9.10	76.37	3,788
Jiangxi 江西	4	116	805	-13	-0.08	-13.89	6.92	99.41	14,858
Shandong 山東	11	382	8,986	124	0.39	3.48	23.50	88.74	31,537
Central-South 中南	30	107	3,988	101	1.57	2.86	37.22	45.14	6,466
Henan 河南	9	38	1,509	53	3.10	9.78	39.71	68.28	1,720
Hubei 湖北	5	118	6,296	238	5.94	495.83	53.18	98.80	4,008
Hunan 湖南	7	69	1,449	24	1.91	4.14	21.13	53.72	1,269
Guangdong 廣東	4	106	13,373	478	2.65	5.12	126.45	48.21	18,020
Guangxi 廣西	5	275	2,188	-142	-0.92	-1.19	7.94	22.81	15,502
Hainan 海南									
Southwest 西南	7	179	4,271	-417	-8.58	-43.52	23.81	80.29	4,864
Chongqing 重慶	1	26	295	124	61.99	-1597.93	10.99	103.88	200
Sichuan 四川	3	271	6,992	785	11.21	88.31	25.80	87.30	7,004
Guizhou 貴州	1	261	7,920	-450	-4.67	-27.27	30.34	82.88	9,640
Yunnan 雲南	2	78	355	5	0.31	0.42	4.55	25.00	1,600
Tibet 西藏									
Northwest 西北	3	33	323	-143	-6.31	-24.57	9.90	74.30	2,270
Shaanxi 陝西	1	20	450	40	16.00	16.00	22.50		250
Gansu 甘肅	2	39	260	-235	-7.16	-31.33	6.67	77.13	3,280
Qinghai 青海									
Ningxia 寧夏									
Xinjiang 新疆									

1769: Other Flax, Ramie and Jute Spinning and Weaving 其他麻紡織業

Year 年份	Number of firms 企業個數	Rate of change 每年變化 (%)	Number of employees 職工人數 (人)	Rate of change 每年變化 (%)	Total revenue (mil. RMB) 總銷售收入 (百萬元)	Rate of change 每年變化 (%)	Total profit (mil. RMB) 總利潤 (百萬元)	Rate of change 每年變化 (%)
1993	149		17,650		323		-9	
1994	125	-16.11%	19,009	7.70%	384	18.95%	-2	71.84%
1995	136	8.80%	18,874	-0.71%	478	24.55%	-3	-7.11%
1996	116	-14.71%	15,601	-17.34%	496	3.76%	12	552.66%

3 Major products* 3 種主要產品 *	Output 產量	Sales volume 銷售量	Unit 單位
a) Jute, Kenaf & Abutilon Yarn 黃、洋、青麻紗線	9,447	8,503	ton 噸
b) Jute, Kenaf & Abutilon Wrapper 黃、洋、青麻包布	1,385	1,329	10,000 metre 萬米
c) Gunny Bag 麻袋	2,695	2,776	10,000 piece 萬條

Top 10 firms by revenue (year founded) 收入排名前 10 家企業 (創辦年份)	City 城市	Province 省	Telephone / fax 電話 / 傳真	Number of employees 職工人數	Ownership 產業所有權	Revenue ('000 RMB) 銷售收入 (千元)	Profit ('000 RMB) (rank) 利潤 (千元) (排名)	Total assets ('000 RMB) 總資產 (千元)	Major products 主要產品
Taishan Hemp Textile Group General Co. 泰山大麻紡織集團總公司(1990)	Tai'an 泰安市	Shandong 山東省	(0538)8417957 (0538)8417958	1,382	State-owned 國有	34,762	261(18)	116,141	o
Shandong Dongping Hemp Textile General Factory 山東省東平大麻紡織總廠(1993)	Tai'an 泰安市	Shandong 山東省	(0538)2822625 (0538)2821834	1,930	Foreign-funded 外資	28,866	1508(3)	190,213	o
Guangzhou Hao Li Bu Fabric Co. Ltd. 廣州豪力不織物有限公司(1989)	Guangzhou 廣州市	Guangdong 廣東省	(020)82211792 (020)82212587	145	Overseas Chinese-funded 港澳台資	26,618	127(25)	30,719	o
Naxi Wuding Textile Co. Ltd. 納溪縣五頂實業公司	Luzhou 瀘州市	Sichuan 四川省	(0830)4292640	724	Collectively-owned 集體	18,534	-1979(50)	19,184	c
Liu'an Ma Tou Zhen Refined Flax Factory 六安市馬頭鎮大麻纖維廠(1994)	Liu'an 六安市	Anhui 安徽省	(0564)3215399	371	Collectively-owned 集體	18,240	1200(6)	13,960	o
Guangzhou Sheng Li Bu Woven Cloth Co. Ltd. 廣州勝力不織布有限公司(1993)	Guangzhou 廣州市	Guangdong 廣東省	(020)82214160 (020)82222493	65	Overseas Chinese-funded 港澳台資	17,647	1769(2)	31,466	o
Zhangjiagang Jiu Zhou Hemp Textile Factory 張家港市九州麻紡廠(1988)	Suzhou 蘇州市	Jiangsu 江蘇省	(0512)8592270	250	Collectively-owned 集體	15,670	5(35)	16,045	o
Liu'an Tuan Jie Hemp Thread Factory 六安市團結大麻線廠(1993)	Liu'an 六安市	Anhui 安徽省		61	Collectively-owned 集體	14,988	1489(4)	2,756	o
Laohekou Zan Yang Office Hemp Cord Factory 老河口市贊陽辦事處麻繩廠(1988)	Xiangfan 襄樊市	Hubei 湖北省	(0710)8221293	36	Collectively-owned 集體	13,590	790(9)	2,110	c
Wuxian Fuyu Bleaching & Dyeing Factory 吳縣市富裕漂染廠(1992)	Suzhou 蘇州市	Jiangsu 江蘇省	(0512)5010188	130	Collectively-owned 集體	12,651	4(37)	15,846	o

Top 10 Cities by Production Output 產出排名前 10 位城市	Province 省	Market share 市場份額	Number of firms 企業個數
Tai'an 泰安市	Shandong 山東省	19.20%	5
Suzhou 蘇州市	Jiangsu 江蘇省	19.02%	6
Guangzhou 廣州市	Guangdong 廣東省	9.30%	2
Shanghai 上海市	Shanghai 上海市	8.55%	4
Suihua 綏化市	Heilongjiang 黑龍江省	3.03%	2
Liu'an 六安市	Anhui 安徽省	2.88%	12
Zhanjiang 湛江市	Guangdong 廣東省	2.42%	1
Guichi 貴池市	Anhui 安徽省	2.18%	1
Ji'nan 濟南市	Shandong 山東省	2.04%	1
Jinhua 金華市	Zhejiang 浙江省	1.85%	1

10 Major Wholesalers 10 家主要批發商	City 城市	Province 省	Telephone / Fax 電話 / 傳真
Anhui Clothing Import & Export Company 安徽省服裝進出口公司	Hefei 合肥市	Anhui 安徽省	(0551)3632212 (0551)3632002
Qingdao Textile Clothing Industrial Group Company 青島紡織服裝實業集團公司	Qingdao 青島市	Shandong 山東省	(0532)2877853 (0532)2869315
Hebei Textile Import & Export (Group) Company 河北省紡織品進出口(集團)公司	Shijiazhuang 石家莊市	Hebei 河北省	(0311)7028530 (0311)7027781
Zhong Fang Pledget Import & Export Company 中紡紗布進出口公司	Beijing 北京市	Beijing 北京市	(010)65124718 (010)65124713
Shaoxing Import & Export Company 紹興市進出口公司	Shaoxing 紹興市	Zhejiang 浙江省	(0575)5132822 (0575)5141577
Hunan Hua Xiang Import & Export (Group) Company 湖南省華湘進出口(集團)公司	Changsha 長沙市	Hunan 湖南省	(0731)2282440 (0731)2286995
City's Import & Export Company Trade Dept. 市進出口公司貿易部	Yichang 宜昌市	Hubei 湖北省	(0717)6450778 (0717)6441875
Shanghai Pu Dong Xinqu Import & Export Company 上海浦東新區進出口公司	Shanghai 上海市	Shanghai 上海市	(021)58878801 (021)58827444
Ningbo Yinxian Import & Export Company 寧波市鄞縣進出口公司	Ningbo 寧波市	Zhejiang 浙江省	(0574)7875205 (0574)7873168
Zhejiang Silk Import & Export Company 浙江省絲綢進出口公司	Hangzhou 杭州市	Zhejiang 浙江省	(0571)5195588 (0571)5192542

*Also include sales by firms outside this industry.包括本行業以外廠家的銷售。"o" stands for "others". "o" 代表"其他產品"。

1771: Silk Reeling 繅絲業

The industry accounts for 0.204% of the total revenue of China's industrial sector in 1996. The revenue growth rate of the industry is -13.4% from 1995, as compared to the growth rate of China's industrial sector, 9.51%. The rate of return on asset is -9.69%. 50.46% of all firms in the industry made a profit while 42.74% had negative returns. The top province in terms of the industry's revenue is Jiangsu, accounting for 27.98% of the total revenue.
本行業在1996年佔全行業總產值0.204%，行業年增長率為-13.4%（全國工業年增長率9.51%）。行業的資產回報率-9.69%，50.46%的企業盈利，42.74%的企業虧損。銷售收入最高的省份為江蘇省，佔本行業的27.98%。

	Total number of firms 企業總數	Total number of employees 職工總數	Total revenue (mil. RMB) 總銷售收入（百萬元）	Total profit (mil. RMB) 總利潤（百萬元）	Return on assets 資產利潤率 (%)	Return on equity 權益利潤率 (%)	Labour productivity ('000 RMB / worker) 勞動生產率（千元／人）	Debts / assets 資產負債率 (%)	Total assets (mil. RMB) 總資產（百萬元）
Industry Overall 行業總體	1,221	533,176	11,823	-1,791	-9.69	-286.27	22.17	96.62	18,497

	Number of firms 企業個數	Average number of employees 平均職工人數	Average revenue ('000 RMB) 平均銷售收入（千元）	Average profit ('000 RMB) 平均利潤（千元）	Return on assets 資產利潤率 (%)	Return on equity 權益利潤率 (%)	Labour productivity ('000 RMB / worker) 勞動生產率（千元／人）	Average debts / assets 平均資產負債率(%)	Average Total assets ('000 RMB) 平均總資產（千元）
By ownership 產業所有權									
State-owned 國有	249	905	18,072	-3,775	-11.26	-192.23	19.97	94.14	33,518
Collectively-owned 集體	916	312	7,533	-856	-8.43	-1387.39	24.11	99.39	10,158
Privately-owned 私有	2	42	1,330	64	7.58	7.72	31.66	1.78	842
Domestic JVs 聯營	16	298	6,267	-1,002	-10.28	-119.15	21.00	91.38	9,748
Joint stock 股份制	24	473	9,815	-1,536	-7.96	-73.80	20.75	89.21	19,280
Foreign-funded 外資	4	330	4,476	-1,504	-8.74	-111.25	13.56	92.14	17,212
Overseas Chinese-funded 港澳台資	11	421	7,670	-742	-5.18	-90.06	18.21	94.25	14,332
By size 規模									
Large 大型	31	2,060	62,486	-8,011	-7.64	-49.30	30.33	84.50	104,843
Medium 中型	203	955	23,099	-3,365	-9.61	-149.95	24.20	93.59	35,025
Small 小型	971	282	5,410	-885	-10.56	257.23	19.19	104.11	8,380
By regional distribution 地區分布									
Central-North 華北	14	401	7,104	-779	-6.83	-45.65	17.70	85.04	11,418
Beijing 北京									
Tianjin 天津									
Hebei 河北	1	24	1,200	250	18.66	73.53	50.00	74.63	1,340
Shanxi 山西	12	460	8,126	-931	-7.07	-48.38	17.65	85.37	13,161
Inner Mongolia 內蒙	1	71	740	10	1.72	2.13	10.42	18.97	580
Northeast 東北	53	132	2,584	-104	-3.80	-54.02	19.55	92.97	2,736
Liaoning 遼寧	51	131	2,626	1	0.04	0.24	20.07	84.65	2,674
Jilin 吉林	2	166	1,515	-2,780	-64.58	51.77	9.15	224.74	4,305
Heilongjiang 黑龍江									
Central East 華東	631	433	12,808	-952	-5.75	-48.43	29.58	88.13	16,559
Shanghai 上海	1	251	8,150	-100	-0.63	-1.05	32.47	40.10	15,960
Jiangsu 江蘇	230	471	14,381	-708	-4.29	-36.46	30.50	88.22	16,488
Zhejiang 浙江	205	444	14,402	-1,262	-6.14	-36.30	32.46	83.09	20,552
Anhui 安徽	107	334	7,113	-1,271	-12.46	104.54	21.27	111.92	10,199
Fujian 福建	4	61	475	-288	-16.45	-66.09	7.76	74.96	1,748
Jiangxi 江西	46	255	3,732	-1,271	-13.02	126.03	14.61	110.33	9,767
Shandong 山東	38	680	23,136	440	1.90	6.80	34.04	72.03	23,158
Central-South 中南	135	290	6,199	-881	-7.45	-75.44	21.34	90.13	11,836
Henan 河南	49	179	3,901	56	1.11	4.64	21.77	76.13	5,029
Hubei 湖北	24	400	8,976	-445	-2.91	-27.80	22.42	89.52	15,281
Hunan 湖南	5	161	2,882	-1,658	-20.51	42.08	17.86	148.75	8,082
Guangdong 廣東	26	449	10,361	-2,433	-10.73	-105.61	23.09	89.84	22,689
Guangxi 廣西	31	270	4,727	-1,274	-11.14	-194.63	17.54	94.27	11,431
Hainan 海南									
Southwest 西南	361	538	6,825	-2,678	-17.53	122.85	12.68	114.27	15,278
Chongqing 重慶	106	490	5,722	-2,404	-19.15	93.03	11.66	120.59	12,554
Sichuan 四川	237	570	7,421	-2,866	-17.08	130.50	13.00	113.09	16,779
Guizhou 貴州	8	115	551	-374	-13.20	-251.26	4.79	94.75	2,833
Yunnan 雲南	9	623	9,766	-3,017	-15.79	-306.43	15.67	94.85	19,099
Tibet 西藏									
Northwest 西北	27	512	7,560	-3,283	-14.06	465.84	14.77	103.02	23,344
Shaanxi 陝西	18	602	9,790	-3,757	-15.16	461.95	16.26	103.28	24,789
Gansu 甘肅	1	6							6,420
Qinghai 青海									
Ningxia 寧夏	1	230	1,610				7.00	104.94	8,900
Xinjiang 新疆	7	393	3,757	-3,003	-12.45	202.70	9.57	106.14	24,110

1771: Silk Reeling 繅絲業

Year 年份	Number of firms 企業個數	Rate of change 每年變化 (%)	Number of employees 職工人數 (人)	Rate of change 每年變化 (%)	Total revenue (mil. RMB) 總銷售收入 (百萬元)	Rate of change 每年變化 (%)	Total profit (mil. RMB) 總利潤 (百萬元)	Rate of change 每年變化 (%)
1993	898		467,353		12,938		345	
1994	1,081	20.38%	621,511	32.99%	14,563	12.56%	-154	-144.69%
1995	1,325	22.57%	663,429	6.74%	13,653	-6.25%	-2,150	-1293.07%
1996	1,221	-7.85%	533,176	-19.63%	11,823	-13.40%	-1,791	16.68%

3 Major products* 3種主要產品*	Output 產量	Sales volume 銷售量	Unit 單位
a) Mulberry Silk 桑蠶絲	59,790	57,996	ton 噸
b) Tussah Silk 柞蠶絲	3,534	1,131	ton 噸
c) Mulberry Silk & Their Union Products 桑蠶絲及其交織品	11,350	11,236	10,000 metre 萬米

Top 10 firms by revenue (year founded) 收入排名前10家企業 (創辦年份)	City 城市	Province 省	Telephone / fax 電話 / 傳真	Number of employees 職工人數	Ownership 產業所有權	Revenue ('000 RMB) 銷售收入 (千元)	Profit ('000 RMB) (rank) 利潤(千元) (排名)	Total assets ('000 RMB) 總資產 (千元)	Major products 主要產品
Jiangsu Jin Feng Group Co. 江蘇金蜂集團公司(1993)	Suzhou 蘇州市	Jiangsu 江蘇省	(0512)3731161 (0512)3731424	1,270	Collectively-owned 集體	156,493	866(39)	79,809	a,c
Zhejiang Fortune Silk Group Co. Zhejiang Silk No.2 Factory 浙江富泉絲綢集團公司浙絲二廠(1946)	Huzhou 湖州市	Zhejiang 浙江省	(0572)3941539 (0572)3941539	1,857	State-owned 國有	154,690	-19226(845)	228,314	a,c
Hangzhou Xin Hua Silk Mill 杭州新華絲廠(1928)	Hangzhou 杭州市	Zhejiang 浙江省	(0571)6372477	2,410	State-owned 國有	129,940	-12530(832)	187,560	a,c
Zhejiang San Huan Silk (Group) Co. 浙江三環絲綢集團公司(1969)	Jiaxing 嘉興市	Zhejiang 浙江省	(0573)6032024 (0573)6021678	1,935	State-owned 國有	101,919	608(55)	150,575	a,c
Zhejiang Misai Silk Group Co. 浙江米賽絲綢集團公司(1921)	Jiaxing 嘉興市	Zhejiang 浙江省	(0573)7411600 (0573)7411275	2,349	State-owned 國有	99,360	180(135)	134,450	a
Jiangsu Hua Hong Silk Co. Ltd. 江蘇省華宏絲綢股份有限公司(1994)	Yancheng 鹽城市	Jiangsu 江蘇省	(0515)6511888 (0515)6511493	1,031	Collectively-owned 集體	93,300	2580(13)	83,090	a
Rushan Silk Reeling Factory 乳山製絲廠(1967)	Weihai 威海市	Shandong 山東省	(0896)6624161 (0896)6623484	1,840	State-owned 國有	81,480	4030(5)	92,690	a
Haining Zhong Si No.3 Factory 海寧中絲三廠(1926)	Jiaxing 嘉興市	Zhejiang 浙江省	(0573)7024028 (0573)7024028	1,546	State-owned 國有	79,859	18(230)	71,912	a
Yancheng Silk Reeling No.2 Factory 鹽城繅絲二廠(1984)	Yancheng 鹽城市	Jiangsu 江蘇省	(0515)8701188	750	Collectively-owned 集體	79,700	2080(18)	22,350	a
Suqian Silk Industry Co. Ltd. 宿遷市絲綢工業公司(1985)	Suqian 宿遷市	Jiangsu 江蘇省	(0527)4880008	1,800	Collectively-owned 集體	77,762	-1685(570)	46,783	o

Top 10 Cities by Production Output 產出排名前10位城市	Province 省	Market share 市場份額	Number of firms 企業個數
Jiaxing 嘉興市	Zhejiang 浙江省	12.08%	74
Huzhou 湖州市	Zhejiang 浙江省	7.29%	72
Nantong 南通市	Jiangsu 江蘇省	6.12%	46
Yancheng 鹽城市	Jiangsu 江蘇省	5.97%	35
Suzhou 蘇州市	Jiangsu 江蘇省	5.62%	29
Chongqing 重慶市	Chongqing 重慶市	4.89%	116
Xuzhou 徐州市	Jiangsu 江蘇省	3.82%	40
Nanchong 南充市	Sichuan 四川省	3.34%	44
Hangzhou 杭州市	Zhejiang 浙江省	2.84%	31
Liu'an 六安市	Anhui 安徽省	2.65%	59

10 Major Wholesalers 10家主要批發商	City 城市	Province 省	Telephone / Fax 電話 / 傳真
Anhui Clothing Import & Export Company 安徽省服裝進出口公司	Hefei 合肥市	Anhui 安徽省	(0551)3632212 (0551)3632002
Qingdao Textile Clothing Industrial Group Company 青島紡織服裝實業集團公司	Qingdao 青島市	Shandong 山東省	(0532)2877853 (0532)2869315
Hebei Textile Import & Export (Group) Company 河北省紡織品進出口(集團)公司	Shijiazhuang 石家莊市	Hebei 河北省	(0311)7028530 (0311)7027781
Zhong Fang Pledget Import & Export Company 中紡紗布進出口公司	Beijing 北京市	Beijing 北京市	(010)65124718 (010)65124713
Shaoxing Import & Export Company 紹興市進出口公司	Shaoxing 紹興市	Zhejiang 浙江省	(0575)5132822 (0575)5141577
Hunan Hua Xiang Import & Export (Group) Company 湖南省華湘進出口(集團)公司	Changsha 長沙市	Hunan 湖南省	(0731)2282440 (0731)2286995
City's Import & Export Company Trade Dept. 市進出口公司貿易部	Yichang 宜昌市	Hubei 湖北省	(0717)6450778 (0717)6441875
Shanghai Pu Dong Xinqu Import & Export Company 上海浦東新區進出口公司	Shanghai 上海市	Shanghai 上海市	(021)58878801 (021)58827444
Ningbo Yinxian Import & Export Company 寧波市鄞縣進出口公司	Ningbo 寧波市	Zhejiang 浙江省	(0574)7875205 (0574)7873168
Zhejiang Silk Import & Export Company 浙江省絲綢進出口公司	Hangzhou 杭州市	Zhejiang 浙江省	(0571)5195588 (0571)5192542

*Also include sales by firms outside this industry.包括本行業以外廠家的銷售。"o" stands for "others". "o" 代表 "其他產品"。

1772: Silk Spinning 絹紡業

The industry accounts for 0.085% of the total revenue of China's industrial sector in 1996. The revenue growth rate of the industry is 2.1% from 1995, as compared to the growth rate of China's industrial sector, 9.51%. The rate of return on asset is -3.54%. 52.57% of all firms in the industry made a profit while 39.15% had negative returns. The top province in terms of the industry's revenue is Zhejiang, accounting for 41.39% of the total revenue.
本行業在1996年佔全行業總產值0.085%，行業年增長率為2.1%（全國工業年增長率9.51%）。行業的資產回報率-3.54%，52.57%的企業盈利，39.15%的企業虧損。銷售收入最高的省份為浙江省，佔本行業的41.39%。

	Total number of firms 企業總數	Total number of employees 職工總數	Total revenue (mil. RMB) 總銷售收入（百萬元）	Total profit (mil. RMB) 總利潤（百萬元）	Return on assets 資產利潤率 (%)	Return on equity 權益利潤率 (%)	Labour productivity ('000 RMB / worker) 勞動生產率（千元/人）	Debts / assets 資產負債率 (%)	Total assets (mil. RMB) 總資產（百萬元）
Industry Overall 行業總體	187	101,796	4,927	-192	-3.54	-14.40	48.40	75.42	5,435

	Number of firms 企業個數	Average number of employees 平均職工人數	Average revenue ('000 RMB) 平均銷售收入（千元）	Average profit ('000 RMB) 平均利潤（千元）	Return on assets 資產利潤率 (%)	Return on equity 權益利潤率 (%)	Labour productivity ('000 RMB / worker) 勞動生產率（千元/人）	Average debts / assets 平均資產負債率(%)	Average Total assets ('000 RMB) 平均總資產（千元）
By ownership 產業所有權									
State-owned 國有	34	1,228	27,059	-5,441	-9.49	-54.73	22.04	82.66	57,324
Collectively-owned 集體	140	371	25,018	-103	-0.50	-2.11	67.52	76.15	20,562
Privately-owned 私有									
Domestic JVs 聯營	2	87	3,065	-943	-6.91	178.88	35.44	103.86	13,654
Joint stock 股份制	1	3,980	198,650	14,392	4.68	7.01	49.91	33.28	307,843
Foreign-funded 外資	2	223	65,211	1,222	3.08	5.22	292.43	41.08	39,726
Overseas Chinese-funded 港澳台資	9	397	18,840	-833	-3.87	-12.36	47.48	68.68	21,498
By size 規模									
Large 大型	13	2,737	104,642	-6,914	-4.05	-12.20	38.23	66.79	170,584
Medium 中型	20	1,172	35,628	-4,175	-7.82	-46.23	30.39	83.08	53,389
Small 小型	152	279	18,778	-122	-0.87	-4.44	67.31	80.51	14,148
By regional distribution 地區分布									
Central-North 華北	3	420	1,847	-790	-15.56	-60.77	4.40	74.33	5,077
Beijing 北京									
Tianjin 天津									
Hebei 河北									
Shanxi 山西	1	380	4,100	-770	-8.56	100.00	10.79	108.56	9,000
Inner Mongolia 內蒙	2	440	720	-800	-25.68	-34.26	1.64	24.88	3,115
Northeast 東北	15	390	11,090	-414	-2.15	-3.81	28.41	43.66	19,269
Liaoning 遼寧	14	418	11,882	-444	-2.15	-3.81	28.43	43.66	20,645
Jilin 吉林									
Heilongjiang 黑龍江	1	4							
Central East 華東	128	540	34,135	-289	-0.89	-3.08	63.23	71.22	32,615
Shanghai 上海	5	442	32,384	398	0.70	1.81	73.33	61.36	56,798
Jiangsu 江蘇	48	490	41,390	-43	-0.14	-0.55	84.52	73.89	29,581
Zhejiang 浙江	62	591	32,892	309	0.88	2.69	55.66	67.24	35,104
Anhui 安徽	7	522	7,929	-7,476	-44.92	159.84	15.20	128.10	16,643
Fujian 福建									
Jiangxi 江西	2	159	2,295	-540	-6.52	42.86	14.48	115.22	8,280
Shandong 山東	4	696	30,318	-678	-1.68	-6.28	43.58	73.28	40,328
Central-South 中南	8	966	15,176	-275	-0.76	8.53	15.71	108.91	36,196
Henan 河南	2	550	16,060	870	3.37	16.46	29.23	79.56	25,830
Hubei 湖北	4	1,096	18,328	-985	-2.13	8.75	16.72	124.36	46,223
Hunan 湖南									
Guangdong 廣東									
Guangxi 廣西	2	1,123	7,990				7.12	83.63	26,510
Hainan 海南									
Southwest 西南	31	549	8,260	-4,545	-22.29	1003.56	15.04	102.22	20,388
Chongqing 重慶	19	539	6,814	-5,299	-35.28	447.25	12.62	107.89	15,020
Sichuan 四川	11	564	10,626	-3,310	-11.35	-443.95	18.84	97.44	29,172
Guizhou 貴州									
Yunnan 雲南									
Tibet 西藏									
Northwest 西北	2	411	4,235	-1,840	-10.71	-49.66	10.30	78.43	17,180
Shaanxi 陝西	2	411	4,235	-1,840	-10.71	-49.66	10.30	78.43	17,180
Gansu 甘肅									
Qinghai 青海									
Ningxia 寧夏									
Xinjiang 新疆									

1772: Silk Spinning 絹紡業

Year 年份	Number of firms 企業個數	Rate of change 每年變化 (%)	Number of employees 職工人數 (人)	Rate of change 每年變化 (%)	Total revenue (mil. RMB) 總銷售收入 (百萬元)	Rate of change 每年變化 (%)	Total profit (mil. RMB) 總利潤 (百萬元)	Rate of change 每年變化 (%)
1993	139		71,727		2,852		107	
1994	144	3.60%	98,037	36.68%	4,653	63.16%	26	-75.50%
1995	194	34.72%	104,214	6.30%	4,828	3.76%	-181	-791.87%
1996	187	-3.61%	101,796	-2.32%	4,927	2.05%	-192	-6.09%

3 Major products* 3 種主要產品 *	Output 產量	Sales volume 銷售量	Unit 單位
a) Spun Silk 絹紡絲	16,532	16,532	ton 噸
b) Spun Silk & Their Union Products 絹絲及其交織品	4,947	4,897	10,000 metre 萬米
c) Scouring & Bleaching Silk Products 煉白絲織品	1,708	1,725	10,000 metre 萬米

Top 10 firms by revenue (year founded) 收入排名前 10 家企業 (創辦年份)	City 城市	Province 省	Telephone / fax 電話 / 傳真	Number of employees 職工人數	Ownership 產業所有權	Revenue ('000 RMB) 銷售收入 (千元)	Profit ('000 RMB) (rank) 利潤 (千元) (排名)	Total assets ('000 RMB) 總資產 (千元)	Major products 主要產品
Jiangsu Yi Long Spun Textile Group Co. 江蘇藝龍絹紡集團公司(1994)	Suzhou 蘇州市	Jiangsu 江蘇省	(0512)3771818 (0512)3772055	1,043	Collectively-owned 集體	420,144	19821(1)	71,013	o
Jiangsu Ding Qiu Industrial Co. Ltd. 江蘇鼎球實業股份有限公司(1986)	Wuxi 無錫市	Jiangsu 江蘇省	(0510)7381472 (0510)7381652	1,600	Collectively-owned 集體	290,718	7213(3)	217,749	a
Jiangsu Cai Wen Silk Group Co. 江蘇彩雯絲綢集團公司(1984)	Wuxi 無錫市	Jiangsu 江蘇省	(0510)7382366 (0510)7382366	1,376	Collectively-owned 集體	289,954	6578(4)	108,414	a,b
Siyang Schappe Spinning Factory 泗陽縣絹紡廠(1961)	Suqian 宿遷市	Jiangsu 江蘇省	(0527)5213311 (0527)5213748	3,672	State-owned 國有	152,684	405(29)	170,565	a,b
Jiangsu Donghu Silk Group Company 江蘇東湖絲綢集團公司(1980)	Wuxi 無錫市	Jiangsu 江蘇省	(0510)8791593	1,040	Collectively-owned 集體	151,580	-1050(110)	207,340	b,c
Jiaxing Spun Textile Mill 嘉興絹紡廠(1923)	Jiaxing 嘉興市	Zhejiang 浙江省	(0573)2080951 (0573)2088297	2,989	State-owned 國有	150,851	226(38)	308,222	a,c
Zhejiang Wei Hua Group Company 浙江威華集團公司(1987)	Huzhou 湖州市	Zhejiang 浙江省	(0572)3952070 (0572)3952858	120	Collectively-owned 集體	131,507	7271(2)	104,091	a
Zhejiang Feng Shu Group Co. Ltd 浙江省楓樹集團有限責任公司(1981)	Jiaxing 嘉興市	Zhejiang 浙江省	(0573)8677118 (0573)8677091	2,123	Collectively-owned 集體	114,604	209(40)	146,555	a,b,c
Zhejiang Jiaxing Hao Long Group Corp., Ltd. 浙江嘉興豪龍集團公司(1992)	Jiaxing 嘉興市	Zhejiang 浙江省	(0573)8591983 (0573)8591136	921	Collectively-owned 集體	107,110	1508(14)	77,652	o
Zhejiang Tongxiang Spun Silk & Flax Textile Factory 浙江省桐鄉市絹麻紡織廠(1984)	Jiaxing 嘉興市	Zhejiang 浙江省	(0573)8677158 (0573)8677047	1,325	Collectively-owned 集體	104,127	580(27)	85,638	a

Top 10 Cities by Production Output 產出排名前 10 位城市	Province 省	Market share 市場份額	Number of firms 企業個數
Wuxi 無錫市	Jiangsu 江蘇省	25.92%	27
Jiaxing 嘉興市	Zhejiang 浙江省	20.39%	34
Suzhou 蘇州市	Jiangsu 江蘇省	12.98%	37
Huzhou 湖州市	Zhejiang 浙江省	9.48%	21
Yancheng 鹽城市	Jiangsu 江蘇省	3.82%	12
Shanghai 上海市	Shanghai 上海市	3.21%	8
Suqian 宿遷市	Jiangsu 江蘇省	2.96%	5
Hangzhou 杭州市	Zhejiang 浙江省	2.80%	11
Chongqing 重慶市	Chongqing 重慶市	2.33%	18
Nantong 南通市	Jiangsu 江蘇省	1.55%	5

10 Major Wholesalers 10 家主要批發商	City 城市	Province 省	Telephone / Fax 電話 / 傳真
Anhui Clothing Import & Export Company 安徽省服裝進出口公司	Hefei 合肥市	Anhui 安徽省	(0551)3632212 (0551)3632002
Qingdao Textile Clothing Industrial Group Company 青島紡織服裝實業集團公司	Qingdao 青島市	Shandong 山東省	(0532)2877853 (0532)2869315
Hebei Textile Import & Export (Group) Company 河北省紡織品進出口(集團)公司	Shijiazhuang 石家莊市	Hebei 河北省	(0311)7028530 (0311)7027781
Zhong Fang Pledget Import & Export Company 中紡紗布進出口公司	Beijing 北京市	Beijing 北京市	(010)65124718 (010)65124713
Shaoxing Import & Export Company 紹興市進出口公司	Shaoxing 紹興市	Zhejiang 浙江省	(0575)5132822 (0575)5141577
Hunan Hua Xiang Import & Export (Group) Company 湖南省華湘進出口(集團)公司	Changsha 長沙市	Hunan 湖南省	(0731)2282440 (0731)2286995
City's Import & Export Company Trade Dept. 市進出口公司貿易部	Yichang 宜昌市	Hubei 湖北省	(0717)6450778 (0717)6441875
Shanghai Pu Dong Xinqu Import & Export Company 上海浦東新區進出口公司	Shanghai 上海市	Shanghai 上海市	(021)58878801 (021)58827444
Ningbo Yinxian Import & Export Company 寧波市鄞縣進出口公司	Ningbo 寧波市	Zhejiang 浙江省	(0574)7875205 (0574)7873168
Zhejiang Silk Import & Export Company 浙江省絲綢進出口公司	Hangzhou 杭州市	Zhejiang 浙江省	(0571)5195588 (0571)5192542

*Also include sales by firms outside this industry.包括本行業以外廠家的銷售。"o" stands for "others". "o" 代表"其他產品"。

1773: Silk Weaving 絲織業

The industry accounts for 0.442% of the total revenue of China's industrial sector in 1996. The revenue growth rate of the industry is 4.9% from 1995, as compared to the growth rate of China's industrial sector, 9.51%. The rate of return on asset is -1.52%. 55.59% of all firms in the industry made a profit while 38.44% had negative returns. The top province in terms of the industry's revenue is Zhejiang, accounting for 48.21% of the total revenue.
本行業在1996年佔全行業總產值0.442%，行業年增長率為4.9%（全國工業年增長率9.51%）。行業的資產回報率-1.52%，55.59%的企業盈利，38.44%的企業虧損。銷售收入最高的省份為浙江省，佔本行業的48.21%。

	Total number of firms 企業總數	Total number of employees 職工總數	Total revenue (mil. RMB) 總銷售收入（百萬元）	Total profit (mil. RMB) 總利潤（百萬元）	Return on assets 資產利潤率 (%)	Return on equity 權益利潤率 (%)	Labour productivity ('000 RMB / worker) 勞動生產率（千元/人）	Debts / assets 資產負債率 (%)	Total assets (mil. RMB) 總資產（百萬元）
Industry Overall 行業總體	1,353	561,549	25,630	-601	-1.52	-7.72	45.64	80.38	39,642

	Number of firms 企業個數	Average number of employees 平均職工人數	Average revenue ('000 RMB) 平均銷售收入（千元）	Average profit ('000 RMB) 平均利潤（千元）	Return on assets 資產利潤率 (%)	Return on equity 權益利潤率 (%)	Labour productivity ('000 RMB / worker) 勞動生產率（千元/人）	Average debts / assets 平均資產負債率(%)	Average Total assets ('000 RMB) 平均總資產（千元）
By ownership 產業所有權									
State-owned 國有	253	1,074	29,142	-2,375	-3.54	-27.56	27.13	87.16	67,158
Collectively-owned 集體	976	264	16,429				62.26	77.16	19,151
Privately-owned 私有	10	117	6,368				54.25	89.05	7,702
Domestic JVs 聯營	22	224	12,790				57.04	81.18	14,087
Joint stock 股份制	8	1,003	21,707				21.65	68.83	77,888
Foreign-funded 外資	32	280	20,634				73.67	68.91	43,579
Overseas Chinese-funded 港澳台資	52	226	20,045				88.74	59.38	29,763
By size 規模									
Large 大型	72	1,997	117,260	-2,036	-0.97	-4.23	58.71	77.02	209,321
Medium 中型	155	1,050	44,865	-1,278	-1.81	-10.01	42.75	81.91	70,554
Small 小型	1,117	230	9,160	-229	-1.88	-10.97	39.87	82.87	12,205
By regional distribution 地區分布									
Central-North 華北	52	348	6,867	-442	-1.44	-7.89	19.73	81.82	30,794
Beijing 北京	2	836	24,960	-7,180	-3.48	-14.58	29.87	76.16	206,500
Tianjin 天津	17	346	10,204	369	0.91	5.32	29.46	82.88	40,564
Hebei 河北	22	299	5,503	-467	-2.89	-27.62	18.43	89.55	16,166
Shanxi 山西	9	365	1,072	-187	-1.52	-5.00	2.94	69.61	12,286
Inner Mongolia 內蒙	2	344	1,490	-1,475	-9.09	-77.02	4.34	88.17	16,235
Northeast 東北	40	700	6,945	-1,695	-5.18	397.42	9.93	101.30	32,750
Liaoning 遼寧	33	729	7,101	-1,994	-5.87	118.60	9.73	104.95	33,965
Jilin 吉林	3	675	3,707	-377	-2.09	-9.69	5.49	78.40	17,997
Heilongjiang 黑龍江	4	472	8,088	-215	-0.64	-3.21	17.14	80.19	33,795
Central East 華東	998	369	22,658	-76	-0.25	-1.06	61.46	76.77	30,988
Shanghai 上海	24	576	17,333	-633	-1.42	-7.41	30.08	80.81	44,540
Jiangsu 江蘇	220	497	36,246	-31	-0.06	-0.27	72.92	76.49	48,198
Zhejiang 浙江	602	309	20,527	170	0.64	2.43	66.34	73.71	26,569
Anhui 安徽	63	362	8,935	-1,655	-10.96	101.58	24.70	110.79	15,108
Fujian 福建	10	173	6,282	-389	-2.10	-13.58	36.23	84.54	18,524
Jiangxi 江西	19	304	3,370	-575	-4.11	2484.09	11.07	100.17	13,989
Shandong 山東	60	469	19,593	-620	-2.00	-10.45	41.80	80.83	30,940
Central-South 中南	104	776	15,225	-799	-2.74	-22.27	19.62	87.69	29,139
Henan 河南	34	378	6,910	-70	-0.41	-4.10	18.30	90.00	17,168
Hubei 湖北	30	315	8,409	-102	-0.52	-4.11	26.70	87.46	19,867
Hunan 湖南	10	358	1,233	-1,367	-15.52	28.82	3.45	153.86	8,808
Guangdong 廣東	24	2,206	43,889	-2,096	-3.01	-17.73	19.89	83.02	69,649
Guangxi 廣西	5	341	2,486	-2,678	-25.21	426.43	7.29	105.91	10,622
Hainan 海南	1	198	18,160	-230	-0.61	-3.47	91.72	82.55	37,930
Southwest 西南	139	407	4,898	-2,142	-12.56	639.56	12.04	101.96	17,063
Chongqing 重慶	19	442	7,024	-2,909	-14.94	237.53	15.88	106.29	19,472
Sichuan 四川	110	412	4,854	-2,069	-11.84	907.84	11.77	101.30	17,470
Guizhou 貴州	6	300	353	-1,885	-22.71	-1119.80	1.18	97.97	8,300
Yunnan 雲南	3	167	1,837	-413	-10.43	-87.32	11.00	88.14	3,963
Tibet 西藏									
Northwest 西北	20	515	5,943	-2,653	-13.18	642.37	11.53	102.05	20,126
Shaanxi 陝西	13	467	6,495	-1,879	-9.09	146.20	13.91	106.22	20,680
Gansu 甘肅	3	178	140	-40	-2.23	-10.53	0.79	78.81	1,793
Qinghai 青海									
Ningxia 寧夏	1	59	440				7.46	141.27	1,260
Xinjiang 新疆	3	1,215	11,187	-9,503	-22.44	-364.58	9.21	93.84	42,347

1773: Silk Weaving 絲織業

Year 年份	Number of firms 企業個數	Rate of change 每年變化 (%)	Number of employees 職工人數 (人)	Rate of change 每年變化 (%)	Total revenue (mil. RMB) 總銷售收入 (百萬元)	Rate of change 每年變化 (%)	Total profit (mil. RMB) 總利潤 (百萬元)	Rate of change 每年變化 (%)
1993	1,596		564,229		26,275		485	
1994	1,581	-0.94%	619,848	9.86%	24,455	-6.93%	-173	-135.65%
1995	1,532	-3.10%	577,532	-6.83%	24,439	-0.07%	-896	-417.56%
1996	1,353	-11.68%	561,549	-2.77%	25,630	4.87%	-601	32.90%

3 Major products* 3種主要產品*	Output 產量	Sales volume 銷售量	Unit 單位
a) Synthetic Fibre & Their Union Products 合纖絲及其交織品	295,133	268,571	10,000 metre 萬米
b) Rayon & Their Union Products 人造絲及其交織品	23,145	18,979	10,000 metre 萬米
c) Mulberry Silk & Their Union Products 桑蠶絲及其交織品	39,378	38,985	10,000 metre 萬米

Top 10 firms by revenue (year founded) 收入排名前10家企業 (創辦年份)	City 城市	Province 省	Telephone / fax 電話 / 傳真	Number of employees 職工人數	Ownership 產業所有權	Revenue ('000 RMB) 銷售收入 (千元)	Profit ('000 RMB) (rank) 利潤 (千元) (排名)	Total assets ('000 RMB) 總資產 (千元)	Major products 主要產品
Wujiang Silk Group Company 吳江絲綢集團公司(1991)	Suzhou 蘇州市	Jiangsu 江蘇省	(0512)3557239	13,869	State-owned 國有	1,156,113	14261(5)	2,095,807	o
Suzhou Silk Group Co. Ltd. 蘇州絲綢集團有限責任公司(1996)	Suzhou 蘇州市	Jiangsu 江蘇省	(0512)7291497 (0512)7295487	13,080	State-owned 國有	1,149,238	10796(11)	1,541,386	a,b,c
Wujiang Silk & Craft Factory 吳江工藝織造廠(1972)	Suzhou 蘇州市	Jiangsu 江蘇省	(0512)3558998 (0512)3550617	3,188	Collectively-owned 集體	765,213	63487(1)	909,874	a
Chun Hua Polyamide Fibre Textile Co. Ltd. 春華錦綸紡織有限公司(1986)	Yangjiang 陽江市	Guangdong 廣東省	(0662)7733978 (0662)7734380	2,200	Overseas Chinese-funded 港澳台資	485,498	850(130)	255,961	o
Zhejiang Long Chao Textile Group Co. 浙江龍巢紡織集團公司(1975)	Huzhou 湖州市	Zhejiang 浙江省	(0572)3940788 (0572)3940752	835	Collectively-owned 集體	331,911	22880(2)	268,339	a
Zhe Jiangnan Fang Enterprise Group Company 浙江南方企業集團公司(1993)	Shaoxing 紹興市	Zhejiang 浙江省	(0575)4061888 (0575)4061646	1,252	Collectively-owned 集體	320,808	16194(4)	513,516	a
Jiangsu Su Feng Group Co. 江蘇蘇楓集團公司(1993)	Suzhou 蘇州市	Jiangsu 江蘇省	(0512)5362158 (0512)5361663	850	Collectively-owned 集體	304,200	-8314(888)	112,777	o
Zhejiang Jin Lai Enterprise Group Company 浙江金來企業集團公司(1994)	Shaoxing 紹興市	Zhejiang 浙江省	(0575)4362457 (0575)4361170	9	Collectively-owned 集體	293,030	20006(3)	165,757	a
Jiangsu Que Ling Velvet Group Co. 江蘇雀翎絲絨(集團)公司(1983)	Suzhou 蘇州市	Jiangsu 江蘇省	(0512)8674357	1,130	Collectively-owned 集體	289,608	13092(7)	166,344	c
Zhejiang Saili Silk Group Co. 浙江賽麗絲綢集團公司(1973)	Shaoxing 紹興市	Zhejiang 浙江省	(0575)6023720 (0575)6023461	3,153	State-owned 國有	211,788	5600(27)	151,881	c

Top 10 Cities by Production Output 產出排名前10位城市	Province 省	Market share 市場份額	Number of firms 企業個數
Shaoxing 紹興市	Zhejiang 浙江省	23.50%	280
Suzhou 蘇州市	Jiangsu 江蘇省	22.68%	286
Hangzhou 杭州市	Zhejiang 浙江省	8.61%	236
Huzhou 湖州市	Zhejiang 浙江省	8.11%	116
Baoding 保定市	Hebei 河北省	4.65%	4
Jiaxing 嘉興市	Zhejiang 浙江省	3.65%	111
Shanghai 上海市	Shanghai 上海市	3.47%	35
Yangjiang 陽江市	Guangdong 廣東省	2.61%	2
Changzhou 常州市	Jiangsu 江蘇省	2.16%	18
Nantong 南通市	Jiangsu 江蘇省	1.63%	43

10 Major Wholesalers 10家主要批發商	City 城市	Province 省	Telephone / Fax 電話 / 傳真
Anhui Clothing Import & Export Company 安徽省服裝進出口公司	Hefei 合肥市	Anhui 安徽省	(0551)3632212 (0551)3632002
Qingdao Textile Clothing Industrial Group Company 青島紡織服裝實業集團公司	Qingdao 青島市	Shandong 山東省	(0532)2877853 (0532)2869315
Hebei Textile Import & Export (Group) Company 河北省紡織品進出口(集團)公司	Shijiazhuang 石家莊市	Hebei 河北省	(0311)7028530 (0311)7027781
Zhong Fang Pledget Import & Export Company 中紡紗布進出口公司	Beijing 北京市	Beijing 北京市	(010)65124718 (010)65124713
Shaoxing Import & Export Company 紹興市進出口公司	Shaoxing 紹興市	Zhejiang 浙江省	(0575)5132822 (0575)5141577
Hunan Hua Xiang Import & Export (Group) Company 湖南省華湘進出口(集團)公司	Changsha 長沙市	Hunan 湖南省	(0731)2282440 (0731)2286995
City's Import & Export Company Trade Dept. 市進出口公司貿易部	Yichang 宜昌市	Hubei 湖北省	(0717)6450778 (0717)6441875
Shanghai Pu Dong Xinqu Import & Export Company 上海浦東新區進出口公司	Shanghai 上海市	Shanghai 上海市	(021)58878801 (021)58827444
Ningbo Yinxian Import & Export Company 寧波市鄞縣進出口公司	Ningbo 寧波市	Zhejiang 浙江省	(0574)7875205 (0574)7873168
Zhejiang Silk Import & Export Company 浙江省絲綢進出口公司	Hangzhou 杭州市	Zhejiang 浙江省	(0571)5195588 (0571)5192542

*Also include sales by firms outside this industry.包括本行業以外廠家的銷售。"o" stands for "others"."o"代表"其他產品"。

1774: Silk Printing and Dyeing 絲印染業

The industry accounts for 0.126% of the total revenue of China's industrial sector in 1996. The revenue growth rate of the industry is -8.6% from 1995, as compared to the growth rate of China's industrial sector, 9.51%. The rate of return on asset is 0.72%. 51.57% of all firms in the industry made a profit while 42.52% had negative returns. The top province in terms of the industry's revenue is Jiangsu, accounting for 42.53% of the total revenue.
本行業在1996年佔全行業總產值0.126%，行業年增長率為-8.6%（全國工業年增長率9.51%）。行業的資產回報率0.72%，51.57%的企業盈利，42.52%的企業虧損。銷售收入最高的省份為江蘇省，佔本行業的42.53%。

	Total number of firms 企業總數	Total number of employees 職工總數	Total revenue (mil. RMB) 總銷售收入（百萬元）	Total profit (mil. RMB) 總利潤（百萬元）	Return on assets 資產利潤率 (%)	Return on equity 權益利潤率 (%)	Labour productivity ('000 RMB / worker) 勞動生產率（千元/人）	Debts / assets 資產負債率 (%)	Total assets (mil. RMB) 總資產（百萬元）
Industry Overall 行業總體	244	82,063	7,286	79	0.72	2.09	88.79	65.44	10,898

	Number of firms 企業個數	Average number of employees 平均職工人數	Average revenue ('000 RMB) 平均銷售收入（千元）	Average profit ('000 RMB) 平均利潤（千元）	Return on assets 資產利潤率 (%)	Return on equity 權益利潤率 (%)	Labour productivity ('000 RMB / worker) 勞動生產率（千元/人）	Average debts / assets 平均資產負債率(%)	Average Total assets ('000 RMB) 平均總資產（千元）
By ownership 產業所有權									
State-owned 國有	41	740	36,927	-1,951	-2.17	-9.48	49.91	77.16	90,122
Collectively-owned 集體	140	304	34,651	860	2.23	5.79	113.95	61.46	38,524
Privately-owned 私有	1	43	2,179	59	3.54	7.43	50.67	52.37	1,679
Domestic JVs 聯營	4	100	6,778	-730	-4.58	-7.76	67.78	41.05	15,957
Joint stock 股份制									
Foreign-funded 外資	15	86	14,561	165	1.16	2.18	168.92	46.56	14,141
Overseas Chinese-funded 港澳台資	41	168	15,513	905	2.93	6.02	92.08	51.32	30,890
By size 規模									
Large 大型	26	1,106	119,843	1,891	0.95	2.50	108.39	62.16	199,995
Medium 中型	46	587	49,469	488	0.69	2.37	84.22	71.06	71,194
Small 小型	167	156	11,348	44	0.30	0.87	72.79	64.89	14,512
By regional distribution 地區分布									
Central-North 華北	8	159	7,253	58	0.35	2.86	45.51	87.83	16,536
Beijing 北京	1	24	1,370	-670	-15.06	-670.00	57.08	97.75	4,450
Tianjin 天津	5	228	4,158	-330	-1.31	-10.44	18.22	87.45	25,178
Hebei 河北	1	110	35,860	2,780	142.56	1390.00	326.00	89.74	1,950
Shanxi 山西									
Inner Mongolia 內蒙	1								
Northeast 東北	6	714	17,590	-3,545	-7.63	174.06	24.62	104.39	46,443
Liaoning 遼寧	4	610	25,925	-3,715	-7.63	-111.98	42.50	93.19	48,685
Jilin 吉林	2	923	920	-3,205	-7.64	25.15	1.00	130.37	41,960
Heilongjiang 黑龍江									
Central East 華東	190	347	33,873	746	1.55	4.13	97.67	62.54	48,160
Shanghai 上海	10	487	24,776	-173	-0.29	-1.42	50.92	79.70	59,939
Jiangsu 江蘇	41	457	75,579	1,479	1.92	4.26	165.33	55.03	77,207
Zhejiang 浙江	127	290	22,956	652	1.70	4.74	79.05	64.13	38,325
Anhui 安徽	1	61	5,390	-90	-0.75	-0.90	88.36	16.67	11,940
Fujian 福建	4	126	14,373	1,820	10.07	17.21	113.84	41.48	18,070
Jiangxi 江西									
Shandong 山東	7	692	15,880	-1,019	-1.64	-8.42	22.95	80.48	62,010
Central-South 中南	32	251	19,841	-365	-1.05	-3.55	79.18	70.53	34,874
Henan 河南	5	420	9,804	66	0.18	1.53	23.35	87.97	35,840
Hubei 湖北	2	246	13,905	-2,375	-5.28	47.60	56.52	111.11	44,940
Hunan 湖南									
Guangdong 廣東	23	196	23,533	-93	-0.26	-0.65	120.36	59.82	35,332
Guangxi 廣西	2	466	8,415	-2,560	-14.95	55.90	18.08	126.74	17,125
Hainan 海南									
Southwest 西南	8	323	6,500	-3,800	-13.76	-596.08	20.12	97.70	27,608
Chongqing 重慶	2	64	2,090	-5,521	-23.33	66.67	32.26	135.00	23,662
Sichuan 四川	6	409	7,970	-3,226	-11.16	-89.45	19.48	87.53	28,923
Guizhou 貴州									
Yunnan 雲南									
Tibet 西藏									
Northwest 西北									
Shaanxi 陝西									
Gansu 甘肅									
Qinghai 青海									
Ningxia 寧夏									
Xinjiang 新疆									

1774: Silk Printing and Dyeing 絲印染業

Year 年份	Number of firms 企業個數	Rate of change 每年變化 (%)	Number of employees 職工人數 (人)	Rate of change 每年變化 (%)	Total revenue (mil. RMB) 總銷售收入 (百萬元)	Rate of change 每年變化 (%)	Total profit (mil. RMB) 總利潤 (百萬元)	Rate of change 每年變化 (%)
1993	243		93,996		7,181		273	
1994	266	9.47%	99,978	6.36%	7,519	4.71%	236	-13.42%
1995	273	2.63%	99,842	-0.14%	7,971	6.02%	150	-36.36%
1996	244	-10.62%	82,063	-17.81%	7,286	-8.59%	79	-47.44%

3 Major products* 3 種主要產品 *	Output 產量	Sales volume 銷售量	Unit 單位
a) Printing Silk Fabric 印花絲織品	34,467	32,743	10,000 metre 萬米
b) Dyeing Silk Fabric 染色絲織品	129,885	119,494	10,000 metre 萬米
c) Scouring & Bleaching Silk Products 煉白絲織品	21,987	22,206	10,000 metre 萬米

Top 10 firms by revenue (year founded) 收入排名前 10 家企業 (創辦年份)	City 城市	Province 省	Telephone / fax 電話 / 傳真	Number of employees 職工人數	Ownership 產業所有權	Revenue ('000 RMB) 銷售收入 (千元)	Profit ('000 RMB) (rank) 利潤 (千元) (排名)	Total assets ('000 RMB) 總資產 (千元)	Major products 主要產品
China Ying Xiang Corp. 中國鷹翔集團(1981)	Suzhou 蘇州市	Jiangsu 江蘇省	(0512)3555588 (0512)3554265	3,242	Collectively-owned 集體	1,313,941	68031(1)	1,203,864	a,b,c
Jiangsu Chui Hong Group Co. 江蘇垂虹集團公司(1994)	Suzhou 蘇州市	Jiangsu 江蘇省	(0512)3412137	1,232	Collectively-owned 集體	562,088	1003(45)	153,600	b
Guangdong Xinhui Victory City Co. Ltd. 廣東省新會市冠華針織有限公司(1992)	Jiangmen 江門市	Guangdong 廣東省	(0750)6488623 (0750)6488247	796	Foreign-funded 外資	232,344	1050(44)	128,067	o
Zhejiang Tian Chang Group Company 浙江天昌集團公司(1938)	Huzhou 湖州市	Zhejiang 浙江省	(0572)2022424 (0572)2033224	314	State-owned 國有	145,124	-28182(186)	383,196	a,b,c
Zhejiang Ya Ma Silk Group Co. Ltd. 浙江省亞馬絲綢集團有限公司(1979)	Jiaxing 嘉興市	Zhejiang 浙江省	(0573)4028464 (0573)4028992	134	State-owned 國有	128,613	28(106)	155,967	a,b,c
Zhejiang Shaoxing Yong Sheng Industrial Development Company 浙江紹興永盛實業發展公司(1993)	Shaoxing 紹興市	Zhejiang 浙江省	(0575)4051988 (0575)4056356	838	Collectively-owned 集體	125,846	-4138(175)	152,524	a,b
Wuxi Silk Printing & Dyeing General Factory 無錫市絲綢印染廠(1953)	Wuxi 無錫市	Jiangsu 江蘇省	(0510)3709171 (0510)3707298	974	State-owned 國有	125,699	1(118)	324,513	a,b,c
Zhejiang Ji Shan Printing & Dyeing Factory 浙江稽山印染廠(1985)	Shaoxing 紹興市	Zhejiang 浙江省	(0575)4022668 (0575)4021130	662	Collectively-owned 集體	120,227	5025(13)	126,826	a,b
Hangzhou Silk Refining and Dyeing Factory 杭州絲綢煉染廠(1927)	Hangzhou 杭州市	Zhejiang 浙江省	(0571)5190843 (0571)5193765	1,078	State-owned 國有	117,331	10(113)	132,155	b,c
Suzhou Silk Refining and Dyeing No.1 Factory 蘇州綢緞煉染一廠(1934)	Suzhou 蘇州市	Jiangsu 江蘇省	(0512)5251318 (0512)5252277	1,364	State-owned 國有	100,882	13(112)	205,810	a,b,c

Top 10 Cities by Production Output 產出排名前 10 位城市	Province 省	Market share 市場份額	Number of firms 企業個數
Suzhou 蘇州市	Jiangsu 江蘇省	30.37%	41
Shaoxing 紹興市	Zhejiang 浙江省	26.29%	69
Dandong 丹東市	Liaoning 遼寧省	9.05%	2
Hangzhou 杭州市	Zhejiang 浙江省	6.72%	47
Huzhou 湖州市	Zhejiang 浙江省	3.73%	25
Shanghai 上海市	Shanghai 上海市	3.54%	18
Wuxi 無錫市	Jiangsu 江蘇省	3.40%	10
Jiaxing 嘉興市	Zhejiang 浙江省	3.33%	27
Jiangmen 江門市	Guangdong 廣東省	2.70%	1
Changzhou 常州市	Jiangsu 江蘇省	1.85%	5

10 Major Wholesalers 10 家主要批發商	City 城市	Province 省	Telephone / Fax 電話 / 傳真
Anhui Clothing Import & Export Company 安徽省服裝進出口公司	Hefei 合肥市	Anhui 安徽省	(0551)3632212 (0551)3632002
Qingdao Textile Clothing Industrial Group Company 青島紡織服裝實業集團公司	Qingdao 青島市	Shandong 山東省	(0532)2877853 (0532)2869315
Hebei Textile Import & Export (Group) Company 河北省紡織品進出口(集團)公司	Shijiazhuang 石家莊市	Hebei 河北省	(0311)7028530 (0311)7027781
Zhong Fang Pledget Import & Export Company 中紡紗布進出口公司	Beijing 北京市	Beijing 北京市	(010)65124718 (010)65124713
Shaoxing Import & Export Company 紹興市進出口公司	Shaoxing 紹興市	Zhejiang 浙江省	(0575)5132822 (0575)5141577
Hunan Hua Xiang Import & Export (Group) Company 湖南省華湘進出口(集團)公司	Changsha 長沙市	Hunan 湖南省	(0731)2282440 (0731)2286995
City's Import & Export Company Trade Dept. 市進出口公司貿易部	Yichang 宜昌市	Hubei 湖北省	(0717)6450778 (0717)6441875
Shanghai Pu Dong Xinqu Import & Export Company 上海浦東新區進出口公司	Shanghai 上海市	Shanghai 上海市	(021)58878801 (021)58827444
Ningbo Yinxian Import & Export Company 寧波市鄞縣進出口公司	Ningbo 寧波市	Zhejiang 浙江省	(0574)7875205 (0574)7873168
Zhejiang Silk Import & Export Company 浙江省絲綢進出口公司	Hangzhou 杭州市	Zhejiang 浙江省	(0571)5195588 (0571)5192542

*Also include sales by firms outside this industry.包括本行業以外廠家的銷售。"o" stands for "others". "o" 代表 "其他產品" 。

1775: Silk Products 絲製品業

The industry accounts for 0.037% of the total revenue of China's industrial sector in 1996. The revenue growth rate of the industry is 1.7% from 1995, as compared to the growth rate of China's industrial sector, 9.51%. The rate of return on asset is -1.10%. 62.89% of all firms in the industry made a profit while 32.56% had negative returns. The top province in terms of the industry's revenue is Jiangsu, accounting for 23.63% of the total revenue.
本行業在 1996 年佔全行業總產值 0.037%，行業年增長率為 1.7%（全國工業年增長率 9.51%）。行業的資產回報率 -1.10%，62.89% 的企業盈利，32.56% 的企業虧損。銷售收入最高的省份為江蘇省，佔本行業的 23.63%。

	Total number of firms 企業總數	Total number of employees 職工總數	Total revenue (mil. RMB) 總銷售收入（百萬元）	Total profit (mil. RMB) 總利潤（百萬元）	Return on assets 資產利潤率 (%)	Return on equity 權益利潤率 (%)	Labour productivity ('000 RMB / worker) 勞動生產率（千元/人）	Debts / assets 資產負債率 (%)	Total assets (mil. RMB) 總資產（百萬元）
Industry Overall 行業總體	376	47,389	2,119	-28	-1.10	-4.13	44.72	73.41	2,507

	Number of firms 企業個數	Average number of employees 平均職工人數	Average revenue ('000 RMB) 平均銷售收入（千元）	Average profit ('000 RMB) 平均利潤（千元）	Return on assets 資產利潤率 (%)	Return on equity 權益利潤率 (%)	Labour productivity ('000 RMB / worker) 勞動生產率（千元/人）	Average debts / assets 平均資產負債率(%)	Average Total assets ('000 RMB) 平均總資產（千元）
By ownership 產業所有權									
State-owned 國有	44	217	4,659	-1,000	-9.17	-258.82	21.52	96.46	10,909
Collectively-owned 集體	248	120	5,071	-56	-1.20	-6.10	42.11	80.35	4,712
Privately-owned 私有	2	80	10,456	155	7.95	11.33	131.52	29.82	1,950
Domestic JVs 聯營	4	116	5,104	179	3.13	11.39	44.00	72.47	5,700
Joint stock 股份制	2	42	3,143	120	5.86	16.97	75.73	65.45	2,046
Foreign-funded 外資	31	124	8,622	-1	-0.01	-0.02	69.30	51.96	12,579
Overseas Chinese-funded 港澳台資	45	87	7,595	640	6.57	12.92	87.01	49.16	9,737
By size 規模									
Large 大型									
Medium 中型	8	1,356	51,385	-3,567	-6.19	-216.71	37.88	97.14	57,615
Small 小型	360	102	4,744	1	0.03	0.08	46.69	68.05	5,685
By regional distribution 地區分布									
Central-North 華北	21	43	909	2	0.07	0.18	21.04	64.03	2,927
Beijing 北京	9	12	1,079	-37	-1.34	-2.27	86.70	41.16	2,740
Tianjin 天津	4	162	1,738	105	1.48	12.10	10.74	87.76	7,090
Hebei 河北	6	20	342	-10	-0.78	-1.24	16.80	37.16	1,278
Shanxi 山西	1	8	130				16.25	80.00	150
Inner Mongolia 內蒙	1	18	240	10	1.59	-1.41	13.33	214.29	630
Northeast 東北	9	30	873	17	2.52	6.05	29.55	58.32	661
Liaoning 遼寧	7	24	1,003	21	4.78	13.39	42.55	64.33	449
Jilin 吉林	1	101	840				8.32	51.60	2,810
Heilongjiang 黑龍江	1								
Central East 華東	239	136	6,308	138	2.05	6.56	46.31	68.74	6,739
Shanghai 上海	22	48	3,290	115	2.93	5.30	69.00	44.77	3,926
Jiangsu 江蘇	68	169	7,363	-79	-1.08	-7.24	43.46	85.07	7,264
Zhejiang 浙江	83	140	4,331	220	3.50	8.46	31.03	58.55	6,292
Anhui 安徽	16	199	22,418	1,025	11.36	50.93	112.62	77.69	9,019
Fujian 福建	12	74	5,388	267	2.55	4.16	72.89	38.80	10,468
Jiangxi 江西	11	45	744	-13	-0.38	-3.95	16.49	90.38	3,344
Shandong 山東	27	142	5,313	-71	-0.95	-3.61	37.46	73.71	7,464
Central-South 中南	62	88	5,553	30	0.46	1.57	62.81	70.45	6,454
Henan 河南	14	61	1,569	79	4.32	14.71	25.56	70.59	1,819
Hubei 湖北	11	195	1,826	-115	-2.80	-153.66	9.38	98.18	4,095
Hunan 湖南	8	51	629	-89	-4.89	-22.98	12.27	78.72	1,815
Guangdong 廣東	25	82	11,852	108	0.86	2.56	144.96	66.25	12,557
Guangxi 廣西	4	7	225	5	1.64	2.20	34.62	25.41	305
Hainan 海南									
Southwest 西南	41	196	5,816	-1,529	-14.69	-318.61	29.62	95.39	10,403
Chongqing 重慶	9	121	4,162	466	12.28	116.25	34.22	89.44	3,798
Sichuan 四川	26	222	7,211	-2,339	-18.31	1510.50	32.35	101.21	12,774
Guizhou 貴州	1	56	120	-20	-2.90	-40.00	2.14	92.75	690
Yunnan 雲南	4	227	1,705	-1,073	-8.82	-21.36	7.52	58.71	12,158
Tibet 西藏									
Northwest 西北	4	33	463	20	3.64	14.04	13.91	74.09	550
Shaanxi 陝西	2	59	845	35	3.41	15.91	14.44	78.54	1,025
Gansu 甘肅									
Qinghai 青海									
Ningxia 寧夏									
Xinjiang 新疆	2	8	80	5	6.67	7.69	10.00	13.33	75

Year 年份	Number of firms 企業個數	Rate of change 每年變化 (%)	Number of employees 職工人數 (人)	Rate of change 每年變化 (%)	Total revenue (mil. RMB) 總銷售收入 (百萬元)	Rate of change 每年變化 (%)	Total profit (mil. RMB) 總利潤 (百萬元)	Rate of change 每年變化 (%)
1993	366		49,014		1,609		53	
1994	353	-3.55%	71,183	45.23%	1,874	16.45%	34	-36.48%
1995	396	12.18%	51,990	-26.96%	2,084	11.19%	-37	-211.83%
1996	376	-5.05%	47,389	-8.85%	2,119	1.68%	-28	25.29%

3 Major products* 3 種主要產品 *	Output 產量	Sales volume 銷售量	Unit 單位
a) Silk Headscarf 絲綢頭圍巾	4,276,995	4,191,455	piece 條
b) Hand-dyed & Woven Handicraft 手工染織工藝品	86,581	96,970	1,000 yuan 千元
c) Silk Necktie 絲綢領帶	1,174,760	1,151,265	piece 條

Top 10 firms by revenue (year founded) 收入排名前 10 家企業 (創辦年份)	City 城市	Province 省	Telephone / fax 電話 / 傳真	Number of employees 職工人數	Ownership 產業所有權	Revenue ('000 RMB) 銷售收入 (千元)	Profit ('000 RMB) (rank) 利潤 (千元) (排名)	Total assets ('000 RMB) 總資產 (千元)	Major products 主要產品
Anhui Huaibei Hang Huai Silk Mill 安徽省淮北市杭淮絲綢廠(1985)	Huaibei 淮北市	Anhui 安徽省	(0561)4041041 (0561)4041040	1,017	Collectively-owned 集體	248,579	11984(1)	65,136	o
Jiedong Silk Jin Fiber Industrial Co. Ltd. 揭東縣錦絲錦纖維工業有限公司(1995)	Jieyang 揭陽市	Guangdong 廣東省	(0663)3264461	170	Foreign-funded 外資	112,134	1342(9)	73,094	o
Zhong Jiang Silk Co. Ltd. 中江絲綢有限公司(1992)	Chaohu 巢湖市	Anhui 安徽省	(0565)7322479	200	Foreign-funded 外資	71,220	2380(7)	58,662	o
Yangzhou Lan Guang Group Co. 揚州藍光集團公司(1974)	Yangzhou 揚州市	Jiangsu 江蘇省	(0514)7261088 (0514)7261980	729	Collectively-owned 集體	62,654	1492(8)	33,903	b
Dafeng Mnricipal Silk Cloth General Factory 大豐市絲綢總廠(1971)	Yancheng 鹽城市	Jiangsu 江蘇省	(0515)3513511 (0515)3513511	2,311	State-owned 國有	54,810	-2980(170)	83,170	o
Shanghai Fu Hao Zipper Co. Ltd. 上海福豪拉鏈有限公司(1995)	Shanghai 上海市	Shanghai 上海市	(021)58116253 (021)58116253	50	Overseas Chinese-funded 港澳台資	48,110	626(30)	68,585	o
Suzhou Thread & Belt Group Corp., Ltd. 蘇州線帶集團有限責任公司(1956)	Suzhou 蘇州市	Jiangsu 江蘇省	(0512)5251309 (0512)5257626	434	Collectively-owned 集體	44,241	5(110)	21,378	o
Guangdong Zhaoqing Unification Silk Socks Factory 廣東省肇慶市統一絲襪廠(1989)	Zhaoqing 肇慶市	Guangdong 廣東省	(0757)2718645 (0757)2727144	480	Overseas Chinese-funded 港澳台資	42,720	0(125)	59,932	o
Sichuan Ew Textiles Co. Ltd. 四川依格爾紡織品有限公司	Nanchong 南充市	Sichuan 四川省	(0817)3631553	628	Foreign-funded 外資	42,620	-484(149)	76,051	a,c
Fuzhou Xin Li Sen Spinning and Weaving Co. Ltd. 福州鑫利森紡織有限公司(1993)	Fuzhou 福州市	Fujian 福建省	(0591)3662430 (0591)3660862	415	Overseas Chinese-funded 港澳台資	40,694	4114(3)	59,549	o

Top 10 Cities by Production Output 產出排名前 10 位城市	Province 省	Market share 市場份額	Number of firms 企業個數
Shanghai 上海市	Shanghai 上海市	7.21%	31
Suzhou 蘇州市	Jiangsu 江蘇省	6.78%	42
Shaoxing 紹興市	Zhejiang 浙江省	6.09%	29
Jieyang 揭陽市	Guangdong 廣東省	5.20%	3
Hangzhou 杭州市	Zhejiang 浙江省	4.94%	26
Yangzhou 揚州市	Jiangsu 江蘇省	4.79%	5
Rizhao 日照市	Shandong 山東省	4.63%	3
Wuxi 無錫市	Jiangsu 江蘇省	4.25%	7
Ningbo 寧波市	Zhejiang 浙江省	3.62%	6
Foshan 佛山市	Guangdong 廣東省	3.31%	2

10 Major Wholesalers 10 家主要批發商	City 城市	Province 省	Telephone / Fax 電話 / 傳真
Anhui Clothing Import & Export Company 安徽省服裝進出口公司	Hefei 合肥市	Anhui 安徽省	(0551)3632212 (0551)3632002
Qingdao Textile Clothing Industrial Group Company 青島紡織服裝實業集團公司	Qingdao 青島市	Shandong 山東省	(0532)2877853 (0532)2869315
Hebei Textile Import & Export (Group) Company 河北省紡織品進出口(集團)公司	Shijiazhuang 石家莊市	Hebei 河北省	(0311)7028530 (0311)7027781
Zhong Fang Pledget Import & Export Company 中紡紗布進出口公司	Beijing 北京市	Beijing 北京市	(010)65124718 (010)65124713
Shaoxing Import & Export Company 紹興市進出口公司	Shaoxing 紹興市	Zhejiang 浙江省	(0575)5132822 (0575)5141577
Hunan Hua Xiang Import & Export (Group) Company 湖南省華湘進出口(集團)公司	Changsha 長沙市	Hunan 湖南省	(0731)2282440 (0731)2286995
City's Import & Export Company Trade Dept. 市進出口公司貿易部	Yichang 宜昌市	Hubei 湖北省	(0717)6450778 (0717)6441875
Shanghai Pu Dong Xinqu Import & Export Company 上海浦東新區進出口公司	Shanghai 上海市	Shanghai 上海市	(021)58878801 (021)58827444
Ningbo Yinxian Import & Export Company 寧波市鄞縣進出口公司	Ningbo 寧波市	Zhejiang 浙江省	(0574)7875205 (0574)7873168
Zhejiang Silk Import & Export Company 浙江省絲綢進出口公司	Hangzhou 杭州市	Zhejiang 浙江省	(0571)5195588 (0571)5192542

*Also include sales by firms outside this industry.包括本行業以外廠家的銷售。"o" stands for "others". "o" 代表"其他產品"。

1779: Other Silk Fabrics 其他絲絹紡織業

The industry accounts for 0.015% of the total revenue of China's industrial sector in 1996. The revenue growth rate of the industry is 2.9% from 1995, as compared to the growth rate of China's industrial sector, 9.51%. The rate of return on asset is -0.61%. 67.12% of all firms in the industry made a profit while 29.75% had negative returns. The top province in terms of the industry's revenue is Guangdong, accounting for 25.82% of the total revenue.
本行業在1996年佔全行業總產值0.015%，行業年增長率為2.9%（全國工業年增長率9.51%）。行業的資產回報率-0.61%，67.12%的企業盈利，29.75%的企業虧損。銷售收入最高的省份為廣東省，佔本行業的25.82%。

	Total number of firms 企業總數	Total number of employees 職工總數	Total revenue (mil. RMB) 總銷售收入（百萬元）	Total profit (mil. RMB) 總利潤（百萬元）	Return on assets 資產利潤率 (%)	Return on equity 權益利潤率 (%)	Labour productivity ('000 RMB / worker) 勞動生產率（千元/人）	Debts / assets 資產負債率 (%)	Total assets (mil. RMB) 總資產（百萬元）
Industry Overall 行業總體	159	18,650	885	-13	-0.61	-3.18	47.45	80.69	2,172

	Number of firms 企業個數	Average number of employees 平均職工人數	Average revenue ('000 RMB) 平均銷售收入（千元）	Average profit ('000 RMB) 平均利潤（千元）	Return on assets 資產利潤率 (%)	Return on equity 權益利潤率 (%)	Labour productivity ('000 RMB / worker) 勞動生產率（千元/人）	Average debts / assets 平均資產負債率(%)	Average Total assets ('000 RMB) 平均總資產（千元）
By ownership 產業所有權									
State-owned 國有	8	262	1,750	-375	-3.49	-42.86	6.69	91.86	10,750
Collectively-owned 集體	120	104	4,841	21	0.38	35.45	46.49	98.94	5,697
Privately-owned 私有	2	61	4,194	-278	-0.36	-0.50	69.32	26.44	76,341
Domestic JVs 聯營	1	35	850	-184	-6.42	25.75	24.27	124.95	2,869
Joint stock 股份制	1	261	15,278	82	0.40	2.68	58.53	85.08	20,533
Foreign-funded 外資	13	108	6,902	-24	-0.18	-0.35	63.64	47.72	13,234
Overseas Chinese-funded 港澳台資	15	149	11,713	-773	-1.10	-5.79	78.58	81.01	70,285
By size 規模									
Large 大型									
Medium 中型	2	1,091	55,395	289	0.22	1.54	50.80	85.73	131,639
Small 小型	155	106	4,994	-88	-0.71	-3.56	47.04	80.02	12,314
By regional distribution 地區分布									
Central-North 華北	8	62	1,183	43	1.42	5.35	19.00	73.49	2,994
Beijing 北京	3								
Tianjin 天津	1	67	3,450	560	39.72	93.33	51.49	57.45	1,410
Hebei 河北	2	33	725	-110	-4.65	-8.66	21.97	46.30	2,365
Shanxi 山西									
Inner Mongolia 內蒙	2	183	2,280				12.49	81.98	8,905
Northeast 東北	12	247	7,004	201	2.58	14.38	28.34	82.04	7,773
Liaoning 遼寧	8	304	9,896	256	2.73	13.53	32.54	79.87	9,401
Jilin 吉林	2	241	485	10	0.12	1.52	2.02	92.37	8,650
Heilongjiang 黑龍江	2	26	1,955	170	44.16	117.24	75.19	62.34	385
Central East 華東	78	105	6,402	143	1.57	5.54	60.71	71.60	9,091
Shanghai 上海	4	54	10,025	848	7.19	19.08	186.51	62.34	11,790
Jiangsu 江蘇	23	101	9,599	217	1.43	4.68	94.59	69.36	15,104
Zhejiang 浙江	28	128	5,438	31	0.53	2.99	42.40	82.21	5,845
Anhui 安徽	4	160	4,225	148	2.57	25.32	26.41	89.84	5,733
Fujian 福建	3	22	1,443	-927	-14.79	-27.63	65.61	46.49	6,267
Jiangxi 江西	3	105	500	17	12.20	100.00	4.76	87.80	137
Shandong 山東	13	82	4,882	312	3.72	11.37	59.65	67.24	8,364
Central-South 中南	35	138	7,656	-674	-1.81	-12.42	55.43	85.40	37,168
Henan 河南	7	41	571	30	1.62	3.72	13.79	56.38	1,847
Hubei 湖北	3	33	3,913	67	2.31	17.09	117.40	86.51	2,890
Hunan 湖南	3	20	497	-87	-4.91	-216.67	24.83	97.92	1,763
Guangdong 廣東	17	184	13,440	-1,100	-1.53	-10.97	72.95	86.04	71,791
Guangxi 廣西	5	250	4,452	-1,010	-9.43	-40.05	17.78	76.47	10,712
Hainan 海南									
Southwest 西南	24	72	1,028	-151	-8.21	-73.13	14.21	88.77	1,837
Chongqing 重慶	8	136	1,198	-344	-9.45	250.46	8.76	103.77	3,637
Sichuan 四川	13	42	1,073	-53	-5.41	-11.79	25.00	54.08	983
Guizhou 貴州	2								
Yunnan 雲南									
Tibet 西藏									
Northwest 西北	2	196						100.00	300
Shaanxi 陝西	2	196						100.00	300
Gansu 甘肅									
Qinghai 青海									
Ningxia 寧夏									
Xinjiang 新疆									

1779: Other Silk Fabrics 其他絲綢紡織業

Year 年份	Number of firms 企業個數	Rate of change 每年變化 (%)	Number of employees 職工人數 (人)	Rate of change 每年變化 (%)	Total revenue (mil. RMB) 總銷售收入 (百萬元)	Rate of change 每年變化 (%)	Total profit (mil. RMB) 總利潤 (百萬元)	Rate of change 每年變化 (%)
1993	160		14,030		527		11	
1994	175	9.38%	21,304	51.85%	715	35.83%	-24	-327.31%
1995	177	1.14%	20,042	-5.92%	860	20.20%	-19	21.55%
1996	159	-10.17%	18,650	-6.95%	885	2.91%	-13	31.62%

3 Major products* 3種主要產品 *	Output 產量	Sales volume 銷售量	Unit 單位
a) Synthetic Filament Fabric 合纖長絲機織物	2,227	2,183	ton 噸
b) Silk Necktie 絲綢領帶	133,853	131,176	piece 條
c) Polyester Processing Silk 滌綸加工絲	4,412	4,103	ton 噸

Top 10 firms by revenue (year founded) 收入排名前10家企業 (創辦年份)	City 城市	Province 省	Telephone / fax 電話 / 傳真	Number of employees 職工人數	Ownership 產業所有權	Revenue ('000 RMB) 銷售收入 (千元)	Profit ('000 RMB) (rank) 利潤(千元) (排名)	Total assets ('000 RMB) 總資產 (千元)	Major products 主要產品
Wuxi Yu Tong Weaving Co. Ltd. 無錫裕通織造有限公司(1992)	Wuxi 無錫市	Jiangsu 江蘇省	(0510)3880579 (0510)3880879	560	Collectively-owned 集體	108,598	5197(1)	284,480	o
Guangdong Zhu Jiang Silk Co. Ltd. 廣東珠江絲綢有限公司(1992)	Jiangmen 江門市	Guangdong 廣東省	(0750)6677400 (0750)6677400	587	Overseas Chinese-funded 港澳台資	75,989	-8498(63)	439,823	a
Zhuanghe Jin Yuan Spinning and Weaving Factory 裝河市金元紡織廠(1995)	Dalian 大連市	Liaoning 遼寧省	(0411)8420283	360	Collectively-owned 集體	66,280	2130(3)	27,410	o
Shunde Li De Textile Clothing Co. Ltd. 順德市麗德紡織服裝有限公司(1993)	Foshan 佛山市	Guangdong 廣東省	(0757)8893633 (0757)8882560	497	Overseas Chinese-funded 港澳台資	59,988	-13859(64)	663,410	c
Wujiang Ba Du Silk Twisting Factory 吳江市八都捻絲廠(1995)	Suzhou 蘇州市	Jiangsu 江蘇省	(0512)3870228	140	Collectively-owned 集體	54,976	42(39)	20,571	o
China Yin Li Lai Co. Ltd. 中國銀利來有限公司(1984)	Meizhou 梅州市	Guangdong 廣東省	(0752)2223390 (0752)2234170	72	Foreign-funded 外資	32,416	1760(5)	32,928	b
Shanghai Min De Textile Co. Ltd. 上海民德紡織品有限公司(1995)	Shanghai 上海市	Shanghai 上海市	(021)64111651	50	Overseas Chinese-funded 港澳台資	22,880	222(22)	24,443	o
Lufeng Stone Table Knitting No.2 Factory 陸豐市碣石針織二廠(1985)	Shanwei 汕尾市	Guangdong 廣東省	(0660)8861556	764	Collectively-owned 集體	19,900	768(8)	4,030	o
Shanghai Tian Lu Knitting Co. Ltd. 上海天祿針織有限公司(1992)	Shanghai 上海市	Shanghai 上海市	(021)56064220 (021)56054092	184	Foreign-funded 外資	17,219	3164(2)	22,721	o
Taierzhuang Xue Zhuang Xiang Silkworm Cocoon Station 台兒莊區薛莊鄉蠶繭站(1978)	Zaozhuang 棗莊市	Shandong 山東省	(0632)8900231 (0632)8900231	105	Collectively-owned 集體	15,510	1260(6)	6,680	o

Top 10 Cities by Production Output 產出排名前10位城市	Province 省	Market share 市場份額	Number of firms 企業個數
Foshan 佛山市	Guangdong 廣東省	31.14%	4
Wuxi 無錫市	Jiangsu 江蘇省	11.67%	5
Shanghai 上海市	Shanghai 上海市	7.85%	16
Jiangmen 江門市	Guangdong 廣東省	6.22%	1
Suzhou 宿州市	Anhui 安徽省	4.87%	1
Suzhou 蘇州市	Jiangsu 江蘇省	4.25%	10
Meizhou 梅州市	Guangdong 廣東省	2.47%	1
Dalian 大連市	Liaoning 遼寧省	2.04%	1
Zaozhuang 棗莊市	Shandong 山東省	1.93%	2
Ningbo 寧波市	Zhejiang 浙江省	1.70%	1

10 Major Wholesalers 10家主要批發商	City 城市	Province 省	Telephone / Fax 電話 / 傳真
Anhui Clothing Import & Export Company 安徽省服裝進出口公司	Hefei 合肥市	Anhui 安徽省	(0551)3632212 (0551)3632002
Qingdao Textile Clothing Industrial Group Company 青島紡織服裝實業集團公司	Qingdao 青島市	Shandong 山東省	(0532)2877853 (0532)2869315
Hebei Textile Import & Export (Group) Company 河北省紡織品進出口(集團)公司	Shijiazhuang 石家莊市	Hebei 河北省	(0311)7028530 (0311)7027781
Zhong Fang Pledget Import & Export Company 中紡紗布進出口公司	Beijing 北京市	Beijing 北京市	(010)65124718 (010)65124713
Shaoxing Import & Export Company 紹興市進出口公司	Shaoxing 紹興市	Zhejiang 浙江省	(0575)5132822 (0575)5141577
Hunan Hua Xiang Import & Export (Group) Company 湖南省華湘進出口(集團)公司	Changsha 長沙市	Hunan 湖南省	(0731)2282440 (0731)2286995
City's Import & Export Company Trade Dept. 市進出口公司貿易部	Yichang 宜昌市	Hubei 湖北省	(0717)6450778 (0717)6441875
Shanghai Pu Dong Xinqu Import & Export Company 上海浦東新區進出口公司	Shanghai 上海市	Shanghai 上海市	(021)58878801 (021)58827444
Ningbo Yinxian Import & Export Company 寧波市鄞縣進出口公司	Ningbo 寧波市	Zhejiang 浙江省	(0574)7875205 (0574)7873168
Zhejiang Silk Import & Export Company 浙江省絲綢進出口公司	Hangzhou 杭州市	Zhejiang 浙江省	(0571)5195588 (0571)5192542

*Also include sales by firms outside this industry.包括本行業以外廠家的銷售。"o" stands for "others". "o" 代表"其他產品"。

1781: Cotton Knitwear 棉針織品業

The industry accounts for 0.439% of the total revenue of China's industrial sector in 1996. The revenue growth rate of the industry is 1.8% from 1995, as compared to the growth rate of China's industrial sector, 9.51%. The rate of return on asset is -0.48%. 59.16% of all firms in the industry made a profit while 33.38% had negative returns. The top province in terms of the industry's revenue is Shanghai, accounting for 18.10% of the total revenue.
本行業在1996年佔全行業總產值0.439%，行業年增長率為1.8%（全國工業年增長率9.51%）。行業的資產回報率-0.48%，59.16%的企業盈利，33.38%的企業虧損。銷售收入最高的省份為上海市，佔本行業的18.10%。

	Total number of firms 企業總數	Total number of employees 職工總數	Total revenue (mil. RMB) 總銷售收入（百萬元）	Total profit (mil. RMB) 總利潤（百萬元）	Return on assets 資產利潤率 (%)	Return on equity 權益利潤率 (%)	Labour productivity ('000 RMB / worker) 勞動生產率（千元/人）	Debts / assets 資產負債率 (%)	Total assets (mil. RMB) 總資產（百萬元）
Industry Overall 行業總體	2,416	485,751	25,464	-164	-0.48	-2.17	52.42	77.87	34,066

	Number of firms 企業個數	Average number of employees 平均職工人數	Average revenue ('000 RMB) 平均銷售收入（千元）	Average profit ('000 RMB) 平均利潤（千元）	Return on assets 資產利潤率 (%)	Return on equity 權益利潤率 (%)	Labour productivity ('000 RMB / worker) 勞動生產率（千元/人）	Average debts / assets 平均資產負債率(%)	Average Total assets ('000 RMB) 平均總資產（千元）
By ownership 產業所有權									
State-owned 國有	368	556	19,891	-989	-2.41	-21.03	35.81	88.52	40,984
Collectively-owned 集體	1,441	133	6,128	-25	-0.42	-2.33	46.14	81.92	5,979
Privately-owned 私有	19	50	6,637	260	6.55	17.04	132.33	61.54	3,969
Domestic JVs 聯營	26	215	20,928	185	1.48	5.03	97.55	70.64	12,553
Joint stock 股份制	13	349	19,458	2,152	8.32	21.31	55.73	60.97	25,879
Foreign-funded 外資	194	191	16,531	558	3.08	7.86	86.69	60.87	18,131
Overseas Chinese-funded 港澳台資	351	134	14,727	258	1.48	3.46	109.59	57.17	17,382
By size 規模									
Large 大型	60	1,461	101,992	1,115	0.75	3.54	69.80	78.93	149,679
Medium 中型	155	736	33,266	-941	-1.63	-10.32	45.19	84.18	57,613
Small 小型	2,166	132	6,551	-39	-0.53	-2.01	49.79	73.80	7,457
By regional distribution 地區分布									
Central-North 華北	288	195	4,516	-304	-2.42	-12.11	23.15	80.01	12,544
Beijing 北京	71	106	2,584	-346	-4.96	-19.35	24.38	74.35	6,975
Tianjin 天津	81	168	5,516	-315	-2.35	-16.82	32.92	86.01	13,396
Hebei 河北	78	233	5,677	-125	-0.93	-4.25	24.32	78.06	13,397
Shanxi 山西	37	340	3,524	-779	-3.97	-16.60	10.36	76.05	19,597
Inner Mongolia 內蒙	21	204	4,620	58	0.46	2.99	22.61	84.55	12,488
Northeast 東北	223	195	3,708	-312	-3.16	-23.58	19.03	86.58	9,873
Liaoning 遼寧	116	231	5,186	-322	-2.70	-20.02	22.42	86.53	11,938
Jilin 吉林	46	163	2,407	-502	-7.07	62.21	14.77	111.36	7,108
Heilongjiang 黑龍江	61	150	1,877	-151	-1.88	-6.31	12.55	70.19	8,030
Central East 華東	1,114	212	15,132	175	1.09	4.45	71.35	75.46	16,000
Shanghai 上海	149	264	30,931	1,105	3.42	15.21	117.33	77.52	32,324
Jiangsu 江蘇	294	218	15,158	56	0.45	1.75	69.63	74.62	12,669
Zhejiang 浙江	192	191	17,683	288	1.69	5.92	92.63	71.35	17,018
Anhui 安徽	101	218	6,858	-609	-8.11	-80.23	31.40	89.89	7,504
Fujian 福建	122	92	5,476	116	1.45	3.24	59.26	55.18	7,973
Jiangxi 江西	69	196	4,271	-484	-6.45	-37.43	21.84	82.77	7,507
Shandong 山東	187	265	14,659	208	1.03	4.81	55.38	78.55	20,145
Central-South 中南	574	194	10,182	-185	-1.24	-5.45	52.60	77.24	14,941
Henan 河南	128	175	3,460	-22	-0.34	-2.01	19.74	82.85	6,329
Hubei 湖北	102	300	13,266	-113	-0.71	-4.35	44.16	83.62	15,907
Hunan 湖南	60	215	2,093	-548	-8.69	62.02	9.73	114.00	6,307
Guangdong 廣東	232	169	15,846	-172	-0.74	-2.63	94.04	71.88	23,199
Guangxi 廣西	49	120	4,522	-376	-5.09	-28.28	37.71	81.99	7,376
Hainan 海南	3	56	8,303	-307	-4.20	-4.27	149.16	1.69	7,307
Southwest 西南	121	149	2,677	-204	-3.13	-14.70	17.96	78.71	6,519
Chongqing 重慶	40	142	1,913	-230	-4.32	-20.96	13.39	79.41	5,337
Sichuan 四川	53	132	2,799	-8	-0.17	-0.54	21.13	68.67	4,756
Guizhou 貴州	11	142	1,520	-638	-7.91	-331.13	10.73	97.61	8,064
Yunnan 雲南	16	225	5,004	-495	-3.45	-19.04	22.26	81.87	14,336
Tibet 西藏									
Northwest 西北	96	216	3,242	-731	-6.60	-247.39	15.03	97.33	11,069
Shaanxi 陝西	50	177	1,656	-391	-9.54	345.66	9.34	102.76	4,093
Gansu 甘肅	20	239	2,722	-1,419	-13.40	318.05	11.38	104.23	10,582
Qinghai 青海	1	392	4,290	-940	-15.82	-78.99	10.94	80.13	5,940
Ningxia 寧夏	4	243	1,470	-2,225	-12.69	41.51	6.05	130.57	17,533
Xinjiang 新疆	21	272	7,801	-591	-2.18	-19.66	28.72	88.92	27,154

1781: Cotton Knitwear 棉針織品業

Year 年份	Number of firms 企業個數	Rate of change 每年變化 (%)	Number of employees 職工人數 (人)	Rate of change 每年變化 (%)	Total revenue (mil. RMB) 總銷售收入 (百萬元)	Rate of change 每年變化 (%)	Total profit (mil. RMB) 總利潤 (百萬元)	Rate of change 每年變化 (%)
1993	2,687		643,505		19,329		-179	
1994	2,733	1.71%	582,080	-9.55%	24,942	29.04%	-54	70.06%
1995	2,502	-8.45%	521,815	-10.35%	25,023	0.32%	-200	-273.26%
1996	2,416	-3.44%	485,751	-6.91%	25,464	1.76%	-164	18.10%

3 Major products* 3 種主要產品 *	Output 產量	Sales volume 銷售量	Unit 單位
a) Knitted Gloves 針織手套	28,602	30,604	10,000 pair 萬付
b) Knitted Dress 針織服裝	79,377	79,377	10,000 piece 萬件

Top 10 firms by revenue (year founded) 收入排名前 10 家企業 (創辦年份)	City 城市	Province 省	Telephone / fax 電話 / 傳真	Number of employees 職工人數	Ownership 產業所有權	Revenue ('000 RMB) 銷售收入 (千元)	Profit ('000 RMB) (rank) 利潤 (千元) (排名)	Total assets ('000 RMB) 總資產 (千元)	Major products 主要產品
Shanghai No.9 Knitting Mill 上海針纖九廠(1958)	Shanghai 上海市	Shanghai 上海市	(021)63737888 (021)63202936	4,259	State-owned 國有	1,191,993	68719(1)	1,000,648	b
Jimo Hair Products Group Co. 即墨市發製品集團公司(1955)	Qingdao 青島市	Shandong 山東省	(0532)8513493 (0532)8514298	1,780	Collectively-owned 集體	388,116	19955(6)	178,672	a,b
Zhejiang Fu Run Spinning and Weaving Group Co. Ltd. 浙江富潤紡织集團有限責任公司(1982)	Shaoxing 紹興市	Zhejiang 浙江省	(0575)7222043 (0575)7223018	5,652	State-owned 國有	314,251	24343(4)	351,452	b
Shanghai Three Gun Knitting Garment Co. Ltd. 上海三槍製衣有限公司(1991)	Shanghai 上海市	Shanghai 上海市	(021)64376281 (021)64338142	1,200	Overseas Chinese-funded 港澳台資	283,861	29573(3)	225,981	b
Jiangsu Fei Yu Group Co. 江蘇飛宇集團公司(1964)	Wuxi 無錫市	Jiangsu 江蘇省	(0510)6621905 (0510)6621030	600	Collectively-owned 集體	282,926	19749(7)	124,124	b
Ningbo Bu Li Jie Knitting Group Co. 寧波布利傑集團公司(1953)	Ningbo 寧波市	Zhejiang 浙江省	(0574)8443501 (0574)8443417	1,770	Collectively-owned 集體	266,291	6198(27)	160,471	b
Zhonghua No.1 Cotton Spinning & Knitting Mill 上海第一棉紡針織廠(1914)	Shanghai 上海市	Shanghai 上海市	(021)65419660 (021)65458528	1,356	State-owned 國有	254,907	10169(14)	254,400	b
Hangzhou Wan Shi Li Knitting Co. Ltd. 杭州萬事利針織有限公司(1995)	Hangzhou 杭州市	Zhejiang 浙江省	(0571)5140666 (0571)5140688	135	Overseas Chinese-funded 港澳台資	254,110	6624(22)	217,719	b
Shanghai Song Xing Textile Co. Ltd. 上海松興紡織品有限公司(1992)	Shanghai 上海市	Shanghai 上海市	(021)57833266 (021)57836653	1,048	Overseas Chinese-funded 港澳台資	241,176	40334(2)	281,470	b
Shanghai Jing Fu Knitting Factory 上海景福針織廠(1937)	Shanghai 上海市	Shanghai 上海市	(021)64372173 (021)64335694	1,793	State-owned 國有	222,677	2036(73)	371,886	b

Top 10 Cities by Production Output 產出排名前 10 位城市	Province 省	Market share 市場份額	Number of firms 企業個數
Shanghai 上海市	Shanghai 上海市	21.55%	228
Dongguan 東莞市	Guangdong 廣東省	7.27%	21
Ningbo 寧波市	Zhejiang 浙江省	5.08%	61
Qingdao 青島市	Shandong 山東省	4.90%	57
Suzhou 蘇州市	Jiangsu 江蘇省	4.53%	103
Wuxi 無錫市	Jiangsu 江蘇省	3.54%	89
Guangzhou 廣州市	Guangdong 廣東省	2.98%	56
Nantong 南通市	Jiangsu 江蘇省	2.97%	113
Shaoxing 紹興市	Zhejiang 浙江省	2.84%	46
Yancheng 鹽城市	Jiangsu 江蘇省.	2.39%	43

10 Major Wholesalers 10 家主要批發商	City 城市	Province 省	Telephone / Fax 電話 / 傳真
Anhui Clothing Import & Export Company 安徽省服裝進出口公司	Hefei 合肥市	Anhui 安徽省	(0551)3632212 (0551)3632002
Qingdao Textile Clothing Industrial Group Company 青島紡織服裝實業集團公司	Qingdao 青島市	Shandong 山東省	(0532)2877853 (0532)2869315
Hebei Textile Import & Export (Group) Company 河北省紡織品進出口(集團)公司	Shijiazhuang 石家莊市	Hebei 河北省	(0311)7028530 (0311)7027781
Zhong Fang Pledget Import & Export Company 中紡紗布進出口公司	Beijing 北京市	Beijing 北京市	(010)65124718 (010)65124713
Shaoxing Import & Export Company 紹興市進出口公司	Shaoxing 紹興市	Zhejiang 浙江省	(0575)5132822 (0575)5141577
Hunan Hua Xiang Import & Export (Group) Company 湖南省華湘進出口(集團)公司	Changsha 長沙市	Hunan 湖南省	(0731)2282440 (0731)2286995
City's Import & Export Company Trade Dept. 市進出口公司貿易部	Yichang 宜昌市	Hubei 湖北省	(0717)6450778 (0717)6441875
Shanghai Pu Dong Xinqu Import & Export Company 上海浦東新區進出口公司	Shanghai 上海市	Shanghai 上海市	(021)58878801 (021)58827444
Ningbo Yinxian Import & Export Company 寧波市鄞縣進出口公司	Ningbo 寧波市	Zhejiang 浙江省	(0574)7875205 (0574)7873168
Zhejiang Silk Import & Export Company 浙江省絲綢進出口公司	Hangzhou 杭州市	Zhejiang 浙江省	(0571)5195588 (0571)5192542

*Also include sales by firms outside this industry.包括本行業以外廠家的銷售。"o" stands for "others". "o" 代表"其他產品"。

1782: Wool Knitwear 毛針織品業

The industry accounts for 0.232% of the total revenue of China's industrial sector in 1996. The revenue growth rate of the industry is 14.2% from 1995, as compared to the growth rate of China's industrial sector, 9.51%. The rate of return on asset is 1.60%. 66.34% of all firms in the industry made a profit while 27.92% had negative returns. The top province in terms of the industry's revenue is Jiangsu, accounting for 19.11% of the total revenue.
本行業在1996年佔全行業總產值0.232%，行業年增長率為14.2%（全國工業年增長率9.51%）。行業的資產回報率1.60%，66.34%的企業盈利，27.92%的企業虧損。銷售收入最高的省份為江蘇省，佔本行業的19.11%。

	Total number of firms 企業總數	Total number of employees 職工總數	Total revenue (mil. RMB) 總銷售收入（百萬元）	Total profit (mil. RMB) 總利潤（百萬元）	Return on assets 資產利潤率 (%)	Return on equity 權益利潤率 (%)	Labour productivity ('000 RMB / worker) 勞動生產率（千元/人）	Debts / assets 資產負債率 (%)	Total assets (mil. RMB) 總資產（百萬元）
Industry Overall 行業總體	1,824	259,843	13,471	253	1.60	5.03	51.84	68.21	15,846

	Number of firms 企業個數	Average number of employees 平均職工人數	Average revenue ('000 RMB) 平均銷售收入（千元）	Average profit ('000 RMB) 平均利潤（千元）	Return on assets 資產利潤率 (%)	Return on equity 權益利潤率 (%)	Labour productivity ('000 RMB / worker) 勞動生產率（千元/人）	Average debts / assets 平均資產負債率(%)	Average Total assets ('000 RMB) 平均總資產（千元）
By ownership 產業所有權									
State-owned 國有	124	234	7,282	-129	-0.85	-7.44	31.17	88.53	15,113
Collectively-owned 集體	1,122	116	4,727	67	1.46	4.97	40.71	70.68	4,632
Privately-owned 私有	9	94	3,535	146	3.16	8.06	37.43	60.75	4,611
Domestic JVs 聯營	30	373	27,212	399	1.19	6.27	73.04	80.98	33,459
Joint stock 股份制	18	97	3,198	95	1.75	4.15	32.99	57.81	5,446
Foreign-funded 外資	175	144	11,207	219	1.99	4.32	78.03	53.88	10,988
Overseas Chinese-funded 港澳台資	343	189	12,782	408	2.46	6.49	67.61	62.12	16,590
By size 規模									
Large 大型	4	2,444	341,996	22,251	3.98	17.03	139.92	76.62	559,015
Medium 中型	31	572	37,815	928	1.36	5.17	66.07	73.75	68,336
Small 小型	1,767	133	6,185	79	1.21	3.52	46.61	65.61	6,496
By regional distribution 地區分布									
Central-North 華北	260	132	6,649	120	1.21	5.94	50.45	79.68	9,945
Beijing 北京	87	169	11,000	124	0.72	4.05	64.90	82.20	17,266
Tianjin 天津	51	117	5,322	16	0.29	1.16	45.52	75.48	5,774
Hebei 河北	44	121	4,760	414	8.86	21.50	39.22	58.78	4,669
Shanxi 山西	3	30	150	10	0.98	8.82	5.06	88.85	1,017
Inner Mongolia 內蒙	75	108	3,873	17	0.22	1.28	35.74	82.65	7,740
Northeast 東北	113	164	2,768	-245	-4.67	-44.97	16.92	89.62	5,253
Liaoning 遼寧	51	143	3,799	-134	-2.57	-10.62	26.52	75.82	5,210
Jilin 吉林	43	139	1,564	-298	-9.41	110.51	11.22	108.51	3,172
Heilongjiang 黑龍江	19	273	2,724	-424	-4.21	-89.74	9.99	95.31	10,074
Central East 華東	934	136	8,239	161	1.94	6.14	60.38	68.37	8,314
Shanghai 上海	180	147	12,547	188	1.68	4.99	85.40	66.25	11,180
Jiangsu 江蘇	233	168	11,047	167	1.72	6.29	65.56	72.57	9,655
Zhejiang 浙江	294	93	5,045	31	0.46	1.51	54.51	69.90	6,817
Anhui 安徽	22	103	3,597	150	5.02	25.96	34.92	80.67	2,989
Fujian 福建	126	186	6,592	264	3.84	8.12	35.43	52.64	6,867
Jiangxi 江西	19	42	811	29	2.87	5.52	19.41	47.90	1,025
Shandong 山東	60	134	7,567	531	5.81	25.67	56.67	77.37	9,139
Central-South 中南	406	148	7,017	210	2.86	5.45	47.30	47.57	7,339
Henan 河南	29	131	3,483	11	0.26	0.56	26.56	53.19	4,239
Hubei 湖北	12	218	21,038	3,566	8.45	17.61	96.47	52.06	42,223
Hunan 湖南	11	153	1,729	-196	-8.59	-17.01	11.31	49.50	2,286
Guangdong 廣東	342	149	7,204	131	1.98	3.67	48.42	45.95	6,605
Guangxi 廣西	10	92	863	-53	-1.58	-4.61	9.38	65.73	3,353
Hainan 海南	2	159	1,970	-15	-0.09	-0.18	12.39	48.70	16,160
Southwest 西南	21	206	1,263	-644	-6.49	164.00	6.14	103.95	9,933
Chongqing 重慶	6	180	1,043	-234	-4.53	-18.51	5.76	75.55	5,174
Sichuan 四川	6	106	468	-404	-8.36	-36.88	4.41	77.33	4,838
Guizhou 貴州	4	356	1,650	-725	-2.75	37.42	4.63	107.35	26,320
Yunnan 雲南	2	304	3,410	-1,910	-15.88	41.03	11.22	138.71	12,025
Tibet 西藏	2	226	1,765	-1,290	-17.99	39.88	7.81	145.12	7,170
Northwest 西北	90	168	9,545	304	1.60	6.21	56.82	74.30	19,036
Shaanxi 陝西	11	59	526	-107	-4.18	287.80	8.91	101.45	2,567
Gansu 甘肅	27	150	1,716	-54	-1.04	-5.55	11.45	81.31	5,209
Qinghai 青海	12	128	3,590	256	2.91	14.77	28.08	80.31	8,801
Ningxia 寧夏	3	84	1,603	-117	-1.77	-7.95	19.16	77.81	6,610
Xinjiang 新疆	37	233	20,516	737	1.92	7.01	87.88	72.57	38,350

1782: Wool Knitwear 毛針織品業

Year 年份	Number of firms 企業個數	Rate of change 每年變化 (%)	Number of employees 職工人數 (人)	Rate of change 每年變化 (%)	Total revenue (mil. RMB) 總銷售收入 (百萬元)	Rate of change 每年變化 (%)	Total profit (mil. RMB) 總利潤 (百萬元)	Rate of change 每年變化 (%)
1993	1,737		355,785		8,485		297	
1994	1,799	3.57%	296,806	-16.58%	10,764	26.86%	249	-16.15%
1995	1,970	9.51%	285,228	-3.90%	11,800	9.62%	142	-42.91%
1996	1,824	-7.41%	259,843	-8.90%	13,471	14.16%	253	78.11%

3 Major products* 3 種主要產品 *	Output 產量	Sales volume 銷售量	Unit 單位
a) Knitted Dress 針織服裝	307,652	307,652	10,000 piece 萬件
b) Pure Wool Floss For Embroidery 純毛絨線	7,309	6,505	ton 噸
c) Kniting Floss For Embroidery 針織絨線	13,263	12,069	ton 噸

Top 10 firms by revenue (year founded) 收入排名前 10 家企業 (創辦年份)	City 城市	Province 省	Telephone / fax 電話 / 傳真	Number of employees 職工人數	Ownership 產業所有權	Revenue ('000 RMB) 銷售收入 (千元)	Profit ('000 RMB) (rank) 利潤 (千元) (排名)	Total assets ('000 RMB) 總資產 (千元)	Major products 主要產品
Xinjiang Tianshan Wool Textile Co. Ltd. 新疆天山毛紡織股份有限公司(1981)	Urumqi 烏魯木齊市	Xinjiang 新疆	(0991)4841866 (0991)4840472	2,810	Overseas Chinese-funded 港澳台資	601,998	45812(1)	914,322	a,b,c
Beijing San Huan Wool Spinning & Knitting Group 北京市三環毛紡針織集團公司(1958)	Beijing 北京市	Beijing 北京市	(010)64014488 (010)64011074	5,715	Domestic JVs 聯營	447,894	11326(6)	673,845	a,b,c
Shanghai Fumin Wool Spinning & Knitting Development Company 上海富民毛紡針織發展公司(1994)	Shanghai 上海市	Shanghai 上海市	(021)59820295	1,394	Collectively-owned 集體	408,940	12678(5)	61,035	a
Chinese-foreign Joint Venture Jiangsu Hong Da Decoration Rong Co. Ltd. 中外合資江蘇宏大裝飾絨有限公司(1992)	Yancheng 鹽城市	Jiangsu 江蘇省	(0515)8593597 (0515)8593637	1,301	Foreign-funded 外資	344,750	22010(3)	227,020	a
Yunfu Group Co. 江蘇雲蝠集團公司(1978)	Wuxi 無錫市	Jiangsu 江蘇省	(0510)6321999 (0510)6321600	1,639	Collectively-owned 集體	331,588	9372(9)	127,092	a
Shanghai Fa Qi Wool Spinning & Knitting Factory 上海發啟毛紡針織廠(1996)	Shanghai 上海市	Shanghai 上海市	(021)57852479 (021)57854703	285	Collectively-owned 集體	213,142	942(104)	95,963	a
Beijing Xue Lian Cashmere Co. Ltd. 北京雪蓮羊絨有限公司(1988)	Beijing 北京市	Beijing 北京市	(010)64664443 (010)64668812	1,310	Overseas Chinese-funded 港澳台資	200,609	9386(8)	339,373	a,b,c
Shanghai Sungung Plush Co. Ltd. 上海申光毛絨實業有限公司(1989)	Shanghai 上海市	Shanghai 上海市	(021)58593993 (021)58593993	980	Overseas Chinese-funded 港澳台資	192,186	8002(10)	199,681	o
Wendeng Rui Yi Clothing Co. Ltd. 文登市瑞一服裝有限公司(1993)	Weihai 威海市	Shandong 山東省	(0896)8861269 (0896)8861268	260	Foreign-funded 外資	179,660	24800(2)	45,780	a
Shandou Shengping Zhong Xing Industrial Company 汕頭市升平區中興工業公司(1963)	Shantou 汕頭市	Guangdong 廣東省	(0754)8273162	2,125	Collectively-owned 集體	176,616	2484(41)	67,866	a

Top 10 Cities by Production Output 產出排名前 10 位城市	Province 省	Market share 市場份額	Number of firms 企業個數
Shanghai 上海市	Shanghai 上海市	16.25%	252
Suzhou 蘇州市	Jiangsu 江蘇省	11.27%	127
Beijing 北京市	Beijing 北京市	7.57%	72
Wuxi 無錫市	Jiangsu 江蘇省	4.01%	42
Jiaxing 嘉興市	Zhejiang 浙江省	3.76%	120
Shantou 汕頭市	Guangdong 廣東省	3.71%	65
Tianjin 天津市	Tianjin 天津市	3.42%	59
Nantong 南通市	Jiangsu 江蘇省	2.83%	104
Huizhou 惠州市	Guangdong 廣東省	2.66%	57
Quanzhou 泉州市	Fujian 福建省	2.63%	91

10 Major Wholesalers 10 家主要批發商	City 城市	Province 省	Telephone / Fax 電話 / 傳真
Anhui Clothing Import & Export Company 安徽省服裝進出口公司	Hefei 合肥市	Anhui 安徽省	(0551)3632212 (0551)3632002
Qingdao Textile Clothing Industrial Group Company 青島紡織服裝實業集團公司	Qingdao 青島市	Shandong 山東省	(0532)2877853 (0532)2869315
Hebei Textile Import & Export (Group) Company 河北省紡織品進出口(集團)公司	Shijiazhuang 石家莊市	Hebei 河北省	(0311)7028530 (0311)7027781
Zhong Fang Pledget Import & Export Company 中紡紗布進出口公司	Beijing 北京市	Beijing 北京市	(010)65124718 (010)65124713
Shaoxing Import & Export Company 紹興市進出口公司	Shaoxing 紹興市	Zhejiang 浙江省	(0575)5132822 (0575)5141577
Hunan Hua Xiang Import & Export (Group) Company 湖南省華湘進出口(集團)公司	Changsha 長沙市	Hunan 湖南省	(0731)2282440 (0731)2286995
City's Import & Export Company Trade Dept. 市進出口公司貿易部	Yichang 宜昌市	Hubei 湖北省	(0717)6450778 (0717)6441875
Shanghai Pu Dong Xinqu Import & Export Company 上海浦東新區進出口公司	Shanghai 上海市	Shanghai 上海市	(021)58878801 (021)58827444
Ningbo Yinxian Import & Export Company 寧波市鄞縣進出口公司	Ningbo 寧波市	Zhejiang 浙江省	(0574)7875205 (0574)7873168
Zhejiang Silk Import & Export Company 浙江省絲綢進出口公司	Hangzhou 杭州市	Zhejiang 浙江省	(0571)5195588 (0571)5192542

*Also include sales by firms outside this industry.包括本行業以外廠家的銷售。"o" stands for "others". "o" 代表"其他產品"。

1783: Silk Knitwear 絲針織品業

The industry accounts for 0.064% of the total revenue of China's industrial sector in 1996. The revenue growth rate of the industry is -19.3% from 1995, as compared to the growth rate of China's industrial sector, 9.51%. The rate of return on asset is -1.20%. 60.64% of all firms in the industry made a profit while 34.69% had negative returns. The top province in terms of the industry's revenue is Zhejiang, accounting for 31.36% of the total revenue.
本行業在1996年佔全行業總產值0.064%，行業年增長率為-19.3%（全國工業年增長率9.51%）。行業的資產回報率-1.20%，60.64%的企業盈利，34.69%的企業虧損。銷售收入最高的省份為浙江省，佔本行業的31.36%。

	Total number of firms 企業總數	Total number of employees 職工總數	Total revenue (mil. RMB) 總銷售收入（百萬元）	Total profit (mil. RMB) 總利潤（百萬元）	Return on assets 資產利潤率 (%)	Return on equity 權益利潤率 (%)	Labour productivity ('000 RMB / worker) 勞動生產率（千元/人）	Debts / assets 資產負債率 (%)	Total assets (mil. RMB) 總資產（百萬元）
Industry Overall 行業總體	428	77,632	3,721	-82	-1.20	-4.86	47.93	75.28	6,791

	Number of firms 企業個數	Average number of employees 平均職工人數	Average revenue ('000 RMB) 平均銷售收入（千元）	Average profit ('000 RMB) 平均利潤（千元）	Return on assets 資產利潤率 (%)	Return on equity 權益利潤率 (%)	Labour productivity ('000 RMB / worker) 勞動生產率（千元/人）	Average debts / assets 平均資產負債率(%)	Average Total assets ('000 RMB) 平均總資產（千元）
By ownership 產業所有權									
State-owned 國有	69	486	12,029	-1,478	-4.44	-87.93	24.77	94.95	33,319
Collectively-owned 集體	250	116	4,500	-14	-0.19	-1.42	38.89	86.72	7,237
Privately-owned 私有	1	54	4,149	115	4.91	7.76	76.83	36.66	2,334
Domestic JVs 聯營	3	294	7,357	-157	-0.89	-9.14	25.05	90.26	17,632
Joint stock 股份制	4	315	11,666	144	1.47	3.21	37.01	54.19	9,818
Foreign-funded 外資	42	177	29,716	555	1.63	2.85	167.55	42.84	34,077
Overseas Chinese-funded 港澳台資	59	100	7,542	-2	-0.01	-0.03	75.21	58.52	19,613
By size 規模									
Large 大型	10	987	62,943	-3,116	-2.24	-15.90	63.79	85.91	139,112
Medium 中型	35	545	16,475	-2,037	-4.25	-44.47	30.23	90.43	47,886
Small 小型	380	127	6,618	54	0.55	1.55	52.13	64.48	9,800
By regional distribution 地區分布									
Central-North 華北	47	197	4,633	-286	-1.86	-13.40	23.55	86.10	15,367
Beijing 北京	4	79	6,648	-73	-0.73	-4.70	83.88	84.45	9,923
Tianjin 天津	16	158	4,494	-284	-2.44	-12.03	28.52	79.71	11,653
Hebei 河北	17	333	6,379	-526	-1.89	-17.80	19.13	89.41	27,895
Shanxi 山西	6	44	1,050	7	0.26	1.58	23.95	83.86	2,613
Inner Mongolia 內蒙	4	119	1,125	70	4.50	7.63	9.47	41.00	1,555
Northeast 東北	46	257	3,377	-619	-4.21	-163.38	13.16	97.42	14,692
Liaoning 遼寧	30	227	2,828	-486	-3.89	-108.65	12.47	96.42	12,472
Jilin 吉林	9	425	2,563	-152	-1.07	-16.41	6.03	93.49	14,261
Heilongjiang 黑龍江	7	169	6,777	-1,789	-7.22	288.48	40.14	102.50	24,764
Central East 華東	208	162	10,942	85	0.53	1.55	67.40	65.91	16,185
Shanghai 上海	20	392	16,713	-1,507	-4.18	-28.20	42.61	85.17	36,011
Jiangsu 江蘇	43	148	7,680	-13	-0.12	-0.43	51.72	71.38	10,092
Zhejiang 浙江	93	131	12,546	492	3.03	8.56	95.78	64.56	16,213
Anhui 安徽	10	137	1,662	-329	-5.21	498.48	12.15	101.05	6,312
Fujian 福建	18	49	4,559	91	1.40	2.30	93.46	38.99	6,490
Jiangxi 江西	5	49	1,404	-100	-3.08	-28.25	28.77	89.08	3,242
Shandong 山東	19	256	17,835	256	0.96	1.57	69.65	39.08	26,763
Central-South 中南	87	188	11,805	-576	-2.69	-12.69	62.63	78.80	21,395
Henan 河南	12	193	2,095	-273	-3.48	-16.69	10.84	79.14	7,850
Hubei 湖北	22	182	2,160	-128	-1.65	-7.39	11.86	77.69	7,776
Hunan 湖南	9	268	1,844	-576	-9.27	24.12	6.89	138.43	6,208
Guangdong 廣東	38	182	24,150	-603	-1.61	-6.63	132.40	75.67	37,339
Guangxi 廣西	6	122	3,340	-2,652	-13.12	-121.64	27.45	89.22	20,215
Hainan 海南									
Southwest 西南	28	182	1,224	-228	-4.85	-54.35	6.71	91.09	4,695
Chongqing 重慶	4	111	633	-174	-6.85	-19.37	5.69	64.63	2,538
Sichuan 四川	18	197	1,042	-339	-8.96	73.72	5.26	112.15	3,786
Guizhou 貴州	3	253	2,600	20	0.14	0.52	10.26	72.09	13,890
Yunnan 雲南	1	186	3,180	130	1.95	5.86	17.10	66.77	6,650
Tibet 西藏	1	14	1,300	460	23.00	23.00	92.86		2,000
Northwest 西北	12	109	906	-78	-2.77	-13.17	8.30	78.99	2,828
Shaanxi 陝西	5	125	900	-188	-6.62	-22.71	7.22	70.85	2,840
Gansu 甘肅	3	19	163	10	1.76	8.57	8.75	79.41	567
Qinghai 青海	1	317	4,260	80	1.38	3.81	13.44	63.86	5,810
Ningxia 寧夏	1	218	1,260	-100	-1.22	-5.08	5.78	76.03	8,220
Xinjiang 新疆	2	48	180	-5	-0.25	0.70	3.79	135.75	2,000

Year 年份	Number of firms 企業個數	Rate of change 每年變化 (%)	Number of employees 職工人數 (人)	Rate of change 每年變化 (%)	Total revenue (mil. RMB) 總銷售收入 (百萬元)	Rate of change 每年變化 (%)	Total profit (mil. RMB) 總利潤 (百萬元)	Rate of change 每年變化 (%)
1993	409		110,141		2,802		-37	
1994	428	4.65%	105,003	-4.67%	3,045	8.67%	-53	-42.22%
1995	486	13.55%	106,624	1.54%	4,609	51.35%	-50	6.60%
1996	428	-11.93%	77,632	-27.19%	3,721	-19.27%	-82	-65.58%

3 Major products* 3 種主要產品 *	Output 產量	Sales volume 銷售量	Unit 單位
a) Hosiery 襪子	54,672	47,018	10,000 pair 萬雙
b) Synthetic Filament Fabric 合纖長絲機織物	1,201	1,177	ton 噸

Top 10 firms by revenue (year founded) 收入排名前 10 家企業 (創辦年份)	City 城市	Province 省	Telephone / fax 電話 / 傳真	Number of employees 職工人數	Ownership 產業所有權	Revenue ('000 RMB) 銷售收入 (千元)	Profit ('000 RMB) (rank) 利潤 (千元) (排名)	Total assets ('000 RMB) 總資產 (千元)	Major products 主要產品
Shunde De Run Textile Industrial Co. 順德市德潤紡織實業公司(1953)	Foshan 佛山市	Guangdong 廣東省	(0757)8869333 (0757)8861482	1,887	State-owned 國有	459,744	2457(11)	418,375	o
Qingdao Nan Nan Nylon Co. Ltd. 青島南南尼龍有限公司(1993)	Qingdao 青島市	Shandong 山東省	(0532)4817651 (0532)4817654	1,610	Foreign-funded 外資	176,598	13487(2)	92,407	a
Shanghai Huazhong Socks Co. Ltd. 上海華鐘襪子有限公司(1988)	Shanghai 上海市	Shanghai 上海市	(021)65395448 (021)65455754	424	Foreign-funded 外資	113,661	12448(3)	88,101	a
Shaoxing Hong Da Knitting Factory 紹興宏大針織廠(1984)	Shaoxing 紹興市	Zhejiang 浙江省	(0575)4069979 (0575)4069158	192	Collectively-owned 集體	100,859	5088(6)	260,741	b
Xinhui Hong Da Decorative Fabrics Co. Ltd. 新會宏達裝飾織物有限公司(1994)	Jiangmen 江門市	Guangdong 廣東省	(0750)6678678 (0750)6672243	412	Overseas Chinese-funded 港澳台資	98,313	5129(5)	204,611	o
Linhai Wei Cheng Bleaching & Dyeing (Tai Zhou) Co. Ltd. 臨海市偉程漂染(台州)有限公司(1993)	Taizhou 臺州市	Zhejiang 浙江省	(0576)5222848 (0576)5222748	208	Overseas Chinese-funded 港澳台資	81,781	2147(14)	71,481	o
Shanghai Vocal Knitting Co. Ltd. 上海華高針織有限公司(1987)	Shanghai 上海市	Shanghai 上海市	(021)64625600 (021)64301316	500	Foreign-funded 外資	75,728	-18454(214)	222,980	a
Shanghai Hua Yuan Co. Ltd. Xi Shan Weaving Branch 上海華源股份有限公司錫山織造分公司(1992)	Wuxi 無錫市	Jiangsu 江蘇省	(0510)3761632	376	Joint stock 股份制	74,800	5533(4)	61,077	o
Zhongshan Fu Wei Socks Industry Co. Ltd. 中山市富威襪業有限公司(1991)	Zhongshan 中山市	Guangdong 廣東省	(0760)8807693 (0760)8807931	616	Overseas Chinese-funded 港澳台資	73,040	-3980(205)	135,408	a
Zhejiang Hong Da Warp Knitting Industrial Company 浙江宏達經編實業公司(1985)	Jiaxing 嘉興市	Zhejiang 浙江省	(0573)7567888 (0573)7566616	188	Collectively-owned 集體	70,229	3032(9)	63,243	o

Top 10 Cities by Production Output 產出排名前 10 位城市	Province 省	Market share 市場份額	Number of firms 企業個數
Foshan 佛山市	Guangdong 廣東省	12.74%	1
Shanghai 上海市	Shanghai 上海市	10.69%	34
Suzhou 蘇州市	Jiangsu 江蘇省	10.19%	35
Jiaxing 嘉興市	Zhejiang 浙江省	9.83%	29
Shaoxing 紹興市	Zhejiang 浙江省	8.58%	33
Wenzhou 溫州市	Zhejiang 浙江省	4.41%	70
Jiangmen 江門市	Guangdong 廣東省	4.31%	6
Zhongshan 中山市	Guangdong 廣東省	2.61%	4
Taiyuan 太原市	Shanxi 山西省	2.59%	3
Hangzhou 杭州市	Zhejiang 浙江省	2.39%	13

10 Major Wholesalers 10 家主要批發商	City 城市	Province 省	Telephone / Fax 電話 / 傳真
Anhui Clothing Import & Export Company 安徽省服裝進出口公司	Hefei 合肥市	Anhui 安徽省	(0551)3632212 (0551)3632002
Qingdao Textile Clothing Industrial Group Company 青島紡織服裝實業集團公司	Qingdao 青島市	Shandong 山東省	(0532)2877853 (0532)2869315
Hebei Textile Import & Export (Group) Company 河北省紡織品進出口(集團)公司	Shijiazhuang 石家莊市	Hebei 河北省	(0311)7028530 (0311)7027781
Zhong Fang Pledget Import & Export Company 中紡紗布進出口公司	Beijing 北京市	Beijing 北京市	(010)65124718 (010)65124713
Shaoxing Import & Export Company 紹興市進出口公司	Shaoxing 紹興市	Zhejiang 浙江省	(0575)5132822 (0575)5141577
Hunan Hua Xiang Import & Export (Group) Company 湖南省華湘進出口(集團)公司	Changsha 長沙市	Hunan 湖南省	(0731)2282440 (0731)2286995
City's Import & Export Company Trade Dept. 市進出口公司貿易部	Yichang 宜昌市	Hubei 湖北省	(0717)6450778 (0717)6441875
Shanghai Pu Dong Xinqu Import & Export Company 上海浦東新區進出口公司	Shanghai 上海市	Shanghai 上海市	(021)58878801 (021)58827444
Ningbo Yinxian Import & Export Company 寧波市鄞縣進出口公司	Ningbo 寧波市	Zhejiang 浙江省	(0574)7875205 (0574)7873168
Zhejiang Silk Import & Export Company 浙江省絲綢進出口公司	Hangzhou 杭州市	Zhejiang 浙江省	(0571)5195588 (0571)5192542

*Also include sales by firms outside this industry.包括本行業以外廠家的銷售。"o" stands for "others". "o" 代表"其他產品"。

1789: Other Knitwear 其他針織業

The industry accounts for 0.079% of the total revenue of China's industrial sector in 1996. The revenue growth rate of the industry is 28.3% from 1995, as compared to the growth rate of China's industrial sector, 9.51%. The rate of return on asset is -0.08%. 65.85% of all firms in the industry made a profit while 29.02% had negative returns. The top province in terms of the industry's revenue is Jiangsu, accounting for 30.11% of the total revenue.
本行業在1996年佔全行業總產值0.079%，行業年增長率為28.3%（全國工業年增長率9.51%）。行業的資產回報率-0.08%，65.85%的企業盈利，29.02%的企業虧損。銷售收入最高的省份為江蘇省，佔本行業的30.11%。

	Total number of firms 企業總數	Total number of employees 職工總數	Total revenue (mil. RMB) 總銷售收入（百萬元）	Total profit (mil. RMB) 總利潤（百萬元）	Return on assets 資產利潤率 (%)	Return on equity 權益利潤率 (%)	Labour productivity ('000 RMB / worker) 勞動生產率（千元/人）	Debts / assets 資產負債率 (%)	Total assets (mil. RMB) 總資產（百萬元）
Industry Overall 行業總體	649	84,550	4,554	-5	-0.08	-0.29	53.86	71.30	6,118

	Number of firms 企業個數	Average number of employees 平均職工人數	Average revenue ('000 RMB) 平均銷售收入（千元）	Average profit ('000 RMB) 平均利潤（千元）	Return on assets 資產利潤率 (%)	Return on equity 權益利潤率 (%)	Labour productivity ('000 RMB / worker) 勞動生產率（千元/人）	Average debts / assets 平均資產負債率(%)	Average Total assets ('000 RMB) 平均總資產（千元）
By ownership 產業所有權									
State-owned 國有	76	348	9,211	-632	-2.84	-15.64	26.46	81.86	22,263
Collectively-owned 集體	410	93	5,009	165	3.68	17.66	53.58	79.19	4,503
Privately-owned 私有	2	55	909	-218	-44.46	-269.64	16.68	83.51	491
Domestic JVs 聯營	5	478	32,445	-11,263	-26.40	894.16	67.82	102.95	42,663
Joint stock 股份制	2	1,746	65,815	15,662	7.98	34.69	37.70	77.00	196,285
Foreign-funded 外資	35	94	9,876	-751	-7.22	-12.05	105.10	40.12	10,402
Overseas Chinese-funded 港澳台資	119	98	9,737	226	1.67	3.52	99.76	52.59	13,520
By size 規模									
Large 大型	4	1,890	83,989	-264	-0.13	-0.97	44.43	86.40	199,307
Medium 中型	26	636	31,913	-124	-0.23	-1.05	50.14	78.42	54,575
Small 小型	614	100	5,519	-1	-0.02	-0.05	55.38	65.62	6,355
By regional distribution 地區分布									
Central-North 華北	75	154	4,855	-187	-1.71	-8.24	31.46	79.30	10,986
Beijing 北京	4	30	2,833	60	6.08	48.98	96.02	87.59	988
Tianjin 天津	15	27	2,237	19	0.69	1.86	81.43	62.95	2,713
Hebei 河北	28	270	7,472	-658	-3.18	-46.79	27.69	93.20	20,666
Shanxi 山西	9	339	11,391	437	2.08	3.43	33.57	39.26	20,950
Inner Mongolia 內蒙	19	23	396	-5	-0.83	-9.01	17.25	90.74	636
Northeast 東北	75	163	2,488	-152	-2.17	-28.96	15.23	92.52	7,014
Liaoning 遼寧	54	136	2,572		-0.01	-0.04	18.86	85.52	6,093
Jilin 吉林	10	337	2,494	-827	-7.98	62.75	7.41	112.71	10,364
Heilongjiang 黑龍江	11	138	2,067	-282	-3.32	-63.79	14.98	94.80	8,495
Central East 華東	323	142	8,750	59	0.62	1.77	61.71	65.15	9,521
Shanghai 上海	33	63	5,619	139	2.19	5.80	88.81	62.24	6,363
Jiangsu 江蘇	92	148	14,904	-26	-0.20	-0.52	100.58	61.81	12,923
Zhejiang 浙江	62	98	5,910	-50	-0.60	-1.85	60.29	67.68	8,405
Anhui 安徽	21	203	3,072	-793	-12.25	-2975.00	15.11	99.59	6,477
Fujian 福建	66	81	5,313	80	1.13	2.49	65.34	54.63	7,072
Jiangxi 江西	10	38	774	-77	-9.91	-28.00	20.48	64.61	777
Shandong 山東	39	359	12,319	821	5.88	20.65	34.35	71.54	13,968
Central-South 中南	134	92	8,599	50	0.43	1.55	93.87	72.19	11,715
Henan 河南	29	89	2,788	53	1.35	4.21	31.25	67.95	3,907
Hubei 湖北	14	202	33,423	1,661	8.87	81.44	165.87	89.11	18,740
Hunan 湖南	10	105	1,396	-216	-10.07	-62.61	13.36	83.87	2,145
Guangdong 廣東	66	82	8,374	-209	-1.25	-3.78	102.61	67.05	16,770
Guangxi 廣西	13	17	587	-140	-4.03	-63.19	34.37	93.63	3,477
Hainan 海南	2	108	14,650	-130	-1.25	-44.07	136.28	97.11	10,365
Southwest 西南	16	93	798	-318	-5.95	-15.38	8.59	61.33	5,348
Chongqing 重慶	4	50	328	-285	-20.35	287.42	6.53	107.08	1,402
Sichuan 四川	6	112	1,133	-538	-5.25	-10.27	10.04	48.88	10,260
Guizhou 貴州	4	130	1,060	-100	-2.50	-26.14	8.15	90.44	4,003
Yunnan 雲南	1	30							
Tibet 西藏									
Northwest 西北	26	45	469	-12	-0.83	-6.38	10.49	87.11	1,445
Shaanxi 陝西	6	88	633	125	13.11	-65.79	7.22	120.10	953
Gansu 甘肅	8	30	296	4	1.18	4.35	9.88	72.94	319
Qinghai 青海	3	20	507	-47	-6.83	175.00	24.92	103.90	683
Ningxia 寧夏	2	41	1,070	-245	-3.79	-350.00	26.10	98.99	6,460
Xinjiang 新疆	7	36	337	-66	-3.21	-8.76	9.33	63.34	2,046

1789: Other Knitwear 其他針織業

Year 年份	Number of firms 企業個數	Rate of change 每年變化 (%)	Number of employees 職工人數 (人)	Rate of change 每年變化 (%)	Total revenue (mil. RMB) 總銷售收入 (百萬元)	Rate of change 每年變化 (%)	Total profit (mil. RMB) 總利潤 (百萬元)	Rate of change 每年變化 (%)
1993	704		81,706		3,396		-3	
1994	695	-1.28%	84,640	3.59%	4,185	23.25%	61	2252.03%
1995	674	-3.02%	85,975	1.58%	3,549	-15.20%	-28	-145.61%
1996	649	-3.71%	84,550	-1.66%	4,554	28.32%	-5	82.15%

3 Major products* 3 種主要產品 *	Output 產量	Sales volume 銷售量	Unit 單位
a) Knitted Gloves 針織手套	29,479	31,542	10,000 pair 萬付
b) Hosiery 襪子	19,783	17,014	10,000 pair 萬雙
c) Knitted Dress 針織服裝	3,375	3,375	10,000 piece 萬件

Top 10 firms by revenue (year founded) 收入排名前 10 家企業 (創辦年份)	City 城市	Province 省	Telephone / fax 電話 / 傳真	Number of employees 職工人數	Ownership 產業所有權	Revenue ('000 RMB) 銷售收入 (千元)	Profit ('000 RMB) (rank) 利潤 (千元) (排名)	Total assets ('000 RMB) 總資產 (千元)	Major products 主要產品
Shandong Yishui Spinning and Weaving Factory 山東省沂水紡織廠(1988)	Linyi 臨沂市	Shandong 山東省	(0539)2251220 (0539)2251220	1,500	State-owned 國有	149,704	5097(7)	114,554	o
Zeng Yi Weaving Co. Ltd. 增益織造有限公司(1989)	Guangzhou 廣州市	Guangdong 廣東省	(020)82755882	142	Foreign-funded 外資	149,523	-5766(269)	543,984	o
Shanghai Shen Da Industry & Trade Company 上海申大工貿公司(1993)	Shanghai 上海市	Shanghai 上海市	(021)57642928 (021)57642928	80	Domestic JVs 聯營	147,181	6610(6)	25,668	o
Nantong Dong Sheng Plush Products Co. Ltd. 南通東升長毛絨製品有限公司(1992)	Nantong 南通市	Jiangsu 江蘇省	(0513)4522113 (0513)4523217	239	Overseas Chinese-funded 港澳台資	139,881	12011(1)	96,939	o
Suzhou Da Hua Artistic Blanket Co. Ltd. 蘇州大華工藝毯有限公司(1992)	Suzhou 蘇州市	Jiangsu 江蘇省	(0512)3528010 (0512)3528199	130	Collectively-owned 集體	125,000	8000(4)	11,890	o
Zhucheng Clothing Knitting Co. Ltd. 諸城市服裝針織股份有限公司(1956)	Weifang 濰坊市	Shandong 山東省	(0536)6212934 (0536)6212934	1,243	Joint stock 股份制	121,280	10397(2)	146,767	c
Jiangsu Jin Ji Group Co. 江蘇金雞集團公司(1993)	Suzhou 蘇州市	Jiangsu 江蘇省	(0512)2391412	1,266	Collectively-owned 集體	96,742	2331(17)	136,004	b,c
Xiong Ying Knitgoods Printing & Dyeing Co. Ltd. 雄鷹針織品印染有限公司(1995)	Suzhou 蘇州市	Jiangsu 江蘇省	(0512)2521988	292	Foreign-funded 外資	93,392	3214(10)	68,588	o
Nan'an Nan Tai Fashionable Dress Knitting Co. Ltd. 南安南泰時裝針織有限公司(1993)	Quanzhou 泉州市	Fujian 福建省	(0595)6908600 (0595)6908601	332	Overseas Chinese-funded 港澳台資	66,063	6820(5)	17,445	c
Hai Men Tian Ma Textile Ornament Co. Ltd. 海門市天馬紡織裝飾品有限責任公司(1995)	Nantong 南通市	Jiangsu 江蘇省	(0513)2282023	13	Collectively-owned 集體	55,639	253(87)	2,675	o

Top 10 Cities by Production Output 產出排名前 10 位城市	Province 省	Market share 市場份額	Number of firms 企業個數
Quanzhou 泉州市	Fujian 福建省	67.43%	41
Shanghai 上海市	Shanghai 上海市	2.97%	55
Jiaxing 嘉興市	Zhejiang 浙江省	2.74%	26
Suzhou 蘇州市	Jiangsu 江蘇省	2.64%	37
Guangzhou 廣州市	Guangdong 廣東省	2.14%	14
Nantong 南通市	Jiangsu 江蘇省	1.90%	23
Linyi 臨沂市	Shandong 山東省	1.71%	2
Yancheng 鹽城市	Jiangsu 江蘇省	1.05%	2
Ningbo 寧波市	Zhejiang 浙江省	0.91%	14
Zhuhai 珠海市	Guangdong 廣東省	0.73%	4

10 Major Wholesalers 10 家主要批發商	City 城市	Province 省	Telephone / Fax 電話 / 傳真
Anhui Clothing Import & Export Company 安徽省服裝進出口公司	Hefei 合肥市	Anhui 安徽省	(0551)3632212 (0551)3632002
Qingdao Textile Clothing Industrial Group Company 青島紡織服裝實業集團公司	Qingdao 青島市	Shandong 山東省	(0532)2877853 (0532)2869315
Hebei Textile Import & Export (Group) Company 河北省紡織品進出口(集團)公司	Shijiazhuang 石家莊市	Hebei 河北省	(0311)7028530 (0311)7027781
Zhong Fang Pledget Import & Export Company 中紡紗布進出口公司	Beijing 北京市	Beijing 北京市	(010)65124718 (010)65124713
Shaoxing Import & Export Company 紹興市進出口公司	Shaoxing 紹興市	Zhejiang 浙江省	(0575)5132822 (0575)5141577
Hunan Hua Xiang Import & Export (Group) Company 湖南省華湘進出口(集團)公司	Changsha 長沙市	Hunan 湖南省	(0731)2282440 (0731)2286995
City's Import & Export Company Trade Dept. 市進出口公司貿易部	Yichang 宜昌市	Hubei 湖北省	(0717)6450778 (0717)6441875
Shanghai Pu Dong Xinqu Import & Export Company 上海浦東新區進出口公司	Shanghai 上海市	Shanghai 上海市	(021)58878801 (021)58827444
Ningbo Yinxian Import & Export Company 寧波市鄞縣進出口公司	Ningbo 寧波市	Zhejiang 浙江省	(0574)7875205 (0574)7873168
Zhejiang Silk Import & Export Company 浙江省絲綢進出口公司	Hangzhou 杭州市	Zhejiang 浙江省	(0571)5195588 (0571)5192542

*Also include sales by firms outside this industry.包括本行業以外廠家的銷售。"o" stands for "others". "o" 代表 "其他產品" 。

1790: Other Textiles 其他紡織業

The industry accounts for 0.173% of the total revenue of China's industrial sector in 1996. The revenue growth rate of the industry is 21.8% from 1995, as compared to the growth rate of China's industrial sector, 9.51%. The rate of return on asset is 0.77%. 64.84% of all firms in the industry made a profit while 28.34% had negative returns. The top province in terms of the industry's revenue is Jiangsu, accounting for 31.11% of the total revenue.
本行業在1996年佔全行業總產值0.173%，行業年增長率為21.8%（全國工業年增長率9.51%）。行業的資產回報率0.77%，64.84%的企業盈利，28.34%的企業虧損。銷售收入最高的省份為江蘇省，佔本行業的31.11%。

	Total number of firms 企業總數	Total number of employees 職工總數	Total revenue (mil. RMB) 總銷售收入（百萬元）	Total profit (mil. RMB) 總利潤（百萬元）	Return on assets 資產利潤率 (%)	Return on equity 權益利潤率 (%)	Labour productivity ('000 RMB / worker) 勞動生產率（千元/人）	Debts / assets 資產負債率 (%)	Total assets (mil. RMB) 總資產（百萬元）
Industry Overall 行業總體	1,078	115,877	10,013	120	0.77	2.49	86.41	68.94	15,498

	Number of firms 企業個數	Average number of employees 平均職工人數	Average revenue ('000 RMB) 平均銷售收入（千元）	Average profit ('000 RMB) 平均利潤（千元）	Return on assets 資產利潤率 (%)	Return on equity 權益利潤率 (%)	Labour productivity ('000 RMB / worker) 勞動生產率（千元/人）	Average debts / assets 平均資產負債率(%)	Average Total assets ('000 RMB) 平均總資產（千元）
By ownership 產業所有權									
State-owned 國有	91	308	15,242	-659	-1.54	-15.15	49.43	89.84	42,846
Collectively-owned 集體	687	92	7,726	184	2.36	10.15	83.76	76.77	7,811
Privately-owned 私有	4	23	785	-76	-7.51	-93.06	34.91	91.93	1,018
Domestic JVs 聯營	18	69	6,965	-219	-2.89	-6.82	100.95	57.61	7,585
Joint stock 股份制	12	240	25,803	1,354	2.47	4.42	107.66	44.09	54,815
Foreign-funded 外資	74	93	12,813	-129	-0.59	-1.15	137.70	49.06	21,970
Overseas Chinese-funded 港澳台資	191	74	10,112	267	1.34	2.66	136.16	49.66	19,946
By size 規模									
Large 大型	16	987	113,174	1,757	1.02	3.99	114.72	74.48	172,578
Medium 中型	41	554	42,228	797	0.85	4.50	76.17	81.02	93,301
Small 小型	991	77	6,529	60	0.66	1.75	84.52	62.04	8,993
By regional distribution 地區分布									
Central-North 華北	147	97	6,798	267	2.47	9.40	70.40	73.78	10,832
Beijing 北京	35	46	2,968	-20	-0.25	-0.54	64.16	54.51	7,999
Tianjin 天津	28	96	13,695	1,176	6.54	30.07	142.60	78.24	17,983
Hebei 河北	61	94	5,822	227	2.61	12.92	62.16	79.80	8,686
Shanxi 山西	8	55	1,419	-60	-1.53	-7.64	26.03	80.03	3,930
Inner Mongolia 內蒙	15	249	9,699	-422	-2.56	-9.40	38.92	72.79	16,505
Northeast 東北	106	101	2,433	-405	-5.29	-40.45	24.17	86.93	7,665
Liaoning 遼寧	63	73	2,766	-299	-5.18	-17.44	37.72	70.33	5,776
Jilin 吉林	20	235	1,852	-1,180	-6.92	85.97	7.88	108.06	17,044
Heilongjiang 黑龍江	23	59	2,027	-23	-0.50	-2.10	34.57	76.15	4,685
Central East 華東	525	117	12,463	257	1.68	4.29	106.12	60.77	15,304
Shanghai 上海	59	91	10,754	472	3.02	5.53	118.00	45.39	15,605
Jiangsu 江蘇	166	141	18,763	314	1.49	4.60	133.11	67.61	21,116
Zhejiang 浙江	124	117	11,070	392	2.85	7.06	94.75	59.62	13,761
Anhui 安徽	48	46	4,021	-133	-2.99	-14.64	87.05	79.57	4,460
Fujian 福建	50	84	10,290	177	1.11	1.53	123.12	27.57	15,966
Jiangxi 江西	20	17	964	-18	-1.28	-3.85	57.90	66.85	1,371
Shandong 山東	58	201	11,972	76	0.51	2.27	59.53	77.55	14,873
Central-South 中南	227	103	8,828	-8	-0.04	-0.18	85.88	77.51	20,638
Henan 河南	59	66	2,411	57	1.52	5.44	36.33	71.98	3,773
Hubei 湖北	40	116	8,331	330	4.35	9.91	72.03	56.08	7,575
Hunan 湖南	12	109	1,210	-173	-7.70	41.24	11.08	118.67	2,241
Guangdong 廣東	103	125	13,665	-138	-0.37	-1.77	109.51	79.03	37,294
Guangxi 廣西	11	38	2,451	-337	-9.40	-16.78	64.65	43.98	3,588
Hainan 海南	2	105	39,730	790	0.63	4.46	378.38	85.90	125,775
Southwest 西南	37	114	4,223	-132	-1.72	-11.21	37.15	84.65	7,649
Chongqing 重慶	4	101	7,136	7	0.07	0.31	70.16	75.92	9,392
Sichuan 四川	25	136	4,680	-187	-2.18	-16.25	34.31	86.58	8,594
Guizhou 貴州	5	29	516				17.92	79.33	3,126
Yunnan 雲南	2	68	875	-85	-2.92	-40.48	12.87	92.80	2,915
Tibet 西藏									
Northwest 西北	36	50	1,458	-139	-5.53	-12.02	28.88	53.99	2,515
Shaanxi 陝西	18	55	2,008	-292	-7.60	-17.46	36.78	56.45	3,844
Gansu 甘肅	12	55	1,135	44	3.60	5.27	20.48	31.82	1,228
Qinghai 青海	2	22	180	-120	-9.30	-33.80	8.37	72.48	1,290
Ningxia 寧夏									
Xinjiang 新疆	4	32	588	-10	-0.99	-5.19	18.65	80.94	1,010

Year 年份	Number of firms 企業個數	Rate of change 每年變化 (%)	Number of employees 職工人數 (人)	Rate of change 每年變化 (%)	Total revenue (mil. RMB) 總銷售收入 (百萬元)	Rate of change 每年變化 (%)	Total profit (mil. RMB) 總利潤 (百萬元)	Rate of change 每年變化 (%)
1993	896		94,660		4,347		102	
1994	991	10.60%	100,248	5.90%	5,461	25.62%	63	-38.76%
1995	1,062	7.16%	117,933	17.64%	8,224	50.59%	92	46.83%
1996	1,078	1.51%	115,877	-1.74%	10,013	21.75%	120	30.49%

3 Major products* 3種主要產品 *	Output 產量	Sales volume 銷售量	Unit 單位
a) Pure Chemical Fabric 純化纖布	16,727	15,890	10,000 metre 萬米
b) Printing & Dyeing Cloth 印染布	20,662	19,629	10,000 metre 萬米
c) Blended Yarn 混紡紗	18,346	12,842	ton 噸

Top 10 firms by revenue (year founded) 收入排名前10家企業 (創辦年份)	City 城市	Province 省	Telephone / fax 電話 / 傳真	Number of employees 職工人數	Ownership 產業所有權	Revenue ('000 RMB) 銷售收入 (千元)	Profit ('000 RMB) (rank) 利潤 (千元) (排名)	Total assets ('000 RMB) 總資產 (千元)	Major products 主要產品
Jiangsu Tong Yu Textile Group Co. 江蘇通裕紡織集團公司(1958)	Yangzhou 揚州市	Jiangsu 江蘇省	(0514)7885512 (0514)7887765	3,490	Collectively-owned 集體	480,202	6226(20)	361,714	c
Zhejiang Hongshan Textile Printing & Dyeing Co. Ltd. 浙江紅山紡織印染有限公司(1994)	Hangzhou 杭州市	Zhejiang 浙江省	(0571)2699116 (0571)2699149	1,384	Collectively-owned 集體	305,457	1723(49)	290,463	a,b
Hangzhou Jinjiang Group Company 杭州錦江集團公司(1990)	Hangzhou 杭州市	Zhejiang 浙江省	(0571)3716788	1,407	Collectively-owned 集體	266,034	10004(6)	494,543	b
Hua Cheng Weaving & Dyeing Co. Ltd. 華成織染有限公司(1995)	Suzhou 蘇州市	Jiangsu 江蘇省	(0512)7671386 (0512)7671389	681	Overseas Chinese-funded 港澳台資	237,620	0(338)	484,829	a
Qidong Xin Jie Clothing Auxiliary Mererial Co. Ltd. 啟東市欣捷服裝輔料有限公司(1993)	Nantong 南通市	Jiangsu 江蘇省	(0513)3388876 (0513)3388273	153	Overseas Chinese-funded 港澳台資	225,864	4067(27)	49,900	o
Jiangsu Zhenyang Group Co. Ltd. 江蘇振陽集團公司(1987)	Yancheng 鹽城市	Jiangsu 江蘇省	(0515)2323314	1,230	Overseas Chinese-funded 港澳台資	220,000	18000(3)	220,130	o
Shanghai Met (Group) Corp. 上海望春花實業股份有限公司(1979)	Shanghai 上海市	Shanghai 上海市	(021)62748803 (021)62749024	901	Joint stock 股份制	211,536	27826(2)	368,555	b
Panyu Printing & Dyeing General Factory 番禺市印染總廠(1952)	Guangzhou 廣州市	Guangdong 廣東省	(020)84856370 (020)84858313	891	State-owned 國有	176,481	-10369(510)	197,823	b
Rui Xiang Group 瑞祥集團(1979)	Weifang 濰坊市	Shandong 山東省	(0536)7251570 (0536)7251106	2,769	State-owned 國有	160,104	1924(45)	216,958	a,c
Guangdong Yu Long Weaving & Dyeing Factory Co. Ltd. 廣東裕隆織染廠有限公司(1995)	Jiangmen 江門市	Guangdong 廣東省	(0750)6673807 (0750)6679688	787	Foreign-funded 外資	150,506	-5341(501)	644,956	b

Top 10 Cities by Production Output 產出排名前10位城市	Province 省	Market share 市場份額	Number of firms 企業個數
Shanghai 上海市	Shanghai 上海市	8.66%	85
Hangzhou 杭州市	Zhejiang 浙江省	6.82%	22
Suzhou 蘇州市	Jiangsu 江蘇省	6.69%	70
Yangzhou 揚州市	Jiangsu 江蘇省	5.34%	11
Yancheng 鹽城市	Jiangsu 江蘇省	4.86%	11
Jiaxing 嘉興市	Zhejiang 浙江省	4.67%	30
Jiangmen 江門市	Guangdong 廣東省	3.99%	17
Nantong 南通市	Jiangsu 江蘇省	3.70%	59
Xianyang 咸陽市	Shaanxi 陝西省	3.03%	2
Shaoxing 紹興市	Zhejiang 浙江省	2.84%	24

10 Major Wholesalers 10家主要批發商	City 城市	Province 省	Telephone / Fax 電話 / 傳真
Anhui Clothing Import & Export Company 安徽省服裝進出口公司	Hefei 合肥市	Anhui 安徽省	(0551)3632212 (0551)3632002
Qingdao Textile Clothing Industrial Group Company 青島紡織服裝實業集團公司	Qingdao 青島市	Shandong 山東省	(0532)2877853 (0532)2869315
Hebei Textile Import & Export (Group) Company 河北省紡織品進出口(集團)公司	Shijiazhuang 石家莊市	Hebei 河北省	(0311)7028530 (0311)7027781
Zhong Fang Pledget Import & Export Company 中紡紗布進出口公司	Beijing 北京市	Beijing 北京市	(010)65124718 (010)65124713
Shaoxing Import & Export Company 紹興市進出口公司	Shaoxing 紹興市	Zhejiang 浙江省	(0575)5132822 (0575)5141577
Hunan Hua Xiang Import & Export (Group) Company 湖南省華湘進出口(集團)公司	Changsha 長沙市	Hunan 湖南省	(0731)2282440 (0731)2286995
City's Import & Export Company Trade Dept. 市進出口公司貿易部	Yichang 宜昌市	Hubei 湖北省	(0717)6450778 (0717)6441875
Shanghai Pu Dong Xinqu Import & Export Company 上海浦東新區進出口公司	Shanghai 上海市	Shanghai 上海市	(021)58878801 (021)58827444
Ningbo Yinxian Import & Export Company 寧波市鄞縣進出口公司	Ningbo 寧波市	Zhejiang 浙江省	(0574)7875205 (0574)7873168
Zhejiang Silk Import & Export Company 浙江省絲綢進出口公司	Hangzhou 杭州市	Zhejiang 浙江省	(0571)5195588 (0571)5192542

*Also include sales by firms outside this industry.包括本行業以外廠家的銷售。"o" stands for "others". "o" 代表 "其他產品"。

1810: Apparel 服裝製造業

The industry accounts for 2.264% of the total revenue of China's industrial sector in 1996. The revenue growth rate of the industry is 11.0% from 1995, as compared to the growth rate of China's industrial sector, 9.51%. The rate of return on asset is 2.54%. 67.84% of all firms in the industry made a profit while 25.43% had negative returns. The top province in terms of the industry's revenue is Guangdong, accounting for 22.95% of the total revenue.
本行業在1996年佔全行業總產值2.264%，行業年增長率為11.0%（全國工業年增長率9.51%）。行業的資產回報率2.54%，67.84%的企業盈利，25.43%的企業虧損。銷售收入最高的省份為廣東省，佔本行業的22.95%。

	Total number of firms 企業總數	Total number of employees 職工總數	Total revenue (mil. RMB) 總銷售收入（百萬元）	Total profit (mil. RMB) 總利潤（百萬元）	Return on assets 資產利潤率 (%)	Return on equity 權益利潤率 (%)	Labour productivity ('000 RMB / worker) 勞動生產率（千元/人）	Debts / assets 資產負債率 (%)	Total assets (mil. RMB) 總資產（百萬元）
Industry Overall 行業總體	16,468	2,235,047	131,217	3,113	2.54	7.09	58.71	64.25	122,717

	Number of firms 企業個數	Average number of employees 平均職工人數	Average revenue ('000 RMB) 平均銷售收入（千元）	Average profit ('000 RMB) 平均利潤（千元）	Return on assets 資產利潤率 (%)	Return on equity 權益利潤率 (%)	Labour productivity ('000 RMB / worker) 勞動生產率（千元/人）	Average debts / assets 平均資產負債率(%)	Average Total assets ('000 RMB) 平均總資產（千元）
By ownership 產業所有權									
State-owned 國有	1,005	204	7,996	-97	-0.73	-2.42	39.24	70.04	13,300
Collectively-owned 集體	10,362	116	5,258	106	2.29	7.15	45.25	67.99	4,609
Privately-owned 私有	60	121	6,633	96	1.12	1.86	55.04	40.08	8,620
Domestic JVs 聯營	150	293	16,864	236	1.77	5.07	57.59	64.99	13,301
Joint stock 股份制	89	361	39,821	4,642	11.10	26.97	110.37	58.85	41,825
Foreign-funded 外資	1,667	182	17,318	623	4.40	11.20	95.29	60.69	14,156
Overseas Chinese-funded 港澳台資	3,114	152	10,673	200	1.97	4.89	70.42	59.79	10,170
By size 規模									
Large 大型	57	1,796	200,344	16,596	7.05	16.42	111.57	57.03	235,302
Medium 中型	257	793	61,245	2,390	3.83	10.57	77.22	63.73	62,370
Small 小型	15,743	123	6,622	99	1.67	4.81	53.71	65.38	5,923
By regional distribution 地區分布									
Central-North 華北	2,419	135	5,510	189	3.28	10.26	40.84	68.05	5,752
Beijing 北京	824	135	5,023	12	0.18	0.57	37.29	68.69	6,597
Tianjin 天津	569	141	7,233	378	6.43	20.71	51.15	68.96	5,870
Hebei 河北	603	166	6,925	344	5.45	15.45	41.65	64.73	6,308
Shanxi 山西	176	98	1,908	-42	-1.40	-4.56	19.41	69.36	2,993
Inner Mongolia 內蒙	247	70	2,279	129	3.96	15.65	32.47	74.71	3,265
Northeast 東北	1,527	123	3,920		0.01	0.02	31.74	68.32	4,397
Liaoning 遼寧	838	166	5,805	43	0.70	1.99	35.06	64.81	6,122
Jilin 吉林	298	107	2,219	-129	-3.63	-18.24	20.79	80.11	3,564
Heilongjiang 黑龍江	391	46	1,176	8	0.57	2.69	25.54	78.88	1,337
Central East 華東	6,451	144	10,759	318	3.33	9.11	74.82	63.47	9,544
Shanghai 上海	1,025	153	13,467	416	3.11	8.42	87.78	62.99	13,371
Jiangsu 江蘇	1,413	194	16,119	428	3.61	9.75	82.99	62.97	11,867
Zhejiang 浙江	1,445	136	12,062	372	3.25	9.49	88.51	65.74	11,458
Anhui 安徽	331	170	6,451	113	2.08	8.89	37.92	76.54	5,423
Fujian 福建	1,157	81	6,204	260	5.58	10.16	76.99	45.05	4,657
Jiangxi 江西	302	66	2,877	-5	-0.16	-1.30	43.75	88.07	3,199
Shandong 山東	778	166	6,700	183	2.23	6.98	40.24	68.06	8,216
Central-South 中南	4,714	147	8,561	145	1.86	4.99	58.23	62.77	7,780
Henan 河南	564	77	2,100	31	1.26	4.64	27.26	72.84	2,455
Hubei 湖北	623	188	11,692	587	6.24	21.26	62.33	70.66	9,402
Hunan 湖南	341	90	2,346	-59	-2.57	-7.79	26.08	66.99	2,280
Guangdong 廣東	2,930	164	10,279	117	1.23	3.10	62.83	60.21	9,457
Guangxi 廣西	228	88	3,526	-76	-2.24	-7.12	39.92	68.52	3,395
Hainan 海南	28	93	5,944	-198	-3.24	-17.94	63.97	81.94	6,095
Southwest 西南	746	72	1,538	-55	-1.98	-5.67	21.43	65.07	2,799
Chongqing 重慶	147	61	1,132	-136	-8.37	-51.32	18.37	83.69	1,626
Sichuan 四川	323	83	1,945	-78	-1.98	-5.88	23.15	66.35	3,929
Guizhou 貴州	109	60	1,667	67	2.97	6.50	27.60	54.27	2,256
Yunnan 雲南	151	67	1,084	-27	-1.28	-2.91	16.23	56.19	2,118
Tibet 西藏	15	27	355	26	3.54	4.00	13.10	11.62	735
Northwest 西北	611	75	1,628	-55	-1.92	-7.82	21.64	75.51	2,873
Shaanxi 陝西	292	82	1,855	-70	-2.52	-8.50	22.50	70.31	2,787
Gansu 甘肅	144	62	847	-22	-1.42	-6.13	13.65	76.82	1,572
Qinghai 青海	35	108	3,832	44	0.55	-177.91	35.60	100.31	7,887
Ningxia 寧夏	31	73	1,196	-55	-1.97	-8.85	16.48	77.68	2,810
Xinjiang 新疆	109	64	1,467	-89	-2.75	-8.25	23.07	66.71	3,229

1810: Apparel 服裝製造業

Year 年份	Number of firms 企業個數	Rate of change 每年變化 (%)	Number of employees 職工人數 (人)	Rate of change 每年變化 (%)	Total revenue (mil. RMB) 總銷售收入 (百萬元)	Rate of change 每年變化 (%)	Total profit (mil. RMB) 總利潤 (百萬元)	Rate of change 每年變化 (%)
1993	14,984		2,248,208		69,791		2,756	
1994	15,891	6.05%	2,302,324	2.41%	105,826	51.63%	2,298	-16.60%
1995	16,870	6.16%	2,359,453	2.48%	118,225	11.72%	2,291	-0.31%
1996	16,468	-2.38%	2,235,047	-5.27%	131,217	10.99%	3,113	35.88%

3 Major products* 3 種主要產品 *	Output 產量	Sales volume 銷售量	Unit 單位
a) Shuttlloom Costume 梭織服裝	682,793	689,621	10,000 piece 萬件
b) Down Costume 羽絨服裝	2,912	2,475	10,000 piece 萬件
c) Knitted Dress 針織服裝	91,055	91,055	10,000 piece 萬件

Top 10 firms by revenue (year founded) 收入排名前 10 家企業 (創辦年份)	City 城市	Province 省	Telephone / fax 電話 / 傳真	Number of employees 職工人數	Ownership 產業所有權	Revenue ('000 RMB) 銷售收入 (千元)	Profit ('000 RMB) (rank) 利潤 (千元) (排名)	Total assets ('000 RMB) 總資產 (千元)	Major products 主要產品
Jiangsu Hua Xi Group Co. 江蘇華西集團公司(1984)	Wuxi 無錫市	Jiangsu 江蘇省	(0510)6201349 (0510)6201744	3,525	Collectively-owned 集體	1,894,710	180259(1)	1,113,219	a,c
Hong Dou Group Co. 紅豆集團公司(1993)	Wuxi 無錫市	Jiangsu 江蘇省	(0510)8761888	6,011	Collectively-owned 集體	889,409	55124(4)	718,630	a,c
Gaoming Gaofeng United Textiles Ltd. 高豐紡織染聯合企業有限公司(1991)	Foshan 佛山市	Guangdong 廣東省	(0757)8826112 (0757)8881510	4,290	Overseas Chinese-funded 港澳台資	742,514	-5925(7130)	971,841	a
Ningbo Youngor Group Co. Ltd. 寧波雅戈爾(集團)股份有限公司(1979)	Ningbo 寧波市	Zhejiang 浙江省	(0574)7425873 (0574)7425873	4,017	Collectively-owned 集體	709,109	111641(2)	611,068	a
Da Yang Enterprise Group 大楊企業集團(1979)	Dalian 大連市	Liaoning 遼寧省	(0411)9450258 (0411)9450189	6,198	Foreign-funded 外資	627,840	42990(5)	682,130	a,c
Pinghu Mo Zhi Hua Industrial Group Co. Ltd. 平湖茉織華實業有限公司(1990)	Jiaxing 嘉興市	Zhejiang 浙江省	(0573)5700777 (0573)5700188	950	Foreign-funded 外資	620,573	33803(8)	192,282	a
Unitex (Huizhou) Knitting Industries Ltd. 裕泰(惠州)針織實業有限公司(1993)	Huizhou 惠州市	Guangdong 廣東省	(0751)2223485 (0751)2223424	2,110	Overseas Chinese-funded 港澳台資	534,220	1753(576)	315,719	c
Shanghai Xie Tong (Group) Company 上海協通(集團)公司(1993)	Shanghai 上海市	Shanghai 上海市	(021)59598888 (021)59598888	2,678	Foreign-funded 外資	519,560	38130(7)	363,921	c
Shanghai Kai Tuo (Group) Co. Ltd. 上海凱托(集團)有限公司(1991)	Shanghai 上海市	Shanghai 上海市	(021)57410893	3,374	Collectively-owned 集體	501,358	20915(20)	878,817	a
Ningbo Shan Shan Group Co. Ltd. 寧波杉杉集團有限公司(1980)	Ningbo 寧波市	Zhejiang 浙江省	(0574)7711333 (0574)7716363	1,762	Joint stock 股份制	500,415	98368(3)	715,606	a,c

Top 10 Cities by Production Output 產出排名前 10 位城市	Province 省	Market share 市場份額	Number of firms 企業個數
Shanghai 上海市	Shanghai 上海市	14.39%	1669
Ningbo 寧波市	Zhejiang 浙江省	5.42%	342
Suzhou 蘇州市	Jiangsu 江蘇省	4.43%	635
Guangzhou 廣州市	Guangdong 廣東省	4.34%	1048
Quanzhou 泉州市	Fujian 福建省	4.27%	1209
Beijing 北京市	Beijing 北京市	3.57%	652
Jiaxing 嘉興市	Zhejiang 浙江省	3.11%	254
Tianjin 天津市	Tianjin 天津市	3.02%	673
Wuxi 無錫市	Jiangsu 江蘇省	2.89%	398
Nantong 南通市	Jiangsu 江蘇省	2.69%	385

10 Major Wholesalers 10 家主要批發商	City 城市	Province 省	Telephone / Fax 電話 / 傳真
Bao Xiang Hebei Import & Export Group Company 葆祥河北進出口集團公司	Shijiazhuang 石家莊市	Hebei 河北省	(0311)7768648 (0311)7752705
Henan Clothing Import & Export Company 河南省服裝進出口公司	Zhengzhou 鄭州市	Henan 河南省	(0371)5958892
Jiangsu Clothing Import & Export Group Co. Ltd. 江蘇省服裝進出口集團股份有限公司	Nanjing 南京市	Jiangsu 江蘇省	(025)7714688 (025)3361837
Beijing Clothing Import & Export Co. 北京市服裝進出口股份有限公司	Beijing 北京市	Beijing 北京市	(010)64269728 (010)64269496
Zhong Fang Clothing Import & Export Company 中紡服裝進出口公司	Beijing 北京市	Beijing 北京市	(010)65123010 (010)65124768
Tianjin Clothing Import & Export Company 天津服裝進出口公司	Tianjin 天津市	Tianjin 天津市	(022)28328888 (022)28326166
Guangzhou Textiles Import & Export Co. 廣州市紡織進出口公司	Guangzhou 廣州市	Guangdong 廣東省	(020)83348898 (020)83343898
Jiangsu Overseas Enterprise Group Co. Ltd. 江蘇省海外企業集團有限公司	Nanjing 南京市	Jiangsu 江蘇省	(025)7710880 (025)7711532
Weihai Import & Export Company 威海市進出口公司	Weihai 威海市	Shandong 山東省	(0896)5232228 (0896)5232014
Suzhou Foreign Trade Company 蘇州市對外貿易公司	Suzhou 蘇州市	Jiangsu 江蘇省	(0512)5205488 (0512)5205232

*Also include sales by firms outside this industry.包括本行業以外廠家的銷售。"o" stands for "others". "o" 代表"其他產品"。

1820: Hats 製帽業

The industry accounts for 0.029% of the total revenue of China's industrial sector in 1996. The revenue growth rate of the industry is 12.7% from 1995, as compared to the growth rate of China's industrial sector, 9.51%. The rate of return on asset is 0.90%. 64.51% of all firms in the industry made a profit while 25.00% had negative returns. The top province in terms of the industry's revenue is Jiangsu, accounting for 27.50% of the total revenue.
本行業在1996年佔全行業總產值0.029%，行業年增長率為12.7%（全國工業年增長率9.51%）。行業的資產回報率0.90%，64.51%的企業盈利，25.00%的企業虧損。銷售收入最高的省份為江蘇省，佔本行業的27.50%。

	Total number of firms 企業總數	Total number of employees 職工總數	Total revenue (mil. RMB) 總銷售收入（百萬元）	Total profit (mil. RMB) 總利潤（百萬元）	Return on assets 資產利潤率 (%)	Return on equity 權益利潤率 (%)	Labour productivity ('000 RMB / worker) 勞動生產率（千元/人）	Debts / assets 資產負債率 (%)	Total assets (mil. RMB) 總資產（百萬元）
Industry Overall 行業總體	351	42,692	1,703	16	0.90	2.42	39.89	62.94	1,754

	Number of firms 企業個數	Average number of employees 平均職工人數	Average revenue ('000 RMB) 平均銷售收入（千元）	Average profit ('000 RMB) 平均利潤（千元）	Return on assets 資產利潤率 (%)	Return on equity 權益利潤率 (%)	Labour productivity ('000 RMB / worker) 勞動生產率（千元/人）	Average debts / assets 平均資產負債率(%)	Average Total assets ('000 RMB) 平均總資產（千元）
By ownership 產業所有權									
State-owned 國有	24	221	13,042	208	1.13	4.10	59.15	72.40	18,417
Collectively-owned 集體	259	110	3,190	77	2.75	8.51	28.92	67.72	2,786
Privately-owned 私有									
Domestic JVs 聯營	8	209	15,737	477	2.80	6.59	75.43	57.44	17,020
Joint stock 股份制	2	28							
Foreign-funded 外資	18	127	10,153	-259	-2.58	-5.38	79.91	52.17	10,059
Overseas Chinese-funded 港澳台資	39	134	6,511	-244	-3.50	-6.39	48.62	45.21	6,972
By size 規模									
Large 大型									
Medium 中型	1	681	56,276	2,908	5.53	13.24	82.64	58.20	52,556
Small 小型	343	123	4,803	38	0.77	2.08	39.01	63.09	4,962
By regional distribution 地區分布									
Central-North 華北	58	128	3,043	145	3.26	9.09	23.84	64.15	4,438
Beijing 北京	14	90	3,345	244	4.47	13.95	37.08	68.00	5,455
Tianjin 天津	19	116	3,669	227	6.80	23.18	31.60	70.65	3,342
Hebei 河北	18	172	2,929	74	1.34	2.89	17.04	53.74	5,572
Shanxi 山西	3	126	743	-117	-5.24	-16.43	5.90	68.11	2,227
Inner Mongolia 內蒙	4	116	1,250	-83	-3.12	-48.53	10.78	93.48	2,645
Northeast 東北	48	82	1,323	-90	-3.43	-8.37	16.09	58.94	2,626
Liaoning 遼寧	19	99	2,356	-104	-2.82	-10.53	23.87	73.22	3,696
Jilin 吉林	11	72	535	-16	-0.50	-0.69	7.48	28.23	3,295
Heilongjiang 黑龍江	18	71	715	-121	-11.08	-31.27	10.01	64.57	1,088
Central East 華東	119	126	7,671	74	1.24	3.32	60.66	62.73	6,022
Shanghai 上海	22	107	7,602	113	1.38	3.62	71.32	61.87	8,157
Jiangsu 江蘇	41	179	11,423	125	1.58	4.64	63.95	66.02	7,921
Zhejiang 浙江	19	78	4,221	45	0.99	3.49	54.04	71.50	4,501
Anhui 安徽	11	64	1,580	34	4.75	-37.37	24.51	112.71	708
Fujian 福建	10	111	2,555	-152	-3.91	-8.31	22.96	52.93	3,886
Jiangxi 江西	2	47	695	-15	-1.12	-2.03	14.79	44.98	1,345
Shandong 山東	14	142	10,913	114	2.05	3.52	77.08	41.77	5,541
Central-South 中南	102	140	5,097	31	0.53	1.44	36.42	63.21	5,842
Henan 河南	22	122	2,176	105	4.96	10.71	17.78	53.68	2,116
Hubei 湖北	18	101	1,553	-13	-0.63	-2.87	15.39	78.16	2,038
Hunan 湖南	8	77	491	-108	-11.57	124.64	6.39	109.29	929
Guangdong 廣東	51	174	8,572	47	0.48	1.27	49.21	62.29	9,831
Guangxi 廣西	3	89	983	-153	-11.89	-35.38	11.09	66.41	1,290
Hainan 海南									
Southwest 西南	10	97	1,388	10	0.38	0.73	14.29	47.44	2,622
Chongqing 重慶	3	109	1,542	-22	-1.63	-3.73	14.06	56.39	1,367
Sichuan 四川	3	82	1,588	18	0.90	1.62	19.28	44.37	2,027
Guizhou 貴州	2	118	1,450	50	0.73	1.47	12.34	50.04	6,805
Yunnan 雲南	2	81	795	5	0.41	0.55	9.88	25.51	1,215
Tibet 西藏									
Northwest 西北	14	75	1,194	-29	-1.28	-6.89	15.99	81.37	2,281
Shaanxi 陝西	5	49	194	32	3.60	18.39	3.94	80.41	888
Gansu 甘肅	4	86	2,065	168	8.90	23.93	24.08	62.82	1,883
Qinghai 青海	1	159	410	-210	-14.58	2100.00	2.58	100.69	1,440
Ningxia 寧夏									
Xinjiang 新疆	4	74	1,768	-258	-5.56	-44.98	23.80	87.63	4,630

1820: Hats 製帽業

Year 年份	Number of firms 企業個數	Rate of change 每年變化 (%)	Number of employees 職工人數 (人)	Rate of change 每年變化 (%)	Total revenue (mil. RMB) 總銷售收入 (百萬元)	Rate of change 每年變化 (%)	Total profit (mil. RMB) 總利潤 (百萬元)	Rate of change 每年變化 (%)
1993	304		36,453		959		28	
1994	304		38,702	6.17%	1,069	11.49%	17	-38.29%
1995	358	17.76%	46,424	19.95%	1,511	41.32%	7	-57.28%
1996	351	-1.96%	42,692	-8.04%	1,703	12.71%	16	120.48%

3 Major products* 3 種主要產品 *	Output 產量	Sales volume 銷售量	Unit 單位
a) Suture Cap 縫製帽	37,299	36,553	10,000 piece 萬頂

Top 10 firms by revenue (year founded) 收入排名前 10 家企業 (創辦年份)	City 城市	Province 省	Telephone / fax 電話 / 傳真	Number of employees 職工人數	Ownership 產業所有權	Revenue ('000 RMB) 銷售收入 (千元)	Profit ('000 RMB) (rank) 利潤 (千元) (排名)	Total assets ('000 RMB) 總資產 (千元)	Major products 主要產品
Zhangjiagang Jin Zhou Group Co. 張家港市金洲集團公司(1992)	Suzhou 蘇州市	Jiangsu 江蘇省	(0512)8291228 (0512)8291813	845	State-owned 國有	157,196	3875(1)	117,851	a
Qingdao Pai Chang Clothing Co. Ltd. 青島派昌服裝有限公司(1995)	Qingdao 青島市	Shandong 山東省	(0532)3869435 (0532)3869420	60	Foreign-funded 外資	90,400	-1150(156)	22,350	o
Heshan Zhong Ao Enterprise (Group) Co. 鶴山市中奧企業(集團)公司(1984)	Jiangmen 江門市	Guangdong 廣東省	(0750)8883368 (0750)8889078	770	State-owned 國有	65,810	650(21)	169,961	a
Shang Hai & Changshu Artistic Hat Joint Venture Factory 上海市常熟市工藝帽聯營廠(1964)	Suzhou 蘇州市	Jiangsu 江蘇省	(0512)2787924	769	Domestic JVs 聯營	58,600	1290(8)	56,708	a
Shanghai Kang Hua Cap Making Co. Ltd. 上海康華製帽有限公司(1996)	Shanghai 上海市	Shanghai 上海市	(021)64781065	100	Overseas Chinese-funded 港澳台資	49,807	996(10)	11,497	o
Shi An Da Clothes & Cap Co. 時安達服裝製帽公司(1992)	Guangzhou 廣州市	Guangdong 廣東省	(020)82765223 (020)82765904	198	Foreign-funded 外資	44,845	447(28)	17,293	a
Yangxi De Cheng Hat Industry Co. Ltd. 陽西縣德誠帽業有限公司	Yangjiang 陽江市	Guangdong 廣東省	(0662)5553217	510	Foreign-funded 外資	33,663	3063(2)	14,515	a
Zhangjiagang Hat 張家港市禮帽廠(1981)	Suzhou 蘇州市	Jiangsu 江蘇省	(0512)8450108	236	Collectively-owned 集體	31,808	836(13)	23,370	o
Jurong Knitting Cap Making Factory 句容縣針織製帽廠(1983)	Zhenjiang 鎮江市	Jiangsu 江蘇省	(0511)7671028	500	Collectively-owned 集體	31,264	408(32)	8,656	a
Heyuan Wan Meng Medical Care Articles Co. Ltd. 河源市萬盟醫保用品有限公司(1994)	Heyuan 河源市	Guangdong 廣東省	(0762)3326270 (0762)3326269	125	Overseas Chinese-funded 港澳台資	29,880	-752(153)	4,360	o

Top 10 Cities by Production Output 產出排名前 10 位城市	Province 省	Market share 市場份額	Number of firms 企業個數
Shanghai 上海市	Shanghai 上海市	13.18%	30
Suzhou 蘇州市	Jiangsu 江蘇省	12.32%	12
Nanjing 南京市	Jiangsu 江蘇省	5.21%	12
Tianjin 天津市	Tianjin 天津市	4.83%	27
Beijing 北京市	Beijing 北京市	4.72%	14
Guangzhou 廣州市	Guangdong 廣東省	4.60%	13
Jiangmen 江門市	Guangdong 廣東省	4.36%	3
Zhenjiang 鎮江市	Jiangsu 江蘇省	4.34%	9
Yangjiang 陽江市	Guangdong 廣東省	4.21%	13
Nantong 南通市	Jiangsu 江蘇省	3.32%	13

10 Major Wholesalers 10 家主要批發商	City 城市	Province 省	Telephone / Fax 電話 / 傳真
Beijing Foreign Trade Import & Export Company 北京市對外貿易進出口公司	Beijing 北京市	Beijing 北京市	(010)65081589 (010)65043755
Fujian Putian Foreign Trade Company 福建省莆田市對外貿易公司	Putian 莆田市	Fujian 福建省	(0594)2398702 (0594)2292681
Hunan Light Industry General Company Import & Export Products Company 湖南省輕工業總公司進出品公司	Changsha 長沙市	Hunan 湖南省	(0731)2287932 (0731)2287844
Jiangxi Handicrafts Import & Export Company 江西省工藝品進出口公司	Nanchang 南昌市	Jiangxi 江西省	(0791)6246932 (0791)6223383
Jiangyin Shoes and Cap General Co. 江蘇江陰市鞋帽總公司	Wuxi 無錫市	Jiangsu 江蘇省	(0510)6804355 (0510)6803479
Jinhua Jin Hai Industrial Company 金華市金海實業公司	Jinhua 金華市	Zhejiang 浙江省	(0579)2324590
Guangdong Nanhai Handicrafts Import & Export Company 廣東南海市工藝品進出口公司	Foshan 佛山市	Guangdong 廣東省	(0757)6338620 (0757)6220225
Guangzhou Light Industry Products Shoes, Cap, Box, Bag Import & Export Co. 廣州市輕工業品鞋帽箱包進出口公司	Guangzhou 廣州市	Guangdong 廣東省	(020)83337522 (020)83339145
Nanjing Foreign Trade Company 南京市對外貿易公司	Nanjing 南京市	Jiangsu 江蘇省	(025)4403991 (025)4403700

*Also include sales by firms outside this industry.包括本行業以外廠家的銷售。"o" stands for "others". "o" 代表 "其他產品"。

1830: Shoes 製鞋業

The industry accounts for 0.172% of the total revenue of China's industrial sector in 1996. The revenue growth rate of the industry is 0.8% from 1995, as compared to the growth rate of China's industrial sector, 9.51%. The rate of return on asset is 1.14%. 65.52% of all firms in the industry made a profit while 26.59% had negative returns. The top province in terms of the industry's revenue is Jiangsu, accounting for 22.61% of the total revenue.
本行業在1996年佔全行業總產值0.172%，行業年增長率為0.8%（全國工業年增長率9.51%）。行業的資產回報率1.14%，65.52%的企業盈利，26.59%的企業虧損。銷售收入最高的省份為江蘇省，佔本行業的22.61%。

	Total number of firms 企業總數	Total number of employees 職工總數	Total revenue (mil. RMB) 總銷售收入（百萬元）	Total profit (mil. RMB) 總利潤（百萬元）	Return on assets 資產利潤率 (%)	Return on equity 權益利潤率 (%)	Labour productivity ('000 RMB / worker) 勞動生產率（千元/人）	Debts / assets 資產負債率 (%)	Total assets (mil. RMB) 總資產（百萬元）
Industry Overall 行業總體	1,621	249,542	9,987	112	1.14	4.54	40.02	74.96	9,818

	Number of firms 企業個數	Average number of employees 平均職工人數	Average revenue ('000 RMB) 平均銷售收入（千元）	Average profit ('000 RMB) 平均利潤（千元）	Return on assets 資產利潤率 (%)	Return on equity 權益利潤率 (%)	Labour productivity ('000 RMB / worker) 勞動生產率（千元/人）	Average debts / assets 平均資產負債率(%)	Average Total assets ('000 RMB) 平均總資產（千元）
By ownership 產業所有權									
State-owned 國有	82	286	11,049	85	0.64	2.76	38.62	76.74	13,317
Collectively-owned 集體	1,273	124	3,715	32	0.83	4.24	29.95	80.34	3,856
Privately-owned 私有	12	94	5,067	401	17.23	26.23	54.05	34.31	2,329
Domestic JVs 聯營	18	158	5,822	18	0.32	1.19	36.75	72.66	5,585
Joint stock 股份制	14	447	37,547	2,229	5.00	11.22	84.08	55.46	44,591
Foreign-funded 外資	82	278	17,277	38	0.25	0.96	62.25	74.05	15,271
Overseas Chinese-funded 港澳台資	138	264	16,245	172	1.31	4.05	61.61	67.58	13,098
By size 規模									
Large 大型	2	2,243	247,291	25,267	8.80	18.77	110.25	53.11	287,049
Medium 中型	20	1,010	69,868	319	0.58	1.86	69.16	68.94	55,275
Small 小型	1,583	141	5,113	35	0.68	2.99	36.18	77.32	5,141
By regional distribution 地區分布									
Central-North 華北	277	77	1,568	12	0.47	3.29	20.39	85.85	2,514
Beijing 北京	65	67	1,479	-53	-1.54	-11.02	22.02	86.03	3,460
Tianjin 天津	24	120	2,135	-11	-0.36	-4.71	17.75	92.28	2,979
Hebei 河北	93	90	2,618	108	3.89	17.98	29.22	78.37	2,790
Shanxi 山西	43	72	533	-35	-1.81	-47.15	7.40	96.15	1,910
Inner Mongolia 內蒙	52	50	392	-32	-2.81	-71.00	7.82	96.02	1,122
Northeast 東北	165	104	1,360	-182	-6.90	-163.49	13.11	95.78	2,640
Liaoning 遼寧	54	123	2,004	-302	-8.65	-63.03	16.32	86.27	3,495
Jilin 吉林	40	152	1,637	-352	-9.77	77.91	10.78	112.54	3,599
Heilongjiang 黑龍江	71	62	714	5	0.34	3.32	11.51	89.77	1,450
Central East 華東	639	205	10,117	190	2.02	6.99	49.25	71.02	9,408
Shanghai 上海	30	229	10,547	168	1.44	4.89	46.01	70.56	11,639
Jiangsu 江蘇	127	255	17,783	458	3.42	11.29	69.62	69.72	13,399
Zhejiang 浙江	117	206	5,618	51	1.21	3.83	27.31	68.33	4,175
Anhui 安徽	51	140	3,765	113	3.97	66.36	26.86	94.02	2,845
Fujian 福建	148	178	10,116	85	0.97	3.03	56.84	68.02	8,805
Jiangxi 江西	34	53	451	-9	-1.25	-5.61	8.47	77.63	704
Shandong 山東	132	247	11,576	261	1.72	6.40	46.92	73.07	15,154
Central-South 中南	347	176	7,424	103	1.67	7.30	42.25	77.14	6,191
Henan 河南	99	136	4,155	272	6.20	17.93	30.55	65.40	4,382
Hubei 湖北	51	125	3,592	61	1.37	13.04	28.73	89.46	4,465
Hunan 湖南	59	88	1,667	-3	-0.18	-1.66	19.01	89.41	1,926
Guangdong 廣東	128	274	13,974	52	0.50	2.24	51.05	77.56	10,292
Guangxi 廣西	10	92	9,456	-62	-1.12	-6.70	102.67	83.32	5,551
Hainan 海南									
Southwest 西南	108	105	1,820	-104	-3.81	-19.87	17.32	80.83	2,739
Chongqing 重慶	22	113	926	-223	-13.62	171.04	8.16	107.96	1,640
Sichuan 四川	42	92	1,425	-93	-3.66	-17.46	15.37	79.04	2,553
Guizhou 貴州	22	86	1,276	-28	-1.66	-9.37	14.83	82.26	1,668
Yunnan 雲南	18	158	4,785	-94	-1.51	-5.84	30.33	74.12	6,253
Tibet 西藏	3	40	360	27	5.37	5.44	9.00	1.34	497
Northwest 西北	85	89	1,076	-92	-3.40	-15.35	12.08	77.83	2,706
Shaanxi 陝西	40	96	978	-92	-3.44	-31.05	10.15	88.92	2,670
Gansu 甘肅	26	90	1,622	-113	-3.60	-10.31	18.07	65.15	3,133
Qinghai 青海	3	131	660	-510	-26.80	82.70	5.04	132.40	1,903
Ningxia 寧夏	8	69	364	-74	-3.67	-20.63	5.26	82.22	2,011
Xinjiang 新疆	8	55	658	111	4.46	9.12	12.06	51.13	2,494

1830: Shoes 製鞋業

Year 年份	Number of firms 企業個數	Rate of change 每年變化 (%)	Number of employees 職工人數 (人)	Rate of change 每年變化 (%)	Total revenue (mil. RMB) 總銷售收入 (百萬元)	Rate of change 每年變化 (%)	Total profit (mil. RMB) 總利潤 (百萬元)	Rate of change 每年變化 (%)
1993	1,817		255,092		6,442		9	
1994	1,846	1.60%	309,057	21.16%	9,751	51.36%	73	688.62%
1995	1,710	-7.37%	274,669	-11.13%	9,905	1.58%	54	-25.53%
1996	1,621	-5.20%	249,542	-9.15%	9,987	0.83%	112	106.11%

3 Major products* 3 種主要產品 *	Output 產量	Sales volume 銷售量	Unit 單位
a) Cloth Shoes 布鞋	117,358	113,837	10,000 pair 萬雙
b) Rubber Shoes 膠鞋	10,425	9,800	10,000 pair 萬雙
c) Leather Shoes 皮鞋	11,416	11,073	10,000 pair 萬雙

Top 10 firms by revenue (year founded) 收入排名前 10 家企業 (創辦年份)	City 城市	Province 省	Telephone / fax 電話 / 傳真	Number of employees 職工人數	Ownership 產業所有權	Revenue ('000 RMB) 銷售收入 (千元)	Profit ('000 RMB) (rank) 利潤 (千元) (排名)	Total assets ('000 RMB) 總資產 (千元)	Major products 主要產品
Shandong Shen Yue Shoes Industry Group Co. 山東聲樂鞋業集團公司(1953)	Linyi 臨沂市	Shandong 山東省	(0539)3221280 (0539)3221510	3,270	Joint stock 股份制	392,356	28800(2)	436,123	a,c
Shunde Bai Wool Shoes Industry Co. Ltd. 順德百茂鞋業有限公司(1991)	Foshan 佛山市	Guangdong 廣東省	(0757)2282012 (0757)2282312	3,890	State-owned 國有	356,153	14424(4)	128,796	a,c
Fujian Li Feng Shoes Industry Development Co. Ltd. 福建荔豐鞋業開發有限公司(1988)	Putian 莆田市	Fujian 福建省	(0594)3991088	3,760	Foreign-funded 外資	324,170	9883(7)	251,356	o
Qingdao San Hu Shoe Making Co. Ltd. 青島三湖製鞋有限公司(1993)	Qingdao 青島市	Shandong 山東省	(0532)2590101 (0532)2590102	4,510	Foreign-funded 外資	245,423	-17056(570)	240,837	o
Huizhou Passport Shoes Industry Co. Ltd. 惠州市通行鞋業有限公司(1991)	Huizhou 惠州市	Guangdong 廣東省	(0751)2508652 (0751)2508886	1,008	Overseas Chinese-funded 港澳台資	231,580	6850(9)	75,240	a,c
Taicang Xiang Tang Group Co. Ltd. 太倉市香塘集團(1980)	Suzhou 蘇州市	Jiangsu 江蘇省	(0512)3293126 (0512)3295321	435	Collectively-owned 集體	215,000	29860(1)	205,000	a
Nanhai Tong Li Shoes Industry Co. Ltd. 南海市同立鞋業有限公司(1992)	Foshan 佛山市	Guangdong 廣東省	(0757)6775783 (0757)6775784	2,049	Overseas Chinese-funded 港澳台資	200,966	3143(23)	79,720	o
Jiangsu Bei Bei Group Company 江蘇貝貝集團公司(1973)	Suzhou 蘇州市	Jiangsu 江蘇省	(0512)8450140	2,191	Collectively-owned 集體	188,714	5921(10)	143,005	b,c
Forlic Pacific Footwear (fujian) Co. Ltd. 景新太平鞋業(福建)有限公司(1990)	Fuzhou 福州市	Fujian 福建省	(0591)5380572 (0591)5380132	2,800	Overseas Chinese-funded 港澳台資	186,300	-9000(569)	153,129	a
Shanghai Da Shun Toy Co. Ltd. 上海大順玩具有限公司(1995)	Shanghai 上海市	Shanghai 上海市	(021)62211170 (021)62211748	700	Overseas Chinese-funded 港澳台資	170,902	4201(18)	73,339	o

Top 10 Cities by Production Output 產出排名前 10 位城市	Province 省	Market share 市場份額	Number of firms 企業個數
Putian 莆田市	Fujian 福建省	15.08%	54
Foshan 佛山市	Guangdong 廣東省	8.61%	25
Guangzhou 廣州市	Guangdong 廣東省	7.24%	40
Suzhou 蘇州市	Jiangsu 江蘇省	6.24%	28
Huizhou 惠州市	Guangdong 廣東省	5.25%	15
Shanghai 上海市	Shanghai 上海市	4.08%	58
Yangzhou 揚州市	Jiangsu 江蘇省	3.72%	49
Quanzhou 泉州市	Fujian 福建省	2.47%	52
Yantai 煙台市	Shandong 山東省	2.28%	21
Tianjin 天津市	Tianjin 天津市	2.26%	33

10 Major Wholesalers 10 家主要批發商	City 城市	Province 省	Telephone / Fax 電話 / 傳真
Beijing Foreign Trade Import & Export Company 北京市對外貿易進出口公司	Beijing 北京市	Beijing 北京市	(010)65081589 (010)65043755
Fujian Putian Foreign Trade Company 福建省莆田市對外貿易公司	Putian 莆田市	Fujian 福建省	(0594)2398702 (0594)2292681
Hunan Light Industry General Company Import & Export Products Company 湖南省輕工業總公司進出品公司	Changsha 長沙市	Hunan 湖南省	(0731)2287932 (0731)2287844
Jiangxi Handicrafts Import & Export Company 江西省工藝品進出口公司	Nanchang 南昌市	Jiangxi 江西省	(0791)6246932 (0791)6223383
Jiangyin Shoes and Cap General Co. 江蘇江陰市鞋帽總公司	Wuxi 無錫市	Jiangsu 江蘇省	(0510)6804355 (0510)6803479
Jinhua Jin Hai Industrial Company 金華市金海實業公司	Jinhua 金華市	Zhejiang 浙江省	(0579)2324590
Guangdong Nanhai Handicrafts Import & Export Company 廣東南海市工藝品進出口公司	Foshan 佛山市	Guangdong 廣東省	(0757)6338620 (0757)6220225
Guangzhou Light Industry Products Shoes, Cap, Box, Bag Import & Export Co. 廣州市輕工業品鞋帽箱包進出口公司	Guangzhou 廣州市	Guangdong 廣東省	(020)83337522 (020)83339145
Nanjing Foreign Trade Company 南京市對外貿易公司	Nanjing 南京市	Jiangsu 江蘇省	(025)4403991 (025)4403700

*Also include sales by firms outside this industry.包括本行業以外廠家的銷售。"o" stands for "others". "o" 代表 "其他產品"。

1890: Other Apparel 其他纖維製品業

The industry accounts for 0.108% of the total revenue of China's industrial sector in 1996. The revenue growth rate of the industry is 12.6% from 1995, as compared to the growth rate of China's industrial sector, 9.51%. The rate of return on asset is 1.35%. 66.38% of all firms in the industry made a profit while 25.35% had negative returns. The top province in terms of the industry's revenue is Guangdong, accounting for 20.05% of the total revenue.
本行業在1996年佔全行業總產值0.108%，行業年增長率為12.6%（全國工業年增長率9.51%）。行業的資產回報率1.35%，66.38%的企業盈利，25.35%的企業虧損。銷售收入最高的省份為廣東省，佔本行業的20.05%。

	Total number of firms 企業總數	Total number of employees 職工總數	Total revenue (mil. RMB) 總銷售收入（百萬元）	Total profit (mil. RMB) 總利潤（百萬元）	Return on assets 資產利潤率 (%)	Return on equity 權益利潤率 (%)	Labour productivity ('000 RMB / worker) 勞動生產率（千元/人）	Debts / assets 資產負債率 (%)	Total assets (mil. RMB) 總資產（百萬元）
Industry Overall 行業總體	1,062	82,502	6,239	73	1.35	3.55	75.62	62.05	5,437

	Number of firms 企業個數	Average number of employees 平均職工人數	Average revenue ('000 RMB) 平均銷售收入（千元）	Average profit ('000 RMB) 平均利潤（千元）	Return on assets 資產利潤率 (%)	Return on equity 權益利潤率 (%)	Labour productivity ('000 RMB / worker) 勞動生產率（千元/人）	Average debts / assets 平均資產負債率(%)	Average Total assets ('000 RMB) 平均總資產（千元）
By ownership 產業所有權									
State-owned 國有	66	114	5,379	-91	-1.22	-4.03	47.19	69.78	7,470
Collectively-owned 集體	738	62	3,416	66	2.41	7.10	54.69	66.11	2,722
Privately-owned 私有	4	64	4,143	17	1.27	7.45	64.74	82.96	1,333
Domestic JVs 聯營	8	109	7,327	116	2.64	8.26	67.37	68.07	4,392
Joint stock 股份制	2	31	4,573	11	0.60	1.27	147.52	52.44	1,866
Foreign-funded 外資	90	155	18,337	306	2.02	4.63	118.62	56.40	15,164
Overseas Chinese-funded 港澳台資	153	93	10,579	11	0.11	0.28	113.40	59.17	9,929
By size 規模									
Large 大型	1	1,802	146,113	547	0.32	0.54	81.08	39.79	169,145
Medium 中型	11	436	64,442	887	1.51	3.41	147.68	55.75	58,853
Small 小型	1,032	73	5,217	61	1.36	3.74	71.45	63.75	4,478
By regional distribution 地區分布									
Central-North 華北	131	63	3,108	-26	-0.73	-2.04	49.45	64.15	3,596
Beijing 北京	44	29	2,199	-78	-2.68	-10.29	75.46	73.99	2,929
Tianjin 天津	27	127	6,806	-102	-1.34	-2.96	53.58	54.84	7,643
Hebei 河北	35	81	3,159	77	2.38	8.75	39.02	72.85	3,259
Shanxi 山西	6	38	1,028	18	1.40	1.96	26.83	28.32	1,307
Inner Mongolia 內蒙	19	24	524	-3	-0.36	-0.90	21.68	59.93	732
Northeast 東北	167	40	1,993	36	1.66	4.49	49.48	62.99	2,146
Liaoning 遼寧	86	55	2,877	63	1.92	4.91	52.31	60.94	3,275
Jilin 吉林	26	37	1,430	18	1.23	4.65	38.46	73.61	1,506
Heilongjiang 黑龍江	55	19	878	1	0.21	0.65	46.83	67.29	683
Central East 華東	416	91	8,330	212	3.06	7.31	91.80	58.20	6,946
Shanghai 上海	77	127	15,499	648	5.11	10.31	122.29	50.44	12,674
Jiangsu 江蘇	122	90	8,528	45	0.64	1.89	94.43	66.10	6,972
Zhejiang 浙江	64	61	8,178	435	7.33	19.06	134.04	61.53	5,925
Anhui 安徽	26	71	6,332	164	2.90	5.97	89.52	51.50	5,672
Fujian 福建	57	92	4,282	49	1.28	2.58	46.38	50.45	3,801
Jiangxi 江西	25	21	1,400	-97	-7.79	-20.07	65.81	61.20	1,242
Shandong 山東	45	121	5,873	12	0.19	0.55	48.64	65.74	6,414
Central-South 中南	235	94	7,899	7	0.11	0.31	84.04	63.60	5,934
Henan 河南	26	30	1,579	-123	-4.98	-29.86	52.91	83.32	2,479
Hubei 湖北	32	77	3,642	25	0.72	1.62	47.01	55.56	3,430
Hunan 湖南	40	64	1,605	-46	-2.35	-9.69	24.92	75.76	1,937
Guangdong 廣東	116	115	10,785	113	1.26	3.29	93.76	61.73	8,957
Guangxi 廣西	21	139	18,257	-347	-7.02	-23.07	131.57	69.57	4,939
Hainan 海南									
Southwest 西南	50	79	1,423	-18	-1.14	-4.98	18.12	77.04	1,576
Chongqing 重慶	10	126	2,105	173	6.38	23.52	16.65	72.89	2,705
Sichuan 四川	22	92	1,605	-3	-0.16	-0.83	17.43	80.92	1,756
Guizhou 貴州	9	43	843	86	13.80	44.77	19.41	69.00	620
Yunnan 雲南	7	16	747	6	0.78	4.35	45.48	81.96	729
Tibet 西藏	1	10	150	40	20.00	20.00	15.00		200
Northwest 西北	63	60	1,691	-289	-7.43	-63.30	28.24	88.27	3,886
Shaanxi 陝西	32	55	1,805	-1	-0.10	-0.53	32.86	81.84	970
Gansu 甘肅	10	80	341	-287	-9.25	-41.00	4.26	77.51	3,104
Qinghai 青海	6	19	373	-80	-16.38	69.57	20.18	123.21	488
Ningxia 寧夏									
Xinjiang 新疆	15	74	2,876	-987	-8.23	-88.25	39.04	90.67	11,985

1890: Other Apparel 其他纖維製品業

Year 年份	Number of firms 企業個數	Rate of change 每年變化 (%)	Number of employees 職工人數 (人)	Rate of change 每年變化 (%)	Total revenue (mil. RMB) 總銷售收入 (百萬元)	Rate of change 每年變化 (%)	Total profit (mil. RMB) 總利潤 (百萬元)	Rate of change 每年變化 (%)
1993	895		86,546		3,663		150	
1994	1,015	13.41%	82,182	-5.04%	4,994	36.30%	140	-6.29%
1995	1,070	5.42%	85,727	4.31%	5,541	10.97%	86	-38.76%
1996	1,062	-0.75%	82,502	-3.76%	6,239	12.60%	73	-14.99%

3 Major products* 3 種主要產品 *	Output 產量	Sales volume 銷售量	Unit 單位
a) Coverlet 被罩	78,081	76,519	10,000 piece 萬個
b) Leather Handbag & Bag 皮包、袋	19,478	19,088	10,000 piece 萬個
c) Blanket 毛毯	1,149,305	1,034,375	piece 條

Top 10 firms by revenue (year founded) 收入排名前 10 家企業 (創辦年份)	City 城市	Province 省	Telephone / fax 電話 / 傳真	Number of employees 職工人數	Ownership 產業所有權	Revenue ('000 RMB) 銷售收入 (千元)	Profit ('000 RMB) (rank) 利潤 (千元) (排名)	Total assets ('000 RMB) 總資產 (千元)	Major products 主要產品
Yulin Jiangnan Clothing Factory 玉林市江南服裝廠(1978)	Yulin 玉林市	Guangxi 廣西	(0775)3838743	2,145	Collectively-owned 集體	362,060	0(284)	18,450	o
Shanghai Xin Min Privately Owned Economic Development Company 上海新閔私營經濟開發公司(1994)	Shanghai 上海市	Shanghai 上海市	(021)57642307	1,450	其他經濟	183,294	16102(2)	37,200	o
Nanhai Zhu Jiang Plush Co. Ltd. 南海市珠江長毛絨有限公司(1988)	Foshan 佛山市	Guangdong 廣東省	(0757)6334143 (0757)6330081	437	Collectively-owned 集體	144,816	16736(5)	76,752	o
Nanjing Harness Factory 南京裝具廠(1941)	Nanjing 南京市	Jiangsu 江蘇省	(025)4593521 (025)4583521	1,900	State-owned 國有	142,647	228(123)	187,650	o
Su Long Jie Long Jia Mei Wool & Velvet Cloth Factory 素龍捷龍佳美毛絨布廠(1979)	Yunfu 雲浮市	Guangdong 廣東省		525	Collectively-owned 集體	124,410	2520(15)	104,010	c
Bengbu Cigarette Material Factory 蚌埠卷煙材料廠(1981)	Bengbu 蚌埠市	Anhui 安徽省	(0552)4083623 (0552)4083567	762	Collectively-owned 集體	121,585	3584(10)	128,077	o
Zheng Zhang Textile Products Factory 正章紡織製品廠 (1970)	Shanghai 上海市	Shanghai 上海市	(021)65030796 (021)65036907	520	Collectively-owned 集體	111,354	11134(3)	93,564	o
Dangyang Bei Hua Group Co. Ltd. 丹陽市蓓花集團有限公司(1986)	Zhenjiang 鎮江市	Jiangsu 江蘇省	(0511)2456887	809	Collectively-owned 集體	108,802	2470(16)	51,958	a
Tang Xin Fiber Co. Ltd. 唐昕纖維有限公司(1992)	Foshan 佛山市	Guangdong 廣東省	(0757)3351050 (0757)3351070	225	Foreign-funded 外資	102,824	-193(353)	36,872	o
Jia Yi Textile Products Co. Ltd. 佳誼紡織製品有限公司(1993)	Shanghai 上海市	Shanghai 上海市	(021)65300187 (021)65301022	14	Overseas Chinese-funded 港澳台資	97,579	914(47)	35,229	a

Top 10 Cities by Production Output 產出排名前 10 位城市	Province 省	Market share 市場份額	Number of firms 企業個數
Shanghai 上海市	Shanghai 上海市	9.73%	102
Suzhou 蘇州市	Jiangsu 江蘇省	7.92%	29
Nantong 南通市	Jiangsu 江蘇省	6.89%	55
Quanzhou 泉州市	Fujian 福建省	6.42%	77
Foshan 佛山市	Guangdong 廣東省	5.32%	18
Jinhua 金華市	Zhejiang 浙江省	4.03%	27
Guangzhou 廣州市	Guangdong 廣東省	3.52%	36
Tianjin 天津市	Tianjin 天津市	3.27%	34
Huizhou 惠州市	Guangdong 廣東省	2.96%	20
Nanjing 南京市	Jiangsu 江蘇省	2.85%	12

10 Major Wholesalers 10 家主要批發商	City 城市	Province 省	Telephone / Fax 電話 / 傳真
Anhui Clothing Import & Export Company 安徽省服裝進出口公司	Hefei 合肥市	Anhui 安徽省	(0551)3632212 (0551)3632002
Qingdao Textile Clothing Industrial Group Company 青島紡織服裝實業集團公司	Qingdao 青島市	Shandong 山東省	(0532)2877853 (0532)2869315
Hebei Textile Import & Export (Group) Company 河北省紡織品進出口(集團)公司	Shijiazhuang 石家莊市	Hebei 河北省	(0311)7028530 (0311)7027781
Zhong Fang Pledget Import & Export Company 中紡紗布進出口公司	Beijing 北京市	Beijing 北京市	(010)65124718 (010)65124713
Shaoxing Import & Export Company 紹興市進出口公司	Shaoxing 紹興市	Zhejiang 浙江省	(0575)5132822 (0575)5141577
Hunan Hua Xiang Import & Export (Group) Company 湖南省華湘進出口(集團)公司	Changsha 長沙市	Hunan 湖南省	(0731)2282440 (0731)2286995
City's Import & Export Company Trade Dept. 市進出口公司貿易部	Yichang 宜昌市	Hubei 湖北省	(0717)6450778 (0717)6441875
Shanghai Pu Dong Xinqu Import & Export Company 上海浦東新區進出口公司	Shanghai 上海市	Shanghai 上海市	(021)58878801 (021)58827444
Ningbo Yinxian Import & Export Company 寧波市鄞縣進出口公司	Ningbo 寧波市	Zhejiang 浙江省	(0574)7875205 (0574)7873168
Zhejiang Silk Import & Export Company 浙江省絲綢進出口公司	Hangzhou 杭州市	Zhejiang 浙江省	(0571)5195588 (0571)5192542

*Also include sales by firms outside this industry.包括本行業以外廠家的銷售。"o" stands for "others". "o" 代表 "其他產品"。

1911: Light Leather 輕革業

The industry accounts for 0.257% of the total revenue of China's industrial sector in 1996. The revenue growth rate of the industry is 2.5% from 1995, as compared to the growth rate of China's industrial sector, 9.51%. The rate of return on asset is 0.88%. 63.58% of all firms in the industry made a profit while 27.46% had negative returns. The top province in terms of the industry's revenue is Zhejiang, accounting for 24.93% of the total revenue.
本行業在1996年佔全行業總產值0.257%，行業年增長率為2.5%（全國工業年增長率9.51%）。行業的資產回報率0.88%，63.58%的企業盈利，27.46%的企業虧損。銷售收入最高的省份為浙江省，佔本行業的24.93%。

	Total number of firms 企業總數	Total number of employees 職工總數	Total revenue (mil. RMB) 總銷售收入（百萬元）	Total profit (mil. RMB) 總利潤（百萬元）	Return on assets 資產利潤率 (%)	Return on equity 權益利潤率 (%)	Labour productivity ('000 RMB / worker) 勞動生產率（千元／人）	Debts / assets 資產負債率 (%)	Total assets (mil. RMB) 總資產（百萬元）
Industry Overall 行業總體	1,061	146,245	14,902	149	0.88	4.34	101.90	79.77	17,007

	Number of firms 企業個數	Average number of employees 平均職工人數	Average revenue ('000 RMB) 平均銷售收入（千元）	Average profit ('000 RMB) 平均利潤（千元）	Return on assets 資產利潤率 (%)	Return on equity 權益利潤率 (%)	Labour productivity ('000 RMB / worker) 勞動生產率（千元／人）	Average debts / assets 平均資產負債率(%)	Average Total assets ('000 RMB) 平均總資產（千元）
By ownership 產業所有權									
State-owned 國有	141	321	8,738	-1,610	-5.36	-74.92	27.18	92.85	30,043
Collectively-owned 集體	715	104	11,491	478	5.10	20.99	110.08	75.70	9,368
Privately-owned 私有	8	40	10,477	789	15.63	23.11	261.12	32.38	5,047
Domestic JVs 聯營	8	313	17,940	-279	-1.04	-2.92	57.39	64.39	26,791
Joint stock 股份制	11	188	25,561	-186	-0.53	-2.50	136.16	78.72	34,956
Foreign-funded 外資	54	99	19,888	-420	-1.66	-6.67	201.49	75.04	25,211
Overseas Chinese-funded 港澳台資	121	135	31,721	413	1.23	5.08	234.19	75.84	33,592
By size 規模									
Large 大型	7	935	147,484	-231	-0.11	-0.52	157.81	79.13	211,741
Medium 中型	88	521	56,048	828	1.19	5.64	107.65	78.89	69,521
Small 小型	945	99	9,457	82	0.83	4.26	95.80	80.57	9,937
By regional distribution 地區分布									
Central-North 華北	96	149	6,824	-117	-0.87	-6.12	45.66	85.72	13,350
Beijing 北京	5	270	4,092	-2,668	-5.53	-23.25	15.16	76.24	48,274
Tianjin 天津	12	170	10,284	173	0.85	3.11	60.41	72.54	20,219
Hebei 河北	47	130	9,998	334	2.93	25.35	76.73	88.43	11,402
Shanxi 山西	8	139	1,505	-90	-0.81	-2.52	10.81	67.78	11,066
Inner Mongolia 內蒙	24	155	1,220	-622	-8.62	47.49	7.88	118.16	7,216
Northeast 東北	58	153	5,964	-587	-3.06	-25.57	38.98	88.04	19,193
Liaoning 遼寧	22	183	6,945	-438	-1.66	-11.65	37.89	85.74	26,367
Jilin 吉林	15	130	2,467	-354	-3.00	-31.22	19.01	90.39	11,803
Heilongjiang 黑龍江	21	138	7,434	-910	-5.37	-57.13	53.92	90.61	16,955
Central East 華東	394	153	21,793	552	2.78	11.36	142.76	75.50	19,843
Shanghai 上海	16	190	11,483	-1,216	-3.80	-17.16	60.56	77.87	32,024
Jiangsu 江蘇	65	129	17,805	-203	-1.13	-5.75	138.38	80.34	17,944
Zhejiang 浙江	150	135	24,764	681	3.71	11.53	183.06	67.84	18,359
Anhui 安徽	40	187	23,542	861	3.89	36.28	125.87	89.28	22,138
Fujian 福建	26	118	14,283	118	0.73	2.92	121.16	74.94	16,066
Jiangxi 江西	34	82	2,258	-172	-3.26	-58.33	27.54	94.41	5,279
Shandong 山東	63	240	33,983	1,850	6.12	24.39	141.55	74.90	30,204
Central-South 中南	337	109	12,675	281	2.07	8.53	116.22	75.74	13,592
Henan 河南	146	77	8,751	347	4.00	20.46	114.36	80.43	8,669
Hubei 湖北	36	165	9,211	268	2.44	6.49	55.95	62.39	10,963
Hunan 湖南	63	162	12,039	-176	-1.28	-5.58	74.46	77.00	13,715
Guangdong 廣東	72	98	23,999	787	3.28	12.98	245.02	74.75	23,999
Guangxi 廣西	19	126	9,244	-579	-3.37	-13.86	73.64	75.70	17,196
Hainan 海南	1	34	360	-70	-4.46	-10.29	10.59	57.32	1,570
Southwest 西南	111	145	6,141	-490	-4.63	-42.37	42.46	89.06	10,581
Chongqing 重慶	12	166	4,998	-2,757	-18.78	60.66	30.07	130.96	14,682
Sichuan 四川	65	146	8,042	-214	-1.96	-10.70	54.71	81.63	10,872
Guizhou 貴州	15	117	1,211	-72	-0.93	-4.68	10.38	80.23	7,781
Yunnan 雲南	18	144	4,076	-317	-3.50	-19.49	28.26	82.07	9,076
Tibet 西藏									
Northwest 西北	65	155	5,565	-978	-6.12	200.44	35.94	103.05	15,984
Shaanxi 陝西	16	127	13,536	408	1.67	11.18	106.90	85.09	24,444
Gansu 甘肅	22	121	2,231	-807	-12.68	116.31	18.47	110.89	6,367
Qinghai 青海	5	189	6,060	-4,024	-15.94	310.02	32.00	105.14	25,238
Ningxia 寧夏	3	105	1,227	-2,237	-13.43	-86.47	11.68	84.47	16,653
Xinjiang 新疆	19	217	3,267	-1,342	-7.69	33.53	15.07	122.93	17,455

Year 年份	Number of firms 企業個數	Rate of change 每年變化 (%)	Number of employees 職工人數（人）	Rate of change 每年變化 (%)	Total revenue (mil. RMB) 總銷售收入（百萬元）	Rate of change 每年變化 (%)	Total profit (mil. RMB) 總利潤（百萬元）	Rate of change 每年變化 (%)
1993	877		126,151		8,119		66	
1994	1,017	15.96%	127,032	0.70%	10,565	30.12%	-14	-121.14%
1995	1,133	11.41%	165,298	30.12%	14,534	37.57%	157	1235.04%
1996	1,061	-6.35%	146,245	-11.53%	14,902	2.53%	149	-5.33%

3 Major products* 3種主要產品*	Output 產量	Sales volume 銷售量	Unit 單位
a) Tanning Leather 鞣製皮革	77,898,062	74,782,140	piece 張
b) Light Leather 輕革	169,653,310	186,618,641	square metre 平方米
c) Leather Costume 革皮服裝	4,795,225	4,555,464	piece 件

Top 10 firms by revenue (year founded) 收入排名前10家企業（創辦年份）	City 城市	Province 省	Telephone / fax 電話／傳真	Number of employees 職工人數	Ownership 產業所有權	Revenue ('000 RMB) 銷售收入（千元）	Profit ('000 RMB) (rank) 利潤（千元）（排名）	Total assets ('000 RMB) 總資產（千元）	Major products 主要產品
Sichuan Chengdu Quan Xing Distillery 四川省成都全興酒廠(1950)	Chengdu 成都市	Sichuan 四川省	(028)7513999 (028)4430727	2,789	State-owned 國有	1,075,027	193524(1)	1,003,567	o
Nanhai Leather Co. Ltd. 南海皮革有限公司(1991)	Foshan 佛山市	Guangdong 廣東省	(0757)6441908 (0757)6441701	788	Overseas Chinese-funded 港澳台資	510,458	31242(5)	350,431	a,b,c
Haining Ka Sen Leather Group Corp., Ltd. 海寧市卡森皮革集團有限責任公司(1988)	Jiaxing 嘉興市	Zhejiang 浙江省	(0573)7788388 (0573)7788157	330	Collectively-owned 集體	374,783	36942(2)	248,209	a,b,c
Zhejiang Fu Bang Leather Co. Ltd. 浙江富邦皮革有限公司(1993)	Jiaxing 嘉興市	Zhejiang 浙江省	(0573)7533498 (0573)7533336	888	Overseas Chinese-funded 港澳台資	341,821	13682(9)	258,162	a,b,c
Zhejiang Long Chang Leather Group Corp., Ltd. 浙江龍昌皮革集團有限責任公司(1987)	Jiaxing 嘉興市	Zhejiang 浙江省	(0573)8911508 (0573)8911674	1,142	Collectively-owned 集體	324,221	3846(33)	194,727	a,c
Wendeng Tannery 文登市製革廠(1953)	Weihai 威海市	Shandong 山東省	(0896)8251667 (0896)8251667	1,397	Collectively-owned 集體	241,710	36427(3)	212,585	a,b
Zhongshan Nan Yi Tannery Co. Ltd. 中山市南藝製革廠有限公司(1988)	Zhongshan 中山市	Guangdong 廣東省	(0760)3115878 (0760)3116132	418	Overseas Chinese-funded 港澳台資	218,655	33499(4)	134,811	a,b
Funan Nan Yang Tannery Co. Ltd. 阜南縣南洋製革有限公司(1994)	Fuyang 阜陽市	Anhui 安徽省	(0558)6712306	267	Domestic JVs 聯營	206,600	1815(59)	93,586	a
Quzhou Tian Yi Industrial Co. Tannery 衢州天一實業公司製革廠(1965)	Quzhou 衢州市	Zhejiang 浙江省	(0570)3021492 (0570)3021214	615	Collectively-owned 集體	197,372	5916(20)	188,842	a,b
Guangzhou Di Wei Leather Co. Ltd. 廣州迪威皮革有限公司(1994)	Guangzhou 廣州市	Guangdong 廣東省	(020)82309586 (020)82300646	740	Overseas Chinese-funded 港澳台資	194,216	-16946(612)	349,463	a,b

Top 10 Cities by Production Output 產出排名前10位城市	Province 省	Market share 市場份額	Number of firms 企業個數
Wenzhou 温州市	Zhejiang 浙江省	11.52%	434
Chengdu 成都市	Sichuan 四川省	8.30%	21
Jiaxing 嘉興市	Zhejiang 浙江省	7.85%	26
Zhoukou 周口市	Henan 河南省	5.57%	51
Nantong 南通市	Jiangsu 江蘇省	4.22%	23
Weihai 威海市	Shandong 山東省	3.66%	5
Suzhou 蘇州市	Jiangsu 江蘇省	3.15%	19
Fuyang 阜陽市	Anhui 安徽省	2.32%	20
Zhongshan 中山市	Guangdong 廣東省	2.14%	7
Quzhou 衢州市	Zhejiang 浙江省	2.00%	4

10 Major Wholesalers 10家主要批發商	City 城市	Province 省	Telephone / Fax 電話／傳真
Ningbo Local Products Animal Products Import & Export Company 寧波市土產畜產進出口公司	Ningbo 寧波市	Zhejiang 浙江省	(0574)7319525 (0574)7320262
Jiangmen Local Products Import & Export Co 江門市土產進出口公司	Jiangmen 江門市	Guangdong 廣東省	(0759)3353805 (0759)3351104
Jiang Men Handicrafts Import & Export Company 江門市工藝品進出口公司	Jiangmen 江門市	Guangdong 廣東省	(0759)3534021 (0759)3535342
Shandong Animal Products Import & Export Company 山東省畜產進出口公司	Qingdao 青島市	Shandong 山東省	(0532)2971790 (0532)2971838
Hunan Local Products Animal Products Import & Export Company 湖南省土產畜產進出口公司	Changsha 長沙市	Hunan 湖南省	(0731)4727265 (0731)4726674
Zhejiang Local Products Animal Products Import & Export Company 浙江省土產畜產進出口公司	Hangzhou 杭州市	Zhejiang 浙江省	(0571)5178390 (0571)5152310
Jiangsu Dong Xing Import & Export (Group) Co. Ltd. 江蘇省東星進出口(集團)股份有限公司	Nanjing 南京市	Jiangsu 江蘇省	(025)6617488 (025)6616141
Jiang Men Cooking Oil Mill Import & Export Company 江門市糧油進出口公司	Jiangmen 江門市	Guangdong 廣東省	(0759)3366449 (0759)3369323
Guangzhou Animal Products Import & Export Company 廣州市畜產進出口公司	Guangzhou 廣州市	Guangdong 廣東省	(020)83852888 (020)83824187
Tianjin Animal Products Import & Export Company 天津畜產進出口公司	Tianjin 天津市	Tianjin 天津市	(022)23310832 (022)23317312

*Also include sales by firms outside this industry.包括本行業以外廠家的銷售。"o" stands for "others". "o" 代表"其他產品"。

1912: Heavy Leather 重革業

The industry accounts for 0.012% of the total revenue of China's industrial sector in 1996. The revenue growth rate of the industry is 0.7% from 1995, as compared to the growth rate of China's industrial sector, 9.51%. The rate of return on asset is -1.43%. 78.94% of all firms in the industry made a profit while 14.81% had negative returns. The top province in terms of the industry's revenue is Jiangsu, accounting for 57.71% of the total revenue.
本行業在1996年佔全行業總產值0.012%，行業年增長率為0.7%（全國工業年增長率9.51%）。行業的資產回報率-1.43%，78.94%的企業盈利，14.81%的企業虧損。銷售收入最高的省份為江蘇省，佔本行業的57.71%。

	Total number of firms 企業總數	Total number of employees 職工總數	Total revenue (mil. RMB) 總銷售收入（百萬元）	Total profit (mil. RMB) 總利潤（百萬元）	Return on assets 資產利潤率 (%)	Return on equity 權益利潤率 (%)	Labour productivity ('000 RMB / worker) 勞動生產率（千元/人）	Debts / assets 資產負債率 (%)	Total assets (mil. RMB) 總資產（百萬元）
Industry Overall 行業總體	85	6,055	683	-8	-1.43	-6.19	112.80	76.82	590

	Number of firms 企業個數	Average number of employees 平均職工人數	Average revenue ('000 RMB) 平均銷售收入（千元）	Average profit ('000 RMB) 平均利潤（千元）	Return on assets 資產利潤率 (%)	Return on equity 權益利潤率 (%)	Labour productivity ('000 RMB / worker) 勞動生產率（千元/人）	Average debts / assets 平均資產負債率(%)	Average Total assets ('000 RMB) 平均總資產（千元）
By ownership 產業所有權									
State-owned 國有	7	244	5,286	-1,286	-4.59	-25.71	21.65	82.14	28,000
Collectively-owned 集體	71	50	2,613	-4,257	-190.73	-701.99	52.43	72.83	2,232
Privately-owned 私有	1	25	5,134	-8,875	-595.08	-1186.09	205.36	49.83	1,491
Domestic JVs 聯營									
Joint stock 股份制	1	99	6,091	-12,750	-279.60	-1028.50	61.53	72.81	4,560
Foreign-funded 外資	1	338	410,885	339,690	227.71	803.71	1215.64	71.67	149,174
Overseas Chinese-funded 港澳台資	4	99	9,587	-3,703	-18.46	-100.94	97.33	81.71	20,061
By size 規模									
Large 大型									
Medium 中型	2	573	12,286	-1,558	-1.82	-5.83	21.46	68.76	85,509
Small 小型	82	60	8,030	-60	-1.17	-5.84	133.34	80.05	5,109
By regional distribution 地區分布									
Central-North 華北	7	88	9,319	1,269	18.90	48.08	105.38	60.67	6,713
Beijing 北京									
Tianjin 天津	2	148	21,990	2,990	32.12	51.29	148.58	37.33	9,310
Hebei 河北	2	150	10,325	1,445	10.31	43.46	69.06	76.27	14,010
Shanxi 山西									
Inner Mongolia 內蒙	3	8	200	3	2.86	6.25	25.00	54.29	117
Northeast 東北	6	173	4,040	-1,513	-10.91	-38.94	23.42	71.99	13,872
Liaoning 遼寧	5	205	4,848	-1,820	-10.99	-39.38	23.60	72.08	16,554
Jilin 吉林									
Heilongjiang 黑龍江	1	8		20	4.35	9.52		56.52	460
Central East 華東	43	57	11,187	-117	-1.53	-8.79	196.42	82.57	7,621
Shanghai 上海	1	28	1,000	40	4.94	23.53	35.71	79.01	810
Jiangsu 江蘇	4	275	98,538	-1,350	-2.01	-14.97	358.32	86.60	67,298
Zhejiang 浙江	35	36	2,415	9	0.55	1.53	66.92	64.12	1,611
Anhui 安徽	1	45	550	20	2.25	6.45	12.22	65.17	890
Fujian 福建	1	13	810	10	2.33	3.03	62.31	23.26	430
Jiangxi 江西									
Shandong 山東	1								
Central-South 中南	14	66	5,811	142	3.15	5.24	87.47	39.85	4,510
Henan 河南	5	31	10,956	68	2.39	4.81	358.04	50.25	2,842
Hubei 湖北	3	60	1,500	30	2.98	-8.57	25.14	134.77	1,007
Hunan 湖南	1	35	220	30	2.54	4.55	6.29	44.07	1,180
Guangdong 廣東	4	141	5,463	383	3.42	4.89	38.81	30.02	11,183
Guangxi 廣西	1								
Hainan 海南									
Southwest 西南	14	69	2,204	-375	-7.69	1693.55	31.74	100.47	4,879
Chongqing 重慶	2	11	200	-126	-42.97	21.92	18.03	296.06	292
Sichuan 四川	5	115	3,940	-846	-10.72	136.59	33.97	107.85	7,892
Guizhou 貴州	2	13	110	15	6.82	13.04	8.80	50.00	220
Yunnan 雲南	4	74	2,273	-108	-1.72	-10.02	30.61	82.83	6,248
Tibet 西藏									
Northwest 西北	1	50	300				6.00	70.21	470
Shaanxi 陝西									
Gansu 甘肅	1	50	300				6.00	70.21	470
Qinghai 青海									
Ningxia 寧夏									
Xinjiang 新疆									

1912: Heavy Leather 重革業

Year 年份	Number of firms 企業個數	Rate of change 每年變化 (%)	Number of employees 職工人數（人）	Rate of change 每年變化 (%)	Total revenue (mil. RMB) 總銷售收入（百萬元）	Rate of change 每年變化 (%)	Total profit (mil. RMB) 總利潤（百萬元）	Rate of change 每年變化 (%)
1993	51		5,311		219		-15	
1994	55	7.84%	7,571	42.55%	410	86.98%	-9	37.40%
1995	86	56.36%	5,745	-24.12%	678	65.61%	-9	-0.13%
1996	85	-1.16%	6,055	5.40%	683	0.70%	-8	14.71%

3 Major products* 3 種主要產品 *	Output 產量	Sales volume 銷售量	Unit 單位
a) Heavy Leather 重革	5,863	5,218	ton 噸
b) Tanning Leather 鞣製皮革	1,691,059	1,623,416	piece 張
c) Light Leather 輕革	1,279,213	1,407,135	square metre 平方米

Top 10 firms by revenue (year founded) 收入排名前 10 家企業（創辦年份）	City 城市	Province 省	Telephone / fax 電話 / 傳真	Number of employees 職工人數	Ownership 產業所有權	Revenue ('000 RMB) 銷售收入（千元）	Profit ('000 RMB) (rank) 利潤（千元）（排名）	Total assets ('000 RMB) 總資產（千元）	Major products 主要產品
Nantong Dong Xing Leather Co. Ltd. 南通東星皮革有限公司(1993)	Nantong 南通市	Jiangsu 江蘇省	(0513)3596889 (0513)3596891	430	Foreign-funded 外資	374,369	4093(2)	130,829	b,c
Zhenping Jia Song Zhen Food Series Leather Factory 鎮平縣賈宋鎮食品系列皮革廠(1995)	Nanyang 南陽市	Henan 河南省		50	Joint stock 股份制	45,471	0(23)	7,650	b
Chengguanzhen Niu Si Tai Er Shoes Industry Co. Ltd. 城關鎮紐斯泰爾鞋業有限公司(1993)	Tianjin 天津市	Tianjin 天津市	(022)29461337	280	Foreign-funded 外資	43,710	6240(1)	17,110	o
Shenyang Jin Fu Shoes Industry Co. Ltd. 瀋陽金福鞋業有限公司(1994)	Shenyang 瀋陽市	Liaoning 遼寧省	(024)89570803 (024)89570242	500	Overseas Chinese-funded 港澳台資	17,493	-9103(31)	23,799	o
Wenzhou Dong Qiao Tan Company 温州市洞橋製革公司(1987)	Wenzhou 温州市	Zhejiang 浙江省	(0577)8793143	14	Collectively-owned 集體	17,400	176(9)	1,929	o
Hengshui Leather Shoes Material Factory 衡水市皮鞋材料廠(1971)	Hengshui 衡水市	Hebei 河北省	(0318)2022976 (0318)2023767	268	State-owned 國有	17,348	2618(3)	26,792	o
Guangdong Nanhai Tan Factory 廣東省南海製革廠(1965)	Foshan 佛山市	Guangdong 廣東省	(0757)6441483 (0757)6443370	101	Collectively-owned 集體	16,080	1140(4)	37,860	b
Chongqing Ke Er Shi Shoes Industry Co. Ltd. 重慶科而士鞋業有限公司	Chongqing 重慶市	Chongqing 重慶市	(023)68832788 (023)68833988	275	Private-owned 私營	11,266	227(8)	17,219	o
Xuzhou Globe-eagle Leather Group Co. 徐州鷹球皮革集團公司(1950)	Xuzhou 徐州市	Jiangsu 江蘇省	(0516)7768794 (0516)7767618	570	State-owned 國有	11,170	-9143(32)	96,393	a,b
Wenzhou Lucheng Flourishing Tan Factory 温州市鹿城繁榮製革廠(1992)	Wenzhou 温州市	Zhejiang 浙江省	(0577)8785301	18	Collectively-owned 集體	9,365	77(10)	10,643	o

Top 10 Cities by Production Output 產出排名前 10 位城市	Province 省	Market share 市場份額	Number of firms 企業個數
Fuyang 阜陽市	Anhui 安徽省	21.75%	5
Guangzhou 廣州市	Guangdong 廣東省	20.82%	4
Foshan 佛山市	Guangdong 廣東省	19.98%	2
Wenzhou 温州市	Zhejiang 浙江省	13.92%	33
Nanyang 南陽市	Henan 河南省	8.05%	2
Xuzhou 徐州市	Jiangsu 江蘇省	2.53%	1
Fuzhou 福州市	Fujian 福建省	2.03%	1
Chongqing 重慶市	Chongqing 重慶市	1.85%	3
Zhangzhou 漳州市	Fujian 福建省	1.78%	1
Nantong 南通市	Jiangsu 江蘇省	1.36%	1

10 Major Wholesalers 10 家主要批發商	City 城市	Province 省	Telephone / Fax 電話 / 傳真
Ningbo Local Products Animal Products Import & Export Company 寧波市土產畜產進出口公司	Ningbo 寧波市	Zhejiang 浙江省	(0574)7319525 (0574)7320262
Jiangmen Local Products Import & Export Co 江門市土產進出口公司	Jiangmen 江門市	Guangdong 廣東省	(0759)3353805 (0759)3351104
Jiangmen Handicrafts Import & Export Company 江門市工藝品進出口公司	Jiangmen 江門市	Guangdong 廣東省	(0759)3534021 (0759)3535342
Shandong Animal Products Import & Export Company 山東省畜產進出口公司	Qingdao 青島市	Shandong 山東省	(0532)2971790 (0532)2971838
Hunan Local Products Animal Products Import & Export Company 湖南省土產畜產進出口公司	Changsha 長沙市	Hunan 湖南省	(0731)4727265 (0731)4726674
Zhejiang Local Products Animal Products Import & Export Company 浙江省土產畜產進出口公司	Hangzhou 杭州市	Zhejiang 浙江省	(0571)5178390 (0571)5152310
Jiangsu Dong Xing Import & Export (Group) Co. Ltd. 江蘇省東星進出口(集團)股份有限公司	Nanjing 南京市	Jiangsu 江蘇省	(025)6617488 (025)6616141
Jiangmen Cooking Oil Mill Import & Export Company 江門市糧油進出口公司	Jiangmen 江門市	Guangdong 廣東省	(0759)3366449 (0759)3369323
Guangzhou Animal Products Import & Export Company 廣州市畜產進出口公司	Guangzhou 廣州市	Guangdong 廣東省	(020)83852888 (020)83824187
Tianjin Animal Products Import & Export Company 天津畜產進出口公司	Tianjin 天津市	Tianjin 天津市	(022)23310832 (022)23317312

*Also include sales by firms outside this industry.包括本行業以外廠家的銷售。"o" stands for "others". "o" 代表"其他產品"。

1919: Other Leather 其他製革業

The industry accounts for 0.042% of the total revenue of China's industrial sector in 1996. The revenue growth rate of the industry is 77.6% from 1995, as compared to the growth rate of China's industrial sector, 9.51%. The rate of return on asset is 1.63%. 70.57% of all firms in the industry made a profit while 21.10% had negative returns. The top province in terms of the industry's revenue is Guangdong, accounting for 33.44% of the total revenue.
本行業在1996年佔全行業總產值0.042%，行業年增長率為77.6%（全國工業年增長率9.51%）。行業的資產回報率1.63%，70.57%的企業盈利，21.10%的企業虧損。銷售收入最高的省份為廣東省，佔本行業的33.44%。

	Total number of firms 企業總數	Total number of employees 職工總數	Total revenue (mil. RMB) 總銷售收入（百萬元）	Total profit (mil. RMB) 總利潤（百萬元）	Return on assets 資產利潤率 (%)	Return on equity 權益利潤率 (%)	Labour productivity ('000 RMB / worker) 勞動生產率（千元/人）	Debts / assets 資產負債率 (%)	Total assets (mil. RMB) 總資產（百萬元）
Industry Overall 行業總體	267	21,675	2,430	44	1.63	4.82	112.11	66.22	2,675

	Number of firms 企業個數	Average number of employees 平均職工人數	Average revenue ('000 RMB) 平均銷售收入（千元）	Average profit ('000 RMB) 平均利潤（千元）	Return on assets 資產利潤率 (%)	Return on equity 權益利潤率 (%)	Labour productivity ('000 RMB / worker) 勞動生產率（千元/人）	Average debts / assets 平均資產負債率(%)	Average Total assets ('000 RMB) 平均總資產（千元）
By ownership 產業所有權									
State-owned 國有	18	39	1,111	-667	-9.68	34.29	28.69	128.23	6,889
Collectively-owned 集體	174	73	6,404	157	2.47	8.97	87.33	72.44	6,366
Privately-owned 私有	1	124	2,940	99	7.43	7.43	23.71		1,332
Domestic JVs 聯營	1	28							
Joint stock 股份制	4	81	4,349	12	0.11	0.59	53.85	80.55	10,189
Foreign-funded 外資	34	176	29,363	137	0.52	1.46	167.14	64.26	26,200
Overseas Chinese-funded 港澳台資	34	78	8,183	700	4.65	7.77	104.29	40.12	15,058
By size 規模									
Large 大型	1	771	84,164	-7,913	-2.32	-10.32	109.16	77.53	341,298
Medium 中型									
Small 小型	258	82	9,097	201	2.22	6.27	110.60	64.55	9,050
By regional distribution 地區分布									
Central-North 華北	28	49	8,429	165	2.43	6.93	172.02	64.90	6,789
Beijing 北京	5	32	1,680	-1,408	-14.22	-30.60	52.17	53.52	9,900
Tianjin 天津	2	204	90,860	4,925	11.58	28.74	445.39	59.71	42,525
Hebei 河北	11	56	3,970	225	6.53	79.42	71.47	91.78	3,438
Shanxi 山西	3	23	217	-7	-0.58	-7.41	9.42	92.20	1,153
Inner Mongolia 內蒙	7	18	224	-91	-4.49	-10.60	12.76	57.54	2,036
Northeast 東北	17	20	746	-4	-0.13	-0.32	37.77	59.57	2,705
Liaoning 遼寧	10	23	1,076	-6	-0.21	-0.97	47.40	78.46	2,865
Jilin 吉林	2	16	105	-10	-3.85	-7.69	6.77	48.08	260
Heilongjiang 黑龍江	5	16	344	4	0.12	0.16	22.05	27.72	3,362
Central East 華東	73	91	8,477	310	2.92	8.75	93.48	66.65	10,641
Shanghai 上海	9	37	2,053	-692	-15.08	84.30	56.00	117.89	4,589
Jiangsu 江蘇	9	49	4,639	31	0.62	3.98	95.54	84.50	5,040
Zhejiang 浙江	17	85	12,262	385	4.52	13.20	143.67	65.77	8,529
Anhui 安徽	7	163	1,794	13	0.12	4.29	11.01	97.16	10,551
Fujian 福建	9	81	21,044	1,988	6.82	12.01	261.24	43.25	29,167
Jiangxi 江西	5	14	168	-32	-1.71	-21.05	11.67	91.90	1,876
Shandong 山東	17	145	8,668	249	2.13	7.32	59.81	70.94	11,729
Central-South 中南	113	99	11,499	130	1.09	3.13	116.59	65.32	11,957
Henan 河南	30	72	8,760	-22	-0.21	8.26	121.16	102.52	10,410
Hubei 湖北	7	74	2,650	53	2.71	12.46	35.88	78.21	1,947
Hunan 湖南	21	65	9,348	41	0.89	4.94	143.19	81.97	4,596
Guangdong 廣東	47	146	17,287	298	1.53	3.08	118.78	50.48	19,502
Guangxi 廣西	8	31	1,155	14	0.91	4.93	37.26	81.67	1,514
Hainan 海南									
Southwest 西南	23	59	6,636	-65	-0.67	-2.33	113.05	71.09	9,666
Chongqing 重慶	2	18	17,696	2	0.05	0.11	941.29	57.48	3,397
Sichuan 四川	15	79	6,733	-80	-0.60	-2.11	85.18	71.68	13,403
Guizhou 貴州	2	10	110	-5	-0.56	-12.50	11.00	95.51	890
Yunnan 雲南	2	17	630	-190	-7.17	-31.15	37.06	76.98	2,650
Tibet 西藏	1	30	350	110	11.00	11.00	11.67		1,000
Northwest 西北	13	66	8,460	241	3.55	12.00	129.08	70.42	6,787
Shaanxi 陝西	3	111	19,337	1,393	17.28	32.73	173.68	47.17	8,063
Gansu 甘肅	5	78	2,212	-234	-2.37	-20.00	28.36	88.13	9,872
Qinghai 青海	2	13	150	25	11.90	11.90	12.00		210
Ningxia 寧夏									
Xinjiang 新疆	3	34	13,537	23	0.49	0.99	394.27	50.63	4,753

1919: Other Leather 其他製革業

Year 年份	Number of firms 企業個數	Rate of change 每年變化 (%)	Number of employees 職工人數 (人)	Rate of change 每年變化 (%)	Total revenue (mil. RMB) 總銷售收入 (百萬元)	Rate of change 每年變化 (%)	Total profit (mil. RMB) 總利潤 (百萬元)	Rate of change 每年變化 (%)
1993	187		12,850		701		-14	
1994	213	13.90%	17,304	34.66%	1,537	119.40%	-5	66.39%
1995	203	-4.70%	17,002	-1.75%	1,368	-10.97%	16	429.20%
1996	267	31.53%	21,675	27.49%	2,430	77.63%	44	183.83%

3 Major products* 3種主要產品*	Output 產量	Sales volume 銷售量	Unit 單位
a) Light Leather 輕革	25,283,274	27,811,602	square metre 平方米
b) Tanning Leather 鞣製皮革	6,614,369	6,349,794	piece 張

Top 10 firms by revenue (year founded) 收入排名前10家企業 (創辦年份)	City 城市	Province 省	Telephone / fax 電話 / 傳真	Number of employees 職工人數	Ownership 產業所有權	Revenue ('000 RMB) 銷售收入 (千元)	Profit ('000 RMB) (rank) 利潤 (千元) (排名)	Total assets ('000 RMB) 總資產 (千元)	Major products 主要產品
Tianjin Shun Cheng Tourism Articles Co. Ltd. 天津市順成旅遊用品有限公司(1994)	Tianjin 天津市	Tianjin 天津市	(022)25536010	380	Overseas Chinese-funded 港澳台資	178,330	9180(4)	83,850	o
Henan Great Wall Group Company 河南長城集團公司(1987)	Jiaozuo 焦作市	Henan 河南省	(0391)5693475 (0391)5695006	920	Collectively-owned 集體	175,804	9554(2)	174,879	b
Jiang Retail Sales Mei Mei Artificial Leather Factory Co. Ltd. 江門市美美人造皮廠有限公司(1988)	Jiangmen 江門市	Guangdong 廣東省	(0750)3796938 (0750)3795113	648	Overseas Chinese-funded 港澳台資	135,274	9413(3)	194,474	o
Kaiping Sha Gang Meilin Products Factory 開平沙岡美林製品廠(1984)	Jiangmen 江門市	Guangdong 廣東省	(0750)2298056	1,382	Foreign-funded 外資	125,810	284(37)	12,359	o
Enxin Plastic Leather Industrial Co. Ltd. 恩新塑料皮革實業公司(1989)	Jiangmen 江門市	Guangdong 廣東省	(0750)4423691	485	Foreign-funded 外資	105,750	1676(12)	37,228	a
Xinhui Hua Lian Leather Tanning Industrial Co. Ltd. 新會市華聯製皮工業有限公司(1995)	Jiangmen 江門市	Guangdong 廣東省		350	Overseas Chinese-funded 港澳台資	101,247	-198(105)	294,231	a
Hangzhou Fu Ke Da Leather Industry Co. Ltd. 杭州富可達皮業有限公司(1986)	Hangzhou 杭州市	Zhejiang 浙江省	(0571)2406388 (0571)2406748	650	Foreign-funded 外資	100,039	4258(6)	32,538	o
Shandong Laiwu Zhen Hua Industrial (Group) Company 山東省萊蕪市振華實業(集團)公司(1986)	Laiwu 萊蕪市	Shandong 山東省	(0634)6212943 (0634)6212943	931	Collectively-owned 集體	85,494	3976(7)	119,019	o
Sihui Jin Bao Li Xie Factory 四會市金寶利鞋廠(1987)	Zhaoqing 肇慶市	Guangdong 廣東省	(0757)3321601 (0757)3321818	480	Overseas Chinese-funded 港澳台資	78,799	180(46)	22,998	o
Fujian Xianyou Xing Wei Shoes Industry Co. Ltd. 福建仙遊幸偉鞋業有限公司(1989)	Putian 莆田市	Fujian 福建省	(0594)7692266 (0594)7693066	65	Overseas Chinese-funded 港澳台資	75,043	17840(1)	8,161	o

Top 10 Cities by Production Output 產出排名前10位城市	Province 省	Market share 市場份額	Number of firms 企業個數
Jiangmen 江門市	Guangdong 廣東省	13.05%	8
Xiangtan 湘潭市	Hunan 湖南省	9.14%	12
Jiaozuo 焦作市	Henan 河南省	9.13%	1
Hangzhou 杭州市	Zhejiang 浙江省	5.15%	4
Foshan 佛山市	Guangdong 廣東省	4.95%	5
Guangzhou 廣州市	Guangdong 廣東省	4.86%	26
Shantou 汕頭市	Guangdong 廣東省	4.11%	3
Zhaoqing 肇慶市	Guangdong 廣東省	3.92%	4
Laiwu 萊蕪市	Shandong 山東省	3.71%	1
Huizhou 惠州市	Guangdong 廣東省	3.10%	14

10 Major Wholesalers 10家主要批發商	City 城市	Province 省	Telephone / Fax 電話 / 傳真
Ningbo Local Products Animal Products Import & Export Company 寧波市土產畜產進出口公司	Ningbo 寧波市	Zhejiang 浙江省	(0574)7319525 (0574)7320262
Jiangmen Local Products Import & Export Co 江門市土產進出口公司	Jiangmen 江門市	Guangdong 廣東省	(0759)3353805 (0759)3351104
Jiangmen Handicrafts Import & Export Company 江門市工藝品進出口公司	Jiangmen 江門市	Guangdong 廣東省	(0759)3534021 (0759)3535342
Shandong Animal Products Import & Export Company 山東省畜產進出口公司	Qingdao 青島市	Shandong 山東省	(0532)2971790 (0532)2971838
Hunan Local Products Animal Products Import & Export Company 湖南省土產畜產進出口公司	Changsha 長沙市	Hunan 湖南省	(0731)4727265 (0731)4726674
Zhejiang Local Products Animal Products Import & Export Company 浙江省土產畜產進出口公司	Hangzhou 杭州市	Zhejiang 浙江省	(0571)5178390 (0571)5152310
Jiangsu Dong Xing Import & Export (Group) Co. Ltd. 江蘇省東星進出口(集團)股份有限公司	Nanjing 南京市	Jiangsu 江蘇省	(025)6617488 (025)6616141
Jiangmen Cooking Oil Mill Import & Export Company 江門市糧油進出口公司	Jiangmen 江門市	Guangdong 廣東省	(0759)3366449 (0759)3369323
Guangzhou Animal Products Import & Export Company 廣州市畜產進出口公司	Guangzhou 廣州市	Guangdong 廣東省	(020)83852888 (020)83824187
Tianjin Animal Products Import & Export Company 天津畜產進出口公司	Tianjin 天津市	Tianjin 天津市	(022)23310832 (022)23317312

*Also include sales by firms outside this industry.包括本行業以外廠家的銷售。"o" stands for "others". "o" 代表"其他產品"。

1921: Leather Shoes 皮鞋製造業

The industry accounts for 0.662% of the total revenue of China's industrial sector in 1996. The revenue growth rate of the industry is 4.5% from 1995, as compared to the growth rate of China's industrial sector, 9.51%. The rate of return on asset is 1.66%. 68.58% of all firms in the industry made a profit while 24.77% had negative returns. The top province in terms of the industry's revenue is Guangdong, accounting for 34.76% of the total revenue.
本行業在1996年佔全行業總產值0.662%，行業年增長率為4.5%（全國工業年增長率9.51%）。行業的資產回報率1.66%，68.58%的企業盈利，24.77%的企業虧損。銷售收入最高的省份為廣東省，佔本行業的34.76%。

	Total number of firms 企業總數	Total number of employees 職工總數	Total revenue (mil. RMB) 總銷售收入（百萬元）	Total profit (mil. RMB) 總利潤（百萬元）	Return on assets 資產利潤率 (%)	Return on equity 權益利潤率 (%)	Labour productivity ('000 RMB / worker) 勞動生產率（千元／人）	Debts / assets 資產負債率 (%)	Total assets (mil. RMB) 總資產（百萬元）
Industry Overall 行業總體	3,689	664,943	38,403	586	1.66	5.29	57.75	68.53	35,212

	Number of firms 企業個數	Average number of employees 平均職工人數	Average revenue ('000 RMB) 平均銷售收入（千元）	Average profit ('000 RMB) 平均利潤（千元）	Return on assets 資產利潤率 (%)	Return on equity 權益利潤率 (%)	Labour productivity ('000 RMB / worker) 勞動生產率（千元／人）	Average debts / assets 平均資產負債率(%)	Average Total assets ('000 RMB) 平均總資產（千元）
By ownership 產業所有權									
State-owned 國有	251	334	11,060	-163	-0.81	-3.27	33.16	75.15	20,120
Collectively-owned 集體	2,501	94	3,363	305	8.90	30.71	35.87	71.02	3,427
Privately-owned 私有	8	53	1,269	-137	-5.77	-25.51	24.17	77.37	2,373
Domestic JVs 聯營	38	392	25,186	1,970	8.49	28.55	64.29	70.25	23,197
Joint stock 股份制	51	212	9,832	1,456	7.73	18.14	46.44	57.41	18,845
Foreign-funded 外資	295	282	20,791	97	0.51	1.48	73.84	65.48	19,048
Overseas Chinese-funded 港澳台資	541	454	36,214	-580	-2.22	-6.65	79.83	66.53	26,067
By size 規模									
Large 大型	13	2,674	170,560	14,448	5.34	13.92	63.79	61.64	270,667
Medium 中型	59	973	70,827	3,841	4.96	18.66	72.78	73.39	77,383
Small 小型	3,544	161	9,030	48	0.63	2.01	55.96	68.61	7,655
By regional distribution 地區分布									
Central-North 華北	293	151	5,760	-125	-1.22	-4.75	38.27	74.31	10,251
Beijing 北京	61	133	4,100	-219	-1.48	-5.92	30.93	75.07	14,859
Tianjin 天津	82	181	11,153	-70	-0.53	-1.49	61.74	64.50	13,357
Hebei 河北	67	207	6,514	-182	-1.67	-9.99	31.41	83.31	10,921
Shanxi 山西	21	137	1,188	-250	-4.38	-25.80	8.66	83.02	5,695
Inner Mongolia 內蒙	62	71	992	-1	-0.05	-0.49	13.89	90.51	2,429
Northeast 東北	360	161	2,920	-147	-3.40	-24.76	18.15	86.28	4,317
Liaoning 遼寧	144	273	4,886	-150	-2.47	-11.44	17.90	78.38	6,071
Jilin 吉林	65	117	1,468	-246	-4.95	381.19	12.53	101.30	4,980
Heilongjiang 黑龍江	151	73	1,669	-101	-4.26	-53.41	22.94	92.02	2,358
Central East 華東	1,633	179	12,164	313	3.05	8.31	68.14	63.31	10,272
Shanghai 上海	145	175	16,379	366	2.27	7.92	93.59	71.29	16,098
Jiangsu 江蘇	313	157	11,153	198	2.29	7.63	71.24	70.01	8,645
Zhejiang 浙江	463	77	6,191	159	3.14	8.73	80.33	64.00	5,054
Anhui 安徽	80	96	3,788	-41	-0.98	-5.27	39.43	81.37	4,209
Fujian 福建	324	360	25,770	656	3.39	7.08	71.62	52.15	19,357
Jiangxi 江西	115	50	846	-66	-5.17	-27.73	16.79	81.36	1,279
Shandong 山東	193	266	12,342	627	4.59	16.37	46.33	71.99	13,667
Central-South 中南	935	250	16,155	213	1.64	5.50	64.55	70.23	13,044
Henan 河南	179	110	3,991	157	2.77	9.61	36.35	71.20	5,672
Hubei 湖北	128	108	4,485	104	2.51	11.17	41.55	77.55	4,150
Hunan 湖南	177	63	1,868	-25	-1.18	-5.14	29.45	77.03	2,158
Guangdong 廣東	389	474	34,319	458	1.78	5.86	72.40	69.64	25,742
Guangxi 廣西	60	82	2,262	-259	-6.13	-17.05	27.64	64.07	4,232
Hainan 海南	2								
Southwest 西南	309	79	1,394	-98	-2.92	-18.23	17.57	84.00	3,355
Chongqing 重慶	82	66	1,080	-94	-5.36	-29.90	16.24	82.09	1,760
Sichuan 四川	111	96	1,980	-80	-1.68	-14.12	20.45	88.09	4,755
Guizhou 貴州	53	50	703	-55	-2.90	-29.23	14.07	90.08	1,901
Yunnan 雲南	59	88	1,290	-202	-5.80	-38.39	14.63	84.89	3,478
Tibet 西藏	3	117	2,377	400	2.21	3.37	20.31	34.36	18,100
Northwest 西北	159	81	1,667	-33	-0.80	-3.59	20.57	77.74	4,079
Shaanxi 陝西	45	108	3,894	272	3.68	10.98	36.10	66.50	7,382
Gansu 甘肅	53	69	831	-85	-3.17	-7.95	12.01	60.18	2,690
Qinghai 青海	15	108	1,501	-423	-14.62	82.90	13.91	117.63	2,896
Ningxia 寧夏	8	101	543	-184	-3.00	-27.53	5.35	89.12	6,124
Xinjiang 新疆	38	51	498	-133	-6.22	23.64	9.79	126.31	2,140

1921: Leather Shoes 皮鞋製造業

Year 年份	Number of firms 企業個數	Rate of change 每年變化 (%)	Number of employees 職工人數 (人)	Rate of change 每年變化 (%)	Total revenue (mil. RMB) 總銷售收入 (百萬元)	Rate of change 每年變化 (%)	Total profit (mil. RMB) 總利潤 (百萬元)	Rate of change 每年變化 (%)
1993	4,128		712,728		20,544		434	
1994	4,339	5.11%	683,993	-4.03%	27,674	34.70%	374	-13.88%
1995	4,161	-4.10%	758,655	10.92%	36,759	32.83%	133	-64.34%
1996	3,689	-11.34%	664,943	-12.35%	38,403	4.47%	586	339.72%

3 Major products* 3 種主要產品 *	Output 產量	Sales volume 銷售量	Unit 單位
a) Cow Leather Upper Shoes 牛面皮鞋	69,754	66,964	10,000 pair 萬雙
b) Composition Leather Shoes 合成革、人造革皮鞋	77,807	77,029	10,000 pair 萬雙
c) Other Leather Shoes 其他皮鞋	12,395	11,899	10,000 pair 萬雙

Top 10 firms by revenue (year founded) 收入排名前 10 家企業 (創辦年份)	City 城市	Province 省	Telephone / fax 電話 / 傳真	Number of employees 職工人數	Ownership 產業所有權	Revenue ('000 RMB) 銷售收入 (千元)	Profit ('000 RMB) (rank) 利潤 (千元) (排名)	Total assets ('000 RMB) 總資產 (千元)	Major products 主要產品
Fujian Xie Feng Footwear Co. Ltd. 福建協豐鞋業有限公司(1989)	Putian 莆田市	Fujian 福建省	(0594)2894210 (0594)2893130	4,472	Overseas Chinese-funded 港澳台資	857,232	39140(3)	325,401	a
Fujian San Feng Shoes Industry Co. Ltd. 福建省三豐鞋業有限公司	Fuzhou 福州市	Fujian 福建省	(0591)3497668	4,671	Foreign-funded 外資	823,800	25050(6)	439,220	o
Fujian Qing Lu Shoes Industry Co. Ltd. 福州市清祿鞋業有限公司(1991)	Fuzhou 福州市	Fujian 福建省	(0591)3688888 (0591)3681040	10,483	Overseas Chinese-funded 港澳台資	696,060	11308(22)	314,635	a
Jiangsu Sen Da Group of Co. 江蘇森達集團公司(1976)	Yancheng 鹽城市	Jiangsu 江蘇省	(0515)6213511 (0515)6210044	2,910	Collectively-owned 集體	641,590	35990(4)	403,010	a
Guangzhou Haifeng Shoes Industry Co. Ltd. 廣州海豐鞋業有限公司(1989)	Guangzhou 廣州市	Guangdong 廣東省	(020)85516772 (020)85516776	4,961	Overseas Chinese-funded 港澳台資	630,685	14777(15)	135,565	b
Zhuhai Sez Maystar Footwear Co. Ltd. 珠海經濟特區美星製鞋有限公司(1988)	Zhuhai 珠海市	Guangdong 廣東省	(0756)8610198 (0756)8620468	4,318	Overseas Chinese-funded 港澳台資	531,901	-6796(1430)	1,050,605	a
Panyu Lan He Zhen Foreign Ecnomy Industrial Company 番禺市欖核鎮對外經濟工業公司	Guangzhou 廣州市	Guangdong 廣東省	(020)84928173 (020)84928200	2,408	Collectively-owned 集體	492,002	740(261)	204,450	o
Guangzhou Rong Cheng Shoes Industry Co. Ltd. 廣州榮誠鞋業有限公司(1990)	Guangzhou 廣州市	Guangdong 廣東省	(020)86622469 (020)86412026	3,000	Overseas Chinese-funded 港澳台資	469,268	7270(31)	223,982	a
Guangzhou Xin Chang Shoes Industry Co. Ltd. 廣州欣昌鞋業有限公司(1990)	Guangzhou 廣州市	Guangdong 廣東省	(020)82386985 (020)82396984	2,525	Overseas Chinese-funded 港澳台資	383,814	5306(43)	166,099	a,c
Guangzhou Guang Rong Shoes Industry Co. Ltd. 廣州市廣榮鞋業有限公司(1988)	Guangzhou 廣州市	Guangdong 廣東省	(020)86621289 (020)86627405	3,433	Overseas Chinese-funded 港澳台資	363,116	17392(11)	198,819	a

Top 10 Cities by Production Output 產出排名前 10 位城市	Province 省	Market share 市場份額	Number of firms 企業個數
Guangzhou 廣州市	Guangdong 廣東省	15.97%	161
Shanghai 上海市	Shanghai 上海市	11.06%	266
Wenzhou 溫州市	Zhejiang 浙江省	6.24%	906
Fuzhou 福州市	Fujian 福建省	4.90%	39
Putian 莆田市	Fujian 福建省	4.79%	23
Dongguan 東莞市	Guangdong 廣東省	4.65%	38
Foshan 佛山市	Guangdong 廣東省	2.75%	46
Zhaoqing 肇慶市	Guangdong 廣東省	2.68%	27
Zhuhai 珠海市	Guangdong 廣東省	2.47%	18
Quanzhou 泉州市	Fujian 福建省	2.46%	107

10 Major Wholesalers 10 家主要批發商	City 城市	Province 省	Telephone / Fax 電話 / 傳真
Beijing Foreign Trade Import & Export Company 北京市對外貿易進出口公司	Beijing 北京市	Beijing 北京市	(010)65081589 (010)65043755
Fujian Putian Foreign Trade Company 福建省莆田市對外貿易公司	Putian 莆田市	Fujian 福建省	(0594)2398702 (0594)2292681
Hunan Light Industry General Company Import & Export Products Company 湖南省輕工業總公司進出品公司	Changsha 長沙市	Hunan 湖南省	(0731)2287932 (0731)2287844
Jiangxi Handicrafts Import & Export Company 江西省工藝品進出口公司	Nanchang 南昌市	Jiangxi 江西省	(0791)6246932 (0791)6223383
Jiangyin Shoes and Cap General Co. 江蘇江陰市鞋帽總公司	Wuxi 無錫市	Jiangsu 江蘇省	(0510)6804355 (0510)6803479
Jinhua Jin Hai Industrial Company 金華市金海實業公司	Jinhua 金華市	Zhejiang 浙江省	(0579)2324590
Guangdong Nanhai Handicrafts Import & Export Company 廣東南海市工藝品進出口公司	Foshan 佛山市	Guangdong 廣東省	(0757)6338620 (0757)6220225
Guangzhou Light Industry Products Shoes, Cap, Box, Bag Import & Export Co. 廣州市輕工業品鞋帽箱包進出口公司	Guangzhou 廣州市	Guangdong 廣東省	(020)83337522 (020)83339145
Nanjing Foreign Trade Company 南京市對外貿易公司	Nanjing 南京市	Jiangsu 江蘇省	(025)4403991 (025)4403700

*Also include sales by firms outside this industry.包括本行業以外廠家的銷售。"o" stands for "others". "o" 代表"其他產品"。

1923: Leather Apparel 革皮服裝製造業

The industry accounts for 0.185% of the total revenue of China's industrial sector in 1996. The revenue growth rate of the industry is 15.6% from 1995, as compared to the growth rate of China's industrial sector, 9.51%. The rate of return on asset is 3.30%. 68.23% of all firms in the industry made a profit while 25.31% had negative returns. The top province in terms of the industry's revenue is Zhejiang, accounting for 27.92% of the total revenue.
本行業在1996年佔全行業總產值0.185%，行業年增長率為15.6%（全國工業年增長率9.51%）。行業的資產回報率3.30%，68.23%的企業盈利，25.31%的企業虧損。銷售收入最高的省份為浙江省，佔本行業的27.92%。

	Total number of firms 企業總數	Total number of employees 職工總數	Total revenue (mil. RMB) 總銷售收入 (百萬元)	Total profit (mil. RMB) 總利潤 (百萬元)	Return on assets 資產利潤率 (%)	Return on equity 權益利潤率 (%)	Labour productivity ('000 RMB / worker) 勞動生產率 (千元/人)	Debts / assets 資產負債率 (%)	Total assets (mil. RMB) 總資產 (百萬元)
Industry Overall 行業總體	1,068	136,704	10,708	312	3.30	12.11	78.33	72.74	9,459

	Number of firms 企業個數	Average number of employees 平均職工人數	Average revenue ('000 RMB) 平均銷售收入（千元）	Average profit ('000 RMB) 平均利潤（千元）	Return on assets 資產利潤率 (%)	Return on equity 權益利潤率 (%)	Labour productivity ('000 RMB / worker) 勞動生產率 (千元/人)	Average debts / assets 平均資產負債率(%)	Average Total assets ('000 RMB) 平均總資產 (千元)
By ownership 產業所有權									
State-owned 國有	89	147	4,371	-292	-3.33	-38.24	29.67	91.28	8,764
Collectively-owned 集體	723	109	7,996	360	4.99	16.77	73.50	70.25	7,219
Privately-owned 私有	3	64	3,282	13	0.82	2.57	51.29	68.19	1,609
Domestic JVs 聯營	10	158	9,705	-413	-3.36	-12.10	61.50	72.27	12,315
Joint stock 股份制	7	107	3,849	-38	-0.38	-1.09	36.07	64.56	9,992
Foreign-funded 外資	111	216	23,656	308	2.04	7.31	109.75	72.08	15,082
Overseas Chinese-funded 港澳台資	124	156	14,343	386	3.01	11.10	91.76	72.89	12,812
By size 規模									
Large 大型	1	1,241	233,415	15,687	7.67	13.48	188.09	43.07	204,435
Medium 中型	12	886	76,652	3,760	3.61	14.12	86.56	74.47	104,270
Small 小型	1,041	120	9,179	241	3.14	11.72	76.75	73.22	7,688
By regional distribution 地區分布									
Central-North 華北	216	104	8,081	713	14.85	38.62	77.47	61.55	4,798
Beijing 北京	31	22	3,255	165	5.51	16.17	151.29	65.96	3,006
Tianjin 天津	24	86	6,244	217	3.37	10.14	72.36	66.73	6,421
Hebei 河北	79	184	17,728	1,882	26.99	49.61	96.55	45.61	6,975
Shanxi 山西	21	66	1,745	61	1.83	6.86	26.40	73.38	3,363
Inner Mongolia 內蒙	61	64	942	-105	-3.83	214.38	14.74	101.79	2,744
Northeast 東北	98	79	4,478	115	1.70	10.23	56.90	83.41	6,796
Liaoning 遼寧	42	129	8,639	94	0.81	4.89	66.89	83.44	11,560
Jilin 吉林	18	45	1,104	338	4.99	-146.51	24.65	103.40	6,773
Heilongjiang 黑龍江	38	39	1,477	34	2.20	3.77	37.87	41.53	1,541
Central East 華東	409	173	16,413	400	3.10	10.53	95.09	70.53	12,874
Shanghai 上海	16	70	7,121	88	2.25	8.21	101.81	72.59	3,913
Jiangsu 江蘇	67	145	16,151	286	2.27	7.22	111.14	68.49	12,578
Zhejiang 浙江	168	135	17,797	418	2.92	10.63	131.35	72.52	14,317
Anhui 安徽	17	236	13,231	1,216	6.12	21.89	56.18	72.03	19,865
Fujian 福建	21	180	13,070	1,043	11.07	29.45	72.73	62.40	9,419
Jiangxi 江西	15	51	2,366	-14	-0.34	-2.86	46.09	88.21	4,155
Shandong 山東	105	271	18,973	288	2.23	7.00	70.08	68.19	12,925
Central-South 中南	226	110	6,446	33	0.45	1.84	58.41	75.84	7,512
Henan 河南	79	87	5,287	156	1.66	7.48	60.93	77.82	9,387
Hubei 湖北	20	155	5,272	195	1.72	13.98	34.10	87.69	11,337
Hunan 湖南	56	108	5,496	-87	-2.15	-10.73	51.12	79.98	4,040
Guangdong 廣東	69	130	9,064	-55	-0.75	-2.19	69.88	65.76	7,287
Guangxi 廣西	2	13	245	-10	-4.17	-7.69	19.60	43.75	240
Hainan 海南									
Southwest 西南	43	125	5,704	-305	-2.95	-11.61	45.78	74.55	10,323
Chongqing 重慶	6	139	3,458	-924	-18.69	-150.33	24.77	87.57	4,946
Sichuan 四川	25	161	8,570	-211	-1.37	-4.93	53.02	72.14	15,338
Guizhou 貴州	3	23	270	-140	-7.08	-420.00	11.57	98.15	1,977
Yunnan 雲南	7	39	661	-163	-6.64	-148.05	16.96	95.46	2,453
Tibet 西藏	1								
Northwest 西北	76	73	1,433	-140	-3.04	219.83	19.56	101.40	4,602
Shaanxi 陝西	13	138	2,703	2	0.03	0.24	19.61	87.76	7,887
Gansu 甘肅	22	58	1,718	-11	-0.41	7.43	29.58	105.60	2,652
Qinghai 青海	4	41	1,120	-55	-2.63	14.86	27.32	117.66	2,095
Ningxia 寧夏	7	30	397	-43	-4.04	12.88	13.05	131.36	1,061
Xinjiang 新疆	30	71	958	-330	-5.73	95.75	13.54	105.98	5,769

Year 年份	Number of firms 企業個數	Rate of change 每年變化 (%)	Number of employees 職工人數 (人)	Rate of change 每年變化 (%)	Total revenue (mil. RMB) 總銷售收入 (百萬元)	Rate of change 每年變化 (%)	Total profit (mil. RMB) 總利潤 (百萬元)	Rate of change 每年變化 (%)
1993	876		102,465		4,845		123	
1994	1,011	15.41%	119,927	17.04%	6,769	39.72%	136	10.28%
1995	1,065	5.34%	129,945	8.35%	9,263	36.84%	165	21.44%
1996	1,068	0.28%	136,704	5.20%	10,708	15.60%	312	89.46%

3 Major products* 3 種主要產品 *	Output 產量	Sales volume 銷售量	Unit 單位
a) Leather Costume 革皮服裝	29,498,807	28,023,867	piece 件
b) Leather Gloves 皮手套	2,163	2,141	10,000 pair 萬副
c) Tanning Leather 鞣製皮革	4,105,121	3,940,916	piece 張

Top 10 firms by revenue (year founded) 收入排名前 10 家企業 (創辦年份)	City 城市	Province 省	Telephone / fax 電話 / 傳真	Number of employees 職工人數	Ownership 產業所有權	Revenue ('000 RMB) 銷售收入 (千元)	Profit ('000 RMB) (rank) 利潤 (千元) (排名)	Total assets ('000 RMB) 總資產 (千元)	Major products 主要產品
Hebei Xinji China Leather Commerce Cheng Group Company 河北省辛集市中國皮革商業城集團公司(1993)	Shijiazhuang 石家莊市	Hebei 河北省	(0311)3215436	8,010	Collectively-owned 集體	690,800	108110(1)	265,000	o
Xue Bao Group Co. 海寧市雪豹集團公司(1984)	Jiaxing 嘉興市	Zhejiang 浙江省	(0573)7411067 (0573)7411067	222	Collectively-owned 集體	451,134	17961(4)	406,703	a,b,c
Zhejiang Shou Wang Group Company 浙江獸王集團公司(1988)	Hangzhou 杭州市	Zhejiang 浙江省	(0571)5232508	838	Collectively-owned 集體	388,994	18039(3)	178,753	a
Jiangsu Fu Chang Group Co. 江蘇富昌集團公司(1984)	Wuxi 無錫市	Jiangsu 江蘇省	(0510)6341391 (0510)6341116	1,185	Collectively-owned 集體	303,599	9231(8)	151,603	a
Qingdao Xin Yu Leather Co. Ltd. 青島信宇皮革有限公司(1992)	Qingdao 青島市	Shandong 山東省	(0532)4821260 (0532)4815305	986	Foreign-funded 外資	256,480	140(220)	64,980	o
Qingdao Shuanglong Clothing Co. Ltd. 青島雙龍服裝有限公司(1994)	Qingdao 青島市	Shandong 山東省	(0532)8516341 (0532)8516340	1,100	Foreign-funded 外資	242,505	517(112)	85,340	a
Zhenjiang Pi Lu Dan Fashionable Dress Co. Ltd. 鎮江皮鹿丹時裝有限公司(1994)	Zhenjiang 鎮江市	Jiangsu 江蘇省	(0511)8888989 (0511)8888887	638	Overseas Chinese-funded 港澳台資	220,587	8940(9)	112,979	a
Cosie Leather & Coat Products Ltd. 富隆革裘製品有限公司(1988)	Hangzhou 杭州市	Zhejiang 浙江省	(0571)3591621 (0571)3591570	435	Overseas Chinese-funded 港澳台資	195,998	2500(30)	202,088	o
Shandong Yuncheng Su Ge Leather (Group) Co. Ltd. 山東省鄆城縣蘇閣皮革(集團)有限公司(1995)	Heze 菏澤市	Shandong 山東省	(0530)6321008 (0530)6321033	1,395	Collectively-owned 集體	191,943	10060(6)	121,680	a,c
Qinhuangdao Xiang Lin Leather Co. Ltd. 秦皇島相林皮革有限公司(1992)	Qinhuangdao 秦皇島市	Hebei 河北省	(0335)8051457 (0335)8051133	600	Foreign-funded 外資	184,440	29(308)	38,903	o

Top 10 Cities by Production Output 產出排名前 10 位城市	Province 省	Market share 市場份額	Number of firms 企業個數
Hangzhou 杭州市	Zhejiang 浙江省	15.24%	59
Jiaxing 嘉興市	Zhejiang 浙江省	10.37%	115
Wuxi 無錫市	Jiangsu 江蘇省	5.78%	23
Weifang 濰坊市	Shandong 山東省	4.25%	14
Heze 菏澤市	Shandong 山東省	3.93%	14
Shenyang 瀋陽市	Liaoning 遼寧省	3.79%	12
Jiangmen 江門市	Guangdong 廣東省	3.66%	22
Shijiazhuang 石家莊市	Hebei 河北省	2.69%	21
Nantong 南通市	Jiangsu 江蘇省	2.27%	22
Chengdu 成都市	Sichuan 四川省	2.25%	23

10 Major Wholesalers 10 家主要批發商	City 城市	Province 省	Telephone / Fax 電話 / 傳真
Bao Xiang Hebei Import & Export Group Company 葆祥河北進出口集團公司	Shijiazhuang 石家莊市	Hebei 河北省	(0311)7768648 (0311)7752705
Henan Clothing Import & Export Company 河南省服裝進出口公司	Zhengzhou 鄭州市	Henan 河南省	(0371)5958892
Jiangsu Clothing Import & Export Group Co. Ltd. 江蘇省服裝進出口集團股份有限公司	Nanjing 南京市	Jiangsu 江蘇省	(025)7714688 (025)3361837
Beijing Clothing Import & Export Co. 北京市服裝進出口股份有限公司	Beijing 北京市	Beijing 北京市	(010)64269728 (010)64269496
Zhong Fang Clothing Import & Export Company 中紡服裝進出口公司	Beijing 北京市	Beijing 北京市	(010)65123010 (010)65124768
Tianjin Clothing Import & Export Company 天津服裝進出口公司	Tianjin 天津市	Tianjin 天津市	(022)28328888 (022)28326166
Guangzhou Textiles Import & Export Co. 廣州市紡織進出口公司	Guangzhou 廣州市	Guangdong 廣東省	(020)83348898 (020)83343898
Jiangsu Overseas Enterprise Group Co. Ltd. 江蘇省海外企業集團有限公司	Nanjing 南京市	Jiangsu 江蘇省	(025)7710880 (025)7711532
Weihai Import & Export Company 威海市進出口公司	Weihai 威海市	Shandong 山東省	(0896)5232228 (0896)5232014
Suzhou Foreign Trade Company 蘇州市對外貿易公司	Suzhou 蘇州市	Jiangsu 江蘇省	(0512)5205488 (0512)5205232

*Also include sales by firms outside this industry.包括本行業以外廠家的銷售。"o" stands for "others". "o" 代表 "其他產品"。

1924: Leather Luggage and Handbags 皮箱製造業

The industry accounts for 0.044% of the total revenue of China's industrial sector in 1996. The revenue growth rate of the industry is 7.2% from 1995, as compared to the growth rate of China's industrial sector, 9.51%. The rate of return on asset is 1.11%. 70.28% of all firms in the industry made a profit while 22.49% had negative returns. The top province in terms of the industry's revenue is Jiangsu, accounting for 20.57% of the total revenue.
本行業在1996年佔全行業總產值0.044%，行業年增長率為7.2%（全國工業年增長率9.51%）。行業的資產回報率1.11%，70.28%的企業盈利，22.49%的企業虧損。銷售收入最高的省份為江蘇省，佔本行業的20.57%。

	Total number of firms 企業總數	Total number of employees 職工總數	Total revenue (mil. RMB) 總銷售收入（百萬元）	Total profit (mil. RMB) 總利潤（百萬元）	Return on assets 資產利潤率 (%)	Return on equity 權益利潤率 (%)	Labour productivity ('000 RMB / worker) 勞動生產率（千元/人）	Debts / assets 資產負債率 (%)	Total assets (mil. RMB) 總資產（百萬元）
Industry Overall 行業總體	360	35,741	2,573	27	1.11	5.76	71.99	80.68	2,433

	Number of firms 企業個數	Average number of employees 平均職工人數	Average revenue ('000 RMB) 平均銷售收入（千元）	Average profit ('000 RMB) 平均利潤（千元）	Return on assets 資產利潤率 (%)	Return on equity 權益利潤率 (%)	Labour productivity ('000 RMB / worker) 勞動生產率（千元/人）	Average debts / assets 平均資產負債率(%)	Average Total assets ('000 RMB) 平均總資產（千元）
By ownership 產業所有權									
State-owned 國有	14	129	4,143	-357	-4.72	83.33	32.10	105.66	7,571
Collectively-owned 集體	263	87	4,070	44	1.13	6.01	46.61	81.19	3,879
Privately-owned 私有	2	23	2,655	46	3.71	-478.14	117.98	100.78	1,251
Domestic JVs 聯營	3	278	22,517	-195	-0.71	12.34	81.00	105.77	27,440
Joint stock 股份制	1	33	6,988	106	2.56	13.29	211.75	80.75	4,144
Foreign-funded 外資	28	118	20,319	237	1.40	10.87	172.41	87.13	16,941
Overseas Chinese-funded 港澳台資	48	142	16,504	297	1.92	6.27	116.04	69.37	15,466
By size 規模									
Large 大型	1	403	57,061	-1,687	-2.29	-3.15	141.59	27.43	73,748
Medium 中型	8	586	47,361	-74	-0.12	-0.89	80.89	86.67	62,311
Small 小型	342	89	6,249	86	1.57	8.36	69.94	81.19	5,443
By regional distribution 地區分布									
Central-North 華北	34	116	4,947	-132	-1.82	-7.93	42.81	77.05	7,242
Beijing 北京	10	126	6,135	24	0.23	0.79	48.88	70.28	10,280
Tianjin 天津	9	101	2,437	-471	-13.50	-63.38	24.23	78.69	3,489
Hebei 河北	11	141	7,545	-44	-0.50	-2.65	53.58	81.27	8,778
Shanxi 山西	3	67	527				7.86	94.00	4,610
Inner Mongolia 內蒙	1	19	350				18.42	79.27	1,640
Northeast 東北	20	144	8,778	-19	-0.27	-1.71	61.11	84.05	6,979
Liaoning 遼寧	9	221	18,954	137	0.99	4.75	85.94	79.08	13,757
Jilin 吉林	6	129	232	-285	-11.78	40.24	1.80	129.29	2,418
Heilongjiang 黑龍江	5	23	716	20	8.00	16.39	31.40	51.20	250
Central East 華東	158	103	10,147	159	2.01	7.01	98.40	71.40	7,926
Shanghai 上海	23	184	16,613	9	0.06	0.24	90.29	75.23	14,861
Jiangsu 江蘇	38	129	13,930	223	3.46	13.09	108.27	73.56	6,443
Zhejiang 浙江	41	81	11,853	448	4.21	14.60	146.38	71.16	10,628
Anhui 安徽	13	27	833	13	2.03	4.28	30.34	52.63	643
Fujian 福建	22	83	5,577	-99	-1.99	-5.31	67.34	62.51	4,975
Jiangxi 江西	11	29	474	15	1.26	3.70	16.49	66.09	1,158
Shandong 山東	10	136	6,703	-6	-0.06	-0.18	49.40	66.04	9,931
Central-South 中南	117	98	5,239	78	1.21	40.18	53.31	96.98	6,406
Henan 河南	10	68	3,023	186	5.33	19.87	44.46	73.18	3,490
Hubei 湖北	31	85	3,322	-22	-0.68	-5.31	38.89	87.16	3,168
Hunan 湖南	30	52	683	6	0.54	2.36	13.06	77.13	1,048
Guangdong 廣東	39	156	11,061	177	1.21	-58.34	70.85	102.07	14,635
Guangxi 廣西	7	73	3,976	119	5.87	15.81	54.36	62.87	2,020
Hainan 海南									
Southwest 西南	18	22	299	15	3.05	8.08	13.44	62.26	492
Chongqing 重慶	6	26	162	-8	-3.93	-10.63	6.21	63.06	210
Sichuan 四川	7	22	434	40	4.94	15.02	19.42	67.08	813
Guizhou 貴州	3	21	223				10.63	21.62	247
Yunnan 雲南	1	8	310	10	2.33	5.56	38.75	58.14	430
Tibet 西藏									
Northwest 西北	13	58	561	-192	-6.83	-34.20	9.75	80.03	2,805
Shaanxi 陝西	6	81	467	-393	-10.74	224.76	5.75	104.78	3,662
Gansu 甘肅	3	70	587	-50	-1.21	-1.91	8.42	36.33	4,120
Qinghai 青海	2	9	40				4.44	94.59	185
Ningxia 寧夏									
Xinjiang 新疆	2	17	1,325	10	1.14	4.55	77.94	75.00	880

1924: Leather Luggage and Handbags 皮箱製造業

Year 年份	Number of firms 企業個數	Rate of change 每年變化 (%)	Number of employees 職工人數 (人)	Rate of change 每年變化 (%)	Total revenue (mil. RMB) 總銷售收入 (百萬元)	Rate of change 每年變化 (%)	Total profit (mil. RMB) 總利潤 (百萬元)	Rate of change 每年變化 (%)
1993	393		47,508		1,555		43	
1994	384	-2.29%	43,632	-8.16%	1,913	23.00%	7	-84.13%
1995	381	-0.78%	42,982	-1.49%	2,401	25.48%	16	142.51%
1996	360	-5.51%	35,741	-16.85%	2,573	7.16%	27	63.83%

3 Major products* 3 種主要產品 *	Output 產量	Sales volume 銷售量	Unit 單位
a) Leather Suitcase 皮箱	30,114,864	29,813,715	piece 只
b) Leather Handbag & Bag 皮包、袋	21,719	21,285	10,000 piece 萬個

Top 10 firms by revenue (year founded) 收入排名前 10 家企業 (創辦年份)	City 城市	Province 省	Telephone / fax 電話 / 傳真	Number of employees 職工人數	Ownership 產業所有權	Revenue ('000 RMB) 銷售收入 (千元)	Profit ('000 RMB) (rank) 利潤 (千元) (排名)	Total assets ('000 RMB) 總資產 (千元)	Major products 主要產品
Fu Li Leather Products Co. Ltd. 富利皮革製品有限公司(1993)	Suzhou 蘇州市	Jiangsu 江蘇省	(0512)6551783	337	Foreign-funded 外資	134,200	306(38)	24,980	b
Daewoo (Dalian) Bag & Tent Manufacturing Co. Ltd. 大宇(大連)箱包帳篷製作有限公司(1992)	Dalian 大連市	Liaoning 遼寧省	(0411)7614576 (0411)7614577	448	Foreign-funded 外資	110,781	2313(6)	70,721	o
Jiaxing Tian Tian Box and Bag Co. Ltd. 嘉興天天箱包有限公司(1995)	Jiaxing 嘉興市	Zhejiang 浙江省	(0573)2088187 (0573)2082719	122	Foreign-funded 外資	84,993	8965(1)	29,654	o
Shanghai Fei Ou Industrial Co. Ltd. 上海飛鷗實業有限公司(1995)	Shanghai 上海市	Shanghai 上海市	(021)57491365 (021)57491708	581	Collectively-owned 集體	84,719	3598(3)	41,405	b
Zhongshan Huang Guan Leather Articles Co. Ltd. 中山皇冠皮件有限公司(1992)	Zhongshan 中山市	Guangdong 廣東省	(0760)6683756 (0760)6683758	400	Overseas Chinese-funded 港澳台資	76,914	964(22)	83,225	a
Hubei Yong Xiang Plastic Cement Co. Ltd. 湖北永祥塑膠有限公司(1990)	Jingsha 荊沙市	Hubei 湖北省	(0716)4223216 (0716)224438	280	State-owned 國有	70,120	310(36)	29,050	a,b
Haining Fan Tai Box and Bag Co. Ltd. 海寧泛太箱包製品有限公司(1995)	Jiaxing 嘉興市	Zhejiang 浙江省	(0573)7404376 (0573)7404376	320	Foreign-funded 外資	64,126	333(34)	63,257	o
Shanghai Tai Feng Box and Bag Co. Ltd. 上海泰豐箱包有限公司(1995)	Shanghai 上海市	Shanghai 上海市	(021)59763666 (021)59760138	250	Foreign-funded 外資	59,485	-1053(161)	90,204	a
Dongguan Chashan Chang Long Fur Products Co. Ltd. 東莞茶山昌隆皮件有限公司(1993)	Dongguan 東莞市	Guangdong 廣東省	(0769)6641671 (0769)6641142	450	Collectively-owned 集體	52,679	318(35)	66,588	b
Guangzhou Wu Yang Cases & Bags Factory 廣州市五羊箱包廠(1984)	Guangzhou 廣州市	Guangdong 廣東省	(020)81983545 (020)81982243	486	Collectively-owned 集體	51,948	129(61)	28,988	a

Top 10 Cities by Production Output 產出排名前 10 位城市	Province 省	Market share 市場份額	Number of firms 企業個數
Shanghai 上海市	Shanghai 上海市	18.80%	42
Jiaxing 嘉興市	Zhejiang 浙江省	6.98%	9
Guangzhou 廣州市	Guangdong 廣東省	5.85%	14
Suzhou 蘇州市	Jiangsu 江蘇省	5.71%	12
Zhongshan 中山市	Guangdong 廣東省	5.26%	3
Wenzhou 溫州市	Zhejiang 浙江省	4.41%	30
Dalian 大連市	Liaoning 遼寧省	4.29%	2
Jiangmen 江門市	Guangdong 廣東省	4.05%	5
Nantong 南通市	Jiangsu 江蘇省	3.15%	10
Beijing 北京市	Beijing 北京市	2.45%	8

10 Major Wholesalers 10 家主要批發商	City 城市	Province 省	Telephone / Fax 電話 / 傳真
Changzhou General Merchandise Wholesale General Company 常州百貨批發總公司	Changzhou 常州市	Jiangsu 江蘇省	(0519)6680488 (0519)6680488
Suzhou General Merchandise General Co. 蘇州百貨總公司	Suzhou 蘇州市	Jiangsu 江蘇省	(0512)5222288 (0512)5222247
Guangzhou Yue Xiu Enterprise (Holdings) Co. 廣州越秀企業(集團)公司	Guangzhou 廣州市	Guangdong 廣東省	(020)86662828 (020)86672634
Wunan Commercial Group Corp. 湖南省商業集團總公司	Changsha 長沙市	Hunan 湖南省	(0731)4442765
Kunming General Merchandise Purchase Supply Station Kunming General Merchandise Company 昆明百貨採購供應站昆明市百貨公司	Kunming 昆明市	Yunnan 雲南省	(0871)3314883 (0871)3314961
Nanjing General Merchandise General Company 南京市百貨總公司	Nanjing 南京市	Jiangsu 江蘇省	(025)6664681 (025)6643927
Guangzhou Shang Ling Trade Co. Ltd. 廣州商菱貿易有限公司	Guangzhou 廣州市	Guangdong 廣東省	(020)86677190 (020)86673971
Beijing Light Industry Product Import & Export Company 北京市輕工業品進出口公司	Beijing 北京市	Beijing 北京市	(010)64057425 (010)64057427
Xi Shan Shi Commerce Group Company 錫山市商業集團公司	Wuxi 無錫市	Jiangsu 江蘇省	(0510)2442982
Yixing Su Nan Commercial Building 宜興市蘇南商廈	Wuxi 無錫市	Jiangsu 江蘇省	(0510)7904407 (0510)7904754

*Also include sales by firms outside this industry.包括本行業以外廠家的銷售。"o" stands for "others". "o" 代表 "其他產品"。

1925: Leather Bags 皮包製造業

The industry accounts for 0.117% of the total revenue of China's industrial sector in 1996. The revenue growth rate of the industry is 5.2% from 1995, as compared to the growth rate of China's industrial sector, 9.51%. The rate of return on asset is 4.68%. 66.64% of all firms in the industry made a profit while 26.34% had negative returns. The top province in terms of the industry's revenue is Guangdong, accounting for 53.33% of the total revenue.
本行業在1996年佔全行業總產值0.117%，行業年增長率為5.2%（全國工業年增長率9.51%）。行業的資產回報率4.68%，66.64%的企業盈利，26.34%的企業虧損。銷售收入最高的省份為廣東省，佔本行業的53.33%。

	Total number of firms 企業總數	Total number of employees 職工總數	Total revenue (mil. RMB) 總銷售收入（百萬元）	Total profit (mil. RMB) 總利潤（百萬元）	Return on assets 資產利潤率 (%)	Return on equity 權益利潤率 (%)	Labour productivity ('000 RMB / worker) 勞動生產率（千元/人）	Debts / assets 資產負債率 (%)	Total assets (mil. RMB) 總資產（百萬元）
Industry Overall 行業總體	838	112,752	6,775	270	4.68	11.71	60.09	60.00	5,763

	Number of firms 企業個數	Average number of employees 平均職工人數	Average revenue ('000 RMB) 平均銷售收入（千元）	Average profit ('000 RMB) 平均利潤（千元）	Return on assets 資產利潤率 (%)	Return on equity 權益利潤率 (%)	Labour productivity ('000 RMB / worker) 勞動生產率（千元/人）	Average debts / assets 平均資產負債率(%)	Average Total assets ('000 RMB) 平均總資產（千元）
By ownership 產業所有權									
State-owned 國有	28	206	6,036	107	1.38	4.69	29.37	70.64	7,786
Collectively-owned 集體	488	100	3,627	167	4.56	9.25	36.43	50.71	3,663
Privately-owned 私有									
Domestic JVs 聯營	3	62	3,926	61	1.10	-17.04	63.66	106.44	5,557
Joint stock 股份制									
Foreign-funded 外資	108	203	22,117	1,398	8.88	26.68	108.96	66.71	15,740
Overseas Chinese-funded 港澳台資	212	173	11,492	161	1.68	4.30	66.28	61.04	9,628
By size 規模									
Large 大型									
Medium 中型	4	277	71,216	9,119	15.42	35.79	257.10	56.92	59,144
Small 小型	813	136	7,984	288	4.24	10.63	58.53	60.08	6,781
By regional distribution 地區分布									
Central-North 華北	46	80	5,670	453	7.48	20.42	70.97	63.35	6,060
Beijing 北京	24	65	4,343	27	0.70	3.50	66.65	80.00	3,870
Tianjin 天津	9	120	12,689	1,750	10.43	23.43	105.94	55.51	16,784
Hebei 河北	11	92	3,638	395	12.92	26.70	39.51	51.57	3,060
Shanxi 山西	1	20	2,350	110	9.32	137.50	117.50	93.22	1,180
Inner Mongolia 內蒙	1								
Northeast 東北	31	180	3,792	118	5.32	13.49	21.02	60.57	2,219
Liaoning 遼寧	16	86	5,349	224	8.48	17.21	61.88	50.75	2,639
Jilin 吉林	6	29	317	-97	-6.93	-31.35	10.80	77.90	1,395
Heilongjiang 黑龍江	9	448	3,340	73	3.63	14.73	7.45	75.38	2,022
Central East 華東	310	103	8,406	383	5.74	15.69	81.64	63.38	6,659
Shanghai 上海	63	128	15,276	1,231	10.30	25.33	119.12	59.32	11,946
Jiangsu 江蘇	40	67	8,028	368	9.56	29.89	120.35	68.01	3,852
Zhejiang 浙江	74	66	3,966	50	1.57	6.12	60.38	74.35	3,179
Anhui 安徽	15	54	1,404	39	3.16	8.15	26.06	61.20	1,223
Fujian 福建	56	89	6,326	165	2.42	7.69	70.92	68.52	6,809
Jiangxi 江西	8	60	99	-74	-5.16	30.73	1.65	116.80	1,429
Shandong 山東	54	186	12,089	248	2.62	6.24	65.11	57.96	9,471
Central-South 中南	423	166	8,933	323	4.15	9.60	53.77	56.77	7,790
Henan 河南	14	34	1,678	111	7.67	20.31	49.77	62.17	1,452
Hubei 湖北	17	72	3,911	136	6.13	13.85	54.63	55.76	2,227
Hunan 湖南	11	35	609	-105	-7.21	-31.42	17.59	77.05	1,450
Guangdong 廣東	368	183	9,819	353	4.10	9.43	53.61	56.57	8,620
Guangxi 廣西	12	58	3,802	340	13.78	31.75	65.73	56.59	2,467
Hainan 海南	1	113	22,980				203.36	70.20	19,430
Southwest 西南	19	26	229	-6	-2.07	-5.04	8.72	58.89	305
Chongqing 重慶	2	13	331	34	19.96	37.41	23.78	46.64	171
Sichuan 四川	9	36	176	-13	-3.64	-8.16	4.79	55.34	355
Guizhou 貴州	3	9	213	13	6.35	7.84	23.70	17.46	210
Yunnan 雲南	4	22	300	-33	-9.49	-92.86	13.95	90.51	343
Tibet 西藏									
Northwest 西北	9	88	860	-1,092	-19.61	141.85	9.80	113.84	5,571
Shaanxi 陝西	2	145	635	-655	-13.11	-94.24	4.39	86.09	4,995
Gansu 甘肅	1	165	2,200	-6,640	-32.45	62.35	13.33	152.10	20,460
Qinghai 青海	1	117	380	-320	-28.32	66.67	3.25	142.48	1,130
Ningxia 寧夏									
Xinjiang 新疆	5	44	778	-312	-8.41	-55.52	17.76	84.86	3,712

1925: Leather Bags 皮包製造業

Year 年份	Number of firms 企業個數	Rate of change 每年變化 (%)	Number of employees 職工人數 (人)	Rate of change 每年變化 (%)	Total revenue (mil. RMB) 總銷售收入 (百萬元)	Rate of change 每年變化 (%)	Total profit (mil. RMB) 總利潤 (百萬元)	Rate of change 每年變化 (%)
1993	596		84,747		2,659		105	
1994	709	18.96%	106,618	25.81%	3,663	37.75%	146	39.00%
1995	912	28.63%	129,742	21.69%	6,439	75.78%	214	46.93%
1996	838	-8.11%	112,752	-13.10%	6,775	5.22%	270	26.25%

3 Major products* 3 種主要產品 *	Output 產量	Sales volume 銷售量	Unit 單位
a) Leather Handbag & Bag 皮包、袋	53,580	52,508	10,000 piece 萬個
b) Leather Suitcase 皮箱	2,592,918	2,566,989	piece 只
c) Light Leather 輕革	1,138,124	1,251,936	square metre 平方米

Top 10 firms by revenue (year founded) 收入排名前 10 家企業 (創辦年份)	City 城市	Province 省	Telephone / fax 電話 / 傳真	Number of employees 職工人數	Ownership 產業所有權	Revenue ('000 RMB) 銷售收入 (千元)	Profit ('000 RMB) (rank) 利潤 (千元) (排名)	Total assets ('000 RMB) 總資產 (千元)	Major products 主要產品
Panyu Shi Men Handbag Co. Ltd. 番禺世門手袋有限公司(1992)	Guangzhou 廣州市	Guangdong 廣東省	(020)84754777 (020)84755459	1,500	Foreign-funded 外資	423,194	9673(7)	87,510	a
Shanghai Ace Travel Goods Co. Ltd. 上海愛思旅遊用品有限公司(1989)	Shanghai 上海市	Shanghai 上海市	(021)65422410 (021)65442717	1,073	Foreign-funded 外資	312,546	50036(1)	202,849	a,b
Shanghai Qingpu Ace Luggage & Bags Co. Ltd. 上海青浦愛思箱包有限公司(1994)	Shanghai 上海市	Shanghai 上海市	(021)59770016	634	Foreign-funded 外資	165,278	20184(3)	94,371	a
Yangzhou A Pai Si Leather Co. Ltd. 揚州市阿派司皮革有限公司(1994)	Yangzhou 揚州市	Jiangsu 江蘇省	(0514)7531467 (0514)7531995	205	Foreign-funded 外資	127,390	5880(11)	17,736	a
Huadu Yong Sheng Leather Articles Co. Ltd. 花都市永盛皮件有限公司(1991)	Guangzhou 廣州市	Guangdong 廣東省	(020)86843265 (020)86843666	756	Overseas Chinese-funded 港澳台資	114,120	12100(4)	3,484	a
Enping Niu Jiang Jiang Hong Leather Products Co. Ltd. 恩平牛江江鴻皮革製品有限公司(1991)	Jiangmen 江門市	Guangdong 廣東省	(0750)7631583	443	Foreign-funded 外資	101,050	980(70)	39,630	a
Ju Mei (Huiyang) Handbag Co. Ltd. 聚美(惠陽)手袋有限公司(1995)	Huizhou 惠州市	Guangdong 廣東省	(0751)3332445 (0751)3332445	1,400	Overseas Chinese-funded 港澳台資	99,652	1474(45)	105,247	a
Weihai Yong Bai Leather Products Co. Ltd. 威海永柏革製品有限公司(1994)	Weihai 威海市	Shandong 山東省	(0896)8545080 (0896)8545177	350	Foreign-funded 外資	91,000	11600(5)	30,240	a
Meizhou Gold Lion (China) Dress & Adornment Leather Utensil Co. Ltd. 金利來服飾皮具有限公司(1991)	Meizhou 梅州市	Guangdong 廣東省	(0752)2222413 (0752)2234170	99	Foreign-funded 外資	89,860	22641(2)	532,033	a
Dinghu Sha Pu Leather Products Factory 鼎湖區沙浦鎮皮革製品廠(1987)	Zhaoqing 肇慶市	Guangdong 廣東省	(0757)2631038	750	Foreign-funded 外資	78,430	4020(22)	23,456	a

Top 10 Cities by Production Output 產出排名前 10 位城市	Province 省	Market share 市場份額	Number of firms 企業個數
Shanghai 上海市	Shanghai 上海市	16.43%	86
Guangzhou 廣州市	Guangdong 廣東省	15.45%	73
Shenzhen 深圳市	Guangdong 廣東省	10.36%	40
Huizhou 惠州市	Guangdong 廣東省	9.25%	113
Suzhou 蘇州市	Jiangsu 江蘇省	4.88%	20
Dongguan 東莞市	Guangdong 廣東省	4.32%	26
Zhaoqing 肇慶市	Guangdong 廣東省	3.69%	10
Foshan 佛山市	Guangdong 廣東省	3.58%	20
Jiangmen 江門市	Guangdong 廣東省	3.30%	24
Hangzhou 杭州市	Zhejiang 浙江省	2.59%	25

10 Major Wholesalers 10 家主要批發商	City 城市	Province 省	Telephone / Fax 電話 / 傳真
Changzhou General Merchandise Wholesale General Company 常州百貨批發總公司	Changzhou 常州市	Jiangsu 江蘇省	(0519)6680488 (0519)6680488
Suzhou General Merchandise General Co. 蘇州百貨總公司	Suzhou 蘇州市	Jiangsu 江蘇省	(0512)5222288 (0512)5222247
Guangzhou Yue Xiu Enterprise (Holdings) Co. 廣州越秀企業(集團)公司	Guangzhou 廣州市	Guangdong 廣東省	(020)86662828 (020)86672634
Wunan Commercial Group Corp. 湖南省商業集團總公司	Changsha 長沙市	Hunan 湖南省	(0731)4442765
Kunming General Merchandise Purchase Supply Station Kunming General Merchandise Company 昆明百貨採購供應站昆明市百貨公司	Kunming 昆明市	Yunnan 雲南省	(0871)3314883 (0871)3314961
Nanjing General Merchandise General Company 南京市百貨總公司	Nanjing 南京市	Jiangsu 江蘇省	(025)6664681 (025)6643927
Guangzhou Shang Ling Trade Co. Ltd. 廣州商菱貿易有限公司	Guangzhou 廣州市	Guangdong 廣東省	(020)86677190 (020)86673971
Beijing Light Industry Product Import & Export Company 北京市輕工業品進出口公司	Beijing 北京市	Beijing 北京市	(010)64057425 (010)64057427
Xi Shan Shi Commerce Group Company 錫山市商業集團公司	Wuxi 無錫市	Jiangsu 江蘇省	(0510)2442982
Yixing Su Nan Commercial Building 宜興市蘇南商廈	Wuxi 無錫市	Jiangsu 江蘇省	(0510)7904407 (0510)7904754

*Also include sales by firms outside this industry.包括本行業以外廠家的銷售。"o" stands for "others". "o" 代表 "其他產品" 。

1929: Other Leather Products 其他類未包括的皮革製品業

The industry accounts for 0.092% of the total revenue of China's industrial sector in 1996. The revenue growth rate of the industry is 11.4% from 1995, as compared to the growth rate of China's industrial sector, 9.51%. The rate of return on asset is 1.73%. 68.11% of all firms in the industry made a profit while 24.96% had negative returns. The top province in terms of the industry's revenue is Guangdong, accounting for 23.72% of the total revenue.
本行業在1996年佔全行業總產值0.092%，行業年增長率為11.4%（全國工業年增長率9.51%）。行業的資產回報率1.73%，68.11%的企業盈利，24.96%的企業虧損。銷售收入最高的省份為廣東省，佔本行業的23.72%。

	Total number of firms 企業總數	Total number of employees 職工總數	Total revenue (mil. RMB) 總銷售收入（百萬元）	Total profit (mil. RMB) 總利潤（百萬元）	Return on assets 資產利潤率 (%)	Return on equity 權益利潤率 (%)	Labour productivity ('000 RMB / worker) 勞動生產率（千元/人）	Debts / assets 資產負債率 (%)	Total assets (mil. RMB) 總資產（百萬元）
Industry Overall 行業總體	777	84,687	5,306	71	1.73	4.77	62.65	63.69	4,097

	Number of firms 企業個數	Average number of employees 平均職工人數	Average revenue ('000 RMB) 平均銷售收入（千元）	Average profit ('000 RMB) 平均利潤（千元）	Return on assets 資產利潤率 (%)	Return on equity 權益利潤率 (%)	Labour productivity ('000 RMB / worker) 勞動生產率（千元/人）	Average debts / assets 平均資產負債率(%)	Average Total assets ('000 RMB) 平均總資產（千元）
By ownership 產業所有權									
State-owned 國有	30	137	3,033	-133	-2.44	-11.11	22.13	78.05	5,467
Collectively-owned 集體	527	92	4,229	49	1.64	5.11	46.21	67.95	2,963
Privately-owned 私有	5	57	4,482	579	30.36	54.27	79.18	44.06	1,908
Domestic JVs 聯營	9	221	10,953	11	0.07	0.13	49.54	49.88	17,173
Joint stock 股份制	6	268	15,906	141	3.32	13.06	59.42	74.62	4,259
Foreign-funded 外資	101	170	16,664	418	3.58	10.10	98.01	64.59	11,682
Overseas Chinese-funded 港澳台資	99	122	10,975	34	0.34	0.76	89.86	55.64	10,122
By size 規模									
Large 大型									
Medium 中型	6	679	47,509	1,002	2.06	4.33	69.93	52.50	48,709
Small 小型	748	107	6,713	87	1.71	4.82	62.76	64.54	5,087
By regional distribution 地區分布									
Central-North 華北	81	55	2,447	-16	-0.65	-2.14	44.76	69.73	2,399
Beijing 北京	15	21	1,528	-30	-1.25	-3.96	72.08	68.44	2,400
Tianjin 天津	30	66	3,451	-94	-2.95	-8.76	52.69	66.33	3,187
Hebei 河北	22	61	2,784	68	2.88	14.24	45.57	79.80	2,353
Shanxi 山西	5	49	1,186	40	4.39	13.89	24.40	68.42	912
Inner Mongolia 內蒙	9	62	506	36	5.03	9.58	8.15	47.33	707
Northeast 東北	81	56	1,831	-93	-5.17	-29.27	32.85	82.33	1,801
Liaoning 遼寧	35	97	3,898	-198	-5.97	-30.74	40.21	80.58	3,321
Jilin 吉林	22	21	260	-11	-1.48	-16.22	12.14	90.86	736
Heilongjiang 黑龍江	24	27	255	-15	-2.75	-21.39	9.45	87.22	561
Central East 華東	286	132	10,829	182	2.08	5.96	81.99	65.06	8,758
Shanghai 上海	54	133	11,083	209	2.85	9.00	83.26	68.33	7,347
Jiangsu 江蘇	83	163	13,895	250	2.29	5.97	85.49	61.62	10,900
Zhejiang 浙江	54	95	5,161	75	1.02	2.35	54.34	56.71	7,337
Anhui 安徽	9	131	7,748	-457	-8.63	-69.90	59.04	87.66	5,293
Fujian 福建	34	136	17,954	431	2.94	9.97	132.42	70.54	14,686
Jiangxi 江西	31	99	4,751	94	2.91	10.40	48.05	71.98	3,232
Shandong 山東	21	148	11,385	123	1.62	5.20	76.90	68.91	7,621
Central-South 中南	301	121	5,993	94	2.37	5.43	49.64	56.44	3,980
Henan 河南	33	98	2,658	82	2.54	10.35	27.26	75.48	3,246
Hubei 湖北	32	142	11,257	343	6.71	28.48	79.06	76.44	5,115
Hunan 湖南	26	62	1,448	-1	-0.07	-0.89	23.25	92.62	1,172
Guangdong 廣東	192	127	6,554	82	1.94	3.52	51.56	44.87	4,230
Guangxi 廣西	14	159	4,014	-314	-6.85	-61.80	25.32	88.91	4,587
Hainan 海南	4	79	903	823	16.20	-4112.50	11.39	100.39	5,078
Southwest 西南	17	41	2,439	-28	-1.47	-11.74	59.58	87.48	1,922
Chongqing 重慶	5	56	4,944	-76	-2.90	6.72	88.15	143.18	2,627
Sichuan 四川	4	51	2,503	-18	-0.51	-0.86	48.50	41.02	3,532
Guizhou 貴州	5	28	662	6	1.42	8.57	23.48	83.41	422
Yunnan 雲南	2	10	55	-10	-25.00	-28.57	5.79	12.50	40
Tibet 西藏									
Northwest 西北	11	85	1,548	-14	-0.70	-8.38	18.12	91.73	1,956
Shaanxi 陝西	6	64	1,420	5	0.37	3.45	22.13	89.52	1,368
Gansu 甘肅	4	133	2,103	-43	-1.28	-18.68	15.87	93.16	3,325
Qinghai 青海									
Ningxia 寧夏									
Xinjiang 新疆	1	25	100	-10	-100.00	-100.00	4.00		10

1929: Other Leather Products 其他類未包括的皮革製品業

Year 年份	Number of firms 企業個數	Rate of change 每年變化 (%)	Number of employees 職工人數 (人)	Rate of change 每年變化 (%)	Total revenue (mil. RMB) 總銷售收入 (百萬元)	Rate of change 每年變化 (%)	Total profit (mil. RMB) 總利潤 (百萬元)	Rate of change 每年變化 (%)
1993	800		98,535		2,812		55	
1994	876	9.50%	119,690	21.47%	3,973	41.26%	61	10.30%
1995	845	-3.54%	102,969	-13.97%	4,762	19.86%	43	-29.36%
1996	777	-8.05%	84,687	-17.75%	5,306	11.42%	71	65.43%

3 Major products* 3 種主要產品 *	Output 產量	Sales volume 銷售量	Unit 單位
a) Leather Gloves 皮手套	34,323	33,980	10,000 pair 萬副
b) Leather Handbag & Bag 皮包、袋	24,292	23,806	10,000 piece 萬個
c) Tanning Leather 鞣製皮革	805,025	772,824	piece 張

Top 10 firms by revenue (year founded) 收入排名前 10 家企業 (創辦年份)	City 城市	Province 省	Telephone / fax 電話 / 傳真	Number of employees 職工人數	Ownership 產業所有權	Revenue ('000 RMB) 銷售收入 (千元)	Profit ('000 RMB) (rank) 利潤 (千元) (排名)	Total assets ('000 RMB) 總資產 (千元)	Major products 主要產品
Huaxia Shan'er (Xiamen) Leather Products Co. Ltd. 華夏山二(廈門)皮革製品有限公司(1989)	Xiamen 廈門市	Fujian 福建省	(0592)7033456 (0592)7023800	1,279	Foreign-funded 外資	237,072	8342(2)	170,100	b
Wuxi Bai Le Fur Products Group Company 無錫百樂皮件集團公司(1979)	Wuxi 無錫市	Jiangsu 江蘇省	(0510)3201798 (0510)3201740	1,105	Collectively-owned 集體	222,350	8583(1)	81,317	o
Jiangsu Meidiyang (Group) Co. 江蘇美迪洋集團公司(1994)	Suzhou 蘇州市	Jiangsu 江蘇省	(0512)2381318	1,366	Foreign-funded 外資	189,413	4697(4)	190,000	b,c
Wanyi Leather (Xia Men) Co. Ltd 萬益皮革(廈門)有限公司(1990)	Xiamen 廈門市	Fujian 福建省	(0592)7023371 (0592)7022782	691	Overseas Chinese-funded 港澳台資	126,494	701(57)	78,262	o
Chaoyang Chun Tian Group Company 潮陽市春田集團公司(1995)	Shantou 汕頭市	Guangdong 廣東省	(0754)6646986 (0754)6645581	100	Collectively-owned 集體	99,500	620(65)	39,430	o
Primo Leather Articles Co. Ltd. Zhongshan 中山泳盟皮件有限公司(1990)	Zhongshan 中山市	Guangdong 廣東省	(0760)6632015 (0760)6632525	900	Overseas Chinese-funded 港澳台資	93,650	166(124)	56,448	b
Jiangxi Chang Sheng Light Industrial Products Joint Venture Co. Ltd. 江西昌盛輕工業品聯營有限公司(1985)	Nanchang 南昌市	Jiangxi 江西省	(0791)8331640 (0791)8333787	852	Collectively-owned 集體	93,000	2633(9)	37,173	o
Yantai Hua Sheng Leather Products Co. Ltd. 煙台華盛革製品有限公司(1987)	Yantai 煙台市	Shandong 山東省	(0535)6372729 (0535)6372418	204	Collectively-owned 集體	87,006	1340(34)	10,377	a
Yingkou Xin Guo Cases & Bags Co. Ltd. 營口新國箱包有限公司(1992)	Yingkou 營口市	Liaoning 遼寧省	(0417)6259100 (0417)6259101	650	Foreign-funded 外資	81,124	460(75)	32,060	o
Suzhou Die Ka Men Ge Fur Products Co. Ltd. 蘇州碟卡門格皮件有限公司(1991)	Suzhou 蘇州市	Jiangsu 江蘇省	(0512)8201228 (0512)8202538	100	Overseas Chinese-funded 港澳台資	75,570	3759(5)	26,243	o

Top 10 Cities by Production Output 產出排名前 10 位城市	Province 省	Market share 市場份額	Number of firms 企業個數
Shanghai 上海市	Shanghai 上海市	14.28%	78
Suzhou 蘇州市	Jiangsu 江蘇省	10.22%	34
Huizhou 惠州市	Guangdong 廣東省	5.08%	44
Maoming 茂名市	Guangdong 廣東省	4.85%	32
Suizhou 隨州市	Hubei 湖北省	4.82%	4
Guangzhou 廣州市	Guangdong 廣東省	3.87%	42
Wuxi 無錫市	Jiangsu 江蘇省	3.64%	12
Nanchang 南昌市	Jiangxi 江西省	3.60%	9
Zhongshan 中山市	Guangdong 廣東省	3.08%	12
Nantong 南通市	Jiangsu 江蘇省	3.01%	30

10 Major Wholesalers 10 家主要批發商	City 城市	Province 省	Telephone / Fax 電話 / 傳真
Changzhou General Merchandise Wholesale General Company 常州百貨批發總公司	Changzhou 常州市	Jiangsu 江蘇省	(0519)6680488 (0519)6680488
Suzhou General Merchandise General Co. 蘇州百貨總公司	Suzhou 蘇州市	Jiangsu 江蘇省	(0512)5222288 (0512)5222247
Guangzhou Yue Xiu Enterprise (Holdings) Co. 廣州越秀企業(集團)公司	Guangzhou 廣州市	Guangdong 廣東省	(020)86662828 (020)86672634
Wunan Commercial Group Corp. 湖南省商業集團總公司	Changsha 長沙市	Hunan 湖南省	(0731)4442765
Kunming General Merchandise Purchase Supply Station Kunming General Merchandise Company 昆明百貨採購供應站昆明市百貨公司	Kunming 昆明市	Yunnan 雲南省	(0871)3314883 (0871)3314961
Nanjing General Merchandise General Company 南京市百貨總公司	Nanjing 南京市	Jiangsu 江蘇省	(025)6664681 (025)6643927
Guangzhou Shang Ling Trade Co. Ltd. 廣州商菱貿易有限公司	Guangzhou 廣州市	Guangdong 廣東省	(020)86677190 (020)86673971
Beijing Light Industry Product Import & Export Company 北京市輕工業品進出口公司	Beijing 北京市	Beijing 北京市	(010)64057425 (010)64057427
Xi Shan Shi Commerce Group Company 錫山市商業集團公司	Wuxi 無錫市	Jiangsu 江蘇省	(0510)2442982
Yixing Su Nan Commercial Building 宜興市蘇南商廈	Wuxi 無錫市	Jiangsu 江蘇省	(0510)7904407 (0510)7904754

*Also include sales by firms outside this industry.包括本行業以外廠家的銷售。"o" stands for "others". "o" 代表 "其他產品" 。

1931: Fur Tanning 毛皮鞣製業

The industry accounts for 0.035% of the total revenue of China's industrial sector in 1996. The revenue growth rate of the industry is -1.5% from 1995, as compared to the growth rate of China's industrial sector, 9.51%. The rate of return on asset is 2.60%. 73.61% of all firms in the industry made a profit while 17.22% had negative returns. The top province in terms of the industry's revenue is Henan, accounting for 13.86% of the total revenue.
本行業在 1996 年佔全行業總產值 0.035% ，行業年增長率為 -1.5%（全國工業年增長率 9.51%）。行業的資產回報率 2.60% ，73.61% 的企業盈利，17.22% 的企業虧損。銷售收入最高的省份為河南省，佔本行業的 13.86% 。

	Total number of firms 企業總數	Total number of employees 職工總數	Total revenue (mil. RMB) 總銷售收入（百萬元）	Total profit (mil. RMB) 總利潤（百萬元）	Return on assets 資產利潤率 (%)	Return on equity 權益利潤率 (%)	Labour productivity ('000 RMB / worker) 勞動生產率（千元 / 人）	Debts / assets 資產負債率 (%)	Total assets (mil. RMB) 總資產（百萬元）
Industry Overall 行業總體	255	27,992	2,033	53	2.60	10.59	72.63	75.40	2,030

	Number of firms 企業個數	Average number of employees 平均職工人數	Average revenue ('000 RMB) 平均銷售收入（千元）	Average profit ('000 RMB) 平均利潤（千元）	Return on assets 資產利潤率 (%)	Return on equity 權益利潤率 (%)	Labour productivity ('000 RMB / worker) 勞動生產率（千元 / 人）	Average debts / assets 平均資產負債率(%)	Average Total assets ('000 RMB) 平均總資產（千元）
By ownership 產業所有權									
State-owned 國有	29	248	10,552	-483	-2.10	-10.22	42.49	79.46	23,000
Collectively-owned 集體	197	83	4,800	185	4.37	27.86	57.96	84.33	4,235
Privately-owned 私有									
Domestic JVs 聯營									
Joint stock 股份制	4	36	1,371	7	0.14	0.84	38.34	82.83	5,110
Foreign-funded 外資	9	175	17,568	-595	-3.51	-9.98	100.65	64.85	16,961
Overseas Chinese-funded 港澳台資	16	173	38,661	2,243	10.09	20.61	223.88	51.06	22,241
By size 規模									
Large 大型	1	2,240	115,442	8,003	3.83	9.35	51.54	59.01	208,940
Medium 中型	5	583	39,291	-646	-1.43	-6.44	67.37	77.74	45,064
Small 小型	245	93	7,028	197	3.02	13.28	75.61	77.24	6,514
By regional distribution 地區分布									
Central-North 華北	64	81	4,107	222	4.82	19.79	50.44	75.64	4,612
Beijing 北京	2	18	725				41.43	70.56	2,480
Tianjin 天津	6	29	1,702	107	3.36	14.68	58.68	77.04	3,172
Hebei 河北	30	91	6,366	483	9.22	53.97	70.14	82.91	5,233
Shanxi 山西	3	132	2,667	27	0.68	9.88	20.15	93.13	3,930
Inner Mongolia 內蒙	23	82	2,270	-42	-0.95	-2.52	27.73	62.46	4,451
Northeast 東北	13	88	9,602	-885	-11.81	-113.19	109.21	89.56	7,488
Liaoning 遼寧	6	156	18,943	-1,972	-19.18	-448.11	121.43	95.72	10,278
Jilin 吉林	1	40	470	-150	-3.33	-9.62	11.75	65.41	4,510
Heilongjiang 黑龍江	6	28	1,783	80	1.54	8.05	64.07	80.88	5,195
Central East 華東	55	201	12,363	359	3.57	11.33	61.53	68.52	10,056
Shanghai 上海	1	1,150	46,760	-9,970	-10.12	-36.18	40.66	72.04	98,540
Jiangsu 江蘇	8	110	4,260	-41	-1.34	-7.40	38.73	81.90	3,074
Zhejiang 浙江	12	54	3,591	-153	-2.94	-15.02	67.12	80.43	5,216
Anhui 安徽	14	43	15,854	1,859	35.91	99.16	370.53	63.78	5,175
Fujian 福建	7	191	15,911	1,060	7.25	20.53	83.31	64.67	14,614
Jiangxi 江西	3	20	2,860	120	14.94	49.32	143.00	69.71	803
Shandong 山東	10	638	21,415	-192	-1.01	-2.88	33.54	64.90	19,022
Central-South 中南	78	69	8,852	374	4.66	18.97	128.51	75.42	8,013
Henan 河南	57	59	4,944	354	7.08	24.95	84.47	71.60	4,996
Hubei 湖北	4	55	605	75	19.48	32.61	10.95	40.91	385
Hunan 湖南	1	70	12,480	1,870	28.81	415.56	178.29	92.91	6,490
Guangdong 廣東	13	105	18,717	582	4.56	12.32	179.04	63.00	12,753
Guangxi 廣西	3	129	50,160	-253	-0.46	-7.54	388.84	93.95	55,487
Hainan 海南									
Southwest 西南	9	86	7,272	-511	-8.65	128.13	84.13	106.75	5,910
Chongqing 重慶	3	35	297	-110	-51.26	-86.41	8.41	40.67	214
Sichuan 四川	5	133	12,911	-854	-8.13	107.55	96.35	107.56	10,510
Guizhou 貴州	1								
Yunnan 雲南									
Tibet 西藏									
Northwest 西北	36	123	5,823	163	1.44	6.29	47.27	77.08	11,279
Shaanxi 陝西	3	124	3,733	-733	-8.61	-59.62	30.03	85.55	8,513
Gansu 甘肅	15	173	11,584	1,307	7.48	21.68	67.11	65.52	17,487
Qinghai 青海	4	89	895	-630	-9.63	132.63	10.03	107.26	6,540
Ningxia 寧夏	2	28	490				17.82	95.16	2,275
Xinjiang 新疆	12	88	1,674	-753	-10.33	-1532.20	18.95	99.33	7,292

1931: Fur Tanning 毛皮鞣製業

Year 年份	Number of firms 企業個數	Rate of change 每年變化 (%)	Number of employees 職工人數 (人)	Rate of change 每年變化 (%)	Total revenue (mil. RMB) 總銷售收入 (百萬元)	Rate of change 每年變化 (%)	Total profit (mil. RMB) 總利潤 (百萬元)	Rate of change 每年變化 (%)
1993	207		24,432		1,046		-1	
1994	253	22.22%	19,226	-21.31%	1,397	33.52%	-1	-177.97%
1995	268	5.93%	25,670	33.52%	2,063	47.68%	77	5496.49%
1996	255	-4.85%	27,992	9.05%	2,033	-1.45%	53	-31.13%

3 Major products* 3 種主要產品 *	Output 產量	Sales volume 銷售量	Unit 單位
a) Fur 毛皮	1,503,107	1,367,828	piece 張
b) Tanning Leather 鞣製皮革	6,242,741	5,993,031	piece 張
c) Light Leather 輕革	3,374,395	3,711,835	square metre 平方米

Top 10 firms by revenue (year founded) 收入排名前 10 家企業 (創辦年份)	City 城市	Province 省	Telephone / fax 電話 / 傳真	Number of employees 職工人數	Ownership 產業所有權	Revenue ('000 RMB) 銷售收入 (千元)	Profit ('000 RMB) (rank) 利潤 (千元) (排名)	Total assets ('000 RMB) 總資產 (千元)	Major products 主要產品
Heze Dongcheng Society Welfare Processing Factory 菏澤市東城社會福利加工廠(1989)	Heze 菏澤市	Shandong 山東省	(0530)5334596	5,320	Collectively-owned 集體	176,540	0(87)	60,350	b
Beihai Ke Hong Tan Co. Ltd. 北海科紅製革有限公司(1991)	Beihai 北海市	Guangxi 廣西	(0779)7285511	369	Overseas Chinese-funded 港澳台資	150,091	-784(111)	166,037	b,c
Jingyi (Zhuhai) Leather Factory Co. Ltd. 精藝(珠海)皮革廠有限公司(1988)	Zhuhai 珠海市	Guangdong 廣東省	(0756)2261043 (0756)2261040	90	Overseas Chinese-funded 港澳台資	90,659	-462(109)	34,159	a
Anhui Jieshou Zhongyuan Tan Factory 安徽省界首市中原製革廠(1993)	Fuyang 阜陽市	Anhui 安徽省		128	Collectively-owned 集體	85,030	11040(2)	8,400	b
Yingkou Rahsung Leather Co. Ltd. 營口羅興皮革有限公司(1993)	Yingkou 營口市	Liaoning 遼寧省	(0417)6252644 (0417)6252340	238	Foreign-funded 外資	83,450	-10167(120)	40,894	o
Fujian Xianyou Nan Tai Tannery Co. Ltd. 福建仙遊南泰製鞋有限公司(1991)	Putian 莆田市	Fujian 福建省	(0594)7396014 (0594)7396024	254	Overseas Chinese-funded 港澳台資	77,900	6229(3)	50,694	b
Wutongqiao Xinhua Tan Factory 五通橋區新華製革廠	Leshan 樂山市	Sichuan 四川省	(0833)3354349		Collectively-owned 集體	60,498	-4865(117)	50,598	b
Gucheng Jun Tun Xiang Ji Nan Nap Factory 故城縣軍屯鄉冀南絨毛廠(1990)	Hengshui 衡水市	Hebei 河北省		120	Collectively-owned 集體	56,830	5050(4)	19,980	o
Shanghai Fur General Factory 上海皮毛總廠(1958)	Shanghai 上海市	Shanghai 上海市	(021)62505450 (021)62506603	1,114	State-owned 國有	46,760	-9971(119)	98,540	o
Schmidt-toll Leather (Boluo) Ltd. 寶利皮革(博羅)有限公司(1990)	Huizhou 惠州市	Guangdong 廣東省		60	Overseas Chinese-funded 港澳台資	44,000	3960(6)	9,190	o

Top 10 Cities by Production Output 產出排名前 10 位城市	Province 省	Market share 市場份額	Number of firms 企業個數
Zhumadian 駐馬店市	Henan 河南省	13.16%	19
Beihai 北海市	Guangxi 廣西	9.69%	2
Suzhou 宿州市	Anhui 安徽省	9.50%	9
Zhuhai 珠海市	Guangdong 廣東省	5.82%	1
Putian 莆田市	Fujian 福建省	4.59%	2
Wenzhou 溫州市	Zhejiang 浙江省	4.26%	13
Fuyang 阜陽市	Anhui 安徽省	3.62%	6
Hengshui 衡水市	Hebei 河北省	3.28%	2
Huludao 葫蘆島市	Liaoning 遼寧省	3.15%	2
Huizhou 惠州市	Guangdong 廣東省	3.13%	6

10 Major Wholesalers 10 家主要批發商	City 城市	Province 省	Telephone / Fax 電話 / 傳真
Ningbo Local Products Animal Products Import & Export Company 寧波市土產畜產進出口公司	Ningbo 寧波市	Zhejiang 浙江省	(0574)7319525 (0574)7320262
Jiangmen Local Products Import & Export Co. 江門市土產進出口公司	Jiangmen 江門市	Guangdong 廣東省	(0759)3353805 (0759)3351104
Jiangmen Handicrafts Import & Export Company 江門市工藝品進出口公司	Jiangmen 江門市	Guangdong 廣東省	(0759)3534021 (0759)3535342
Shandong Animal Products Import & Export Company 山東省畜產進出口公司	Qingdao 青島市	Shandong 山東省	(0532)2971790 (0532)2971838
Hunan Local Products Animal Products Import & Export Company 湖南省土產畜產進出口公司	Changsha 長沙市	Hunan 湖南省	(0731)4727265 (0731)4726674
Zhejiang Local Products Animal Products Import & Export Company 浙江省土產畜產進出口公司	Hangzhou 杭州市	Zhejiang 浙江省	(0571)5178390 (0571)5152310
Jiangsu Dong Xing Import & Export (Group) Co. Ltd. 江蘇省東星進出口(集團)股份有限公司	Nanjing 南京市	Jiangsu 江蘇省	(025)6617488 (025)6616141
Jiangmen Cooking Oil Mill Import & Export Company 江門市糧油進出口公司	Jiangmen 江門市	Guangdong 廣東省	(0759)3366449 (0759)3369323
Guangzhou Animal Products Import & Export Company 廣州市畜產進出口公司	Guangzhou 廣州市	Guangdong 廣東省	(020)83852888 (020)83824187
Tianjin Animal Products Import & Export Company 天津畜產進出口公司	Tianjin 天津市	Tianjin 天津市	(022)23310832 (022)23317312

*Also include sales by firms outside this industry.包括本行業以外廠家的銷售。"o" stands for "others". "o" 代表 "其他產品"。

1932: Fur Clothes 毛皮服裝業

The industry accounts for 0.044% of the total revenue of China's industrial sector in 1996. The revenue growth rate of the industry is 38.8% from 1995, as compared to the growth rate of China's industrial sector, 9.51%. The rate of return on asset is 8.05%. 74.90% of all firms in the industry made a profit while 19.89% had negative returns. The top province in terms of the industry's revenue is Hebei, accounting for 34.06% of the total revenue.
本行業在1996年佔全行業總產值0.044%，行業年增長率為38.8%（全國工業年增長率9.51%）。行業的資產回報率8.05%，74.90%的企業盈利，19.89%的企業虧損。銷售收入最高的省份為河北省，佔本行業的34.06%。

	Total number of firms 企業總數	Total number of employees 職工總數	Total revenue (mil. RMB) 總銷售收入（百萬元）	Total profit (mil. RMB) 總利潤（百萬元）	Return on assets 資產利潤率 (%)	Return on equity 權益利潤率 (%)	Labour productivity ('000 RMB / worker) 勞動生產率（千元/人）	Debts / assets 資產負債率 (%)	Total assets (mil. RMB) 總資產（百萬元）
Industry Overall 行業總體	191	30,915	2,535	165	8.05	28.17	82.00	71.42	2,053

	Number of firms 企業個數	Average number of employees 平均職工人數	Average revenue ('000 RMB) 平均銷售收入（千元）	Average profit ('000 RMB) 平均利潤（千元）	Return on assets 資產利潤率 (%)	Return on equity 權益利潤率 (%)	Labour productivity ('000 RMB / worker) 勞動生產率（千元/人）	Average debts / assets 平均資產負債率(%)	Average Total assets ('000 RMB) 平均總資產（千元）
By ownership 產業所有權									
State-owned 國有	25	241	29,080	480	1.45	7.84	120.68	81.52	33,120
Collectively-owned 集體	132	149	9,591	1,134	20.70	94.30	64.33	78.05	5,477
Privately-owned 私有	1	76	10,091	462	20.64	153.73	132.78	86.57	2,236
Domestic JVs 聯營									
Joint stock 股份制	2	82	2,224	-13	-0.57	-7.78	27.12	92.65	2,260
Foreign-funded 外資	10	139	17,909	57	0.80	2.29	128.66	65.18	7,178
Overseas Chinese-funded 港澳台資	21	176	16,638	112	0.56	0.94	94.33	41.04	20,164
By size 規模									
Large 大型									
Medium 中型	5	926	47,676	1,220	2.10	12.04	51.51	82.53	57,983
Small 小型	185	142	12,421	859	9.01	29.63	87.38	69.58	9,530
By regional distribution 地區分布									
Central-North 華北	68	113	14,436	635	4.84	16.73	127.82	71.07	13,119
Beijing 北京	8	102	4,656	-354	-3.02	-5.73	45.54	47.30	11,716
Tianjin 天津	9	117	4,112	447	8.91	20.08	35.25	55.65	5,013
Hebei 河北	42	102	20,557	935	5.76	23.92	202.15	75.91	16,219
Shanxi 山西	2	76	3,025	60	1.75	5.61	39.80	68.80	3,430
Inner Mongolia 內蒙	7	198	5,424	374	4.02	11.68	27.34	65.57	9,314
Northeast 東北	27	86	3,619	182	4.26	-77.20	41.89	105.52	4,269
Liaoning 遼寧	14	103	5,409	424	7.08	139.11	52.51	94.91	5,991
Jilin 吉林	5	39	3,056	48	1.37	-7.36	78.76	118.58	3,510
Heilongjiang 黑龍江	8	87	840	-159	-9.18	17.23	9.64	153.29	1,729
Central East 華東	42	207	11,134	115	1.10	5.52	53.91	79.99	10,440
Shanghai 上海	1	309	14,310	-3,560	-6.50	125.35	46.31	105.17	54,790
Jiangsu 江蘇	10	272	22,642	1,097	5.41	24.19	83.37	77.65	20,291
Zhejiang 浙江	8	44	2,595	1	0.04	0.14	59.15	71.92	3,076
Anhui 安徽	6	52	3,140	-263	-11.51	113.67	60.19	110.12	2,288
Fujian 福建	1	91	4,230	-890	-4.28	-16.15	46.48	73.50	20,790
Jiangxi 江西									
Shandong 山東	16	306	11,442	-7	-0.09	-0.32	37.41	71.89	7,603
Central-South 中南	34	293	26,329	3,366	29.04	52.44	90.00	44.62	11,592
Henan 河南	15	476	43,242	6,773	44.06	70.61	90.87	37.60	15,371
Hubei 湖北	2	36	665	40	1.66	-23.53	18.73	106.85	2,410
Hunan 湖南	3	102	410	23	3.37	3.45	4.03	2.40	693
Guangdong 廣東	14	174	17,427	908	8.11	17.48	100.32	53.59	11,191
Guangxi 廣西									
Hainan 海南									
Southwest 西南	4	50	335	-285	-11.68	950.00	6.67	101.23	2,440
Chongqing 重慶		18							
Sichuan 四川	3	57	419	-356	-11.68	949.62	7.23	101.23	3,050
Guizhou 貴州									
Yunnan 雲南									
Tibet 西藏									
Northwest 西北	16	130	5,714	-59	-0.46	-3.22	43.93	85.65	12,728
Shaanxi 陝西	3	52	1,010	-193	-8.38	46.03	19.30	118.21	2,307
Gansu 甘肅	7	36	1,723	291	20.24	49.28	47.48	58.93	1,440
Qinghai 青海	1	6	130	-30	-1.81	2.91	21.67	162.05	1,660
Ningxia 寧夏	2	15	125				8.33	42.11	380
Xinjiang 新疆	3	545	25,317	-790	-1.29	-8.80	46.48	85.38	61,410

1932: Fur Clothes 毛皮服裝業

Year 年份	Number of firms 企業個數	Rate of change 每年變化 (%)	Number of employees 職工人數 (人)	Rate of change 每年變化 (%)	Total revenue (mil. RMB) 總銷售收入 (百萬元)	Rate of change 每年變化 (%)	Total profit (mil. RMB) 總利潤 (百萬元)	Rate of change 每年變化 (%)
1993	215		31,603		1,577		65	
1994	235	9.30%	36,444	15.32%	1,891	19.89%	58	-9.39%
1995	213	-9.36%	28,281	-22.40%	1,826	-3.41%	110	88.80%
1996	191	-10.33%	30,915	9.31%	2,535	38.83%	165	49.46%

3 Major products* 3 種主要產品 *	Output 產量	Sales volume 銷售量	Unit 單位
a) Fur 毛皮	4,362,473	3,969,850	piece 張
b) Fur Costume 毛皮服裝	1,258,044	1,245,464	piece 件
c) Leather Costume 革皮服裝	1,261,088	1,198,034	piece 件

Top 10 firms by revenue (year founded) 收入排名前 10 家企業 (創辦年份)	City 城市	Province 省	Telephone / fax 電話 / 傳真	Number of employees 職工人數	Ownership 產業所有權	Revenue ('000 RMB) 銷售收入 (千元)	Profit ('000 RMB) (rank) 利潤 (千元) (排名)	Total assets ('000 RMB) 總資產 (千元)	Major products 主要產品
Mengzhou Nanzhuang Fur & Leather Corp. 孟州市南裝雪洋皮毛公司(1993)	Jiaozuo 焦作市	Henan 河南省	(0391)8190438	5,580	Collectively-owned 集體	579,340	99230(1)	154,980	c
Bao Xiang International Garment Center Pilot Plant 葆祥國際服裝中心試驗廠(1993)	Shijiazhuang 石家莊市	Hebei 河北省	(0311)7768648 (0311)7752705	423	State-owned 國有	553,959	21674(2)	432,553	o
Huilai Kui Keng Leather Factory Co. Ltd. 惠來縣葵鏗皮革廠有限公司(1991)	Jieyang 揭陽市	Guangdong 廣東省	(0663)6682578 (0663)6682558	300	Overseas Chinese-funded 港澳台資	99,010	31(67)	29,042	b
Dingtao Nanguan Leather Factory 定陶縣南關皮廠(1969)	Heze 菏澤市	Shandong 山東省	(0530)2212174 (0530)2741007	886	Collectively-owned 集體	80,150	250(51)	16,700	a,b,c
Hebei Xinji Lan Dun Bei Zhuang Factory 河北省辛集市藍盾被裝廠(1987)	Shijiazhuang 石家莊市	Hebei 河北省	(0311)3221316	1,260	Collectively-owned 集體	76,890	5178(4)	80,422	o
Xinjiang Altay Leather Group Co. Ltd 新疆阿勒泰地區皮革集團有限公司(1957)	Altay 阿勒泰市	Xinjiang 新疆	(0906)2123536	1,242	State-owned 國有	70,388	2581(9)	158,639	a,b,c
Jiangdu Fur Mill 江都皮毛廠(1959)	Yangzhou 揚州市	Jiangsu 江蘇省	(0514)6899051 (0514)6899075	582	Collectively-owned 集體	66,169	3282(7)	96,169	b
Yangchun Bai Xue Fashionable Dress Co. Ltd. 陽春白雪時裝有限公司(1993)	Yangjiang 陽江市	Guangdong 廣東省	(0662)7738779	62	Overseas Chinese-funded 港澳台資	65,910	285(46)	21,253	b
Yangzhou Shen Yang Joint Venture Fur Coat & Leather Clothing Mill 揚州市申揚聯營裘皮服裝廠(1964)	Yangzhou 揚州市	Jiangsu 江蘇省	(0514)7461260 (0514)7461259	745	Collectively-owned 集體	61,039	3219(8)	46,106	a,b
Gucheng Jun Tun Xiang Zhen Hua Qiu Hua Clothing Factory 故城縣軍屯鄉振華裘華服裝廠(1984)	Hengshui 衡水市	Hebei 河北省	(0318)5425624	180	Collectively-owned 集體	34,270	4040(5)	12,150	o

Top 10 Cities by Production Output 產出排名前 10 位城市	Province 省	Market share 市場份額	Number of firms 企業個數
Jiaozuo 焦作市	Henan 河南省	33.45%	2
Hengshui 衡水市	Hebei 河北省	7.48%	30
Yangzhou 揚州市	Jiangsu 江蘇省	6.62%	6
Heze 菏澤市	Shandong 山東省	6.61%	6
Jieyang 揭陽市	Guangdong 廣東省	5.73%	3
Shijiazhuang 石家莊市	Hebei 河北省	5.52%	2
Altay 阿勒泰市	Xinjiang 新疆	3.74%	1
Guangzhou 廣州市	Guangdong 廣東省	3.25%	5
Huludao 葫蘆島市	Liaoning 遼寧省	2.87%	1
Beijing 北京市	Beijing 北京市	1.88%	8

10 Major Wholesalers 10 家主要批發商	City 城市	Province 省	Telephone / Fax 電話 / 傳真
Bao Xiang Hebei Import & Export Group Company 葆祥河北進出口集團公司	Shijiazhuang 石家莊市	Hebei 河北省	(0311)7768648 (0311)7752705
Henan Clothing Import & Export Company 河南省服裝進出口公司	Zhengzhou 鄭州市	Henan 河南省	(0371)5958892
Jiangsu Clothing Import & Export Group Co. Ltd. 江蘇省服裝進出口集團股份有限公司	Nanjing 南京市	Jiangsu 江蘇省	(025)7714688 (025)3361837
Beijing Clothing Import & Export Co. 北京市服裝進出口股份有限公司	Beijing 北京市	Beijing 北京市	(010)64269728 (010)64269496
Zhong Fang Clothing Import & Export Company 中紡服裝進出口公司	Beijing 北京市	Beijing 北京市	(010)65123010 (010)65124768
Tianjin Clothing Import & Export Company 天津服裝進出口公司	Tianjin 天津市	Tianjin 天津市	(022)28328888 (022)28326166
Guangzhou Textiles Import & Export Co. 廣州市紡織進出口公司	Guangzhou 廣州市	Guangdong 廣東省	(020)83348898 (020)83343898
Jiangsu Overseas Enterprise Group Co. Ltd. 江蘇省海外企業集團有限公司	Nanjing 南京市	Jiangsu 江蘇省	(025)7710880 (025)7711532
Weihai Import & Export Company 威海市進出口公司	Weihai 威海市	Shandong 山東省	(0896)5232228 (0896)5232014
Suzhou Foreign Trade Company 蘇州市對外貿易公司	Suzhou 蘇州市	Jiangsu 江蘇省	(0512)5205488 (0512)5205232

*Also include sales by firms outside this industry.包括本行業以外廠家的銷售。"o" stands for "others". "o" 代表 "其他產品" 。

1939: Other Fur Products Manufacturing 其他毛皮製品業

The industry accounts for 0.022% of the total revenue of China's industrial sector in 1996. The revenue growth rate of the industry is 22.4% from 1995, as compared to the growth rate of China's industrial sector, 9.51%. The rate of return on asset is -0.08%. 63.62% of all firms in the industry made a profit while 28.13% had negative returns. The top province in terms of the industry's revenue is Hebei, accounting for 29.66% of the total revenue.
本行業在1996年佔全行業總產值0.022%，行業年增長率為22.4%（全國工業年增長率9.51%）。行業的資產回報率-0.08%，63.62%的企業盈利，28.13%的企業虧損。銷售收入最高的省份為河北省，佔本行業的29.66%。

	Total number of firms 企業總數	Total number of employees 職工總數	Total revenue (mil. RMB) 總銷售收入（百萬元）	Total profit (mil. RMB) 總利潤（百萬元）	Return on assets 資產利潤率 (%)	Return on equity 權益利潤率 (%)	Labour productivity ('000 RMB / worker) 勞動生產率（千元/人）	Debts / assets 資產負債率 (%)	Total assets (mil. RMB) 總資產（百萬元）
Industry Overall 行業總體	269	27,061	1,297	-1	-0.08	-0.50	47.93	83.24	1,567

	Number of firms 企業個數	Average number of employees 平均職工人數	Average revenue ('000 RMB) 平均銷售收入（千元）	Average profit ('000 RMB) 平均利潤（千元）	Return on assets 資產利潤率 (%)	Return on equity 權益利潤率 (%)	Labour productivity ('000 RMB / worker) 勞動生產率（千元/人）	Average debts / assets 平均資產負債率(%)	Average Total assets ('000 RMB) 平均總資產（千元）
By ownership 產業所有權									
State-owned 國有	36	197	4,389	-1,000	-7.44	73.47	22.25	110.12	13,444
Collectively-owned 集體	185	70	3,036	86	2.69	12.44	43.42	78.34	3,200
Privately-owned 私有	1	12	261	-355	-45.12	2173.90	21.73	102.08	787
Domestic JVs 聯營	1	34	1,128	194	49.19	77.80	33.19	36.77	395
Joint stock 股份制									
Foreign-funded 外資	23	174	14,596	2,555	23.32	48.32	84.07	51.75	10,959
Overseas Chinese-funded 港澳台資	23	130	10,483	-1,720	-16.61	-63.80	80.78	73.96	10,354
By size 規模									
Large 大型	1	872	78,506	-155	-0.16	-1.29	90.03	87.97	99,402
Medium 中型	4	417	20,316	-236	-0.58	2.32	48.75	125.00	40,773
Small 小型	264	93	4,311	0	0.01	0.03	46.41	77.63	4,943
By regional distribution 地區分布									
Central-North 華北	118	92	5,467	76	1.19	6.67	59.31	82.09	6,367
Beijing 北京	9	47	2,426	-28	-0.49	-2.00	51.36	75.36	5,638
Tianjin 天津	6	188	16,967	-2,075	-8.30	-75.64	90.33	89.03	25,013
Hebei 河北	52	77	7,397	586	14.35	70.93	96.11	79.77	4,080
Shanxi 山西	9	91	5,263	74	0.62	4.38	57.63	85.92	12,070
Inner Mongolia 內蒙	42	107	2,130	-225	-4.11	-19.94	19.88	79.36	5,469
Northeast 東北	39	106	1,662	-666	-9.47	49.40	15.71	119.18	7,025
Liaoning 遼寧	17	121	2,420	-1,232	-16.56	62.57	20.02	126.46	7,442
Jilin 吉林	9	102	1,079	-133	-5.78	14.07	10.54	141.11	2,306
Heilongjiang 黑龍江	13	89	1,075	-293	-3.01	36.15	12.15	108.32	9,748
Central East 華東	46	108	7,154	334	5.78	13.54	66.34	57.32	5,777
Shanghai 上海	2	13	380	-90	-4.17	-22.22	30.40	81.25	2,160
Jiangsu 江蘇	17	127	13,858	725	7.12	17.37	109.27	59.02	10,182
Zhejiang 浙江	7	41	3,404	80	2.38	7.50	83.32	68.29	3,366
Anhui 安徽	5	54	4,862	122	6.12	17.18	89.38	64.36	1,992
Fujian 福建	4	292	4,588	378	10.81	13.90	15.71	22.26	3,493
Jiangxi 江西									
Shandong 山東	11	96	2,388	49	1.32	2.73	24.92	51.53	3,712
Central-South 中南	42	130	5,103	87	1.81	5.19	39.12	65.13	4,807
Henan 河南	28	154	5,789	130	2.34	6.86	37.61	65.95	5,565
Hubei 湖北	5	119	6,386	222	6.40	8.75	53.84	26.86	3,470
Hunan 湖南									
Guangdong 廣東	8	69	2,431	-96	-2.86	-14.67	35.36	80.48	3,361
Guangxi 廣西	1	25	830	-330	-17.84	55.93	33.20	131.89	1,850
Hainan 海南									
Southwest 西南	6	26	467	-160	-9.00	-28.66	17.95	68.70	1,778
Chongqing 重慶	2	26	993	-410	-11.10	-30.67	37.22	63.82	3,694
Sichuan 四川	1	4	192	-5	-4.14	-7.21	38.76	42.50	122
Guizhou 貴州	1	65							
Yunnan 雲南	1	20	110	30	1.86	150.00	5.50	98.76	1,610
Tibet 西藏									
Northwest 西北	18	81	2,284	-132	-3.78	35.74	28.12	110.57	3,501
Shaanxi 陝西	2	126	10,920	820	26.58	780.95	86.67	96.60	3,085
Gansu 甘肅	2	232	4,350	-840	-14.35	21.00	18.75	168.32	5,855
Qinghai 青海	1	12	120	40	66.67	66.67	10.00		60
Ningxia 寧夏	5	81	1,474	-356	-5.28	-142.40	18.29	96.29	6,738
Xinjiang 新疆	8	41	385	-75	-5.27	333.33	9.31	101.58	1,423

1939: Other Fur Products Manufacturing 其他毛皮製品業

Year 年份	Number of firms 企業個數	Rate of change 每年變化 (%)	Number of employees 職工人數 (人)	Rate of change 每年變化 (%)	Total revenue (mil. RMB) 總銷售收入 (百萬元)	Rate of change 每年變化 (%)	Total profit (mil. RMB) 總利潤 (百萬元)	Rate of change 每年變化 (%)
1993	262		24,707		1,006		-5	
1994	300	14.50%	28,743	16.34%	1,383	37.52%	28	703.16%
1995	275	-8.33%	31,293	8.87%	1,060	-23.33%	-17	-162.02%
1996	269	-2.18%	27,061	-13.52%	1,297	22.36%	-1	94.26%

3 Major products* 3 種主要產品 *	Output 產量	Sales volume 銷售量	Unit 單位
a) Sheep Wool & Skin 綿羊毛皮	1,071,775	1,296,847	piece 張
b) Leather Gloves 皮手套	423	419	10,000 pair 萬副
c) Soft Furniture 軟體傢具	15,080	14,628	piece 件

Top 10 firms by revenue (year founded) 收入排名前 10 家企業 (創辦年份)	City 城市	Province 省	Telephone / fax 電話 / 傳真	Number of employees 職工人數	Ownership 產業所有權	Revenue ('000 RMB) 銷售收入 (千元)	Profit ('000 RMB) (rank) 利潤 (千元) (排名)	Total assets ('000 RMB) 總資產 (千元)	Major products 主要產品
Hua Tat Lee Furniture (China) Co. Ltd. 華達利傢具有限公司(1994)	Suzhou 蘇州市	Jiangsu 江蘇省	(0512)7631691 (0512)7631686	208	Foreign-funded 外資	84,100	7500(1)	75,586	c
Hua Ao Fur Factory 華澳皮毛廠(1989)	Xingtai 邢臺市	Hebei 河北省	(0319)5385465	175	Foreign-funded 外資	63,750	6547(2)	10,197	o
Tianjin Fei Long Livestock Products Co. Ltd. 天津飛龍畜產製品有限公司(1993)	Tianjin 天津市	Tianjin 天津市	(022)25328458 (022)25326989	55	Overseas Chinese-funded 港澳台資	57,194	815(18)	48,234	o
Wuxi Xin Yuan Plush Co. Ltd. 無錫鑫源長毛絨有限公司(1990)	Wuxi 無錫市	Jiangsu 江蘇省	(0510)8150519	181	Overseas Chinese-funded 港澳台資	51,000	830(17)	22,200	o
Suning Hua Si Fur Coat & Leather Products Co. Ltd. 肅寧縣華斯裘革製品有限公司(1991)	Cangzhou 滄州市	Hebei 河北省	(0317)5099896	178	Foreign-funded 外資	49,239	4329(4)	17,584	o
Suzhou Ai Da Gloves Co. Ltd. 蘇州愛達手套有限公司(1993)	Suzhou 蘇州市	Jiangsu 江蘇省	(0512)3611511 (0512)3611945	251	Foreign-funded 外資	41,200	2520(7)	9,400	o
Henan Fugou Woollen Products Factory 河南省扶溝縣毛製品廠(1992)	Zhoukou 周口市	Henan 河南省	(0394)6221569 (0394)6222675	552	State-owned 國有	35,892	430(29)	20,795	o
Tianjin Livestock Products Import & Export Co. Leather & Fur Processing Factory 天津畜產品進出口公司皮毛加工廠(1949)	Tianjin 天津市	Tianjin 天津市	(022)24313700 (022)24312003	921	State-owned 國有	33,590	-13782(97)	91,503	o
Gucheng Jun Tun Xiang Tian Xiang Industrial Co. Ltd. 故城縣軍屯鄉天祥實業有限公司(1979)	Hengshui 衡水市	Hebei 河北省	(0318)5425099	40	Collectively-owned 集體	29,160	3070(6)	1,363	o
Datong Fur Mill 大同市皮毛廠(1949)	Datong 大同市	Shanxi 山西省	(0352)5022646 (0352)5022645	363	State-owned 國有	28,012	268(42)	75,219	a

Top 10 Cities by Production Output 產出排名前 10 位城市	Province 省	Market share 市場份額	Number of firms 企業個數
Tianjin 天津市	Tianjin 天津市	10.60%	7
Zhangjiakou 張家口市	Hebei 河北省	7.75%	19
Jiaozuo 焦作市	Henan 河南省	7.19%	9
Zhoukou 周口市	Henan 河南省	6.89%	6
Hengshui 衡水市	Hebei 河北省	6.12%	18
Suzhou 蘇州市	Jiangsu 江蘇省	5.84%	2
Cangzhou 滄州市	Hebei 河北省	5.49%	3
Datong 大同市	Shanxi 山西省	4.39%	6
Chifeng 赤峯市	Inner Mong 內蒙	4.18%	5
Zhenjiang 鎮江市	Jiangsu 江蘇省	2.86%	5

10 Major Wholesalers 10 家主要批發商	City 城市	Province 省	Telephone / Fax 電話 / 傳真
Ningbo Local Products Animal Products Import & Export Company 寧波市土產畜產進出口公司	Ningbo 寧波市	Zhejiang 浙江省	(0574)7319525 (0574)7320262
Jiangmen Local Products Import & Export Co. 江門市土產進出口公司	Jiangmen 江門市	Guangdong 廣東省	(0759)3353805 (0759)3351104
Jiangmen Handicrafts Import & Export Company 江門市工藝品進出口公司	Jiangmen 江門市	Guangdong 廣東省	(0759)3534021 (0759)3535342
Shandong Animal Products Import & Export Company 山東省畜產進出口公司	Qingdao 青島市	Shandong 山東省	(0532)2971790 (0532)2971838
Hunan Local Products Animal Products Import & Export Company 湖南省土產畜產進出口公司	Changsha 長沙市	Hunan 湖南省	(0731)4727265 (0731)4726674
Zhejiang Local Products Animal Products Import & Export Company 浙江省土產畜產進出口公司	Hangzhou 杭州市	Zhejiang 浙江省	(0571)5178390 (0571)5152310
Jiangsu Dong Xing Import & Export (Group) Co. Ltd. 江蘇省東星進出口(集團)股份有限公司	Nanjing 南京市	Jiangsu 江蘇省	(025)6617488 (025)6616141
Jiangmen Cooking Oil Mill Import & Export Company 江門市糧油進出口公司	Jiangmen 江門市	Guangdong 廣東省	(0759)3366449 (0759)3369323
Guangzhou Animal Products Import & Export Company 廣州市畜產進出口公司	Guangzhou 廣州市	Guangdong 廣東省	(020)83852888 (020)83824187
Tianjin Animal Products Import & Export Company 天津畜產進出口公司	Tianjin 天津市	Tianjin 天津市	(022)23310832 (022)23317312

*Also include sales by firms outside this industry.包括本行業以外廠家的銷售。"o" stands for "others". "o" 代表 "其他產品"。

1951: Feather (Down) Processing 羽毛（絨）加工業

The industry accounts for 0.041% of the total revenue of China's industrial sector in 1996. The revenue growth rate of the industry is -15.3% from 1995, as compared to the growth rate of China's industrial sector, 9.51%. The rate of return on asset is 1.90%. 83.06% of all firms in the industry made a profit while 16.32% had negative returns. The top province in terms of the industry's revenue is Anhui, accounting for 25.31% of the total revenue.
本行業在1996年佔全行業總產值0.041%，行業年增長率為-15.3%（全國工業年增長率9.51%）。行業的資產回報率1.90%，83.06%的企業盈利，16.32%的企業虧損。銷售收入最高的省份為安徽省，佔本行業的25.31%。

	Total number of firms 企業總數	Total number of employees 職工總數	Total revenue (mil. RMB) 總銷售收入（百萬元）	Total profit (mil. RMB) 總利潤（百萬元）	Return on assets 資產利潤率 (%)	Return on equity 權益利潤率 (%)	Labour productivity ('000 RMB / worker) 勞動生產率（千元/人）	Debts / assets 資產負債率 (%)	Total assets (mil. RMB) 總資產（百萬元）
Industry Overall 行業總體	320	18,836	2,357	31	1.90	7.88	125.13	75.90	1,658

	Number of firms 企業個數	Average number of employees 平均職工人數	Average revenue ('000 RMB) 平均銷售收入（千元）	Average profit ('000 RMB) 平均利潤（千元）	Return on assets 資產利潤率 (%)	Return on equity 權益利潤率 (%)	Labour productivity ('000 RMB / worker) 勞動生產率（千元/人）	Average debts / assets 平均資產負債率(%)	Average Total assets ('000 RMB) 平均總資產（千元）
By ownership 產業所有權									
State-owned 國有	16	199	6,250	-1,938	-12.25	140.91	31.49	108.70	15,813
Collectively-owned 集體	265	51	5,762	174	5.63	23.49	113.25	76.04	3,091
Privately-owned 私有	2	22	1,637	45	1.60	12.11	74.43	86.81	2,819
Domestic JVs 聯營	4	25	34,880	-192	-0.84	-6.25	1423.65	86.63	22,958
Joint stock 股份制	4	171	25,651	775	4.59	18.73	149.79	75.49	16,886
Foreign-funded 外資	15	61	14,914	247	1.70	3.89	242.64	56.35	14,576
Overseas Chinese-funded 港澳台資	13	50	20,076	752	4.82	9.69	401.52	50.28	15,606
By size 規模									
Large 大型	3	519	40,540	-2,443	-4.30	-16.75	78.06	74.36	56,879
Medium 中型	3	264	29,011	120	0.21	1.02	109.75	79.37	57,012
Small 小型	308	53	6,974	123	2.88	11.83	130.67	75.62	4,275
By regional distribution 地區分布									
Central-North 華北	49	54	6,747	697	38.56	69.05	124.47	44.15	1,807
Beijing 北京	3								
Tianjin 天津	2	50	25,700	2,620	26.04	49.16	514.00	47.02	10,060
Hebei 河北	38	65	7,303	763	45.63	75.13	112.90	39.27	1,673
Shanxi 山西									
Inner Mongolia 內蒙	6	16	282	-15	-1.84	-45.00	17.24	95.90	813
Northeast 東北	22	26	3,316	8	0.27	0.38	128.22	28.18	2,813
Liaoning 遼寧	7	21	617	-124	-10.41	-13.62	29.19	23.56	1,194
Jilin 吉林	5	66	9,838	-36	-0.39	-0.51	149.51	23.45	9,270
Heilongjiang 黑龍江	10	9	1,945	122	16.99	47.29	211.41	64.07	718
Central East 華東	156	57	6,772	130	2.90	16.37	119.03	82.29	4,497
Shanghai 上海									
Jiangsu 江蘇	45	66	6,639	-142	-2.23	-10.02	101.28	77.77	6,396
Zhejiang 浙江	8	29	11,468	-33	-0.21	-1.31	398.87	84.10	15,616
Anhui 安徽	79	58	7,551	330	10.39	116.32	130.16	91.07	3,176
Fujian 福建	7	33	2,943	-6	-0.38	-0.93	88.03	59.19	1,509
Jiangxi 江西	9	48	3,336	79	7.03	10.41	69.65	32.48	1,122
Shandong 山東	8	56	2,340	33	1.51	3.80	41.88	60.19	2,148
Central-South 中南	57	75	12,828	-173	-1.50	-5.57	171.37	73.10	11,522
Henan 河南	12	96	5,272	345	8.16	20.99	55.01	61.12	4,227
Hubei 湖北	6	70	3,283	68	3.75	5.70	47.02	34.16	1,820
Hunan 湖南	5	79	4,236	-1,084	-14.42	-384.40	53.48	96.25	7,518
Guangdong 廣東	20	91	27,508	-321	-1.29	-4.20	302.45	69.38	24,899
Guangxi 廣西	13	37	5,917	-197	-4.30	62.44	159.25	106.87	4,582
Hainan 海南	1								
Southwest 西南	27	82	5,810	-460	-8.83	-236.76	70.99	96.28	5,211
Chongqing 重慶	2	45	1,496	65	2.70	-28.36	33.16	109.51	2,391
Sichuan 四川	24	85	6,228	-511	-9.31	-217.70	72.78	95.72	5,484
Guizhou 貴州									
Yunnan 雲南									
Tibet 西藏									
Northwest 西北	9	29	960	-99	-10.50	185.42	33.36	105.78	942
Shaanxi 陝西	2	24	1,725	5	0.25	7.14	73.40	96.81	2,035
Gansu 甘肅	2	45	605	50	14.49	26.32	13.44	44.93	345
Qinghai 青海	1	37	910	40	4.35	400.00	24.59	98.91	920
Ningxia 寧夏	3	20	400	3	3.23	4.76	20.00	32.26	103
Xinjiang 新疆	1	25	1,870	-1,050	-42.17	86.07	74.80	149.00	2,490

1951: Feather (Down) Processing 羽毛（絨）加工業

Year 年份	Number of firms 企業個數	Rate of change 每年變化 (%)	Number of employees 職工人數 (人)	Rate of change 每年變化 (%)	Total revenue (mil. RMB) 總銷售收入 (百萬元)	Rate of change 每年變化 (%)	Total profit (mil. RMB) 總利潤 (百萬元)	Rate of change 每年變化 (%)
1993	219		12,262		2,013		4	
1994	278	26.94%	18,988	54.85%	1,895	-5.87%	19	374.74%
1995	329	18.35%	24,826	30.75%	2,784	46.86%	46	136.90%
1996	320	-2.74%	18,836	-24.13%	2,357	-15.34%	31	-32.32%

3 Major products* 3 種主要產品 *	Output 產量	Sales volume 銷售量	Unit 單位
a) Down 羽毛	3,634,389	3,343,638	piece 條
b) Badminton 羽毛球	5,537	5,315	10,000 piece 萬個
c) Down Quilt 羽絨被	197,246	193,301	piece 條

Top 10 firms by revenue (year founded) 收入排名前 10 家企業 (創辦年份)	City 城市	Province 省	Telephone / fax 電話 / 傳真	Number of employees 職工人數	Ownership 產業所有權	Revenue ('000 RMB) 銷售收入 (千元)	Profit ('000 RMB) (rank) 利潤（千元）(排名)	Total assets ('000 RMB) 總資產 (千元)	Major products 主要產品
Zhan Mao Joint Washed Down Mill 湛茂聯合水洗羽絨廠(1989)	Zhanjiang 湛江市	Guangdong 廣東省	(0758)3380066 (0758)3380338	98	Domestic JVs 聯營	198,470	-1365(150)	199,851	a
Huazhou Chang Qi Zhen Chang Yi Down Products Co. Ltd. 化州市長岐鎮長益羽絨製品有限公司(1988)	Maoming 茂名市	Guangdong 廣東省	(0668)7860396	55	Collectively-owned 集體	117,080	6090(2)	28,770	a
Sichuan Down Mill 四川省雙流羽絨廠(1984)	Chengdu 成都市	Sichuan 四川省	(028)5822091	349	Collectively-owned 集體	78,047	370(63)	62,523	o
Zhanjiang Li Bao Down Products Co. Ltd. 湛江麗寶羽絨製品有限公司(1991)	Zhanjiang 湛江市	Guangdong 廣東省	(0758)3381688 (0758)3380338	58	Foreign-funded 外資	65,073	-210(144)	41,433	a
Guangzhou Panyu Wen Hua Down Products Factory 廣州市番禺文華羽絨製品廠(1991)	Guangzhou 廣州市	Guangdong 廣東省	(020)84913638 (020)84913688	141	Overseas Chinese-funded 港澳台資	62,647	484(49)	24,520	a
Yulin Zhangmu Zhen Down Factory 玉林市樟木鎮羽絨廠(1994)	Yulin 玉林市	Guangxi 廣西	(0775)2277188	60	Collectively-owned 集體	53,000	2490(7)	24,630	a
Xiaoshan Lin Pu Feather Co. Ltd. 蕭山市臨浦羽毛有限公司(1995)	Hangzhou 杭州市	Zhejiang 浙江省	(0571)9066965	99	Private-owned 私營	48,165	67(111)	43,459	o
Tianjin Hai De Local & Livestock Products Co. Ltd. 天津市海德土蓄產有限公司(1992)	Tianjin 天津市	Tianjin 天津市	(022)28589972	50	Collectively-owned 集體	48,150	4920(3)	18,720	o
Tongcheng Decoration Flannelette Factory 桐城縣裝飾絨布廠(1990)	Anqing 安慶市	Anhui 安徽省	(0556)6127218	272	Collectively-owned 集體	48,000	6190(1)	25,430	o
Jilin Xin Fa Down Development Co. Ltd. 吉林市新法羽絨開發有限公司(1993)	Jilin 吉林市	Jilin 吉林省	(0432)8942359	65	Foreign-funded 外資	46,629	33(124)	43,250	a,c

Top 10 Cities by Production Output 產出排名前 10 位城市	Province 省	Market share 市場份額	Number of firms 企業個數
Liu'an 六安市	Anhui 安徽省	20.50%	59
Zhanjiang 湛江市	Guangdong 廣東省	18.74%	8
Nanjing 南京市	Jiangsu 江蘇省	5.58%	23
Maoming 茂名市	Guangdong 廣東省	5.51%	1
Huaiyin 淮陰市	Jiangsu 江蘇省	5.15%	16
Hangzhou 杭州市	Zhejiang 浙江省	4.18%	4
Chongqing 重慶市	Chongqing 重慶市	3.58%	4
Yancheng 鹽城市	Jiangsu 江蘇省	2.74%	3
Chuzhou 滁州市	Anhui 安徽省	2.66%	12
Langfang 廊坊市	Hebei 河北省	2.34%	1

10 Major Wholesalers 10 家主要批發商	City 城市	Province 省	Telephone / Fax 電話 / 傳真
Ningbo Local Products Animal Products Import & Export Company 寧波市土產畜產進出口公司	Ningbo 寧波市	Zhejiang 浙江省	(0574)7319525 (0574)7320262
Jiangmen Local Products Import & Export Co 江門市土產進出口公司	Jiangmen 江門市	Guangdong 廣東省	(0759)3353805 (0759)3351104
Jiangmen Handicrafts Import & Export Company 江門市工藝品進出口公司	Jiangmen 江門市	Guangdong 廣東省	(0759)3534021 (0759)3535342
Shandong Animal Products Import & Export Company 山東省畜產進出口公司	Qingdao 青島市	Shandong 山東省	(0532)2971790 (0532)2971838
Hunan Local Products Animal Products Import & Export Company 湖南省土產畜產進出口公司	Changsha 長沙市	Hunan 湖南省	(0731)4727265 (0731)4726674
Zhejiang Local Products Animal Products Import & Export Company 浙江省土產畜產進出口公司	Hangzhou 杭州市	Zhejiang 浙江省	(0571)5178390 (0571)5152310
Jiangsu Dong Xing Import & Export (Group) Co. Ltd. 江蘇省東星進出口(集團)股份有限公司	Nanjing 南京市	Jiangsu 江蘇省	(025)6617488 (025)6616141
Jiangmen Cooking Oil Mill Import & Export Company 江門市糧油進出口公司	Jiangmen 江門市	Guangdong 廣東省	(0759)3366449 (0759)3369323
Guangzhou Animal Products Import & Export Company 廣州市畜產進出口公司	Guangzhou 廣州市	Guangdong 廣東省	(020)83852888 (020)83824187
Tianjin Animal Products Import & Export Company 天津畜產進出口公司	Tianjin 天津市	Tianjin 天津市	(022)23310832 (022)23317312

*Also include sales by firms outside this industry.包括本行業以外廠家的銷售。"o" stands for "others". "o" 代表 "其他產品"。

1952: Feather (Down) Products 羽毛（絨）製品業

The industry accounts for 0.104% of the total revenue of China's industrial sector in 1996. The revenue growth rate of the industry is 0.6% from 1995, as compared to the growth rate of China's industrial sector, 9.51%. The rate of return on asset is 0.66%. 61.71% of all firms in the industry made a profit while 30.60% had negative returns. The top province in terms of the industry's revenue is Jiangsu, accounting for 22.93% of the total revenue.
本行業在1996年佔全行業總產值0.104%，行業年增長率為0.6%（全國工業年增長率9.51%）。行業的資產回報率0.66%，61.71%的企業盈利，30.60%的企業虧損。銷售收入最高的省份為江蘇省，佔本行業的22.93%。

	Total number of firms 企業總數	Total number of employees 職工總數	Total revenue (mil. RMB) 總銷售收入（百萬元）	Total profit (mil. RMB) 總利潤（百萬元）	Return on assets 資產利潤率 (%)	Return on equity 權益利潤率 (%)	Labour productivity ('000 RMB / worker) 勞動生產率（千元/人）	Debts / assets 資產負債率 (%)	Total assets (mil. RMB) 總資產（百萬元）
Industry Overall 行業總體	548	87,828	6,008	47	0.66	2.49	68.41	73.57	7,137

	Number of firms 企業個數	Average number of employees 平均職工人數	Average revenue ('000 RMB) 平均銷售收入（千元）	Average profit ('000 RMB) 平均利潤（千元）	Return on assets 資產利潤率 (%)	Return on equity 權益利潤率 (%)	Labour productivity ('000 RMB / worker) 勞動生產率（千元/人）	Average debts / assets 平均資產負債率(%)	Average Total assets ('000 RMB) 平均總資產（千元）
By ownership 產業所有權									
State-owned 國有	80	318	10,488	-550	-2.32	-21.57	32.99	89.23	23,688
Collectively-owned 集體	363	107	7,509	135	1.93	7.90	70.00	75.50	6,954
Privately-owned 私有	1	26	8,336	700	25.61	41.29	320.62	37.97	2,735
Domestic JVs 聯營	10	160	8,626	-512	-4.27	-14.20	54.05	69.89	11,973
Joint stock 股份制	6	565	85,593	6,809	4.56	8.48	151.40	46.25	149,314
Foreign-funded 外資	42	215	16,731	741	4.21	11.54	77.87	63.50	17,584
Overseas Chinese-funded 港澳台資	46	209	24,629	-552	-2.64	-9.23	117.85	71.40	20,899
By size 規模									
Large 大型	3	2,371	213,066	32,656	7.89	18.83	89.88	58.12	414,024
Medium 中型	21	689	45,993	-403	-0.60	-2.56	66.74	76.43	66,911
Small 小型	521	127	8,452	-82	-0.95	-4.11	66.49	76.96	8,619
By regional distribution 地區分布									
Central-North 華北	40	132	4,989	337	3.45	12.40	37.88	72.15	9,771
Beijing 北京	15	177	7,521	673	3.30	12.31	42.38	73.17	20,391
Tianjin 天津	5	154	5,796	-2	-0.03	-0.07	37.54	63.38	7,816
Hebei 河北	10	116	3,756	273	7.91	24.62	32.44	67.87	3,452
Shanxi 山西	3	23	453	-3	-0.24	0.41	20.00	160.15	1,363
Inner Mongolia 內蒙	7	87	2,689	97	9.34	17.80	31.00	47.53	1,040
Northeast 東北	55	104	2,649	-33	-0.54	-4.46	25.57	87.92	6,075
Liaoning 遼寧	25	62	1,456	-2	-0.09	-0.37	23.61	75.22	2,200
Jilin 吉林	14	232	3,471	-222	-1.32	-16.78	14.98	92.14	16,831
Heilongjiang 黑龍江	16	57	3,792	85	3.13	16.57	66.67	81.12	2,718
Central East 華東	270	198	16,009	70	0.42	1.80	81.03	76.55	16,600
Shanghai 上海	17	147	13,142	-802	-3.93	-17.52	89.40	77.56	20,409
Jiangsu 江蘇	68	192	20,262	197	1.20	5.15	105.60	76.70	16,410
Zhejiang 浙江	47	194	25,073	94	0.43	1.65	129.39	74.01	21,837
Anhui 安徽	39	177	16,311	357	4.28	64.06	91.95	93.32	8,345
Fujian 福建	34	101	6,136	-249	-3.68	-12.11	60.99	69.65	6,782
Jiangxi 江西	37	353	9,882	-355	-1.28	-6.64	28.01	80.79	27,813
Shandong 山東	28	189	11,868	803	5.52	14.33	62.72	61.52	14,562
Central-South 中南	129	119	5,909	76	1.29	5.54	49.73	76.77	5,885
Henan 河南	26	137	2,852	140	2.38	11.15	20.88	78.63	5,892
Hubei 湖北	19	184	10,923	245	2.86	37.31	59.25	92.32	8,561
Hunan 湖南	40	78	3,372	139	6.96	22.60	43.43	69.20	1,997
Guangdong 廣東	30	135	7,152	-293	-3.65	-12.91	52.93	71.74	8,040
Guangxi 廣西	10	44	7,790	361	10.04	23.23	177.85	56.73	3,594
Hainan 海南	4	169	13,295	273	1.26	4.78	78.79	73.61	21,583
Southwest 西南	50	161	11,505	130	0.56	1.28	71.25	56.40	23,299
Chongqing 重慶	12	114	11,472	148	0.82	2.74	100.13	70.14	18,077
Sichuan 四川	29	214	14,265	164	0.52	1.11	66.39	52.68	31,247
Guizhou 貴州	4	36	1,895	65	3.00	11.61	52.64	74.19	2,170
Yunnan 雲南	4	39	870	-110	-5.07	-21.89	22.60	76.82	2,168
Tibet 西藏									
Northwest 西北	4	30	705	5	0.35	1.13	23.70	69.50	1,443
Shaanxi 陝西	2	27	420	15	0.87	2.59	15.85	66.76	1,730
Gansu 甘肅									
Qinghai 青海									
Ningxia 寧夏									
Xinjiang 新疆	2	33	990	-5	-0.43	-1.64	30.00	73.59	1,155

1952: Feather (Down) Products 羽毛（絨）製品業

Year 年份	Number of firms 企業個數	Rate of change 每年變化 (%)	Number of employees 職工人數（人）	Rate of change 每年變化 (%)	Total revenue (mil. RMB) 總銷售收入（百萬元）	Rate of change 每年變化 (%)	Total profit (mil. RMB) 總利潤（百萬元）	Rate of change 每年變化 (%)
1993	467		77,428		3,919		157	
1994	510	9.21%	84,869	9.61%	5,111	30.42%	108	-31.15%
1995	598	17.25%	101,812	19.96%	5,971	16.83%	14	-86.98%
1996	548	-8.36%	87,828	-13.74%	6,008	0.62%	47	233.43%

3 Major products* 3 種主要產品 *	Output 產量	Sales volume 銷售量	Unit 單位
a) Down Pillow 羽絨枕頭	4,633,992	4,541,313	piece 只
b) Down Quilt 絨被	4,772,298	4,676,852	piece 條
c) Down Costume 羽絨服裝	2,748	2,336	10,000 piece 萬件

Top 10 firms by revenue (year founded) 收入排名前 10 家企業（創辦年份）	City 城市	Province 省	Telephone / fax 電話 / 傳真	Number of employees 職工人數	Ownership 產業所有權	Revenue ('000 RMB) 銷售收入（千元）	Profit ('000 RMB) (rank) 利潤（千元）（排名）	Total assets ('000 RMB) 總資產（千元）	Major products 主要產品
Zhejiang Natural Group Co. Ltd. 浙江天然集團股份有限公司(1985)	Shaoxing 紹興市	Zhejiang 浙江省	(0575)5114798 (0575)5126892	2,104	Joint stock 股份制	349,476	10057(3)	339,108	a,b,c
Jiangxi Gong Qing Down Mill 江西共青羽絨廠(1970)	Nanchang 南昌市	Jiangxi 江西省	(0791)4342520 (0791)4341446		State-owned 國有	220,608	1010(36)	661,186	b,c
Wujiang Dong Ya Down Products Co. Ltd. 吳江市東亞羽絨製品有限公司(1992)	Suzhou 蘇州市	Jiangsu 江蘇省	(0512)3291723	450	Overseas Chinese-funded 港澳台資	176,000	5920(10)	24,275	b
Snowdown Merchandise Co. Ltd. 光隆羽絨製品公司(1993)	Suzhou 蘇州市	Jiangsu 江蘇省	(0512)7631510 (0512)7631632	580	Overseas Chinese-funded 港澳台資	162,032	0(166)	202,095	b
Jiangsu Meierzi Group Co. 江蘇美爾姿集團公司(1983)	Yancheng 鹽城市	Jiangsu 江蘇省	(0515)2722220 (0515)2722011	1,986	State-owned 國有	159,400	4700(12)	150,230	c
Sichuan Tiange Group Corp., Ltd. 四川天歌集團股份有限公司(1983)	Nanchong 南充市	Sichuan 四川省	(0817)2228189 (0817)2223200	2,463	Joint stock 股份制	152,857	10092(2)	544,310	a,b,c
Zhejiang San Hong International Feather Co. Ltd. 浙江三弘國際羽毛有限公司(1995)	Hangzhou 杭州市	Zhejiang 浙江省	(0571)2475666 (0571)2475679	200	Foreign-funded 外資	130,600	1320(23)	37,326	o
Anhui Guan Zhen Down General Factory 安徽省官鎮羽絨總廠(1985)	Chaohu 巢湖市	Anhui 安徽省	(0565)6321743 (0565)6321781	248	Collectively-owned 集體	114,123	8322(4)	42,479	a,b,c
Zhejiang Bei Tian E Group Co. 浙江北天鵝集團公司(1991)	Hangzhou 杭州市	Zhejiang 浙江省	(0571)2726888 (0571)2726828	95	Collectively-owned 集體	100,637	454(63)	100,560	b,c
Diadem International (Xiamen) Co. Ltd. 廈門廣懋國際有限公司(1987)	Xiamen 廈門市	Fujian 福建省	(0592)6217290 (0592)6217298	613	Overseas Chinese-funded 港澳台資	93,795	1011(35)	76,340	b,c

Top 10 Cities by Production Output 產出排名前 10 位城市	Province 省	Market share 市場份額	Number of firms 企業個數
Shaoxing 紹興市	Zhejiang 浙江省	11.61%	14
Hangzhou 杭州市	Zhejiang 浙江省	7.50%	16
Shanghai 上海市	Shanghai 上海市	7.21%	28
Suzhou 蘇州市	Jiangsu 江蘇省	5.68%	20
Yangzhou 揚州市	Jiangsu 江蘇省	5.66%	17
Beijing 北京市	Beijing 北京市	4.86%	13
Jiujiang 九江市	Jiangxi 江西省	4.77%	12
Chongqing 重慶市	Chongqing 重慶市	3.71%	24
Yancheng 鹽城市	Jiangsu 江蘇省	3.62%	11
Jining 濟寧市	Shandong 山東省	3.47%	10

10 Major Wholesalers 10 家主要批發商	City 城市	Province 省	Telephone / Fax 電話 / 傳真
Ningbo Local Products Animal Products Import & Export Company 寧波市土產畜產進出口公司	Ningbo 寧波市	Zhejiang 浙江省	(0574)7319525 (0574)7320262
Jiangmen Local Products Import & Export Co 江門市土產進出口公司	Jiangmen 江門市	Guangdong 廣東省	(0759)3353805 (0759)3351104
Jiangmen Handicrafts Import & Export Company 江門市工藝品進出口公司	Jiangmen 江門市	Guangdong 廣東省	(0759)3534021 (0759)3535342
Shandong Animal Products Import & Export Company 山東省畜產進出口公司	Qingdao 青島市	Shandong 山東省	(0532)2971790 (0532)2971838
Hunan Local Products Animal Products Import & Export Company 湖南省土產畜產進出口公司	Changsha 長沙市	Hunan 湖南省	(0731)4727265 (0731)4726674
Zhejiang Local Products Animal Products Import & Export Company 浙江省土產畜產進出口公司	Hangzhou 杭州市	Zhejiang 浙江省	(0571)5178390 (0571)5152310
Jiangsu Dong Xing Import & Export (Group) Co. Ltd. 江蘇省東星進出口(集團)股份有限公司	Nanjing 南京市	Jiangsu 江蘇省	(025)6617488 (025)6616141
Jiangmen Cooking Oil Mill Import & Export Company 江門市糧油進出口公司	Jiangmen 江門市	Guangdong 廣東省	(0759)3366449 (0759)3369323
Guangzhou Animal Products Import & Export Company 廣州市畜產進出口公司	Guangzhou 廣州市	Guangdong 廣東省	(020)83852888 (020)83824187
Tianjin Animal Products Import & Export Company 天津畜產進出口公司	Tianjin 天津市	Tianjin 天津市	(022)23310832 (022)23317312

*Also include sales by firms outside this industry.包括本行業以外廠家的銷售。"o" stands for "others". "o" 代表"其他產品"。

2011: Sawing Lumber Processing 鋸材加工業

The industry accounts for 0.120% of the total revenue of China's industrial sector in 1996. The revenue growth rate of the industry is 5.0% from 1995, as compared to the growth rate of China's industrial sector, 9.51%. The rate of return on asset is 0.46%. 82.67% of all firms in the industry made a profit while 12.12% had negative returns. The top province in terms of the industry's revenue is Helongjiang, accounting for 18.34% of the total revenue.
本行業在1996年佔全行業總產值0.120%，行業年增長率為5.0%（全國工業年增長率9.51%）。行業的資產回報率0.46%，82.67%的企業盈利，12.12%的企業虧損。銷售收入最高的省份為黑龍江省，佔本行業的18.34%。

	Total number of firms 企業總數	Total number of employees 職工總數	Total revenue (mil. RMB) 總銷售收入（百萬元）	Total profit (mil. RMB) 總利潤（百萬元）	Return on assets 資產利潤率 (%)	Return on equity 權益利潤率 (%)	Labour productivity ('000 RMB / worker) 勞動生產率（千元／人）	Debts / assets 資產負債率 (%)	Total assets (mil. RMB) 總資產（百萬元）
Industry Overall 行業總體	3,734	219,188	6,952	42	0.46	1.43	31.72	67.91	9,157

	Number of firms 企業個數	Average number of employees 平均職工人數	Average revenue ('000 RMB) 平均銷售收入（千元）	Average profit ('000 RMB) 平均利潤（千元）	Return on assets 資產利潤率 (%)	Return on equity 權益利潤率 (%)	Labour productivity ('000 RMB / worker) 勞動生產率（千元／人）	Average debts / assets 平均資產負債率(%)	Average Total assets ('000 RMB) 平均總資產（千元）
By ownership 產業所有權									
State-owned 國有	308	208	4,698	-455	-2.92	-9.78	22.60	70.12	15,558
Collectively-owned 集體	3,290	45	1,429	63	6.54	21.19	31.71	69.16	957
Privately-owned 私有	16	10	950	79	21.39	66.08	95.57	67.63	369
Domestic JVs 聯營	18	47	3,770	-282	-8.38	-36.70	79.64	77.18	3,371
Joint stock 股份制	12	22	3,298	103	9.47	18.55	150.49	48.96	1,090
Foreign-funded 外資	36	98	9,341	158	1.07	2.47	95.62	56.68	14,814
Overseas Chinese-funded 港澳台資	50	61	6,707	-541	-4.51	-9.61	110.35	53.05	11,983
By size 規模									
Large 大型	6	1,793	78,176	-4,957	-2.34	-6.40	43.59	63.50	212,280
Medium 中型	18	1,086	31,041	-2,041	-1.96	-8.43	28.58	76.72	103,986
Small 小型	3,681	51	1,608	29	1.80	5.32	31.37	66.11	1,633
By regional distribution 地區分布									
Central-North 華北	205	145	2,352	-93	-1.45	-3.41	16.19	57.41	6,366
Beijing 北京	17	81	5,972	-29	-0.30	-0.58	73.83	47.74	9,701
Tianjin 天津	18	119	11,173	-1,155	-3.05	-6.03	94.16	49.33	37,810
Hebei 河北	27	25	827	43	4.32	11.36	33.05	62.03	987
Shanxi 山西	12	16	200	7	4.35	7.84	12.90	44.57	153
Inner Mongolia 內蒙	131	194	1,182	8	0.25	0.95	6.09	73.64	3,290
Northeast 東北	1,156	92	1,880	-7	-0.26	-1.52	20.45	82.67	2,836
Liaoning 遼寧	251	33	2,270	108	4.61	28.66	68.47	83.91	2,335
Jilin 吉林	311	129	1,059	-36	-1.63	-4.97	8.20	67.20	2,182
Heilongjiang 黑龍江	594	97	2,146	-41	-1.22	-9.79	22.05	87.51	3,390
Central East 華東	1,082	34	2,071	52	2.68	6.80	61.76	60.60	1,941
Shanghai 上海	28	49	3,647	-150	-2.70	-8.73	74.05	69.11	5,550
Jiangsu 江蘇	83	66	4,171	-2	-0.05	-0.15	63.25	63.72	4,244
Zhejiang 浙江	182	33	1,801	-4	-0.14	-0.27	54.54	48.85	2,788
Anhui 安徽	300	28	2,473	159	18.74	62.80	89.14	70.15	851
Fujian 福建	275	31	1,505	-3	-0.15	-0.42	49.22	64.80	1,705
Jiangxi 江西	158	18	742	28	3.49	6.49	42.25	46.31	810
Shandong 山東	56	70	3,421	174	4.19	11.89	48.97	64.75	4,159
Central-South 中南	836	27	1,823	83	6.50	14.59	66.72	55.44	1,277
Henan 河南	86	40	2,979	216	9.30	26.54	75.11	64.98	2,326
Hubei 湖北	86	43	3,245	128	4.63	7.36	75.09	37.03	2,774
Hunan 湖南	272	18	1,038	57	12.07	27.76	56.29	56.50	468
Guangdong 廣東	164	25	2,000	65	6.01	18.33	80.79	67.19	1,085
Guangxi 廣西	219	27	1,438	48	4.00	7.55	52.95	47.05	1,200
Hainan 海南	9	77	7,072	358	5.26	120.60	91.71	95.64	6,807
Southwest 西南	282	61	1,396	-156	-4.61	-12.67	22.98	63.62	3,386
Chongqing 重慶	20	63	650	-118	-7.93	-42.98	10.26	81.54	1,490
Sichuan 四川	141	50	1,631	-128	-4.41	-14.31	32.38	69.17	2,908
Guizhou 貴州	50	29	570	-5	-0.32	-0.62	19.36	48.06	1,625
Yunnan 雲南	61	107	1,520	-457	-7.67	-21.72	14.25	64.69	5,963
Tibet 西藏	9	73	3,159	532	7.07	10.85	43.08	34.83	7,526
Northwest 西北	173	40	795	-69	-2.64	-7.25	20.07	63.64	2,608
Shaanxi 陝西	89	19	529	31	7.66	18.64	27.94	58.94	404
Gansu 甘肅	61	40	597	-73	-5.20	-14.70	15.04	64.67	1,413
Qinghai 青海	3	202	7,187	-1,550	-6.66	-28.63	35.58	76.74	23,270
Ningxia 寧夏	2	4	5				1.43		90
Xinjiang 新疆	18	119	1,806	-306	-2.13	-5.38	15.22	60.46	14,391

2011: Sawing Lumber Processing 鋸材加工業

Year 年份	Number of firms 企業個數	Rate of change 每年變化 (%)	Number of employees 職工人數 (人)	Rate of change 每年變化 (%)	Total revenue (mil. RMB) 總銷售收入 (百萬元)	Rate of change 每年變化 (%)	Total profit (mil. RMB) 總利潤 (百萬元)	Rate of change 每年變化 (%)
1993								
1994	2,761		274,797		4,525		-47	
1995	4,205	52.30%	283,201	3.06%	6,618	46.23%	58	222.17%
1996	3,734	-11.20%	219,188	-22.60%	6,952	5.05%	42	-27.39%

3 Major products* 3 種主要產品 *	Output 產量	Sales volume 銷售量	Unit 單位
a) Special Sawmilling 特種鋸材	313,996	270,036	cubic metre 立方米
b) Common Sawmilling 普通鋸材	3,423,392	3,252,223	cubic metre 立方米
c) Manmade Board 人造板	328,845	299,249	cubic metre 立方米

Top 10 firms by revenue (year founded) 收入排名前 10 家企業 (創辦年份)	City 城市	Province 省	Telephone / fax 電話 / 傳真	Number of employees 職工人數	Ownership 產業所有權	Revenue ('000 RMB) 銷售收入 (千元)	Profit ('000 RMB) (rank) 利潤 (千元) (排名)	Total assets ('000 RMB) 總資產 (千元)	Major products 主要產品
Wan Xi Wood & Bamboo Group Co. 皖西木竹集團公司(1993)	Liu'an 六安市	Anhui 安徽省	(0564)6496434	1,800	Collectively-owned 集體	95,930	11030(1)	17,190	b
Paulownia Timber Processing Factory 桐板加工廠(1990)	Fuyang 阜陽市	Anhui 安徽省		64	Collectively-owned 集體	79,510	10220(2)	30,280	b
Wenzhou Timber Group Co. 温州木材集團公司(1952)	Wenzhou 温州市	Zhejiang 浙江省	(0577)8781506 (0577)8781425	1,098	State-owned 國有	79,040	1221(32)	144,862	c
Railway Department Wuhan Wood Preservation Mill 鐵道部武漢市木材防腐廠(1954)	Wuhan 武漢市	Hubei 湖北省	(027)84844827 (027)84844827	855	State-owned 國有	72,849	500(101)	157,755	o
Tianjin American Type Furniture Co. Ltd. 天津美式傢具有限公司(1993)	Tianjin 天津市	Tianjin 天津市	(022)5324745 (022)5324744	373	Overseas Chinese-funded 港澳台資	71,319	-16449(691)	258,814	c
Zhengyanghe General Wood Multiple Processing Plant 正陽河木材綜合加工廠(1958)	Harbin 哈爾濱市	Heilongjiang 黑龍江省	(0451)4603514 (0451)4601387	3,021	State-owned 國有	71,152	-4465(680)	214,340	b,c
The Ministry of Railways Harbin Timber Antiseptic Mill 鐵道部哈爾濱木材防腐廠(1935)	Harbin 哈爾濱市	Heilongjiang 黑龍江省	(0451)7600818 (0451)7671173	686	State-owned 國有	69,290	620(78)	134,320	b
Shenyang Eurasia Wooden Products Co. Ltd. 瀋陽市歐亞木製品有限公司(1994)	Shenyang 瀋陽市	Liaoning 遼寧省	(024)22903937	38	Foreign-funded 外資	62,813	4928(3)	14,818	o
The Ministry of Railways Liuzhou Timber Antiseptic Mill 鐵道部柳州木材防腐廠(1957)	Liuzhou 柳州市	Guangxi 廣西	(0772)3836642 (0772)3836642	450	State-owned 國有	59,520	50(464)	132,848	a
Jiangyin Nan Zha Da Qiao Timber Factory 江陰市南閘大橋木材廠(1989)	Wuxi 無錫市	Jiangsu 江蘇省	(0510)6181692	300	Collectively-owned 集體	55,843	1003(41)	38,540	o

Top 10 Cities by Production Output 產出排名前 10 位城市	Province 省	Market share 市場份額	Number of firms 企業個數
Suzhou 蘇州市	Jiangsu 江蘇省	4.86%	24
Tianjin 天津市	Tianjin 天津市	4.22%	22
Harbin 哈爾濱市	Heilongjiang 黑龍江省	4.18%	56
Yichun 伊春市	Heilongjiang 黑龍江省	3.91%	58
Shuangcheng 雙城市	Heilongjiang 黑龍江省	3.28%	158
Zhaoqing 肇慶市	Guangdong 廣東省	2.74%	36
Sanming 三明市	Fujian 福建省	2.66%	111
Shanghai 上海市	Shanghai 上海市	2.60%	47
Kaifeng 開封市	Henan 河南省	2.24%	22
Beijing 北京市	Beijing 北京市	2.08%	16

10 Major Wholesalers 10 家主要批發商	City 城市	Province 省	Telephone / Fax 電話 / 傳真
Jilin Forestry Import & Export Company 吉林省林業進出口公司	Changchun 長春市	Jilin 吉林省	(0431)5629740 (0431)5638250
Shanghai Local Products Goods & Materials General Co. 上海市土產物資總公司	Shanghai 上海市	Shanghai 上海市	(021)63200857 (021)63200857
Kunming Import & Export Company 昆明市進出口公司	Kunming 昆明市	Yunnan 雲南省	(0871)5155192 (0871)5155193
Wujin Supply & Marketing Cooperative Means of Production General Company 武進市供銷社生產資料總公司	Changzhou 常州市	Jiangsu 江蘇省	(0519)6609079 (0519)6609079
China Timber Import & Export Company 中國木材進出口公司	Beijing 北京市	Beijing 北京市	(010)65132383 (010)65124788
Jinchen Urban Goods & Materials General Company Timber Company 晉城市城區物資總公司木材公司	Jincheng 晉城市	Shanxi 山西省	
Zhangjiagang Timber General Company 張家港市木材總公司	Suzhou 蘇州市	Jiangsu 江蘇省	(0512)8223241
Wujiang Timber General Company 吳江市木材總公司	Suzhou 蘇州市	Jiangsu 江蘇省	(0512)3422179
China Forest Products Marketing Company 中國林產品經銷公司	Beijing 北京市	Beijing 北京市	(010)64228370 (010)64216443
Yangzhou Timber General Company 揚州市木材總公司	Yangzhou 揚州市	Jiangsu 江蘇省	(0514)7246917 (0514)7247383

*Also include sales by firms outside this industry.包括本行業以外廠家的銷售。"o" stands for "others". "o" 代表 "其他產品"。

2012: Wood Chip Processing 木片加工業

The industry accounts for 0.029% of the total revenue of China's industrial sector in 1996. The revenue growth rate of the industry is 33.4% from 1995, as compared to the growth rate of China's industrial sector, 9.51%. The rate of return on asset is 4.24%. 82.59% of all firms in the industry made a profit while 11.04% had negative returns. The top province in terms of the industry's revenue is Guangdong, accounting for 22.58% of the total revenue.
本行業在1996年佔全行業總產值0.029%，行業年增長率為33.4%（全國工業年增長率9.51%）。行業的資產回報率4.24%，82.59%的企業盈利，11.04%的企業虧損。銷售收入最高的省份為廣東省，佔本行業的22.58%。

	Total number of firms 企業總數	Total number of employees 職工總數	Total revenue (mil. RMB) 總銷售收入（百萬元）	Total profit (mil. RMB) 總利潤（百萬元）	Return on assets 資產利潤率 (%)	Return on equity 權益利潤率 (%)	Labour productivity ('000 RMB / worker) 勞動生產率（千元/人）	Debts / assets 資產負債率 (%)	Total assets (mil. RMB) 總資產（百萬元）
Industry Overall 行業總體	624	22,874	1,654	53	4.24	12.04	72.31	64.74	1,249

	Number of firms 企業個數	Average number of employees 平均職工人數	Average revenue ('000 RMB) 平均銷售收入（千元）	Average profit ('000 RMB) 平均利潤（千元）	Return on assets 資產利潤率 (%)	Return on equity 權益利潤率 (%)	Labour productivity ('000 RMB / worker) 勞動生產率（千元/人）	Average debts / assets 平均資產負債率(%)	Average Total assets ('000 RMB) 平均總資產（千元）
By ownership 產業所有權									
State-owned 國有	43	63	3,488	-326	-4.68	-20.00	55.51	76.59	6,953
Collectively-owned 集體	538	34	2,140	88	7.15	18.58	63.43	61.53	1,238
Privately-owned 私有	3	48	4,067	46	2.04	2.58	84.72	21.00	2,237
Domestic JVs 聯營	3	12	2,038	259	16.63	33.77	174.70	50.74	1,558
Joint stock 股份制	3	56	4,849	303	9.05	48.14	86.08	81.19	3,343
Foreign-funded 外資	17	46	7,566	373	5.69	13.93	165.55	59.15	6,552
Overseas Chinese-funded 港澳台資	16	56	12,000	702	7.45	19.16	214.29	61.11	9,414
By size 規模									
Large 大型									
Medium 中型	1	19	5,335	713	15.99	29.17	280.81	45.17	4,456
Small 小型	607	37	2,718	86	4.20	11.95	73.62	64.84	2,050
By regional distribution 地區分布									
Central-North 華北	45	30	713	43	5.85	12.55	24.02	53.29	736
Beijing 北京	6	4	335	20	13.48	60.00	95.71	76.40	148
Tianjin 天津	1	30	30	-20	-2.63	-50.00	1.00	94.74	760
Hebei 河北	27	17	688	39	5.73	14.29	40.48	59.89	672
Shanxi 山西									
Inner Mongolia 內蒙	11	75	1,041	73	6.00	10.08	13.88	40.40	1,213
Northeast 東北	117	37	2,194	92	4.82	15.25	58.66	68.36	1,910
Liaoning 遼寧	47	33	3,686	164	5.34	19.37	112.85	72.45	3,081
Jilin 吉林	28	29	1,223	76	6.95	19.69	42.39	64.72	1,100
Heilongjiang 黑龍江	42	48	1,173	22	1.90	4.56	24.22	58.32	1,139
Central East 華東	205	45	3,680	164	6.81	18.28	81.70	62.74	2,415
Shanghai 上海	4	35	3,318	113	2.73	6.57	94.11	58.50	4,120
Jiangsu 江蘇	41	93	8,265	261	8.07	27.93	89.20	71.10	3,239
Zhejiang 浙江	13	25	1,617	-69	-5.26	183.67	65.69	102.87	1,315
Anhui 安徽	26	37	7,795	861	52.74	73.07	208.94	27.82	1,633
Fujian 福建	43	17	1,305	-32	-2.93	-4.04	75.65	27.35	1,094
Jiangxi 江西	54	18	418	11	2.18	11.61	23.16	81.22	484
Shandong 山東	24	95	4,160	78	0.88	2.67	43.66	67.13	8,880
Central-South 中南	188	32	2,950	72	3.41	7.86	93.54	56.56	2,105
Henan 河南	35	34	2,100	121	7.28	21.00	61.20	65.33	1,657
Hubei 湖北	13	41	1,379	105	4.47	6.39	33.96	30.01	2,355
Hunan 湖南	28	23	1,298	45	5.35	9.67	57.12	44.67	834
Guangdong 廣東	58	41	6,439	163	4.41	9.90	158.04	55.46	3,707
Guangxi 廣西	52	19	925	-41	-4.34	-9.67	48.07	55.10	952
Hainan 海南	2	101	2,680	-330	-3.41	126.92	26.67	102.64	9,665
Southwest 西南	38	24	1,153	-90	-5.05	-44.30	48.92	88.59	1,783
Chongqing 重慶	2	19	343	-2,898	-214.23	-772.28	17.51	72.26	1,353
Sichuan 四川	22	23	1,667	414	16.74	176.25	71.48	90.50	2,473
Guizhou 貴州	10	19	252	-28	-5.66	-560.00	13.13	98.79	495
Yunnan 雲南	3	39	837				21.45	56.30	1,137
Tibet 西藏									
Northwest 西北	31	36	389	-112	-10.17	35.23	10.95	128.87	1,101
Shaanxi 陝西	21	25	342	-168	-12.08	33.24	13.60	136.38	1,391
Gansu 甘肅	8	55	389	4	0.76	7.69	7.10	89.87	494
Qinghai 青海									
Ningxia 寧夏									
Xinjiang 新疆	2	68	890	15	3.16	7.89	13.09	60.00	475

2012: Wood Chip Processing 木片加工業

Year 年份	Number of firms 企業個數	Rate of change 每年變化 (%)	Number of employees 職工人數 (人)	Rate of change 每年變化 (%)	Total revenue (mil. RMB) 總銷售收入 (百萬元)	Rate of change 每年變化 (%)	Total profit (mil. RMB) 總利潤 (百萬元)	Rate of change 每年變化 (%)
1993								
1994	475		21,257		1,018		44	
1995	576	21.26%	24,385	14.72%	1,240	21.80%	53	19.36%
1996	624	8.33%	22,874	-6.20%	1,654	33.39%	53	0.37%

3 Major products* 3種主要產品*	Output 產量	Sales volume 銷售量	Unit 單位
a) Wood Chip 木片	1,714,086	1,679,804	cubic metre 立方米
b) Common Sawmilling 普通鋸材	156,114	148,309	cubic metre 立方米
c) Repressed Manmade Board 人造板二次加工裝飾板	1,703,314	1,618,148	square metre 平方米

Top 10 firms by revenue (year founded) 收入排名前10家企業 (創辦年份)	City 城市	Province 省	Telephone / fax 電話 / 傳真	Number of employees 職工人數	Ownership 產業所有權	Revenue ('000 RMB) 銷售收入 (千元)	Profit ('000 RMB) (rank) 利潤 (千元) (排名)	Total assets ('000 RMB) 總資產 (千元)	Major products 主要產品
Bozhou Zhangji Xun Da Wood Products Co. Ltd. 亳州市張集鎮迅達木製品有限公司(1988)	Fuyang 阜陽市	Anhui 安徽省	(0558)5501037 (0558)5501025	290	Collectively-owned 集體	86,220	10350(1)	12,370	b
Guangdong Yunan Du Cheng Industry Development Co. 廣東省郁南縣都城工業發展公司(1992)	Yunfu 雲浮市	Guangdong 廣東省	(0766)7592100 (0766)7592100	284	Collectively-owned 集體	82,160	35(113)	16,430	o
Pizhou Jinhu Timber Industry Co. Ltd. 邳州金湖木業有限公司(1996)	Xuzhou 徐州市	Jiangsu 江蘇省	(0516)6441306	646	Collectively-owned 集體	76,450	2810(5)	14,040	o
Pizhou Guanhu Yong Hua Industrial Co. 邳州市官湖鎮永華實業公司(1991)	Xuzhou 徐州市	Jiangsu 江蘇省	(0516)6441306	543	Collectively-owned 集體	52,010	1570(7)	16,278	a
Bozhou Hao Sen Timber Industry Co. Ltd. 亳州市豪森木業有限公司(1955)	Fuyang 阜陽市	Anhui 安徽省	(0558)5521174 (0558)5521174	50	Collectively-owned 集體	50,310	6600(2)	8,610	b
Hai City Li Hua Wooden Products Processing Factory 海城市利華木製品加工廠(1993)	Anshan 鞍山市	Liaoning 遼寧省	(0412)3764128	200	Collectively-owned 集體	48,390	1300(9)	10,400	o
Jinzhou Jianhua Forestry Industry Co. Ltd. 錦州建華林產工業公司(1992)	Jinzhou 錦州市	Liaoning 遼寧省	(0416)5141254 (0416)5141254	260	Overseas Chinese-funded 港澳台資	47,160	5709(3)	20,451	o
Zhanjiang Sheng Ye Eucalyptus Develpment Co. Ltd. 湛江盛業桉樹發展有限公司(1994)	Zhanjiang 湛江市	Guangdong 廣東省	(0758)7765291	86	Overseas Chinese-funded 港澳台資	31,510	-520(146)	17,350	a
Lianjiang Wood Chip Co. 廉江市木片公司(1992)	Zhanjiang 湛江市	Guangdong 廣東省	(0758)6255727	116	State-owned 國有	29,340	500(32)	13,270	a
Weifang Chang Yi Tung Wooden Products Co. Ltd. 濰坊昌藝桐木製品有限公司(1990)	Weifang 濰坊市	Shandong 山東省	(0536)8900231 (0536)8900231	750	Foreign-funded 外資	27,517	1490(8)	69,574	o

Top 10 Cities by Production Output 產出排名前10位城市	Province 省	Market share 市場份額	Number of firms 企業個數
Zhanjiang 湛江市	Guangdong 廣東省	12.94%	12
Fuyang 阜陽市	Anhui 安徽省	12.86%	13
Shaoyang 邵陽市	Hunan 湖南省	4.73%	37
Yunfu 雲浮市	Guangdong 廣東省	4.70%	4
Anshan 鞍山市	Liaoning 遼寧省	3.35%	2
Qingdao 青島市	Shandong 山東省	3.05%	4
Jiangmen 江門市	Guangdong 廣東省	2.86%	2
Xuzhou 徐州市	Jiangsu 江蘇省	2.80%	17
Jinzhou 錦州市	Liaoning 遼寧省	2.42%	5
Zhaoqing 肇慶市	Guangdong 廣東省	2.36%	7

10 Major Wholesalers 10家主要批發商	City 城市	Province 省	Telephone / Fax 電話 / 傳真
Jilin Forestry Import & Export Company 吉林省林業進出口公司	Changchun 長春市	Jilin 吉林省	(0431)5629740 (0431)5638250
Shanghai Local Products Goods & Materials General Co. 上海市土產物資總公司	Shanghai 上海市	Shanghai 上海市	(021)63200857 (021)63200857
Kunming Import & Export Company 昆明市進出口公司	Kunming 昆明市	Yunnan 雲南省	(0871)5155192 (0871)5155193
Wujin Supply & Marketing Cooperative Means of Production General Company 武進市供銷社生產資料總公司	Changzhou 常州市	Jiangsu 江蘇省	(0519)6609079 (0519)6609079
China Timber Import & Export Company 中國木材進出口公司	Beijing 北京市	Beijing 北京市	(010)65132383 (010)65124788
Jinchen Urban Goods & Materials General Company Timber Company 晉城市城區物資總公司木材公司	Jincheng 晉城市	Shanxi 山西省	
Zhangjiagang Timber General Company 張家港市木材總公司	Suzhou 蘇州市	Jiangsu 江蘇省	(0512)8223241
Wujiang Timber General Company 吳江市木材總公司	Suzhou 蘇州市	Jiangsu 江蘇省	(0512)3422179
China Forest Products Marketing Company 中國林產品經銷公司	Beijing 北京市	Beijing 北京市	(010)64228370 (010)64216443
Yangzhou Timber General Company 揚州市木材總公司	Yangzhou 揚州市	Jiangsu 江蘇省	(0514)7246917 (0514)7247383

*Also include sales by firms outside this industry.包括本行業以外廠家的銷售。"o" stands for "others". "o" 代表 "其他產品"。

2021: Plywood 膠合板製造業

The industry accounts for 0.168% of the total revenue of China's industrial sector in 1996. The revenue growth rate of the industry is 8.5% from 1995, as compared to the growth rate of China's industrial sector, 9.51%. The rate of return on asset is 0.44%. 70.99% of all firms in the industry made a profit while 23.37% had negative returns. The top province in terms of the industry's revenue is Jiangsu, accounting for 18.41% of the total revenue.
本行業在1996年佔全行業總產值0.168%，行業年增長率為8.5%（全國工業年增長率9.51%）。行業的資產回報率0.44%，70.99%的企業盈利，23.37%的企業虧損。銷售收入最高的省份為江蘇省，佔本行業的18.41%。

	Total number of firms 企業總數	Total number of employees 職工總數	Total revenue (mil. RMB) 總銷售收入（百萬元）	Total profit (mil. RMB) 總利潤（百萬元）	Return on assets 資產利潤率 (%)	Return on equity 權益利潤率 (%)	Labour productivity ('000 RMB / worker) 勞動生產率（千元/人）	Debts / assets 資產負債率 (%)	Total assets (mil. RMB) 總資產（百萬元）
Industry Overall 行業總體	1,335	172,922	9,752	55	0.44	1.66	56.40	73.32	12,476

	Number of firms 企業個數	Average number of employees 平均職工人數	Average revenue ('000 RMB) 平均銷售收入（千元）	Average profit ('000 RMB) 平均利潤（千元）	Return on assets 資產利潤率 (%)	Return on equity 權益利潤率 (%)	Labour productivity ('000 RMB / worker) 勞動生產率（千元/人）	Average debts / assets 平均資產負債率(%)	Average Total assets ('000 RMB) 平均總資產（千元）
By ownership 產業所有權									
State-owned 國有	176	272	8,869	-602	-2.91	-12.35	32.62	76.42	20,670
Collectively-owned 集體	957	90	3,451	56	1.81	8.35	38.32	78.38	3,121
Privately-owned 私有	24	59	3,313	605	33.35	58.14	56.03	42.63	1,814
Domestic JVs 聯營	22	106	3,884	-116	-2.08	-4.53	36.60	54.12	5,589
Joint stock 股份制	23	156	5,784	-248	-3.58	-11.76	37.00	69.58	6,933
Foreign-funded 外資	48	289	40,911	2,480	5.31	17.29	141.73	69.31	46,745
Overseas Chinese-funded 港澳台資	82	243	31,927	-202	-0.51	-1.65	131.25	69.20	39,890
By size 規模									
Large 大型	14	1,493	180,610	-1,717	-0.74	-3.50	120.94	78.74	230,536
Medium 中型	22	1,098	36,044	2,782	4.65	31.49	32.83	85.22	59,787
Small 小型	1,268	100	5,071	14	0.22	0.73	50.49	69.15	6,256
By regional distribution 地區分布									
Central-North 華北	94	73	9,814	1,055	10.95	33.07	133.89	66.90	9,640
Beijing 北京	8	115	3,526	-185	-2.19	-8.03	30.73	72.74	8,450
Tianjin 天津	7	231	85,557	11,227	14.28	42.44	370.38	66.35	78,621
Hebei 河北	55	52	5,131	458	12.09	31.00	98.42	61.01	3,791
Shanxi 山西	8	46	406	-8	-0.34	-0.68	8.83	49.69	2,186
Inner Mongolia 內蒙	16	70	623	-192	-4.93	-49.20	8.90	89.96	3,889
Northeast 東北	166	292	5,128	-221	-2.26	-10.65	17.53	78.77	9,801
Liaoning 遼寧	21	52	7,043	348	4.79	7.94	135.95	39.76	7,274
Jilin 吉林	61	451	6,209	-499	-3.50	-14.42	13.76	75.74	14,250
Heilongjiang 黑龍江	84	237	3,864	-163	-2.26	-32.20	16.29	92.99	7,201
Central East 華東	610	113	7,969	61	0.72	2.57	70.47	71.77	8,385
Shanghai 上海	14	394	32,584	679	1.75	9.11	82.62	80.83	38,901
Jiangsu 江蘇	69	177	26,019	904	4.95	12.15	146.72	59.25	18,265
Zhejiang 浙江	55	86	7,262	129	1.50	4.79	84.01	68.69	8,630
Anhui 安徽	54	131	7,367	52	0.88	2.23	56.20	60.70	5,951
Fujian 福建	185	75	3,421	-312	-5.29	-30.14	45.38	82.44	5,890
Jiangxi 江西	147	115	3,021	-167	-2.64	-12.25	26.19	78.43	6,307
Shandong 山東	86	99	8,553	435	7.53	23.44	86.61	67.87	5,779
Central-South 中南	333	97	8,032	-9	-0.07	-0.30	82.44	75.65	11,854
Henan 河南	106	56	3,113	15	0.25	1.06	55.94	76.44	6,062
Hubei 湖北	30	133	16,183	994	7.51	29.70	121.74	74.71	13,237
Hunan 湖南	83	102	2,815	-241	-4.41	-11.95	27.63	63.07	5,461
Guangdong 廣東	41	232	35,255	377	0.71	2.94	151.66	75.72	52,877
Guangxi 廣西	68	60	2,523	-439	-11.94	-396.94	41.83	96.99	3,677
Hainan 海南	5	93	1,688	24	0.33	1.45	18.11	77.31	7,316
Southwest 西南	104	137	4,053	-353	-4.68	-14.64	29.51	68.06	7,545
Chongqing 重慶	8	83	1,361	-96	-2.05	-9.26	16.31	77.86	4,676
Sichuan 四川	65	115	2,749	-129	-2.63	-8.71	23.79	69.84	4,899
Guizhou 貴州	8	121	2,665	70	2.20	4.48	22.02	50.83	3,178
Yunnan 雲南	19	263	10,955	-1,473	-7.04	-21.30	41.61	66.94	20,917
Tibet 西藏	3	8	7	-3	-0.86	-0.96	0.83	10.34	387
Northwest 西北	28	63	733	-171	-5.02	-17.44	11.59	71.20	3,413
Shaanxi 陝西	18	81	843	-277	-6.42	-27.75	10.45	76.87	4,319
Gansu 甘肅	7	36	691	26	1.17	2.07	19.21	43.47	2,199
Qinghai 青海									
Ningxia 寧夏									
Xinjiang 新疆	3	23	170	3	0.41	1.19	7.50	65.43	810

Year 年份	Number of firms 企業個數	Rate of change 每年變化 (%)	Number of employees 職工人數 (人)	Rate of change 每年變化 (%)	Total revenue (mil. RMB) 總銷售收入 (百萬元)	Rate of change 每年變化 (%)	Total profit (mil. RMB) 總利潤 (百萬元)	Rate of change 每年變化 (%)
1993	875		148,994		6,931		355	
1994	1,106	26.40%	189,931	27.48%	7,200	3.89%	107	-69.97%
1995	1,351	22.15%	192,445	1.32%	8,987	24.82%	-101	-194.81%
1996	1,335	-1.18%	172,922	-10.14%	9,752	8.51%	55	154.45%

3 Major products* 3 種主要產品 *	Output 產量	Sales volume 銷售量	Unit 單位
a) Plywood 膠合板	3,596,228	3,200,643	cubic metre 立方米
b) Veneered Strip-glued Board 細木工板	469,425	403,705	cubic metre 立方米
c) Fibre Board 纖維板	219,741	197,767	cubic metre 立方米

Top 10 firms by revenue (year founded) 收入排名前 10 家企業 (創辦年份)	City 城市	Province 省	Telephone / fax 電話 / 傳真	Number of employees 職工人數	Ownership 產業所有權	Revenue ('000 RMB) 銷售收入 (千元)	Profit ('000 RMB) (rank) 利潤 (千元) (排名)	Total assets ('000 RMB) 總資產 (千元)	Major products 主要產品
Shenzhen Guang Da Timber Industrial Co. Ltd. 深圳光大木材工業有限公司(1988)	Shenzhen 深圳市	Guangdong 廣東省	(0755)6695030 (0755)6695036	2,701	Overseas Chinese-funded 港澳台資	763,270	34757(4)	867,923	a,c
Tianjin Fujin Timber Co. Ltd. 天津福津木業有限公司(1990)	Tianjin 天津市	Tianjin 天津市	(022)28300060 (022)28308193	1,231	Overseas Chinese-funded 港澳台資	575,383	54739(1)	452,652	a,b,c
Shanghai Fuhai (Timber) Enterprise Co. Ltd. 上海福海(木業)企業有限公司(1988)	Shanghai 上海市	Shanghai 上海市	(021)58911188 (021)63724824	1,200	Foreign-funded 外資	571,549	45596(2)	429,555	o
China Jiang Hai Timber Industry Co. Ltd. 中國江海木業有限公司(1981)	Wuxi 無錫市	Jiangsu 江蘇省	(0510)3753992	1,276	Foreign-funded 外資	398,481	42941(3)	188,276	a,b
Nantong Plywood Industry Co. Ltd. 南通合板工業有限公司(1992)	Nantong 南通市	Jiangsu 江蘇省	(0513)3596318 (0513)3596320	1,016	Foreign-funded 外資	283,748	3302(21)	274,519	a
Guangdong Yuzhu Forestry Group Co. Ltd. 廣東省魚珠木材集團有限公司(1952)	Guangzhou 廣州市	Guangdong 廣東省	(020)92273285 (020)82277070	1,636	State-owned 國有	240,699	3363(20)	374,295	a,c
Hubei Fu Han Timber Industry Co. Ltd. 湖北福漢木業有限公司(1991)	Wuhan 武漢市	Hubei 湖北省	(027)88116110 (027)88113327	478	Foreign-funded 外資	197,610	21118(5)	143,994	a,b
Yangzhou Kuai Le Racket Factory 揚州市快樂球拍廠(1984)	Yangzhou 揚州市	Jiangsu 江蘇省	(0514)6716217 (0514)6716217	1,500	Collectively-owned 集體	176,148	3967(16)	71,335	a
Shanghai Artificial Board Factory 上海人造板廠(1959)	Shanghai 上海市	Shanghai 上海市	(021)64083551 (021)64700748	1,261	State-owned 國有	152,396	800(90)	96,376	a,c
Jiangsu Xi Wei Timber Industry Group Company 江蘇錫威木業集團公司(1992)	Wuxi 無錫市	Jiangsu 江蘇省	(0510)8741402	1,404	Collectively-owned 集體	150,933	2403(34)	126,741	a

Top 10 Cities by Production Output 產出排名前 10 位城市	Province 省	Market share 市場份額	Number of firms 企業個數
Tianjin 天津市	Tianjin 天津市	7.30%	16
Wuxi 無錫市	Jiangsu 江蘇省	7.22%	14
Heze 菏澤市	Shandong 山東省	4.93%	41
Yining 伊寧市	Xinjiang 新疆	4.87%	1
Suzhou 蘇州市	Jiangsu 江蘇省	4.32%	13
Shanghai 上海市	Shanghai 上海市	4.03%	19
Shenzhen 深圳市	Guangdong 廣東省	3.96%	5
Sanming 三明市	Fujian 福建省	3.68%	48
Guangzhou 廣州市	Guangdong 廣東省	3.42%	14
Jiaxing 嘉興市	Zhejiang 浙江省	2.67%	10

10 Major Wholesalers 10 家主要批發商	City 城市	Province 省	Telephone / Fax 電話 / 傳真
Jilin Forestry Import & Export Company 吉林省林業進出口公司	Changchun 長春市	Jilin 吉林省	(0431)5629740 (0431)5638250
Shanghai Local Products Goods & Materials General Co. 上海市土產物資總公司	Shanghai 上海市	Shanghai 上海市	(021)63200857 (021)63200857
Kunming Import & Export Company 昆明市進出口公司	Kunming 昆明市	Yunnan 雲南省	(0871)5155192 (0871)5155193
Wujin Supply & Marketing Cooperative Means of Production General Company 武進市供銷社生產資料總公司	Changzhou 常州市	Jiangsu 江蘇省	(0519)6609079 (0519)6609079
China Timber Import & Export Company 中國木材進出口公司	Beijing 北京市	Beijing 北京市	(010)65132383 (010)65124788
Jinchen Urban Goods & Materials General Company Timber Company 晉城市城區物資總公司木材公司	Jincheng 晉城市	Shanxi 山西省	
Zhangjiagang Timber General Company 張家港市木材總公司	Suzhou 蘇州市	Jiangsu 江蘇省	(0512)8223241
Wujiang Timber General Company 吳江市木材總公司	Suzhou 蘇州市	Jiangsu 江蘇省	(0512)3422179
China Forest Products Marketing Company 中國林產品經銷公司	Beijing 北京市	Beijing 北京市	(010)64228370 (010)64216443
Yangzhou Timber General Company 揚州市木材總公司	Yangzhou 揚州市	Jiangsu 江蘇省	(0514)7246917 (0514)7247383

*Also include sales by firms outside this industry.包括本行業以外廠家的銷售。"o" stands for "others". "o" 代表 "其他產品"。

2022: Fibreboard 纖維板製造業

The industry accounts for 0.052% of the total revenue of China's industrial sector in 1996. The revenue growth rate of the industry is 32.7% from 1995, as compared to the growth rate of China's industrial sector, 9.51%. The rate of return on asset is 1.63%. 54.82% of all firms in the industry made a profit while 33.06% had negative returns. The top province in terms of the industry's revenue is Guangdong, accounting for 26.86% of the total revenue.
本行業在1996年佔全行業總產值0.052%，行業年增長率為32.7%（全國工業年增長率9.51%）。行業的資產回報率1.63%，54.82%的企業盈利，33.06%的企業虧損。銷售收入最高的省份為廣東省，佔本行業的26.86%。

	Total number of firms 企業總數	Total number of employees 職工總數	Total revenue (mil. RMB) 總銷售收入（百萬元）	Total profit (mil. RMB) 總利潤（百萬元）	Return on assets 資產利潤率 (%)	Return on equity 權益利潤率 (%)	Labour productivity ('000 RMB / worker) 勞動生產率（千元/人）	Debts / assets 資產負債率 (%)	Total assets (mil. RMB) 總資產（百萬元）
Industry Overall 行業總體	258	55,763	3,029	105	1.63	6.37	54.32	74.33	6,437

	Number of firms 企業個數	Average number of employees 平均職工人數	Average revenue ('000 RMB) 平均銷售收入（千元）	Average profit ('000 RMB) 平均利潤（千元）	Return on assets 資產利潤率 (%)	Return on equity 權益利潤率 (%)	Labour productivity ('000 RMB / worker) 勞動生產率（千元/人）	Average debts / assets 平均資產負債率(%)	Average Total assets ('000 RMB) 平均總資產（千元）
By ownership 產業所有權									
State-owned 國有	110	307	9,473	245	0.90	3.51	30.88	74.25	27,182
Collectively-owned 集體	113	144	9,425	-17,852	-104.70	-442.09	65.34	76.32	17,050
Privately-owned 私有									
Domestic JVs 聯營	3	140	8,575	4,211	37.70	113.88	61.25	66.90	11,170
Joint stock 股份制	6	209	9,677	38,579	318.04	690.35	46.38	53.93	12,130
Foreign-funded 外資	13	93	11,925	60,875	334.79	977.05	128.12	65.73	18,183
Overseas Chinese-funded 港澳台資	13	255	52,582	81,522	89.92	352.86	205.89	74.52	90,663
By size 規模									
Large 大型	6	1,537	160,244	69,898	24.20	102.39	104.29	76.37	288,875
Medium 中型	17	533	26,510	-2,773	-3.67	-13.27	49.69	72.37	75,653
Small 小型	212	170	7,628	-1,261	-7.82	-30.12	44.82	74.04	16,124
By regional distribution 地區分布									
Central-North 華北	37	156	4,166	286	2.27	7.18	26.67	68.36	12,569
Beijing 北京	2	39	1,570	50	4.72	6.80	40.78	30.19	1,060
Tianjin 天津	2	96	4,785	750	12.22	80.21	49.84	84.76	6,135
Hebei 河北	19	193	6,284	465	2.57	8.29	32.57	69.00	18,113
Shanxi 山西	8	92	1,159	-126	-2.45	-13.32	12.56	81.62	5,155
Inner Mongolia 內蒙	6	184	2,128	190	1.75	3.86	11.55	54.79	10,882
Northeast 東北	33	466	9,067	325	1.17	7.16	19.46	83.69	27,817
Liaoning 遼寧	14	136	9,863	1,661	7.27	24.69	72.41	70.55	22,836
Jilin 吉林	4	307	3,545	-413	-2.64	-198.80	11.54	98.67	15,628
Heilongjiang 黑龍江	15	816	9,796	-725	-2.03	-19.89	12.01	89.79	35,717
Central East 華東	85	189	15,734	504	1.63	6.22	83.12	73.78	30,875
Shanghai 上海	2	167	7,010	-115	-1.02	-2.02	41.98	49.31	11,245
Jiangsu 江蘇	10	278	64,853	162	0.15	1.08	232.95	86.53	110,850
Zhejiang 浙江	9	397	25,289	1,230	3.20	8.79	63.70	63.57	38,401
Anhui 安徽	9	100	5,532	-179	-4.47	-13.51	55.08	66.87	4,001
Fujian 福建	19	147	10,220	1,312	3.74	10.24	69.60	63.46	35,053
Jiangxi 江西	22	157	4,686	197	1.80	4.00	29.82	54.90	10,946
Shandong 山東	14	161	7,155	192	1.31	7.16	44.58	81.66	14,637
Central-South 中南	55	172	18,843	1,090	3.48	11.45	109.83	69.63	31,358
Henan 河南	13	105	2,568	34	1.00	3.61	24.47	72.14	3,368
Hubei 湖北	14	235	9,879	101	0.75	2.68	42.13	71.90	13,364
Hunan 湖南	9	159	3,878	-589	-3.93	-9.38	24.39	58.10	14,981
Guangdong 廣東	14	191	58,124	4,529	4.74	16.05	303.63	70.49	95,598
Guangxi 廣西	5	136	3,216				23.72	63.71	4,122
Hainan 海南									
Southwest 西南	25	213	4,192	-474	-3.27	-11.58	19.71	71.77	14,506
Chongqing 重慶									
Sichuan 四川	13	150	3,898	-58	-1.00	-6.56	25.99	84.69	5,778
Guizhou 貴州	2	686	6,950	-4,345	-11.01	-84.12	10.13	86.91	39,455
Yunnan 雲南	10	200	4,022	-242	-1.16	-3.00	20.16	61.39	20,863
Tibet 西藏									
Northwest 西北	23	164	4,228	-303	-2.04	-16.88	25.79	87.93	14,877
Shaanxi 陝西	13	137	4,646	-42	-0.45	-2.67	33.80	83.04	9,161
Gansu 甘肅	2	356	1,895	-845	-2.07	-7.63	5.33	72.88	40,855
Qinghai 青海									
Ningxia 寧夏	1	84	2,700	210	2.69	3.19	32.14	15.73	7,820
Xinjiang 新疆	7	170	4,336	-707	-3.71	64.62	25.55	105.74	19,080

Year 年份	Number of firms 企業個數	Rate of change 每年變化 (%)	Number of employees 職工人數 (人)	Rate of change 每年變化 (%)	Total revenue (mil. RMB) 總銷售收入 (百萬元)	Rate of change 每年變化 (%)	Total profit (mil. RMB) 總利潤 (百萬元)	Rate of change 每年變化 (%)
1993	223		43,802		1,644		143	
1994	265	18.83%	72,736	66.06%	1,921	16.86%	104	-27.43%
1995	276	4.15%	63,908	-12.14%	2,283	18.84%	28	-72.76%
1996	258	-6.52%	55,763	-12.74%	3,029	32.68%	105	271.44%

3 Major products* 3種主要產品*	Output 產量	Sales volume 銷售量	Unit 單位
a) Fibre Board 纖維板	1,078,238	970,414	cubic metre 立方米
b) Plywood 膠合板	137,042	121,967	cubic metre 立方米
c) Repressed Manmade Board 人造板二次加工裝飾板	3,033,104	2,881,449	square metre 平方米

Top 10 firms by revenue (year founded) 收入排名前10家企業 (創辦年份)	City 城市	Province 省	Telephone / fax 電話 / 傳真	Number of employees 職工人數	Ownership 產業所有權	Revenue ('000 RMB) 銷售收入 (千元)	Profit ('000 RMB) (rank) 利潤 (千元) (排名)	Total assets ('000 RMB) 總資產 (千元)	Major products 主要產品
Wei De Timber Industry (Suzhou) Co. Ltd. 維德木業(蘇州)有限公司(1993)	Suzhou 蘇州市	Jiangsu 江蘇省	(0512)5392094 (0512)5392093	1,255	Overseas Chinese-funded 港澳台資	539,035	8950(8)	757,232	b,c
Guangdong Zhaoqing Kang Lan Medium Density Board Enterprise Group Co. 廣東肇慶康藍中密板企業集團公司(1990)	Zhaoqing 肇慶市	Guangdong 廣東省	(0757)7765388 (0757)7763826	408	Collectively-owned 集體	213,641	20399(3)	201,214	a
Fuzhou Artificial Board Plant 福州人造板廠(1979)	Fuzhou 福州市	Fujian 福建省	(0591)3662395 (0591)3662464	798	State-owned 國有	147,373	32088(1)	509,608	o
Nanhai Yuehua Decoratire Timber Factory 南海粵華裝飾板材廠(1994)	Foshan 佛山市	Guangdong 廣東省	(0757)6003888 (0757)6001020	300	Collectively-owned 集體	125,718	610(26)	160,769	o
Heilong Jiang Nancha Timber Hydrolysis Factory 黑龍江省南岔木材水解廠(1962)	Yichun 伊春市	Heilongjiang 黑龍江省	(0458)3412951 (0458)3413913	8,346	State-owned 國有	117,857	-4641(131)	364,751	a
Foshan Taisong Fibreboard Manufacture Co. Ltd. 佛山市泰嵩纖維內底板有限公司(1994)	Foshan 佛山市	Guangdong 廣東省	(0757)2260144 (0757)2266144	78	Foreign-funded 外資	100,730	10386(7)	108,207	o
Fengkai Ming Zhu Industrial (Group) Company 封開明珠實業(集團)公司(1993)	Zhaoqing 肇慶市	Guangdong 廣東省	(0757)6663422 (0757)6663327	861	State-owned 國有	99,166	16060(4)		a,c
Guangzhou San Xing Fibreboard Enterprise Co. Ltd. 廣州三興纖維板企業有限公司(1988)	Guangzhou 廣州市	Guangdong 廣東省	(020)84563443 (020)84563443	316	Overseas Chinese-funded 港澳台資	86,223	1009(19)	154,594	a
Huaiji Nan You Joint Venture Medium Density Board Factory 懷集縣南油聯營中密板廠(1991)	Zhaoqing 肇慶市	Guangdong 廣東省	(0757)5522676 (0757)5522676	243	State-owned 國有	85,070	14500(5)	111,276	a
Shun Long Medium-density Fibre Board Co. Ltd. 順龍中密度纖維板有限公司(1991)	Foshan 佛山市	Guangdong 廣東省	(0757)2291183 (0757)2291921	267	Collectively-owned 集體	78,158	80(56)	291,600	a

Top 10 Cities by Production Output 產出排名前10位城市	Province 省	Market share 市場份額	Number of firms 企業個數
Zhaoqing 肇慶市	Guangdong 廣東省	14.40%	3
Foshan 佛山市	Guangdong 廣東省	12.32%	4
Zhenjiang 鎮江市	Jiangsu 江蘇省	11.83%	1
Fuzhou 福州市	Fujian 福建省	5.78%	1
Guangzhou 廣州市	Guangdong 廣東省	3.72%	4
Lishui 麗水市	Zhejiang 浙江省	3.36%	4
Benxi 本溪市	Liaoning 遼寧省	2.56%	2
Quzhou 衢州市	Zhejiang 浙江省	2.49%	2
Shijiazhuang 石家莊市	Hebei 河北省	2.44%	4
Shenyang 瀋陽市	Liaoning 遼寧省	2.32%	1

10 Major Wholesalers 10家主要批發商	City 城市	Province 省	Telephone / Fax 電話 / 傳真
Jilin Forestry Import & Export Company 吉林省林業進出口公司	Changchun 長春市	Jilin 吉林省	(0431)5629740 (0431)5638250
Shanghai Local Products Goods & Materials General Co. 上海市土產物資總公司	Shanghai 上海市	Shanghai 上海市	(021)63200857 (021)63200857
Kunming Import & Export Company 昆明市進出口公司	Kunming 昆明市	Yunnan 雲南省	(0871)5155192 (0871)5155193
Wujin Supply & Marketing Cooperative Means of Production General Company 武進市供銷社生產資料總公司	Changzhou 常州市	Jiangsu 江蘇省	(0519)6609079 (0519)6609079
China Timber Import & Export Company 中國木材進出口公司	Beijing 北京市	Beijing 北京市	(010)65132383 (010)65124788
Jinchen Urban Goods & Materials General Company Timber Company 晉城市城區物資總公司木材公司	Jincheng 晉城市	Shanxi 山西省	
Zhangjiagang Timber General Company 張家港市木材總公司	Suzhou 蘇州市	Jiangsu 江蘇省	(0512)8223241
Wujiang Timber General Company 吳江市木材總公司	Suzhou 蘇州市	Jiangsu 江蘇省	(0512)3422179
China Forest Products Marketing Company 中國林產品經銷公司	Beijing 北京市	Beijing 北京市	(010)64228370 (010)64216443
Yangzhou Timber General Company 揚州市木材總公司	Yangzhou 揚州市	Jiangsu 江蘇省	(0514)7246917 (0514)7247383

*Also include sales by firms outside this industry.包括本行業以外廠家的銷售。"o" stands for "others". "o" 代表 "其他產品"。

2023: Chipboard 刨花板製造業

The industry accounts for 0.040% of the total revenue of China's industrial sector in 1996. The revenue growth rate of the industry is 20.9% from 1995, as compared to the growth rate of China's industrial sector, 9.51%. The rate of return on asset is -0.22%. 64.30% of all firms in the industry made a profit while 27.11% had negative returns. The top province in terms of the industry's revenue is Hunan, accounting for 10.49% of the total revenue.
本行業在1996年佔全行業總產值0.040%，行業年增長率為20.9%（全國工業年增長率9.51%）。行業的資產回報率-0.22%，64.30%的企業盈利，27.11%的企業虧損。銷售收入最高的省份為湖南省，佔本行業的10.49%。

	Total number of firms 企業總數	Total number of employees 職工總數	Total revenue (mil. RMB) 總銷售收入（百萬元）	Total profit (mil. RMB) 總利潤（百萬元）	Return on assets 資產利潤率 (%)	Return on equity 權益利潤率 (%)	Labour productivity ('000 RMB / worker) 勞動生產率（千元/人）	Debts / assets 資產負債率 (%)	Total assets (mil. RMB) 總資產（百萬元）
Industry Overall 行業總體	350	54,200	2,334	-15	-0.22	-0.93	43.06	76.57	6,730

	Number of firms 企業個數	Average number of employees 平均職工人數	Average revenue ('000 RMB) 平均銷售收入（千元）	Average profit ('000 RMB) 平均利潤（千元）	Return on assets 資產利潤率 (%)	Return on equity 權益利潤率 (%)	Labour productivity ('000 RMB / worker) 勞動生產率（千元/人）	Average debts / assets 平均資產負債率(%)	Average Total assets ('000 RMB) 平均總資產（千元）
By ownership 產業所有權									
State-owned 國有	78	370	16,103	-641	-1.06	-5.42	43.47	80.50	60,679
Collectively-owned 集體	220	80	2,691	-96	-2.23	-8.58	33.58	74.05	4,336
Privately-owned 私有	7	88	4,785	-2,934	-80.33	-96.57	54.64	16.82	3,652
Domestic JVs 聯營	4	111	1,467	306	4.59	6.49	13.22	29.18	6,660
Joint stock 股份制	13	193	8,252	622	3.03	12.84	42.75	76.40	20,517
Foreign-funded 外資	10	151	12,483	18,104	51.38	165.73	82.61	69.00	35,237
Overseas Chinese-funded 港澳台資	17	159	12,626	-6,681	-30.49	-58.45	79.20	47.83	21,911
By size 規模									
Large 大型	10	1,014	63,829	-1,097	-0.51	-3.20	62.95	84.23	217,107
Medium 中型	9	431	35,488	378	0.44	2.26	82.36	80.60	86,035
Small 小型	316	125	4,355	-24	-0.20	-0.69	34.71	71.35	11,980
By regional distribution 地區分布									
Central-North 華北	52	99	4,376	148	1.28	5.41	44.06	76.37	11,531
Beijing 北京	1								
Tianjin 天津	2	240	41,065	4,605	10.00	19.06	171.46	47.56	46,060
Hebei 河北	27	82	2,498	-8	-0.07	-0.63	30.59	89.56	11,799
Shanxi 山西	8	99	4,341	124	2.29	5.62	44.07	59.13	5,395
Inner Mongolia 內蒙	14	121	3,090	-166	-1.59	-5.46	25.55	70.84	10,413
Northeast 東北	47	217	6,196	93	0.55	1.98	28.56	71.95	16,821
Liaoning 遼寧	14	149	3,281	-432	-3.82	-26.65	21.96	85.66	11,311
Jilin 吉林	15	168	4,821	687	5.55	13.26	28.74	58.13	12,369
Heilongjiang 黑龍江	18	310	9,608	7	0.03	0.11	30.95	72.83	24,816
Central East 華東	96	118	6,850	149	0.84	4.33	57.84	80.56	17,655
Shanghai 上海									
Jiangsu 江蘇	17	88	5,228	-32	-0.84	-3.77	59.61	77.76	3,859
Zhejiang 浙江	5	98	2,834	-136	-2.72	-6.95	28.80	60.93	5,006
Anhui 安徽	16	110	8,501	1,124	10.56	20.35	77.06	48.10	10,641
Fujian 福建	18	145	9,439	232	1.02	3.35	65.12	69.50	22,726
Jiangxi 江西	18	124	3,374	-448	-3.03	-16.11	27.20	81.18	14,786
Shandong 山東	22	126	8,541	65	0.19	3.39	67.62	94.48	34,490
Central-South 中南	94	147	8,930	-139	-0.51	-2.41	60.83	78.70	27,093
Henan 河南	36	106	3,878	122	2.16	8.21	36.66	73.75	5,643
Hubei 湖北	15	103	4,505	-436	-5.03	-10.09	43.63	50.18	8,676
Hunan 湖南	16	291	15,304	189	0.32	1.22	52.60	73.61	58,792
Guangdong 廣東	17	113	11,013	-10	-0.04	-0.27	97.31	85.81	26,120
Guangxi 廣西	9	152	17,466	-803	-1.24	-6.07	114.82	79.63	64,941
Hainan 海南	1	494	42,910	-6,520	-2.67	109.03	86.86	102.45	244,260
Southwest 西南	34	306	7,181	-220	-1.03	-3.67	23.47	71.98	21,362
Chongqing 重慶	4	911	13,615	-1,015	-1.80	-5.13	14.94	65.01	56,512
Sichuan 四川	14	225	7,554	-55	-0.43	-2.82	33.48	84.91	12,933
Guizhou 貴州	7	27	484	-70	-3.65	-36.30	18.13	89.93	1,916
Yunnan 雲南	8	335	8,555	-173	-0.53	-1.72	25.56	69.09	32,521
Tibet 西藏									
Northwest 西北	27	121	2,729	-755	-5.49	-14.79	22.54	62.92	13,759
Shaanxi 陝西	10	121	1,400	-1,186	-8.74	-21.69	11.57	59.69	13,564
Gansu 甘肅	5	80	1,730	-22	-0.50	-1.27	21.52	60.92	4,412
Qinghai 青海									
Ningxia 寧夏	4	262	7,093	-1,198	-3.38	-8.01	27.07	57.78	35,415
Xinjiang 新疆	8	76	2,831	-453	-5.02	-24.71	37.25	79.69	9,018

Year 年份	Number of firms 企業個數	Rate of change 每年變化 (%)	Number of employees 職工人數 (人)	Rate of change 每年變化 (%)	Total revenue (mil. RMB) 總銷售收入 (百萬元)	Rate of change 每年變化 (%)	Total profit (mil. RMB) 總利潤 (百萬元)	Rate of change 每年變化 (%)
1993	144		23,178		1,225		134	
1994	188	30.56%	34,300	47.99%	1,394	13.81%	48	-64.10%
1995	347	84.57%	53,775	56.78%	1,930	38.43%	-54	-211.88%
1996	350	0.86%	54,200	0.79%	2,334	20.93%	-15	72.08%

3 Major products* 3 種主要產品*	Output 產量	Sales volume 銷售量	Unit 單位
a) Chipboard 刨花板	1,788,956	1,681,618	cubic metre 立方米
b) Veneered Strip-glued Board 细木工板	77,536	66,681	cubic metre 立方米
c) Repressed Manmade Board 人造板二次加工裝飾板	6,923,890	6,577,695	square metre 平方米

Top 10 firms by revenue (year founded) 收入排名前 10 家企業 (創辦年份)	City 城市	Province 省	Telephone / fax 電話 / 傳真	Number of employees 職工人數	Ownership 產業所有權	Revenue ('000 RMB) 銷售收入 (千元)	Profit ('000 RMB) (rank) 利潤 (千元) (排名)	Total assets ('000 RMB) 總資產 (千元)	Major products 主要產品
Hangzhou Timber General Factory 杭州木材總廠(1951)	Hangzhou 杭州市	Zhejiang 浙江省	(0571)6051344 (0571)6051806	2,306	State-owned 國有	131,390	661(24)	257,446	a,c
Guangxi Zhuangzu Autonomous Region Wuzhou Timber Mill 廣西壯族自治區梧州木材廠(1954)	Wuzhou 梧州市	Guangxi 廣西	(0774)3827180 (0774)3825168	563	State-owned 國有	115,111	822(21)	366,004	a,c
Mudanjiang Comprehensive Wood Processing Plant 國營牡丹江木材綜合加工廠(1933)	Mudanjiang 牡丹江市	Heilongjiang 黑龍江省	(0453)6613388 (0453)6614614	3,086	State-owned 國有	103,226	-3149(155)	286,668	a,b,c
Tianjin Fu Jia Furniture Co. Ltd. 天津福家傢具有限公司(1993)	Tianjin 天津市	Tianjin 天津市	(022)28333808 (022)28333808	473	Overseas Chinese-funded 港澳台資	81,817	9206(3)	92,121	a
Luyi Furniture Factory 鹿邑縣傢具廠(1989)	Zhoukou 周口市	Henan 河南省	(0394)7223837	210	Collectively-owned 集體	76,500	9660(2)	28,900	o
Anhui Chuzhou Huaneng Artificial Board Co. Ltd. 安徽省滁州華能人造板有限責任公司(1989)	Chuzhou 滁州市	Anhui 安徽省	(0550)3056622 (0550)3055935	644	State-owned 國有	67,496	11728(1)	85,627	a,c
Fujian Shaowu Timber Yard 福建省邵武貯木場(1957)	Nangping 南平市	Fujian 福建省	(0599)6522911 (0599)6523722	1,114	State-owned 國有	67,317	128(62)	219,729	a,b
Huaiji Wei Li Ban Factory 懷集縣微粒板廠(1987)	Zhaoqing 肇慶市	Guangdong 廣東省	(0757)5522742 (0757)5521198	251	State-owned 國有	51,960	6130(4)	63,048	a
Shandong Shouguang Artificial Board Factory 山東壽光人造板廠(1991)	Weifang 濰坊市	Shandong 山東省	(0536)5222751 (0536)5222642	498	Foreign-funded 外資	50,085	0(110)	129,635	a
Nanjing Li Rong Brush Making Co. Ltd. 南京利榮製刷有限公司(1991)	Nanjing 南京市	Jiangsu 江蘇省	(025)8852099 (025)8852098	600	Overseas Chinese-funded 港澳台資	48,190	0(113)	10,331	o

Top 10 Cities by Production Output 產出排名前 10 位城市	Province 省	Market share 市場份額	Number of firms 企業個數
Taizhou 臺州市	Zhejiang 浙江省	8.72%	4
Zhoukou 周口市	Henan 河南省	6.32%	10
Changsha 長沙市	Hunan 湖南省	5.81%	1
Mudanjiang 牡丹江市	Heilongjiang 黑龍江省	5.33%	5
Hangzhou 杭州市	Zhejiang 浙江省	5.01%	3
Wuzhou 梧州市	Guangxi 廣西	4.35%	6
Nangping 南平市	Fujian 福建省	4.19%	7
Tianjin 天津市	Tianjin 天津市	3.11%	2
Harbin 哈爾濱市	Heilongjiang 黑龍江省	3.08%	5
Chuzhou 滁州市	Anhui 安徽省	2.70%	3

10 Major Wholesalers 10 家主要批發商	City 城市	Province 省	Telephone / Fax 電話 / 傳真
Jilin Forestry Import & Export Company 吉林省林業進出口公司	Changchun 長春市	Jilin 吉林省	(0431)5629740 (0431)5638250
Shanghai Local Products Goods & Materials General Co. 上海市土產物資總公司	Shanghai 上海市	Shanghai 上海市	(021)63200857 (021)63200857
Kunming Import & Export Company 昆明市進出口公司	Kunming 昆明市	Yunnan 雲南省	(0871)5155192 (0871)5155193
Wujin Supply & Marketing Cooperative Means of Production General Company 武進市供銷社生產資料總公司	Changzhou 常州市	Jiangsu 江蘇省	(0519)6609079 (0519)6609079
China Timber Import & Export Company 中國木材進出口公司	Beijing 北京市	Beijing 北京市	(010)65132383 (010)65124788
Jinchen Urban Goods & Materials General Company Timber Company 晉城市城區物資總公司木材公司	Jincheng 晉城市	Shanxi 山西省	
Zhangjiagang Timber General Company 張家港市木材總公司	Suzhou 蘇州市	Jiangsu 江蘇省	(0512)8223241
Wujiang Timber General Company 吳江市木材總公司	Suzhou 蘇州市	Jiangsu 江蘇省	(0512)3422179
China Forest Products Marketing Company 中國林產品經銷公司	Beijing 北京市	Beijing 北京市	(010)64228370 (010)64216443
Yangzhou Timber General Company 揚州市木材總公司	Yangzhou 揚州市	Jiangsu 江蘇省	(0514)7246917 (0514)7247383

*Also include sales by firms outside this industry.包括本行業以外廠家的銷售。"o" stands for "others". "o" 代表 "其他產品"。

2029: Other Artificial Boards 其他人造板製造業

The industry accounts for 0.048% of the total revenue of China's industrial sector in 1996. The revenue growth rate of the industry is 27.5% from 1995, as compared to the growth rate of China's industrial sector, 9.51%. The rate of return on asset is 1.55%. 75.08% of all firms in the industry made a profit while 18.45% had negative returns. The top province in terms of the industry's revenue is Shanghai, accounting for 14.68% of the total revenue.
本行業在1996年佔全行業總產值0.048%，行業年增長率為27.5%（全國工業年增長率9.51%）。行業的資產回報率1.55%，75.08%的企業盈利，18.45%的企業虧損。銷售收入最高的省份為上海市，佔本行業的14.68%。

	Total number of firms 企業總數	Total number of employees 職工總數	Total revenue (mil. RMB) 總銷售收入（百萬元）	Total profit (mil. RMB) 總利潤（百萬元）	Return on assets 資產利潤率 (%)	Return on equity 權益利潤率 (%)	Labour productivity ('000 RMB / worker) 勞動生產率（千元/人）	Debts / assets 資產負債率 (%)	Total assets (mil. RMB) 總資產（百萬元）
Industry Overall 行業總體	534	46,987	2,778	52	1.55	4.84	59.12	67.96	3,364

	Number of firms 企業個數	Average number of employees 平均職工人數	Average revenue ('000 RMB) 平均銷售收入（千元）	Average profit ('000 RMB) 平均利潤（千元）	Return on assets 資產利潤率 (%)	Return on equity 權益利潤率 (%)	Labour productivity ('000 RMB / worker) 勞動生產率（千元/人）	Average debts / assets 平均資產負債率(%)	Average Total assets ('000 RMB) 平均總資產（千元）
By ownership 產業所有權									
State-owned 國有	38	148	5,000	-132	-1.19	-5.49	33.83	78.33	11,053
Collectively-owned 集體	372	79	3,485	503	15.20	65.90	44.27	76.94	3,308
Privately-owned 私有	5	88	4,724	3,283	39.42	124.49	53.44	68.34	8,329
Domestic JVs 聯營	11	59	5,058	-255	-3.18	-4.89	85.47	34.90	8,029
Joint stock 股份制	7	101	2,938	-976	-28.77	-154.70	29.08	81.40	3,391
Foreign-funded 外資	49	91	7,047	-1,291	-12.63	-25.14	77.80	49.78	10,222
Overseas Chinese-funded 港澳台資	52	117	16,289	-1,415	-6.95	-19.53	139.80	64.43	20,369
By size 規模									
Large 大型	2	1,182	18,436	8,900	10.51	106.63	15.60	90.14	84,674
Medium 中型	3	499	99,299	-7,181	-7.05	-17.00	198.86	58.55	101,910
Small 小型	499	84	4,898	112	1.93	5.98	58.02	67.68	5,782
By regional distribution 地區分布									
Central-North 華北	53	69	6,836	276	4.62	13.61	99.38	66.02	5,970
Beijing 北京	8	37	1,613	-166	-2.76	-6.77	43.29	59.30	6,029
Tianjin 天津	10	53	12,143	201	2.17	5.55	230.42	61.01	9,284
Hebei 河北	20	30	5,468	402	16.14	33.85	181.95	52.29	2,490
Shanxi 山西	5	243	16,606	8	0.05	0.33	68.39	86.13	17,668
Inner Mongolia 內蒙	10	101	3,562	587	15.78	37.46	35.41	57.86	3,721
Northeast 東北	111	128	3,749	11	0.16	0.46	29.21	64.23	6,440
Liaoning 遼寧	28	56	2,754	4	0.08	0.16	49.49	50.27	4,796
Jilin 吉林	23	338	6,937	143	1.07	2.66	20.55	59.90	13,426
Heilongjiang 黑龍江	60	82	2,992	-37	-0.82	-3.43	36.45	76.06	4,529
Central East 華東	195	84	6,853	177	2.43	8.29	81.92	70.69	7,281
Shanghai 上海	12	283	33,991	1,358	2.72	8.82	120.04	69.18	49,999
Jiangsu 江蘇	36	69	6,105	139	2.20	7.81	88.98	71.84	6,319
Zhejiang 浙江	14	142	23,581	839	5.83	17.69	165.82	67.05	14,381
Anhui 安徽	20	44	4,616	142	6.30	18.56	104.67	66.08	2,254
Fujian 福建	32	50	1,380	-147	-4.28	-12.21	27.49	64.95	3,425
Jiangxi 江西	48	29	624	-21	-2.53	-15.97	21.21	84.11	847
Shandong 山東	33	138	6,428	132	2.22	10.67	46.58	79.21	5,931
Central-South 中南	132	64	4,362	-15	-0.26	-0.89	67.92	71.18	5,871
Henan 河南	43	43	1,745	27	1.09	4.09	40.13	73.32	2,516
Hubei 湖北	13	66	4,524	-129	-3.31	-12.57	68.86	73.68	3,905
Hunan 湖南	29	52	2,347	126	7.30	19.76	45.22	63.09	1,730
Guangdong 廣東	35	118	10,437	-117	-0.75	-2.55	88.51	70.72	15,713
Guangxi 廣西	12	10	716	-87	-6.57	-66.24	70.99	90.14	1,318
Hainan 海南									
Southwest 西南	25	33	2,018	80	2.18	3.58	61.52	39.26	3,674
Chongqing 重慶		89	1,731	-445	-12.47	-236.30	19.27	94.72	3,568
Sichuan 四川	10	38	3,087	4	0.08	0.13	79.53	38.35	5,069
Guizhou 貴州	8	10	193	13	8.77	13.16	18.78	33.33	143
Yunnan 雲南	6	46	2,648	360	6.00	9.52	57.57	36.98	5,998
Tibet 西藏									
Northwest 西北	18	194	2,070	107	4.17	9.96	10.69	58.15	2,558
Shaanxi 陝西	11	294	1,494	15	0.53	1.07	5.08	50.59	2,929
Gansu 甘肅	6	42	3,472	292	12.66	52.08	83.65	75.76	2,303
Qinghai 青海									
Ningxia 寧夏									
Xinjiang 新疆	1								

2029: Other Artificial Boards 其他人造板製造業

Year 年份	Number of firms 企業個數	Rate of change 每年變化 (%)	Number of employees 職工人數 (人)	Rate of change 每年變化 (%)	Total revenue (mil. RMB) 總銷售收入 (百萬元)	Rate of change 每年變化 (%)	Total profit (mil. RMB) 總利潤 (百萬元)	Rate of change 每年變化 (%)
1993	354		22,486		1,552		17	
1994	469	32.49%	33,528	49.11%	1,706	9.95%	-3	-116.89%
1995	504	7.46%	41,099	22.58%	2,179	27.72%	-9	-197.61%
1996	534	5.95%	46,987	14.33%	2,778	27.49%	52	706.48%

3 Major products* 3 種主要產品 *	Output 產量	Sales volume 銷售量	Unit 單位
a) Repressed Manmade Board 人造板二次加工裝飾板	68,901,521	65,456,445	square metre 平方米
b) Wood Articles For Production 生產用木製品	378,188	329,024	1,000 yuan 千元
c) Plywood 膠合板	76,586	68,162	cubic metre 立方米

Top 10 firms by revenue (year founded) 收入排名前 10 家企業 (創辦年份)	City 城市	Province 省	Telephone / fax 電話 / 傳真	Number of employees 職工人數	Ownership 產業所有權	Revenue ('000 RMB) 銷售收入 (千元)	Profit ('000 RMB) (rank) 利潤 (千元) (排名)	Total assets ('000 RMB) 總資產 (千元)	Major products 主要產品
Shanghai Sen Da Timber Industry Co. Ltd. 上海森大木業有限公司(1990)	Shanghai 上海市	Shanghai 上海市	(021)64087592 (021)64700331	805	Overseas Chinese-funded 港澳台資	157,266	9199(1)	135,655	a
Shanghai Fumeijia Decoratire Material Co. Ltd. 上海富美家裝飾材料有限公司(1994)	Shanghai 上海市	Shanghai 上海市	(021)59201143 (021)59201142	155	Foreign-funded 外資	122,009	5185(3)	168,382	o
Zhejiang De Hua Decorative Materials Co. Ltd. 浙江德華裝飾材料有限公司(1993)	Huzhou 湖州市	Zhejiang 浙江省	(0572)8405171	480	Overseas Chinese-funded 港澳台資	120,751	5329(2)	60,387	a
Lu Qiao Qu Zhejiang Guo Mei Decorative Materials Co. Ltd. 路橋區浙江國美裝潢材料有限公司(1994)	Taizhou 臺州市	Zhejiang 浙江省	(0576)2448000 (0576)2441967	693	Foreign-funded 外資	99,021	2777(7)	45,983	o
Guangdong Shi Long Timber Mill 廣東省石龍木材廠(1952)	Dongguan 東莞市	Guangdong 廣東省	(0769)6611121 (0769)6612883	650	State-owned 國有	72,516	1721(13)	108,419	a
Shanghai Xin Jia Timber Industry Company 上海新加木業公司(1996)	Shanghai 上海市	Shanghai 上海市	(021)58120888 (021)58120128	2,000	Collectively-owned 集體	48,346	281(65)	193,463	a
Jiashan San Xian Timber Industry Co. Ltd. 嘉善縣三仙木業有限公司(1994)	Jiaxing 嘉興市	Zhejiang 浙江省	(0573)4611603 (0573)4611602	167	Overseas Chinese-funded 港澳台資	48,018	3062(5)	27,387	o
Panyu Zhu Jiang Wooden Products Industrial Co. 番禺市珠江木製品工業公司(1985)	Guangzhou 廣州市	Guangdong 廣東省	(020)84838406 (020)84833255	405	Collectively-owned 集體	45,192	316(60)	92,823	a
Zibo Jin Cheng Industrial Co. Ltd. Light-weight Board Factory 淄博金城實業股份有限公司輕體板廠(1993)	Zibo 淄博市	Shandong 山東省	(0533)5410164 (0533)5410164	305	Collectively-owned 集體	41,350	1640(16)	14,080	b
Jiangmen Timber Products Co. Ltd. 江門市木材製品有限公司(1987)	Jiangmen 江門市	Guangdong 廣東省	(0750)3360120 (0750)3365530	243	Overseas Chinese-funded 港澳台資	36,919	-4869(201)	75,783	c

Top 10 Cities by Production Output 產出排名前 10 位城市	Province 省	Market share 市場份額	Number of firms 企業個數
Shanghai 上海市	Shanghai 上海市	14.16%	21
Huzhou 湖州市	Zhejiang 浙江省	4.88%	3
Guangzhou 廣州市	Guangdong 廣東省	4.86%	13
Dalian 大連市	Liaoning 遼寧省	4.56%	7
Jiaxing 嘉興市	Zhejiang 浙江省	4.04%	2
Dongguan 東莞市	Guangdong 廣東省	3.63%	4
Tianjin 天津市	Tianjin 天津市	3.31%	7
Wuhan 武漢市	Hubei 湖北省	2.99%	7
Wuxi 無錫市	Jiangsu 江蘇省	2.18%	9
Jiangmen 江門市	Guangdong 廣東省	2.06%	3

10 Major Wholesalers 10 家主要批發商	City 城市	Province 省	Telephone / Fax 電話 / 傳真
Jilin Forestry Import & Export Company 吉林省林業進出口公司	Changchun 長春市	Jilin 吉林省	(0431)5629740 (0431)5638250
Shanghai Local Products Goods & Materials General Co. 上海市土產物資總公司	Shanghai 上海市	Shanghai 上海市	(021)63200857 (021)63200857
Kunming Import & Export Company 昆明市進出口公司	Kunming 昆明市	Yunnan 雲南省	(0871)5155192 (0871)5155193
Wujin Supply & Marketing Cooperative Means of Production General Company 武進市供銷社生產資料總公司	Changzhou 常州市	Jiangsu 江蘇省	(0519)6609079 (0519)6609079
China Timber Import & Export Company 中國木材進出口公司	Beijing 北京市	Beijing 北京市	(010)65132383 (010)65124788
Jinchen Urban Goods & Materials General Company Timber Company 晉城市城區物資總公司木材公司	Jincheng 晉城市	Shanxi 山西省	
Zhangjiagang Timber General Company 張家港市木材總公司	Suzhou 蘇州市	Jiangsu 江蘇省	(0512)8223241
Wujiang Timber General Company 吳江市木材總公司	Suzhou 蘇州市	Jiangsu 江蘇省	(0512)3422179
China Forest Products Marketing Company 中國林產品經銷公司	Beijing 北京市	Beijing 北京市	(010)64228370 (010)64216443
Yangzhou Timber General Company 揚州市木材總公司	Yangzhou 揚州市	Jiangsu 江蘇省	(0514)7246917 (0514)7247383

*Also include sales by firms outside this industry.包括本行業以外廠家的銷售。"o" stands for "others". "o" 代表 "其他產品"。

2031: Industrial Wood Products 生產用木製品業

The industry accounts for 0.140% of the total revenue of China's industrial sector in 1996. The revenue growth rate of the industry is 20.3% from 1995, as compared to the growth rate of China's industrial sector, 9.51%. The rate of return on asset is 1.46%. 77.15% of all firms in the industry made a profit while 15.81% had negative returns. The top province in terms of the industry's revenue is Helongjiang, accounting for 13.07% of the total revenue.
本行業在1996年佔全行業總產值0.140%，行業年增長率為20.3%（全國工業年增長率9.51%）。行業的資產回報率1.46%，77.15%的企業盈利，15.81%的企業虧損。銷售收入最高的省份為黑龍江省，佔本行業的13.07%。

	Total number of firms 企業總數	Total number of employees 職工總數	Total revenue (mil. RMB) 總銷售收入（百萬元）	Total profit (mil. RMB) 總利潤（百萬元）	Return on assets 資產利潤率 (%)	Return on equity 權益利潤率 (%)	Labour productivity ('000 RMB / worker) 勞動生產率（千元/人）	Debts / assets 資產負債率 (%)	Total assets (mil. RMB) 總資產（百萬元）
Industry Overall 行業總體	4,482	209,378	8,110	139	1.46	4.23	38.73	65.57	9,517

	Number of firms 企業個數	Average number of employees 平均職工人數	Average revenue ('000 RMB) 平均銷售收入（千元）	Average profit ('000 RMB) 平均利潤（千元）	Return on assets 資產利潤率 (%)	Return on equity 權益利潤率 (%)	Labour productivity ('000 RMB / worker) 勞動生產率（千元/人）	Average debts / assets 平均資產負債率(%)	Average Total assets ('000 RMB) 平均總資產（千元）
By ownership 產業所有權									
State-owned 國有	308	106	2,419	-130	-1.63	-5.83	22.84	72.03	7,964
Collectively-owned 集體	3,781	40	1,519	57	5.25	17.03	38.38	69.15	1,087
Privately-owned 私有	34	24	2,926	163	11.53	16.98	122.50	32.08	1,411
Domestic JVs 聯營	17	109	5,085	173	4.15	12.95	46.68	67.96	4,170
Joint stock 股份制	40	65	2,465	12	0.34	1.52	38.08	77.33	3,577
Foreign-funded 外資	131	85	4,826	-233	-2.35	-5.45	56.76	56.83	9,928
Overseas Chinese-funded 港澳台資	167	69	4,199	-92	-1.10	-2.27	60.71	51.59	8,334
By size 規模									
Large 大型	1	1,967	70,634	167	0.08	0.28	35.91	72.55	215,628
Medium 中型	8	745	36,278	404	0.68	2.17	48.67	68.89	59,710
Small 小型	4,382	45	1,768	31	1.54	4.42	38.87	65.22	2,013
By regional distribution 地區分布									
Central-North 華北	373	110	1,943	57	1.53	4.72	17.72	67.62	3,748
Beijing 北京	89	48	1,240	-49	-1.28	-4.94	25.83	74.11	3,815
Tianjin 天津	81	51	2,199	78	1.98	4.68	43.43	57.77	3,936
Hebei 河北	75	37	3,421	261	7.36	19.29	92.93	61.82	3,540
Shanxi 山西	25	55	970	-43	-2.52	-5.97	17.75	57.77	1,698
Inner Mongolia 內蒙	103	276	1,507	9	0.22	0.86	5.47	74.32	4,191
Northeast 東北	1,131	54	1,673	19	0.88	3.34	30.95	73.61	2,153
Liaoning 遼寧	309	37	1,666	2	0.09	0.30	44.45	71.56	1,885
Jilin 吉林	191	65	1,664	-14	-0.34	-2.36	25.68	85.75	4,305
Heilongjiang 黑龍江	631	59	1,680	38	2.30	6.59	28.50	65.07	1,632
Central East 華東	1,457	38	1,925	24	1.10	3.43	50.70	67.97	2,141
Shanghai 上海	87	70	3,804	-92	-0.94	-3.55	54.13	73.48	9,803
Jiangsu 江蘇	177	61	4,762	63	1.35	3.53	77.74	61.84	4,661
Zhejiang 浙江	212	25	1,217	4	0.30	1.02	49.01	70.70	1,209
Anhui 安徽	175	31	1,694	25	2.57	13.39	54.34	80.83	992
Fujian 福建	334	27	986	13	1.78	3.76	36.57	52.61	755
Jiangxi 江西	352	32	794	18	2.67	9.50	25.20	71.90	683
Shandong 山東	120	63	3,902	125	2.90	9.24	61.98	68.67	4,329
Central-South 中南	976	33	2,191	82	5.20	10.82	67.04	51.94	1,576
Henan 河南	102	28	1,370	64	4.51	11.62	48.66	61.21	1,421
Hubei 湖北	199	41	2,036	81	5.40	13.13	49.80	58.89	1,500
Hunan 湖南	275	29	1,472	34	4.38	10.76	50.50	59.26	779
Guangdong 廣東	199	42	4,742	214	6.01	10.67	111.79	43.69	3,566
Guangxi 廣西	191	21	1,252	29	3.60	8.58	58.82	58.06	805
Hainan 海南	10	38	644	-20	-1.19	-2.27	17.17	47.72	1,685
Southwest 西南	300	42	1,324	-65	-2.62	-6.14	31.66	57.32	2,468
Chongqing 重慶	42	55	966	-79	-4.72	-9.41	17.34	49.86	1,675
Sichuan 四川	130	38	1,544	-14	-0.61	-1.24	39.75	50.62	2,281
Guizhou 貴州	69	23	412	4	0.51	1.41	17.64	63.39	872
Yunnan 雲南	55	61	2,249	-270	-4.83	-13.70	36.67	64.73	5,586
Tibet 西藏	3	26	847	127	9.07	12.71	32.56	28.88	1,397
Northwest 西北	245	31	618	4	0.32	0.72	20.03	55.75	1,169
Shaanxi 陝西	203	29	628	3	0.25	0.53	21.71	52.00	1,143
Gansu 甘肅	24	49	673	3	0.21	0.61	13.71	66.21	1,412
Qinghai 青海	3	6	40				6.67	197.18	237
Ningxia 寧夏	7	48	666	41	1.88	7.82	13.87	75.92	2,201
Xinjiang 新疆	8	19	371	-5	-0.91	-4.44	19.41	79.77	550

2031: Industrial Wood Products 生產用木製品業

Year 年份	Number of firms 企業個數	Rate of change 每年變化 (%)	Number of employees 職工人數（人）	Rate of change 每年變化 (%)	Total revenue (mil. RMB) 總銷售收入（百萬元）	Rate of change 每年變化 (%)	Total profit (mil. RMB) 總利潤（百萬元）	Rate of change 每年變化 (%)
1993	4,236		151,322		4,159		137	
1994	4,550	7.41%	223,715	47.84%	5,290	27.17%	143	4.84%
1995	4,375	-3.85%	201,450	-9.95%	6,739	27.40%	125	-12.62%
1996	4,482	2.45%	209,378	3.94%	8,110	20.34%	139	10.86%

3 Major products* 3 種主要產品 *	Output 產量	Sales volume 銷售量	Unit 單位
a) Common Sawmilling 普通鋸材	848,919	806,473	cubic metre 立方米
b) Repressed Manmade Board 人造板二次加工裝飾板	6,415,634	6,094,852	square metre 平方米
c) Wooden Furniture 木製傢具	6,199,630	5,889,648	piece 件

Top 10 firms by revenue (year founded) 收入排名前 10 家企業 (創辦年份)	City 城市	Province 省	Telephone / fax 電話 / 傳真	Number of employees 職工人數	Ownership 產業所有權	Revenue ('000 RMB) 銷售收入（千元）	Profit ('000 RMB) (rank) 利潤（千元）（排名）	Total assets ('000 RMB) 總資產（千元）	Major products 主要產品
Guangdong Yi Hua Enterprise (Group) Co. Ltd. 廣東省宜華企業(集團)有限公司(1995)	Shantou 汕頭市	Guangdong 廣東省	(0754)5744898 (0754)5741881	853	Overseas Chinese-funded 港澳台資	302,590	12020(1)	220,915	b
Danjiangkou Wu Dang Shan Development Zone Handicrafts Company 丹江口市武當山開發區工藝製品公司(1993)	Shiyan 十堰市	Hubei 湖北省	(0719)665569	7	State-owned 國有	136,800	2160(19)	250,290	o
Changshu Jiang Wan Group Co. Ltd 常熟市江灣集團有限公司(1988)	Suzhou 蘇州市	Jiangsu 江蘇省	(0512)2571328	264	Collectively-owned 集體	108,977	3460(9)	69,489	a
Shenyang Shen Hai Wooden Products Factory 瀋陽市沈海木製品廠(1988)	Shenyang 瀋陽市	Liaoning 遼寧省	(024)88120069	19	Collectively-owned 集體	61,141	2691(14)	5,114	o
The Ministry of Railways Chengdu Timber Antiseptic Factory 鐵道部成都木材防腐廠(1958)	Chengdu 成都市	Sichuan 四川省	(028)3335535 (028)3335535	436	State-owned 國有	60,920	500(131)	142,530	o
Nanjing Sheng Hong Timber Industry Co. Ltd. 南京盛弘木業有限公司(1993)	Nanjing 南京市	Jiangsu 江蘇省	(025)2418524 (025)2418478	95	Foreign-funded 外資	56,040	674(92)	10,194	o
Zhongshan Jia Hua Loudspeaker Carbinet Co. Ltd. 中山市嘉華音箱有限公司(1992)	Zhongshan 中山市	Guangdong 廣東省	(0760)8337040 (0760)8337041	236	Overseas Chinese-funded 港澳台資	54,245	10874(3)	44,861	o
Yan Bian Chang Baishan Integrated Cai Factory 延邊長白山集成材廠(1989)	Yanji 延吉市	Jilin 吉林省	(0433)5823620 (0433)5823309	467	State-owned 國有	52,590	720(84)	81,680	o
Huoshan Wooden Floor General Company 霍山縣木地板總公司(1992)	Liu'an 六安市	Anhui 安徽省	(0564)5023608	508	Collectively-owned 集體	52,451	972(59)	28,700	o
Shanghai Kai Fu Wooden Articles Factory 上海凱福木器廠(1988)	Shanghai 上海市	Shanghai 上海市	(021)64881060	140	Collectively-owned 集體	50,695	15(659)	25,414	o

Top 10 Cities by Production Output 產出排名前 10 位城市	Province 省	Market share 市場份額	Number of firms 企業個數
Shanghai 上海市	Shanghai 上海市	7.59%	185
Shantou 汕頭市	Guangdong 廣東省	5.33%	13
Shuangcheng 雙城市	Heilongjiang 黑龍江省	3.78%	76
Liuzhou 柳州市	Guangxi 廣西	2.41%	46
Tianjin 天津市	Tianjin 天津市	2.28%	93
Mudanjiang 牡丹江市	Heilongjiang 黑龍江省	2.25%	116
Beijing 北京市	Beijing 北京市	2.16%	75
Wuxi 無錫市	Jiangsu 江蘇省	2.04%	43
Jiangmen 江門市	Guangdong 廣東省	1.99%	12
Kunming 昆明市	Yunnan 雲南省	1.79%	38

10 Major Wholesalers 10 家主要批發商	City 城市	Province 省	Telephone / Fax 電話 / 傳真
Jilin Forestry Import & Export Company 吉林省林業進出口公司	Changchun 長春市	Jilin 吉林省	(0431)5629740 (0431)5638250
Shanghai Local Products Goods & Materials General Co. 上海市土產物資總公司	Shanghai 上海市	Shanghai 上海市	(021)63200857 (021)63200857
Kunming Import & Export Company 昆明市進出口公司	Kunming 昆明市	Yunnan 雲南省	(0871)5155192 (0871)5155193
Wujin Supply & Marketing Cooperative Means of Production General Company 武進市供銷社生產資料總公司	Changzhou 常州市	Jiangsu 江蘇省	(0519)6609079 (0519)6609079
China Timber Import & Export Company 中國木材進出口公司	Beijing 北京市	Beijing 北京市	(010)65132383 (010)65124788
Jinchen Urban Goods & Materials General Company Timber Company 晉城市城區物資總公司木材公司	Jincheng 晉城市	Shanxi 山西省	
Zhangjiagang Timber General Company 張家港市木材總公司	Suzhou 蘇州市	Jiangsu 江蘇省	(0512)8223241
Wujiang Timber General Company 吳江市木材總公司	Suzhou 蘇州市	Jiangsu 江蘇省	(0512)3422179
China Forest Products Marketing Company 中國林產品經銷公司	Beijing 北京市	Beijing 北京市	(010)64228370 (010)64216443
Yangzhou Timber General Company 揚州市木材總公司	Yangzhou 揚州市	Jiangsu 江蘇省	(0514)7246917 (0514)7247383

*Also include sales by firms outside this industry.包括本行業以外廠家的銷售。"o" stands for "others". "o" 代表 "其他產品"。

2033: Domestic Wood Products 生活用木製品業

The industry accounts for 0.067% of the total revenue of China's industrial sector in 1996. The revenue growth rate of the industry is 23.8% from 1995, as compared to the growth rate of China's industrial sector, 9.51%. The rate of return on asset is 1.12%. 74.52% of all firms in the industry made a profit while 18.78% had negative returns. The top province in terms of the industry's revenue is Helongjiang, accounting for 21.40% of the total revenue.
本行業在1996年佔全行業總產值0.067%，行業年增長率為23.8%（全國工業年增長率9.51%）。行業的資產回報率1.12%，74.52%的企業盈利，18.78%的企業虧損。銷售收入最高的省份為黑龍江省，佔本行業的21.40%。

	Total number of firms 企業總數	Total number of employees 職工總數	Total revenue (mil. RMB) 總銷售收入（百萬元）	Total profit (mil. RMB) 總利潤（百萬元）	Return on assets 資產利潤率 (%)	Return on equity 權益利潤率 (%)	Labour productivity ('000 RMB / worker) 勞動生產率（千元/人）	Debts / assets 資產負債率 (%)	Total assets (mil. RMB) 總資產（百萬元）
Industry Overall 行業總體	1,904	100,890	3,865	47	1.12	3.34	38.31	66.31	4,144

	Number of firms 企業個數	Average number of employees 平均職工人數	Average revenue ('000 RMB) 平均銷售收入（千元）	Average profit ('000 RMB) 平均利潤（千元）	Return on assets 資產利潤率 (%)	Return on equity 權益利潤率 (%)	Labour productivity ('000 RMB / worker) 勞動生產率（千元/人）	Average debts / assets 平均資產負債率(%)	Average Total assets ('000 RMB) 平均總資產（千元）
By ownership 產業所有權									
State-owned 國有	114	78	947	-70	-2.72	-17.78	12.11	84.69	2,579
Collectively-owned 集體	1,443	47	1,563	38	3.22	11.36	33.30	71.66	1,184
Privately-owned 私有	27	18	1,553	146	18.54	30.43	85.25	39.06	789
Domestic JVs 聯營	10	16	421	-28	-2.61	-7.03	26.16	62.88	1,091
Joint stock 股份制	20	59	1,788	169	8.28	23.50	30.54	64.78	2,045
Foreign-funded 外資	149	90	4,498	-22	-0.33	-0.88	49.76	62.57	6,660
Overseas Chinese-funded 港澳台資	137	69	5,460	-27	-0.34	-0.80	78.75	56.84	7,833
By size 規模									
Large 大型	1	41	1,227	-881	-20.62	-1173.80	29.93	98.24	4,274
Medium 中型	1	235	30,747	7,277	9.35	17.22	130.84	45.72	77,848
Small 小型	1,867	54	2,053	22	1.00	3.00	38.27	66.67	2,176
By regional distribution 地區分布									
Central-North 華北	118	42	1,583	-34	-1.58	-5.33	38.04	70.45	2,152
Beijing 北京	17	16	619	-41	-2.35	-4.84	37.84	51.41	1,751
Tianjin 天津	24	55	4,188	-60	-1.23	-4.65	75.63	73.53	4,913
Hebei 河北	39	43	1,278	-38	-2.18	-6.86	30.02	68.23	1,729
Shanxi 山西	14	27	679	26	4.43	15.79	25.54	71.83	581
Inner Mongolia 內蒙	24	53	685	-31	-2.41	-13.05	12.93	81.54	1,280
Northeast 東北	499	97	2,902	19	0.52	1.90	29.80	72.90	3,611
Liaoning 遼寧	131	51	3,037	18	0.60	1.86	59.24	67.91	2,955
Jilin 吉林	118	91	1,891	-26	-0.92	-4.10	20.83	77.51	2,787
Heilongjiang 黑龍江	250	125	3,309	40	0.92	3.45	26.54	73.27	4,343
Central East 華東	729	37	1,800	44	2.66	6.67	48.91	60.21	1,647
Shanghai 上海	22	66	4,088	-48	-1.04	-3.01	61.60	65.56	4,610
Jiangsu 江蘇	46	70	7,210	336	4.44	10.02	102.36	55.65	7,554
Zhejiang 浙江	105	25	1,210	7	0.64	2.10	47.81	69.60	1,029
Anhui 安徽	69	25	1,471	39	5.26	15.78	59.91	66.65	738
Fujian 福建	276	39	1,550	8	0.63	1.32	39.87	52.39	1,283
Jiangxi 江西	169	25	453	1	0.29	1.25	18.40	77.70	516
Shandong 山東	42	69	3,760	277	7.71	22.97	54.55	66.45	3,596
Central-South 中南	425	39	1,852	22	1.52	3.81	47.18	59.97	1,465
Henan 河南	37	32	1,652	-48	-2.45	-9.38	51.10	73.87	1,952
Hubei 湖北	46	50	1,556	59	6.63	16.76	31.22	60.45	895
Hunan 湖南	72	36	1,329	26	3.28	10.77	37.10	69.60	797
Guangdong 廣東	163	43	2,672	49	2.56	5.98	61.70	57.18	1,908
Guangxi 廣西	102	32	950	-21	-1.96	-4.71	29.80	58.29	1,093
Hainan 海南	5	61	5,256	176	3.01	5.20	86.16	42.21	5,856
Southwest 西南	65	31	1,311	-11	-0.44	-0.99	41.86	55.75	2,568
Chongqing 重慶	8	12	147	1	0.27	1.79	12.14	84.85	521
Sichuan 四川	25	36	2,628	4	0.15	0.46	72.60	66.15	2,295
Guizhou 貴州	13	13	165	6	2.74	4.04	12.51	31.85	225
Yunnan 雲南	18	47	854	-51	-0.90	-1.76	18.35	49.19	5,639
Tibet 西藏									
Northwest 西北	68	27	661	10	0.67	2.08	24.60	67.69	1,444
Shaanxi 陝西	60	28	702	10	0.61	1.92	25.43	68.38	1,563
Gansu 甘肅	4	39	683	25	2.53	5.85	17.50	57.07	990
Qinghai 青海									
Ningxia 寧夏	2								
Xinjiang 新疆	2	8	50	-5	-2.38	-2.78	6.67	11.90	210

2033: Domestic Wood Products 生活用木製品業

Year 年份	Number of firms 企業個數	Rate of change 每年變化 (%)	Number of employees 職工人數（人）	Rate of change 每年變化 (%)	Total revenue (mil. RMB) 總銷售收入（百萬元）	Rate of change 每年變化 (%)	Total profit (mil. RMB) 總利潤（百萬元）	Rate of change 每年變化 (%)
1993	1,416		49,813		1,852		34	
1994	1,650	16.53%	100,182	101.12%	2,504	35.17%	44	28.83%
1995	1,778	7.76%	123,433	23.21%	3,121	24.64%	33	-24.46%
1996	1,904	7.09%	100,890	-18.26%	3,865	23.84%	47	41.00%

3 Major products* 3種主要產品*	Output 產量	Sales volume 銷售量	Unit 單位
a) Manmade Board 人造板	160,994	146,504	cubic metre 立方米
b) Wooden Furniture 木製傢具	4,526,434	4,300,113	piece 件
c) Wood Chip 木片	8,031	7,871	cubic metre 立方米

Top 10 firms by revenue (year founded) 收入排名前10家企業（創辦年份）	City 城市	Province 省	Telephone / fax 電話 / 傳真	Number of employees 職工人數	Ownership 產業所有權	Revenue ('000 RMB) 銷售收入（千元）	Profit ('000 RMB) (rank) 利潤（千元）（排名）	Total assets ('000 RMB) 總資產（千元）	Major products 主要產品
Zhangjiagang Hua Xing Decorative Materials Factory 張家港市華興裝潢材料廠(1994)	Suzhou 蘇州市	Jiangsu 江蘇省	(0512)8201261	202	Collectively-owned 集體	84,660	4805(3)	129,230	o
Changshu Chaoyang Timber Industry Co. Ltd. 常熟市朝陽木業有限公司(1995)	Suzhou 蘇州市	Jiangsu 江蘇省	(0512)2347788 (0512)2347454	250	Overseas Chinese-funded 港澳台資	84,490	7220(2)	78,940	o
Heilongjiang Chang An Wooden Products Co. Ltd. 黑龍江常安木製品有限公司(1989)	Harbin 哈爾濱市	Heilongjiang 黑龍江省	(0451)6802734 (0451)6802713	180	Foreign-funded 外資	76,798	9798(1)	75,871	b
Dandong Foreign Trade Youyi Comprehensive Factory 丹東市外貿友誼綜合廠(1988)	Dandong 丹東市	Liaoning 遼寧省	(0415)7609293 (0415)7609202	820	Collectively-owned 集體	62,213	1046(20)	54,056	o
Xiamen Uptrade Furnishing Industry Co. Ltd. 廈門尚貿家飾工業有限公司(1992)	Xiamen 廈門市	Fujian 福建省	(0592)6025725 (0592)6025726	240	Overseas Chinese-funded 港澳台資	57,728	3705(5)	53,326	o
Harbin Jin Luan Timber Industry Co. Ltd. 哈爾濱市金鑾木業有限公司(1995)	Harbin 哈爾濱市	Heilongjiang 黑龍江省	(0451)4101824	61	Collectively-owned 集體	50,688	1760(14)	2,220	o
Sichuan Xindu Furniture General Factory 四川省新都縣傢具總廠	Chengdu 成都市	Sichuan 四川省	(028)3972573	326	Collectively-owned 集體	42,529	1003(24)	35,488	o
Bao Tong (Huizhou) Teak Floor Co. Ltd. 寶通(惠州)柚木地板有限公司(1991)	Huizhou 惠州市	Guangdong 廣東省	(0751)2103001	321	Overseas Chinese-funded 港澳台資	36,700	-14(343)	2,194	o
Tianjin Tian Li Forest Products Co. Ltd. 天津天立林產品有限公司(1989)	Tianjin 天津市	Tianjin 天津市	(022)25323739 (022)25329271	127	Foreign-funded 外資	36,417	309(93)	28,255	c
Zhuhai Zheng Feng Wooden Articles Co. Ltd. 珠海政豐木器有限公司(1990)	Zhuhai 珠海市	Guangdong 廣東省	(0756)3311622 (0756)3311623	115	Foreign-funded 外資	30,634	-181(356)	9,660	o

Top 10 Cities by Production Output 產出排名前10位城市	Province 省	Market share 市場份額	Number of firms 企業個數
Shanghai 上海市	Shanghai 上海市	7.03%	58
Dalian 大連市	Liaoning 遼寧省	4.85%	34
Shuangcheng 雙城市	Heilongjiang 黑龍江省	4.53%	25
Tianjin 天津市	Tianjin 天津市	4.48%	26
Dandong 丹東市	Liaoning 遼寧省	4.10%	20
Zhaoqing 肇慶市	Guangdong 廣東省	3.89%	45
Nangping 南平市	Fujian 福建省	3.61%	144
Huizhou 惠州市	Guangdong 廣東省	3.01%	9
Suzhou 蘇州市	Jiangsu 江蘇省	2.24%	22
Chengdu 成都市	Sichuan 四川省	2.12%	15

10 Major Wholesalers 10家主要批發商	City 城市	Province 省	Telephone / Fax 電話 / 傳真
Jilin Forestry Import & Export Company 吉林省林業進出口公司	Changchun 長春市	Jilin 吉林省	(0431)5629740 (0431)5638250
Shanghai Local Products Goods & Materials General Co. 上海市土產物資總公司	Shanghai 上海市	Shanghai 上海市	(021)63200857 (021)63200857
Kunming Import & Export Company 昆明市進出口公司	Kunming 昆明市	Yunnan 雲南省	(0871)5155192 (0871)5155193
Wujin Supply & Marketing Cooperative Means of Production General Company 武進市供銷社生產資料總公司	Changzhou 常州市	Jiangsu 江蘇省	(0519)6609079 (0519)6609079
China Timber Import & Export Company 中國木材進出口公司	Beijing 北京市	Beijing 北京市	(010)65132383 (010)65124788
Jinchen Urban Goods & Materials General Company Timber Company 晉城市城區物資總公司木材公司	Jincheng 晉城市	Shanxi 山西省	
Zhangjiagang Timber General Company 張家港市木材總公司	Suzhou 蘇州市	Jiangsu 江蘇省	(0512)8223241
Wujiang Timber General Company 吳江市木材總公司	Suzhou 蘇州市	Jiangsu 江蘇省	(0512)3422179
China Forest Products Marketing Company 中國林產品經銷公司	Beijing 北京市	Beijing 北京市	(010)64228370 (010)64216443
Yangzhou Timber General Company 揚州市木材總公司	Yangzhou 揚州市	Jiangsu 江蘇省	(0514)7246917 (0514)7247383

*Also include sales by firms outside this industry.包括本行業以外廠家的銷售。"o" stands for "others". "o" 代表"其他產品"。

2040: Bamboo, Rattan, Palm and Straw Products 竹、藤、棕、草製品業

The industry accounts for 0.073% of the total revenue of China's industrial sector in 1996. The revenue growth rate of the industry is 24.8% from 1995, as compared to the growth rate of China's industrial sector, 9.51%. The rate of return on asset is 2.52%. 79.57% of all firms in the industry made a profit while 15.61% had negative returns. The top province in terms of the industry's revenue is Zhejiang, accounting for 16.71% of the total revenue.
本行業在1996年佔全行業總產值0.073%，行業年增長率為24.8%（全國工業年增長率9.51%）。行業的資產回報率2.52%，79.57%的企業盈利，15.61%的企業虧損。銷售收入最高的省份為浙江省，佔本行業的16.71%。

	Total number of firms 企業總數	Total number of employees 職工總數	Total revenue (mil. RMB) 總銷售收入（百萬元）	Total profit (mil. RMB) 總利潤（百萬元）	Return on assets 資產利潤率 (%)	Return on equity 權益利潤率 (%)	Labour productivity ('000 RMB / worker) 勞動生產率（千元/人）	Debts / assets 資產負債率 (%)	Total assets (mil. RMB) 總資產（百萬元）
Industry Overall 行業總體	2,037	103,555	4,219	95	2.52	6.94	40.74	63.71	3,770

	Number of firms 企業個數	Average number of employees 平均職工人數	Average revenue ('000 RMB) 平均銷售收入（千元）	Average profit ('000 RMB) 平均利潤（千元）	Return on assets 資產利潤率 (%)	Return on equity 權益利潤率 (%)	Labour productivity ('000 RMB / worker) 勞動生產率（千元/人）	Average debts / assets 平均資產負債率(%)	Average Total assets ('000 RMB) 平均總資產（千元）
By ownership 產業所有權									
State-owned 國有	79	55	1,646	-253	-6.23	-21.74	29.72	71.34	4,063
Collectively-owned 集體	1,683	46	1,742	118	11.11	33.77	37.87	67.11	1,066
Privately-owned 私有	16	56	1,850	85	2.49	12.49	32.93	80.07	3,397
Domestic JVs 聯營	16	82	2,160	37	2.01	5.98	26.22	66.38	1,832
Joint stock 股份制	8	61	2,432	-477	-9.58	-30.87	39.63	68.97	4,977
Foreign-funded 外資	72	78	3,953	-291	-4.32	-10.03	50.86	56.90	6,735
Overseas Chinese-funded 港澳台資	163	86	4,835	-378	-5.89	-13.89	56.11	57.59	6,414
By size 規模									
Large 大型									
Medium 中型	1	49	36,308	6	0.01	0.04	740.99	74.32	54,143
Small 小型	2,024	51	2,066	47	2.56	7.02	40.34	63.56	1,835
By regional distribution 地區分布									
Central-North 華北	52	51	1,543	55	3.78	9.75	30.37	61.24	1,455
Beijing 北京	8	10	181	-48	-2.31	-2.93	19.08	21.06	2,054
Tianjin 天津	5	15	2,146	192	11.62	23.59	139.35	50.73	1,652
Hebei 河北	23	75	2,761	84	4.42	19.09	36.96	76.86	1,909
Shanxi 山西	4	19	200				10.81	41.67	150
Inner Mongolia 內蒙	12	58	313	28	5.26	19.10	5.38	72.49	539
Northeast 東北	50	43	1,243	74	5.48	15.13	28.60	63.73	1,342
Liaoning 遼寧	26	49	657	-13	-0.71	-1.95	13.53	63.77	1,799
Jilin 吉林	9	21	3,143	272	42.53	80.33	150.48	46.88	640
Heilongjiang 黑龍江	15	48	1,118	104	10.71	36.03	23.23	70.26	971
Central East 華東	1,066	53	2,444	71	3.43	9.03	46.24	62.05	2,083
Shanghai 上海	11	97	4,994	-201	-2.21	-6.49	51.72	65.85	9,071
Jiangsu 江蘇	40	77	5,243	18	0.45	1.93	68.45	76.78	3,897
Zhejiang 浙江	174	54	4,051	103	2.47	6.69	75.71	63.14	4,185
Anhui 安徽	142	99	4,681	273	12.77	38.07	47.12	66.47	2,140
Fujian 福建	339	36	1,541	24	1.63	3.49	42.95	53.39	1,461
Jiangxi 江西	320	33	746	13	1.73	4.87	22.86	64.50	777
Shandong 山東	40	154	5,234	211	4.48	10.19	33.89	56.05	4,719
Central-South 中南	706	52	1,969	29	1.67	5.16	38.05	67.65	1,751
Henan 河南	39	68	3,194	150	5.93	29.63	47.31	79.98	2,525
Hubei 湖北	93	78	2,463	153	10.44	20.25	31.40	48.43	1,465
Hunan 湖南	309	37	1,189	15	2.02	5.24	32.37	61.55	748
Guangdong 廣東	138	73	3,235	-15	-0.33	-1.27	44.51	74.17	4,484
Guangxi 廣西	120	42	1,806	-17	-1.40	-3.50	43.20	59.99	1,221
Hainan 海南	7	29	817	-3	-0.38	-0.75	27.90	49.81	757
Southwest 西南	129	39	567	-66	-5.36	-12.61	14.65	57.55	1,241
Chongqing 重慶	12	55	592	-20	-2.27	-4.99	10.76	54.41	894
Sichuan 四川	58	39	681	-41	-3.88	-11.91	17.39	67.42	1,047
Guizhou 貴州	42	30	474	-61	-6.49	-48.76	15.92	86.69	939
Yunnan 雲南	15	49	371	-231	-7.26	-9.31	7.54	22.05	3,187
Tibet 西藏	1	24	390	70	20.00	20.00	16.25		350
Northwest 西北	34	26	246	9	3.04	8.12	9.46	62.87	310
Shaanxi 陝西	14	23	276	16	4.68	8.30	11.98	43.79	351
Gansu 甘肅	16	27	248	-2	-0.59	-4.76	9.32	87.99	318
Qinghai 青海									
Ningxia 寧夏	2	21	175	20	22.22	22.22	8.54		90
Xinjiang 新疆	2	48	90	40	22.22	22.22	1.89		180

2040: Bamboo, Rattan, Palm and Straw Products 竹、藤、棕、草製品業

Year 年份	Number of firms 企業個數	Rate of change 每年變化 (%)	Number of employees 職工人數 (人)	Rate of change 每年變化 (%)	Total revenue (mil. RMB) 總銷售收入 (百萬元)	Rate of change 每年變化 (%)	Total profit (mil. RMB) 總利潤 (百萬元)	Rate of change 每年變化 (%)
1993	2,025		85,346		1,846		95	
1994	2,174	7.36%	110,263	29.20%	2,844	54.05%	102	8.02%
1995	2,067	-4.92%	108,860	-1.27%	3,380	18.86%	46	-55.02%
1996	2,037	-1.45%	103,555	-4.87%	4,219	24.82%	95	106.28%

3 Major products* 3種主要產品*	Output 產量	Sales volume 銷售量	Unit 單位
a) Bamboo Furniture 竹製傢具	601,690	571,606	piece 件

Top 10 firms by revenue (year founded) 收入排名前10家企業 (創辦年份)	City 城市	Province 省	Telephone / fax 電話 / 傳真	Number of employees 職工人數	Ownership 產業所有權	Revenue ('000 RMB) 銷售收入 (千元)	Profit ('000 RMB) (rank) 利潤(千元) (排名)	Total assets ('000 RMB) 總資產 (千元)	Major products 主要產品
Shouxian Banqiao Straw Mat General Co. 壽縣板橋鎮草席總公司(1992)	Liu'an 六安市	Anhui 安徽省	(0564)405906	1,946	Collectively-owned 集體	126,260	10710(1)	27,410	o
Shanghai Chun De Bamboo Products Co. Ltd. 上海春德竹製品有限公司(1993)	Shanghai 上海市	Shanghai 上海市	(021)64780590	93	Overseas Chinese-funded 港澳台資	93,021	4705(4)	23,157	o
Ningbo Gaoqiao Lin-straw Products (Group) Corp. 寧波高橋藺草集團公司(1988)	Ningbo 寧波市	Zhejiang 浙江省	(0574)8447253 (0574)8447351	283	Collectively-owned 集體	65,583	5455(2)	47,113	o
Anhui Hefei Yi Yuan Group 安徽省合肥義苑集團(1984)	Hefei 合肥市	Anhui 安徽省	(0551)4841622	406	Collectively-owned 集體	58,200	5080(3)	12,870	o
Haiyang Handicrafts Group Co. 海陽市工藝品集團公司(1996)	Yantai 煙台市	Shandong 山東省	(0535)3221876 (0535)3222871	1,500	Collectively-owned 集體	52,698	802(36)	75,793	o
Xiamen Hua He Co. Ltd. 廈門華和有限公司(1987)	Xiamen 廈門市	Fujian 福建省	(0592)6021516 (0592)6021515	59	Foreign-funded 外資	49,388	482(62)	17,208	o
Henan Grass Products Group Company 河南省草製品集團公司(1994)	Zhoukou 周口市	Henan 河南省	(0394)7223548	450	Collectively-owned 集體	46,750	3900(5)	12,640	o
Bobai Yong Fa Mang Bamboo Woven Company 博白縣永發芒竹編公司(1989)	Yulin 玉林市	Guangxi 廣西		25	Collectively-owned 集體	46,150	1340(18)	6,880	o
Ying He Straw Mat Company 迎河草席公司(1994)	Liu'an 六安市	Anhui 安徽省	(0564)405005	328	Collectively-owned 集體	41,324	1388(16)	8,882	o
White Bamboo & Wood (Fuqing) Co. Ltd. 百竹行(福清)竹木有限公司(1994)	Fuzhou 福州市	Fujian 福建省	(0591)5380917 (0591)5380937	312	Overseas Chinese-funded 港澳台資	36,527	264(120)	41,320	o

Top 10 Cities by Production Output 產出排名前10位城市	Province 省	Market share 市場份額	Number of firms 企業個數
Liu'an 六安市	Anhui 安徽省	9.70%	63
Ningbo 寧波市	Zhejiang 浙江省	7.15%	43
Huzhou 湖州市	Zhejiang 浙江省	6.21%	51
Zhaoqing 肇慶市	Guangdong 廣東省	4.37%	30
Taizhou 臺州市	Zhejiang 浙江省	3.89%	87
Nangping 南平市	Fujian 福建省	3.65%	108
Yulin 玉林市	Guangxi 廣西	3.13%	30
Shanghai 上海市	Shanghai 上海市	2.82%	17
Zhoukou 周口市	Henan 河南省	2.34%	2
Lingchuan 靈川縣	Guangxi 廣西	2.21%	41

10 Major Wholesalers 10家主要批發商	City 城市	Province 省	Telephone / Fax 電話 / 傳真
Chengdu Great Wall Electric Appliance Company 成都長城電器公司	Chengdu 成都市	Sichuan 四川省	(028)6662132 (028)6671975
Shandou Ceramics (Group) Company 汕頭陶瓷(集團)公司	Shantou 汕頭市	Guangdong 廣東省	(0754)8255441 (0754)8255442
Guangdong Puning Local Products Import & Export Company 廣東省普寧土產進出口公司	Jieyang 揭陽市	Guangdong 廣東省	(0663)2226744
Yixing Sundry Goods General Co. 宜興市土產雜品總公司	Wuxi 無錫市	Jiangsu 江蘇省	(0510)7903683 (0510)7903683
Sujiang Qu Zhe Jiang Dongda Group Company 椒江區浙江東大集團公司	Taizhou 臺州市	Zhejiang 浙江省	(0576)8881477 (0576)8881672
Jiangsu New Suzhou Co. Ltd. Suzhou Daily Goods General Co. 江蘇新蘇州股份有限公司蘇州日用雜品總公司	Suzhou 蘇州市	Jiangsu 江蘇省	(0512)7276630 (0512)7275964
Shandong Daily Use General Merchandise Import & Export Company 山東省日用百貨進出口公司	Qingdao 青島市	Shandong 山東省	(0532)5849141 (0532)5849207
Guangdong Yangjiang Light Industry Ye Pin Import & Export (Group) Company 廣東陽江輕工業品進出口(集團)公司	Yangjiang 陽江市	Guangdong 廣東省	(0662)3222497 (0662)3222976
Hebei Artts & Crtfts Imp. & Exp. Corp. 河北工藝品進出口公司	Shijiazhuang 石家莊市	Hebei 河北省	(0311)7756124 (0311)7755347
Shandong Handicrafts Import & Export Products Group Linyi Craft Co. Ltd. 山東工藝品進出品集團臨沂工藝有限公司	Linyi 臨沂市	Shandong 山東省	(0539)8310001 (0539)8315396

*Also include sales by firms outside this industry.包括本行業以外廠家的銷售。"o" stands for "others". "o" 代表"其他產品"。

2110: Wood Furniture 木製傢具製造業

The industry accounts for 0.278% of the total revenue of China's industrial sector in 1996. The revenue growth rate of the industry is 25.8% from 1995, as compared to the growth rate of China's industrial sector, 9.51%. The rate of return on asset is 2.21%. 74.94% of all firms in the industry made a profit while 18.61% had negative returns. The top province in terms of the industry's revenue is Guangdong, accounting for 16.81% of the total revenue.
本行業在1996年佔全行業總產值0.278%，行業年增長率為25.8%（全國工業年增長率9.51%）。行業的資產回報率2.21%，74.94%的企業盈利，18.61%的企業虧損。銷售收入最高的省份為廣東省，佔本行業的16.81%。

	Total number of firms 企業總數	Total number of employees 職工總數	Total revenue (mil. RMB) 總銷售收入（百萬元）	Total profit (mil. RMB) 總利潤（百萬元）	Return on assets 資產利潤率 (%)	Return on equity 權益利潤率 (%)	Labour productivity ('000 RMB / worker) 勞動生產率（千元/人）	Debts / assets 資產負債率 (%)	Total assets (mil. RMB) 總資產（百萬元）
Industry Overall 行業總體	6,912	379,954	16,115	454	2.21	6.79	42.41	67.43	20,522

	Number of firms 企業個數	Average number of employees 平均職工人數	Average revenue ('000 RMB) 平均銷售收入（千元）	Average profit ('000 RMB) 平均利潤（千元）	Return on assets 資產利潤率 (%)	Return on equity 權益利潤率 (%)	Labour productivity ('000 RMB / worker) 勞動生產率（千元/人）	Average debts / assets 平均資產負債率(%)	Average Total assets ('000 RMB) 平均總資產（千元）
By ownership 產業所有權									
State-owned 國有	490	84	2,780	-51	-0.90	-3.29	33.01	72.60	5,661
Collectively-owned 集體	5,796	47	1,577	61	3.70	11.45	33.76	67.72	1,660
Privately-owned 私有	49	84	5,917	207	4.91	11.93	70.80	58.81	4,220
Domestic JVs 聯營	35	102	9,093	379	4.52	11.77	89.12	61.62	8,390
Joint stock 股份制	44	88	6,630	1,098	10.68	27.97	75.22	61.81	10,273
Foreign-funded 外資	183	115	8,719	-327	-2.14	-7.73	75.95	72.27	15,279
Overseas Chinese-funded 港澳台資	311	120	10,003	359	2.55	6.68	83.49	61.81	14,054
By size 規模									
Large 大型	11	1,167	113,754	12,405	5.32	26.32	97.51	79.78	233,042
Medium 中型	29	564	27,891	-579	-0.99	-3.49	49.46	71.80	58,772
Small 小型	6,780	51	2,072	49	2.06	5.88	40.30	65.02	2,396
By regional distribution 地區分布									
Central-North 華北	951	55	1,952	58	1.93	6.76	35.70	71.37	3,018
Beijing 北京	257	56	1,894	-32	-0.87	-3.90	33.98	77.68	3,619
Tianjin 天津	75	62	4,503	355	7.18	18.35	72.94	60.87	4,941
Hebei 河北	284	69	2,796	129	3.71	12.43	40.42	70.13	3,480
Shanxi 山西	144	44	939	-3	-0.16	-0.65	21.27	75.78	1,863
Inner Mongolia 內蒙	191	37	538	4	0.24	0.69	14.59	65.24	1,639
Northeast 東北	698	73	2,279	15	0.32	1.16	31.33	72.48	4,762
Liaoning 遼寧	241	71	2,561	-166	-2.63	-8.98	35.85	70.69	6,311
Jilin 吉林	176	67	1,263	-51	-1.48	-10.37	18.81	85.75	3,437
Heilongjiang 黑龍江	281	77	2,673	212	4.97	15.55	34.55	68.04	4,264
Central East 華東	2,306	55	2,868	107	3.18	9.31	52.58	65.83	3,378
Shanghai 上海	140	98	6,506	208	2.55	6.72	66.11	62.02	8,171
Jiangsu 江蘇	315	75	4,668	95	1.78	6.33	62.44	71.96	5,327
Zhejiang 浙江	224	48	2,630	24	0.73	2.32	54.44	68.56	3,309
Anhui 安徽	370	41	2,288	155	11.33	26.00	55.67	56.42	1,366
Fujian 福建	357	34	1,492	-22	-1.05	-2.31	43.33	54.27	2,059
Jiangxi 江西	422	30	593	11	1.84	6.60	19.73	72.06	605
Shandong 山東	478	78	4,214	270	4.73	14.42	53.77	67.19	5,712
Central-South 中南	1,906	59	2,708	67	2.48	7.32	45.71	66.16	2,717
Henan 河南	350	41	1,372	34	1.84	5.86	33.31	68.53	1,850
Hubei 湖北	378	46	2,971	98	5.78	19.05	64.76	69.63	1,697
Hunan 湖南	345	30	1,363	51	8.11	23.40	46.12	65.35	634
Guangdong 廣東	586	105	4,624	117	2.11	5.74	44.00	63.31	5,542
Guangxi 廣西	214	36	1,060	-17	-1.40	-6.15	29.48	77.31	1,221
Hainan 海南	33	52	4,611	-98	-1.98	-11.76	89.51	83.17	4,927
Southwest 西南	519	35	774	9	0.79	1.91	22.05	58.87	1,083
Chongqing 重慶	107	33	600	12	2.08	4.87	18.13	57.37	584
Sichuan 四川	215	29	717	4	0.48	1.35	23.94	64.27	922
Guizhou 貴州	98	27	378	-13	-2.51	-5.34	13.97	52.95	532
Yunnan 雲南	86	47	1,570	32	1.32	3.52	33.31	62.59	2,394
Tibet 西藏	12	118	885	68	1.89	2.53	7.48	25.36	3,572
Northwest 西北	532	38	922	13	0.89	2.36	24.20	62.17	1,499
Shaanxi 陝西	253	33	598	14	1.80	9.12	17.89	80.22	786
Gansu 甘肅	148	41	919	19	1.33	2.71	22.21	51.14	1,467
Qinghai 青海	21	42	284	-76	-8.24	-34.34	6.73	76.00	919
Ningxia 寧夏	32	43	692	22	2.02	4.06	16.18	50.20	1,083
Xinjiang 新疆	78	44	2,247	20	0.47	1.14	51.00	58.96	4,199

2110: Wood Furniture 木製傢具製造業

Year 年份	Number of firms 企業個數	Rate of change 每年變化 (%)	Number of employees 職工人數 (人)	Rate of change 每年變化 (%)	Total revenue (mil. RMB) 總銷售收入 (百萬元)	Rate of change 每年變化 (%)	Total profit (mil. RMB) 總利潤 (百萬元)	Rate of change 每年變化 (%)
1993	6,098		335,171		8,792		322	
1994	6,607	8.35%	372,214	11.05%	11,070	25.90%	343	6.36%
1995	6,938	5.01%	378,449	1.68%	12,807	15.70%	281	-17.95%
1996	6,912	-0.37%	379,954	0.40%	16,115	25.83%	454	61.48%

3 Major products* 3 種主要產品 *	Output 產量	Sales volume 銷售量	Unit 單位
a) Wooden Furniture 木製傢具	151,323,808	143,757,617	piece 件
b) Soft Furniture 軟體傢具	3,105,208	3,012,052	piece 件
c) Steel-wood Furniture 鋼木傢具	1,927,571	1,889,019	piece 件

Top 10 firms by revenue (year founded) 收入排名前 10 家企業 (創辦年份)	City 城市	Province 省	Telephone / fax 電話 / 傳真	Number of employees 職工人數	Ownership 產業所有權	Revenue ('000 RMB) 銷售收入 (千元)	Profit ('000 RMB) (rank) 利潤 (千元) (排名)	Total assets ('000 RMB) 總資產 (千元)	Major products 主要產品
Jilin Chia Tai Co. Ltd. 吉林正大有限公司(1986)	Changchun 長春市	Jilin 吉林省	(0431)8583838 (0431)8583838	789	Foreign-funded 外資	365,384	20027(4)	207,378	o
Guang Ming Furniture Group Co. Ltd. 光明傢具集團股份有限公司(1985)	Yichun 伊春市	Heilongjiang 黑龍江省	(0458)3605088 (0458)3602181	1,707	Overseas Chinese-funded 港澳台資	220,606	52758(1)	465,148	a
Dalian Hua Feng Furniture Co. Ltd. 大連華豐傢具有限公司(1988)	Dalian 大連市	Liaoning 遼寧省	(0411)8614156 (0411)8613307	606	Foreign-funded 外資	214,703	-23130(1551)	577,072	o
Shanghai Furniture General Company 上海傢具總公司(1993)	Shanghai 上海市	Shanghai 上海市	(021)63216948 (021)63218564	1,048	State-owned 國有	157,510	5553(18)	188,167	a,b
Ji'nan Concentrated Feedstuff Factory 濟南濃縮飼料廠(1987)	Ji'nan 濟南市	Shandong 山東省	(0531)7994193 (0531)7994193	198	State-owned 國有	152,729	6585(12)	52,181	o
Shandong Zibo Feng Yang Co. Ltd. 山東淄博鳳陽股份有限公司(1964)	Zibo 淄博市	Shandong 山東省	(0533)6182436 (0533)6182520	621	Joint stock 股份制	149,080	21123(3)	277,680	a,b
Jilin Timber General Co. 吉林市木業總公司(1952)	Jilin 吉林市	Jilin 吉林省	(0432)2553679	1,643	State-owned 國有	111,070	-800(1479)	43,997	a
Qidong Chang Long Economic Industrial Company 啟東市長龍經濟實業公司(1994)	Nantong 南通市	Jiangsu 江蘇省	(0513)3318430	614	Collectively-owned 集體	109,989	1591(87)	27,508	o
Guangzhou Huan Mei Furniture Co. Ltd. 廣州環美傢具有限公司(1992)	Guangzhou 廣州市	Guangdong 廣東省	(020)82214068 (020)82216994	614	Overseas Chinese-funded 港澳台資	105,287	-1262(1504)	138,183	a,b
Zhaoqing Europe & America Furniture Factory 肇慶歐美傢俬廠(1993)	Zhaoqing 肇慶市	Guangdong 廣東省	(0757)8471241 (0757)8471241	374	Overseas Chinese-funded 港澳台資	99,930	3960(30)	43,677	a

Top 10 Cities by Production Output 產出排名前 10 位城市	Province 省	Market share 市場份額	Number of firms 企業個數
Shanghai 上海市	Shanghai 上海市	8.51%	308
Zhaoqing 肇慶市	Guangdong 廣東省	3.86%	79
Beijing 北京市	Beijing 北京市	3.78%	194
Guangzhou 廣州市	Guangdong 廣東省	3.21%	139
Tianjin 天津市	Tianjin 天津市	2.76%	102
Suzhou 蘇州市	Jiangsu 江蘇省	2.63%	125
Dalian 大連市	Liaoning 遼寧省	2.35%	53
Yichun 伊春市	Heilongjiang 黑龍江省	2.23%	19
Foshan 佛山市	Guangdong 廣東省	2.21%	54
Zibo 淄博市	Shandong 山東省	1.90%	31

10 Major Wholesalers 10 家主要批發商	City 城市	Province 省	Telephone / Fax 電話 / 傳真
Changzhou General Merchandise Wholesale General Company 常州百貨批發總公司	Changzhou 常州市	Jiangsu 江蘇省	(0519)6680488 (0519)6680488
Suzhou General Merchandise General Co. 蘇州百貨總公司	Suzhou 蘇州市	Jiangsu 江蘇省	(0512)5222288 (0512)5222247
Guangzhou Yue Xiu Enterprise (Holdings) Co. 廣州越秀企業(集團)公司	Guangzhou 廣州市	Guangdong 廣東省	(020)86662828 (020)86672634
Wunan Commercial Group Corp. 湖南省商業集團總公司	Changsha 長沙市	Hunan 湖南省	(0731)4442765
Kunming General Merchandise Purchase Supply Station Kunming General Merchandise Company 昆明百貨採購供應站昆明市百貨公司	Kunming 昆明市	Yunnan 雲南省	(0871)3314883 (0871)3314961
Nanjing General Merchandise General Company 南京市百貨總公司	Nanjing 南京市	Jiangsu 江蘇省	(025)6664681 (025)6643927
Guangzhou Shang Ling Trade Co. Ltd. 廣州商菱貿易有限公司	Guangzhou 廣州市	Guangdong 廣東省	(020)86677190 (020)86673971
Beijing Light Industry Product Import & Export Company 北京市輕工業品進出口公司	Beijing 北京市	Beijing 北京市	(010)64057425 (010)64057427
Xi Shan Shi Commerce Group Company 錫山市商業集團公司	Wuxi 無錫市	Jiangsu 江蘇省	(0510)2442982
Yixing Su Nan Commercial Building 宜興市蘇南商廈	Wuxi 無錫市	Jiangsu 江蘇省	(0510)7904407 (0510)7904754

*Also include sales by firms outside this industry.包括本行業以外廠家的銷售。"o" stands for "others". "o" 代表"其他產品"。

2120: Bamboo and Rattan Furniture 竹、藤傢具製造業

The industry accounts for 0.011% of the total revenue of China's industrial sector in 1996. The revenue growth rate of the industry is -1.8% from 1995, as compared to the growth rate of China's industrial sector, 9.51%. The rate of return on asset is 2.92%. 80.29% of all firms in the industry made a profit while 16.01% had negative returns. The top province in terms of the industry's revenue is Guangdong, accounting for 49.65% of the total revenue.
本行業在 1996 年佔全行業總產值 0.011%，行業年增長率為 -1.8%（全國工業年增長率 9.51%）。行業的資產回報率 2.92%，80.29% 的企業盈利，16.01% 的企業虧損。銷售收入最高的省份為廣東省，佔本行業的 49.65%。

	Total number of firms 企業總數	Total number of employees 職工總數	Total revenue (mil. RMB) 總銷售收入（百萬元）	Total profit (mil. RMB) 總利潤（百萬元）	Return on assets 資產利潤率 (%)	Return on equity 權益利潤率 (%)	Labour productivity ('000 RMB / worker) 勞動生產率（千元/人）	Debts / assets 資產負債率 (%)	Total assets (mil. RMB) 總資產（百萬元）
Industry Overall 行業總體	330	12,508	665	14	2.92	8.62	53.17	66.09	481

	Number of firms 企業個數	Average number of employees 平均職工人數	Average revenue ('000 RMB) 平均銷售收入（千元）	Average profit ('000 RMB) 平均利潤（千元）	Return on assets 資產利潤率 (%)	Return on equity 權益利潤率 (%)	Labour productivity ('000 RMB / worker) 勞動生產率（千元/人）	Average debts / assets 平均資產負債率(%)	Average Total assets ('000 RMB) 平均總資產（千元）
By ownership 產業所有權									
State-owned 國有	15	17	867				50.58	91.67	800
Collectively-owned 集體	287	35	1,352	32	2.43	7.65	38.38	68.27	1,337
Privately-owned 私有	3	49	3,579	314	33.95	35.89	73.55	5.43	925
Domestic JVs 聯營	3	12	99	5	5.10	10.03	8.26	49.20	94
Joint stock 股份制	1	88	376	52	18.44	105.48	4.28	82.52	283
Foreign-funded 外資	5	34	1,228	70	5.50	10.44	35.91	47.31	1,268
Overseas Chinese-funded 港澳台資	15	116	16,414	222	4.41	9.77	141.67	54.91	5,042
By size 規模									
Large 大型									
Medium 中型	1	981	62,440	6	0.00	0.02	63.65	79.89	160,815
Small 小型	327	35	1,842	43	4.37	10.71	52.32	59.19	979
By regional distribution 地區分布									
Central-North 華北	4	100	880	48	12.58	59.38	8.84	78.81	378
Beijing 北京									
Tianjin 天津	1								
Hebei 河北	3	133	1,173	63	12.58	59.38	8.84	78.81	503
Shanxi 山西									
Inner Mongolia 內蒙									
Northeast 東北	1	20						85.69	5,380
Liaoning 遼寧									
Jilin 吉林	1	20						85.69	5,380
Heilongjiang 黑龍江									
Central East 華東	154	28	1,239	44	3.82	9.14	44.42	58.22	1,144
Shanghai 上海	1	13	60	-20	-5.41	-100.00	4.62	94.59	370
Jiangsu 江蘇	6	30	1,092	35	5.11	20.79	35.99	75.67	685
Zhejiang 浙江	18	38	1,639	11	0.57	2.70	43.13	78.80	1,845
Anhui 安徽	12	29	1,798	121	19.75	42.52	61.66	53.54	612
Fujian 福建	47	33	1,353	13	0.95	2.13	41.45	55.36	1,389
Jiangxi 江西	61	18	374	10	2.23	11.25	20.97	80.17	455
Shandong 山東	9	50	5,193	407	9.62	13.32	104.80	27.82	4,229
Central-South 中南	125	49	3,644	74	3.54	11.20	74.11	68.41	2,101
Henan 河南	14	45	2,596	272	30.63	89.65	57.42	65.84	889
Hubei 湖北	28	38	1,442	47	7.54	22.84	38.30	66.97	625
Hunan 湖南	29	18	943	63	11.89	16.46	53.75	27.84	534
Guangdong 廣東	38	91	8,688	44	0.87	3.45	95.39	74.66	5,058
Guangxi 廣西	15	32	1,411	43	2.59	4.91	44.55	47.21	1,647
Hainan 海南	1	15	150				10.00	100.00	290
Southwest 西南	42	36	334	-49	-6.13	-38.64	9.29	84.13	792
Chongqing 重慶	6	20	238	-3	-0.86	-4.37	11.82	80.38	390
Sichuan 四川	25	41	417	-72	-7.96	-51.91	10.00	84.67	904
Guizhou 貴州	4	27	173	18	5.83	13.21	6.33	55.83	300
Yunnan 雲南	6	38	203	-47	-4.16	-37.33	5.40	88.86	1,122
Tibet 西藏									
Northwest 西北	4	35	368	-23	-4.69	-69.23	10.58	92.71	480
Shaanxi 陜西	4	35	368	-23	-4.69	-69.23	10.58	92.71	480
Gansu 甘肅									
Qinghai 青海									
Ningxia 寧夏									
Xinjiang 新疆									

2120: Bamboo and Rattan Furniture 竹、藤傢具製造業

Year 年份	Number of firms 企業個數	Rate of change 每年變化 (%)	Number of employees 職工人數 (人)	Rate of change 每年變化 (%)	Total revenue (mil. RMB) 總銷售收入 (百萬元)	Rate of change 每年變化 (%)	Total profit (mil. RMB) 總利潤 (百萬元)	Rate of change 每年變化 (%)
1993	361		12,871		383		7	
1994	422	16.90%	19,941	54.93%	606	58.02%	23	222.19%
1995	305	-27.73%	17,500	-12.24%	677	11.76%	12	-48.02%
1996	330	8.20%	12,508	-28.53%	665	-1.79%	14	15.28%

3 Major products* 3 種主要產品 *	Output 產量	Sales volume 銷售量	Unit 單位
a) Bamboo Furniture 竹製傢具	491,619	467,038	piece 件
b) Soft Furniture 軟體傢具	42,425	41,152	piece 件
c) Wooden Furniture 木製傢具	493,152	468,495	piece 件

Top 10 firms by revenue (year founded) 收入排名前 10 家企業 (創辦年份)	City 城市	Province 省	Telephone / fax 電話 / 傳真	Number of employees 職工人數	Ownership 產業所有權	Revenue ('000 RMB) 銷售收入 (千元)	Profit ('000 RMB) (rank) 利潤 (千元) (排名)	Total assets ('000 RMB) 總資產 (千元)	Major products 主要產品
Guangzhou Nan Fang Furniture Co. Ltd. 廣州市南方傢具有限公司(1993)	Guangzhou 廣州市	Guangdong 廣東省	(020)84905844 (020)84905804	59	Overseas Chinese-funded 港澳台資	123,678	2283(3)	60,665	o
Feicui Furniture (Huiyang) Co. Ltd. 翡翠傢具(惠陽)有限公司(1992)	Huizhou 惠州市	Guangdong 廣東省	(0751)3559817 (0751)3559094	800	Overseas Chinese-funded 港澳台資	97,034	2344(2)	6,860	o
Jiangmen Pengjiangqu Rattan Wares Furniture Factory 江門市蓬江區藤器傢俬廠(1966)	Jiangmen 江門市	Guangdong 廣東省	(0750)3512397	266	Collectively-owned 集體	28,877	25(40)	39,882	o
Bo'ai Jin Cheng Craft Weaving Mill 博愛金城工藝編織廠(1975)	Jiaozuo 焦作市	Henan 河南省		36	Collectively-owned 集體	27,120	3470(1)	2,500	o
Huadu Shennanpeng Bamboo & Wood Products Factory 花都市深南鵬竹木製品廠(1993)	Guangzhou 廣州市	Guangdong 廣東省	(020)86831716 (020)86847173	450	Overseas Chinese-funded 港澳台資	20,752	299(20)	6,194	o
Xiamen Xihua Furniture Co. Ltd. 廈門市西華傢具有限公司(1992)	Xiamen 廈門市	Fujian 福建省	(0592)5770919 (0592)5770687	336	Overseas Chinese-funded 港澳台資	17,174	1030(6)	23,262	o
Guangdong Guang Zhi Rattan Bamboo & Wood Products Co. Ltd. 廣東廣植藤竹木製品有限公司(1990)	Guangzhou 廣州市	Guangdong 廣東省	(020)82279355 (020)82275091	250	Overseas Chinese-funded 港澳台資	15,966	256(21)	13,331	o
Tai'an Rattan Furniture Welfare Factory 泰安市藤木傢具福利廠(1985)	Tai'an 泰安市	Shandong 山東省	(0538)8414630 (0538)8414630	106	Collectively-owned 集體	14,928	1772(4)	11,790	b
Shandong Nan Yang Rattan Industry Co. Ltd. 山東南洋藤業有限公司(1995)	Binzhou 濱州市	Shandong 山東省	(0543)4551098 (0543)4551098	96	Collectively-owned 集體	13,210	526(12)	1,888	c
Ningbo Fu Kang Grass Products Co. Ltd. 寧波富康草製品有限公司(1993)	Ningbo 寧波市	Zhejiang 浙江省	(0574)2950826	240	Collectively-owned 集體	11,698	177(23)	12,932	o

Top 10 Cities by Production Output 產出排名前 10 位城市	Province 省	Market share 市場份額	Number of firms 企業個數
Guangzhou 廣州市	Guangdong 廣東省	29.22%	6
Ningbo 寧波市	Zhejiang 浙江省	6.91%	10
Jiangmen 江門市	Guangdong 廣東省	6.58%	2
Jiaozuo 焦作市	Henan 河南省	5.72%	2
Huizhou 惠州市	Guangdong 廣東省	3.98%	8
Tai'an 泰安市	Shandong 山東省	3.43%	3
Lingchuan 靈川縣	Guangxi 廣西	2.97%	7
Longyan 龍巖市	Fujian 福建省	2.91%	9
Shanwei 汕尾市	Guangdong 廣東省	2.69%	4
Binzhou 濱州市	Shandong 山東省	2.26%	3

10 Major Wholesalers 10 家主要批發商	City 城市	Province 省	Telephone / Fax 電話 / 傳真
Changzhou General Merchandise Wholesale General Company 常州百貨批發總公司	Changzhou 常州市	Jiangsu 江蘇省	(0519)6680488 (0519)6680488
Suzhou General Merchandise General Co. 蘇州百貨總公司	Suzhou 蘇州市	Jiangsu 江蘇省	(0512)5222288 (0512)5222247
Guangzhou Yue Xiu Enterprise (Holdings) Co. 廣州越秀企業(集團)公司	Guangzhou 廣州市	Guangdong 廣東省	(020)86662828 (020)86672634
Wunan Commercial Group Corp. 湖南省商業集團總公司	Changsha 長沙市	Hunan 湖南省	(0731)4442765
Kunming General Merchandise Purchase Supply Station Kunming General Merchandise Company 昆明百貨採購供應站昆明市百貨公司	Kunming 昆明市	Yunnan 雲南省	(0871)3314883 (0871)3314961
Nanjing General Merchandise General Company 南京市百貨總公司	Nanjing 南京市	Jiangsu 江蘇省	(025)6664681 (025)6643927
Guangzhou Shang Ling Trade Co. Ltd. 廣州商菱貿易有限公司	Guangzhou 廣州市	Guangdong 廣東省	(020)86677190 (020)86673971
Beijing Light Industry Product Import & Export Company 北京市輕工業品進出口公司	Beijing 北京市	Beijing 北京市	(010)64057425 (010)64057427
Xi Shan Shi Commerce Group Company 錫山市商業集團公司	Wuxi 無錫市	Jiangsu 江蘇省	(0510)2442982
Yixing Su Nan Commercial Building 宜興市蘇南商廈	Wuxi 無錫市	Jiangsu 江蘇省	(0510)7904407 (0510)7904754

*Also include sales by firms outside this industry.包括本行業以外廠家的銷售。"o" stands for "others". "o" 代表"其他產品"。

2130: Metal Furniture 金屬傢具製造業

The industry accounts for 0.080% of the total revenue of China's industrial sector in 1996. The revenue growth rate of the industry is -2.4% from 1995, as compared to the growth rate of China's industrial sector, 9.51%. The rate of return on asset is 1.32%. 68.13% of all firms in the industry made a profit while 26.30% had negative returns. The top province in terms of the industry's revenue is Zhejiang, accounting for 19.61% of the total revenue.
本行業在 1996 年佔全行業總產值 0.080%，行業年增長率為 -2.4%（全國工業年增長率 9.51%）。行業的資產回報率 1.32%，68.13% 的企業盈利，26.30% 的企業虧損。銷售收入最高的省份為浙江省，佔本行業的 19.61%。

	Total number of firms 企業總數	Total number of employees 職工總數	Total revenue (mil. RMB) 總銷售收入（百萬元）	Total profit (mil. RMB) 總利潤（百萬元）	Return on assets 資產利潤率 (%)	Return on equity 權益利潤率 (%)	Labour productivity ('000 RMB / worker) 勞動生產率（千元/人）	Debts / assets 資產負債率 (%)	Total assets (mil. RMB) 總資產（百萬元）
Industry Overall 行業總體	1,018	80,277	4,633	70	1.32	4.72	57.71	72.08	5,309

	Number of firms 企業個數	Average number of employees 平均職工人數	Average revenue ('000 RMB) 平均銷售收入（千元）	Average profit ('000 RMB) 平均利潤（千元）	Return on assets 資產利潤率 (%)	Return on equity 權益利潤率 (%)	Labour productivity ('000 RMB / worker) 勞動生產率（千元/人）	Average debts / assets 平均資產負債率(%)	Average Total assets ('000 RMB) 平均總資產（千元）
By ownership 產業所有權									
State-owned 國有	78	103	3,013	-103	-1.80	-8.89	29.24	79.73	5,692
Collectively-owned 集體	843	76	3,730	74	1.87	7.36	48.84	74.57	3,965
Privately-owned 私有	7	50	3,887	40	1.66	5.33	78.18	68.80	2,404
Domestic JVs 聯營	3	143	6,746	-956	-10.53	467.10	47.06	102.25	9,083
Joint stock 股份制	4	22	1,363	8	0.64	0.92	61.26	31.08	1,279
Foreign-funded 外資	28	85	12,493	-14	-0.10	-0.38	146.24	73.11	13,988
Overseas Chinese-funded 港澳台資	55	94	15,472	335	1.70	4.30	164.75	60.37	19,653
By size 規模									
Large 大型	1	2,012	344,551	8,742	3.76	12.76	171.25	70.50	232,281
Medium 中型	16	426	25,313	-455	-1.23	-5.34	59.38	77.02	37,128
Small 小型	991	72	3,919	69	1.53	5.37	54.23	71.51	4,522
By regional distribution 地區分布									
Central-North 華北	191	79	4,416	161	3.22	10.23	55.58	68.53	4,993
Beijing 北京	67	60	2,786	114	2.99	10.65	46.12	71.89	3,810
Tianjin 天津	30	90	6,001	168	2.05	5.76	66.34	64.42	8,195
Hebei 河北	47	109	8,265	390	6.01	15.79	75.95	61.91	6,477
Shanxi 山西	30	86	2,438	8	0.20	1.21	28.50	83.87	4,084
Inner Mongolia 內蒙	17	43	887	-31	-2.07	-10.17	20.60	79.67	1,508
Northeast 東北	91	88	1,877	55	2.20	11.56	21.22	80.94	2,518
Liaoning 遼寧	34	85	1,666	47	1.28	19.14	19.67	93.29	3,662
Jilin 吉林	16	77	996	-54	-3.60	-23.69	12.97	84.79	1,492
Heilongjiang 黑龍江	41	96	2,396	105	5.34	13.60	24.92	60.75	1,969
Central East 華東	346	79	6,061	112	1.84	5.60	76.84	67.21	6,096
Shanghai 上海	52	90	4,305	-327	-4.25	-20.46	47.97	79.22	7,699
Jiangsu 江蘇	60	81	5,903	308	5.02	12.62	73.30	60.19	6,132
Zhejiang 浙江	81	90	11,219	358	4.21	10.17	125.00	58.55	8,499
Anhui 安徽	42	91	5,602	270	5.75	23.54	61.56	75.57	4,691
Fujian 福建	51	44	4,514	97	2.79	5.59	103.52	50.12	3,480
Jiangxi 江西	25	40	816	7	0.57	2.67	20.49	78.72	1,269
Shandong 山東	35	100	3,559	-234	-3.32	-24.74	35.75	86.57	7,033
Central-South 中南	261	86	4,837	-5	-0.07	-0.37	56.51	80.37	6,419
Henan 河南	55	57	1,014	13	0.79	3.88	17.73	79.70	1,686
Hubei 湖北	67	129	4,360	9	0.21	2.37	33.71	91.33	4,499
Hunan 湖南	24	57	1,941	-258	-12.13	-40.39	34.03	69.98	2,123
Guangdong 廣東	99	87	8,661	48	0.39	1.78	99.14	77.89	12,190
Guangxi 廣西	12	38	572	-106	-7.71	-112.39	15.08	93.14	1,373
Hainan 海南	4	15	930	35	2.01	20.00	62.00	89.83	1,745
Southwest 西南	71	68	2,557	-18	-0.56	-1.28	37.81	56.02	3,138
Chongqing 重慶	16	65	1,694	-144	-5.26	-9.10	25.67	42.21	2,736
Sichuan 四川	37	64	3,030	149	4.15	11.98	46.94	65.40	3,602
Guizhou 貴州	12	37	943	5	0.48	0.83	25.38	42.45	1,048
Yunnan 雲南	4	205	7,203	450	6.11	10.36	35.22	41.02	7,368
Tibet 西藏	1	18	230	20	2.44	4.55	12.78	46.34	820
Northwest 西北	58	45	1,329	-35	-1.72	-10.10	29.49	82.97	2,053
Shaanxi 陝西	29	50	1,697	-42	-1.69	-12.90	33.61	86.93	2,474
Gansu 甘肅	7	43	709	-44	-2.16	-12.97	16.32	83.40	2,049
Qinghai 青海	4	86	985	-33	-1.77	40.63	11.52	104.37	1,833
Ningxia 寧夏	2	35	1,495	65	4.11	4.98	42.71	17.41	1,580
Xinjiang 新疆	16	27	999	-33	-2.35	-8.51	36.84	72.34	1,408

2130: Metal Furniture 金屬傢具製造業

Year 年份	Number of firms 企業個數	Rate of change 每年變化 (%)	Number of employees 職工人數 (人)	Rate of change 每年變化 (%)	Total revenue (mil. RMB) 總銷售收入 (百萬元)	Rate of change 每年變化 (%)	Total profit (mil. RMB) 總利潤 (百萬元)	Rate of change 每年變化 (%)
1993	934		90,565		2,914		62	
1994	1,010	8.14%	87,850	-3.00%	3,037	4.21%	92	48.77%
1995	1,037	2.67%	94,818	7.93%	4,745	56.25%	96	4.44%
1996	1,018	-1.83%	80,277	-15.34%	4,633	-2.36%	70	-27.20%

3 Major products* 3 種主要產品 *	Output 產量	Sales volume 銷售量	Unit 單位
a) All Steel Furniture 全鋼傢具	9,429,476	9,335,181	piece 件
b) Light Metal Furniture 輕金屬傢具	2,920,685	2,803,858	piece 件
c) Steel-wood Furniture 鋼木傢具	26,333,813	25,807,137	piece 件

Top 10 firms by revenue (year founded) 收入排名前 10 家企業 (創辦年份)	City 城市	Province 省	Telephone / fax 電話 / 傳真	Number of employees 職工人數	Ownership 產業所有權	Revenue ('000 RMB) 銷售收入 (千元)	Profit ('000 RMB) (rank) 利潤 (千元) (排名)	Total assets ('000 RMB) 總資產 (千元)	Major products 主要產品
Zhejiang Ya Xia Ornaments Group Co. Ltd 浙江亞廈裝飾集團有限公司(1988)	Shaoxing 紹興市	Zhejiang 浙江省	(0575)2096888 (0575)2096888	600	Collectively-owned 集體	298,547	17385(1)	99,977	c
Himark Furniture Industrial Corp. Ltd. 浙江華欣傢具工業有限公司(1990)	Hangzhou 杭州市	Zhejiang 浙江省	(0571)2727703 (0571)2726609	162	Overseas Chinese-funded 港澳台資	139,898	3477(12)	71,254	o
Hebei Tangshan Tian Hai Metal Products Industrial Co. 河北省唐山市天海金屬製品工業公司(1972)	Tangshan 唐山市	Hebei 河北省	(0315)5598086 (0315)5598039	805	Collectively-owned 集體	127,158	8293(4)	78,761	a
Guangzhou Jin Pin Furniture Co. Ltd. 廣州金品傢具有限公司(1990)	Guangzhou 廣州市	Guangdong 廣東省	(020)75757719 (020)75757722	655	Overseas Chinese-funded 港澳台資	119,500	2665(19)	379,785	c
Hefei Hua Lian Industrial Co. 合肥華聯實業公司(1984)	Liu'an 六安市	Anhui 安徽省	(0564)3414902 (0564)3414902	153	Collectively-owned 集體	86,850	7820(5)	73,170	b
Tianjin Bo Ke Lai Family Articles For Use Industrial Co. Ltd. 天津博克來家庭用品實業有限公司(1992)	Tianjin 天津市	Tianjin 天津市	(022)28581426 (022)28589007	500	Foreign-funded 外資	85,001	429(75)	126,902	o
Dachang Hui Zu Autonomous County Ya Meng Metal Handicrafts Factory 大廠回族自治縣亞萌金屬工藝品廠(1992)	Langfang 廊坊市	Hebei 河北省	(0316)8823738 (0316)8823738	418	Collectively-owned 集體	82,610	9830(2)	24,100	o
Zhe Jianghua Bang Furniture Industrial Co. Ltd. 浙江華邦傢具工業有限公司(1995)	Hangzhou 杭州市	Zhejiang 浙江省	(0571)2618242	385	Foreign-funded 外資	75,316	2956(14)	32,544	o
Mai Zhi Xi Bai Light Industry Products Co. Ltd. 麥芝西柏輕工製品有限公司(1994)	Suzhou 蘇州市	Jiangsu 江蘇省	(0520)2852868	613	Overseas Chinese-funded 港澳台資	71,930	7690(6)	95,110	o
Guangdong Metal Furniture Factory 羅定市金屬傢具廠(1975)	Yunfu 雲浮市	Guangdong 廣東省	(0766)3722788	280	Collectively-owned 集體	70,511	690(52)	21,577	b

Top 10 Cities by Production Output 產出排名前 10 位城市	Province 省	Market share 市場份額	Number of firms 企業個數
Shanghai 上海市	Shanghai 上海市	6.35%	67
Shaoxing 紹興市	Zhejiang 浙江省	6.07%	6
Tianjin 天津市	Tianjin 天津市	5.37%	31
Hangzhou 杭州市	Zhejiang 浙江省	5.06%	22
Beijing 北京市	Beijing 北京市	4.27%	56
Langfang 廊坊市	Hebei 河北省	3.97%	12
Guangzhou 廣州市	Guangdong 廣東省	3.84%	38
Huzhou 湖州市	Zhejiang 浙江省	3.60%	33
Suzhou 蘇州市	Jiangsu 江蘇省	3.35%	31
Foshan 佛山市	Guangdong 廣東省	3.24%	11

10 Major Wholesalers 10 家主要批發商	City 城市	Province 省	Telephone / Fax 電話 / 傳真
Changzhou General Merchandise Wholesale General Company 常州百貨批發總公司	Changzhou 常州市	Jiangsu 江蘇省	(0519)6680488 (0519)6680488
Suzhou General Merchandise General Co. 蘇州百貨總公司	Suzhou 蘇州市	Jiangsu 江蘇省	(0512)5222288 (0512)5222247
Guangzhou Yue Xiu Enterprise (Holdings) Co. 廣州越秀企業(集團)公司	Guangzhou 廣州市	Guangdong 廣東省	(020)86662828 (020)86672634
Wunan Commercial Group Corp. 湖南省商業集團總公司	Changsha 長沙市	Hunan 湖南省	(0731)4442765
Kunming General Merchandise Purchase Supply Station Kunming General Merchandise Company 昆明百貨採購供應站昆明市百貨公司	Kunming 昆明市	Yunnan 雲南省	(0871)3314883 (0871)3314961
Nanjing General Merchandise General Company 南京市百貨總公司	Nanjing 南京市	Jiangsu 江蘇省	(025)6664681 (025)6643927
Guangzhou Shang Ling Trade Co. Ltd. 廣州商菱貿易有限公司	Guangzhou 廣州市	Guangdong 廣東省	(020)86677190 (020)86673971
Beijing Light Industry Product Import & Export Company 北京市輕工業品進出口公司	Beijing 北京市	Beijing 北京市	(010)64057425 (010)64057427
Xi Shan Shi Commerce Group Company 錫山市商業集團公司	Wuxi 無錫市	Jiangsu 江蘇省	(0510)2442982
Yixing Su Nan Commercial Building 宜興市蘇南商廈	Wuxi 無錫市	Jiangsu 江蘇省	(0510)7904407 (0510)7904754

*Also include sales by firms outside this industry.包括本行業以外廠家的銷售。"o" stands for "others". "o" 代表"其他產品"。

2140: Plastic Furniture 塑料傢具製造業

The industry accounts for 0.001% of the total revenue of China's industrial sector in 1996. The revenue growth rate of the industry is -35.2% from 1995, as compared to the growth rate of China's industrial sector, 9.51%. The rate of return on asset is -1.19%. 78.24% of all firms in the industry made a profit while 11.76% had negative returns. The top province in terms of the industry's revenue is Zhejiang, accounting for 26.52% of the total revenue.
本行業在1996年佔全行業總產值0.001%，行業年增長率為-35.2%（全國工業年增長率9.51%）。行業的資產回報率-1.19%，78.24%的企業盈利，11.76%的企業虧損。銷售收入最高的省份為浙江省，佔本行業的26.52%。

	Total number of firms 企業總數	Total number of employees 職工總數	Total revenue (mil. RMB) 總銷售收入（百萬元）	Total profit (mil. RMB) 總利潤（百萬元）	Return on assets 資產利潤率 (%)	Return on equity 權益利潤率 (%)	Labour productivity ('000 RMB / worker) 勞動生產率（千元/人）	Debts / assets 資產負債率 (%)	Total assets (mil. RMB) 總資產（百萬元）
Industry Overall 行業總體	41	1,584	85	-2	-1.19	-3.97	53.66	70.12	167

	Number of firms 企業個數	Average number of employees 平均職工人數	Average revenue ('000 RMB) 平均銷售收入（千元）	Average profit ('000 RMB) 平均利潤（千元）	Return on assets 資產利潤率 (%)	Return on equity 權益利潤率 (%)	Labour productivity ('000 RMB / worker) 勞動生產率（千元/人）	Average debts / assets 平均資產負債率(%)	Average Total assets ('000 RMB) 平均總資產（千元）
By ownership 產業所有權									
State-owned 國有	1	3	6,000				2000.00	71.43	7,000
Collectively-owned 集體	32	42	1,973	-52	-1.90	-15.89	46.74	88.06	2,723
Privately-owned 私有									
Domestic JVs 聯營									
Joint stock 股份制									
Foreign-funded 外資	2	25	811	-17	0.22	-0.23	32.44	4.60	7,623
Overseas Chinese-funded 港澳台資	6	30	2,370	-52	-0.54	-1.36	78.55	59.99	9,600
By size 規模									
Large 大型									
Medium 中型	1	153	18,559	240	0.89	-14.62	121.30	106.07	27,069
Small 小型	40	36	1,660	-56	-1.60	-4.34	46.41	63.09	3,498
By regional distribution 地區分布									
Central-North 華北	1	16	670	-110	-4.62	100.00	41.88	104.62	2,380
Beijing 北京									
Tianjin 天津									
Hebei 河北	1	16	670	-110	-4.62	100.00	41.88	104.62	2,380
Shanxi 山西									
Inner Mongolia 內蒙									
Northeast 東北	4	19	28	5	3.51	13.33	1.49	73.68	143
Liaoning 遼寧	2								
Jilin 吉林	2	37	55	10	3.51	13.33	1.49	73.68	285
Heilongjiang 黑龍江									
Central East 華東	17	46	3,162	18	0.31	0.91	68.47	66.16	5,716
Shanghai 上海									
Jiangsu 江蘇	2	14	1,185	-105	-2.16	-2.51	84.64	14.01	4,855
Zhejiang 浙江	5	60	4,508	86	1.72	7.85	74.88	78.13	5,012
Anhui 安徽	2	71	5,625	100	2.85	13.70	79.23	79.20	3,510
Fujian 福建	4	43	4,158	-13	-0.17	-0.33	97.82	47.39	7,228
Jiangxi 江西	2	2	20	5	7.69	10.00	10.00	15.38	65
Shandong 山東	2	70	460	-40	-0.30	-3.51	6.57	91.35	13,175
Central-South 中南	13	47	1,979	-97	-2.80	-17.14	42.18	83.67	3,466
Henan 河南	7	23	1,466	34	1.89	6.90	62.94	72.58	1,813
Hubei 湖北	2	68	3,555	85	3.67	8.67	52.67	57.67	2,315
Hunan 湖南	1	50	180	-180	-24.32	41.86	3.60	156.76	740
Guangdong 廣東	3	87	2,727	-497	-5.52	-63.68	31.22	91.33	9,000
Guangxi 廣西									
Hainan 海南									
Southwest 西南	4	18	1,115	-238	-4.46	-10.07	61.94	55.73	5,320
Chongqing 重慶									
Sichuan 四川									
Guizhou 貴州									
Yunnan 雲南	1	62	4,460	-950	-4.46	-10.07	71.94	55.73	21,280
Tibet 西藏									
Northwest 西北	2	14	90	15	9.09	21.43	6.67	57.58	165
Shaanxi 陝西									
Gansu 甘肅	2	14	90	15	9.09	21.43	6.67	57.58	165
Qinghai 青海									
Ningxia 寧夏									
Xinjiang 新疆									

2140: Plastic Furniture 塑料傢具製造業

Year 年份	Number of firms 企業個數	Rate of change 每年變化 (%)	Number of employees 職工人數 (人)	Rate of change 每年變化 (%)	Total revenue (mil. RMB) 總銷售收入 (百萬元)	Rate of change 每年變化 (%)	Total profit (mil. RMB) 總利潤 (百萬元)	Rate of change 每年變化 (%)
1993	48		1,876		121		-5	
1994	38	-20.83%	4,246	126.33%	185	52.34%	5	202.02%
1995	44	15.79%	2,281	-46.28%	131	-29.11%	4	-25.22%
1996	41	-6.82%	1,584	-30.56%	85	-35.17%	-2	-148.66%

3 Major products* 3 種主要產品 *	Output 產量	Sales volume 銷售量	Unit 單位
a) Plastic Furniture 塑料傢具	828,647	638,058	piece 件
b) Light Metal Furniture 輕金屬傢具	382,661	367,354	piece 件

Top 10 firms by revenue (year founded) 收入排名前 10 家企業 (創辦年份)	City 城市	Province 省	Telephone / fax 電話 / 傳真	Number of employees 職工人數	Ownership 產業所有權	Revenue ('000 RMB) 銷售收入 (千元)	Profit ('000 RMB) (rank) 利潤（千元）(排名)	Total assets ('000 RMB) 總資產 (千元)	Major products 主要產品
Sing Fung Decoration Furniture (Fuqing) Co. Ltd. 誠豐裝飾傢具(福清)有限公司(1993)	Fuzhou 福州市	Fujian 福建省	(0591)5380255 (0591)5380606	70	Overseas Chinese-funded 港澳台資	11,646	-241(8)	20,529	a
Ministry of Metallurgical Industry Ma'anshan Mine Research Institute Qianshan Magnetic Materials Factory 冶金部馬鞍山礦山研究院濳山磁性材料廠(1988)	Anqing 安慶市	Anhui 安徽省	(0556)8951215	80	Collectively-owned 集體	10,200	185(2)	5,449	o
Shunde Gui Zhou Household Appliances Factory 順德市桂洲家用電器廠(1984)	Foshan 佛山市	Guangdong 廣東省	(0757)8886002 (0757)8883069	227	Collectively-owned 集體	4,605	-1514(10)	26,085	a,b
Yunnan Ya Di Plastic Products Co. Ltd. 雲南雅棣塑料製品有限公司(1993)	Gejiu 個舊市	Yunnan 雲南省	(0873)2122686 (0873)2122686	62	Overseas Chinese-funded 港澳台資	4,455	-953(9)	21,284	a
Jiaxing Bo Ai Detergent Factory 嘉興市博愛裝飾洗滌用品廠(1991)	Jiaxing 嘉興市	Zhejiang 浙江省	(0573)2085477 (0573)2085477	64	Collectively-owned 集體	4,403	300(1)	9,073	o
Meizhou Nan Jia Industrial Co. Ltd. 梅州市南佳實業有限公司(1996)	Meizhou 梅州市	Guangdong 廣東省	(0752)2242084	35	Collectively-owned 集體	3,570	22(6)	912	o
Hangzhou Yuhang Jia Li Cosmetic Case Factory 杭州市余杭佳麗美容柜廠(1994)	Hangzhou 杭州市	Zhejiang 浙江省	(0571)8551345	52	Collectively-owned 集體	2,781	0(7)	13,552	o
Shishi Hui Da Plastic Cement Products Co. Ltd. 石獅市輝達塑膠製品有限公司(1992)	Quanzhou 泉州市	Fujian 福建省	(0595)8781417 (0595)8884502	30	Foreign-funded 外資	2,585	150(3)	7,920	a
Zhao'an Hong Fa Mahogany Handicraft Factory 詔安縣宏發紅木工藝廠(1995)	Zhangzhou 漳州市	Fujian 福建省	(0596)3313019	30	Collectively-owned 集體	2,400	37(4)	463	o

Top 10 Cities by Production Output 產出排名前 10 位城市	Province 省	Market share 市場份額	Number of firms 企業個數
Dongguan 東莞市	Guangdong 廣東省	12.27%	2
Changzhou 常州市	Jiangsu 江蘇省	12.03%	2
Suzhou 蘇州市	Jiangsu 江蘇省	10.88%	1
Jiaxing 嘉興市	Zhejiang 浙江省	10.02%	1
Nanjing 南京市	Jiangsu 江蘇省	8.63%	2
Foshan 佛山市	Guangdong 廣東省	8.43%	2
Chengdu 成都市	Sichuan 四川省	7.95%	3
Gejiu 個舊市	Yunnan 雲南省	5.62%	1
Siping 四平市	Jilin 吉林省	4.62%	1
Hangzhou 杭州市	Zhejiang 浙江省	4.01%	1

10 Major Wholesalers 10 家主要批發商	City 城市	Province 省	Telephone / Fax 電話 / 傳真
Changzhou General Merchandise Wholesale General Company 常州百貨批發總公司	Changzhou 常州市	Jiangsu 江蘇省	(0519)6680488 (0519)6680488
Suzhou General Merchandise General Co. 蘇州百貨總公司	Suzhou 蘇州市	Jiangsu 江蘇省	(0512)5222288 (0512)5222247
Guangzhou Yue Xiu Enterprise (Holdings) Co. 廣州越秀企業(集團)公司	Guangzhou 廣州市	Guangdong 廣東省	(020)86662828 (020)86672634
Wunan Commercial Group Corp. 湖南省商業集團總公司	Changsha 長沙市	Hunan 湖南省	(0731)4442765
Kunming General Merchandise Purchase Supply Station Kunming General Merchandise Company 昆明百貨採購供應站昆明市百貨公司	Kunming 昆明市	Yunnan 雲南省	(0871)3314883 (0871)3314961
Nanjing General Merchandise General Company 南京市百貨總公司	Nanjing 南京市	Jiangsu 江蘇省	(025)6664681 (025)6643927
Guangzhou Shang Ling Trade Co. Ltd. 廣州商菱貿易有限公司	Guangzhou 廣州市	Guangdong 廣東省	(020)86677190 (020)86673971
Beijing Light Industry Product Import & Export Company 北京市輕工業品進出口公司	Beijing 北京市	Beijing 北京市	(010)64057425 (010)64057427
Xi Shan Shi Commerce Group Company 錫山市商業集團公司	Wuxi 無錫市	Jiangsu 江蘇省	(0510)2442982
Yixing Su Nan Commercial Building 宜興市蘇南商廈	Wuxi 無錫市	Jiangsu 江蘇省	(0510)7904407 (0510)7904754

*Also include sales by firms outside this industry.包括本行業以外廠家的銷售。"o" stands for "others". "o" 代表"其他產品"。

2190: Other Furniture 其他傢具製造業

The industry accounts for 0.035% of the total revenue of China's industrial sector in 1996. The revenue growth rate of the industry is 17.1% from 1995, as compared to the growth rate of China's industrial sector, 9.51%. The rate of return on asset is 6.93%. 68.60% of all firms in the industry made a profit while 21.08% had negative returns. The top province in terms of the industry's revenue is Sichuan, accounting for 22.46% of the total revenue.
本行業在1996年佔全行業總產值0.035%，行業年增長率為17.1%（全國工業年增長率9.51%）。行業的資產回報率6.93%，68.60%的企業盈利，21.08%的企業虧損。銷售收入最高的省份為四川省，佔本行業的22.46%。

	Total number of firms 企業總數	Total number of employees 職工總數	Total revenue (mil. RMB) 總銷售收入（百萬元）	Total profit (mil. RMB) 總利潤（百萬元）	Return on assets 資產利潤率 (%)	Return on equity 權益利潤率 (%)	Labour productivity ('000 RMB / worker) 勞動生產率（千元／人）	Debts / assets 資產負債率 (%)	Total assets (mil. RMB) 總資產（百萬元）
Industry Overall 行業總體	415	22,904	2,023	128	6.93	16.48	88.33	57.98	1,850

	Number of firms 企業個數	Average number of employees 平均職工人數	Average revenue ('000 RMB) 平均銷售收入（千元）	Average profit ('000 RMB) 平均利潤（千元）	Return on assets 資產利潤率 (%)	Return on equity 權益利潤率 (%)	Labour productivity ('000 RMB / worker) 勞動生產率（千元／人）	Average debts / assets 平均資產負債率(%)	Average Total assets ('000 RMB) 平均總資產（千元）
By ownership 產業所有權									
State-owned 國有	31	53	3,161	-290	-7.38	-15.52	59.36	52.46	3,935
Collectively-owned 集體	299	50	3,489	134	4.49	11.72	69.63	61.70	2,982
Privately-owned 私有	4	42	2,495	88	4.13	4.93	59.06	16.25	2,120
Domestic JVs 聯營	4	62	3,722	72	1.61	4.01	60.27	59.93	4,496
Joint stock 股份制	7	93	7,580	1,596	17.51	79.94	81.26	78.10	9,118
Foreign-funded 外資	22	48	4,127	-232	-3.63	-6.82	85.73	46.85	6,399
Overseas Chinese-funded 港澳台資	50	89	14,275	1,805	14.91	32.90	159.64	54.67	12,103
By size 規模									
Large 大型									
Medium 中型	6	325	64,944	11,239	24.70	47.55	199.83	48.06	45,508
Small 小型	395	53	4,137	153	3.84	9.53	77.78	59.72	3,992
By regional distribution 地區分布									
Central-North 華北	57	69	4,359	476	11.60	28.01	63.25	58.56	4,102
Beijing 北京	22	57	5,474	302	5.98	14.98	96.03	60.09	5,055
Tianjin 天津	9	38	7,841	1,944	42.72	58.16	203.96	26.54	4,551
Hebei 河北	13	86	3,738	242	7.07	17.99	43.55	60.73	3,418
Shanxi 山西	7	123	551	-80	-3.86	-57.73	4.47	93.31	2,070
Inner Mongolia 內蒙	6	58	835	67	1.76	10.05	14.40	82.42	3,782
Northeast 東北	35	31	1,978	214	6.03	13.24	63.40	54.46	3,550
Liaoning 遼寧	23	33	2,523	322	6.48	13.45	75.94	51.83	4,966
Jilin 吉林	1	153	410	-280	-8.43	25.45	2.68	133.13	3,320
Heilongjiang 黑龍江	11	16	982	34	5.50	13.91	61.71	60.33	612
Central East 華東	160	41	3,208	150	4.29	11.07	77.73	61.22	3,492
Shanghai 上海	19	29	3,238	35	1.07	2.45	111.67	56.30	3,299
Jiangsu 江蘇	36	81	6,458	399	5.30	14.05	79.79	62.29	7,539
Zhejiang 浙江	28	25	2,383	37	1.55	5.60	95.06	72.29	2,394
Anhui 安徽	21	36	3,083	167	11.55	34.48	85.20	66.54	1,447
Fujian 福建	21	22	1,397	2	0.11	0.21	64.34	49.83	2,229
Jiangxi 江西	15	16	347	5	1.09	1.76	21.85	37.91	427
Shandong 山東	20	49	2,660	214	5.78	13.93	54.16	58.50	3,703
Central-South 中南	103	62	6,195	439	8.26	20.13	100.49	58.98	5,316
Henan 河南	19	58	3,067	-38	-0.89	-4.91	52.73	81.83	4,311
Hubei 湖北	14	77	3,115	132	5.34	24.28	40.42	77.99	2,473
Hunan 湖南	12	68	6,964	555	17.63	53.62	101.91	67.13	3,148
Guangdong 廣東	45	69	9,604	808	9.68	19.58	138.56	50.57	8,344
Guangxi 廣西	10	17	1,734	77	9.47	23.91	104.46	60.39	813
Hainan 海南	3	20	1,040	107	3.32	36.78	51.15	90.97	3,210
Southwest 西南	28	125	16,409	730	7.60	14.83	131.19	48.74	9,603
Chongqing 重慶	5	48	3,736	370	23.32	48.81	77.53	52.23	1,587
Sichuan 四川	12	246	34,944	1,468	7.29	14.29	141.88	48.98	20,145
Guizhou 貴州	5	5	72				13.85	26.45	1,104
Yunnan 雲南	5	25	210	4	0.82	2.20	8.54	62.55	486
Tibet 西藏									
Northwest 西北	32	45	2,944	123	3.35	8.71	65.93	61.59	3,659
Shaanxi 陝西	19	48	4,075	197	4.36	10.65	85.09	59.06	4,513
Gansu 甘肅	8	32	411	28	3.01	10.19	12.95	70.49	915
Qinghai 青海	1	17	150	50	31.25	35.71	8.82	12.50	160
Ningxia 寧夏	1	130	10,610	290	1.52	5.16	81.62	70.55	19,050
Xinjiang 新疆	3	39	913	-127	-7.92	-19.39	23.22	59.38	1,600

2190: Other Furniture 其他傢具製造業

Year 年份	Number of firms 企業個數	Rate of change 每年變化 (%)	Number of employees 職工人數 (人)	Rate of change 每年變化 (%)	Total revenue (mil. RMB) 總銷售收入 (百萬元)	Rate of change 每年變化 (%)	Total profit (mil. RMB) 總利潤 (百萬元)	Rate of change 每年變化 (%)
1993	321		14,853		1,143		77	
1994	394	22.74%	23,919	61.04%	1,569	37.27%	106	38.51%
1995	436	10.66%	23,306	-2.56%	1,728	10.17%	96	-10.09%
1996	415	-4.82%	22,904	-1.72%	2,023	17.07%	128	33.87%

3 Major products* 3 種主要產品 *	Output 產量	Sales volume 銷售量	Unit 單位
a) Soft Furniture 軟體傢具	3,322,330	3,222,660	piece 件
b) Copper Pipe 銅管材	50,684	43,588	ton 噸
c) Light Metal Furniture 輕金屬傢具	674,228	647,258	piece 件

Top 10 firms by revenue (year founded) 收入排名前 10 家企業 (創辦年份)	City 城市	Province 省	Telephone / fax 電話 / 傳真	Number of employees 職工人數	Ownership 產業所有權	Revenue ('000 RMB) 銷售收入 (千元)	Profit ('000 RMB) (rank) 利潤 (千元) (排名)	Total assets ('000 RMB) 總資產 (千元)	Major products 主要產品
Chengdu Ba Yi Furniture Industrial Co. 成都八一傢具實業公司(1985)	Chengdu 成都市	Sichuan 四川省	(028)5170416 (028)5189553	213	Collectively-owned 集體	284,360	7730(5)	121,357	a
Guangzhou Eurasia Mattress Furniture Co. Ltd. 廣州市歐亞床墊傢具有限公司(1992)	Guangzhou 廣州市	Guangdong 廣東省	(020)81821638 (020)81957173	484	Overseas Chinese-funded 港澳台資	187,943	36669(1)	134,734	a
Chengdu Ao Long Industrial Co. Ltd. 成都市奧龍實業有限公司	Chengdu 成都市	Sichuan 四川省	(028)5183501	409	Collectively-owned 集體	151,609	12068(3)	103,480	a
Yangchun Yi Ya Furniture Co. Ltd. 陽春市怡雅傢具有限公司(1992)	Yangjiang 陽江市	Guangdong 廣東省	(0662)7738023 (0662)7738023	138	Overseas Chinese-funded 港澳台資	73,938	1426(19)	26,701	a
Suzhou Suzhou Xinqu Le Xing Industry & Commerce Industrial Co. 蘇州市蘇州新區樂星工商實業公司(1992)	Suzhou 蘇州市	Jiangsu 江蘇省	(0512)8252499	396	Collectively-owned 集體	73,437	3028(8)	75,736	b
Beijing Jiu Zhou Lan Yue Bedclothes Company 北京市九洲攬月床具公司(1994)	Beijing 北京市	Beijing 北京市	(010)69576167 (010)69576165	401	Collectively-owned 集體	70,290	5180(6)	34,480	a
Tianjin Eurasia Mattress Furniture Co. Ltd. 天津歐亞床墊傢具有限公司(1993)	Tianjin 天津市	Tianjin 天津市	(022)26974341 (022)26974341	173	Foreign-funded 外資	63,405	18980(2)	30,751	a
Nanjing Qi Lin Bedclothes General Factory 南京麒麟床具總廠(1985)	Nanjing 南京市	Jiangsu 江蘇省	(025)8842870 (025)8840858	250	State-owned 國有	52,614	8216(4)	41,302	a
Flower Furniture Co. Ltd. 福樂傢具有限公司(1992)	Xi'an 西安市	Shaanxi 陝西省	(029)7284103 (029)7217788	292	Overseas Chinese-funded 港澳台資	48,369	2579(10)	46,875	o
Hangzhou Xin Fu Mei Fashionable Dress Co. Ltd. 杭州新富美時裝有限公司(1993)	Hangzhou 杭州市	Zhejiang 浙江省	(0571)3313079 (0571)3313079	110	Overseas Chinese-funded 港澳台資	32,490	910(24)	16,040	o

Top 10 Cities by Production Output 產出排名前 10 位城市	Province 省	Market share 市場份額	Number of firms 企業個數
Guangzhou 廣州市	Guangdong 廣東省	14.81%	22
Chengdu 成都市	Sichuan 四川省	14.58%	10
Shanghai 上海市	Shanghai 上海市	7.82%	42
Nanjing 南京市	Jiangsu 江蘇省	6.78%	8
Beijing 北京市	Beijing 北京市	5.14%	20
Xi'an 西安市	Shaanxi 陝西省	4.63%	10
Tianjin 天津市	Tianjin 天津市	4.47%	13
Hangzhou 杭州市	Zhejiang 浙江省	3.34%	16
Changsha 長沙市	Hunan 湖南省	2.99%	1
Yantai 煙台市	Shandong 山東省	2.60%	7

10 Major Wholesalers 10 家主要批發商	City 城市	Province 省	Telephone / Fax 電話 / 傳真
Changzhou General Merchandise Wholesale General Company 常州百貨批發總公司	Changzhou 常州市	Jiangsu 江蘇省	(0519)6680488 (0519)6680488
Suzhou General Merchandise General Co. 蘇州百貨總公司	Suzhou 蘇州市	Jiangsu 江蘇省	(0512)5222288 (0512)5222247
Guangzhou Yue Xiu Enterprise (Holdings) Co. 廣州越秀企業(集團)公司	Guangzhou 廣州市	Guangdong 廣東省	(020)86662828 (020)86672634
Wunan Commercial Group Corp. 湖南省商業集團總公司	Changsha 長沙市	Hunan 湖南省	(0731)4442765
Kunming General Merchandise Purchase Supply Station Kunming General Merchandise Company 昆明百貨採購供應站昆明市百貨公司	Kunming 昆明市	Yunnan 雲南省	(0871)3314883 (0871)3314961
Nanjing General Merchandise General Company 南京市百貨總公司	Nanjing 南京市	Jiangsu 江蘇省	(025)6664681 (025)6643927
Guangzhou Shang Ling Trade Co. Ltd. 廣州商菱貿易有限公司	Guangzhou 廣州市	Guangdong 廣東省	(020)86677190 (020)86673971
Beijing Light Industry Product Import & Export Company 北京市輕工業品進出口公司	Beijing 北京市	Beijing 北京市	(010)64057425 (010)64057427
Xi Shan Shi Commerce Group Company 錫山市商業集團公司	Wuxi 無錫市	Jiangsu 江蘇省	(0510)2442982
Yixing Su Nan Commercial Building 宜興市蘇南商廈	Wuxi 無錫市	Jiangsu 江蘇省	(0510)7904407 (0510)7904754

*Also include sales by firms outside this industry.包括本行業以外廠家的銷售。"o" stands for "others". "o" 代表 "其他產品"。

2210: Paper Pulp 紙漿製造業

The industry accounts for 0.021% of the total revenue of China's industrial sector in 1996. The revenue growth rate of the industry is 55.0% from 1995, as compared to the growth rate of China's industrial sector, 9.51%. The rate of return on asset is -1.82%. 68.49% of all firms in the industry made a profit while 25.26% had negative returns. The top province in terms of the industry's revenue is Guangdong, accounting for 15.61% of the total revenue.
本行業在1996年佔全行業總產值0.021%，行業年增長率為55.0%（全國工業年增長率9.51%）。行業的資產回報率-1.82%，68.49%的企業盈利，25.26%的企業虧損。銷售收入最高的省份為廣東省，佔本行業的15.61%。

	Total number of firms 企業總數	Total number of employees 職工總數	Total revenue (mil. RMB) 總銷售收入（百萬元）	Total profit (mil. RMB) 總利潤（百萬元）	Return on assets 資產利潤率 (%)	Return on equity 權益利潤率 (%)	Labour productivity ('000 RMB / worker) 勞動生產率（千元/人）	Debts / assets 資產負債率 (%)	Total assets (mil. RMB) 總資產（百萬元）
Industry Overall 行業總體	218	26,783	1,194	-70	-1.82	-9.18	44.58	80.14	3,866

	Number of firms 企業個數	Average number of employees 平均職工人數	Average revenue ('000 RMB) 平均銷售收入（千元）	Average profit ('000 RMB) 平均利潤（千元）	Return on assets 資產利潤率 (%)	Return on equity 權益利潤率 (%)	Labour productivity ('000 RMB / worker) 勞動生產率（千元/人）	Average debts / assets 平均資產負債率(%)	Average Total assets ('000 RMB) 平均總資產（千元）
By ownership 產業所有權									
State-owned 國有	28	482	16,321				33.84	84.76	104,071
Collectively-owned 集體	165	71	3,849	-226	-4.73	-19.22	54.37	75.40	4,783
Privately-owned 私有									
Domestic JVs 聯營									
Joint stock 股份制	7	54	3,014	-579	-28.56	-237.36	56.12	87.97	2,027
Foreign-funded 外資	3	54	15,972	-553	-11.54	-28.18	297.61	59.06	4,794
Overseas Chinese-funded 港澳台資	13	126	5,146	-2,045	-20.89	-22.84	40.86	8.53	9,787
By size 規模									
Large 大型	3	947						102.74	232,916
Medium 中型	10	392	25,869	-6,139	-5.79	-23.74	65.98	75.63	106,118
Small 小型	192	97	4,871	-45	-0.41	-1.63	50.46	74.91	10,980
By regional distribution 地區分布									
Central-North 華北	12	47	1,018	-39	-1.46	-2.44	21.59	40.05	2,680
Beijing 北京	4	33	1,908				57.37	25.20	3,115
Tianjin 天津									
Hebei 河北	4	43	468	25	2.32	4.29	10.94	45.94	1,078
Shanxi 山西	2	48							
Inner Mongolia 內蒙	2	84	1,360	-285	-3.70	-7.48	16.29	50.42	7,695
Northeast 東北	20	208	7,371	247	2.12	20.96	35.48	89.88	11,624
Liaoning 遼寧	8	80	2,263	96	3.33	24.52	28.24	86.42	2,890
Jilin 吉林	3	225	1,217	-10	-0.05	1.54	5.41	103.00	21,553
Heilongjiang 黑龍江	9	315	13,962	466	2.90	18.76	44.26	84.57	16,078
Central East 華東	56	72	5,081	157	3.13	7.75	71.07	59.57	5,003
Shanghai 上海	1	60	2,770				46.17	52.42	1,240
Jiangsu 江蘇	4	114	2,783	93	1.57	21.39	24.35	92.65	5,888
Zhejiang 浙江	3	64	1,950	-423	-20.58	26.74	30.63	176.99	2,057
Anhui 安徽	14	86	5,075	385	18.38	29.73	58.96	38.15	2,095
Fujian 福建	17	34	5,680	31	0.52	0.69	164.78	24.05	5,952
Jiangxi 江西	1	30	360	20	5.71	15.38	12.00	62.86	350
Shandong 山東	16	92	6,053	234	3.16	18.17	65.65	82.62	7,396
Central-South 中南	95	142	6,694	-655	-2.33	-17.92	47.18	87.02	28,167
Henan 河南	21	168	7,428	305	1.69	7.49	44.23	77.40	18,030
Hubei 湖北	19	166	6,224	-1,165	-9.32	-101.51	37.53	90.82	12,496
Hunan 湖南	14	182	5,049	109	1.40	4.24	27.76	66.92	7,797
Guangdong 廣東	20	85	9,320	41	0.09	0.91	110.09	90.64	47,529
Guangxi 廣西	21	122	4,980	-2,327	-4.89	-42.55	40.86	88.52	47,621
Hainan 海南									
Southwest 西南	17	204	5,793	-1,216	-3.44	-8.03	28.45	57.15	35,360
Chongqing 重慶	3	52	1,936	308	16.38	182.78	36.99	91.04	1,880
Sichuan 四川	4	254	9,084	1,202	2.96	10.83	35.66	72.71	40,660
Guizhou 貴州									
Yunnan 雲南	10	229	5,633	-1,495	-3.45	-7.03	24.62	50.86	43,284
Tibet 西藏									
Northwest 西北	18	62	881	-42	-1.71	-11.30	14.15	84.84	2,433
Shaanxi 陝西	7	58	737	-130	-6.10	94.79	12.80	106.43	2,131
Gansu 甘肅	5	104	1,938	66	2.03	7.45	18.71	72.77	3,254
Qinghai 青海									
Ningxia 寧夏	1	3							10
Xinjiang 新疆	5	39	200	-34	-1.35	-5.38	5.10	74.90	2,518

Year 年份	Number of firms 企業個數	Rate of change 每年變化 (%)	Number of employees 職工人數 (人)	Rate of change 每年變化 (%)	Total revenue (mil. RMB) 總銷售收入 (百萬元)	Rate of change 每年變化 (%)	Total profit (mil. RMB) 總利潤 (百萬元)	Rate of change 每年變化 (%)
1993	147		16,272		445		2	
1994	161	9.52%	16,900	3.86%	624	40.09%	2	-5.12%
1995	157	-2.49%	25,023	48.07%	770	23.46%	19	1074.65%
1996	218	38.85%	26,783	7.03%	1,194	55.03%	-70	-473.85%

3 Major products* 3種主要產品 *	Output 產量	Sales volume 銷售量	Unit 單位
a) Machine-made Paper Pulp 機製紙漿	350,207	325,693	ton 噸
b) Packing Paper 包裝用紙	79,321	75,355	ton 噸
c) Machine-made Paper & Paper Board 機製紙及紙板	233,481	210,133	ton 噸

Top 10 firms by revenue (year founded) 收入排名前10家企業 (創辦年份)	City 城市	Province 省	Telephone / fax 電話 / 傳真	Number of employees 職工人數	Ownership 產業所有權	Revenue ('000 RMB) 銷售收入 (千元)	Profit ('000 RMB) (rank) 利潤 (千元) (排名)	Total assets ('000 RMB) 總資產 (千元)	Major products 主要產品
Zhejiang Ya Lun Co. Ltd. 浙江亞倫股份有限公司(1960)	Quzhou 衢州市	Zhejiang 浙江省	(0570)7022912 (0570)7022117	2,575	Joint stock 股份制	238,077	10035(1)	225,953	a,b,c
Guangxi He Zhi Co. Ltd. 廣西賀紙有限責任公司(1996)	Cenxi 岑溪縣	Guangxi 廣西	(0774)5101175 (0774)5283054	1,210	State-owned 國有	76,084	-48317(80)	932,946	o
Fujian Yan Jin Paper Industry Co. Ltd. 福建延金紙業有限公司(1993)	Nangping 南平市	Fujian 福建省	(0599)8801888	110	Foreign-funded 外資	56,005	-350(67)	77,659	o
Huihua Packing Industry General Co. 惠華包裝工業總公司(1988)	Huizhou 惠州市	Guangdong 廣東省	(0751)2224142 (0751)2234450	275	State-owned 國有	45,657	490(19)	43,300	a,b,c
Guangdong Guangning Paper Pulp Factory 廣東省廣寧縣紙漿廠(1996)	Zhaoqing 肇慶市	Guangdong 廣東省	(0757)8623888	635	State-owned 國有	44,700	4660(2)	736,233	a
Hegang Paper Pulp Factory 鶴崗市紙漿廠(1958)	Hegang 鶴崗市	Heilongjiang 黑龍江省	(0454)3682888	1,252	State-owned 國有	39,656	561(17)	57,994	a,c
Dengfeng Tang Zhuang Pulp Board General Company 登封市唐裝板紙總公司(1988)	Zhengzhou 鄭州市	Henan 河南省	(0371)2981168	150	Collectively-owned 集體	32,995	1300(7)	9,822	o
Yu City Hong Ma Paper Pulp Factory 禹城市紅麻紙漿廠(1990)	Dezhou 德州市	Shandong 山東省	(0534)7221420 (0534)7221420	469	State-owned 國有	30,500	1817(5)	74,392	a
Tancheng Sheng Li Xiang Yongxing Industrial Company 郯城縣勝利鄉永興實業公司(1992)	Linyi 臨沂市	Shandong 山東省	(0539)6731099 (0539)6731099	230	Collectively-owned 集體	29,367	974(8)	9,689	o
Dongguan Chang'an Zhen Qian Tai Paper Industry Co. Ltd. 東莞長安鎮謙泰紙業有限公司(1995)	Dongguan 東莞市	Guangdong 廣東省	(0769)5537598 (0769)5539783	52	Overseas Chinese-funded 港澳台資	28,123	-3222(77)	120,406	a,b,c

Top 10 Cities by Production Output 產出排名前10位城市	Province 省	Market share 市場份額	Number of firms 企業個數
Zhenjiang 鎮江市	Jiangsu 江蘇省	16.49%	2
Quzhou 衢州市	Zhejiang 浙江省	14.68%	1
Cenxi 岑溪縣	Guangxi 廣西	4.24%	5
Huizhou 惠州市	Guangdong 廣東省	4.22%	1
Nangping 南平市	Fujian 福建省	4.11%	5
Anqing 安慶市	Anhui 安徽省	2.90%	5
Xinyang 信陽市	Henan 河南省	2.86%	2
Jingsha 荊沙市	Hubei 湖北省	2.83%	4
Suzhou 宿州市	Anhui 安徽省	2.52%	7
Fuyang 阜陽市	Anhui 安徽省	2.48%	3

10 Major Wholesalers 10家主要批發商	City 城市	Province 省	Telephone / Fax 電話 / 傳真
Zhong Hua Singbo Import & Export Company 中化寧波進出口公司	Ningbo 寧波市	Zhejiang 浙江省	(0574)7346764 (0574)7366775
China Chemical Supply & Marketing Hua Nan Company 中國化工供銷華南公司	Guangzhou 廣州市	Guangdong 廣東省	(020)87654477 (020)87784414
China Agriculture Means of Production Chengdu Company 中國農業生產資料成都公司	Chengdu 成都市	Sichuan 四川省	(028)3333909 (028)3331202
Shanxi Agriculture Means of Production Company 山西省農業生產資料公司	Taiyuan 太原市	Shanxi 山西省	(0351)4040255 (0351)4040231
Beijing Chemical Light Industry General Company 北京市化工輕工總公司	Beijing 北京市	Beijing 北京市	(010)64224837 (010)64219301
Beijing Chemical Industry Group Company Supply & Marketing Company 北京化學工業集團公司供銷公司	Beijing 北京市	Beijing 北京市	(010)67714610 (010)67714058
Zhong Hua Jiangsu Import & Export Company 中化江蘇進出口公司	Nanjing 南京市	Jiangsu 江蘇省	(025)2258718 (025)2257789
Yunnan Chemical Import & Export Company 雲南省化工進出口公司	Kunming 昆明市	Yunnan 雲南省	(0871)3314002 (0871)3314931
Fujian Jiu Zhou Group Co. Ltd. 福建九州集團股份有限公司	Xiamen 廈門市	Fujian 福建省	(0592)5055818 (0592)5052033
China Chemical Industry Commission Agent Hua Dong Co. 中國化工供銷華東公司	Shanghai 上海市	Shanghai 上海市	(021)62514123

*Also include sales by firms outside this industry.包括本行業以外廠家的銷售。"o" stands for "others". "o" 代表"其他產品"。

2221: Machine-made Paper and Paperboard 機製紙及紙板製造業

The industry accounts for 1.180% of the total revenue of China's industrial sector in 1996. The revenue growth rate of the industry is 6.2% from 1995, as compared to the growth rate of China's industrial sector, 9.51%. The rate of return on asset is 1.50%. 68.58% of all firms in the industry made a profit while 25.15% had negative returns. The top province in terms of the industry's revenue is Shandong, accounting for 16.45% of the total revenue.
本行業在1996年佔全行業總產值1.180%，行業年增長率為6.2%（全國工業年增長率9.51%）。行業的資產回報率1.50%，68.58%的企業盈利，25.15%的企業虧損。銷售收入最高的省份為山東省，佔本行業的16.45%。

	Total number of firms 企業總數	Total number of employees 職工總數	Total revenue (mil. RMB) 總銷售收入（百萬元）	Total profit (mil. RMB) 總利潤（百萬元）	Return on assets 資產利潤率 (%)	Return on equity 權益利潤率 (%)	Labour productivity ('000 RMB / worker) 勞動生產率（千元/人）	Debts / assets 資產負債率 (%)	Total assets (mil. RMB) 總資產（百萬元）
Industry Overall 行業總體	5,517	1,244,674	68,433	1,728	1.50	5.54	54.98	72.81	114,861

	Number of firms 企業個數	Average number of employees 平均職工人數	Average revenue ('000 RMB) 平均銷售收入（千元）	Average profit ('000 RMB) 平均利潤（千元）	Return on assets 資產利潤率 (%)	Return on equity 權益利潤率 (%)	Labour productivity ('000 RMB / worker) 勞動生產率（千元/人）	Average debts / assets 平均資產負債率(%)	Average Total assets ('000 RMB) 平均總資產（千元）
By ownership 產業所有權									
State-owned 國有	1,062	603	31,187	281	0.46	1.90	51.70	76.00	61,485
Collectively-owned 集體	4,042	119	5,627	216	3.82	16.09	47.20	76.25	5,649
Privately-owned 私有	56	66	3,765	516	18.39	52.80	57.33	65.18	2,806
Domestic JVs 聯營	34	157	9,725	84	0.85	2.26	61.97	62.67	9,919
Joint stock 股份制	59	931	79,731	6,263	4.13	14.04	85.67	70.60	151,759
Foreign-funded 外資	104	289	30,296	283	0.31	0.60	104.90	49.44	92,913
Overseas Chinese-funded 港澳台資	155	217	26,370	768	1.58	5.03	121.41	68.48	48,464
By size 規模									
Large 大型	114	2,431	207,245	7,555	1.74	5.24	85.25	66.84	434,796
Medium 中型	378	874	44,390	855	1.16	5.77	50.77	79.94	73,861
Small 小型	4,949	128	5,704	110	1.46	5.92	44.62	75.40	7,551
By regional distribution 地區分布									
Central-North 華北	764	195	10,469	363	2.06	6.30	53.73	67.26	17,613
Beijing 北京	57	188	11,647	105	0.52	1.99	61.80	73.99	20,245
Tianjin 天津	53	319	15,187	-244	-0.38	-0.61	47.67	37.97	64,575
Hebei 河北	421	189	12,456	631	4.33	17.84	65.99	75.71	14,554
Shanxi 山西	166	137	3,614	27	0.42	1.68	26.45	75.05	6,506
Inner Mongolia 內蒙	67	285	10,233	218	0.87	6.50	35.93	86.55	24,969
Northeast 東北	507	477	14,900	-80	-0.26	-1.04	31.24	75.50	31,358
Liaoning 遼寧	194	758	15,882	258	0.84	3.48	20.96	75.80	30,603
Jilin 吉林	146	336	14,738	-335	-0.96	-3.74	43.87	74.29	34,836
Heilongjiang 黑龍江	167	274	13,901	-250	-0.86	-3.63	50.70	76.41	29,195
Central East 華東	1,490	258	18,805	860	2.76	9.52	72.86	70.95	31,118
Shanghai 上海	52	316	31,528	-853	-1.58	-8.66	99.80	81.73	53,913
Jiangsu 江蘇	172	319	22,024	168	0.56	2.27	69.12	75.15	29,704
Zhejiang 浙江	218	232	20,052	547	1.11	3.13	86.46	64.44	49,054
Anhui 安徽	240	205	10,647	96	0.72	3.57	52.05	79.76	13,268
Fujian 福建	266	149	11,895	128	0.57	2.12	79.66	73.01	22,322
Jiangxi 江西	230	151	5,413	-131	-0.94	-5.71	35.83	83.48	13,854
Shandong 山東	312	446	36,079	3,691	7.45	22.52	80.84	66.91	49,525
Central-South 中南	1,753	155	9,817	152	1.09	3.99	63.23	72.65	13,907
Henan 河南	525	165	7,730	445	4.49	17.62	46.86	74.53	9,924
Hubei 湖北	238	198	10,551	-37	-0.24	-1.35	53.25	82.03	15,358
Hunan 湖南	465	151	6,882	-51	-0.54	-1.79	45.72	69.53	9,333
Guangdong 廣東	287	142	18,613	226	0.83	2.56	131.13	67.78	27,401
Guangxi 廣西	226	118	9,031	26	0.19	0.74	76.49	74.59	14,026
Hainan 海南	12	81	4,695	-506	-4.33	-28.90	58.26	85.00	11,672
Southwest 西南	587	215	9,322	-89	-0.53	-2.65	43.41	80.19	16,893
Chongqing 重慶	107	213	7,524	-32	-0.29	-3.43	35.27	91.56	11,012
Sichuan 四川	310	238	10,674	225	1.20	5.82	44.77	79.39	18,718
Guizhou 貴州	97	107	3,111	-97	-1.93	-10.81	28.98	82.15	5,035
Yunnan 雲南	72	257	14,528	330	0.98	4.11	56.52	76.21	33,731
Tibet 西藏									
Northwest 西北	416	171	5,237	-11	-0.10	-0.58	30.61	83.00	11,646
Shaanxi 陝西	266	132	3,716	-79	-1.11	-7.14	28.13	84.44	7,141
Gansu 甘肅	64	187	3,978	-235	-2.36	-10.66	21.25	77.86	9,959
Qinghai 青海	8	201	4,769	-233	-2.56	-27.84	23.71	90.80	9,080
Ningxia 寧夏	36	314	12,666	828	2.73	14.13	40.35	80.69	30,331
Xinjiang 新疆	42	265	10,510	82	0.30	2.04	39.61	85.19	27,222

2221: Machine-made Paper and Paperboard 機製紙及紙板製造業

Year 年份	Number of firms 企業個數	Rate of change 每年變化 (%)	Number of employees 職工人數 (人)	Rate of change 每年變化 (%)	Total revenue (mil. RMB) 總銷售收入 (百萬元)	Rate of change 每年變化 (%)	Total profit (mil. RMB) 總利潤 (百萬元)	Rate of change 每年變化 (%)
1993	4,478		967,232		38,210		-285	
1994	4,834	7.95%	1,027,983	6.28%	42,450	11.10%	-312	-9.58%
1995	5,642	16.71%	1,237,938	20.42%	64,414	51.74%	1,767	665.89%
1996	5,517	-2.22%	1,244,674	0.54%	68,433	6.24%	1,728	-2.21%

3 Major products* 3 種主要產品 *	Output 產量	Sales volume 銷售量	Unit 單位
a) Printing Paper 印刷用紙	3,816,505	3,473,019	ton 噸
b) Writing Paper 書寫用紙	2,223,149	2,089,760	ton 噸
c) Technology Matching Paper 技術配套用紙	301,178	313,225	ton 噸

Top 10 firms by revenue (year founded) 收入排名前 10 家企業 (創辦年份)	City 城市	Province 省	Telephone / fax 電話 / 傳真	Number of employees 職工人數	Ownership 產業所有權	Revenue ('000 RMB) 銷售收入 (千元)	Profit ('000 RMB) (rank) 利潤 (千元) (排名)	Total assets ('000 RMB) 總資產 (千元)	Major products 主要產品
Guangzhou Paper Ltd. 廣州造紙有限公司(1994)	Guangzhou 廣州市	Guangdong 廣東省	(020)84366415 (020)84356618	4,755	Overseas Chinese-funded 港澳台資	977,201	80331(3)	1,763,392	a
Fujian Nangping Papermarking Mill 福建省南平造紙廠(1958)	Nangping 南平市	Fujian 福建省	(0599)8801888 (0599)8801296	5,053	State-owned 國有	812,324	34840(11)	1,205,587	a
Jilin Paper Industrial Co. Ltd. 吉林市紙業股份有限公司(1943)	Jilin 吉林市	Jilin 吉林省	(0432)2777787 (0432)2772858	9,319	State-owned 國有	764,466	20047(23)	1,753,174	a
Fujian Qingshan Paper Industrial Co. Ltd. 福建省青山紙業股份有限公司(1970)	Sanming 三明市	Fujian 福建省	(0598)5656261 (0598)5653336	4,830	Joint stock 股份制	655,206	1035(464)	2,256,574	o
Jin Cheng Paper Making (Group) Co. Ltd. 金城造紙(集團)有限責任公司(1942)	Jinzhou 錦州市	Liaoning 遼寧省	(0416)8120015 (0416)8124702	7,686	State-owned 國有	630,051	10048(52)	797,518	o
Shi Xian Paper Mill 石峴造紙廠(1938)	Yanji 延吉市	Jilin 吉林省	(0433)7868351 (0433)7868007	6,791	State-owned 國有	560,080	4250(148)	1,078,670	a,c
Shouguang Paper Making Group Co. Ltd. 壽光造紙集團股份有限公司(1958)	Weifang 濰坊市	Shandong 山東省	(0536)5221053 (0536)5221843	3,001	Joint stock 股份制	553,047	150202(1)	647,725	a,b,c
Baoding Bank Note Paper Mill 保定鈔票紙廠(1959)	Baoding 保定市	Hebei 河北省	(0312)3176982 (0312)3178167	3,457	State-owned 國有	523,369	47010(7)	610,635	o
Yingkou Paper Making Factory 營口造紙廠(1936)	Yingkou 營口市	Liaoning 遼寧省	(0417)3842717 (0417)3842195	6,303	State-owned 國有	488,409	3013(193)	1,383,101	o
Ya Lv Jiang Paper Making Factory 鴨綠江造紙廠(1951)	Dandong 丹東市	Liaoning 遼寧省	(0415)4143849 (0415)4144774	4,235	State-owned 國有	449,886	8206(72)	607,704	o

Top 10 Cities by Production Output 產出排名前 10 位城市	Province 省	Market share 市場份額	Number of firms 企業個數
Weifang 濰坊市	Shandong 山東省	4.39%	60
Shanghai 上海市	Shanghai 上海市	4.32%	102
Guangzhou 廣州市	Guangdong 廣東省	2.43%	30
Tangshan 唐山市	Hebei 河北省	2.14%	63
Ji'nan 濟南市	Shandong 山東省	1.83%	24
Jiaxing 嘉興市	Zhejiang 浙江省	1.82%	28
Jining 濟寧市	Shandong 山東省	1.68%	46
Jiangmen 江門市	Guangdong 廣東省	1.58%	27
Hangzhou 杭州市	Zhejiang 浙江省	1.56%	48
Dezhou 德州市	Shandong 山東省	1.54%	50

10 Major Wholesalers 10 家主要批發商	City 城市	Province 省	Telephone / Fax 電話 / 傳真
Zhong Hua Singbo Import & Export Company 中化寧波進出口公司	Ningbo 寧波市	Zhejiang 浙江省	(0574)7346764 (0574)7366775
China Chemical Supply & Marketing Hua Nan Company 中國化工供銷華南公司	Guangzhou 廣州市	Guangdong 廣東省	(020)87654477 (020)87784414
China Agriculture Means of Production Chengdu Company 中國農業生產資料成都公司	Chengdu 成都市	Sichuan 四川省	(028)3333909 (028)3331202
Shanxi Agriculture Means of Production Company 山西省農業生產資料公司	Taiyuan 太原市	Shanxi 山西省	(0351)4040255 (0351)4040231
Beijing Chemical Light Industry General Company 北京市化工輕工總公司	Beijing 北京市	Beijing 北京市	(010)64224837 (010)64219301
Beijing Chemical Industry Group Company Supply & Marketing Company 北京化學工業集團公司供銷公司	Beijing 北京市	Beijing 北京市	(010)67714610 (010)67714058
Zhong Hua Jiangsu Import & Export Company 中化江蘇進出口公司	Nanjing 南京市	Jiangsu 江蘇省	(025)2258718 (025)2257789
Yunnan Chemical Import & Export Company 雲南省化工進出口公司	Kunming 昆明市	Yunnan 雲南省	(0871)3314002 (0871)3314931
Fujian Jiu Zhou Group Co. Ltd. 福建九州集團股份有限公司	Xiamen 廈門市	Fujian 福建省	(0592)5055818 (0592)5052033
China Chemical Industry Commission Agent Hua Dong Co. 中國化工供銷華東公司	Shanghai 上海市	Shanghai 上海市	(021)62514123

*Also include sales by firms outside this industry.包括本行業以外廠家的銷售。"o" stands for "others". "o" 代表 "其他產品"。

2223: Hand-made Paper 手工紙製造業

The industry accounts for 0.010% of the total revenue of China's industrial sector in 1996. The revenue growth rate of the industry is 31.3% from 1995, as compared to the growth rate of China's industrial sector, 9.51%. The rate of return on asset is 5.28%. 82.98% of all firms in the industry made a profit while 14.58% had negative returns. The top province in terms of the industry's revenue is Jiangsu, accounting for 45.84% of the total revenue.
本行業在1996年佔全行業總產值0.010%，行業年增長率為31.3%（全國工業年增長率9.51%）。行業的資產回報率5.28%，82.98%的企業盈利，14.58%的企業虧損。銷售收入最高的省份為江蘇省，佔本行業的45.84%。

	Total number of firms 企業總數	Total number of employees 職工總數	Total revenue (mil. RMB) 總銷售收入 (百萬元)	Total profit (mil. RMB) 總利潤 (百萬元)	Return on assets 資產利潤率 (%)	Return on equity 權益利潤率 (%)	Labour productivity ('000 RMB / worker) 勞動生產率 (千元/人)	Debts / assets 資產負債率 (%)	Total assets (mil. RMB) 總資產 (百萬元)
Industry Overall 行業總體	215	11,864	597	29	5.28	10.04	50.32	47.38	545

	Number of firms 企業個數	Average number of employees 平均職工人數	Average revenue ('000 RMB) 平均銷售收入 (千元)	Average profit ('000 RMB) 平均利潤 (千元)	Return on assets 資產利潤率 (%)	Return on equity 權益利潤率 (%)	Labour productivity ('000 RMB / worker) 勞動生產率 (千元/人)	Average debts / assets 平均資產負債率(%)	Average Total assets ('000 RMB) 平均總資產 (千元)
By ownership 產業所有權									
State-owned 國有	10	138	1,000	-300	-5.56	12.33	7.27	100.00	5,400
Collectively-owned 集體	193	46	1,097	124	10.66	23.23	23.99	54.12	1,163
Privately-owned 私有									
Domestic JVs 聯營									
Joint stock 股份制									
Foreign-funded 外資	1	420	324,412	23,783	18.29	26.83	772.41	31.85	130,048
Overseas Chinese-funded 港澳台資	10	124	5,086	-1,571	-11.51	-16.48	41.11	30.12	13,647
By size 規模									
Large 大型	1	1,661	51,616	14,879	10.29	14.82	31.08	30.60	144,625
Medium 中型									
Small 小型	212	48	2,572	67	3.53	7.57	53.81	53.39	1,887
By regional distribution 地區分布									
Central-North 華北	7	10	263	4	2.03	21.43	26.29	90.54	211
Beijing 北京	4	3	60	10	9.52	57.14	20.00	83.33	105
Tianjin 天津									
Hebei 河北	1	12	140	10	11.11	20.00	11.67	44.44	90
Shanxi 山西	2	23	730	-10	-2.06	-100.00	31.74	97.94	485
Inner Mongolia 內蒙									
Northeast 東北	8	133	2,321	53	1.26	11.44	17.47	88.97	4,171
Liaoning 遼寧	5	179	1,378	52	0.93	25.24	7.68	96.32	5,592
Jilin 吉林	1	32	170	-80	-9.76	61.54	5.31	114.63	820
Heilongjiang 黑龍江	2	67	5,755	120	5.23	8.66	85.90	39.65	2,295
Central East 華東	79	90	5,933	322	5.81	9.78	65.73	40.60	5,550
Shanghai 上海									
Jiangsu 江蘇	5	131	54,732	1,696	7.73	13.67	417.80	43.40	21,930
Zhejiang 浙江	5	47	1,672	2	0.08	0.14	35.42	42.28	2,512
Anhui 安徽	25	191	5,206	802	7.64	11.78	27.29	35.15	10,506
Fujian 福建	21	43	1,884	-188	-8.76	-23.04	44.06	61.99	2,142
Jiangxi 江西	19	28	840	45	11.87	27.87	30.23	57.40	377
Shandong 山東	4	12	258				22.39	54.86	360
Central-South 中南	48	39	1,940	57	5.03	12.48	50.29	59.72	1,139
Henan 河南	1	2							
Hubei 湖北	20	35	600	28	4.64	21.54	17.37	78.48	604
Hunan 湖南	15	35	1,695	-21	-2.18	-6.83	49.00	68.14	948
Guangdong 廣東	7	25	5,763	267	19.77	22.24	229.20	11.10	1,351
Guangxi 廣西	5	93	3,074	126	3.33	9.72	33.13	65.73	3,782
Hainan 海南									
Southwest 西南	33	34	305	-5	-1.27	13.08	8.92	109.79	405
Chongqing 重慶	10	14	162	1	0.56	-1.69	10.92	133.11	111
Sichuan 四川	15	21	310	-9	-2.29	24.59	14.25	109.31	382
Guizhou 貴州	5	90	488	-40	-5.46	22.47	5.43	124.32	732
Yunnan 雲南	2	100	555	-55	-4.25	-20.75	5.58	79.92	1,295
Tibet 西藏									
Northwest 西北	40	15	115	8	8.29	16.84	7.43	50.52	97
Shaanxi 陝西	39	16	114	8	8.31	17.13	7.28	51.47	96
Gansu 甘肅									
Qinghai 青海									
Ningxia 寧夏	1	8	150	10	7.69	11.11	18.75	23.08	130
Xinjiang 新疆									

2223: Hand-made Paper 手工紙製造業

Year 年份	Number of firms 企業個數	Rate of change 每年變化 (%)	Number of employees 職工人數 (人)	Rate of change 每年變化 (%)	Total revenue (mil. RMB) 總銷售收入 (百萬元)	Rate of change 每年變化 (%)	Total profit (mil. RMB) 總利潤 (百萬元)	Rate of change 每年變化 (%)
1993	251		9,481		216		0	
1994	286	13.94%	12,621	33.12%	358	65.47%	12	3569.17%
1995	235	-17.83%	10,891	-13.71%	455	27.14%	21	65.52%
1996	215	-8.51%	11,864	8.93%	597	31.33%	29	40.29%

3 Major products* 3 種主要產品 *	Output 產量	Sales volume 銷售量	Unit 單位
a) Hand-made Paper 手工紙	6,129	6,068	ton 噸
b) Other Machine-made Paper 其他機製紙	3,726	3,540	ton 噸

Top 10 firms by revenue (year founded) 收入排名前 10 家企業 (創辦年份)	City 城市	Province 省	Telephone / fax 電話 / 傳真	Number of employees 職工人數	Ownership 產業所有權	Revenue ('000 RMB) 銷售收入 (千元)	Profit ('000 RMB) (rank) 利潤 (千元) (排名)	Total assets ('000 RMB) 總資產 (千元)	Major products 主要產品
Wuxi Hai Jiang Printing & Dyeing Co. Ltd. 無錫海江印染有限公司(1992)	Wuxi 無錫市	Jiangsu 江蘇省	(0510)6321128 (0510)6321688	375	Foreign-funded 外資	243,400	7581(2)	83,562	o
China Xuan Paper Group Co. 中國宣紙集團公司(1951)	Xuanzhou 宣州市	Anhui 安徽省	(0563)5022837 (0563)5022053	1,525	Joint stock 股份制	52,570	19769(1)	189,837	a
Xinyi Heshui Multiple-producing Factory 信宜市合水綜合廠(1965)	Maoming 茂名市	Guangdong 廣東省	(0668)8128289	103	Collectively-owned 集體	30,800	1680(3)	6,020	a
Jiangyin Jintong Weaving Co. Ltd. 江陰市金潼紡織有限公司(1994)	Wuxi 無錫市	Jiangsu 江蘇省	(0510)6131312	170	Overseas Chinese-funded 港澳台資	20,900	480(7)	20,671	o
Jie Long Ma Ya Commerce Table and System Co. Ltd. 界龍摩亞商業表格和系統有限公司(1996)	Shanghai 上海市	Shanghai 上海市	(021)58921863 (021)58921864	88	Foreign-funded 外資	18,313	-6559(41)	103,233	o
A City Fei Ke Tu Paper Making Factory 阿城市蜚克圖造紙廠(1954)	Harbin 哈爾濱市	Heilongjiang 黑龍江省	(0451)3861921	3	Collectively-owned 集體	11,500	235(12)	3,319	o
Langxi Ya Shan Paper Making Factory 郎溪縣鴉山造紙廠(1957)	Xuanzhou 宣州市	Anhui 安徽省	(0563)7082053	600	Collectively-owned 集體	10,200	0(32)	792	a,b
Du'an Yao Zu Autonomous County Painting & Calligraphy Paper Factory 都安瑤族自治縣書畫紙廠(1981)	Hechi 河池市	Guangxi 廣西	(0778)5212435	415	Collectively-owned 集體	8,468	503(6)	9,866	a
Anhui Jingxian Xiao Ling Xuan Paper Factory 安徽省涇縣小嶺宣紙廠(1961)	Xuanzhou 宣州市	Anhui 安徽省	(0563)5071510	409	Collectively-owned 集體	8,005	12(29)	12,376	a
Longhai Lv Yang Paper Industry Co. Ltd. 龍海市綠陽紙業有限公司(1993)	Zhangzhou 漳州市	Fujian 福建省	(0596)6778379 (0596)6775699	154	Overseas Chinese-funded 港澳台資	7,700	-2296(40)	9,605	a

Top 10 Cities by Production Output 產出排名前 10 位城市	Province 省	Market share 市場份額	Number of firms 企業個數
Xuanzhou 宣州市	Anhui 安徽省	29.70%	14
Suzhou 蘇州市	Jiangsu 江蘇省	12.14%	9
Maoming 茂名市	Guangdong 廣東省	10.55%	1
Shanghai 上海市	Shanghai 上海市	5.17%	7
Linyi 臨沂市	Shandong 山東省	3.74%	1
Hengyang 衡陽市	Hunan 湖南省	3.35%	2
Hechi 河池市	Guangxi 廣西	3.11%	2
Zhaoqing 肇慶市	Guangdong 廣東省	2.67%	2
Yingkou 營口市	Liaoning 遼寧省	2.40%	1
Huaying 華鎣市	Sichuan 四川省	2.14%	2

10 Major Wholesalers 10 家主要批發商	City 城市	Province 省	Telephone / Fax 電話 / 傳真
Shandong Stationary & Sporting Goods Import & Export Company 山東省文教體育用品進出口公司	Qingdao 青島市	Shandong 山東省	(0532)2826827 (0532)3831971
Henan Printing Goods & Materials General Company 河南省印刷物資總公司	Zhengzhou 鄭州市	Henan 河南省	(0371)5967060 (0371)5947912
China Packing Import & Export Singbo Company 中國包裝進出口寧波公司	Ningbo 寧波市	Zhejiang 浙江省	(0574)7367512 (0574)7361096
Tianjin Stationary & Sporting Goods Import & Export Company 天津文教體育用品進出口公司	Tianjin 天津市	Tianjin 天津市	(022)23112048 (022)23112054
China Packing Import & Export Liaoning Company 中國包裝進出口遼寧公司	Dalian 大連市	Liaoning 遼寧省	(0411)4687657 (0411)4687644
Hunan Printing Goods & Materials General Company 湖南省印刷物資總公司	Changsha 長沙市	Hunan 湖南省	(0731)4444618 (0731)4446936
Guangzhou Stationery Co. 廣州市文化用品公司	Guangzhou 廣州市	Guangdong 廣東省	(020)81889089 (020)81861964
Casio Electronics (Shenzhen) Co. Ltd. 卡西歐電子(深圳)有限公司	Shenzhen 深圳市	Guangdong 廣東省	(0755)3590620 (0755)3590565
Changsha Keven Group Co. 長沙市科文集團公司	Changsha 長沙市	Hunan 湖南省	(0731)4444108
Hunan Firecrackers Fireworks Import & Export Company 湖南省鞭炮煙花進出口公司	Changsha 長沙市	Hunan 湖南省	(0731)4439580

*Also include sales by firms outside this industry.包括本行業以外廠家的銷售。"o" stands for "others". "o" 代表 "其他產品" 。

2224: Processed Paper 加工紙製造業

The industry accounts for 0.073% of the total revenue of China's industrial sector in 1996. The revenue growth rate of the industry is 22.4% from 1995, as compared to the growth rate of China's industrial sector, 9.51%. The rate of return on asset is 3.90%. 70.08% of all firms in the industry made a profit while 24.17% had negative returns. The top province in terms of the industry's revenue is Guangdong, accounting for 24.88% of the total revenue.
本行業在1996年佔全行業總產值0.073%，行業年增長率為22.4%（全國工業年增長率9.51%）。行業的資產回報率3.90%，70.08%的企業盈利，24.17%的企業虧損。銷售收入最高的省份為廣東省，佔本行業的24.88%。

	Total number of firms 企業總數	Total number of employees 職工總數	Total revenue (mil. RMB) 總銷售收入（百萬元）	Total profit (mil. RMB) 總利潤（百萬元）	Return on assets 資產利潤率 (%)	Return on equity 權益利潤率 (%)	Labour productivity ('000 RMB / worker) 勞動生產率（千元/人）	Debts / assets 資產負債率 (%)	Total assets (mil. RMB) 總資產（百萬元）
Industry Overall 行業總體	529	42,855	4,209	207	3.90	11.69	98.21	66.60	5,294

	Number of firms 企業個數	Average number of employees 平均職工人數	Average revenue ('000 RMB) 平均銷售收入（千元）	Average profit ('000 RMB) 平均利潤（千元）	Return on assets 資產利潤率 (%)	Return on equity 權益利潤率 (%)	Labour productivity ('000 RMB / worker) 勞動生產率（千元/人）	Average debts / assets 平均資產負債率(%)	Average Total assets ('000 RMB) 平均總資產（千元）
By ownership 產業所有權									
State-owned 國有	57	248	15,561	88	0.38	1.52	62.67	75.15	23,158
Collectively-owned 集體	349	61	4,341	93	2.02	7.16	71.14	71.75	4,619
Privately-owned 私有	7	29	1,489	137	4.82	16.30	51.10	70.42	2,837
Domestic JVs 聯營	10	152	16,829	1,227	12.79	32.49	111.08	60.65	9,597
Joint stock 股份制	5	30	7,538	186	5.97	15.25	247.97	60.89	3,113
Foreign-funded 外資	37	90	28,230	5,586	14.71	38.78	312.73	62.06	37,971
Overseas Chinese-funded 港澳台資	61	50	7,784	-955	-7.51	-15.00	156.54	49.96	12,722
By size 規模									
Large 大型	6	1,310	123,698	8,622	5.10	16.67	94.44	69.40	168,979
Medium 中型	10	419	56,763	273	0.36	1.13	135.47	68.35	76,134
Small 小型	496	62	5,845	308	4.33	12.54	94.59	65.42	7,094
By regional distribution 地區分布									
Central-North 華北	83	65	10,007	1,370	14.50	34.74	154.13	58.27	9,450
Beijing 北京	24	21	15,511	3,102	21.67	62.51	727.09	65.33	14,315
Tianjin 天津	23	77	3,342	62	1.37	9.52	43.63	85.64	4,517
Hebei 河北	28	97	13,461	1,356	11.54	19.96	138.87	42.16	11,743
Shanxi 山西	6	59	640				10.85	61.41	1,132
Inner Mongolia 內蒙	2	24	350	-65	-9.77	-27.66	14.89	64.66	665
Northeast 東北	42	66	1,950	7	0.23	1.25	29.38	81.25	2,838
Liaoning 遼寧	13	28	2,825	259	11.64	23.52	101.16	50.50	2,227
Jilin 吉林	14	102	1,431	-272	-5.51	-99.48	13.99	94.46	4,935
Heilongjiang 黑龍江	15	66	1,675	48	3.40	17.18	25.32	80.21	1,411
Central East 華東	188	123	9,108	133	1.15	3.63	73.97	68.25	11,548
Shanghai 上海	35	180	18,873	448	2.34	7.07	105.10	66.96	19,188
Jiangsu 江蘇	34	158	11,497	89	0.64	2.15	72.59	70.37	13,935
Zhejiang 浙江	29	122	8,019	-73	-0.62	-2.01	65.84	69.38	11,869
Anhui 安徽	19	61	2,332	73	3.08	9.91	37.93	68.90	2,356
Fujian 福建	27	71	5,235	217	4.11	7.70	74.24	46.69	5,278
Jiangxi 江西	18	33	2,833	148	3.55	9.22	86.59	61.50	4,161
Shandong 山東	26	165	7,369	-56	-0.35	-1.41	44.70	75.49	16,128
Central-South 中南	156	58	8,972	434	3.44	10.51	154.47	67.24	12,587
Henan 河南	29	72	4,997	161	2.95	12.49	69.50	76.39	5,470
Hubei 湖北	22	64	4,563	134	2.67	12.08	71.05	77.91	5,027
Hunan 湖南	23	53	2,052	-128	-5.08	-34.34	38.59	85.20	2,523
Guangdong 廣東	65	57	16,110	933	3.77	10.75	280.37	64.88	24,711
Guangxi 廣西	16	37	3,749	146	7.73	26.45	102.53	70.79	1,885
Hainan 海南	1	20							
Southwest 西南	31	41	4,461	6	0.11	0.29	108.38	63.71	6,046
Chongqing 重慶	1	8	188	66	34.42	37.26	21.79	7.62	193
Sichuan 四川	11	34	856	-4	-0.52	-1.57	24.52	66.68	725
Guizhou 貴州	7	40	1,571	-49	-2.15	-6.43	39.43	66.48	2,254
Yunnan 雲南	11	53	10,648	54	0.36	0.99	200.22	63.39	14,816
Tibet 西藏									
Northwest 西北	29	41	1,611	-6	-0.24	-0.90	39.16	73.94	2,348
Shaanxi 陝西	19	52	1,637	-62	-2.20	-9.77	31.68	77.46	2,821
Gansu 甘肅	5	16	1,034	180	39.82	69.23	64.63	42.48	452
Qinghai 青海									
Ningxia 寧夏	2	43	4,015	45	0.95	2.21	94.47	56.93	4,725
Xinjiang 新疆	3	15	803	10	1.08	10.34	52.39	89.53	923

2224: Processed Paper 加工紙製造業

Year 年份	Number of firms 企業個數	Rate of change 每年變化 (%)	Number of employees 職工人數 (人)	Rate of change 每年變化 (%)	Total revenue (mil. RMB) 總銷售收入 (百萬元)	Rate of change 每年變化 (%)	Total profit (mil. RMB) 總利潤 (百萬元)	Rate of change 每年變化 (%)
1993	554		56,708		2,441		33	
1994	565	1.99%	49,962	-11.90%	2,810	15.14%	25	-23.65%
1995	517	-8.50%	40,895	-18.15%	3,438	22.33%	67	166.41%
1996	529	2.32%	42,855	4.79%	4,209	22.43%	207	208.37%

3 Major products* 3種主要產品*	Output 產量	Sales volume 銷售量	Unit 單位
a) Processed Paper 加工紙	324,416	314,684	ton 噸
b) Technology Matching Paper 技術配套用紙	16,510	17,170	ton 噸
c) Printing Paper 印刷用紙	53,542	48,724	ton 噸

Top 10 firms by revenue (year founded) 收入排名前10家企業 (創辦年份)	City 城市	Province 省	Telephone / fax 電話 / 傳真	Number of employees 職工人數	Ownership 產業所有權	Revenue ('000 RMB) 銷售收入 (千元)	Profit ('000 RMB) (rank) 利潤 (千元) (排名)	Total assets ('000 RMB) 總資產 (千元)	Major products 主要產品
Zhuhai Sez Hong Ta Ren Heng Paper Products Co. Ltd. 珠海經濟特區紅塔仁恒紙製品有限公司(1991)	Zhuhai 珠海市	Guangdong 廣東省	(0756)8610208 (0756)8615037	430	Overseas Chinese-funded 港澳台資	407,986	70577(2)	753,254	o
Kimberly-clark Cbg Hygienic Products (Group) Co. Limted, Handan 邯鄲金佰利舒而美衛生用品(集團)有限公司(1992)	Handan 邯鄲市	Hebei 河北省	(0310)7020908 (0310)7029055	1,800	Foreign-funded 外資	312,000	34670(3)	268,680	a
Beijing Tetra Pall Packing Co. Ltd. 北京利樂包裝有限公司(1995)	Beijing 北京市	Beijing 北京市	(010)67741155 (010)67748806	164	Foreign-funded 外資	289,594	73142(1)	251,882	a
Jiang Nan Papermaking Mill 江南造紙廠(1925)	Shanghai 上海市	Shanghai 上海市	(021)62440266 (021)62443841	1,108	State-owned 國有	189,455	7014(5)	213,693	a,b,c
Hangzhou Wu Lin Paper Industry Industrial General Company 杭州武林紙業實業總公司(1996)	Hangzhou 杭州市	Zhejiang 浙江省	(0571)8084724 (0571)8088402	1,173	State-owned 國有	118,724	1058(36)	147,500	a,b,c
Yangzhou No.3 Cloth Factory 揚州市第三布廠(1970)	Yangzhou 揚州市	Jiangsu 江蘇省	(0514)7610726 (0514)7610877	1,509	Collectively-owned 集體	109,888	3427(8)	38,662	o
Shanghai Tian Zhang Record Paper Mill 上海天章記錄紙廠(1884)	Shanghai 上海市	Shanghai 上海市	(021)65462370 (021)65125594	1,297	State-owned 國有	107,874	1635(19)	129,701	a,b,c
Shanghai Hua Li Art Paper Mill 上海華麗銅版紙廠(1935)	Shanghai 上海市	Shanghai 上海市	(021)65035977 (021)65030946	1,226	State-owned 國有	96,098	-7257(260)	80,199	a,b,c
Zhanjiang Guan Hao Paper Industry Co. Ltd. 湛江冠豪紙業有限公司(1994)	Zhanjiang 湛江市	Guangdong 廣東省	(0758)3386011 (0758)3382109	198	Overseas Chinese-funded 港澳台資	92,384	435(63)	214,820	o
State-owned Qingdao Paper Making Mill 國營青島造紙廠(1941)	Qingdao 青島市	Shandong 山東省	(0532)4851203 (0532)4863637	1,047	State-owned 國有	61,023	1501(24)	110,688	a,b

Top 10 Cities by Production Output 產出排名前10位城市	Province 省	Market share 市場份額	Number of firms 企業個數
Shanghai 上海市	Shanghai 上海市	12.42%	67
Zhuhai 珠海市	Guangdong 廣東省	12.00%	4
Beijing 北京市	Beijing 北京市	6.33%	18
Hangzhou 杭州市	Zhejiang 浙江省	3.82%	6
Handan 邯鄲市	Hebei 河北省	3.25%	2
Yangzhou 揚州市	Jiangsu 江蘇省	3.16%	8
Zhanjiang 湛江市	Guangdong 廣東省	2.97%	3
Dongguan 東莞市	Guangdong 廣東省	2.77%	2
Jiaxing 嘉興市	Zhejiang 浙江省	2.32%	6
Guangzhou 廣州市	Guangdong 廣東省	2.26%	20

10 Major Wholesalers 10家主要批發商	City 城市	Province 省	Telephone / Fax 電話 / 傳真
Shandong Stationary & Sporting Goods Import & Export Company 山東省文教體育用品進出口公司	Qingdao 青島市	Shandong 山東省	(0532)2826827 (0532)3831971
Henan Printing Goods & Materials General Company 河南省印刷物資總公司	Zhengzhou 鄭州市	Henan 河南省	(0371)5967060 (0371)5947912
China Packing Import & Export Singbo Company 中國包裝進出口寧波公司	Ningbo 寧波市	Zhejiang 浙江省	(0574)7367512 (0574)7361096
Tianjin Stationary & Sporting Goods Import & Export Company 天津文教體育用品進出口公司	Tianjin 天津市	Tianjin 天津市	(022)23112048 (022)23112054
China Packing Import & Export Liaoning Company 中國包裝進出口遼寧公司	Dalian 大連市	Liaoning 遼寧省	(0411)4687657 (0411)4687644
Hunan Printing Goods & Materials General Company 湖南省印刷物資總公司	Changsha 長沙市	Hunan 湖南省	(0731)4444618 (0731)4446936
Guangzhou Stationery Co. 廣州市文化用品公司	Guangzhou 廣州市	Guangdong 廣東省	(020)81889089 (020)81861964
Casio Electronics (Shenzhen) Co. Ltd. 卡西歐電子(深圳)有限公司	Shenzhen 深圳市	Guangdong 廣東省	(0755)3590620 (0755)3590565
Changsha Keven Group Co. 長沙市科文集團公司	Changsha 長沙市	Hunan 湖南省	(0731)4444108
Hunan Firecrackers Fireworks Import & Export Company 湖南省鞭炮煙花進出口公司	Changsha 長沙市	Hunan 湖南省	(0731)4439580

*Also include sales by firms outside this industry.包括本行業以外廠家的銷售。"o" stands for "others". "o" 代表 "其他產品"。

2230: Paper Products 紙製品業

The industry accounts for 0.555% of the total revenue of China's industrial sector in 1996. The revenue growth rate of the industry is 17.6% from 1995, as compared to the growth rate of China's industrial sector, 9.51%. The rate of return on asset is 2.44%. 70.77% of all firms in the industry made a profit while 23.78% had negative returns. The top province in terms of the industry's revenue is Guangdong, accounting for 23.84% of the total revenue.
本行業在1996年佔全行業總產值0.555%，行業年增長率為17.6%（全國工業年增長率9.51%）。行業的資產回報率2.44%，70.77%的企業盈利，23.78%的企業虧損。銷售收入最高的省份為廣東省，佔本行業的23.84%。

	Total number of firms 企業總數	Total number of employees 職工總數	Total revenue (mil. RMB) 總銷售收入（百萬元）	Total profit (mil. RMB) 總利潤（百萬元）	Return on assets 資產利潤率 (%)	Return on equity 權益利潤率 (%)	Labour productivity ('000 RMB / worker) 勞動生產率（千元/人）	Debts / assets 資產負債率 (%)	Total assets (mil. RMB) 總資產（百萬元）
Industry Overall 行業總體	7,414	531,417	32,159	824	2.44	7.18	60.52	66.05	33,802

	Number of firms 企業個數	Average number of employees 平均職工人數	Average revenue ('000 RMB) 平均銷售收入（千元）	Average profit ('000 RMB) 平均利潤（千元）	Return on assets 資產利潤率 (%)	Return on equity 權益利潤率 (%)	Labour productivity ('000 RMB / worker) 勞動生產率（千元/人）	Average debts / assets 平均資產負債率(%)	Average Total assets ('000 RMB) 平均總資產（千元）
By ownership 產業所有權									
State-owned 國有	638	104	4,168	-45	-0.69	-2.45	40.24	71.94	6,613
Collectively-owned 集體	5,991	67	3,295	69	2.33	8.71	49.05	73.26	2,972
Privately-owned 私有	28	26	1,647	115	15.03	45.81	63.80	67.19	762
Domestic JVs 聯營	64	111	9,213	448	5.67	15.35	82.70	63.05	7,898
Joint stock 股份制	72	123	9,966	507	4.96	14.40	80.96	65.55	10,218
Foreign-funded 外資	179	94	16,951	918	4.17	8.07	179.91	48.39	22,034
Overseas Chinese-funded 港澳台資	431	72	12,394	476	3.14	6.76	172.90	53.59	15,175
By size 規模									
Large 大型	14	553	194,271	20,389	8.19	16.97	351.30	51.75	249,045
Medium 中型	76	432	43,800	449	0.74	2.23	101.49	66.93	60,813
Small 小型	7,242	68	3,605	70	1.96	6.10	53.23	67.83	3,547
By regional distribution 地區分布									
Central-North 華北	943	62	2,948	160	4.91	12.72	47.35	61.36	3,255
Beijing 北京	185	31	1,889	49	1.98	5.17	60.37	61.72	2,470
Tianjin 天津	181	60	4,531	311	5.43	10.25	74.99	46.99	5,714
Hebei 河北	357	78	3,713	238	7.58	26.20	47.47	71.05	3,137
Shanxi 山西	123	61	1,167	32	1.75	5.30	19.17	66.89	1,813
Inner Mongolia 內蒙	97	68	1,461	-34	-1.40	-5.08	21.52	72.48	2,421
Northeast 東北	847	81	2,394	-1	-0.04	-0.16	29.54	73.34	2,757
Liaoning 遼寧	444	82	2,883	25	0.76	2.79	35.31	72.87	3,256
Jilin 吉林	205	83	1,304	-71	-3.38	-14.77	15.67	77.14	2,096
Heilongjiang 黑龍江	198	77	2,426	13	0.56	1.95	31.35	71.28	2,321
Central East 華東	2,667	76	4,995	128	2.67	7.63	65.94	65.03	4,779
Shanghai 上海	229	95	7,922	307	3.14	7.69	83.47	59.23	9,784
Jiangsu 江蘇	448	94	6,856	103	1.69	5.48	72.65	69.18	6,078
Zhejiang 浙江	453	55	5,225	139	2.73	8.29	95.48	67.04	5,082
Anhui 安徽	292	87	3,622	147	7.48	21.74	41.48	65.59	1,968
Fujian 福建	527	46	3,416	28	0.76	1.81	73.99	57.83	3,629
Jiangxi 江西	253	65	1,787	-20	-0.84	-4.51	27.32	81.22	2,442
Shandong 山東	465	101	5,936	234	4.57	13.15	58.88	65.23	5,109
Central-South 中南	2,015	68	5,647	176	2.83	7.98	83.09	64.67	6,208
Henan 河南	387	59	2,301	49	1.76	6.03	38.94	70.87	2,768
Hubei 湖北	282	81	4,213	113	3.56	14.30	51.71	75.10	3,172
Hunan 湖南	321	62	2,766	-13	-0.54	-2.65	44.49	79.63	2,401
Guangdong 廣東	761	75	10,074	402	3.41	8.78	134.29	61.31	11,782
Guangxi 廣西	243	53	2,740	5	0.17	0.54	51:22	67.80	2,870
Hainan 海南	21	50	3,812	2	0.04	0.12	75.53	68.98	5,156
Southwest 西南	521	77	3,736	-30	-0.71	-2.76	48.69	74.33	4,201
Chongqing 重慶	112	71	3,589	-50	-1.07	-5.62	50.27	80.93	4,682
Sichuan 四川	268	80	3,834	-51	-1.37	-4.81	47.48	71.63	3,761
Guizhou 貴州	86	64	1,992	20	0.79	3.85	31.31	79.44	2,585
Yunnan 雲南	54	91	6,332	38	0.48	1.60	69.78	70.00	7,964
Tibet 西藏									
Northwest 西北	421	60	1,670	-9	-0.41	-1.72	28.00	76.19	2,267
Shaanxi 陝西	260	58	1,451	6	0.32	1.44	24.95	77.62	1,950
Gansu 甘肅	95	62	1,743	7	0.32	1.16	28.16	72.34	2,189
Qinghai 青海	8	48	1,308	6	0.35	2.56	27.38	86.50	1,805
Ningxia 寧夏	11	99	1,979	28	0.93	2.63	19.90	64.58	3,026
Xinjiang 新疆	47	56	2,718	-140	-3.43	-15.47	48.76	77.83	4,081

2230: Paper Products 紙製品業

Year 年份	Number of firms 企業個數	Rate of change 每年變化 (%)	Number of employees 職工人數 (人)	Rate of change 每年變化 (%)	Total revenue (mil. RMB) 總銷售收入 (百萬元)	Rate of change 每年變化 (%)	Total profit (mil. RMB) 總利潤 (百萬元)	Rate of change 每年變化 (%)
1993	6,488		492,710		20,947		1,039	
1994	6,995	7.81%	545,949	10.81%	19,798	-5.49%	530	-49.03%
1995	7,338	4.90%	548,120	0.40%	27,354	38.16%	433	-18.30%
1996	7,414	1.04%	531,417	-3.05%	32,159	17.57%	824	90.43%

3 Major products* 3 種主要產品 *	Output 產量	Sales volume 銷售量	Unit 單位
a) Monochrome Printed Product 單色印刷品	16,809	16,305	10,000 ream 萬令
b) Wrapping Paper Board 包裝紙板	1,037,213	985,352	ton 噸

Top 10 firms by revenue (year founded) 收入排名前 10 家企業 (創辦年份)	City 城市	Province 省	Telephone / fax 電話 / 傳真	Number of employees 職工人數	Ownership 產業所有權	Revenue ('000 RMB) 銷售收入 (千元)	Profit ('000 RMB) (rank) 利潤 (千元) (排名)	Total assets ('000 RMB) 總資產 (千元)	Major products 主要產品
Procter & Gamble Paper (Guangzhou) Ltd. 廣州寶潔紙品有限公司(1990)	Guangzhou 廣州市	Guangdong 廣東省	(020)82218828 (020)82215594	237	Foreign-funded 外資	760,403	131023(1)	550,319	o
Shenzhen Good Luck Corrugated Carton Ltd. 深圳順豐瓦通紙品有限公司(1987)	Shenzhen 深圳市	Guangdong 廣東省	(0755)2263323 (0755)2260736	750	Overseas Chinese-funded 港澳台資	484,458	17010(7)	468,329	o
Hua Xin Li Le (Foshan) Packing Co. Ltd. 佛山市華新複合材料有限公司(1995)	Foshan 佛山市	Guangdong 廣東省	(0757)3831023 (0757)3831023	203	Foreign-funded 外資	384,135	128366(2)	665,023	o
Shenzhen Jiu Hui Industrial Co. Ltd. 深圳九輝實業有限公司(1993)	Shenzhen 深圳市	Guangdong 廣東省	(0755)7607999	700	Foreign-funded 外資	309,411	13225(9)	532,764	o
Zhejiang Xiaoshan Sheng Da Group Co. Ltd. 浙江蕭山勝達集團有限公司(1994)	Hangzhou 杭州市	Zhejiang 浙江省	(0571)2473022 (0571)2473062	778	Collectively-owned 集體	231,633	10068(13)	119,150	o
Shenzhen Hua Li Packing & Trade Co. Ltd. 深圳華力包裝貿易有限公司(1986)	Shenzhen 深圳市	Guangdong 廣東省	(0755)6600212 (0755)6600213	396	Overseas Chinese-funded 港澳台資	221,987	31653(3)	166,096	o
Shandong De Chang Group General Co. 山東省德昌集團總公司(1982)	Jining 濟寧市	Shandong 山東省	(0537)2514675 (0537)2514675	1,092	Collectively-owned 集體	204,936	15064(8)	107,297	o
Shanghai Shen Yong Gilding Materials Co. Ltd. 上海申永燙金材料有限公司(1992)	Shanghai 上海市	Shanghai 上海市	(021)56653620 (021)56654351	322	Overseas Chinese-funded 港澳台資	178,243	20248(4)	196,030	o
Shaoxing Dong Fang Paper Industrial Packing Group Co. 紹興東方紙業包裝集團公司(1967)	Shaoxing 紹興市	Zhejiang 浙江省	(0575)2076079	460	Collectively-owned 集體	174,271	9057(15)	60,546	b
Shanghai Fu Jian Packing Co. 上海市復建包裝公司(1955)	Shanghai 上海市	Shanghai 上海市	(021)59529435 (021)59528079	1,288	Collectively-owned 集體	164,378	13124(10)	167,655	o

Top 10 Cities by Production Output 產出排名前 10 位城市	Province 省	Market share 市場份額	Number of firms 企業個數
Zhenjiang 鎮江市	Jiangsu 江蘇省	18.22%	68
Guangzhou 廣州市	Guangdong 廣東省	5.93%	185
Shanghai 上海市	Shanghai 上海市	5.64%	348
Foshan 佛山市	Guangdong 廣東省	4.51%	79
Shenzhen 深圳市	Guangdong 廣東省	2.60%	42
Tianjin 天津市	Tianjin 天津市	2.52%	227
Hangzhou 杭州市	Zhejiang 浙江省	2.08%	143
Dongguan 東莞市	Guangdong 廣東省	2.06%	70
Shaoxing 紹興市	Zhejiang 浙江省	1.99%	44
Suzhou 蘇州市	Jiangsu 江蘇省	1.90%	123

10 Major Wholesalers 10 家主要批發商	City 城市	Province 省	Telephone / Fax 電話 / 傳真
Shandong Stationary & Sporting Goods Import & Export Company 山東省文教體育用品進出口公司	Qingdao 青島市	Shandong 山東省	(0532)2826827 (0532)3831971
Henan Printing Goods & Materials General Company 河南省印刷物資總公司	Zhengzhou 鄭州市	Henan 河南省	(0371)5967060 (0371)5947912
China Packing Import & Export Singbo Company 中國包裝進出口寧波公司	Ningbo 寧波市	Zhejiang 浙江省	(0574)7367512 (0574)7361096
Tianjin Stationary & Sporting Goods Import & Export Company 天津文教體育用品進出口公司	Tianjin 天津市	Tianjin 天津市	(022)23112048 (022)23112054
China Packing Import & Export Liaoning Company 中國包裝進出口遼寧公司	Dalian 大連市	Liaoning 遼寧省	(0411)4687657 (0411)4687644
Hunan Printing Goods & Materials General Company 湖南省印刷物資總公司	Changsha 長沙市	Hunan 湖南省	(0731)4444618 (0731)4446936
Guangzhou Stationery Co. 廣州市文化用品公司	Guangzhou 廣州市	Guangdong 廣東省	(020)81889089 (020)81861964
Casio Electronics (Shenzhen) Co. Ltd. 卡西歐電子(深圳)有限公司	Shenzhen 深圳市	Guangdong 廣東省	(0755)3590620 (0755)3590565
Changsha Keven Group Co. 長沙市科文集團公司	Changsha 長沙市	Hunan 湖南省	(0731)4444108
Hunan Firecrackers Fireworks Import & Export Company 湖南省鞭炮煙花進出口公司	Changsha 長沙市	Hunan 湖南省	(0731)4439580

*Also include sales by firms outside this industry.包括本行業以外廠家的銷售。"o" stands for "others". "o" 代表 "其他產品"。

2311: Book, Newspaper, and Magazine Printing 書、報、刊印刷業

The industry accounts for 0.234% of the total revenue of China's industrial sector in 1996. The revenue growth rate of the industry is 23.5% from 1995, as compared to the growth rate of China's industrial sector, 9.51%. The rate of return on asset is 0.42%. 69.46% of all firms in the industry made a profit while 25.38% had negative returns. The top province in terms of the industry's revenue is Guangdong, accounting for 13.12% of the total revenue.
本行業在1996年佔全行業總產值0.234%，行業年增長率為23.5%（全國工業年增長率9.51%）。行業的資產回報率0.42%，69.46%的企業盈利，25.38%的企業虧損。銷售收入最高的省份為廣東省，佔本行業的13.12%。

	Total number of firms 企業總數	Total number of employees 職工總數	Total revenue (mil. RMB) 總銷售收入（百萬元）	Total profit (mil. RMB) 總利潤（百萬元）	Return on assets 資產利潤率 (%)	Return on equity 權益利潤率 (%)	Labour productivity ('000 RMB / worker) 勞動生產率（千元/人）	Debts / assets 資產負債率 (%)	Total assets (mil. RMB) 總資產（百萬元）
Industry Overall 行業總體	4,156	455,764	13,567	99	0.42	1.04	29.77	59.25	23,385

	Number of firms 企業個數	Average number of employees 平均職工人數	Average revenue ('000 RMB) 平均銷售收入（千元）	Average profit ('000 RMB) 平均利潤（千元）	Return on assets 資產利潤率 (%)	Return on equity 權益利潤率 (%)	Labour productivity ('000 RMB / worker) 勞動生產率（千元/人）	Average debts / assets 平均資產負債率(%)	Average Total assets ('000 RMB) 平均總資產（千元）
By ownership 產業所有權									
State-owned 國有	1,624	190	5,177	-18	-0.18	-0.42	27.20	58.28	10,490
Collectively-owned 集體	2,382	56	1,645	81	4.73	14.66	29.48	67.75	1,715
Privately-owned 私有	6	34	1,190	134	12.73	21.30	35.18	40.24	1,057
Domestic JVs 聯營	11	71	4,542	597	17.36	33.29	64.39	47.86	3,441
Joint stock 股份制	36	139	2,555	-169	-3.76	-12.62	18.35	70.16	4,490
Foreign-funded 外資	31	100	15,267	-3,406	-10.20	-22.42	152.37	54.49	33,375
Overseas Chinese-funded 港澳台資	60	70	10,048	653	3.87	7.09	143.75	45.33	16,857
By size 規模									
Large 大型	38	1,027	47,721	951	0.92	1.90	46.48	51.39	102,993
Medium 中型	140	576	19,819	489	1.14	2.39	34.43	52.20	42,769
Small 小型	3,967	85	2,263	-1	-0.04	-0.12	26.67	64.67	3,399
By regional distribution 地區分布									
Central-North 華北	795	109	2,810	43	0.71	1.44	25.78	50.53	6,036
Beijing 北京	268	111	3,788	127	1.26	2.04	34.18	38.39	10,109
Tianjin 天津	50	95	3,099	172	3.34	5.83	32.50	42.74	5,163
Hebei 河北	228	115	3,258	-5	-0.10	-0.35	28.25	70.69	5,135
Shanxi 山西	136	121	1,315	-24	-0.96	-2.82	10.86	65.86	2,511
Inner Mongolia 內蒙	113	83	1,258	-36	-1.29	-4.25	15.09	69.59	2,822
Northeast 東北	515	92	1,810	-28	-0.75	-2.03	19.69	62.96	3,680
Liaoning 遼寧	212	104	2,254	-6	-0.12	-0.29	21.75	60.46	4,817
Jilin 吉林	167	85	1,482	-106	-3.76	-15.05	17.44	75.04	2,815
Heilongjiang 黑龍江	136	82	1,522	34	1.13	2.52	18.49	55.22	2,968
Central East 華東	1,135	120	3,967	44	0.77	2.13	33.13	64.03	5,683
Shanghai 上海	98	127	4,717	191	2.73	5.12	37.08	46.65	6,991
Jiangsu 江蘇	241	153	4,117	-17	-0.35	-1.17	26.83	70.44	5,004
Zhejiang 浙江	193	67	3,115	88	1.90	4.42	46.28	56.89	4,596
Anhui 安徽	116	114	4,784	309	6.81	18.48	41.84	63.16	4,541
Fujian 福建	159	71	2,257	53	1.60	3.59	31.93	55.56	3,314
Jiangxi 江西	132	118	2,613	75	1.79	6.32	22.23	71.77	4,175
Shandong 山東	196	171	6,059	-184	-1.75	-5.71	35.51	69.43	10,545
Central-South 中南	1,072	100	3,935	37	0.62	1.68	39.47	63.07	5,940
Henan 河南	211	116	2,946	43	0.84	2.47	25.50	65.93	5,084
Hubei 湖北	233	110	3,226	47	0.95	3.33	29.27	71.38	4,881
Hunan 湖南	228	81	2,251	-13	-0.39	-0.93	27.65	58.68	3,290
Guangdong 廣東	211	99	8,439	127	1.07	2.78	84.98	61.35	11,795
Guangxi 廣西	149	92	2,961		0.01	0.02	32.03	60.77	4,412
Hainan 海南	40	88	2,754	-104	-1.59	-3.17	31.18	49.82	6,520
Southwest 西南	364	124	2,500	-26	-0.41	-0.82	20.14	49.68	6,225
Chongqing 重慶	48	167	1,810	-178	-3.34	-6.87	10.80	51.43	5,336
Sichuan 四川	180	136	2,744	-22	-0.47	-1.36	20.11	65.60	4,721
Guizhou 貴州	75	85	1,682	-51	-0.51	-0.74	19.85	30.90	9,986
Yunnan 雲南	55	106	3,275	108	1.62	3.46	31.03	53.10	6,675
Tibet 西藏	5	51	4,064	210	2.71	3.30	79.38	17.94	7,760
Northwest 西北	275	123	2,802	-3	-0.05	-0.12	22.80	60.06	5,850
Shaanxi 陝西	117	128	3,110	-39	-0.63	-1.95	24.27	67.62	6,242
Gansu 甘肅	52	142	2,827	44	0.73	1.61	19.87	54.77	6,051
Qinghai 青海	14	126	2,277	-63	-1.19	-3.03	18.11	60.73	5,282
Ningxia 寧夏	16	120	1,750	-91	-1.33	-4.28	14.54	68.81	6,793
Xinjiang 新疆	76	102	2,629	51	1.02	1.94	25.88	47.32	5,017

2311: Book, Newspaper, and Magazine Printing 書、報、刊印刷業

Year 年份	Number of firms 企業個數	Rate of change 每年變化 (%)	Number of employees 職工人數 (人)	Rate of change 每年變化 (%)	Total revenue (mil. RMB) 總銷售收入 (百萬元)	Rate of change 每年變化 (%)	Total profit (mil. RMB) 總利潤 (百萬元)	Rate of change 每年變化 (%)
1993	4,019		473,224		9,415		403	
1994	4,244	5.60%	459,884	-2.82%	9,205	-2.22%	53	-86.92%
1995	3,941	-7.14%	442,802	-3.72%	10,988	19.36%	70	33.14%
1996	4,156	5.46%	455,764	2.93%	13,567	23.47%	99	41.05%

3 Major products* 3 種主要產品 *	Output 產量	Sales volume 銷售量	Unit 單位
a) Monochrome Printed Product 單色印刷品	66,460	64,466	10,000 ream 萬令
b) Multichrome Printed Product 多色印刷品	130,496	123,971	10,000 ream 萬對開色令

Top 10 firms by revenue (year founded) 收入排名前 10 家企業 (創辦年份)	City 城市	Province 省	Telephone / fax 電話 / 傳真	Number of employees 職工人數	Ownership 產業所有權	Revenue ('000 RMB) 銷售收入 (千元)	Profit ('000 RMB) (rank) 利潤 (千元) (排名)	Total assets ('000 RMB) 總資產 (千元)	Major products 主要產品
Shenzhen Goodyear Enterprise Co. Ltd. 深圳嘉年實業股份有限公司(1983)	Shenzhen 深圳市	Guangdong 廣東省	(0755)3366233 (0755)3366267	449	Overseas Chinese-funded 港澳台資	213,168	19936(1)	236,655	b
State-owned Qingdao Ren Min Printing House 國營青島人民印刷廠(1956)	Qingdao 青島市	Shandong 山東省	(0532)4630577 (0532)4843510	1,050	State-owned 國有	136,943	582(148)	248,795	b
Zhejiang Printing Group Co. Ltd. 浙江印刷集團公司(1993)	Hangzhou 杭州市	Zhejiang 浙江省	(0571)5152032 (0571)5152032	982	State-owned 國有	117,647	2949(28)	219,513	a,b
Heze Xicheng Printing Factory 菏澤市西城印刷廠(1993)	Heze 菏澤市	Shandong 山東省		3,880	Collectively-owned 集體	115,000	9000(4)	40,000	o
Jiangxi Printing Co. 江西印刷集團公司(1952)	Nanchang 南昌市	Jiangxi 江西省	(0791)6223112 (0791)6222864	1,220	State-owned 國有	106,298	5522(7)	131,978	a,b
Hefei Science & Technology Commission Xiao Xing Printing Factory 合肥市科委曉星印刷廠(1979)	Hefei 合肥市	Anhui 安徽省	(0551)4841490	245	Collectively-owned 集體	96,400	16350(2)	8,980	a,b
Shenzhen Dang Na Li Xu Ri Printing Co. Ltd. 深圳當納利旭日印刷有限公司(1994)	Shenzhen 深圳市	Guangdong 廣東省	(0755)8892821 (0755)8892014	427	Foreign-funded 外資	95,458	-42103(1278)	251,712	b
Shannxi Printing House 陝西省印刷廠(1949)	Xi'an 西安市	Shaanxi 陝西省	(029)7322707 (029)7225237	1,221	State-owned 國有	91,189	64(571)	177,072	o
Shandong Heze Printing Factory 山東菏澤印刷廠(1952)	Heze 菏澤市	Shandong 山東省	(0530)5625612 (0530)5625713	2,240	State-owned 國有	86,111	-58535(1279)	186,071	b
Lufeng Donghai Color Printing Co. Ltd. 陸豐市東海彩印有限公司(1995)	Shanwei 汕尾市	Guangdong 廣東省	(0660)8821642	725	Collectively-owned 集體	83,280	5450(10)	6,830	o

Top 10 Cities by Production Output 產出排名前 10 位城市	Province 省	Market share 市場份額	Number of firms 企業個數
Beijing 北京市	Beijing 北京市	9.70%	238
Shanghai 上海市	Shanghai 上海市	4.89%	211
Guangzhou 廣州市	Guangdong 廣東省	3.34%	128
Hangzhou 杭州市	Zhejiang 浙江省	3.09%	100
Hefei 合肥市	Anhui 安徽省	2.85%	63
Xi'an 西安市	Shaanxi 陝西省	2.29%	77
Zhengzhou 鄭州市	Henan 河南省	2.00%	47
Shenyang 瀋陽市	Liaoning 遼寧省	1.79%	98
Chengdu 成都市	Sichuan 四川省	1.57%	102
Changchun 長春市	Jilin 吉林省	1.51%	99

10 Major Wholesalers 10 家主要批發商	City 城市	Province 省	Telephone / Fax 電話 / 傳真
Sichuan Xinhua Bookstore 四川省新華書店	Chengdu 成都市	Sichuan 四川省	(028)6627757 (028)6624760
Hebei Xinhua Bookstore 河北省新華書店	Shijiazhuang 石家莊市	Hebei 河北省	(0311)6048270
Zhejiang Xinhua Bookstore 浙江省新華書店	Hangzhou 杭州市	Zhejiang 浙江省	(0571)8088568 (0571)8066331
Anhui Xinhua Bookstore 安徽省新華書店	Hefei 合肥市	Anhui 安徽省	(0551)2640292
Jiangsu Xinhua Bookstore 江蘇省新華書店	Nanjing 南京市	Jiangsu 江蘇省	(025)2713234 (025)2213941
Hunan Xinhua Bookstore 湖南省新華書店	Changsha 長沙市	Hunan 湖南省	(0731)4432142 (0731)4415250
Fujian Xinhua Bookstore 福建省新華書店	Fuzhou 福州市	Fujian 福建省	(0591)7559404 (0591)7559404
Guangxi Xinhua Bookstore 廣西壯族自治區新華書店	Nanning 南寧市	Guangxi 廣西	(0771)5853442 (0771)5867011
Henan Xinhua Bookstore 河南省新華書店	Zhengzhou 鄭州市	Henan 河南省	(0371)6230424 (0371)6227350
Guangdong Xinhua Bookstore 廣東省新華書店	Guangzhou 廣州市	Guangdong 廣東省	(020)83837158 (020)83837287

*Also include sales by firms outside this industry.包括本行業以外廠家的銷售。"o" stands for "others". "o" 代表 "其他產品"。

2312: Packaging Printing 包裝裝潢印刷業

The industry accounts for 0.322% of the total revenue of China's industrial sector in 1996. The revenue growth rate of the industry is 25.6% from 1995, as compared to the growth rate of China's industrial sector, 9.51%. The rate of return on asset is 3.28%. 67.64% of all firms in the industry made a profit while 24.93% had negative returns. The top province in terms of the industry's revenue is Guangdong, accounting for 17.41% of the total revenue.
本行業在1996年佔全行業總產值0.322%，行業年增長率為25.6%（全國工業年增長率9.51%）。行業的資產回報率3.28%，67.64%的企業盈利，24.93%的企業虧損。銷售收入最高的省份為廣東省，佔本行業的17.41%。

	Total number of firms 企業總數	Total number of employees 職工總數	Total revenue (mil. RMB) 總銷售收入（百萬元）	Total profit (mil. RMB) 總利潤（百萬元）	Return on assets 資產利潤率 (%)	Return on equity 權益利潤率 (%)	Labour productivity ('000 RMB / worker) 勞動生產率（千元/人）	Debts / assets 資產負債率 (%)	Total assets (mil. RMB) 總資產（百萬元）
Industry Overall 行業總體	2,508	249,114	18,664	914	3.28	8.92	74.92	63.19	27,823

	Number of firms 企業個數	Average number of employees 平均職工人數	Average revenue ('000 RMB) 平均銷售收入（千元）	Average profit ('000 RMB) 平均利潤（千元）	Return on assets 資產利潤率 (%)	Return on equity 權益利潤率 (%)	Labour productivity ('000 RMB / worker) 勞動生產率（千元/人）	Average debts / assets 平均資產負債率(%)	Average Total assets ('000 RMB) 平均總資產（千元）
By ownership 產業所有權									
State-owned 國有	442	217	10,787	143	0.63	2.14	49.62	70.35	22,493
Collectively-owned 集體	1,638	68	4,805	233	4.90	16.01	70.21	69.38	4,751
Privately-owned 私有	17	47	4,194	-111	-1.60	-8.95	88.36	82.17	6,930
Domestic JVs 聯營	26	124	10,368	-40	-0.23	-0.53	83.58	55.78	17,171
Joint stock 股份制	46	207	21,820	3,105	7.12	14.32	105.32	50.31	43,633
Foreign-funded 外資	125	88	16,413	1,620	6.02	11.58	186.09	48.02	26,909
Overseas Chinese-funded 港澳台資	209	86	12,586	598	3.02	6.47	145.52	53.31	19,819
By size 規模									
Large 大型	32	733	97,847	14,577	9.09	18.70	133.55	51.41	160,378
Medium 中型	127	420	33,189	1,491	2.51	7.68	79.10	67.30	59,381
Small 小型	2,294	75	4,979	113	1.70	4.89	66.41	65.13	6,603
By regional distribution 地區分布									
Central-North 華北	241	107	5,350	281	2.58	6.18	49.94	58.16	10,865
Beijing 北京	65	77	6,514	101	0.70	1.36	84.33	48.79	14,443
Tianjin 天津	64	122	5,245	897	6.97	16.85	43.13	58.61	12,870
Hebei 河北	75	103	5,681	111	1.30	4.00	55.30	67.42	8,498
Shanxi 山西	14	273	5,062	-260	-2.28	-7.14	18.54	68.09	11,412
Inner Mongolia 內蒙	23	65	1,443	-42	-1.65	-6.32	22.33	73.90	2,557
Northeast 東北	240	93	3,714	99	1.32	4.24	39.78	68.95	7,550
Liaoning 遼寧	113	99	5,881	525	4.39	12.82	59.19	65.74	11,953
Jilin 吉林	57	98	2,215	-202	-3.87	-16.31	22.68	76.24	5,212
Heilongjiang 黑龍江	70	80	1,438	-342	-14.57	-81.46	17.93	82.12	2,347
Central East 華東	1,044	90	7,648	391	3.71	9.51	84.88	60.98	10,541
Shanghai 上海	146	98	10,101	485	2.74	6.30	102.68	56.57	17,737
Jiangsu 江蘇	234	117	11,920	879	6.86	18.00	101.93	61.88	12,817
Zhejiang 浙江	264	58	4,588	141	2.33	5.57	79.30	58.27	6,064
Anhui 安徽	49	93	5,600	196	4.39	25.55	60.25	82.82	4,473
Fujian 福建	143	48	4,099	208	2.71	6.05	85.90	55.22	7,679
Jiangxi 江西	73	65	1,553	-61	-1.47	-3.82	23.91	61.60	4,151
Shandong 山東	135	155	11,374	441	2.71	8.35	73.31	67.52	16,256
Central-South 中南	643	108	8,409	315	2.52	7.17	77.64	64.89	12,508
Henan 河南	164	94	4,368	192	3.46	10.09	46.71	65.71	5,545
Hubei 湖北	104	118	5,690	229	2.10	4.63	48.20	54.73	10,929
Hunan 湖南	107	102	6,021	-3	-0.04	-0.10	59.18	59.91	7,792
Guangdong 廣東	222	123	14,635	728	3.44	10.41	119.14	66.97	21,160
Guangxi 廣西	44	85	4,499	-263	-2.76	-11.94	52.88	76.92	9,530
Hainan 海南	2	65	3,710	-1,185	-5.15	-15.53	57.08	66.83	23,020
Southwest 西南	268	109	10,139	816	6.19	18.17	92.74	65.92	13,174
Chongqing 重慶	51	113	6,040	-23	-0.29	-1.42	53.10	79.68	8,054
Sichuan 四川	124	99	5,143	203	2.77	8.07	51.44	65.61	7,329
Guizhou 貴州	37	71	5,086	40	0.53	1.77	71.42	69.91	7,502
Yunnan 雲南	55	151	28,689	3,511	10.03	26.76	190.29	62.52	35,017
Tibet 西藏									
Northwest 西北	72	109	5,198	-104	-0.92	-2.87	47.50	67.97	11,316
Shaanxi 陝西	41	122	7,490	27	0.17	0.46	61.62	63.11	15,712
Gansu 甘肅	14	87	1,540	-46	-1.18	-2.93	17.61	59.78	3,942
Qinghai 青海									
Ningxia 寧夏	7	117	2,711	-694	-7.64	118.83	23.09	106.43	9,083
Xinjiang 新疆	10	85	2,661	-307	-5.92	-58.93	31.31	89.93	5,182

2312: Packaging Printing 包裝裝潢印刷業

Year 年份	Number of firms 企業個數	Rate of change 每年變化 (%)	Number of employees 職工人數 (人)	Rate of change 每年變化 (%)	Total revenue (mil. RMB) 總銷售收入 (百萬元)	Rate of change 每年變化 (%)	Total profit (mil. RMB) 總利潤 (百萬元)	Rate of change 每年變化 (%)
1993	2,025		258,445		9,656		519	
1994	2,293	13.23%	225,790	-12.64%	11,427	18.34%	422	-18.65%
1995	2,388	4.14%	261,253	15.71%	14,860	30.05%	344	-18.64%
1996	2,508	5.03%	249,114	-4.65%	18,664	25.60%	914	166.00%

3 Major products* 3 種主要產品 *	Output 產量	Sales volume 銷售量	Unit 單位
a) Multichrome Printed Product 多色印刷品	125,240	118,978	10,000 ream 萬對開色令

Top 10 firms by revenue (year founded) 收入排名前 10 家企業 (創辦年份)	City 城市	Province 省	Telephone / fax 電話 / 傳真	Number of employees 職工人數	Ownership 產業所有權	Revenue ('000 RMB) 銷售收入 (千元)	Profit ('000 RMB) (rank) 利潤 (千元) (排名)	Total assets ('000 RMB) 總資產 (千元)	Major products 主要產品
Dalian Sheng Dao Group Co. Ltd. 大連盛道集團有限公司(1995)	Dalian 大連市	Liaoning 遼寧省	(0411)3672193 (0411)2687794	2,330	State-owned 國有	399,065	54651(3)	981,094	o
Shenzhen Jiu Xing Printing & Package Center 深圳九星印刷包裝中心(1990)	Shenzhen 深圳市	Guangdong 廣東省	(0755)3354806 (0755)3345970	372	Overseas Chinese-funded 港澳台資	350,432	15116(19)	251,116	o
Jiangsu Lian Tong Group Corp. 江蘇聯通集團公司(1994)	Wuxi 無錫市	Jiangsu 江蘇省	(0510)6885441 (0510)6886013	1,105	Collectively-owned 集體	342,660	49139(6)	372,429	a
Shandou Shengping Ji Xiang Industry General Company 汕頭市升平區吉祥工業總公司(1984)	Shantou 汕頭市	Guangdong 廣東省	(0754)8273387	2,620	Collectively-owned 集體	292,000	7880(36)	76,760	a
Yuxi Globle Colour Printing Paper Carton Co. Ltd. 玉溪環球印紙盒有限公司(1994)	Yuxi 玉溪市	Yunnan 雲南省	(0877)2051818 (0877)2052288	305	Foreign-funded 外資	290,114	79151(1)	258,351	a
Shanghai No.8 Ren Min Printing House 上海人民印刷八廠(1932)	Shanghai 上海市	Shanghai 上海市	(021)63260670 (021)63202997	1,256	State-owned 國有	210,350	11131(24)	329,218	a
Zhongshan Hong Xing Printing & Packing Co. Ltd. 中山鴻興印刷包裝有限公司(1992)	Zhongshan 中山市	Guangdong 廣東省	(0760)5597288 (0760)5597882	480	Foreign-funded 外資	205,272	30920(8)	184,270	a
Dongguan Xinzhou Printing Co. Ltd. 東莞新洲印刷有限公司(1992)	Dongguan 東莞市	Guangdong 廣東省	(0769)3354419 (0769)3351422	650	Overseas Chinese-funded 港澳台資	191,645	15331(18)	163,537	o
Qingdao Li Ma Dun Packing Co. Ltd. 青島黎馬敦包裝有限公司(1995)	Qingdao 青島市	Shandong 山東省	(0532)4854279 (0532)4854279	224	Foreign-funded 外資	182,312	27477(10)	269,186	o
Shanghai Embossing Color Printing General Corp. 上海凹凸彩印廠(1933)	Shanghai 上海市	Shanghai 上海市	(021)63201920 (021)63201922	1,127	State-owned 國有	170,417	9457(26)	368,223	a

Top 10 Cities by Production Output 產出排名前 10 位城市	Province 省	Market share 市場份額	Number of firms 企業個數
Shanghai 上海市	Shanghai 上海市	10.73%	291
Wuxi 無錫市	Jiangsu 江蘇省	6.94%	153
Dalian 大連市	Liaoning 遼寧省	4.52%	17
Wenzhou 温州市	Zhejiang 浙江省	2.97%	201
Guangzhou 廣州市	Guangdong 廣東省	2.92%	116
Yuxi 玉溪市	Yunnan 雲南省	2.84%	9
Chengdu 成都市	Sichuan 四川省	2.68%	75
Foshan 佛山市	Guangdong 廣東省	2.59%	25
Shantou 汕頭市	Guangdong 廣東省	2.28%	61
Tianjin 天津市	Tianjin 天津市	2.27%	68

10 Major Wholesalers 10 家主要批發商	City 城市	Province 省	Telephone / Fax 電話 / 傳真
Sichuan Xinhua Bookstore 四川省新華書店	Chengdu 成都市	Sichuan 四川省	(028)6627757 (028)6624760
Hebei Xinhua Bookstore 河北省新華書店	Shijiazhuang 石家莊市	Hebei 河北省	(0311)6048270
Zhejiang Xinhua Bookstore 浙江省新華書店	Hangzhou 杭州市	Zhejiang 浙江省	(0571)8088568 (0571)8066331
Anhui Xinhua Bookstore 安徽省新華書店	Hefei 合肥市	Anhui 安徽省	(0551)2640292
Jiangsu Xinhua Bookstore 江蘇省新華書店	Nanjing 南京市	Jiangsu 江蘇省	(025)2713234 (025)2213941
Hunan Xinhua Bookstore 湖南省新華書店	Changsha 長沙市	Hunan 湖南省	(0731)4432142 (0731)4415250
Fujian Xinhua Bookstore 福建省新華書店	Fuzhou 福州市	Fujian 福建省	(0591)7559404 (0591)7559404
Guangxi Xinhua Bookstore 廣西壯族自治區新華書店	Nanning 南寧市	Guangxi 廣西	(0771)5853442 (0771)5867011
Henan Xinhua Bookstore 河南省新華書店	Zhengzhou 鄭州市	Henan 河南省	(0371)6230424 (0371)6227350
Guangdong Xinhua Bookstore 廣東省新華書店	Guangzhou 廣州市	Guangdong 廣東省	(020)83837158 (020)83837287

*Also include sales by firms outside this industry.包括本行業以外廠家的銷售。"o" stands for "others". "o" 代表 "其他產品" 。

2319: Other Printing Industries 其他印刷業

The industry accounts for 0.237% of the total revenue of China's industrial sector in 1996. The revenue growth rate of the industry is 16.5% from 1995, as compared to the growth rate of China's industrial sector, 9.51%. The rate of return on asset is 5.65%. 70.28% of all firms in the industry made a profit while 22.97% had negative returns. The top province in terms of the industry's revenue is Guangdong, accounting for 10.45% of the total revenue.
本行業在1996年佔全行業總產值0.237%，行業年增長率為16.5%（全國工業年增長率9.51%）。行業的資產回報率5.65%，70.28%的企業盈利，22.97%的企業虧損。銷售收入最高的省份為廣東省，佔本行業的10.45%。

	Total number of firms 企業總數	Total number of employees 職工總數	Total revenue (mil. RMB) 總銷售收入（百萬元）	Total profit (mil. RMB) 總利潤（百萬元）	Return on assets 資產利潤率 (%)	Return on equity 權益利潤率 (%)	Labour productivity ('000 RMB / worker) 勞動生產率（千元/人）	Debts / assets 資產負債率 (%)	Total assets (mil. RMB) 總資產（百萬元）
Industry Overall 行業總體	8,614	385,285	13,713	1,012	5.65	13.59	35.59	58.45	17,933

	Number of firms 企業個數	Average number of employees 平均職工人數	Average revenue ('000 RMB) 平均銷售收入（千元）	Average profit ('000 RMB) 平均利潤（千元）	Return on assets 資產利潤率 (%)	Return on equity 權益利潤率 (%)	Labour productivity ('000 RMB / worker) 勞動生產率（千元/人）	Average debts / assets 平均資產負債率(%)	Average Total assets ('000 RMB) 平均總資產（千元）
By ownership 產業所有權									
State-owned 國有	1,509	93	2,827	214	4.21	10.04	30.55	58.04	5,083
Collectively-owned 集體	6,693	34	1,112	77	7.48	22.60	33.05	66.89	1,034
Privately-owned 私有	22	18	1,689	54	6.50	22.29	92.68	70.82	833
Domestic JVs 聯營	36	66	3,326	373	7.72	14.62	50.25	47.23	4,838
Joint stock 股份制	34	82	3,735	391	9.31	20.14	45.73	53.76	4,195
Foreign-funded 外資	114	45	4,497	996	10.91	18.72	99.24	41.74	9,130
Overseas Chinese-funded 港澳台資	195	55	6,155	150	1.50	2.51	111.97	40.28	10,033
By size 規模									
Large 大型	12	1,404	179,103	48,584	14.62	29.96	127.60	51.21	332,321
Medium 中型	20	417	26,973	2,363	4.48	12.69	64.62	64.71	52,751
Small 小型	8,544	42	1,290	45	2.96	7.44	30.56	60.18	1,508
By regional distribution 地區分布									
Central-North 華北	1,156	43	1,817	163	5.50	11.59	42.52	52.57	2,960
Beijing 北京	296	47	3,796	341	4.91	10.08	80.82	51.29	6,946
Tianjin 天津	176	26	736	55	7.59	16.79	28.00	54.80	725
Hebei 河北	250	48	2,378	232	7.99	20.45	49.10	60.95	2,899
Shanxi 山西	176	68	873	98	4.93	7.97	12.77	38.16	1,995
Inner Mongolia 內蒙	258	26	383	9	1.39	3.56	14.72	60.84	628
Northeast 東北	1,626	49	802	9	0.87	2.78	16.44	68.59	1,055
Liaoning 遼寧	720	43	906	27	2.47	6.56	20.89	62.32	1,091
Jilin 吉林	478	42	597	-27	-2.43	-11.47	14.34	78.78	1,112
Heilongjiang 黑龍江	428	66	856	20	2.13	6.53	12.99	67.37	932
Central East 華東	2,705	41	1,925	239	11.33	27.84	46.96	59.29	2,109
Shanghai 上海	322	53	3,493	424	9.74	20.20	66.00	51.81	4,351
Jiangsu 江蘇	549	46	2,245	63	2.87	9.53	49.07	69.93	2,201
Zhejiang 浙江	476	33	1,927	78	3.87	9.01	59.16	57.03	2,025
Anhui 安徽	325	46	1,391	1,083	99.05	264.35	29.96	62.53	1,093
Fujian 福建	350	30	1,302	23	1.78	3.47	43.83	48.54	1,299
Jiangxi 江西	312	34	1,194	168	9.81	17.57	34.70	44.15	1,709
Shandong 山東	371	46	1,756	70	3.28	12.62	38.39	74.01	2,126
Central-South 中南	1,634	45	1,871	2	0.07	0.19	42.00	62.69	2,449
Henan 河南	404	41	1,135	27	1.71	6.17	27.90	72.28	1,586
Hubei 湖北	245	40	1,585	13	1.00	3.72	40.12	73.22	1,270
Hunan 湖南	389	47	1,309	-18	-1.33	-4.74	27.72	71.86	1,346
Guangdong 廣東	416	51	3,446	19	0.37	0.82	67.66	54.51	4,963
Guangxi 廣西	172	39	1,453	-72	-2.89	-9.87	36.81	70.69	2,502
Hainan 海南	8	43	2,259	53	1.33	2.14	53.15	37.83	3,955
Southwest 西南	987	36	1,194	29	1.37	3.05	32.84	54.94	2,109
Chongqing 重慶	223	33	903	-1,315	-106.77	-419.35	27.32	74.54	1,231
Sichuan 四川	414	40	1,461	630	20.30	38.73	35.94	47.59	3,106
Guizhou 貴州	199	29	1,129	-15	-1.17	-2.90	38.51	59.78	1,276
Yunnan 雲南	148	37	982	-1	-0.05	-0.15	26.63	65.78	1,785
Tibet 西藏	2	8	115				14.38	39.13	115
Northwest 西北	506	73	1,714	260	13.06	24.50	23.42	46.71	1,989
Shaanxi 陝西	239	117	2,874	535	17.52	30.59	24.48	42.71	3,051
Gansu 甘肅	103	42	646	-3	-0.22	-0.54	15.53	59.23	1,330
Qinghai 青海	29	34	662	19	1.72	4.27	19.33	59.64	1,100
Ningxia 寧夏	22	31	511	6	0.92	1.82	16.28	49.29	642
Xinjiang 新疆	113	27	739	28	3.42	7.57	27.81	54.76	832

2319: Other Printing Industries 其他印刷業

Year 年份	Number of firms 企業個數	Rate of change 每年變化 (%)	Number of employees 職工人數 (人)	Rate of change 每年變化 (%)	Total revenue (mil. RMB) 總銷售收入 (百萬元)	Rate of change 每年變化 (%)	Total profit (mil. RMB) 總利潤 (百萬元)	Rate of change 每年變化 (%)
1993	7,018		517,165		8,363		659	
1994	7,312	4.19%	373,599	-27.76%	9,823	17.45%	507	-22.97%
1995	9,006	23.17%	394,626	5.63%	11,770	19.83%	437	-13.95%
1996	8,614	-4.35%	385,285	-2.37%	13,713	16.51%	1,012	131.84%

3 Major products* 3 種主要產品 *	Output 產量	Sales volume 銷售量	Unit 單位
a) Multichrome Printed Product 多色印刷品	26,083	24,778	10,000 ream 萬對開色令

Top 10 firms by revenue (year founded) 收入排名前 10 家企業 (創辦年份)	City 城市	Province 省	Telephone / fax 電話 / 傳真	Number of employees 職工人數	Ownership 產業所有權	Revenue ('000 RMB) 銷售收入 (千元)	Profit ('000 RMB) (rank) 利潤 (千元) (排名)	Total assets ('000 RMB) 總資產 (千元)	Major products 主要產品
Xi'an Printing Paper Money Factory 西安印鈔廠(1952)	Xi'an 西安市	Shaanxi 陝西省	(029)4262320 (029)4262066	2,279	State-owned 國有	409,167	102784(2)	400,925	o
Shanghai Printing Paper Money Factory 上海印鈔廠(1941)	Shanghai 上海市	Shanghai 上海市	(021)62440542 (021)62440060	2,669	State-owned 國有	400,346	88177(3)	565,395	o
Chengdu Printing Paper Money Company 成都印鈔公司(1970)	Chengdu 成都市	Sichuan 四川省	(028)2722138 (028)2722138	3,024	State-owned 國有	255,078	38450(5)	927,077	o
Nanchang Printing Paper Money Factory 南昌印鈔廠(1990)	Nanchang 南昌市	Jiangxi 江西省	(0791)5233154 (0791)5232461	1,079	State-owned 國有	210,571	48573(4)	274,753	o
Shijiazhuang Printing Paper Money Factory 石家莊印鈔廠(1988)	Shijiazhuang 石家莊市	Hebei 河北省	(0311)5051875 (0311)5052872	1,173	State-owned 國有	195,129	36532(6)	323,164	o
Kunshan Zhang Pu Color Printing House 昆山市張浦彩印廠(1977)	Suzhou 蘇州市	Jiangsu 江蘇省	(0512)7441723 (0512)7441009	236	Collectively-owned 集體	152,468	14889(11)	129,128	o
Baoding Geology Picture Printing & Making Factory 保定地質圖製印廠(1939)	Baoding 保定市	Hebei 河北省	(0312)3135971 (0312)3137480	1,118	State-owned 國有	139,707	11076(13)	108,398	o
Shanghai Zi Hua Bai Mao Color Printing Co. Ltd. 上海紫華白貓彩印有限公司(1995)	Shanghai 上海市	Shanghai 上海市	(021)64891997 (021)64891799	374	Overseas Chinese-funded 港澳台資	120,037	20229(9)	188,925	o
Dongguan Hu Men Color Printing Co. Ltd. 東莞市虎門彩色印刷有限公司(1988)	Dongguan 東莞市	Guangdong 廣東省	(0769)5513189 (0769)5514119	395	Overseas Chinese-funded 港澳台資	117,962	2540(38)	129,775	a
Sichuan Printing & Making Plate Center 四川省印刷製版中心(1956)	Chengdu 成都市	Sichuan 四川省	(028)3972895	489	State-owned 國有	102,174	2321(40)	167,955	a

Top 10 Cities by Production Output 產出排名前 10 位城市	Province 省	Market share 市場份額	Number of firms 企業個數
Shanghai 上海市	Shanghai 上海市	10.19%	520
Beijing 北京市	Beijing 北京市	6.95%	265
Wenzhou 溫州市	Zhejiang 浙江省	5.68%	343
Shenzhen 深圳市	Guangdong 廣東省	4.11%	51
Xi'an 西安市	Shaanxi 陝西省	4.03%	93
Chengdu 成都市	Sichuan 四川省	3.61%	154
Suzhou 蘇州市	Jiangsu 江蘇省	3.43%	226
Guangzhou 廣州市	Guangdong 廣東省	2.76%	459
Nanchang 南昌市	Jiangxi 江西省	2.06%	55
Shijiazhuang 石家莊市	Hebei 河北省	2.01%	29

10 Major Wholesalers 10 家主要批發商	City 城市	Province 省	Telephone / Fax 電話 / 傳真
Sichuan Xinhua Bookstore 四川省新華書店	Chengdu 成都市	Sichuan 四川省	(028)6627757 (028)6624760
Hebei Xinhua Bookstore 河北省新華書店	Shijiazhuang 石家莊市	Hebei 河北省	(0311)6048270
Zhejiang Xinhua Bookstore 浙江省新華書店	Hangzhou 杭州市	Zhejiang 浙江省	(0571)8088568 (0571)8066331
Anhui Xinhua Bookstore 安徽省新華書店	Hefei 合肥市	Anhui 安徽省	(0551)2640292
Jiangsu Xinhua Bookstore 江蘇省新華書店	Nanjing 南京市	Jiangsu 江蘇省	(025)2713234 (025)2213941
Hunan Xinhua Bookstore 湖南省新華書店	Changsha 長沙市	Hunan 湖南省	(0731)4432142 (0731)4415250
Fujian Xinhua Bookstore 福建省新華書店	Fuzhou 福州市	Fujian 福建省	(0591)7559404 (0591)7559404
Guangxi Xinhua Bookstore 廣西壯族自治區新華書店	Nanning 南寧市	Guangxi 廣西	(0771)5853442 (0771)5867011
Henan Xinhua Bookstore 河南省新華書店	Zhengzhou 鄭州市	Henan 河南省	(0371)6230424 (0371)6227350
Guangdong Xinhua Bookstore 廣東省新華書店	Guangzhou 廣州市	Guangdong 廣東省	(020)83837158 (020)83837287

*Also include sales by firms outside this industry.包括本行業以外廠家的銷售。"o" stands for "others". "o" 代表"其他產品"。

2320: Recording Media Duplicating 記錄媒介的複製

The industry accounts for 0.020% of the total revenue of China's industrial sector in 1996. The revenue growth rate of the industry is 5.4% from 1995, as compared to the growth rate of China's industrial sector, 9.51%. The rate of return on asset is 3.35%. 69.14% of all firms in the industry made a profit while 28.42% had negative returns. The top province in terms of the industry's revenue is Guangdong, accounting for 60.22% of the total revenue.
本行業在1996年佔全行業總產值0.020%，行業年增長率為5.4%（全國工業年增長率9.51%）。行業的資產回報率3.35%，69.14%的企業盈利，28.42%的企業虧損。銷售收入最高的省份為廣東省，佔本行業的60.22%。

	Total number of firms 企業總數	Total number of employees 職工總數	Total revenue (mil. RMB) 總銷售收入（百萬元）	Total profit (mil. RMB) 總利潤（百萬元）	Return on assets 資產利潤率 (%)	Return on equity 權益利潤率 (%)	Labour productivity ('000 RMB / worker) 勞動生產率（千元/人）	Debts / assets 資產負債率 (%)	Total assets (mil. RMB) 總資產（百萬元）
Industry Overall 行業總體	100	9,885	1,139	84	3.35	7.75	115.23	56.69	2,501

	Number of firms 企業個數	Average number of employees 平均職工人數	Average revenue ('000 RMB) 平均銷售收入（千元）	Average profit ('000 RMB) 平均利潤（千元）	Return on assets 資產利潤率 (%)	Return on equity 權益利潤率 (%)	Labour productivity ('000 RMB / worker) 勞動生產率（千元/人）	Average debts / assets 平均資產負債率(%)	Average Total assets ('000 RMB) 平均總資產（千元）
By ownership 產業所有權									
State-owned 國有	21	259	21,762	1,905	4.98	9.78	83.96	49.07	38,238
Collectively-owned 集體	32	51	1,787	-40	-1.20	-5.65	35.38	78.81	3,361
Privately-owned 私有									
Domestic JVs 聯營	1	9	646	10	0.65	0.76	71.80	14.71	1,547
Joint stock 股份制									
Foreign-funded 外資	17	62	20,415	2,636	4.53	10.41	328.04	56.46	58,190
Overseas Chinese-funded 港澳台資	30	62	9,246	15	0.08	0.21	148.17	63.45	20,014
By size 規模									
Large 大型	2	619	80,616	7,364	2.55	7.58	130.24	66.42	289,282
Medium 中型	6	232	45,058	3,611	3.90	8.40	193.94	53.60	92,688
Small 小型	88	83	8,042	541	3.48	7.54	96.34	53.84	15,536
By regional distribution 地區分布									
Central-North 華北	22	75	5,505	170	1.30	2.25	73.84	42.15	13,104
Beijing 北京	16	65	4,330	96	0.70	1.05	66.36	33.26	13,766
Tianjin 天津	4	84	9,310	453	3.02	10.86	110.50	72.13	14,965
Hebei 河北	1	214	14,280	490	9.70	15.36	66.73	36.83	5,050
Shanxi 山西	1	45	300	-90	-2.88	112.50	6.67	102.56	3,120
Inner Mongolia 內蒙									
Northeast 東北	10	85	1,031	-165	-3.35	-21.21	12.09	84.20	4,925
Liaoning 遼寧	3	88	1,077	-90	-2.56	-18.00	12.19	85.78	3,517
Jilin 吉林	4	136	1,678	-335	-4.46	-30.59	12.33	85.43	7,515
Heilongjiang 黑龍江	3	15	123	-13	-0.46	-2.11	8.41	78.01	2,880
Central East 華東	16	162	16,804	383	1.30	3.12	103.49	58.27	29,394
Shanghai 上海	3	360	29,453	1,420	2.48	3.11	81.89	20.39	57,360
Jiangsu 江蘇	1	48	5,470	-570	-9.25	1900.00	113.96	100.49	6,160
Zhejiang 浙江	4	29	1,488	-23	-0.76	-1.73	50.85	55.86	2,945
Anhui 安徽	2	17	880	20	1.68	3.54	53.33	52.52	1,190
Fujian 福建	4	296	40,383	635	0.96	5.58	136.66	82.73	65,915
Jiangxi 江西									
Shandong 山東	2	70	2,895	-25	-0.35	-0.67	41.65	47.89	7,120
Central-South 中南	44	93	16,410	1,795	4.86	11.48	175.68	57.64	36,910
Henan 河南	1	200	30,000	-120	-0.32	-0.47	150.00	32.69	37,630
Hubei 湖北	3	53	1,770	7	0.21	0.30	33.19	30.47	3,217
Hunan 湖南									
Guangdong 廣東	39	96	17,588	2,025	5.01	12.05	182.92	58.39	40,391
Guangxi 廣西	1		780	120	7.95	40.00		80.13	1,510
Hainan 海南									
Southwest 西南	3	193	4,523	-1,107	-5.03	-14.61	23.44	65.55	21,993
Chongqing 重慶									
Sichuan 四川	3	193	4,523	-1,107	-5.03	-14.61	23.44	65.55	21,993
Guizhou 貴州									
Yunnan 雲南									
Tibet 西藏									
Northwest 西北	5	21	626	2	0.37	0.67	29.81	45.39	542
Shaanxi 陝西	5	21	626	2	0.37	0.67	29.81	45.39	542
Gansu 甘肅									
Qinghai 青海									
Ningxia 寧夏									
Xinjiang 新疆									

2320: Recording Media Duplicating 記錄媒介的複製

Year 年份	Number of firms 企業個數	Rate of change 每年變化 (%)	Number of employees 職工人數 (人)	Rate of change 每年變化 (%)	Total revenue (mil. RMB) 總銷售收入 (百萬元)	Rate of change 每年變化 (%)	Total profit (mil. RMB) 總利潤 (百萬元)	Rate of change 每年變化 (%)
1993	89		16,021		596		12	
1994	96	7.87%	10,629	-33.66%	631	5.85%	25	110.94%
1995	102	6.25%	10,673	0.41%	1,081	71.47%	64	151.82%
1996	100	-1.96%	9,885	-7.38%	1,139	5.37%	84	32.02%

3 Major products* 3 種主要產品 *	Output 產量	Sales volume 銷售量	Unit 單位
a) Laser Disc 激光盤	42,035,657	36,991,378	piece 片
b) Video Tape 像帶	13,169,873	11,062,693	box 盒

Top 10 firms by revenue (year founded) 收入排名前 10 家企業 (創辦年份)	City 城市	Province 省	Telephone / fax 電話 / 傳真	Number of employees 職工人數	Ownership 產業所有權	Revenue ('000 RMB) 銷售收入 (千元)	Profit ('000 RMB) (rank) 利潤 (千元) (排名)	Total assets ('000 RMB) 總資產 (千元)	Major products 主要產品
Foshan Nan Fang Electronic Audiovideo Co. 佛山市南方電子音像公司(1975)	Foshan 佛山市	Guangdong 廣東省	(0757)2810411 (0757)2812575	384	State-owned 國有	166,450	36046(1)	235,349	a,b
Indesen (Fujian) Magnetic Co. Ltd. 永德信(福建)磁帶有限公司(1991)	Fuzhou 福州市	Fujian 福建省	(0591)5380178 (0591)5380176	308	Overseas Chinese-funded 港澳台資	128,852	2429(7)	220,037	o
Foshan Jin Sheng Electronics Co. Ltd. 佛山金聲電子有限公司(1993)	Foshan 佛山市	Guangdong 廣東省	(0757)2212770 (0757)2212770	230	Overseas Chinese-funded 港澳台資	97,540	24310(2)	291,050	a
Meizhou Radio Factory Huiyang Branch 梅州市無線電廠惠陽分廠(1992)	Huizhou 惠州市	Guangdong 廣東省	(0751)3361646	735	State-owned 國有	79,600	7525(4)	39,779	o
China Record Shanghai Corp. 中國唱片上海公司(1952)	Shanghai 上海市	Shanghai 上海市	(021)64724470 (021)64724814	988	State-owned 國有	67,394	1074(10)	114,092	o
Shenzhen Shen Fei Laser Optical System Co. Ltd. 深圳深飛激光光學系統有限公司(1988)	Shenzhen 深圳市	Guangdong 廣東省	(0755)2260482 (0755)2264423	310	Foreign-funded 外資	60,224	1673(9)	500,507	a
Guangzhou Yong Tong Audiovisual Making Co. Ltd. 廣州永通音像製作有限公司(1991)	Guangzhou 廣州市	Guangdong 廣東省	(020)84879406 (020)84870470	93	Overseas Chinese-funded 港澳台資	40,486	2778(6)	68,568	a
Nanhai Ming Zhu Audio and Video Company 南海市明珠影音公司(1985)	Foshan 佛山市	Guangdong 廣東省	(0757)6332889 (0757)6220000	171	Overseas Chinese-funded 港澳台資	31,975	77(22)	35,222	a
Zhengzhou Mai Di Ya Record Technology Co. Ltd. 鄭州麥迪亞記錄技術有限公司(1996)	Zhengzhou 鄭州市	Henan 河南省	(0371)7981710 (0371)7981433	238	Foreign-funded 外資	30,000	-117(31)	37,634	o
Xinhui Pei Si Photoelectricity Co. Ltd. 新會佩斯光電有限公司(1993)	Jiangmen 江門市	Guangdong 廣東省	(0750)6698218 (0750)6693629	48	Overseas Chinese-funded 港澳台資	29,430	16504(3)	72,104	a

Top 10 Cities by Production Output 產出排名前 10 位城市	Province 省	Market share 市場份額	Number of firms 企業個數
Jiangmen 江門市	Guangdong 廣東省	23.02%	1
Foshan 佛山市	Guangdong 廣東省	22.80%	7
Huizhou 惠州市	Guangdong 廣東省	9.97%	9
Shanghai 上海市	Shanghai 上海市	7.65%	11
Shenzhen 深圳市	Guangdong 廣東省	6.60%	7
Guangzhou 廣州市	Guangdong 廣東省	6.37%	11
Beijing 北京市	Beijing 北京市	4.54%	16
Hangzhou 杭州市	Zhejiang 浙江省	2.65%	3
Fuzhou 福州市	Fujian 福建省	2.61%	3
Tianjin 天津市	Tianjin 天津市	2.55%	6

10 Major Wholesalers 10 家主要批發商	City 城市	Province 省	Telephone / Fax 電話 / 傳真
Sichuan Xinhua Bookstore 四川省新華書店	Chengdu 成都市	Sichuan 四川省	(028)6627757 (028)6624760
Hebei Xinhua Bookstore 河北省新華書店	Shijiazhuang 石家莊市	Hebei 河北省	(0311)6048270
Zhejiang Xinhua Bookstore 浙江省新華書店	Hangzhou 杭州市	Zhejiang 浙江省	(0571)8088568 (0571)8066331
Anhui Xinhua Bookstore 安徽省新華書店	Hefei 合肥市	Anhui 安徽省	(0551)2640292
Jiangsu Xinhua Bookstore 江蘇省新華書店	Nanjing 南京市	Jiangsu 江蘇省	(025)2713234 (025)2213941
Hunan Xinhua Bookstore 湖南省新華書店	Changsha 長沙市	Hunan 湖南省	(0731)4432142 (0731)4415250
Fujian Xinhua Bookstore 福建省新華書店	Fuzhou 福州市	Fujian 福建省	(0591)7559404 (0591)7559404
Guangxi Xinhua Bookstore 廣西壯族自治區新華書店	Nanning 南寧市	Guangxi 廣西	(0771)5853442 (0771)5867011
Henan Xinhua Bookstore 河南省新華書店	Zhengzhou 鄭州市	Henan 河南省	(0371)6230424 (0371)6227350
Guangdong Xinhua Bookstore 廣東省新華書店	Guangzhou 廣州市	Guangdong 廣東省	(020)83837158 (020)83837287

*Also include sales by firms outside this industry.包括本行業以外廠家的銷售。"o" stands for "others". "o" 代表 "其他產品"。

2411: Stationery Products 文具製造業

The industry accounts for 0.036% of the total revenue of China's industrial sector in 1996. The revenue growth rate of the industry is -11.5% from 1995, as compared to the growth rate of China's industrial sector, 9.51%. The rate of return on asset is 2.62%. 68.80% of all firms in the industry made a profit while 24.95% had negative returns. The top province in terms of the industry's revenue is Shanghai, accounting for 26.71% of the total revenue.
本行業在1996年佔全行業總產值0.036%，行業年增長率為-11.5%（全國工業年增長率9.51%）。行業的資產回報率2.62%，68.80%的企業盈利，24.95%的企業虧損。銷售收入最高的省份為上海市，佔本行業的26.71%。

	Total number of firms 企業總數	Total number of employees 職工總數	Total revenue (mil. RMB) 總銷售收入（百萬元）	Total profit (mil. RMB) 總利潤（百萬元）	Return on assets 資產利潤率 (%)	Return on equity 權益利潤率 (%)	Labour productivity ('000 RMB / worker) 勞動生產率（千元/人）	Debts / assets 資產負債率 (%)	Total assets (mil. RMB) 總資產（百萬元）
Industry Overall 行業總體	569	41,904	2,074	68	2.62	6.89	49.49	61.93	2,592

	Number of firms 企業個數	Average number of employees 平均職工人數	Average revenue ('000 RMB) 平均銷售收入（千元）	Average profit ('000 RMB) 平均利潤（千元）	Return on assets 資產利潤率 (%)	Return on equity 權益利潤率 (%)	Labour productivity ('000 RMB / worker) 勞動生產率（千元/人）	Average debts / assets 平均資產負債率(%)	Average Total assets ('000 RMB) 平均總資產（千元）
By ownership 產業所有權									
State-owned 國有	47	175	6,404				36.61	67.52	15,000
Collectively-owned 集體	415	60	2,064	60	2.63	7.54	34.40	65.12	2,297
Privately-owned 私有	1	22	532	27	5.91	16517.16	24.18	99.96	456
Domestic JVs 聯營	7	139	6,825	99	1.81	4.61	48.95	60.67	5,483
Joint stock 股份制	3	25	537	-4	-0.37	-0.84	21.75	56.04	1,138
Foreign-funded 外資	39	80	7,230	483	6.09	13.28	90.31	54.12	7,921
Overseas Chinese-funded 港澳台資	56	93	10,435	417	4.02	8.75	112.40	54.11	10,398
By size 規模									
Large 大型	2	435	50,240	6,796	7.51	21.22	115.63	64.63	90,523
Medium 中型	3	836	45,086	2,699	3.01	8.84	53.93	65.90	89,599
Small 小型	554	70	3,318	84	2.16	5.57	47.46	61.19	3,867
By regional distribution 地區分布									
Central-North 華北	91	81	2,618	-24	-0.56	-1.99	32.45	71.69	4,253
Beijing 北京	23	100	3,548	-30	-0.39	-1.23	35.64	68.14	7,643
Tianjin 天津	44	89	3,003	-39	-0.95	-4.28	33.56	77.83	4,139
Hebei 河北	9	44	1,650	21	2.24	3.54	37.88	36.79	942
Shanxi 山西	9	57	864	4	0.25	0.61	15.14	59.52	1,803
Inner Mongolia 內蒙	6	35	313	2	0.23	0.80	9.00	71.78	738
Northeast 東北	60	54	1,221	-64	-3.00	-9.20	22.78	67.39	2,140
Liaoning 遼寧	23	68	2,238	-60	-1.47	-3.38	33.02	56.62	4,087
Jilin 吉林	14	68	409	-227	-17.08	53.27	6.01	132.06	1,330
Heilongjiang 黑龍江	23	31	697	31	4.51	10.06	22.75	55.20	685
Central East 華東	241	86	5,250	280	4.19	10.77	61.22	61.06	6,672
Shanghai 上海	46	178	12,042	586	2.79	7.98	67.59	64.99	20,990
Jiangsu 江蘇	46	80	5,067	360	8.25	19.90	63.15	58.56	4,372
Zhejiang 浙江	66	71	3,691	125	3.39	8.43	52.21	59.76	3,672
Anhui 安徽	17	75	1,614	51	2.61	6.76	21.56	61.32	1,936
Fujian 福建	30	57	5,883	487	11.85	18.39	103.08	35.60	4,114
Jiangxi 江西	20	26	343	-24	-6.41	-129.73	13.38	95.06	375
Shandong 山東	16	39	1,499	42	1.90	4.54	38.68	58.06	2,199
Central-South 中南	126	64	3,394	60	2.06	4.71	53.00	56.33	2,912
Henan 河南	14	70	1,736	-242	-9.34	-56.69	24.96	83.53	2,594
Hubei 湖北	18	78	2,417	102	6.31	20.70	30.92	69.55	1,611
Hunan 湖南	19	48	1,272	-38	-3.22	-13.16	26.50	75.57	1,178
Guangdong 廣東	67	67	4,912	164	4.15	8.35	73.48	50.30	3,947
Guangxi 廣西	7	40	913	-169	-8.52	-14.46	22.90	41.16	1,979
Hainan 海南	1	17	130	20	2.41	5.88	7.65	59.04	830
Southwest 西南	29	55	1,862	-40	-1.55	-3.15	33.83	50.68	2,574
Chongqing 重慶	8	50	1,797	-2,144	-67.13	-199.15	35.83	66.29	3,194
Sichuan 四川	13	48	1,521	1,344	78.10	157.24	31.47	50.33	1,720
Guizhou 貴州	3	90	2,540	50	1.29	2.02	28.22	36.03	3,867
Yunnan 雲南	4	64	2,670	-40	-1.21	-1.82	41.88	33.46	3,303
Tibet 西藏									
Northwest 西北	22	46	720	9	0.73	1.66	15.61	55.97	1,245
Shaanxi 陝西	10	57	848	-2	-0.14	-0.32	14.90	56.75	1,452
Gansu 甘肅	6	31	383	17	2.33	9.71	12.30	76.05	717
Qinghai 青海	1	70	2,570	40	2.17	5.06	36.71	56.52	1,840
Ningxia 寧夏	3	27	267	3	0.82	2.38	9.88	65.57	407
Xinjiang 新疆	2	54	840	35	1.27	1.98	15.70	35.93	2,755

2411: Stationery Products 文具製造業

Year 年份	Number of firms 企業個數	Rate of change 每年變化 (%)	Number of employees 職工人數 (人)	Rate of change 每年變化 (%)	Total revenue (mil. RMB) 總銷售收入 (百萬元)	Rate of change 每年變化 (%)	Total profit (mil. RMB) 總利潤 (百萬元)	Rate of change 每年變化 (%)
1993	578		63,321		1,550		65	
1994	596	3.11%	82,142	29.72%	2,160	39.38%	75	15.46%
1995	586	-1.68%	47,375	-42.33%	2,344	8.51%	76	1.41%
1996	569	-2.90%	41,904	-11.55%	2,074	-11.52%	68	-10.50%

3 Major products* 3 種主要產品 *	Output 產量	Sales volume 銷售量	Unit 單位

Top 10 firms by revenue (year founded) 收入排名前 10 家企業 (創辦年份)	City 城市	Province 省	Telephone / fax 電話 / 傳真	Number of employees 職工人數	Ownership 產業所有權	Revenue ('000 RMB) 銷售收入 (千元)	Profit ('000 RMB) (rank) 利潤 (千元) (排名)	Total assets ('000 RMB) 總資產 (千元)	Major products 主要產品
Shanghai Stationary & Sporting Goods Corp. 上海文教體育用品總公司(1956)	Shanghai 上海市	Shanghai 上海市	(021)63215728 (021)63217219	1,945	State-owned 國有	126,173	5805(5)	428,300	o
Fuzhou Xin Yao Stationery Co. Ltd. 福州新曜文具有限公司(1994)	Fuzhou 福州市	Fujian 福建省	(0591)3432574 (0591)3428040	460	Foreign-funded 外資	98,654	14462(1)	46,118	o
Guangzhou Huaxing Stationery Co. Ltd. 廣州華興文具有限公司(1989)	Guangzhou 廣州市	Guangdong 廣東省	(020)84781908 (020)84781808	478	Overseas Chinese-funded 港澳台資	85,905	119(93)	51,975	o
Shanghai Jun Quan Stationary Co. Ltd. 上海俊泉文教用品有限公司(1994)	Shanghai 上海市	Shanghai 上海市	(021)59155414 (021)59157583	131	Overseas Chinese-funded 港澳台資	84,080	5182(6)	23,693	o
E&g Electronic (Shenzhen) Ltd. 業全電子(深圳)有限公司(1991)	Shenzhen 深圳市	Guangdong 廣東省	(0755)5511770 (0755)5501205	287	Overseas Chinese-funded 港澳台資	68,218	9295(3)	53,719	o
Shanghai Industrial Ma Li Drawing Materials Co. Ltd. 上海實業馬利畫材有限公司(1993)	Shanghai 上海市	Shanghai 上海市	(021)62580610 (021)62562003	600	Overseas Chinese-funded 港澳台資	66,812	12057(2)	89,880	o
Shanghai Great Wall Stationery Corp., Ltd. 上海長城文化用品有限公司(1994)	Shanghai 上海市	Shanghai 上海市	(021)62850805 (021)62330382	123	Overseas Chinese-funded 港澳台資	64,781	3832(8)	35,063	o
Bao Hua Printing Factory 寶華印刷廠(1995)	Zhenjiang 鎮江市	Jiangsu 江蘇省		165	Collectively-owned 集體	41,100	830(27)	14,740	o
Tianjin Artistic Pigment Factory 天津市美術顏料廠(1956)	Tianjin 天津市	Tianjin 天津市	(022)27362015 (022)27362015	610	Collectively-owned 集體	37,516	806(29)	30,355	o
Union Chemical (Tianjin) Co. Ltd. 聯合化學(天津)有限公司(1992)	Tianjin 天津市	Tianjin 天津市	(022)26372095	80	Foreign-funded 外資	34,058	-1083(202)	26,322	o

Top 10 Cities by Production Output 產出排名前 10 位城市	Province 省	Market share 市場份額	Number of firms 企業個數
Shanghai 上海市	Shanghai 上海市	26.40%	79
Guangzhou 廣州市	Guangdong 廣東省	13.94%	38
Ningbo 寧波市	Zhejiang 浙江省	6.80%	17
Tianjin 天津市	Tianjin 天津市	6.73%	51
Quanzhou 泉州市	Fujian 福建省	5.02%	23
Beijing 北京市	Beijing 北京市	3.59%	19
Suzhou 蘇州市	Jiangsu 江蘇省	2.72%	9
Hangzhou 杭州市	Zhejiang 浙江省	2.64%	12
Wuxi 無錫市	Jiangsu 江蘇省	2.27%	15
Wenzhou 溫州市	Zhejiang 浙江省	2.10%	37

10 Major Wholesalers 10 家主要批發商	City 城市	Province 省	Telephone / Fax 電話 / 傳真
Shandong Stationary & Sporting Goods Import & Export Company 山東省文教體育用品進出口公司	Qingdao 青島市	Shandong 山東省	(0532)2826827 (0532)3831971
Henan Printing Goods & Materials General Company 河南省印刷物資總公司	Zhengzhou 鄭州市	Henan 河南省	(0371)5967060 (0371)5947912
China Packing Import & Export Singbo Company 中國包裝進出口寧波公司	Ningbo 寧波市	Zhejiang 浙江省	(0574)7367512 (0574)7361096
Tianjin Stationary & Sporting Goods Import & Export Company 天津文教體育用品進出口公司	Tianjin 天津市	Tianjin 天津市	(022)23112048 (022)23112054
China Packing Import & Export Liaoning Company 中國包裝進出口遼寧公司	Dalian 大連市	Liaoning 遼寧省	(0411)4687657 (0411)4687644
Hunan Printing Goods & Materials General Company 湖南省印刷物資總公司	Changsha 長沙市	Hunan 湖南省	(0731)4444618 (0731)4446936
Guangzhou Stationery Co. 廣州市文化用品公司	Guangzhou 廣州市	Guangdong 廣東省	(020)81889089 (020)81861964
Casio Electronics (Shenzhen) Co. Ltd. 卡西歐電子(深圳)有限公司	Shenzhen 深圳市	Guangdong 廣東省	(0755)3590620 (0755)3590565
Changsha Keven Group Co. 長沙市科文集團公司	Changsha 長沙市	Hunan 湖南省	(0731)4444108
Hunan Firecrackers Fireworks Import & Export Company 湖南省鞭炮煙花進出口公司	Changsha 長沙市	Hunan 湖南省	(0731)4439580

*Also include sales by firms outside this industry.包括本行業以外廠家的銷售。"o" stands for "others". "o" 代表"其他產品"。

2413: Notebooks 本冊製造業

The industry accounts for 0.037% of the total revenue of China's industrial sector in 1996. The revenue growth rate of the industry is 44.5% from 1995, as compared to the growth rate of China's industrial sector, 9.51%. The rate of return on asset is 3.51%. 79.60% of all firms in the industry made a profit while 17.33% had negative returns. The top province in terms of the industry's revenue is Jiangsu, accounting for 15.12% of the total revenue.
本行業在1996年佔全行業總產值0.037%，行業年增長率為44.5%（全國工業年增長率9.51%）。行業的資產回報率3.51%，79.60%的企業盈利，17.33%的企業虧損。銷售收入最高的省份為江蘇省，佔本行業的15.12%。

	Total number of firms 企業總數	Total number of employees 職工總數	Total revenue (mil. RMB) 總銷售收入（百萬元）	Total profit (mil. RMB) 總利潤（百萬元）	Return on assets 資產利潤率 (%)	Return on equity 權益利潤率 (%)	Labour productivity ('000 RMB / worker) 勞動生產率（千元/人）	Debts / assets 資產負債率 (%)	Total assets (mil. RMB) 總資產（百萬元）
Industry Overall 行業總體	1,138	48,839	2,137	75	3.51	8.76	43.76	59.91	2,139

	Number of firms 企業個數	Average number of employees 平均職工人數	Average revenue ('000 RMB) 平均銷售收入（千元）	Average profit ('000 RMB) 平均利潤（千元）	Return on assets 資產利潤率 (%)	Return on equity 權益利潤率 (%)	Labour productivity ('000 RMB / worker) 勞動生產率（千元/人）	Average debts / assets 平均資產負債率(%)	Average Total assets ('000 RMB) 平均總資產（千元）
By ownership 產業所有權									
State-owned 國有	115	70	1,409	-26	-0.84	-2.61	20.01	67.88	3,113
Collectively-owned 集體	981	36	1,553	70	6.12	17.58	43.36	65.21	1,150
Privately-owned 私有	3	8	667	36	19.12	32.79	83.42	41.69	191
Domestic JVs 聯營	3	335	33,503	715	2.81	5.58	100.11	49.67	25,461
Joint stock 股份制	3	91	15,194	4,774	16.23	18.77	166.97	13.57	29,423
Foreign-funded 外資	14	184	11,020	211	1.60	2.58	59.80	38.06	13,233
Overseas Chinese-funded 港澳台資	17	105	8,498	-641	-3.62	-9.15	80.66	60.41	17,690
By size 規模									
Large 大型									
Medium 中型	3	460	10,834	4	0.01	0.08	23.57	87.24	36,733
Small 小型	1,130	42	1,863	66	3.70	8.89	44.42	58.40	1,795
By regional distribution 地區分布									
Central-North 華北	122	57	1,869	75	2.51	5.94	32.59	57.81	3,013
Beijing 北京	32	47	1,976	70	1.35	2.34	42.32	42.36	5,172
Tianjin 天津	28	107	3,353	110	2.05	8.42	31.32	75.64	5,350
Hebei 河北	34	54	1,754	99	9.27	21.04	32.65	55.89	1,069
Shanxi 山西	4	30	788	25	7.41	11.36	26.47	34.81	338
Inner Mongolia 內蒙	24	23	338	18	3.01	7.02	14.53	57.07	610
Northeast 東北	146	40	486	-5	-0.71	-3.48	12.12	79.47	642
Liaoning 遼寧	53	44	570	-8	-1.38	-8.15	13.06	83.04	559
Jilin 吉林	42	35	398	7	1.15	4.07	11.45	71.72	580
Heilongjiang 黑龍江	51	41	471	-11	-1.36	-7.37	11.55	81.57	780
Central East 華東	331	46	3,290	156	6.92	15.45	71.65	55.23	2,254
Shanghai 上海	22	111	4,330	17	0.33	0.75	39.07	56.18	5,149
Jiangsu 江蘇	66	56	4,897	325	12.50	51.73	87.50	75.84	2,598
Zhejiang 浙江	55	52	3,567	65	1.96	4.83	68.75	59.38	3,310
Anhui 安徽	40	43	7,057	579	25.13	34.24	162.33	26.61	2,303
Fujian 福建	54	21	815	8	0.71	0.85	38.45	16.12	1,065
Jiangxi 江西	54	23	500	29	6.06	11.49	21.57	47.31	471
Shandong 山東	40	52	3,026	29	1.09	2.86	58.27	61.81	2,607
Central-South 中南	305	46	1,917	56	2.53	6.33	41.45	60.07	2,218
Henan 河南	66	17	462	15	2.68	8.29	26.97	67.67	571
Hubei 湖北	56	53	2,463	78	4.60	13.65	46.29	66.30	1,692
Hunan 湖南	102	44	1,126	31	3.03	6.70	25.75	54.78	1,033
Guangdong 廣東	65	80	4,380	116	1.78	4.39	54.62	59.43	6,529
Guangxi 廣西	15	22	1,094	63	7.01	17.34	50.49	59.58	894
Hainan 海南	1		320	50	6.67	6.67			750
Southwest 西南	123	29	881	-25	-1.71	-6.16	29.87	72.26	1,452
Chongqing 重慶	14	27	529	-70	-6.05	-59.44	19.41	89.83	1,150
Sichuan 四川	68	29	645	37	3.88	10.41	21.97	62.77	965
Guizhou 貴州	31	30	1,560	-54	-2.07	-8.45	51.68	75.46	2,612
Yunnan 雲南	9	32	893	22	1.34	6.02	28.01	77.74	1,652
Tibet 西藏									
Northwest 西北	111	28	506	8	1.22	3.18	18.35	61.65	688
Shaanxi 陝西	41	25	394	13	1.96	5.15	15.78	61.95	646
Gansu 甘肅	29	28	458	22	3.54	8.02	16.55	55.74	613
Qinghai 青海	4	42	675	-10	-1.97	-4.35	16.07	54.68	508
Ningxia 寧夏	21	28	410	-15	-2.31	-6.13	14.84	62.34	660
Xinjiang 新疆	16	30	965	9	0.86	2.69	31.70	67.94	1,014

Year 年份	Number of firms 企業個數	Rate of change 每年變化 (%)	Number of employees 職工人數 (人)	Rate of change 每年變化 (%)	Total revenue (mil. RMB) 總銷售收入 (百萬元)	Rate of change 每年變化 (%)	Total profit (mil. RMB) 總利潤 (百萬元)	Rate of change 每年變化 (%)
1993	1,063		46,360		1,002		32	
1994	1,141	7.34%	55,530	19.78%	1,096	9.36%	32	-0.51%
1995	1,327	16.30%	51,109	-7.96%	1,479	34.90%	52	63.40%
1996	1,138	-14.24%	48,839	-4.44%	2,137	44.49%	75	43.45%

3 Major products* 3 種主要產品 *	Output 產量	Sales volume 銷售量	Unit 單位
a) Monochrome Printed Product 單色印刷品	740	718	10,000 ream 萬令

Top 10 firms by revenue (year founded) 收入排名前 10 家企業 (創辦年份)	City 城市	Province 省	Telephone / fax 電話 / 傳真	Number of employees 職工人數	Ownership 產業所有權	Revenue ('000 RMB) 銷售收入 (千元)	Profit ('000 RMB) (rank) 利潤 (千元) (排名)	Total assets ('000 RMB) 總資產 (千元)	Major products 主要產品
Bozhou Welfare General Factory 亳州市福利總廠(1986)	Fuyang 阜陽市	Anhui 安徽省	(0558)5526162	468	Collectively-owned 集體	220,000	20180(1)	58,981	a
Xi Shan Shi An Zhen School-run Tiao Factory 錫山市安鎮校辦條線廠(1980)	Wuxi 無錫市	Jiangsu 江蘇省	(0510)8781888	58	Collectively-owned 集體	169,660	17510(2)	45,000	o
Zhongshan Zhong Rong Paper Printing Products Co. Ltd. 中山中榮紙類印刷製品有限公司(1978)	Zhongshan 中山市	Guangdong 廣東省	(0760)5591388 (0760)5596788	361	Overseas Chinese-funded 港澳台資	116,362	13560(3)	103,867	o
Jiaxing Seagull Paper Products Factory 嘉興市海鷗紙品廠(1984)	Jiaxing 嘉興市	Zhejiang 浙江省	(0573)2083844 (0573)2071469	303	Domestic JVs 聯營	47,633	731(19)	45,206	o
Pingyang Education Industrial Company 平陽縣教育實業公司(1993)	Wenzhou 溫州市	Zhejiang 浙江省	(0577)3725185	50	Collectively-owned 集體	36,001	456(31)	14,186	o
Chao'an Hong He Stationery Co. Ltd. 潮安縣紅盒文具有限公司(1993)	Chaozhou 潮州市	Guangdong 廣東省	(0768)6618899 (0768)6611388	213	Foreign-funded 外資	31,994	-6081(228)	93,225	o
Ji'nan Center No.3 Printing Factory 濟南市市中印刷三廠(1971)	Ji'nan 濟南市	Shandong 山東省	(0531)2975441	232	Collectively-owned 集體	27,890	194(73)	17,768	o
Shanghai Quan Wei Handle Official Business Stationary Co. Ltd. 上海權偉辦公文教用品有限公司(1993)	Shanghai 上海市	Shanghai 上海市	(021)59596118 (021)59597789	175	Overseas Chinese-funded 港澳台資	27,586	388(40)	16,989	o
Dongguan Yi Zhi Gao Paper Products Manufacture Factory Co. Ltd. 東莞市意志高紙品製造有限公司(1995)	Dongguan 東莞市	Guangdong 廣東省	(0769)2259730 (0769)2259735	600	Overseas Chinese-funded 港澳台資	26,392	102(105)	37,568	o
Ninghe Education Bureau School-run Industrial Company 寧河縣教育局校辦工業公司(1988)	Tianjin 天津市	Tianjin 天津市	(022)5593633	9	State-owned 國有	25,160	1732(5)	25,991	o

Top 10 Cities by Production Output 產出排名前 10 位城市	Province 省	Market share 市場份額	Number of firms 企業個數
Shanghai 上海市	Shanghai 上海市	11.36%	34
Zhongshan 中山市	Guangdong 廣東省	7.44%	2
Tianjin 天津市	Tianjin 天津市	6.04%	32
Jiaxing 嘉興市	Zhejiang 浙江省	4.74%	8
Wenzhou 溫州市	Zhejiang 浙江省	4.10%	109
Dongguan 東莞市	Guangdong 廣東省	3.64%	4
Beijing 北京市	Beijing 北京市	2.93%	28
Anqing 安慶市	Anhui 安徽省	2.69%	19
Chaozhou 潮州市	Guangdong 廣東省	2.01%	2
Wuxi 無錫市	Jiangsu 江蘇省	1.93%	10

10 Major Wholesalers 10 家主要批發商	City 城市	Province 省	Telephone / Fax 電話 / 傳真
Shandong Stationary & Sporting Goods Import & Export Company 山東省文教體育用品進出口公司	Qingdao 青島市	Shandong 山東省	(0532)2826827 (0532)3831971
Henan Printing Goods & Materials General Company 河南省印刷物資總公司	Zhengzhou 鄭州市	Henan 河南省	(0371)5967060 (0371)5947912
China Packing Import & Export Singbo Company 中國包裝進出口寧波公司	Ningbo 寧波市	Zhejiang 浙江省	(0574)7367512 (0574)7361096
Tianjin Stationary & Sporting Goods Import & Export Company 天津文教體育用品進出口公司	Tianjin 天津市	Tianjin 天津市	(022)23112048 (022)23112054
China Packing Import & Export Liaoning Company 中國包裝進出口遼寧公司	Dalian 大連市	Liaoning 遼寧省	(0411)4687657 (0411)4687644
Hunan Printing Goods & Materials General Company 湖南省印刷物資總公司	Changsha 長沙市	Hunan 湖南省	(0731)4444618 (0731)4446936
Guangzhou Stationery Co. 廣州市文化用品公司	Guangzhou 廣州市	Guangdong 廣東省	(020)81889089 (020)81861964
Casio Electronics (Shenzhen) Co. Ltd. 卡西歐電子(深圳)有限公司	Shenzhen 深圳市	Guangdong 廣東省	(0755)3590620 (0755)3590565
Changsha Keven Group Co. 長沙市科文集團公司	Changsha 長沙市	Hunan 湖南省	(0731)4444108
Hunan Firecrackers Fireworks Import & Export Company 湖南省鞭炮煙花進出口公司	Changsha 長沙市	Hunan 湖南省	(0731)4439580

*Also include sales by firms outside this industry.包括本行業以外廠家的銷售。"o" stands for "others". "o" 代表"其他產品"。

2415: Pens 筆製造業

The industry accounts for 0.067% of the total revenue of China's industrial sector in 1996. The revenue growth rate of the industry is 8.8% from 1995, as compared to the growth rate of China's industrial sector, 9.51%. The rate of return on asset is 3.95%. 67.77% of all firms in the industry made a profit while 26.73% had negative returns. The top province in terms of the industry's revenue is Shanghai, accounting for 51.29% of the total revenue.

本行業在1996年佔全行業總產值0.067%，行業年增長率為8.8%（全國工業年增長率9.51%）。行業的資產回報率3.95%，67.77%的企業盈利，26.73%的企業虧損。銷售收入最高的省份為上海市，佔本行業的51.29%。

	Total number of firms 企業總數	Total number of employees 職工總數	Total revenue (mil. RMB) 總銷售收入（百萬元）	Total profit (mil. RMB) 總利潤（百萬元）	Return on assets 資產利潤率 (%)	Return on equity 權益利潤率 (%)	Labour productivity ('000 RMB / worker) 勞動生產率（千元/人）	Debts / assets 資產負債率 (%)	Total assets (mil. RMB) 總資產（百萬元）
Industry Overall 行業總體	443	77,605	3,889	243	3.95	8.97	50.11	56.02	6,165

	Number of firms 企業個數	Average number of employees 平均職工人數	Average revenue ('000 RMB) 平均銷售收入（千元）	Average profit ('000 RMB) 平均利潤（千元）	Return on assets 資產利潤率 (%)	Return on equity 權益利潤率 (%)	Labour productivity ('000 RMB / worker) 勞動生產率（千元/人）	Average debts / assets 平均資產負債率(%)	Average Total assets ('000 RMB) 平均總資產（千元）
By ownership 產業所有權									
State-owned 國有	70	551	15,457	-571	-2.20	-9.01	28.08	75.63	26,029
Collectively-owned 集體	284	77	3,540	168	5.36	14.64	45.89	63.37	3,127
Privately-owned 私有	3	42	4,508	181	6.68	33.31	107.33	79.93	2,707
Domestic JVs 聯營	10	211	10,404	237	2.23	6.70	49.26	66.73	10,619
Joint stock 股份制	12	707	80,795	14,436	6.89	11.63	114.36	40.82	209,675
Foreign-funded 外資	25	110	8,680	380	4.50	7.09	78.99	36.46	8,428
Overseas Chinese-funded 港澳台資	35	112	8,981	354	2.95	7.23	80.14	59.25	12,001
By size 規模									
Large 大型	7	1,714	189,646	19,328	5.23	10.07	110.66	48.10	369,799
Medium 中型	15	1,048	39,152	2,059	2.34	6.04	37.35	61.25	88,001
Small 小型	412	122	4,793	186	3.40	8.97	39.43	62.06	5,476
By regional distribution 地區分布									
Central-North 華北	44	429	3,895	-54	-0.59	-1.93	9.07	69.15	9,103
Beijing 北京	15	1,010	4,019	-231	-1.61	-7.56	3.98	78.67	14,349
Tianjin 天津	23	101	3,767	133	2.03	4.30	37.23	52.80	6,532
Hebei 河北	2	328	9,135	-145	-1.76	-7.46	27.85	76.42	8,250
Shanxi 山西	3	250	2,067	-557	-9.00	-58.39	8.26	84.58	6,183
Inner Mongolia 內蒙	1								
Northeast 東北	42	211	2,256	-582	-5.55	-22.01	10.69	74.78	10,487
Liaoning 遼寧	20	210	1,646	-579	-4.20	-12.53	7.84	66.45	13,768
Jilin 吉林	5	378	3,924	-876	-13.09	353.23	10.39	103.71	6,692
Heilongjiang 黑龍江	17	163	2,485	-500	-6.46	-42.61	15.20	84.85	7,744
Central East 華東	275	150	12,617	1,050	5.77	12.17	83.87	52.61	18,207
Shanghai 上海	64	260	31,165	3,798	6.97	13.80	119.95	49.46	54,468
Jiangsu 江蘇	47	144	8,713	191	2.25	6.03	60.52	62.69	8,501
Zhejiang 浙江	57	107	8,957	417	5.63	14.39	83.34	60.89	7,408
Anhui 安徽	20	149	3,634	-533	-8.59	-68.16	24.37	87.39	6,202
Fujian 福建	18	170	9,136	-39	-0.24	-0.37	53.70	36.08	16,361
Jiangxi 江西	47	40	2,437	98	9.61	59.51	60.67	83.83	1,018
Shandong 山東	22	178	9,240	894	8.45	23.17	51.89	63.54	10,576
Central-South 中南	53	116	2,481	-268	-5.68	-16.68	21.30	65.97	4,716
Henan 河南	5	60	326	20	5.88	18.18	5.45	67.65	340
Hubei 湖北	8	128	1,934	-329	-9.27	-17.09	15.09	45.75	3,546
Hunan 湖南	23	124	1,998	-177	-6.30	-23.97	16.12	73.70	2,814
Guangdong 廣東	14	98	3,599	-544	-5.85	-17.35	36.86	66.26	9,287
Guangxi 廣西	3	210	6,007	10	0.12	0.36	28.65	67.24	8,383
Hainan 海南									
Southwest 西南	21	104	1,014	-212	-6.78	-24.02	9.78	71.77	3,132
Chongqing 重慶	12	107	833	-260	-10.55	-31.27	7.71	66.25	2,463
Sichuan 四川	6	42	623	-83	-6.57	-24.76	14.83	73.47	1,266
Guizhou 貴州	3	212	2,517	-280	-2.94	-12.77	11.87	77.00	9,537
Yunnan 雲南									
Tibet 西藏									
Northwest 西北	8	17	79				4.70	51.90	198
Shaanxi 陝西	4	22	5	-3	-1.20	-4.55	0.23	73.49	208
Gansu 甘肅	3	15	203	3	1.35	1.92	13.26	28.38	247
Qinghai 青海									
Ningxia 寧夏									
Xinjiang 新疆	1	1							10

Year 年份	Number of firms 企業個數	Rate of change 每年變化 (%)	Number of employees 職工人數（人）	Rate of change 每年變化 (%)	Total revenue (mil. RMB) 總銷售收入（百萬元）	Rate of change 每年變化 (%)	Total profit (mil. RMB) 總利潤（百萬元）	Rate of change 每年變化 (%)
1993	399		120,795		2,386		184	
1994	400	0.25%	75,775	-37.27%	2,933	22.91%	204	10.97%
1995	479	19.75%	74,525	-1.65%	3,576	21.92%	269	31.50%
1996	443	-7.52%	77,605	4.13%	3,889	8.75%	243	-9.50%

3 Major products* 3 種主要產品 *	Output 產量	Sales volume 銷售量	Unit 單位
a) Fountain Pen 自來水筆	20,432	20,227	10,000 piece 萬支
b) Pencil 鉛筆	704,143	612,604	10,000 piece 萬支

Top 10 firms by revenue (year founded) 收入排名前 10 家企業 (創辦年份)	City 城市	Province 省	Telephone / fax 電話 / 傳真	Number of employees 職工人數	Ownership 產業所有權	Revenue ('000 RMB) 銷售收入（千元）	Profit ('000 RMB) (rank) 利潤（千元）（排名）	Total assets ('000 RMB) 總資產（千元）	Major products 主要產品
Shanghai Pens Making Industrial General Co. 上海製筆實業總公司(1925)	Shanghai 上海市	Shanghai 上海市	(021)63230535 (021)63230224	4,086	State-owned 國有	608,844	5602(10)	501,252	a
Shanghai Hero Co. Ltd. 上海英雄股份有限公司(1931)	Shanghai 上海市	Shanghai 上海市	(021)62506261 (021)62506181	2,028	Joint stock 股份制	407,128	69061(1)	831,473	a,b
China First Pencil Co. Ltd. 中國第一鉛筆股份有限公司(1935)	Shanghai 上海市	Shanghai 上海市	(021)65416940 (021)65458009	996	Joint stock 股份制	173,967	58228(2)	476,549	b
Shanghai Feng Hua Ball-pen Co. Ltd. 上海豐華圓珠筆股份有限公司(1948)	Shanghai 上海市	Shanghai 上海市	(021)58811688 (021)58811023	1,275	Joint stock 股份制	160,494	22025(4)	485,877	a
Shanghai Yong Sheng Co. Ltd. 上海永生股份有限公司(1948)	Shanghai 上海市	Shanghai 上海市	(021)63254537 (021)63248014	981	Joint stock 股份制	120,321	18816(5)	490,559	a
Shanghai Fu Si Te Pen Industry Co. Ltd. 上海福斯特筆業有限公司(1994)	Shanghai 上海市	Shanghai 上海市	(021)58549624 (021)58992997	240	Foreign-funded 外資	111,493	37018(3)	123,558	b
Ningbo Bei Fa Recreation & Sports Craft Tourism Articles Manufacture Co. Ltd. 寧波貝發文體工藝旅遊用品製造有限公司(1994)	Ningbo 寧波市	Zhejiang 浙江省	(0574)6156888 (0574)6155295	208	Foreign-funded 外資	95,794	2026(22)	20,481	o
Jin Xing Stationery Gifts (Yuyao) Co. Ltd. 金星文具禮品(余姚)有限公司(1994)	Ningbo 寧波市	Zhejiang 浙江省	(0574)2595529 (0574)2595500	184	Overseas Chinese-funded 港澳台資	89,000	5340(12)	42,916	o
Shanghai Three Star Stationery Industry Co. 上海三星文教實業公司(1931)	Shanghai 上海市	Shanghai 上海市	(021)58716572 (021)58716485	1,227	State-owned 國有	80,040	1786(27)	124,614	a,b
Jiangsu Pai Di Quality Fountain Pen Group Co. 江蘇派迪金筆集團公司(1985)	Wuxi 無錫市	Jiangsu 江蘇省	(0510)6601062 (0510)6601062	638	Collectively-owned 集體	77,118	4170(14)	50,226	a

Top 10 Cities by Production Output 產出排名前 10 位城市	Province 省	Market share 市場份額	Number of firms 企業個數
Shanghai 上海市	Shanghai 上海市	61.20%	90
Suzhou 蘇州市	Jiangsu 江蘇省	3.77%	38
Ningbo 寧波市	Zhejiang 浙江省	3.71%	14
Wenzhou 溫州市	Zhejiang 浙江省	3.10%	22
Lishui 麗水市	Zhejiang 浙江省	2.97%	9
Tianjin 天津市	Tianjin 天津市	2.16%	22
Ji'nan 濟南市	Shandong 山東省	1.95%	5
Beijing 北京市	Beijing 北京市	1.72%	15
Qingdao 青島市	Shandong 山東省	1.37%	5
Yangzhou 揚州市	Jiangsu 江蘇省	1.20%	17

10 Major Wholesalers 10 家主要批發商	City 城市	Province 省	Telephone / Fax 電話 / 傳真
Shandong Stationary & Sporting Goods Import & Export Company 山東省文教體育用品進出口公司	Qingdao 青島市	Shandong 山東省	(0532)2826827 (0532)3831971
Henan Printing Goods & Materials General Company 河南省印刷物資總公司	Zhengzhou 鄭州市	Henan 河南省	(0371)5967060 (0371)5947912
China Packing Import & Export Singbo Company 中國包裝進出口寧波公司	Ningbo 寧波市	Zhejiang 浙江省	(0574)7367512 (0574)7361096
Tianjin Stationary & Sporting Goods Import & Export Company 天津文教體育用品進出口公司	Tianjin 天津市	Tianjin 天津市	(022)23112048 (022)23112054
China Packing Import & Export Liaoning Company 中國包裝進出口遼寧公司	Dalian 大連市	Liaoning 遼寧省	(0411)4687657 (0411)4687644
Hunan Printing Goods & Materials General Company 湖南省印刷物資總公司	Changsha 長沙市	Hunan 湖南省	(0731)4444618 (0731)4446936
Guangzhou Stationery Co. 廣州市文化用品公司	Guangzhou 廣州市	Guangdong 廣東省	(020)81889089 (020)81861964
Casio Electronics (Shenzhen) Co. Ltd. 卡西歐電子(深圳)有限公司	Shenzhen 深圳市	Guangdong 廣東省	(0755)3590620 (0755)3590565
Changsha Keven Group Co. 長沙市科文集團公司	Changsha 長沙市	Hunan 湖南省	(0731)4444108
Hunan Firecrackers Fireworks Import & Export Company 湖南省鞭炮煙花進出口公司	Changsha 長沙市	Hunan 湖南省	(0731)4439580

*Also include sales by firms outside this industry.包括本行業以外廠家的銷售。"o" stands for "others". "o" 代表"其他產品"。

2417: Teaching Samples and Models 教學標本、模型製造業

The industry accounts for 0.023% of the total revenue of China's industrial sector in 1996. The revenue growth rate of the industry is 108.4% from 1995, as compared to the growth rate of China's industrial sector, 9.51%. The rate of return on asset is 15.88%. 71.92% of all firms in the industry made a profit while 12.93% had negative returns. The top province in terms of the industry's revenue is Zhejiang, accounting for 79.85% of the total revenue.
本行業在1996年佔全行業總產值0.023%，行業年增長率為108.4%（全國工業年增長率9.51%）。行業的資產回報率15.88%，71.92%的企業盈利，12.93%的企業虧損。銷售收入最高的省份為浙江省，佔本行業的79.85%。

	Total number of firms 企業總數	Total number of employees 職工總數	Total revenue (mil. RMB) 總銷售收入（百萬元）	Total profit (mil. RMB) 總利潤（百萬元）	Return on assets 資產利潤率 (%)	Return on equity 權益利潤率 (%)	Labour productivity ('000 RMB / worker) 勞動生產率（千元/人）	Debts / assets 資產負債率 (%)	Total assets (mil. RMB) 總資產（百萬元）
Industry Overall 行業總體	168	7,542	1,305	146	15.88	41.04	173.03	61.30	918

	Number of firms 企業個數	Average number of employees 平均職工人數	Average revenue ('000 RMB) 平均銷售收入（千元）	Average profit ('000 RMB) 平均利潤（千元）	Return on assets 資產利潤率 (%)	Return on equity 權益利潤率 (%)	Labour productivity ('000 RMB / worker) 勞動生產率（千元/人）	Average debts / assets 平均資產負債率(%)	Average Total assets ('000 RMB) 平均總資產（千元）
By ownership 產業所有權									
State-owned 國有	35	36	1,029	86	6.52	14.29	28.59	54.35	1,314
Collectively-owned 集體	128	48	9,856	1,114	16.40	42.95	204.91	61.82	6,793
Privately-owned 私有	1	10							
Domestic JVs 聯營									
Joint stock 股份制									
Foreign-funded 外資	1	19							
Overseas Chinese-funded 港澳台資	1	39	4,078	-63	-4.32	-5.57	104.56	22.45	1,460
By size 規模									
Large 大型									
Medium 中型	1	929	83,083	4,255	5.15	14.63	89.43	64.77	82,554
Small 小型	166	40	7,359	854	16.97	43.50	184.88	60.99	5,032
By regional distribution 地區分布									
Central-North 華北	14	19	372	44	6.23	12.37	19.37	49.64	699
Beijing 北京	5	5	22	18	10.71	16.36	4.07	34.52	168
Tianjin 天津	2	73						8.33	60
Hebei 河北	3	9	940	70	5.88	15.91	104.44	63.31	1,190
Shanxi 山西	1	42	1,100	50	3.21	7.69	26.19	58.33	1,560
Inner Mongolia 內蒙	3	9	393	87	7.03	11.30	42.14	37.57	1,233
Northeast 東北	16	16	719	129	17.86	44.04	44.61	59.45	724
Liaoning 遼寧	8	15	598	29	5.02	8.75	40.17	42.58	573
Jilin 吉林	4	30	338	13	1.41	3.85	11.34	63.38	888
Heilongjiang 黑龍江	4	5	1,345	448	51.73	232.47	269.00	77.75	865
Central East 華東	72	77	16,968	1,946	16.91	42.93	221.60	60.62	11,512
Shanghai 上海	9	80	2,316	22	0.89	3.38	28.86	73.75	2,506
Jiangsu 江蘇	6	117	18,737	315	2.30	11.75	160.83	80.43	13,692
Zhejiang 浙江	24	132	43,416	5,641	19.53	46.47	328.81	57.97	28,876
Anhui 安徽	8	27	2,393	205	25.83	47.26	88.61	45.35	794
Fujian 福建	11	27	905	41	3.35	7.49	33.99	55.32	1,223
Jiangxi 江西	3	32	1,067	73	5.91	12.72	33.68	53.49	1,240
Shandong 山東	11	29	1,283	32	4.61	18.62	44.23	75.23	690
Central-South 中南	48	25	1,189	46	4.57	13.24	47.50	65.50	1,004
Henan 河南	16	22	1,075	33	3.50	12.90	50.00	72.86	928
Hubei 湖北	2	33	4,440	240	22.54	64.86	136.62	65.26	1,065
Hunan 湖南	18	27	905	26	3.00	8.49	33.24	64.60	851
Guangdong 廣東	10	25	1,209	58	3.96	9.02	48.95	56.05	1,463
Guangxi 廣西	2	28	1,295	80	12.80		47.09	100.00	625
Hainan 海南									
Southwest 西南	13	13	370	28	5.39	11.35	28.29	52.48	528
Chongqing 重慶	3	7	160	35	8.71	21.73	20.19	59.90	406
Sichuan 四川	5	18	548	30	4.35	14.65	29.84	70.30	680
Guizhou 貴州	3	9							
Yunnan 雲南	1	18	1,340	80	4.52	5.03	74.44	10.17	1,770
Tibet 西藏									
Northwest 西北	5	26	1,000	92	3.47	-95.83	38.17	103.70	2,650
Shaanxi 陝西	3	28	1,427	130	3.31	-35.78	50.35	109.34	3,927
Gansu 甘肅	1	30	390	80	7.48	15.38	13.00	51.40	1,070
Qinghai 青海									
Ningxia 寧夏	1	16	330	-10	-2.50	-11.11	20.63	77.50	400
Xinjiang 新疆									

2417: Teaching Samples and Models 教學標本、模型製造業

Year 年份	Number of firms 企業個數	Rate of change 每年變化 (%)	Number of employees 職工人數 (人)	Rate of change 每年變化 (%)	Total revenue (mil. RMB) 總銷售收入 (百萬元)	Rate of change 每年變化 (%)	Total profit (mil. RMB) 總利潤 (百萬元)	Rate of change 每年變化 (%)
1993	107		3,961		98		5	
1994	101	-5.61%	4,709	18.88%	122	24.80%	5	1.19%
1995	149	47.52%	6,285	33.47%	626	412.00%	115	2041.90%
1996	168	12.75%	7,542	20.00%	1,305	108.39%	146	27.39%

3 Major products* 3 種主要產品 *	Output 產量	Sales volume 銷售量	Unit 單位
a) Glass Steel Products 玻璃鋼製品	223,021	211,870	ton 噸

Top 10 firms by revenue (year founded) 收入排名前 10 家企業 (創辦年份)	City 城市	Province 省	Telephone / fax 電話 / 傳真	Number of employees 職工人數	Ownership 產業所有權	Revenue ('000 RMB) 銷售收入 (千元)	Profit ('000 RMB) (rank) 利潤 (千元) (排名)	Total assets ('000 RMB) 總資產 (千元)	Major products 主要產品
Ningbo Hua Mao Group Co. Ltd. 寧波華茂集團股份有限公司(1980)	Ningbo 寧波市	Zhejiang 浙江省	(0574)8449417 (0574)8440232	380	Joint stock 股份制	861,446	116902(1)	532,665	o
Suzhou Medical Science Education Model Factory 蘇州市醫學模型廠(1972)	Suzhou 蘇州市	Jiangsu 江蘇省	(0512)8620065 (0512)8620216	390	Collectively-owned 集體	92,541	1491(5)	65,841	a
Hangzhou Pingyao Stationery Factory 杭州市瓶窯文教用品廠(1983)	Hangzhou 杭州市	Zhejiang 浙江省	(0571)8541876	283	Collectively-owned 集體	26,574	4607(3)	19,598	o
Zhangjiagang Le Yu School-run Co. 張家港市樂余校辦工業公司(1979)	Suzhou 蘇州市	Jiangsu 江蘇省	(0512)8660795	103	Collectively-owned 集體	16,160	10(25)	13,020	a
Anhui Tongling Li Xin Education Instrument Plant 安徽省銅陵縣立新教學儀器廠(1975)	Tongling 銅陵市	Anhui 安徽省	(0562)8891466	111	Collectively-owned 集體	16,000	1430(6)	3,490	o
Shanghai Sample Model Factory 上海標本模型廠(1952)	Shanghai 上海市	Shanghai 上海市	(021)56036700 (021)56038256	455	State-owned 國有	9,205	20(24)	11,787	o
Henan Shen Qiuxian Mechanize Wool Scouring Factory 河南省沈丘縣機械化洗毛廠(1992)	Zhoukou 周口市	Henan 河南省	(0394)5551188	29	Collectively-owned 集體	9,100	121(19)	4,634	o
Zhejiang San He Science & Education Instrument Co. Ltd. 浙江三和科教儀器有限公司(1995)	Wenzhou 溫州市	Zhejiang 浙江省	(0577)7391668	78	Collectively-owned 集體	8,913	1050(7)	11,194	o
Zhejiang Longyou Education Instrument General Factory 浙江省龍游縣教學儀器總廠(1979)	Quzhou 衢州市	Zhejiang 浙江省	(0570)7022760 (0570)7021464	130	Collectively-owned 集體	7,963	297(12)	9,500	o
Xiangshan Education Instrument Factory 象山縣教學儀器廠(1981)	Ningbo 寧波市	Zhejiang 浙江省	(0574)5810054 (0574)5810267	101	Collectively-owned 集體	5,620	190(17)	5,366	o

Top 10 Cities by Production Output 產出排名前 10 位城市	Province 省	Market share 市場份額	Number of firms 企業個數
Ningbo 寧波市	Zhejiang 浙江省	72.78%	7
Suzhou 蘇州市	Jiangsu 江蘇省	6.04%	7
Hangzhou 杭州市	Zhejiang 浙江省	2.77%	4
Wenzhou 溫州市	Zhejiang 浙江省	2.02%	12
Shanghai 上海市	Shanghai 上海市	1.72%	12
Tianjin 天津市	Tianjin 天津市	1.46%	3
Huaiyin 淮陰市	Jiangsu 江蘇省	1.38%	2
Shenzhen 深圳市	Guangdong 廣東省	1.20%	2
Zhoukou 周口市	Henan 河南省	1.08%	3
Yiyang 益陽市	Hunan 湖南省	1.05%	9

10 Major Wholesalers 10 家主要批發商	City 城市	Province 省	Telephone / Fax 電話 / 傳真
Shandong Stationary & Sporting Goods Import & Export Company 山東省文教體育用品進出口公司	Qingdao 青島市	Shandong 山東省	(0532)2826827 (0532)3831971
Henan Printing Goods & Materials General Company 河南省印刷物資總公司	Zhengzhou 鄭州市	Henan 河南省	(0371)5967060 (0371)5947912
China Packing Import & Export Singbo Company 中國包裝進出口寧波公司	Ningbo 寧波市	Zhejiang 浙江省	(0574)7367512 (0574)7361096
Tianjin Stationary & Sporting Goods Import & Export Company 天津文教體育用品進出口公司	Tianjin 天津市	Tianjin 天津市	(022)23112048 (022)23112054
China Packing Import & Export Liaoning Company 中國包裝進出口遼寧公司	Dalian 大連市	Liaoning 遼寧省	(0411)4687657 (0411)4687644
Hunan Printing Goods & Materials General Company 湖南省印刷物資總公司	Changsha 長沙市	Hunan 湖南省	(0731)4444618 (0731)4446936
Guangzhou Stationery Co. 廣州市文化用品公司	Guangzhou 廣州市	Guangdong 廣東省	(020)81889089 (020)81861964
Casio Electronics (Shenzhen) Co. Ltd. 卡西歐電子(深圳)有限公司	Shenzhen 深圳市	Guangdong 廣東省	(0755)3590620 (0755)3590565
Changsha Keven Group Co. 長沙市科文集團公司	Changsha 長沙市	Hunan 湖南省	(0731)4444108
Hunan Firecrackers Fireworks Import & Export Company 湖南省鞭炮煙花進出口公司	Changsha 長沙市	Hunan 湖南省	(0731)4439580

*Also include sales by firms outside this industry.包括本行業以外廠家的銷售。"o" stands for "others". "o" 代表 "其他產品"。

2419: Other Cultural and Educational Products 其他文化用品製造業

The industry accounts for 0.015% of the total revenue of China's industrial sector in 1996. The revenue growth rate of the industry is -1.2% from 1995, as compared to the growth rate of China's industrial sector, 9.51%. The rate of return on asset is 2.15%. 68.28% of all firms in the industry made a profit while 28.81% had negative returns. The top province in terms of the industry's revenue is Jiangsu, accounting for 35.48% of the total revenue.
本行業在1996年佔全行業總產值0.015%，行業年增長率為-1.2%（全國工業年增長率9.51%）。行業的資產回報率2.15%，68.28%的企業盈利，28.81%的企業虧損。銷售收入最高的省份為江蘇省，佔本行業的35.48%。

	Total number of firms 企業總數	Total number of employees 職工總數	Total revenue (mil. RMB) 總銷售收入（百萬元）	Total profit (mil. RMB) 總利潤（百萬元）	Return on assets 資產利潤率 (%)	Return on equity 權益利潤率 (%)	Labour productivity ('000 RMB / worker) 勞動生產率（千元/人）	Debts / assets 資產負債率 (%)	Total assets (mil. RMB) 總資產（百萬元）
Industry Overall 行業總體	253	18,497	871	21	2.15	6.48	47.09	66.83	971

	Number of firms 企業個數	Average number of employees 平均職工人數	Average revenue ('000 RMB) 平均銷售收入（千元）	Average profit ('000 RMB) 平均利潤（千元）	Return on assets 資產利潤率 (%)	Return on equity 權益利潤率 (%)	Labour productivity ('000 RMB / worker) 勞動生產率（千元/人）	Average debts / assets 平均資產負債率(%)	Average Total assets ('000 RMB) 平均總資產（千元）
By ownership 產業所有權									
State-owned 國有	39	163	5,974				36.67	71.68	8,692
Collectively-owned 集體	186	58	2,445	41	1.97	5.88	42.46	66.49	2,081
Privately-owned 私有	2	52	505	-35	-4.71	-14.48	9.80	67.49	750
Domestic JVs 聯營	1	19	1,047	24	2.46	4.41	55.13	44.22	972
Joint stock 股份制	2	188	24,560	2,374	12.87	24.55	130.99	47.58	18,447
Foreign-funded 外資	7	33	2,686	1,198	31.45	54.15	82.48	41.92	3,811
Overseas Chinese-funded 港澳台資	16	70	7,078	17	0.16	0.46	100.76	66.22	11,203
By size 規模									
Large 大型									
Medium 中型	3	459	29,607	293	0.89	2.40	64.50	62.69	32,802
Small 小型	245	71	3,192	82	2.30	7.05	45.23	67.31	3,564
By regional distribution 地區分布									
Central-North 華北	31	51	2,284	84	3.08	8.98	44.78	65.70	2,713
Beijing 北京	14	30	972	-20	-1.45	-5.86	32.95	75.14	1,376
Tianjin 天津	9	108	6,108	301	4.36	11.61	56.67	62.40	6,903
Hebei 河北	3	19	520	60	32.73	51.43	26.90	36.36	183
Shanxi 山西	1	7							
Inner Mongolia 內蒙	4	33	163	-5	-0.93	-5.71	4.89	83.72	538
Northeast 東北	40	53	1,197	29	1.07	3.21	22.71	66.54	2,722
Liaoning 遼寧	14	45	1,044	81	4.68	11.17	23.41	58.05	1,739
Jilin 吉林	11	83	1,982	-42	-0.68	-2.27	23.96	70.02	6,149
Heilongjiang 黑龍江	15	38	763	33	2.90	8.25	19.98	64.87	1,127
Central East 華東	130	99	5,264	105	1.94	6.09	53.26	68.13	5,423
Shanghai 上海	19	137	6,683	11	0.13	0.45	48.93	70.78	8,385
Jiangsu 江蘇	30	185	10,301	180	1.80	6.46	55.74	72.14	10,000
Zhejiang 浙江	35	57	3,318	108	3.47	12.53	58.18	72.34	3,115
Anhui 安徽	10	89	2,241	-14	-0.35	-0.89	25.12	60.38	3,968
Fujian 福建	16	62	5,329	218	5.08	7.90	86.39	35.66	4,294
Jiangxi 江西	15	48	1,333	34	2.04	16.67	27.50	87.75	1,665
Shandong 山東	5	21	908	86	13.31	30.71	42.43	56.66	646
Central-South 中南	35	30	1,208	50	4.18	11.01	40.27	62.07	1,203
Henan 河南	2	13	5,835	650	81.76	99.24	448.85	18.24	795
Hubei 湖北	4	49	2,373	205	11.71	53.95	48.42	78.43	1,750
Hunan 湖南	16	32	608	-13	-1.37	-9.86	18.91	86.13	960
Guangdong 廣東	8	22	1,281	4	0.19	0.30	59.25	37.52	1,973
Guangxi 廣西	5	28	230	-36	-7.59	-15.38	8.16	50.63	474
Hainan 海南									
Southwest 西南	12	66	2,025	143	5.82	10.95	30.57	46.85	2,448
Chongqing 重慶	6	76	2,227	43	1.48	2.99	29.05	50.47	2,919
Sichuan 四川	2	66	2,285	39	1.52	2.48	34.17	38.80	2,566
Guizhou 貴州	1	63							
Yunnan 雲南	2	34	2,055	665	33.59	58.08	60.44	42.17	1,980
Tibet 西藏									
Northwest 西北	5	23	254	-4	-1.40	-4.17	10.95	66.43	286
Shaanxi 陝西	3	27	157	-13	-5.88	-33.33	5.88	82.35	227
Gansu 甘肅	1	30	700	20	3.13	7.69	23.33	59.38	640
Qinghai 青海									
Ningxia 寧夏									
Xinjiang 新疆	1	6	100				16.67	9.09	110

2419: Other Cultural and Educational Products 其他文化用品製造業

Year 年份	Number of firms 企業個數	Rate of change 每年變化 (%)	Number of employees 職工人數（人）	Rate of change 每年變化 (%)	Total revenue (mil. RMB) 總銷售收入（百萬元）	Rate of change 每年變化 (%)	Total profit (mil. RMB) 總利潤（百萬元）	Rate of change 每年變化 (%)
1993	300		24,325		545		21	
1994	290	-3.33%	23,761	-2.32%	759	39.27%	74	257.61%
1995	302	4.14%	23,379	-1.61%	881	16.10%	18	-75.95%
1996	253	-16.23%	18,497	-20.88%	871	-1.17%	21	17.32%

3 Major products* 3 種主要產品 *	Output 產量	Sales volume 銷售量	Unit 單位
a) Ink 墨水	6,363	6,235	ton 噸
b) Various Kinds of Chesses 各種棋	2,298,369	2,298,369	pair 付

Top 10 firms by revenue (year founded) 收入排名前 10 家企業（創辦年份）	City 城市	Province 省	Telephone / fax 電話 / 傳真	Number of employees 職工人數	Ownership 產業所有權	Revenue ('000 RMB) 銷售收入（千元）	Profit ('000 RMB) (rank) 利潤（千元）（排名）	Total assets ('000 RMB) 總資產（千元）	Major products 主要產品
Fuzhou No.5 Printing Factory 福州市第五印刷廠(1956)	Fuzhou 福州市	Fujian 福建省	(0591)3259511	764	Collectively-owned 集體	56,735	2088(5)	29,575	o
Taicang Paper Products Factory 太倉市紙品廠(1989)	Suzhou 蘇州市	Jiangsu 江蘇省	(0512)3645178	236	Collectively-owned 集體	45,550	820(13)	14,350	o
Ningbo Ya Ning Printing Co. Ltd. 寧波雅寧印刷有限公司(1984)	Ningbo 寧波市	Zhejiang 浙江省	(0574)7344542	358	Foreign-funded 外資	43,589	4807(1)	22,356	o
Jiangyan People Printing Factory 姜堰市人民印刷廠(1955)	Yangzhou 揚州市	Jiangsu 江蘇省	(0514)8213287	630	State-owned 國有	36,276	-3(87)	59,068	o
Taizhou You Yi Printing General Factory 泰州市友誼印刷總廠(1980)	Taizhou 泰州市	Jiangsu 江蘇省	(0523)6223830 (0523)6223830	777	State-owned 國有	31,272	0(84)	30,726	o
Hangzhou Stationery Industrial Co. 杭州文化用品工業公司(1958)	Hangzhou 杭州市	Zhejiang 浙江省	(0571)7027842 (0571)7027842	670	Collectively-owned 集體	30,201	455(29)	18,440	o
Jiangdu Fumin Cutural and Sporting Industrial Co. 江都市富民文體實業公司(1995)	Yangzhou 揚州市	Jiangsu 江蘇省	(0514)6651425	102	Collectively-owned 集體	28,393	232(40)	11,194	o
Tianjin Ink Factory 天津墨水廠(1945)	Tianjin 天津市	Tianjin 天津市	(022)27623400 (022)27622524	407	State-owned 國有	28,105	3103(2)	28,253	a
Shanghai Playing Cards Factory 上海撲克牌廠(1980)	Shanghai 上海市	Shanghai 上海市	(021)56629630 (021)56639146	660	State-owned 國有	23,179	-5517(103)	34,434	o
Shanghai Mingtai Chemical Industry Co. Ltd. 上海明台化學工業有限公司(1989)	Shanghai 上海市	Shanghai 上海市	(021)56620697 (021)56632086	125	Overseas Chinese-funded 港澳台資	23,131	2501(4)	48,312	o

Top 10 Cities by Production Output 產出排名前 10 位城市	Province 省	Market share 市場份額	Number of firms 企業個數
Shanghai 上海市	Shanghai 上海市	15.39%	26
Taizhou 泰州市	Jiangsu 江蘇省	12.00%	13
Fuzhou 福州市	Fujian 福建省	6.98%	9
Hangzhou 杭州市	Zhejiang 浙江省	6.56%	15
Tianjin 天津市	Tianjin 天津市	6.22%	10
Quanzhou 泉州市	Fujian 福建省	4.72%	8
Jinhua 金華市	Zhejiang 浙江省	4.44%	10
Ningbo 寧波市	Zhejiang 浙江省	4.22%	15
Jiamusi 佳木斯市	Heilongjiang 黑龍江省	3.83%	5
Suzhou 蘇州市	Jiangsu 江蘇省	3.17%	11

10 Major Wholesalers 10 家主要批發商	City 城市	Province 省	Telephone / Fax 電話 / 傳真
Shandong Stationary & Sporting Goods Import & Export Company 山東省文教體育用品進出口公司	Qingdao 青島市	Shandong 山東省	(0532)2826827 (0532)3831971
Henan Printing Goods & Materials General Company 河南省印刷物資總公司	Zhengzhou 鄭州市	Henan 河南省	(0371)5967060 (0371)5947912
China Packing Import & Export Singbo Company 中國包裝進出口寧波公司	Ningbo 寧波市	Zhejiang 浙江省	(0574)7367512 (0574)7361096
Tianjin Stationary & Sporting Goods Import & Export Company 天津文教體育用品進出口公司	Tianjin 天津市	Tianjin 天津市	(022)23112048 (022)23112054
China Packing Import & Export Liaoning Company 中國包裝進出口遼寧公司	Dalian 大連市	Liaoning 遼寧省	(0411)4687657 (0411)4687644
Hunan Printing Goods & Materials General Company 湖南省印刷物資總公司	Changsha 長沙市	Hunan 湖南省	(0731)4444618 (0731)4446936
Guangzhou Stationery Co. 廣州市文化用品公司	Guangzhou 廣州市	Guangdong 廣東省	(020)81889089 (020)81861964
Casio Electronics (Shenzhen) Co. Ltd. 卡西歐電子(深圳)有限公司	Shenzhen 深圳市	Guangdong 廣東省	(0755)3590620 (0755)3590565
Changsha Keven Group Co. 長沙市科文集團公司	Changsha 長沙市	Hunan 湖南省	(0731)4444108
Hunan Firecrackers Fireworks Import & Export Company 湖南省鞭炮煙花進出口公司	Changsha 長沙市	Hunan 湖南省	(0731)4439580

*Also include sales by firms outside this industry.包括本行業以外廠家的銷售。"o" stands for "others". "o" 代表 "其他產品" 。

2421: Balls 各種球類製造業

The industry accounts for 0.028% of the total revenue of China's industrial sector in 1996. The revenue growth rate of the industry is 38.8% from 1995, as compared to the growth rate of China's industrial sector, 9.51%. The rate of return on asset is 0.61%. 67.11% of all firms in the industry made a profit while 29.73% had negative returns. The top province in terms of the industry's revenue is Fujian, accounting for 25.52% of the total revenue.
本行業在1996年佔全行業總產值0.028%，行業年增長率為38.8%（全國工業年增長率9.51%）。行業的資產回報率0.61%，67.11%的企業盈利，29.73%的企業虧損。銷售收入最高的省份為福建省，佔本行業的25.52%。

	Total number of firms 企業總數	Total number of employees 職工總數	Total revenue (mil. RMB) 總銷售收入（百萬元）	Total profit (mil. RMB) 總利潤（百萬元）	Return on assets 資產利潤率 (%)	Return on equity 權益利潤率 (%)	Labour productivity ('000 RMB / worker) 勞動生產率（千元/人）	Debts / assets 資產負債率 (%)	Total assets (mil. RMB) 總資產（百萬元）
Industry Overall 行業總體	158	22,391	1,600	9	0.61	1.77	71.46	65.43	1,441

	Number of firms 企業個數	Average number of employees 平均職工人數	Average revenue ('000 RMB) 平均銷售收入（千元）	Average profit ('000 RMB) 平均利潤（千元）	Return on assets 資產利潤率 (%)	Return on equity 權益利潤率 (%)	Labour productivity ('000 RMB / worker) 勞動生產率（千元/人）	Average debts / assets 平均資產負債率(%)	Average Total assets ('000 RMB) 平均總資產（千元）
By ownership 產業所有權									
State-owned 國有	15	290	16,200				55.95	79.94	21,267
Collectively-owned 集體	79	100	6,122	-42	-1.20	-4.85	61.27	75.33	3,485
Privately-owned 私有									
Domestic JVs 聯營	1	144	8,467	-239	-3.24	-6.29	58.80	48.53	7,379
Joint stock 股份制	1	141	11,962	-8	-0.10	-0.77	84.84	87.27	8,440
Foreign-funded 外資	21	130	17,921	258	1.67	3.37	137.50	50.38	15,450
Overseas Chinese-funded 港澳台資	40	177	11,607	183	1.47	3.66	65.68	59.81	12,392
By size 規模									
Large 大型	1	1,606	152,737	-92	-0.08	-0.28	95.10	72.31	118,249
Medium 中型	1	286	43,324	-1,173	-3.43	-5.28	151.48	35.11	34,253
Small 小型	152	134	9,242	68	0.80	2.32	68.81	65.62	8,480
By regional distribution 地區分布									
Central-North 華北	18	82	4,518	153	3.40	17.27	55.32	80.30	4,510
Beijing 北京	2	71	7,950	-130	-0.82	-8.97	111.97	90.84	15,835
Tianjin 天津	9	87	4,214	12	0.30	0.79	48.63	62.51	4,126
Hebei 河北	6	90	4,567	485	23.64	-338.37	50.83	106.99	2,052
Shanxi 山西	1	9	90				10.00	57.14	70
Inner Mongolia 內蒙									
Northeast 東北	3	85	2,243	-920	-22.60	-202.94	26.29	88.86	4,070
Liaoning 遼寧	3	85	2,243	-920	-22.60	-202.94	26.29	88.86	4,070
Jilin 吉林									
Heilongjiang 黑龍江									
Central East 華東	102	150	11,718	154	1.58	3.79	78.37	58.43	9,747
Shanghai 上海	9	307	15,602	684	3.86	11.48	50.86	66.36	17,719
Jiangsu 江蘇	26	104	8,177	250	5.43	13.62	78.45	60.10	4,601
Zhejiang 浙江	24	140	8,538	112	1.41	4.40	61.00	67.88	7,897
Anhui 安徽	10	78	5,034	233	10.72	230.69	64.37	95.35	2,174
Fujian 福建	21	170	19,441	101	0.67	1.52	114.11	55.93	15,069
Jiangxi 江西	2	43	765				18.00	71.83	710
Shandong 山東	10	198	17,718	-413	-2.22	-3.75	89.67	40.77	18,598
Central-South 中南	28	165	10,609	-249	-2.13	-10.50	64.48	79.70	11,669
Henan 河南	1		2,010	90	3.98	13.24		69.91	2,260
Hubei 湖北									
Hunan 湖南	5	148	12,188	-246	-1.40	17.42	82.57	108.05	17,532
Guangdong 廣東	21	176	10,951	-278	-2.51	-8.27	62.06	69.65	11,076
Guangxi 廣西	1	163	4,110	20	0.48	0.95	25.21	50.12	4,210
Hainan 海南									
Southwest 西南	5	106	1,426	-24	-0.83	5.45	13.48	115.30	2,888
Chongqing 重慶	3	102	1,895	-32	-1.06	3.26	18.55	132.62	2,983
Sichuan 四川	2	112	723	-12	-0.45	-3.49	6.47	87.06	2,745
Guizhou 貴州									
Yunnan 雲南									
Tibet 西藏									
Northwest 西北	2	139	6,265	145	2.28	7.97	45.07	71.48	6,365
Shaanxi 陝西									
Gansu 甘肅	2	139	6,265	145	2.28	7.97	45.07	71.48	6,365
Qinghai 青海									
Ningxia 寧夏									
Xinjiang 新疆									

2421: Balls 各種球類製造業

Year 年份	Number of firms 企業個數	Rate of change 每年變化 (%)	Number of employees 職工人數（人）	Rate of change 每年變化 (%)	Total revenue (mil. RMB) 總銷售收入（百萬元）	Rate of change 每年變化 (%)	Total profit (mil. RMB) 總利潤（百萬元）	Rate of change 每年變化 (%)
1993	126		28,146		840		19	
1994	139	10.32%	24,967	-11.30%	1,075	27.96%	11	-45.33%
1995	151	8.63%	23,470	-6.00%	1,153	7.27%	-20	-288.10%
1996	158	4.64%	22,391	-4.60%	1,600	38.77%	9	144.94%

3 Major products* 3 種主要產品 *	Output 產量	Sales volume 銷售量	Unit 單位
a) Table Tennis Ball 乒乓球	85,132	108,969	10,000 piece 萬個
b) Various Kinds of Basket Balls, Volleyballs & Football 各種籃排足球	43,349,089	39,447,671	piece 個
c) Badminton 羽毛球	9,522	9,141	10,000 piece 萬個

Top 10 firms by revenue (year founded) 收入排名前 10 家企業 (創辦年份)	City 城市	Province 省	Telephone / fax 電話 / 傳真	Number of employees 職工人數	Ownership 產業所有權	Revenue ('000 RMB) 銷售收入（千元）	Profit ('000 RMB) (rank) 利潤（千元）（排名）	Total assets ('000 RMB) 總資產（千元）	Major products 主要產品
Qingdao Xin Xin Sports Products Co. Ltd. 青島新新體育用品有限公司(1991)	Qingdao 青島市	Shandong 山東省	(0532)7899354 (0532)897724	941	Foreign-funded 外資	122,998	-1091(88)	92,109	b
Shanghai United Ball Enterprises Corp. 上海製球聯合公司(1949)	Shanghai 上海市	Shanghai 上海市	(021)58835039 (021)58801737	1,488	State-owned 國有	90,591	4007(2)	104,285	b
Shunde Jun An Wei Li Sporting Goods Factory 順德市均安威利體育用品廠(1991)	Foshan 佛山市	Guangdong 廣東省	(0757)5576279	1,252	Collectively-owned 集體	78,741	-356(82)	70,487	b
Tai Hui (Xiamen) Sports Equipment Co. Ltd. 台慧(廈門)運動器材有限公司(1994)	Xiamen 廈門市	Fujian 福建省	(0592)7021928 (0592)7023436	453	Foreign-funded 外資	75,335	97(43)	14,685	o
Longhai Zhuyi Table Ball Products Co. Ltd. 龍海珠益桌球製品有限公司(1992)	Zhangzhou 漳州市	Fujian 福建省	(0596)6777200 (0596)6777209	381	Overseas Chinese-funded 港澳台資	69,500	842(14)	18,166	o
Yi Fu (Longhai) Sports Products Co. Ltd. 義福(龍海)體育用品有限公司(1993)	Zhangzhou 漳州市	Fujian 福建省	(0596)6778017 (0596)6777942	280	Overseas Chinese-funded 港澳台資	62,000	-1252(90)	19,977	o
Nanjing Da Tong Li Sports Products Co. Ltd. 南京大桐利體育用品有限公司(1993)	Nanjing 南京市	Jiangsu 江蘇省	(025)6615735 (025)6615735	260	Foreign-funded 外資	61,105	2448(5)	12,075	o
Shaoxing Dong Feng Physical Culture Articles Factory 紹興市東風體育用品廠(1958)	Shaoxing 紹興市	Zhejiang 浙江省	(0575)5133474 (0575)5133474	566	Collectively-owned 集體	50,183	812(17)	32,092	o
Tian Long Tennis Ball Co. Ltd. 天龍網球有限公司(1988)	Wenzhou 温州市	Zhejiang 浙江省	(0577)6351702 (0577)6353488	170	Foreign-funded 外資	49,250	2050(6)	37,597	o
Xiamen You Lai Si Ball Industry Co. Ltd. 廈門悠來斯球業有限公司(1989)	Xiamen 廈門市	Fujian 福建省	(0592)7029600 (0592)7127392	383	Overseas Chinese-funded 港澳台資	46,476	1977(7)	40,721	b

Top 10 Cities by Production Output 產出排名前 10 位城市	Province 省	Market share 市場份額	Number of firms 企業個數
Shanghai 上海市	Shanghai 上海市	25.12%	16
Guangzhou 廣州市	Guangdong 廣東省	9.82%	15
Wuxi 無錫市	Jiangsu 江蘇省	9.52%	3
Wenzhou 温州市	Zhejiang 浙江省	6.57%	8
Changsha 長沙市	Hunan 湖南省	5.12%	4
Nanjing 南京市	Jiangsu 江蘇省	4.85%	9
Foshan 佛山市	Guangdong 廣東省	4.13%	2
Ningbo 寧波市	Zhejiang 浙江省	4.09%	5
Shaoxing 紹興市	Zhejiang 浙江省	3.98%	1
Yangzhou 揚州市	Jiangsu 江蘇省	3.27%	7

10 Major Wholesalers 10 家主要批發商	City 城市	Province 省	Telephone / Fax 電話 / 傳真
Shandong Stationary & Sporting Goods Import & Export Company 山東省文教體育用品進出口公司	Qingdao 青島市	Shandong 山東省	(0532)2826827 (0532)3831971
Henan Printing Goods & Materials General Company 河南省印刷物資總公司	Zhengzhou 鄭州市	Henan 河南省	(0371)5967060 (0371)5947912
China Packing Import & Export Singbo Company 中國包裝進出口寧波公司	Ningbo 寧波市	Zhejiang 浙江省	(0574)7367512 (0574)7361096
Tianjin Stationary & Sporting Goods Import & Export Company 天津文教體育用品進出口公司	Tianjin 天津市	Tianjin 天津市	(022)23112048 (022)23112054
China Packing Import & Export Liaoning Company 中國包裝進出口遼寧公司	Dalian 大連市	Liaoning 遼寧省	(0411)4687657 (0411)4687644
Hunan Printing Goods & Materials General Company 湖南省印刷物資總公司	Changsha 長沙市	Hunan 湖南省	(0731)4444618 (0731)4446936
Guangzhou Stationery Co. 廣州市文化用品公司	Guangzhou 廣州市	Guangdong 廣東省	(020)81889089 (020)81861964
Casio Electronics (Shenzhen) Co. Ltd. 卡西歐電子(深圳)有限公司	Shenzhen 深圳市	Guangdong 廣東省	(0755)3590620 (0755)3590565
Changsha Keven Group Co. 長沙市科文集團公司	Changsha 長沙市	Hunan 湖南省	(0731)4444108
Hunan Firecrackers Fireworks Import & Export Company 湖南省鞭炮煙花進出口公司	Changsha 長沙市	Hunan 湖南省	(0731)4439580

*Also include sales by firms outside this industry.包括本行業以外廠家的銷售。"o" stands for "others". "o" 代表"其他產品"。

2423: Sports Equipment 各種體育器材製造業

The industry accounts for 0.038% of the total revenue of China's industrial sector in 1996. The revenue growth rate of the industry is 17.6% from 1995, as compared to the growth rate of China's industrial sector, 9.51%. The rate of return on asset is 2.67%. 63.80% of all firms in the industry made a profit while 32.32% had negative returns. The top province in terms of the industry's revenue is Fujian, accounting for 30.26% of the total revenue.
本行業在1996年佔全行業總產值0.038%，行業年增長率為17.6%（全國工業年增長率9.51%）。行業的資產回報率2.67%，63.80%的企業盈利，32.32%的企業虧損。銷售收入最高的省份為福建省，佔本行業的30.26%。

	Total number of firms 企業總數	Total number of employees 職工總數	Total revenue (mil. RMB) 總銷售收入（百萬元）	Total profit (mil. RMB) 總利潤（百萬元）	Return on assets 資產利潤率 (%)	Return on equity 權益利潤率 (%)	Labour productivity ('000 RMB / worker) 勞動生產率（千元/人）	Debts / assets 資產負債率 (%)	Total assets (mil. RMB) 總資產（百萬元）
Industry Overall 行業總體	269	27,082	2,190	62	2.67	7.00	80.87	61.80	2,312

	Number of firms 企業個數	Average number of employees 平均職工人數	Average revenue ('000 RMB) 平均銷售收入（千元）	Average profit ('000 RMB) 平均利潤（千元）	Return on assets 資產利潤率 (%)	Return on equity 權益利潤率 (%)	Labour productivity ('000 RMB / worker) 勞動生產率（千元/人）	Average debts / assets 平均資產負債率(%)	Average Total assets ('000 RMB) 平均總資產（千元）
By ownership 產業所有權									
State-owned 國有	16	96	2,063	125	1.21	2.63	21.48	53.94	10,313
Collectively-owned 集體	150	63	2,949	-229	-8.97	-24.22	46.85	62.95	2,550
Privately-owned 私有	1	21	1,307	-530	-39.84	-87.70	62.25	54.57	1,331
Domestic JVs 聯營	1	47	563	-89	-5.30	-5.30	11.97		1,679
Joint stock 股份制									
Foreign-funded 外資	21	165	16,242	-104	-0.59	-2.02	98.47	70.72	17,622
Overseas Chinese-funded 港澳台資	80	159	17,146	1,214	6.98	17.50	107.56	60.14	17,402
By size 規模									
Large 大型	1	1,081	61,992	-9,605	-5.54	-29.34	57.35	81.11	173,288
Medium 中型	2	665	80,724	-41	-0.07	-0.15	121.39	53.50	58,695
Small 小型	259	94	7,593	277	3.55	9.01	80.81	60.64	7,807
By regional distribution 地區分布									
Central-North 華北	40	58	4,703	607	11.60	26.86	81.50	56.81	5,233
Beijing 北京	10	35	5,212	754	13.13	35.85	149.77	63.37	5,741
Tianjin 天津	13	83	7,212	1,072	16.75	36.00	86.65	53.49	6,398
Hebei 河北	9	24	1,372	128	10.12	16.99	56.65	40.40	1,262
Shanxi 山西	7	94	4,269	237	2.90	6.98	45.27	58.43	8,171
Inner Mongolia 內蒙	1							17.65	170
Northeast 東北	26	139	4,438	93	0.59	2.35	32.02	74.86	15,746
Liaoning 遼寧	7	97	1,446	-586	-9.51	-19.72	14.97	51.77	6,159
Jilin 吉林	4	52	898	-30	-2.39	-30.00	17.26	92.03	1,255
Heilongjiang 黑龍江	15	181	6,779	443	1.84	8.13	37.38	77.38	24,084
Central East 華東	133	112	11,200	242	2.60	6.72	100.15	61.24	9,301
Shanghai 上海	16	105	13,730	205	2.10	6.40	130.45	67.12	9,746
Jiangsu 江蘇	25	101	6,685	59	1.13	3.05	65.95	62.90	5,201
Zhejiang 浙江	24	35	2,210	29	1.28	4.33	63.43	70.44	2,244
Anhui 安徽	5	60	4,088	142	7.07	22.90	68.59	69.22	2,008
Fujian 福建	40	160	16,565	167	0.98	2.72	103.71	64.04	17,067
Jiangxi 江西	5	64	2,472	154	8.27	28.52	38.63	71.00	1,862
Shandong 山東	18	156	19,690	1,034	9.54	16.51	125.99	42.25	10,841
Central-South 中南	52	113	7,497	68	0.80	1.71	66.07	53.16	8,547
Henan 河南	2	25	1,155	70	5.58	16.67	46.20	66.53	1,255
Hubei 湖北	1	20	1,520	190	22.62	41.30	76.00	45.24	840
Hunan 湖南	7	46	411	3	0.40	0.60	9.03	33.60	714
Guangdong 廣東	40	132	9,529	108	1.01	2.12	72.05	52.25	10,606
Guangxi 廣西	2	111	980	-550	-9.27	-114.58	8.87	91.91	5,930
Hainan 海南									
Southwest 西南	15	20	417	-27	-4.44	-25.15	20.90	82.45	615
Chongqing 重慶	3	8	247	-72	-9.55	-91.33	31.10	89.54	751
Sichuan 四川	8	21	498	-5	-1.25	725.14	23.31	100.17	434
Guizhou 貴州	3	29	487	-57	-4.74	-11.97	16.59	60.72	1,197
Yunnan 雲南	1	18							
Tibet 西藏									
Northwest 西北	3	32	253	-70	-8.17	-33.87	7.84	75.88	857
Shaanxi 陝西	1	45	290	-220	-12.29	-2200.00	6.44	99.44	1,790
Gansu 甘肅	1	34	90				2.65	100.00	10
Qinghai 青海	1	18	380	10	1.30	1.64	21.11	20.78	770
Ningxia 寧夏									
Xinjiang 新疆									

2423: Sports Equipment 各種體育器材製造業

Year 年份	Number of firms 企業個數	Rate of change 每年變化 (%)	Number of employees 職工人數 (人)	Rate of change 每年變化 (%)	Total revenue (mil. RMB) 總銷售收入 (百萬元)	Rate of change 每年變化 (%)	Total profit (mil. RMB) 總利潤 (百萬元)	Rate of change 每年變化 (%)
1993	189		19,381		703		18	
1994	216	14.29%	22,553	16.37%	1,108	57.73%	15	-20.55%
1995	243	12.50%	28,275	25.37%	1,863	68.13%	-19	-228.93%
1996	269	10.70%	27,082	-4.22%	2,190	17.55%	62	429.26%

3 Major products* 3 種主要產品 *	Output 產量	Sales volume 銷售量	Unit 單位
a) Badminton Racket 羽毛球拍	3,780,360	3,553,538	piece 支
b) Jogging Health Apparatus 跑步機	351,721	330,617	set 台
c) Tennis Racket 網球拍	2,795,568	2,739,656	piece 支

Top 10 firms by revenue (year founded) 收入排名前 10 家企業 (創辦年份)	City 城市	Province 省	Telephone / fax 電話 / 傳真	Number of employees 職工人數	Ownership 產業所有權	Revenue ('000 RMB) 銷售收入 (千元)	Profit ('000 RMB) (rank) 利潤 (千元) (排名)	Total assets ('000 RMB) 總資產 (千元)	Major products 主要產品
Xiamen Keentech Composite Technology Co. Ltd. 廈門新凱複材科技有限公司(1993)	Xiamen 廈門市	Fujian 福建省	(0592)6077452 (0592)6077450	568	Foreign-funded 外資	165,601	4083(5)	103,624	c
Xiamen Qiao Xing Industrial Co. Ltd. 廈門僑興工業有限公司(1988)	Xiamen 廈門市	Fujian 福建省	(0592)6022020 (0592)6022038	1,034	Overseas Chinese-funded 港澳台資	124,692	1019(23)	80,745	c
Qingdao Ri Ding Sporting Equipment Co. Ltd. 青島日鼎運動器材有限公司(1994)	Qingdao 青島市	Shandong 山東省	(0532)7891431 (0532)7891434	456	Overseas Chinese-funded 港澳台資	107,824	-260(111)	60,440	b
Qingdao Impex Gymnasium Equipment Co. Ltd. 青島英派斯健身器材有限公司(1992)	Qingdao 青島市	Shandong 山東省	(0532)7867666 (0532)7867255	247	Overseas Chinese-funded 港澳台資	99,390	13920(1)	22,895	o
Qiqiha'er Sports Skates Industrial Co. Ltd. 齊齊哈爾冰刀工業有限公司(1989)	Qiqiha'er 齊齊哈爾市	Heilongjiang 黑龍江省	(0452)2713969 (0452)2714827	1,129	Foreign-funded 外資	87,490	4302(4)	232,468	o
Qingdao Gao Li Sports Products Co. Ltd. 青島高麗體育用品有限公司(1996)	Qingdao 青島市	Shandong 山東省	(0532)7871347 (0532)7871345	1,149	Foreign-funded 外資	73,944	1361(19)	47,040	o
Zhongshan Worldmark Sporting Equipment Co. Ltd. 中山廣盛運動器材有限公司(1992)	Zhongshan 中山市	Guangdong 廣東省	(0760)5596821 (0760)5596825	650	Overseas Chinese-funded 港澳台資	71,600	1043(21)	83,723	o
Xiamen Feipeng Sporting Equipment Co. Ltd. 廈門飛鵬運動器材有限公司(1992)	Xiamen 廈門市	Fujian 福建省	(0592)6260792 (0592)6260790	1,403	Overseas Chinese-funded 港澳台資	64,340	8807(3)	90,930	o
Shanghai Yu Xin Precision Casting Co. Ltd. 上海玉鑫精密鑄造有限公司(1996)	Shanghai 上海市	Shanghai 上海市	(021)59733711	102	Overseas Chinese-funded 港澳台資	57,000	1800(15)	16,730	o
Shanghai Superior Sports Co. Ltd. 上海日櫻運動用品有限公司(1993)	Shanghai 上海市	Shanghai 上海市	(021)59791141 (021)59791142	254	Overseas Chinese-funded 港澳台資	55,702	-483(115)	35,090	o

Top 10 Cities by Production Output 產出排名前 10 位城市	Province 省	Market share 市場份額	Number of firms 企業個數
Guangzhou 廣州市	Guangdong 廣東省	17.09%	14
Xiamen 廈門市	Fujian 福建省	12.59%	4
Shanghai 上海市	Shanghai 上海市	9.98%	21
Huizhou 惠州市	Guangdong 廣東省	8.44%	3
Qiqiha'er 齊齊哈爾市	Heilongjiang 黑龍江省	5.46%	6
Dezhou 德州市	Shandong 山東省	5.22%	2
Zhongshan 中山市	Guangdong 廣東省	4.62%	2
Hangzhou 杭州市	Zhejiang 浙江省	3.71%	10
Suzhou 蘇州市	Jiangsu 江蘇省	2.88%	4
Jiangmen 江門市	Guangdong 廣東省	2.84%	4

10 Major Wholesalers 10 家主要批發商	City 城市	Province 省	Telephone / Fax 電話 / 傳真
Shandong Stationary & Sporting Goods Import & Export Company 山東省文教體育用品進出口公司	Qingdao 青島市	Shandong 山東省	(0532)2826827 (0532)3831971
Henan Printing Goods & Materials General Company 河南省印刷物資總公司	Zhengzhou 鄭州市	Henan 河南省	(0371)5967060 (0371)5947912
China Packing Import & Export Singbo Company 中國包裝進出口寧波公司	Ningbo 寧波市	Zhejiang 浙江省	(0574)7367512 (0574)7361096
Tianjin Stationary & Sporting Goods Import & Export Company 天津文教體育用品進出口公司	Tianjin 天津市	Tianjin 天津市	(022)23112048 (022)23112054
China Packing Import & Export Liaoning Company 中國包裝進出口遼寧公司	Dalian 大連市	Liaoning 遼寧省	(0411)4687657 (0411)4687644
Hunan Printing Goods & Materials General Company 湖南省印刷物資總公司	Changsha 長沙市	Hunan 湖南省	(0731)4444618 (0731)4446936
Guangzhou Stationery Co. 廣州市文化用品公司	Guangzhou 廣州市	Guangdong 廣東省	(020)81889089 (020)81861964
Casio Electronics (Shenzhen) Co. Ltd. 卡西歐電子(深圳)有限公司	Shenzhen 深圳市	Guangdong 廣東省	(0755)3590620 (0755)3590565
Changsha Keven Group Co. 長沙市科文集團公司	Changsha 長沙市	Hunan 湖南省	(0731)4444108
Hunan Firecrackers Fireworks Import & Export Company 湖南省鞭炮煙花進出口公司	Changsha 長沙市	Hunan 湖南省	(0731)4439580

*Also include sales by firms outside this industry.包括本行業以外廠家的銷售。"o" stands for "others". "o" 代表 "其他產品" 。

2429: Other Sports Products 其他體育用品製造業

The industry accounts for 0.038% of the total revenue of China's industrial sector in 1996. The revenue growth rate of the industry is -0.3% from 1995, as compared to the growth rate of China's industrial sector, 9.51%. The rate of return on asset is 1.66%. 63.19% of all firms in the industry made a profit while 29.59% had negative returns. The top province in terms of the industry's revenue is Guangdong, accounting for 23.71% of the total revenue.
本行業在 1996 年佔全行業總產值 0.038% ，行業年增長率為 -0.3%（全國工業年增長率 9.51%）。行業的資產回報率 1.66% ，63.19% 的企業盈利，29.59% 的企業虧損。銷售收入最高的省份為廣東省，佔本行業的 23.71% 。

	Total number of firms 企業總數	Total number of employees 職工總數	Total revenue (mil. RMB) 總銷售收入（百萬元）	Total profit (mil. RMB) 總利潤（百萬元）	Return on assets 資產利潤率 (%)	Return on equity 權益利潤率 (%)	Labour productivity ('000 RMB / worker) 勞動生產率（千元／人）	Debts / assets 資產負債率 (%)	Total assets (mil. RMB) 總資產（百萬元）
Industry Overall 行業總體	195	25,223	2,210	39	1.66	4.26	87.62	61.08	2,326

	Number of firms 企業個數	Average number of employees 平均職工人數	Average revenue ('000 RMB) 平均銷售收入（千元）	Average profit ('000 RMB) 平均利潤（千元）	Return on assets 資產利潤率 (%)	Return on equity 權益利潤率 (%)	Labour productivity ('000 RMB / worker) 勞動生產率（千元／人）	Average debts / assets 平均資產負債率(%)	Average Total assets ('000 RMB) 平均總資產（千元）
By ownership 產業所有權									
State-owned 國有	15	265	15,533	400	1.74	10.71	58.63	83.72	22,933
Collectively-owned 集體	115	97	4,335	94	1.47	3.90	44.81	62.24	6,360
Privately-owned 私有	1	17	10	-64	-4.68	-4.68	0.60		1,374
Domestic JVs 聯營	3	141	6,356	-334	-2.36	-7.94	45.08	70.30	14,155
Joint stock 股份制									
Foreign-funded 外資	26	139	13,754	565	4.39	10.45	99.19	57.94	12,848
Overseas Chinese-funded 港澳台資	32	192	34,440	269	0.99	2.06	179.44	52.07	27,273
By size 規模									
Large 大型	1	2,005	94,284	5,553	2.92	10.05	47.02	70.99	190,494
Medium 中型	5	625	44,271	1,260	2.12	6.74	70.86	68.60	59,520
Small 小型	187	108	10,132	145	1.48	3.59	93.93	58.85	9,832
By regional distribution 地區分布									
Central-North 華北	48	81	3,714	20	0.33	0.94	45.84	64.83	6,019
Beijing 北京	14	73	4,397	-84	-1.20	-1.75	60.06	31.36	6,997
Tianjin 天津	18	47	736	-17	-1.50	-5.93	15.78	74.76	1,151
Hebei 河北	10	95	2,671	29	0.67	2.28	28.26	70.48	4,306
Shanxi 山西	6	180	12,797	360	1.70	13.15	71.09	87.09	21,195
Inner Mongolia 內蒙									
Northeast 東北	16	33	2,991	418	13.95	36.22	91.16	61.49	2,998
Liaoning 遼寧	9	29	826	63	9.16	48.31	28.69	81.03	691
Jilin 吉林	2	4	45				12.86	91.67	120
Heilongjiang 黑龍江	5	52	8,068	1,224	14.75	35.44	155.75	58.39	8,300
Central East 華東	85	182	16,535	498	3.07	7.30	90.75	57.91	16,223
Shanghai 上海	19	154	14,328	696	4.76	9.90	93.20	51.95	14,639
Jiangsu 江蘇	26	180	14,226	216	1.71	5.04	79.20	66.05	12,604
Zhejiang 浙江	14	273	29,089	1,598	5.18	8.67	106.50	40.21	30,828
Anhui 安徽	4	30	2,698	158	18.21	73.26	90.67	75.43	865
Fujian 福建	9	85	5,912	-254	-4.96	-14.10	69.28	64.84	5,132
Jiangxi 江西	2	55	2,025	130	14.44	30.59	36.82	52.78	900
Shandong 山東	11	280	26,190	233	0.88	4.31	93.66	79.51	26,368
Central-South 中南	38	135	14,989	-295	-1.87	-5.58	111.23	66.56	15,797
Henan 河南	7	36	1,584	13	0.39	1.40	43.83	72.43	3,337
Hubei 湖北	2	286	4,770	5	0.05	-0.19	16.68	123.92	11,035
Hunan 湖南	4	77	5,025	-1,360	-6.87	-97.32	65.47	92.94	19,783
Guangdong 廣東	23	167	22,785	280	1.45	3.29	136.83	55.92	19,270
Guangxi 廣西	2	80	2,410	-6,150	-37.82	897.81	30.31	104.21	16,260
Hainan 海南									
Southwest 西南	4	24	348	-145	-9.54	-33.53	14.63	71.71	1,520
Chongqing 重慶	2	50	724	318	9.60	33.46	14.49	71.31	3,315
Sichuan 四川	2	8	90	-684	-190.77	-1396.19	11.20	86.34	359
Guizhou 貴州	1	8	170	-30	-5.26	-13.04	21.25	61.40	570
Yunnan 雲南									
Tibet 西藏									
Northwest 西北	4	26	1,963	100	9.73	15.94	74.76	39.17	1,028
Shaanxi 陝西	2	33	3,750	290	18.13	27.88	115.38	35.00	1,600
Gansu 甘肅	1	10	170	30	23.08	23.08	17.00		130
Qinghai 青海									
Ningxia 寧夏									
Xinjiang 新疆	1	30	180	-210	-26.92	-70.00	6.00	62.82	780

2429: Other Sports Products 其他體育用品製造業

Year 年份	Number of firms 企業個數	Rate of change 每年變化 (%)	Number of employees 職工人數 (人)	Rate of change 每年變化 (%)	Total revenue (mil. RMB) 總銷售收入 (百萬元)	Rate of change 每年變化 (%)	Total profit (mil. RMB) 總利潤 (百萬元)	Rate of change 每年變化 (%)
1993	168		11,975		436		16	
1994	192	14.29%	18,843	57.35%	1,062	143.58%	14	-11.44%
1995	212	10.42%	23,851	26.58%	2,216	108.53%	26	85.91%
1996	195	-8.02%	25,223	5.75%	2,210	-0.27%	39	50.86%

3 Major products* 3 種主要產品 *	Output 產量	Sales volume 銷售量	Unit 單位
a) Health Vehicle 健身車	774,849	790,346	set 台
b) Health Apparatus For Single Man 單人單站位健身訓練器	405,527	356,864	set 台
c) Jogging Health Apparatus 跑步機	109,498	102,928	set 台

Top 10 firms by revenue (year founded) 收入排名前 10 家企業 (創辦年份)	City 城市	Province 省	Telephone / fax 電話 / 傳真	Number of employees 職工人數	Ownership 產業所有權	Revenue ('000 RMB) 銷售收入 (千元)	Profit ('000 RMB) (rank) 利潤 (千元) (排名)	Total assets ('000 RMB) 總資產 (千元)	Major products 主要產品
Shengli (China) Group Corp. 浙江生力集團公司(1991)	Huzhou 湖州市	Zhejiang 浙江省	(0572)3915769 (0572)3911888	425	Collectively-owned 集體	300,205	14957(1)	344,310	a,b,c
Huan Qiu Fishing Tackle Industrial Co. Ltd. 山東威海環球漁具實業有限公司(1985)	Weihai 威海市	Shandong 山東省	(0896)5251213 (0896)5251216	1,998	State-owned 國有	123,050	4164(6)	161,548	o
Long Yi Sporting Equipment (Shenzhen) Co. Ltd. 龍億運動器材(深圳)有限公司(1994)	Shenzhen 深圳市	Guangdong 廣東省	(0755)8861304 (0755)8863435	600	Overseas Chinese-funded 港澳台資	109,535	3054(7)	77,758	o
Guang Hua Industries Co. Ltd. 光華工業股份公司(1990)	Guangzhou 廣州市	Guangdong 廣東省	(020)82767997	620	Overseas Chinese-funded 港澳台資	106,674	1144(19)	116,802	o
Jiangsu Shun Tong Group Co. Ltd 江蘇順通集團有限公司(1990)	Xuzhou 徐州市	Jiangsu 江蘇省	(0516)6720118 (0516)6720418	830	Foreign-funded 外資	106,500	7159(4)	91,273	o
Huizhou Jadom Sporting Equipment Co. Ltd. 惠州經迪運動器材有限公司(1992)	Huizhou 惠州市	Guangdong 廣東省	(0751)3320563 (0751)3320562	325	Overseas Chinese-funded 港澳台資	96,000	-657(84)	2,900	o
Shang Yang Fan Industrial General Company 上海洋帆實業總公司(1976)	Shanghai 上海市	Shanghai 上海市	(021)58426153 (021)58423336	236	Collectively-owned 集體	89,426	1147(18)	75,977	o
Shanghai Hong Shuang Xi Guan Du Sports Products Co. Ltd. 上海紅雙喜冠都體育用品有限公司(1996)	Shanghai 上海市	Shanghai 上海市	(021)62598611 (021)62747912	1,186	Overseas Chinese-funded 港澳台資	74,530	9006(2)	119,024	o
Shanxi Changzhi Ao Rui Te Body-building Equipments General Factory 山西長治澳瑞特健身器材總廠(1991)	Changzhi 長治市	Shanxi 山西省	(0355)2029004 (0355)2021961	911	State-owned 國有	73,302	2279(8)	119,317	a,b,c
Zhejiang Tonglu Fu Chun Jiang Furniture General Factory 浙江省桐盧富春江傢具總廠(1980)	Hangzhou 杭州市	Zhejiang 浙江省	(0571)4623157 (0571)4623157	294	Collectively-owned 集體	69,533	8482(3)	38,197	o

Top 10 Cities by Production Output 產出排名前 10 位城市	Province 省	Market share 市場份額	Number of firms 企業個數
Zhenjiang 鎮江市	Jiangsu 江蘇省	24.90%	5
Shanghai 上海市	Shanghai 上海市	10.03%	17
Huzhou 湖州市	Zhejiang 浙江省	9.21%	1
Weihai 威海市	Shandong 山東省	5.54%	5
Hangzhou 杭州市	Zhejiang 浙江省	5.01%	9
Beijing 北京市	Beijing 北京市	4.46%	11
Shaoxing 紹興市	Zhejiang 浙江省	4.31%	4
Guangzhou 廣州市	Guangdong 廣東省	3.70%	14
Changzhi 長治市	Shanxi 山西省	3.69%	4
Yangzhou 揚州市	Jiangsu 江蘇省	3.63%	23

10 Major Wholesalers 10 家主要批發商	City 城市	Province 省	Telephone / Fax 電話 / 傳真
Shandong Stationary & Sporting Goods Import & Export Company 山東省文教體育用品進出口公司	Qingdao 青島市	Shandong 山東省	(0532)2826827 (0532)3831971
Henan Printing Goods & Materials General Company 河南省印刷物資總公司	Zhengzhou 鄭州市	Henan 河南省	(0371)5967060 (0371)5947912
China Packing Import & Export Singbo Company 中國包裝進出口寧波公司	Ningbo 寧波市	Zhejiang 浙江省	(0574)7367512 (0574)7361096
Tianjin Stationary & Sporting Goods Import & Export Company 天津文教體育用品進出口公司	Tianjin 天津市	Tianjin 天津市	(022)23112048 (022)23112054
China Packing Import & Export Liaoning Company 中國包裝進出口遼寧公司	Dalian 大連市	Liaoning 遼寧省	(0411)4687657 (0411)4687644
Hunan Printing Goods & Materials General Company 湖南省印刷物資總公司	Changsha 長沙市	Hunan 湖南省	(0731)4444618 (0731)4446936
Guangzhou Stationery Co. 廣州市文化用品公司	Guangzhou 廣州市	Guangdong 廣東省	(020)81889089 (020)81861964
Casio Electronics (Shenzhen) Co. Ltd. 卡西歐電子(深圳)有限公司	Shenzhen 深圳市	Guangdong 廣東省	(0755)3590620 (0755)3590565
Changsha Keven Group Co. 長沙市科文集團公司	Changsha 長沙市	Hunan 湖南省	(0731)4444108
Hunan Firecrackers Fireworks Import & Export Company 湖南省鞭炮煙花進出口公司	Changsha 長沙市	Hunan 湖南省	(0731)4439580

*Also include sales by firms outside this industry.包括本行業以外廠家的銷售。"o" stands for "others". "o" 代表 "其他產品"。

2431: Chinese Musical Instruments 中樂器製造業

The industry accounts for 0.003% of the total revenue of China's industrial sector in 1996. The revenue growth rate of the industry is 46.6% from 1995, as compared to the growth rate of China's industrial sector, 9.51%. The rate of return on asset is 2.29%. 79.69% of all firms in the industry made a profit while 20.31% had negative returns. The top province in terms of the industry's revenue is Tianjin, accounting for 24.50% of the total revenue.
本行業在1996年佔全行業總產值0.003%，行業年增長率為46.6%（全國工業年增長率9.51%）。行業的資產回報率2.29%，79.69%的企業盈利，20.31%的企業虧損。銷售收入最高的省份為天津市，佔本行業的24.50%。

	Total number of firms 企業總數	Total number of employees 職工總數	Total revenue (mil. RMB) 總銷售收入（百萬元）	Total profit (mil. RMB) 總利潤（百萬元）	Return on assets 資產利潤率 (%)	Return on equity 權益利潤率 (%)	Labour productivity ('000 RMB / worker) 勞動生產率（千元/人）	Debts / assets 資產負債率 (%)	Total assets (mil. RMB) 總資產（百萬元）
Industry Overall 行業總體	62	4,492	167	5	2.29	6.06	37.18	62.16	222

	Number of firms 企業個數	Average number of employees 平均職工人數	Average revenue ('000 RMB) 平均銷售收入（千元）	Average profit ('000 RMB) 平均利潤（千元）	Return on assets 資產利潤率 (%)	Return on equity 權益利潤率 (%)	Labour productivity ('000 RMB / worker) 勞動生產率（千元/人）	Average debts / assets 平均資產負債率(%)	Average Total assets ('000 RMB) 平均總資產（千元）
By ownership 產業所有權									
State-owned 國有	3	95	2,333				24.65	91.30	7,667
Collectively-owned 集體	53	74	2,688	-24	-0.69	-1.78	36.31	61.01	3,416
Privately-owned 私有									
Domestic JVs 聯營									
Joint stock 股份制									
Foreign-funded 外資	3	21	1,372	1,371	57.97	83.83	65.31	30.84	2,365
Overseas Chinese-funded 港澳台資	4	55	3,340	536	19.86	33.08	60.45	39.97	2,699
By size 規模									
Large 大型									
Medium 中型									
Small 小型	60	73	2,783	83	2.25	5.95	37.89	62.16	3,700
By regional distribution 地區分布									
Central-North 華北	27	41	2,078	186	6.93	11.23	50.64	38.28	2,679
Beijing 北京	9	9	142	-4	-2.08		15.24	100.00	213
Tianjin 天津	11	67	3,719	314	6.26	8.19	55.66	23.57	5,014
Hebei 河北	4	55	3,213	395	13.18	99.37	58.68	86.74	2,998
Shanxi 山西	2	35	535	10	0.61	2.25	15.29	72.48	1,635
Inner Mongolia 內蒙	1								
Northeast 東北	3	13	520	57	15.45	27.42	39.00	43.64	367
Liaoning 遼寧	1	4	580	70	116.67	116.67	145.00		60
Jilin 吉林	2	18	490	50	9.62	17.86	27.22	46.15	520
Heilongjiang 黑龍江									
Central East 華東	11	160	5,195	8	0.10	0.53	32.51	80.65	8,009
Shanghai 上海	4	194	8,283	38	0.29	1.26	42.64	77.15	13,053
Jiangsu 江蘇	3	287	7,317	13	0.13	0.87	25.52	84.77	10,003
Zhejiang 浙江	1	54	1,160	10	0.88	2.78	21.48	68.42	1,140
Anhui 安徽									
Fujian 福建	1	35	240	-110	-2.46	-550.00	6.86	99.33	4,470
Jiangxi 江西	1	32	670				20.94	40.74	270
Shandong 山東	1								
Central-South 中南	14	79	2,809	111	3.55	9.21	35.75	61.54	3,142
Henan 河南	3	97	3,463	27	0.39	1.78	35.70	77.95	6,773
Hubei 湖北	3	54	6,450	450	22.43	56.25	119.44	60.13	2,007
Hunan 湖南	3	86	510	3	0.94	3.45	5.93	73.58	353
Guangdong 廣東	5	78	1,610	24	0.72	1.23	20.69	41.17	3,318
Guangxi 廣西									
Hainan 海南									
Southwest 西南	3	81	3,520	173	6.39	13.07	43.46	51.35	2,713
Chongqing 重慶									
Sichuan 四川	1	158	2,640	250	6.17	14.53	16.71	57.53	4,050
Guizhou 貴州	1	30	230	10	1.41	2.13	7.67	35.21	710
Yunnan 雲南	1	55	7,690	260	7.69	14.61	139.82	47.34	3,380
Tibet 西藏									
Northwest 西北	4	61	573	-565	-28.29	-342.42	9.42	91.86	1,998
Shaanxi 陝西	2	56		-20	-23.53	-100.00		82.35	85
Gansu 甘肅									
Qinghai 青海	1	20	440				22.00	34.09	440
Ningxia 寧夏									
Xinjiang 新疆	1	111	1,850	-2,220	-30.08	-672.73	16.67	95.53	7,380

2431: Chinese Musical Instruments 中樂器製造業

Year 年份	Number of firms 企業個數	Rate of change 每年變化 (%)	Number of employees 職工人數 (人)	Rate of change 每年變化 (%)	Total revenue (mil. RMB) 總銷售收入 (百萬元)	Rate of change 每年變化 (%)	Total profit (mil. RMB) 總利潤 (百萬元)	Rate of change 每年變化 (%)
1993	53		6,938		104		2	
1994	67	26.42%	5,512	-20.55%	136	30.42%	-2	-187.15%
1995	65	-2.99%	4,332	-21.41%	114	-16.14%	1	149.21%
1996	62	-4.62%	4,492	3.69%	167	46.65%	5	416.53%

3 Major products* 3 種主要產品 *	Output 產量	Sales volume 銷售量	Unit 單位
a) National Wind Instrument 民族吹管樂器	877,247	973,744	piece 支
b) National Percussion Instrument 民族打擊樂器	539,841	442,670	piece 件
c) National Stringed Instrument 民族弦樂器	123,822	144,872	piece 把

Top 10 firms by revenue (year founded) 收入排名前 10 家企業 (創辦年份)	City 城市	Province 省	Telephone / fax 電話 / 傳真	Number of employees 職工人數	Ownership 產業所有權	Revenue ('000 RMB) 銷售收入 (千元)	Profit ('000 RMB) (rank) 利潤 (千元) (排名)	Total assets ('000 RMB) 總資產 (千元)	Major products 主要產品
Tianjin Jms Musical Instrument Co. Ltd. 天津傑麥詩樂器有限公司(1995)	Tianjin 天津市	Tianjin 天津市	(022)29332742 (022)29345974	150	Overseas Chinese-funded 港澳台資	27,036	2304(1)	33,428	o
Shanghai No.1 National Musical Instruments Factory 上海民族樂器一廠(1958)	Shanghai 上海市	Shanghai 上海市	(021)64921440 (021)64880351	364	Collectively-owned 集體	18,203	464(6)	23,979	a,c
Huangpi Gantang Gao Jia He Gong Factory 黃陂高家河鑼廠(1984)	Wuhan 武漢市	Hubei 湖北省	(027)85943605	110	Collectively-owned 集體	17,000	1270(2)	4,850	o
Suzhou No.1 National Musical Instrument Factory 蘇州市民族樂器一廠(1954)	Suzhou 蘇州市	Jiangsu 江蘇省	(0512)5224238	525	Collectively-owned 集體	16,979	142(13)	20,819	a,b,c
Tianjin Shen Lao Musical Instrument Co. Ltd. 天津沈勞樂器有限公司(1995)	Tianjin 天津市	Tianjin 天津市	(022)9333242 (022)9333242	246	Foreign-funded 外資	11,372	1179(3)	17,212	o
Hebei Huailai Gong Factory 河北省懷來縣鑼廠(1992)	Zhangjiakou 張家口市	Hebei 河北省	(0313)6815481	42	Collectively-owned 集體	8,400	1008(4)	1,490	o
Kunming Musical Instrument Factory 昆明市樂器廠(1960)	Kunming 昆明市	Yunnan 雲南省	(0871)3610896	55	Collectively-owned 集體	7,689	260(10)	3,379	b,c
Shanghai Dun Huang Musical Instrument Co. Ltd. 上海敦煌樂器有限公司(1993)	Shanghai 上海市	Shanghai 上海市	(021)64885371 (021)64880351	42	Overseas Chinese-funded 港澳台資	6,671	413(7)	3,688	a,b,c
Shanghai Nation Musical Instrument No.1 Factory 上海民族樂器一廠(1986)	Shanghai 上海市	Shanghai 上海市	(021)58082182	146	Domestic JVs 聯營	6,293	563(5)	1,972	c
Shanghai Fiddle Factory 上海提琴廠(1951)	Shanghai 上海市	Shanghai 上海市	(021)56778377 (021)56778379	207	State-owned 國有	5,948	3(17)	20,312	o

Top 10 Cities by Production Output 產出排名前 10 位城市	Province 省	Market share 市場份額	Number of firms 企業個數
Tianjin 天津市	Tianjin 天津市	33.16%	12
Shanghai 上海市	Shanghai 上海市	18.21%	4
Suzhou 蘇州市	Jiangsu 江蘇省	12.20%	6
Beijing 北京市	Beijing 北京市	6.91%	8
Guangzhou 廣州市	Guangdong 廣東省	5.16%	5
Pingdingshan 平頂山市	Henan 河南省	3.27%	1
Hengshui 衡水市	Hebei 河北省	2.68%	2
Kaifeng 開封市	Henan 河南省	2.48%	1
Zhangjiakou 張家口市	Hebei 河北省	2.07%	1
Chengdu 成都市	Sichuan 四川省	1.93%	1

10 Major Wholesalers 10 家主要批發商	City 城市	Province 省	Telephone / Fax 電話 / 傳真
Shandong Stationary & Sporting Goods Import & Export Company 山東省文教體育用品進出口公司	Qingdao 青島市	Shandong 山東省	(0532)2826827 (0532)3831971
Henan Printing Goods & Materials General Company 河南省印刷物資總公司	Zhengzhou 鄭州市	Henan 河南省	(0371)5967060 (0371)5947912
China Packing Import & Export Singbo Company 中國包裝進出口寧波公司	Ningbo 寧波市	Zhejiang 浙江省	(0574)7367512 (0574)7361096
Tianjin Stationary & Sporting Goods Import & Export Company 天津文教體育用品進出口公司	Tianjin 天津市	Tianjin 天津市	(022)23112048 (022)23112054
China Packing Import & Export Liaoning Company 中國包裝進出口遼寧公司	Dalian 大連市	Liaoning 遼寧省	(0411)4687657 (0411)4687644
Hunan Printing Goods & Materials General Company 湖南省印刷物資總公司	Changsha 長沙市	Hunan 湖南省	(0731)4444618 (0731)4446936
Guangzhou Stationery Co. 廣州市文化用品公司	Guangzhou 廣州市	Guangdong 廣東省	(020)81889089 (020)81861964
Casio Electronics (Shenzhen) Co. Ltd. 卡西歐電子(深圳)有限公司	Shenzhen 深圳市	Guangdong 廣東省	(0755)3590620 (0755)3590565
Changsha Keven Group Co. 長沙市科文集團公司	Changsha 長沙市	Hunan 湖南省	(0731)4444108
Hunan Firecrackers Fireworks Import & Export Company 湖南省鞭炮煙花進出口公司	Changsha 長沙市	Hunan 湖南省	(0731)4439580

*Also include sales by firms outside this industry.包括本行業以外廠家的銷售。"o" stands for "others". "o" 代表"其他產品"。

2433: Western Musical Instruments 西樂器製造業

The industry accounts for 0.026% of the total revenue of China's industrial sector in 1996. The revenue growth rate of the industry is 8.1% from 1995, as compared to the growth rate of China's industrial sector, 9.51%. The rate of return on asset is 3.01%. 61.12% of all firms in the industry made a profit while 31.53% had negative returns. The top province in terms of the industry's revenue is Guangdong, accounting for 33.09% of the total revenue.
本行業在1996年佔全行業總產值0.026%，行業年增長率為8.1%（全國工業年增長率9.51%）。行業的資產回報率3.01%，61.12%的企業盈利，31.53%的企業虧損。銷售收入最高的省份為廣東省，佔本行業的33.09%。

	Total number of firms 企業總數	Total number of employees 職工總數	Total revenue (mil. RMB) 總銷售收入（百萬元）	Total profit (mil. RMB) 總利潤（百萬元）	Return on assets 資產利潤率 (%)	Return on equity 權益利潤率 (%)	Labour productivity ('000 RMB / worker) 勞動生產率（千元/人）	Debts / assets 資產負債率 (%)	Total assets (mil. RMB) 總資產（百萬元）
Industry Overall 行業總體	115	23,743	1,529	77	3.01	8.64	64.40	65.17	2,559

	Number of firms 企業個數	Average number of employees 平均職工人數	Average revenue ('000 RMB) 平均銷售收入（千元）	Average profit ('000 RMB) 平均利潤（千元）	Return on assets 資產利潤率 (%)	Return on equity 權益利潤率 (%)	Labour productivity ('000 RMB / worker) 勞動生產率（千元/人）	Average debts / assets 平均資產負債率(%)	Average Total assets ('000 RMB) 平均總資產（千元）
By ownership 產業所有權									
State-owned 國有	27	512	37,667	2,815	4.41	15.45	73.53	71.46	63,852
Collectively-owned 集體	60	121	5,254	8	0.10	0.25	43.38	58.69	8,005
Privately-owned 私有									
Domestic JVs 聯營	1	87	328	0	0.01	0.03	3.77	69.43	4,836
Joint stock 股份制	1	217	9,936	53	0.15	0.21	45.79	29.98	35,345
Foreign-funded 外資	10	130	5,906	47	0.72	1.26	45.57	42.88	6,508
Overseas Chinese-funded 港澳台資	16	128	8,004	-1	0.00	-0.01	62.78	45.03	15,630
By size 規模									
Large 大型	5	1,732	198,706	15,493	4.54	12.95	114.74	64.98	341,519
Medium 中型	2	751	27,866	-2,564	-5.58	-15.61	37.11	64.26	45,948
Small 小型	106	131	4,532	44	0.61	1.79	34.69	65.75	7,171
By regional distribution 地區分布									
Central-North 華北	46	174	10,742	368	2.43	8.04	61.79	69.80	15,167
Beijing 北京	15	260	20,529	1,033	3.37	12.38	79.08	72.78	30,653
Tianjin 天津	22	148	7,184	-22	-0.23	-0.80	48.56	70.95	9,346
Hebei 河北	8	104	3,483	239	5.98	7.47	33.37	19.94	3,993
Shanxi 山西	1	12	270	10	2.94	4.55	22.50	35.29	340
Inner Mongolia 內蒙									
Northeast 東北	9	415	10,588	70	0.18	1.91	25.53	90.48	38,436
Liaoning 遼寧	6	507	15,540	237	0.46	4.51	30.65	89.91	52,002
Jilin 吉林	2	303	895	-320	-2.10	-112.28	2.95	98.13	15,215
Heilongjiang 黑龍江	1	85	260	-150	-4.31	-17.24	3.06	75.00	3,480
Central East 華東	41	180	10,367	37	0.22	0.62	57.44	64.58	16,921
Shanghai 上海	9	337	21,970	-551	-1.37	-4.15	65.28	66.91	40,089
Jiangsu 江蘇	12	207	12,778	629	4.37	9.96	61.75	56.09	14,390
Zhejiang 浙江	10	71	1,289	-72	-1.37	-6.36	18.10	78.45	5,254
Anhui 安徽									
Fujian 福建	4	102	7,960	213	2.26	3.96	78.04	42.93	9,410
Jiangxi 江西	3	94	1,393	17	0.55	4.13	14.77	86.71	3,010
Shandong 山東	3	162	8,357	-417	-2.05	-7.56	51.69	72.91	20,353
Central-South 中南	17	250	29,765	3,476	7.31	14.94	119.29	51.06	47,542
Henan 河南	1	291							
Hubei 湖北									
Hunan 湖南									
Guangdong 廣東	16	247	31,626	3,694	7.31	14.94	128.07	51.06	50,514
Guangxi 廣西									
Hainan 海南									
Southwest 西南	2	186	4,140	-590	-8.70	-18.44	22.26	52.73	6,780
Chongqing 重慶									
Sichuan 四川	2	186	4,140	590	8.70	18.41	22.26	52.73	6,780
Guizhou 貴州									
Yunnan 雲南									
Tibet 西藏									
Northwest 西北									
Shaanxi 陝西									
Gansu 甘肅									
Qinghai 青海									
Ningxia 寧夏									
Xinjiang 新疆									

2433: Western Musical Instruments 西樂器製造業

Year 年份	Number of firms 企業個數	Rate of change 每年變化 (%)	Number of employees 職工人數 (人)	Rate of change 每年變化 (%)	Total revenue (mil. RMB) 總銷售收入 (百萬元)	Rate of change 每年變化 (%)	Total profit (mil. RMB) 總利潤 (百萬元)	Rate of change 每年變化 (%)
1993	109		33,500		940		69	
1994	118	8.26%	26,208	-21.77%	1,293	37.49%	80	17.47%
1995	112	-5.09%	24,444	-6.73%	1,414	9.40%	72	-9.92%
1996	115	2.68%	23,743	-2.87%	1,529	8.13%	77	6.23%

3 Major products* 3 種主要產品 *	Output 產量	Sales volume 銷售量	Unit 單位
a) Accordion 手風琴	99,700	94,715	set 架
b) Western Keyboard Instrument 西樂鍵盤樂器	576,753	570,985	set 架
c) Guitar 結他	1,209,657	1,137,078	piece 把

Top 10 firms by revenue (year founded) 收入排名前 10 家企業 (創辦年份)	City 城市	Province 省	Telephone / fax 電話 / 傳真	Number of employees 職工人數	Ownership 產業所有權	Revenue ('000 RMB) 銷售收入 (千元)	Profit ('000 RMB) (rank) 利潤 (千元) (排名)	Total assets ('000 RMB) 總資產 (千元)	Major products 主要產品
Guangzhou Pearl Piano Group Ltd. 廣州市珠江鋼琴集團有限公司(1956)	Guangzhou 廣州市	Guangdong 廣東省	(020)81502729 (020)81509247	2,257	State-owned 國有	355,792	65024(1)	570,429	b
Beijing Xing Hai Musical Instruments Co. Ltd. 北京星海樂器有限責任公司(1994)	Beijing 北京市	Beijing 北京市	(010)67781853 (010)67711318	3,153	State-owned 國有	272,583	13100(2)	417,827	b
Shanghai Piano Co. 上海鋼琴公司(1895)	Shanghai 上海市	Shanghai 上海市	(021)65416510 (021)65450065	1,163	State-owned 國有	96,094	-2769(65)	194,686	b
Yingkou Dong Bei Piano (Group) Co. 營口東北鋼琴(集團)公司(1980)	Yingkou 營口市	Liaoning 遼寧省	(0417)4838502 (0417)4839057	1,775	State-owned 國有	82,110	1184(9)	284,383	o
Yangzhou Chang Jiang Mouth Organ General Factory 揚州市長江口琴總廠(1983)	Taizhou 泰州市	Jiangsu 江蘇省	(0523)4580155 (0523)4580238	524	Collectively-owned 集體	76,457	3819(4)	111,888	o
Tianjin Musical Instrument Factory 天津市樂器廠(1952)	Tianjin 天津市	Tianjin 天津市	(022)24386556	1,219	State-owned 國有	50,794	0(53)	35,008	a,b
Guangdong Musical Instrument Factory 廣州市廣東樂器廠(1957)	Guangzhou 廣州市	Guangdong 廣東省	(020)84415173 (020)84415173	250	State-owned 國有	48,708	1609(7)	45,495	c
Tianjin Jin Bao Musical Instrument Factory 天津市津寶樂器廠(1986)	Tianjin 天津市	Tianjin 天津市	(022)29241326	300	Collectively-owned 集體	43,000	6000(3)	10,360	o
Yantai Longfeng Piano Co. Ltd. 煙台龍鳳鋼琴有限公司	Yantai 煙台市	Shandong 山東省	(0535)6371909 (0535)6371909	479	Overseas Chinese-funded 港澳台資	25,013	-1238(62)	60,816	b
Shanghai Zhong Ya Piano Co. Ltd. 上海中雅鋼琴有限公司(1994)	Shanghai 上海市	Shanghai 上海市	(021)64103930 (021)64766310	185	Overseas Chinese-funded 港澳台資	24,058	549(15)	62,303	b

Top 10 Cities by Production Output 產出排名前 10 位城市	Province 省	Market share 市場份額	Number of firms 企業個數
Guangzhou 廣州市	Guangdong 廣東省	38.24%	13
Shanghai 上海市	Shanghai 上海市	13.38%	14
Tianjin 天津市	Tianjin 天津市	12.81%	22
Taizhou 泰州市	Jiangsu 江蘇省	11.07%	6
Yingkou 營口市	Liaoning 遼寧省	7.43%	5
Beijing 北京市	Beijing 北京市	2.48%	12
Yantai 煙台市	Shandong 山東省	2.07%	1
Wuxi 無錫市	Jiangsu 江蘇省	1.93%	4
Fuzhou 福州市	Fujian 福建省	1.64%	1
Langfang 廊坊市	Hebei 河北省	0.91%	5

10 Major Wholesalers 10 家主要批發商	City 城市	Province 省	Telephone / Fax 電話 / 傳真
Shandong Stationary & Sporting Goods Import & Export Company 山東省文教體育用品進出口公司	Qingdao 青島市	Shandong 山東省	(0532)2826827 (0532)3831971
Henan Printing Goods & Materials General Company 河南省印刷物資總公司	Zhengzhou 鄭州市	Henan 河南省	(0371)5967060 (0371)5947912
China Packing Import & Export Singbo Company 中國包裝進出口寧波公司	Ningbo 寧波市	Zhejiang 浙江省	(0574)7367512 (0574)7361096
Tianjin Stationary & Sporting Goods Import & Export Company 天津文教體育用品進出口公司	Tianjin 天津市	Tianjin 天津市	(022)23112048 (022)23112054
China Packing Import & Export Liaoning Company 中國包裝進出口遼寧公司	Dalian 大連市	Liaoning 遼寧省	(0411)4687657 (0411)4687644
Hunan Printing Goods & Materials General Company 湖南省印刷物資總公司	Changsha 長沙市	Hunan 湖南省	(0731)4444618 (0731)4446936
Guangzhou Stationery Co. 廣州市文化用品公司	Guangzhou 廣州市	Guangdong 廣東省	(020)81889089 (020)81861964
Casio Electronics (Shenzhen) Co. Ltd. 卡西歐電子(深圳)有限公司	Shenzhen 深圳市	Guangdong 廣東省	(0755)3590620 (0755)3590565
Changsha Keven Group Co. 長沙市科文集團公司	Changsha 長沙市	Hunan 湖南省	(0731)4444108
Hunan Firecrackers Fireworks Import & Export Company 湖南省鞭炮煙花進出口公司	Changsha 長沙市	Hunan 湖南省	(0731)4439580

*Also include sales by firms outside this industry.包括本行業以外廠家的銷售。"o" stands for "others". "o" 代表 "其他產品" 。

2435: Electrical Musical Instruments 電子樂器製造業

The industry accounts for 0.018% of the total revenue of China's industrial sector in 1996. The revenue growth rate of the industry is 22.9% from 1995, as compared to the growth rate of China's industrial sector, 9.51%. The rate of return on asset is 6.90%. 82.61% of all firms in the industry made a profit while 17.39% had negative returns. The top province in terms of the industry's revenue is Tianjin, accounting for 73.21% of the total revenue.
本行業在1996年佔全行業總產值0.018%，行業年增長率為22.9%（全國工業年增長率9.51%）。行業的資產回報率6.90%，82.61%的企業盈利，17.39%的企業虧損。銷售收入最高的省份為天津市，佔本行業的73.21%。

	Total number of firms 企業總數	Total number of employees 職工總數	Total revenue (mil. RMB) 總銷售收入（百萬元）	Total profit (mil. RMB) 總利潤（百萬元）	Return on assets 資產利潤率 (%)	Return on equity 權益利潤率 (%)	Labour productivity ('000 RMB / worker) 勞動生產率（千元/人）	Debts / assets 資產負債率 (%)	Total assets (mil. RMB) 總資產（百萬元）
Industry Overall 行業總體	23	3,390	1,035	34	6.90	17.36	305.31	60.25	500

	Number of firms 企業個數	Average number of employees 平均職工人數	Average revenue ('000 RMB) 平均銷售收入（千元）	Average profit ('000 RMB) 平均利潤（千元）	Return on assets 資產利潤率 (%)	Return on equity 權益利潤率 (%)	Labour productivity ('000 RMB / worker) 勞動生產率（千元/人）	Average debts / assets 平均資產負債率(%)	Average Total assets ('000 RMB) 平均總資產（千元）
By ownership 產業所有權									
State-owned 國有	2	140	10,000	500	4.00	33.33	71.68	88.00	12,500
Collectively-owned 集體	7	39	2,946	162	3.52	11.38	76.38	69.05	4,587
Privately-owned 私有									
Domestic JVs 聯營	1	610	15,832	-131	-0.27	-1.61	25.95	83.19	48,204
Joint stock 股份制									
Foreign-funded 外資	7	231	121,159	2,760	5.86	11.85	525.15	50.53	47,077
Overseas Chinese-funded 港澳台資	7	126	18,632	1,811	19.46	84.88	147.37	77.08	9,306
By size 規模									
Large 大型	1	885	811,355	24,473	9.62	20.71	916.79	53.52	254,282
Medium 中型									
Small 小型	21	125	10,649	454	3.88	11.79	85.45	67.11	11,700
By regional distribution 地區分布									
Central-North 華北	6	230	126,683	5,068	11.75	25.53	550.00	53.98	43,148
Beijing 北京	3	9	260	27	12.70	28.57	30.00	53.97	210
Tianjin 天津	2	673	378,870	15,115	11.78	25.49	562.96	53.79	128,335
Hebei 河北	1	10	1,580	100	6.29	41.67	158.00	84.91	1,590
Shanxi 山西									
Inner Mongolia 內蒙									
Northeast 東北	2	59	1,005	-155	-2.91	-7.24	17.18	59.98	5,335
Liaoning 遼寧									
Jilin 吉林	1	97	70	-50	-0.69	-3.03	0.72	77.08	7,200
Heilongjiang 黑龍江	1	20	1,940	-260	-7.49	-9.89	97.00	24.50	3,470
Central East 華東	11	124	12,373	603	4.47	16.76	100.15	73.32	13,485
Shanghai 上海	3	123	20,943	2,250	13.67	94.27	169.81	85.50	16,457
Jiangsu 江蘇	3	145	2,603	-410	-5.86	-19.40	17.91	69.80	6,997
Zhejiang 浙江	2	120	16,820	585	2.84	11.54	140.17	75.35	20,565
Anhui 安徽									
Fujian 福建	2	104	15,910	-30	-0.16	-0.38	152.98	56.76	18,420
Jiangxi 江西									
Shandong 山東	1	105							
Central-South 中南	4	133	34,083	-555	-2.71	-6.21	256.26	56.43	20,503
Henan 河南									
Hubei 湖北									
Hunan 湖南									
Guangdong 廣東	4	133	34,083	-555	-2.71	-6.21	256.26	56.43	20,503
Guangxi 廣西									
Hainan 海南									
Southwest 西南									
Chongqing 重慶									
Sichuan 四川									
Guizhou 貴州									
Yunnan 雲南									
Tibet 西藏									
Northwest 西北									
Shaanxi 陝西									
Gansu 甘肅									
Qinghai 青海									
Ningxia 寧夏									
Xinjiang 新疆									

2435: Electrical Musical Instruments 電子樂器製造業

Year 年份	Number of firms 企業個數	Rate of change 每年變化 (%)	Number of employees 職工人數 (人)	Rate of change 每年變化 (%)	Total revenue (mil. RMB) 總銷售收入 (百萬元)	Rate of change 每年變化 (%)	Total profit (mil. RMB) 總利潤 (百萬元)	Rate of change 每年變化 (%)
1993	19		4,827		273		30	
1994	25	31.58%	3,247	-32.73%	410	50.25%	11	-62.37%
1995	21	-16.00%	2,895	-10.84%	842	105.51%	28	148.08%
1996	23	9.52%	3,390	17.10%	1,035	22.91%	34	22.11%

3 Major products* 3 種主要產品 *	Output 產量	Sales volume 銷售量	Unit 單位
a) Electronic Organ 電子琴	1,813,643	1,922,462	set 架
b) Guitar 結他	9,059	8,515	piece 把

Top 10 firms by revenue (year founded) 收入排名前 10 家企業 (創辦年份)	City 城市	Province 省	Telephone / fax 電話 / 傳真	Number of employees 職工人數	Ownership 產業所有權	Revenue ('000 RMB) 銷售收入 (千元)	Profit ('000 RMB) (rank) 利潤 (千元) (排名)	Total assets ('000 RMB) 總資產 (千元)	Major products 主要產品
Tianjin Yamaha Electronic Musical Instruments Co. Ltd. 天津雅馬哈電子樂器有限公司(1990)	Tianjin 天津市	Tianjin 天津市	(022)25329379 (022)25329143	777	Foreign-funded 外資	757,744	30229(1)	256,672	a
Casio Electronics (Zhuhai) Co. Ltd. 卡西歐電子(珠海)有限公司(1995)	Zhuhai 珠海市	Guangdong 廣東省	(0756)8670888 (0756)8670578	134	Foreign-funded 外資	67,834	-5059(11)	39,175	a
Shanghai Xin Li Electronics Co. Ltd. 上海新理電子有限公司(1993)	Shanghai 上海市	Shanghai 上海市	(021)58840000 (021)58840558	327	Overseas Chinese-funded 港澳台資	61,290	6747(2)	44,204	a
Shenzhen Tong Li Electronics Co. Ltd. 深圳通理電子有限公司(1989)	Shenzhen 深圳市	Guangdong 廣東省	(0755)6613071 (0755)6611841	210	Overseas Chinese-funded 港澳台資	40,120	3535(3)	19,169	a
Xiangcheng Ya Ge Musical Instrument (Zhangzhou) Co. Ltd. 薌城雅歌樂器(漳州)有限公司(1993)	Zhangzhou 漳州市	Fujian 福建省	(0596)2590086 (0596)2590018	104	Overseas Chinese-funded 港澳台資	26,551	-490(8)	30,735	b
Chaoyang Liang Ying Great Wall Electron Co. Ltd. 潮陽市兩英長城電子有限公司(1993)	Shantou 汕頭市	Guangdong 廣東省	(0754)5575268	188	Collectively-owned 集體	24,350	30(7)	2,215	a
Xihu Electronics Group Co. Sound Equipment Factory 西湖電子集團公司音響設備廠(1991)	Hangzhou 杭州市	Zhejiang 浙江省	(0571)5122034 (0571)5123722	160	State-owned 國有	20,100	606(4)	18,176	o
Ningbo Dong Fang Steel Qin Components General Company 寧波東方鋼琴部件總公司(1987)	Ningbo 寧波市	Zhejiang 浙江省	(0574)3549321	59	Collectively-owned 集體	13,543	560(5)	22,954	o
Nan'an Wan Lian Electronics Co. Ltd. 南安市萬聯電子有限公司(1991)	Quanzhou 泉州市	Fujian 福建省	(0595)6781397	87	Overseas Chinese-funded 港澳台資	5,269	428(6)	6,103	o
Xintongmei Electrial Co. Ltd. 新通美電子有限公司(1980)	Nantong 南通市	Jiangsu 江蘇省	(0513)5545410	384	Domestic JVs 聯營	5,211	-1045(10)	13,155	a

Top 10 Cities by Production Output 產出排名前 10 位城市	Province 省	Market share 市場份額	Number of firms 企業個數
Tianjin 天津市	Tianjin 天津市	70.76%	2
Shanghai 上海市	Shanghai 上海市	15.68%	3
Zhuhai 珠海市	Guangdong 廣東省	5.80%	1
Shenzhen 深圳市	Guangdong 廣東省	1.89%	1
Hangzhou 杭州市	Zhejiang 浙江省	1.78%	1
Nantong 南通市	Jiangsu 江蘇省	1.45%	2
Yangzhou 揚州市	Jiangsu 江蘇省	0.66%	1
Weifang 濰坊市	Shandong 山東省	0.65%	1
Zhaoqing 肇慶市	Guangdong 廣東省	0.56%	1
Shantou 汕頭市	Guangdong 廣東省	0.36%	1

10 Major Wholesalers 10 家主要批發商	City 城市	Province 省	Telephone / Fax 電話 / 傳真
Shandong Stationary & Sporting Goods Import & Export Company 山東省文教體育用品進出口公司	Qingdao 青島市	Shandong 山東省	(0532)2826827 (0532)3831971
Henan Printing Goods & Materials General Company 河南省印刷物資總公司	Zhengzhou 鄭州市	Henan 河南省	(0371)5967060 (0371)5947912
China Packing Import & Export Singbo Company 中國包裝進出口寧波公司	Ningbo 寧波市	Zhejiang 浙江省	(0574)7367512 (0574)7361096
Tianjin Stationary & Sporting Goods Import & Export Company 天津文教體育用品進出口公司	Tianjin 天津市	Tianjin 天津市	(022)23112048 (022)23112054
China Packing Import & Export Liaoning Company 中國包裝進出口遼寧公司	Dalian 大連市	Liaoning 遼寧省	(0411)4687657 (0411)4687644
Hunan Printing Goods & Materials General Company 湖南省印刷物資總公司	Changsha 長沙市	Hunan 湖南省	(0731)4444618 (0731)4446936
Guangzhou Stationery Co. 廣州市文化用品公司	Guangzhou 廣州市	Guangdong 廣東省	(020)81889089 (020)81861964
Casio Electronics (Shenzhen) Co. Ltd. 卡西歐電子(深圳)有限公司	Shenzhen 深圳市	Guangdong 廣東省	(0755)3590620 (0755)3590565
Changsha Keven Group Co. 長沙市科文集團公司	Changsha 長沙市	Hunan 湖南省	(0731)4444108
Hunan Firecrackers Fireworks Import & Export Company 湖南省鞭炮煙花進出口公司	Changsha 長沙市	Hunan 湖南省	(0731)4439580

*Also include sales by firms outside this industry.包括本行業以外廠家的銷售。"o" stands for "others". "o" 代表"其他產品"。

2439: Other Musical Instruments 其他樂器及文娛用品製造業

The industry accounts for 0.004% of the total revenue of China's industrial sector in 1996. The revenue growth rate of the industry is 169.6% from 1995, as compared to the growth rate of China's industrial sector, 9.51%. The rate of return on asset is 5.34%. 80.43% of all firms in the industry made a profit while 19.57% had negative returns. The top province in terms of the industry's revenue is Zhejiang, accounting for 52.80% of the total revenue.
本行業在1996年佔全行業總產值0.004%，行業年增長率為169.6%（全國工業年增長率9.51%）。行業的資產回報率5.34%，80.43%的企業盈利，19.57%的企業虧損。銷售收入最高的省份為浙江省，佔本行業的52.80%。

	Total number of firms 企業總數	Total number of employees 職工總數	Total revenue (mil. RMB) 總銷售收入（百萬元）	Total profit (mil. RMB) 總利潤（百萬元）	Return on assets 資產利潤率 (%)	Return on equity 權益利潤率 (%)	Labour productivity ('000 RMB / worker) 勞動生產率（千元/人）	Debts / assets 資產負債率 (%)	Total assets (mil. RMB) 總資產（百萬元）
Industry Overall 行業總體	43	3,765	255	21	5.34	11.89	67.73	55.12	385

	Number of firms 企業個數	Average number of employees 平均職工人數	Average revenue ('000 RMB) 平均銷售收入（千元）	Average profit ('000 RMB) 平均利潤（千元）	Return on assets 資產利潤率 (%)	Return on equity 權益利潤率 (%)	Labour productivity ('000 RMB / worker) 勞動生產率（千元/人）	Average debts / assets 平均資產負債率(%)	Average Total assets ('000 RMB) 平均總資產（千元）
By ownership 產業所有權									
State-owned 國有	3	117	2,333				19.94	91.67	4,000
Collectively-owned 集體	32	93	4,995	506	9.49	19.94	53.77	52.38	5,331
Privately-owned 私有									
Domestic JVs 聯營									
Joint stock 股份制									
Foreign-funded 外資	7	58	12,591	686	2.37	5.29	218.71	55.16	28,910
Overseas Chinese-funded 港澳台資	1	38							
By size 規模									
Large 大型									
Medium 中型									
Small 小型	42	89	6,070	500	5.46	12.14	68.33	55.06	9,166
By regional distribution 地區分布									
Central-North 華北	14	40	1,696	189	13.17	24.93	42.32	47.21	1,431
Beijing 北京	5	17	804	60	6.06	14.29	48.43	57.78	990
Tianjin 天津	7	53	2,739	339	25.99	41.29	51.26	37.17	1,303
Hebei 河北									
Shanxi 山西	1	86	70				0.81	91.75	3,030
Inner Mongolia 內蒙	1	18	480	-30	-1.02	-1.20	26.67	14.63	2,940
Northeast 東北	6	72	3,537	-342	-2.68	-13.20	49.46	79.71	12,755
Liaoning 遼寧	3	25	807	657	74.62	182.41	32.27	59.09	880
Jilin 吉林	1	20	1,920	-220	-25.58	-57.89	96.00	55.81	860
Heilongjiang 黑龍江	2	167	8,440	-1,900	-5.20	-27.01	50.54	80.73	36,515
Central East 華東	15	130	11,825	1,306	7.59	14.64	91.01	48.11	17,197
Shanghai 上海	2	219	4,510	35	0.54	2.01	20.64	72.90	6,440
Jiangsu 江蘇	3	43	3,330	290	4.39	11.13	76.85	60.53	6,613
Zhejiang 浙江	3	375	44,877	6,110	8.97	15.63	119.78	42.64	68,147
Anhui 安徽									
Fujian 福建	3	31	1,533	-60	-2.97	-8.22	49.46	63.86	2,020
Jiangxi 江西									
Shandong 山東	4	41	4,785	125	3.39	16.23	116.00	79.10	3,685
Central-South 中南	8	103	4,131	48	1.24	2.95	40.01	57.84	3,825
Henan 河南	3	76	270	17	2.65	12.20	3.57	78.31	630
Hubei 湖北									
Hunan 湖南									
Guangdong 廣東	5	120	6,448	66	1.15	2.64	53.82	56.50	5,742
Guangxi 廣西									
Hainan 海南									
Southwest 西南									
Chongqing 重慶									
Sichuan 四川									
Guizhou 貴州									
Yunnan 雲南									
Tibet 西藏									
Northwest 西北									
Shaanxi 陝西									
Gansu 甘肅									
Qinghai 青海									
Ningxia 寧夏									
Xinjiang 新疆									

2439: Other Musical Instruments 其他樂器及文娛用品製造業

Year 年份	Number of firms 企業個數	Rate of change 每年變化 (%)	Number of employees 職工人數 (人)	Rate of change 每年變化 (%)	Total revenue (mil. RMB) 總銷售收入 (百萬元)	Rate of change 每年變化 (%)	Total profit (mil. RMB) 總利潤 (百萬元)	Rate of change 每年變化 (%)
1993	58		4,150		110		3	
1994	67	15.52%	4,867	17.28%	186	68.88%	13	292.29%
1995	41	-38.81%	2,909	-40.23%	95	-49.24%	3	-78.03%
1996	43	4.88%	3,765	29.43%	255	169.57%	21	654.58%

3 Major products* 3 種主要產品 *	Output 產量	Sales volume 銷售量	Unit 單位
a) Guitar 結他	233,058	219,075	piece 把
b) Western Stringed Instrument 西弦樂器	200,691	190,656	piece 把
c) National Stringed Instrument 民族弦樂器	4,098	4,795	piece 把

Top 10 firms by revenue (year founded) 收入排名前 10 家企業 (創辦年份)	City 城市	Province 省	Telephone / fax 電話 / 傳真	Number of employees 職工人數	Ownership 產業所有權	Revenue ('000 RMB) 銷售收入 (千元)	Profit ('000 RMB) (rank) 利潤 (千元) (排名)	Total assets ('000 RMB) 總資產 (千元)	Major products 主要產品
Ningbo Yun Sheng Co. Ltd. 寧波韻聲股份有限公司(1991)	Ningbo 寧波市	Zhejiang 浙江省	(0574)7371128	774	Joint stock 股份制	131,592	18433(1)	200,549	o
Tianjin Xiang Jin Musical Instrument Co. Ltd. 天津相進樂器有限公司(1996)	Tianjin 天津市	Tianjin 天津市	(022)29579083	256	Foreign-funded 外資	16,790	2570(2)	5,660	a,b
Harbin Samaick Musical Instruments Co. Ltd. 哈爾濱三益樂器有限公司(1993)	Harbin 哈爾濱市	Heilongjiang 黑龍江省	(0451)7351379	197	Foreign-funded 外資	16,379	-3824(22)	71,149	o
Weifang Yong Xin Injection Moulding Products Co. Ltd. 濰坊永鑫注塑製品有限公司(1993)	Weifang 濰坊市	Shandong 山東省	(0536)7588138 (0536)7588138	20	Overseas Chinese-funded 港澳台資	16,118	414(6)	11,545	o
Guangzhou Zhu Jiang Musical Instrument Industrial Company 廣州珠江樂器實業公司(1993)	Guangzhou 廣州市	Guangdong 廣東省	(020)81891331 (020)81586037	188	Collectively-owned 集體	13,729	75(11)	4,582	o
Shanghai Hua Yue Piano Industrial Co. Ltd. 上海華粵琴業有限公司(1992)	Shanghai 上海市	Shanghai 上海市	(021)58370779 (021)58377958	110	Overseas Chinese-funded 港澳台資	10,467	1758(3)	17,215	o
Yan Bian Li Yi Wooden Products Co. Ltd. 延邊利誼木製品有限公司(1994)	Yanji 延吉市	Jilin 吉林省	(0433)8812278	166	Foreign-funded 外資	9,480	10(16)	8,030	o
Guangzhou String Factory 廣州琴弦廠(1956)	Guangzhou 廣州市	Guangdong 廣東省	(020)87706095	282	Collectively-owned 集體	8,777	100(9)	16,830	o
Conghua Ji Sheng Piano Factory 從化市吉聲琴廠(1966)	Guangzhou 廣州市	Guangdong 廣東省	(020)87921143	27	Collectively-owned 集體	8,075	626(5)	1,770	o
Shanghai Ai Ke Shen Piano Components Factory 上海愛克申鋼琴部件廠(1993)	Shanghai 上海市	Shanghai 上海市	(021)56043112	80	Collectively-owned 集體	6,190	379(8)	9,200	o

Top 10 Cities by Production Output 產出排名前 10 位城市	Province 省	Market share 市場份額	Number of firms 企業個數
Ningbo 寧波市	Zhejiang 浙江省	50.83%	3
Guangzhou 廣州市	Guangdong 廣東省	14.67%	12
Weifang 濰坊市	Shandong 山東省	7.32%	1
Harbin 哈爾濱市	Heilongjiang 黑龍江省	6.89%	2
Shanghai 上海市	Shanghai 上海市	4.75%	5
Tianjin 天津市	Tianjin 天津市	3.72%	7
Nanjing 南京市	Jiangsu 江蘇省	3.35%	4
Beijing 北京市	Beijing 北京市	2.55%	5
Quanzhou 泉州市	Fujian 福建省	1.66%	1
Wuxi 無錫市	Jiangsu 江蘇省	1.01%	2

10 Major Wholesalers 10 家主要批發商	City 城市	Province 省	Telephone / Fax 電話 / 傳真
Shandong Stationary & Sporting Goods Import & Export Company 山東省文教體育用品進出口公司	Qingdao 青島市	Shandong 山東省	(0532)2826827 (0532)3831971
Henan Printing Goods & Materials General Company 河南省印刷物資總公司	Zhengzhou 鄭州市	Henan 河南省	(0371)5967060 (0371)5947912
China Packing Import & Export Singbo Company 中國包裝進出口寧波公司	Ningbo 寧波市	Zhejiang 浙江省	(0574)7367512 (0574)7361096
Tianjin Stationary & Sporting Goods Import & Export Company 天津文教體育用品進出口公司	Tianjin 天津市	Tianjin 天津市	(022)23112048 (022)23112054
China Packing Import & Export Liaoning Company 中國包裝進出口遼寧公司	Dalian 大連市	Liaoning 遼寧省	(0411)4687657 (0411)4687644
Hunan Printing Goods & Materials General Company 湖南省印刷物資總公司	Changsha 長沙市	Hunan 湖南省	(0731)4444618 (0731)4446936
Guangzhou Stationery Co. 廣州市文化用品公司	Guangzhou 廣州市	Guangdong 廣東省	(020)81889089 (020)81861964
Casio Electronics (Shenzhen) Co. Ltd. 卡西歐電子(深圳)有限公司	Shenzhen 深圳市	Guangdong 廣東省	(0755)3590620 (0755)3590565
Changsha Keven Group Co. 長沙市科文集團公司	Changsha 長沙市	Hunan 湖南省	(0731)4444108
Hunan Firecrackers Fireworks Import & Export Company 湖南省鞭炮煙花進出口公司	Changsha 長沙市	Hunan 湖南省	(0731)4439580

*Also include sales by firms outside this industry.包括本行業以外廠家的銷售。"o" stands for "others". "o" 代表"其他產品"。

2440: Toys 玩具製造業

The industry accounts for 0.299% of the total revenue of China's industrial sector in 1996. The revenue growth rate of the industry is 4.6% from 1995, as compared to the growth rate of China's industrial sector, 9.51%. The rate of return on asset is 3.24%. 70.42% of all firms in the industry made a profit while 24.02% had negative returns. The top province in terms of the industry's revenue is Guangdong, accounting for 45.78% of the total revenue.
本行業在1996年佔全行業總產值0.299%，行業年增長率為4.6%（全國工業年增長率9.51%）。行業的資產回報率3.24%，70.42%的企業盈利，24.02%的企業虧損。銷售收入最高的省份為廣東省，佔本行業的45.78%。

	Total number of firms 企業總數	Total number of employees 職工總數	Total revenue (mil. RMB) 總銷售收入（百萬元）	Total profit (mil. RMB) 總利潤（百萬元）	Return on assets 資產利潤率 (%)	Return on equity 權益利潤率 (%)	Labour productivity ('000 RMB / worker) 勞動生產率（千元/人）	Debts / assets 資產負債率 (%)	Total assets (mil. RMB) 總資產（百萬元）
Industry Overall 行業總體	1,536	360,124	17,308	545	3.24	7.58	48.06	57.19	16,808

	Number of firms 企業個數	Average number of employees 平均職工人數	Average revenue ('000 RMB) 平均銷售收入（千元）	Average profit ('000 RMB) 平均利潤（千元）	Return on assets 資產利潤率 (%)	Return on equity 權益利潤率 (%)	Labour productivity ('000 RMB / worker) 勞動生產率（千元/人）	Average debts / assets 平均資產負債率(%)	Average Total assets ('000 RMB) 平均總資產（千元）
By ownership 產業所有權									
State-owned 國有	79	192	4,899	-671	-5.64	-33.13	25.47	82.96	11,886
Collectively-owned 集體	901	219	6,738	359	4.79	11.40	30.72	57.96	7,499
Privately-owned 私有	9	57	3,763	-32	-0.75	-2.28	66.16	66.98	4,184
Domestic JVs 聯營	17	173	8,811	171	2.16	8.80	50.84	75.41	7,895
Joint stock 股份制	5	559	30,616	5,992	16.05	28.40	54.81	43.49	37,332
Foreign-funded 外資	160	253	18,916	283	1.88	4.40	74.69	57.13	15,025
Overseas Chinese-funded 港澳台資	365	288	20,511	538	3.09	6.51	71.26	52.54	17,397
By size 規模									
Large 大型	3	1,183	129,453	2,763	1.91	5.70	109.40	66.41	144,404
Medium 中型	22	1,165	84,380	2,119	2.48	6.48	72.41	61.73	85,374
Small 小型	1,460	227	10,309	336	3.39	7.77	45.36	56.40	9,903
By regional distribution 地區分布									
Central-North 華北	107	88	2,739	-52	-0.87	-3.18	31.21	72.74	6,029
Beijing 北京	51	73	2,518	-152	-2.40	-7.46	34.51	67.89	6,349
Tianjin 天津	24	85	4,458	-23	-0.29	-1.32	52.63	78.17	7,974
Hebei 河北	28	89	1,930	98	2.55	11.45	21.78	77.75	3,840
Shanxi 山西	2	56	280	-10	-0.44	-1.87	5.00	76.27	2,255
Inner Mongolia 內蒙	2	521	1,505				2.89	71.35	8,935
Northeast 東北	25	85	2,938	135	3.85	10.95	34.50	64.86	3,513
Liaoning 遼寧	15	112	4,410	215	4.91	12.92	39.30	61.97	4,383
Jilin 吉林	2	40	130	-140	-8.21	-28.87	3.29	71.55	1,705
Heilongjiang 黑龍江	8	46	881	54	2.30	8.78	19.21	73.81	2,334
Central East 華東	846	173	10,349	229	3.03	8.99	59.82	66.34	7,563
Shanghai 上海	133	177	11,152	-11	-0.09	-0.35	63.11	73.64	11,846
Jiangsu 江蘇	244	233	15,038	373	3.90	10.89	64.61	64.15	9,547
Zhejiang 浙江	154	96	8,551	134	2.11	6.44	89.00	67.21	6,357
Anhui 安徽	81	160	4,687	214	9.85	27.56	29.27	64.27	2,176
Fujian 福建	107	116	7,770	457	7.48	16.93	67.21	55.79	6,100
Jiangxi 江西	27	45	2,419	38	1.49	2.47	54.10	39.63	2,561
Shandong 山東	100	247	10,100	162	2.62	8.57	40.85	69.38	6,161
Central-South 中南	526	380	15,450	684	3.76	7.48	40.66	49.74	18,207
Henan 河南	23	75	3,314	69	2.93	9.65	44.06	69.61	2,358
Hubei 湖北	18	196	4,192	96	1.12	38.05	21.38	97.05	8,502
Hunan 湖南	17	25	342				13.64	88.82	531
Guangdong 廣東	456	423	17,377	783	3.83	7.47	41.05	48.65	20,418
Guangxi 廣西	9	111	4,796	76	2.05	8.21	43.16	75.08	3,691
Hainan 海南	3	58	643	-283	-5.05	-30.69	11.03	83.54	5,610
Southwest 西南	23	58	2,103	-200	-6.24	-23.76	36.21	73.77	3,207
Chongqing 重慶	5	72	4,966	169	13.21	31.83	69.11	58.52	1,282
Sichuan 四川	13	64	1,526	-398	-9.64	-53.24	23.98	81.89	4,130
Guizhou 貴州	2	23	210	15	4.23	10.34	9.13	59.15	355
Yunnan 雲南	3	35	927	-127	-2.84	-5.66	26.23	49.81	4,457
Tibet 西藏									
Northwest 西北	9	113	1,229	-171	-5.87	-50.49	10.88	88.37	2,913
Shaanxi 陝西	8	126	1,376	-193	-5.88	-50.66	10.90	88.40	3,276
Gansu 甘肅	1	7	50				7.14		10
Qinghai 青海									
Ningxia 寧夏									
Xinjiang 新疆									

Year 年份	Number of firms 企業個數	Rate of change 每年變化 (%)	Number of employees 職工人數 (人)	Rate of change 每年變化 (%)	Total revenue (mil. RMB) 總銷售收入 (百萬元)	Rate of change 每年變化 (%)	Total profit (mil. RMB) 總利潤 (百萬元)	Rate of change 每年變化 (%)
1993	1,470		458,267		9,649		593	
1994	1,629	10.82%	538,993	17.62%	12,221	26.65%	439	-25.86%
1995	1,624	-0.31%	399,337	-25.91%	16,548	35.40%	517	17.66%
1996	1,536	-5.42%	360,124	-9.82%	17,308	4.59%	545	5.40%

3 Major products* 3 種主要產品 *	Output 產量	Sales volume 銷售量	Unit 單位
a) Cloth & Flannelette Toy 布絨玩具	6,404,636	6,212,497	1,000 yuan 千元
b) Plastic Toy 塑料玩具	6,964,679	6,477,152	1,000 yuan 千元
c) Childern's Cart 童車	1,433,781	1,448,119	1,000 yuan 千元

Top 10 firms by revenue (year founded) 收入排名前 10 家企業 (創辦年份)	City 城市	Province 省	Telephone / fax 電話 / 傳真	Number of employees 職工人數	Ownership 產業所有權	Revenue ('000 RMB) 銷售收入 (千元)	Profit ('000 RMB) (rank) 利潤 (千元) (排名)	Total assets ('000 RMB) 總資產 (千元)	Major products 主要產品
Guangdong Getta Co. Ltd. 鎮泰廣州有限公司(1993)	Guangzhou 廣州市	Guangdong 廣東省	(020)86621998 (020)86627186	5,150	Overseas Chinese-funded 港澳台資	554,620	44460(2)	226,470	b
Ningbo Hai Wei Group Co. Ltd. 寧波海威集團有限公司(1989)	Ningbo 寧波市	Zhejiang 浙江省	(0574)3601128 (0574)3603060	510	Collectively-owned 集體	505,020	16710(11)	131,703	c
Dongguan Longchang Toys Co. Ltd. 東莞龍昌玩具有限公司(1988)	Dongguan 東莞市	Guangdong 廣東省	(0769)2261414 (0769)2262253	2,740	Overseas Chinese-funded 港澳台資	481,377	10574(18)	223,516	b
Good Baby Group Co. 江蘇好孩子集團公司(1975)	Suzhou 蘇州市	Jiangsu 江蘇省	(0512)7671798 (0512)7671558	2,928	Collectively-owned 集體	423,756	48267(1)	337,036	c
Hao Hai Zi Childern's Cart Factory 好孩子童車廠(1985)	Suzhou 蘇州市	Jiangsu 江蘇省		2,500	Collectively-owned 集體	345,150	19440(9)	255,710	o
Zhongshan International Toys Co. Ltd. 中山國際玩具有限公司(1989)	Zhongshan 中山市	Guangdong 廣東省	(0760)5596778 (0760)5596716	5,400	Foreign-funded 外資	322,060	3200(48)	371,233	b
Bai Ke Xing Privately Owned Economic Development Co. Ltd. 百顆星私營經濟開發有限公司(1994)	Shanghai 上海市	Shanghai 上海市		2,724		310,350	23900(6)	174,622	a
Can Ming Industrial (Shenzhen) Co. Ltd. 燦明實業(深圳)有限公司(1993)	Shenzhen 深圳市	Guangdong 廣東省	(0755)5556356 (0755)5554030	1,347	Overseas Chinese-funded 港澳台資	260,038	36567(3)	446,157	a
Jiangsu Le Kai Group Company 江蘇樂凱集團公司(1981)	Yangzhou 揚州市	Jiangsu 江蘇省	(0514)7304241 (0514)7301583	3,275	Overseas Chinese-funded 港澳台資	256,007	4680(33)	193,507	a
Guangzhou Ri Cheng Toy Products Co. Ltd. 廣州日成玩具製品有限公司(1994)	Guangzhou 廣州市	Guangdong 廣東省	(020)87429040 (020)87422893	2,600	Overseas Chinese-funded 港澳台資	235,354	481(219)	58,007	a

Top 10 Cities by Production Output 產出排名前 10 位城市	Province 省	Market share 市場份額	Number of firms 企業個數
Wuxi 無錫市	Jiangsu 江蘇省	49.85%	18
Shanghai 上海市	Shanghai 上海市	7.62%	196
Guangzhou 廣州市	Guangdong 廣東省	4.85%	79
Zhongshan 中山市	Guangdong 廣東省	4.46%	44
Yangzhou 揚州市	Jiangsu 江蘇省	3.54%	86
Shenzhen 深圳市	Guangdong 廣東省	3.11%	54
Ningbo 寧波市	Zhejiang 浙江省	2.53%	30
Suzhou 蘇州市	Jiangsu 江蘇省	2.31%	32
Foshan 佛山市	Guangdong 廣東省	2.28%	27
Huizhou 惠州市	Guangdong 廣東省	1.99%	77

10 Major Wholesalers 10 家主要批發商	City 城市	Province 省	Telephone / Fax 電話 / 傳真
Jiangsu Light Industry Product Import & Export Group Co. Ltd. 江蘇省輕工業品進出口集團股份有限公司	Nanjing 南京市	Jiangsu 江蘇省	(025)4403618 (025)4407398
Ningbo Light Industry Product Import & Export Company 寧波市輕工業品進出口公司	Ningbo 寧波市	Zhejiang 浙江省	(0574)7324652 (0574)7297985
Shenyang Wishing Cosmetic Articles Company 瀋陽洗滌化妝用品公司	Shenyang 瀋陽市	Liaoning 遼寧省	(024)22523549 (024)22527600
Toy Import & Export Company 玩具進出口公司	Shanghai 上海市	Shanghai 上海市	(021)63262640
Dalian Light Industry Product Import & Export Company 大連輕工業品進出口公司	Dalian 大連市	Liaoning 遼寧省	(0411)4301268 (0411)4308560
Shanghai La Wei Industry & Trade Co. Ltd. Dress Fitting Parts Factory 上海拉維工貿有限公司服飾配件廠	Shanghai 上海市	Shanghai 上海市	(021)63262778
Shandong Light Industry Product Import & Export Company 山東省輕工業品進出口公司	Qingdao 青島市	Shandong 山東省	(0532)3869751 (0532)3869758
Guangdong Qing Chu General Merchandise Co. Ltd. 廣東輕出百貨有限公司	Guangzhou 廣州市	Guangdong 廣東省	(020)83326338 (020)83355241
Guangdong Qing Chu Household Appliances Co. Ltd. 廣東輕出家電有限公司	Guangzhou 廣州市	Guangdong 廣東省	(020)83379166 (020)83376675
Guangdong Qing Chu Box and Bag Co. Ltd. 廣東輕出箱包有限公司	Guangzhou 廣州市	Guangdong 廣東省	(020)83355247 (020)83332183

*Also include sales by firms outside this industry.包括本行業以外廠家的銷售。"o" stands for "others". "o" 代表 "其他產品"。

2450: Game Machines 遊藝器材製造業

The industry accounts for 0.007% of the total revenue of China's industrial sector in 1996. The revenue growth rate of the industry is -64.0% from 1995, as compared to the growth rate of China's industrial sector, 9.51%. The rate of return on asset is 1.45%. 75.00% of all firms in the industry made a profit while 25.00% had negative returns. The top province in terms of the industry's revenue is Guangdong, accounting for 41.42% of the total revenue.
本行業在1996年佔全行業總產值0.007%，行業年增長率為-64.0%（全國工業年增長率9.51%）。行業的資產回報率1.45%，75.00%的企業盈利，25.00%的企業虧損。銷售收入最高的省份為廣東省，佔本行業的41.42%。

	Total number of firms 企業總數	Total number of employees 職工總數	Total revenue (mil. RMB) 總銷售收入（百萬元）	Total profit (mil. RMB) 總利潤（百萬元）	Return on assets 資產利潤率 (%)	Return on equity 權益利潤率 (%)	Labour productivity ('000 RMB / worker) 勞動生產率（千元/人）	Debts / assets 資產負債率 (%)	Total assets (mil. RMB) 總資產（百萬元）
Industry Overall 行業總體	77	6,539	384	6	1.45	3.62	58.72	59.98	396

	Number of firms 企業個數	Average number of employees 平均職工人數	Average revenue ('000 RMB) 平均銷售收入（千元）	Average profit ('000 RMB) 平均利潤（千元）	Return on assets 資產利潤率 (%)	Return on equity 權益利潤率 (%)	Labour productivity ('000 RMB / worker) 勞動生產率（千元/人）	Average debts / assets 平均資產負債率(%)	Average Total assets ('000 RMB) 平均總資產（千元）
By ownership 產業所有權									
State-owned 國有	8	116	3,500	-375	-6.00	-50.00	30.27	88.00	6,250
Collectively-owned 集體	45	98	7,099	212	3.78	9.75	72.29	61.21	5,614
Privately-owned 私有									
Domestic JVs 聯營									
Joint stock 股份制	1	5	45	4	1.11	1.27	8.92	12.91	353
Foreign-funded 外資	9	38	819	-90	-5.26	-9.37	21.42	43.82	1,712
Overseas Chinese-funded 港澳台資	14	65	2,096	18	0.32	0.55	32.35	41.97	5,542
By size 規模									
Large 大型									
Medium 中型	3	310	34,121	294	0.73	1.82	110.19	59.85	40,240
Small 小型	70	80	4,027	73	1.86	4.67	50.55	60.21	3,932
By regional distribution 地區分布									
Central-North 華北	17	57	3,280	48	1.07	2.29	57.31	53.56	4,526
Beijing 北京	9	71	4,049	-9	-0.15	-0.29	57.39	48.04	5,988
Tianjin 天津	1								
Hebei 河北	7	48	2,760	129	3.90	11.64	57.16	66.46	3,293
Shanxi 山西									
Inner Mongolia 內蒙									
Northeast 東北	4	8	78	5	4.35	5.56	9.69	21.74	115
Liaoning 遼寧	2	6	155	10	4.44	5.71	25.83	22.22	225
Jilin 吉林	1	20							10
Heilongjiang 黑龍江	1								
Central East 華東	29	56	5,027	247	5.16	11.56	89.06	55.36	4,777
Shanghai 上海	9	97	10,706	661	5.66	12.32	110.62	54.07	11,682
Jiangsu 江蘇	4	58	4,478	5	0.19	0.38	77.87	49.90	2,630
Zhejiang 浙江	9	48	1,469	21	1.58	4.32	30.82	63.49	1,339
Anhui 安徽									
Fujian 福建	4	15	2,870	165	10.89	13.78	188.20	20.96	1,515
Jiangxi 江西									
Shandong 山東	3	15	2,277	110	6.92	-36.67	148.48	119.08	1,590
Central-South 中南	22	165	8,056	-96	-1.23	-3.90	48.76	68.39	7,809
Henan 河南	3	166	2,247	-47	-1.42	-7.22	13.51	80.32	3,287
Hubei 湖北	2	176	3,780	55	0.60	-8.03	21.48	107.52	9,105
Hunan 湖南									
Guangdong 廣東	14	192	11,362	-1	-0.01	-0.04	59.13	59.57	9,720
Guangxi 廣西	3	31	1,290	-690	-27.09	161.72	41.17	116.75	2,547
Hainan 海南									
Southwest 西南	3	71	597	-60	-3.06	-4.10	8.40	25.34	1,960
Chongqing 重慶									
Sichuan 四川	3	71	597	-60	-3.06	-4.10	8.41	25.34	1,960
Guizhou 貴州									
Yunnan 雲南									
Tibet 西藏									
Northwest 西北	2	25	1,435	40	3.92	4.68	58.57	16.67	1,020
Shaanxi 陝西	2	25	1,435	40	3.92	4.68	58.57	16.67	1,020
Gansu 甘肅									
Qinghai 青海									
Ningxia 寧夏									
Xinjiang 新疆									

2450: Game Machines 遊藝器材製造業

Year 年份	Number of firms 企業個數	Rate of change 每年變化 (%)	Number of employees 職工人數（人）	Rate of change 每年變化 (%)	Total revenue (mil. RMB) 總銷售收入（百萬元）	Rate of change 每年變化 (%)	Total profit (mil. RMB) 總利潤（百萬元）	Rate of change 每年變化 (%)
1993	55		5,127		233		0	
1994	63	14.55%	4,153	-19.00%	157	-32.68%	2	2097.83%
1995	79	25.40%	8,504	104.77%	1,066	581.37%	11	494.18%
1996	77	-2.53%	6,539	-23.11%	384	-63.98%	6	-45.06%

3 Major products* 3 種主要產品 *	Output 產量	Sales volume 銷售量	Unit 單位
a) Electronic Toy 電子玩具	57,220	53,215	1,000 yuan 千元

Top 10 firms by revenue (year founded) 收入排名前 10 家企業 (創辦年份)	City 城市	Province 省	Telephone / fax 電話 / 傳真	Number of employees 職工人數	Ownership 產業所有權	Revenue ('000 RMB) 銷售收入（千元）	Profit ('000 RMB) (rank) 利潤（千元）（排名）	Total assets ('000 RMB) 總資產（千元）	Major products 主要產品
Zhuhai Sez Li Ming Electronics Co. Ltd. 珠海經濟特區利明電子有限公司(1991)	Zhuhai 珠海市	Guangdong 廣東省	(0756)8621938 (0756)8614936	201	Collectively-owned 集體	72,195	778(3)	9,138	o
Shanghai Hua Chang Tourism Handicrafts Co. Ltd. 上海華菖旅遊工藝用品有限公司(1995)	Shanghai 上海市	Shanghai 上海市	(021)57832478 (021)57832549	407	Overseas Chinese-funded 港澳台資	67,888	5650(1)	65,506	o
Beijing Shi Bao Lai Amusement Facilities Manufacture Company 北京實寶來遊樂設施製造公司(1994)	Beijing 北京市	Beijing 北京市	(010)64373552 (010)64363272	309	Collectively-owned 集體	27,052	560(7)	37,567	o
Zhongshan Yue Zhong Electron Co. Ltd. 中山粵中電子有限公司(1992)	Zhongshan 中山市	Guangdong 廣東省	(0760)5596228 (0760)5598553	481	Foreign-funded 外資	26,296	-132(24)	51,096	a
Shanghai Xi Du Nei He Engineering Ship Building and Repair Factory 上海西渡內河工程船舶修造廠(1950)	Shanghai 上海市	Shanghai 上海市	(021)64356658 (021)57150452	260	State-owned 國有	14,748	-372(26)	20,510	o
Dongguan Shi Jia Electronic Toy Co. Ltd. 東莞世佳電子玩具有限公司(1994)	Dongguan 東莞市	Guangdong 廣東省	(0769)3342857 (0769)3342857	200	Overseas Chinese-funded 港澳台資	13,000	575(6)	13,705	a
Dongguan Qiaotuo Zhongxing Electric Appliance Factory 東莞橋頭中星電器廠(1988)	Dongguan 東莞市	Guangdong 廣東省	(0769)3341334 (0769)3343324	1,400	Collectively-owned 集體	12,272	1008(2)	13,736	o
Shishi Da Xin Electronics Development Co. Ltd. 石獅市達新電子發展有限公司(1920)	Quanzhou 泉州市	Fujian 福建省	(0595)8789113 (0595)8789115	52	Overseas Chinese-funded 港澳台資	11,260	660(5)	6,024	o
Zhongshan Ming Xun Electron Co. Ltd. 中山明迅電子有限公司(1994)	Zhongshan 中山市	Guangdong 廣東省	(0760)6632213 (0760)6632214	56	Overseas Chinese-funded 港澳台資	9,573	-74(23)	11,492	o
Da Feng Da Zhong School-run Enterprise Group Company 大豐市大中校辦企業集團公司(1993)	Yancheng 鹽城市	Jiangsu 江蘇省	(0515)3513164	126	Collectively-owned 集體	8,970	120(12)	1,660	o

Top 10 Cities by Production Output 產出排名前 10 位城市	Province 省	Market share 市場份額	Number of firms 企業個數
Zhuhai 珠海市	Guangdong 廣東省	22.70%	2
Shanghai 上海市	Shanghai 上海市	20.09%	17
Zhongshan 中山市	Guangdong 廣東省	12.99%	4
Beijing 北京市	Beijing 北京市	8.77%	9
Guangzhou 廣州市	Guangdong 廣東省	7.92%	9
Baoding 保定市	Hebei 河北省	2.72%	2
Jiangmen 江門市	Guangdong 廣東省	2.41%	1
Hengshui 衡水市	Hebei 河北省	2.28%	1
Guilin 桂林市	Guangxi 廣西	2.02%	3
Liuzhou 柳州市	Guangxi 廣西	1.97%	3

10 Major Wholesalers 10 家主要批發商	City 城市	Province 省	Telephone / Fax 電話 / 傳真
Jiangsu Light Industry Product Import & Export Group Co. Ltd. 江蘇省輕工業品進出口集團股份有限公司	Nanjing 南京市	Jiangsu 江蘇省	(025)4403618 (025)4407398
Ningbo Light Industry Product Import & Export Company 寧波市輕工業品進出口公司	Ningbo 寧波市	Zhejiang 浙江省	(0574)7324652 (0574)7297985
Shenyang Wishing Cosmetic Articles Company 瀋陽洗滌化妝用品公司	Shenyang 瀋陽市	Liaoning 遼寧省	(024)22523549 (024)22527600
Toy Import & Export Company 玩具進出口公司	Shanghai 上海市	Shanghai 上海市	(021)63262640
Dalian Light Industry Product Import & Export Company 大連輕工業品進出口公司	Dalian 大連市	Liaoning 遼寧省	(0411)4301268 (0411)4308560
Shanghai La Wei Industry & Trade Co. Ltd. Dress Fitting Parts Factory 上海拉維工貿有限公司服飾配件廠	Shanghai 上海市	Shanghai 上海市	(021)63262778
Shandong Light Industry Product Import & Export Company 山東省輕工業品進出口公司	Qingdao 青島市	Shandong 山東省	(0532)3869751 (0532)3869758
Guangdong Qing Chu General Merchandise Co. Ltd. 廣東輕出百貨有限公司	Guangzhou 廣州市	Guangdong 廣東省	(020)83326338 (020)83355241
Guangdong Qing Chu Household Appliances Co. Ltd. 廣東輕出家電有限公司	Guangzhou 廣州市	Guangdong 廣東省	(020)83379166 (020)83376675
Guangdong Qing Chu Box and Bag Co. Ltd. 廣東輕出箱包有限公司	Guangzhou 廣州市	Guangdong 廣東省	(020)83355247 (020)83332183

*Also include sales by firms outside this industry.包括本行業以外廠家的銷售。"o" stands for "others". "o" 代表"其他產品"。

2490: Other Cultural, Educational and Sports Products
其他類未包括的文教體育用品製造業

The industry accounts for 0.021% of the total revenue of China's industrial sector in 1996. The revenue growth rate of the industry is 18.3% from 1995, as compared to the growth rate of China's industrial sector, 9.51%. The rate of return on asset is 2.24%. 67.25% of all firms in the industry made a profit while 23.13% had negative returns. The top province in terms of the industry's revenue is Fujian, accounting for 53.40% of the total revenue.
本行業在1996年佔全行業總產值0.021%，行業年增長率為18.3%（全國工業年增長率9.51%）。行業的資產回報率2.24%，67.25%的企業盈利，23.13%的企業虧損。銷售收入最高的省份為福建省，佔本行業的53.40%。

	Total number of firms 企業總數	Total number of employees 職工總數	Total revenue (mil. RMB) 總銷售收入（百萬元）	Total profit (mil. RMB) 總利潤（百萬元）	Return on assets 資產利潤率 (%)	Return on equity 權益利潤率 (%)	Labour productivity ('000 RMB / worker) 勞動生產率（千元/人）	Debts / assets 資產負債率 (%)	Total assets (mil. RMB) 總資產（百萬元）
Industry Overall 行業總體	155	10,065	1,236	27	2.24	7.11	122.80	68.50	1,214

	Number of firms 企業個數	Average number of employees 平均職工人數	Average revenue ('000 RMB) 平均銷售收入（千元）	Average profit ('000 RMB) 平均利潤（千元）	Return on assets 資產利潤率 (%)	Return on equity 權益利潤率 (%)	Labour productivity ('000 RMB / worker) 勞動生產率（千元/人）	Average debts / assets 平均資產負債率(%)	Average Total assets ('000 RMB) 平均總資產（千元）
By ownership 產業所有權									
State-owned 國有	13	136	7,615	231	1.92	2.86	55.96	32.69	12,000
Collectively-owned 集體	106	34	1,930	92	4.89	12.32	56.94	60.30	1,890
Privately-owned 私有	1	111	21,567	1,481	14.65	61.67	194.30	76.25	10,107
Domestic JVs 聯營	4	75	6,423	609	11.64	45.19	85.92	74.24	5,229
Joint stock 股份制	1	41	130				3.18	98.82	944
Foreign-funded 外資	15	214	55,027	680	1.36	6.35	257.38	78.53	49,883
Overseas Chinese-funded 港澳台資	15	104	4,043	5	0.10	0.28	38.97	62.59	5,178
By size 規模									
Large 大型	1	484	56,372	4,845	4.57	7.26	116.47	37.11	106,117
Medium 中型									
Small 小型	151	64	7,819	147	2.00	7.03	121.72	71.54	7,337
By regional distribution 地區分布									
Central-North 華北	27	38	2,085	19	0.64	2.42	55.58	73.52	2,949
Beijing 北京	16	32	1,494	38	1.15	4.45	47.16	74.08	3,309
Tianjin 天津	6	39	5,015	-10	-0.29	-1.06	128.59	72.31	3,413
Hebei 河北	2	52	335	-30	-1.49	-11.54	6.50	87.06	2,010
Shanxi 山西									
Inner Mongolia 內蒙	3	56	543	7	0.92	1.72	9.64	46.08	723
Northeast 東北	16	18	489	73	8.85	26.98	26.69	67.18	819
Liaoning 遼寧	10	17	560	40	4.19	10.64	33.94	60.63	955
Jilin 吉林	3	9	213	7	4.65	10.53	24.62	55.81	143
Heilongjiang 黑龍江	3	34	527	247	23.72	211.43	15.49	88.78	1,040
Central East 華東	56	94	17,369	399	2.45	9.21	184.63	73.43	16,285
Shanghai 上海	10	112	8,700	-276	-2.24	-3.75	77.54	40.26	12,321
Jiangsu 江蘇	8	69	7,178	-31	-0.75	-2.39	103.46	68.75	4,176
Zhejiang 浙江	11	64	5,833	771	12.10	39.74	91.27	69.54	6,370
Anhui 安徽	7	10	461	4	1.51	3.80	47.50	60.30	284
Fujian 福建	12	174	55,000	1,066	2.01	10.85	316.24	81.51	53,138
Jiangxi 江西	2	46	1,305	235	27.49	39.50	28.68	29.82	855
Shandong 山東	6	107	16,370	593	8.11	20.89	152.99	61.18	7,317
Central-South 中南	42	70	3,714	50	1.47	2.90	52.92	49.21	3,368
Henan 河南	5	23	540	32	5.33	17.20	23.08	69.00	600
Hubei 湖北	4	160	5,908	93	0.78	1.16	36.98	32.81	11,888
Hunan 湖南	11	52	3,927	45	1.92	5.66	76.19	66.07	2,320
Guangdong 廣東	13	110	6,398	70	1.62	3.15	58.05	48.65	4,332
Guangxi 廣西	9	21	366	17	1.65	10.87	17.14	84.67	1,008
Hainan 海南									
Southwest 西南	9	14	3,303	108	2.16	2.59	237.84	16.78	5,000
Chongqing 重慶	3	3	997	34	5.48	8.73	343.00	37.23	616
Sichuan 四川	4	17	6,626	202	1.86	2.19	379.15	15.10	10,860
Guizhou 貴州	2	25	430	40	9.41	20.51	17.20	54.12	425
Yunnan 雲南									
Tibet 西藏									
Northwest 西北	5	84	2,624	30	0.65	2.76	31.39	76.49	4,620
Shaanxi 陝西	4	103	3,213	25	0.45	2.07	31.19	78.44	5,600
Gansu 甘肅									
Qinghai 青海	1	6	270	50	7.14	8.33	45.00	14.29	700
Ningxia 寧夏									
Xinjiang 新疆									

2490: Other Cultural, Educational and Sports Products
其他類未包括的文教體育用品製造業

Year 年份	Number of firms 企業個數	Rate of change 每年變化 (%)	Number of employees 職工人數 (人)	Rate of change 每年變化 (%)	Total revenue (mil. RMB) 總銷售收入 (百萬元)	Rate of change 每年變化 (%)	Total profit (mil. RMB) 總利潤 (百萬元)	Rate of change 每年變化 (%)
1993	128		11,227		183		10	
1994	161	25.78%	10,185	-9.28%	481	163.57%	9	-9.65%
1995	174	8.07%	12,531	23.03%	1,045	117.28%	22	147.86%
1996	155	-10.92%	10,065	-19.68%	1,236	18.28%	27	20.49%

3 Major products* 3種主要產品*	Output 產量	Sales volume 銷售量	Unit 單位
a) Various Kinds of Chesses 各種棋	9,061,585	9,061,585	pair 付
b) Fishing Rod 釣魚竿	1,658,636	1,658,636	piece 支

Top 10 firms by revenue (year founded) 收入排名前10家企業 (創辦年份)	City 城市	Province 省	Telephone / fax 電話 / 傳真	Number of employees 職工人數	Ownership 產業所有權	Revenue ('000 RMB) 銷售收入 (千元)	Profit ('000 RMB) (rank) 利潤 (千元) (排名)	Total assets ('000 RMB) 總資產 (千元)	Major products 主要產品
Xiamen Jinwoong Enterprise Co. Ltd. 廈門進雄企業有限公司(1988)	Xiamen 廈門市	Fujian 福建省	(0592)6022106 (0592)6022108	1,214	Foreign-funded 外資	624,017	14500(1)	613,903	o
Shanghai Film Technology Plant 上海電影技術廠(1954)	Shanghai 上海市	Shanghai 上海市	(021)56628742 (021)56639888	453	State-owned 國有	47,746	1554(4)	76,213	o
Ningbo Beilun Hatty Precision Machinery Manufacture Co. Ltd. 寧波市北侖海伯精密機械製造有限公司(1990)	Ningbo 寧波市	Zhejiang 浙江省	(0574)6887504 (0574)6882132	271	Collectively-owned 集體	41,361	6863(2)	45,078	o
Qingdao Jason Sporting Goods Co. Ltd. 青島財李孫體育用品有限公司(1991)	Qingdao 青島市	Shandong 山東省	(0532)7896484 (0532)7897748	280	Foreign-funded 外資	36,005	914(7)	17,856	o
Qingdao Gold Star Sporting Goods Co. Ltd. 青島金星體育用品有限公司(1993)	Qingdao 青島市	Shandong 山東省	(0532)7893953 (0532)7893953	150	Foreign-funded 外資	33,878	-24(41)	11,641	o
Yixing Fang Zhuang Science & Education Instrument Factory 宜興市芳裝科教儀器廠(1989)	Wuxi 無錫市	Jiangsu 江蘇省	(0510)7971523	56	Collectively-owned 集體	26,180	0(37)	4,620	o
Tianjin Tian Shi Fallow Articles Co. Ltd. 天津天石休閑用品有限公司(1994)	Tianjin 天津市	Tianjin 天津市	(022)23393086	150	Foreign-funded 外資	25,053	-195(46)	11,063	o
Chengdu Tuo Fei Sports Equipment Co. Ltd. 成都拓菲體育運動器材有限公司(1993)	Chengdu 成都市	Sichuan 四川省	(028)5187550	38	Foreign-funded 外資	24,680	736(8)	31,600	o
Weihai Huan Qiu Fishing Tackle Industrial Co. Ltd. Feng Da Jointly-operated Fishing Tackle Factory 威海環球漁具實業有限公司馮達聯營釣具廠(1989)	Weihai 威海市	Shandong 山東省	(0896)6466052 (0896)6466052	137	Collectively-owned 集體	22,600	2480(3)	12,000	b
Yangjiang No.2 Light Industry Managenment Office 陽江市二輕工業管理所	Yangjiang 陽江市	Guangdong 廣東省	(0662)322569	200	Collectively-owned 集體	21,231	363(11)	13,648	o

Top 10 Cities by Production Output 產出排名前10位城市	Province 省	Market share 市場份額	Number of firms 企業個數
Shanghai 上海市	Shanghai 上海市	10.75%	18
Quanzhou 泉州市	Fujian 福建省	10.68%	3
Ningbo 寧波市	Zhejiang 浙江省	8.68%	3
Beijing 北京市	Beijing 北京市	7.99%	13
Tianjin 天津市	Tianjin 天津市	6.88%	12
Chengdu 成都市	Sichuan 四川省	5.64%	7
Weihai 威海市	Shandong 山東省	4.95%	2
Changsha 長沙市	Hunan 湖南省	4.59%	1
Shiyan 十堰市	Hubei 湖北省	4.39%	1
Zhongshan 中山市	Guangdong 廣東省	3.74%	1

10 Major Wholesalers 10家主要批發商	City 城市	Province 省	Telephone / Fax 電話 / 傳真
Shandong Stationary & Sporting Goods Import & Export Company 山東省文教體育用品進出口公司	Qingdao 青島市	Shandong 山東省	(0532)2826827 (0532)3831971
Henan Printing Goods & Materials General Company 河南省印刷物資總公司	Zhengzhou 鄭州市	Henan 河南省	(0371)5967060 (0371)5947912
China Packing Import & Export Singbo Company 中國包裝進出口寧波公司	Ningbo 寧波市	Zhejiang 浙江省	(0574)7367512 (0574)7361096
Tianjin Stationary & Sporting Goods Import & Export Company 天津文教體育用品進出口公司	Tianjin 天津市	Tianjin 天津市	(022)23112048 (022)23112054
China Packing Import & Export Liaoning Company 中國包裝進出口遼寧公司	Dalian 大連市	Liaoning 遼寧省	(0411)4687657 (0411)4687644
Hunan Printing Goods & Materials General Company 湖南省印刷物資總公司	Changsha 長沙市	Hunan 湖南省	(0731)4444618 (0731)4446936
Guangzhou Stationery Co. 廣州市文化用品公司	Guangzhou 廣州市	Guangdong 廣東省	(020)81889089 (020)81861964
Casio Electronics (Shenzhen) Co. Ltd. 卡西歐電子(深圳)有限公司	Shenzhen 深圳市	Guangdong 廣東省	(0755)3590620 (0755)3590565
Changsha Keven Group Co. 長沙市科文集團公司	Changsha 長沙市	Hunan 湖南省	(0731)4444108
Hunan Firecrackers Fireworks Import & Export Company 湖南省鞭炮煙花進出口公司	Changsha 長沙市	Hunan 湖南省	(0731)4439580

*Also include sales by firms outside this industry.包括本行業以外廠家的銷售。"o" stands for "others". "o" 代表 "其他產品"。

2510: Artificial Crude Oil Production 人造原油生產業

The industry accounts for 0.019% of the total revenue of China's industrial sector in 1996. The revenue growth rate of the industry is 20.4% from 1995, as compared to the growth rate of China's industrial sector, 9.51%. The rate of return on asset is 0.84%. 69.47% of all firms in the industry made a profit while 10.53% had negative returns. The top province in terms of the industry's revenue is Shanxi, accounting for 79.12% of the total revenue.
本行業在 1996 年佔全行業總產值 0.019% ，行業年增長率為 20.4%（全國工業年增長率 9.51%）。行業的資產回報率 0.84% ，69.47% 的企業盈利， 10.53% 的企業虧損。銷售收入最高的省份為山西省，佔本行業的 79.12% 。

	Total number of firms 企業總數	Total number of employees 職工總數	Total revenue (mil. RMB) 總銷售收入（百萬元）	Total profit (mil. RMB) 總利潤（百萬元）	Return on assets 資產利潤率 (%)	Return on equity 權益利潤率 (%)	Labour productivity ('000 RMB / worker) 勞動生產率（千元／人）	Debts / assets 資產負債率 (%)	Total assets (mil. RMB) 總資產（百萬元）
Industry Overall 行業總體	46	14,166	1,127	20	0.84	1.56	79.56	45.99	2,320

	Number of firms 企業個數	Average number of employees 平均職工人數	Average revenue ('000 RMB) 平均銷售收入（千元）	Average profit ('000 RMB) 平均利潤（千元）	Return on assets 資產利潤率 (%)	Return on equity 權益利潤率 (%)	Labour productivity ('000 RMB / worker) 勞動生產率（千元／人）	Average debts / assets 平均資產負債率(%)	Average Total assets ('000 RMB) 平均總資產（千元）
By ownership 產業所有權									
State-owned 國有	6	2,078	143,000	1,167	0.35	0.62	68.82	43.65	336,000
Collectively-owned 集體	33	45	6,458	387	5.13	12.94	144.58	60.34	7,540
Privately-owned 私有									
Domestic JVs 聯營	2	32	18,053	293	1.73	3.92	573.11	55.96	16,978
Joint stock 股份制	1	72							
Foreign-funded 外資	2	35	9,684	83	0.97	3.23	280.70	70.13	8,615
Overseas Chinese-funded 港澳台資									
By size 規模									
Large 大型	1	11,630	850,880	10,086	0.48	0.86	73.16	44.46	2,117,746
Medium 中型									
Small 小型	42	57	6,574	236	4.88	12.82	115.92	61.93	4,838
By regional distribution 地區分布									
Central-North 華北	14	936	68,692	562	0.38	0.68	73.43	44.17	148,669
Beijing 北京	6	6	3,935	7	0.28	2.04	674.57	86.12	2,353
Tianjin 天津	1								
Hebei 河北	4	62	11,603	50	1.01	5.57	186.39	81.96	4,960
Shanxi 山西	3	4,271	297,223	2,543	0.37	0.66	69.59	43.52	682,470
Inner Mongolia 內蒙									
Northeast 東北	15	34	3,755	433	4.32	9.54	108.96	54.70	10,021
Liaoning 遼寧	11	34	4,277	587	14.84	26.10	125.80	43.18	3,958
Jilin 吉林	3	44	2,950				66.54	59.52	35,503
Heilongjiang 黑龍江	1	10	430	40	14.81	17.39	43.00	14.81	270
Central East 華東	7	37	8,619	759	11.79	56.37	232.04	79.09	6,436
Shanghai 上海									
Jiangsu 江蘇	3	50	3,447	40	0.85	10.71	68.48	92.02	4,680
Zhejiang 浙江									
Anhui 安徽	1	45	5,660	660	33.00	64.71	125.78	49.00	2,000
Fujian 福建									
Jiangxi 江西									
Shandong 山東	3	21	14,777	1,510	15.62	62.23	692.66	74.91	9,670
Central-South 中南	3	22	7,113	43	0.56	1.92	318.51	71.14	7,807
Henan 河南	1	10	1,910	80	3.72	12.31	191.00	70.23	2,150
Hubei 湖北	1	50	19,370	50	0.24	0.83	387.40	71.50	21,050
Hunan 湖南									
Guangdong 廣東									
Guangxi 廣西	1	7	60				8.57	45.45	220
Hainan 海南									
Southwest 西南	4	22	4,743	-240	-9.51	-58.18	215.57	83.85	2,523
Chongqing 重慶	0	8	367	41	21.40	41.09	45.64	47.92	191
Sichuan 四川	2	25	9,904	442	8.63	46.70	399.53	81.53	5,122
Guizhou 貴州									
Yunnan 雲南	2	23	1,170	-105	-14.09	-700.00	52.00	98.66	745
Tibet 西藏									
Northwest 西北	3	46	2,937	230	7.17	13.56	64.31	47.14	3,210
Shaanxi 陝西									
Gansu 甘肅	3	46	2,937	230	7.17	13.56	64.31	47.14	3,210
Qinghai 青海									
Ningxia 寧夏									
Xinjiang 新疆									

2510: Artificial Crude Oil Production 人造原油生產業

Year 年份	Number of firms 企業個數	Rate of change 每年變化(%)	Number of employees 職工人數(人)	Rate of change 每年變化(%)	Total revenue (mil. RMB) 總銷售收入(百萬元)	Rate of change 每年變化(%)	Total profit (mil. RMB) 總利潤(百萬元)	Rate of change 每年變化(%)
1993	68		4,072		191		6	
1994	76	11.76%	2,539	-37.65%	160	-16.08%	9	49.19%
1995	72	-5.26%	14,802	482.99%	936	485.41%	13	46.14%
1996	46	-36.11%	14,166	-4.30%	1,127	20.37%	20	57.99%

3 Major products* 3 種主要產品 *	Output 產量	Sales volume 銷售量	Unit 單位
a) Lubricating Grease 潤滑脂	4,562	4,425	ton 噸
b) Coke 焦炭	1,521,206	851,875	ton 噸
c) Lubricating Oil 潤滑油	19,780	17,208	ton 噸

Top 10 firms by revenue (year founded) 收入排名前 10 家企業(創辦年份)	City 城市	Province 省	Telephone / fax 電話 / 傳真	Number of employees 職工人數	Ownership 產業所有權	Revenue ('000 RMB) 銷售收入(千元)	Profit ('000 RMB) (rank) 利潤(千元)(排名)	Total assets ('000 RMB) 總資產(千元)	Major products 主要產品
Taiyuan Coal Gasify General Co. 太原煤炭氣化總公司(1982)	Taiyuan 太原市	Shanxi 山西省	(0351)6019214 (0351)6040001	12,313	State-owned 國有	853,188	7086(1)	2,002,700	b
Rushan San You Lubricant Oil Co. Ltd. 乳山三友潤滑油有限公司(1985)	Weihai 威海市	Shandong 山東省	(0896)6466062 (0896)6466061	64	Foreign-funded 外資	44,330	4530(3)	29,010	a,c
Qinhuangdao Yu Li Petroleum Products Co. Ltd. 秦皇島譽利石油製品有限公司(1993)	Qinhuangdao 秦皇島市	Hebei 河北省	(0335)3012304	20	Overseas Chinese-funded 港澳台資	38,200	-282(14)	8,308	o
Xiangyuan Chemical Group General Co. 襄垣縣化工集團總公司(1993)	Changzhi 長治市	Shanxi 山西省	(0355)7426011	500	Collectively-owned 集體	38,000	530(5)	43,020	o
Shenyang Ao Ji Na Fine Chemical Company 瀋陽市奧吉娜精細化學公司(1991)	Shenyang 瀋陽市	Liaoning 遼寧省	(024)25810501	60	Collectively-owned 集體	37,431	5830(2)	19,882	c
Chengdu Fei Da Petrochemical Co. Ltd. 成都菲達石油化工有限公司	Chengdu 成都市	Sichuan 四川省	(028)5558138	39	Foreign-funded 外資	16,522	-754(15)	8,508	c
Jilin Ji Yuan Petroleum Natural Gas Development Co. Ltd. 吉林省吉原石油天然氣開發有限責任公司(1995)	Changchun 長春市	Jilin 吉林省	(0431)4630070 (0431)4630070	111	Joint stock 股份制	8,800	0(11)	103,733	o
Nanjing Nan Jiang Petrochemical Plant 南京市南江化工廠(1990)	Nanjing 南京市	Jiangsu 江蘇省	(025)6414825	116	Collectively-owned 集體	7,001	116(10)	13,310	o
Fuyang Great Wall Grease Company 阜陽市長城潤滑油脂公司(1993)	Fuyang 阜陽市	Anhui 安徽省	(0558)2257814	45	Collectively-owned 集體	5,660	660(4)	2,000	o
Lanzhou Jin Chen No.2 Chemical Plant 蘭州金晨化工二廠(1989)	Lanzhou 蘭州市	Gansu 甘肅省	(0931)7556639	70	Collectively-owned 集體	5,520	480(6)	4,940	o

Top 10 Cities by Production Output 產出排名前 10 位城市	Province 省	Market share 市場份額	Number of firms 企業個數
Daqing 大慶市	Heilongjiang 黑龍江省	24.69%	1
Qinhuangdao 秦皇島市	Hebei 河北省	17.96%	2
Shenyang 瀋陽市	Liaoning 遼寧省	16.74%	5
Lanzhou 蘭州市	Gansu 甘肅省	13.60%	3
Yuncheng 運城市	Shanxi 山西省	4.09%	1
Shijiazhuang 石家莊市	Hebei 河北省	3.63%	2
Nanjing 南京市	Jiangsu 江蘇省	3.32%	2
Weihai 威海市	Shandong 山東省	3.19%	3
Beijing 北京市	Beijing 北京市	2.75%	5
Changzhi 長治市	Shanxi 山西省	2.60%	1

10 Major Wholesalers 10 家主要批發商	City 城市	Province 省	Telephone / Fax 電話 / 傳真
Zhong Hua Liaoning Import & Export Company 中化遼寧進出口公司	Dalian 大連市	Liaoning 遼寧省	(0411)2821888 (0411)2639378
Huzhou Petrochemical Marketing General Company 湖州市石化銷售總公司	Huzhou 湖州市	Zhejiang 浙江省	(0572)2067002
Xinjiang Wei Wu Er Autonomous Region Petroleum General Company Urumqi Branch 新疆維吾爾自治區石油總公司烏魯木齊分公司	Urumqi 烏魯木齊市	Xinjiang 新疆	(0991)6897333
Shanghai Petroleum (Group) Co. Ltd. 上海石油(集團)有限公司	Shanghai 上海市	Shanghai 上海市	(021)63219490
Guangzhou Development Zone Zhong Sui Petrochemical Products Supply & Marketing Company 廣州開發區中穗石油化工產品供銷公司	Guangzhou 廣州市	Guangdong 廣東省	(020)82393431 (020)82398354
China Petrochemical Marketing Maoming Company 中國石化銷售茂名公司	Maoming 茂名市	Guangdong 廣東省	(0668)2245836 (0668)2269297
Zhejiang Petroleum General Co. 浙江省石油總公司	Hangzhou 杭州市	Zhejiang 浙江省	(0571)7805026 (0571)7805201
Guangdong Petroleum Enterprise Group Co. 廣東省石油企業集團公司	Guangzhou 廣州市	Guangdong 廣東省	(020)81850888 (020)81856088
China Shipping Fuel Supply Shanghai Company 中國船舶燃料供應上海公司	Shanghai 上海市	Shanghai 上海市	(021)63290555
Zhejiang Petroleum General Company Singbo Branch 浙江省石油總公司寧波分公司	Ningbo 寧波市	Zhejiang 浙江省	(0574)7267937 (0574)7268027

*Also include sales by firms outside this industry.包括本行業以外廠家的銷售。"o" stands for "others". "o" 代表"其他產品"。

2520: Processing of Crude Oil 原油加工業

The industry accounts for 3.540% of the total revenue of China's industrial sector in 1996. The revenue growth rate of the industry is 9.1% from 1995, as compared to the growth rate of China's industrial sector, 9.51%. The rate of return on asset is 2.77%. 80.63% of all firms in the industry made a profit while 14.67% had negative returns. The top province in terms of the industry's revenue is Liaoning, accounting for 16.81% of the total revenue.
本行業在1996年佔全行業總產值3.540%，行業年增長率為9.1%（全國工業年增長率9.51%）。行業的資產回報率2.77%，80.63%的企業盈利，14.67%的企業虧損。銷售收入最高的省份為遼寧省，佔本行業的16.81%。

	Total number of firms 企業總數	Total number of employees 職工總數	Total revenue (mil. RMB) 總銷售收入（百萬元）	Total profit (mil. RMB) 總利潤（百萬元）	Return on assets 資產利潤率 (%)	Return on equity 權益利潤率 (%)	Labour productivity ('000 RMB / worker) 勞動生產率（千元/人）	Debts / assets 資產負債率 (%)	Total assets (mil. RMB) 總資產（百萬元）
Industry Overall 行業總體	940	532,543	205,217	5,502	2.77	6.24	385.35	55.57	198,530

	Number of firms 企業個數	Average number of employees 平均職工人數	Average revenue ('000 RMB) 平均銷售收入（千元）	Average profit ('000 RMB) 平均利潤（千元）	Return on assets 資產利潤率 (%)	Return on equity 權益利潤率 (%)	Labour productivity ('000 RMB / worker) 勞動生產率（千元/人）	Average debts / assets 平均資產負債率(%)	Average Total assets ('000 RMB) 平均總資產（千元）
By ownership 產業所有權									
State-owned 國有	168	2,752	1,099,714	25,357	2.45	5.47	399.60	55.09	1,032,952
Collectively-owned 集體	707	69	10,046	447	3.45	19.37	146.63	82.16	12,945
Privately-owned 私有	5	80	20,722	329	1.56	373.33	257.73	99.58	21,093
Domestic JVs 聯營	11	40	11,302	481	4.45	38.33	283.20	88.40	10,829
Joint stock 股份制	14	1,188	767,729	72,163	7.72	11.67	646.31	33.87	935,182
Foreign-funded 外資	23	171	102,105	-3,965	-3.68	150.48	598.02	102.45	107,744
Overseas Chinese-funded 港澳台資	11	31	3,547	-6	-0.15	-0.36	113.08	57.00	4,134
By size 規模									
Large 大型	39	11,601	4,862,034	134,808	2.91	6.40	419.10	54.59	4,636,050
Medium 中型	20	1,079	349,863	-4,400	-1.11	-3.75	324.26	70.44	396,952
Small 小型	855	66	10,059	389	3.40	8.84	151.52	61.55	11,443
By regional distribution 地區分布									
Central-North 華北	127	622	236,353	8,888	4.75	8.53	379.87	44.28	186,913
Beijing 北京	23	1,660	708,559	28,827	5.49	9.57	426.75	42.60	525,052
Tianjin 天津	15	1,670	499,594	7,743	1.81	3.19	299.11	43.39	428,597
Hebei 河北	67	184	71,882	5,836	10.72	16.82	390.16	36.27	54,446
Shanxi 山西	8	31	15,025	-188	-2.01	-32.47	492.62	93.81	9,348
Inner Mongolia 內蒙	14	228	92,126	-2,853	-2.64	-12.24	404.44	78.39	107,866
Northeast 東北	323	443	168,317	5,179	2.50	6.56	380.33	61.98	207,522
Liaoning 遼寧	188	453	183,511	7,429	3.32	9.84	405.15	66.26	223,777
Jilin 吉林	23	338	94,517	-1,294	-1.72	-4.20	279.78	59.14	75,391
Heilongjiang 黑龍江	112	447	157,969	2,731	1.32	2.89	353.70	54.43	207,372
Central East 華東	222	714	304,031	9,029	3.40	6.74	425.60	49.58	265,847
Shanghai 上海	22	756	435,486	7,156	2.09	4.49	576.11	53.37	342,018
Jiangsu 江蘇	61	505	224,030	3,271	2.46	4.79	443.22	48.76	133,231
Zhejiang 浙江	12	1,066	833,792	74,636	9.25	15.30	782.54	39.55	806,918
Anhui 安徽	20	753	263,085	365	0.16	0.51	349.59	69.39	234,751
Fujian 福建	6	532	568,513	-17,513	-2.67	-16.99	1069.30	84.26	654,905
Jiangxi 江西	8	947	427,956	4,661	1.85	3.45	452.09	46.47	252,108
Shandong 山東	93	780	238,134	8,735	3.53	6.20	305.36	43.16	247,765
Central-South 中南	141	748	278,307	2,366	0.99	2.38	371.87	58.58	239,771
Henan 河南	75	183	69,728	3,912	6.04	12.96	381.61	53.38	64,741
Hubei 湖北	36	581	230,051	2,320	1.62	3.29	396.30	50.90	143,537
Hunan 湖南	6	6,382	1,381,413	4,880	0.29	0.93	216.47	68.27	1,661,050
Guangdong 廣東	14	2,219	1,230,687	-6,321	-0.65	-1.50	554.67	56.71	972,739
Guangxi 廣西	10	157	21,178	1,595	7.97	11.06	134.81	27.90	20,010
Hainan 海南									
Southwest 西南	37	60	3,490	-40	-0.86	-2.01	58.27	57.26	4,661
Chongqing 重慶	6	25	1,056	-19	-1.12	-1.77	42.89	36.74	1,710
Sichuan 四川	25	76	4,705	69	1.09	2.58	61.63	57.76	6,284
Guizhou 貴州	4	21	1,475	25	1.66	8.33	71.95	80.27	1,508
Yunnan 雲南	2	50							
Tibet 西藏									
Northwest 西北	90	492	155,209	4,041	2.46	6.42	315.69	61.65	164,042
Shaanxi 陝西	24	140	70,079	6,560	9.16	20.26	501.16	54.76	71,584
Gansu 甘肅	26	819	270,323	6,199	3.07	7.73	329.88	60.24	201,619
Qinghai 青海									
Ningxia 寧夏	7	488	118,220	5,880	5.41	10.11	242.11	46.47	108,620
Xinjiang 新疆	33	490	134,272	119	0.06	0.16	274.04	66.03	213,436

2520: Processing of Crude Oil 原油加工業

Year 年份	Number of firms 企業個數	Rate of change 每年變化 (%)	Number of employees 職工人數（人）	Rate of change 每年變化 (%)	Total revenue (mil. RMB) 總銷售收入（百萬元）	Rate of change 每年變化 (%)	Total profit (mil. RMB) 總利潤（百萬元）	Rate of change 每年變化 (%)
1993	846		505,619		128,713		6,944	
1994	919	8.63%	536,368	6.08%	143,853	11.76%	4,082	-41.21%
1995	919	0	546,882	1.96%	188,140	30.79%	7,116	74.30%
1996	940	2.29%	532,543	-2.62%	205,217	9.08%	5,502	-22.68%

3 Major products* 3 種主要產品 *	Output 產量	Sales volume 銷售量	Unit 單位
a) Parffin War 石蠟	1,023,723	972,537	ton 噸
b) Kerosene 煤油	4,776,350	3,964,371	ton 噸
c) Disel Oil 柴油	36,830,913	37,935,841	ton 噸

Top 10 firms by revenue (year founded) 收入排名前 10 家企業 (創辦年份)	City 城市	Province 省	Telephone / fax 電話 / 傳真	Number of employees 職工人數	Ownership 產業所有權	Revenue ('000 RMB) 銷售收入（千元）	Profit ('000 RMB) (rank) 利潤（千元）（排名）	Total assets ('000 RMB) 總資產（千元）	Major products 主要產品
China Petrochemical Beijing Yan Shan Petrochemical Co. 中國石化北京燕山石油化工公司(1969)	Beijing 北京市	Beijing 北京市	(010)69342281 (010)69342736	41,553	State-owned 國有	16,244,299	662274(2)	12,045,599	a,b,c
China Petrochemical Qi Lu Petrochemical Co. 中國石油化工總公司齊魯石油化工公司(1967)	Zibo 淄博市	Shandong 山東省	(0533)7180777 (0533)7180406	50,540	State-owned 國有	14,692,365	150290(11)	16,877,977	b,c
China Petrochemical Fushun Petrochemical Co. 中國石油化工公司撫順公司(1928)	Fushun 撫順市	Liaoning 遼寧省	(0413)2622484 (0413)2622484	32,273	State-owned 國有	14,169,629	9607(44)	21,229,480	b,c
China Petrochemical Jin Ling Petrochemical Co. 中國石化金陵石油化工公司(1982)	Nanjing 南京市	Jiangsu 江蘇省	(025)5097076 (025)5410537	22,187	State-owned 國有	11,877,064	180595(9)	6,916,341	b,c
China Petrochemical Daqing Petrochemical General Plant 中國石化大慶石油化工總廠(1963)	Daqing 大慶市	Heilongjiang 黑龍江省	(0459)6763228 (0459)6250208	39,235	State-owned 國有	11,272,414	50085(21)	17,207,990	a,b,c
China Petrochemical Shanghai Gao Qiao Petrochemical Co. 中國石化上海高橋石油化工公司(1945)	Shanghai 上海市	Shanghai 上海市	(021)58711001 (021)58712207	16,417	State-owned 國有	9,308,300	150014(12)	7,323,928	a,b,c
Zhenhai Refining & Chemical Co. Ltd. 鎮海煉油化工股份有限公司(1978)	Ningbo 寧波市	Zhejiang 浙江省	(0574)6444213 (0574)6270015	6,129	Joint stock 股份制	9,233,531	850507(1)	8,859,749	b,c
Sinopec Maominig Petrochemical Co. 中國石化茂名石油化工公司(1965)	Maoming 茂名市	Guangdong 廣東省	(0668)2242241 (0668)2269317	18,352	State-owned 國有	8,889,233	-49981(443)	7,560,410	a,b,c
China Ba Ling Petrochemical Company 中國巴陵石油化工公司(1971)	Yueyang 岳陽市	Hunan 湖南省	(0730)8844512 (0730)8843613	39,291	State-owned 國有	8,277,372	29010(28)	9,962,266	b,c
China Petrochemical Tianjin Petrochemical Co. 中國石化天津石油化工公司(1976)	Tianjin 天津市	Tianjin 天津市	(022)27356622 (022)25990965	21,246	State-owned 國有	7,217,152	74534(16)	6,347,673	b,c

Top 10 Cities by Production Output 產出排名前 10 位城市	Province 省	Market share 市場份額	Number of firms 企業個數
Yueyang 岳陽市	Hunan 湖南省	8.96%	4
Maoming 茂名市	Guangdong 廣東省	6.54%	2
Shanghai 上海市	Shanghai 上海市	6.44%	42
Ningbo 寧波市	Zhejiang 浙江省	5.93%	2
Nanjing 南京市	Jiangsu 江蘇省	5.50%	17
Tianjin 天津市	Tianjin 天津市	5.02%	15
Dalian 大連市	Liaoning 遼寧省	4.90%	8
Beijing 北京市	Beijing 北京市	4.63%	15
Lanzhou 蘭州市	Gansu 甘肅省	3.80%	9
Anqing 安慶市	Anhui 安徽省	3.47%	2

10 Major Wholesalers 10 家主要批發商	City 城市	Province 省	Telephone / Fax 電話 / 傳真
Zhong Hua Liaoning Import & Export Company 中化遼寧進出口公司	Dalian 大連市	Liaoning 遼寧省	(0411)2821888 (0411)2639378
Huzhou Petrochemical Marketing General Company 湖州市石化銷售總公司	Huzhou 湖州市	Zhejiang 浙江省	(0572)2067002
Xinjiang Wei Wu Er Autonomous Region Petroleum General Company Urumqi Branch 新疆維吾爾自治區石油總公司烏魯木齊分公司	Urumqi 烏魯木齊市	Xinjiang 新疆	(0991)6897333
Shanghai Petroleum (Group) Co. Ltd. 上海石油(集團)有限公司	Shanghai 上海市	Shanghai 上海市	(021)63219490
Guangzhou Development Zone Zhong Sui Petrochemical Products Supply & Marketing Company 廣州開發區中穗石油化工產品供銷公司	Guangzhou 廣州市	Guangdong 廣東省	(020)82393431 (020)82398354
China Petrochemical Marketing Maoming Company 中國石化銷售茂名公司	Maoming 茂名市	Guangdong 廣東省	(0668)2245836 (0668)2269297
Zhejiang Petroleum General Co. 浙江省石油總公司	Hangzhou 杭州市	Zhejiang 浙江省	(0571)7805026 (0571)7805201
Guangdong Petroleum Enterprise Group Co. 廣東省石油企業集團公司	Guangzhou 廣州市	Guangdong 廣東省	(020)81850888 (020)81856088
China Shipping Fuel Supply Shanghai Company 中國船舶燃料供應上海公司	Shanghai 上海市	Shanghai 上海市	(021)63290555
Zhejiang Petroleum General Company Singbo Branch 浙江省石油總公司寧波分公司	Ningbo 寧波市	Zhejiang 浙江省	(0574)7267937 (0574)7268027

*Also include sales by firms outside this industry.包括本行業以外廠家的銷售。"o" stands for "others". "o" 代表 "其他產品"。

2530: Petroleum Products 石油製品業

The industry accounts for 0.160% of the total revenue of China's industrial sector in 1996. The revenue growth rate of the industry is 20.8% from 1995, as compared to the growth rate of China's industrial sector, 9.51%. The rate of return on asset is 4.06%. 74.00% of all firms in the industry made a profit while 19.65% had negative returns. The top province in terms of the industry's revenue is Shandong, accounting for 14.40% of the total revenue.
本行業在1996年佔全行業總產值0.160%，行業年增長率為20.8%（全國工業年增長率9.51%）。行業的資產回報率4.06%，74.00%的企業盈利，19.65%的企業虧損。銷售收入最高的省份為山東省，佔本行業的14.40%。

	Total number of firms 企業總數	Total number of employees 職工總數	Total revenue (mil. RMB) 總銷售收入（百萬元）	Total profit (mil. RMB) 總利潤（百萬元）	Return on assets 資產利潤率 (%)	Return on equity 權益利潤率 (%)	Labour productivity ('000 RMB / worker) 勞動生產率（千元/人）	Debts / assets 資產負債率 (%)	Total assets (mil. RMB) 總資產（百萬元）
Industry Overall 行業總體	837	80,501	9,261	337	4.06	10.90	115.04	62.70	8,300

	Number of firms 企業個數	Average number of employees 平均職工人數	Average revenue ('000 RMB) 平均銷售收入（千元）	Average profit ('000 RMB) 平均利潤（千元）	Return on assets 資產利潤率 (%)	Return on equity 權益利潤率 (%)	Labour productivity ('000 RMB / worker) 勞動生產率（千元/人）	Average debts / assets 平均資產負債率(%)	Average Total assets ('000 RMB) 平均總資產（千元）
By ownership 產業所有權									
State-owned 國有	115	192	24,922	800	3.21	9.61	129.95	66.56	24,887
Collectively-owned 集體	623	85	7,654	320	5.33	13.97	90.54	61.81	6,004
Privately-owned 私有	12	42	4,457	206	5.93	12.06	106.76	50.84	3,481
Domestic JVs 聯營	18	42	22,999	131	0.89	3.69	552.71	75.91	14,703
Joint stock 股份制	6	256	54,594	2,204	3.62	6.32	213.40	42.72	60,852
Foreign-funded 外資	33	49	7,465	10	0.06	0.14	152.15	55.34	16,375
Overseas Chinese-funded 港澳台資	28	71	20,601	937	5.59	15.60	291.78	64.20	16,767
By size 規模									
Large 大型	3	2,794	286,500	21,332	8.97	16.88	102.53	46.85	237,773
Medium 中型	10	813	99,831	2,634	2.20	5.43	122.84	59.55	119,850
Small 小型	796	79	9,300	310	3.86	11.05	117.08	65.06	8,026
By regional distribution 地區分布									
Central-North 華北	159	95	13,487	524	4.16	9.87	142.67	57.82	12,574
Beijing 北京	63	56	12,867	827	7.35	13.95	229.70	47.31	11,253
Tianjin 天津	23	141	3,661	33	0.54	0.99	25.99	45.82	6,149
Hebei 河北	53	123	20,684	700	3.95	11.76	168.65	66.39	17,700
Shanxi 山西	9	138	13,482	-653	-3.55	-9.03	98.01	60.65	18,390
Inner Mongolia 內蒙	11	48	2,910	-74	-1.79	-6.39	61.09	72.03	4,125
Northeast 東北	270	93	7,492	393	5.07	11.55	80.28	56.13	7,746
Liaoning 遼寧	159	103	8,059	545	6.44	12.84	78.11	49.83	8,468
Jilin 吉林	50	85	4,628	5	0.09	0.26	54.26	63.55	5,740
Heilongjiang 黑龍江	61	74	8,361	312	4.15	13.82	112.69	69.97	7,510
Central East 華東	178	93	16,094	678	5.14	14.61	172.27	64.80	13,178
Shanghai 上海	18	96	9,686	266	3.06	8.84	100.78	65.36	8,668
Jiangsu 江蘇	51	102	13,878	55	0.39	1.35	135.80	71.16	14,179
Zhejiang 浙江	17	69	27,869	1,407	8.17	21.24	402.52	61.54	17,226
Anhui 安徽	19	31	4,434	259	17.70	45.35	144.99	60.97	1,466
Fujian 福建	11	21	6,096	150	3.82	13.85	289.05	72.42	3,926
Jiangxi 江西	11	28	2,167	-33	-1.64	-5.27	76.17	68.87	1,995
Shandong 山東	51	145	26,150	1,626	7.67	19.71	180.62	61.06	21,192
Central-South 中南	138	128	12,660	142	1.51	6.75	98.71	77.55	9,386
Henan 河南	62	223	7,103	129	2.12	7.48	31.84	71.63	6,058
Hubei 湖北	19	55	8,362	104	2.09	5.81	153.36	64.11	4,969
Hunan 湖南	14	57	4,176	12	0.22	0.56	73.92	60.40	5,454
Guangdong 廣東	33	35	13,462	206	1.94	7.08	384.30	72.65	10,647
Guangxi 廣西	10	89	64,514	270	0.68	11.27	726.51	93.97	39,758
Hainan 海南									
Southwest 西南	23	86	7,554	-203	-2.25	-4.45	87.79	49.39	9,041
Chongqing 重慶	5	294	23,444	-715	-2.21	-3.82	79.71	42.21	32,409
Sichuan 四川	16	31	3,480	-68	-2.45	-10.24	112.94	76.08	2,760
Guizhou 貴州	2	2	25				12.50	46.30	270
Yunnan 雲南									
Tibet 西藏									
Northwest 西北	69	57	4,460	180	3.45	10.99	77.62	68.60	5,224
Shaanxi 陝西	19	49	3,397	48	1.49	5.31	69.63	71.86	3,239
Gansu 甘肅	9	57	7,221	538	15.83	82.03	127.68	80.67	3,398
Qinghai 青海	5	162	4,696	-2	-0.03	-0.23	29.06	84.97	5,760
Ningxia 寧夏									
Xinjiang 新疆	36	48	4,298	186	2.79	7.81	89.91	64.26	6,654

2530: Petroleum Products 石油製品業

Year 年份	Number of firms 企業個數	Rate of change 每年變化 (%)	Number of employees 職工人數 (人)	Rate of change 每年變化 (%)	Total revenue (mil. RMB) 總銷售收入 (百萬元)	Rate of change 每年變化 (%)	Total profit (mil. RMB) 總利潤 (百萬元)	Rate of change 每年變化 (%)
1993	390		65,517		9,272		426	
1994	569	45.90%	77,005	17.53%	10,960	18.20%	531	24.65%
1995	874	53.60%	80,604	4.67%	7,669	-30.02%	394	-25.83%
1996	837	-4.23%	80,501	-0.13%	9,261	20.76%	337	-14.38%

3 Major products* 3 種主要產品 *	Output 產量	Sales volume 銷售量	Unit 單位
a) Lubricating Grease 潤滑脂	72,216	70,050	ton 噸
b) Internal-combustion Engine Lubricating Oil 內燃機用油	272,998	264,808	ton 噸
c) Lubricating Oil 潤滑油	497,200	432,564	ton 噸

Top 10 firms by revenue (year founded) 收入排名前 10 家企業 (創辦年份)	City 城市	Province 省	Telephone / fax 電話 / 傳真	Number of employees 職工人數	Ownership 產業所有權	Revenue ('000 RMB) 銷售收入 (千元)	Profit ('000 RMB) (rank) 利潤 (千元) (排名)	Total assets ('000 RMB) 總資產 (千元)	Major products 主要產品
Beihai Petrochemical Plant 北海石油化工廠(1991)	Beihai 北海市	Guangxi 廣西	(0779)3034502 (0779)3035519	832	State-owned 國有	619,549	2548(29)	362,780	o
Great Wall High Quality Lubricating Oil Co. Sinopec. 中國石化長城高級潤滑油公司(1962)	Beijing 北京市	Beijing 北京市	(010)62913781 (010)62913311	1,256	State-owned 國有	574,800	44867(1)	487,462	b,c
Shandong Guangrao Petrochemical Group Co. Ltd. 山東省廣饒石化集團股份有限公司(1991)	Dongying 東營市	Shandong 山東省	(0546)6261072 (0546)6261072	1,172	Joint stock 股份制	343,372	11560(11)	200,349	o
Shan Dongsheng Tong Group Co. Ltd. 山東勝通集團有限公司(1986)	Dongying 東營市	Shandong 山東省	(0546)8742178 (0546)2061326	1,180	Collectively-owned 集體	249,693	21182(5)	170,406	o
Wenzhou Long Da Liquefied Petroleum Gas Company 溫州龍達石油液化氣公司(1994)	Wenzhou 溫州市	Zhejiang 浙江省	(0577)4208408 (0577)4201048	48	Collectively-owned 集體	220,013	2147(32)	34,204	o
Tianjin Hangu Petrochemical Plant 天津市漢沽石油化學廠(1949)	Tianjin 天津市	Tianjin 天津市	(022)25693644 (022)25693644	1,088	State-owned 國有	217,589	1618(46)	222,665	a,b,c
Panshan Asphalt Factory 盤山縣瀝青廠(1978)	Panjin 盤錦市	Liaoning 遼寧省	(0427)7580129	580	State-owned 國有	205,869	23145(3)	186,937	o
Jinzhou Petrochemical Tian Yuan Group Co. 錦州石化天元集團公司(1979)	Jinzhou 錦州市	Liaoning 遼寧省	(0416)4168298 (0416)4166095	5,488	Collectively-owned 集體	197,740	29580(2)	343,803	o
Qinhuangdao Funing Oil Refining Factory 秦皇島撫寧煉油廠(1994)	Qinhuangdao 秦皇島市	Hebei 河北省	(0335)6015945	352	Joint stock 股份制	193,187	306(133)	139,136	o
Cangzhou Oil Refining Factory Industry & Trade Industrial General Company 滄州煉油廠工貿實業總公司(1981)	Cangzhou 滄州市	Hebei 河北省	(0317)2042350	847	Collectively-owned 集體	181,888	4145(15)	51,591	o

Top 10 Cities by Production Output 產出排名前 10 位城市	Province 省	Market share 市場份額	Number of firms 企業個數
Quanzhou 泉州市	Fujian 福建省	31.82%	2
Beijing 北京市	Beijing 北京市	6.20%	42
Dongying 東營市	Shandong 山東省	5.29%	11
Tianjin 天津市	Tianjin 天津市	5.11%	22
Taizhou 泰州市	Jiangsu 江蘇省	4.28%	6
Jinzhou 錦州市	Liaoning 遼寧省	2.60%	12
Daqing 大慶市	Heilongjiang 黑龍江省	2.50%	18
Shanghai 上海市	Shanghai 上海市	2.11%	41
Wuxi 無錫市	Jiangsu 江蘇省	1.98%	33
Wenzhou 溫州市	Zhejiang 浙江省	1.92%	10

10 Major Wholesalers 10 家主要批發商	City 城市	Province 省	Telephone / Fax 電話 / 傳真
Zhong Hua Liaoning Import & Export Company 中化遼寧進出口公司	Dalian 大連市	Liaoning 遼寧省	(0411)2821888 (0411)2639378
Huzhou Petrochemical Marketing General Company 湖州市石化銷售總公司	Huzhou 湖州市	Zhejiang 浙江省	(0572)2067002
Xinjiang Wei Wu Er Autonomous Region Petroleum General Company Urumqi Branch 新疆維吾爾自治區石油總公司烏魯木齊分公司	Urumqi 烏魯木齊市	Xinjiang 新疆	(0991)6897333
Shanghai Petroleum (Group) Co. Ltd. 上海石油(集團)有限公司	Shanghai 上海市	Shanghai 上海市	(021)63219490
Guangzhou Development Zone Zhong Sui Petrochemical Products Supply & Marketing Company 廣州開發區中穗石油化工產品供銷公司	Guangzhou 廣州市	Guangdong 廣東省	(020)82393431 (020)82398354
China Petrochemical Marketing Maoming Company 中國石化銷售茂名公司	Maoming 茂名市	Guangdong 廣東省	(0668)2245836 (0668)2269297
Zhejiang Petroleum General Co. 浙江省石油總公司	Hangzhou 杭州市	Zhejiang 浙江省	(0571)7805026 (0571)7805201
Guangdong Petroleum Enterprise Group Co. 廣東省石油企業集團公司	Guangzhou 廣州市	Guangdong 廣東省	(020)81850888 (020)81856088
China Shipping Fuel Supply Shanghai Company 中國船舶燃料供應上海公司	Shanghai 上海市	Shanghai 上海市	(021)63290555
Zhejiang Petroleum General Company Singbo Branch 浙江省石油總公司寧波分公司	Ningbo 寧波市	Zhejiang 浙江省	(0574)7267937 (0574)7268027

*Also include sales by firms outside this industry.包括本行業以外廠家的銷售。"o" stands for "others". "o" 代表"其他產品"。

2570: Coking 煉焦業

The industry accounts for 0.165% of the total revenue of China's industrial sector in 1996. The revenue growth rate of the industry is 19.0% from 1995, as compared to the growth rate of China's industrial sector, 9.51%. The rate of return on asset is -0.02%. 71.88% of all firms in the industry made a profit while 18.98% had negative returns. The top province in terms of the industry's revenue is Shanxi, accounting for 32.08% of the total revenue.
本行業在1996年佔全行業總產值0.165%，行業年增長率為19.0%（全國工業年增長率9.51%）。行業的資產回報率-0.02%，71.88%的企業盈利，18.98%的企業虧損。銷售收入最高的省份為山西省，佔本行業的32.08%。

	Total number of firms 企業總數	Total number of employees 職工總數	Total revenue (mil. RMB) 總銷售收入（百萬元）	Total profit (mil. RMB) 總利潤（百萬元）	Return on assets 資產利潤率 (%)	Return on equity 權益利潤率 (%)	Labour productivity ('000 RMB / worker) 勞動生產率（千元/人）	Debts / assets 資產負債率 (%)	Total assets (mil. RMB) 總資產（百萬元）
Industry Overall 行業總體	789	138,989	9,582	-3	-0.02	-0.09	68.94	75.30	15,149

	Number of firms 企業個數	Average number of employees 平均職工人數	Average revenue ('000 RMB) 平均銷售收入（千元）	Average profit ('000 RMB) 平均利潤（千元）	Return on assets 資產利潤率 (%)	Return on equity 權益利潤率 (%)	Labour productivity ('000 RMB / worker) 勞動生產率（千元/人）	Average debts / assets 平均資產負債率(%)	Average Total assets ('000 RMB) 平均總資產（千元）
By ownership 產業所有權									
State-owned 國有	114	619	40,140	-1,386	-1.55	-6.81	64.90	77.18	89,167
Collectively-owned 集體	626	95	6,410	237	3.96	14.23	67.31	72.16	5,995
Privately-owned 私有	8	46	4,811	480	16.46	40.26	103.73	59.12	2,914
Domestic JVs 聯營	7	35	2,295	508	23.73	35.89	65.04	33.88	2,143
Joint stock 股份制	12	230	13,515	1,990	7.75	15.95	58.78	51.42	25,670
Foreign-funded 外資	12	346	49,948	1,271	2.54	12.18	144.36	79.14	50,052
Overseas Chinese-funded 港澳台資	10	142	17,775	-4,022	-14.16	-48.56	125.27	70.85	28,413
By size 規模									
Large 大型	5	3,751	497,567	-338	-0.05	-0.16	132.66	72.51	746,864
Medium 中型	24	1,351	102,424	66	0.04	0.15	75.83	76.43	185,408
Small 小型	735	118	6,308	-4	-0.04	-0.17	53.39	76.05	9,448
By regional distribution 地區分布									
Central-North 華北	439	145	10,898	292	2.12	7.71	75.35	72.51	13,790
Beijing 北京									
Tianjin 天津	1	290	375,100	15,450	41.66	109.42	1293.45	61.93	37,090
Hebei 河北	48	313	24,363	-687	-1.54	-8.66	77.81	82.18	44,536
Shanxi 山西	354	126	8,684	386	3.89	11.14	69.16	65.08	9,917
Inner Mongolia 內蒙	36	103	4,597	260	2.54	21.57	44.45	88.21	10,234
Northeast 東北	27	420	25,842	321	0.54	2.25	61.56	76.09	59,557
Liaoning 遼寧	8	296	11,089	-423	-1.92	-12.26	37.43	84.31	21,969
Jilin 吉林	3	90	883	-577	-11.61	98.30	9.81	111.81	4,967
Heilongjiang 黑龍江	16	543	37,899	861	0.97	3.84	69.75	74.70	88,587
Central East 華東	32	696	57,728	-3,963	-3.58	-15.08	82.92	76.22	110,550
Shanghai 上海									
Jiangsu 江蘇	5	1,040	114,840	-4,770	-2.56	-9.62	110.44	73.37	186,118
Zhejiang 浙江									
Anhui 安徽	2	1,439	106,805	-4,615	-2.14	-6.74	74.25	68.22	215,350
Fujian 福建									
Jiangxi 江西	3	734	104,713	3,687	1.80	6.09	142.66	70.41	204,640
Shandong 山東	22	545	33,880	-4,764	-6.71	-38.14	62.12	82.41	71,017
Central-South 中南	51	271	18,438	-469	-1.57	-8.89	67.94	82.31	29,845
Henan 河南	25	326	27,320	-548	-1.15	-7.66	83.74	85.04	47,819
Hubei 湖北	5	261	16,788	22	0.08	0.21	64.22	63.30	27,900
Hunan 湖南	18	241	9,483	-614	-5.97	-29.12	39.36	79.48	10,276
Guangdong 廣東									
Guangxi 廣西	3	13	900	233	32.26	57.38	67.50	43.78	723
Hainan 海南									
Southwest 西南	176	67	2,508	33	1.15	4.18	37.47	72.51	2,827
Chongqing 重慶	9	47	1,257	-6	-1.42	-61.86	26.70	97.71	398
Sichuan 四川	53	129	6,232	88	1.29	4.06	48.21	68.20	6,822
Guizhou 貴州	105	32	452	29	6.16	14.70	14.32	58.13	473
Yunnan 雲南	9	132	5,947	-211	-2.25	-125.83	44.90	98.21	9,373
Tibet 西藏									
Northwest 西北	64	254	13,612	73	0.24	1.05	53.55	76.90	30,156
Shaanxi 陝西	29	320	17,055	281	0.66	3.38	53.34	80.52	42,650
Gansu 甘肅	9	197	6,302	-1,449	-8.25	-84.68	31.92	90.26	17,558
Qinghai 青海	2	14	230	5	1.43	2.04	16.43	30.00	350
Ningxia 寧夏	11	315	14,138	98	0.35	1.42	44.90	75.15	27,824
Xinjiang 新疆	13	133	12,604	651	3.70	7.50	94.93	50.58	17,567

Year 年份	Number of firms 企業個數	Rate of change 每年變化 (%)	Number of employees 職工人數 (人)	Rate of change 每年變化 (%)	Total revenue (mil. RMB) 總銷售收入 (百萬元)	Rate of change 每年變化 (%)	Total profit (mil. RMB) 總利潤 (百萬元)	Rate of change 每年變化 (%)
1993	552		82,201		5,453		143	
1994	650	17.75%	103,992	26.51%	6,379	16.98%	155	7.99%
1995	869	33.69%	148,034	42.35%	8,053	26.24%	63	-59.16%
1996	789	-9.21%	138,989	-6.11%	9,582	18.99%	-3	-104.75%

3 Major products* 3 種主要產品 *	Output 產量	Sales volume 銷售量	Unit 單位
a) Coke of Mechanize Coke Oven Production 機械化焦爐生產的焦炭	10,018,174	4,508,178	ton 噸
b) Crude Benzene 粗苯	65,881	65,222	ton 噸
c) Fine Coal Washing 洗精煤	8,791,163	8,615,339	ton 噸

Top 10 firms by revenue (year founded) 收入排名前 10 家企業 (創辦年份)	City 城市	Province 省	Telephone / fax 電話 / 傳真	Number of employees 職工人數	Ownership 產業所有權	Revenue ('000 RMB) 銷售收入 (千元)	Profit ('000 RMB) (rank) 利潤 (千元) (排名)	Total assets ('000 RMB) 總資產 (千元)	Major products 主要產品
Shijiazhuang Coking Plant 石家莊焦化廠(1914)	Shijiazhuang 石家莊市	Hebei 河北省	(0311)5051996 (0311)5053276	3,885	State-owned 國有	527,335	-17569(402)	1,039,082	a
Heilong Jiang Chemical General Plant 黑龍江化工總廠(1970)	Qiqiha'er 齊齊哈爾市	Heilongjiang 黑龍江省	(0452)6817114 (0452)6884895	5,247	State-owned 國有	415,269	13816(5)	956,624	a,b
Tianjin Hua Hai Petrochemical General Factory 天津市華海石油化工總廠(1987)	Tianjin 天津市	Tianjin 天津市	(022)27350725	283	Collectively-owned 集體	375,100	15450(3)	37,090	o
Shanxi San Jia Carbonization Co. Ltd. 山西三佳煤化有限公司(1990)	Yuci 榆次市	Shanxi 山西省	(0354)7536391 (0354)7536563	2,050	Foreign-funded 外資	369,120	2600(20)	259,773	c
Jingdezhen Coking Gas General Plant 景德鎮市焦化煤氣總廠(1986)	Jingdezhen 景德鎮市	Jiangxi 江西省	(0798)8551282 (0798)8551618	3,776	State-owned 國有	292,063	11061(6)	593,382	a,b
Jining Coal & Chemical Industrial Co. 濟寧市煤炭化學工業公司(1965)	Jining 濟寧市	Shandong 山東省	(0537)2315241 (0537)2311534	2,799	Collectively-owned 集體	223,221	-9805(394)	462,770	a,b
Wuxi Coking Plant 無錫市焦化廠(1958)	Wuxi 無錫市	Jiangsu 江蘇省	(0510)5213889 (0510)5217884	1,907	State-owned 國有	215,905	18(269)	218,758	a,b
Shanxi Rui Yu De Carbonization Co. Ltd. 山西瑞玉德煤化有限公司(1988)	Yuci 榆次市	Shanxi 山西省	(0354)7536447	2,084	Collectively-owned 集體	185,000	1500(33)	94,000	c
Shanxi Hongdong Zhao Cheng Coking Industrial Group 山西省洪洞縣趙城焦化實業集團(1986)	Linfen 臨汾市	Shanxi 山西省	(0357)6664125	428	Collectively-owned 集體	161,000	16980(2)	91,700	c
Xinjiang Iron & Steel Company Coking Factory 新疆鋼鐵公司焦化廠(1996)	Urumqi 烏魯木齊市	Xinjiang 新疆	(0991)3894378 (0991)3894378	1,203	State-owned 國有	151,306	9673(7)	184,085	a,b

Top 10 Cities by Production Output 產出排名前 10 位城市	Province 省	Market share 市場份額	Number of firms 企業個數
Shanghai 上海市	Shanghai 上海市	34.24%	3
Yuci 榆次市	Shanxi 山西省	6.58%	75
Pingdingshan 平頂山市	Henan 河南省	5.29%	17
Shijiazhuang 石家莊市	Hebei 河北省	4.56%	10
Qiqiha'er 齊齊哈爾市	Heilongjiang 黑龍江省	3.48%	2
Jingdezhen 景德鎮市	Jiangxi 江西省	3.11%	1
Jining 濟寧市	Shandong 山東省	2.53%	4
Linfen 臨汾市	Shanxi 山西省	2.50%	99
Weinan 渭南市	Shaanxi 陝西省	2.38%	9
Taiyuan 太原市	Shanxi 山西省	2.25%	74

10 Major Wholesalers 10 家主要批發商	City 城市	Province 省	Telephone / Fax 電話 / 傳真
Zhong Hua Liaoning Import & Export Company 中化遼寧進出口公司	Dalian 大連市	Liaoning 遼寧省	(0411)2821888 (0411)2639378
Huzhou Petrochemical Marketing General Company 湖州市石化銷售總公司	Huzhou 湖州市	Zhejiang 浙江省	(0572)2067002
Xinjiang Wei Wu Er Autonomous Region Petroleum General Company Urumqi Branch 新疆維吾爾自治區石油總公司烏魯木齊分公司	Urumqi 烏魯木齊市	Xinjiang 新疆	(0991)6897333
Shanghai Petroleum (Group) Co. Ltd. 上海石油(集團)有限公司	Shanghai 上海市	Shanghai 上海市	(021)63219490
Guangzhou Development Zone Zhong Sui Petrochemical Products Supply & Marketing Company 廣州開發區中穗石油化工產品供銷公司	Guangzhou 廣州市	Guangdong 廣東省	(020)82393431 (020)82398354
China Petrochemical Marketing Maoming Company 中國石化銷售茂名公司	Maoming 茂名市	Guangdong 廣東省	(0668)2245836 (0668)2269297
Zhejiang Petroleum General Co. 浙江省石油總公司	Hangzhou 杭州市	Zhejiang 浙江省	(0571)7805026 (0571)7805201
Guangdong Petroleum Enterprise Group Co. 廣東省石油企業集團公司	Guangzhou 廣州市	Guangdong 廣東省	(020)81850888 (020)81856088
China Shipping Fuel Supply Shanghai Company 中國船舶燃料供應上海公司	Shanghai 上海市	Shanghai 上海市	(021)63290555
Zhejiang Petroleum General Company Singbo Branch 浙江省石油總公司寧波分公司	Ningbo 寧波市	Zhejiang 浙江省	(0574)7267937 (0574)7268027

*Also include sales by firms outside this industry.包括本行業以外廠家的銷售。"o" stands for "others". "o" 代表"其他產品"。

2611: Inorganic Acids 無機酸製造業

The industry accounts for 0.138% of the total revenue of China's industrial sector in 1996. The revenue growth rate of the industry is 8.6% from 1995, as compared to the growth rate of China's industrial sector, 9.51%. The rate of return on asset is 0.84%. 66.51% of all firms in the industry made a profit while 25.78% had negative returns. The top province in terms of the industry's revenue is Shanxi, accounting for 19.49% of the total revenue.
本行業在1996年佔全行業總產值0.138%，行業年增長率為8.6%（全國工業年增長率9.51%）。行業的資產回報率0.84%，66.51%的企業盈利，25.78%的企業虧損。銷售收入最高的省份為山西省，佔本行業的19.49%。

	Total number of firms 企業總數	Total number of employees 職工總數	Total revenue (mil. RMB) 總銷售收入（百萬元）	Total profit (mil. RMB) 總利潤（百萬元）	Return on assets 資產利潤率 (%)	Return on equity 權益利潤率 (%)	Labour productivity ('000 RMB / worker) 勞動生產率（千元/人）	Debts / assets 資產負債率 (%)	Total assets (mil. RMB) 總資產（百萬元）
Industry Overall 行業總體	708	136,744	8,002	125	0.84	2.74	58.52	69.39	14,877

	Number of firms 企業個數	Average number of employees 平均職工人數	Average revenue ('000 RMB) 平均銷售收入（千元）	Average profit ('000 RMB) 平均利潤（千元）	Return on assets 資產利潤率 (%)	Return on equity 權益利潤率 (%)	Labour productivity ('000 RMB / worker) 勞動生產率（千元/人）	Average debts / assets 平均資產負債率(%)	Average Total assets ('000 RMB) 平均總資產（千元）
By ownership 產業所有權									
State-owned 國有	137	632	28,832	-234	-0.37	-1.14	45.63	67.87	63,496
Collectively-owned 集體	519	71	5,433	109	1.71	7.48	76.71	77.12	6,383
Privately-owned 私有	7	25	2,495	165	12.78	21.16	98.13	39.59	1,294
Domestic JVs 聯營	11	64	5,620	226	3.53	7.67	87.56	54.03	6,419
Joint stock 股份制	10	858	81,626	7,718	5.76	12.72	95.12	54.71	134,001
Foreign-funded 外資	11	146	12,760	225	1.86	2.78	87.23	32.93	12,095
Overseas Chinese-funded 港澳台資	12	227	16,444	1,417	1.29	6.36	72.36	79.65	109,440
By size 規模									
Large 大型	9	4,980	316,077	4,011	0.56	1.33	63.47	57.91	717,231
Medium 中型	39	900	43,522	878	0.88	3.68	48.38	75.95	99,279
Small 小型	641	88	5,399	85	1.20	6.03	61.37	80.08	7,100
By regional distribution 地區分布									
Central-North 華北	131	353	19,337	530	1.33	3.31	54.74	59.81	39,792
Beijing 北京	25	69	2,876	-162	-3.97	-16.45	41.55	75.85	4,068
Tianjin 天津	18	159	23,923	2,607	10.53	27.69	150.67	61.96	24,756
Hebei 河北	53	103	6,301	375	5.27	29.93	61.33	82.40	7,110
Shanxi 山西	23	1,447	67,796	183	0.10	0.23	46.84	55.34	174,806
Inner Mongolia 內蒙	12	246	11,451	203	0.91	6.22	46.61	85.36	22,343
Northeast 東北	89	142	3,829	-380	-4.28	-27.23	26.95	84.28	8,868
Liaoning 遼寧	53	136	3,241	-253	-3.22	-20.65	23.78	84.41	7,855
Jilin 吉林	22	135	3,183	-334	-3.83	-15.30	23.57	74.99	8,715
Heilongjiang 黑龍江	14	175	7,069	-931	-7.20	-116.53	40.38	93.82	12,939
Central East 華東	194	158	12,539	401	2.39	8.24	79.30	70.94	16,742
Shanghai 上海	16	230	18,239	1,368	4.80	19.92	79.32	75.91	28,496
Jiangsu 江蘇	65	101	11,409	190	1.72	5.60	113.24	69.25	11,016
Zhejiang 浙江	25	93	7,430	54	0.54	1.32	80.17	59.34	10,046
Anhui 安徽	13	575	22,598	-58	-0.11	-0.35	39.30	67.61	51,058
Fujian 福建	13	187	10,962	142	1.04	3.04	58.64	65.59	13,547
Jiangxi 江西	19	48	2,767	138	4.53	20.98	57.40	78.40	3,044
Shandong 山東	43	170	16,851	894	4.15	17.19	99.12	75.89	21,561
Central-South 中南	148	149	8,101	-474	-3.37	-18.74	54.39	82.02	14,081
Henan 河南	48	144	6,337	54	0.65	3.24	43.99	79.82	8,319
Hubei 湖北	32	94	6,432	153	2.86	12.56	68.47	77.22	5,352
Hunan 湖南	33	151	9,185	-314	-3.02	-51.01	60.63	94.08	10,382
Guangdong 廣東	20	205	12,701	-48	-0.19	-0.84	61.83	76.90	24,873
Guangxi 廣西	15	201	8,787	-4,428	-9.86	-55.33	43.72	82.17	44,891
Hainan 海南									
Southwest 西南	90	172	11,263	801	2.76	9.72	65.62	71.60	29,026
Chongqing 重慶	15	135	3,248	418	0.64	4.51	24.00	85.80	65,359
Sichuan 四川	55	217	16,741	1,201	4.24	11.23	77.03	62.30	28,368
Guizhou 貴州	15	58	1,296	76	4.79	16.19	22.27	70.47	1,587
Yunnan 雲南	5	110	4,380	-308	-2.76	-21.57	39.75	87.19	11,146
Tibet 西藏									
Northwest 西北	56	173	8,628	170	1.02	3.48	50.01	70.55	16,625
Shaanxi 陝西	22	131	6,371	169	1.96	5.89	48.79	66.78	8,639
Gansu 甘肅	16	217	14,191	844	3.21	8.20	65.27	60.85	26,288
Qinghai 青海	7	94	1,671	-143	-3.70	-65.36	17.84	94.34	3,860
Ningxia 寧夏	2	35	1,875				53.57	87.04	2,700
Xinjiang 新疆	9	287	11,168	-743	-2.32	-15.16	38.91	84.67	31,990

2611: Inorganic Acids 無機酸製造業

Year 年份	Number of firms 企業個數	Rate of change 每年變化 (%)	Number of employees 職工人數 (人)	Rate of change 每年變化 (%)	Total revenue (mil. RMB) 總銷售收入 (百萬元)	Rate of change 每年變化 (%)	Total profit (mil. RMB) 總利潤 (百萬元)	Rate of change 每年變化 (%)
1993	644		124,319		4,404		-16	
1994	697	8.23%	129,596	4.24%	5,472	24.27%	-38	-137.88%
1995	664	-4.74%	143,398	10.65%	7,371	34.70%	158	517.79%
1996	708	6.63%	136,744	-4.64%	8,002	8.56%	125	-20.75%

3 Major products* 3 種主要產品 *	Output 產量	Sales volume 銷售量	Unit 單位
a) Sulfuric Acid 硫酸	3,373,662	1,821,778	ton 噸
b) Phosphate Fertilize 磷肥	254,998	239,698	ton 噸

Top 10 firms by revenue (year founded) 收入排名前 10 家企業 (創辦年份)	City 城市	Province 省	Telephone / fax 電話 / 傳真	Number of employees 職工人數	Ownership 產業所有權	Revenue ('000 RMB) 銷售收入 (千元)	Profit ('000 RMB) (rank) 利潤 (千元) (排名)	Total assets ('000 RMB) 總資產 (千元)	Major products 主要產品
Taiyuan Chemical Industry Group Corporation 太原化學工業集團公司(1982)	Taiyuan 太原市	Shanxi 山西省	(0351)6071261 (0351)6070565	29,815	State-owned 國有	1,408,861	-5280(344)	3,753,698	a,b
Sichuan Jinlu Group Co. Ltd. 四川省金路股份公司	Deyang 德陽市	Sichuan 四川省	(0838)2302554	4,350	Joint stock 股份制	486,382	83084(1)	854,247	o
Tianjin Greatwall Chemical Plant 天津市長城化工廠(1989)	Tianjin 天津市	Tianjin 天津市	(022)27393835	480	Collectively-owned 集體	161,570	22470(2)	78,150	o
Shanghai Sulfuric Acid Plant 上海硫酸廠(1948)	Shanghai 上海市	Shanghai 上海市	(021)56995888 (021)56754417	2,193	State-owned 國有	153,281	57(191)	255,504	a
Ma'anshan Goldstar Chemical Industrial (Group) Co. Ltd. 馬鞍山市金星化工(集團)有限公司(1972)	Ma'anshan 馬鞍山市	Anhui 安徽省	(0555)2473764 (0555)2475765	1,226	State-owned 國有	128,190	839(65)	254,216	a,b
Sichuan Sulfuric Acid Plant 四川省硫酸廠(1965)	Neijiang 內江市	Sichuan 四川省	(0832)5522680 (0832)5522791	2,032	State-owned 國有	115,168	129(158)	137,867	a,b
Jiangsu Tai Ping Yang Chemistry Co. 江蘇太平洋化學公司(1973)	Zhenjiang 鎮江市	Jiangsu 江蘇省	(0511)7223080 (0511)7223993	540	Collectively-owned 集體	113,140	163(141)	131,589	b
Liuzhou Longcheng Chemical General Factory 柳州市龍城化工總廠(1985)	Liuzhou 柳州市	Guangxi 廣西	(0772)3123468 (0772)2823298	2,239	Collectively-owned 集體	106,959	-65161(350)	636,857	a
Lixian Chemical No.2 Factory 澧縣化工二廠(1970)	Changde 常德市	Hunan 湖南省	(0736)3466028	600	Collectively-owned 集體	104,350	2369(26)	21,316	a
Sichuan Hong Da Chemical Co. Ltd. 四川宏達化工有限公司	Deyang 德陽市	Sichuan 四川省	(0838)8601193 (0838)8203240	968	Joint stock 股份制	100,112	11112(5)	177,585	a,b

Top 10 Cities by Production Output 產出排名前 10 位城市	Province 省	Market share 市場份額	Number of firms 企業個數
Taiyuan 太原市	Shanxi 山西省	14.21%	5
Shanghai 上海市	Shanghai 上海市	5.11%	26
Tianjin 天津市	Tianjin 天津市	4.89%	13
Suzhou 蘇州市	Jiangsu 江蘇省	4.60%	27
Zibo 淄博市	Shandong 山東省	2.74%	10
Jiaozuo 焦作市	Henan 河南省	2.66%	6
Tai'an 泰安市	Shandong 山東省	2.15%	4
Zhenjiang 鎮江市	Jiangsu 江蘇省	2.05%	6
Weifang 濰坊市	Shandong 山東省	2.03%	12
Beijing 北京市	Beijing 北京市	1.95%	23

10 Major Wholesalers 10 家主要批發商	City 城市	Province 省	Telephone / Fax 電話 / 傳真
Changzhou Hardware Alternating-current Appliance and Chemical Wholesale General Company 常州五金交電化工批發總公司	Changzhou 常州市	Jiangsu 江蘇省	(0519)6609929 (0519)6609925
Suzhou Hardware & Alternating Electricity Co. Ltd. 蘇州五金交電股份有限公司	Suzhou 蘇州市	Jiangsu 江蘇省	(0512)5239572 (0512)5213248
Tianjin Foreign Trade General Company 天津市對外貿易總公司	Tianjin 天津市	Tianjin 天津市	(022)23310922
Chongqing International Trade Center 重慶國際貿易中心	Chongqing 重慶市	Chongqing 重慶市	(023)67853232 (023)67850402
China Chemical Plastics Co. Ltd. 中化塑料有限公司	Beijing 北京市	Beijing 北京市	(010)68569863 (010)68569041
Ningbo Hualian Group Co. Ltd. 寧波華聯集團股份有限公司	Ningbo 寧波市	Zhejiang 浙江省	(0574)7367626 (0574)7367652
Xiamen Kaiyuan Wei Wei Electromechanical Building Materials Marketing Dept. 廈門市開元區威威機電建材經營部	Xiamen 廈門市	Fujian 福建省	(0592)2071044
Rudong Industry Product General Company 如東縣工業品總公司	Nantong 南通市	Jiangsu 江蘇省	(0513)4516110 (0513)4516110
Fujian Fu Ri Group Company 福建福日集團公司	Fuzhou 福州市	Fujian 福建省	(0591)3269325 (0591)3270426
Guangdong Hardware & Alternating Electrical Co. 廣東省五金交電公司	Guangzhou 廣州市	Guangdong 廣東省	(020)81884078 (020)81861287

*Also include sales by firms outside this industry.包括本行業以外廠家的銷售。"o" stands for "others". "o" 代表 "其他產品"。

2613: Caustic Soda 燒鹼製造業

The industry accounts for 0.301% of the total revenue of China's industrial sector in 1996. The revenue growth rate of the industry is 0.9% from 1995, as compared to the growth rate of China's industrial sector, 9.51%. The rate of return on asset is 1.05%. 68.02% of all firms in the industry made a profit while 28.95% had negative returns. The top province in terms of the industry's revenue is Shandong, accounting for 13.50% of the total revenue.
本行業在1996年佔全行業總產值0.301%，行業年增長率為0.9%（全國工業年增長率9.51%）。行業的資產回報率1.05%，68.02%的企業盈利，28.95%的企業虧損。銷售收入最高的省份為山東省，佔本行業的13.50%。

	Total number of firms 企業總數	Total number of employees 職工總數	Total revenue (mil. RMB) 總銷售收入（百萬元）	Total profit (mil. RMB) 總利潤（百萬元）	Return on assets 資產利潤率 (%)	Return on equity 權益利潤率 (%)	Labour productivity ('000 RMB / worker) 勞動生產率（千元/人）	Debts / assets 資產負債率 (%)	Total assets (mil. RMB) 總資產（百萬元）
Industry Overall 行業總體	262	226,969	17,477	319	1.05	3.66	77.00	71.32	30,363

	Number of firms 企業個數	Average number of employees 平均職工人數	Average revenue ('000 RMB) 平均銷售收入（千元）	Average profit ('000 RMB) 平均利潤（千元）	Return on assets 資產利潤率 (%)	Return on equity 權益利潤率 (%)	Labour productivity ('000 RMB / worker) 勞動生產率（千元/人）	Average debts / assets 平均資產負債率(%)	Average Total assets ('000 RMB) 平均總資產（千元）
By ownership 產業所有權									
State-owned 國有	122	1,516	106,877	1,000	0.52	1.75	70.49	70.62	194,074
Collectively-owned 集體	123	132	8,239	168	1.81	11.48	62.54	84.27	9,297
Privately-owned 私有									
Domestic JVs 聯營	3	390	27,361	641	1.50	4.40	70.10	65.96	42,845
Joint stock 股份制	6	3,150	436,192	21,947	3.35	11.97	138.48	72.00	654,719
Foreign-funded 外資	4	1,306	176,147	8,437	2.77	8.84	134.85	68.71	304,891
Overseas Chinese-funded 港澳台資	5	95	27,702	1,792	3.36	19.05	290.38	82.35	53,285
By size 規模									
Large 大型	37	3,867	339,918	6,744	1.15	3.72	87.90	69.05	586,095
Medium 中型	64	961	67,437	1,141	1.04	4.49	70.19	76.79	109,441
Small 小型	154	134	5,946	-24	-0.22	-0.98	44.36	77.81	10,868
By regional distribution 地區分布									
Central-North 華北	59	694	63,298	2,043	1.64	6.67	91.18	75.38	124,390
Beijing 北京	1	30	6,120	40	1.55	3.33	204.00	53.49	2,580
Tianjin 天津	25	693	86,804	932	0.58	2.27	125.22	74.29	159,785
Hebei 河北	12	850	85,977	5,713	3.62	11.54	101.20	68.61	157,743
Shanxi 山西	7	134	3,450	111	1.69	18.01	25.77	90.63	6,599
Inner Mongolia 內蒙	14	891	35,894	1,993	1.99	15.48	40.30	87.15	100,195
Northeast 東北	30	1,473	103,428	668	0.35	1.10	70.20	68.15	190,252
Liaoning 遼寧	17	1,180	106,651	5,624	3.57	7.89	90.40	54.79	157,618
Jilin 吉林	6	2,500	82,147	-6,457	-2.73	-31.37	32.86	91.28	236,142
Heilongjiang 黑龍江	7	1,306	113,843	-5,263	-2.29	-7.63	87.19	70.02	230,173
Central East 華東	78	779	66,777	1,310	1.28	4.21	85.76	69.50	101,976
Shanghai 上海	2	65	12,875	765	18.84	45.27	198.08	58.37	4,060
Jiangsu 江蘇	17	630	57,926	1,608	2.43	6.83	91.96	64.41	66,193
Zhejiang 浙江	6	458	39,567	2,100	4.13	9.62	86.42	57.13	50,897
Anhui 安徽	5	1,586	100,678	-2,464	-1.56	-8.41	63.48	81.51	158,386
Fujian 福建	10	727	72,887	387	0.50	0.99	100.24	49.12	77,168
Jiangxi 江西	6	1,767	61,600	-11,912	-5.73	-111.72	34.86	94.88	208,038
Shandong 山東	32	667	73,714	4,395	3.80	10.92	110.52	65.23	115,736
Central-South 中南	48	989	75,034	2,483	2.20	6.38	75.90	65.57	113,115
Henan 河南	23	434	23,491	1,155	2.88	13.08	54.19	78.01	40,153
Hubei 湖北	4	3,620	226,715	18,923	4.87	12.78	62.63	61.91	388,613
Hunan 湖南	9	1,096	86,572	11	0.01	0.05	78.99	80.61	111,093
Guangdong 廣東	8	746	98,374	1,566	1.22	2.80	131.89	56.47	128,428
Guangxi 廣西	4	1,793	147,083	1,078	0.47	1.00	82.04	53.16	231,070
Hainan 海南									
Southwest 西南	28	808	42,265	-770	-1.01	-4.62	52.31	78.11	76,074
Chongqing 重慶	8	822	35,850	-578	-0.67	-3.29	43.63	79.53	85,796
Sichuan 四川	10	1,036	58,610	1,009	1.06	5.45	56.59	80.53	95,172
Guizhou 貴州	2	899	68,845	30	0.03	0.09	76.58	63.65	87,580
Yunnan 雲南	8	480	20,790	-1,961	-4.99	-20.47	43.32	75.60	39,266
Tibet 西藏									
Northwest 西北	19	579	33,971	-1,134	-1.19	-6.67	58.67	82.09	94,878
Shaanxi 陝西	9	524	39,848	-382	-0.43	-2.10	76.03	79.62	89,500
Gansu 甘肅	5	519	25,856	154	0.27	0.70	49.84	61.26	57,140
Qinghai 青海	2	798	10,350	-10,370	-10.54	155.12	12.98	106.79	98,395
Ningxia 寧夏	2	544	52,610	210	0.23	5.24	96.80	95.62	91,600
Xinjiang 新疆	1	1,009	31,620	1,450	0.44	2.72	31.34	83.92	331,490

2613: Caustic Soda 燒鹼製造業

Year 年份	Number of firms 企業個數	Rate of change 每年變化 (%)	Number of employees 職工人數 (人)	Rate of change 每年變化 (%)	Total revenue (mil. RMB) 總銷售收入 (百萬元)	Rate of change 每年變化 (%)	Total profit (mil. RMB) 總利潤 (百萬元)	Rate of change 每年變化 (%)
1993	262		277,929		14,046		313	
1994	283	8.02%	222,887	-19.81%	12,593	-10.35%	73	-76.67%
1995	267	-5.65%	231,770	3.99%	17,327	37.60%	510	599.87%
1996	262	-1.87%	226,969	-2.07%	17,477	0.87%	319	-37.50%

3 Major products* 3 種主要產品 *	Output 產量	Sales volume 銷售量	Unit 單位
a) Liquid Chlorine Commodity 商品液氯	924,263	628,499	ton 噸
b) Sodium Hydrate 氫氧化鈉	3,044,821	2,648,994	ton 噸
c) Hydrochloric Acid 酸	2,046,804	1,514,635	ton 噸

Top 10 firms by revenue (year founded) 收入排名前 10 家企業 (創辦年份)	City 城市	Province 省	Telephone / fax 電話 / 傳真	Number of employees 職工人數	Ownership 產業所有權	Revenue ('000 RMB) 銷售收入 (千元)	Profit ('000 RMB) (rank) 利潤 (千元) (排名)	Total assets ('000 RMB) 總資產 (千元)	Major products 主要產品
Bohai Chemical Industry (Group) Co. Ltd. Tianjin Chemical Plant 渤海化工(集團)股份有限公司天津化工廠(1938)	Tianjin 天津市	Tianjin 天津市	(022)25602448 (022)25694533	7,056	Joint stock 股份制	1,217,340	25000(6)	1,764,035	a,b,c
Jinhua Chemical (Group) Corp. 錦化化工集團有限責任公司(1949)	Huludao 葫蘆島市	Liaoning 遼寧省	(0429)2709164 (0429)2127294	15,865	State-owned 國有	1,078,796	15020(8)	1,764,949	o
Bo Hai Chemical (Group) Co. Ltd. Tianjin Da Gu Chemical Plant 渤海化工(集團)股份有限公司天津大沽化工廠(1942)	Tianjin 天津市	Tianjin 天津市	(022)25392414 (022)25387908	5,914	Joint stock 股份制	842,861	17631(7)	1,964,981	a,b,c
Wuhan Ge Hua Industry Group Company 武漢葛化工業集團公司(1959)	Wuhan 武漢市	Hubei 湖北省	(027)87601819 (027)87600357	6,285	State-owned 國有	842,158	75531(2)	1,396,349	a,b,c
Shenyang Chemical Co. Ltd. 永新 - 瀋陽化工股份有限公司(1938)	Shenyang 瀋陽市	Liaoning 遼寧省	(024)25820516 (024)25854973	4,281	Foreign-funded 外資	704,796	80018(1)	892,675	a,b,c
Hunan Zhuzhou Chemical Factory 湖南省株洲化工廠(1959)	Zhuzhou 株洲市	Hunan 湖南省	(0733)8361806 (0733)8630056	7,246	State-owned 國有	659,783	175(90)	790,851	a,b,c
Shandong Binzhou Chemical Factory 山東濱州化工廠(1970)	Binzhou 濱州市	Shandong 山東省	(0543)3316888 (0543)3324544	2,333	State-owned 國有	568,120	8202(14)	464,509	b,c
Fuzhou No.2 Chemical Group Co. Ltd. 福州二化集團有限公司(1959)	Fuzhou 福州市	Fujian 福建省	(0591)7555403 (0591)7555403	4,477	State-owned 國有	500,640	1786(39)	559,486	o
Hebei Cangzhou Chemical Industrial (Group) Co. Ltd. 河北省滄州化工實業集團公司(1979)	Cangzhou 滄州市	Hebei 河北省	(0317)3041831 (0317)3042321	3,871	State-owned 國有	477,989	45037(3)	1,006,093	a,b,c
Nanning Chemical Industry Group Co. Ltd. 南寧化學工業集團公司(1964)	Nanning 南寧市	Guangxi 廣西	(0771)4821223 (0771)4835643	4,546	State-owned 國有	451,133	11423(10)	609,601	a,b,c

Top 10 Cities by Production Output 產出排名前 10 位城市	Province 省	Market share 市場份額	Number of firms 企業個數
Tianjin 天津市	Tianjin 天津市	13.02%	32
Huludao 葫蘆島市	Liaoning 遼寧省	6.28%	5
Shenyang 瀋陽市	Liaoning 遼寧省	4.31%	2
Zhuzhou 株洲市	Hunan 湖南省	4.26%	3
Weifang 濰坊市	Shandong 山東省	4.23%	4
Cangzhou 滄州市	Hebei 河北省	3.28%	4
Binzhou 濱州市	Shandong 山東省	3.17%	1
Fuzhou 福州市	Fujian 福建省	2.73%	1
Qiqiha'er 齊齊哈爾市	Heilongjiang 黑龍江省	2.54%	4
Nanning 南寧市	Guangxi 廣西	2.44%	1

10 Major Wholesalers 10 家主要批發商	City 城市	Province 省	Telephone / Fax 電話 / 傳真
Changzhou Hardware Alternating-current Appliance and Chemical Wholesale General Company 常州五金交電化工批發總公司	Changzhou 常州市	Jiangsu 江蘇省	(0519)6609929 (0519)6609925
Suzhou Hardware & Alternating Electricity Co. Ltd. 蘇州五金交電股份有限公司	Suzhou 蘇州市	Jiangsu 江蘇省	(0512)5239572 (0512)5213248
Tianjin Foreign Trade General Company 天津市對外貿易總公司	Tianjin 天津市	Tianjin 天津市	(022)23310922
Chongqing International Trade Center 重慶國際貿易中心	Chongqing 重慶市	Chongqing 重慶市	(023)67853232 (023)67850402
China Chemical Plastics Co. Ltd. 中化塑料有限公司	Beijing 北京市	Beijing 北京市	(010)68569863 (010)68569041
Ningbo Hualian Group Co. Ltd. 寧波華聯集團股份有限公司	Ningbo 寧波市	Zhejiang 浙江省	(0574)7367626 (0574)7367652
Xiamen Kaiyuan Wei Wei Electromechanical Building Materials Marketing Dept. 廈門市開元區威威機電建材經營部	Xiamen 廈門市	Fujian 福建省	(0592)2071044
Rudong Industry Product General Company 如東縣工業品總公司	Nantong 南通市	Jiangsu 江蘇省	(0513)4516110 (0513)4516110
Fujian Fu Ri Group Company 福建福日集團公司	Fuzhou 福州市	Fujian 福建省	(0591)3269325 (0591)3270426
Guangdong Hardware & Alternating Electrical Co. 廣東省五金交電公司	Guangzhou 廣州市	Guangdong 廣東省	(020)81884078 (020)81861287

*Also include sales by firms outside this industry.包括本行業以外廠家的銷售。"o" stands for "others". "o" 代表"其他產品"。

2615: Soda Ash 純鹼製造業

The industry accounts for 0.182% of the total revenue of China's industrial sector in 1996. The revenue growth rate of the industry is 23.7% from 1995, as compared to the growth rate of China's industrial sector, 9.51%. The rate of return on asset is 1.89%. 65.58% of all firms in the industry made a profit while 21.92% had negative returns. The top province in terms of the industry's revenue is Shandong, accounting for 18.18% of the total revenue.
本行業在1996年佔全行業總產值0.182%，行業年增長率為23.7%（全國工業年增長率9.51%）。行業的資產回報率1.89%，65.58%的企業盈利，21.92%的企業虧損。銷售收入最高的省份為山東省，佔本行業的18.18%。

	Total number of firms 企業總數	Total number of employees 職工總數	Total revenue (mil. RMB) 總銷售收入（百萬元）	Total profit (mil. RMB) 總利潤（百萬元）	Return on assets 資產利潤率 (%)	Return on equity 權益利潤率 (%)	Labour productivity ('000 RMB / worker) 勞動生產率（千元/人）	Debts / assets 資產負債率 (%)	Total assets (mil. RMB) 總資產（百萬元）
Industry Overall 行業總體	283	132,666	10,533	473	1.89	5.98	79.39	68.42	25,057

	Number of firms 企業個數	Average number of employees 平均職工人數	Average revenue ('000 RMB) 平均銷售收入（千元）	Average profit ('000 RMB) 平均利潤（千元）	Return on assets 資產利潤率 (%)	Return on equity 權益利潤率 (%)	Labour productivity ('000 RMB / worker) 勞動生產率（千元/人）	Average debts / assets 平均資產負債率(%)	Average Total assets ('000 RMB) 平均總資產（千元）
By ownership 產業所有權									
State-owned 國有	57	1,585	115,772	5,263	1.72	5.63	73.04	69.47	306,351
Collectively-owned 集體	208	94	5,234	116	2.59	50.23	55.40	94.85	4,498
Privately-owned 私有	2	89	2,320	-233	-6.99	50.73	26.21	113.79	3,325
Domestic JVs 聯營	2	46	2,169	-151	-3.12	8.85	47.68	135.28	4,829
Joint stock 股份制	7	3,029	549,027	20,979	2.24	5.84	181.23	61.65	936,227
Foreign-funded 外資	3	100	2,361	151	1.58	5.51	23.69	71.28	9,562
Overseas Chinese-funded 港澳台資	4	670	16,070	528	3.52	13.41	23.99	73.79	15,031
By size 規模									
Large 大型	13	6,077	730,028	29,570	1.95	5.46	120.13	64.23	1,512,633
Medium 中型	18	1,497	91,445	5,200	3.35	16.09	61.07	79.15	155,028
Small 小型	249	122	5,744	-20	-0.19	-1.69	47.17	88.58	10,453
By regional distribution 地區分布									
Central-North 華北	52	514	47,088	3,349	2.85	7.46	91.61	61.84	117,667
Beijing 北京	1	24	1,230				51.25	165.29	1,700
Tianjin 天津	7	1,170	142,324	7,554	2.68	5.62	121.60	52.28	281,590
Hebei 河北	15	542	64,824	3,655	2.25	5.13	119.53	56.09	162,297
Shanxi 山西	11	147	5,185	-25	-0.25	-1.02	35.27	75.61	10,252
Inner Mongolia 內蒙	18	487	23,426	3,708	4.17	22.32	48.14	81.30	88,812
Northeast 東北	39	848	48,578	677	0.36	1.24	57.28	70.62	185,879
Liaoning 遼寧	23	1,373	81,078	1,136	0.36	1.24	59.06	70.56	312,136
Jilin 吉林	5	109	940	6	0.07	0.29	8.61	77.44	9,034
Heilongjiang 黑龍江	11	87	2,276	23	1.00	3.95	26.17	74.67	2,272
Central East 華東	76	383	41,754	2,433	3.31	8.15	108.98	59.39	73,542
Shanghai 上海	3	599	38,363	23	0.06	0.19	64.05	67.74	37,247
Jiangsu 江蘇	18	283	36,965	973	1.46	6.59	130.41	77.78	66,417
Zhejiang 浙江	12	235	22,603	1,766	7.06	14.33	96.22	50.76	25,018
Anhui 安徽	10	56	2,741	8	0.28	-4.88	49.39	105.82	2,819
Fujian 福建	8	279	21,444	348	1.53	4.45	76.96	65.52	22,664
Jiangxi 江西	6	46	1,210	-17	-0.80	-3.65	26.12	78.03	2,078
Shandong 山東	19	860	100,809	7,546	3.81	8.16	117.23	53.28	197,883
Central-South 中南	68	340	25,471	1,077	2.02	9.90	74.87	79.57	53,274
Henan 河南	27	259	17,834	710	2.51	9.38	68.89	73.30	28,344
Hubei 湖北	17	571	48,312	3,291	5.09	12.75	84.58	60.10	64,686
Hunan 湖南	15	312	17,352	-48	-0.19	-2.14	55.67	90.89	24,676
Guangdong 廣東	6	277	27,868	3		0.03	100.49	95.37	229,348
Guangxi 廣西	3	31	557	-387	-10.15	161.11	17.77	106.30	3,810
Hainan 海南									
Southwest 西南	21	515	43,440	2,264	4.19	15.09	84.41	72.22	53,988
Chongqing 重慶	2	59	998	16	1.23	11.77	16.86	89.59	1,329
Sichuan 四川	18	599	51,082	2,668	4.20	15.07	85.28	72.16	63,579
Guizhou 貴州	1	35	1,920	80	15.69	80.00	54.86	80.39	510
Yunnan 雲南									
Tibet 西藏									
Northwest 西北	27	363	13,774	-1,222	-2.46	-26.54	37.95	90.75	49,765
Shaanxi 陝西	12	208	7,432	-574	-3.08	-70.81	35.67	95.65	18,655
Gansu 甘肅	5	689	40,748	1,074	1.32	4.65	59.11	71.51	81,110
Qinghai 青海	1	673	10,580	-8,820	-4.01	-114.10	15.72	96.49	220,100
Ningxia 寧夏	3	50	1,440	190	8.62	24.78	28.99	65.20	2,203
Xinjiang 新疆	6	505	10,682	-3,870	-4.76	210.71	21.14	102.26	81,257

2615: Soda Ash 純鹼製造業

Year 年份	Number of firms 企業個數	Rate of change 每年變化 (%)	Number of employees 職工人數 (人)	Rate of change 每年變化 (%)	Total revenue (mil. RMB) 總銷售收入 (百萬元)	Rate of change 每年變化 (%)	Total profit (mil. RMB) 總利潤 (百萬元)	Rate of change 每年變化 (%)
1993	325		115,664		7,709		347	
1994	357	9.85%	110,324	-4.62%	7,638	-0.93%	325	-6.43%
1995	297	-16.81%	116,991	6.04%	8,515	11.48%	410	26.06%
1996	283	-4.71%	132,666	13.40%	10,533	23.70%	473	15.41%

3 Major products* 3 種主要產品 *	Output 產量	Sales volume 銷售量	Unit 單位
a) Sodium Bicarbonate 碳酸氫鈉	248,422	238,485	ton 噸
b) Sodium Carbonate 碳酸鈉	5,675,646	4,824,299	ton 噸
c) Sodium Silicate 硅酸鈉	325,058	318,557	ton 噸

Top 10 firms by revenue (year founded) 收入排名前 10 家企業 (創辦年份)	City 城市	Province 省	Telephone / fax 電話 / 傳真	Number of employees 職工人數	Ownership 產業所有權	Revenue ('000 RMB) 銷售收入 (千元)	Profit ('000 RMB) (rank) 利潤 (千元) (排名)	Total assets ('000 RMB) 總資產 (千元)	Major products 主要產品
Dahua Group Co. Ltd. 大化集團有限責任公司(1935)	Dalian 大連市	Liaoning 遼寧省	(0411)6672312 (0411)6671199	11,000	State-owned 國有	1,833,969	30240(6)	7,113,692	b
Shandong Hai Yang Chemical Industry Group General Co. 山東海洋化工集團總公司	Weifang 濰坊市	Shandong 山東省	(0536)5331631 (0536)5331634	11,930	State-owned 國有	1,322,211	124401(1)	2,805,597	a,b
Bo Hai Chemical Industry (Group) Co. Ltd. Tianjin Alkali Mill 渤海化工(集團)股份有限公司天津鹼廠(1924)	Tianjin 天津市	Tianjin 天津市	(022)25893951 (022)25895881	7,596	Joint stock 股份制	974,829	51683(3)	1,526,743	a,b,c
Tangshan Alkali Mill 河北省唐山鹼廠(1989)	Tangshan 唐山市	Hebei 河北省	(0315)8511173	5,709	Joint stock 股份制	771,208	41983(5)	2,162,412	b
Honghe Chemical Inc., Zigong 自貢鴻鶴化工股份有限公司(1994)	Zigong 自貢市	Sichuan 四川省	(0813)2204951 (0813)2206209	6,846	State-owned 國有	691,959	48006(4)	797,705	a,b
Hubei Shuang Huan Chemical Group Company 湖北雙環化工集團公司(1970)	Xiaogan 孝感市	Hubei 湖北省	(0712)3591222 (0712)3591188	5,817	State-owned 國有	649,213	61530(2)	835,253	a,b
Nanjing Chemical Industry Group Company Lianyungang Alkali Factory 南京化學工業集團公司連雲港鹼廠(1989)	Lianyungang 連雲港市	Jiangsu 江蘇省	(0518)2310301 (0518)2311440	3,684	State-owned 國有	606,401	21470(7)	1,134,810	o
Qingdao Alkali Industrial Co. Ltd. 青島鹼業股份有限公司(1965)	Qingdao 青島市	Shandong 山東省	(0532)4817791 (0532)4812049	3,494	Joint stock 股份制	540,853	17221(9)	887,443	a,b
Hangzhou Longshan Chemical General Factory 杭州龍山化工總廠(1960)	Hangzhou 杭州市	Zhejiang 浙江省	(0571)6617638 (0571)6618654	1,820	State-owned 國有	221,284	20030(8)	255,707	a,b
Jinchang Chemical General Factory 金昌化工總廠(1967)	Jinchang 金昌市	Gansu 甘肅省	(0935)7321223 (0935)7322525	3,297	State-owned 國有	202,469	5261(11)	400,848	b

Top 10 Cities by Production Output 產出排名前 10 位城市	Province 省	Market share 市場份額	Number of firms 企業個數
Weifang 濰坊市	Shandong 山東省	14.85%	7
Dalian 大連市	Liaoning 遼寧省	14.12%	1
Tianjin 天津市	Tianjin 天津市	10.71%	8
Zigong 自貢市	Sichuan 四川省	8.45%	4
Tangshan 唐山市	Hebei 河北省	7.81%	3
Xiaogan 孝感市	Hubei 湖北省	6.90%	4
Lianyungang 連雲港市	Jiangsu 江蘇省	5.16%	3
Jiaozuo 焦作市	Henan 河南省	3.37%	3
Hangzhou 杭州市	Zhejiang 浙江省	2.72%	4
Guangzhou 廣州市	Guangdong 廣東省	2.43%	3

10 Major Wholesalers 10 家主要批發商	City 城市	Province 省	Telephone / Fax 電話 / 傳真
Changzhou Hardware Alternating-current Appliance and Chemical Wholesale General Company 常州五金交電化工批發總公司	Changzhou 常州市	Jiangsu 江蘇省	(0519)6609929 (0519)6609925
Suzhou Hardware & Alternating Electricity Co. Ltd. 蘇州五金交電股份有限公司	Suzhou 蘇州市	Jiangsu 江蘇省	(0512)5239572 (0512)5213248
Tianjin Foreign Trade General Company 天津市對外貿易總公司	Tianjin 天津市	Tianjin 天津市	(022)23310922
Chongqing International Trade Center 重慶國際貿易中心	Chongqing 重慶市	Chongqing 重慶市	(023)67853232 (023)67850402
China Chemical Plastics Co. Ltd. 中化塑料有限公司	Beijing 北京市	Beijing 北京市	(010)68569863 (010)68569041
Ningbo Hualian Group Co. Ltd. 寧波華聯集團股份有限公司	Ningbo 寧波市	Zhejiang 浙江省	(0574)7367626 (0574)7367652
Xiamen Kaiyuan Wei Wei Electromechanical Building Materials Marketing Dept. 廈門市開元區威威機電建材經營部	Xiamen 廈門市	Fujian 福建省	(0592)2071044
Rudong Industry Product General Company 如東縣工業品總公司	Nantong 南通市	Jiangsu 江蘇省	(0513)4516110 (0513)4516110
Fujian Fu Ri Group Company 福建福日集團公司	Fuzhou 福州市	Fujian 福建省	(0591)3269325 (0591)3270426
Guangdong Hardware & Alternating Electrical Co. 廣東省五金交電公司	Guangzhou 廣州市	Guangdong 廣東省	(020)81884078 (020)81861287

*Also include sales by firms outside this industry.包括本行業以外廠家的銷售。"o" stands for "others". "o" 代表 "其他產品"。

2617: Inorganic Salts 無機鹽製造業

The industry accounts for 0.288% of the total revenue of China's industrial sector in 1996. The revenue growth rate of the industry is 6.2% from 1995, as compared to the growth rate of China's industrial sector, 9.51%. The rate of return on asset is 0.75%. 66.78% of all firms in the industry made a profit while 26.32% had negative returns. The top province in terms of the industry's revenue is Jiangsu, accounting for 11.83% of the total revenue.
本行業在1996年佔全行業總產值0.288%，行業年增長率為6.2%（全國工業年增長率9.51%）。行業的資產回報率0.75%，66.78%的企業盈利，26.32%的企業虧損。銷售收入最高的省份為江蘇省，佔本行業的11.83%。

	Total number of firms 企業總數	Total number of employees 職工總數	Total revenue (mil. RMB) 總銷售收入（百萬元）	Total profit (mil. RMB) 總利潤（百萬元）	Return on assets 資產利潤率 (%)	Return on equity 權益利潤率 (%)	Labour productivity ('000 RMB / worker) 勞動生產率（千元/人）	Debts / assets 資產負債率 (%)	Total assets (mil. RMB) 總資產（百萬元）
Industry Overall 行業總體	1,970	288,027	16,669	185	0.75	2.68	57.87	72.12	24,719

	Number of firms 企業個數	Average number of employees 平均職工人數	Average revenue ('000 RMB) 平均銷售收入（千元）	Average profit ('000 RMB) 平均利潤（千元）	Return on assets 資產利潤率 (%)	Return on equity 權益利潤率 (%)	Labour productivity ('000 RMB / worker) 勞動生產率（千元/人）	Average debts / assets 平均資產負債率(%)	Average Total assets ('000 RMB) 平均總資產（千元）
By ownership 產業所有權									
State-owned 國有	320	404	22,672	-250	-0.54	-2.06	56.05	73.78	46,363
Collectively-owned 集體	1,519	93	5,049	124	2.42	8.53	54.54	71.58	5,119
Privately-owned 私有	13	40	2,339	100	4.27	17.58	58.02	75.73	2,339
Domestic JVs 聯營	28	77	5,468	-36	-0.67	-2.19	70.91	69.44	5,438
Joint stock 股份制	20	376	27,250	1,956	4.69	12.61	72.52	62.84	41,729
Foreign-funded 外資	29	114	15,018	785	5.61	11.52	131.34	51.32	13,985
Overseas Chinese-funded 港澳台資	40	158	14,470	357	2.10	6.21	91.67	66.24	17,062
By size 規模									
Large 大型	22	2,406	187,315	3,131	0.96	2.43	77.84	60.60	326,637
Medium 中型	88	784	45,103	-132	-0.18	-0.81	57.55	77.81	73,220
Small 小型	1,812	91	4,735	70	1.15	4.85	52.14	76.28	6,120
By regional distribution 地區分布									
Central-North 華北	325	196	10,522	496	2.69	9.37	53.70	71.27	18,453
Beijing 北京	18	52	2,268	70	2.10	4.64	43.48	54.71	3,329
Tianjin 天津	73	107	6,364	49	0.18	0.90	59.60	79.71	26,859
Hebei 河北	138	146	9,687	508	5.01	17.46	66.51	71.33	10,154
Shanxi 山西	61	395	19,351	1,381	5.08	11.96	48.97	57.54	27,208
Inner Mongolia 內蒙	35	307	11,350	60	0.23	1.09	36.98	79.11	26,161
Northeast 東北	202	160	5,956	-98	-0.92	-4.56	37.29	79.84	10,645
Liaoning 遼寧	125	173	6,460	-101	-0.88	-3.47	37.34	74.64	11,421
Jilin 吉林	46	122	4,210	-85	-1.15	-10.18	34.51	88.71	7,378
Heilongjiang 黑龍江	31	162	6,514	-107	-0.87	-10.00	40.20	91.34	12,366
Central East 華東	516	135	11,027	257	2.15	6.88	81.42	68.79	11,952
Shanghai 上海	38	176	16,800	-13	-0.09	-0.29	95.20	68.23	14,158
Jiangsu 江蘇	162	122	12,177	481	5.20	14.75	99.82	64.72	9,241
Zhejiang 浙江	70	53	4,665	57	1.50	3.77	87.78	60.13	3,795
Anhui 安徽	48	157	9,615	226	2.47	9.09	61.36	72.85	9,170
Fujian 福建	41	68	7,419	142	1.46	4.95	108.32	70.56	9,717
Jiangxi 江西	55	103	4,747	204	2.48	8.97	46.19	72.42	8,242
Shandong 山東	102	233	16,916	227	0.90	3.06	72.76	70.56	25,242
Central-South 中南	454	111	6,103	-17	-0.21	-0.91	55.03	77.14	8,267
Henan 河南	119	81	2,800	58	1.41	4.60	34.47	69.33	4,146
Hubei 湖北	66	128	10,118	124	1.02	5.25	78.76	80.58	12,204
Hunan 湖南	170	119	5,978	13	0.19	0.79	50.10	75.62	6,860
Guangdong 廣東	58	88	6,794	-209	-1.66	-13.60	76.79	87.77	12,546
Guangxi 廣西	40	165	8,985	-327	-2.41	-7.53	54.41	68.05	13,601
Hainan 海南	1	183	10	-30	-0.18	-0.93	0.05	80.54	16,600
Southwest 西南	311	144	8,757	-66	-0.46	-1.42	60.92	67.24	14,232
Chongqing 重慶	61	178	8,527	-61	-0.46	-2.00	47.82	76.99	13,170
Sichuan 四川	168	137	6,146	143	1.43	6.96	44.86	79.48	10,029
Guizhou 貴州	43	115	8,351	29	0.30	1.88	72.31	83.93	9,550
Yunnan 雲南	39	152	20,814	-36	-0.09	-0.17	136.66	44.12	39,166
Tibet 西藏									
Northwest 西北	162	167	5,320	-376	-2.74	-12.13	31.76	77.41	13,732
Shaanxi 陝西	61	106	4,182	-75	-1.06	-4.85	39.47	78.16	7,109
Gansu 甘肅	39	153	4,686	-134	-1.09	-4.64	30.62	76.54	12,267
Qinghai 青海	16	159	2,491	-2,109	-16.54	-483.38	15.63	96.58	12,748
Ningxia 寧夏	14	253	11,119	869	3.10	6.59	43.95	52.98	28,039
Xinjiang 新疆	32	269	7,139	-924	-4.13	-28.42	26.53	85.46	22,374

Year 年份	Number of firms 企業個數	Rate of change 每年變化 (%)	Number of employees 職工人數 (人)	Rate of change 每年變化 (%)	Total revenue (mil. RMB) 總銷售收入 (百萬元)	Rate of change 每年變化 (%)	Total profit (mil. RMB) 總利潤 (百萬元)	Rate of change 每年變化 (%)
1993	1,581		259,498		9,667		-29	
1994	1,731	9.49%	276,089	6.39%	11,161	15.45%	9	129.43%
1995	2,068	19.47%	313,977	13.72%	15,700	40.67%	243	2723.34%
1996	1,970	-4.74%	288,027	-8.26%	16,669	6.17%	185	-23.79%

3 Major products* 3種主要產品 *	Output 產量	Sales volume 銷售量	Unit 單位
a) Anhydride Chromate 鉻酸酐	31,069	32,933	ton 噸
b) Base Sulifide 硫化鹼	444,258	390,947	ton 噸
c) Sodium Tripolyphosphate 三聚磷酸鈉	369,334	336,094	ton 噸

Top 10 firms by revenue (year founded) 收入排名前10家企業 (創辦年份)	City 城市	Province 省	Telephone / fax 電話 / 傳真	Number of employees 職工人數	Ownership 產業所有權	Revenue ('000 RMB) 銷售收入 (千元)	Profit ('000 RMB) (rank) 利潤 (千元) (排名)	Total assets ('000 RMB) 總資產 (千元)	Major products 主要產品
Zhongqing Yilan Group Corp. Ltd. 中輕依蘭集團有限公司(1986)	Kunming 昆明市	Yunnan 雲南省	(0871)8590319 (0871)8590023	2,518	State-owned 國有	637,878	4105(24)	1,268,115	c
Shanxi Nan Feng Chemical Group Co. Ltd. 山西省南風化工集團股份有限公司(1996)	Yuncheng 運城市	Shanxi 山西省	(0359)2017022 (0359)2023302	10,840	Joint stock 股份制	462,818	52722(1)	553,049	o
Jiangsu Cheng Xing Phosphorization Group Co. 江蘇澄星磷化工集團公司(1995)	Wuxi 無錫市	Jiangsu 江蘇省	(0510)6285288 (0510)6281884	457	Collectively-owned 集體	438,300	22693(4)	210,460	c
Qingdao Hong Xing Chemical Group Co. 青島紅星化工集團公司(1959)	Qingdao 青島市	Shandong 山東省	(0532)4816630 (0532)4816920	3,498	State-owned 國有	292,402	3280(36)	451,784	b
Hebei Xinji Barium Salt Group Co. Ltd. 河北辛集市鋇鹽集團有限責任公司(1947)	Shijiazhuang 石家莊市	Hebei 河北省	(0311)3222622 (0311)3225039	3,716	State-owned 國有	253,349	25027(3)	458,902	b
Hefei Chemical Fertilizer Plant 合肥化肥廠(1958)	Hefei 合肥市	Anhui 安徽省	(0551)3635195 (0551)3633570	1,964	State-owned 國有	212,287	8230(8)	250,609	c
Ji'nan Yu Xing Chemical General Factory 濟南裕興化工總廠(1919)	Ji'nan 濟南市	Shandong 山東省	(0531)5952322 (0531)5951148	3,039	State-owned 國有	210,171	20(529)	565,029	a
Guangxi Phosphate Chemical Factory 廣西磷酸鹽化工廠(1975)	Liuzhou 柳州市	Guangxi 廣西	(0772)7612433 (0772)2826304	2,272	State-owned 國有	164,508	59(460)	191,231	c
Chongqing Dongfeng Chemical Factory 重慶東風化工廠	Chongqing 重慶市	Chongqing 重慶市	(023)65152409 (023)65313170	1,282	State-owned 國有	158,299	652(153)	217,849	a
Fuzhou No.1 Chemical Factory 福州第一化工廠(1958)	Fuzhou 福州市	Fujian 福建省	(0591)3660183 (0591)3660140	930	State-owned 國有	151,322	7167(11)	161,498	o

Top 10 Cities by Production Output 產出排名前10位城市	Province 省	Market share 市場份額	Number of firms 企業個數
Yuncheng 運城市	Shanxi 山西省	5.08%	14
Kunming 昆明市	Yunnan 雲南省	4.65%	12
Chongqing 重慶市	Chongqing 重慶市	3.64%	74
Tianjin 天津市	Tianjin 天津市	3.46%	98
Shanghai 上海市	Shanghai 上海市	3.32%	47
Qingdao 青島市	Shandong 山東省	3.04%	12
Changsha 長沙市	Hunan 湖南省	2.65%	20
Shijiazhuang 石家莊市	Hebei 河北省	2.52%	41
Suzhou 蘇州市	Jiangsu 江蘇省	2.28%	59
Zibo 淄博市	Shandong 山東省	2.03%	21

10 Major Wholesalers 10家主要批發商	City 城市	Province 省	Telephone / Fax 電話 / 傳真
Changzhou Hardware Alternating-current Appliance and Chemical Wholesale General Company 常州五金交電化工批發總公司	Changzhou 常州市	Jiangsu 江蘇省	(0519)6609929 (0519)6609925
Suzhou Hardware & Alternating Electricity Co. Ltd. 蘇州五金交電股份有限公司	Suzhou 蘇州市	Jiangsu 江蘇省	(0512)5239572 (0512)5213248
Tianjin Foreign Trade General Company 天津市對外貿易總公司	Tianjin 天津市	Tianjin 天津市	(022)23310922
Chongqing International Trade Center 重慶國際貿易中心	Chongqing 重慶市	Chongqing 重慶市	(023)67853232 (023)67850402
China Chemical Plastics Co. Ltd. 中化塑料有限公司	Beijing 北京市	Beijing 北京市	(010)68569863 (010)68569041
Ningbo Hualian Group Co. Ltd. 寧波華聯集團股份有限公司	Ningbo 寧波市	Zhejiang 浙江省	(0574)7367626 (0574)7367652
Xiamen Kaiyuan Wei Wei Electromechanical Building Materials Marketing Dept. 廈門市開元區威威機電建材經營部	Xiamen 廈門市	Fujian 福建省	(0592)2071044
Rudong Industry Product General Company 如東縣工業品總公司	Nantong 南通市	Jiangsu 江蘇省	(0513)4516110 (0513)4516110
Fujian Fu Ri Group Company 福建福日集團公司	Fuzhou 福州市	Fujian 福建省	(0591)3269325 (0591)3270426
Guangdong Hardware & Alternating Electrical Co. 廣東省五金交電公司	Guangzhou 廣州市	Guangdong 廣東省	(020)81884078 (020)81861287

*Also include sales by firms outside this industry.包括本行業以外廠家的銷售。"o" stands for "others". "o" 代表 "其他產品"。

2619: Other Basic Chemical Raw Materials 其他基本化學原料製造業

The industry accounts for 0.251% of the total revenue of China's industrial sector in 1996. The revenue growth rate of the industry is 24.2% from 1995, as compared to the growth rate of China's industrial sector, 9.51%. The rate of return on asset is 1.25%. 63.86% of all firms in the industry made a profit while 27.58% had negative returns. The top province in terms of the industry's revenue is Jiangsu, accounting for 10.91% of the total revenue.
本行業在1996年佔全行業總產值0.251%，行業年增長率為24.2%（全國工業年增長率9.51%）。行業的資產回報率1.25%，63.86%的企業盈利，27.58%的企業虧損。銷售收入最高的省份為江蘇省，佔本行業的10.91%。

	Total number of firms 企業總數	Total number of employees 職工總數	Total revenue (mil. RMB) 總銷售收入（百萬元）	Total profit (mil. RMB) 總利潤（百萬元）	Return on assets 資產利潤率 (%)	Return on equity 權益利潤率 (%)	Labour productivity ('000 RMB / worker) 勞動生產率（千元/人）	Debts / assets 資產負債率 (%)	Total assets (mil. RMB) 總資產（百萬元）
Industry Overall 行業總體	2,145	253,085	14,557	289	1.25	4.15	57.52	69.84	23,074

	Number of firms 企業個數	Average number of employees 平均職工人數	Average revenue ('000 RMB) 平均銷售收入（千元）	Average profit ('000 RMB) 平均利潤（千元）	Return on assets 資產利潤率 (%)	Return on equity 權益利潤率 (%)	Labour productivity ('000 RMB / worker) 勞動生產率（千元/人）	Average debts / assets 平均資產負債率(%)	Average Total assets ('000 RMB) 平均總資產（千元）
By ownership 產業所有權									
State-owned 國有	411	283	13,448	-34	-0.12	-0.53	47.50	76.44	27,440
Collectively-owned 集體	1,552	77	4,508	127	2.69	10.94	58.72	75.42	4,729
Privately-owned 私有	7	19	2,540	243	16.17	35.35	135.72	54.26	1,503
Domestic JVs 聯營	41	107	10,088	102	0.75	1.83	94.17	58.83	13,465
Joint stock 股份制	31	188	15,062	445	2.07	10.26	80.05	79.85	21,515
Foreign-funded 外資	57	96	16,174	1,389	2.89	4.29	168.94	32.63	48,089
Overseas Chinese-funded 港澳台資	45	53	4,670	150	1.39	2.38	88.48	41.41	10,779
By size 規模									
Large 大型	16	1,571	123,524	178	0.06	0.25	78.62	74.09	274,208
Medium 中型	71	704	45,761	1,198	1.56	4.57	65.04	66.01	77,025
Small 小型	2,011	87	4,640	100	1.53	5.10	53.05	70.08	6,550
By regional distribution 地區分布									
Central-North 華北	331	129	5,946	174	1.89	5.05	46.23	62.65	9,218
Beijing 北京	38	98	7,971	33	0.15	0.30	81.27	49.35	21,168
Tianjin 天津	30	81	5,364	535	4.81	10.68	66.09	54.94	11,113
Hebei 河北	116	83	6,282	261	3.59	10.50	75.48	65.75	7,274
Shanxi 山西	117	197	5,668	70	0.92	3.29	28.73	72.07	7,666
Inner Mongolia 內蒙	30	123	3,751	57	0.99	4.05	30.57	75.48	5,747
Northeast 東北	266	92	2,983	-33	-0.55	-1.36	32.38	59.22	6,019
Liaoning 遼寧	148	111	3,655	-98	-1.14	-2.60	32.85	56.11	8,589
Jilin 吉林	66	68	2,384	44	1.35	5.86	35.03	77.04	3,300
Heilongjiang 黑龍江	52	68	1,828	52	2.40	6.00	26.81	59.96	2,154
Central East 華東	567	121	8,356	177	1.37	4.41	69.19	68.88	12,860
Shanghai 上海	50	229	24,277	1,110	2.17	6.58	106.02	67.01	51,131
Jiangsu 江蘇	151	166	10,514	-100	-0.74	-2.05	63.44	63.83	13,519
Zhejiang 浙江	80	62	4,073	-5	-0.07	-0.20	65.59	65.37	6,988
Anhui 安徽	59	131	6,419	177	2.79	14.85	49.07	81.23	6,351
Fujian 福建	51	28	1,572	-14	-0.53	-1.48	56.15	63.90	2,687
Jiangxi 江西	54	100	3,306	82	1.49	6.02	33.15	75.18	5,469
Shandong 山東	122	103	7,977	377	3.47	15.31	77.82	77.34	10,884
Central-South 中南	539	96	6,500	182	1.88	6.01	67.80	68.70	9,698
Henan 河南	139	110	6,581	164	1.59	7.70	59.98	79.38	10,310
Hubei 湖北	125	126	7,774	194	1.77	6.88	61.68	74.28	10,932
Hunan 湖南	126	82	4,031	105	2.08	5.74	48.95	63.81	5,080
Guangdong 廣東	95	74	10,090	494	3.06	6.87	136.81	55.43	16,135
Guangxi 廣西	48	62	2,919	-196	-4.19	-15.72	47.35	73.32	4,664
Hainan 海南	6	55	1,780	90	1.75	3.65	32.56	52.06	5,145
Southwest 西南	313	155	9,263	209	1.48	5.60	59.87	73.55	14,134
Chongqing 重慶	50	122	7,692	4	0.04	0.08	63.09	54.71	10,413
Sichuan 四川	105	153	6,161	0	0.00	-0.02	40.25	85.33	10,822
Guizhou 貴州	91	109	7,956	432	3.78	10.43	72.89	63.73	11,424
Yunnan 雲南	66	247	17,325	396	1.51	6.71	70.02	77.44	26,158
Tibet 西藏	1	10	110	-40	-3.96	-4.04	11.00	2.97	1,010
Northwest 西北	129	135	5,078	-185	-1.61	-26.13	37.58	93.83	11,468
Shaanxi 陝西	50	117	4,505	-567	-6.12	-68.15	38.39	91.03	9,264
Gansu 甘肅	33	174	5,315	-48	-0.27	10.92	30.63	102.44	18,121
Qinghai 青海	9	55	1,043	-7	-0.10	1.46	18.89	106.67	6,847
Ningxia 寧夏	25	161	7,356	22	0.20	1.16	45.59	82.91	10,878
Xinjiang 新疆	12	109	5,090	465	6.60	25.43	46.84	74.06	7,049

2619: Other Basic Chemical Raw Materials 其他基本化學原料製造業

Year 年份	Number of firms 企業個數	Rate of change 每年變化 (%)	Number of employees 職工人數 (人)	Rate of change 每年變化 (%)	Total revenue (mil. RMB) 總銷售收入 (百萬元)	Rate of change 每年變化 (%)	Total profit (mil. RMB) 總利潤 (百萬元)	Rate of change 每年變化 (%)
1993	2,009		281,043		8,803		162	
1994	2,089	3.98%	253,048	-9.96%	10,635	20.82%	161	-0.66%
1995	1,998	-4.36%	246,022	-2.78%	11,717	10.17%	227	40.79%
1996	2,145	7.36%	253,085	2.87%	14,557	24.24%	289	27.47%

3 Major products* 3 種主要產品 *	Output 產量	Sales volume 銷售量	Unit 單位
a) Yellow Phosphorus 黃磷	287,228	241,272	ton 噸
b) Calcium Carbide 碳化鈣	816,248	587,699	ton 噸
c) Phosphoric Acid 磷酸	123,607	65,512	ton 噸

Top 10 firms by revenue (year founded) 收入排名前 10 家企業 (創辦年份)	City 城市	Province 省	Telephone / fax 電話 / 傳真	Number of employees 職工人數	Ownership 產業所有權	Revenue ('000 RMB) 銷售收入 (千元)	Profit ('000 RMB) (rank) 利潤 (千元) (排名)	Total assets ('000 RMB) 總資產 (千元)	Major products 主要產品
Shanghai Wu Song Chemical General Factory 上海吳淞化工總廠(1933)	Shanghai 上海市	Shanghai 上海市	(021)56993888 (021)56754337	3,630	State-owned 國有	309,211	1031(128)	979,113	b
Shandong Longhai Group Co. Ltd. 山東龍海集團有限公司(1995)	Yantai 煙台市	Shandong 山東省	(0535)8591181 (0535)8591181	1,335	Collectively-owned 集體	233,099	23283(1)	105,624	o
Yunnan Dian Dong Phosphor Chemical Company 雲南滇東磷化工公司(1965)	Qujing 曲靖市	Yunnan 雲南省	(0874)7123558 (0874)7122601	3,201	State-owned 國有	219,427	4721(24)	235,390	a,c
Yunnan Chengjiang Phosphorus Industry Chemical Co. 雲南省澄江縣磷業化工公司(1986)	Yuxi 玉溪市	Yunnan 雲南省	(0877)6913393 (0877)6913140	1,745	Collectively-owned 集體	166,027	6399(13)	259,946	a,c
Kaiyang Shuang Liu Yellow Phosphorus Factory 開陽縣雙流黃磷廠(1990)	Guiyang 貴陽市	Guizhou 貴州省	(0851)7552258 (0851)5819268	1,063	Joint stock 股份制	158,880	5827(15)	130,989	a,c
Wu Song Chemical Fertilizer Factory 吳淞化肥廠(1956)	Shanghai 上海市	Shanghai 上海市	(021)56671701 (021)63209672	1,444	State-owned 國有	147,420	506(198)	232,284	o
State-owned Torch Chemical Factory 國營火炬化工廠(1976)	Luzhou 瀘州市	Sichuan 四川省	(0830)4188000	3,216	State-owned 國有	138,700	816(150)	341,923	o
Hebei Cheng Xin Co. Ltd. 河北誠信有限責任公司(1989)	Shijiazhuang 石家莊市	Hebei 河北省	(0311)4623437	360	State-owned 國有	123,540	14013(5)	63,954	o
Guangzhou Zhu Jiang Electrochemical Plant 廣州市珠江電化廠(1952)	Guangzhou 廣州市	Guangdong 廣東省	(020)81891357 (020)81891357	964	Domestic JVs 聯營	121,407	2821(43)	192,038	o
Sichuan Chuan Xi Phosphorization Group 四川川西磷化工集團(1979)	Deyang 德陽市	Sichuan 四川省	(0838)8204048 (0838)8204537	3,088	Joint stock 股份制	115,567	3358(34)	286,603	a,c

Top 10 Cities by Production Output 產出排名前 10 位城市	Province 省	Market share 市場份額	Number of firms 企業個數
Taizhou 泰州市	Jiangsu 江蘇省	13.26%	18
Shanghai 上海市	Shanghai 上海市	8.80%	94
Changzhi 長治市	Shanxi 山西省	5.71%	21
Suzhou 蘇州市	Jiangsu 江蘇省	3.07%	39
Yantai 煙台市	Shandong 山東省	2.69%	17
Qujing 曲靖市	Yunnan 雲南省	2.50%	9
Yuxi 玉溪市	Yunnan 雲南省	2.49%	7
Guangzhou 廣州市	Guangdong 廣東省	2.37%	18
Jiaozuo 焦作市	Henan 河南省	1.93%	18
Nanjing 南京市	Jiangsu 江蘇省	1.84%	26

10 Major Wholesalers 10 家主要批發商	City 城市	Province 省	Telephone / Fax 電話 / 傳真
Changzhou Hardware Alternating-current Appliance and Chemical Wholesale General Company 常州五金交電化工批發總公司	Changzhou 常州市	Jiangsu 江蘇省	(0519)6609929 (0519)6609925
Suzhou Hardware & Alternating Electricity Co. Ltd. 蘇州五金交電股份有限公司	Suzhou 蘇州市	Jiangsu 江蘇省	(0512)5239572 (0512)5213248
Tianjin Foreign Trade General Company 天津市對外貿易總公司	Tianjin 天津市	Tianjin 天津市	(022)23310922
Chongqing International Trade Center 重慶國際貿易中心	Chongqing 重慶市	Chongqing 重慶市	(023)67853232 (023)67850402
China Chemical Plastics Co. Ltd. 中化塑料有限公司	Beijing 北京市	Beijing 北京市	(010)68569863 (010)68569041
Ningbo Hualian Group Co. Ltd. 寧波華聯集團股份有限公司	Ningbo 寧波市	Zhejiang 浙江省	(0574)7367626 (0574)7367652
Xiamen Kaiyuan Wei Wei Electromechanical Building Materials Marketing Dept. 廈門市開元區威威機電建材經營部	Xiamen 廈門市	Fujian 福建省	(0592)2071044
Rudong Industry Product General Company 如東縣工業品總公司	Nantong 南通市	Jiangsu 江蘇省	(0513)4516110 (0513)4516110
Fujian Fu Ri Group Company 福建福日集團公司	Fuzhou 福州市	Fujian 福建省	(0591)3269325 (0591)3270426
Guangdong Hardware & Alternating Electrical Co. 廣東省五金交電公司	Guangzhou 廣州市	Guangdong 廣東省	(020)81884078 (020)81861287

*Also include sales by firms outside this industry.包括本行業以外廠家的銷售。"o" stands for "others". "o" 代表 "其他產品"。

2621: Nitrogenous Fertilizer 氮肥製造業

The industry accounts for 1.054% of the total revenue of China's industrial sector in 1996. The revenue growth rate of the industry is 15.5% from 1995, as compared to the growth rate of China's industrial sector, 9.51%. The rate of return on asset is 2.93%. 53.58% of all firms in the industry made a profit while 42.94% had negative returns. The top province in terms of the industry's revenue is Shandong, accounting for 11.48% of the total revenue.
本行業在1996年佔全行業總產值1.054%，行業年增長率為15.5%（全國工業年增長率9.51%）。行業的資產回報率2.93%，53.58%的企業盈利，42.94%的企業虧損。銷售收入最高的省份為山東省，佔本行業的11.48%。

	Total number of firms 企業總數	Total number of employees 職工總數	Total revenue (mil. RMB) 總銷售收入（百萬元）	Total profit (mil. RMB) 總利潤（百萬元）	Return on assets 資產利潤率 (%)	Return on equity 權益利潤率 (%)	Labour productivity ('000 RMB / worker) 勞動生產率（千元/人）	Debts / assets 資產負債率 (%)	Total assets (mil. RMB) 總資產（百萬元）
Industry Overall 行業總體	890	900,287	61,084	2,881	2.93	9.00	67.85	67.49	98,463

	Number of firms 企業個數	Average number of employees 平均職工人數	Average revenue ('000 RMB) 平均銷售收入（千元）	Average profit ('000 RMB) 平均利潤（千元）	Return on assets 資產利潤率 (%)	Return on equity 權益利潤率 (%)	Labour productivity ('000 RMB / worker) 勞動生產率（千元/人）	Average debts / assets 平均資產負債率(%)	Average Total assets ('000 RMB) 平均總資產（千元）
By ownership 產業所有權									
State-owned 國有	813	1,051	70,086	3,488	3.11	9.60	66.68	67.60	112,181
Collectively-owned 集體	51	260	23,065	37	0.11	0.32	88.82	67.19	35,624
Privately-owned 私有									
Domestic JVs 聯營									
Joint stock 股份制	26	1,221	112,673	1,657	0.79	2.31	92.28	65.68	209,377
Foreign-funded 外資									
Overseas Chinese-funded 港澳台資									
By size 規模									
Large 大型	65	3,480	350,440	20,767	3.15	8.08	100.69	61.06	660,190
Medium 中型	277	1,165	78,106	3,631	3.04	10.52	67.02	71.06	119,288
Small 小型	540	639	30,871	974	2.34	9.17	48.34	74.50	41,682
By regional distribution 地區分布									
Central-North 華北	164	845	52,297	3,439	3.85	13.05	61.89	70.50	89,374
Beijing 北京	5	1,687	108,212	854	0.36	1.55	64.15	76.43	234,272
Tianjin 天津	2	820	81,315	2,060	1.59	19.94	99.16	92.02	129,375
Hebei 河北	75	952	68,863	5,212	4.68	15.97	72.34	70.71	111,413
Shanxi 山西	69	652	32,142	2,142	3.59	11.06	49.28	67.50	59,594
Inner Mongolia 內蒙	13	931	37,728	1,307	2.24	7.00	40.53	68.02	58,401
Northeast 東北	33	1,410	111,851	4,351	2.01	5.10	79.33	60.60	216,418
Liaoning 遼寧	20	1,404	133,398	4,970	1.90	4.60	95.00	58.68	261,589
Jilin 吉林	8	1,611	71,078	-2,754	-1.93	-6.96	44.11	72.32	142,973
Heilongjiang 黑龍江	5	1,110	90,902	13,240	8.64	19.74	81.88	56.24	153,250
Central East 華東	262	1,086	77,289	3,366	3.16	10.56	71.17	70.11	106,661
Shanghai 上海	6	653	47,097	187	0.43	1.32	72.12	67.13	43,090
Jiangsu 江蘇	55	1,141	84,073	-48	-0.05	-0.20	73.72	75.93	100,522
Zhejiang 浙江	21	1,762	127,844	5,035	2.22	5.97	72.57	62.90	227,156
Anhui 安徽	51	951	64,976	1,300	1.57	5.96	68.34	73.62	82,665
Fujian 福建	34	802	45,585	635	1.07	3.03	56.83	64.64	59,214
Jiangxi 江西	16	872	49,089	-503	-0.54	-2.16	56.27	74.96	92,956
Shandong 山東	79	1,154	88,727	8,833	7.22	23.49	76.90	69.28	122,421
Central-South 中南	255	969	59,483	1,925	2.12	6.33	61.38	66.53	90,825
Henan 河南	94	1,120	66,732	3,890	3.88	14.08	59.58	72.47	100,337
Hubei 湖北	52	992	63,170	1,157	1.23	4.26	63.68	71.06	93,763
Hunan 湖南	70	794	45,445	913	1.61	6.37	57.21	74.70	56,726
Guangdong 廣東	18	962	66,609	-797	-0.81	-2.25	69.24	63.96	98,377
Guangxi 廣西	20	835	60,991	642	0.67	1.42	73.08	52.77	95,705
Hainan 海南	1	629	10,490	2,510	0.21	0.21	16.68		1,197,430
Southwest 西南	130	1,085	79,473	4,228	2.76	9.05	73.24	69.50	153,208
Chongqing 重慶	23	977	76,223	-1,436	-0.75	-9.80	78.02	92.37	191,902
Sichuan 四川	72	1,045	67,183	3,581	3.27	8.06	64.26	59.36	109,376
Guizhou 貴州	13	1,047	83,005	5,724	3.63	9.78	79.29	62.90	157,682
Yunnan 雲南	22	1,352	121,103	11,324	4.45	14.08	89.59	68.39	254,461
Tibet 西藏									
Northwest 西北	46	924	66,664	5,457	4.45	9.33	72.12	52.30	122,624
Shaanxi 陝西	29	831	48,814	1,613	2.38	7.34	58.71	67.55	67,707
Gansu 甘肅	4	1,249	110,823	2,775	1.75	4.12	88.73	57.60	158,960
Qinghai 青海	1	962	20,370	510	0.51	2.09	21.17	75.66	100,450
Ningxia 寧夏	10	949	100,593	18,906	7.11	11.90	106.04	40.30	266,065
Xinjiang 新疆	2	1,481	90,670	1,795	1.28	2.10	61.22	38.93	140,130

2621: Nitrogenous Fertilizer 氮肥製造業

Year 年份	Number of firms 企業個數	Rate of change 每年變化 (%)	Number of employees 職工人數（人）	Rate of change 每年變化 (%)	Total revenue (mil. RMB) 總銷售收入（百萬元）	Rate of change 每年變化 (%)	Total profit (mil. RMB) 總利潤（百萬元）	Rate of change 每年變化 (%)
1993	978		835,472		28,876		12	
1994	919	-6.03%	733,942	-12.15%	35,938	24.46%	681	5625.81%
1995	924	0.54%	911,658	24.21%	52,868	47.11%	2,547	273.85%
1996	890	-3.68%	900,287	-1.25%	61,084	15.54%	2,881	13.11%

3 Major products* 3 種主要產品 *	Output 產量	Sales volume 銷售量	Unit 單位
a) Ammonium Hydrogen Carbonate 碳酸氫銨	8,966,960	12,015,726	ton 噸
b) Synthetic Ammonia 合成氨	22,797,918	8,435,230	ton 噸
c) Nitrogen Fertilizer 氮肥	15,552,794	15,241,738	ton 噸

Top 10 firms by revenue (year founded) 收入排名前 10 家企業（創辦年份）	City 城市	Province 省	Telephone / fax 電話 / 傳真	Number of employees 職工人數	Ownership 產業所有權	Revenue ('000 RMB) 銷售收入（千元）	Profit ('000 RMB) (rank) 利潤（千元）（排名）	Total assets ('000 RMB) 總資產（千元）	Major products 主要產品
Juhua Group Corp. 衢化集團公司(1958)	Quzhou 衢州市	Zhejiang 浙江省	(0570)3096232 (0570)3021716	23,529	State-owned 國有	1,773,712	80300(7)	3,551,344	a,b,c
Panjin Liaohe Chemical (Group) Corp. 盤錦遼河化工集團有限責任公司(1976)	Panjin 盤錦市	Liaoning 遼寧省	(0427)5855242	8,560	Joint stock 股份制	1,384,654	81930(5)	2,046,751	o
Sichuan Chemical (Group) Corp. 川化集團有限責任公司(1959)	Chengdu 成都市	Sichuan 四川省	(028)3302000 (028)3301647	10,170	State-owned 國有	959,106	81064(6)	1,209,740	b,c
Lutianhua Group Corp. 瀘天化(集團)有限責任公司(1964)	Luzhou 瀘州市	Sichuan 四川省	(0830)4122222 (0830)4122500	8,312	State-owned 國有	890,001	122882(2)	1,622,721	b,c
Jiangsu Xin Yuan Group Company 江蘇新苑集團公司(1965)	Wuxi 無錫市	Jiangsu 江蘇省	(0510)3311460	3,500	State-owned 國有	732,730	4734(131)	1,002,716	a,b,c
Fujian Sanming Chemical General Factory 福建省三明化工總廠(1958)	Sanming 三明市	Fujian 福建省	(0598)8222801 (0598)8224896	8,771	State-owned 國有	698,316	2093(237)	848,417	o
Hebei Cangzhou Dahua Group Co. Ltd. 河北滄州大化集團有限責任公司(1977)	Cangzhou 滄州市	Hebei 河北省	(0317)2046486 (0317)3022527	3,835	State-owned 國有	697,752	75021(8)	1,156,948	b,c
Jinxi Natural Gas Chemical General Factory 錦西天然氣化工總廠(1993)	Huludao 葫蘆島市	Liaoning 遼寧省	(0429)2709524 (0429)2120079	1,811	State-owned 國有	659,477	29633(15)	2,140,124	o
China Petrochemical Ningxia Chemical Plant 中國石化寧夏化工廠(1989)	Yinchuan 銀川市	Ningxia 寧夏	(0951)2021963 (0951)2021379	2,183	State-owned 國有	655,433	172287(1)	2,006,770	b,c
Yuntian Chemical Industry Group Co. Ltd. 天雲化工集團有限公司(1977)	Zhaotong 昭通市	Yunnan 雲南省	(0870)8636088 (0870)8636337	3,553	State-owned 國有	640,313	122526(3)	1,312,126	b,c

Top 10 Cities by Production Output 產出排名前 10 位城市	Province 省	Market share 市場份額	Number of firms 企業個數
Chongqing 重慶市	Chongqing 重慶市	10.93%	22
Baoji 寶雞市	Shaanxi 陝西省	7.55%	3
Quzhou 衢州市	Zhejiang 浙江省	2.47%	2
Luzhou 瀘州市	Sichuan 四川省	2.19%	7
Chengdu 成都市	Sichuan 四川省	1.97%	15
Yueyang 岳陽市	Hunan 湖南省	1.95%	8
Panjin 盤錦市	Liaoning 遼寧省	1.88%	2
Shijiazhuang 石家莊市	Hebei 河北省	1.81%	14
Yichang 宜昌市	Hubei 湖北省	1.63%	7
Qujing 曲靖市	Yunnan 雲南省	1.40%	5

10 Major Wholesalers 10 家主要批發商	City 城市	Province 省	Telephone / Fax 電話 / 傳真
China Agricultural Machinery Hua Bei Company 中國農業機械華北公司	Tianjin 天津市	Tianjin 天津市	(022)23394240 (022)23304247
Shandong Agriculture Means of Production Company 山東省農業生產資料公司	Ji'nan 濟南市	Shandong 山東省	(0531)8957052 (0531)8957142
Yantai Agriculture Means of Production General Company 煙台市農業生產資料總公司	Yantai 煙台市	Shandong 山東省	(0535)6216668 (0535)6211348
Sichuan Agriculture Means of Production General Company 四川省農業生產資料總公司	Chengdu 成都市	Sichuan 四川省	(028)6751135 (028)6751646
Heilongjiang Agriculture Means of Production Company 黑龍江省農業生產資料公司	Harbin 哈爾濱市	Heilongjiang 黑龍江省	(0451)8989948 (0451)8382367
Shannxi Agriculture Means of Production General Company 陝西省農業生產資料總公司	Xi'an 西安市	Shaanxi 陝西省	(029)7422104 (029)7411799
Gansu Agriculture Means of Production General Company 甘肅省農業生產資料總公司	Lanzhou 蘭州市	Gansu 甘肅省	(0931)8822971
Yitong Man Zu Autonomous County Agricultural Goods & Materials Co. Ltd. 伊通滿族自治縣農用物資有限責任公司	Siping 四平市	Jilin 吉林省	(0434)4223146
Langfang Agriculture Means of Production Company 廊坊市農業生產資料公司	Langfang 廊坊市	Hebei 河北省	(0316)2013148
Anhui Agriculture Means of Production Company 安徽省農業生產資料公司	Hefei 合肥市	Anhui 安徽省	(0551)2656541 (0551)2655720

*Also include sales by firms outside this industry.包括本行業以外廠家的銷售。"o" stands for "others". "o" 代表"其他產品"。

2622: Phosphate Fertilizer 磷肥製造業

The industry accounts for 0.274% of the total revenue of China's industrial sector in 1996. The revenue growth rate of the industry is 1.8% from 1995, as compared to the growth rate of China's industrial sector, 9.51%. The rate of return on asset is 0.72%. 68.94% of all firms in the industry made a profit while 25.02% had negative returns. The top province in terms of the industry's revenue is Jiangsu, accounting for 14.97% of the total revenue.
本行業在1996年佔全行業總產值0.274%，行業年增長率為1.8%（全國工業年增長率9.51%）。行業的資產回報率0.72%，68.94%的企業盈利，25.02%的企業虧損。銷售收入最高的省份為江蘇省，佔本行業的14.97%。

	Total number of firms 企業總數	Total number of employees 職工總數	Total revenue (mil. RMB) 總銷售收入（百萬元）	Total profit (mil. RMB) 總利潤（百萬元）	Return on assets 資產利潤率 (%)	Return on equity 權益利潤率 (%)	Labour productivity ('000 RMB / worker) 勞動生產率（千元/人）	Debts / assets 資產負債率 (%)	Total assets (mil. RMB) 總資產（百萬元）
Industry Overall 行業總體	1,222	311,362	15,895	166	0.72	2.50	51.05	71.30	23,209

	Number of firms 企業個數	Average number of employees 平均職工人數	Average revenue ('000 RMB) 平均銷售收入（千元）	Average profit ('000 RMB) 平均利潤（千元）	Return on assets 資產利潤率 (%)	Return on equity 權益利潤率 (%)	Labour productivity ('000 RMB / worker) 勞動生產率（千元/人）	Average debts / assets 平均資產負債率(%)	Average Total assets ('000 RMB) 平均總資產（千元）
By ownership 產業所有權									
State-owned 國有	428	584	27,465	58	0.13	0.45	47.04	71.92	45,785
Collectively-owned 集體	756	65	4,462	127	3.77	13.79	68.37	72.64	3,358
Privately-owned 私有	5	56	2,021	17	0.71	2.25	36.21	68.42	2,447
Domestic JVs 聯營	11	77	7,092	275	5.75	24.19	92.22	76.21	4,787
Joint stock 股份制	19	581	35,458	2,212	4.22	9.57	61.07	55.91	52,458
Foreign-funded 外資	1	47	2,025	-7	-0.06	-0.08	43.08	25.24	11,623
Overseas Chinese-funded 港澳台資	1	21							
By size 規模									
Large 大型	11	5,135	309,240	2,493	0.45	1.30	60.22	65.43	555,163
Medium 中型	98	954	51,160	663	0.83	2.74	53.62	69.76	79,987
Small 小型	1,103	144	6,781	67	0.79	3.38	47.06	76.47	8,399
By regional distribution 地區分布									
Central-North 華北	96	182	8,638	271	1.86	9.06	47.50	79.46	14,587
Beijing 北京	2	106	5,645	10	0.12	0.35	53.25	65.64	8,250
Tianjin 天津	3	167	5,543	467	3.17	8.26	33.26	61.66	14,727
Hebei 河北	60	169	9,644	399	2.62	13.14	57.10	80.02	15,207
Shanxi 山西	29	208	6,918	123	1.06	4.76	33.31	77.74	11,656
Inner Mongolia 內蒙	2	295	11,050	-1,445	-3.24	-38.33	37.46	91.55	44,635
Northeast 東北	38	225	5,157	-326	-2.00	-6.68	22.95	70.09	16,323
Liaoning 遼寧	23	204	4,343	-277	-2.37	-9.30	21.32	74.57	11,707
Jilin 吉林	2	192	1,780	-605	-10.82	-864.29	9.30	98.75	5,590
Heilongjiang 黑龍江	13	267	7,117	-370	-1.42	-4.11	26.65	65.60	26,142
Central East 華東	381	296	16,207	124	0.54	1.73	54.73	68.89	23,051
Shanghai 上海	2	609	58,860	2,020	3.11	10.58	96.65	70.61	64,970
Jiangsu 江蘇	86	530	27,662	-288	-0.71	-2.25	52.15	68.29	40,365
Zhejiang 浙江	23	341	26,519	-297	-1.08	-3.94	77.71	72.64	27,535
Anhui 安徽	144	209	11,424	246	1.50	5.03	54.66	70.25	16,424
Fujian 福建	18	325	18,197	37	0.14	0.33	55.95	56.42	25,791
Jiangxi 江西	39	245	10,503	271	1.67	6.44	42.86	74.12	16,264
Shandong 山東	69	183	9,944	408	2.60	8.05	54.28	67.73	15,712
Central-South 中南	323	260	14,756	237	1.26	4.19	56.71	69.95	18,787
Henan 河南	82	228	11,344	234	1.55	7.45	49.76	79.13	15,080
Hubei 湖北	139	190	13,816	509	3.73	12.67	72.61	70.54	13,643
Hunan 湖南	50	344	14,483	-153	-0.76	-2.31	42.06	67.11	20,049
Guangdong 廣東	22	447	27,400	-30	-0.07	-0.20	61.27	63.71	41,386
Guangxi 廣西	29	391	18,946	-184	-0.54	-1.59	48.45	66.16	34,264
Hainan 海南	1	515	39,240	100	0.35	0.95	76.19	63.23	28,720
Southwest 西南	225	316	14,305	144	0.64	2.43	45.25	73.88	22,682
Chongqing 重慶	20	353	12,620	-102	-0.57	-2.34	35.79	75.70	18,017
Sichuan 四川	102	277	11,597	228	1.24	6.30	41.90	80.35	18,427
Guizhou 貴州	69	189	5,410	-1	-0.01	-0.02	28.65	60.37	10,272
Yunnan 雲南	34	672	41,481	1,582	2.50	9.04	61.74	72.38	63,370
Tibet 西藏									
Northwest 西北	159	109	4,468	-22	-0.28	-1.15	40.96	75.76	7,767
Shaanxi 陝西	64	120	4,707	58	0.70	2.34	39.30	69.95	8,323
Gansu 甘肅	78	54	3,195	134	4.33	13.43	59.04	67.73	3,101
Qinghai 青海	1	1,304	11,490	-13,610	-10.46	-264.79	8.81	96.05	130,080
Ningxia 寧夏	14	255	9,302	-364	-1.74	-14.00	36.55	87.59	20,937
Xinjiang 新疆	2	294	9,100	515	2.77	5.24	30.95	47.12	18,590

2622: Phosphate Fertilizer 磷肥製造業

Year 年份	Number of firms 企業個數	Rate of change 每年變化 (%)	Number of employees 職工人數（人）	Rate of change 每年變化 (%)	Total revenue (mil. RMB) 總銷售收入（百萬元）	Rate of change 每年變化 (%)	Total profit (mil. RMB) 總利潤（百萬元）	Rate of change 每年變化 (%)
1993	1,168		285,289		9,062		-139	
1994	1,162	-0.51%	304,108	6.60%	11,937	31.72%	129	192.85%
1995	1,249	7.49%	329,343	8.30%	15,621	30.86%	385	199.09%
1996	1,222	-2.16%	311,362	-5.46%	15,895	1.75%	166	-56.85%

3 Major products* 3種主要產品*	Output 產量	Sales volume 銷售量	Unit 單位
a) Phosphate Fertilizer 磷肥	4,198,223	3,946,330	ton 噸
b) Sulfuric Acid 硫酸	8,270,002	4,465,801	ton 噸

Top 10 firms by revenue (year founded) 收入排名前10家企業 (創辦年份)	City 城市	Province 省	Telephone / fax 電話 / 傳真	Number of employees 職工人數	Ownership 產業所有權	Revenue ('000 RMB) 銷售收入（千元）	Profit ('000 RMB) (rank) 利潤（千元）（排名）	Total assets ('000 RMB) 總資產（千元）	Major products 主要產品
Nanjing Chemical Industries Group Co. Ltd. 南京化學工業(集團)公司(1934)	Nanjing 南京市	Jiangsu 江蘇省	(025)7792455 (025)7792812	24,902	State-owned 國有	1,226,078	1070(90)	2,125,252	a,b
Tongling Chemical Industry Group Co. Ltd. 銅陵化學工業集團公司(1962)	Tongling 銅陵市	Anhui 安徽省	(0562)2863215 (0562)2831031	13,105	State-owned 國有	819,675	5063(15)	1,609,523	a,b
Yunnan Phosphate Fertilizer Factory 雲南磷肥廠(1982)	Kunming 昆明市	Yunnan 雲南省	(0871)8590611 (0871)8590530	3,267	State-owned 國有	313,130	20725(2)	656,873	a,b
Sichuan Yinshan Chemical Industry (Group) Co. Ltd. 四川銀山化工集團股份有限公司(1963)	Neijiang 內江市	Sichuan 四川省	(0832)5452211	3,350	Joint stock 股份制	175,040	20800(1)	309,636	a,b
Shannxi Bao Jia Phosphate Fertilizer General Factory 陝西省寶嘉磷肥總廠(1968)	Baoji 寶雞市	Shaanxi 陝西省	(0917)6217115	2,367	State-owned 國有	169,912	6787(8)	181,232	o
Guangdong Zhan Hua Enterprise Co. Ltd. 廣東湛化企業股份有限公司(1962)	Zhanjiang 湛江市	Guangdong 廣東省	(0758)2280322 (0758)2284066	2,983	Joint stock 股份制	147,296	3186(26)	291,852	a,b
Guangxi Zhuang Zu Autonomous Region Luzhai Chemical Fertilizer General Factory 廣西壯族自治區鹿寨化肥總廠(1964)	Heshan 合山市	Guangxi 廣西	(0772)6892085 (0772)6892888	4,519	State-owned 國有	143,899	-8057(673)	198,582	a,b
Yunnan Kun Yang Phosphate Fertilizer Factory 雲南昆陽磷肥廠(1957)	Kunming 昆明市	Yunnan 雲南省	(0871)7891617 (0871)7891597	2,895	State-owned 國有	135,952	2081(43)	188,217	a,b
Hubei Wuxue Chemical General Factory 湖北省武穴市化工總廠(1970)	Huanggang 黃岡市	Hubei 湖北省	(0713)542581 (0713)542455	1,048	State-owned 國有	133,170	14477(3)	114,405	a,b
Shifang Ying Feng Industrial General Company 什邡鍙峯實業總公司(1975)	Deyang 德陽市	Sichuan 四川省	(0838)8209420 (0838)8801470	938	State-owned 國有	130,527	13114(4)	147,394	a,b

Top 10 Cities by Production Output 產出排名前10位城市	Province 省	Market share 市場份額	Number of firms 企業個數
Nanjing 南京市	Jiangsu 江蘇省	9.51%	6
Kunming 昆明市	Yunnan 雲南省	4.44%	26
Deyang 德陽市	Sichuan 四川省	2.70%	39
Chongqing 重慶市	Chongqing 重慶市	2.68%	27
Yichang 宜昌市	Hubei 湖北省	2.65%	11
Gejiu 個舊市	Yunnan 雲南省	1.99%	5
Hefei 合肥市	Anhui 安徽省	1.83%	11
Luohe 漯河市	Henan 河南省	1.59%	2
Jingmen 荊門市	Hubei 湖北省	1.55%	27
Neijiang 內江市	Sichuan 四川省	1.51%	8

10 Major Wholesalers 10家主要批發商	City 城市	Province 省	Telephone / Fax 電話 / 傳真
China Agricultural Machinery Hua Bei Company 中國農業機械華北公司	Tianjin 天津市	Tianjin 天津市	(022)23394240 (022)23304247
Shandong Agriculture Means of Production Company 山東省農業生產資料公司	Ji'nan 濟南市	Shandong 山東省	(0531)8957052 (0531)8957142
Yantai Agriculture Means of Production General Company 煙台市農業生產資料總公司	Yantai 煙台市	Shandong 山東省	(0535)6216668 (0535)6211348
Sichuan Agriculture Means of Production General Company 四川省農業生產資料總公司	Chengdu 成都市	Sichuan 四川省	(028)6751135 (028)6751646
Heilongjiang Agriculture Means of Production Company 黑龍江省農業生產資料公司	Harbin 哈爾濱市	Heilongjiang 黑龍江省	(0451)8989948 (0451)8382367
Shannxi Agriculture Means of Production General Company 陝西省農業生產資料總公司	Xi'an 西安市	Shaanxi 陝西省	(029)7422104 (029)7411799
Gansu Agriculture Means of Production General Company 甘肅省農業生產資料總公司	Lanzhou 蘭州市	Gansu 甘肅省	(0931)8822971
Yitong Man Zu Autonomous County Agricultural Goods & Materials Co. Ltd. 伊通滿族自治縣農用物資有限責任公司	Siping 四平市	Jilin 吉林省	(0434)4223146
Langfang Agriculture Means of Production Company 廊坊市農業生產資料公司	Langfang 廊坊市	Hebei 河北省	(0316)2013148
Anhui Agriculture Means of Production Company 安徽省農業生產資料公司	Hefei 合肥市	Anhui 安徽省	(0551)2656541 (0551)2655720

*Also include sales by firms outside this industry.包括本行業以外廠家的銷售。"o" stands for "others". "o" 代表 "其他產品" 。

2623: Potash Fertilizer 鉀肥製造業

The industry accounts for 0.004% of the total revenue of China's industrial sector in 1996. The revenue growth rate of the industry is -55.3% from 1995, as compared to the growth rate of China's industrial sector, 9.51%. The rate of return on asset is 0.21%. 74.77% of all firms in the industry made a profit while 17.54% had negative returns. The top province in terms of the industry's revenue is Zhejiang, accounting for 30.73% of the total revenue.
本行業在1996年佔全行業總產值0.004%，行業年增長率為-55.3%（全國工業年增長率9.51%）。行業的資產回報率0.21%，74.77%的企業盈利，17.54%的企業虧損。銷售收入最高的省份為浙江省，佔本行業的30.73%。

	Total number of firms 企業總數	Total number of employees 職工總數	Total revenue (mil. RMB) 總銷售收入（百萬元）	Total profit (mil. RMB) 總利潤（百萬元）	Return on assets 資產利潤率 (%)	Return on equity 權益利潤率 (%)	Labour productivity ('000 RMB / worker) 勞動生產率（千元／人）	Debts / assets 資產負債率 (%)	Total assets (mil. RMB) 總資產（百萬元）
Industry Overall 行業總體	57	11,483	206	1	0.21	0.82	17.94	74.25	432

	Number of firms 企業個數	Average number of employees 平均職工人數	Average revenue ('000 RMB) 平均銷售收入（千元）	Average profit ('000 RMB) 平均利潤（千元）	Return on assets 資產利潤率 (%)	Return on equity 權益利潤率 (%)	Labour productivity ('000 RMB / worker) 勞動生產率（千元／人）	Average debts / assets 平均資產負債率(%)	Average Total assets ('000 RMB) 平均總資產（千元）
By ownership 產業所有權									
State-owned 國有	15	623	6,733				10.80	76.64	21,400
Collectively-owned 集體	37	54	2,525	30	1.49	4.96	46.46	69.94	2,045
Privately-owned 私有									
Domestic JVs 聯營	1	24							
Joint stock 股份制	1	8							
Foreign-funded 外資	1	31	1,419	-154	-1.82	-9.00	45.77	79.73	8,420
Overseas Chinese-funded 港澳台資	2	55	5,063	13	0.10	0.22	92.89	57.53	13,694
By size 規模									
Large 大型	2	2,841	50,430	280	0.17	0.79	17.75	78.09	162,680
Medium 中型	2	1,003	10,825	-80	-0.38	-1.12	10.80	65.89	21,130
Small 小型	50	76	1,670	12	0.93	2.37	22.01	60.73	1,291
By regional distribution 地區分布									
Central-North 華北	1	20	760				38.00	107.32	410
Beijing 北京									
Tianjin 天津									
Hebei 河北	1	20	760				38.00	107.32	410
Shanxi 山西									
Inner Mongolia 內蒙									
Northeast 東北	6	27	3,720	38	0.51	1.63	140.38	68.77	7,537
Liaoning 遼寧	2	34	10,510	115	0.61	1.70	309.12	63.90	18,765
Jilin 吉林	2	41	650				16.05	92.59	3,845
Heilongjiang 黑龍江	2	5							
Central East 華東	15	246	7,441	9	0.05	0.20	30.29	76.56	20,317
Shanghai 上海									
Jiangsu 江蘇	11	37	3,971	119	8.38	39.10	107.85	78.57	1,421
Zhejiang 浙江	1	3,152	63,310	-1,230	-0.43	-1.83	20.09	76.26	283,240
Anhui 安徽	2	49	1,035	-100	-6.92	-60.61	21.12	88.58	1,445
Fujian 福建									
Jiangxi 江西									
Shandong 山東	1	30	2,550	260	8.67	52.00	85.00	83.33	3,000
Central-South 中南	8	66	5,406	106	2.51	11.01	82.38	77.22	4,236
Henan 河南	5	98	8,518	314	4.77	18.92	86.74	74.76	6,578
Hubei 湖北	1	18	570	-120	-18.75	-600.00	31.67	96.88	640
Hunan 湖南	1	16	90	-600	-166.67	100.00	5.63	266.67	360
Guangdong 廣東									
Guangxi 廣西	1								
Hainan 海南									
Southwest 西南	12	77	1,730	-80	-2.33	-5.63	22.37	58.71	3,439
Chongqing 重慶	2	31	531	38	9.26	158.80	16.97	94.17	405
Sichuan 四川	4	145	4,337	-289	-7.94	-33.94	29.94	76.59	3,635
Guizhou 貴州	5	52	118	10	0.26	0.39	2.29	33.35	3,892
Yunnan 雲南	1	29	1,760	70	1.08	11.29	60.69	90.40	6,460
Tibet 西藏									
Northwest 西北	15	411	485	46	10.45	71.13	1.18	85.30	440
Shaanxi 陝西	2	45	3,640	345	10.45	71.13	80.89	85.30	3,300
Gansu 甘肅									
Qinghai 青海	13	467							
Ningxia 寧夏									
Xinjiang 新疆									

2623: Potash Fertilizer 鉀肥製造業

Year 年份	Number of firms 企業個數	Rate of change 每年變化 (%)	Number of employees 職工人數（人）	Rate of change 每年變化 (%)	Total revenue (mil. RMB) 總銷售收入（百萬元）	Rate of change 每年變化 (%)	Total profit (mil. RMB) 總利潤（百萬元）	Rate of change 每年變化 (%)
1993	37		6,695		233		7	
1994	38	2.70%	2,278	-65.98%	250	7.27%	8	9.21%
1995	60	57.89%	11,846	420.02%	461	84.63%	13	62.70%
1996	57	-5.00%	11,483	-3.06%	206	-55.29%	1	-92.50%

3 Major products* 3種主要產品 *	Output 產量	Sales volume 銷售量	Unit 單位
a) Potassium Fertilizer 鉀肥	84,731	73,716	ton 噸
b) Feedstuff Additive 飼料添加劑	364	357	ton 噸

Top 10 firms by revenue (year founded) 收入排名前10家企業（創辦年份）	City 城市	Province 省	Telephone / fax 電話 / 傳真	Number of employees 職工人數	Ownership 產業所有權	Revenue ('000 RMB) 銷售收入（千元）	Profit ('000 RMB) (rank) 利潤（千元）（排名）	Total assets ('000 RMB) 總資產（千元）	Major products 主要產品
Qinghai Salt Lake Industry Group Co. Ltd. 青海鹽湖工業集團有限公司(1958)	Golmud 格爾木市	Qinghai 青海省	(0979)413233 (0979)413621	4,520	State-owned 國有	156,620	-109766(26)	2,588,466	o
Zhejiang Wenzhou Chemical General Factory 浙江省溫州化工總廠(1958)	Wenzhou 溫州市	Zhejiang 浙江省	(0577)8781471	2,845	State-owned 國有	63,307	-1230(25)	283,236	o
Puyang Organic Chemical Plant 濮陽市有機化工廠(1993)	Puyang 濮陽市	Henan 河南省	(0393)7222021	422	State-owned 國有	30,722	1210(1)	24,840	o
Panjin Yong Xing Chemical Industrial Co. Ltd 盤錦永興化學工業有限公司(1992)	Panjin 盤錦市	Liaoning 遼寧省	(0427)2852144 (0427)2852642	34	Overseas Chinese-funded 港澳台資	20,275	220(11)	34,807	o
Henan Xiping Song Ji Xiang Bone Meal Factory 河南省西平縣宋集鄉骨粉廠(1992)	Zhumadian 駐馬店市	Henan 河南省	(0396)63883862	35	Collectively-owned 集體	9,230	560(2)	2,320	b
Lianyungang Haizhou Experiment Chemical Factory 連雲港市海州實驗化工廠(1992)	Lianyungang 連雲港市	Jiangsu 江蘇省	(0518)5430275	36	Collectively-owned 集體	7,600	343(6)	3,149	a
Lianyungang Xing Fu Chemical Factory 連雲港市幸福化工廠(1992)	Lianyungang 連雲港市	Jiangsu 江蘇省	(0518)5402756	20	Collectively-owned 集體	7,307	223(10)	1,105	o
Qinghai Chai Da Mu Salt Chemical Industry Shi Li General Company 青海省柴達木鹽化工業實力總公司(1977)	Golmud 格爾木市	Qinghai 青海省	(0979)412134	327	Collectively-owned 集體	7,119	465(4)	16,770	a
Golmud Potash & Magnesium Factory 格爾木市鉀鎂廠(1987)	Golmud 格爾木市	Qinghai 青海省	(0979)413016	706	State-owned 國有	6,829	530(3)	113,090	a
Lianyungang Yu Dong Chemical Factory 連雲港市宇東化工廠(1993)	Lianyungang 連雲港市	Jiangsu 江蘇省	(0518)5431065	17	Collectively-owned 集體	5,088	-8(21)	2,606	o

Top 10 Cities by Production Output 產出排名前10位城市	Province 省	Market share 市場份額	Number of firms 企業個數
Golmud 格爾木市	Qinghai 青海省	45.68%	11
Wenzhou 溫州市	Zhejiang 浙江省	17.66%	2
Puyang 濮陽市	Henan 河南省	8.18%	1
Panjin 盤錦市	Liaoning 遼寧省	3.92%	1
Xining 西寧市	Qinghai 青海省	3.86%	1
Linyi 臨沂市	Shandong 山東省	3.07%	1
Lianyungang 連雲港市	Jiangsu 江蘇省	2.50%	8
Zhumadian 駐馬店市	Henan 河南省	2.46%	2
Yan'an 延安市	Shaanxi 陝西省	1.47%	1
Suzhou 宿州市	Anhui 安徽省	1.21%	2

10 Major Wholesalers 10家主要批發商	City 城市	Province 省	Telephone / Fax 電話 / 傳真
China Agricultural Machinery Hua Bei Company 中國農業機械華北公司	Tianjin 天津市	Tianjin 天津市	(022)23394240 (022)23304247
Shandong Agriculture Means of Production Company 山東省農業生產資料公司	Ji'nan 濟南市	Shandong 山東省	(0531)8957052 (0531)8957142
Yantai Agriculture Means of Production General Company 煙台市農業生產資料總公司	Yantai 煙台市	Shandong 山東省	(0535)6216668 (0535)6211348
Sichuan Agriculture Means of Production General Company 四川省農業生產資料總公司	Chengdu 成都市	Sichuan 四川省	(028)6751135 (028)6751646
Heilongjiang Agriculture Means of Production Company 黑龍江省農業生產資料公司	Harbin 哈爾濱市	Heilongjiang 黑龍江省	(0451)8989948 (0451)8382367
Shannxi Agriculture Means of Production General Company 陝西省農業生產資料總公司	Xi'an 西安市	Shaanxi 陝西省	(029)7422104 (029)7411799
Gansu Agriculture Means of Production General Company 甘肅省農業生產資料總公司	Lanzhou 蘭州市	Gansu 甘肅省	(0931)8822971
Yitong Man Zu Autonomous County Agricultural Goods & Materials Co. Ltd. 伊通滿族自治縣農用物資有限責任公司	Siping 四平市	Jilin 吉林省	(0434)4223146
Langfang Agriculture Means of Production Company 廊坊市農業生產資料公司	Langfang 廊坊市	Hebei 河北省	(0316)2013148
Anhui Agriculture Means of Production Company 安徽省農業生產資料公司	Hefei 合肥市	Anhui 安徽省	(0551)2656541 (0551)2655720

*Also include sales by firms outside this industry.包括本行業以外廠家的銷售。"o" stands for "others". "o" 代表"其他產品"。

2624: Compound Fertilizer 複合肥料製造業

The industry accounts for 0.197% of the total revenue of China's industrial sector in 1996. The revenue growth rate of the industry is 31.9% from 1995, as compared to the growth rate of China's industrial sector, 9.51%. The rate of return on asset is 3.62%. 72.02% of all firms in the industry made a profit while 20.70% had negative returns. The top province in terms of the industry's revenue is Jiangsu, accounting for 20.21% of the total revenue.
本行業在1996年佔全行業總產值0.197%，行業年增長率為31.9%（全國工業年增長率9.51%）。行業的資產回報率3.62%，72.02%的企業盈利，20.70%的企業虧損。銷售收入最高的省份為江蘇省，佔本行業的20.21%。

	Total number of firms 企業總數	Total number of employees 職工總數	Total revenue (mil. RMB) 總銷售收入（百萬元）	Total profit (mil. RMB) 總利潤（百萬元）	Return on assets 資產利潤率 (%)	Return on equity 權益利潤率 (%)	Labour productivity ('000 RMB / worker) 勞動生產率（千元／人）	Debts / assets 資產負債率 (%)	Total assets (mil. RMB) 總資產（百萬元）
Industry Overall 行業總體	1,129	112,146	11,425	466	3.62	12.21	101.88	70.32	12,864

	Number of firms 企業個數	Average number of employees 平均職工人數	Average revenue ('000 RMB) 平均銷售收入（千元）	Average profit ('000 RMB) 平均利潤（千元）	Return on assets 資產利潤率 (%)	Return on equity 權益利潤率 (%)	Labour productivity ('000 RMB / worker) 勞動生產率（千元／人）	Average debts / assets 平均資產負債率(%)	Average Total assets ('000 RMB) 平均總資產（千元）
By ownership 產業所有權									
State-owned 國有	166	300	24,578	1,096	2.42	7.92	82.03	69.46	45,313
Collectively-owned 集體	875	59	6,017	207	5.61	18.11	101.73	69.02	3,681
Privately-owned 私有	7	79	7,192	158	4.73	12.13	90.54	60.96	3,343
Domestic JVs 聯營	21	56	10,874	444	6.99	27.18	192.87	74.28	6,355
Joint stock 股份制	26	245	20,868	354	1.12	3.89	85.01	71.22	31,608
Foreign-funded 外資	15	90	58,368	4,565	8.19	53.16	647.57	84.59	55,709
Overseas Chinese-funded 港澳台資	18	66	22,327	896	5.37	14.50	337.71	63.00	16,690
By size 規模									
Large 大型	9	2,275	295,458	21,541	4.81	14.24	129.85	66.20	447,575
Medium 中型	12	985	84,183	4,248	4.01	18.11	85.43	77.86	105,928
Small 小型	1,068	74	7,573	207	2.92	10.17	102.69	71.25	7,083
By regional distribution 地區分布									
Central-North 華北	79	147	19,604	1,410	6.61	27.89	133.02	76.30	21,333
Beijing 北京	16	65	2,948	-125	-2.02	-13.74	45.65	85.27	6,177
Tianjin 天津	18	70	7,778	644	8.06	17.02	110.51	52.66	8,000
Hebei 河北	32	169	34,996	2,080	7.07	50.60	207.16	86.03	29,413
Shanxi 山西	8	457	28,611	4,540	7.52	19.92	62.68	62.23	60,349
Inner Mongolia 內蒙	5	57	2,554	-220	-5.97	-39.29	44.81	84.82	3,688
Northeast 東北	152	68	4,263	492	8.74	22.20	63.01	60.63	5,630
Liaoning 遼寧	60	81	4,696	323	4.52	8.16	58.18	44.57	7,134
Jilin 吉林	25	95	3,106	-69	-1.13	-5.45	32.55	79.27	6,090
Heilongjiang 黑龍江	67	46	4,307	853	20.74	83.87	94.44	75.27	4,112
Central East 華東	338	121	15,767	777	4.77	13.99	130.37	65.86	16,264
Shanghai 上海	1	664	80,680	2,040	2.01	4.22	121.51	52.29	101,310
Jiangsu 江蘇	109	126	21,180	662	4.24	12.17	167.48	65.21	15,637
Zhejiang 浙江	12	71	6,383	78	1.48	6.07	89.80	75.57	5,225
Anhui 安徽	125	66	8,976	395	10.08	33.28	136.60	69.72	3,919
Fujian 福建	27	110	6,923	96	2.47	5.05	63.02	51.15	3,890
Jiangxi 江西	1	2,351	342,310				145.60	91.18	1,016,910
Shandong 山東	63	191	19,242	2,148	6.71	14.54	100.63	53.86	32,016
Central-South 中南	234	64	6,897	131	2.51	9.35	108.56	73.11	5,222
Henan 河南	53	62	4,085	136	3.51	13.65	66.09	74.31	3,885
Hubei 湖北	53	120	15,085	288	2.70	10.99	125.37	75.44	10,657
Hunan 湖南	58	47	3,293	45	2.18	6.32	70.39	65.54	2,068
Guangdong 廣東	54	42	7,072	103	1.76	6.14	169.87	71.28	5,826
Guangxi 廣西	9								
Hainan 海南	7	36	3,584	14	0.60	1.87	99.17	68.16	2,396
Southwest 西南	249	94	6,636	-10	-0.10	-0.37	70.83	73.95	10,516
Chongqing 重慶	28	162	10,161	782	5.76	19.07	62.54	69.79	13,563
Sichuan 四川	116	101	6,835	-3	-0.02	-0.11	67.78	77.87	11,481
Guizhou 貴州	90	41	2,328	57	2.65	10.00	57.20	73.52	2,152
Yunnan 雲南	15	228	24,281	946	1.99	6.43	106.43	69.01	47,490
Tibet 西藏									
Northwest 西北	77	145	8,216	-140	-1.09	-5.54	56.77	80.33	12,799
Shaanxi 陝西	26	233	15,822	170	0.82	4.99	67.96	83.62	20,766
Gansu 甘肅	24	75	5,530	185	5.78	14.31	74.23	59.66	3,201
Qinghai 青海	2	252	4,665	-2,120	-6.07	170.97	18.55	103.55	34,905
Ningxia 寧夏	4	43	1,693	-140	-4.32	90.32	39.13	104.78	3,243
Xinjiang 新疆	21	125	3,451	-705	-5.18	-19.08	27.59	72.88	13,619

2624: Compound Fertilizer 複合肥料製造業

Year 年份	Number of firms 企業個數	Rate of change 每年變化 (%)	Number of employees 職工人數 (人)	Rate of change 每年變化 (%)	Total revenue (mil. RMB) 總銷售收入 (百萬元)	Rate of change 每年變化 (%)	Total profit (mil. RMB) 總利潤 (百萬元)	Rate of change 每年變化 (%)
1993	692		60,670		3,349		-23	
1994	786	13.58%	68,750	13.32%	4,740	41.50%	118	611.43%
1995	1,055	34.22%	108,387	57.65%	8,664	82.80%	349	196.98%
1996	1,129	7.01%	112,146	3.47%	11,425	31.87%	466	33.48%

3 Major products* 3 種主要產品 *	Output 產量	Sales volume 銷售量	Unit 單位
a) Phosphate Fertilizer 磷肥	679,756	638,971	ton 噸
b) Sulfuric Acid 硫酸	1,449,595	782,782	ton 噸

Top 10 firms by revenue (year founded) 收入排名前 10 家企業 (創辦年份)	City 城市	Province 省	Telephone / fax 電話 / 傳真	Number of employees 職工人數	Ownership 產業所有權	Revenue ('000 RMB) 銷售收入 (千元)	Profit ('000 RMB) (rank) 利潤 (千元) (排名)	Total assets ('000 RMB) 總資產 (千元)	Major products 主要產品
Sino – Arab Chemical Fertilizer Co. Ltd. 中國－阿拉伯化肥有限公司(1985)	Qinhuangdao 秦皇島市	Hebei 河北省	(0335)3013245 (0335)3015779	335	Foreign-funded 外資	855,390	64741(2)	632,988	a
Jiangsu Hua Chang Group Company 江蘇華昌集團公司(1972)	Suzhou 蘇州市	Jiangsu 江蘇省	(0512)8683240 (0512)8684850	2,050	State-owned 國有	462,020	29382(4)	306,499	o
Shandong Lu Bei Enterprise Group General Co. 山東省魯北企業集團總公司(1977)	Binzhou 濱州市	Shandong 山東省	(0543)6581341 (0543)6581341	2,218	State-owned 國有	378,957	80004(1)	1,163,546	a,b
Jiangxi Guixi Chemical Fertilizer Plant 江西貴溪化肥廠(1991)	Yingtan 鷹潭市	Jiangxi 江西省	(0701)3771124	2,509	State-owned 國有	342,305	0(462)	1,016,911	a
Shannxi Hua Shan Chemical Fertilizer General Factory 陝西省華山化肥總廠(1976)	Weinan 渭南市	Shaanxi 陝西省	(0913)4016515	4,398	State-owned 國有	338,273	3028(28)	465,992	o
Ningguo Chemical Fertilizer Factory 寧國化肥廠(1994)	Xuanzhou 宣州市	Anhui 安徽省	(0563)4024324	167	Joint stock 股份制	271,994	4797(21)	46,513	o
Yunnan Honghe Ha Ni Zu Yi Zu Autonomous Prefecture Phosphate Fertilizer Factory 雲南省紅河哈尼族彝族自治州磷肥廠(1971)	Gejiu 個舊市	Yunnan 雲南省	(0873)7171412 (0873)7171380	2,496	State-owned 國有	243,878	8017(12)	545,062	a,b
Shanxi Liyi Chemical General Factory 山西省臨猗縣化工總廠(1974)	Yuncheng 運城市	Shanxi 山西省	(0359)4022408	3,377	State-owned 國有	222,088	36232(3)	458,896	o
Wujin Fertilizer Factory 武進市複合肥廠(1986)	Changzhou 常州市	Jiangsu 江蘇省	(0519)3801103	256	Collectively-owned 集體	215,980	2435(33)	83,561	o
Sichuan Shihua Group Co. 四川什化集團公司(1958)	Deyang 德陽市	Sichuan 四川省	(0838)8801528 (0838)8801154	1,356	State-owned 國有	212,541	-42018(563)	614,728	a,b

Top 10 Cities by Production Output 產出排名前 10 位城市	Province 省	Market share 市場份額	Number of firms 企業個數
Suzhou 蘇州市	Jiangsu 江蘇省	5.61%	8
Weinan 渭南市	Shaanxi 陝西省	4.07%	5
Yingtan 鷹潭市	Jiangxi 江西省	3.77%	1
Linyi 臨沂市	Shandong 山東省	3.36%	9
Changzhou 常州市	Jiangsu 江蘇省	3.17%	17
Chongqing 重慶市	Chongqing 重慶市	3.03%	26
Lianyungang 連雲港市	Jiangsu 江蘇省	3.00%	27
Fuyang 阜陽市	Anhui 安徽省	2.91%	33
Deyang 德陽市	Sichuan 四川省	2.81%	16
Gejiu 個舊市	Yunnan 雲南省	2.74%	2

10 Major Wholesalers 10 家主要批發商	City 城市	Province 省	Telephone / Fax 電話 / 傳真
China Agricultural Machinery Hua Bei Company 中國農業機械華北公司	Tianjin 天津市	Tianjin 天津市	(022)23394240 (022)23304247
Shandong Agriculture Means of Production Company 山東省農業生產資料公司	Ji'nan 濟南市	Shandong 山東省	(0531)8957052 (0531)8957142
Yantai Agriculture Means of Production General Company 煙台市農業生產資料總公司	Yantai 煙台市	Shandong 山東省	(0535)6216668 (0535)6211348
Sichuan Agriculture Means of Production General Company 四川省農業生產資料總公司	Chengdu 成都市	Sichuan 四川省	(028)6751135 (028)6751646
Heilongjiang Agriculture Means of Production Company 黑龍江省農業生產資料公司	Harbin 哈爾濱市	Heilongjiang 黑龍江省	(0451)8989948 (0451)8382367
Shannxi Agriculture Means of Production General Company 陝西省農業生產資料總公司	Xi'an 西安市	Shaanxi 陝西省	(029)7422104 (029)7411799
Gansu Agriculture Means of Production General Company 甘肅省農業生產資料總公司	Lanzhou 蘭州市	Gansu 甘肅省	(0931)8822971
Yitong Man Zu Autonomous County Agricultural Goods & Materials Co. Ltd. 伊通滿族自治縣農用物資有限責任公司	Siping 四平市	Jilin 吉林省	(0434)4223146
Langfang Agriculture Means of Production Company 廊坊市農業生產資料公司	Langfang 廊坊市	Hebei 河北省	(0316)2013148
Anhui Agriculture Means of Production Company 安徽省農業生產資料公司	Hefei 合肥市	Anhui 安徽省	(0551)2656541 (0551)2655720

*Also include sales by firms outside this industry.包括本行業以外廠家的銷售。"o" stands for "others". "o" 代表"其他產品"。

2625: Trace Element Fertilizer 微量元素肥料製造業

The industry accounts for 0.004% of the total revenue of China's industrial sector in 1996. The revenue growth rate of the industry is 44.5% from 1995, as compared to the growth rate of China's industrial sector, 9.51%. The rate of return on asset is 2.40%. 60.84% of all firms in the industry made a profit while 27.16% had negative returns. The top province in terms of the industry's revenue is Hebei, accounting for 24.03% of the total revenue.
本行業在1996年佔全行業總產值0.004%，行業年增長率為44.5%（全國工業年增長率9.51%）。行業的資產回報率2.40%，60.84%的企業盈利，27.16%的企業虧損。銷售收入最高的省份為河北省，佔本行業的24.03%。

	Total number of firms 企業總數	Total number of employees 職工總數	Total revenue (mil. RMB) 總銷售收入（百萬元）	Total profit (mil. RMB) 總利潤（百萬元）	Return on assets 資產利潤率 (%)	Return on equity 權益利潤率 (%)	Labour productivity ('000 RMB / worker) 勞動生產率（千元/人）	Debts / assets 資產負債率 (%)	Total assets (mil. RMB) 總資產（百萬元）
Industry Overall 行業總體	99	3,551	205	6	2.40	9.18	57.73	73.79	260

	Number of firms 企業個數	Average number of employees 平均職工人數	Average revenue ('000 RMB) 平均銷售收入（千元）	Average profit ('000 RMB) 平均利潤（千元）	Return on assets 資產利潤率 (%)	Return on equity 權益利潤率 (%)	Labour productivity ('000 RMB / worker) 勞動生產率（千元/人）	Average debts / assets 平均資產負債率(%)	Average Total assets ('000 RMB) 平均總資產（千元）
By ownership 產業所有權									
State-owned 國有	16	66	3,375				50.90	86.57	4,188
Collectively-owned 集體	67	29	1,521	67	3.06	13.33	52.11	77.04	2,202
Privately-owned 私有									
Domestic JVs 聯營	4	67	6,572	318	5.76	12.93	98.09	55.46	5,516
Joint stock 股份制	1	46	1,779	-119	-5.50	-6.16	38.68	10.72	2,156
Foreign-funded 外資	4	27	326	-42	-1.50	-2.75	11.98	45.27	2,802
Overseas Chinese-funded 港澳台資	6	18	3,279	83	5.02	6.93	178.83	27.52	1,662
By size 規模									
Large 大型									
Medium 中型									
Small 小型	96	36	2,135	63	2.31	8.82	58.61	73.85	2,708
By regional distribution 地區分布									
Central-North 華北	10	66	5,038	5	0.08	0.35	76.22	77.62	6,391
Beijing 北京	3								
Tianjin 天津									
Hebei 河北	5	98	9,852	48	0.53	3.92	100.74	86.47	9,064
Shanxi 山西	1	147	1,120	100	0.89	6.62	7.62	86.49	11,180
Inner Mongolia 內蒙	1	25		-290	-3.91	-4.35		10.12	7,410
Northeast 東北	9	17	560	18	2.70	17.20	33.83	84.49	659
Liaoning 遼寧	3	32	1,167	3	0.25	2.56	36.46	90.23	1,330
Jilin 吉林	2	9	145	20	8.33	40.00	16.11	81.25	240
Heilongjiang 黑龍江	4	9	313	28	7.53	25.00	35.71	69.86	365
Central East 華東	24	42	3,074	110	2.60	9.52	73.41	72.74	4,219
Shanghai 上海	1	75	11,840	650	8.31	13.89	157.87	40.15	7,820
Jiangsu 江蘇	2	37	3,745	50	1.04	3.76	101.22	72.20	4,785
Zhejiang 浙江	3	9	1,263	40	1.04	2.13	140.37	51.13	3,840
Anhui 安徽	4	72	3,583	75	2.02	13.39	49.58	85.01	3,720
Fujian 福建									
Jiangxi 江西									
Shandong 山東	14	39	2,595	104	2.54	11.77	67.28	78.42	4,104
Central-South 中南	29	41	2,122	127	5.68	16.63	51.29	65.85	2,241
Henan 河南	15	43	2,195	221	7.45	17.27	51.20	56.85	2,962
Hubei 湖北	4	97	5,225	93	2.33	20.11	53.73	88.43	3,975
Hunan 湖南	1	64	2,040	10	0.39		31.88	100.00	2,570
Guangdong 廣東	1								
Guangxi 廣西	8	13	711				54.71	43.27	260
Hainan 海南									
Southwest 西南	16	19	456	-26	-2.71	-17.80	24.66	84.71	969
Chongqing 重慶	4	29	572	-99	-4.81	53.83	19.87	108.94	2,062
Sichuan 四川	9	14	391	-38	-7.56	-143.01	27.98	94.71	508
Guizhou 貴州	1								
Yunnan 雲南	1	22	1,080	100	9.26	21.28	49.09	56.48	1,080
Tibet 西藏	1	45	500	200	8.70	8.70	11.11		2,300
Northwest 西北	11	22	635	15	2.01	26.23	29.13	92.36	725
Shaanxi 陝西	7	25	259	9	1.92	75.00	10.28	97.44	447
Gansu 甘肅	2	21	2,305	45	3.01	42.86	112.44	92.98	1,495
Qinghai 青海	1								
Ningxia 寧夏									
Xinjiang 新疆	1	23	570	10	0.54	3.13	24.78	82.80	1,860

2625: Trace Element Fertilizer 微量元素肥料製造業

Year 年份	Number of firms 企業個數	Rate of change 每年變化 (%)	Number of employees 職工人數（人）	Rate of change 每年變化 (%)	Total revenue (mil. RMB) 總銷售收入（百萬元）	Rate of change 每年變化 (%)	Total profit (mil. RMB) 總利潤（百萬元）	Rate of change 每年變化 (%)
1993	78		3,245		113		4	
1994	71	-8.98%	2,326	-28.32%	116	2.53%	6	32.13%
1995	85	19.72%	3,423	47.16%	142	22.48%	7	19.75%
1996	99	16.47%	3,551	3.74%	205	44.54%	6	-11.96%

3 Major products* 3 種主要產品 *	Output 產量	Sales volume 銷售量	Unit 單位
a) Nitrogen Fertilizer 氮肥	16,875	16,537	ton 噸

Top 10 firms by revenue (year founded) 收入排名前 10 家企業（創辦年份）	City 城市	Province 省	Telephone / fax 電話／傳真	Number of employees 職工人數	Ownership 產業所有權	Revenue ('000 RMB) 銷售收入（千元）	Profit ('000 RMB) (rank) 利潤（千元）（排名）	Total assets ('000 RMB) 總資產（千元）	Major products 主要產品
Hebei Xingtai Metallurgy & Chemistry General Factory 河北省邢臺冶化總廠(1975)	Xingtai 邢臺市	Hebei 河北省	(0319)2995543 (0319)2995542	391	State-owned 國有	43,474	261(7)	41,542	o
Shandong Zaozhuang Quan Yuan Chemical Fertilizer Factory 山東省棗裝市全元化肥廠(1992)	Zaozhuang 棗莊市	Shandong 山東省	(0632)3315195	38	Collectively-owned 集體	16,000	320(5)	4,138	a
Jilin Bei Fang Peace Green Engineering Co. Ltd. 吉林省北方和平綠色工程有限公司(1994)	Changchun 長春市	Jilin 吉林省	(0431)4646974 (0431)4644062	42	Foreign-funded 外資	12,916	3747(1)	18,973	o
Shanghai Da Tong Applied Chemistry Research Institute Experiment Factory 上海大通應用化學研究所實驗廠(1992)	Shanghai 上海市	Shanghai 上海市	(021)59760037 (021)9760464	75	Domestic JVs 聯營	11,837	652(3)	7,816	o
Yuexi Zhuang Zhong Chemical Fertilizer Co. Ltd. 岳西縣撞鐘化肥有限責任公司(1985)	Anqing 安慶市	Anhui 安徽省	(0556)2104213	130	Domestic JVs 聯營	9,800	240(9)	12,624	o
Fugou Shen Nong Technology Development Co. Ltd. 扶溝神農技術發展有限公司(1995)	Zhoukou 周口市	Henan 河南省	(0394)6221423	86	Overseas Chinese-funded 港澳台資	7,327	3100(2)	9,026	o
Xiangshui Guan He Formula Fertilizer Factory 響水縣灌河配方肥料廠(1992)	Yancheng 鹽城市	Jiangsu 江蘇省	(0515)6862035	47	Collectively-owned 集體	5,350	50(14)	8,760	o
Shandong Tian Run Bao Development Group General Company 山東田潤寶開發集團總公司(1990)	Linyi 臨沂市	Shandong 山東省	(0539)2253216 (0539)2258399	191	Collectively-owned 集體	5,309	2(21)	25,952	o
Ji'nan Shi Feng Active Calcium Fertilizer Factory 濟南世豐活性鈣肥廠(1995)	Ji'nan 濟南市	Shandong 山東省	(0531)8992364	31	Collectively-owned 集體	4,570	450(4)	3,430	o
Silver Silver Qu Wuchuan Multiple Chemical Factory 白銀市白銀區武川綜合化工廠(1992)	Baiyin 白銀市	Gansu 甘肅省	(0943)8846235	25	Collectively-owned 集體	4,550	80(12)	1,320	o

Top 10 Cities by Production Output 產出排名前 10 位城市	Province 省	Market share 市場份額	Number of firms 企業個數
Shangrao 上饒市	Jiangxi 江西省	17.57%	2
Baiyin 白銀市	Gansu 甘肅省	15.60%	1
Xingtai 邢臺市	Hebei 河北省	14.67%	1
Zaozhuang 棗莊市	Shandong 山東省	5.33%	1
Taiyuan 太原市	Shanxi 山西省	4.06%	2
Yancheng 鹽城市	Jiangsu 江蘇省	3.85%	1
Anqing 安慶市	Anhui 安徽省	3.27%	1
Suizhou 隨州市	Hubei 湖北省	3.27%	2
Kunming 昆明市	Yunnan 雲南省	2.85%	3
Zhoukou 周口市	Henan 河南省	2.51%	2

10 Major Wholesalers 10 家主要批發商	City 城市	Province 省	Telephone / Fax 電話／傳真
China Agricultural Machinery Hua Bei Company 中國農業機械華北公司	Tianjin 天津市	Tianjin 天津市	(022)23394240 (022)23304247
Shandong Agriculture Means of Production Company 山東省農業生產資料公司	Ji'nan 濟南市	Shandong 山東省	(0531)8957052 (0531)8957142
Yantai Agriculture Means of Production General Company 煙台市農業生產資料總公司	Yantai 煙台市	Shandong 山東省	(0535)6216668 (0535)6211348
Sichuan Agriculture Means of Production General Company 四川省農業生產資料總公司	Chengdu 成都市	Sichuan 四川省	(028)6751135 (028)6751646
Heilongjiang Agriculture Means of Production Company 黑龍江省農業生產資料公司	Harbin 哈爾濱市	Heilongjiang 黑龍江省	(0451)8989948 (0451)8382367
Shannxi Agriculture Means of Production General Company 陝西省農業生產資料總公司	Xi'an 西安市	Shaanxi 陝西省	(029)7422104 (029)7411799
Gansu Agriculture Means of Production General Company 甘肅省農業生產資料總公司	Lanzhou 蘭州市	Gansu 甘肅省	(0931)8822971
Yitong Man Zu Autonomous County Agricultural Goods & Materials Co. Ltd. 伊通滿族自治縣農用物資有限責任公司	Siping 四平市	Jilin 吉林省	(0434)4223146
Langfang Agriculture Means of Production Company 廊坊市農業生產資料公司	Langfang 廊坊市	Hebei 河北省	(0316)2013148
Anhui Agriculture Means of Production Company 安徽省農業生產資料公司	Hefei 合肥市	Anhui 安徽省	(0551)2656541 (0551)2655720

*Also include sales by firms outside this industry.包括本行業以外廠家的銷售。"o" stands for "others". "o" 代表 "其他產品"。

2629: Other Chemical Fertilizer 其他化學肥料製造業

The industry accounts for 0.048% of the total revenue of China's industrial sector in 1996. The revenue growth rate of the industry is 39.2% from 1995, as compared to the growth rate of China's industrial sector, 9.51%. The rate of return on asset is 2.10%. 72.10% of all firms in the industry made a profit while 18.54% had negative returns. The top province in terms of the industry's revenue is Guangxi, accounting for 12.08% of the total revenue.
本行業在1996年佔全行業總產值0.048%，行業年增長率為39.2%（全國工業年增長率9.51%）。行業的資產回報率2.10%，72.10%的企業盈利，18.54%的企業虧損。銷售收入最高的省份為廣西省，佔本行業的12.08%。

	Total number of firms 企業總數	Total number of employees 職工總數	Total revenue (mil. RMB) 總銷售收入（百萬元）	Total profit (mil. RMB) 總利潤（百萬元）	Return on assets 資產利潤率 (%)	Return on equity 權益利潤率 (%)	Labour productivity ('000 RMB / worker) 勞動生產率（千元/人）	Debts / assets 資產負債率 (%)	Total assets (mil. RMB) 總資產（百萬元）
Industry Overall 行業總體	610	39,127	2,803	58	2.10	7.50	71.64	72.05	2,751

	Number of firms 企業個數	Average number of employees 平均職工人數	Average revenue ('000 RMB) 平均銷售收入（千元）	Average profit ('000 RMB) 平均利潤（千元）	Return on assets 資產利潤率 (%)	Return on equity 權益利潤率 (%)	Labour productivity ('000 RMB / worker) 勞動生產率（千元/人）	Average debts / assets 平均資產負債率(%)	Average Total assets ('000 RMB) 平均總資產（千元）
By ownership 產業所有權									
State-owned 國有	102	148	7,275	49	0.42	1.79	49.12	76.38	11,578
Collectively-owned 集體	436	47	3,837	139	6.02	23.37	82.43	74.23	2,307
Privately-owned 私有	2	61	1,319	-106	-7.16	-493.24	21.62	98.55	1,480
Domestic JVs 聯營	17	51	7,113	191	3.48	9.14	140.29	61.98	5,485
Joint stock 股份制	12	64	10,065	299	4.57	8.98	157.27	49.18	6,557
Foreign-funded 外資	23	35	2,554	-178	-3.18	-6.07	73.43	47.61	5,595
Overseas Chinese-funded 港澳台資	18	65	4,757	-562	-3.87	-11.48	72.93	66.26	14,507
By size 規模									
Large 大型	1	1,639	92,869	2,332	1.77	9.44	56.66	81.27	131,886
Medium 中型	5	514	37,652	-508	-1.04	-13.09	73.31	92.08	48,959
Small 小型	577	59	4,372	101	2.45	8.03	73.56	69.47	4,116
By regional distribution 地區分布									
Central-North 華北	58	74	4,270	215	4.02	13.51	57.78	70.22	5,350
Beijing 北京	8	16	686	166	12.37	84.71	43.23	85.40	1,344
Tianjin 天津	3	25	617	-287	-6.07	-11.20	25.00	45.76	4,720
Hebei 河北	27	92	5,954	323	4.13	14.90	64.80	72.30	7,815
Shanxi 山西	14	108	5,586	241	5.05	15.04	51.89	66.39	4,762
Inner Mongolia 內蒙	6	16	225	-12	-0.91	-3.04	13.92	70.13	1,283
Northeast 東北	62	37	1,884	50	2.42	7.83	50.44	69.08	2,051
Liaoning 遼寧	15	41	2,227	-141	-7.30	-1009.52	53.71	99.28	1,936
Jilin 吉林	14	57	1,861	52	1.77	8.14	32.62	78.23	2,944
Heilongjiang 黑龍江	33	27	1,737	135	7.85	14.83	64.11	47.05	1,725
Central East 華東	196	75	6,180	156	2.99	12.00	81.86	75.10	5,229
Shanghai 上海	1	16	10	-180	-6.52	-18.00	0.63	63.77	2,760
Jiangsu 江蘇	22	123	11,712	-330	-3.99	-14.59	95.04	72.64	8,258
Zhejiang 浙江	6	190	22,722	1,530	7.54	12.81	119.38	41.12	20,280
Anhui 安徽	28	54	5,150	164	4.59	19.62	95.93	76.61	3,571
Fujian 福建	21	86	5,110	108	1.99	4.69	59.55	57.67	5,441
Jiangxi 江西	88	41	3,422	115	3.81	28.85	82.64	86.80	3,009
Shandong 山東	30	133	8,823	398	4.98	45.60	66.52	89.08	7,988
Central-South 中南	195	62	5,284	82	1.88	6.48	84.91	70.97	4,360
Henan 河南	27	67	3,385	101	3.76	8.72	50.16	56.85	2,698
Hubei 湖北	35	82	7,381	193	3.87	12.67	89.76	69.46	4,978
Hunan 湖南	34	66	4,896	63	1.88	5.59	74.38	66.46	3,356
Guangdong 廣東	21	65	8,364	-33	-0.39	-2.14	127.92	81.78	8,535
Guangxi 廣西	78	49	4,341	65	1.64	5.55	88.54	70.55	3,973
Hainan 海南									
Southwest 西南	76	55	1,998	1	0.04	0.09	36.54	60.09	3,589
Chongqing 重慶	4	48	1,251	-75	-4.83	17.22	26.08	128.05	1,544
Sichuan 四川	24	68	1,683	-77	-1.95	-5.97	24.88	67.29	3,965
Guizhou 貴州	39	39	1,318	104	15.05	39.26	33.54	61.68	692
Yunnan 雲南	9	89	6,103	-201	-1.26	-2.63	68.92	52.22	15,987
Tibet 西藏									
Northwest 西北	23	63	1,957	-200	-2.78	-17.57	31.28	84.22	7,189
Shaanxi 陝西	11	56	1,051	-529	-6.34	-83.50	18.65	92.40	8,341
Gansu 甘肅	7	31	1,557	199	11.14	31.24	50.46	64.50	1,783
Qinghai 青海									
Ningxia 寧夏									
Xinjiang 新疆	5	121	4,510	-32	-0.26	-1.09	37.40	75.95	12,224

2629: Other Chemical Fertilizer 其他化學肥料製造業

Year 年份	Number of firms 企業個數	Rate of change 每年變化 (%)	Number of employees 職工人數（人）	Rate of change 每年變化 (%)	Total revenue (mil. RMB) 總銷售收入（百萬元）	Rate of change 每年變化 (%)	Total profit (mil. RMB) 總利潤（百萬元）	Rate of change 每年變化 (%)
1993	250		15,003		532		-3	
1994	319	27.60%	19,518	30.09%	989	86.00%	28	1133.25%
1995	534	67.40%	31,658	62.20%	2,014	103.65%	37	34.94%
1996	610	14.23%	39,127	23.59%	2,803	39.18%	58	55.91%

3 Major products* 3 種主要產品 *	Output 產量	Sales volume 銷售量	Unit 單位
a) Ammonium Hydrogen Carbonate 碳酸氫銨	105,397	141,232	ton 噸
b) Phosphate Fertilizer 磷肥	65,768	61,822	ton 噸

Top 10 firms by revenue (year founded) 收入排名前 10 家企業（創辦年份）	City 城市	Province 省	Telephone / fax 電話 / 傳真	Number of employees 職工人數	Ownership 產業所有權	Revenue ('000 RMB) 銷售收入（千元）	Profit ('000 RMB) (rank) 利潤（千元）（排名）	Total assets ('000 RMB) 總資產（千元）	Major products 主要產品
Zhongshan Zhong Heng Compound Fertilizer Co. Ltd. 中山市中橫實業(複合)有限公司(1994)	Zhongshan 中山市	Guangdong 廣東省	(0760)7612388 (0760)7767123	209	Overseas Chinese-funded 港澳台資	71,449	3454(3)	82,771	o
Zhejiang Tian Ma Industrial Co. Ltd. 浙江天馬實業股份有限公司(1993)	Hangzhou 杭州市	Zhejiang 浙江省	(0571)2623862 (0571)2623861	135	Joint stock 股份制	68,510	2518(9)	37,177	o
Di Fang State-owned Tongxiang Chemical Fertilizer Factory 地方國營桐鄉化肥廠(1966)	Jiaxing 嘉興市	Zhejiang 浙江省	(0573)8411613 (0573)8411816	1,010	State-owned 國有	67,557	6684(1)	83,220	a
Hunan Zhuzhou Chemical Fertilizer Factory 湖南省株洲市化肥廠(1976)	Zhuzhou 株洲市	Hunan 湖南省	(0733)8631299 (0733)8632754	380	Collectively-owned 集體	65,275	-520(218)	42,406	o
Fujian Taining Synthetic Ammonia Factory 福建省泰寧縣合成氨廠(1972)	Sanming 三明市	Fujian 福建省	(0598)7832358	1,015	State-owned 國有	54,170	1768(12)	74,889	a
Jiangxi No.3 Pharmaceutical Factory 江西第三製藥廠(1988)	Shangrao 上饒市	Jiangxi 江西省	(0793)3271107 (0793)3271085	528	State-owned 國有	52,668	2599(8)	76,556	o
Laizhou Chemical General Factory 萊州市化工總廠(1972)	Yantai 煙台市	Shandong 山東省	(0535)2212917 (0535)2212917	974	State-owned 國有	47,391	360(61)	65,035	b
Hubei Jiayu Chemical Fertilizer Factory 嘉魚縣化肥廠(1975)	Xianning 咸寧市	Hubei 湖北省	(0715)323503	765	State-owned 國有	47,372	1042(27)	82,982	a
Shandong Haiyang Chemical Fertilizer Factory 山東省海陽市化肥廠(1973)	Yantai 煙台市	Shandong 山東省	(0535)3861231 (0535)3861231	763	State-owned 國有	46,377	690(38)	77,771	a,b
Huaihua Phosphor Chemical General Factory 懷化磷化工總廠(1967)	Huaihua 懷化市	Hunan 湖南省	(0745)2883452 (0745)2883475	998	State-owned 國有	42,699	60(125)	45,513	b

Top 10 Cities by Production Output 產出排名前 10 位城市	Province 省	Market share 市場份額	Number of firms 企業個數
Nanjing 南京市	Jiangsu 江蘇省	9.48%	12
Yantai 煙台市	Shandong 山東省	6.29%	6
Guangzhou 廣州市	Guangdong 廣東省	6.19%	6
Ji'an 吉安市	Jiangxi 江西省	3.32%	14
Hangzhou 杭州市	Zhejiang 浙江省	3.09%	2
Yangquan 陽泉市	Shanxi 山西省	3.09%	2
Zhuzhou 株洲市	Hunan 湖南省	2.79%	2
Jiaxing 嘉興市	Zhejiang 浙江省	2.77%	1
Huaihua 懷化市	Hunan 湖南省	2.56%	10
Sanming 三明市	Fujian 福建省	2.40%	2

10 Major Wholesalers 10 家主要批發商	City 城市	Province 省	Telephone / Fax 電話 / 傳真
China Agricultural Machinery Hua Bei Company 中國農業機械華北公司	Tianjin 天津市	Tianjin 天津市	(022)23394240 (022)23304247
Shandong Agriculture Means of Production Company 山東省農業生產資料公司	Ji'nan 濟南市	Shandong 山東省	(0531)8957052 (0531)8957142
Yantai Agriculture Means of Production General Company 煙台市農業生產資料總公司	Yantai 煙台市	Shandong 山東省	(0535)6216668 (0535)6211348
Sichuan Agriculture Means of Production General Company 四川省農業生產資料總公司	Chengdu 成都市	Sichuan 四川省	(028)6751135 (028)6751646
Heilongjiang Agriculture Means of Production Company 黑龍江省農業生產資料公司	Harbin 哈爾濱市	Heilongjiang 黑龍江省	(0451)8989948 (0451)8382367
Shannxi Agriculture Means of Production General Company 陝西省農業生產資料總公司	Xi'an 西安市	Shaanxi 陝西省	(029)7422104 (029)7411799
Gansu Agriculture Means of Production General Company 甘肅省農業生產資料總公司	Lanzhou 蘭州市	Gansu 甘肅省	(0931)8822971
Yitong Man Zu Autonomous County Agricultural Goods & Materials Co. Ltd. 伊通滿族自治縣農用物資有限責任公司	Siping 四平市	Jilin 吉林省	(0434)4223146
Langfang Agriculture Means of Production Company 廊坊市農業生產資料公司	Langfang 廊坊市	Hebei 河北省	(0316)2013148
Anhui Agriculture Means of Production Company 安徽省農業生產資料公司	Hefei 合肥市	Anhui 安徽省	(0551)2656541 (0551)2655720

*Also include sales by firms outside this industry.包括本行業以外廠家的銷售。"o" stands for "others". "o" 代表 "其他產品"。

2631: Agricultural Chemical Materials 農藥原藥製造業

The industry accounts for 0.240% of the total revenue of China's industrial sector in 1996. The revenue growth rate of the industry is 14.2% from 1995, as compared to the growth rate of China's industrial sector, 9.51%. The rate of return on asset is 3.27%. 74.25% of all firms in the industry made a profit while 22.19% had negative returns. The top province in terms of the industry's revenue is Jiangsu, accounting for 33.72% of the total revenue.
本行業在1996年佔全行業總產值0.240%，行業年增長率為14.2%（全國工業年增長率9.51%）。行業的資產回報率3.27%，74.25%的企業盈利，22.19%的企業虧損。銷售收入最高的省份為江蘇省，佔本行業的33.72%。

	Total number of firms 企業總數	Total number of employees 職工總數	Total revenue (mil. RMB) 總銷售收入（百萬元）	Total profit (mil. RMB) 總利潤（百萬元）	Return on assets 資產利潤率 (%)	Return on equity 權益利潤率 (%)	Labour productivity ('000 RMB / worker) 勞動生產率（千元/人）	Debts / assets 資產負債率 (%)	Total assets (mil. RMB) 總資產（百萬元）
Industry Overall 行業總體	363	123,636	13,923	516	3.27	9.65	112.61	66.13	15,782

	Number of firms 企業個數	Average number of employees 平均職工人數	Average revenue ('000 RMB) 平均銷售收入（千元）	Average profit ('000 RMB) 平均利潤（千元）	Return on assets 資產利潤率 (%)	Return on equity 權益利潤率 (%)	Labour productivity ('000 RMB / worker) 勞動生產率（千元/人）	Average debts / assets 平均資產負債率(%)	Average Total assets ('000 RMB) 平均總資產（千元）
By ownership 產業所有權									
State-owned 國有	120	641	62,800	892	1.22	4.07	97.92	69.97	72,950
Collectively-owned 集體	199	116	12,725	445	3.92	14.79	109.90	73.48	11,346
Privately-owned 私有	2	32	5,186	-21	-0.68	-3.29	164.63	79.18	3,044
Domestic JVs 聯營	6	202	31,982	3,509	9.18	19.10	158.59	51.97	38,241
Joint stock 股份制	11	1,788	260,593	26,396	7.96	17.08	145.71	53.39	331,572
Foreign-funded 外資	14	133	45,803	-1,039	-1.94	-5.74	343.28	66.15	53,495
Overseas Chinese-funded 港澳台資	10	89	14,479	2,358	17.12	45.73	162.32	62.57	13,778
By size 規模									
Large 大型	23	2,121	285,823	12,530	3.59	8.92	134.73	59.79	349,485
Medium 中型	52	793	79,523	2,249	2.54	8.84	100.23	71.20	88,374
Small 小型	277	120	11,573	473	4.21	17.20	96.59	75.55	11,238
By regional distribution 地區分布									
Central-North 華北	45	333	30,841	1,455	3.43	10.67	92.73	67.85	42,427
Beijing 北京	3	130	13,897	823	7.37	11.67	106.90	36.82	11,170
Tianjin 天津	9	375	40,216	3,372	5.31	11.29	107.34	53.02	63,550
Hebei 河北	22	379	38,898	1,410	2.85	11.60	102.66	75.48	49,573
Shanxi 山西	11	261	11,679	147	0.76	2.87	44.78	73.50	19,378
Inner Mongolia 內蒙									
Northeast 東北	34	229	12,540	37	0.16	0.60	54.77	74.01	23,462
Liaoning 遼寧	19	302	19,015	562	1.69	5.15	62.94	67.27	33,304
Jilin 吉林	3	87	4,737	333	2.71	9.73	54.65	72.16	12,310
Heilongjiang 黑龍江	12	149	4,238	-868	-8.14	103.99	28.51	107.83	10,667
Central East 華東	168	409	51,436	1,864	3.54	10.54	125.70	66.39	52,625
Shanghai 上海	5	176	51,890	3,000	3.85	25.69	294.83	85.03	77,958
Jiangsu 江蘇	72	453	65,204	2,139	3.78	10.54	143.95	64.17	56,632
Zhejiang 浙江	27	517	73,667	2,591	3.38	10.13	142.61	66.60	76,586
Anhui 安徽	16	217	11,564	-631	-3.59	-27.89	53.31	87.13	17,566
Fujian 福建	9	450	48,400	3,859	7.94	19.60	107.48	59.50	48,623
Jiangxi 江西	12	306	14,103	412	1.45	7.42	46.11	80.51	28,488
Shandong 山東	27	375	33,639	1,655	3.59	9.28	89.81	61.31	46,121
Central-South 中南	84	325	37,356	1,606	3.46	9.02	114.97	61.68	46,435
Henan 河南	28	133	9,266	295	2.69	8.98	69.54	70.08	10,997
Hubei 湖北	16	674	94,269	7,180	6.32	13.57	139.84	53.41	113,591
Hunan 湖南	14	625	57,537	1,789	2.42	6.14	92.02	60.51	73,841
Guangdong 廣東	16	209	31,338	-816	-2.02	-9.97	149.99	79.77	40,425
Guangxi 廣西	9	52	7,013	74	0.88	2.84	135.45	69.07	8,461
Hainan 海南	1	212	90	-930	-5.03	13.46	0.42	137.34	18,480
Southwest 西南	26	173	12,106	25	0.20	1.24	70.15	83.71	12,400
Chongqing 重慶	3	842	69,043	126	0.20	0.93	82.04	78.61	63,574
Sichuan 四川	17	80	3,761	-55	-1.19	12.11	47.18	109.79	4,653
Guizhou 貴州	5	6	258				43.00	62.38	202
Yunnan 雲南	1	570	42,420	100	0.19	0.52	74.42	63.02	51,570
Tibet 西藏									
Northwest 西北	6	60	2,445	20	1.04	2.21	40.75	52.74	1,915
Shaanxi 陝西	5	25	962	66	6.50	8.75	39.11	25.98	1,016
Gansu 甘肅	1	237	9,860	-210	-3.28	-12.57	41.60	73.95	6,410
Qinghai 青海									
Ningxia 寧夏									
Xinjiang 新疆									

2631: Agricultural Chemical Materials 農藥原藥製造業

Year 年份	Number of firms 企業個數	Rate of change 每年變化 (%)	Number of employees 職工人數 (人)	Rate of change 每年變化 (%)	Total revenue (mil. RMB) 總銷售收入 (百萬元)	Rate of change 每年變化 (%)	Total profit (mil. RMB) 總利潤 (百萬元)	Rate of change 每年變化 (%)
1993	361		109,187		6,995		80	
1994	350	-3.05%	112,010	2.59%	7,403	5.83%	29	-64.13%
1995	359	2.57%	124,777	11.40%	12,191	64.67%	318	1007.69%
1996	363	1.11%	123,636	-0.91%	13,923	14.21%	516	62.02%

3 Major products* 3 種主要產品 *	Output 產量	Sales volume 銷售量	Unit 單位
a) Pesticide Emulsion 農藥乳劑	113,039	108,518	ton 噸
b) Organophosphorus Insecticide 有機磷殺蟲劑	163,139	151,719	ton 噸
c) Herbicide 除草劑	32,226	27,714	ton 噸

Top 10 firms by revenue (year founded) 收入排名前 10 家企業 (創辦年份)	City 城市	Province 省	Telephone / fax 電話 / 傳真	Number of employees 職工人數	Ownership 產業所有權	Revenue ('000 RMB) 銷售收入 (千元)	Profit ('000 RMB) (rank) 利潤 (千元) (排名)	Total assets ('000 RMB) 總資產 (千元)	Major products 主要產品
Sanonda Group Co. 沙隆達集團公司(1994)	Jingsha 荊沙市	Hubei 湖北省	(0716)8314802 (0716)8315265	3,910	Joint stock 股份制	1,118,553	105708(1)	1,433,996	b,c
Jiangsu Chemical Pesticide Group Co. 江蘇化工農藥集團公司(1956)	Suzhou 蘇州市	Jiangsu 江蘇省	(0512)5251605 (0512)5251980	3,174	State-owned 國有	708,872	25230(5)	619,290	a,b,c
Jiangsu Eternal Union Group Corp. 江蘇永聯集團公司(1975)	Wuxi 無錫市	Jiangsu 江蘇省	(0510)6501359 (0510)6501359	2,553	State-owned 國有	414,064	5310(25)	441,241	c
Yangzhou Pesticide Factory 揚州農藥廠(1958)	Yangzhou 揚州市	Jiangsu 江蘇省	(0514)7813243 (0514)7814008	2,166	State-owned 國有	392,570	12629(11)	313,174	b
Zhejiang Xin An Chemical Industrial Group Co. Ltd. 浙江新安江化工集團股份有限公司(1965)	Hangzhou 杭州市	Zhejiang 浙江省	(0571)4723891 (0571)4721344	2,016	Joint stock 股份制	386,474	30169(4)	298,091	a,b,c
Zhejiang Ling Hua Enterprise Group Co. 浙江菱化企業集團公司(1946)	Huzhou 湖州市	Zhejiang 浙江省	(0572)3944201 (0572)3941402	1,917	State-owned 國有	348,822	12096(12)	285,905	b,c
Shandong Pesticide Industry Co. Ltd. 山東農藥工業股份有限公司(1949)	Zibo 淄博市	Shandong 山東省	(0533)2183042 (0533)2184511	3,255	Joint stock 股份制	333,417	33493(3)	508,413	a,b
Nantong Pesticide Factory 南通農藥廠(1958)	Nantong 南通市	Jiangsu 江蘇省	(0513)3513131 (0513)5510690	1,665	State-owned 國有	300,310	11320(14)	247,850	a,b,c
Hangzhou Pesticide General Factory 杭州農藥總廠(1957)	Hangzhou 杭州市	Zhejiang 浙江省	(0571)6992951 (0571)6046335	1,372	State-owned 國有	298,380	6270(22)	245,090	a,b,c
Fujian San Nong Chemical Co. Ltd. 福建省三農化學股份有限公司(1966)	Sanming 三明市	Fujian 福建省	(0598)8238008 (0598)8242852	1,753	Joint stock 股份制	284,640	34440(2)	287,326	a,b

Top 10 Cities by Production Output 產出排名前 10 位城市	Province 省	Market share 市場份額	Number of firms 企業個數
Suzhou 蘇州市	Jiangsu 江蘇省	10.96%	14
Jingsha 荊沙市	Hubei 湖北省	6.75%	5
Nantong 南通市	Jiangsu 江蘇省	5.02%	15
Wuxi 無錫市	Jiangsu 江蘇省	3.77%	9
Huzhou 湖州市	Zhejiang 浙江省	3.45%	2
Hangzhou 杭州市	Zhejiang 浙江省	3.44%	6
Jiaxing 嘉興市	Zhejiang 浙江省	3.39%	7
Tianjin 天津市	Tianjin 天津市	3.05%	10
Yangzhou 揚州市	Jiangsu 江蘇省	3.05%	2
Zibo 淄博市	Shandong 山東省	2.83%	1

10 Major Wholesalers 10 家主要批發商	City 城市	Province 省	Telephone / Fax 電話 / 傳真
China Agricultural Machinery Hua Bei Company 中國農業機械華北公司	Tianjin 天津市	Tianjin 天津市	(022)23394240 (022)23304247
Shandong Agriculture Means of Production Company 山東省農業生產資料公司	Ji'nan 濟南市	Shandong 山東省	(0531)8957052 (0531)8957142
Yantai Agriculture Means of Production General Company 煙台市農業生產資料總公司	Yantai 煙台市	Shandong 山東省	(0535)6216668 (0535)6211348
Sichuan Agriculture Means of Production General Company 四川省農業生產資料總公司	Chengdu 成都市	Sichuan 四川省	(028)6751135 (028)6751646
Heilongjiang Agriculture Means of Production Company 黑龍江省農業生產資料公司	Harbin 哈爾濱市	Heilongjiang 黑龍江省	(0451)8989948 (0451)8382367
Shannxi Agriculture Means of Production General Company 陝西省農業生產資料總公司	Xi'an 西安市	Shaanxi 陝西省	(029)7422104 (029)7411799
Gansu Agriculture Means of Production General Company 甘肅省農業生產資料總公司	Lanzhou 蘭州市	Gansu 甘肅省	(0931)8822971
Yitong Man Zu Autonomous County Agricultural Goods & Materials Co. Ltd. 伊通滿族自治縣農用物資有限責任公司	Siping 四平市	Jilin 吉林省	(0434)4223146
Langfang Agriculture Means of Production Company 廊坊市農業生產資料公司	Langfang 廊坊市	Hebei 河北省	(0316)2013148
Anhui Agriculture Means of Production Company 安徽省農業生產資料公司	Hefei 合肥市	Anhui 安徽省	(0551)2656541 (0551)2655720

*Also include sales by firms outside this industry.包括本行業以外廠家的銷售。"o" stands for "others". "o" 代表"其他產品"。

2633: Agricultural Chemical Products 農藥製劑製造業

The industry accounts for 0.145% of the total revenue of China's industrial sector in 1996. The revenue growth rate of the industry is 17.3% from 1995, as compared to the growth rate of China's industrial sector, 9.51%. The rate of return on asset is 3.85%. 71.63% of all firms in the industry made a profit while 21.11% had negative returns. The top province in terms of the industry's revenue is Jiangsu, accounting for 18.50% of the total revenue.
本行業在1996年佔全行業總產值0.145%，行業年增長率為17.3%（全國工業年增長率9.51%）。行業的資產回報率3.85%，71.63%的企業盈利，21.11%的企業虧損。銷售收入最高的省份為江蘇省，佔本行業的18.50%。

	Total number of firms 企業總數	Total number of employees 職工總數	Total revenue (mil. RMB) 總銷售收入（百萬元）	Total profit (mil. RMB) 總利潤（百萬元）	Return on assets 資產利潤率 (%)	Return on equity 權益利潤率 (%)	Labour productivity ('000 RMB / worker) 勞動生產率（千元/人）	Debts / assets 資產負債率 (%)	Total assets (mil. RMB) 總資產（百萬元）
Industry Overall 行業總體	719	76,933	8,382	352	3.85	13.86	108.95	72.22	9,150

	Number of firms 企業個數	Average number of employees 平均職工人數	Average revenue ('000 RMB) 平均銷售收入（千元）	Average profit ('000 RMB) 平均利潤（千元）	Return on assets 資產利潤率 (%)	Return on equity 權益利潤率 (%)	Labour productivity ('000 RMB / worker) 勞動生產率（千元/人）	Average debts / assets 平均資產負債率(%)	Average Total assets ('000 RMB) 平均總資產（千元）
By ownership 產業所有權									
State-owned 國有	158	238	18,703	101	0.43	2.49	78.73	82.59	23,373
Collectively-owned 集體	498	69	8,610	500	6.81	20.06	125.42	66.05	7,341
Privately-owned 私有	3	56	4,336	318	12.80	18.85	77.89	32.09	2,484
Domestic JVs 聯營	6	57	8,795	288	4.03	8.84	155.67	54.39	7,155
Joint stock 股份制	9	286	70,050	4,871	3.41	10.25	245.03	66.74	142,843
Foreign-funded 外資	23	56	12,114	1,348	10.29	23.03	217.50	55.32	13,098
Overseas Chinese-funded 港澳台資	20	41	8,252	472	5.77	13.33	199.08	56.70	8,185
By size 規模									
Large 大型	5	1,820	351,921	15,448	3.13	8.52	193.32	63.21	492,832
Medium 中型	27	610	64,081	2,126	2.88	11.88	104.97	75.75	73,839
Small 小型	673	76	7,270	323	4.63	18.87	96.14	75.45	6,972
By regional distribution 地區分布									
Central-North 華北	95	108	9,838	497	4.61	22.37	91.15	79.38	10,780
Beijing 北京	14	32	2,591	44	1.16	3.15	81.90	63.04	3,803
Tianjin 天津	17	38	4,591	478	11.71	28.11	121.94	58.34	4,079
Hebei 河北	46	192	17,423	833	4.35	24.05	90.84	81.89	19,125
Shanxi 山西	10	17	1,581	3	0.29	1.96	94.67	85.01	1,021
Inner Mongolia 內蒙	8	23	371	19	1.30	8.67	16.50	85.01	1,443
Northeast 東北	62	61	3,733	109	1.90	8.38	61.06	77.31	5,750
Liaoning 遼寧	34	62	4,251	130	2.12	8.24	68.62	74.29	6,147
Jilin 吉林	8	114	3,863	-66	-0.64	-5.14	33.81	87.63	10,415
Heilongjiang 黑龍江	20	39	2,803	144	4.49	17.10	72.70	73.77	3,209
Central East 華東	277	127	16,924	652	4.12	15.38	133.26	73.19	15,824
Shanghai 上海	7	635	120,160	2,126	1.39	6.52	189.23	78.68	152,996
Jiangsu 江蘇	105	118	14,770	444	3.25	11.01	124.74	70.47	13,665
Zhejiang 浙江	47	125	21,278	595	3.34	12.87	169.62	74.07	17,818
Anhui 安徽	33	121	13,495	811	16.41	52.68	111.47	68.84	4,943
Fujian 福建	9	43	4,997	38	0.78	2.13	116.20	63.33	4,836
Jiangxi 江西	20	92	6,705	574	7.31	22.83	72.88	67.98	7,844
Shandong 山東	56	110	11,988	940	7.78	27.84	108.58	72.06	12,079
Central-South 中南	195	117	11,678	614	4.09	12.00	100.05	65.93	15,015
Henan 河南	68	87	6,769	588	6.64	29.05	77.42	77.13	8,845
Hubei 湖北	32	178	13,080	136	1.00	6.26	73.48	84.08	13,637
Hunan 湖南	26	254	20,080	34	0.17	0.62	79.02	73.49	20,428
Guangdong 廣東	37	99	21,898	2,034	5.72	11.99	221.19	52.27	35,528
Guangxi 廣西	31	27	2,046	-24	-1.66	-3.31	76.98	49.72	1,417
Hainan 海南	1	25	2,580	20	3.45	13.33	103.20	72.41	580
Southwest 西南	62	43	2,483	-38	-1.09	-8.67	58.10	87.44	3,493
Chongqing 重慶	16	37	1,462	-50	-3.25	-37.74	39.38	91.38	1,531
Sichuan 四川	27	51	3,007	-178	-5.57	-75.68	58.64	92.64	3,188
Guizhou 貴州	15	32	950	14	0.71	2.49	29.69	71.37	1,965
Yunnan 雲南	4	49	8,788	760	3.97	29.46	179.34	86.53	19,135
Tibet 西藏									
Northwest 西北	28	82	3,482	8	0.09	0.44	42.37	79.40	8,638
Shaanxi 陝西	13	105	5,048	-41	-0.44	-4.54	48.15	90.34	9,294
Gansu 甘肅	11	84	2,715	38	0.35	1.13	32.35	68.97	10,845
Qinghai 青海									
Ningxia 寧夏									
Xinjiang 新疆	4	4	500	83	18.75	28.95	133.33	35.23	440

2633: Agricultural Chemical Products 農藥製劑製造業

Year 年份	Number of firms 企業個數	Rate of change 每年變化 (%)	Number of employees 職工人數 (人)	Rate of change 每年變化 (%)	Total revenue (mil. RMB) 總銷售收入 (百萬元)	Rate of change 每年變化 (%)	Total profit (mil. RMB) 總利潤 (百萬元)	Rate of change 每年變化 (%)
1993	543		79,098		3,620		19	
1994	595	9.58%	71,607	-9.47%	4,261	17.69%	17	-10.44%
1995	686	15.29%	75,229	5.06%	7,146	67.71%	281	1577.48%
1996	719	4.81%	76,933	2.27%	8,382	17.30%	352	25.19%

3 Major products* 3 種主要產品 *	Output 產量	Sales volume 銷售量	Unit 單位
a) Plant Growth Regulator 植物生長調節劑	10,125	8,505	ton 噸
b) Pyrthrin 除蟲菊酯殺蟲劑	4,501	4,051	ton 噸
c) Insecticide 殺蟲劑	90,979	83,701	ton 噸

Top 10 firms by revenue (year founded) 收入排名前 10 家企業 (創辦年份)	City 城市	Province 省	Telephone / fax 電話 / 傳真	Number of employees 職工人數	Ownership 產業所有權	Revenue ('000 RMB) 銷售收入 (千元)	Profit ('000 RMB) (rank) 利潤（千元）（排名）	Total assets ('000 RMB) 總資產 (千元)	Major products 主要產品
Zhongshan Kai Da Fine Chemical Industry Industrial Co. Ltd. 中山凱達精細化工實業有限公司(1966)	Zhongshan 中山市	Guangdong 廣東省	(0760)8700113 (0760)8700139	1,832	Foreign-funded 外資	551,269	69716(1)	884,702	b,c
Asia Pacific Agricultural Chemical (Group) Co. 上海亞太農用化學(集團)公司(1952)	Shanghai 上海市	Shanghai 上海市	(021)58611010 (021)58611767	3,370	State-owned 國有	467,673	-9879(372)	294,481	a,b,c
Shanghai Zhong Xi Pharmaceutical Co. Ltd. 中西藥業股份有限公司(1952)	Shanghai 上海市	Shanghai 上海市	(021)56082188 (021)56083743	563	Joint stock 股份制	317,043	23502(2)	703,471	b,c
Lanxi Pesticide Factory 蘭溪農藥廠(1963)	Jinhua 金華市	Zhejiang 浙江省	(0579)8824647 (0579)8825843	1,230	State-owned 國有	197,456	3156(32)	154,748	o
Hangzhou Well-done Chemical Co. Ltd. 杭州威爾達化工有限公司(1984)	Hangzhou 杭州市	Zhejiang 浙江省	(0571)6375868	160	Collectively-owned 集體	134,618	8180(11)	58,658	o
Hebi Tian Yuan Co. Ltd. 鶴壁市天元股份有限公司(1994)	Hebi 鶴壁市	Henan 河南省	(0392)3311100 (0392)33110782	807	Collectively-owned 集體	129,545	10796(7)	145,386	o
Shandong Liang You Group Co. Ltd. 山東良友集團有限公司(1979)	Yantai 煙台市	Shandong 山東省	(0535)5911538 (0535)5911538	538	Collectively-owned 集體	127,550	13930(4)	75,341	c
Hebei Kang Da Co. Ltd. 河北康達有限公司(1989)	Baoding 保定市	Hebei 河北省	(0312)3160302 (0312)3163407	195	Joint stock 股份制	125,810	20590(3)	57,827	o
Gaomi Pesticide Chemical General Factory 高密市農藥化工總廠(1974)	Weifang 濰坊市	Shandong 山東省	(0536)2323133 (0536)2323133	742	State-owned 國有	125,350	4769(22)	72,010	c
Anhui Guoyang Chemical General Factory 安徽省渦陽縣化工總廠(1970)	Fuyang 阜陽市	Anhui 安徽省	(0558)7212366	460	Collectively-owned 集體	113,440	1192(69)	31,730	o

Top 10 Cities by Production Output 產出排名前 10 位城市	Province 省	Market share 市場份額	Number of firms 企業個數
Shanghai 上海市	Shanghai 上海市	8.29%	11
Zhongshan 中山市	Guangdong 廣東省	7.13%	4
Hangzhou 杭州市	Zhejiang 浙江省	4.58%	15
Jinhua 金華市	Zhejiang 浙江省	3.36%	6
Changzhou 常州市	Jiangsu 江蘇省	3.25%	20
Yancheng 鹽城市	Jiangsu 江蘇省	3.16%	25
Hengyang 衡陽市	Hunan 湖南省	2.76%	3
Weifang 濰坊市	Shandong 山東省	2.56%	18
Suqian 宿遷市	Jiangsu 江蘇省	2.48%	3
Yiyang 益陽市	Hunan 湖南省	2.11%	6

10 Major Wholesalers 10 家主要批發商	City 城市	Province 省	Telephone / Fax 電話 / 傳真
China Agricultural Machinery Hua Bei Company 中國農業機械華北公司	Tianjin 天津市	Tianjin 天津市	(022)23394240 (022)23304247
Shandong Agriculture Means of Production Company 山東省農業生產資料公司	Ji'nan 濟南市	Shandong 山東省	(0531)8957052 (0531)8957142
Yantai Agriculture Means of Production General Company 煙台市農業生產資料總公司	Yantai 煙台市	Shandong 山東省	(0535)6216668 (0535)6211348
Sichuan Agriculture Means of Production General Company 四川省農業生產資料總公司	Chengdu 成都市	Sichuan 四川省	(028)6751135 (028)6751646
Heilongjiang Agriculture Means of Production Company 黑龍江省農業生產資料公司	Harbin 哈爾濱市	Heilongjiang 黑龍江省	(0451)8989948 (0451)8382367
Shannxi Agriculture Means of Production General Company 陝西省農業生產資料總公司	Xi'an 西安市	Shaanxi 陝西省	(029)7422104 (029)7411799
Gansu Agriculture Means of Production General Company 甘肅省農業生產資料總公司	Lanzhou 蘭州市	Gansu 甘肅省	(0931)8822971
Yitong Man Zu Autonomous County Agricultural Goods & Materials Co. Ltd. 伊通滿族自治縣農用物資有限責任公司	Siping 四平市	Jilin 吉林省	(0434)4223146
Langfang Agriculture Means of Production Company 廊坊市農業生產資料公司	Langfang 廊坊市	Hebei 河北省	(0316)2013148
Anhui Agriculture Means of Production Company 安徽省農業生產資料公司	Hefei 合肥市	Anhui 安徽省	(0551)2656541 (0551)2655720

*Also include sales by firms outside this industry.包括本行業以外廠家的銷售。"o" stands for "others". "o" 代表"其他產品"。

2651: Industrial Organic Chemical 有機化工原料製造業

The industry accounts for 0.776% of the total revenue of China's industrial sector in 1996. The revenue growth rate of the industry is -3.8% from 1995, as compared to the growth rate of China's industrial sector, 9.51%. The rate of return on asset is 1.17%. 67.50% of all firms in the industry made a profit while 24.92% had negative returns. The top province in terms of the industry's revenue is Jiangsu, accounting for 29.81% of the total revenue.
本行業在1996年佔全行業總產值0.776%，行業年增長率為-3.8%（全國工業年增長率9.51%）。行業的資產回報率1.17%，67.50%的企業盈利，24.92%的企業虧損。銷售收入最高的省份為江蘇省，佔本行業的29.81%。

	Total number of firms 企業總數	Total number of employees 職工總數	Total revenue (mil. RMB) 總銷售收入（百萬元）	Total profit (mil. RMB) 總利潤（百萬元）	Return on assets 資產利潤率 (%)	Return on equity 權益利潤率 (%)	Labour productivity ('000 RMB / worker) 勞動生產率（千元/人）	Debts / assets 資產負債率 (%)	Total assets (mil. RMB) 總資產（百萬元）
Industry Overall 行業總體	1,351	385,759	44,984	1,015	1.17	3.37	116.61	65.37	87,052

	Number of firms 企業個數	Average number of employees 平均職工人數	Average revenue ('000 RMB) 平均銷售收入（千元）	Average profit ('000 RMB) 平均利潤（千元）	Return on assets 資產利潤率 (%)	Return on equity 權益利潤率 (%)	Labour productivity ('000 RMB / worker) 勞動生產率（千元/人）	Average debts / assets 平均資產負債率(%)	Average Total assets ('000 RMB) 平均總資產（千元）
By ownership 產業所有權									
State-owned 國有	272	915	120,011	2,254	0.84	2.38	131.11	64.74	268,533
Collectively-owned 集體	925	113	9,396	426	5.10	16.53	83.03	69.13	8,354
Privately-owned 私有	7	25	2,909	242	18.87	38.44	115.71	50.91	1,281
Domestic JVs 聯營	19	234	11,529	-427	-1.63	-5.47	49.19	70.23	26,231
Joint stock 股份制	23	568	54,196	2,752	4.67	9.53	95.45	51.01	58,957
Foreign-funded 外資	48	159	19,136	-2,808	-6.99	-27.67	120.68	74.73	40,151
Overseas Chinese-funded 港澳台資	58	142	21,479	1,505	3.50	12.49	150.99	71.96	42,971
By size 規模									
Large 大型	30	6,749	1,034,300	30,327	1.35	3.58	153.26	62.21	2,244,645
Medium 中型	89	684	55,612	345	0.40	1.58	81.32	74.71	86,322
Small 小型	1,203	97	7,486	62	0.62	2.72	77.08	77.07	10,000
By regional distribution 地區分布									
Central-North 華北	214	212	31,782	904	2.03	7.57	150.18	73.15	44,502
Beijing 北京	27	760	170,307	3,440	1.40	4.55	224.00	69.28	246,403
Tianjin 天津	34	117	18,372	430	1.77	6.97	156.87	74.63	24,308
Hebei 河北	113	125	11,867	741	6.14	37.66	95.21	83.71	12,077
Shanxi 山西	30	138	4,489	239	3.53	26.77	32.63	86.82	6,775
Inner Mongolia 內蒙	10	257	10,268	-494	-1.04	-9.01	40.00	88.48	47,607
Northeast 東北	204	675	59,503	86	0.05	0.15	88.09	68.69	183,725
Liaoning 遼寧	121	372	7,293	-807	-3.16	-11.56	19.62	72.70	25,582
Jilin 吉林	44	1,941	243,854	2,506	0.34	1.02	125.62	66.87	741,921
Heilongjiang 黑龍江	39	190	13,502	127	0.29	6.63	71.23	95.69	44,612
Central East 華東	595	241	37,407	1,255	2.23	5.41	155.36	58.76	56,316
Shanghai 上海	42	644	81,135	-669	-0.39	-1.80	125.93	78.07	169,834
Jiangsu 江蘇	263	222	50,995	2,533	3.41	6.63	230.14	48.47	74,188
Zhejiang 浙江	81	128	17,182	-312	-1.47	-5.44	134.19	72.91	21,203
Anhui 安徽	43	187	15,618	979	4.41	7.25	83.57	39.11	22,190
Fujian 福建	9	21	7,320	479	7.01	9.86	343.13	28.84	6,827
Jiangxi 江西	26	107	4,060	-106	-1.47	-10.88	37.92	86.54	7,218
Shandong 山東	131	279	24,449	691	2.30	8.33	87.66	72.44	30,098
Central-South 中南	224	146	10,039	345	2.12	6.38	68.87	66.82	16,286
Henan 河南	108	136	8,453	499	4.25	17.26	62.14	75.35	11,717
Hubei 湖北	33	221	20,090	1,287	3.97	8.99	91.01	55.85	32,407
Hunan 湖南	45	151	8,645	-34	-0.19	-0.47	57.07	59.25	17,518
Guangdong 廣東	24	85	6,923	-417	-4.75	-23.64	81.72	79.92	8,776
Guangxi 廣西	13	113	7,525	-589	-3.30	-19.36	66.87	82.96	17,866
Hainan 海南	1	360	19,760	60	0.07	0.26	54.89	71.91	81,940
Southwest 西南	56	244	11,573	-437	-1.76	-7.62	47.38	76.93	24,883
Chongqing 重慶	18	202	10,646	-524	-2.33	-16.12	52.62	85.52	22,431
Sichuan 四川	24	103	6,114	-72	-0.72	-3.39	59.19	78.79	10,048
Guizhou 貴州	9	709	29,621	109	0.15	0.43	41.77	64.47	70,791
Yunnan 雲南	5	235	8,516	-2,852	-12.97	97.34	36.24	113.32	21,994
Tibet 西藏									
Northwest 西北	58	226	15,358	78	0.30	0.89	68.02	66.31	25,855
Shaanxi 陝西	27	173	11,993	-490	-2.14	-11.34	69.37	81.10	22,848
Gansu 甘肅	9	547	40,392	889	1.64	3.14	73.80	47.77	54,201
Qinghai 青海	5	58	950	-68	-2.06	20.00	16.49	110.30	3,300
Ningxia 寧夏	4	440	28,660	1,725	2.87	9.08	65.21	68.41	60,150
Xinjiang 新疆	13	112	6,465	244	2.30	5.32	57.77	56.78	10,600

2651: Industrial Organic Chemical 有機化工原料製造業

Year 年份	Number of firms 企業個數	Rate of change 每年變化 (%)	Number of employees 職工人數 (人)	Rate of change 每年變化 (%)	Total revenue (mil. RMB) 總銷售收入 (百萬元)	Rate of change 每年變化 (%)	Total profit (mil. RMB) 總利潤 (百萬元)	Rate of change 每年變化 (%)
1993	1,166		458,047		27,294		761	
1994	1,300	11.49%	437,620	-4.46%	36,993	35.53%	951	24.94%
1995	1,389	6.85%	426,571	-2.53%	46,755	26.39%	1,775	86.70%
1996	1,351	-2.74%	385,759	-9.57%	44,984	-3.79%	1,015	-42.82%

3 Major products* 3種主要產品 *	Output 產量	Sales volume 銷售量	Unit 單位
a) Acetaldehyde 乙醛	164,263	164,263	ton 噸
b) Glacial Acetic Acid 冰醋酸	283,899	187,374	ton 噸
c) Ethylene Glycol 乙二醇	226,057	79,120	ton 噸

Top 10 firms by revenue (year founded) 收入排名前10家企業 (創辦年份)	City 城市	Province 省	Telephone / fax 電話 / 傳真	Number of employees 職工人數	Ownership 產業所有權	Revenue ('000 RMB) 銷售收入 (千元)	Profit ('000 RMB) (rank) 利潤 (千元) (排名)	Total assets ('000 RMB) 總資產 (千元)	Major products 主要產品
Ji Hua Group Co. 吉化集團公司(1957)	Jilin 吉林市	Jilin 吉林省	(0432)3038752 (0432)3038752	63,722	State-owned 國有	10,543,396	110494(2)	32,190,066	a,b,c
Sinopec Yangzi Petrochenical Corp. 揚子石油化工公司(1986)	Nanjing 南京市	Jiangsu 江蘇省	(025)7782946 (025)7791214	19,751	State-owned 國有	8,433,451	551877(1)	15,112,296	a,b,c
Beijing Chemical Industry Group Co. 北京化學工業集團有限責任公司(1991)	Beijing 北京市	Beijing 北京市	(010)63022806 (010)63012342	19,794	State-owned 國有	4,518,899	91616(3)	6,546,003	b,c
Shanghai Tai Ping Yang Chemical (Group) Co. Ltd. 上海太平洋化工(集團)有限公司(1956)	Shanghai 上海市	Shanghai 上海市	(021)64343649 (021)64345588	16,186	State-owned 國有	2,212,055	-22343(776)	5,084,917	b
Shanghai Gao Qiao Petrochemical Acrylic Acid Factory 上海高橋石化丙烯酸廠(1994)	Shanghai 上海市	Shanghai 上海市	(021)58611739 (021)58612283	652	State-owned 國有	390,505	1810(91)	1,138,037	o
Ji'nan Petrochemical (Group) Co. Ltd. 濟南石化(集團)股份有限公司(1959)	Ji'nan 濟南市	Shandong 山東省	(0531)8988401 (0531)8985196	1,870	Joint stock 股份制	343,019	1281(114)	208,839	o
Lanzhou San Ye Co. 蘭州三葉公司(1990)	Lanzhou 蘭州市	Gansu 甘肅省	(0931)7558994 (0931)7557631	5,114	Collectively-owned 集體	318,935	6602(29)	436,692	o
Shandong Kui Xing Chemical Company 山東魁星化工公司(1958)	Tai'an 泰安市	Shandong 山東省	(0538)5811500	3,194	State-owned 國有	318,321	508(213)	572,775	o
Sishan City No.2 Organic Plant 錫山市有機化二廠(1987)	Wuxi 無錫市	Jiangsu 江蘇省	(0510)8781931 (0510)8781931	500	Collectively-owned 集體	280,030	25580(6)	51,260	o
Guizhou Organic Chemical General Plant 貴州有機化工總廠(1971)	Guiyang 貴陽市	Guizhou 貴州省	(0851)2561328 (0851)2561222	5,894	State-owned 國有	260,737	616(190)	625,381	a,b

Top 10 Cities by Production Output 產出排名前10位城市	Province 省	Market share 市場份額	Number of firms 企業個數
Beijing 北京市	Beijing 北京市	19.07%	26
Nanjing 南京市	Jiangsu 江蘇省	8.14%	45
Shanghai 上海市	Shanghai 上海市	5.33%	63
Suzhou 蘇州市	Jiangsu 江蘇省	4.50%	69
Tianjin 天津市	Tianjin 天津市	4.33%	46
Wuxi 無錫市	Jiangsu 江蘇省	3.33%	50
Shijiazhuang 石家莊市	Hebei 河北省	2.79%	50
Changzhou 常州市	Jiangsu 江蘇省	2.59%	54
Jilin 吉林市	Jilin 吉林省	2.21%	19
Taizhou 臺州市	Zhejiang 浙江省	2.11%	42

10 Major Wholesalers 10家主要批發商	City 城市	Province 省	Telephone / Fax 電話 / 傳真
Changzhou Hardware Alternating-current Appliance and Chemical Wholesale General Company 常州五金交電化工批發總公司	Changzhou 常州市	Jiangsu 江蘇省	(0519)6609929 (0519)6609925
Suzhou Hardware & Alternating Electricity Co. Ltd. 蘇州五金交電股份有限公司	Suzhou 蘇州市	Jiangsu 江蘇省	(0512)5239572 (0512)5213248
Tianjin Foreign Trade General Company 天津市對外貿易總公司	Tianjin 天津市	Tianjin 天津市	(022)23310922
Chongqing International Trade Center 重慶國際貿易中心	Chongqing 重慶市	Chongqing 重慶市	(023)67853232 (023)67850402
China Chemical Plastics Co. Ltd. 中化塑料有限公司	Beijing 北京市	Beijing 北京市	(010)68569863 (010)68569041
Ningbo Hualian Group Co. Ltd. 寧波華聯集團股份有限公司	Ningbo 寧波市	Zhejiang 浙江省	(0574)7367626 (0574)7367652
Xiamen Kaiyuan Wei Wei Electromechanical Building Materials Marketing Dept. 廈門市開元區威威機電建材經營部	Xiamen 廈門市	Fujian 福建省	(0592)2071044
Rudong Industry Product General Company 如東縣工業品總公司	Nantong 南通市	Jiangsu 江蘇省	(0513)4516110 (0513)4516110
Fujian Fu Ri Group Company 福建福日集團公司	Fuzhou 福州市	Fujian 福建省	(0591)3269325 (0591)3270426
Guangdong Hardware & Alternating Electrical Co. 廣東省五金交電公司	Guangzhou 廣州市	Guangdong 廣東省	(020)81884078 (020)81861287

*Also include sales by firms outside this industry.包括本行業以外廠家的銷售。"o" stands for "others". "o" 代表 "其他產品"。

2652: Paint 塗料製造業

The industry accounts for 0.375% of the total revenue of China's industrial sector in 1996. The revenue growth rate of the industry is 11.2% from 1995, as compared to the growth rate of China's industrial sector, 9.51%. The rate of return on asset is 3.99%. 71.74% of all firms in the industry made a profit while 21.49% had negative returns. The top province in terms of the industry's revenue is Shanghai, accounting for 19.96% of the total revenue.
本行業在1996年佔全行業總產值0.375%，行業年增長率為11.2%（全國工業年增長率9.51%）。行業的資產回報率3.99%，71.74%的企業盈利，21.49%的企業虧損。銷售收入最高的省份為上海市，佔本行業的19.96%。

	Total number of firms 企業總數	Total number of employees 職工總數	Total revenue (mil. RMB) 總銷售收入（百萬元）	Total profit (mil. RMB) 總利潤（百萬元）	Return on assets 資產利潤率 (%)	Return on equity 權益利潤率 (%)	Labour productivity ('000 RMB / worker) 勞動生產率（千元/人）	Debts / assets 資產負債率 (%)	Total assets (mil. RMB) 總資產（百萬元）
Industry Overall 行業總體	3,005	188,894	21,740	1,000	3.99	10.25	115.09	61.06	25,052

	Number of firms 企業個數	Average number of employees 平均職工人數	Average revenue ('000 RMB) 平均銷售收入（千元）	Average profit ('000 RMB) 平均利潤（千元）	Return on assets 資產利潤率 (%)	Return on equity 權益利潤率 (%)	Labour productivity ('000 RMB / worker) 勞動生產率（千元/人）	Average debts / assets 平均資產負債率(%)	Average Total assets ('000 RMB) 平均總資產（千元）
By ownership 產業所有權									
State-owned 國有	340	153	16,565	-21	-0.09	-0.25	108.55	64.29	23,171
Collectively-owned 集體	2,327	48	4,414	264	6.68	17.97	92.87	62.81	3,951
Privately-owned 私有	14	38	2,843	-12	-0.28	-1.35	73.99	79.62	4,421
Domestic JVs 聯營	36	56	9,531	729	7.23	17.11	170.70	57.72	10,081
Joint stock 股份制	42	314	40,802	2,533	4.64	10.13	130.11	54.21	54,589
Foreign-funded 外資	103	59	19,316	790	3.02	7.31	328.58	58.73	26,188
Overseas Chinese-funded 港澳台資	139	51	12,477	1,285	7.02	15.10	242.50	53.47	18,289
By size 規模									
Large 大型	15	1,797	352,044	32,391	8.06	17.35	195.92	53.52	401,721
Medium 中型	56	601	84,321	1,138	1.13	3.05	140.28	62.92	100,484
Small 小型	2,880	45	4,075	156	3.36	9.26	91.47	63.68	4,652
By regional distribution 地區分布									
Central-North 華北	503	57	5,342	179	2.56	7.27	94.51	64.81	7,006
Beijing 北京	191	38	3,041	-161	-2.83	-7.79	81.08	63.70	5,678
Tianjin 天津	61	104	15,198	1,247	6.04	14.41	145.61	58.08	20,628
Hebei 河北	166	64	6,122	266	4.62	16.54	95.47	72.09	5,752
Shanxi 山西	39	44	1,418	-16	-0.84	-3.00	32.21	72.00	1,925
Inner Mongolia 內蒙	46	55	2,334	29	0.89	4.31	42.32	79.25	3,282
Northeast 東北	486	61	2,611	-33	-0.68	-2.43	42.91	72.12	4,811
Liaoning 遼寧	240	59	2,519	56	1.39	4.16	42.37	66.57	4,035
Jilin 吉林	110	53	2,398	-166	-2.54	-9.68	44.88	73.72	6,527
Heilongjiang 黑龍江	136	69	2,945	-81	-1.69	-7.89	42.50	78.61	4,793
Central East 華東	958	72	11,342	678	5.96	14.46	157.71	58.76	11,365
Shanghai 上海	112	113	38,750	4,244	10.05	20.23	343.19	50.33	42,227
Jiangsu 江蘇	236	100	12,318	255	2.48	6.79	123.65	63.54	10,310
Zhejiang 浙江	135	50	9,099	272	3.36	7.65	181.49	56.06	8,078
Anhui 安徽	130	54	4,901	113	2.83	12.16	91.24	76.75	3,999
Fujian 福建	112	32	2,687	93	2.70	5.69	85.28	52.56	3,445
Jiangxi 江西	75	46	2,594	88	1.99	7.14	56.68	72.11	4,422
Shandong 山東	158	76	7,960	287	3.25	11.98	104.57	72.88	8,847
Central-South 中南	676	63	7,622	324	3.54	8.75	121.69	59.55	9,151
Henan 河南	158	39	2,879	70	2.49	8.11	73.68	69.27	2,804
Hubei 湖北	150	73	6,044	171	2.38	5.12	82.24	53.37	7,213
Hunan 湖南	114	68	4,677	54	1.05	2.37	68.55	55.64	5,130
Guangdong 廣東	184	70	15,168	929	4.76	12.08	218.13	60.55	19,492
Guangxi 廣西	60	68	6,805	78	1.20	3.28	99.94	63.51	6,551
Hainan 海南	10	49	5,888	30	0.31	0.68	120.41	54.51	9,697
Southwest 西南	199	46	5,339	185	3.19	8.19	115.03	61.00	5,789
Chongqing 重慶	43	73	9,187	607	4.71	10.22	125.58	53.96	12,905
Sichuan 四川	107	38	4,842	188	5.88	16.00	128.16	63.23	3,194
Guizhou 貴州	35	29	1,557	-241	-7.78	-97.46	53.53	92.02	3,101
Yunnan 雲南	14	73	6,672	-82	-0.80	-1.98	91.04	59.64	10,276
Tibet 西藏									
Northwest 西北	183	57	3,842	113	2.16	4.93	67.48	56.28	5,264
Shaanxi 陝西	79	49	2,287	13	0.42	1.26	47.15	66.88	3,116
Gansu 甘肅	47	69	6,581	464	5.19	9.47	94.99	45.23	8,945
Qinghai 青海	6	47	1,900	-22	-0.85	-4.47	40.86	81.02	2,547
Ningxia 寧夏	12	48	906	-270	-10.25	-53.03	18.94	80.65	2,635
Xinjiang 新疆	39	64	4,895	33	0.52	1.30	77.00	59.85	6,405

2652: Paint 塗料製造業

Year 年份	Number of firms 企業個數	Rate of change 每年變化 (%)	Number of employees 職工人數 (人)	Rate of change 每年變化 (%)	Total revenue (mil. RMB) 總銷售收入 (百萬元)	Rate of change 每年變化 (%)	Total profit (mil. RMB) 總利潤 (百萬元)	Rate of change 每年變化 (%)
1993	2,716		202,319		13,158		463	
1994	3,018	11.12%	210,100	3.85%	15,569	18.32%	707	52.58%
1995	3,118	3.31%	197,241	-6.12%	19,556	25.61%	724	2.35%
1996	3,005	-3.62%	188,894	-4.23%	21,740	11.17%	1,000	38.21%

3 Major products* 3 種主要產品 *	Output 產量	Sales volume 銷售量	Unit 單位
a) Amino Resin Lacquer 氨基樹脂漆類	102,871	96,699	ton 噸
b) Polyurethane Lacquer 聚氨基甲酸脂漆類	103,729	106,841	ton 噸
c) Alkyd Resin Lacquer 醇酸樹脂漆類	338,726	335,339	ton 噸

Top 10 firms by revenue (year founded) 收入排名前 10 家企業 (創辦年份)	City 城市	Province 省	Telephone / fax 電話 / 傳真	Number of employees 職工人數	Ownership 產業所有權	Revenue ('000 RMB) 銷售收入 (千元)	Profit ('000 RMB) (rank) 利潤 (千元) (排名)	Total assets ('000 RMB) 總資產 (千元)	Major products 主要產品
Shanghai Hua Sheng Chemical Industry Co. 上海華生化工公司(1982)	Shanghai 上海市	Shanghai 上海市	(021)63215693 (021)63216210	686	Collectively-owned 集體	1,224,376	354655(1)	913,580	a,b,c
Shanghai Hui Li Group Co. 上海匯麗集團公司(1973)	Shanghai 上海市	Shanghai 上海市	(021)58113390 (021)58113390	1,906	State-owned 國有	1,094,053	16501(11)	1,389,536	a
Shanghai Coatings Co. Ltd. 上海塗料有限公司(1996)	Shanghai 上海市	Shanghai 上海市	(021)62710407 (021)62710400	2,632	State-owned 國有	566,348	3350(58)	515,269	a,b,c
Chongqing San Xia Paint Co. Ltd. 重慶三峽油漆股份有限公司	Chongqing 重慶市	Chongqing 重慶市	(023)68825420 (023)68820710	1,719	Joint stock 股份制	381,827	18735(9)	347,886	a,b,c
Tianjin Dengta Coatings Co. Ltd. 天津燈塔塗料股份有限公司(1916)	Tianjin 天津市	Tianjin 天津市	(022)26340772 (022)26340776	2,515	Joint stock 股份制	372,933	24093(7)	519,793	a,b,c
Hempel-hai Hong Coatings (Shenzhen) Co. Ltd. 海虹老人牌塗料(深圳)有限公司(1992)	Shenzhen 深圳市	Guangdong 廣東省	(0755)6680688 (0755)6687288	162	Overseas Chinese-funded 港澳台資	336,283	62164(2)	403,706	c
Bu Nei Men Tai Gu Paint (China) Co. Ltd. 卜內門太古漆油(中國)有限公司(1992)	Guangzhou 廣州市	Guangdong 廣東省	(020)82217755 (020)82217745	310	Foreign-funded 外資	333,559	38803(4)	450,106	o
Shanghai International Paint Co. Ltd. 上海國際油漆有限公司(1990)	Shanghai 上海市	Shanghai 上海市	(021)58993845 (021)58990360	167	Foreign-funded 外資	330,410	48912(3)	236,508	b,c
Guangzhou Guangqi Paint Chemical Industrial Co. Ltd. 廣州廣漆化工實業有限公司(1933)	Guangzhou 廣州市	Guangdong 廣東省	(020)81891210 (020)81891207	1,081	State-owned 國有	299,434	3249(61)	216,703	a,b,c
Jiangsu San Mu Group Company 江蘇三木集團公司(1996)	Wuxi 無錫市	Jiangsu 江蘇省	(0510)7231685	685	Collectively-owned 集體	285,070	15370(12)	105,340	o

Top 10 Cities by Production Output 產出排名前 10 位城市	Province 省	Market share 市場份額	Number of firms 企業個數
Nanjing 南京市	Jiangsu 江蘇省	20.65%	44
Shanghai 上海市	Shanghai 上海市	17.57%	208
Guangzhou 廣州市	Guangdong 廣東省	4.87%	57
Tianjin 天津市	Tianjin 天津市	3.75%	76
Suzhou 蘇州市	Jiangsu 江蘇省	2.63%	100
Weifang 濰坊市	Shandong 山東省	2.16%	23
Wuxi 無錫市	Jiangsu 江蘇省	2.07%	89
Chongqing 重慶市	Chongqing 重慶市	2.06%	75
Hangzhou 杭州市	Zhejiang 浙江省	1.76%	47
Foshan 佛山市	Guangdong 廣東省	1.76%	21

10 Major Wholesalers 10 家主要批發商	City 城市	Province 省	Telephone / Fax 電話 / 傳真
Zhong Hua Singbo Import & Export Company 中化寧波進出口公司	Ningbo 寧波市	Zhejiang 浙江省	(0574)7346764 (0574)7366775
China Chemical Supply & Marketing Hua Nan Company 中國化工供銷華南公司	Guangzhou 廣州市	Guangdong 廣東省	(020)87654477 (020)87784414
China Agriculture Means of Production Chengdu Company 中國農業生產資料成都公司	Chengdu 成都市	Sichuan 四川省	(028)3333909 (028)3331202
Shanxi Agriculture Means of Production Company 山西省農業生產資料公司	Taiyuan 太原市	Shanxi 山西省	(0351)4040255 (0351)4040231
Beijing Chemical Light Industry General Company 北京市化工輕工總公司	Beijing 北京市	Beijing 北京市	(010)64224837 (010)64219301
Beijing Chemical Industry Group Company Supply & Marketing Company 北京化學工業集團公司供銷公司	Beijing 北京市	Beijing 北京市	(010)67714610 (010)67714058
Zhong Hua Jiangsu Import & Export Company 中化江蘇進出口公司	Nanjing 南京市	Jiangsu 江蘇省	(025)2258718 (025)2257789
Yunnan Chemical Import & Export Company 雲南省化工進出口公司	Kunming 昆明市	Yunnan 雲南省	(0871)3314002 (0871)3314931
Fujian Jiu Zhou Group Co. Ltd. 福建九州集團股份有限公司	Xiamen 廈門市	Fujian 福建省	(0592)5055818 (0592)5052033
China Chemical Industry Commission Agent Hua Dong Co. 中國化工供銷華東公司	Shanghai 上海市	Shanghai 上海市	(021)62514123

*Also include sales by firms outside this industry.包括本行業以外廠家的銷售。"o" stands for "others". "o" 代表 "其他產品"。

2653: Printing Ink 油墨製造業

The industry accounts for 0.044% of the total revenue of China's industrial sector in 1996. The revenue growth rate of the industry is 13.5% from 1995, as compared to the growth rate of China's industrial sector, 9.51%. The rate of return on asset is 1.96%. 67.92% of all firms in the industry made a profit while 28.05% had negative returns. The top province in terms of the industry's revenue is Guangdong, accounting for 22.01% of the total revenue.
本行業在1996年佔全行業總產值0.044%，行業年增長率為13.5%（全國工業年增長率9.51%）。行業的資產回報率1.96%，67.92%的企業盈利，28.05%的企業虧損。銷售收入最高的省份為廣東省，佔本行業的22.01%。

	Total number of firms 企業總數	Total number of employees 職工總數	Total revenue (mil. RMB) 總銷售收入（百萬元）	Total profit (mil. RMB) 總利潤（百萬元）	Return on assets 資產利潤率 (%)	Return on equity 權益利潤率 (%)	Labour productivity ('000 RMB / worker) 勞動生產率（千元/人）	Debts / assets 資產負債率 (%)	Total assets (mil. RMB) 總資產（百萬元）
Industry Overall 行業總體	254	21,408	2,575	81	1.96	4.13	120.28	52.47	4,130

	Number of firms 企業個數	Average number of employees 平均職工人數	Average revenue ('000 RMB) 平均銷售收入（千元）	Average profit ('000 RMB) 平均利潤（千元）	Return on assets 資產利潤率 (%)	Return on equity 權益利潤率 (%)	Labour productivity ('000 RMB / worker) 勞動生產率（千元/人）	Average debts / assets 平均資產負債率(%)	Average Total assets ('000 RMB) 平均總資產（千元）
By ownership 產業所有權									
State-owned 國有	39	191	10,718	51	0.21	0.82	56.11	74.04	24,103
Collectively-owned 集體	162	46	3,311	86	2.22	5.81	71.75	61.87	3,889
Privately-owned 私有									
Domestic JVs 聯營	6	158	26,788	891	3.67	6.55	169.73	43.91	24,243
Joint stock 股份制	10	126	33,052	2,072	2.87	4.70	262.73	38.92	72,215
Foreign-funded 外資	19	225	54,383	2,270	3.08	5.54	242.04	44.45	73,796
Overseas Chinese-funded 港澳台資	17	33	5,669	-246	-1.44	-2.36	171.80	38.93	17,067
By size 規模									
Large 大型	4	801	199,675	439	0.15	0.28	249.20	46.38	287,593
Medium 中型	6	662	81,806	5,892	5.58	14.66	123.67	61.95	105,637
Small 小型	239	60	5,380	184	1.87	3.97	89.26	52.89	9,814
By regional distribution 地區分布									
Central-North 華北	37	123	13,264	723	2.64	3.51	107.93	24.90	27,410
Beijing 北京	11	44	2,205	64	1.06	2.22	49.82	52.32	6,025
Tianjin 天津	13	229	25,205	1,129	1.80	2.23	109.95	19.35	62,777
Hebei 河北	9	60	6,223	504	11.99	31.46	103.72	61.89	4,207
Shanxi 山西	2	228	40,930	4,220	9.79	13.25	179.91	26.12	43,120
Inner Mongolia 內蒙	2	43	485	-810	-21.04	25.84	11.41	181.56	3,850
Northeast 東北	27	52	3,605	146	3.25	18.21	69.73	82.18	4,503
Liaoning 遼寧	14	36	1,976	121	4.63	11.37	55.21	59.29	2,607
Jilin 吉林	5	85	1,512	-60	-0.54	-3.32	17.70	83.88	11,214
Heilongjiang 黑龍江	8	59	7,765	320	8.82	-115.32	132.74	107.69	3,626
Central East 華東	105	77	11,140	333	2.34	4.96	144.61	52.75	14,225
Shanghai 上海	10	203	50,218	856	1.11	2.04	247.26	45.82	77,432
Jiangsu 江蘇	23	61	5,360	84	2.78	6.63	87.75	58.16	3,038
Zhejiang 浙江	22	75	13,854	796	5.31	11.27	183.94	52.85	14,976
Anhui 安徽	8	68	5,263	128	2.88	9.77	77.96	70.53	4,429
Fujian 福建	17	37	7,009	186	2.12	5.46	187.34	61.25	8,813
Jiangxi 江西	9	87	2,483	93	1.95	20.79	28.62	90.62	4,787
Shandong 山東	16	65	3,493	121	2.11	6.65	53.78	68.32	5,724
Central-South 中南	66	51	9,599	223	1.70	5.13	190.08	66.81	13,097
Henan 河南	23	31	1,319	11	0.48	1.87	42.36	74.31	2,260
Hubei 湖北	4	111	1,500	-28	-0.37	-1.95	13.57	80.89	7,393
Hunan 湖南	12	61	2,477	-39	-1.18	-2.28	40.66	48.44	3,333
Guangdong 廣東	23	62	24,640	655	2.04	6.10	398.54	66.61	32,175
Guangxi 廣西	4	6	190	-3	-0.35	-4.76	34.55	92.58	708
Hainan 海南									
Southwest 西南	12	157	8,856	28	0.07	0.20	56.53	63.96	37,967
Chongqing 重慶	3	319	15,868	139	0.32	0.97	49.73	66.88	43,361
Sichuan 四川	6	85	4,860	-132	-0.58	-2.77	57.30	78.94	22,585
Guizhou 貴州	1	24	350				14.58	96.77	620
Yunnan 雲南	2	163	13,075	15	0.02	0.03	80.46	51.04	91,860
Tibet 西藏									
Northwest 西北	7	309	10,990	57	0.22	1.76	35.57	87.42	25,784
Shaanxi 陝西	3	24	450	-173	-10.28	25.00	19.01	141.11	1,687
Gansu 甘肅	2	1,033	37,650	520	0.60	4.24	36.45	85.98	87,365
Qinghai 青海									
Ningxia 寧夏									
Xinjiang 新疆	2	13	140	-60	-17.14	-41.38	10.77	58.57	350

2653: Printing Ink 油墨製造業

Year 年份	Number of firms 企業個數	Rate of change 每年變化 (%)	Number of employees 職工人數 (人)	Rate of change 每年變化 (%)	Total revenue (mil. RMB) 總銷售收入 (百萬元)	Rate of change 每年變化 (%)	Total profit (mil. RMB) 總利潤 (百萬元)	Rate of change 每年變化 (%)
1993	185		20,964		1,306		42	
1994	221	19.46%	17,470	-16.67%	1,753	34.14%	29	-30.74%
1995	246	11.31%	20,762	18.84%	2,269	29.46%	45	56.02%
1996	254	3.25%	21,408	3.11%	2,575	13.49%	81	78.65%

3 Major products* 3 種主要產品 *	Output 產量	Sales volume 銷售量	Unit 單位
a) Ink 油墨	129,832	122,042	ton 噸
b) Alkyd Resin Lacquer 醇酸樹脂漆類	4,389	4,345	ton 噸

Top 10 firms by revenue (year founded) 收入排名前 10 家企業 (創辦年份)	City 城市	Province 省	Telephone / fax 電話 / 傳真	Number of employees 職工人數	Ownership 產業所有權	Revenue ('000 RMB) 銷售收入 (千元)	Profit ('000 RMB) (rank) 利潤 (千元) (排名)	Total assets ('000 RMB) 總資產 (千元)	Major products 主要產品
Shanghai Kele-sicap Printing Ink Chemical Co. Ltd. 上海克勒錫克拜油墨化工有限公司(1994)	Shanghai 上海市	Shanghai 上海市	(021)62506860 (021)62505508	754	Foreign-funded 外資	247,723	-9136(124)	394,949	a
Tianjin Toyo Printing Ink Co. Ltd. 天津東洋油墨有限公司(1993)	Tianjin 天津市	Tianjin 天津市	(022)27472463 (022)27472463	1,674	Foreign-funded 外資	185,837	5112(9)	537,347	a
Hang Hua Printing Ink Chemical Co. Ltd. 杭華油墨化學有限公司(1988)	Hangzhou 杭州市	Zhejiang 浙江省	(0571)8092399 (0571)8091144	404	Foreign-funded 外資	175,465	14970(1)	155,412	a
Shenzhen --dic Co. Ltd. 深圳深日油墨有限公司(1987)	Shenzhen 深圳市	Guangdong 廣東省	(0755)6640294 (0755)6640133	108	Foreign-funded 外資	125,389	7135(7)	117,515	a
Shanghai Min Xing Company 上海閔星公司(1995)	Shanghai 上海市	Shanghai 上海市	(021)11111111	50	Collectively-owned 集體	122,100	10421(2)	17,719	o
Shunde Jin Long Jing Da Printing Ink Co. Ltd. 順德金龍景達油墨有限公司(1985)	Foshan 佛山市	Guangdong 廣東省	(0757)2291101 (0757)2291201	297	Joint stock 股份制	116,491	-160(110)	138,222	a,b
Shanghai Hui Bo Industrial General Company 上海會波實業總公司(1994)	Shanghai 上海市	Shanghai 上海市	(021)57612166 (021)57611258	637	Domestic JVs 聯營	106,816	4797(10)	158,658	o
Jiang Retail Sales Printing Ink Chemical Co. Ltd. 江門市油墨化工有限公司(1976)	Jiangmen 江門市	Guangdong 廣東省	(0750)3532618 (0750)3558265	183	Foreign-funded 外資	93,785	7571(6)	185,406	a
Shanghai Xiang Le Tian Cun Electrochemical Industrial Co. Ltd. 上海祥樂田村電化工業有限公司(1994)	Shanghai 上海市	Shanghai 上海市	(021)62717198 (021)62717200	71	Foreign-funded 外資	92,253	7599(5)	76,176	o
Shanghai Printing Ink Si Lian Chemical Factory 上海油墨泗聯化工廠(1996)	Shanghai 上海市	Shanghai 上海市	(021)57610282 (021)57611198	419	Domestic JVs 聯營	81,180	2620(13)	69,403	a

Top 10 Cities by Production Output 產出排名前 10 位城市	Province 省	Market share 市場份額	Number of firms 企業個數
Shanghai 上海市	Shanghai 上海市	18.77%	22
Tianjin 天津市	Tianjin 天津市	11.49%	14
Hangzhou 杭州市	Zhejiang 浙江省	8.64%	6
Foshan 佛山市	Guangdong 廣東省	5.95%	3
Guangzhou 廣州市	Guangdong 廣東省	4.45%	10
Jiangmen 江門市	Guangdong 廣東省	4.08%	2
Shenzhen 深圳市	Guangdong 廣東省	3.82%	4
Taiyuan 太原市	Shanxi 山西省	3.68%	4
Chengdu 成都市	Sichuan 四川省	3.27%	6
Tianshui 天水市	Gansu 甘肅省	3.19%	2

10 Major Wholesalers 10 家主要批發商	City 城市	Province 省	Telephone / Fax 電話 / 傳真
Zhong Hua Singbo Import & Export Company 中化寧波進出口公司	Ningbo 寧波市	Zhejiang 浙江省	(0574)7346764 (0574)7366775
China Chemical Supply & Marketing Hua Nan Company 中國化工供銷華南公司	Guangzhou 廣州市	Guangdong 廣東省	(020)87654477 (020)87784414
China Agriculture Means of Production Chengdu Company 中國農業生產資料成都公司	Chengdu 成都市	Sichuan 四川省	(028)3333909 (028)3331202
Shanxi Agriculture Means of Production Company 山西省農業生產資料公司	Taiyuan 太原市	Shanxi 山西省	(0351)4040255 (0351)4040231
Beijing Chemical Light Industry General Company 北京市化工輕工總公司	Beijing 北京市	Beijing 北京市	(010)64224837 (010)64219301
Beijing Chemical Industry Group Company Supply & Marketing Company 北京化學工業集團公司供銷公司	Beijing 北京市	Beijing 北京市	(010)67714610 (010)67714058
Zhong Hua Jiangsu Import & Export Company 中化江蘇進出口公司	Nanjing 南京市	Jiangsu 江蘇省	(025)2258718 (025)2257789
Yunnan Chemical Import & Export Company 雲南省化工進出口公司	Kunming 昆明市	Yunnan 雲南省	(0871)3314002 (0871)3314931
Fujian Jiu Zhou Group Co. Ltd. 福建九州集團股份有限公司	Xiamen 廈門市	Fujian 福建省	(0592)5055818 (0592)5052033
China Chemical Industry Commission Agent Hua Dong Co. 中國化工供銷華東公司	Shanghai 上海市	Shanghai 上海市	(021)62514123

*Also include sales by firms outside this industry.包括本行業以外廠家的銷售。"o" stands for "others". "o" 代表 "其他產品"。

2654: Pigment 顏料製造業

The industry accounts for 0.063% of the total revenue of China's industrial sector in 1996. The revenue growth rate of the industry is 9.0% from 1995, as compared to the growth rate of China's industrial sector, 9.51%. The rate of return on asset is 1.68%. 67.71% of all firms in the industry made a profit while 25.00% had negative returns. The top province in terms of the industry's revenue is Jiangsu, accounting for 20.68% of the total revenue.
本行業在1996年佔全行業總產值0.063%，行業年增長率為9.0%（全國工業年增長率9.51%）。行業的資產回報率1.68%，67.71%的企業盈利，25.00%的企業虧損。銷售收入最高的省份為江蘇省，佔本行業的20.68%。

	Total number of firms 企業總數	Total number of employees 職工總數	Total revenue (mil. RMB) 總銷售收入（百萬元）	Total profit (mil. RMB) 總利潤（百萬元）	Return on assets 資產利潤率 (%)	Return on equity 權益利潤率 (%)	Labour productivity ('000 RMB / worker) 勞動生產率（千元/人）	Debts / assets 資產負債率 (%)	Total assets (mil. RMB) 總資產（百萬元）
Industry Overall 行業總體	393	43,348	3,652	74	1.68	5.76	84.25	70.88	4,444

	Number of firms 企業個數	Average number of employees 平均職工人數	Average revenue ('000 RMB) 平均銷售收入（千元）	Average profit ('000 RMB) 平均利潤（千元）	Return on assets 資產利潤率 (%)	Return on equity 權益利潤率 (%)	Labour productivity ('000 RMB / worker) 勞動生產率（千元/人）	Average debts / assets 平均資產負債率(%)	Average Total assets ('000 RMB) 平均總資產（千元）
By ownership 產業所有權									
State-owned 國有	56	313	18,161	-339	-1.03	-4.24	58.01	75.82	33,089
Collectively-owned 集體	279	74	7,316	286	4.33	15.21	98.83	71.54	6,608
Privately-owned 私有	1	28	1,376	-422	-25.73	87.85	49.13	129.29	1,638
Domestic JVs 聯營	5	48	5,749	331	3.90	10.61	118.79	63.20	8,471
Joint stock 股份制	4	299	28,768	510	1.19	3.67	96.13	67.51	42,721
Foreign-funded 外資	20	85	8,815	101	0.90	1.73	103.46	48.22	11,230
Overseas Chinese-funded 港澳台資	27	74	10,109	293	2.57	5.89	137.01	56.38	11,426
By size 規模									
Large 大型	1	555	30,164	3	0.00	0.01	54.35	80.41	119,594
Medium 中型	14	685	70,469	981	0.95	2.88	102.87	67.01	103,114
Small 小型	367	88	7,183	164	2.09	7.59	81.28	72.43	7,851
By regional distribution 地區分布									
Central-North 華北	77	82	6,885	361	4.89	22.86	83.84	78.60	7,379
Beijing 北京	5	25	2,144	38	1.80	4.73	85.08	61.84	2,112
Tianjin 天津	14	108	5,102	231	4.22	18.66	47.37	77.39	5,466
Hebei 河北	50	87	8,774	483	5.18	25.27	100.30	79.52	9,321
Shanxi 山西	4	32	1,910	143	7.19	11.56	59.22	37.83	1,983
Inner Mongolia 內蒙	4	47	415	-83	-4.67	220.00	8.92	102.12	1,768
Northeast 東北	27	122	3,958	-22	-0.47	-3.01	32.55	84.30	4,623
Liaoning 遼寧	21	149	4,805	-40	-0.72	-4.64	32.27	84.53	5,638
Jilin 吉林	1	12						66.67	540
Heilongjiang 黑龍江	5	29	1,192	52	4.42	23.42	41.39	81.12	1,176
Central East 華東	151	115	11,239	154	1.12	3.84	98.03	70.73	13,721
Shanghai 上海	17	159	11,809	-215	-0.76	-2.00	74.21	61.98	28,296
Jiangsu 江蘇	44	153	17,163	305	1.87	7.89	111.99	76.36	16,369
Zhejiang 浙江	33	81	10,316	138	1.37	4.26	127.98	67.77	10,041
Anhui 安徽	14	53	3,638	5	0.15	0.74	69.01	80.38	3,430
Fujian 福建	2	32	1,690	-235	-7.09	-13.70	52.81	48.27	3,315
Jiangxi 江西	10	44	3,392	162	5.21	115.71	76.57	95.53	3,111
Shandong 山東	31	128	10,080	248	1.70	5.83	78.93	70.86	14,627
Central-South 中南	106	126	11,352	282	2.07	5.86	90.13	64.74	13,655
Henan 河南	20	160	16,645	1,550	9.47	22.93	104.26	58.71	16,366
Hubei 湖北	15	124	7,553	70	0.90	5.61	61.08	83.90	7,753
Hunan 湖南	33	100	7,071	70	1.07	4.70	70.86	77.22	6,541
Guangdong 廣東	28	117	14,449	79	0.35	0.86	123.95	59.67	22,627
Guangxi 廣西	10	175	11,926	-663	-4.29	-12.78	68.30	66.41	15,445
Hainan 海南									
Southwest 西南	20	95	4,756	-254	-3.37	-17.25	49.85	80.45	7,526
Chongqing 重慶	5	291	10,268	-2,497	-11.95	-48.16	35.27	75.19	20,899
Sichuan 四川	11	35	2,935	578	18.91	243.72	82.88	92.24	3,057
Guizhou 貴州	1	67	12,680				189.25	90.89	16,910
Yunnan 雲南	3	25	413	7	1.39	1.96	16.76	29.86	480
Tibet 西藏									
Northwest 西北	12	98	1,662	-68	-1.01	-12.58	17.03	91.97	6,778
Shaanxi 陝西	6	64	1,803				28.25	63.68	3,185
Gansu 甘肅	4	170	2,140	3	0.02	0.81	12.61	97.70	13,455
Qinghai 青海									
Ningxia 寧夏	1	59	560	-830	-16.34	50.00	9.49	132.48	5,080
Xinjiang 新疆	1	50						100.00	3,320

2654: Pigment 顏料製造業

Year 年份	Number of firms 企業個數	Rate of change 每年變化 (%)	Number of employees 職工人數 (人)	Rate of change 每年變化 (%)	Total revenue (mil. RMB) 總銷售收入 (百萬元)	Rate of change 每年變化 (%)	Total profit (mil. RMB) 總利潤 (百萬元)	Rate of change 每年變化 (%)
1993	256		38,023		1,682		38	
1994	317	23.83%	35,071	-7.76%	2,208	31.30%	2	-95.38%
1995	437	37.85%	46,417	32.35%	3,351	51.77%	45	2477.38%
1996	393	-10.07%	43,348	-6.61%	3,652	8.98%	74	65.67%

3 Major products* 3 種主要產品 *	Output 產量	Sales volume 銷售量	Unit 單位
a) Organic Pigment 有機顏料	37,820	59,377	ton 噸
b) Inorganic Pigment 無機顏料	343,197	319,173	ton 噸
c) Reactive Dye 活性染料	2,551	2,424	ton 噸

Top 10 firms by revenue (year founded) 收入排名前 10 家企業 (創辦年份)	City 城市	Province 省	Telephone / fax 電話 / 傳真	Number of employees 職工人數	Ownership 產業所有權	Revenue ('000 RMB) 銷售收入 (千元)	Profit ('000 RMB) (rank) 利潤 (千元) (排名)	Total assets ('000 RMB) 總資產 (千元)	Major products 主要產品
Guangzhou Hua Li Pigment Chemical Industrial Co. 廣州華立顏料化工實業公司(1959)	Guangzhou 廣州市	Guangdong 廣東省	(020)82232001 (020)82233382	1,402	State-owned 國有	198,555	1097(23)	253,550	b
Zhenjiang Titanium White Co. Ltd. 鎮江鈦白粉股份有限公司(1948)	Zhenjiang 鎮江市	Jiangsu 江蘇省	(0511)5271180 (0511)5273715	1,118	Joint stock 股份制	121,794	2057(13)	156,111	b
Yixing Fei Da Chemical Plant 宜興市菲達化工廠(1988)	Wuxi 無錫市	Jiangsu 江蘇省	(0510)7551818 (0510)7551187	220	Collectively-owned 集體	93,640	3540(3)	43,350	c
Shengxian Jin Shen Jointly-operated Pigment Chemical Factory 深州市津深聯營顏料化工廠(1986)	Hengshui 衡水市	Hebei 河北省	(0318)3319687	570	Collectively-owned 集體	76,025	6850(1)	64,500	a
Guangzhou Titanium White Plant 廣州鈦白粉廠(1959)	Guangzhou 廣州市	Guangdong 廣東省	(020)82270065 (020)82270569	408	State-owned 國有	61,404	-607(229)	149,749	b
Yixing Hong Ta Social Welfare Factory 宜興市紅塔社會福利廠(1978)	Wuxi 無錫市	Jiangsu 江蘇省	(0510)7533666 (0510)7533688	738	Collectively-owned 集體	56,170	14(165)	62,930	o
Shanghai Dyestuff Chemical No.12 Factory 上海染料化工十二廠(1946)	Shanghai 上海市	Shanghai 上海市	(021)65414976 (021)65129058	458	State-owned 國有	55,028	32(156)	33,520	a,b
Zibo Sai De Ke Ceramics Pigment Co. Ltd. 淄博賽德克陶瓷顏料有限公司(1995)	Zibo 淄博市	Shandong 山東省	(0533)5781171 (0533)5780377	156	Foreign-funded 外資	52,147	295(88)	83,515	b
Hangzhou Lily Chemical Co. Ltd. 杭州百合化工有限公司(1989)	Hangzhou 杭州市	Zhejiang 浙江省	(0571)2120664 (0571)2120680	200	Collectively-owned 集體	50,190	2487(7)	38,406	o
Doumen Dong Yang Chemical Co. Ltd. 斗門縣東洋化工有限公司(1993)	Zhuhai 珠海市	Guangdong 廣東省	(0756)5501452	82	Foreign-funded 外資	49,710	2033(14)	131,304	o

Top 10 Cities by Production Output 產出排名前 10 位城市	Province 省	Market share 市場份額	Number of firms 企業個數
Xinxiang 新鄉市	Henan 河南省	7.26%	4
Guangzhou 廣州市	Guangdong 廣東省	6.49%	11
Shanghai 上海市	Shanghai 上海市	6.47%	34
Yantai 煙台市	Shandong 山東省	6.07%	8
Wuxi 無錫市	Jiangsu 江蘇省	5.76%	13
Suzhou 蘇州市	Jiangsu 江蘇省	5.64%	23
Hangzhou 杭州市	Zhejiang 浙江省	5.23%	17
Hengshui 衡水市	Hebei 河北省	4.44%	14
Zibo 淄博市	Shandong 山東省	3.36%	13
Shijiazhuang 石家莊市	Hebei 河北省	2.95%	26

10 Major Wholesalers 10 家主要批發商	City 城市	Province 省	Telephone / Fax 電話 / 傳真
Zhong Hua Singbo Import & Export Company 中化寧波進出口公司	Ningbo 寧波市	Zhejiang 浙江省	(0574)7346764 (0574)7366775
China Chemical Supply & Marketing Hua Nan Company 中國化工供銷華南公司	Guangzhou 廣州市	Guangdong 廣東省	(020)87654477 (020)87784414
China Agriculture Means of Production Chengdu Company 中國農業生產資料成都公司	Chengdu 成都市	Sichuan 四川省	(028)3333909 (028)3331202
Shanxi Agriculture Means of Production Company 山西省農業生產資料公司	Taiyuan 太原市	Shanxi 山西省	(0351)4040255 (0351)4040231
Beijing Chemical Light Industry General Company 北京市化工輕工總公司	Beijing 北京市	Beijing 北京市	(010)64224837 (010)64219301
Beijing Chemical Industry Group Company Supply & Marketing Company 北京化學工業集團公司供銷公司	Beijing 北京市	Beijing 北京市	(010)67714610 (010)67714058
Zhong Hua Jiangsu Import & Export Company 中化江蘇進出口公司	Nanjing 南京市	Jiangsu 江蘇省	(025)2258718 (025)2257789
Yunnan Chemical Import & Export Company 雲南省化工進出口公司	Kunming 昆明市	Yunnan 雲南省	(0871)3314002 (0871)3314931
Fujian Jiu Zhou Group Co. Ltd. 福建九州集團股份有限公司	Xiamen 廈門市	Fujian 福建省	(0592)5055818 (0592)5052033
China Chemical Industry Commission Agent Hua Dong Co. 中國化工供銷華東公司	Shanghai 上海市	Shanghai 上海市	(021)62514123

*Also include sales by firms outside this industry.包括本行業以外廠家的銷售。"o" stands for "others". "o" 代表"其他產品"。

2655: Dyestuff 染料製造業

The industry accounts for 0.133% of the total revenue of China's industrial sector in 1996. The revenue growth rate of the industry is -8.8% from 1995, as compared to the growth rate of China's industrial sector, 9.51%. The rate of return on asset is -0.30%. 69.23% of all firms in the industry made a profit while 25.05% had negative returns. The top province in terms of the industry's revenue is Jiangsu, accounting for 24.59% of the total revenue.
本行業在1996年佔全行業總產值0.133%，行業年增長率為-8.8%（全國工業年增長率9.51%）。行業的資產回報率-0.30%，69.23%的企業盈利，25.05%的企業虧損。銷售收入最高的省份為江蘇省，佔本行業的24.59%。

	Total number of firms 企業總數	Total number of employees 職工總數	Total revenue (mil. RMB) 總銷售收入（百萬元）	Total profit (mil. RMB) 總利潤（百萬元）	Return on assets 資產利潤率 (%)	Return on equity 權益利潤率 (%)	Labour productivity ('000 RMB / worker) 勞動生產率（千元/人）	Debts / assets 資產負債率 (%)	Total assets (mil. RMB) 總資產（百萬元）
Industry Overall 行業總體	530	95,303	7,692	-35	-0.30	-1.07	80.71	71.88	11,450

	Number of firms 企業個數	Average number of employees 平均職工人數	Average revenue ('000 RMB) 平均銷售收入（千元）	Average profit ('000 RMB) 平均利潤（千元）	Return on assets 資產利潤率 (%)	Return on equity 權益利潤率 (%)	Labour productivity ('000 RMB / worker) 勞動生產率（千元/人）	Average debts / assets 平均資產負債率(%)	Average Total assets ('000 RMB) 平均總資產（千元）
By ownership 產業所有權									
State-owned 國有	67	606	29,627	-1,881	-3.19	-12.45	48.85	74.41	59,030
Collectively-owned 集體	397	119	11,726	379	3.10	12.51	98.55	75.20	12,213
Privately-owned 私有	3	38	2,197	51	1.57	7.61	57.81	79.37	3,251
Domestic JVs 聯營	10	103	15,689	214	1.40	3.00	151.88	53.44	15,312
Joint stock 股份制	7	193	26,603	-1,206	-4.86	-48.41	137.84	89.95	24,786
Foreign-funded 外資	21	187	24,426	-2,120	-2.16	-5.20	130.32	58.46	98,087
Overseas Chinese-funded 港澳台資	25	59	7,578	-349	-3.48	-14.74	129.15	76.40	10,023
By size 規模									
Large 大型	14	1,967	160,221	-1,407	-0.42	-1.17	81.44	64.00	333,371
Medium 中型	29	796	41,649	-2,648	-2.94	-11.45	52.34	74.33	90,128
Small 小型	482	93	8,799	128	1.47	7.07	94.52	79.15	8,650
By regional distribution 地區分布									
Central-North 華北	162	138	13,262	695	6.13	23.74	96.35	74.17	11,333
Beijing 北京	8	216	7,428	-734	-5.58	156.53	34.39	103.57	13,149
Tianjin 天津	55	203	19,677	936	5.14	17.71	96.72	70.99	18,225
Hebei 河北	91	83	10,383	731	11.00	40.72	124.86	72.99	6,644
Shanxi 山西	7	259	8,843	67	0.38	1.96	34.14	80.63	17,687
Inner Mongolia 內蒙	1								
Northeast 東北	38	216	4,734	-759	-5.67	-27.16	21.87	79.12	13,382
Liaoning 遼寧	30	109	3,571	-293	-3.73	-13.99	32.71	73.31	7,847
Jilin 吉林	8	619	9,098	-2,505	-7.34	-46.25	14.70	84.13	34,138
Heilongjiang 黑龍江									
Central East 華東	251	190	18,598	-137	-0.45	-1.51	98.00	70.03	30,195
Shanghai 上海	31	279	23,055	-2,758	-2.71	-8.44	82.75	67.84	101,600
Jiangsu 江蘇	113	169	16,737	158	0.84	2.87	98.78	70.84	18,834
Zhejiang 浙江	49	143	20,445	17	0.09	0.32	142.65	71.70	18,956
Anhui 安徽	16	163	13,696	992	8.26	200.38	84.25	95.88	12,009
Fujian 福建	6	24	2,825	48	2.50	3.16	116.10	20.64	1,930
Jiangxi 江西	2	63	1,000	10	0.26	2.90	15.87	91.04	3,795
Shandong 山東	34	293	24,181	478	1.40	4.55	82.59	69.25	34,142
Central-South 中南	69	128	3,961	-527	-4.20	-14.66	30.95	71.34	12,554
Henan 河南	29	114	3,756	-33	-0.58	-2.24	32.87	74.23	5,788
Hubei 湖北	7	327	7,401	-3,173	-14.77	-263.78	22.64	94.41	21,487
Hunan 湖南	18	137	4,804	-504	-3.82	-10.56	35.04	63.85	13,206
Guangdong 廣東	14	53	1,831	-296	-1.34	-3.74	34.65	64.17	22,039
Guangxi 廣西	1	21	450				21.43	91.28	1,720
Hainan 海南									
Southwest 西南	6	1,345	67,903	-7,755	-7.31	-38.58	50.49	81.06	106,115
Chongqing 重慶	6	1,345	67,903	-7,755	-7.31	-38.59	50.49	81.06	106,115
Sichuan 四川									
Guizhou 貴州									
Yunnan 雲南									
Tibet 西藏									
Northwest 西北	4	61	3,628	-255	-4.29	73.38	59.47	105.85	5,940
Shaanxi 陝西	4	61	3,628	-255	-4.29	73.38	59.47	105.85	5,940
Gansu 甘肅									
Qinghai 青海									
Ningxia 寧夏									
Xinjiang 新疆									

Year 年份	Number of firms 企業個數	Rate of change 每年變化 (%)	Number of employees 職工人數 (人)	Rate of change 每年變化 (%)	Total revenue (mil. RMB) 總銷售收入 (百萬元)	Rate of change 每年變化 (%)	Total profit (mil. RMB) 總利潤 (百萬元)	Rate of change 每年變化 (%)
1993	449		126,819		5,718		63	
1994	552	22.94%	111,725	-11.90%	6,822	19.31%	21	-67.64%
1995	547	-0.91%	111,270	-0.41%	8,432	23.59%	-36	-277.64%
1996	530	-3.11%	95,303	-14.35%	7,692	-8.78%	-35	4.06%

3 Major products* 3 種主要產品 *	Output 產量	Sales volume 銷售量	Unit 單位
a) Reactive Dye 活性染料	26,900	25,555	ton 噸
b) Acid Dyeing 酸性染料	32,721	29,449	ton 噸
c) Disperse Dye 分散染料	51,085	46,999	ton 噸

Top 10 firms by revenue (year founded) 收入排名前 10 家企業 (創辦年份)	City 城市	Province 省	Telephone / fax 電話 / 傳真	Number of employees 職工人數	Ownership 產業所有權	Revenue ('000 RMB) 銷售收入 (千元)	Profit ('000 RMB) (rank) 利潤 (千元) (排名)	Total assets ('000 RMB) 總資產 (千元)	Major products 主要產品
State-owned Qingdao Dyestuff Factory 國營青島染料廠(1919)	Qingdao 青島市	Shandong 山東省	(0532)3731234 (0532)3734209	2,784	State-owned 國有	264,854	527(97)	496,831	b,c
Tianjin Jin Xi Jing Mei Multiple Utilization Welfare Chemical Factory 天津市津西境美綜合利用福利化工廠(1988)	Tianjin 天津市	Tianjin 天津市	(022)27392569	236	Collectively-owned 集體	250,730	26410(1)	27,270	o
Suzhou Lintong Dyestuff Chemical Group Co. 蘇州林通染料化工集團公司(1976)	Suzhou 蘇州市	Jiangsu 江蘇省	(0512)5252072 (0512)5252487	600	Collectively-owned 集體	237,930	18400(3)	68,450	o
Shanghai No.8 Dyestuff Chemical Plant 上海染料化工八廠(1947)	Shanghai 上海市	Shanghai 上海市	(021)62506833 (021)62506148	1,740	State-owned 國有	220,909	600(87)	294,771	a
Sichuan Dyestuff Factory 四川染料廠(1965)	Chongqing 重慶市	Chongqing 重慶市	(023)40612001 (023)40245141	5,007	State-owned 國有	208,444	-39584(366)	429,061	c
Zhe Jiang Dong Gang Industry & Trade Group Co. Ltd. 浙江東港工貿集團有限公司(1981)	Taizhou 臺州市	Zhejiang 浙江省	(0576)8881534 (0576)8881534	598	Collectively-owned 集體	196,243	9617(5)	106,256	o
Tianjin Hua Shi Chemical Co. Ltd. 天津華士化工有限公司(1995)	Tianjin 天津市	Tianjin 天津市	(022)28340961 (022)28342155	1,232	Foreign-funded 外資	157,710	1288(54)	112,969	c
Chongqing Chuan Qing Chemical Plant 重慶川慶化工廠(1971)	Chongqing 重慶市	Chongqing 重慶市	(023)67381604 (023)67381559	1,997	State-owned 國有	147,796	73(187)	108,130	b
Hebei Zaoqiang Zao Ning Joint Dyestuff Chemical Factory 河北省棗強縣棗寧聯合染化廠(1988)	Hengshui 衡水市	Hebei 河北省	(0318)8224158	390	Collectively-owned 集體	124,070	1180(59)	36,850	o
Tianjin Dyestuff Factory Branch 天津市染料廠分廠(1977)	Tianjin 天津市	Tianjin 天津市	(022)23981376	559	Collectively-owned 集體	108,630	6440(9)	48,410	o

Top 10 Cities by Production Output 產出排名前 10 位城市	Province 省	Market share 市場份額	Number of firms 企業個數
Tianjin 天津市	Tianjin 天津市	14.50%	57
Shanghai 上海市	Shanghai 上海市	9.87%	38
Chongqing 重慶市	Chongqing 重慶市	6.16%	6
Suzhou 蘇州市	Jiangsu 江蘇省	5.61%	59
Taizhou 臺州市	Zhejiang 浙江省	4.59%	16
Qingdao 青島市	Shandong 山東省	4.58%	10
Hengshui 衡水市	Hebei 河北省	4.28%	21
Wuxi 無錫市	Jiangsu 江蘇省	3.31%	17
Dalian 大連市	Liaoning 遼寧省	3.16%	3
Wenzhou 溫州市	Zhejiang 浙江省	3.12%	21

10 Major Wholesalers 10 家主要批發商	City 城市	Province 省	Telephone / Fax 電話 / 傳真
Zhong Hua Singbo Import & Export Company 中化寧波進出口公司	Ningbo 寧波市	Zhejiang 浙江省	(0574)7346764 (0574)7366775
China Chemical Supply & Marketing Hua Nan Company 中國化工供銷華南公司	Guangzhou 廣州市	Guangdong 廣東省	(020)87654477 (020)87784414
China Agriculture Means of Production Chengdu Company 中國農業生產資料成都公司	Chengdu 成都市	Sichuan 四川省	(028)3333909 (028)3331202
Shanxi Agriculture Means of Production Company 山西省農業生產資料公司	Taiyuan 太原市	Shanxi 山西省	(0351)4040255 (0351)4040231
Beijing Chemical Light Industry General Company 北京市化工輕工總公司	Beijing 北京市	Beijing 北京市	(010)64224837 (010)64219301
Beijing Chemical Industry Group Company Supply & Marketing Company 北京化學工業集團公司供銷公司	Beijing 北京市	Beijing 北京市	(010)67714610 (010)67714058
Zhong Hua Jiangsu Import & Export Company 中化江蘇進出口公司	Nanjing 南京市	Jiangsu 江蘇省	(025)2258718 (025)2257789
Yunnan Chemical Import & Export Company 雲南省化工進出口公司	Kunming 昆明市	Yunnan 雲南省	(0871)3314002 (0871)3314931
Fujian Jiu Zhou Group Co. Ltd. 福建九州集團股份有限公司	Xiamen 廈門市	Fujian 福建省	(0592)5055818 (0592)5052033
China Chemical Industry Commission Agent Hua Dong Co. 中國化工供銷華東公司	Shanghai 上海市	Shanghai 上海市	(021)62514123

*Also include sales by firms outside this industry.包括本行業以外廠家的銷售。"o" stands for "others". "o" 代表 "其他產品"。

2659: Other Organic Chemical Products 其他有機化學產品製造業

The industry accounts for 0.144% of the total revenue of China's industrial sector in 1996. The revenue growth rate of the industry is 5.4% from 1995, as compared to the growth rate of China's industrial sector, 9.51%. The rate of return on asset is 1.28%. 69.44% of all firms in the industry made a profit while 24.60% had negative returns. The top province in terms of the industry's revenue is Jiangsu, accounting for 24.18% of the total revenue.
本行業在1996年佔全行業總產值0.144%，行業年增長率為5.4%（全國工業年增長率9.51%）。行業的資產回報率1.28%，69.44%的企業盈利，24.60%的企業虧損。銷售收入最高的省份為江蘇省，佔本行業的24.18%。

	Total number of firms 企業總數	Total number of employees 職工總數	Total revenue (mil. RMB) 總銷售收入（百萬元）	Total profit (mil. RMB) 總利潤（百萬元）	Return on assets 資產利潤率 (%)	Return on equity 權益利潤率 (%)	Labour productivity ('000 RMB / worker) 勞動生產率（千元/人）	Debts / assets 資產負債率 (%)	Total assets (mil. RMB) 總資產（百萬元）
Industry Overall 行業總體	1,042	103,148	8,333	129	1.28	4.36	80.79	70.61	10,095

	Number of firms 企業個數	Average number of employees 平均職工人數	Average revenue ('000 RMB) 平均銷售收入（千元）	Average profit ('000 RMB) 平均利潤（千元）	Return on assets 資產利潤率 (%)	Return on equity 權益利潤率 (%)	Labour productivity ('000 RMB / worker) 勞動生產率（千元/人）	Average debts / assets 平均資產負債率(%)	Average Total assets ('000 RMB) 平均總資產（千元）
By ownership 產業所有權									
State-owned 國有	161	253	17,280	-68	-0.26	-1.02	68.22	74.33	26,180
Collectively-owned 集體	782	70	5,218	96	1.82	6.26	74.57	70.98	5,298
Privately-owned 私有	2	43	2,145	15	1.13	1.95	49.89	42.29	1,377
Domestic JVs 聯營	5	42	5,336	221	3.88	6.14	127.66	36.84	5,686
Joint stock 股份制	7	373	56,493	2,994	4.18	8.47	151.34	50.68	71,667
Foreign-funded 外資	42	61	11,927	344	2.36	7.30	196.90	67.68	14,559
Overseas Chinese-funded 港澳台資	42	68	12,924	671	4.76	12.92	189.39	63.19	14,111
By size 規模									
Large 大型	4	1,743	120,021	2,305	1.22	4.95	68.88	75.43	189,449
Medium 中型	36	744	67,087	690	0.82	2.83	90.20	70.90	83,923
Small 小型	986	70	5,515	96	1.50	4.99	78.77	69.89	6,405
By regional distribution 地區分布									
Central-North 華北	164	89	7,188	337	3.73	15.03	80.55	75.19	9,033
Beijing 北京	31	53	9,307	764	8.02	16.23	176.26	50.58	9,521
Tianjin 天津	26	110	8,873	247	1.99	8.82	80.58	77.38	12,385
Hebei 河北	79	72	6,565	335	4.72	26.31	91.71	82.07	7,098
Shanxi 山西	23	141	5,333	-25	-0.29	-1.47	37.87	80.11	8,630
Inner Mongolia 內蒙	5	248	3,670	-152	-0.72	-8.69	14.79	91.66	20,998
Northeast 東北	208	110	3,760	-11	-0.19	-0.55	34.18	65.86	5,967
Liaoning 遼寧	128	152	5,177			0.01	34.14	63.64	8,336
Jilin 吉林	52	36	1,201	13	0.65	3.75	33.11	82.56	1,942
Heilongjiang 黑龍江	28	57	2,039	-109	-4.17	-16.83	35.88	75.20	2,610
Central East 華東	386	99	10,265	227	2.13	7.13	103.47	70.19	10,664
Shanghai 上海	37	124	13,969	716	4.54	10.72	112.51	57.70	15,791
Jiangsu 江蘇	166	118	12,138	117	0.93	3.37	103.25	72.24	12,467
Zhejiang 浙江	51	61	7,961	-66	-0.96	-2.54	129.67	62.33	6,880
Anhui 安徽	26	97	5,686	311	3.15	8.73	58.80	63.91	9,861
Fujian 福建	12	63	1,278	-152	-3.36	-6.18	20.32	45.56	4,511
Jiangxi 江西	25	79	4,208	70	1.38	3.38	53.00	59.31	5,116
Shandong 山東	69	84	10,959	536	5.50	37.25	130.36	85.24	9,758
Central-South 中南	204	98	10,355	105	0.83	2.65	105.71	68.74	12,607
Henan 河南	63	51	3,041	74	2.04	12.45	60.10	83.62	3,652
Hubei 湖北	35	83	4,481	-357	-7.70	-1374.73	53.71	99.45	4,644
Hunan 湖南	53	94	5,407	-22	-0.34	-1.28	57.63	73.35	6,303
Guangdong 廣東	43	118	27,175	425	1.26	3.77	229.80	66.71	33,850
Guangxi 廣西	8	468	36,270	1,525	3.28	6.52	77.54	49.71	46,481
Hainan 海南	2	38	9,345	-95	-1.07	-3.94	245.92	72.88	8,885
Southwest 西南	54	69	3,890	-212	-3.23	-15.37	56.54	78.99	6,554
Chongqing 重慶	14	54	5,094	-342	-7.98	66.04	94.54	112.08	4,290
Sichuan 四川	25	74	3,765	-130	-1.66	-5.17	50.75	67.92	7,822
Guizhou 貴州	8	27	981	-146	-9.38	-56.25	36.18	83.32	1,559
Yunnan 雲南	7	127	5,286	-321	-2.64	-13.86	41.48	80.96	12,174
Tibet 西藏									
Northwest 西北	26	140	3,337	-806	-6.34	-29.84	23.87	78.76	12,713
Shaanxi 陝西	8	49	1,981	-173	-3.45	-19.41	40.13	82.20	4,994
Gansu 甘肅	10	43	1,184	37	1.46	5.25	27.60	72.12	2,529
Qinghai 青海	1	2,566	51,000	-16,910	-6.99	-30.91	19.88	77.39	241,890
Ningxia 寧夏	4	10	655	-163	-9.19	-37.79	68.95	75.81	1,768
Xinjiang 新疆	3	69	1,813	-793	-14.56	643.24	26.41	102.26	5,450

2659: Other Organic Chemical Products 其他有機化學產品製造業

Year 年份	Number of firms 企業個數	Rate of change 每年變化 (%)	Number of employees 職工人數 (人)	Rate of change 每年變化 (%)	Total revenue (mil. RMB) 總銷售收入 (百萬元)	Rate of change 每年變化 (%)	Total profit (mil. RMB) 總利潤 (百萬元)	Rate of change 每年變化 (%)
1993	1,312		141,602		6,585		99	
1994	1,298	-1.07%	135,461	-4.34%	7,424	12.74%	143	45.26%
1995	1,070	-17.57%	111,046	-18.02%	7,907	6.50%	146	1.69%
1996	1,042	-2.62%	103,148	-7.11%	8,333	5.39%	129	-11.51%

3 Major products* 3 種主要產品 *	Output 產量	Sales volume 銷售量	Unit 單位
a) Ethyl Acetate 醋酸乙酯	10,472	9,529	ton 噸
b) Formaldehyde 甲醛	124,776	116,041	ton 噸

Top 10 firms by revenue (year founded) 收入排名前 10 家企業 (創辦年份)	City 城市	Province 省	Telephone / fax 電話 / 傳真	Number of employees 職工人數	Ownership 產業所有權	Revenue ('000 RMB) 銷售收入 (千元)	Profit ('000 RMB) (rank) 利潤 (千元) (排名)	Total assets ('000 RMB) 總資產 (千元)	Major products 主要產品
Guangxi Vinylion Plant 廣西維尼綸廠(1980)	Hechi 河池市	Guangxi 廣西	(0778)3212235 (0778)3211945	3,583	State-owned 國有	271,599	12008(3)	366,161	o
Shandong Zibo Bao Feng Group Co. 山東淄博寶灃集團公司(1979)	Zibo 淄博市	Shandong 山東省	(0533)2081420 (0533)2081420	400	Collectively-owned 集體	266,550	8550(4)	137,340	o
No.5 Mine Changzhou Synthetic Chemical General Plant 五礦常州合成化工總廠(1959)	Changzhou 常州市	Jiangsu 江蘇省	(0519)5212622 (0519)5210023	1,472	State-owned 國有	257,336	1871(36)	324,038	o
Beijing Eastern Rohm & Hass Co. Ltd. 北京市東方羅門哈斯有限公司(1993)	Beijing 北京市	Beijing 北京市	(010)69550554 (010)69547747	190	Foreign-funded 外資	207,756	19073(1)	157,714	o
Guangdong Xinhui Charming Fibre Master Batch Stock Ltd. 廣東新會彩艷纖維母粒股份有限公司(1993)	Jiangmen 江門市	Guangdong 廣東省	(0750)6692273 (0750)6697575	565	Joint stock 股份制	187,911	3670(22)	237,186	o
Guangzhou Solvent Plant 廣州溶劑廠(1956)	Guangzhou 廣州市	Guangdong 廣東省	(020)82231074 (020)82231074	490	State-owned 國有	158,054	2612(25)	118,120	a,b
Nanjing Jin Xing Petrochemical Industrial Co. Ltd. 南京金星石化實業有限公司(1991)	Nanjing 南京市	Jiangsu 江蘇省	(025)5761244 (025)5762960	643	Foreign-funded 外資	150,089	7700(8)	185,173	o
Jiangsu Nan Yuan Chemical Group Company 江蘇南苑化工集團公司(1969)	Taizhou 泰州市	Jiangsu 江蘇省	(0523)3232405 (0523)3231420	2,359	State-owned 國有	123,439	-7164(468)	203,555	o
Shanghai Leather Chemical Factory 上海皮革化工廠(1959)	Shanghai 上海市	Shanghai 上海市	(021)62506580 (021)62506317	599	State-owned 國有	120,311	8026(6)	63,626	o
Huaiji Wei Da Industry (Group) Company 懷集縣威達工業(集團)公司(1992)	Zhaoqing 肇慶市	Guangdong 廣東省	(0757)5527952	225	State-owned 國有	110,973	8230(5)	159,641	o

Top 10 Cities by Production Output 產出排名前 10 位城市	Province 省	Market share 市場份額	Number of firms 企業個數
Nanjing 南京市	Jiangsu 江蘇省	12.66%	21
Shanghai 上海市	Shanghai 上海市	6.35%	63
Guangzhou 廣州市	Guangdong 廣東省	4.57%	19
Changzhou 常州市	Jiangsu 江蘇省	4.01%	38
Beijing 北京市	Beijing 北京市	3.55%	30
Jiangmen 江門市	Guangdong 廣東省	3.45%	4
Hechi 河池市	Guangxi 廣西	3.29%	1
Taizhou 泰州市	Jiangsu 江蘇省	3.28%	21
Yangzhou 揚州市	Jiangsu 江蘇省	2.69%	33
Taiyuan 太原市	Shanxi 山西省	2.46%	11

10 Major Wholesalers 10 家主要批發商	City 城市	Province 省	Telephone / Fax 電話 / 傳真
Zhong Hua Singbo Import & Export Company 中化寧波進出口公司	Ningbo 寧波市	Zhejiang 浙江省	(0574)7346764 (0574)7366775
China Chemical Supply & Marketing Hua Nan Company 中國化工供銷華南公司	Guangzhou 廣州市	Guangdong 廣東省	(020)87654477 (020)87784414
China Agriculture Means of Production Chengdu Company 中國農業生產資料成都公司	Chengdu 成都市	Sichuan 四川省	(028)3333909 (028)3331202
Shanxi Agriculture Means of Production Company 山西省農業生產資料公司	Taiyuan 太原市	Shanxi 山西省	(0351)4040255 (0351)4040231
Beijing Chemical Light Industry General Company 北京市化工輕工總公司	Beijing 北京市	Beijing 北京市	(010)64224837 (010)64219301
Beijing Chemical Industry Group Company Supply & Marketing Company 北京化學工業集團公司供銷公司	Beijing 北京市	Beijing 北京市	(010)67714610 (010)67714058
Zhong Hua Jiangsu Import & Export Company 中化江蘇進出口公司	Nanjing 南京市	Jiangsu 江蘇省	(025)2258718 (025)2257789
Yunnan Chemical Import & Export Company 雲南省化工進出口公司	Kunming 昆明市	Yunnan 雲南省	(0871)3314002 (0871)3314931
Fujian Jiu Zhou Group Co. Ltd. 福建九州集團股份有限公司	Xiamen 廈門市	Fujian 福建省	(0592)5055818 (0592)5052033
China Chemical Industry Commission Agent Hua Dong Co. 中國化工供銷華東公司	Shanghai 上海市	Shanghai 上海市	(021)62514123

*Also include sales by firms outside this industry.包括本行業以外廠家的銷售。"o" stands for "others". "o" 代表 "其他產品"。

2661: Polyolefin Plastic 聚烯烴塑料製造業

The industry accounts for 0.170% of the total revenue of China's industrial sector in 1996. The revenue growth rate of the industry is 13.3% from 1995, as compared to the growth rate of China's industrial sector, 9.51%. The rate of return on asset is 2.84%. 73.81% of all firms in the industry made a profit while 24.29% had negative returns. The top province in terms of the industry's revenue is Gansu, accounting for 32.99% of the total revenue.
本行業在1996年佔全行業總產值0.170%，行業年增長率為13.3%（全國工業年增長率9.51%）。行業的資產回報率2.84%，73.81%的企業盈利，24.29%的企業虧損。銷售收入最高的省份為甘肅，佔本行業的32.99%。

	Total number of firms 企業總數	Total number of employees 職工總數	Total revenue (mil. RMB) 總銷售收入（百萬元）	Total profit (mil. RMB) 總利潤（百萬元）	Return on assets 資產利潤率 (%)	Return on equity 權益利潤率 (%)	Labour productivity ('000 RMB / worker) 勞動生產率（千元/人）	Debts / assets 資產負債率 (%)	Total assets (mil. RMB) 總資產（百萬元）
Industry Overall 行業總體	201	82,901	9,877	423	2.84	9.27	119.14	69.38	14,900

	Number of firms 企業個數	Average number of employees 平均職工人數	Average revenue ('000 RMB) 平均銷售收入（千元）	Average profit ('000 RMB) 平均利潤（千元）	Return on assets 資產利潤率 (%)	Return on equity 權益利潤率 (%)	Labour productivity ('000 RMB / worker) 勞動生產率（千元/人）	Average debts / assets 平均資產負債率(%)	Average Total assets ('000 RMB) 平均總資產（千元）
By ownership 產業所有權									
State-owned 國有	37	1,557	179,108	865	0.28	1.03	115.07	72.97	310,784
Collectively-owned 集體	121	183	15,312	1,421	10.99	24.53	83.90	55.20	12,933
Privately-owned 私有	1	59	5,064	213	5.79	26.47	85.82	78.11	3,670
Domestic JVs 聯營	6	41	8,381	-192	-3.86	-12.30	202.76	68.63	4,988
Joint stock 股份制	6	231	119,728	28,951	16.99	52.70	519.05	67.75	170,350
Foreign-funded 外資	8	39	6,794	113	1.77	3.45	175.33	48.84	6,392
Overseas Chinese-funded 港澳台資	23	55	24,793	1,967	6.20	11.68	451.14	46.95	31,733
By size 規模									
Large 大型	13	4,251	523,213	8,455	1.06	3.67	123.08	71.05	795,132
Medium 中型	9	697	87,314	16,057	13.52	33.60	125.27	59.74	118,718
Small 小型	172	116	13,317	980	4.82	14.78	114.83	67.39	20,324
By regional distribution 地區分布									
Central-North 華北	31	314	25,208	1,329	3.09	9.55	80.22	67.66	43,025
Beijing 北京	15	99	11,923	576	3.05	39.17	119.87	92.22	18,911
Tianjin 天津	2	12	385	-10	-3.17	-8.33	32.08	61.90	315
Hebei 河北	13	378	27,735	1,518	3.63	15.86	73.31	77.08	41,764
Shanxi 山西	1	3,307	241,280	12,840	2.53	4.51	72.96	43.82	506,560
Inner Mongolia 內蒙									
Northeast 東北	20	747	119,076	3,909	2.13	8.04	159.34	73.46	183,126
Liaoning 遼寧	12	530	127,522	1,069	0.47	2.70	240.46	82.66	228,027
Jilin 吉林	3	2,351	112,920	3,513	1.91	4.55	48.02	58.15	184,337
Heilongjiang 黑龍江	5	306	102,498	10,962	14.69	20.60	335.40	28.71	74,638
Central East 華東	65	183	19,365	532	1.94	6.92	105.62	71.93	27,367
Shanghai 上海	6	45	5,057	57	0.98	3.75	113.21	73.77	5,763
Jiangsu 江蘇	14	470	40,684	190	0.25	0.98	86.63	74.27	75,454
Zhejiang 浙江	13	43	21,169	1,985	14.38	32.18	490.55	55.31	13,805
Anhui 安徽	7	229	9,696	-1,074	-6.27	-20.87	42.34	69.96	17,134
Fujian 福建	4	12	3,998	155	4.03	7.47	333.13	46.06	3,843
Jiangxi 江西	3	521	49,773	1,347	2.44	11.83	95.60	79.35	55,130
Shandong 山東	18	72	8,358	479	4.15	14.45	115.72	71.28	11,541
Central-South 中南	60	193	28,144	3,913	10.85	36.94	145.77	70.62	36,060
Henan 河南	19	394	19,941	1,188	4.12	9.48	50.60	56.55	28,853
Hubei 湖北	9	266	86,338	20,374	27.42	54.52	324.99	49.70	74,306
Hunan 湖南	7	50	15,343	4,247	19.74	1670.22	308.62	98.81	21,510
Guangdong 廣東	20	44	19,137	-103	-0.27	-4.20	438.42	93.63	38,476
Guangxi 廣西	4	112	10,228	273	4.30	12.04	91.73	64.26	6,330
Hainan 海南	1	38	1,650	80	6.45	6.45	43.42		1,240
Southwest 西南	5	130	5,828	-474	-5.24	-16.23	44.83	67.74	9,052
Chongqing 重慶	1	150	10,529	441	5.34	19.06	70.19	72.00	8,259
Sichuan 四川	3	19	855	-879	-25.68	-240.29	45.61	89.31	3,423
Guizhou 貴州	1	470	17,980	90	0.32	0.78	38.26	58.19	27,700
Yunnan 雲南									
Tibet 西藏									
Northwest 西北	20	1,703	186,877	1,830	0.62	1.82	109.72	66.04	295,792
Shaanxi 陝西	10	316	3,277	-425	-5.88	-80.04	10.38	92.65	7,224
Gansu 甘肅	3	8,706	1,086,077	19,437	1.11	3.08	124.75	63.90	1,748,273
Qinghai 青海	1								
Ningxia 寧夏	1	1,861	89,640	-18,250	-6.61	-82.54	48.17	91.99	275,970
Xinjiang 新疆	5	585	71,378	156	0.24	0.88	122.01	72.62	64,562

2661: Polyolefin Plastic 聚烯烴塑料製造業

Year 年份	Number of firms 企業個數	Rate of change 每年變化 (%)	Number of employees 職工人數 (人)	Rate of change 每年變化 (%)	Total revenue (mil. RMB) 總銷售收入 (百萬元)	Rate of change 每年變化 (%)	Total profit (mil. RMB) 總利潤 (百萬元)	Rate of change 每年變化 (%)
1993	168		58,960		4,726		195	
1994	166	-1.19%	67,356	14.24%	5,710	20.81%	223	13.92%
1995	202	21.69%	94,643	40.51%	8,715	52.63%	433	94.43%
1996	201	-0.50%	82,901	-12.41%	9,877	13.33%	423	-2.28%

3 Major products* 3 種主要產品 *	Output 產量	Sales volume 銷售量	Unit 單位
a) Polypropylene Resin 聚丙烯樹脂	168,362	168,362	ton 噸
b) Polyolefine Resin 聚烯烴樹脂	392,510	372,884	ton 噸

Top 10 firms by revenue (year founded) 收入排名前 10 家企業 (創辦年份)	City 城市	Province 省	Telephone / fax 電話 / 傳真	Number of employees 職工人數	Ownership 產業所有權	Revenue ('000 RMB) 銷售收入 (千元)	Profit ('000 RMB) (rank) 利潤 (千元) (排名)	Total assets ('000 RMB) 總資產 (千元)	Major products 主要產品
Lanzhou Chemical Industrial Co. Sinopec 蘭州化學工業公司(1958)	Lanzhou 蘭州市	Gansu 甘肅省	(0931)7555981 (0931)7555851	33,782	State-owned 國有	3,034,292	3101(15)	4,875,943	b
Panjin Ethylene Industrial Co. 盤錦乙烯工業公司(1990)	Panjin 盤錦市	Liaoning 遼寧省	(0427)5851668	5,507	State-owned 國有	1,398,357	6(79)	2,653,459	o
Hubei Xing Hua Co. Ltd. 湖北興化股份有限公司(1989)	Jingmen 荊門市	Hubei 湖北省	(0724)211501 (0724)210632	810	Joint stock 股份制	600,922	183373(1)	483,246	a,b
Mudanjiang Petrochemical Plant 牡丹江石油化工廠(1977)	Mudanjiang 牡丹江市	Heilongjiang 黑龍江省	(0453)6331766 (0453)6332271	1,324	State-owned 國有	449,687	32933(3)	319,223	o
Jiangsu Bei Fang Chlor-alkali Group Co. 江蘇北方氯鹼集團公司(1958)	Xuzhou 徐州市	Jiangsu 江蘇省	(0516)7767055 (0516)7767151	4,424	State-owned 國有	353,638	5623(10)	844,506	b
Dushanzi Petrochemistry General Factory Tianli Enterprise Group Co. 新疆獨山子石化天利企業集團公司(1983)	Karamay 克拉瑪依市	Xinjiang 新疆	(0990)867431 (0990)682773	2,580	Collectively-owned 集體	321,623	202(45)	292,202	b
Guangzhou Silver Pear Polypropylene Co. Ltd. 廣州銀珠聚丙烯有限公司(1995)	Guangzhou 廣州市	Guangdong 廣東省	(020)82124523 (020)82124535	213	State-owned 國有	271,176	139(54)	678,720	a,b
Shanxi Sanwei Group Co. Ltd 山西三維集團股份有限公司(1984)	Linfen 臨汾市	Shanxi 山西省	(0357)6662602 (0357)6222727	3,307	State-owned 國有	241,285	12835(8)	506,560	o
Ningbo He Qiao Chemical Co. Ltd. 寧波和橋化工有限公司(1993)	Ningbo 寧波市	Zhejiang 浙江省	(0574)6222211 (0574)6221715	74	Overseas Chinese-funded 港澳台資	208,232	23728(4)	104,531	o
Jilin Chemical Industrial Co. Chang Song Chemical Plant 吉林化學工業公司長松化工廠(1963)	Jilin 吉林市	Jilin 吉林省	(0432)3970928 (0432)3038875	4,277	Collectively-owned 集體	188,923	3379(14)	357,598	a,b

Top 10 Cities by Production Output 產出排名前 10 位城市	Province 省	Market share 市場份額	Number of firms 企業個數
Lanzhou 蘭州市	Gansu 甘肅省	39.35%	3
Panjin 盤錦市	Liaoning 遼寧省	15.59%	1
Mudanjiang 牡丹江市	Heilongjiang 黑龍江省	5.12%	1
Xuzhou 徐州市	Jiangsu 江蘇省	4.11%	1
Guangzhou 廣州市	Guangdong 廣東省	3.27%	7
Linfen 臨汾市	Shanxi 山西省	2.92%	1
Nanjing 南京市	Jiangsu 江蘇省	2.92%	3
Shanghai 上海市	Shanghai 上海市	1.89%	20
Jiujiang 九江市	Jiangxi 江西省	1.79%	3
Shijiazhuang 石家莊市	Hebei 河北省	1.67%	4

10 Major Wholesalers 10 家主要批發商	City 城市	Province 省	Telephone / Fax 電話 / 傳真
Zhong Hua Singbo Import & Export Company 中化寧波進出口公司	Ningbo 寧波市	Zhejiang 浙江省	(0574)7346764 (0574)7366775
China Chemical Supply & Marketing Hua Nan Company 中國化工供銷華南公司	Guangzhou 廣州市	Guangdong 廣東省	(020)87654477 (020)87784414
China Agriculture Means of Production Chengdu Company 中國農業生產資料成都公司	Chengdu 成都市	Sichuan 四川省	(028)3333909 (028)3331202
Shanxi Agriculture Means of Production Company 山西省農業生產資料公司	Taiyuan 太原市	Shanxi 山西省	(0351)4040255 (0351)4040231
Beijing Chemical Light Industry General Company 北京市化工輕工總公司	Beijing 北京市	Beijing 北京市	(010)64224837 (010)64219301
Beijing Chemical Industry Group Company Supply & Marketing Company 北京化學工業集團公司供銷公司	Beijing 北京市	Beijing 北京市	(010)67714610 (010)67714058
Zhong Hua Jiangsu Import & Export Company 中化江蘇進出口公司	Nanjing 南京市	Jiangsu 江蘇省	(025)2258718 (025)2257789
Yunnan Chemical Import & Export Company 雲南省化工進出口公司	Kunming 昆明市	Yunnan 雲南省	(0871)3314002 (0871)3314931
Fujian Jiu Zhou Group Co. Ltd. 福建九州集團股份有限公司	Xiamen 廈門市	Fujian 福建省	(0592)5055818 (0592)5052033
China Chemical Industry Commission Agent Hua Dong Co. 中國化工供銷華東公司	Shanghai 上海市	Shanghai 上海市	(021)62514123

*Also include sales by firms outside this industry.包括本行業以外廠家的銷售。"o" stands for "others". "o" 代表 "其他產品"。

2662: Resinoid and Plastic 熱固性樹脂及塑料製造業

The industry accounts for 0.089% of the total revenue of China's industrial sector in 1996. The revenue growth rate of the industry is -5.9% from 1995, as compared to the growth rate of China's industrial sector, 9.51%. The rate of return on asset is 1.88%. 68.56% of all firms in the industry made a profit while 27.62% had negative returns. The top province in terms of the industry's revenue is Shanghai, accounting for 57.36% of the total revenue.
本行業在1996年佔全行業總產值0.089%，行業年增長率為-5.9%（全國工業年增長率9.51%）。行業的資產回報率1.88%，68.56%的企業盈利，27.62%的企業虧損。銷售收入最高的省份為上海市，佔本行業的57.36%。

	Total number of firms 企業總數	Total number of employees 職工總數	Total revenue (mil. RMB) 總銷售收入（百萬元）	Total profit (mil. RMB) 總利潤（百萬元）	Return on assets 資產利潤率 (%)	Return on equity 權益利潤率 (%)	Labour productivity ('000 RMB / worker) 勞動生產率（千元/人）	Debts / assets 資產負債率 (%)	Total assets (mil. RMB) 總資產（百萬元）
Industry Overall 行業總體	300	43,146	5,149	164	1.88	4.23	119.34	55.69	8,728

	Number of firms 企業個數	Average number of employees 平均職工人數	Average revenue ('000 RMB) 平均銷售收入（千元）	Average profit ('000 RMB) 平均利潤（千元）	Return on assets 資產利潤率 (%)	Return on equity 權益利潤率 (%)	Labour productivity ('000 RMB / worker) 勞動生產率（千元/人）	Average debts / assets 平均資產負債率(%)	Average Total assets ('000 RMB) 平均總資產（千元）
By ownership 產業所有權									
State-owned 國有	54	310	23,370	-519	-1.87	-11.38	75.34	83.57	27,722
Collectively-owned 集體	197	68	5,265	123	1.96	7.09	76.86	72.39	6,278
Privately-owned 私有									
Domestic JVs 聯營	5	80	7,747	258	1.36	1.77	97.32	23.40	18,968
Joint stock 股份制	4	2,443	566,065	44,532	3.47	5.95	231.71	41.73	1,284,918
Foreign-funded 外資	20	62	13,328	-349	-2.14	-7.03	214.63	69.52	16,297
Overseas Chinese-funded 港澳台資	19	104	14,782	-244	-1.07	-4.11	141.71	74.04	22,839
By size 規模									
Large 大型	4	3,626	750,375	47,800	3.31	5.94	206.97	44.22	1,442,128
Medium 中型	11	673	38,116	-747	-1.16	-5.76	56.65	79.80	64,245
Small 小型	278	76	6,218	-68	-0.84	-3.75	81.37	77.50	8,104
By regional distribution 地區分布									
Central-North 華北	37	70	3,716	-17	-0.39	-1.75	53.16	77.94	4,470
Beijing 北京	8	30	2,190	44	0.75	2.38	73.00	68.57	5,843
Tianjin 天津	2	13	1,315	70	6.51	70.00	101.15	90.70	1,075
Hebei 河北	18	55	1,824	47	1.96	6.07	33.37	67.72	2,382
Shanxi 山西	3	246	19,013	-403	-4.60	-38.29	77.39	87.99	8,770
Inner Mongolia 內蒙	6	100	4,575	-127	-1.61	-16.52	45.83	90.28	7,888
Northeast 東北	38	111	2,671	-132	-2.57	-28.95	24.12	91.11	5,131
Liaoning 遼寧	21	128	2,915	-41	-0.87	-5.70	22.69	84.71	4,699
Jilin 吉林	13	107	2,708	-333	-4.88	268.94	25.31	101.81	6,824
Heilongjiang 黑龍江	4	30	1,270	43	2.24	4.42	42.69	49.21	1,895
Central East 華東	138	189	30,847	2,167	4.43	8.32	163.15	46.78	48,943
Shanghai 上海	15	932	196,913	19,181	5.40	9.12	211.30	40.78	355,177
Jiangsu 江蘇	31	206	21,759	137	0.60	2.01	105.56	70.28	22,863
Zhejiang 浙江	27	59	8,138	146	1.91	5.76	139.06	66.90	7,673
Anhui 安徽	15	103	5,992	-96	-0.99	-2.57	58.14	61.61	9,719
Fujian 福建	12	53	12,868	21	0.19	0.55	241.64	65.95	11,152
Jiangxi 江西	11	23	815	-93	-6.85	-44.93	35.04	84.74	1,353
Shandong 山東	27	63	5,769	196	2.45	9.39	91.51	73.88	8,003
Central-South 中南	72	105	8,288	-1,676	-8.10	-58.92	79.04	86.25	20,679
Henan 河南	25	98	3,276	-197	-3.46	-22.66	33.30	84.71	5,693
Hubei 湖北	11	62	5,605	115	3.65	13.73	90.00	73.41	3,138
Hunan 湖南	10	121	4,494	-402	-6.96	-89.14	37.14	92.21	5,773
Guangdong 廣東	24	131	16,914	-4,707	-9.03	-66.89	128.75	86.51	52,140
Guangxi 廣西	2	21	1,145	-5	-0.34	-2.13	54.52	84.12	1,480
Hainan 海南									
Southwest 西南	11	236	4,966	-810	-7.20	-64.19	21.07	88.78	11,245
Chongqing 重慶	4	436	7,960	-2,115	-13.22	-84.46	18.27	84.35	16,001
Sichuan 四川	7	122	3,255	-64	-0.75	-11.66	26.70	93.53	8,527
Guizhou 貴州									
Yunnan 雲南									
Tibet 西藏									
Northwest 西北	4	30	410	10	6.25	7.55	13.90	17.19	160
Shaanxi 陝西	2	37							
Gansu 甘肅	1	24	1,640	40	6.25	7.55	68.33	17.19	640
Qinghai 青海	1	20							
Ningxia 寧夏									
Xinjiang 新疆									

2662: Resinoid and Plastic 熱固性樹脂及塑料製造業

Year 年份	Number of firms 企業個數	Rate of change 每年變化 (%)	Number of employees 職工人數 (人)	Rate of change 每年變化 (%)	Total revenue (mil. RMB) 總銷售收入 (百萬元)	Rate of change 每年變化 (%)	Total profit (mil. RMB) 總利潤 (百萬元)	Rate of change 每年變化 (%)
1993	215		37,643		2,066		9	
1994	240	11.63%	48,362	28.48%	5,990	189.83%	251	2623.96%
1995	280	16.67%	45,079	-6.79%	5,471	-8.66%	262	4.30%
1996	300	7.14%	43,146	-4.29%	5,149	-5.89%	164	-37.40%

3 Major products* 3 種主要產品 *	Output 產量	Sales volume 銷售量	Unit 單位
a) Unsaturaled Polyester Resin 不飽和聚酯樹脂	31,705	29,168	ton 噸
b) Polyvinyl Chloride Resin 聚氯乙烯樹脂	296,255	231,079	ton 噸
c) Polyolefine Resin 聚烯烴樹脂	357,241	339,379	ton 噸

Top 10 firms by revenue (year founded) 收入排名前 10 家企業 (創辦年份)	City 城市	Province 省	Telephone / fax 電話 / 傳真	Number of employees 職工人數	Ownership 產業所有權	Revenue ('000 RMB) 銷售收入 (千元)	Profit ('000 RMB) (rank) 利潤 (千元) (排名)	Total assets ('000 RMB) 總資產 (千元)	Major products 主要產品
Shanghai Chlor-alkali Chemical Co. Ltd., Shanghai Tian Yuan (Group) Corp. 上海氯鹼化工股份有限公司(1960)	Shanghai 上海市	Shanghai 上海市	(021)64340000 (021)64341341	9,155	Joint stock 股份制	2,242,000	270000(1)	4,781,489	b,c
Shanghai Tian Yuan (Group) Co. Ltd. Tian Yuan Factory 上海天原(集團)有限公司天原廠(1949)	Shanghai 上海市	Shanghai 上海市	(021)62745100 (021)62747295	3,140	State-owned 國有	600,593	15008(2)	423,264	b,c
Zhongshan Da Xin Chemical Plastics Industrial Co. 中山市大新化工塑料實業公司(1976)	Zhongshan 中山市	Guangdong 廣東省	(0760)7793503 (0760)7797921	357	State-owned 國有	96,280	-20978(156)	151,896	c
Fujian Sanming Yuan Fa Resin Co. Ltd. 福建三明元發樹脂有限公司(1991)	Sanming 三明市	Fujian 福建省	(0598)8221827 (0598)8242336	65	Foreign-funded 外資	90,584	268(48)	53,625	o
Nantong Resin Plant 南通市樹脂廠(1970)	Nantong 南通市	Jiangsu 江蘇省	(0513)5517151 (0513)3513252	988	Collectively-owned 集體	79,239	73(79)	106,540	b,c
Jiangsu Jin Yi Group Co. 江蘇金益集團公司(1970)	Zhenjiang 鎮江市	Jiangsu 江蘇省	(0511)3361470 (0511)3361969	1,363	Collectively-owned 集體	79,203	2031(6)	118,643	o
Taishan Phosphate Fertilizer Factory 台山市磷肥廠(1965)	Jiangmen 江門市	Guangdong 廣東省	(0750)5411496 (0750)5411496	931	State-owned 國有	76,577	1804(8)	109,986	o
Nanjing Composite Material General Factory 南京複合材料總廠(1955)	Nanjing 南京市	Jiangsu 江蘇省	(025)2411504 (025)2411504	586	Collectively-owned 集體	72,417	100(75)	68,978	a
Jinling D.s.m Resin Co. Ltd. 金陵巴斯夫樹脂有限公司(1992)	Nanjing 南京市	Jiangsu 江蘇省	(025)5562925 (025)5564848	50	Foreign-funded 外資	69,830	-2899(151)	87,941	a
Jiangyin Ma Zhen Resin Factory 江陰市馬鎮樹脂廠(1988)	Wuxi 無錫市	Jiangsu 江蘇省	(0510)6521173	150	Collectively-owned 集體	60,260	2350(4)	6,720	a

Top 10 Cities by Production Output 產出排名前 10 位城市	Province 省	Market share 市場份額	Number of firms 企業個數
Shanghai 上海市	Shanghai 上海市	16.81%	26
Zhenjiang 鎮江市	Jiangsu 江蘇省	6.54%	10
Wuxi 無錫市	Jiangsu 江蘇省	5.67%	10
Zhongshan 中山市	Guangdong 廣東省	4.85%	7
Nanjing 南京市	Jiangsu 江蘇省	4.54%	7
Nantong 南通市	Jiangsu 江蘇省	3.33%	6
Taizhou 臺州市	Zhejiang 浙江省	3.18%	31
Sanming 三明市	Fujian 福建省	3.17%	3
Jiangmen 江門市	Guangdong 廣東省	3.09%	2
Wuhu 蕪湖市	Anhui 安徽省	3.01%	5

10 Major Wholesalers 10 家主要批發商	City 城市	Province 省	Telephone / Fax 電話 / 傳真
Zhong Hua Singbo Import & Export Company 中化寧波進出口公司	Ningbo 寧波市	Zhejiang 浙江省	(0574)7346764 (0574)7366775
China Chemical Supply & Marketing Hua Nan Company 中國化工供銷華南公司	Guangzhou 廣州市	Guangdong 廣東省	(020)87654477 (020)87784414
China Agriculture Means of Production Chengdu Company 中國農業生產資料成都公司	Chengdu 成都市	Sichuan 四川省	(028)3333909 (028)3331202
Shanxi Agriculture Means of Production Company 山西省農業生產資料公司	Taiyuan 太原市	Shanxi 山西省	(0351)4040255 (0351)4040231
Beijing Chemical Light Industry General Company 北京市化工輕工總公司	Beijing 北京市	Beijing 北京市	(010)64224837 (010)64219301
Beijing Chemical Industry Group Company Supply & Marketing Company 北京化學工業集團公司供銷公司	Beijing 北京市	Beijing 北京市	(010)67714610 (010)67714058
Zhong Hua Jiangsu Import & Export Company 中化江蘇進出口公司	Nanjing 南京市	Jiangsu 江蘇省	(025)2258718 (025)2257789
Yunnan Chemical Import & Export Company 雲南省化工進出口公司	Kunming 昆明市	Yunnan 雲南省	(0871)3314002 (0871)3314931
Fujian Jiu Zhou Group Co. Ltd. 福建九州集團股份有限公司	Xiamen 廈門市	Fujian 福建省	(0592)5055818 (0592)5052033
China Chemical Industry Commission Agent Hua Dong Co. 中國化工供銷華東公司	Shanghai 上海市	Shanghai 上海市	(021)62514123

*Also include sales by firms outside this industry.包括本行業以外廠家的銷售。"o" stands for "others". "o" 代表"其他產品"。

2663: Engineering Plastic 工程塑料製造業

The industry accounts for 0.035% of the total revenue of China's industrial sector in 1996. The revenue growth rate of the industry is 35.7% from 1995, as compared to the growth rate of China's industrial sector, 9.51%. The rate of return on asset is 0.53%. 60.31% of all firms in the industry made a profit while 29.80% had negative returns. The top province in terms of the industry's revenue is Jiangsu, accounting for 43.01% of the total revenue.
本行業在 1996 年佔全行業總產值 0.035%，行業年增長率為 35.7%（全國工業年增長率 9.51%）。行業的資產回報率 0.53%，60.31% 的企業盈利，29.80% 的企業虧損。銷售收入最高的省份為江蘇省，佔本行業的 43.01%。

	Total number of firms 企業總數	Total number of employees 職工總數	Total revenue (mil. RMB) 總銷售收入（百萬元）	Total profit (mil. RMB) 總利潤（百萬元）	Return on assets 資產利潤率 (%)	Return on equity 權益利潤率 (%)	Labour productivity ('000 RMB / worker) 勞動生產率（千元/人）	Debts / assets 資產負債率 (%)	Total assets (mil. RMB) 總資產（百萬元）
Industry Overall 行業總體	216	20,927	2,037	15	0.53	1.83	97.34	71.03	2,770

	Number of firms 企業個數	Average number of employees 平均職工人數	Average revenue ('000 RMB) 平均銷售收入（千元）	Average profit ('000 RMB) 平均利潤（千元）	Return on assets 資產利潤率 (%)	Return on equity 權益利潤率 (%)	Labour productivity ('000 RMB / worker) 勞動生產率（千元/人）	Average debts / assets 平均資產負債率(%)	Average Total assets ('000 RMB) 平均總資產（千元）
By ownership 產業所有權									
State-owned 國有	22	445	21,955	-636	-1.67	-13.46	49.33	87.59	38,091
Collectively-owned 集體	139	64	8,580	234	2.86	7.19	133.99	60.23	8,202
Privately-owned 私有	1	43	60,987	1,560	5.25	14.85	1418.30	64.62	29,706
Domestic JVs 聯營	5	23	4,469	-57	-0.91	-5.69	191.00	84.00	6,257
Joint stock 股份制	2	57	2,342	-207	-0.74	-1.14	41.45	34.91	27,828
Foreign-funded 外資	29	42	3,939	-104	-0.99	-2.33	94.25	57.42	10,489
Overseas Chinese-funded 港澳台資	18	53	8,863	-79	-0.38	-2.24	165.84	82.92	20,704
By size 規模									
Large 大型	2	3,340	424,327	9,610	2.33	6.29	127.04	62.96	412,320
Medium 中型	7	372	22,919	-1,067	-2.21	-20.84	61.54	89.42	48,395
Small 小型	198	56	5,194	16	0.20	0.71	92.25	71.32	8,121
By regional distribution 地區分布									
Central-North 華北	40	57	3,516	-131	-1.56	-6.10	62.21	74.38	8,387
Beijing 北京	19	69	3,961	8	0.07	0.26	57.53	74.53	12,930
Tianjin 天津	5	56	2,522	-1,266	-18.29	-39.37	45.20	53.53	6,920
Hebei 河北	14	42	3,754	66	1.79	20.99	88.78	91.46	3,704
Shanxi 山西	2	41	115				2.80	14.97	1,670
Inner Mongolia 內蒙									
Northeast 東北	34	56	2,600	-371	-3.88	-18.31	46.68	78.82	9,560
Liaoning 遼寧	22	24	1,126	-420	-4.63	-20.30	46.84	77.19	9,080
Jilin 吉林	3	35	187	50	5.00	10.42	5.33	52.00	1,000
Heilongjiang 黑龍江	9	140	7,008	-389	-2.86	-16.03	50.06	82.15	13,586
Central East 華東	83	134	18,378	471	2.85	9.37	137.14	69.64	16,539
Shanghai 上海	13	384	35,678	-632	-1.35	-9.75	93.01	86.18	46,860
Jiangsu 江蘇	28	142	31,289	1,697	8.45	16.66	220.79	49.30	20,087
Zhejiang 浙江	10	39	4,772	-185	-3.08	-7.61	121.42	59.54	6,004
Anhui 安徽	4	64	11,563	593	7.95	81.44	180.66	90.23	7,450
Fujian 福建	3	25	7,403	390	6.91	13.00	292.24	46.81	5,640
Jiangxi 江西	7	22	1,034	-14	-1.15	-5.49	47.63	79.15	1,247
Shandong 山東	18	72	3,448	-102	-2.14	-19.53	48.07	89.06	4,757
Central-South 中南	46	90	5,482	28	0.20	0.59	61.09	65.83	13,995
Henan 河南	22	108	1,272	10	0.67	2.56	11.74	73.96	1,501
Hubei 湖北	4	52	2,733	-140	-1.08	-1.64	52.30	34.17	12,978
Hunan 湖南	7	66	4,049	89	2.34	4.61	61.21	49.15	3,781
Guangdong 廣東	12	31	14,283	6	0.01	0.04	454.62	69.10	43,768
Guangxi 廣西	1	695	13,520	940	13.17	63.95	19.45	79.41	7,140
Hainan 海南									
Southwest 西南	9	144	2,591	-874	-9.36	-89.13	17.98	89.50	9,347
Chongqing 重慶	3	222	1,615	-27,060	-262.30	7896.92	7.28	103.32	10,316
Sichuan 四川	5	102	3,782	19,680	195.52	1318.67	37.02	85.17	10,066
Guizhou 貴州									
Yunnan 雲南	1	100						1.08	2,790
Tibet 西藏									
Northwest 西北	4	56	1,715	15	0.66	2.75	30.63	75.86	2,258
Shaanxi 陝西	3	23	543	10	1.48	4.76	23.97	68.47	677
Gansu 甘肅	1	156	5,230	30	0.43	1.94	33.53	78.00	7,000
Qinghai 青海									
Ningxia 寧夏									
Xinjiang 新疆									

2663: Engineering Plastic 工程塑料製造業

Year 年份	Number of firms 企業個數	Rate of change 每年變化 (%)	Number of employees 職工人數 (人)	Rate of change 每年變化 (%)	Total revenue (mil. RMB) 總銷售收入 (百萬元)	Rate of change 每年變化 (%)	Total profit (mil. RMB) 總利潤 (百萬元)	Rate of change 每年變化 (%)
1993	126		40,860		1,174		24	
1994	135	7.14%	21,030	-48.53%	1,180	0.48%	-1	-106.16%
1995	195	44.44%	20,776	-1.21%	1,501	27.21%	17	1245.24%
1996	216	10.77%	20,927	0.73%	2,037	35.71%	15	-10.23%

3 Major products* 3種主要產品 *	Output 產量	Sales volume 銷售量	Unit 單位
a) Phenolic Plastic 酚醛塑料	41,484	38,580	ton 噸
b) Amino Plastics 氨基塑料	12,883	12,883	ton 噸
c) Polyamide Resin 聚酰胺樹脂	1,038	914	ton 噸

Top 10 firms by revenue (year founded) 收入排名前10家企業(創辦年份)	City 城市	Province 省	Telephone / fax 電話 / 傳真	Number of employees 職工人數	Ownership 產業所有權	Revenue ('000 RMB) 銷售收入(千元)	Profit ('000 RMB) (rank) 利潤(千元)(排名)	Total assets ('000 RMB) 總資產(千元)	Major products 主要產品
Jiangsu Li Qiang Group Co. 江蘇力強集團公司(1994)	Changzhou 常州市	Jiangsu 江蘇省	(0519)7690266 (0519)7690099	2,314	Collectively-owned 集體	553,360	22010(1)	335,120	a,b
Shanghai Plastics Industry Co. Ltd. 上海塑料工業聯合公司(1992)	Shanghai 上海市	Shanghai 上海市	(021)64376893 (021)64330937	3,591	State-owned 國有	336,518	361(25)	334,562	c
American General Electric Appliance Plastics China Co. Ltd. 美國通用電器塑料中國有限公司(1994)	Guangzhou 廣州市	Guangdong 廣東省	(020)84980148 (020)84980148	97	Foreign-funded 外資	150,172	729(18)	496,222	o
Jiangyin Organic Chemical Plant 江陰市有機化工廠(1970)	Wuxi 無錫市	Jiangsu 江蘇省	(0510)6331801 (0510)6331672	403	Collectively-owned 集體	128,979	20587(2)	78,578	o
Beijing Fan Wei Engineering Plastics Co. Ltd. 北京泛威工程塑料有限公司(1989)	Beijing 北京市	Beijing 北京市	(010)67383894 (010)62544070	264	Overseas Chinese-funded 港澳台資	57,168	753(16)	88,616	o
Nanjing Jiangning Chemical Fibre Material Factory 南京江寧化纖材料廠(1982)	Nanjing 南京市	Jiangsu 江蘇省	(025)2721664	103	Collectively-owned 集體	49,320	880(13)	15,050	o
Anhui Zhong Lu Plastic Cement Co. Ltd. 安徽省中路塑膠有限公司	Chaohu 巢湖市	Anhui 安徽省	(0565)5312920	134	Collectively-owned 集體	44,940	2350(5)	27,860	o
Shanghai Zhong Lian Chemical Plant 上海中聯化工廠(1948)	Shanghai 上海市	Shanghai 上海市	(021)56635919 (021)56636015	809	State-owned 國有	35,546	-206(75)	112,480	o
Xi Shan Shi Plastics No.1 Factory 錫山市塑料一廠(1986)	Wuxi 無錫市	Jiangsu 江蘇省	(0510)3311984 (0510)3311379	120	Collectively-owned 集體	26,430	570(23)	26,930	o
Hebei Longrao An Li Da Chemical Factory 河北省隆堯縣安利達化工廠(1995)	Xingtai 邢臺市	Hebei 河北省		40	Private-owned 私營	25,000	0(64)	3,100	o

Top 10 Cities by Production Output 產出排名前10位城市	Province 省	Market share 市場份額	Number of firms 企業個數
Shanghai 上海市	Shanghai 上海市	51.88%	36
Guangzhou 廣州市	Guangdong 廣東省	9.05%	7
Changzhou 常州市	Jiangsu 江蘇省	7.20%	8
Shenzhen 深圳市	Guangdong 廣東省	4.38%	4
Beijing 北京市	Beijing 北京市	2.75%	18
Wuxi 無錫市	Jiangsu 江蘇省	2.21%	15
Nanjing 南京市	Jiangsu 江蘇省	1.83%	6
Suzhou 蘇州市	Jiangsu 江蘇省	1.31%	12
Weifang 濰坊市	Shandong 山東省	1.01%	4
Zhenjiang 鎮江市	Jiangsu 江蘇省	0.96%	10

10 Major Wholesalers 10家主要批發商	City 城市	Province 省	Telephone / Fax 電話 / 傳真
Zhong Hua Singbo Import & Export Company 中化寧波進出口公司	Ningbo 寧波市	Zhejiang 浙江省	(0574)7346764 (0574)7366775
China Chemical Supply & Marketing Hua Nan Company 中國化工供銷華南公司	Guangzhou 廣州市	Guangdong 廣東省	(020)87654477 (020)87784414
China Agriculture Means of Production Chengdu Company 中國農業生產資料成都公司	Chengdu 成都市	Sichuan 四川省	(028)3333909 (028)3331202
Shanxi Agriculture Means of Production Company 山西省農業生產資料公司	Taiyuan 太原市	Shanxi 山西省	(0351)4040255 (0351)4040231
Beijing Chemical Light Industry General Company 北京市化工輕工總公司	Beijing 北京市	Beijing 北京市	(010)64224837 (010)64219301
Beijing Chemical Industry Group Company Supply & Marketing Company 北京化學工業集團公司供銷公司	Beijing 北京市	Beijing 北京市	(010)67714610 (010)67714058
Zhong Hua Jiangsu Import & Export Company 中化江蘇進出口公司	Nanjing 南京市	Jiangsu 江蘇省	(025)2258718 (025)2257789
Yunnan Chemical Import & Export Company 雲南省化工進出口公司	Kunming 昆明市	Yunnan 雲南省	(0871)3314002 (0871)3314931
Fujian Jiu Zhou Group Co. Ltd. 福建九州集團股份有限公司	Xiamen 廈門市	Fujian 福建省	(0592)5055818 (0592)5052033
China Chemical Industry Commission Agent Hua Dong Co. 中國化工供銷華東公司	Shanghai 上海市	Shanghai 上海市	(021)62514123

*Also include sales by firms outside this industry.包括本行業以外廠家的銷售。"o" stands for "others". "o" 代表"其他產品"。

2664: Functional Polymer 功能高分子製造業

The industry accounts for 0.046% of the total revenue of China's industrial sector in 1996. The revenue growth rate of the industry is 44.4% from 1995, as compared to the growth rate of China's industrial sector, 9.51%. The rate of return on asset is 3.73%. 68.91% of all firms in the industry made a profit while 23.53% had negative returns. The top province in terms of the industry's revenue is Jiangsu, accounting for 36.76% of the total revenue.
本行業在 1996 年佔全行業總產值 0.046% ，行業年增長率為 44.4%（全國工業年增長率 9.51%）。行業的資產回報率 3.73% ，68.91% 的企業盈利，23.53% 的企業虧損。銷售收入最高的省份為江蘇省，佔本行業的 36.76% 。

	Total number of firms 企業總數	Total number of employees 職工總數	Total revenue (mil. RMB) 總銷售收入（百萬元）	Total profit (mil. RMB) 總利潤（百萬元）	Return on assets 資產利潤率 (%)	Return on equity 權益利潤率 (%)	Labour productivity ('000 RMB / worker) 勞動生產率（千元／人）	Debts / assets 資產負債率 (%)	Total assets (mil. RMB) 總資產（百萬元）
Industry Overall 行業總體	241	19,923	2,686	96	3.73	10.06	134.82	62.92	2,575

	Number of firms 企業個數	Average number of employees 平均職工人數	Average revenue ('000 RMB) 平均銷售收入（千元）	Average profit ('000 RMB) 平均利潤（千元）	Return on assets 資產利潤率 (%)	Return on equity 權益利潤率 (%)	Labour productivity ('000 RMB / worker) 勞動生產率（千元／人）	Average debts / assets 平均資產負債率(%)	Average Total assets ('000 RMB) 平均總資產（千元）
By ownership 產業所有權									
State-owned 國有	28	146	4,571	-357	-3.76	-10.20	31.30	63.16	9,500
Collectively-owned 集體	171	75	11,854	602	6.51	18.35	157.71	64.54	9,258
Privately-owned 私有	1	26	817	16	0.58	0.58	31.42		2,707
Domestic JVs 聯營	7	94	3,659	-410	-4.32	-7.12	38.87	39.26	9,478
Joint stock 股份制	3	61	427	-8	-0.22	-0.97	7.03	77.33	3,597
Foreign-funded 外資	11	92	16,543	-494	-1.44	-3.75	179.28	61.68	34,383
Overseas Chinese-funded 港澳台資	19	76	16,919	595	4.21	10.72	221.85	60.71	14,130
By size 規模									
Large 大型									
Medium 中型	6	616	55,991	-1,065	-1.29	-3.65	90.97	64.57	82,288
Small 小型	223	72	10,539	459	4.92	13.12	146.92	62.52	9,335
By regional distribution 地區分布									
Central-North 華北	28	82	4,080	300	8.23	18.39	49.72	55.27	3,650
Beijing 北京	10	21	1,450	99	2.85	7.71	70.05	63.02	3,475
Tianjin 天津	5	276	3,970	206	6.66	23.52	14.38	71.73	3,092
Hebei 河北	10	64	7,884	639	12.93	22.93	123.00	43.62	4,943
Shanxi 山西	2	35	530				15.14	75.49	1,285
Inner Mongolia 內蒙	1								
Northeast 東北	31	99	5,951	27	0.27	0.75	60.21	64.44	10,157
Liaoning 遼寧	20	110	6,734	-272	-2.17	-6.47	61.41	66.48	12,530
Jilin 吉林	5	95	424	-20	-1.27	-3.77	4.47	66.20	1,574
Heilongjiang 黑龍江	6	66	7,950	1,063	11.31	25.22	120.15	55.15	9,402
Central East 華東	99	93	18,972	967	6.12	14.32	203.47	57.26	15,800
Shanghai 上海	8	79	13,038	-591	-4.52	-14.74	165.03	69.34	13,079
Jiangsu 江蘇	29	111	34,047	2,032	7.50	14.58	307.01	48.55	27,100
Zhejiang 浙江	20	101	11,742	58	0.32	0.76	116.32	58.12	18,156
Anhui 安徽	9	50	4,127	126	4.50	10.90	82.53	58.66	2,790
Fujian 福建	5	38	7,784	38	1.68	5.14	204.84	67.43	2,266
Jiangxi 江西	4	58	1,450	-90	-7.53	-72.00	25.00	89.75	1,195
Shandong 山東	24	104	19,578	1,643	14.64	60.18	188.55	75.68	11,222
Central-South 中南	65	67	7,040	-124	-1.52	-8.74	104.42	82.60	8,127
Henan 河南	25	32	1,434	87	5.00	14.03	44.60	64.33	1,743
Hubei 湖北	6	91	6,690	237	9.46	80.68	73.52	88.27	2,502
Hunan 湖南	10	145	7,505	282	5.18	13.13	51.87	60.56	5,446
Guangdong 廣東	23	68	13,269	-547	-3.09	-24.21	196.01	87.25	17,730
Guangxi 廣西	1	28	1,340	-1,860	-25.07	-166.07	47.86	84.91	7,420
Hainan 海南									
Southwest 西南	12	45	1,135	-8	-0.38	-0.78	25.46	51.03	2,195
Chongqing 重慶	1	7							
Sichuan 四川	10	53	1,362	-10	-0.38	-0.77	25.62	51.03	2,635
Guizhou 貴州	1								
Yunnan 雲南									
Tibet 西藏									
Northwest 西北	6	69	6,262	-133	-2.04	-3.35	90.97	39.14	6,532
Shaanxi 陝西	4	20	1,773	-48	-4.20	-9.90	90.90	57.74	1,130
Gansu 甘肅									
Qinghai 青海									
Ningxia 寧夏									
Xinjiang 新疆	2	168	15,240	-305	-1.76	-2.78	90.99	36.72	17,335

2664: Functional Polymer 功能高分子製造業

Year 年份	Number of firms 企業個數	Rate of change 每年變化 (%)	Number of employees 職工人數（人）	Rate of change 每年變化 (%)	Total revenue (mil. RMB) 總銷售收入（百萬元）	Rate of change 每年變化 (%)	Total profit (mil. RMB) 總利潤（百萬元）	Rate of change 每年變化 (%)
1993	119		11,129		708		42	
1994	121	1.68%	9,218	-17.17%	953	34.50%	26	-39.31%
1995	209	72.73%	16,325	77.10%	1,860	95.25%	66	157.29%
1996	241	15.31%	19,923	22.04%	2,686	44.41%	96	44.98%

3 Major products* 3種主要產品*	Output 產量	Sales volume 銷售量	Unit 單位
a) Ion-exchange Resin 離子交換樹脂	14,635	12,586	ton 噸
b) Unsaturaled Polyester Resin 不飽和聚酯樹脂	34,183	31,448	ton 噸
c) Polyurethane Plastics 聚氨酯塑料	9,774	9,677	ton 噸

Top 10 firms by revenue (year founded) 收入排名前10家企業（創辦年份）	City 城市	Province 省	Telephone / fax 電話／傳真	Number of employees 職工人數	Ownership 產業所有權	Revenue ('000 RMB) 銷售收入（千元）	Profit ('000 RMB) (rank) 利潤（千元）（排名）	Total assets ('000 RMB) 總資產（千元）	Major products 主要產品
Starlite Resin Products (Kunshan) Co. Ltd. 星光樹脂有限公司(1994)	Suzhou 蘇州市	Jiangsu 江蘇省	(0512)7831220	760	Foreign-funded 外資	231,820	11000(4)	205,000	o
Jiangsu Fu Li Chemical Group Co. 江蘇富麗化工集團公司(1994)	Wuxi 無錫市	Jiangsu 江蘇省	(0510)6651029 (0510)6651333	250	Collectively-owned 集體	212,222	24489(1)	138,491	b
Ji'nan Sheng Quan Group Co. Ltd. 濟南聖泉集團股份有限公司(1979)	Ji'nan 濟南市	Shandong 山東省	(0531)3511076 (0531)3511356	510	Collectively-owned 集體	183,440	17590(2)	88,972	o
Jiangsu Ji Yang Chemical Group Co. Ltd 江蘇暨陽化工集團有限公司(1976)	Wuxi 無錫市	Jiangsu 江蘇省	(0510)6651031 (0510)6651031	406	Collectively-owned 集體	180,344	11970(3)	86,081	b
Hangzhou Zheng Guang Chemical Group Company 杭州爭光化工集團公司(1993)	Hangzhou 杭州市	Zhejiang 浙江省	(0571)6373478	589	Collectively-owned 集體	116,910	1170(24)	208,254	o
Jiangsu De Fa Resin Co. Ltd. 江蘇德發樹脂有限公司(1994)	Yancheng 鹽城市	Jiangsu 江蘇省	(0515)2322500	56	Overseas Chinese-funded 港澳台資	104,180	8220(6)	73,460	o
Zhucheng Si Da Insulating Material Co. Ltd. 諸城市四達絕緣材料股份有限公司(1966)	Weifang 濰坊市	Shandong 山東省	(0536)6213175 (0536)6111058	383	Joint stock 股份制	69,901	8665(5)	33,177	o
Ri Dong Electric Engineering Co. Ltd. 日東電工有限公司(1995)	Shanghai 上海市	Shanghai 上海市	(021)58663802 (021)58663710	84	Foreign-funded 外資	57,984	-5864(118)	56,743	o
Xishan Resin Plant 錫山市樹脂廠(1994)	Wuxi 無錫市	Jiangsu 江蘇省	(0510)5380679	287	Collectively-owned 集體	54,610	2160(16)	29,970	o
Shandong Huantai Chemical Factory 山東省桓台縣化工廠(1976)	Zibo 淄博市	Shandong 山東省	(0533)8880088 (0533)8880088	200	Collectively-owned 集體	52,360	2660(11)	27,760	o

Top 10 Cities by Production Output 產出排名前10位城市	Province 省	Market share 市場份額	Number of firms 企業個數
Shantou 汕頭市	Guangdong 廣東省	21.18%	7
Changzhou 常州市	Jiangsu 江蘇省	10.23%	7
Shanghai 上海市	Shanghai 上海市	7.77%	32
Ji'nan 濟南市	Shandong 山東省	5.94%	9
Yancheng 鹽城市	Jiangsu 江蘇省	3.32%	3
Guangzhou 廣州市	Guangdong 廣東省	3.25%	7
Xuzhou 徐州市	Jiangsu 江蘇省	2.86%	2
Wuxi 無錫市	Jiangsu 江蘇省	2.81%	14
Hangzhou 杭州市	Zhejiang 浙江省	2.64%	6
Weifang 濰坊市	Shandong 山東省	2.19%	7

10 Major Wholesalers 10家主要批發商	City 城市	Province 省	Telephone / Fax 電話／傳真
Zhong Hua Singbo Import & Export Company 中化寧波進出口公司	Ningbo 寧波市	Zhejiang 浙江省	(0574)7346764 (0574)7366775
China Chemical Supply & Marketing Hua Nan Company 中國化工供銷華南公司	Guangzhou 廣州市	Guangdong 廣東省	(020)87654477 (020)87784414
China Agriculture Means of Production Chengdu Company 中國農業生產資料成都公司	Chengdu 成都市	Sichuan 四川省	(028)3333909 (028)3331202
Shanxi Agriculture Means of Production Company 山西省農業生產資料公司	Taiyuan 太原市	Shanxi 山西省	(0351)4040255 (0351)4040231
Beijing Chemical Light Industry General Company 北京市化工輕工總公司	Beijing 北京市	Beijing 北京市	(010)64224837 (010)64219301
Beijing Chemical Industry Group Company Supply & Marketing Company 北京化學工業集團公司供銷公司	Beijing 北京市	Beijing 北京市	(010)67714610 (010)67714058
Zhong Hua Jiangsu Import & Export Company 中化江蘇進出口公司	Nanjing 南京市	Jiangsu 江蘇省	(025)2258718 (025)2257789
Yunnan Chemical Import & Export Company 雲南省化工進出口公司	Kunming 昆明市	Yunnan 雲南省	(0871)3314002 (0871)3314931
Fujian Jiu Zhou Group Co. Ltd. 福建九州集團股份有限公司	Xiamen 廈門市	Fujian 福建省	(0592)5055818 (0592)5052033
China Chemical Industry Commission Agent Hua Dong Co. 中國化工供銷華東公司	Shanghai 上海市	Shanghai 上海市	(021)62514123

*Also include sales by firms outside this industry.包括本行業以外廠家的銷售。"o" stands for "others". "o" 代表"其他產品"。

2665: Organic Silicofluoride Material 有機硅氟材料製造業

The industry accounts for 0.021% of the total revenue of China's industrial sector in 1996. The revenue growth rate of the industry is 56.4% from 1995, as compared to the growth rate of China's industrial sector, 9.51%. The rate of return on asset is 1.57%. 67.31% of all firms in the industry made a profit while 27.52% had negative returns. The top province in terms of the industry's revenue is Beijing, accounting for 20.45% of the total revenue.
本行業在1996年佔全行業總產值0.021%，行業年增長率為56.4%（全國工業年增長率9.51%）。行業的資產回報率1.57%，67.31%的企業盈利，27.52%的企業虧損。銷售收入最高的省份為北京市，佔本行業的20.45%。

	Total number of firms 企業總數	Total number of employees 職工總數	Total revenue (mil. RMB) 總銷售收入（百萬元）	Total profit (mil. RMB) 總利潤（百萬元）	Return on assets 資產利潤率 (%)	Return on equity 權益利潤率 (%)	Labour productivity ('000 RMB / worker) 勞動生產率（千元/人）	Debts / assets 資產負債率 (%)	Total assets (mil. RMB) 總資產（百萬元）
Industry Overall 行業總體	122	15,589	1,202	31	1.57	5.97	77.11	73.77	1,954

	Number of firms 企業個數	Average number of employees 平均職工人數	Average revenue ('000 RMB) 平均銷售收入（千元）	Average profit ('000 RMB) 平均利潤（千元）	Return on assets 資產利潤率 (%)	Return on equity 權益利潤率 (%)	Labour productivity ('000 RMB / worker) 勞動生產率（千元/人）	Average debts / assets 平均資產負債率(%)	Average Total assets ('000 RMB) 平均總資產（千元）
By ownership 產業所有權									
State-owned 國有	17	518	28,765	-765	-1.10	-7.98	55.51	86.22	69,588
Collectively-owned 集體	85	52	5,810	320	7.58	28.46	111.71	73.38	4,223
Privately-owned 私有									
Domestic JVs 聯營	3	64	1,867	-320	-2.79	-3.89	29.02	28.34	11,472
Joint stock 股份制	1	1,123	82,956	10,455	5.41	6.45	73.87	16.18	193,331
Foreign-funded 外資	9	91	5,556	-1,216	-8.10	-27.12	61.05	70.12	15,002
Overseas Chinese-funded 港澳台資	7	40	11,498	2,606	36.82	66.45	286.43	44.59	7,078
By size 規模									
Large 大型	2	2,753	120,068	-3,678	-0.88	-17.77	43.62	95.04	417,176
Medium 中型	1	730	21,583	-3,513	-12.23	39.39	29.57	131.06	28,712
Small 小型	111	83	8,471	377	3.84	8.71	102.34	55.96	9,831
By regional distribution 地區分布									
Central-North 華北	15	192	17,626	95	0.46	1.67	91.67	72.74	20,793
Beijing 北京	3	848	81,933	73	0.08	0.29	96.58	73.88	96,193
Tianjin 天津	6	35	2,442	152	5.08	11.64	70.43	56.31	2,983
Hebei 河北	5	22	706	52	5.06	14.36	31.80	64.79	1,028
Shanxi 山西	1	20	410	30	11.11		20.50	100.00	270
Inner Mongolia 內蒙									
Northeast 東北	17	141	5,531	-345	-1.82	-24.14	39.31	92.47	18,993
Liaoning 遼寧	14	158	6,297	-453	-2.41	-50.68	39.95	95.24	18,767
Jilin 吉林	1	30	480				16.00	100.00	130
Heilongjiang 黑龍江	2	78	2,695	235	0.78	3.98	34.77	80.32	30,005
Central East 華東	56	143	11,121	492	2.47	7.58	77.93	67.39	19,898
Shanghai 上海	5	255	18,500	1,248	2.52	3.04	72.44	17.08	49,496
Jiangsu 江蘇	12	113	13,985	559	4.24	13.15	123.67	67.77	13,193
Zhejiang 浙江	11	42	7,345	-89	-1.51	-4.10	176.78	63.31	5,919
Anhui 安徽	4	79	22,563	3,838	28.17	43.40	286.51	35.08	13,625
Fujian 福建	10	37	2,117	-26	-0.54	-2.46	56.76	78.13	4,832
Jiangxi 江西	4	85	2,068	-233	-5.52	22.46	24.47	124.58	4,210
Shandong 山東	10	388	16,199	142	0.27	3.43	41.80	92.09	52,372
Central-South 中南	23	77	8,196	483	7.66	27.95	106.14	72.59	6,311
Henan 河南	4	81	6,355	138	2.74	34.59	78.94	92.07	5,015
Hubei 湖北	7	71	7,733	199	3.65	16.16	109.35	77.44	5,440
Hunan 湖南	6	111	3,678	33	1.09	7.75	33.14	85.92	3,053
Guangdong 廣東	4	36	20,833	2,198	14.23	37.66	578.68	62.21	15,448
Guangxi 廣西	2	75	1,780	95	2.75	5.16	23.89	46.74	3,455
Hainan 海南									
Southwest 西南	5	23	2,004	-966	-14.76	79.97	86.38	118.42	6,546
Chongqing 重慶									
Sichuan 四川	4	28	1,648	123	6.30	-446.67	58.86	101.41	1,953
Guizhou 貴州	1	5	3,430	-5,320	-21.35	89.86	686.00	123.76	24,920
Yunnan 雲南									
Tibet 西藏									
Northwest 西北	6	72	3,682	202	4.49	19.97	51.49	77.54	4,490
Shaanxi 陝西	3	55	3,190	113	4.56	-13.77	58.35	133.24	2,487
Gansu 甘肅	1	200	8,740	490	3.62	9.55	43.70	62.14	13,550
Qinghai 青海									
Ningxia 寧夏									
Xinjiang 新疆	2	33	1,890	190	6.41	11.18	58.15	42.66	2,965

2665: Organic Silicofluoride Material 有機硅氟材料製造業

Year 年份	Number of firms 企業個數	Rate of change 每年變化 (%)	Number of employees 職工人數 (人)	Rate of change 每年變化 (%)	Total revenue (mil. RMB) 總銷售收入 (百萬元)	Rate of change 每年變化 (%)	Total profit (mil. RMB) 總利潤 (百萬元)	Rate of change 每年變化 (%)
1993	74		14,906		485		18	
1994	92	24.32%	11,095	-25.57%	521	7.30%	-43	-338.00%
1995	100	8.70%	12,873	16.03%	769	47.61%	17	138.63%
1996	122	22.00%	15,589	21.10%	1,202	56.38%	31	85.56%

3 Major products* 3種主要產品*	Output 產量	Sales volume 銷售量	Unit 單位
a) Flouride Polymer 含氟聚合物	12,661	12,028	ton 噸
b) Anhydrous Hydrogen Fluoride 無水氟化氫	5,702	5,132	ton 噸
c) Disperse Dye 分散染料	4,684	4,309	ton 噸

Top 10 firms by revenue (year founded) 收入排名前10家企業 (創辦年份)	City 城市	Province 省	Telephone / fax 電話 / 傳真	Number of employees 職工人數	Ownership 產業所有權	Revenue ('000 RMB) 銷售收入 (千元)	Profit ('000 RMB) (rank) 利潤 (千元) (排名)	Total assets ('000 RMB) 總資產 (千元)	Major products 主要產品
Beijing Dyestuff Factory 北京染料廠(1952)	Beijing 北京市	Beijing 北京市	(010)67383777 (010)67364145	2,173	State-owned 國有	245,397	161(29)	287,200	c
Changshu Refrigeration Agent Factory 常熟市致冷劑廠(1975)	Suzhou 蘇州市	Jiangsu 江蘇省	(0512)2621544 (0512)2621243	680	Collectively-owned 集體	112,631	2830(4)	119,107	a
Ji'nan Chemical Plant 濟南化工廠(1914)	Ji'nan 濟南市	Shandong 山東省	(0531)5952244 (0531)5951373	2,995	State-owned 國有	86,936	0(45)	453,720	a,b
Anhui Zhong Ding Xi Wei Artificial Crystal Co. Ltd. 安徽中鼎烯煒人工晶體有限公司(1985)	Xuanzhou 宣州市	Anhui 安徽省	(0563)4074800	150	Domestic JVs 聯營	80,000	15000(1)	43,070	o
Shanghai 3f New Materials Co. Ltd. 上海三愛富新材料股份有限公司(1960)	Shanghai 上海市	Shanghai 上海市	(021)64340430 (021)64345915	820	Joint stock 股份制	71,492	6357(3)	188,943	a
Shenzhen Tian Yu High Polymer Materials Co. Ltd. 深圳天玉高分子材料有限公司(1993)	Shenzhen 深圳市	Guangdong 廣東省	(0755)6674566 (0755)6684699	99	Overseas Chinese-funded 港澳台資	69,428	9892(2)	41,198	o
Fuxin Fluorine Chemical General Factory 阜新氟化學總廠(1972)	Fuxin 阜新市	Liaoning 遼寧省	(0418)2852957 (0418)2852956	1,465	State-owned 國有	61,553	-4985(57)	211,040	o
Zhejiang Linhai Li Min Chemical Factory 浙江省臨海市利民化工廠(1988)	Taizhou 臺州市	Zhejiang 浙江省	(0576)5111058 (0576)5111058	127	Collectively-owned 集體	38,545	188(26)	16,659	o
Ningbo Yong Da Industrial General Company 寧波永大實業總公司(1977)	Ningbo 寧波市	Zhejiang 浙江省	(0574)3813942 (0574)3812818	105	State-owned 國有	27,254	140(32)	26,716	o
The Chinese Academy of Sciences Shanghai Organic Chemical Research Institute Development Co.中科院上海有機所開發公司(1958)	Shanghai 上海市	Shanghai 上海市	(021)62412403 (021)62747223	366	State-owned 國有	19,203	159(30)	36,252	o

Top 10 Cities by Production Output 產出排名前10位城市	Province 省	Market share 市場份額	Number of firms 企業個數
Beijing 北京市	Beijing 北京市	21.68%	3
Shanghai 上海市	Shanghai 上海市	12.18%	10
Nantong 南通市	Jiangsu 江蘇省	9.81%	2
Ji'nan 濟南市	Shandong 山東省	8.43%	3
Fuxin 阜新市	Liaoning 遼寧省	5.54%	2
Taizhou 臺州市	Zhejiang 浙江省	3.91%	3
Zhenjiang 鎮江市	Jiangsu 江蘇省	3.24%	9
Ningbo 寧波市	Zhejiang 浙江省	2.50%	1
Hangzhou 杭州市	Zhejiang 浙江省	1.95%	6
Taizhou 泰州市	Jiangsu 江蘇省	1.92%	2

10 Major Wholesalers 10家主要批發商	City 城市	Province 省	Telephone / Fax 電話 / 傳真
Zhong Hua Singbo Import & Export Company 中化寧波進出口公司	Ningbo 寧波市	Zhejiang 浙江省	(0574)7346764 (0574)7366775
China Chemical Supply & Marketing Hua Nan Company 中國化工供銷華南公司	Guangzhou 廣州市	Guangdong 廣東省	(020)87654477 (020)87784414
China Agriculture Means of Production Chengdu Company 中國農業生產資料成都公司	Chengdu 成都市	Sichuan 四川省	(028)3333909 (028)3331202
Shanxi Agriculture Means of Production Company 山西省農業生產資料公司	Taiyuan 太原市	Shanxi 山西省	(0351)4040255 (0351)4040231
Beijing Chemical Light Industry General Company 北京市化工輕工總公司	Beijing 北京市	Beijing 北京市	(010)64224837 (010)64219301
Beijing Chemical Industry Group Company Supply & Marketing Company 北京化學工業集團公司供銷公司	Beijing 北京市	Beijing 北京市	(010)67714610 (010)67714058
Zhong Hua Jiangsu Import & Export Company 中化江蘇進出口公司	Nanjing 南京市	Jiangsu 江蘇省	(025)2258718 (025)2257789
Yunnan Chemical Import & Export Company 雲南省化工進出口公司	Kunming 昆明市	Yunnan 雲南省	(0871)3314002 (0871)3314931
Fujian Jiu Zhou Group Co. Ltd. 福建九州集團股份有限公司	Xiamen 廈門市	Fujian 福建省	(0592)5055818 (0592)5052033
China Chemical Industry Commission Agent Hua Dong Co. 中國化工供銷華東公司	Shanghai 上海市	Shanghai 上海市	(021)62514123

*Also include sales by firms outside this industry.包括本行業以外廠家的銷售。"o" stands for "others". "o" 代表 "其他產品"。

2666: Synthetic Rubber 合成橡膠製造業

The industry accounts for 0.036% of the total revenue of China's industrial sector in 1996. The revenue growth rate of the industry is 32.1% from 1995, as compared to the growth rate of China's industrial sector, 9.51%. The rate of return on asset is 4.33%. 66.53% of all firms in the industry made a profit while 21.88% had negative returns. The top province in terms of the industry's revenue is Chongqing, accounting for 19.00% of the total revenue.
本行業在1996年佔全行業總產值0.036%，行業年增長率為32.1%（全國工業年增長率9.51%）。行業的資產回報率4.33%，66.53%的企業盈利，21.88%的企業虧損。銷售收入最高的省份為重慶市，佔本行業的19.00%。

	Total number of firms 企業總數	Total number of employees 職工總數	Total revenue (mil. RMB) 總銷售收入（百萬元）	Total profit (mil. RMB) 總利潤（百萬元）	Return on assets 資產利潤率 (%)	Return on equity 權益利潤率 (%)	Labour productivity ('000 RMB / worker) 勞動生產率（千元/人）	Debts / assets 資產負債率 (%)	Total assets (mil. RMB) 總資產（百萬元）
Industry Overall 行業總體	191	20,742	2,089	103	4.33	12.11	100.71	64.23	2,371

	Number of firms 企業個數	Average number of employees 平均職工人數	Average revenue ('000 RMB) 平均銷售收入（千元）	Average profit ('000 RMB) 平均利潤（千元）	Return on assets 資產利潤率 (%)	Return on equity 權益利潤率 (%)	Labour productivity ('000 RMB / worker) 勞動生產率（千元/人）	Average debts / assets 平均資產負債率(%)	Average Total assets ('000 RMB) 平均總資產（千元）
By ownership 產業所有權									
State-owned 國有	10	1,181	68,700	200	0.16	0.50	58.17	67.64	123,000
Collectively-owned 集體	148	37	3,246	182	9.13	30.44	86.90	70.00	1,988
Privately-owned 私有									
Domestic JVs 聯營	5	113	3,565	-307	-4.30	-55.58	31.61	92.27	7,136
Joint stock 股份制	1	49	1,617	-5	-0.30	4.96	33.00	105.98	1,837
Foreign-funded 外資	11	206	68,944	6,652	12.76	28.77	334.83	55.63	52,119
Overseas Chinese-funded 港澳台資	15	41	9,660	166	1.05	2.37	235.61	55.67	15,793
By size 規模									
Large 大型	3	4,122	246,622	2,251	0.62	2.07	59.83	70.22	365,070
Medium 中型	1	109	213,185	11,210	6.10	10.83	1955.83	43.71	183,924
Small 小型	177	45	6,424	480	7.78	20.31	142.37	61.69	6,175
By regional distribution 地區分布									
Central-North 華北	31	172	10,632	224	1.18	2.09	61.69	43.69	19,034
Beijing 北京	7	9	810	-40	-4.40	-41.18	94.50	89.31	909
Tianjin 天津	5	19	2,784	118	13.79	421.43	143.51	96.73	856
Hebei 河北	15	62	2,949	217	3.20	6.70	47.36	52.14	6,761
Shanxi 山西	3	1,402	88,440	1,183	0.75	1.26	63.08	40.61	158,203
Inner Mongolia 內蒙	1	46	460	-160	-4.72	-15.24	10.00	69.03	3,390
Northeast 東北	32	38	1,316	43	2.56	11.72	34.69	78.15	1,695
Liaoning 遼寧	18	50	1,182	45	2.09	13.55	23.61	84.59	2,156
Jilin 吉林	6	29	2,688	37	2.61	4.97	93.78	47.63	1,407
Heilongjiang 黑龍江	8	18	589	45	5.15	24.83	33.40	79.26	874
Central East 華東	65	61	11,343	1,065	11.86	25.69	186.24	53.82	8,976
Shanghai 上海	4	60	46,900	5,415	10.69	16.68	781.67	35.91	50,640
Jiangsu 江蘇	23	58	12,438	1,728	20.45	52.68	214.28	61.19	8,450
Zhejiang 浙江	6	22	4,943	127	9.05	30.40	223.01	70.24	1,400
Anhui 安徽	5	76	29,868	916	10.98	18.62	390.94	41.01	8,340
Fujian 福建	10	28	1,801	-213	-3.56	-8.93	63.42	60.13	5,982
Jiangxi 江西									
Shandong 山東	17	93	3,919	271	6.01	34.87	42.04	82.75	4,509
Central-South 中南	40	57	12,641	619	7.11	22.42	223.23	68.30	8,705
Henan 河南	10	36	3,433	116	4.39	11.30	94.57	61.17	2,642
Hubei 湖北	10	78	15,770	533	7.91	34.79	202.96	77.26	6,741
Hunan 湖南	4	40	2,883	165	9.82	18.86	71.61	47.92	1,680
Guangdong 廣東	13	69	22,952	1,401	7.90	25.80	331.17	69.37	17,722
Guangxi 廣西	3	21	1,227	-203	-3.53	-5.70	58.41	37.98	5,757
Hainan 海南									
Southwest 西南	15	496	29,365	78	0.16	0.99	59.16	84.32	50,108
Chongqing 重慶	2	3,648	198,438	99	0.03	0.17	54.39	84.11	362,337
Sichuan 四川	8	5	1,562	2	1.66	3.69	287.90	55.00	91
Guizhou 貴州	2	1	10,280	275	3.67	35.48	20560.00	89.67	7,500
Yunnan 雲南	3	35	3,517	137	3.65	46.59	100.48	92.16	3,740
Tibet 西藏									
Northwest 西北	8	64	4,176	-94	-1.73	-11.79	64.87	85.32	5,415
Shaanxi 陝西	7	35	3,164	319	13.22	40.62	90.78	67.46	2,410
Gansu 甘肅									
Qinghai 青海									
Ningxia 寧夏									
Xinjiang 新疆	1	271	11,260	-2,980	-11.27	-342.53	41.55	96.71	26,450

Year 年份	Number of firms 企業個數	Rate of change 每年變化 (%)	Number of employees 職工人數 (人)	Rate of change 每年變化 (%)	Total revenue (mil. RMB) 總銷售收入 (百萬元)	Rate of change 每年變化 (%)	Total profit (mil. RMB) 總利潤 (百萬元)	Rate of change 每年變化 (%)
1993	176		8,596		568		26	
1994	199	13.07%	19,441	126.16%	1,086	91.45%	48	86.78%
1995	152	-23.62%	19,004	-2.25%	1,581	45.55%	86	77.92%
1996	191	25.66%	20,742	9.15%	2,089	32.13%	103	19.88%

3 Major products* 3種主要產品*	Output 產量	Sales volume 銷售量	Unit 單位
a) Chlorobutadiene Rubber 氯丁橡膠	24,039	23,318	ton 噸
b) Skin Glue 皮膠	1,035	973	ton 噸
c) Butadiene Styrene Rubber 丁苯橡膠	13,933	13,515	ton 噸

Top 10 firms by revenue (year founded) 收入排名前10家企業 (創辦年份)	City 城市	Province 省	Telephone / fax 電話 / 傳真	Number of employees 職工人數	Ownership 產業所有權	Revenue ('000 RMB) 銷售收入 (千元)	Profit ('000 RMB) (rank) 利潤 (千元) (排名)	Total assets ('000 RMB) 總資產 (千元)	Major products 主要產品
Changshou Chemical General Factory 長壽化工總廠(1945)	Chongqing 重慶市	Chongqing 重慶市	(023)40262651 (023)40510596	7,174	State-owned 國有	405,736	231(37)	721,584	a
Shanxi Chemical Factory 山西省化工廠(1960)	Datong 大同市	Shanxi 山西省	(0352)2892078 (0352)2892055	4,143	State-owned 國有	263,837	3528(6)	472,798	a
Vnion Carbide (Guangdong, Zhongshan) Co. Ltd. 聯合碳化(廣東中山)有限公司(1992)	Zhongshan 中山市	Guangdong 廣東省	(0760)2101288 (0760)2100823	84	Foreign-funded 外資	185,844	13449(3)	110,153	o
Shanghai Gao Qiao Basf Dispersions Co. Ltd. 上海高橋巴斯夫分散體有限公司(1993)	Shanghai 上海市	Shanghai 上海市	(021)58670303 (021)58675050	101	Foreign-funded 外資	144,326	18341(2)	154,217	c
Nantong Sandexing Electronic Industry Co. Ltd. 南通三德興電子工業有限公司(1991)	Nantong 南通市	Jiangsu 江蘇省	(0513)3596388 (0513)3596678	100	Foreign-funded 外資	138,068	36884(1)	111,120	o
Anhui Zhong Ding Group Rubber Factory 安徽中鼎集團煉膠廠(1993)	Xuanzhou 宣州市	Anhui 安徽省	(0563)4074888	250	Collectively-owned 集體	120,000	1500(10)	33,810	o
Zaoyang Longkou Chemical Factory 棗陽市龍口化工廠(1986)	Xiangfan 襄樊市	Hubei 湖北省	(0710)6226592	230	Collectively-owned 集體	110,876	4106(4)	44,393	o
Guang Sheng Toy (Shenzhen) Co. Ltd. 光晟玩具(深圳)有限公司(1992)	Shenzhen 深圳市	Guangdong 廣東省	(0755)7401000 (0755)7400111	440	Overseas Chinese-funded 港澳台資	68,434	4106(5)	35,726	o
Wuxian Che Fang Emulsiod Factory 吳縣市車坊乳膠廠(1992)	Suzhou 蘇州市	Jiangsu 江蘇省	(0512)5911754	189	Collectively-owned 集體	38,670	30(49)	4,810	o
Shanghai Gaoqiao Basf Latex Co. Ltd. 上海高橋——巴斯夫膠乳有限公司(1987)	Shanghai 上海市	Shanghai 上海市	(021)58670303 (021)58675050	42	Foreign-funded 外資	35,744	3106(7)	33,248	c

Top 10 Cities by Production Output 產出排名前10位城市	Province 省	Market share 市場份額	Number of firms 企業個數
Yueyang 岳陽市	Hunan 湖南省	53.78%	1
Datong 大同市	Shanxi 山西省	10.12%	1
Zhongshan 中山市	Guangdong 廣東省	7.13%	1
Xiangfan 襄樊市	Hubei 湖北省	4.26%	5
Shanghai 上海市	Shanghai 上海市	2.82%	25
Zhenjiang 鎮江市	Jiangsu 江蘇省	1.59%	5
Suzhou 蘇州市	Jiangsu 江蘇省	1.43%	6
Baoding 保定市	Hebei 河北省	1.05%	2
Foshan 佛山市	Guangdong 廣東省	0.96%	3
Luohe 漯河市	Henan 河南省	0.82%	1

10 Major Wholesalers 10家主要批發商	City 城市	Province 省	Telephone / Fax 電話 / 傳真
Zhong Hua Singbo Import & Export Company 中化寧波進出口公司	Ningbo 寧波市	Zhejiang 浙江省	(0574)7346764 (0574)7366775
China Chemical Supply & Marketing Hua Nan Company 中國化工供銷華南公司	Guangzhou 廣州市	Guangdong 廣東省	(020)87654477 (020)87784414
China Agriculture Means of Production Chengdu Company 中國農業生產資料成都公司	Chengdu 成都市	Sichuan 四川省	(028)3333909 (028)3331202
Shanxi Agriculture Means of Production Company 山西省農業生產資料公司	Taiyuan 太原市	Shanxi 山西省	(0351)4040255 (0351)4040231
Beijing Chemical Light Industry General Company 北京市化工輕工總公司	Beijing 北京市	Beijing 北京市	(010)64224837 (010)64219301
Beijing Chemical Industry Group Company Supply & Marketing Company 北京化學工業集團公司供銷公司	Beijing 北京市	Beijing 北京市	(010)67714610 (010)67714058
Zhong Hua Jiangsu Import & Export Company 中化江蘇進出口公司	Nanjing 南京市	Jiangsu 江蘇省	(025)2258718 (025)2257789
Yunnan Chemical Import & Export Company 雲南省化工進出口公司	Kunming 昆明市	Yunnan 雲南省	(0871)3314002 (0871)3314931
Fujian Jiu Zhou Group Co. Ltd. 福建九州集團股份有限公司	Xiamen 廈門市	Fujian 福建省	(0592)5055818 (0592)5052033
China Chemical Industry Commission Agent Hua Dong Co. 中國化工供銷華東公司	Shanghai 上海市	Shanghai 上海市	(021)62514123

*Also include sales by firms outside this industry.包括本行業以外廠家的銷售。"o" stands for "others". "o" 代表"其他產品"。

2667: Synthetic Fibre 合成纖維單（聚合）體製造業

The industry accounts for 0.161% of the total revenue of China's industrial sector in 1996. The revenue growth rate of the industry is 3.6% from 1995, as compared to the growth rate of China's industrial sector, 9.51%. The rate of return on asset is -1.97%. 68.75% of all firms in the industry made a profit while 31.25% had negative returns. The top province in terms of the industry's revenue is Liaoning, accounting for 53.09% of the total revenue.
本行業在1996年佔全行業總產值0.161%，行業年增長率為3.6%（全國工業年增長率9.51%）。行業的資產回報率-1.97%，68.75%的企業盈利，31.25%的企業虧損。銷售收入最高的省份為遼寧省，佔本行業的53.09%。

	Total number of firms 企業總數	Total number of employees 職工總數	Total revenue (mil. RMB) 總銷售收入（百萬元）	Total profit (mil. RMB) 總利潤（百萬元）	Return on assets 資產利潤率 (%)	Return on equity 權益利潤率 (%)	Labour productivity ('000 RMB / worker) 勞動生產率（千元/人）	Debts / assets 資產負債率 (%)	Total assets (mil. RMB) 總資產（百萬元）
Industry Overall 行業總體	65	43,933	9,326	-353	-1.97	-6.31	212.28	68.78	17,950

	Number of firms 企業個數	Average number of employees 平均職工人數	Average revenue ('000 RMB) 平均銷售收入（千元）	Average profit ('000 RMB) 平均利潤（千元）	Return on assets 資產利潤率 (%)	Return on equity 權益利潤率 (%)	Labour productivity ('000 RMB / worker) 勞動生產率（千元/人）	Average debts / assets 平均資產負債率(%)	Average Total assets ('000 RMB) 平均總資產（千元）
By ownership 產業所有權									
State-owned 國有	10	3,300	542,800	7,900	0.99	1.90	164.50	47.87	798,000
Collectively-owned 集體	34	73	8,731	-1,386	-20.62	-87.56	119.13	76.45	6,721
Privately-owned 私有									
Domestic JVs 聯營									
Joint stock 股份制	3	461	3,944	-237	-0.08	-0.43	8.56	80.89	287,990
Foreign-funded 外資	8	382	267,133	-23,488	-3.78	-32.34	699.53	88.30	620,870
Overseas Chinese-funded 港澳台資	11	363	132,621	-17,840	-5.02	-30.47	364.89	83.53	355,531
By size 規模									
Large 大型	8	4,370	1,071,842	-66,037	-4.30	-10.11	245.27	57.52	1,537,241
Medium 中型	4	762	98,488	12,666	4.55	24.32	129.33	81.29	278,460
Small 小型	49	115	29,182	2,543	2.75	72.67	254.16	96.22	92,621
By regional distribution 地區分布									
Central-North 華北	12	79	13,387	794	15.97	79.15	169.09	79.83	4,974
Beijing 北京	2	87	2,820	-35	-1.08	-2.85	32.41	61.94	3,245
Tianjin 天津	5	99	27,050	1,380	17.48	322.43	274.34	94.60	7,894
Hebei 河北	2	107	9,405	1,350	23.77	42.99	88.31	44.72	5,680
Shanxi 山西	2	35	470				13.43	51.05	1,185
Inner Mongolia 內蒙	1								
Northeast 東北	1	26,476	4,951,270	16,630	0.26	0.46	187.01	44.66	6,466,040
Liaoning 遼寧	1	26,476	4,951,270	16,630	0.26	0.46	187.01	44.66	6,466,040
Jilin 吉林									
Heilongjiang 黑龍江									
Central East 華東	29	334	85,397	-4,057	-1.76	-10.22	255.36	82.76	230,286
Shanghai 上海	2	192	332,720	5,040	1.07	2.72	1732.92	60.56	469,055
Jiangsu 江蘇	18	196	39,683	-8,079	-6.10	829.08	202.69	100.74	132,363
Zhejiang 浙江	1	1,762	641,450	12,300	0.69	3.00	364.05	77.02	1,783,150
Anhui 安徽	1	215	28,000	1,860	26.38	75.00	130.23	64.82	7,050
Fujian 福建	2	738	112,210	8,880	1.93	6.89	152.15	71.93	459,335
Jiangxi 江西									
Shandong 山東	5	468	40,582	-2,848	-2.19	-11.07	86.79	80.18	129,756
Central-South 中南	19	175	79,553	-18,592	-8.86	-111.77	453.50	92.08	209,959
Henan 河南	5	21	1,444	16	3.27	10.67	68.76	69.39	490
Hubei 湖北									
Hunan 湖南	3	9	3	-7	-3.03	-28.57	0.36	89.39	220
Guangdong 廣東	10	293	121,653	-36,339	-11.25	-227.13	415.06	95.05	323,090
Guangxi 廣西									
Hainan 海南	1	269	287,750	10,080	1.33	6.49	1069.70	79.45	755,210
Southwest 西南	3	1,152	75,220	30,550	12.13	16.74	65.31	27.55	251,823
Chongqing 重慶									
Sichuan 四川	1	708			0.68	3.44		80.26	
Guizhou 貴州	1	233	22,950	100	0.18	0.21	98.50	12.27	55,270
Yunnan 雲南	1	2,514	202,710	91,550	13.07	18.35	80.63	28.76	700,200
Tibet 西藏									
Northwest 西北	1	21	110	-290	-26.85	93.55	5.24	128.70	1,080
Shaanxi 陝西									
Gansu 甘肅									
Qinghai 青海									
Ningxia 寧夏									
Xinjiang 新疆	1	21	110	-290	-26.85	93.55	5.24	128.70	1,080

2667: Synthetic Fibre 合成纖維單（聚合）體製造業

Year 年份	Number of firms 企業個數	Rate of change 每年變化 (%)	Number of employees 職工人數 (人)	Rate of change 每年變化 (%)	Total revenue (mil. RMB) 總銷售收入 (百萬元)	Rate of change 每年變化 (%)	Total profit (mil. RMB) 總利潤 (百萬元)	Rate of change 每年變化 (%)
1993	50		62,936		5,292		20	
1994	62	24.00%	41,094	-34.71%	5,382	1.70%	114	472.94%
1995	66	6.45%	44,576	8.47%	9,006	67.32%	258	127.27%
1996	65	-1.52%	43,933	-1.44%	9,326	3.55%	-353	-236.68%

3 Major products* 3種主要產品*	Output 產量	Sales volume 銷售量	Unit 單位
a) Polyester 聚酯	386,819	309,455	ton 噸
b) Ammonium Sulphate 硫酸銨	70,822	69,405	ton 噸
c) Polyvinyl Alcohol 聚乙烯醇	17,893	13,062	ton 噸

Top 10 firms by revenue (year founded) 收入排名前10家企業 (創辦年份)	City 城市	Province 省	Telephone / fax 電話 / 傳真	Number of employees 職工人數	Ownership 產業所有權	Revenue ('000 RMB) 銷售收入 (千元)	Profit ('000 RMB) (rank) 利潤（千元）(排名)	Total assets ('000 RMB) 總資產 (千元)	Major products 主要產品
Liaoyang Petroleum Chemical Fibre Co. 遼陽石油化纖公司(1983)	Liaoyang 遼陽市	Liaoning 遼寧省	(0419)5152589 (0419)5154911	27,042	State-owned 國有	4,951,270	16630(3)	6,466,040	o
Shanghai Lian He Synthetic Fibre Co. Ltd. 上海聯合化纖有限公司(1994)	Shanghai 上海市	Shanghai 上海市	(021)57502751 (021)57502644	335	Foreign-funded 外資	652,752	10111(5)	927,631	a
Zhejiang Chemical Fibre Joint Group Co. Ltd. 浙江化纖聯合集團股份有限公司(1984)	Shaoxing 紹興市	Zhejiang 浙江省	(0575)8064167 (0575)8067783	1,841	Joint stock 股份制	641,447	12299(4)	1,783,154	a
Foshan Polyester Chip Co. Ltd. 佛山市聚酯切片有限公司(1986)	Foshan 佛山市	Guangdong 廣東省	(0757)2814411 (0757)2812522	398	Overseas Chinese-funded 港澳台資	509,390	-77886(40)	304,922	a
Nanjing Dongfang Chemical Co. Ltd. 南京東方化工有限公司(1988)	Nanjing 南京市	Jiangsu 江蘇省	(025)7791216 (025)7791216	1,444	Foreign-funded 外資	415,793	-146369(43)	1,828,457	b
Guangzhou Yamei Polyester Co. Ltd. 廣州亞美聚酯有限公司(1994)	Guangzhou 廣州市	Guangdong 廣東省	(020)82215863 (020)82212921	244	Foreign-funded 外資	384,209	-114558(42)	503,917	a
Xiamen Li Heng Co. Ltd. 廈門利恒股份有限公司(1985)	Xiamen 廈門市	Fujian 福建省	(0592)6214450 (0592)6210529	1,436	Overseas Chinese-funded 港澳台資	209,831	17416(2)	867,591	a
Yunnan Polyvinyl Alcohol Fibre Mill 雲南維尼綸廠(1980)	Qujing 曲靖市	Yunnan 雲南省	(0874)3068899 (0874)3068590	2,367	State-owned 國有	202,713	91549(1)	700,202	c
Yuxing Polyester Chip Co. Ltd. 裕興聚酯切片有限公司(1992)	Zhuhai 珠海市	Guangdong 廣東省	(0756)3311868 (0756)3311483	267	Overseas Chinese-funded 港澳台資	171,822	-86553(41)	561,624	a
Zibo Petrochemical Plant 淄博石油化工廠(1968)	Zibo 淄博市	Shandong 山東省	(0533)2980406 (0533)2980211	1,605	State-owned 國有	158,939	-14492(37)	568,808	b

Top 10 Cities by Production Output 產出排名前10位城市	Province 省	Market share 市場份額	Number of firms 企業個數
Liaoyang 遼陽市	Liaoning 遼寧省	32.81%	1
Guangzhou 廣州市	Guangdong 廣東省	25.23%	5
Foshan 佛山市	Guangdong 廣東省	10.35%	2
Chongqing 重慶市	Chongqing 重慶市	6.99%	1
Shanghai 上海市	Shanghai 上海市	4.95%	12
Shaoxing 紹興市	Zhejiang 浙江省	4.26%	1
Yueyang 岳陽市	Hunan 湖南省	4.03%	1
Nanjing 南京市	Jiangsu 江蘇省	3.42%	2
Zhuhai 珠海市	Guangdong 廣東省	2.03%	3
Wuxi 無錫市	Jiangsu 江蘇省	1.40%	15

10 Major Wholesalers 10家主要批發商	City 城市	Province 省	Telephone / Fax 電話 / 傳真
Zhong Hua Singbo Import & Export Company 中化寧波進出口公司	Ningbo 寧波市	Zhejiang 浙江省	(0574)7346764 (0574)7366775
China Chemical Supply & Marketing Hua Nan Company 中國化工供銷華南公司	Guangzhou 廣州市	Guangdong 廣東省	(020)87654477 (020)87784414
China Agriculture Means of Production Chengdu Company 中國農業生產資料成都公司	Chengdu 成都市	Sichuan 四川省	(028)3333909 (028)3331202
Shanxi Agriculture Means of Production Company 山西省農業生產資料公司	Taiyuan 太原市	Shanxi 山西省	(0351)4040255 (0351)4040231
Beijing Chemical Light Industry General Company 北京市化工輕工總公司	Beijing 北京市	Beijing 北京市	(010)64224837 (010)64219301
Beijing Chemical Industry Group Company Supply & Marketing Company 北京化學工業集團公司供銷公司	Beijing 北京市	Beijing 北京市	(010)67714610 (010)67714058
Zhong Hua Jiangsu Import & Export Company 中化江蘇進出口公司	Nanjing 南京市	Jiangsu 江蘇省	(025)2258718 (025)2257789
Yunnan Chemical Import & Export Company 雲南省化工進出口公司	Kunming 昆明市	Yunnan 雲南省	(0871)3314002 (0871)3314931
Fujian Jiu Zhou Group Co. Ltd. 福建九州集團股份有限公司	Xiamen 廈門市	Fujian 福建省	(0592)5055818 (0592)5052033
China Chemical Industry Commission Agent Hua Dong Co. 中國化工供銷華東公司	Shanghai 上海市	Shanghai 上海市	(021)62514123

*Also include sales by firms outside this industry.包括本行業以外廠家的銷售。"o" stands for "others". "o" 代表"其他產品"。

2669: Other Synthetic Materials 其他合成材料製造業

The industry accounts for 0.069% of the total revenue of China's industrial sector in 1996. The revenue growth rate of the industry is 11.1% from 1995, as compared to the growth rate of China's industrial sector, 9.51%. The rate of return on asset is -0.11%. 65.92% of all firms in the industry made a profit while 28.00% had negative returns. The top province in terms of the industry's revenue is Jiangsu, accounting for 29.12% of the total revenue.
本行業在1996年佔全行業總產值0.069%，行業年增長率為11.1%（全國工業年增長率9.51%）。行業的資產回報率-0.11%，65.92%的企業盈利，28.00%的企業虧損。銷售收入最高的省份為江蘇省，佔本行業的29.12%。

	Total number of firms 企業總數	Total number of employees 職工總數	Total revenue (mil. RMB) 總銷售收入（百萬元）	Total profit (mil. RMB) 總利潤（百萬元）	Return on assets 資產利潤率 (%)	Return on equity 權益利潤率 (%)	Labour productivity ('000 RMB / worker) 勞動生產率（千元/人）	Debts / assets 資產負債率 (%)	Total assets (mil. RMB) 總資產（百萬元）
Industry Overall 行業總體	290	40,804	4,021	-6	-0.11	-0.38	98.54	70.48	5,737

	Number of firms 企業個數	Average number of employees 平均職工人數	Average revenue ('000 RMB) 平均銷售收入（千元）	Average profit ('000 RMB) 平均利潤（千元）	Return on assets 資產利潤率 (%)	Return on equity 權益利潤率 (%)	Labour productivity ('000 RMB / worker) 勞動生產率（千元/人）	Average debts / assets 平均資產負債率(%)	Average Total assets ('000 RMB) 平均總資產（千元）
By ownership 產業所有權									
State-owned 國有	47	365	22,021	-681	-1.41	-6.06	60.28	76.81	48,447
Collectively-owned 集體	190	103	10,057	50	0.57	1.61	97.53	64.62	8,812
Privately-owned 私有									
Domestic JVs 聯營	2	145	27,741	270	1.26	2.42	191.32	48.13	21,511
Joint stock 股份制	5	20	306	1	0.29	0.39	15.45	24.91	478
Foreign-funded 外資	21	87	14,255	-1,268	-3.84	-7.30	164.49	47.39	33,029
Overseas Chinese-funded 港澳台資	24	74	32,485	1,715	3.98	22.85	436.77	82.59	43,116
By size 規模									
Large 大型	10	1,645	212,942	-449	-0.14	-0.47	129.47	71.29	332,717
Medium 中型	7	603	98,394	-29	-0.02	-0.13	163.14	82.11	128,168
Small 小型	268	75	5,285	-5	-0.09	-0.23	70.87	61.78	5,644
By regional distribution 地區分布									
Central-North 華北	53	160	7,521	-8	-0.07	-0.22	46.96	66.35	10,582
Beijing 北京	12	575	10,907	159	0.79	5.27	18.98	85.06	20,207
Tianjin 天津	18	38	9,911	-342	-2.50	-4.64	264.28	46.19	13,692
Hebei 河北	18	45	4,852	213	5.53	19.64	107.02	71.86	3,849
Shanxi 山西	3	25	473				18.68	90.09	740
Inner Mongolia 內蒙	2	12	300				25.00	58.54	205
Northeast 東北	34	98	3,223	-398	-1.78	-22.09	32.77	91.95	22,407
Liaoning 遼寧	23	130	4,512	-594	-1.85	-23.42	34.69	92.12	32,213
Jilin 吉林	8	38	466	6	0.25	2.24	12.23	88.71	2,469
Heilongjiang 黑龍江	3	16	690	27	6.67	11.43	43.13	40.83	400
Central East 華東	120	148	17,490	47	0.26	0.74	117.80	65.46	18,204
Shanghai 上海	16	170	23,493	344	1.76	5.07	138.45	65.36	19,608
Jiangsu 江蘇	37	201	31,650	15	0.05	0.17	157.23	72.46	30,999
Zhejiang 浙江	27	103	12,780	628	6.18	20.15	123.99	69.32	10,160
Anhui 安徽	10	73	4,888	-80	-1.79	-6.07	67.05	70.51	4,469
Fujian 福建	12	16	2,937	-739	-9.56	-20.77	178.88	54.01	7,735
Jiangxi 江西	7	47	1,070	-110	-15.04	22.06	22.91	168.16	731
Shandong 山東	11	329	10,467	-634	-2.27	-3.61	31.83	37.00	27,899
Central-South 中南	62	64	19,272	87	0.31	1.06	302.11	70.91	28,269
Henan 河南	18	39	2,125	144	5.78	17.68	54.41	67.30	2,489
Hubei 湖北	7	61	5,274	-79	-1.91	500.00	86.67	100.42	4,120
Hunan 湖南	9	33	2,196	-20	-0.90	-4.09	65.65	78.04	2,227
Guangdong 廣東	25	99	43,985	147	0.22	0.75	442.51	70.41	66,221
Guangxi 廣西	3	13	97	-43	-3.75	-13.00	7.25	71.47	1,157
Hainan 海南									
Southwest 西南	12	494	14,073	-22	-0.10	-0.25	28.51	60.82	21,853
Chongqing 重慶	2	24	896	5	1.15	3.35	37.89	65.56	454
Sichuan 四川	10	588	16,708	25	0.10	0.25	28.41	60.80	26,133
Guizhou 貴州									
Yunnan 雲南									
Tibet 西藏									
Northwest 西北	9	142	5,578	-361	-1.52	-4.26	39.31	64.40	23,830
Shaanxi 陝西	8	157	6,168	-384	-1.44	-4.04	39.25	64.37	26,685
Gansu 甘肅									
Qinghai 青海									
Ningxia 寧夏									
Xinjiang 新疆	1	20	860	-180	-18.18	-60.00	43.00	70.71	990

2669: Other Synthetic Materials 其他合成材料製造業

Year 年份	Number of firms 企業個數	Rate of change 每年變化 (%)	Number of employees 職工人數 (人)	Rate of change 每年變化 (%)	Total revenue (mil. RMB) 總銷售收入 (百萬元)	Rate of change 每年變化 (%)	Total profit (mil. RMB) 總利潤 (百萬元)	Rate of change 每年變化 (%)
1993	278		44,000		2,727		98	
1994	289	3.96%	39,952	-9.20%	2,811	3.05%	61	-37.55%
1995	290	0.35%	34,857	-12.75%	3,619	28.76%	157	155.55%
1996	290		40,804	17.06%	4,021	11.11%	-6	-103.82%

3 Major products* 3 種主要產品 *	Output 產量	Sales volume 銷售量	Unit 單位
a) Epoxide Resin 環氧樹脂	9,860	9,071	ton 噸
b) Unsaturaled Polyester Resin 不飽和聚酯樹脂	5,670	5,216	ton 噸
c) Polyolefine Resin 聚烯烴樹脂	136,262	129,449	ton 噸

Top 10 firms by revenue (year founded) 收入排名前 10 家企業 (創辦年份)	City 城市	Province 省	Telephone / fax 電話 / 傳真	Number of employees 職工人數	Ownership 產業所有權	Revenue ('000 RMB) 銷售收入 (千元)	Profit ('000 RMB) (rank) 利潤 (千元) (排名)	Total assets ('000 RMB) 總資產 (千元)	Major products 主要產品
Shandou Sez Ocean No.1 Polyphenyl Resin Co. Ltd. 汕頭經濟特區海洋第一聚苯樹脂有限公司(1991)	Shantou 汕頭市	Guangdong 廣東省	(0754)8897218 (0754)8894538	268	Foreign-funded 外資	557,436	58610(1)	597,438	c
Jiangsu Yabang Group Co. 江蘇亞邦集團公司(1993)	Changzhou 常州市	Jiangsu 江蘇省	(0519)6391051	1,402	Collectively-owned 集體	382,635	266(43)	258,463	o
Wuxi Petrochemical General Factory 無錫市石油化工總廠(1958)	Wuxi 無錫市	Jiangsu 江蘇省	(0510)2406736 (0510)2401228	1,816	State-owned 國有	350,081	1791(12)	411,117	a,b
Ningbo Zhenhai Smelting Industry Trade Jointly-operated General Company 寧波市鎮海煉化工業貿易聯營總公司(1979)	Ningbo 寧波市	Zhejiang 浙江省	(0574)6444951 (0574)6262534	1,446	Collectively-owned 集體	152,374	11110(2)	108,048	o
Chenguang Research Institute of Chemical Industry The Ministry of Chemical Industry 化工部晨光化工研究院(1965)	Zigong 自貢市	Sichuan 四川省	(0813)7100180 (0813)7101124	5,354	State-owned 國有	125,529	300(41)	226,196	a
Jiangmen Hua Nan Plastics Development Co. 江門華南塑料發展公司(1991)	Jiangmen 江門市	Guangdong 廣東省	(0750)3372385 (0750)3382111	506	Collectively-owned 集體	101,522	5068(6)	72,286	o
Foshan Tian Ma Polyester Slices Co. Ltd. 佛山市天馬聚酯切片有限公司(1988)	Foshan 佛山市	Guangdong 廣東省	(0757)2814411 (0757)2812522	236	Overseas Chinese-funded 港澳台資	99,670	-41108(148)	335,611	o
Shanghai Pens Making Chemical Plant 上海製筆化工廠(1947)	Shanghai 上海市	Shanghai 上海市	(021)58112690 (021)58112582	827	State-owned 國有	98,196	305(39)	54,753	c
Shandou Sez Ocean No.1 Polyester Resin Co. Ltd. 汕頭經濟特區海洋第一聚脂樹脂有限公司(1990)	Shantou 汕頭市	Guangdong 廣東省	(0754)8896140 (0754)8892695	204	Foreign-funded 外資	89,948	-24108(147)	262,622	o
Wujin Niu Tang Chemical Factory 武進市牛塘化工廠(1969)	Changzhou 常州市	Jiangsu 江蘇省	(0519)6391149	500	Collectively-owned 集體	82,506	0(107)	130,000	o

Top 10 Cities by Production Output 產出排名前 10 位城市	Province 省	Market share 市場份額	Number of firms 企業個數
Changzhou 常州市	Jiangsu 江蘇省	20.18%	18
Wuxi 無錫市	Jiangsu 江蘇省	14.01%	25
Foshan 佛山市	Guangdong 廣東省	11.38%	4
Nanjing 南京市	Jiangsu 江蘇省	11.12%	5
Shanghai 上海市	Shanghai 上海市	5.89%	24
Zigong 自貢市	Sichuan 四川省	3.69%	1
Jiangmen 江門市	Guangdong 廣東省	3.66%	4
Suzhou 蘇州市	Jiangsu 江蘇省	3.63%	8
Tianjin 天津市	Tianjin 天津市	2.78%	14
Jiaxing 嘉興市	Zhejiang 浙江省	2.24%	8

10 Major Wholesalers 10 家主要批發商	City 城市	Province 省	Telephone / Fax 電話 / 傳真
Zhong Hua Singbo Import & Export Company 中化寧波進出口公司	Ningbo 寧波市	Zhejiang 浙江省	(0574)7346764 (0574)7366775
China Chemical Supply & Marketing Hua Nan Company 中國化工供銷華南公司	Guangzhou 廣州市	Guangdong 廣東省	(020)87654477 (020)87784414
China Agriculture Means of Production Chengdu Company 中國農業生產資料成都公司	Chengdu 成都市	Sichuan 四川省	(028)3333909 (028)3331202
Shanxi Agriculture Means of Production Company 山西省農業生產資料公司	Taiyuan 太原市	Shanxi 山西省	(0351)4040255 (0351)4040231
Beijing Chemical Light Industry General Company 北京市化工輕工總公司	Beijing 北京市	Beijing 北京市	(010)64224837 (010)64219301
Beijing Chemical Industry Group Company Supply & Marketing Company 北京化學工業集團公司供銷公司	Beijing 北京市	Beijing 北京市	(010)67714610 (010)67714058
Zhong Hua Jiangsu Import & Export Company 中化江蘇進出口公司	Nanjing 南京市	Jiangsu 江蘇省	(025)2258718 (025)2257789
Yunnan Chemical Import & Export Company 雲南省化工進出口公司	Kunming 昆明市	Yunnan 雲南省	(0871)3314002 (0871)3314931
Fujian Jiu Zhou Group Co. Ltd. 福建九州集團股份有限公司	Xiamen 廈門市	Fujian 福建省	(0592)5055818 (0592)5052033
China Chemical Industry Commission Agent Hua Dong Co. 中國化工供銷華東公司	Shanghai 上海市	Shanghai 上海市	(021)62514123

*Also include sales by firms outside this industry.包括本行業以外廠家的銷售。"o" stands for "others". "o" 代表"其他產品"。

2671: Chemical Reagent and Auxiliaries 化學試劑、助劑製造業

The industry accounts for 0.362% of the total revenue of China's industrial sector in 1996. The revenue growth rate of the industry is 21.3% from 1995, as compared to the growth rate of China's industrial sector, 9.51%. The rate of return on asset is 2.34%. 69.21% of all firms in the industry made a profit while 24.06% had negative returns. The top province in terms of the industry's revenue is Jiangsu, accounting for 24.99% of the total revenue.
本行業在1996年佔全行業總產值0.362%，行業年增長率為21.3%（全國工業年增長率9.51%）。行業的資產回報率2.34%，69.21%的企業盈利，24.06%的企業虧損。銷售收入最高的省份為江蘇省，佔本行業的24.99%。

	Total number of firms 企業總數	Total number of employees 職工總數	Total revenue (mil. RMB) 總銷售收入（百萬元）	Total profit (mil. RMB) 總利潤（百萬元）	Return on assets 資產利潤率 (%)	Return on equity 權益利潤率 (%)	Labour productivity ('000 RMB / worker) 勞動生產率（千元/人）	Debts / assets 資產負債率 (%)	Total assets (mil. RMB) 總資產（百萬元）
Industry Overall 行業總體	2,350	266,359	20,987	567	2.34	7.51	78.79	68.89	24,255

	Number of firms 企業個數	Average number of employees 平均職工人數	Average revenue ('000 RMB) 平均銷售收入（千元）	Average profit ('000 RMB) 平均利潤（千元）	Return on assets 資產利潤率 (%)	Return on equity 權益利潤率 (%)	Labour productivity ('000 RMB / worker) 勞動生產率（千元/人）	Average debts / assets 平均資產負債率(%)	Average Total assets ('000 RMB) 平均總資產（千元）
By ownership 產業所有權									
State-owned 國有	351	320	22,989	-17	-0.05	-0.20	71.77	73.79	32,584
Collectively-owned 集體	1,774	74	5,592	236	4.69	15.48	75.46	69.68	5,022
Privately-owned 私有	6	20	1,843	75	10.75	-33.77	92.94	131.83	694
Domestic JVs 聯營	32	94	12,369	1,292	10.98	31.88	131.93	65.57	11,768
Joint stock 股份制	31	323	31,977	1,973	5.84	13.58	99.14	57.00	33,786
Foreign-funded 外資	74	90	12,483	318	1.50	2.75	138.04	45.39	21,160
Overseas Chinese-funded 港澳台資	81	56	8,165	327	2.93	6.50	145.74	54.98	11,152
By size 規模									
Large 大型	17	2,422	279,503	2,357	0.89	3.00	115.38	70.47	265,781
Medium 中型	77	747	59,469	1,440	1.75	5.50	79.59	68.23	82,396
Small 小型	2,205	75	5,285	189	3.11	9.93	70.11	68.67	6,066
By regional distribution 地區分布									
Central-North 華北	373	71	5,778	243	2.67	8.34	81.38	67.96	9,099
Beijing 北京	109	65	7,574	251	1.71	5.95	116.65	71.26	14,668
Tianjin 天津	94	87	6,352	106	0.90	2.28	73.06	60.45	11,787
Hebei 河北	118	62	4,681	378	9.39	33.99	75.12	72.37	4,021
Shanxi 山西	38	58	2,745	105	2.54	8.86	46.97	71.29	4,141
Inner Mongolia 內蒙	14	118	5,406	343	8.70	36.01	45.68	75.84	3,941
Northeast 東北	442	118	4,813	-86	-1.13	-4.44	40.92	74.52	7,557
Liaoning 遼寧	276	114	4,571	-74	-1.03	-2.93	40.02	64.86	7,169
Jilin 吉林	86	157	5,262	98	1.19	4.77	33.50	74.96	8,233
Heilongjiang 黑龍江	80	87	5,164	-324	-3.97	119.34	59.39	103.32	8,170
Central East 華東	907	133	13,622	546	4.07	11.41	102.64	64.30	13,410
Shanghai 上海	87	108	15,556	986	5.41	17.79	143.64	69.59	18,222
Jiangsu 江蘇	305	132	17,195	465	3.19	8.06	130.49	60.39	14,566
Zhejiang 浙江	224	98	13,288	732	5.49	14.15	135.40	61.18	13,331
Anhui 安徽	45	86	5,023	-740	-19.84	64.41	58.25	130.80	3,728
Fujian 福建	45	61	7,646	32	0.54	1.99	125.03	72.77	5,941
Jiangxi 江西	48	39	1,334	31	1.56	6.26	34.54	75.03	1,999
Shandong 山東	153	263	14,031	877	5.13	14.96	53.27	65.75	17,109
Central-South 中南	442	100	7,865	97	1.07	4.56	78.62	76.42	9,023
Henan 河南	186	88	6,288	265	3.23	12.25	71.17	73.59	8,181
Hubei 湖北	81	121	9,558	225	3.04	13.59	78.97	77.66	7,411
Hunan 湖南	69	171	11,399	-441	-2.99	-21.62	66.49	86.16	14,733
Guangdong 廣東	89	66	8,007	56	0.62	2.11	120.76	70.69	9,139
Guangxi 廣西	16	15	2,078	51	2.25	3.26	135.67	30.91	2,277
Hainan 海南	1								
Southwest 西南	108	109	4,978	-244	-3.07	-15.40	45.58	80.07	7,948
Chongqing 重慶	30	205	10,434	-746	-4.41	-28.49	50.93	84.54	16,931
Sichuan 四川	51	87	3,597	58	1.05	3.99	41.51	73.72	5,498
Guizhou 貴州	20	55	1,426	-197	-8.23	-31.15	25.90	73.57	2,394
Yunnan 雲南	7	26	2,089	-456	-12.47	-49.00	80.33	74.56	3,656
Tibet 西藏									
Northwest 西北	78	147	4,308	25	0.38	1.27	29.21	70.20	6,560
Shaanxi 陝西	39	213	2,376	-4	-0.11	-0.32	11.16	64.51	3,418
Gansu 甘肅	15	150	9,680	-170	-0.99	-3.60	64.50	72.60	17,226
Qinghai 青海	1	20	860	50	8.77	33.33	43.00	73.68	570
Ningxia 寧夏	2	115	2,205	610	12.83	28.71	19.17	55.31	4,755
Xinjiang 新疆	21	33	4,423	160	3.07	11.26	132.50	72.74	5,232

2671: Chemical Reagent and Auxiliaries 化學試劑、助劑製造業

Year 年份	Number of firms 企業個數	Rate of change 每年變化 (%)	Number of employees 職工人數 (人)	Rate of change 每年變化 (%)	Total revenue (mil. RMB) 總銷售收入 (百萬元)	Rate of change 每年變化 (%)	Total profit (mil. RMB) 總利潤 (百萬元)	Rate of change 每年變化 (%)
1993	1,959		210,474		10,642		239	
1994	2,176	11.08%	215,557	2.42%	12,276	15.35%	244	2.48%
1995	2,328	6.99%	244,102	13.24%	17,295	40.88%	395	61.69%
1996	2,350	0.95%	266,359	9.12%	20,987	21.35%	567	43.44%

3 Major products* 3 種主要產品 *	Output 產量	Sales volume 銷售量	Unit 單位
a) Chemical Reagent 化學試劑	159,629	154,840	ton 噸
b) Plastic Auxiliary 塑料助劑	324,188	295,011	ton 噸

Top 10 firms by revenue (year founded) 收入排名前 10 家企業 (創辦年份)	City 城市	Province 省	Telephone / fax 電話 / 傳真	Number of employees 職工人數	Ownership 產業所有權	Revenue ('000 RMB) 銷售收入 (千元)	Profit ('000 RMB) (rank) 利潤 (千元) (排名)	Total assets ('000 RMB) 總資產 (千元)	Major products 主要產品
Nanjing Chemical Plant 南京化工廠(1949)	Nanjing 南京市	Jiangsu 江蘇省	(025)53154145 (025)5302204	5,159	State-owned 國有	634,511	20208(7)	539,697	o
Jiangsu Lingguang Group 江蘇陵光集團(1995)	Taizhou 泰州市	Jiangsu 江蘇省	(0523)6558888 (0523)6558088	1,762	State-owned 國有	500,528	8386(23)	330,817	o
Xiangxiang Aluminium Factory 湘鄉鋁廠(1960)	Xiangtan 湘潭市	Hunan 湖南省	(0732)6771001 (0732)6775013	3,393	State-owned 國有	481,328	1037(151)	527,485	o
Zibo Plasticizer Plant 淄博增塑劑廠(1990)	Zibo 淄博市	Shandong 山東省	(0533)7580688 (0533)7580606	347	Collectively-owned 集體	472,531	36207(2)	297,818	b
Zhejiang Long Sheng Group Co. 浙江龍盛集團公司(1970)	Shaoxing 紹興市	Zhejiang 浙江省	(0575)2042778 (0575)2042878	635	Collectively-owned 集體	450,932	48550(1)	178,102	o
Suzhou Fine Chemical Industry Group Co. Ltd. 蘇州精細化工集團公司(1923)	Suzhou 蘇州市	Jiangsu 江蘇省	(0512)7273601 (0512)7248490	2,141	State-owned 國有	440,824	20399(6)	322,678	o
Wuxi Chemical Group Co. Ltd. 無錫化工集團股份有限公司(1958)	Wuxi 無錫市	Jiangsu 江蘇省	(0510)3101601 (0510)3101678	3,144	State-owned 國有	394,565	12184(15)	395,924	o
Hangzhou Electrochemical Group Company 杭州電化集團公司(1994)	Hangzhou 杭州市	Zhejiang 浙江省	(0571)6617799 (0571)6617811	406	State-owned 國有	390,920	31862(3)	479,354	a,b
Shanghai General Chemical Reagent Plant 上海試劑總廠(1940)	Shanghai 上海市	Shanghai 上海市	(021)62593768 (021)62748123	3,081	State-owned 國有	355,898	101(510)	295,967	a
Zhejiang Run Tu Chemical Group Company 浙江潤土化工集團公司(1986)	Shaoxing 紹興市	Zhejiang 浙江省	(0575)2042874 (0575)2041188	440	Collectively-owned 集體	291,524	30574(4)	120,568	o

Top 10 Cities by Production Output 產出排名前 10 位城市	Province 省	Market share 市場份額	Number of firms 企業個數
Taizhou 泰州市	Jiangsu 江蘇省	22.73%	32
Shanghai 上海市	Shanghai 上海市	6.32%	167
Suzhou 蘇州市	Jiangsu 江蘇省	5.69%	139
Wuxi 無錫市	Jiangsu 江蘇省	4.64%	123
Shaoxing 紹興市	Zhejiang 浙江省	3.77%	39
Nanjing 南京市	Jiangsu 江蘇省	3.46%	44
Zibo 淄博市	Shandong 山東省	3.13%	26
Beijing 北京市	Beijing 北京市	2.92%	99
Tianjin 天津市	Tianjin 天津市	2.88%	113
Wenzhou 溫州市	Zhejiang 浙江省	2.19%	56

10 Major Wholesalers 10 家主要批發商	City 城市	Province 省	Telephone / Fax 電話 / 傳真
Zhong Hua Singbo Import & Export Company 中化寧波進出口公司	Ningbo 寧波市	Zhejiang 浙江省	(0574)7346764 (0574)7366775
China Chemical Supply & Marketing Hua Nan Company 中國化工供銷華南公司	Guangzhou 廣州市	Guangdong 廣東省	(020)87654477 (020)87784414
China Agriculture Means of Production Chengdu Company 中國農業生產資料成都公司	Chengdu 成都市	Sichuan 四川省	(028)3333909 (028)3331202
Shanxi Agriculture Means of Production Company 山西省農業生產資料公司	Taiyuan 太原市	Shanxi 山西省	(0351)4040255 (0351)4040231
Beijing Chemical Light Industry General Company 北京市化工輕工總公司	Beijing 北京市	Beijing 北京市	(010)64224837 (010)64219301
Beijing Chemical Industry Group Company Supply & Marketing Company 北京化學工業集團公司供銷公司	Beijing 北京市	Beijing 北京市	(010)67714610 (010)67714058
Zhong Hua Jiangsu Import & Export Company 中化江蘇進出口公司	Nanjing 南京市	Jiangsu 江蘇省	(025)2258718 (025)2257789
Yunnan Chemical Import & Export Company 雲南省化工進出口公司	Kunming 昆明市	Yunnan 雲南省	(0871)3314002 (0871)3314931
Fujian Jiu Zhou Group Co. Ltd. 福建九州集團股份有限公司	Xiamen 廈門市	Fujian 福建省	(0592)5055818 (0592)5052033
China Chemical Industry Commission Agent Hua Dong Co. 中國化工供銷華東公司	Shanghai 上海市	Shanghai 上海市	(021)62514123

*Also include sales by firms outside this industry.包括本行業以外廠家的銷售。"o" stands for "others". "o" 代表"其他產品"。

2673: Forest Chemical Products 林產化學產品製造業

The industry accounts for 0.070% of the total revenue of China's industrial sector in 1996. The revenue growth rate of the industry is 18.9% from 1995, as compared to the growth rate of China's industrial sector, 9.51%. The rate of return on asset is 1.80%. 77.69% of all firms in the industry made a profit while 18.95% had negative returns. The top province in terms of the industry's revenue is Guangxi, accounting for 32.69% of the total revenue.
本行業在1996年佔全行業總產值0.070%，行業年增長率為18.9%（全國工業年增長率9.51%）。行業的資產回報率1.80%，77.69%的企業盈利，18.95%的企業虧損。銷售收入最高的省份為廣西省，佔本行業的32.69%。

	Total number of firms 企業總數	Total number of employees 職工總數	Total revenue (mil. RMB) 總銷售收入（百萬元）	Total profit (mil. RMB) 總利潤（百萬元）	Return on assets 資產利潤率 (%)	Return on equity 權益利潤率 (%)	Labour productivity ('000 RMB / worker) 勞動生產率（千元/人）	Debts / assets 資產負債率 (%)	Total assets (mil. RMB) 總資產（百萬元）
Industry Overall 行業總體	1,039	60,841	4,051	81	1.80	6.60	66.58	72.78	4,493

	Number of firms 企業個數	Average number of employees 平均職工人數	Average revenue ('000 RMB) 平均銷售收入（千元）	Average profit ('000 RMB) 平均利潤（千元）	Return on assets 資產利潤率 (%)	Return on equity 權益利潤率 (%)	Labour productivity ('000 RMB / worker) 勞動生產率（千元/人）	Average debts / assets 平均資產負債率(%)	Average Total assets ('000 RMB) 平均總資產（千元）
By ownership 產業所有權									
State-owned 國有	266	146	8,662	49	0.40	1.58	59.15	74.95	12,335
Collectively-owned 集體	720	24	1,891	81	7.69	25.20	77.55	69.47	1,046
Privately-owned 私有	1	30							
Domestic JVs 聯營	13	23	2,103	13	0.75	1.64	90.82	54.42	1,804
Joint stock 股份制	11	191	24,778	2,142	8.19	23.83	129.61	65.65	26,175
Foreign-funded 外資	18	68	2,396	-597	-12.34	-27.75	35.01	55.55	4,837
Overseas Chinese-funded 港澳台資	10	66	4,188	-297	-4.89	-13.01	63.36	62.38	6,071
By size 規模									
Large 大型	2	2,362	69,688	-95,856	-41.55	-276.30	29.51	84.96	230,718
Medium 中型	8	706	87,261	9,432	11.13	52.92	123.58	78.96	84,710
Small 小型	1,020	49	3,150	193	5.88	19.50	64.03	69.86	3,289
By regional distribution 地區分布									
Central-North 華北	27	182	3,697	-641	-5.14	-22.59	20.27	77.22	12,471
Beijing 北京	4	33	2,308	90	2.21	29.03	69.40	92.34	4,078
Tianjin 天津	1	15	490				32.67	82.35	170
Hebei 河北	13	33	894	17	1.39	11.76	26.84	88.16	1,215
Shanxi 山西	6	59	2,293	118	4.61	7.95	39.20	41.98	2,565
Inner Mongolia 內蒙	3	1,331	21,577	-6,203	-6.44	-28.80	16.21	77.65	96,353
Northeast 東北	39	58	2,088	45	2.23	26.56	36.22	91.61	2,005
Liaoning 遼寧	14	51	2,759	94	7.41	65.50	54.55	88.68	1,262
Jilin 吉林	14	65	2,706	-9	-0.30	-16.44	41.35	98.17	2,850
Heilongjiang 黑龍江	11	57	450	50	2.67	14.40	7.92	81.43	1,875
Central East 華東	483	42	2,306	46	1.85	4.96	54.28	62.65	2,464
Shanghai 上海	2	45	3,350	45	1.10	2.20	74.44	49.82	4,085
Jiangsu 江蘇	8	46	4,254	105	3.69	11.24	92.98	67.19	2,846
Zhejiang 浙江	35	45	2,535	54	1.51	5.62	55.95	73.10	3,593
Anhui 安徽	23	30	2,265	14	0.80	2.56	76.51	68.90	1,749
Fujian 福建	217	42	2,849	84	3.03	7.38	68.59	59.00	2,779
Jiangxi 江西	190	44	1,575	4	0.20	0.50	35.77	60.19	1,889
Shandong 山東	8	52	1,806	-8	-0.19	1.70	35.07	111.27	3,904
Central-South 中南	394	63	6,131	110	1.96	8.56	96.85	77.11	5,590
Henan 河南	10	92	2,767	5	0.11	0.37	30.24	69.68	4,432
Hubei 湖北	21	68	2,044	-25	-0.48	5.99	30.06	108.04	5,243
Hunan 湖南	84	24	1,355	-15	-1.17	-4.76	56.00	75.43	1,303
Guangdong 廣東	83	84	10,409	274	2.50	11.93	123.50	79.07	10,980
Guangxi 廣西	170	53	7,789	176	3.54	12.09	146.59	70.70	4,976
Hainan 海南	26	175	1,659	-300	-4.30	-22.78	9.50	81.14	6,983
Southwest 西南	76	88	4,129	481	6.53	24.54	46.74	73.37	7,360
Chongqing 重慶	8	48	598	-38	-0.94	-2.72	12.35	65.44	3,997
Sichuan 四川	22	53	1,406	-13	-0.44	2.77	26.35	115.83	3,036
Guizhou 貴州	15	44	955	-15	-0.57	-3.83	21.63	85.09	2,567
Yunnan 雲南	31	145	8,517	1,167	8.58	25.44	58.64	66.29	13,607
Tibet 西藏									
Northwest 西北	20	75	1,321	-275	-4.36	-13.05	17.67	66.62	6,301
Shaanxi 陝西	12	95	1,779	-408	-4.40	-12.63	18.71	65.17	9,283
Gansu 甘肅	8	44	633	-74	-4.04	-18.10	14.29	77.69	1,826
Qinghai 青海									
Ningxia 寧夏									
Xinjiang 新疆									

2673: Forest Chemical Products 林產化學產品製造業

Year 年份	Number of firms 企業個數	Rate of change 每年變化 (%)	Number of employees 職工人數（人）	Rate of change 每年變化 (%)	Total revenue (mil. RMB) 總銷售收入（百萬元）	Rate of change 每年變化 (%)	Total profit (mil. RMB) 總利潤（百萬元）	Rate of change 每年變化 (%)
1993	668		34,106		2,572		45	
1994	812	21.56%	46,245	35.59%	2,563	-0.35%	10	-78.80%
1995	995	22.54%	60,749	31.36%	3,408	32.96%	10	1.75%
1996	1,039	4.42%	60,841	0.15%	4,051	18.87%	81	728.81%

3 Major products* 3 種主要產品 *	Output 產量	Sales volume 銷售量	Unit 單位
a) Rosin 松香	473,459	473,459	ton 噸
b) Abies Oil 松節油	51,995	49,396	ton 噸
c) Active Carbon 活性炭	18,327	17,594	ton 噸

Top 10 firms by revenue (year founded) 收入排名前 10 家企業 (創辦年份)	City 城市	Province 省	Telephone / fax 電話 / 傳真	Number of employees 職工人數	Ownership 產業所有權	Revenue ('000 RMB) 銷售收入（千元）	Profit ('000 RMB) (rank) 利潤（千元）（排名）	Total assets ('000 RMB) 總資產（千元）	Major products 主要產品
Guangdong Deqing Chemical Industry of Forest Products (Group) Co. Ltd. 廣東省德慶林產化工(集團)股份有限公司(1969)	Zhaoqing 肇慶市	Guangdong 廣東省	(0757)7762712 (0757)7765461	893	Joint stock 股份制	165,524	6650(4)	189,706	a,b
Guangxi Wuzhou Rosin Plant 廣西壯族自治區梧州松脂廠(1950)	Wuzhou 梧州市	Guangxi 廣西	(0774)3827991 (0774)3828660	1,096	State-owned 國有	145,197	4332(5)	183,555	a,b
Jinggu Forestry Enterprise Group General Company 景谷縣林業企業集團總公司(1972)	Simao 思茅市	Yunnan 雲南省	(0879)5224485	1,858	State-owned 國有	133,156	25789(1)	174,781	a,b
Xinyi Rosin Factory 信宜縣松香廠(1955)	Maoming 茂名市	Guangdong 廣東省	(0668)8885299	467	State-owned 國有	121,746	827(31)	64,056	a,b
Fengkai Forest Products Industry Group Co. 封開縣林產工業集團公司(1952)	Zhaoqing 肇慶市	Guangdong 廣東省	(0757)6662231 (0757)6662858	819	State-owned 國有	120,930	7530(3)	154,300	a,b
Guangxi Cangwu County Rosin Plant 廣西蒼梧縣松脂廠(1986)	Wuzhou 梧州市	Guangxi 廣西	(0774)2682134 (0774)2683737	314	State-owned 國有	81,586	1835(16)	49,961	a,b
Guangxi Ningming Rosin Co. Ltd. 廣西寧明松香股份有限公司(1969)	Pingxiang 憑祥市	Guangxi 廣西	(0771)8628105 (0771)8628193	408	Joint stock 股份制	80,984	15144(2)	48,031	a,b
Guangxi Tengxian Pine Resin Factory 廣西藤縣松脂廠(1969)	Cenxi 岑溪縣	Guangxi 廣西	(0774)7281668 (0774)7283860	310	State-owned 國有	70,883	-2875(326)	25,939	a,b
Tengxian Taiping Pine Resin Factory 藤縣太平松脂廠(1984)	Cenxi 岑溪縣	Guangxi 廣西	(0774)7602496 (0774)7602496	243	State-owned 國有	62,899	292(78)	30,555	a,b
Cenxi Rosin Factory 岑溪市松香廠(1968)	Cenxi 岑溪縣	Guangxi 廣西	(0774)8222390 (0774)8221642	546	State-owned 國有	62,206	479(51)	53,723	a,b

Top 10 Cities by Production Output 產出排名前 10 位城市	Province 省	Market share 市場份額	Number of firms 企業個數
Zhaoqing 肇慶市	Guangdong 廣東省	11.77%	12
Cenxi 岑溪縣	Guangxi 廣西	8.40%	30
Wuzhou 梧州市	Guangxi 廣西	5.92%	2
Sanming 三明市	Fujian 福建省	4.88%	105
Longyan 龍巖市	Fujian 福建省	4.83%	37
Maoming 茂名市	Guangdong 廣東省	3.80%	8
Yunfu 雲浮市	Guangdong 廣東省	3.39%	11
Simao 思茅市	Yunnan 雲南省	3.38%	12
Nangping 南平市	Fujian 福建省	3.25%	57
Fangchenggang 防城港市	Guangxi 廣西	3.10%	14

10 Major Wholesalers 10 家主要批發商	City 城市	Province 省	Telephone / Fax 電話 / 傳真
Zhong Hua Singbo Import & Export Company 中化寧波進出口公司	Ningbo 寧波市	Zhejiang 浙江省	(0574)7346764 (0574)7366775
China Chemical Supply & Marketing Hua Nan Company 中國化工供銷華南公司	Guangzhou 廣州市	Guangdong 廣東省	(020)87654477 (020)87784414
China Agriculture Means of Production Chengdu Company 中國農業生產資料成都公司	Chengdu 成都市	Sichuan 四川省	(028)3333909 (028)3331202
Shanxi Agriculture Means of Production Company 山西省農業生產資料公司	Taiyuan 太原市	Shanxi 山西省	(0351)4040255 (0351)4040231
Beijing Chemical Light Industry General Company 北京市化工輕工總公司	Beijing 北京市	Beijing 北京市	(010)64224837 (010)64219301
Beijing Chemical Industry Group Company Supply & Marketing Company 北京化學工業集團公司供銷公司	Beijing 北京市	Beijing 北京市	(010)67714610 (010)67714058
Zhong Hua Jiangsu Import & Export Company 中化江蘇進出口公司	Nanjing 南京市	Jiangsu 江蘇省	(025)2258718 (025)2257789
Yunnan Chemical Import & Export Company 雲南省化工進出口公司	Kunming 昆明市	Yunnan 雲南省	(0871)3314002 (0871)3314931
Fujian Jiu Zhou Group Co. Ltd. 福建九州集團股份有限公司	Xiamen 廈門市	Fujian 福建省	(0592)5055818 (0592)5052033
China Chemical Industry Commission Agent Hua Dong Co. 中國化工供銷華東公司	Shanghai 上海市	Shanghai 上海市	(021)62514123

*Also include sales by firms outside this industry.包括本行業以外廠家的銷售。"o" stands for "others". "o" 代表"其他產品"。

2675: Information Chemical Products 信息化學品製造業

The industry accounts for 0.069% of the total revenue of China's industrial sector in 1996. The revenue growth rate of the industry is -15.6% from 1995, as compared to the growth rate of China's industrial sector, 9.51%. The rate of return on asset is -1.24%. 64.42% of all firms in the industry made a profit while 31.82% had negative returns. The top province in terms of the industry's revenue is Guangdong, accounting for 41.19% of the total revenue.
本行業在1996年佔全行業總產值0.069%，行業年增長率為-15.6%（全國工業年增長率9.51%）。行業的資產回報率-1.24%，64.42%的企業盈利，31.82%的企業虧損。銷售收入最高的省份為廣東省，佔本行業的41.19%。

	Total number of firms 企業總數	Total number of employees 職工總數	Total revenue (mil. RMB) 總銷售收入（百萬元）	Total profit (mil. RMB) 總利潤（百萬元）	Return on assets 資產利潤率 (%)	Return on equity 權益利潤率 (%)	Labour productivity ('000 RMB / worker) 勞動生產率（千元/人）	Debts / assets 資產負債率 (%)	Total assets (mil. RMB) 總資產（百萬元）
Industry Overall 行業總體	281	55,082	4,025	-175	-1.24	-5.39	73.07	77.03	14,128

	Number of firms 企業個數	Average number of employees 平均職工人數	Average revenue ('000 RMB) 平均銷售收入（千元）	Average profit ('000 RMB) 平均利潤（千元）	Return on assets 資產利潤率 (%)	Return on equity 權益利潤率 (%)	Labour productivity ('000 RMB / worker) 勞動生產率（千元/人）	Average debts / assets 平均資產負債率(%)	Average Total assets ('000 RMB) 平均總資產（千元）
By ownership 產業所有權									
State-owned 國有	54	521	27,037	-1,426	-0.97	-7.54	51.87	87.09	146,407
Collectively-owned 集體	88	78	3,275	775	13.99	38.06	41.84	63.23	5,539
Privately-owned 私有	1	11							
Domestic JVs 聯營	5	138	14,292	12,269	60.71	140.82	103.72	56.89	20,209
Joint stock 股份制									
Foreign-funded 外資	45	105	11,281	-3,646	-10.07	-89.91	107.21	88.79	36,190
Overseas Chinese-funded 港澳台資	87	180	19,520	-730	-1.59	-3.49	108.24	54.59	46,040
By size 規模									
Large 大型	7	2,562	165,175	-8,159	-0.83	-7.70	64.48	89.18	979,357
Medium 中型	17	340	12,365	-1,875	-2.87	-17.09	36.37	83.20	65,320
Small 小型	244	128	10,898	-352	-1.40	-3.71	85.13	62.41	25,256
By regional distribution 地區分布									
Central-North 華北	41	241	16,600	25	0.06	0.17	68.94	62.49	38,305
Beijing 北京	16	23	1,198	-1	-0.03	-0.10	52.96	69.51	4,250
Tianjin 天津	14	215	9,172	-358	-1.36	-4.12	42.66	66.99	26,290
Hebei 河北	7	762	72,517	1,027	0.73	1.71	95.18	57.02	139,841
Shanxi 山西	2	460	530	-340	-0.61	-13.18	1.15	95.34	55,385
Inner Mongolia 內蒙	2	124	12,175	-235	-1.05	-2.24	98.19	53.19	22,400
Northeast 東北	22	45	1,578	-660	-5.52	-23.70	35.14	76.71	11,962
Liaoning 遼寧	14	25	2,068	-927	-9.82	-22.77	83.19	56.85	9,438
Jilin 吉林	6	28	110	-230	-5.10	-21.20	3.95	75.90	4,508
Heilongjiang 黑龍江	2	237	2,555	-80	-0.15	7.11	10.80	102.16	51,995
Central East 華東	98	162	11,706	-561	-0.99	-6.41	72.21	84.52	56,524
Shanghai 上海	14	205	9,310	-1,689	-4.45	-16.01	45.32	72.17	37,904
Jiangsu 江蘇	24	199	23,767	-448	-0.52	-3.31	119.46	84.28	86,095
Zhejiang 浙江	17	166	2,818	104	1.91	3.95	16.98	51.55	5,444
Anhui 安徽	4	51	19,165	638	5.51	21.57	373.95	74.45	11,565
Fujian 福建	23	171	11,810	-158	-0.14	-1.31	69.07	89.14	110,708
Jiangxi 江西	5	50	702	-776	-7.73	-30.19	14.15	74.41	10,036
Shandong 山東	11	94	4,250	-1,585	-8.42	-44.69	45.43	81.17	18,828
Central-South 中南	105	240	20,086	-879	-1.43	-5.45	83.62	73.83	61,663
Henan 河南	15	334	22,201	101	0.22	0.61	66.54	64.11	46,221
Hubei 湖北	9	213	7,058	-656	-1.98	-4.67	33.12	57.55	33,039
Hunan 湖南	2	51	3,000	-3,890	-20.73	-172.89	58.82	88.01	18,765
Guangdong 廣東	72	245	23,026	-989	-1.35	-5.40	94.03	74.93	73,070
Guangxi 廣西	5	36	1,106	-298	-3.83	-11.82	30.72	67.59	7,776
Hainan 海南	2	192	21,555	-3,700	-5.05	43.84	112.27	111.52	73,270
Southwest 西南	8	288	3,615	-479	-3.22	-55.91	12.54	94.24	14,845
Chongqing 重慶	1	252	13,191	-4,107	-5.32	-36.12	52.32	85.26	77,157
Sichuan 四川	5	393	3,113	-137	-1.26	29.57	7.93	104.25	10,866
Guizhou 貴州									
Yunnan 雲南	2	28	1,340	-15	-0.78	-4.05	47.86	80.78	1,925
Tibet 西藏									
Northwest 西北	7	115	3,481	-1,467	-6.37	-28.40	30.24	77.57	23,036
Shaanxi 陝西	3	193	2,200	-2,650	-12.12	779.41	11.40	101.56	21,857
Gansu 甘肅	1	15	500	-260	-5.75	-10.83	33.33	46.90	4,520
Qinghai 青海									
Ningxia 寧夏	1	178	16,670	20	0.03	0.12	93.65	73.83	65,600
Xinjiang 新疆	2	17	300	-1,040	-8.14	-11.81	17.65	31.06	12,780

2675: Information Chemical Products 信息化學品製造業

Year 年份	Number of firms 企業個數	Rate of change 每年變化 (%)	Number of employees 職工人數（人）	Rate of change 每年變化 (%)	Total revenue (mil. RMB) 總銷售收入（百萬元）	Rate of change 每年變化 (%)	Total profit (mil. RMB) 總利潤（百萬元）	Rate of change 每年變化 (%)
1993	190		55,182		3,312		-128	
1994	229	20.53%	55,090	-0.17%	4,342	31.09%	-91	28.83%
1995	300	31.00%	61,191	11.07%	4,771	9.89%	-80	11.80%
1996	281	-6.33%	55,082	-9.98%	4,025	-15.64%	-175	-117.55%

3 Major products* 3種主要產品*	Output 產量	Sales volume 銷售量	Unit 單位
a) Photosensitive Paper 感光紙	169	163	10,000 square metre 萬平方米
b) Magnetic Tape 磁帶	12,811,948	12,427,590	10,000 metre 萬米
c) Diskette 軟磁盤	160	154	10,000 piece 萬片

Top 10 firms by revenue (year founded) 收入排名前10家企業（創辦年份）	City 城市	Province 省	Telephone / fax 電話 / 傳真	Number of employees 職工人數	Ownership 產業所有權	Revenue ('000 RMB) 銷售收入（千元）	Profit ('000 RMB) (rank) 利潤（千元）（排名）	Total assets ('000 RMB) 總資產（千元）	Major products 主要產品
China Lucky Film Corp. 中國樂凱膠片公司(1960)	Baoding 保定市	Hebei 河北省	(0312)3027901 (0312)3026296	4,657	State-owned 國有	431,617	172(42)	874,079	a,b,c
Ben Lu Ke Si Industrial Co. Ltd. 本魯克斯實業股份有限公司(1988)	Shenzhen 深圳市	Guangdong 廣東省	(0755)6649025 (0755)6649031	719	Overseas Chinese-funded 港澳台資	232,590	12900(3)	258,800	b,c
Shenzhen Ge Le Electromagnetism Co. Ltd. 深圳歌樂電磁有限公司(1993)	Shenzhen 深圳市	Guangdong 廣東省	(0755)8503234 (0755)8502119	2,200	Overseas Chinese-funded 港澳台資	222,300	2986(6)	86,153	b
Wei Wang (Zhuhai) Magnetic Communication Co. Ltd. 威望(珠海)磁訊有限公司(1988)	Zhuhai 珠海市	Guangdong 廣東省	(0756)8613941 (0756)8613947	2,188	Overseas Chinese-funded 港澳台資	219,190	-82649(133)	1,083,879	c
Nantong Si Ta Wei Data Co. Ltd. 南通斯塔維數據有限公司(1992)	Nantong 南通市	Jiangsu 江蘇省	(0513)5537338 (0513)5519595	1,114	Foreign-funded 外資	160,329	1308(18)	502,060	c
Xiamen Fu Da Sensitization Materials Co. Ltd. 廈門福達感光材料有限公司(1984)	Xiamen 廈門市	Fujian 福建省	(0592)5051001 (0592)5051055	2,399	State-owned 國有	157,122	425(33)	2,334,627	a
Fuyuan Handle Official Business Automation Products Shenzhen Co. Ltd. 富源辦公自動化產品深圳有限公司(1993)	Shenzhen 深圳市	Guangdong 廣東省	(0755)5512888 (0755)5515463	738	Overseas Chinese-funded 港澳台資	136,251	15158(1)	162,039	c
Tianjin Sensitization Material Company 天津感光材料公司(1958)	Tianjin 天津市	Tianjin 天津市	(022)28342936 (022)28341945	2,607	State-owned 國有	114,571	4(75)	208,918	a
Wuxi A Er Mei Sensitization Chemical Co. 無錫阿爾梅感光化學公司(1972)	Wuxi 無錫市	Jiangsu 江蘇省	(0510)5501110 (0510)5502527	1,276	State-owned 國有	111,841	502(32)	566,144	o
Jiangyin Da Ya Electron Co. Ltd. 江陰達芽電子有限公司(1992)	Wuxi 無錫市	Jiangsu 江蘇省	(0510)6531818 (0510)6531818	488	Overseas Chinese-funded 港澳台資	95,575	-1764(113)	37,435	c

Top 10 Cities by Production Output 產出排名前10位城市	Province 省	Market share 市場份額	Number of firms 企業個數
Shanghai 上海市	Shanghai 上海市	13.36%	25
Shenzhen 深圳市	Guangdong 廣東省	11.57%	33
Shantou 汕頭市	Guangdong 廣東省	9.76%	40
Baoding 保定市	Hebei 河北省	9.26%	1
Zhuhai 珠海市	Guangdong 廣東省	8.25%	10
Nantong 南通市	Jiangsu 江蘇省	6.20%	5
Nanyang 南陽市	Henan 河南省	5.96%	1
Wuxi 無錫市	Jiangsu 江蘇省	3.86%	13
Xiamen 廈門市	Fujian 福建省	3.30%	3
Tianjin 天津市	Tianjin 天津市	2.73%	14

10 Major Wholesalers 10家主要批發商	City 城市	Province 省	Telephone / Fax 電話 / 傳真
Zhong Hua Singbo Import & Export Company 中化寧波進出口公司	Ningbo 寧波市	Zhejiang 浙江省	(0574)7346764 (0574)7366775
China Chemical Supply & Marketing Hua Nan Company 中國化工供銷華南公司	Guangzhou 廣州市	Guangdong 廣東省	(020)87654477 (020)87784414
China Agriculture Means of Production Chengdu Company 中國農業生產資料成都公司	Chengdu 成都市	Sichuan 四川省	(028)3333909 (028)3331202
Shanxi Agriculture Means of Production Company 山西省農業生產資料公司	Taiyuan 太原市	Shanxi 山西省	(0351)4040255 (0351)4040231
Beijing Chemical Light Industry General Company 北京市化工輕工總公司	Beijing 北京市	Beijing 北京市	(010)64224837 (010)64219301
Beijing Chemical Industry Group Company Supply & Marketing Company 北京化學工業集團公司供銷公司	Beijing 北京市	Beijing 北京市	(010)67714610 (010)67714058
Zhong Hua Jiangsu Import & Export Company 中化江蘇進出口公司	Nanjing 南京市	Jiangsu 江蘇省	(025)2258718 (025)2257789
Yunnan Chemical Import & Export Company 雲南省化工進出口公司	Kunming 昆明市	Yunnan 雲南省	(0871)3314002 (0871)3314931
Fujian Jiu Zhou Group Co. Ltd. 福建九州集團股份有限公司	Xiamen 廈門市	Fujian 福建省	(0592)5055818 (0592)5052033
China Chemical Industry Commission Agent Hua Dong Co. 中國化工供銷華東公司	Shanghai 上海市	Shanghai 上海市	(021)62514123

*Also include sales by firms outside this industry.包括本行業以外廠家的銷售。"o" stands for "others"."o" 代表"其他產品"。

2677: Chemical Additive 添加劑製造業

The industry accounts for 0.057% of the total revenue of China's industrial sector in 1996. The revenue growth rate of the industry is 52.4% from 1995, as compared to the growth rate of China's industrial sector, 9.51%. The rate of return on asset is 4.32%. 72.30% of all firms in the industry made a profit while 21.85% had negative returns. The top province in terms of the industry's revenue is Jiangsu, accounting for 14.59% of the total revenue.
本行業在1996年佔全行業總產值0.057% ，行業年增長率為52.4%（全國工業年增長率9.51%）。行業的資產回報率4.32% ，72.30%的企業盈利，21.85%的企業虧損。銷售收入最高的省份為江蘇省，佔本行業的14.59%。

	Total number of firms 企業總數	Total number of employees 職工總數	Total revenue (mil. RMB) 總銷售收入 (百萬元)	Total profit (mil. RMB) 總利潤 (百萬元)	Return on assets 資產利潤率 (%)	Return on equity 權益利潤率 (%)	Labour productivity ('000 RMB / worker) 勞動生產率 (千元/人)	Debts / assets 資產負債率 (%)	Total assets (mil. RMB) 總資產 (百萬元)
Industry Overall 行業總體	495	31,827	3,323	148	4.32	12.86	104.41	66.45	3,430

	Number of firms 企業個數	Average number of employees 平均職工人數	Average revenue ('000 RMB) 平均銷售收入（千元）	Average profit ('000 RMB) 平均利潤（千元）	Return on assets 資產利潤率 (%)	Return on equity 權益利潤率 (%)	Labour productivity ('000 RMB / worker) 勞動生產率 (千元/人)	Average debts / assets 平均資產負債率(%)	Average Total assets ('000 RMB) 平均總資產（千元）
By ownership 產業所有權									
State-owned 國有	84	72	4,560	48	0.55	1.74	62.90	68.28	8,631
Collectively-owned 集體	317	62	6,499	240	4.74	16.20	104.31	70.71	5,065
Privately-owned 私有	4	31	2,209	170	8.71	49.51	71.83	82.41	1,946
Domestic JVs 聯營	9	53	16,268	1,866	11.26	18.10	305.65	37.80	16,577
Joint stock 股份制	6	117	2,430	284	22.43	43.97	20.86	49.00	1,265
Foreign-funded 外資	40	69	9,081	548	3.37	9.59	130.75	64.89	16,275
Overseas Chinese-funded 港澳台資	33	57	10,188	829	9.84	22.12	180.27	55.51	8,419
By size 規模									
Large 大型	2	869	121,383	7,749	4.32	8.27	139.76	47.73	179,228
Medium 中型	8	513	63,571	2,838	4.32	13.78	123.86	68.66	65,718
Small 小型	456	55	5,642	241	4.31	13.74	103.17	68.62	5,584
By regional distribution 地區分布									
Central-North 華北	80	46	5,095	209	4.17	11.35	109.95	63.22	5,014
Beijing 北京	25	10	720	-108	-6.60	-28.78	70.04	77.04	1,636
Tianjin 天津	17	84	9,236	626	7.23	17.71	110.34	59.18	8,669
Hebei 河北	27	37	2,806	239	12.62	43.07	74.93	70.69	1,896
Shanxi 山西	4	52	2,468	340	7.28	37.16	47.45	80.40	4,668
Inner Mongolia 內蒙	7	115	20,994	139	0.68	1.64	181.88	58.53	20,433
Northeast 東北	57	49	3,558	145	7.71	16.93	73.27	54.51	1,876
Liaoning 遼寧	30	46	2,418	-62	-3.08	-7.75	52.34	60.32	2,004
Jilin 吉林	9	19	709	56	14.79	42.37	37.53	65.09	376
Heilongjiang 黑龍江	18	67	6,883	533	22.08	40.62	102.22	45.64	2,413
Central East 華東	161	82	9,877	420	4.47	15.34	120.39	70.86	9,397
Shanghai 上海	16	86	11,895	338	2.81	6.09	138.11	53.80	11,996
Jiangsu 江蘇	34	119	14,255	449	4.73	19.91	119.38	76.23	9,496
Zhejiang 浙江	25	118	14,684	1,049	4.24	20.27	124.19	79.11	24,764
Anhui 安徽	19	104	12,942	911	11.61	40.76	124.63	71.51	7,847
Fujian 福建	14	33	7,890	-309	-7.44	-24.11	237.55	69.16	4,159
Jiangxi 江西	19	42	1,495	89	5.89	27.69	35.46	78.71	1,518
Shandong 山東	34	46	4,806	177	4.22	7.59	103.69	44.37	4,202
Central-South 中南	102	62	6,263	367	4.07	10.34	100.55	60.68	9,030
Henan 河南	36	70	5,325	482	10.76	40.77	76.59	73.60	4,478
Hubei 湖北	12	33	1,773	122	7.12	47.40	53.04	84.98	1,709
Hunan 湖南	10	11	840	27	4.27	15.34	75.00	72.15	632
Guangdong 廣東	32	40	7,132	323	2.62	6.76	176.65	61.18	12,307
Guangxi 廣西	12	170	15,768	671	2.37	4.97	92.53	52.28	28,272
Hainan 海南									
Southwest 西南	67	73	6,320	264	4.24	12.73	86.42	66.71	6,232
Chongqing 重慶	6	48	4,609	1,127	19.78	28.94	96.35	31.63	5,698
Sichuan 四川	43	96	9,127	281	3.22	10.65	95.29	69.74	8,714
Guizhou 貴州	7	8	31	-4	-7.50	-33.33	3.73	77.50	57
Yunnan 雲南	11	40	249	-96	-13.32	-47.32	6.20	71.86	724
Tibet 西藏									
Northwest 西北	28	32	2,161	10	0.40	2.24	68.00	82.20	2,511
Shaanxi 陝西	9	38	3,098	-68	-2.04	-19.18	82.24	89.38	3,328
Gansu 甘肅	10	42	2,177	61	2.53	6.89	51.71	63.35	2,415
Qinghai 青海	1	22	730	30	12.50	13.64	33.18	8.33	240
Ningxia 寧夏	2	14	410	50	7.04	17.86	29.29	61.27	710
Xinjiang 新疆	6	13	1,553	25	1.03	-51.72	116.50	101.99	2,423

2677: Chemical Additive 添加劑製造業

Year 年份	Number of firms 企業個數	Rate of change 每年變化 (%)	Number of employees 職工人數 (人)	Rate of change 每年變化 (%)	Total revenue (mil. RMB) 總銷售收入 (百萬元)	Rate of change 每年變化 (%)	Total profit (mil. RMB) 總利潤 (百萬元)	Rate of change 每年變化 (%)
1993								
1994	319		20,743		1,206		46	
1995	434	36.05%	31,703	52.84%	2,181	80.78%	76	63.56%
1996	495	14.06%	31,827	0.39%	3,323	52.36%	148	95.48%

3 Major products* 3 種主要產品 *	Output 產量	Sales volume 銷售量	Unit 單位
a) Food Additive 食品添加劑	300,350	288,336	ton 噸
b) Petroleum Additive 石油添加劑	17,640	17,993	ton 噸
c) Feedstuff Additive 飼料添加劑	1,175	1,152	ton 噸

Top 10 firms by revenue (year founded) 收入排名前 10 家企業 (創辦年份)	City 城市	Province 省	Telephone / fax 電話 / 傳真	Number of employees 職工人數	Ownership 產業所有權	Revenue ('000 RMB) 銷售收入 (千元)	Profit ('000 RMB) (rank) 利潤 (千元) (排名)	Total assets ('000 RMB) 總資產 (千元)	Major products 主要產品
Sheng Hua Group Co. 德清縣升華集團(生物化學總公司)(1984)	Huzhou 湖州市	Zhejiang 浙江省	(0572)8401212 (0572)8401258	586	Collectively-owned 集體	209,020	20983(1)	396,147	o
Guangxi Lysine Factory 廣西賴氨酸廠(1987)	Nanning 南寧市	Guangxi 廣西	(0771)4831307 (0771)4820506	1,348	State-owned 國有	105,296	5968(5)	282,359	c
Sichuan Mianzhu Long Mang Mineral Group Co. Ltd 四川省綿竹龍蟒礦物資飼料集團有限公司(1985)	Deyang 德陽市	Sichuan 四川省	(0838)6205484 (0838)6204188	2,232	Collectively-owned 集體	105,050	14390(2)	172,500	o
Jianhu Dyestuff Chemical General Factory 建湖縣染料化工總廠(1981)	Yancheng 鹽城市	Jiangsu 江蘇省	(0515)6411388 (0515)6410948	237	Collectively-owned 集體	96,100	4280(8)	48,330	o
Harbin Nangang Wang Gang Grains of Bone Processing Factory 哈爾濱市南崗王崗骨粒加工廠(1988)	Harbin 哈爾濱市	Heilongjiang 黑龍江省		30	Collectively-owned 集體	94,140	4560(7)	7,963	o
Xiamen Zhong Run Grain & Oil Feed Industrial Co. Ltd. 廈門市中潤糧油飼料工業有限公司(1996)	Xiamen 廈門市	Fujian 福建省	(0592)5626785 (0592)5626833	18	Domestic JVs 聯營	78,586	-52(158)	24,071	o
Tianjin North Foods Co. Ltd. 天津北方食品有限公司(1993)	Tianjin 天津市	Tianjin 天津市	(022)24392925 (022)24395189	287	Foreign-funded 外資	57,670	3718(10)	46,065	a
Xi Shan Shi Petroleum Additive Factory 錫山市石油添加劑廠(1977)	Wuxi 無錫市	Jiangsu 江蘇省	(0510)3260836	330	Collectively-owned 集體	56,388	3603(12)	29,912	b
Guilin Hongxing Chemical Factory 桂林市紅星化工總廠(1958)	Guilin 桂林市	Guangxi 廣西	(0773)2829674	253	Collectively-owned 集體	55,881	2107(21)	18,358	o
Wujin Zhai Qiao Ji Ti Accessory Material Factory 武進市寨橋機體輔助材料廠(1995)	Changzhou 常州市	Jiangsu 江蘇省	(0519)6261019	495	Collectively-owned 集體	55,831	30(128)	1,183	o

Top 10 Cities by Production Output 產出排名前 10 位城市	Province 省	Market share 市場份額	Number of firms 企業個數
Shanghai 上海市	Shanghai 上海市	7.56%	29
Tianjin 天津市	Tianjin 天津市	7.20%	30
Hohhot 呼和浩特市	Inner Mong 內蒙	6.91%	3
Deyang 德陽市	Sichuan 四川省	5.08%	4
Xiamen 廈門市	Fujian 福建省	3.81%	3
Wuxi 無錫市	Jiangsu 江蘇省	3.61%	11
Guangzhou 廣州市	Guangdong 廣東省	3.32%	18
Huzhou 湖州市	Zhejiang 浙江省	3.09%	5
Guilin 桂林市	Guangxi 廣西	3.07%	6
Shantou 汕頭市	Guangdong 廣東省	2.81%	5

10 Major Wholesalers 10 家主要批發商	City 城市	Province 省	Telephone / Fax 電話 / 傳真
Zhejiang Cereal & Oils Food Import & Export Co. Ltd. 浙江省糧油食品進出口股份有限公司	Hangzhou 杭州市	Zhejiang 浙江省	(0571)5152515 (0571)5152514
Henan Cereal & Oils Food Import & Export Company 河南省糧油食品進出口公司	Zhengzhou 鄭州市	Henan 河南省	(0371)3942915 (0371)3942790
Shanghai Land Reclamation & Cultivation Cooking Oil Mill Marketing Company 上海市農墾糧油食品經營公司	Shanghai 上海市	Shanghai 上海市	(021)64714931
Changtu Da Chang Cooking Oil Mill Trade Jointly-operated Company 昌圖縣大昌糧油貿易聯營公司	Tieling 鐵嶺市	Liaoning 遼寧省	(0410)5824099
China Vegetable Oil Company 中國植物油公司	Beijing 北京市	Beijing 北京市	(010)66038248
Zhong Liang Shandong Cooking Oil Mill Import & Export Company 中糧山東糧油進出口公司	Qingdao 青島市	Shandong 山東省	(0532)2972342 (0532)2972379
Zhejiang Cooking Oil Mill Storage & Transport Trade Company 浙江省糧油儲運貿易公司	Hangzhou 杭州市	Zhejiang 浙江省	(0571)5161408 (0571)5161411
Anhui Cereal & Oils Food Import & Export (Group) Company 安徽省糧油食品進出口(集團)公司	Hefei 合肥市	Anhui 安徽省	(0551)2653731 (0551)2652831
Shanghai Farm, Industry & Commerce Group Cooking Oil Mill General Company 上海農工商集團糧油總公司	Shanghai 上海市	Shanghai 上海市	(021)62593423 (021)62748578
Sichuan Chang Jiang Enterprise Co. Ltd. 四川省長江企業股份有限公司	Chengdu 成都市	Sichuan 四川省	(028)3339888 (028)3333896

*Also include sales by firms outside this industry.包括本行業以外廠家的銷售。"o" stands for "others". "o" 代表 "其他產品"。

2681: Soap, Washing Powder and Synthetic Detergent
肥皂及皂粉、合成洗滌劑製造業

The industry accounts for 0.389% of the total revenue of China's industrial sector in 1996. The revenue growth rate of the industry is 17.8% from 1995, as compared to the growth rate of China's industrial sector, 9.51%. The rate of return on asset is 6.93%. 67.56% of all firms in the industry made a profit while 23.95% had negative returns. The top province in terms of the industry's revenue is Guangdong, accounting for 29.65% of the total revenue.
本行業在1996年佔全行業總產值0.389%，行業年增長率為17.8%（全國工業年增長率9.51%）。行業的資產回報率6.93%，67.56%的企業盈利，23.95%的企業虧損。銷售收入最高的省份為廣東省，佔本行業的29.65%。

	Total number of firms 企業總數	Total number of employees 職工總數	Total revenue (mil. RMB) 總銷售收入（百萬元）	Total profit (mil. RMB) 總利潤（百萬元）	Return on assets 資產利潤率 (%)	Return on equity 權益利潤率 (%)	Labour productivity ('000 RMB / worker) 勞動生產率（千元／人）	Debts / assets 資產負債率 (%)	Total assets (mil. RMB) 總資產（百萬元）
Industry Overall 行業總體	1,361	142,089	22,535	1,785	6.93	16.01	158.60	56.72	25,758

	Number of firms 企業個數	Average number of employees 平均職工人數	Average revenue ('000 RMB) 平均銷售收入（千元）	Average profit ('000 RMB) 平均利潤（千元）	Return on assets 資產利潤率 (%)	Return on equity 權益利潤率 (%)	Labour productivity ('000 RMB / worker) 勞動生產率（千元／人）	Average debts / assets 平均資產負債率(%)	Average Total assets ('000 RMB) 平均總資產（千元）
By ownership 產業所有權									
State-owned 國有	218	327	24,807	-372	-0.83	-2.49	75.80	66.68	44,794
Collectively-owned 集體	910	36	1,766	23	1.31	4.94	49.36	73.48	1,766
Privately-owned 私有	6	21	1,386	49	3.24	7.73	67.63	58.13	1,520
Domestic JVs 聯營	17	62	10,108	122	2.44	7.62	163.19	67.98	5,019
Joint stock 股份制	27	515	119,301	7,927	7.32	15.70	231.72	53.35	108,245
Foreign-funded 外資	102	159	96,380	15,556	16.99	31.33	605.34	45.76	91,538
Overseas Chinese-funded 港澳台資	75	117	31,448	584	2.16	4.34	269.83	50.28	27,035
By size 規模									
Large 大型	47	1,108	336,824	37,985	11.46	25.33	303.93	54.76	331,455
Medium 中型	42	681	62,648	275	0.33	0.80	92.01	58.22	82,388
Small 小型	1,230	49	3,897	-9	-0.16	-0.39	79.42	60.50	5,462
By regional distribution 地區分布									
Central-North 華北	240	89	10,931	-5	-0.03	-0.09	122.66	64.15	14,371
Beijing 北京	81	47	7,307	97	0.81	1.73	156.79	53.33	12,011
Tianjin 天津	73	90	16,876	-34	-0.21	-0.63	187.17	67.31	16,606
Hebei 河北	51	90	8,966	-118	-1.14	-2.48	99.74	54.19	10,406
Shanxi 山西	17	283	17,071	11	0.03	0.16	60.31	80.23	33,429
Inner Mongolia 內蒙	18	91	2,893	-34	-0.38	-2.02	31.89	81.40	9,156
Northeast 東北	210	89	4,177	-259	-2.63	-9.00	47.07	70.77	9,850
Liaoning 遼寧	97	108	5,551	-185	-1.46	-3.88	51.38	62.23	12,629
Jilin 吉林	49	91	2,971	-560	-4.89	-19.75	32.66	75.23	11,447
Heilongjiang 黑龍江	64	58	3,019	-141	-3.20	-298.68	52.21	98.93	4,416
Central East 華東	382	120	21,829	475	2.32	5.72	182.22	59.35	20,423
Shanghai 上海	54	130	67,290	2,218	3.73	7.98	518.28	53.29	59,476
Jiangsu 江蘇	80	94	10,967	123	1.20	3.74	116.19	67.81	10,167
Zhejiang 浙江	47	171	26,750	1,274	4.80	11.62	156.61	58.70	26,531
Anhui 安徽	57	163	21,383	32	0.19	0.57	131.13	67.44	17,389
Fujian 福建	43	38	2,704	-216	-3.81	-15.23	71.51	75.00	5,670
Jiangxi 江西	36	81	5,756	-101	-1.14	-4.14	70.98	72.41	8,848
Shandong 山東	65	144	15,820	46	0.31	0.71	110.19	56.64	15,014
Central-South 中南	337	111	26,435	4,901	16.89	32.82	237.13	48.54	29,019
Henan 河南	67	109	9,152	169	1.37	4.21	83.84	67.34	12,278
Hubei 湖北	61	146	10,751	678	3.61	9.02	73.88	59.92	18,760
Hunan 湖南	45	113	10,096	-441	-3.78	-17.31	89.19	78.15	11,668
Guangdong 廣東	115	106	58,100	14,159	24.84	42.24	549.87	41.20	57,005
Guangxi 廣西	43	82	10,919	-141	-0.91	-1.93	133.92	52.60	15,438
Hainan 海南	6	105	5,703	-545	-4.80	-15.08	54.58	68.18	11,357
Southwest 西南	145	88	8,599	111	0.85	2.14	98.07	60.25	13,007
Chongqing 重慶	35	121	7,091	-12	-0.09	-0.40	58.57	77.07	12,966
Sichuan 四川	70	86	11,395	229	1.40	3.08	132.00	54.48	16,352
Guizhou 貴州	26	43	1,872	-21	-0.44	-0.96	43.93	53.70	4,695
Yunnan 雲南	14	94	10,976	76	0.64	1.53	116.32	58.33	11,891
Tibet 西藏									
Northwest 西北	47	128	11,496	-177	-1.07	-2.35	89.77	54.30	16,452
Shaanxi 陝西	17	119	12,967	-641	-2.73	-5.70	109.13	52.05	23,454
Gansu 甘肅	15	110	8,879	-185	-1.71	-3.69	81.02	53.62	10,829
Qinghai 青海	4	73	9,258	35	0.34	1.03	126.38	67.17	10,318
Ningxia 寧夏	2	405	36,065	565	1.64	4.48	89.05	63.47	34,515
Xinjiang 新疆	9	139	8,612	454	4.02	8.51	61.91	52.78	11,313

2681: Soap, Washing Powder and Synthetic Detergent
肥皂及皂粉、合成洗滌劑製造業

Year 年份	Number of firms 企業個數	Rate of change 每年變化 (%)	Number of employees 職工人數 (人)	Rate of change 每年變化 (%)	Total revenue (mil. RMB) 總銷售收入 (百萬元)	Rate of change 每年變化 (%)	Total profit (mil. RMB) 總利潤 (百萬元)	Rate of change 每年變化 (%)
1993	1,001		147,455		12,438		332	
1994	1,159	15.78%	139,448	-5.43%	15,211	22.29%	604	81.79%
1995	1,294	11.65%	144,240	3.44%	19,132	25.78%	1,216	101.36%
1996	1,361	5.18%	142,089	-1.49%	22,535	17.79%	1,785	46.79%

3 Major products* 3種主要產品*	Output 產量	Sales volume 銷售量	Unit 單位
a) Soap 肥皂	710,788	682,356	ton 噸
b) Synthetic Detergent 合成洗滌劑	2,184,677	2,119,136	ton 噸
c) Fine Glycerin 精甘油	27,924	21,502	ton 噸

Top 10 firms by revenue (year founded) 收入排名前10家企業 (創辦年份)	City 城市	Province 省	Telephone / fax 電話 / 傳真	Number of employees 職工人數	Ownership 產業所有權	Revenue ('000 RMB) 銷售收入 (千元)	Profit ('000 RMB) (rank) 利潤 (千元) (排名)	Total assets ('000 RMB) 總資產 (千元)	Major products 主要產品
Procter & Gamble (Guangzhou) Ltd. 廣州寶潔有限公司(1988)	Guangzhou 廣州市	Guangdong 廣東省	(020)82218828 (020)82215594	1,362	Foreign-funded 外資	3,995,887	1581886(1)	2,992,290	b
Shanghai White-cat Co. Ltd. 上海白貓有限公司(1993)	Shanghai 上海市	Shanghai 上海市	(021)64700249 (021)64756025	1,363	Overseas Chinese-funded 港澳台資	1,238,194	30792(5)	647,895	b
Shanghai Li Hua Co. Ltd. 上海利華有限公司(1986)	Shanghai 上海市	Shanghai 上海市	(021)65390810 (021)65191940	735	Foreign-funded 外資	1,128,672	115657(2)	701,936	a,b
Amway (China) Daily Articles Co. Ltd. 安利(中國)日用品有限公司(1995)	Guangzhou 廣州市	Guangdong 廣東省	(020)87596868 (020)87536589	587	Foreign-funded 外資	890,046	-1062(392)	1,124,015	b
Zhejiang Nice Chemical Industry Co. Ltd. 浙江納愛斯化工股份有限公司(1968)	Lishui 麗水市	Zhejiang 浙江省	(0578)2133451 (0578)2135514	1,085	Joint stock 股份制	636,175	53617(3)	281,096	o
Procter & Gamble (Tianjing) Ltd. 天津寶潔有限公司(1994)	Tianjin 天津市	Tianjin 天津市	(022)28309603 (022)28309602	422	Foreign-funded 外資	602,274	11124(11)	361,338	a
Shanghai Soap Co. Ltd. 上海製皂有限公司(1995)	Shanghai 上海市	Shanghai 上海市	(021)65431130 (021)65439829	1,727	Foreign-funded 外資	529,894	8387(13)	539,549	a
Guangzhou Lang Qi Industrial Co. Ltd. 廣州市浪奇實業股份有限公司(1959)	Guangzhou 廣州市	Guangdong 廣東省	(020)82305694 (020)82305104	860	Joint stock 股份制	466,587	41453(4)	664,644	a,b,c
Tianjin Hankel Detergents & Cleaning Products Co. Ltd. 天津漢高洗滌劑有限公司(1992)	Tianjin 天津市	Tianjin 天津市	(022)24373622 (022)24373318	1,009	Foreign-funded 外資	453,981	-3435(416)	302,829	b
Shanghai Unilever Co. Ltd. 上海聯合利華有限公司(1993)	Shanghai 上海市	Shanghai 上海市	(021)64307228 (021)64306357	322	Foreign-funded 外資	442,340	-36713(436)	718,984	b

Top 10 Cities by Production Output 產出排名前10位城市	Province 省	Market share 市場份額	Number of firms 企業個數
Shanghai 上海市	Shanghai 上海市	25.87%	87
Guangzhou 廣州市	Guangdong 廣東省	11.60%	58
Tianjin 天津市	Tianjin 天津市	7.04%	89
Beijing 北京市	Beijing 北京市	3.78%	65
Lishui 麗水市	Zhejiang 浙江省	3.33%	4
Chengdu 成都市	Sichuan 四川省	2.76%	21
Changsha 長沙市	Hunan 湖南省	1.74%	3
Chongqing 重慶市	Chongqing 重慶市	1.61%	41
Hangzhou 杭州市	Zhejiang 浙江省	1.55%	22
Jingsha 荊沙市	Hubei 湖北省	1.52%	11

10 Major Wholesalers 10家主要批發商	City 城市	Province 省	Telephone / Fax 電話 / 傳真
Changzhou General Merchandise Wholesale General Company 常州百貨批發總公司	Changzhou 常州市	Jiangsu 江蘇省	(0519)6680488 (0519)6680488
Suzhou General Merchandise General Co. 蘇州百貨總公司	Suzhou 蘇州市	Jiangsu 江蘇省	(0512)5222288 (0512)5222247
Guangzhou Yue Xiu Enterprise (Holdings) Co. 廣州越秀企業(集團)公司	Guangzhou 廣州市	Guangdong 廣東省	(020)86662828 (020)86672634
Wunan Commercial Group Corp. 湖南省商業集團總公司	Changsha 長沙市	Hunan 湖南省	(0731)4442765
Kunming General Merchandise Purchase Supply Station Kunming General Merchandise Company 昆明百貨採購供應站昆明市百貨公司	Kunming 昆明市	Yunnan 雲南省	(0871)3314883 (0871)3314961
Nanjing General Merchandise General Company 南京市百貨總公司	Nanjing 南京市	Jiangsu 江蘇省	(025)6664681 (025)6643927
Guangzhou Shang Ling Trade Co. Ltd. 廣州商菱貿易有限公司	Guangzhou 廣州市	Guangdong 廣東省	(020)86677190 (020)86673971
Beijing Light Industry Product Import & Export Company 北京市輕工業品進出口公司	Beijing 北京市	Beijing 北京市	(010)64057425 (010)64057427
Xi Shan Shi Commerce Group Company 錫山市商業集團公司	Wuxi 無錫市	Jiangsu 江蘇省	(0510)2442982
Yixing Su Nan Commercial Building 宜興市蘇南商廈	Wuxi 無錫市	Jiangsu 江蘇省	(0510)7904407 (0510)7904754

*Also include sales by firms outside this industry.包括本行業以外廠家的銷售。"o" stands for "others". "o" 代表"其他產品"。

2682: Synthetic Fatty Acid 合成脂肪酸製造業

The industry accounts for 0.005% of the total revenue of China's industrial sector in 1996. The revenue growth rate of the industry is 39.9% from 1995, as compared to the growth rate of China's industrial sector, 9.51%. The rate of return on asset is 2.58%. 68.95% of all firms in the industry made a profit while 20.34% had negative returns. The top province in terms of the industry's revenue is Shandong, accounting for 34.76% of the total revenue.
本行業在 1996 年佔全行業總產值 0.005% ，行業年增長率為 39.9%（全國工業年增長率 9.51%）。行業的資產回報率 2.58% ， 68.95% 的企業盈利， 20.34% 的企業虧損。銷售收入最高的省份為山東省，佔本行業的 34.76% 。

	Total number of firms 企業總數	Total number of employees 職工總數	Total revenue (mil. RMB) 總銷售收入（百萬元）	Total profit (mil. RMB) 總利潤（百萬元）	Return on assets 資產利潤率 (%)	Return on equity 權益利潤率 (%)	Labour productivity ('000 RMB / worker) 勞動生產率（千元／人）	Debts / assets 資產負債率 (%)	Total assets (mil. RMB) 總資產（百萬元）
Industry Overall 行業總體	61	4,589	292	15	2.58	24.42	63.63	89.41	566

	Number of firms 企業個數	Average number of employees 平均職工人數	Average revenue ('000 RMB) 平均銷售收入（千元）	Average profit ('000 RMB) 平均利潤（千元）	Return on assets 資產利潤率 (%)	Return on equity 權益利潤率 (%)	Labour productivity ('000 RMB / worker) 勞動生產率（千元／人）	Average debts / assets 平均資產負債率(%)	Average Total assets ('000 RMB) 平均總資產（千元）
By ownership 產業所有權									
State-owned 國有	11	191	3,909	364	1.27	100.00	20.52	98.73	28,727
Collectively-owned 集體	47	48	4,158	178	3.89	16.47	87.21	76.37	4,578
Privately-owned 私有	1	80	12,755	1,008	8.75	34.33	159.43	74.50	11,511
Domestic JVs 聯營	1	140	40,771	1,616	6.96	73.78	291.22	90.57	23,223
Joint stock 股份制	1	32							
Foreign-funded 外資									
Overseas Chinese-funded 港澳台資									
By size 規模									
Large 大型									
Medium 中型	2	653	12,579	11	0.01	0.22	19.26	96.82	159,200
Small 小型	58	56	4,600	258	6.05	30.05	81.89	79.86	4,268
By regional distribution 地區分布									
Central-North 華北	8	28	1,419	25	1.37	4.69	51.59	70.65	1,819
Beijing 北京	1								
Tianjin 天津	4	19	430	18	0.72	7.45	22.63	90.40	2,448
Hebei 河北	2	37	3,935	65	5.96	7.93	106.35	24.31	1,090
Shanxi 山西									
Inner Mongolia 內蒙	1	70	1,760				25.14	34.88	2,580
Northeast 東北	5	167	4,360	744	1.86	-60.78	26.17	103.06	40,036
Liaoning 遼寧	2	33	1,430	210	6.23	45.16	44.00	86.20	3,370
Jilin 吉林	3	256	6,313	1,100	1.71	-46.81	24.66	103.64	64,480
Heilongjiang 黑龍江									
Central East 華東	28	71	7,050	323	3.73	18.17	99.95	79.48	8,651
Shanghai 上海									
Jiangsu 江蘇	11	34	5,496	146	3.70	19.63	159.53	81.13	3,951
Zhejiang 浙江	3	3	197				65.56	86.90	967
Anhui 安徽	4	53	6,745	373	6.88	122.13	128.48	94.36	5,413
Fujian 福建	1								
Jiangxi 江西	1	165	7,870	10	0.07	0.18	47.70	57.72	13,410
Shandong 山東	8	152	12,689	740	3.68	17.29	83.75	78.71	20,101
Central-South 中南	15	95	3,713	117	1.65	16.01	39.17	89.68	7,057
Henan 河南	7	138	4,687	263	2.25	19.76	33.86	88.62	11,687
Hubei 湖北	5	66	4,112	242	9.49	29.37	62.68	67.69	2,550
Hunan 湖南	1	40	1,460	120	8.05	-100.00	36.50	108.05	1,490
Guangdong 廣東	1	46	870	-1,420	-14.48	59.66	18.91	124.26	9,810
Guangxi 廣西	1	39							
Hainan 海南									
Southwest 西南	1	23	2,920				126.96	33.82	680
Chongqing 重慶									
Sichuan 四川	1	23	2,920				126.96	33.82	680
Guizhou 貴州									
Yunnan 雲南									
Tibet 西藏									
Northwest 西北	4	29	748	-10	-1.43	-5.48	25.78	74.29	700
Shaanxi 陝西	1	60	2,630	10	1.16	1.54	43.83	24.42	860
Gansu 甘肅	2	11	95	-30	-5.77	-120.00	8.64	95.19	520
Qinghai 青海									
Ningxia 寧夏									
Xinjiang 新疆	1	34	170	10	1.11	33.33	5.00	97.78	900

2682: Synthetic Fatty Acid 合成脂肪酸製造業

Year 年份	Number of firms 企業個數	Rate of change 每年變化(%)	Number of employees 職工人數(人)	Rate of change 每年變化(%)	Total revenue (mil. RMB) 總銷售收入(百萬元)	Rate of change 每年變化(%)	Total profit (mil. RMB) 總利潤(百萬元)	Rate of change 每年變化(%)
1993	58		4,684		293		18	
1994	60	3.45%	3,463	-26.07%	221	-24.68%	4	-76.86%
1995	63	5.00%	3,631	4.85%	209	-5.33%	5	24.98%
1996	61	-3.17%	4,589	26.38%	292	39.87%	15	180.43%

3 Major products* 3 種主要產品 *	Output 產量	Sales volume 銷售量	Unit 單位
a) Soap Synthetic Fatty Acid 皂用合成脂肪酸	5,798	5,567	ton 噸
b) Cotadecanoic Acid 硬脂酸	4,823	4,678	ton 噸
c) Fine Glycerin 精甘油	181	139	ton 噸

Top 10 firms by revenue (year founded) 收入排名前 10 家企業 (創辦年份)	City 城市	Province 省	Telephone / fax 電話 / 傳真	Number of employees 職工人數	Ownership 產業所有權	Revenue ('000 RMB) 銷售收入(千元)	Profit ('000 RMB) (rank) 利潤(千元)(排名)	Total assets ('000 RMB) 總資產(千元)	Major products 主要產品
Feicheng Rui Tai Fine Chemical Industry Co. Ltd. 肥城瑞泰精細化工有限公司(1993)	Tai'an 泰安市	Shandong 山東省	(0538)3850243 (0538)3850249	570	Collectively-owned 集體	48,380	1360(4)	92,020	b
Liyang Yong An Fine Chemical Refinery 溧陽市永安精細化工廠(1995)	Changzhou 常州市	Jiangsu 江蘇省	(0519)7620315	54	Collectively-owned 集體	21,916	1352(5)	11,345	o
Dingyuan Special Chemical Plant 定遠縣特種化工廠(1991)	Chuzhou 滁州市	Anhui 安徽省	(0550)4022338	60	Collectively-owned 集體	21,610	1680(2)	9,240	o
Shangqiu Wangwen Oils & Fats Chemical Plant 商丘縣王墳鄉油脂化學廠(1982)	Shangqiu 商丘市	Henan 河南省	(0370)3314334	80	Collectively-owned 集體	21,000	1560(3)	10,651	o
Zibo Zhoucun Fat Chemical Factory 淄博市周村油脂化學廠(1972)	Zibo 淄博市	Shandong 山東省	(0533)6889212 (0533)6889212	69	Collectively-owned 集體	18,080	2800(1)	8,570	b
Zibo Linzi Fat Chemical Industry Factory 淄博市臨淄油脂化工廠(1991)	Zibo 淄博市	Shandong 山東省	(0533)7580581 (0533)7580581	152	Collectively-owned 集體	17,132	703(6)	12,766	a,c
Lianyungang Wan Da Chemical Company 連雲港市萬達化工公司(1989)	Lianyungang 連雲港市	Jiangsu 江蘇省	(0518)5300054	23	Collectively-owned 集體	9,634	413(11)	1,957	b
Funing Fupin Welfare Fat Chemical Industry Factory 阜寧縣扶貧福利油脂化工廠(1992)	Yancheng 鹽城市	Jiangsu 江蘇省	(0515)7213291	54	Collectively-owned 集體	8,900	540(8)	12,790	a
Jiangxi Xin Long Enterprise Group Chemical Factory 江西省鑫龍企業集團化工廠(1987)	Yichun 宜春市	Jiangxi 江西省	(0795)2769424	60	State-owned 國有	7,873	14(18)	13,406	o
Lu Nan Chemical Factory 魯南化工廠(1992)	Jining 濟寧市	Shandong 山東省	(0537)2080674 (0537)2080674	256	State-owned 國有	6,404	-137(27)	31,757	o

Top 10 Cities by Production Output 產出排名前 10 位城市	Province 省	Market share 市場份額	Number of firms 企業個數
Shanghai 上海市	Shanghai 上海市	28.99%	1
Suzhou 蘇州市	Jiangsu 江蘇省	14.70%	4
Tai'an 泰安市	Shandong 山東省	7.90%	1
Binzhou 濱州市	Shandong 山東省	7.90%	1
Zibo 淄博市	Shandong 山東省	7.37%	2
Shangqiu 商丘市	Henan 河南省	6.02%	2
Jining 濟寧市	Shandong 山東省	4.21%	2
Nantong 南通市	Jiangsu 江蘇省	2.28%	3
Tangshan 唐山市	Hebei 河北省	1.66%	1
Xinxiang 新鄉市	Henan 河南省	1.53%	2

10 Major Wholesalers 10 家主要批發商	City 城市	Province 省	Telephone / Fax 電話 / 傳真
Changzhou General Merchandise Wholesale General Company 常州百貨批發總公司	Changzhou 常州市	Jiangsu 江蘇省	(0519)6680488 (0519)6680488
Suzhou General Merchandise General Co. 蘇州百貨總公司	Suzhou 蘇州市	Jiangsu 江蘇省	(0512)5222288 (0512)5222247
Guangzhou Yue Xiu Enterprise (Holdings) Co. 廣州越秀企業(集團)公司	Guangzhou 廣州市	Guangdong 廣東省	(020)86662828 (020)86672634
Wunan Commercial Group Corp. 湖南省商業集團總公司	Changsha 長沙市	Hunan 湖南省	(0731)4442765
Kunming General Merchandise Purchase Supply Station Kunming General Merchandise Company 昆明百貨採購供應站昆明市百貨公司	Kunming 昆明市	Yunnan 雲南省	(0871)3314883 (0871)3314961
Nanjing General Merchandise General Company 南京市百貨總公司	Nanjing 南京市	Jiangsu 江蘇省	(025)6664681 (025)6643927
Guangzhou Shang Ling Trade Co. Ltd. 廣州商菱貿易有限公司	Guangzhou 廣州市	Guangdong 廣東省	(020)86677190 (020)86673971
Beijing Light Industry Product Import & Export Company 北京市輕工業品進出口公司	Beijing 北京市	Beijing 北京市	(010)64057425 (010)64057427
Xi Shan Shi Commerce Group Company 錫山市商業集團公司	Wuxi 無錫市	Jiangsu 江蘇省	(0510)2442982
Yixing Su Nan Commercial Building 宜興市蘇南商廈	Wuxi 無錫市	Jiangsu 江蘇省	(0510)7904407 (0510)7904754

*Also include sales by firms outside this industry.包括本行業以外廠家的銷售。"o" stands for "others". "o" 代表"其他產品"。

2683: Stearic Acid and Stearin Oil 硬脂酸、硬化油製造業

The industry accounts for 0.015% of the total revenue of China's industrial sector in 1996. The revenue growth rate of the industry is 0.3% from 1995, as compared to the growth rate of China's industrial sector, 9.51%. The rate of return on asset is 1.85%. 62.81% of all firms in the industry made a profit while 26.85% had negative returns. The top province in terms of the industry's revenue is Jiangsu, accounting for 27.22% of the total revenue.
本行業在1996年佔全行業總產值0.015%，行業年增長率為0.3%（全國工業年增長率9.51%）。行業的資產回報率1.85%，62.81%的企業盈利，26.85%的企業虧損。銷售收入最高的省份為江蘇省，佔本行業的27.22%。

	Total number of firms 企業總數	Total number of employees 職工總數	Total revenue (mil. RMB) 總銷售收入（百萬元）	Total profit (mil. RMB) 總利潤（百萬元）	Return on assets 資產利潤率 (%)	Return on equity 權益利潤率 (%)	Labour productivity ('000 RMB / worker) 勞動生產率（千元/人）	Debts / assets 資產負債率 (%)	Total assets (mil. RMB) 總資產（百萬元）
Industry Overall 行業總體	115	9,782	878	20	1.85	6.96	89.76	73.49	1,060

	Number of firms 企業個數	Average number of employees 平均職工人數	Average revenue ('000 RMB) 平均銷售收入（千元）	Average profit ('000 RMB) 平均利潤（千元）	Return on assets 資產利潤率 (%)	Return on equity 權益利潤率 (%)	Labour productivity ('000 RMB / worker) 勞動生產率（千元/人）	Average debts / assets 平均資產負債率(%)	Average Total assets ('000 RMB) 平均總資產（千元）
By ownership 產業所有權									
State-owned 國有	22	243	12,227	-318	-1.39	-5.26	50.31	73.51	22,818
Collectively-owned 集體	84	47	5,247	256	5.71	23.86	112.42	76.06	4,488
Privately-owned 私有									
Domestic JVs 聯營	1	163	30,973	659	2.22	7.02	190.02	68.43	29,739
Joint stock 股份制	2	37	24,406	126	1.96	44.06	659.62	95.56	6,423
Foreign-funded 外資	2	57	6,267	2	0.02	0.15	110.91	86.32	7,432
Overseas Chinese-funded 港澳台資	4	93	18,971	1,138	3.69	9.95	203.99	62.97	30,880
By size 規模									
Large 大型									
Medium 中型	5	636	45,959	477	0.62	1.96	72.31	68.22	76,446
Small 小型	108	60	6,001	163	2.60	11.05	99.91	76.46	6,275
By regional distribution 地區分布									
Central-North 華北	13	61	3,816	69	1.67	22.28	62.64	92.50	4,152
Beijing 北京	3	88	5,157	-133	-2.66	-40.82	58.38	93.49	5,020
Tianjin 天津	1								
Hebei 河北	7	58	3,180	183	4.29	-474.07	54.43	100.87	4,261
Shanxi 山西	1	103	11,690	20	0.24	0.70	113.50	65.04	8,210
Inner Mongolia 內蒙	1	15	190				12.67	47.13	870
Northeast 東北	13	193	4,877	-540	-2.90	-34.75	25.29	91.66	18,618
Liaoning 遼寧	10	216	5,291	-546	-2.70	-34.06	24.48	92.07	20,205
Jilin 吉林									
Heilongjiang 黑龍江	3	115	3,497	-520	-3.90	-37.41	30.32	89.57	13,330
Central East 華東	56	70	9,871	460	5.09	14.28	140.36	64.39	9,044
Shanghai 上海	3	74	15,493	-140	-0.97	-4.35	209.37	77.80	14,507
Jiangsu 江蘇	16	96	14,938	918	6.51	14.13	155.60	53.93	14,110
Zhejiang 浙江	9	110	12,918	442	3.72	9.51	117.55	60.93	11,897
Anhui 安徽	6	23	1,547	-8	-0.81	0.62	67.25	231.13	1,033
Fujian 福建	9	28	3,589	216	3.66	10.03	127.67	63.49	5,889
Jiangxi 江西	2	72	500	-275	-39.86	211.54	6.99	118.84	690
Shandong 山東	11	60	9,857	561	8.88	44.36	165.04	80.01	6,320
Central-South 中南	28	78	7,013	208	3.18	10.57	89.45	69.89	6,539
Henan 河南	10	20	2,689	366	23.52	80.62	131.81	70.82	1,556
Hubei 湖北	12	113	11,825	186	1.98	5.15	104.72	61.49	9,376
Hunan 湖南	4	153	6,590	10	0.08	0.70	43.21	89.21	13,228
Guangdong 廣東	2	13	600	-50	-4.76	-6.41	46.15	26.19	1,050
Guangxi 廣西									
Hainan 海南									
Southwest 西南	2	12							
Chongqing 重慶									
Sichuan 四川					1.84	2.59	6.20	28.80	
Guizhou 貴州	2	12							
Yunnan 雲南									
Tibet 西藏									
Northwest 西北	3	109	5,203	-1,967	-7.92	-27.78	47.74	71.48	24,823
Shaanxi 陝西	1	110	11,870	-4,940	-14.98	-28.07	107.91	46.62	32,970
Gansu 甘肅	1	217	3,740	-960	-2.71	-41.03	17.24	93.39	35,380
Qinghai 青海									
Ningxia 寧夏									
Xinjiang 新疆	1							78.76	6,120

2683: Stearic Acid and Stearin Oil 硬脂酸、硬化油製造業

Year 年份	Number of firms 企業個數	Rate of change 每年變化 (%)	Number of employees 職工人數 (人)	Rate of change 每年變化 (%)	Total revenue (mil. RMB) 總銷售收入 (百萬元)	Rate of change 每年變化 (%)	Total profit (mil. RMB) 總利潤 (百萬元)	Rate of change 每年變化 (%)
1993	112		10,337		610		0	
1994	124	10.71%	12,631	22.19%	643	5.33%	-4	-1514.68%
1995	124		11,131	-11.88%	876	36.24%	16	537.50%
1996	115	-7.26%	9,782	-12.12%	878	0.27%	20	28.23%

3 Major products* 3 種主要產品 *	Output 產量	Sales volume 銷售量	Unit 單位
a) Cotadecanoic Acid 硬脂酸	47,568	46,141	ton 噸
b) Fine Glycerin 精甘油	3,433	2,644	ton 噸
c) Lubricating Oil 潤滑油	10,848	9,438	ton 噸

Top 10 firms by revenue (year founded) 收入排名前 10 家企業 (創辦年份)	City 城市	Province 省	Telephone / fax 電話 / 傳真	Number of employees 職工人數	Ownership 產業所有權	Revenue ('000 RMB) 銷售收入 (千元)	Profit ('000 RMB) (rank) 利潤 (千元) (排名)	Total assets ('000 RMB) 總資產 (千元)	Major products 主要產品
Hangzhou Fat Chemical Industry Factory 杭州油脂化工廠(1973)	Hangzhou 杭州市	Zhejiang 浙江省	(0571)6617528 (0571)6617540	768	State-owned 國有	86,227	1944(6)	70,778	a,b
Zhangjiagang Zhongding Oils & Fats Chemical Industry Co. Ltd. 張家港中鼎油脂化工有限公司(1976)	Suzhou 蘇州市	Jiangsu 江蘇省	(0512)8450193	248	Collectively-owned 集體	80,971	10890(1)	63,166	a,b
Wuhan No.2 Chemical Plant 武漢化工二廠(1975)	Wuhan 武漢市	Hubei 湖北省	(027)87601768 (027)87600104	856	State-owned 國有	52,751	-2718(56)	77,673	a,b
Shanghai Coking General Factory Yan An Oils & Fats Factory Jiading Branch 上海焦化總廠延安油脂廠嘉定分廠(1994)	Shanghai 上海市	Shanghai 上海市	(021)59540446	180	Domestic JVs 聯營	41,332	0(41)	33,250	a
Shenyang Sanway Oils & Fats Co. Ltd. 瀋陽三威油脂有限公司(1988)	Shenyang 瀋陽市	Liaoning 遼寧省	(024)25824981 (024)25824978	282	Overseas Chinese-funded 港澳台資	35,551	-1814(54)	89,380	o
Jiangsu Kunbao Group Co. Ltd. 江蘇昆寶集團有限責任公司(1971)	Suzhou 蘇州市	Jiangsu 江蘇省	(0512)7891304	183	Collectively-owned 集體	28,965	1683(7)	37,712	o
Kunshan Zheng Da Rubber & Plastics Factory 昆山市正大橡塑廠(1991)	Suzhou 蘇州市	Jiangsu 江蘇省	(0512)7891125	143	Collectively-owned 集體	26,143	3056(3)	8,738	a,b
Shandong Gaomi Fat Chemical Industry Factory 山東省高密市油脂化工廠(1986)	Weifang 濰坊市	Shandong 山東省	(0536)2733198 (0536)2733049	130	Collectively-owned 集體	23,116	456(14)	5,736	a,b
Mayang Miao Zu Autonomous County Tu Qiang Fat Chemical General Company 麻陽苗族自治縣圖強油脂化學總公司(1973)	Huaihua 懷化市	Hunan 湖南省	(0745)5823815 (0745)5824258	382	State-owned 國有	21,462	15(35)	40,615	a,b
Shandong Anqiu Lubricant Factory 山東省安丘市潤滑劑廠(1980)	Weifang 濰坊市	Shandong 山東省	(0536)4681036 (0536)4681036	50	Collectively-owned 集體	20,500	2476(4)	4,046	o

Top 10 Cities by Production Output 產出排名前 10 位城市	Province 省	Market share 市場份額	Number of firms 企業個數
Suzhou 蘇州市	Jiangsu 江蘇省	13.81%	11
Fuyang 阜陽市	Anhui 安徽省	10.50%	5
Hangzhou 杭州市	Zhejiang 浙江省	7.78%	2
Huaiyin 淮陰市	Jiangsu 江蘇省	7.78%	3
Wuhan 武漢市	Hubei 湖北省	4.93%	2
Baoding 保定市	Hebei 河北省	3.92%	4
Shenyang 瀋陽市	Liaoning 遼寧省	3.34%	1
Weifang 濰坊市	Shandong 山東省	3.25%	4
Shanghai 上海市	Shanghai 上海市	2.96%	3
Jiaxing 嘉興市	Zhejiang 浙江省	2.66%	5

10 Major Wholesalers 10 家主要批發商	City 城市	Province 省	Telephone / Fax 電話 / 傳真
Changzhou General Merchandise Wholesale General Company 常州百貨批發總公司	Changzhou 常州市	Jiangsu 江蘇省	(0519)6680488 (0519)6680488
Suzhou General Merchandise General Co. 蘇州百貨總公司	Suzhou 蘇州市	Jiangsu 江蘇省	(0512)5222288 (0512)5222247
Guangzhou Yue Xiu Enterprise (Holdings) Co. 廣州越秀企業(集團)公司	Guangzhou 廣州市	Guangdong 廣東省	(020)86662828 (020)86672634
Wunan Commercial Group Corp. 湖南省商業集團總公司	Changsha 長沙市	Hunan 湖南省	(0731)4442765
Kunming General Merchandise Purchase Supply Station Kunming General Merchandise Company 昆明百貨採購供應站昆明市百貨公司	Kunming 昆明市	Yunnan 雲南省	(0871)3314883 (0871)3314961
Nanjing General Merchandise General Company 南京市百貨總公司	Nanjing 南京市	Jiangsu 江蘇省	(025)6664681 (025)6643927
Guangzhou Shang Ling Trade Co. Ltd. 廣州商菱貿易有限公司	Guangzhou 廣州市	Guangdong 廣東省	(020)86677190 (020)86673971
Beijing Light Industry Product Import & Export Company 北京市輕工業品進出口公司	Beijing 北京市	Beijing 北京市	(010)64057425 (010)64057427
Xi Shan Shi Commerce Group Company 錫山市商業集團公司	Wuxi 無錫市	Jiangsu 江蘇省	(0510)2442982
Yixing Su Nan Commercial Building 宜興市蘇南商廈	Wuxi 無錫市	Jiangsu 江蘇省	(0510)7904407 (0510)7904754

*Also include sales by firms outside this industry.包括本行業以外廠家的銷售。"o" stands for "others". "o" 代表"其他產品"。

2684: Perfumes and Essences 香料、香精製造業

The industry accounts for 0.059% of the total revenue of China's industrial sector in 1996. The revenue growth rate of the industry is 3.9% from 1995, as compared to the growth rate of China's industrial sector, 9.51%. The rate of return on asset is 2.39%. 69.00% of all firms in the industry made a profit while 26.26% had negative returns. The top province in terms of the industry's revenue is Guangdong, accounting for 21.55% of the total revenue.
本行業在1996年佔全行業總產值0.059%，行業年增長率為3.9%（全國工業年增長率9.51%）。行業的資產回報率2.39%，69.00%的企業盈利，26.26%的企業虧損。銷售收入最高的省份為廣東省，佔本行業的21.55%。

	Total number of firms 企業總數	Total number of employees 職工總數	Total revenue (mil. RMB) 總銷售收入（百萬元）	Total profit (mil. RMB) 總利潤（百萬元）	Return on assets 資產利潤率 (%)	Return on equity 權益利潤率 (%)	Labour productivity ('000 RMB / worker) 勞動生產率（千元/人）	Debts / assets 資產負債率 (%)	Total assets (mil. RMB) 總資產（百萬元）
Industry Overall 行業總體	410	30,001	3,396	95	2.39	6.32	113.20	62.25	3,987

	Number of firms 企業個數	Average number of employees 平均職工人數	Average revenue ('000 RMB) 平均銷售收入（千元）	Average profit ('000 RMB) 平均利潤（千元）	Return on assets 資產利潤率 (%)	Return on equity 權益利潤率 (%)	Labour productivity ('000 RMB / worker) 勞動生產率（千元/人）	Average debts / assets 平均資產負債率(%)	Average Total assets ('000 RMB) 平均總資產（千元）
By ownership 產業所有權									
State-owned 國有	79	159	12,772	-63	-0.36	-1.43	80.21	74.91	17,658
Collectively-owned 集體	263	50	5,103	162	3.30	9.11	101.55	63.81	4,915
Privately-owned 私有	2	56	12,464	106	4.19	11.92	224.58	64.81	2,516
Domestic JVs 聯營	11	59	5,116	-95	-2.75	-9.71	86.32	71.64	3,462
Joint stock 股份制	9	75	23,442	854	3.91	11.99	313.02	67.36	21,813
Foreign-funded 外資	21	98	25,811	1,755	4.53	7.31	262.36	38.03	38,734
Overseas Chinese-funded 港澳台資	25	49	8,451	547	5.55	12.83	171.21	56.78	9,859
By size 規模									
Large 大型	3	700	138,119	5,692	2.22	4.82	197.22	54.04	256,869
Medium 中型	13	500	65,647	2,198	2.49	5.42	131.27	54.03	88,174
Small 小型	384	56	5,544	129	2.38	7.91	99.77	69.86	5,393
By regional distribution 地區分布									
Central-North 華北	36	138	4,326	16	0.22	0.72	31.37	69.84	7,191
Beijing 北京	2	8	380	-5	-1.16	-3.45	47.50	66.28	430
Tianjin 天津	15	136	8,328	85	0.59	1.90	61.21	69.08	14,387
Hebei 河北	8	32	1,623	81	3.91	7.28	51.30	46.30	2,079
Shanxi 山西	9	27	1,779	-162	-6.10	-292.00	65.35	97.87	2,659
Inner Mongolia 內蒙	2	1,205	525	55	6.71	6.83	0.44	1.83	820
Northeast 東北	17	94	4,376	53	0.61	1.47	46.70	58.38	8,639
Liaoning 遼寧	6	131	6,737	492	3.00	7.13	51.29	57.95	16,408
Jilin 吉林	6	60	2,785	18	0.50	0.96	46.29	48.01	3,683
Heilongjiang 黑龍江	5	89	3,452	-432	-8.21	-26.25	38.87	68.72	5,262
Central East 華東	160	93	11,325	318	2.40	6.81	122.29	64.68	13,208
Shanghai 上海	19	174	33,633	1,829	5.84	16.25	193.65	64.08	31,329
Jiangsu 江蘇	43	84	10,207	82	0.74	3.81	121.67	80.51	11,060
Zhejiang 浙江	25	99	11,937	612	2.74	4.65	121.01	41.12	22,359
Anhui 安徽	19	116	9,952	-244	-2.81	-38.57	85.45	92.71	8,694
Fujian 福建	25	64	5,063	1	0.01	0.03	79.40	62.47	8,037
Jiangxi 江西	20	60	4,883	-65	-1.45	-10.58	81.18	86.25	4,471
Shandong 山東	9	48	2,480	348	11.19	28.25	51.43	60.34	3,107
Central-South 中南	153	41	7,591	364	4.77	12.02	183.07	60.35	7,641
Henan 河南	43	40	4,347	112	2.78	9.79	110.01	71.54	4,009
Hubei 湖北	13	47	3,633	152	7.68	31.33	78.07	75.48	1,983
Hunan 湖南	14	35	4,504	204	5.77	22.03	128.67	73.81	3,541
Guangdong 廣東	53	46	13,806	886	6.27	13.90	301.99	54.90	14,136
Guangxi 廣西	27	37	4,356	-62	-1.16	-4.70	116.79	75.40	5,345
Hainan 海南	3	40	4,967	263	2.83	3.62	124.17	21.71	9,290
Southwest 西南	38	57	4,987	-341	-4.39	-8.41	87.12	47.78	7,766
Chongqing 重慶	3	99	3,479	61	1.31	1.71	35.28	23.59	4,689
Sichuan 四川	9	98	3,513	-92	-1.30	-2.86	35.92	54.46	7,061
Guizhou 貴州	12	27	2,666	178	5.67	27.66	100.28	79.50	3,130
Yunnan 雲南	14	49	8,246	-1,030	-8.03	-13.51	169.52	40.51	12,821
Tibet 西藏									
Northwest 西北	6	18	463	32	5.76	11.59	25.74	50.30	550
Shaanxi 陝西	3	15	723	47	10.29	22.58	47.17	54.41	453
Gansu 甘肅	3	21	203	17	2.58	4.90	9.84	47.42	647
Qinghai 青海									
Ningxia 寧夏									
Xinjiang 新疆									

2684: Perfumes and Essences 香料、香精製造業

Year 年份	Number of firms 企業個數	Rate of change 每年變化 (%)	Number of employees 職工人數 (人)	Rate of change 每年變化 (%)	Total revenue (mil. RMB) 總銷售收入 (百萬元)	Rate of change 每年變化 (%)	Total profit (mil. RMB) 總利潤 (百萬元)	Rate of change 每年變化 (%)
1993	343		38,375		2,335		81	
1994	358	4.37%	25,073	-34.66%	2,671	14.37%	55	-31.58%
1995	421	17.60%	31,161	24.28%	3,267	22.34%	108	94.45%
1996	410	-2.61%	30,001	-3.72%	3,396	3.95%	95	-11.69%

3 Major products* 3 種主要產品 *	Output 產量	Sales volume 銷售量	Unit 單位
a) Perfumery 香料	55,310	50,332	ton 噸
b) Flavouring Essence 香精	66,876	65,539	ton 噸
c) Ethyl Acetate 醋酸乙酯	1,014	923	ton 噸

Top 10 firms by revenue (year founded) 收入排名前 10 家企業 (創辦年份)	City 城市	Province 省	Telephone / fax 電話 / 傳真	Number of employees 職工人數	Ownership 產業所有權	Revenue ('000 RMB) 銷售收入 (千元)	Profit ('000 RMB) (rank) 利潤 (千元) (排名)	Total assets ('000 RMB) 總資產 (千元)	Major products 主要產品
International Perfumery (China) Co. Ltd. 國際香料(中國)有限公司(1990)	Guangzhou 廣州市	Guangdong 廣東省	(020)82219838 (020)82219828	88	Foreign-funded 外資	249,659	21446(2)	279,762	b
Shanghai Peacock Essence & Perfumery Co. Ltd. 上海孔雀香精香料有限公司(1912)	Shanghai 上海市	Shanghai 上海市	(021)56902608 (021)56639028	580	State-owned 國有	160,841	12026(3)	122,090	a,b
Guangzhou Baihua Perfumery Co. Ltd. 廣州百花香料股份有限公司(1956)	Guangzhou 廣州市	Guangdong 廣東省	(020)81890431 (020)81890420	523	Joint stock 股份制	145,724	10005(5)	192,237	a,b
Shanghai Haarmann & Reimer Cosfra Essence Ltd. 上海高仕香精有限公司(1982)	Shanghai 上海市	Shanghai 上海市	(021)56931088 (021)56935815	226	Foreign-funded 外資	122,783	25405(1)	87,139	a,b
Hangzhou Perfumery Factory 杭州香料廠(1958)	Hangzhou 杭州市	Zhejiang 浙江省	(0571)6064075 (0571)6064232	778	State-owned 國有	102,685	7873(6)	109,775	a,b
Shanghai Xin Hua Perfumery Factory 上海新華香料廠(1937)	Shanghai 上海市	Shanghai 上海市	(021)58816690 (021)58815281	585	State-owned 國有	101,800	-3776(229)	68,461	a
Nantong Peppermint Factory 南通薄荷廠(1960)	Nantong 南通市	Jiangsu 江蘇省	(0513)5516184 (0513)5537011	580	State-owned 國有	95,929	98(118)	135,141	a,b
International Essence & Perfumery (Hangzhou) Co. Ltd. 國際香料香精杭州有限公司(1982)	Hangzhou 杭州市	Zhejiang 浙江省	(0571)4721406 (0571)4726848	353	Foreign-funded 外資	85,125	6069(7)	292,918	o
Shanghai Pu Fa Perfumery Co. Ltd. 上海浦發香料有限公司(1994)	Shanghai 上海市	Shanghai 上海市	(021)58661118 (021)58661718	61	Overseas Chinese-funded 港澳台資	69,936	3459(10)	87,840	a
Suzhou Fen Mei Yi Essence Co. Ltd. 蘇州芬美意香精有限公司(1989)	Suzhou 蘇州市	Jiangsu 江蘇省	(0512)5334282 (0512)5334282	36	Foreign-funded 外資	62,852	567(54)	64,860	b

Top 10 Cities by Production Output 產出排名前 10 位城市	Province 省	Market share 市場份額	Number of firms 企業個數
Shanghai 上海市	Shanghai 上海市	26.00%	37
Guangzhou 廣州市	Guangdong 廣東省	13.33%	10
Hangzhou 杭州市	Zhejiang 浙江省	6.51%	6
Suzhou 蘇州市	Jiangsu 江蘇省	6.19%	37
Tianjin 天津市	Tianjin 天津市	5.78%	18
Kaifeng 開封市	Henan 河南省	2.50%	17
Maoming 茂名市	Guangdong 廣東省	2.46%	11
Jilin 吉林市	Jilin 吉林省	2.25%	2
Kunming 昆明市	Yunnan 雲南省	2.02%	11
Nantong 南通市	Jiangsu 江蘇省	1.87%	5

10 Major Wholesalers 10 家主要批發商	City 城市	Province 省	Telephone / Fax 電話 / 傳真
Changzhou General Merchandise Wholesale General Company 常州百貨批發總公司	Changzhou 常州市	Jiangsu 江蘇省	(0519)6680488 (0519)6680488
Suzhou General Merchandise General Co. 蘇州百貨總公司	Suzhou 蘇州市	Jiangsu 江蘇省	(0512)5222288 (0512)5222247
Guangzhou Yue Xiu Enterprise (Holdings) Co. 廣州越秀企業(集團)公司	Guangzhou 廣州市	Guangdong 廣東省	(020)86662828 (020)86672634
Wunan Commercial Group Corp. 湖南省商業集團總公司	Changsha 長沙市	Hunan 湖南省	(0731)4442765
Kunming General Merchandise Purchase Supply Station Kunming General Merchandise Company 昆明百貨採購供應站昆明市百貨公司	Kunming 昆明市	Yunnan 雲南省	(0871)3314883 (0871)3314961
Nanjing General Merchandise General Company 南京市百貨總公司	Nanjing 南京市	Jiangsu 江蘇省	(025)6664681 (025)6643927
Guangzhou Shang Ling Trade Co. Ltd. 廣州商菱貿易有限公司	Guangzhou 廣州市	Guangdong 廣東省	(020)86677190 (020)86673971
Beijing Light Industry Product Import & Export Company 北京市輕工業品進出口公司	Beijing 北京市	Beijing 北京市	(010)64057425 (010)64057427
Xi Shan Shi Commerce Group Company 錫山市商業集團公司	Wuxi 無錫市	Jiangsu 江蘇省	(0510)2442982
Yixing Su Nan Commercial Building 宜興市蘇南商廈	Wuxi 無錫市	Jiangsu 江蘇省	(0510)7904407 (0510)7904754

*Also include sales by firms outside this industry.包括本行業以外廠家的銷售。"o" stands for "others". "o"代表"其他產品"。

2685: Cosmetics 化妝品製造業

The industry accounts for 0.162% of the total revenue of China's industrial sector in 1996. The revenue growth rate of the industry is 2.1% from 1995, as compared to the growth rate of China's industrial sector, 9.51%. The rate of return on asset is 4.00%. 64.84% of all firms in the industry made a profit while 26.77% had negative returns. The top province in terms of the industry's revenue is Shanghai, accounting for 34.97% of the total revenue.
本行業在1996年佔全行業總產值0.162%，行業年增長率為2.1%（全國工業年增長率9.51%）。行業的資產回報率4.00%，64.84%的企業盈利，26.77%的企業虧損。銷售收入最高的省份為上海市，佔本行業的34.97%。

	Total number of firms 企業總數	Total number of employees 職工總數	Total revenue (mil. RMB) 總銷售收入（百萬元）	Total profit (mil. RMB) 總利潤（百萬元）	Return on assets 資產利潤率 (%)	Return on equity 權益利潤率 (%)	Labour productivity ('000 RMB / worker) 勞動生產率（千元/人）	Debts / assets 資產負債率 (%)	Total assets (mil. RMB) 總資產（百萬元）
Industry Overall 行業總體	732	58,063	9,379	509	4.00	10.89	161.53	63.29	12,742

	Number of firms 企業個數	Average number of employees 平均職工人數	Average revenue ('000 RMB) 平均銷售收入（千元）	Average profit ('000 RMB) 平均利潤（千元）	Return on assets 資產利潤率 (%)	Return on equity 權益利潤率 (%)	Labour productivity ('000 RMB / worker) 勞動生產率（千元/人）	Average debts / assets 平均資產負債率(%)	Average Total assets ('000 RMB) 平均總資產（千元）
By ownership 產業所有權									
State-owned 國有	75	158	12,480	160	0.58	1.86	78.83	68.98	27,680
Collectively-owned 集體	414	66	9,155	767	7.58	19.82	138.09	61.77	10,122
Privately-owned 私有	5	44	12,730	424	7.04	16.57	289.31	57.51	6,019
Domestic JVs 聯營	8	79	20,733	282	0.84	2.41	262.85	65.21	33,665
Joint stock 股份制	7	73	10,975	-131	-0.62	-1.63	151.23	61.67	20,977
Foreign-funded 外資	102	90	29,164	-712	-1.97	-5.04	324.26	60.93	36,170
Overseas Chinese-funded 港澳台資	122	78	11,244	2,037	10.62	30.03	143.90	64.63	19,182
By size 規模									
Large 大型	12	697	270,300	3,288	0.97	2.49	387.90	61.02	338,260
Medium 中型	18	490	84,162	7,174	5.35	13.11	171.60	59.20	134,133
Small 小型	662	62	6,980	514	5.43	16.13	113.11	66.33	9,469
By regional distribution 地區分布									
Central-North 華北	117	92	7,775	11	0.08	0.21	84.17	61.30	13,523
Beijing 北京	59	94	7,528	737	4.63	11.40	80.21	59.35	15,897
Tianjin 天津	34	105	9,394	-1,346	-9.86	-25.82	89.74	61.82	13,648
Hebei 河北	16	77	7,994	218	3.45	10.69	104.49	67.75	6,308
Shanxi 山西	4	90	4,163	418	2.77	6.91	46.38	59.91	15,068
Inner Mongolia 內蒙	4	32	395	-390	-8.18	54.93	12.34	114.88	4,770
Northeast 東北	54	82	2,732	27	0.43	2.91	33.16	85.26	6,250
Liaoning 遼寧	25	74	5,136	52	0.48	3.69	69.56	87.08	10,838
Jilin 吉林	15	40	959	16	0.43	1.99	23.97	78.28	3,713
Heilongjiang 黑龍江	14	143	339	-6	-0.74	-3.01	2.37	75.51	776
Central East 華東	312	101	19,249	896	3.60	8.93	189.75	59.72	24,904
Shanghai 上海	75	155	43,725	2,544	3.97	9.44	281.69	57.99	64,150
Jiangsu 江蘇	78	128	21,882	889	3.80	10.52	170.55	63.86	23,373
Zhejiang 浙江	53	70	8,962	1,078	9.12	17.90	128.13	49.07	11,822
Anhui 安徽	27	83	10,053	-1,718	-25.05	184.09	121.39	113.61	6,859
Fujian 福建	53	55	4,023	65	1.30	2.53	72.53	48.72	5,023
Jiangxi 江西	10	35	366	68	3.37	7.84	10.46	57.06	2,019
Shandong 山東	16	48	3,502	282	11.99	41.07	73.05	70.81	2,351
Central-South 中南	186	40	9,191	977	7.37	25.92	228.25	71.57	13,252
Henan 河南	28	25	1,200	-3	-0.15	-0.54	47.81	72.77	1,713
Hubei 湖北	16	77	4,730	89	2.08	9.65	61.83	78.46	4,299
Hunan 湖南	25	22	807	10	1.10	2.56	36.96	56.94	943
Guangdong 廣東	100	46	15,705	1,809	7.83	27.46	344.10	71.48	23,098
Guangxi 廣西	15	28	563	-59	-7.07	-23.16	19.98	69.48	830
Hainan 海南	2	15	605	15	1.29	10.00	40.33	87.07	1,160
Southwest 西南	43	70	13,208	1,200	9.78	29.97	189.76	67.36	12,263
Chongqing 重慶	16	86	26,543	3,243	15.92	40.34	309.19	60.54	20,371
Sichuan 四川	16	76	8,794	63	0.54	2.66	115.10	79.88	11,812
Guizhou 貴州	5	22	442	10	1.15	1.84	19.73	37.70	870
Yunnan 雲南	6	47	1,338	3	0.17	0.38	28.58	55.51	1,952
Tibet 西藏									
Northwest 西北	20	34	1,924	-318	-10.60	-53.00	57.09	80.02	3,000
Shaanxi 陝西	10	42	3,035	45	1.47	3.47	72.26	57.71	3,067
Gansu 甘肅	4	18	1,148	68	15.43	27.84	62.88	45.14	438
Qinghai 青海	1	37	480	-120	-10.53	-80.00	12.97	86.84	1,140
Ningxia 寧夏									
Xinjiang 新疆	5	29	612	-1,392	-26.32	333.01	21.25	107.90	5,288

2685: Cosmetics 化妝品製造業

Year 年份	Number of firms 企業個數	Rate of change 每年變化 (%)	Number of employees 職工人數 (人)	Rate of change 每年變化 (%)	Total revenue (mil. RMB) 總銷售收入 (百萬元)	Rate of change 每年變化 (%)	Total profit (mil. RMB) 總利潤 (百萬元)	Rate of change 每年變化 (%)
1993	760		109,889		6,118		381	
1994	775	1.97%	61,023	-44.47%	6,843	11.85%	217	-43.12%
1995	797	2.84%	66,939	9.69%	9,190	34.29%	341	57.27%
1996	732	-8.16%	58,063	-13.26%	9,379	2.06%	509	49.30%

3 Major products* 3種主要產品*	Output 產量	Sales volume 銷售量	Unit 單位
a) Cosmetics 化妝品	9,845,421	8,762,425	1,000 yuan 千元
b) Synthetic Detergent 合成洗滌劑	13,058	12,666	ton 噸

Top 10 firms by revenue (year founded) 收入排名前10家企業 (創辦年份)	City 城市	Province 省	Telephone / fax 電話 / 傳真	Number of employees 職工人數	Ownership 產業所有權	Revenue ('000 RMB) 銷售收入 (千元)	Profit ('000 RMB) (rank) 利潤 (千元) (排名)	Total assets ('000 RMB) 總資產 (千元)	Major products 主要產品
Shanghai Jahwa Co. Ltd. 上海家化有限公司(1996)	Shanghai 上海市	Shanghai 上海市	(021)65456400 (021)65458990	986	Foreign-funded 外資	688,589	48944(4)	864,054	a,b
Shanghai Kao Corp. 上海花王有限公司(1994)	Shanghai 上海市	Shanghai 上海市	(021)64090071 (021)64090072	400	Foreign-funded 外資	628,067	39544(7)	721,226	a
Shanghai Sc Johnson Co. Ltd. 上海莊臣有限公司(1987)	Shanghai 上海市	Shanghai 上海市	(021)58994833 (021)58990288	888	Foreign-funded 外資	614,472	22942(10)	516,950	a,b
Guangzhou Avon Co. Ltd. 廣州雅芳有限公司(1991)	Guangzhou 廣州市	Guangdong 廣東省	(020)87610088 (020)87663531	444	Foreign-funded 外資	587,441	24472(8)	519,878	a
Chongqing Olive Cosmetics Co. Ltd. 重慶奧妮化妝品有限公司	Chongqing 重慶市	Chongqing 重慶市	(023)67855640 (023)67862138	478	Overseas Chinese-funded 港澳台資	454,954	57619(3)	264,135	a
Shanghai Pond's Co. Ltd. 上海旁氏有限公司(1989)	Shanghai 上海市	Shanghai 上海市	(021)62414480 (021)62748183	320	Foreign-funded 外資	363,807	40297(6)	264,515	a
Shanghai Phoenix Daily Chemical Co. Ltd. 上海鳳凰日用化學有限公司(1930)	Shanghai 上海市	Shanghai 上海市	(021)62410500 (021)62748425	954	State-owned 國有	236,149	14027(17)	231,609	a,b
Shanghai Hankel - Kemeng Cosmetics Co. Ltd. 上海漢高－可蒙化妝品有限公司(1996)	Shanghai 上海市	Shanghai 上海市	(021)65432690	484	Foreign-funded 外資	194,297	9006(20)	301,047	o
Anhui Tai Dao Group Co. Ltd. 安徽太島集團有限責任公司(1990)	Fuyang 阜陽市	Anhui 安徽省	(0558)8623344 (0558)8621558	193	Collectively-owned 集體	185,500	-9854(307)	37,270	a
Beijing Li Yuan Co. 北京麗源公司(1961)	Beijing 北京市	Beijing 北京市	(010)67145298 (010)67115534	2,141	State-owned 國有	181,025	8503(21)	502,191	a,b

Top 10 Cities by Production Output 產出排名前10位城市	Province 省	Market share 市場份額	Number of firms 企業個數
Shanghai 上海市	Shanghai 上海市	40.11%	110
Guangzhou 廣州市	Guangdong 廣東省	7.67%	76
Suzhou 蘇州市	Jiangsu 江蘇省	7.56%	37
Taizhou 泰州市	Jiangsu 江蘇省	6.65%	16
Chongqing 重慶市	Chongqing 重慶市	6.16%	16
Beijing 北京市	Beijing 北京市	4.68%	48
Tianjin 天津市	Tianjin 天津市	3.86%	42
Jiangmen 江門市	Guangdong 廣東省	1.76%	9
Zhuhai 珠海市	Guangdong 廣東省	1.73%	16
Hangzhou 杭州市	Zhejiang 浙江省	1.66%	13

10 Major Wholesalers 10家主要批發商	City 城市	Province 省	Telephone / Fax 電話 / 傳真
Changzhou General Merchandise Wholesale General Company 常州百貨批發總公司	Changzhou 常州市	Jiangsu 江蘇省	(0519)6680488 (0519)6680488
Suzhou General Merchandise General Co. 蘇州百貨總公司	Suzhou 蘇州市	Jiangsu 江蘇省	(0512)5222288 (0512)5222247
Guangzhou Yue Xiu Enterprise (Holdings) Co. 廣州越秀企業(集團)公司	Guangzhou 廣州市	Guangdong 廣東省	(020)86662828 (020)86672634
Wunan Commercial Group Corp. 湖南省商業集團總公司	Changsha 長沙市	Hunan 湖南省	(0731)4442765
Kunming General Merchandise Purchase Supply Station Kunming General Merchandise Company 昆明百貨採購供應站昆明市百貨公司	Kunming 昆明市	Yunnan 雲南省	(0871)3314883 (0871)3314961
Nanjing General Merchandise General Company 南京市百貨總公司	Nanjing 南京市	Jiangsu 江蘇省	(025)6664681 (025)6643927
Guangzhou Shang Ling Trade Co. Ltd. 廣州商菱貿易有限公司	Guangzhou 廣州市	Guangdong 廣東省	(020)86677190 (020)86673971
Beijing Light Industry Product Import & Export Company 北京市輕工業品進出口公司	Beijing 北京市	Beijing 北京市	(010)64057425 (010)64057427
Xi Shan Shi Commerce Group Company 錫山市商業集團公司	Wuxi 無錫市	Jiangsu 江蘇省	(0510)2442982
Yixing Su Nan Commercial Building 宜興市蘇南商廈	Wuxi 無錫市	Jiangsu 江蘇省	(0510)7904407 (0510)7904754

*Also include sales by firms outside this industry.包括本行業以外廠家的銷售。"o" stands for "others". "o" 代表"其他產品"。

2686: Toothpaste 牙膏製造業

The industry accounts for 0.064% of the total revenue of China's industrial sector in 1996. The revenue growth rate of the industry is 32.8% from 1995, as compared to the growth rate of China's industrial sector, 9.51%. The rate of return on asset is 2.14%. 68.75% of all firms in the industry made a profit while 31.25% had negative returns. The top province in terms of the industry's revenue is Shanghai, accounting for 32.22% of the total revenue.

本行業在1996年佔全行業總產值0.064%，行業年增長率為32.8%（全國工業年增長率9.51%）。行業的資產回報率2.14%，68.75%的企業盈利，31.25%的企業虧損。銷售收入最高的省份為上海市，佔本行業的32.22%。

	Total number of firms 企業總數	Total number of employees 職工總數	Total revenue (mil. RMB) 總銷售收入（百萬元）	Total profit (mil. RMB) 總利潤（百萬元）	Return on assets 資產利潤率 (%)	Return on equity 權益利潤率 (%)	Labour productivity ('000 RMB / worker) 勞動生產率（千元/人）	Debts / assets 資產負債率 (%)	Total assets (mil. RMB) 總資產（百萬元）
Industry Overall 行業總體	54	18,037	3,693	88	2.14	6.39	204.75	66.55	4,135

	Number of firms 企業個數	Average number of employees 平均職工人數	Average revenue ('000 RMB) 平均銷售收入（千元）	Average profit ('000 RMB) 平均利潤（千元）	Return on assets 資產利潤率 (%)	Return on equity 權益利潤率 (%)	Labour productivity ('000 RMB / worker) 勞動生產率（千元/人）	Average debts / assets 平均資產負債率(%)	Average Total assets ('000 RMB) 平均總資產（千元）
By ownership 產業所有權									
State-owned 國有	14	577	65,000	3,786	4.71	11.70	112.62	59.77	80,429
Collectively-owned 集體	27	124	14,811	127	1.07	4.12	119.34	74.08	11,864
Privately-owned 私有									
Domestic JVs 聯營	2	159	23,252	266	1.59	3.17	146.24	49.76	16,716
Joint stock 股份制	3	1,021	315,042	15,279	3.77	9.49	308.66	60.29	405,661
Foreign-funded 外資	4	674	347,040	-3,279	-0.98	-4.14	515.28	76.41	335,775
Overseas Chinese-funded 港澳台資	3	266	1,445	-561	-1.75	-5.55	5.43	68.40	31,960
By size 規模									
Large 大型	8	990	354,946	11,781	3.31	8.65	358.49	61.71	355,538
Medium 中型	8	644	57,606	45	0.06	0.31	89.48	80.41	73,874
Small 小型	38	131	10,358	-174	-0.94	-3.70	79.36	74.54	18,431
By regional distribution 地區分布									
Central-North 華北	3	675	72,417	-223	-0.32	-1.23	107.34	73.91	69,653
Beijing 北京									
Tianjin 天津	3	675	72,417	-223	-0.32	-1.23	107.34	73.91	69,653
Hebei 河北									
Shanxi 山西									
Inner Mongolia 內蒙									
Northeast 東北	8	258	7,539	-1,010	-4.34	-21.40	29.21	79.75	23,296
Liaoning 遼寧	2	539	16,185	-2,470	-5.74	-47.91	30.03	88.01	42,995
Jilin 吉林	3	174	5,950	-813	-4.25	-25.42	34.13	83.29	19,127
Heilongjiang 黑龍江	3	155	3,363	-233	-1.63	-3.92	21.75	58.51	14,333
Central East 華東	24	327	69,182	1,683	2.53	7.70	211.62	67.09	66,411
Shanghai 上海	7	376	170,004	6,319	4.33	11.85	452.48	63.47	146,043
Jiangsu 江蘇	8	283	32,945	285	0.89	4.20	116.57	78.92	32,173
Zhejiang 浙江	4	244	23,415	488	1.86	6.21	95.96	69.98	26,143
Anhui 安徽									
Fujian 福建	2	150	9,270	-4,510	-12.73	-58.19	62.01	78.13	35,430
Jiangxi 江西	2	478	33,320	465	0.91	2.11	69.78	57.06	51,360
Shandong 山東	1	725	27,930	30	0.08	0.51	38.52	83.60	36,040
Central-South 中南	13	327	114,869	1,842	1.26	3.84	350.87	67.15	146,172
Henan 河南	1	395	50,660	1,130	2.07	10.25	128.25	79.80	54,550
Hubei 湖北	1	15	1,150				76.67	71.96	1,070
Hunan 湖南									
Guangdong 廣東	8	259	124,195	-10,689	-6.42	-25.00	479.98	74.31	166,408
Guangxi 廣西	2	820	220,965	55,130	22.57	41.05	269.47	45.01	244,210
Hainan 海南	1	136	6,000	-1,930	-7.74	-82.13	44.12	90.58	24,940
Southwest 西南	5	317	50,234	6,570	14.94	23.98	158.67	37.72	43,982
Chongqing 重慶	2	573	114,888	17,453	22.13	29.77	200.65	25.68	78,875
Sichuan 四川	2	91	378	-1,533	-6.71	-40.97	4.13	83.63	22,861
Guizhou 貴州									
Yunnan 雲南	1	254	20,640	1,010	6.14	8.24	81.26	25.55	16,440
Tibet 西藏									
Northwest 西北	1	263	10,780	20	0.08	0.39	40.99	79.55	25,380
Shaanxi 陝西	1	263	10,780	20	0.08	0.39	40.99	79.55	25,380
Gansu 甘肅									
Qinghai 青海									
Ningxia 寧夏									
Xinjiang 新疆									

2686: Toothpaste 牙膏製造業

Year 年份	Number of firms 企業個數	Rate of change 每年變化 (%)	Number of employees 職工人數（人）	Rate of change 每年變化 (%)	Total revenue (mil. RMB) 總銷售收入（百萬元）	Rate of change 每年變化 (%)	Total profit (mil. RMB) 總利潤（百萬元）	Rate of change 每年變化 (%)
1993	44		22,456		1,793		88	
1994	48	9.09%	16,316	-27.34%	2,234	24.59%	160	81.30%
1995	50	4.17%	16,690	2.29%	2,781	24.50%	122	-23.45%
1996	54	8.00%	18,037	8.07%	3,693	32.79%	88	-28.06%

3 Major products* 3 種主要產品 *	Output 產量	Sales volume 銷售量	Unit 單位
a) Toothpaste 牙膏	260,211	265,415	10,000 piece 萬支
b) Flavouring Essences 香精	1,491	1,462	ton 噸
c) Synthetic Detergent 合成洗滌劑	22,811	22,127	ton 噸

Top 10 firms by revenue (year founded) 收入排名前 10 家企業 (創辦年份)	City 城市	Province 省	Telephone / fax 電話 / 傳真	Number of employees 職工人數	Ownership 產業所有權	Revenue ('000 RMB) 銷售收入（千元）	Profit ('000 RMB) (rank) 利潤（千元）（排名）	Total assets ('000 RMB) 總資產（千元）	Major products 主要產品
Unilever (Shanghai) Toothpaste Co. Ltd. 上海聯合利華牙膏有限公司(1994)	Shanghai 上海市	Shanghai 上海市	(021)62773020 (021)62773689	1,174	Foreign-funded 外資	825,567	14455(5)	539,156	a,b
Guangzhou Colgate Co. Ltd. 廣州高露潔有限公司(1991)	Guangzhou 廣州市	Guangdong 廣東省	(020)87551991 (020)87550727	684	Foreign-funded 外資	490,878	-19998(32)	456,958	a
Liuzhou Liang Mian Zhen Co. Ltd. 柳州兩面針股份有限公司(1980)	Liuzhou 柳州市	Guangxi 廣西	(0772)2513750 (0772)2513419	1,615	Joint stock 股份制	441,627	110279(1)	487,189	a
Guangzhou Mansson Co. Ltd. 廣州美晨股份有限公司(1993)	Guangzhou 廣州市	Guangdong 廣東省	(020)86646596 (020)86626484	1,166	Joint stock 股份制	429,633	61861(2)	487,999	a,c
Chongqing Toothpaste Factory 重慶牙膏廠(1964)	Chongqing 重慶市	Chongqing 重慶市	(023)37852258 (023)67852258	933	State-owned 國有	223,551	33214(3)	163,314	a
Shanghai Toothpaste Factory 上海牙膏廠(1912)	Shanghai 上海市	Shanghai 上海市	(021)62775188 (021)62775175	540	State-owned 國有	191,373	16037(4)	371,262	a,b,c
Tianjin Toothpaste Factory 天津市牙膏廠(1956)	Tianjin 天津市	Tianjin 天津市	(022)24328842 (022)24328846	1,390	State-owned 國有	178,561	2000(11)	118,143	a,c
Suzhou Yue Zhong Gui Daily Chemical General Factory 蘇州市月中桂日用化工總廠(1956)	Suzhou 蘇州市	Jiangsu 江蘇省	(0512)5624017 (0512)5232195	449	Collectively-owned 集體	139,839	2040(10)	85,293	a,c
Hangzhou Toothpaste Factory 杭州牙膏廠(1973)	Hangzhou 杭州市	Zhejiang 浙江省	(0571)6064368 (0571)6064175	647	State-owned 國有	89,500	2502(8)	72,001	a
Nanchang Daily Chemical General Factory 南昌日用化工總廠(1970)	Nanchang 南昌市	Jiangxi 江西省	(0791)8211345 (0791)8213254	478	State-owned 國有	66,643	925(16)	102,720	a,b

Top 10 Cities by Production Output 產出排名前 10 位城市	Province 省	Market share 市場份額	Number of firms 企業個數
Shanghai 上海市	Shanghai 上海市	25.97%	9
Guangzhou 廣州市	Guangdong 廣東省	24.83%	8
Liuzhou 柳州市	Guangxi 廣西	21.62%	5
Tianjin 天津市	Tianjin 天津市	5.52%	3
Chongqing 重慶市	Chongqing 重慶市	5.15%	1
Hefei 合肥市	Anhui 安徽省	3.61%	1
Suzhou 蘇州市	Jiangsu 江蘇省	3.46%	6
Hangzhou 杭州市	Zhejiang 浙江省	2.33%	4
Zhengzhou 鄭州市	Henan 河南省	1.29%	1
Dandong 丹東市	Liaoning 遼寧省	0.84%	2

10 Major Wholesalers 10 家主要批發商	City 城市	Province 省	Telephone / Fax 電話 / 傳真
Changzhou General Merchandise Wholesale General Company 常州百貨批發總公司	Changzhou 常州市	Jiangsu 江蘇省	(0519)6680488 (0519)6680488
Suzhou General Merchandise General Co. 蘇州百貨總公司	Suzhou 蘇州市	Jiangsu 江蘇省	(0512)5222288 (0512)5222247
Guangzhou Yue Xiu Enterprise (Holdings) Co. 廣州越秀企業(集團)公司	Guangzhou 廣州市	Guangdong 廣東省	(020)86662828 (020)86672634
Wunan Commercial Group Corp. 湖南省商業集團總公司	Changsha 長沙市	Hunan 湖南省	(0731)4442765
Kunming General Merchandise Purchase Supply Station Kunming General Merchandise Company 昆明百貨採購供應站昆明市百貨公司	Kunming 昆明市	Yunnan 雲南省	(0871)3314883 (0871)3314961
Nanjing General Merchandise General Company 南京市百貨總公司	Nanjing 南京市	Jiangsu 江蘇省	(025)6664681 (025)6643927
Guangzhou Shang Ling Trade Co. Ltd. 廣州商菱貿易有限公司	Guangzhou 廣州市	Guangdong 廣東省	(020)86677190 (020)86673971
Beijing Light Industry Product Import & Export Company 北京市輕工業品進出口公司	Beijing 北京市	Beijing 北京市	(010)64057425 (010)64057427
Xi Shan Shi Commerce Group Company 錫山市商業集團公司	Wuxi 無錫市	Jiangsu 江蘇省	(0510)2442982
Yixing Su Nan Commercial Building 宜興市蘇南商廈	Wuxi 無錫市	Jiangsu 江蘇省	(0510)7904407 (0510)7904754

*Also include sales by firms outside this industry.包括本行業以外廠家的銷售。"o" stands for "others". "o" 代表"其他產品"。

2687: Matches 火柴製造業

The industry accounts for 0.018% of the total revenue of China's industrial sector in 1996. The revenue growth rate of the industry is -11.3% from 1995, as compared to the growth rate of China's industrial sector, 9.51%. The rate of return on asset is -5.67%. 46.09% of all firms in the industry made a profit while 45.75% had negative returns. The top province in terms of the industry's revenue is Hebei, accounting for 14.64% of the total revenue.
本行業在1996年佔全行業總產值0.018%，行業年增長率為-11.3%（全國工業年增長率9.51%）。行業的資產回報率-5.67%，46.09%的企業盈利，45.75%的企業虧損。銷售收入最高的省份為河北省，佔本行業的14.64%。

	Total number of firms 企業總數	Total number of employees 職工總數	Total revenue (mil. RMB) 總銷售收入（百萬元）	Total profit (mil. RMB) 總利潤（百萬元）	Return on assets 資產利潤率 (%)	Return on equity 權益利潤率 (%)	Labour productivity ('000 RMB / worker) 勞動生產率（千元/人）	Debts / assets 資產負債率 (%)	Total assets (mil. RMB) 總資產（百萬元）
Industry Overall 行業總體	180	63,674	1,071	-110	-5.67	-16.66	16.82	65.97	1,945

	Number of firms 企業個數	Average number of employees 平均職工人數	Average revenue ('000 RMB) 平均銷售收入（千元）	Average profit ('000 RMB) 平均利潤（千元）	Return on assets 資產利潤率 (%)	Return on equity 權益利潤率 (%)	Labour productivity ('000 RMB / worker) 勞動生產率（千元/人）	Average debts / assets 平均資產負債率(%)	Average Total assets ('000 RMB) 平均總資產（千元）
By ownership 產業所有權									
State-owned 國有	108	514	7,685	-1,083	-6.93	-22.16	14.96	68.72	15,630
Collectively-owned 集體	68	117	3,384	28	0.84	1.73	29.01	51.53	3,396
Privately-owned 私有									
Domestic JVs 聯營	1	41	249				6.08	39.35	2,237
Joint stock 股份制	3	104	3,550	1,688	20.57	23.93	34.03	14.02	8,204
Foreign-funded 外資									
Overseas Chinese-funded 港澳台資									
By size 規模									
Large 大型	3	1,636	53,399	1,902	2.31	3.67	32.63	36.93	82,211
Medium 中型	17	1,053	17,787	-2,244	-7.35	-37.31	16.89	80.29	30,506
Small 小型	160	257	3,803	-485	-6.57	-19.18	14.80	65.74	7,377
By regional distribution 地區分布									
Central-North 華北	13	523	14,683	567	2.33	4.09	28.06	43.17	24,368
Beijing 北京									
Tianjin 天津	2	305	295	-5	-0.02	-0.03	0.97	27.15	23,185
Hebei 河北	6	689	26,130	1,463	4.31	7.01	37.95	38.55	33,950
Shanxi 山西	2	702	13,375	-500	-3.37	-5.31	19.05	36.50	14,835
Inner Mongolia 內蒙	3	219	2,253	-133	-1.08	-17.94	10.29	93.98	12,347
Northeast 東北	22	425	5,532	-489	-4.52	-25.53	13.01	82.32	10,820
Liaoning 遼寧	6	503	8,297	-370	-2.36	-13.06	16.50	81.91	15,650
Jilin 吉林	6	520	4,647	-660	-4.42	-22.98	8.94	80.79	14,948
Heilongjiang 黑龍江	10	322	4,405	-457	-8.39	-57.99	13.67	85.54	5,444
Central East 華東	51	407	6,010	-882	-7.00	-27.42	14.78	74.45	12,591
Shanghai 上海	1	353	2,480	-3,170	-29.19	100.32	7.03	129.01	10,860
Jiangsu 江蘇	6	412	5,323	-1,518	-11.96	-114.59	12.93	89.58	12,700
Zhejiang 浙江	4	340	8,870	-150	-1.23	-2.41	26.09	49.16	12,220
Anhui 安徽	11	477	9,679	-2,448	-15.85	-112.58	20.30	85.92	15,444
Fujian 福建	5	476	3,206	-184	-1.75	-4.36	6.74	59.76	10,486
Jiangxi 江西	13	289	3,044	-148	-2.51	-6.80	10.52	63.10	5,885
Shandong 山東	11	470	6,776	-211	-1.12	-3.79	14.41	70.51	18,853
Central-South 中南	42	335	6,634	-610	-6.47	-18.04	19.81	64.16	9,442
Henan 河南	9	587	13,902	37	0.26	0.50	23.69	49.00	14,368
Hubei 湖北	7	233	6,250	71	0.82	2.10	26.82	60.97	8,716
Hunan 湖南	11	286	3,214	-1,476	-19.22	-127.77	11.25	84.96	7,683
Guangdong 廣東	7	185	3,317	-566	-9.77	-70.84	17.96	86.21	5,793
Guangxi 廣西	7	374	7,203	-856	-7.75	-17.76	19.24	56.36	11,037
Hainan 海南	1	100	780	-280	-7.16	-77.78	7.80	90.79	3,910
Southwest 西南	39	218	2,945	-449	-8.38	-30.04	13.50	72.10	5,363
Chongqing 重慶	9	228	2,767	-522	-12.06	-94.73	12.12	87.27	4,332
Sichuan 四川	20	202	2,648	-446	-9.84	-40.36	13.11	75.62	4,530
Guizhou 貴州	4	254	2,933	-363	-4.48	-14.84	11.56	69.80	8,088
Yunnan 雲南	5	260	4,966	-480	-5.81	-12.15	19.09	52.17	8,262
Tibet 西藏	1	104	430	-80	-1.37	-4.91	4.13	72.01	5,860
Northwest 西北	13	323	4,505	-1,445	-13.22	-24.99	13.95	47.10	10,935
Shaanxi 陝西	3	285	3,267	-607	-10.89	-50.70	11.45	78.53	5,573
Gansu 甘肅	7	294	4,439	-2,200	-21.71	-42.84	15.12	49.32	10,136
Qinghai 青海	1	314	3,360	-1,590	-17.81	-88.83	10.70	79.96	8,930
Ningxia 寧夏	1	302							
Xinjiang 新疆	1	670	14,330	20	0.04	0.06	21.39	25.68	45,560

2687: Matches 火柴製造業

Year 年份	Number of firms 企業個數	Rate of change 每年變化 (%)	Number of employees 職工人數 (人)	Rate of change 每年變化 (%)	Total revenue (mil. RMB) 總銷售收入 (百萬元)	Rate of change 每年變化 (%)	Total profit (mil. RMB) 總利潤 (百萬元)	Rate of change 每年變化 (%)
1993	203		76,549		1,264		-76	
1994	195	-3.94%	65,199	-14.83%	1,046	-17.26%	-75	0.86%
1995	196	0.51%	76,971	18.06%	1,207	15.34%	-81	-7.59%
1996	180	-8.16%	63,674	-17.28%	1,071	-11.27%	-110	-35.49%

3 Major products* 3 種主要產品 *	Output 產量	Sales volume 銷售量	Unit 單位
a) Match 火柴	23,861,722	21,952,784	piece 件
b) Chipboard 刨花板	31,560	29,666	cubic metre 立方米
c) Manmade Board 人造板	58,357	53,105	cubic metre 立方米

Top 10 firms by revenue (year founded) 收入排名前 10 家企業 (創辦年份)	City 城市	Province 省	Telephone / fax 電話 / 傳真	Number of employees 職工人數	Ownership 產業所有權	Revenue ('000 RMB) 銷售收入 (千元)	Profit ('000 RMB) (rank) 利潤 (千元) (排名)	Total assets ('000 RMB) 總資產 (千元)	Major products 主要產品
Botou Match Factory 泊頭火柴廠(1912)	Cangzhou 滄州市	Hebei 河北省	(0317)8222467	1,957	State-owned 國有	66,111	2254(2)	63,898	a,b,c
Shenzhou Match Factory 深州市火柴廠(1991)	Hengshui 衡水市	Hebei 河北省	(0318)368376	390	Collectively-owned 集體	61,960	5097(1)	13,120	o
Shandong Jining Match Factory 山東省濟寧市火柴廠(1917)	Jining 濟寧市	Shandong 山東省	(0537)2219901 (0537)2216585	2,184	State-owned 國有	49,280	-1481(78)	102,944	a,c
Anhui Bengbu Match Factory 安徽省蚌埠市火柴廠(1954)	Bengbu 蚌埠市	Anhui 安徽省	(0552)4081596 (0552)4081596	1,297	State-owned 國有	36,592	909(3)	35,689	a,b,c
Benxi Match Factory 本溪火柴廠(1970)	Benxi 本溪市	Liaoning 遼寧省	(0414)6823289	976	State-owned 國有	28,605	28(19)	55,096	a,c
Hangzhou Match Factory 杭州火柴廠(1910)	Hangzhou 杭州市	Zhejiang 浙江省	(0571)6082313 (0571)6082313	826	State-owned 國有	27,485	352(9)	31,035	a
Pingyao Match Factory 平遙火柴廠(1892)	Yuci 榆次市	Shanxi 山西省	(0354)5623792	1,378	State-owned 國有	26,446	-996(70)	28,292	a,b,c
Jingxian Match Factory 涇縣火柴廠(1926)	Xuanzhou 宣州市	Anhui 安徽省	(0563)5022465 (0563)5025123	700	State-owned 國有	25,552	265(11)	52,855	a
Tianshui Match Factory 天水火柴廠(1956)	Tianshui 天水市	Gansu 甘肅省	(0938)212943	905	State-owned 國有	20,634	157(13)	45,500	a
Wuzhou Wu Long Industry General Company 梧州市舞龍工業總公司(1921)	Wuzhou 梧州市	Guangxi 廣西	(0774)3834541 (0774)3834541	969	State-owned 國有	19,755	-1458(77)	26,532	a

Top 10 Cities by Production Output 產出排名前 10 位城市	Province 省	Market share 市場份額	Number of firms 企業個數
Jining 濟寧市	Shandong 山東省	6.31%	1
Anyang 安陽市	Henan 河南省	6.24%	2
Kaifeng 開封市	Henan 河南省	5.49%	1
Hengshui 衡水市	Hebei 河北省	4.11%	2
Bengbu 蚌埠市	Anhui 安徽省	3.60%	1
Shanghai 上海市	Shanghai 上海市	2.95%	5
Zhenjiang 鎮江市	Jiangsu 江蘇省	2.87%	1
Hangzhou 杭州市	Zhejiang 浙江省	2.83%	3
Yuci 榆次市	Shanxi 山西省	2.53%	1
Benxi 本溪市	Liaoning 遼寧省	2.51%	1

10 Major Wholesalers 10 家主要批發商	City 城市	Province 省	Telephone / Fax 電話 / 傳真
Changzhou General Merchandise Wholesale General Company 常州百貨批發總公司	Changzhou 常州市	Jiangsu 江蘇省	(0519)6680488 (0519)6680488
Suzhou General Merchandise General Co. 蘇州百貨總公司	Suzhou 蘇州市	Jiangsu 江蘇省	(0512)5222288 (0512)5222247
Guangzhou Yue Xiu Enterprise (Holdings) Co. 廣州越秀企業(集團)公司	Guangzhou 廣州市	Guangdong 廣東省	(020)86662828 (020)86672634
Wunan Commercial Group Corp. 湖南省商業集團總公司	Changsha 長沙市	Hunan 湖南省	(0731)4442765
Kunming General Merchandise Purchase Supply Station Kunming General Merchandise Company 昆明百貨採購供應站昆明市百貨公司	Kunming 昆明市	Yunnan 雲南省	(0871)3314883 (0871)3314961
Nanjing General Merchandise General Company 南京市百貨總公司	Nanjing 南京市	Jiangsu 江蘇省	(025)6664681 (025)6643927
Guangzhou Shang Ling Trade Co. Ltd. 廣州商菱貿易有限公司	Guangzhou 廣州市	Guangdong 廣東省	(020)86677190 (020)86673971
Beijing Light Industry Product Import & Export Company 北京市輕工業品進出口公司	Beijing 北京市	Beijing 北京市	(010)64057425 (010)64057427
Xi Shan Shi Commerce Group Company 錫山市商業集團公司	Wuxi 無錫市	Jiangsu 江蘇省	(0510)2442982
Yixing Su Nan Commercial Building 宜興市蘇南商廈	Wuxi 無錫市	Jiangsu 江蘇省	(0510)7904407 (0510)7904754

*Also include sales by firms outside this industry.包括本行業以外廠家的銷售。"o" stands for "others". "o" 代表"其他產品"。

2688: Animal Jelly 動物膠製造業

The industry accounts for 0.022% of the total revenue of China's industrial sector in 1996. The revenue growth rate of the industry is 20.8% from 1995, as compared to the growth rate of China's industrial sector, 9.51%. The rate of return on asset is 1.52%. 74.14% of all firms in the industry made a profit while 21.19% had negative returns. The top province in terms of the industry's revenue is Shandong, accounting for 21.03% of the total revenue.
本行業在1996年佔全行業總產值0.022%，行業年增長率為20.8%（全國工業年增長率9.51%）。行業的資產回報率1.52%，74.14%的企業盈利，21.19%的企業虧損。銷售收入最高的省份為山東省，佔本行業的21.03%。

	Total number of firms 企業總數	Total number of employees 職工總數	Total revenue (mil. RMB) 總銷售收入（百萬元）	Total profit (mil. RMB) 總利潤（百萬元）	Return on assets 資產利潤率 (%)	Return on equity 權益利潤率 (%)	Labour productivity ('000 RMB / worker) 勞動生產率（千元/人）	Debts / assets 資產負債率 (%)	Total assets (mil. RMB) 總資產（百萬元）
Industry Overall 行業總體	255	25,383	1,296	38	1.52	5.93	51.06	74.27	2,522

	Number of firms 企業個數	Average number of employees 平均職工人數	Average revenue ('000 RMB) 平均銷售收入（千元）	Average profit ('000 RMB) 平均利潤（千元）	Return on assets 資產利潤率 (%)	Return on equity 權益利潤率 (%)	Labour productivity ('000 RMB / worker) 勞動生產率（千元/人）	Average debts / assets 平均資產負債率(%)	Average Total assets ('000 RMB) 平均總資產（千元）
By ownership 產業所有權									
State-owned 國有	53	196	8,340	151	0.61	2.27	42.61	73.29	24,868
Collectively-owned 集體	180	67	3,574	159	4.68	18.76	53.19	75.06	3,393
Privately-owned 私有	3	67	3,305	123	2.49	6.51	49.58	61.67	4,947
Domestic JVs 聯營	2	81	1,824	-326	-0.79	-5.84	22.52	86.41	41,025
Joint stock 股份制	2	873	71,495	884	0.41	1.75	81.94	76.49	215,192
Foreign-funded 外資	5	76	2,446	-59	-2.19	-6.31	32.27	65.39	2,709
Overseas Chinese-funded 港澳台資	9	56	4,714	26	0.43	1.04	83.68	58.25	5,887
By size 規模									
Large 大型	3	739	63,911	975	0.44	1.97	86.52	77.78	222,140
Medium 中型	9	369	22,975	-864	-1.56	-6.17	62.21	74.66	55,279
Small 小型	238	83	3,773	180	3.15	11.43	45.58	72.40	5,709
By regional distribution 地區分布									
Central-North 華北	41	64	2,579	72	0.97	4.17	40.14	76.77	7,430
Beijing 北京	10	9	797	13	2.00	8.61	86.63	76.73	649
Tianjin 天津	1	55	4,620	560	19.05	58.33	84.00	67.35	2,940
Hebei 河北	19	64	3,632	341	4.59	10.38	56.57	55.72	7,413
Shanxi 山西	4	94	3,778	-15	-0.11	-1.23	40.19	91.24	13,958
Inner Mongolia 內蒙	7	127	1,290	-593	-4.21	-399.04	10.13	98.94	14,077
Northeast 東北	43	70	1,709	-17	-0.49	-2.11	24.25	76.69	3,357
Liaoning 遼寧	6	103	4,543	117	1.78	2.84	44.33	37.54	6,567
Jilin 吉林	20	81	876	-99	-3.91	-160.98	10.88	97.57	2,529
Heilongjiang 黑龍江	17	47	1,689	34	1.05	7.30	35.63	85.63	3,197
Central East 華東	89	122	8,132	512	3.90	17.19	66.63	77.33	13,132
Shanghai 上海	3	91	9,547	2,420	8.88	50.98	105.29	82.58	27,247
Jiangsu 江蘇	9	139	7,272	-92	-1.20	-4.84	52.40	75.23	7,697
Zhejiang 浙江	17	95	7,788	201	3.15	7.28	82.23	56.70	6,382
Anhui 安徽	18	125	11,301	1,053	11.57	44.63	90.65	74.08	9,103
Fujian 福建	4	15	1,555	-188	-5.61	-47.77	103.67	88.18	3,343
Jiangxi 江西	13	41	1,158	-46	-1.48	-2.86	28.47	48.31	3,119
Shandong 山東	25	196	10,903	724	2.62	14.88	55.64	82.41	27,660
Central-South 中南	40	84	5,930	138	1.65	4.47	70.89	63.15	8,371
Henan 河南	22	83	5,997	216	2.91	11.09	72.41	73.80	7,430
Hubei 湖北	4	17	3,250	-65	-5.36	-15.85	194.03	66.19	1,213
Hunan 湖南	8	61	915	-125	-3.95	-37.31	15.12	89.42	3,165
Guangdong 廣東	3	268	24,190	663	1.66	2.81	90.26	40.91	39,937
Guangxi 廣西	3	56	4,127	13	0.19	0.73	73.25	74.54	7,137
Hainan 海南									
Southwest 西南	26	122	2,526	-269	-4.46	-26.22	20.71	82.98	6,024
Chongqing 重慶	8	102	1,261	-202	-9.61	67.00	12.34	114.35	2,105
Sichuan 四川	10	153	4,089	-279	-2.54	-10.15	26.75	75.00	10,996
Guizhou 貴州	2	153	780	-235	-5.14	-117.50	5.11	95.62	4,570
Yunnan 雲南	6	89	2,410	-358	-8.65	-82.06	26.98	89.50	4,143
Tibet 西藏									
Northwest 西北	16	146	5,662	-490	-1.90	-6.07	38.75	68.67	25,788
Shaanxi 陝西	5	55	582	24	3.00	7.19	10.54	58.25	800
Gansu 甘肅	6	181	4,782	-1,142	-5.41	-44.63	26.39	87.87	21,120
Qinghai 青海	3	229	17,427	-303	-0.35	-0.85	75.99	59.46	87,800
Ningxia 寧夏	1	64	910	-230	-10.04	56.10	14.22	117.47	2,290
Xinjiang 新疆	1	223	5,800	30	0.19	0.51	26.01	63.87	16,190

2688: Animal Jelly 動物膠製造業

Year 年份	Number of firms 企業個數	Rate of change 每年變化 (%)	Number of employees 職工人數 (人)	Rate of change 每年變化 (%)	Total revenue (mil. RMB) 總銷售收入 (百萬元)	Rate of change 每年變化 (%)	Total profit (mil. RMB) 總利潤 (百萬元)	Rate of change 每年變化 (%)
1993	228		24,500		626		-17	
1994	230	0.88%	24,059	-1.80%	762	21.61%	-5	68.39%
1995	250	8.70%	27,946	16.16%	1,073	40.95%	22	507.97%
1996	255	2.00%	25,383	-9.17%	1,296	20.78%	38	75.51%

3 Major products* 3種主要產品*	Output 產量	Sales volume 銷售量	Unit 單位
a) Bone Glue 骨膠	28,481	27,342	ton 噸
b) Skin Glue 皮膠	2,650	2,491	ton 噸
c) Jelly 明膠	15,879	14,450	ton 噸

Top 10 firms by revenue (year founded) 收入排名前10家企業 (創辦年份)	City 城市	Province 省	Telephone / fax 電話 / 傳真	Number of employees 職工人數	Ownership 產業所有權	Revenue ('000 RMB) 銷售收入 (千元)	Profit ('000 RMB) (rank) 利潤 (千元) (排名)	Total assets ('000 RMB) 總資產 (千元)	Major products 主要產品
Shandong Fu Jiao Group Co. Ltd. 山東福膠集團有限公司	Ji'nan 濟南市	Shandong 山東省	(0531)7871793	645	State-owned 國有	62,752	8061(2)	143,262	o
Guang Dongming Zhu Organism Industrial Co. Ltd. 廣東明珠生物工業有限公司(1996)	Jiangmen 江門市	Guangdong 廣東省	(0750)2212323 (0750)2292119	648	Foreign-funded 外資	62,119	830(19)	88,040	a,b,c
Jieshou Capsule General Factory 界首市膠囊總廠(1995)	Fuyang 阜陽市	Anhui 安徽省	(0558)4812428	150	Collectively-owned 集體	52,500	5224(5)	22,422	o
Qinghai Gum Making General Co. 青海製膠總公司	Xining 西寧市	Qinghai 青海省	(0971)6144491 (0971)8149106	682	State-owned 國有	52,280	-905(100)	263,403	a,c
Anhui Guoyang Bone Glue Factory 安徽省渦陽縣骨膠廠(1988)	Fuyang 阜陽市	Anhui 安徽省	(0558)7471617	410	Collectively-owned 集體	50,580	5937(3)	10,719	o
Anhui Bengbu Gelatin Factory 安徽省蚌埠明膠廠(1957)	Bengbu 蚌埠市	Anhui 安徽省	(0552)2045674	762	State-owned 國有	37,530	118(54)	73,812	a,c
Qingdao Guo Jian Co. Ltd. 青島國箭股份有限公司(1919)	Qingdao 青島市	Shandong 山東省	(0532)3834715 (0532)3833633	973	Joint stock 股份制	33,836	601(25)	232,227	c
Shandong Dong Fang Donkey-hide Gelatin Products Industrial Co. 山東東方阿膠製品工業公司(1992)	Ji'nan 濟南市	Shandong 山東省	(0531)7625888 (0531)7625653	245	Collectively-owned 集體	22,960	1670(9)	12,930	o
Shandong Yishui Gum Making Factory 山東省沂水縣製膠廠(1976)	Linyi 臨沂市	Shandong 山東省	(0539)2252535 (0539)2252583	508	State-owned 國有	21,851	0(81)	88,626	b,c
Anqiu Biochemistry Products Factory 安丘市生化製品廠(1988)	Weifang 濰坊市	Shandong 山東省		173	Collectively-owned 集體	21,088	1008(14)	948	o

Top 10 Cities by Production Output 產出排名前10位城市	Province 省	Market share 市場份額	Number of firms 企業個數
Jiangmen 江門市	Guangdong 廣東省	6.69%	2
Wenzhou 溫州市	Zhejiang 浙江省	6.39%	10
Jiaozuo 焦作市	Henan 河南省	5.95%	3
Fuyang 阜陽市	Anhui 安徽省	5.67%	3
Xining 西寧市	Qinghai 青海省	5.42%	3
Liaocheng 聊城市	Shandong 山東省	5.41%	2
Yuci 榆次市	Shanxi 山西省	2.90%	3
Chongqing 重慶市	Chongqing 重慶市	2.85%	11
Qingdao 青島市	Shandong 山東省	2.71%	2
Hangzhou 杭州市	Zhejiang 浙江省	2.61%	3

10 Major Wholesalers 10家主要批發商	City 城市	Province 省	Telephone / Fax 電話 / 傳真
Changzhou General Merchandise Wholesale General Company 常州百貨批發總公司	Changzhou 常州市	Jiangsu 江蘇省	(0519)6680488 (0519)6680488
Suzhou General Merchandise General Co. 蘇州百貨總公司	Suzhou 蘇州市	Jiangsu 江蘇省	(0512)5222288 (0512)5222247
Guangzhou Yue Xiu Enterprise (Holdings) Co. 廣州越秀企業(集團)公司	Guangzhou 廣州市	Guangdong 廣東省	(020)86662828 (020)86672634
Wunan Commercial Group Corp. 湖南省商業集團總公司	Changsha 長沙市	Hunan 湖南省	(0731)4442765
Kunming General Merchandise Purchase Supply Station Kunming General Merchandise Company 昆明百貨採購供應站昆明市百貨公司	Kunming 昆明市	Yunnan 雲南省	(0871)3314883 (0871)3314961
Nanjing General Merchandise General Company 南京市百貨總公司	Nanjing 南京市	Jiangsu 江蘇省	(025)6664681 (025)6643927
Guangzhou Shang Ling Trade Co. Ltd. 廣州商菱貿易有限公司	Guangzhou 廣州市	Guangdong 廣東省	(020)86677190 (020)86673971
Beijing Light Industry Product Import & Export Company 北京市輕工業品進出口公司	Beijing 北京市	Beijing 北京市	(010)64057425 (010)64057427
Xi Shan Shi Commerce Group Company 錫山市商業集團公司	Wuxi 無錫市	Jiangsu 江蘇省	(0510)2442982
Yixing Su Nan Commercial Building 宜興市蘇南商廈	Wuxi 無錫市	Jiangsu 江蘇省	(0510)7904407 (0510)7904754

*Also include sales by firms outside this industry.包括本行業以外廠家的銷售。"o" stands for "others". "o" 代表"其他產品"。

2689: Other Household Chemical Products 其他日用化學產品製造業

The industry accounts for 0.052% of the total revenue of China's industrial sector in 1996. The revenue growth rate of the industry is 25.6% from 1995, as compared to the growth rate of China's industrial sector, 9.51%. The rate of return on asset is 0.15%. 73.21% of all firms in the industry made a profit while 20.68% had negative returns. The top province in terms of the industry's revenue is Guangdong, accounting for 19.60% of the total revenue.
本行業在1996年佔全行業總產值0.052%，行業年增長率為25.6%（全國工業年增長率9.51%）。行業的資產回報率0.15%，73.21%的企業盈利，20.68%的企業虧損。銷售收入最高的省份為廣東省，佔本行業的19.60%。

	Total number of firms 企業總數	Total number of employees 職工總數	Total revenue (mil. RMB) 總銷售收入（百萬元）	Total profit (mil. RMB) 總利潤（百萬元）	Return on assets 資產利潤率 (%)	Return on equity 權益利潤率 (%)	Labour productivity ('000 RMB / worker) 勞動生產率（千元/人）	Debts / assets 資產負債率 (%)	Total assets (mil. RMB) 總資產（百萬元）
Industry Overall 行業總體	808	40,793	3,034	5	0.15	0.46	74.38	66.73	3,440

	Number of firms 企業個數	Average number of employees 平均職工人數	Average revenue ('000 RMB) 平均銷售收入（千元）	Average profit ('000 RMB) 平均利潤（千元）	Return on assets 資產利潤率 (%)	Return on equity 權益利潤率 (%)	Labour productivity ('000 RMB / worker) 勞動生產率（千元/人）	Average debts / assets 平均資產負債率(%)	Average Total assets ('000 RMB) 平均總資產（千元）
By ownership 產業所有權									
State-owned 國有	50	70	3,880	-160	-2.19	-9.52	55.30	76.99	7,300
Collectively-owned 集體	644	47	3,440	21	0.58	1.73	73.46	66.48	3,646
Privately-owned 私有	6	16	503	2	0.50	1.12	30.81	55.17	400
Domestic JVs 聯營	8	68	6,948	46	0.94	2.72	102.55	65.48	4,881
Joint stock 股份制	5	26	852	-11	-0.79	-9.59	32.53	91.81	1,435
Foreign-funded 外資	37	74	3,915	6	0.10	0.25	52.95	60.25	6,034
Overseas Chinese-funded 港澳台資	56	71	7,393	-20	-0.25	-0.67	104.19	62.57	8,051
By size 規模									
Large 大型	1	1,280	129,966	288	0.18	0.84	101.54	78.86	161,454
Medium 中型	5	620	74,531	396	0.65	1.42	120.25	54.52	61,310
Small 小型	783	46	3,232	3	0.09	0.28	70.81	67.35	3,797
By regional distribution 地區分布									
Central-North 華北	120	41	2,843	41	0.85	2.87	69.63	70.21	4,760
Beijing 北京	41	27	789	8	0.65	1.94	29.52	66.18	1,230
Tianjin 天津	29	50	5,765	-97	-0.78	-2.76	114.59	71.92	12,493
Hebei 河北	25	55	4,590	230	5.67	23.16	83.63	75.53	4,059
Shanxi 山西	7	61	2,704	301	9.53	16.36	44.65	41.71	3,161
Inner Mongolia 內蒙	18	30	439	-28	-1.44	-3.67	14.42	60.88	1,936
Northeast 東北	86	48	2,638	120	5.76	15.20	55.14	62.13	2,075
Liaoning 遼寧	40	52	3,585	160	7.06	14.46	69.40	51.21	2,271
Jilin 吉林	20	44	1,423	-14	-0.79	-10.11	32.12	92.24	1,779
Heilongjiang 黑龍江	26	45	2,118	160	7.97	20.24	47.34	60.61	2,002
Central East 華東	319	46	4,146	140	4.44	12.35	89.84	64.06	3,144
Shanghai 上海	26	63	4,219	-52	-0.90	-2.46	67.42	63.46	5,767
Jiangsu 江蘇	54	67	6,692	125	2.10	8.63	100.33	75.62	5,921
Zhejiang 浙江	32	58	11,328	946	15.99	31.29	195.31	48.90	5,917
Anhui 安徽	33	28	1,610	134	17.73	46.57	57.32	61.94	754
Fujian 福建	98	50	3,593	10	0.40	0.95	72.12	57.86	2,552
Jiangxi 江西	48	19	439	19	4.67	12.45	23.37	62.39	397
Shandong 山東	28	33	2,239	92	5.16	28.91	67.78	82.15	1,778
Central-South 中南	209	66	5,042	-49	-0.67	-2.00	75.93	66.49	7,323
Henan 河南	25	28	1,180	54	5.97	17.31	42.10	65.54	898
Hubei 湖北	33	58	3,816	140	4.94	11.07	65.89	55.35	2,839
Hunan 湖南	50	71	3,940	135	3.73	13.27	55.88	71.93	3,618
Guangdong 廣東	72	99	8,259	-456	-2.90	-9.23	83.68	68.56	15,697
Guangxi 廣西	25	20	4,092	397	10.86	19.19	204.17	43.39	3,653
Hainan 海南	4	33	1,088	-18	-0.59	-1.30	32.71	54.90	2,983
Southwest 西南	28	50	1,113	-209	-8.16	-76.17	22.14	89.27	2,561
Chongqing 重慶	3	113	2,386	-1,107	-20.33	-59.07	21.17	65.58	5,442
Sichuan 四川	16	54	1,293	-196	-7.23	64.71	23.95	111.17	2,709
Guizhou 貴州	4	29	173	20	2.00	8.89	5.90	77.56	1,003
Yunnan 雲南	5	24	618	30	1.64	2.18	26.19	24.42	1,826
Tibet 西藏									
Northwest 西北	46	39	1,272	-832	-44.93	-148.43	33.01	69.71	1,851
Shaanxi 陝西	16	31	2,369	-2,433	-88.90	-395.93	75.97	77.55	2,736
Gansu 甘肅	16	55	726	9	0.58	2.14	13.22	73.00	1,628
Qinghai 青海	3	51	593	-3	-0.79	-2.78	11.63	71.65	423
Ningxia 寧夏	3	4	20				5.45	111.11	30
Xinjiang 新疆	8	29	894	66	3.80	6.18	30.95	38.54	1,745

2689: Other Household Chemical Products 其他日用化學產品製造業

Year 年份	Number of firms 企業個數	Rate of change 每年變化 (%)	Number of employees 職工人數 (人)	Rate of change 每年變化 (%)	Total revenue (mil. RMB) 總銷售收入 (百萬元)	Rate of change 每年變化 (%)	Total profit (mil. RMB) 總利潤 (百萬元)	Rate of change 每年變化 (%)
1993	827		50,568		2,235		109	
1994	880	6.41%	51,953	2.74%	2,663	19.15%	74	-32.37%
1995	752	-14.55%	43,303	-16.65%	2,416	-9.29%	72	-2.27%
1996	808	7.45%	40,793	-5.80%	3,034	25.58%	5	-93.06%

3 Major products* 3 種主要產品 *	Output 產量	Sales volume 銷售量	Unit 單位
a) White Oil 白色油	26,303	24,725	ton 噸
b) Pyrthrin 除蟲菊酯殺蟲劑	778	700	ton 噸
c) Parffin War 石蠟	40,173	38,165	ton 噸

Top 10 firms by revenue (year founded) 收入排名前 10 家企業 (創辦年份)	City 城市	Province 省	Telephone / fax 電話 / 傳真	Number of employees 職工人數	Ownership 產業所有權	Revenue ('000 RMB) 銷售收入 (千元)	Profit ('000 RMB) (rank) 利潤 (千元) (排名)	Total assets ('000 RMB) 總資產 (千元)	Major products 主要產品
China Petrochemical Maoming Petrochemical Company Hua Yue Enterprise Group Company 中國石化茂名石油化工公司華粵企業集團公司(1980)	Maoming 茂名市	Guangdong 廣東省	(0668)2284059 (0668)2286942	3,650	Collectively-owned 集體	272,420	13596(2)	311,846	a,c
Zhejiang Li Zi Industrial Group Co. Ltd 浙江李字實業集團有限公司(1988)	Shaoxing 紹興市	Zhejiang 浙江省	(0575)7051747 (0575)7051209	500	Collectively-owned 集體	249,992	24622(1)	79,835	o
Ji Wei Daily Chemistry (Tianjin) Co. Ltd. 奇偉日用化學(天津)有限公司(1994)	Tianjin 天津市	Tianjin 天津市	(022)24340127 (022)24342819	652	Foreign-funded 外資	112,473	-6999(227)	234,502	o
Shunde Hua Bao Fine Chemical Industry Factory 順德市華寶精細化工廠(1992)	Foshan 佛山市	Guangdong 廣東省	(0757)2293888 (0757)2291160	458	Collectively-owned 集體	93,275	-49266(229)	412,887	o
Changzhou Kang Da Industrial General Co. 常州康達工業總公司(1971)	Changzhou 常州市	Jiangsu 江蘇省	(0519)3681081	280	State-owned 國有	74,450	4030(5)	46,220	o
Pingle Mosquito-repellent Incense Factory 平樂縣蚊香廠(1968)	Lingchuan 靈川縣	Guangxi 廣西	(0773)7882218	812	Collectively-owned 集體	73,030	9604(3)	72,698	o
Fujian Jin Lu Group Co. 福建省金鹿集團公司(1981)	Quanzhou 泉州市	Fujian 福建省	(0595)6682168 (0595)6682718	339	Collectively-owned 集體	60,355	4868(4)	19,515	o
Nanjing Ninggang Mosquito-repellent Incense Developing Co. Ltd. 南京寧港蚊香開發有限公司(1992)	Nanjing 南京市	Jiangsu 江蘇省	(025)2415741 (025)2415331	438	Overseas Chinese-funded 港澳台資	55,794	1411(16)	43,141	o
Xiamen Fang Yuan Plastic Cement Industrial Co. Ltd. 廈門芳源塑膠工業有限公司(1994)	Xiamen 廈門市	Fujian 福建省	(0592)5129801 (0592)5129080	46	Foreign-funded 外資	35,315	68(125)	25,394	o
Shanghai Fengxian Feng Cheng Gao Qiao Shoeshine Factory 上海奉賢奉城高橋鞋油廠(1991)	Shanghai 上海市	Shanghai 上海市	(021)57523631	106	Collectively-owned 集體	33,638	1842(13)	8,203	o

Top 10 Cities by Production Output 產出排名前 10 位城市	Province 省	Market share 市場份額	Number of firms 企業個數
Shanghai 上海市	Shanghai 上海市	22.70%	45
Shaoxing 紹興市	Zhejiang 浙江省	9.72%	5
Maoming 茂名市	Guangdong 廣東省	7.95%	3
Tianjin 天津市	Tianjin 天津市	4.90%	27
Nanjing 南京市	Jiangsu 江蘇省	4.22%	17
Changde 常德市	Hunan 湖南省	3.65%	14
Foshan 佛山市	Guangdong 廣東省	2.93%	7
Changzhou 常州市	Jiangsu 江蘇省	2.33%	8
Guangzhou 廣州市	Guangdong 廣東省	2.18%	27
Quanzhou 泉州市	Fujian 福建省	1.96%	13

10 Major Wholesalers 10 家主要批發商	City 城市	Province 省	Telephone / Fax 電話 / 傳真
Changzhou General Merchandise Wholesale General Company 常州百貨批發總公司	Changzhou 常州市	Jiangsu 江蘇省	(0519)6680488 (0519)6680488
Suzhou General Merchandise General Co. 蘇州百貨總公司	Suzhou 蘇州市	Jiangsu 江蘇省	(0512)5222288 (0512)5222247
Guangzhou Yue Xiu Enterprise (Holdings) Co. 廣州越秀企業(集團)公司	Guangzhou 廣州市	Guangdong 廣東省	(020)86662828 (020)86672634
Wunan Commercial Group Corp. 湖南省商業集團總公司	Changsha 長沙市	Hunan 湖南省	(0731)4442765
Kunming General Merchandise Purchase Supply Station Kunming General Merchandise Company 昆明百貨採購供應站昆明市百貨公司	Kunming 昆明市	Yunnan 雲南省	(0871)3314883 (0871)3314961
Nanjing General Merchandise General Company 南京市百貨總公司	Nanjing 南京市	Jiangsu 江蘇省	(025)6664681 (025)6643927
Guangzhou Shang Ling Trade Co. Ltd. 廣州商菱貿易有限公司	Guangzhou 廣州市	Guangdong 廣東省	(020)86677190 (020)86673971
Beijing Light Industry Product Import & Export Company 北京市輕工業品進出口公司	Beijing 北京市	Beijing 北京市	(010)64057425 (010)64057427
Xi Shan Shi Commerce Group Company 錫山市商業集團公司	Wuxi 無錫市	Jiangsu 江蘇省	(0510)2442982
Yixing Su Nan Commercial Building 宜興市蘇南商廈	Wuxi 無錫市	Jiangsu 江蘇省	(0510)7904407 (0510)7904754

*Also include sales by firms outside this industry.包括本行業以外廠家的銷售。"o" stands for "others". "o" 代表 "其他產品"。

2710: Medicines and Chemical Reagents 化學藥品原藥製造業

The industry accounts for 0.599% of the total revenue of China's industrial sector in 1996. The revenue growth rate of the industry is 10.3% from 1995, as compared to the growth rate of China's industrial sector, 9.51%. The rate of return on asset is 0.73%. 62.16% of all firms in the industry made a profit while 32.56% had negative returns. The top province in terms of the industry's revenue is Hebei, accounting for 14.61% of the total revenue.
本行業在1996年佔全行業總產值0.599%，行業年增長率為10.3%（全國工業年增長率9.51%）。行業的資產回報率0.73%，62.16%的企業盈利，32.56%的企業虧損。銷售收入最高的省份為河北省，佔本行業的14.61%。

	Total number of firms 企業總數	Total number of employees 職工總數	Total revenue (mil. RMB) 總銷售收入（百萬元）	Total profit (mil. RMB) 總利潤（百萬元）	Return on assets 資產利潤率 (%)	Return on equity 權益利潤率 (%)	Labour productivity ('000 RMB / worker) 勞動生產率（千元/人）	Debts / assets 資產負債率 (%)	Total assets (mil. RMB) 總資產（百萬元）
Industry Overall 行業總體	986	410,734	34,711	436	0.73	2.61	84.51	72.02	59,567

	Number of firms 企業個數	Average number of employees 平均職工人數	Average revenue ('000 RMB) 平均銷售收入（千元）	Average profit ('000 RMB) 平均利潤（千元）	Return on assets 資產利潤率 (%)	Return on equity 權益利潤率 (%)	Labour productivity ('000 RMB / worker) 勞動生產率（千元/人）	Average debts / assets 平均資產負債率(%)	Average Total assets ('000 RMB) 平均總資產（千元）
By ownership 產業所有權									
State-owned 國有	348	785	55,284	-606	-0.60	-2.55	70.44	76.52	101,282
Collectively-owned 集體	462	128	11,281	129	0.89	4.22	87.94	78.97	14,539
Privately-owned 私有	2	55	792				14.54	84.06	6,439
Domestic JVs 聯營	31	182	25,616	71	0.24	0.79	140.77	69.21	29,351
Joint stock 股份制	30	1,778	228,633	17,056	4.12	9.58	128.59	56.93	413,526
Foreign-funded 外資	54	237	25,192	902	2.10	5.64	106.15	62.73	42,955
Overseas Chinese-funded 港澳台資	57	145	21,669	442	1.31	5.31	149.08	75.23	33,597
By size 規模									
Large 大型	88	2,482	250,591	5,242	1.17	3.73	100.97	68.66	447,919
Medium 中型	130	704	44,717	-347	-0.44	-2.26	63.51	80.34	78,156
Small 小型	731	135	9,366	27	0.20	0.86	69.55	76.83	13,666
By regional distribution 地區分布									
Central-North 華北	128	532	53,253	3,303	3.25	10.62	100.02	69.44	101,753
Beijing 北京	26	168	10,242	298	2.08	6.08	60.88	65.77	14,312
Tianjin 天津	21	425	43,348	3,121	5.69	12.53	102.06	54.56	54,810
Hebei 河北	46	848	110,234	9,475	4.35	14.58	129.98	70.17	217,873
Shanxi 山西	16	503	14,252	-4,482	-9.13	-33.35	28.34	72.61	49,072
Inner Mongolia 內蒙	19	410	17,945	-768	-2.10	-11.70	43.73	82.02	36,523
Northeast 東北	103	533	41,175	-898	-0.94	-4.10	77.19	76.99	95,131
Liaoning 遼寧	54	619	39,591	-782	-0.76	-2.48	63.91	69.23	102,361
Jilin 吉林	19	365	24,916	866	1.89	3.71	68.28	48.98	45,792
Heilongjiang 黑龍江	30	485	54,324	-2,223	-1.96	-60.40	111.95	96.75	113,363
Central East 華東	369	383	39,991	544	0.99	3.30	104.51	70.10	55,131
Shanghai 上海	51	401	59,022	672	0.74	3.20	147.17	76.80	90,527
Jiangsu 江蘇	121	312	33,092	-582	-1.54	-4.99	106.18	69.15	37,830
Zhejiang 浙江	86	232	27,941	1,140	3.62	11.53	120.22	68.62	31,521
Anhui 安徽	21	501	25,504	-5,416	-12.93	-122.26	50.92	89.42	41,875
Fujian 福建	11	507	52,159	620	1.14	4.54	102.95	74.87	54,336
Jiangxi 江西	27	542	25,992	7	0.01	0.04	47.98	75.03	73,929
Shandong 山東	52	622	67,857	4,721	4.94	12.23	109.17	59.58	95,486
Central-South 中南	244	343	24,622	67	0.15	0.58	71.76	74.48	45,050
Henan 河南	77	388	26,699	419	1.11	5.81	68.75	80.82	37,549
Hubei 湖北	72	328	22,411	-171	-0.52	-1.87	68.39	72.40	33,204
Hunan 湖南	35	343	17,969	-1,174	-3.84	-21.87	52.34	82.46	30,599
Guangdong 廣東	48	274	29,440	-19	-0.02	-0.08	107.31	71.12	83,073
Guangxi 廣西	11	401	26,486	3,543	6.47	16.13	66.02	59.91	54,794
Hainan 海南	1	626	5,050	-610	-1.24	-6.32	8.07	80.31	49,000
Southwest 西南	81	523	25,726	-804	-1.73	-5.67	49.20	69.40	46,354
Chongqing 重慶	29	679	33,777	257	0.36	1.09	49.76	67.13	71,445
Sichuan 四川	38	541	26,199	497	1.28	3.80	48.44	66.37	38,932
Guizhou 貴州	9	153	5,716	-3,102	-21.06	238.84	37.44	108.82	14,731
Yunnan 雲南	5	157	11,884	-2,166	-13.53	72.20	75.79	118.75	16,014
Tibet 西藏									
Northwest 西北	61	334	13,193	-763	-2.81	-11.77	39.50	76.10	27,114
Shaanxi 陝西	49	356	13,679	-648	-2.30	-10.19	38.47	77.47	28,219
Gansu 甘肅	5	417	16,714	-2,918	-8.56	-29.55	40.06	71.03	34,094
Qinghai 青海	1	142	3,050	-2,010	-32.42	87.39	21.48	137.10	6,200
Ningxia 寧夏	1								
Xinjiang 新疆	5	145	9,580	364	1.92	4.96	65.98	61.18	18,910

2710: Medicines and Chemical Reagents 化學藥品原藥製造業

Year 年份	Number of firms 企業個數	Rate of change 每年變化 (%)	Number of employees 職工人數 (人)	Rate of change 每年變化 (%)	Total revenue (mil. RMB) 總銷售收入 (百萬元)	Rate of change 每年變化 (%)	Total profit (mil. RMB) 總利潤 (百萬元)	Rate of change 每年變化 (%)
1993	819		377,200		20,431		618	
1994	834	1.83%	323,462	-14.25%	25,658	25.58%	1,118	80.92%
1995	1,001	20.02%	391,998	21.19%	31,470	22.65%	1,021	-8.65%
1996	986	-1.50%	410,734	4.78%	34,711	10.30%	436	-57.30%

3 Major products* 3 種主要產品 *	Output 產量	Sales volume 銷售量	Unit 單位
a) Antipyretic Analgesic 解熱鎮痛藥	41,732	40,480	ton 噸
b) Vitamin 維生素類	35,084	32,277	ton 噸
c) Anti-infective 抗感染藥類	44,367	36,825	ton 噸

Top 10 firms by revenue (year founded) 收入排名前 10 家企業 (創辦年份)	City 城市	Province 省	Telephone / fax 電話 / 傳真	Number of employees 職工人數	Ownership 產業所有權	Revenue ('000 RMB) 銷售收入 (千元)	Profit ('000 RMB) (rank) 利潤 (千元) (排名)	Total assets ('000 RMB) 總資產 (千元)	Major products 主要產品
North China Pharmaceutical Group Corp. 華北製藥集團有限責任公司(1958)	Shijiazhuang 石家莊市	Hebei 河北省	(0311)6062875 (0311)5053560	17,054	Joint stock 股份制	2,650,237	279571(1)	6,001,070	b,c
Shandong Xinhua Medicine Group Company 山東新華醫藥集團公司(1943)	Zibo 淄博市	Shandong 山東省	(0533)2184223 (0533)2183499	7,228	State-owned 國有	1,372,103	118962(2)	1,660,795	a,c
Harbin Pharmaceutical Factory 哈爾濱製藥廠(1949)	Harbin 哈爾濱市	Heilongjiang 黑龍江省	(0451)6664526 (0451)6664526	5,012	Joint stock 股份制	941,980	43000(5)	859,316	c
Notheeast General Pharmaceutical Factory 東北製藥總廠(1946)	Shenyang 瀋陽市	Liaoning 遼寧省	(024)25806833	12,852	State-owned 國有	909,913	16749(19)	2,217,166	o
Shandong Lu Kang Medicine Enterprise Group Co. 山東魯抗醫藥企業集團公司(1968)	Jining 濟寧市	Shandong 山東省	(0537)2213961 (0537)2218814	6,516	State-owned 國有	785,274	79280(4)	1,236,343	c
Shijiazhuang Pharmaceutical Group Company 石家莊製藥集團公司(1938)	Shijiazhuang 石家莊市	Hebei 河北省	(0311)7027976 (0311)7026170	3,954	State-owned 國有	657,452	28804(9)	921,286	a,b,c
State-owned Jingjiang Glucose Refinery 國營靖江葡萄糖廠(1959)	Taizhou 泰州市	Jiangsu 江蘇省	(0523)4816224 (0523)4813411	4,507	State-owned 國有	609,417	-38356(602)	1,275,624	b
Shanghai Sunv3 Pharmaceutical Co. Ltd. 上海三維製藥有限公司(1958)	Shanghai 上海市	Shanghai 上海市	(021)62506900 (021)62508020	2,645	State-owned 國有	517,292	5224(44)	801,422	b,c
Hebei Pharmaceutical Factory 河北製藥(集團)有限公司(1972)	Shijiazhuang 石家莊市	Hebei 河北省	(0311)6827658 (0311)6827629	2,560	State-owned 國有	498,639	87489(3)	742,638	c
Shanghai Pioneer Pharmaceutical Company 上海先鋒藥業公司(1953)	Shanghai 上海市	Shanghai 上海市	(021)58552452 (021)58552671	1,875	State-owned 國有	451,485	296(224)	1,048,070	b,c

Top 10 Cities by Production Output 產出排名前 10 位城市	Province 省	Market share 市場份額	Number of firms 企業個數
Shijiazhuang 石家莊市	Hebei 河北省	10.84%	12
Shanghai 上海市	Shanghai 上海市	10.82%	80
Harbin 哈爾濱市	Heilongjiang 黑龍江省	9.01%	10
Dalian 大連市	Liaoning 遼寧省	6.12%	6
Zibo 淄博市	Shandong 山東省	3.81%	9
Jining 濟寧市	Shandong 山東省	3.52%	5
Shenyang 瀋陽市	Liaoning 遼寧省	3.27%	23
Suzhou 蘇州市	Jiangsu 江蘇省	2.58%	43
Taizhou 臺州市	Zhejiang 浙江省	2.26%	46
Wuxi 無錫市	Jiangsu 江蘇省	2.00%	21

10 Major Wholesalers 10 家主要批發商	City 城市	Province 省	Telephone / Fax 電話 / 傳真
Nanjing Medicine (Group) Company 南京醫藥(集團)公司	Nanjing 南京市	Jiangsu 江蘇省	(025)4404068 (025)4523033
Sichuan Medicine Company 四川省醫藥公司	Chengdu 成都市	Sichuan 四川省	(028)7763010 (028)7763010
Guangzhou Medicine Co. 廣州市醫藥公司	Guangzhou 廣州市	Guangdong 廣東省	(020)81811491 (020)81811492
Hangzhou Medicine Station Co. Ltd. 杭州醫藥站股份有限公司	Hangzhou 杭州市	Zhejiang 浙江省	(0571)5159638 (0571)5178578
Zhejiang Medical Health Care Product Import & Export Company 浙江省醫藥保健品進出口公司	Hangzhou 杭州市	Zhejiang 浙江省	(0571)5100288 (0571)5100777
Singbo Medicine Co. Ltd. 寧波醫藥股份有限公司	Ningbo 寧波市	Zhejiang 浙江省	(0574)7267909 (0574)7265934
Jiangsu Medical Health Care Product Import & Export (Group) Company 江蘇省醫藥保健品進出口(集團)公司	Nanjing 南京市	Jiangsu 江蘇省	(025)3729500 (025)3721996
Chang Zhou Pharmaceutical Co. Ltd. 常州藥業股份有限公司	Changzhou 常州市	Jiangsu 江蘇省	(0519)6606394 (0519)6604810
Shenyang Medicine Group Company 瀋陽醫藥集團公司	Shenyang 瀋陽市	Liaoning 遼寧省	(024)23832115 (024)23834228
Shandong Weifang Medicine Group Co. Ltd. 山東濰坊醫藥集團股份有限公司	Weifang 濰坊市	Shandong 山東省	(0536)8324797 (0536)8324791

*Also include sales by firms outside this industry.包括本行業以外廠家的銷售。"o" stands for "others". "o" 代表 "其他產品"。

2720: Pharmaceutical Preparations 化學藥品製劑製造業

The industry accounts for 0.531% of the total revenue of China's industrial sector in 1996. The revenue growth rate of the industry is 8.5% from 1995, as compared to the growth rate of China's industrial sector, 9.51%. The rate of return on asset is 4.28%. 63.53% of all firms in the industry made a profit while 30.76% had negative returns. The top province in terms of the industry's revenue is Guangdong, accounting for 15.00% of the total revenue.
本行業在1996年佔全行業總產值0.531%，行業年增長率為8.5%（全國工業年增長率9.51%）。行業的資產回報率4.28%，63.53%的企業盈利，30.76%的企業虧損。銷售收入最高的省份為廣東省，佔本行業的15.00%。

	Total number of firms 企業總數	Total number of employees 職工總數	Total revenue (mil. RMB) 總銷售收入（百萬元）	Total profit (mil. RMB) 總利潤（百萬元）	Return on assets 資產利潤率 (%)	Return on equity 權益利潤率 (%)	Labour productivity ('000 RMB / worker) 勞動生產率（千元/人）	Debts / assets 資產負債率 (%)	Total assets (mil. RMB) 總資產（百萬元）
Industry Overall 行業總體	1,308	335,482	30,761	2,135	4.28	12.57	91.69	65.92	49,849

	Number of firms 企業個數	Average number of employees 平均職工人數	Average revenue ('000 RMB) 平均銷售收入（千元）	Average profit ('000 RMB) 平均利潤（千元）	Return on assets 資產利潤率 (%)	Return on equity 權益利潤率 (%)	Labour productivity ('000 RMB / worker) 勞動生產率（千元/人）	Average debts / assets 平均資產負債率(%)	Average Total assets ('000 RMB) 平均總資產（千元）
By ownership 產業所有權									
State-owned 國有	597	357	26,335	781	1.81	7.31	73.85	75.22	43,102
Collectively-owned 集體	413	166	10,927	358	2.37	7.78	65.90	69.59	15,138
Privately-owned 私有	6	54	9,131	474	4.58	-32.26	168.05	114.21	10,336
Domestic JVs 聯營	26	121	12,294	357	2.17	6.19	101.86	64.88	16,430
Joint stock 股份制	48	471	49,593	4,921	5.27	13.37	105.34	60.62	93,443
Foreign-funded 外資	113	134	46,778	8,313	12.81	23.91	347.94	46.42	64,887
Overseas Chinese-funded 港澳台資	103	132	23,841	3,221	6.00	11.58	181.00	48.20	53,691
By size 規模									
Large 大型	46	1,233	224,421	29,875	8.56	19.80	182.04	56.76	349,010
Medium 中型	177	616	52,663	2,839	3.47	12.54	85.43	72.33	81,807
Small 小型	1,023	164	10,867	253	1.34	4.29	66.36	68.72	18,880
By regional distribution 地區分布									
Central-North 華北	210	252	21,172	3,275	9.32	23.29	84.13	59.99	35,142
Beijing 北京	43	223	19,785	430	0.85	2.86	88.83	70.22	50,523
Tianjin 天津	25	352	70,604	23,514	23.34	35.36	200.46	33.98	100,729
Hebei 河北	68	235	16,532	1,044	4.75	15.98	70.35	70.27	21,972
Shanxi 山西	50	301	11,460	375	1.94	8.07	38.03	75.95	19,303
Inner Mongolia 內蒙	24	143	5,550	-347	-3.62	25.17	38.94	114.38	9,578
Northeast 東北	218	246	10,949	128	0.45	1.92	44.58	76.35	28,304
Liaoning 遼寧	95	235	11,418	202	0.68	2.55	48.50	73.25	29,644
Jilin 吉林	67	223	8,004	-392	-1.41	-7.14	35.89	80.28	27,820
Heilongjiang 黑龍江	56	290	13,675	626	2.35	10.37	47.17	77.30	26,612
Central East 華東	404	284	29,718	1,520	3.70	10.62	104.71	65.19	41,115
Shanghai 上海	51	273	60,124	3,063	3.69	10.10	220.58	63.47	83,040
Jiangsu 江蘇	99	372	41,244	3,779	7.23	18.88	110.90	61.72	52,307
Zhejiang 浙江	76	211	21,140	175	0.49	1.19	99.96	59.13	35,829
Anhui 安徽	61	264	16,721	32	0.15	1.62	63.34	90.56	20,706
Fujian 福建	37	167	12,812	350	2.19	6.88	76.73	68.22	16,018
Jiangxi 江西	22	210	11,913	-230	-1.11	-10.73	56.76	89.63	20,669
Shandong 山東	58	362	25,754	1,044	2.80	7.70	71.22	63.66	37,303
Central-South 中南	308	259	26,681	1,148	2.39	7.36	103.10	67.53	48,046
Henan 河南	97	344	16,796	767	2.65	11.00	48.78	75.93	28,966
Hubei 湖北	50	236	12,676	14	0.06	0.23	53.76	73.78	22,889
Hunan 湖南	38	203	7,363	6	0.04	0.16	36.27	73.69	13,753
Guangdong 廣東	77	260	59,914	2,786	2.51	7.31	230.67	65.68	111,068
Guangxi 廣西	25	159	19,538	419	1.87	5.44	122.94	65.59	22,356
Hainan 海南	21	135	27,293	2,533	4.40	9.45	202.60	53.48	57,630
Southwest 西南	100	204	16,630	458	1.82	5.73	81.58	68.23	25,136
Chongqing 重慶	21	309	29,614	49	0.12	0.37	95.90	68.96	42,075
Sichuan 四川	33	215	14,463	267	1.16	4.79	67.38	75.76	23,017
Guizhou 貴州	18	85	4,764	-164	-1.43	-3.87	56.38	63.00	11,432
Yunnan 雲南	28	190	17,159	1,387	5.82	14.64	90.55	60.27	23,847
Tibet 西藏									
Northwest 西北	68	211	30,016	5,976	17.10	34.10	142.38	49.86	34,950
Shaanxi 陝西	45	173	37,268	9,060	26.24	43.65	215.64	39.88	34,523
Gansu 甘肅	11	276	11,746	-417	-1.73	-4.92	42.55	64.90	24,174
Qinghai 青海	1	1,138	84,100	10,530	6.99	18.72	73.90	62.67	150,640
Ningxia 寧夏	3	361	26,373	803	1.67	8.41	73.06	80.14	48,087
Xinjiang 新疆	8	163	8,948	-1,215	-3.71	-12.22	55.06	69.67	32,781

2720: Pharmaceutical Preparations 化學藥品製劑製造業

Year 年份	Number of firms 企業個數	Rate of change 每年變化 (%)	Number of employees 職工人數 (人)	Rate of change 每年變化 (%)	Total revenue (mil. RMB) 總銷售收入 (百萬元)	Rate of change 每年變化 (%)	Total profit (mil. RMB) 總利潤 (百萬元)	Rate of change 每年變化 (%)
1993	1,059		327,674		21,049		1,090	
1994	1,167	10.20%	311,672	-4.88%	24,261	15.26%	1,236	13.36%
1995	1,347	15.42%	361,727	16.06%	28,353	16.87%	1,553	25.61%
1996	1,308	-2.90%	335,482	-7.26%	30,761	8.49%	2,135	37.48%

3 Major products* 3 種主要產品 *	Output 產量	Sales volume 銷售量	Unit 單位
a) Medicine for Respiration System 呼吸系統用藥	662	490	ton 噸
b) Medicine for Central Nervous System 中樞神經系統用藥	2,954	2,924	ton 噸
c) Anti-infective 抗感染藥類	8,440	7,005	ton 噸

Top 10 firms by revenue (year founded) 收入排名前 10 家企業 (創辦年份)	City 城市	Province 省	Telephone / fax 電話 / 傳真	Number of employees 職工人數	Ownership 產業所有權	Revenue ('000 RMB) 銷售收入 (千元)	Profit ('000 RMB) (rank) 利潤 (千元) (排名)	Total assets ('000 RMB) 總資產 (千元)	Major products 主要產品
Xian-janssen Pharmaceutical Ltd. 西安楊森製藥有限公司(1985)	Xi'an 西安市	Shaanxi 陝西省	(029)3234455 (029)3235161	650	Foreign-funded 外資	1,434,723	407880(2)	1,182,806	o
Sino-american Tianjin Smith Kline & French Labs. Ltd. 中美天津史克製藥有限公司(1984)	Tianjin 天津市	Tianjin 天津市	(022)24700088 (022)24700666	764	Foreign-funded 外資	1,179,523	575153(1)	1,291,484	o
Guangzhou Baiyunshan Enterprise Group Co. 廣州白雲山企業集團公司(1988)	Guangzhou 廣州市	Guangdong 廣東省	(020)87706688 (020)87705599	2,331	State-owned 國有	1,175,441	45008(10)	1,745,479	c
Livzon Pharmaceutical Group Inc. 麗珠醫藥集團股份有限公司(1985)	Zhuhai 珠海市	Guangdong 廣東省	(0756)8112535 (0756)8886002	1,380	Overseas Chinese-funded 港澳台資	769,667	122903(3)	1,398,569	c
Sino-u.s.a Shanghai Skuibb Pharmaceutical Co. Ltd. 中美上海施貴寶製藥有限公司(1985)	Shanghai 上海市	Shanghai 上海市	(021)64302740 (021)64301498	851	Foreign-funded 外資	623,480	30113(12)	571,090	o
Qi Lu Pharmaceutical Factory 齊魯製藥廠(1959)	Ji'nan 濟南市	Shandong 山東省	(0531)8962118 (0531)8967329	1,872	State-owned 國有	450,638	22279(16)	465,350	c
Hangzhou Min Sheng Pharmacy Industry Group Co. 杭州民生藥業集團公司(1926)	Hangzhou 杭州市	Zhejiang 浙江省	(0571)8074824 (0571)8072129	2,900	State-owned 國有	349,120	7250(50)	464,820	a,b,c
Pfizer Pharmaceutical Dalian Co. Ltd. 輝瑞製藥大連有限公司(1993)	Dalian 大連市	Liaoning 遼寧省	(0411)7615400 (0411)7615444	503	Foreign-funded 外資	324,943	74121(6)	457,682	o
Shanghai New Asiatic Medical Industry Company 上海新亞藥業公司(1926)	Shanghai 上海市	Shanghai 上海市	(021)58563780 (021)58563797	824	State-owned 國有	318,384	2501(111)	472,156	a,b
Astra (Wuxi) Pharmaceutical Co. Ltd. 阿斯特拉(無錫)製藥有限公司(1994)	Wuxi 無錫市	Jiangsu 江蘇省	(0510)5211633 (0510)5210064	449	Foreign-funded 外資	304,158	24898(15)	328,659	o

Top 10 Cities by Production Output 產出排名前 10 位城市	Province 省	Market share 市場份額	Number of firms 企業個數
Shanghai 上海市	Shanghai 上海市	10.76%	72
Tianjin 天津市	Tianjin 天津市	5.77%	32
Xi'an 西安市	Shaanxi 陝西省	5.46%	26
Guangzhou 廣州市	Guangdong 廣東省	4.18%	29
Hangzhou 杭州市	Zhejiang 浙江省	3.17%	12
Nanjing 南京市	Jiangsu 江蘇省	2.89%	14
Suzhou 蘇州市	Jiangsu 江蘇省	2.76%	20
Beijing 北京市	Beijing 北京市	2.28%	39
Chongqing 重慶市	Chongqing 重慶市	2.23%	24
Taizhou 臺州市	Zhejiang 浙江省	2.03%	21

10 Major Wholesalers 10 家主要批發商	City 城市	Province 省	Telephone / Fax 電話 / 傳真
Nanjing Medicine (Group) Company 南京醫藥(集團)公司	Nanjing 南京市	Jiangsu 江蘇省	(025)4404068 (025)4523033
Sichuan Medicine Company 四川省醫藥公司	Chengdu 成都市	Sichuan 四川省	(028)7763010 (028)7763010
Guangzhou Medicine Co. 廣州市醫藥公司	Guangzhou 廣州市	Guangdong 廣東省	(020)81811491 (020)81811492
Hangzhou Medicine Station Co. Ltd. 杭州醫藥站股份有限公司	Hangzhou 杭州市	Zhejiang 浙江省	(0571)5159638 (0571)5178578
Zhejiang Medical Health Care Product Import & Export Company 浙江省醫藥保健品進出口公司	Hangzhou 杭州市	Zhejiang 浙江省	(0571)5100288 (0571)5100777
Singbo Medicine Co. Ltd. 寧波醫藥股份有限公司	Ningbo 寧波市	Zhejiang 浙江省	(0574)7267909 (0574)7265934
Jiangsu Medical Health Care Product Import & Export (Group) Company 江蘇省醫藥保健品進出口(集團)公司	Nanjing 南京市	Jiangsu 江蘇省	(025)3729500 (025)3721996
Chang Zhou Pharmaceutical Co. Ltd. 常州藥業股份有限公司	Changzhou 常州市	Jiangsu 江蘇省	(0519)6606394 (0519)6604810
Shenyang Medicine Group Company 瀋陽醫藥集團公司	Shenyang 瀋陽市	Liaoning 遼寧省	(024)23832115 (024)23834228
Shandong Weifang Medicine Group Co. Ltd. 山東濰坊醫藥集團股份有限公司	Weifang 濰坊市	Shandong 山東省	(0536)8324797 (0536)8324791

*Also include sales by firms outside this industry.包括本行業以外廠家的銷售。"o" stands for "others". "o" 代表 "其他產品" 。

2730: Chinese Medicines 中藥材及中成藥加工業

The industry accounts for 0.452% of the total revenue of China's industrial sector in 1996. The revenue growth rate of the industry is 25.5% from 1995, as compared to the growth rate of China's industrial sector, 9.51%. The rate of return on asset is 4.79%. 64.57% of all firms in the industry made a profit while 30.16% had negative returns. The top province in terms of the industry's revenue is Guangdong, accounting for 18.10% of the total revenue.
本行業在 1996 年佔全行業總產值 0.452% ，行業年增長率為 25.5%（全國工業年增長率 9.51%）。行業的資產回報率 4.79% ， 64.57% 的企業盈利， 30.16% 的企業虧損。銷售收入最高的省份為廣東省，佔本行業的 18.10% 。

	Total number of firms 企業總數	Total number of employees 職工總數	Total revenue (mil. RMB) 總銷售收入（百萬元）	Total profit (mil. RMB) 總利潤（百萬元）	Return on assets 資產利潤率 (%)	Return on equity 權益利潤率 (%)	Labour productivity ('000 RMB / worker) 勞動生產率（千元 / 人）	Debts / assets 資產負債率 (%)	Total assets (mil. RMB) 總資產（百萬元）
Industry Overall 行業總體	2,000	341,082	26,231	2,155	4.79	13.35	76.91	64.14	44,974

	Number of firms 企業個數	Average number of employees 平均職工人數	Average revenue ('000 RMB) 平均銷售收入（千元）	Average profit ('000 RMB) 平均利潤（千元）	Return on assets 資產利潤率 (%)	Return on equity 權益利潤率 (%)	Labour productivity ('000 RMB / worker) 勞動生產率（千元 / 人）	Average debts / assets 平均資產負債率(%)	Average Total assets ('000 RMB) 平均總資產（千元）
By ownership 產業所有權									
State-owned 國有	769	263	15,579	698	2.43	9.21	59.23	73.68	28,795
Collectively-owned 集體	769	90	6,471	293	4.09	12.96	71.83	68.42	7,152
Privately-owned 私有	9	203	23,967	2,766	10.42	34.90	118.07	70.14	26,542
Domestic JVs 聯營	37	76	7,642	107	1.16	2.62	100.73	55.70	9,227
Joint stock 股份制	91	296	39,444	7,990	12.50	24.60	133.22	49.19	63,916
Foreign-funded 外資	156	141	17,755	1,690	3.98	7.39	125.56	46.17	42,495
Overseas Chinese-funded 港澳台資	162	99	14,898	2,321	8.82	21.00	150.58	58.01	26,313
By size 規模									
Large 大型	25	1,442	281,576	31,039	6.98	16.17	195.21	56.81	444,405
Medium 中型	136	627	47,650	5,493	5.76	15.40	76.02	62.57	95,295
Small 小型	1,770	123	7,340	375	3.17	10.24	59.71	69.01	11,809
By regional distribution 地區分布									
Central-North 華北	216	167	14,542	263	1.16	4.36	86.97	73.40	22,673
Beijing 北京	60	175	31,090	1,068	2.66	9.31	177.62	71.46	40,192
Tianjin 天津	26	256	20,075	-557	-1.37	-4.82	78.38	71.60	40,637
Hebei 河北	63	167	8,007	243	1.89	7.78	47.86	75.68	12,824
Shanxi 山西	35	130	4,747	-65	-0.61	-2.39	36.38	74.50	10,656
Inner Mongolia 內蒙	32	120	2,602	-182	-2.34	-25.29	21.62	90.74	7,763
Northeast 東北	439	165	6,795	622	3.33	11.35	41.17	70.65	18,663
Liaoning 遼寧	157	132	4,331	-274	-2.05	-8.86	32.87	76.82	13,368
Jilin 吉林	223	178	8,044	1,257	5.58	16.91	45.15	66.99	22,523
Heilongjiang 黑龍江	59	204	8,626	605	3.33	13.73	42.28	75.74	18,163
Central East 華東	439	169	18,064	1,702	6.82	19.73	106.75	65.58	24,951
Shanghai 上海	49	205	43,943	984	2.37	15.83	214.87	85.06	41,603
Jiangsu 江蘇	39	194	17,133	505	2.34	6.99	88.13	66.51	21,568
Zhejiang 浙江	67	161	16,418	1,747	6.01	14.16	102.29	57.57	29,083
Anhui 安徽	75	166	16,769	1,067	6.95	23.97	101.03	71.00	15,349
Fujian 福建	60	71	9,585	3,088	19.66	34.42	134.12	42.88	15,707
Jiangxi 江西	93	177	11,166	1,171	5.79	15.31	62.93	63.13	20,221
Shandong 山東	56	227	20,310	3,360	8.75	23.78	89.62	63.22	38,412
Central-South 中南	504	171	16,311	1,340	4.86	11.41	95.30	57.37	27,550
Henan 河南	90	181	7,434	336	2.14	8.86	41.13	75.83	15,668
Hubei 湖北	60	285	13,434	79	0.31	1.46	47.12	79.02	25,870
Hunan 湖南	72	131	8,282	425	2.63	6.23	63.36	57.80	16,175
Guangdong 廣東	167	166	28,429	3,650	8.24	14.99	170.80	45.04	44,315
Guangxi 廣西	99	148	11,867	297	1.49	5.04	80.37	70.37	19,868
Hainan 海南	16	66	14,174	-1,818	-7.45	-26.21	214.35	71.58	24,412
Southwest 西南	204	259	14,220	1,928	7.78	17.98	54.87	56.71	24,769
Chongqing 重慶	22	550	20,374	970	2.31	7.64	37.04	69.79	42,016
Sichuan 四川	77	388	20,990	3,828	11.51	23.46	54.05	50.94	33,261
Guizhou 貴州	54	92	8,854	619	4.56	15.94	96.27	71.40	13,566
Yunnan 雲南	45	129	7,870	942	5.10	9.70	60.82	47.39	18,472
Tibet 西藏	6	23	682	160	17.98	21.97	29.85	18.16	890
Northwest 西北	198	96	5,331	46	0.46	1.67	55.28	72.66	10,062
Shaanxi 陝西	96	111	6,543	257	2.37	9.51	58.76	75.05	10,821
Gansu 甘肅	49	70	3,898	102	1.34	4.01	56.07	66.58	7,592
Qinghai 青海	3	77	1,750	-823	-12.39	-40.96	22.73	69.76	6,647
Ningxia 寧夏	12	98	2,807	-193	-3.93	-16.28	28.66	75.85	4,921
Xinjiang 新疆	38	95	5,196	-414	-3.13	-11.17	54.95	71.97	13,222

2730: Chinese Medicines 中藥材及中成藥加工業

Year 年份	Number of firms 企業個數	Rate of change 每年變化 (%)	Number of employees 職工人數 (人)	Rate of change 每年變化 (%)	Total revenue (mil. RMB) 總銷售收入 (百萬元)	Rate of change 每年變化 (%)	Total profit (mil. RMB) 總利潤 (百萬元)	Rate of change 每年變化 (%)
1993	1,545		311,649		20,216		2,131	
1994	1,682	8.87%	286,758	-7.99%	20,164	-0.26%	1,916	-10.13%
1995	1,975	17.42%	325,142	13.39%	20,898	3.64%	1,448	-24.40%
1996	2,000	1.27%	341,082	4.90%	26,231	25.52%	2,155	48.83%

3 Major products* 3種主要產品*	Output 產量	Sales volume 銷售量	Unit 單位
a) Powder Preparation to be Taken after being Mixed with Boiling Water, Wine, Etc. 沖劑	64,611	74,303	ton 噸
b) Peroral Fluid 口服液	60,055	58,253	ton 噸
c) Tablet 片劑	38,208	34,769	ton 噸

Top 10 firms by revenue (year founded) 收入排名前10家企業 (創辦年份)	City 城市	Province 省	Telephone / fax 電話 / 傳真	Number of employees 職工人數	Ownership 產業所有權	Revenue ('000 RMB) 銷售收入 (千元)	Profit ('000 RMB) (rank) 利潤 (千元) (排名)	Total assets ('000 RMB) 總資產 (千元)	Major products 主要產品
China Beijing Tong Ren Tang Group Co. 中國北京同仁堂集團公司(1955)	Beijing 北京市	Beijing 北京市	(010)67027281 (010)67012376	5,956	State-owned 國有	1,589,564	36799(15)	1,799,385	a,b,c
Shanghai Crude Drugs (Group) Co. 上海藥材(集團)公司(1955)	Shanghai 上海市	Shanghai 上海市	(021)63237578 (021)63230929	4,985	State-owned 國有	1,500,616	15319(37)	1,341,220	a,b,c
Shenzhen Nan Fang Pharmaceutical Factory 深圳南方製藥廠(1986)	Shenzhen 深圳市	Guangdong 廣東省	(0755)3360999 (0755)3350888	1,262	Foreign-funded 外資	1,416,525	210462(1)	2,417,288	a
Chinese Academy of Sciences Chengdu Di Ao Pharmaceutical Company 中科院成都地奧製藥公司(1989)	Chengdu 成都市	Sichuan 四川省	(028)5181354 (028)5181354	950	State-owned 國有	458,952	183653(2)	543,262	c
Tai Ji Industrial Group Co. Ltd. 太極實業集團股份有限公司	Chongqing 重慶市	Chongqing 重慶市	(023)2221516 (023)2221513	1,310	Joint stock 股份制	374,572	53573(12)	495,277	b
Bozhou Nanshi Weiwu Industrial General Co. 亳州市南市區魏武實業總公司(1993)	Fuyang 阜陽市	Anhui 安徽省	(0558)5522218	2,670	Collectively-owned 集體	361,000	61600(11)	167,790	o
China Tonghua Dong Bao Industrial Group Co. 中國通化東寶實業股份有限公司(1985)	Tonghua 通化市	Jilin 吉林省	(0435)5858018 (0435)5858055	816	Joint stock 股份制	287,223	166091(4)	725,882	b,c
Shenzhen Tai Tai Pharmacy Industry Co. Ltd. 深圳太太藥業有限公司(1992)	Shenzhen 深圳市	Guangdong 廣東省	(0755)3389948 (0755)3389949	700	Overseas Chinese-funded 港澳台資	282,672	114269(5)	250,144	o
Zheng Da Qing Chun Bao Pharmacy Industry Co. Ltd. 正大青春寶藥業有限公司(1992)	Hangzhou 杭州市	Zhejiang 浙江省	(0571)5121024 (0571)5152635	1,079	Foreign-funded 外資	275,066	65740(10)	297,600	a,b,c
Zhangzhou Pian Zi Huang Group Company 漳州片仔癀集團公司(1956)	Zhangzhou 漳州市	Fujian 福建省	(0596)2025448 (0596)2026435	553	State-owned 國有	272,328	169587(3)	471,584	a,c

Top 10 Cities by Production Output 產出排名前10位城市	Province 省	Market share 市場份額	Number of firms 企業個數
Beijing 北京市	Beijing 北京市	8.55%	58
Guangzhou 廣州市	Guangdong 廣東省	5.33%	26
Shenzhen 深圳市	Guangdong 廣東省	4.21%	14
Chengdu 成都市	Sichuan 四川省	3.74%	33
Nanchang 南昌市	Jiangxi 江西省	3.32%	19
Tonghua 通化市	Jilin 吉林省	3.29%	67
Chongqing 重慶市	Chongqing 重慶市	2.87%	27
Hangzhou 杭州市	Zhejiang 浙江省	2.81%	18
Shanghai 上海市	Shanghai 上海市	2.76%	69
Tianjin 天津市	Tianjin 天津市	2.54%	32

10 Major Wholesalers 10家主要批發商	City 城市	Province 省	Telephone / Fax 電話 / 傳真
Shanghai Medical Health Care Product Import & Export Company 上海市醫藥保健品進出口公司	Shanghai 上海市	Shanghai 上海市	(021)63290161
Shenzhen San Jiu Trade Company 深圳三九貿易公司	Shenzhen 深圳市	Guangdong 廣東省	(0755)3360999 (0755)3350988
Nanjing Pharmacy Industry Co. Ltd. 南京藥業股份有限公司	Nanjing 南京市	Jiangsu 江蘇省	(025)4522541 (025)4522541
Puning Medicine Company 普寧市醫藥公司	Jieyang 揭陽市	Guangdong 廣東省	(0663)2225633
Shandong Medical Health Care Product Import & Export Company 山東省醫藥保健品進出口公司	Qingdao 青島市	Shandong 山東省	(0532)2816868 (0532)2844748
Guangzhou Chinese-medicine Corporation 廣州市藥材公司	Guangzhou 廣州市	Guangdong 廣東省	(020)81888782 (020)81861355
Guangdong Crude Medicines Co. 廣東省藥材公司	Guangzhou 廣州市	Guangdong 廣東省	(020)81889725 (020)81861349
Tianjin Crude Medicines Group Co. Ltd. 天津藥材集團有限公司	Tianjin 天津市	Tianjin 天津市	(022)23312858 (022)23312858
Jiangsu Wuxi Crude Drugs Purchase Supply Station 江蘇省無錫藥材採購供應站	Wuxi 無錫市	Jiangsu 江蘇省	(0510)2709196 (0510)2709196
Hubei Medical Health Care Product Import & Export Company 湖北省醫藥保健品進出口公司	Wuhan 武漢市	Hubei 湖北省	(027)85791259 (027)85771260

*Also include sales by firms outside this industry.包括本行業以外廠家的銷售。"o" stands for "others". "o" 代表"其他產品"。

2740: Veterinary Medicines 動物藥品製造業

The industry accounts for 0.071% of the total revenue of China's industrial sector in 1996. The revenue growth rate of the industry is 1.0% from 1995, as compared to the growth rate of China's industrial sector, 9.51%. The rate of return on asset is 2.49%. 60.81% of all firms in the industry made a profit while 32.82% had negative returns. The top province in terms of the industry's revenue is Hubei, accounting for 18.82% of the total revenue.
本行業在1996年佔全行業總產值0.071%，行業年增長率為1.0%（全國工業年增長率9.51%）。行業的資產回報率2.49%，60.81%的企業盈利，32.82%的企業虧損。銷售收入最高的省份為湖北省，佔本行業的18.82%。

	Total number of firms 企業總數	Total number of employees 職工總數	Total revenue (mil. RMB) 總銷售收入（百萬元）	Total profit (mil. RMB) 總利潤（百萬元）	Return on assets 資產利潤率 (%)	Return on equity 權益利潤率 (%)	Labour productivity ('000 RMB / worker) 勞動生產率（千元／人）	Debts / assets 資產負債率 (%)	Total assets (mil. RMB) 總資產（百萬元）
Industry Overall 行業總體	669	51,597	4,093	112	2.49	7.56	79.33	67.07	4,493

	Number of firms 企業個數	Average number of employees 平均職工人數	Average revenue ('000 RMB) 平均銷售收入（千元）	Average profit ('000 RMB) 平均利潤（千元）	Return on assets 資產利潤率 (%)	Return on equity 權益利潤率 (%)	Labour productivity ('000 RMB / worker) 勞動生產率（千元／人）	Average debts / assets 平均資產負債率(%)	Average Total assets ('000 RMB) 平均總資產（千元）
By ownership 產業所有權									
State-owned 國有	200	100	5,455	45	0.52	1.61	54.72	67.52	8,620
Collectively-owned 集體	402	66	5,016	158	3.44	12.47	75.96	72.37	4,585
Privately-owned 私有	4	29	2,310	8	0.35	0.96	79.66	63.90	2,232
Domestic JVs 聯營	11	64	11,099	860	10.38	31.76	173.91	67.34	8,286
Joint stock 股份制	11	105	10,644	1,340	13.84	28.28	101.82	51.07	9,682
Foreign-funded 外資	23	84	16,135	6	0.02	0.06	192.88	59.90	22,762
Overseas Chinese-funded 港澳台資	17	81	21,466	895	7.81	13.19	264.44	40.78	11,465
By size 規模									
Large 大型	3	620	44,893	-5,010	-5.38	-14.97	72.45	64.04	93,068
Medium 中型	10	502	74,083	3,470	6.81	12.65	147.61	46.11	50,915
Small 小型	634	70	5,075	146	2.49	8.35	72.52	70.17	5,844
By regional distribution 地區分布									
Central-North 華北	91	55	2,921	59	1.20	3.04	52.88	60.50	4,931
Beijing 北京	19	43	3,721	15	0.34	0.61	87.38	44.28	4,318
Tianjin 天津	11	46	3,298	-55	-1.04	-5.97	71.84	82.52	5,226
Hebei 河北	32	71	3,314	161	2.16	5.09	46.88	57.56	7,446
Shanxi 山西	13	41	2,254	92	4.85	17.00	54.87	71.53	1,888
Inner Mongolia 內蒙	16	57	1,466	-40	-1.38	-4.79	25.61	71.18	2,899
Northeast 東北	51	97	3,313	-165	-2.38	-9.29	34.29	74.34	6,929
Liaoning 遼寧	16	101	2,298	-433	-9.71	-113.42	22.71	91.44	4,459
Jilin 吉林	17	71	2,963	251	4.51	18.30	41.46	75.35	5,567
Heilongjiang 黑龍江	18	116	4,547	-320	-3.07	-9.41	39.09	67.33	10,411
Central East 華東	230	90	8,241	310	3.26	9.32	91.61	65.02	9,517
Shanghai 上海	15	123	25,766	1,366	5.67	14.78	210.05	61.61	24,083
Jiangsu 江蘇	61	108	6,456	54	0.71	2.49	59.67	71.58	7,659
Zhejiang 浙江	32	70	4,655	-28	-0.38	-1.07	66.09	64.90	7,414
Anhui 安徽	24	85	8,941	664	12.27	41.14	104.93	70.17	5,408
Fujian 福建	18	59	5,997	-64	-0.61	-1.77	101.36	65.53	10,483
Jiangxi 江西	22	56	1,468	-111	-3.74	-86.52	26.10	95.67	2,968
Shandong 山東	58	97	10,538	623	4.88	11.87	108.24	58.85	12,751
Central-South 中南	195	69	7,647	227	4.20	12.57	111.58	66.59	5,401
Henan 河南	50	69	3,522	131	3.52	15.65	51.08	77.52	3,734
Hubei 湖北	22	96	35,023	1,071	13.57	42.57	365.69	68.13	7,896
Hunan 湖南	30	76	2,565	-194	-4.38	-20.66	33.71	78.82	4,434
Guangdong 廣東	42	47	4,470	128	2.23	7.31	95.64	69.53	5,749
Guangxi 廣西	49	72	5,708	296	4.58	9.54	79.10	51.99	6,472
Hainan 海南	2	14	120				8.57	53.78	595
Southwest 西南	79	64	2,294	-28	-0.73	-3.70	35.70	80.12	3,825
Chongqing 重慶	15	64	1,804	-16	-0.44	-9.59	28.08	95.46	3,672
Sichuan 四川	50	65	2,695	9	0.21	0.92	41.32	76.83	4,010
Guizhou 貴州	6	70	852	-180	-6.88	-308.57	12.14	97.77	2,617
Yunnan 雲南	8	55	1,746	-121	-3.15	-9.24	32.04	65.86	3,845
Tibet 西藏									
Northwest 西北	23	109	3,916	64	1.01	4.34	35.81	76.70	6,373
Shaanxi 陝西	14	88	3,849	46	1.00	7.32	43.88	86.39	4,589
Gansu 甘肅	4	297	7,968	263	1.44	4.50	26.87	67.89	18,173
Qinghai 青海									
Ningxia 寧夏	1	40	450	-20	-0.78	-1.01	11.25	22.66	2,560
Xinjiang 新疆	4	15	965	-48	-2.68	-211.11	63.28	98.73	1,773

2740: Veterinary Medicines 動物藥品製造業

Year 年份	Number of firms 企業個數	Rate of change 每年變化 (%)	Number of employees 職工人數 (人)	Rate of change 每年變化 (%)	Total revenue (mil. RMB) 總銷售收入 (百萬元)	Rate of change 每年變化 (%)	Total profit (mil. RMB) 總利潤 (百萬元)	Rate of change 每年變化 (%)
1993	486		41,618		2,105		67	
1994	521	7.20%	45,341	8.95%	2,281	8.37%	60	-10.40%
1995	669	28.41%	59,016	30.16%	4,051	77.53%	136	125.11%
1996	669		51,597	-12.57%	4,093	1.04%	112	-17.69%

3 Major products* 3 種主要產品 *	Output 產量	Sales volume 銷售量	Unit 單位
a) Animal Medicine 畜用製劑藥品	1,180,681	1,062,613	1,000 yuan 千元
b) Antimicrobial Chemical Raw Material Medicine for Animal 畜用抗微生物化學原料藥	32,560	31,257	ton 噸
c) Feedstuff Additive 飼料添加劑	906	888	ton 噸

Top 10 firms by revenue (year founded) 收入排名前 10 家企業 (創辦年份)	City 城市	Province 省	Telephone / fax 電話 / 傳真	Number of employees 職工人數	Ownership 產業所有權	Revenue ('000 RMB) 銷售收入 (千元)	Profit ('000 RMB) (rank) 利潤 (千元) (排名)	Total assets ('000 RMB) 總資產 (千元)	Major products 主要產品
Shanghai Tongren Pharmaceutical Co. Ltd. 上海同仁藥業有限公司(1946)	Shanghai 上海市	Shanghai 上海市	(021)62512430 (021)62512051	722	State-owned 國有	164,204	6613(5)	101,630	a,c
Beiliu Shentong Group Co. 北流市神通獸藥集團公司(1993)	Yulin 玉林市	Guangxi 廣西	(0775)90050444	1,088	Collectively-owned 集體	147,980	15010(1)	61,030	a
Ji Xing Medical Chemistry Group Co. Ltd. 濟興醫化集團有限責任公司(1971)	Jining 濟寧市	Shandong 山東省	(0537)2514249 (0537)2514249	827	Collectively-owned 集體	144,390	12058(2)	130,863	a
Shanghai Qi Ba – Jia Ji Poultry & Stock Health Care Co. Ltd. 上海汽巴—嘉基禽畜保健有限公司(1990)	Shanghai 上海市	Shanghai 上海市	(021)62196598 (021)62196617	257	Foreign-funded 外資	89,121	4078(9)	160,825	a
Shandong Shengwang Group Ltd. 山東聖旺集團總公司(1993)	Jining 濟寧市	Shandong 山東省	(0537)4415160 (0537)4413350	326	State-owned 國有	85,244	8008(3)	74,757	o
Shanghai Sunv3 Pharmacy Co. Bao Ling Pharmaceutical Factory 上海三維製藥公司寶靈製藥廠(1990)	Shanghai 上海市	Shanghai 上海市	(021)56043995 (021)56042763	191	Domestic JVs 聯營	74,812	2506(14)	40,448	o
Pucheng Biochemistry Co. Ltd. 浦城縣生化有限公司(1989)	Nangping 南平市	Fujian 福建省	(0599)2833324 (0599)2823294	512	Foreign-funded 外資	62,088	-1323(259)	126,546	o
Nanjing Medical Equipment Factory 南京藥械廠(1950)	Nanjing 南京市	Jiangsu 江蘇省	(025)2416171 (025)2414586	986	State-owned 國有	59,554	1418(27)	78,736	a
Jiangsu Animal's Medicine Factory 江蘇動物藥品廠(1972)	Yangzhou 揚州市	Jiangsu 江蘇省	(0514)8661136 (0514)8662140	977	Collectively-owned 集體	59,359	-3404(265)	76,075	a
Zhejiang Jinhua Pharmaceutical Factory 浙江金華製藥廠(1958)	Jinhua 金華市	Zhejiang 浙江省	(0579)2341767	996	State-owned 國有	56,650	-1060(258)	119,600	o

Top 10 Cities by Production Output 產出排名前 10 位城市	Province 省	Market share 市場份額	Number of firms 企業個數
Shanghai 上海市	Shanghai 上海市	11.56%	24
Jining 濟寧市	Shandong 山東省	6.30%	6
Yulin 玉林市	Guangxi 廣西	5.33%	21
Guangzhou 廣州市	Guangdong 廣東省	4.73%	19
Ji'nan 濟南市	Shandong 山東省	4.45%	17
Changzhou 常州市	Jiangsu 江蘇省	3.73%	15
Taizhou 泰州市	Jiangsu 江蘇省	3.43%	13
Nanning 南寧市	Guangxi 廣西	3.13%	8
Harbin 哈爾濱市	Heilongjiang 黑龍江省	2.09%	7
Hefei 合肥市	Anhui 安徽省	1.81%	8

10 Major Wholesalers 10 家主要批發商	City 城市	Province 省	Telephone / Fax 電話 / 傳真
Nanjing Medicine (Group) Company 南京醫藥(集團)公司	Nanjing 南京市	Jiangsu 江蘇省	(025)4404068 (025)4523033
Sichuan Medicine Company 四川省醫藥公司	Chengdu 成都市	Sichuan 四川省	(028)7763010 (028)7763010
Guangzhou Medicine Co. 廣州市醫藥公司	Guangzhou 廣州市	Guangdong 廣東省	(020)81811491 (020)81811492
Hangzhou Medicine Station Co. Ltd. 杭州醫藥站股份有限公司	Hangzhou 杭州市	Zhejiang 浙江省	(0571)5159638 (0571)5178578
Zhejiang Medical Health Care Product Import & Export Company 浙江省醫藥保健品進出口公司	Hangzhou 杭州市	Zhejiang 浙江省	(0571)5100288 (0571)5100777
Singbo Medicine Co. Ltd. 寧波醫藥股份有限公司	Ningbo 寧波市	Zhejiang 浙江省	(0574)7267909 (0574)7265934
Jiangsu Medical Health Care Product Import & Export (Group) Company 江蘇省醫藥保健品進出口(集團)公司	Nanjing 南京市	Jiangsu 江蘇省	(025)3729500 (025)3721996
Chang Zhou Pharmaceutical Co. Ltd. 常州藥業股份有限公司	Changzhou 常州市	Jiangsu 江蘇省	(0519)6606394 (0519)6604810
Shenyang Medicine Group Company 瀋陽醫藥集團公司	Shenyang 瀋陽市	Liaoning 遼寧省	(024)23832115 (024)23834228
Shandong Weifang Medicine Group Co. Ltd. 山東濰坊醫藥集團股份有限公司	Weifang 濰坊市	Shandong 山東省	(0536)8324797 (0536)8324791

*Also include sales by firms outside this industry.包括本行業以外廠家的銷售。"o" stands for "others". "o" 代表 "其他產品" 。

2750: Biological Products 生物製造業

The industry accounts for 0.147% of the total revenue of China's industrial sector in 1996. The revenue growth rate of the industry is 105.7% from 1995, as compared to the growth rate of China's industrial sector, 9.51%. The rate of return on asset is 18.73%. 69.90% of all firms in the industry made a profit while 24.09% had negative returns. The top province in terms of the industry's revenue is Shandong, accounting for 44.81% of the total revenue.
本行業在1996年佔全行業總產值0.147%，行業年增長率為105.7%（全國工業年增長率9.51%）。行業的資產回報率18.73%，69.90%的企業盈利，24.09%的企業虧損。銷售收入最高的省份為山東省，佔本行業的44.81%。

	Total number of firms 企業總數	Total number of employees 職工總數	Total revenue (mil. RMB) 總銷售收入（百萬元）	Total profit (mil. RMB) 總利潤（百萬元）	Return on assets 資產利潤率 (%)	Return on equity 權益利潤率 (%)	Labour productivity ('000 RMB / worker) 勞動生產率（千元/人）	Debts / assets 資產負債率 (%)	Total assets (mil. RMB) 總資產（百萬元）
Industry Overall 行業總體	433	47,613	8,539	1,748	18.73	35.80	179.34	47.69	9,334

	Number of firms 企業個數	Average number of employees 平均職工人數	Average revenue ('000 RMB) 平均銷售收入（千元）	Average profit ('000 RMB) 平均利潤（千元）	Return on assets 資產利潤率 (%)	Return on equity 權益利潤率 (%)	Labour productivity ('000 RMB / worker) 勞動生產率（千元/人）	Average debts / assets 平均資產負債率(%)	Average Total assets ('000 RMB) 平均總資產（千元）
By ownership 產業所有權									
State-owned 國有	130	197	15,500	1,023	3.20	5.87	78.83	45.49	31,962
Collectively-owned 集體	143	54	8,416	619	10.45	23.33	156.08	55.21	5,921
Privately-owned 私有	1	4,828	2,773,281	1,109,568	86.97	170.63	574.42	49.03	1,275,765
Domestic JVs 聯營	22	57	7,413	867	7.70	15.32	129.02	49.77	11,271
Joint stock 股份制	22	77	13,038	6,310	36.81	63.20	168.83	41.75	17,142
Foreign-funded 外資	52	62	21,312	3,650	16.19	30.77	341.52	47.38	22,544
Overseas Chinese-funded 港澳台資	63	60	15,711	1,095	5.47	10.99	262.82	50.17	20,003
By size 規模									
Large 大型	9	1,235	219,339	43,060	13.85	23.61	177.55	41.33	310,869
Medium 中型	9	370	36,825	-704	-1.57	-3.84	99.50	59.00	44,719
Small 小型	381	85	16,363	3,585	22.27	44.39	192.79	49.84	16,102
By regional distribution 地區分布									
Central-North 華北	80	69	9,559	2,456	15.94	27.94	139.26	42.96	15,408
Beijing 北京	42	72	6,864	1,245	7.42	12.19	94.93	39.12	16,777
Tianjin 天津	21	28	16,934	6,090	38.72	62.21	606.86	37.76	15,726
Hebei 河北	7	116	3,347	123	1.31	5.55	28.78	76.36	9,361
Shanxi 山西	5	179	18,728	2,930	12.37	35.89	104.51	65.54	23,690
Inner Mongolia 內蒙	5	32	742	158	5.73	6.44	23.48	10.96	2,756
Northeast 東北	50	107	9,990	1,533	6.81	11.84	93.00	42.50	22,528
Liaoning 遼寧	27	60	9,662	1,614	8.84	16.76	159.95	47.21	18,249
Jilin 吉林	15	202	11,639	1,575	4.18	6.73	57.53	37.87	37,659
Heilongjiang 黑龍江	8	88	8,005	1,183	13.75	25.81	90.84	46.72	8,599
Central East 華東	166	121	31,721	7,666	34.73	65.29	262.60	46.81	22,075
Shanghai 上海	28	143	19,584	3,271	8.42	15.99	137.33	47.33	38,837
Jiangsu 江蘇	37	101	11,309	191	1.79	6.46	112.12	72.35	10,708
Zhejiang 浙江	25	63	7,210	1,614	11.19	18.00	115.26	37.85	14,425
Anhui 安徽	9	149	15,049	863	5.98	27.29	101.07	78.10	14,446
Fujian 福建	32	36	3,386	1,213	16.40	31.95	93.40	48.66	7,397
Jiangxi 江西	7	64	6,967	967	8.70	26.33	108.62	66.98	11,123
Shandong 山東	28	279	136,646	38,578	78.52	124.59	489.65	36.98	49,131
Central-South 中南	90	102	16,661	2,091	9.06	18.70	162.86	51.53	23,074
Henan 河南	25	99	5,104	24	0.32	0.97	51.79	66.84	7,368
Hubei 湖北	16	227	47,858	10,624	27.72	49.15	210.71	43.61	38,334
Hunan 湖南	5	95	4,962	30	0.12	0.16	52.34	25.03	25,460
Guangdong 廣東	34	65	16,616	513	1.62	3.96	254.26	58.98	31,588
Guangxi 廣西	9	44	1,818				41.63	17.82	7,920
Hainan 海南	1	20						23.04	6,510
Southwest 西南	29	134	11,956	445	1.79	4.01	89.52	55.27	24,811
Chongqing 重慶	6	18	1,927	-497	-8.32	-57.27	109.04	85.47	5,970
Sichuan 四川	16	172	19,387	1,178	3.00	6.30	112.70	52.41	39,300
Guizhou 貴州	6	80	475	-172	-8.60	-27.91	5.96	69.20	1,997
Yunnan 雲南	1	489	16,930	-2,430	-7.35	-28.83	34.62	74.52	33,050
Tibet 西藏									
Northwest 西北	18	201	9,048	62	0.22	0.44	45.00	50.46	28,568
Shaanxi 陝西	8	61	1,911	-601	-6.49	-13.33	31.53	51.28	9,258
Gansu 甘肅	3	737	41,050	3,917	3.23	5.67	55.70	42.99	121,173
Qinghai 青海	1	225	7,580	370	1.70	2.48	33.69	31.56	21,800
Ningxia 寧夏	2	65	2,180	-1,005	-12.09	773.08	33.80	101.56	8,310
Xinjiang 新疆	4	142	3,120	-1,048	-10.96	129.32	21.93	108.48	9,558

2750: Biological Products 生物製造業

Year 年份	Number of firms 企業個數	Rate of change 每年變化 (%)	Number of employees 職工人數 (人)	Rate of change 每年變化 (%)	Total revenue (mil. RMB) 總銷售收入 (百萬元)	Rate of change 每年變化 (%)	Total profit (mil. RMB) 總利潤 (百萬元)	Rate of change 每年變化 (%)
1993	269		43,291		2,209		376	
1994	300	11.52%	39,293	-9.24%	2,745	24.27%	366	-2.63%
1995	397	32.33%	45,806	16.58%	4,151	51.22%	664	81.60%
1996	433	9.07%	47,613	3.94%	8,539	105.71%	1,748	163.15%

3 Major products* 3種主要產品 *	Output 產量	Sales volume 銷售量	Unit 單位
a) Biological Products 生物製品	1,676,973	1,576,355	1,000 yuan 千元
b) Peroral Fluid 口服液	5,302	5,143	ton 噸
c) Chinese Patent Medicine 中成藥	5,153	4,895	ton 噸

Top 10 firms by revenue (year founded) 收入排名前10家企業 (創辦年份)	City 城市	Province 省	Telephone / fax 電話 / 傳真	Number of employees 職工人數	Ownership 產業所有權	Revenue ('000 RMB) 銷售收入 (千元)	Profit ('000 RMB) (rank) 利潤 (千元) (排名)	Total assets ('000 RMB) 總資產 (千元)	Major products 主要產品
Ji'nan San Zhu Co. Ltd. 濟南三株藥業有限公司(1993)	Ji'nan 濟南市	Shandong 山東省	(0531)8903029 (0531)8912747	5,811	Private-owned 私營	3,645,043	1093101(1)	1,006,245	o
Tianjin Shang He Health-care Articles Co. Ltd. 天津尚赫保健用品有限公司(1993)	Tianjin 天津市	Tianjin 天津市	(022)23124496 (022)23123488	87	Foreign-funded 外資	308,677	122858(2)	233,530	o
Shenzhen Jiu Kai Biological Products Factory 深圳九開生物製品廠(1992)	Shenzhen 深圳市	Guangdong 廣東省	(0755)3360999 (0755)2413999	380	State-owned 國有	302,480	13047(13)	172,788	b,c
Chengdu Institute of Biological Products, Ministry of Public Health 衛生部成都生物製品研究所(1958)	Chengdu 成都市	Sichuan 四川省	(028)4418882 (028)4419060	1,485	State-owned 國有	169,527	15607(8)	318,738	o
Shanghai Lai Shi Blood Products Co. Ltd. 上海萊士血製品有限公司(1992)	Shanghai 上海市	Shanghai 上海市	(021)64303911 (021)64301713	303	Foreign-funded 外資	158,867	43556(3)	229,759	a
Shanghai Institute of Biological Products, Ministry of Health 衛生部上海生物製品研究所(1949)	Shanghai 上海市	Shanghai 上海市	(021)62803189 (021)62801807	1,638	State-owned 國有	149,528	2862(40)	417,604	a
Sichuan Shu Yang Enterprise(group) Co. Ltd. 四川蜀陽企業集團有限公司(1985)	Chengdu 成都市	Sichuan 四川省	(028)6699140 (028)6699131	654	State-owned 國有	127,965	2085(46)	242,998	o
Wuhan Institute of Biological Products, Ministry of Public Health 衛生部武漢生物製品研究所(1950)	Wuhan 武漢市	Hubei 湖北省	(027)88845077 (027)88842261	1,505	State-owned 國有	125,030	15516(9)	259,011	a
Suzhou Kang Da Pharmaceutical Co. Ltd. 宿州市康達製藥有限公司(1994)	Suzhou 宿州市	Anhui 安徽省	(0557)2010741	781	State-owned 國有	120,640	13260(12)	106,046	o
Ministry of Public Health Lanzhou Institute of Biological Products 衛生部蘭州生物製品研究所(1934)	Lanzhou 蘭州市	Gansu 甘肅省	(0931)8888311 (0931)8417199	2,116	State-owned 國有	120,000	12000(14)	356,300	a

Top 10 Cities by Production Output 產出排名前10位城市	Province 省	Market share 市場份額	Number of firms 企業個數
Shanghai 上海市	Shanghai 上海市	18.37%	75
Tianjin 天津市	Tianjin 天津市	9.88%	25
Chengdu 成都市	Sichuan 四川省	7.12%	15
Beijing 北京市	Beijing 北京市	6.05%	32
Shenzhen 深圳市	Guangdong 廣東省	4.65%	18
Wuhan 武漢市	Hubei 湖北省	3.83%	9
Fuzhou 福州市	Fujian 福建省	3.48%	13
Changchun 長春市	Jilin 吉林省	3.34%	7
Hangzhou 杭州市	Zhejiang 浙江省	3.04%	16
Lanzhou 蘭州市	Gansu 甘肅省	2.64%	2

10 Major Wholesalers 10家主要批發商	City 城市	Province 省	Telephone / Fax 電話 / 傳真
Nanjing Medicine (Group) Company 南京醫藥(集團)公司	Nanjing 南京市	Jiangsu 江蘇省	(025)4404068 (025)4523033
Sichuan Medicine Company 四川省醫藥公司	Chengdu 成都市	Sichuan 四川省	(028)7763010 (028)7763010
Guangzhou Medicine Co. 廣州市醫藥公司	Guangzhou 廣州市	Guangdong 廣東省	(020)81811491 (020)81811492
Hangzhou Medicine Station Co. Ltd. 杭州醫藥站股份有限公司	Hangzhou 杭州市	Zhejiang 浙江省	(0571)5159638 (0571)5178578
Zhejiang Medical Health Care Product Import & Export Company 浙江省醫藥保健品進出口公司	Hangzhou 杭州市	Zhejiang 浙江省	(0571)5100288 (0571)5100777
Singbo Medicine Co. Ltd. 寧波醫藥股份有限公司	Ningbo 寧波市	Zhejiang 浙江省	(0574)7267909 (0574)7265934
Jiangsu Medical Health Care Product Import & Export (Group) Company 江蘇省醫藥保健品進出口(集團)公司	Nanjing 南京市	Jiangsu 江蘇省	(025)3729500 (025)3721996
Chang Zhou Pharmaceutical Co. Ltd. 常州藥業股份有限公司	Changzhou 常州市	Jiangsu 江蘇省	(0519)6606394 (0519)6604810
Shenyang Medicine Group Company 瀋陽醫藥集團公司	Shenyang 瀋陽市	Liaoning 遼寧省	(024)23832115 (024)23834228
Shandong Weifang Medicine Group Co. Ltd. 山東濰坊醫藥集團股份有限公司	Weifang 濰坊市	Shandong 山東省	(0536)8324797 (0536)8324791

*Also include sales by firms outside this industry.包括本行業以外廠家的銷售。"o" stands for "others". "o" 代表 "其他產品"。

2811: Synthetic Fibre Pulp 化纖漿粕製造業

The industry accounts for 0.027% of the total revenue of China's industrial sector in 1996. The revenue growth rate of the industry is -18.2% from 1995, as compared to the growth rate of China's industrial sector, 9.51%. The rate of return on asset is -2.19%. 67.70% of all firms in the industry made a profit while 26.42% had negative returns. The top province in terms of the industry's revenue is Jilin, accounting for 23.28% of the total revenue.
本行業在1996年佔全行業總產值0.027%，行業年增長率為-18.2%（全國工業年增長率9.51%）。行業的資產回報率-2.19%，67.70%的企業盈利，26.42%的企業虧損。銷售收入最高的省份為吉林省，佔本行業的23.28%。

	Total number of firms 企業總數	Total number of employees 職工總數	Total revenue (mil. RMB) 總銷售收入（百萬元）	Total profit (mil. RMB) 總利潤（百萬元）	Return on assets 資產利潤率 (%)	Return on equity 權益利潤率 (%)	Labour productivity ('000 RMB / worker) 勞動生產率（千元/人）	Debts / assets 資產負債率 (%)	Total assets (mil. RMB) 總資產（百萬元）
Industry Overall 行業總體	59	19,886	1,571	-61	-2.19	-12.00	79.00	81.73	2,766

	Number of firms 企業個數	Average number of employees 平均職工人數	Average revenue ('000 RMB) 平均銷售收入（千元）	Average profit ('000 RMB) 平均利潤（千元）	Return on assets 資產利潤率 (%)	Return on equity 權益利潤率 (%)	Labour productivity ('000 RMB / worker) 勞動生產率（千元/人）	Average debts / assets 平均資產負債率(%)	Average Total assets ('000 RMB) 平均總資產（千元）
By ownership 產業所有權									
State-owned 國有	18	860	66,667	-2,000	-1.63	-9.94	77.49	83.58	122,500
Collectively-owned 集體	34	113	10,363	-537	-3.68	-19.22	92.02	80.85	14,594
Privately-owned 私有									
Domestic JVs 聯營	1	40	1,270	-910	-68.46	-133.55	31.76	48.74	1,329
Joint stock 股份制									
Foreign-funded 外資	3	139	4,777	-4,702	-32.97	-36.55	34.29	9.79	14,260
Overseas Chinese-funded 港澳台資	3	35	1,135	2,780	38.63	94.85	32.42	59.28	7,197
By size 規模									
Large 大型	6	1,644	142,630	-9,113	-3.96	-14.42	86.74	72.54	230,127
Medium 中型	9	454	34,478	266	0.31	4.09	75.89	92.49	86,570
Small 小型	43	137	9,424	-203	-1.44	-12.93	68.61	88.89	14,110
By regional distribution 地區分布									
Central-North 華北	9	223	15,600	303	0.72	2.40	69.92	70.07	42,272
Beijing 北京	4	24	573	-318	-14.87	-423.33	24.36	96.49	2,135
Tianjin 天津	1	200	16,670	2,450	6.08	7.03	83.35	13.54	40,320
Hebei 河北	4	429	30,360	388	0.47	1.97	70.85	76.27	82,898
Shanxi 山西									
Inner Mongolia 內蒙									
Northeast 東北	6	1,166	61,435	-6,975	-4.67	-23.22	52.67	79.87	149,265
Liaoning 遼寧	5	28	568	40	1.74	13.99	20.00	87.50	2,304
Jilin 吉林	1	6,856	365,770	-42,050	-4.76	-23.52	53.35	79.78	884,070
Heilongjiang 黑龍江									
Central East 華東	32	224	21,549	-562	-1.93	-12.05	96.20	83.98	29,093
Shanghai 上海	4	62	5,283	-500	-11.53	-23.26	85.55	50.46	4,335
Jiangsu 江蘇	14	234	21,321	-1,246	-4.07	-35.43	91.12	88.50	30,571
Zhejiang 浙江	5	119	7,952	-1,244	-11.94	-1054.24	67.05	98.87	10,420
Anhui 安徽	2	582	48,550	-2,725	-2.69	-25.25	83.49	89.35	101,245
Fujian 福建	1								
Jiangxi 江西									
Shandong 山東	6	315	38,845	2,190	5.69	18.99	123.38	70.05	38,507
Central-South 中南	10	332	34,125	-518	-1.07	-11.11	102.76	90.40	48,603
Henan 河南	6	531	47,083	-1,063	-1.48	-20.38	88.64	92.73	71,763
Hubei 湖北									
Hunan 湖南									
Guangdong 廣東	3	34	18,910	393	2.21	7.81	556.18	71.70	17,810
Guangxi 廣西	1	32	2,020	20	0.99	9.52	63.13	89.60	2,020
Hainan 海南									
Southwest 西南									
Chongqing 重慶									
Sichuan 四川									
Guizhou 貴州									
Yunnan 雲南									
Tibet 西藏									
Northwest 西北	2	196	15,825	820	2.26	10.73	80.95	78.93	36,255
Shaanxi 陝西									
Gansu 甘肅	1	61	2,320	150	2.38	6.67	38.03	64.23	6,290
Qinghai 青海									
Ningxia 寧夏									
Xinjiang 新疆	1	330	29,330	1,490	2.25	11.44	88.88	80.32	66,220

2811: Synthetic Fibre Pulp 化纖漿粕製造業

Year 年份	Number of firms 企業個數	Rate of change 每年變化 (%)	Number of employees 職工人數 (人)	Rate of change 每年變化 (%)	Total revenue (mil. RMB) 總銷售收入 (百萬元)	Rate of change 每年變化 (%)	Total profit (mil. RMB) 總利潤 (百萬元)	Rate of change 每年變化 (%)
1993	40		18,537		896		12	
1994	41	2.50%	18,370	-0.90%	1,305	45.72%	12	-1.77%
1995	41		19,778	7.66%	1,920	47.14%	31	151.16%
1996	59	43.90%	19,886	0.55%	1,571	-18.18%	-61	-298.72%

3 Major products* 3 種主要產品 *	Output 產量	Sales volume 銷售量	Unit 單位
a) Wood Pulp 木漿粕	29,643	25,789	ton 噸
b) Other Pulp 其他漿粕	4,767	3,719	ton 噸
c) Pulp for Cotton Velvet 棉絨漿粕	132,833	134,162	ton 噸

Top 10 firms by revenue (year founded) 收入排名前 10 家企業 (創辦年份)	City 城市	Province 省	Telephone / fax 電話 / 傳真	Number of employees 職工人數	Ownership 產業所有權	Revenue ('000 RMB) 銷售收入 (千元)	Profit ('000 RMB) (rank) 利潤 (千元) (排名)	Total assets ('000 RMB) 總資產 (千元)	Major products 主要產品
Kaishan Chemical Fibre Mill 開山屯化學纖維漿廠(1938)	Yanji 延吉市	Jilin 吉林省	(0433)3402876 (0433)3405454	6,881	State-owned 國有	365,770	-42050(34)	884,070	a
Shandong Gaomi Chemical Fibre General Factory 山東高密化學纖維總廠(1972)	Weifang 濰坊市	Shandong 山東省	(0536)2323121 (0536)2323187	1,362	State-owned 國有	216,253	13077(1)	165,070	c
Dafeng Chemical Fibre Mill 大豐化學纖維廠(1992)	Yancheng 鹽城市	Jiangsu 江蘇省	(0515)3514801 (0515)3514810	772	State-owned 國有	84,410	-970(27)	169,220	c
Dantu Jianmin Chemical Fibre Co. Ltd. 丹徒縣化纖廠(1980)	Zhenjiang 鎮江市	Jiangsu 江蘇省	(0511)3301450	801	Collectively-owned 集體	73,640	-13300(33)	62,432	c
Hebei Ji Gao Joint Chemical Fibre Thick Liquid Mill 河北吉藁聯合化纖漿廠(1989)	Shijiazhuang 石家莊市	Hebei 河北省	(0311)8043142 (0311)8048224	1,231	State-owned 國有	71,978	9538(2)	198,338	b,c
Anhui Suzhou Chemical Fibre Mill 安徽省宿州化纖廠(1991)	Suzhou 宿州市	Anhui 安徽省	(0557)3032736 (0557)3032457	723	State-owned 國有	70,610	11(18)	119,576	c
Sanshui Union Chemical Industrial Co. Ltd. 三水市聯邦化工實業有限公司(1989)	Foshan 佛山市	Guangdong 廣東省	(0757)7518788	43	Overseas Chinese-funded 港澳台資	48,384	854(7)	49,344	o
Jia Yi (Lianyungang) Glue Co. Ltd. 甲乙(連雲港)粘膠有限公司(1995)	Lianyungang 連雲港市	Jiangsu 江蘇省	(0518)5150851 (0518)5150014	482	Foreign-funded 外資	40,241	-4419(29)	104,592	o
Di Fang State-owned Shangyu Chemical Fibre Factory 地方國營上虞化纖廠(1970)	Shaoxing 紹興市	Zhejiang 浙江省	(0575)2012636 (0575)2012636	498	State-owned 國有	37,060	-5803(31)	46,868	c
Tongzhou Nan Sai Cellulose Factory 通州市南賽纖維素廠(1994)	Nantong 南通市	Jiangsu 江蘇省	(0513)2521306 (0513)2521305	239	Collectively-owned 集體	35,090	1290(5)	19,770	o

Top 10 Cities by Production Output 產出排名前 10 位城市	Province 省	Market share 市場份額	Number of firms 企業個數
Yanji 延吉市	Jilin 吉林省	21.20%	1
Weifang 濰坊市	Shandong 山東省	17.28%	2
Sanmenxia 三門峽市	Henan 河南省	13.33%	2
Yancheng 鹽城市	Jiangsu 江蘇省	6.19%	3
Zhenjiang 鎮江市	Jiangsu 江蘇省	5.95%	1
Suzhou 蘇州市	Jiangsu 江蘇省	5.34%	3
Shanghai 上海市	Shanghai 上海市	4.18%	8
Suzhou 宿州市	Anhui 安徽省	3.95%	1
Shijiazhuang 石家莊市	Hebei 河北省	3.65%	1
Nanyang 南陽市	Henan 河南省	2.64%	1

10 Major Wholesalers 10 家主要批發商	City 城市	Province 省	Telephone / Fax 電話 / 傳真
Anhui Clothing Import & Export Company 安徽省服裝進出口公司	Hefei 合肥市	Anhui 安徽省	(0551)3632212 (0551)3632002
Qingdao Textile Clothing Industrial Group Company 青島紡織服裝實業集團公司	Qingdao 青島市	Shandong 山東省	(0532)2877853 (0532)2869315
Hebei Textile Import & Export (Group) Company 河北省紡織品進出口(集團)公司	Shijiazhuang 石家莊市	Hebei 河北省	(0311)7028530 (0311)7027781
Zhong Fang Pledget Import & Export Company 中紡紗布進出口公司	Beijing 北京市	Beijing 北京市	(010)65124718 (010)65124713
Shaoxing Import & Export Company 紹興市進出口公司	Shaoxing 紹興市	Zhejiang 浙江省	(0575)5132822 (0575)5141577
Hunan Hua Xiang Import & Export (Group) Company 湖南省華湘進出口(集團)公司	Changsha 長沙市	Hunan 湖南省	(0731)2282440 (0731)2286995
City's Import & Export Company Trade Dept. 市進出口公司貿易部	Yichang 宜昌市	Hubei 湖北省	(0717)6450778 (0717)6441875
Shanghai Pu Dong Xinqu Import & Export Company 上海浦東新區進出口公司	Shanghai 上海市	Shanghai 上海市	(021)58878801 (021)58827444
Ningbo Yinxian Import & Export Company 寧波市鄞縣進出口公司	Ningbo 寧波市	Zhejiang 浙江省	(0574)7875205 (0574)7873168
Zhejiang Silk Import & Export Company 浙江省絲綢進出口公司	Hangzhou 杭州市	Zhejiang 浙江省	(0571)5195588 (0571)5192542

*Also include sales by firms outside this industry.包括本行業以外廠家的銷售。"o" stands for "others". "o"代表"其他產品"。

2812: Rayon Fibre 粘膠纖維製造業

The industry accounts for 0.131% of the total revenue of China's industrial sector in 1996. The revenue growth rate of the industry is -14.6% from 1995, as compared to the growth rate of China's industrial sector, 9.51%. The rate of return on asset is -0.39%. 67.69% of all firms in the industry made a profit while 25.37% had negative returns. The top province in terms of the industry's revenue is Zhejiang, accounting for 15.22% of the total revenue.
本行業在1996年佔全行業總產值0.131%，行業年增長率為-14.6%（全國工業年增長率9.51%）。行業的資產回報率-0.39%，67.69%的企業盈利，25.37%的企業虧損。銷售收入最高的省份為浙江省，佔本行業的15.22%。

	Total number of firms 企業總數	Total number of employees 職工總數	Total revenue (mil. RMB) 總銷售收入（百萬元）	Total profit (mil. RMB) 總利潤（百萬元）	Return on assets 資產利潤率 (%)	Return on equity 權益利潤率 (%)	Labour productivity ('000 RMB / worker) 勞動生產率（千元/人）	Debts / assets 資產負債率 (%)	Total assets (mil. RMB) 總資產（百萬元）
Industry Overall 行業總體	131	96,987	7,593	-53	-0.39	-1.18	78.29	67.29	13,729

	Number of firms 企業個數	Average number of employees 平均職工人數	Average revenue ('000 RMB) 平均銷售收入（千元）	Average profit ('000 RMB) 平均利潤（千元）	Return on assets 資產利潤率 (%)	Return on equity 權益利潤率 (%)	Labour productivity ('000 RMB / worker) 勞動生產率（千元/人）	Average debts / assets 平均資產負債率(%)	Average Total assets ('000 RMB) 平均總資產（千元）
By ownership 產業所有權									
State-owned 國有	25	2,827	185,320	-6,920	-1.72	-5.83	65.56	70.52	402,760
Collectively-owned 集體	64	82	9,459	54	0.59	3.74	115.83	84.13	9,062
Privately-owned 私有	1	36	5,888	-85	-2.13	-5.28	163.55	59.56	3,982
Domestic JVs 聯營									
Joint stock 股份制	5	2,557	274,335	16,003	4.68	10.01	107.28	53.20	341,630
Foreign-funded 外資	6	227	46,059	984	1.73	5.16	203.35	66.40	56,809
Overseas Chinese-funded 港澳台資	30	233	23,367	1,024	2.99	5.96	100.46	49.82	34,240
By size 規模									
Large 大型	13	5,284	389,025	-3,793	-0.51	-1.50	73.62	65.92	743,290
Medium 中型	16	1,320	118,197	-102	-0.05	-0.18	89.56	70.72	193,488
Small 小型	98	73	6,579	-21	-0.21	-0.71	89.88	69.94	9,904
By regional distribution 地區分布									
Central-North 華北	17	886	49,594	851	0.64	1.63	55.97	60.55	132,592
Beijing 北京	5	27	1,334	-72	-2.24	-25.00	49.78	91.03	3,212
Tianjin 天津	3	485	35,450	-2,210	-11.54	-25.43	73.04	54.64	19,157
Hebei 河北	6	1,379	88,567	8,887	3.47	7.30	64.22	52.41	255,965
Shanxi 山西	2	1,467	65,650	100	0.06	0.20	44.75	69.89	166,380
Inner Mongolia 內蒙	1	2,265	67,380	-32,070	-10.28	-104.43	29.75	90.16	311,990
Northeast 東北	8	1,090	102,163	8,251	5.11	11.08	93.72	53.86	161,445
Liaoning 遼寧	5	17	312	14	4.76	10.14	18.14	53.06	294
Jilin 吉林	1	6,791	733,470	85,940	8.21	15.69	108.01	47.67	1,046,570
Heilongjiang 黑龍江	2	922	41,135	-10,000	-8.21	-42.01	44.61	80.45	121,760
Central East 華東	49	825	76,883	-2,039	-1.66	-6.04	93.19	72.58	123,048
Shanghai 上海	5	165	12,236	-3,312	-16.04	-53.82	74.34	70.20	20,650
Jiangsu 江蘇	10	550	88,265	3,555	4.33	11.77	160.37	63.22	82,152
Zhejiang 浙江	17	519	67,975	693	0.81	2.17	130.97	62.77	85,837
Anhui 安徽	1	11	1,200	10	2.27	3.13	109.09	27.27	440
Fujian 福建	6	474	32,120	1,043	3.37	7.49	67.72	54.97	30,938
Jiangxi 江西	3	3,419	168,787	-18,327	-3.61	-19.13	49.37	81.12	507,240
Shandong 山東	7	1,738	138,224	-11,711	-4.23	-20.21	79.54	79.06	276,796
Central-South 中南	48	567	37,683	-492	-0.71	-1.90	66.42	62.97	69,763
Henan 河南	16	570	42,020	1,473	2.25	4.07	73.75	44.83	65,571
Hubei 湖北	6	2,161	127,068	-1,593	-0.67	-2.02	58.80	66.93	239,012
Hunan 湖南	7	384	18,713	14	0.04	0.13	48.75	70.22	37,886
Guangdong 廣東	17	139	14,199	-2,215	-6.37	-35.33	101.85	81.96	34,761
Guangxi 廣西	2	47	825	-30	-0.65	-4.55	17.74	85.88	4,640
Hainan 海南									
Southwest 西南	6	879	57,878	-587	-0.46	-2.98	65.88	84.39	126,183
Chongqing 重慶									
Sichuan 四川	4	1,053	71,173	38	0.02	0.18	67.59	87.18	168,403
Guizhou 貴州									
Yunnan 雲南	2	531	31,290	-1,835	-4.40	-11.54	58.98	61.90	41,745
Tibet 西藏									
Northwest 西北	3	90	3,157	-2,170	-13.45	125.92	34.94	110.66	16,133
Shaanxi 陝西	1	250	9,180	-6,510	-13.64	122.14	36.72	111.17	47,720
Gansu 甘肅	2	11	145				13.81	75.00	340
Qinghai 青海									
Ningxia 寧夏									
Xinjiang 新疆									

2812: Rayon Fibre 粘膠纖維製造業

Year 年份	Number of firms 企業個數	Rate of change 每年變化 (%)	Number of employees 職工人數（人）	Rate of change 每年變化 (%)	Total revenue (mil. RMB) 總銷售收入（百萬元）	Rate of change 每年變化 (%)	Total profit (mil. RMB) 總利潤（百萬元）	Rate of change 每年變化 (%)
1993	116		73,299		4,796		373	
1994	149	28.45%	79,699	8.73%	6,100	27.19%	380	1.71%
1995	120	-19.46%	92,185	15.67%	8,888	45.69%	533	40.37%
1996	131	9.17%	96,987	5.21%	7,593	-14.57%	-53	-109.94%

3 Major products* 3 種主要產品 *	Output 產量	Sales volume 銷售量	Unit 單位
a) Viscose Fibre 粘膠纖維	278,216	250,394	ton 噸
b) Pulp for Cotton Velvet 棉絨漿粕	154,366	155,910	ton 噸
c) Polymide Fibre 錦綸纖維	4,759	4,521	ton 噸

Top 10 firms by revenue (year founded) 收入排名前 10 家企業 (創辦年份)	City 城市	Province 省	Telephone / fax 電話 / 傳真	Number of employees 職工人數	Ownership 產業所有權	Revenue ('000 RMB) 銷售收入（千元）	Profit ('000 RMB) (rank) 利潤（千元）（排名）	Total assets ('000 RMB) 總資產（千元）	Major products 主要產品
Weifang Chemical Fibre Factory 濰坊化學纖維廠(1986)	Weifang 濰坊市	Shandong 山東省	(0536)7251481 (0536)7251388	11,282	State-owned 國有	874,082	-82172(72)	1,793,421	o
Baoding Swan Chemical Fibre Group Co. Ltd 保定天鵝化纖集團有限公司(1957)	Baoding 保定市	Hebei 河北省	(0312)3136736 (0312)3137013	8,158	State-owned 國有	521,203	52828(1)	1,525,188	a
Hangzhou Bp Chemical Fibre Co. Ltd. 杭州蘭孔雀化學纖維(股份)有限公司(1993)	Hangzhou 杭州市	Zhejiang 浙江省	(0571)8093188 (0571)8095538	4,468	Overseas Chinese-funded 港澳台資	416,399	2143(12)	621,731	a,b,c
Hubei Chemical Fibre Group Co. Ltd 湖北化纖集團有限公司(1972)	Xiangfan 襄樊市	Hubei 湖北省	(0710)3225390 (0710)3225398	6,150	State-owned 國有	393,569	-13911(66)	1,018,224	a,b
Yuyao Chemical Fibre (Group) Corp., Zhejiang 余姚化纖集團公司(1963)	Ningbo 寧波市	Zhejiang 浙江省	(0574)2633092 (0574)2635172	2,088	State-owned 國有	372,952	3760(8)	440,731	a,b
Yicheng Da Yan Industrial Co. 宜城大雁工業公司(1966)	Xiangfan 襄樊市	Hubei 湖北省	(0710)4393570 (0710)4393630	3,600	State-owned 國有	311,810	19764(3)	300,359	a,b
Zhangjiagang Jin Hua Group No.1 Factory 張家港市錦花集團一廠(1951)	Suzhou 蘇州市	Jiangsu 江蘇省	(0512)8550592 (0512)8550217	1,074	Overseas Chinese-funded 港澳台資	310,323	1962(14)	144,539	a,b
Jiujiang Chemical Fibre Mill 九江化學纖維廠(1962)	Jiujiang 九江市	Jiangxi 江西省	(0792)8234601 (0792)8234629	5,081	State-owned 國有	299,732	-58684(71)	1,228,297	a,b
Nanjing Chemical Fibre Co. Ltd. 南京化纖股份有限公司(1964)	Nanjing 南京市	Jiangsu 江蘇省	(025)5561011 (025)5562252	3,040	Joint stock 股份制	283,894	27561(2)	412,339	a,b
Jiangxi Chemical Fibre Factory 江西化學纖維廠(1942)	Nanchang 南昌市	Jiangxi 江西省	(0791)8626996 (0791)8624005	5,188	State-owned 國有	206,630	3700(9)	293,424	a

Top 10 Cities by Production Output 產出排名前 10 位城市	Province 省	Market share 市場份額	Number of firms 企業個數
Jilin 吉林市	Jilin 吉林省	10.76%	2
Xiangfan 襄樊市	Hubei 湖北省	10.51%	4
Hangzhou 杭州市	Zhejiang 浙江省	8.54%	8
Baoding 保定市	Hebei 河北省	7.76%	3
Xinxiang 新鄉市	Henan 河南省	6.99%	4
Nanjing 南京市	Jiangsu 江蘇省	5.55%	2
Weifang 濰坊市	Shandong 山東省	5.44%	2
Shanghai 上海市	Shanghai 上海市	4.93%	16
Jiujiang 九江市	Jiangxi 江西省	4.25%	2
Ningbo 寧波市	Zhejiang 浙江省	3.62%	1

10 Major Wholesalers 10 家主要批發商	City 城市	Province 省	Telephone / Fax 電話 / 傳真
Anhui Clothing Import & Export Company 安徽省服裝進出口公司	Hefei 合肥市	Anhui 安徽省	(0551)3632212 (0551)3632002
Qingdao Textile Clothing Industrial Group Company 青島紡織服裝實業集團公司	Qingdao 青島市	Shandong 山東省	(0532)2877853 (0532)2869315
Hebei Textile Import & Export (Group) Company 河北省紡織品進出口(集團)公司	Shijiazhuang 石家莊市	Hebei 河北省	(0311)7028530 (0311)7027781
Zhong Fang Pledget Import & Export Company 中紡紗布進出口公司	Beijing 北京市	Beijing 北京市	(010)65124718 (010)65124713
Shaoxing Import & Export Company 紹興市進出口公司	Shaoxing 紹興市	Zhejiang 浙江省	(0575)5132822 (0575)5141577
Hunan Hua Xiang Import & Export (Group) Company 湖南省華湘進出口(集團)公司	Changsha 長沙市	Hunan 湖南省	(0731)2282440 (0731)2286995
City's Import & Export Company Trade Dept. 市進出口公司貿易部	Yichang 宜昌市	Hubei 湖北省	(0717)6450778 (0717)6441875
Shanghai Pu Dong Xinqu Import & Export Company 上海浦東新區進出口公司	Shanghai 上海市	Shanghai 上海市	(021)58878801 (021)58827444
Ningbo Yinxian Import & Export Company 寧波市鄞縣進出口公司	Ningbo 寧波市	Zhejiang 浙江省	(0574)7875205 (0574)7873168
Zhejiang Silk Import & Export Company 浙江省絲綢進出口公司	Hangzhou 杭州市	Zhejiang 浙江省	(0571)5195588 (0571)5192542

*Also include sales by firms outside this industry.包括本行業以外廠家的銷售。"o" stands for "others". "o" 代表"其他產品"。

2819: Cellulose Fibre 其他纖維素纖維製造業

The industry accounts for 0.024% of the total revenue of China's industrial sector in 1996. The revenue growth rate of the industry is 75.1% from 1995, as compared to the growth rate of China's industrial sector, 9.51%. The rate of return on asset is 15.58%. 64.93% of all firms in the industry made a profit while 27.66% had negative returns. The top province in terms of the industry's revenue is Jiangsu, accounting for 64.20% of the total revenue.
本行業在1996年佔全行業總產值0.024%，行業年增長率為75.1%（全國工業年增長率9.51%）。行業的資產回報率15.58%，64.93%的企業盈利，27.66%的企業虧損。銷售收入最高的省份為江蘇省，佔本行業的64.20%。

	Total number of firms 企業總數	Total number of employees 職工總數	Total revenue (mil. RMB) 總銷售收入（百萬元）	Total profit (mil. RMB) 總利潤（百萬元）	Return on assets 資產利潤率 (%)	Return on equity 權益利潤率 (%)	Labour productivity ('000 RMB / worker) 勞動生產率（千元/人）	Debts / assets 資產負債率 (%)	Total assets (mil. RMB) 總資產（百萬元）
Industry Overall 行業總體	61	5,246	1,376	307	15.58	27.16	262.30	42.63	1,972

	Number of firms 企業個數	Average number of employees 平均職工人數	Average revenue ('000 RMB) 平均銷售收入（千元）	Average profit ('000 RMB) 平均利潤（千元）	Return on assets 資產利潤率 (%)	Return on equity 權益利潤率 (%)	Labour productivity ('000 RMB / worker) 勞動生產率（千元/人）	Average debts / assets 平均資產負債率(%)	Average Total assets ('000 RMB) 平均總資產（千元）
By ownership 產業所有權									
State-owned 國有	11	108	7,273	-636	-4.43	-35.00	67.17	87.34	14,364
Collectively-owned 集體	41	46	2,338	-72	-2.63	-7.66	50.31	65.68	2,759
Privately-owned 私有	1	44	3,245	228	9.23	10.39	73.75	11.17	2,468
Domestic JVs 聯營									
Joint stock 股份制									
Foreign-funded 外資	6	328	198,736	53,201	18.96	30.07	606.21	36.92	280,531
Overseas Chinese-funded 港澳台資	2	70	2,242	-1,233	-15.99	-29.27	32.03	45.37	7,713
By size 規模									
Large 大型	1	1,321	1,258,431	315,892	18.00	29.50	952.64	38.99	1,754,844
Medium 中型									
Small 小型	57	55	2,062	-156	-4.09	-14.72	37.77	72.20	3,813
By regional distribution 地區分布									
Central-North 華北	8	43	2,903	195	10.15	19.24	67.89	47.17	1,921
Beijing 北京	4	52	1,048	13	0.64	1.38	20.34	53.63	1,963
Tianjin 天津	1	28	1,560	300	19.23	27.78	55.71	30.77	1,560
Hebei 河北	3	36	5,823	403	20.30	35.59	161.76	42.95	1,987
Shanxi 山西									
Inner Mongolia 內蒙									
Northeast 東北	7	64	1,850	-903	-19.79	96.93	28.97	120.44	4,563
Liaoning 遼寧	4	65	2,043	-148	-6.67	-62.11	31.42	89.27	2,213
Jilin 吉林	1	40	10				0.25	98.16	1,630
Heilongjiang 黑龍江	2	74	2,385	-2,865	-26.70	76.30	32.45	135.00	10,730
Central East 華東	26	123	37,563	10,460	22.80	38.08	305.87	40.14	45,885
Shanghai 上海									
Jiangsu 江蘇	4	544	220,845	66,335	23.63	38.87	405.78	39.22	280,783
Zhejiang 浙江	4	49	2,970	63	1.78	6.94	60.30	74.43	3,520
Anhui 安徽	1	54	11,000	1,490	55.60	85.14	203.70	34.70	2,680
Fujian 福建	3	5	33				6.67	71.43	70
Jiangxi 江西	4	25	478	60	32.00	96.00	19.10	68.00	188
Shandong 山東	10	65	6,837	463	8.87	17.92	105.18	50.49	5,217
Central-South 中南	13	61	3,880	-134	-1.30	-16.62	63.29	92.19	10,318
Henan 河南	5	12	1,108	4	0.29	0.90	90.82	68.05	1,396
Hubei 湖北									
Hunan 湖南	5	49	1,476	-16	-0.63	-3.70	30.37	82.86	2,520
Guangdong 廣東	3	164	12,507	-560	-1.47	-27.63	76.11	94.69	38,183
Guangxi 廣西									
Hainan 海南									
Southwest 西南	6	76	52,038	6,983	7.01	10.34	686.22	32.18	99,568
Chongqing 重慶	3	16	227	3	4.48	-44.78	14.19	110.00	67
Sichuan 四川									
Guizhou 貴州	1								
Yunnan 雲南	2	204	155,775	20,945	7.01	10.34	763.60	32.15	298,605
Tibet 西藏									
Northwest 西北	1	12	640	-20	-3.17	-7.41	53.33	57.14	630
Shaanxi 陝西									
Gansu 甘肅									
Qinghai 青海									
Ningxia 寧夏									
Xinjiang 新疆	1	12	640	-20	-3.17	-7.41	53.33	57.14	630

2819: Cellulose Fibre 其他纖維素纖維製造業

Year 年份	Number of firms 企業個數	Rate of change 每年變化 (%)	Number of employees 職工人數 (人)	Rate of change 每年變化 (%)	Total revenue (mil. RMB) 總銷售收入 (百萬元)	Rate of change 每年變化 (%)	Total profit (mil. RMB) 總利潤 (百萬元)	Rate of change 每年變化 (%)
1993								
1994	17		2,113		39		4	
1995	48	182.35%	3,595	70.14%	786	1917.53%	157	4098.61%
1996	61	27.08%	5,246	45.92%	1,376	75.08%	307	95.98%

3 Major products* 3 種主要產品 *	Output 產量	Sales volume 銷售量	Unit 單位
a) Cellulose Resin 纖維素樹脂	792	705	ton 噸
b) Other Synthetic Fibre 其他合成纖維	22,274	21,383	ton 噸
c) Polypropylene Fibre 丙綸纖維	4,921	3,937	ton 噸

Top 10 firms by revenue (year founded) 收入排名前 10 家企業 (創辦年份)	City 城市	Province 省	Telephone / fax 電話 / 傳真	Number of employees 職工人數	Ownership 產業所有權	Revenue ('000 RMB) 銷售收入 (千元)	Profit ('000 RMB) (rank) 利潤（千元）(排名)	Total assets ('000 RMB) 總資產 (千元)	Major products 主要產品
Nantong Cellulose Fibres Co. Ltd. 南通醋酸纖維有限公司(1990)	Nantong 南通市	Jiangsu 江蘇省	(0513)3560512 (0513)3560794	985	Foreign-funded 外資	797,851	265152(1)	964,545	b
Kunming Acetic Acid Co. Ltd. 昆明醋酸有限公司(1995)	Kunming 昆明市	Yunnan 雲南省	(0871)5631028 (0871)5627158	389	Foreign-funded 外資	311,545	41894(2)	597,205	o
Xuzhou Chemical Fibre Factory 徐州化纖廠(1989)	Xuzhou 徐州市	Jiangsu 江蘇省	(0516)4623394 (0516)4621022	792	State-owned 國有	67,025	-677(25)	126,801	c
Zengcheng Yi Da Enterprise Group Co. Ltd 增城市一大企業集團有限公司(1986)	Guangzhou 廣州市	Guangdong 廣東省	(020)82753423 (020)82730715	483	Joint stock 股份制	37,143	-1521(26)	109,918	o
Anqiu Cellulose Factory 安丘市纖維素廠(1985)	Weifang 濰坊市	Shandong 山東省	(0536)4641113 (0536)4641113	124	Collectively-owned 集體	25,495	1492(3)	8,083	a
Jianhu Chemical Fibre Plant 建湖縣化纖廠(1988)	Yancheng 鹽城市	Jiangsu 江蘇省	(0515)6511898	262	Collectively-owned 集體	18,160	900(5)	29,460	o
Mengcheng San Yi Zhen Cellulose Factory 蒙城縣三義鎮纖維素廠(1993)	Fuyang 阜陽市	Anhui 安徽省	(0558)7791038	54	Collectively-owned 集體	11,000	1490(4)	2,680	o
Zhaoxian Pledget Factory 趙縣脱脂棉廠(1985)	Shijiazhuang 石家莊市	Hebei 河北省	(0311)4935006	40	Collectively-owned 集體	9,400	480(7)	3,500	o
Shandong Laizhou Saltern 山東省萊州市鹽場(1978)	Yantai 煙台市	Shandong 山東省	(0535)2331152 (0535)2331153	131	Collectively-owned 集體	8,705	183(15)	18,218	o
Wenzhou Ouhai Daily Chemical Co. Ltd. 温州市甌海日用化工有限公司(1986)	Wenzhou 温州市	Zhejiang 浙江省	(0577)6265075	24	Joint stock 股份制	8,350	160(16)	8,727	o

Top 10 Cities by Production Output 產出排名前 10 位城市	Province 省	Market share 市場份額	Number of firms 企業個數
Nantong 南通市	Jiangsu 江蘇省	50.93%	4
Kunming 昆明市	Yunnan 雲南省	25.04%	2
Suzhou 蘇州市	Jiangsu 江蘇省	8.72%	8
Xuzhou 徐州市	Jiangsu 江蘇省	3.43%	1
Xiamen 廈門市	Fujian 福建省	2.08%	2
Shanghai 上海市	Shanghai 上海市	1.67%	3
Shijiazhuang 石家莊市	Hebei 河北省	1.01%	2
Weifang 濰坊市	Shandong 山東省	0.79%	1
Binzhou 濱州市	Shandong 山東省	0.74%	2
Xi'an 西安市	Shaanxi 陝西省	0.49%	2

10 Major Wholesalers 10 家主要批發商	City 城市	Province 省	Telephone / Fax 電話 / 傳真
Anhui Clothing Import & Export Company 安徽省服裝進出口公司	Hefei 合肥市	Anhui 安徽省	(0551)3632212 (0551)3632002
Qingdao Textile Clothing Industrial Group Company 青島紡織服裝實業集團公司	Qingdao 青島市	Shandong 山東省	(0532)2877853 (0532)2869315
Hebei Textile Import & Export (Group) Company 河北省紡織品進出口(集團)公司	Shijiazhuang 石家莊市	Hebei 河北省	(0311)7028530 (0311)7027781
Zhong Fang Pledget Import & Export Company 中紡紗布進出口公司	Beijing 北京市	Beijing 北京市	(010)65124718 (010)65124713
Shaoxing Import & Export Company 紹興市進出口公司	Shaoxing 紹興市	Zhejiang 浙江省	(0575)5132822 (0575)5141577
Hunan Hua Xiang Import & Export (Group) Company 湖南省華湘進出口(集團)公司	Changsha 長沙市	Hunan 湖南省	(0731)2282440 (0731)2286995
City's Import & Export Company Trade Dept. 市進出口公司貿易部	Yichang 宜昌市	Hubei 湖北省	(0717)6450778 (0717)6441875
Shanghai Pu Dong Xinqu Import & Export Company 上海浦東新區進出口公司	Shanghai 上海市	Shanghai 上海市	(021)58878801 (021)58827444
Ningbo Yinxian Import & Export Company 寧波市鄞縣進出口公司	Ningbo 寧波市	Zhejiang 浙江省	(0574)7875205 (0574)7873168
Zhejiang Silk Import & Export Company 浙江省絲綢進出口公司	Hangzhou 杭州市	Zhejiang 浙江省	(0571)5195588 (0571)5192542

*Also include sales by firms outside this industry.包括本行業以外廠家的銷售。"o" stands for "others". "o" 代表 "其他產品"。

2821: Polyamide Fibre 錦綸纖維製造業

The industry accounts for 0.103% of the total revenue of China's industrial sector in 1996. The revenue growth rate of the industry is 30.5% from 1995, as compared to the growth rate of China's industrial sector, 9.51%. The rate of return on asset is -0.20%. 58.03% of all firms in the industry made a profit while 36.56% had negative returns. The top province in terms of the industry's revenue is Guangdong, accounting for 24.65% of the total revenue.
本行業在1996年佔全行業總產值0.103%，行業年增長率為30.5%（全國工業年增長率9.51%）。行業的資產回報率-0.20%，58.03%的企業盈利，36.56%的企業虧損。銷售收入最高的省份為廣東省，佔本行業的24.65%。

	Total number of firms 企業總數	Total number of employees 職工總數	Total revenue (mil. RMB) 總銷售收入（百萬元）	Total profit (mil. RMB) 總利潤（百萬元）	Return on assets 資產利潤率 (%)	Return on equity 權益利潤率 (%)	Labour productivity ('000 RMB / worker) 勞動生產率（千元/人）	Debts / assets 資產負債率 (%)	Total assets (mil. RMB) 總資產（百萬元）
Industry Overall 行業總體	102	53,940	5,970	-26	-0.20	-0.70	110.68	71.06	13,014

	Number of firms 企業個數	Average number of employees 平均職工人數	Average revenue ('000 RMB) 平均銷售收入（千元）	Average profit ('000 RMB) 平均利潤（千元）	Return on assets 資產利潤率 (%)	Return on equity 權益利潤率 (%)	Labour productivity ('000 RMB / worker) 勞動生產率（千元/人）	Average debts / assets 平均資產負債率(%)	Average Total assets ('000 RMB) 平均總資產（千元）
By ownership 產業所有權									
State-owned 國有	27	1,288	98,370	2,185	0.88	2.15	76.35	58.98	247,556
Collectively-owned 集體	54	206	11,169	-847	-5.09	145.48	54.18	103.50	16,627
Privately-owned 私有									
Domestic JVs 聯營	2	281	26,312	2,775	14.99	45.84	93.80	67.29	18,507
Joint stock 股份制	3	944	531,764	76,500	12.55	26.57	563.11	52.79	609,772
Foreign-funded 外資	7	228	29,401	-14,827	-16.13	-129.83	128.87	87.58	91,921
Overseas Chinese-funded 港澳台資	9	336	95,288	-18,958	-5.84	-171.00	283.78	96.59	324,712
By size 規模									
Large 大型	4	3,644	807,306	-10,213	-0.70	-1.20	221.57	41.74	1,461,919
Medium 中型	21	1,028	79,089	533	0.25	4.34	76.97	94.25	213,757
Small 小型	75	217	14,404	49	0.14	3.62	66.44	96.23	35,699
By regional distribution 地區分布									
Central-North 華北	11	661	23,983	-609	-0.81	-6.35	36.27	87.27	75,343
Beijing 北京	3	237	14,133	30	0.32	0.87	59.72	62.95	9,347
Tianjin 天津	1	1,486	74,620	500	0.17	1.08	50.22	84.53	298,030
Hebei 河北	2	271	7,460	-1,590	-1.35	29.89	27.58	104.53	117,555
Shanxi 山西	5	907	26,374	-822	-1.54	-6.89	29.07	77.70	53,518
Inner Mongolia 內蒙									
Northeast 東北	18	529	20,682	-352	-0.74	-2.15	39.06	65.43	47,326
Liaoning 遼寧	16	587	23,262	-376	-0.71	-2.04	39.64	65.27	53,193
Jilin 吉林	2	71	45	-160	-41.03	29.91	0.64	237.18	390
Heilongjiang 黑龍江									
Central East 華東	48	396	47,768	355	0.47	2.02	120.53	76.51	74,811
Shanghai 上海	3	173	9,083	-620	-4.10	-8.10	52.50	49.36	15,113
Jiangsu 江蘇	9	621	120,654	2,410	2.22	23.46	194.33	90.55	108,746
Zhejiang 浙江	17	346	30,978	-232	-0.79	-5.27	89.59	85.04	29,419
Anhui 安徽	5	432	17,736	-3,070	-3.53	-13.96	41.04	74.71	86,942
Fujian 福建	5	41	1,826	52	2.10	3.58	44.32	41.37	2,480
Jiangxi 江西									
Shandong 山東	9	519	61,700	1,806	1.00	3.03	118.86	66.89	179,962
Central-South 中南	21	809	144,420	-793	-0.22	-0.64	178.48	66.24	364,183
Henan 河南	5	1,619	247,210	27,702	5.17	6.58	152.71	21.35	535,554
Hubei 湖北	3	647	44,753	-13,770	-10.45	90.93	69.17	111.50	131,760
Hunan 湖南	3	671	51,913	-14,470	-7.56	52.75	77.33	114.33	191,447
Guangdong 廣東	8	508	183,921	-3,755	-1.09	-6.90	362.41	84.26	345,668
Guangxi 廣西	1	100	4,350	-1,070	-7.40	-16.56	43.50	55.36	14,450
Hainan 海南	1	784	31,060	-39,330	-3.22	-24.33	39.62	86.76	1,220,670
Southwest 西南	3	369	2,703	-4,523	-14.35	22.80	7.33	162.95	31,523
Chongqing 重慶	2	553	4,055	-6,785	-14.35	22.79	7.33	162.95	47,285
Sichuan 四川									
Guizhou 貴州	1								
Yunnan 雲南									
Tibet 西藏									
Northwest 西北	1	13	50	30	13.04	15.00	3.85	13.04	230
Shaanxi 陝西	1	13	50	30	13.04	15.00	3.85	13.04	230
Gansu 甘肅									
Qinghai 青海									
Ningxia 寧夏									
Xinjiang 新疆									

2821: Polyamide Fibre 錦綸纖維製造業

Year 年份	Number of firms 企業個數	Rate of change 每年變化 (%)	Number of employees 職工人數 (人)	Rate of change 每年變化 (%)	Total revenue (mil. RMB) 總銷售收入 (百萬元)	Rate of change 每年變化 (%)	Total profit (mil. RMB) 總利潤 (百萬元)	Rate of change 每年變化 (%)
1993	110		47,966		2,762		6	
1994	101	-8.18%	42,296	-11.82%	2,726	-1.29%	-185	-3456.85%
1995	93	-7.92%	46,679	10.36%	4,573	67.72%	115	162.48%
1996	102	9.68%	53,940	15.56%	5,970	30.55%	-26	-122.53%

3 Major products* 3 種主要產品 *	Output 產量	Sales volume 銷售量	Unit 單位
a) Polymide Fibre 錦綸纖維	84,479	80,255	ton 噸
b) Polypropylene Fibre 丙綸纖維	8,170	6,536	ton 噸
c) Polyamide Elastic Yarn 錦綸彈力絲	853	836	ton 噸

Top 10 firms by revenue (year founded) 收入排名前 10 家企業 (創辦年份)	City 城市	Province 省	Telephone / fax 電話 / 傳真	Number of employees 職工人數	Ownership 產業所有權	Revenue ('000 RMB) 銷售收入 (千元)	Profit ('000 RMB) (rank) 利潤 (千元) (排名)	Total assets ('000 RMB) 總資產 (千元)	Major products 主要產品
Guangdong Xinhui Mestt Polyamide Fibre Group Co. 廣東新會美達錦綸集團公司(1993)	Jiangmen 江門市	Guangdong 廣東省	(0750)6129328 (0750)6120975	1,915	Joint stock 股份制	1,059,820	61163(1)	1,146,833	a
Jiangsu Wei Li Da Chemical Fibre Group Company 江蘇威利達化纖集團公司(1990)	Wuxi 無錫市	Jiangsu 江蘇省	(0510)3221764	1,363	Collectively-owned 集體	555,563	20311(2)	201,456	o
Gaoyao Nglon Plant Co. Ltd. 高要錦綸廠有限公司(1994)	Zhaoqing 肇慶市	Guangdong 廣東省	(0757)8393088 (0757)8391035	671	Overseas Chinese-funded 港澳台資	256,039	1303(9)	644,368	a
Yingkou Chemical Fibre Factory 營口化學纖維廠(1986)	Yingkou 營口市	Liaoning 遼寧省	(0417)3810201 (0417)3842382	4,486	State-owned 國有	239,407	1083(12)	634,711	o
Zhejiang Anji Chemical Fibre General Factory 浙江省安吉化纖總廠(1972)	Huzhou 湖州市	Zhejiang 浙江省	(0572)5022283 (0572)5022284	985	State-owned 國有	199,107	6969(4)	120,610	o
Jiangsu Qing Jiang Synthetic Fibre Factory 江蘇省清江合成纖維廠(1973)	Huaiyin 淮陰市	Jiangsu 江蘇省	(0517)3964468 (0517)3964468	2,208	State-owned 國有	182,653	112(31)	421,915	a,b,c
Yan Tai Polyamide Fibre Co. Ltd. 煙台華潤錦綸有限公司(1988)	Yantai 煙台市	Shandong 山東省	(0535)6371688 (0535)6372777	744	Overseas Chinese-funded 港澳台資	178,015	16225(3)	489,492	a,c
Qingdao Zhongda Chemical Fibre Co. Ltd. 青島中達化纖有限公司(1991)	Qingdao 青島市	Shandong 山東省	(0532)6898043 (0532)6897751	467	Foreign-funded 外資	154,213	-576(56)	427,146	a
Xi Shan Shi Chemical Fibre Factory 錫山市化纖廠(1978)	Wuxi 無錫市	Jiangsu 江蘇省	(0510)5061161	728	Collectively-owned 集體	151,472	299(26)	166,356	o
Zhongshan Xin Hua Synthetic Fibre Co. Ltd. 中山市新華合成纖維有限公司(1989)	Zhongshan 中山市	Guangdong 廣東省	(0760)5596930 (0760)5598500	530	Overseas Chinese-funded 港澳台資	127,880	-79230(74)	601,580	a,c

Top 10 Cities by Production Output 產出排名前 10 位城市	Province 省	Market share 市場份額	Number of firms 企業個數
Pingdingshan 平頂山市	Henan 河南省	21.94%	2
Shanghai 上海市	Shanghai 上海市	16.56%	5
Wuxi 無錫市	Jiangsu 江蘇省	7.01%	11
Huzhou 湖州市	Zhejiang 浙江省	4.49%	3
Zibo 淄博市	Shandong 山東省	4.47%	1
Yingkou 營口市	Liaoning 遼寧省	4.38%	2
Yangzhou 揚州市	Jiangsu 江蘇省	4.37%	2
Zhaoqing 肇慶市	Guangdong 廣東省	3.75%	3
Yantai 煙台市	Shandong 山東省	3.68%	3
Huaiyin 淮陰市	Jiangsu 江蘇省	3.28%	2

10 Major Wholesalers 10 家主要批發商	City 城市	Province 省	Telephone / Fax 電話 / 傳真
Anhui Clothing Import & Export Company 安徽省服裝進出口公司	Hefei 合肥市	Anhui 安徽省	(0551)3632212 (0551)3632002
Qingdao Textile Clothing Industrial Group Company 青島紡織服裝實業集團公司	Qingdao 青島市	Shandong 山東省	(0532)2877853 (0532)2869315
Hebei Textile Import & Export (Group) Company 河北省紡織品進出口(集團)公司	Shijiazhuang 石家莊市	Hebei 河北省	(0311)7028530 (0311)7027781
Zhong Fang Pledget Import & Export Company 中紡紗布進出口公司	Beijing 北京市	Beijing 北京市	(010)65124718 (010)65124713
Shaoxing Import & Export Company 紹興市進出口公司	Shaoxing 紹興市	Zhejiang 浙江省	(0575)5132822 (0575)5141577
Hunan Hua Xiang Import & Export (Group) Company 湖南省華湘進出口(集團)公司	Changsha 長沙市	Hunan 湖南省	(0731)2282440 (0731)2286995
City's Import & Export Company Trade Dept. 市進出口公司貿易部	Yichang 宜昌市	Hubei 湖北省	(0717)6450778 (0717)6441875
Shanghai Pu Dong Xinqu Import & Export Company 上海浦東新區進出口公司	Shanghai 上海市	Shanghai 上海市	(021)58878801 (021)58827444
Ningbo Yinxian Import & Export Company 寧波市鄞縣進出口公司	Ningbo 寧波市	Zhejiang 浙江省	(0574)7875205 (0574)7873168
Zhejiang Silk Import & Export Company 浙江省絲綢進出口公司	Hangzhou 杭州市	Zhejiang 浙江省	(0571)5195588 (0571)5192542

*Also include sales by firms outside this industry.包括本行業以外廠家的銷售。"o" stands for "others". "o" 代表"其他產品"。

2822: Polyester Fibre 滌綸纖維製造業

The industry accounts for 0.832% of the total revenue of China's industrial sector in 1996. The revenue growth rate of the industry is -6.6% from 1995, as compared to the growth rate of China's industrial sector, 9.51%. The rate of return on asset is 1.97%. 64.81% of all firms in the industry made a profit while 30.03% had negative returns. The top province in terms of the industry's revenue is Shanghai, accounting for 28.60% of the total revenue.
本行業在 1996 年佔全行業總產值 0.832% ，行業年增長率為 -6.6%（全國工業年增長率 9.51%） 。行業的資產回報率 1.97% ， 64.81% 的企業盈利， 30.03% 的企業虧損。銷售收入最高的省份為上海市，佔本行業的 28.60% 。

	Total number of firms 企業總數	Total number of employees 職工總數	Total revenue (mil. RMB) 總銷售收入（百萬元）	Total profit (mil. RMB) 總利潤（百萬元）	Return on assets 資產利潤率 (%)	Return on equity 權益利潤率 (%)	Labour productivity ('000 RMB / worker) 勞動生產率（千元/人）	Debts / assets 資產負債率 (%)	Total assets (mil. RMB) 總資產（百萬元）
Industry Overall 行業總體	382	275,921	48,207	1,767	1.97	4.66	174.71	57.79	89,892

	Number of firms 企業個數	Average number of employees 平均職工人數	Average revenue ('000 RMB) 平均銷售收入（千元）	Average profit ('000 RMB) 平均利潤（千元）	Return on assets 資產利潤率 (%)	Return on equity 權益利潤率 (%)	Labour productivity ('000 RMB / worker) 勞動生產率（千元/人）	Average debts / assets 平均資產負債率(%)	Average Total assets ('000 RMB) 平均總資產（千元）
By ownership 產業所有權									
State-owned 國有	87	1,358	117,425	-3,736	-1.36	-6.48	86.45	78.97	274,161
Collectively-owned 集體	191	313	49,655	353	0.55	1.90	158.67	71.05	64,219
Privately-owned 私有									
Domestic JVs 聯營	10	280	21,506	-1,647	-4.28	-25.41	76.73	83.16	38,467
Joint stock 股份制	23	3,463	1,070,566	92,459	4.70	8.00	309.11	41.22	1,967,041
Foreign-funded 外資	22	222	30,259	-357	-0.58	-1.10	136.24	47.72	62,045
Overseas Chinese-funded 港澳台資	49	232	61,294	-1,572	-1.14	-3.84	264.45	70.44	138,428
By size 規模									
Large 大型	39	3,803	847,351	47,835	3.11	6.32	222.84	50.71	1,536,438
Medium 中型	88	817	102,048	-200	-0.10	-0.31	124.92	68.20	204,399
Small 小型	244	196	25,260	-330	-0.69	-3.06	129.02	77.58	48,121
By regional distribution 地區分布									
Central-North 華北	31	454	24,820	-1,369	-1.52	-6.96	54.70	78.19	90,223
Beijing 北京	10	378	12,117	-4,577	-7.33	-60.66	32.03	87.91	62,421
Tianjin 天津	8	243	22,853	3,245	6.36	11.72	94.24	45.72	51,021
Hebei 河北	10	482	34,403	1,633	1.68	7.83	71.36	78.53	97,109
Shanxi 山西	3	1,174	40,470	-12,983	-4.91	-37.27	34.46	86.83	264,480
Inner Mongolia 內蒙									
Northeast 東北	24	1,186	87,901	-2,815	-1.31	-4.92	74.13	73.46	215,575
Liaoning 遼寧	17	1,175	58,582	-2,765	-1.93	-8.21	49.87	76.50	143,331
Jilin 吉林	4	720	44,270	-6,230	-3.99	-12.88	61.51	69.04	156,200
Heilongjiang 黑龍江	3	1,870	312,217	1,450	0.21	0.72	166.93	71.27	704,127
Central East 華東	234	811	164,308	8,911	3.28	6.72	202.54	51.25	272,080
Shanghai 上海	21	2,588	656,484	66,810	6.50	10.09	253.62	35.62	1,028,477
Jiangsu 江蘇	89	644	146,424	6,536	2.54	4.92	227.32	48.29	257,033
Zhejiang 浙江	72	514	82,305	1,346	1.24	3.82	160.11	67.65	108,878
Anhui 安徽	7	1,067	79,660	-47	-0.04	-0.10	74.67	64.80	128,734
Fujian 福建	13	672	206,835	-2,186	-0.71	-2.05	307.97	65.40	307,991
Jiangxi 江西	5	838	63,278	124	0.07	0.34	75.49	78.50	167,514
Shandong 山東	27	768	79,311	1,170	0.56	3.57	103.24	84.21	207,814
Central-South 中南	75	455	83,102	-1,444	-0.68	-2.52	182.50	72.93	212,033
Henan 河南	12	502	24,493	-39	-0.07	-0.28	48.77	74.73	55,291
Hubei 湖北	10	421	33,117	-5,918	-8.47	613.26	78.59	101.38	69,864
Hunan 湖南	5	421	32,014	42	0.05	0.16	76.04	67.37	81,004
Guangdong 廣東	39	432	127,057	232	0.08	0.29	294.15	73.80	306,384
Guangxi 廣西	2	1,014	84,585	-14,000	-6.24	-30.28	83.46	79.39	224,280
Hainan 海南	7	419	46,161	-4,274	-1.72	-3.78	110.21	54.44	248,257
Southwest 西南	11	564	42,974	-6,613	-4.38	-12.40	76.19	64.66	150,882
Chongqing 重慶	2	417	3,254	-770	-2.21	5.19	7.80	142.67	34,746
Sichuan 四川	8	495	48,397	-315	-0.22	-0.50	97.78	56.20	144,524
Guizhou 貴州	1	1,141	51,190	-18,490	-5.31	-14.45	44.86	63.25	348,270
Yunnan 雲南	1	727	53,660	-57,770	-32.94	-958.04	73.81	96.56	175,380
Tibet 西藏									
Northwest 西北	7	459	24,974	-3,874	-3.92	-80.52	54.44	95.14	98,926
Shaanxi 陝西	2	822	31,420	-5,620	-6.40	-60.40	38.22	89.41	87,855
Gansu 甘肅	1	16	520	30	14.29	15.79	32.50	9.52	210
Qinghai 青海									
Ningxia 寧夏	1	859	63,490	-9,740	-4.87	1411.59	73.91	100.34	200,140
Xinjiang 新疆	3	231	15,990	-2,057	-1.95	-39.63	69.32	95.08	105,473

2822: Polyester Fibre 滌綸纖維製造業

Year 年份	Number of firms 企業個數	Rate of change 每年變化 (%)	Number of employees 職工人數 （人）	Rate of change 每年變化 (%)	Total revenue (mil. RMB) 總銷售收入 （百萬元）	Rate of change 每年變化 (%)	Total profit (mil. RMB) 總利潤 （百萬元）	Rate of change 每年變化 (%)
1993	286		532,627		31,040		2,588	
1994	316	10.49%	287,376	-46.05%	40,988	32.05%	3,499	35.20%
1995	390	23.42%	272,088	-5.32%	51,605	25.90%	3,704	5.87%
1996	382	-2.05%	275,921	1.41%	48,207	-6.58%	1,767	-52.29%

3 Major products* 3種主要產品 *	Output 產量	Sales volume 銷售量	Unit 單位
a) Polyester Fibre 滌綸纖維	1,998,614	1,738,794	ton 噸
b) Polyester Processing Sill 滌綸加工絲	438,232	407,556	ton 噸
c) Polyester 聚酯	1,141,470	913,176	ton 噸

Top 10 firms by revenue (year founded) 收入排名前10家企業 (創辦年份)	City 城市	Province 省	Telephone / fax 電話 / 傳真	Number of employees 職工人數	Ownership 產業所有權	Revenue ('000 RMB) 銷售收入 （千元）	Profit ('000 RMB) (rank) 利潤（千元） （排名）	Total assets ('000 RMB) 總資產 （千元）	Major products 主要產品
Shanghai Petrochemical Co. Ltd. 上海石油化工股份有限公司(1975)	Shanghai 上海市	Shanghai 上海市	(021)57941941 (021)57942267	38,790	Joint stock 股份制	11,599,793	1404867(1)	18,155,514	a,b,c
Yizheng Chemical Fibre Co. Ltd. 儀征化纖股份有限公司(1993)	Yangzhou 揚州市	Jiangsu 江蘇省	(0514)3232235 (0514)3233880	15,404	Joint stock 股份制	6,340,460	437580(2)	13,541,860	a,c
Kaiping Polyester Enterprise Group Co. Ltd. Guangdong 廣東省開平滌綸企業集團股份有限公司(1986)	Jiangmen 江門市	Guangdong 廣東省	(0750)2213758 (0750)2218807	3,516	Joint stock 股份制	2,291,850	237913(3)	4,175,021	a,b,c
Xianglu Polyester Fibres (Xiamen) Co. Ltd. 翔鷺滌綸紡織(廈門)有限公司(1989)	Xiamen 廈門市	Fujian 福建省	(0592)6051111 (0592)6051281	1,346	Overseas Chinese-funded 港澳台資	2,012,082	-30537(303)	2,900,023	a,c
Shanghai Chemical Fibre Co. Ltd. (Group) 上海化學纖維(集團)有限公司(1923)	Shanghai 上海市	Shanghai 上海市	(021)62800200 (021)62809639	11,540	State-owned 國有	1,484,523	3028(54)	2,087,774	a,b,c
China Ji'nan Chemical Fibre General Corp. 中國濟南化纖總公司(1990)	Ji'nan 濟南市	Shandong 山東省	(0531)8902560 (0531)8902560	12,199	State-owned 國有	1,104,378	12507(17)	3,501,044	a,b,c
Heilong Jiang Long Di Group Co. Ltd 黑龍江龍滌集團有限公司(1980)	Harbin 哈爾濱市	Heilongjiang 黑龍江省	(0451)3722601 (0451)3721949	4,796	State-owned 國有	932,417	4271(43)	2,110,750	a,b
Dandong Chemical Fibre (Group) Corp. 丹東化學纖維工業(集團)總公司(1941)	Dandong 丹東市	Liaoning 遼寧省	(0415)6162385 (0415)6160297	11,615	State-owned 國有	824,177	10264(22)	1,574,569	o
Zhejiang Xiao Xiao Enterprise General Co. 浙江小小企業總公司(1992)	Shaoxing 紹興市	Zhejiang 浙江省	(0575)4091275 (0575)4092140	5,228	Collectively-owned 集體	700,102	30042(7)	1,384,713	a,b
Zhejiang Da Pu Chemical Fibre Group Co. 浙江大普化纖集團公司(1985)	Shaoxing 紹興市	Zhejiang 浙江省	(0575)2083788 (0575)2083080	1,391	Collectively-owned 集體	458,797	22198(9)	272,070	o

Top 10 Cities by Production Output 產出排名前10位城市	Province 省	Market share 市場份額	Number of firms 企業個數
Yangzhou 揚州市	Jiangsu 江蘇省	22.89%	15
Shanghai 上海市	Shanghai 上海市	9.77%	33
Suzhou 蘇州市	Jiangsu 江蘇省	9.40%	62
Shaoxing 紹興市	Zhejiang 浙江省	7.83%	26
Wuxi 無錫市	Jiangsu 江蘇省	5.53%	34
Xiamen 廈門市	Fujian 福建省	5.44%	5
Jiaxing 嘉興市	Zhejiang 浙江省	4.49%	19
Jiangmen 江門市	Guangdong 廣東省	4.10%	5
Foshan 佛山市	Guangdong 廣東省	3.43%	13
Ji'nan 濟南市	Shandong 山東省	2.27%	6

10 Major Wholesalers 10家主要批發商	City 城市	Province 省	Telephone / Fax 電話 / 傳真
Anhui Clothing Import & Export Company 安徽省服裝進出口公司	Hefei 合肥市	Anhui 安徽省	(0551)3632212 (0551)3632002
Qingdao Textile Clothing Industrial Group Company 青島紡織服裝實業集團公司	Qingdao 青島市	Shandong 山東省	(0532)2877853 (0532)2869315
Hebei Textile Import & Export (Group) Company 河北省紡織品進出口(集團)公司	Shijiazhuang 石家莊市	Hebei 河北省	(0311)7028530 (0311)7027781
Zhong Fang Pledget Import & Export Company 中紡紗布進出口公司	Beijing 北京市	Beijing 北京市	(010)65124718 (010)65124713
Shaoxing Import & Export Company 紹興市進出口公司	Shaoxing 紹興市	Zhejiang 浙江省	(0575)5132822 (0575)5141577
Hunan Hua Xiang Import & Export (Group) Company 湖南省華湘進出口(集團)公司	Changsha 長沙市	Hunan 湖南省	(0731)2282440 (0731)2286995
City's Import & Export Company Trade Dept. 市進出口公司貿易部	Yichang 宜昌市	Hubei 湖北省	(0717)6450778 (0717)6441875
Shanghai Pu Dong Xinqu Import & Export Company 上海浦東新區進出口公司	Shanghai 上海市	Shanghai 上海市	(021)58878801 (021)58827444
Ningbo Yinxian Import & Export Company 寧波市鄞縣進出口公司	Ningbo 寧波市	Zhejiang 浙江省	(0574)7875205 (0574)7873168
Zhejiang Silk Import & Export Company 浙江省絲綢進出口公司	Hangzhou 杭州市	Zhejiang 浙江省	(0571)5195588 (0571)5192542

*Also include sales by firms outside this industry.包括本行業以外廠家的銷售。"o" stands for "others". "o" 代表"其他產品"。

2823: Acrylic Fibre 腈綸纖維製造業

The industry accounts for 0.036% of the total revenue of China's industrial sector in 1996. The revenue growth rate of the industry is 7.3% from 1995, as compared to the growth rate of China's industrial sector, 9.51%. The rate of return on asset is -1.01%. 60.05% of all firms in the industry made a profit while 21.43% had negative returns. The top province in terms of the industry's revenue is Shandong, accounting for 31.12% of the total revenue.
本行業在 1996 年佔全行業總產值0.036% ，行業年增長率為 7.3%（全國工業年增長率 9.51%）。行業的資產回報率 -1.01% ， 60.05% 的企業盈利， 21.43% 的企業虧損。銷售收入最高的省份為山東省，佔本行業的 31.12% 。

	Total number of firms 企業總數	Total number of employees 職工總數	Total revenue (mil. RMB) 總銷售收入（百萬元）	Total profit (mil. RMB) 總利潤（百萬元）	Return on assets 資產利潤率 (%)	Return on equity 權益利潤率 (%)	Labour productivity ('000 RMB / worker) 勞動生產率（千元/人）	Debts / assets 資產負債率 (%)	Total assets (mil. RMB) 總資產（百萬元）
Industry Overall 行業總體	46	18,701	2,112	-60	-1.01	-6.28	112.94	83.88	5,968

	Number of firms 企業個數	Average number of employees 平均職工人數	Average revenue ('000 RMB) 平均銷售收入（千元）	Average profit ('000 RMB) 平均利潤（千元）	Return on assets 資產利潤率 (%)	Return on equity 權益利潤率 (%)	Labour productivity ('000 RMB / worker) 勞動生產率（千元/人）	Average debts / assets 平均資產負債率(%)	Average Total assets ('000 RMB) 平均總資產（千元）
By ownership 產業所有權									
State-owned 國有	7	1,735	211,571	-8,857	-1.18	-8.42	121.94	86.04	753,000
Collectively-owned 集體	29	125	8,007	7	0.13	2.91	64.04	95.59	5,786
Privately-owned 私有									
Domestic JVs 聯營	1	84	60,155	109	0.55	1.33	716.13	58.38	19,744
Joint stock 股份制	1	20	1,485	5	0.83	4.86	74.25	82.93	656
Foreign-funded 外資	2	23	1,033	9	0.08	0.10	45.92	21.92	11,124
Overseas Chinese-funded 港澳台資	6	487	55,970	276	0.34	0.86	114.85	60.37	81,137
By size 規模									
Large 大型	3	2,577	333,051	-26,181	-2.00	-15.76	129.26	87.29	1,307,512
Medium 中型	4	1,091	193,981	1,211	0.29	1.45	177.84	80.23	421,343
Small 小型	38	203	8,881	360	3.80	10.51	43.84	63.82	9,482
By regional distribution 地區分布									
Central-North 華北	5	620	92,892	194	0.08	0.14	149.83	44.35	254,282
Beijing 北京									
Tianjin 天津									
Hebei 河北	4	673	114,858	243	0.08	0.14	170.79	44.26	317,340
Shanxi 山西	1	410	5,030				12.27	100.00	2,050
Inner Mongolia 內蒙									
Northeast 東北	7	225	33,797	257	1.19	2.57	149.92	53.64	21,599
Liaoning 遼寧	3	498	77,627	533	1.10	2.33	155.77	52.85	48,580
Jilin 吉林									
Heilongjiang 黑龍江	4	21	925	50	3.67	14.49	44.58	74.68	1,363
Central East 華東	28	370	44,198	-2,373	-1.55	-74.93	119.53	97.93	153,146
Shanghai 上海	4	414	114,013	2,518	1.00	13.42	275.23	92.52	250,808
Jiangsu 江蘇	8	184	12,259	164	1.79	13.34	66.76	86.59	9,164
Zhejiang 浙江	6	73	4,155	-10	-0.24	-0.61	56.92	60.67	4,153
Anhui 安徽	1	31	1,140				36.77	103.51	570
Fujian 福建									
Jiangxi 江西									
Shandong 山東	9	751	73,039	-8,640	-2.44	1300.33	97.27	100.19	354,006
Central-South 中南	4	746	34,493	1,573	3.23	7.85	46.27	58.78	48,615
Henan 河南									
Hubei 湖北	1	123	6,410	240	7.34	18.32	52.11	59.94	3,270
Hunan 湖南	1	25	260				10.40	100.00	200
Guangdong 廣東	2	1,417	65,650	3,025	3.17	7.67	46.33	58.72	95,495
Guangxi 廣西									
Hainan 海南									
Southwest 西南	1	548	21,730	-4,190	-7.15	-31.36	39.65	77.20	58,600
Chongqing 重慶									
Sichuan 四川	1	548	21,730	-4,190	-7.15	-31.36	39.65	77.20	58,600
Guizhou 貴州									
Yunnan 雲南									
Tibet 西藏									
Northwest 西北	1	140	13,800	1,200	29.93	58.25	98.57	48.63	4,010
Shaanxi 陝西									
Gansu 甘肅	1	140	13,800	1,200	29.93	58.25	98.57	48.63	4,010
Qinghai 青海									
Ningxia 寧夏									
Xinjiang 新疆									

2823: Acrylic Fibre 腈綸纖維製造業

Year 年份	Number of firms 企業個數	Rate of change 每年變化 (%)	Number of employees 職工人數 (人)	Rate of change 每年變化 (%)	Total revenue (mil. RMB) 總銷售收入 (百萬元)	Rate of change 每年變化 (%)	Total profit (mil. RMB) 總利潤 (百萬元)	Rate of change 每年變化 (%)
1993	33		12,497		818		40	
1994	33		13,839	10.74%	1,008	23.31%	-25	-163.05%
1995	49	48.48%	18,775	35.67%	1,968	95.27%	-77	-207.61%
1996	46	-6.12%	18,701	-0.39%	2,112	7.32%	-60	21.77%

3 Major products* 3 種主要產品 *	Output 產量	Sales volume 銷售量	Unit 單位
a) Acrylic Fibre 腈綸纖維	99,951	78,961	ton 噸
b) Polymide Fibre 錦綸纖維	17,545	16,668	ton 噸
c) Pure Synthetic Yarn 純化纖紗	24,348	19,235	ton 噸

Top 10 firms by revenue (year founded) 收入排名前 10 家企業 (創辦年份)	City 城市	Province 省	Telephone / fax 電話 / 傳真	Number of employees 職工人數	Ownership 產業所有權	Revenue ('000 RMB) 銷售收入 (千元)	Profit ('000 RMB) (rank) 利潤 (千元) (排名)	Total assets ('000 RMB) 總資產 (千元)	Major products 主要產品
Hebei Qinhuangdao Acrylic Fibre Factory 河北省秦皇島腈綸廠(1991)	Qinhuangdao 秦皇島市	Hebei 河北省	(0335)3016152 (0335)3011549	2,527	State-owned 國有	433,116	0(19)	1,248,291	a
Shanghai Jin Yang Acrylic Fibre Factory 上海金陽腈綸廠(1992)	Shanghai 上海市	Shanghai 上海市	(021)57940940 (021)57940413	1,232	State-owned 國有	404,618	16598(1)	864,724	a
Shandong Xueyin Chemical Fibre Group Co. Ltd. 山東雪銀化纖集團股份有限公司(1977)	Zibo 淄博市	Shandong 山東省	(0533)3980131 (0533)3980001	2,001	State-owned 國有	373,381	15632(2)	719,736	a,b
Shandong Zibo Chemical Fibre General Factory 山東淄博化學纖維總廠(1990)	Zibo 淄博市	Shandong 山東省	(0533)3581651 (0533)3580811	3,451	State-owned 國有	226,020	-95229(27)	2,380,448	a
Shenyang Dong Fang Textile Co. Ltd. 瀋陽東方紡織有限公司(1992)	Shenyang 瀋陽市	Liaoning 遼寧省	(024)25813575 (024)25813920	1,378	Foreign-funded 外資	224,848	1106(7)	137,665	c
Shenzhen Xin Hua Textile Co. Ltd. 深圳新華紡織有限公司(1989)	Shenzhen 深圳市	Guangdong 廣東省	(0755)6600980 (0755)6600994	1,035	Overseas Chinese-funded 港澳台資	131,298	6048(3)	190,994	c
Shanghai Gao Kai Acrylic Fibre Co. Ltd. 上海高凱腈綸有限公司(1996)	Shanghai 上海市	Shanghai 上海市	(021)58611682 (021)58848019	266	Foreign-funded 外資	39,223	-9057(26)	111,621	o
Yixing Tong Da Chemical Fibre Co. Ltd. 宜興通達化纖有限公司(1993)	Wuxi 無錫市	Jiangsu 江蘇省	(0510)7902783 (0510)7901407	250	Overseas Chinese-funded 港澳台資	37,000	690(11)	19,120	b
Wujin No.3 Textile Mill 武進市第三紡織廠(1984)	Changzhou 常州市	Jiangsu 江蘇省	(0519)3661226	440	Collectively-owned 集體	29,012	41(15)	9,889	c
Hebei Pingxiang Wool Manufacturing Factory 河北省平鄉縣毛紡織廠(1976)	Xingtai 邢臺市	Hebei 河北省	(0319)7832968	70	State-owned 國有	24,090	893(9)	18,958	o

Top 10 Cities by Production Output 產出排名前 10 位城市	Province 省	Market share 市場份額	Number of firms 企業個數
Wuxi 無錫市	Jiangsu 江蘇省	74.98%	4
Shanghai 上海市	Shanghai 上海市	5.94%	15
Qinhuangdao 秦皇島市	Hebei 河北省	4.20%	2
Anqing 安慶市	Anhui 安徽省	4.10%	1
Zibo 淄博市	Shandong 山東省	3.77%	4
Shenyang 瀋陽市	Liaoning 遼寧省	2.21%	2
Ningbo 寧波市	Zhejiang 浙江省	1.13%	2
Foshan 佛山市	Guangdong 廣東省	0.84%	1
Jiaxing 嘉興市	Zhejiang 浙江省	0.40%	3
Changzhou 常州市	Jiangsu 江蘇省	0.38%	2

10 Major Wholesalers 10 家主要批發商	City 城市	Province 省	Telephone / Fax 電話 / 傳真
Anhui Clothing Import & Export Company 安徽省服裝進出口公司	Hefei 合肥市	Anhui 安徽省	(0551)3632212 (0551)3632002
Qingdao Textile Clothing Industrial Group Company 青島紡織服裝實業集團公司	Qingdao 青島市	Shandong 山東省	(0532)2877853 (0532)2869315
Hebei Textile Import & Export (Group) Company 河北省紡織品進出口(集團)公司	Shijiazhuang 石家莊市	Hebei 河北省	(0311)7028530 (0311)7027781
Zhong Fang Pledget Import & Export Company 中紡紗布進出口公司	Beijing 北京市	Beijing 北京市	(010)65124718 (010)65124713
Shaoxing Import & Export Company 紹興市進出口公司	Shaoxing 紹興市	Zhejiang 浙江省	(0575)5132822 (0575)5141577
Hunan Hua Xiang Import & Export (Group) Company 湖南省華湘進出口(集團)公司	Changsha 長沙市	Hunan 湖南省	(0731)2282440 (0731)2286995
City's Import & Export Company Trade Dept. 市進出口公司貿易部	Yichang 宜昌市	Hubei 湖北省	(0717)6450778 (0717)6441875
Shanghai Pu Dong Xinqu Import & Export Company 上海浦東新區進出口公司	Shanghai 上海市	Shanghai 上海市	(021)58878801 (021)58827444
Ningbo Yinxian Import & Export Company 寧波市鄞縣進出口公司	Ningbo 寧波市	Zhejiang 浙江省	(0574)7875205 (0574)7873168
Zhejiang Silk Import & Export Company 浙江省絲綢進出口公司	Hangzhou 杭州市	Zhejiang 浙江省	(0571)5195588 (0571)5192542

*Also include sales by firms outside this industry.包括本行業以外廠家的銷售。"o" stands for "others". "o" 代表 "其他產品"。

2824: Polyvinyl Alcohol Fibre 維綸纖維製造業

The industry accounts for 0.035% of the total revenue of China's industrial sector in 1996. The revenue growth rate of the industry is -22.5% from 1995, as compared to the growth rate of China's industrial sector, 9.51%. The rate of return on asset is 0.23%. 83.81% of all firms in the industry made a profit while 9.52% had negative returns. The top province in terms of the industry's revenue is Chongqing, accounting for 53.60% of the total revenue.
本行業在 1996 年佔全行業總產值 0.035%，行業年增長率為 -22.5%（全國工業年增長率 9.51%）。行業的資產回報率 0.23%，83.81% 的企業盈利，9.52% 的企業虧損。銷售收入最高的省份為重慶市，佔本行業的 53.60%。

	Total number of firms 企業總數	Total number of employees 職工總數	Total revenue (mil. RMB) 總銷售收入（百萬元）	Total profit (mil. RMB) 總利潤（百萬元）	Return on assets 資產利潤率 (%)	Return on equity 權益利潤率 (%)	Labour productivity ('000 RMB / worker) 勞動生產率（千元／人）	Debts / assets 資產負債率 (%)	Total assets (mil. RMB) 總資產（百萬元）
Industry Overall 行業總體	24	23,330	2,046	11	0.23	0.53	87.70	56.26	4,735

	Number of firms 企業個數	Average number of employees 平均職工人數	Average revenue ('000 RMB) 平均銷售收入（千元）	Average profit ('000 RMB) 平均利潤（千元）	Return on assets 資產利潤率 (%)	Return on equity 權益利潤率 (%)	Labour productivity ('000 RMB / worker) 勞動生產率（千元／人）	Average debts / assets 平均資產負債率(%)	Average Total assets ('000 RMB) 平均總資產（千元）
By ownership 產業所有權									
State-owned 國有	6	3,665	315,000	1,000	0.13	0.29	85.96	55.94	771,333
Collectively-owned 集體	17	70	7,014	292	6.65	24.20	100.37	72.51	4,385
Privately-owned 私有									
Domestic JVs 聯營									
Joint stock 股份制									
Foreign-funded 外資									
Overseas Chinese-funded 港澳台資	2	77	19,248	20	0.12	0.34	251.60	64.25	16,805
By size 規模									
Large 大型	8	2,844	250,724	1,353	0.23	0.53	88.15	55.90	583,686
Medium 中型									
Small 小型	16	36	2,541	11	0.26	1.42	70.59	81.51	4,134
By regional distribution 地區分布									
Central-North 華北	2	919	31,860	-15,985	-18.72	-1486.98	34.69	98.74	85,375
Beijing 北京	1	1,781	62,460	-32,000	-18.95	-2580.65	35.07	99.27	168,840
Tianjin 天津									
Hebei 河北	1	56	1,260	30	1.57	3.30	22.50	52.36	1,910
Shanxi 山西									
Inner Mongolia 內蒙									
Northeast 東北									
Liaoning 遼寧									
Jilin 吉林									
Heilongjiang 黑龍江									
Central East 華東	9	360	38,349	1,036	2.15	4.43	106.49	51.49	48,172
Shanghai 上海									
Jiangsu 江蘇	5	104	10,848	1,062	14.00	76.29	104.11	81.65	7,586
Zhejiang 浙江	1	22	750	60	8.57	8.96	34.09	5.71	700
Anhui 安徽									
Fujian 福建									
Jiangxi 江西	1	2,598	272,610	3,240	0.83	1.61	104.93	48.30	390,150
Shandong 山東	2	50	8,770	355	14.88	71.72	175.40	79.45	2,385
Central-South 中南	9	494	40,220	1,136	1.96	3.80	81.44	48.56	58,071
Henan 河南	1	25							
Hubei 湖北	1	12	7,590	310	7.29	31.00	632.50	76.24	4,250
Hunan 湖南	2	2,018	140,945	5,600	2.41	4.48	69.84	46.18	232,355
Guangdong 廣東	4	93	18,103	-233	-1.80	-5.49	194.65	67.21	12,923
Guangxi 廣西	1		90	-360	-18.09	-44.44		59.30	1,990
Hainan 海南									
Southwest 西南	2	5,043	548,290	10,490	0.70	1.50	108.73	53.26	1,495,180
Chongqing 重慶	2	5,043	548,290	10,490	0.70	1.50	108.72	53.26	1,495,180
Sichuan 四川									
Guizhou 貴州									
Yunnan 雲南									
Tibet 西藏									
Northwest 西北	2	1,861	89,335	1,240	0.40	1.29	48.00	68.87	308,850
Shaanxi 陝西									
Gansu 甘肅	2	1,861	89,335	1,240	0.40	1.29	48.00	68.87	308,850
Qinghai 青海									
Ningxia 寧夏									
Xinjiang 新疆									

2824: Polyvinyl Alcohol Fibre 維綸纖維製造業

Year 年份	Number of firms 企業個數	Rate of change 每年變化 (%)	Number of employees 職工人數 (人)	Rate of change 每年變化 (%)	Total revenue (mil. RMB) 總銷售收入 (百萬元)	Rate of change 每年變化 (%)	Total profit (mil. RMB) 總利潤 (百萬元)	Rate of change 每年變化 (%)
1993	26		12,962		810		40	
1994	26		23,128	78.43%	1,679	107.33%	35	-12.22%
1995	19	-26.92%	26,356	13.96%	2,639	57.18%	137	294.68%
1996	24	26.32%	23,330	-11.48%	2,046	-22.47%	11	-91.97%

3 Major products* 3種主要產品*	Output 產量	Sales volume 銷售量	Unit 單位
a) Vinylon Fibre 維綸纖維	24,599	21,155	ton 噸
b) Polyvinyl Alcohol 聚乙烯醇	99,668	72,757	ton 噸
c) Polyester Fibre 滌綸纖維	23,126	20,119	ton 噸

Top 10 firms by revenue (year founded) 收入排名前10家企業 (創辦年份)	City 城市	Province 省	Telephone / fax 電話 / 傳真	Number of employees 職工人數	Ownership 產業所有權	Revenue ('000 RMB) 銷售收入 (千元)	Profit ('000 RMB) (rank) 利潤 (千元) (排名)	Total assets ('000 RMB) 總資產 (千元)	Major products 主要產品
Sinopec Sichuan Vinylon Works 中國石化四川維尼綸廠(1979)	Chongqing 重慶市	Chongqing 重慶市	(023)68974716 (023)68974999	10,069	State-owned 國有	1,095,975	21172(1)	2,980,424	a,b,c
Xiang Wei Co. Ltd. 湘維有限公司(1971)	Huaihua 懷化市	Hunan 湖南省	(0745)3222115 (0745)3225569	3,953	State-owned 國有	281,182	12351(2)	463,917	a,b
Jiangxi Chemical Fibre and Chemical Co. Ltd. 江西化纖化工有限公司(1978)	Jingdezhen 景德鎮市	Jiangxi 江西省	(0798)6832400 (0798)6834994	2,585	State-owned 國有	272,614	3239(4)	390,148	b,c
Lanzhou Vinylion Plant 蘭州維尼綸廠(1979)	Lanzhou 蘭州市	Gansu 甘肅省	(0931)7912200 (0931)7912389	3,749	State-owned 國有	178,120	2460(5)	617,000	a,b,c
Beijing Vinylon Plant 北京維尼綸廠(1966)	Beijing 北京市	Beijing 北京市	(010)69411293 (010)69411828	2,049	State-owned 國有	62,463	-32001(15)	168,837	a,c
Xi Shan Shi Taihu Vinylon Bu Factory 錫山市太湖維綸布廠(1993)	Wuxi 無錫市	Jiangsu 江蘇省	(0510)8791908	340	Collectively-owned 集體	44,750	5040(3)	22,440	o
Fanya Chemical Fibre Cotton Factory 泛亞化纖綿廠(1989)	Guangzhou 廣州市	Guangdong 廣東省	(020)82752199 (020)82752616	60	Overseas Chinese-funded 港澳台資	35,340	-1(13)	15,927	o
Zhongshan De Xi Box and Bag Industrial Co. Ltd. 中山得喜箱包工業有限公司(1990)	Zhongshan 中山市	Guangdong 廣東省	(0760)6652607 (0760)6652609	205	Overseas Chinese-funded 港澳台資	31,534	1093(6)	16,596	o
Shandong Junan Belt-weaving Factory 山東省莒南縣織帶廠(1987)	Linyi 臨沂市	Shandong 山東省	(0539)7212843 (0539)7212843	48	Collectively-owned 集體	10,170	410(7)	1,176	o
Zaoyang Jacquard Pattern Carpet Factory 棗陽市提花地毯徑紗廠(1995)	Xiangfan 襄樊市	Hubei 湖北省	(0710)6223928	44	Collectively-owned 集體	7,591	312(8)	4,246	o

Top 10 Cities by Production Output 產出排名前10位城市	Province 省	Market share 市場份額	Number of firms 企業個數
Chaohu 巢湖市	Anhui 安徽省	35.67%	1
Huaihua 懷化市	Hunan 湖南省	27.30%	1
Lanzhou 蘭州市	Gansu 甘肅省	14.77%	1
Beijing 北京市	Beijing 北京市	14.19%	1
Guangzhou 廣州市	Guangdong 廣東省	3.65%	4
Wuxi 無錫市	Jiangsu 江蘇省	1.65%	2
Tai'an 泰安市	Shandong 山東省	0.68%	1
Suzhou 蘇州市	Jiangsu 江蘇省	0.50%	2
Zhenjiang 鎮江市	Jiangsu 江蘇省	0.39%	1
Linyi 臨沂市	Shandong 山東省	0.26%	1

10 Major Wholesalers 10家主要批發商	City 城市	Province 省	Telephone / Fax 電話 / 傳真
Anhui Clothing Import & Export Company 安徽省服裝進出口公司	Hefei 合肥市	Anhui 安徽省	(0551)3632212 (0551)3632002
Qingdao Textile Clothing Industrial Group Company 青島紡織服裝實業集團公司	Qingdao 青島市	Shandong 山東省	(0532)2877853 (0532)2869315
Hebei Textile Import & Export (Group) Company 河北省紡織品進出口(集團)公司	Shijiazhuang 石家莊市	Hebei 河北省	(0311)7028530 (0311)7027781
Zhong Fang Pledget Import & Export Company 中紡紗布進出口公司	Beijing 北京市	Beijing 北京市	(010)65124718 (010)65124713
Shaoxing Import & Export Company 紹興市進出口公司	Shaoxing 紹興市	Zhejiang 浙江省	(0575)5132822 (0575)5141577
Hunan Hua Xiang Import & Export (Group) Company 湖南省華湘進出口(集團)公司	Changsha 長沙市	Hunan 湖南省	(0731)2282440 (0731)2286995
City's Import & Export Company Trade Dept. 市進出口公司貿易部	Yichang 宜昌市	Hubei 湖北省	(0717)6450778 (0717)6441875
Shanghai Pu Dong Xinqu Import & Export Company 上海浦東新區進出口公司	Shanghai 上海市	Shanghai 上海市	(021)58878801 (021)58827444
Ningbo Yinxian Import & Export Company 寧波市鄞縣進出口公司	Ningbo 寧波市	Zhejiang 浙江省	(0574)7875205 (0574)7873168
Zhejiang Silk Import & Export Company 浙江省絲綢進出口公司	Hangzhou 杭州市	Zhejiang 浙江省	(0571)5195588 (0571)5192542

*Also include sales by firms outside this industry.包括本行業以外廠家的銷售。"o" stands for "others". "o" 代表"其他產品"。

2829: Other Synthetic Fibre 其他合成纖維製造業

The industry accounts for 0.065% of the total revenue of China's industrial sector in 1996. The revenue growth rate of the industry is -8.2% from 1995, as compared to the growth rate of China's industrial sector, 9.51%. The rate of return on asset is 1.36%. 61.59% of all firms in the industry made a profit while 30.13% had negative returns. The top province in terms of the industry's revenue is Jiangsu, accounting for 30.54% of the total revenue.
本行業在1996年佔全行業總產值0.065%，行業年增長率為-8.2%（全國工業年增長率9.51%）。行業的資產回報率1.36%，61.59%的企業盈利，30.13%的企業虧損。銷售收入最高的省份為江蘇省，佔本行業的30.54%。

	Total number of firms 企業總數	Total number of employees 職工總數	Total revenue (mil. RMB) 總銷售收入（百萬元）	Total profit (mil. RMB) 總利潤（百萬元）	Return on assets 資產利潤率 (%)	Return on equity 權益利潤率 (%)	Labour productivity ('000 RMB / worker) 勞動生產率（千元/人）	Debts / assets 資產負債率 (%)	Total assets (mil. RMB) 總資產（百萬元）
Industry Overall 行業總體	263	38,242	3,791	93	1.36	5.34	99.13	74.48	6,791

	Number of firms 企業個數	Average number of employees 平均職工人數	Average revenue ('000 RMB) 平均銷售收入（千元）	Average profit ('000 RMB) 平均利潤（千元）	Return on assets 資產利潤率 (%)	Return on equity 權益利潤率 (%)	Labour productivity ('000 RMB / worker) 勞動生產率（千元/人）	Average debts / assets 平均資產負債率(%)	Average Total assets ('000 RMB) 平均總資產（千元）
By ownership 產業所有權									
State-owned 國有	36	352	18,833	-417	-0.83	-5.86	53.54	85.77	49,972
Collectively-owned 集體	147	119	12,846	350	2.12	10.11	107.70	78.99	16,500
Privately-owned 私有									
Domestic JVs 聯營	2	449	70,970	1,013	0.99	2.94	158.24	66.23	101,835
Joint stock 股份制	3	248	59,500	16,351	10.43	14.28	240.24	26.93	156,739
Foreign-funded 外資	20	79	9,457	331	1.75	4.74	120.32	63.18	18,985
Overseas Chinese-funded 港澳台資	56	88	13,292	-22	-0.08	-0.29	151.33	72.56	27,028
By size 規模									
Large 大型	6	777	117,750	-206,154	-118.35	-505.25	151.54	76.58	174,197
Medium 中型	24	492	44,992	18,045	16.37	62.20	91.38	73.69	110,259
Small 小型	224	97	9,476	4,004	28.93	113.23	98.14	74.45	13,840
By regional distribution 地區分布									
Central-North 華北	40	111	7,838	-52	-0.29	-0.89	70.63	67.54	17,992
Beijing 北京	18	70	2,801	-781	-6.31	-12.58	39.79	49.87	12,376
Tianjin 天津	9	48	8,838	1,234	17.16	33.14	182.43	48.23	7,194
Hebei 河北	8	296	19,684	-35	-0.07	-0.34	66.47	80.40	52,305
Shanxi 山西	2	160	12,315	505	7.72	17.35	76.97	55.54	6,545
Inner Mongolia 內蒙	3	16	490	40	19.67	21.05	31.28	6.56	203
Northeast 東北	26	241	6,512	-863	-3.91	-22.70	27.05	82.76	22,050
Liaoning 遼寧	16	245	5,090	-1,244	-7.85	-96.18	20.74	91.84	15,851
Jilin 吉林	8	183	3,199	-464	-2.42	-15.41	17.48	84.28	19,143
Heilongjiang 黑龍江	2	435	31,145	595	0.71	2.20	71.68	67.55	83,270
Central East 華東	130	147	17,741	940	3.40	12.12	120.60	71.92	27,628
Shanghai 上海	7	143	17,246	907	3.81	10.02	120.96	61.94	23,796
Jiangsu 江蘇	47	184	24,636	697	1.94	7.44	133.87	73.90	35,879
Zhejiang 浙江	26	115	10,538	-313	-1.16	-4.11	91.76	71.73	26,943
Anhui 安徽	5	47	1,142	-192	-7.36	-45.93	24.19	83.97	2,608
Fujian 福建	4	18	5,360	-313	-7.26	-18.33	297.78	60.39	4,305
Jiangxi 江西	1	308	22,300	150	2.48	35.71	72.40	93.06	6,050
Shandong 山東	40	147	17,606	2,333	9.31	31.34	119.87	70.29	25,050
Central-South 中南	53	119	16,649	110	0.37	1.66	139.35	77.90	30,183
Henan 河南	18	131	9,339	860	3.51	31.58	71.17	88.90	24,528
Hubei 湖北	4	162	4,505	-635	-3.62	29.53	27.89	112.25	17,533
Hunan 湖南	4	60	2,480	-1,640	-14.95	-24.74	41.51	39.58	10,973
Guangdong 廣東	26	118	26,315	-7	-0.02	-0.07	223.22	72.82	39,906
Guangxi 廣西	1	20	2,150	-340	-5.14	-7.62	107.50	32.53	6,610
Hainan 海南									
Southwest 西南	9	187	11,844	-1,066	-3.62	-28.60	63.23	87.33	29,396
Chongqing 重慶	4	194	16,017	-94	-0.40	-1.75	82.35	77.31	23,778
Sichuan 四川	4	232	9,960	-2,580	-5.77	-96.11	43.00	93.99	44,684
Guizhou 貴州	1								
Yunnan 雲南									
Tibet 西藏									
Northwest 西北	5	80	2,612	-284	-3.35	-27.36	32.49	87.77	8,484
Shaanxi 陝西	3	56	3,143				56.13	97.66	9,837
Gansu 甘肅	1	170	890				5.24	75.47	1,060
Qinghai 青海									
Ningxia 寧夏									
Xinjiang 新疆	1	64	2,740	-1,420	-11.98	-33.49	42.81	64.22	11,850

2829: Other Synthetic Fibre 其他合成纖維製造業

Year 年份	Number of firms 企業個數	Rate of change 每年變化 (%)	Number of employees 職工人數 (人)	Rate of change 每年變化 (%)	Total revenue (mil. RMB) 總銷售收入 (百萬元)	Rate of change 每年變化 (%)	Total profit (mil. RMB) 總利潤 (百萬元)	Rate of change 每年變化 (%)
1993	245		43,892		3,044		152	
1994	254	3.67%	45,327	3.27%	3,773	23.94%	153	0.38%
1995	274	7.87%	48,278	6.51%	4,130	9.47%	-3	-102.05%
1996	263	-4.01%	38,242	-20.79%	3,791	-8.21%	93	3074.10%

3 Major products* 3種主要產品*	Output 產量	Sales volume 銷售量	Unit 單位
a) Polypropylene Fibre 丙綸纖維	114,219	91,375	ton 噸
b) Tobacco Tow 煙用絲束	87,311	81,200	ton 噸
c) Other Synthetic Fibre 其他合成纖維	1,674	1,607	ton 噸

Top 10 firms by revenue (year founded) 收入排名前10家企業 (創辦年份)	City 城市	Province 省	Telephone / fax 電話 / 傳真	Number of employees 職工人數	Ownership 產業所有權	Revenue ('000 RMB) 銷售收入 (千元)	Profit ('000 RMB) (rank) 利潤(千元)(排名)	Total assets ('000 RMB) 總資產 (千元)	Major products 主要產品
Wendeng Li Xiang Industrial Co. Ltd. 文登市力象實業集團有限公司(1953)	Weihai 威海市	Shandong 山東省	(0896)8898988 (0896)8898988	700	Collectively-owned 集體	300,150	55120(1)	159,470	a
Nantong Palypropylene Fibre Co. of China Tobacco 中煙南通丙綸纖維公司(1989)	Nantong 南通市	Jiangsu 江蘇省	(0513)4541540 (0513)4541728	737	Collectively-owned 集體	132,120	7568(10)	95,814	b
Lianyungang Zhongshan Polyurethane Fibre Co. Ltd. 連雲港鐘山氨綸有限公司(1988)	Lianyungang 連雲港市	Jiangsu 江蘇省	(0518)2340647 (0518)2340750	253	Foreign-funded 外資	129,862	24302(2)	398,610	c
Shenzhen Petrochemical Chemical Fibres Co. Ltd. 深圳石化東宏化纖有限公司(1991)	Shenzhen 深圳市	Guangdong 廣東省	(0755)3311007 (0755)3310110	417	Overseas Chinese-funded 港澳台資	128,754	10539(6)	127,524	a
Zhongshan Yue Heng Chemical Fibre Co. Ltd. 中山粵輕化纖有限公司(1989)	Zhongshan 中山市	Guangdong 廣東省	(0760)8337283 (0760)8317686	312	Overseas Chinese-funded 港澳台資	126,056	4594(12)	84,332	a
Changzhou No.2 Synthetic Fibre Factory 常州市第二合成纖維廠(1985)	Changzhou 常州市	Jiangsu 江蘇省	(0519)3731131	800	Collectively-owned 集體	113,637	91(79)	179,816	a
Changshu Polypropylene Fibre Factory 常熟市丙綸廠(1980)	Suzhou 蘇州市	Jiangsu 江蘇省	(0512)2772500 (0512)2772224	944	Domestic JVs 聯營	109,620	1340(21)	218,270	a
Zhuhai Sez Cigarette Filter Medium Company 珠海特區卷煙濾材公司(1991)	Zhuhai 珠海市	Guangdong 廣東省	(0756)2263298 (0756)2263743	231	State-owned 國有	101,361	10285(7)	184,692	o
Nanjing Cigarette Filter Tows Factory 南京煙濾嘴絲束廠(1987)	Nanjing 南京市	Jiangsu 江蘇省	(025)2495930	420	Collectively-owned 集體	95,620	2040(15)	56,930	o
Henan Zhong Zhou Burang Tai Ke Si Chemical Fibre Industrial Co. Ltd. 河南省中州普蘭太克斯化纖工業有限公司(1984)	Zhengzhou 鄭州市	Henan 河南省	(0371)4234126	702	Foreign-funded 外資	94,546	10878(5)	176,587	b

Top 10 Cities by Production Output 產出排名前10位城市	Province 省	Market share 市場份額	Number of firms 企業個數
Weihai 威海市	Shandong 山東省	8.31%	2
Suzhou 蘇州市	Jiangsu 江蘇省	7.80%	11
Shanghai 上海市	Shanghai 上海市	7.25%	13
Zhongshan 中山市	Guangdong 廣東省	6.31%	8
Changzhou 常州市	Jiangsu 江蘇省	6.13%	13
Nantong 南通市	Jiangsu 江蘇省	5.74%	11
Binzhou 濱州市	Shandong 山東省	3.69%	26
Wuxi 無錫市	Jiangsu 江蘇省	3.68%	13
Shenzhen 深圳市	Guangdong 廣東省	3.67%	6
Guangzhou 廣州市	Guangdong 廣東省	3.00%	7

10 Major Wholesalers 10家主要批發商	City 城市	Province 省	Telephone / Fax 電話 / 傳真
Anhui Clothing Import & Export Company 安徽省服裝進出口公司	Hefei 合肥市	Anhui 安徽省	(0551)3632212 (0551)3632002
Qingdao Textile Clothing Industrial Group Company 青島紡織服裝實業集團公司	Qingdao 青島市	Shandong 山東省	(0532)2877853 (0532)2869315
Hebei Textile Import & Export (Group) Company 河北省紡織品進出口(集團)公司	Shijiazhuang 石家莊市	Hebei 河北省	(0311)7028530 (0311)7027781
Zhong Fang Pledget Import & Export Company 中紡紗布進出口公司	Beijing 北京市	Beijing 北京市	(010)65124718 (010)65124713
Shaoxing Import & Export Company 紹興市進出口公司	Shaoxing 紹興市	Zhejiang 浙江省	(0575)5132822 (0575)5141577
Hunan Hua Xiang Import & Export (Group) Company 湖南省華湘進出口(集團)公司	Changsha 長沙市	Hunan 湖南省	(0731)2282440 (0731)2286995
City's Import & Export Company Trade Dept. 市進出口公司貿易部	Yichang 宜昌市	Hubei 湖北省	(0717)6450778 (0717)6441875
Shanghai Pu Dong Xinqu Import & Export Company 上海浦東新區進出口公司	Shanghai 上海市	Shanghai 上海市	(021)58878801 (021)58827444
Ningbo Yinxian Import & Export Company 寧波市鄞縣進出口公司	Ningbo 寧波市	Zhejiang 浙江省	(0574)7875205 (0574)7873168
Zhejiang Silk Import & Export Company 浙江省絲綢進出口公司	Hangzhou 杭州市	Zhejiang 浙江省	(0571)5195588 (0571)5192542

*Also include sales by firms outside this industry.包括本行業以外廠家的銷售。"o" stands for "others". "o" 代表 "其他產品" 。

2851: Fishing Tackle Wire 漁具用絲製造業

The industry accounts for 0.002% of the total revenue of China's industrial sector in 1996. The revenue growth rate of the industry is -40.3% from 1995, as compared to the growth rate of China's industrial sector, 9.51%. The rate of return on asset is 0.34%. 76.19% of all firms in the industry made a profit while 23.81% had negative returns. The top province in terms of the industry's revenue is Shanghai, accounting for 21.91% of the total revenue.
本行業在1996年佔全行業總產值0.002%，行業年增長率為-40.3%（全國工業年增長率9.51%）。行業的資產回報率0.34%，76.19%的企業盈利，23.81%的企業虧損。銷售收入最高的省份為上海市，佔本行業的21.91%。

	Total number of firms 企業總數	Total number of employees 職工總數	Total revenue (mil. RMB) 總銷售收入（百萬元）	Total profit (mil. RMB) 總利潤（百萬元）	Return on assets 資產利潤率 (%)	Return on equity 權益利潤率 (%)	Labour productivity ('000 RMB / worker) 勞動生產率（千元/人）	Debts / assets 資產負債率 (%)	Total assets (mil. RMB) 總資產（百萬元）
Industry Overall 行業總體	21	3,091	112	1	0.34	1.34	36.23	74.43	155

	Number of firms 企業個數	Average number of employees 平均職工人數	Average revenue ('000 RMB) 平均銷售收入（千元）	Average profit ('000 RMB) 平均利潤（千元）	Return on assets 資產利潤率 (%)	Return on equity 權益利潤率 (%)	Labour productivity ('000 RMB / worker) 勞動生產率（千元/人）	Average debts / assets 平均資產負債率(%)	Average Total assets ('000 RMB) 平均總資產（千元）
By ownership 產業所有權									
State-owned 國有	5	405	10,200	-400	-1.98	-10.00	25.20	80.20	20,200
Collectively-owned 集體	14	61	3,083	80	3.01	7.93	50.60	62.12	2,673
Privately-owned 私有									
Domestic JVs 聯營									
Joint stock 股份制									
Foreign-funded 外資	1	124	6,459	2,452	24.90	91.21	52.09	72.70	9,846
Overseas Chinese-funded 港澳台資	1	90	11,367	-576	-8.55	-18.37	126.30	53.43	6,735
By size 規模									
Large 大型									
Medium 中型	2	653	19,622	152	0.47	2.37	30.05	80.02	32,030
Small 小型	19	94	3,829	37	0.77	2.56	40.76	70.09	4,786
By regional distribution 地區分布									
Central-North 華北	2	54	2,410	30	1.92	21.43	45.05	91.05	1,565
Beijing 北京									
Tianjin 天津									
Hebei 河北	2	54	2,410	30	1.92	21.43	45.05	91.05	1,565
Shanxi 山西									
Inner Mongolia 內蒙									
Northeast 東北	2	35	965	40	1.70	50.00	27.97	96.82	2,355
Liaoning 遼寧	1	34	1,330	80	1.90	-22.86	39.12	108.57	4,200
Jilin 吉林									
Heilongjiang 黑龍江	1	35	600				17.14		510
Central East 華東	10	204	6,067	21	0.18	0.83	29.71	78.73	11,836
Shanghai 上海	1	992	24,540	-1,950	-3.28	85.53	24.74	103.83	59,540
Jiangsu 江蘇	1	30	1,410	200	15.15	28.17	47.00	45.45	1,320
Zhejiang 浙江	1	509	14,750	120	0.57	1.05	28.98	45.43	20,890
Anhui 安徽	2	33	1,990	165	8.62	11.58	60.30	25.59	1,915
Fujian 福建									
Jiangxi 江西									
Shandong 山東	5	89	3,198	302	4.61	12.10	35.93	61.93	6,556
Central-South 中南	6	144	7,405	27	0.57	1.15	51.48	50.76	4,698
Henan 河南	1	456	10,490	-170	-0.85	-1.61	23.00	47.13	20,010
Hubei 湖北	1	280	21,870	120	2.69	20.00	78.11	86.55	4,460
Hunan 湖南	1	32	1,640	90	20.45	300.00	51.25	93.18	440
Guangdong 廣東	3	32	3,477	40	3.66	4.49	109.79	18.60	1,093
Guangxi 廣西									
Hainan 海南									
Southwest 西南	1	10	230	10	6.25	20.00	23.00	68.75	160
Chongqing 重慶	1	10	230	10	6.25	20.00	23.00	68.75	160
Sichuan 四川									
Guizhou 貴州									
Yunnan 雲南									
Tibet 西藏									
Northwest 西北									
Shaanxi 陝西									
Gansu 甘肅									
Qinghai 青海									
Ningxia 寧夏									
Xinjiang 新疆									

2851: Fishing Tackle Wire 漁具用絲製造業

Year 年份	Number of firms 企業個數	Rate of change 每年變化 (%)	Number of employees 職工人數 (人)	Rate of change 每年變化 (%)	Total revenue (mil. RMB) 總銷售收入 (百萬元)	Rate of change 每年變化 (%)	Total profit (mil. RMB) 總利潤 (百萬元)	Rate of change 每年變化 (%)
1993	22		7,768		118		-4	
1994	19	-13.64%	4,226	-45.60%	166	40.34%	-11	-190.95%
1995	29	52.63%	4,185	-0.97%	188	13.14%	-6	38.65%
1996	21	-27.59%	3,091	-26.14%	112	-40.29%	1	115.51%

3 Major products* 3 種主要產品 *	Output 產量	Sales volume 銷售量	Unit 單位
a) Polythylene Products 聚乙烯製品	6,359	6,232	ton 噸
b) Polypropylene Products 聚丙烯製品	2,608	2,191	ton 噸

Top 10 firms by revenue (year founded) 收入排名前 10 家企業 (創辦年份)	City 城市	Province 省	Telephone / fax 電話 / 傳真	Number of employees 職工人數	Ownership 產業所有權	Revenue ('000 RMB) 銷售收入 (千元)	Profit ('000 RMB) (rank) 利潤 (千元) (排名)	Total assets ('000 RMB) 總資產 (千元)	Major products 主要產品
Shanghai Rope Net Factory 上海繩網廠(1939)	Shanghai 上海市	Shanghai 上海市	(021)65025760 (021)65028464	950	State-owned 國有	24,537	-1950(8)	59,544	b
Hubei Jiayu Pai Zhou Chemical Plant 湖北省嘉魚縣牌洲化工廠(1986)	Xianning 咸寧市	Hubei 湖北省	(0715)516296	91	Collectively-owned 集體	21,872	124(4)	4,462	o
Wenling Fishery Plastics Chemical Factory 浙江省温嶺漁業塑料化工廠(1966)	Taizhou 臺州市	Zhejiang 浙江省	(0576)6111970 (0576)6111970	530	State-owned 國有	14,753	124(5)	20,885	o
Weihai Plastics Net Thread Factory 威海市塑料網線廠(1984)	Weihai 威海市	Shandong 山東省	(0896)5817991 (0896)5817991	250	Collectively-owned 集體	12,676	1294(1)	29,987	a
Huilai Huicheng Mei Xing Plastic Products Factory 惠來縣惠城梅興塑料製品廠(1989)	Jieyang 揭陽市	Guangdong 廣東省	(0663)6681067	80	Collectively-owned 集體	9,600	120(6)	2,200	a
Hejian Chemical Fibre Factory 河間市化纖廠(1991)	Cangzhou 滄州市	Hebei 河北省	(0317)3225309	40	Collectively-owned 集體	3,480	117(7)	2,211	o
Caohu Hai Bin Fishing Net Coir Thread Factory 巢湖市海濱漁網綜絲廠(1995)	Chaohu 巢湖市	Anhui 安徽省		40	Collectively-owned 集體	3,000	306(2)	3,567	o
Leling Hu Jia Xiang Welfare Fishing Net Wire Factory 樂陵市胡家鄉福利漁網絲廠(1992)	Dezhou 德州市	Shandong 山東省	(0534)6323138 (0534)6323138	90	Collectively-owned 集體	2,630	150(3)	1,350	o

Top 10 Cities by Production Output 產出排名前 10 位城市	Province 省	Market share 市場份額	Number of firms 企業個數
Chaohu 巢湖市	Anhui 安徽省	49.39%	4
Tianjin 天津市	Tianjin 天津市	12.19%	2
Taizhou 臺州市	Zhejiang 浙江省	10.16%	2
Weihai 威海市	Shandong 山東省	7.41%	1
Pingdingshan 平頂山市	Henan 河南省	6.30%	1
Zhanjiang 湛江市	Guangdong 廣東省	5.53%	1
Cangzhou 滄州市	Hebei 河北省	2.55%	2
Ningbo 寧波市	Zhejiang 浙江省	1.94%	1
Shanghai 上海市	Shanghai 上海市	1.27%	1
Maoming 茂名市	Guangdong 廣東省	0.74%	1

10 Major Wholesalers 10 家主要批發商	City 城市	Province 省	Telephone / Fax 電話 / 傳真
China Agricultural Machinery Hua Bei Company 中國農業機械華北公司	Tianjin 天津市	Tianjin 天津市	(022)23394240 (022)23304247
Shandong Agriculture Means of Production Company 山東省農業生產資料公司	Ji'nan 濟南市	Shandong 山東省	(0531)8957052 (0531)8957142
Yantai Agriculture Means of Production General Company 煙台市農業生產資料總公司	Yantai 煙台市	Shandong 山東省	(0535)6216668 (0535)6211348
Sichuan Agriculture Means of Production General Company 四川省農業生產資料總公司	Chengdu 成都市	Sichuan 四川省	(028)6751135 (028)6751646
Heilongjiang Agriculture Means of Production Company 黑龍江省農業生產資料公司	Harbin 哈爾濱市	Heilongjiang 黑龍江省	(0451)8989948 (0451)8382367
Shannxi Agriculture Means of Production General Company 陝西省農業生產資料總公司	Xi'an 西安市	Shaanxi 陝西省	(029)7422104 (029)7411799
Gansu Agriculture Means of Production General Company 甘肅省農業生產資料總公司	Lanzhou 蘭州市	Gansu 甘肅省	(0931)8822971
Yitong Man Zu Autonomous County Agricultural Goods & Materials Co. Ltd. 伊通滿族自治縣農用物資有限責任公司	Siping 四平市	Jilin 吉林省	(0434)4223146
Langfang Agriculture Means of Production Company 廊坊市農業生產資料公司	Langfang 廊坊市	Hebei 河北省	(0316)2013148
Anhui Agriculture Means of Production Company 安徽省農業生產資料公司	Hefei 合肥市	Anhui 安徽省	(0551)2656541 (0551)2655720

*Also include sales by firms outside this industry.包括本行業以外廠家的銷售。"o" stands for "others". "o" 代表"其他產品"。

2852: Fishing Tackle Thread 漁具用線製造業

The industry accounts for 0.001% of the total revenue of China's industrial sector in 1996. The revenue growth rate of the industry is -53.2% from 1995, as compared to the growth rate of China's industrial sector, 9.51%. The rate of return on asset is -0.89%. 80.00% of all firms in the industry made a profit while 20.00% had negative returns. The top province in terms of the industry's revenue is Jiangsu, accounting for 62.59% of the total revenue.
本行業在1996年佔全行業總產值0.001%，行業年增長率為-53.2%（全國工業年增長率9.51%）。行業的資產回報率-0.89%，80.00%的企業盈利，20.00%的企業虧損。銷售收入最高的省份為江蘇省，佔本行業的62.59%。

	Total number of firms 企業總數	Total number of employees 職工總數	Total revenue (mil. RMB) 總銷售收入（百萬元）	Total profit (mil. RMB) 總利潤（百萬元）	Return on assets 資產利潤率 (%)	Return on equity 權益利潤率 (%)	Labour productivity ('000 RMB / worker) 勞動生產率（千元/人）	Debts / assets 資產負債率 (%)	Total assets (mil. RMB) 總資產（百萬元）
Industry Overall 行業總體	7	686	42		-0.89	-8.45	61.22	89.41	34

	Number of firms 企業個數	Average number of employees 平均職工人數	Average revenue ('000 RMB) 平均銷售收入（千元）	Average profit ('000 RMB) 平均利潤（千元）	Return on assets 資產利潤率 (%)	Return on equity 權益利潤率 (%)	Labour productivity ('000 RMB / worker) 勞動生產率（千元/人）	Average debts / assets 平均資產負債率(%)	Average Total assets ('000 RMB) 平均總資產（千元）
By ownership 產業所有權									
State-owned 國有					-7.74	-111.63	28.09	93.07	
Collectively-owned 集體	5	99	6,176				62.14	101.50	3,588
Privately-owned 私有									
Domestic JVs 聯營									
Joint stock 股份制									
Foreign-funded 外資	2	95	5,559				58.82	73.41	8,028
Overseas Chinese-funded 港澳台資									
By size 規模									
Large 大型									
Medium 中型									
Small 小型	7	98	6,000				61.22	88.24	4,857
By regional distribution 地區分布									
Central-North 華北	2	49	3,390	570	27.14	102.70	69.18	73.57	2,100
Beijing 北京									
Tianjin 天津	2	49	3,390	570	27.14	102.70	69.18	73.57	2,100
Hebei 河北									
Shanxi 山西									
Inner Mongolia 內蒙									
Northeast 東北	1	192	7,400	-1,850	-20.29	64.24	38.54	131.58	9,120
Liaoning 遼寧	1	192	7,400	-1,850	-20.29	64.24	38.54	131.58	9,120
Jilin 吉林									
Heilongjiang 黑龍江									
Central East 華東	4	99	7,048	103	2.03	7.71	71.19	73.63	5,053
Shanghai 上海									
Jiangsu 江蘇	3	127	8,763	127	1.95	7.88	68.82	75.23	6,500
Zhejiang 浙江									
Anhui 安徽									
Fujian 福建	1	14	1,900	30	4.23	6.00	135.71	29.58	710
Jiangxi 江西									
Shandong 山東									
Central-South 中南									
Henan 河南									
Hubei 湖北									
Hunan 湖南									
Guangdong 廣東									
Guangxi 廣西									
Hainan 海南									
Southwest 西南									
Chongqing 重慶									
Sichuan 四川									
Guizhou 貴州									
Yunnan 雲南									
Tibet 西藏									
Northwest 西北									
Shaanxi 陝西									
Gansu 甘肅									
Qinghai 青海									
Ningxia 寧夏									
Xinjiang 新疆									

Year 年份	Number of firms 企業個數	Rate of change 每年變化 (%)	Number of employees 職工人數 (人)	Rate of change 每年變化 (%)	Total revenue (mil. RMB) 總銷售收入 (百萬元)	Rate of change 每年變化 (%)	Total profit (mil. RMB) 總利潤 (百萬元)	Rate of change 每年變化 (%)
1993	14		2,364		71		0	
1994	16	14.29%	2,706	14.47%	70	-1.53%	-2	-491.05%
1995	10	-37.50%	1,282	-52.62%	90	29.07%	-7	-329.96%
1996	7	-30.00%	686	-46.49%	42	-53.22%		100.00%

3 Major products* 3種主要產品 *	Output 產量	Sales volume 銷售量	Unit 單位
a) Plastic Products 塑料製品	2,361	2,479	ton 噸

Top 10 firms by revenue (year founded) 收入排名前10家企業 (創辦年份)	City 城市	Province 省	Telephone / fax 電話 / 傳真	Number of employees 職工人數	Ownership 產業所有權	Revenue ('000 RMB) 銷售收入 (千元)	Profit ('000 RMB) (rank) 利潤 (千元) (排名)	Total assets ('000 RMB) 總資產 (千元)	Major products 主要產品
Rugao Technology Ply Yarn Mill 如皋市工藝拼線廠(1980)	Nantong 南通市	Jiangsu 江蘇省	(0513)7533573	200	Collectively-owned 集體	22,254	350(2)	13,965	o
Pulandian Dalian Net Tools Factory 普蘭店市大連網具廠(1984)	Dalian 大連市	Liaoning 遼寧省	(0411)9614976	195	Collectively-owned 集體	7,401	-1851(6)	9,120	a
Jinbao Yinda Plastics Hardware Products Factory 津寶銀達塑料五金製品廠(1984)	Tianjin 天津市	Tianjin 天津市	(022)29237007	60	Collectively-owned 集體	6,200	1200(1)	2,600	o
Nanjing Ocean Rope & Net Factory 南京遠洋繩網廠(1990)	Nanjing 南京市	Jiangsu 江蘇省	(025)7630211	135	其他經濟	2,660	8(3)	2,435	o
Zhoushan Zhe Hua Group Co. Ltd. 舟山市浙華集團有限公司(1995)	Zhoushan 舟山市	Zhejiang 浙江省	(0580)2038683 / (0580)2027497	22	Collectively-owned 集體	2,571	-189(5)	16,581	o

Top 10 Cities by Production Output 產出排名前10位城市	Province 省	Market share 市場份額	Number of firms 企業個數
Nantong 南通市	Jiangsu 江蘇省	71.98%	4
Tianjin 天津市	Tianjin 天津市	9.92%	2
Dalian 大連市	Liaoning 遼寧省	6.05%	1
Tai'an 泰安市	Shandong 山東省	3.98%	1
Binzhou 濱州市	Shandong 山東省	3.31%	1
Zhoushan 舟山市	Zhejiang 浙江省	3.26%	1
Fuzhou 福州市	Fujian 福建省	1.20%	1
Nanjing 南京市	Jiangsu 江蘇省	0.29%	1

10 Major Wholesalers 10家主要批發商	City 城市	Province 省	Telephone / Fax 電話 / 傳真
China Agricultural Machinery Hua Bei Company 中國農業機械華北公司	Tianjin 天津市	Tianjin 天津市	(022)23394240 / (022)23304247
Shandong Agriculture Means of Production Company 山東省農業生產資料公司	Ji'nan 濟南市	Shandong 山東省	(0531)8957052 / (0531)8957142
Yantai Agriculture Means of Production General Company 煙台市農業生產資料總公司	Yantai 煙台市	Shandong 山東省	(0535)6216668 / (0535)6211348
Sichuan Agriculture Means of Production General Company 四川省農業生產資料總公司	Chengdu 成都市	Sichuan 四川省	(028)6751135 / (028)6751646
Heilongjiang Agriculture Means of Production Company 黑龍江省農業生產資料公司	Harbin 哈爾濱市	Heilongjiang 黑龍江省	(0451)8989948 / (0451)8382367
Shannxi Agriculture Means of Production General Company 陝西省農業生產資料總公司	Xi'an 西安市	Shaanxi 陝西省	(029)7422104 / (029)7411799
Gansu Agriculture Means of Production General Company 甘肅省農業生產資料總公司	Lanzhou 蘭州市	Gansu 甘肅省	(0931)8822971
Yitong Man Zu Autonomous County Agricultural Goods & Materials Co. Ltd. 伊通滿族自治縣農用物資有限責任公司	Siping 四平市	Jilin 吉林省	(0434)4223146
Langfang Agriculture Means of Production Company 廊坊市農業生產資料公司	Langfang 廊坊市	Hebei 河北省	(0316)2013148
Anhui Agriculture Means of Production Company 安徽省農業生產資料公司	Hefei 合肥市	Anhui 安徽省	(0551)2656541 / (0551)2655720

*Also include sales by firms outside this industry.包括本行業以外廠家的銷售。"o" stands for "others". "o" 代表"其他產品"。

2853: Fishing Tackle Rope 漁具用繩製造業

The industry accounts for 0.002% of the total revenue of China's industrial sector in 1996. The revenue growth rate of the industry is -24.1% from 1995, as compared to the growth rate of China's industrial sector, 9.51%. The rate of return on asset is -7.03%. 68.42% of all firms in the industry made a profit while 31.58% had negative returns. The top province in terms of the industry's revenue is Jiangsu, accounting for 48.38% of the total revenue.
本行業在1996年佔全行業總產值0.002%，行業年增長率為-24.1%（全國工業年增長率9.51%）。行業的資產回報率-7.03%，68.42%的企業盈利，31.58%的企業虧損。銷售收入最高的省份為江蘇省，佔本行業的48.38%。

	Total number of firms 企業總數	Total number of employees 職工總數	Total revenue (mil. RMB) 總銷售收入（百萬元）	Total profit (mil. RMB) 總利潤（百萬元）	Return on assets 資產利潤率 (%)	Return on equity 權益利潤率 (%)	Labour productivity ('000 RMB / worker) 勞動生產率（千元/人）	Debts / assets 資產負債率 (%)	Total assets (mil. RMB) 總資產（百萬元）
Industry Overall 行業總體	23	2,746	90	-12	-7.03	-30.30	32.77	76.80	177

	Number of firms 企業個數	Average number of employees 平均職工人數	Average revenue ('000 RMB) 平均銷售收入（千元）	Average profit ('000 RMB) 平均利潤（千元）	Return on assets 資產利潤率 (%)	Return on equity 權益利潤率 (%)	Labour productivity ('000 RMB / worker) 勞動生產率（千元/人）	Average debts / assets 平均資產負債率(%)	Average Total assets ('000 RMB) 平均總資產（千元）
By ownership 產業所有權									
State-owned 國有	4	253	7,500	-2,000	-13.56	-80.00	29.67	83.05	14,750
Collectively-owned 集體	16	57	1,885	-54	-2.55	-87.97	33.22	97.10	2,137
Privately-owned 私有	1	8	93	5	9.01	9.01	11.59		53
Domestic JVs 聯營									
Joint stock 股份制									
Foreign-funded 外資	1	795	28,843	-2,847	-4.27	-16.07	36.28	73.45	66,735
Overseas Chinese-funded 港澳台資	1	23	896	-287	-1.68	-2.34	38.96	28.10	17,023
By size 規模									
Large 大型	1	934	28,349	-6,493	-8.95	-40.18	30.35	77.73	72,555
Medium 中型	1	351	24,351	186	0.58	1.71	69.38	65.90	31,884
Small 小型	21	70	1,776	-271	-7.85	-40.77	25.53	80.75	3,454
By regional distribution 地區分布									
Central-North 華北	1								
Beijing 北京									
Tianjin 天津									
Hebei 河北									
Shanxi 山西									
Inner Mongolia 內蒙	1								
Northeast 東北	4	155	6,710	-995	-10.60	-46.12	43.22	77.02	9,390
Liaoning 遼寧	4	155	6,710	-995	-10.60	-46.12	43.22	77.02	9,390
Jilin 吉林									
Heilongjiang 黑龍江									
Central East 華東	10	146	5,211	-479	-5.56	-32.39	35.62	82.84	8,612
Shanghai 上海									
Jiangsu 江蘇	4	317	10,885	-1,353	-7.04	-50.37	34.39	86.03	19,208
Zhejiang 浙江	1	30	870	-30	-5.00	-9.09	29.00	45.00	600
Anhui 安徽									
Fujian 福建									
Jiangxi 江西									
Shandong 山東	5	33	1,540	130	7.48	17.47	46.11	57.19	1,738
Central-South 中南	8	83	1,335	-459	-6.92	-20.86	16.13	66.87	6,634
Henan 河南									
Hubei 湖北	1	220	2,220	-150	-2.49	-8.88	10.09	71.93	6,020
Hunan 湖南									
Guangdong 廣東	5	64	1,390	-124	-2.11	-3.64	21.72	42.15	5,884
Guangxi 廣西	2	61	755	-1,450	-16.45	258.93	12.38	106.41	8,815
Hainan 海南									
Southwest 西南									
Chongqing 重慶									
Sichuan 四川									
Guizhou 貴州									
Yunnan 雲南									
Tibet 西藏									
Northwest 西北									
Shaanxi 陝西									
Gansu 甘肅									
Qinghai 青海									
Ningxia 寧夏									
Xinjiang 新疆									

2853: Fishing Tackle Rope 漁具用繩製造業

Year 年份	Number of firms 企業個數	Rate of change 每年變化 (%)	Number of employees 職工人數 (人)	Rate of change 每年變化 (%)	Total revenue (mil. RMB) 總銷售收入 (百萬元)	Rate of change 每年變化 (%)	Total profit (mil. RMB) 總利潤 (百萬元)	Rate of change 每年變化 (%)
1993	19		2,279		68		-6	
1994	25	31.58%	2,042	-10.40%	69	1.65%	-2	56.81%
1995	26	4.00%	3,606	76.59%	119	72.45%	-11	-349.41%
1996	23	-11.54%	2,746	-23.85%	90	-24.08%	-12	-9.03%

3 Major products* 3 種主要產品 *	Output 產量	Sales volume 銷售量	Unit 單位
a) Plastic Artificial Leather 塑料人造革	212	193	ton 噸
b) Polythylene Products 聚乙烯製品	76	75	ton 噸

Top 10 firms by revenue (year founded) 收入排名前 10 家企業 (創辦年份)	City 城市	Province 省	Telephone / fax 電話 / 傳真	Number of employees 職工人數	Ownership 產業所有權	Revenue ('000 RMB) 銷售收入 (千元)	Profit ('000 RMB) (rank) 利潤 (千元) (排名)	Total assets ('000 RMB) 總資產 (千元)	Major products 主要產品
Taizhou Nanyang Rope & Net Co. Ltd. 泰州南陽繩網有限公司(1993)	Taizhou 泰州市	Jiangsu 江蘇省	(0523)6224320 (0523)6234163	1,192	Foreign-funded 外資	40,435	-5454(7)	72,711	o
Dalian Rope & Net Factory 大連繩網廠(1935)	Dalian 大連市	Liaoning 遼寧省	(0411)6658870 (0411)6658505	463	State-owned 國有	22,930	-4070(6)	32,273	o
Rongcheng Xunshan Net Knitting Factory 榮成市尋山織網廠(1986)	Weihai 威海市	Shandong 山東省		70	Collectively-owned 集體	5,280	506(1)	2,453	a
Shantou Fishery Articles for Use Import & Export Co. Fishery Articles Factory 汕頭漁業用品進出口公司漁業用品廠(1956)	Shantou 汕頭市	Guangdong 廣東省	(0754)8222158	243	State-owned 國有	3,547	-579(5)	5,206	o
Donggang Xin Gang Net Tools Factory 東港市新港網具廠(1993)	Dandong 丹東市	Liaoning 遼寧省	(0415)7104172	108	Collectively-owned 集體	3,349	81(2)	4,407	o
Honghu Fishing Tackle Factory 洪湖市漁具廠(1958)	Jingsha 荊沙市	Hubei 湖北省	(0716)8422718	220	State-owned 國有	2,218	-150(4)	6,017	o
Guanyun Yi Shan Zhen Yi Synthetic Fibre Net Factory 灌雲縣伊山鎮乙綸絲網廠(1973)	Lianyungang 連雲港市	Jiangsu 江蘇省	(0518)88165270 (0518)8812532	40	Collectively-owned 集體	2,171	52(3)	1,512	b

Top 10 Cities by Production Output 產出排名前 10 位城市	Province 省	Market share 市場份額	Number of firms 企業個數
Xiamen 廈門市	Fujian 福建省	29.28%	1
Taizhou 泰州市	Jiangsu 江蘇省	27.68%	1
Dalian 大連市	Liaoning 遼寧省	15.13%	2
Shanghai 上海市	Shanghai 上海市	6.30%	1
Yantai 煙台市	Shandong 山東省	3.37%	3
Dandong 丹東市	Liaoning 遼寧省	2.86%	2
Jingsha 荊沙市	Hubei 湖北省	2.37%	1
Nantong 南通市	Jiangsu 江蘇省	2.36%	2
Weifang 濰坊市	Shandong 山東省	2.22%	2
Weihai 威海市	Shandong 山東省	1.77%	2

10 Major Wholesalers 10 家主要批發商	City 城市	Province 省	Telephone / Fax 電話 / 傳真
China Agricultural Machinery Hua Bei Company 中國農業機械華北公司	Tianjin 天津市	Tianjin 天津市	(022)23394240 (022)23304247
Shandong Agriculture Means of Production Company 山東省農業生產資料公司	Ji'nan 濟南市	Shandong 山東省	(0531)8957052 (0531)8957142
Yantai Agriculture Means of Production General Company 煙台市農業生產資料總公司	Yantai 煙台市	Shandong 山東省	(0535)6216668 (0535)6211348
Sichuan Agriculture Means of Production General Company 四川省農業生產資料總公司	Chengdu 成都市	Sichuan 四川省	(028)6751135 (028)6751646
Heilongjiang Agriculture Means of Production Company 黑龍江省農業生產資料公司	Harbin 哈爾濱市	Heilongjiang 黑龍江省	(0451)8989948 (0451)8382367
Shannxi Agriculture Means of Production General Company 陝西省農業生產資料總公司	Xi'an 西安市	Shaanxi 陝西省	(029)7422104 (029)7411799
Gansu Agriculture Means of Production General Company 甘肅省農業生產資料總公司	Lanzhou 蘭州市	Gansu 甘肅省	(0931)8822971
Yitong Man Zu Autonomous County Agricultural Goods & Materials Co. Ltd. 伊通滿族自治縣農用物資有限責任公司	Siping 四平市	Jilin 吉林省	(0434)4223146
Langfang Agriculture Means of Production Company 廊坊市農業生產資料公司	Langfang 廊坊市	Hebei 河北省	(0316)2013148
Anhui Agriculture Means of Production Company 安徽省農業生產資料公司	Hefei 合肥市	Anhui 安徽省	(0551)2656541 (0551)2655720

*Also include sales by firms outside this industry.包括本行業以外廠家的銷售。"o" stands for "others". "o" 代表"其他產品"。

2854: Fishing Net 漁網製造業

The industry accounts for 0.019% of the total revenue of China's industrial sector in 1996. The revenue growth rate of the industry is 6.7% from 1995, as compared to the growth rate of China's industrial sector, 9.51%. The rate of return on asset is 0.42%. 57.20% of all firms in the industry made a profit while 35.90% had negative returns. The top province in terms of the industry's revenue is Guangdong, accounting for 27.44% of the total revenue.
本行業在1996年佔全行業總產值0.019%，行業年增長率為6.7%（全國工業年增長率9.51%）。行業的資產回報率0.42%，57.20%的企業盈利，35.90%的企業虧損。銷售收入最高的省份為廣東省，佔本行業的27.44%。

	Total number of firms 企業總數	Total number of employees 職工總數	Total revenue (mil. RMB) 總銷售收入（百萬元）	Total profit (mil. RMB) 總利潤（百萬元）	Return on assets 資產利潤率 (%)	Return on equity 權益利潤率 (%)	Labour productivity ('000 RMB / worker) 勞動生產率（千元/人）	Debts / assets 資產負債率 (%)	Total assets (mil. RMB) 總資產（百萬元）
Industry Overall 行業總體	167	24,523	1,095	7	0.42	1.29	44.65	67.18	1,588

	Number of firms 企業個數	Average number of employees 平均職工人數	Average revenue ('000 RMB) 平均銷售收入（千元）	Average profit ('000 RMB) 平均利潤（千元）	Return on assets 資產利潤率 (%)	Return on equity 權益利潤率 (%)	Labour productivity ('000 RMB / worker) 勞動生產率（千元/人）	Average debts / assets 平均資產負債率(%)	Average Total assets ('000 RMB) 平均總資產（千元）
By ownership 產業所有權									
State-owned 國有	21	204	4,238				20.75	68.68	16,571
Collectively-owned 集體	113	119	6,568	163	2.56	10.27	55.07	75.03	6,361
Privately-owned 私有	1	117	6,776	39	0.61	-5.12	57.91	111.98	6,287
Domestic JVs 聯營									
Joint stock 股份制									
Foreign-funded 外資	11	173	6,461	-252	-1.83	-4.84	37.44	62.27	13,807
Overseas Chinese-funded 港澳台資	21	226	8,854	-414	-2.39	-4.94	39.21	51.55	17,297
By size 規模									
Large 大型	1	62							
Medium 中型	8	386	22,164	504	1.87	4.96	57.46	62.30	26,940
Small 小型	157	136	5,845	19	0.22	0.67	42.99	67.96	8,743
By regional distribution 地區分布									
Central-North 華北	13	235	13,965	536	3.92	13.82	59.31	71.65	13,690
Beijing 北京									
Tianjin 天津	3	691	44,537	1,443	4.02	10.99	64.42	63.38	35,877
Hebei 河北	10	99	4,794	264	3.75	23.91	48.57	84.29	7,034
Shanxi 山西									
Inner Mongolia 內蒙									
Northeast 東北	8	100	3,325	-194	-3.46	-7.72	33.25	55.11	5,598
Liaoning 遼寧	4	137	3,980	-403	-4.26	-9.27	29.10	54.00	9,440
Jilin 吉林	2	46	840	-155	-8.83	129.17	18.46	106.84	1,755
Heilongjiang 黑龍江	2	81	4,500	185	10.54	12.46	55.56	15.38	1,755
Central East 華東	86	107	5,934	169	2.21	6.85	55.67	67.69	7,634
Shanghai 上海	2	37	5,200	80	1.74	66.67	142.47	97.39	4,600
Jiangsu 江蘇	36	122	6,476	87	1.21	2.94	53.06	58.78	7,157
Zhejiang 浙江	12	103	6,047	290	2.21	6.30	58.47	64.91	13,113
Anhui 安徽	10	168	9,800	650	5.83	34.82	58.30	83.25	11,143
Fujian 福建	8	19	963	-9	-0.67	-1.37	51.33	51.24	1,315
Jiangxi 江西	1	24	3,200	100	8.55	22.22	133.33	61.54	1,170
Shandong 山東	17	94	5,020	74	1.14	4.76	53.20	75.96	6,425
Central-South 中南	57	196	6,084	-249	-2.22	-6.52	31.08	66.00	11,228
Henan 河南	1	26	1,280	60	4.17	13.95	49.23	70.14	1,440
Hubei 湖北	3	104	6,390	-303	-7.17	-39.06	61.44	81.65	4,233
Hunan 湖南	6	130	3,160	-88	-1.53	-17.04	24.31	90.99	5,755
Guangdong 廣東	43	197	6,988	-274	-2.07	-5.65	35.48	63.30	13,237
Guangxi 廣西	2	761	2,875	-505	-5.16	-45.50	3.78	88.66	9,790
Hainan 海南	2	25	565				22.60	75.97	1,290
Southwest 西南	1	243	27,380	790	1.21	4.17	112.67	71.04	65,460
Chongqing 重慶	1	243	27,380	790	1.21	4.17	112.67	71.04	65,460
Sichuan 四川									
Guizhou 貴州									
Yunnan 雲南									
Tibet 西藏									
Northwest 西北	2	47	1,255	90	4.95	8.96	26.99	44.78	1,820
Shaanxi 陝西	1	87	2,300	180	5.33	9.18	26.44	42.01	3,380
Gansu 甘肅									
Qinghai 青海									
Ningxia 寧夏									
Xinjiang 新疆	1	6	210				35.00	80.77	260

2854: Fishing Net 漁網製造業

Year 年份	Number of firms 企業個數	Rate of change 每年變化 (%)	Number of employees 職工人數 (人)	Rate of change 每年變化 (%)	Total revenue (mil. RMB) 總銷售收入 (百萬元)	Rate of change 每年變化 (%)	Total profit (mil. RMB) 總利潤 (百萬元)	Rate of change 每年變化 (%)
1993	142		15,262		386		8	
1994	150	5.63%	21,358	39.94%	528	36.81%	-1	-118.51%
1995	170	13.33%	24,672	15.52%	1,026	94.47%	16	1158.14%
1996	167	-1.76%	24,523	-0.60%	1,095	6.73%	7	-55.69%

3 Major products* 3 種主要產品 *	Output 產量	Sales volume 銷售量	Unit 單位
a) Polythylene Products 聚乙烯製品	41,393	40, 5	ton 噸
b) Polyvinyl Chloride Products 聚氯乙烯製品	3,720	3,423	ton 噸

Top 10 firms by revenue (year founded) 收入排名前 10 家企業 (創辦年份)	City 城市	Province 省	Telephone / fax 電話 / 傳真	Number of employees 職工人數	Ownership 產業所有權	Revenue ('000 RMB) 銷售收入 (千元)	Profit ('000 RMB) (rank) 利潤 (千元) (排名)	Total assets ('000 RMB) 總資產 (千元)	Major products 主要產品
Tianjin Fishnet Making Factory 天津市漁網廠(1981)	Tianjin 天津市	Tianjin 天津市	(022)25623317	2,120	Collectively-owned 集體	132,630	4350(1)	106,990	o
Huilai Hua Hu Fishing Net Factory 惠來縣華湖漁網廠(1983)	Jieyang 揭陽市	Guangdong 廣東省	(0663)6686689	590	Collectively-owned 集體	72,038	-1233(83)	26,420	a
King Chou Net Mfg. Co. Ltd. 金洲製網有限公司(1992)	Suzhou 蘇州市	Jiangsu 江蘇省	(0512)7301219	400	Overseas Chinese-funded 港澳台資	52,741	4342(2)	61,652	o
Jinhu Fishnet Making Factory 金湖縣漁網廠(1982)	Huaiyin 淮陰市	Jiangsu 江蘇省	(0517)6551234	399	Collectively-owned 集體	38,682	898(14)	15,207	o
Chinese-foreign Joint Venture Anhui Jin Long Net Tools Co. Ltd. 中外合資安徽省金龍網具有限公司(1994)	Liu'an 六安市	Anhui 安徽省	(0564)3316918	284	Collectively-owned 集體	36,042	2463(4)	42,495	b
Chaoyang Plastics Rope Making Factory 潮陽市塑料製繩廠(1954)	Shantou 汕頭市	Guangdong 廣東省	(0754)8862457	230	Collectively-owned 集體	28,895	-125(66)	26,900	a
Chongqing Changshou Hu Joint Enterprise Co. 重慶市長壽湖聯合企業公司	Chongqing 重慶市	Chongqing 重慶市	(023)40751125 (023)40751106	864	State-owned 國有	27,382	793(17)	65,464	o
Rui'an Hua Bin Fishnet Making Factory 瑞安市華濱漁網廠(1989)	Wenzhou 温州市	Zhejiang 浙江省	(0577)5507012 (0577)5502088	175	Collectively-owned 集體	27,181	2075(6)	58,399	o
Caohu Huai Lin Zhen Hua Bin Fishing Net Factory 巢湖市槐林鎮華濱漁網廠(1994)	Chaohu 巢湖市	Anhui 安徽省	(0565)8372204	188	Collectively-owned 集體	26,500	2090(5)	12,550	o
Panyu Qing Sheng Fishery Net Tools Co. Ltd. 番禺慶盛漁業網具有限公司(1993)	Guangzhou 廣州市	Guangdong 廣東省	(020)84754656 (020)84754655	150	Overseas Chinese-funded 港澳台資	25,031	1386(7)	76,228	o

Top 10 Cities by Production Output 產出排名前 10 位城市	Province 省	Market share 市場份額	Number of firms 企業個數
Jieyang 揭陽市	Guangdong 廣東省	14.27%	11
Tianjin 天津市	Tianjin 天津市	13.31%	4
Shantou 汕頭市	Guangdong 廣東省	9.84%	13
Zhanjiang 湛江市	Guangdong 廣東省	7.59%	14
Liu'an 六安市	Anhui 安徽省	6.41%	6
Suzhou 蘇州市	Jiangsu 江蘇省	4.16%	7
Wenzhou 温州市	Zhejiang 浙江省	4.10%	7
Huaiyin 淮陰市	Jiangsu 江蘇省	3.24%	2
Lianyungang 連雲港市	Jiangsu 江蘇省	3.10%	6
Taizhou 泰州市	Jiangsu 江蘇省	2.85%	4

10 Major Wholesalers 10 家主要批發商	City 城市	Province 省	Telephone / Fax 電話 / 傳真
China Agricultural Machinery Hua Bei Company 中國農業機械華北公司	Tianjin 天津市	Tianjin 天津市	(022)23394240 (022)23304247
Shandong Agriculture Means of Production Company 山東省農業生產資料公司	Ji'nan 濟南市	Shandong 山東省	(0531)8957052 (0531)8957142
Yantai Agriculture Means of Production General Company 煙台市農業生產資料總公司	Yantai 煙台市	Shandong 山東省	(0535)6216668 (0535)6211348
Sichuan Agriculture Means of Production General Company 四川省農業生產資料總公司	Chengdu 成都市	Sichuan 四川省	(028)6751135 (028)6751646
Heilongjiang Agriculture Means of Production Company 黑龍江省農業生產資料公司	Harbin 哈爾濱市	Heilongjiang 黑龍江省	(0451)8989948 (0451)8382367
Shannxi Agriculture Means of Production General Company 陝西省農業生產資料總公司	Xi'an 西安市	Shaanxi 陝西省	(029)7422104 (029)7411799
Gansu Agriculture Means of Production General Company 甘肅省農業生產資料總公司	Lanzhou 蘭州市	Gansu 甘肅省	(0931)8822971
Yitong Man Zu Autonomous County Agricultural Goods & Materials Co. Ltd. 伊通滿族自治縣農用物資有限責任公司	Siping 四平市	Jilin 吉林省	(0434)4223146
Langfang Agriculture Means of Production Company 廊坊市農業生產資料公司	Langfang 廊坊市	Hebei 河北省	(0316)2013148
Anhui Agriculture Means of Production Company 安徽省農業生產資料公司	Hefei 合肥市	Anhui 安徽省	(0551)2656541 (0551)2655720

*Also include sales by firms outside this industry.包括本行業以外廠家的銷售。"o" stands for "others". "o" 代表"其他產品"。

2859: Other Fishing Tackle Products 其他漁具製造業

The industry accounts for 0.013% of the total revenue of China's industrial sector in 1996. The revenue growth rate of the industry is 103.3% from 1995, as compared to the growth rate of China's industrial sector, 9.51%. The rate of return on asset is 6.51%. 71.20% of all firms in the industry made a profit while 26.58% had negative returns. The top province in terms of the industry's revenue is Shandong, accounting for 39.99% of the total revenue.
本行業在1996年佔全行業總產值0.013%，行業年增長率為103.3%（全國工業年增長率9.51%）。行業的資產回報率6.51%，71.20%的企業盈利，26.58%的企業虧損。銷售收入最高的省份為山東省，佔本行業的39.99%。

	Total number of firms 企業總數	Total number of employees 職工總數	Total revenue (mil. RMB) 總銷售收入（百萬元）	Total profit (mil. RMB) 總利潤（百萬元）	Return on assets 資產利潤率 (%)	Return on equity 權益利潤率 (%)	Labour productivity ('000 RMB / worker) 勞動生產率（千元／人）	Debts / assets 資產負債率 (%)	Total assets (mil. RMB) 總資產（百萬元）
Industry Overall 行業總體	88	10,433	740	54	6.51	15.09	70.93	56.82	833

	Number of firms 企業個數	Average number of employees 平均職工人數	Average revenue ('000 RMB) 平均銷售收入（千元）	Average profit ('000 RMB) 平均利潤（千元）	Return on assets 資產利潤率 (%)	Return on equity 權益利潤率 (%)	Labour productivity ('000 RMB / worker) 勞動生產率（千元／人）	Average debts / assets 平均資產負債率(%)	Average Total assets ('000 RMB) 平均總資產（千元）
By ownership 產業所有權									
State-owned 國有	2	265	9,000	500	2.08	5.26	33.96	60.42	24,000
Collectively-owned 集體	41	95	4,712	444	9.26	22.57	49.35	58.99	4,798
Privately-owned 私有									
Domestic JVs 聯營									
Joint stock 股份制	1	175	8,053				46.02	79.39	14,184
Foreign-funded 外資	18	156	13,364	796	6.00	13.46	85.51	55.38	13,261
Overseas Chinese-funded 港澳台資	25	127	11,205	818	6.10	13.56	88.17	55.01	13,413
By size 規模									
Large 大型									
Medium 中型	1	841	103,272	12,113	8.66	21.82	122.80	60.33	139,917
Small 小型	80	117	7,958	524	6.04	13.76	68.11	56.07	8,662
By regional distribution 地區分布									
Central-North 華北	10	91	3,734	319	7.22	15.80	41.03	54.29	4,419
Beijing 北京									
Tianjin 天津	9	98	4,113	361	7.43	16.16	41.83	53.98	4,858
Hebei 河北	1	25	320	-60	-12.77	-75.00	12.80	82.98	470
Shanxi 山西									
Inner Mongolia 內蒙									
Northeast 東北	6	95	4,358	125	3.13	13.61	46.04	77.04	4,000
Liaoning 遼寧	6	95	4,358	125	3.13	13.61	46.04	77.04	4,000
Jilin 吉林									
Heilongjiang 黑龍江									
Central East 華東	51	140	11,479	819	5.99	14.54	81.83	58.78	13,661
Shanghai 上海	5	76	2,756	290	16.29	24.13	36.36	32.36	1,780
Jiangsu 江蘇	13	155	14,516	574	3.92	13.62	93.79	71.23	14,645
Zhejiang 浙江	5	94	8,732	-212	-1.43	-4.65	93.29	69.31	14,872
Anhui 安徽	2	20	535	75	13.51	37.50	26.75	64.86	555
Fujian 福建	4	133	10,563	408	6.55	14.10	79.72	53.52	6,218
Jiangxi 江西	1								
Shandong 山東	21	177	14,093	1,530	8.09	16.76	79.45	51.74	18,909
Central-South 中南	20	90	4,536	430	12.63	18.41	50.65	31.40	3,402
Henan 河南									
Hubei 湖北	1	20	610	30	60.00	75.00	30.50	20.00	50
Hunan 湖南	8	33	1,005	169	16.23	48.04	30.45	66.23	1,040
Guangdong 廣東	10	151	8,207	721	12.09	16.45	54.46	26.55	5,966
Guangxi 廣西	1								
Hainan 海南									
Southwest 西南	1	10	60				6.00	40.00	100
Chongqing 重慶									
Sichuan 四川	1	10	60				6.00	40.00	100
Guizhou 貴州									
Yunnan 雲南									
Tibet 西藏									
Northwest 西北									
Shaanxi 陝西									
Gansu 甘肅									
Qinghai 青海									
Ningxia 寧夏									
Xinjiang 新疆									

2859: Other Fishing Tackle Products 其他漁具製造業

Year 年份	Number of firms 企業個數	Rate of change 每年變化 (%)	Number of employees 職工人數 (人)	Rate of change 每年變化 (%)	Total revenue (mil. RMB) 總銷售收入 (百萬元)	Rate of change 每年變化 (%)	Total profit (mil. RMB) 總利潤 (百萬元)	Rate of change 每年變化 (%)
1993	42		5,326		135		8	
1994	51	21.43%	5,794	8.79%	281	109.08%	16	112.60%
1995	64	25.49%	7,261	25.32%	364	29.37%	14	-13.40%
1996	88	37.50%	10,433	43.69%	740	103.29%	54	280.55%

3 Major products* 3 種主要產品 *	Output 產量	Sales volume 銷售量	Unit 單位
a) Fishing Rod 釣魚竿	2,783,881	2,783,881	piece 支
b) Fishery Machinery 漁業機械	364	327	set 台
c) Other Plastic Products 其他塑料製品	2,118	2,033	ton 噸

Top 10 firms by revenue (year founded) 收入排名前 10 家企業 (創辦年份)	City 城市	Province 省	Telephone / fax 電話 / 傳真	Number of employees 職工人數	Ownership 產業所有權	Revenue ('000 RMB) 銷售收入 (千元)	Profit ('000 RMB) (rank) 利潤 (千元) (排名)	Total assets ('000 RMB) 總資產 (千元)	Major products 主要產品
Yang Kou Fishery Company 羊口漁業公司	Weifang 濰坊市	Shandong 山東省	(0536)8900231 (0536)8900231	2,188	Collectively-owned 集體	136,159	27601(1)	249,874	o
Yangzhou Jiu Yang Fishing Tackle Co. Ltd. 揚州久揚漁具有限公司(1992)	Yangzhou 揚州市	Jiangsu 江蘇省	(0514)7301118 (0514)7301458	350	Overseas Chinese-funded 港澳台資	80,353	4123(3)	102,817	a
Gamakaisu Shantou Co. Ltd. 汕頭伽瑪卡兹有限公司(1989)	Shantou 汕頭市	Guangdong 廣東省	(0754)8362806	900	Foreign-funded 外資	63,600	6885(2)	30,739	o
Suzhou Ji Xing Fishing Tackle Co. Ltd. 蘇州吉星漁具有限公司(1992)	Suzhou 蘇州市	Jiangsu 江蘇省	(0512)3616888 (0512)3615899	240	Foreign-funded 外資	38,455	2036(5)	16,560	o
Zhucheng Fishery Machinery Co. Ltd. 諸城市漁業機械股份有限公司(1974)	Weifang 濰坊市	Shandong 山東省	(0536)6213932	362	Joint stock 股份制	36,984	1006(9)	15,529	b
Wuxi Sanwei Fishing Tackle Co. Ltd. 無錫三威漁具有限公司(1992)	Wuxi 無錫市	Jiangsu 江蘇省	(0510)5995965 (0510)5995142	370	Foreign-funded 外資	30,365	626(10)	23,077	a
Weihai Qiao Tou Fishing Tackle Factory 威海市橋頭漁具廠(1982)	Weihai 威海市	Shandong 山東省	(0896)5521081 (0896)5521081	100	Collectively-owned 集體	30,000	600(12)	5,940	a,c
Ningbo Ever Winner Industrial Fishing Tackle Co. Ltd. 寧波達金興業漁具有限公司(1993)	Ningbo 寧波市	Zhejiang 浙江省	(0574)6881232	200	Foreign-funded 外資	26,294	-1341(45)	53,275	o
Fujian Dongshan Fu Huang Hardware Products Co. Ltd. 福建東山縣福煌五金製造有限公司(1992)	Zhangzhou 漳州市	Fujian 福建省	(0596)5620560 (0596)5620385	307	Overseas Chinese-funded 港澳台資	23,968	80(24)	11,544	o
Shenyang New World Products Co. Ltd. 瀋陽新世界物產有限公司(1995)	Shenyang 瀋陽市	Liaoning 遼寧省	(024)23702848 (024)23702842	200	Foreign-funded 外資	22,720	479(15)	18,782	o

Top 10 Cities by Production Output 產出排名前 10 位城市	Province 省	Market share 市場份額	Number of firms 企業個數
Shantou 汕頭市	Guangdong 廣東省	13.60%	1
Yangzhou 揚州市	Jiangsu 江蘇省	13.45%	7
Weifang 濰坊市	Shandong 山東省	8.48%	2
Shanghai 上海市	Shanghai 上海市	7.96%	7
Tianjin 天津市	Tianjin 天津市	7.85%	6
Weihai 威海市	Shandong 山東省	7.08%	4
Shenyang 瀋陽市	Liaoning 遼寧省	5.83%	3
Zibo 淄博市	Shandong 山東省	5.42%	3
Wuxi 無錫市	Jiangsu 江蘇省	5.05%	4
Hangzhou 杭州市	Zhejiang 浙江省	4.63%	3

10 Major Wholesalers 10 家主要批發商	City 城市	Province 省	Telephone / Fax 電話 / 傳真
China Agricultural Machinery Hua Bei Company 中國農業機械華北公司	Tianjin 天津市	Tianjin 天津市	(022)23394240 (022)23304247
Shandong Agriculture Means of Production Company 山東省農業生產資料公司	Ji'nan 濟南市	Shandong 山東省	(0531)8957052 (0531)8957142
Yantai Agriculture Means of Production General Company 煙台市農業生產資料總公司	Yantai 煙台市	Shandong 山東省	(0535)6216668 (0535)6211348
Sichuan Agriculture Means of Production General Company 四川省農業生產資料總公司	Chengdu 成都市	Sichuan 四川省	(028)6751135 (028)6751646
Heilongjiang Agriculture Means of Production Company 黑龍江省農業生產資料公司	Harbin 哈爾濱市	Heilongjiang 黑龍江省	(0451)8989948 (0451)8382367
Shannxi Agriculture Means of Production General Company 陕西省農業生產資料總公司	Xi'an 西安市	Shaanxi 陝西省	(029)7422104 (029)7411799
Gansu Agriculture Means of Production General Company 甘肅省農業生產資料總公司	Lanzhou 蘭州市	Gansu 甘肅省	(0931)8822971
Yitong Man Zu Autonomous County Agricultural Goods & Materials Co. Ltd. 伊通滿族自治縣農用物資有限責任公司	Siping 四平市	Jilin 吉林省	(0434)4223146
Langfang Agriculture Means of Production Company 廊坊市農業生產資料公司	Langfang 廊坊市	Hebei 河北省	(0316)2013148
Anhui Agriculture Means of Production Company 安徽省農業生產資料公司	Hefei 合肥市	Anhui 安徽省	(0551)2656541 (0551)2655720

*Also include sales by firms outside this industry.包括本行業以外廠家的銷售。"o" stands for "others". "o" 代表 "其他產品"。

2910: Tires 輪胎製造業

The industry accounts for 0.483% of the total revenue of China's industrial sector in 1996. The revenue growth rate of the industry is 14.4% from 1995, as compared to the growth rate of China's industrial sector, 9.51%. The rate of return on asset is 0.91%. 67.16% of all firms in the industry made a profit while 26.69% had negative returns. The top province in terms of the industry's revenue is Shandong, accounting for 22.50% of the total revenue.
本行業在1996年佔全行業總產值0.483%，行業年增長率為14.4%（全國工業年增長率9.51%）。行業的資產回報率0.91%，67.16%的企業盈利，26.69%的企業虧損。銷售收入最高的省份為山東省，佔本行業的22.50%。

	Total number of firms 企業總數	Total number of employees 職工總數	Total revenue (mil. RMB) 總銷售收入（百萬元）	Total profit (mil. RMB) 總利潤（百萬元）	Return on assets 資產利潤率 (%)	Return on equity 權益利潤率 (%)	Labour productivity ('000 RMB / worker) 勞動生產率（千元/人）	Debts / assets 資產負債率 (%)	Total assets (mil. RMB) 總資產（百萬元）
Industry Overall 行業總體	257	212,108	28,015	392	0.91	2.77	132.08	67.28	43,168

	Number of firms 企業個數	Average number of employees 平均職工人數	Average revenue ('000 RMB) 平均銷售收入（千元）	Average profit ('000 RMB) 平均利潤（千元）	Return on assets 資產利潤率 (%)	Return on equity 權益利潤率 (%)	Labour productivity ('000 RMB / worker) 勞動生產率（千元/人）	Average debts / assets 平均資產負債率(%)	Average Total assets ('000 RMB) 平均總資產（千元）
By ownership 產業所有權									
State-owned 國有	81	1,526	171,654	1,222	0.44	1.74	112.45	74.82	279,494
Collectively-owned 集體	128	216	21,799	1,929	10.00	35.35	100.97	71.72	19,291
Privately-owned 私有	3	310	16,524	415	3.60	6.37	53.36	43.49	11,523
Domestic JVs 聯營	6	304	54,780	8,287	21.41	55.04	180.50	61.10	38,700
Joint stock 股份制	9	2,237	467,412	20,744	2.71	5.61	208.91	51.74	766,205
Foreign-funded 外資	18	1,403	254,028	-9,780	-2.71	-6.41	181.10	57.77	361,011
Overseas Chinese-funded 港澳台資	10	1,170	227,039	-4,779	-1.13	-3.28	194.05	65.71	424,823
By size 規模									
Large 大型	40	3,143	530,210	27,800	3.52	9.75	168.71	63.96	790,852
Medium 中型	40	1,155	101,469	-15,025	-7.79	-44.08	87.85	82.32	192,757
Small 小型	170	233	19,949	-700	-3.11	-8.75	85.45	64.40	22,494
By regional distribution 地區分布									
Central-North 華北	38	584	60,289	287	0.27	0.98	103.18	72.12	104,999
Beijing 北京	5	915	122,272	-1,170	-0.55	-3.20	133.63	82.85	213,494
Tianjin 天津	12	377	60,358	574	0.46	1.70	160.28	72.94	124,900
Hebei 河北	15	485	32,414	198	0.54	1.80	66.82	69.97	36,679
Shanxi 山西	4	912	99,180	1,863	1.01	2.30	108.81	56.36	185,310
Inner Mongolia 內蒙	2	1,094	36,195	-280	-0.42	-1.61	33.10	73.66	66,125
Northeast 東北	31	1,018	93,446	-4,308	-1.96	-15.18	91.82	87.10	220,007
Liaoning 遼寧	19	884	71,675	-5,126	-2.81	-15.81	81.12	82.21	182,175
Jilin 吉林	5	692	40,304	-9,258	-4.22	63.54	58.26	106.65	219,158
Heilongjiang 黑龍江	7	1,615	190,499	1,449	0.45	3.01	117.98	85.11	323,299
Central East 華東	110	830	129,008	3,726	2.04	5.34	155.42	61.84	182,810
Shanghai 上海	7	2,349	583,357	22,083	2.67	6.44	248.30	58.53	826,390
Jiangsu 江蘇	13	855	99,292	900	0.60	1.55	116.10	61.11	149,409
Zhejiang 浙江	4	1,620	295,905	6,975	2.22	6.01	182.69	63.05	314,285
Anhui 安徽	9	529	75,629	2,819	1.40	1.93	142.97	27.51	201,034
Fujian 福建	5	1,074	108,040	1,302	1.02	2.98	100.60	65.84	127,746
Jiangxi 江西	2	2,004	54,150	-6,680	-3.78	-17.88	27.03	78.85	176,705
Shandong 山東	70	616	90,055	2,816	2.37	8.04	146.17	70.56	118,907
Central-South 中南	49	746	104,945	827	0.53	1.43	140.65	63.01	156,140
Henan 河南	19	663	103,875	4,717	4.50	11.28	156.76	60.13	104,936
Hubei 湖北	7	967	151,157	439	0.16	0.59	156.38	72.84	275,150
Hunan 湖南	6	393	24,655	-1,115	-2.51	-29.23	62.74	91.41	44,398
Guangdong 廣東	12	466	101,884	-1,993	-0.97	-2.43	218.79	59.84	204,488
Guangxi 廣西	3	2,814	233,547	-4,113	-1.35	-2.46	82.98	45.19	304,817
Hainan 海南	2	409	19,695	-4,605	-9.56	-374.39	48.21	97.45	48,175
Southwest 西南	19	944	91,188	363	0.26	0.98	96.61	73.23	138,178
Chongqing 重慶	6	1,076	52,063	-1,508	-1.45	-4.76	48.38	69.44	103,749
Sichuan 四川	3	929	71,548	207	0.39	1.11	77.03	64.97	53,351
Guizhou 貴州	5	978	182,336	2,354	1.15	3.11	186.48	63.02	204,818
Yunnan 雲南	5	760	58,776	-2,658	-1.62	-17.05	77.36	90.48	163,750
Tibet 西藏									
Northwest 西北	10	1,255	176,180	5,714	2.90	6.19	140.37	53.16	197,230
Shaanxi 陝西	3	1,372	32,290	-5,997	-8.12	-46.02	23.53	82.36	73,833
Gansu 甘肅	2	593	15,315	-6,180	-9.43	-55.38	25.83	82.99	65,570
Qinghai 青海									
Ningxia 寧夏	2	2,267	597,600	41,845	7.58	11.23	263.67	32.47	551,940
Xinjiang 新疆	3	905	146,367	1,267	0.74	3.25	161.73	77.33	171,927

2910: Tires 輪胎製造業

Year 年份	Number of firms 企業個數	Rate of change 每年變化 (%)	Number of employees 職工人數 (人)	Rate of change 每年變化 (%)	Total revenue (mil. RMB) 總銷售收入 (百萬元)	Rate of change 每年變化 (%)	Total profit (mil. RMB) 總利潤 (百萬元)	Rate of change 每年變化 (%)
1993	209		269,087		17,838		934	
1994	227	8.61%	184,965	-31.26%	19,088	7.01%	437	-53.20%
1995	230	1.32%	214,356	15.89%	24,484	28.27%	69	-84.32%
1996	257	11.74%	212,108	-1.05%	28,015	14.42%	392	471.73%

3 Major products* 3 種主要產品 *	Output 產量	Sales volume 銷售量	Unit 單位
a) Tire Cover 輪胎外胎	74,710,827	70,228,177	piece 條
b) Tire Tube 輪胎內胎	78,212,426	71,173,307	piece 條
c) Rickshaw Cover 力車胎外胎	26,656	26,123	10,000 piece 萬條

Top 10 firms by revenue (year founded) 收入排名前 10 家企業 (創辦年份)	City 城市	Province 省	Telephone / fax 電話 / 傳真	Number of employees 職工人數	Ownership 產業所有權	Revenue ('000 RMB) 銷售收入 (千元)	Profit ('000 RMB) (rank) 利潤 (千元) (排名)	Total assets ('000 RMB) 總資產 (千元)	Major products 主要產品
Shanghai Tires & Rubber Group Co. Ltd. 上海輪胎橡膠(集團)股份有限公司(1927)	Shanghai 上海市	Shanghai 上海市	(021)63290433 (021)63299609	11,837	Joint stock 股份制	3,520,052	150462(1)	5,303,619	a,b
Shandong Cheng Shan Rubber (Group) Co. Ltd. 山東成山橡膠集團股份有限公司(1976)	Weihai 威海市	Shandong 山東省	(0896)7571754	5,299	State-owned 國有	1,405,898	68861(3)	2,130,480	a,b
Qingdao No.2 Rubber Plant 青島第二橡膠廠(1935)	Qingdao 青島市	Shandong 山東省	(0532)4842493 (0532)4842493	6,502	State-owned 國有	1,358,379	15269(10)	2,428,132	a,b
Mudanjiang Hua Lin Group Co. Ltd. 牡丹江樺林集團有限責任公司(1938)	Mudanjiang 牡丹江市	Heilongjiang 黑龍江省	(0453)6245660 (0453)6245666	9,876	State-owned 國有	1,315,052	10833(15)	2,219,718	a,b
Shandong Tires Plant 山東輪胎廠(1978)	Weihai 威海市	Shandong 山東省	(0896)5322983 (0896)5322983	4,929	State-owned 國有	1,233,669	46340(5)	1,336,691	a,b
Yinchuan C.s.I (Great Wall) Rubber Co. Ltd. 銀川中策長城橡膠有限公司(1993)	Yinchuan 銀川市	Ningxia 寧夏	(0951)2076491 (0951)3015491	3,974	Foreign-funded 外資	1,194,088	83807(2)	1,098,814	a,b
Hangzhou Zhongce Rubber (Ltd.) Co. Ltd. 杭州中策橡膠股份有限公司(1958)	Hangzhou 杭州市	Zhejiang 浙江省	(0571)6053939 (0571)6053191	5,732	Overseas Chinese-funded 港澳台資	1,136,010	32659(6)	1,186,454	a,b,c
Dong Feng Jin Shi Tires Co. Ltd. 東風金獅輪胎有限公司(1993)	Shiyan 十堰市	Hubei 湖北省	(0719)665211 (0719)665650	5,207	Foreign-funded 外資	958,761	-693(144)	1,788,568	a,b
Guizhou Tyre Co. Ltd. 貴州輪胎股份有限公司(1995)	Guiyang 貴陽市	Guizhou 貴州省	(0851)4842490 (0851)4844248	4,535	Joint stock 股份制	906,800	11750(13)	1,016,960	a,b
Liaoning Tires Plant 遼寧輪胎廠(1932)	Chaoyang 朝陽市	Liaoning 遼寧省	(0421)3815801 (0421)3814146	4,728	State-owned 國有	906,174	27601(7)	1,598,581	o

Top 10 Cities by Production Output 產出排名前 10 位城市	Province 省	Market share 市場份額	Number of firms 企業個數
Shanghai 上海市	Shanghai 上海市	14.94%	15
Weihai 威海市	Shandong 山東省	10.97%	8
Qingdao 青島市	Shandong 山東省	5.77%	25
Yinchuan 銀川市	Ningxia 寧夏	4.99%	2
Mudanjiang 牡丹江市	Heilongjiang 黑龍江省	4.77%	1
Guangzhou 廣州市	Guangdong 廣東省	4.39%	9
Hangzhou 杭州市	Zhejiang 浙江省	4.22%	2
Chaoyang 朝陽市	Liaoning 遼寧省	3.91%	4
Jiaozuo 焦作市	Henan 河南省	3.72%	6
Yantai 煙台市	Shandong 山東省	3.57%	8

10 Major Wholesalers 10 家主要批發商	City 城市	Province 省	Telephone / Fax 電話 / 傳真
Shanghai Auto Parts Company 上海市汽車配件公司	Shanghai 上海市	Shanghai 上海市	(021)62564400
China Automobile Trade Hua Bei Company 中國汽車貿易華北公司	Beijing 北京市	Beijing 北京市	(010)68518091 (010)68513546
China Yan Xing Tianjin Company 中國燕興天津公司	Tianjin 天津市	Tianjin 天津市	(022)28310131
China Automobile Industry Import & Export Guizhou Company 中國汽車工業進出口貴州公司	Guiyang 貴陽市	Guizhou 貴州省	(0851)5869068 (0851)5869008
Jining Automobile Marketing General Company 濟寧市汽車銷售總公司	Jining 濟寧市	Shandong 山東省	(0537)2313628 (0537)2314301
Shanghai Automobile Trade Company 上海汽車貿易公司	Shanghai 上海市	Shanghai 上海市	(021)58752443 (021)58753520
Shanghai Automobile Import & Export Company 上海汽車進出口公司	Shanghai 上海市	Shanghai 上海市	(021)63724288 (021)63724643
Fuyang Tyre Rubber General Company 富陽市輪胎橡膠總公司	Hangzhou 杭州市	Zhejiang 浙江省	(0571)3319574 (0571)3326835
Jilin Electromechanical Equipment General Company 吉林省機電設備總公司	Changchun 長春市	Jilin 吉林省	(0431)8717107 (0431)8743523
Chongqing Chang Jiang Business General Company 重慶長江商務總公司	Chongqing 重慶市	Chongqing 重慶市	(023)62810558 (023)62804041

*Also include sales by firms outside this industry.包括本行業以外廠家的銷售。"o" stands for "others". "o" 代表 "其他產品"。

2920: Inner Tubes 內車胎製造業

The industry accounts for 0.084% of the total revenue of China's industrial sector in 1996. The revenue growth rate of the industry is 14.9% from 1995, as compared to the growth rate of China's industrial sector, 9.51%. The rate of return on asset is 1.32%. 67.00% of all firms in the industry made a profit while 29.25% had negative returns. The top province in terms of the industry's revenue is Fujian, accounting for 17.45% of the total revenue.
本行業在1996年佔全行業總產值0.084%，行業年增長率為14.9%（全國工業年增長率9.51%）。行業的資產回報率1.32%，67.00%的企業盈利，29.25%的企業虧損。銷售收入最高的省份為福建省，佔本行業的17.45%。

	Total number of firms 企業總數	Total number of employees 職工總數	Total revenue (mil. RMB) 總銷售收入（百萬元）	Total profit (mil. RMB) 總利潤（百萬元）	Return on assets 資產利潤率 (%)	Return on equity 權益利潤率 (%)	Labour productivity ('000 RMB / worker) 勞動生產率（千元/人）	Debts / assets 資產負債率 (%)	Total assets (mil. RMB) 總資產（百萬元）
Industry Overall 行業總體	119	64,490	4,884	88	1.32	4.07	75.73	67.48	6,624

	Number of firms 企業個數	Average number of employees 平均職工人數	Average revenue ('000 RMB) 平均銷售收入（千元）	Average profit ('000 RMB) 平均利潤（千元）	Return on assets 資產利潤率 (%)	Return on equity 權益利潤率 (%)	Labour productivity ('000 RMB / worker) 勞動生產率（千元/人）	Average debts / assets 平均資產負債率(%)	Average Total assets ('000 RMB) 平均總資產（千元）
By ownership 產業所有權									
State-owned 國有	30	888	39,500	-3,167	-4.55	-23.63	44.50	80.77	69,667
Collectively-owned 集體	74	332	23,604	754	3.58	11.87	71.11	69.83	21,050
Privately-owned 私有	2	72	4,497	142	2.24	2.58	62.46	13.16	6,333
Domestic JVs 聯營	2	1,435	239,512	4,765	1.98	6.12	166.97	67.66	240,607
Joint stock 股份制	4	1,273	108,504	5,268	4.81	9.70	85.24	50.38	109,481
Foreign-funded 外資	3	534	64,690	1,017	1.54	4.13	121.14	62.80	66,210
Overseas Chinese-funded 港澳台資	4	978	209,080	23,325	5.05	11.32	213.84	55.35	461,675
By size 規模									
Large 大型	9	2,436	254,878	6,488	1.72	5.49	104.63	68.76	378,018
Medium 中型	20	1,174	80,143	296	0.31	0.98	68.27	68.30	94,996
Small 小型	89	217	11,094	266	1.79	4.84	51.21	63.01	14,863
By regional distribution 地區分布									
Central-North 華北	16	642	33,837	-987	-2.21	-6.87	52.68	67.78	44,566
Beijing 北京	2	1,219	124,085	-9,000	-8.14	-53.25	101.83	84.72	110,595
Tianjin 天津	4	1,052	38,675	168	0.28	0.57	36.77	51.94	60,815
Hebei 河北	5	491	25,834	308	1.07	3.54	52.66	69.83	28,820
Shanxi 山西	5	236	1,870				7.92	65.97	20,900
Inner Mongolia 內蒙									
Northeast 東北	7	663	2,760	-6,353	-19.13	355.76	4.16	105.37	33,209
Liaoning 遼寧	4	968	2,845	-11,133	-22.08	289.72	2.94	107.62	50,418
Jilin 吉林	2	275	3,155	5	0.04	0.68	11.47	94.77	13,955
Heilongjiang 黑龍江	1	220	1,630	50	1.74	3.55	7.41	50.69	2,880
Central East 華東	54	590	55,473	1,821	2.41	7.20	93.95	66.48	75,509
Shanghai 上海	14	558	39,026	388	0.80	3.14	69.93	74.67	48,702
Jiangsu 江蘇	9	668	71,726	830	0.85	2.26	107.37	62.21	97,278
Zhejiang 浙江	10	653	56,143	1,400	2.11	6.03	85.95	64.98	66,278
Anhui 安徽	6	267	8,170	38	0.41	2.28	30.62	82.12	9,405
Fujian 福建	3	992	284,107	24,897	5.88	14.26	286.40	58.76	423,270
Jiangxi 江西									
Shandong 山東	12	579	28,405	-289	-0.65	-3.57	49.04	81.68	44,259
Central-South 中南	31	442	37,774	1,539	3.44	9.47	85.39	63.70	44,786
Henan 河南	3	672	31,337	1,197	3.24	15.57	46.63	79.22	36,963
Hubei 湖北	10	306	11,179	-6	-0.05	-0.13	36.56	61.30	11,844
Hunan 湖南	6	283	18,885	-750	-3.63	-11.63	66.65	68.79	20,662
Guangdong 廣東	10	680	84,717	4,872	4.76	12.40	124.64	61.58	102,307
Guangxi 廣西	1	108	1,800	-40	-1.19	-8.89	16.67	86.65	3,370
Hainan 海南	1	34	2,910				85.59	65.89	8,620
Southwest 西南	5	310	26,554	284	0.96	3.36	85.66	71.58	29,708
Chongqing 重慶	1	24	933	30	3.82	7.07	39.06	46.01	786
Sichuan 四川	1	40	527				13.13	84.69	494
Guizhou 貴州									
Yunnan 雲南	3	496	43,770	463	0.94	3.33	88.31	71.67	49,087
Tibet 西藏									
Northwest 西北	6	404	4,070	77	0.72	1.92	10.07	62.58	10,648
Shaanxi 陝西	2	793	6,060	35	0.25	0.76	7.65	66.73	13,900
Gansu 甘肅	2	186	2,525	-240	-3.25	-7.05	13.61	53.99	7,390
Qinghai 青海	1	232	6,320	-440	-2.81	-10.21	27.24	72.45	15,680
Ningxia 寧夏	1	237	930	1,310	23.27	37.01	3.92	37.12	5,630
Xinjiang 新疆									

Year 年份	Number of firms 企業個數	Rate of change 每年變化 (%)	Number of employees 職工人數 (人)	Rate of change 每年變化 (%)	Total revenue (mil. RMB) 總銷售收入 (百萬元)	Rate of change 每年變化 (%)	Total profit (mil. RMB) 總利潤 (百萬元)	Rate of change 每年變化 (%)
1993	78		66,244		2,964		9	
1994	96	23.08%	58,322	-11.96%	2,899	-2.17%	0	-94.73%
1995	119	23.96%	62,240	6.72%	4,249	46.54%	142	31342.48%
1996	119		64,490	3.62%	4,884	14.94%	88	-38.08%

3 Major products* 3種主要產品 *	Output 產量	Sales volume 銷售量	Unit 單位
a) Bicycle Tire 自行車外胎	16,061	15,900	10,000 piece 萬條
b) Motorcycle Cover 摩托車輪胎外胎	17,814,250	17,279,822	piece 條
c) Motorcycle Tire Tube 摩托車輪胎內胎	18,160,786	16,707,923	piece 條

Top 10 firms by revenue (year founded) 收入排名前10家企業 (創辦年份)	City 城市	Province 省	Telephone / fax 電話 / 傳真	Number of employees 職工人數	Ownership 產業所有權	Revenue ('000 RMB) 銷售收入 (千元)	Profit ('000 RMB) (rank) 利潤 (千元) (排名)	Total assets ('000 RMB) 總資產 (千元)	Major products 主要產品
Cheng Shin Rubber (Xiamen) Ind., Ltd. 廈門正新橡膠工業有限公司(1991)	Xiamen 廈門市	Fujian 福建省	(0592)6211606 (0592)6214649	2,365	Overseas Chinese-funded 港澳台資	850,057	75840(1)	1,260,444	a,b,c
Jian Tai Rubber (Shenzhen) Co. Ltd. 建泰橡膠(深圳)有限公司(1990)	Shenzhen 深圳市	Guangdong 廣東省	(0755)7748172 (0755)7748171	1,450	Overseas Chinese-funded 港澳台資	400,100	65600(2)	390,433	a,b,c
Wuxi Rubber Group Co. 無錫橡膠集團有限責任公司(1957)	Wuxi 無錫市	Jiangsu 江蘇省	(0510)5753152 (0510)5759816	2,680	Domestic JVs 聯營	371,689	4584(6)	571,674	a,b,c
Zhejiang Hang Tong Enterprise Group (Co.) 浙江杭通企業集團公司(1986)	Jinhua 金華市	Zhejiang 浙江省	(0579)4661570 (0579)4664082	2,314	Collectively-owned 集體	248,853	3261(8)	414,130	o
Beijing Rubber No.1 Factory 北京橡膠一廠(1950)	Beijing 北京市	Beijing 北京市	(010)68181144 (010)68187381	2,437	State-owned 國有	248,167	-17996(79)	221,194	a,b
State-owned Qingdao Tong Tai Rubber Plant 國營青島同泰橡膠廠(1932)	Qingdao 青島市	Shandong 山東省	(0532)3833431 (0532)3833346	3,352	State-owned 國有	174,372	-10975(77)	368,774	a,b,c
Jiangsu Fei Chi Co. Ltd. 江蘇飛馳股份有限公司(1965)	Yancheng 鹽城市	Jiangsu 江蘇省	(0515)8364109 (0515)8364217	1,490	Joint stock 股份制	166,290	10260(3)	173,760	o
Tianjin Jin Tai Rubber Co. Ltd. 天津津泰橡膠股份有限公司(1993)	Tianjin 天津市	Tianjin 天津市	(022)27924958 (022)27924646	3,428	Joint stock 股份制	142,172	0(59)	221,018	a,b,c
Shanghai Flywheel Rubber General Plant 上海飛輪橡膠廠(1988)	Shanghai 上海市	Shanghai 上海市	(021)58900660 (021)58984894	1,068	Collectively-owned 集體	135,754	5103(5)	136,192	a,b
Zhejiang Pinghu Rubber Plant 浙江平湖橡膠廠(1958)	Jiaxing 嘉興市	Zhejiang 浙江省	(0573)5022904 (0573)5022916	1,358	Collectively-owned 集體	100,060	10(52)	83,686	a

Top 10 Cities by Production Output 產出排名前10位城市	Province 省	Market share 市場份額	Number of firms 企業個數
Shanghai 上海市	Shanghai 上海市	13.50%	13
Wuxi 無錫市	Jiangsu 江蘇省	12.91%	4
Guangzhou 廣州市	Guangdong 廣東省	10.39%	8
Jinhua 金華市	Zhejiang 浙江省	8.84%	3
Beijing 北京市	Beijing 北京市	7.00%	2
Qingdao 青島市	Shandong 山東省	5.33%	6
Yancheng 鹽城市	Jiangsu 江蘇省	4.25%	2
Tianjin 天津市	Tianjin 天津市	4.11%	3
Jiaxing 嘉興市	Zhejiang 浙江省	2.90%	1
Maoming 茂名市	Guangdong 廣東省	2.76%	1

10 Major Wholesalers 10家主要批發商	City 城市	Province 省	Telephone / Fax 電話 / 傳真
Changzhou Hardware Alternating-current Appliance and Chemical Wholesale General Company 常州五金交電化工批發總公司	Changzhou 常州市	Jiangsu 江蘇省	(0519)6609929 (0519)6609925
Suzhou Hardware & Alternating Electricity Co. Ltd. 蘇州五金交電股份有限公司	Suzhou 蘇州市	Jiangsu 江蘇省	(0512)5239572 (0512)5213248
Tianjin Foreign Trade General Company 天津市對外貿易總公司	Tianjin 天津市	Tianjin 天津市	(022)23310922
Chongqing International Trade Center 重慶國際貿易中心	Chongqing 重慶市	Chongqing 重慶市	(023)67853232 (023)67850402
China Chemical Plastics Co. Ltd. 中化塑料有限公司	Beijing 北京市	Beijing 北京市	(010)68569863 (010)68569041
Ningbo Hualian Group Co. Ltd. 寧波華聯集團股份有限公司	Ningbo 寧波市	Zhejiang 浙江省	(0574)7367626 (0574)7367652
Xia Retail Sales Kaiyuan Wei Wei Electromechanical Building Materials Marketing Dept. 廈門市開元區威威機電建材經營部	Xiamen 廈門市	Fujian 福建省	(0592)2071044
Rudong Industry Product General Company 如東縣工業品總公司	Nantong 南通市	Jiangsu 江蘇省	(0513)4516110 (0513)4516110
Fujian Fu Ri Group Company 福建福日集團公司	Fuzhou 福州市	Fujian 福建省	(0591)3269325 (0591)3270426
Guangdong Hardware & Alternating Electrical Co. 廣東省五金交電公司	Guangzhou 廣州市	Guangdong 廣東省	(020)81884078 (020)81861287

*Also include sales by firms outside this industry.包括本行業以外廠家的銷售。"o" stands for "others". "o" 代表"其他產品"。

2930: Rubber Sheet, Tube and Belt Products 橡膠板、管、帶製造業

The industry accounts for 0.143% of the total revenue of China's industrial sector in 1996. The revenue growth rate of the industry is 15.5% from 1995, as compared to the growth rate of China's industrial sector, 9.51%. The rate of return on asset is 1.41%. 71.59% of all firms in the industry made a profit while 23.64% had negative returns. The top province in terms of the industry's revenue is Shandong, accounting for 16.48% of the total revenue.
本行業在1996年佔全行業總產值0.143%，行業年增長率為15.5%（全國工業年增長率9.51%）。行業的資產回報率1.41%，71.59%的企業盈利，23.64%的企業虧損。銷售收入最高的省份為山東省，佔本行業的16.48%。

	Total number of firms 企業總數	Total number of employees 職工總數	Total revenue (mil. RMB) 總銷售收入（百萬元）	Total profit (mil. RMB) 總利潤（百萬元）	Return on assets 資產利潤率 (%)	Return on equity 權益利潤率 (%)	Labour productivity ('000 RMB / worker) 勞動生產率（千元/人）	Debts / assets 資產負債率 (%)	Total assets (mil. RMB) 總資產（百萬元）
Industry Overall 行業總體	859	154,587	8,296	175	1.41	4.60	53.67	69.42	12,415

	Number of firms 企業個數	Average number of employees 平均職工人數	Average revenue ('000 RMB) 平均銷售收入（千元）	Average profit ('000 RMB) 平均利潤（千元）	Return on assets 資產利潤率 (%)	Return on equity 權益利潤率 (%)	Labour productivity ('000 RMB / worker) 勞動生產率（千元/人）	Average debts / assets 平均資產負債率(%)	Average Total assets ('000 RMB) 平均總資產（千元）
By ownership 產業所有權									
State-owned 國有	128	522	25,945	-211	-0.43	-1.59	49.67	73.17	49,406
Collectively-owned 集體	658	108	5,475	182	3.17	10.99	50.82	71.15	5,745
Privately-owned 私有	3	147	9,658	2,131	18.96	24.66	65.55	23.12	11,239
Domestic JVs 聯營	7	240	17,723	-1,032	-5.54	-16.72	73.98	66.88	18,629
Joint stock 股份制	14	523	46,519	4,547	5.41	12.06	88.96	55.16	84,090
Foreign-funded 外資	23	117	10,442	370	2.82	7.20	89.22	60.81	13,125
Overseas Chinese-funded 港澳台資	26	204	12,649	415	1.62	3.67	61.98	55.97	25,684
By size 規模									
Large 大型	10	2,537	209,736	11,074	2.76	8.54	82.68	67.65	400,841
Medium 中型	42	801	51,732	-977	-1.29	-4.08	64.62	68.47	75,930
Small 小型	800	119	5,032	132	2.02	7.04	42.12	71.35	6,523
By regional distribution 地區分布									
Central-North 華北	153	180	8,023	309	3.52	13.32	44.50	73.57	8,768
Beijing 北京	12	290	11,582	151	0.62	6.87	39.93	90.99	24,387
Tianjin 天津	22	159	5,362	272	3.42	18.66	33.75	81.65	7,940
Hebei 河北	87	185	9,434	427	5.44	14.53	50.99	62.58	7,854
Shanxi 山西	23	131	5,663	110	1.77	7.96	43.14	77.81	6,224
Inner Mongolia 內蒙	9	166	2,176	-26	-0.48	-2.64	13.10	81.78	5,311
Northeast 東北	186	148	5,135	110	1.15	4.56	34.65	74.71	9,542
Liaoning 遼寧	117	162	6,738	348	3.20	9.20	41.69	65.25	10,903
Jilin 吉林	35	99	2,096	-201	-3.43	-19.18	21.09	82.11	5,852
Heilongjiang 黑龍江	34	152	2,743	-391	-4.51	42.90	18.05	110.52	8,660
Central East 華東	307	181	13,452	364	1.82	5.87	74.35	69.00	20,017
Shanghai 上海	26	300	25,343	907	2.05	5.98	84.49	65.63	44,130
Jiangsu 江蘇	79	198	13,530	248	1.81	6.56	68.21	72.42	13,714
Zhejiang 浙江	57	89	7,630	276	2.36	5.81	85.92	59.33	11,681
Anhui 安徽	33	192	10,353	69	0.48	3.13	53.81	84.56	14,360
Fujian 福建	15	91	4,288	-119	-1.65	-6.23	47.29	73.50	7,227
Jiangxi 江西	22	214	8,800	-126	-0.54	-1.59	41.04	66.16	23,352
Shandong 山東	75	195	18,232	735	2.56	8.29	93.74	69.10	28,703
Central-South 中南	148	210	10,793	95	0.55	1.49	51.49	62.93	17,092
Henan 河南	50	228	11,915	282	1.77	7.98	52.23	77.83	15,924
Hubei 湖北	27	319	14,448	-189	-0.59	-1.20	45.22	50.61	31,853
Hunan 湖南	28	148	6,218	-10	-0.16	-0.76	41.99	79.62	6,658
Guangdong 廣東	30	165	11,494	196	1.06	2.27	69.55	53.11	18,438
Guangxi 廣西	9	153	9,097	166	1.43	4.71	59.54	69.58	11,549
Hainan 海南	4	129	2,670	-515	-6.90	-27.36	20.78	74.78	7,465
Southwest 西南	30	233	7,246	-661	-5.25	-32.23	31.05	83.72	12,596
Chongqing 重慶	13	289	8,620	-1,572	-8.27	-116.45	29.81	92.90	19,008
Sichuan 四川	10	68	2,173	-12	-0.61	-1.40	32.00	56.17	1,925
Guizhou 貴州	3	306	117				0.38	65.38	87
Yunnan 雲南	4	390	20,135	343	1.32	3.89	51.63	66.19	26,040
Tibet 西藏									
Northwest 西北	35	168	4,819	28	0.39	1.10	28.72	64.11	7,024
Shaanxi 陝西	20	141	3,136	-2	-0.04	-0.12	22.30	66.35	3,849
Gansu 甘肅	6	265	8,213	105	0.69	1.51	31.05	54.35	15,225
Qinghai 青海									
Ningxia 寧夏	5	222	9,904	238	1.99	7.25	44.65	72.54	11,954
Xinjiang 新疆	4	91	1,788	-205	-4.62	-19.48	19.64	76.27	4,435

2930: Rubber Sheet, Tube and Belt Products 橡膠板、管、帶製造業

Year 年份	Number of firms 企業個數	Rate of change 每年變化 (%)	Number of employees 職工人數（人）	Rate of change 每年變化 (%)	Total revenue (mil. RMB) 總銷售收入（百萬元）	Rate of change 每年變化 (%)	Total profit (mil. RMB) 總利潤（百萬元）	Rate of change 每年變化 (%)
1993	795		155,420		5,300		82	
1994	865	8.81%	150,022	-3.47%	5,612	5.88%	54	-33.82%
1995	895	3.47%	160,282	6.84%	7,182	27.98%	70	29.03%
1996	859	-4.02%	154,587	-3.55%	8,296	15.51%	175	150.82%

3 Major products* 3 種主要產品 *	Output 產量	Sales volume 銷售量	Unit 單位
a) Steel Wire Braided Hose 鋼絲編織管	76,402	72,582	10,000 metre 萬標米
b) Feed Belt 輸送帶	63,015,883	47,261,912	square metre 平方米
c) Automotive V-belt 車V帶	9,146,022	8,688,721	piece 條

Top 10 firms by revenue (year founded) 收入排名前 10 家企業 (創辦年份)	City 城市	Province 省	Telephone / fax 電話 / 傳真	Number of employees 職工人數	Ownership 產業所有權	Revenue ('000 RMB) 銷售收入（千元）	Profit ('000 RMB) (rank) 利潤（千元）（排名）	Total assets ('000 RMB) 總資產（千元）	Major products 主要產品
Qingdao No.6 Rubber Plant 青島第六橡膠廠(1952)	Qingdao 青島市	Shandong 山東省	(0532)4843079 (0532)3835611	2,824	State-owned 國有	398,249	2801(25)	714,427	a,b
Shanghai Rubber Belt Co. Ltd. 上海膠帶股份有限公司(1948)	Shanghai 上海市	Shanghai 上海市	(021)65415210 (021)65123671	2,110	Joint stock 股份制	275,871	15611(3)	530,826	b,c
Yanzhou Huaxi Rubber Belt Factory 兗州市華西膠帶廠(1989)	Jining 濟寧市	Shandong 山東省	(0537)3413320 (0537)3413315	512	Collectively-owned 集體	263,882	33682(1)	146,514	b
Shanghai Rubber Products Co. Ltd. 上海橡膠製品有限公司(1946)	Shanghai 上海市	Shanghai 上海市	(021)62506531 (021)62505695	2,637	State-owned 國有	197,390	178(181)	297,772	a,b
Zaozhuang Rubber Plant 棗裝市橡膠廠(1973)	Zaozhuang 棗莊市	Shandong 山東省	(0632)3318702 (0632)3315019	2,433	State-owned 國有	192,318	3720(20)	477,335	a,b
Shenyang No.4 Rubber Plant 瀋陽第四橡膠廠(1938)	Shenyang 瀋陽市	Liaoning 遼寧省	(024)25804401 (024)25850327	1,062	State-owned 國有	175,523	103(210)	355,276	o
Fuxin Rubber General Plant 阜新橡膠總廠(1955)	Fuxin 阜新市	Liaoning 遼寧省	(0418)2904474 (0418)2900927	1,850	State-owned 國有	160,044	13563(5)	264,810	o
Shenyang Rubber Hose Factory 瀋陽膠管廠(1949)	Shenyang 瀋陽市	Liaoning 遼寧省	(024)25875237 (024)25855217	1,653	State-owned 國有	157,005	9472(8)	251,732	a
Wuxi Rubber Plant 無錫市橡膠廠(1950)	Wuxi 無錫市	Jiangsu 江蘇省	(0510)3708541 (0510)3707295	1,204	State-owned 國有	133,579	1900(37)	196,501	b,c
Zhejiang Shuang Niu Rubber Co. Ltd. 浙江雙牛橡膠股份有限公司(1966)	Jinhua 金華市	Zhejiang 浙江省	(0579)8886945 (0579)8886980	689	Joint stock 股份制	117,807	10109(7)	309,525	o

Top 10 Cities by Production Output 產出排名前 10 位城市	Province 省	Market share 市場份額	Number of firms 企業個數
Shanghai 上海市	Shanghai 上海市	8.56%	37
Qingdao 青島市	Shandong 山東省	5.50%	19
Hengshui 衡水市	Hebei 河北省	4.53%	42
Shenyang 瀋陽市	Liaoning 遼寧省	4.47%	54
Wuxi 無錫市	Jiangsu 江蘇省	4.06%	17
Jining 濟寧市	Shandong 山東省	3.82%	6
Jinhua 金華市	Zhejiang 浙江省	3.10%	9
Suzhou 蘇州市	Jiangsu 江蘇省	3.00%	11
Yichang 宜昌市	Hubei 湖北省	2.81%	1
Kaifeng 開封市	Henan 河南省	2.73%	5

10 Major Wholesalers 10 家主要批發商	City 城市	Province 省	Telephone / Fax 電話 / 傳真
Zhong Hua Singbo Import & Export Company 中化寧波進出口公司	Ningbo 寧波市	Zhejiang 浙江省	(0574)7346764 (0574)7366775
China Chemical Supply & Marketing Hua Nan Company 中國化工供銷華南公司	Guangzhou 廣州市	Guangdong 廣東省	(020)87654477 (020)87784414
China Agriculture Means of Production Chengdu Company 中國農業生產資料成都公司	Chengdu 成都市	Sichuan 四川省	(028)3333909 (028)3331202
Shanxi Agriculture Means of Production Company 山西省農業生產資料公司	Taiyuan 太原市	Shanxi 山西省	(0351)4040255 (0351)4040231
Beijing Chemical Light Industry General Company 北京市化工輕工總公司	Beijing 北京市	Beijing 北京市	(010)64224837 (010)64219301
Beijing Chemical Industry Group Company Supply & Marketing Company 北京化學工業集團公司供銷公司	Beijing 北京市	Beijing 北京市	(010)67714610 (010)67714058
Zhong Hua Jiangsu Import & Export Company 中化江蘇進出口公司	Nanjing 南京市	Jiangsu 江蘇省	(025)2258718 (025)2257789
Yunnan Chemical Import & Export Company 雲南省化工進出口公司	Kunming 昆明市	Yunnan 雲南省	(0871)3314002 (0871)3314931
Fujian Jiu Zhou Group Co. Ltd. 福建九州集團股份有限公司	Xiamen 廈門市	Fujian 福建省	(0592)5055818 (0592)5052033
China Chemical Industry Commission Agent Hua Dong Co. 中國化工供銷華東公司	Shanghai 上海市	Shanghai 上海市	(021)62514123

*Also include sales by firms outside this industry.包括本行業以外廠家的銷售。"o" stands for "others". "o" 代表 "其他產品"。

2940: Rubber Parts 橡膠零件製品業

The industry accounts for 0.054% of the total revenue of China's industrial sector in 1996. The revenue growth rate of the industry is 7.3% from 1995, as compared to the growth rate of China's industrial sector, 9.51%. The rate of return on asset is 2.19%. 74.38% of all firms in the industry made a profit while 19.78% had negative returns. The top province in terms of the industry's revenue is Jiangsu, accounting for 19.69% of the total revenue.
本行業在1996年佔全行業總產值0.054%，行業年增長率為7.3%（全國工業年增長率9.51%）。行業的資產回報率2.19%，74.38%的企業盈利，19.78%的企業虧損。銷售收入最高的省份為江蘇省，佔本行業的19.69%。

	Total number of firms 企業總數	Total number of employees 職工總數	Total revenue (mil. RMB) 總銷售收入（百萬元）	Total profit (mil. RMB) 總利潤（百萬元）	Return on assets 資產利潤率 (%)	Return on equity 權益利潤率 (%)	Labour productivity ('000 RMB / worker) 勞動生產率（千元/人）	Debts / assets 資產負債率 (%)	Total assets (mil. RMB) 總資產（百萬元）
Industry Overall 行業總體	925	79,062	3,117	110	2.19	5.73	39.42	61.78	5,045

	Number of firms 企業個數	Average number of employees 平均職工人數	Average revenue ('000 RMB) 平均銷售收入（千元）	Average profit ('000 RMB) 平均利潤（千元）	Return on assets 資產利潤率 (%)	Return on equity 權益利潤率 (%)	Labour productivity ('000 RMB / worker) 勞動生產率（千元/人）	Average debts / assets 平均資產負債率(%)	Average Total assets ('000 RMB) 平均總資產（千元）
By ownership 產業所有權									
State-owned 國有	74	262	7,135	81	0.45	1.58	27.26	71.81	18,216
Collectively-owned 集體	776	60	2,006	54	2.09	6.45	33.24	67.65	2,581
Privately-owned 私有	3	22	1,102	48	5.64	16.68	49.34	66.18	852
Domestic JVs 聯營	9	169	6,195	6	0.05	0.12	36.66	60.51	12,935
Joint stock 股份制	9	336	16,124	113	0.34	1.60	48.05	78.88	33,336
Foreign-funded 外資	25	243	22,810	2,289	6.85	11.62	93.87	41.05	33,429
Overseas Chinese-funded 港澳台資	28	102	9,194	133	0.85	1.25	90.01	32.39	15,701
By size 規模									
Large 大型	3	1,965	57,079	-2,910	-1.83	-16.85	29.05	89.11	158,625
Medium 中型	17	889	46,510	3,025	3.28	7.12	52.30	53.95	92,255
Small 小型	889	65	2,424	76	2.24	5.83	37.22	61.54	3,376
By regional distribution 地區分布									
Central-North 華北	136	103	3,198	175	3.26	10.10	31.05	67.72	5,354
Beijing 北京	33	177	3,438	-64	-0.68	-2.70	19.37	74.79	9,383
Tianjin 天津	27	51	1,125	136	6.54	28.24	22.08	76.84	2,085
Hebei 河北	49	105	5,425	416	6.29	15.32	51.58	58.95	6,614
Shanxi 山西	21	69	1,115	88	5.07	17.72	16.16	71.40	1,738
Inner Mongolia 內蒙	6	28	297	-8	-3.11	-10.64	10.60	70.19	268
Northeast 東北	198	70	1,525	38	1.39	3.75	21.90	63.06	2,765
Liaoning 遼寧	135	59	1,288	25	1.07	2.43	21.81	55.99	2,382
Jilin 吉林	35	91	2,572	84	1.87	9.87	28.22	81.07	4,497
Heilongjiang 黑龍江	28	94	1,355	43	1.77	3.91	14.48	54.81	2,444
Central East 華東	331	101	5,571	214	2.31	5.57	55.18	58.48	9,242
Shanghai 上海	50	87	4,532	-91	-1.00	-2.13	52.18	53.05	9,086
Jiangsu 江蘇	98	137	6,262	164	1.65	4.44	45.75	62.82	9,958
Zhejiang 浙江	58	83	4,521	202	3.07	7.91	54.22	61.19	6,587
Anhui 安徽	39	70	7,121	1,126	9.27	17.75	101.02	47.77	12,144
Fujian 福建	23	108	9,578	-27	-0.22	-0.42	88.36	47.22	12,323
Jiangxi 江西	24	43	1,074	-1	-0.04	-0.21	25.00	78.14	1,855
Shandong 山東	39	117	5,581	107	0.94	3.01	47.82	68.77	11,417
Central-South 中南	121	70	3,221	91	2.51	7.27	46.01	65.51	3,627
Henan 河南	29	36	1,472	24	1.01	3.36	40.76	69.98	2,392
Hubei 湖北	38	108	5,341	223	4.94	11.73	49.24	57.87	4,522
Hunan 湖南	19	46	1,262	-1	-0.07	-0.19	27.18	62.44	1,504
Guangdong 廣東	20	90	4,708	79	1.09	3.61	52.46	69.67	7,175
Guangxi 廣西	14	43	1,841	19	1.03	7.14	42.60	85.58	1,804
Hainan 海南	1	19	210				11.05	30.56	360
Southwest 西南	102	73	1,113	-36	-1.79	-7.02	15.29	74.48	2,014
Chongqing 重慶	17	66	926	-152	-7.92	-76.78	14.13	89.68	1,923
Sichuan 四川	49	72	1,481	-24	-0.85	-3.03	20.70	72.01	2,775
Guizhou 貴州	30	76	406	11	1.60	5.55	5.34	71.01	665
Yunnan 雲南	6	85	2,188	-37	-1.30	-4.17	25.85	68.72	2,813
Tibet 西藏									
Northwest 西北	37	53	884	28	1.57	6.08	16.68	74.23	1,777
Shaanxi 陝西	30	52	894	41	2.54	10.38	17.19	75.50	1,627
Gansu 甘肅	5	59	780	-32	-1.22	-3.18	13.18	61.77	2,626
Qinghai 青海									
Ningxia 寧夏	1	101	1,990	-50	-1.36	125.00	19.70	101.08	3,690
Xinjiang 新疆	1	5	10				2.00	100.00	100

2940: Rubber Parts 橡膠零件製品業

Year 年份	Number of firms 企業個數	Rate of change 每年變化 (%)	Number of employees 職工人數（人）	Rate of change 每年變化 (%)	Total revenue (mil. RMB) 總銷售收入（百萬元）	Rate of change 每年變化 (%)	Total profit (mil. RMB) 總利潤（百萬元）	Rate of change 每年變化 (%)
1993	839		92,541		2,275		106	
1994	947	12.87%	92,026	-0.56%	2,263	-0.56%	17	-84.45%
1995	903	-4.65%	86,942	-5.53%	2,906	28.41%	105	533.52%
1996	925	2.44%	79,062	-9.06%	3,117	7.26%	110	5.20%

3 Major products* 3 種主要產品 *	Output 產量	Sales volume 銷售量	Unit 單位
a) Seal Part 密封件	105,956	91,122	10,000 piece 萬件
b) Rubber Roller 膠輥	3,845,622	3,730,254	kg 公斤

Top 10 firms by revenue (year founded) 收入排名前 10 家企業（創辦年份）	City 城市	Province 省	Telephone / fax 電話 / 傳真	Number of employees 職工人數	Ownership 產業所有權	Revenue ('000 RMB) 銷售收入（千元）	Profit ('000 RMB) (rank) 利潤（千元）（排名）	Total assets ('000 RMB) 總資產（千元）	Major products 主要產品
Ningguo Zhong Ding Co. Ltd. 寧國縣中鼎股份有限公司(1980)	Xuanzhou 宣州市	Anhui 安徽省	(0563)4674803 (0563)4674880	3,120	Foreign-funded 外資	201,780	40430(1)	391,610	a
Shijiazhuang No.1 Rubber Co. Ltd. 石家莊第一橡膠股份有限公司(1965)	Shijiazhuang 石家莊市	Hebei 河北省	(0311)5054458 (0311)5052706	1,856	Joint stock 股份制	70,103	843(52)	165,128	o
Xiamen Xia Hui Rubber Metal Industrial Co. Ltd. 廈門廈暉橡膠金屬工業有限公司(1990)	Xiamen 廈門市	Fujian 福建省	(0592)6210902 (0592)6210901	335	Overseas Chinese-funded 港澳台資	66,590	5670(5)	62,600	o
Ninghai Seal Components Factory 寧海縣密封件廠(1988)	Ningbo 寧波市	Zhejiang 浙江省	(0574)5291538 (0574)5291538	560	Private-owned 私營	62,236	2509(15)	47,202	o
Wuxi No.2 Rubber Co. Ltd. 無錫第二橡膠股份有限公司(1971)	Wuxi 無錫市	Jiangsu 江蘇省	(0510)2703862 (0510)2706675	1,360	State-owned 國有	56,090	1068(39)	113,648	b
Ezhou Seal Components General Factory 鄂州市密封件總廠(1975)	Ezhou 鄂州市	Hubei 湖北省	(0711)2331164	450	Collectively-owned 集體	53,900	2070(21)	19,870	o
Nanjing Rubber Plant 南京橡膠廠(1958)	Nanjing 南京市	Jiangsu 江蘇省	(025)3436383 (025)3418217	1,103	State-owned 國有	49,472	51(176)	79,629	b
Beijing Chemical Industry Group Rubber Plastic Products Factory 北京化學工業集團公司橡膠塑料製品廠(1956)	Beijing 北京市	Beijing 北京市	(010)69503104 (010)69501509	1,993	State-owned 國有	47,665	-7996(291)	206,273	b
Changshu Rubber Factory 常熟市橡膠廠(1968)	Suzhou 蘇州市	Jiangsu 江蘇省	(0512)2880021 (0512)2882141	327	Collectively-owned 集體	46,021	1013(43)	37,546	o
Xiamen Bai Ma Rubber & Plastics Metal Industrial Co. Ltd. 廈門白馬橡塑金屬工業有限公司(1992)	Xiamen 廈門市	Fujian 福建省	(0592)6076575 (0592)6076576	280	Overseas Chinese-funded 港澳台資	43,184	959(47)	63,452	o

Top 10 Cities by Production Output 產出排名前 10 位城市	Province 省	Market share 市場份額	Number of firms 企業個數
Xuanzhou 宣州市	Anhui 安徽省	8.69%	12
Shanghai 上海市	Shanghai 上海市	7.86%	82
Wuxi 無錫市	Jiangsu 江蘇省	6.04%	68
Taizhou 臺州市	Zhejiang 浙江省	5.30%	48
Ningbo 寧波市	Zhejiang 浙江省	4.17%	17
Xingtai 邢臺市	Hebei 河北省	3.66%	15
Qingdao 青島市	Shandong 山東省	2.76%	19
Shijiazhuang 石家莊市	Hebei 河北省	2.71%	6
Nanjing 南京市	Jiangsu 江蘇省	2.71%	17
Suzhou 蘇州市	Jiangsu 江蘇省	2.54%	23

10 Major Wholesalers 10 家主要批發商	City 城市	Province 省	Telephone / Fax 電話 / 傳真
Zhong Hua Singbo Import & Export Company 中化寧波進出口公司	Ningbo 寧波市	Zhejiang 浙江省	(0574)7346764 (0574)7366775
China Chemical Supply & Marketing Hua Nan Company 中國化工供銷華南公司	Guangzhou 廣州市	Guangdong 廣東省	(020)87654477 (020)87784414
China Agriculture Means of Production Chengdu Company 中國農業生產資料成都公司	Chengdu 成都市	Sichuan 四川省	(028)3333909 (028)3331202
Shanxi Agriculture Means of Production Company 山西省農業生產資料公司	Taiyuan 太原市	Shanxi 山西省	(0351)4040255 (0351)4040231
Beijing Chemical Light Industry General Company 北京市化工輕工總公司	Beijing 北京市	Beijing 北京市	(010)64224837 (010)64219301
Beijing Chemical Industry Group Company Supply & Marketing Company 北京化學工業集團公司供銷公司	Beijing 北京市	Beijing 北京市	(010)67714610 (010)67714058
Zhong Hua Jiangsu Import & Export Company 中化江蘇進出口公司	Nanjing 南京市	Jiangsu 江蘇省	(025)2258718 (025)2257789
Yunnan Chemical Import & Export Company 雲南省化工進出口公司	Kunming 昆明市	Yunnan 雲南省	(0871)3314002 (0871)3314931
Fujian Jiu Zhou Group Co. Ltd. 福建九州集團股份有限公司	Xiamen 廈門市	Fujian 福建省	(0592)5055818 (0592)5052033
China Chemical Industry Commission Agent Hua Dong Co. 中國化工供銷華東公司	Shanghai 上海市	Shanghai 上海市	(021)62514123

*Also include sales by firms outside this industry.包括本行業以外廠家的銷售。"o" stands for "others". "o" 代表 "其他產品"。

2950: Recycled Rubber 再生橡膠製品業

The industry accounts for 0.025% of the total revenue of China's industrial sector in 1996. The revenue growth rate of the industry is 20.8% from 1995, as compared to the growth rate of China's industrial sector, 9.51%. The rate of return on asset is 2.35%. 69.65% of all firms in the industry made a profit while 24.14% had negative returns. The top province in terms of the industry's revenue is Hebei, accounting for 20.62% of the total revenue.
本行業在1996年佔全行業總產值0.025%，行業年增長率為20.8%（全國工業年增長率9.51%）。行業的資產回報率2.35%，69.65%的企業盈利，24.14%的企業虧損。銷售收入最高的省份為河北省，佔本行業的20.62%。

	Total number of firms 企業總數	Total number of employees 職工總數	Total revenue (mil. RMB) 總銷售收入（百萬元）	Total profit (mil. RMB) 總利潤（百萬元）	Return on assets 資產利潤率 (%)	Return on equity 權益利潤率 (%)	Labour productivity ('000 RMB / worker) 勞動生產率（千元/人）	Debts / assets 資產負債率 (%)	Total assets (mil. RMB) 總資產（百萬元）
Industry Overall 行業總體	357	29,263	1,438	39	2.35	9.66	49.14	75.68	1,664

	Number of firms 企業個數	Average number of employees 平均職工人數	Average revenue ('000 RMB) 平均銷售收入（千元）	Average profit ('000 RMB) 平均利潤（千元）	Return on assets 資產利潤率 (%)	Return on equity 權益利潤率 (%)	Labour productivity ('000 RMB / worker) 勞動生產率（千元/人）	Average debts / assets 平均資產負債率(%)	Average Total assets ('000 RMB) 平均總資產（千元）
By ownership 產業所有權									
State-owned 國有	37	188	5,676	-216	-1.79	-8.42	30.23	78.70	12,054
Collectively-owned 集體	298	68	3,676	139	4.18	19.50	54.37	78.58	3,333
Privately-owned 私有	1	18	2,460	285	16.13	17.48	136.65	7.72	1,769
Domestic JVs 聯營	5	116	6,493	80	0.62	1.51	55.98	59.21	13,020
Joint stock 股份制	4	301	12,983	438	2.62	7.86	43.20	66.70	16,738
Foreign-funded 外資	4	50	5,233	476	3.01	5.67	105.72	46.88	15,800
Overseas Chinese-funded 港澳台資	7	44	3,650	168	4.23	8.88	82.95	52.36	3,971
By size 規模									
Large 大型									
Medium 中型	3	443	12,718	-4,493	-10.35	-112.71	28.73	90.82	43,411
Small 小型	345	81	4,060	152	3.42	13.35	50.33	74.37	4,446
By regional distribution 地區分布									
Central-North 華北	75	77	4,681	302	6.84	28.81	61.01	76.26	4,412
Beijing 北京	5	13	524	106	1.42	18.15	40.31	92.18	7,468
Tianjin 天津	6	126	5,623	-52	-0.86	-5.32	44.81	83.76	5,983
Hebei 河北	54	81	5,492	397	9.38	34.73	68.13	73.00	4,233
Shanxi 山西	7	64	1,890	110	3.43	11.27	29.73	69.54	3,203
Inner Mongolia 內蒙	3	46	1,623	70	3.15	16.80	35.29	81.11	2,223
Northeast 東北	43	89	1,977	-18	-0.41	-4.27	22.12	90.36	4,465
Liaoning 遼寧	25	71	2,231	-76	-1.64	-33.99	31.46	95.18	4,618
Jilin 吉林	11	135	2,140	183	3.74	20.18	15.80	81.47	4,885
Heilongjiang 黑龍江	7	83	811	-130	-3.99	-30.54	9.79	86.92	3,256
Central East 華東	121	79	4,395	94	1.83	7.67	55.88	76.17	5,120
Shanghai 上海	8	62	4,243	181	3.46	8.73	68.84	60.37	5,233
Jiangsu 江蘇	17	115	7,132	-88	-1.07	-6.04	62.08	82.27	8,234
Zhejiang 浙江	25	77	4,049	116	1.72	6.12	52.45	71.91	6,740
Anhui 安徽	7	87	7,127	139	6.89	43.89	81.79	84.29	2,010
Fujian 福建	23	33	1,521	23	2.11	6.75	46.76	68.81	1,094
Jiangxi 江西	26	91	3,924	148	2.93	14.50	43.25	79.77	5,049
Shandong 山東	15	95	5,903	208	3.16	14.02	62.18	77.43	6,576
Central-South 中南	78	90	4,274	129	3.04	9.13	47.75	66.73	4,246
Henan 河南	26	103	3,897	299	6.06	19.79	37.76	69.39	4,935
Hubei 湖北	7	201	13,856	317	3.59	9.43	69.08	61.96	8,837
Hunan 湖南	17	94	3,994	-11	-0.29	-1.62	42.59	82.21	3,886
Guangdong 廣東	23	52	2,844	29	0.95	1.84	54.97	48.41	3,073
Guangxi 廣西	5	22	358	-82	-9.62	50.00	16.13	119.48	852
Hainan 海南									
Southwest 西南	24	67	4,046	-148	-3.52	-21.94	59.98	83.97	4,203
Chongqing 重慶	2	50	2,401	-832	-10.57	904.14	48.10	101.17	7,877
Sichuan 四川	13	86	6,339	-105	-2.18	-12.55	73.69	82.64	4,828
Guizhou 貴州	5	10	246	-22	-1.35	28.21	24.12	104.79	1,630
Yunnan 雲南	4	84	1,843	-163	-4.28	-11.73	22.07	63.55	3,800
Tibet 西藏									
Northwest 西北	16	97	2,462	-36	-0.63	-1.69	25.45	62.53	5,628
Shaanxi 陝西	9	92	1,272	-161	-5.11	-15.44	13.88	66.90	3,152
Gansu 甘肅	2	165	3,575	185	1.24	3.33	21.73	62.68	14,900
Qinghai 青海	1	65	4,020				61.85	50.67	4,500
Ningxia 寧夏									
Xinjiang 新疆	4	82	4,193	128	1.86	4.63	50.97	59.77	6,843

2950: Recycled Rubber 再生橡膠製品業

Year 年份	Number of firms 企業個數	Rate of change 每年變化 (%)	Number of employees 職工人數（人）	Rate of change 每年變化 (%)	Total revenue (mil. RMB) 總銷售收入（百萬元）	Rate of change 每年變化 (%)	Total profit (mil. RMB) 總利潤（百萬元）	Rate of change 每年變化 (%)
1993	252		25,026		608		2	
1994	294	16.67%	25,213	0.75%	893	46.79%	14	552.51%
1995	347	18.03%	29,047	15.21%	1,190	33.36%	25	73.74%
1996	357	2.88%	29,263	0.74%	1,438	20.84%	39	55.73%

3 Major products* 3 種主要產品 *	Output 產量	Sales volume 銷售量	Unit 單位
a) Regenerated Rubber 再生膠	336,189	279,036	ton 噸
b) Other Synthetic Rubber 其他合成橡膠	14,261	13,548	ton 噸

Top 10 firms by revenue (year founded) 收入排名前 10 家企業 (創辦年份)	City 城市	Province 省	Telephone / fax 電話 / 傳真	Number of employees 職工人數	Ownership 產業所有權	Revenue ('000 RMB) 銷售收入（千元）	Profit ('000 RMB) (rank) 利潤（千元）（排名）	Total assets ('000 RMB) 總資產（千元）	Major products 主要產品
Nantong Hui Li Rubber Industrial General Company 南通市回力橡膠實業總公司(1915)	Nantong 南通市	Jiangsu 江蘇省	(0513)2671668 (0513)2671708	330	Collectively-owned 集體	62,998	5380(2)	38,099	a
Bo'ai Welfare Rubber Plant 博愛縣福利橡膠製品廠(1992)	Jiaozuo 焦作市	Henan 河南省	(0391)8693533	120	Collectively-owned 集體	42,059	6109(1)	12,647	o
Renqiu Jing Dong Rubber Factory 任丘市京東橡膠廠(1986)	Cangzhou 滄州市	Hebei 河北省	(0317)2223278	390	Collectively-owned 集體	30,776	2544(4)	12,731	o
Anhui Chuzhou No.2 Rubber Plant 安徽省滁州市橡膠二廠(1972)	Chuzhou 滁州市	Anhui 安徽省	(0550)3701583	80	Collectively-owned 集體	29,380	80(83)	2,990	a
Pinghu No.1 Rubber Plant 平湖橡膠一廠(1979)	Jiaxing 嘉興市	Zhejiang 浙江省	(0573)5022986 (0573)5022988	436	State-owned 國有	26,369	875(22)	60,706	o
Huangshi No.2 Rubber Plant 黃石市第二橡膠廠(1976)	Huangshi 黃石市	Hubei 湖北省	(0714)6224273 (0714)6223833	591	State-owned 國有	25,671	-886(152)	30,095	a
Jiaozhou Reclaimed Rubber Factory 膠州市再生膠廠(1986)	Qingdao 青島市	Shandong 山東省	(0532)7212667	60	Collectively-owned 集體	23,589	2241(5)	8,987	a
Weixian Ya Tai Rubber & Plastic Products Co. Ltd. 威縣亞泰橡塑製品有限公司(1993)	Xingtai 邢臺市	Hebei 河北省		765	Collectively-owned 集體	21,702	3261(3)	12,834	o
Shandong Gaomi Reclaimed Rubber Co. Ltd. 山東高密再生膠股份有限公司(1978)	Weifang 濰坊市	Shandong 山東省	(0536)2322686 (0536)2320710	580	Joint stock 股份制	20,187	33(95)	38,719	a
Shaoxing Jin Long Rubber & Plastics Group Co. Ltd. 紹興金龍橡塑集團有限公司(1993)	Shaoxing 紹興市	Zhejiang 浙江省	(0575)8084904 (0575)8082688		Collectively-owned 集體	20,004	602(36)	39,821	o

Top 10 Cities by Production Output 產出排名前 10 位城市	Province 省	Market share 市場份額	Number of firms 企業個數
Dongguan 東莞市	Guangdong 廣東省	7.67%	3
Tangshan 唐山市	Hebei 河北省	7.16%	21
Nantong 南通市	Jiangsu 江蘇省	5.69%	13
Xingtai 邢臺市	Hebei 河北省	4.69%	11
Jiaozuo 焦作市	Henan 河南省	4.07%	7
Nanchang 南昌市	Jiangxi 江西省	3.80%	9
Bengbu 蚌埠市	Anhui 安徽省	3.78%	1
Shaoxing 紹興市	Zhejiang 浙江省	3.15%	4
Cangzhou 滄州市	Hebei 河北省	2.54%	6
Xuchang 許昌市	Henan 河南省	2.39%	4

10 Major Wholesalers 10 家主要批發商	City 城市	Province 省	Telephone / Fax 電話 / 傳真
Zhong Hua Singbo Import & Export Company 中化寧波進出口公司	Ningbo 寧波市	Zhejiang 浙江省	(0574)7346764 (0574)7366775
China Chemical Supply & Marketing Hua Nan Company 中國化工供銷華南公司	Guangzhou 廣州市	Guangdong 廣東省	(020)87654477 (020)87784414
China Agriculture Means of Production Chengdu Company 中國農業生產資料成都公司	Chengdu 成都市	Sichuan 四川省	(028)3333909 (028)3331202
Shanxi Agriculture Means of Production Company 山西省農業生產資料公司	Taiyuan 太原市	Shanxi 山西省	(0351)4040255 (0351)4040231
Beijing Chemical Light Industry General Company 北京市化工輕工總公司	Beijing 北京市	Beijing 北京市	(010)64224837 (010)64219301
Beijing Chemical Industry Group Company Supply & Marketing Company 北京化學工業集團公司供銷公司	Beijing 北京市	Beijing 北京市	(010)67714610 (010)67714058
Zhong Hua Jiangsu Import & Export Company 中化江蘇進出口公司	Nanjing 南京市	Jiangsu 江蘇省	(025)2258718 (025)2257789
Yunnan Chemical Import & Export Company 雲南省化工進出口公司	Kunming 昆明市	Yunnan 雲南省	(0871)3314002 (0871)3314931
Fujian Jiu Zhou Group Co. Ltd. 福建九州集團股份有限公司	Xiamen 廈門市	Fujian 福建省	(0592)5055818 (0592)5052033
China Chemical Industry Commission Agent Hua Dong Co. 中國化工供銷華東公司	Shanghai 上海市	Shanghai 上海市	(021)62514123

*Also include sales by firms outside this industry.包括本行業以外廠家的銷售。"o" stands for "others". "o" 代表"其他產品"。

2960: Rubber Shoes 橡膠靴鞋製造業

The industry accounts for 0.262% of the total revenue of China's industrial sector in 1996. The revenue growth rate of the industry is 6.0% from 1995, as compared to the growth rate of China's industrial sector, 9.51%. The rate of return on asset is 1.60%. 66.26% of all firms in the industry made a profit while 30.48% had negative returns. The top province in terms of the industry's revenue is Zhejiang, accounting for 14.48% of the total revenue.
本行業在1996年佔全行業總產值0.262%，行業年增長率為6.0%（全國工業年增長率9.51%）。行業的資產回報率1.60%，66.26%的企業盈利，30.48%的企業虧損。銷售收入最高的省份為浙江省，佔本行業的14.48%。

	Total number of firms 企業總數	Total number of employees 職工總數	Total revenue (mil. RMB) 總銷售收入（百萬元）	Total profit (mil. RMB) 總利潤（百萬元）	Return on assets 資產利潤率 (%)	Return on equity 權益利潤率 (%)	Labour productivity ('000 RMB / worker) 勞動生產率（千元/人）	Debts / assets 資產負債率 (%)	Total assets (mil. RMB) 總資產（百萬元）
Industry Overall 行業總體	673	285,825	15,214	250	1.60	5.80	53.23	72.40	15,617

	Number of firms 企業個數	Average number of employees 平均職工人數	Average revenue ('000 RMB) 平均銷售收入（千元）	Average profit ('000 RMB) 平均利潤（千元）	Return on assets 資產利潤率 (%)	Return on equity 權益利潤率 (%)	Labour productivity ('000 RMB / worker) 勞動生產率（千元/人）	Average debts / assets 平均資產負債率(%)	Average Total assets ('000 RMB) 平均總資產（千元）
By ownership 產業所有權									
State-owned 國有	115	996	46,626	304	0.52	2.46	46.80	79.00	58,974
Collectively-owned 集體	399	247	12,245	1,339	12.41	42.71	49.49	70.94	10,788
Privately-owned 私有	3	447	17,172	-2,882	-14.36	-40.76	38.42	64.77	20,067
Domestic JVs 聯營	17	686	42,369	-6,828	-12.55	-37.61	61.77	66.64	54,415
Joint stock 股份制	17	726	45,808	9,862	23.76	63.67	63.07	62.67	41,499
Foreign-funded 外資	42	449	30,093	-11,220	-43.58	-110.17	67.10	60.44	25,745
Overseas Chinese-funded 港澳台資	79	375	27,247	1,379	6.19	17.74	72.59	65.08	22,268
By size 規模									
Large 大型	17	2,524	196,068	12,323	6.10	18.91	77.68	67.73	201,905
Medium 中型	85	1,082	58,651	803	1.29	5.11	54.20	74.74	62,241
Small 小型	567	265	12,163	-49	-0.40	-1.49	45.90	72.93	12,160
By regional distribution 地區分布									
Central-North 華北	59	532	31,285	1,113	3.08	10.68	58.84	71.17	36,130
Beijing 北京	8	74	2,491	-210	-1.70	-7.61	33.78	77.68	12,369
Tianjin 天津	20	490	23,719	229	0.66	2.44	48.37	73.08	34,817
Hebei 河北	24	632	46,043	2,018	4.75	16.16	72.90	70.63	42,525
Shanxi 山西	4	1,230	58,610	3,880	5.29	14.62	47.66	63.84	73,410
Inner Mongolia 內蒙	3	299	4,007	-407	-5.51	127.08	13.42	104.38	7,377
Northeast 東北	64	409	11,277	-614	-3.14	-137.30	27.55	97.72	19,583
Liaoning 遼寧	31	460	13,588	-569	-2.54	-37.17	29.51	93.17	22,433
Jilin 吉林	12	288	2,987	-1,558	-11.08	42.19	10.36	126.26	14,066
Heilongjiang 黑龍江	21	403	12,604	-141	-0.76	-11.63	31.27	93.46	18,529
Central East 華東	362	387	21,399	348	1.79	5.78	55.32	69.12	19,504
Shanghai 上海	38	480	30,558	256	0.93	4.63	63.71	79.81	27,423
Jiangsu 江蘇	58	409	25,124	786	3.88	11.45	61.37	66.10	20,243
Zhejiang 浙江	148	264	14,881	216	1.72	4.22	56.46	59.35	12,600
Anhui 安徽	18	648	20,516	-600	-2.40	-23.86	31.65	89.93	24,971
Fujian 福建	32	249	12,618	-606	-5.06	-24.07	50.75	78.99	11,979
Jiangxi 江西	17	306	4,242	-408	-4.43	1875.68	13.85	100.24	9,218
Shandong 山東	51	671	40,792	1,487	3.81	11.02	60.79	65.40	39,020
Central-South 中南	129	443	24,689	125	0.52	1.81	55.68	70.95	23,818
Henan 河南	25	397	13,395	102	0.58	2.77	33.73	79.10	17,685
Hubei 湖北	16	413	22,460	-299	-1.36	-7.72	54.44	82.38	22,016
Hunan 湖南	22	645	35,376	1,265	4.10	9.82	54.82	58.23	30,851
Guangdong 廣東	59	376	24,413	-82	-0.36	-1.37	64.95	73.46	22,528
Guangxi 廣西	6	621	44,395	87	0.21	0.51	71.49	59.26	41,532
Hainan 海南	1	569	5,580	-5,200	-24.70	-1625.00	9.81	98.48	21,050
Southwest 西南	47	533	32,001	1,656	4.20	14.61	60.05	71.24	39,405
Chongqing 重慶	15	579	26,940	1,550	6.78	33.89	46.52	80.00	22,869
Sichuan 四川	11	293	8,998	-381	-3.00	-20.72	30.73	85.52	12,715
Guizhou 貴州	11	651	66,071	4,728	4.56	13.31	101.49	65.73	103,685
Yunnan 雲南	10	598	27,421	675	2.95	12.75	45.85	76.85	22,860
Tibet 西藏									
Northwest 西北	12	499	17,560	323	1.57	6.24	35.22	74.91	20,590
Shaanxi 陝西	7	610	21,739	479	2.04	9.22	35.63	77.92	23,516
Gansu 甘肅	2	440	13,265	135	0.53	1.50	30.18	64.88	25,710
Qinghai 青海	1	157	1,810	-230	-6.93	42.59	11.53	116.57	3,320
Ningxia 寧夏									
Xinjiang 新疆	2	338	15,105	240	1.73	5.89	44.69	70.61	13,865

2960: Rubber Shoes 橡膠靴鞋製造業

Year 年份	Number of firms 企業個數	Rate of change 每年變化 (%)	Number of employees 職工人數 (人)	Rate of change 每年變化 (%)	Total revenue (mil. RMB) 總銷售收入 (百萬元)	Rate of change 每年變化 (%)	Total profit (mil. RMB) 總利潤 (百萬元)	Rate of change 每年變化 (%)
1993	572		291,164		9,145		-151	
1994	628	9.79%	275,141	-5.50%	10,570	15.59%	-39	74.29%
1995	646	2.87%	314,711	14.38%	14,355	35.81%	101	360.96%
1996	673	4.18%	285,825	-9.18%	15,214	5.98%	250	147.60%

3 Major products* 3 種主要產品*	Output 產量	Sales volume 銷售量	Unit 單位
a) Rubber Shoes 膠鞋	130,681	122,840	10,000 pair 萬雙
b) Cloth Shoes 布鞋	19,219	18,643	10,000 pair 萬雙
c) Regenerated Rubber 再生膠	18,578	15,420	ton 噸

Top 10 firms by revenue (year founded) 收入排名前 10 家企業 (創辦年份)	City 城市	Province 省	Telephone / fax 電話 / 傳真	Number of employees 職工人數	Ownership 產業所有權	Revenue ('000 RMB) 銷售收入 (千元)	Profit ('000 RMB) (rank) 利潤 (千元) (排名)	Total assets ('000 RMB) 總資產 (千元)	Major products 主要產品
Guangzhou Panyu Da Xing Footwear Industry & Commerce Co. Ltd. 廣州番禺大興製鞋實業有限公司(1989)	Guangzhou 廣州市	Guangdong 廣東省	(020)84937909 (020)84933389	5,562	Overseas Chinese-funded 港澳台資	586,433	2852(36)	273,476	a
Guizhou Galoshes Factory 貴州膠鞋廠(1958)	Guiyang 貴陽市	Guizhou 貴州省	(0851)3813037	1,733	Collectively-owned 集體	380,506	17202(7)	817,815	a
Wenzhou Rong Guang Group Co. 溫州榮光集團公司(1987)	Wenzhou 溫州市	Zhejiang 浙江省	(0577)5600888 (0577)5600388	3,500	Collectively-owned 集體	344,021	11711(13)	175,586	a
Shanghai Rubber Shoes Co. 上海膠鞋公司(1932)	Shanghai 上海市	Shanghai 上海市	(021)63043846 (021)63046795	2,332	State-owned 國有	313,765	2842(37)	169,821	a
Hebei Zaoqiang Xing Da Chemical General Company 河北省棗強縣興達化工總公司(1989)	Hengshui 衡水市	Hebei 河北省	(0318)8225088	1,050	Collectively-owned 集體	239,360	19451(5)	69,516	o
Jiangsu Jinteng Group Corp. 江蘇金騰集團公司(1992)	Suzhou 蘇州市	Jiangsu 江蘇省	(0512)8740918	2,680	Collectively-owned 集體	237,440	12048(12)	143,865	a
Guangxi Nanning Rubber Plant 廣西南寧橡膠廠(1959)	Nanning 南寧市	Guangxi 廣西	(0771)3833961 (0771)3823731	2,937	State-owned 國有	221,650	382(136)	214,283	a,c
Hangzhou Zhonghua Rubber Factory 杭州中華橡膠總廠(1984)	Hangzhou 杭州市	Zhejiang 浙江省	(0571)8111251 (0571)8111531	2,351	Collectively-owned 集體	212,928	9754(16)	253,721	o
Hunan Rubber Factory 湖南橡膠廠(1958)	Changsha 長沙市	Hunan 湖南省	(0731)5563566 (0731)5563831	3,275	State-owned 國有	181,271	109(220)	188,993	a,c
Yunnan Nan Hu Rubber Factory 雲南省南湖橡膠廠(1973)	Gejiu 個舊市	Yunnan 雲南省	(0873)3848063 (0873)3848063	2,760	State-owned 國有	158,855	6729(18)	99,841	a

Top 10 Cities by Production Output 產出排名前 10 位城市	Province 省	Market share 市場份額	Number of firms 企業個數
Wenzhou 溫州市	Zhejiang 浙江省	11.36%	156
Shanghai 上海市	Shanghai 上海市	9.92%	57
Guangzhou 廣州市	Guangdong 廣東省	9.26%	24
Qingdao 青島市	Shandong 山東省	5.21%	21
Hangzhou 杭州市	Zhejiang 浙江省	3.92%	15
Tianjin 天津市	Tianjin 天津市	3.64%	22
Changzhou 常州市	Jiangsu 江蘇省	2.83%	12
Suzhou 蘇州市	Jiangsu 江蘇省	2.52%	18
Nantong 南通市	Jiangsu 江蘇省	2.35%	30
Hengshui 衡水市	Hebei 河北省	2.04%	3

10 Major Wholesalers 10 家主要批發商	City 城市	Province 省	Telephone / Fax 電話 / 傳真
Zhong Hua Singbo Import & Export Company 中化寧波進出口公司	Ningbo 寧波市	Zhejiang 浙江省	(0574)7346764 (0574)7366775
China Chemical Supply & Marketing Hua Nan Company 中國化工供銷華南公司	Guangzhou 廣州市	Guangdong 廣東省	(020)87654477 (020)87784414
China Agriculture Means of Production Chengdu Company 中國農業生產資料成都公司	Chengdu 成都市	Sichuan 四川省	(028)3333909 (028)3331202
Shanxi Agriculture Means of Production Company 山西省農業生產資料公司	Taiyuan 太原市	Shanxi 山西省	(0351)4040255 (0351)4040231
Beijing Chemical Light Industry General Company 北京市化工輕工總公司	Beijing 北京市	Beijing 北京市	(010)64224837 (010)64219301
Beijing Chemical Industry Group Company Supply & Marketing Company 北京化學工業集團公司供銷公司	Beijing 北京市	Beijing 北京市	(010)67714610 (010)67714058
Zhong Hua Jiangsu Import & Export Company 中化江蘇進出口公司	Nanjing 南京市	Jiangsu 江蘇省	(025)2258718 (025)2257789
Yunnan Chemical Import & Export Company 雲南省化工進出口公司	Kunming 昆明市	Yunnan 雲南省	(0871)3314002 (0871)3314931
Fujian Jiu Zhou Group Co. Ltd. 福建九州集團股份有限公司	Xiamen 廈門市	Fujian 福建省	(0592)5055818 (0592)5052033
China Chemical Industry Commission Agent Hua Dong Co. 中國化工供銷華東公司	Shanghai 上海市	Shanghai 上海市	(021)62514123

*Also include sales by firms outside this industry.包括本行業以外廠家的銷售。"o" stands for "others". "o" 代表 "其他產品"。

2970: Household Rubber Products 日用橡膠製品業

The industry accounts for 0.029% of the total revenue of China's industrial sector in 1996. The revenue growth rate of the industry is 6.6% from 1995, as compared to the growth rate of China's industrial sector, 9.51%. The rate of return on asset is 0.32%. 70.30% of all firms in the industry made a profit while 21.94% had negative returns. The top province in terms of the industry's revenue is Guangdong, accounting for 27.92% of the total revenue.
本行業在1996年佔全行業總產值0.029%，行業年增長率為6.6%（全國工業年增長率9.51%）。行業的資產回報率0.32%，70.30%的企業盈利，21.94%的企業虧損。銷售收入最高的省份為廣東省，佔本行業的27.92%。

	Total number of firms 企業總數	Total number of employees 職工總數	Total revenue (mil. RMB) 總銷售收入（百萬元）	Total profit (mil. RMB) 總利潤（百萬元）	Return on assets 資產利潤率 (%)	Return on equity 權益利潤率 (%)	Labour productivity ('000 RMB / worker) 勞動生產率（千元/人）	Debts / assets 資產負債率 (%)	Total assets (mil. RMB) 總資產（百萬元）
Industry Overall 行業總體	301	33,974	1,693	8	0.32	0.87	49.83	63.55	2,590

	Number of firms 企業個數	Average number of employees 平均職工人數	Average revenue ('000 RMB) 平均銷售收入（千元）	Average profit ('000 RMB) 平均利潤（千元）	Return on assets 資產利潤率 (%)	Return on equity 權益利潤率 (%)	Labour productivity ('000 RMB / worker) 勞動生產率（千元/人）	Average debts / assets 平均資產負債率(%)	Average Total assets ('000 RMB) 平均總資產（千元）
By ownership 產業所有權									
State-owned 國有	37	263	14,162	-135	-0.53	-2.60	53.77	79.47	25,270
Collectively-owned 集體	211	79	3,101	10	0.22	0.51	39.27	57.44	4,464
Privately-owned 私有	2	25	449	4	0.32	0.57	17.96	44.07	1,125
Domestic JVs 聯營	4	202	14,530	324	1.76	3.69	72.02	52.34	18,422
Joint stock 股份制	4	172	15,500	424	2.44	5.15	90.25	52.65	17,390
Foreign-funded 外資	14	96	10,434	-186	-1.29	-2.14	108.52	39.55	14,367
Overseas Chinese-funded 港澳台資	30	167	8,266	352	2.88	6.59	49.59	56.29	12,224
By size 規模									
Large 大型									
Medium 中型	11	786	49,186	11,996	13.31	43.59	62.61	69.47	90,144
Small 小型	282	90	4,086	-440	-7.75	-19.32	45.48	59.88	5,670
By regional distribution 地區分布									
Central-North 華北	43	138	5,838	47	0.65	2.66	42.45	75.56	7,186
Beijing 北京	5	91	6,632	62	1.30	3.04	73.20	57.29	4,776
Tianjin 天津	22	197	9,010	157	1.46	6.09	45.65	75.99	10,747
Hebei 河北	10	68	1,635	-183	-5.07	-38.13	24.12	86.70	3,610
Shanxi 山西	3	63	807	13	0.83	1.53	12.80	45.53	1,603
Inner Mongolia 內蒙	3	84	297	10	0.39	2.68	3.53	85.62	2,597
Northeast 東北	33	95	2,243	59	1.01	2.49	23.67	59.37	5,848
Liaoning 遼寧	16	146	4,092	119	1.06	2.64	28.10	59.74	11,216
Jilin 吉林	7	50	814	21	2.33	5.43	16.38	56.99	920
Heilongjiang 黑龍江	10	45	285	-11	-1.56	-3.25	6.35	52.19	707
Central East 華東	124	87	5,431	25	0.33	1.16	62.30	71.33	7,516
Shanghai 上海	15	209	16,793	-113	-0.39	-1.73	80.30	77.48	28,891
Jiangsu 江蘇	38	74	3,953	-72	-1.65	-4.79	53.28	65.55	4,371
Zhejiang 浙江	26	63	3,835	132	2.63	8.25	60.83	68.07	4,994
Anhui 安徽	6	189	5,040	-125	-1.64	-3.91	26.74	57.94	7,605
Fujian 福建	17	18	1,431	154	5.54	10.20	77.70	45.70	2,783
Jiangxi 江西	7	30	404	17	1.68	7.64	13.61	78.07	1,023
Shandong 山東	15	104	7,614	141	2.07	8.65	73.12	76.11	6,837
Central-South 中南	77	164	8,488	-7	-0.05	-0.11	51.85	54.73	14,399
Henan 河南	11	53	2,288	291	7.96	9.56	43.40	16.67	3,653
Hubei 湖北	10	164	6,118	-307	-4.51	-18.67	37.30	75.86	6,809
Hunan 湖南	10	63	1,697	65	3.22	12.87	26.81	74.98	2,018
Guangdong 廣東	39	230	12,121	87	0.43	0.84	52.68	48.06	20,069
Guangxi 廣西	2	88	1,705	35	3.11	14.00	19.49	77.78	1,125
Hainan 海南	5	121	14,834	-958	-2.45	-11.99	122.60	79.55	39,074
Southwest 西南	20	62	1,841	77	3.96	8.24	29.55	51.94	1,945
Chongqing 重慶	8	70	1,914	79	4.72	8.51	27.54	44.55	1,670
Sichuan 四川	7	38	1,008	10	0.79	1.92	26.47	58.96	1,256
Guizhou 貴州	2	78	2,580	-15	-0.82	-2.83	33.08	71.12	1,835
Yunnan 雲南	3	86	3,073	287	6.60	13.07	35.74	49.50	4,343
Tibet 西藏									
Northwest 西北	4	68	1,058	35	1.72	5.98	15.55	71.32	2,040
Shaanxi 陝西	2	59	1,435	190	7.31	29.23	24.53	75.00	2,600
Gansu 甘肅									
Qinghai 青海	2	78	680	-120	-8.11	-23.08	8.77	64.86	1,480
Ningxia 寧夏									
Xinjiang 新疆									

2970: Household Rubber Products 日用橡膠製品業

Year 年份	Number of firms 企業個數	Rate of change 每年變化 (%)	Number of employees 職工人數 (人)	Rate of change 每年變化 (%)	Total revenue (mil. RMB) 總銷售收入 (百萬元)	Rate of change 每年變化 (%)	Total profit (mil. RMB) 總利潤 (百萬元)	Rate of change 每年變化 (%)
1993	349		49,386		1,351		14	
1994	382	9.46%	47,783	-3.25%	1,462	8.19%	-1	-103.53%
1995	321	-15.97%	38,951	-18.48%	1,588	8.60%	-1	-12.18%
1996	301	-6.23%	33,974	-12.78%	1,693	6.61%	8	1501.05%

3 Major products* 3 種主要產品 *	Output 產量	Sales volume 銷售量	Unit 單位
a) Rubber Roller 膠輥	133,266	129,268	kg 公斤
b) Daily Plastic Products 日用塑料製品	14,105	14,951	ton 噸
c) Polythylene Products 聚乙烯製品	7,159	7,016	ton 噸

Top 10 firms by revenue (year founded) 收入排名前 10 家企業 (創辦年份)	City 城市	Province 省	Telephone / fax 電話 / 傳真	Number of employees 職工人數	Ownership 產業所有權	Revenue ('000 RMB) 銷售收入 (千元)	Profit ('000 RMB) (rank) 利潤 (千元) (排名)	Total assets ('000 RMB) 總資產 (千元)	Major products 主要產品
World Plastic Mat (Bao'an) Co. Ltd. 世界塑膠餐墊(寶安)有限公司(1989)	Shenzhen 深圳市	Guangdong 廣東省	(0755)8826481 (0755)8826449	4,000	Overseas Chinese-funded 港澳台資	90,810	330(31)	242,540	b,c
Guangzhou No.11 Rubber Plant 廣州第十一橡膠廠(1956)	Guangzhou 廣州市	Guangdong 廣東省	(020)84369694 (020)84323190	1,026	State-owned 國有	62,614	95(52)	115,696	o
Nan Hainan Lian Rubber Item Co. Ltd. 南海南聯橡膠製品有限公司(1991)	Foshan 佛山市	Guangdong 廣東省	(0757)5771131 (0757)5771042	237	Overseas Chinese-funded 港澳台資	61,429	5598(1)	102,640	o
Shanghai Emulsion Plant 上海乳膠廠(1959)	Shanghai 上海市	Shanghai 上海市	(021)65480975 (021)65491248	729	State-owned 國有	60,344	-247(90)	70,896	o
Tianjin No.1 Rubber Products Factory 天津市橡膠製品一廠(1941)	Tianjin 天津市	Tianjin 天津市	(022)27382095 (022)27382095	1,082	State-owned 國有	55,683	0(73)	41,249	o
Shanghai Poseidon Plastic Cement Products Co. Ltd. 上海佳運塑膠製品有限公司(1994)	Shanghai 上海市	Shanghai 上海市	(021)57271018 (021)57271018	180	Foreign-funded 外資	52,496	2518(5)	84,158	o
Shanghai Xiang Mao Co. Ltd. 上海翔茂有限公司(1996)	Shanghai 上海市	Shanghai 上海市	(021)57271789	480	Collectively-owned 集體	52,161	-4323(116)	129,015	o
Qingdao Emulsion Co. Ltd. 青島乳膠股份有限公司(1956)	Qingdao 青島市	Shandong 山東省	(0532)3610595 (0532)3617653	541	Joint stock 股份制	48,708	840(12)	47,775	o
Tianjin No.3 Rubber Products Factory 天津市橡膠製品三廠(1953)	Tianjin 天津市	Tianjin 天津市	(022)26353310 (022)26276454	560	State-owned 國有	48,097	-800(106)	58,243	o
Tianjin Emulsion Plant 天津市乳膠廠(1951)	Tianjin 天津市	Tianjin 天津市	(022)26352964 (022)26351624	877	State-owned 國有	47,367	0(75)	77,164	o

Top 10 Cities by Production Output 產出排名前 10 位城市	Province 省	Market share 市場份額	Number of firms 企業個數
Shanghai 上海市	Shanghai 上海市	13.44%	35
Tianjin 天津市	Tianjin 天津市	11.05%	25
Guangzhou 廣州市	Guangdong 廣東省	8.48%	18
Suzhou 蘇州市	Jiangsu 江蘇省	8.20%	8
Yangzhou 揚州市	Jiangsu 江蘇省	7.99%	13
Qingdao 青島市	Shandong 山東省	4.69%	11
Zhongshan 中山市	Guangdong 廣東省	3.84%	4
Haikou 海口市	Hainan 海南省	3.41%	2
Zhanjiang 湛江市	Guangdong 廣東省	3.27%	8
Foshan 佛山市	Guangdong 廣東省	3.07%	2

10 Major Wholesalers 10 家主要批發商	City 城市	Province 省	Telephone / Fax 電話 / 傳真
Zhong Hua Singbo Import & Export Company 中化寧波進出口公司	Ningbo 寧波市	Zhejiang 浙江省	(0574)7346764 (0574)7366775
China Chemical Supply & Marketing Hua Nan Company 中國化工供銷華南公司	Guangzhou 廣州市	Guangdong 廣東省	(020)87654477 (020)87784414
China Agriculture Means of Production Chengdu Company 中國農業生產資料成都公司	Chengdu 成都市	Sichuan 四川省	(028)3333909 (028)3331202
Shanxi Agriculture Means of Production Company 山西省農業生產資料公司	Taiyuan 太原市	Shanxi 山西省	(0351)4040255 (0351)4040231
Beijing Chemical Light Industry General Company 北京市化工輕工總公司	Beijing 北京市	Beijing 北京市	(010)64224837 (010)64219301
Beijing Chemical Industry Group Company Supply & Marketing Company 北京化學工業集團公司供銷公司	Beijing 北京市	Beijing 北京市	(010)67714610 (010)67714058
Zhong Hua Jiangsu Import & Export Company 中化江蘇進出口公司	Nanjing 南京市	Jiangsu 江蘇省	(025)2258718 (025)2257789
Yunnan Chemical Import & Export Company 雲南省化工進出口公司	Kunming 昆明市	Yunnan 雲南省	(0871)3314002 (0871)3314931
Fujian Jiu Zhou Group Co. Ltd. 福建九州集團股份有限公司	Xiamen 廈門市	Fujian 福建省	(0592)5055818 (0592)5052033
China Chemical Industry Commission Agent Hua Dong Co. 中國化工供銷華東公司	Shanghai 上海市	Shanghai 上海市	(021)62514123

*Also include sales by firms outside this industry.包括本行業以外廠家的銷售。"o" stands for "others". "o" 代表"其他產品"。

2981: Tire Recycling 輪胎翻新業

The industry accounts for 0.009% of the total revenue of China's industrial sector in 1996. The revenue growth rate of the industry is 4.8% from 1995, as compared to the growth rate of China's industrial sector, 9.51%. The rate of return on asset is -1.57%. 57.15% of all firms in the industry made a profit while 32.85% had negative returns. The top province in terms of the industry's revenue is Sichuan, accounting for 10.41% of the total revenue.
本行業在1996年佔全行業總產值0.009%，行業年增長率為4.8%（全國工業年增長率9.51%）。行業的資產回報率-1.57%，57.15%的企業盈利，32.85%的企業虧損。銷售收入最高的省份為四川省，佔本行業的10.41%。

	Total number of firms 企業總數	Total number of employees 職工總數	Total revenue (mil. RMB) 總銷售收入（百萬元）	Total profit (mil. RMB) 總利潤（百萬元）	Return on assets 資產利潤率 (%)	Return on equity 權益利潤率 (%)	Labour productivity ('000 RMB / worker) 勞動生產率（千元/人）	Debts / assets 資產負債率 (%)	Total assets (mil. RMB) 總資產（百萬元）
Industry Overall 行業總體	308	21,441	528	-16	-1.57	-4.60	24.63	65.77	988

	Number of firms 企業個數	Average number of employees 平均職工人數	Average revenue ('000 RMB) 平均銷售收入（千元）	Average profit ('000 RMB) 平均利潤（千元）	Return on assets 資產利潤率 (%)	Return on equity 權益利潤率 (%)	Labour productivity ('000 RMB / worker) 勞動生產率（千元/人）	Average debts / assets 平均資產負債率(%)	Average Total assets ('000 RMB) 平均總資產（千元）
By ownership 產業所有權									
State-owned 國有	56	140	2,411	-161	-2.33	-5.33	17.16	56.33	6,911
Collectively-owned 集體	234	54	1,565	-20	-0.96	-3.48	28.78	72.43	2,054
Privately-owned 私有									
Domestic JVs 聯營									
Joint stock 股份制	7	88	2,639	-79	-1.41	-3.59	29.90	60.63	5,554
Foreign-funded 外資	6	25	1,069	-250	-2.40	-12.31	43.62	80.52	10,421
Overseas Chinese-funded 港澳台資	6	14	263	-57	-1.83	-3.85	19.25	52.37	3,114
By size 規模									
Large 大型									
Medium 中型	1	285	5,219	-1,057	-4.83	10.52	18.31	145.92	21,884
Small 小型	301	70	1,736	-50	-1.55	-4.29	24.83	63.97	3,209
By regional distribution 地區分布									
Central-North 華北	44	50	1,261	-45	-1.47	-2.50	25.04	41.08	3,056
Beijing 北京	12	49	1,297	-178	-2.73	-3.93	26.74	30.56	6,496
Tianjin 天津	2	129	5,440	160	2.86	3.99	42.33	28.30	5,600
Hebei 河北	11	49	1,924	9	0.42	1.36	39.26	69.06	2,165
Shanxi 山西	6	28	452	-15	-1.88	-4.64	16.33	59.21	797
Inner Mongolia 內蒙	13	52	398	-14	-1.08	-2.33	7.69	53.65	1,285
Northeast 東北	77	49	1,111	-13	-0.63	-2.47	22.71	74.59	2,029
Liaoning 遼寧	23	89	2,204	-62	-1.60	-7.63	24.71	78.99	3,876
Jilin 吉林	14	49	556	4	0.26	0.92	11.34	71.20	1,349
Heilongjiang 黑龍江	40	26	677	10	0.83	2.58	26.32	67.78	1,205
Central East 華東	66	84	2,227	-56	-1.50	-4.26	26.40	64.88	3,723
Shanghai 上海	3	72	2,667	-557	-8.94	-36.62	37.21	75.66	6,230
Jiangsu 江蘇	8	79	2,676	254	7.54	13.84	34.09	45.51	3,365
Zhejiang 浙江	5	56	2,318	-18	-0.37	-0.88	41.39	58.21	4,872
Anhui 安徽	10	83	1,275	-52	-2.11	-7.75	15.44	72.77	2,464
Fujian 福建	20	64	2,061	-72	-2.44	-6.15	32.15	60.33	2,952
Jiangxi 江西	14	107	442	-155	-7.33	-55.64	4.12	86.82	2,114
Shandong 山東	6	139	7,633	30	0.29	0.79	54.98	63.40	10,415
Central-South 中南	40	87	3,046	20	0.41	1.79	35.11	77.25	4,975
Henan 河南	10	128	1,893	-31	-0.95	-3.57	14.85	73.37	3,259
Hubei 湖北	6	119	4,015	25	0.30	2.24	33.83	86.46	8,245
Hunan 湖南	8	60	1,875	-124	-5.60	-30.46	31.19	81.55	2,209
Guangdong 廣東	10	44	5,325	217	2.83	12.97	119.93	78.16	7,660
Guangxi 廣西	4	123	2,485	-28	-0.54	-1.17	20.16	54.07	5,100
Hainan 海南	2	33	320	-50	-4.41	-18.87	9.70	76.65	1,135
Southwest 西南	55	92	1,867	-86	-2.48	-6.47	20.22	61.72	3,472
Chongqing 重慶	10	116	2,276	-105	-3.17	-7.74	19.60	59.08	3,304
Sichuan 四川	24	109	2,290	-118	-2.36	-6.49	21.05	63.65	5,006
Guizhou 貴州	10	86	897	-166	-8.19	-22.83	10.49	64.13	2,027
Yunnan 雲南	11	41	1,455	72	4.42	9.04	35.82	51.15	1,626
Tibet 西藏									
Northwest 西北	26	52	598	-193	-8.14	-34.38	11.57	76.35	2,378
Shaanxi 陝西	5	49	1,016	-116	-5.79	-62.37	20.82	90.62	2,004
Gansu 甘肅	11	50	555	-10	-0.76	-1.90	11.01	59.94	1,307
Qinghai 青海	2	135	240	-1,120	-19.46	-224.00	1.78	91.23	5,755
Ningxia 寧夏	2	34	590	5	0.84	1.16	17.35	27.73	595
Xinjiang 新疆	6	34	448	-352	-8.54	-34.88	13.06	75.53	4,120

Year 年份	Number of firms 企業個數	Rate of change 每年變化 (%)	Number of employees 職工人數 (人)	Rate of change 每年變化 (%)	Total revenue (mil. RMB) 總銷售收入 (百萬元)	Rate of change 每年變化 (%)	Total profit (mil. RMB) 總利潤 (百萬元)	Rate of change 每年變化 (%)
1993	339		29,078		626		-1	
1994	351	3.54%	37,345	28.43%	507	-18.89%	-36	-5260.96%
1995	329	-6.27%	27,943	-25.18%	504	-0.76%	-28	22.53%
1996	308	-6.38%	21,441	-23.27%	528	4.84%	-16	42.15%

3 Major products* 3 種主要產品 *	Output 產量	Sales volume 銷售量	Unit 單位
a) Tire Tube 輪胎內胎	801,357	729,235	piece 條
b) Regenerated Rubber 再生膠	2,002	1,661	ton 噸
c) Tire Cover 輪胎外胎	46,670	43,870	piece 條

Top 10 firms by revenue (year founded) 收入排名前 10 家企業 (創辦年份)	City 城市	Province 省	Telephone / fax 電話 / 傳真	Number of employees 職工人數	Ownership 產業所有權	Revenue ('000 RMB) 銷售收入 (千元)	Profit ('000 RMB) (rank) 利潤 (千元) (排名)	Total assets ('000 RMB) 總資產 (千元)	Major products 主要產品
Qingdao No.2 Rubber Plant Jimo Retread Branch 青島第二橡膠廠即墨翻胎分廠(1974)	Qingdao 青島市	Shandong 山東省	(0532)2590345 (0532)2590345	424	Joint stock 股份制	38,419	0(50)	34,341	a
Guangzhou Da Li Tyre Factory Co. Ltd. 廣州大利輪胎廠有限公司(1996)	Guangzhou 廣州市	Guangdong 廣東省	(020)87891854	50	Foreign-funded 外資	23,090	1480(2)	9,540	o
Dalian Rubber Item Company 大連橡膠製品公司(1994)	Dalian 大連市	Liaoning 遼寧省	(0411)6641889 (0411)6656328	423	Collectively-owned 集體	15,301	4(41)	24,963	o
Shenyang Bei Fang Rubber General Company 瀋陽北方橡膠總公司(1993)	Shenyang 瀋陽市	Liaoning 遼寧省	(024)23780275	216	Collectively-owned 集體	15,213	1110(3)	28,384	o
Henan Nanyang Rubber Plant 河南省南陽市橡膠廠(1959)	Nanyang 南陽市	Henan 河南省	(0377)3134014	685	State-owned 國有	12,949	24(32)	19,847	o
Tianjin Tires Renovating Factory 天津市輪胎翻修廠(1937)	Tianjin 天津市	Tianjin 天津市	(022)26351520	237	State-owned 國有	10,879	322(9)	7,382	o
Dongguan Shi Pai Zhen Tyre Renovating Factory 東莞市石排鎮輪胎翻新廠(1987)	Dongguan 東莞市	Guangdong 廣東省	(0769)6651642	54	Collectively-owned 集體	10,475	617(6)	9,066	o
Wujin Hu Ning Tyre Renovating Factory 武進市滬寧輪胎翻修廠(1984)	Changzhou 常州市	Jiangsu 江蘇省	(0519)6543281	135	Collectively-owned 集體	10,229	2001(1)	6,005	o
Sichuan Chongqing Retread Factory 四川省重慶翻胎廠(1944)	Chongqing 重慶市	Chongqing 重慶市	(023)62801338	429	State-owned 國有	8,058	184(13)	18,973	o
Fujian Yongchun Shun Fa Rubber Factory 福建省永春順發橡膠廠(1993)	Quanzhou 泉州市	Fujian 福建省	(0595)3822218	25	Collectively-owned 集體	7,000	120(16)	1,960	o

Top 10 Cities by Production Output 產出排名前 10 位城市	Province 省	Market share 市場份額	Number of firms 企業個數
Qingdao 青島市	Shandong 山東省	7.80%	4
Chongqing 重慶市	Chongqing 重慶市	5.59%	11
Dalian 大連市	Liaoning 遼寧省	4.81%	3
Guangzhou 廣州市	Guangdong 廣東省	4.32%	1
Putian 莆田市	Fujian 福建省	3.89%	3
Nanyang 南陽市	Henan 河南省	2.73%	1
Tianjin 天津市	Tianjin 天津市	2.45%	2
Longyan 龍巖市	Fujian 福建省	2.38%	6
Beijing 北京市	Beijing 北京市	2.29%	12
Sanming 三明市	Fujian 福建省	2.29%	3

10 Major Wholesalers 10 家主要批發商	City 城市	Province 省	Telephone / Fax 電話 / 傳真
Zhong Hua Singbo Import & Export Company 中化寧波進出口公司	Ningbo 寧波市	Zhejiang 浙江省	(0574)7346764 (0574)7366775
China Chemical Supply & Marketing Hua Nan Company 中國化工供銷華南公司	Guangzhou 廣州市	Guangdong 廣東省	(020)87654477 (020)87784414
China Agriculture Means of Production Chengdu Company 中國農業生產資料成都公司	Chengdu 成都市	Sichuan 四川省	(028)3333909 (028)3331202
Shanxi Agriculture Means of Production Company 山西省農業生產資料公司	Taiyuan 太原市	Shanxi 山西省	(0351)4040255 (0351)4040231
Beijing Chemical Light Industry General Company 北京市化工輕工總公司	Beijing 北京市	Beijing 北京市	(010)64224837 (010)64219301
Beijing Chemical Industry Group Company Supply & Marketing Company 北京化學工業集團公司供銷公司	Beijing 北京市	Beijing 北京市	(010)67714610 (010)67714058
Zhong Hua Jiangsu Import & Export Company 中化江蘇進出口公司	Nanjing 南京市	Jiangsu 江蘇省	(025)2258718 (025)2257789
Yunnan Chemical Import & Export Company 雲南省化工進出口公司	Kunming 昆明市	Yunnan 雲南省	(0871)3314002 (0871)3314931
Fujian Jiu Zhou Group Co. Ltd. 福建九州集團股份有限公司	Xiamen 廈門市	Fujian 福建省	(0592)5055818 (0592)5052033
China Chemical Industry Commission Agent Hua Dong Co. 中國化工供銷華東公司	Shanghai 上海市	Shanghai 上海市	(021)62514123

*Also include sales by firms outside this industry.包括本行業以外廠家的銷售。"o" stands for "others". "o" 代表 "其他產品"。

2989: Other Rubber Products Repairing 其他橡膠製品翻修業

The industry accounts for 0.001% of the total revenue of China's industrial sector in 1996. The revenue growth rate of the industry is -45.6% from 1995, as compared to the growth rate of China's industrial sector, 9.51%. The rate of return on asset is 6.60%. 52.38% of all firms in the industry made a profit while 19.05% had negative returns. The top province in terms of the industry's revenue is Fujian, accounting for 56.96% of the total revenue.
本行業在1996年佔全行業總產值0.001%，行業年增長率為-45.6%（全國工業年增長率9.51%）。行業的資產回報率6.60%，52.38%的企業盈利，19.05%的企業虧損。銷售收入最高的省份為福建省，佔本行業的56.96%。

	Total number of firms 企業總數	Total number of employees 職工總數	Total revenue (mil. RMB) 總銷售收入（百萬元）	Total profit (mil. RMB) 總利潤（百萬元）	Return on assets 資產利潤率 (%)	Return on equity 權益利潤率 (%)	Labour productivity ('000 RMB / worker) 勞動生產率（千元/人）	Debts / assets 資產負債率 (%)	Total assets (mil. RMB) 總資產（百萬元）
Industry Overall 行業總體	45	1,976	79	3	6.60	15.30	39.98	56.87	40

	Number of firms 企業個數	Average number of employees 平均職工人數	Average revenue ('000 RMB) 平均銷售收入（千元）	Average profit ('000 RMB) 平均利潤（千元）	Return on assets 資產利潤率 (%)	Return on equity 權益利潤率 (%)	Labour productivity ('000 RMB / worker) 勞動生產率（千元/人）	Average debts / assets 平均資產負債率(%)	Average Total assets ('000 RMB) 平均總資產（千元）
By ownership 產業所有權									
State-owned 國有					-25.68	-223.81	17.24	88.52	
Collectively-owned 集體	45	45	1,755	67	7.50	17.65	38.66	57.50	889
Privately-owned 私有									
Domestic JVs 聯營									
Joint stock 股份制									
Foreign-funded 外資									
Overseas Chinese-funded 港澳台資									
By size 規模									
Large 大型									
Medium 中型									
Small 小型	45	45	1,755	67	7.51	17.66	38.80	57.50	888
By regional distribution 地區分布									
Central-North 華北	5	14	148	-12	-4.62	-6.98	10.72	33.08	260
Beijing 北京									
Tianjin 天津									
Hebei 河北	2	17	110	-35	-8.24	-14.89	6.47	44.71	425
Shanxi 山西	2	14	135				9.64		170
Inner Mongolia 內蒙	1	7	250	10	9.09	20.00	35.71	45.45	110
Northeast 東北	6	27	1,027	50	6.79	26.55	38.74	74.66	737
Liaoning 遼寧	5	13	1,026	58	9.27	27.36	80.16	66.45	626
Jilin 吉林	1	95	1,030	10	0.78	14.29	10.84	94.57	1,290
Heilongjiang 黑龍江									
Central East 華東	18	66	3,304	125	15.76	40.76	49.73	61.34	793
Shanghai 上海	1	4	80	50	125.00	166.67	20.00	25.00	40
Jiangsu 江蘇	3	12	300	7	1.67	7.41	25.71	77.50	400
Zhejiang 浙江	3	26	943				35.82	69.47	1,070
Anhui 安徽	1	198	8,260	260	4.56	9.56	41.72	52.28	5,700
Fujian 福建	2	363	22,500	925	90.24	217.65	62.07	58.54	1,025
Jiangxi 江西	6	21	330	12	4.46	15.56	15.84	71.34	262
Shandong 山東	2	15	215				14.33	56.86	255
Central-South 中南	8	29	918	14	1.26	7.38	31.50	82.87	1,088
Henan 河南	3	18	1,067	50	4.49	14.85	58.18	69.76	1,113
Hubei 湖北	2	38	225	15	0.85	-25.00	6.00	103.39	1,770
Hunan 湖南	2	52	1,845	-35	-3.85	-11.67	35.83	67.03	910
Guangdong 廣東	1								
Guangxi 廣西									
Hainan 海南									
Southwest 西南	6	47	765	10	0.64	0.82	16.39	21.97	1,570
Chongqing 重慶									
Sichuan 四川	3	32	103				3.22	12.58	1,007
Guizhou 貴州	3	62	1,427	20	0.94	1.27	23.14	26.41	2,133
Yunnan 雲南									
Tibet 西藏									
Northwest 西北	2	20	445	5	0.48	1.02	22.82	52.66	1,035
Shaanxi 陝西	1	27	850				31.48	29.90	970
Gansu 甘肅	1	12	40	10	0.91	3.33	3.33	72.73	1,100
Qinghai 青海									
Ningxia 寧夏									
Xinjiang 新疆									

2989: Other Rubber Products Repairing 其他橡膠製品翻修業

Year 年份	Number of firms 企業個數	Rate of change 每年變化 (%)	Number of employees 職工人數（人）	Rate of change 每年變化 (%)	Total revenue (mil. RMB) 總銷售收入（百萬元）	Rate of change 每年變化 (%)	Total profit (mil. RMB) 總利潤（百萬元）	Rate of change 每年變化 (%)
1993	40		1,703		27		0	
1994	44	10.00%	2,220	30.36%	164	511.10%	12	60980.00%
1995	34	-22.73%	1,327	-40.23%	145	-11.21%	13	4.13%
1996	45	32.35%	1,976	48.91%	79	-45.62%	3	-76.42%

3 Major products* 3 種主要產品 *	Output 產量	Sales volume 銷售量	Unit 單位

Top 10 firms by revenue (year founded) 收入排名前 10 家企業 (創辦年份)	City 城市	Province 省	Telephone / fax 電話 / 傳真	Number of employees 職工人數	Ownership 產業所有權	Revenue ('000 RMB) 銷售收入（千元）	Profit ('000 RMB) (rank) 利潤（千元）（排名）	Total assets ('000 RMB) 總資產（千元）	Major products 主要產品
Fujian Xianyou Feng Ting Enterprise Multiple Co. 福建省仙遊縣楓亭鎮企業綜合公司(1985)	Putian 莆田市	Fujian 福建省	(0594)7692142	85	Collectively-owned 集體	45,000	1850(1)	2,050	o
Chuzhou Welfare Tires Renovating Factory 滁州市福利輪胎翻修廠(1971)	Chuzhou 滁州市	Anhui 安徽省	(0550)3022957	232	Collectively-owned 集體	8,264	257(4)	5,700	o
Shanghai Lei Fa Industrial Company 上海蕾發實業公司(1993)	Shanghai 上海市	Shanghai 上海市	(021)64110497	40	Collectively-owned 集體	7,257	1009(2)	1,299	o
Shenyang Si Da Friction Sealing Material Factory 瀋陽市斯達摩擦密封材料廠(1996)	Shenyang 瀋陽市	Liaoning 遼寧省	(024)24317549	8	Collectively-owned 集體	3,962	280(3)	1,079	o
Hengyang Chengbei Welfare Rubber Factory 衡陽市城北福利橡膠廠(1979)	Hengyang 衡陽市	Hunan 湖南省	(0734)8225406	20	Collectively-owned 集體	3,687	-70(7)	1,819	o
Huishui Regeneration Rubber Plant 惠水縣再生橡膠廠(1993)	Duyun 都勻市	Guizhou 貴州省	(0854)428018	55	Collectively-owned 集體	2,851	0(5)	5,358	o

Top 10 Cities by Production Output 產出排名前 10 位城市	Province 省	Market share 市場份額	Number of firms 企業個數
Shanghai 上海市	Shanghai 上海市	63.06%	5
Hengyang 衡陽市	Hunan 湖南省	7.80%	2
Duyun 都勻市	Guizhou 貴州省	3.15%	2
Zhoukou 周口市	Henan 河南省	2.88%	1
Huzhou 湖州市	Zhejiang 浙江省	2.37%	1
Dalian 大連市	Liaoning 遼寧省	2.11%	2
Shangrao 上饒市	Jiangxi 江西省	2.03%	3
Huanggang 黃岡市	Hubei 湖北省	1.81%	2
Suzhou 蘇州市	Jiangsu 江蘇省	1.69%	1
Foshan 佛山市	Guangdong 廣東省	1.59%	1

10 Major Wholesalers 10 家主要批發商	City 城市	Province 省	Telephone / Fax 電話 / 傳真
Zhong Hua Singbo Import & Export Company 中化寧波進出口公司	Ningbo 寧波市	Zhejiang 浙江省	(0574)7346764 (0574)7366775
China Chemical Supply & Marketing Hua Nan Company 中國化工供銷華南公司	Guangzhou 廣州市	Guangdong 廣東省	(020)87654477 (020)87784414
China Agriculture Means of Production Chengdu Company 中國農業生產資料成都公司	Chengdu 成都市	Sichuan 四川省	(028)3333909 (028)3331202
Shanxi Agriculture Means of Production Company 山西省農業生產資料公司	Taiyuan 太原市	Shanxi 山西省	(0351)4040255 (0351)4040231
Beijing Chemical Light Industry General Company 北京市化工輕工總公司	Beijing 北京市	Beijing 北京市	(010)64224837 (010)64219301
Beijing Chemical Industry Group Company Supply & Marketing Company 北京化學工業集團公司供銷公司	Beijing 北京市	Beijing 北京市	(010)67714610 (010)67714058
Zhong Hua Jiangsu Import & Export Company 中化江蘇進出口公司	Nanjing 南京市	Jiangsu 江蘇省	(025)2258718 (025)2257789
Yunnan Chemical Import & Export Company 雲南省化工進出口公司	Kunming 昆明市	Yunnan 雲南省	(0871)3314002 (0871)3314931
Fujian Jiu Zhou Group Co. Ltd. 福建九州集團股份有限公司	Xiamen 廈門市	Fujian 福建省	(0592)5055818 (0592)5052033
China Chemical Industry Commission Agent Hua Dong Co. 中國化工供銷華東公司	Shanghai 上海市	Shanghai 上海市	(021)62514123

*Also include sales by firms outside this industry.包括本行業以外廠家的銷售。"o" stands for "others". "o" 代表 "其他產品"。

2990: Other Rubber Products 其他橡膠製品業

The industry accounts for 0.050% of the total revenue of China's industrial sector in 1996. The revenue growth rate of the industry is 22.9% from 1995, as compared to the growth rate of China's industrial sector, 9.51%. The rate of return on asset is 0.59%. 72.31% of all firms in the industry made a profit while 21.75% had negative returns. The top province in terms of the industry's revenue is Shandong, accounting for 12.92% of the total revenue.
本行業在1996年佔全行業總產值0.050%，行業年增長率為22.9%（全國工業年增長率9.51%）。行業的資產回報率0.59%，72.31%的企業盈利，21.75%的企業虧損。銷售收入最高的省份為山東省，佔本行業的12.92%。

	Total number of firms 企業總數	Total number of employees 職工總數	Total revenue (mil. RMB) 總銷售收入（百萬元）	Total profit (mil. RMB) 總利潤（百萬元）	Return on assets 資產利潤率 (%)	Return on equity 權益利潤率 (%)	Labour productivity ('000 RMB / worker) 勞動生產率（千元/人）	Debts / assets 資產負債率 (%)	Total assets (mil. RMB) 總資產（百萬元）
Industry Overall 行業總體	812	60,654	2,882	23	0.59	1.77	47.52	66.74	3,938

	Number of firms 企業個數	Average number of employees 平均職工人數	Average revenue ('000 RMB) 平均銷售收入（千元）	Average profit ('000 RMB) 平均利潤（千元）	Return on assets 資產利潤率 (%)	Return on equity 權益利潤率 (%)	Labour productivity ('000 RMB / worker) 勞動生產率（千元/人）	Average debts / assets 平均資產負債率(%)	Average Total assets ('000 RMB) 平均總資產（千元）
By ownership 產業所有權									
State-owned 國有	63	156	4,254	-381	-3.59	-19.20	27.23	81.32	10,619
Collectively-owned 集體	658	65	2,870	80	2.34	7.30	44.35	67.90	3,419
Privately-owned 私有	2	89	10,858	89	3.06	7.60	122.69	59.71	2,892
Domestic JVs 聯營	11	96	6,014	144	1.69	4.95	62.64	65.82	8,500
Joint stock 股份制	5	326	9,361	461	3.37	13.14	28.70	74.34	13,686
Foreign-funded 外資	25	77	6,637	284	2.45	6.36	85.88	61.53	11,601
Overseas Chinese-funded 港澳台資	47	84	9,037	-360	-3.01	-5.65	107.72	46.62	11,927
By size 規模									
Large 大型	2	809	27,573	-2,451	-1.50	-4.37	34.10	65.69	163,505
Medium 中型	5	925	49,492	239	0.29	1.48	53.50	80.66	83,283
Small 小型	788	69	3,275	34	0.84	2.39	47.56	65.03	4,053
By regional distribution 地區分布									
Central-North 華北	115	94	3,857	-46	-0.84	-3.33	41.13	74.86	5,495
Beijing 北京	21	118	7,096	-1,005	-10.17	-72.53	60.09	85.98	9,880
Tianjin 天津	29	68	2,638	223	5.02	15.12	39.04	66.82	4,449
Hebei 河北	47	82	4,139	226	4.79	13.73	50.20	65.11	4,722
Shanxi 山西	9	97	1,852	1	0.03	0.11	19.12	76.22	4,088
Inner Mongolia 內蒙	9	177	763	-144	-3.53	-162.50	4.30	97.80	4,087
Northeast 東北	164	69	2,503	22	0.56	1.99	36.09	71.83	3,910
Liaoning 遼寧	113	66	2,847	16	0.36	1.23	43.45	70.72	4,465
Jilin 吉林	18	59	644	-16	-1.26	-3.42	10.84	63.12	1,279
Heilongjiang 黑龍江	33	88	2,341	62	1.81	8.43	26.61	78.52	3,447
Central East 華東	289	66	4,250	108	2.10	5.33	64.87	60.68	5,129
Shanghai 上海	32	79	6,089	43	0.42	0.91	77.17	54.02	10,269
Jiangsu 江蘇	88	76	3,891	49	1.33	4.02	51.28	66.98	3,693
Zhejiang 浙江	48	71	4,801	79	1.35	2.87	67.34	53.06	5,894
Anhui 安徽	26	45	1,464	61	4.06	14.61	32.39	72.24	1,507
Fujian 福建	25	17	1,262	-2	-0.13	-0.28	76.00	54.02	1,223
Jiangxi 江西	18	25	1,033	8	0.98	22.73	41.33	95.68	849
Shandong 山東	52	82	7,162	382	4.31	11.97	87.20	63.97	8,858
Central-South 中南	148	94	3,786	-49	-0.95	-3.19	40.49	70.26	5,138
Henan 河南	37	50	1,893	62	1.61	5.01	37.62	67.92	3,834
Hubei 湖北	23	117	3,507	-661	-6.56	-27.15	30.03	75.85	10,077
Hunan 湖南	24	62	1,345	85	3.95	14.16	21.53	72.13	2,165
Guangdong 廣東	55	134	6,755	67	1.13	3.47	50.31	67.39	5,925
Guangxi 廣西	4	32	755	-33	-3.07	-16.25	23.59	81.09	1,058
Hainan 海南	5	56	570	18	1.89	2.89	10.22	34.87	952
Southwest 西南	50	73	3,162	-30	-0.57	-2.13	43.22	73.01	5,186
Chongqing 重慶	11	115	2,588	8	0.44	1.63	22.54	73.29	1,929
Sichuan 四川	28	68	3,051	-56	-0.88	-2.82	44.56	68.88	6,351
Guizhou 貴州	6	27	542	-10	-1.03	-1.42	19.82	27.07	967
Yunnan 雲南	5	63	8,226	2	0.02	0.19	130.99	90.56	11,226
Tibet 西藏									
Northwest 西北	46	45	1,766	55	1.56	2.78	39.41	44.06	3,547
Shaanxi 陝西	35	43	1,952	67	1.80	3.27	45.18	45.12	3,756
Gansu 甘肅	3	63	1,273	63	1.53	2.27	20.32	32.39	4,127
Qinghai 青海									
Ningxia 寧夏	1	12	540	30	7.50	10.71	45.00	30.00	400
Xinjiang 新疆	7	50	1,221	-6	-0.21	-0.38	24.50	44.59	2,704

2990: Other Rubber Products 其他橡膠製品業

Year 年份	Number of firms 企業個數	Rate of change 每年變化 (%)	Number of employees 職工人數 (人)	Rate of change 每年變化 (%)	Total revenue (mil. RMB) 總銷售收入 (百萬元)	Rate of change 每年變化 (%)	Total profit (mil. RMB) 總利潤 (百萬元)	Rate of change 每年變化 (%)
1993	676		68,593		1,533		26	
1994	775	14.64%	62,565	-8.79%	1,773	15.64%	38	48.30%
1995	839	8.26%	62,678	0.18%	2,345	32.25%	41	6.60%
1996	812	-3.22%	60,654	-3.23%	2,882	22.90%	23	-43.77%

3 Major products* 3 種主要產品 *	Output 產量	Sales volume 銷售量	Unit 單位
a)Rubber Roller 膠輥	2,651,098	2,571,566	kg 公斤
b)Other Synthetic Rubber 其他合成橡膠	6,762	6,424	ton 噸

Top 10 firms by revenue (year founded) 收入排名前 10 家企業 (創辦年份)	City 城市	Province 省	Telephone / fax 電話 / 傳真	Number of employees 職工人數	Ownership 產業所有權	Revenue ('000 RMB) 銷售收入 (千元)	Profit ('000 RMB) (rank) 利潤 (千元) (排名)	Total assets ('000 RMB) 總資產 (千元)	Major products 主要產品
Shenyang Chang Qiao Adhesive Tape Co. Ltd. 瀋陽長橋膠帶有限公司(1956)	Shenyang 瀋陽市	Liaoning 遼寧省	(024)86801106 (024)86800072	1,944	Overseas Chinese-funded 港澳台資	147,672	1048(24)	268,012	o
Beijing No.10 Rubber Plant 北京橡膠十廠(1958)	Beijing 北京市	Beijing 北京市	(010)69544525 (010)69547362	1,614	State-owned 國有	121,794	0(210)	119,862	o
Wendeng Kou Zi Rubber Factory 文登市口子橡膠廠(1982)	Weihai 威海市	Shandong 山東省	(0896)8631049 (0896)8631049	120	Collectively-owned 集體	78,400	9000(1)	12,680	o
Panyu Nan Sha He Qun Rubber Factory 番禺南沙合羣橡膠廠(1993)	Guangzhou 廣州市	Guangdong 廣東省	(020)84988542 (020)84988593	3,000	Foreign-funded 外資	63,399	-699(267)	5,638	o
Shanghai Pengpu Rubber Products General Factory 上海彭浦橡膠製品總廠(1963)	Shanghai 上海市	Shanghai 上海市	(021)56953731 (021)56050999	507	Collectively-owned 集體	61,173	7845(2)	70,480	o
Zhuhai Doumen Lian Yue Xiang Gen Thread & Belt Factory 珠海市斗門縣聯悅橡根線帶廠(1994)	Zhuhai 珠海市	Guangdong 廣東省	(0756)5571525 (0756)5571319	50	Overseas Chinese-funded 港澳台資	51,770	904(31)	7,463	o
Ji'nan Pingyin Rubber Factory 濟南市平陰橡膠廠(1985)	Ji'nan 濟南市	Shandong 山東省	(0531)7872604	195	Collectively-owned 集體	49,950	3990(6)	45,430	b
New Energy Chemical (Shenzhen) Co. Ltd. 新能源化工(深圳)有限公司(1994)	Shenzhen 深圳市	Guangdong 廣東省	(0755)6692379 (0755)6695803	89	Overseas Chinese-funded 港澳台資	39,788	-2089(281)	47,426	b
Hangzhou Yong Gu Rain-proof Products Factory 杭州永固防雨製品廠(1984)	Hangzhou 杭州市	Zhejiang 浙江省	(0571)6063925 (0571)6051044	279	Collectively-owned 集體	39,505	201(112)	54,002	o
Jining Rubber Factory 濟寧市橡膠廠(1981)	Jining 濟寧市	Shandong 山東省	(0537)2219801 (0537)2118318	646	Collectively-owned 集體	39,000	1800(13)	34,168	o

Top 10 Cities by Production Output 產出排名前 10 位城市	Province 省	Market share 市場份額	Number of firms 企業個數
Shanghai 上海市	Shanghai 上海市	10.84%	75
Shenzhen 深圳市	Guangdong 廣東省	6.89%	12
Shenyang 瀋陽市	Liaoning 遼寧省	6.61%	56
Beijing 北京市	Beijing 北京市	5.41%	19
Taizhou 泰州市	Jiangsu 江蘇省	4.19%	10
Wuxi 無錫市	Jiangsu 江蘇省	3.56%	42
Weihai 威海市	Shandong 山東省	3.32%	4
Guangzhou 廣州市	Guangdong 廣東省	2.90%	34
Hengshui 衡水市	Hebei 河北省	2.40%	18
Fuzhou 福州市	Fujian 福建省	2.07%	9

10 Major Wholesalers 10 家主要批發商	City 城市	Province 省	Telephone / Fax 電話 / 傳真
Zhong Hua Singbo Import & Export Company 中化寧波進出口公司	Ningbo 寧波市	Zhejiang 浙江省	(0574)7346764 (0574)7366775
China Chemical Supply & Marketing Hua Nan Company 中國化工供銷華南公司	Guangzhou 廣州市	Guangdong 廣東省	(020)87654477 (020)87784414
China Agriculture Means of Production Chengdu Company 中國農業生產資料成都公司	Chengdu 成都市	Sichuan 四川省	(028)3333909 (028)3331202
Shanxi Agriculture Means of Production Company 山西省農業生產資料公司	Taiyuan 太原市	Shanxi 山西省	(0351)4040255 (0351)4040231
Beijing Chemical Light Industry General Company 北京市化工輕工總公司	Beijing 北京市	Beijing 北京市	(010)64224837 (010)64219301
Beijing Chemical Industry Group Company Supply & Marketing Company 北京化學工業集團公司供銷公司	Beijing 北京市	Beijing 北京市	(010)67714610 (010)67714058
Zhong Hua Jiangsu Import & Export Company 中化江蘇進出口公司	Nanjing 南京市	Jiangsu 江蘇省	(025)2258718 (025)2257789
Yunnan Chemical Import & Export Company 雲南省化工進出口公司	Kunming 昆明市	Yunnan 雲南省	(0871)3314002 (0871)3314931
Fujian Jiu Zhou Group Co. Ltd. 福建九州集團股份有限公司	Xiamen 廈門市	Fujian 福建省	(0592)5055818 (0592)5052033
China Chemical Industry Commission Agent Hua Dong Co. 中國化工供銷華東公司	Shanghai 上海市	Shanghai 上海市	(021)62514123

*Also include sales by firms outside this industry.包括本行業以外廠家的銷售。"o" stands for "others". "o" 代表"其他產品"。

3010: Plastic Films 塑料薄膜製造業

The industry accounts for 0.380% of the total revenue of China's industrial sector in 1996. The revenue growth rate of the industry is 10.2% from 1995, as compared to the growth rate of China's industrial sector, 9.51%. The rate of return on asset is 1.53%. 63.84% of all firms in the industry made a profit while 28.74% had negative returns. The top province in terms of the industry's revenue is Guangdong, accounting for 18.24% of the total revenue.
本行業在1996年佔全行業總產值0.380%，行業年增長率為10.2%（全國工業年增長率9.51%）。行業的資產回報率1.53%，63.84%的企業盈利，28.74%的企業虧損。銷售收入最高的省份為廣東省，佔本行業的18.24%。

	Total number of firms 企業總數	Total number of employees 職工總數	Total revenue (mil. RMB) 總銷售收入（百萬元）	Total profit (mil. RMB) 總利潤（百萬元）	Return on assets 資產利潤率 (%)	Return on equity 權益利潤率 (%)	Labour productivity ('000 RMB / worker) 勞動生產率（千元/人）	Debts / assets 資產負債率 (%)	Total assets (mil. RMB) 總資產（百萬元）
Industry Overall 行業總體	2,077	238,277	22,021	470	1.53	4.91	92.42	68.77	30,677

	Number of firms 企業個數	Average number of employees 平均職工人數	Average revenue ('000 RMB) 平均銷售收入（千元）	Average profit ('000 RMB) 平均利潤（千元）	Return on assets 資產利潤率 (%)	Return on equity 權益利潤率 (%)	Labour productivity ('000 RMB / worker) 勞動生產率（千元/人）	Average debts / assets 平均資產負債率(%)	Average Total assets ('000 RMB) 平均總資產（千元）
By ownership 產業所有權									
State-owned 國有	275	228	17,225	124	0.36	1.50	75.70	76.10	34,505
Collectively-owned 集體	1,473	96	7,375	200	2.35	7.58	76.81	69.06	8,508
Privately-owned 私有	7	26	4,121	-56	-1.20	-2.31	155.93	48.00	4,633
Domestic JVs 聯營	20	106	8,040	-98	-0.90	-2.81	76.21	68.11	10,939
Joint stock 股份制	23	427	58,113	4,899	7.36	17.42	136.01	57.72	66,517
Foreign-funded 外資	110	85	15,862	643	2.53	6.46	186.67	60.89	25,441
Overseas Chinese-funded 港澳台資	167	81	18,731	-239	-1.00	-2.50	230.70	60.09	24,004
By size 規模									
Large 大型	56	777	146,661	9,382	4.80	14.94	188.70	67.88	195,540
Medium 中型	108	450	33,051	-809	-1.41	-5.14	73.41	72.59	57,359
Small 小型	1,893	77	5,409	17	0.24	0.73	70.13	67.74	7,149
By regional distribution 地區分布									
Central-North 華北	271	123	6,575	-38	-0.24	-1.07	53.59	77.26	15,579
Beijing 北京	54	161	10,290	-214	-0.60	-2.38	63.97	74.80	35,781
Tianjin 天津	45	89	4,967	-150	-1.38	-7.81	55.62	82.36	10,916
Hebei 河北	95	108	6,772	123	1.06	4.84	62.81	78.16	11,610
Shanxi 山西	29	225	8,385	-74	-0.47	-2.19	37.30	78.53	15,703
Inner Mongolia 內蒙	48	79	2,423	-30	-0.60	-3.01	30.71	80.08	5,005
Northeast 東北	309	109	6,968	-22	-0.22	-1.00	64.00	78.54	10,161
Liaoning 遼寧	114	106	6,585	-132	-1.30	-6.86	62.40	81.04	10,179
Jilin 吉林	59	164	11,427	38	0.25	1.11	69.62	77.87	15,616
Heilongjiang 黑龍江	136	88	5,354	45	0.57	2.43	61.06	76.37	7,779
Central East 華東	730	125	12,571	393	2.79	8.32	100.85	66.47	14,100
Shanghai 上海	64	114	10,167	326	2.45	7.12	88.99	65.52	13,270
Jiangsu 江蘇	125	130	14,601	244	1.47	3.97	112.08	63.05	16,612
Zhejiang 浙江	136	80	13,215	330	2.66	9.25	166.09	71.26	12,401
Anhui 安徽	101	107	9,815	384	4.11	16.60	91.39	75.27	9,349
Fujian 福建	111	59	10,605	272	2.66	6.61	180.66	59.82	10,247
Jiangxi 江西	52	101	3,092	-59	-0.93	-3.08	30.75	69.93	6,417
Shandong 山東	141	241	18,259	886	3.83	11.21	75.74	65.85	23,160
Central-South 中南	463	96	13,368	367	1.78	4.86	139.57	63.41	20,645
Henan 河南	102	96	8,451	73	0.78	2.90	87.85	73.14	9,435
Hubei 湖北	62	167	12,835	569	3.14	11.71	77.06	73.14	18,082
Hunan 湖南	63	80	3,218	-452	-8.04	-60.77	40.31	86.77	5,621
Guangdong 廣東	177	87	22,699	863	2.33	5.52	260.72	57.71	37,012
Guangxi 廣西	54	60	4,246	-47	-0.63	-2.79	70.25	77.55	7,472
Hainan 海南	5	101	16,390	1,072	3.22	18.12	162.60	82.21	33,248
Southwest 西南	164	97	7,853	68	0.77	2.14	80.71	63.89	8,814
Chongqing 重慶	32	85	3,875	-6	-0.15	-0.39	45.75	62.07	3,823
Sichuan 四川	78	106	7,661	25	0.26	0.70	72.13	62.88	9,544
Guizhou 貴州	19	94	10,733	410	3.75	9.46	113.79	60.37	10,943
Yunnan 雲南	34	91	10,630	44	0.40	1.27	117.15	68.50	10,861
Tibet 西藏	1	58	130	140	82.35	140.00	2.24	41.18	170
Northwest 西北	140	143	10,228	138	0.96	4.06	71.31	76.43	14,416
Shaanxi 陝西	47	95	3,937	-138	-1.94	-8.28	41.43	76.52	7,111
Gansu 甘肅	43	177	9,895	171	0.99	3.97	55.84	75.15	17,375
Qinghai 青海	4	198	2,783	-1,360	-15.81	55.85	14.09	128.31	8,600
Ningxia 寧夏	11	131	4,537	-137	-1.71	-9.90	34.61	82.74	8,031
Xinjiang 新疆	35	165	21,725	726	3.12	12.33	131.92	74.68	23,261

3010: Plastic Films 塑料薄膜製造業

Year 年份	Number of firms 企業個數	Rate of change 每年變化 (%)	Number of employees 職工人數 (人)	Rate of change 每年變化 (%)	Total revenue (mil. RMB) 總銷售收入 (百萬元)	Rate of change 每年變化 (%)	Total profit (mil. RMB) 總利潤 (百萬元)	Rate of change 每年變化 (%)
1993	1,558		203,988		12,104		152	
1994	1,717	10.21%	205,703	0.84%	13,823	14.21%	136	-10.44%
1995	2,073	20.73%	232,067	12.82%	19,974	44.50%	233	71.04%
1996	2,077	0.19%	238,277	2.68%	22,021	10.25%	470	101.58%

3 Major products* 3 種主要產品 *	Output 產量	Sales volume 銷售量	Unit 單位
a) Polythylene Products 聚乙烯製品	1,301,536	1,275,506	ton 噸
b) Polypropylene Products 聚丙烯製品	544,451	457,339	ton 噸
c) Polyvinyl Chloride Products 聚氯乙烯製品	675,666	621,613	ton 噸

Top 10 firms by revenue (year founded) 收入排名前 10 家企業 (創辦年份)	City 城市	Province 省	Telephone / fax 電話 / 傳真	Number of employees 職工人數	Ownership 產業所有權	Revenue ('000 RMB) 銷售收入 (千元)	Profit ('000 RMB) (rank) 利潤 (千元) (排名)	Total assets ('000 RMB) 總資產 (千元)	Major products 主要產品
Qilu Shihua Qi Hua Industry & Trade Group General Co. 齊魯石化齊華工貿集團總公司(1988)	Zibo 淄博市	Shandong 山東省	(0533)8900231 (0533)8900231	15,542	Collectively-owned 集體	891,329	81128(1)	1,079,582	c
Unitex Pvc (Fujian) Co. Ltd. 太平洋塑膠(福建)有限公司(1988)	Fuzhou 福州市	Fujian 福建省	(0591)5380111 (0591)5380109	634	Overseas Chinese-funded 港澳台資	683,888	17652(9)	498,250	c
Zhejiang Da Dong Ya Plastic Cement Group Co. 浙江大東南塑膠集團公司(1975)	Shaoxing 紹興市	Zhejiang 浙江省	(0575)7091468 (0575)7091508	885	Collectively-owned 集體	581,563	60205(2)	323,768	a,b
Foshan Dong Fang Packing Material Co. Ltd. 佛山東方包裝材料有限公司(1956)	Foshan 佛山市	Guangdong 廣東省	(0757)2212635 (0757)2217245	910	State-owned 國有	492,346	46588(3)	874,112	a,b
Dongguan Tian Shi Chemical Plant Co. Ltd. 東莞田氏化工廠有限公司(1992)	Dongguan 東莞市	Guangdong 廣東省	(0769)5518638 (0769)5518639	430	Overseas Chinese-funded 港澳台資	345,780	36937(5)	152,012	c
Wuhan Plastics Industry Group Co. Ltd. 武漢塑料工業集團股份有限公司(1965)	Wuhan 武漢市	Hubei 湖北省	(027)85780911 (027)85795900	2,189	Joint stock 股份制	263,587	25005(8)	319,741	a,b,c
Foshan Dupont Hong Ji Film Co. Ltd. 佛山杜邦鴻基薄膜有限公司(1996)	Foshan 佛山市	Guangdong 廣東省	(0757)2211988 (0757)2211016	458	Foreign-funded 外資	241,511	38074(4)	698,967	o
Jieyang Yun Tong Plastic Packag Co. Ltd. 揭陽市運通塑料包裝有限公司(1989)	Jieyang 揭陽市	Guangdong 廣東省	(0663)8812938	238	Foreign-funded 外資	239,290	2800(50)	402,060	b
Xi Feng Plastics Co. Ltd. Baishan 白山市喜豐塑料股份有限公司(1966)	Baishan 白山市	Jilin 吉林省	(0439)3222970	1,387	Joint stock 股份制	229,130	11507(10)	235,842	a,b,c
Ji'nan Plastics No.3 Factory 濟南塑料三廠(1954)	Ji'nan 濟南市	Shandong 山東省	(0531)6943668 (0531)6952316	1,197	Collectively-owned 集體	224,732	11008(12)	210,500	a,c

Top 10 Cities by Production Output 產出排名前 10 位城市	Province 省	Market share 市場份額	Number of firms 企業個數
Wuxi 無錫市	Jiangsu 江蘇省	9.61%	27
Foshan 佛山市	Guangdong 廣東省	7.09%	23
Beijing 北京市	Beijing 北京市	3.28%	45
Shaoxing 紹興市	Zhejiang 浙江省	2.90%	10
Shanghai 上海市	Shanghai 上海市	2.65%	102
Changzhou 常州市	Jiangsu 江蘇省	2.50%	33
Guangzhou 廣州市	Guangdong 廣東省	2.11%	42
Zhongshan 中山市	Guangdong 廣東省	2.04%	10
Wenzhou 温州市	Zhejiang 浙江省	1.97%	80
Jiaxing 嘉興市	Zhejiang 浙江省	1.78%	26

10 Major Wholesalers 10 家主要批發商	City 城市	Province 省	Telephone / Fax 電話 / 傳真
Zhong Hua Singbo Import & Export Company 中化寧波進出口公司	Ningbo 寧波市	Zhejiang 浙江省	(0574)7346764 (0574)7366775
China Chemical Supply & Marketing Hua Nan Company 中國化工供銷華南公司	Guangzhou 廣州市	Guangdong 廣東省	(020)87654477 (020)87784414
China Agriculture Means of Production Chengdu Company 中國農業生產資料成都公司	Chengdu 成都市	Sichuan 四川省	(028)3333909 (028)3331202
Shanxi Agriculture Means of Production Company 山西省農業生產資料公司	Taiyuan 太原市	Shanxi 山西省	(0351)4040255 (0351)4040231
Beijing Chemical Light Industry General Company 北京市化工輕工總公司	Beijing 北京市	Beijing 北京市	(010)64224837 (010)64219301
Beijing Chemical Industry Group Company Supply & Marketing Company 北京化學工業集團公司供銷公司	Beijing 北京市	Beijing 北京市	(010)67714610 (010)67714058
Zhong Hua Jiangsu Import & Export Company 中化江蘇進出口公司	Nanjing 南京市	Jiangsu 江蘇省	(025)2258718 (025)2257789
Yunnan Chemical Import & Export Company 雲南省化工進出口公司	Kunming 昆明市	Yunnan 雲南省	(0871)3314002 (0871)3314931
Fujian Jiu Zhou Group Co. Ltd. 福建九州集團股份有限公司	Xiamen 廈門市	Fujian 福建省	(0592)5055818 (0592)5052033
China Chemical Industry Commission Agent Hua Dong Co. 中國化工供銷華東公司	Shanghai 上海市	Shanghai 上海市	(021)62514123

*Also include sales by firms outside this industry.包括本行業以外廠家的銷售。"o" stands for "others". "o" 代表"其他產品"。

3020: Plastic Sheet, Pipe and Rods 塑料板、管、棒材製造業

The industry accounts for 0.234% of the total revenue of China's industrial sector in 1996. The revenue growth rate of the industry is 18.6% from 1995, as compared to the growth rate of China's industrial sector, 9.51%. The rate of return on asset is 0.51%. 64.72% of all firms in the industry made a profit while 27.17% had negative returns. The top province in terms of the industry's revenue is Jiangsu, accounting for 24.25% of the total revenue.
本行業在1996年佔全行業總產值0.234%，行業年增長率為18.6%（全國工業年增長率9.51%）。行業的資產回報率0.51%，64.72%的企業盈利，27.17%的企業虧損。銷售收入最高的省份為江蘇省，佔本行業的24.25%。

	Total number of firms 企業總數	Total number of employees 職工總數	Total revenue (mil. RMB) 總銷售收入（百萬元）	Total profit (mil. RMB) 總利潤（百萬元）	Return on assets 資產利潤率 (%)	Return on equity 權益利潤率 (%)	Labour productivity ('000 RMB / worker) 勞動生產率（千元/人）	Debts / assets 資產負債率 (%)	Total assets (mil. RMB) 總資產（百萬元）
Industry Overall 行業總體	2,324	197,484	13,553	117	0.51	1.55	68.63	67.19	22,988

	Number of firms 企業個數	Average number of employees 平均職工人數	Average revenue ('000 RMB) 平均銷售收入（千元）	Average profit ('000 RMB) 平均利潤（千元）	Return on assets 資產利潤率 (%)	Return on equity 權益利潤率 (%)	Labour productivity ('000 RMB / worker) 勞動生產率（千元/人）	Average debts / assets 平均資產負債率(%)	Average Total assets ('000 RMB) 平均總資產（千元）
By ownership 產業所有權									
State-owned 國有	207	241	9,217	-367	-1.42	-6.37	38.26	77.63	25,783
Collectively-owned 集體	1,726	67	4,079	-93	-1.86	-8.01	60.54	76.74	4,990
Privately-owned 私有	9	51	6,188	-2,523	-96.60	-400.63	120.81	75.89	2,611
Domestic JVs 聯營	21	198	10,567	4,691	33.92	136.00	53.38	75.06	13,830
Joint stock 股份制	30	92	7,859	-12,244	-65.77	-122.04	85.83	46.11	18,617
Foreign-funded 外資	117	70	9,144	635	2.90	6.07	130.21	52.30	21,924
Overseas Chinese-funded 港澳台資	210	75	13,057	3,273	13.28	27.21	173.88	51.18	24,638
By size 規模									
Large 大型	17	855	111,256	-6,561	-3.61	-11.45	130.12	68.43	181,550
Medium 中型	78	463	33,203	1,179	1.77	7.78	71.64	77.19	66,453
Small 小型	2,172	67	4,176	63	0.93	2.54	62.29	63.41	6,776
By regional distribution 地區分布									
Central-North 華北	326	110	5,124	-13	-0.09	-0.34	46.43	72.78	13,531
Beijing 北京	75	128	6,845	-274	-1.19	-4.81	53.27	75.23	22,956
Tianjin 天津	57	80	4,995	-56	-0.45	-1.80	62.66	74.96	12,433
Hebei 河北	126	77	5,339	311	2.90	10.14	69.76	71.43	10,745
Shanxi 山西	32	333	5,111	-566	-3.31	-9.37	15.37	64.70	17,130
Inner Mongolia 內蒙	36	42	998	-42	-1.91	-9.11	23.76	78.99	2,191
Northeast 東北	383	75	1,865	-33	-0.63	-2.56	25.01	75.28	5,182
Liaoning 遼寧	177	87	2,102	-101	-1.92	-10.08	24.15	80.99	5,261
Jilin 吉林	107	69	1,830	92	2.07	5.07	26.71	59.17	4,429
Heilongjiang 黑龍江	99	59	1,478	-46	-0.78	-3.75	25.13	79.26	5,857
Central East 華東	835	95	8,560	145	1.19	3.21	90.20	62.87	12,184
Shanghai 上海	53	91	9,987	-226	-1.48	-4.70	109.23	68.45	15,256
Jiangsu 江蘇	255	111	12,888	345	2.42	6.42	116.42	62.33	14,243
Zhejiang 浙江	174	90	7,911	46	0.41	1.13	87.85	63.55	11,156
Anhui 安徽	72	85	4,225	3	0.03	0.08	49.64	57.19	8,004
Fujian 福建	63	39	3,234	-45	-0.37	-0.72	82.54	48.98	12,140
Jiangxi 江西	44	43	866	-135	-4.62	-16.09	20.26	71.29	2,927
Shandong 山東	174	115	8,100	264	1.98	5.95	70.39	66.73	13,345
Central-South 中南	499	72	6,474	90	0.91	2.77	89.63	66.99	9,863
Henan 河南	152	52	2,990	99	2.87	9.04	57.01	68.25	3,448
Hubei 湖北	65	107	5,172	52	0.78	1.98	48.34	60.84	6,745
Hunan 湖南	73	69	2,543	-136	-3.79	-29.61	36.82	87.20	3,595
Guangdong 廣東	172	85	12,500	216	1.04	3.05	147.76	65.91	20,785
Guangxi 廣西	33	41	3,032	6	0.20	0.79	73.25	75.33	3,254
Hainan 海南	4	38	973	-230	-6.47	-11.72	25.42	44.76	3,553
Southwest 西南	200	55	3,074	-60	-1.24	-3.88	55.42	67.96	4,786
Chongqing 重慶	33	74	2,110	-182	-4.96	-23.05	28.62	78.46	3,661
Sichuan 四川	112	62	4,297	-75	-1.16	-3.94	68.83	70.63	6,438
Guizhou 貴州	34	16	425	-7	-0.76	-1.40	26.11	45.53	924
Yunnan 雲南	21	52	2,371	131	3.27	5.30	45.94	38.26	4,000
Tibet 西藏									
Northwest 西北	81	81	2,167	-256	-3.84	-14.56	26.69	73.67	6,664
Shaanxi 陝西	37	59	1,825	-268	-4.17	-12.51	30.98	66.68	6,416
Gansu 甘肅	15	71	2,443	-203	-2.65	-6.92	34.32	61.65	7,634
Qinghai 青海	4	163	3,423	-1,173	-11.98	31.99	20.96	137.44	9,790
Ningxia 寧夏	7	228	2,441	-231	-2.71	-15.21	10.69	82.16	8,527
Xinjiang 新疆	18	60	2,252	-81	-1.63	-6.27	37.74	74.02	4,944

3020: Plastic Sheet, Pipe and Rods 塑料板、管、棒材製造業

Year 年份	Number of firms 企業個數	Rate of change 每年變化 (%)	Number of employees 職工人數 (人)	Rate of change 每年變化 (%)	Total revenue (mil. RMB) 總銷售收入 (百萬元)	Rate of change 每年變化 (%)	Total profit (mil. RMB) 總利潤 (百萬元)	Rate of change 每年變化 (%)
1993	1,852		160,735		7,062		191	
1994	2,082	12.42%	170,973	6.37%	7,872	11.47%	54	-71.92%
1995	2,343	12.54%	190,830	11.61%	11,431	45.21%	-58	-208.60%
1996	2,324	-0.81%	197,484	3.49%	13,553	18.56%	117	300.56%

3 Major products* 3 種主要產品 *	Output 產量	Sales volume 銷售量	Unit 單位
a) Plastic Plate-piece Materia 塑料板片材	413,478	388,669	ton 噸
b) Polystyrol Products 聚苯乙烯製品	1,079,564	1,057,972	ton 噸

Top 10 firms by revenue (year founded) 收入排名前 10 家企業 (創辦年份)	City 城市	Province 省	Telephone / fax 電話 / 傳真	Number of employees 職工人數	Ownership 產業所有權	Revenue ('000 RMB) 銷售收入 (千元)	Profit ('000 RMB) (rank) 利潤 (千元) (排名)	Total assets ('000 RMB) 總資產 (千元)	Major products 主要產品
Jiangsu Jiangyin Moulding Group General Co. 江蘇江陰模塑集團總公司(1984)	Wuxi 無錫市	Jiangsu 江蘇省	(0510)6221226 (0510)6222388	790	Overseas Chinese-funded 港澳台資	610,700	41227(2)	647,548	o
Capital Aerospace Machinery Co. 首都航天機械公司(1951)	Beijing 北京市	Beijing 北京市	(010)68750017 (010)68383476	6,600	State-owned 國有	358,709	1582(66)	1,336,886	o
Shantou Plastic Cement Decoration Material Manufacturing Plant 汕頭市塑膠裝飾材料製造廠(1987)	Shantou 汕頭市	Guangdong 廣東省	(0754)8330740 (0754)8330734	318	Overseas Chinese-funded 港澳台資	289,254	61377(1)	262,501	o
Jiangsu Yin Shan Industrial Group Co. Ltd. 江蘇省銀杉實業集團有限公司(1989)	Nanjing 南京市	Jiangsu 江蘇省	(025)4128699	551	Collectively-owned 集體	221,593	7296(13)	233,202	o
Changzhou Ju Li Plastics Industrial General Co. 常州市巨力塑料實業總公司(1964)	Changzhou 常州市	Jiangsu 江蘇省	(0519)6970267 (0519)6968554	497	其他經濟	221,445	20419(3)	215,386	a,b
Hebei Bao Su Group Co. Ltd. 河北保塑集團有限公司(1957)	Baoding 保定市	Hebei 河北省	(0312)3036307 (0312)3137545	2,394	State-owned 國有	212,312	11255(7)	508,129	o
Jiangsu Qiong Hua Plastics (Group) Factory 江蘇瓊花塑料(集團)廠(1984)	Yangzhou 揚州市	Jiangsu 江蘇省	(0514)7271301 (0514)7273004	484	Collectively-owned 集體	201,950	13076(5)	152,859	a
China Zhong Light Industry Group Company 中國中輕工業集團公司(1988)	Ningbo 寧波市	Zhejiang 浙江省	(0574)3601368 (0574)3601217	715	Collectively-owned 集體	197,828	2201(49)	425,646	a,b
Shenzhen Petrochemical Plastics Corp., Ltd. 深圳石化塑膠股份有限公司(1983)	Shenzhen 深圳市	Guangdong 廣東省	(0755)5515013 (0755)5530195	544	Overseas Chinese-funded 港澳台資	192,231	11694(6)	245,115	a
Hangzhou Plastics Industrial Co. 杭州塑料工業公司(1958)	Hangzhou 杭州市	Zhejiang 浙江省	(0571)8088788 (0571)8086419	1,217	State-owned 國有	167,365	1003(98)	212,366	a

Top 10 Cities by Production Output 產出排名前 10 位城市	Province 省	Market share 市場份額	Number of firms 企業個數
Shenzhen 深圳市	Guangdong 廣東省	9.91%	13
Wuxi 無錫市	Jiangsu 江蘇省	6.14%	90
Shanghai 上海市	Shanghai 上海市	4.13%	111
Guangzhou 廣州市	Guangdong 廣東省	3.94%	47
Foshan 佛山市	Guangdong 廣東省	3.76%	34
Hangzhou 杭州市	Zhejiang 浙江省	3.65%	47
Changzhou 常州市	Jiangsu 江蘇省	3.52%	40
Baoding 保定市	Hebei 河北省	2.44%	16
Tianjin 天津市	Tianjin 天津市	2.33%	71
Suzhou 蘇州市	Jiangsu 江蘇省	2.22%	48

10 Major Wholesalers 10 家主要批發商	City 城市	Province 省	Telephone / Fax 電話 / 傳真
Zhong Hua Singbo Import & Export Company 中化寧波進出口公司	Ningbo 寧波市	Zhejiang 浙江省	(0574)7346764 (0574)7366775
China Chemical Supply & Marketing Hua Nan Company 中國化工供銷華南公司	Guangzhou 廣州市	Guangdong 廣東省	(020)87654477 (020)87784414
China Agriculture Means of Production Chengdu Company 中國農業生產資料成都公司	Chengdu 成都市	Sichuan 四川省	(028)3333909 (028)3331202
Shanxi Agriculture Means of Production Company 山西省農業生產資料公司	Taiyuan 太原市	Shanxi 山西省	(0351)4040255 (0351)4040231
Beijing Chemical Light Industry General Company 北京市化工輕工總公司	Beijing 北京市	Beijing 北京市	(010)64224837 (010)64219301
Beijing Chemical Industry Group Company Supply & Marketing Company 北京化學工業集團公司供銷公司	Beijing 北京市	Beijing 北京市	(010)67714610 (010)67714058
Zhong Hua Jiangsu Import & Export Company 中化江蘇進出口公司	Nanjing 南京市	Jiangsu 江蘇省	(025)2258718 (025)2257789
Yunnan Chemical Import & Export Company 雲南省化工進出口公司	Kunming 昆明市	Yunnan 雲南省	(0871)3314002 (0871)3314931
Fujian Jiu Zhou Group Co. Ltd. 福建九州集團股份有限公司	Xiamen 廈門市	Fujian 福建省	(0592)5055818 (0592)5052033
China Chemical Industry Commission Agent Hua Dong Co. 中國化工供銷華東公司	Shanghai 上海市	Shanghai 上海市	(021)62514123

*Also include sales by firms outside this industry.包括本行業以外廠家的銷售。"o" stands for "others". "o" 代表 "其他產品"。

3030: Plastic Thread, Rope and Knitted Products 塑料絲、繩及編織品製造業

The industry accounts for 0.340% of the total revenue of China's industrial sector in 1996. The revenue growth rate of the industry is 19.0% from 1995, as compared to the growth rate of China's industrial sector, 9.51%. The rate of return on asset is 1.01%. 67.93% of all firms in the industry made a profit while 26.41% had negative returns. The top province in terms of the industry's revenue is Zhejiang, accounting for 15.52% of the total revenue.
本行業在1996年佔全行業總產值0.340%，行業年增長率為19.0%（全國工業年增長率9.51%）。行業的資產回報率1.01%，67.93%的企業盈利，26.41%的企業虧損。銷售收入最高的省份為浙江省，佔本行業的15.52%。

	Total number of firms 企業總數	Total number of employees 職工總數	Total revenue (mil. RMB) 總銷售收入（百萬元）	Total profit (mil. RMB) 總利潤（百萬元）	Return on assets 資產利潤率 (%)	Return on equity 權益利潤率 (%)	Labour productivity ('000 RMB / worker) 勞動生產率（千元/人）	Debts / assets 資產負債率 (%)	Total assets (mil. RMB) 總資產（百萬元）
Industry Overall 行業總體	3,934	363,897	19,692	225	1.01	3.55	54.11	71.59	22,242

	Number of firms 企業個數	Average number of employees 平均職工人數	Average revenue ('000 RMB) 平均銷售收入（千元）	Average profit ('000 RMB) 平均利潤（千元）	Return on assets 資產利潤率 (%)	Return on equity 權益利潤率 (%)	Labour productivity ('000 RMB / worker) 勞動生產率（千元/人）	Average debts / assets 平均資產負債率(%)	Average Total assets ('000 RMB) 平均總資產（千元）
By ownership 產業所有權									
State-owned 國有	350	142	4,746	-171	-1.64	-11.72	33.33	85.99	10,443
Collectively-owned 集體	3,193	84	4,307	43	1.06	3.86	51.11	72.64	4,101
Privately-owned 私有	16	55	3,445	157	7.24	17.53	62.35	58.73	2,167
Domestic JVs 聯營	35	131	9,670	-208	-1.89	-5.78	73.98	67.38	11,039
Joint stock 股份制	47	116	5,435	153	3.59	12.68	46.66	71.70	4,274
Foreign-funded 外資	114	115	13,932	324	1.89	4.74	121.12	60.14	17,142
Overseas Chinese-funded 港澳台資	177	120	11,498	606	3.70	8.66	95.60	57.26	16,385
By size 規模									
Large 大型	23	938	88,542	9,034	6.62	26.48	94.44	74.98	136,376
Medium 中型	82	462	23,740	-4,038	-8.87	-38.20	51.42	76.77	45,504
Small 小型	3,790	80	4,144	92	2.27	7.46	51.73	69.64	4,057
By regional distribution 地區分布									
Central-North 華北	437	75	2,995	112	3.16	11.78	40.12	73.20	3,535
Beijing 北京	66	49	2,767	-6	-0.16	-0.38	56.97	59.17	3,792
Tianjin 天津	75	100	4,038	152	3.35	19.91	40.41	83.16	4,526
Hebei 河北	182	77	3,494	194	5.57	20.57	45.16	72.92	3,474
Shanxi 山西	59	80	1,688	14	0.40	1.84	21.22	78.34	3,574
Inner Mongolia 內蒙	55	57	1,591	31	1.53	4.52	27.85	66.24	2,037
Northeast 東北	419	132	4,342	36	0.49	2.53	32.83	80.53	7,326
Liaoning 遼寧	228	151	5,756	128	1.47	5.86	38.11	74.97	8,730
Jilin 吉林	89	103	2,179	-133	-2.57	7425.00	21.14	100.03	5,200
Heilongjiang 黑龍江	102	116	3,070	-21	-0.36	-2.20	26.53	83.83	6,043
Central East 華東	1,703	91	6,285	103	1.84	5.69	69.30	67.65	5,577
Shanghai 上海	54	120	10,471	269	2.16	4.84	87.39	55.43	12,472
Jiangsu 江蘇	263	126	6,164	-113	-1.58	-6.85	48.92	76.89	7,136
Zhejiang 浙江	609	63	5,019	37	1.24	3.56	79.59	65.08	2,993
Anhui 安徽	203	111	10,689	487	6.86	18.59	95.92	63.09	7,106
Fujian 福建	140	59	3,377	6	0.15	0.36	57.39	59.40	4,105
Jiangxi 江西	149	66	1,562	-16	-0.75	-4.88	23.56	84.59	2,142
Shandong 山東	285	125	9,070	245	2.51	7.88	72.38	68.16	9,782
Central-South 中南	907	90	5,306	47	0.71	2.39	58.83	70.37	6,665
Henan 河南	199	90	3,142	60	1.39	5.29	35.09	73.63	4,335
Hubei 湖北	181	95	5,808	191	4.86	21.59	61.06	77.48	3,936
Hunan 湖南	168	100	3,951	-42	-0.89	-4.82	39.68	81.61	4,700
Guangdong 廣東	216	98	9,407	20	0.15	0.46	95.89	67.44	13,526
Guangxi 廣西	132	60	2,761	-15	-0.34	-0.85	45.82	59.96	4,386
Hainan 海南	11	81	6,888	65	0.40	0.95	84.85	58.47	16,338
Southwest 西南	269	84	2,197	-142	-3.49	-16.74	26.09	79.15	4,076
Chongqing 重慶	46	72	1,234	-135	-5.25	-36.80	17.25	85.73	2,567
Sichuan 四川	119	92	2,178	-160	-4.76	-43.71	23.76	89.12	3,367
Guizhou 貴州	54	63	1,819	-15	-0.26	-0.97	28.77	73.40	5,668
Yunnan 雲南	50	101	3,547	-245	-4.50	-14.11	35.10	68.10	5,442
Tibet 西藏									
Northwest 西北	199	85	2,297	-93	-1.88	-8.66	26.97	78.27	4,967
Shaanxi 陝西	86	70	1,725	-78	-2.73	-14.00	24.82	80.51	2,843
Gansu 甘肅	47	119	3,397	21	0.26	0.63	28.57	58.96	8,115
Qinghai 青海	8	71	1,068	-318	-9.29	66.32	15.12	113.98	3,416
Ningxia 寧夏	19	119	3,312	-494	-5.58	59.54	27.93	109.38	8,849
Xinjiang 新疆	39	66	1,991	-25	-0.58	-3.21	30.26	81.91	4,283

3030: Plastic Thread, Rope and Knitted Products 塑料絲、繩及編織品製造業

Year 年份	Number of firms 企業個數	Rate of change 每年變化 (%)	Number of employees 職工人數 (人)	Rate of change 每年變化 (%)	Total revenue (mil. RMB) 總銷售收入 (百萬元)	Rate of change 每年變化 (%)	Total profit (mil. RMB) 總利潤 (百萬元)	Rate of change 每年變化 (%)
1993	3,302		305,875		9,990		27	
1994	3,459	4.75%	323,161	5.65%	11,348	13.59%	-40	-247.14%
1995	3,747	8.33%	379,434	17.41%	16,545	45.79%	42	205.70%
1996	3,934	4.99%	363,897	-4.09%	19,692	19.02%	225	432.27%

3 Major products* 3 種主要產品 *	Output 產量	Sales volume 銷售量	Unit 單位
a) Polypropylene Products 聚丙烯製品	695,421	584,154	ton 噸
b) Polythylene Products 聚乙烯製品	656,118	642,996	ton 噸

Top 10 firms by revenue (year founded) 收入排名前 10 家企業 (創辦年份)	City 城市	Province 省	Telephone / fax 電話 / 傳真	Number of employees 職工人數	Ownership 產業所有權	Revenue ('000 RMB) 銷售收入 (千元)	Profit ('000 RMB) (rank) 利潤 (千元) (排名)	Total assets ('000 RMB) 總資產 (千元)	Major products 主要產品
Qingdao Jiao He Plastics Co. Ltd. 青島交河塑料有限公司(1991)	Qingdao 青島市	Shandong 山東省	(0532)7881424 (0532)7881403	1,490	Foreign-funded 外資	489,410	4450(23)	305,070	o
Dalian Beihai Plastic Package Co. Ltd. 大連北海塑料包裝有限公司(1991)	Dalian 大連市	Liaoning 遼寧省	(0411)2648888	288	Overseas Chinese-funded 港澳台資	378,130	30710(1)	200,805	o
Anhui Tian Da Enterprise Group Co. 安徽天大企業集團公司(1972)	Chuzhou 滁州市	Anhui 安徽省	(0550)7511022 (0550)511023	1,214	Collectively-owned 集體	332,548	23904(2)	278,560	a,b
Foshan No.8 Plastics Factory Co. Ltd. 佛山市塑料八廠(1970)	Foshan 佛山市	Guangdong 廣東省	(0757)2810212 (0757)2816308	1,081	Collectively-owned 集體	317,864	8100(9)	406,688	a,b
Chenghai Nan Yang Industry City Group Corp. Ltd. 澄海市南洋工業城實業總公司(1993)	Shantou 汕頭市	Guangdong 廣東省	(0754)5743888 (0754)5743831	1,350	Collectively-owned 集體	265,046	3417(33)	508,067	b
Anhui Taihe Pi Tiao Sun Zhen Plastics Processing Factory 安徽省太和縣皮條孫鎮塑料加工廠(1987)	Fuyang 阜陽市	Anhui 安徽省	(0558)8203017 (0558)8203066	210	Collectively-owned 集體	207,280	16100(3)	26,660	a,b
Anhui Shuang Jin Group 安徽雙津集團(1986)	Xuanzhou 宣州市	Anhui 安徽省	(0563)4022812 (0563)4023526	1,014	State-owned 國有	171,532	11559(6)	116,548	o
Taihe Pi Tiao Sun Zhen Plastic Products General Factory 太和縣皮條孫鎮塑料製品總廠(1991)	Fuyang 阜陽市	Anhui 安徽省	(0558)8683016	137	Collectively-owned 集體	142,800	5480(19)	20,970	b
Anhui Taihe Pi Tiao Sun Rope & Net Factory 安徽省太和縣皮條孫繩網廠(1992)	Fuyang 阜陽市	Anhui 安徽省	(0558)8683015	110	Collectively-owned 集體	136,860	4810(21)	18,460	b
Qi Lu Ethylene Plastic Febric Co. Ltd. 齊魯乙烯塑編廠有限公司(1987)	Zibo 淄博市	Shandong 山東省	(0533)7188666 (0533)7181521	1,185	Overseas Chinese-funded 港澳台資	125,037	6569(15)	243,362	o

Top 10 Cities by Production Output 產出排名前 10 位城市	Province 省	Market share 市場份額	Number of firms 企業個數
Wenzhou 温州市	Zhejiang 浙江省	16.14%	742
Wuxi 無錫市	Jiangsu 江蘇省	8.73%	36
Shanghai 上海市	Shanghai 上海市	4.00%	103
Shantou 汕頭市	Guangdong 廣東省	3.19%	53
Chuzhou 滁州市	Anhui 安徽省	2.73%	30
Changzhou 常州市	Jiangsu 江蘇省	2.70%	50
Fuyang 阜陽市	Anhui 安徽省	2.31%	52
Foshan 佛山市	Guangdong 廣東省	2.24%	16
Yantai 煙台市	Shandong 山東省	2.08%	54
Jiangmen 江門市	Guangdong 廣東省	1.97%	21

10 Major Wholesalers 10 家主要批發商	City 城市	Province 省	Telephone / Fax 電話 / 傳真
Zhong Hua Singbo Import & Export Company 中化寧波進出口公司	Ningbo 寧波市	Zhejiang 浙江省	(0574)7346764 (0574)7366775
China Chemical Supply & Marketing Hua Nan Company 中國化工供銷華南公司	Guangzhou 廣州市	Guangdong 廣東省	(020)87654477 (020)87784414
China Agriculture Means of Production Chengdu Company 中國農業生產資料成都公司	Chengdu 成都市	Sichuan 四川省	(028)3333909 (028)3331202
Shanxi Agriculture Means of Production Company 山西省農業生產資料公司	Taiyuan 太原市	Shanxi 山西省	(0351)4040255 (0351)4040231
Beijing Chemical Light Industry General Company 北京市化工輕工總公司	Beijing 北京市	Beijing 北京市	(010)64224837 (010)64219301
Beijing Chemical Industry Group Company Supply & Marketing Company 北京化學工業集團公司供銷公司	Beijing 北京市	Beijing 北京市	(010)67714610 (010)67714058
Zhong Hua Jiangsu Import & Export Company 中化江蘇進出口公司	Nanjing 南京市	Jiangsu 江蘇省	(025)2258718 (025)2257789
Yunnan Chemical Import & Export Company 雲南省化工進出口公司	Kunming 昆明市	Yunnan 雲南省	(0871)3314002 (0871)3314931
Fujian Jiu Zhou Group Co. Ltd. 福建九州集團股份有限公司	Xiamen 廈門市	Fujian 福建省	(0592)5055818 (0592)5052033
China Chemical Industry Commission Agent Hua Dong Co. 中國化工供銷華東公司	Shanghai 上海市	Shanghai 上海市	(021)62514123

*Also include sales by firms outside this industry.包括本行業以外廠家的銷售。"o" stands for "others". "o" 代表"其他產品"。

3040: Aerated Plastics, Imitation Leather, and Synthetic Leather
泡沫塑料及人造革、合成革製造業

The industry accounts for 0.311% of the total revenue of China's industrial sector in 1996. The revenue growth rate of the industry is 6.6% from 1995, as compared to the growth rate of China's industrial sector, 9.51%. The rate of return on asset is 0.60%. 69.60% of all firms in the industry made a profit while 26.40% had negative returns. The top province in terms of the industry's revenue is Guangdong, accounting for 25.80% of the total revenue.
本行業在1996年佔全行業總產值0.311%，行業年增長率為6.6%（全國工業年增長率9.51%）。行業的資產回報率0.60%，69.60%的企業盈利，26.40%的企業虧損。銷售收入最高的省份為廣東省，佔本行業的25.80%。

	Total number of firms 企業總數	Total number of employees 職工總數	Total revenue (mil. RMB) 總銷售收入（百萬元）	Total profit (mil. RMB) 總利潤（百萬元）	Return on assets 資產利潤率 (%)	Return on equity 權益利潤率 (%)	Labour productivity ('000 RMB / worker) 勞動生產率（千元/人）	Debts / assets 資產負債率 (%)	Total assets (mil. RMB) 總資產（百萬元）
Industry Overall 行業總體	1,772	157,503	18,040	136	0.60	1.83	114.54	67.55	22,920

	Number of firms 企業個數	Average number of employees 平均職工人數	Average revenue ('000 RMB) 平均銷售收入（千元）	Average profit ('000 RMB) 平均利潤（千元）	Return on assets 資產利潤率 (%)	Return on equity 權益利潤率 (%)	Labour productivity ('000 RMB / worker) 勞動生產率（千元/人）	Average debts / assets 平均資產負債率(%)	Average Total assets ('000 RMB) 平均總資產（千元）
By ownership 產業所有權									
State-owned 國有	171	178	12,094	117	0.51	1.45	68.01	64.66	22,854
Collectively-owned 集體	1,180	76	6,461	-252	-3.46	-12.16	85.47	71.57	7,283
Privately-owned 私有	14	75	2,348	-397	-21.90	-62.42	31.33	64.92	1,813
Domestic JVs 聯營	21	87	4,805	-537	-13.68	-28.30	55.04	51.65	3,927
Joint stock 股份制	19	156	32,947	-1,180	-3.03	-10.09	210.77	69.96	38,920
Foreign-funded 外資	106	92	19,278	3,604	12.35	44.48	210.01	72.24	29,185
Overseas Chinese-funded 港澳台資	255	90	21,718	262	1.03	2.70	241.04	61.64	25,321
By size 規模									
Large 大型	19	839	149,050	35,432	14.77	46.13	177.75	67.99	239,927
Medium 中型	68	447	54,130	-1,920	-2.55	-7.29	121.04	65.08	75,389
Small 小型	1,653	67	6,973	-246	-3.07	-9.71	103.72	68.35	8,006
By regional distribution 地區分布									
Central-North 華北	229	84	6,277	12	0.14	0.47	74.64	69.48	8,801
Beijing 北京	67	73	6,174	-311	-2.91	-10.55	84.08	72.43	10,704
Tianjin 天津	32	102	6,185	257	3.72	11.72	60.47	68.29	6,918
Hebei 河北	81	95	9,100	230	2.07	5.92	95.32	64.97	11,109
Shanxi 山西	29	89	2,274	-118	-2.53	-14.25	25.60	82.27	4,681
Inner Mongolia 內蒙	20	38	1,137	13	0.63	3.32	30.03	81.05	2,069
Northeast 東北	187	74	3,861	4	0.09	0.34	52.05	74.81	5,191
Liaoning 遼寧	91	63	3,601	29	0.65	2.81	57.39	76.96	4,497
Jilin 吉林	42	115	4,346	-30	-0.45	-2.06	37.75	78.10	6,550
Heilongjiang 黑龍江	54	62	3,922	-11	-0.20	-0.64	63.66	68.59	5,303
Central East 華東	796	101	12,281	198	1.36	3.51	121.97	61.32	14,569
Shanghai 上海	67	120	11,902	-356	-1.58	-4.96	99.54	68.16	22,518
Jiangsu 江蘇	198	117	18,199	499	3.16	8.93	155.95	64.57	15,764
Zhejiang 浙江	155	96	13,031	70	0.50	1.30	135.33	61.28	13,983
Anhui 安徽	92	80	8,077	276	3.07	8.63	101.34	64.40	8,989
Fujian 福建	122	72	7,776	-86	-0.78	-1.65	107.27	52.45	11,024
Jiangxi 江西	39	79	2,407	-321	-3.63	-10.16	30.44	64.23	8,844
Shandong 山東	123	121	12,757	562	3.03	6.89	105.69	56.05	18,560
Central-South 中南	400	86	14,244	-23	-0.12	-0.50	166.22	75.30	18,949
Henan 河南	63	55	4,852	218	5.52	13.07	88.65	57.76	3,954
Hubei 湖北	60	119	7,577	141	1.23	2.77	63.84	55.67	11,510
Hunan 湖南	32	78	5,978	-192	-1.80	-5.57	77.14	67.65	10,654
Guangdong 廣東	214	94	21,746	-116	-0.41	-1.86	231.61	78.08	28,466
Guangxi 廣西	27	37	3,239	-10	-0.14	-2.68	86.67	94.78	7,423
Hainan 海南	4	32	1,275	-85	-4.94	-6.49	40.16	23.84	1,720
Southwest 西南	84	58	2,889	-90	-2.38	-8.10	49.75	70.60	3,796
Chongqing 重慶	21	53	2,558	-4	-0.14	-0.54	48.54	73.14	2,938
Sichuan 四川	45	72	3,208	-176	-4.11	-13.15	44.42	68.74	4,272
Guizhou 貴州	15	21	858	11	1.08	2.69	41.38	60.01	1,052
Yunnan 雲南	2	116	15,545	95	0.39	1.84	134.01	78.78	24,360
Tibet 西藏	1	4	640	30	6.67	6.67	160.00		450
Northwest 西北	76	67	2,170	-99	-1.72	-5.99	32.54	71.22	5,771
Shaanxi 陝西	37	91	2,441	-322	-4.51	-26.08	26.72	82.70	7,141
Gansu 甘肅	12	63	1,043	5	0.16	0.42	16.61	62.61	3,160
Qinghai 青海	1	10							
Ningxia 寧夏	6	21	270	-13	-1.94	61.54	13.06	102.91	687
Xinjiang 新疆	20	40	3,024	219	3.31	6.59	75.51	49.80	6,619

3040: Aerated Plastics, Imitation Leather, and Synthetic Leather
泡沫塑料及人造革、合成革製造業

Year 年份	Number of firms 企業個數	Rate of change 每年變化 (%)	Number of employees 職工人數 (人)	Rate of change 每年變化 (%)	Total revenue (mil. RMB) 總銷售收入 (百萬元)	Rate of change 每年變化 (%)	Total profit (mil. RMB) 總利潤 (百萬元)	Rate of change 每年變化 (%)
1993	1,260		145,162		9,673		312	
1994	1,388	10.16%	151,120	4.10%	11,592	19.85%	205	-34.23%
1995	1,766	27.23%	160,706	6.34%	16,917	45.93%	-24	-111.53%
1996	1,772	0.34%	157,503	-1.99%	18,040	6.64%	136	674.98%

3 Major products* 3種主要產品*	Output 產量	Sales volume 銷售量	Unit 單位
a) Plastic Artificial Leather 塑料人造革	318,063	289,437	ton 噸
b) Plastic Synthetic Leather 塑料合成革	47,953	120,841	ton 噸
c) Aerated Plastics 泡沫塑料	387,321	367,955	ton 噸

Top 10 firms by revenue (year founded) 收入排名前10家企業 (創辦年份)	City 城市	Province 省	Telephone / fax 電話 / 傳真	Number of employees 職工人數	Ownership 產業所有權	Revenue ('000 RMB) 銷售收入 (千元)	Profit ('000 RMB) (rank) 利潤 (千元) (排名)	Total assets ('000 RMB) 總資產 (千元)	Major products 主要產品
Yantai Wan Hua Synthetic Leather Group Co. Ltd 煙台萬華合成革集團有限公司(1985)	Yantai 煙台市	Shandong 山東省	(0535)6532468 (0535)6530594	5,448	State-owned 國有	654,061	28678(1)	1,182,250	a,b
Gaoming Plastics No.2 Factory 高明市塑料二廠(1986)	Foshan 佛山市	Guangdong 廣東省	(0757)8821111 (0757)8823152	202	Joint stock 股份制	500,651	12981(5)	373,151	a
Shenda Group Corp. 江蘇申達包裝集團公司(1986)	Wuxi 無錫市	Jiangsu 江蘇省	(0510)6621666 (0510)6621021	508	Collectively-owned 集體	300,101	24861(2)	168,072	o
Guangdong Yu Lan Wall Paper Factory 廣東玉蘭牆紙廠(1984)	Dongguan 東莞市	Guangdong 廣東省	(0769)2465856 (0769)2452784	271	Collectively-owned 集體	272,431	562(225)	309,320	o
Foshan No.2 Plastics Facory 佛山市塑料二廠(1965)	Foshan 佛山市	Guangdong 廣東省	(0757)2819988 (0757)2817149	937	Collectively-owned 集體	242,867	8005(11)	368,641	a
Chaozhou Hua Da Li Industrial Co. Ltd. 潮州市華達利實業有限公司(1988)	Chaozhou 潮州市	Guangdong 廣東省	(0768)6872013 (0768)6873813	518	Overseas Chinese-funded 港澳台資	240,457	3310(40)	125,887	a
Xishan Xing Da Plastic Foam Materials Factory 錫山市興達泡塑材料廠(1992)	Wuxi 無錫市	Jiangsu 江蘇省	(0510)8701598 (0510)8701598	388	Collectively-owned 集體	240,147	17001(4)	106,467	c
Zhejiang Shaoxing Artificial Leather Factory 浙江紹興市人造革廠(1980)	Shaoxing 紹興市	Zhejiang 浙江省	(0575)4021346 (0575)4021978	268	Collectively-owned 集體	209,137	9880(7)	132,979	a,b
Jiangyin Composite Material Factory 江陰市複合材料廠(1958)	Wuxi 無錫市	Jiangsu 江蘇省	(0510)62059496 (0510)6201333	338	Collectively-owned 集體	181,169	11606(6)	99,684	a
Wan Li Plastic Cement (Shenzhen) Co. Ltd. 萬利塑膠(深圳)有限公司(1992)	Shenzhen 深圳市	Guangdong 廣東省	(0755)8022811 (0755)8022681	119	Overseas Chinese-funded 港澳台資	169,526	1346(104)	26,688	o

Top 10 Cities by Production Output 產出排名前10位城市	Province 省	Market share 市場份額	Number of firms 企業個數
Foshan 佛山市	Guangdong 廣東省	8.76%	42
Suzhou 蘇州市	Jiangsu 江蘇省	7.31%	58
Wuxi 無錫市	Jiangsu 江蘇省	4.35%	56
Shanghai 上海市	Shanghai 上海市	4.31%	103
Dongguan 東莞市	Guangdong 廣東省	4.12%	28
Yangzhou 揚州市	Jiangsu 江蘇省	4.00%	31
Yantai 煙台市	Shandong 山東省	3.98%	51
Hangzhou 杭州市	Zhejiang 浙江省	3.83%	63
Shaoxing 紹興市	Zhejiang 浙江省	3.69%	13
Wenzhou 温州市	Zhejiang 浙江省	2.75%	67

10 Major Wholesalers 10家主要批發商	City 城市	Province 省	Telephone / Fax 電話 / 傳真
Zhong Hua Singbo Import & Export Company 中化寧波進出口公司	Ningbo 寧波市	Zhejiang 浙江省	(0574)7346764 (0574)7366775
China Chemical Supply & Marketing Hua Nan Company 中國化工供銷華南公司	Guangzhou 廣州市	Guangdong 廣東省	(020)87654477 (020)87784414
China Agriculture Means of Production Chengdu Company 中國農業生產資料成都公司	Chengdu 成都市	Sichuan 四川省	(028)3333909 (028)3331202
Shanxi Agriculture Means of Production Company 山西省農業生產資料公司	Taiyuan 太原市	Shanxi 山西省	(0351)4040255 (0351)4040231
Beijing Chemical Light Industry General Company 北京市化工輕工總公司	Beijing 北京市	Beijing 北京市	(010)64224837 (010)64219301
Beijing Chemical Industry Group Company Supply & Marketing Company 北京化學工業集團公司供銷公司	Beijing 北京市	Beijing 北京市	(010)67714610 (010)67714058
Zhong Hua Jiangsu Import & Export Company 中化江蘇進出口公司	Nanjing 南京市	Jiangsu 江蘇省	(025)2258718 (025)2257789
Yunnan Chemical Import & Export Company 雲南省化工進出口公司	Kunming 昆明市	Yunnan 雲南省	(0871)3314002 (0871)3314931
Fujian Jiu Zhou Group Co. Ltd. 福建九州集團股份有限公司	Xiamen 廈門市	Fujian 福建省	(0592)5055818 (0592)5052033
China Chemical Industry Commission Agent Hua Dong Co. 中國化工供銷華東公司	Shanghai 上海市	Shanghai 上海市	(021)62514123

*Also include sales by firms outside this industry.包括本行業以外廠家的銷售。"o" stands for "others". "o" 代表"其他產品"。

3050: Plastic Containers 塑料包裝箱及容器製造業

The industry accounts for 0.137% of the total revenue of China's industrial sector in 1996. The revenue growth rate of the industry is 15.5% from 1995, as compared to the growth rate of China's industrial sector, 9.51%. The rate of return on asset is 1.19%. 63.71% of all firms in the industry made a profit while 30.16% had negative returns. The top province in terms of the industry's revenue is Guangdong, accounting for 26.59% of the total revenue.
本行業在1996年佔全行業總產值0.137%，行業年增長率為15.5%（全國工業年增長率9.51%）。行業的資產回報率1.19%，63.71%的企業盈利，30.16%的企業虧損。銷售收入最高的省份為廣東省，佔本行業的26.59%。

	Total number of firms 企業總數	Total number of employees 職工總數	Total revenue (mil. RMB) 總銷售收入（百萬元）	Total profit (mil. RMB) 總利潤（百萬元）	Return on assets 資產利潤率 (%)	Return on equity 權益利潤率 (%)	Labour productivity ('000 RMB / worker) 勞動生產率（千元/人）	Debts / assets 資產負債率 (%)	Total assets (mil. RMB) 總資產（百萬元）
Industry Overall 行業總體	1,365	119,961	7,963	134	1.19	3.59	66.38	66.93	11,267

	Number of firms 企業個數	Average number of employees 平均職工人數	Average revenue ('000 RMB) 平均銷售收入（千元）	Average profit ('000 RMB) 平均利潤（千元）	Return on assets 資產利潤率 (%)	Return on equity 權益利潤率 (%)	Labour productivity ('000 RMB / worker) 勞動生產率（千元/人）	Average debts / assets 平均資產負債率(%)	Average Total assets ('000 RMB) 平均總資產（千元）
By ownership 產業所有權									
State-owned 國有	129	126	4,481	-527	-4.35	-34.52	35.64	87.40	12,116
Collectively-owned 集體	1,008	84	4,326	30	0.63	2.62	51.32	75.97	4,792
Privately-owned 私有	11	47	3,350	150	14.17	27.67	71.42	48.80	1,059
Domestic JVs 聯營	18	140	13,673	481	1.99	5.77	97.59	65.48	24,139
Joint stock 股份制	14	174	48,687	4,601	7.70	16.40	280.61	53.08	59,774
Foreign-funded 外資	61	95	10,685	555	2.92	6.07	112.44	51.92	19,017
Overseas Chinese-funded 港澳台資	123	69	11,448	512	2.59	4.99	164.88	48.08	19,759
By size 規模									
Large 大型	10	463	133,485	4,953	2.21	6.12	288.18	63.90	224,039
Medium 中型	36	425	25,826	209	0.51	1.97	60.78	74.26	41,177
Small 小型	1,297	77	4,393	59	1.02	3.04	56.76	66.39	5,816
By regional distribution 地區分布									
Central-North 華北	181	53	3,309	-50	-1.02	-4.56	62.16	77.68	4,890
Beijing 北京	71	28	1,410	-158	-5.74	-24.14	51.23	76.22	2,747
Tianjin 天津	35	103	7,706	-234	-2.00	-10.02	74.65	80.02	11,700
Hebei 河北	58	53	3,432	182	4.89	19.50	64.49	74.94	3,721
Shanxi 山西	11	63	2,179	33	0.67	2.60	34.39	74.36	4,910
Inner Mongolia 內蒙	6	47	1,005	-88	-4.93	-37.06	21.31	86.70	1,792
Northeast 東北	178	121	2,371	-246	-4.55	-19.32	19.62	76.47	5,420
Liaoning 遼寧	106	146	1,615	-279	-5.69	-40.12	11.09	85.81	4,909
Jilin 吉林	38	70	2,241	-435	-12.21	-31.61	32.16	61.35	3,559
Heilongjiang 黑龍江	34	101	4,870	67	0.74	2.26	48.36	67.36	9,095
Central East 華東	525	94	6,995	165	1.82	5.39	74.48	66.23	9,076
Shanghai 上海	71	118	11,588	446	2.57	6.57	98.07	60.92	17,374
Jiangsu 江蘇	123	118	12,541	400	3.18	8.18	106.48	61.06	12,552
Zhejiang 浙江	133	76	4,793	46	0.70	2.27	62.79	68.97	6,592
Anhui 安徽	44	121	4,590	62	1.24	3.96	37.80	68.64	4,983
Fujian 福建	52	43	2,624	-26	-0.73	-1.74	61.10	57.99	3,526
Jiangxi 江西	35	67	1,542	-225	-6.26	-684.35	23.06	99.09	3,594
Shandong 山東	67	95	4,139	93	1.07	5.82	43.60	81.67	8,693
Central-South 中南	339	84	8,330	361	3.16	8.28	99.57	61.88	11,432
Henan 河南	73	59	2,113	118	4.97	15.60	35.70	68.15	2,382
Hubei 湖北	69	84	5,127	103	2.25	7.60	61.00	70.39	4,562
Hunan 湖南	46	78	2,076	-253	-6.18	-28.80	26.72	78.53	4,089
Guangdong 廣東	122	105	17,354	982	3.97	9.74	165.46	59.28	24,742
Guangxi 廣西	24	62	3,468	-80	-1.47	-7.63	56.31	80.73	5,463
Hainan 海南	5	78	3,978	80	0.81	1.18	51.00	31.01	9,828
Southwest 西南	96	88	4,100	-229	-3.42	-12.70	46.72	73.11	6,712
Chongqing 重慶	23	104	3,988	-923	-13.52	-90.76	38.47	85.10	6,826
Sichuan 四川	51	76	3,985	849	12.65	47.65	52.10	73.45	6,710
Guizhou 貴州	12	123	5,383	-200	-2.40	-7.38	43.92	67.47	8,329
Yunnan 雲南	10	66	3,401	215	4.76	8.07	51.30	41.07	4,519
Tibet 西藏									
Northwest 西北	46	59	1,132	-10	-0.33	-1.04	19.09	67.86	2,869
Shaanxi 陝西	21	87	1,559	51	1.14	3.16	17.82	63.94	4,472
Gansu 甘肅	7	50	824	1	0.13	0.57	16.58	76.56	1,073
Qinghai 青海	2	98	990	-690	-13.23	306.67	10.10	104.31	5,215
Ningxia 寧夏	3	15	167	-233	-8.74	-76.92	10.87	88.64	2,670
Xinjiang 新疆	13	23	853	43	4.63	8.85	36.97	47.69	931

3050: Plastic Containers 塑料包裝箱及容器製造業

Year 年份	Number of firms 企業個數	Rate of change 每年變化 (%)	Number of employees 職工人數 (人)	Rate of change 每年變化 (%)	Total revenue (mil. RMB) 總銷售收入 (百萬元)	Rate of change 每年變化 (%)	Total profit (mil. RMB) 總利潤 (百萬元)	Rate of change 每年變化 (%)
1993	1,234		120,998		4,517		96	
1994	1,324	7.29%	115,441	-4.59%	5,439	20.42%	151	57.45%
1995	1,325	0.08%	110,636	-4.16%	6,892	26.70%	240	58.47%
1996	1,365	3.02%	119,961	8.43%	7,963	15.54%	134	-44.13%

3 Major products* 3種主要產品*	Output 產量	Sales volume 銷售量	Unit 單位
a) Plastic Packing Box & Container 塑料包裝箱及容器	348,728	292,931	ton 噸
b) Daily Plastic Products 日用塑料製品	163,951	173,789	ton 噸
c) Other Plastic Products 其他塑料製品	44,862	43,068	ton 噸

Top 10 firms by revenue (year founded) 收入排名前10家企業 (創辦年份)	City 城市	Province 省	Telephone / fax 電話 / 傳真	Number of employees 職工人數	Ownership 產業所有權	Revenue ('000 RMB) 銷售收入 (千元)	Profit ('000 RMB) (rank) 利潤 (千元) (排名)	Total assets ('000 RMB) 總資產 (千元)	Major products 主要產品
Zhuhai Sez Zhongfu Industrial Co. Ltd. 珠海經濟特區中富實業股份有限公司(1986)	Zhuhai 珠海市	Guangdong 廣東省	(0756)8821449 (0756)8822046	867	Joint stock 股份制	470,185	75252(1)	631,849	a
Shanghai Zi Jiang Enterprise Co. Ltd. 上海紫江企業有限公司(1989)	Shanghai 上海市	Shanghai 上海市	(021)64921636	364	Overseas Chinese-funded 港澳台資	383,579	22005(3)	551,512	a
Sanshui Jian Li Bao Plastic Products Co. Ltd. 三水市健力寶塑料製品有限公司(1994)	Foshan 佛山市	Guangdong 廣東省	(0757)7737668 (0757)7733474	410	Overseas Chinese-funded 港澳台資	247,717	6825(9)	179,195	a
Shandou Shengping Guo Ping Industry Development General Company 汕頭市升平區國平工業發展總公司(1967)	Shantou 汕頭市	Guangdong 廣東省	(0754)8273173	2,103	Collectively-owned 集體	230,727	2103(37)	58,380	a,b
Yangzhou Auto Plastic Parts Co. Ltd. 揚州汽車塑料件製造公司(1989)	Yangzhou 揚州市	Jiangsu 江蘇省	(0514)7247481 (0514)7245777	620	Domestic JVs 聯營	193,412	18034(4)	231,785	a,b
He Yi Packing Products (Shenzhen) Co. Ltd. 合益包裝製品(深圳)有限公司(1984)	Shenzhen 深圳市	Guangdong 廣東省	(0755)6694322 (0755)6674280	192	Overseas Chinese-funded 港澳台資	133,257	30722(2)	140,148	o
Tianjin Zhongfu Container Co. Ltd. 天津中富容器有限公司(1992)	Tianjin 天津市	Tianjin 天津市	(022)25325731 (022)25325729	231	Overseas Chinese-funded 港澳台資	127,443	-6776(551)	169,483	a
Jianhu Heng Feng Group Company 建湖縣恒豐集團公司(1981)	Yancheng 鹽城市	Jiangsu 江蘇省	(0515)6381052 (0515)6381344	235	Collectively-owned 集體	108,260	3360(20)	63,630	a
Wuxian Wei Tang No.7 Plastic Products Factory 吳縣市渭塘塑料製品七廠(1986)	Suzhou 蘇州市	Jiangsu 江蘇省	(0512)5401236	600	Collectively-owned 集體	105,010	2550(26)	128,180	o
Zhuhai Zhong Fu Jiao Gai Co. Ltd. 珠海市中富膠蓋有限公司(1994)	Zhuhai 珠海市	Guangdong 廣東省	(0756)8823513 (0756)8823011	105	Overseas Chinese-funded 港澳台資	97,677	14893(6)	158,353	c

Top 10 Cities by Production Output 產出排名前10位城市	Province 省	Market share 市場份額	Number of firms 企業個數
Shanghai 上海市	Shanghai 上海市	12.23%	114
Zhuhai 珠海市	Guangdong 廣東省	9.56%	12
Foshan 佛山市	Guangdong 廣東省	5.97%	14
Suzhou 蘇州市	Jiangsu 江蘇省	4.36%	50
Shenzhen 深圳市	Guangdong 廣東省	4.29%	17
Shantou 汕頭市	Guangdong 廣東省	3.98%	39
Tianjin 天津市	Tianjin 天津市	3.69%	44
Guangzhou 廣州市	Guangdong 廣東省	3.18%	38
Changzhou 常州市	Jiangsu 江蘇省	2.66%	54
Wuxi 無錫市	Jiangsu 江蘇省	2.34%	35

10 Major Wholesalers 10家主要批發商	City 城市	Province 省	Telephone / Fax 電話 / 傳真
Zhong Hua Singbo Import & Export Company 中化寧波進出口公司	Ningbo 寧波市	Zhejiang 浙江省	(0574)7346764 (0574)7366775
China Chemical Supply & Marketing Hua Nan Company 中國化工供銷華南公司	Guangzhou 廣州市	Guangdong 廣東省	(020)87654477 (020)87784414
China Agriculture Means of Production Chengdu Company 中國農業生產資料成都公司	Chengdu 成都市	Sichuan 四川省	(028)3333909 (028)3331202
Shanxi Agriculture Means of Production Company 山西省農業生產資料公司	Taiyuan 太原市	Shanxi 山西省	(0351)4040255 (0351)4040231
Beijing Chemical Light Industry General Company 北京市化工輕工總公司	Beijing 北京市	Beijing 北京市	(010)64224837 (010)64219301
Beijing Chemical Industry Group Company Supply & Marketing Company 北京化學工業集團公司供銷公司	Beijing 北京市	Beijing 北京市	(010)67714610 (010)67714058
Zhong Hua Jiangsu Import & Export Company 中化江蘇進出口公司	Nanjing 南京市	Jiangsu 江蘇省	(025)2258718 (025)2257789
Yunnan Chemical Import & Export Company 雲南省化工進出口公司	Kunming 昆明市	Yunnan 雲南省	(0871)3314002 (0871)3314931
Fujian Jiu Zhou Group Co. Ltd. 福建九州集團股份有限公司	Xiamen 廈門市	Fujian 福建省	(0592)5055818 (0592)5052033
China Chemical Industry Commission Agent Hua Dong Co. 中國化工供銷華東公司	Shanghai 上海市	Shanghai 上海市	(021)62514123

*Also include sales by firms outside this industry.包括本行業以外廠家的銷售。"o" stands for "others". "o" 代表"其他產品"。

3060: Plastic Shoes 塑料鞋製造業

The industry accounts for 0.072% of the total revenue of China's industrial sector in 1996. The revenue growth rate of the industry is 10.9% from 1995, as compared to the growth rate of China's industrial sector, 9.51%. The rate of return on asset is 0.52%. 69.50% of all firms in the industry made a profit while 26.26% had negative returns. The top province in terms of the industry's revenue is Fujian, accounting for 30.79% of the total revenue.
本行業在1996年佔全行業總產值0.072%，行業年增長率為10.9%（全國工業年增長率9.51%）。行業的資產回報率0.52%，69.50%的企業盈利，26.26%的企業虧損。銷售收入最高的省份為福建省，佔本行業的30.79%。

	Total number of firms 企業總數	Total number of employees 職工總數	Total revenue (mil. RMB) 總銷售收入（百萬元）	Total profit (mil. RMB) 總利潤（百萬元）	Return on assets 資產利潤率 (%)	Return on equity 權益利潤率 (%)	Labour productivity ('000 RMB / worker) 勞動生產率（千元／人）	Debts / assets 資產負債率 (%)	Total assets (mil. RMB) 總資產（百萬元）
Industry Overall 行業總體	669	77,092	4,145	21	0.52	1.59	53.77	66.99	4,084

	Number of firms 企業個數	Average number of employees 平均職工人數	Average revenue ('000 RMB) 平均銷售收入（千元）	Average profit ('000 RMB) 平均利潤（千元）	Return on assets 資產利潤率 (%)	Return on equity 權益利潤率 (%)	Labour productivity ('000 RMB / worker) 勞動生產率（千元／人）	Average debts / assets 平均資產負債率(%)	Average Total assets ('000 RMB) 平均總資產（千元）
By ownership 產業所有權									
State-owned 國有	32	326	9,000	-469	-2.30	-22.39	27.57	89.74	20,406
Collectively-owned 集體	438	91	3,486	28	0.82	3.04	38.11	73.10	3,386
Privately-owned 私有	7	26	2,000	134	12.76	28.29	75.68	54.92	1,049
Domestic JVs 聯營	8	65	3,109	14	0.62	1.22	47.65	49.33	2,315
Joint stock 股份制	9	146	8,874	215	3.21	5.43	60.73	40.91	6,685
Foreign-funded 外資	29	111	6,915	74	1.40	2.77	62.08	49.43	5,299
Overseas Chinese-funded 港澳台資	145	150	13,824	126	1.08	2.44	92.21	55.91	11,731
By size 規模									
Large 大型									
Medium 中型	11	641	25,068	-2,483	-5.84	-41.21	39.08	85.83	42,542
Small 小型	640	110	6,046	75	1.34	3.77	54.90	64.56	5,650
By regional distribution 地區分布									
Central-North 華北	40	85	3,300	60	1.78	4.92	38.72	63.76	3,368
Beijing 北京	9	56	1,328	-100	-4.44	43.90	23.62	110.06	2,253
Tianjin 天津	12	119	1,594	-293	-12.68	-18.64	13.42	31.96	2,313
Hebei 河北	18	81	5,579	378	7.88	21.29	68.60	62.99	4,801
Shanxi 山西									
Inner Mongolia 內蒙	1	14	480	10	3.57	100.00	34.29	96.43	280
Northeast 東北	22	158	3,677	115	1.14	16.33	23.22	93.00	10,104
Liaoning 遼寧	15	191	4,376	199	1.52	29.11	22.88	94.78	13,119
Jilin 吉林	2	122	45	-640	-12.61	206.45	0.37	106.11	5,075
Heilongjiang 黑龍江	5	74	3,032	166	5.41	14.07	40.75	61.54	3,068
Central East 華東	359	120	6,426	78	1.24	4.19	53.75	70.38	6,253
Shanghai 上海	20	97	3,572	-156	-2.51	-14.12	36.82	82.23	6,220
Jiangsu 江蘇	35	133	6,103	-43	-0.49	-2.68	45.95	81.76	8,757
Zhejiang 浙江	30	325	15,315	124	1.29	3.54	47.11	63.58	9,634
Anhui 安徽	25	250	4,889	101	1.47	6.14	19.57	76.14	6,880
Fujian 福建	224	80	5,698	94	2.02	5.84	71.42	65.45	4,644
Jiangxi 江西	16	83	5,400	531	6.26	12.55	64.82	50.07	8,471
Shandong 山東	9	126	8,630	-361	-1.83	-24.00	68.73	92.36	19,697
Central-South 中南	192	113	7,637	-54	-0.90	-2.29	67.64	60.81	6,036
Henan 河南	33	59	2,678	64	2.15	8.93	45.51	75.88	2,982
Hubei 湖北	10	116	8,224	197	4.47	13.05	70.65	65.74	4,408
Hunan 湖南	19	75	1,265	-177	-7.32	25.28	16.82	128.95	2,423
Guangdong 廣東	116	138	10,426	-92	-1.18	-2.61	75.31	54.67	7,749
Guangxi 廣西	13	82	4,755	-47	-0.89	-2.96	57.98	69.81	5,255
Hainan 海南	1	15	340	100	3.15	16.95	22.67	81.39	3,170
Southwest 西南	45	95	3,046	-33	-0.53	-0.94	31.97	43.15	6,122
Chongqing 重慶	13	161	5,848	-89	-0.68	-1.10	36.27	37.75	13,120
Sichuan 四川	19	84	1,552	-12	-0.27	-0.48	18.54	42.95	4,237
Guizhou 貴州	8	30	361	-33	-4.61	-104.00	12.25	95.39	705
Yunnan 雲南	5	65	5,446	40	1.26	8.55	83.53	85.24	3,170
Tibet 西藏									
Northwest 西北	11	120	1,979	48	1.11	6.57	16.56	83.10	4,347
Shaanxi 陝西	7	50	590	-19	-1.44	-11.71	11.87	87.60	1,290
Gansu 甘肅	1	436	12,380				28.39	92.73	24,470
Qinghai 青海									
Ningxia 寧夏	1	75	120	-150	-10.79	-214.29	1.60	94.96	1,390
Xinjiang 新疆	2	228	2,570	405	6.26	15.85	11.27	60.48	6,465

3060: Plastic Shoes 塑料鞋製造業

Year 年份	Number of firms 企業個數	Rate of change 每年變化 (%)	Number of employees 職工人數（人）	Rate of change 每年變化 (%)	Total revenue (mil. RMB) 總銷售收入（百萬元）	Rate of change 每年變化 (%)	Total profit (mil. RMB) 總利潤（百萬元）	Rate of change 每年變化 (%)
1993	521		67,675		2,106		-14	
1994	535	2.69%	72,754	7.50%	2,550	21.04%	-50	-258.53%
1995	608	13.64%	73,663	1.25%	3,736	46.51%	13	125.46%
1996	669	10.03%	77,092	4.65%	4,145	10.95%	21	65.76%

3 Major products* 3 種主要產品 *	Output 產量	Sales volume 銷售量	Unit 單位
a) Plastic Shoes 塑料鞋	189,975	178,577	ton 噸
b) Other Plastic Products 其他塑料製品	30,157	28,951	ton 噸

Top 10 firms by revenue (year founded) 收入排名前 10 家企業（創辦年份）	City 城市	Province 省	Telephone / fax 電話 / 傳真	Number of employees 職工人數	Ownership 產業所有權	Revenue ('000 RMB) 銷售收入（千元）	Profit ('000 RMB) (rank) 利潤（千元）（排名）	Total assets ('000 RMB) 總資產（千元）	Major products 主要產品
Rui'an Plastic & Rubber Shoes General Factory 瑞安市塑膠鞋總廠(1991)	Wenzhou 温州市	Zhejiang 浙江省	(0577)5580535	2,140	Collectively-owned 集體	221,228	3583(6)	43,550	o
Nanhai Wei Li Shoes Industry Co. Ltd. 南海市偉麗鞋業有限公司(1989)	Foshan 佛山市	Guangdong 廣東省	(0757)5226024 (0757)6220000	1,531	Overseas Chinese-funded 港澳台資	152,976	-317(287)	29,015	o
Nanhai Hong Ji Shoes Industry Co. Ltd. 南海市弘基鞋業有限公司(1992)	Foshan 佛山市	Guangdong 廣東省	(0757)5886619 (0757)5886699	870	Overseas Chinese-funded 港澳台資	141,901	714(50)	33,123	o
Putian Qia Shun Plastic Products Co. Ltd. 莆田洽順塑膠製品有限公司(1993)	Putian 莆田市	Fujian 福建省	(0594)5897577 (0594)5897273	170	Overseas Chinese-funded 港澳台資	99,600	-146(271)	63,779	a
Fuzhou No.2 Plastics Factory 福州市第二塑料廠(1956)	Fuzhou 福州市	Fujian 福建省	(0591)3727817 (0591)3728317	1,253	State-owned 國有	79,149	206(104)	53,089	a,b
Putian Achievement Shoes Industry Co. Ltd. 莆田市成果鞋業有限公司(1990)	Putian 莆田市	Fujian 福建省	(0594)2295129 (0594)2295128	856	Overseas Chinese-funded 港澳台資	79,130	670(51)	35,422	b
Guangzhou Da Xin Plastics Co. Ltd. 廣州大新塑料有限公司(1992)	Guangzhou 廣州市	Guangdong 廣東省	(020)86645191 (020)86636000	770	Overseas Chinese-funded 港澳台資	73,234	1407(17)	55,462	b
Dongguan Huang Cun Wan Xin Shoes Industry Co. Ltd. 東莞篁村萬鑫鞋業有限公司(1991)	Dongguan 東莞市	Guangdong 廣東省	(0769)2404912 (0769)2403830	1,500	Overseas Chinese-funded 港澳台資	72,552	274(93)	34,639	o
Fujian Xianyou Yi Hua Shoes Industry Co. Ltd. 福建仙遊儀樺鞋業有限公司(1989)	Putian 莆田市	Fujian 福建省	(0594)7692811 (0594)7693428	135	Overseas Chinese-funded 港澳台資	69,368	15043(1)	30,504	o
Guangzhou Xie Feng Plastic & Rubber Shoes Co. Ltd. 廣州協豐塑膠鞋業有限公司(1990)	Guangzhou 廣州市	Guangdong 廣東省	(020)87573728 (020)85512917	380	Overseas Chinese-funded 港澳台資	57,088	1282(22)	90,178	o

Top 10 Cities by Production Output 產出排名前 10 位城市	Province 省	Market share 市場份額	Number of firms 企業個數
Wenzhou 温州市	Zhejiang 浙江省	16.26%	161
Fuzhou 福州市	Fujian 福建省	13.02%	81
Putian 莆田市	Fujian 福建省	10.92%	60
Guangzhou 廣州市	Guangdong 廣東省	9.29%	27
Quanzhou 泉州市	Fujian 福建省	5.04%	60
Shanghai 上海市	Shanghai 上海市	3.17%	35
Yangzhou 揚州市	Jiangsu 江蘇省	3.03%	9
Chaozhou 潮州市	Guangdong 廣東省	2.57%	34
Taizhou 臺州市	Zhejiang 浙江省	2.15%	48
Pingxiang 萍鄉市	Jiangxi 江西省	2.14%	8

10 Major Wholesalers 10 家主要批發商	City 城市	Province 省	Telephone / Fax 電話 / 傳真
Beijing Foreign Trade Import & Export Company 北京市對外貿易進出口公司	Beijing 北京市	Beijing 北京市	(010)65081589 (010)65043755
Fujian Putian Foreign Trade Company 福建省莆田市對外貿易公司	Putian 莆田市	Fujian 福建省	(0594)2398702 (0594)2292681
Hunan Light Industry General Company Import & Export Products Company 湖南省輕工業總公司進出品公司	Changsha 長沙市	Hunan 湖南省	(0731)2287932 (0731)2287844
Jiangxi Handicrafts Import & Export Company 江西省工藝品進出口公司	Nanchang 南昌市	Jiangxi 江西省	(0791)6246932 (0791)6223383
Jiangyin Shoes and Cap General Co. 江蘇江陰市鞋帽總公司	Wuxi 無錫市	Jiangsu 江蘇省	(0510)6804355 (0510)6803479
Jinhua Jin Hai Industrial Company 金華市金海實業公司	Jinhua 金華市	Zhejiang 浙江省	(0579)2324590
Guangdong Nanhai Handicrafts Import & Export Company 廣東南海市工藝品進出口公司	Foshan 佛山市	Guangdong 廣東省	(0757)6338620 (0757)6220225
Guangzhou Light Industry Products Shoes, Cap, Box, Bag Import & Export Co. 廣州市輕工業品鞋帽箱包進出口公司	Guangzhou 廣州市	Guangdong 廣東省	(020)83337522 (020)83339145
Nanjing Foreign Trade Company 南京市對外貿易公司	Nanjing 南京市	Jiangsu 江蘇省	(025)4403991 (025)4403700

*Also include sales by firms outside this industry.包括本行業以外廠家的銷售。"o" stands for "others". "o" 代表"其他產品"。

3070: Household Plastic Goods 日用塑料雜品製造業

The industry accounts for 0.109% of the total revenue of China's industrial sector in 1996. The revenue growth rate of the industry is -3.8% from 1995, as compared to the growth rate of China's industrial sector, 9.51%. The rate of return on asset is 1.46%. 72.18% of all firms in the industry made a profit while 22.82% had negative returns. The top province in terms of the industry's revenue is Guangdong, accounting for 31.18% of the total revenue.
本行業在 1996 年佔全行業總產值 0.109% ，行業年增長率為 -3.8%（全國工業年增長率 9.51%） 。行業的資產回報率 1.46% ， 72.18% 的企業盈利， 22.82% 的企業虧損。銷售收入最高的省份為廣東省，佔本行業的 31.18% 。

	Total number of firms 企業總數	Total number of employees 職工總數	Total revenue (mil. RMB) 總銷售收入（百萬元）	Total profit (mil. RMB) 總利潤（百萬元）	Return on assets 資產利潤率 (%)	Return on equity 權益利潤率 (%)	Labour productivity ('000 RMB / worker) 勞動生產率（千元/人）	Debts / assets 資產負債率 (%)	Total assets (mil. RMB) 總資產（百萬元）
Industry Overall 行業總體	1,636	95,114	6,315	111	1.46	3.70	66.39	60.44	7,567

	Number of firms 企業個數	Average number of employees 平均職工人數	Average revenue ('000 RMB) 平均銷售收入（千元）	Average profit ('000 RMB) 平均利潤（千元）	Return on assets 資產利潤率 (%)	Return on equity 權益利潤率 (%)	Labour productivity ('000 RMB / worker) 勞動生產率（千元/人）	Average debts / assets 平均資產負債率(%)	Average Total assets ('000 RMB) 平均總資產（千元）
By ownership 產業所有權									
State-owned 國有	84	103	2,548	-60	-0.85	-5.10	24.74	83.42	7,036
Collectively-owned 集體	1,264	51	2,930	132	4.96	13.90	57.32	64.34	2,668
Privately-owned 私有	9	35	1,393	264	45.68	79.92	40.30	42.84	578
Domestic JVs 聯營	10	124	6,367	17	0.23	0.77	51.51	70.50	7,549
Joint stock 股份制	13	126	5,771	340	4.24	11.06	45.63	61.63	8,016
Foreign-funded 外資	83	59	6,144	-257	-2.64	-5.48	104.35	51.91	9,745
Overseas Chinese-funded 港澳台資	168	84	10,323	-220	-1.41	-2.98	122.51	52.53	15,522
By size 規模									
Large 大型	6	430	55,464	9,595	9.07	22.55	129.14	59.76	105,749
Medium 中型	13	457	48,142	2,805	4.75	15.85	105.41	70.04	59,079
Small 小型	1,592	54	3,356	12	0.30	0.74	61.98	59.38	3,860
By regional distribution 地區分布									
Central-North 華北	161	51	1,975		-0.01	-0.03	38.92	66.18	4,056
Beijing 北京	44	34	1,878	49	1.56	3.90	56.07	60.03	3,137
Tianjin 天津	41	73	2,886	-112	-1.35	-3.43	39.59	60.57	8,256
Hebei 河北	43	48	2,141	50	1.89	10.13	44.64	81.35	2,623
Shanxi 山西	22	55	761	-5	-0.23	-1.44	13.74	84.28	2,406
Inner Mongolia 內蒙	11	39	752	32	3.24	12.24	19.32	73.40	981
Northeast 東北	141	37	1,601	-35	-1.33	-3.54	43.49	62.48	2,638
Liaoning 遼寧	72	33	1,548	12	0.63	1.15	46.27	45.14	1,929
Jilin 吉林	29	56	1,405	-198	-3.39	-13.39	25.19	74.70	5,844
Heilongjiang 黑龍江	40	29	1,838	-2	-0.13	-0.39	63.21	67.79	1,588
Central East 華東	660	52	4,508	92	2.05	5.86	87.12	65.06	4,494
Shanghai 上海	64	81	4,444	-150	-1.30	-4.27	55.09	69.61	11,571
Jiangsu 江蘇	101	73	9,855	11	0.21	0.62	134.91	66.62	5,500
Zhejiang 浙江	206	43	3,214	147	4.70	12.70	74.15	63.00	3,138
Anhui 安徽	95	44	3,499	226	17.62	62.08	80.14	71.61	1,280
Fujian 福建	105	38	2,754	-16	-0.48	-1.01	72.89	51.93	3,248
Jiangxi 江西	32	26	750	-31	-4.07	-17.10	29.01	76.17	759
Shandong 山東	57	66	6,802	350	3.72	10.94	103.72	65.99	9,416
Central-South 中南	530	80	5,048	112	1.75	3.86	62.95	54.60	6,412
Henan 河南	60	44	2,220	183	11.54	26.40	50.42	56.30	1,586
Hubei 湖北	72	80	4,743	137	3.05	10.30	59.14	70.42	4,479
Hunan 湖南	77	31	1,672	-5	-0.52	-1.83	53.46	71.58	974
Guangdong 廣東	267	113	7,375	145	1.36	2.85	65.14	52.11	10,659
Guangxi 廣西	51	26	1,981	50	5.29	13.26	77.11	60.14	942
Hainan 海南	3	44	560	-733	-18.49	-85.27	12.73	78.32	3,967
Southwest 西南	94	38	900	-38	-2.69	-7.84	23.76	65.72	1,406
Chongqing 重慶	27	27	652	5	0.40	1.20	24.08	66.58	1,156
Sichuan 四川	46	41	1,074	-70	-4.58	-14.89	26.01	69.26	1,523
Guizhou 貴州	11	41	699	26	5.23	14.87	16.98	64.80	504
Yunnan 雲南	10	48	999	-79	-3.11	-6.93	20.73	55.14	2,541
Tibet 西藏									
Northwest 西北	50	31	724	-20	-2.24	-12.33	23.43	81.81	910
Shaanxi 陜西	19	29	727	-30	-3.63	-36.31	25.40	90.00	826
Gansu 甘肅	13	27	362	12	4.00	13.04	13.27	69.33	288
Qinghai 青海	1	12	130	10	4.00	6.67	10.83	40.00	250
Ningxia 寧夏	3	52	777	7	0.67	1.64	15.03	59.33	1,000
Xinjiang 新疆	14	34	1,086	-45	-2.76	-15.07	31.75	81.64	1,630

3070: Household Plastic Goods 日用塑料雜品製造業

Year 年份	Number of firms 企業個數	Rate of change 每年變化 (%)	Number of employees 職工人數 (人)	Rate of change 每年變化 (%)	Total revenue (mil. RMB) 總銷售收入 (百萬元)	Rate of change 每年變化 (%)	Total profit (mil. RMB) 總利潤 (百萬元)	Rate of change 每年變化 (%)
1993	1,709		118,721		4,314		134	
1994	1,720	0.64%	112,395	-5.33%	4,807	11.43%	76	-43.55%
1995	1,718	-0.12%	113,153	0.67%	6,566	36.58%	58	-23.68%
1996	1,636	-4.77%	95,114	-15.94%	6,315	-3.82%	111	92.63%

3 Major products* 3 種主要產品 *	Output 產量	Sales volume 銷售量	Unit 單位
a) Polyurethane Products 聚氨酯製品	63,611	52,797	ton 噸
b) Daily Plastic Products 日用塑料製品	573,916	608,350	ton 噸
c) Other Plastic Products 其他塑料製品	163,651	157,105	ton 噸

Top 10 firms by revenue (year founded) 收入排名前 10 家企業 (創辦年份)	City 城市	Province 省	Telephone / fax 電話 / 傳真	Number of employees 職工人數	Ownership 產業所有權	Revenue ('000 RMB) 銷售收入 (千元)	Profit ('000 RMB) (rank) 利潤 (千元) (排名)	Total assets ('000 RMB) 總資產 (千元)	Major products 主要產品
Wujiang Plastics Decoration Material Factory 吳江市塑料裝飾材料廠(1992)	Suzhou 蘇州市	Jiangsu 江蘇省	(0512)3616599	42	Collectively-owned 集體	392,690	281(147)	2,900	c
Shandou Dahao Dang Shi Street Office Industry & Communication Office 汕頭市達濠區宕石街道辦事處工交辦公室(1978)	Shantou 汕頭市	Guangdong 廣東省	(0754)7490059	985	Collectively-owned 集體	270,664	14421(2)	287,636	o
Shanghai Zi Jiang Color Printing & Packing Co. Ltd. 上海紫江彩印包裝有限公司(1991)	Shanghai 上海市	Shanghai 上海市	(021)64090018 (021)64090909	610	Overseas Chinese-funded 港澳台資	230,161	35951(1)	341,701	o
Linyi Lan Shan Qu Zhong Lian Packing Co. Ltd. 臨沂市蘭山區中聯包裝有限公司(1996)	Linyi 臨沂市	Shandong 山東省	(0539)8234513	612	Overseas Chinese-funded 港澳台資	144,658	13685(3)	225,459	o
Taizhou Chunan Rubber & Plastic Corp. 泰州春蘭橡塑公司(1971)	Taizhou 泰州市	Jiangsu 江蘇省	(0523)6238898 (0523)6238848	614	Domestic JVs 聯營	141,247	2895(15)	119,138	o
Dazhong Plastic Cement Products Co. Ltd. 大中塑膠製品有限公司(1989)	Qingyuan 清遠市	Guangdong 廣東省	(0763)5810510 (0763)5810513	450	Overseas Chinese-funded 港澳台資	77,167	544(77)	48,263	b
Shandou Jin Field Jin Xia Industry General Company 汕頭市金園區金廈工業總公司(1990)	Shantou 汕頭市	Guangdong 廣東省	(0754)8553461	1,000	Collectively-owned 集體	75,910	82(240)	2,900	c
Jiangsu Suqian Su Cheng Xing Fu Multiple-producing Factory 江蘇省宿遷市宿城幸福綜合廠(1974)	Suqian 宿遷市	Jiangsu 江蘇省	(0527)4212283	382	Collectively-owned 集體	72,953	371(120)	14,901	b
Suzhou Plastics No.9 Factory 蘇州塑料九廠(1956)	Suzhou 蘇州市	Jiangsu 江蘇省	(0512)7275033 (0512)7273537	509	Collectively-owned 集體	71,328	2080(24)	43,931	o
Laian Plastics No.2 Factory 來安縣塑料二廠(1979)	Chuzhou 滁州市	Anhui 安徽省	(0550)5692031	240	Collectively-owned 集體	68,350	4130(9)	7,140	b

Top 10 Cities by Production Output 產出排名前 10 位城市	Province 省	Market share 市場份額	Number of firms 企業個數
Shenzhen 深圳市	Guangdong 廣東省	10.55%	21
Shanghai 上海市	Shanghai 上海市	5.77%	95
Guangzhou 廣州市	Guangdong 廣東省	4.98%	107
Shantou 汕頭市	Guangdong 廣東省	4.55%	84
Ningbo 寧波市	Zhejiang 浙江省	3.61%	31
Huizhou 惠州市	Guangdong 廣東省	3.51%	35
Jiangmen 江門市	Guangdong 廣東省	3.50%	24
Yangzhou 揚州市	Jiangsu 江蘇省	3.42%	23
Taizhou 臺州市	Zhejiang 浙江省	2.93%	119
Suzhou 蘇州市	Jiangsu 江蘇省	2.77%	28

10 Major Wholesalers 10 家主要批發商	City 城市	Province 省	Telephone / Fax 電話 / 傳真
Chengdu Great Wall Electric Appliance Company 成都長城電器公司	Chengdu 成都市	Sichuan 四川省	(028)6662132 (028)6671975
Shandou Ceramics (Group) Company 汕頭陶瓷（集團）公司	Shantou 汕頭市	Guangdong 廣東省	(0754)8255441 (0754)8255442
Guangdong Puning Local Products Import & Export Company 廣東省普寧土產進出口公司	Jieyang 揭陽市	Guangdong 廣東省	(0663)2226744
Yixing Sundry Goods General Co. 宜興市土產雜品總公司	Wuxi 無錫市	Jiangsu 江蘇省	(0510)7903683 (0510)7903683
Sujiang Qu Zhe Jiang Dongda Group Company 椒江區浙江東大集團公司	Taizhou 臺州市	Zhejiang 浙江省	(0576)8881477 (0576)8881672
Jiangsu New Suzhou Co. Ltd. Suzhou Daily Goods General Co. 江蘇新蘇州股份有限公司蘇州日用雜品總公司	Suzhou 蘇州市	Jiangsu 江蘇省	(0512)7276630 (0512)7275964
Shandong Daily Use General Merchandise Import & Export Company 山東省日用百貨進出口公司	Qingdao 青島市	Shandong 山東省	(0532)5849141 (0532)5849207
Guangdong Yangjiang Light Industrial Products Import & Export (Group) Company 廣東陽江輕工業品進出口(集團)公司	Yangjiang 陽江市	Guangdong 廣東省	(0662)3222497 (0662)3222976
Hebei Artts & Crtfts Import & Export Corp. 河北工藝品進出口公司	Shijiazhuang 石家莊市	Hebei 河北省	(0311)7756124 (0311)7755347
Shandong Handicrafts Import & Export Products Group Linyi Craft Co. Ltd. 山東工藝品進出品集團臨沂工藝有限公司	Linyi 臨沂市	Shandong 山東省	(0539)8310001 (0539)8315396

*Also include sales by firms outside this industry.包括本行業以外廠家的銷售。"o" stands for "others". "o" 代表 "其他產品"。

3080: Plastic Parts 塑料零件製造業

The industry accounts for 0.092% of the total revenue of China's industrial sector in 1996. The revenue growth rate of the industry is 25.1% from 1995, as compared to the growth rate of China's industrial sector, 9.51%. The rate of return on asset is 3.21%. 72.84% of all firms in the industry made a profit while 23.62% had negative returns. The top province in terms of the industry's revenue is Zhejiang, accounting for 31.02% of the total revenue.
本行業在1996年佔全行業總產值0.092%，行業年增長率為25.1%（全國工業年增長率9.51%）。行業的資產回報率3.21%，72.84%的企業盈利，23.62%的企業虧損。銷售收入最高的省份為浙江省，佔本行業的31.02%。

	Total number of firms 企業總數	Total number of employees 職工總數	Total revenue (mil. RMB) 總銷售收入（百萬元）	Total profit (mil. RMB) 總利潤（百萬元）	Return on assets 資產利潤率 (%)	Return on equity 權益利潤率 (%)	Labour productivity ('000 RMB / worker) 勞動生產率（千元/人）	Debts / assets 資產負債率 (%)	Total assets (mil. RMB) 總資產（百萬元）
Industry Overall 行業總體	998	64,279	5,311	209	3.21	7.49	82.62	57.14	6,501

	Number of firms 企業個數	Average number of employees 平均職工人數	Average revenue ('000 RMB) 平均銷售收入（千元）	Average profit ('000 RMB) 平均利潤（千元）	Return on assets 資產利潤率 (%)	Return on equity 權益利潤率 (%)	Labour productivity ('000 RMB / worker) 勞動生產率（千元/人）	Average debts / assets 平均資產負債率(%)	Average Total assets ('000 RMB) 平均總資產（千元）
By ownership 產業所有權									
State-owned 國有	74	59	2,068				35.03	68.29	4,730
Collectively-owned 集體	782	58	3,755	146	3.43	9.72	64.45	64.68	4,266
Privately-owned 私有	10	23	1,150	118	13.31	24.08	49.15	44.71	885
Domestic JVs 聯營	14	113	17,962	1,945	10.84	20.55	158.75	47.23	17,941
Joint stock 股份制	7	227	29,720	2,811	8.13	15.42	130.84	47.28	34,570
Foreign-funded 外資	36	97	14,635	-216	-0.87	-1.55	150.49	43.68	24,720
Overseas Chinese-funded 港澳台資	72	109	16,917	751	3.84	7.44	155.15	48.38	19,572
By size 規模									
Large 大型	3	486	48,174	-5,256	-4.13	-15.92	99.06	74.05	127,201
Medium 中型	13	437	39,421	2,423	3.83	10.08	90.22	62.04	63,298
Small 小型	971	59	4,793	199	3.65	8.14	81.36	55.17	5,454
By regional distribution 地區分布									
Central-North 華北	95	65	3,005	284	6.56	13.15	46.58	50.12	4,328
Beijing 北京	24	41	2,854	-33	-0.81	-2.37	70.33	65.74	4,007
Tianjin 天津	40	87	3,463	320	6.76	11.11	39.65	39.13	4,732
Hebei 河北	20	59	3,605	756	14.45	29.83	60.68	51.57	5,230
Shanxi 山西	7	58	643	-26	-1.01	-3.72	11.17	72.72	2,540
Inner Mongolia 內蒙	4	18	460	5	0.60	1.40	26.29	57.44	840
Northeast 東北	87	50	1,452	-219	-5.53	-28.97	28.81	80.92	3,954
Liaoning 遼寧	55	49	1,361	-351	-8.89	-38.79	27.65	77.09	3,949
Jilin 吉林	18	60	2,376	4	0.06	0.20	39.52	67.98	6,168
Heilongjiang 黑龍江	14	43	624	16	1.40	-1.12	14.64	225.05	1,124
Central East 華東	605	57	4,937	271	4.43	10.52	86.71	57.89	6,117
Shanghai 上海	61	59	4,757	442	4.91	10.48	80.29	53.13	8,999
Jiangsu 江蘇	95	67	6,149	366	5.51	11.61	92.19	52.51	6,643
Zhejiang 浙江	337	54	4,888	255	4.44	10.34	90.04	57.04	5,748
Anhui 安徽	26	58	3,170	83	3.87	11.88	54.33	67.46	2,149
Fujian 福建	29	44	2,309	-36	-0.68	-2.57	52.02	73.67	5,308
Jiangxi 江西	11	17	575	31	4.42	20.36	32.92	78.41	699
Shandong 山東	46	70	6,732	319	4.01	13.46	96.59	70.25	7,962
Central-South 中南	132	108	13,110	335	2.96	6.05	121.71	51.07	11,329
Henan 河南	17	46	1,936	-2	-0.06	-0.21	41.88	69.72	2,801
Hubei 湖北	13	91	3,172	-298	-1.95	-3.27	34.73	40.50	15,293
Hunan 湖南	19	33	1,244	-34	-1.59	-5.23	37.46	69.59	2,118
Guangdong 廣東	76	152	21,413	641	4.05	8.35	140.90	51.55	15,831
Guangxi 廣西	7	9	764	20	2.51	3.66	82.31	31.24	796
Hainan 海南									
Southwest 西南	65	71	2,620	-110	-1.34	-3.22	36.94	58.36	8,193
Chongqing 重慶	31	70	2,916	-17	-0.25	-0.69	41.90	63.57	6,916
Sichuan 四川	23	45	1,652	-215	-3.64	-8.95	36.81	59.29	5,891
Guizhou 貴州	7	66	2,326	19	0.14	0.26	35.16	46.85	13,467
Yunnan 雲南	4	247	6,450	-433	-1.95	-4.51	26.17	56.64	22,133
Tibet 西藏									
Northwest 西北	14	35	831	-39	-3.20	-17.14	23.71	81.36	1,207
Shaanxi 陝西	12	38	911	-38	-3.53	-16.14	23.81	78.13	1,086
Gansu 甘肅	1	20	190				9.50	88.27	1,620
Qinghai 青海									
Ningxia 寧夏	1	12	520	-80	-3.56	-72.73	43.33	95.11	2,250
Xinjiang 新疆									

3080: Plastic Parts 塑料零件製造業

Year 年份	Number of firms 企業個數	Rate of change 每年變化 (%)	Number of employees 職工人數（人）	Rate of change 每年變化 (%)	Total revenue (mil. RMB) 總銷售收入（百萬元）	Rate of change 每年變化 (%)	Total profit (mil. RMB) 總利潤（百萬元）	Rate of change 每年變化 (%)
1993	957		84,526		2,671		151	
1994	938	-1.99%	61,493	-27.25%	3,233	21.05%	172	14.01%
1995	932	-0.64%	66,841	8.70%	4,247	31.36%	137	-20.45%
1996	998	7.08%	64,279	-3.83%	5,311	25.05%	209	52.33%

3 Major products* 3 種主要產品 *	Output 產量	Sales volume 銷售量	Unit 單位
a) Other Plastic Products 其他塑料製品	62,189	59,702	ton 噸
b) Daily Plastic Products 日用塑料製品	104,862	111,154	ton 噸

Top 10 firms by revenue (year founded) 收入排名前 10 家企業（創辦年份）	City 城市	Province 省	Telephone / fax 電話 / 傳真	Number of employees 職工人數	Ownership 產業所有權	Revenue ('000 RMB) 銷售收入（千元）	Profit ('000 RMB) (rank) 利潤（千元）（排名）	Total assets ('000 RMB) 總資產（千元）	Major products 主要產品
Huizhou Market Shanyang Industrial Co. Ltd. 惠州麥科特山陽工業有限公司(1995)	Huizhou 惠州市	Guangdong 廣東省	(0751)3322767 (0751)3321284	512	Overseas Chinese-funded 港澳台資	329,162	1322(47)	86,969	o
Ningbo Hua Xiang Group Company 寧波華翔集團公司(1980)	Ningbo 寧波市	Zhejiang 浙江省	(0574)5836055 (0574)5837000	1,042	Joint stock 股份制	326,957	40059(1)	208,614	o
Shenzhen Mei Yang Injection Co. Ltd. 深圳美陽注塑有限公司(1992)	Shenzhen 深圳市	Guangdong 廣東省	(0755)3308459 (0755)3305500	596	Foreign-funded 外資	188,375	7093(9)	117,433	o
Zi Yan Die Set Shaping Co. Ltd. 紫燕模具成型有限公司(1993)	Shanghai 上海市	Shanghai 上海市	(021)64590050 (021)64193320	493	Foreign-funded 外資	150,818	7622(8)	183,352	o
Shanghai Zhao He Plastics Co. Ltd. 上海昭和塑料有限公司(1994)	Shanghai 上海市	Shanghai 上海市	(021)62211180 (021)62211250	370	Foreign-funded 外資	137,920	1500(43)	36,010	o
Hui Huang Plastic Cement Die Set Manufacturing (Huizhou) Co. Ltd. 輝煌塑膠模具製造(惠州)有限公司(1992)	Huizhou 惠州市	Guangdong 廣東省	(0751)2602515 (0751)2602535	1,020	Overseas Chinese-funded 港澳台資	126,020	70(216)	62,333	a
Taishan Fu Cheng Zhen Ji Lian Electric Wire Factory 台山市附城鎮吉聯電線廠(1993)	Jiangmen 江門市	Guangdong 廣東省	(0750)5511789	67	Collectively-owned 集體	122,400	160(167)	13,620	o
Wujin Jian Hu Hardware Plastics Factory 武進市劍湖五金塑料廠(1988)	Changzhou 常州市	Jiangsu 江蘇省	(0519)8771878	382	Collectively-owned 集體	113,011	22251(2)	87,012	a
Zhongshan Kawa Plastic Co. Ltd. 中山市嘉華塑料有限公司(1993)	Zhongshan 中山市	Guangdong 廣東省	(0760)8322415	442	Foreign-funded 外資	79,628	17950(3)	97,807	b
Nanjing Jia Jia Le Household Appliances Factory 南京家家樂家用電器廠(1990)	Nanjing 南京市	Jiangsu 江蘇省	(025)4432580	279	Domestic JVs 聯營	75,000	2090(27)	18,696	a

Top 10 Cities by Production Output 產出排名前 10 位城市	Province 省	Market share 市場份額	Number of firms 企業個數
Wuxi 無錫市	Jiangsu 江蘇省	63.88%	68
Ningbo 寧波市	Zhejiang 浙江省	7.73%	215
Shanghai 上海市	Shanghai 上海市	3.18%	108
Shenzhen 深圳市	Guangdong 廣東省	2.58%	16
Foshan 佛山市	Guangdong 廣東省	2.29%	19
Huizhou 惠州市	Guangdong 廣東省	1.98%	19
Changzhou 常州市	Jiangsu 江蘇省	1.94%	70
Zhongshan 中山市	Guangdong 廣東省	1.53%	7
Qingdao 青島市	Shandong 山東省	1.48%	23
Jiangmen 江門市	Guangdong 廣東省	0.99%	4

10 Major Wholesalers 10 家主要批發商	City 城市	Province 省	Telephone / Fax 電話 / 傳真
Zhong Hua Singbo Import & Export Company 中化寧波進出口公司	Ningbo 寧波市	Zhejiang 浙江省	(0574)7346764 (0574)7366775
China Chemical Supply & Marketing Hua Nan Company 中國化工供銷華南公司	Guangzhou 廣州市	Guangdong 廣東省	(020)87654477 (020)87784414
China Agriculture Means of Production Chengdu Company 中國農業生產資料成都公司	Chengdu 成都市	Sichuan 四川省	(028)3333909 (028)3331202
Shanxi Agriculture Means of Production Company 山西省農業生產資料公司	Taiyuan 太原市	Shanxi 山西省	(0351)4040255 (0351)4040231
Beijing Chemical Light Industry General Company 北京市化工輕工總公司	Beijing 北京市	Beijing 北京市	(010)64224837 (010)64219301
Beijing Chemical Industry Group Company Supply & Marketing Company 北京化學工業集團公司供銷公司	Beijing 北京市	Beijing 北京市	(010)67714610 (010)67714058
Zhong Hua Jiangsu Import & Export Company 中化江蘇進出口公司	Nanjing 南京市	Jiangsu 江蘇省	(025)2258718 (025)2257789
Yunnan Chemical Import & Export Company 雲南省化工進出口公司	Kunming 昆明市	Yunnan 雲南省	(0871)3314002 (0871)3314931
Fujian Jiu Zhou Group Co. Ltd. 福建九州集團股份有限公司	Xiamen 廈門市	Fujian 福建省	(0592)5055818 (0592)5052033
China Chemical Industry Commission Agent Hua Dong Co. 中國化工供銷華東公司	Shanghai 上海市	Shanghai 上海市	(021)62514123

*Also include sales by firms outside this industry.包括本行業以外廠家的銷售。"o" stands for "others". "o" 代表"其他產品"。

3090: Other Plastic Products 其他塑料製品業

The industry accounts for 0.336% of the total revenue of China's industrial sector in 1996. The revenue growth rate of the industry is 8.3% from 1995, as compared to the growth rate of China's industrial sector, 9.51%. The rate of return on asset is 1.52%. 73.41% of all firms in the industry made a profit while 22.08% had negative returns. The top province in terms of the industry's revenue is Guangdong, accounting for 30.18% of the total revenue.
本行業在1996年佔全行業總產值0.336%，行業年增長率為8.3%（全國工業年增長率9.51%）。行業的資產回報率1.52%，73.41%的企業盈利，22.08%的企業虧損。銷售收入最高的省份為廣東省，佔本行業的30.18%。

	Total number of firms 企業總數	Total number of employees 職工總數	Total revenue (mil. RMB) 總銷售收入（百萬元）	Total profit (mil. RMB) 總利潤（百萬元）	Return on assets 資產利潤率 (%)	Return on equity 權益利潤率 (%)	Labour productivity ('000 RMB / worker) 勞動生產率（千元/人）	Debts / assets 資產負債率 (%)	Total assets (mil. RMB) 總資產（百萬元）
Industry Overall 行業總體	4,657	278,275	19,480	349	1.52	3.95	70.00	61.30	22,969

	Number of firms 企業個數	Average number of employees 平均職工人數	Average revenue ('000 RMB) 平均銷售收入（千元）	Average profit ('000 RMB) 平均利潤（千元）	Return on assets 資產利潤率 (%)	Return on equity 權益利潤率 (%)	Labour productivity ('000 RMB / worker) 勞動生產率（千元/人）	Average debts / assets 平均資產負債率(%)	Average Total assets ('000 RMB) 平均總資產（千元）
By ownership 產業所有權									
State-owned 國有	345	88	4,510	6	0.07	0.22	51.52	68.54	8,403
Collectively-owned 集體	3,424	52	2,787	96	3.67	10.56	53.99	65.26	2,623
Privately-owned 私有	26	68	4,973	64	1.13	2.23	73.38	49.31	5,652
Domestic JVs 聯營	29	70	7,667	299	3.84	18.43	110.29	79.14	7,783
Joint stock 股份制	32	91	7,070	-353	-4.19	-10.79	77.72	61.16	8,429
Foreign-funded 外資	242	70	10,531	368	2.64	5.88	150.61	55.12	13,948
Overseas Chinese-funded 港澳台資	553	93	9,475	-126	-0.99	-2.25	102.31	55.98	12,760
By size 規模									
Large 大型	7	593	81,182	8,812	5.23	9.63	136.93	45.75	168,641
Medium 中型	44	315	38,434	1,376	2.63	6.54	122.09	59.79	52,370
Small 小型	4,514	58	3,815	50	1.16	3.10	65.86	62.42	4,316
By regional distribution 地區分布									
Central-North 華北	561	38	1,828	25	0.73	1.88	47.86	61.22	3,450
Beijing 北京	198	30	1,434	-55	-1.63	-3.90	47.96	58.12	3,381
Tianjin 天津	142	33	1,781	111	2.89	6.81	53.40	57.53	3,841
Hebei 河北	159	54	2,807	64	1.59	4.85	51.66	67.20	4,001
Shanxi 山西	29	47	674	35	2.15	6.72	14.40	68.01	1,621
Inner Mongolia 內蒙	33	24	703	-58	-5.11	-12.99	29.67	60.59	1,126
Northeast 東北	491	50	1,784	28	0.76	1.91	36.03	60.11	3,657
Liaoning 遼寧	275	55	2,120	20	0.44	0.89	38.35	50.35	4,451
Jilin 吉林	118	32	769	14	0.98	4.12	24.10	76.22	1,443
Heilongjiang 黑龍江	98	54	2,060	67	1.63	9.65	37.86	83.06	4,094
Central East 華東	2,096	57	4,838	89	1.68	4.64	84.28	63.66	5,263
Shanghai 上海	289	66	5,473	243	2.88	6.29	83.19	54.21	8,431
Jiangsu 江蘇	417	72	6,748	16	0.22	0.64	93.33	66.34	7,291
Zhejiang 浙江	673	48	3,756	62	1.66	5.52	78.56	69.93	3,723
Anhui 安徽	164	45	3,442	197	8.84	27.83	76.47	68.22	2,226
Fujian 福建	277	62	6,462	27	0.45	1.15	103.84	60.84	6,069
Jiangxi 江西	100	28	807	-35	-2.92	-8.28	28.88	64.71	1,185
Shandong 山東	176	66	4,438	177	3.53	10.38	67.60	66.04	5,019
Central-South 中南	1,195	84	5,843	115	1.84	4.35	69.45	57.18	6,272
Henan 河南	127	31	1,607	34	1.67	5.31	52.20	68.50	2,015
Hubei 湖北	143	61	3,735	89	2.63	8.92	61.12	70.49	3,370
Hunan 湖南	133	44	1,241	-5	-0.38	-0.96	27.92	60.44	1,280
Guangdong 廣東	678	116	8,671	183	1.96	4.43	74.94	55.18	9,342
Guangxi 廣西	109	30	1,544	21	1.19	3.27	51.88	63.71	1,809
Hainan 海南	5	56	6,302	-944	-8.50	-54.25	111.74	84.34	11,110
Southwest 西南	210	36	1,300	-11	-0.61	-2.16	35.86	71.80	1,856
Chongqing 重慶	55	43	1,415	43	2.71	22.69	32.96	88.04	1,592
Sichuan 四川	114	37	1,511	1	0.06	0.19	40.72	68.12	2,368
Guizhou 貴州	25	18	381	-1	-0.26	-0.49	20.72	46.94	457
Yunnan 雲南	16	38	840	17	1.30	3.75	21.96	65.22	1,294
Tibet 西藏									
Northwest 西北	104	39	1,763	1	0.02	0.06	44.96	70.60	3,113
Shaanxi 陝西	61	44	2,140	24	0.64	1.96	48.11	67.50	3,800
Gansu 甘肅	21	40	1,641	-55	-1.91	-14.52	41.47	86.91	2,867
Qinghai 青海	1								
Ningxia 寧夏	6	33	978	-17	-1.29	-4.31	30.10	70.06	1,292
Xinjiang 新疆	15	23	833	-11	-0.71	-1.77	36.84	59.80	1,599

3090: Other Plastic Products 其他塑料製品業

Year 年份	Number of firms 企業個數	Rate of change 每年變化 (%)	Number of employees 職工人數 (人)	Rate of change 每年變化 (%)	Total revenue (mil. RMB) 總銷售收入 (百萬元)	Rate of change 每年變化 (%)	Total profit (mil. RMB) 總利潤 (百萬元)	Rate of change 每年變化 (%)
1993	4,081		255,430		9,907		323	
1994	4,431	8.58%	290,030	13.55%	12,901	30.21%	311	-3.74%
1995	4,740	6.97%	307,543	6.04%	17,981	39.38%	208	-32.96%
1996	4,657	-1.75%	278,275	-9.52%	19,480	8.34%	349	67.50%

3 Major products* 3 種主要產品 *	Output 產量	Sales volume 銷售量	Unit 單位
a) Other Plastic Products 其他塑料製品	499,408	479,431	ton 噸
b) Daily Plastic Products 日用塑料製品	918,183	973,274	ton 噸
c) Polyvinyl Chloride Products 聚氯乙烯製品	298,868	274,959	ton 噸

Top 10 firms by revenue (year founded) 收入排名前 10 家企業 (創辦年份)	City 城市	Province 省	Telephone / fax 電話 / 傳真	Number of employees 職工人數	Ownership 產業所有權	Revenue ('000 RMB) 銷售收入 (千元)	Profit ('000 RMB) (rank) 利潤 (千元) (排名)	Total assets ('000 RMB) 總資產 (千元)	Major products 主要產品
Ming Da Plastic Cement (Fujian) Co. Ltd. 福清市明達塑膠(福建)有限公司(1990)	Fuzhou 福州市	Fujian 福建省	(0591)5380123 (0591)5380101	2,271	Foreign-funded 外資	741,382	19998(5)	336,755	a,c
Shanghai Chemical Plant Co. Ltd. 上海化工廠有限公司(1949)	Shanghai 上海市	Shanghai 上海市	(021)65193960 (021)65190090	1,840	State-owned 國有	330,806	2222(62)	328,464	a,c
Hou Hong Daily Use Products (Shenzhen) Co. Ltd. 厚宏日用製品(深圳)有限公司(1991)	Shenzhen 深圳市	Guangdong 廣東省	(0755)7706666 (0755)7701243	1,000	Overseas Chinese-funded 港澳台資	179,071	2179(65)	111,901	o
Shandou Dahao Zhen Industrial Company 汕頭市達濠區市鎮工業公司(1990)	Shantou 汕頭市	Guangdong 廣東省	(0754)7380537	910	Collectively-owned 集體	178,870	3037(40)	57,052	o
Guangzhou Yong Fa Plastic Products Co. Ltd. 廣州永發塑料製品有限公司(1989)	Guangzhou 廣州市	Guangdong 廣東省	(020)82232378 (020)82232330	1,434	Overseas Chinese-funded 港澳台資	176,077	457(323)	402,331	b
Jiangyin Shen Gang School-run Factory 江陰市申港校辦廠(1994)	Wuxi 無錫市	Jiangsu 江蘇省	(0510)6621527	180	Collectively-owned 集體	152,060	6210(13)	24,240	c
Shunde Large Scale Injection Products Factory 順德市大型注塑製品廠(1988)	Foshan 佛山市	Guangdong 廣東省	(0757)2291280 (0757)2291501	758	Collectively-owned 集體	150,447	-2560(1570)	179,579	a
Jiangmen Yu Hua Wall Paper Factory 江門市裕華牆紙廠(1991)	Jiangmen 江門市	Guangdong 廣東省	(0750)3894059 (0750)3897423	198	State-owned 國有	134,490	1961(75)	78,493	a
Hua De Plastic Products Co. Ltd. 華德塑料製品有限公司(1988)	Shanghai 上海市	Shanghai 上海市	(021)58745615 (021)58839694	216	Foreign-funded 外資	134,481	31926(1)	148,705	a
De Kui Industrial Co. Ltd. 德奎實業有限公司(1992)	Shanghai 上海市	Shanghai 上海市	(021)57575430 (021)57576617	833	Overseas Chinese-funded 港澳台資	129,569	26599(2)	326,784	o

Top 10 Cities by Production Output 產出排名前 10 位城市	Province 省	Market share 市場份額	Number of firms 企業個數
Shanghai 上海市	Shanghai 上海市	10.13%	435
Shenzhen 深圳市	Guangdong 廣東省	9.23%	94
Suzhou 蘇州市	Jiangsu 江蘇省	5.30%	178
Guangzhou 廣州市	Guangdong 廣東省	4.82%	215
Taizhou 臺州市	Zhejiang 浙江省	4.01%	193
Wenzhou 溫州市	Zhejiang 浙江省	3.79%	314
Huizhou 惠州市	Guangdong 廣東省	3.70%	92
Foshan 佛山市	Guangdong 廣東省	3.61%	60
Ningbo 寧波市	Zhejiang 浙江省	3.44%	205
Wuxi 無錫市	Jiangsu 江蘇省	2.94%	146

10 Major Wholesalers 10 家主要批發商	City 城市	Province 省	Telephone / Fax 電話 / 傳真
Zhong Hua Singbo Import & Export Company 中化寧波進出口公司	Ningbo 寧波市	Zhejiang 浙江省	(0574)7346764 (0574)7366775
China Chemical Supply & Marketing Hua Nan Company 中國化工供銷華南公司	Guangzhou 廣州市	Guangdong 廣東省	(020)87654477 (020)87784414
China Agriculture Means of Production Chengdu Company 中國農業生產資料成都公司	Chengdu 成都市	Sichuan 四川省	(028)3333909 (028)3331202
Shanxi Agriculture Means of Production Company 山西省農業生產資料公司	Taiyuan 太原市	Shanxi 山西省	(0351)4040255 (0351)4040231
Beijing Chemical Light Industry General Company 北京市化工輕工總公司	Beijing 北京市	Beijing 北京市	(010)64224837 (010)64219301
Beijing Chemical Industry Group Company Supply & Marketing Company 北京化學工業集團公司供銷公司	Beijing 北京市	Beijing 北京市	(010)67714610 (010)67714058
Zhong Hua Jiangsu Import & Export Company 中化江蘇進出口公司	Nanjing 南京市	Jiangsu 江蘇省	(025)2258718 (025)2257789
Yunnan Chemical Import & Export Company 雲南省化工進出口公司	Kunming 昆明市	Yunnan 雲南省	(0871)3314002 (0871)3314931
Fujian Jiu Zhou Group Co. Ltd. 福建九州集團股份有限公司	Xiamen 廈門市	Fujian 福建省	(0592)5055818 (0592)5052033
China Chemical Industry Commission Agent Hua Dong Co. 中國化工供銷華東公司	Shanghai 上海市	Shanghai 上海市	(021)62514123

*Also include sales by firms outside this industry.包括本行業以外廠家的銷售。"o" stands for "others". "o" 代表 "其他產品"。

3110: Cement 水泥製造業

The industry accounts for 1.836% of the total revenue of China's industrial sector in 1996. The revenue growth rate of the industry is 7.6% from 1995, as compared to the growth rate of China's industrial sector, 9.51%. The rate of return on asset is -1.01%. 53.31% of all firms in the industry made a profit while 40.79% had negative returns. The top province in terms of the industry's revenue is Guangdong, accounting for 12.01% of the total revenue.
本行業在1996年佔全行業總產值1.836%，行業年增長率為7.6%（全國工業年增長率9.51%）。行業的資產回報率-1.01%，53.31%的企業盈利，40.79%的企業虧損。銷售收入最高的省份為廣東省，佔本行業的12.01%。

	Total number of firms 企業總數	Total number of employees 職工總數	Total revenue (mil. RMB) 總銷售收入（百萬元）	Total profit (mil. RMB) 總利潤（百萬元）	Return on assets 資產利潤率 (%)	Return on equity 權益利潤率 (%)	Labour productivity ('000 RMB / worker) 勞動生產率（千元/人）	Debts / assets 資產負債率 (%)	Total assets (mil. RMB) 總資產（百萬元）
Industry Overall 行業總體	6,609	2,227,945	106,452	-2,295	-1.01	-3.14	47.78	67.81	227,295

	Number of firms 企業個數	Average number of employees 平均職工人數	Average revenue ('000 RMB) 平均銷售收入（千元）	Average profit ('000 RMB) 平均利潤（千元）	Return on assets 資產利潤率 (%)	Return on equity 權益利潤率 (%)	Labour productivity ('000 RMB / worker) 勞動生產率（千元/人）	Average debts / assets 平均資產負債率(%)	Average Total assets ('000 RMB) 平均總資產（千元）
By ownership 產業所有權									
State-owned 國有	2,110	526	22,237	-658	-1.18	-3.61	42.29	67.17	55,558
Collectively-owned 集體	3,928	228	11,156	100	0.56	2.55	49.02	77.96	17,813
Privately-owned 私有	39	137	7,771	-768	-7.71	-18.80	56.80	58.97	9,956
Domestic JVs 聯營	105	193	9,133	2,059	8.32	17.09	47.42	51.34	24,755
Joint stock 股份制	205	586	36,127	-5,087	-6.52	-14.36	61.68	54.59	78,012
Foreign-funded 外資	102	456	44,415	-6,194	-4.32	-8.74	97.34	50.62	143,504
Overseas Chinese-funded 港澳台資	116	304	21,838	1,622	2.94	5.69	71.73	48.34	55,206
By size 規模									
Large 大型	96	2,210	186,234	-47,304	-9.47	-22.53	84.28	57.96	499,547
Medium 中型	543	956	54,183	-2,958	-2.66	-7.67	56.69	65.37	111,302
Small 小型	5,824	254	10,188	661	3.24	12.01	40.06	73.02	20,415
By regional distribution 地區分布									
Central-North 華北	794	313	12,809	432	1.36	3.76	40.95	63.96	31,895
Beijing 北京	44	802	51,426	-928	-0.69	-2.06	64.13	66.73	135,415
Tianjin 天津	20	331	19,274	829	1.56	2.95	58.19	47.27	53,219
Hebei 河北	354	328	14,836	849	2.51	6.51	45.19	61.46	33,800
Shanxi 山西	263	232	5,332	165	1.10	3.74	22.97	70.63	15,049
Inner Mongolia 內蒙	113	258	7,679	209	0.99	2.92	29.73	65.99	21,054
Northeast 東北	452	424	15,092	-814	-2.04	-7.17	35.62	71.54	39,931
Liaoning 遼寧	248	406	14,852	-402	-1.07	-3.12	36.60	65.84	37,740
Jilin 吉林	92	474	15,721	-253	-0.51	-2.24	33.13	77.38	49,831
Heilongjiang 黑龍江	112	421	15,105	-2,188	-5.97	-27.16	35.84	78.03	36,649
Central East 華東	1,976	363	22,048	232	0.61	1.68	60.69	63.60	37,974
Shanghai 上海	28	432	48,204	2,729	2.86	6.92	111.58	58.59	95,260
Jiangsu 江蘇	352	447	27,953	6	0.01	0.03	62.51	61.12	49,251
Zhejiang 浙江	337	402	29,144	-35	-0.08	-0.21	72.55	63.32	46,308
Anhui 安徽	298	350	16,849	629	2.30	5.72	48.08	59.77	27,346
Fujian 福建	343	172	10,619	-475	-2.10	-5.85	61.59	64.16	22,674
Jiangxi 江西	206	312	12,084	219	0.91	2.92	38.71	68.91	24,097
Shandong 山東	412	449	27,678	783	1.74	5.26	61.59	66.91	44,993
Central-South 中南	1,912	337	16,605	-1,416	-3.57	-12.83	49.21	72.19	39,661
Henan 河南	404	323	13,553	306	1.10	3.65	41.93	69.85	27,858
Hubei 湖北	258	375	15,559	27	0.08	0.23	41.46	63.61	32,447
Hunan 湖南	494	295	9,832	-667	-3.49	-12.87	33.38	72.87	19,092
Guangdong 廣東	466	369	27,424	-4,411	-6.07	-24.64	74.25	75.39	72,633
Guangxi 廣西	267	347	15,650	-1,692	-3.80	-14.45	45.09	73.69	44,524
Hainan 海南	23	322	19,288	-80	-0.18	-0.29	59.84	39.21	45,140
Southwest 西南	946	286	9,947	35	0.16	0.47	34.73	65.09	21,500
Chongqing 重慶	180	291	9,345	222	1.39	4.23	32.12	67.11	15,940
Sichuan 四川	362	336	11,810	-74	-0.30	-1.00	35.16	69.69	24,507
Guizhou 貴州	217	186	4,586	140	1.40	3.03	24.61	53.86	9,984
Yunnan 雲南	180	296	12,783	55	0.16	0.43	43.22	61.96	33,428
Tibet 西藏	7	441	22,190	826	1.40	3.23	50.28	56.54	58,781
Northwest 西北	529	291	8,952	-104	-0.43	-1.61	30.71	73.31	24,037
Shaanxi 陝西	237	238	6,152	-408	-2.47	-14.15	25.85	82.53	16,516
Gansu 甘肅	152	271	8,440	296	1.43	4.25	31.16	66.31	20,624
Qinghai 青海	27	292	6,191	-379	-2.13	-9.54	21.22	77.68	17,772
Ningxia 寧夏	25	412	13,207	-595	-1.50	-5.57	32.05	73.05	39,600
Xinjiang 新疆	88	437	17,013	251	0.53	1.73	38.95	69.51	47,686

Year 年份	Number of firms 企業個數	Rate of change 每年變化 (%)	Number of employees 職工人數 (人)	Rate of change 每年變化 (%)	Total revenue (mil. RMB) 總銷售收入 (百萬元)	Rate of change 每年變化 (%)	Total profit (mil. RMB) 總利潤 (百萬元)	Rate of change 每年變化 (%)
1993	5,485		1,581,255		82,581		10,774	
1994	6,061	10.50%	1,840,047	16.37%	86,519	4.77%	5,022	-53.38%
1995	6,618	9.19%	2,311,814	25.64%	98,934	14.35%	537	-89.31%
1996	6,609	-0.14%	2,227,945	-3.63%	106,452	7.60%	-2,295	-527.49%

3 Major products* 3 種主要產品 *	Output 產量	Sales volume 銷售量	Unit 單位
a) Cement Clinker 水泥熟料	35,443	29,772	10,000 ton 萬噸
b) Limestone 石灰石	36,343	29,801	10,000 ton 萬噸

Top 10 firms by revenue (year founded) 收入排名前 10 家企業 (創辦年份)	City 城市	Province 省	Telephone / fax 電話 / 傳真	Number of employees 職工人數	Ownership 產業所有權	Revenue ('000 RMB) 銷售收入 (千元)	Profit ('000 RMB) (rank) 利潤 (千元) (排名)	Total assets ('000 RMB) 總資產 (千元)	Major products 主要產品
Beijing Building Materials Group Co. Ltd. 北京建築材料集團有限責任公司(1992)	Beijing 北京市	Beijing 北京市	(010)63021485 (010)63021372	20,560	State-owned 國有	1,702,518	32316(12)	4,189,056	a,b
Shandong Cong Lin Group Co. 山東叢林集團公司(1983)	Yantai 煙台市	Shandong 山東省	(0535)8561241 (0535)8561337	3,776	Collectively-owned 集體	1,157,700	103550(2)	1,038,294	a
Liuzhou Cement Plant 柳州水泥廠(1964)	Liuzhou 柳州市	Guangxi 廣西	(0772)3883889 (0772)339347	3,811	State-owned 國有	514,721	16029(29)	1,266,439	a
Anhui Ningguo Cement Plant 安徽省寧國水泥廠(1985)	Xuanzhou 宣州市	Anhui 安徽省	(0563)4888114 (0563)4888514	3,101	Foreign-funded 外資	502,211	90111(3)	2,171,109	a
Suzhou Golden Cat Cement Co. Ltd. 蘇州金貓水泥有限公司(1994)	Suzhou 蘇州市	Jiangsu 江蘇省	(0512)6262015 (0512)6265155	2,558	Foreign-funded 外資	482,180	-49390(4878)	1,277,270	a
Dalian Huaneng – onoda Cement Co. Ltd. 大連華能－小野田水泥有限公司(1992)	Dalian 大連市	Liaoning 遼寧省	(0411)6681888 (0411)6681627	609	Foreign-funded 外資	447,358	7810(79)	1,454,802	a
Tangshan Jidong Cement Co. Ltd 河北省冀東水泥廠(1985)	Tangshan 唐山市	Hebei 河北省	(0315)3241822 (0315)3243444	2,936	State-owned 國有	446,195	177603(1)	2,478,012	a
Guangzhou Zhu Jiang Cement Plant 廣州市珠江水泥廠(1989)	Guangzhou 廣州市	Guangdong 廣東省	(020)86607692 (020)86607915	1,507	Overseas Chinese-funded 港澳台資	428,443	57168(4)	1,101,953	a
Hebei Taihang Group Company 河北太行集團公司(1969)	Handan 邯鄲市	Hebei 河北省	(0310)5013722 (0310)5015761	3,103	State-owned 國有	427,959	30945(15)	969,616	a
Anhui Fanchang Di Gang Cement Factory 安徽省繁昌縣荻港水泥廠(1978)	Wuhu 蕪湖市	Anhui 安徽省	(0553)7892688 (0553)7892836	1,316	Collectively-owned 集體	356,706	8185(74)	106,081	a

Top 10 Cities by Production Output 產出排名前 10 位城市	Province 省	Market share 市場份額	Number of firms 企業個數
Beijing 北京市	Beijing 北京市	3.08%	45
Yantai 煙台市	Shandong 山東省	2.37%	47
Hangzhou 杭州市	Zhejiang 浙江省	2.26%	101
Guangzhou 廣州市	Guangdong 廣東省	2.24%	63
Zaozhuang 棗莊市	Shandong 山東省	2.14%	75
Huzhou 湖州市	Zhejiang 浙江省	1.95%	60
Jiangmen 江門市	Guangdong 廣東省	1.77%	42
Jiaxing 嘉興市	Zhejiang 浙江省	1.73%	60
Nanjing 南京市	Jiangsu 江蘇省	1.65%	36
Suzhou 蘇州市	Jiangsu 江蘇省	1.65%	49

10 Major Wholesalers 10 家主要批發商	City 城市	Province 省	Telephone / Fax 電話 / 傳真
Chengdu Sheng Xing Trade Company 成都盛興商貿公司	Chengdu 成都市	Sichuan 四川省	(028)7762591
Shanghai Municipal Administration Engineering Material Company 上海市市政工程材料公司	Shanghai 上海市	Shanghai 上海市	(021)64372632
Shanghai Construction Engineering Material Co. 上海市建築工程材料公司	Shanghai 上海市	Shanghai 上海市	(021)63298630
Yixing Jin San Jiao Zhao Bazaar 宜興市金三角招商城	Wuxi 無錫市	Jiangsu 江蘇省	(0510)7935138 (0510)7935138
Fujian Hua Fu Import & Export Company 福建省華福進出口公司	Fuzhou 福州市	Fujian 福建省	(0591)7810477 (0591)7810485
China Building Goods & Materials Company 中國建築物資公司	Beijing 北京市	Beijing 北京市	(010)68586253
Dalian Jinzhou Xin Gang Industry & Trade Company 大連金州新港工貿公司	Dalian 大連市	Liaoning 遼寧省	(0411)7624747
Shanghai Zhan Dong Industrial Co. Ltd. 上海展東實業有限公司	Shanghai 上海市	Shanghai 上海市	(021)58201778 (021)58200874
China Building Materials and Equipment Import & Export Company 中國建築材料及設備進出口公司	Beijing 北京市	Beijing 北京市	(010)68393420
Dandong Chemical Light Industry Material Company Chemical Construction Material Marketing Station 丹東市化工輕工材料公司化工建材經銷站	Dandong 丹東市	Liaoning 遼寧省	(0415)2146396

*Also include sales by firms outside this industry.包括本行業以外廠家的銷售。"o" stands for "others". "o" 代表"其他產品"。

3121: Cement Products 水泥製品業

The industry accounts for 0.305% of the total revenue of China's industrial sector in 1996. The revenue growth rate of the industry is 12.7% from 1995, as compared to the growth rate of China's industrial sector, 9.51%. The rate of return on asset is 1.02%. 77.81% of all firms in the industry made a profit while 16.04% had negative returns. The top province in terms of the industry's revenue is Jiangsu, accounting for 19.88% of the total revenue.
本行業在1996年佔全行業總產值0.305%，行業年增長率為12.7%（全國工業年增長率9.51%）。行業的資產回報率1.02%，77.81%的企業盈利，16.04%的企業虧損。銷售收入最高的省份為江蘇省，佔本行業的19.88%。

	Total number of firms 企業總數	Total number of employees 職工總數	Total revenue (mil. RMB) 總銷售收入（百萬元）	Total profit (mil. RMB) 總利潤（百萬元）	Return on assets 資產利潤率 (%)	Return on equity 權益利潤率 (%)	Labour productivity ('000 RMB / worker) 勞動生產率（千元/人）	Debts / assets 資產負債率 (%)	Total assets (mil. RMB) 總資產（百萬元）
Industry Overall 行業總體	5,289	349,537	17,683	240	1.02	2.73	50.59	62.78	23,655

	Number of firms 企業個數	Average number of employees 平均職工人數	Average revenue ('000 RMB) 平均銷售收入（千元）	Average profit ('000 RMB) 平均利潤（千元）	Return on assets 資產利潤率 (%)	Return on equity 權益利潤率 (%)	Labour productivity ('000 RMB / worker) 勞動生產率（千元/人）	Average debts / assets 平均資產負債率(%)	Average Total assets ('000 RMB) 平均總資產（千元）
By ownership 產業所有權									
State-owned 國有	724	177	5,511	-264	-1.95	-5.17	31.05	62.28	13,522
Collectively-owned 集體	4,349	47	2,709	81	3.55	12.34	57.12	71.26	2,283
Privately-owned 私有	21	51	5,401	262	17.63	34.97	104.92	49.59	1,488
Domestic JVs 聯營	64	67	8,403	700	5.88	13.05	125.42	54.97	11,910
Joint stock 股份制	43	69	2,587	-46	-0.89	-2.05	37.65	56.62	5,132
Foreign-funded 外資	35	89	11,667	152	0.42	0.58	131.05	26.76	35,914
Overseas Chinese-funded 港澳台資	48	80	15,174	521	1.50	2.84	189.53	47.04	34,663
By size 規模									
Large 大型	13	1,676	78,484	-5,064	-2.44	-5.38	46.83	54.73	207,733
Medium 中型	66	692	35,024	489	0.69	1.73	50.59	59.93	70,386
Small 小型	5,171	54	2,775	53	1.68	4.78	51.13	64.93	3,154
By regional distribution 地區分布									
Central-North 華北	581	78	3,399	27	0.47	1.29	43.53	63.77	5,768
Beijing 北京	108	101	5,595	76	0.75	2.20	55.61	66.12	10,223
Tianjin 天津	35	94	8,790	-185	-1.02	-2.20	93.82	53.88	18,258
Hebei 河北	198	79	3,577	128	3.19	10.72	45.38	70.28	4,034
Shanxi 山西	76	108	2,393	-134	-2.41	-5.87	22.15	59.01	5,568
Inner Mongolia 內蒙	164	45	1,053	-8	-0.35	-0.99	23.33	65.13	2,356
Northeast 東北	409	86	2,144	-28	-0.56	-1.62	25.00	65.36	4,998
Liaoning 遼寧	188	92	2,790			-0.01	30.34	62.96	5,731
Jilin 吉林	81	105	2,171	-116	-1.80	-6.99	20.59	74.25	6,434
Heilongjiang 黑龍江	140	66	1,262	-15	-0.46	-1.17	19.10	60.76	3,182
Central East 華東	2,191	66	4,269	163	3.63	9.73	64.88	62.73	4,501
Shanghai 上海	70	112	15,582	150	0.55	1.25	139.68	56.44	27,460
Jiangsu 江蘇	643	76	5,468	151	2.90	8.21	72.42	64.71	5,216
Zhejiang 浙江	218	64	2,762	65	1.88	5.91	43.19	68.11	3,425
Anhui 安徽	703	42	2,696	217	15.31	38.35	63.59	60.07	1,416
Fujian 福建	105	51	3,490	10	0.14	0.34	68.36	58.50	7,057
Jiangxi 江西	132	54	1,182	7	0.27	0.84	22.06	67.93	2,421
Shandong 山東	320	99	5,394	255	4.58	13.42	54.60	65.86	5,570
Central-South 中南	1,318	60	3,073	-86	-2.00	-5.42	51.06	63.11	4,325
Henan 河南	326	40	1,715	12	0.51	1.43	43.35	64.60	2,274
Hubei 湖北	371	83	4,602	114	3.05	8.33	55.41	63.42	3,754
Hunan 湖南	320	57	1,896	-104	-4.07	-12.44	33.31	67.31	2,559
Guangdong 廣東	164	74	5,543	-724	-5.32	-14.29	74.90	62.79	13,623
Guangxi 廣西	111	41	2,221	-51	-1.46	-3.82	54.79	61.69	3,482
Hainan 海南	26	29	818	-89	-1.83	-2.76	28.01	33.57	4,868
Southwest 西南	469	53	1,901	19	0.59	1.44	35.86	59.15	3,150
Chongqing 重慶	85	38	1,003	3	0.23	0.84	26.56	72.91	1,251
Sichuan 四川	217	55	2,034	3	0.09	0.20	37.13	57.26	3,504
Guizhou 貴州	119	55	1,834	42	1.25	2.85	33.19	56.23	3,406
Yunnan 雲南	45	68	3,120	78	1.91	5.98	45.90	68.04	4,089
Tibet 西藏	3	55	2,017	-217	-3.10	-4.84	36.45	36.06	6,997
Northwest 西北	321	65	1,672	-52	-1.35	-3.30	25.84	58.99	3,804
Shaanxi 陝西	149	68	1,744	-81	-2.08	-6.55	25.52	68.23	3,885
Gansu 甘肅	92	46	1,134	48	2.34	4.66	24.74	49.86	2,049
Qinghai 青海	11	89	1,820	-24	-0.49	-1.26	20.39	61.17	4,830
Ningxia 寧夏	19	53	1,719	53	1.75	4.41	32.53	60.44	3,044
Xinjiang 新疆	50	88	2,396	-193	-2.82	-5.40	27.31	47.83	6,856

3121: Cement Products 水泥製品業

Year 年份	Number of firms 企業個數	Rate of change 每年變化 (%)	Number of employees 職工人數（人）	Rate of change 每年變化 (%)	Total revenue (mil. RMB) 總銷售收入（百萬元）	Rate of change 每年變化 (%)	Total profit (mil. RMB) 總利潤（百萬元）	Rate of change 每年變化 (%)
1993	4,539		333,243		13,295		844	
1994	5,192	14.39%	387,283	16.22%	14,567	9.57%	514	-39.07%
1995	5,480	5.55%	359,946	-7.06%	15,694	7.74%	357	-30.49%
1996	5,289	-3.49%	349,537	-2.89%	17,683	12.67%	240	-32.85%

3 Major products* 3 種主要產品 *	Output 產量	Sales volume 銷售量	Unit 單位
a) Drain Cement Pipe 水泥排水管	3,184,664	3,025,431	ton 噸
b) Cement Sleeper 水泥軌枕	1,591,499	1,416,434	ton 噸
c) Cement Pole 水泥電桿	5,511,545	5,346,198	piece 根

Top 10 firms by revenue (year founded) 收入排名前 10 家企業（創辦年份）	City 城市	Province 省	Telephone / fax 電話 / 傳真	Number of employees 職工人數	Ownership 產業所有權	Revenue ('000 RMB) 銷售收入（千元）	Profit ('000 RMB) (rank) 利潤（千元）（排名）	Total assets ('000 RMB) 總資產（千元）	Major products 主要產品
Hefei Hong Qi Cement General Factory 合肥紅旗水泥總廠(1976)	Hefei 合肥市	Anhui 安徽省	(0551)4483965	1,074	Collectively-owned 集體	294,240	31780(1)	92,150	a
Zhangjiagang Hou Cheng Building Materials Factory 張家港市后塍建築材料廠(1992)	Suzhou 蘇州市	Jiangsu 江蘇省	(0512)8771088	300	Collectively-owned 集體	155,000	5872(11)	131,308	o
Ningbo Zhe Dong Cement Products Factory 寧波浙東水泥製品有限公司(1986)	Ningbo 寧波市	Zhejiang 浙江省	(0574)8412769 (0574)8412229	500	Collectively-owned 集體	141,734	5518(13)	42,502	o
Jiangsu Oasis Group 江蘇綠洲集團(1990)	Wuxi 無錫市	Jiangsu 江蘇省	(0510)5739080	363	Collectively-owned 集體	141,701	5271(17)	79,839	o
Xi Si Er (Tianjin) Concrete Industrial Co. Ltd. 西斯爾(天津)混凝土工業有限公司(1995)	Tianjin 天津市	Tianjin 天津市	(022)23280812 (022)23280819	576	Foreign-funded 外資	140,481	-18105(1462)	342,593	o
Jiangyin Dong Fang Building Group Co. 江陰東方建築集團公司(1964)	Wuxi 無錫市	Jiangsu 江蘇省	(0510)6221664	1,215	Collectively-owned 集體	138,864	13714(3)	158,206	o
Zhuzhou Bridge Factory 株洲橋樑廠(1959)	Zhuzhou 株洲市	Hunan 湖南省	(0733)8332931 (0733)8331063	3,071	State-owned 國有	130,270	-14990(1460)	298,900	b,c
Rongcheng Li Dao Building Materials General Factory 榮成市俚島建材總廠(1991)	Weihai 威海市	Shandong 山東省	(0896)7661146 (0896)7661146	432	Collectively-owned 集體	130,130	13000(4)	63,990	o
Shanghai Cement Product Manufacturing Factory 上海水泥成品廠(1905)	Shanghai 上海市	Shanghai 上海市	(021)56610292 (021)56952613	799	State-owned 國有	124,316	215(536)	234,437	a
Jiangsu Sha Xia Group Co. Ltd. 江蘇沙霞集團有限公司(1996)	Suzhou 蘇州市	Jiangsu 江蘇省	(0512)2502588 (0512)2501381	1,102	Collectively-owned 集體	120,220	6030(9)	218,740	o

Top 10 Cities by Production Output 產出排名前 10 位城市	Province 省	Market share 市場份額	Number of firms 企業個數
Shanghai 上海市	Shanghai 上海市	9.81%	133
Beijing 北京市	Beijing 北京市	4.25%	96
Suzhou 蘇州市	Jiangsu 江蘇省	3.77%	101
Linyi 臨沂市	Shandong 山東省	2.92%	29
Yantai 煙台市	Shandong 山東省	2.50%	24
Wuxi 無錫市	Jiangsu 江蘇省	2.35%	53
Huaiyin 淮陰市	Jiangsu 江蘇省	2.24%	119
Tianjin 天津市	Tianjin 天津市	2.22%	41
Yancheng 鹽城市	Jiangsu 江蘇省	1.88%	77
Guangzhou 廣州市	Guangdong 廣東省	1.72%	28

10 Major Wholesalers 10 家主要批發商	City 城市	Province 省	Telephone / Fax 電話 / 傳真
Chengdu Sheng Xing Trade Company 成都盛興商貿公司	Chengdu 成都市	Sichuan 四川省	(028)7762591
Shanghai Municipal Administration Engineering Material Company 上海市市政工程材料公司	Shanghai 上海市	Shanghai 上海市	(021)64372632
Shanghai Construction Engineering Material Co. 上海市建築工程材料公司	Shanghai 上海市	Shanghai 上海市	(021)63298630
Yixing Jin San Jiao Zhao Bazaar 宜興市金三角招商城	Wuxi 無錫市	Jiangsu 江蘇省	(0510)7935138 (0510)7935138
Fujian Hua Fu Import & Export Company 福建省華福進出口公司	Fuzhou 福州市	Fujian 福建省	(0591)7810477 (0591)7810485
China Building Goods & Materials Company 中國建築物資公司	Beijing 北京市	Beijing 北京市	(010)68586253
Dalian Jinzhou Xin Gang Industry & Trade Company 大連金州新港工貿公司	Dalian 大連市	Liaoning 遼寧省	(0411)7624747
Shanghai Zhan Dong Industrial Co. Ltd. 上海展東實業有限公司	Shanghai 上海市	Shanghai 上海市	(021)58201778 (021)58200874
China Building Materials and Equipment Import & Export Company 中國建築材料及設備進出口公司	Beijing 北京市	Beijing 北京市	(010)68393420
Dandong Chemical Light Industry Material Company Chemical Construction Material Marketing Station 丹東市化工輕工材料公司化工建材經銷站	Dandong 丹東市	Liaoning 遼寧省	(0415)2146396

*Also include sales by firms outside this industry.包括本行業以外廠家的銷售。"o" stands for "others". "o" 代表"其他產品"。

3123: Concrete Construction Member 混凝土結構構件製造業

The industry accounts for 0.203% of the total revenue of China's industrial sector in 1996. The revenue growth rate of the industry is 18.8% from 1995, as compared to the growth rate of China's industrial sector, 9.51%. The rate of return on asset is 3.01%. 82.37% of all firms in the industry made a profit while 12.27% had negative returns. The top province in terms of the industry's revenue is Jiangsu, accounting for 16.34% of the total revenue.
本行業在1996年佔全行業總產值0.203%，行業年增長率為18.8%（全國工業年增長率9.51%）。行業的資產回報率3.01%，82.37%的企業盈利，12.27%的企業虧損。銷售收入最高的省份為江蘇省，佔本行業的16.34%。

	Total number of firms 企業總數	Total number of employees 職工總數	Total revenue (mil. RMB) 總銷售收入（百萬元）	Total profit (mil. RMB) 總利潤（百萬元）	Return on assets 資產利潤率 (%)	Return on equity 權益利潤率 (%)	Labour productivity ('000 RMB / worker) 勞動生產率（千元/人）	Debts / assets 資產負債率 (%)	Total assets (mil. RMB) 總資產（百萬元）
Industry Overall 行業總體	5,089	241,028	11,792	386	3.01	8.93	48.92	66.30	12,829

	Number of firms 企業個數	Average number of employees 平均職工人數	Average revenue ('000 RMB) 平均銷售收入（千元）	Average profit ('000 RMB) 平均利潤（千元）	Return on assets 資產利潤率 (%)	Return on equity 權益利潤率 (%)	Labour productivity ('000 RMB / worker) 勞動生產率（千元/人）	Average debts / assets 平均資產負債率(%)	Average Total assets ('000 RMB) 平均總資產（千元）
By ownership 產業所有權									
State-owned 國有	325	168	6,240	15	0.10	0.31	37.06	66.81	14,871
Collectively-owned 集體	4,668	38	1,926	91	6.56	18.88	50.18	65.24	1,388
Privately-owned 私有	13	36	3,034	45	3.06	8.32	84.27	63.19	1,480
Domestic JVs 聯營	22	67	8,113	264	2.99	7.28	121.67	58.91	8,814
Joint stock 股份制	28	95	5,806	200	2.99	8.31	61.23	63.98	6,683
Foreign-funded 外資	11	112	11,319	-1,673	-4.33	-15.47	100.66	72.03	38,646
Overseas Chinese-funded 港澳台資	18	88	14,399	-2,103	-5.55	-19.85	164.46	72.04	37,901
By size 規模									
Large 大型	6	2,359	179,280	902	0.37	1.09	76.00	66.38	246,492
Medium 中型	23	665	38,121	709	1.06	3.11	57.28	66.07	67,110
Small 小型	5,047	42	1,949	72	3.72	11.03	46.83	66.33	1,943
By regional distribution 地區分布									
Central-North 華北	447	83	2,867	100	1.92	5.77	34.63	66.76	5,198
Beijing 北京	68	162	5,809	130	0.88	2.72	35.75	67.59	14,725
Tianjin 天津	25	237	8,391	207	1.06	2.65	35.43	59.96	19,520
Hebei 河北	192	51	2,501	169	8.22	25.04	49.51	67.18	2,056
Shanxi 山西	72	60	1,288	3	0.12	0.38	21.36	68.20	2,209
Inner Mongolia 內蒙	90	67	1,155	-23	-0.74	-2.86	17.31	74.22	3,115
Northeast 東北	404	70	2,311	78	2.10	6.30	33.22	66.58	3,729
Liaoning 遼寧	172	75	2,682	104	2.11	5.56	35.63	61.99	4,923
Jilin 吉林	80	72	1,540	65	2.08	7.92	21.41	73.76	3,104
Heilongjiang 黑龍江	152	62	2,297	57	2.10	7.43	37.13	71.69	2,706
Central East 華東	1,525	57	3,502	134	4.00	13.28	61.53	69.88	3,356
Shanghai 上海	56	180	18,903	634	2.72	12.85	104.85	78.88	23,368
Jiangsu 江蘇	502	55	3,838	78	1.88	6.43	69.19	70.69	4,166
Zhejiang 浙江	222	37	2,361	120	4.16	13.58	63.24	69.35	2,876
Anhui 安徽	434	46	2,163	122	14.41	32.99	47.31	56.31	846
Fujian 福建	18	25	3,021	43	1.91	5.95	119.78	67.90	2,267
Jiangxi 江西	87	33	538	8	0.61	1.13	16.37	46.20	1,378
Shandong 山東	206	84	3,839	237	8.84	22.35	45.44	60.44	2,681
Central-South 中南	1,509	34	2,200	64	3.63	9.16	65.29	60.33	1,762
Henan 河南	481	25	1,289	60	5.22	15.25	51.86	65.75	1,142
Hubei 湖北	375	56	4,345	214	9.71	19.50	77.05	50.21	2,202
Hunan 湖南	589	25	1,320	62	11.88	26.10	52.13	54.50	521
Guangdong 廣東	35	58	7,653	-1,404	-5.70	-18.51	132.54	69.20	24,638
Guangxi 廣西	29	28	855	14	0.37	0.83	30.72	56.02	3,957
Hainan 海南									
Southwest 西南	801	29	700	6	0.71	2.16	23.97	67.19	805
Chongqing 重慶	231	17	417	6	1.98	4.85	24.59	59.24	282
Sichuan 四川	496	32	744	9	1.02	2.79	23.48	63.36	891
Guizhou 貴州	52	36	944	-38	-3.50	-33.73	26.01	89.61	1,078
Yunnan 雲南	22	99	2,095	43	1.16	5.48	21.14	78.92	3,695
Tibet 西藏									
Northwest 西北	403	37	883	9	0.66	1.59	23.92	58.47	1,432
Shaanxi 陝西	210	36	875	4	0.32	0.85	24.61	62.46	1,336
Gansu 甘肅	81	49	1,269	47	2.37	4.47	26.13	47.02	1,963
Qinghai 青海	11	41	119	-4	-1.52	-5.97	2.93	74.62	240
Ningxia 寧夏	20	42	910	-16	-0.82	-1.89	21.84	56.54	1,884
Xinjiang 新疆	81	27	615	-6	-0.53	-1.57	22.65	65.99	1,200

3123: Concrete Construction Member 混凝土結構構件製造業

Year 年份	Number of firms 企業個數	Rate of change 每年變化 (%)	Number of employees 職工人數（人）	Rate of change 每年變化 (%)	Total revenue (mil. RMB) 總銷售收入（百萬元）	Rate of change 每年變化 (%)	Total profit (mil. RMB) 總利潤（百萬元）	Rate of change 每年變化 (%)
1993	4,864		252,437		7,746		340	
1994	5,031	3.43%	257,373	1.96%	9,311	20.21%	384	12.69%
1995	5,182	3.00%	244,217	-5.11%	9,928	6.62%	309	-19.36%
1996	5,089	-1.79%	241,028	-1.31%	11,792	18.78%	386	24.80%

3 Major products* 3 種主要產品 *	Output 產量	Sales volume 銷售量	Unit 單位
a) Pressure Cement Pip 水泥壓力管	11,893	10,942	1,000 metre 千米
b) Cement Drain Pipe 水泥排水管	25,960	25,182	1,000 metre 千米
c) Cement Prefabricated Member 水泥預製構件	30,472,842	30,777,570	cubic metre 立方米

Top 10 firms by revenue (year founded) 收入排名前 10 家企業（創辦年份）	City 城市	Province 省	Telephone / fax 電話 / 傳真	Number of employees 職工人數	Ownership 產業所有權	Revenue ('000 RMB) 銷售收入（千元）	Profit ('000 RMB) (rank) 利潤（千元）（排名）	Total assets ('000 RMB) 總資產（千元）	Major products 主要產品
Shanghai Building Components Products Co. 上海市建築構件製品公司(1993)	Shanghai 上海市	Shanghai 上海市	(021)64366761 (021)65436700	3,916	State-owned 國有	388,542	2085(26)	360,283	c
Jiangsu Xing Ye Building Group Co. 江蘇興業建築集團公司(1964)	Wuxi 無錫市	Jiangsu 江蘇省	(0510)6891678 (0510)6891678	1,360	Collectively-owned 集體	280,800	6140(5)	107,410	c
Changyi Xin Ying Industrial General Company 昌邑市新營實業總公司(1983)	Weifang 濰坊市	Shandong 山東省	(0536)7832068	850	Collectively-owned 集體	191,720	11680(2)	41,290	c
Shanghai San Hang Concrete Products Co. 上海三航混凝土製品公司(1958)	Shanghai 上海市	Shanghai 上海市	(021)58610278 (021)58610771	653	State-owned 國有	161,404	4002(9)	183,972	a,c
Suzhou Jin Yu Construction Group Co. 蘇州市金宇建設集團公司(1971)	Suzhou 蘇州市	Jiangsu 江蘇省	(0512)2751343 (0512)7240110	1,384	Collectively-owned 集體	150,727	3905(10)	354,170	c
Shanghai Residence Construction Components and Fittings General Company 上海住宅建設構配件總公司(1982)	Shanghai 上海市	Shanghai 上海市	(021)58837060 (021)58800722	843	State-owned 國有	129,558	10013(3)	251,060	c
Tianjin Building Components Co. 天津市建築構件公司(1964)	Tianjin 天津市	Tianjin 天津市	(022)24312963 (022)24312963	3,817	State-owned 國有	94,348	-1976(1168)	272,876	o
Dalian Building Components Engineering Co. 大連建築構件工程公司(1952)	Dalian 大連市	Liaoning 遼寧省	(0411)4304968 (0411)4345234	1,868	State-owned 國有	82,176	88(666)	286,325	c
Jiangyin West Suburb Prefabricated Components Factory 江陰市西郊預製構件廠(1976)	Wuxi 無錫市	Jiangsu 江蘇省	(0510)6883973	450	Collectively-owned 集體	79,956	1736(36)	107,019	c
Changzhou Building Components General Factory 常州建築構件總廠(1954)	Changzhou 常州市	Jiangsu 江蘇省	(0519)6602611 (0519)6600285	931	State-owned 國有	69,847	353(241)	118,736	c

Top 10 Cities by Production Output 產出排名前 10 位城市	Province 省	Market share 市場份額	Number of firms 企業個數
Beijing 北京市	Beijing 北京市	18.02%	65
Shanghai 上海市	Shanghai 上海市	10.43%	76
Changzhou 常州市	Jiangsu 江蘇省	2.31%	40
Tianjin 天津市	Tianjin 天津市	2.30%	24
Weifang 濰坊市	Shandong 山東省	2.15%	21
Zhumadian 駐馬店市	Henan 河南省	1.88%	81
Hangzhou 杭州市	Zhejiang 浙江省	1.81%	39
Chuzhou 滁州市	Anhui 安徽省	1.71%	85
Fuyang 阜陽市	Anhui 安徽省	1.61%	102
Guangzhou 廣州市	Guangdong 廣東省	1.50%	10

10 Major Wholesalers 10 家主要批發商	City 城市	Province 省	Telephone / Fax 電話 / 傳真
Chengdu Sheng Xing Trade Company 成都盛興商貿公司	Chengdu 成都市	Sichuan 四川省	(028)7762591
Shanghai Municipal Administration Engineering Material Company 上海市市政工程材料公司	Shanghai 上海市	Shanghai 上海市	(021)64372632
Shanghai Construction Engineering Material Co. 上海市建築工程材料公司	Shanghai 上海市	Shanghai 上海市	(021)63298630
Yixing Jin San Jiao Zhao Bazaar 宜興市金三角招商城	Wuxi 無錫市	Jiangsu 江蘇省	(0510)7935138 (0510)7935138
Fujian Hua Fu Import & Export Company 福建省華福進出口公司	Fuzhou 福州市	Fujian 福建省	(0591)7810477 (0591)7810485
China Building Goods & Materials Company 中國建築物資公司	Beijing 北京市	Beijing 北京市	(010)68586253
Dalian Jinzhou Xin Gang Industry & Trade Company 大連金州新港工貿公司	Dalian 大連市	Liaoning 遼寧省	(0411)7624747
Shanghai Zhan Dong Industrial Co. Ltd. 上海展東實業有限公司	Shanghai 上海市	Shanghai 上海市	(021)58201778 (021)58200874
China Building Materials and Equipment Import & Export Company 中國建築材料及設備進出口公司	Beijing 北京市	Beijing 北京市	(010)68393420
Dandong Chemical Light Industry Material Company Chemical Construction Material Marketing Station 丹東市化工輕工材料公司化工建材經銷站	Dandong 丹東市	Liaoning 遼寧省	(0415)2146396

*Also include sales by firms outside this industry.包括本行業以外廠家的銷售。"o" stands for "others". "o" 代表"其他產品"。

3124: Asbestos Cement Products 石棉水泥製品業

The industry accounts for 0.026% of the total revenue of China's industrial sector in 1996. The revenue growth rate of the industry is 2.3% from 1995, as compared to the growth rate of China's industrial sector, 9.51%. The rate of return on asset is 1.64%. 70.53% of all firms in the industry made a profit while 21.21% had negative returns. The top province in terms of the industry's revenue is Jiangsu, accounting for 20.63% of the total revenue.

本行業在1996年佔全行業總產值0.026%，行業年增長率為2.3%（全國工業年增長率9.51%）。行業的資產回報率1.64%，70.53%的企業盈利，21.21%的企業虧損。銷售收入最高的省份為江蘇省，佔本行業的20.63%。

	Total number of firms 企業總數	Total number of employees 職工總數	Total revenue (mil. RMB) 總銷售收入（百萬元）	Total profit (mil. RMB) 總利潤（百萬元）	Return on assets 資產利潤率 (%)	Return on equity 權益利潤率 (%)	Labour productivity ('000 RMB / worker) 勞動生產率（千元/人）	Debts / assets 資產負債率 (%)	Total assets (mil. RMB) 總資產（百萬元）
Industry Overall 行業總體	279	30,210	1,497	33	1.64	4.11	49.55	60.00	1,999

	Number of firms 企業個數	Average number of employees 平均職工人數	Average revenue ('000 RMB) 平均銷售收入（千元）	Average profit ('000 RMB) 平均利潤（千元）	Return on assets 資產利潤率 (%)	Return on equity 權益利潤率 (%)	Labour productivity ('000 RMB / worker) 勞動生產率（千元/人）	Average debts / assets 平均資產負債率(%)	Average Total assets ('000 RMB) 平均總資產（千元）
By ownership 產業所有權									
State-owned 國有	32	224	7,125	-94	-0.55	-1.22	31.85	54.71	16,906
Collectively-owned 集體	236	88	4,455	174	3.54	10.00	50.63	64.64	4,914
Privately-owned 私有	2	110	5,226	-11	-0.15	-0.37	47.51	60.78	7,308
Domestic JVs 聯營	3	59	2,350	266	10.78	61.45	39.84	82.47	2,472
Joint stock 股份制	1	548	20,431	2,320	8.50	17.54	37.28	51.55	27,296
Foreign-funded 外資	4	309	36,221	-1,704	-3.15	-5.20	117.31	39.42	54,121
Overseas Chinese-funded 港澳台資	1	108	34,745	-1,294	-4.00	19.90	321.71	120.13	32,317
By size 規模									
Large 大型									
Medium 中型	10	702	35,826	-9,619	-15.29	-28.35	51.04	46.08	62,927
Small 小型	266	87	4,281	486	9.43	28.04	49.22	66.37	5,149
By regional distribution 地區分布									
Central-North 華北	34	78	3,151	95	2.13	5.11	40.66	58.26	4,467
Beijing 北京	5	10	788	-20	-1.45	-2.61	77.25	44.57	1,382
Tianjin 天津	3	259	4,570	-247	-2.35	-4.02	17.62	41.39	10,477
Hebei 河北	19	76	4,152	208	4.04	10.75	54.82	62.43	5,159
Shanxi 山西	3	49	780	37	1.77	4.26	16.03	58.52	2,073
Inner Mongolia 內蒙	4	55	2,065	3	0.11	0.58	37.38	81.29	2,325
Northeast 東北	58	137	4,321	20	0.30	1.19	31.48	74.56	6,702
Liaoning 遼寧	24	136	3,566	-98	-1.18	-9.17	26.31	87.19	8,293
Jilin 吉林	15	200	5,981	-3	-0.03	-0.09	29.91	63.13	8,381
Heilongjiang 黑龍江	19	90	3,965	187	5.57	13.17	44.08	57.72	3,366
Central East 華東	77	121	8,076	318	3.28	7.63	66.60	57.05	9,709
Shanghai 上海	3	88	4,560	80	1.61	4.41	51.62	63.59	4,980
Jiangsu 江蘇	24	152	12,866	205	1.88	4.98	84.81	62.23	10,910
Zhejiang 浙江	2	98	8,495	500	4.94	22.17	86.68	77.72	10,120
Anhui 安徽	23	55	4,089	487	21.00	55.20	74.70	61.96	2,317
Fujian 福建	4	154	11,173	353	1.87	8.69	72.67	78.45	18,830
Jiangxi 江西	8	98	2,986	23	0.81	2.42	30.36	66.52	2,778
Shandong 山東	13	198	9,213	427	1.85	3.30	46.53	43.85	23,054
Central-South 中南	69	74	4,811	88	1.44	2.42	64.90	40.65	6,124
Henan 河南	25	63	2,346	76	3.54	17.90	37.21	80.22	2,158
Hubei 湖北	18	44	2,269	29	1.58	5.62	51.89	71.98	1,869
Hunan 湖南	12	120	5,367	101	2.88	5.51	44.72	47.73	3,501
Guangdong 廣東	8	134	18,976	249	0.72	1.00	141.75	27.47	34,428
Guangxi 廣西	6	40	2,708	72	2.45	4.78	67.43	48.75	2,927
Hainan 海南									
Southwest 西南	30	141	5,373	-102	-1.26	-7.10	38.17	82.24	8,059
Chongqing 重慶	4	187	4,283	-889	-9.30	-64.83	22.89	85.65	9,560
Sichuan 四川	17	88	3,062	53	1.31	-25.81	34.80	105.07	4,081
Guizhou 貴州	3	187	9,677	47	0.35	0.83	51.84	58.62	13,527
Yunnan 雲南	6	238	10,533	-118	-0.75	-2.90	44.26	74.14	15,763
Tibet 西藏									
Northwest 西北	11	85	2,195	85	2.00	4.12	25.71	51.55	4,236
Shaanxi 陝西	7	82	1,726	37	1.39	4.48	21.05	69.07	2,679
Gansu 甘肅	2	9	300	5	2.08	9.09	35.29	77.08	240
Qinghai 青海									
Ningxia 寧夏	2	174	5,730	330	2.41	3.96	32.93	39.09	13,685
Xinjiang 新疆									

3124: Asbestos Cement Products 石棉水泥製品業

Year 年份	Number of firms 企業個數	Rate of change 每年變化 (%)	Number of employees 職工人數 (人)	Rate of change 每年變化 (%)	Total revenue (mil. RMB) 總銷售收入 (百萬元)	Rate of change 每年變化 (%)	Total profit (mil. RMB) 總利潤 (百萬元)	Rate of change 每年變化 (%)
1993	264		23,842		1,043		46	
1994	276	4.55%	29,821	25.08%	1,041	-0.12%	9	-79.93%
1995	296	7.25%	32,901	10.33%	1,463	40.43%	7	-26.40%
1996	279	-5.74%	30,210	-8.18%	1,497	2.32%	33	387.80%

3 Major products* 3 種主要產品 *	Output 產量	Sales volume 銷售量	Unit 單位
a) Asbestos Cement Shingle 石棉水泥瓦	90,138,690	86,533,142	square metre 平方米
b) Cement Prefabricated Member 水泥預製構件	190,217	192,120	cubic metre 立方米

Top 10 firms by revenue (year founded) 收入排名前 10 家企業 (創辦年份)	City 城市	Province 省	Telephone / fax 電話 / 傳真	Number of employees 職工人數	Ownership 產業所有權	Revenue ('000 RMB) 銷售收入 (千元)	Profit ('000 RMB) (rank) 利潤 (千元) (排名)	Total assets ('000 RMB) 總資產 (千元)	Major products 主要產品
Guangzhou Eternit Co. Ltd. 廣州埃特尼特有限公司(1987)	Guangzhou 廣州市	Guangdong 廣東省	(020)81587551 (020)81803536	363	Foreign-funded 外資	80,037	3066(3)	78,077	a
Yancheng New Type Plate Factory 鹽城新型板材廠(1986)	Yancheng 鹽城市	Jiangsu 江蘇省	(0515)8621222	306	Domestic JVs 聯營	49,410	2180(5)	27,670	o
Jiangsu Lan Ying Group Co. Ltd. 江蘇藍鷹集團有限公司(1956)	Suzhou 蘇州市	Jiangsu 江蘇省	(0512)8500819 (0512)8500819	276	Collectively-owned 集體	47,100	3080(2)	49,906	o
Zhuzhou Fibre Cement Products Factory 株洲纖維水泥製品廠(1962)	Zhuzhou 株洲市	Hunan 湖南省	(0733)8221168 (0733)8222287	800	State-owned 國有	46,236	105(66)	32,320	a
Fujian Jian Ming Building Materials Group Sanming New Type Building Materials General Factory 福建建明建材集團三明新型建材總廠(1980)	Sanming 三明市	Fujian 福建省	(0598)8223874 (0598)8224457	558	Domestic JVs 聯營	44,348	1402(7)	72,981	a
Yantai Ishikawa Industry Co. Ltd. 煙台石川實業有限公司(1994)	Yantai 煙台市	Shandong 山東省	(0535)6531648 (0535)6536245	755	Foreign-funded 外資	41,936	2309(4)	113,572	o
Nanjing Xie He Asbestos Cement Products Factory 南京協和石棉水泥製品廠(1993)	Nanjing 南京市	Jiangsu 江蘇省	(025)2290301	107	Collectively-owned 集體	41,720	1530(6)	13,060	o
Dongguan Nan Ying Rock Wool Pipe Making Factory Co. Ltd. 東莞南鷹岩棉製管廠有限公司(1992)	Dongguan 東莞市	Guangdong 廣東省	(0769)2233743	243	Overseas Chinese-funded 港澳台資	41,354	-486(114)	137,308	o
Jilin Song Jiang Building Materials Industrial Co. 吉林市松江建築材料工業公司(1980)	Jilin 吉林市	Jilin 吉林省	(0432)2732036	1,316	Collectively-owned 集體	32,249	-1233(119)	36,984	a
Wujiang New Building Materials Factory 吳江市新型建築材料廠(1964)	Suzhou 蘇州市	Jiangsu 江蘇省	(0512)3330357	518	Collectively-owned 集體	31,786	121(62)	57,131	a

Top 10 Cities by Production Output 產出排名前 10 位城市	Province 省	Market share 市場份額	Number of firms 企業個數
Changchun 長春市	Jilin 吉林省	5.29%	3
Suzhou 蘇州市	Jiangsu 江蘇省	5.23%	2
Zhuzhou 株洲市	Hunan 湖南省	4.03%	1
Shanghai 上海市	Shanghai 上海市	4.01%	8
Sanming 三明市	Fujian 福建省	3.86%	1
Qingdao 青島市	Shandong 山東省	3.61%	2
Yancheng 鹽城市	Jiangsu 江蘇省	3.01%	5
Yantai 煙台市	Shandong 山東省	3.00%	3
Shenyang 瀋陽市	Liaoning 遼寧省	2.91%	6
Guangzhou 廣州市	Guangdong 廣東省	2.90%	2

10 Major Wholesalers 10 家主要批發商	City 城市	Province 省	Telephone / Fax 電話 / 傳真
Chengdu Sheng Xing Trade Company 成都盛興商貿公司	Chengdu 成都市	Sichuan 四川省	(028)7762591
Shanghai Municipal Administration Engineering Material Company 上海市市政工程材料公司	Shanghai 上海市	Shanghai 上海市	(021)64372632
Shanghai Construction Engineering Material Co. 上海市建築工程材料公司	Shanghai 上海市	Shanghai 上海市	(021)63298630
Yixing Jin San Jiao Zhao Bazaar 宜興市金三角招商城	Wuxi 無錫市	Jiangsu 江蘇省	(0510)7935138 (0510)7935138
Fujian Hua Fu Import & Export Company 福建省華福進出口公司	Fuzhou 福州市	Fujian 福建省	(0591)7810477 (0591)7810485
China Building Goods & Materials Company 中國建築物資公司	Beijing 北京市	Beijing 北京市	(010)68586253
Dalian Jinzhou Xin Gang Industry & Trade Company 大連金州新港工貿公司	Dalian 大連市	Liaoning 遼寧省	(0411)7624747
Shanghai Zhan Dong Industrial Co. Ltd. 上海展東實業有限公司	Shanghai 上海市	Shanghai 上海市	(021)58201778 (021)58200874
China Building Materials and Equipment Import & Export Company 中國建築材料及設備進出口公司	Beijing 北京市	Beijing 北京市	(010)68393420
Dandong Chemical Light Industry Material Company Chemical Construction Material Marketing Station 丹東市化工輕工材料公司化工建材經銷站	Dandong 丹東市	Liaoning 遼寧省	(0415)2146396

*Also include sales by firms outside this industry.包括本行業以外廠家的銷售。"o" stands for "others". "o" 代表 "其他產品"。

3129: Other Cement and Asbestos Products 其他水泥及石棉製品業

The industry accounts for 0.007% of the total revenue of China's industrial sector in 1996. The revenue growth rate of the industry is 10.6% from 1995, as compared to the growth rate of China's industrial sector, 9.51%. The rate of return on asset is 3.33%. 65.71% of all firms in the industry made a profit while 18.01% had negative returns. The top province in terms of the industry's revenue is Liaoning, accounting for 15.55% of the total revenue.
本行業在1996年佔全行業總產值0.007%，行業年增長率為10.6%（全國工業年增長率9.51%）。行業的資產回報率3.33%，65.71%的企業盈利，18.01%的企業虧損。銷售收入最高的省份為遼寧省，佔本行業的15.55%。

	Total number of firms 企業總數	Total number of employees 職工總數	Total revenue (mil. RMB) 總銷售收入（百萬元）	Total profit (mil. RMB) 總利潤（百萬元）	Return on assets 資產利潤率 (%)	Return on equity 權益利潤率 (%)	Labour productivity ('000 RMB / worker) 勞動生產率（千元/人）	Debts / assets 資產負債率 (%)	Total assets (mil. RMB) 總資產（百萬元）
Industry Overall 行業總體	176	10,231	426	15	3.33	10.42	41.64	68.05	441

	Number of firms 企業個數	Average number of employees 平均職工人數	Average revenue ('000 RMB) 平均銷售收入（千元）	Average profit ('000 RMB) 平均利潤（千元）	Return on assets 資產利潤率 (%)	Return on equity 權益利潤率 (%)	Labour productivity ('000 RMB / worker) 勞動生產率（千元/人）	Average debts / assets 平均資產負債率(%)	Average Total assets ('000 RMB) 平均總資產（千元）
By ownership 產業所有權									
State-owned 國有	15	19	400				20.91	53.33	1,000
Collectively-owned 集體	144	60	1,881	202	14.68	46.68	31.27	68.54	1,376
Privately-owned 私有	2	67	1,252	371	75.06	282.59	18.69	73.44	494
Domestic JVs 聯營	5	123	11,576	539	4.64	8.71	93.96	46.75	11,623
Joint stock 股份制	1	24	1,198	64	8.16	15.93	49.92	48.79	787
Foreign-funded 外資	6	56	5,372	-5,078	-26.45	-75.33	95.93	64.89	19,200
Overseas Chinese-funded 港澳台資	3	57	18,409	4,292	24.41	-3308.51	324.86	100.74	17,586
By size 規模									
Large 大型									
Medium 中型	2	490	30,838	-312	-1.47	-2.78	62.94	47.33	21,278
Small 小型	173	53	2,106	90	3.92	13.18	39.43	70.24	2,303
By regional distribution 地區分布									
Central-North 華北	33	35	1,415	71	4.53	8.85	40.88	48.87	1,572
Beijing 北京	11	32	1,111	8	0.43	2.15	34.42	80.18	1,917
Tianjin 天津	7	13	1,787	136	7.52	12.01	139.00	37.42	1,806
Hebei 河北	4	17	543	75	18.18	52.63	32.39	65.45	413
Shanxi 山西	3	31	770	-23	-2.17	-8.54	25.11	74.84	1,073
Inner Mongolia 內蒙	8	67	2,184	135	8.13	8.27	32.47	1.73	1,661
Northeast 東北	28	77	3,929	146	5.45	20.07	50.89	72.85	2,682
Liaoning 遼寧	11	156	6,022	249	4.83	24.84	38.71	80.54	5,158
Jilin 吉林	8	30	1,176	39	3.58	7.11	38.72	49.71	1,084
Heilongjiang 黑龍江	9	23	3,819	116	10.74	20.84	165.24	48.45	1,076
Central East 華東	57	67	3,028	196	5.05	13.24	44.93	61.83	3,877
Shanghai 上海	10	36	3,039	302	6.13	17.05	83.95	64.04	4,928
Jiangsu 江蘇	13	71	3,676	-21	-0.45	-1.42	51.44	68.34	4,633
Zhejiang 浙江	9	25	2,468	27	0.97	2.82	99.60	65.69	2,762
Anhui 安徽	5	219	1,218	40	5.35	7.52	5.56	28.88	748
Fujian 福建	9	22	2,618	89	3.02	3.49	118.99	13.41	2,942
Jiangxi 江西	4	17	708	-18	-3.43	53.85	42.88	106.37	510
Shandong 山東	7	138	5,674	1,036	13.33	53.35	41.08	75.01	7,769
Central-South 中南	33	44	1,861	-142	-9.08	46.75	42.73	119.44	1,559
Henan 河南	3	32	277	13	1.99	7.27	8.65	73.13	670
Hubei 湖北	16	46	3,068	89	9.40	29.79	66.78	68.44	951
Hunan 湖南	6	72	850	80	37.50	960.00	11.86	96.09	213
Guangdong 廣東	7	23	897	-947	-20.32	42.23	38.53	148.12	4,661
Guangxi 廣西									
Hainan 海南	1	13	120	10	3.23	3.23	9.23		310
Southwest 西南	16	51	1,028	25	1.76	3.49	20.27	49.76	1,424
Chongqing 重慶	2	33	544	-53	-8.33	-11.52	16.43	27.70	636
Sichuan 四川	9	47	855	33	3.17	4.32	18.15	26.71	1,046
Guizhou 貴州	4	14	353	43	12.59	25.00	26.11	49.63	338
Yunnan 雲南	1	269	6,380	380	3.47	12.26	23.72	71.76	10,940
Tibet 西藏									
Northwest 西北	9	93	2,068	151	7.17	16.61	22.21	56.83	2,108
Shaanxi 陝西	5	67	2,574	254	10.88	23.83	38.42	54.33	2,334
Gansu 甘肅	4	126	1,435	23	1.23	3.15	11.41	60.82	1,825
Qinghai 青海									
Ningxia 寧夏									
Xinjiang 新疆									

3129: Other Cement and Asbestos Products 其他水泥及石棉製品業

Year 年份	Number of firms 企業個數	Rate of change 每年變化 (%)	Number of employees 職工人數（人）	Rate of change 每年變化 (%)	Total revenue (mil. RMB) 總銷售收入（百萬元）	Rate of change 每年變化 (%)	Total profit (mil. RMB) 總利潤（百萬元）	Rate of change 每年變化 (%)
1993	179		9,283		439		15	
1994	215	20.11%	11,341	22.17%	849	93.31%	28	88.72%
1995	188	-12.56%	10,329	-8.92%	385	-54.64%	3	-90.63%
1996	176	-6.38%	10,231	-0.95%	426	10.60%	15	462.01%

3 Major products* 3種主要產品*	Output 產量	Sales volume 銷售量	Unit 單位
a) Asbestos Cement Shingle 石棉水泥瓦	370,542	355,721	square metre 平方米
b) Cement Prefabricated Member 水泥預製構件	196,558	198,524	cubic metre 立方米

Top 10 firms by revenue (year founded) 收入排名前10家企業（創辦年份）	City 城市	Province 省	Telephone / fax 電話／傳真	Number of employees 職工人數	Ownership 產業所有權	Revenue ('000 RMB) 銷售收入（千元）	Profit ('000 RMB) (rank) 利潤（千元）（排名）	Total assets ('000 RMB) 總資產（千元）	Major products 主要產品
Liao He Oil Field Liao Nan Industrial General Company 遼河油田遼南實業總公司(1992)	Panjin 盤錦市	Liaoning 遼寧省	(0427)7541171	432	Collectively-owned 集體	55,000	1330(4)	37,400	o
Municipal Administration Er Company Tong Component Qibao Branch 市政二公司砼構件七寶分廠(1995)	Shanghai 上海市	Shanghai 上海市	(021)64195247	70	Domestic JVs 聯營	37,662	0(33)	3,253	o
Pingyuan Building Materials General Factory 平原縣建築材料總廠(1970)	Dezhou 德州市	Shandong 山東省	(0534)4211260 (0534)4211260	305	Collectively-owned 集體	20,449	100(20)	29,999	o
Dongshan Kang Mei Zhen Construction Material Products Factory 東山縣康美鎮建材製品廠(1987)	Zhangzhou 漳州市	Fujian 福建省	(0596)5620235	26	Private-owned 私營	18,000	850(8)	7,759	o
Shanghai Ba Zao Industrial General Company 上海八灶實業總公司(1992)	Shanghai 上海市	Shanghai 上海市	(021)58592828 (021)58590587	278	Collectively-owned 集體	16,601	-611(42)	65,015	o
Changqing Changtai Group 長清縣長泰集團(1990)	Ji'nan 濟南市	Shandong 山東省		382	Collectively-owned 集體	14,960	6840(1)	22,030	b
Wujin No.4 Building Materials Component Factory 武進市第四建材構件廠(1976)	Changzhou 常州市	Jiangsu 江蘇省	(0519)3311175	165	Collectively-owned 集體	13,620	57(24)	10,787	b
Nanjing Fibre Cement Products Factory 南京纖維水泥製品廠(1989)	Nanjing 南京市	Jiangsu 江蘇省	(025)7530347	180	Domestic JVs 聯營	9,360	0(35)	22,429	a
Yuyao Municipal Administration Engineering Company 余姚市市政工程公司(1979)	Ningbo 寧波市	Zhejiang 浙江省	(0574)2640177	32	Collectively-owned 集體	9,066	152(15)	18,637	o
Shanghai Qingpu Trade General Company 上海青浦物貿置業總公司(1996)	Shanghai 上海市	Shanghai 上海市	(021)59291387	19	Collectively-owned 集體	8,829	1448(3)	17,324	o

Top 10 Cities by Production Output 產出排名前10位城市	Province 省	Market share 市場份額	Number of firms 企業個數
Suzhou 蘇州市	Jiangsu 江蘇省	19.88%	9
Shanghai 上海市	Shanghai 上海市	11.58%	21
Chaohu 巢湖市	Anhui 安徽省	11.48%	2
Linyi 臨沂市	Shandong 山東省	6.04%	2
Dezhou 德州市	Shandong 山東省	5.54%	3
Beijing 北京市	Beijing 北京市	5.20%	11
Dalian 大連市	Liaoning 遼寧省	4.55%	2
Liu'an 六安市	Anhui 安徽省	4.07%	4
Nanjing 南京市	Jiangsu 江蘇省	2.44%	2
Hangzhou 杭州市	Zhejiang 浙江省	2.42%	3

10 Major Wholesalers 10家主要批發商	City 城市	Province 省	Telephone / Fax 電話／傳真
Chengdu Sheng Xing Trade Company 成都盛興商貿公司	Chengdu 成都市	Sichuan 四川省	(028)7762591
Shanghai Municipal Administration Engineering Material Company 上海市市政工程材料公司	Shanghai 上海市	Shanghai 上海市	(021)64372632
Shanghai Construction Engineering Material Co. 上海市建築工程材料公司	Shanghai 上海市	Shanghai 上海市	(021)63298630
Yixing Jin San Jiao Zhao Bazaar 宜興市金三角招商城	Wuxi 無錫市	Jiangsu 江蘇省	(0510)7935138 (0510)7935138
Fujian Hua Fu Import & Export Company 福建省華福進出口公司	Fuzhou 福州市	Fujian 福建省	(0591)7810477 (0591)7810485
China Building Goods & Materials Company 中國建築物資公司	Beijing 北京市	Beijing 北京市	(010)68586253
Dalian Jinzhou Xin Gang Industry & Trade Company 大連金州新港工貿公司	Dalian 大連市	Liaoning 遼寧省	(0411)7624747
Shanghai Zhan Dong Industrial Co. Ltd. 上海展東實業有限公司	Shanghai 上海市	Shanghai 上海市	(021)58201778 (021)58200874
China Building Materials and Equipment Import & Export Company 中國建築材料及設備進出口公司	Beijing 北京市	Beijing 北京市	(010)68393420
Dandong Chemical Light Industry Material Company Chemical Construction Material Marketing Station 丹東市化工輕工材料公司化工建材經銷站	Dandong 丹東市	Liaoning 遼寧省	(0415)2146396

*Also include sales by firms outside this industry.包括本行業以外廠家的銷售。"o" stands for "others". "o" 代表"其他產品"。

3131: Brick and Tile 磚瓦製造業

The industry accounts for 0.721% of the total revenue of China's industrial sector in 1996. The revenue growth rate of the industry is 12.2% from 1995, as compared to the growth rate of China's industrial sector, 9.51%. The rate of return on asset is 3.71%. 79.99% of all firms in the industry made a profit while 14.28% had negative returns. The top province in terms of the industry's revenue is Jiangsu, accounting for 15.12% of the total revenue.
本行業在 1996 年佔全行業總產值 0.721%，行業年增長率為 12.2%（全國工業年增長率 9.51%）。行業的資產回報率 3.71%，79.99% 的企業盈利，14.28% 的企業虧損。銷售收入最高的省份為江蘇省，佔本行業的 15.12%。

	Total number of firms 企業總數	Total number of employees 職工總數	Total revenue (mil. RMB) 總銷售收入（百萬元）	Total profit (mil. RMB) 總利潤（百萬元）	Return on assets 資產利潤率 (%)	Return on equity 權益利潤率 (%)	Labour productivity ('000 RMB / worker) 勞動生產率（千元/人）	Debts / assets 資產負債率 (%)	Total assets (mil. RMB) 總資產（百萬元）
Industry Overall 行業總體	20,953	2,067,264	41,774	1,590	3.71	9.43	20.21	60.64	42,830

	Number of firms 企業個數	Average number of employees 平均職工人數	Average revenue ('000 RMB) 平均銷售收入（千元）	Average profit ('000 RMB) 平均利潤（千元）	Return on assets 資產利潤率 (%)	Return on equity 權益利潤率 (%)	Labour productivity ('000 RMB / worker) 勞動生產率（千元/人）	Average debts / assets 平均資產負債率(%)	Average Total assets ('000 RMB) 平均總資產（千元）
By ownership 產業所有權									
State-owned 國有	1,262	198	2,668	-157	-1.62	-3.62	13.46	55.36	9,699
Collectively-owned 集體	19,245	93	1,942	93	6.22	16.85	20.97	63.06	1,497
Privately-owned 私有	82	58	1,659	96	9.72	19.84	28.37	51.03	988
Domestic JVs 聯營	184	78	1,719	43	1.96	3.60	22.15	45.65	2,207
Joint stock 股份制	100	107	2,336	98	4.56	11.79	21.86	61.35	2,145
Foreign-funded 外資	34	98	3,513	-470	-2.99	-5.32	35.88	43.81	15,728
Overseas Chinese-funded 港澳台資	36	91	4,697	-417	-3.09	-16.98	51.45	81.82	13,524
By size 規模									
Large 大型	7	1,033	26,265	-5,939	-4.65	-35.18	25.44	86.77	127,590
Medium 中型	57	777	14,956	-737	-1.16	-2.19	19.24	47.05	63,452
Small 小型	20,757	97	1,962	81	4.37	11.30	20.23	61.31	1,845
By regional distribution 地區分布									
Central-North 華北	2,243	97	2,015	169	6.78	14.40	20.78	52.90	2,494
Beijing 北京	121	161	2,775	80	1.55	3.57	17.29	56.57	5,158
Tianjin 天津	129	176	4,181	535	6.94	10.48	23.74	33.78	7,718
Hebei 河北	1,124	95	2,377	225	12.48	32.40	25.01	61.50	1,806
Shanxi 山西	268	74	1,137	46	1.76	3.22	15.46	45.49	2,614
Inner Mongolia 內蒙	601	81	1,111	58	2.82	6.48	13.67	56.53	2,070
Northeast 東北	2,423	105	1,566	55	2.45	7.08	14.92	65.38	2,237
Liaoning 遼寧	759	93	1,246	1	0.05	0.32	13.43	85.26	1,939
Jilin 吉林	673	104	1,463	49	1.80	3.52	14.06	48.93	2,740
Heilongjiang 黑龍江	991	115	1,881	100	4.70	13.78	16.37	65.89	2,124
Central East 華東	7,403	116	2,476	93	4.09	10.42	21.36	60.76	2,266
Shanghai 上海	118	184	3,383	3	0.07	0.20	18.43	65.31	4,873
Jiangsu 江蘇	1,731	159	3,650	74	2.16	6.52	22.92	66.79	3,424
Zhejiang 浙江	761	157	2,939	-38	-0.98	-2.97	18.71	66.99	3,831
Anhui 安徽	1,923	124	2,525	176	12.13	25.82	20.42	53.02	1,454
Fujian 福建	506	28	1,321	96	3.87	6.07	46.61	36.19	2,483
Jiangxi 江西	1,079	51	851	16	1.56	3.84	16.70	59.26	1,034
Shandong 山東	1,285	105	2,283	140	8.23	20.42	21.84	59.68	1,702
Central-South 中南	5,288	84	2,174	71	3.80	9.52	25.90	60.10	1,879
Henan 河南	1,178	81	1,641	57	3.19	10.33	20.19	69.15	1,790
Hubei 湖北	1,157	136	3,346	114	4.37	12.71	24.69	65.61	2,603
Hunan 湖南	1,093	79	2,045	85	6.54	15.86	25.98	58.78	1,298
Guangdong 廣東	811	58	2,432	81	4.37	9.78	41.61	55.29	1,850
Guangxi 廣西	993	55	1,435	25	1.51	2.92	25.98	48.29	1,671
Hainan 海南	56	57	1,102	-84	-1.98	-2.85	19.30	30.57	4,221
Southwest 西南	2,119	87	1,160	-17	-1.08	-3.71	13.28	70.91	1,566
Chongqing 重慶	382	98	1,482	31	1.45	4.94	15.11	70.63	2,103
Sichuan 四川	1,243	91	1,159	25	1.78	7.70	12.68	76.90	1,384
Guizhou 貴州	246	61	695	13	0.93	1.87	11.37	50.01	1,341
Yunnan 雲南	242	80	1,150	9	0.48	1.40	14.29	65.58	1,856
Tibet 西藏	6	47	522	102	4.16	5.06	11.02	17.79	2,445
Northwest 西北	1,477	73	795	35	2.85	6.11	10.87	53.33	1,211
Shaanxi 陝西	611	66	716	34	4.80	11.37	10.77	57.76	698
Gansu 甘肅	482	92	931	43	2.96	6.76	10.15	56.18	1,441
Qinghai 青海	63	86	963	-14	-0.34	-0.54	11.16	36.86	4,067
Ningxia 寧夏	87	68	557	23	2.00	3.94	8.21	49.21	1,136
Xinjiang 新疆	234	51	764	38	2.85	6.43	15.09	55.73	1,336

3131: Brick and Tile 磚瓦製造業

Year 年份	Number of firms 企業個數	Rate of change 每年變化 (%)	Number of employees 職工人數（人）	Rate of change 每年變化 (%)	Total revenue (mil. RMB) 總銷售收入（百萬元）	Rate of change 每年變化 (%)	Total profit (mil. RMB) 總利潤（百萬元）	Rate of change 每年變化 (%)
1993	18,340		1,292,030		22,340		1,139	
1994	20,486	11.70%	1,986,527	53.75%	29,132	30.40%	1,401	23.00%
1995	20,458	-0.14%	2,112,244	6.33%	37,247	27.86%	1,985	41.67%
1996	20,953	2.42%	2,067,264	-2.13%	41,774	12.15%	1,590	-19.90%

3 Major products* 3 種主要產品 *	Output 產量	Sales volume 銷售量	Unit 單位
a) Brick 磚	70,704,832	68,583,687	10,000 chip 萬塊
b) Tile 瓦	6,783,041	6,240,398	10,000 piece 萬片
c) Terrazzo Slab 水磨石板材	1,541,666	1,310,416	square metre 平方米

Top 10 firms by revenue (year founded) 收入排名前 10 家企業 (創辦年份)	City 城市	Province 省	Telephone / fax 電話 / 傳真	Number of employees 職工人數	Ownership 產業所有權	Revenue ('000 RMB) 銷售收入（千元）	Profit ('000 RMB) (rank) 利潤（千元）（排名）	Total assets ('000 RMB) 總資產（千元）	Major products 主要產品
Xuzhou Mine Administrative Bureau Varied Marketing General Company 徐州礦務局多種經營總公司(1979)	Xuzhou 徐州市	Jiangsu 江蘇省	(0516)5753940 (0516)5702342	13,896	Collectively-owned 集體	164,320	-3760(6089)	186,958	a
Hao Sheng (Fujian) Co. Ltd. 豪盛(福建)股份有限公司(1989)	Quanzhou 泉州市	Fujian 福建省	(0595)2688168	563	Joint stock 股份制	151,842	29963(1)	697,493	o
Yulin Nanjiang Zhen Red Brick No.2 Factory 玉林市南江鎮紅磚二廠(1982)	Yulin 玉林市	Guangxi 廣西	(0775)3835285	492	Collectively-owned 集體	141,090	12093(4)	41,833	a
Zhangjiagang Si Gang Jian Hong Industrial Company 張家港市泗港建紅實業公司(1986)	Suzhou 蘇州市	Jiangsu 江蘇省	(0512)8581378	265	Collectively-owned 集體	127,863	13633(2)	96,781	o
San Jue Zhen Da Zhuang Bricks Kiln Factory 三覺鎮大裝輪窯廠(1987)	Liu'an 六安市	Anhui 安徽省	(0564)408004	550	Private-owned 私營	98,940	2070(50)	14,030	a
Jianhu Xin Yu Group Company 建湖縣新宇集團公司(1974)	Yancheng 鹽城市	Jiangsu 江蘇省	(0515)6381053	580	Collectively-owned 集體	86,590	3390(23)	42,890	a
Xiamen San Rong Ceramics Development Co. Ltd. 廈門三榮陶瓷開發有限公司(1993)	Xiamen 廈門市	Fujian 福建省	(0592)7076109 (0592)7076113	108	Foreign-funded 外資	85,669	1651(83)	135,574	o
Dantu Building Materials Factory 丹徒縣建築材料廠(1956)	Zhenjiang 鎮江市	Jiangsu 江蘇省	(0511)3371142	740	Collectively-owned 集體	78,073	2505(35)	38,683	a,b
Huazhou Na Wu Zhen Building Materials Multiple Factory 化州市那務鎮建材綜合廠(1981)	Maoming 茂名市	Guangdong 廣東省	(0668)7570385	198	Collectively-owned 集體	66,520	3620(21)	4,510	a
Henan Shangcai Body Building Galoshes Factory 河南上蔡縣健美膠鞋廠(1993)	Zhumadian 駐馬店市	Henan 河南省	(0396)6922183	2,890	Collectively-owned 集體	64,475	726(389)	8,364	o

Top 10 Cities by Production Output 產出排名前 10 位城市	Province 省	Market share 市場份額	Number of firms 企業個數
Huaiyin 淮陰市	Jiangsu 江蘇省	23.86%	303
Nantong 南通市	Jiangsu 江蘇省	3.37%	343
Maoming 茂名市	Guangdong 廣東省	1.99%	135
Jiaxing 嘉興市	Zhejiang 浙江省	1.98%	174
Yancheng 鹽城市	Jiangsu 江蘇省	1.95%	221
Suzhou 蘇州市	Jiangsu 江蘇省	1.94%	202
Liu'an 六安市	Anhui 安徽省	1.54%	538
Chongqing 重慶市	Chongqing 重慶市	1.26%	424
Suihua 綏化市	Heilongjiang 黑龍江省	1.20%	199
Shanghai 上海市	Shanghai 上海市	1.19%	162

10 Major Wholesalers 10 家主要批發商	City 城市	Province 省	Telephone / Fax 電話 / 傳真
Chengdu Sheng Xing Trade Company 成都盛興商貿公司	Chengdu 成都市	Sichuan 四川省	(028)7762591
Shanghai Municipal Administration Engineering Material Company 上海市市政工程材料公司	Shanghai 上海市	Shanghai 上海市	(021)64372632
Shanghai Construction Engineering Material Co. 上海市建築工程材料公司	Shanghai 上海市	Shanghai 上海市	(021)63298630
Yixing Jin San Jiao Zhao Bazaar 宜興市金三角招商城	Wuxi 無錫市	Jiangsu 江蘇省	(0510)7935138 (0510)7935138
Fujian Hua 盈 Import & Export Company 福建省華福進出口公司	Fuzhou 福州市	Fujian 福建省	(0591)7810477 (0591)7810485
China Building Goods & Materials Company 中國建築物資公司	Beijing 北京市	Beijing 北京市	(010)68586253
Dalian Jinzhou Xin Gang Industry & Trade Company 大連金州新港工貿公司	Dalian 大連市	Liaoning 遼寧省	(0411)7624747
Shanghai Zhan Dong Industrial Co. Ltd. 上海展東實業有限公司	Shanghai 上海市	Shanghai 上海市	(021)58201778 (021)58200874
China Building Materials and Equipment Import & Export Company 中國建築材料及設備進出口公司	Beijing 北京市	Beijing 北京市	(010)68393420
Dandong Chemical Light Industry Material Company Chemical Construction Material Marketing Station 丹東市化工輕工材料公司化工建材經銷站	Dandong 丹東市	Liaoning 遼寧省	(0415)2146396

*Also include sales by firms outside this industry.包括本行業以外廠家的銷售。"o" stands for "others". "o" 代表 "其他產品"。

3132: Lime 石灰製造業

The industry accounts for 0.059% of the total revenue of China's industrial sector in 1996. The revenue growth rate of the industry is 38.4% from 1995, as compared to the growth rate of China's industrial sector, 9.51%. The rate of return on asset is 4.77%. 84.82% of all firms in the industry made a profit while 9.92% had negative returns. The top province in terms of the industry's revenue is Hubei, accounting for 13.17% of the total revenue.
本行業在1996年佔全行業總產值0.059%，行業年增長率為38.4%（全國工業年增長率9.51%）。行業的資產回報率4.77%，84.82%的企業盈利，9.92%的企業虧損。銷售收入最高的省份為湖北省，佔本行業的13.17%。

	Total number of firms 企業總數	Total number of employees 職工總數	Total revenue (mil. RMB) 總銷售收入（百萬元）	Total profit (mil. RMB) 總利潤（百萬元）	Return on assets 資產利潤率 (%)	Return on equity 權益利潤率 (%)	Labour productivity ('000 RMB / worker) 勞動生產率（千元/人）	Debts / assets 資產負債率 (%)	Total assets (mil. RMB) 總資產（百萬元）
Industry Overall 行業總體	1,922	96,335	3,427	115	4.77	13.83	35.57	65.54	2,410

	Number of firms 企業個數	Average number of employees 平均職工人數	Average revenue ('000 RMB) 平均銷售收入（千元）	Average profit ('000 RMB) 平均利潤（千元）	Return on assets 資產利潤率 (%)	Return on equity 權益利潤率 (%)	Labour productivity ('000 RMB / worker) 勞動生產率（千元/人）	Average debts / assets 平均資產負債率(%)	Average Total assets ('000 RMB) 平均總資產（千元）
By ownership 產業所有權									
State-owned 國有	100	121	2,370	-70	-1.15	-3.54	19.52	67.54	6,100
Collectively-owned 集體	1,796	46	1,749	66	6.80	19.41	37.66	64.94	977
Privately-owned 私有	8	40	2,103	46	4.92	19.24	52.75	74.45	928
Domestic JVs 聯營	6	44	1,131	182	9.18	33.82	25.51	72.85	1,987
Joint stock 股份制	7	49	2,496	125	5.31	16.37	50.65	67.56	2,351
Foreign-funded 外資									
Overseas Chinese-funded 港澳台資	2	98	4,163	142	2.65	4.19	42.48	36.70	5,354
By size 規模									
Large 大型									
Medium 中型	3	799	15,179	-426	-0.74	-1.72	19.01	57.12	57,860
Small 小型	1,911	49	1,769	61	5.20	15.39	35.99	66.22	1,170
By regional distribution 地區分布									
Central-North 華北	251	49	1,499	76	4.79	16.06	30.70	70.20	1,582
Beijing 北京	40	29	870	-14	-1.34	-5.48	29.69	75.46	1,041
Tianjin 天津	9	53	1,057	43	1.42	4.16	20.06	65.94	3,053
Hebei 河北	98	63	2,589	176	9.18	28.54	41.09	67.84	1,912
Shanxi 山西	41	34	952	11	0.77	3.14	27.65	75.49	1,397
Inner Mongolia 內蒙	63	48	623	24	1.85	6.29	12.98	70.63	1,323
Northeast 東北	259	54	1,080	-1	-0.07	-0.30	20.03	75.14	1,557
Liaoning 遼寧	111	46	1,151	-24	-1.61	-6.46	25.28	75.00	1,512
Jilin 吉林	69	54	888	8	0.56	2.13	16.50	73.85	1,382
Heilongjiang 黑龍江	79	66	1,148	24	1.34	5.64	17.43	76.20	1,772
Central East 華東	561	48	2,413	98	8.05	21.85	50.29	63.18	1,214
Shanghai 上海	13	57	2,806	119	4.96	16.35	49.10	69.63	2,402
Jiangsu 江蘇	83	82	4,175	36	1.56	4.12	51.01	62.07	2,276
Zhejiang 浙江	61	48	2,413	41	2.19	5.64	50.30	61.19	1,871
Anhui 安徽	133	48	2,447	175	22.61	56.17	50.98	59.75	775
Fujian 福建	42	25	839	28	3.49	12.95	33.67	73.01	811
Jiangxi 江西	158	36	997	65	12.46	33.15	28.08	62.42	522
Shandong 山東	71	48	4,298	183	10.24	29.82	89.38	65.66	1,789
Central-South 中南	680	52	1,805	59	5.20	13.19	34.78	60.58	1,128
Henan 河南	91	26	1,606	73	6.60	17.89	60.61	63.13	1,103
Hubei 湖北	163	67	2,768	102	6.11	15.40	41.46	60.31	1,663
Hunan 湖南	264	64	1,275	56	6.99	14.96	20.05	53.26	795
Guangdong 廣東	96	29	2,051	-25	-1.68	-6.76	69.77	75.24	1,486
Guangxi 廣西	65	37	1,487	68	10.37	18.41	40.41	43.66	654
Hainan 海南	1		60					42.47	730
Southwest 西南	78	64	1,495	2	0.12	0.37	23.30	67.85	1,287
Chongqing 重慶	23	128	2,794	10	0.33	1.07	21.88	69.36	2,928
Sichuan 四川	40	31	1,011	-1	-0.15	-0.53	32.50	70.88	480
Guizhou 貴州	10	40	802	22	3.56	5.02	20.10	29.29	618
Yunnan 雲南	4	107	1,088	-65	-3.15	-13.98	10.21	77.45	2,063
Tibet 西藏	1								
Northwest 西北	93	31	786	15	2.25	5.20	25.24	56.68	654
Shaanxi 陝西	51	28	963	7	1.14	2.73	34.22	58.42	656
Gansu 甘肅	21	34	564	23	5.70	15.12	16.81	62.17	409
Qinghai 青海	9	28	512	3	0.39	0.82	18.51	51.71	847
Ningxia 寧夏	6	67	853	57	13.93	17.71	12.74	21.31	407
Xinjiang 新疆	6	18	407	22	1.49	3.62	23.02	58.83	1,453

3132: Lime 石灰製造業

Year 年份	Number of firms 企業個數	Rate of change 每年變化 (%)	Number of employees 職工人數（人）	Rate of change 每年變化 (%)	Total revenue (mil. RMB) 總銷售收入（百萬元）	Rate of change 每年變化 (%)	Total profit (mil. RMB) 總利潤（百萬元）	Rate of change 每年變化 (%)
1993	1,977		77,834		1,748		69	
1994	2,044	3.39%	104,966	34.86%	2,356	34.80%	88	28.51%
1995	1,840	-9.98%	92,933	-11.46%	2,476	5.08%	100	13.31%
1996	1,922	4.46%	96,335	3.66%	3,427	38.41%	115	14.84%

3 Major products* 3種主要產品 *	Output 產量	Sales volume 銷售量	Unit 單位
a) Building Lime 建築用石灰	8,221,515	8,221,515	ton 噸
b) Limestone 石灰石	16,768	13,750	10,000 ton 萬噸
c) Light Calcium Carbonate 輕質碳酸鈣	88,824	84,383	ton 噸

Top 10 firms by revenue (year founded) 收入排名前10家企業（創辦年份）	City 城市	Province 省	Telephone / fax 電話／傳真	Number of employees 職工人數	Ownership 產業所有權	Revenue ('000 RMB) 銷售收入（千元）	Profit ('000 RMB) (rank) 利潤（千元）（排名）	Total assets ('000 RMB) 總資產（千元）	Major products 主要產品
Fengyang Hong Xin Zhen Quarrying Factory 鳳陽縣紅心鎮採石廠(1978)	Chuzhou 滁州市	Anhui 安徽省		485	Collectively-owned 集體	57,680	6730(1)	10,910	b
Jia Xing Yin Xin Industry & Trade Co. Ltd. 加興銀鑫工貿有限責任公司(1996)	Jiaxing 嘉興市	Zhejiang 浙江省	(0573)4866717 (0573)4866735	5	Collectively-owned 集體	52,159	1438(10)	38,882	o
Chong Gang Industrial Co. Furnace Charge General Factory 重鋼產業公司爐料總廠	Chongqing 重慶市	Chongqing 重慶市	(023)68846571	552	Collectively-owned 集體	42,132	519(49)	56,311	o
Yixing Shan Juan Lime Chemical Plant 宜興市善卷石灰化工廠(1976)	Wuxi 無錫市	Jiangsu 江蘇省	(0510)7391261	205	Collectively-owned 集體	41,860	800(22)	16,360	a,b,c
Tancheng Jin Lei Building Materials Group 郯城縣金磊建材集團(1995)	Linyi 臨沂市	Shandong 山東省	(0539)8900231 (0539)8900231	56	Collectively-owned 集體	38,520	1050(15)	1,990	a
Yi Xing Guo Tai Building & Installing Group 宜興國泰建築安裝集團(1988)	Wuxi 無錫市	Jiangsu 江蘇省	(0510)7301670	130	Collectively-owned 集體	35,267	196(163)	5,506	a
Enping Heng Pi Building Materials Multiple-producing Factory 恩平橫陂鎮建材綜合廠(1969)	Jiangmen 江門市	Guangdong 廣東省	(0750)7221268	100	Collectively-owned 集體	32,340	-30(390)	6,000	a
Tancheng Lan Shan Building Materials Group 郯城縣蘭山建材集團(1994)	Linyi 臨沂市	Shandong 山東省	(0539)8900231 (0539)8900231	49	Collectively-owned 集體	30,270	1100(13)	1,690	a
Hebei Xingtai Lime Powder Factory 河北省邢台石灰粉廠(1991)	Xingtai 邢臺市	Hebei 河北省	(0319)2995311	650	Collectively-owned 集體	28,500	2850(3)	14,100	o
Panzhihua Xixian Pingjiang Building Materials Company 攀枝花市西區平江建材公司(1987)	Panzhihua 攀枝花市	Sichuan 四川省		420	Collectively-owned 集體	27,760	2120(4)	13,310	a,b

Top 10 Cities by Production Output 產出排名前10位城市	Province 省	Market share 市場份額	Number of firms 企業個數
Beijing 北京市	Beijing 北京市	73.27%	40
Jiangmen 江門市	Guangdong 廣東省	0.89%	8
Linyi 臨沂市	Shandong 山東省	0.82%	8
Zhumadian 駐馬店市	Henan 河南省	0.67%	22
Suzhou 蘇州市	Jiangsu 江蘇省	0.63%	15
Changsha 長沙市	Hunan 湖南省	0.62%	24
Shanghai 上海市	Shanghai 上海市	0.60%	21
Hengyang 衡陽市	Hunan 湖南省	0.59%	40
Xingtai 邢臺市	Hebei 河北省	0.53%	7
Wuxi 無錫市	Jiangsu 江蘇省	0.52%	12

10 Major Wholesalers 10家主要批發商	City 城市	Province 省	Telephone / Fax 電話／傳真
Chengdu Sheng Xing Trade Company 成都盛興商貿公司	Chengdu 成都市	Sichuan 四川省	(028)7762591
Shanghai Municipal Administration Engineering Material Company 上海市市政工程材料公司	Shanghai 上海市	Shanghai 上海市	(021)64372632
Shanghai Construction Engineering Material Co. 上海市建築工程材料公司	Shanghai 上海市	Shanghai 上海市	(021)63298630
Yixing Jin San Jiao Zhao Bazaar 宜興市金三角招商城	Wuxi 無錫市	Jiangsu 江蘇省	(0510)7935138 (0510)7935138
Fujian Hua Fu Import & Export Company 福建省華福進出口公司	Fuzhou 福州市	Fujian 福建省	(0591)7810477 (0591)7810485
China Building Goods & Materials Company 中國建築物資公司	Beijing 北京市	Beijing 北京市	(010)68586253
Dalian Jinzhou Xin Gang Industry & Trade Company 大連金州新港工貿公司	Dalian 大連市	Liaoning 遼寧省	(0411)7624747
Shanghai Zhan Dong Industrial Co. Ltd. 上海展東實業有限公司	Shanghai 上海市	Shanghai 上海市	(021)58201778 (021)58200874
China Building Materials and Equipment Import & Export Company 中國建築材料及設備進出口公司	Beijing 北京市	Beijing 北京市	(010)68393420
Dandong Chemical Light Industry Material Company Chemical Construction Material Marketing Station 丹東市化工輕工材料公司化工建材經銷站	Dandong 丹東市	Liaoning 遼寧省	(0415)2146396

*Also include sales by firms outside this industry.包括本行業以外廠家的銷售。"o" stands for "others". "o" 代表"其他產品"。

3133: Construction Stone 建築用石加工業

The industry accounts for 0.207% of the total revenue of China's industrial sector in 1996. The revenue growth rate of the industry is 24.5% from 1995, as compared to the growth rate of China's industrial sector, 9.51%. The rate of return on asset is 3.04%. 78.51% of all firms in the industry made a profit while 16.05% had negative returns. The top province in terms of the industry's revenue is Shandong, accounting for 18.21% of the total revenue.

本行業在1996年佔全行業總產值0.207%，行業年增長率為24.5%（全國工業年增長率9.51%）。行業的資產回報率3.04%，78.51%的企業盈利，16.05%的企業虧損。銷售收入最高的省份為山東省，佔本行業的18.21%。

	Total number of firms 企業總數	Total number of employees 職工總數	Total revenue (mil. RMB) 總銷售收入（百萬元）	Total profit (mil. RMB) 總利潤（百萬元）	Return on assets 資產利潤率 (%)	Return on equity 權益利潤率 (%)	Labour productivity ('000 RMB / worker) 勞動生產率（千元/人）	Debts / assets 資產負債率 (%)	Total assets (mil. RMB) 總資產（百萬元）
Industry Overall 行業總體	4,471	206,840	11,994	401	3.04	7.98	57.99	61.88	13,205

	Number of firms 企業個數	Average number of employees 平均職工人數	Average revenue ('000 RMB) 平均銷售收入（千元）	Average profit ('000 RMB) 平均利潤（千元）	Return on assets 資產利潤率 (%)	Return on equity 權益利潤率 (%)	Labour productivity ('000 RMB / worker) 勞動生產率（千元/人）	Average debts / assets 平均資產負債率(%)	Average Total assets ('000 RMB) 平均總資產（千元）
By ownership 產業所有權									
State-owned 國有	360	102	1,944	-64	-0.81	-3.19	19.08	74.51	7,856
Collectively-owned 集體	3,497	39	2,480	164	10.21	27.91	64.09	63.43	1,604
Privately-owned 私有	49	15	1,091	45	8.39	17.02	71.19	50.70	542
Domestic JVs 聯營	62	32	1,753	-8	-0.37	-0.77	54.84	51.65	2,206
Joint stock 股份制	63	81	2,607	197	7.92	14.36	32.07	44.86	2,490
Foreign-funded 外資	210	64	5,987	-294	-2.40	-4.73	93.04	49.38	12,271
Overseas Chinese-funded 港澳台資	228	61	4,537	-443	-5.43	-12.85	74.07	57.73	8,165
By size 規模									
Large 大型	8	590	44,150	-2,866	-2.44	-7.55	74.89	67.64	117,352
Medium 中型	22	262	10,122	-1,141	-2.74	-9.20	38.60	70.25	41,699
Small 小型	4,350	45	2,624	103	3.96	10.07	58.63	60.72	2,609
By regional distribution 地區分布									
Central-North 華北	409	43	1,496	25	0.89	2.78	34.45	67.54	2,770
Beijing 北京	79	27	982	-33	-0.71	-3.13	36.79	75.62	4,586
Tianjin 天津	15	80	3,099	76	1.00	1.81	38.77	44.73	7,597
Hebei 河北	152	41	2,013	68	3.18	9.17	49.12	65.28	2,141
Shanxi 山西	76	72	1,571	-13	-0.52	-2.55	21.94	79.50	2,387
Inner Mongolia 內蒙	87	32	718	24	1.41	3.18	22.45	55.76	1,723
Northeast 東北	321	57	1,315	28	1.17	5.25	23.15	77.65	2,420
Liaoning 遼寧	172	43	1,184	85	4.76	18.37	27.68	74.10	1,784
Jilin 吉林	65	117	934	-66	-2.37	-26.70	7.96	91.13	2,779
Heilongjiang 黑龍江	84	39	1,877	-14	-0.42	-1.55	48.62	72.99	3,444
Central East 華東	1,553	55	3,818	160	3.91	9.87	69.43	60.42	4,107
Shanghai 上海	25	88	8,597	612	5.72	14.70	98.05	61.14	10,701
Jiangsu 江蘇	128	73	4,182	128	4.74	18.22	57.06	73.97	2,703
Zhejiang 浙江	146	27	1,816	15	0.65	1.68	67.95	61.49	2,398
Anhui 安徽	164	56	3,237	168	10.36	44.80	57.78	76.87	1,617
Fujian 福建	524	37	3,898	96	2.40	4.72	104.18	49.21	4,023
Jiangxi 江西	206	25	762	36	2.71	9.49	31.05	71.49	1,326
Shandong 山東	360	100	6,068	360	4.69	13.17	60.54	64.40	7,689
Central-South 中南	1,669	38	2,477	86	4.16	10.08	65.29	58.73	2,076
Henan 河南	330	51	2,259	128	6.51	16.73	44.24	61.09	1,974
Hubei 湖北	204	66	2,657	61	2.17	6.31	40.47	65.66	2,792
Hunan 湖南	150	38	1,359	17	1.37	2.81	36.18	51.33	1,237
Guangdong 廣東	799	20	1,777	60	3.28	7.92	88.67	58.53	1,838
Guangxi 廣西	175	61	6,944	229	8.28	15.38	113.58	46.18	2,769
Hainan 海南	11	66	700	-135	-1.41	-7.13	10.58	80.23	9,546
Southwest 西南	368	41	1,961	2	0.09	0.24	48.37	62.63	2,222
Chongqing 重慶	19	80	1,327	-6	-0.59	-1.13	16.66	47.73	1,093
Sichuan 四川	264	39	2,422	12	0.51	1.38	61.72	63.06	2,405
Guizhou 貴州	59	37	625	-4	-0.25	-0.62	16.98	59.62	1,481
Yunnan 雲南	25	39	790	-98	-3.37	-10.21	20.19	66.96	2,904
Tibet 西藏	1	16	550	380	16.31	37.25	34.38	56.22	2,330
Northwest 西北	151	48	1,156	-79	-1.89	-5.15	24.22	63.33	4,206
Shaanxi 陝西	78	55	1,291	-21	-0.75	-3.71	23.32	79.72	2,726
Gansu 甘肅	40	36	788	-118	-3.99	-13.06	21.65	69.45	2,951
Qinghai 青海	3	21	123	-23	-3.76	31.82	5.78	111.83	620
Ningxia 寧夏	6	25	240				9.73	49.86	1,170
Xinjiang 新疆	24	51	1,688	-234	-1.90	-3.74	33.21	49.10	12,313

3133: Construction Stone 建築用石加工業

Year 年份	Number of firms 企業個數	Rate of change 每年變化 (%)	Number of employees 職工人數（人）	Rate of change 每年變化 (%)	Total revenue (mil. RMB) 總銷售收入（百萬元）	Rate of change 每年變化 (%)	Total profit (mil. RMB) 總利潤（百萬元）	Rate of change 每年變化 (%)
1993	3,302		147,745		4,988		271	
1994	3,727	12.87%	182,615	23.60%	6,961	39.54%	215	-20.44%
1995	4,014	7.70%	209,572	14.76%	9,630	38.35%	151	-29.83%
1996	4,471	11.39%	206,840	-1.30%	11,994	24.55%	401	165.52%

3 Major products* 3種主要產品*	Output 產量	Sales volume 銷售量	Unit 單位
a) Marble Slab 大理石板材	47,843,870	44,016,360	square metre 平方米
b) Granite Slab 花崗石板材	15,972,737	15,972,737	square metre 平方米
c) Rough Granite Material 花崗石荒料	6,131,847	6,070,529	cubic metre 立方米

Top 10 firms by revenue (year founded) 收入排名前10家企業（創辦年份）	City 城市	Province 省	Telephone / fax 電話／傳真	Number of employees 職工人數	Ownership 產業所有權	Revenue ('000 RMB) 銷售收入（千元）	Profit ('000 RMB) (rank) 利潤（千元）（排名）	Total assets ('000 RMB) 總資產（千元）	Major products 主要產品
Cenxi Gui Yi Graniteslab Development Company 岑溪市歸義花崗岩板材開發公司(1992)	Cenxi 岑溪縣	Guangxi 廣西	(0774)8411278	1,600	Collectively-owned 集體	472,010	18920(2)	49,940	b
Guangxi Cenxi Cen Cheng Stone Material Industrial Zone 廣西岑溪市岑城石材工業區(1992)	Cenxi 岑溪縣	Guangxi 廣西	(0774)8222025	710	Collectively-owned 集體	135,000	5750(13)	32,750	b
Cenxi Nuo Tong Zhen Stone Material Development Company 岑溪市糯垌鎮石材開發公司(1990)	Cenxi 岑溪縣	Guangxi 廣西		658	Collectively-owned 集體	120,740	5200(16)	10,250	b
Cenxi Camphorwood Granite Plates Mill 岑溪市樟木鎮花崗岩板材廠(1992)	Cenxi 岑溪縣	Guangxi 廣西	(0774)8222546	474	Collectively-owned 集體	108,640	5570(14)	10,990	b
Xiamen Hui Xing Stone Material Co. Ltd. 廈門匯興石材有限公司(1988)	Xiamen 廈門市	Fujian 福建省	(0592)6021628 (0592)6021629	341	Foreign-funded 外資	105,793	7124(9)	274,308	b
Wendeng Ming Hui Construction Engineering Group Company 文登市明輝建工集團公司(1993)	Weihai 威海市	Shandong 山東省	(0896)8842042 (0896)8842042	339	Collectively-owned 集體	103,870	8830(5)	22,120	o
Wendeng Dong Yi Stone Material Co. Ltd. 文登市東意石材有限公司(1974)	Weihai 威海市	Shandong 山東省	(0896)8881196 (0896)8881047	150	Foreign-funded 外資	103,610	7130(8)	39,319	o
Wendeng Stone Material Industry Group Co. 文登市石材集團公司(1994)	Weihai 威海市	Shandong 山東省	(0896)8832030 (0896)8832088	176	Collectively-owned 集體	96,310	12850(4)	22,930	o
Huada (Fuzhou) Stone Products Co. Ltd. 華達(福州)石材有限公司(1993)	Fuzhou 福州市	Fujian 福建省	(0591)7832866 (0591)7835333	66	Foreign-funded 外資	88,930	-215(1128)	38,385	b
Dianbai Sha Yuan Zhen Quarrying Joint Company 電白縣沙院鎮採石聯合公司(1985)	Maoming 茂名市	Guangdong 廣東省	(0668)5811100	1,157	Collectively-owned 集體	79,600	7850(6)	53,970	o

Top 10 Cities by Production Output 產出排名前10位城市	Province 省	Market share 市場份額	Number of firms 企業個數
Beijing 北京市	Beijing 北京市	17.79%	74
Quanzhou 泉州市	Fujian 福建省	9.62%	479
Cenxi 岑溪縣	Guangxi 廣西	6.52%	41
Weihai 威海市	Shandong 山東省	3.57%	53
Fuzhou 福州市	Fujian 福建省	3.10%	86
Maoming 茂名市	Guangdong 廣東省	3.08%	53
Ji'nan 濟南市	Shandong 山東省	2.86%	51
Yunfu 雲浮市	Guangdong 廣東省	2.36%	185
Linyi 臨沂市	Shandong 山東省	2.09%	97
Zhaoqing 肇慶市	Guangdong 廣東省	1.98%	73

10 Major Wholesalers 10家主要批發商	City 城市	Province 省	Telephone / Fax 電話／傳真
Chengdu Sheng Xing Trade Company 成都盛興商貿公司	Chengdu 成都市	Sichuan 四川省	(028)7762591
Shanghai Municipal Administration Engineering Material Company 上海市市政工程材料公司	Shanghai 上海市	Shanghai 上海市	(021)64372632
Shanghai Construction Engineering Material Co. 上海市建築工程材料公司	Shanghai 上海市	Shanghai 上海市	(021)63298630
Yixing Jin San Jiao Zhao Bazaar 宜興市金三角招商城	Wuxi 無錫市	Jiangsu 江蘇省	(0510)7935138 (0510)7935138
Fujian Hua Fu Import & Export Company 福建省華福進出口公司	Fuzhou 福州市	Fujian 福建省	(0591)7810477 (0591)7810485
China Building Goods & Materials Company 中國建築物資公司	Beijing 北京市	Beijing 北京市	(010)68586253
Dalian Jinzhou Xin Gang Industry & Trade Company 大連金州新港工貿公司	Dalian 大連市	Liaoning 遼寧省	(0411)7624747
Shanghai Zhan Dong Industrial Co. Ltd. 上海展東實業有限公司	Shanghai 上海市	Shanghai 上海市	(021)58201778 (021)58200874
China Building Materials and Equipment Import & Export Company 中國建築材料及設備進出口公司	Beijing 北京市	Beijing 北京市	(010)68393420
Dandong Chemical Light Industry Material Company Chemical Construction Material Marketing Station 丹東市化工輕工材料公司化工建材經銷站	Dandong 丹東市	Liaoning 遼寧省	(0415)2146396

*Also include sales by firms outside this industry.包括本行業以外廠家的銷售。"o" stands for "others". "o"代表"其他產品"。

3134: Light Construction Materials 輕質建築材料製造業

The industry accounts for 0.045% of the total revenue of China's industrial sector in 1996. The revenue growth rate of the industry is 5.4% from 1995, as compared to the growth rate of China's industrial sector, 9.51%. The rate of return on asset is 1.86%. 70.22% of all firms in the industry made a profit while 21.98% had negative returns. The top province in terms of the industry's revenue is Beijing, accounting for 18.43% of the total revenue.
本行業在1996年佔全行業總產值0.045%，行業年增長率為5.4%（全國工業年增長率9.51%）。行業的資產回報率1.86%，70.22%的企業盈利，21.98%的企業虧損。銷售收入最高的省份為北京市，佔本行業的18.43%。

	Total number of firms 企業總數	Total number of employees 職工總數	Total revenue (mil. RMB) 總銷售收入（百萬元）	Total profit (mil. RMB) 總利潤（百萬元）	Return on assets 資產利潤率 (%)	Return on equity 權益利潤率 (%)	Labour productivity ('000 RMB / worker) 勞動生產率（千元/人）	Debts / assets 資產負債率 (%)	Total assets (mil. RMB) 總資產（百萬元）
Industry Overall 行業總體	888	48,991	2,636	97	1.86	4.57	53.81	59.21	5,219

	Number of firms 企業個數	Average number of employees 平均職工人數	Average revenue ('000 RMB) 平均銷售收入（千元）	Average profit ('000 RMB) 平均利潤（千元）	Return on assets 資產利潤率 (%)	Return on equity 權益利潤率 (%)	Labour productivity ('000 RMB / worker) 勞動生產率（千元/人）	Average debts / assets 平均資產負債率(%)	Average Total assets ('000 RMB) 平均總資產（千元）
By ownership 產業所有權									
State-owned 國有	102	178	7,578	471	1.93	3.68	42.47	47.44	24,343
Collectively-owned 集體	689	39	1,934	41	1.58	6.75	50.01	76.67	2,574
Privately-owned 私有	3	10	1,967	123	13.19	13.44	190.33	1.82	933
Domestic JVs 聯營	20	37	3,946	40	0.74	1.63	107.97	54.57	5,405
Joint stock 股份制	11	35	948	-144	-3.49	-12.35	27.03	71.75	4,123
Foreign-funded 外資	37	52	6,302	275	2.53	4.67	121.88	45.69	10,848
Overseas Chinese-funded 港澳台資	26	62	7,776	434	2.79	8.83	124.95	68.46	15,595
By size 規模									
Large 大型	9	670	65,204	3,720	2.64	6.25	97.38	57.67	140,691
Medium 中型	18	468	21,079	1,528	2.59	4.76	45.06	45.54	58,923
Small 小型	830	41	2,012	43	1.25	3.55	49.37	64.89	3,485
By regional distribution 地區分布									
Central-North 華北	223	59	3,555	310	3.84	7.20	60.60	46.66	8,078
Beijing 北京	64	71	7,591	659	4.28	7.71	107.17	44.43	15,382
Tianjin 天津	38	76	3,619	611	5.89	12.39	47.66	52.50	10,387
Hebei 河北	55	49	2,056	47	1.50	4.65	42.11	67.80	3,130
Shanxi 山西	37	53	815	15	0.28	0.36	15.51	20.16	5,141
Inner Mongolia 內蒙	29	36	907	23	1.14	3.58	25.39	68.29	2,064
Northeast 東北	86	58	2,119	23	0.48	1.15	36.36	57.75	4,748
Liaoning 遼寧	44	54	1,219	-74	-1.39	-2.97	22.63	53.13	5,294
Jilin 吉林	15	47	834	-24	-0.92	-4.20	17.64	78.13	2,615
Heilongjiang 黑龍江	27	72	4,300	207	4.10	10.20	60.07	59.79	5,041
Central East 華東	191	62	4,977	282	4.04	11.03	79.85	63.40	6,985
Shanghai 上海	15	87	9,617	733	4.50	14.18	110.37	68.26	16,299
Jiangsu 江蘇	43	65	8,663	148	2.05	6.15	132.37	66.65	7,199
Zhejiang 浙江	14	75	3,164	64	0.92	1.79	42.42	48.60	6,923
Anhui 安徽	20	39	1,620	144	15.58	46.30	41.96	66.41	925
Fujian 福建	25	16	1,365	100	4.37	7.58	84.46	42.38	2,299
Jiangxi 江西	20	55	1,184	1	0.01	0.02	21.39	44.17	5,684
Shandong 山東	54	83	5,545	559	6.12	19.50	67.18	68.61	9,139
Central-South 中南	199	47	2,343	8	0.16	0.56	49.89	70.54	4,946
Henan 河南	37	22	1,117	9	0.49	1.73	50.96	71.56	1,865
Hubei 湖北	47	91	3,935	90	1.50	3.57	43.44	57.89	5,993
Hunan 湖南	52	48	1,793	53	3.55	11.96	37.55	70.29	1,478
Guangdong 廣東	32	35	2,798	-36	-0.48	-1.77	79.02	73.03	7,605
Guangxi 廣西	27	19	1,923	-76	-3.78	-9.38	103.45	59.70	1,999
Hainan 海南	4	40	1,338	-620	-0.96	-5.98	33.23	84.01	64,880
Southwest 西南	68	65	2,040	-290	-7.45	-33.81	31.18	77.96	3,891
Chongqing 重慶	14	50	1,011	-91	-4.30	-17.50	20.08	75.42	2,111
Sichuan 四川	43	77	2,827	-425	-8.06	-37.24	36.51	78.37	5,280
Guizhou 貴州	4	43	160	30	5.88	10.62	3.76	44.61	510
Yunnan 雲南	6	35	245	-15	-2.01	-17.31	7.00	88.37	745
Tibet 西藏	1								
Northwest 西北	121	43	867	-80	-2.26	-6.06	20.20	62.74	3,521
Shaanxi 陝西	17	93	1,293	-473	-6.15	-11.79	13.95	47.83	7,688
Gansu 甘肅	47	32	572		0.03	0.11	18.00	71.62	1,319
Qinghai 青海	7	18	417	6	1.99	2.84	22.99	29.85	287
Ningxia 寧夏	17	47	1,241	-62	-1.20	-5.56	26.31	78.48	5,161
Xinjiang 新疆	33	36	972	-18	-0.41	-1.12	26.78	63.31	4,354

3134: Light Construction Materials 輕質建築材料製造業

Year 年份	Number of firms 企業個數	Rate of change 每年變化 (%)	Number of employees 職工人數 (人)	Rate of change 每年變化 (%)	Total revenue (mil. RMB) 總銷售收入 (百萬元)	Rate of change 每年變化 (%)	Total profit (mil. RMB) 總利潤 (百萬元)	Rate of change 每年變化 (%)
1993	615		46,641		1,530		79	
1994	822	33.66%	57,095	22.41%	2,075	35.58%	99	25.03%
1995	817	-0.61%	60,100	5.26%	2,500	20.48%	107	7.74%
1996	888	8.69%	48,991	-18.48%	2,636	5.44%	97	-9.41%

3 Major products* 3 種主要產品 *	Output 產量	Sales volume 銷售量	Unit 單位
a) Gypsum Board 石膏板	62,660,894	57,021,413	square metre 平方米
b) Aerocrete 加氣混凝土	961,673	884,739	cubic metre 立方米
c) Mineral Wool Products 礦物棉製品	18,195	8,733	ton 噸

Top 10 firms by revenue (year founded) 收入排名前 10 家企業 (創辦年份)	City 城市	Province 省	Telephone / fax 電話 / 傳真	Number of employees 職工人數	Ownership 產業所有權	Revenue ('000 RMB) 銷售收入 (千元)	Profit ('000 RMB) (rank) 利潤 (千元) (排名)	Total assets ('000 RMB) 總資產 (千元)	Major products 主要產品
Bei Xin Building Materials (Group) Co. Ltd. 北新建材(集團)有限公司(1984)	Beijing 北京市	Beijing 北京市	(010)62913831 (010)62912658	2,115	State-owned 國有	321,332	41760(1)	671,408	a,c
An Mei Gu Building Materials Industry (Suzhou) Co. Ltd. 安美固建材工業(蘇州)有限公司(1996)	Suzhou 蘇州市	Jiangsu 江蘇省		31	Foreign-funded 外資	207,935	2961(7)	125,270	o
Shandong Taian Taishan Paperboard Plaster Splint Factory 山東省泰安泰山紙面石膏板總廠(1988)	Tai'an 泰安市	Shandong 山東省	(0538)8711439 (0538)8711439	1,144	State-owned 國有	127,083	28405(2)	118,382	a
Shanghai Xiao Bao Light Building Material Co. Ltd. 上海曉寶輕質建材有限公司(1989)	Shanghai 上海市	Shanghai 上海市	(021)65243072 (021)65327645	118	Overseas Chinese-funded 港澳台資	66,929	5687(4)	83,886	o
Tianjin Wan Li Building Plate Co. Ltd. 天津萬力建築板材有限公司(1994)	Tianjin 天津市	Tianjin 天津市	(022)22316368 (022)22316374	84	Foreign-funded 外資	51,259	15709(3)	80,348	o
Sichuan Pengshan Hua Xi Concrete Additive Factory 四川省彭山縣華西混凝土外加劑廠	Leshan 樂山市	Sichuan 四川省	(0833)660362	395	Collectively-owned 集體	47,302	639(35)	14,404	o
Shandong Linyi Paper-faced Gypsum Board Factory 山東臨沂紙面石膏板廠(1995)	Linyi 臨沂市	Shandong 山東省	(0539)8591612 (0539)8591519	252	Domestic JVs 聯營	40,841	248(69)	34,192	a
Harbin New Type Building Material General Factory 哈爾濱新型建築材料總廠(1954)	Harbin 哈爾濱市	Heilongjiang 黑龍江省	(0451)6663951	940	State-owned 國有	36,210	129(95)	66,952	a
Beijing Xi Si Er Gypsum Slab Co. Ltd. 北京西斯爾石膏板有限公司(1995)	Beijing 北京市	Beijing 北京市	(010)69256781	180	Foreign-funded 外資	33,458	-12597(218)	96,518	a
Heilongjiang Muling Ba Mian Tong Ceramsite Factory 黑龍江省穆棱市八面通陶粒廠(1986)	Mudanjiang 牡丹江市	Heilongjiang 黑龍江省	(0453)3122261	155	Collectively-owned 集體	32,850	965(25)	7,400	o

Top 10 Cities by Production Output 產出排名前 10 位城市	Province 省	Market share 市場份額	Number of firms 企業個數
Wuxi 無錫市	Jiangsu 江蘇省	28.29%	11
Beijing 北京市	Beijing 北京市	14.34%	59
Tianjin 天津市	Tianjin 天津市	5.03%	43
Tai'an 泰安市	Shandong 山東省	3.71%	9
Shanghai 上海市	Shanghai 上海市	3.49%	26
Linyi 臨沂市	Shandong 山東省	2.71%	11
Zibo 淄博市	Shandong 山東省	2.25%	4
Harbin 哈爾濱市	Heilongjiang 黑龍江省	1.55%	11
Zhenjiang 鎮江市	Jiangsu 江蘇省	1.51%	8
Wuhan 武漢市	Hubei 湖北省	1.34%	7

10 Major Wholesalers 10 家主要批發商	City 城市	Province 省	Telephone / Fax 電話 / 傳真
Chengdu Sheng Xing Trade Company 成都盛興商貿公司	Chengdu 成都市	Sichuan 四川省	(028)7762591
Shanghai Municipal Administration Engineering Material Company 上海市市政工程材料公司	Shanghai 上海市	Shanghai 上海市	(021)64372632
Shanghai Construction Engineering Material Co. 上海市建築工程材料公司	Shanghai 上海市	Shanghai 上海市	(021)63298630
Yixing Jin San Jiao Zhao Bazaar 宜興市金三角招商城	Wuxi 無錫市	Jiangsu 江蘇省	(0510)7935138 (0510)7935138
Fujian Hua Fu Import & Export Company 福建省華福進出口公司	Fuzhou 福州市	Fujian 福建省	(0591)7810477 (0591)7810485
China Building Goods & Materials Company 中國建築物資公司	Beijing 北京市	Beijing 北京市	(010)68586253
Dalian Jinzhou Xin Gang Industry & Trade Company 大連金州新港工貿公司	Dalian 大連市	Liaoning 遼寧省	(0411)7624747
Shanghai Zhan Dong Industrial Co. Ltd. 上海展東實業有限公司	Shanghai 上海市	Shanghai 上海市	(021)58201778 (021)58200874
China Building Materials and Equipment Import & Export Company 中國建築材料及設備進出口公司	Beijing 北京市	Beijing 北京市	(010)68393420
Dandong Chemical Light Industry Material Company Chemical Construction Material Marketing Station 丹東市化工輕工材料公司化工建材經銷站	Dandong 丹東市	Liaoning 遼寧省	(0415)2146396

*Also include sales by firms outside this industry.包括本行業以外廠家的銷售。"o" stands for "others". "o" 代表 "其他產品"。

3135: Water-proof Construction Materials 防水密封建築材料製造業

The industry accounts for 0.065% of the total revenue of China's industrial sector in 1996. The revenue growth rate of the industry is 9.0% from 1995, as compared to the growth rate of China's industrial sector, 9.51%. The rate of return on asset is 0.27%. 72.15% of all firms in the industry made a profit while 21.81% had negative returns. The top province in terms of the industry's revenue is Hebei, accounting for 21.38% of the total revenue.
本行業在1996年佔全行業總產值0.065%，行業年增長率為9.0%（全國工業年增長率9.51%）。行業的資產回報率0.27%，72.15%的企業盈利，21.81%的企業虧損。銷售收入最高的省份為河北省，佔本行業的21.38%。

	Total number of firms 企業總數	Total number of employees 職工總數	Total revenue (mil. RMB) 總銷售收入（百萬元）	Total profit (mil. RMB) 總利潤（百萬元）	Return on assets 資產利潤率 (%)	Return on equity 權益利潤率 (%)	Labour productivity ('000 RMB / worker) 勞動生產率（千元／人）	Debts / assets 資產負債率 (%)	Total assets (mil. RMB) 總資產（百萬元）
Industry Overall 行業總體	913	63,556	3,778	12	0.27	0.95	59.44	71.82	4,449

	Number of firms 企業個數	Average number of employees 平均職工人數	Average revenue ('000 RMB) 平均銷售收入（千元）	Average profit ('000 RMB) 平均利潤（千元）	Return on assets 資產利潤率 (%)	Return on equity 權益利潤率 (%)	Labour productivity ('000 RMB / worker) 勞動生產率（千元／人）	Average debts / assets 平均資產負債率(%)	Average Total assets ('000 RMB) 平均總資產（千元）
By ownership 產業所有權									
State-owned 國有	104	192	12,481	-510	-2.44	-8.88	64.89	72.51	20,885
Collectively-owned 集體	751	51	2,532	82	4.05	16.43	49.72	75.32	2,012
Privately-owned 私有	4	50	4,091	584	35.68	60.19	81.81	40.71	1,635
Domestic JVs 聯營	6	37	6,779	845	13.38	24.42	183.22	45.19	6,310
Joint stock 股份制	10	135	11,082	54	0.41	1.09	81.85	61.99	12,952
Foreign-funded 外資	22	107	13,237	54	0.26	0.68	124.29	62.44	20,926
Overseas Chinese-funded 港澳台資	17	81	7,027	-316	-4.06	-14.34	87.01	71.68	7,780
By size 規模									
Large 大型	8	903	129,956	150	0.09	0.34	143.98	74.25	170,981
Medium 中型	14	532	29,886	-1,139	-1.95	-5.27	56.15	62.98	58,352
Small 小型	884	55	2,624	30	1.18	4.46	47.55	73.53	2,561
By regional distribution 地區分布									
Central-North 華北	123	80	8,899	348	4.42	10.72	110.83	58.74	7,857
Beijing 北京	41	47	4,594	95	1.69	5.60	98.62	69.82	5,631
Tianjin 天津	8	119	6,759	-281	-2.03	-5.73	56.86	64.53	13,833
Hebei 河北	37	135	21,831	1,056	7.05	13.99	161.97	49.59	14,968
Shanxi 山西	18	45	1,016	99	5.15	33.78	22.48	84.72	1,919
Inner Mongolia 內蒙	19	64	1,374	14	0.74	5.05	21.48	85.30	1,919
Northeast 東北	162	64	2,587	-198	-3.49	-18.27	40.32	80.92	5,665
Liaoning 遼寧	83	65	2,707	-261	-4.05	-25.48	41.36	84.11	6,456
Jilin 吉林	42	71	1,684	-218	-4.01	-53.82	23.59	92.54	5,429
Heilongjiang 黑龍江	37	53	3,344	-31	-0.75	-1.59	62.99	52.57	4,161
Central East 華東	247	75	4,651	127	2.64	8.62	62.00	69.34	4,811
Shanghai 上海	12	129	14,080	1,009	4.47	10.53	109.22	57.52	22,557
Jiangsu 江蘇	62	85	4,959	10	0.22	0.75	58.08	70.77	4,339
Zhejiang 浙江	19	90	5,062	-403	-3.58	-14.15	56.11	74.67	11,249
Anhui 安徽	52	62	3,925	265	15.00	64.65	63.71	76.80	1,768
Fujian 福建	15	27	1,323	11	0.75	2.19	49.72	65.84	1,427
Jiangxi 江西	32	62	1,127	-32	-1.45	-5.54	18.04	73.85	2,221
Shandong 山東	55	79	5,747	244	5.36	19.37	72.32	72.31	4,556
Central-South 中南	257	69	3,322	-99	-2.61	-12.33	47.82	78.80	3,795
Henan 河南	62	36	2,160	50	2.05	6.54	60.07	68.70	2,426
Hubei 湖北	62	143	6,198	-17	-0.33	-1.19	43.21	72.33	5,149
Hunan 湖南	94	61	2,970	-203	-4.73	-46.26	49.03	89.78	4,302
Guangdong 廣東	14	28	1,821	-256	-6.63	-17.12	64.56	61.28	3,856
Guangxi 廣西	25	26	1,240	-193	-10.21	-52.91	48.05	80.71	1,889
Hainan 海南									
Southwest 西南	80	40	1,886	-70	-2.39	-7.92	46.63	69.86	2,926
Chongqing 重慶	19	38	1,080	-154	-3.52	-24.14	28.42	85.42	4,375
Sichuan 四川	42	44	2,550	-62	-2.13	-6.23	58.28	65.85	2,906
Guizhou 貴州	11	36	675	7	0.63	1.15	18.60	45.27	1,153
Yunnan 雲南	8	36	1,909	-23	-1.08	-1.86	52.47	42.11	2,093
Tibet 西藏									
Northwest 西北	44	83	2,518	19	0.51	2.25	30.22	77.31	3,789
Shaanxi 陝西	23	98	2,062	-44	-1.01	-7.83	21.05	87.14	4,358
Gansu 甘肅	8	69	3,491	223	10.70	19.33	50.42	44.68	2,079
Qinghai 青海	3	73	2,273	-147	-5.31	-28.57	31.00	81.42	2,763
Ningxia 寧夏	3	15	597	-17	-3.23	-125.00	38.91	96.77	517
Xinjiang 新疆	7	85	3,836	81	1.42	4.03	45.20	64.63	5,716

3135: Water-proof Construction Materials 防水密封建築材料製造業

Year 年份	Number of firms 企業個數	Rate of change 每年變化 (%)	Number of employees 職工人數 (人)	Rate of change 每年變化 (%)	Total revenue (mil. RMB) 總銷售收入 (百萬元)	Rate of change 每年變化 (%)	Total profit (mil. RMB) 總利潤 (百萬元)	Rate of change 每年變化 (%)
1993	849		71,692		2,535		65	
1994	928	9.31%	78,224	9.11%	2,917	15.07%	26	-60.58%
1995	933	0.54%	71,957	-8.01%	3,465	18.77%	21	-19.35%
1996	913	-2.14%	63,556	-11.68%	3,778	9.03%	12	-42.17%

3 Major products* 3 種主要產品 *	Output 產量	Sales volume 銷售量	Unit 單位
a) Felt Paper 油氈油紙	37,287,726	35,423,340	roll 卷
b) Cement Block 水泥磚	28,722,113	28,147,671	block 塊
c) Petroluem Asphalt 石油瀝青	81,756	80,938	ton 噸

Top 10 firms by revenue (year founded) 收入排名前 10 家企業 (創辦年份)	City 城市	Province 省	Telephone / fax 電話 / 傳真	Number of employees 職工人數	Ownership 產業所有權	Revenue ('000 RMB) 銷售收入 (千元)	Profit ('000 RMB) (rank) 利潤 (千元) (排名)	Total assets ('000 RMB) 總資產 (千元)	Major products 主要產品
Hebei Baoding Petrochemical Plant 河北省保定石油化工廠(1972)	Baoding 保定市	Hebei 河北省	(0312)3135911 (0312)3111701	2,163	State-owned 國有	593,976	25546(1)	378,555	c
Beijing-oakland Building Waterproof Material Co. Ltd. 北京一奧克蘭建築防水材料有限公司(1988)	Beijing 北京市	Beijing 北京市	(010)67991831 (010)67991960	921	Foreign-funded 外資	126,686	1019(31)	143,685	a
Shanghai Building Waterproof Material (Group) Co. 上海建築防水材料(集團)公司(1991)	Shanghai 上海市	Shanghai 上海市	(021)64387777 (021)64383622	974	State-owned 國有	81,431	4326(5)	193,888	a
Jiangsu Hua Xin Construction Engineering Group Company Heng Jing Branch 江蘇省華新建設工程集團公司橫涇分公司(1959)	Suzhou 蘇州市	Jiangsu 江蘇省	(0512)6201963	1,400	Collectively-owned 集體	78,715	126(113)	22,340	o
Feicheng Social Welfare Linoleum Factory 山東省肥城市社會福利油毯廠(1979)	Tai'an 泰安市	Shandong 山東省	(0538)3680286 (0538)3680286	190	Collectively-owned 集體	64,481	4810(2)	17,165	a
Wuhan Waterproof Material Co. Ltd. 武漢防水材料股份有限公司(1953)	Wuhan 武漢市	Hubei 湖北省	(027)82315807 (027)82871434	1,273	Joint stock 股份制	60,490	-6573(262)	94,054	a
Tianjin Asphalt Felt Factory 天津市油氈廠(1951)	Tianjin 天津市	Tianjin 天津市	(022)28335482 (022)28335520	722	State-owned 國有	52,266	-1971(250)	100,844	a
Panjin New Type Water-proofer Factory 盤錦市新型防水材料廠(1989)	Panjin 盤錦市	Liaoning 遼寧省	(0427)2854811 (0427)2854043	783	State-owned 國有	46,430	-15220(264)	184,600	o
Sichuan Zigong Asphalt Felt Factory 四川省自貢市油氈廠(1965)	Zigong 自貢市	Sichuan 四川省	(0813)3301238 (0813)3301238	886	State-owned 國有	46,314	41(153)	67,392	a
Laian Waterproof Anticorrosion General Company 來安縣防水防腐總公司(1991)	Chuzhou 滁州市	Anhui 安徽省	(0550)5681020	310	Collectively-owned 集體	44,400	3600(9)	9,830	o

Top 10 Cities by Production Output 產出排名前 10 位城市	Province 省	Market share 市場份額	Number of firms 企業個數
Baoding 保定市	Hebei 河北省	18.29%	6
Shanghai 上海市	Shanghai 上海市	5.51%	21
Suzhou 蘇州市	Jiangsu 江蘇省	3.67%	18
Shijiazhuang 石家莊市	Hebei 河北省	2.65%	7
Wuhan 武漢市	Hubei 湖北省	2.55%	11
Beijing 北京市	Beijing 北京市	2.46%	37
Ningbo 寧波市	Zhejiang 浙江省	2.30%	8
Panjin 盤錦市	Liaoning 遼寧省	2.20%	3
Weihai 威海市	Shandong 山東省	2.17%	5
Tongliao 通遼市	Inner Mong 內蒙	2.11%	2

10 Major Wholesalers 10 家主要批發商	City 城市	Province 省	Telephone / Fax 電話 / 傳真
Chengdu Sheng Xing Trade Company 成都盛興商貿公司	Chengdu 成都市	Sichuan 四川省	(028)7762591
Shanghai Municipal Administration Engineering Material Company 上海市市政工程材料公司	Shanghai 上海市	Shanghai 上海市	(021)64372632
Shanghai Construction Engineering Material Co. 上海市建築工程材料公司	Shanghai 上海市	Shanghai 上海市	(021)63298630
Yixing Jin San Jiao Zhao Bazaar 宜興市金三角招商城	Wuxi 無錫市	Jiangsu 江蘇省	(0510)7935138 (0510)7935138
Fujian Hua Fu Import & Export Company 福建省華福進出口公司	Fuzhou 福州市	Fujian 福建省	(0591)7810477 (0591)7810485
China Building Goods & Materials Company 中國建築物資公司	Beijing 北京市	Beijing 北京市	(010)68586253
Dalian Jinzhou Xin Gang Industry & Trade Company 大連金州新港工貿公司	Dalian 大連市	Liaoning 遼寧省	(0411)7624747
Shanghai Zhan Dong Industrial Co. Ltd. 上海展東實業有限公司	Shanghai 上海市	Shanghai 上海市	(021)58201778 (021)58200874
China Building Materials and Equipment Import & Export Company 中國建築材料及設備進出口公司	Beijing 北京市	Beijing 北京市	(010)68393420
Dandong Chemical Light Industry Material Company Chemical Construction Material Marketing Station 丹東市化工輕工材料公司化工建材經銷站	Dandong 丹東市	Liaoning 遼寧省	(0415)2146396

*Also include sales by firms outside this industry.包括本行業以外廠家的銷售。"o" stands for "others". "o" 代表 "其他產品"。

3136: Heat-barrier Materials 隔熱保溫材料製造業

The industry accounts for 0.051% of the total revenue of China's industrial sector in 1996. The revenue growth rate of the industry is 47.1% from 1995, as compared to the growth rate of China's industrial sector, 9.51%. The rate of return on asset is 2.37%. 74.83% of all firms in the industry made a profit while 19.69% had negative returns. The top province in terms of the industry's revenue is Jiangsu, accounting for 24.46% of the total revenue.
本行業在1996年佔全行業總產值0.051%，行業年增長率為47.1%（全國工業年增長率9.51%）。行業的資產回報率2.37%，74.83%的企業盈利，19.69%的企業虧損。銷售收入最高的省份為江蘇省，佔本行業的24.46%。

	Total number of firms 企業總數	Total number of employees 職工總數	Total revenue (mil. RMB) 總銷售收入（百萬元）	Total profit (mil. RMB) 總利潤（百萬元）	Return on assets 資產利潤率 (%)	Return on equity 權益利潤率 (%)	Labour productivity ('000 RMB / worker) 勞動生產率（千元/人）	Debts / assets 資產負債率 (%)	Total assets (mil. RMB) 總資產（百萬元）
Industry Overall 行業總體	913	48,835	2,947	92	2.37	6.57	60.35	63.96	3,898

	Number of firms 企業個數	Average number of employees 平均職工人數	Average revenue ('000 RMB) 平均銷售收入（千元）	Average profit ('000 RMB) 平均利潤（千元）	Return on assets 資產利潤率 (%)	Return on equity 權益利潤率 (%)	Labour productivity ('000 RMB / worker) 勞動生產率（千元/人）	Average debts / assets 平均資產負債率(%)	Average Total assets ('000 RMB) 平均總資產（千元）
By ownership 產業所有權									
State-owned 國有	83	118	2,566	-181	-1.23	-5.60	21.79	78.10	14,747
Collectively-owned 集體	777	48	3,299	143	5.06	12.94	69.16	60.89	2,831
Privately-owned 私有	9	24	2,645	115	4.96	7.78	109.19	36.23	2,321
Domestic JVs 聯營	7	19	608	-39	-3.09	-5.52	32.25	43.98	1,260
Joint stock 股份制	9	56	4,708	639	10.81	24.05	84.24	55.04	5,909
Foreign-funded 外資	13	41	2,872	-824	-3.21	-5.26	70.30	38.98	25,696
Overseas Chinese-funded 港澳台資	13	50	4,830	-14	-0.31	-0.59	96.74	46.52	4,359
By size 規模									
Large 大型	2	351	54,120	1,475	1.13	4.73	154.19	76.16	130,819
Medium 中型	11	267	41,535	4,591	7.16	16.77	155.61	57.33	64,143
Small 小型	887	51	2,685	43	1.32	3.70	53.06	64.46	3,304
By regional distribution 地區分布									
Central-North 華北	187	50	2,444	88	1.96	5.86	49.18	66.54	4,468
Beijing 北京	40	44	2,671	1	0.01	0.02	61.05	50.40	7,608
Tianjin 天津	14	51	714	-41	-3.42	-9.08	14.03	62.37	1,192
Hebei 河北	74	63	3,879	267	5.26	18.68	61.66	71.83	5,078
Shanxi 山西	20	49	1,457	-70	-3.31	-7.41	29.92	55.33	2,116
Inner Mongolia 內蒙	39	31	613	-37	-1.50	60.92	19.95	102.47	2,472
Northeast 東北	215	42	1,243	19	0.83	3.44	29.57	75.98	2,313
Liaoning 遼寧	99	41	1,242	12	0.62	3.06	30.59	79.90	1,872
Jilin 吉林	49	40	1,147	1	0.05	0.36	28.36	87.20	2,683
Heilongjiang 黑龍江	67	45	1,317	43	1.61	4.45	29.00	63.78	2,695
Central East 華東	229	71	6,083	395	6.08	16.61	86.05	63.40	6,496
Shanghai 上海	10	130	8,364	-37	-0.18	-1.20	64.59	85.29	20,982
Jiangsu 江蘇	66	86	10,923	679	7.56	15.53	127.69	51.35	8,986
Zhejiang 浙江	27	103	4,806	136	1.75	4.77	46.68	63.25	7,779
Anhui 安徽	33	36	4,053	304	13.50	37.27	112.21	63.79	2,252
Fujian 福建	9	19	418	-109	-7.99	-29.97	22.12	73.35	1,363
Jiangxi 江西	15	13	327	15	1.70	10.48	24.43	83.78	863
Shandong 山東	69	71	4,582	479	8.81	28.58	64.47	69.16	5,438
Central-South 中南	149	52	2,685	-104	-2.13	-4.31	51.89	50.59	4,876
Henan 河南	61	37	1,435	6	0.28	1.17	38.34	75.75	2,194
Hubei 湖北	30	84	3,813	44	0.57	1.19	45.20	52.13	7,701
Hunan 湖南	30	52	1,136	-30	-2.25	-21.23	21.69	89.41	1,334
Guangdong 廣東	20	46	7,150	-839	-5.53	-8.04	156.97	31.24	15,173
Guangxi 廣西	5	46	4,080	168	5.43	79.25	89.47	93.15	3,096
Hainan 海南	3	61	193	-113	-12.78	-17.44	3.17	26.69	887
Southwest 西南	47	88	2,249	-120	-3.51	-17.50	25.47	79.95	3,407
Chongqing 重慶	15	181	4,192	-8	-0.16	-1.00	23.22	84.01	5,059
Sichuan 四川	19	47	1,380	83	3.34	18.17	29.60	81.61	2,485
Guizhou 貴州	8	49	2,068	-485	-11.69	-30.74	41.87	61.98	4,149
Yunnan 雲南	5	45	250	-48	-4.84	20.34	5.53	123.79	992
Tibet 西藏									
Northwest 西北	86	29	3,770	29	1.31	3.58	132.02	63.33	2,225
Shaanxi 陝西	30	36	813	19	1.35	2.38	22.90	43.19	1,408
Gansu 甘肅	13	38	21,544	214	4.41	7.34	563.52	39.94	4,850
Qinghai 青海	3	23	223	7	0.30	1.41	9.85	78.58	2,210
Ningxia 寧夏	7	16	463	27	16.38	24.68	29.19	33.62	166
Xinjiang 新疆	33	22	481	-32	-1.34	-17.18	22.18	92.18	2,373

3136: Heat-barrier Materials 隔熱保溫材料製造業

Year 年份	Number of firms 企業個數	Rate of change 每年變化 (%)	Number of employees 職工人數（人）	Rate of change 每年變化 (%)	Total revenue (mil. RMB) 總銷售收入（百萬元）	Rate of change 每年變化 (%)	Total profit (mil. RMB) 總利潤（百萬元）	Rate of change 每年變化 (%)
1993	700		35,668		1,128		34	
1994	839	19.86%	56,338	57.95%	1,500	32.93%	53	56.26%
1995	908	8.22%	56,443	0.19%	2,003	33.53%	81	51.62%
1996	913	0.55%	48,835	-13.48%	2,947	47.13%	92	13.82%

3 Major products* 3 種主要產品 *	Output 產量	Sales volume 銷售量	Unit 單位
a) Expanded Perlite Products 膨脹珍珠岩製品	174,199	172,457	ton 噸
b) Mineral Wool Products 礦物棉製品	48,234	23,152	ton 噸
c) Refractory Material Products 耐火材料製品	172,010	120,407	ton 噸

Top 10 firms by revenue (year founded) 收入排名前 10 家企業（創辦年份）	City 城市	Province 省	Telephone / fax 電話 / 傳真	Number of employees 職工人數	Ownership 產業所有權	Revenue ('000 RMB) 銷售收入（千元）	Profit ('000 RMB) (rank) 利潤（千元）（排名）	Total assets ('000 RMB) 總資產（千元）	Major products 主要產品
Jiangsu De Sheng New Type Building Materials Group Co. 江蘇得勝新型建材集團公司(1975)	Wuxi 無錫市	Jiangsu 江蘇省	(0510)7871688 (0510)7871128	380	Collectively-owned 集體	168,021	23287(1)	88,135	o
Nantong Jin Yang Xing Wang Group Co. Ltd. 南通金洋興旺集團有限公司(1995)	Nantong 南通市	Jiangsu 江蘇省	(0513)3797016	420	Collectively-owned 集體	100,160	3210(9)	34,990	o
Jiangsu Wuxian Calcium Silicate Plate Factory 江蘇省吳縣市硅酸鈣板廠(1989)	Suzhou 蘇州市	Jiangsu 江蘇省	(0512)5401141 (0512)5402257	295	Collectively-owned 集體	92,700	7310(3)	74,150	o
Jiangsu Xiao Jin Group Co. 江蘇曉金集團公司(1956)	Wuxi 無錫市	Jiangsu 江蘇省	(0510)7561101 (0510)7561101	170	Collectively-owned 集體	85,752	6328(4)	34,344	o
Jintan Building Erection Work Company Anticorrosion Thermal Insulation No.2 Engineering Dept. 金壇市建築安裝工程公司防腐保温第二工程處(1992)	Changzhou 常州市	Jiangsu 江蘇省	(0519)2461368	175	Collectively-owned 集體	52,350	74(133)	2,962	o
Hebei Jizhou Zhenxing Thermal Insulating Material Factory 河北省冀州市振興保温材料廠(1991)	Hengshui 衡水市	Hebei 河北省	(0318)8837258	100	Collectively-owned 集體	50,960	4860(6)	300	o
Xi Si Er (Guangdong) Glass Wool Products Co. Ltd. 西斯爾(廣東)玻璃棉製品有限公司(1995)	Zhuhai 珠海市	Guangdong 廣東省	(0756)5511448 (0756)5511449	175	Foreign-funded 外資	49,573	-17956(219)	247,552	o
Beijing Yi Suo Wei Er Glass Fibre Co. Ltd. 北京依索維爾玻璃棉有限公司(1995)	Beijing 北京市	Beijing 北京市	(010)65758236	196	Foreign-funded 外資	46,117	-609(201)	136,171	o
Shenyang Refractory Factory Zibo Branch 瀋陽耐火材料廠淄博分廠(1976)	Zibo 淄博市	Shandong 山東省	(0533)5518315 (0533)5518315	430	Collectively-owned 集體	44,900	4340(7)	13,210	c
Lujiang Special Type Building Materials Factory 廬江特種建築材料廠(1985)	Chaohu 巢湖市	Anhui 安徽省		150	Collectively-owned 集體	42,030	263(81)	25,540	o

Top 10 Cities by Production Output 產出排名前 10 位城市	Province 省	Market share 市場份額	Number of firms 企業個數
Zibo 淄博市	Shandong 山東省	18.55%	6
Nantong 南通市	Jiangsu 江蘇省	16.05%	15
Shanghai 上海市	Shanghai 上海市	4.87%	25
Beijing 北京市	Beijing 北京市	3.60%	40
Wuxi 無錫市	Jiangsu 江蘇省	3.49%	33
Zhuhai 珠海市	Guangdong 廣東省	2.65%	4
Changzhou 常州市	Jiangsu 江蘇省	2.56%	15
Chongqing 重慶市	Chongqing 重慶市	2.44%	22
Huzhou 湖州市	Zhejiang 浙江省	2.31%	5
Hengshui 衡水市	Hebei 河北省	2.18%	7

10 Major Wholesalers 10 家主要批發商	City 城市	Province 省	Telephone / Fax 電話 / 傳真
Chengdu Sheng Xing Trade Company 成都盛興商貿公司	Chengdu 成都市	Sichuan 四川省	(028)7762591
Shanghai Municipal Administration Engineering Material Company 上海市市政工程材料公司	Shanghai 上海市	Shanghai 上海市	(021)64372632
Shanghai Construction Engineering Material Co. 上海市建築工程材料公司	Shanghai 上海市	Shanghai 上海市	(021)63298630
Yixing Jin San Jiao Zhao Bazaar 宜興市金三角招商城	Wuxi 無錫市	Jiangsu 江蘇省	(0510)7935138 (0510)7935138
Fujian Hua Fu Import & Export Company 福建省華福進出口公司	Fuzhou 福州市	Fujian 福建省	(0591)7810477 (0591)7810485
China Building Goods & Materials Company 中國建築物資公司	Beijing 北京市	Beijing 北京市	(010)68586253
Dalian Jinzhou Xin Gang Industry & Trade Company 大連金州新港工貿公司	Dalian 大連市	Liaoning 遼寧省	(0411)7624747
Shanghai Zhan Dong Industrial Co. Ltd. 上海展東實業有限公司	Shanghai 上海市	Shanghai 上海市	(021)58201778 (021)58200874
China Building Materials and Equipment Import & Export Company 中國建築材料及設備進出口公司	Beijing 北京市	Beijing 北京市	(010)68393420
Dandong Chemical Light Industry Material Company Chemical Construction Material Marketing Station 丹東市化工輕工材料公司化工建材經銷站	Dandong 丹東市	Liaoning 遼寧省	(0415)2146396

*Also include sales by firms outside this industry.包括本行業以外廠家的銷售。"o" stands for "others". "o" 代表 "其他產品"。

3139: Other Bricks and Tiles, Lime and Light Construction Materials
其他磚瓦、石灰和輕質建築材料製造業

The industry accounts for 0.031% of the total revenue of China's industrial sector in 1996. The revenue growth rate of the industry is 18.0% from 1995, as compared to the growth rate of China's industrial sector, 9.51%. The rate of return on asset is 0.51%. 74.78% of all firms in the industry made a profit while 17.14% had negative returns. The top province in terms of the industry's revenue is Hubei, accounting for 13.17% of the total revenue.
本行業在1996年佔全行業總產值0.031%，行業年增長率為18.0%（全國工業年增長率9.51%）。行業的資產回報率0.51%，74.78%的企業盈利，17.14%的企業虧損。銷售收入最高的省份為湖北省，佔本行業的13.17%。

	Total number of firms 企業總數	Total number of employees 職工總數	Total revenue (mil. RMB) 總銷售收入（百萬元）	Total profit (mil. RMB) 總利潤（百萬元）	Return on assets 資產利潤率 (%)	Return on equity 權益利潤率 (%)	Labour productivity ('000 RMB / worker) 勞動生產率（千元/人）	Debts / assets 資產負債率 (%)	Total assets (mil. RMB) 總資產（百萬元）
Industry Overall 行業總體	766	51,897	1,792	13	0.51	1.49	34.53	65.80	2,603

	Number of firms 企業個數	Average number of employees 平均職工人數	Average revenue ('000 RMB) 平均銷售收入（千元）	Average profit ('000 RMB) 平均利潤（千元）	Return on assets 資產利潤率 (%)	Return on equity 權益利潤率 (%)	Labour productivity ('000 RMB / worker) 勞動生產率（千元/人）	Average debts / assets 平均資產負債率(%)	Average Total assets ('000 RMB) 平均總資產（千元）
By ownership 產業所有權									
State-owned 國有	76	124	3,711	-158	-1.62	-4.07	29.96	60.14	9,737
Collectively-owned 集體	631	61	1,904	-25	-1.40	-6.06	31.12	76.88	1,804
Privately-owned 私有	9	47	2,324	-63	-3.97	-17.35	48.99	77.14	1,584
Domestic JVs 聯營	9	69	3,135	-138	-2.24	-6.03	45.59	62.80	6,139
Joint stock 股份制	7	44	586	-68	-3.08	-4.04	13.36	23.61	2,203
Foreign-funded 外資	18	108	12,259	442	1.94	4.67	113.68	58.50	22,793
Overseas Chinese-funded 港澳台資	16	40	2,210	2,205	15.29	27.92	54.99	45.22	14,416
By size 規模									
Large 大型	1	767	111,666	-7,124	-6.20	-11.57	145.59	46.38	114,870
Medium 中型	6	718	19,832	1,701	3.46	7.29	27.62	52.58	49,201
Small 小型	744	62	2,099	13	0.45	1.44	33.81	68.61	2,949
By regional distribution 地區分布									
Central-North 華北	149	65	2,591	106	2.47	5.63	40.17	56.06	4,301
Beijing 北京	21	86	3,983	108	1.13	2.51	46.42	55.06	9,559
Tianjin 天津	22	80	5,868	158	1.55	3.33	73.23	53.40	10,190
Hebei 河北	51	63	2,413	163	5.86	13.47	38.02	56.48	2,779
Shanxi 山西	28	55	1,063	54	4.26	11.14	19.46	61.73	1,258
Inner Mongolia 內蒙	27	47	760	11	0.77	2.55	16.02	69.85	1,445
Northeast 東北	121	64	1,660	21	1.01	4.32	25.96	76.60	2,045
Liaoning 遼寧	56	88	2,433	37	1.31	4.03	27.63	67.45	2,832
Jilin 吉林	40	49	1,028	-12	-0.74	-21.66	20.97	96.61	1,598
Heilongjiang 黑龍江	25	34	943	36	3.58	21.65	27.79	83.49	996
Central East 華東	198	84	2,775	76	2.14	7.02	32.87	69.57	3,556
Shanghai 上海	16	72	2,935	7	0.18	0.54	40.98	67.22	3,865
Jiangsu 江蘇	29	203	4,389	77	1.43	6.08	21.61	76.49	5,401
Zhejiang 浙江	16	49	856	22	0.68	2.36	17.54	71.20	3,214
Anhui 安徽	23	78	4,176	191	9.78	31.00	53.30	68.45	1,951
Fujian 福建	26	21	1,796	-29	-1.87	-3.53	84.30	46.87	1,560
Jiangxi 江西	45	48	872	-16	-1.58	-8.80	18.18	82.07	1,042
Shandong 山東	43	102	4,176	220	3.13	9.62	40.93	67.46	7,021
Central-South 中南	177	69	3,224	-97	-2.03	-6.04	46.43	66.43	4,798
Henan 河南	35	63	4,240	182	2.79	5.13	67.37	45.62	6,529
Hubei 湖北	35	114	6,743	264	7.00	24.55	59.30	71.48	3,775
Hunan 湖南	45	45	1,306	34	2.49	11.94	28.72	79.14	1,348
Guangdong 廣東	37	59	2,446	-653	-7.77	-65.13	41.19	88.08	8,411
Guangxi 廣西	25	75	1,477	-408	-8.73	-13.89	19.81	37.12	4,666
Hainan 海南									
Southwest 西南	65	54	780	-51	-3.20	-10.44	14.33	69.36	1,597
Chongqing 重慶	14	53	434	-188	-26.20	-706.83	8.12	96.29	719
Sichuan 四川	29	44	808	126	10.44	29.56	18.38	64.69	1,207
Guizhou 貴州	8	38	429	20	4.30	10.67	11.28	59.68	465
Yunnan 雲南	15	83	1,225	-162	-4.34	-13.65	14.69	68.21	3,733
Tibet 西藏									
Northwest 西北	56	36	612	8	0.80	2.36	17.15	66.06	1,024
Shaanxi 陝西	22	46	831	-5	-0.43	-2.22	17.91	80.76	1,174
Gansu 甘肅	16	31	593	26	2.51	5.04	19.04	50.21	1,022
Qinghai 青海	7	31	186	-77	-7.07	-24.22	6.07	70.81	1,091
Ningxia 寧夏	6	27	443	97	12.18	19.53	16.22	37.61	793
Xinjiang 新疆	5	20	508	24	4.30	10.34	25.15	58.42	558

3139: Other Bricks and Tiles, Lime and Light Construction Materials
其他磚瓦、石灰和輕質建築材料製造業

Year 年份	Number of firms 企業個數	Rate of change 每年變化 (%)	Number of employees 職工人數 (人)	Rate of change 每年變化 (%)	Total revenue (mil. RMB) 總銷售收入 (百萬元)	Rate of change 每年變化 (%)	Total profit (mil. RMB) 總利潤 (百萬元)	Rate of change 每年變化 (%)
1993	897		55,945		1,531		72	
1994	933	4.01%	58,668	4.87%	1,548	1.13%	62	-13.84%
1995	729	-21.87%	51,775	-11.75%	1,519	-1.87%	-20	-131.79%
1996	766	5.08%	51,897	0.24%	1,792	17.97%	13	165.58%

3 Major products* 3 種主要產品 *	Output 產量	Sales volume 銷售量	Unit 單位
a) Cement Block 水泥磚	24,785,496	24,289,786	block 塊
b) Light Calcium Carbonate 輕質碳酸鈣	60,508	57,483	ton 噸
c) Glazed Brick 釉面磚	139	114	10,000 square metre 萬平方米

Top 10 firms by revenue (year founded) 收入排名前 10 家企業 (創辦年份)	City 城市	Province 省	Telephone / fax 電話 / 傳真	Number of employees 職工人數	Ownership 產業所有權	Revenue ('000 RMB) 銷售收入 (千元)	Profit ('000 RMB) (rank) 利潤 (千元) (排名)	Total assets ('000 RMB) 總資產 (千元)	Major products 主要產品
Tianjin Bao Ming Group Co. Ltd. 天津市豹鳴集團有限公司(1995)	Tianjin 天津市	Tianjin 天津市	(022)9341402 (022)9342402	93	State-owned 國有	79,853	6162(1)	121,748	o
Henan Zhongmo Zheng An Sand Factory 河南省中牟縣鄭庵砂廠(1979)	Zhengzhou 鄭州市	Henan 河南省	(0371)2262055	278	Collectively-owned 集體	60,580	2780(6)	25,250	o
Longkou Dong Jiang Building Ceramics Factory 龍口市東江建築陶瓷廠(1985)	Yantai 煙台市	Shandong 山東省	(0535)8619019	1,319	Collectively-owned 集體	57,690	2000(10)	39,680	c
Xin Artistic Ceramics Ci Industrial Co. Ltd. Zhengzhou Branch 新美陶瓷工業有限公司鄭州分公司(1995)	Zhengzhou 鄭州市	Henan 河南省	(0371)2568347	470	Foreign-funded 外資	48,580	2470(8)	155,394	o
Xiaogan Guangsha Industrial General Co. 孝感市廣廈實業有限公司	Xiaogan 孝感市	Hubei 湖北省	(0712)2410048	865	Collectively-owned 集體	47,650	1591(11)	12,439	o
Xiangyang Xiang Xi Building Materials Co. 襄陽襄西建材綜合有限公司	Xiangfan 襄樊市	Hubei 湖北省		168	Collectively-owned 集體	45,098	4490(2)	27,380	o
Xiao Chi Chemical Construction Co. Ltd. 小池化建有限公司(1975)	Huanggang 黃岡市	Hubei 湖北省	(0713)3436490	257	Collectively-owned 集體	43,760	264(59)	15,366	o
Guangde Xin Hang Zhen Glazed Tile Factory 廣德縣新杭鎮琉璃瓦廠(1993)	Xuanzhou 宣州市	Anhui 安徽省	(0563)6086195	34	Collectively-owned 集體	32,481	8(136)	582	o
Linyi Tian Ren Architectural Pottery Co. Ltd. 臨沂天仁建陶有限公司(1994)	Linyi 臨沂市	Shandong 山東省	(0539)8241052 (0539)8241990	322	Overseas Chinese-funded 港澳台資	31,360	3158(4)	45,449	o
Fushun Shun Tong Industrial Co. Ltd. 撫順市順通工業有限公司(1987)	Fushun 撫順市	Liaoning 遼寧省	(0413)4071218 (0413)4071258	350	Foreign-funded 外資	30,638	587(29)	24,538	o

Top 10 Cities by Production Output 產出排名前 10 位城市	Province 省	Market share 市場份額	Number of firms 企業個數
Suzhou 蘇州市	Jiangsu 江蘇省	12.36%	13
Beijing 北京市	Beijing 北京市	7.87%	19
Zhengzhou 鄭州市	Henan 河南省	7.63%	7
Shanghai 上海市	Shanghai 上海市	4.88%	23
Shaoxing 紹興市	Zhejiang 浙江省	3.80%	6
Wuxi 無錫市	Jiangsu 江蘇省	2.46%	10
Fushun 撫順市	Liaoning 遼寧省	2.37%	5
Changzhou 常州市	Jiangsu 江蘇省	2.36%	4
Linyi 臨沂市	Shandong 山東省	2.28%	4
Liu'an 六安市	Anhui 安徽省	2.13%	10

10 Major Wholesalers 10 家主要批發商	City 城市	Province 省	Telephone / Fax 電話 / 傳真
Chengdu Sheng Xing Trade Company 成都盛興商貿公司	Chengdu 成都市	Sichuan 四川省	(028)7762591
Shanghai Municipal Administration Engineering Material Company 上海市市政工程材料公司	Shanghai 上海市	Shanghai 上海市	(021)64372632
Shanghai Construction Engineering Material Co. 上海市建築工程材料公司	Shanghai 上海市	Shanghai 上海市	(021)63298630
Yixing Jin San Jiao Zhao Bazaar 宜興市金三角招商城	Wuxi 無錫市	Jiangsu 江蘇省	(0510)7935138 (0510)7935138
Fujian Hua Fu Import & Export Company 福建省華福進出口公司	Fuzhou 福州市	Fujian 福建省	(0591)7810477 (0591)7810485
China Building Goods & Materials Company 中國建築物資公司	Beijing 北京市	Beijing 北京市	(010)68586253
Dalian Jinzhou Xin Gang Industry & Trade Company 大連金州新港工貿公司	Dalian 大連市	Liaoning 遼寧省	(0411)7624747
Shanghai Zhan Dong Industrial Co. Ltd. 上海展東實業有限公司	Shanghai 上海市	Shanghai 上海市	(021)58201778 (021)58200874
China Building Materials and Equipment Import & Export Company 中國建築材料及設備進出口公司	Beijing 北京市	Beijing 北京市	(010)68393420
Dandong Chemical Light Industry Material Company Chemical Construction Material Marketing Station 丹東市化工輕工材料公司化工建材經銷站	Dandong 丹東市	Liaoning 遼寧省	(0415)2146396

*Also include sales by firms outside this industry.包括本行業以外廠家的銷售。"o" stands for "others". "o" 代表"其他產品"。

3141: Construction Glass 建築用玻璃製品業

The industry accounts for 0.212% of the total revenue of China's industrial sector in 1996. The revenue growth rate of the industry is -16.2% from 1995, as compared to the growth rate of China's industrial sector, 9.51%. The rate of return on asset is -0.72%. 62.06% of all firms in the industry made a profit while 30.20% had negative returns. The top province in terms of the industry's revenue is Guangdong, accounting for 11.11% of the total revenue.
本行業在1996年佔全行業總產值0.212%，行業年增長率為-16.2%（全國工業年增長率9.51%）。行業的資產回報率-0.72%，62.06%的企業盈利，30.20%的企業虧損。銷售收入最高的省份為廣東省，佔本行業的11.11%。

	Total number of firms 企業總數	Total number of employees 職工總數	Total revenue (mil. RMB) 總銷售收入（百萬元）	Total profit (mil. RMB) 總利潤（百萬元）	Return on assets 資產利潤率 (%)	Return on equity 權益利潤率 (%)	Labour productivity ('000 RMB / worker) 勞動生產率（千元/人）	Debts / assets 資產負債率 (%)	Total assets (mil. RMB) 總資產（百萬元）
Industry Overall 行業總體	577	199,142	12,300	-239	-0.72	-1.68	61.76	57.28	33,216

	Number of firms 企業個數	Average number of employees 平均職工人數	Average revenue ('000 RMB) 平均銷售收入（千元）	Average profit ('000 RMB) 平均利潤（千元）	Return on assets 資產利潤率 (%)	Return on equity 權益利潤率 (%)	Labour productivity ('000 RMB / worker) 勞動生產率（千元/人）	Average debts / assets 平均資產負債率(%)	Average Total assets ('000 RMB) 平均總資產（千元）
By ownership 產業所有權									
State-owned 國有	111	1,010	45,027	-2,450	-1.67	-3.87	44.59	56.92	146,793
Collectively-owned 集體	315	185	10,045	22	0.12	0.49	54.27	74.35	17,584
Privately-owned 私有	31	97	2,700	10	0.35	0.47	27.73	24.21	2,859
Domestic JVs 聯營	11	97	3,006	-5	-0.08	-0.24	30.88	66.06	5,690
Joint stock 股份制	20	423	62,170	597	0.37	0.62	146.97	39.49	160,144
Foreign-funded 外資	39	255	43,809	198	0.14	0.33	171.73	56.17	136,951
Overseas Chinese-funded 港澳台資	48	177	21,930	131	0.24	0.45	123.77	48.07	55,343
By size 規模									
Large 大型	45	2,451	186,522	-4,841	-0.91	-1.86	76.11	51.06	532,393
Medium 中型	32	1,027	48,903	-231	-0.21	-0.95	47.62	77.93	110,496
Small 小型	485	114	4,719	-23	-0.21	-0.72	41.56	70.86	11,175
By regional distribution 地區分布									
Central-North 華北	139	323	14,931	443	0.92	1.67	46.21	45.09	48,311
Beijing 北京	27	244	7,306	-310	-0.68	-4.34	29.96	84.31	45,569
Tianjin 天津	5	487	24,856	-196	-0.33	-0.53	51.06	36.70	58,538
Hebei 河北	89	319	15,083	825	1.96	3.16	47.22	37.88	42,092
Shanxi 山西	8	386	23,811	151	0.15	0.21	61.65	30.04	103,195
Inner Mongolia 內蒙	10	438	22,093	-366	-0.59	-0.91	50.50	34.86	62,037
Northeast 東北	58	601	25,335	-6,194	-6.41	-20.69	42.14	69.05	96,699
Liaoning 遼寧	36	521	28,914	-7,533	-6.20	-17.52	55.54	64.63	121,551
Jilin 吉林	8	654	16,660	-2,989	-7.69	-310.92	25.48	97.53	38,850
Heilongjiang 黑龍江	14	778	21,090	-4,584	-6.96	-35.50	27.10	80.39	65,849
Central East 華東	130	358	32,336	1,778	2.33	4.78	90.40	51.18	76,228
Shanghai 上海	11	782	101,216	18,437	6.77	9.74	129.39	30.48	272,227
Jiangsu 江蘇	28	386	35,071	-738	-1.05	-2.90	90.91	63.62	69,989
Zhejiang 浙江	22	203	20,406	1,148	2.34	6.38	100.70	63.31	49,024
Anhui 安徽	20	193	11,370	294	1.28	2.41	58.79	47.10	23,020
Fujian 福建	6	388	48,258	3,243	2.26	4.88	124.32	53.72	143,665
Jiangxi 江西	10	241	7,350	-1,351	-11.05	79.38	30.56	113.92	12,224
Shandong 山東	33	425	32,393	360	0.49	1.16	76.17	57.99	73,707
Central-South 中南	171	278	20,829	-752	-1.66	-4.60	74.79	63.95	45,316
Henan 河南	61	266	17,276	630	1.73	4.68	64.95	63.08	36,452
Hubei 湖北	18	338	20,411	56	0.17	0.43	60.48	60.98	33,138
Hunan 湖南	21	552	28,291	-4,510	-6.55	-27.91	51.24	76.54	68,890
Guangdong 廣東	58	189	23,569	-1,106	-2.16	-5.88	124.63	63.29	51,275
Guangxi 廣西	11	242	15,264	-272	-0.70	-0.97	63.00	27.55	38,583
Hainan 海南	2	46	5,710	-3,060	-7.29	-375.46	124.13	98.06	41,960
Southwest 西南	49	253	11,387	-408	-1.03	-2.66	45.02	61.40	39,782
Chongqing 重慶	9	262	7,058	-1,745	-14.32	-67.79	26.96	78.88	12,190
Sichuan 四川	26	231	14,187	1,237	2.48	6.23	61.53	60.16	49,828
Guizhou 貴州	5	270	5,596	-1,316	-7.51	-17.49	20.74	57.08	17,534
Yunnan 雲南	9	297	11,223	179	0.34	0.88	37.85	61.28	52,719
Tibet 西藏									
Northwest 西北	30	428	14,394	-789	-1.84	-6.21	33.62	70.29	42,796
Shaanxi 陝西	14	417	12,134	-1,249	-3.19	-14.00	29.13	77.21	39,139
Gansu 甘肅	10	524	21,483	68	0.12	0.29	41.01	60.21	58,808
Qinghai 青海	1	712	22,750	120	0.20	2.02	31.95	89.95	59,230
Ningxia 寧夏	2	412	9,590	-3,735	-9.63	-77.33	23.30	87.53	38,775
Xinjiang 新疆	3	80	1,730	160	4.33	6.87	21.54	36.91	3,693

3141: Construction Glass 建築用玻璃製品業

Year 年份	Number of firms 企業個數	Rate of change 每年變化 (%)	Number of employees 職工人數 (人)	Rate of change 每年變化 (%)	Total revenue (mil. RMB) 總銷售收入 (百萬元)	Rate of change 每年變化 (%)	Total profit (mil. RMB) 總利潤 (百萬元)	Rate of change 每年變化 (%)
1993	346		217,325		13,309		2,465	
1994	467	34.97%	190,177	-12.49%	14,220	6.84%	2,495	1.21%
1995	589	26.12%	222,958	17.24%	14,670	3.17%	1,928	-22.74%
1996	577	-2.04%	199,142	-10.68%	12,300	-16.16%	-239	-112.40%

3 Major products* 3 種主要產品 *	Output 產量	Sales volume 銷售量	Unit 單位
a) Float Glass 浮法玻璃	311,302,659	261,494,233	square metre 平方米
b) Vertical Drawn Glass 垂直引上法玻璃	56,197,101	46,643,594	weight box 重量箱
c) Other Glass 其他玻璃	19,687,456	19,687,456	weight box 重量箱

Top 10 firms by revenue (year founded) 收入排名前 10 家企業 (創辦年份)	City 城市	Province 省	Telephone / fax 電話 / 傳真	Number of employees 職工人數	Ownership 產業所有權	Revenue ('000 RMB) 銷售收入 (千元)	Profit ('000 RMB) (rank) 利潤 (千元) (排名)	Total assets ('000 RMB) 總資產 (千元)	Major products 主要產品
China Yao Hua Glass Group Co. 中國耀華玻璃集團公司(1922)	Qinhuangdao 秦皇島市	Hebei 河北省	(0335)3033844 (0335)3033998	11,730	State-owned 國有	603,949	41373(4)	2,503,986	a,b
Shanghai Yaohua Pilkington Glass Co. Ltd. 上海耀華皮爾金頓玻璃有限公司(1983)	Shanghai 上海市	Shanghai 上海市	(021)58839305 (021)58801554	944	Joint stock 股份制	589,534	126737(1)	1,893,819	a
Jiangsu Hua Run Group Co. 江蘇華潤集團公司(1970)	Suzhou 蘇州市	Jiangsu 江蘇省	(0512)8550102 (0512)8550252	2,666	Collectively-owned 集體	504,266	43381(3)	733,390	a
Shenyang Xing Guang Building Materials Group Co. 瀋陽星光建築材料集團公司(1993)	Shenyang 瀋陽市	Liaoning 遼寧省	(024)23239175 (024)23239177	1,302	State-owned 國有	394,444	-50371(308)	2,069,260	o
Guangdong Float Glass Co. Ltd. 廣東浮法玻璃有限公司(1985)	Shenzhen 深圳市	Guangdong 廣東省	(0755)6692135 (0755)6696593	546	Foreign-funded 外資	333,830	-20873(303)	597,827	a
Zhuzhou Glass Factory 株洲玻璃廠(1959)	Zhuzhou 株洲市	Hunan 湖南省	(0733)8305686 (0733)8331439	6,861	State-owned 國有	288,502	-86911(309)	677,519	a,b
Zhongshan Chen Xing Glass Co. Ltd. 中山市晨星玻璃股份有限公司(1993)	Zhongshan 中山市	Guangdong 廣東省	(0760)8634141 (0760)8639149	3,229	Joint stock 股份制	283,883	2092(25)	548,915	o
Hangzhou Float Glass Industrial Co. Ltd. 杭州浮法玻璃工業有限公司(1993)	Hangzhou 杭州市	Zhejiang 浙江省	(0571)8144501 (0571)8145649	1,273	Overseas Chinese-funded 港澳台資	277,424	25215(6)	724,074	a,b
Ming Da Glass (Xiamen) Co. Ltd. 明達玻璃(廈門)有限公司(1993)	Xiamen 廈門市	Fujian 福建省	(0592)6211168 (0592)6212364	2,195	Foreign-funded 外資	276,469	19093(8)	848,946	a,b
Qingdao Float Glass Co. Ltd. 青島浮法玻璃有限公司(1993)	Qingdao 青島市	Shandong 山東省	(0532)3161177 (0532)3161203	750	Foreign-funded 外資	228,525	-32558(306)	630,518	a

Top 10 Cities by Production Output 產出排名前 10 位城市	Province 省	Market share 市場份額	Number of firms 企業個數
Shanghai 上海市	Shanghai 上海市	10.17%	21
Qinhuangdao 秦皇島市	Hebei 河北省	6.17%	6
Luoyang 洛陽市	Henan 河南省	5.76%	5
Suzhou 蘇州市	Jiangsu 江蘇省	4.81%	12
Dalian 大連市	Liaoning 遼寧省	3.42%	5
Zhongshan 中山市	Guangdong 廣東省	3.14%	7
Shangqiu 商丘市	Henan 河南省	3.12%	4
Shenzhen 深圳市	Guangdong 廣東省	3.05%	4
Jiaozuo 焦作市	Henan 河南省	3.03%	5
Qingdao 青島市	Shandong 山東省	2.80%	4

10 Major Wholesalers 10 家主要批發商	City 城市	Province 省	Telephone / Fax 電話 / 傳真
Chengdu Sheng Xing Trade Company 成都盛興商貿公司	Chengdu 成都市	Sichuan 四川省	(028)7762591
Shanghai Municipal Administration Engineering Material Company 上海市市政工程材料公司	Shanghai 上海市	Shanghai 上海市	(021)64372632
Shanghai Construction Engineering Material Co. 上海市建築工程材料公司	Shanghai 上海市	Shanghai 上海市	(021)63298630
Yixing Jin San Jiao Zhao Bazaar 宜興市金三角招商城	Wuxi 無錫市	Jiangsu 江蘇省	(0510)7935138 (0510)7935138
Fujian Hua Fu Import & Export Company 福建省華福進出口公司	Fuzhou 福州市	Fujian 福建省	(0591)7810477 (0591)7810485
China Building Goods & Materials Company 中國建築物資公司	Beijing 北京市	Beijing 北京市	(010)68586253
Dalian Jinzhou Xin Gang Industry & Trade Company 大連金州新港工貿公司	Dalian 大連市	Liaoning 遼寧省	(0411)7624747
Shanghai Zhan Dong Industrial Co. Ltd. 上海展東實業有限公司	Shanghai 上海市	Shanghai 上海市	(021)58201778 (021)58200874
China Building Materials and Equipment Import & Export Company 中國建築材料及設備進出口公司	Beijing 北京市	Beijing 北京市	(010)68393420
Dandong Chemical Light Industry Material Company Chemical Construction Material Marketing Station 丹東市化工輕工材料公司化工建材經銷站	Dandong 丹東市	Liaoning 遼寧省	(0415)2146396

*Also include sales by firms outside this industry.包括本行業以外廠家的銷售。"o" stands for "others". "o" 代表"其他產品"。

3142: Industrial Glass 工業技術用玻璃製造業

The industry accounts for 0.053% of the total revenue of China's industrial sector in 1996. The revenue growth rate of the industry is 3.0% from 1995, as compared to the growth rate of China's industrial sector, 9.51%. The rate of return on asset is 2.37%. 64.94% of all firms in the industry made a profit while 29.63% had negative returns. The top province in terms of the industry's revenue is Guangdong, accounting for 49.08% of the total revenue.
本行業在1996年佔全行業總產值0.053%，行業年增長率為3.0%（全國工業年增長率9.51%）。行業的資產回報率2.37%，64.94%的企業盈利，29.63%的企業虧損。銷售收入最高的省份為廣東省，佔本行業的49.08%。

	Total number of firms 企業總數	Total number of employees 職工總數	Total revenue (mil. RMB) 總銷售收入（百萬元）	Total profit (mil. RMB) 總利潤（百萬元）	Return on assets 資產利潤率 (%)	Return on equity 權益利潤率 (%)	Labour productivity ('000 RMB / worker) 勞動生產率（千元/人）	Debts / assets 資產負債率 (%)	Total assets (mil. RMB) 總資產（百萬元）
Industry Overall 行業總體	289	29,893	3,067	175	2.37	7.67	102.60	69.15	7,400

	Number of firms 企業個數	Average number of employees 平均職工人數	Average revenue ('000 RMB) 平均銷售收入（千元）	Average profit ('000 RMB) 平均利潤（千元）	Return on assets 資產利潤率 (%)	Return on equity 權益利潤率 (%)	Labour productivity ('000 RMB / worker) 勞動生產率（千元/人）	Average debts / assets 平均資產負債率(%)	Average Total assets ('000 RMB) 平均總資產（千元）
By ownership 產業所有權									
State-owned 國有	35	208	3,829	-714	-4.09	-23.58	18.42	82.68	17,486
Collectively-owned 集體	179	67	3,794	22	0.35	1.44	56.28	75.84	6,202
Privately-owned 私有	3	37	836	-112	-0.85	-1.51	22.79	43.69	13,218
Domestic JVs 聯營	5	64	11,084	1,386	8.45	28.79	172.64	70.64	16,400
Joint stock 股份制	4	506	18,569	-10,100	-7.68	-22.79	36.73	66.30	131,484
Foreign-funded 外資	24	127	19,330	1,804	4.37	7.03	152.20	37.92	41,326
Overseas Chinese-funded 港澳台資	39	130	42,518	4,785	4.62	17.45	328.16	73.52	103,567
By size 規模									
Large 大型	5	742	287,176	36,135	5.12	21.90	387.24	76.62	705,805
Medium 中型	12	506	22,479	-3,520	-3.75	-10.48	44.44	64.18	93,793
Small 小型	262	75	5,197	140	1.34	3.51	69.12	61.87	10,427
By regional distribution 地區分布									
Central-North 華北	42	70	6,346	702	4.46	10.39	90.32	57.06	15,737
Beijing 北京	12	82	2,339	-336	-4.03	-9.78	28.70	58.78	8,329
Tianjin 天津	7	28	6,703	1,637	9.70	62.79	238.17	84.55	16,876
Hebei 河北	21	80	8,663	1,082	5.82	10.60	108.22	45.08	18,580
Shanxi 山西	1		630	-1,220	-2.54	-12.79		80.13	48,020
Inner Mongolia 內蒙	1	95	9,000	560	11.94	100.00	94.74	88.06	4,690
Northeast 東北	61	117	2,637	-101	-1.26	-3.05	22.51	58.62	8,051
Liaoning 遼寧	45	121	2,681	-7	-0.10	-0.31	22.23	68.65	6,821
Jilin 吉林	13	114	2,720	-445	-3.33	-5.58	23.91	40.35	13,369
Heilongjiang 黑龍江	3	80	1,630	-37	-1.06	-3.30	20.29	68.05	3,463
Central East 華東	80	104	11,706	602	2.20	5.01	112.59	56.08	27,347
Shanghai 上海	9	76	15,852	572	2.20	5.11	209.81	57.01	26,062
Jiangsu 江蘇	27	134	8,249	-83	-0.65	-3.21	61.59	79.62	12,746
Zhejiang 浙江	11	106	9,113	1,057	5.35	13.17	85.68	59.39	19,772
Anhui 安徽	1	66	230	-20	-1.79	-5.00	3.48	65.18	1,120
Fujian 福建	14	115	27,707	2,141	2.50	4.47	240.04	43.97	85,509
Jiangxi 江西	7	60	1,579	-113	-2.85	-23.44	26.18	87.85	3,963
Shandong 山東	11	68	6,517	405	2.69	16.42	95.84	83.59	15,053
Central-South 中南	72	118	22,564	1,518	2.86	14.02	190.77	79.59	53,043
Henan 河南	18	86	2,342	66	1.68	7.95	27.24	78.89	3,905
Hubei 湖北	9	68	1,871	-601	-13.35	1001.85	27.70	101.33	4,501
Hunan 湖南	13	75	1,618	-82	-2.49	-13.47	21.54	81.52	3,276
Guangdong 廣東	29	172	51,910	3,899	3.19	17.29	301.50	81.53	122,069
Guangxi 廣西	3	130	13,053	517	1.23	1.50	100.41	17.61	41,913
Hainan 海南									
Southwest 西南	28	103	2,685	-196	-2.34	-10.53	26.18	77.74	8,384
Chongqing 重慶	7	107	4,049	-58	-0.57	-2.80	37.80	79.64	10,153
Sichuan 四川	14	141	3,145	-367	-3.25	-14.13	22.23	77.03	11,311
Guizhou 貴州	7	19	400	7	0.94	3.52	21.05	73.22	763
Yunnan 雲南									
Tibet 西藏									
Northwest 西北	6	15	577	-3	-0.31	-0.60	38.02	47.88	1,062
Shaanxi 陝西	2	15	220	-35	-3.02	-25.00	14.67	87.93	1,160
Gansu 甘肅	1								
Qinghai 青海									
Ningxia 寧夏									
Xinjiang 新疆	3	20	1,007	17	1.23	1.65	49.51	24.94	1,350

3142: Industrial Glass 工業技術用玻璃製造業

Year 年份	Number of firms 企業個數	Rate of change 每年變化 (%)	Number of employees 職工人數 (人)	Rate of change 每年變化 (%)	Total revenue (mil. RMB) 總銷售收入 (百萬元)	Rate of change 每年變化 (%)	Total profit (mil. RMB) 總利潤 (百萬元)	Rate of change 每年變化 (%)
1993	241		30,855		1,039		106	
1994	258	7.05%	29,467	-4.50%	2,077	99.78%	118	11.01%
1995	297	15.12%	34,860	18.30%	2,979	43.45%	178	51.07%
1996	289	-2.69%	29,893	-14.25%	3,067	2.95%	175	-1.79%

3 Major products* 3 種主要產品 *	Output 產量	Sales volume 銷售量	Unit 單位
a) Colour Trasislor Glass Shell 彩色晶體管玻殼	10,176,563	8,853,609	piece 只
b) Plane Tempered Glass 平面鋼化玻璃	3,921,143	3,842,721	square metre 平方米
c) Cured Tempered Glass 彎型鋼化玻璃	4,042,179	3,233,744	square metre 平方米

Top 10 firms by revenue (year founded) 收入排名前 10 家企業 (創辦年份)	City 城市	Province 省	Telephone / fax 電話 / 傳真	Number of employees 職工人數	Ownership 產業所有權	Revenue ('000 RMB) 銷售收入 (千元)	Profit ('000 RMB) (rank) 利潤 (千元) (排名)	Total assets ('000 RMB) 總資產 (千元)	Major products 主要產品
Shenzhen Cnedc-conic Glass Co. Ltd. 深圳中康玻璃有限公司(1989)	Shenzhen 深圳市	Guangdong 廣東省	(0755)3311988 (0755)3310743	2,022	Overseas Chinese-funded 港澳台資	877,506	103501(1)	2,274,390	a
Fuyao Glass Industring Group Co. Ltd. 福建省耀華玻璃工業股份有限公司(1988)	Fuzhou 福州市	Fujian 福建省	(0591)5383562 (0591)5383666	576	Foreign-funded 外資	228,350	37171(2)	636,777	c
Fujian Wan Da Automobile Glass Industrial Co. Ltd. 福建省萬達汽車玻璃工業有限公司(1996)	Fuzhou 福州市	Fujian 福建省	(0591)5382726 (0591)5382719	436	Overseas Chinese-funded 港澳台資	129,160	-1650(117)	474,521	o
Shanghai Fu Hua Glass Co. Ltd. 上海福華玻璃有限公司(1994)	Shanghai 上海市	Shanghai 上海市	(021)58836224 (021)58742817	424	Foreign-funded 外資	124,985	4894(12)	210,030	b,c
Qinhuangdao Hai Yan Safety Glass Co. Ltd. 秦皇島海燕安全玻璃有限公司(1992)	Qinhuangdao 秦皇島市	Hebei 河北省	(0335)3063752 (0335)3066239	475	Foreign-funded 外資	100,134	19801(4)	163,651	b,c
Shenzhen Nan Xing Glass Processing Co. Ltd. 深圳南星玻璃加工有限公司(1988)	Shenzhen 深圳市	Guangdong 廣東省	(0755)6693379 (0755)6696223	87	Overseas Chinese-funded 港澳台資	63,960	25266(3)	68,176	b
Taishan Jin An Glass Craft Co. Ltd. 台山金安玻璃工藝有限公司(1995)	Jiangmen 江門市	Guangdong 廣東省	(0750)5527000	120	Collectively-owned 集體	63,166	255(49)	10,320	o
Shenzhen Nan Bo Spandrel & Tempglass Co. Ltd. 深圳南玻彩釉鋼化玻璃有限公司(1993)	Shenzhen 深圳市	Guangdong 廣東省	(0755)6685713 (0755)6682401	57	Overseas Chinese-funded 港澳台資	62,517	7220(8)	43,135	b
Guangdong Lunjiao Automobile Glass Factory 廣東倫教汽車玻璃廠(1978)	Foshan 佛山市	Guangdong 廣東省	(0757)7759375 (0757)7759103	388	Collectively-owned 集體	61,589	2382(18)	73,700	b,c
Hangzhou Safety Glass Co. Ltd. 杭州安全玻璃有限公司(1986)	Hangzhou 杭州市	Zhejiang 浙江省	(0571)8144501 (0571)8145938	270	Foreign-funded 外資	58,642	11022(7)	99,961	o

Top 10 Cities by Production Output 產出排名前 10 位城市	Province 省	Market share 市場份額	Number of firms 企業個數
Fuzhou 福州市	Fujian 福建省	11.97%	1
Shanghai 上海市	Shanghai 上海市	9.81%	17
Guangzhou 廣州市	Guangdong 廣東省	7.43%	13
Foshan 佛山市	Guangdong 廣東省	7.11%	6
Qinhuangdao 秦皇島市	Hebei 河北省	6.43%	11
Nantong 南通市	Jiangsu 江蘇省	4.46%	5
Hangzhou 杭州市	Zhejiang 浙江省	3.39%	6
Jiangmen 江門市	Guangdong 廣東省	3.32%	2
Shenyang 瀋陽市	Liaoning 遼寧省	2.62%	20
Suzhou 蘇州市	Jiangsu 江蘇省	2.55%	8

10 Major Wholesalers 10 家主要批發商	City 城市	Province 省	Telephone / Fax 電話 / 傳真
Chengdu Sheng Xing Trade Company 成都盛興商貿公司	Chengdu 成都市	Sichuan 四川省	(028)7762591
Shanghai Municipal Administration Engineering Material Company 上海市市政工程材料公司	Shanghai 上海市	Shanghai 上海市	(021)64372632
Shanghai Construction Engineering Material Co. 上海市建築工程材料公司	Shanghai 上海市	Shanghai 上海市	(021)63298630
Yixing Jin San Jiao Zhao Bazaar 宜興市金三角招商城	Wuxi 無錫市	Jiangsu 江蘇省	(0510)7935138 (0510)7935138
Fujian Hua Fu Import & Export Company 福建省華福進出口公司	Fuzhou 福州市	Fujian 福建省	(0591)7810477 (0591)7810485
China Building Goods & Materials Company 中國建築物資公司	Beijing 北京市	Beijing 北京市	(010)68586253
Dalian Jinzhou Xin Gang Industry & Trade Company 大連金州新港工貿公司	Dalian 大連市	Liaoning 遼寧省	(0411)7624747
Shanghai Zhan Dong Industrial Co. Ltd. 上海展東實業有限公司	Shanghai 上海市	Shanghai 上海市	(021)58201778 (021)58200874
China Building Materials and Equipment Import & Export Company 中國建築材料及設備進出口公司	Beijing 北京市	Beijing 北京市	(010)68393420
Dandong Chemical Light Industry Material Company Chemical Construction Material Marketing Station 丹東市化工輕工材料公司化工建材經銷站	Dandong 丹東市	Liaoning 遼寧省	(0415)2146396

*Also include sales by firms outside this industry.包括本行業以外廠家的銷售。"o" stands for "others". "o" 代表"其他產品"。

3143: Optical Glass 光學玻璃製造業

The industry accounts for 0.014% of the total revenue of China's industrial sector in 1996. The revenue growth rate of the industry is 2.4% from 1995, as compared to the growth rate of China's industrial sector, 9.51%. The rate of return on asset is 2.60%. 66.92% of all firms in the industry made a profit while 25.81% had negative returns. The top province in terms of the industry's revenue is Sichuan, accounting for 18.68% of the total revenue.
本行業在1996年佔全行業總產值0.014%，行業年增長率為2.4%（全國工業年增長率9.51%）。行業的資產回報率2.60%，66.92%的企業盈利，25.81%的企業虧損。銷售收入最高的省份為四川省，佔本行業的18.68%。

	Total number of firms 企業總數	Total number of employees 職工總數	Total revenue (mil. RMB) 總銷售收入（百萬元）	Total profit (mil. RMB) 總利潤（百萬元）	Return on assets 資產利潤率 (%)	Return on equity 權益利潤率 (%)	Labour productivity ('000 RMB / worker) 勞動生產率（千元/人）	Debts / assets 資產負債率 (%)	Total assets (mil. RMB) 總資產（百萬元）
Industry Overall 行業總體	120	15,274	808	47	2.60	5.08	52.90	48.85	1,801

	Number of firms 企業個數	Average number of employees 平均職工人數	Average revenue ('000 RMB) 平均銷售收入（千元）	Average profit ('000 RMB) 平均利潤（千元）	Return on assets 資產利潤率 (%)	Return on equity 權益利潤率 (%)	Labour productivity ('000 RMB / worker) 勞動生產率（千元/人）	Average debts / assets 平均資產負債率(%)	Average Total assets ('000 RMB) 平均總資產（千元）
By ownership 產業所有權									
State-owned 國有	11	545	27,273	2,364	2.86	5.49	50.04	47.85	82,636
Collectively-owned 集體	73	74	2,767	59	2.86	6.79	37.45	57.90	2,061
Privately-owned 私有	1	24	5,160	32	3.66	11.98	214.98	69.43	883
Domestic JVs 聯營	3	127	1,757	6	0.19	0.39	13.84	50.78	3,209
Joint stock 股份制	2	120	2,076	-51	-1.30	-2.15	17.30	39.68	3,909
Foreign-funded 外資	14	148	8,553	322	2.44	3.17	57.87	23.00	13,169
Overseas Chinese-funded 港澳台資	17	95	10,098	720	2.27	5.27	106.75	56.94	31,726
By size 規模									
Large 大型	4	1,063	87,085	10,098	5.05	8.54	81.90	40.82	199,911
Medium 中型									
Small 小型	110	99	4,178	60	0.66	1.47	42.21	55.28	9,108
By regional distribution 地區分布									
Central-North 華北	16	42	1,184	-93	-3.76	-5.51	28.07	31.70	2,459
Beijing 北京	7	18	1,233	-39	-2.91	-3.40	68.49	14.35	1,324
Tianjin 天津	4	84	2,333	-280	-4.63	-7.71	27.69	40.00	6,050
Hebei 河北	2	39							1,650
Shanxi 山西	2	30	405	-35	-4.09	-11.86	13.50	65.50	855
Inner Mongolia 內蒙	1	75	180	-20	-2.33	-3.92	2.40	39.53	860
Northeast 東北	6	43	1,775	-457	-9.35	-16.98	41.76	44.93	4,885
Liaoning 遼寧	2	18	35	5	0.09	0.10	1.94	15.34	5,770
Jilin 吉林	4	55	2,645	-688	-15.48	-43.17	48.31	64.15	4,443
Heilongjiang 黑龍江									
Central East 華東	50	107	4,659	-216	-2.10	-5.67	43.46	62.98	10,282
Shanghai 上海	7	222	10,186	203	1.58	9.17	45.94	82.81	12,874
Jiangsu 江蘇	18	77	2,255	-46	-1.22	-3.90	29.14	68.82	3,747
Zhejiang 浙江	10	71	2,864	209	5.55	13.84	40.17	59.92	3,767
Anhui 安徽	4	139	2,873	5	0.03	0.05	20.63	38.74	15,920
Fujian 福建	6	162	11,403	-2,623	-6.58	-17.16	70.54	61.67	39,883
Jiangxi 江西									
Shandong 山東	5	35	2,502	448	14.10	28.11	71.49	49.84	3,178
Central-South 中南	29	162	11,540	1,820	7.84	13.84	71.22	43.39	23,230
Henan 河南	6	202	10,923	1,073	6.01	9.19	54.03	34.63	17,870
Hubei 湖北	3	657	42,677	8,057	6.68	12.43	64.92	46.24	120,590
Hunan 湖南	7	89	426	7	0.65	0.84	4.76	23.16	1,104
Guangdong 廣東	12	69	11,501	1,844	11.25	19.98	166.68	43.71	16,397
Guangxi 廣西	1	60	100				1.67	50.00	200
Hainan 海南									
Southwest 西南	16	244	12,308	586	1.78	3.21	50.39	44.47	32,890
Chongqing 重慶	5	181	4,879	20	0.15	0.26	26.96	43.24	13,684
Sichuan 四川	8	336	18,870	807	1.48	2.65	56.16	43.96	54,391
Guizhou 貴州									
Yunnan 雲南	3	116	8,120	990	9.63	21.05	69.80	54.23	10,277
Tibet 西藏									
Northwest 西北	3	126	4,740	-120	-1.99	-2.54	37.72	21.64	6,023
Shaanxi 陝西	3	126	4,740	-120	-1.99	-2.54	37.72	21.64	6,023
Gansu 甘肅									
Qinghai 青海									
Ningxia 寧夏									
Xinjiang 新疆									

3143: Optical Glass 光學玻璃製造業

Year 年份	Number of firms 企業個數	Rate of change 每年變化 (%)	Number of employees 職工人數（人）	Rate of change 每年變化 (%)	Total revenue (mil. RMB) 總銷售收入（百萬元）	Rate of change 每年變化 (%)	Total profit (mil. RMB) 總利潤（百萬元）	Rate of change 每年變化 (%)
1993	104		25,027		635		55	
1994	100	-3.85%	14,272	-42.97%	618	-2.77%	51	-7.85%
1995	126	26.00%	17,510	22.69%	789	27.75%	88	73.58%
1996	120	-4.76%	15,274	-12.77%	808	2.41%	47	-46.74%

3 Major products* 3種主要產品 *	Output 產量	Sales volume 銷售量	Unit 單位
a) Optical Instrument 光學儀器	160,518	141,255	set 台
b) Quartz Glass 石英玻璃	1,979	1,781	ton 噸
c) Daily Glass Products 日用玻璃製品	8,759	8,321	ton 噸

Top 10 firms by revenue (year founded) 收入排名前10家企業（創辦年份）	City 城市	Province 省	Telephone / fax 電話 / 傳真	Number of employees 職工人數	Ownership 產業所有權	Revenue ('000 RMB) 銷售收入（千元）	Profit ('000 RMB) (rank) 利潤（千元）（排名）	Total assets ('000 RMB) 總資產（千元）	Major products 主要產品
Hubei Hua Guang Materials Factory 湖北華光器材廠(1983)	Xiangfan 襄樊市	Hubei 湖北省	(0710)3249087 (0710)4212300	1,841	State-owned 國有	119,260	22080(1)	344,750	o
Chengdu Guang Ming Material Plant 成都光明器材廠(1959)	Chengdu 成都市	Sichuan 四川省	(028)4331612 (028)4332218	1,983	State-owned 國有	99,740	4290(4)	411,050	c
Shenzhen Wei Guang Conducting Electricity Film Co. Ltd. 深圳偉光導電膜有限公司(1993)	Shenzhen 深圳市	Guangdong 廣東省	(0755)6693157 (0755)6678963	50	Overseas Chinese-funded 港澳台資	74,454	19234(2)	111,392	o
Shanghai Xin Hu Glass Factory 上海新滬玻璃廠(1960)	Shanghai 上海市	Shanghai 上海市	(021)59530272 (021)59528160	945	State-owned 國有	53,034	81(30)	70,680	b,c
Nanyang Li Da Photoelectricity Co. Ltd. 南陽利達光電有限公司(1995)	Nanyang 南陽市	Henan 河南省	(0377)3152375 (0377)3167800	828	Foreign-funded 外資	44,715	4888(3)	74,963	c
Foshan Hua Guo Optics Equipment Co. Ltd. 佛山華國光學器材有限公司(1992)	Foshan 佛山市	Guangdong 廣東省	(0757)6488657 (0757)6488434	120	Overseas Chinese-funded 港澳台資	31,756	2690(8)	18,813	c
Shanghai Jia Guang – Si Mi Ke Optics Co. Ltd. 上海嘉光－斯米克光學有限公司(1990)	Shanghai 上海市	Shanghai 上海市	(021)62507952 (021)62505697	250	Foreign-funded 外資	30,480	3515(5)	27,428	o
Fuzhou Ke Teng Photoelectricity Technology Co. Ltd. 福州市科騰光電技術有限公司(1995)	Fuzhou 福州市	Fujian 福建省	(0591)3624948 (0591)3623454	116	Overseas Chinese-funded 港澳台資	30,051	-10402(55)	106,895	o
Shanghai Jing Hua Guang Electric Element Factory 上海靜華光電元件廠(1995)	Shanghai 上海市	Shanghai 上海市	(021)59124065	150	Domestic JVs 聯營	29,940	1458(11)	23,870	o
Genius Electronic Optical (Xiamen) Co. Ltd. 玉晶光電(廈門)有限公司(1994)	Xiamen 廈門市	Fujian 福建省	(0592)6026012 (0592)6026013	280	Overseas Chinese-funded 港澳台資	26,997	-806(50)	90,810	o

Top 10 Cities by Production Output 產出排名前10位城市	Province 省	Market share 市場份額	Number of firms 企業個數
Chengdu 成都市	Sichuan 四川省	21.06%	6
Xiangfan 襄樊市	Hubei 湖北省	14.07%	1
Shanghai 上海市	Shanghai 上海市	12.71%	12
Nanyang 南陽市	Henan 河南省	7.36%	3
Fuzhou 福州市	Fujian 福建省	4.52%	3
Foshan 佛山市	Guangdong 廣東省	4.20%	1
Kunming 昆明市	Yunnan 雲南省	3.72%	8
Nantong 南通市	Jiangsu 江蘇省	3.52%	10
Yantai 煙台市	Shandong 山東省	3.13%	3
Ezhou 鄂州市	Hubei 湖北省	2.94%	2

10 Major Wholesalers 10家主要批發商	City 城市	Province 省	Telephone / Fax 電話 / 傳真
Chengdu Sheng Xing Trade Company 成都盛興商貿公司	Chengdu 成都市	Sichuan 四川省	(028)7762591
Shanghai Municipal Administration Engineering Material Company 上海市市政工程材料公司	Shanghai 上海市	Shanghai 上海市	(021)64372632
Shanghai Construction Engineering Material Co. 上海市建築工程材料公司	Shanghai 上海市	Shanghai 上海市	(021)63298630
Yixing Jin San Jiao Zhao Bazaar 宜興市金三角招商城	Wuxi 無錫市	Jiangsu 江蘇省	(0510)7935138 (0510)7935138
Fujian Hua Fu Import & Export Company 福建省華福進出口公司	Fuzhou 福州市	Fujian 福建省	(0591)7810477 (0591)7810485
China Building Goods & Materials Company 中國建築物資公司	Beijing 北京市	Beijing 北京市	(010)68586253
Dalian Jinzhou Xin Gang Industry & Trade Company 大連金州新港工貿公司	Dalian 大連市	Liaoning 遼寧省	(0411)7624747
Shanghai Zhan Dong Industrial Co. Ltd. 上海展東實業有限公司	Shanghai 上海市	Shanghai 上海市	(021)58201778 (021)58200874
China Building Materials and Equipment Import & Export Company 中國建築材料及設備進出口公司	Beijing 北京市	Beijing 北京市	(010)68393420
Dandong Chemical Light Industry Material Company Chemical Construction Material Marketing Station 丹東市化工輕工材料公司化工建材經銷站	Dandong 丹東市	Liaoning 遼寧省	(0415)2146396

*Also include sales by firms outside this industry.包括本行業以外廠家的銷售。"o" stands for "others". "o" 代表"其他產品"。

3145: Glass Instruments 玻璃儀器製造業

The industry accounts for 0.008% of the total revenue of China's industrial sector in 1996. The revenue growth rate of the industry is 16.7% from 1995, as compared to the growth rate of China's industrial sector, 9.51%. The rate of return on asset is 0.75%. 81.04% of all firms in the industry made a profit while 16.79% had negative returns. The top province in terms of the industry's revenue is Jiangsu, accounting for 32.45% of the total revenue.
本行業在1996年佔全行業總產值0.008%，行業年增長率為16.7%（全國工業年增長率9.51%）。行業的資產回報率0.75%，81.04%的企業盈利，16.79%的企業虧損。銷售收入最高的省份為江蘇省，佔本行業的32.45%。

	Total number of firms 企業總數	Total number of employees 職工總數	Total revenue (mil. RMB) 總銷售收入（百萬元）	Total profit (mil. RMB) 總利潤（百萬元）	Return on assets 資產利潤率 (%)	Return on equity 權益利潤率 (%)	Labour productivity ('000 RMB / worker) 勞動生產率（千元/人）	Debts / assets 資產負債率 (%)	Total assets (mil. RMB) 總資產（百萬元）
Industry Overall 行業總體	160	18,215	436	4	0.75	3.99	23.94	81.15	525

	Number of firms 企業個數	Average number of employees 平均職工人數	Average revenue ('000 RMB) 平均銷售收入（千元）	Average profit ('000 RMB) 平均利潤（千元）	Return on assets 資產利潤率 (%)	Return on equity 權益利潤率 (%)	Labour productivity ('000 RMB / worker) 勞動生產率（千元/人）	Average debts / assets 平均資產負債率(%)	Average Total assets ('000 RMB) 平均總資產（千元）
By ownership 產業所有權									
State-owned 國有	11	382	11,273	-182	-0.81	-14.29	29.50	94.33	22,455
Collectively-owned 集體	147	95	2,112	41	2.19	7.23	22.28	69.69	1,868
Privately-owned 私有									
Domestic JVs 聯營									
Joint stock 股份制									
Foreign-funded 外資	1	57	1,245				21.83	46.65	3,176
Overseas Chinese-funded 港澳台資									
By size 規模									
Large 大型	2	1,552	16,957	2,950	3.88	28.61	10.93	86.45	76,133
Medium 中型	2	1,006	39,140	-1,120	-3.03	-1057.88	38.93	99.71	36,955
Small 小型	155	84	2,088	2	0.11	0.43	24.72	73.84	1,927
By regional distribution 地區分布									
Central-North 華北	22	112	3,902	58	1.07	23.23	34.74	95.40	5,435
Beijing 北京	10	76	1,269	15	0.91	5.21	16.70	82.57	1,647
Tianjin 天津	1	1,318	62,710	810	0.83	130.65	47.58	99.36	97,150
Hebei 河北	9	43	1,157	36	5.51	15.92	26.83	65.40	646
Shanxi 山西									
Inner Mongolia 內蒙	2	3	20				8.00	100.00	65
Northeast 東北	29	29	1,333	104	18.57	56.87	45.85	67.40	561
Liaoning 遼寧	24	29	1,134	120	20.15	67.53	39.62	70.15	593
Jilin 吉林	2	43	135				3.14	91.14	395
Heilongjiang 黑龍江	3	23	3,720	50	12.20	15.15	159.43	20.33	410
Central East 華東	55	190	3,893	29	0.73	3.03	20.52	76.06	4,060
Shanghai 上海	4	434	10,593	-335	-1.73	-38.62	24.39	95.53	19,410
Jiangsu 江蘇	29	78	4,878	88	2.14	6.21	62.31	65.55	4,111
Zhejiang 浙江	5	42	1,128	42	3.46	9.81	26.60	64.74	1,214
Anhui 安徽	10	594	2,141	58	4.82	13.91	3.60	65.37	1,204
Fujian 福建	2	25	30	-60	-5.26	-8.96	1.20	41.23	1,140
Jiangxi 江西	3	39	490	-113	-7.05	-32.69	12.46	78.42	1,607
Shandong 山東	2	53	850	40	6.50	33.33	16.19	81.30	615
Central-South 中南	37	60	1,497	57	2.29	9.99	24.88	77.09	2,503
Henan 河南	12	54	1,026	56	4.15	11.67	18.97	64.44	1,345
Hubei 湖北	5	79	2,046	10	0.36	1.34	25.83	73.00	2,770
Hunan 湖南	14	74	1,332	61	3.78	17.03	17.97	77.88	1,627
Guangdong 廣東	1	138	11,950	440	1.11	6.63	86.59	83.19	39,490
Guangxi 廣西	5	1	448	20	27.78	166.67	448.00	83.33	72
Hainan 海南									
Southwest 西南	15	147	2,768	-273	-5.64	-31.61	18.82	82.14	4,833
Chongqing 重慶	6	151	3,894	-64	-4.15	-17.82	25.73	76.71	1,548
Sichuan 四川	8	163	2,303	-455	-5.85	-34.23	14.15	82.91	7,772
Guizhou 貴州	1								
Yunnan 雲南									
Tibet 西藏									
Northwest 西北	2	17	115	10	2.44	3.70	6.97	34.15	410
Shaanxi 陝西	2	17	115	10	2.44	3.70	6.97	34.15	410
Gansu 甘肅									
Qinghai 青海									
Ningxia 寧夏									
Xinjiang 新疆									

3145: Glass Instruments 玻璃儀器製造業

Year 年份	Number of firms 企業個數	Rate of change 每年變化 (%)	Number of employees 職工人數（人）	Rate of change 每年變化 (%)	Total revenue (mil. RMB) 總銷售收入（百萬元）	Rate of change 每年變化 (%)	Total profit (mil. RMB) 總利潤（百萬元）	Rate of change 每年變化 (%)
1993	150		24,528		306		3	
1994	182	21.33%	19,128	-22.02%	407	32.78%	4	17.82%
1995	155	-14.84%	16,519	-13.64%	374	-8.14%	-3	-185.44%
1996	160	3.23%	18,215	10.27%	436	16.73%	4	220.45%

3 Major products* 3 種主要產品 *	Output 產量	Sales volume 銷售量	Unit 單位
a) Daily Glass Products 日用玻璃製品	35,038	33,286	ton 噸
b) Other Packing Products from Metal 其他金屬製包裝用品	200	196	ton 噸

Top 10 firms by revenue (year founded) 收入排名前 10 家企業 (創辦年份)	City 城市	Province 省	Telephone / fax 電話 / 傳真	Number of employees 職工人數	Ownership 產業所有權	Revenue ('000 RMB) 銷售收入（千元）	Profit ('000 RMB) (rank) 利潤（千元）(排名)	Total assets ('000 RMB) 總資產（千元）	Major products 主要產品
Tianjin Glass Instrument Factory 天津玻璃儀器廠(1938)	Tianjin 天津市	Tianjin 天津市	(022)27326956 (022)27326956	1,329	State-owned 國有	62,706	809(2)	97,145	a
Jiangsu Guo Tai Medicine Packaging Group Co. 江蘇國泰醫藥包裝集團公司(1993)	Zhenjiang 鎮江市	Jiangsu 江蘇省	(0511)6632386	540	Collectively-owned 集體	61,659	475(7)	44,745	o
Shanghai Ya Tai Technology Glass Co. 上海亞太技術玻璃公司(1958)	Shanghai 上海市	Shanghai 上海市	(021)56756277 (021)56755051	1,357	State-owned 國有	38,524	-1500(44)	74,112	a
Yixin Boiler Accessory Instrument Factory 宜興市鍋爐輔機儀表廠(1958)	Wuxi 無錫市	Jiangsu 江蘇省	(0510)7391072	100	Collectively-owned 集體	14,880	320(13)	4,670	o
Tongcheng Glass Container Factory 桐城縣玻璃容器廠(1992)	Anqing 安慶市	Anhui 安徽省	(0556)6106655	394	Collectively-owned 集體	13,500	290(14)	6,940	b
Guangdong Ling Nan Industry General Company Zhuhai Company 廣東省嶺南工業總公司珠海公司(1986)	Zhuhai 珠海市	Guangdong 廣東省	(0756)3357053 (0756)3334800	138	State-owned 國有	11,949	440(10)	39,489	o
Taixing Glass Instrument Factory 泰興市玻璃儀器廠(1965)	Yangzhou 揚州市	Jiangsu 江蘇省	(0514)7770457	124	Collectively-owned 集體	11,233	483(6)	9,548	o
Wan Bao Company 萬寶公司(1996)	Huaiyin 淮陰市	Jiangsu 江蘇省	(0517)7542100	120	Collectively-owned 集體	10,025	546(5)	5,822	o
Harbin Elm Bus Boxcar Back Factory 哈爾濱市榆樹客車棚罪廠(1993)	Harbin 哈爾濱市	Heilongjiang 黑龍江省	(0451)6662691	53	Collectively-owned 集體	9,860	70(21)	400	o
Deyang Glass Instrument Factory 德陽市玻璃儀器廠(1970)	Deyang 德陽市	Sichuan 四川省	(0838)3640080 (0838)3640079	320	Collectively-owned 集體	6,698	-1654(45)	16,211	o

Top 10 Cities by Production Output 產出排名前 10 位城市	Province 省	Market share 市場份額	Number of firms 企業個數
Shanghai 上海市	Shanghai 上海市	26.10%	16
Tianjin 天津市	Tianjin 天津市	15.93%	2
Nantong 南通市	Jiangsu 江蘇省	5.41%	7
Yangzhou 揚州市	Jiangsu 江蘇省	4.90%	6
Yongzhou 永州市	Hunan 湖南省	3.85%	8
Beijing 北京市	Beijing 北京市	3.53%	10
Chuzhou 滁州市	Anhui 安徽省	3.40%	10
Zhuhai 珠海市	Guangdong 廣東省	2.90%	1
Taizhou 泰州市	Jiangsu 江蘇省	2.89%	14
Chengdu 成都市	Sichuan 四川省	2.86%	5

10 Major Wholesalers 10 家主要批發商	City 城市	Province 省	Telephone / Fax 電話 / 傳真
Chengdu Sheng Xing Trade Company 成都盛興商貿公司	Chengdu 成都市	Sichuan 四川省	(028)7762591
Shanghai Municipal Administration Engineering Material Company 上海市市政工程材料公司	Shanghai 上海市	Shanghai 上海市	(021)64372632
Shanghai Construction Engineering Material Co. 上海市建築工程材料公司	Shanghai 上海市	Shanghai 上海市	(021)63298630
Yixing Jin San Jiao Zhao Bazaar 宜興市金三角招商城	Wuxi 無錫市	Jiangsu 江蘇省	(0510)7935138 (0510)7935138
Fujian Hua Fu Import & Export Company 福建省華福進出口公司	Fuzhou 福州市	Fujian 福建省	(0591)7810477 (0591)7810485
China Building Goods & Materials Company 中國建築物資公司	Beijing 北京市	Beijing 北京市	(010)68586253
Dalian Jinzhou Xin Gang Industry & Trade Company 大連金州新港工貿公司	Dalian 大連市	Liaoning 遼寧省	(0411)7624747
Shanghai Zhan Dong Industrial Co. Ltd. 上海展東實業有限公司	Shanghai 上海市	Shanghai 上海市	(021)58201778 (021)58200874
China Building Materials and Equipment Import & Export Company 中國建築材料及設備進出口公司	Beijing 北京市	Beijing 北京市	(010)68393420
Dandong Chemical Light Industry Material Company Chemical Construction Material Marketing Station 丹東市化工輕工材料公司化工建材經銷站	Dandong 丹東市	Liaoning 遼寧省	(0415)2146396

*Also include sales by firms outside this industry.包括本行業以外廠家的銷售。"o" stands for "others". "o" 代表 "其他產品"。

3147: Household Glass Products 日用玻璃製品業

The industry accounts for 0.198% of the total revenue of China's industrial sector in 1996. The revenue growth rate of the industry is 11.7% from 1995, as compared to the growth rate of China's industrial sector, 9.51%. The rate of return on asset is 0.52%. 66.42% of all firms in the industry made a profit while 26.06% had negative returns. The top province in terms of the industry's revenue is Shandong, accounting for 18.92% of the total revenue.
本行業在1996年佔全行業總產值0.198%，行業年增長率為11.7%（全國工業年增長率9.51%）。行業的資產回報率0.52%，66.42%的企業盈利，26.06%的企業虧損。銷售收入最高的省份為山東省，佔本行業的18.92%。

	Total number of firms 企業總數	Total number of employees 職工總數	Total revenue (mil. RMB) 總銷售收入（百萬元）	Total profit (mil. RMB) 總利潤（百萬元）	Return on assets 資產利潤率 (%)	Return on equity 權益利潤率 (%)	Labour productivity ('000 RMB / worker) 勞動生產率（千元/人）	Debts / assets 資產負債率 (%)	Total assets (mil. RMB) 總資產（百萬元）
Industry Overall 行業總體	1,128	280,139	11,507	104	0.52	2.07	41.08	74.99	19,989

	Number of firms 企業個數	Average number of employees 平均職工人數	Average revenue ('000 RMB) 平均銷售收入（千元）	Average profit ('000 RMB) 平均利潤（千元）	Return on assets 資產利潤率 (%)	Return on equity 權益利潤率 (%)	Labour productivity ('000 RMB / worker) 勞動生產率（千元/人）	Average debts / assets 平均資產負債率(%)	Average Total assets ('000 RMB) 平均總資產（千元）
By ownership 產業所有權									
State-owned 國有	254	597	20,083	-465	-0.96	-5.99	33.63	84.01	48,520
Collectively-owned 集體	773	142	5,885	267	5.21	18.30	41.39	71.50	5,129
Privately-owned 私有	1	14	776	103	38.73	38.73	55.46		265
Domestic JVs 聯營	11	250	17,045	762	4.22	21.54	68.21	80.41	18,073
Joint stock 股份制	11	341	17,185	-2,134	-7.05	19.59	50.44	135.97	30,270
Foreign-funded 外資	33	223	19,023	-410	-0.81	-1.45	85.18	44.39	50,820
Overseas Chinese-funded 港澳台資	43	207	19,804	1,018	2.94	4.18	95.61	29.77	34,674
By size 規模									
Large 大型	31	1,649	100,329	-971	-0.39	-1.22	60.86	67.89	248,618
Medium 中型	84	845	37,519	1,022	1.61	7.03	44.41	77.05	63,336
Small 小型	990	160	5,293	51	0.74	3.89	33.04	81.02	6,967
By regional distribution 地區分布									
Central-North 華北	161	274	9,325	243	1.13	5.42	34.05	79.05	21,419
Beijing 北京	21	520	16,746	556	0.76	2.53	32.18	69.82	72,914
Tianjin 天津	12	269	14,858	-3	-0.02	-0.28	55.25	94.29	20,651
Hebei 河北	80	202	7,965	286	2.40	14.84	39.44	83.83	11,899
Shanxi 山西	33	278	5,739	91	0.66	4.12	20.65	83.91	13,650
Inner Mongolia 內蒙	15	307	9,653	111	0.62	8.41	31.44	92.60	17,805
Northeast 東北	105	241	4,494	-424	-2.71	-25.71	18.62	89.46	15,641
Liaoning 遼寧	55	280	3,982	-632	-3.23	-58.37	14.23	94.46	19,537
Jilin 吉林	32	217	6,268	-310	-2.13	-12.11	28.86	82.38	14,523
Heilongjiang 黑龍江	18	167	2,905	8	0.14	0.44	17.41	69.25	5,727
Central East 華東	400	263	14,093	395	1.84	6.35	53.60	71.05	21,472
Shanghai 上海	34	261	18,739	392	0.96	2.84	71.78	66.30	40,958
Jiangsu 江蘇	113	230	11,002	105	0.80	2.73	47.77	70.71	13,106
Zhejiang 浙江	60	124	5,274	-6	-0.07	-0.20	42.66	62.61	8,557
Anhui 安徽	52	315	16,757	836	3.84	12.33	53.22	68.84	21,748
Fujian 福建	29	206	10,631	704	4.90	10.21	51.57	52.04	14,388
Jiangxi 江西	40	113	2,091	-220	-3.81	-191.72	18.47	98.01	5,777
Shandong 山東	72	500	30,238	1,083	2.28	9.35	60.53	75.63	47,537
Central-South 中南	258	205	9,535	-159	-0.98	-3.33	46.54	70.67	16,329
Henan 河南	69	256	7,787	9	0.08	1.05	30.41	92.38	11,437
Hubei 湖北	44	216	5,478	-218	-2.11	-19.65	25.32	89.28	10,335
Hunan 湖南	53	118	4,077	25	0.44	2.04	34.52	78.29	5,667
Guangdong 廣東	66	188	17,240	-440	-1.31	-3.10	91.74	57.72	33,649
Guangxi 廣西	26	269	12,605	-170	-0.99	-3.60	46.81	72.65	17,219
Hainan 海南									
Southwest 西南	154	283	8,057	-36	-0.34	-2.11	28.48	84.04	10,851
Chongqing 重慶	40	260	8,417	104	0.99	6.13	32.32	83.85	10,535
Sichuan 四川	92	317	8,965	2	0.01	0.09	28.24	83.25	10,839
Guizhou 貴州	18	160	2,457	-606	-5.18	-57.45	15.34	91.00	11,712
Yunnan 雲南	4	281	8,858	235	2.24	7.37	31.52	69.55	10,475
Tibet 西藏									
Northwest 西北	50	182	3,916	-40	-0.47	-1.72	21.47	72.77	8,504
Shaanxi 陝西	28	200	3,221	-251	-3.35	-15.15	16.08	77.92	7,514
Gansu 甘肅	10	181	4,760	89	0.84	3.65	26.31	76.99	10,585
Qinghai 青海	1								
Ningxia 寧夏	2	34	70	-70	-8.48	1400.00	2.06	100.61	825
Xinjiang 新疆	9	182	6,430	478	4.01	9.57	35.37	58.10	11,921

3147: Household Glass Products 日用玻璃製品業

Year 年份	Number of firms 企業個數	Rate of change 每年變化 (%)	Number of employees 職工人數 (人)	Rate of change 每年變化 (%)	Total revenue (mil. RMB) 總銷售收入 (百萬元)	Rate of change 每年變化 (%)	Total profit (mil. RMB) 總利潤 (百萬元)	Rate of change 每年變化 (%)
1993	910		231,768		6,881		-115	
1994	1,032	13.41%	250,396	8.04%	8,068	17.25%	-29	74.59%
1995	1,205	16.76%	309,853	23.75%	10,299	27.65%	78	364.36%
1996	1,128	-6.39%	280,139	-9.59%	11,507	11.73%	104	34.10%

3 Major products* 3 種主要產品 *	Output 產量	Sales volume 銷售量	Unit 單位
a) Daily Glass Products 日用玻璃製品	6,954,670	6,606,937	ton 噸
b) Rolled Glass 壓延玻璃	3,762,000	3,498,660	square metre 標準平方米
c) Vacuum Glass Container 玻璃保溫容器	2,118	2,055	10,000 piece 萬個

Top 10 firms by revenue (year founded) 收入排名前 10 家企業 (創辦年份)	City 城市	Province 省	Telephone / fax 電話 / 傳真	Number of employees 職工人數	Ownership 產業所有權	Revenue ('000 RMB) 銷售收入 (千元)	Profit ('000 RMB) (rank) 利潤 (千元) (排名)	Total assets ('000 RMB) 總資產 (千元)	Major products 主要產品
Aci-guangdong Glass Co. Ltd. 廣東澳聯玻璃有限公司(1994)	Guangzhou 廣州市	Guangdong 廣東省	(020)85525021 (020)85524207	1,437	Overseas Chinese-funded 港澳台資	329,026	2410(41)	831,298	a
Beijing Glass Group Co. 北京玻璃集團公司(1964)	Beijing 北京市	Beijing 北京市	(010)67711645 (010)67711645	9,348	State-owned 國有	277,763	51(320)	1,388,009	a
Bozhou Zhang Ji Glass Products Co. Ltd. 亳州市張集玻璃製品有限公司(1996)	Fuyang 阜陽市	Anhui 安徽省	(0558)5501115	440	Collectively-owned 集體	220,310	26430(2)	55,570	o
Aci-shanghai Glass Co. Ltd. 上海澳聯玻璃有限公司(1993)	Shanghai 上海市	Shanghai 上海市	(021)64779638 (021)64766547	548	Foreign-funded 外資	219,713	9453(11)	489,441	a
Dezhou Jing Feng Group General Co. 德州晶峯集團總公司(1955)	Dezhou 德州市	Shandong 山東省	(0534)2324924 (0534)2348984	2,645	State-owned 國有	162,273	19027(5)	226,926	a
Shandong Chang Sheng Tai Group Co. 山東長盛泰集團公司(1980)	Weifang 濰坊市	Shandong 山東省	(0536)2576437 (0536)2576135	1,462	Collectively-owned 集體	150,597	850(101)	93,463	a
Shandong Medical Glass Co. Ltd. 山東省藥用玻璃股份有限公司(1970)	Zibo 淄博市	Shandong 山東省	(0533)3242312 (0533)3243376	2,727	Joint stock 股份制	143,320	20190(4)	200,228	a
Shanghai Glass Plant 上海玻璃廠(1953)	Shanghai 上海市	Shanghai 上海市	(021)56627988 (021)56633129	2,238	State-owned 國有	119,504	-1532(544)	287,020	a
Weifang Anqiu Glass Co. Ltd. 濰坊市安丘玻璃股份有限公司(1959)	Weifang 濰坊市	Shandong 山東省	(0536)4221938 (0536)4222923	1,461	Joint stock 股份制	105,819	720(112)	75,589	a
Anhui Bengbu Glass Factory 安徽省蚌埠市玻璃廠(1954)	Bengbu 蚌埠市	Anhui 安徽省	(0552)4017913 (0552)4013357	2,463	State-owned 國有	103,427	203(221)	129,291	a,c

Top 10 Cities by Production Output 產出排名前 10 位城市	Province 省	Market share 市場份額	Number of firms 企業個數
Qingdao 青島市	Shandong 山東省	4.93%	12
Guangzhou 廣州市	Guangdong 廣東省	4.43%	25
Chongqing 重慶市	Chongqing 重慶市	3.70%	62
Beijing 北京市	Beijing 北京市	3.11%	20
Qinhuangdao 秦皇島市	Hebei 河北省	2.86%	4
Zibo 淄博市	Shandong 山東省	2.59%	13
Weifang 濰坊市	Shandong 山東省	2.48%	4
Shanghai 上海市	Shanghai 上海市	2.41%	54
Nantong 南通市	Jiangsu 江蘇省	2.04%	33
Dezhou 德州市	Shandong 山東省	1.98%	5

10 Major Wholesalers 10 家主要批發商	City 城市	Province 省	Telephone / Fax 電話 / 傳真
Chengdu Sheng Xing Trade Company 成都盛興商貿公司	Chengdu 成都市	Sichuan 四川省	(028)7762591
Shanghai Municipal Administration Engineering Material Company 上海市市政工程材料公司	Shanghai 上海市	Shanghai 上海市	(021)64372632
Shanghai Construction Engineering Material Co. 上海市建築工程材料公司	Shanghai 上海市	Shanghai 上海市	(021)63298630
Yixing Jin San Jiao Zhao Bazaar 宜興市金三角招商城	Wuxi 無錫市	Jiangsu 江蘇省	(0510)7935138 (0510)7935138
Fujian Hua Fu Import & Export Company 福建省華福進出口公司	Fuzhou 福州市	Fujian 福建省	(0591)7810477 (0591)7810485
China Building Goods & Materials Company 中國建築物資公司	Beijing 北京市	Beijing 北京市	(010)68586253
Dalian Jinzhou Xin Gang Industry & Trade Company 大連金州新港工貿公司	Dalian 大連市	Liaoning 遼寧省	(0411)7624747
Shanghai Zhan Dong Industrial Co. Ltd. 上海展東實業有限公司	Shanghai 上海市	Shanghai 上海市	(021)58201778 (021)58200874
China Building Materials and Equipment Import & Export Company 中國建築材料及設備進出口公司	Beijing 北京市	Beijing 北京市	(010)68393420
Dandong Chemical Light Industry Material Company Chemical Construction Material Marketing Station 丹東市化工輕工材料公司化工建材經銷站	Dandong 丹東市	Liaoning 遼寧省	(0415)2146396

*Also include sales by firms outside this industry.包括本行業以外廠家的銷售。"o" stands for "others". "o" 代表 "其他產品"。

3148: Glass Thermal Containers 玻璃保溫容器製造業

The industry accounts for 0.032% of the total revenue of China's industrial sector in 1996. The revenue growth rate of the industry is -22.2% from 1995, as compared to the growth rate of China's industrial sector, 9.51%. The rate of return on asset is -2.93%. 40.82% of all firms in the industry made a profit while 48.65% had negative returns. The top province in terms of the industry's revenue is Shanghai, accounting for 12.84% of the total revenue.
本行業在1996年佔全行業總產值0.032%，行業年增長率為-22.2%（全國工業年增長率9.51%）。行業的資產回報率-2.93%，40.82%的企業盈利，48.65%的企業虧損。銷售收入最高的省份為上海市，佔本行業的12.84%。

	Total number of firms 企業總數	Total number of employees 職工總數	Total revenue (mil. RMB) 總銷售收入（百萬元）	Total profit (mil. RMB) 總利潤（百萬元）	Return on assets 資產利潤率 (%)	Return on equity 權益利潤率 (%)	Labour productivity ('000 RMB / worker) 勞動生產率（千元/人）	Debts / assets 資產負債率 (%)	Total assets (mil. RMB) 總資產（百萬元）
Industry Overall 行業總體	107	53,987	1,867	-80	-2.93	-11.06	34.58	73.54	2,720

	Number of firms 企業個數	Average number of employees 平均職工人數	Average revenue ('000 RMB) 平均銷售收入（千元）	Average profit ('000 RMB) 平均利潤（千元）	Return on assets 資產利潤率 (%)	Return on equity 權益利潤率 (%)	Labour productivity ('000 RMB / worker) 勞動生產率（千元/人）	Average debts / assets 平均資產負債率(%)	Average Total assets ('000 RMB) 平均總資產（千元）
By ownership 產業所有權									
State-owned 國有	32	1,149	33,813	-2,406	-4.10	-16.38	29.42	74.96	58,656
Collectively-owned 集體	58	282	10,111	-67	-0.65	-1.91	35.82	65.89	10,334
Privately-owned 私有									
Domestic JVs 聯營									
Joint stock 股份制	1	243	8,443	-108	-1.03	69.98	34.75	101.47	10,490
Foreign-funded 外資	4	124	24,234	-834	-4.66	-20.58	195.83	77.34	17,879
Overseas Chinese-funded 港澳台資	12	105	7,765	362	2.69	14.72	74.19	81.75	13,473
By size 規模									
Large 大型	7	1,539	57,821	392	0.43	1.49	37.57	70.88	90,239
Medium 中型	24	1,145	37,635	-3,511	-6.06	-25.83	32.86	76.56	57,960
Small 小型	75	212	7,454	20	0.22	0.72	35.15	69.90	9,297
By regional distribution 地區分布									
Central-North 華北	19	431	13,441	-757	-3.59	-44.76	31.20	91.98	21,093
Beijing 北京	5	598	29,600	176	0.54	2.11	49.51	74.54	32,712
Tianjin 天津	9	255	7,838	-377	-2.44	-21.68	30.76	88.75	15,441
Hebei 河北	4	723	9,208	-2,968	-12.09	47.07	12.74	125.69	24,545
Shanxi 山西	1	11							60
Inner Mongolia 內蒙									
Northeast 東北	4	429	3,103	-3,850	-26.08	178.65	7.24	114.56	14,765
Liaoning 遼寧	1	28	7,500	820	42.93	92.13	267.86	52.88	1,910
Jilin 吉林	1	1,096	3,160	-12,080	-37.92	58.61	2.88	164.66	31,860
Heilongjiang 黑龍江	2	295	875	-2,070	-16.37	-37.30	2.97	56.11	12,645
Central East 華東	48	513	18,021	-429	-1.80	-6.81	35.13	73.54	23,837
Shanghai 上海	8	482	29,961	576	1.59	10.56	62.21	84.91	36,166
Jiangsu 江蘇	10	457	16,964	-878	-4.37	-17.80	37.12	75.44	20,080
Zhejiang 浙江	11	119	6,850	-178	-1.96	-7.80	57.56	74.88	9,097
Anhui 安徽	9	1,004	24,651	-204	-0.77	-2.74	24.56	71.74	26,388
Fujian 福建	3	54	1,290	-557	-7.20	-12.09	24.04	40.45	7,730
Jiangxi 江西	3	586	18,083	-2,383	-33.54	-112.60	30.88	70.22	7,107
Shandong 山東	4	985	25,090	-955	-1.40	-3.92	25.49	64.20	67,995
Central-South 中南	23	509	22,425	-45	-0.16	-0.47	44.04	65.66	28,140
Henan 河南	7	577	20,699	126	0.52	1.60	35.87	67.31	24,011
Hubei 湖北	5	859	38,000	-250	-0.53	-1.12	44.23	52.59	47,076
Hunan 湖南	3	571	20,707	3	0.01	0.09	36.29	83.90	23,637
Guangdong 廣東	8	208	14,846	-85	-0.39	-1.53	71.38	74.37	21,606
Guangxi 廣西									
Hainan 海南									
Southwest 西南	8	528	21,065	-79	-0.26	-0.64	39.90	58.95	29,836
Chongqing 重慶	3	736	30,292	-1,901	-4.08	-8.46	41.15	51.78	46,634
Sichuan 四川	3	344	17,024	1,385	5.85	14.43	49.51	59.48	23,686
Guizhou 貴州									
Yunnan 雲南	2	492	13,285	-1,090	-7.86	-127.49	27.00	93.83	13,865
Tibet 西藏									
Northwest 西北	5	706	9,928	-5,502	-11.97	-37.69	14.05	68.24	45,956
Shaanxi 陝西	1	1,081	4,850	-7,660	-10.44	-29.59	4.49	64.72	73,380
Gansu 甘肅	1	1,666	37,390	-11,720	-13.98	-50.87	22.44	72.52	83,820
Qinghai 青海									
Ningxia 寧夏									
Xinjiang 新疆	3	262	2,467	-2,710	-11.20	-33.79	9.43	66.85	24,193

3148: Glass Thermal Containers 玻璃保溫容器製造業

Year 年份	Number of firms 企業個數	Rate of change 每年變化 (%)	Number of employees 職工人數 (人)	Rate of change 每年變化 (%)	Total revenue (mil. RMB) 總銷售收入 (百萬元)	Rate of change 每年變化 (%)	Total profit (mil. RMB) 總利潤 (百萬元)	Rate of change 每年變化 (%)
1993	106		68,586		1,789		-13	
1994	115	8.49%	63,963	-6.74%	2,182	21.92%	1	110.31%
1995	111	-3.48%	65,006	1.63%	2,401	10.03%	-22	-1685.83%
1996	107	-3.60%	53,987	-16.95%	1,867	-22.24%	-80	-266.62%

3 Major products* 3 種主要產品 *	Output 產量	Sales volume 銷售量	Unit 單位
a) Vacuum Flask 保温瓶	21,388	17,966	10,000 piece 萬個
b) Daily Glass Products 日用玻璃製品	84,028	79,827	ton 噸

Top 10 firms by revenue (year founded) 收入排名前 10 家企業 (創辦年份)	City 城市	Province 省	Telephone / fax 電話 / 傳真	Number of employees 職工人數	Ownership 產業所有權	Revenue ('000 RMB) 銷售收入 (千元)	Profit ('000 RMB) (rank) 利潤 (千元) (排名)	Total assets ('000 RMB) 總資產 (千元)	Major products 主要產品
Beijing Vacuum-bottle Industrial Co. 北京保温瓶工業公司(1962)	Beijing 北京市	Beijing 北京市	(010)69771061 (010)69771239	3,035	Collectively-owned 集體	147,608	1017(5)	159,290	a
Hubei Jing Jiang Co. Ltd. 湖北荊江股份有限公司(1994)	Jingsha 荊沙市	Hubei 湖北省	(0716)8213434	2,616	State-owned 國有	110,155	2343(3)	163,924	a
Chongqing Thermos General Factory 重慶熱水瓶總廠	Chongqing 重慶市	Chongqing 重慶市	(023)68822938 (023)68826500	2,024	State-owned 國有	88,816	434(12)	137,868	a
Anhui Wuhu Guang Hua Glass Factory 安徽省蕪湖市光華玻璃廠(1954)	Wuhu 蕪湖市	Anhui 安徽省	(0553)3835906 (0553)3839028	2,960	State-owned 國有	81,700	203(16)	133,082	a,b
Shanghai Vacuum-bottle Glass Liner General Factory 上海保温瓶瓶膽總廠(1983)	Shanghai 上海市	Shanghai 上海市	(021)56882511 (021)56880867	1,472	State-owned 國有	77,266	-298(50)	99,237	a
Shanghai Jia Sheng Vacuum Container Co. Ltd. 上海嘉盛保温容器有限公司(1991)	Shanghai 上海市	Shanghai 上海市	(021)56973705 (021)56630545	118	Foreign-funded 外資	76,918	9553(1)	38,458	a
Xuzhou Vacuum-bottle Factory 徐州保温瓶廠(1954)	Xuzhou 徐州市	Jiangsu 江蘇省	(0516)3573283 (0516)3573283	1,950	State-owned 國有	67,543	-3828(67)	72,462	a
Wuhan Vacuum-bottle Factory 武漢市武漢保温瓶廠(1970)	Wuhan 武漢市	Hubei 湖北省	(027)87803877	1,416	State-owned 國有	62,883	-3869(68)	56,318	a
Changsha Vacuum-bottle General Factory 長沙保温瓶總廠(1953)	Changsha 長沙市	Hunan 湖南省	(0731)4221748 (0731)4322484	1,586	State-owned 國有	60,886	9(30)	69,170	a
Nanchang Chang E Industrial Company 南昌市嫦娥實業公司(1994)	Nanchang 南昌市	Jiangxi 江西省	(0791)5211481 (0791)5211484	1,560	Collectively-owned 集體	51,589	-7182(71)	18,043	a

Top 10 Cities by Production Output 產出排名前 10 位城市	Province 省	Market share 市場份額	Number of firms 企業個數
Shanghai 上海市	Shanghai 上海市	15.52%	17
Beijing 北京市	Beijing 北京市	12.00%	4
Jingsha 荊沙市	Hubei 湖北省	5.48%	1
Xinxiang 新鄉市	Henan 河南省	5.14%	1
Wuhu 蕪湖市	Anhui 安徽省	5.09%	4
Chongqing 重慶市	Chongqing 重慶市	4.69%	4
Bengbu 蚌埠市	Anhui 安徽省	4.31%	8
Tianjin 天津市	Tianjin 天津市	4.31%	11
Wuhan 武漢市	Hubei 湖北省	3.53%	2
Dalian 大連市	Liaoning 遼寧省	3.00%	2

10 Major Wholesalers 10 家主要批發商	City 城市	Province 省	Telephone / Fax 電話 / 傳真
Changzhou General Merchandise Wholesale General Company 常州百貨批發總公司	Changzhou 常州市	Jiangsu 江蘇省	(0519)6680488 (0519)6680488
Suzhou General Merchandise General Co. 蘇州百貨總公司	Suzhou 蘇州市	Jiangsu 江蘇省	(0512)5222288 (0512)5222247
Guangzhou Yue Xiu Enterprise (Holdings) Co. 廣州越秀企業(集團)公司	Guangzhou 廣州市	Guangdong 廣東省	(020)86662828 (020)86672634
Wunan Commercial Group Corp. 湖南省商業集團總公司	Changsha 長沙市	Hunan 湖南省	(0731)4442765
Kunming General Merchandise Purchase Supply Station Kunming General Merchandise Company 昆明百貨採購供應站昆明市百貨公司	Kunming 昆明市	Yunnan 雲南省	(0871)3314883 (0871)3314961
Nanjing General Merchandise General Company 南京市百貨總公司	Nanjing 南京市	Jiangsu 江蘇省	(025)6664681 (025)6643927
Guangzhou Shang Ling Trade Co. Ltd. 廣州商菱貿易有限公司	Guangzhou 廣州市	Guangdong 廣東省	(020)86677190 (020)86673971
Beijing Light Industry Product Import & Export Company 北京市輕工業品進出口公司	Beijing 北京市	Beijing 北京市	(010)64057425 (010)64057427
Xi Shan Shi Commerce Group Company 錫山市商業集團公司	Wuxi 無錫市	Jiangsu 江蘇省	(0510)2442982
Yixing Su Nan Commercial Building 宜興市蘇南商廈	Wuxi 無錫市	Jiangsu 江蘇省	(0510)7904407 (0510)7904754

*Also include sales by firms outside this industry.包括本行業以外廠家的銷售。"o" stands for "others". "o" 代表 "其他產品"。

3149: Other Glass and Glass Products 其他玻璃及玻璃製品業

The industry accounts for 0.045% of the total revenue of China's industrial sector in 1996. The revenue growth rate of the industry is 44.3% from 1995, as compared to the growth rate of China's industrial sector, 9.51%. The rate of return on asset is 2.94%. 65.90% of all firms in the industry made a profit while 26.71% had negative returns. The top province in terms of the industry's revenue is Guangdong, accounting for 24.96% of the total revenue.
本行業在 1996 年佔全行業總產值 0.045%，行業年增長率為 44.3%（全國工業年增長率 9.51%）。行業的資產回報率 2.94%，65.90% 的企業盈利，26.71% 的企業虧損。銷售收入最高的省份為廣東省，佔本行業的 24.96%。

	Total number of firms 企業總數	Total number of employees 職工總數	Total revenue (mil. RMB) 總銷售收入（百萬元）	Total profit (mil. RMB) 總利潤（百萬元）	Return on assets 資產利潤率 (%)	Return on equity 權益利潤率 (%)	Labour productivity ('000 RMB / worker) 勞動生產率（千元/人）	Debts / assets 資產負債率 (%)	Total assets (mil. RMB) 總資產（百萬元）
Industry Overall 行業總體	545	47,910	2,606	99	2.94	8.72	54.39	66.26	3,380

	Number of firms 企業個數	Average number of employees 平均職工人數	Average revenue ('000 RMB) 平均銷售收入（千元）	Average profit ('000 RMB) 平均利潤（千元）	Return on assets 資產利潤率 (%)	Return on equity 權益利潤率 (%)	Labour productivity ('000 RMB / worker) 勞動生產率（千元/人）	Average debts / assets 平均資產負債率(%)	Average Total assets ('000 RMB) 平均總資產（千元）
By ownership 產業所有權									
State-owned 國有	59	237	4,949	-661	-4.96	-57.35	20.84	91.36	13,339
Collectively-owned 集體	394	68	3,715	44	1.09	3.52	54.53	69.13	4,016
Privately-owned 私有	4	70	3,760	161	5.30	14.86	53.91	64.34	3,048
Domestic JVs 聯營	7	212	5,137	-505	-4.65	-9.56	24.25	51.34	10,851
Joint stock 股份制	4	77	10,043	-4,020	-29.54	-93.19	130.43	68.30	13,610
Foreign-funded 外資	29	65	7,027	46	0.76	1.29	108.00	41.19	6,042
Overseas Chinese-funded 港澳台資	47	70	11,817	2,946	20.01	32.82	167.84	39.02	14,719
By size 規模									
Large 大型	3	1,536	150,916	32,095	15.68	33.09	98.25	52.62	204,716
Medium 中型	9	722	24,994	300	0.86	2.60	34.62	66.82	34,785
Small 小型	520	70	3,708	0	0.00	0.00	53.21	69.62	4,718
By regional distribution 地區分布									
Central-North 華北	85	59	2,348	86	2.01	7.17	39.51	71.92	4,298
Beijing 北京	16	11	744	54	3.24	5.45	65.03	40.48	1,658
Tianjin 天津	22	36	2,333	199	8.63	22.34	63.99	61.37	2,301
Hebei 河北	32	112	3,757	57	0.71	2.97	33.47	76.24	8,110
Shanxi 山西	9	30	1,180	20	0.95	4.15	39.04	77.06	2,102
Inner Mongolia 內蒙	6	34	917	18	1.13	8.94	27.36	87.40	1,627
Northeast 東北	69	95	1,923	-189	-4.12	-35.61	20.17	88.43	4,594
Liaoning 遼寧	39	109	2,160	-301	-6.08	-37.11	19.75	83.61	4,941
Jilin 吉林	16	102	2,550	143	2.30	66.86	24.95	96.55	6,186
Heilongjiang 黑龍江	14	48	546	-259	-14.28	-214.20	11.27	93.33	1,811
Central East 華東	182	85	6,249	209	3.41	8.97	73.57	62.01	6,138
Shanghai 上海	23	57	6,228	266	3.62	8.20	109.35	55.90	7,356
Jiangsu 江蘇	59	107	7,561	299	4.29	12.98	70.65	66.95	6,967
Zhejiang 浙江	28	65	1,578	-80	-4.13	-16.87	24.44	75.53	1,947
Anhui 安徽	22	104	7,524	393	8.58	16.12	72.47	46.78	4,584
Fujian 福建	12	27	908	-152	-5.46	-6.64	33.30	17.71	2,776
Jiangxi 江西	16	52	1,096	-59	-6.63	41.13	20.99	116.12	896
Shandong 山東	22	117	14,088	486	3.20	8.78	120.04	63.51	15,177
Central-South 中南	143	83	6,583	661	8.78	17.88	79.44	50.90	7,530
Henan 河南	33	76	6,038	336	8.86	23.10	79.41	61.65	3,790
Hubei 湖北	22	57	2,075	3	0.14	0.50	36.14	72.60	1,995
Hunan 湖南	27	75	1,357	-97	-4.34	-49.15	18.05	91.17	2,228
Guangdong 廣東	48	120	13,553	1,774	10.18	18.56	113.06	45.13	17,424
Guangxi 廣西	13	23	718	66	7.59	18.94	31.73	59.93	872
Hainan 海南									
Southwest 西南	45	119	3,401	29	0.46	2.14	28.56	78.44	6,362
Chongqing 重慶	14	239	7,753	481	3.35	11.21	32.44	70.10	14,339
Sichuan 四川	19	69	1,982	-189	-6.29	-655.11	28.62	99.04	3,003
Guizhou 貴州	10	53	354	-172	-10.80	73.19	6.68	114.75	1,593
Yunnan 雲南	2	80	1,240	-105	-1.91	-7.22	15.60	73.56	5,485
Tibet 西藏									
Northwest 西北	21	172	2,008	-1,371	-13.24	211.54	11.67	106.26	10,357
Shaanxi 陝西	6	364	4,340	-4,568	-16.65	91.40	11.92	118.22	27,440
Gansu 甘肅	5	69	780	-60	-4.08	7.50	11.27	154.35	1,472
Qinghai 青海	2	129	2,055	15	0.44	11.54	15.93	96.16	3,385
Ningxia 寧夏	1	140	820				5.86	15.23	7,750
Xinjiang 新疆	7	98	1,041	-159	-3.58	-8.19	10.66	56.25	4,424

3149: Other Glass and Glass Products 其他玻璃及玻璃製品業

Year 年份	Number of firms 企業個數	Rate of change 每年變化 (%)	Number of employees 職工人數 (人)	Rate of change 每年變化 (%)	Total revenue (mil. RMB) 總銷售收入 (百萬元)	Rate of change 每年變化 (%)	Total profit (mil. RMB) 總利潤 (百萬元)	Rate of change 每年變化 (%)
1993	728		100,402		2,560		48	
1994	678	-6.87%	79,295	-21.02%	2,431	-5.04%	28	-41.45%
1995	508	-25.07%	48,440	-38.91%	1,806	-25.70%	84	200.01%
1996	545	7.28%	47,910	-1.09%	2,606	44.30%	99	18.29%

3 Major products* 3 種主要產品 *	Output 產量	Sales volume 銷售量	Unit 單位
a) Coated Glass 鍍膜玻璃	2,649,246	2,490,291	square metre 平方米
b) Glass Mosaic 玻璃馬賽克	11,522,622	10,946,491	square metre 平方米
c) Daily Glass Products 日用玻璃製品	126,818	120,477	ton 噸

Top 10 firms by revenue (year founded) 收入排名前 10 家企業 (創辦年份)	City 城市	Province 省	Telephone / fax 電話 / 傳真	Number of employees 職工人數	Ownership 產業所有權	Revenue ('000 RMB) 銷售收入 (千元)	Profit ('000 RMB) (rank) 利潤 (千元) (排名)	Total assets ('000 RMB) 總資產 (千元)	Major products 主要產品
Shenzhen Wei Guang Coated Glass Co. Ltd. 深圳偉光鍍膜玻璃有限公司(1987)	Shenzhen 深圳市	Guangdong 廣東省	(0755)6693157 (0755)6678963	120	Overseas Chinese-funded 港澳台資	164,065	73954(1)	190,650	a
Qufu Tian Mu Group General Co. 曲阜市天幕集團總公司	Jining 濟寧市	Shandong 山東省	(0537)8900231 (0537)8900231	1,200	Collectively-owned 集體	159,080	7590(4)	157,410	o
Wuxi Plexiglass General Factory 無錫市有機玻璃總廠(1985)	Wuxi 無錫市	Jiangsu 江蘇省	(0510)3791003 (0510)3791511	585	Collectively-owned 集體	149,308	6297(6)	89,789	o
Jiangmen Yeebo Semiconductor Co. Ltd. 江門市億都半導體有限公司(1992)	Jiangmen 江門市	Guangdong 廣東省	(0750)3365188 (0750)3365138	1,043	Overseas Chinese-funded 港澳台資	124,724	-1555(193)	122,483	o
De Urban No.1 Glass Fibre Reinforced Plastic Factory 德城區第一玻璃鋼廠(1992)	Dezhou 德州市	Shandong 山東省	(0534)2743105	145	Private-owned 私營	92,490	1250(21)	118,564	o
Henan Linying Hua De Industrial Co. Ltd. 河南省臨穎縣華德實業有限公司(1992)	Luohe 漯河市	Henan 河南省	(0395)8862092	350	其他經濟	84,661	6770(5)	25,618	o
Chongqing Beibei Glass Instrument General Factory 重慶北碚玻璃儀器總廠	Chongqing 重慶市	Chongqing 重慶市	(023)68862021 (023)68863310	1,901	State-owned 國有	76,848	5037(7)	143,225	c
Shanghai Mei Te Building Materials High Science & Technology Co. Ltd. 上海美特建材高科技有限公司(1994)	Shanghai 上海市	Shanghai 上海市	(021)58863323 (021)58742165	156	Foreign-funded 外資	73,328	7931(3)	60,138	o
Tianhe Shahe Glass Handicrafts Factory 天河區沙河玻璃工藝製品廠(1987)	Guangzhou 廣州市	Guangdong 廣東省	(020)87705314	1,272	Collectively-owned 集體	62,531	9204(2)	41,338	b
Jiangyin Shang Ren Middle School-run Factory 江陰市尚仁中學校辦廠(1968)	Wuxi 無錫市	Jiangsu 江蘇省	(0510)6501287 (0510)6501218	190	Collectively-owned 集體	45,879	3223(9)	23,587	o

Top 10 Cities by Production Output 產出排名前 10 位城市	Province 省	Market share 市場份額	Number of firms 企業個數
Shijiazhuang 石家莊市	Hebei 河北省	15.74%	4
Wuxi 無錫市	Jiangsu 江蘇省	9.71%	14
Shanghai 上海市	Shanghai 上海市	7.17%	37
Jiangmen 江門市	Guangdong 廣東省	6.83%	8
Guangzhou 廣州市	Guangdong 廣東省	5.20%	14
Shenzhen 深圳市	Guangdong 廣東省	4.70%	10
Beijing 北京市	Beijing 北京市	2.68%	16
Tieling 鐵嶺市	Liaoning 遼寧省	2.01%	3
Tai'an 泰安市	Shandong 山東省	1.80%	2
Hangzhou 杭州市	Zhejiang 浙江省	1.64%	15

10 Major Wholesalers 10 家主要批發商	City 城市	Province 省	Telephone / Fax 電話 / 傳真
Chengdu Sheng Xing Trade Company 成都盛興商貿公司	Chengdu 成都市	Sichuan 四川省	(028)7762591
Shanghai Municipal Administration Engineering Material Company 上海市市政工程材料公司	Shanghai 上海市	Shanghai 上海市	(021)64372632
Shanghai Construction Engineering Material Co. 上海市建築工程材料公司	Shanghai 上海市	Shanghai 上海市	(021)63298630
Yixing Jin San Jiao Zhao Bazaar 宜興市金三角招商城	Wuxi 無錫市	Jiangsu 江蘇省	(0510)7935138 (0510)7935138
Fujian Hua Fu Import & Export Company 福建省華福進出口公司	Fuzhou 福州市	Fujian 福建省	(0591)7810477 (0591)7810485
China Building Goods & Materials Company 中國建築物資公司	Beijing 北京市	Beijing 北京市	(010)68586253
Dalian Jinzhou Xin Gang Industry & Trade Company 大連金州新港工貿公司	Dalian 大連市	Liaoning 遼寧省	(0411)7624747
Shanghai Zhan Dong Industrial Co. Ltd. 上海展東實業有限公司	Shanghai 上海市	Shanghai 上海市	(021)58201778 (021)58200874
China Building Materials and Equipment Import & Export Company 中國建築材料及設備進出口公司	Beijing 北京市	Beijing 北京市	(010)68393420
Dandong Chemical Light Industry Material Company Chemical Construction Material Marketing Station 丹東市化工輕工材料公司化工建材經銷站	Dandong 丹東市	Liaoning 遼寧省	(0415)2146396

*Also include sales by firms outside this industry.包括本行業以外廠家的銷售。"o" stands for "others". "o" 代表"其他產品"。

3151: Construction and Hygienic Ceramics 建築、衛生陶瓷製造業

The industry accounts for 0.293% of the total revenue of China's industrial sector in 1996. The revenue growth rate of the industry is 5.6% from 1995, as compared to the growth rate of China's industrial sector, 9.51%. The rate of return on asset is -2.15%. 57.55% of all firms in the industry made a profit while 36.22% had negative returns. The top province in terms of the industry's revenue is Guangdong, accounting for 43.98% of the total revenue.
本行業在1996年佔全行業總產值0.293%，行業年增長率為5.6%（全國工業年增長率9.51%）。行業的資產回報率-2.15%，57.55%的企業盈利，36.22%的企業虧損。銷售收入最高的省份為廣東省，佔本行業的43.98%。

	Total number of firms 企業總數	Total number of employees 職工總數	Total revenue (mil. RMB) 總銷售收入（百萬元）	Total profit (mil. RMB) 總利潤（百萬元）	Return on assets 資產利潤率 (%)	Return on equity 權益利潤率 (%)	Labour productivity ('000 RMB / worker) 勞動生產率（千元/人）	Debts / assets 資產負債率 (%)	Total assets (mil. RMB) 總資產（百萬元）
Industry Overall 行業總體	1,466	357,503	17,010	-1,066	-2.15	-8.23	47.58	73.89	49,656

	Number of firms 企業個數	Average number of employees 平均職工人數	Average revenue ('000 RMB) 平均銷售收入（千元）	Average profit ('000 RMB) 平均利潤（千元）	Return on assets 資產利潤率 (%)	Return on equity 權益利潤率 (%)	Labour productivity ('000 RMB / worker) 勞動生產率（千元/人）	Average debts / assets 平均資產負債率(%)	Average Total assets ('000 RMB) 平均總資產（千元）
By ownership 產業所有權									
State-owned 國有	272	501	9,956	-1,107	-2.50	-13.61	19.85	81.62	44,246
Collectively-owned 集體	841	174	8,248	-333	-2.03	-11.29	47.31	82.03	16,389
Privately-owned 私有	3	89	4,929	151	4.69	3074.59	55.18	99.85	3,215
Domestic JVs 聯營	15	232	11,814	-3,465	-14.32	-44.97	50.99	68.15	24,195
Joint stock 股份制	32	539	54,305	6,316	5.86	15.98	100.83	63.30	107,715
Foreign-funded 外資	106	192	16,769	155	0.26	0.64	87.43	59.02	58,830
Overseas Chinese-funded 港澳台資	191	179	19,146	-3,416	-4.73	-15.03	106.68	68.50	72,157
By size 規模									
Large 大型	89	894	64,295	3,275	1.72	6.22	71.88	72.37	190,633
Medium 中型	103	679	25,950	-2,702	-3.51	-15.94	38.20	77.96	76,892
Small 小型	1,193	170	7,220	-905	-4.38	-16.70	42.40	73.76	20,648
By regional distribution 地區分布									
Central-North 華北	186	284	8,320	-124	-0.45	-1.33	29.29	66.42	27,716
Beijing 北京	11	120	10,125	-2,264	-3.61	-10.15	84.37	64.40	62,622
Tianjin 天津	7	214	13,843	-4,684	-7.54	-17.30	64.69	56.43	62,133
Hebei 河北	120	322	9,340	318	1.26	3.68	29.01	65.70	25,162
Shanxi 山西	27	139	3,714	77	0.62	1.96	26.67	68.17	12,379
Inner Mongolia 內蒙	21	363	5,627	-263	-0.82	-3.58	15.48	77.21	32,276
Northeast 東北	70	304	2,747	-428	-2.18	-13.95	9.02	84.35	19,624
Liaoning 遼寧	34	486	3,355	-389	-1.54	-15.55	6.90	90.09	25,253
Jilin 吉林	11	213	4,883	-933	-2.68	-12.23	22.94	78.11	34,836
Heilongjiang 黑龍江	25	98	979	-259	-4.91	-14.10	10.02	65.20	5,275
Central East 華東	515	191	9,935	20	0.08	0.21	51.95	63.95	26,530
Shanghai 上海	12	235	37,503	5,202	4.99	9.22	159.93	45.83	104,175
Jiangsu 江蘇	40	264	22,195	-975	-1.53	-4.56	84.07	66.48	63,765
Zhejiang 浙江	121	84	5,336	-274	-2.09	-5.84	63.18	64.15	13,077
Anhui 安徽	41	245	6,222	-922	-6.15	-30.73	25.36	79.99	14,993
Fujian 福建	131	78	6,217	289	2.25	3.60	80.19	37.52	12,840
Jiangxi 江西	70	352	8,056	-367	-1.27	-7.35	22.86	82.76	28,921
Shandong 山東	100	300	14,995	457	1.15	3.50	49.97	67.07	39,590
Central-South 中南	500	280	18,098	-1,804	-3.54	-17.22	64.53	79.46	50,998
Henan 河南	125	192	5,772	-13	-0.08	-0.28	30.02	72.50	17,187
Hubei 湖北	64	314	6,884	-546	-2.33	-13.24	21.94	82.38	23,420
Hunan 湖南	52	219	3,609	-533	-4.41	-17.93	16.51	75.38	12,081
Guangdong 廣東	219	345	34,158	-3,279	-3.63	-17.51	98.89	79.28	90,422
Guangxi 廣西	37	223	5,281	-3,205	-9.83	-169.11	23.68	94.19	32,621
Hainan 海南	3	283	7,707	-250	-0.35	-1.33	27.20	73.74	71,393
Southwest 西南	147	229	6,271	-617	-2.89	-12.68	27.34	77.18	21,325
Chongqing 重慶	30	190	5,496	-329	-1.58	-4.23	28.89	62.67	20,847
Sichuan 四川	93	266	7,478	-789	-3.44	-19.85	28.16	82.68	22,958
Guizhou 貴州	13	133	2,025	-242	-2.32	-6.78	15.28	65.81	10,447
Yunnan 雲南	11	152	3,259	-394	-1.81	-6.73	21.38	73.08	21,737
Tibet 西藏									
Northwest 西北	48	227	3,819	-652	-3.77	-22.91	16.79	83.54	17,295
Shaanxi 陝西	16	178	5,724	-1,283	-5.92	-42.93	32.13	86.21	21,672
Gansu 甘肅	14	363	4,109	-209	-1.31	-6.08	11.33	78.49	15,935
Qinghai 青海	1								
Ningxia 寧夏	7	170	2,034	-164	-1.41	-5.41	11.94	73.85	11,619
Xinjiang 新疆	10	180	1,994	-671	-3.75	-34.32	11.11	89.08	17,897

3151: Construction and Hygienic Ceramics 建築、衛生陶瓷製造業

Year 年份	Number of firms 企業個數	Rate of change 每年變化 (%)	Number of employees 職工人數 (人)	Rate of change 每年變化 (%)	Total revenue (mil. RMB) 總銷售收入 (百萬元)	Rate of change 每年變化 (%)	Total profit (mil. RMB) 總利潤 (百萬元)	Rate of change 每年變化 (%)
1993	1,232		321,028		9,777		324	
1994	1,338	8.60%	359,019	11.83%	11,573	18.38%	-136	-142.04%
1995	1,537	14.87%	433,531	20.75%	16,112	39.21%	-583	-327.82%
1996	1,466	-4.62%	357,503	-17.54%	17,010	5.57%	-1,066	-82.99%

3 Major products* 3種主要產品*	Output 產量	Sales volume 銷售量	Unit 單位
a) Sanitary Ceramics 衛生陶瓷	52,166,168	50,601,183	piece 件
b) Glazed Brick 釉面磚	48,394	39,683	10,000 square metre 萬平方米
c) Wall-ground Brick 牆地磚	65,265	58,738	10,000 square metre 萬平方米

Top 10 firms by revenue (year founded) 收入排名前10家企業 (創辦年份)	City 城市	Province 省	Telephone / fax 電話 / 傳真	Number of employees 職工人數	Ownership 產業所有權	Revenue ('000 RMB) 銷售收入 (千元)	Profit ('000 RMB) (rank) 利潤 (千元) (排名)	Total assets ('000 RMB) 總資產 (千元)	Major products 主要產品
Tangshan Victory Ceramic Group Co. Ltd. 唐山勝利陶瓷集團有限責任公司(1990)	Tangshan 唐山市	Hebei 河北省	(0315)2837707 (0315)2811728	9,946	State-owned 國有	355,190	20827(7)	1,484,712	a,b,c
Foshan Shiwan Jian Guo Ceramics Factory 佛山市石灣建國陶瓷廠(1974)	Foshan 佛山市	Guangdong 廣東省	(0757)2272268 (0757)2271215	2,300	Joint stock 股份制	327,523	10109(15)	713,525	b
Zibo Hua Chen Group General Co. 淄博華辰集團總公司(1993)	Zibo 淄博市	Shandong 山東省	(0533)8900231 (0533)8900231	2,816	Foreign-funded 外資	295,505	24818(5)	945,148	b,c
Nanhai Ming Zhu High-grade Decoration Brick Factory 南海市明珠高級裝飾磚廠(1993)	Foshan 佛山市	Guangdong 廣東省	(0757)5332328 (0757)5333142	1,596	Collectively-owned 集體	204,014	2922(53)	295,551	c
Foshan Shiwan Pai Hua Yi Ceramics Co. Ltd. 佛山市石灣牌華益陶瓷有限公司(1993)	Foshan 佛山市	Guangdong 廣東省	(0757)2262363 (0757)2271664	459	Overseas Chinese-funded 港澳台資	193,760	57325(1)	148,717	c
Nanhai Nan Zhuang Hua Xiong Architectural Pottery Factory 南海市南裝華雄建陶廠(1990)	Foshan 佛山市	Guangdong 廣東省	(0757)5332054 (0757)5334260	1,200	Collectively-owned 集體	157,414	2228(63)	96,809	c
Luo Ma Ceramic Tile Co. Ltd. 羅馬瓷磚有限公司(1993)	Suzhou 蘇州市	Jiangsu 江蘇省	(0512)5010712 (0512)5010715	296	Foreign-funded 外資	154,377	1112(96)	296,635	c
Zhongshan Gu Zhen Color Porcelain Brick Factory 中山市古鎮彩瓷磚廠(1991)	Zhongshan 中山市	Guangdong 廣東省	(0760)2356448	490	Collectively-owned 集體	148,030	7155(21)	138,415	b
Shanghai Fu Xiang Ceramics Co. Ltd. 上海福祥陶瓷有限公司(1995)	Shanghai 上海市	Shanghai 上海市	(021)64345555 (021)64345987	365	Overseas Chinese-funded 港澳台資	139,203	51992(3)	308,369	b
Foshan Shiwan Dongping Ceramics Group Company Hua Peng Ceramics Factory 佛山市石灣東平陶瓷集團公司華鵬陶瓷廠(1993)	Foshan 佛山市	Guangdong 廣東省	(0757)2271564 (0757)2268323	935	Collectively-owned 集體	138,157	10260(14)	186,491	b,c

Top 10 Cities by Production Output 產出排名前10位城市	Province 省	Market share 市場份額	Number of firms 企業個數
Foshan 佛山市	Guangdong 廣東省	32.64%	112
Zibo 淄博市	Shandong 山東省	5.29%	38
Tangshan 唐山市	Hebei 河北省	5.23%	65
Quanzhou 泉州市	Fujian 福建省	4.08%	140
Shanghai 上海市	Shanghai 上海市	2.88%	26
Yichun 宜春市	Jiangxi 江西省	2.19%	26
Wenzhou 溫州市	Zhejiang 浙江省	2.10%	310
Suzhou 蘇州市	Jiangsu 江蘇省	2.05%	18
Linyi 臨沂市	Shandong 山東省	2.03%	21
Zhaoqing 肇慶市	Guangdong 廣東省	1.96%	16

10 Major Wholesalers 10家主要批發商	City 城市	Province 省	Telephone / Fax 電話 / 傳真
Chengdu Sheng Xing Trade Company 成都盛興商貿公司	Chengdu 成都市	Sichuan 四川省	(028)7762591
Shanghai Municipal Administration Engineering Material Company 上海市市政工程材料公司	Shanghai 上海市	Shanghai 上海市	(021)64372632
Shanghai Construction Engineering Material Co. 上海市建築工程材料公司	Shanghai 上海市	Shanghai 上海市	(021)63298630
Yixing Jin San Jiao Zhao Bazaar 宜興市金三角招商城	Wuxi 無錫市	Jiangsu 江蘇省	(0510)7935138 (0510)7935138
Fujian Hua Fu Import & Export Company 福建省華福進出口公司	Fuzhou 福州市	Fujian 福建省	(0591)7810477 (0591)7810485
China Building Goods & Materials Company 中國建築物資公司	Beijing 北京市	Beijing 北京市	(010)68586253
Dalian Jinzhou Xin Gang Industry & Trade Company 大連金州新港工貿公司	Dalian 大連市	Liaoning 遼寧省	(0411)7624747
Shanghai Zhan Dong Industrial Co. Ltd. 上海展東實業有限公司	Shanghai 上海市	Shanghai 上海市	(021)58201778 (021)58200874
China Building Materials and Equipment Import & Export Company 中國建築材料及設備進出口公司	Beijing 北京市	Beijing 北京市	(010)68393420
Dandong Chemical Light Industry Material Company Chemical Construction Material Marketing Station 丹東市化工輕工材料公司化工建材經銷站	Dandong 丹東市	Liaoning 遼寧省	(0415)2146396

*Also include sales by firms outside this industry.包括本行業以外廠家的銷售。"o" stands for "others". "o" 代表"其他產品"。

3153: Industrial Ceramics 工業用陶瓷製造業

The industry accounts for 0.045% of the total revenue of China's industrial sector in 1996. The revenue growth rate of the industry is 35.8% from 1995, as compared to the growth rate of China's industrial sector, 9.51%. The rate of return on asset is 0.43%. 61.92% of all firms in the industry made a profit while 32.85% had negative returns. The top province in terms of the industry's revenue is Henan, accounting for 18.99% of the total revenue.
本行業在1996年佔全行業總產值0.045%，行業年增長率為35.8%（全國工業年增長率9.51%）。行業的資產回報率0.43%，61.92%的企業盈利，32.85%的企業虧損。銷售收入最高的省份為河南省，佔本行業的18.99%。

	Total number of firms 企業總數	Total number of employees 職工總數	Total revenue (mil. RMB) 總銷售收入（百萬元）	Total profit (mil. RMB) 總利潤（百萬元）	Return on assets 資產利潤率 (%)	Return on equity 權益利潤率 (%)	Labour productivity ('000 RMB / worker) 勞動生產率（千元／人）	Debts / assets 資產負債率 (%)	Total assets (mil. RMB) 總資產（百萬元）
Industry Overall 行業總體	378	74,580	2,615	25	0.43	1.26	35.06	65.74	5,801

	Number of firms 企業個數	Average number of employees 平均職工人數	Average revenue ('000 RMB) 平均銷售收入（千元）	Average profit ('000 RMB) 平均利潤（千元）	Return on assets 資產利潤率 (%)	Return on equity 權益利潤率 (%)	Labour productivity ('000 RMB / worker) 勞動生產率（千元／人）	Average debts / assets 平均資產負債率(%)	Average Total assets ('000 RMB) 平均總資產（千元）
By ownership 產業所有權									
State-owned 國有	89	456	12,000	-843	-2.07	-7.88	26.32	73.67	40,629
Collectively-owned 集體	249	123	4,222	577	10.75	25.97	34.21	58.63	5,366
Privately-owned 私有	1	103	1,098	1,962	42.94	100.59	10.66	57.31	4,570
Domestic JVs 聯營	3	121	13,604	-5,415	-127.98	-168.72	112.43	24.15	4,231
Joint stock 股份制	3	190	9,647	-2,286	-11.02	-28.67	50.69	61.57	20,744
Foreign-funded 外資	18	61	10,421	-1,296	-4.99	-9.57	171.30	47.82	25,946
Overseas Chinese-funded 港澳台資	14	106	17,073	64	0.29	0.44	160.85	32.95	21,672
By size 規模									
Large 大型	4	3,280	227,657	-2,696	-0.54	-1.52	69.41	64.88	503,471
Medium 中型	16	909	33,311	325	0.38	1.24	36.63	69.08	84,818
Small 小型	346	135	3,388	88	1.26	3.55	25.13	64.61	7,026
By regional distribution 地區分布									
Central-North 華北	33	146	3,161	15	0.17	0.59	21.71	71.04	8,673
Beijing 北京	4								
Tianjin 天津	8	103	2,866	55	0.99	2.20	27.73	54.93	5,544
Hebei 河北	15	200	4,683	-37	-0.30	-1.07	23.42	72.16	12,360
Shanxi 山西	5	195	2,226	120	1.06	5.32	11.39	80.02	11,294
Inner Mongolia 內蒙	1								
Northeast 東北	36	407	10,276	-204	-0.58	-2.23	25.25	73.79	34,924
Liaoning 遼寧	24	493	13,637	-205	-0.47	-1.59	27.65	70.67	44,036
Jilin 吉林	5	194	1,994	-372	-5.37	-44.82	10.27	88.01	6,922
Heilongjiang 黑龍江	7	264	4,667	-80	-0.34	-3.64	17.71	90.72	23,684
Central East 華東	168	183	5,868	-150	-1.03	-2.87	32.04	64.19	14,612
Shanghai 上海	11	79	2,324	95	1.05	1.28	29.38	18.46	9,026
Jiangsu 江蘇	31	251	12,862	-215	-0.61	-1.79	51.17	65.78	35,127
Zhejiang 浙江	27	140	2,194	-119	-2.60	-8.44	15.70	69.23	4,562
Anhui 安徽	4	248	4,423	-185	-1.44	-9.48	17.85	84.86	12,878
Fujian 福建	31	111	2,700	-178	-2.05	-3.48	24.22	40.91	8,681
Jiangxi 江西	50	164	2,538	-408	-6.70	-115.11	15.53	94.18	6,100
Shandong 山東	14	408	19,568	736	1.99	5.08	47.99	60.78	36,982
Central-South 中南	113	158	9,322	608	4.72	10.78	59.17	56.20	12,870
Henan 河南	15	130	33,099	3,998	10.98	17.76	255.13	38.16	36,406
Hubei 湖北	8	194	2,664	-163	-1.74	-9.90	13.75	82.47	9,365
Hunan 湖南	66	189	5,047	-46	-0.56	-2.06	26.69	72.94	8,308
Guangdong 廣東	22	72	8,952	645	5.07	10.34	124.10	50.97	12,715
Guangxi 廣西	2	121	2,770	-575	-22.07	-191.67	22.99	88.68	2,605
Hainan 海南									
Southwest 西南	14	240	4,941	-200	2.02	11.41	20.11	82.31	13,028
Chongqing 重慶	5	99	700	-584	-20.65	154.42	7.06	113.37	2,826
Sichuan 四川	5	299	7,118	-254	-2.36	-10.49	23.77	77.52	10,761
Guizhou 貴州	3	148	3,070	127	1.45	4.55	20.74	68.13	8,733
Yunnan 雲南	1	926	18,410				19.88	85.18	85,200
Tibet 西藏									
Northwest 西北	14	223	2,325	-561	-4.73	-29.09	10.44	83.75	11,880
Shaanxi 陝西	10	202	1,934	-332	-3.11	-23.50	9.58	86.76	10,672
Gansu 甘肅	2	247	3,890	90	0.65	2.29	15.75	71.73	13,885
Qinghai 青海	1	154	850				5.52	45.16	10,650
Ningxia 寧夏	1	450	4,580	-4,720	-22.29	590.00	10.18	103.78	21,180
Xinjiang 新疆									

3153: Industrial Ceramics 工業用陶瓷製造業

Year 年份	Number of firms 企業個數	Rate of change 每年變化 (%)	Number of employees 職工人數 (人)	Rate of change 每年變化 (%)	Total revenue (mil. RMB) 總銷售收入 (百萬元)	Rate of change 每年變化 (%)	Total profit (mil. RMB) 總利潤 (百萬元)	Rate of change 每年變化 (%)
1993	343		68,947		2,005		60	
1994	344	0.29%	71,382	3.53%	1,930	-3.76%	40	-32.85%
1995	356	3.49%	74,352	4.16%	1,925	-0.24%	-25	-162.27%
1996	378	6.18%	74,580	0.31%	2,615	35.84%	25	199.32%

3 Major products* 3 種主要產品 *	Output 產量	Sales volume 銷售量	Unit 單位
a) Industrial Ceramics 工業陶瓷	539,561,699	485,605,530	piece 件
b) Acid-proof Brick 耐酸磚	138,725	133,176	ton 噸
c) High Voltage Isolator 高壓隔離開關	17,150	15,950	set 組

Top 10 firms by revenue (year founded) 收入排名前 10 家企業 (創辦年份)	City 城市	Province 省	Telephone / fax 電話 / 傳真	Number of employees 職工人數	Ownership 產業所有權	Revenue ('000 RMB) 銷售收入 (千元)	Profit ('000 RMB) (rank) 利潤 (千元) (排名)	Total assets ('000 RMB) 總資產 (千元)	Major products 主要產品
Ge Tian Group Co. Ltd. Henan Prov. 河南省葛天集團有限責任公司(1993)	Xuchang 許昌市	Henan 河南省	(0374)6611088	5,590	Collectively-owned 集體	396,140	38922(1)	231,455	o
Linyi Industry Enamel Co. Ltd. 臨沂市羅裝區工業搪瓷股份有限公司(1985)	Linyi 臨沂市	Shandong 山東省	(0539)8241767 (0539)8241720	3,268	Joint stock 股份制	223,740	13205(3)	372,014	o
Fushun Electric Ceramics Factory 撫順電瓷廠(1936)	Fushun 撫順市	Liaoning 遼寧省	(0413)2424053 (0413)2423906	4,281	State-owned 國有	160,291	307(39)	580,328	o
Nanjing Thunder-lighting (Group) Co. Ltd. 南京雷電(集團)有限責任公司(1948)	Nanjing 南京市	Jiangsu 江蘇省	(025)5504222 (025)5501634	3,122	State-owned 國有	149,680	-9880(172)	641,310	o
Dalian Electric Ceramics Factory 大連電瓷廠(1915)	Dalian 大連市	Liaoning 遼寧省	(0411)3636229 (0411)3633530	2,240	State-owned 國有	98,220	21(82)	245,652	o
Suzhou Electric Ceramics Factory 蘇州電瓷廠(1959)	Suzhou 蘇州市	Jiangsu 江蘇省	(0512)5204747 (0512)5252289	1,157	State-owned 國有	65,966	311(38)	146,091	c
Liling Electric Ceramics Factory 醴陵市電瓷廠(1946)	Zhuzhou 株洲市	Hunan 湖南省	(0733)3232311 (0733)3233160	2,644	State-owned 國有	65,356	-1368(156)	186,352	a
Luoyang Hai Deng Huang Ge Fine Ceramics Co. Ltd. 洛陽海登皇格精細陶瓷有限公司(1993)	Luoyang 洛陽市	Henan 河南省	(0379)4311110 (0379)4311107	79	Overseas Chinese-funded 港澳台資	57,910	21177(2)	132,574	o
Fo Tao Group Ceramics Research Institute 佛陶集團陶瓷研究所(1958)	Foshan 佛山市	Guangdong 廣東省	(0757)2273883 (0757)2275583	260	Joint stock 股份制	55,381	10488(4)	79,249	a
Fujian Minqing Electric Ceramics General Factory 福建省閩清電瓷總廠(1958)	Fuzhou 福州市	Fujian 福建省	(0591)2332263 (0591)2333539	1,125	State-owned 國有	48,839	-3626(169)	91,810	a

Top 10 Cities by Production Output 產出排名前 10 位城市	Province 省	Market share 市場份額	Number of firms 企業個數
Xuchang 許昌市	Henan 河南省	15.55%	3
Linyi 臨沂市	Shandong 山東省	15.37%	2
Nanjing 南京市	Jiangsu 江蘇省	9.39%	5
Zhuzhou 株洲市	Hunan 湖南省	8.94%	49
Fushun 撫順市	Liaoning 遼寧省	6.87%	4
Wuxi 無錫市	Jiangsu 江蘇省	5.09%	21
Foshan 佛山市	Guangdong 廣東省	4.79%	7
Suzhou 蘇州市	Jiangsu 江蘇省	4.42%	15
Dalian 大連市	Liaoning 遼寧省	3.91%	5
Guangzhou 廣州市	Guangdong 廣東省	3.10%	5

10 Major Wholesalers 10 家主要批發商	City 城市	Province 省	Telephone / Fax 電話 / 傳真
Chengdu Sheng Xing Trade Company 成都盛興商貿公司	Chengdu 成都市	Sichuan 四川省	(028)7762591
Shanghai Municipal Administration Engineering Material Company 上海市市政工程材料公司	Shanghai 上海市	Shanghai 上海市	(021)64372632
Shanghai Construction Engineering Material Co. 上海市建築工程材料公司	Shanghai 上海市	Shanghai 上海市	(021)63298630
Yixing Jin San Jiao Zhao Bazaar 宜興市金三角招商城	Wuxi 無錫市	Jiangsu 江蘇省	(0510)7935138 (0510)7935138
Fujian Hua Fu Import & Export Company 福建省華福進出口公司	Fuzhou 福州市	Fujian 福建省	(0591)7810477 (0591)7810485
China Building Goods & Materials Company 中國建築物資公司	Beijing 北京市	Beijing 北京市	(010)68586253
Dalian Jinzhou Xin Gang Industry & Trade Company 大連金州新港工貿公司	Dalian 大連市	Liaoning 遼寧省	(0411)7624747
Shanghai Zhan Dong Industrial Co. Ltd. 上海展東實業有限公司	Shanghai 上海市	Shanghai 上海市	(021)58201778 (021)58200874
China Building Materials and Equipment Import & Export Company 中國建築材料及設備進出口公司	Beijing 北京市	Beijing 北京市	(010)68393420
Dandong Chemical Light Industry Material Company Chemical Construction Material Marketing Station 丹東市化工輕工材料公司化工建材經銷站	Dandong 丹東市	Liaoning 遼寧省	(0415)2146396

*Also include sales by firms outside this industry.包括本行業以外廠家的銷售。"o" stands for "others". "o" 代表"其他產品"。

3155: Household Ceramics 日用陶瓷製造業

The industry accounts for 0.140% of the total revenue of China's industrial sector in 1996. The revenue growth rate of the industry is 9.2% from 1995, as compared to the growth rate of China's industrial sector, 9.51%. The rate of return on asset is -0.96%. 70.42% of all firms in the industry made a profit while 23.33% had negative returns. The top province in terms of the industry's revenue is Guangdong, accounting for 17.05% of the total revenue.
本行業在 1996 年佔全行業總產值 0.140% ，行業年增長率為 9.2%（全國工業年增長率 9.51%） 。行業的資產回報率 -0.96% ， 70.42% 的企業盈利， 23.33% 的企業虧損。銷售收入最高的省份為廣東省，佔本行業的 17.05% 。

	Total number of firms 企業總數	Total number of employees 職工總數	Total revenue (mil. RMB) 總銷售收入（百萬元）	Total profit (mil. RMB) 總利潤（百萬元）	Return on assets 資產利潤率 (%)	Return on equity 權益利潤率 (%)	Labour productivity ('000 RMB / worker) 勞動生產率（千元/人）	Debts / assets 資產負債率 (%)	Total assets (mil. RMB) 總資產（百萬元）
Industry Overall 行業總體	1,794	423,591	8,093	-155	-0.96	-3.37	19.11	71.44	16,134

	Number of firms 企業個數	Average number of employees 平均職工人數	Average revenue ('000 RMB) 平均銷售收入（千元）	Average profit ('000 RMB) 平均利潤（千元）	Return on assets 資產利潤率 (%)	Return on equity 權益利潤率 (%)	Labour productivity ('000 RMB / worker) 勞動生產率（千元/人）	Average debts / assets 平均資產負債率(%)	Average Total assets ('000 RMB) 平均總資產（千元）
By ownership 產業所有權									
State-owned 國有	320	786	11,694	-600	-1.90	-6.99	14.88	72.80	31,563
Collectively-owned 集體	1,285	96	1,959	-141	-6.29	-30.52	20.51	79.40	2,242
Privately-owned 私有	2	37							
Domestic JVs 聯營	4	108	1,816	2,696	41.80	168.35	16.85	75.17	6,450
Joint stock 股份制	13	593	19,504	4,701	12.55	41.70	32.89	69.90	37,451
Foreign-funded 外資	52	268	10,030	-3,076	-22.24	-51.24	37.37	56.60	13,830
Overseas Chinese-funded 港澳台資	117	236	9,095	2,620	15.97	38.23	38.62	58.22	16,405
By size 規模									
Large 大型	20	4,030	113,750	939	0.35	1.06	28.23	66.61	265,390
Medium 中型	82	1,364	21,783	-1,451	-2.97	-12.54	15.97	76.29	48,782
Small 小型	1,669	138	2,478	-33	-0.80	-2.91	17.90	72.35	4,090
By regional distribution 地區分布									
Central-North 華北	148	494	9,191	396	1.53	4.72	18.61	67.54	25,826
Beijing 北京	12	28	1,157	70	2.95	11.44	41.31	74.23	2,373
Tianjin 天津	5	90	3,118	320	7.46	18.39	34.57	59.46	4,292
Hebei 河北	61	947	19,859	945	1.73	5.37	20.98	67.76	54,571
Shanxi 山西	62	223	1,840	-28	-0.42	-1.22	8.26	65.27	6,557
Inner Mongolia 內蒙	8	93	654	23	0.49	1.73	7.03	71.89	4,625
Northeast 東北	44	303	2,998	-190	-2.38	-9.41	9.89	74.73	8,006
Liaoning 遼寧	22	257	2,048	-84	-1.50	-8.65	7.96	82.65	5,574
Jilin 吉林	7	651	7,709	-974	-4.16	-12.76	11.85	67.42	23,431
Heilongjiang 黑龍江	15	209	2,194	19	0.43	1.96	10.52	78.19	4,373
Central East 華東	622	231	4,477	-146	-1.56	-5.25	19.40	70.30	9,366
Shanghai 上海	6	138	4,628	-363	-5.20	-13.40	33.62	61.21	6,990
Jiangsu 江蘇	28	905	26,875	-1,187	-2.07	-6.47	29.70	68.02	57,345
Zhejiang 浙江	42	187	4,194	36	0.45	1.23	22.48	63.28	7,886
Anhui 安徽	58	156	2,434	-202	-4.46	-44.02	15.64	89.86	4,532
Fujian 福建	165	105	2,427	-28	-0.84	-1.50	23.07	44.12	3,299
Jiangxi 江西	260	186	1,441	-237	-4.78	-30.94	7.76	84.54	4,947
Shandong 山東	63	554	14,480	331	1.19	3.80	26.14	68.67	27,834
Central-South 中南	731	222	4,702	-138	-1.96	-7.74	21.18	74.66	7,034
Henan 河南	72	272	6,101	265	3.00	11.44	22.43	73.76	8,814
Hubei 湖北	65	63	1,278				20.34	76.98	1,670
Hunan 湖南	218	363	4,853	-171	-2.06	-9.11	13.35	77.43	8,337
Guangdong 廣東	273	133	5,055	-205	-2.96	-10.30	37.98	71.25	6,908
Guangxi 廣西	95	234	4,957	-268	-3.76	-16.91	21.21	77.74	7,110
Hainan 海南	8	114	806	-165	-6.55	-14.62	7.10	55.19	2,519
Southwest 西南	181	120	1,662	-41	-1.11	-4.98	13.84	77.67	3,720
Chongqing 重慶	58	105	1,716	-56	-0.96	-3.76	16.28	74.55	5,817
Sichuan 四川	76	115	1,216	-76	-3.30	-92.48	10.55	96.43	2,288
Guizhou 貴州	19	15	370	-2	-0.41	-0.88	24.41	53.88	516
Yunnan 雲南	27	242	3,725	47	0.86	2.55	15.37	66.40	5,536
Tibet 西藏	1	80	1,500	300	7.50	7.50	18.75		4,000
Northwest 西北	68	140	1,143	-92	-1.96	-6.58	8.15	70.17	4,673
Shaanxi 陝西	42	116	756	-81	-2.27	-8.96	6.50	74.63	3,580
Gansu 甘肅	11	203	1,774	-108	-1.66	-5.15	8.74	67.87	6,530
Qinghai 青海	3	19	100				5.26	26.77	3,810
Ningxia 寧夏	7	267	2,306	-263	-3.17	-14.32	8.65	77.85	8,287
Xinjiang 新疆	5	99	2,008	42	0.80	1.70	20.32	52.76	5,220

3155: Household Ceramics 日用陶瓷製造業

Year 年份	Number of firms 企業個數	Rate of change 每年變化 (%)	Number of employees 職工人數 (人)	Rate of change 每年變化 (%)	Total revenue (mil. RMB) 總銷售收入 (百萬元)	Rate of change 每年變化 (%)	Total profit (mil. RMB) 總利潤 (百萬元)	Rate of change 每年變化 (%)
1993	1,661		379,052		4,859		-5	
1994	1,817	9.39%	426,502	12.52%	5,733	17.99%	-132	-2468.12%
1995	1,950	7.32%	466,170	9.30%	7,411	29.27%	-233	-76.68%
1996	1,794	-8.00%	423,591	-9.13%	8,093	9.20%	-155	33.38%

3 Major products* 3 種主要產品 *	Output 產量	Sales volume 銷售量	Unit 單位
a) Household Ceramics 日用陶瓷	928,538	872,826	10,000 piece 萬件
b) Industrial Ceramics 工業陶瓷	24,649,236	24,156,252	ton 噸
c) Sanitary Ceramics 衛生陶瓷	2,406,497	2,334,302	piece 件

Top 10 firms by revenue (year founded) 收入排名前 10 家企業 (創辦年份)	City 城市	Province 省	Telephone / fax 電話 / 傳真	Number of employees 職工人數	Ownership 產業所有權	Revenue ('000 RMB) 銷售收入 (千元)	Profit ('000 RMB) (rank) 利潤（千元）(排名)	Total assets ('000 RMB) 總資產 (千元)	Major products 主要產品
Handan Ceramics Group General Co. 邯鄲陶瓷集團總公司(1952)	Handan 邯鄲市	Hebei 河北省	(0310)5022122 (0310)5022659	19,759	State-owned 國有	485,560	11290(6)	1,255,280	a,b,c
Tangshan Ceramics Group Co. Ltd. 唐山陶瓷集團有限公司(1962)	Tangshan 唐山市	Hebei 河北省	(0315)3271011 (0315)3271595	18,821	State-owned 國有	454,820	38200(1)	1,395,470	a,c
Jiangsu Yixing Ceramics Co. 江蘇省宜興陶瓷公司(1956)	Wuxi 無錫市	Jiangsu 江蘇省	(0510)7401426 (0510)7404640	17,001	State-owned 國有	427,357	-51987(528)	1,181,801	a,b,c
Hua Guang Ceramics Group Co. Ltd 華光陶瓷集團有限公司(1995)	Zibo 淄博市	Shandong 山東省	(0533)2010593 (0533)2011404	2,983	Joint stock 股份制	181,002	22239(2)	423,275	a
Shandong Zibo Wan Feng Group General Company 山東淄博萬灃集團總公司(1994)	Zibo 淄博市	Shandong 山東省	(0533)2081334 (0533)2081340	2,520	Collectively-owned 集體	160,380	7980(8)	146,280	a
Yixing Han Guang Group 宜興市漢光集團(1986)	Wuxi 無錫市	Jiangsu 江蘇省	(0510)7451263	360	Collectively-owned 集體	104,291	12358(4)	63,067	o
Liling Guo Guang Porcelain Industry Co. Ltd. 醴陵市國光瓷業股份有限公司(1958)	Zhuzhou 株洲市	Hunan 湖南省	(0733)3232911 (0733)3225111	4,010	Domestic JVs 聯營	101,484	19397(3)	219,528	a
Shandong Boshan Ceramics Factory 山東博山陶瓷廠(1949)	Zibo 淄博市	Shandong 山東省	(0533)4408463 (0533)4408657	5,148	State-owned 國有	83,352	-3886(506)	192,298	a
Shandong Linyi Ceramics Enterprise Group 山東臨沂陶瓷企業集團(1957)	Linyi 臨沂市	Shandong 山東省	(0539)8241123 (0539)8241840	2,111	State-owned 國有	76,434	3939(12)	122,283	a
Jiangsu Gaochun Ceramics Co. Ltd. 江蘇高淳陶瓷股份有限公司(1958)	Nanjing 南京市	Jiangsu 江蘇省	(025)7377231 (025)7377688	1,884	State-owned 國有	75,386	11480(5)	103,178	a

Top 10 Cities by Production Output 產出排名前 10 位城市	Province 省	Market share 市場份額	Number of firms 企業個數
Wuxi 無錫市	Jiangsu 江蘇省	10.41%	36
Tangshan 唐山市	Hebei 河北省	8.25%	17
Handan 邯鄲市	Hebei 河北省	6.09%	7
Zibo 淄博市	Shandong 山東省	5.97%	35
Chaozhou 潮州市	Guangdong 廣東省	5.74%	157
Quanzhou 泉州市	Fujian 福建省	5.48%	164
Zhuzhou 株洲市	Hunan 湖南省	4.38%	46
Yulin 玉林市	Guangxi 廣西	3.09%	31
Jingdezhen 景德鎮市	Jiangxi 江西省	3.07%	108
Hengyang 衡陽市	Hunan 湖南省	2.90%	31

10 Major Wholesalers 10 家主要批發商	City 城市	Province 省	Telephone / Fax 電話 / 傳真
Chengdu Great Wall Electric Appliance Company 成都長城電器公司	Chengdu 成都市	Sichuan 四川省	(028)6662132 (028)6671975
Shandou Ceramics (Group) Company 汕頭陶瓷(集團)公司	Shantou 汕頭市	Guangdong 廣東省	(0754)8255441 (0754)8255442
Guangdong Puning Local Products Import & Export Company 廣東省普寧土產進出口公司	Jieyang 揭陽市	Guangdong 廣東省	(0663)2226744
Yixing Sundry Goods General Co. 宜興市土產雜品總公司	Wuxi 無錫市	Jiangsu 江蘇省	(0510)7903683 (0510)7903683
Sujiang Qu Zhe Jiang Dongda Group Company 椒江區浙江東大集團公司	Taizhou 臺州市	Zhejiang 浙江省	(0576)8881477 (0576)8881672
Jiangsu New Suzhou Co. Ltd. Suzhou Daily Goods General Co. 江蘇新蘇州股份有限公司蘇州日用雜品總公司	Suzhou 蘇州市	Jiangsu 江蘇省	(0512)7276630 (0512)7275964
Shandong Daily Use General Merchandise Import & Export Company 山東省日用百貨進出口公司	Qingdao 青島市	Shandong 山東省	(0532)5849141 (0532)5849207
Guangdong Yangjiang Light Industrial Products Import & Export (Group) Company 廣東陽江輕工業品進出口(集團)公司	Yangjiang 陽江市	Guangdong 廣東省	(0662)3222497 (0662)3222976
Hebei Artts & Crtfts Import & Export Corp. 河北工藝品進出口公司	Shijiazhuang 石家莊市	Hebei 河北省	(0311)7756124 (0311)7755347
Shandong Handicrafts Import & Export Products Group Linyi Craft Co. Ltd. 山東工藝品進出品集團臨沂工藝有限公司	Linyi 臨沂市	Shandong 山東省	(0539)8310001 (0539)8315396

*Also include sales by firms outside this industry.包括本行業以外廠家的銷售。"o" stands for "others". "o" 代表"其他產品"。

3159: Other Ceramics 其他陶瓷製造業

The industry accounts for 0.013% of the total revenue of China's industrial sector in 1996. The revenue growth rate of the industry is 34.2% from 1995, as compared to the growth rate of China's industrial sector, 9.51%. The rate of return on asset is -0.76%. 70.56% of all firms in the industry made a profit while 20.51% had negative returns. The top province in terms of the industry's revenue is Guangdong, accounting for 45.24% of the total revenue.
本行業在1996年佔全行業總產值0.013%，行業年增長率為34.2%（全國工業年增長率9.51%）。行業的資產回報率-0.76%，70.56%的企業盈利，20.51%的企業虧損。銷售收入最高的省份為廣東省，佔本行業的45.24%。

	Total number of firms 企業總數	Total number of employees 職工總數	Total revenue (mil. RMB) 總銷售收入（百萬元）	Total profit (mil. RMB) 總利潤（百萬元）	Return on assets 資產利潤率 (%)	Return on equity 權益利潤率 (%)	Labour productivity ('000 RMB / worker) 勞動生產率（千元／人）	Debts / assets 資產負債率 (%)	Total assets (mil. RMB) 總資產（百萬元）
Industry Overall 行業總體	183	14,459	772	-8	-0.76	-2.16	53.39	64.59	1,005

	Number of firms 企業個數	Average number of employees 平均職工人數	Average revenue ('000 RMB) 平均銷售收入（千元）	Average profit ('000 RMB) 平均利潤（千元）	Return on assets 資產利潤率 (%)	Return on equity 權益利潤率 (%)	Labour productivity ('000 RMB / worker) 勞動生產率（千元／人）	Average debts / assets 平均資產負債率(%)	Average Total assets ('000 RMB) 平均總資產（千元）
By ownership 產業所有權									
State-owned 國有	20	143	2,500	-50	-0.96	-2.56	17.46	62.50	5,200
Collectively-owned 集體	112	53	3,000	-288	-9.06	-40.78	56.31	77.79	3,182
Privately-owned 私有									
Domestic JVs 聯營	3	140	3,699				26.42	48.77	11,654
Joint stock 股份制	1	17	789	-96	-14.13	-23.40	46.41	39.61	678
Foreign-funded 外資	19	108	7,591	-199	-3.85	-6.85	70.18	43.86	5,164
Overseas Chinese-funded 港澳台資	27	116	8,511	1,079	7.09	17.72	73.23	59.97	15,215
By size 規模									
Large 大型	2	664	64,353	3,338	2.17	16.55	96.99	86.87	153,571
Medium 中型	2	401	15,239	-18	-0.07	-0.14	38.05	53.59	27,202
Small 小型	173	71	3,542	-85	-2.28	-5.07	50.16	54.98	3,706
By regional distribution 地區分布									
Central-North 華北	17	99	2,741	139	6.35	10.60	27.62	40.10	2,196
Beijing 北京	7	183	1,640	109	12.48	32.20	8.95	61.25	870
Tianjin 天津	1	35	3,150	-410	-47.13	-241.18	90.00	80.46	870
Hebei 河北	9	41	3,552	224	6.65	10.19	86.41	34.71	3,374
Shanxi 山西									
Inner Mongolia 內蒙									
Northeast 東北	12	103	2,253	-22	-0.39	-0.95	21.97	58.74	5,550
Liaoning 遼寧	7	132	2,356	-61	-0.78	-1.94	17.79	59.68	7,841
Jilin 吉林	3	47	450	23	1.51	1.84	9.57	18.10	1,547
Heilongjiang 黑龍江	2	82	4,600	50	1.41	6.45	56.44	78.08	3,535
Central East 華東	70	67	3,807	59	1.99	4.45	57.06	55.15	2,966
Shanghai 上海	2	44	840	-395	-9.48	-28.11	19.31	66.27	4,165
Jiangsu 江蘇	9	151	13,152	279	4.94	14.65	86.97	66.27	5,642
Zhejiang 浙江	12	102	5,059	39	0.90	2.30	49.76	61.06	4,368
Anhui 安徽	3	24	170	-10	-1.42	60.00	7.08	102.36	707
Fujian 福建	18	43	2,228	28	0.77	1.10	51.62	30.61	3,703
Jiangxi 江西	16	39	699	24	3.52	17.04	17.82	79.37	676
Shandong 山東	10	53	3,395	109	6.59	25.12	64.54	73.74	1,653
Central-South 中南	59	103	6,746	-231	-2.11	-7.14	65.63	70.39	10,902
Henan 河南	14	106	2,056	-3	-0.08	-0.22	19.45	64.62	3,717
Hubei 湖北	4	35	940	80	22.54	200.00	27.25	88.73	355
Hunan 湖南	7	54	1,686	126	5.02	13.37	31.13	62.46	2,504
Guangdong 廣東	29	124	12,044	-468	-2.43	-8.45	97.51	71.21	19,240
Guangxi 廣西	3	135	1,350	-357	-9.71	-27.09	9.98	64.25	3,673
Hainan 海南	2	40	180	-60	-3.68	-16.00	4.50	76.69	1,630
Southwest 西南	18	29	1,617	-27	-1.13	-2.47	55.24	54.23	2,407
Chongqing 重慶	7	39	1,727	-86	-2.14	-3.43	44.53	37.67	4,026
Sichuan 四川	10	25	1,689	12	0.84	7.84	67.10	89.34	1,434
Guizhou 貴州	1	8	120	20	33.33	33.33	15.00		60
Yunnan 雲南									
Tibet 西藏									
Northwest 西北	7	40	746	24	2.54	6.72	18.78	62.18	956
Shaanxi 陝西	5	37	722	22	3.18	12.22	19.41	73.99	692
Gansu 甘肅	1	22	460	10	1.61	5.26	20.91	69.35	620
Qinghai 青海									
Ningxia 寧夏									
Xinjiang 新疆	1	70	1,150	50	1.92	3.47	16.43	44.83	2,610

3159: Other Ceramics 其他陶瓷製造業

Year 年份	Number of firms 企業個數	Rate of change 每年變化 (%)	Number of employees 職工人數 (人)	Rate of change 每年變化 (%)	Total revenue (mil. RMB) 總銷售收入 (百萬元)	Rate of change 每年變化 (%)	Total profit (mil. RMB) 總利潤 (百萬元)	Rate of change 每年變化 (%)
1993	221		20,291		438		12	
1994	217	-1.81%	18,532	-8.67%	483	10.39%	6	-52.56%
1995	163	-24.89%	15,758	-14.97%	575	19.09%	2	-56.64%
1996	183	12.27%	14,459	-8.24%	772	34.22%	-8	-424.68%

3 Major products* 3 種主要產品 *	Output 產量	Sales volume 銷售量	Unit 單位
a) Industrial Ceramics 工業陶瓷	115,475	113,166	ton 噸
b) Toy 玩具	59,472	57,688	1,000 yuan 千元
c) Household Ceramics 日用陶瓷	720	677	10,000 piece 萬件

Top 10 firms by revenue (year founded) 收入排名前 10 家企業 (創辦年份)	City 城市	Province 省	Telephone / fax 電話 / 傳真	Number of employees 職工人數	Ownership 產業所有權	Revenue ('000 RMB) 銷售收入 (千元)	Profit ('000 RMB) (rank) 利潤 (千元) (排名)	Total assets ('000 RMB) 總資產 (千元)	Major products 主要產品
Dongguan Building Decorating Materials Factory 東莞市建築裝飾材料廠(1991)	Dongguan 東莞市	Guangdong 廣東省	(0769)2469008 (0769)2469008	850	Collectively-owned 集體	129,173	-7824(55)	205,563	o
Dongsheng Art Ceramics Co. 東生藝術陶瓷公司(1992)	Guangzhou 廣州市	Guangdong 廣東省	(020)82765229	450	Overseas Chinese-funded 港澳台資	48,348	300(15)	18,800	c
Nanhai Hua Nan Color Enamelled Mosaic Factory 南海市華南彩釉馬賽克廠(1992)	Foshan 佛山市	Guangdong 廣東省	(0757)5388868 (0757)5388495	494	Collectively-owned 集體	46,158	-8284(56)	251,479	o
Dinghu Fenghuang Ceramics Craft Company 鼎湖區鳳凰陶瓷工藝公司(1993)	Zhaoqing 肇慶市	Guangdong 廣東省	(0757)2692088	450	Collectively-owned 集體	30,090	1190(3)	11,323	c
Nanjing Song Fu Ceramics Co. Ltd. 南京松富陶瓷有限公司(1995)	Nanjing 南京市	Jiangsu 江蘇省	(025)2741933	250	Overseas Chinese-funded 港澳台資	29,570	210(21)	3,510	o
Shang Hai Tai Ping Yang Ceramics Co. Ltd. Yixing Branch 上海太平洋陶瓷有限公司宜興分公司(1992)	Wuxi 無錫市	Jiangsu 江蘇省	(0510)7401205	250	Foreign-funded 外資	28,400	1350(2)	6,450	o
Sheng Zhou Shi Cheng Industrial Ceramics Factory 嵊州市城工業陶瓷廠(1993)	Shaoxing 紹興市	Zhejiang 浙江省	(0575)3180389	18	Collectively-owned 集體	26,862	449(12)	18,390	o
Cixian Ceramics Factory 磁縣陶瓷廠(1987)	Handan 邯鄲市	Hebei 河北省	(0310)2325524	120	Collectively-owned 集體	25,250	1130(4)	15,037	o
Dianbai Ceramics Frit Raw Materials Factory 電白縣陶瓷熔塊原料廠(1992)	Maoming 茂名市	Guangdong 廣東省	(0668)5529633	68	Collectively-owned 集體	22,500	1575(1)	7,520	o
Jiedong Lian Feng Porcelain Industry Co. Ltd. 揭東縣聯豐瓷業有限公司(1992)	Jieyang 揭陽市	Guangdong 廣東省	(0663)3266668	300	Foreign-funded 外資	20,885	250(16)	13,614	b

Top 10 Cities by Production Output 產出排名前 10 位城市	Province 省	Market share 市場份額	Number of firms 企業個數
Foshan 佛山市	Guangdong 廣東省	11.27%	6
Zibo 淄博市	Shandong 山東省	8.14%	6
Quanzhou 泉州市	Fujian 福建省	6.85%	10
Jieyang 揭陽市	Guangdong 廣東省	6.78%	3
Zhaoqing 肇慶市	Guangdong 廣東省	5.99%	1
Maoming 茂名市	Guangdong 廣東省	5.31%	1
Zhengzhou 鄭州市	Henan 河南省	5.02%	4
Nanjing 南京市	Jiangsu 江蘇省	4.06%	3
Hangzhou 杭州市	Zhejiang 浙江省	3.23%	5
Baiyin 白銀市	Gansu 甘肅省	2.62%	1

10 Major Wholesalers 10 家主要批發商	City 城市	Province 省	Telephone / Fax 電話 / 傳真
Chengdu Sheng Xing Trade Company 成都盛興商貿公司	Chengdu 成都市	Sichuan 四川省	(028)7762591
Shanghai Municipal Administration Engineering Material Company 上海市市政工程材料公司	Shanghai 上海市	Shanghai 上海市	(021)64372632
Shanghai Construction Engineering Material Co. 上海市建築工程材料公司	Shanghai 上海市	Shanghai 上海市	(021)63298630
Yixing Jin San Jiao Zhao Bazaar 宜興市金三角招商城	Wuxi 無錫市	Jiangsu 江蘇省	(0510)7935138 (0510)7935138
Fujian Hua Fu Import & Export Company 福建省華福進出口公司	Fuzhou 福州市	Fujian 福建省	(0591)7810477 (0591)7810485
China Building Goods & Materials Company 中國建築物資公司	Beijing 北京市	Beijing 北京市	(010)68586253
Dalian Jinzhou Xin Gang Industry & Trade Company 大連金州新港工貿公司	Dalian 大連市	Liaoning 遼寧省	(0411)7624747
Shanghai Zhan Dong Industrial Co. Ltd. 上海展東實業有限公司	Shanghai 上海市	Shanghai 上海市	(021)58201778 (021)58200874
China Building Materials and Equipment Import & Export Company 中國建築材料及設備進出口公司	Beijing 北京市	Beijing 北京市	(010)68393420
Dandong Chemical Light Industry Material Company Chemical Construction Material Marketing Station 丹東市化工輕工材料公司化工建材經銷站	Dandong 丹東市	Liaoning 遼寧省	(0415)2146396

*Also include sales by firms outside this industry.包括本行業以外廠家的銷售。"o" stands for "others". "o" 代表"其他產品"。

3161: Asbestos Products 石棉製品業

The industry accounts for 0.028% of the total revenue of China's industrial sector in 1996. The revenue growth rate of the industry is 14.4% from 1995, as compared to the growth rate of China's industrial sector, 9.51%. The rate of return on asset is -0.11%. 67.82% of all firms in the industry made a profit while 25.51% had negative returns. The top province in terms of the industry's revenue is Zhejiang, accounting for 21.32% of the total revenue.
本行業在1996年佔全行業總產值0.028%，行業年增長率為14.4%（全國工業年增長率9.51%）。行業的資產回報率-0.11%，67.82%的企業盈利，25.51%的企業虧損。銷售收入最高的省份為浙江省，佔本行業的21.32%。

	Total number of firms 企業總數	Total number of employees 職工總數	Total revenue (mil. RMB) 總銷售收入（百萬元）	Total profit (mil. RMB) 總利潤（百萬元）	Return on assets 資產利潤率 (%)	Return on equity 權益利潤率 (%)	Labour productivity ('000 RMB / worker) 勞動生產率（千元／人）	Debts / assets 資產負債率 (%)	Total assets (mil. RMB) 總資產（百萬元）
Industry Overall 行業總體	480	41,722	1,632	-3	-0.11	-0.44	39.12	74.93	2,445

	Number of firms 企業個數	Average number of employees 平均職工人數	Average revenue ('000 RMB) 平均銷售收入（千元）	Average profit ('000 RMB) 平均利潤（千元）	Return on assets 資產利潤率 (%)	Return on equity 權益利潤率 (%)	Labour productivity ('000 RMB / worker) 勞動生產率（千元／人）	Average debts / assets 平均資產負債率(%)	Average Total assets ('000 RMB) 平均總資產（千元）
By ownership 產業所有權									
State-owned 國有	60	338	6,533	-817	-4.02	-20.68	19.30	80.57	20,333
Collectively-owned 集體	399	46	2,418	81	3.44	11.88	53.07	71.01	2,352
Privately-owned 私有									
Domestic JVs 聯營	3	20	291	13	4.97	11.40	14.30	56.37	264
Joint stock 股份制	3	147	9,368	1,393	9.54	20.10	63.58	52.55	14,612
Foreign-funded 外資	4	175	18,258	-119	-0.78	-2.68	104.48	70.95	15,332
Overseas Chinese-funded 港澳台資	10	201	16,307	951	5.33	14.63	81.21	63.55	17,822
By size 規模									
Large 大型	3	1,417	50,858	440	0.40	2.12	35.90	81.07	109,913
Medium 中型	13	920	29,247	-824	-1.35	-5.22	31.79	74.05	60,848
Small 小型	463	55	2,375	14	0.48	1.85	42.93	73.93	2,862
By regional distribution 地區分布									
Central-North 華北	82	56	2,404	39	1.24	4.95	42.59	75.03	3,127
Beijing 北京	16	80	1,288	-243	-2.97	-23.55	16.02	87.38	8,181
Tianjin 天津	9	118	776	-439	-11.44	-62.50	6.55	81.73	3,838
Hebei 河北	37	35	3,872	292	18.36	48.85	109.77	62.43	1,590
Shanxi 山西	11	74	2,101	20	0.80	1.28	28.39	37.79	2,514
Inner Mongolia 內蒙	9	18	357	-1	-0.22	-0.53	20.19	58.13	499
Northeast 東北	98	82	2,653	-35	-0.68	-4.55	32.22	85.01	5,181
Liaoning 遼寧	58	65	2,607	5	0.11	0.47	40.13	75.83	4,086
Jilin 吉林	27	135	2,904	-122	-1.40	-19.76	21.57	92.91	8,730
Heilongjiang 黑龍江	13	51	2,336	-33	-1.23	-20.09	45.53	93.90	2,698
Central East 華東	144	112	5,296	-2	-0.04	-0.12	47.39	70.94	6,900
Shanghai 上海	9	80	2,938	-326	-5.06	-19.47	36.77	73.99	6,429
Jiangsu 江蘇	44	106	5,249	58	0.83	2.61	49.46	68.30	6,992
Zhejiang 浙江	40	126	8,697	60	0.69	2.17	69.29	68.36	8,710
Anhui 安徽	11	106	2,171	-277	-6.96	-46.35	20.53	85.00	3,983
Fujian 福建	5	51	1,358	-208	-6.52	-11.35	26.73	42.61	3,192
Jiangxi 江西	6	31	588	-18	-1.92	-7.19	18.98	73.25	953
Shandong 山東	29	141	4,249	63	0.86	3.78	30.18	77.29	7,385
Central-South 中南	85	74	2,809	63	1.45	5.42	38.13	73.16	4,359
Henan 河南	56	44	2,098	112	4.20	15.71	47.27	73.27	2,675
Hubei 湖北	16	191	6,726	139	1.21	4.66	35.19	73.99	11,489
Hunan 湖南	7	55	734	-17	-1.34	-4.12	13.28	67.59	1,283
Guangdong 廣東	4	42	523	-778	-14.87	-95.99	12.51	84.51	5,228
Guangxi 廣西	2	83	3,215	50	1.43	1.84	38.97	22.21	3,490
Hainan 海南									
Southwest 西南	33	81	3,114	-128	-2.85	-11.60	38.57	75.42	4,498
Chongqing 重慶	15	113	5,147	254	3.15	15.14	45.51	79.19	8,056
Sichuan 四川	17	58	1,590	30	1.70	4.42	27.45	61.46	1,786
Guizhou 貴州	1	10	130				13.00		80
Yunnan 雲南									
Tibet 西藏									
Northwest 西北	38	105	1,866	-84	-1.90	-6.63	17.71	71.34	4,430
Shaanxi 陝西	20	100	1,515	54	1.91	5.81	15.15	67.07	2,797
Gansu 甘肅	11	153	3,287	-268	-3.72	-14.31	21.42	73.96	7,201
Qinghai 青海	3	62	977	-317	-5.01	-9.52	15.67	47.39	6,323
Ningxia 寧夏									
Xinjiang 新疆	4	32	383	-93	-2.60	47.44	11.86	105.48	3,558

3161: Asbestos Products 石棉製品業

Year 年份	Number of firms 企業個數	Rate of change 每年變化 (%)	Number of employees 職工人數 (人)	Rate of change 每年變化 (%)	Total revenue (mil. RMB) 總銷售收入 (百萬元)	Rate of change 每年變化 (%)	Total profit (mil. RMB) 總利潤 (百萬元)	Rate of change 每年變化 (%)
1993	471		50,756		1,502		55	
1994	493	4.67%	46,631	-8.13%	1,381	-8.05%	5	-91.64%
1995	469	-4.87%	42,909	-7.98%	1,427	3.31%	-7	-241.04%
1996	480	2.35%	41,722	-2.77%	1,632	14.37%	-3	53.86%

3 Major products* 3 種主要產品 *	Output 產量	Sales volume 銷售量	Unit 單位
a) Asbestos Cement Shingle 石棉水泥瓦	8,191,720	8,027,886	piece 實物張
b) Mineral Wool Products 礦物棉製品	8,204	3,938	ton 噸

Top 10 firms by revenue (year founded) 收入排名前 10 家企業 (創辦年份)	City 城市	Province 省	Telephone / fax 電話 / 傳真	Number of employees 職工人數	Ownership 產業所有權	Revenue ('000 RMB) 銷售收入 (千元)	Profit ('000 RMB) (rank) 利潤 (千元) (排名)	Total assets ('000 RMB) 總資產 (千元)	Major products 主要產品
Shangyu Cotton Knitgoods Joint General Factory 上虞市針綿織品聯合總廠(1990)	Shaoxing 紹興市	Zhejiang 浙江省	(0575)2091055	490	Collectively-owned 集體	128,100	2010(6)	42,430	o
Hang Cheng Friction Material Co. Ltd. 杭城摩擦材料有限公司(1988)	Hangzhou 杭州市	Zhejiang 浙江省	(0571)5154724 (0571)5153187	1,299	Overseas Chinese-funded 港澳台資	89,644	4270(2)	118,123	o
Jiangsu Wei Te Group 江蘇威特集團(1972)	Yancheng 鹽城市	Jiangsu 江蘇省	(0515)8334884 (0515)8335644	390	Collectively-owned 集體	54,600	3720(4)	53,530	o
Hubei Friction Sealing Material General Factory 湖北摩擦密封材料總廠(1970)	Xiangfan 襄樊市	Hubei 湖北省	(0710)6222390 (0710)225002	1,874	State-owned 國有	47,497	17(106)	128,783	o
China Non-metal Mine Industry General Co. Changchun Asbestos Products Factory 中國非金屬礦工業總公司長春石棉製品廠(1937)	Changchun 長春市	Jilin 吉林省	(0431)4716180 (0431)4713567	1,392	State-owned 國有	38,282	-3972(161)	103,826	o
Yingkou Asbestos Board Making Factory 營口市石棉製板廠(1992)	Yingkou 營口市	Liaoning 遼寧省	(0417)3800815	32	Collectively-owned 集體	35,340	6000(1)	29,300	o
Gansu Friction Sealing Material Factory 甘肅省摩擦密封材料廠(1972)	Tianshui 天水市	Gansu 甘肅省	(0938)5621007 (0938)5624662	1,220	State-owned 國有	28,170	-2597(156)	64,574	o
Shenyang Friction Sealing Material General Factory 瀋陽磨擦密封材料總廠(1952)	Shenyang 瀋陽市	Liaoning 遼寧省	(024)86722453 (024)86724331	1,298	State-owned 國有	27,035	-8775(165)	112,519	o
Jilin Liuhe Asbestos Products Factory 吉林省柳河縣石棉製品廠(1937)	Tonghua 通化市	Jilin 吉林省	(0435)5222632 (0435)5222632	1,071	State-owned 國有	26,778	1304(13)	52,592	o
Qingdao Asbestos Products General Factory 青島石棉製品總廠(1950)	Qingdao 青島市	Shandong 山東省	(0532)5624503 (0532)5627622	1,132	State-owned 國有	25,377	-1383(152)	82,411	o

Top 10 Cities by Production Output 產出排名前 10 位城市	Province 省	Market share 市場份額	Number of firms 企業個數
Chaoyang 朝陽市	Liaoning 遼寧省	18.39%	2
Shaoxing 紹興市	Zhejiang 浙江省	7.26%	3
Yancheng 鹽城市	Jiangsu 江蘇省	5.36%	6
Hangzhou 杭州市	Zhejiang 浙江省	4.63%	6
Wuxi 無錫市	Jiangsu 江蘇省	4.19%	70
Shanghai 上海市	Shanghai 上海市	4.16%	15
Changchun 長春市	Jilin 吉林省	3.38%	10
Xiangfan 襄樊市	Hubei 湖北省	3.32%	5
Ningbo 寧波市	Zhejiang 浙江省	3.16%	18
Guangzhou 廣州市	Guangdong 廣東省	2.87%	7

10 Major Wholesalers 10 家主要批發商	City 城市	Province 省	Telephone / Fax 電話 / 傳真
Chengdu Sheng Xing Trade Company 成都盛興商貿公司	Chengdu 成都市	Sichuan 四川省	(028)7762591
Shanghai Municipal Administration Engineering Material Company 上海市市政工程材料公司	Shanghai 上海市	Shanghai 上海市	(021)64372632
Shanghai Construction Engineering Material Co. 上海市建築工程材料公司	Shanghai 上海市	Shanghai 上海市	(021)63298630
Yixing Jin San Jiao Zhao Bazaar 宜興市金三角招商城	Wuxi 無錫市	Jiangsu 江蘇省	(0510)7935138 (0510)7935138
Fujian Hua Fu Import & Export Company 福建省華福進出口公司	Fuzhou 福州市	Fujian 福建省	(0591)7810477 (0591)7810485
China Building Goods & Materials Company 中國建築物資公司	Beijing 北京市	Beijing 北京市	(010)68586253
Dalian Jinzhou Xin Gang Industry & Trade Company 大連金州新港工貿公司	Dalian 大連市	Liaoning 遼寧省	(0411)7624747
Shanghai Zhan Dong Industrial Co. Ltd. 上海展東實業有限公司	Shanghai 上海市	Shanghai 上海市	(021)58201778 (021)58200874
China Building Materials and Equipment Import & Export Company 中國建築材料及設備進出口公司	Beijing 北京市	Beijing 北京市	(010)68393420
Dandong Chemical Light Industry Material Company Chemical Construction Material Marketing Station 丹東市化工輕工材料公司化工建材經銷站	Dandong 丹東市	Liaoning 遼寧省	(0415)2146396

*Also include sales by firms outside this industry.包括本行業以外廠家的銷售。"o" stands for "others". "o" 代表"其他產品"。

3163: Mica Products 雲母製品業

The industry accounts for 0.006% of the total revenue of China's industrial sector in 1996. The revenue growth rate of the industry is 30.2% from 1995, as compared to the growth rate of China's industrial sector, 9.51%. The rate of return on asset is -0.64%. 73.53% of all firms in the industry made a profit while 17.65% had negative returns. The top province in terms of the industry's revenue is Hebei, accounting for 24.23% of the total revenue.
本行業在1996年佔全行業總產值0.006%，行業年增長率為30.2%（全國工業年增長率9.51%）。行業的資產回報率-0.64%，73.53%的企業盈利，17.65%的企業虧損。銷售收入最高的省份為河北省，佔本行業的24.23%。

	Total number of firms 企業總數	Total number of employees 職工總數	Total revenue (mil. RMB) 總銷售收入（百萬元）	Total profit (mil. RMB) 總利潤（百萬元）	Return on assets 資產利潤率 (%)	Return on equity 權益利潤率 (%)	Labour productivity ('000 RMB / worker) 勞動生產率（千元/人）	Debts / assets 資產負債率 (%)	Total assets (mil. RMB) 總資產（百萬元）
Industry Overall 行業總體	113	9,723	323	-4	-0.64	-2.77	33.22	77.10	589

	Number of firms 企業個數	Average number of employees 平均職工人數	Average revenue ('000 RMB) 平均銷售收入（千元）	Average profit ('000 RMB) 平均利潤（千元）	Return on assets 資產利潤率 (%)	Return on equity 權益利潤率 (%)	Labour productivity ('000 RMB / worker) 勞動生產率（千元/人）	Average debts / assets 平均資產負債率(%)	Average Total assets ('000 RMB) 平均總資產（千元）
By ownership 產業所有權									
State-owned 國有	24	211	5,667	-625	-4.03	-23.44	26.87	82.80	15,500
Collectively-owned 集體	80	50	1,499	9	0.50	1.86	29.76	73.14	1,837
Privately-owned 私有	1	71	2,610	609	27.78	39.77	36.76	30.15	2,194
Domestic JVs 聯營	2	32						58.72	587
Joint stock 股份制	1	207	5,588	150	1.91	9.86	27.00	80.67	7,885
Foreign-funded 外資	2	40	402	-2,068	-14.86	-28.92	10.05	48.60	13,913
Overseas Chinese-funded 港澳台資	3	70	19,341	4,546	44.18	99.86	276.29	55.76	10,291
By size 規模									
Large 大型									
Medium 中型	2	1,166	26,657	-2,911	-3.69	-121.33	22.86	96.96	78,898
Small 小型	110	67	2,451	17	0.42	1.40	36.73	69.81	3,920
By regional distribution 地區分布									
Central-North 華北	40	66	2,456	143	4.01	19.97	37.08	79.92	3,573
Beijing 北京	3	40	1,300	83	5.04	12.08	32.50	58.27	1,653
Tianjin 天津									
Hebei 河北	18	69	4,348	262	4.78	22.41	62.66	78.66	5,483
Shanxi 山西	3	311	4,090	23	0.28	2.88	13.17	90.13	8,203
Inner Mongolia 內蒙	16	22	237	43	4.71	22.04	10.89	78.63	916
Northeast 東北	18	43	833	187	16.45	44.74	19.18	63.34	1,135
Liaoning 遼寧	13	50	812	246	20.28	48.56	16.40	58.30	1,214
Jilin 吉林	5	28	888	32	3.44	17.39	32.17	80.43	930
Heilongjiang 黑龍江									
Central East 華東	17	68	4,605	15	0.26	0.80	67.95	67.09	5,803
Shanghai 上海	2	141	12,495	105	0.59	1.98	88.62	70.03	17,670
Jiangsu 江蘇	7	59	4,593	-51	-1.60	-6.95	78.41	77.05	3,224
Zhejiang 浙江	3	111	4,947	-53	-0.41	-0.98	44.43	57.85	12,930
Anhui 安徽	2	24	1,390	95	33.93	79.17	57.92	57.14	280
Fujian 福建									
Jiangxi 江西	1	20	160	10	25.00	25.00	8.00		40
Shandong 山東	2	29	1,680	185	27.41	528.57	57.93	94.81	675
Central-South 中南	21	63	3,201	166	3.30	10.47	50.51	68.54	5,040
Henan 河南	5	83	1,930	-22	-0.62	-2.64	23.14	76.72	3,574
Hubei 湖北	3	58	1,487	190	10.05	48.72	25.49	79.37	1,890
Hunan 湖南	6	78	1,067	-317	-8.74	-68.59	13.76	87.31	3,625
Guangdong 廣東	6	42	7,673	818	8.21	19.73	182.70	58.39	9,965
Guangxi 廣西	1	22	680	20	2.60	6.06	30.91	57.14	770
Hainan 海南									
Southwest 西南	8	286	3,921	-1,074	-10.30	-55.46	13.70	81.43	10,429
Chongqing 重慶									
Sichuan 四川	8	286	3,921	-1,074	-10.30	-55.46	13.71	81.43	10,429
Guizhou 貴州									
Yunnan 雲南									
Tibet 西藏									
Northwest 西北	9	169	3,624	-886	-5.80	-45.78	21.46	87.34	15,273
Shaanxi 陝西	2	63	735	-75	-3.07	-7.65	11.76	59.92	2,445
Gansu 甘肅	1	16	400	10	0.27	0.29	25.00	4.11	3,650
Qinghai 青海									
Ningxia 寧夏									
Xinjiang 新疆	6	230	5,125	-1,305	-6.07	-65.52	22.30	90.74	21,487

3163: Mica Products 雲母製品業

Year 年份	Number of firms 企業個數	Rate of change 每年變化 (%)	Number of employees 職工人數 (人)	Rate of change 每年變化 (%)	Total revenue (mil. RMB) 總銷售收入 (百萬元)	Rate of change 每年變化 (%)	Total profit (mil. RMB) 總利潤 (百萬元)	Rate of change 每年變化 (%)
1993	103		10,732		207		14	
1994	110	6.80%	10,567	-1.54%	285	37.36%	9	-34.11%
1995	110		10,525	-0.40%	248	-12.82%	-5	-160.43%
1996	113	2.73%	9,723	-7.62%	323	30.19%	-4	25.65%

3 Major products* 3 種主要產品 *	Output 產量	Sales volume 銷售量	Unit 單位
a) Mica Paper Products 雲母紙製品	2,537,070	3,196,708	kg 千克
b) Industrial Raw Material Mica 工業原料雲母	1,464	1,405	ton 噸
c) Insulation Products 絕緣製品	750	727	ton 噸

Top 10 firms by revenue (year founded) 收入排名前 10 家企業 (創辦年份)	City 城市	Province 省	Telephone / fax 電話 / 傳真	Number of employees 職工人數	Ownership 產業所有權	Revenue ('000 RMB) 銷售收入 (千元)	Profit ('000 RMB) (rank) 利潤 (千元) (排名)	Total assets ('000 RMB) 總資產 (千元)	Major products 主要產品
Shenzhen Mai Ka Electrical Appliances Co. Ltd. 深圳麥卡電工器材有限公司(1989)	Shenzhen 深圳市	Guangdong 廣東省	(0755)5535258 (0755)5535158	115	Overseas Chinese-funded 港澳台資	25,195	3802(1)	16,717	a
Shanghai Electric Machinery (Group) Co. 上海電機(集團)公司(1951)	Shanghai 上海市	Shanghai 上海市	(021)56624032 (021)56637287	235	State-owned 國有	23,234	154(14)	34,640	a
Shahe Paper Making China Clay Factory 沙河市造紙瓷土廠(1988)	Xingtai 邢臺市	Hebei 河北省	(0319)8804585	322	State-owned 國有	22,885	71(18)	58,469	a
Xinjiang Yun Yang Electrical Appliance Industrial Co. 新疆雲洋電器工業公司(1965)	Urumqi 烏魯木齊市	Xinjiang 新疆	(0991)4521811	734	State-owned 國有	22,067	-4522(33)	88,050	o
China Non-metal Mine Industrial General Co. Ya'an Mica Co. 中國非金屬礦工業總公司雅安雲母公司(1952)	Ya'an 雅安市	Sichuan 四川省	(0835)2222541 (0835)2225244	1,529	State-owned 國有	21,017	-7888(34)	56,581	a
Danyang Insulating Material Factory 丹陽市絕緣材料廠(1975)	Zhenjiang 鎮江市	Jiangsu 江蘇省	(0511)6387451	169	Collectively-owned 集體	20,718	-281(31)	8,904	c
Xin Ji Cheng Electrical Material (Shenzhen) Co. Ltd. 新集誠電工材料(深圳)有限公司(1994)	Shenzhen 深圳市	Guangdong 廣東省	(0755)5534438 (0755)7745417	92	Overseas Chinese-funded 港澳台資	18,201	2966(2)	11,087	o
Yan Chuan Xiang Mica Factory 燕川鄉雲母廠(1982)	Shijiazhuang 石家莊市	Hebei 河北省		90	Collectively-owned 集體	15,980	1710(4)	800	o
Hangzhou Mica Paper Factory 杭州雲母紙廠(1973)	Hangzhou 杭州市	Zhejiang 浙江省	(0571)3597219 (0571)3597219	242	State-owned 國有	11,500	210(11)	26,100	o
Ta Shang Mica Factory 塔上雲母廠	Shijiazhuang 石家莊市	Hebei 河北省		120	Collectively-owned 集體	8,000	840(5)	700	o

Top 10 Cities by Production Output 產出排名前 10 位城市	Province 省	Market share 市場份額	Number of firms 企業個數
Xingtai 邢臺市	Hebei 河北省	12.43%	5
Shanghai 上海市	Shanghai 上海市	10.42%	2
Shenzhen 深圳市	Guangdong 廣東省	9.16%	1
Urumqi 烏魯木齊市	Xinjiang 新疆	8.11%	1
Ya'an 雅安市	Sichuan 四川省	7.90%	1
Shijiazhuang 石家莊市	Hebei 河北省	5.47%	6
Chuzhou 滁州市	Anhui 安徽省	5.01%	1
Hangzhou 杭州市	Zhejiang 浙江省	4.30%	2
Zhenjiang 鎮江市	Jiangsu 江蘇省	4.25%	3
Huaiyin 淮陰市	Jiangsu 江蘇省	2.71%	3

10 Major Wholesalers 10 家主要批發商	City 城市	Province 省	Telephone / Fax 電話 / 傳真
Chengdu Sheng Xing Trade Company 成都盛興商貿公司	Chengdu 成都市	Sichuan 四川省	(028)7762591
Shanghai Municipal Administration Engineering Material Company 上海市市政工程材料公司	Shanghai 上海市	Shanghai 上海市	(021)64372632
Shanghai Construction Engineering Material Co. 上海市建築工程材料公司	Shanghai 上海市	Shanghai 上海市	(021)63298630
Yixing Jin San Jiao Zhao Bazaar 宜興市金三角招商城	Wuxi 無錫市	Jiangsu 江蘇省	(0510)7935138 (0510)7935138
Fujian Hua Fu Import & Export Company 福建省華福進出口公司	Fuzhou 福州市	Fujian 福建省	(0591)7810477 (0591)7810485
China Building Goods & Materials Company 中國建築物資公司	Beijing 北京市	Beijing 北京市	(010)68586253
Dalian Jinzhou Xin Gang Industry & Trade Company 大連金州新港工貿公司	Dalian 大連市	Liaoning 遼寧省	(0411)7624747
Shanghai Zhan Dong Industrial Co. Ltd. 上海展東實業有限公司	Shanghai 上海市	Shanghai 上海市	(021)58201778 (021)58200874
China Building Materials and Equipment Import & Export Company 中國建築材料及設備進出口公司	Beijing 北京市	Beijing 北京市	(010)68393420
Dandong Chemical Light Industry Material Company Chemical Construction Material Marketing Station 丹東市化工輕工材料公司化工建材經銷站	Dandong 丹東市	Liaoning 遼寧省	(0415)2146396

*Also include sales by firms outside this industry.包括本行業以外廠家的銷售。"o" stands for "others". "o" 代表"其他產品"。

3169: Other Fireproof Materials 其他耐火材料製品業

The industry accounts for 0.210% of the total revenue of China's industrial sector in 1996. The revenue growth rate of the industry is 12.4% from 1995, as compared to the growth rate of China's industrial sector, 9.51%. The rate of return on asset is 0.97%. 68.17% of all firms in the industry made a profit while 23.79% had negative returns. The top province in terms of the industry's revenue is Henan, accounting for 26.76% of the total revenue.
本行業在1996年佔全行業總產值0.210%，行業年增長率為12.4%（全國工業年增長率9.51%）。行業的資產回報率0.97%，68.17%的企業盈利，23.79%的企業虧損。銷售收入最高的省份為河南省，佔本行業的26.76%。

	Total number of firms 企業總數	Total number of employees 職工總數	Total revenue (mil. RMB) 總銷售收入（百萬元）	Total profit (mil. RMB) 總利潤（百萬元）	Return on assets 資產利潤率 (%)	Return on equity 權益利潤率 (%)	Labour productivity ('000 RMB / worker) 勞動生產率（千元/人）	Debts / assets 資產負債率 (%)	Total assets (mil. RMB) 總資產（百萬元）
Industry Overall 行業總體	1,928	270,713	12,154	200	0.97	3.14	44.90	69.12	20,602

	Number of firms 企業個數	Average number of employees 平均職工人數	Average revenue ('000 RMB) 平均銷售收入（千元）	Average profit ('000 RMB) 平均利潤（千元）	Return on assets 資產利潤率 (%)	Return on equity 權益利潤率 (%)	Labour productivity ('000 RMB / worker) 勞動生產率（千元/人）	Average debts / assets 平均資產負債率(%)	Average Total assets ('000 RMB) 平均總資產（千元）
By ownership 產業所有權									
State-owned 國有	233	454	10,880	-1,288	-3.43	-12.48	23.95	72.49	37,502
Collectively-owned 集體	1,582	93	5,285	273	4.47	14.46	56.88	69.11	6,118
Privately-owned 私有	7	32	1,248	166	11.08	17.37	38.50	36.21	1,498
Domestic JVs 聯營	15	70	5,883	256	3.41	8.38	84.28	59.30	7,498
Joint stock 股份制	30	324	19,500	997	2.28	5.59	60.10	59.29	43,776
Foreign-funded 外資	33	142	12,253	853	5.23	10.50	86.57	50.18	16,314
Overseas Chinese-funded 港澳台資	19	100	7,178	64	0.62	1.15	71.90	46.40	10,448
By size 規模									
Large 大型	24	2,608	95,788	-5,216	-1.93	-6.29	36.72	69.27	270,013
Medium 中型	46	788	53,657	2,564	3.13	11.33	68.12	72.33	81,802
Small 小型	1,840	93	4,015	113	2.00	6.22	43.08	67.86	5,629
By regional distribution 地區分布									
Central-North 華北	332	95	3,246	96	1.71	5.81	34.13	70.51	5,596
Beijing 北京	27	60	4,942	109	1.30	3.42	82.27	62.10	8,419
Tianjin 天津	16	144	6,316	27	0.26	1.20	43.76	78.28	10,302
Hebei 河北	107	129	4,509	218	2.70	8.81	34.97	69.37	8,078
Shanxi 山西	161	76	1,923	21	0.65	2.34	25.17	72.25	3,290
Inner Mongolia 內蒙	21	74	2,441	80	2.36	11.93	33.11	80.21	3,412
Northeast 東北	406	199	7,976	305	2.00	7.10	40.06	71.80	15,218
Liaoning 遼寧	334	215	9,384	379	2.16	7.55	43.57	71.34	17,489
Jilin 吉林	39	90	1,025	8	0.24	1.22	11.40	80.34	3,514
Heilongjiang 黑龍江	33	163	1,937	-93	-1.53	-7.47	11.89	79.45	6,063
Central East 華東	418	142	7,897	114	0.97	2.80	55.67	65.15	11,685
Shanghai 上海	22	357	17,975	-2,021	-6.20	-19.51	50.38	68.20	32,578
Jiangsu 江蘇	129	125	9,489	216	2.10	7.95	75.70	73.58	10,279
Zhejiang 浙江	85	87	7,015	371	4.11	10.57	80.80	61.13	9,031
Anhui 安徽	37	105	3,014	157	4.37	14.48	28.62	69.79	3,584
Fujian 福建	28	44	1,091	-21	-0.96	-1.54	24.89	37.46	2,195
Jiangxi 江西	47	98	1,742	-389	-6.57	-21.49	17.79	69.44	5,926
Shandong 山東	70	260	12,302	654	2.86	6.92	47.40	58.67	22,877
Central-South 中南	499	136	7,566	131	1.12	3.63	55.48	69.28	11,697
Henan 河南	315	159	10,326	382	2.55	8.53	64.95	70.13	14,964
Hubei 湖北	40	78	2,580	65	1.61	4.47	32.93	63.99	4,009
Hunan 湖南	89	128	3,133	-110	-1.84	-7.98	24.48	76.91	5,952
Guangdong 廣東	35	71	2,946	-1,244	-12.07	-23.32	41.68	48.30	10,300
Guangxi 廣西	19	44	1,863	-186	-6.14	-26.86	42.34	77.13	3,033
Hainan 海南	1	131	1,990	-800	-5.32	-15.81	15.19	66.29	15,040
Southwest 西南	211	106	2,949	-248	-3.93	-13.26	27.92	70.34	6,295
Chongqing 重慶	26	120	3,184	-29	-0.56	-2.38	26.58	76.42	5,159
Sichuan 四川	115	98	3,193	-294	-4.38	-17.16	32.61	74.49	6,706
Guizhou 貴州	47	122	2,239	-375	-6.10	-16.85	18.41	63.78	6,140
Yunnan 雲南	23	96	2,912	-7	-0.12	-0.26	30.40	54.59	5,867
Tibet 西藏									
Northwest 西北	62	140	2,246	-265	-3.18	-9.02	16.03	64.74	8,326
Shaanxi 陝西	30	169	2,679	-491	-5.45	-21.58	15.83	74.74	9,001
Gansu 甘肅	7	128	1,816	30	0.51	2.36	14.19	78.41	5,901
Qinghai 青海	2	315	3,525	685	4.88	36.63	11.21	86.71	14,030
Ningxia 寧夏	13	74	1,272	-358	-4.10	-7.38	17.23	44.40	8,715
Xinjiang 新疆	10	113	2,258	137	2.16	3.59	20.05	39.96	6,354

3169: Other Fireproof Materials 其他耐火材料製品業

Year 年份	Number of firms 企業個數	Rate of change 每年變化 (%)	Number of employees 職工人數 (人)	Rate of change 每年變化 (%)	Total revenue (mil. RMB) 總銷售收入 (百萬元)	Rate of change 每年變化 (%)	Total profit (mil. RMB) 總利潤 (百萬元)	Rate of change 每年變化 (%)
1993	1,366		269,242		7,361		285	
1994	1,593	16.62%	240,304	-10.75%	8,464	14.99%	275	-3.31%
1995	1,871	17.45%	283,079	17.80%	10,816	27.78%	284	3.32%
1996	1,928	3.05%	270,713	-4.37%	12,154	12.37%	200	-29.67%

3 Major products* 3 種主要產品 *	Output 產量	Sales volume 銷售量	Unit 單位
a) Refractory Material Products 耐火材料製品	19,381,034	13,566,724	ton 噸
b) Refractory Aggregate 耐火集料	834,647	801,261	ton 噸
c) Acid-proof Brick 耐酸磚	733,665	704,318	ton 噸

Top 10 firms by revenue (year founded) 收入排名前 10 家企業 (創辦年份)	City 城市	Province 省	Telephone / fax 電話 / 傳真	Number of employees 職工人數	Ownership 產業所有權	Revenue ('000 RMB) 銷售收入 (千元)	Profit ('000 RMB) (rank) 利潤 (千元) (排名)	Total assets ('000 RMB) 總資產 (千元)	Major products 主要產品
Haicheng Hua Mei Industrial Co. 海城市鏵鎂實業公司(1992)	Anshan 鞍山市	Liaoning 遼寧省	(0412)3248791 (0412)3248300	3,106	Collectively-owned 集體	319,540	27210(3)	216,390	a
Shanghai Tai Shan Refractories Co. Ltd. 上海泰山耐火材料有限公司(1921)	Shanghai 上海市	Shanghai 上海市	(021)56636600 (021)56639852	5,238	State-owned 國有	246,026	-49964(770)	573,615	a,b
Hai City Qingshan Industrial Company 海城市青山實業公司(1993)	Anshan 鞍山市	Liaoning 遼寧省	(0412)3248052 (0412)3248065	2,675	Collectively-owned 集體	232,900	29600(2)	75,280	a
Zhengzhou Hua Yu Refractory Group Company 鄭州華宇耐火材料集團公司(1974)	Zhengzhou 鄭州市	Henan 河南省	(0371)4157028 (0371)4157027	938	Collectively-owned 集體	200,760	0(565)	52,978	a
Hai City Xi Yang Refractory Company 海城市西洋耐火材料公司(1988)	Anshan 鞍山市	Liaoning 遼寧省	(0412)3277388 (0412)3277060	1,738	Collectively-owned 集體	200,150	36060(1)	509,100	a
Dengfeng Daye Zhen No.2 Refractory General Factory 登封市大冶鎮第二耐火材料總廠(1963)	Zhengzhou 鄭州市	Henan 河南省	(0371)2931278	842	Collectively-owned 集體	162,290	9640(11)	101,850	o
Zhengzhou Zhen Zhong Industrial Group Co. Ltd. 鄭州振中實業集團股份有限公司(1987)	Zhengzhou 鄭州市	Henan 河南省	(0371)9551188	1,436	Joint stock 股份制	155,080	8210(14)	206,735	a
Shandong Refractories Corp. 山東省耐火原材料公司(1993)	Zibo 淄博市	Shandong 山東省	(0533)2282029 (0533)2289531	6,000	State-owned 國有	152,660	-15585(764)	451,711	a,b
Dashiqiao Household Electric Appliances Material Factory 大石橋市家用電器材料廠(1980)	Yingkou 營口市	Liaoning 遼寧省	(0417)5812283 (0417)5817524	435	Collectively-owned 集體	140,557	11418(10)	144,531	o
Ji'nan Magnesia & Carbon Brick Factory 濟南市鎂碳磚廠(1987)	Ji'nan 濟南市	Shandong 山東省	(0531)8991172 (0531)8991327	488	Collectively-owned 集體	135,180	13510(7)	128,963	a

Top 10 Cities by Production Output 產出排名前 10 位城市	Province 省	Market share 市場份額	Number of firms 企業個數
Zhengzhou 鄭州市	Henan 河南省	19.28%	122
Anshan 鞍山市	Liaoning 遼寧省	15.67%	105
Wuxi 無錫市	Jiangsu 江蘇省	6.31%	86
Shanghai 上海市	Shanghai 上海市	6.29%	39
Yingkou 營口市	Liaoning 遼寧省	5.54%	54
Huzhou 湖州市	Zhejiang 浙江省	3.39%	60
Zibo 淄博市	Shandong 山東省	3.04%	32
Luoyang 洛陽市	Henan 河南省	2.97%	28
Jiaozuo 焦作市	Henan 河南省	2.19%	24
Shenyang 瀋陽市	Liaoning 遼寧省	1.71%	29

10 Major Wholesalers 10 家主要批發商	City 城市	Province 省	Telephone / Fax 電話 / 傳真
Chengdu Sheng Xing Trade Company 成都盛興商貿公司	Chengdu 成都市	Sichuan 四川省	(028)7762591
Shanghai Municipal Administration Engineering Material Company 上海市市政工程材料公司	Shanghai 上海市	Shanghai 上海市	(021)64372632
Shanghai Construction Engineering Material Co. 上海市建築工程材料公司	Shanghai 上海市	Shanghai 上海市	(021)63298630
Yixing Jin San Jiao Zhao Bazaar 宜興市金三角招商城	Wuxi 無錫市	Jiangsu 江蘇省	(0510)7935138 (0510)7935138
Fujian Hua Fu Import & Export Company 福建省華福進出口公司	Fuzhou 福州市	Fujian 福建省	(0591)7810477 (0591)7810485
China Building Goods & Materials Company 中國建築物資公司	Beijing 北京市	Beijing 北京市	(010)68586253
Dalian Jinzhou Xin Gang Industry & Trade Company 大連金州新港工貿公司	Dalian 大連市	Liaoning 遼寧省	(0411)7624747
Shanghai Zhan Dong Industrial Co. Ltd. 上海展東實業有限公司	Shanghai 上海市	Shanghai 上海市	(021)58201778 (021)58200874
China Building Materials and Equipment Import & Export Company 中國建築材料及設備進出口公司	Beijing 北京市	Beijing 北京市	(010)68393420
Dandong Chemical Light Industry Material Company Chemical Construction Material Marketing Station 丹東市化工輕工材料公司化工建材經銷站	Dandong 丹東市	Liaoning 遼寧省	(0415)2146396

*Also include sales by firms outside this industry.包括本行業以外廠家的銷售。"o" stands for "others". "o" 代表 "其他產品" 。

3171: Metallurgical Coke 冶金用碳素製品業

The industry accounts for 0.072% of the total revenue of China's industrial sector in 1996. The revenue growth rate of the industry is 17.1% from 1995, as compared to the growth rate of China's industrial sector, 9.51%. The rate of return on asset is -0.18%. 68.58% of all firms in the industry made a profit while 24.54% had negative returns. The top province in terms of the industry's revenue is Jilin, accounting for 16.49% of the total revenue.
本行業在1996年佔全行業總產值0.072%，行業年增長率為17.1%（全國工業年增長率9.51%）。行業的資產回報率-0.18%，68.58%的企業盈利，24.54%的企業虧損。銷售收入最高的省份為吉林省，佔本行業的16.49%。

	Total number of firms 企業總數	Total number of employees 職工總數	Total revenue (mil. RMB) 總銷售收入（百萬元）	Total profit (mil. RMB) 總利潤（百萬元）	Return on assets 資產利潤率 (%)	Return on equity 權益利潤率 (%)	Labour productivity ('000 RMB / worker) 勞動生產率（千元/人）	Debts / assets 資產負債率 (%)	Total assets (mil. RMB) 總資產（百萬元）
Industry Overall 行業總體	401	79,610	4,194	-15	-0.18	-0.61	52.68	70.69	8,332

	Number of firms 企業個數	Average number of employees 平均職工人數	Average revenue ('000 RMB) 平均銷售收入（千元）	Average profit ('000 RMB) 平均利潤（千元）	Return on assets 資產利潤率 (%)	Return on equity 權益利潤率 (%)	Labour productivity ('000 RMB / worker) 勞動生產率（千元/人）	Average debts / assets 平均資產負債率(%)	Average Total assets ('000 RMB) 平均總資產（千元）
By ownership 產業所有權									
State-owned 國有	71	642	32,803	-831	-0.98	-3.43	51.12	71.42	84,662
Collectively-owned 集體	304	98	5,418	89	1.35	4.81	55.45	71.88	6,575
Privately-owned 私有	4	30	2,392	-5	-0.22	-0.60	79.73	63.46	2,071
Domestic JVs 聯營	5	165	14,674	218	1.67	4.03	88.93	58.60	13,069
Joint stock 股份制	5	451	16,315	1,157	3.11	5.74	36.14	45.91	37,266
Foreign-funded 外資	1	67	11,457	264	2.50	7.60	171.00	67.08	10,537
Overseas Chinese-funded 港澳台資	10	108	4,269	985	18.77	35.20	39.67	46.69	5,246
By size 規模									
Large 大型	12	2,754	163,512	-1,385	-0.35	-1.10	59.37	68.32	397,274
Medium 中型	16	820	25,723	-825	-0.91	-3.42	31.38	73.24	90,265
Small 小型	365	91	4,990	41	0.70	2.72	55.00	74.27	5,811
By regional distribution 地區分布									
Central-North 華北	71	156	9,051	131	0.88	3.28	57.94	73.25	14,899
Beijing 北京	3	44	873	-63	-7.22	-11.24	20.00	35.36	877
Tianjin 天津	11	130	11,561	-68	-0.60	-1.96	88.81	69.40	11,389
Hebei 河北	21	156	8,127	409	2.74	23.44	52.14	88.33	14,954
Shanxi 山西	27	187	11,444	73	0.40	1.02	61.14	60.88	18,124
Inner Mongolia 內蒙	9	133	3,689	-36	-0.25	-2.15	27.64	88.25	14,058
Northeast 東北	91	236	10,663	39	0.14	0.43	45.26	66.72	26,853
Liaoning 遼寧	48	127	5,351	121	1.21	3.77	41.97	67.86	10,003
Jilin 吉林	35	402	19,764	-2		-0.01	49.14	68.41	52,226
Heilongjiang 黑龍江	8	155	2,719	-279	-1.65	-2.74	17.50	39.86	16,945
Central East 華東	63	251	18,008	-370	-1.42	-5.28	71.74	73.07	25,979
Shanghai 上海	6	385	33,992	-602	-0.93	-2.91	88.37	68.20	64,978
Jiangsu 江蘇	21	216	16,589	366	1.99	8.77	76.84	77.32	18,379
Zhejiang 浙江	4	35	2,565	38	0.52	1.38	72.77	62.00	7,165
Anhui 安徽	3	1,080	67,610	-14,653	-12.39	-54.17	62.60	77.12	118,260
Fujian 福建	5	14	428	-4	-1.20	-4.08	31.47	70.66	334
Jiangxi 江西	6	60	3,185	-2	-0.04	-0.09	53.53	60.74	4,500
Shandong 山東	18	287	19,326	916	3.67	13.06	67.32	71.89	24,931
Central-South 中南	97	163	7,787	-22	-0.15	-0.50	47.77	70.04	14,656
Henan 河南	45	182	9,891	245	1.64	5.56	54.29	70.48	14,950
Hubei 湖北	12	329	9,371	-1,248	-4.12	-13.68	28.47	69.85	30,270
Hunan 湖南	33	86	4,124	97	1.33	3.93	48.09	66.09	7,299
Guangdong 廣東	1	633	55,600	140	0.11	0.51	87.84	77.85	123,900
Guangxi 廣西	6	34	1,022	-258	-7.43	-17.69	30.50	57.96	3,477
Hainan 海南									
Southwest 西南	42	79	2,377	-42	-0.63	-3.95	30.25	83.96	6,651
Chongqing 重慶	6	14	427	-41	-4.88	14.15	29.85	134.50	840
Sichuan 四川	19	89	3,626	-133	-1.07	-6.16	40.60	82.57	12,423
Guizhou 貴州	15	89	1,566	84	5.49	16.30	17.64	66.30	1,529
Yunnan 雲南	2	81	2,070	-120	-1.90	8.30	25.56	122.83	6,330
Tibet 西藏									
Northwest 西北	37	328	15,980	-12	-0.03	-0.10	48.66	70.93	40,356
Shaanxi 陝西	3	341	16,963	-337	-0.85	234.88	49.75	100.36	39,483
Gansu 甘肅	11	832	43,750	112	0.10	0.31	52.61	65.92	106,513
Qinghai 青海	2	43	1,970	-45	-1.28		46.35	100.00	3,510
Ningxia 寧夏	16	112	3,233	-26	-0.22	-1.29	28.96	82.76	11,817
Xinjiang 新疆	5	22	692	-30	-2.14	-5.79	31.45	63.14	1,400

3171: Metallurgical Coke 冶金用碳素製品業

Year 年份	Number of firms 企業個數	Rate of change 每年變化 (%)	Number of employees 職工人數 (人)	Rate of change 每年變化 (%)	Total revenue (mil. RMB) 總銷售收入 (百萬元)	Rate of change 每年變化 (%)	Total profit (mil. RMB) 總利潤 (百萬元)	Rate of change 每年變化 (%)
1993	286		78,238		2,845		68	
1994	301	5.24%	67,688	-13.49%	3,229	13.50%	88	28.38%
1995	386	28.24%	78,425	15.86%	3,583	10.98%	-32	-136.19%
1996	401	3.89%	79,610	1.51%	4,194	17.05%	-15	52.69%

3 Major products* 3種主要產品*	Output 產量	Sales volume 銷售量	Unit 單位
a) Aluminium 礦產鋁	505,857	455,272	ton 噸
b) Graphite 石墨	352,404	341,832	ton 噸

Top 10 firms by revenue (year founded) 收入排名前10家企業 (創辦年份)	City 城市	Province 省	Telephone / fax 電話 / 傳真	Number of employees 職工人數	Ownership 產業所有權	Revenue ('000 RMB) 銷售收入 (千元)	Profit ('000 RMB) (rank) 利潤 (千元) (排名)	Total assets ('000 RMB) 總資產 (千元)	Major products 主要產品
Jilin Carbon General Factory 吉林炭素總廠(1955)	Jilin 吉林市	Jilin 吉林省	(0432)2738590 (0432)2738464	8,900	State-owned 國有	548,319	5207(4)	1,427,484	o
Lanzhou Carbon Factory 蘭州炭素廠(1966)	Lanzhou 蘭州市	Gansu 甘肅省	(0931)6211511 (0931)6213833	7,168	State-owned 國有	380,722	3603(7)	1,021,528	o
Hefei Carbon Factory (Hefei Aluminium Manufacturer) 合肥炭素廠(1960)	Hefei 合肥市	Anhui 安徽省	(0551)5526001 (0551)5548356	2,745	State-owned 國有	185,552	-43464(189)	322,008	a
Shanghai Carbon Factory 上海碳素廠(1958)	Shanghai 上海市	Shanghai 上海市	(021)64342130 (021)64345534	1,775	State-owned 國有	180,317	28(115)	322,406	o
Jining Carbon Industry General Co. 濟寧碳素工業總公司(1992)	Jining 濟寧市	Shandong 山東省	(0537)8900231 (0537)8900231	931	Collectively-owned 集體	112,809	8333(1)	92,513	o
Nantong Carbon Factory 南通碳素廠(1967)	Nantong 南通市	Jiangsu 江蘇省	(0513)5544623 (0513)5544806	1,962	State-owned 國有	97,010	1080(26)	189,460	o
Shandong No.83 Factory 山東省生建八三廠(1958)	Zibo 淄博市	Shandong 山東省	(0533)6680412 (0533)6680418	2,676	State-owned 國有	84,562	-932(170)	200,809	o
Fushun Carbon Factory 撫順市炭素廠(1958)	Fushun 撫順市	Liaoning 遼寧省	(0413)6689982 (0413)6689700	1,587	State-owned 國有	80,815	17(118)	210,851	o
Jilin Songjiang Carbon Factory 吉林松江炭素廠(1970)	Jilin 吉林市	Jilin 吉林省	(0432)2738591 (0432)2778382	2,410	Collectively-owned 集體	78,496	-4138(186)	210,103	o
Pingyin Aluminium Manufacturer Carbon Factory 平陰鋁廠炭素廠(1989)	Ji'nan 濟南市	Shandong 山東省	(0531)7745914	298	Collectively-owned 集體	72,980	5470(3)	38,230	o

Top 10 Cities by Production Output 產出排名前10位城市	Province 省	Market share 市場份額	Number of firms 企業個數
Jilin 吉林市	Jilin 吉林省	14.75%	23
Lanzhou 蘭州市	Gansu 甘肅省	9.79%	11
Shanghai 上海市	Shanghai 上海市	5.41%	13
Ji'nan 濟南市	Shandong 山東省	5.06%	3
Hefei 合肥市	Anhui 安徽省	4.85%	2
Jiaozuo 焦作市	Henan 河南省	4.41%	8
Tianjin 天津市	Tianjin 天津市	3.26%	10
Fushun 撫順市	Liaoning 遼寧省	2.99%	14
Jining 濟寧市	Shandong 山東省	2.96%	5
Nantong 南通市	Jiangsu 江蘇省	2.80%	6

10 Major Wholesalers 10家主要批發商	City 城市	Province 省	Telephone / Fax 電話 / 傳真
Chengdu Sheng Xing Trade Company 成都盛興商貿公司	Chengdu 成都市	Sichuan 四川省	(028)7762591
Shanghai Municipal Administration Engineering Material Company 上海市市政工程材料公司	Shanghai 上海市	Shanghai 上海市	(021)64372632
Shanghai Construction Engineering Material Co. 上海市建築工程材料公司	Shanghai 上海市	Shanghai 上海市	(021)63298630
Yixing Jin San Jiao Zhao Bazaar 宜興市金三角招商城	Wuxi 無錫市	Jiangsu 江蘇省	(0510)7935138 (0510)7935138
Fujian Hua Fu Import & Export Company 福建省華福進出口公司	Fuzhou 福州市	Fujian 福建省	(0591)7810477 (0591)7810485
China Building Goods & Materials Company 中國建築物資公司	Beijing 北京市	Beijing 北京市	(010)68586253
Dalian Jinzhou Xin Gang Industry & Trade Company 大連金州新港工貿公司	Dalian 大連市	Liaoning 遼寧省	(0411)7624747
Shanghai Zhan Dong Industrial Co. Ltd. 上海展東實業有限公司	Shanghai 上海市	Shanghai 上海市	(021)58201778 (021)58200874
China Building Materials and Equipment Import & Export Company 中國建築材料及設備進出口公司	Beijing 北京市	Beijing 北京市	(010)68393420
Dandong Chemical Light Industry Material Company Chemical Construction Material Marketing Station 丹東市化工輕工材料公司化工建材經銷站	Dandong 丹東市	Liaoning 遼寧省	(0415)2146396

*Also include sales by firms outside this industry.包括本行業以外廠家的銷售。"o" stands for "others". "o" 代表"其他產品"。

3172: Graphite Products 石墨製品業

The industry accounts for 0.008% of the total revenue of China's industrial sector in 1996. The revenue growth rate of the industry is -1.0% from 1995, as compared to the growth rate of China's industrial sector, 9.51%. The rate of return on asset is 0.50%. 73.01% of all firms in the industry made a profit while 18.10% had negative returns. The top province in terms of the industry's revenue is Liaoning, accounting for 21.00% of the total revenue.
本行業在 1996 年佔全行業總產值 0.008%，行業年增長率為 -1.0%（全國工業年增長率 9.51%）。行業的資產回報率 0.50%，73.01% 的企業盈利，18.10% 的企業虧損。銷售收入最高的省份為遼寧省，佔本行業的 21.00%。

	Total number of firms 企業總數	Total number of employees 職工總數	Total revenue (mil. RMB) 總銷售收入（百萬元）	Total profit (mil. RMB) 總利潤（百萬元）	Return on assets 資產利潤率 (%)	Return on equity 權益利潤率 (%)	Labour productivity ('000 RMB / worker) 勞動生產率（千元/人）	Debts / assets 資產負債率 (%)	Total assets (mil. RMB) 總資產（百萬元）
Industry Overall 行業總體	116	14,299	448	5	0.50	1.16	31.33	57.04	1,012

	Number of firms 企業個數	Average number of employees 平均職工人數	Average revenue ('000 RMB) 平均銷售收入（千元）	Average profit ('000 RMB) 平均利潤（千元）	Return on assets 資產利潤率 (%)	Return on equity 權益利潤率 (%)	Labour productivity ('000 RMB / worker) 勞動生產率（千元/人）	Average debts / assets 平均資產負債率(%)	Average Total assets ('000 RMB) 平均總資產（千元）
By ownership 產業所有權									
State-owned 國有	14	341	5,000	-500	-2.44	-7.87	14.65	68.99	20,500
Collectively-owned 集體	91	60	2,085	34	1.41	6.59	34.86	78.55	2,430
Privately-owned 私有	2	15	2,432	125	6.40	7.89	162.13	18.86	1,946
Domestic JVs 聯營	1	430	16,984	-1	-0.01	-0.03	39.50	79.01	10,880
Joint stock 股份制	1	2,596	65,843	2,824	0.91	1.60	25.36	43.17	309,994
Foreign-funded 外資	6	160	16,302	961	3.30	4.98	102.10	33.69	29,099
Overseas Chinese-funded 港澳台資	1	64	2,657	35	0.77	3.02	41.51	74.41	4,467
By size 規模									
Large 大型	2	2,351	46,107	-11,451	-4.64	-9.52	19.62	51.25	246,879
Medium 中型	5	581	24,380	2,709	5.30	11.59	41.96	54.30	51,146
Small 小型	107	62	2,186	134	5.47	18.55	35.30	70.50	2,453
By regional distribution 地區分布									
Central-North 華北	12	36	981	-28	-1.08	-3.59	27.18	70.11	2,632
Beijing 北京	2	28	945	-245	-4.14	-102.08	33.75	96.03	5,925
Tianjin 天津	7	25	526	-10	-1.26	-2.76	21.27	54.58	796
Hebei 河北	2	77	2,255	110	1.68	3.58	29.29	53.16	6,565
Shanxi 山西									
Inner Mongolia 內蒙	1	50	1,690				33.80	71.84	1,030
Northeast 東北	26	146	5,168	-236	-2.17	-6.05	35.44	64.24	10,907
Liaoning 遼寧	12	85	7,841	75	1.65	3.50	92.06	52.84	4,538
Jilin 吉林	8	30	526	-3	-0.12	-0.39	17.69	70.20	2,160
Heilongjiang 黑龍江	6	422	6,012	-1,170	-3.31	-9.95	14.25	66.68	35,308
Central East 華東	40	58	3,575	271	4.40	9.13	61.58	51.85	6,158
Shanghai 上海	4	133	11,638	1,965	5.72	9.61	87.66	40.52	34,383
Jiangsu 江蘇	18	44	1,226	-13	-0.53	-1.58	27.90	66.50	2,411
Zhejiang 浙江	4	17	1,128	123	15.17	30.25	66.32	50.15	808
Anhui 安徽	2	10	260	10	5.88	66.67	26.00	91.18	170
Fujian 福建	2	14	575	-50	-13.89	-62.50	41.07	77.78	360
Jiangxi 江西	3	20	333	-47	-5.91	-38.89	16.67	84.81	790
Shandong 山東	7	118	9,599	419	4.99	14.56	81.54	65.76	8,391
Central-South 中南	26	147	2,995	18	0.36	1.38	20.44	74.08	4,951
Henan 河南	10	240	3,349	23	0.36	1.33	13.97	73.22	6,452
Hubei 湖北	5	52	2,702	380	10.22	28.49	51.56	64.07	3,718
Hunan 湖南	10	68	1,625	-129	-3.78	-17.41	23.76	78.30	3,415
Guangdong 廣東	1	467	14,630	-380	-3.32	-19.10	31.33	82.64	11,460
Guangxi 廣西									
Hainan 海南									
Southwest 西南	11	355	7,331	43	0.15	0.27	20.65	46.27	29,088
Chongqing 重慶	3	345	5,472	-77	-0.68	-5.06	15.85	86.51	11,233
Sichuan 四川	7	388	8,388	84	0.21	0.36	21.60	40.94	39,504
Guizhou 貴州	1	150	5,090	90	1.58	9.57	33.93	83.51	5,700
Yunnan 雲南									
Tibet 西藏									
Northwest 西北	1	36	550	-210	-12.35		15.28	100.00	1,700
Shaanxi 陝西									
Gansu 甘肅									
Qinghai 青海	1	36	550	-210	-12.35		15.28	100.00	1,700
Ningxia 寧夏									
Xinjiang 新疆									

3172: Graphite Products 石墨製品業

Year 年份	Number of firms 企業個數	Rate of change 每年變化 (%)	Number of employees 職工人數 (人)	Rate of change 每年變化 (%)	Total revenue (mil. RMB) 總銷售收入 (百萬元)	Rate of change 每年變化 (%)	Total profit (mil. RMB) 總利潤 (百萬元)	Rate of change 每年變化 (%)
1993	113		14,109		432		39	
1994	114	0.88%	13,744	-2.59%	433	0.19%	42	10.06%
1995	120	5.26%	16,236	18.13%	452	4.59%	2	-94.27%
1996	116	-3.33%	14,299	-11.93%	448	-0.97%	5	105.51%

3 Major products* 3 種主要產品 *	Output 產量	Sales volume 銷售量	Unit 單位
a) Abradant 磨料	9,411	8,941	ton 噸

Top 10 firms by revenue (year founded) 收入排名前 10 家企業 (創辦年份)	City 城市	Province 省	Telephone / fax 電話 / 傳真	Number of employees 職工人數	Ownership 產業所有權	Revenue ('000 RMB) 銷售收入 (千元)	Profit ('000 RMB) (rank) 利潤 (千元) (排名)	Total assets ('000 RMB) 總資產 (千元)	Major products 主要產品
Dalian Aupac Co. Ltd. 大連奧巴克有限公司(1988)	Dalian 大連市	Liaoning 遼寧省	(0411)7611450 (0411)7611452	387	Foreign-funded 外資	55,433	164(19)	26,541	o
Dong Xin Electric Carbon Co. Ltd. 東新電碳股份有限公司(1970)	Zigong 自貢市	Sichuan 四川省	(0813)2600758 (0813)2600861	2,680	Joint stock 股份制	54,290	364(10)	277,139	o
Shanghai Ma Gen Carbon Products Co. Ltd. 上海摩根碳製品有限公司(1992)	Shanghai 上海市	Shanghai 上海市	(021)64343350 (021)64020793	378	Foreign-funded 外資	32,711	6942(1)	121,095	o
Shenyang Teng Fei Carbon Factory 瀋陽市騰飛炭素廠(1995)	Shenyang 瀋陽市	Liaoning 遼寧省	(024)29814410	30	Collectively-owned 集體	32,250	1150(6)	12,250	o
Harbin Electric Carbon Factory 哈爾濱電碳廠(1958)	Harbin 哈爾濱市	Heilongjiang 黑龍江省	(0451)5303490 (0451)5303394	2,559	State-owned 國有	28,086	-7477(45)	208,862	o
Tengzhou Power Supply Bureau Carborundum Factory 滕州市供電局碳化硅廠(1986)	Zaozhuang 棗莊市	Shandong 山東省	(0632)5582868	234	Collectively-owned 集體	26,758	-5(40)	15,530	a
Hebi Carbon No.2 Factory 鶴壁市碳素二廠(1992)	Hebi 鶴壁市	Henan 河南省	(0392)2813235	540	Collectively-owned 集體	20,240	1645(4)	5,540	o
Weihai Xin Xing Graphite Products Factory 威海市新興石墨製品廠(1980)	Weihai 威海市	Shandong 山東省	(0896)5704017 (0896)5704017	120	Collectively-owned 集體	20,050	1819(2)	9,108	o
Guangzhou Fogang Carbon Plant 廣州市佛岡炭素公司(1987)	Qingyuan 清遠市	Guangdong 廣東省	(0763)4721338	467	Domestic JVs 聯營	14,634	-376(43)	11,456	o
Fengjie Carbon Factory 奉節縣炭素廠	Chongqing 重慶市	Chongqing 重慶市	(023)522776 (023)522300	582	State-owned 國有	8,591	249(15)	17,399	o

Top 10 Cities by Production Output 產出排名前 10 位城市	Province 省	Market share 市場份額	Number of firms 企業個數
Zigong 自貢市	Sichuan 四川省	13.40%	5
Shanghai 上海市	Shanghai 上海市	12.77%	9
Dalian 大連市	Liaoning 遼寧省	12.55%	2
Harbin 哈爾濱市	Heilongjiang 黑龍江省	9.19%	8
Hebi 鶴壁市	Henan 河南省	5.75%	2
Anyang 安陽市	Henan 河南省	5.33%	5
Nantong 南通市	Jiangsu 江蘇省	4.65%	17
Ji'nan 濟南市	Shandong 山東省	3.61%	2
Qingyuan 清遠市	Guangdong 廣東省	3.24%	1
Binzhou 濱州市	Shandong 山東省	2.93%	1

10 Major Wholesalers 10 家主要批發商	City 城市	Province 省	Telephone / Fax 電話 / 傳真
Chengdu Sheng Xing Trade Company 成都盛興商貿公司	Chengdu 成都市	Sichuan 四川省	(028)7762591
Shanghai Municipal Administration Engineering Material Company 上海市市政工程材料公司	Shanghai 上海市	Shanghai 上海市	(021)64372632
Shanghai Construction Engineering Material Co. 上海市建築工程材料公司	Shanghai 上海市	Shanghai 上海市	(021)63298630
Yixing Jin San Jiao Zhao Bazaar 宜興市金三角招商城	Wuxi 無錫市	Jiangsu 江蘇省	(0510)7935138 (0510)7935138
Fujian Hua Fu Import & Export Company 福建省華福進出口公司	Fuzhou 福州市	Fujian 福建省	(0591)7810477 (0591)7810485
China Building Goods & Materials Company 中國建築物資公司	Beijing 北京市	Beijing 北京市	(010)68586253
Dalian Jinzhou Xin Gang Industry & Trade Company 大連金州新港工貿公司	Dalian 大連市	Liaoning 遼寧省	(0411)7624747
Shanghai Zhan Dong Industrial Co. Ltd. 上海展東實業有限公司	Shanghai 上海市	Shanghai 上海市	(021)58201778 (021)58200874
China Building Materials and Equipment Import & Export Company 中國建築材料及設備進出口公司	Beijing 北京市	Beijing 北京市	(010)68393420
Dandong Chemical Light Industry Material Company Chemical Construction Material Marketing Station 丹東市化工輕工材料公司化工建材經銷站	Dandong 丹東市	Liaoning 遼寧省	(0415)2146396

*Also include sales by firms outside this industry.包括本行業以外廠家的銷售。"o" stands for "others". "o" 代表 "其他產品"。

3179: Other Graphite and Carbon Products 其他石墨及碳素製品業

The industry accounts for 0.023% of the total revenue of China's industrial sector in 1996. The revenue growth rate of the industry is 41.2% from 1995, as compared to the growth rate of China's industrial sector, 9.51%. The rate of return on asset is 3.07%. 74.40% of all firms in the industry made a profit while 20.80% had negative returns. The top province in terms of the industry's revenue is Anhui, accounting for 22.26% of the total revenue.
本行業在1996年佔全行業總產值0.023%，行業年增長率為41.2%（全國工業年增長率9.51%）。行業的資產回報率3.07%，74.40%的企業盈利，20.80%的企業虧損。銷售收入最高的省份為安徽省，佔本行業的22.26%。

	Total number of firms 企業總數	Total number of employees 職工總數	Total revenue (mil. RMB) 總銷售收入（百萬元）	Total profit (mil. RMB) 總利潤（百萬元）	Return on assets 資產利潤率 (%)	Return on equity 權益利潤率 (%)	Labour productivity ('000 RMB / worker) 勞動生產率（千元/人）	Debts / assets 資產負債率 (%)	Total assets (mil. RMB) 總資產（百萬元）
Industry Overall 行業總體	346	26,153	1,336	55	3.07	8.60	51.08	64.33	1,805

	Number of firms 企業個數	Average number of employees 平均職工人數	Average revenue ('000 RMB) 平均銷售收入（千元）	Average profit ('000 RMB) 平均利潤（千元）	Return on assets 資產利潤率 (%)	Return on equity 權益利潤率 (%)	Labour productivity ('000 RMB / worker) 勞動生產率（千元/人）	Average debts / assets 平均資產負債率(%)	Average Total assets ('000 RMB) 平均總資產（千元）
By ownership 產業所有權									
State-owned 國有	42	116	3,690	48	0.48	1.57	31.87	69.83	10,024
Collectively-owned 集體	274	70	3,919	213	5.00	14.49	55.92	65.46	4,264
Privately-owned 私有	1	36	934	21	0.76	0.95	25.94	20.29	2,739
Domestic JVs 聯營	5	169	4,869	-792	-7.71	-16.95	28.81	54.49	10,266
Joint stock 股份制	2	21	1,725	-445	-12.70	69.96	84.14	118.15	3,506
Foreign-funded 外資	9	46	3,381	119	1.65	2.62	73.68	36.89	7,201
Overseas Chinese-funded 港澳台資	11	52	3,528	-89	-1.24	-2.04	67.84	39.19	7,198
By size 規模									
Large 大型	1	1,218	169,471	37,651	38.01	47.05	139.14	19.21	99,058
Medium 中型	2	436	34,367	1,221	1.75	3.02	78.91	42.12	69,961
Small 小型	332	71	3,306	45	0.95	3.08	46.72	69.15	4,721
By regional distribution 地區分布									
Central-North 華北	52	49	1,684	95	3.11	8.33	34.29	62.71	3,057
Beijing 北京	8	10	1,136	80	3.37	8.82	119.61	61.75	2,373
Tianjin 天津	3	63	1,993	97	3.93	8.03	31.64	51.08	2,460
Hebei 河北	16	64	2,209	226	8.07	32.12	34.55	74.88	2,796
Shanxi 山西	15	67	1,793	57	1.74	4.82	26.79	63.86	3,291
Inner Mongolia 內蒙	10	26	1,026	-46	-1.19	-2.38	39.16	49.79	3,850
Northeast 東北	62	106	2,179	64	2.51	10.96	20.51	77.12	2,540
Liaoning 遼寧	26	163	2,694	212	10.09	24.16	16.57	58.24	2,104
Jilin 吉林	25	62	1,286	-120	-3.96	766.67	20.75	100.52	3,024
Heilongjiang 黑龍江	11	73	2,989	129	5.23	10.46	40.69	50.04	2,469
Central East 華東	119	77	6,119	361	5.29	12.74	79.85	58.50	6,825
Shanghai 上海	6	48	2,180	5	0.10	0.12	45.73	15.04	5,065
Jiangsu 江蘇	36	40	3,323	90	3.03	8.74	83.72	65.34	2,981
Zhejiang 浙江	18	61	4,989	72	1.10	3.58	81.65	69.26	6,513
Anhui 安徽	17	115	17,494	1,705	13.33	25.05	152.66	46.76	12,789
Fujian 福建	11	23	1,207	-85	-3.33	-3.78	53.33	12.14	2,569
Jiangxi 江西	3	99	1,937	117	4.69	20.47	19.63	77.11	2,490
Shandong 山東	28	136	6,755	356	3.28	10.41	49.63	68.53	10,861
Central-South 中南	66	78	4,200	47	0.58	1.80	53.67	67.96	8,177
Henan 河南	25	40	2,151	19	0.63	2.88	53.57	78.11	3,040
Hubei 湖北	8	177	5,460	56	0.32	2.02	30.91	84.19	17,611
Hunan 湖南	22	105	6,691	98	1.00	3.24	63.56	69.18	9,798
Guangdong 廣東	8	21	1,404	-121	-2.48	-4.29	68.06	42.11	4,883
Guangxi 廣西	3	89	7,103	333	1.47	2.23	79.81	34.05	22,720
Hainan 海南									
Southwest 西南	27	61	2,991	-39	-1.01	-4.88	48.70	79.23	3,803
Chongqing 重慶	1	48	1,535	0	0.01	0.03	31.82	50.20	1,742
Sichuan 四川	20	70	3,830	-22	-0.49	-2.35	54.64	79.10	4,500
Guizhou 貴州	3	5	437	27	21.62	21.62	81.88		123
Yunnan 雲南	3	66	473	-227	-6.36	-53.97	7.21	88.12	3,563
Tibet 西藏									
Northwest 西北	20	54	1,370	76	4.42	8.70	25.56	49.22	1,721
Shaanxi 陝西	6	34	230	-38	-7.67	-12.78	6.76	40.00	500
Gansu 甘肅	5	41	3,054	164	5.49	11.05	75.22	50.30	2,986
Qinghai 青海	1	20							
Ningxia 寧夏	7	88	1,536	133	8.99	11.82	17.37	23.96	1,479
Xinjiang 新疆	1	26						93.65	6,140

3179: Other Graphite and Carbon Products 其他石墨及碳素製品業

Year 年份	Number of firms 企業個數	Rate of change 每年變化 (%)	Number of employees 職工人數 (人)	Rate of change 每年變化 (%)	Total revenue (mil. RMB) 總銷售收入 (百萬元)	Rate of change 每年變化 (%)	Total profit (mil. RMB) 總利潤 (百萬元)	Rate of change 每年變化 (%)
1993	298		23,487		741		28	
1994	345	15.77%	24,938	6.18%	889	19.95%	34	22.77%
1995	329	-4.64%	20,930	-16.07%	946	6.40%	25	-25.74%
1996	346	5.17%	26,153	24.95%	1,336	41.23%	55	116.76%

3 Major products* 3 種主要產品 *	Output 產量	Sales volume 銷售量	Unit 單位
a) Calcium Carbide 碳化鈣	18,058	13,002	ton 噸
b) Seal Part 密封件	501	431	10,000 piece 萬件

Top 10 firms by revenue (year founded) 收入排名前 10 家企業 (創辦年份)	City 城市	Province 省	Telephone / fax 電話 / 傳真	Number of employees 職工人數	Ownership 產業所有權	Revenue ('000 RMB) 銷售收入 (千元)	Profit ('000 RMB) (rank) 利潤 (千元) (排名)	Total assets ('000 RMB) 總資產 (千元)	Major products 主要產品
Bozhou Diamond Factory 亳州市金剛石廠(1985)	Fuyang 阜陽市	Anhui 安徽省	(0558)5523921 (0558)5520466	986	Collectively-owned 集體	201,349	29580(1)	107,312	o
Changsha Wu Xing Industrial Group Co. Ltd 長沙五星實業集團有限公司(1993)	Changsha 長沙市	Hunan 湖南省	(0731)8530016	486	Collectively-owned 集體	78,900	1820(7)	50,640	a
Qingdao Hei Li Graphite Industrial Co. 青島黑鯉石墨工業公司(1970)	Qingdao 青島市	Shandong 山東省	(0532)7362628 (0532)7361601	1,126	State-owned 國有	50,014	308(49)	104,244	o
Qingdao Pingdu Tian Zhuang Graphite Mine 青島市平度田裝石墨礦(1979)	Qingdao 青島市	Shandong 山東省	(0532)6383050 (0532)6383132	760	Foreign-funded 外資	45,311	3106(3)	38,743	o
Anhui Chang Jiang Ultrahard Material Group Co. 安徽長江超硬材料集團公司(1986)	Chuzhou 滁州市	Anhui 安徽省	(0550)5255498 (0550)5255408	403	Collectively-owned 集體	43,897	-3214(125)	71,471	o
Zigong Yantan Shun Li Multiple Material Factory 自貢市沿灘區順利綜合材料廠	Zigong 自貢市	Sichuan 四川省		50	Collectively-owned 集體	31,776	2(96)	3,230	o
Nantong Long Deng Chemical Co. Ltd. 南通龍燈化工有限公司(1995)	Nantong 南通市	Jiangsu 江蘇省	(0513)3518891 (0513)3518892	36	Foreign-funded 外資	26,515	3257(2)	16,399	o
Hunan Changsha Xin Xing Electric Carbon Group Company 湖南省長沙新星電碳集團公司(1966)	Changsha 長沙市	Hunan 湖南省	(0731)8550017	879	Collectively-owned 集體	24,697	1301(8)	62,925	a
Zibo He Da Co. Ltd. 淄博赫達股份有限公司(1972)	Zibo 淄博市	Shandong 山東省	(0533)6680818 (0533)6680066	340	Joint stock 股份制	22,910	1110(11)	33,939	o
Anhui Dingyuan Machinery Seal Maker 安徽省定遠縣機械密封件廠(1969)	Chuzhou 滁州市	Anhui 安徽省	(0550)4021345	21	Collectively-owned 集體	18,050	937(17)	7,347	b

Top 10 Cities by Production Output 產出排名前 10 位城市	Province 省	Market share 市場份額	Number of firms 企業個數
Fuyang 阜陽市	Anhui 安徽省	18.29%	4
Changsha 長沙市	Hunan 湖南省	9.56%	7
Qingdao 青島市	Shandong 山東省	7.66%	12
Ningbo 寧波市	Zhejiang 浙江省	7.31%	16
Wuxi 無錫市	Jiangsu 江蘇省	2.76%	7
Yichang 宜昌市	Hubei 湖北省	2.74%	3
Xining 西寧市	Qinghai 青海省	2.42%	1
Chongqing 重慶市	Chongqing 重慶市	2.25%	3
Nantong 南通市	Jiangsu 江蘇省	2.10%	15
Hanzhong 漢中市	Shaanxi 陝西省	1.83%	2

10 Major Wholesalers 10 家主要批發商	City 城市	Province 省	Telephone / Fax 電話 / 傳真
Chengdu Sheng Xing Trade Company 成都盛興商貿公司	Chengdu 成都市	Sichuan 四川省	(028)7762591
Shanghai Municipal Administration Engineering Material Company 上海市市政工程材料公司	Shanghai 上海市	Shanghai 上海市	(021)64372632
Shanghai Construction Engineering Material Co. 上海市建築工程材料公司	Shanghai 上海市	Shanghai 上海市	(021)63298630
Yixing Jin San Jiao Zhao Bazaar 宜興市金三角招商城	Wuxi 無錫市	Jiangsu 江蘇省	(0510)7935138 (0510)7935138
Fujian Hua Fu Import & Export Company 福建省華福進出口公司	Fuzhou 福州市	Fujian 福建省	(0591)7810477 (0591)7810485
China Building Goods & Materials Company 中國建築物資公司	Beijing 北京市	Beijing 北京市	(010)68586253
Dalian Jinzhou Xin Gang Industry & Trade Company 大連金州新港工貿公司	Dalian 大連市	Liaoning 遼寧省	(0411)7624747
Shanghai Zhan Dong Industrial Co. Ltd. 上海展東實業有限公司	Shanghai 上海市	Shanghai 上海市	(021)58201778 (021)58200874
China Building Materials and Equipment Import & Export Company 中國建築材料及設備進出口公司	Beijing 北京市	Beijing 北京市	(010)68393420
Dandong Chemical Light Industry Material Company Chemical Construction Material Marketing Station 丹東市化工輕工材料公司化工建材經銷站	Dandong 丹東市	Liaoning 遼寧省	(0415)2146396

*Also include sales by firms outside this industry.包括本行業以外廠家的銷售。"o" stands for "others". "o" 代表 "其他產品"。

3181: Fibreglass Products 玻璃纖維及其製品業

The industry accounts for 0.070% of the total revenue of China's industrial sector in 1996. The revenue growth rate of the industry is 23.5% from 1995, as compared to the growth rate of China's industrial sector, 9.51%. The rate of return on asset is 1.06%. 64.01% of all firms in the industry made a profit while 23.71% had negative returns. The top province in terms of the industry's revenue is Henan, accounting for 17.29% of the total revenue.
本行業在1996年佔全行業總產值0.070%，行業年增長率為23.5%（全國工業年增長率9.51%）。行業的資產回報率1.06%，64.01%的企業盈利，23.71%的企業虧損。銷售收入最高的省份為河南省，佔本行業的17.29%。

	Total number of firms 企業總數	Total number of employees 職工總數	Total revenue (mil. RMB) 總銷售收入（百萬元）	Total profit (mil. RMB) 總利潤（百萬元）	Return on assets 資產利潤率 (%)	Return on equity 權益利潤率 (%)	Labour productivity ('000 RMB / worker) 勞動生產率（千元/人）	Debts / assets 資產負債率 (%)	Total assets (mil. RMB) 總資產（百萬元）
Industry Overall 行業總體	594	105,716	4,053	107	1.06	2.50	38.34	57.73	10,080

	Number of firms 企業個數	Average number of employees 平均職工人數	Average revenue ('000 RMB) 平均銷售收入（千元）	Average profit ('000 RMB) 平均利潤（千元）	Return on assets 資產利潤率 (%)	Return on equity 權益利潤率 (%)	Labour productivity ('000 RMB / worker) 勞動生產率（千元/人）	Average debts / assets 平均資產負債率(%)	Average Total assets ('000 RMB) 平均總資產（千元）
By ownership 產業所有權									
State-owned 國有	78	702	20,205	538	0.64	1.20	28.80	46.73	84,526
Collectively-owned 集體	480	93	3,741	171	4.18	21.09	40.23	80.20	4,098
Privately-owned 私有	1	14	2,624	167	6.69	10.55	187.42	36.54	2,503
Domestic JVs 聯營	7	84	7,691	201	3.06	10.33	91.87	70.37	6,568
Joint stock 股份制	4	167	10,314	944	7.93	37.99	61.76	79.12	11,900
Foreign-funded 外資	10	161	22,322	-3,309	-5.00	-9.16	138.73	45.44	66,193
Overseas Chinese-funded 港澳台資	14	266	25,780	757	1.39	-39.66	96.79	103.51	54,444
By size 規模									
Large 大型	6	3,754	137,301	16,610	3.65	7.37	36.58	50.45	455,064
Medium 中型	25	996	51,228	-505	-0.35	-0.93	51.45	62.10	143,473
Small 小型	554	105	3,519	36	0.53	1.29	33.54	58.84	6,792
By regional distribution 地區分布									
Central-North 華北	90	184	4,089	22	0.24	0.61	22.18	61.05	9,107
Beijing 北京	14	82	1,492	-26	-0.24	-0.32	18.10	23.69	10,539
Tianjin 天津	7	605	3,877	81	0.28	0.99	6.41	71.98	29,311
Hebei 河北	49	184	5,984	35	0.44	1.24	32.46	65.02	8,108
Shanxi 山西	10	148	1,380	-1	-0.02	-0.12	9.36	83.78	5,148
Inner Mongolia 內蒙	10	70	1,300	2	0.11	1.09	18.54	89.85	1,812
Northeast 東北	54	109	2,035	66	1.20	6.85	18.70	82.55	5,511
Liaoning 遼寧	30	108	1,934	-65	-1.93	-6.37	17.97	69.68	3,347
Jilin 吉林	15	106	2,662	464	3.93	30.20	25.22	86.98	11,801
Heilongjiang 黑龍江	9	118	1,328	-162	-7.24	93.59	11.23	107.73	2,241
Central East 華東	242	154	7,649	316	2.94	8.19	49.53	64.12	10,751
Shanghai 上海	10	107	6,071	150	2.43	9.60	56.90	74.69	6,175
Jiangsu 江蘇	58	174	10,352	175	1.07	2.30	59.62	53.41	16,371
Zhejiang 浙江	51	149	6,710	510	3.88	10.65	45.05	63.59	13,145
Anhui 安徽	38	109	4,406	139	4.31	9.07	40.57	52.52	3,227
Fujian 福建	6	29	427	17	2.86	7.04	14.55	59.43	583
Jiangxi 江西	47	114	2,979	87	1.80	15.16	26.15	88.11	4,803
Shandong 山東	32	281	16,806	918	5.17	20.25	59.85	74.49	17,759
Central-South 中南	116	224	9,934	121	0.28	0.53	44.31	47.92	43,940
Henan 河南	42	393	16,683	1,326	1.43	2.20	42.41	35.11	92,962
Hubei 湖北	16	184	6,906	139	1.31	4.90	37.61	73.25	10,631
Hunan 湖南	34	90	2,024	-8	-0.36	-1.47	22.60	75.35	2,276
Guangdong 廣東	17	117	15,414	-2,249	-4.22	-96.30	131.22	95.62	53,288
Guangxi 廣西	7	215	1,467	-767	-13.69	-32.66	6.83	58.09	5,604
Hainan 海南									
Southwest 西南	62	243	7,628	140	0.78	3.49	31.41	77.76	18,081
Chongqing 重慶	12	105	4,508	-2,751	-18.89	44.87	42.95	142.10	14,564
Sichuan 四川	38	338	10,502	586	2.49	7.37	31.02	66.23	23,513
Guizhou 貴州	9	12	201	-107	-5.16	-12.57	16.76	59.02	2,069
Yunnan 雲南	3	247	5,310	7	0.06	0.23	21.50	72.01	10,373
Tibet 西藏									
Northwest 西北	30	160	3,308	67	1.40	3.81	20.65	63.37	4,770
Shaanxi 陝西	14	285	6,555	146	1.62	4.11	23.02	60.61	8,991
Gansu 甘肅	11	58	619	15	1.54	10.00	10.62	84.73	946
Qinghai 青海	1	64	20	-150	-5.77	-23.81	0.31	75.77	2,600
Ningxia 寧夏	2	41	280	-30	-1.50	-9.84	6.91	84.79	2,005
Xinjiang 新疆	2	17	40	5	4.76	100.00	2.42	100.00	105

3181: Fibreglass Products 玻璃纖維及其製品業

Year 年份	Number of firms 企業個數	Rate of change 每年變化 (%)	Number of employees 職工人數（人）	Rate of change 每年變化 (%)	Total revenue (mil. RMB) 總銷售收入（百萬元）	Rate of change 每年變化 (%)	Total profit (mil. RMB) 總利潤（百萬元）	Rate of change 每年變化 (%)
1993	700		94,250		2,240		55	
1994	669	-4.43%	336,286	256.80%	2,063	-7.87%	-20	-136.35%
1995	646	-3.44%	99,915	-70.29%	3,282	59.05%	52	360.20%
1996	594	-8.05%	105,716	5.81%	4,053	23.49%	107	104.45%

3 Major products* 3 種主要產品 *	Output 產量	Sales volume 銷售量	Unit 單位
a) Glass Fibre Cloth 玻璃纖維布	60,000	60,000	10,000 metre 萬米
b) Glass Fibre Yarn 玻璃纖維紗	200,548	130,356	ton 噸
c) Unsaturaled Polyester Resin 不飽和聚酯樹脂	16,969	15,611	ton 噸

Top 10 firms by revenue (year founded) 收入排名前 10 家企業 (創辦年份)	City 城市	Province 省	Telephone / fax 電話 / 傳真	Number of employees 職工人數	Ownership 產業所有權	Revenue ('000 RMB) 銷售收入（千元）	Profit ('000 RMB) (rank) 利潤（千元）（排名）	Total assets ('000 RMB) 總資產（千元）	Major products 主要產品
Weihai Guang Wei Fishing Tackle (Group) Co. Ltd. 威海光威漁具(集團)有限責任公司(1992)	Weihai 威海市	Shandong 山東省	(0896)5251625 (0896)5817474	2,412	Collectively-owned 集體	253,153	10606(4)	146,821	o
Sichuan Kang Da Industry General Corp. 國營四川省威遠縣康達實業總公司(1958)	Neijiang 內江市	Sichuan 四川省	(0832)822031 (0832)822938	5,468	State-owned 國有	224,629	22230(3)	592,233	a,b,c
Tian Ma Group Co. 天馬集團公司(1960)	Changzhou 常州市	Jiangsu 江蘇省	(0519)5212676 (0519)5210145	2,338	State-owned 國有	210,635	7532(5)	585,821	a,b,c
Glass Fibre Enterprise Co. Ltd. of Zhuhai Sez 珠海經濟特區玻璃纖維企業有限公司(1985)	Zhuhai 珠海市	Guangdong 廣東省	(0756)8611796 (0756)8612095	705	Overseas Chinese-funded 港澳台資	178,287	38282(1)	499,235	a,b
Tongxiang Ju Shi Group Co. Ltd. 桐鄉市巨石集團有限公司(1954)	Jiaxing 嘉興市	Zhejiang 浙江省	(0573)8101805 (0573)8102124	1,642	Collectively-owned 集體	117,369	22242(2)	365,189	b
Tongcheng Fibrous Glass Industrial Company 桐城縣玻纖工業公司(1981)	Anqing 安慶市	Anhui 安徽省	(0556)6010021 (0556)6010341	1,100	Collectively-owned 集體	82,952	7082(6)	59,010	a,b
Shannxi Glass Fibre General Factory 陝西玻璃纖維總廠(1966)	Xianyang 咸陽市	Shaanxi 陝西省	(0910)8822901 (0910)8822946	3,410	State-owned 國有	82,179	1720(17)	104,722	o
Rugao Glass Fibre Plant 如皋市玻璃纖維廠(1972)	Nantong 南通市	Jiangsu 江蘇省	(0513)7513392 (0513)7513082	786	Collectively-owned 集體	72,325	482(48)	77,506	a,b
Hangzhou Hang Fibrous Glass Wei Industrial Co. Ltd. 杭州杭玻纖維工業有限公司(1994)	Hangzhou 杭州市	Zhejiang 浙江省	(0571)8144501 (0571)8145649	2,138	Overseas Chinese-funded 港澳台資	69,119	1243(27)	91,510	o
Qinhuangdao Glass Fibre General Factory 秦皇島玻璃纖維總廠(1960)	Qinhuangdao 秦皇島市	Hebei 河北省	(0335)3034501 (0335)3031991	3,903	State-owned 國有	68,772	-9878(227)	149,852	a,b

Top 10 Cities by Production Output 產出排名前 10 位城市	Province 省	Market share 市場份額	Number of firms 企業個數
Weihai 威海市	Shandong 山東省	8.52%	16
Neijiang 內江市	Sichuan 四川省	7.07%	1
Nantong 南通市	Jiangsu 江蘇省	6.47%	11
Zhuhai 珠海市	Guangdong 廣東省	5.19%	1
Jiaxing 嘉興市	Zhejiang 浙江省	4.81%	8
Shanghai 上海市	Shanghai 上海市	4.69%	28
Qinhuangdao 秦皇島市	Hebei 河北省	3.99%	14
Deyang 德陽市	Sichuan 四川省	2.75%	11
Hangzhou 杭州市	Zhejiang 浙江省	2.71%	8
Xianyang 咸陽市	Shaanxi 陝西省	2.68%	5

10 Major Wholesalers 10 家主要批發商	City 城市	Province 省	Telephone / Fax 電話 / 傳真
Chengdu Sheng Xing Trade Company 成都盛興商貿公司	Chengdu 成都市	Sichuan 四川省	(028)7762591
Shanghai Municipal Administration Engineering Material Company 上海市市政工程材料公司	Shanghai 上海市	Shanghai 上海市	(021)64372632
Shanghai Construction Engineering Material Co. 上海市建築工程材料公司	Shanghai 上海市	Shanghai 上海市	(021)63298630
Yixing Jin San Jiao Zhao Bazaar 宜興市金三角招商城	Wuxi 無錫市	Jiangsu 江蘇省	(0510)7935138 (0510)7935138
Fujian Hua Fu Import & Export Company 福建省華福進出口公司	Fuzhou 福州市	Fujian 福建省	(0591)7810477 (0591)7810485
China Building Goods & Materials Company 中國建築物資公司	Beijing 北京市	Beijing 北京市	(010)68586253
Dalian Jinzhou Xin Gang Industry & Trade Company 大連金州新港工貿公司	Dalian 大連市	Liaoning 遼寧省	(0411)7624747
Shanghai Zhan Dong Industrial Co. Ltd. 上海展東實業有限公司	Shanghai 上海市	Shanghai 上海市	(021)58201778 (021)58200874
China Building Materials and Equipment Import & Export Company 中國建築材料及設備進出口公司	Beijing 北京市	Beijing 北京市	(010)68393420
Dandong Chemical Light Industry Material Company Chemical Construction Material Marketing Station 丹東市化工輕工材料公司化工建材經銷站	Dandong 丹東市	Liaoning 遼寧省	(0415)2146396

*Also include sales by firms outside this industry.包括本行業以外廠家的銷售。"o" stands for "others". "o" 代表 "其他產品"。

3182: Glass Fibre Reinforced Plastic 玻璃鋼製品業

The industry accounts for 0.078% of the total revenue of China's industrial sector in 1996. The revenue growth rate of the industry is 26.3% from 1995, as compared to the growth rate of China's industrial sector, 9.51%. The rate of return on asset is 3.17%. 75.38% of all firms in the industry made a profit while 19.36% had negative returns. The top province in terms of the industry's revenue is Zhejiang, accounting for 25.52% of the total revenue.
本行業在 1996 年佔全行業總產值 0.078%，行業年增長率為 26.3%（全國工業年增長率 9.51%）。行業的資產回報率 3.17%，75.38% 的企業盈利，19.36% 的企業虧損。銷售收入最高的省份為浙江省，佔本行業的 25.52%。

	Total number of firms 企業總數	Total number of employees 職工總數	Total revenue (mil. RMB) 總銷售收入（百萬元）	Total profit (mil. RMB) 總利潤（百萬元）	Return on assets 資產利潤率 (%)	Return on equity 權益利潤率 (%)	Labour productivity ('000 RMB / worker) 勞動生產率（千元/人）	Debts / assets 資產負債率 (%)	Total assets (mil. RMB) 總資產（百萬元）
Industry Overall 行業總體	800	59,575	4,545	167	3.17	9.81	76.29	67.70	5,268

	Number of firms 企業個數	Average number of employees 平均職工人數	Average revenue ('000 RMB) 平均銷售收入（千元）	Average profit ('000 RMB) 平均利潤（千元）	Return on assets 資產利潤率 (%)	Return on equity 權益利潤率 (%)	Labour productivity ('000 RMB / worker) 勞動生產率（千元/人）	Average debts / assets 平均資產負債率(%)	Average Total assets ('000 RMB) 平均總資產（千元）
By ownership 產業所有權									
State-owned 國有	87	146	15,793	103	0.67	1.92	108.45	65.18	15,483
Collectively-owned 集體	627	65	3,940	205	4.80	17.89	60.75	73.17	4,277
Privately-owned 私有	7	22	1,560	153	17.40	44.59	71.83	60.97	878
Domestic JVs 聯營	4	75	11,938	168	0.87	8.02	159.70	89.14	19,316
Joint stock 股份制	7	180	27,198	1,422	3.67	12.68	151.34	71.04	38,753
Foreign-funded 外資	38	75	8,331	315	1.72	3.64	111.58	52.61	18,260
Overseas Chinese-funded 港澳台資	31	57	4,369	181	2.94	5.88	77.08	50.03	6,147
By size 規模									
Large 大型	3	2,316	416,902	16,181	5.71	14.34	180.01	60.16	283,238
Medium 中型	9	388	35,615	2,309	3.14	13.10	91.82	76.03	73,493
Small 小型	768	63	3,872	127	2.60	8.11	61.12	67.93	4,891
By regional distribution 地區分布									
Central-North 華北	113	58	5,502	254	2.76	6.51	95.28	57.53	9,178
Beijing 北京	25	34	3,554	-171	-1.46	-2.91	104.78	49.91	11,742
Tianjin 天津	20	69	1,412	-70	-1.00	-1.35	20.35	25.89	6,959
Hebei 河北	50	76	9,753	672	5.84	18.33	127.89	68.12	11,505
Shanxi 山西	5	39	2,350	124	8.54	44.93	60.88	80.99	1,452
Inner Mongolia 內蒙	13	22	402	8	0.46	1.82	18.42	74.84	1,682
Northeast 東北	113	35	1,296	13	0.56	1.70	37.02	67.10	2,330
Liaoning 遼寧	78	30	1,024	38	2.39	7.02	34.31	65.98	1,585
Jilin 吉林	17	56	1,262	6	0.18	1.28	22.42	86.26	3,347
Heilongjiang 黑龍江	18	37	2,506	-88	-1.91	-4.30	67.23	55.61	4,597
Central East 華東	329	109	8,695	276	3.44	12.10	79.79	71.56	8,031
Shanghai 上海	18	91	7,582	108	0.46	3.29	83.62	86.10	23,592
Jiangsu 江蘇	129	116	6,343	120	1.87	6.68	54.53	71.97	6,418
Zhejiang 浙江	41	113	28,292	1,023	6.81	20.06	249.83	66.05	15,023
Anhui 安徽	18	65	2,241	20	1.04	7.71	34.32	86.53	1,926
Fujian 福建	16	90	5,374	660	9.89	29.65	59.54	66.65	6,674
Jiangxi 江西	24	164	3,059	-795	-9.13	-32.89	18.63	72.23	8,699
Shandong 山東	83	97	6,583	478	9.37	25.95	68.20	63.88	5,101
Central-South 中南	171	56	4,278	254	4.43	14.00	75.97	68.34	5,725
Henan 河南	68	68	6,445	797	19.43	54.97	95.14	64.66	4,102
Hubei 湖北	29	54	3,497	228	9.18	35.57	65.01	74.19	2,486
Hunan 湖南	24	40	1,283	-3	-0.15	-0.56	32.03	72.83	2,202
Guangdong 廣東	40	54	3,648	-398	-3.26	-11.53	67.00	71.77	12,234
Guangxi 廣西	8	35	981	-180	-1.82	-3.95	27.74	53.99	9,903
Hainan 海南	2	21	3,700	20	0.61	1.06	176.19	42.20	3,270
Southwest 西南	50	54	2,691	18	0.34	1.10	49.77	69.13	5,426
Chongqing 重慶	13	43	1,161	-60	-2.73	-22.28	26.93	87.75	2,210
Sichuan 四川	28	71	4,293	-10	-0.12	-0.37	60.81	67.13	8,665
Guizhou 貴州	7	19	271	6	1.08	2.67	14.39	59.68	531
Yunnan 雲南	3	24	30	-57	-10.06	-31.48	1.25	68.05	563
Tibet 西藏									
Northwest 西北	24	38	2,087	68	2.17	5.50	54.97	60.62	3,151
Shaanxi 陝西	14	31	2,199	89	3.15	7.79	71.09	59.59	2,812
Gansu 甘肅	5	48	1,446	110	8.62	19.86	30.38	56.74	1,276
Qinghai 青海									
Ningxia 寧夏	1	40	940	10	1.03	20.00	23.50	94.85	970
Xinjiang 新疆	4	50	2,783	-40	-0.55	-1.45	55.65	61.74	7,228

3182: Glass Fibre Reinforced Plastic 玻璃鋼製品業

Year 年份	Number of firms 企業個數	Rate of change 每年變化 (%)	Number of employees 職工人數 (人)	Rate of change 每年變化 (%)	Total revenue (mil. RMB) 總銷售收入 (百萬元)	Rate of change 每年變化 (%)	Total profit (mil. RMB) 總利潤 (百萬元)	Rate of change 每年變化 (%)
1993	589		47,134		1,816		85	
1994	643	9.17%	44,543	-5.50%	2,118	16.64%	80	-5.16%
1995	805	25.19%	56,510	26.87%	3,598	69.82%	149	85.12%
1996	800	-0.62%	59,575	5.42%	4,545	26.32%	167	12.40%

3 Major products* 3 種主要產品 *	Output 產量	Sales volume 銷售量	Unit 單位
a) Glass Steel Products 玻璃鋼製品	174,226	165,515	ton 噸
b) Glass Fibre Cloth 玻璃纖維布	6,129	6,129	10,000 metre 萬米
c) Glass Fibre Yarn 玻璃纖維紗	5,295	3,442	ton 噸

Top 10 firms by revenue (year founded) 收入排名前 10 家企業 (創辦年份)	City 城市	Province 省	Telephone / fax 電話 / 傳真	Number of employees 職工人數	Ownership 產業所有權	Revenue ('000 RMB) 銷售收入 (千元)	Profit ('000 RMB) (rank) 利潤 (千元) (排名)	Total assets ('000 RMB) 總資產 (千元)	Major products 主要產品
Zhejiang Dong Fang Group Co. 浙江東方集團公司(1975)	Wenzhou 温州市	Zhejiang 浙江省	(0577)8336707 (0577)8332287	2,289	State-owned 國有	1,065,447	40216(1)	456,167	o
Hebei Zhong Yi Glass Fibre Reinforced Plastic Co. Ltd. 河北省中意玻璃鋼有限公司(1987)	Hengshui 衡水市	Hebei 河北省	(0318)8613754 (0318)8612721	252	Foreign-funded 外資	176,293	14082(2)	122,492	a
Shanghai Water – Supply Equipment & Engineering Co. 上海自來水給水設備工程公司(1964)	Shanghai 上海市	Shanghai 上海市	(021)56959993 (021)56050884	990	Collectively-owned 集體	97,516	2859(23)	332,805	o
Wendeng Tai Yang Fishing Tackle Co. Ltd. 文登市太陽漁具有限公司(1991)	Weihai 威海市	Shandong 山東省	(0896)8545161 (0896)8545162	410	Foreign-funded 外資	93,500	11200(3)	38,180	o
Wendeng Bao Li Fishing Tackle Co. Ltd. 文登市寶利漁具有限公司(1989)	Weihai 威海市	Shandong 山東省	(0896)8545085 (0896)8545085	700	Overseas Chinese-funded 港澳台資	81,400	9880(7)	71,140	o
Hebei Sino-italy Glass Fibre Reinforced Plastic Co. Ltd. 河北中意玻璃鋼有限公司(1992)	Shijiazhuang 石家莊市	Hebei 河北省	(0311)3826203	770	Foreign-funded 外資	78,029	2024(32)	221,580	o
Zhong Dian Jointly-operated Qinyang Tai Xing Chemical Equipment General Factory 中電聯營沁陽市太行化工設備總廠(1986)	Jiaozuo 焦作市	Henan 河南省	(0391)5098006	300	Collectively-owned 集體	76,480	9689(8)	41,900	a
Qinyang Di Building Chemical Engineering General Co. 沁陽市地建化工程總公司(1995)	Jiaozuo 焦作市	Henan 河南省	(0391)5099491	200	Collectively-owned 集體	69,945	10734(5)	10,996	a
Yixing Li Da Group 宜興市利達集團(1979)	Wuxi 無錫市	Jiangsu 江蘇省	(0510)7501780 (0510)7502889	238	Collectively-owned 集體	63,970	5270(12)	43,490	o
Jiangxi Chang Jiang Chemical Plant 江西長江化工廠(1960)	Jiujiang 九江市	Jiangxi 江西省	(0792)8252331 (0792)8252717	2,798	State-owned 國有	60,520	-19410(285)	189,410	a,b,c

Top 10 Cities by Production Output 產出排名前 10 位城市	Province 省	Market share 市場份額	Number of firms 企業個數
Wenzhou 温州市	Zhejiang 浙江省	25.35%	22
Jiaozuo 焦作市	Henan 河南省	9.15%	42
Hengshui 衡水市	Hebei 河北省	5.17%	36
Shanghai 上海市	Shanghai 上海市	4.28%	31
Dezhou 德州市	Shandong 山東省	4.24%	87
Nantong 南通市	Jiangsu 江蘇省	3.78%	34
Wuxi 無錫市	Jiangsu 江蘇省	3.72%	44
Changzhou 常州市	Jiangsu 江蘇省	3.21%	47
Suzhou 蘇州市	Jiangsu 江蘇省	3.00%	80
Weihai 威海市	Shandong 山東省	2.70%	12

10 Major Wholesalers 10 家主要批發商	City 城市	Province 省	Telephone / Fax 電話 / 傳真
Chengdu Sheng Xing Trade Company 成都盛興商貿公司	Chengdu 成都市	Sichuan 四川省	(028)7762591
Shanghai Municipal Administration Engineering Material Company 上海市市政工程材料公司	Shanghai 上海市	Shanghai 上海市	(021)64372632
Shanghai Construction Engineering Material Co. 上海市建築工程材料公司	Shanghai 上海市	Shanghai 上海市	(021)63298630
Yixing Jin San Jiao Zhao Bazaar 宜興市金三角招商城	Wuxi 無錫市	Jiangsu 江蘇省	(0510)7935138 (0510)7935138
Fujian Hua Fu Import & Export Company 福建省華福進出口公司	Fuzhou 福州市	Fujian 福建省	(0591)7810477 (0591)7810485
China Building Goods & Materials Company 中國建築物資公司	Beijing 北京市	Beijing 北京市	(010)68586253
Dalian Jinzhou Xin Gang Industry & Trade Company 大連金州新港工貿公司	Dalian 大連市	Liaoning 遼寧省	(0411)7624747
Shanghai Zhan Dong Industrial Co. Ltd. 上海展東實業有限公司	Shanghai 上海市	Shanghai 上海市	(021)58201778 (021)58200874
China Building Materials and Equipment Import & Export Company 中國建築材料及設備進出口公司	Beijing 北京市	Beijing 北京市	(010)68393420
Dandong Chemical Light Industry Material Company Chemical Construction Material Marketing Station 丹東市化工輕工材料公司化工建材經銷站	Dandong 丹東市	Liaoning 遼寧省	(0415)2146396

*Also include sales by firms outside this industry.包括本行業以外廠家的銷售。"o" stands for "others". "o" 代表 "其他產品" 。

3189: Other Mineral Fibre Products 其他礦物纖維及其製品業

The industry accounts for 0.005% of the total revenue of China's industrial sector in 1996. The revenue growth rate of the industry is 75.1% from 1995, as compared to the growth rate of China's industrial sector, 9.51%. The rate of return on asset is -0.50%. 83.93% of all firms in the industry made a profit while 16.07% had negative returns. The top province in terms of the industry's revenue is Shanghai, accounting for 36.17% of the total revenue.
本行業在1996年佔全行業總產值0.005%，行業年增長率為75.1%（全國工業年增長率9.51%）。行業的資產回報率-0.50%，83.93%的企業盈利，16.07%的企業虧損。銷售收入最高的省份為上海市，佔本行業的36.17%。

	Total number of firms 企業總數	Total number of employees 職工總數	Total revenue (mil. RMB) 總銷售收入（百萬元）	Total profit (mil. RMB) 總利潤（百萬元）	Return on assets 資產利潤率 (%)	Return on equity 權益利潤率 (%)	Labour productivity ('000 RMB / worker) 勞動生產率（千元/人）	Debts / assets 資產負債率 (%)	Total assets (mil. RMB) 總資產（百萬元）
Industry Overall 行業總體	65	5,894	308	-2	-0.50	-1.36	52.26	62.97	361

	Number of firms 企業個數	Average number of employees 平均職工人數	Average revenue ('000 RMB) 平均銷售收入（千元）	Average profit ('000 RMB) 平均利潤（千元）	Return on assets 資產利潤率 (%)	Return on equity 權益利潤率 (%)	Labour productivity ('000 RMB / worker) 勞動生產率（千元/人）	Average debts / assets 平均資產負債率(%)	Average Total assets ('000 RMB) 平均總資產（千元）
By ownership 產業所有權									
State-owned 國有	8	222	7,500	-1,125	-5.26	-10.47	33.78	49.71	21,375
Collectively-owned 集體	52	77	4,685	139	4.10	17.82	60.86	76.99	3,378
Privately-owned 私有									
Domestic JVs 聯營									
Joint stock 股份制									
Foreign-funded 外資	2	57	1,698	37	0.72	1.12	30.05	35.73	5,144
Overseas Chinese-funded 港澳台資	3	20	314	-93	-7.03	-29.55	15.96	76.19	1,324
By size 規模									
Large 大型									
Medium 中型	2	1,115	27,662	-133	-0.18	-0.36	24.82	50.45	74,650
Small 小型	61	60	4,141	-28	-0.82	-2.89	68.98	71.65	3,469
By regional distribution 地區分布									
Central-North 華北	12	99	2,281	-555	-10.41	-43.33	22.94	76.00	5,333
Beijing 北京	2	76	3,475	-450	-13.24	65.69	45.72	120.15	3,400
Tianjin 天津	1								
Hebei 河北	4	40	4,170	508	24.00	127.67	104.25	81.32	2,115
Shanxi 山西	5	176	748	-1,558	-15.99	-51.42	4.25	68.91	9,746
Inner Mongolia 內蒙									
Northeast 東北	10	102	2,557	-65	-4.55	-29.82	25.09	84.59	1,428
Liaoning 遼寧	3	275	550	-150	-7.59	-18.52	2.00	58.85	1,977
Jilin 吉林	5	35	4,658	-60	-3.92	41.67	131.58	109.27	1,532
Heilongjiang 黑龍江	2	9	315	50	14.49	21.28	35.00	31.88	345
Central East 華東	20	71	9,151	241	3.50	13.32	129.16	73.70	6,866
Shanghai 上海	3	226	37,137	93	0.30	1.25	164.56	76.29	31,447
Jiangsu 江蘇	6	57	6,060	173	8.41	17.28	106.63	51.33	2,062
Zhejiang 浙江	2	38	790				21.07	60.50	1,810
Anhui 安徽	3	71	10,270	1,137	19.20	130.65	143.97	85.30	5,920
Fujian 福建	2	13	605	5	2.56	5.88	48.40	56.41	195
Jiangxi 江西									
Shandong 山東	4	21	413	18	0.79	2.00	19.41	60.29	2,210
Central-South 中南	15	110	3,327	33	0.51	0.95	30.15	46.12	6,396
Henan 河南	5	192	1,692	28	0.94	5.38	8.83	82.52	2,974
Hubei 湖北	2	15	1,825	55	15.07	39.29	121.67	60.27	365
Hunan 湖南	3	59	1,237	43	3.81	5.53	21.08	30.79	1,137
Guangdong 廣東	4	123	8,193	10	0.05	0.09	66.74	39.78	19,055
Guangxi 廣西	1		1,310	70	9.86	12.96		23.94	710
Hainan 海南									
Southwest 西南	2	14	315	35	9.33	38.89	22.50	76.00	375
Chongqing 重慶									
Sichuan 四川	2	14	315	35	9.33	38.89	22.50	76.00	375
Guizhou 貴州									
Yunnan 雲南									
Tibet 西藏									
Northwest 西北	6	97	3,595	15	0.19	0.32	37.06	42.16	8,060
Shaanxi 陝西	3	93	2,263	-133	-2.07	-3.08	24.34	32.76	6,430
Gansu 甘肅	1	150	11,990	1,200	51.06	97.56	79.93	47.66	2,350
Qinghai 青海									
Ningxia 寧夏	1	130	710	-1,090	-4.81	-10.04	5.46	52.07	22,660
Xinjiang 新疆	1	23	2,080	380	9.36	13.06	90.43	28.33	4,060

3189: Other Mineral Fibre Products 其他礦物纖維及其製品業

Year 年份	Number of firms 企業個數	Rate of change 每年變化 (%)	Number of employees 職工人數 (人)	Rate of change 每年變化 (%)	Total revenue (mil. RMB) 總銷售收入 (百萬元)	Rate of change 每年變化 (%)	Total profit (mil. RMB) 總利潤 (百萬元)	Rate of change 每年變化 (%)
1993	74		4,543		168		4	
1994	84	13.51%	6,367	40.15%	234	38.84%	12	197.03%
1995	61	-27.38%	4,355	-31.60%	176	-24.72%	4	-64.66%
1996	65	6.56%	5,894	35.34%	308	75.07%	-2	-148.41%

3 Major products* 3 種主要產品 *	Output 產量	Sales volume 銷售量	Unit 單位
a) Mineral Wool Products 礦物棉製品	1,489	715	ton 噸
b) Polyurethane Plastics 聚氨酯塑料	77	76	ton 噸
c) Soap Stone for Industrial Raw Material 工業原料滑石	6,683	8,354	ton 噸

Top 10 firms by revenue (year founded) 收入排名前 10 家企業 (創辦年份)	City 城市	Province 省	Telephone / fax 電話 / 傳真	Number of employees 職工人數	Ownership 產業所有權	Revenue ('000 RMB) 銷售收入 (千元)	Profit ('000 RMB) (rank) 利潤 (千元) (排名)	Total assets ('000 RMB) 總資產 (千元)	Major products 主要產品
Shanghai Dongjia Industrial Co. 上海東佳實業公司(1993)	Shanghai 上海市	Shanghai 上海市	(021)64110208	500	Collectively-owned 集體	107,682	2263(2)	74,707	o
Zhanjiang Additive Factory 湛江外加劑廠(1970)	Zhanjiang 湛江市	Guangdong 廣東省	(0758)2302367 (0758)2303682	469	State-owned 國有	32,033	4(11)	75,812	o
Chaohu Magnesite Products Factory 巢湖市菱鎂製品廠(1987)	Chaohu 巢湖市	Anhui 安徽省	(0565)8361218	130	Collectively-owned 集體	30,487	3415(1)	11,380	o
Jiangyin Huang Tang Polyester Plastic Granule Making Factory 江陰市璜塘滌塑造粒廠(1993)	Wuxi 無錫市	Jiangsu 江蘇省	(0510)6531436	196	Collectively-owned 集體	27,932	428(7)	3,624	o
Tonghua Industry Silicon Company 通化市工業硅公司(1995)	Tonghua 通化市	Jilin 吉林省	(0435)3617998	85	State-owned 國有	18,370	-317(15)	4,010	o
Lanzhou Carbon Fibre Factory 蘭州炭素纖維廠(1992)	Lanzhou 蘭州市	Gansu 甘肅省	(0931)8488445 (0931)8488445	29	Collectively-owned 集體	11,993	1200(3)	2,350	o
Hejian Chang Cheng Thermal Insulation Materials Plant 河間市長城保温材料廠(1991)	Cangzhou 滄州市	Hebei 河北省	(0317)3815032	80	Collectively-owned 集體	8,600	1200(4)	1,100	o
Hebei Wuji Gaotou Diamond Factory 河北省無極縣高頭鄉金剛石廠(1986)	Shijiazhuang 石家莊市	Hebei 河北省		65	Collectively-owned 集體	6,650	700(5)	7,084	o
Dengfeng Xin Xing Industrial Co. Ltd. 登封市新星實業有限責任公司(1995)	Zhengzhou 鄭州市	Henan 河南省		60	Collectively-owned 集體	4,310	190(9)	6,632	o
Tonghua Kang Tai Industry Silicon Factory 通化市康泰工業硅廠(1996)	Tonghua 通化市	Jilin 吉林省	(0435)3618015	52	Collectively-owned 集體	3,548	-96(13)	2,216	o

Top 10 Cities by Production Output 產出排名前 10 位城市	Province 省	Market share 市場份額	Number of firms 企業個數
Ji'nan 濟南市	Shandong 山東省	21.78%	1
Lanzhou 蘭州市	Gansu 甘肅省	18.22%	1
Zhanjiang 湛江市	Guangdong 廣東省	13.55%	2
Nantong 南通市	Jiangsu 江蘇省	9.35%	1
Shijiazhuang 石家莊市	Hebei 河北省	5.24%	2
Tonghua 通化市	Jilin 吉林省	3.91%	1
Wuxi 無錫市	Jiangsu 江蘇省	3.08%	6
Zhengzhou 鄭州市	Henan 河南省	2.89%	2
Beijing 北京市	Beijing 北京市	2.65%	2
Cangzhou 滄州市	Hebei 河北省	2.64%	1

10 Major Wholesalers 10 家主要批發商	City 城市	Province 省	Telephone / Fax 電話 / 傳真
Chengdu Sheng Xing Trade Company 成都盛興商貿公司	Chengdu 成都市	Sichuan 四川省	(028)7762591
Shanghai Municipal Administration Engineering Material Company 上海市市政工程材料公司	Shanghai 上海市	Shanghai 上海市	(021)64372632
Shanghai Construction Engineering Material Co. 上海市建築工程材料公司	Shanghai 上海市	Shanghai 上海市	(021)63298630
Yixing Jin San Jiao Zhao Bazaar 宜興市金三角招商城	Wuxi 無錫市	Jiangsu 江蘇省	(0510)7935138 (0510)7935138
Fujian Hua Fu Import & Export Company 福建省華福進出口公司	Fuzhou 福州市	Fujian 福建省	(0591)7810477 (0591)7810485
China Building Goods & Materials Company 中國建築物資公司	Beijing 北京市	Beijing 北京市	(010)68586253
Dalian Jinzhou Xin Gang Industry & Trade Company 大連金州新港工貿公司	Dalian 大連市	Liaoning 遼寧省	(0411)7624747
Shanghai Zhan Dong Industrial Co. Ltd. 上海展東實業有限公司	Shanghai 上海市	Shanghai 上海市	(021)58201778 (021)58200874
China Building Materials and Equipment Import & Export Company 中國建築材料及設備進出口公司	Beijing 北京市	Beijing 北京市	(010)68393420
Dandong Chemical Light Industry Material Company Chemical Construction Material Marketing Station 丹東市化工輕工材料公司化工建材經銷站	Dandong 丹東市	Liaoning 遼寧省	(0415)2146396

*Also include sales by firms outside this industry.包括本行業以外廠家的銷售。"o" stands for "others". "o" 代表"其他產品"。

3190: Other Non-metal Mineral Products 其他類未包括的非金屬礦物製品業

The industry accounts for 0.156% of the total revenue of China's industrial sector in 1996. The revenue growth rate of the industry is 8.9% from 1995, as compared to the growth rate of China's industrial sector, 9.51%. The rate of return on asset is 1.35%. 67.54% of all firms in the industry made a profit while 24.80% had negative returns. The top province in terms of the industry's revenue is Henan, accounting for 17.34% of the total revenue.
本行業在1996年佔全行業總產值0.156%，行業年增長率為8.9%（全國工業年增長率9.51%）。行業的資產回報率1.35%，67.54%的企業盈利，24.80%的企業虧損。銷售收入最高的省份為河南省，佔本行業的17.34%。

	Total number of firms 企業總數	Total number of employees 職工總數	Total revenue (mil. RMB) 總銷售收入（百萬元）	Total profit (mil. RMB) 總利潤（百萬元）	Return on assets 資產利潤率 (%)	Return on equity 權益利潤率 (%)	Labour productivity ('000 RMB / worker) 勞動生產率（千元/人）	Debts / assets 資產負債率 (%)	Total assets (mil. RMB) 總資產（百萬元）
Industry Overall 行業總體	2,029	193,739	9,048	198	1.35	4.38	46.70	69.14	14,666

	Number of firms 企業個數	Average number of employees 平均職工人數	Average revenue ('000 RMB) 平均銷售收入（千元）	Average profit ('000 RMB) 平均利潤（千元）	Return on assets 資產利潤率 (%)	Return on equity 權益利潤率 (%)	Labour productivity ('000 RMB / worker) 勞動生產率（千元/人）	Average debts / assets 平均資產負債率(%)	Average Total assets ('000 RMB) 平均總資產（千元）
By ownership 產業所有權									
State-owned 國有	268	228	7,019	-328	-1.71	-6.43	30.80	73.33	19,153
Collectively-owned 集體	1,531	69	3,230	94	2.46	9.90	47.01	75.10	3,829
Privately-owned 私有	10	65	3,532	133	5.09	13.60	54.34	62.59	2,620
Domestic JVs 聯營	32	94	5,844	9	0.14	0.37	61.90	61.03	6,166
Joint stock 股份制	33	413	24,881	1,464	2.64	5.93	60.31	55.39	55,372
Foreign-funded 外資	83	71	6,898	202	1.82	3.74	96.79	51.31	11,092
Overseas Chinese-funded 港澳台資	70	72	8,632	1,068	10.76	21.62	120.29	50.24	9,922
By size 規模									
Large 大型	13	2,072	106,472	4,230	1.58	3.90	51.39	59.60	268,314
Medium 中型	37	713	28,273	-289	-0.45	-1.87	39.67	75.80	63,772
Small 小型	1,944	72	3,404	79	1.74	6.04	47.35	71.13	4,536
By regional distribution 地區分布									
Central-North 華北	270	81	3,055	79	1.56	5.31	37.50	70.57	5,065
Beijing 北京	49	49	1,731	40	1.13	2.66	35.63	57.52	3,553
Tianjin 天津	40	106	3,082	8	0.10	0.29	28.95	66.30	8,431
Hebei 河北	129	56	3,520	124	3.96	10.74	62.42	63.12	3,129
Shanxi 山西	30	221	3,029	13	0.12	0.63	13.73	80.42	10,768
Inner Mongolia 內蒙	22	67	3,264	122	2.07	99.26	49.04	97.91	5,886
Northeast 東北	329	128	3,668	22	0.36	1.42	28.68	74.26	6,041
Liaoning 遼寧	210	125	3,169	64	1.44	4.60	25.37	68.61	4,440
Jilin 吉林	68	163	5,173	-149	-1.31	-6.34	31.73	79.27	11,325
Heilongjiang 黑龍江	51	94	3,720	76	1.37	6.58	39.76	79.20	5,589
Central East 華東	615	88	4,957	126	1.66	4.97	56.41	66.58	7,613
Shanghai 上海	24	143	12,493	41	0.19	1.14	87.54	83.08	21,417
Jiangsu 江蘇	173	90	5,607	97	1.61	4.84	62.46	66.63	6,038
Zhejiang 浙江	75	107	4,913	3	0.03	0.11	46.07	73.36	10,741
Anhui 安徽	62	78	5,453	249	4.39	13.71	70.20	67.99	5,680
Fujian 福建	67	49	2,967	51	1.18	2.16	60.74	45.33	4,296
Jiangxi 江西	104	60	1,587	-85	-2.25	-7.47	26.62	69.83	3,758
Shandong 山東	110	116	6,440	451	3.85	9.42	55.34	59.10	11,703
Central-South 中南	558	82	5,331	238	3.14	9.06	64.90	65.31	7,568
Henan 河南	230	100	6,823	511	5.39	15.15	68.16	64.40	9,472
Hubei 湖北	87	96	5,558	133	2.86	8.92	58.02	67.96	4,658
Hunan 湖南	120	57	2,638	-48	-1.55	-9.57	46.08	83.81	3,116
Guangdong 廣東	60	52	6,093	245	1.95	4.78	117.25	59.24	12,570
Guangxi 廣西	59	73	3,957	-91	-1.10	-2.97	54.07	62.81	8,263
Hainan 海南	2	86	3,085	75	0.63	1.50	36.08	57.72	11,860
Southwest 西南	157	117	4,176	-86	-0.77	-3.03	35.67	74.73	11,189
Chongqing 重慶	11	104	2,273	-93	-2.76	-19.26	21.91	85.65	3,351
Sichuan 四川	54	92	2,344	-137	-2.64	-8.89	25.45	70.35	5,213
Guizhou 貴州	83	135	5,586	-39	-0.24	-0.96	41.34	74.79	16,155
Yunnan 雲南	9	118	4,492	-201	-1.87	-10.77	38.03	82.67	10,776
Tibet 西藏									
Northwest 西北	100	114	3,373	-272	-4.19	-19.57	29.58	78.58	6,494
Shaanxi 陝西	35	113	2,786	-643	-9.09	-81.18	24.60	88.80	7,077
Gansu 甘肅	12	156	2,585	-147	-2.72	-7.18	16.58	62.13	5,395
Qinghai 青海	27	115	4,214	7	0.10	0.30	36.51	67.67	6,814
Ningxia 寧夏	14	140	5,712	-15	-0.17	-1.07	40.95	84.37	8,954
Xinjiang 新疆	12	41	1,247	-243	-10.54	-37.31	30.16	71.74	2,300

3190: Other Non-metal Mineral Products 其他類未包括的非金屬礦物製品業

Year 年份	Number of firms 企業個數	Rate of change 每年變化 (%)	Number of employees 職工人數 (人)	Rate of change 每年變化 (%)	Total revenue (mil. RMB) 總銷售收入 (百萬元)	Rate of change 每年變化 (%)	Total profit (mil. RMB) 總利潤 (百萬元)	Rate of change 每年變化 (%)
1993	1,491		168,389		6,046		259	
1994	1,730	16.03%	152,923	-9.19%	6,324	4.60%	127	-50.86%
1995	2,019	16.71%	195,991	28.16%	8,309	31.38%	239	87.50%
1996	2,029	0.50%	193,739	-1.15%	9,048	8.89%	198	-17.15%

3 Major products* 3種主要產品*	Output 產量	Sales volume 銷售量	Unit 單位
a) Abrasive Tool 磨具	1,240,814	1,215,998	ton 噸
b) Abradant 磨料	1,329,310	1,262,845	ton 噸

Top 10 firms by revenue (year founded) 收入排名前10家企業 (創辦年份)	City 城市	Province 省	Telephone / fax 電話 / 傳真	Number of employees 職工人數	Ownership 產業所有權	Revenue ('000 RMB) 銷售收入 (千元)	Profit ('000 RMB) (rank) 利潤 (千元) (排名)	Total assets ('000 RMB) 總資產 (千元)	Major products 主要產品
Henan Kai Xiang Enterprise Co. Ltd. 河南省凱祥企業有限公司(1974)	Jiaozuo 焦作市	Henan 河南省	(0391)8191819	520	Overseas Chinese-funded 港澳台資	295,850	56764(1)	82,344	a
Shanghai Grinding Wheel Factory 上海砂輪廠(1952)	Shanghai 上海市	Shanghai 上海市	(021)58890015 (021)58811181	1,450	State-owned 國有	222,026	1655(36)	394,441	a,b
Zhuhai Sez Color Bead Industrial General Co. 珠海彩珠實業總公司(1994)	Zhuhai 珠海市	Guangdong 廣東省	(0756)3330668 (0756)3334763	1	Collectively-owned 集體	180,891	17644(3)	288,283	o
Shandong Tai'an Abrasive & Apparatus Co. Ltd. 山東泰山磨料磨具股份有限公司(1950)	Zibo 淄博市	Shandong 山東省	(0533)2980151 (0533)2980151	2,464	Joint stock 股份制	173,877	21841(2)	350,750	a,b
Hua Bei Petroleum Supply Dept. Farm, Industry & Commerce Industrial Company 華北石油供應處農工商實業公司(1977)	Cangzhou 滄州市	Hebei 河北省	(0317)2725413	800	Collectively-owned 集體	152,197	-862(738)	49,370	o
China Qisha Group Co. Ltd. 中國七砂集團有限責任公司(1967)	Guiyang 貴陽市	Guizhou 貴州省	(0851)2550002	2,853	State-owned 國有	134,985	4535(10)	524,907	a,b
Zhe Jiangdong Yang Magnetic Enterprise Group Company Huoshan General Factory 浙江東陽磁性企業集團公司霍山總廠(1989)	Liu'an 六安市	Anhui 安徽省	(0564)5022881 (0564)5022881	612	Collectively-owned 集體	109,875	7748(6)	41,944	o
Zhejiang Crystal Factory 浙江水晶廠(1984)	Taizhou 臺州市	Zhejiang 浙江省	(0576)8224183 (0576)8881475	1,758	Collectively-owned 集體	91,148	1913(29)	238,542	o
Shenyang Municipal Administration Engineering Material Company 瀋陽市市政工程材料公司(1964)	Shenyang 瀋陽市	Liaoning 遼寧省	(024)22827753 (024)22827622	1,501	State-owned 國有	83,160	10(509)	124,410	o
Guilin Metallurgy Machine General Factory 桂林冶金機械總廠(1967)	Guilin 桂林市	Guangxi 廣西	(0773)2602860 (0773)2602343	1,529	State-owned 國有	75,117	1163(57)	237,317	o

Top 10 Cities by Production Output 產出排名前10位城市	Province 省	Market share 市場份額	Number of firms 企業個數
Zhengzhou 鄭州市	Henan 河南省	12.44%	81
Shanghai 上海市	Shanghai 上海市	5.25%	66
Zibo 淄博市	Shandong 山東省	4.87%	25
Jiaozuo 焦作市	Henan 河南省	4.75%	15
Guiyang 貴陽市	Guizhou 貴州省	3.63%	39
Shenyang 瀋陽市	Liaoning 遼寧省	2.73%	46
Taiyuan 太原市	Shanxi 山西省	2.27%	8
Anshan 鞍山市	Liaoning 遼寧省	2.21%	29
Linyi 臨沂市	Shandong 山東省	1.81%	24
Lianyungang 連雲港市	Jiangsu 江蘇省	1.68%	51

10 Major Wholesalers 10家主要批發商	City 城市	Province 省	Telephone / Fax 電話 / 傳真
Chengdu Sheng Xing Trade Company 成都盛興商貿公司	Chengdu 成都市	Sichuan 四川省	(028)7762591
Shanghai Municipal Administration Engineering Material Company 上海市市政工程材料公司	Shanghai 上海市	Shanghai 上海市	(021)64372632
Shanghai Construction Engineering Material Co. 上海市建築工程材料公司	Shanghai 上海市	Shanghai 上海市	(021)63298630
Yixing Jin San Jiao Zhao Bazaar 宜興市金三角招商城	Wuxi 無錫市	Jiangsu 江蘇省	(0510)7935138 (0510)7935138
Fujian Hua Fu Import & Export Company 福建省華福進出口公司	Fuzhou 福州市	Fujian 福建省	(0591)7810477 (0591)7810485
China Building Goods & Materials Company 中國建築物資公司	Beijing 北京市	Beijing 北京市	(010)68586253
Dalian Jinzhou Xin Gang Industry & Trade Company 大連金州新港工貿公司	Dalian 大連市	Liaoning 遼寧省	(0411)7624747
Shanghai Zhan Dong Industrial Co. Ltd. 上海展東實業有限公司	Shanghai 上海市	Shanghai 上海市	(021)58201778 (021)58200874
China Building Materials and Equipment Import & Export Company 中國建築材料及設備進出口公司	Beijing 北京市	Beijing 北京市	(010)68393420
Dandong Chemical Light Industry Material Company Chemical Construction Material Marketing Station 丹東市化工輕工材料公司化工建材經銷站	Dandong 丹東市	Liaoning 遼寧省	(0415)2146396

*Also include sales by firms outside this industry.包括本行業以外廠家的銷售。"o" stands for "others". "o" 代表"其他產品"。

3210: Iron Smelting 煉鐵業

The industry accounts for 0.526% of the total revenue of China's industrial sector in 1996. The revenue growth rate of the industry is 4.7% from 1995, as compared to the growth rate of China's industrial sector, 9.51%. The rate of return on asset is -0.38%. 64.45% of all firms in the industry made a profit while 23.73% had negative returns. The top province in terms of the industry's revenue is Hebei, accounting for 23.77% of the total revenue.
本行業在1996年佔全行業總產值0.526%，行業年增長率為4.7%（全國工業年增長率9.51%）。行業的資產回報率-0.38%，64.45%的企業盈利，23.73%的企業虧損。銷售收入最高的省份為河北省，佔本行業的23.77%。

	Total number of firms 企業總數	Total number of employees 職工總數	Total revenue (mil. RMB) 總銷售收入（百萬元）	Total profit (mil. RMB) 總利潤（百萬元）	Return on assets 資產利潤率 (%)	Return on equity 權益利潤率 (%)	Labour productivity ('000 RMB / worker) 勞動生產率（千元/人）	Debts / assets 資產負債率 (%)	Total assets (mil. RMB) 總資產（百萬元）
Industry Overall 行業總體	1,397	524,848	30,476	-211	-0.38	-1.25	58.07	69.36	55,062

	Number of firms 企業個數	Average number of employees 平均職工人數	Average revenue ('000 RMB) 平均銷售收入（千元）	Average profit ('000 RMB) 平均利潤（千元）	Return on assets 資產利潤率 (%)	Return on equity 權益利潤率 (%)	Labour productivity ('000 RMB / worker) 勞動生產率（千元/人）	Average debts / assets 平均資產負債率(%)	Average Total assets ('000 RMB) 平均總資產（千元）
By ownership 產業所有權									
State-owned 國有	257	1,374	77,759	-1,502	-0.94	-3.01	56.59	68.84	160,070
Collectively-owned 集體	1,001	141	7,748	-50	-0.53	-1.81	54.76	70.77	9,425
Privately-owned 私有	26	55	4,069	-680	-26.41	-79.83	74.19	66.92	2,575
Domestic JVs 聯營	33	144	6,376	1,482	14.60	38.56	44.14	62.15	10,152
Joint stock 股份制	40	260	29,618	-1,097	-3.25	-9.44	113.72	65.61	33,756
Foreign-funded 外資	17	357	36,741	9,130	9.64	30.43	102.90	68.32	94,724
Overseas Chinese-funded 港澳台資	23	343	26,346	3,676	7.53	49.68	76.83	84.85	48,828
By size 規模									
Large 大型	11	11,944	1,067,413	22,338	1.10	3.18	89.37	65.47	2,034,444
Medium 中型	60	2,323	121,773	-117	-0.05	-0.16	52.41	70.18	246,939
Small 小型	1,287	196	8,880	-349	-2.52	-9.52	45.33	73.55	13,882
By regional distribution 地區分布									
Central-North 華北	563	392	23,475	-27	-0.07	-0.23	59.83	71.41	40,204
Beijing 北京	6	38	2,010	10	0.28	9.09	53.36	96.86	3,560
Tianjin 天津	11	1,986	193,495	2,315	0.65	2.13	97.42	69.31	354,842
Hebei 河北	189	560	38,325	-6	-0.01	-0.04	68.46	73.26	62,882
Shanxi 山西	329	259	10,831	-40	-0.21	-0.65	41.82	67.99	18,967
Inner Mongolia 內蒙	28	278	9,599	-939	-4.49	-26.77	34.49	83.22	20,904
Northeast 東北	120	484	37,256	274	0.39	1.16	76.91	66.12	69,756
Liaoning 遼寧	86	415	40,048	755	1.05	2.61	96.57	59.70	71,850
Jilin 吉林	13	357	18,263	-559	-1.62	-6.15	51.17	73.68	34,546
Heilongjiang 黑龍江	21	849	37,579	-1,182	-1.42	-10.91	44.27	86.94	82,976
Central East 華東	191	574	36,800	378	0.57	1.47	64.06	61.16	66,258
Shanghai 上海	4	6,670	628,488	12,503	0.79	1.97	94.22	59.95	1,583,953
Jiangsu 江蘇	33	516	38,808	-451	-0.84	-3.23	75.20	74.10	53,919
Zhejiang 浙江	39	61	7,300	-21	-0.36	-1.18	120.17	69.39	5,902
Anhui 安徽	21	1,361	34,847	677	1.38	3.43	25.60	59.83	49,082
Fujian 福建	44	139	9,949	-91	-0.57	-1.11	71.51	48.21	15,858
Jiangxi 江西	10	57	3,645	-19	-0.67	-3.73	63.95	82.02	2,831
Shandong 山東	40	709	43,588	698	1.09	2.62	61.47	58.25	63,830
Central-South 中南	213	236	11,288	-301	-1.46	-4.89	47.88	70.04	20,561
Henan 河南	81	321	13,776	-36	-0.14	-0.40	42.91	65.68	26,003
Hubei 湖北	33	84	6,719	225	5.51	19.70	80.42	72.03	4,082
Hunan 湖南	32	372	17,331	-205	-0.63	-2.29	46.58	72.53	32,659
Guangdong 廣東	35	98	8,334	-39	-0.31	-1.15	84.65	73.03	12,490
Guangxi 廣西	30	179	6,710	-1,363	-7.86	-38.97	37.50	79.83	17,330
Hainan 海南	2	369	9,610	-9,925	-14.54	-47.81	26.08	69.58	68,240
Southwest 西南	230	263	10,711	-789	-3.66	-17.68	40.71	79.27	21,525
Chongqing 重慶	14	429	16,391	-1,424	-4.88	-28.39	38.25	82.82	29,207
Sichuan 四川	88	371	11,770	-1,128	-4.26	-24.82	31.70	82.82	26,462
Guizhou 貴州	93	85	5,664	3	0.04	0.13	66.61	71.11	8,605
Yunnan 雲南	35	399	19,227	-1,787	-4.42	-19.24	48.13	77.01	40,394
Tibet 西藏									
Northwest 西北	80	317	11,152	-699	-2.70	-17.89	35.15	84.91	25,884
Shaanxi 陝西	43	259	13,820	-108	-0.38	-3.15	53.39	87.78	28,096
Gansu 甘肅	7	331	16,451	161	0.69	2.13	49.70	67.45	23,236
Qinghai 青海	1	1							
Ningxia 寧夏	4	409	6,980	195	0.94	2.52	17.06	62.75	20,740
Xinjiang 新疆	25	412	6,194	-2,127	-8.62	-65.62	15.04	86.87	24,681

3210: Iron Smelting 煉鐵業

Year 年份	Number of firms 企業個數	Rate of change 每年變化 (%)	Number of employees 職工人數（人）	Rate of change 每年變化 (%)	Total revenue (mil. RMB) 總銷售收入（百萬元）	Rate of change 每年變化 (%)	Total profit (mil. RMB) 總利潤（百萬元）	Rate of change 每年變化 (%)
1993	1,089		523,928		29,345		2,507	
1994	1,283	17.81%	507,758	-3.09%	28,208	-3.88%	1,011	-59.67%
1995	1,471	14.65%	551,031	8.52%	29,105	3.18%	-128	-112.63%
1996	1,397	-5.03%	524,848	-4.75%	30,476	4.71%	-211	-65.20%

3 Major products* 3 種主要產品 *	Output 產量	Sales volume 銷售量	Unit 單位
a) Casting Pig Iron 鑄造生鐵	15,106,031	12,991,187	ton 噸
b) Substandard Pig Iron 出格生鐵	96,474	85,862	ton 噸
c) Basic Pig Iron 煉鋼生鐵	12,745,167	2,803,937	ton 噸

Top 10 firms by revenue (year founded) 收入排名前 10 家企業（創辦年份）	City 城市	Province 省	Telephone / fax 電話 / 傳真	Number of employees 職工人數	Ownership 產業所有權	Revenue ('000 RMB) 銷售收入（千元）	Profit ('000 RMB) (rank) 利潤（千元）（排名）	Total assets ('000 RMB) 總資產（千元）	Major products 主要產品
Bei Tai Iron & Steel Group Co. Ltd. 北台鋼鐵總廠(1964)	Benxi 本溪市	Liaoning 遼寧省	(0414)2531246 (0414)2531826	6,493	State-owned 國有	2,939,397	55343(1)	5,128,839	o
Shanghai Mei Shan (Group) Co. Ltd. 上海梅山(集團)有限公司(1970)	Nanjing 南京市	Jiangsu 江蘇省	(025)6701885 (025)6703644	26,014	State-owned 國有	2,486,140	50600(2)	6,260,251	a,b,c
Xuanhua Iron & Steel Co. Ltd. 宣化鋼鐵公司(1919)	Zhangjiakou 張家口市	Hebei 河北省	(0313)8674513 (0313)3014502	37,086	State-owned 國有	2,053,672	-163323(795)	4,414,214	a,b,c
Tianjin Tian Tie Steel-smelting Group Co. Ltd. 天津天鐵冶金集團有限公司(1970)	Tianjin 天津市	Tianjin 天津市	(022)23973288 (022)23972812	20,430	State-owned 國有	2,002,140	20180(5)	3,142,480	a,b,c
Hebei Xingtai Iron & Steel Corp. Ltd. 河北省邢台鋼鐵公司(1958)	Xingtai 邢臺市	Hebei 河北省	(0319)2042053 (0319)2624517	13,758	State-owned 國有	1,023,285	5068(27)	2,041,631	a,c
Xuzhou Iron & Steel General Factory 徐州鋼鐵總廠(1958)	Xuzhou 徐州市	Jiangsu 江蘇省	(0516)7773980 (0516)7773817	6,555	State-owned 國有	650,347	10656(10)	1,041,132	a,b,c
Zhangdian Iron & Steel Factory 張店鋼鐵廠(1958)	Zibo 淄博市	Shandong 山東省	(0533)3183123 (0533)3183728	3,860	State-owned 國有	529,189	9(449)	457,846	a,c
Han Jiang Steel Factory 漢江鋼鐵廠(1986)	Hanzhong 漢中市	Shaanxi 陝西省	(0916)3212641 (0916)3213232	4,900	State-owned 國有	410,200	302(227)	903,754	a,b,c
Shanxi Hai Xin Iron & Steel Co. Ltd. 山西省海鑫鋼鐵有限公司(1993)	Yuncheng 運城市	Shanxi 山西省	(0359)7080916	4,245	Joint stock 股份制	319,473	6698(21)	613,738	c
Handan Fu Jiang Iron & Steel Co. Ltd. 邯鄲富江鋼鐵有限公司(1995)	Handan 邯鄲市	Hebei 河北省	(0310)6072101	262	Foreign-funded 外資	298,461	49688(3)	139,779	o

Top 10 Cities by Production Output 產出排名前 10 位城市	Province 省	Market share 市場份額	Number of firms 企業個數
Taiyuan 太原市	Shanxi 山西省	19.46%	24
Zhangjiakou 張家口市	Hebei 河北省	6.69%	8
Jiayuguan 嘉峪關市	Gansu 甘肅省	6.48%	3
Tianjin 天津市	Tianjin 天津市	5.92%	12
Benxi 本溪市	Liaoning 遼寧省	5.41%	16
Guangzhou 廣州市	Guangdong 廣東省	5.23%	1
Handan 邯鄲市	Hebei 河北省	4.57%	54
Xingtai 邢臺市	Hebei 河北省	3.00%	9
Tangshan 唐山市	Hebei 河北省	2.57%	56
Linfen 臨汾市	Shanxi 山西省	2.05%	105

10 Major Wholesalers 10 家主要批發商	City 城市	Province 省	Telephone / Fax 電話 / 傳真
China Goods & Materials Storage & Transport Wuhan Company 中國物資儲運武漢公司	Wuhan 武漢市	Hubei 湖北省	(027)82821763 (027)82832856
China Light Industry Goods & Materials Supply & Marketing Hua Dong Company 中國輕工業物資供銷華東公司	Shanghai 上海市	Shanghai 上海市	(021)63216677 (021)63290262
Xinjiang Corps Products Group Company 新疆兵團物產集團公司	Urumqi 烏魯木齊市	Xinjiang 新疆	(0991)2841540
Anshan Iron & Steel Corporation Group International Economic Trade Company 鞍鋼集團國際經濟貿易公司	Anshan 鞍山市	Liaoning 遼寧省	(0412)6311645 (0412)6323413
Shanghai Pu Dong Goods & Materials General Company 上海浦東物資總公司	Shanghai 上海市	Shanghai 上海市	(021)58885013 (021)58889664
China Railway Goods & Materials Tianjin Company 中國鐵路物資天津公司	Tianjin 天津市	Tianjin 天津市	(022)24215754 (022)24215754
Wuhan Metal Material General Company 武漢市金屬材料總公司	Wuhan 武漢市	Hubei 湖北省	(027)82813443 (027)82818158
Jiangyin Steel Materials Supply & Marketing General Company 江陰市鋼材供銷總公司	Wuxi 無錫市	Jiangsu 江蘇省	(0510)6807676 (0510)6806909
Zhejiang Goods & Materials Development General Company 浙江物資開發總公司	Hangzhou 杭州市	Zhejiang 浙江省	(0571)7054562 (0571)5151675
China Metallurgy Import & Export Baotou Iron & Steel Company 中國冶金進出口包鋼公司	Baotou 包頭市	Inner Mong 內蒙	(0472)2185648 (0472)2183708

*Also include sales by firms outside this industry.包括本行業以外廠家的銷售。"o" stands for "others". "o" 代表"其他產品"。

3220: Steel Smelting 煉鋼業

The industry accounts for 2.566% of the total revenue of China's industrial sector in 1996. The revenue growth rate of the industry is -12.0% from 1995, as compared to the growth rate of China's industrial sector, 9.51%. The rate of return on asset is 0.87%. 71.00% of all firms in the industry made a profit while 22.19% had negative returns. The top province in terms of the industry's revenue is Liaoning, accounting for 15.12% of the total revenue.
本行業在1996年佔全行業總產值2.566%，行業年增長率為-12.0%（全國工業年增長率9.51%）。行業的資產回報率0.87%，71.00%的企業盈利，22.19%的企業虧損。銷售收入最高的省份為遼寧省，佔本行業的15.12%。

	Total number of firms 企業總數	Total number of employees 職工總數	Total revenue (mil. RMB) 總銷售收入（百萬元）	Total profit (mil. RMB) 總利潤（百萬元）	Return on assets 資產利潤率 (%)	Return on equity 權益利潤率 (%)	Labour productivity ('000 RMB / worker) 勞動生產率（千元/人）	Debts / assets 資產負債率 (%)	Total assets (mil. RMB) 總資產（百萬元）
Industry Overall 行業總體	779	1,418,478	148,756	2,653	0.87	2.02	104.87	56.68	303,887

	Number of firms 企業個數	Average number of employees 平均職工人數	Average revenue ('000 RMB) 平均銷售收入（千元）	Average profit ('000 RMB) 平均利潤（千元）	Return on assets 資產利潤率 (%)	Return on equity 權益利潤率 (%)	Labour productivity ('000 RMB / worker) 勞動生產率（千元/人）	Average debts / assets 平均資產負債率(%)	Average Total assets ('000 RMB) 平均總資產（千元）
By ownership 產業所有權									
State-owned 國有	121	10,219	1,044,215	19,455	0.90	2.14	102.18	57.88	2,159,281
Collectively-owned 集體	566	92	9,955	90	0.95	2.76	108.51	65.48	9,497
Privately-owned 私有	26	58	10,071	84	0.89	9.26	172.49	90.38	9,390
Domestic JVs 聯營	21	165	19,184	-791	-2.85	-6.01	116.27	52.62	27,758
Joint stock 股份制	18	6,143	642,279	2,571	0.15	0.29	104.56	47.35	1,713,680
Foreign-funded 外資	6	146	16,735	-7,017	-9.50	-16.49	114.36	42.41	73,885
Overseas Chinese-funded 港澳台資	19	699	229,734	13,760	5.19	8.92	328.74	41.85	265,311
By size 規模									
Large 大型	44	27,713	3,042,760	65,310	1.03	2.33	109.80	55.97	6,359,285
Medium 中型	32	3,767	249,345	-7,276	-1.48	-4.08	66.20	63.73	491,092
Small 小型	690	112	9,994	18	0.15	0.45	89.24	67.26	12,121
By regional distribution 地區分布									
Central-North 華北	127	1,332	127,313	8,478	3.29	7.69	95.61	57.24	257,872
Beijing 北京	5	57	2,236	-132	-4.12	29.86	39.51	113.80	3,202
Tianjin 天津	11	1,719	191,431	-1,605	-0.40	-1.64	111.39	75.46	400,096
Hebei 河北	81	1,302	146,179	14,309	4.90	10.24	112.31	52.13	292,017
Shanxi 山西	18	2,122	118,503	-320	-0.13	-0.35	55.86	62.01	238,045
Inner Mongolia 內蒙	12	525	6,528	-4,851	-14.76	258.14	12.43	105.72	32,874
Northeast 東北	131	2,212	201,669	2,698	0.56	1.18	91.18	52.38	481,429
Liaoning 遼寧	55	4,368	408,870	7,202	0.70	1.42	93.60	50.67	1,026,175
Jilin 吉林	39	889	82,814	811	0.63	1.78	93.14	64.73	129,058
Heilongjiang 黑龍江	37	400	18,946	-2,008	-4.66	-17.98	47.40	74.08	43,090
Central East 華東	169	1,815	247,388	822	0.22	0.51	136.33	57.36	380,630
Shanghai 上海	11	5,289	1,443,284	21,851	1.40	5.32	272.89	73.69	1,561,639
Jiangsu 江蘇	20	1,490	223,851	-1,646	-0.49	-1.00	150.19	50.93	336,619
Zhejiang 浙江	29	804	110,107	1,700	1.00	1.81	136.91	44.66	169,428
Anhui 安徽	23	2,501	316,256	5,254	0.66	0.99	126.43	33.35	795,744
Fujian 福建	19	59	4,928	88	2.36	9.36	83.91	74.77	3,745
Jiangxi 江西	44	1,700	93,334	-7,287	-4.32	-20.28	54.89	78.72	168,803
Shandong 山東	23	2,691	295,133	3,493	0.83	2.60	109.67	68.16	421,828
Central-South 中南	205	1,406	182,668	5,804	1.43	3.00	129.93	52.22	405,448
Henan 河南	43	1,216	125,387	9,613	4.95	7.63	103.12	35.15	194,295
Hubei 湖北	38	3,123	537,020	15,719	1.13	2.60	171.98	56.59	1,393,749
Hunan 湖南	42	1,424	103,620	-686	-0.30	-0.60	72.78	49.69	226,339
Guangdong 廣東	55	615	97,097	4,092	2.95	6.21	157.92	52.50	138,787
Guangxi 廣西	27	876	72,450	-631	-0.37	-0.59	82.72	37.88	172,601
Hainan 海南									
Southwest 西南	94	2,878	217,517	-787	-0.17	-0.50	75.57	66.86	473,616
Chongqing 重慶	24	821	45,059	3	0.00	0.01	54.86	70.91	150,865
Sichuan 四川	53	3,280	268,826	-6	0.00	0.00	81.95	67.04	549,170
Guizhou 貴州	16	2,660	113,308	-14,020	-4.02	-23.29	42.60	82.72	348,438
Yunnan 雲南	1	34,617	3,318,400	150,570	2.41	4.78	95.86	49.51	6,243,030
Tibet 西藏									
Northwest 西北	53	1,778	122,007	-596	-0.20	-0.55	68.64	64.45	303,901
Shaanxi 陝西	34	934	40,458	-4,575	-3.98	-22.87	43.30	82.59	114,916
Gansu 甘肅	9	3,941	237,616	3,594	0.44	0.93	60.30	52.56	813,452
Qinghai 青海	2	6,420	602,670	555	0.04	0.13	93.88	69.52	1,373,095
Ningxia 寧夏	1								
Xinjiang 新疆	7	2,019	249,561	12,929	4.24	12.30	123.61	65.51	304,619

3220: Steel Smelting 煉鋼業

Year 年份	Number of firms 企業個數	Rate of change 每年變化 (%)	Number of employees 職工人數 (人)	Rate of change 每年變化 (%)	Total revenue (mil. RMB) 總銷售收入 (百萬元)	Rate of change 每年變化 (%)	Total profit (mil. RMB) 總利潤 (百萬元)	Rate of change 每年變化 (%)
1993	874		2,036,251		170,952		16,912	
1994	888	1.60%	1,877,293	-7.81%	188,729	10.40%	18,400	8.79%
1995	862	-2.93%	1,743,600	-7.12%	169,085	-10.41%	6,671	-63.74%
1996	779	-9.63%	1,418,478	-18.65%	148,756	-12.02%	2,653	-60.23%

3 Major products* 3 種主要產品 *	Output 產量	Sales volume 銷售量	Unit 單位
a) Plain Carbon Steel 普通碳素鋼	30,591,231	6,424,158	ton 噸
b) Billet Steel 鋼坯	21,027,462	4,836,316	ton 噸
c) Plain Low-alloy Steel 普通低合金鋼	11,439,879	3,660,761	ton 噸

Top 10 firms by revenue (year founded) 收入排名前 10 家企業 (創辦年份)	City 城市	Province 省	Telephone / fax 電話 / 傳真	Number of employees 職工人數	Ownership 產業所有權	Revenue ('000 RMB) 銷售收入 (千元)	Profit ('000 RMB) (rank) 利潤 (千元) (排名)	Total assets ('000 RMB) 總資產 (千元)	Major products 主要產品
Anshan Iron & Steel (Group) Co. 鞍山鋼鐵集團公司(1919)	Anshan 鞍山市	Liaoning 遼寧省	(0412)6728866 (0412)6723090	197,962	State-owned 國有	19,742,640	350980(3)	49,265,560	a,b,c
Wuhan Iron & Steel (Group) Co. 武漢鋼鐵(集團)公司(1958)	Wuhan 武漢市	Hubei 湖北省	(027)86865180 (027)86862325	135,399	State-owned 國有	15,500,610	750910(1)	41,117,380	o
Panzhihua Iron & Steel (Group) Co. 攀鋼(集團)公司(1970)	Panzhihua 攀枝花市	Sichuan 四川省	(0812)3394261 (0812)2224103	105,877	State-owned 國有	8,839,776	2000(53)	15,363,422	a,b,c
Ma'anshan Iron & Steel Co. Ltd. 馬鞍山鋼鐵股份有限公司(1993)	Ma'anshan 馬鞍山市	Anhui 安徽省	(0555)2883492 (0555)2324350	53,986	Joint stock 股份制	6,795,336	104013(12)	17,864,990	a,b,c
Shanghai No.1 Iron & Steel (Group) Co. Ltd. 上海第一鋼鐵(集團)有限公司(1943)	Shanghai 上海市	Shanghai 上海市	(021)56758000 (021)56759804	21,337	State-owned 國有	5,441,231	150472(8)	5,235,971	a,b,c
Shanghai Pudong Iron & Steel (Group) Co. Ltd. 上海浦東鋼鐵(集團)有限公司(1918)	Shanghai 上海市	Shanghai 上海市	(021)58839180 (021)63201284	14,145	State-owned 國有	5,403,886	59221(14)	6,595,137	a,b,c
Ji'nan Iron & Steel Group General Company 濟南鋼鐵集團總公司(1958)	Ji'nan 濟南市	Shandong 山東省	(0531)8985901 (0531)8982126	37,798	State-owned 國有	4,725,590	172138(5)	6,043,369	a,b,c
Shanghai Wugang (Group) Co. Ltd. 上海五鋼(集團)有限公司(1958)	Shanghai 上海市	Shanghai 上海市	(021)56679080 (021)56679920	19,728	State-owned 國有	4,715,844	40684(16)	4,920,905	a,b,c
Tangshan Iron & Steel Group Co. Ltd. 唐山鋼鐵集團有限責任公司(1944)	Tangshan 唐山市	Hebei 河北省	(0315)2822357 (0315)2827527	53,557	State-owned 國有	4,527,510	250990(4)	10,655,400	a,b,c
Handan Iron & Steel Group Co. Ltd. 邯鄲鋼鐵集團有限責任公司(1958)	Handan 邯鄲市	Hebei 河北省	(0310)4042342 (0310)4041970	28,000	State-owned 國有	4,405,564	701685(2)	8,831,836	a,b

Top 10 Cities by Production Output 產出排名前 10 位城市	Province 省	Market share 市場份額	Number of firms 企業個數
Shanghai 上海市	Shanghai 上海市	14.11%	32
Anshan 鞍山市	Liaoning 遼寧省	8.12%	9
Panzhihua 攀枝花市	Sichuan 四川省	6.64%	6
Ma'anshan 馬鞍山市	Anhui 安徽省	5.65%	2
Handan 邯鄲市	Hebei 河北省	5.01%	15
Wuhan 武漢市	Hubei 湖北省	4.72%	5
Tangshan 唐山市	Hebei 河北省	4.64%	47
Anyang 安陽市	Henan 河南省	3.36%	6
Tonghua 通化市	Jilin 吉林省	2.61%	2
Chengdu 成都市	Sichuan 四川省	2.54%	14

10 Major Wholesalers 10 家主要批發商	City 城市	Province 省	Telephone / Fax 電話 / 傳真
China Goods & Materials Storage & Transport Wuhan Company 中國物資儲運武漢公司	Wuhan 武漢市	Hubei 湖北省	(027)82821763 (027)82832856
China Light Industry Goods & Materials Supply & Marketing Hua Dong Company 中國輕工業物資供銷華東公司	Shanghai 上海市	Shanghai 上海市	(021)63216677 (021)63290262
Xinjiang Corps Products Group Company 新疆兵團物產集團公司	Urumqi 烏魯木齊市	Xinjiang 新疆	(0991)2841540
Anshan Iron & Steel Corporation Group International Economic Trade Company 鞍鋼集團國際經濟貿易公司	Anshan 鞍山市	Liaoning 遼寧省	(0412)6311645 (0412)6323413
Shanghai Pu Dong Goods & Materials General Company 上海浦東物資總公司	Shanghai 上海市	Shanghai 上海市	(021)58885013 (021)58889664
China Railway Goods & Materials Tianjin Company 中國鐵路物資天津公司	Tianjin 天津市	Tianjin 天津市	(022)24215754 (022)24215754
Wuhan Metal Material General Company 武漢市金屬材料總公司	Wuhan 武漢市	Hubei 湖北省	(027)82813443 (027)82818158
Jiangyin Steel Materials Supply & Marketing General Company 江陰市鋼材供銷總公司	Wuxi 無錫市	Jiangsu 江蘇省	(0510)6807676 (0510)6806909
Zhejiang Goods & Materials Development General Company 浙江物資開發總公司	Hangzhou 杭州市	Zhejiang 浙江省	(0571)7054562 (0571)5151675
China Metallurgy Import & Export Baotou Iron & Steel Company 中國冶金進出口包鋼公司	Baotou 包頭市	Inner Mong 內蒙	(0472)2185648 (0472)2183708

*Also include sales by firms outside this industry.包括本行業以外廠家的銷售。"o" stands for "others". "o" 代表"其他產品"。

3240: Steel Rolling 鋼壓延加工業

The industry accounts for 2.889% of the total revenue of China's industrial sector in 1996. The revenue growth rate of the industry is 3.8% from 1995, as compared to the growth rate of China's industrial sector, 9.51%. The rate of return on asset is 1.19%. 66.35% of all firms in the industry made a profit while 27.68% had negative returns. The top province in terms of the industry's revenue is Shanghai, accounting for 20.17% of the total revenue.

本行業在1996年佔全行業總產值2.889%，行業年增長率為3.8%（全國工業年增長率9.51%）。行業的資產回報率1.19%，66.35%的企業盈利，27.68%的企業虧損。銷售收入最高的省份為上海市，佔本行業的20.17%。

	Total number of firms 企業總數	Total number of employees 職工總數	Total revenue (mil. RMB) 總銷售收入（百萬元）	Total profit (mil. RMB) 總利潤（百萬元）	Return on assets 資產利潤率 (%)	Return on equity 權益利潤率 (%)	Labour productivity ('000 RMB / worker) 勞動生產率（千元/人）	Debts / assets 資產負債率 (%)	Total assets (mil. RMB) 總資產（百萬元）
Industry Overall 行業總體	3,485	1,430,912	167,497	4,065	1.19	2.68	117.06	55.65	342,628

	Number of firms 企業個數	Average number of employees 平均職工人數	Average revenue ('000 RMB) 平均銷售收入（千元）	Average profit ('000 RMB) 平均利潤（千元）	Return on assets 資產利潤率 (%)	Return on equity 權益利潤率 (%)	Labour productivity ('000 RMB / worker) 勞動生產率（千元/人）	Average debts / assets 平均資產負債率(%)	Average Total assets ('000 RMB) 平均總資產（千元）
By ownership 產業所有權									
State-owned 國有	388	2,284	285,023	8,165	1.16	2.42	124.81	52.30	706,680
Collectively-owned 集體	2,764	170	15,590	207	1.27	4.27	91.89	70.32	16,366
Privately-owned 私有	21	54	4,422	108	3.11	8.23	82.11	62.23	3,485
Domestic JVs 聯營	79	153	20,943	215	1.03	3.11	137.05	66.92	20,891
Joint stock 股份制	53	515	84,940	2,057	1.21	2.97	164.93	59.33	170,336
Foreign-funded 外資	69	176	57,884	1,426	1.81	6.25	328.43	71.07	78,913
Overseas Chinese-funded 港澳台資	106	235	32,338	981	1.52	5.51	137.88	72.36	64,435
By size 規模									
Large 大型	51	12,155	1,714,896	77,643	1.73	3.39	141.08	48.95	4,490,287
Medium 中型	165	1,738	224,506	-368	-0.11	-0.32	129.15	65.84	340,892
Small 小型	3,214	161	13,377	52	0.29	1.05	83.12	72.41	17,851
By regional distribution 地區分布									
Central-North 華北	637	699	80,303	1,815	0.99	2.41	114.89	58.80	182,734
Beijing 北京	53	2,566	342,341	5,471	0.75	1.53	133.41	50.67	725,031
Tianjin 天津	88	387	58,936	729	0.28	1.26	152.18	77.82	261,783
Hebei 河北	371	271	29,313	805	1.97	5.94	107.98	66.77	40,773
Shanxi 山西	56	1,347	133,441	3,610	1.17	2.36	99.08	50.64	309,734
Inner Mongolia 內蒙	69	1,435	137,318	4,363	1.34	2.92	95.68	54.14	325,599
Northeast 東北	632	505	30,613	-610	-0.78	-2.50	60.59	68.68	77,845
Liaoning 遼寧	460	532	35,136	-563	-0.64	-1.92	66.07	66.90	88,646
Jilin 吉林	71	622	15,846	-2,117	-4.79	-47.43	25.46	89.90	44,185
Heilongjiang 黑龍江	101	302	20,392	239	0.46	1.51	67.45	69.84	52,313
Central East 華東	1,119	322	64,530	3,495	2.86	5.08	200.51	43.66	122,171
Shanghai 上海	115	578	293,822	30,094	3.96	5.88	508.32	32.68	760,590
Jiangsu 江蘇	321	352	64,424	484	0.62	1.57	182.79	60.70	78,677
Zhejiang 浙江	153	176	28,034	366	1.20	3.24	159.50	62.82	30,432
Anhui 安徽	150	291	23,199	378	1.51	4.92	79.77	69.36	25,069
Fujian 福建	139	181	20,625	362	1.36	2.79	113.76	51.34	26,624
Jiangxi 江西	101	119	7,691	-61	-0.69	-2.31	64.80	69.95	8,823
Shandong 山東	140	520	45,188	988	1.26	4.25	86.89	70.34	78,415
Central-South 中南	583	205	19,395	-839	-2.49	-10.31	94.66	75.86	33,713
Henan 河南	113	246	18,439	-1,624	-4.19	-17.07	74.86	75.44	38,739
Hubei 湖北	137	273	22,170	-543	-1.92	-12.16	81.13	84.21	28,279
Hunan 湖南	93	239	19,489	-494	-1.60	-7.59	81.44	78.97	30,941
Guangdong 廣東	165	140	23,935	-601	-1.56	-4.60	171.07	65.96	38,383
Guangxi 廣西	69	117	4,629	-352	-3.11	-8.56	39.55	63.60	11,298
Hainan 海南	6	128	17,540	-10,357	-4.40	-466.52	136.85	99.06	235,437
Southwest 西南	388	413	30,026	-67	-0.16	-0.48	72.64	67.02	42,678
Chongqing 重慶	76	814	49,520	47	0.05	0.18	60.83	72.15	95,569
Sichuan 四川	232	317	28,617	12	0.04	0.11	90.33	64.18	32,181
Guizhou 貴州	38	202	4,954	-294	-2.68	-10.71	24.56	74.95	10,977
Yunnan 雲南	42	416	25,381	-203	-0.60	-1.28	60.95	53.62	34,125
Tibet 西藏									
Northwest 西北	126	209	14,530	-808	-2.48	-7.52	69.44	67.00	32,580
Shaanxi 陝西	43	174	14,270	-109	-0.27	-1.17	81.78	77.41	41,037
Gansu 甘肅	41	328	26,153	-1,251	-2.93	-6.08	79.85	51.81	42,687
Qinghai 青海	6	320	6,698	-4,560	-11.43	-125.22	20.95	90.87	39,885
Ningxia 寧夏	7	210	4,870	-1,979	-6.25	-29.53	23.17	78.84	31,666
Xinjiang 新疆	29	70	2,435	-161	-3.61	-10.60	34.56	65.95	4,463

3240: Steel Rolling 鋼壓延加工業

Year 年份	Number of firms 企業個數	Rate of change 每年變化 (%)	Number of employees 職工人數 (人)	Rate of change 每年變化 (%)	Total revenue (mil. RMB) 總銷售收入 (百萬元)	Rate of change 每年變化 (%)	Total profit (mil. RMB) 總利潤 (百萬元)	Rate of change 每年變化 (%)
1993	3,080		1,510,566		124,311		10,506	
1994	3,709	20.42%	1,311,422	-13.18%	155,506	25.09%	14,685	39.78%
1995	3,886	4.77%	1,448,556	10.46%	161,440	3.82%	6,506	-55.70%
1996	3,485	-10.32%	1,430,912	-1.22%	167,497	3.75%	4,065	-37.52%

3 Major products* 3種主要產品*	Output 產量	Sales volume 銷售量	Unit 單位
a) Cold Prosessing Steels 冷加工材	7,959,991	7,561,992	ton 噸
b) Steel Strip 鋼帶	3,436,596	3,299,132	ton 噸
c) Thin Steel Plate 薄鋼板	8,585,834	4,550,492	ton 噸

Top 10 firms by revenue (year founded) 收入排名前10家企業 (創辦年份)	City 城市	Province 省	Telephone / fax 電話 / 傳真	Number of employees 職工人數	Ownership 產業所有權	Revenue ('000 RMB) 銷售收入 (千元)	Profit ('000 RMB) (rank) 利潤 (千元) (排名)	Total assets ('000 RMB) 總資產 (千元)	Major products 主要產品
Baoshan Iron & Steel (Group) Co. Ltd. 寶山鋼鐵(集團)公司(1982)	Shanghai 上海市	Shanghai 上海市	(021)56648648 (021)56648046	17,244	State-owned 國有	23,662,404	3136206(1)	75,365,574	a,b,c
Capital Iron & Steel Coporation General Co. 首鋼總公司(1919)	Beijing 北京市	Beijing 北京市	(010)68293520 (010)68293080	59,410	State-owned 國有	17,109,916	182616(4)	36,473,609	a,b,c
Benxi Iron & Steel (Group) Co. Ltd. 本溪鋼鐵(集團)有限責任公司(1905)	Benxi 本溪市	Liaoning 遼寧省	(0414)2843191 (0414)2842074	85,678	State-owned 國有	7,484,148	158010(6)	20,731,114	b,c
Taiyuan Iron & Steel (Group) Ltd. 太原鋼鐵(集團)公司(1934)	Taiyuan 太原市	Shanxi 山西省	(0351)3044984 (0351)3044170	67,776	State-owned 國有	7,003,358	201305(2)	16,749,742	a,b,c
Chongqing Iron & Steel (Group) Co. Ltd. 重慶鋼鐵(集團)有限責任公司	Chongqing 重慶市	Chongqing 重慶市	(023)68846080 (023)68849988	17,119	State-owned 國有	3,518,737	60274(13)	6,881,932	a,b,c
Jiangsu Sha Gang Group Co. Ltd. 江蘇沙鋼集團有限公司(1975)	Suzhou 蘇州市	Jiangsu 江蘇省	(0512)8550801 (0512)8550818	4,868	State-owned 國有	3,163,312	63139(12)	3,847,866	o
Laiwu Iron & Steel General Factory 萊蕪鋼鐵總廠(1961)	Laiwu 萊蕪市	Shandong 山東省	(0634)6820222 (0634)6821407	33,760	State-owned 國有	2,969,553	102882(8)	6,461,030	a,b
Nanjing Iron & Steel Group Co. Ltd. 南京鋼鐵集團有限公司(1958)	Nanjing 南京市	Jiangsu 江蘇省	(025)7791615 (025)7792159	23,078	State-owned 國有	2,504,479	46296(17)	5,313,802	b,c
Fushun Special Steel Co. Ltd. 撫順特殊鋼有限公司(1938)	Fushun 撫順市	Liaoning 遼寧省	(0413)6681441 (0413)6686258	23,758	State-owned 國有	2,033,158	10231(51)	4,136,679	c
Tianjin Steel Tube Company 天津鋼管公司(1992)	Tianjin 天津市	Tianjin 天津市	(022)24802122 (022)34361109	7,029	State-owned 國有	1,810,505	180004(5)	16,434,399	o

Top 10 Cities by Production Output 產出排名前10位城市	Province 省	Market share 市場份額	Number of firms 企業個數
Shanghai 上海市	Shanghai 上海市	13.03%	158
Wuxi 無錫市	Jiangsu 江蘇省	7.46%	133
Baotou 包頭市	Inner Mong 內蒙	6.93%	24
Benxi 本溪市	Liaoning 遼寧省	6.31%	54
Suzhou 蘇州市	Jiangsu 江蘇省	5.13%	127
Tianjin 天津市	Tianjin 天津市	4.32%	95
Beijing 北京市	Beijing 北京市	3.94%	50
Ji'nan 濟南市	Shandong 山東省	3.41%	17
Chongqing 重慶市	Chongqing 重慶市	2.82%	101
Laiwu 萊蕪市	Shandong 山東省	2.63%	7

10 Major Wholesalers 10家主要批發商	City 城市	Province 省	Telephone / Fax 電話 / 傳真
China Goods & Materials Storage & Transport Wuhan Company 中國物資儲運武漢公司	Wuhan 武漢市	Hubei 湖北省	(027)82821763 (027)82832856
China Light Industry Goods & Materials Supply & Marketing Hua Dong Company 中國輕工業物資供銷華東公司	Shanghai 上海市	Shanghai 上海市	(021)63216677 (021)63290262
Xinjiang Corps Products Group Company 新疆兵團物產集團公司	Urumqi 烏魯木齊市	Xinjiang 新疆	(0991)2841540
Anshan Iron & Steel Corporation Group International Economic Trade Company 鞍鋼集團國際經濟貿易公司	Anshan 鞍山市	Liaoning 遼寧省	(0412)6311645 (0412)6323413
Shanghai Pu Dong Goods & Materials General Company 上海浦東物資總公司	Shanghai 上海市	Shanghai 上海市	(021)58885013 (021)58889664
China Railway Goods & Materials Tianjin Company 中國鐵路物資天津公司	Tianjin 天津市	Tianjin 天津市	(022)24215754 (022)24215754
Wuhan Metal Material General Company 武漢市金屬材料總公司	Wuhan 武漢市	Hubei 湖北省	(027)82813443 (027)82818158
Jiangyin Steel Materials Supply & Marketing General Company 江陰市鋼材供銷總公司	Wuxi 無錫市	Jiangsu 江蘇省	(0510)6807676 (0510)6806909
Zhejiang Goods & Materials Development General Company 浙江物資開發總公司	Hangzhou 杭州市	Zhejiang 浙江省	(0571)7054562 (0571)5151675
China Metallurgy Import & Export Baotou Iron & Steel Company 中國冶金進出口包鋼公司	Baotou 包頭市	Inner Mong 內蒙	(0472)2185648 (0472)2183708

*Also include sales by firms outside this industry.包括本行業以外廠家的銷售。"o" stands for "others". "o" 代表"其他產品"。

3260: Ferroalloy Smelting and Refining 鐵合金冶煉業

The industry accounts for 0.279% of the total revenue of China's industrial sector in 1996. The revenue growth rate of the industry is -3.4% from 1995, as compared to the growth rate of China's industrial sector, 9.51%. The rate of return on asset is -1.18%. 55.18% of all firms in the industry made a profit while 35.41% had negative returns. The top province in terms of the industry's revenue is Liaoning, accounting for 9.19% of the total revenue.
本行業在1996年佔全行業總產值0.279%，行業年增長率為-3.4%（全國工業年增長率9.51%）。行業的資產回報率-1.18%，55.18%的企業盈利，35.41%的企業虧損。銷售收入最高的省份為遼寧省，佔本行業的9.19%。

	Total number of firms 企業總數	Total number of employees 職工總數	Total revenue (mil. RMB) 總銷售收入（百萬元）	Total profit (mil. RMB) 總利潤（百萬元）	Return on assets 資產利潤率 (%)	Return on equity 權益利潤率 (%)	Labour productivity ('000 RMB / worker) 勞動生產率（千元/人）	Debts / assets 資產負債率 (%)	Total assets (mil. RMB) 總資產（百萬元）
Industry Overall 行業總體	1,069	235,236	16,158	-299	-1.18	-4.92	68.69	75.97	25,284

	Number of firms 企業個數	Average number of employees 平均職工人數	Average revenue ('000 RMB) 平均銷售收入（千元）	Average profit ('000 RMB) 平均利潤（千元）	Return on assets 資產利潤率 (%)	Return on equity 權益利潤率 (%)	Labour productivity ('000 RMB / worker) 勞動生產率（千元/人）	Average debts / assets 平均資產負債率(%)	Average Total assets ('000 RMB) 平均總資產（千元）
By ownership 產業所有權									
State-owned 國有	280	458	27,486	-1,218	-2.26	-9.69	60.03	76.66	53,839
Collectively-owned 集體	677	115	7,407	30	0.39	1.82	64.39	78.60	7,815
Privately-owned 私有	9	60	2,221	-72	-1.65	-9.21	36.95	82.12	4,345
Domestic JVs 聯營	31	108	11,638	2	0.02	0.08	108.12	81.43	11,615
Joint stock 股份制	18	869	59,436	399	0.30	0.85	68.42	64.78	133,703
Foreign-funded 外資	21	147	36,314	147	0.38	1.89	247.03	79.66	38,149
Overseas Chinese-funded 港澳台資	31	245	39,823	378	0.89	3.45	162.48	74.07	42,275
By size 規模									
Large 大型	20	3,654	283,235	95,263	15.55	63.37	77.51	75.46	612,617
Medium 中型	27	1,087	79,794	-22,055	-20.13	-76.66	73.38	73.74	109,549
Small 小型	1,000	132	8,339	-1,609	-15.97	-70.17	63.10	77.24	10,074
By regional distribution 地區分布									
Central-North 華北	95	236	17,092	-156	-0.64	-2.41	72.34	73.61	24,566
Beijing 北京	8	62	9,110	224	1.73	7.99	147.23	78.40	12,969
Tianjin 天津	3	238	18,330	70	0.29	0.54	77.12	46.64	24,137
Hebei 河北	19	242	22,189	-759	-2.48	-22.08	91.77	88.79	30,663
Shanxi 山西	47	325	20,851	-46	-0.15	-0.46	64.10	68.31	31,221
Inner Mongolia 內蒙	18	75	5,239	-15	-0.25	-1.10	69.49	77.28	5,978
Northeast 東北	108	359	26,583	-484	-1.01	-3.79	74.11	73.22	47,724
Liaoning 遼寧	65	324	22,851	-64	-0.17	-0.61	70.63	72.50	38,282
Jilin 吉林	36	473	37,275	-1,397	-1.91	-7.27	78.86	73.72	73,151
Heilongjiang 黑龍江	7	99	6,256	316	6.82	60.22	62.92	88.68	4,630
Central East 華東	155	170	19,912	109	0.49	1.73	117.29	71.74	22,181
Shanghai 上海	18	367	63,479	1,156	1.66	7.46	172.99	77.78	69,782
Jiangsu 江蘇	32	240	26,498	-1,267	-4.40	-24.10	110.51	81.76	28,828
Zhejiang 浙江	12	376	34,890	13	0.03	0.06	92.85	60.22	51,873
Anhui 安徽	8	87	6,776	244	5.27	11.93	78.11	55.89	4,628
Fujian 福建	58	71	4,665	70	1.31	2.79	65.96	52.98	5,349
Jiangxi 江西	12	23	955	28	1.76	6.52	42.29	72.97	1,560
Shandong 山東	15	164	22,728	2,003	11.09	27.48	138.59	59.65	18,065
Central-South 中南	265	183	12,752	-262	-1.41	-5.75	69.64	75.56	18,651
Henan 河南	54	160	10,255	369	2.88	16.91	64.17	82.96	12,794
Hubei 湖北	36	270	17,281	74	0.35	2.18	63.99	83.71	20,844
Hunan 湖南	106	198	10,459	-740	-4.12	-20.14	52.93	79.52	17,936
Guangdong 廣東	18	48	2,598	-440	-9.05	-37.55	54.63	75.89	4,859
Guangxi 廣西	51	164	20,546	-112	-0.38	-1.03	125.24	63.15	29,659
Hainan 海南									
Southwest 西南	261	188	11,381	-415	-2.04	-9.86	60.45	79.31	20,354
Chongqing 重慶	16	352	13,773	-176	-0.63	-4.81	39.10	86.87	27,835
Sichuan 四川	70	216	13,124	363	1.19	3.47	60.70	65.74	30,512
Guizhou 貴州	108	203	12,099	-551	-2.76	-25.54	59.54	89.19	19,948
Yunnan 雲南	66	96	7,881	-420	-4.89	-34.05	82.01	85.64	8,592
Tibet 西藏	1		4,410	1,240	11.80	-33.42		135.30	10,510
Northwest 西北	185	271	12,041	-383	-1.73	-8.84	44.49	80.46	22,177
Shaanxi 陝西	43	295	7,363	-793	-5.91	-161.92	25.00	96.35	13,427
Gansu 甘肅	57	236	12,556	125	0.50	1.96	53.28	74.35	24,861
Qinghai 青海	46	311	12,564	-611	-2.31	-9.16	40.36	74.83	26,503
Ningxia 寧夏	34	265	17,628	-433	-1.71	-13.47	66.49	87.26	25,245
Xinjiang 新疆	5	128	3,606	-218	-3.54	-100.00	28.08	96.46	6,160

3260: Ferroalloy Smelting and Refining 鐵合金冶煉業

Year 年份	Number of firms 企業個數	Rate of change 每年變化 (%)	Number of employees 職工人數 (人)	Rate of change 每年變化 (%)	Total revenue (mil. RMB) 總銷售收入 (百萬元)	Rate of change 每年變化 (%)	Total profit (mil. RMB) 總利潤 (百萬元)	Rate of change 每年變化 (%)
1993	758		195,769		12,433		240	
1994	807	6.46%	234,886	19.98%	11,843	-4.75%	15	-93.84%
1995	1,080	33.83%	250,296	6.56%	16,726	41.23%	16	10.87%
1996	1,069	-1.02%	235,236	-6.02%	16,158	-3.40%	-299	-1923.50%

3 Major products* 3 種主要產品 *	Output 產量	Sales volume 銷售量	Unit 單位
a) Ferrochrome 鉻鐵	708,681	510,250	ton 噸
b) Manganese-silicon Alloy 錳硅合金	750,492	600,394	ton 噸
c) Ferrosilicium 硅鐵	1,104,588	1,027,267	ton 噸

Top 10 firms by revenue (year founded) 收入排名前 10 家企業 (創辦年份)	City 城市	Province 省	Telephone / fax 電話 / 傳真	Number of employees 職工人數	Ownership 產業所有權	Revenue ('000 RMB) 銷售收入 (千元)	Profit ('000 RMB) (rank) 利潤(千元) (排名)	Total assets ('000 RMB) 總資產 (千元)	Major products 主要產品
Shanghai Shenjia Ferroalloys Co. Ltd. 上海申佳鐵合金有限公司(1993)	Shanghai 上海市	Shanghai 上海市	(021)56758675 (021)56751108	3,629	Overseas Chinese-funded 港澳台資	684,974	5078(8)	912,020	a,b
Zunyi Ferroalloys Plant 遵義鐵合金廠(1950)	Zunyi 遵義市	Guizhou 貴州省	(0852)222930	9,065	State-owned 國有	680,150	-3642(683)	1,243,878	a,b,c
Jilin Ferroalloys Plant 吉林鐵合金廠(1956)	Jilin 吉林市	Jilin 吉林省	(0432)2733634 (0432)2738326	7,610	State-owned 國有	637,366	-40841(712)	1,797,053	a,b,c
Jinzhou Ferroalloys Group Co. Ltd. 錦州鐵合金(集團)股份公司(1942)	Jinzhou 錦州市	Liaoning 遼寧省	(0416)2583173 (0416)5139270	8,883	Joint stock 股份制	547,533	163(237)	1,094,560	o
Jilin Lin Bao Ferroalloys Co. Ltd. 吉林林寶鐵合金有限公司(1993)	Jilin 吉林市	Jilin 吉林省	(0432)2736571 (0432)2736574	436	Foreign-funded 外資	371,302	-5422(695)	392,685	a,b
Liaoyang Ferroalloys Plant 遼陽鐵合金廠(1949)	Liaoyang 遼陽市	Liaoning 遼寧省	(0419)3303585 (0419)3303264	4,182	State-owned 國有	356,557	3204(14)	750,350	o
Guangxi Ba Yi Ferroalloys General Plant 廣西八一鐵合金廠(1959)	Heshan 合山市	Guangxi 廣西	(0772)4812266 (0772)4812267	3,002	State-owned 國有	299,327	2605(21)	392,526	b
Xibei Ferroalloys Plant 西北鐵合金廠(1984)	Lanzhou 蘭州市	Gansu 甘肅省	(0931)6311188 (0931)6312660	5,149	State-owned 國有	290,842	681(92)	826,922	c
Shanxi Yangquan Iron & Steel Co. 山西陽泉鋼鐵公司(1926)	Yangquan 陽泉市	Shanxi 山西省	(0353)2022880 (0353)2025235	5,524	State-owned 國有	286,939	-18963(705)	739,207	b
E Mei Ferro Alloy (Group) Co. Ltd. 峨眉鐵合金(集團)股份有限公司(1970)	Leshan 樂山市	Sichuan 四川省	(0833)5576169 (0833)5525357	5,146	Joint stock 股份制	272,063	16(395)	1,069,638	a,b,c

Top 10 Cities by Production Output 產出排名前 10 位城市	Province 省	Market share 市場份額	Number of firms 企業個數
Jilin 吉林市	Jilin 吉林省	9.45%	10
Shanghai 上海市	Shanghai 上海市	7.17%	27
Zunyi 遵義市	Guizhou 貴州省	5.78%	37
Jinzhou 錦州市	Liaoning 遼寧省	4.06%	4
Heshan 合山市	Guangxi 廣西	3.18%	6
Yangquan 陽泉市	Shanxi 山西省	2.92%	7
Leshan 樂山市	Sichuan 四川省	2.82%	12
Liaoyang 遼陽市	Liaoning 遼寧省	2.80%	5
Lingchuan 靈川縣	Guangxi 廣西	2.53%	16
Lanzhou 蘭州市	Gansu 甘肅省	2.50%	37

10 Major Wholesalers 10 家主要批發商	City 城市	Province 省	Telephone / Fax 電話 / 傳真
China Goods & Materials Storage & Transport Wuhan Company 中國物資儲運武漢公司	Wuhan 武漢市	Hubei 湖北省	(027)82821763 (027)82832856
China Light Industry Goods & Materials Supply & Marketing Hua Dong Company 中國輕工業物資供銷華東公司	Shanghai 上海市	Shanghai 上海市	(021)63216677 (021)63290262
Xinjiang Corps Products Group Company 新疆兵團物產集團公司	Urumqi 烏魯木齊市	Xinjiang 新疆	(0991)2841540
Anshan Iron & Steel Corporation Group International Economic Trade Company 鞍鋼集團國際經濟貿易公司	Anshan 鞍山市	Liaoning 遼寧省	(0412)6311645 (0412)6323413
Shanghai Pu Dong Goods & Materials General Company 上海浦東物資總公司	Shanghai 上海市	Shanghai 上海市	(021)58885013 (021)58889664
China Railway Goods & Materials Tianjin Company 中國鐵路物資天津公司	Tianjin 天津市	Tianjin 天津市	(022)24215754 (022)24215754
Wuhan Metal Material General Company 武漢市金屬材料總公司	Wuhan 武漢市	Hubei 湖北省	(027)82813443 (027)82818158
Jiangyin Steel Materials Supply & Marketing General Company 江陰市鋼材供銷總公司	Wuxi 無錫市	Jiangsu 江蘇省	(0510)6807676 (0510)6806909
Zhejiang Goods & Materials Development General Company 浙江物資開發總公司	Hangzhou 杭州市	Zhejiang 浙江省	(0571)7054562 (0571)5151675
China Metallurgy Import & Export Baotou Iron & Steel Company 中國冶金進出口包鋼公司	Baotou 包頭市	Inner Mong 內蒙	(0472)2185648 (0472)2183708

*Also include sales by firms outside this industry.包括本行業以外廠家的銷售。"o" stands for "others". "o" 代表 "其他產品"。

3410: Metal Structures 金屬結構製造業

The industry accounts for 0.208% of the total revenue of China's industrial sector in 1996. The revenue growth rate of the industry is 16.5% from 1995, as compared to the growth rate of China's industrial sector, 9.51%. The rate of return on asset is 2.09%. 73.56% of all firms in the industry made a profit while 20.47% had negative returns. The top province in terms of the industry's revenue is Jiangsu, accounting for 18.07% of the total revenue.
本行業在1996年佔全行業總產值0.208%，行業年增長率為16.5%（全國工業年增長率9.51%）。行業的資產回報率2.09%，73.56%的企業盈利，20.47%的企業虧損。銷售收入最高的省份為江蘇省，佔本行業的18.07%。

	Total number of firms 企業總數	Total number of employees 職工總數	Total revenue (mil. RMB) 總銷售收入（百萬元）	Total profit (mil. RMB) 總利潤（百萬元）	Return on assets 資產利潤率 (%)	Return on equity 權益利潤率 (%)	Labour productivity ('000 RMB / worker) 勞動生產率（千元/人）	Debts / assets 資產負債率 (%)	Total assets (mil. RMB) 總資產（百萬元）
Industry Overall 行業總體	2,187	209,313	12,052	333	2.09	5.96	57.58	64.85	15,911

	Number of firms 企業個數	Average number of employees 平均職工人數	Average revenue ('000 RMB) 平均銷售收入（千元）	Average profit ('000 RMB) 平均利潤（千元）	Return on assets 資產利潤率 (%)	Return on equity 權益利潤率 (%)	Labour productivity ('000 RMB / worker) 勞動生產率（千元/人）	Average debts / assets 平均資產負債率(%)	Average Total assets ('000 RMB) 平均總資產（千元）
By ownership 產業所有權									
State-owned 國有	280	149	7,539	-64	-0.43	-1.25	50.70	65.37	14,832
Collectively-owned 集體	1,696	88	4,452	115	2.48	8.13	50.51	69.55	4,656
Privately-owned 私有	10	57	2,957	-28	-1.29	-5.43	51.61	76.17	2,140
Domestic JVs 聯營	38	80	7,132	480	3.48	7.77	89.03	55.26	13,811
Joint stock 股份制	24	104	13,223	2,165	10.74	17.78	127.19	39.63	20,166
Foreign-funded 外資	65	120	17,580	706	2.96	6.15	147.10	51.89	23,873
Overseas Chinese-funded 港澳台資	70	75	8,342	397	2.38	6.53	111.72	63.50	16,668
By size 規模									
Large 大型	4	1,718	79,154	-13,348	-5.84	-16.67	46.08	64.98	228,673
Medium 中型	42	691	41,501	958	1.24	2.82	60.09	55.88	77,100
Small 小型	2,108	82	4,740	164	2.94	9.01	57.85	67.31	5,578
By regional distribution 地區分布									
Central-North 華北	527	82	3,608	116	2.07	6.31	43.91	67.25	5,622
Beijing 北京	307	38	1,775	28	0.76	2.92	46.37	74.10	3,691
Tianjin 天津	56	77	5,883	189	2.08	7.69	76.47	72.95	9,084
Hebei 河北	101	119	6,857	524	6.43	14.11	57.62	54.45	8,153
Shanxi 山西	34	403	8,245	-295	-2.28	-6.98	20.46	67.34	12,937
Inner Mongolia 內蒙	29	52	1,862	-29	-1.46	-4.13	35.48	64.72	1,990
Northeast 東北	392	81	3,522	-5	-0.11	-0.36	43.22	68.93	4,795
Liaoning 遼寧	294	75	3,401	2	0.04	0.12	45.62	65.93	4,278
Jilin 吉林	33	142	6,174	-226	-1.74	-6.00	43.62	71.05	12,993
Heilongjiang 黑龍江	65	82	2,726	74	2.50	15.48	33.06	83.83	2,969
Central East 華東	593	107	7,888	219	2.24	6.60	73.42	66.10	9,784
Shanghai 上海	137	84	8,734	289	2.30	6.68	104.50	65.55	12,569
Jiangsu 江蘇	191	150	11,403	343	2.63	7.88	76.01	66.67	13,071
Zhejiang 浙江	58	67	6,042	201	2.44	5.96	90.72	58.98	8,239
Anhui 安徽	48	85	3,585	-5	-0.13	-0.52	42.28	75.06	3,664
Fujian 福建	35	39	5,119	-70	-1.08	-2.91	132.32	62.78	6,491
Jiangxi 江西	30	119	1,708	-182	-3.59	-12.95	14.41	72.30	5,072
Shandong 山東	94	115	5,856	225	3.85	12.10	51.11	68.19	5,858
Central-South 中南	417	94	6,919	346	4.18	9.96	73.81	58.01	8,277
Henan 河南	91	74	2,596	9	0.32	1.18	34.96	73.07	2,799
Hubei 湖北	140	98	4,943	46	0.91	2.76	50.64	66.86	5,013
Hunan 湖南	38	102	7,183	411	5.31	19.75	70.35	73.12	7,731
Guangdong 廣東	126	103	12,827	954	5.86	11.63	124.59	49.61	16,266
Guangxi 廣西	20	86	2,939	-31	-0.45	-2.24	34.07	79.76	6,730
Hainan 海南	2	44	4,535	945	10.98	20.88	103.07	47.44	8,610
Southwest 西南	164	142	5,836	45	0.57	1.67	41.09	66.13	7,965
Chongqing 重慶	35	142	3,668	-3	-0.08	-0.20	25.86	60.71	3,187
Sichuan 四川	94	160	7,296	-93	-0.89	-2.69	45.64	67.16	10,563
Guizhou 貴州	16	43	1,514	18	1.68	3.77	34.95	55.42	1,078
Yunnan 雲南	19	137	6,193	-94	-0.97	-2.77	45.29	64.81	9,610
Tibet 西藏									
Northwest 西北	94	85	2,662	-78	-1.44	-4.09	31.41	64.74	5,415
Shaanxi 陝西	49	69	2,794	35	0.76	2.51	40.51	69.92	4,641
Gansu 甘肅	23	116	2,780	46	0.63	1.07	23.93	40.79	7,201
Qinghai 青海	5	94	3,250	-668	-10.24	-96.53	34.65	89.39	6,524
Ningxia 寧夏	5	64	1,040	-56	-2.39	-32.18	16.35	92.67	2,346
Xinjiang 新疆	12	94	2,329	-542	-9.08	-74.97	24.73	87.89	5,967

3410: Metal Structures 金屬結構製造業

Year 年份	Number of firms 企業個數	Rate of change 每年變化 (%)	Number of employees 職工人數 (人)	Rate of change 每年變化 (%)	Total revenue (mil. RMB) 總銷售收入 (百萬元)	Rate of change 每年變化 (%)	Total profit (mil. RMB) 總利潤 (百萬元)	Rate of change 每年變化 (%)
1993	1,476		184,646		8,046		362	
1994	1,712	15.99%	170,488	-7.67%	10,312	28.16%	341	-5.78%
1995	1,948	13.79%	193,751	13.64%	10,347	0.34%	241	-29.45%
1996	2,187	12.27%	209,313	8.03%	12,052	16.48%	333	38.36%

3 Major products* 3 種主要產品 *	Output 產量	Sales volume 銷售量	Unit 單位
a) Metal Structure Products 金屬結構製品	1,352,486	1,217,237	ton 噸
b) Welded Steel Pipe 焊接鋼管	149,148	135,725	ton 噸
c) Metal Window & Door 金屬門窗	79,313	74,554	ton 噸

Top 10 firms by revenue (year founded) 收入排名前 10 家企業 (創辦年份)	City 城市	Province 省	Telephone / fax 電話 / 傳真	Number of employees 職工人數	Ownership 產業所有權	Revenue ('000 RMB) 銷售收入 (千元)	Profit ('000 RMB) (rank) 利潤 (千元) (排名)	Total assets ('000 RMB) 總資產 (千元)	Major products 主要產品
Shenzhen Fang Da Industrial Co. Ltd. 深圳市方大實業股份有限公司(1994)	Shenzhen 深圳市	Guangdong 廣東省	(0755)6608572 (0755)6608353	444	Joint stock 股份制	242,472	114975(1)	457,544	a
Chengdu Iron Tower Factory 成都鐵塔廠(1958)	Chengdu 成都市	Sichuan 四川省	(028)4332123 (028)4334194	1,085	State-owned 國有	193,197	3137(37)	235,039	o
Jiangsu Yangzhou Buses Manufacturing General Factory Special Vehicle Factory 江蘇省揚州市客車製造總廠特種車輛廠(1993)	Yangzhou 揚州市	Jiangsu 江蘇省	(0514)7301898 (0514)7302878	998	Domestic JVs 聯營	171,743	10191(5)	90,888	o
Chengdu ShuangLiu Great Wall Metallurgy Enterprise Company 成都市雙流長城冶金企業公司	Chengdu 成都市	Sichuan 四川省	(028)5822280	1,200	Collectively-owned 集體	170,982	4081(30)	91,017	b
Xuzhou Fei Hong Net Frame Group Company 徐州飛虹網架集團公司(1973)	Xuzhou 徐州市	Jiangsu 江蘇省	(0516)5757965 (0516)5758184	846	State-owned 國有	167,804	6182(18)	310,869	a
Tianjin Hai Tong Industry & Trade General Company 天津市海通工貿總公司(1993)	Tianjin 天津市	Tianjin 天津市	(022)25990275	840	Collectively-owned 集體	162,760	5150(25)	188,590	b
Anshan Steel Tower Manufacturing General Plant 鞍山鐵塔製造總廠(1953)	Anshan 鞍山市	Liaoning 遼寧省	(0412)6211430 (0412)6211827	1,264	State-owned 國有	134,560	-32120(838)	303,170	a
Chenzhou Highway Engineering Machinery General Factory 郴州公路工程機械總廠(1958)	Chenzhou 郴州市	Hunan 湖南省	(0735)2255539	412	State-owned 國有	131,125	18095(2)	101,831	a
Zhe Jiangdong Nan Net Frame Group Co. Ltd. 浙江東南網架集團有限公司(1966)	Hangzhou 杭州市	Zhejiang 浙江省	(0571)2648318	856	Collectively-owned 集體	122,554	7084(13)	203,289	a
Fenxi Mine Administrative Bureau Industry & Trade General Company 汾西礦務局工貿總公司(1979)	Yuci 榆次市	Shanxi 山西省	(0354)3547191	9,031	Collectively-owned 集體	121,088	-8598(832)	198,637	o

Top 10 Cities by Production Output 產出排名前 10 位城市	Province 省	Market share 市場份額	Number of firms 企業個數
Shanghai 上海市	Shanghai 上海市	13.03%	278
Beijing 北京市	Beijing 北京市	6.35%	292
Wuhan 武漢市	Hubei 湖北省	4.69%	67
Wuxi 無錫市	Jiangsu 江蘇省	4.58%	85
Guangzhou 廣州市	Guangdong 廣東省	4.15%	117
Suzhou 蘇州市	Jiangsu 江蘇省	2.89%	109
Chengdu 成都市	Sichuan 四川省	2.64%	51
Dongguan 東莞市	Guangdong 廣東省	2.40%	6
Anshan 鞍山市	Liaoning 遼寧省	2.27%	51
Taizhou 泰州市	Jiangsu 江蘇省	1.95%	30

10 Major Wholesalers 10 家主要批發商	City 城市	Province 省	Telephone / Fax 電話 / 傳真
China Goods & Materials Storage & Transport Wuhan Company 中國物資儲運武漢公司	Wuhan 武漢市	Hubei 湖北省	(027)82821763 (027)82832856
China Light Industry Goods & Materials Supply & Marketing Hua Dong Company 中國輕工業物資供銷華東公司	Shanghai 上海市	Shanghai 上海市	(021)63216677 (021)63290262
Xinjiang Corps Products Group Company 新疆兵團物產集團公司	Urumqi 烏魯木齊市	Xinjiang 新疆	(0991)2841540
Anshan Iron & Steel Corporation Group International Economic Trade Company 鞍鋼集團國際經濟貿易公司	Anshan 鞍山市	Liaoning 遼寧省	(0412)6311645 (0412)6323413
Shanghai Pu Dong Goods & Materials General Company 上海浦東物資總公司	Shanghai 上海市	Shanghai 上海市	(021)58885013 (021)58889664
China Railway Goods & Materials Tianjin Company 中國鐵路物資天津公司	Tianjin 天津市	Tianjin 天津市	(022)24215754 (022)24215754
Wuhan Metal Material General Company 武漢市金屬材料總公司	Wuhan 武漢市	Hubei 湖北省	(027)82813443 (027)82818158
Jiangyin Steel Materials Supply & Marketing General Company 江陰市鋼材供銷總公司	Wuxi 無錫市	Jiangsu 江蘇省	(0510)6807676 (0510)6806909
Zhejiang Goods & Materials Development General Company 浙江物資開發總公司	Hangzhou 杭州市	Zhejiang 浙江省	(0571)7054562 (0571)5151675
China Metallurgy Import & Export Baotou Iron & Steel Company 中國冶金進出口包鋼公司	Baotou 包頭市	Inner Mong 內蒙	(0472)2185648 (0472)2183708

*Also include sales by firms outside this industry.包括本行業以外廠家的銷售。"o" stands for "others". "o" 代表 "其他產品"。

3420: Cast Iron Pipe 鑄鐵管製造業

The industry accounts for 0.108% of the total revenue of China's industrial sector in 1996. The revenue growth rate of the industry is 23.0% from 1995, as compared to the growth rate of China's industrial sector, 9.51%. The rate of return on asset is 1.83%. 70.58% of all firms in the industry made a profit while 22.88% had negative returns. The top province in terms of the industry's revenue is Jiangsu, accounting for 13.67% of the total revenue.
本行業在1996年佔全行業總產值0.108%，行業年增長率為23.0%（全國工業年增長率9.51%）。行業的資產回報率1.83%，70.58%的企業盈利，22.88%的企業虧損。銷售收入最高的省份為江蘇省，佔本行業的13.67%。

	Total number of firms 企業總數	Total number of employees 職工總數	Total revenue (mil. RMB) 總銷售收入（百萬元）	Total profit (mil. RMB) 總利潤（百萬元）	Return on assets 資產利潤率 (%)	Return on equity 權益利潤率 (%)	Labour productivity ('000 RMB / worker) 勞動生產率（千元/人）	Debts / assets 資產負債率 (%)	Total assets (mil. RMB) 總資產（百萬元）
Industry Overall 行業總體	1,141	95,762	6,273	130	1.83	7.17	65.51	74.54	7,121

	Number of firms 企業個數	Average number of employees 平均職工人數	Average revenue ('000 RMB) 平均銷售收入（千元）	Average profit ('000 RMB) 平均利潤（千元）	Return on assets 資產利潤率 (%)	Return on equity 權益利潤率 (%)	Labour productivity ('000 RMB / worker) 勞動生產率（千元/人）	Average debts / assets 平均資產負債率(%)	Average Total assets ('000 RMB) 平均總資產（千元）
By ownership 產業所有權									
State-owned 國有	93	190	6,720	-312	-1.78	-13.36	35.40	86.69	17,527
Collectively-owned 集體	975	69	4,777	176	4.71	17.22	69.07	72.67	3,746
Privately-owned 私有	4	34	2,300	107	5.32	6.55	67.14	18.77	2,017
Domestic JVs 聯營	9	42	3,676	270	3.91	6.39	87.29	38.83	6,905
Joint stock 股份制	21	200	15,675	94	0.38	1.60	78.49	76.42	24,759
Foreign-funded 外資	16	116	10,302	-854	-2.38	-4.34	88.52	45.28	35,909
Overseas Chinese-funded 港澳台資	21	208	21,279	-170	-0.53	-3.05	102.19	82.56	31,911
By size 規模									
Large 大型	1	1,567	195,309	181	0.06	2.73	124.64	97.78	297,840
Medium 中型	9	866	66,159	-31	-0.03	-0.18	76.41	83.05	102,121
Small 小型	1,118	77	4,904	116	2.20	7.88	63.66	72.04	5,281
By regional distribution 地區分布									
Central-North 華北	199	105	4,525	94	1.59	8.61	43.14	81.48	5,883
Beijing 北京	23	130	4,388	-273	-3.54	-33.64	33.79	89.49	7,722
Tianjin 天津	4	55	1,498	-78	-3.35	-24.03	27.35	86.07	2,315
Hebei 河北	71	122	7,367	375	5.18	33.09	60.26	84.35	7,236
Shanxi 山西	67	89	2,988	79	1.73	6.23	33.53	72.28	4,546
Inner Mongolia 內蒙	34	89	2,069	-194	-3.99	-20.61	23.31	80.65	4,869
Northeast 東北	150	77	4,190	86	1.65	9.62	54.26	82.80	5,188
Liaoning 遼寧	71	95	5,056	8	0.10	1.08	53.46	90.43	7,644
Jilin 吉林	30	67	3,986	263	5.07	15.02	59.61	66.24	5,180
Heilongjiang 黑龍江	49	58	3,061	91	5.54	15.08	52.39	63.27	1,636
Central East 華東	310	85	7,864	302	3.99	13.01	92.09	69.32	7,569
Shanghai 上海	8	193	25,855	279	0.89	3.92	134.05	77.34	31,356
Jiangsu 江蘇	68	114	12,614	427	4.88	16.35	110.52	70.13	8,750
Zhejiang 浙江	43	49	7,889	500	7.11	25.47	161.01	72.07	7,021
Anhui 安徽	41	149	11,245	842	8.17	36.78	75.26	77.80	10,316
Fujian 福建	42	25	1,717	48	3.59	5.50	69.48	34.72	1,326
Jiangxi 江西	51	32	1,158	1	0.07	0.70	36.11	90.13	1,134
Shandong 山東	57	110	7,749	76	0.66	1.64	70.56	59.98	11,617
Central-South 中南	289	80	6,450	73	1.00	3.84	80.14	73.99	7,270
Henan 河南	66	74	4,286	229	5.04	17.69	57.81	71.50	4,538
Hubei 湖北	82	102	6,938	250	3.99	28.29	68.14	85.90	6,269
Hunan 湖南	75	60	3,712	57	1.99	10.71	62.28	81.41	2,846
Guangdong 廣東	37	91	16,058	-482	-1.99	-5.83	177.09	65.82	24,194
Guangxi 廣西	25	71	3,247	-98	-1.81	-8.66	46.04	79.05	5,378
Hainan 海南	4	107	14,600	355	3.20	9.67	136.13	66.88	11,090
Southwest 西南	106	67	2,097	-92	-2.78	-9.48	31.30	70.69	3,327
Chongqing 重慶	28	80	1,598	3	0.11	0.42	19.96	74.22	2,648
Sichuan 四川	42	68	2,565	-138	-3.93	-15.01	37.62	73.83	3,518
Guizhou 貴州	23	39	1,549	-58	-2.42	-7.17	40.08	66.16	2,403
Yunnan 雲南	13	86	2,656	-215	-3.69	-10.38	30.83	64.46	5,840
Tibet 西藏									
Northwest 西北	87	74	2,524	-73	-1.70	-6.83	33.92	75.07	4,275
Shaanxi 陝西	41	73	2,080	-100	-2.26	-7.52	28.53	69.93	4,441
Gansu 甘肅	23	63	3,738	117	3.65	9.86	59.50	63.04	3,207
Qinghai 青海	1	437	14,470	-1,790	-5.03	-19.02	33.11	73.54	35,560
Ningxia 寧夏	7	25	1,383	101	6.76	17.97	55.63	62.38	1,500
Xinjiang 新疆	15	95	1,611	-255	-5.46	143.61	16.91	103.80	4,668

3420: Cast Iron Pipe 鑄鐵管製造業

Year 年份	Number of firms 企業個數	Rate of change 每年變化 (%)	Number of employees 職工人數 (人)	Rate of change 每年變化 (%)	Total revenue (mil. RMB) 總銷售收入 (百萬元)	Rate of change 每年變化 (%)	Total profit (mil. RMB) 總利潤 (百萬元)	Rate of change 每年變化 (%)
1993	1,049		88,423		4,147		164	
1994	1,124	7.15%	100,216	13.34%	4,949	19.33%	97	-40.59%
1995	1,130	0.53%	98,984	-1.23%	5,099	3.04%	75	-23.03%
1996	1,141	0.97%	95,762	-3.26%	6,273	23.02%	130	73.72%

3 Major products* 3 種主要產品 *	Output 產量	Sales volume 銷售量	Unit 單位
a) Cast Iorn Pipe 鑄鐵管	1,881,735	1,561,840	ton 噸
b) Remade Steels 改製鋼材	59,224	55,078	ton 噸
c) Iron Casting 鑄鐵件	45,553	44,642	ton 噸

Top 10 firms by revenue (year founded) 收入排名前 10 家企業 (創辦年份)	City 城市	Province 省	Telephone / fax 電話 / 傳真	Number of employees 職工人數	Ownership 產業所有權	Revenue ('000 RMB) 銷售收入 (千元)	Profit ('000 RMB) (rank) 利潤 (千元) (排名)	Total assets ('000 RMB) 總資產 (千元)	Major products 主要產品
Zhanjiang Shang Zhan Steel Tube Co. Ltd. 湛江上湛鋼管有限公司(1992)	Zhanjiang 湛江市	Guangdong 廣東省	(0758)2300171	223	Overseas Chinese-funded 港澳台資	230,830	-8093(428)	244,216	o
Dalian Cheerglory Cast Iron Pipe Co. Ltd. 大連企榮鑄鐵管有限公司(1989)	Dalian 大連市	Liaoning 遼寧省	(0411)6671526 (0411)6671721	1,615	Overseas Chinese-funded 港澳台資	182,054	61(235)	303,495	o
Xinle Xie Shen Xiang Repair & Assembly Factory 新樂市協神鄉修配廠(1984)	Shijiazhuang 石家莊市	Hebei 河北省		1,210	Collectively-owned 集體	121,350	12120(2)	21,000	o
Yuyao Steel Tube Factory 余姚市鋼管廠(1993)	Ningbo 寧波市	Zhejiang 浙江省	(0574)2465383	74	Collectively-owned 集體	116,435	6986(5)	43,221	o
Zhangjiagang Galvanization Factory 張家港市鍍鋅廠(1980)	Suzhou 蘇州市	Jiangsu 江蘇省	(0512)8490347	221	Collectively-owned 集體	111,000	5880(7)	25,400	o
Hefei Cast Tube Plant 合肥市鑄管廠(1972)	Hefei 合肥市	Anhui 安徽省	(0551)4484561	247	Collectively-owned 集體	105,270	15663(1)	27,722	o
Nanhai Song Gang Stainless Steel Products Co. Ltd. 南海市松崗不銹鋼製品有限公司(1989)	Foshan 佛山市	Guangdong 廣東省	(0757)5228848 (0757)6522818	350	Overseas Chinese-funded 港澳台資	89,954	0(334)	26,470	o
Laohekou Casting Factory 老河口市鑄造廠(1968)	Xiangfan 襄樊市	Hubei 湖北省	(0710)8223606	80	Collectively-owned 集體	83,210	6780(6)	2,580	c
Jiangsu Jianhu Cast Tube Factory 江蘇省建湖鑄管廠(1993)	Yancheng 鹽城市	Jiangsu 江蘇省	(0515)6210494	747	Collectively-owned 集體	81,710	2500(18)	55,860	c
Nanjing Jin Tong Cast Tube Industrial Co. Ltd. 南京金通鑄管實業有限公司(1975)	Nanjing 南京市	Jiangsu 江蘇省	(025)2295720	290	Collectively-owned 集體	73,500	2260(22)	25,700	a,c

Top 10 Cities by Production Output 產出排名前 10 位城市	Province 省	Market share 市場份額	Number of firms 企業個數
Suzhou 蘇州市	Jiangsu 江蘇省	7.15%	43
Shanghai 上海市	Shanghai 上海市	4.70%	33
Ji'nan 濟南市	Shandong 山東省	3.51%	9
Nanjing 南京市	Jiangsu 江蘇省	3.28%	18
Shijiazhuang 石家莊市	Hebei 河北省	2.85%	14
Benxi 本溪市	Liaoning 遼寧省	2.73%	6
Ningbo 寧波市	Zhejiang 浙江省	2.46%	3
Loudi 婁底市	Hunan 湖南省	2.33%	10
Weifang 濰坊市	Shandong 山東省	2.32%	11
Dalian 大連市	Liaoning 遼寧省	2.31%	8

10 Major Wholesalers 10 家主要批發商	City 城市	Province 省	Telephone / Fax 電話 / 傳真
China Goods & Materials Storage & Transport Wuhan Company 中國物資儲運武漢公司	Wuhan 武漢市	Hubei 湖北省	(027)82821763 (027)82832856
China Light Industry Goods & Materials Supply & Marketing Hua Dong Company 中國輕工業物資供銷華東公司	Shanghai 上海市	Shanghai 上海市	(021)63216677 (021)63290262
Xinjiang Corps Products Group Company 新疆兵團物產集團公司	Urumqi 烏魯木齊市	Xinjiang 新疆	(0991)2841540
Anshan Iron & Steel Corporation Group International Economic Trade Company 鞍鋼集團國際經濟貿易公司	Anshan 鞍山市	Liaoning 遼寧省	(0412)6311645 (0412)6323413
Shanghai Pu Dong Goods & Materials General Company 上海浦東物資總公司	Shanghai 上海市	Shanghai 上海市	(021)58885013 (021)58889664
China Railway Goods & Materials Tianjin Company 中國鐵路物資天津公司	Tianjin 天津市	Tianjin 天津市	(022)24215754 (022)24215754
Wuhan Metal Material General Company 武漢市金屬材料總公司	Wuhan 武漢市	Hubei 湖北省	(027)82813443 (027)82818158
Jiangyin Steel Materials Supply & Marketing General Company 江陰市鋼材供銷總公司	Wuxi 無錫市	Jiangsu 江蘇省	(0510)6807676 (0510)6806909
Zhejiang Goods & Materials Development General Company 浙江物資開發總公司	Hangzhou 杭州市	Zhejiang 浙江省	(0571)7054562 (0571)5151675
China Metallurgy Import & Export Baotou Iron & Steel Company 中國冶金進出口包鋼公司	Baotou 包頭市	Inner Mong 內蒙	(0472)2185648 (0472)2183708

*Also include sales by firms outside this industry.包括本行業以外廠家的銷售。"o" stands for "others". "o" 代表"其他產品"。

3431: Cutting Tools 切削工具製造業

The industry accounts for 0.089% of the total revenue of China's industrial sector in 1996. The revenue growth rate of the industry is 10.4% from 1995, as compared to the growth rate of China's industrial sector, 9.51%. The rate of return on asset is -0.38%. 72.27% of all firms in the industry made a profit while 24.17% had negative returns. The top province in terms of the industry's revenue is Shanghai, accounting for 14.87% of the total revenue.
本行業在1996年佔全行業總產值0.089%，行業年增長率為10.4%（全國工業年增長率9.51%）。行業的資產回報率-0.38%，72.27%的企業盈利，24.17%的企業虧損。銷售收入最高的省份為上海市，佔本行業的14.87%。

	Total number of firms 企業總數	Total number of employees 職工總數	Total revenue (mil. RMB) 總銷售收入（百萬元）	Total profit (mil. RMB) 總利潤（百萬元）	Return on assets 資產利潤率 (%)	Return on equity 權益利潤率 (%)	Labour productivity ('000 RMB / worker) 勞動生產率（千元/人）	Debts / assets 資產負債率 (%)	Total assets (mil. RMB) 總資產（百萬元）
Industry Overall 行業總體	885	139,001	5,184	-38	-0.38	-1.40	37.29	73.07	10,150

	Number of firms 企業個數	Average number of employees 平均職工人數	Average revenue ('000 RMB) 平均銷售收入（千元）	Average profit ('000 RMB) 平均利潤（千元）	Return on assets 資產利潤率 (%)	Return on equity 權益利潤率 (%)	Labour productivity ('000 RMB / worker) 勞動生產率（千元/人）	Average debts / assets 平均資產負債率(%)	Average Total assets ('000 RMB) 平均總資產（千元）
By ownership 產業所有權									
State-owned 國有	143	540	13,063	-692	-1.59	-6.84	24.17	76.75	43,517
Collectively-owned 集體	633	82	3,967	68	1.64	5.68	48.33	71.13	4,119
Privately-owned 私有	5	33	2,320	37	2.13	4.21	70.73	49.43	1,731
Domestic JVs 聯營	16	230	8,085	29	0.19	0.51	35.18	62.69	15,289
Joint stock 股份制	13	54	2,052	24	0.69	1.39	38.17	50.36	3,490
Foreign-funded 外資	37	75	7,933	114	0.70	2.15	105.09	67.46	16,260
Overseas Chinese-funded 港澳台資	34	68	9,719	379	3.21	6.18	142.93	47.97	11,781
By size 規模									
Large 大型	10	3,334	112,305	351	0.10	0.40	33.69	74.84	350,434
Medium 中型	40	839	25,059	57	0.09	0.36	29.87	75.52	64,777
Small 小型	816	88	3,748	-54	-1.08	-3.60	42.61	69.99	4,969
By regional distribution 地區分布									
Central-North 華北	157	126	4,648	79	0.82	3.30	36.90	75.25	9,627
Beijing 北京	49	44	1,030	10	0.31	1.09	23.42	71.19	3,175
Tianjin 天津	31	172	3,820	-217	-1.48	-15.19	22.26	90.26	14,653
Hebei 河北	56	109	7,426	333	3.23	10.20	67.95	68.34	10,323
Shanxi 山西	18	324	7,796	-4	-0.02	-0.07	24.04	68.46	17,268
Inner Mongolia 內蒙	3	114	1,567	-10	-0.24	-0.78	13.70	69.55	4,237
Northeast 東北	138	242	4,799	-263	-1.52	-7.05	19.84	78.51	17,347
Liaoning 遼寧	71	120	2,640	-38	-0.64	-2.47	21.98	74.00	5,949
Jilin 吉林	14	197	2,333	-669	-6.19	69.25	11.84	108.93	10,821
Heilongjiang 黑龍江	53	417	8,341	-456	-1.33	-5.79	20.01	77.02	34,339
Central East 華東	334	118	6,100	128	1.64	5.78	51.76	71.70	7,826
Shanghai 上海	55	189	14,013	577	3.79	17.62	74.02	78.49	15,225
Jiangsu 江蘇	116	106	5,414	14	0.19	0.54	51.11	64.30	7,167
Zhejiang 浙江	52	103	4,174	-58	-0.80	-2.75	40.36	70.80	7,179
Anhui 安徽	25	90	5,600	480	20.61	47.38	62.03	56.50	2,331
Fujian 福建	25	36	1,982	54	1.06	2.80	55.19	62.18	5,067
Jiangxi 江西	20	188	2,583	74	1.05	9.07	13.77	88.44	7,053
Shandong 山東	41	107	4,399	-58	-0.97	-3.71	41.16	73.89	5,996
Central-South 中南	154	106	6,532	-107	-1.13	-3.93	61.46	71.23	9,444
Henan 河南	31	45	2,364	175	6.21	17.52	52.22	64.53	2,820
Hubei 湖北	29	116	5,893	160	2.41	7.71	50.76	68.70	6,621
Hunan 湖南	37	172	2,314	-150	-2.82	-12.34	13.45	77.17	5,335
Guangdong 廣東	41	100	16,028	-401	-1.84	-6.63	160.31	72.25	21,824
Guangxi 廣西	14	67	1,144	-309	-6.25	-15.96	17.08	60.87	4,939
Hainan 海南	2	99	1,510	-95	-1.39	-2.71	15.33	48.91	6,850
Southwest 西南	69	264	6,499	-234	-1.26	-3.38	24.65	62.73	18,595
Chongqing 重慶	14	155	3,292	430	5.55	14.21	21.22	60.95	7,761
Sichuan 四川	45	277	7,678	-467	-2.10	-5.57	27.70	62.26	22,209
Guizhou 貴州	7	332	5,356	89	0.56	1.55	16.11	64.05	15,879
Yunnan 雲南	3	412	6,630	-650	-2.97	-10.08	16.09	70.56	21,897
Tibet 西藏									
Northwest 西北	33	361	9,101	-745	-2.75	-11.81	25.20	76.70	27,082
Shaanxi 陝西	25	341	7,894	-743	-3.01	-14.81	23.18	79.69	24,696
Gansu 甘肅	4	434	5,635	-1,508	-6.14	-17.72	12.98	65.34	24,538
Qinghai 青海	2	822	31,325	145	0.20	0.80	38.13	74.72	71,500
Ningxia 寧夏									
Xinjiang 新疆	2	12	8,900	-140	-0.80	-2.22	773.91	64.04	17,575

3431: Cutting Tools 切削工具製造業

Year 年份	Number of firms 企業個數	Rate of change 每年變化 (%)	Number of employees 職工人數 (人)	Rate of change 每年變化 (%)	Total revenue (mil. RMB) 總銷售收入 (百萬元)	Rate of change 每年變化 (%)	Total profit (mil. RMB) 總利潤 (百萬元)	Rate of change 每年變化 (%)
1993	636		144,279		4,111		205	
1994	685	7.70%	134,219	-6.97%	4,550	10.68%	174	-15.24%
1995	870	27.01%	146,675	9.28%	4,694	3.16%	72	-58.46%
1996	885	1.72%	139,001	-5.23%	5,184	10.44%	-38	-152.63%

3 Major products* 3 種主要產品 *	Output 產量	Sales volume 銷售量	Unit 單位
a) Metal Cutting Tool 金屬切削工具	129,708	132,302	10,000 piece 萬件
b) Measuring Instrument 量具	3,432,347	3,672,612	piece 件
c) Remade Steels 改製鋼材	232,288	216,028	ton 噸

Top 10 firms by revenue (year founded) 收入排名前 10 家企業 (創辦年份)	City 城市	Province 省	Telephone / fax 電話 / 傳真	Number of employees 職工人數	Ownership 產業所有權	Revenue ('000 RMB) 銷售收入 (千元)	Profit ('000 RMB) (rank) 利潤 (千元) (排名)	Total assets ('000 RMB) 總資產 (千元)	Major products 主要產品
Bao Ling Tong Li Co. Ltd. 寶菱同利有限公司(1988)	Shenzhen 深圳市	Guangdong 廣東省	(0755)7803456 (0755)7803455	150	Foreign-funded 外資	482,373	-12824(363)	499,715	c
Shanghai Zheng Feng Industrial Co. Ltd. 上海正峯電器有限公司(1993)	Shanghai 上海市	Shanghai 上海市	(021)64193480 (021)64190055	325	Overseas Chinese-funded 港澳台資	276,450	20410(1)	26,625	o
Shanghai Machinery & Measuring Tool General Co. 上海機械工具量具總公司(1949)	Shanghai 上海市	Shanghai 上海市	(021)65038055 (021)65411877	3,219	State-owned 國有	212,953	1752(17)	349,759	a
Chengdu Cheng Liang Group Co. 成都成量集團公司(1957)	Chengdu 成都市	Sichuan 四川省	(028)3331923 (028)3333941	6,213	State-owned 國有	146,206	-7177(362)	690,347	a,b
Harbin Measuring and Cutting Tools Plant 哈爾濱量具刃具廠(1955)	Harbin 哈爾濱市	Heilongjiang 黑龍江省	(0451)2623021 (0451)2623555	6,650	State-owned 國有	140,320	501(80)	635,053	a,b
Shanghai Yu Suo Hardware Tools Co. Ltd. 上海鈺梭五金工具有限公司(1996)	Shanghai 上海市	Shanghai 上海市		80	Overseas Chinese-funded 港澳台資	130,176	159(160)	6,697	o
Harbin No.1 Tool Factory 哈爾濱第一工具廠(1948)	Harbin 哈爾濱市	Heilongjiang 黑龍江省	(0451)8350840 (0451)8351595	5,399	State-owned 國有	122,948	-22719(365)	673,635	a
Han Jiang Tools Factory 漢江工具廠(1974)	Hanzhong 漢中市	Shaanxi 陝西省	(0916)2206010 (0916)2206555	2,954	State-owned 國有	96,643	500(82)	244,480	a
Shanxi Taihang Saw Blade Factory 山西省太行鋸條廠(1956)	Changzhi 長治市	Shanxi 山西省	(0355)5052152 (0355)5052480	2,562	Collectively-owned 集體	85,670	0(272)	167,847	a
Jiangyin Cheng Gong Group Company 江陰市澄工集團公司(1972)	Wuxi 無錫市	Jiangsu 江蘇省	(0510)6805117 (0510)6803999	281	Collectively-owned 集體	67,447	1372(27)	27,323	o

Top 10 Cities by Production Output 產出排名前 10 位城市	Province 省	Market share 市場份額	Number of firms 企業個數
Shanghai 上海市	Shanghai 上海市	12.58%	91
Harbin 哈爾濱市	Heilongjiang 黑龍江省	6.05%	27
Hangzhou 杭州市	Zhejiang 浙江省	5.73%	16
Chengdu 成都市	Sichuan 四川省	4.42%	32
Xingtai 邢臺市	Hebei 河北省	4.16%	16
Beijing 北京市	Beijing 北京市	3.33%	42
Zhenjiang 鎮江市	Jiangsu 江蘇省	3.13%	39
Tianjin 天津市	Tianjin 天津市	2.88%	34
Hanzhong 漢中市	Shaanxi 陝西省	2.43%	4
Suzhou 蘇州市	Jiangsu 江蘇省	2.32%	25

10 Major Wholesalers 10 家主要批發商	City 城市	Province 省	Telephone / Fax 電話 / 傳真
Liaoning Automobile Trade Group Corp. 遼寧省汽車貿易集團	Shenyang 瀋陽市	Liaoning 遼寧省	(024)23835494 (024)23838338
China Post and Telecommunication Equipment General Company 中國郵電器材總公司	Beijing 北京市	Beijing 北京市	(010)63523715 (010)63525935
Jiangsu Electromechanical Products General Company 江蘇省機電產品總公司	Nanjing 南京市	Jiangsu 江蘇省	(025)7713642 (025)7711036
Xi Nan Technology Import & Export Company 西南技術進出口公司	Chongqing 重慶市	Chongqing 重慶市	(023)63850185 (023)63850026
Changzhou Economic Technology Industrial Development Zone Tian Ming Trade Company 常州經濟技術產業開發區天明貿易公司	Changzhou 常州市	Jiangsu 江蘇省	(0519)8829882 (0519)8829882
Shanxi Mechanical Equipment Import & Export Company 山西省機械設備進出口公司	Taiyuan 太原市	Shanxi 山西省	(0351)4040713 (0351)4043981
Ningbo Five Mining Machinery Import & Export Company 寧波市五礦機械進出口公司	Ningbo 寧波市	Zhejiang 浙江省	(0574)7311255 (0574)7320322
Tianjin Jin Huan Electromechanical Complete Sets of Equipment Factory 天津市津環機電成套設備廠	Tianjin 天津市	Tianjin 天津市	(022)26371628
Yunnan Machinery Import & Export Company 雲南省機械進出口公司	Kunming 昆明市	Yunnan 雲南省	(0871)3164879 (0871)3136829
Tianjin Da Qiu Zhuang Yi Yuan Trade Center 天津市大丘莊億源商貿中心	Tianjin 天津市	Tianjin 天津市	(022)28899478 (022)28899046

*Also include sales by firms outside this industry.包括本行業以外廠家的銷售。"o" stands for "others". "o" 代表 "其他產品"。

3434: Moulds 模具製造業

The industry accounts for 0.061% of the total revenue of China's industrial sector in 1996. The revenue growth rate of the industry is 18.7% from 1995, as compared to the growth rate of China's industrial sector, 9.51%. The rate of return on asset is 1.17%. 69.65% of all firms in the industry made a profit while 24.52% had negative returns. The top province in terms of the industry's revenue is Guangdong, accounting for 27.73% of the total revenue.
本行業在1996年佔全行業總產值0.061%，行業年增長率為18.7%（全國工業年增長率9.51%）。行業的資產回報率1.17%，69.65%的企業盈利，24.52%的企業虧損。銷售收入最高的省份為廣東省，佔本行業的27.73%。

	Total number of firms 企業總數	Total number of employees 職工總數	Total revenue (mil. RMB) 總銷售收入（百萬元）	Total profit (mil. RMB) 總利潤（百萬元）	Return on assets 資產利潤率 (%)	Return on equity 權益利潤率 (%)	Labour productivity ('000 RMB / worker) 勞動生產率（千元/人）	Debts / assets 資產負債率 (%)	Total assets (mil. RMB) 總資產（百萬元）
Industry Overall 行業總體	1,295	78,334	3,560	75	1.17	3.12	45.45	62.62	6,446

	Number of firms 企業個數	Average number of employees 平均職工人數	Average revenue ('000 RMB) 平均銷售收入（千元）	Average profit ('000 RMB) 平均利潤（千元）	Return on assets 資產利潤率 (%)	Return on equity 權益利潤率 (%)	Labour productivity ('000 RMB / worker) 勞動生產率（千元/人）	Average debts / assets 平均資產負債率(%)	Average Total assets ('000 RMB) 平均總資產（千元）
By ownership 產業所有權									
State-owned 國有	164	127	3,530	-226	-1.80	-7.74	27.85	76.72	12,518
Collectively-owned 集體	899	47	1,996	61	2.79	7.77	42.07	64.08	2,174
Privately-owned 私有	7	20	1,164	15	0.61	1.06	59.50	42.54	2,534
Domestic JVs 聯營	18	89	4,314	347	4.26	10.36	48.35	58.86	8,146
Joint stock 股份制	16	92	7,960	803	6.22	22.09	86.88	71.86	12,908
Foreign-funded 外資	60	97	7,321	596	3.78	7.55	75.12	49.89	15,759
Overseas Chinese-funded 港澳台資	127	55	4,149	20	0.22	0.40	75.64	44.22	8,729
By size 規模									
Large 大型	2	385	48,232	7,221	4.55	11.75	125.28	61.28	158,698
Medium 中型	26	454	19,664	287	0.50	1.84	43.28	72.67	56,947
Small 小型	1,235	53	2,391	43	1.14	2.82	45.12	59.50	3,763
By regional distribution 地區分布									
Central-North 華北	275	46	1,463	-67	-1.95	-4.72	31.61	58.68	3,415
Beijing 北京	102	24	626	14	1.06	3.29	25.81	67.69	1,290
Tianjin 天津	101	52	1,205	-331	-5.97	-14.12	22.96	57.69	5,538
Hebei 河北	51	69	3,975	337	11.03	23.24	58.01	52.54	3,058
Shanxi 山西	9	102	676	-333	-8.78	100.67	6.59	108.72	3,796
Inner Mongolia 內蒙	12	45	663	-43	-0.89	-1.37	14.75	34.80	4,845
Northeast 東北	178	63	2,085	21	0.58	1.51	33.33	62.00	3,614
Liaoning 遼寧	124	61	2,296	50	1.27	3.25	37.71	60.97	3,898
Jilin 吉林	24	76	1,283	-115	-2.92	-12.87	16.83	77.28	3,947
Heilongjiang 黑龍江	30	59	1,856	11	0.51	0.96	31.70	47.42	2,175
Central East 華東	472	62	3,088	131	2.78	7.70	49.80	63.83	4,694
Shanghai 上海	72	73	2,620	160	2.45	8.32	36.01	70.55	6,539
Jiangsu 江蘇	89	64	4,758	61	1.03	2.42	74.57	57.40	5,920
Zhejiang 浙江	135	47	1,985	13	0.42	1.30	42.17	67.87	3,023
Anhui 安徽	27	136	6,313	297	3.58	13.71	46.49	73.85	8,289
Fujian 福建	56	44	2,671	343	8.55	15.53	61.39	44.96	4,017
Jiangxi 江西	13	42	981	18	1.44	6.73	23.10	78.64	1,232
Shandong 山東	80	67	3,058	194	4.49	12.78	45.81	64.83	4,316
Central-South 中南	261	67	4,397	111	1.28	3.35	65.39	61.93	8,710
Henan 河南	45	37	1,388	4	0.17	0.38	37.06	55.26	2,499
Hubei 湖北	27	75	1,835	57	1.49	4.25	24.57	65.10	3,815
Hunan 湖南	23	70	1,666	-127	-2.91	-8.67	23.78	66.42	4,359
Guangdong 廣東	160	74	6,170	195	1.61	4.19	83.07	61.64	12,146
Guangxi 廣西	6	59	1,672	-162	-6.76	-9700.00	28.33	99.93	2,390
Hainan 海南									
Southwest 西南	84	77	1,885	-16	-0.40	-1.43	24.40	72.11	4,078
Chongqing 重慶	20	44	825	-17	-0.79	-1.63	18.85	51.72	2,143
Sichuan 四川	51	97	2,647	-23	-0.40	-1.64	27.17	75.65	5,660
Guizhou 貴州	11	47	471	-10	-1.19	-3.37	9.98	64.75	838
Yunnan 雲南	2	58	1,210	130	8.07	18.06	21.04	55.28	1,610
Tibet 西藏									
Northwest 西北	25	46	931	20	1.58	3.36	20.05	52.97	1,267
Shaanxi 陝西	16	37	861	30	3.92	9.80	23.16	60.03	766
Gansu 甘肅	5	105	1,668	4	0.11	0.21	15.89	46.74	3,654
Qinghai 青海									
Ningxia 寧夏	1								
Xinjiang 新疆	3	14	387				28.29	76.52	383

3434: Moulds 模具製造業

Year 年份	Number of firms 企業個數	Rate of change 每年變化 (%)	Number of employees 職工人數 (人)	Rate of change 每年變化 (%)	Total revenue (mil. RMB) 總銷售收入 (百萬元)	Rate of change 每年變化 (%)	Total profit (mil. RMB) 總利潤 (百萬元)	Rate of change 每年變化 (%)
1993	1,017		105,444		2,537		135	
1994	1,155	13.57%	80,287	-23.86%	2,824	11.32%	69	-49.16%
1995	1,216	5.28%	84,332	5.04%	2,999	6.20%	95	38.51%
1996	1,295	6.50%	78,334	-7.11%	3,560	18.71%	75	-21.39%

3 Major products* 3種主要產品*	Output 產量	Sales volume 銷售量	Unit 單位
a) Mould 模具	3,102,787	3,102,787	set 套
b) Abrasive Tool 磨具	46,833	45,897	ton 噸
c) Abradant 磨料	8,187	7,778	ton 噸

Top 10 firms by revenue (year founded) 收入排名前10家企業 (創辦年份)	City 城市	Province 省	Telephone / fax 電話 / 傳真	Number of employees 職工人數	Ownership 產業所有權	Revenue ('000 RMB) 銷售收入 (千元)	Profit ('000 RMB) (rank) 利潤 (千元) (排名)	Total assets ('000 RMB) 總資產 (千元)	Major products 主要產品
China The Second Abrasive Wheel Factory's Shenzhen Associated Corp. 第二砂輪廠深圳聯合公司(1984)	Shenzhen 深圳市	Guangdong 廣東省	(0755)5530025 (0755)5530238	397	State-owned 國有	91,991	6396(6)	99,581	b,c
Punch Industry (Dalian) Co. Ltd. 盤起工業(大連)有限公司(1990)	Dalian 大連市	Liaoning 遼寧省	(0411)7613051 (0411)7613050	572	Foreign-funded 外資	77,773	2707(18)	169,521	o
Anhui Zhong Ding Group Die Set Factory 安徽中鼎集團模具廠(1984)	Xuanzhou 宣州市	Anhui 安徽省	(0563)4074800	300	Collectively-owned 集體	75,000	1200(34)	21,680	o
Xian Jin Precision Work Co. 先進精工公司(1995)	Shenzhen 深圳市	Guangdong 廣東省	(0755)5351811	500	Overseas Chinese-funded 港澳台資	66,335	14492(2)	101,931	o
Jiedong Tyre Die Set Factory 揭東縣輪胎模具廠(1980)	Jieyang 揭陽市	Guangdong 廣東省	(0663)3351575	260	Collectively-owned 集體	65,400	3100(15)	47,430	a
Qingdao Plastic Mould Industrial Co. 青島塑料模具實業公司(1966)	Qingdao 青島市	Shandong 山東省	(0532)5621385 (0532)5621385	417	Joint stock 股份制	54,789	6432(5)	116,235	a
Zhuhai Machinery Industry Group Corp. 珠海市機械工業集團公司(1988)	Zhuhai 珠海市	Guangdong 廣東省	(0756)2220234 (0756)2228252	955	State-owned 國有	52,568	-1933(398)	239,483	a
Hong Zhun Precise Die Set (Kunshan) Co. Ltd. 鴻准精密模具(昆山)有限公司(1996)	Suzhou 蘇州市	Jiangsu 江蘇省	(0520)7792239 (0520)7791044	100	Foreign-funded 外資	48,920	610(63)	33,940	o
Huizhou Huang Xiang Precise Plastic Model Products Co. Ltd. 惠州皇翔精密塑膠模具製品有限公司	Huizhou 惠州市	Guangdong 廣東省	(0751)2790520	55	Overseas Chinese-funded 港澳台資	48,530	3470(14)	46,340	o
Shanghai Shen Lian Science & Technology Development General Company 上海申聯科技發展總公司(1991)	Shanghai 上海市	Shanghai 上海市	(021)63774094 (021)63762999	190	Domestic JVs 聯營	42,886	3603(12)	34,779	o

Top 10 Cities by Production Output 產出排名前10位城市	Province 省	Market share 市場份額	Number of firms 企業個數
Shenzhen 深圳市	Guangdong 廣東省	12.64%	48
Shanghai 上海市	Shanghai 上海市	8.31%	166
Guangzhou 廣州市	Guangdong 廣東省	4.97%	145
Dalian 大連市	Liaoning 遼寧省	4.08%	22
Taizhou 臺州市	Zhejiang 浙江省	3.85%	85
Tianjin 天津市	Tianjin 天津市	3.77%	124
Foshan 佛山市	Guangdong 廣東省	3.48%	29
Beijing 北京市	Beijing 北京市	3.46%	90
Huizhou 惠州市	Guangdong 廣東省	2.53%	20
Qingdao 青島市	Shandong 山東省	2.43%	47

10 Major Wholesalers 10家主要批發商	City 城市	Province 省	Telephone / Fax 電話 / 傳真
Liaoning Automobile Trade Group Corp. 遼寧省汽車貿易集團	Shenyang 瀋陽市	Liaoning 遼寧省	(024)23835494 (024)23838338
China Post and Telecommunication Equipment General Company 中國郵電器材總公司	Beijing 北京市	Beijing 北京市	(010)63523715 (010)63525935
Jiangsu Electromechanical Products General Company 江蘇省機電產品總公司	Nanjing 南京市	Jiangsu 江蘇省	(025)7713642 (025)7711036
Xi Nan Technology Import & Export Company 西南技術進出口公司	Chongqing 重慶市	Chongqing 重慶市	(023)63850185 (023)63850026
Changzhou Economic Technology Industrial Development Zone Tian Ming Trade Company 常州經濟技術產業開發區天明貿易公司	Changzhou 常州市	Jiangsu 江蘇省	(0519)8829882 (0519)8829882
Shanxi Mechanical Equipment Import & Export Company 山西省機械設備進出口公司	Taiyuan 太原市	Shanxi 山西省	(0351)4040713 (0351)4043981
Ningbo Five Mining Machinery Import & Export Company 寧波市五礦機械進出口公司	Ningbo 寧波市	Zhejiang 浙江省	(0574)7311255 (0574)7320322
Tianjin Jin Huan Electromechanical Complete Sets of Equipment Factory 天津市津環機電成套設備廠	Tianjin 天津市	Tianjin 天津市	(022)26371628
Yunnan Machinery Import & Export Company 雲南省機械進出口公司	Kunming 昆明市	Yunnan 雲南省	(0871)3164879 (0871)3136829
Tianjin Da Qiu Zhuang Yi Yuan Trade Center 天津市大丘莊億源商貿中心	Tianjin 天津市	Tianjin 天津市	(022)28899478 (022)28899046

*Also include sales by firms outside this industry.包括本行業以外廠家的銷售。"o" stands for "others". "o" 代表 "其他產品"。

3435: Hand Tools 手工具製造業

The industry accounts for 0.097% of the total revenue of China's industrial sector in 1996. The revenue growth rate of the industry is 0.0% from 1995, as compared to the growth rate of China's industrial sector, 9.51%. The rate of return on asset is 0.12%. 59.48% of all firms in the industry made a profit while 32.36% had negative returns. The top province in terms of the industry's revenue is Shandong, accounting for 20.28% of the total revenue.
本行業在1996年佔全行業總產值0.097%，行業年增長率為0.0%（全國工業年增長率9.51%）。行業的資產回報率0.12%，59.48%的企業盈利，32.36%的企業虧損。銷售收入最高的省份為山東省，佔本行業的20.28%。

	Total number of firms 企業總數	Total number of employees 職工總數	Total revenue (mil. RMB) 總銷售收入（百萬元）	Total profit (mil. RMB) 總利潤（百萬元）	Return on assets 資產利潤率 (%)	Return on equity 權益利潤率 (%)	Labour productivity ('000 RMB / worker) 勞動生產率（千元/人）	Debts / assets 資產負債率 (%)	Total assets (mil. RMB) 總資產（百萬元）
Industry Overall 行業總體	1,049	164,585	5,595	10	0.12	0.43	33.99	72.42	8,055

	Number of firms 企業個數	Average number of employees 平均職工人數	Average revenue ('000 RMB) 平均銷售收入（千元）	Average profit ('000 RMB) 平均利潤（千元）	Return on assets 資產利潤率 (%)	Return on equity 權益利潤率 (%)	Labour productivity ('000 RMB / worker) 勞動生產率（千元/人）	Average debts / assets 平均資產負債率(%)	Average Total assets ('000 RMB) 平均總資產（千元）
By ownership 產業所有權									
State-owned 國有	82	337	9,415	37	0.18	0.72	27.92	74.43	19,793
Collectively-owned 集體	883	137	4,454	5	0.09	0.36	32.41	75.93	5,905
Privately-owned 私有	7	26	465	0	-0.03	-0.07	17.80	61.35	1,523
Domestic JVs 聯營	8	367	14,177	22	0.14	0.54	38.64	74.38	16,044
Joint stock 股份制	10	227	10,101	59	0.43	1.26	44.50	66.04	13,797
Foreign-funded 外資	20	111	7,067	-3	-0.03	-0.06	63.81	44.44	10,078
Overseas Chinese-funded 港澳台資	40	237	13,271	44	0.24	0.50	56.01	51.77	18,460
By size 規模									
Large 大型	5	1,862	109,458	1,002	0.62	1.44	58.78	56.92	162,048
Medium 中型	40	726	26,845	51	0.11	0.42	36.99	74.09	47,088
Small 小型	998	127	3,981	3	0.05	0.21	31.28	74.17	5,372
By regional distribution 地區分布									
Central-North 華北	161	137	3,951	59	0.78	2.50	28.84	68.98	7,548
Beijing 北京	29	103	2,743	-190	-2.92	-11.74	26.62	75.17	6,530
Tianjin 天津	53	139	5,801	175	1.80	4.23	41.68	57.44	9,695
Hebei 河北	49	150	3,849	122	1.68	8.10	25.61	79.28	7,272
Shanxi 山西	26	156	2,248	16	0.29	1.11	14.37	74.29	5,638
Inner Mongolia 內蒙	4	64	498	-175	-7.60	269.23	7.74	102.93	2,303
Northeast 東北	112	127	1,513	-214	-4.05	-81.19	11.87	95.02	5,278
Liaoning 遼寧	53	141	1,977	-331	-4.58	-90.60	14.03	94.94	7,221
Jilin 吉林	31	143	1,365	-186	-3.82	2890.00	9.52	100.13	4,884
Heilongjiang 黑龍江	28	84	798	-21	-1.05	-5.83	9.47	81.95	2,038
Central East 華東	501	181	7,557	78	0.79	2.60	41.81	69.53	9,847
Shanghai 上海	63	239	9,535	248	1.53	4.84	39.93	68.27	16,160
Jiangsu 江蘇	112	182	9,232	29	0.33	1.21	50.62	72.72	8,793
Zhejiang 浙江	120	143	6,579	22	0.24	0.66	46.05	62.77	8,837
Anhui 安徽	23	128	4,230	-57	-1.10	-5.04	33.08	78.13	5,203
Fujian 福建	32	51	2,321	-56	-1.91	-5.97	45.10	68.04	2,917
Jiangxi 江西	49	80	1,138	-87	-3.58	-19.26	14.29	81.40	2,415
Shandong 山東	102	289	11,125	245	1.63	5.70	38.52	71.49	15,085
Central-South 中南	172	139	4,437	44	0.88	3.50	31.81	74.71	5,017
Henan 河南	42	180	5,716	227	3.17	10.45	31.73	69.63	7,155
Hubei 湖北	38	180	6,152	292	4.96	26.74	34.17	81.44	5,874
Hunan 湖南	43	107	2,154	-169	-5.94	-50.35	20.17	88.21	2,852
Guangdong 廣東	40	122	4,813	-147	-2.74	-8.44	39.29	67.53	5,370
Guangxi 廣西	9	10	457	20	10.23	13.33	46.70	23.30	196
Hainan 海南									
Southwest 西南	81	153	2,710	-269	-5.39	-27.55	17.69	80.42	4,980
Chongqing 重慶	25	113	1,550	-311	-11.95	428.56	13.66	102.79	2,604
Sichuan 四川	48	187	3,528	-282	-4.28	-19.86	18.89	78.48	6,602
Guizhou 貴州	4	44	200				4.60	4.35	690
Yunnan 雲南	4	105	2,490	-103	-2.37	-4.34	23.66	45.44	4,330
Tibet 西藏									
Northwest 西北	22	59	940	-40	-1.82	-6.05	15.92	69.98	2,229
Shaanxi 陝西	15	57	855	-61	-3.17	-17.49	15.02	81.85	1,932
Gansu 甘肅	2	19	210	-25	-4.00	-18.52	11.35	78.40	625
Qinghai 青海									
Ningxia 寧夏	2	47	1,245	-10	-0.43	-2.08	26.49	79.31	2,320
Xinjiang 新疆	3	105	1,647	33	0.71	1.22	15.73	41.88	4,720

Year 年份	Number of firms 企業個數	Rate of change 每年變化 (%)	Number of employees 職工人數（人）	Rate of change 每年變化 (%)	Total revenue (mil. RMB) 總銷售收入（百萬元）	Rate of change 每年變化 (%)	Total profit (mil. RMB) 總利潤（百萬元）	Rate of change 每年變化 (%)
1993	1,041		204,607		5,026		126	
1994	1,170	12.39%	180,091	-11.98%	5,026	0.02%	43	-65.55%
1995	1,071	-8.46%	177,760	-1.30%	5,594	11.29%	51	16.99%
1996	1,049	-2.05%	164,585	-7.41%	5,595	0.02%	10	-80.33%

3 Major products* 3 種主要產品 *	Output 產量	Sales volume 銷售量	Unit 單位
a) Spanner 扳手	41,779	40,526	10,000 piece 萬把
b) Hammer 錘子	7,690	7,690	10,000 piece 萬把
c) Pincers 鉗子	18,305	16,841	10,000 piece 萬把

Top 10 firms by revenue (year founded) 收入排名前 10 家企業 (創辦年份)	City 城市	Province 省	Telephone / fax 電話 / 傳真	Number of employees 職工人數	Ownership 產業所有權	Revenue ('000 RMB) 銷售收入（千元）	Profit ('000 RMB) (rank) 利潤（千元）(排名)	Total assets ('000 RMB) 總資產（千元）	Major products 主要產品
Wuxi Hardware Tools Group Co. 無錫市五金工具集團公司(1954)	Wuxi 無錫市	Jiangsu 江蘇省	(0510)2700394 (0510)2705668	1,134	Domestic JVs 聯營	108,650	3(296)	83,861	a,c
Rizhao Hardware Industrial Group Co. Ltd. 日照市五金工業集團公司(1993)	Rizhao 日照市	Shandong 山東省	(0633)8331979 (0633)8331979	1,120	Collectively-owned 集體	100,467	8000(4)	122,585	b
Tianjin South China Tools (Holdings) Co. Ltd. 天津南華工具(集團)有限公司(1994)	Tianjin 天津市	Tianjin 天津市	(022)28227745 (022)28227724	2,471	Overseas Chinese-funded 港澳台資	97,287	-2596(481)	179,633	a,b,c
Hangzhou Qianjiang Hardware Tools Factory 杭州錢江五金工具廠(1952)	Hangzhou 杭州市	Zhejiang 浙江省	(0571)6224182	1,331	State-owned 國有	83,918	3457(9)	102,511	a,c
Wendeng Wei Li Tools Group Co. 文登市威力工具集團公司(1968)	Weihai 威海市	Shandong 山東省	(0896)8252421 (0896)8256059	1,538	Overseas Chinese-funded 港澳台資	80,016	8117(3)	96,183	a
Shanghai Laodong Machinery Plant 上海市勞動機械廠(1949)	Shanghai 上海市	Shanghai 上海市	(021)65560609 (021)65560808	1,297	State-owned 國有	79,283	5513(5)	170,793	a
Shanghai Dong Wu Tool Co. Ltd. 上海東吳工具有限公司(1994)	Shanghai 上海市	Shanghai 上海市	(021)64883105	150	Domestic JVs 聯營	74,430	1800(24)	92,154	o
Xuzhou Hardware Tools General Factory 徐州五金工具總廠(1958)	Xuzhou 徐州市	Jiangsu 江蘇省	(0516)6531158	750	Collectively-owned 集體	67,520	1900(22)	21,578	c
Chenghai Yongjia Enterprise (Group) Co. Ltd. 澄海永嘉企業(集團)有限公司(1995)	Shantou 汕頭市	Guangdong 廣東省	(0754)5751402 (0754)5753528	1,493	Joint stock 股份制	66,267	-2816(482)	101,901	o
Wuhan Iron & Steel Corp. Steel-smelting Tool Repair General Factory 武鋼實業公司冶金設備修造總廠(1981)	Wuhan 武漢市	Hubei 湖北省	(027)86899150	1,142	Collectively-owned 集體	50,822	10559(2)	41,384	o

Top 10 Cities by Production Output 產出排名前 10 位城市	Province 省	Market share 市場份額	Number of firms 企業個數
Shanghai 上海市	Shanghai 上海市	11.26%	85
Suzhou 蘇州市	Jiangsu 江蘇省	6.12%	29
Hangzhou 杭州市	Zhejiang 浙江省	5.12%	27
Tianjin 天津市	Tianjin 天津市	4.32%	52
Yangzhou 揚州市	Jiangsu 江蘇省	3.89%	36
Changzhou 常州市	Jiangsu 江蘇省	3.79%	38
Qingdao 青島市	Shandong 山東省	3.66%	26
Ningbo 寧波市	Zhejiang 浙江省	3.44%	39
Yantai 煙台市	Shandong 山東省	2.95%	16
Weihai 威海市	Shandong 山東省	2.88%	5

10 Major Wholesalers 10 家主要批發商	City 城市	Province 省	Telephone / Fax 電話 / 傳真
Liaoning Automobile Trade Group Corp. 遼寧省汽車貿易集團	Shenyang 瀋陽市	Liaoning 遼寧省	(024)23835494 (024)23838338
China Post and Telecommunication Equipment General Company 中國郵電器材總公司	Beijing 北京市	Beijing 北京市	(010)63523715 (010)63525935
Jiangsu Electromechanical Products General Company 江蘇省機電產品總公司	Nanjing 南京市	Jiangsu 江蘇省	(025)7713642 (025)7711036
Xi Nan Technology Import & Export Company 西南技術進出口公司	Chongqing 重慶市	Chongqing 重慶市	(023)63850185 (023)63850026
Changzhou Economic Technology Industrial Development Zone Tian Ming Trade Company 常州經濟技術產業開發區天明貿易公司	Changzhou 常州市	Jiangsu 江蘇省	(0519)8829882 (0519)8829882
Shanxi Mechanical Equipment Import & Export Company 山西省機械設備進出口公司	Taiyuan 太原市	Shanxi 山西省	(0351)4040713 (0351)4043981
Ningbo Five Mining Machinery Import & Export Company 寧波市五礦機械進出口公司	Ningbo 寧波市	Zhejiang 浙江省	(0574)7311255 (0574)7320322
Tianjin Jin Huan Electromechanical Complete Sets of Equipment Factory 天津市津環機電成套設備廠	Tianjin 天津市	Tianjin 天津市	(022)26371628
Yunnan Machinery Import & Export Company 雲南省機械進出口公司	Kunming 昆明市	Yunnan 雲南省	(0871)3164879 (0871)3136829
Tianjin Da Qiu Zhuang Yi Yuan Trade Center 天津市大丘莊億源商貿中心	Tianjin 天津市	Tianjin 天津市	(022)28899478 (022)28899046

*Also include sales by firms outside this industry.包括本行業以外廠家的銷售。"o" stands for "others". "o" 代表"其他產品"。

3439: Other Tools 其他工具製造業

The industry accounts for 0.019% of the total revenue of China's industrial sector in 1996. The revenue growth rate of the industry is 5.1% from 1995, as compared to the growth rate of China's industrial sector, 9.51%. The rate of return on asset is 0.58%. 63.35% of all firms in the industry made a profit while 31.22% had negative returns. The top province in terms of the industry's revenue is Zhejiang, accounting for 23.08% of the total revenue.
本行業在1996年佔全行業總產值0.019%，行業年增長率為5.1%（全國工業年增長率9.51%）。行業的資產回報率0.58%，63.35%的企業盈利，31.22%的企業虧損。銷售收入最高的省份為浙江省，佔本行業的23.08%。

	Total number of firms 企業總數	Total number of employees 職工總數	Total revenue (mil. RMB) 總銷售收入（百萬元）	Total profit (mil. RMB) 總利潤（百萬元）	Return on assets 資產利潤率 (%)	Return on equity 權益利潤率 (%)	Labour productivity ('000 RMB / worker) 勞動生產率（千元/人）	Debts / assets 資產負債率 (%)	Total assets (mil. RMB) 總資產（百萬元）
Industry Overall 行業總體	246	28,482	1,103	10	0.58	1.76	38.73	67.23	1,819

	Number of firms 企業個數	Average number of employees 平均職工人數	Average revenue ('000 RMB) 平均銷售收入（千元）	Average profit ('000 RMB) 平均利潤（千元）	Return on assets 資產利潤率 (%)	Return on equity 權益利潤率 (%)	Labour productivity ('000 RMB / worker) 勞動生產率（千元/人）	Average debts / assets 平均資產負債率(%)	Average Total assets ('000 RMB) 平均總資產（千元）
By ownership 產業所有權									
State-owned 國有	19	272	5,053	-316	-2.33	-15.38	18.57	84.82	13,526
Collectively-owned 集體	195	107	4,268	57	0.85	2.55	39.75	66.44	6,630
Privately-owned 私有									
Domestic JVs 聯營	7	90	1,357	-67	-1.43	-4.25	15.05	66.23	4,662
Joint stock 股份制	3	112	13,650	356	3.66	7.55	122.24	51.47	9,724
Foreign-funded 外資	9	49	9,533	429	2.71	6.03	194.99	55.05	15,845
Overseas Chinese-funded 港澳台資	12	81	3,216	40	0.75	1.43	39.66	47.73	5,378
By size 規模									
Large 大型									
Medium 中型	8	647	23,421	-380	-0.54	-1.56	36.22	65.62	71,023
Small 小型	235	99	3,896	55	1.04	3.25	39.45	67.97	5,323
By regional distribution 地區分布									
Central-North 華北	45	96	2,890	-166	-2.97	-6.70	30.11	55.59	5,574
Beijing 北京	11	95	2,055	-219	-4.73	-16.70	21.71	71.66	4,629
Tianjin 天津	26	92	3,480	-208	-3.63	-7.27	37.86	50.07	5,718
Hebei 河北	5	36	402	-10	-1.34	-3.68	11.17	63.44	744
Shanxi 山西	3	236	4,987	133	0.84	1.87	21.13	54.99	15,840
Inner Mongolia 內蒙									
Northeast 東北	45	119	2,297	-22	-0.37	-1.96	19.37	81.02	5,782
Liaoning 遼寧	23	107	2,248	43	1.04	3.64	20.95	71.29	4,121
Jilin 吉林	7	76	876	-311	-10.64	83.52	11.59	112.74	2,926
Heilongjiang 黑龍江	15	156	3,035	15	0.15	0.89	19.47	82.90	9,661
Central East 華東	101	123	7,218	303	3.17	9.39	58.80	66.25	9,567
Shanghai 上海	21	83	2,497	-110	-1.60	-5.68	30.08	71.82	6,900
Jiangsu 江蘇	23	158	6,549	120	1.19	3.67	41.42	67.72	10,085
Zhejiang 浙江	30	85	8,484	388	4.64	12.19	99.96	61.95	8,372
Anhui 安徽	1	10	5,700	30	4.76	42.86	570.00	88.89	630
Fujian 福建	5	34	996	-76	-3.54	-5.48	29.47	35.26	2,144
Jiangxi 江西	9	36	881	64	9.98	20.35	24.33	50.95	646
Shandong 山東	12	331	21,072	1,525	5.70	17.44	63.72	67.32	26,756
Central-South 中南	36	130	1,818	-182	-4.70	-13.39	13.99	64.90	3,877
Henan 河南	4	78	1,210	15	0.82	3.97	15.46	79.32	1,825
Hubei 湖北	10	209	3,025	6	0.19	1.15	14.45	83.54	3,178
Hunan 湖南	8	204	1,549	-489	-6.86	-27.36	7.61	74.93	7,125
Guangdong 廣東	12	51	1,328	-231	-6.43	-9.96	26.13	35.40	3,588
Guangxi 廣西	2	16	1,005				64.84	65.91	220
Hainan 海南									
Southwest 西南	15	111	4,910	-359	-2.69	-9.08	44.39	70.38	13,354
Chongqing 重慶	11	95	5,102	-582	-3.52	-12.80	53.47	72.47	16,503
Sichuan 四川	4	153	4,397	235	4.73	9.82	28.83	51.81	4,956
Guizhou 貴州									
Yunnan 雲南									
Tibet 西藏									
Northwest 西北	4	23	403	65	15.95	33.77	17.31	52.76	408
Shaanxi 陝西	4	23	403	65	15.95	33.77	17.31	52.76	408
Gansu 甘肅									
Qinghai 青海									
Ningxia 寧夏									
Xinjiang 新疆									

3439: Other Tools 其他工具製造業

Year 年份	Number of firms 企業個數	Rate of change 每年變化 (%)	Number of employees 職工人數 (人)	Rate of change 每年變化 (%)	Total revenue (mil. RMB) 總銷售收入 (百萬元)	Rate of change 每年變化 (%)	Total profit (mil. RMB) 總利潤 (百萬元)	Rate of change 每年變化 (%)
1993	253		33,437		917		47	
1994	250	-1.19%	25,994	-22.26%	855	-6.71%	17	-64.50%
1995	222	-11.20%	29,620	13.95%	1,049	22.66%	20	17.85%
1996	246	10.81%	28,482	-3.84%	1,103	5.15%	10	-49.48%

3 Major products* 3 種主要產品 *	Output 產量	Sales volume 銷售量	Unit 單位
a) Measuring Instrument 量具	27,181,194	29,083,877	piece 件

Top 10 firms by revenue (year founded) 收入排名前 10 家企業 (創辦年份)	City 城市	Province 省	Telephone / fax 電話 / 傳真	Number of employees 職工人數	Ownership 產業所有權	Revenue ('000 RMB) 銷售收入 (千元)	Profit ('000 RMB) (rank) 利潤 (千元) (排名)	Total assets ('000 RMB) 總資產 (千元)	Major products 主要產品
Shandong Hua Rong Group General Company Zibo Tool Factory 山東華榮集團總公司淄博工具廠(1956)	Zibo 淄博市	Shandong 山東省	(0533)5310290 (0533)5310290	737	Collectively-owned 集體	114,890	9090(1)	83,590	o
Jiangsu Jian Yu Table Clamp Factory 江蘇劍魚台鉗廠(1966)	Yangzhou 揚州市	Jiangsu 江蘇省	(0514)8431722	913	Collectively-owned 集體	80,573	3052(5)	78,287	o
Shandong Zhen Long Group Co. 山東振龍集團公司(1976)	Yantai 煙台市	Shandong 山東省	(0535)5911421 (0535)5911421	1,528	Collectively-owned 集體	77,588	7456(2)	149,070	o
Shanghai Min Sheng Bucket Making Factory 上海民生製桶廠(1995)	Shanghai 上海市	Shanghai 上海市	(021)64781414	79	Collectively-owned 集體	67,814	279(32)	31,814	o
Ningbo Longxing Group Co. 寧波隆興集團公司(1987)	Ningbo 寧波市	Zhejiang 浙江省	(0574)8472178 (0574)8471304	595	Collectively-owned 集體	60,966	5017(3)	52,508	o
Ningbo Electronic Equipment and Material No.1 Factory 寧波電子器材一廠(1971)	Ningbo 寧波市	Zhejiang 浙江省	(0574)6100417 (0574)6100384	297	Collectively-owned 集體	42,453	1552(8)	25,027	o
Ningbo Great Wall Precision Work Bend Tape Manufacturing Co. Ltd. 寧波長城精工卷尺製造有限公司(1994)	Ningbo 寧波市	Zhejiang 浙江省	(0574)2811913 (0574)2815376	213	Overseas Chinese-funded 港澳台資	42,256	4997(4)	70,069	o
Tianjin Hua Zhu Metal Products Co. Ltd. 天津市華住金屬製品有限公司(1995)	Tianjin 天津市	Tianjin 天津市	(022)29332501 (022)29332502	29	Foreign-funded 外資	35,231	-7236(92)	76,218	o
Chongqing Jiang Nan Bend Tape Factory 重慶江南卷尺廠	Chongqing 重慶市	Chongqing 重慶市	(023)62511508 (023)62511508	127	Collectively-owned 集體	33,250	1411(10)	16,625	o
Jiaxing Datong Machinery Factory 嘉興市大通機械廠(1980)	Jiaxing 嘉興市	Zhejiang 浙江省	(0573)3166238 (0573)2086963	225	Collectively-owned 集體	28,234	155(37)	14,551	o

Top 10 Cities by Production Output 產出排名前 10 位城市	Province 省	Market share 市場份額	Number of firms 企業個數
Yantai 煙台市	Shandong 山東省	14.20%	2
Ningbo 寧波市	Zhejiang 浙江省	12.51%	9
Tianjin 天津市	Tianjin 天津市	11.14%	29
Taizhou 泰州市	Jiangsu 江蘇省	6.72%	3
Shanghai 上海市	Shanghai 上海市	6.08%	29
Chongqing 重慶市	Chongqing 重慶市	4.58%	6
Yancheng 鹽城市	Jiangsu 江蘇省	3.75%	7
Jiaxing 嘉興市	Zhejiang 浙江省	3.17%	4
Mudanjiang 牡丹江市	Heilongjiang 黑龍江省	2.98%	7
Wuhan 武漢市	Hubei 湖北省	2.87%	6

10 Major Wholesalers 10 家主要批發商	City 城市	Province 省	Telephone / Fax 電話 / 傳真
Liaoning Automobile Trade Group Corp. 遼寧省汽車貿易集團	Shenyang 瀋陽市	Liaoning 遼寧省	(024)23835494 (024)23838338
China Post and Telecommunication Equipment General Company 中國郵電器材總公司	Beijing 北京市	Beijing 北京市	(010)63523715 (010)63525935
Jiangsu Electromechanical Products General Company 江蘇省機電產品總公司	Nanjing 南京市	Jiangsu 江蘇省	(025)7713642 (025)7711036
Xi Nan Technology Import & Export Company 西南技術進出口公司	Chongqing 重慶市	Chongqing 重慶市	(023)63850185 (023)63850026
Changzhou Economic Technology Industrial Development Zone Tian Ming Trade Company 常州經濟技術產業開發區天明貿易公司	Changzhou 常州市	Jiangsu 江蘇省	(0519)8829882 (0519)8829882
Shanxi Mechanical Equipment Import & Export Company 山西省機械設備進出口公司	Taiyuan 太原市	Shanxi 山西省	(0351)4040713 (0351)4043981
Ningbo Five Mining Machinery Import & Export Company 寧波市五礦機械進出口公司	Ningbo 寧波市	Zhejiang 浙江省	(0574)7311255 (0574)7320322
Tianjin Jin Huan Electromechanical Complete Sets of Equipment Factory 天津市津環機電成套設備廠	Tianjin 天津市	Tianjin 天津市	(022)26371628
Yunnan Machinery Import & Export Company 雲南省機械進出口公司	Kunming 昆明市	Yunnan 雲南省	(0871)3164879 (0871)3136829
Tianjin Da Qiu Zhuang Yi Yuan Trade Center 天津市大丘莊億源商貿中心	Tianjin 天津市	Tianjin 天津市	(022)28899478 (022)28899046

*Also include sales by firms outside this industry.包括本行業以外廠家的銷售。"o" stands for "others". "o" 代表"其他產品"。

3441: Containers 集裝箱製造業

The industry accounts for 0.190% of the total revenue of China's industrial sector in 1996. The revenue growth rate of the industry is 1.5% from 1995, as compared to the growth rate of China's industrial sector, 9.51%. The rate of return on asset is -1.04%. 56.01% of all firms in the industry made a profit while 36.05% had negative returns. The top province in terms of the industry's revenue is Guangdong, accounting for 30.15% of the total revenue.
本行業在 1996 年佔全行業總產值 0.190%，行業年增長率為 1.5%（全國工業年增長率 9.51%）。行業的資產回報率 -1.04%，56.01% 的企業盈利，36.05% 的企業虧損。銷售收入最高的省份為廣東省，佔本行業的 30.15%。

	Total number of firms 企業總數	Total number of employees 職工總數	Total revenue (mil. RMB) 總銷售收入（百萬元）	Total profit (mil. RMB) 總利潤（百萬元）	Return on assets 資產利潤率 (%)	Return on equity 權益利潤率 (%)	Labour productivity ('000 RMB / worker) 勞動生產率（千元/人）	Debts / assets 資產負債率 (%)	Total assets (mil. RMB) 總資產（百萬元）
Industry Overall 行業總體	81	26,653	11,038	-107	-1.04	-5.22	414.14	80.15	10,360

	Number of firms 企業個數	Average number of employees 平均職工人數	Average revenue ('000 RMB) 平均銷售收入（千元）	Average profit ('000 RMB) 平均利潤（千元）	Return on assets 資產利潤率 (%)	Return on equity 權益利潤率 (%)	Labour productivity ('000 RMB / worker) 勞動生產率（千元/人）	Average debts / assets 平均資產負債率(%)	Average Total assets ('000 RMB) 平均總資產（千元）
By ownership 產業所有權									
State-owned 國有	10	166	5,600	-1,500	-3.50	40.54	33.80	108.64	42,800
Collectively-owned 集體	28	165	30,567	-222	-0.81	-2.85	185.06	71.73	27,530
Privately-owned 私有									
Domestic JVs 聯營	1	251	22,307				88.87	40.33	15,721
Joint stock 股份制									
Foreign-funded 外資	28	444	190,502	-978	-0.50	-3.41	429.44	85.36	196,098
Overseas Chinese-funded 港澳台資	15	583	317,999	-3,893	-1.60	-5.50	545.08	70.94	243,646
By size 規模									
Large 大型	13	629	425,331	-4,871	-1.28	-5.53	676.70	76.79	379,591
Medium 中型	10	644	211,056	-1,078	-0.62	-2.74	327.83	77.30	173,273
Small 小型	53	227	64,120	-620	-0.89	-6.36	283.08	86.00	69,671
By regional distribution 地區分布									
Central-North 華北	11	222	69,624	-4,093	-6.46	-47.55	313.49	86.41	63,338
Beijing 北京	3	7	87	7	1.25	4.08	13.00	69.38	533
Tianjin 天津	4	318	150,138	-1,480	-1.33	-5.05	472.87	73.73	111,665
Hebei 河北	2	406	79,805	-19,600	-16.76	131.99	196.81	112.69	116,940
Shanxi 山西	1	179	3,290				18.38	57.73	12,490
Inner Mongolia 內蒙	1	163	2,150	80	3.83	6.30	13.19	39.23	2,090
Northeast 東北	8	336	120,514	-681	-0.45	-2.68	358.54	83.11	150,180
Liaoning 遼寧	7	358	137,286	-633	-0.37	-2.18	383.48	82.95	170,434
Jilin 吉林	1	183	3,110	-1,020	-12.14	261.54	16.99	104.64	8,400
Heilongjiang 黑龍江									
Central East 華東	41	328	142,091	-2,736	-2.09	-8.96	433.75	76.69	130,985
Shanghai 上海	18	309	118,314	-5,117	-4.37	-14.27	382.55	69.37	117,063
Jiangsu 江蘇	12	447	231,373	3,633	1.98	8.03	518.00	75.31	183,359
Zhejiang 浙江	2	4	170				42.50	73.08	130
Anhui 安徽	1	20	710				35.50	92.86	420
Fujian 福建	1	735	216,470	-43,390	-15.44	439.61	294.52	103.51	281,010
Jiangxi 江西									
Shandong 山東	7	249	100,297	-2,896	-2.59	-27.73	403.26	90.64	111,606
Central-South 中南	18	441	193,312	3,077	1.80	11.07	438.18	83.77	171,321
Henan 河南	2	74	715	15	1.52	4.92	9.66	69.19	990
Hubei 湖北	4	79	10,658	-185	-0.86	-1.37	134.48	37.26	21,473
Hunan 湖南									
Guangdong 廣東	11	630	302,557	5,099	1.99	12.81	480.53	84.47	256,396
Guangxi 廣西	1	550	107,420				195.31	95.52	175,540
Hainan 海南									
Southwest 西南									
Chongqing 重慶									
Sichuan 四川									
Guizhou 貴州									
Yunnan 雲南									
Tibet 西藏									
Northwest 西北	3	50	997	-30	-1.13	-1.40	20.07	19.25	2,650
Shaanxi 陝西	2	36	1,135	85	12.23	18.48	31.97	33.81	695
Gansu 甘肅	1	78	720	-260	-3.96	-4.72	9.23	16.16	6,560
Qinghai 青海									
Ningxia 寧夏									
Xinjiang 新疆									

3441: Containers 集裝箱製造業

Year 年份	Number of firms 企業個數	Rate of change 每年變化 (%)	Number of employees 職工人數 (人)	Rate of change 每年變化 (%)	Total revenue (mil. RMB) 總銷售收入 (百萬元)	Rate of change 每年變化 (%)	Total profit (mil. RMB) 總利潤 (百萬元)	Rate of change 每年變化 (%)
1993	58		39,620		2,942		202	
1994	73	25.86%	21,256	-46.35%	6,732	128.77%	516	155.22%
1995	83	13.70%	28,263	32.96%	10,873	61.51%	345	-33.07%
1996	81	-2.41%	26,653	-5.70%	11,038	1.52%	-107	-130.98%

3 Major products* 3 種主要產品 *	Output 產量	Sales volume 銷售量	Unit 單位
a) Metal Container 金屬集裝箱	25,668,165	23,614,711	cubic metre 立方米
b) Metal Structure Products 金屬結構製品	10,310	9,279	ton 噸
c) Ferro Alloy 鐵合金	1,672	1,421	ton 噸

Top 10 firms by revenue (year founded) 收入排名前 10 家企業 (創辦年份)	City 城市	Province 省	Telephone / fax 電話 / 傳真	Number of employees 職工人數	Ownership 產業所有權	Revenue ('000 RMB) 銷售收入 (千元)	Profit ('000 RMB) (rank) 利潤 (千元) (排名)	Total assets ('000 RMB) 總資產 (千元)	Major products 主要產品
Shenzhen Nan Fang Zhong Si Container Manufacture Co. Ltd. 深圳南方中絲集裝箱製造有限公司(1983)	Shenzhen 深圳市	Guangdong 廣東省	(0755)6691131 (0755)6693975	1,332	Foreign-funded 外資	1,033,477	87493(1)	522,246	a
Nantong Smooth Sail Container Co. Ltd. 南通順達集裝箱有限公司(1991)	Nantong 南通市	Jiangsu 江蘇省	(0513)5562116 (0513)5564961	529	Overseas Chinese-funded 港澳台資	963,572	27398(2)	430,992	o
Guangzhou Gindo Container Co. Ltd. 廣州進道集裝箱有限公司(1992)	Guangzhou 廣州市	Guangdong 廣東省	(020)84861085 (020)84861185	1,050	Foreign-funded 外資	671,326	-20394(56)	487,100	a
Shanghai Pacific International Container Co. Ltd. 上海太平國際貨柜有限公司(1990)	Shanghai 上海市	Shanghai 上海市	(021)59528050 (021)59529745	841	Overseas Chinese-funded 港澳台資	636,314	-31584(59)	472,405	a
Jiangsu Hua Yi Machinery Group Co. 江蘇華億機械集團公司(1985)	Suzhou 蘇州市	Jiangsu 江蘇省	(0512)8684300 (0512)8681069	1,263	Collectively-owned 集體	626,185	15474(6)	362,396	a
Xinhui Zhong Ji Container Co. Ltd. 新會中集集裝箱有限公司(1992)	Jiangmen 江門市	Guangdong 廣東省	(0750)6255905	862	Foreign-funded 外資	586,200	660(22)	385,920	a
Joint Chinese-foreign Yangzhou Tong Yun Container Co. Ltd. 中外合資揚州通運集裝箱有限公司(1990)	Yangzhou 揚州市	Jiangsu 江蘇省	(0514)7231691 (0514)7231207	1,117	Foreign-funded 外資	563,940	6050(8)	855,440	o
Guangdong Modern Container Manufacture Co. Ltd. 廣東現代集裝箱製造有限公司(1992)	Jiangmen 江門市	Guangdong 廣東省	(0750)6864128 (0750)6864635	1,146	Foreign-funded 外資	518,671	601(24)	511,816	a
Shanghai Yuan Dong Container Co. Ltd. 上海遠東集裝箱有限公司(1992)	Shanghai 上海市	Shanghai 上海市	(021)58991280 (021)58991188	894	Overseas Chinese-funded 港澳台資	469,034	16203(5)	417,528	a
Shunde Shun Anda Container Manufacture Factory Co. Ltd. 順德市順安達集裝箱製造廠有限公司(1993)	Foshan 佛山市	Guangdong 廣東省	(0757)5563373 (0757)5566159	1,029	Overseas Chinese-funded 港澳台資	421,915	1316(18)	474,966	a

Top 10 Cities by Production Output 產出排名前 10 位城市	Province 省	Market share 市場份額	Number of firms 企業個數
Shanghai 上海市	Shanghai 上海市	22.67%	22
Jiangmen 江門市	Guangdong 廣東省	12.96%	3
Yangzhou 揚州市	Jiangsu 江蘇省	7.96%	7
Dalian 大連市	Liaoning 遼寧省	7.63%	3
Nantong 南通市	Jiangsu 江蘇省	7.50%	5
Guangzhou 廣州市	Guangdong 廣東省	6.58%	1
Tianjin 天津市	Tianjin 天津市	6.42%	3
Suzhou 蘇州市	Jiangsu 江蘇省	6.05%	4
Foshan 佛山市	Guangdong 廣東省	5.32%	1
Qingdao 青島市	Shandong 山東省	4.41%	2

10 Major Wholesalers 10 家主要批發商	City 城市	Province 省	Telephone / Fax 電話 / 傳真
Liaoning Automobile Trade Group Corp. 遼寧省汽車貿易集團	Shenyang 瀋陽市	Liaoning 遼寧省	(024)23835494 (024)23838338
China Post and Telecommunication Equipment General Company 中國郵電器材總公司	Beijing 北京市	Beijing 北京市	(010)63523715 (010)63525935
Jiangsu Electromechanical Products General Company 江蘇省機電產品總公司	Nanjing 南京市	Jiangsu 江蘇省	(025)7713642 (025)7711036
Xi Nan Technology Import & Export Company 西南技術進出口公司	Chongqing 重慶市	Chongqing 重慶市	(023)63850185 (023)63850026
Changzhou Economic Technology Industrial Development Zone Tian Ming Trade Company 常州經濟技術產業開發區天明貿易公司	Changzhou 常州市	Jiangsu 江蘇省	(0519)8829882 (0519)8829882
Shanxi Mechanical Equipment Import & Export Company 山西省機械設備進出口公司	Taiyuan 太原市	Shanxi 山西省	(0351)4040713 (0351)4043981
Ningbo Five Mining Machinery Import & Export Company 寧波市五礦機械進出口公司	Ningbo 寧波市	Zhejiang 浙江省	(0574)7311255 (0574)7320322
Tianjin Jin Huan Electromechanical Complete Sets of Equipment Factory 天津市津環機電成套設備廠	Tianjin 天津市	Tianjin 天津市	(022)26371628
Yunnan Machinery Import & Export Company 雲南省機械進出口公司	Kunming 昆明市	Yunnan 雲南省	(0871)3164879 (0871)3136829
Tianjin Da Qiu Zhuang Yi Yuan Trade Center 天津市大丘莊億源商貿中心	Tianjin 天津市	Tianjin 天津市	(022)28899478 (022)28899046

*Also include sales by firms outside this industry.包括本行業以外廠家的銷售。"o" stands for "others". "o" 代表"其他產品"。

3442: Metal Packing Goods and Containers 金屬包裝物品及容器製造業

The industry accounts for 0.269% of the total revenue of China's industrial sector in 1996. The revenue growth rate of the industry is 7.0% from 1995, as compared to the growth rate of China's industrial sector, 9.51%. The rate of return on asset is 0.29%. 66.60% of all firms in the industry made a profit while 27.21% had negative returns. The top province in terms of the industry's revenue is Guangdong, accounting for 21.16% of the total revenue.

本行業在1996年佔全行業總產值0.269%，行業年增長率為7.0%（全國工業年增長率9.51%）。行業的資產回報率0.29%，66.60%的企業盈利，27.21%的企業虧損。銷售收入最高的省份為廣東省，佔本行業的21.16%。

	Total number of firms 企業總數	Total number of employees 職工總數	Total revenue (mil. RMB) 總銷售收入（百萬元）	Total profit (mil. RMB) 總利潤（百萬元）	Return on assets 資產利潤率 (%)	Return on equity 權益利潤率 (%)	Labour productivity ('000 RMB / worker) 勞動生產率（千元/人）	Debts / assets 資產負債率 (%)	Total assets (mil. RMB) 總資產（百萬元）
Industry Overall 行業總體	1,862	191,667	15,610	71	0.29	0.81	81.44	63.65	24,023

	Number of firms 企業個數	Average number of employees 平均職工人數	Average revenue ('000 RMB) 平均銷售收入（千元）	Average profit ('000 RMB) 平均利潤（千元）	Return on assets 資產利潤率 (%)	Return on equity 權益利潤率 (%)	Labour productivity ('000 RMB / worker) 勞動生產率（千元/人）	Average debts / assets 平均資產負債率(%)	Average Total assets ('000 RMB) 平均總資產（千元）
By ownership 產業所有權									
State-owned 國有	182	202	7,313	-615	-3.91	-16.30	36.26	76.00	15,731
Collectively-owned 集體	1,458	88	4,792	30	0.57	2.07	54.47	72.63	5,338
Privately-owned 私有	7	54	2,303	27	1.32	2.33	42.43	43.34	2,004
Domestic JVs 聯營	29	77	6,379	83	1.12	2.37	82.55	52.95	7,475
Joint stock 股份制	16	253	20,847	217	0.49	1.46	82.32	66.24	43,949
Foreign-funded 外資	68	133	37,734	374	0.50	1.14	283.68	55.97	74,313
Overseas Chinese-funded 港澳台資	100	118	41,905	1,076	1.46	3.22	355.61	54.70	73,814
By size 規模									
Large 大型	16	518	214,944	1,593	0.41	1.17	414.60	65.26	390,373
Medium 中型	51	554	43,829	45	0.06	0.17	79.13	63.77	74,215
Small 小型	1,771	88	5,610	24	0.31	0.83	63.95	62.90	7,901
By regional distribution 地區分布									
Central-North 華北	256	91	6,219	72	0.78	2.51	68.06	68.96	9,240
Beijing 北京	67	73	7,009	-214	-1.41	-5.56	96.38	74.69	15,249
Tianjin 天津	50	84	8,406	66	0.52	1.58	99.83	67.20	12,662
Hebei 河北	92	93	6,313	310	5.12	12.48	68.21	59.00	6,066
Shanxi 山西	20	121	3,686	98	3.02	12.69	30.55	76.16	3,224
Inner Mongolia 內蒙	27	125	1,771	-36	-1.09	-4.03	14.14	72.97	3,264
Northeast 東北	353	111	2,971	-42	-0.92	-3.32	26.77	72.32	4,545
Liaoning 遼寧	192	131	3,351	10	0.20	0.65	25.65	69.61	5,178
Jilin 吉林	72	72	1,566	-76	-2.84	-15.26	21.82	81.42	2,674
Heilongjiang 黑龍江	89	100	3,287	-127	-2.70	-10.60	32.76	74.58	4,694
Central East 華東	623	113	11,488	155	0.91	2.28	101.63	59.94	17,015
Shanghai 上海	73	151	18,039	-104	-0.35	-1.05	119.20	66.71	29,710
Jiangsu 江蘇	181	141	13,762	107	0.59	1.61	97.80	63.24	18,057
Zhejiang 浙江	100	94	8,274	70	0.54	1.29	88.20	58.04	12,898
Anhui 安徽	38	96	5,015	73	1.66	5.20	52.31	68.17	4,420
Fujian 福建	84	54	12,195	711	2.84	4.69	225.14	39.36	25,000
Jiangxi 江西	60	109	3,022	-814	-12.77	-200.25	27.82	93.53	6,370
Shandong 山東	87	113	12,937	740	5.26	14.96	114.69	64.84	14,059
Central-South 中南	376	102	13,003	-9	-0.04	-0.12	127.69	63.93	20,821
Henan 河南	65	56	3,367	125	3.22	9.01	60.45	64.26	3,891
Hubei 湖北	75	161	11,786	463	4.18	10.77	73.25	61.21	11,086
Hunan 湖南	54	76	2,863	-167	-3.95	-24.26	37.62	83.72	4,222
Guangdong 廣東	128	115	25,801	-440	-0.91	-2.45	225.22	62.92	48,514
Guangxi 廣西	44	64	6,991	466	7.93	38.72	108.73	79.52	5,873
Hainan 海南	10	100	2,154	-134	-2.78	-7.29	21.56	61.80	4,814
Southwest 西南	134	75	2,912	-133	-2.22	-7.21	38.88	69.17	5,966
Chongqing 重慶	31	86	3,725	-466	-6.08	-20.02	43.38	69.65	7,670
Sichuan 四川	60	74	2,995	-52	-0.75	-2.66	40.52	71.71	6,919
Guizhou 貴州	19	48	1,335	56	2.92	6.15	27.57	52.45	1,908
Yunnan 雲南	24	84	2,903	-51	-1.12	-3.11	34.70	64.08	4,592
Tibet 西藏									
Northwest 西北	120	86	4,444	-71	-1.03	-3.57	51.55	71.20	6,877
Shaanxi 陝西	57	60	5,729	-242	-3.22	-12.39	95.32	73.99	7,524
Gansu 甘肅	21	163	3,990	78	1.36	3.51	24.41	61.35	5,754
Qinghai 青海	6	102	742	-640	-16.88	-165.52	7.28	89.80	3,792
Ningxia 寧夏	8	133	1,771	-10	-0.22	-0.62	13.34	64.62	4,561
Xinjiang 新疆	28	65	3,725	272	3.52	11.87	57.50	70.32	7,723

3442: Metal Packing Goods and Containers 金屬包裝物品及容器製造業

Year 年份	Number of firms 企業個數	Rate of change 每年變化 (%)	Number of employees 職工人數（人）	Rate of change 每年變化 (%)	Total revenue (mil. RMB) 總銷售收入（百萬元）	Rate of change 每年變化 (%)	Total profit (mil. RMB) 總利潤（百萬元）	Rate of change 每年變化 (%)
1993	1,579		166,870		10,341		463	
1994	1,720	8.93%	184,583	10.61%	10,262	-0.76%	581	25.42%
1995	1,884	9.53%	189,770	2.81%	14,589	42.16%	520	-10.40%
1996	1,862	-1.17%	191,667	1.00%	15,610	7.00%	71	-86.36%

3 Major products* 3 種主要產品 *	Output 產量	Sales volume 銷售量	Unit 單位
a) Gas Storage Tank from Metal 金屬製氣體貯藏罐	35,358,430	34,297,677	piece 個
b) Packing Tin, Tank & Box from Metal 金屬製包裝用錫、罐、盒	788,429	725,355	ton 噸
c) Liquid Storage Tank from Metal 金屬製液體貯藏罐	230,026	234,626	ton 噸

Top 10 firms by revenue (year founded) 收入排名前 10 家企業 (創辦年份)	City 城市	Province 省	Telephone / fax 電話 / 傳真	Number of employees 職工人數	Ownership 產業所有權	Revenue ('000 RMB) 銷售收入（千元）	Profit ('000 RMB) (rank) 利潤（千元）（排名）	Total assets ('000 RMB) 總資產（千元）	Major products 主要產品
Sanshui Jianlibao Ftb Packaging Co. Ltd. 三水健力寶富特容器有限公司(1992)	Foshan 佛山市	Guangdong 廣東省	(0757)7826988 (0757)7831888	569	Overseas Chinese-funded 港澳台資	745,639	86018(1)	869,622	b
Guangzhou M.C. Packaging Ltd. 廣州美特容器有限公司(1985)	Guangzhou 廣州市	Guangdong 廣東省	(020)82212458 (020)82212458	536	Foreign-funded 外資	408,327	-47582(839)	749,390	b
Shandong Huan Ri Group General Company 山東環日集團總公司(1985)	Yantai 煙台市	Shandong 山東省	(0535)2331056 (0535)2331262	2,320	Collectively-owned 集體	405,300	34060(3)	198,780	a,c
Shanghai Crown Packaging Co. Ltd. 上海皇冠包裝有限公司(1995)	Shanghai 上海市	Shanghai 上海市	(021)58995108 (021)58995106	142	Overseas Chinese-funded 港澳台資	277,826	914(132)	312,675	b
Honghu Zhen Sheng Industrial General Company 洪湖市振聲實業總公司(1972)	Jingsha 荊沙市	Hubei 湖北省	(0716)8842232 (0716)8842002	1,500	Collectively-owned 集體	261,200	25960(5)	89,720	o
Xi'an Kun Lun Fu Te Bo Er Container Co. Ltd. 西安昆侖富特波爾容器有限公司(1992)	Xi'an 西安市	Shaanxi 陝西省	(029)3234696 (029)3238433	307	Overseas Chinese-funded 港澳台資	233,831	2026(65)	260,174	o
Dalian North Pacific Can Co. Ltd. 大連北太平洋製罐有限公司(1992)	Dalian 大連市	Liaoning 遼寧省	(0411)7612406 (0411)7628711	237	Overseas Chinese-funded 港澳台資	202,613	3346(38)	260,414	b
Qingdao M.C. Packaging Ltd. 青島美特容器有限公司(1993)	Qingdao 青島市	Shandong 山東省	(0532)4849666 (0532)4845161	252	Overseas Chinese-funded 港澳台資	198,102	0(612)	356,288	b
American National Can (Zhaoqing) Co. Ltd. 美國國家製罐(肇慶)有限公司(1987)	Zhaoqing 肇慶市	Guangdong 廣東省	(0757)2833238 (0757)2836338	211	Foreign-funded 外資	197,990	550(180)	329,992	b
Xi Shan Shi Xi Zhang Silkworm Egg Farm 錫山市西漳蠶種場(1989)	Wuxi 無錫市	Jiangsu 江蘇省	(0510)3751624	1,757	State-owned 國有	191,743	3481(37)	235,651	o

Top 10 Cities by Production Output 產出排名前 10 位城市	Province 省	Market share 市場份額	Number of firms 企業個數
Foshan 佛山市	Guangdong 廣東省	10.19%	26
Shanghai 上海市	Shanghai 上海市	6.84%	109
Yancheng 鹽城市	Jiangsu 江蘇省	6.03%	11
Guangzhou 廣州市	Guangdong 廣東省	4.95%	43
Putian 莆田市	Fujian 福建省	4.23%	4
Suzhou 蘇州市	Jiangsu 江蘇省	4.21%	147
Taizhou 泰州市	Jiangsu 江蘇省	3.73%	32
Beijing 北京市	Beijing 北京市	3.13%	65
Tianjin 天津市	Tianjin 天津市	2.81%	61
Yantai 煙台市	Shandong 山東省	2.55%	14

10 Major Wholesalers 10 家主要批發商	City 城市	Province 省	Telephone / Fax 電話 / 傳真
Liaoning Automobile Trade Group Corp. 遼寧省汽車貿易集團	Shenyang 瀋陽市	Liaoning 遼寧省	(024)23835494 (024)23838338
China Post and Telecommunication Equipment General Company 中國郵電器材總公司	Beijing 北京市	Beijing 北京市	(010)63523715 (010)63525935
Jiangsu Electromechanical Products General Company 江蘇省機電產品總公司	Nanjing 南京市	Jiangsu 江蘇省	(025)7713642 (025)7711036
Xi Nan Technology Import & Export Company 西南技術進出口公司	Chongqing 重慶市	Chongqing 重慶市	(023)63850185 (023)63850026
Changzhou Economic Technology Industrial Development Zone Tian Ming Trade Company 常州經濟技術產業開發區天明貿易公司	Changzhou 常州市	Jiangsu 江蘇省	(0519)8829882 (0519)8829882
Shanxi Mechanical Equipment Import & Export Company 山西省機械設備進出口公司	Taiyuan 太原市	Shanxi 山西省	(0351)4040713 (0351)4043981
Ningbo Five Mining Machinery Import & Export Company 寧波市五礦機械進出口公司	Ningbo 寧波市	Zhejiang 浙江省	(0574)7311255 (0574)7320322
Tianjin Jin Huan Electromechanical Complete Sets of Equipment Factory 天津市津環機電成套設備廠	Tianjin 天津市	Tianjin 天津市	(022)26371628
Yunnan Machinery Import & Export Company 雲南省機械進出口公司	Kunming 昆明市	Yunnan 雲南省	(0871)3164879 (0871)3136829
Tianjin Da Qiu Zhuang Yi Yuan Trade Center 天津市大丘莊億源商貿中心	Tianjin 天津市	Tianjin 天津市	(022)28899478 (022)28899046

*Also include sales by firms outside this industry.包括本行業以外廠家的銷售。"o" stands for "others". "o" 代表"其他產品"。

3450: Metal Wire and Cable 金屬絲繩及其製品業

The industry accounts for 0.302% of the total revenue of China's industrial sector in 1996. The revenue growth rate of the industry is 9.0% from 1995, as compared to the growth rate of China's industrial sector, 9.51%. The rate of return on asset is 0.48%. 66.98% of all firms in the industry made a profit while 26.50% had negative returns. The top province in terms of the industry's revenue is Jiangsu, accounting for 22.97% of the total revenue.
本行業在1996年佔全行業總產值0.302%，行業年增長率為9.0%（全國工業年增長率9.51%）。行業的資產回報率0.48%，66.98%的企業盈利，26.50%的企業虧損。銷售收入最高的省份為江蘇省，佔本行業的22.97%。

	Total number of firms 企業總數	Total number of employees 職工總數	Total revenue (mil. RMB) 總銷售收入（百萬元）	Total profit (mil. RMB) 總利潤（百萬元）	Return on assets 資產利潤率 (%)	Return on equity 權益利潤率 (%)	Labour productivity ('000 RMB / worker) 勞動生產率（千元/人）	Debts / assets 資產負債率 (%)	Total assets (mil. RMB) 總資產（百萬元）
Industry Overall 行業總體	2,485	274,742	17,517	108	0.48	1.89	63.76	74.71	22,439

	Number of firms 企業個數	Average number of employees 平均職工人數	Average revenue ('000 RMB) 平均銷售收入（千元）	Average profit ('000 RMB) 平均利潤（千元）	Return on assets 資產利潤率 (%)	Return on equity 權益利潤率 (%)	Labour productivity ('000 RMB / worker) 勞動生產率（千元/人）	Average debts / assets 平均資產負債率(%)	Average Total assets ('000 RMB) 平均總資產（千元）
By ownership 產業所有權									
State-owned 國有	236	360	17,534	-606	-1.55	-8.71	48.70	82.21	39,102
Collectively-owned 集體	2,017	83	5,211	49	1.01	3.82	62.81	73.61	4,828
Privately-owned 私有	41	31	5,216	476	21.67	37.45	166.28	42.13	2,196
Domestic JVs 聯營	37	138	12,975	974	6.56	18.08	93.82	63.73	14,851
Joint stock 股份制	18	359	31,814	2,394	6.45	16.45	88.58	60.79	37,120
Foreign-funded 外資	48	86	11,348	901	4.75	9.40	131.95	49.49	18,976
Overseas Chinese-funded 港澳台資	87	76	12,139	124	0.86	2.21	160.35	60.93	14,404
By size 規模									
Large 大型	16	1,943	177,795	9,571	2.60	10.40	91.49	75.03	368,577
Medium 中型	46	833	60,258	-1,264	-1.42	-6.59	72.30	78.47	89,104
Small 小型	2,401	85	4,956	5	0.10	0.39	57.96	73.32	5,182
By regional distribution 地區分布									
Central-North 華北	484	119	7,259	39	0.32	1.79	61.08	82.14	12,049
Beijing 北京	57	50	6,121	-14	-0.18	-0.91	121.77	80.30	7,529
Tianjin 天津	111	213	11,923	-305	-1.13	-11.29	55.90	90.01	27,084
Hebei 河北	208	94	6,694	268	2.92	9.40	71.55	68.93	9,169
Shanxi 山西	52	105	1,685	-136	-3.38	-515.33	15.99	99.35	4,023
Inner Mongolia 內蒙	56	108	6,449	84	1.68	7.53	59.74	77.63	5,003
Northeast 東北	360	97	2,909	-107	-2.25	-14.76	29.95	84.74	4,732
Liaoning 遼寧	202	114	3,130	-132	-2.27	-15.37	27.52	85.26	5,804
Jilin 吉林	65	108	1,576	-345	-6.70	-236.21	14.60	97.16	5,152
Heilongjiang 黑龍江	93	53	3,361	114	5.42	13.70	62.88	60.41	2,109
Central East 華東	891	105	8,744	95	1.01	3.23	83.63	68.64	9,345
Shanghai 上海	99	121	8,062	173	1.44	4.73	66.61	69.52	12,029
Jiangsu 江蘇	290	120	13,875	102	0.81	2.55	115.18	68.24	12,565
Zhejiang 浙江	151	86	7,146	-68	-0.76	-2.36	83.40	67.96	9,059
Anhui 安徽	119	109	5,866	38	0.61	2.62	53.71	76.72	6,146
Fujian 福建	46	69	2,479	-106	-3.65	-8.24	35.86	55.69	2,894
Jiangxi 江西	61	61	3,822	403	7.61	13.67	62.82	44.35	5,300
Shandong 山東	125	107	6,762	190	2.54	9.75	62.99	73.96	7,485
Central-South 中南	473	108	6,483	191	2.69	9.70	60.11	72.43	7,118
Henan 河南	137	139	5,489	110	1.99	7.41	39.37	73.10	5,541
Hubei 湖北	110	154	10,353	312	2.69	15.07	67.10	82.12	11,575
Hunan 湖南	74	70	2,626	-144	-6.26	-16.48	37.71	62.04	2,301
Guangdong 廣東	100	68	8,267	-6	-0.06	-0.14	121.17	60.47	10,126
Guangxi 廣西	48	56	2,914	1,056	42.04	187.88	52.49	77.63	2,512
Hainan 海南	4	76	3,673	383	4.95	33.70	48.64	85.32	7,730
Southwest 西南	173	117	7,352	-237	-2.50	-10.21	62.91	75.52	9,473
Chongqing 重慶	39	97	5,959	239	2.97	13.71	61.32	78.35	8,050
Sichuan 四川	90	71	4,526	-550	-11.12	-82.11	63.59	86.46	4,949
Guizhou 貴州	26	346	22,662	14	0.04	0.14	65.43	69.42	32,385
Yunnan 雲南	17	56	2,542	-62	-2.77	-6.82	45.06	59.38	2,229
Tibet 西藏	1	18	150	50	16.67	16.67	8.33		300
Northwest 西北	104	172	7,946	-62	-0.41	-1.50	46.29	72.53	15,118
Shaanxi 陝西	30	181	7,679	-78	-0.38	-1.82	42.44	79.13	20,435
Gansu 甘肅	24	124	2,932	-357	-4.26	-19.87	23.73	78.60	8,390
Qinghai 青海	16	77	3,493	2	0.04	0.19	45.15	77.01	4,303
Ningxia 寧夏	9	717	42,096	214	0.32	0.92	58.74	64.86	66,652
Xinjiang 新疆	25	71	3,636	99	2.78	7.24	51.33	61.56	3,565

3450: Metal Wire and Cable 金屬絲繩及其製品業

Year 年份	Number of firms 企業個數	Rate of change 每年變化 (%)	Number of employees 職工人數 (人)	Rate of change 每年變化 (%)	Total revenue (mil. RMB) 總銷售收入 (百萬元)	Rate of change 每年變化 (%)	Total profit (mil. RMB) 總利潤 (百萬元)	Rate of change 每年變化 (%)
1993	2,284		320,836		15,978		457	
1994	2,687	17.64%	301,671	-5.97%	16,268	1.82%	201	-56.11%
1995	2,635	-1.94%	292,321	-3.10%	16,067	-1.24%	47	-76.51%
1996	2,485	-5.69%	274,742	-6.01%	17,517	9.02%	108	129.10%

3 Major products* 3 種主要產品 *	Output 產量	Sales volume 銷售量	Unit 單位
a) Steel Wire Rope 鋼絲繩	502,150	321,376	ton 噸
b) Quality Steel Wire 優質鋼鋼絲	531,601	494,389	ton 噸
c) Common Steel Nail 普通鋼鋼絲	1,427,332	1,370,239	ton 噸

Top 10 firms by revenue (year founded) 收入排名前 10 家企業 (創辦年份)	City 城市	Province 省	Telephone / fax 電話 / 傳真	Number of employees 職工人數	Ownership 產業所有權	Revenue ('000 RMB) 銷售收入 (千元)	Profit ('000 RMB) (rank) 利潤 (千元) (排名)	Total assets ('000 RMB) 總資產 (千元)	Major products 主要產品
Jiangsu Steel Cable Co. 江蘇鋼繩集團公司(1964)	Wuxi 無錫市	Jiangsu 江蘇省	(0510)6882883 (0510)6806856	3,077	Collectively-owned 集體	1,000,480	30020(2)	778,130	a,c
Guizhou Steel Cable Plant 貴州鋼繩廠(1966)	Zunyi 遵義市	Guizhou 貴州省	(0852)422980	6,580	State-owned 國有	499,591	3028(24)	703,376	a,b,c
Ningxia Shizuishan Iron & Steel Factory 寧夏石嘴山鋼鐵廠(1959)	Shizuishan 石嘴山市	Ningxia 寧夏	(0952)3681920 (0952)3681907	5,781	State-owned 國有	357,635	2166(39)	575,214	a,b,c
Jiangsu Jin Liu Group Co. 江蘇金柳集團公司(1975)	Suzhou 蘇州市	Jiangsu 江蘇省	(0512)8581536	1,330	Collectively-owned 集體	247,031	9734(7)	131,247	o
Hebei Jin Bao Factory 河北金寶集團(1954)	Hengshui 衡水市	Hebei 河北省	(0318)5323503 (0318)5322994	1,519	Collectively-owned 集體	177,706	703(146)	310,725	a,c
Shanghai Shen Jia Metal Products Co. Ltd. 上海申佳金屬製品有限公司(1995)	Shanghai 上海市	Shanghai 上海市	(021)65181928 (021)65195482	212	Overseas Chinese-funded 港澳台資	170,533	18331(4)	213,330	b
Tianjin No.1 Prestressing Force Steel Wire Co. Ltd. 天津市第一預應力鋼絲有限公司(1963)	Tianjin 天津市	Tianjin 天津市	(022)24312521 (022)24312434	1,420	State-owned 國有	150,570	10(659)	373,150	b
Jiangsu Xinghai Group Company 江蘇興海集團公司(1995)	Taizhou 泰州市	Jiangsu 江蘇省	(0523)3781465 (0523)3781518	645	State-owned 國有	148,488	1244(71)	91,694	o
Hangzhou Wan Sheng Steel Cable (Group) Co. 杭州萬勝鋼纜(集團)公司(1958)	Hangzhou 杭州市	Zhejiang 浙江省	(0571)6372323 (0571)6372568	1,057	State-owned 國有	145,392	172(358)	230,408	a,b
Wuxi Steel Cable Plant 無錫市鋼絲繩廠(1958)	Wuxi 無錫市	Jiangsu 江蘇省	(0510)2448291 (0510)2403357	1,239	State-owned 國有	135,170	540(175)	115,950	a,b

Top 10 Cities by Production Output 產出排名前 10 位城市	Province 省	Market share 市場份額	Number of firms 企業個數
Wuxi 無錫市	Jiangsu 江蘇省	9.93%	74
Tianjin 天津市	Tianjin 天津市	9.30%	128
Shanghai 上海市	Shanghai 上海市	6.06%	168
Suzhou 蘇州市	Jiangsu 江蘇省	5.89%	72
Nantong 南通市	Jiangsu 江蘇省	3.49%	88
Shizuishan 石嘴山市	Ningxia 寧夏	2.44%	5
Hengshui 衡水市	Hebei 河北省	2.27%	41
Hangzhou 杭州市	Zhejiang 浙江省	2.07%	52
Xinyu 新余市	Jiangxi 江西省	1.81%	11
Qingdao 青島市	Shandong 山東省	1.75%	32

10 Major Wholesalers 10 家主要批發商	City 城市	Province 省	Telephone / Fax 電話 / 傳真
Liaoning Automobile Trade Group Corp. 遼寧省汽車貿易集團	Shenyang 瀋陽市	Liaoning 遼寧省	(024)23835494 (024)23838338
China Post and Telecommunication Equipment General Company 中國郵電器材總公司	Beijing 北京市	Beijing 北京市	(010)63523715 (010)63525935
Jiangsu Electromechanical Products General Company 江蘇省機電產品總公司	Nanjing 南京市	Jiangsu 江蘇省	(025)7713642 (025)7711036
Xi Nan Technology Import & Export Company 西南技術進出口公司	Chongqing 重慶市	Chongqing 重慶市	(023)63850185 (023)63850026
Changzhou Economic Technology Industrial Development Zone Tian Ming Trade Company 常州經濟技術產業開發區天明貿易公司	Changzhou 常州市	Jiangsu 江蘇省	(0519)8829882 (0519)8829882
Shanxi Mechanical Equipment Import & Export Company 山西省機械設備進出口公司	Taiyuan 太原市	Shanxi 山西省	(0351)4040713 (0351)4043981
Ningbo Five Mining Machinery Import & Export Company 寧波市五礦機械進出口公司	Ningbo 寧波市	Zhejiang 浙江省	(0574)7311255 (0574)7320322
Tianjin Jin Huan Electromechanical Complete Sets of Equipment Factory 天津市津環機電成套設備廠	Tianjin 天津市	Tianjin 天津市	(022)26371628
Yunnan Machinery Import & Export Company 雲南省機械進出口公司	Kunming 昆明市	Yunnan 雲南省	(0871)3164879 (0871)3136829
Tianjin Da Qiu Zhuang Yi Yuan Trade Center 天津市大丘莊億源商貿中心	Tianjin 天津市	Tianjin 天津市	(022)28899478 (022)28899046

*Also include sales by firms outside this industry.包括本行業以外廠家的銷售。"o" stands for "others". "o" 代表"其他產品"。

3461: Metal Construction Hardware 建築小五金製造業

The industry accounts for 0.038% of the total revenue of China's industrial sector in 1996. The revenue growth rate of the industry is 18.4% from 1995, as compared to the growth rate of China's industrial sector, 9.51%. The rate of return on asset is 1.86%. 69.29% of all firms in the industry made a profit while 23.39% had negative returns. The top province in terms of the industry's revenue is Guangdong, accounting for 17.19% of the total revenue.
本行業在1996年佔全行業總產值0.038%，行業年增長率為18.4%（全國工業年增長率9.51%）。行業的資產回報率1.86%，69.29%的企業盈利，23.39%的企業虧損。銷售收入最高的省份為廣東省，佔本行業的17.19%。

	Total number of firms 企業總數	Total number of employees 職工總數	Total revenue (mil. RMB) 總銷售收入（百萬元）	Total profit (mil. RMB) 總利潤（百萬元）	Return on assets 資產利潤率 (%)	Return on equity 權益利潤率 (%)	Labour productivity ('000 RMB / worker) 勞動生產率（千元/人）	Debts / assets 資產負債率 (%)	Total assets (mil. RMB) 總資產（百萬元）
Industry Overall 行業總體	767	59,106	2,184	47	1.86	5.95	36.95	68.79	2,547

	Number of firms 企業個數	Average number of employees 平均職工人數	Average revenue ('000 RMB) 平均銷售收入（千元）	Average profit ('000 RMB) 平均利潤（千元）	Return on assets 資產利潤率 (%)	Return on equity 權益利潤率 (%)	Labour productivity ('000 RMB / worker) 勞動生產率（千元/人）	Average debts / assets 平均資產負債率(%)	Average Total assets ('000 RMB) 平均總資產（千元）
By ownership 產業所有權									
State-owned 國有	60	101	3,333	67	1.02	4.17	33.06	75.45	6,517
Collectively-owned 集體	641	73	2,350	90	3.60	11.17	32.05	67.78	2,494
Privately-owned 私有	3	20	345				17.53	70.88	331
Domestic JVs 聯營	3	131	12,203	59	0.83	2.41	92.92	65.58	7,073
Joint stock 股份制	7	53	1,385	56	3.50	17.95	25.99	80.49	1,608
Foreign-funded 外資	15	67	3,197	114	2.55	5.96	47.57	57.26	4,468
Overseas Chinese-funded 港澳台資	35	120	10,910	-481	-3.69	-11.59	90.99	68.19	13,053
By size 規模									
Large 大型									
Medium 中型	6	682	25,518	4,030	10.81	41.59	37.41	74.00	37,272
Small 小型	757	73	2,683	30	0.98	3.10	36.93	68.29	3,070
By regional distribution 地區分布									
Central-North 華北	116	58	1,503	18	0.92	3.31	26.02	72.20	1,913
Beijing 北京	25	18	368	-76	-5.07	-17.26	20.31	70.62	1,499
Tianjin 天津	21	101	1,757	-171	-4.56	-32.09	17.37	85.81	3,762
Hebei 河北	48	55	2,133	160	10.56	26.40	38.64	59.99	1,511
Shanxi 山西	14	86	1,459	-7	-0.35	-1.22	16.99	71.00	2,024
Inner Mongolia 內蒙	8	34	689	-3	-0.44	-0.90	20.04	50.88	565
Northeast 東北	111	55	1,156	55	3.63	13.95	20.85	74.02	1,523
Liaoning 遼寧	47	46	1,350	97	5.77	23.78	29.38	75.75	1,685
Jilin 吉林	35	59	254	-45	-2.88	-16.83	4.32	82.86	1,545
Heilongjiang 黑龍江	29	67	1,932	108	8.72	20.21	28.88	56.82	1,233
Central East 華東	293	70	4,152	107	2.18	7.26	59.70	70.04	4,933
Shanghai 上海	50	95	4,346	66	0.92	4.41	45.70	79.03	7,184
Jiangsu 江蘇	56	81	4,625	-81	-2.09	-6.60	57.28	68.37	3,876
Zhejiang 浙江	69	38	2,947	-41	-1.16	-4.68	78.51	75.14	3,553
Anhui 安徽	18	146	10,329	929	6.25	20.02	70.83	68.77	14,869
Fujian 福建	38	34	2,407	66	2.17	3.97	70.02	45.34	3,040
Jiangxi 江西	14	47	453	-11	-0.70	-2.45	9.56	71.52	1,638
Shandong 山東	48	82	5,276	342	7.54	21.94	64.64	65.62	4,538
Central-South 中南	179	130	3,483	48	1.34	3.71	26.70	63.80	3,551
Henan 河南	27	48	1,487	6	0.24	0.86	30.72	71.64	2,573
Hubei 湖北	35	49	3,510	165	14.57	45.76	71.26	68.16	1,132
Hunan 湖南	35	49	1,600	-3	-0.21	-0.57	32.86	63.16	1,632
Guangdong 廣東	74	247	5,072	29	0.47	1.28	20.50	63.22	6,060
Guangxi 廣西	8	39	3,654	76	2.90	5.17	93.99	43.81	2,625
Hainan 海南									
Southwest 西南	42	39	719	-5	-0.43	-1.12	18.20	61.34	1,153
Chongqing 重慶	13	47	482	-2	-0.21	-0.64	10.19	67.63	1,135
Sichuan 四川	16	45	1,289	-2	-0.10	-0.30	28.71	64.74	1,631
Guizhou 貴州	11	9	62	-3	-1.78	-4.35	6.80	59.17	154
Yunnan 雲南	2	117	1,325	-120	-4.07	-5.91	11.37	31.07	2,945
Tibet 西藏									
Northwest 西北	26	33	413	-23	-2.27	-8.09	12.53	71.92	1,032
Shaanxi 陝西	11	34	320	-40	-4.37	-25.73	9.41	83.10	915
Gansu 甘肅	6	37	680	-27	-1.71	-6.08	18.38	71.96	1,563
Qinghai 青海	4	45	598				13.35	45.15	748
Ningxia 寧夏	2	31	270	-5	-0.26	-0.94	8.71	72.47	1,925
Xinjiang 新疆	3	7	70				10.50	7.41	180

3461: Metal Construction Hardware 建築小五金製造業

Year 年份	Number of firms 企業個數	Rate of change 每年變化 (%)	Number of employees 職工人數 (人)	Rate of change 每年變化 (%)	Total revenue (mil. RMB) 總銷售收入 (百萬元)	Rate of change 每年變化 (%)	Total profit (mil. RMB) 總利潤 (百萬元)	Rate of change 每年變化 (%)
1993	838		69,091		1,749		42	
1994	927	10.62%	61,774	-10.59%	1,965	12.36%	21	-49.64%
1995	694	-25.14%	52,260	-15.40%	1,844	-6.19%	17	-20.59%
1996	767	10.52%	59,106	13.10%	2,184	18.44%	47	180.20%

3 Major products* 3種主要產品 *	Output 產量	Sales volume 銷售量	Unit 單位
a) Hinge 合頁	82,274	83,919	10,000 pair 萬付
b) Handle 拉手	8,391	3,944	10,000 pair 萬付
c) Steel Nail 鋼釘	45,232	48,850	ton 噸

Top 10 firms by revenue (year founded) 收入排名前10家企業 (創辦年份)	City 城市	Province 省	Telephone / fax 電話 / 傳真	Number of employees 職工人數	Ownership 產業所有權	Revenue ('000 RMB) 銷售收入 (千元)	Profit ('000 RMB) (rank) 利潤 (千元) (排名)	Total assets ('000 RMB) 總資產 (千元)	Major products 主要產品
Anhui Industry & Trading Corp. 安徽工貿實業總公司(1985)	Bengbu 蚌埠市	Anhui 安徽省	(0552)4082788 (0552)4083003	946	Collectively-owned 集體	145,931	14477(1)	218,745	a
Ji'nan Malleable Cast Iron Co. Ltd. 濟南瑪鋼股份有限公司(1962)	Ji'nan 濟南市	Shandong 山東省	(0531)7871102 (0531)7871021	1,176	Collectively-owned 集體	115,621	12324(2)	91,700	o
Xiaolan Hardware & Hinge Factory 小欖鎮五金鉸鏈廠(1966)	Zhongshan 中山市	Guangdong 廣東省	(0760)2273622 (0760)2250190	449	Collectively-owned 集體	63,127	408(37)	84,168	a
Qiang Jue (Nanjing) Hardware Xing Ye Co. Ltd. 強爵(南京)五金興業有限公司(1994)	Nanjing 南京市	Jiangsu 江蘇省	(025)8851946	40	Overseas Chinese-funded 港澳台資	41,500	0(140)	20,900	o
Shanghai Hu Xing Trading Co. 上海滬興實業公司(1993)	Shanghai 上海市	Shanghai 上海市	(021)57943916 (021)57943916	480	Collectively-owned 集體	40,096	194(73)	27,761	a
Shanghai Wusi Machinery General Factory 上海五四機械總廠(1977)	Shanghai 上海市	Shanghai 上海市	(021)57162622 (021)51762068	612	State-owned 國有	33,852	1460(8)	98,278	c
Zhangzhou Changshan Zheng Yi Hardware Industrial Co. Ltd. 漳州常山鉦毅五金工業有限公司(1993)	Zhangzhou 漳州市	Fujian 福建省	(0596)8628500 (0596)8628516	36	Overseas Chinese-funded 港澳台資	32,830	75(99)	12,507	o
Weifang Xiong Feng Hardware Manufacture Co. Ltd. 濰坊雄風五金製造有限公司(1987)	Weifang 濰坊市	Shandong 山東省	(0536)7618265	198	Collectively-owned 集體	31,997	2451(6)	9,680	o
Nan'an Chang Jiang Machinery Industrial Co. Ltd. 南安市長江機械實業有限公司(1987)	Quanzhou 泉州市	Fujian 福建省	(0595)6781888 (0595)6782289	328	Overseas Chinese-funded 港澳台資	30,510	2710(4)	56,376	o
Zhongshan No.5 Mine Hinge Factory 中山市五礦鉸鏈廠(1989)	Zhongshan 中山市	Guangdong 廣東省	(0760)2225845 (0760)2226945	144	State-owned 國有	28,547	1050(18)	13,295	a

Top 10 Cities by Production Output 產出排名前10位城市	Province 省	Market share 市場份額	Number of firms 企業個數
Shanghai 上海市	Shanghai 上海市	21.50%	194
Bengbu 蚌埠市	Anhui 安徽省	6.54%	4
Zhongshan 中山市	Guangdong 廣東省	4.46%	5
Guangzhou 廣州市	Guangdong 廣東省	3.90%	88
Wenzhou 温州市	Zhejiang 浙江省	2.95%	45
Yantai 煙台市	Shandong 山東省	2.50%	11
Suzhou 蘇州市	Jiangsu 江蘇省	2.45%	35
Quanzhou 泉州市	Fujian 福建省	2.29%	21
Hangzhou 杭州市	Zhejiang 浙江省	2.22%	14
Zhuhai 珠海市	Guangdong 廣東省	2.07%	3

10 Major Wholesalers 10家主要批發商	City 城市	Province 省	Telephone / Fax 電話 / 傳真
Chengdu Sheng Xing Trade Company 成都盛興商貿公司	Chengdu 成都市	Sichuan 四川省	(028)7762591
Shanghai Municipal Administration Engineering Material Company 上海市市政工程材料公司	Shanghai 上海市	Shanghai 上海市	(021)64372632
Shanghai Construction Engineering Material Co. 上海市建築工程材料公司	Shanghai 上海市	Shanghai 上海市	(021)63298630
Yixing Jin San Jiao Zhao Bazaar 宜興市金三角招商城	Wuxi 無錫市	Jiangsu 江蘇省	(0510)7935138 (0510)7935138
Fujian Hua Fu Import & Export Company 福建省華福進出口公司	Fuzhou 福州市	Fujian 福建省	(0591)7810477 (0591)7810485
China Building Goods & Materials Company 中國建築物資公司	Beijing 北京市	Beijing 北京市	(010)68586253
Dalian Jinzhou Xin Gang Industry & Trade Company 大連金州新港工貿公司	Dalian 大連市	Liaoning 遼寧省	(0411)7624747
Shanghai Zhan Dong Industrial Co. Ltd. 上海展東實業有限公司	Shanghai 上海市	Shanghai 上海市	(021)58201778 (021)58200874
China Building Materials and Equipment Import & Export Company 中國建築材料及設備進出口公司	Beijing 北京市	Beijing 北京市	(010)68393420
Dandong Chemical Light Industry Material Company Chemical Construction Material Marketing Station 丹東市化工輕工材料公司化工建材經銷站	Dandong 丹東市	Liaoning 遼寧省	(0415)2146396

*Also include sales by firms outside this industry.包括本行業以外廠家的銷售。"o" stands for "others". "o" 代表"其他產品"。

3463: Plumbing Parts 水暖管道零件製造業

The industry accounts for 0.112% of the total revenue of China's industrial sector in 1996. The revenue growth rate of the industry is 6.6% from 1995, as compared to the growth rate of China's industrial sector, 9.51%. The rate of return on asset is 2.42%. 70.67% of all firms in the industry made a profit while 22.50% had negative returns. The top province in terms of the industry's revenue is Hebei, accounting for 21.86% of the total revenue.
本行業在1996年佔全行業總產值0.112%，行業年增長率為6.6%（全國工業年增長率9.51%）。行業的資產回報率2.42%，70.67%的企業盈利，22.50%的企業虧損。銷售收入最高的省份為河北省，佔本行業的21.86%。

	Total number of firms 企業總數	Total number of employees 職工總數	Total revenue (mil. RMB) 總銷售收入（百萬元）	Total profit (mil. RMB) 總利潤（百萬元）	Return on assets 資產利潤率 (%)	Return on equity 權益利潤率 (%)	Labour productivity ('000 RMB / worker) 勞動生產率（千元/人）	Debts / assets 資產負債率 (%)	Total assets (mil. RMB) 總資產（百萬元）
Industry Overall 行業總體	1,249	142,167	6,520	167	2.42	7.28	45.86	66.82	6,898

	Number of firms 企業個數	Average number of employees 平均職工人數	Average revenue ('000 RMB) 平均銷售收入（千元）	Average profit ('000 RMB) 平均利潤（千元）	Return on assets 資產利潤率 (%)	Return on equity 權益利潤率 (%)	Labour productivity ('000 RMB / worker) 勞動生產率（千元/人）	Average debts / assets 平均資產負債率(%)	Average Total assets ('000 RMB) 平均總資產（千元）
By ownership 產業所有權									
State-owned 國有	83	177	4,313	-325	-3.13	-16.56	24.31	81.11	10,398
Collectively-owned 集體	1,077	105	4,857	236	5.73	18.72	46.39	69.38	4,120
Privately-owned 私有	11	120	6,644	136	2.92	7.90	55.20	63.12	4,655
Domestic JVs 聯營	7	88	1,233	-48	-1.11	-3.39	13.99	67.14	4,317
Joint stock 股份制	11	363	19,884	-349	-1.23	-2.21	54.78	44.31	28,358
Foreign-funded 外資	19	196	9,448	-1,282	-8.27	-14.75	48.28	43.95	15,506
Overseas Chinese-funded 港澳台資	40	135	10,733	-842	-3.82	-8.97	79.58	57.43	22,066
By size 規模									
Large 大型	2	1,843	119,846	33,405	28.57	71.62	65.05	60.11	116,920
Medium 中型	14	1,409	77,797	5,036	6.29	14.41	55.23	56.34	80,058
Small 小型	1,220	97	4,255	24	0.54	1.74	43.77	69.22	4,543
By regional distribution 地區分布									
Central-North 華北	351	193	8,500	255	3.17	8.85	44.04	64.15	8,024
Beijing 北京	61	90	2,184	-366	-4.82	-21.02	24.24	77.06	7,580
Tianjin 天津	39	129	5,865	222	2.39	10.66	45.41	77.62	9,314
Hebei 河北	133	185	10,715	447	6.21	17.38	57.79	64.27	7,197
Shanxi 山西	83	366	13,289	433	3.78	7.78	36.31	51.39	11,439
Inner Mongolia 內蒙	35	62	2,670	218	9.06	41.03	43.02	77.91	2,402
Northeast 東北	309	76	2,711	46	1.52	6.18	35.64	75.42	3,024
Liaoning 遼寧	141	82	3,510	40	1.14	5.12	42.72	77.84	3,536
Jilin 吉林	67	72	1,807	-74	-2.47	-17.94	25.05	86.22	2,994
Heilongjiang 黑龍江	101	70	2,194	134	5.74	14.74	31.30	61.08	2,330
Central East 華東	280	94	6,042	167	2.75	7.28	64.17	62.27	6,093
Shanghai 上海	31	127	8,228	-213	-1.90	-4.09	64.62	53.65	11,245
Jiangsu 江蘇	46	79	6,253	41	0.45	1.34	79.22	66.10	9,086
Zhejiang 浙江	72	84	4,256	103	2.57	8.29	50.63	68.93	3,998
Anhui 安徽	17	64	4,682	102	2.82	14.81	72.75	81.01	3,615
Fujian 福建	32	53	3,872	114	2.88	5.65	73.57	49.10	3,964
Jiangxi 江西	17	25	708	21	5.78	13.14	27.85	56.02	366
Shandong 山東	65	146	9,647	591	8.40	22.33	65.86	62.37	7,035
Central-South 中南	177	69	4,122	173	3.16	9.52	59.84	66.87	5,468
Henan 河南	58	54	4,138	490	14.12	45.27	76.74	68.82	3,471
Hubei 湖北	19	159	4,739	173	3.08	10.83	29.83	71.57	5,625
Hunan 湖南	15	102	2,321	-261	-6.65	-26.36	22.86	74.76	3,927
Guangdong 廣東	77	31	2,719	-8	-0.18	-0.45	87.50	60.17	4,382
Guangxi 廣西	7	289	20,069	370	1.38	5.14	69.48	73.11	26,750
Hainan 海南	1	108	14,860	770	1.01	2.76	137.59	63.34	76,100
Southwest 西南	60	110	2,314	-143	-3.92	-21.75	21.02	81.96	3,644
Chongqing 重慶	15	91	1,863	-183	-5.45	-73.63	20.58	92.60	3,357
Sichuan 四川	39	126	2,656	-140	-3.42	-17.30	21.16	80.24	4,108
Guizhou 貴州	3	33	320	-40	-12.90	-23.08	9.60	44.09	310
Yunnan 雲南	3	84	2,050	-83	-3.60	-7.40	24.31	51.37	2,317
Tibet 西藏									
Northwest 西北	72	80	1,927	-78	-2.21	-12.41	24.06	82.17	3,540
Shaanxi 陝西	26	59	1,940	72	3.60	18.84	32.99	80.89	1,987
Gansu 甘肅	14	66	1,905	48	2.47	9.90	28.80	75.09	1,939
Qinghai 青海									
Ningxia 寧夏	3	220	5,627	-1,290	-7.91	270.63	25.54	102.92	16,303
Xinjiang 新疆	29	91	1,543	-148	-3.38	-14.22	16.88	76.22	4,385

Year 年份	Number of firms 企業個數	Rate of change 每年變化 (%)	Number of employees 職工人數（人）	Rate of change 每年變化 (%)	Total revenue (mil. RMB) 總銷售收入（百萬元）	Rate of change 每年變化 (%)	Total profit (mil. RMB) 總利潤（百萬元）	Rate of change 每年變化 (%)
1993	1,197		128,523		4,387		139	
1994	1,299	8.52%	164,348	27.87%	5,430	23.76%	105	-24.60%
1995	1,296	-0.23%	172,044	4.68%	6,118	12.66%	79	-24.43%
1996	1,249	-3.63%	142,167	-17.37%	6,520	6.57%	167	110.51%

3 Major products* 3 種主要產品 *	Output 產量	Sales volume 銷售量	Unit 單位
a) Cast Iron Central Heating Radiator 鑄鐵暖氣片	1,582,616	1,550,964	ton 噸
b) Water-heating Pipeline Parts 水暖管道零件	573,057	567,326	ton 噸
c) Metal Window & Door 金屬門窗	83,851	78,820	ton 噸

Top 10 firms by revenue (year founded) 收入排名前 10 家企業（創辦年份）	City 城市	Province 省	Telephone / fax 電話 / 傳真	Number of employees 職工人數	Ownership 產業所有權	Revenue ('000 RMB) 銷售收入（千元）	Profit ('000 RMB) (rank) 利潤（千元）（排名）	Total assets ('000 RMB) 總資產（千元）	Major products 主要產品
Taiyuan Zhao Jia Bao Enterprise Group Company 太原趙家堡企業集團公司(1996)	Taiyuan 太原市	Shanxi 山西省	(0351)5778060	13,000	Collectively-owned 集體	590,500	46570(1)	475,665	a
China Tianyuan Radiators Group 中國天元散熱器集團(1969)	Hengshui 衡水市	Hebei 河北省	(0318)8462242 (0318)8462233	4,562	Collectively-owned 集體	394,896	19497(4)	233,016	a
Heibei Jizhou Radiator Factory 河北省冀州市暖氣片廠(1971)	Hengshui 衡水市	Hebei 河北省	(0318)8615653	5,000	Collectively-owned 集體	380,500	21800(3)	176,540	a
Shanxi Qingxu Gao Hua Radiator Industrial Company 山西省清徐縣高花暖氣片工業公司(1984)	Taiyuan 太原市	Shanxi 山西省	(0351)5775094	2,000	Collectively-owned 集體	115,260	0(340)	28,000	a
Xinhui Xianhao Plumbing Stock Co. Ltd. 新會市顯浩水暖器材有限公司(1991)	Jiangmen 江門市	Guangdong 廣東省	(0750)6812101 (0750)6811658	654	Foreign-funded 外資	114,971	0(352)	97,181	o
Shanxi Taigu Malleable Cast Iron Factory 山西省太谷縣瑪鋼廠(1956)	Yuci 榆次市	Shanxi 山西省	(0354)6322168 (0354)6322156	3,014	Collectively-owned 集體	111,493	-2929(432)	112,177	b
Sweet-scented Osmanthus Water Supply & Heating Equipment Co. Ltd. 桂花水暖器材股份有限公司	Guiping 桂平市	Guangxi 廣西	(0775)7632328	1,685	Joint stock 股份制	110,884	2910(15)	138,279	o
Xinxiang Pipe Making Galvanization Factory 新鄉縣製管鍍鋅廠(1991)	Xinxiang 新鄉市	Henan 河南省	(0373)2020915	84	Collectively-owned 集體	104,070	26798(2)	17,371	o
Zhangjiagang He Xing Cold Work Installation Team 張家港市合興冷作安裝隊(1972)	Suzhou 蘇州市	Jiangsu 江蘇省	(0512)8500747	500	Collectively-owned 集體	95,380	7510(5)	156,581	o
Zouping Hongwei Industrial Company 鄒平縣宏偉實業公司(1995)	Binzhou 濱州市	Shandong 山東省	(0543)4851283 (0543)4851283	230	Collectively-owned 集體	89,150	5898(7)	11,716	b

Top 10 Cities by Production Output 產出排名前 10 位城市	Province 省	Market share 市場份額	Number of firms 企業個數
Taiyuan 太原市	Shanxi 山西省	12.13%	17
Hengshui 衡水市	Hebei 河北省	10.23%	12
Shanghai 上海市	Shanghai 上海市	4.87%	59
Yuci 榆次市	Shanxi 山西省	4.63%	22
Ji'nan 濟南市	Shandong 山東省	3.49%	11
Beijing 北京市	Beijing 北京市	3.20%	57
Tangshan 唐山市	Hebei 河北省	2.61%	33
Xinxiang 新鄉市	Henan 河南省	2.33%	9
Taizhou 臺州市	Zhejiang 浙江省	2.12%	30
Shenyang 瀋陽市	Liaoning 遼寧省	2.07%	46

10 Major Wholesalers 10 家主要批發商	City 城市	Province 省	Telephone / Fax 電話 / 傳真
Chengdu Sheng Xing Trade Company 成都盛興商貿公司	Chengdu 成都市	Sichuan 四川省	(028)7762591
Shanghai Municipal Administration Engineering Material Company 上海市市政工程材料公司	Shanghai 上海市	Shanghai 上海市	(021)64372632
Shanghai Construction Engineering Material Co. 上海市建築工程材料公司	Shanghai 上海市	Shanghai 上海市	(021)63298630
Yixing Jin San Jiao Zhao Bazaar 宜興市金三角招商城	Wuxi 無錫市	Jiangsu 江蘇省	(0510)7935138 (0510)7935138
Fujian Hua Fu Import & Export Company 福建省華福進出口公司	Fuzhou 福州市	Fujian 福建省	(0591)7810477 (0591)7810485
China Building Goods & Materials Company 中國建築物資公司	Beijing 北京市	Beijing 北京市	(010)68586253
Dalian Jinzhou Xin Gang Industry & Trade Company 大連金州新港工貿公司	Dalian 大連市	Liaoning 遼寧省	(0411)7624747
Shanghai Zhan Dong Industrial Co. Ltd. 上海展東實業有限公司	Shanghai 上海市	Shanghai 上海市	(021)58201778 (021)58200874
China Building Materials and Equipment Import & Export Company 中國建築材料及設備進出口公司	Beijing 北京市	Beijing 北京市	(010)68393420
Dandong Chemical Light Industry Material Company Chemical Construction Material Marketing Station 丹東市化工輕工材料公司化工建材經銷站	Dandong 丹東市	Liaoning 遼寧省	(0415)2146396

*Also include sales by firms outside this industry.包括本行業以外廠家的銷售。"o" stands for "others". "o" 代表"其他產品"。

3465: Metal Doors and Windows 金屬門窗製造業

The industry accounts for 0.199% of the total revenue of China's industrial sector in 1996. The revenue growth rate of the industry is 9.8% from 1995, as compared to the growth rate of China's industrial sector, 9.51%. The rate of return on asset is 1.24%. 74.04% of all firms in the industry made a profit while 19.61% had negative returns. The top province in terms of the industry's revenue is Jiangsu, accounting for 19.67% of the total revenue.
本行業在1996年佔全行業總產值0.199%，行業年增長率為9.8%（全國工業年增長率9.51%）。行業的資產回報率1.24%，74.04%的企業盈利，19.61%的企業虧損。銷售收入最高的省份為江蘇省，佔本行業的19.67%。

	Total number of firms 企業總數	Total number of employees 職工總數	Total revenue (mil. RMB) 總銷售收入（百萬元）	Total profit (mil. RMB) 總利潤（百萬元）	Return on assets 資產利潤率 (%)	Return on equity 權益利潤率 (%)	Labour productivity ('000 RMB / worker) 勞動生產率（千元/人）	Debts / assets 資產負債率 (%)	Total assets (mil. RMB) 總資產（百萬元）
Industry Overall 行業總體	4,084	255,250	11,526	183	1.24	4.46	45.16	72.19	14,771

	Number of firms 企業個數	Average number of employees 平均職工人數	Average revenue ('000 RMB) 平均銷售收入（千元）	Average profit ('000 RMB) 平均利潤（千元）	Return on assets 資產利潤率 (%)	Return on equity 權益利潤率 (%)	Labour productivity ('000 RMB / worker) 勞動生產率（千元/人）	Average debts / assets 平均資產負債率(%)	Average Total assets ('000 RMB) 平均總資產（千元）
By ownership 產業所有權									
State-owned 國有	403	117	2,861	241	3.00	10.96	24.42	72.62	8,020
Collectively-owned 集體	3,421	56	2,597	25	0.90	3.36	46.61	73.30	2,770
Privately-owned 私有	27	46	4,021	18	0.66	1.49	87.70	56.14	2,772
Domestic JVs 聯營	49	77	4,411	93	1.48	7.01	57.02	78.84	6,277
Joint stock 股份制	52	107	5,895	74	1.18	3.69	55.29	67.88	6,259
Foreign-funded 外資	48	80	3,660	-180	-1.49	-4.21	45.69	64.53	12,074
Overseas Chinese-funded 港澳台資	82	54	8,281	8	0.08	0.22	152.56	63.30	9,433
By size 規模									
Large 大型	3	1,260	48,171	-12,209	-7.84	-87.75	38.24	91.07	155,730
Medium 中型	27	615	24,175	-529	-0.88	-3.45	39.28	74.59	60,333
Small 小型	4,016	58	2,670	58	1.85	6.42	45.70	71.22	3,154
By regional distribution 地區分布									
Central-North 華北	748	47	1,698	36	1.22	4.56	36.03	73.20	2,951
Beijing 北京	268	40	1,603	43	1.36	4.62	39.65	70.52	3,164
Tianjin 天津	58	54	3,365	96	1.91	8.53	61.91	77.63	5,002
Hebei 河北	181	53	2,133	58	1.80	6.26	39.92	71.28	3,210
Shanxi 山西	46	107	1,314	-97	-2.26	-12.58	12.23	82.04	4,291
Inner Mongolia 內蒙	195	34	1,020	20	1.33	5.20	29.91	74.47	1,491
Northeast 東北	816	82	2,421	46	1.63	7.88	29.54	79.32	2,844
Liaoning 遼寧	441	96	2,689	52	1.81	10.22	27.98	82.27	2,848
Jilin 吉林	141	67	1,566	5	0.17	0.82	23.24	79.39	3,130
Heilongjiang 黑龍江	234	64	2,432	61	2.30	8.60	37.92	73.30	2,663
Central East 華東	1,157	65	4,177	78	1.66	5.56	64.26	70.13	4,722
Shanghai 上海	118	51	3,586	-36	-0.58	-1.60	70.36	63.54	6,145
Jiangsu 江蘇	348	83	6,514	157	2.87	8.21	78.06	65.06	5,461
Zhejiang 浙江	148	39	2,483	-9	-0.30	-1.01	63.77	70.06	2,847
Anhui 安徽	114	55	3,531	223	9.86	27.35	64.18	63.94	2,260
Fujian 福建	79	31	1,186		-0.01	-0.01	38.50	54.59	1,972
Jiangxi 江西	83	37	1,032	-53	-2.72	-12.82	27.74	78.78	1,936
Shandong 山東	267	85	4,468	78	1.12	5.45	52.82	79.38	6,900
Central-South 中南	642	51	2,874	91	2.65	8.60	56.37	69.16	3,442
Henan 河南	195	55	1,448	29	1.39	5.23	26.50	73.37	2,062
Hubei 湖北	103	63	4,084	87	2.53	8.83	64.96	71.33	3,419
Hunan 湖南	82	53	2,355	14	0.59	5.62	44.70	89.47	2,372
Guangdong 廣東	186	43	4,232	216	3.55	9.83	99.25	63.86	6,073
Guangxi 廣西	67	43	2,156	56	4.53	13.55	49.96	66.52	1,231
Hainan 海南	9	51	1,964	-102	-1.88	-5.36	38.19	64.91	5,430
Southwest 西南	303	61	2,987	-5	-0.15	-0.56	49.29	72.88	3,569
Chongqing 重慶	36	60	4,201	20	1.01	17.61	69.78	94.28	2,018
Sichuan 四川	150	60	3,570	22	0.57	2.46	59.54	76.81	3,934
Guizhou 貴州	46	43	873	-34	-2.50	-5.78	20.13	56.76	1,356
Yunnan 雲南	70	69	2,509	-40	-0.90	-3.14	36.44	71.48	4,512
Tibet 西藏	1	318	2,630	-1,260	-3.11	-3.58	8.27	13.11	40,490
Northwest 西北	418	64	1,667	-70	-1.97	-6.82	26.00	71.15	3,561
Shaanxi 陝西	120	60	1,545	18	0.58	1.79	25.92	67.67	3,049
Gansu 甘肅	136	66	1,682	-65	-1.71	-6.00	25.35	71.58	3,782
Qinghai 青海	25	58	1,371	-76	-2.35	-7.14	23.82	67.04	3,214
Ningxia 寧夏	18	79	1,569	-128	-3.34	-10.12	19.80	66.99	3,826
Xinjiang 新疆	119	65	1,851	-155	-4.02	-15.93	28.36	74.78	3,859

3465: Metal Doors and Windows 金屬門窗製造業

Year 年份	Number of firms 企業個數	Rate of change 每年變化 (%)	Number of employees 職工人數 (人)	Rate of change 每年變化 (%)	Total revenue (mil. RMB) 總銷售收入 (百萬元)	Rate of change 每年變化 (%)	Total profit (mil. RMB) 總利潤 (百萬元)	Rate of change 每年變化 (%)
1993	2,816		213,946		9,421		353	
1994	3,411	21.13%	265,406	24.05%	9,861	4.67%	253	-28.15%
1995	4,091	19.94%	259,997	-2.04%	10,498	6.46%	132	-47.95%
1996	4,084	-0.17%	255,250	-1.83%	11,526	9.79%	183	38.73%

3 Major products* 3種主要產品*	Output 產量	Sales volume 銷售量	Unit 單位
a) Metal Window & Door 金屬門窗	2,376,650	2,234,051	ton 噸
b) Metal Products for Building 建築用金屬品	2,374,240	2,255,528	ton 噸
c) Aluminium Section 鋁型材	27,555	25,075	ton 噸

Top 10 firms by revenue (year founded) 收入排名前10家企業 (創辦年份)	City 城市	Province 省	Telephone / fax 電話 / 傳真	Number of employees 職工人數	Ownership 產業所有權	Revenue ('000 RMB) 銷售收入 (千元)	Profit ('000 RMB) (rank) 利潤 (千元) (排名)	Total assets ('000 RMB) 總資產 (千元)	Major products 主要產品
Anshan Electric Industry Steel-aluminum Alloy Door & Window Factory 鞍山市電業鋼鋁門窗廠(1993)	Anshan 鞍山市	Liaoning 遼寧省	(0412)8311479	668	Collectively-owned 集體	198,900	3330(26)	95,580	a
Jiangyin Jin Nan Building Group Company Aluminium Alloy Window & Door Factory 江陰錦南建築集團公司鋁合金門窗廠(1990)	Wuxi 無錫市	Jiangsu 江蘇省	(0510)6181861	1,685	Collectively-owned 集體	186,784	9066(4)	116,517	o
Liaoning Yingkou Group Co. Ltd 遼寧營口股份集團有限公司(1992)	Yingkou 營口市	Liaoning 遼寧省	(0417)5840654 (0417)5840197	1,404	Collectively-owned 集體	142,867	8995(5)	41,766	o
Chongqing Mei Yu Aluminium Industry Company 重慶市美魚鋁業公司	Chongqing 重慶市	Chongqing 重慶市	(023)65111326	450	Collectively-owned 集體	126,622	582(192)	24,973	c
Shenyang Yuan Da Aluminium Industry Engineering Co. Ltd. 瀋陽遠大鋁業工程有限公司(1993)	Shenyang 瀋陽市	Liaoning 遼寧省	(024)88411227 (024)88416737	421	Overseas Chinese-funded 港澳台資	123,000	1040(106)	141,422	o
Jiangsu Shen Ma Group Co. 江蘇神馬集團公司(1985)	Wuxi 無錫市	Jiangsu 江蘇省	(0510)7541889 (0510)7541888	450	Collectively-owned 集體	118,690	6223(10)	32,832	a,b
Xuzhou Yun Hu Door & Window Group Co. 徐州市雲湖門窗集團公司(1978)	Xuzhou 徐州市	Jiangsu 江蘇省	(0516)5729141 (0516)5729141	456	Collectively-owned 集體	111,631	4499(16)	45,190	a,b
Jiangsu Su Xin Decoration Group Co. 江蘇蘇鑫裝飾集團公司(1987)	Suzhou 蘇州市	Jiangsu 江蘇省	(0512)5481518 (0512)5481518	468	Collectively-owned 集體	109,550	12060(2)	101,060	a
Shandong Hui Ye Group Co. Ltd. 山東匯業集團有限公司(1995)	Yantai 煙台市	Shandong 山東省	(0535)8842296	1,536	Collectively-owned 集體	107,830	7090(7)	46,780	a,b
Shanghai Wan Hao Decorative Engineering Co. Ltd. 上海萬豪裝飾工程有限公司(1995)	Shanghai 上海市	Shanghai 上海市	(021)64732299	69	Overseas Chinese-funded 港澳台資	96,936	14643(1)	50,129	o

Top 10 Cities by Production Output 產出排名前10位城市	Province 省	Market share 市場份額	Number of firms 企業個數
Shanghai 上海市	Shanghai 上海市	5.29%	197
Beijing 北京市	Beijing 北京市	5.06%	244
Wuxi 無錫市	Jiangsu 江蘇省	3.52%	103
Qinhuangdao 秦皇島市	Hebei 河北省	3.51%	15
Shenzhen 深圳市	Guangdong 廣東省	2.81%	28
Binzhou 濱州市	Shandong 山東省	2.81%	7
Yantai 煙台市	Shandong 山東省	2.60%	44
Anshan 鞍山市	Liaoning 遼寧省	2.57%	13
Suzhou 蘇州市	Jiangsu 江蘇省	2.43%	109
Shenyang 瀋陽市	Liaoning 遼寧省	2.38%	223

10 Major Wholesalers 10家主要批發商	City 城市	Province 省	Telephone / Fax 電話 / 傳真
Chengdu Sheng Xing Trade Company 成都盛興商貿公司	Chengdu 成都市	Sichuan 四川省	(028)7762591
Shanghai Municipal Administration Engineering Material Company 上海市市政工程材料公司	Shanghai 上海市	Shanghai 上海市	(021)64372632
Shanghai Construction Engineering Material Co. 上海市建築工程材料公司	Shanghai 上海市	Shanghai 上海市	(021)63298630
Yixing Jin San Jiao Zhao Bazaar 宜興市金三角招商城	Wuxi 無錫市	Jiangsu 江蘇省	(0510)7935138 (0510)7935138
Fujian Hua Fu Import & Export Company 福建省華福進出口公司	Fuzhou 福州市	Fujian 福建省	(0591)7810477 (0591)7810485
China Building Goods & Materials Company 中國建築物資公司	Beijing 北京市	Beijing 北京市	(010)68586253
Dalian Jinzhou Xin Gang Industry & Trade Company 大連金州新港工貿公司	Dalian 大連市	Liaoning 遼寧省	(0411)7624747
Shanghai Zhan Dong Industrial Co. Ltd. 上海展東實業有限公司	Shanghai 上海市	Shanghai 上海市	(021)58201778 (021)58200874
China Building Materials and Equipment Import & Export Company 中國建築材料及設備進出口公司	Beijing 北京市	Beijing 北京市	(010)68393420
Dandong Chemical Light Industry Material Company Chemical Construction Material Marketing Station 丹東市化工輕工材料公司化工建材經銷站	Dandong 丹東市	Liaoning 遼寧省	(0415)2146396

*Also include sales by firms outside this industry.包括本行業以外廠家的銷售。"o" stands for "others". "o" 代表"其他產品"。

3469: Other Metal Products for Construction 其他建築用金屬製品業

The industry accounts for 0.043% of the total revenue of China's industrial sector in 1996. The revenue growth rate of the industry is 38.6% from 1995, as compared to the growth rate of China's industrial sector, 9.51%. The rate of return on asset is 1.55%. 70.34% of all firms in the industry made a profit while 25.81% had negative returns. The top province in terms of the industry's revenue is Guangdong, accounting for 20.43% of the total revenue.
本行業在1996年佔全行業總產值0.043%，行業年增長率為38.6%（全國工業年增長率9.51%）。行業的資產回報率1.55%，70.34%的企業盈利，25.81%的企業虧損。銷售收入最高的省份為廣東省，佔本行業的20.43%。

	Total number of firms 企業總數	Total number of employees 職工總數	Total revenue (mil. RMB) 總銷售收入（百萬元）	Total profit (mil. RMB) 總利潤（百萬元）	Return on assets 資產利潤率 (%)	Return on equity 權益利潤率 (%)	Labour productivity ('000 RMB / worker) 勞動生產率（千元／人）	Debts / assets 資產負債率 (%)	Total assets (mil. RMB) 總資產（百萬元）
Industry Overall 行業總體	440	26,513	2,465	44	1.55	4.72	92.97	67.11	2,803

	Number of firms 企業個數	Average number of employees 平均職工人數	Average revenue ('000 RMB) 平均銷售收入（千元）	Average profit ('000 RMB) 平均利潤（千元）	Return on assets 資產利潤率 (%)	Return on equity 權益利潤率 (%)	Labour productivity ('000 RMB / worker) 勞動生產率（千元／人）	Average debts / assets 平均資產負債率(%)	Average Total assets ('000 RMB) 平均總資產（千元）
By ownership 產業所有權									
State-owned 國有	31	59	2,226				37.89	79.41	3,290
Collectively-owned 集體	335	64	5,395	-7	-0.13	-0.48	84.51	73.12	5,129
Privately-owned 私有	4	23	3,292	900	109.68	270.03	141.57	59.38	820
Domestic JVs 聯營	6	88	6,039	1,680	14.32	29.51	68.50	51.47	11,727
Joint stock 股份制	5	39	6,687	3,244	46.12	107.49	171.47	57.10	7,034
Foreign-funded 外資	26	48	13,913	2,673	11.67	25.79	289.16	54.76	22,915
Overseas Chinese-funded 港澳台資	33	45	4,364	-1,611	-19.11	-44.63	96.07	57.19	8,430
By size 規模									
Large 大型	2	825	41,097	738	0.57	1.93	49.84	70.72	130,446
Medium 中型	3	424	41,425	5,236	8.29	43.77	97.78	81.07	63,200
Small 小型	418	56	5,403	64	1.14	3.31	96.20	65.58	5,628
By regional distribution 地區分布									
Central-North 華北	63	49	3,183	244	7.50	24.42	64.68	69.27	3,247
Beijing 北京	24	23	1,330	59	3.72	10.20	57.62	63.55	1,580
Tianjin 天津	15	87	6,513	639	8.77	43.65	74.86	79.91	7,290
Hebei 河北	16	41	3,820	268	11.07	18.58	93.03	40.43	2,416
Shanxi 山西	4	22	795	15	0.55	10.34	36.98	94.70	2,738
Inner Mongolia 內蒙	4	125	1,648	3	0.13	0.29	13.23	54.94	1,925
Northeast 東北	80	61	2,259	-232	-4.06	-12.98	36.97	68.74	5,709
Liaoning 遼寧	54	63	2,873	-341	-4.30	-14.01	45.81	69.31	7,926
Jilin 吉林	11	37	627	-49	-7.80	-27.69	16.91	71.97	629
Heilongjiang 黑龍江	15	73	1,246	27	1.88	4.32	17.08	56.49	1,453
Central East 華東	152	71	7,183	271	3.46	10.97	101.53	68.45	7,825
Shanghai 上海	35	85	9,176	283	2.91	10.48	108.39	72.24	9,718
Jiangsu 江蘇	37	55	5,388	241	4.13	11.27	98.65	63.36	5,827
Zhejiang 浙江	34	56	10,746	483	6.93	17.63	190.69	60.68	6,962
Anhui 安徽	4	47	4,628	83	5.18	50.77	97.94	89.80	1,593
Fujian 福建	20	21	1,921	74	1.80	2.47	92.80	27.32	4,089
Jiangxi 江西	2	50	600				12.00	8.33	60
Shandong 山東	20	158	7,389	210	1.36	8.62	46.91	84.25	15,437
Central-South 中南	103	48	7,237	86	1.15	3.23	150.44	64.31	7,433
Henan 河南	14	36	1,436	-76	-1.78	-4.27	39.80	58.36	4,256
Hubei 湖北	17	49	10,713	-89	-0.54	-1.90	220.22	71.78	16,699
Hunan 湖南	23	37	1,172	-49	-4.89	-15.18	31.53	67.76	997
Guangdong 廣東	39	63	12,912	288	2.91	7.30	203.79	60.08	9,869
Guangxi 廣西	10	30	1,270	130	9.06	17.86	42.76	49.27	1,435
Hainan 海南									
Southwest 西南	31	64	7,217	-77	-1.58	-4.11	113.33	61.53	4,857
Chongqing 重慶	6	42	7,003	9	0.32	1.47	166.64	78.53	2,845
Sichuan 四川	14	74	10,434	-38	-0.68	-1.40	140.35	51.26	5,586
Guizhou 貴州									
Yunnan 雲南	11	63	3,364	-175	-3.42	-11.37	53.31	69.88	5,125
Tibet 西藏									
Northwest 西北	11	77	2,122	-82	-2.50	-9.29	27.72	73.09	3,277
Shaanxi 陝西	7	104	2,654	-150	-3.27	-12.92	25.56	74.65	4,587
Gansu 甘肅	1	81	2,820	60	2.94	19.35	34.81	84.80	2,040
Qinghai 青海	1	9	210	10	14.29	16.67	23.33	14.29	70
Ningxia 寧夏									
Xinjiang 新疆	2	13	865	40	4.37	6.72	69.20	34.97	915

3469: Other Metal Products for Construction 其他建築用金屬製品業

Year 年份	Number of firms 企業個數	Rate of change 每年變化 (%)	Number of employees 職工人數 (人)	Rate of change 每年變化 (%)	Total revenue (mil. RMB) 總銷售收入 (百萬元)	Rate of change 每年變化 (%)	Total profit (mil. RMB) 總利潤 (百萬元)	Rate of change 每年變化 (%)
1993	386		31,084		1,319		47	
1994	427	10.62%	27,506	-11.51%	1,331	0.90%	32	-31.31%
1995	447	4.68%	32,666	18.76%	1,778	33.51%	5	-85.02%
1996	440	-1.57%	26,513	-18.84%	2,465	38.64%	44	805.91%

3 Major products* 3 種主要產品 *	Output 產量	Sales volume 銷售量	Unit 單位
a) Welded Steel Pipe 焊接鋼管	153,750	139,913	ton 噸
b) Metal Products for Building 建築用金屬品	192,944	183,297	ton 噸
c) Metal Window & Door 金屬門窗	41,837	39,327	ton 噸

Top 10 firms by revenue (year founded) 收入排名前 10 家企業 (創辦年份)	City 城市	Province 省	Telephone / fax 電話 / 傳真	Number of employees 職工人數	Ownership 產業所有權	Revenue ('000 RMB) 銷售收入 (千元)	Profit ('000 RMB) (rank) 利潤 (千元) (排名)	Total assets ('000 RMB) 總資產 (千元)	Major products 主要產品
Jiedong Policy-testing Zone Tai Feng Qiao Metal Products Co. Ltd. 揭東縣試驗區泰豐僑金屬製品有限公司(1993)	Jieyang 揭陽市	Guangdong 廣東省	(0663)3264579	300	Foreign-funded 外資	267,021	3197(7)	174,055	a
Wenzhou Wu Tai Group Co. Ltd. 温州吳泰集團有限公司(1983)	Wenzhou 温州市	Zhejiang 浙江省	(0577)5523688 (0577)5522755	418	Joint stock 股份制	178,252	10334(2)	110,775	o
Chengdu Jin Ma Industrial Company 成都金馬實業公司	Chengdu 成都市	Sichuan 四川省	(028)822619	55	Collectively-owned 集體	143,359	479(40)	27,500	o
Foshan Lan Shi Stainless Steel Section Steel Factory 佛山市瀾石不銹鋼型材廠(1989)	Foshan 佛山市	Guangdong 廣東省	(0757)3312387 (0757)3313541	213	Collectively-owned 集體	71,223	13995(1)	34,991	o
Shanghai Hares Metal Products Co. Ltd. 上海哈瑞克斯金屬製品公司(1993)	Shanghai 上海市	Shanghai 上海市	(021)58582236 (021)58582208	61	Foreign-funded 外資	63,930	5016(6)	106,653	b
Shandong Zibo Hua Sheng Group Co. Ltd. 山東淄博華盛集團有限公司(1954)	Zibo 淄博市	Shandong 山東省	(0533)3181741 (0533)3183741	1,648	Collectively-owned 集體	62,048	1797(14)	240,896	o
Liaoning Longde Group General Company 遼寧隆德集團總公司(1986)	Liaoyang 遼陽市	Liaoning 遼寧省	(0419)7166385	872	Collectively-owned 集體	57,455	-7789(155)	194,257	o
Panjin Hua Fu Electric Appliance Co. Ltd. 盤錦市華孚電器有限公司(1995)	Panjin 盤錦市	Liaoning 遼寧省	(0427)7806643	78	Domestic JVs 聯營	51,440	2338(11)	7,565	o
Yuhang Metal Calendering Factory 余杭市金屬壓延廠(1988)	Hangzhou 杭州市	Zhejiang 浙江省	(0571)6372942	112	Collectively-owned 集體	37,087	-42(125)	16,250	o
Xi Shan Shi Hong Sheng Building Company 錫山市鴻聲建築公司(1990)	Wuxi 無錫市	Jiangsu 江蘇省	(0510)8580209	276	Collectively-owned 集體	35,247	3158(8)	10,370	o

Top 10 Cities by Production Output 產出排名前 10 位城市	Province 省	Market share 市場份額	Number of firms 企業個數
Shanghai 上海市	Shanghai 上海市	16.01%	79
Jieyang 揭陽市	Guangdong 廣東省	14.84%	3
Foshan 佛山市	Guangdong 廣東省	7.54%	5
Tianjin 天津市	Tianjin 天津市	5.37%	16
Zibo 淄博市	Shandong 山東省	5.28%	8
Changzhou 常州市	Jiangsu 江蘇省	4.18%	11
Liaoyang 遼陽市	Liaoning 遼寧省	4.00%	17
Hangzhou 杭州市	Zhejiang 浙江省	3.24%	7
Suzhou 蘇州市	Jiangsu 江蘇省	2.19%	21
Ningbo 寧波市	Zhejiang 浙江省	2.08%	5

10 Major Wholesalers 10 家主要批發商	City 城市	Province 省	Telephone / Fax 電話 / 傳真
Chengdu Sheng Xing Trade Company 成都盛興商貿公司	Chengdu 成都市	Sichuan 四川省	(028)7762591
Shanghai Municipal Administration Engineering Material Company 上海市市政工程材料公司	Shanghai 上海市	Shanghai 上海市	(021)64372632
Shanghai Construction Engineering Material Co. 上海市建築工程材料公司	Shanghai 上海市	Shanghai 上海市	(021)63298630
Yixing Jin San Jiao Zhao Bazaar 宜興市金三角招商城	Wuxi 無錫市	Jiangsu 江蘇省	(0510)7935138 (0510)7935138
Fujian Hua Fu Import & Export Company 福建省華福進出口公司	Fuzhou 福州市	Fujian 福建省	(0591)7810477 (0591)7810485
China Building Goods & Materials Company 中國建築物資公司	Beijing 北京市	Beijing 北京市	(010)68586253
Dalian Jinzhou Xin Gang Industry & Trade Company 大連金州新港工貿公司	Dalian 大連市	Liaoning 遼寧省	(0411)7624747
Shanghai Zhan Dong Industrial Co. Ltd. 上海展東實業有限公司	Shanghai 上海市	Shanghai 上海市	(021)58201778 (021)58200874
China Building Materials and Equipment Import & Export Company 中國建築材料及設備進出口公司	Beijing 北京市	Beijing 北京市	(010)68393420
Dandong Chemical Light Industry Material Company Chemical Construction Material Marketing Station 丹東市化工輕工材料公司化工建材經銷站	Dandong 丹東市	Liaoning 遼寧省	(0415)2146396

*Also include sales by firms outside this industry.包括本行業以外廠家的銷售。"o" stands for "others". "o" 代表 "其他產品" 。

3470: Metal Surface Treatment and Heat Treatment
金屬表面處理及熱處理業

The industry accounts for 0.156% of the total revenue of China's industrial sector in 1996. The revenue growth rate of the industry is 7.3% from 1995, as compared to the growth rate of China's industrial sector, 9.51%. The rate of return on asset is 3.15%. 73.17% of all firms in the industry made a profit while 21.21% had negative returns. The top province in terms of the industry's revenue is Guangdong, accounting for 23.37% of the total revenue.
本行業在1996年佔全行業總產值0.156%，行業年增長率為7.3%（全國工業年增長率9.51%）。行業的資產回報率3.15%，73.17%的企業盈利，21.21%的企業虧損。銷售收入最高的省份為廣東省，佔本行業的23.37%。

	Total number of firms 企業總數	Total number of employees 職工總數	Total revenue (mil. RMB) 總銷售收入（百萬元）	Total profit (mil. RMB) 總利潤（百萬元）	Return on assets 資產利潤率 (%)	Return on equity 權益利潤率 (%)	Labour productivity ('000 RMB / worker) 勞動生產率（千元/人）	Debts / assets 資產負債率 (%)	Total assets (mil. RMB) 總資產（百萬元）
Industry Overall 行業總體	1,978	119,894	9,072	269	3.15	10.41	75.67	69.73	8,555

	Number of firms 企業個數	Average number of employees 平均職工人數	Average revenue ('000 RMB) 平均銷售收入（千元）	Average profit ('000 RMB) 平均利潤（千元）	Return on assets 資產利潤率 (%)	Return on equity 權益利潤率 (%)	Labour productivity ('000 RMB / worker) 勞動生產率（千元/人）	Average debts / assets 平均資產負債率(%)	Average Total assets ('000 RMB) 平均總資產（千元）
By ownership 產業所有權									
State-owned 國有	136	88	3,088	66	1.30	3.47	34.98	62.57	5,088
Collectively-owned 集體	1,657	57	3,412	80	2.62	9.78	59.40	73.18	3,057
Privately-owned 私有	14	28	3,824	328	13.91	70.45	137.27	80.26	2,358
Domestic JVs 聯營	25	106	7,341	195	2.98	6.98	69.13	57.28	6,557
Joint stock 股份制	22	75	5,316	166	1.85	7.15	71.01	74.15	8,982
Foreign-funded 外資	42	66	24,833	1,508	6.04	23.59	378.03	74.38	24,941
Overseas Chinese-funded 港澳台資	82	70	19,499	614	3.72	8.74	280.07	57.41	16,494
By size 規模									
Large 大型	2	430	798,075	48,439	8.97	39.18	1855.99	77.12	540,249
Medium 中型	7	333	68,482	2,909	4.44	11.39	205.56	61.00	65,496
Small 小型	1,943	60	3,601	78	2.16	7.01	60.03	69.16	3,611
By regional distribution 地區分布									
Central-North 華北	328	44	2,096	129	5.88	16.66	47.89	64.72	2,203
Beijing 北京	98	40	1,502	108	4.18	11.50	37.62	63.69	2,594
Tianjin 天津	101	51	1,550	111	5.68	15.81	30.40	64.05	1,946
Hebei 河北	101	41	3,568	199	8.31	25.09	87.67	66.88	2,398
Shanxi 山西	17	47	572	-35	-2.73	-7.56	12.18	63.96	1,273
Inner Mongolia 內蒙	11	34	1,226	104	14.30	28.93	35.59	50.56	725
Northeast 東北	265	60	3,525	210	7.54	27.19	58.56	72.27	2,791
Liaoning 遼寧	170	66	3,859	201	6.18	22.25	58.21	72.24	3,249
Jilin 吉林	30	54	1,174	4	0.23	0.85	21.92	73.23	1,903
Heilongjiang 黑龍江	65	47	3,735	331	16.54	58.99	79.04	71.96	2,002
Central East 華東	807	68	5,026	115	2.65	8.33	74.10	68.13	4,350
Shanghai 上海	144	113	5,139	182	2.84	7.20	45.39	60.55	6,421
Jiangsu 江蘇	230	80	6,943	82	1.48	5.09	87.16	70.86	5,544
Zhejiang 浙江	225	49	3,663	91	2.88	8.45	74.77	65.90	3,158
Anhui 安徽	39	28	1,896	115	12.07	43.55	66.60	72.29	954
Fujian 福建	56	48	5,160	69	1.54	5.15	106.74	70.10	4,509
Jiangxi 江西	39	28	1,089	-69	-3.70	-55.76	39.43	93.37	1,879
Shandong 山東	74	57	6,615	295	9.20	44.13	116.61	79.15	3,206
Central-South 中南	394	65	7,458	189	2.52	8.52	114.86	70.40	7,485
Henan 河南	73	35	3,279	139	5.18	15.99	92.68	67.59	2,677
Hubei 湖北	55	88	6,215	244	5.33	13.98	70.64	61.85	4,582
Hunan 湖南	52	43	3,042	61	2.63	16.95	70.56	84.45	2,307
Guangdong 廣東	191	78	11,101	245	2.06	6.98	141.45	70.56	11,933
Guangxi 廣西	22	42	3,583	38	0.82	3.51	84.84	76.70	4,670
Hainan 海南	1								
Southwest 西南	131	55	3,068	28	0.65	3.45	55.60	81.26	4,273
Chongqing 重慶	39	80	1,676	-189	-6.41	-27.25	21.07	76.49	2,955
Sichuan 四川	62	49	4,672	-132	-2.46	-13.49	94.97	81.80	5,357
Guizhou 貴州	14	21	451	-14	-1.20	-4.64	21.07	74.15	1,191
Yunnan 雲南	16	48	2,590	-732	-12.16	-89.32	54.31	86.39	6,019
Tibet 西藏									
Northwest 西北	53	39	1,012	1	0.10	0.22	26.28	55.61	1,376
Shaanxi 陝西	32	41	883	33	3.04	6.27	21.55	51.52	1,069
Gansu 甘肅	7	50	2,229	-23	-0.83	-2.02	44.57	58.73	2,749
Qinghai 青海									
Ningxia 寧夏	5	25	554	14	1.61	3.06	21.81	47.71	872
Xinjiang 新疆	9	28	777	-98	-5.82	-15.80	27.74	63.19	1,681

3470: Metal Surface Treatment and Heat Treatment
金屬表面處理及熱處理業

Year 年份	Number of firms 企業個數	Rate of change 每年變化 (%)	Number of employees 職工人數 (人)	Rate of change 每年變化 (%)	Total revenue (mil. RMB) 總銷售收入 (百萬元)	Rate of change 每年變化 (%)	Total profit (mil. RMB) 總利潤 (百萬元)	Rate of change 每年變化 (%)
1993	1,977		161,315		6,726		280	
1994	2,453	24.08%	168,668	4.56%	7,510	11.66%	177	-36.77%
1995	2,036	-17.00%	132,925	-21.19%	8,454	12.56%	183	3.12%
1996	1,978	-2.85%	119,894	-9.80%	9,072	7.31%	269	47.20%

3 Major products* 3 種主要產品 *	Output 產量	Sales volume 銷售量	Unit 單位
a) Remade Steels 改製鋼材	809,078	752,443	ton 噸
b) Copper Wire 銅絲材	2,044	1,798	ton 噸
c) Metal Products for Building 建築用金屬品	71,836	68,244	ton 噸

Top 10 firms by revenue (year founded) 收入排名前 10 家企業 (創辦年份)	City 城市	Province 省	Telephone / fax 電話 / 傳真	Number of employees 職工人數	Ownership 產業所有權	Revenue ('000 RMB) 銷售收入 (千元)	Profit ('000 RMB) (rank) 利潤 (千元) (排名)	Total assets ('000 RMB) 總資產 (千元)	Major products 主要產品
Zhongshan Zhong Yue Tinplate Industrial Co. Ltd. 中山中粵馬口鐵工業有限公司(1989)	Zhongshan 中山市	Guangdong 廣東省	(0760)5596487 (0760)5596252	423	Overseas Chinese-funded 港澳台資	752,647	30125(1)	348,380	a
Guangdong Nan Fang Galvanization Plate Co. Ltd. 廣東南方鍍鋅板有限公司(1988)	Foshan 佛山市	Guangdong 廣東省	(0757)7823478 (0757)7835332	523	Foreign-funded 外資	419,788	13615(4)	673,499	a
Zhejiang Jin Zhou Enterprise Group Co. 浙江金洲企業集團公司(1981)	Huzhou 湖州市	Zhejiang 浙江省	(0572)2065988 (0572)2036981	773	Collectively-owned 集體	302,290	12042(5)	179,937	a,b
Shenyang Bei Heng Copper Industry 瀋陽北恒銅業(1993)	Shenyang 瀋陽市	Liaoning 遼寧省	(024)88900204	70	Foreign-funded 外資	129,360	2740(26)	27,629	o
Shandong Jiaxiang Tong Factory 山東省嘉祥銅廠(1992)	Jining 濟寧市	Shandong 山東省	(0537)6822864 (0537)6822864	256	Collectively-owned 集體	112,880	8200(8)	41,456	o
Guangdong Huali Electroplate Industrial Co. 廣東華麗電鍍工業公司(1965)	Foshan 佛山市	Guangdong 廣東省	(0757)6773378 (0757)6772378	2,175	Collectively-owned 集體	111,780	467(167)	89,730	o
Chengdu Bicycle Parts Factory 成都自行車零件廠	Chengdu 成都市	Sichuan 四川省	(028)4852370	92	Collectively-owned 集體	108,000	20600(2)	139,076	c
Jiangyin Special Wire Material Factory 江陰市特種線材廠(1971)	Wuxi 無錫市	Jiangsu 江蘇省	(0510)6361118 (0510)6361145	775	Collectively-owned 集體	104,018	1382(64)	60,646	b
Liyang Xinghong Group Co. Ltd. 溧陽市興宏集團(1988)	Changzhou 常州市	Jiangsu 江蘇省	(0519)7730048 (0519)7851012	500	Collectively-owned 集體	96,391	100(353)	47,092	o
Shanghai Yi Hui Machinery Co. Ltd. 上海易匯機械有限公司(1995)	Shanghai 上海市	Shanghai 上海市	(021)59156205 (021)59155006	501	Overseas Chinese-funded 港澳台資	79,556	7063(9)	17,988	o

Top 10 Cities by Production Output 產出排名前 10 位城市	Province 省	Market share 市場份額	Number of firms 企業個數
Zhongshan 中山市	Guangdong 廣東省	10.05%	13
Shanghai 上海市	Shanghai 上海市	9.56%	241
Foshan 佛山市	Guangdong 廣東省	9.43%	23
Suzhou 蘇州市	Jiangsu 江蘇省	4.74%	105
Changzhou 常州市	Jiangsu 江蘇省	4.69%	74
Huzhou 湖州市	Zhejiang 浙江省	3.77%	13
Wuxi 無錫市	Jiangsu 江蘇省	2.84%	64
Shenzhen 深圳市	Guangdong 廣東省	2.83%	20
Wuhan 武漢市	Hubei 湖北省	2.66%	24
Tianjin 天津市	Tianjin 天津市	2.36%	120

10 Major Wholesalers 10 家主要批發商	City 城市	Province 省	Telephone / Fax 電話 / 傳真
Liaoning Automobile Trade Group Corp. 遼寧省汽車貿易集團	Shenyang 瀋陽市	Liaoning 遼寧省	(024)23835494 (024)23838338
China Post and Telecommunication Equipment General Company 中國郵電器材總公司	Beijing 北京市	Beijing 北京市	(010)63523715 (010)63525935
Jiangsu Electromechanical Products General Company 江蘇省機電產品總公司	Nanjing 南京市	Jiangsu 江蘇省	(025)7713642 (025)7711036
Xi Nan Technology Import & Export Company 西南技術進出口公司	Chongqing 重慶市	Chongqing 重慶市	(023)63850185 (023)63850026
Changzhou Economic Technology Industrial Development Zone Tian Ming Trade Company 常州經濟技術產業開發區天明貿易公司	Changzhou 常州市	Jiangsu 江蘇省	(0519)8829882 (0519)8829882
Shanxi Mechanical Equipment Import & Export Company 山西省機械設備進出口公司	Taiyuan 太原市	Shanxi 山西省	(0351)4040713 (0351)4043981
Ningbo Five Mining Machinery Import & Export Company 寧波市五礦機械進出口公司	Ningbo 寧波市	Zhejiang 浙江省	(0574)7311255 (0574)7320322
Tianjin Jin Huan Electromechanical Complete Sets of Equipment Factory 天津市津環機電成套設備廠	Tianjin 天津市	Tianjin 天津市	(022)26371628
Yunnan Machinery Import & Export Company 雲南省機械進出口公司	Kunming 昆明市	Yunnan 雲南省	(0871)3164879 (0871)3136829
Tianjin Da Qiu Zhuang Yi Yuan Trade Center 天津市大丘莊億源商貿中心	Tianjin 天津市	Tianjin 天津市	(022)28899478 (022)28899046

*Also include sales by firms outside this industry.包括本行業以外廠家的銷售。"o" stands for "others". "o" 代表 "其他產品"。

3481: Enamel Products 日用搪瓷製造業

The industry accounts for 0.059% of the total revenue of China's industrial sector in 1996. The revenue growth rate of the industry is 2.9% from 1995, as compared to the growth rate of China's industrial sector, 9.51%. The rate of return on asset is -1.30%. 62.11% of all firms in the industry made a profit while 31.30% had negative returns. The top province in terms of the industry's revenue is Shanghai, accounting for 14.46% of the total revenue.
本行業在 1996 年佔全行業總產值 0.059% ，行業年增長率為 2.9%（全國工業年增長率 9.51%）。行業的資產回報率 -1.30% ， 62.11% 的企業盈利， 31.30% 的企業虧損。銷售收入最高的省份為上海市，佔本行業的 14.46% 。

	Total number of firms 企業總數	Total number of employees 職工總數	Total revenue (mil. RMB) 總銷售收入（百萬元）	Total profit (mil. RMB) 總利潤（百萬元）	Return on assets 資產利潤率 (%)	Return on equity 權益利潤率 (%)	Labour productivity ('000 RMB / worker) 勞動生產率（千元/人）	Debts / assets 資產負債率 (%)	Total assets (mil. RMB) 總資產（百萬元）
Industry Overall 行業總體	284	74,842	3,400	-69	-1.30	-5.25	45.43	75.26	5,328

	Number of firms 企業個數	Average number of employees 平均職工人數	Average revenue ('000 RMB) 平均銷售收入（千元）	Average profit ('000 RMB) 平均利潤（千元）	Return on assets 資產利潤率 (%)	Return on equity 權益利潤率 (%)	Labour productivity ('000 RMB / worker) 勞動生產率（千元/人）	Average debts / assets 平均資產負債率(%)	Average Total assets ('000 RMB) 平均總資產（千元）
By ownership 產業所有權									
State-owned 國有	55	690	24,000	-1,673	-3.30	-17.39	34.80	81.01	50,636
Collectively-owned 集體	197	147	7,350	70	0.87	3.91	50.17	77.65	8,019
Privately-owned 私有	1	20	6,414	127	27.25	54.99	320.70	50.45	466
Domestic JVs 聯營	9	347	14,230	-285	-1.95	-4.28	41.01	54.50	14,615
Joint stock 股份制	5	1,093	67,387	4,270	3.79	8.61	61.66	56.04	112,789
Foreign-funded 外資	8	88	2,550	-1,225	-6.38	-10.34	29.11	38.29	19,204
Overseas Chinese-funded 港澳台資	9	160	15,564	8	0.06	0.22	97.07	70.88	12,643
By size 規模									
Large 大型	5	1,623	59,470	-10,178	-6.78	-50.46	36.63	86.56	150,099
Medium 中型	29	906	41,766	602	0.87	2.81	46.11	69.17	69,437
Small 小型	247	166	7,657	-144	-1.39	-5.97	46.24	76.74	10,380
By regional distribution 地區分布									
Central-North 華北	40	214	10,105	575	4.18	16.51	47.19	74.71	13,759
Beijing 北京	7	82	1,246	-426	-4.24	-7.87	15.22	46.14	10,037
Tianjin 天津	7	87	9,073	1,590	10.53	56.67	104.80	81.42	15,097
Hebei 河北	17	289	15,968	884	6.16	29.78	55.21	79.30	14,344
Shanxi 山西	6	232	5,743	37	0.25	0.84	24.77	70.56	14,813
Inner Mongolia 內蒙	3	360	8,687	-140	-1.01	-8.27	24.15	87.81	13,890
Northeast 東北	36	290	6,239	-718	-5.51	-121.07	21.54	95.45	13,039
Liaoning 遼寧	23	296	6,526	-360	-3.25	-67.65	22.07	95.19	11,065
Jilin 吉林	5	300	1,072	-3,248	-35.38	40.15	3.57	188.13	9,180
Heilongjiang 黑龍江	8	265	8,644	-168	-0.79	-2.70	32.57	70.67	21,126
Central East 華東	114	277	14,317	-267	-1.19	-4.54	51.76	73.87	22,508
Shanghai 上海	24	407	20,481	-757	-2.51	-10.58	50.29	76.32	30,211
Jiangsu 江蘇	30	256	12,210	-289	-1.03	-3.54	47.67	70.83	27,938
Zhejiang 浙江	21	221	11,208	-121	-0.78	-1.93	50.81	59.45	15,489
Anhui 安徽	11	207	9,969	-360	-2.74	-9.21	48.24	70.29	13,156
Fujian 福建	5	31	8,360	-148	-1.54	-3.43	266.24	55.19	9,636
Jiangxi 江西	4	388	12,128	63	0.24	1.10	31.26	78.41	26,430
Shandong 山東	19	287	17,841	178	0.89	9.69	62.08	90.79	19,939
Central-South 中南	56	247	13,622	-409	-2.18	-7.81	55.14	72.05	18,720
Henan 河南	20	278	11,130	189	1.17	5.18	40.06	77.44	16,176
Hubei 湖北	7	469	15,707	4	0.02	0.13	33.50	82.54	18,459
Hunan 湖南	8	190	8,008	-114	-1.62	-37.76	42.23	95.72	7,041
Guangdong 廣東	18	120	14,566	-1,621	-7.37	-19.30	120.99	61.85	22,002
Guangxi 廣西	2	633	51,740	1,940	2.76	8.87	81.80	68.86	70,220
Hainan 海南	1	47	570	-490	-17.44	-163.33	12.13	89.68	2,810
Southwest 西南	20	330	13,974	-479	-2.16	-10.83	42.38	80.02	22,110
Chongqing 重慶	11	284	13,615	-677	-2.69	-24.71	47.95	89.13	25,216
Sichuan 四川	5	333	12,541	-425	-2.59	-7.86	37.65	67.03	16,397
Guizhou 貴州	1	600	14,640	30	0.11	0.19	24.40	44.98	28,410
Yunnan 雲南	3	407	17,307	27	0.16	0.48	42.49	67.00	16,880
Tibet 西藏									
Northwest 西北	18	216	5,374	-191	-1.36	-3.24	24.87	57.93	14,010
Shaanxi 陝西	13	183	4,412	-104	-0.87	-2.21	24.15	60.42	11,892
Gansu 甘肅	2	293	6,445	-1,205	-7.20	-17.46	22.00	58.77	16,735
Qinghai 青海	1	163	3,210	-220	-2.50	-7.91	19.69	68.37	8,790
Ningxia 寧夏	1	110	860	-270	-7.12	-34.18	7.82	79.42	3,790
Xinjiang 新疆	1	656	22,430	810	1.57	2.94	34.19	46.57	51,530

3481: Enamel Products 日用搪瓷製造業

Year 年份	Number of firms 企業個數	Rate of change 每年變化 (%)	Number of employees 職工人數 (人)	Rate of change 每年變化 (%)	Total revenue (mil. RMB) 總銷售收入 (百萬元)	Rate of change 每年變化 (%)	Total profit (mil. RMB) 總利潤 (百萬元)	Rate of change 每年變化 (%)
1993	279		96,809		2,713		-29	
1994	297	6.45%	76,273	-21.21%	3,114	14.77%	-12	59.07%
1995	290	-2.36%	80,260	5.23%	3,305	6.11%	-29	-144.77%
1996	284	-2.07%	74,842	-6.75%	3,400	2.87%	-69	-140.98%

3 Major products* 3 種主要產品 *	Output 產量	Sales volume 銷售量	Unit 單位
a) Daily Enamel Products 日用搪瓷製品	198,771	188,833	ton 噸
b) Enamel Products for Industrial Accessory 衛生潔具用搪瓷製品	61,367	60,140	ton 噸
c) Enamel Products for Industrial Accessory 工業配套用搪瓷製品	9,074	9,619	ton 噸

Top 10 firms by revenue (year founded) 收入排名前 10 家企業 (創辦年份)	City 城市	Province 省	Telephone / fax 電話 / 傳真	Number of employees 職工人數	Ownership 產業所有權	Revenue ('000 RMB) 銷售收入 (千元)	Profit ('000 RMB) (rank) 利潤 (千元) (排名)	Total assets ('000 RMB) 總資產 (千元)	Major products 主要產品
Shandong Caoxian Hong Wei Group Company 山東省曹縣宏威集團公司(1996)	Heze 菏澤市	Shandong 山東省	(0530)3211873	1,000	Collectively-owned 集體	144,000	10014(2)	97,760	a
Chongqing Enamel General Factory 重慶搪瓷總廠	Chongqing 重慶市	Chongqing 重慶市	(023)67614129 (023)67614095	2,515	State-owned 國有	112,644	-6477(176)	267,055	a,c
Hangzhou Jia Li Industry & Trade General Company 杭州佳力工貿總公司(1955)	Hangzhou 杭州市	Zhejiang 浙江省	(0571)8093214 (0571)8091141	2,222	State-owned 國有	106,793	-3994(173)	134,903	a
Shanghai Light Industry Kitchen Equipment Co. Ltd. 上海輕工廚房設備有限公司(1996)	Shanghai 上海市	Shanghai 上海市	(021)58428999 (021)58422963	1,517	State-owned 國有	101,493	29(94)	184,163	a
Liuzhou Enamel Factory 柳州市搪瓷廠(1961)	Liuzhou 柳州市	Guangxi 廣西	(0772)2511002 (0772)2514893	1,203	State-owned 國有	100,888	4662(3)	130,556	a
Zhengding Hua Zheng Enamel Factory 正定縣華正搪瓷廠(1994)	Shijiazhuang 石家莊市	Hebei 河北省	(0311)8022306	139	Collectively-owned 集體	65,000	4420(6)	63,262	o
Guangzhou Enamel Factory 廣州市搪瓷廠(1963)	Guangzhou 廣州市	Guangdong 廣東省	(020)84412039 (020)84414431	380	Collectively-owned 集體	64,109	608(30)	29,009	a
Shanghai Feng Huang Enamel Electric Equipment Plant 上海鳳凰搪瓷電器廠(1939)	Shanghai 上海市	Shanghai 上海市	(021)62536270 (021)62551430	738	State-owned 國有	59,490	40(88)	105,360	a
Shanghai Bo Bao Metal Products Co. Ltd. 上海波寶金屬製品有限公司(1993)	Shanghai 上海市	Shanghai 上海市	(021)58894066 (021)58812856	350	Overseas Chinese-funded 港澳台資	54,983	4532(5)	39,418	a
Tai Wan Yi Lian Flange Products Co. Ltd. 台灣億聯法朗製品有限公司(1996)	Tianjin 天津市	Tianjin 天津市	(022)29534131	60	Overseas Chinese-funded 港澳台資	52,610	11700(1)	30,210	o

Top 10 Cities by Production Output 產出排名前 10 位城市	Province 省	Market share 市場份額	Number of firms 企業個數
Baoji 寶雞市	Shaanxi 陝西省	24.72%	1
Shanghai 上海市	Shanghai 上海市	11.12%	30
Shijiazhuang 石家莊市	Hebei 河北省	5.01%	9
Chongqing 重慶市	Chongqing 重慶市	4.15%	10
Heze 菏澤市	Shandong 山東省	4.03%	4
Guangzhou 廣州市	Guangdong 廣東省	2.85%	8
Hangzhou 杭州市	Zhejiang 浙江省	2.50%	7
Foshan 佛山市	Guangdong 廣東省	2.33%	5
Kaifeng 開封市	Henan 河南省	2.16%	5
Suzhou 蘇州市	Jiangsu 江蘇省	2.08%	10

10 Major Wholesalers 10 家主要批發商	City 城市	Province 省	Telephone / Fax 電話 / 傳真
Chengdu Great Wall Electric Appliance Company 成都長城電器公司	Chengdu 成都市	Sichuan 四川省	(028)6662132 (028)6671975
Shandou Ceramics (Group) Company 汕頭陶瓷(集團)公司	Shantou 汕頭市	Guangdong 廣東省	(0754)8255441 (0754)8255442
Guangdong Puning Local Products Import & Export Company 廣東省普寧土產進出口公司	Jieyang 揭陽市	Guangdong 廣東省	(0663)2226744
Yixing Sundry Goods General Co. 宜興市土產雜品總公司	Wuxi 無錫市	Jiangsu 江蘇省	(0510)7903683 (0510)7903683
Sujiang Qu Zhe Jiang Dongda Group Company 椒江區浙江東大集團公司	Taizhou 臺州市	Zhejiang 浙江省	(0576)8881477 (0576)8881672
Jiangsu New Suzhou Co. Ltd. Suzhou Daily Goods General Co. 江蘇新蘇州股份有限公司蘇州日用雜品總公司	Suzhou 蘇州市	Jiangsu 江蘇省	(0512)7276630 (0512)7275964
Shandong Daily Use General Merchandise Import & Export Company 山東省日用百貨進出口公司	Qingdao 青島市	Shandong 山東省	(0532)5849141 (0532)5849207
Guangdong Yangjiang Light Industrial Products Import & Export (Group) Company 廣東陽江輕工業品進出口(集團)公司	Yangjiang 陽江市	Guangdong 廣東省	(0662)3222497 (0662)3222976
Hebei Artts & Crtfts Import & Export Corp. 河北工藝品進出口公司	Shijiazhuang 石家莊市	Hebei 河北省	(0311)7756124 (0311)7755347
Shandong Handicrafts Import & Export Products Group Linyi Craft Co. Ltd. 山東工藝品進出品集團臨沂工藝有限公司	Linyi 臨沂市	Shandong 山東省	(0539)8310001 (0539)8315396

*Also include sales by firms outside this industry.包括本行業以外廠家的銷售。"o" stands for "others". "o" 代表 "其他產品"。

3482: Aluminum Products 鋁製品業

The industry accounts for 0.184% of the total revenue of China's industrial sector in 1996. The revenue growth rate of the industry is 24.2% from 1995, as compared to the growth rate of China's industrial sector, 9.51%. The rate of return on asset is 0.62%. 68.73% of all firms in the industry made a profit while 26.00% had negative returns. The top province in terms of the industry's revenue is Guangdong, accounting for 20.63% of the total revenue.
本行業在1996年佔全行業總產值0.184%，行業年增長率為24.2%（全國工業年增長率9.51%）。行業的資產回報率0.62%，68.73%的企業盈利，26.00%的企業虧損。銷售收入最高的省份為廣東省，佔本行業的20.63%。

	Total number of firms 企業總數	Total number of employees 職工總數	Total revenue (mil. RMB) 總銷售收入（百萬元）	Total profit (mil. RMB) 總利潤（百萬元）	Return on assets 資產利潤率 (%)	Return on equity 權益利潤率 (%)	Labour productivity ('000 RMB / worker) 勞動生產率（千元/人）	Debts / assets 資產負債率 (%)	Total assets (mil. RMB) 總資產（百萬元）
Industry Overall 行業總體	1,218	122,270	10,671	86	0.62	2.32	87.27	73.19	13,892

	Number of firms 企業個數	Average number of employees 平均職工人數	Average revenue ('000 RMB) 平均銷售收入（千元）	Average profit ('000 RMB) 平均利潤（千元）	Return on assets 資產利潤率 (%)	Return on equity 權益利潤率 (%)	Labour productivity ('000 RMB / worker) 勞動生產率（千元/人）	Average debts / assets 平均資產負債率(%)	Average Total assets ('000 RMB) 平均總資產（千元）
By ownership 產業所有權									
State-owned 國有	106	234	6,755	-462	-2.70	-11.69	28.90	76.95	17,151
Collectively-owned 集體	961	68	5,023	89	1.87	8.36	73.50	77.61	4,776
Privately-owned 私有	7	46	5,019	209	6.38	19.68	109.78	67.59	3,282
Domestic JVs 聯營	17	950	105,035	2,705	3.36	12.47	110.58	73.06	80,542
Joint stock 股份制	10	351	53,500	460	1.15	3.53	152.33	67.46	40,059
Foreign-funded 外資	40	124	35,063	2,323	5.40	11.92	283.05	54.68	43,017
Overseas Chinese-funded 港澳台資	76	97	17,896	-1,197	-2.30	-9.23	184.69	75.07	51,996
By size 規模									
Large 大型	8	2,438	339,000	21,511	6.02	21.35	139.05	71.79	357,232
Medium 中型	33	599	33,519	-3,457	-5.77	-23.56	55.95	75.52	59,961
Small 小型	1,157	71	5,922	24	0.31	1.15	83.15	73.13	7,826
By regional distribution 地區分布									
Central-North 華北	169	95	6,836	52	0.33	0.90	71.72	63.28	15,631
Beijing 北京	48	94	3,241	-331	-1.66	-4.38	34.46	62.12	19,972
Tianjin 天津	33	182	14,272	84	0.22	0.67	78.38	66.39	37,627
Hebei 河北	52	54	8,581	442	7.90	18.25	159.20	56.69	5,589
Shanxi 山西	14	113	3,426	-110	-1.47	-3.14	30.43	53.30	7,494
Inner Mongolia 內蒙	22	55	1,567	18	0.85	2.65	28.64	67.93	2,084
Northeast 東北	161	77	3,931	202	4.25	16.22	50.79	73.77	4,740
Liaoning 遼寧	104	73	4,833	307	5.85	20.23	65.78	71.10	5,254
Jilin 吉林	23	71	1,492	139	5.40	53.60	21.02	89.93	2,578
Heilongjiang 黑龍江	34	94	2,820	-79	-1.70	-7.39	30.10	76.97	4,633
Central East 華東	467	97	8,872	301	3.18	10.27	91.68	69.00	9,460
Shanghai 上海	43	102	8,059	295	2.68	9.02	78.63	70.26	10,989
Jiangsu 江蘇	103	130	15,100	495	2.94	8.30	116.11	64.58	16,847
Zhejiang 浙江	113	92	10,784	392	4.09	14.58	116.95	71.92	9,575
Anhui 安徽	38	116	9,244	457	7.77	28.41	79.96	72.64	5,874
Fujian 福建	42	63	2,951	16	0.28	0.83	46.73	66.67	5,882
Jiangxi 江西	26	68	2,022	37	0.90	2.12	29.58	57.60	4,142
Shandong 山東	102	80	4,852	133	2.47	11.20	60.74	77.93	5,395
Central-South 中南	317	126	14,115	-253	-1.47	-7.53	111.77	80.50	17,240
Henan 河南	64	84	6,296	57	1.06	3.84	75.08	72.50	5,372
Hubei 湖北	53	299	30,094	691	3.34	9.24	100.78	63.86	20,713
Hunan 湖南	45	83	2,826	-177	-6.10	-25.32	34.06	75.89	2,902
Guangdong 廣東	118	97	18,652	-892	-2.87	-22.05	191.68	87.00	31,113
Guangxi 廣西	35	97	4,204	-207	-3.32	-11.41	43.35	70.94	6,248
Hainan 海南	2	115	595	10	0.68	1.08	5.17	36.95	1,475
Southwest 西南	63	64	2,566	3	0.11	0.37	40.04	70.68	3,220
Chongqing 重慶	16	73	3,106	18	0.99	17.03	42.72	94.17	1,851
Sichuan 四川	24	58	2,656	-29	-0.82	-4.88	45.56	83.23	3,493
Guizhou 貴州	14	19	844	-31	-3.06	-10.09	44.90	69.70	1,004
Yunnan 雲南	9	134	4,052	28	0.33	0.64	30.17	47.58	8,342
Tibet 西藏									
Northwest 西北	41	108	2,522	-378	-3.86	-25.66	23.28	84.95	9,773
Shaanxi 陝西	16	71	1,477	-161	-4.50	-19.11	20.73	76.44	3,584
Gansu 甘肅	11	123	2,045	-266	-5.01	-10.55	16.65	52.59	5,321
Qinghai 青海	2	555	12,495	-3,045	-2.78	-135.63	22.51	97.95	109,380
Ningxia 寧夏	4	112	2,865	-110	-0.96	-2.84	25.70	66.10	11,415
Xinjiang 新疆	8	49	2,603	-430	-16.85	378.02	52.71	104.46	2,553

3482: Aluminum Products 鋁製品業

Year 年份	Number of firms 企業個數	Rate of change 每年變化 (%)	Number of employees 職工人數 (人)	Rate of change 每年變化 (%)	Total revenue (mil. RMB) 總銷售收入 (百萬元)	Rate of change 每年變化 (%)	Total profit (mil. RMB) 總利潤 (百萬元)	Rate of change 每年變化 (%)
1993	984		103,270		4,167		85	
1994	1,094	11.18%	110,791	7.28%	5,517	32.41%	4	-95.53%
1995	1,103	0.82%	120,675	8.92%	8,595	55.79%	44	1072.34%
1996	1,218	10.43%	122,270	1.32%	10,671	24.15%	86	93.45%

3 Major products* 3 種主要產品 *	Output 產量	Sales volume 銷售量	Unit 單位
a) Refined Aluminium Cooker 精鋁鍋	23,464,314	21,117,882	piece 口
b) Refined Aluminium Pressure Cooker 精鋁壓力鍋	10,740,053	9,773,448	piece 口
c) Refined Aluminium Kettle 精鋁燒水壺	15,092,299	13,733,992	piece 個

Top 10 firms by revenue (year founded) 收入排名前 10 家企業 (創辦年份)	City 城市	Province 省	Telephone / fax 電話 / 傳真	Number of employees 職工人數	Ownership 產業所有權	Revenue ('000 RMB) 銷售收入 (千元)	Profit ('000 RMB) (rank) 利潤 (千元) (排名)	Total assets ('000 RMB) 總資產 (千元)	Major products 主要產品
Wuhan Long Wei Industrial Commercial (Group) Co. 武漢龍威實業(集團)公司(1993)	Wuhan 武漢市	Hubei 湖北省	(027)82818103 (027)82833984	10,959	Domestic JVs 聯營	1,309,661	33072(2)	856,941	a
Huadong United Can Co. Ltd. 華東聯合製罐有限公司(1991)	Zhenjiang 鎮江市	Jiangsu 江蘇省	(0511)5625393 (0511)5623378	364	Foreign-funded 外資	408,547	18065(3)	593,664	o
Zhejiang Supor Co. Ltd. 浙江蘇泊爾有限公司(1969)	Taizhou 臺州市	Zhejiang 浙江省	(0576)7332888	804	Joint stock 股份制	296,479	40005(1)	175,109	o
Ningbo Double-circle Group Holding Co. Ltd. 寧波雙圓集團股份有限公司(1956)	Ningbo 寧波市	Zhejiang 浙江省	(0574)7838711 (0574)7832272	1,996	Joint stock 股份制	270,085	1959(30)	198,736	a,b,c
Zhuhai Ftb Container Ltd. 珠海富特波爾容器有限公司(1991)	Zhuhai 珠海市	Guangdong 廣東省	(0756)3331808 (0756)3331712	296	Overseas Chinese-funded 港澳台資	258,175	-13258(531)	470,482	o
Tianjin M.C. Packaging Ltd. 天津美特容器有限公司(1993)	Tianjin 天津市	Tianjin 天津市	(022)25323566 (022)25326392	267	Overseas Chinese-funded 港澳台資	216,436	11538(10)	633,954	o
Shenyang Liao Shen Aluminium Material Factory 瀋陽市遼沈鋁材廠(1992)	Shenyang 瀋陽市	Liaoning 遼寧省	(024)24730583	525	Private-owned 私營	163,100	14680(4)	58,999	o
Shenzhen M.C. Container Co. Ltd. 深圳美特容器有限公司(1993)	Shenzhen 深圳市	Guangdong 廣東省	(0755)5738610 (0755)3321234	193	Overseas Chinese-funded 港澳台資	153,554	-10049(527)	377,955	o
Jiangyin Yu Hua Aluminium Industry Co. Ltd. 江陰裕華鋁業有限公司(1994)	Wuxi 無錫市	Jiangsu 江蘇省	(0510)6321034 (0510)6321986	2,230	Foreign-funded 外資	146,267	13169(7)	137,434	o
Nanhai Zhong Nan Aluminium Processing Co. Ltd. 南海中南鋁加工有限公司(1992)	Foshan 佛山市	Guangdong 廣東省	(0757)5771762 (0757)5776307	413	Overseas Chinese-funded 港澳台資	124,651	0(386)	404,845	o

Top 10 Cities by Production Output 產出排名前 10 位城市	Province 省	Market share 市場份額	Number of firms 企業個數
Foshan 佛山市	Guangdong 廣東省	9.59%	30
Wuhan 武漢市	Hubei 湖北省	8.68%	14
Taizhou 臺州市	Zhejiang 浙江省	8.26%	24
Ningbo 寧波市	Zhejiang 浙江省	5.22%	34
Shanghai 上海市	Shanghai 上海市	4.84%	86
Zhuhai 珠海市	Guangdong 廣東省	4.29%	9
Tianjin 天津市	Tianjin 天津市	4.22%	39
Yantai 煙台市	Shandong 山東省	3.29%	19
Suzhou 蘇州市	Jiangsu 江蘇省	3.14%	37
Shenyang 瀋陽市	Liaoning 遼寧省	2.72%	52

10 Major Wholesalers 10 家主要批發商	City 城市	Province 省	Telephone / Fax 電話 / 傳真
Chengdu Great Wall Electric Appliance Company 成都長城電器公司	Chengdu 成都市	Sichuan 四川省	(028)6662132 (028)6671975
Shandou Ceramics (Group) Company 汕頭陶瓷(集團)公司	Shantou 汕頭市	Guangdong 廣東省	(0754)8255441 (0754)8255442
Guangdong Puning Local Products Import & Export Company 廣東省普寧土產進出口公司	Jieyang 揭陽市	Guangdong 廣東省	(0663)2226744
Yixing Sundry Goods General Co. 宜興市土產雜品總公司	Wuxi 無錫市	Jiangsu 江蘇省	(0510)7903683 (0510)7903683
Sujiang Qu Zhe Jiang Dongda Group Company 椒江區浙江東大集團公司	Taizhou 臺州市	Zhejiang 浙江省	(0576)8881477 (0576)8881672
Jiangsu New Suzhou Co. Ltd. Suzhou Daily Goods General Co. 江蘇新蘇州股份有限公司蘇州日用雜品總公司	Suzhou 蘇州市	Jiangsu 江蘇省	(0512)7276630 (0512)7275964
Shandong Daily Use General Merchandise Import & Export Company 山東省日用百貨進出口公司	Qingdao 青島市	Shandong 山東省	(0532)5849141 (0532)5849207
Guangdong Yangjiang Light Industrial Products Import & Export (Group) Company 廣東陽江輕工業品進出口(集團)公司	Yangjiang 陽江市	Guangdong 廣東省	(0662)3222497 (0662)3222976
Hebei Artts & Crtfts Import & Export Corp. 河北工藝品進出口公司	Shijiazhuang 石家莊市	Hebei 河北省	(0311)7756124 (0311)7755347
Shandong Handicrafts Import & Export Products Group Linyi Craft Co. Ltd. 山東工藝品進出品集團臨沂工藝有限公司	Linyi 臨沂市	Shandong 山東省	(0539)8310001 (0539)8315396

*Also include sales by firms outside this industry.包括本行業以外廠家的銷售。"o" stands for "others". "o" 代表 "其他產品"。

3483: Stainless Steel Products 不銹鋼製品業

The industry accounts for 0.127% of the total revenue of China's industrial sector in 1996. The revenue growth rate of the industry is 4.6% from 1995, as compared to the growth rate of China's industrial sector, 9.51%. The rate of return on asset is 0.19%. 65.72% of all firms in the industry made a profit while 27.11% had negative returns. The top province in terms of the industry's revenue is Guangdong, accounting for 41.39% of the total revenue.
本行業在1996年佔全行業總產值0.127%，行業年增長率為4.6%（全國工業年增長率9.51%）。行業的資產回報率0.19%，65.72%的企業盈利，27.11%的企業虧損。銷售收入最高的省份為廣東省，佔本行業的41.39%。

	Total number of firms 企業總數	Total number of employees 職工總數	Total revenue (mil. RMB) 總銷售收入（百萬元）	Total profit (mil. RMB) 總利潤（百萬元）	Return on assets 資產利潤率 (%)	Return on equity 權益利潤率 (%)	Labour productivity ('000 RMB / worker) 勞動生產率（千元/人）	Debts / assets 資產負債率 (%)	Total assets (mil. RMB) 總資產（百萬元）
Industry Overall 行業總體	912	91,834	7,346	19	0.19	0.69	79.99	72.17	9,934

	Number of firms 企業個數	Average number of employees 平均職工人數	Average revenue ('000 RMB) 平均銷售收入（千元）	Average profit ('000 RMB) 平均利潤（千元）	Return on assets 資產利潤率 (%)	Return on equity 權益利潤率 (%)	Labour productivity ('000 RMB / worker) 勞動生產率（千元/人）	Average debts / assets 平均資產負債率(%)	Average Total assets ('000 RMB) 平均總資產（千元）
By ownership 產業所有權									
State-owned 國有	62	208	12,839	-435	-1.90	-16.07	61.77	88.19	22,952
Collectively-owned 集體	570	92	5,784	31	0.40	1.73	63.20	77.00	7,811
Privately-owned 私有	8	26	2,434	102	3.67	13.14	92.71	72.10	2,776
Domestic JVs 聯營	13	187	7,764	-54	-0.35	-1.17	41.60	70.10	15,565
Joint stock 股份制	8	253	20,834	855	3.36	8.41	82.23	60.07	25,487
Foreign-funded 外資	99	89	6,111	-443	-3.57	-9.09	68.39	60.67	12,389
Overseas Chinese-funded 港澳台資	151	98	15,639	433	2.72	6.94	159.98	60.81	15,917
By size 規模									
Large 大型	4	617	48,927	767	0.66	7.98	79.33	91.72	116,068
Medium 中型	31	627	39,348	-308	-0.54	-2.47	62.79	78.01	56,632
Small 小型	841	83	7,052	30	0.33	1.09	84.78	69.66	9,173
By regional distribution 地區分布									
Central-North 華北	136	101	3,830	-275	-3.14	-12.72	37.92	75.34	8,754
Beijing 北京	42	57	2,193	-235	-4.00	-10.28	38.78	61.12	5,880
Tianjin 天津	55	140	5,069	-581	-4.73	-27.66	36.26	82.90	12,292
Hebei 河北	29	87	4,730	152	2.05	6.57	54.50	68.80	7,412
Shanxi 山西	9	129	1,427	9	0.15	0.54	11.10	71.63	5,847
Inner Mongolia 內蒙	1								
Northeast 東北	72	120	4,532	-548	-6.61	-55.95	37.74	88.19	8,293
Liaoning 遼寧	54	124	4,272	-702	-8.91	-280.12	34.48	96.82	7,881
Jilin 吉林	5	44	762	48	0.74	6.40	17.40	88.48	6,508
Heilongjiang 黑龍江	13	134	7,062	-138	-1.30	-3.38	52.89	61.67	10,689
Central East 華東	403	90	8,143	171	1.60	5.16	90.35	68.92	10,686
Shanghai 上海	88	112	12,153	543	2.92	9.68	108.52	69.86	18,591
Jiangsu 江蘇	115	74	9,017	100	1.05	3.74	121.50	71.93	9,539
Zhejiang 浙江	94	74	4,903	43	0.62	1.82	65.94	65.97	6,964
Anhui 安徽	11	81	3,336	-225	-3.29	-6.15	40.96	46.45	6,845
Fujian 福建	35	78	6,099	26	0.28	0.92	78.31	69.89	9,522
Jiangxi 江西	9	59	1,442	64	2.83	5.65	24.44	49.93	2,274
Shandong 山東	51	133	8,850	133	1.38	4.13	66.46	66.60	9,605
Central-South 中南	263	121	12,070	116	0.82	2.99	100.05	72.64	14,144
Henan 河南	5	9	30	-2	-3.23	-10.00	3.26	67.74	62
Hubei 湖北	14	146	5,827	-365	-3.16	-19.37	40.03	83.67	11,544
Hunan 湖南	15	48	1,696	94	5.59	15.63	35.43	64.22	1,681
Guangdong 廣東	212	135	14,342	150	0.91	3.30	106.60	72.48	16,488
Guangxi 廣西	15	22	1,604	237	12.97	18.91	72.25	31.38	1,829
Hainan 海南	2	36	1,385	-550	-11.14	-77.46	39.01	85.61	4,935
Southwest 西南	31	32	786	-30	-1.67	-6.25	24.65	73.29	1,775
Chongqing 重慶	6	72	436	-71	-4.22	-19.25	6.03	78.08	1,672
Sichuan 四川	15	24	1,056	-1	-0.04	-0.14	44.48	69.08	2,439
Guizhou 貴州	8	16	264	-1	-0.22	-0.67	16.61	67.11	570
Yunnan 雲南	2	48	1,820	-245	-13.50	119.51	38.32	111.57	1,815
Tibet 西藏									
Northwest 西北	7	59	2,626	-401	-4.34	-9.47	44.61	54.20	9,254
Shaanxi 陝西	3	104	4,303	-937	-5.45	-11.83	41.51	53.88	17,173
Gansu 甘肅	1	40	1,950	80	1.05	2.53	48.75	58.48	7,610
Qinghai 青海									
Ningxia 寧夏									
Xinjiang 新疆	3	20	1,173	-27	-1.42	-2.91	57.70	51.33	1,883

3483: Stainless Steel Products 不銹鋼製品業

Year 年份	Number of firms 企業個數	Rate of change 每年變化 (%)	Number of employees 職工人數 (人)	Rate of change 每年變化 (%)	Total revenue (mil. RMB) 總銷售收入 (百萬元)	Rate of change 每年變化 (%)	Total profit (mil. RMB) 總利潤 (百萬元)	Rate of change 每年變化 (%)
1993	572		91,917		3,934		168	
1994	728	27.27%	98,072	6.70%	4,732	20.27%	88	-47.31%
1995	859	17.99%	103,009	5.03%	7,020	48.36%	56	-36.26%
1996	912	6.17%	91,834	-10.85%	7,346	4.64%	19	-66.31%

3 Major products* 3 種主要產品 *	Output 產量	Sales volume 銷售量	Unit 單位
a) Daily Stainless Steel Produc 日用不銹鋼製品	889,914	881,015	ton 噸

Top 10 firms by revenue (year founded) 收入排名前 10 家企業 (創辦年份)	City 城市	Province 省	Telephone / fax 電話 / 傳真	Number of employees 職工人數	Ownership 產業所有權	Revenue ('000 RMB) 銷售收入 (千元)	Profit ('000 RMB) (rank) 利潤 (千元) (排名)	Total assets ('000 RMB) 總資產 (千元)	Major products 主要產品
Xinhui Ri Xin Stainless Steel Material Factory Co. Ltd. 新會市日新不銹鋼材料廠有限公司(1993)	Jiangmen 江門市	Guangdong 廣東省	(0750)6124828 (0750)6138088	88	Overseas Chinese-funded 港澳台資	600,110	15100(2)	169,220	o
Wuxian Dong Wu Industrial Development Co. Ltd. 吳縣東吳產業發展有限公司(1990)	Suzhou 蘇州市	Jiangsu 江蘇省	(0512)5253619 (0512)5289395	180	Collectively-owned 集體	362,970	8560(6)	274,600	o
Guangdong Golden Leaf Stainless Steel Products Co. Ltd. 廣東金葉不銹鋼製品集團公司(1992)	Zhaoqing 肇慶市	Guangdong 廣東省	(0757)2736621 (0757)2736625	1,355	Collectively-owned 集體	227,340	1470(49)	226,854	a
Shanghai Pearl Kitchen Utensils Co. Ltd. 上海珍珠廚房用具有限公司(1994)	Shanghai 上海市	Shanghai 上海市	(021)59624967 (021)59621974	675	Overseas Chinese-funded 港澳台資	180,714	14003(3)	118,258	a
Xinxing Country Three A Stainless Stell Products Co. Ltd. Group 新興縣三 A 不銹鋼製品集團有限公司(1986)	Yunfu 雲浮市	Guangdong 廣東省	(0766)2892822	965	State-owned 國有	165,713	5979(9)	97,628	a
Xin Xingxian Bai Li Feng Stainless Steel Products Co. Ltd. 新興縣百利豐不銹鋼製品有限公司(1993)	Yunfu 雲浮市	Guangdong 廣東省	(0766)2885188	817	Overseas Chinese-funded 港澳台資	155,417	1741(40)	60,992	a
Shanghai Solid Stainless Steel Products Co. Ltd. 上海思樂得不銹鋼製品有限公司(1992)	Shanghai 上海市	Shanghai 上海市	(021)58291077 (021)58292888	308	Overseas Chinese-funded 港澳台資	106,686	25902(1)	103,142	o
Yongjia (Xiamen) Kitchen Articles Co. Ltd. 永嘉(廈門)廚室用品有限公司(1990)	Xiamen 廈門市	Fujian 福建省	(0592)5058358 (0592)5058348	1,531	Overseas Chinese-funded 港澳台資	105,687	1586(46)	177,778	o
Ri Sheng Hardware (Shenzhen) Co. Ltd. 日升五金製品(深圳)有限公司(1991)	Shenzhen 深圳市	Guangdong 廣東省	(0755)4401364 (0755)4400270	763	Overseas Chinese-funded 港澳台資	103,704	4646(11)	97,601	a
Shanghai San Die Stainless Products Co. Ltd. 上海三蝶不銹鋼製品有限公司(1975)	Shanghai 上海市	Shanghai 上海市	(021)59655676 (021)59655522	1,111	State-owned 國有	98,049	2963(20)	109,784	a

Top 10 Cities by Production Output 產出排名前 10 位城市	Province 省	Market share 市場份額	Number of firms 企業個數
Shanghai 上海市	Shanghai 上海市	17.33%	159
Yunfu 雲浮市	Guangdong 廣東省	8.40%	10
Jiangmen 江門市	Guangdong 廣東省	7.63%	35
Guangzhou 廣州市	Guangdong 廣東省	5.86%	137
Foshan 佛山市	Guangdong 廣東省	5.62%	34
Tianjin 天津市	Tianjin 天津市	3.88%	65
Zhaoqing 肇慶市	Guangdong 廣東省	3.44%	3
Ningbo 寧波市	Zhejiang 浙江省	2.86%	38
Yangjiang 陽江市	Guangdong 廣東省	2.82%	21
Shenzhen 深圳市	Guangdong 廣東省	2.67%	22

10 Major Wholesalers 10 家主要批發商	City 城市	Province 省	Telephone / Fax 電話 / 傳真
Chengdu Great Wall Electric Appliance Company 成都長城電器公司	Chengdu 成都市	Sichuan 四川省	(028)6662132 (028)6671975
Shandou Ceramics (Group) Company 汕頭陶瓷(集團)公司	Shantou 汕頭市	Guangdong 廣東省	(0754)8255441 (0754)8255442
Guangdong Puning Local Products Import & Export Company 廣東省普寧土產進出口公司	Jieyang 揭陽市	Guangdong 廣東省	(0663)2226744
Yixing Sundry Goods General Co. 宜興市土產雜品總公司	Wuxi 無錫市	Jiangsu 江蘇省	(0510)7903683 (0510)7903683
Sujiang Qu Zhe Jiang Dongda Group Company 椒江區浙江東大集團公司	Taizhou 臺州市	Zhejiang 浙江省	(0576)8881477 (0576)8881672
Jiangsu New Suzhou Co. Ltd. Suzhou Daily Goods General Co. 江蘇新蘇州股份有限公司蘇州日用雜品總公司	Suzhou 蘇州市	Jiangsu 江蘇省	(0512)7276630 (0512)7275964
Shandong Daily Use General Merchandise Import & Export Company 山東省日用百貨進出口公司	Qingdao 青島市	Shandong 山東省	(0532)5849141 (0532)5849207
Guangdong Yangjiang Light Industrial Products Import & Export (Group) Company 廣東陽江輕工業品進出口(集團)公司	Yangjiang 陽江市	Guangdong 廣東省	(0662)3222497 (0662)3222976
Hebei Artts & Crtfts Import & Export Corp. 河北工藝品進出口公司	Shijiazhuang 石家莊市	Hebei 河北省	(0311)7756124 (0311)7755347
Shandong Handicrafts Import & Export Products Group Linyi Craft Co. Ltd. 山東工藝品進出品集團臨沂工藝有限公司	Linyi 臨沂市	Shandong 山東省	(0539)8310001 (0539)8315396

*Also include sales by firms outside this industry.包括本行業以外廠家的銷售。"o" stands for "others". "o" 代表"其他產品"。

3484: Cutlery 刀剪製造業

The industry accounts for 0.019% of the total revenue of China's industrial sector in 1996. The revenue growth rate of the industry is 20.0% from 1995, as compared to the growth rate of China's industrial sector, 9.51%. The rate of return on asset is 0.36%. 64.44% of all firms in the industry made a profit while 28.63% had negative returns. The top province in terms of the industry's revenue is Zhejiang, accounting for 38.36% of the total revenue.
本行業在 1996 年佔全行業總產值 0.019%，行業年增長率為 20.0%（全國工業年增長率 9.51%）。行業的資產回報率 0.36%，64.44% 的企業盈利，28.63% 的企業虧損。銷售收入最高的省份為浙江省，佔本行業的 38.36%。

	Total number of firms 企業總數	Total number of employees 職工總數	Total revenue (mil. RMB) 總銷售收入（百萬元）	Total profit (mil. RMB) 總利潤（百萬元）	Return on assets 資產利潤率 (%)	Return on equity 權益利潤率 (%)	Labour productivity ('000 RMB / worker) 勞動生產率（千元/人）	Debts / assets 資產負債率 (%)	Total assets (mil. RMB) 總資產（百萬元）
Industry Overall 行業總體	242	28,535	1,081	4	0.36	0.93	37.88	61.29	1,132

	Number of firms 企業個數	Average number of employees 平均職工人數	Average revenue ('000 RMB) 平均銷售收入（千元）	Average profit ('000 RMB) 平均利潤（千元）	Return on assets 資產利潤率 (%)	Return on equity 權益利潤率 (%)	Labour productivity ('000 RMB / worker) 勞動生產率（千元/人）	Average debts / assets 平均資產負債率(%)	Average Total assets ('000 RMB) 平均總資產（千元）
By ownership 產業所有權									
State-owned 國有	16	302	5,375	-375	-3.68	-13.64	17.79	73.01	10,188
Collectively-owned 集體	203	100	3,610	42	1.24	3.25	36.26	61.86	3,418
Privately-owned 私有	1	10	531	242	63.89	104.16	53.11	38.66	379
Domestic JVs 聯營	3	652	39,522	-2,194	-7.32	-16.58	60.65	55.84	29,956
Joint stock 股份制	3	259	22,243	-9,090	-42.68	-104.56	85.88	59.18	21,301
Foreign-funded 外資	4	63	7,539	10,226	77.32	120.43	119.67	35.80	13,226
Overseas Chinese-funded 港澳台資	11	55	4,182	-536	-8.55	-19.83	76.29	56.87	6,265
By size 規模									
Large 大型									
Medium 中型	4	528	35,590	-291	-0.89	-2.02	67.44	56.28	32,841
Small 小型	237	112	3,960	22	0.52	1.36	35.46	61.97	4,226
By regional distribution 地區分布									
Central-North 華北	23	115	1,546	-190	-5.83	-25.00	13.45	76.67	3,262
Beijing 北京	8	110	1,986	-341	-7.72	-27.11	18.12	71.53	4,421
Tianjin 天津	2	302	3,180	-330	-4.34	-12.31	10.53	64.65	7,595
Hebei 河北	10	107	1,252	-92	-4.21	-60.13	11.73	92.99	2,184
Shanxi 山西									
Inner Mongolia 內蒙	3	32	263	-20	-2.29	-11.54	8.32	79.77	873
Northeast 東北	20	94	1,387	-68	-2.02	-8.93	14.72	77.38	3,343
Liaoning 遼寧	13	98	892	-99	-3.84	-110.26	9.06	96.51	2,582
Jilin 吉林	3	42	2,123	-127	-2.49	-6.52	50.96	61.87	5,097
Heilongjiang 黑龍江	4	120	2,445	80	1.78	3.94	20.38	54.89	4,500
Central East 華東	107	143	5,679	22	0.35	0.91	39.85	61.58	6,203
Shanghai 上海	11	183	3,232	-450	-5.23	-15.55	17.64	66.35	8,600
Jiangsu 江蘇	20	101	4,860	-42	-0.95	-3.36	48.31	71.61	4,407
Zhejiang 浙江	51	164	8,131	170	2.44	5.61	49.72	56.44	6,970
Anhui 安徽	6	111	2,127	32	1.79	7.60	19.25	76.42	1,767
Fujian 福建	10	58	845	-74	-4.57	-14.12	14.67	67.67	1,621
Jiangxi 江西	4	186	2,940	-33	-0.45	-1.17	15.83	61.59	7,245
Shandong 山東	5	180	5,452	20	0.14	0.41	30.29	64.96	13,948
Central-South 中南	70	106	5,611	127	2.98	6.29	52.70	52.62	4,249
Henan 河南	4	56	1,415	53	2.96	9.68	25.38	69.39	1,773
Hubei 湖北	15	72	2,923	-38	-2.92	-20.07	40.67	85.47	1,303
Hunan 湖南	6	166	3,567	-95	-1.87	-7.48	21.46	75.01	5,082
Guangdong 廣東	44	115	7,301	223	4.12	7.71	63.48	46.62	5,413
Guangxi 廣西	1	94	640				6.81	45.33	2,140
Hainan 海南									
Southwest 西南	14	69	988	-81	-7.46	-39.51	14.33	81.04	1,081
Chongqing 重慶	3	74	1,186	-209	-16.34	-438.24	15.98	96.27	1,279
Sichuan 四川	3	68	890	-47	-5.75	-17.04	13.13	66.28	817
Guizhou 貴州	5	61	674	10	1.55	10.42	10.98	85.09	644
Yunnan 雲南	3	78	1,410	-137	-7.28	-28.87	18.00	74.78	1,877
Tibet 西藏									
Northwest 西北	8	43	413	-34	-2.02	-4.12	9.68	50.86	1,671
Shaanxi 陝西	4	60	440	-88	-3.00	-6.06	7.39	50.39	2,913
Gansu 甘肅	3	29	487	43	32.50	59.09	16.59	42.50	133
Qinghai 青海									
Ningxia 寧夏									
Xinjiang 新疆	1	15	80	-50	-3.79	-8.93	5.33	57.58	1,320

3484: Cutlery 刀剪製造業

Year 年份	Number of firms 企業個數	Rate of change 每年變化 (%)	Number of employees 職工人數 (人)	Rate of change 每年變化 (%)	Total revenue (mil. RMB) 總銷售收入 (百萬元)	Rate of change 每年變化 (%)	Total profit (mil. RMB) 總利潤 (百萬元)	Rate of change 每年變化 (%)
1993	214		29,702		723		5	
1994	227	6.07%	28,725	-3.29%	681	-5.86%	6	30.59%
1995	227	0	29,691	3.36%	901	32.29%	-8	-218.13%
1996	242	6.61%	28,535	-3.89%	1,081	20.00%	4	152.92%

3 Major products* 3 種主要產品 *	Output 產量	Sales volume 銷售量	Unit 單位
a) Scissors 剪刀	18,208	15,659	100,00 piece 萬把
b) Chopping Knife 菜刀	2,301	2,232	10,000 piece 萬把
c) Pincers 鉗子	202	186	10,000 piece 萬把

Top 10 firms by revenue (year founded) 收入排名前 10 家企業 (創辦年份)	City 城市	Province 省	Telephone / fax 電話 / 傳真	Number of employees 職工人數	Ownership 產業所有權	Revenue ('000 RMB) 銷售收入 (千元)	Profit ('000 RMB) (rank) 利潤 (千元) (排名)	Total assets ('000 RMB) 總資產 (千元)	Major products 主要產品
Hangzhou Zhang Xiao Quan Scissors Plant 杭州張小泉剪刀廠(1953)	Hangzhou 杭州市	Zhejiang 浙江省	(0571)8073733 (0571)8075605	1,326	Domestic JVs 聯營	88,071	204(34)	85,060	a,b
Zhangjiagang Gardens Tools Factory 張家港市園林工具廠(1956)	Suzhou 蘇州市	Jiangsu 江蘇省	(0512)8201841 (0512)8201841	230	Collectively-owned 集體	38,005	1004(4)	22,866	c
Yangjiang Jiangcheng Decorating Hardware Factory 陽江市江城區裝潢五金廠(1972)	Yangjiang 陽江市	Guangdong 廣東省	(0662)3103071 (0662)3101486	350	Collectively-owned 集體	36,110	1744(2)	20,380	o
Yangxi Zhigong Hardware Factory 陽西縣織貢五金廠	Yangjiang 陽江市	Guangdong 廣東省	(0662)5553288	360	Collectively-owned 集體	33,284	145(40)	20,572	o
Yangxi Guang Yang Knife & Scissors Factory Co. Ltd. 陽西縣光陽刀剪廠有限公司	Yangjiang 陽江市	Guangdong 廣東省	(0662)5553878	170	Foreign-funded 外資	31,987	198(36)	17,156	o
Yangjiang Jiangcheng Yong Feng Hardware Craft Cutting Tools Factory 陽江市江城永鋒五金工藝刀具廠(1993)	Yangjiang 陽江市	Guangdong 廣東省	(0662)3315700	105	Collectively-owned 集體	26,910	1330(3)	3,290	o
Ningbo Yong Feng Blade Co. Ltd. 寧波市永鋒刀片有限公司(1985)	Ningbo 寧波市	Zhejiang 浙江省	(0574)7586184 (0574)7586514	206	Foreign-funded 外資	26,218	4865(1)	21,000	o
Wenzhou Zhong Qing Hardware Cutting Tools Co. 温州市中輕五金刀具公司(1992)	Wenzhou 温州市	Zhejiang 浙江省	(0577)8781321 (0577)8781321	407	Domestic JVs 聯營	25,994	421(20)	17,082	o
Hainingtian Ying Nail Clipper General Factory 海寧市天鷹指甲鉗總廠(1980)	Jiaxing 嘉興市	Zhejiang 浙江省	(0573)7411070 (0573)7411070	290	Collectively-owned 集體	24,850	306(26)	9,971	o
Guangzhou Nan Fang Kitchen Utensils Development Co. 廣州市南方廚具發展公司(1796)	Guangzhou 廣州市	Guangdong 廣東省	(020)84320194 (020)84324487	301	State-owned 國有	20,182	249(29)	26,910	b

Top 10 Cities by Production Output 產出排名前 10 位城市	Province 省	Market share 市場份額	Number of firms 企業個數
Yangjiang 陽江市	Guangdong 廣東省	22.49%	23
Suzhou 蘇州市	Jiangsu 江蘇省	10.88%	18
Hangzhou 杭州市	Zhejiang 浙江省	10.74%	9
Ningbo 寧波市	Zhejiang 浙江省	9.30%	10
Wenzhou 温州市	Zhejiang 浙江省	8.41%	25
Shanghai 上海市	Shanghai 上海市	6.02%	15
Jinhua 金華市	Zhejiang 浙江省	4.19%	14
Jiaxing 嘉興市	Zhejiang 浙江省	4.15%	4
Taizhou 臺州市	Zhejiang 浙江省	2.44%	5
Beijing 北京市	Beijing 北京市	2.11%	7

10 Major Wholesalers 10 家主要批發商	City 城市	Province 省	Telephone / Fax 電話 / 傳真
Chengdu Great Wall Electric Appliance Company 成都長城電器公司	Chengdu 成都市	Sichuan 四川省	(028)6662132 (028)6671975
Shandou Ceramics (Group) Company 汕頭陶瓷(集團)公司	Shantou 汕頭市	Guangdong 廣東省	(0754)8255441 (0754)8255442
Guangdong Puning Local Products Import & Export Company 廣東省普寧土產進出口公司	Jieyang 揭陽市	Guangdong 廣東省	(0663)2226744
Yixing Sundry Goods General Co. 宜興市土產雜品總公司	Wuxi 無錫市	Jiangsu 江蘇省	(0510)7903683 (0510)7903683
Sujiang Qu Zhe Jiang Dongda Group Company 椒江區浙江東大集團公司	Taizhou 臺州市	Zhejiang 浙江省	(0576)8881477 (0576)8881672
Jiangsu New Suzhou Co. Ltd. Suzhou Daily Goods General Co. 江蘇新蘇州股份有限公司蘇州日用雜品總公司	Suzhou 蘇州市	Jiangsu 江蘇省	(0512)7276630 (0512)7275964
Shandong Daily Use General Merchandise Import & Export Company 山東省日用百貨進出口公司	Qingdao 青島市	Shandong 山東省	(0532)5849141 (0532)5849207
Guangdong Yangjiang Light Industrial Products Import & Export (Group) Company 廣東陽江輕工業品進出口(集團)公司	Yangjiang 陽江市	Guangdong 廣東省	(0662)3222497 (0662)3222976
Hebei Artts & Crtfts Import & Export Corp. 河北工藝品進出口公司	Shijiazhuang 石家莊市	Hebei 河北省	(0311)7756124 (0311)7755347
Shandong Handicrafts Import & Export Products Group Linyi Craft Co. Ltd. 山東工藝品進出品集團臨沂工藝有限公司	Linyi 臨沂市	Shandong 山東省	(0539)8310001 (0539)8315396

*Also include sales by firms outside this industry.包括本行業以外廠家的銷售。"o" stands for "others". "o" 代表"其他產品"。

3485: Locks 製鎖業

The industry accounts for 0.077% of the total revenue of China's industrial sector in 1996. The revenue growth rate of the industry is -5.6% from 1995, as compared to the growth rate of China's industrial sector, 9.51%. The rate of return on asset is -0.30%. 61.65% of all firms in the industry made a profit while 30.88% had negative returns. The top province in terms of the industry's revenue is Zhejiang, accounting for 22.87% of the total revenue.
本行業在1996年佔全行業總產值0.077%，行業年增長率為-5.6%（全國工業年增長率9.51%）。行業的資產回報率-0.30%，61.65%的企業盈利，30.88%的企業虧損。銷售收入最高的省份為浙江省，佔本行業的22.87%。

	Total number of firms 企業總數	Total number of employees 職工總數	Total revenue (mil. RMB) 總銷售收入（百萬元）	Total profit (mil. RMB) 總利潤（百萬元）	Return on assets 資產利潤率 (%)	Return on equity 權益利潤率 (%)	Labour productivity ('000 RMB / worker) 勞動生產率（千元/人）	Debts / assets 資產負債率 (%)	Total assets (mil. RMB) 總資產（百萬元）
Industry Overall 行業總體	538	113,854	4,483	-16	-0.30	-0.92	39.37	67.60	5,489

	Number of firms 企業個數	Average number of employees 平均職工人數	Average revenue ('000 RMB) 平均銷售收入（千元）	Average profit ('000 RMB) 平均利潤（千元）	Return on assets 資產利潤率 (%)	Return on equity 權益利潤率 (%)	Labour productivity ('000 RMB / worker) 勞動生產率（千元/人）	Average debts / assets 平均資產負債率(%)	Average Total assets ('000 RMB) 平均總資產（千元）
By ownership 產業所有權									
State-owned 國有	42	383	13,881	-405	-1.86	-7.20	36.24	74.18	21,762
Collectively-owned 集體	424	204	7,697	4	0.05	0.15	37.70	68.21	9,275
Privately-owned 私有	4	37	2,974	-29	-1.74	-3.74	80.91	53.33	1,680
Domestic JVs 聯營	7	286	16,262	16	0.15	0.35	56.80	56.02	10,376
Joint stock 股份制	13	196	8,459	-10	-0.11	-0.35	43.12	67.93	9,035
Foreign-funded 外資	13	117	5,648	-55	-0.68	-1.37	48.43	50.44	8,153
Overseas Chinese-funded 港澳台資	35	163	9,358	0	0.00	0.01	57.26	50.94	9,663
By size 規模									
Large 大型	4	1,867	110,039	5,908	5.09	12.04	58.93	57.74	116,062
Medium 中型	23	1,144	68,519	1,608	1.78	5.42	59.88	67.10	90,219
Small 小型	505	159	4,885	-152	-2.60	-8.52	30.66	69.52	5,840
By regional distribution 地區分布									
Central-North 華北	57	191	3,568	-25	-0.44	-2.34	18.64	81.33	5,788
Beijing 北京	8	103	3,943	3	0.05	0.14	38.28	66.97	5,268
Tianjin 天津	22	189	1,429	-270	-7.25	104.40	7.58	106.94	3,719
Hebei 河北	13	178	3,409	-72	-1.71	-12.30	19.14	86.07	4,174
Shanxi 山西	8	165	4,276	633	7.91	16.35	25.86	51.64	8,000
Inner Mongolia 內蒙	6	383	10,308	57	0.39	2.29	26.89	83.09	14,615
Northeast 東北	30	335	3,230	16	0.39	1.49	9.65	73.73	3,994
Liaoning 遼寧	16	405	3,852	73	1.96	6.36	9.51	69.20	3,701
Jilin 吉林	7	288	681	-14	-0.44	1.52	2.37	128.99	3,243
Heilongjiang 黑龍江	7	221	4,359	-84	-1.56	-2.98	19.70	47.72	5,416
Central East 華東	316	183	9,358	-27	-0.29	-1.06	51.07	72.92	9,337
Shanghai 上海	30	214	9,651	-365	-3.11	-17.30	45.08	82.02	11,731
Jiangsu 江蘇	58	226	12,822	14	0.14	0.61	56.65	77.25	10,257
Zhejiang 浙江	154	119	6,659	-26	-0.41	-1.27	55.94	67.67	6,423
Anhui 安徽	12	144	3,612	-308	-7.85	-606.56	25.17	98.71	3,926
Fujian 福建	12	67	892	38	2.24	16.25	13.29	86.23	1,671
Jiangxi 江西	18	77	867	-7	-0.43	-2.09	11.29	79.63	1,563
Shandong 山東	32	503	25,895	283	0.99	3.34	51.45	70.46	28,727
Central-South 中南	105	286	10,766	-8	-0.05	-0.11	37.59	56.68	17,983
Henan 河南	10	165	3,546	66	1.27	5.48	21.53	76.86	5,207
Hubei 湖北	14	188	3,714	6	0.10	0.36	19.80	71.60	5,553
Hunan 湖南	20	196	3,941	-97	-2.06	-12.51	20.09	83.52	4,683
Guangdong 廣東	53	382	17,667	111	0.36	0.76	46.27	52.24	30,575
Guangxi 廣西	8	204	3,473	-699	-12.63	100.36	16.99	112.58	5,534
Hainan 海南									
Southwest 西南	21	174	3,808	-109	-1.49	-3.78	21.86	60.69	7,336
Chongqing 重慶	6	270	10,417	349	2.00	4.00	38.55	50.01	17,443
Sichuan 四川	8	132	1,426	-49	-1.19	-3.73	10.79	68.19	4,092
Guizhou 貴州	4	84	550	-573	-31.03	143.13	6.57	121.54	1,845
Yunnan 雲南	3	226	1,993	-537	-12.94	-137.61	8.81	90.59	4,147
Tibet 西藏									
Northwest 西北	9	142	1,703	-421	-8.19	-50.67	12.02	83.84	5,143
Shaanxi 陝西	3	162	1,980	-373	-6.67	-24.51	12.25	72.77	5,593
Gansu 甘肅	2	102	1,975	45	1.07	3.70	19.36	71.14	4,210
Qinghai 青海	2	131	280	-910	-31.38	57.78	2.15	154.31	2,900
Ningxia 寧夏									
Xinjiang 新疆	2	163	2,440	-470	-6.15	-25.90	15.02	76.26	7,645

3485: Locks 製鎖業

Year 年份	Number of firms 企業個數	Rate of change 每年變化 (%)	Number of employees 職工人數（人）	Rate of change 每年變化 (%)	Total revenue (mil. RMB) 總銷售收入（百萬元）	Rate of change 每年變化 (%)	Total profit (mil. RMB) 總利潤（百萬元）	Rate of change 每年變化 (%)
1993	542		155,087		4,099		41	
1994	538	-0.74%	127,413	-17.85%	4,505	9.90%	15	-64.35%
1995	548	1.86%	125,062	-1.85%	4,747	5.37%	-10	-165.31%
1996	538	-1.82%	113,854	-8.96%	4,483	-5.56%	-16	-67.79%

3 Major products* 3 種主要產品 *	Output 產量	Sales volume 銷售量	Unit 單位
a) Lock 鎖	116,282	113,956	10,000 piece 萬把
b) Copper Bar 銅棒材	8,487	7,214	ton 噸
c) Low Voltage Switch 壓開關板	9,808	10,004	piece 面

Top 10 firms by revenue (year founded) 收入排名前 10 家企業 (創辦年份)	City 城市	Province 省	Telephone / fax 電話 / 傳真	Number of employees 職工人數	Ownership 產業所有權	Revenue ('000 RMB) 銷售收入（千元）	Profit ('000 RMB) (rank) 利潤（千元）（排名）	Total assets ('000 RMB) 總資產（千元）	Major products 主要產品
Ye Lu – Gu Li Bao An Products (Guangdong) Co. Ltd. 耶魯—固力保安製品(廣東)有限公司(1996)	Zhongshan 中山市	Guangdong 廣東省	(0760)2102326 (0760)2100316	2,792	Foreign-funded 外資	249,593	-126(220)	553,474	a
Shandong Tri-circle Lock Mfg Group Corp. 山東省三環製鎖集團公司(1930)	Yantai 煙台市	Shandong 山東省	(0535)6254401 (0535)6244704	3,048	State-owned 國有	200,873	1081(25)	222,633	a
Zhongshan Dong Sheng Industrial (Group) company 中山市東升實業(集團)公司(1995)	Zhongshan 中山市	Guangdong 廣東省	(0760)2106050 (0760)2100301	1,926	Collectively-owned 集體	152,890	1112(22)	101,811	a
Guangdong Guli Lock Making (Group) Corp. 廣東固力製鎖(集團)公司(1992)	Zhongshan 中山市	Guangdong 廣東省	(0760)2102326 (0760)2100316	2,460	Collectively-owned 集體	147,743	182(75)	289,620	a
Guangdong Jian Shi Lock Making Co. Ltd. 廣東堅士製鎖有限公司(1988)	Zhongshan 中山市	Guangdong 廣東省	(0760)2318999 (0760)2318080	1,467	Collectively-owned 集體	113,778	130(91)	97,678	a
Zhaoyuan Hardware Industrial Group Co. 招遠市五金工業集團公司(1974)	Yantai 煙台市	Shandong 山東省	(0535)8215736 (0535)8215225	1,644	Collectively-owned 集體	92,589	438(40)	81,795	a
Shandong Double-link Group Co. Ltd. 山東乳山造鎖集團股份有限公司(1973)	Weihai 威海市	Shandong 山東省	(0896)6623405 (0896)6623405	1,679	Joint stock 股份制	85,830	2240(10)	79,210	a,c
Penglai Fu Chang Lock Making Co. Ltd. 蓬萊福昌製鎖有限公司(1955)	Yantai 煙台市	Shandong 山東省	(0535)5811188 (0535)5811188	572	Overseas Chinese-funded 港澳台資	78,293	2413(9)	64,877	a
Shanghai Xin Xing Lock Making Factory 上海新興鎖廠(1937)	Shanghai 上海市	Shanghai 上海市	(021)65451721 (021)65451597	483	State-owned 國有	72,302	0(178)	40,837	a
Jiangsu Jinchang Group Co. Ltd. 江蘇金昌集團有限公司(1970)	Zhenjiang 鎮江市	Jiangsu 江蘇省	(0511)6462814	881	Collectively-owned 集體	68,420	1530(13)	25,630	o

Top 10 Cities by Production Output 產出排名前 10 位城市	Province 省	Market share 市場份額	Number of firms 企業個數
Zhongshan 中山市	Guangdong 廣東省	17.72%	8
Yantai 煙台市	Shandong 山東省	10.45%	11
Wenzhou 温州市	Zhejiang 浙江省	6.43%	117
Shanghai 上海市	Shanghai 上海市	5.39%	48
Ningbo 寧波市	Zhejiang 浙江省	4.98%	38
Jiaxing 嘉興市	Zhejiang 浙江省	4.44%	21
Huzhou 湖州市	Zhejiang 浙江省	4.20%	16
Zhenjiang 鎮江市	Jiangsu 江蘇省	3.92%	15
Wuxi 無錫市	Jiangsu 江蘇省	3.31%	14
Suzhou 蘇州市	Jiangsu 江蘇省	2.86%	18

10 Major Wholesalers 10 家主要批發商	City 城市	Province 省	Telephone / Fax 電話 / 傳真
Chengdu Great Wall Electric Appliance Company 成都長城電器公司	Chengdu 成都市	Sichuan 四川省	(028)6662132 (028)6671975
Shandou Ceramics (Group) Company 汕頭陶瓷(集團)公司	Shantou 汕頭市	Guangdong 廣東省	(0754)8255441 (0754)8255442
Guangdong Puning Local Products Import & Export Company 廣東省普寧土產進出口公司	Jieyang 揭陽市	Guangdong 廣東省	(0663)2226744
Yixing Sundry Goods General Co. 宜興市土產雜品總公司	Wuxi 無錫市	Jiangsu 江蘇省	(0510)7903683 (0510)7903683
Sujiang Qu Zhe Jiang Dongda Group Company 椒江區浙江東大集團公司	Taizhou 臺州市	Zhejiang 浙江省	(0576)8881477 (0576)8881672
Jiangsu New Suzhou Co. Ltd. Suzhou Daily Goods General Co. 江蘇新蘇州股份有限公司蘇州日用雜品總公司	Suzhou 蘇州市	Jiangsu 江蘇省	(0512)7276630 (0512)7275964
Shandong Daily Use General Merchandise Import & Export Company 山東省日用百貨進出口公司	Qingdao 青島市	Shandong 山東省	(0532)5849141 (0532)5849207
Guangdong Yangjiang Light Industrial Products Import & Export (Group) Company 廣東陽江輕工業品進出口(集團)公司	Yangjiang 陽江市	Guangdong 廣東省	(0662)3222497 (0662)3222976
Hebei Artts & Crtfts Import & Export Corp. 河北工藝品進出口公司	Shijiazhuang 石家莊市	Hebei 河北省	(0311)7756124 (0311)7755347
Shandong Handicrafts Import & Export Products Group Linyi Craft Co. Ltd. 山東工藝品進出品集團臨沂工藝有限公司	Linyi 臨沂市	Shandong 山東省	(0539)8310001 (0539)8315396

*Also include sales by firms outside this industry.包括本行業以外廠家的銷售。"o" stands for "others". "o" 代表 "其他產品"。

3486: Cooking Utensils 炊事用具製造業

The industry accounts for 0.048% of the total revenue of China's industrial sector in 1996. The revenue growth rate of the industry is 13.1% from 1995, as compared to the growth rate of China's industrial sector, 9.51%. The rate of return on asset is 0.33%. 67.99% of all firms in the industry made a profit while 24.72% had negative returns. The top province in terms of the industry's revenue is Shandong, accounting for 15.77% of the total revenue.
本行業在1996年佔全行業總產值0.048%，行業年增長率為13.1%（全國工業年增長率9.51%）。行業的資產回報率0.33%，67.99%的企業盈利，24.72%的企業虧損。銷售收入最高的省份為山東省，佔本行業的15.77%。

	Total number of firms 企業總數	Total number of employees 職工總數	Total revenue (mil. RMB) 總銷售收入（百萬元）	Total profit (mil. RMB) 總利潤（百萬元）	Return on assets 資產利潤率 (%)	Return on equity 權益利潤率 (%)	Labour productivity ('000 RMB / worker) 勞動生產率（千元/人）	Debts / assets 資產負債率 (%)	Total assets (mil. RMB) 總資產（百萬元）
Industry Overall 行業總體	1,158	79,261	2,768	11	0.33	1.22	34.92	73.08	3,357

	Number of firms 企業個數	Average number of employees 平均職工人數	Average revenue ('000 RMB) 平均銷售收入（千元）	Average profit ('000 RMB) 平均利潤（千元）	Return on assets 資產利潤率 (%)	Return on equity 權益利潤率 (%)	Labour productivity ('000 RMB / worker) 勞動生產率（千元/人）	Average debts / assets 平均資產負債率(%)	Average Total assets ('000 RMB) 平均總資產（千元）
By ownership 產業所有權									
State-owned 國有	93	194	4,957	-452	-4.88	-23.08	25.58	78.84	9,247
Collectively-owned 集體	1,014	55	1,857	50	2.50	9.04	33.86	72.39	2,000
Privately-owned 私有	6	91	2,698	150	5.00	9.10	29.54	45.07	2,999
Domestic JVs 聯營	1	24	1,189	-149	-4.65	-13.66	49.54	65.95	3,194
Joint stock 股份制	11	146	4,770	725	9.58	19.73	32.77	51.45	7,573
Foreign-funded 外資	10	111	9,766	267	2.73	8.57	87.91	68.11	9,772
Overseas Chinese-funded 港澳台資	22	122	11,602	-408	-3.37	-11.33	94.89	70.24	12,094
By size 規模									
Large 大型	1	2,308	61,683	-16,714	-10.97	-68.72	26.73	84.04	152,418
Medium 中型	5	589	43,474	-1,082	-1.86	-10.23	73.83	81.84	58,242
Small 小型	1,141	65	2,181	29	1.14	4.02	33.66	71.66	2,551
By regional distribution 地區分布									
Central-North 華北	162	47	2,174	65	2.45	10.48	46.09	76.58	2,646
Beijing 北京	33	27	1,577	74	3.09	9.41	57.45	67.16	2,392
Tianjin 天津	17	54	9,299	125	1.74	7.94	172.21	78.02	7,182
Hebei 河北	44	68	2,427	130	3.95	22.87	35.71	82.71	3,293
Shanxi 山西	33	37	327	2	0.21	1.60	8.90	87.10	735
Inner Mongolia 內蒙	35	46	696	5	0.29	0.88	15.13	66.78	1,670
Northeast 東北	150	77	1,478	-134	-4.59	-22.23	19.20	79.37	2,923
Liaoning 遼寧	63	97	2,089	-220	-4.85	-25.43	21.59	80.92	4,528
Jilin 吉林	36	79	1,094	-57	-3.84	-11.70	13.93	67.18	1,490
Heilongjiang 黑龍江	51	51	994	-83	-4.23	-22.86	19.31	81.49	1,951
Central East 華東	259	76	3,817	68	2.11	5.63	50.31	62.46	3,228
Shanghai 上海	8	61	2,484	-465	-9.94	-19.65	40.88	49.43	4,679
Jiangsu 江蘇	26	134	7,732	-52	-0.59	-1.39	57.79	57.30	8,809
Zhejiang 浙江	20	82	3,146	-136	-3.38	-9.44	38.55	64.22	4,012
Anhui 安徽	46	63	1,767	9	0.66	5.79	28.15	88.68	1,425
Fujian 福建	39	91	3,779	71	2.35	5.51	41.72	57.25	3,017
Jiangxi 江西	72	28	549	12	2.37	8.63	19.55	72.56	493
Shandong 山東	48	117	9,093	446	7.92	21.22	77.83	62.69	5,639
Central-South 中南	258	84	3,245	38	0.89	4.93	38.83	81.97	4,288
Henan 河南	67	84	2,541	155	4.22	17.58	30.30	75.98	3,664
Hubei 湖北	40	152	1,925	-44	-1.58	-7.00	12.65	77.40	2,748
Hunan 湖南	58	62	1,689	-84	-4.02	-28.23	27.10	85.75	2,087
Guangdong 廣東	48	88	8,399	21	0.18	1.22	95.64	85.45	11,586
Guangxi 廣西	40	47	2,196	125	6.92	30.71	46.96	77.46	1,806
Hainan 海南	5	31	220	18	6.04	7.56	7.10	20.13	298
Southwest 西南	144	75	1,605	-56	-2.65	-8.74	21.32	69.71	2,127
Chongqing 重慶	23	92	1,925	-29	-1.09	-4.02	20.96	72.94	2,702
Sichuan 四川	38	116	3,601	217	4.88	18.94	30.99	74.22	4,440
Guizhou 貴州	57	54	333	-9	-1.81	-5.65	6.16	68.00	524
Yunnan 雲南	23	50	1,300	-3	-0.14	-0.28	26.00	51.19	1,908
Tibet 西藏	3	26	357	13	2.37	2.67	13.90	11.83	563
Northwest 西北	185	43	740	7	0.51	1.15	17.05	55.71	1,302
Shaanxi 陝西	56	55	903	15	0.94	2.36	16.30	60.30	1,641
Gansu 甘肅	67	49	913	17	1.25	2.81	18.54	55.75	1,402
Qinghai 青海	21	32	419	-20	-1.88	-4.47	13.13	57.95	1,090
Ningxia 寧夏	14	21	311	-16	-1.56	-2.53	14.68	38.10	1,005
Xinjiang 新疆	27	24	444	-6	-0.83	-1.45	18.12	43.07	673

3486: Cooking Utensils 炊事用具製造業

Year 年份	Number of firms 企業個數	Rate of change 每年變化 (%)	Number of employees 職工人數（人）	Rate of change 每年變化 (%)	Total revenue (mil. RMB) 總銷售收入（百萬元）	Rate of change 每年變化 (%)	Total profit (mil. RMB) 總利潤（百萬元）	Rate of change 每年變化 (%)
1993	1,237		77,602		2,555		64	
1994	1,296	4.77%	93,287	20.21%	2,722	6.54%	37	-41.60%
1995	1,223	-5.63%	81,410	-12.73%	2,448	-10.06%	8	-79.74%
1996	1,158	-5.31%	79,261	-2.64%	2,768	13.07%	11	44.93%

3 Major products* 3 種主要產品 *	Output 產量	Sales volume 銷售量	Unit 單位
a) Cast Iron Cooker 鑄鐵鍋	85,506,208	82,941,021	piece 口
b) Stove Utensils 爐具	10,705,378	8,457,248	piece 個
c) Refined Aluminium Pressure Cooker 精鋁壓力鍋	1,161,219	1,056,710	piece 口

Top 10 firms by revenue (year founded) 收入排名前 10 家企業 (創辦年份)	City 城市	Province 省	Telephone / fax 電話 / 傳真	Number of employees 職工人數	Ownership 產業所有權	Revenue ('000 RMB) 銷售收入（千元）	Profit ('000 RMB) (rank) 利潤（千元）（排名）	Total assets ('000 RMB) 總資產（千元）	Major products 主要產品
Shandong Academy of Sciences Heze High Voltage Container Factory 山東省科學院菏澤市高壓容器廠(1986)	Heze 菏澤市	Shandong 山東省	(0530)5400061	620	Collectively-owned 集體	184,120	10880(1)	53,000	o
Nanfang Hardware Factory 南方五金總廠(1971)	Foshan 佛山市	Guangdong 廣東省	(0757)5936712 (0757)5939075	697	Collectively-owned 集體	110,355	5(160)	293,837	c
Nanhai Casting General Factory 南海市鑄造總廠(1968)	Foshan 佛山市	Guangdong 廣東省	(0757)5551976 (0757)5552544	429	Collectively-owned 集體	80,031	209(61)	100,617	a
South Korea Yuan Jin Industrial Co. Ltd. 韓國源進產業有限公司(1996)	Tianjin 天津市	Tianjin 天津市	(022)29534131	100	Foreign-funded 外資	49,150	9960(2)	22,440	o
Nantong Zi Sheng Commercial Co. Ltd. 南通資生鑄造有限公司(1905)	Nantong 南通市	Jiangsu 江蘇省	(0513)5544332 (0513)5545995	674	State-owned 國有	45,796	-1554(238)	62,464	a
Tianjin Jia Li Fu Cast Iron Enamel Product Co. Ltd. 天津市佳利福鑄鐵搪瓷製品有限公司(1991)	Tianjin 天津市	Tianjin 天津市	(022)27393263 (022)27390560	328	Foreign-funded 外資	45,220	233(56)	30,533	o
Guang Hua Hardware Co. Ltd. 廣華五金製品有限公司(1981)	Guangzhou 廣州市	Guangdong 廣東省	(020)87635451 (020)87635448	200	Overseas Chinese-funded 港澳台資	42,332	2738(6)	16,845	o
Wutongqiao Cooker Factory 五通橋鍋廠(1941)	Leshan 樂山市	Sichuan 四川省	(0833)3351432	634	State-owned 國有	40,165	603(24)	47,795	a
Weifang Fangzi Meng Wei Steel Cylinder Co. Ltd. 濰坊市坊子蒙濰鋼瓶有限責任公司(1992)	Weifang 濰坊市	Shandong 山東省	(0536)7665422	350	Private-owned 私營	38,813	1005(13)	20,793	o
Guangzhou Heng Chang Hardware Plastic Products Co. Ltd. 廣州恒昌五金塑料製品有限公司(1992)	Guangzhou 廣州市	Guangdong 廣東省	(020)87705908	768	Overseas Chinese-funded 港澳台資	38,720	-902(231)	16,542	o

Top 10 Cities by Production Output 產出排名前 10 位城市	Province 省	Market share 市場份額	Number of firms 企業個數
Foshan 佛山市	Guangdong 廣東省	30.81%	8
Heze 菏澤市	Shandong 山東省	6.18%	6
Shenzhen 深圳市	Guangdong 廣東省	4.72%	6
Tianjin 天津市	Tianjin 天津市	2.98%	18
Liuzhou 柳州市	Guangxi 廣西	2.96%	6
Nantong 南通市	Jiangsu 江蘇省	2.51%	7
Shanghai 上海市	Shanghai 上海市	2.37%	32
Linyi 臨沂市	Shandong 山東省	1.91%	8
Guangzhou 廣州市	Guangdong 廣東省	1.88%	33
Beijing 北京市	Beijing 北京市	1.78%	28

10 Major Wholesalers 10 家主要批發商	City 城市	Province 省	Telephone / Fax 電話 / 傳真
Chengdu Great Wall Electric Appliance Company 成都長城電器公司	Chengdu 成都市	Sichuan 四川省	(028)6662132 (028)6671975
Shandou Ceramics (Group) Company 汕頭陶瓷(集團)公司	Shantou 汕頭市	Guangdong 廣東省	(0754)8255441 (0754)8255442
Guangdong Puning Local Products Import & Export Company 廣東省普寧土產進出口公司	Jieyang 揭陽市	Guangdong 廣東省	(0663)2226744
Yixing Sundry Goods General Co. 宜興市土產雜品總公司	Wuxi 無錫市	Jiangsu 江蘇省	(0510)7903683 (0510)7903683
Sujiang Qu Zhe Jiang Dongda Group Company 椒江區浙江東大集團公司	Taizhou 臺州市	Zhejiang 浙江省	(0576)8881477 (0576)8881672
Jiangsu New Suzhou Co. Ltd. Suzhou Daily Goods General Co. 江蘇新蘇州股份有限公司蘇州日用雜品總公司	Suzhou 蘇州市	Jiangsu 江蘇省	(0512)7276630 (0512)7275964
Shandong Daily Use General Merchandise Import & Export Company 山東省日用百貨進出口公司	Qingdao 青島市	Shandong 山東省	(0532)5849141 (0532)5849207
Guangdong Yangjiang Light Industrial Products Import & Export (Group) Company 廣東陽江輕工業品進出口(集團)公司	Yangjiang 陽江市	Guangdong 廣東省	(0662)3222497 (0662)3222976
Hebei Artts & Crtfts Import & Export Corp. 河北工藝品進出口公司	Shijiazhuang 石家莊市	Hebei 河北省	(0311)7756124 (0311)7755347
Shandong Handicrafts Import & Export Products Group Linyi Craft Co. Ltd. 山東工藝品進出品集團臨沂工藝有限公司	Linyi 臨沂市	Shandong 山東省	(0539)8310001 (0539)8315396

*Also include sales by firms outside this industry.包括本行業以外廠家的銷售。"o" stands for "others". "o" 代表"其他產品"。

3487: Gas Utensils 燃氣用具製造業

The industry accounts for 0.072% of the total revenue of China's industrial sector in 1996. The revenue growth rate of the industry is -11.6% from 1995, as compared to the growth rate of China's industrial sector, 9.51%. The rate of return on asset is -0.31%. 64.75% of all firms in the industry made a profit while 31.71% had negative returns. The top province in terms of the industry's revenue is Guangdong, accounting for 37.45% of the total revenue.
本行業在1996年佔全行業總產值0.072%，行業年增長率為-11.6%（全國工業年增長率9.51%）。行業的資產回報率-0.31%，64.75%的企業盈利，31.71%的企業虧損。銷售收入最高的省份為廣東省，佔本行業的37.45%。

	Total number of firms 企業總數	Total number of employees 職工總數	Total revenue (mil. RMB) 總銷售收入（百萬元）	Total profit (mil. RMB) 總利潤（百萬元）	Return on assets 資產利潤率 (%)	Return on equity 權益利潤率 (%)	Labour productivity ('000 RMB / worker) 勞動生產率（千元/人）	Debts / assets 資產負債率 (%)	Total assets (mil. RMB) 總資產（百萬元）
Industry Overall 行業總體	390	52,870	4,187	-19	-0.31	-1.10	79.19	71.79	6,034

	Number of firms 企業個數	Average number of employees 平均職工人數	Average revenue ('000 RMB) 平均銷售收入（千元）	Average profit ('000 RMB) 平均利潤（千元）	Return on assets 資產利潤率 (%)	Return on equity 權益利潤率 (%)	Labour productivity ('000 RMB / worker) 勞動生產率（千元/人）	Average debts / assets 平均資產負債率(%)	Average Total assets ('000 RMB) 平均總資產（千元）
By ownership 產業所有權									
State-owned 國有	40	273	13,700	-1,000	-3.86	-68.97	50.27	94.40	25,900
Collectively-owned 集體	271	110	6,805	-52	-0.58	-2.48	61.65	76.67	9,039
Privately-owned 私有	5	31	1,293	31	1.47	4.06	41.99	63.78	2,086
Domestic JVs 聯營	3	139	19,709	8	0.04	0.58	141.45	93.42	19,982
Joint stock 股份制	6	659	126,988	4,754	2.71	7.10	192.70	61.80	175,236
Foreign-funded 外資	28	150	16,812	-85	-0.27	-0.51	112.43	46.94	31,291
Overseas Chinese-funded 港澳台資	35	102	14,163	255	1.62	4.51	139.13	64.03	15,688
By size 規模									
Large 大型	5	1,107	218,932	-8,621	-2.48	-6.06	197.70	59.08	347,372
Medium 中型	18	800	47,376	672	0.90	3.57	59.23	74.71	74,437
Small 小型	354	92	6,326	34	0.41	1.84	68.51	77.94	8,355
By regional distribution 地區分布									
Central-North 華北	47	85	1,826	-363	-6.33	-744.54	21.47	99.15	5,733
Beijing 北京	23	25	1,562	58	3.05	8.79	63.02	65.30	1,910
Tianjin 天津	8	140	1,483	-276	-7.75	-26.66	10.63	70.94	3,566
Hebei 河北	12	189	3,049	-1,353	-8.31	74.35	16.17	111.18	16,273
Shanxi 山西	2	19	580	20	2.50	7.84	31.35	68.13	800
Inner Mongolia 內蒙	2	6	150	5	8.33	12.50	25.00	33.33	60
Northeast 東北	42	130	3,689	-518	-3.40	-20.40	28.47	83.31	15,213
Liaoning 遼寧	16	298	6,903	-1,358	-3.65	-25.15	23.17	85.50	37,236
Jilin 吉林	8	21	2,485	-5	-0.22	-0.40	116.94	44.48	2,229
Heilongjiang 黑龍江	18	28	1,367	1	0.04	0.10	48.73	59.14	1,407
Central East 華東	154	143	12,615	432	3.23	8.70	88.07	62.85	13,360
Shanghai 上海	16	109	24,112	1,704	5.95	11.41	222.23	47.85	28,632
Jiangsu 江蘇	45	230	19,888	748	4.45	13.75	86.58	67.61	16,804
Zhejiang 浙江	56	96	8,657	144	1.40	3.69	89.86	62.09	10,293
Anhui 安徽	11	66	4,091	295	9.77	22.28	61.98	56.12	3,023
Fujian 福建	9	38	2,104	86	2.78	7.70	55.54	63.91	3,079
Jiangxi 江西	6	210	5,640	28	0.30	1.13	26.84	73.76	9,558
Shandong 山東	11	206	7,222	-609	-4.51	-29.91	35.10	84.92	13,495
Central-South 中南	103	154	17,500	-307	-1.14	-4.10	113.79	72.17	26,910
Henan 河南	9	27	4,370	780	39.91	125.13	161.85	68.16	1,954
Hubei 湖北	8	160	4,698	10	0.07	0.15	29.45	56.50	14,928
Hunan 湖南	14	91	8,886	464	6.37	19.76	97.27	67.76	7,288
Guangdong 廣東	67	184	23,404	-588	-1.59	-5.70	127.10	72.11	36,966
Guangxi 廣西	4	32	2,948	45	2.80	26.87	93.57	89.56	1,605
Hainan 海南	1	580	21,330	-5,990	-12.07	57.38	36.78	121.04	49,630
Southwest 西南	33	140	5,677	-266	-3.63	-16.83	40.67	78.41	7,316
Chongqing 重慶	13	230	6,565	-894	-9.69	-53.24	28.50	81.80	9,233
Sichuan 四川	18	84	5,635	183	2.76	11.19	67.47	75.32	6,627
Guizhou 貴州	1	6	40				6.67		60
Yunnan 雲南	1	42	170				4.05	24.75	1,010
Tibet 西藏									
Northwest 西北	11	84	1,226	-554	-11.07	-108.56	14.60	89.79	5,003
Shaanxi 陝西	4	34	1,450	-15	-1.12	-4.88	42.96	77.01	1,338
Gansu 甘肅	3	218	2,077	-1,823	-13.11	-172.01	9.53	92.40	13,907
Qinghai 青海									
Ningxia 寧夏	1	113	1,020	-640	-17.78	27.23	9.03	165.00	3,600
Xinjiang 新疆	3	7	147	27	1.83	2.25	20.00	18.35	1,453

3487: Gas Utensils 燃氣用具製造業

Year 年份	Number of firms 企業個數	Rate of change 每年變化 (%)	Number of employees 職工人數 (人)	Rate of change 每年變化 (%)	Total revenue (mil. RMB) 總銷售收入 (百萬元)	Rate of change 每年變化 (%)	Total profit (mil. RMB) 總利潤 (百萬元)	Rate of change 每年變化 (%)
1993	299		52,915		4,382		190	
1994	355	18.73%	49,123	-7.17%	3,952	-9.82%	99	-47.60%
1995	416	17.18%	56,913	15.86%	4,739	19.90%	36	-63.84%
1996	390	-6.25%	52,870	-7.10%	4,187	-11.65%	-19	-152.86%

3 Major products* 3 種主要產品 *	Output 產量	Sales volume 銷售量	Unit 單位
a) Gas Rice Cooker 燃氣飯鍋	138,909	138,909	set 台
b) Gas Range 燃氣灶	10,674,270	10,354,042	set 台
c) Gas Water Heater 燃氣熱水器	3,032,413	3,002,089	set 台

Top 10 firms by revenue (year founded) 收入排名前 10 家企業 (創辦年份)	City 城市	Province 省	Telephone / fax 電話 / 傳真	Number of employees 職工人數	Ownership 產業所有權	Revenue ('000 RMB) 銷售收入 (千元)	Profit ('000 RMB) (rank) 利潤 (千元) (排名)	Total assets ('000 RMB) 總資產 (千元)	Major products 主要產品
Guangdong Wanjiale Gas Apparatus Co. Ltd. 廣東省萬家樂燃氣具有限公司(1986)	Foshan 佛山市	Guangdong 廣東省	(0757)2291380 (0757)2291338	2,768	Joint stock 股份制	564,035	21481(2)	907,177	b,c
Shanghai N & N Co. Ltd. 上海水仙能率有限公司(1994)	Shanghai 上海市	Shanghai 上海市	(021)58994746 (021)58994348	386	Foreign-funded 外資	178,096	15084(3)	192,080	c
Local State-owned Baoying Vehicle Plant 地方國營寶應車輛廠(1959)	Yangzhou 揚州市	Jiangsu 江蘇省	(0514)8222974 (0514)8223524	1,143	State-owned 國有	161,810	3185(11)	91,568	o
Zhongshan Gas Appliances Industry Group Corp. Ltd. 中山市燃氣具工業集團有限公司(1954)	Zhongshan 中山市	Guangdong 廣東省	(0760)8312046 (0760)8314364	740	Joint stock 股份制	139,470	1450(19)	212,220	b,c
Jiangsu Guang Mang Group Co. 江蘇光芒集團公司(1975)	Taizhou 泰州市	Jiangsu 江蘇省	(0523)4321299 (0523)4321369	803	Collectively-owned 集體	136,051	5727(7)	84,297	b,c
Wuxi Jin Du Kitchen Equipment Co. Ltd. 無錫市金都廚房設備有限公司(1992)	Wuxi 無錫市	Jiangsu 江蘇省	(0510)5102028 (0510)5102518	2,400	Overseas Chinese-funded 港澳台資	124,780	31230(1)	46,720	o
Shanghai Lin Nei Co. Ltd. 上海林內有限公司(1993)	Shanghai 上海市	Shanghai 上海市	(021)58717179 (021)58717179	400	Foreign-funded 外資	111,711	11399(4)	112,863	c
Feng An Hardware Machinery (Shenzhen) Co. Ltd. 豐安五金機械(深圳)有限公司(1993)	Shenzhen 深圳市	Guangdong 廣東省	(0755)7403290 (0755)7402166	350	Overseas Chinese-funded 港澳台資	102,341	252(65)	55,947	o
Shenzhen Huo Wang Burners Company 深圳市火王燃器具公司(1992)	Shenzhen 深圳市	Guangdong 廣東省	(0755)7900000 (0755)7903042	280	Collectively-owned 集體	102,041	7542(5)	57,690	b
Guangdong Shen Zhou Gas Appliances Co. Ltd. 廣東神州燃氣用具有限公司(1995)	Foshan 佛山市	Guangdong 廣東省	(0757)8861113 (0757)8852750	986	Foreign-funded 外資	97,924	-27946(198)	267,266	b,c

Top 10 Cities by Production Output 產出排名前 10 位城市	Province 省	Market share 市場份額	Number of firms 企業個數
Foshan 佛山市	Guangdong 廣東省	21.82%	12
Shaoxing 紹興市	Zhejiang 浙江省	10.16%	11
Yangzhou 揚州市	Jiangsu 江蘇省	7.17%	10
Zhongshan 中山市	Guangdong 廣東省	6.62%	9
Shanghai 上海市	Shanghai 上海市	5.81%	27
Xiangtan 湘潭市	Hunan 湖南省	4.57%	2
Nanjing 南京市	Jiangsu 江蘇省	4.29%	11
Jiangmen 江門市	Guangdong 廣東省	3.70%	4
Jinhua 金華市	Zhejiang 浙江省	2.89%	17
Shenzhen 深圳市	Guangdong 廣東省	2.85%	5

10 Major Wholesalers 10 家主要批發商	City 城市	Province 省	Telephone / Fax 電話 / 傳真
Chengdu Great Wall Electric Appliance Company 成都長城電器公司	Chengdu 成都市	Sichuan 四川省	(028)6662132 (028)6671975
Shandou Ceramics (Group) Company 汕頭陶瓷(集團)公司	Shantou 汕頭市	Guangdong 廣東省	(0754)8255441 (0754)8255442
Guangdong Puning Local Products Import & Export Company 廣東省普寧土產進出口公司	Jieyang 揭陽市	Guangdong 廣東省	(0663)2226744
Yixing Sundry Goods General Co. 宜興市土產雜品總公司	Wuxi 無錫市	Jiangsu 江蘇省	(0510)7903683 (0510)7903683
Sujiang Qu Zhe Jiang Dongda Group Company 椒江區浙江東大集團公司	Taizhou 臺州市	Zhejiang 浙江省	(0576)8881477 (0576)8881672
Jiangsu New Suzhou Co. Ltd. Suzhou Daily Goods General Co. 江蘇新蘇州股份有限公司蘇州日用雜品總公司	Suzhou 蘇州市	Jiangsu 江蘇省	(0512)7276630 (0512)7275964
Shandong Daily Use General Merchandise Import & Export Company 山東省日用百貨進出口公司	Qingdao 青島市	Shandong 山東省	(0532)5849141 (0532)5849207
Guangdong Yangjiang Light Industrial Products Import & Export (Group) Company 廣東陽江輕工業品進出口(集團)公司	Yangjiang 陽江市	Guangdong 廣東省	(0662)3222497 (0662)3222976
Hebei Artts & Crtfts Import & Export Corp. 河北工藝品進出口公司	Shijiazhuang 石家莊市	Hebei 河北省	(0311)7756124 (0311)7755347
Shandong Handicrafts Import & Export Products Group Linyi Craft Co. Ltd. 山東工藝品進出品集團臨沂工藝有限公司	Linyi 臨沂市	Shandong 山東省	(0539)8310001 (0539)8315396

*Also include sales by firms outside this industry.包括本行業以外廠家的銷售。"o" stands for "others". "o" 代表 "其他產品"。

3488: Hair Cutting Equipment 理髮用具製造業

The industry accounts for 0.020% of the total revenue of China's industrial sector in 1996. The revenue growth rate of the industry is 2.2% from 1995, as compared to the growth rate of China's industrial sector, 9.51%. The rate of return on asset is 3.71%. 75.45% of all firms in the industry made a profit while 18.67% had negative returns. The top province in terms of the industry's revenue is Shanghai, accounting for 37.47% of the total revenue.
本行業在1996年佔全行業總產值0.020%，行業年增長率為2.2%（全國工業年增長率9.51%）。行業的資產回報率3.71%，75.45%的企業盈利，18.67%的企業虧損。銷售收入最高的省份為上海市，佔本行業的37.47%。

	Total number of firms 企業總數	Total number of employees 職工總數	Total revenue (mil. RMB) 總銷售收入（百萬元）	Total profit (mil. RMB) 總利潤（百萬元）	Return on assets 資產利潤率 (%)	Return on equity 權益利潤率 (%)	Labour productivity ('000 RMB / worker) 勞動生產率（千元/人）	Debts / assets 資產負債率 (%)	Total assets (mil. RMB) 總資產（百萬元）
Industry Overall 行業總體	79	12,537	1,134	65	3.71	7.70	90.45	51.82	1,754

	Number of firms 企業個數	Average number of employees 平均職工人數	Average revenue ('000 RMB) 平均銷售收入（千元）	Average profit ('000 RMB) 平均利潤（千元）	Return on assets 資產利潤率 (%)	Return on equity 權益利潤率 (%)	Labour productivity ('000 RMB / worker) 勞動生產率（千元/人）	Average debts / assets 平均資產負債率(%)	Average Total assets ('000 RMB) 平均總資產（千元）
By ownership 產業所有權									
State-owned 國有	9	374	11,111	1,000	2.56	7.50	29.71	65.81	39,000
Collectively-owned 集體	49	97	6,281	-3,000	-53.12	-103.26	64.79	48.56	5,649
Privately-owned 私有									
Domestic JVs 聯營	3	190	15,251	-9,338	-70.72	-245.49	80.27	71.19	13,205
Joint stock 股份制	2	33	3,867	-1,424	-74.59	-192.63	117.19	61.28	1,909
Foreign-funded 外資	10	210	54,107	23,652	25.74	46.03	257.29	44.07	91,876
Overseas Chinese-funded 港澳台資	6	322	22,012	-440	-1.60	-4.68	68.36	65.83	[illegible]
By size 規模									
Large 大型	3	409	102,343	111,713	54.12	137.83	250.23	60.74	206,428
Medium 中型	4	702	35,169	1,225	1.89	8.48	50.13	77.76	64,928
Small 小型	72	123	9,537	-3,820	-31.40	-50.51	77.80	37.84	12,166
By regional distribution 地區分布									
Central-North 華北	6	149	2,640	-228	-3.89	-13.84	17.72	71.84	5,865
Beijing 北京	2	185	5,795	125	1.27	4.73	31.32	73.12	9,840
Tianjin 天津	3	165	1,400	-540	-10.90	-39.04	8.50	72.07	4,953
Hebei 河北	1	30	50				1.67	27.69	650
Shanxi 山西									
Inner Mongolia 內蒙									
Northeast 東北	3	81	13,837	8,390	51.15	59.73	171.53	14.39	16,403
Liaoning 遼寧	3	81	13,837	8,390	51.15	59.73	171.53	14.39	16,403
Jilin 吉林									
Heilongjiang 黑龍江									
Central East 華東	59	141	11,201	682	3.72	8.87	79.64	58.07	18,347
Shanghai 上海	16	208	26,554	2,276	4.99	12.93	127.86	61.44	45,649
Jiangsu 江蘇	5	193	6,544	-76	-0.35	-1.02	33.98	65.46	21,592
Zhejiang 浙江	36	106	5,425	270	4.79	8.72	50.95	45.09	5,635
Anhui 安徽									
Fujian 福建	2	90	3,985	-2,745	-13.31	-23.26	44.53	42.80	20,630
Jiangxi 江西									
Shandong 山東									
Central-South 中南	9	331	45,518	94	0.15	0.25	137.70	42.06	
Henan 河南									
Hubei 湖北									
Hunan 湖南									
Guangdong 廣東	9	331	45,518	94	0.15	0.25	137.70	42.06	64,394
Guangxi 廣西									
Hainan 海南									
Southwest 西南	1	45	3,390	80	2.36	8.08	75.33	70.80	3,390
Chongqing 重慶									
Sichuan 四川	1	45	3,390	80	2.36	8.08	75.33	70.80	3,390
Guizhou 貴州									
Yunnan 雲南									
Tibet 西藏									
Northwest 西北	1	83	2,700	40	1.06	1.80	32.53	41.42	3,790
Shaanxi 陝西									
Gansu 甘肅									
Qinghai 青海									
Ningxia 寧夏									
Xinjiang 新疆	1	83	2,700	40	1.06	1.80	32.53	41.42	3,790

3488: Hair Cutting Equipment 理髮用具製造業

Year 年份	Number of firms 企業個數	Rate of change 每年變化 (%)	Number of employees 職工人數（人）	Rate of change 每年變化 (%)	Total revenue (mil. RMB) 總銷售收入（百萬元）	Rate of change 每年變化 (%)	Total profit (mil. RMB) 總利潤（百萬元）	Rate of change 每年變化 (%)
1993	76		20,920		516		20	
1994	84	10.53%	12,365	-40.89%	593	14.99%	-60	-400.16%
1995	90	7.14%	14,898	20.49%	1,110	87.20%	-8	85.90%
1996	79	-12.22%	12,537	-15.85%	1,134	2.16%	65	872.71%

3 Major products* 3 種主要產品 *	Output 產量	Sales volume 銷售量	Unit 單位
a) Hairdressing Tools 理髮用具	161,908	157,051	10,000 piece 萬把
b) Electric Kettle 電水壺	75,101	78,105	piece 個
c) Daily Stainless Steel Product 日用不銹鋼製品	2,453	2,428	ton 噸

Top 10 firms by revenue (year founded) 收入排名前 10 家企業 (創辦年份)	City 城市	Province 省	Telephone / fax 電話 / 傳真	Number of employees 職工人數	Ownership 產業所有權	Revenue ('000 RMB) 銷售收入（千元）	Profit ('000 RMB) (rank) 利潤（千元）（排名）	Total assets ('000 RMB) 總資產（千元）	Major products 主要產品
Shanghai Gillette Co. Ltd. 上海吉列有限公司(1992)	Shanghai 上海市	Shanghai 上海市	(021)58411030 (021)58411724	766	Foreign-funded 外資	289,892	24057(2)	374,313	a
Matsushita Electric Works-wanbao (Guangzhou) Ltd. 松下電工萬寶電器(廣州)有限公司(1993)	Guangzhou 廣州市	Guangdong 廣東省	(020)84770333 (020)84773033	478	Foreign-funded 外資	230,845	1380(6)	308,655	a
Guangzhou Li Min Electrical Appliance Industrial Co. Ltd. 廣州市利民電器實業有限公司(1986)	Guangzhou 廣州市	Guangdong 廣東省	(020)83878397 (020)83807292	1,114	Overseas Chinese-funded 港澳台資	91,407	902(9)	155,709	o
Shanghai Tableware Factory Jiading Branch 上海餐具廠嘉定分廠(1987)	Shanghai 上海市	Shanghai 上海市	(021)59509479 (021)59507888	198	Domestic JVs 聯營	56,818	704(12)	19,143	c
Zhejiang Chao Ren Group Co. Ltd. 浙江超人集團有限公司(1995)	Jinhua 金華市	Zhejiang 浙江省	(0579)7113455	462	Collectively-owned 集體	47,180	1675(5)	45,660	o
Shenmei Daily Use Products Ltd., Co. 沈美日用品有限公司(1983)	Shenyang 瀋陽市	Liaoning 遼寧省	(024)88323987 (024)88323680	104	Foreign-funded 外資	40,171	25143(1)	42,179	o
Ningbo Fa Yuan Beauty Instrument Co. Ltd. 寧波發源美容器具有限公司(1991)	Ningbo 寧波市	Zhejiang 浙江省	(0574)2055024 (0574)2058012	400	Overseas Chinese-funded 港澳台資	30,017	5815(4)	24,201	o
Jieyang Dongfang Electric Appliance Industrial Company 揭陽試驗區東方電器工業公司(1990)	Jieyang 揭陽市	Guangdong 廣東省	(0663)8779328	180	Collectively-owned 集體	29,200	440(15)	13,250	a
Yangzhou Chang Xing Blades Co. Ltd. 揚州長興刀片有限公司(1993)	Yangzhou 揚州市	Jiangsu 江蘇省	(0514)7587299 (0514)7583364	284	Foreign-funded 外資	19,458	203(20)	91,750	a
Xin Zhong Hua Knives & Scissors Factory 新中華刀剪廠(1927)	Shanghai 上海市	Shanghai 上海市	(021)62803570 (021)62809789	1,251	State-owned 國有	18,849	74(28)	114,948	a

Top 10 Cities by Production Output 產出排名前 10 位城市	Province 省	Market share 市場份額	Number of firms 企業個數
Shanghai 上海市	Shanghai 上海市	35.86%	20
Guangzhou 廣州市	Guangdong 廣東省	29.76%	9
Ningbo 寧波市	Zhejiang 浙江省	5.42%	9
Wenzhou 温州市	Zhejiang 浙江省	5.04%	27
Jinhua 金華市	Zhejiang 浙江省	4.78%	3
Jieyang 揭陽市	Guangdong 廣東省	3.51%	2
Shenyang 瀋陽市	Liaoning 遼寧省	3.10%	2
Dongguan 東莞市	Guangdong 廣東省	2.78%	2
Yangzhou 揚州市	Jiangsu 江蘇省	2.56%	3
Shenzhen 深圳市	Guangdong 廣東省	1.49%	1

10 Major Wholesalers 10 家主要批發商	City 城市	Province 省	Telephone / Fax 電話 / 傳真
Chengdu Great Wall Electric Appliance Company 成都長城電器公司	Chengdu 成都市	Sichuan 四川省	(028)6662132 (028)6671975
Shandou Ceramics (Group) Company 汕頭陶瓷(集團)公司	Shantou 汕頭市	Guangdong 廣東省	(0754)8255441 (0754)8255442
Guangdong Puning Local Products Import & Export Company 廣東省普寧土產進出口公司	Jieyang 揭陽市	Guangdong 廣東省	(0663)2226744
Yixing Sundry Goods General Co. 宜興市土產雜品總公司	Wuxi 無錫市	Jiangsu 江蘇省	(0510)7903683 (0510)7903683
Sujiang Qu Zhe Jiang Dongda Group Company 椒江區浙江東大集團公司	Taizhou 臺州市	Zhejiang 浙江省	(0576)8881477 (0576)8881672
Jiangsu New Suzhou Co. Ltd. Suzhou Daily Goods General Co. 江蘇新蘇州股份有限公司蘇州日用雜品總公司	Suzhou 蘇州市	Jiangsu 江蘇省	(0512)7276630 (0512)7275964
Shandong Daily Use General Merchandise Import & Export Company 山東省日用百貨進出口公司	Qingdao 青島市	Shandong 山東省	(0532)5849141 (0532)5849207
Guangdong Yangjiang Light Industrial Products Import & Export (Group) Company 廣東陽江輕工業品進出口(集團)公司	Yangjiang 陽江市	Guangdong 廣東省	(0662)3222497 (0662)3222976
Hebei Artts & Crtfts Import & Export Corp. 河北工藝品進出口公司	Shijiazhuang 石家莊市	Hebei 河北省	(0311)7756124 (0311)7755347
Shandong Handicrafts Import & Export Products Group Linyi Craft Co. Ltd. 山東工藝品進出品集團臨沂工藝有限公司	Linyi 臨沂市	Shandong 山東省	(0539)8310001 (0539)8315396

*Also include sales by firms outside this industry.包括本行業以外廠家的銷售。"o" stands for "others". "o" 代表"其他產品"。

3489: Other Household Metal Products 其他日用金屬製品業

The industry accounts for 0.090% of the total revenue of China's industrial sector in 1996. The revenue growth rate of the industry is 15.7% from 1995, as compared to the growth rate of China's industrial sector, 9.51%. The rate of return on asset is -0.37%. 65.74% of all firms in the industry made a profit while 27.03% had negative returns. The top province in terms of the industry's revenue is Guangdong, accounting for 29.37% of the total revenue.
本行業在1996年佔全行業總產值0.090%，行業年增長率為15.7%（全國工業年增長率9.51%）。行業的資產回報率-0.37%，65.74%的企業盈利，27.03%的企業虧損。銷售收入最高的省份為廣東省，佔本行業的29.37%。

	Total number of firms 企業總數	Total number of employees 職工總數	Total revenue (mil. RMB) 總銷售收入（百萬元）	Total profit (mil. RMB) 總利潤（百萬元）	Return on assets 資產利潤率 (%)	Return on equity 權益利潤率 (%)	Labour productivity ('000 RMB / worker) 勞動生產率（千元/人）	Debts / assets 資產負債率 (%)	Total assets (mil. RMB) 總資產（百萬元）
Industry Overall 行業總體	1,082	93,866	5,193	-24	-0.37	-1.11	55.32	66.36	6,336

	Number of firms 企業個數	Average number of employees 平均職工人數	Average revenue ('000 RMB) 平均銷售收入（千元）	Average profit ('000 RMB) 平均利潤（千元）	Return on assets 資產利潤率 (%)	Return on equity 權益利潤率 (%)	Labour productivity ('000 RMB / worker) 勞動生產率（千元/人）	Average debts / assets 平均資產負債率(%)	Average Total assets ('000 RMB) 平均總資產（千元）
By ownership 產業所有權									
State-owned 國有	71	218	9,930	-563	-3.26	-12.16	45.58	73.16	17,268
Collectively-owned 集體	844	71	3,053	42	1.42	4.58	42.74	69.00	2,949
Privately-owned 私有	5	48	4,026	-325	-19.37	-22.25	83.19	12.96	1,678
Domestic JVs 聯營	11	211	29,759	688	4.80	16.88	141.34	71.58	14,334
Joint stock 股份制	10	78	3,354	-230	-0.55	-1.04	42.78	47.35	42,127
Foreign-funded 外資	33	90	9,832	378	4.23	9.34	109.80	54.73	8,933
Overseas Chinese-funded 港澳台資	106	124	11,365	-335	-2.04	-5.70	91.71	64.18	16,404
By size 規模									
Large 大型	4	711	96,981	-1,385	-0.70	-1.91	136.35	63.57	199,206
Medium 中型	17	552	42,320	918	1.95	7.22	76.67	72.98	47,041
Small 小型	1,045	78	3,909	-32	-0.71	-2.09	49.81	65.72	4,535
By regional distribution 地區分布									
Central-North 華北	137	69	2,314	144	2.19	5.69	33.52	61.55	6,581
Beijing 北京	26	76	2,892	-60	-0.98	-3.39	38.10	71.22	6,146
Tianjin 天津	41	97	2,742	324	2.33	5.12	28.20	54.46	13,895
Hebei 河北	40	62	2,828	212	5.88	22.05	45.54	73.34	3,599
Shanxi 山西	18	47	741	-28	-2.63	-18.32	15.77	85.65	1,057
Inner Mongolia 內蒙	12	14	248	4	0.55	29.41	17.63	98.14	763
Northeast 東北	77	64	1,890	-129	-3.17	-11.72	29.38	72.96	4,076
Liaoning 遼寧	34	64	1,535	-52	-1.50	-5.89	23.85	74.48	3,464
Jilin 吉林	23	64	1,316	-457	-7.18	-31.68	20.57	77.35	6,362
Heilongjiang 黑龍江	20	65	3,155	116	4.67	10.71	48.73	56.42	2,487
Central East 華東	448	103	6,220	33	0.54	1.72	60.53	68.63	6,073
Shanghai 上海	74	171	13,009	-79	-0.68	-1.91	75.93	64.19	11,548
Jiangsu 江蘇	82	130	8,126	38	0.51	1.96	62.58	74.01	7,493
Zhejiang 浙江	155	39	3,513	177	7.74	22.38	89.00	65.41	2,283
Anhui 安徽	26	110	4,420	-38	-1.24	-5.84	40.37	78.70	3,061
Fujian 福建	50	87	2,682	54	1.68	4.49	30.87	62.50	3,182
Jiangxi 江西	26	49	1,090	10	0.60	1.46	22.33	58.58	1,656
Shandong 山東	35	232	9,585	-342	-1.94	-7.00	41.26	72.25	17,596
Central-South 中南	351	82	5,215	-147	-2.34	-6.83	63.34	65.77	6,300
Henan 河南	18	53	1,917	-1,097	-19.56	119.64	35.97	116.35	5,606
Hubei 湖北	42	87	4,689	38	0.61	2.50	53.74	75.44	6,118
Hunan 湖南	34	49	1,529	-72	-6.57	-32.37	31.45	79.71	1,102
Guangdong 廣東	230	96	6,631	-136	-1.74	-4.49	68.75	61.22	7,794
Guangxi 廣西	27	16	817	4	0.43	1.34	50.27	67.70	859
Hainan 海南									
Southwest 西南	42	75	1,835	143	5.97	10.53	24.63	43.32	2,401
Chongqing 重慶	11	112	2,660	334	10.72	19.26	23.65	44.32	3,118
Sichuan 四川	15	83	1,831	196	8.86	14.91	22.05	40.59	2,209
Guizhou 貴州	11	36	550	10	1.92	3.81	15.13	49.30	520
Yunnan 雲南	5	53	2,930	-126	-2.24	-4.02	55.08	44.23	5,616
Tibet 西藏									
Northwest 西北	27	51	1,343	-87	-2.68	-7.27	26.10	63.05	3,256
Shaanxi 陝西	11	62	1,811	-16	-0.54	-0.92	29.04	41.40	3,030
Gansu 甘肅	8	57	1,061	-71	-2.29	-7.02	18.74	67.39	3,116
Qinghai 青海	2	3	30				10.00	28.57	35
Ningxia 寧夏	3	20	430	13	2.45	10.26	21.15	76.07	543
Xinjiang 新疆	3	61	2,163	-550	-5.90	-37.59	35.46	84.30	9,320

3489: Other Household Metal Products 其他日用金屬製品業

Year 年份	Number of firms 企業個數	Rate of change 每年變化 (%)	Number of employees 職工人數 (人)	Rate of change 每年變化 (%)	Total revenue (mil. RMB) 總銷售收入 (百萬元)	Rate of change 每年變化 (%)	Total profit (mil. RMB) 總利潤 (百萬元)	Rate of change 每年變化 (%)
1993	1,447		140,735		4,394		119	
1994	1,588	9.74%	139,661	-0.76%	5,209	18.56%	103	-13.83%
1995	1,144	-27.96%	103,019	-26.24%	4,488	-13.85%	13	-86.86%
1996	1,082	-5.42%	93,866	-8.88%	5,193	15.71%	-24	-277.95%

3 Major products* 3 種主要產品 *	Output 產量	Sales volume 銷售量	Unit 單位
a) Stove Utensils 爐具	8,546,633	6,751,840	piece 個
b) Cigarette Lighter 打火機	42,346	40,653	10,000 piece 萬個
c) Packing Tin, Tank & Box from Metal 金屬製包裝用錫、罐、盒	271,775,196	222,855,661	piece 個

Top 10 firms by revenue (year founded) 收入排名前 10 家企業 (創辦年份)	City 城市	Province 省	Telephone / fax 電話 / 傳真	Number of employees 職工人數	Ownership 產業所有權	Revenue ('000 RMB) 銷售收入 (千元)	Profit ('000 RMB) (rank) 利潤 (千元) (排名)	Total assets ('000 RMB) 總資產 (千元)	Major products 主要產品
Jiangsu Wan Ma Metal Products Group Co. 江蘇萬馬金屬製品集團公司(1954)	Taizhou 泰州市	Jiangsu 江蘇省	(0523)6552030 (0523)6552030	1,174	Domestic JVs 聯營	291,074	5718(6)	149,072	o
Jiangmen Nanchang Enterprise Group Co. Ltd. 江門市南昌企業集團有限公司(1996)	Jiangmen 江門市	Guangdong 廣東省	(0750)3515963 (0750)3558557	608	Domestic JVs 聯營	278,392	3761(11)	36,892	o
Shanghai Du Yuan Economic Development City 上海都源經濟發展城(1996)	Shanghai 上海市	Shanghai 上海市	(021)59251888	1,000	Collectively-owned 集體	213,680	6159(5)	73,969	o
Shanghai Daily Hardware Co. 上海日用五金公司(1933)	Shanghai 上海市	Shanghai 上海市	(021)63723950 (021)63278427	802	State-owned 國有	199,444	144(134)	210,783	a
Shanghai Zhu Qiao Industry Cheng Industrial General Company 上海祝橋工業城實業總公司(1994)	Shanghai 上海市	Shanghai 上海市	(021)58107321	630	Collectively-owned 集體	127,446	10424(3)	112,570	o
Wenzhou Tung Fong Light Industry Industrial Co. Ltd. 溫州市東方輕工實業有限公司(1993)	Wenzhou 溫州市	Zhejiang 浙江省	(0577)6362082	187	Overseas Chinese-funded 港澳台資	95,608	15711(1)	19,763	o
Shunde Long Jiang Nan Tian Industrial Co. 順德市龍江南天實業公司(1984)	Foshan 佛山市	Guangdong 廣東省	(0757)3368768 (0757)3365776	650	Collectively-owned 集體	73,987	797(44)	89,177	o
Shanghai Fu Li Privately Owned Economic City 上海富利私營經濟城(1996)	Shanghai 上海市	Shanghai 上海市	(021)62210509	450	Collectively-owned 集體	62,000	-302(350)	3,040	o
Shanghai Pressure Lantern Factory 上海汽燈廠(1914)	Shanghai 上海市	Shanghai 上海市	(021)62666984 (021)62665548	620	State-owned 國有	59,253	305(95)	43,314	o
Dongguan Shi Long Zhen Hardware Electroplating Factory 東莞市石龍鎮五金電鍍廠(1978)	Dongguan 東莞市	Guangdong 廣東省	(0769)6611931 (0769)6621302	550	Collectively-owned 集體	57,280	48(205)	36,986	o

Top 10 Cities by Production Output 產出排名前 10 位城市	Province 省	Market share 市場份額	Number of firms 企業個數
Shanghai 上海市	Shanghai 上海市	24.15%	136
Taizhou 泰州市	Jiangsu 江蘇省	7.66%	8
Wenzhou 溫州市	Zhejiang 浙江省	7.06%	127
Guangzhou 廣州市	Guangdong 廣東省	4.88%	132
Zhongshan 中山市	Guangdong 廣東省	3.67%	21
Taizhou 臺州市	Zhejiang 浙江省	3.60%	24
Nantong 南通市	Jiangsu 江蘇省	3.27%	36
Foshan 佛山市	Guangdong 廣東省	3.04%	27
Beijing 北京市	Beijing 北京市	2.16%	25
Chongqing 重慶市	Chongqing 重慶市	2.11%	13

10 Major Wholesalers 10 家主要批發商	City 城市	Province 省	Telephone / Fax 電話 / 傳真
Chengdu Great Wall Electric Appliance Company 成都長城電器公司	Chengdu 成都市	Sichuan 四川省	(028)6662132 (028)6671975
Shandou Ceramics (Group) Company 汕頭陶瓷(集團)公司	Shantou 汕頭市	Guangdong 廣東省	(0754)8255441 (0754)8255442
Guangdong Puning Local Products Import & Export Company 廣東省普寧土產進出口公司	Jieyang 揭陽市	Guangdong 廣東省	(0663)2226744
Yixing Sundry Goods General Co. 宜興市土產雜品總公司	Wuxi 無錫市	Jiangsu 江蘇省	(0510)7903683 (0510)7903683
Sujiang Qu Zhe Jiang Dongda Group Company 椒江區浙江東大集團公司	Taizhou 臺州市	Zhejiang 浙江省	(0576)8881477 (0576)8881672
Jiangsu New Suzhou Co. Ltd. Suzhou Daily Goods General Co. 江蘇新蘇州股份有限公司蘇州日用雜品總公司	Suzhou 蘇州市	Jiangsu 江蘇省	(0512)7276630 (0512)7275964
Shandong Daily Use General Merchandise Import & Export Company 山東省日用百貨進出口公司	Qingdao 青島市	Shandong 山東省	(0532)5849141 (0532)5849207
Guangdong Yangjiang Light Industrial Products Import & Export (Group) Company 廣東陽江輕工業品進出口(集團)公司	Yangjiang 陽江市	Guangdong 廣東省	(0662)3222497 (0662)3222976
Hebei Artts & Crtfts Import & Export Corp. 河北工藝品進出口公司	Shijiazhuang 石家莊市	Hebei 河北省	(0311)7756124 (0311)7755347
Shandong Handicrafts Import & Export Products Group Linyi Craft Co. Ltd. 山東工藝品進出品集團臨沂工藝有限公司	Linyi 臨沂市	Shandong 山東省	(0539)8310001 (0539)8315396

*Also include sales by firms outside this industry.包括本行業以外廠家的銷售。"o" stands for "others". "o" 代表 "其他產品"。

3491: Iron Farming Tools 鐵製小農具製造業

The industry accounts for 0.064% of the total revenue of China's industrial sector in 1996. The revenue growth rate of the industry is 27.8% from 1995, as compared to the growth rate of China's industrial sector, 9.51%. The rate of return on asset is 4.75%. 79.67% of all firms in the industry made a profit while 10.45% had negative returns. The top province in terms of the industry's revenue is Hunan, accounting for 14.79% of the total revenue.
本行業在1996年佔全行業總產值0.064%，行業年增長率為27.8%（全國工業年增長率9.51%）。行業的資產回報率4.75%，79.67%的企業盈利，10.45%的企業虧損。銷售收入最高的省份為湖南省，佔本行業的14.79%。

	Total number of firms 企業總數	Total number of employees 職工總數	Total revenue (mil. RMB) 總銷售收入（百萬元）	Total profit (mil. RMB) 總利潤（百萬元）	Return on assets 資產利潤率 (%)	Return on equity 權益利潤率 (%)	Labour productivity ('000 RMB / worker) 勞動生產率（千元/人）	Debts / assets 資產負債率 (%)	Total assets (mil. RMB) 總資產（百萬元）
Industry Overall 行業總體	2,813	91,650	3,727	136	4.75	14.00	40.67	66.11	2,867

	Number of firms 企業個數	Average number of employees 平均職工人數	Average revenue ('000 RMB) 平均銷售收入（千元）	Average profit ('000 RMB) 平均利潤（千元）	Return on assets 資產利潤率 (%)	Return on equity 權益利潤率 (%)	Labour productivity ('000 RMB / worker) 勞動生產率（千元/人）	Average debts / assets 平均資產負債率(%)	Average Total assets ('000 RMB) 平均總資產（千元）
By ownership 產業所有權									
State-owned 國有	58	100	1,586	-172	-4.12	-16.95	15.93	75.72	4,190
Collectively-owned 集體	2,731	31	1,241	53	6.11	18.61	40.14	67.19	865
Privately-owned 私有	5	33	1,611	71	8.73	13.57	49.41	35.67	814
Domestic JVs 聯營	2	8	389	18	3.13	4.12	48.62	23.97	576
Joint stock 股份制	5	102	4,369	223	3.95	10.05	42.75	60.73	5,642
Foreign-funded 外資	4	50	1,312	-523	-9.29	-14.86	26.24	37.52	5,630
Overseas Chinese-funded 港澳台資	4	160	51,730	483	0.94	1.78	323.31	47.13	51,221
By size 規模									
Large 大型									
Medium 中型	7	848	33,829	866	1.60	8.27	39.91	80.69	54,218
Small 小型	2,803	31	1,245	46	5.22	14.45	40.69	63.87	888
By regional distribution 地區分布									
Central-North 華北	270	46	1,399	72	4.21	13.52	30.64	68.86	1,714
Beijing 北京	7	20	614	19	1.66	7.18	30.07	76.94	1,121
Tianjin 天津	7	176	4,984	693	4.35	10.07	28.27	56.86	15,944
Hebei 河北	98	71	2,687	119	4.41	18.94	37.93	76.71	2,690
Shanxi 山西	32	40	672	-22	-2.41	-10.78	16.91	77.70	895
Inner Mongolia 內蒙	126	22	426	28	6.98	13.52	19.62	48.37	406
Northeast 東北	260	54	1,232	29	2.28	8.62	22.75	73.58	1,273
Liaoning 遼寧	72	75	1,300	33	1.58	4.62	17.26	65.77	2,063
Jilin 吉林	84	55	1,008	4	0.37	4.51	18.38	91.83	1,001
Heilongjiang 黑龍江	104	39	1,367	47	4.96	16.40	35.05	69.77	947
Central East 華東	746	41	2,073	89	6.04	18.24	50.43	66.88	1,478
Shanghai 上海	2	401	8,490	-1,215	-12.96	-37.50	21.17	65.44	9,375
Jiangsu 江蘇	205	46	2,457	51	3.13	10.43	53.65	69.96	1,622
Zhejiang 浙江	28	20	729	20	3.69	11.43	36.45	67.74	543
Anhui 安徽	190	29	2,424	179	22.56	47.34	82.63	52.34	795
Fujian 福建	61	17	300	15	7.83	14.86	17.13	47.26	195
Jiangxi 江西	147	17	353	10	4.33	10.93	21.03	60.43	226
Shandong 山東	113	96	4,197	191	4.00	13.28	43.92	69.90	4,776
Central-South 中南	796	23	1,456	43	5.86	15.18	62.67	61.37	729
Henan 河南	137	29	1,058	42	4.04	13.06	36.70	69.09	1,034
Hubei 湖北	122	31	1,832	80	10.51	31.09	59.72	66.20	762
Hunan 湖南	148	27	3,725	54	4.60	19.38	135.53	76.27	1,178
Guangdong 廣東	184	21	763	30	5.25	8.00	36.66	34.42	572
Guangxi 廣西	191	13	500	26	8.21	13.80	37.63	40.49	319
Hainan 海南	14	26	244	-1	-0.20	-0.43	9.27	54.30	366
Southwest 西南	409	20	468	17	3.39	7.95	22.99	57.31	488
Chongqing 重慶	129	16	196	4	2.35	7.75	12.49	69.68	157
Sichuan 四川	208	19	511	17	3.34	8.10	26.28	58.76	514
Guizhou 貴州	31	16	281	-3	-1.00	-1.90	17.32	47.41	323
Yunnan 雲南	40	41	1,278	67	4.30	9.05	31.39	52.50	1,559
Tibet 西藏	1	16	120	30	25.00	25.00	7.50		120
Northwest 西北	332	23	398	5	0.92	2.66	17.00	65.66	575
Shaanxi 陝西	119	23	285		0.08	0.24	12.26	68.59	446
Gansu 甘肅	174	22	438	5	0.77	2.36	20.06	67.60	651
Qinghai 青海	2	8	65				8.13	11.76	170
Ningxia 寧夏	15	26	767	34	5.08	10.49	29.44	51.49	669
Xinjiang 新疆	22	36	465	15	2.33	4.69	12.95	50.46	645

3491: Iron Farming Tools 鐵製小農具製造業

Year 年份	Number of firms 企業個數	Rate of change 每年變化 (%)	Number of employees 職工人數 (人)	Rate of change 每年變化 (%)	Total revenue (mil. RMB) 總銷售收入 (百萬元)	Rate of change 每年變化 (%)	Total profit (mil. RMB) 總利潤 (百萬元)	Rate of change 每年變化 (%)
1993	4,439		103,736		2,679		114	
1994	4,113	-7.34%	121,554	17.18%	3,293	22.89%	118	3.79%
1995	3,217	-21.79%	98,849	-18.68%	2,916	-11.45%	111	-5.99%
1996	2,813	-12.56%	91,650	-7.28%	3,727	27.81%	136	22.43%

3 Major products* 3 種主要產品 *	Output 產量	Sales volume 銷售量	Unit 單位
a) Iron Mini Agricultural Tools 鐵製小農具	358,608	365,780	10,000 piece 萬件
b) Medium & Small Farm Tools 中小農具	9,082,665	9,082,665	set 台

Top 10 firms by revenue (year founded) 收入排名前10家企業 (創辦年份)	City 城市	Province 省	Telephone / fax 電話 / 傳真	Number of employees 職工人數	Ownership 產業所有權	Revenue ('000 RMB) 銷售收入 (千元)	Profit ('000 RMB) (rank) 利潤 (千元) (排名)	Total assets ('000 RMB) 總資產 (千元)	Major products 主要產品
Shandong Zouping Lathe Utensil Factory 山東省鄒平縣車具廠(1983)	Binzhou 濱州市	Shandong 山東省	(0543)8900231 (0543)8900231	2,910	Collectively-owned 集體	118,990	7159(1)	273,410	o
Tangshan Jing Dong Qiao (Group) Company 唐山京東鍬(集團)公司(1994)	Tangshan 唐山市	Hebei 河北省	(0315)4122135	472	Collectively-owned 集體	69,030	4270(3)	12,485	o
Yixing Nan Fang Group Co. 宜興市南方集團公司(1993)	Wuxi 無錫市	Jiangsu 江蘇省	(0510)7401039	178	Collectively-owned 集體	43,700	2860(5)	20,520	o
Zhai Wang Zhen Economic Commission Luo Jia Multiple Processing Factory 翟王鎮經委羅家綜合加工廠(1988)	Binzhou 濱州市	Shandong 山東省	(0543)8381068 (0543)8381068	50	Collectively-owned 集體	41,650	1447(13)	5,230	o
Zigong Steel Spade Plant 自貢市鋼鍬廠(1966)	Zigong 自貢市	Sichuan 四川省	(0813)3600318 (0813)3600318	694	Collectively-owned 集體	35,551	5656(2)	36,295	a
Dingyuan Ou Tang Zhen Chang Ling Machinery Repair & Assembly Factory 定遠縣藕塘鎮昌嶺機械修配廠(1965)	Chuzhou 滁州市	Anhui 安徽省		25	Collectively-owned 集體	35,200	1109(19)	5,515	b
Yancheng No.4 Machinery Factory 鹽城市第四機械廠(1952)	Yancheng 鹽城市	Jiangsu 江蘇省	(0515)8650149	285	Collectively-owned 集體	35,010	330(97)	18,260	o
Harbin Wan Da Farm Tools Processing Factory 哈爾濱市萬達鐵木加工廠(1994)	Harbin 哈爾濱市	Heilongjiang 黑龍江省		10	Collectively-owned 集體	32,746	526(55)	2,300	o
Dingyuan Ou Tang Gu Yue Machine Repair Factory 定遠縣藕塘古月機修廠(1980)	Chuzhou 滁州市	Anhui 安徽省		15	Collectively-owned 集體	32,000	2520(8)	5,000	o
Luannan Liu Miao Steel Spade Group 灤南縣劉廟鋼鍬集團(1994)	Tangshan 唐山市	Hebei 河北省	(0315)4124021	388	Collectively-owned 集體	31,797	1219(16)	800	o

Top 10 Cities by Production Output 產出排名前10位城市	Province 省	Market share 市場份額	Number of firms 企業個數
Xuzhou 徐州市	Jiangsu 江蘇省	3.98%	26
Tangshan 唐山市	Hebei 河北省	3.87%	17
Fuyang 阜陽市	Anhui 安徽省	3.17%	46
Zhumadian 駐馬店市	Henan 河南省	2.72%	29
Nantong 南通市	Jiangsu 江蘇省	2.48%	40
Suzhou 蘇州市	Jiangsu 江蘇省	2.34%	20
Binzhou 濱州市	Shandong 山東省	2.28%	7
Chuzhou 滁州市	Anhui 安徽省	2.27%	37
Shijiazhuang 石家莊市	Hebei 河北省	2.26%	4
Linyi 臨沂市	Shandong 山東省	2.21%	23

10 Major Wholesalers 10家主要批發商	City 城市	Province 省	Telephone / Fax 電話 / 傳真
Chengdu Great Wall Electric Appliance Company 成都長城電器公司	Chengdu 成都市	Sichuan 四川省	(028)6662132 (028)6671975
Shandou Ceramics (Group) Company 汕頭陶瓷(集團)公司	Shantou 汕頭市	Guangdong 廣東省	(0754)8255441 (0754)8255442
Guangdong Puning Local Products Import & Export Company 廣東省普寧土產進出口公司	Jieyang 揭陽市	Guangdong 廣東省	(0663)2226744
Yixing Sundry Goods General Co. 宜興市土產雜品總公司	Wuxi 無錫市	Jiangsu 江蘇省	(0510)7903683 (0510)7903683
Sujiang Qu Zhe Jiang Dongda Group Company 椒江區浙江東大集團公司	Taizhou 臺州市	Zhejiang 浙江省	(0576)8881477 (0576)8881672
Jiangsu New Suzhou Co. Ltd. Suzhou Daily Goods General Co. 江蘇新蘇州股份有限公司蘇州日用雜品總公司	Suzhou 蘇州市	Jiangsu 江蘇省	(0512)7276630 (0512)7275964
Shandong Daily Use General Merchandise Import & Export Company 山東省日用百貨進出口公司	Qingdao 青島市	Shandong 山東省	(0532)5849141 (0532)5849207
Guangdong Yangjiang Light Industrial Products Import & Export (Group) Company 廣東陽江輕工業品進出口(集團)公司	Yangjiang 陽江市	Guangdong 廣東省	(0662)3222497 (0662)3222976
Hebei Artts & Crtfts Import & Export Corp. 河北工藝品進出口公司	Shijiazhuang 石家莊市	Hebei 河北省	(0311)7756124 (0311)7755347
Shandong Handicrafts Import & Export Products Group Linyi Craft Co. Ltd. 山東工藝品進出品集團臨沂工藝有限公司	Linyi 臨沂市	Shandong 山東省	(0539)8310001 (0539)8315396

*Also include sales by firms outside this industry.包括本行業以外廠家的銷售。"o" stands for "others". "o" 代表"其他產品"。

3495: Welding Rods 焊條製造業

The industry accounts for 0.082% of the total revenue of China's industrial sector in 1996. The revenue growth rate of the industry is 3.8% from 1995, as compared to the growth rate of China's industrial sector, 9.51%. The rate of return on asset is -0.94%. 62.81% of all firms in the industry made a profit while 29.66% had negative returns. The top province in terms of the industry's revenue is Hubei, accounting for 13.00% of the total revenue.
本行業在1996年佔全行業總產值0.082%，行業年增長率為3.8%（全國工業年增長率9.51%）。行業的資產回報率-0.94%，62.81%的企業盈利，29.66%的企業虧損。銷售收入最高的省份為湖北省，佔本行業的13.00%。

	Total number of firms 企業總數	Total number of employees 職工總數	Total revenue (mil. RMB) 總銷售收入（百萬元）	Total profit (mil. RMB) 總利潤（百萬元）	Return on assets 資產利潤率 (%)	Return on equity 權益利潤率 (%)	Labour productivity ('000 RMB / worker) 勞動生產率（千元/人）	Debts / assets 資產負債率 (%)	Total assets (mil. RMB) 總資產（百萬元）
Industry Overall 行業總體	351	62,198	4,763	-60	-0.94	-2.93	76.58	67.98	6,378

	Number of firms 企業個數	Average number of employees 平均職工人數	Average revenue ('000 RMB) 平均銷售收入（千元）	Average profit ('000 RMB) 平均利潤（千元）	Return on assets 資產利潤率 (%)	Return on equity 權益利潤率 (%)	Labour productivity ('000 RMB / worker) 勞動生產率（千元/人）	Average debts / assets 平均資產負債率(%)	Average Total assets ('000 RMB) 平均總資產（千元）
By ownership 產業所有權									
State-owned 國有	50	498	38,460	100	0.16	0.47	77.28	65.30	61,900
Collectively-owned 集體	241	100	5,368	-8	-0.14	-1.24	53.94	88.31	5,699
Privately-owned 私有	1	9							
Domestic JVs 聯營	18	288	27,075	-568	-2.01	-6.35	94.14	68.31	28,195
Joint stock 股份制	7	903	96,767	-8,920	-7.20	-13.16	107.13	45.30	123,955
Foreign-funded 外資	16	75	16,124	-604	-4.16	-13.36	216.43	68.83	14,508
Overseas Chinese-funded 港澳台資	18	56	6,876	1,073	6.39	19.39	123.77	67.03	16,789
By size 規模									
Large 大型	7	1,889	223,954	-16,467	-5.56	-11.68	118.57	52.41	296,262
Medium 中型	17	775	55,473	410	0.56	3.32	71.55	83.24	73,648
Small 小型	315	113	7,151	153	1.58	5.72	63.27	72.31	9,689
By regional distribution 地區分布									
Central-North 華北	57	141	12,589	157	1.16	3.98	89.26	70.74	13,465
Beijing 北京	12	65	3,543	30	0.46	1.49	54.43	68.76	6,456
Tianjin 天津	9	393	54,457	1,138	2.31	6.21	138.41	62.85	49,294
Hebei 河北	23	78	5,197	-80	-1.46	-19.85	66.41	92.63	5,499
Shanxi 山西	9	98	2,734	19	0.33	1.43	27.90	76.98	5,720
Inner Mongolia 內蒙	4	259	10,198	5	0.03	0.14	39.41	78.99	17,113
Northeast 東北	53	195	7,548	-1,517	-9.61	-55.94	38.61	82.82	15,781
Liaoning 遼寧	32	237	10,519	-1,829	-8.98	-39.50	44.31	77.25	20,355
Jilin 吉林	7	154	3,234	-2,169	-16.82	71.30	21.04	123.59	12,894
Heilongjiang 黑龍江	14	121	2,913	-477	-7.05	-39.74	24.17	82.26	6,769
Central East 華東	139	137	13,686	-169	-1.22	-3.74	100.19	67.45	13,866
Shanghai 上海	14	213	32,949	772	2.17	5.63	154.43	61.49	35,621
Jiangsu 江蘇	34	161	16,924	-821	-4.50	-14.03	104.94	67.90	18,227
Zhejiang 浙江	25	60	6,167	114	1.88	6.04	101.97	68.88	6,067
Anhui 安徽	22	116	5,129	-1,552	-20.32	-79.88	44.11	74.56	7,639
Fujian 福建	9	80	11,889	-10	-0.17	-0.47	147.79	63.91	5,887
Jiangxi 江西	6	51	3,467	45	1.08	5.41	67.53	80.08	4,175
Shandong 山東	29	187	16,236	855	6.03	20.29	86.93	70.29	14,180
Central-South 中南	76	241	16,537	211	0.70	1.88	68.56	62.82	30,056
Henan 河南	20	96	3,451	121	3.30	11.91	35.95	72.28	3,649
Hubei 湖北	7	1,340	88,457	7,636	3.79	7.61	66.00	50.24	201,529
Hunan 湖南	19	198	9,064	-234	-1.71	-5.75	45.75	70.22	13,677
Guangdong 廣東	20	75	10,425	-1,449	-7.68	-193.98	138.62	96.04	18,865
Guangxi 廣西	9	177	9,784	-506	-2.89	-13.63	55.18	78.78	17,487
Hainan 海南	1	167	99,830	-1,870	-31.06	-133.57	597.78	76.91	6,020
Southwest 西南	16	220	21,628	1,261	5.91	13.91	98.33	57.53	21,356
Chongqing 重慶	1	402	2,993	4	0.13	0.36	7.44	63.90	3,024
Sichuan 四川	13	225	22,796	969	4.02	10.37	101.38	61.23	24,085
Guizhou 貴州									
Yunnan 雲南	2	75	26,045	3,925	25.07	31.54	349.60	20.50	15,655
Tibet 西藏									
Northwest 西北	10	296	13,986	-120	-0.54	-2.31	47.27	76.48	22,042
Shaanxi 陝西	4	279	9,543	108	0.63	1.42	34.17	55.56	16,988
Gansu 甘肅	3	470	22,753	-407	-1.06	-8.60	48.45	87.71	38,473
Qinghai 青海	1	116	380	-250	-7.53	16.78	3.28	145.18	3,320
Ningxia 寧夏	1	206	32,240	1,260	4.43	15.09	156.50	70.63	28,430
Xinjiang 新疆	1	111	810	-1,420	-26.79	-236.67	7.30	88.68	5,300

3495: Welding Rods 焊條製造業

Year 年份	Number of firms 企業個數	Rate of change 每年變化 (%)	Number of employees 職工人數（人）	Rate of change 每年變化 (%)	Total revenue (mil. RMB) 總銷售收入（百萬元）	Rate of change 每年變化 (%)	Total profit (mil. RMB) 總利潤（百萬元）	Rate of change 每年變化 (%)
1993	279		71,804		4,935		242	
1994	313	12.19%	60,605	-15.60%	5,154	4.44%	222	-8.26%
1995	368	17.57%	60,688	0.14%	4,590	-10.94%	21	-90.34%
1996	351	-4.62%	62,198	2.49%	4,763	3.77%	-60	-380.19%

3 Major products* 3 種主要產品 *	Output 產量	Sales volume 銷售量	Unit 單位
a) Gas Welding Rod 氣焊條	32,324	30,384	ton 噸
b) Electric Welding Rod 電焊條	718,345	689,612	ton 噸
c) Electric Wire 電線	693,907	673,089	km 公里

Top 10 firms by revenue (year founded) 收入排名前 10 家企業（創辦年份）	City 城市	Province 省	Telephone / fax 電話 / 傳真	Number of employees 職工人數	Ownership 產業所有權	Revenue ('000 RMB) 銷售收入（千元）	Profit ('000 RMB) (rank) 利潤（千元）（排名）	Total assets ('000 RMB) 總資產（千元）	Major products 主要產品
Jiangsu Yu Zhou Welding Material Group Co. 江蘇宇宙焊接材料集團公司(1992)	Taizhou 泰州市	Jiangsu 江蘇省	(0523)6558937 (0523)6559019	1,638	Domestic JVs 聯營	281,648	-25144(184)	293,048	b,c
Shanghai Welding Electrode Corp. Ltd. 上海電焊條有限公司(1994)	Shanghai 上海市	Shanghai 上海市	(021)63174073 (021)63170140	1,804	State-owned 國有	272,985	8914(2)	281,734	b
Sichuan Daxiyang Group Co. Ltd. 四川省大西洋集團有限責任公司(1950)	Zigong 自貢市	Sichuan 四川省	(0813)5101327 (0813)5101216	1,541	State-owned 國有	215,102	12853(1)	222,982	b
Tianjin Welding Electrode Co. Ltd. 天津大橋集團公司(1992)	Tianjin 天津市	Tianjin 天津市	(022)28303113 (022)28302756	1,392	State-owned 國有	192,705	0(123)	246,671	b
Tianjin Jin Yan Welding Material Co. Ltd. 天津金燕焊接材料有限公司(1986)	Tianjin 天津市	Tianjin 天津市	(022)26328681 (022)25327826	124	Foreign-funded 外資	131,050	6732(6)	55,511	b
Zhuzhou Welding Electrode General Factory 株洲電焊條總廠(1958)	Zhuzhou 株洲市	Hunan 湖南省	(0733)8413242 (0733)8414449	1,606	State-owned 國有	127,242	767(35)	114,511	b
Bao Gang Group Shenzhen Da Xi Yang Electric Welding Rod General Factory 寶鋼集團深圳大西洋電焊條總廠(1987)	Shenzhen 深圳市	Guangdong 廣東省	(0755)2262249 (0755)2262249	209	State-owned 國有	114,456	8003(4)	87,451	b
Penglai Hardware Group Co. Ltd. 蓬萊市五金集團有限公司(1972)	Yantai 煙台市	Shandong 山東省	(0535)5650439 (0535)5610439	417	Collectively-owned 集體	91,152	4602(7)	43,961	o
Jinzhou Jin Tai Metal Industrial Co. Ltd. 錦州錦泰金屬工業有限公司(1993)	Jinzhou 錦州市	Liaoning 遼寧省	(0416)5179785 (0416)5176907	312	Overseas Chinese-funded 港澳台資	90,304	200(66)	191,569	b
Tianjin Electric Welding Rod Company Da Si Electric Welding Rod Factory 天津市電焊條公司大寺電焊條廠(1988)	Tianjin 天津市	Tianjin 天津市	(022)23972537	800	Collectively-owned 集體	89,790	1520(17)	43,440	b

Top 10 Cities by Production Output 產出排名前 10 位城市	Province 省	Market share 市場份額	Number of firms 企業個數
Yichang 宜昌市	Hubei 湖北省	21.81%	1
Tianjin 天津市	Tianjin 天津市	10.50%	12
Shanghai 上海市	Shanghai 上海市	9.38%	25
Taizhou 泰州市	Jiangsu 江蘇省	4.81%	11
Zigong 自貢市	Sichuan 四川省	4.44%	4
Weifang 濰坊市	Shandong 山東省	3.87%	6
Jinzhou 錦州市	Liaoning 遼寧省	3.08%	5
Zhuzhou 株洲市	Hunan 湖南省	2.66%	4
Yantai 煙台市	Shandong 山東省	2.64%	5
Loudi 婁底市	Hunan 湖南省	1.92%	4

10 Major Wholesalers 10 家主要批發商	City 城市	Province 省	Telephone / Fax 電話 / 傳真
Zhong Hua Singbo Import & Export Company 中化寧波進出口公司	Ningbo 寧波市	Zhejiang 浙江省	(0574)7346764 (0574)7366775
China Chemical Supply & Marketing Hua Nan Company 中國化工供銷華南公司	Guangzhou 廣州市	Guangdong 廣東省	(020)87654477 (020)87784414
China Agriculture Means of Production Chengdu Company 中國農業生產資料成都公司	Chengdu 成都市	Sichuan 四川省	(028)3333909 (028)3331202
Shanxi Agriculture Means of Production Company 山西省農業生產資料公司	Taiyuan 太原市	Shanxi 山西省	(0351)4040255 (0351)4040231
Beijing Chemical Light Industry General Company 北京市化工輕工總公司	Beijing 北京市	Beijing 北京市	(010)64224837 (010)64219301
Beijing Chemical Industry Group Company Supply & Marketing Company 北京化學工業集團公司供銷公司	Beijing 北京市	Beijing 北京市	(010)67714610 (010)67714058
Zhong Hua Jiangsu Import & Export Company 中化江蘇進出口公司	Nanjing 南京市	Jiangsu 江蘇省	(025)2258718 (025)2257789
Yunnan Chemical Import & Export Company 雲南省化工進出口公司	Kunming 昆明市	Yunnan 雲南省	(0871)3314002 (0871)3314931
Fujian Jiu Zhou Group Co. Ltd. 福建九州集團股份有限公司	Xiamen 廈門市	Fujian 福建省	(0592)5055818 (0592)5052033
China Chemical Industry Commission Agent Hua Dong Co. 中國化工供銷華東公司	Shanghai 上海市	Shanghai 上海市	(021)62514123

*Also include sales by firms outside this industry.包括本行業以外廠家的銷售。"o" stands for "others". "o" 代表"其他產品"。

3499: Other Metal Products 其他類未包括的金屬製品業

The industry accounts for 0.139% of the total revenue of China's industrial sector in 1996. The revenue growth rate of the industry is 20.1% from 1995, as compared to the growth rate of China's industrial sector, 9.51%. The rate of return on asset is 5.06%. 72.16% of all firms in the industry made a profit while 21.56% had negative returns. The top province in terms of the industry's revenue is Jiangsu, accounting for 26.50% of the total revenue.
本行業在1996年佔全行業總產值0.139%，行業年增長率為20.1%（全國工業年增長率9.51%）。行業的資產回報率5.06%，72.16%的企業盈利，21.56%的企業虧損。銷售收入最高的省份為江蘇省，佔本行業的26.50%。

	Total number of firms 企業總數	Total number of employees 職工總數	Total revenue (mil. RMB) 總銷售收入（百萬元）	Total profit (mil. RMB) 總利潤（百萬元）	Return on assets 資產利潤率 (%)	Return on equity 權益利潤率 (%)	Labour productivity ('000 RMB / worker) 勞動生產率（千元/人）	Debts / assets 資產負債率 (%)	Total assets (mil. RMB) 總資產（百萬元）
Industry Overall 行業總體	1,572	109,252	8,075	523	5.06	13.60	73.91	62.83	10,344

	Number of firms 企業個數	Average number of employees 平均職工人數	Average revenue ('000 RMB) 平均銷售收入（千元）	Average profit ('000 RMB) 平均利潤（千元）	Return on assets 資產利潤率 (%)	Return on equity 權益利潤率 (%)	Labour productivity ('000 RMB / worker) 勞動生產率（千元/人）	Average debts / assets 平均資產負債率(%)	Average Total assets ('000 RMB) 平均總資產（千元）
By ownership 產業所有權									
State-owned 國有	117	173	12,256	2,402	13.97	29.83	70.83	53.18	17,197
Collectively-owned 集體	1,297	58	3,698	125	3.39	11.18	63.66	69.65	3,693
Privately-owned 私有	6	86	5,202	84	1.93	5.82	60.60	66.81	4,326
Domestic JVs 聯營	14	62	6,807	-44	-0.38	-0.81	110.56	53.16	11,482
Joint stock 股份制	14	86	4,279	249	4.28	10.13	49.67	57.72	5,825
Foreign-funded 外資	51	95	15,924	701	2.03	5.73	167.45	64.57	34,562
Overseas Chinese-funded 港澳台資	72	99	11,751	558	2.66	5.69	118.45	53.25	20,988
By size 規模									
Large 大型	7	1,465	192,975	46,348	17.42	38.33	131.71	54.56	266,127
Medium 中型	11	432	45,508	455	0.55	1.12	105.37	50.53	82,133
Small 小型	1,532	61	4,063	126	2.55	7.59	66.37	66.33	4,946
By regional distribution 地區分布									
Central-North 華北	261	66	2,438	23	0.60	2.61	36.73	76.93	3,812
Beijing 北京	83	27	1,366	39	1.92	5.05	51.36	62.08	2,044
Tianjin 天津	62	81	2,211	-62	-1.65	-6.12	27.38	73.08	3,778
Hebei 河北	80	76	4,106	94	1.67	9.06	53.76	81.62	5,660
Shanxi 山西	24	137	2,011	-39	-0.72	-5.88	14.68	87.72	5,417
Inner Mongolia 內蒙	12	59	767				12.90	64.73	690
Northeast 東北	348	50	2,965	212	6.19	16.52	59.59	62.53	3,420
Liaoning 遼寧	239	48	3,595	303	7.18	18.24	74.70	60.64	4,225
Jilin 吉林	58	57	954	-53	-3.18	-21.66	16.75	85.34	1,656
Heilongjiang 黑龍江	51	49	2,299	83	5.03	12.29	46.71	59.08	1,649
Central East 華東	541	85	8,465	827	7.40	19.00	99.58	61.06	11,174
Shanghai 上海	76	84	12,604	3,175	20.89	40.68	150.80	48.65	15,198
Jiangsu 江蘇	140	126	15,284	1,218	7.08	19.44	121.41	63.60	17,216
Zhejiang 浙江	111	79	4,613	164	2.55	6.66	58.34	61.70	6,440
Anhui 安徽	54	60	4,693	278	11.19	54.82	78.87	79.60	2,486
Fujian 福建	55	49	5,613	-231	-1.09	-2.73	114.29	60.29	21,318
Jiangxi 江西	34	35	1,831	-17	-1.16	-6.24	52.71	81.49	1,476
Shandong 山東	71	87	4,867	219	3.80	14.42	56.25	73.63	5,748
Central-South 中南	279	67	5,724	-1	-0.01	-0.02	84.97	60.98	6,164
Henan 河南	36	36	863	-7	-0.34	-0.77	24.07	55.65	1,950
Hubei 湖北	77	96	9,096	188	4.29	20.63	94.80	79.20	4,388
Hunan 湖南	46	43	2,022	40	1.37	4.74	46.84	71.17	2,894
Guangdong 廣東	100	72	6,977	-168	-1.76	-4.84	96.40	63.64	9,550
Guangxi 廣西	20	45	3,739	29	0.26	0.32	83.73	17.68	11,177
Hainan 海南									
Southwest 西南	100	35	1,316	27	1.86	5.09	37.69	63.52	1,454
Chongqing 重慶	33	36	1,491	-2	-0.14	-0.32	41.26	57.29	1,631
Sichuan 四川	37	40	1,615	-59	-3.15	-8.73	40.69	63.90	1,874
Guizhou 貴州	17	32	693	41	5.55	31.53	21.50	82.32	742
Yunnan 雲南	13	19	842	-21	-2.78	-9.68	43.45	71.30	748
Tibet 西藏									
Northwest 西北	43	147	2,290	-153	-2.63	-7.18	15.54	63.31	5,791
Shaanxi 陝西	18	26	1,096	19	1.77	5.73	41.60	69.18	1,069
Gansu 甘肅	15	359	4,419	-435	-3.48	-9.16	12.30	62.00	12,492
Qinghai 青海									
Ningxia 寧夏	3	57	1,483	93	8.67	12.39	25.87	30.34	1,077
Xinjiang 新疆	7	43	1,146	-94	-1.68	-5.50	26.73	69.40	5,597

3499: Other Metal Products 其他類未包括的金屬製品業

Year 年份	Number of firms 企業個數	Rate of change 每年變化 (%)	Number of employees 職工人數 (人)	Rate of change 每年變化 (%)	Total revenue (mil. RMB) 總銷售收入 (百萬元)	Rate of change 每年變化 (%)	Total profit (mil. RMB) 總利潤 (百萬元)	Rate of change 每年變化 (%)
1993	1,563		112,034		3,819		383	
1994	1,849	18.30%	121,390	8.35%	5,223	36.76%	477	24.57%
1995	1,622	-12.28%	112,446	-7.37%	6,725	28.77%	426	-10.70%
1996	1,572	-3.08%	109,252	-2.84%	8,075	20.07%	523	22.69%

3 Major products* 3 種主要產品 *	Output 產量	Sales volume 銷售量	Unit 單位
a) Stove Utensils 爐具	2,597,492	2,052,018	piece 個
b) Pincers 鉗子	1,339	1,232	10,000 piece 萬把
c) Other Packing Products From Metal 其他金屬製包裝用品	6,980	6,840	ton 噸

Top 10 firms by revenue (year founded) 收入排名前 10 家企業 (創辦年份)	City 城市	Province 省	Telephone / fax 電話 / 傳真	Number of employees 職工人數	Ownership 產業所有權	Revenue ('000 RMB) 銷售收入 (千元)	Profit ('000 RMB) (rank) 利潤 (千元) (排名)	Total assets ('000 RMB) 總資產 (千元)	Major products 主要產品
Shanghai Mint 上海造幣廠(1933)	Shanghai 上海市	Shanghai 上海市	(021)62536200 (021)62551922	1,612	State-owned 國有	486,773	213589(1)	448,811	o
Shenyang Mint 瀋陽造幣廠(1897)	Shenyang 瀋陽市	Liaoning 遼寧省	(024)24313906 (024)24832001	1,774	State-owned 國有	395,666	85489(2)	348,706	o
Shimano (Kunshan) Bicycle Components Co. Ltd. 禧瑪諾(昆山)自行車零件有限公司(1994)	Suzhou 蘇州市	Jiangsu 江蘇省	(0512)7311540	691	Foreign-funded 外資	389,811	10551(7)	404,569	o
Shanghai Jiu Fu Economic Development Zone 上海久富經濟開發區(1994)	Shanghai 上海市	Shanghai 上海市		18	其他經濟	231,672	0(450)	1,508	o
Liu Feng Machinery Industry Co. Ltd. 六豐機械工業有限公司(1993)	Suzhou 蘇州市	Jiangsu 江蘇省	(0512)7312278	465	Overseas Chinese-funded 港澳台資	223,639	75089(3)	239,535	o
Suzhou Cang Qing Metal Products Co. Ltd. 蘇州倉慶金屬製品有限公司(1991)	Suzhou 蘇州市	Jiangsu 江蘇省	(0512)3522491 (0512)3523951	650	Overseas Chinese-funded 港澳台資	208,950	37020(4)	50,000	a
Nanjing Mint 南京造幣廠(1990)	Nanjing 南京市	Jiangsu 江蘇省	(025)2281070 (025)2281511	2,301	State-owned 國有	196,784	4929(15)	295,977	o
Jiangsu Jin Lu Group Co. Ltd. 江蘇金鹿集團公司(1991)	Suzhou 蘇州市	Jiangsu 江蘇省	(0512)8550752	1,288	Collectively-owned 集體	195,190	17010(5)	93,620	b
Xinhui Hui Cheng Zhen Agricultural Machinery Metal Factory 新會市會城鎮農機金屬廠(1995)	Jiangmen 江門市	Guangdong 廣東省	(0750)6127882	180	Collectively-owned 集體	135,000	5500(13)	120,889	o
Shanghai Heng Da (Group) Co. Ltd. 上海恒大(集團)有限公司(1980)	Shanghai 上海市	Shanghai 上海市	(021)58864998 (021)58861576	689	Collectively-owned 集體	112,480	4379(18)	186,877	o

Top 10 Cities by Production Output 產出排名前 10 位城市	Province 省	Market share 市場份額	Number of firms 企業個數
Shanghai 上海市	Shanghai 上海市	9.67%	168
Shenyang 瀋陽市	Liaoning 遼寧省	9.66%	75
Tianjin 天津市	Tianjin 天津市	5.95%	71
Nanjing 南京市	Jiangsu 江蘇省	4.96%	27
Shenzhen 深圳市	Guangdong 廣東省	4.85%	24
Suzhou 蘇州市	Jiangsu 江蘇省	4.71%	60
Ningbo 寧波市	Zhejiang 浙江省	3.46%	34
Jiangmen 江門市	Guangdong 廣東省	3.36%	6
Wuxi 無錫市	Jiangsu 江蘇省	3.25%	68
Cangzhou 滄州市	Hebei 河北省	2.50%	31

10 Major Wholesalers 10 家主要批發商	City 城市	Province 省	Telephone / Fax 電話 / 傳真
Zhong Hua Singbo Import & Export Company 中化寧波進出口公司	Ningbo 寧波市	Zhejiang 浙江省	(0574)7346764 (0574)7366775
China Chemical Supply & Marketing Hua Nan Company 中國化工供銷華南公司	Guangzhou 廣州市	Guangdong 廣東省	(020)87654477 (020)87784414
China Agriculture Means of Production Chengdu Company 中國農業生產資料成都公司	Chengdu 成都市	Sichuan 四川省	(028)3333909 (028)3331202
Shanxi Agriculture Means of Production Company 山西省農業生產資料公司	Taiyuan 太原市	Shanxi 山西省	(0351)4040255 (0351)4040231
Beijing Chemical Light Industry General Company 北京市化工輕工總公司	Beijing 北京市	Beijing 北京市	(010)64224837 (010)64219301
Beijing Chemical Industry Group Company Supply & Marketing Company 北京化學工業集團公司供銷公司	Beijing 北京市	Beijing 北京市	(010)67714610 (010)67714058
Zhong Hua Jiangsu Import & Export Company 中化江蘇進出口公司	Nanjing 南京市	Jiangsu 江蘇省	(025)2258718 (025)2257789
Yunnan Chemical Import & Export Company 雲南省化工進出口公司	Kunming 昆明市	Yunnan 雲南省	(0871)3314002 (0871)3314931
Fujian Jiu Zhou Group Co. Ltd. 福建九州集團股份有限公司	Xiamen 廈門市	Fujian 福建省	(0592)5055818 (0592)5052033
China Chemical Industry Commission Agent Hua Dong Co. 中國化工供銷華東公司	Shanghai 上海市	Shanghai 上海市	(021)62514123

*Also include sales by firms outside this industry.包括本行業以外廠家的銷售。"o" stands for "others". "o" 代表 "其他產品"。

3511: Boilers 鍋爐製造業

The industry accounts for 0.235% of the total revenue of China's industrial sector in 1996. The revenue growth rate of the industry is 10.7% from 1995, as compared to the growth rate of China's industrial sector, 9.51%. The rate of return on asset is 0.89%. 70.85% of all firms in the industry made a profit while 24.45% had negative returns. The top province in terms of the industry's revenue is Jiangsu, accounting for 15.91% of the total revenue.
本行業在1996年佔全行業總產值0.235%，行業年增長率為10.7%（全國工業年增長率9.51%）。行業的資產回報率0.89%，70.85%的企業盈利，24.45%的企業虧損。銷售收入最高的省份為江蘇省，佔本行業的15.91%。

	Total number of firms 企業總數	Total number of employees 職工總數	Total revenue (mil. RMB) 總銷售收入（百萬元）	Total profit (mil. RMB) 總利潤（百萬元）	Return on assets 資產利潤率 (%)	Return on equity 權益利潤率 (%)	Labour productivity ('000 RMB / worker) 勞動生產率（千元/人）	Debts / assets 資產負債率 (%)	Total assets (mil. RMB) 總資產（百萬元）
Industry Overall 行業總體	1,138	258,790	13,608	224	0.89	3.13	52.58	71.56	25,186

	Number of firms 企業個數	Average number of employees 平均職工人數	Average revenue ('000 RMB) 平均銷售收入（千元）	Average profit ('000 RMB) 平均利潤（千元）	Return on assets 資產利潤率 (%)	Return on equity 權益利潤率 (%)	Labour productivity ('000 RMB / worker) 勞動生產率（千元/人）	Average debts / assets 平均資產負債率(%)	Average Total assets ('000 RMB) 平均總資產（千元）
By ownership 產業所有權									
State-owned 國有	199	548	24,186	-472	-0.82	-3.10	44.15	73.36	57,261
Collectively-owned 集體	864	140	6,182	173	2.08	6.94	44.24	70.01	8,326
Privately-owned 私有	9	120	13,101	1,421	6.17	18.02	109.58	65.75	23,020
Domestic JVs 聯營	14	200	16,418	917	4.86	14.85	82.06	67.25	18,858
Joint stock 股份制	17	709	93,035	1,012	0.53	1.87	131.29	71.83	192,098
Foreign-funded 外資	23	341	37,578	1,793	2.46	7.23	110.14	66.01	72,983
Overseas Chinese-funded 港澳台資	12	439	55,036	7,012	7.12	26.15	125.25	72.79	98,553
By size 規模									
Large 大型	20	2,894	289,648	6,070	1.06	4.65	100.07	77.25	574,058
Medium 中型	72	947	44,526	552	0.65	1.91	47.00	65.89	84,571
Small 小型	1,037	127	4,445	61	0.83	2.54	34.87	67.52	7,344
By regional distribution 地區分布									
Central-North 華北	226	166	6,445	104	0.72	2.22	38.78	67.58	14,464
Beijing 北京	50	156	10,487	-9	-0.03	-0.13	67.12	72.58	26,914
Tianjin 天津	23	144	5,671	316	3.36	11.62	39.47	71.08	9,408
Hebei 河北	73	135	5,494	100	0.99	2.34	40.77	57.67	10,091
Shanxi 山西	33	261	4,925	77	0.61	1.96	18.87	68.70	12,575
Inner Mongolia 內蒙	47	170	5,066	146	1.24	3.68	29.82	66.40	11,814
Northeast 東北	313	210	6,836	-303	-1.62	-6.57	32.51	75.36	18,754
Liaoning 遼寧	155	207	4,467	-602	-3.59	-16.01	21.54	77.60	16,780
Jilin 吉林	57	159	4,072	18	0.19	0.52	25.58	64.23	9,954
Heilongjiang 黑龍江	101	244	12,031	-27	-0.10	-0.42	49.38	75.55	26,748
Central East 華東	303	259	21,571	920	3.25	10.45	83.36	68.88	28,294
Shanghai 上海	41	347	41,730	1,446	2.73	10.95	120.35	75.04	52,903
Jiangsu 江蘇	79	284	27,398	1,132	3.82	10.28	96.52	62.81	29,614
Zhejiang 浙江	37	167	12,632	378	2.22	9.60	75.57	76.86	17,022
Anhui 安徽	13	235	10,338	458	2.97	8.91	43.98	66.69	15,449
Fujian 福建	6	151	11,607	257	1.68	4.91	77.12	65.85	15,322
Jiangxi 江西	16	341	15,438	714	2.18	6.07	45.27	64.04	32,722
Shandong 山東	111	236	15,697	874	3.71	11.78	66.57	68.53	23,589
Central-South 中南	143	260	10,830	45	0.20	0.78	41.70	74.83	22,925
Henan 河南	53	149	4,772	81	1.02	5.24	32.06	80.48	7,946
Hubei 湖北	39	490	18,436	200	0.48	2.45	37.61	80.48	41,822
Hunan 湖南	22	221	9,477	-168	-1.15	-5.78	42.83	80.15	14,615
Guangdong 廣東	16	179	13,788	-3	-0.01	-0.02	77.08	59.59	38,679
Guangxi 廣西	12	198	11,808	-168	-0.71	-1.85	59.53	61.49	23,673
Hainan 海南	1	13	5,910	60	3.70	5.66	454.62	34.57	1,620
Southwest 西南	43	517	32,935	656	0.94	3.56	63.73	73.52	69,462
Chongqing 重慶	9	345	8,793	26	0.14	0.41	25.48	66.03	18,749
Sichuan 四川	20	888	66,328	1,420	1.02	4.06	74.68	74.78	138,786
Guizhou 貴州	10	77	1,560	-24	-0.47	-0.83	20.31	44.13	5,149
Yunnan 雲南	4	204	4,560	90	0.91	2.19	22.41	58.46	9,900
Tibet 西藏									
Northwest 西北	110	160	4,642	-160	-1.46	-4.72	28.94	69.11	10,990
Shaanxi 陝西	57	133	3,373	-271	-3.67	-11.61	25.33	68.35	7,378
Gansu 甘肅	15	339	9,487	44	0.20	0.61	27.95	67.70	22,312
Qinghai 青海	8	46	979	30	2.04	8.48	21.51	75.91	1,469
Ningxia 寧夏	4	123	3,368	53	0.76	5.48	27.49	86.23	6,953
Xinjiang 新疆	26	158	5,953	-126	-0.79	-2.61	37.64	69.67	15,929

Year 年份	Number of firms 企業個數	Rate of change 每年變化 (%)	Number of employees 職工人數 (人)	Rate of change 每年變化 (%)	Total revenue (mil. RMB) 總銷售收入 (百萬元)	Rate of change 每年變化 (%)	Total profit (mil. RMB) 總利潤 (百萬元)	Rate of change 每年變化 (%)
1993	915		266,423		11,327		414	
1994	1,005	9.84%	246,151	-7.61%	12,331	8.86%	344	-16.80%
1995	1,047	4.18%	245,354	-0.32%	12,293	-0.31%	311	-9.78%
1996	1,138	8.69%	258,790	5.48%	13,608	10.70%	224	-27.92%

3 Major products* 3 種主要產品 *	Output 產量	Sales volume 銷售量	Unit 單位
a) Power Station Boiler 電站鍋爐	421	421	set 台
b) Steam Boiler 蒸氣鍋爐	23,257	17,675	set 台
c) Hot Water Boiler 熱水鍋爐	38,936	38,157	ton 蒸噸

Top 10 firms by revenue (year founded) 收入排名前 10 家企業 (創辦年份)	City 城市	Province 省	Telephone / fax 電話 / 傳真	Number of employees 職工人數	Ownership 產業所有權	Revenue ('000 RMB) 銷售收入 (千元)	Profit ('000 RMB) (rank) 利潤 (千元) (排名)	Total assets ('000 RMB) 總資產 (千元)	Major products 主要產品
Shanghai Boiler Works 上海鍋爐廠(1921)	Shanghai 上海市	Shanghai 上海市	(021)64302391 (021)64301980	4,762	State-owned 國有	956,062	8525(14)	1,076,627	a,b
Dong Fang Boiler Works 東方鍋爐廠(1970)	Zigong 自貢市	Sichuan 四川省	(0813)2201131 (0813)2203200	8,348	State-owned 國有	862,579	33187(2)	1,895,182	a
Harbin Boiler Co. Ltd. 哈爾濱鍋爐有限責任公司(1954)	Harbin 哈爾濱市	Heilongjiang 黑龍江省	(0451)2681711 (0451)2681689	7,427	Joint stock 股份制	814,499	650(101)	1,972,295	a,b,c
Wuxi Boiler Works 無錫鍋爐廠(1958)	Wuxi 無錫市	Jiangsu 江蘇省	(0510)5215556 (0510)5215605	3,041	State-owned 國有	462,039	30583(4)	709,347	a,b,c
Wuhan Boiler Works 武漢鍋爐廠(1957)	Wuhan 武漢市	Hubei 湖北省	(027)87658464 (027)87883938	6,533	State-owned 國有	419,522	7147(16)	1,137,720	a
Wuxi Tai Hu Boiler Group Co. 無錫太湖鍋爐集團公司(1966)	Wuxi 無錫市	Jiangsu 江蘇省	(0510)5952983	900	Collectively-owned 集體	296,079	24500(5)	177,251	b,c
Hangzhou Fu Chun Boiler Vessel Co. Ltd. 杭州富春鍋爐容器有限公司(1992)	Hangzhou 杭州市	Zhejiang 浙江省	(0571)5371966 (0571)5377420	2,325	Overseas Chinese-funded 港澳台資	289,217	10619(10)	447,978	a,b,c
Babcock & Wilcox Beijing Co. Ltd. (sino-u.s) 北京巴布科克威爾科克斯有限公司(1986)	Beijing 北京市	Beijing 北京市	(010)68862244	3,479	Foreign-funded 外資	254,450	-17201(530)	678,570	a
Jiangsu Hai Lu Boiler Group Co. Ltd 江蘇海陸鍋爐集團公司(1958)	Suzhou 蘇州市	Jiangsu 江蘇省	(0512)8224400	1,265	Collectively-owned 集體	250,972	12133(8)	127,302	b
Shanghai Hang Xing Machinery (Group) Co. Ltd. 上海航星機械(集團)有限公司(1992)	Shanghai 上海市	Shanghai 上海市	(021)57426827	866	Foreign-funded 外資	215,674	30699(3)	197,981	o

Top 10 Cities by Production Output 產出排名前 10 位城市	Province 省	Market share 市場份額	Number of firms 企業個數
Shanghai 上海市	Shanghai 上海市	14.71%	68
Wuxi 無錫市	Jiangsu 江蘇省	9.24%	57
Harbin 哈爾濱市	Heilongjiang 黑龍江省	7.40%	36
Zigong 自貢市	Sichuan 四川省	6.97%	10
Beijing 北京市	Beijing 北京市	5.99%	45
Wuhan 武漢市	Hubei 湖北省	3.56%	22
Hangzhou 杭州市	Zhejiang 浙江省	2.85%	12
Ji'nan 濟南市	Shandong 山東省	2.50%	39
Suzhou 蘇州市	Jiangsu 江蘇省	2.22%	22
Changzhou 常州市	Jiangsu 江蘇省	1.91%	16

10 Major Wholesalers 10 家主要批發商	City 城市	Province 省	Telephone / Fax 電話 / 傳真
Liaoning Automobile Trade Group Corp. 遼寧省汽車貿易集團	Shenyang 瀋陽市	Liaoning 遼寧省	(024)23835494 (024)23838338
China Post and Telecommunication Equipment General Company 中國郵電器材總公司	Beijing 北京市	Beijing 北京市	(010)63523715 (010)63525935
Jiangsu Electromechanical Products General Company 江蘇省機電產品總公司	Nanjing 南京市	Jiangsu 江蘇省	(025)7713642 (025)7711036
Xi Nan Technology Import & Export Company 西南技術進出口公司	Chongqing 重慶市	Chongqing 重慶市	(023)63850185 (023)63850026
Changzhou Economic Technology Industrial Development Zone Tian Ming Trade Company 常州經濟技術產業開發區天明貿易公司	Changzhou 常州市	Jiangsu 江蘇省	(0519)8829882 (0519)8829882
Shanxi Mechanical Equipment Import & Export Company 山西省機械設備進出口公司	Taiyuan 太原市	Shanxi 山西省	(0351)4040713 (0351)4043981
Ningbo Five Mining Machinery Import & Export Company 寧波市五礦機械進出口公司	Ningbo 寧波市	Zhejiang 浙江省	(0574)7311255 (0574)7320322
Tianjin Jin Huan Electromechanical Complete Sets of Equipment Factory 天津市津環機電成套設備廠	Tianjin 天津市	Tianjin 天津市	(022)26371628
Yunnan Machinery Import & Export Company 雲南省機械進出口公司	Kunming 昆明市	Yunnan 雲南省	(0871)3164879 (0871)3136829
Tianjin Da Qiu Zhuang Yi Yuan Trade Center 天津市大丘莊億源商貿中心	Tianjin 天津市	Tianjin 天津市	(022)28899478 (022)28899046

*Also include sales by firms outside this industry.包括本行業以外廠家的銷售。"o" stands for "others". "o" 代表"其他產品"。

3512: Internal Combustion Engines 內燃機製造業

The industry accounts for 0.481% of the total revenue of China's industrial sector in 1996. The revenue growth rate of the industry is -0.1% from 1995, as compared to the growth rate of China's industrial sector, 9.51%. The rate of return on asset is 1.87%. 53.87% of all firms in the industry made a profit while 43.65% had negative returns. The top province in terms of the industry's revenue is Jiangsu, accounting for 35.22% of the total revenue.
本行業在1996年佔全行業總產值0.481%，行業年增長率為-0.1%（全國工業年增長率9.51%）。行業的資產回報率1.87%，53.87%的企業盈利，43.65%的企業虧損。銷售收入最高的省份為江蘇省，佔本行業的35.22%。

	Total number of firms 企業總數	Total number of employees 職工總數	Total revenue (mil. RMB) 總銷售收入（百萬元）	Total profit (mil. RMB) 總利潤（百萬元）	Return on assets 資產利潤率 (%)	Return on equity 權益利潤率 (%)	Labour productivity ('000 RMB / worker) 勞動生產率（千元/人）	Debts / assets 資產負債率 (%)	Total assets (mil. RMB) 總資產（百萬元）
Industry Overall 行業總體	256	305,320	27,855	853	1.87	4.97	91.23	62.44	45,669

	Number of firms 企業個數	Average number of employees 平均職工人數	Average revenue ('000 RMB) 平均銷售收入（千元）	Average profit ('000 RMB) 平均利潤（千元）	Return on assets 資產利潤率 (%)	Return on equity 權益利潤率 (%)	Labour productivity ('000 RMB / worker) 勞動生產率（千元/人）	Average debts / assets 平均資產負債率(%)	Average Total assets ('000 RMB) 平均總資產（千元）
By ownership 產業所有權									
State-owned 國有	139	1,722	132,597	2,388	1.09	3.60	77.00	69.68	218,942
Collectively-owned 集體	72	170	13,371	69	0.43	1.65	78.43	74.24	16,220
Privately-owned 私有									
Domestic JVs 聯營	3	172	24,671	279	2.10	4.41	143.44	52.28	13,286
Joint stock 股份制	13	2,512	405,413	18,554	3.46	7.66	161.41	54.79	535,630
Foreign-funded 外資	16	1,030	167,264	15,978	4.04	6.22	162.39	35.11	395,688
Overseas Chinese-funded 港澳台資	12	330	36,710	1,526	2.49	5.22	111.35	52.23	61,231
By size 規模									
Large 大型	52	3,650	409,202	15,738	2.38	5.85	112.10	59.43	662,544
Medium 中型	75	1,159	60,267	73	0.07	0.26	52.01	74.88	110,008
Small 小型	126	224	16,321	232	0.98	2.65	72.73	62.85	23,545
By regional distribution 地區分布									
Central-North 華北	24	1,307	97,016	-1,895	-0.78	-2.85	74.22	72.53	241,908
Beijing 北京	9	1,590	93,957	-7,713	-2.61	-22.81	59.08	88.56	295,622
Tianjin 天津	5	2,125	275,054	5,682	1.01	2.32	129.44	56.46	561,310
Hebei 河北	8	609	12,294	-449	-1.36	-8.67	20.19	84.26	32,876
Shanxi 山西	2	782	4,580	-435	-1.15	-3.21	5.86	64.16	37,810
Inner Mongolia 內蒙									
Northeast 東北	14	1,557	133,991	4,606	1.85	4.69	86.06	60.50	248,592
Liaoning 遼寧	10	1,426	153,712	11,387	4.14	9.56	107.78	56.67	274,958
Jilin 吉林	2	3,617	132,035	-24,720	-7.63	-31.40	36.50	75.71	324,130
Heilongjiang 黑龍江	2	151	37,340	25	0.06	0.19	248.11	68.76	41,225
Central East 華東	121	1,123	132,409	6,750	4.03	10.36	117.90	61.10	167,525
Shanghai 上海	7	1,477	166,693	17,757	4.43	6.84	112.89	35.29	401,164
Jiangsu 江蘇	43	968	228,125	15,656	7.74	19.57	235.63	60.47	202,372
Zhejiang 浙江	19	663	54,892	994	1.01	3.12	82.82	67.79	98,874
Anhui 安徽	13	1,177	77,575	-322	-0.29	-1.15	65.91	74.69	110,358
Fujian 福建	9	825	32,746	-1,474	-2.14	-6.92	39.71	68.98	68,744
Jiangxi 江西	12	1,305	34,549	-953	-1.05	-3.58	26.48	70.63	90,671
Shandong 山東	18	1,831	126,921	1,623	0.78	2.54	69.33	69.27	207,798
Central-South 中南	61	1,154	74,922	-1,100	-0.66	-1.59	64.93	58.28	166,353
Henan 河南	13	1,000	98,814	5,352	5.33	18.72	98.84	71.52	100,392
Hubei 湖北	11	984	48,715	-657	-0.78	-2.20	49.49	64.78	84,805
Hunan 湖南	16	1,179	39,129	-4,899	-4.14	-13.04	33.19	68.23	118,265
Guangdong 廣東	12	529	34,596	-645	-0.94	-3.93	65.44	76.15	68,782
Guangxi 廣西	9	2,374	189,842	-4,814	-0.83	-1.58	79.98	47.31	576,884
Hainan 海南									
Southwest 西南	32	1,176	84,621	2,829	1.78	4.94	71.97	64.01	159,045
Chongqing 重慶	18	898	58,158	1,362	1.10	2.84	64.74	61.36	124,258
Sichuan 四川	8	1,380	121,992	2,772	1.46	4.53	88.38	67.82	190,283
Guizhou 貴州	2	3,420	66,270	-2,695	-0.87	-3.03	19.38	71.34	310,890
Yunnan 雲南	4	901	139,523	12,338	6.91	16.41	154.85	57.91	178,630
Tibet 西藏									
Northwest 西北	4	2,061	87,715	-1,625	-0.74	-2.79	42.57	73.38	218,833
Shaanxi 陝西	1	6,406	102,180	-18,180	-2.88	-10.73	15.95	73.15	630,720
Gansu 甘肅	2	689	14,540	50	0.10	0.50	21.12	80.27	50,410
Qinghai 青海									
Ningxia 寧夏	1	459	219,600	11,580	8.05	26.46	478.43	69.56	143,790
Xinjiang 新疆									

3512: Internal Combustion Engines 內燃機製造業

Year 年份	Number of firms 企業個數	Rate of change 每年變化 (%)	Number of employees 職工人數 (人)	Rate of change 每年變化 (%)	Total revenue (mil. RMB) 總銷售收入 (百萬元)	Rate of change 每年變化 (%)	Total profit (mil. RMB) 總利潤 (百萬元)	Rate of change 每年變化 (%)
1993	238		355,831		21,068		1,262	
1994	259	8.82%	295,414	-16.98%	22,405	6.35%	1,470	16.50%
1995	268	3.47%	318,694	7.88%	27,878	24.43%	1,652	12.35%
1996	256	-4.48%	305,320	-4.20%	27,855	-0.08%	853	-48.37%

3 Major products* 3 種主要產品 *	Output 產量	Sales volume 銷售量	Unit 單位
a) Diesel Engine 柴油機	8,175,049	7,848,047	set 台
b) Petrol Engine 汽油機	1,486,448	1,248,616	set 台

Top 10 firms by revenue (year founded) 收入排名前 10 家企業 (創辦年份)	City 城市	Province 省	Telephone / fax 電話 / 傳真	Number of employees 職工人數	Ownership 產業所有權	Revenue ('000 RMB) 銷售收入 (千元)	Profit ('000 RMB) (rank) 利潤 (千元) (排名)	Total assets ('000 RMB) 總資產 (千元)	Major products 主要產品
Chang Chai Co. Ltd. 常柴股份有限公司(1913)	Changzhou 常州市	Jiangsu 江蘇省	(0519)6603656 (0519)6670765	4,738	Joint stock 股份制	2,535,431	280331(1)	2,195,830	a
Tianjin Internal Combustion Engine Works 天津市內燃機廠(1938)	Tianjin 天津市	Tianjin 天津市	(022)27375122 (022)27371708	2,588	State-owned 國有	1,151,943	108539(4)	1,203,526	b
Guangxi Yu Chai Machinery Co. Ltd. 廣西玉柴機器股份有限公司(1952)	Yulin 玉林市	Guangxi 廣西	(0775)3289113 (0775)3288168	9,871	Foreign-funded 外資	1,148,800	15455(17)	3,419,770	a
Jiangsu Wu Ling Diesel Engine Plant 江蘇省五菱柴油機有限公司(1956)	Changzhou 常州市	Jiangsu 江蘇省	(0519)6551735	2,717	State-owned 國有	1,074,560	107740(5)	679,070	a
Shanghai Diesel Engine Co. Ltd. 上海柴油機股份有限公司(1993)	Shanghai 上海市	Shanghai 上海市	(021)65493506 (021)63269706	8,609	Joint stock 股份制	1,049,678	159977(2)	2,553,940	a
Jiangsu Xing Xing Machinery Group Company 江蘇行星機械集團公司(1956)	Wuxi 無錫市	Jiangsu 江蘇省	(0510)3311412	3,221	State-owned 國有	1,011,514	9545(26)	795,544	a
Yi Qi Group Wuxi Diesel Engine Factory 一汽集團無錫柴油機廠(1943)	Wuxi 無錫市	Jiangsu 江蘇省	(0510)5014990 (0510)5016785	4,577	State-owned 國有	952,552	70282(6)	769,030	a
Weifang Diesel Engine Co. Ltd. 濰坊柴油機有限責任公司(1946)	Weifang 濰坊市	Shandong 山東省	(0536)8234951 (0536)8231074	13,735	State-owned 國有	822,290	86(93)	1,494,334	o
Bei Nei Group Co. 北內集團總公司(1949)	Beijing 北京市	Beijing 北京市	(010)67715588	12,826	State-owned 國有	803,705	-70421(202)	2,582,036	a,b
China No.1 Automobile Group Dalian Diesel Engine Factory 中國第一汽車集團大連柴油機廠(1951)	Dalian 大連市	Liaoning 遼寧省	(0411)3631588	2,550	State-owned 國有	770,420	111682(3)	937,617	a

Top 10 Cities by Production Output 產出排名前 10 位城市	Province 省	Market share 市場份額	Number of firms 企業個數
Changzhou 常州市	Jiangsu 江蘇省	11.65%	11
Wuxi 無錫市	Jiangsu 江蘇省	8.71%	13
Yulin 玉林市	Guangxi 廣西	6.73%	1
Taizhou 泰州市	Jiangsu 江蘇省	4.66%	12
Tianjin 天津市	Tianjin 天津市	4.63%	5
Beijing 北京市	Beijing 北京市	4.01%	8
Harbin 哈爾濱市	Heilongjiang 黑龍江省	3.77%	1
Shanghai 上海市	Shanghai 上海市	3.53%	20
Chongqing 重慶市	Chongqing 重慶市	3.44%	20
Weifang 濰坊市	Shandong 山東省	3.14%	4

10 Major Wholesalers 10 家主要批發商	City 城市	Province 省	Telephone / Fax 電話 / 傳真
Liaoning Automobile Trade Group Corp. 遼寧省汽車貿易集團	Shenyang 瀋陽市	Liaoning 遼寧省	(024)23835494 (024)23838338
China Post and Telecommunication Equipment General Company 中國郵電器材總公司	Beijing 北京市	Beijing 北京市	(010)63523715 (010)63525935
Jiangsu Electromechanical Products General Company 江蘇省機電產品總公司	Nanjing 南京市	Jiangsu 江蘇省	(025)7713642 (025)7711036
Xi Nan Technology Import & Export Company 西南技術進出口公司	Chongqing 重慶市	Chongqing 重慶市	(023)63850185 (023)63850026
Changzhou Economic Technology Industrial Development Zone Tian Ming Trade Company 常州經濟技術產業開發區天明貿易公司	Changzhou 常州市	Jiangsu 江蘇省	(0519)8829882 (0519)8829882
Shanxi Mechanical Equipment Import & Export Company 山西省機械設備進出口公司	Taiyuan 太原市	Shanxi 山西省	(0351)4040713 (0351)4043981
Ningbo Five Mining Machinery Import & Export Company 寧波市五礦機械進出口公司	Ningbo 寧波市	Zhejiang 浙江省	(0574)7311255 (0574)7320322
Tianjin Jin Huan Electromechanical Complete Sets of Equipment Factory 天津市津環機電成套設備廠	Tianjin 天津市	Tianjin 天津市	(022)26371628
Yunnan Machinery Import & Export Company 雲南省機械進出口公司	Kunming 昆明市	Yunnan 雲南省	(0871)3164879 (0871)3136829
Tianjin Da Qiu Zhuang Yi Yuan Trade Center 天津市大丘莊億源商貿中心	Tianjin 天津市	Tianjin 天津市	(022)28899478 (022)28899046

*Also include sales by firms outside this industry.包括本行業以外廠家的銷售。"o" stands for "others". "o" 代表 "其他產品"。

3513: Steam Turbines 汽輪機製造業

The industry accounts for 0.071% of the total revenue of China's industrial sector in 1996. The revenue growth rate of the industry is 14.0% from 1995, as compared to the growth rate of China's industrial sector, 9.51%. The rate of return on asset is 1.02%. 75.65% of all firms in the industry made a profit while 20.00% had negative returns. The top province in terms of the industry's revenue is Shanghai, accounting for 44.02% of the total revenue.
本行業在1996年佔全行業總產值0.071%，行業年增長率為14.0%（全國工業年增長率9.51%）。行業的資產回報率1.02%，75.65%的企業盈利，20.00%的企業虧損。銷售收入最高的省份為上海市，佔本行業的44.02%。

	Total number of firms 企業總數	Total number of employees 職工總數	Total revenue (mil. RMB) 總銷售收入（百萬元）	Total profit (mil. RMB) 總利潤（百萬元）	Return on assets 資產利潤率 (%)	Return on equity 權益利潤率 (%)	Labour productivity ('000 RMB / worker) 勞動生產率（千元/人）	Debts / assets 資產負債率 (%)	Total assets (mil. RMB) 總資產（百萬元）
Industry Overall 行業總體	55	53,101	4,126	114	1.02	2.49	77.70	59.25	11,191

	Number of firms 企業個數	Average number of employees 平均職工人數	Average revenue ('000 RMB) 平均銷售收入（千元）	Average profit ('000 RMB) 平均利潤（千元）	Return on assets 資產利潤率 (%)	Return on equity 權益利潤率 (%)	Labour productivity ('000 RMB / worker) 勞動生產率（千元/人）	Average debts / assets 平均資產負債率(%)	Average Total assets ('000 RMB) 平均總資產（千元）
By ownership 產業所有權									
State-owned 國有	13	2,013	126,154	5,308	1.21	2.70	62.66	55.32	439,923
Collectively-owned 集體	37	281	14,217	538	3.01	5.98	50.52	49.72	17,908
Privately-owned 私有									
Domestic JVs 聯營									
Joint stock 股份制	4	3,973	478,621	6,805	0.57	1.67	120.48	65.67	1,188,398
Foreign-funded 外資	1	611	47,805	-2,154	-3.79	-5.34	78.24	29.11	56,859
Overseas Chinese-funded 港澳台資									
By size 規模									
Large 大型	11	4,070	341,212	7,649	0.81	2.02	83.84	60.03	948,305
Medium 中型	4	940	19,356	3,009	3.74	7.52	20.60	50.30	80,475
Small 小型	40	114	7,407	445	4.06	7.70	64.85	47.27	10,961
By regional distribution 地區分布									
Central-North 華北	4	78	4,690	-70	-0.99	-12.50	60.13	92.10	7,085
Beijing 北京	3	61	993	-227	-10.10	-283.33	16.37	96.43	2,243
Tianjin 天津									
Hebei 河北	1	130	15,780	400	1.85	20.00	121.38	90.75	21,610
Shanxi 山西									
Inner Mongolia 內蒙									
Northeast 東北	15	813	44,986	307	0.19	0.91	55.36	79.10	161,328
Liaoning 遼寧	1	30	370	10	2.86	12.50	12.33	77.14	350
Jilin 吉林									
Heilongjiang 黑龍江	14	869	48,173	329	0.19	0.91	55.46	79.10	172,826
Central East 華東	30	939	95,150	3,417	1.48	2.99	101.38	50.47	230,430
Shanghai 上海	8	1,386	227,021	5,675	0.98	1.82	163.84	46.35	579,818
Jiangsu 江蘇	10	900	51,403	1,100	0.95	2.44	57.10	61.18	116,335
Zhejiang 浙江	5	829	58,932	5,762	4.14	10.45	71.11	60.34	139,088
Anhui 安徽									
Fujian 福建									
Jiangxi 江西									
Shandong 山東	7	561	32,807	2,471	4.16	8.32	58.51	49.98	59,366
Central-South 中南	5	500	13,316	-2,370	-3.87	-7.82	26.62	50.49	61,198
Henan 河南	1	1,219	14,770	-5,270	-2.70	-5.27	12.12	48.74	195,050
Hubei 湖北									
Hunan 湖南	1	470	5,870	-1,930	-37.40	18.12	12.49	306.20	5,160
Guangdong 廣東	3	271	15,313	-1,550	-4.40	-7.48	56.58	41.26	35,260
Guangxi 廣西									
Hainan 海南									
Southwest 西南	1	9,941	511,650	18,800	1.23	3.94	51.47	68.67	1,523,730
Chongqing 重慶									
Sichuan 四川	1	9,941	511,650	18,800	1.23	3.94	51.47	68.67	1,523,730
Guizhou 貴州									
Yunnan 雲南									
Tibet 西藏									
Northwest 西北									
Shaanxi 陝西									
Gansu 甘肅									
Qinghai 青海									
Ningxia 寧夏									
Xinjiang 新疆									

3513: Steam Turbines 汽輪機製造業

Year 年份	Number of firms 企業個數	Rate of change 每年變化 (%)	Number of employees 職工人數 (人)	Rate of change 每年變化 (%)	Total revenue (mil. RMB) 總銷售收入 (百萬元)	Rate of change 每年變化 (%)	Total profit (mil. RMB) 總利潤 (百萬元)	Rate of change 每年變化 (%)
1993	26		114,881		2,633		58	
1994	28	7.69%	64,344	-43.99%	3,833	45.57%	106	82.35%
1995	45	60.71%	54,029	-16.03%	3,618	-5.60%	84	-21.16%
1996	55	22.22%	53,101	-1.72%	4,126	14.04%	114	36.15%

3 Major products* 3 種主要產品 *	Output 產量	Sales volume 銷售量	Unit 單位
a) Industrical Steam Turbine 工業汽輪機	542,152	75,901	kw 千瓦
b) Power Station Steam Turbine 電站汽輪機	10,372,888	10,580,346	kw 千瓦
c) Auxiliary Machinery of Steam Turbine 汽輪機輔機	20,462	21,076	ton 噸

Top 10 firms by revenue (year founded) 收入排名前 10 家企業 (創辦年份)	City 城市	Province 省	Telephone / fax 電話 / 傳真	Number of employees 職工人數	Ownership 產業所有權	Revenue ('000 RMB) 銷售收入 (千元)	Profit ('000 RMB) (rank) 利潤 (千元) (排名)	Total assets ('000 RMB) 總資產 (千元)	Major products 主要產品
Shanghai Steam Turbine Co. Ltd. 上海汽輪機有限公司(1996)	Shanghai 上海市	Shanghai 上海市	(021)64358331 (021)64355046	6,777	Foreign-funded 外資	1,068,254	26023(2)	2,000,532	a,b,c
Haerbin Turbine Co. Ltd. 哈爾濱汽輪機有限責任公司(1958)	Harbin 哈爾濱市	Heilongjiang 黑龍江省	(0451)2681404 (0451)2681364	9,567	Joint stock 股份制	611,786	309(24)	2,279,795	a,b,c
Shanghai Motive Power Equipment Co. Ltd. 上海動力設備有限公司(1996)	Shanghai 上海市	Shanghai 上海市	(021)65431040 (021)65430371	2,980	Foreign-funded 外資	522,344	13914(4)	813,316	c
Dong Fang Steam Turbine Factory 東方汽輪機廠(1966)	Deyang 德陽市	Sichuan 四川省	(0838)6302192 (0838)6301027	9,679	State-owned 國有	511,649	18795(3)	1,523,732	b
Nanjing Turbine & Electric Machinery (Group) Co. Ltd. 南京汽輪電機集團有限公司(1956)	Nanjing 南京市	Jiangsu 江蘇省	(025)5503264 (025)5502858	5,371	State-owned 國有	373,000	10089(6)	736,900	o
Hangzhou Steam Turbine Power Group Co. Ltd 杭州汽輪動力集團有限公司(1958)	Hangzhou 杭州市	Zhejiang 浙江省	(0571)8144982 (0571)8145409	3,534	State-owned 國有	283,265	28520(1)	686,595	a,c
Qingdao Jie Neng Power Group Co. 青島捷能動力集團公司(1950)	Qingdao 青島市	Shandong 山東省	(0532)4851291 (0532)4857619	3,291	State-owned 國有	168,409	11186(5)	371,487	b
Shanghai Power Station Auxiliary Equipment Works 上海電站輔機廠(1921)	Shanghai 上海市	Shanghai 上海市	(021)65431040 (021)65430371	344	State-owned 國有	120,009	3583(8)	566,580	c
Shanghai Electricity Group Wuxi Vane Factory 上海電氣集團無錫葉片廠(1979)	Wuxi 無錫市	Jiangsu 江蘇省	(0510)5754381 (0510)5759426	1,113	State-owned 國有	71,514	209(31)	335,579	o
Shanghai Turbine Co. 上海汽輪機廠(1946)	Shanghai 上海市	Shanghai 上海市	(021)64358331 (021)64355046	248	State-owned 國有	70,294	1511(11)	1,237,503	o

Top 10 Cities by Production Output 產出排名前 10 位城市	Province 省	Market share 市場份額	Number of firms 企業個數
Shanghai 上海市	Shanghai 上海市	44.98%	12
Harbin 哈爾濱市	Heilongjiang 黑龍江省	14.20%	6
Nanjing 南京市	Jiangsu 江蘇省	14.01%	4
Deyang 德陽市	Sichuan 四川省	11.71%	2
Hangzhou 杭州市	Zhejiang 浙江省	5.33%	2
Qingdao 青島市	Shandong 山東省	3.48%	3
Wuxi 無錫市	Jiangsu 江蘇省	1.79%	7
Taiyuan 太原市	Shanxi 山西省	0.79%	1
Guangzhou 廣州市	Guangdong 廣東省	0.69%	2
Zhenjiang 鎮江市	Jiangsu 江蘇省	0.49%	2

10 Major Wholesalers 10 家主要批發商	City 城市	Province 省	Telephone / Fax 電話 / 傳真
Liaoning Automobile Trade Group Corp. 遼寧省汽車貿易集團	Shenyang 瀋陽市	Liaoning 遼寧省	(024)23835494 (024)23838338
China Post and Telecommunication Equipment General Company 中國郵電器材總公司	Beijing 北京市	Beijing 北京市	(010)63523715 (010)63525935
Jiangsu Electromechanical Products General Company 江蘇省機電產品總公司	Nanjing 南京市	Jiangsu 江蘇省	(025)7713642 (025)7711036
Xi Nan Technology Import & Export Company 西南技術進出口公司	Chongqing 重慶市	Chongqing 重慶市	(023)63850185 (023)63850026
Changzhou Economic Technology Industrial Development Zone Tian Ming Trade Company 常州經濟技術產業開發區天明貿易公司	Changzhou 常州市	Jiangsu 江蘇省	(0519)8829882 (0519)8829882
Shanxi Mechanical Equipment Import & Export Company 山西省機械設備進出口公司	Taiyuan 太原市	Shanxi 山西省	(0351)4040713 (0351)4043981
Ningbo Five Mining Machinery Import & Export Company 寧波市五礦機械進出口公司	Ningbo 寧波市	Zhejiang 浙江省	(0574)7311255 (0574)7320322
Tianjin Jin Huan Electromechanical Complete Sets of Equipment Factory 天津市津環機電成套設備廠	Tianjin 天津市	Tianjin 天津市	(022)26371628
Yunnan Machinery Import & Export Company 雲南省機械進出口公司	Kunming 昆明市	Yunnan 云南省	(0871)3164879 (0871)3136829
Tianjin Da Qiu Zhuang Yi Yuan Trade Center 天津市大丘莊億源商貿中心	Tianjin 天津市	Tianjin 天津市	(022)28899478 (022)28899046

*Also include sales by firms outside this industry.包括本行業以外廠家的銷售。"o" stands for "others". "o" 代表"其他產品"。

3514: Hydraulic Turbines 水輪機製造業

The industry accounts for 0.009% of the total revenue of China's industrial sector in 1996. The revenue growth rate of the industry is 3.8% from 1995, as compared to the growth rate of China's industrial sector, 9.51%. The rate of return on asset is -0.63%. 75.79% of all firms in the industry made a profit while 17.07% had negative returns. The top province in terms of the industry's revenue is Chongqing, accounting for 32.42% of the total revenue.
本行業在 1996 年佔全行業總產值 0.009% ，行業年增長率為 3.8%（全國工業年增長率 9.51%）。行業的資產回報率 -0.63% ， 75.79% 的企業盈利， 17.07% 的企業虧損。銷售收入最高的省份為重慶市，佔本行業的 32.42% 。

	Total number of firms 企業總數	Total number of employees 職工總數	Total revenue (mil. RMB) 總銷售收入（百萬元）	Total profit (mil. RMB) 總利潤（百萬元）	Return on assets 資產利潤率 (%)	Return on equity 權益利潤率 (%)	Labour productivity ('000 RMB / worker) 勞動生產率（千元/人）	Debts / assets 資產負債率 (%)	Total assets (mil. RMB) 總資產（百萬元）
Industry Overall 行業總體	43	17,792	537	-10	-0.63	-2.92	30.18	78.41	1,627

	Number of firms 企業個數	Average number of employees 平均職工人數	Average revenue ('000 RMB) 平均銷售收入（千元）	Average profit ('000 RMB) 平均利潤（千元）	Return on assets 資產利潤率 (%)	Return on equity 權益利潤率 (%)	Labour productivity ('000 RMB / worker) 勞動生產率（千元/人）	Average debts / assets 平均資產負債率(%)	Average Total assets ('000 RMB) 平均總資產（千元）
By ownership 產業所有權									
State-owned 國有	31	534	16,194	-452	-0.89	-4.13	30.33	78.41	50,645
Collectively-owned 集體	12	103	2,915	333	6.97	33.09	28.24	78.93	4,782
Privately-owned 私有									
Domestic JVs 聯營									
Joint stock 股份制									
Foreign-funded 外資									
Overseas Chinese-funded 港澳台資									
By size 規模									
Large 大型	3	2,700	100,166	-5,033	-1.41	-8.35	37.10	83.09	356,569
Medium 中型	5	409	13,373	345	1.02	2.77	32.71	62.99	33,671
Small 小型	36	212	4,711	94	0.87	3.13	22.18	72.29	10,817
By regional distribution 地區分布									
Central-North 華北	2	65	3,945	380	26.86	31.40	60.69	14.49	1,415
Beijing 北京	1	4	10				2.50		50
Tianjin 天津									
Hebei 河北									
Shanxi 山西	1	126	7,880	760	27.34	32.07	62.54	14.75	2,780
Inner Mongolia 內蒙									
Northeast 東北									
Liaoning 遼寧									
Jilin 吉林									
Heilongjiang 黑龍江									
Central East 華東	12	417	15,747	891	2.61	6.16	37.73	57.66	34,149
Shanghai 上海									
Jiangsu 江蘇	1	20	660	60	3.37	13.64	33.00	75.28	1,780
Zhejiang 浙江	4	777	38,775	2,163	2.70	5.90	49.90	54.32	80,203
Anhui 安徽									
Fujian 福建	3	131	2,053	193	3.98	5.78	15.71	31.09	4,857
Jiangxi 江西	4	372	6,760	350	1.93	8.49	18.17	77.30	18,158
Shandong 山東									
Central-South 中南	14	339	9,305	-1,684	-3.27	-44.53	27.42	92.66	51,552
Henan 河南	2	338	3,895	-565	-5.16	-152.70	11.54	96.62	10,950
Hubei 湖北									
Hunan 湖南	2	154	2,420	-835	-8.91	-17.56	15.77	49.28	9,375
Guangdong 廣東	5	564	18,464	-2,640	-2.15	-59.73	32.74	96.39	122,570
Guangxi 廣西	5	190	5,064	-1,514	-11.09	-36.78	26.68	69.84	13,646
Hainan 海南									
Southwest 西南	15	527	14,014	125	0.38	1.53	26.60	75.16	32,816
Chongqing 重慶	5	1,159	34,823	320	0.40	1.69	30.04	76.45	80,359
Sichuan 四川	9	211	3,701	17	0.19	0.66	17.50	71.56	8,978
Guizhou 貴州									
Yunnan 雲南	1	208	2,780	120	1.24	2.56	13.37	51.35	9,640
Tibet 西藏									
Northwest 西北									
Shaanxi 陝西									
Gansu 甘肅									
Qinghai 青海									
Ningxia 寧夏									
Xinjiang 新疆									

3514: Hydraulic Turbines 水輪機製造業

Year 年份	Number of firms 企業個數	Rate of change 每年變化 (%)	Number of employees 職工人數（人）	Rate of change 每年變化 (%)	Total revenue (mil. RMB) 總銷售收入（百萬元）	Rate of change 每年變化 (%)	Total profit (mil. RMB) 總利潤（百萬元）	Rate of change 每年變化 (%)
1993	34		10,482		230		13	
1994	38	11.76%	16,627	58.62%	367	59.93%	9	-29.23%
1995	46	21.05%	18,840	13.31%	517	40.78%	-11	-224.18%
1996	43	-6.52%	17,792	-5.56%	537	3.83%	-10	12.06%

3 Major products* 3 種主要產品 *	Output 產量	Sales volume 銷售量	Unit 單位
a) Hydraulic Turbine of Power Station 電站水輪機	490,187	588,224	kw 千瓦
b) Auxiliary Machinery of Hydraulic Turbine 水輪機輔機	427	666	ton 噸
c) Water Turbine Engine Block 水輪發電機組	699,086	699,086	kw 千瓦

Top 10 firms by revenue (year founded) 收入排名前 10 家企業 (創辦年份)	City 城市	Province 省	Telephone / fax 電話 / 傳真	Number of employees 職工人數	Ownership 產業所有權	Revenue ('000 RMB) 銷售收入（千元）	Profit ('000 RMB) (rank) 利潤（千元）（排名）	Total assets ('000 RMB) 總資產（千元）	Major products 主要產品
Chongqing Water Turbine Works 重慶水輪機廠	Chongqing 重慶市	Chongqing 重慶市	(023)62850301 (023)62851810		State-owned 國有	148,891	1029(5)	341,306	b,c
Zhejiang Fu Chun Jiang Water & Electricity Equipment General Factory 浙江富春江水電設備總廠(1970)	Hangzhou 杭州市	Zhejiang 浙江省	(0571)4651111 (0571)4621950	1,815	State-owned 國有	97,981	1689(2)	219,999	c
Guangdong Kang Li General Electrical Group Co. 廣東康立通用電氣集團公司(1958)	Shaoguan 韶關市	Guangdong 廣東省	(0751)8852944 (0751)8852943	2,020	State-owned 國有	77,370	-15067(28)	427,025	c
Zhejiang Jin Lun Electromechanical Industrial Co. Ltd. Hydraulic Turbine Factory 浙江金輪機電實業有限公司水輪機廠(1958)	Jinhua 金華市	Zhejiang 浙江省	(0579)2341066 (0579)2341066	727	State-owned 國有	30,303	3383(1)	58,649	o
Zhejiang Linhai Machinery Factory 浙江省臨海機械廠(1956)	Taizhou 臺州市	Zhejiang 浙江省	(0576)5114971 (0576)5112406	548	State-owned 國有	22,847	636(7)	39,553	o
Liuzhou Hydraulic Turbine Factory 柳州市水輪機廠(1956)	Liuzhou 柳州市	Guangxi 廣西	(0772)3831271	387	State-owned 國有	10,578	-7796(27)	36,649	a,c
Sichuan Water Turbine Factory 四川水輪機廠	Chongqing 重慶市	Chongqing 重慶市	(023)7541622		State-owned 國有	8,303	1450(4)	24,749	a
Dapu Hydraulic Turbine Factory 大埔縣水輪機廠(1957)	Meizhou 梅州市	Guangdong 廣東省	(0752)5681629	176	State-owned 國有	8,262	122(16)	13,127	a
Changning Hydraulic Turbine Factory 長寧水輪機廠(1958)	Yibin 宜賓市	Sichuan 四川省	(0831)4623949 (0831)4622434	234	State-owned 國有	8,205	501(9)	8,995	a
Sichuan Renshou Water & Electricity Equipment Factory 四川省仁壽水電設備廠(1958)	Leshan 樂山市	Sichuan 四川省	(0833)6201779	510	State-owned 國有	7,883	50(19)	15,461	o

Top 10 Cities by Production Output 產出排名前 10 位城市	Province 省	Market share 市場份額	Number of firms 企業個數
Chongqing 重慶市	Chongqing 重慶市	31.26%	6
Hangzhou 杭州市	Zhejiang 浙江省	18.14%	1
Shaoguan 韶關市	Guangdong 廣東省	17.47%	2
Jinhua 金華市	Zhejiang 浙江省	5.86%	1
Taizhou 臺州市	Zhejiang 浙江省	4.41%	1
Leshan 樂山市	Sichuan 四川省	3.40%	3
Chengdu 成都市	Sichuan 四川省	2.73%	4
Nanchang 南昌市	Jiangxi 江西省	2.36%	1
Meizhou 梅州市	Guangdong 廣東省	1.45%	1
Yibin 宜賓市	Sichuan 四川省	1.31%	1

10 Major Wholesalers 10 家主要批發商	City 城市	Province 省	Telephone / Fax 電話 / 傳真
Liaoning Automobile Trade Group Corp. 遼寧省汽車貿易集團	Shenyang 瀋陽市	Liaoning 遼寧省	(024)23835494 (024)23838338
China Post and Telecommunication Equipment General Company 中國郵電器材總公司	Beijing 北京市	Beijing 北京市	(010)63523715 (010)63525935
Jiangsu Electromechanical Products General Company 江蘇省機電產品總公司	Nanjing 南京市	Jiangsu 江蘇省	(025)7713642 (025)7711036
Xi Nan Technology Import & Export Company 西南技術進出口公司	Chongqing 重慶市	Chongqing 重慶市	(023)63850185 (023)63850026
Changzhou Economic Technology Industrial Development Zone Tian Ming Trade Company 常州經濟技術產業開發區天明貿易公司	Changzhou 常州市	Jiangsu 江蘇省	(0519)8829882 (0519)8829882
Shanxi Mechanical Equipment Import & Export Company 山西省機械設備進出口公司	Taiyuan 太原市	Shanxi 山西省	(0351)4040713 (0351)4043981
Ningbo Five Mining Machinery Import & Export Company 寧波市五礦機械進出口公司	Ningbo 寧波市	Zhejiang 浙江省	(0574)7311255 (0574)7320322
Tianjin Jin Huan Electromechanical Complete Sets of Equipment Factory 天津市津環機電成套設備廠	Tianjin 天津市	Tianjin 天津市	(022)26371628
Yunnan Machinery Import & Export Company 雲南省機械進出口公司	Kunming 昆明市	Yunnan 云南省	(0871)3164879 (0871)3136829
Tianjin Da Qiu Zhuang Yi Yuan Trade Center 天津市大丘莊億源商貿中心	Tianjin 天津市	Tianjin 天津市	(022)28899478 (022)28899046

*Also include sales by firms outside this industry.包括本行業以外廠家的銷售。"o" stands for "others". "o" 代表"其他產品"。

3515: Internal Combustion Engine Parts 內燃機零部件及配件製造業

The industry accounts for 0.167% of the total revenue of China's industrial sector in 1996. The revenue growth rate of the industry is 5.3% from 1995, as compared to the growth rate of China's industrial sector, 9.51%. The rate of return on asset is 0.55%. 67.94% of all firms in the industry made a profit while 27.52% had negative returns. The top province in terms of the industry's revenue is Jiangsu, accounting for 38.20% of the total revenue.
本行業在1996年佔全行業總產值0.167%，行業年增長率為5.3%（全國工業年增長率9.51%）。行業的資產回報率0.55%，67.94%的企業盈利，27.52%的企業虧損。銷售收入最高的省份為江蘇省，佔本行業的38.20%。

	Total number of firms 企業總數	Total number of employees 職工總數	Total revenue (mil. RMB) 總銷售收入（百萬元）	Total profit (mil. RMB) 總利潤（百萬元）	Return on assets 資產利潤率 (%)	Return on equity 權益利潤率 (%)	Labour productivity ('000 RMB / worker) 勞動生產率（千元/人）	Debts / assets 資產負債率 (%)	Total assets (mil. RMB) 總資產（百萬元）
Industry Overall 行業總體	800	238,663	9,708	91	0.55	1.57	40.68	65.20	16,705

	Number of firms 企業個數	Average number of employees 平均職工人數	Average revenue ('000 RMB) 平均銷售收入（千元）	Average profit ('000 RMB) 平均利潤（千元）	Return on assets 資產利潤率 (%)	Return on equity 權益利潤率 (%)	Labour productivity ('000 RMB / worker) 勞動生產率（千元/人）	Average debts / assets 平均資產負債率(%)	Average Total assets ('000 RMB) 平均總資產（千元）
By ownership 產業所有權									
State-owned 國有	210	662	19,381	-252	-0.56	-1.80	29.28	69.08	45,290
Collectively-owned 集體	513	138	7,157	168	2.43	8.91	51.96	72.71	6,908
Privately-owned 私有	7	37	2,478	42	1.06	4.56	66.45	76.84	3,970
Domestic JVs 聯營	17	219	16,992	567	4.07	9.44	77.71	56.90	13,931
Joint stock 股份制	26	704	44,183	1,765	2.07	4.30	62.79	51.85	85,157
Foreign-funded 外資	14	386	27,250	-322	-0.43	-0.65	70.65	33.89	74,591
Overseas Chinese-funded 港澳台資	12	142	10,858	543	5.13	16.35	76.24	68.61	10,572
By size 規模									
Large 大型	21	2,247	96,132	115	0.05	0.10	42.79	55.05	252,435
Medium 中型	85	922	37,157	486	0.77	2.43	40.29	68.39	63,331
Small 小型	684	165	6,625	69	0.79	2.74	40.20	71.29	8,802
By regional distribution 地區分布									
Central-North 華北	71	410	14,100	-10	-0.03	-0.07	34.43	57.91	36,086
Beijing 北京	19	241	14,277	-532	-1.03	-1.62	59.16	36.40	51,781
Tianjin 天津	8	30	1,395	-451	-37.53	546.97	47.29	106.86	1,203
Hebei 河北	34	554	17,105	415	1.15	4.03	30.86	71.53	36,171
Shanxi 山西	8	461	10,179	-191	-0.67	-3.29	22.10	79.58	28,464
Inner Mongolia 內蒙	2	864	27,820	215	0.39	0.76	32.22	48.88	55,575
Northeast 東北	47	262	6,647	-198	-1.75	-8.00	25.38	78.08	11,300
Liaoning 遼寧	36	262	8,051	-263	-1.91	-9.12	30.69	79.02	13,724
Jilin 吉林	1	110	5,580	570	9.95	13.64	50.73	27.05	5,730
Heilongjiang 黑龍江	10	275	1,697	-44	-1.41	-5.12	6.17	72.55	3,129
Central East 華東	433	285	15,300	329	1.51	4.34	53.64	65.15	21,802
Shanghai 上海	18	246	17,596	481	2.02	2.81	71.55	28.00	23,779
Jiangsu 江蘇	162	327	22,890	608	2.31	6.83	70.11	66.16	26,292
Zhejiang 浙江	84	122	4,681	175	2.08	4.98	38.39	58.19	8,422
Anhui 安徽	35	310	8,295	-361	-2.10	-8.84	26.74	76.22	17,179
Fujian 福建	14	215	7,857	-416	-2.49	-7.17	36.51	65.32	16,714
Jiangxi 江西	26	212	3,730	-552	-6.11	-25.48	17.56	76.03	9,041
Shandong 山東	94	389	18,188	570	1.80	5.56	46.79	67.59	31,651
Central-South 中南	153	281	6,816	-214	-1.55	-5.52	24.23	71.98	13,808
Henan 河南	46	323	8,077	-123	-0.97	-4.36	25.01	77.79	12,726
Hubei 湖北	30	293	6,450	-322	-3.12	-19.00	21.99	83.55	10,317
Hunan 湖南	49	322	7,662	-212	-1.19	-3.88	23.76	69.28	17,770
Guangdong 廣東	8	106	3,795	216	1.21	2.76	35.97	56.26	17,911
Guangxi 廣西	20	137	3,599	-435	-4.27	-10.75	26.23	60.32	10,182
Hainan 海南									
Southwest 西南	81	283	7,089	-172	-0.86	-2.24	25.07	61.53	19,943
Chongqing 重慶	9	760	18,659	1,065	1.77	5.06	24.54	65.09	60,334
Sichuan 四川	57	214	6,204	-29	-0.20	-0.42	28.98	53.13	14,651
Guizhou 貴州	10	182	1,709	-194	-1.52	-9.30	9.37	83.69	12,787
Yunnan 雲南	5	379	6,380	-752	-3.92	-24.31	16.83	83.87	19,170
Tibet 西藏									
Northwest 西北	15	522	10,149	364	1.23	4.76	19.45	74.15	29,585
Shaanxi 陝西	10	477	9,597	495	1.74	6.94	20.12	74.91	28,437
Gansu 甘肅	4	585	10,625	120	0.48	1.52	18.17	68.74	25,258
Qinghai 青海	1	719	13,760	30	0.05	0.25	19.14	79.80	58,380
Ningxia 寧夏									
Xinjiang 新疆									

3515: Internal Combustion Engine Parts 內燃機零部件及配件製造業

Year 年份	Number of firms 企業個數	Rate of change 每年變化 (%)	Number of employees 職工人數 (人)	Rate of change 每年變化 (%)	Total revenue (mil. RMB) 總銷售收入 (百萬元)	Rate of change 每年變化 (%)	Total profit (mil. RMB) 總利潤 (百萬元)	Rate of change 每年變化 (%)
1993	714		241,880		7,512		350	
1994	737	3.22%	246,220	1.79%	7,485	-0.36%	124	-64.47%
1995	801	8.68%	255,050	3.59%	9,215	23.11%	117	-5.56%
1996	800	-0.12%	238,663	-6.43%	9,708	5.35%	91	-22.46%

3 Major products* 3 種主要產品 *	Output 產量	Sales volume 銷售量	Unit 單位
a) Tractor & Internal Combustion Engine Fitting Parts 拖拉機內燃機配件	4,071,005	3,786,035	1,000 yuan 千元
b) Medium & Small Farm Tools 中小農具	6,382,199	6,382,199	set 台

Top 10 firms by revenue (year founded) 收入排名前 10 家企業 (創辦年份)	City 城市	Province 省	Telephone / fax 電話 / 傳真	Number of employees 職工人數	Ownership 產業所有權	Revenue ('000 RMB) 銷售收入 (千元)	Profit ('000 RMB) (rank) 利潤 (千元) (排名)	Total assets ('000 RMB) 總資產 (千元)	Major products 主要產品
Wuxi Wei Fu Group Co. Ltd. 無錫威孚集團有限公司(1958)	Wuxi 無錫市	Jiangsu 江蘇省	(0510)2708345 (0510)2702740	3,787	Joint stock 股份制	622,576	32533(1)	954,775	o
Shijiazhuang Internal Combustion Engine Parts General Factory 石家莊內燃機配件總廠(1958)	Shijiazhuang 石家莊市	Hebei 河北省	(0311)5054061 (0311)5051008	4,751	State-owned 國有	230,155	10059(5)	536,121	o
Shandong Piston Factory 山東活塞廠(1951)	Binzhou 濱州市	Shandong 山東省	(0543)3325294 (0543)3325305	1,206	Joint stock 股份制	220,953	3581(18)	313,195	o
Beijing Tianwei Fuel Injection Equipment Inc. 北京天緯油泵油嘴股份有限公司(1994)	Beijing 北京市	Beijing 北京市	(010)63811155	3,250	Foreign-funded 外資	211,600	-6874(459)	879,792	a
Laiyang Xin Fa Group Company 萊陽市信發集團公司(1996)	Yantai 煙台市	Shandong 山東省	(0535)7213068 (0535)7213068	1,483	Collectively-owned 集體	200,535	4793(13)	94,723	o
Wujin Electric Engine Factory 武進電機廠(1959)	Changzhou 常州市	Jiangsu 江蘇省	(0519)6553373	1,086	State-owned 國有	178,710	7030(10)	103,712	o
Shanghai Pu Dong Yi Wei Fuel Spraying Co. Ltd. 上海浦東伊維燃油噴射有限公司(1995)	Shanghai 上海市	Shanghai 上海市	(021)58713907 (021)58712914	1,645	其他經濟	134,149	2631(27)	232,382	o
Dalian Fuel Injection Equipment Factory 大連油泵油嘴廠(1956)	Dalian 大連市	Liaoning 遼寧省	(0411)3634725 (0411)3634725	2,632	State-owned 國有	120,045	1606(46)	212,194	o
Nanjing Piston Ring Factory 南京活塞環廠(1958)	Nanjing 南京市	Jiangsu 江蘇省	(025)7212405 (025)7212406	2,457	State-owned 國有	109,152	2312(32)	175,063	o
Shandong Crank Shaft General Factory 山東曲軸總廠(1954)	Weihai 威海市	Shandong 山東省	(0896)8452462 (0896)8451761	2,022	State-owned 國有	102,161	12562(3)	492,482	o

Top 10 Cities by Production Output 產出排名前 10 位城市	Province 省	Market share 市場份額	Number of firms 企業個數
Changzhou 常州市	Jiangsu 江蘇省	9.54%	41
Wuxi 無錫市	Jiangsu 江蘇省	8.33%	44
Yantai 煙台市	Shandong 山東省	5.28%	27
Shanghai 上海市	Shanghai 上海市	4.97%	40
Nanjing 南京市	Jiangsu 江蘇省	4.82%	22
Shijiazhuang 石家莊市	Hebei 河北省	3.69%	14
Yancheng 鹽城市	Jiangsu 江蘇省	3.53%	31
Xinxiang 新鄉市	Henan 河南省	3.31%	9
Nantong 南通市	Jiangsu 江蘇省	3.22%	23
Weifang 濰坊市	Shandong 山東省	2.76%	26

10 Major Wholesalers 10 家主要批發商	City 城市	Province 省	Telephone / Fax 電話 / 傳真
Liaoning Automobile Trade Group Corp. 遼寧省汽車貿易集團	Shenyang 瀋陽市	Liaoning 遼寧省	(024)23835494 (024)23838338
China Post and Telecommunication Equipment General Company 中國郵電器材總公司	Beijing 北京市	Beijing 北京市	(010)63523715 (010)63525935
Jiangsu Electromechanical Products General Company 江蘇省機電產品總公司	Nanjing 南京市	Jiangsu 江蘇省	(025)7713642 (025)7711036
Xi Nan Technology Import & Export Company 西南技術進出口公司	Chongqing 重慶市	Chongqing 重慶市	(023)63850185 (023)63850026
Changzhou Economic Technology Industrial Development Zone Tian Ming Trade Company 常州經濟技術產業開發區天明貿易公司	Changzhou 常州市	Jiangsu 江蘇省	(0519)8829882 (0519)8829882
Shanxi Mechanical Equipment Import & Export Company 山西省機械設備進出口公司	Taiyuan 太原市	Shanxi 山西省	(0351)4040713 (0351)4043981
Ningbo Five Mining Machinery Import & Export Company 寧波市五礦機械進出口公司	Ningbo 寧波市	Zhejiang 浙江省	(0574)7311255 (0574)7320322
Tianjin Jin Huan Electromechanical Complete Sets of Equipment Factory 天津市津環機電成套設備廠	Tianjin 天津市	Tianjin 天津市	(022)26371628
Yunnan Machinery Import & Export Company 雲南省機械進出口公司	Kunming 昆明市	Yunnan 雲南省	(0871)3164879 (0871)3136829
Tianjin Da Qiu Zhuang Yi Yuan Trade Center 天津市大丘莊億源商貿中心	Tianjin 天津市	Tianjin 天津市	(022)28899478 (022)28899046

*Also include sales by firms outside this industry.包括本行業以外廠家的銷售。"o" stands for "others". "o" 代表"其他產品"。

3519: Other Boiler and Power Generation Equipment
其他鍋爐及原動機製造業

The industry accounts for 0.016% of the total revenue of China's industrial sector in 1996. The revenue growth rate of the industry is -2.2% from 1995, as compared to the growth rate of China's industrial sector, 9.51%. The rate of return on asset is 1.21%. 73.33% of all firms in the industry made a profit while 20.00% had negative returns. The top province in terms of the industry's revenue is Jiangsu, accounting for 23.42% of the total revenue.
本行業在1996年佔全行業總產值0.016%，行業年增長率為-2.2%（全國工業年增長率9.51%）。行業的資產回報率1.21%，73.33%的企業盈利，20.00%的企業虧損。銷售收入最高的省份為江蘇省，佔本行業的23.42%。

	Total number of firms 企業總數	Total number of employees 職工總數	Total revenue (Mil. RMB) 總銷售收入（百萬元）	Total profit (Mil. RMB) 總利潤（百萬元）	Return on assets 資產利潤率 (%)	Return on equity 權益利潤率 (%)	Labour productivity ('000 RMB / worker) 勞動生產率（千元/人）	Debts / assets 資產負債率 (%)	Total assets (Mil. RMB) 總資產（百萬元）
Industry Overall 行業總體	215	20,258	948	19	1.21	3.72	46.80	67.55	1,565

	Number of firms 企業個數	Average number of employees 平均職工人數	Average revenue ('000 RMB) 平均銷售收入（千元）	Average profit ('000 RMB) 平均利潤（千元）	Return on assets 資產利潤率 (%)	Return on equity 權益利潤率 (%)	Labour productivity ('000 RMB / worker) 勞動生產率（千元/人）	Average debts / assets 平均資產負債率(%)	Average Total assets ('000 RMB) 平均總資產（千元）
By ownership 產業所有權									
State-owned 國有	19	174	10,526				60.40	69.47	20,000
Collectively-owned 集體	178	79	3,012	45	1.06	3.15	37.99	66.50	4,283
Privately-owned 私有	5	115	4,847	742	4.34	13.64	42.30	68.16	17,080
Domestic JVs 聯營	2	36	2,036	95	1.75	3.50	56.56	49.83	5,431
Joint stock 股份制	4	497	38,047	923	1.28	4.37	76.52	70.76	72,156
Foreign-funded 外資	2	49	9,597	1,340	11.17	23.80	195.85	53.08	12,001
Overseas Chinese-funded 港澳台資	4	26	3,041	169	4.71	7.93	116.96	40.63	3,592
By size 規模									
Large 大型	2	1,676	142,156	-2,399	-0.87	-3.12	84.82	71.99	274,528
Medium 中型	1	475	31,801	2,357	5.42	9.62	66.95	43.68	43,479
Small 小型	211	78	2,995	102	2.20	6.50	38.46	66.09	4,612
By regional distribution 地區分布									
Central-North 華北	46	64	3,009	112	2.38	6.54	46.86	63.66	4,702
Beijing 北京	12	84	4,361	107	1.20	2.32	51.97	48.26	8,888
Tianjin 天津	3	15	4,733	730	55.30	168.46	315.56	67.17	1,320
Hebei 河北	18	57	1,589	85	3.32	22.08	27.91	84.98	2,563
Shanxi 山西	7	105	5,383	-17	-0.23	-0.97	51.13	76.27	7,447
Inner Mongolia 內蒙	6	23	935	43	3.49	9.19	40.07	61.96	1,240
Northeast 東北	47	63	1,820	42	1.42	4.53	28.97	68.64	2,980
Liaoning 遼寧	22	97	2,030	26	0.61	1.91	20.86	67.98	4,306
Jilin 吉林	13	28	2,351	98	5.27	11.00	84.19	52.06	1,868
Heilongjiang 黑龍江	12	37	861	11	0.62	6.67	23.01	90.73	1,753
Central East 華東	41	169	9,506	345	2.44	8.56	56.19	71.46	14,134
Shanghai 上海	2	133	11,435	1,760	15.06	38.55	85.98	60.93	11,685
Jiangsu 江蘇	11	300	20,181	443	1.22	4.12	67.17	70.32	36,182
Zhejiang 浙江	5	59	2,294	36	1.05	4.64	38.62	77.45	3,442
Anhui 安徽	5	149	3,412	-196	-3.52	-15.24	22.84	76.92	5,572
Fujian 福建	1								
Jiangxi 江西	4	48	2,333	53	2.07	6.69	48.85	69.00	2,533
Shandong 山東	13	164	8,234	489	6.18	25.76	50.25	76.02	7,918
Central-South 中南	37	41	1,541	39	1.99	5.46	37.19	63.66	1,988
Henan 河南	12	30	1,514	17	1.10	3.13	51.18	64.72	1,512
Hubei 湖北	6	61	2,140	172	4.55	10.98	35.27	58.57	3,773
Hunan 湖南	8	46	736	-3	-0.18	-0.71	16.14	74.38	1,371
Guangdong 廣東	7	46	2,336	27	1.09	2.56	50.78	57.45	2,484
Guangxi 廣西	4	32	940	15	1.36	8.11	29.61	83.22	1,103
Hainan 海南									
Southwest 西南	16	125	3,654	-330	-4.00	-8.66	29.19	53.81	8,253
Chongqing 重慶	1	32	1,581	375	25.18	35.17	49.88	28.40	1,491
Sichuan 四川	12	157	4,612	-466	-4.43	-9.68	29.31	54.24	10,522
Guizhou 貴州	2	6	200	25	22.73	125.00	33.33	81.82	110
Yunnan 雲南	1	49	730				14.90	44.25	2,870
Tibet 西藏									
Northwest 西北	28	139	7,822	51	0.34	1.08	56.46	68.79	15,120
Shaanxi 陝西	17	106	1,716	20	0.43	1.87	16.23	77.10	4,675
Gansu 甘肅	4	443	44,385	165	0.20	0.61	100.19	66.68	81,560
Qinghai 青海									
Ningxia 寧夏	3	69	3,017	127	2.44	9.00	43.72	72.91	5,193
Xinjiang 新疆	4	26	810	13	2.43	5.00	31.76	51.46	515

3519: Other Boiler and Power Generation Equipment
其他鍋爐及原動機製造業

Year 年份	Number of firms 企業個數	Rate of change 每年變化 (%)	Number of employees 職工人數 (人)	Rate of change 每年變化 (%)	Total revenue (Mil. RMB) 總銷售收入 (百萬元)	Rate of change 每年變化 (%)	Total profit (Mil. RMB) 總利潤 (百萬元)	Rate of change 每年變化 (%)
1993	195		17,714		558		33	
1994	210	7.69%	17,300	-2.34%	420	-24.71%	8	-77.08%
1995	235	11.90%	23,451	35.55%	969	130.59%	25	233.48%
1996	215	-8.51%	20,258	-13.62%	948	-2.17%	19	-24.12%

3 Major products* 3 種主要產品 *	Output 產量	Sales volume 銷售量	Unit 單位
a) Hot Water Boiler 熱水鍋爐	4,108	3,492	ton 蒸噸
b) Steam Boiler 蒸氣鍋爐	143	116	ton 蒸噸

Top 10 firms by revenue (year founded) 收入排名前 10 家企業 (創辦年份)	City 城市	Province 省	Telephone / fax 電話 / 傳真	Number of employees 職工人數	Ownership 產業所有權	Revenue ('000 RMB) 銷售收入 (千元)	Profit ('000 RMB) (rank) 利潤 (千元) (排名)	Total assets ('000 RMB) 總資產 (千元)	Major products 主要產品
Lanzhou Electric Power Equipment Manufacturer Plant 蘭州電力修造廠(1966)	Lanzhou 蘭州市	Gansu 甘肅省	(0931)2334626 (0931)2310639	1,747	State-owned 國有	170,316	39(42)	311,920	o
Wuxi Power Engineering Co. Ltd. 無錫動力工程股份有限公司(1929)	Wuxi 無錫市	Jiangsu 江蘇省	(0510)5752020 (0510)5759070	1,788	Joint stock 股份制	116,493	1066(8)	278,000	o
Zhucheng Agricultural Machinery Factory 諸城市農業機械廠(1970)	Weifang 濰坊市	Shandong 山東省	(0536)6011088 (0536)6011098	469	Joint stock 股份制	31,855	972(9)	17,678	o
Xi Shan Shi Heating Furnace Manufacture Factory 錫山市加熱爐製造廠(1985)	Wuxi 無錫市	Jiangsu 江蘇省	(0510)5601017 (0510)5601017	365	Collectively-owned 集體	29,307	1955(4)	24,595	o
Huantai Energy-saving Equipment Factory 桓台縣環保節能設備廠(1978)	Zibo 淄博市	Shandong 山東省	(0533)8530367	50	Collectively-owned 集體	27,880	1850(5)	5,220	o
Yangzhou Xing Guang Generate Electricity Equipment Factory 揚州市星光發電設備廠(1973)	Yangzhou 揚州市	Jiangsu 江蘇省	(0514)7791002	105	Collectively-owned 集體	27,859	860(11)	22,888	o
Beijing Chaoyang Boiler Factory 北京朝陽鍋爐廠(1976)	Beijing 北京市	Beijing 北京市	(010)67639152 (010)67639150	89	Collectively-owned 集體	21,597	703(14)	44,640	a
Yan Bian Qing Dong Boiler Co. Ltd. 延邊慶東鍋爐有限公司(1993)	Yanji 延吉市	Jilin 吉林省	(0433)2653177 (0433)2653578	17	Foreign-funded 外資	21,200	-10(59)	9,870	o
Shanghai Meilian Industrial Gasequipment Co. Ltd. 上海美聯工業燃氣設備有限公司(1992)	Shanghai 上海市	Shanghai 上海市	(021)63545789 (021)63545999	80	Foreign-funded 外資	19,743	3520(1)	19,438	o
Xi Shan Shi Luo She Zhen Society Cause Development Company Stripe Factory 錫山市洛社鎮社會事業發展公司條線廠(1980)	Wuxi 無錫市	Jiangsu 江蘇省	(0510)3313849	667	Collectively-owned 集體	19,170	1080(6)	44,000	o

Top 10 Cities by Production Output 產出排名前 10 位城市	Province 省	Market share 市場份額	Number of firms 企業個數
Lanzhou 蘭州市	Gansu 甘肅省	17.45%	9
Wuxi 無錫市	Jiangsu 江蘇省	16.40%	8
Shanghai 上海市	Shanghai 上海市	8.33%	22
Xuzhou 徐州市	Jiangsu 江蘇省	8.02%	3
Ji'nan 濟南市	Shandong 山東省	4.67%	9
Beijing 北京市	Beijing 北京市	4.20%	11
Zibo 淄博市	Shandong 山東省	3.30%	6
Leshan 樂山市	Sichuan 四川省	3.07%	5
Weifang 濰坊市	Shandong 山東省	3.00%	3
Taizhou 泰州市	Jiangsu 江蘇省	2.25%	3

10 Major Wholesalers 10 家主要批發商	City 城市	Province 省	Telephone / Fax 電話 / 傳真
Liaoning Automobile Trade Group Corp. 遼寧省汽車貿易集團	Shenyang 沈陽市	Liaoning 遼寧省	(024)23835494 (024)23838338
China Post and Telecommunication Equipment General Company 中國郵電器材總公司	Beijing 北京市	Beijing 北京市	(010)63523715 (010)63525935
Jiangsu Electromechanical Products General Company 江蘇省機電產品總公司	Nanjing 南京市	Jiangsu 江蘇省	(025)7713642 (025)7711036
Xi Nan Technology Import & Export Company 西南技術進出口公司	Chongqing 重慶市	Chongqing 重慶市	(023)63850185 (023)63850026
Changzhou Economic Technology Industrial Development Zone Tian Ming Trade Company 常州經濟技術產業開發區天明貿易公司	Changzhou 常州市	Jiangsu 江蘇省	(0519)8829882 (0519)8829882
Shanxi Mechanical Equipment Import & Export Company 山西省機械設備進出口公司	Taiyuan 太原市	Shanxi 山西省	(0351)4040713 (0351)4043981
Ningbo Five Mining Machinery Import & Export Company 寧波市五礦機械進出口公司	Ningbo 寧波市	Zhejiang 浙江省	(0574)7311255 (0574)7320322
Tianjin Jin Huan Electromechanical Complete Sets of Equipment Factory 天津市津環機電成套設備廠	Tianjin 天津市	Tianjin 天津市	(022)26371628
Yunnan Machinery Import & Export Company 雲南省機械進出口公司	Kunming 昆明市	Yunnan 雲南省	(0871)3164879 (0871)3136829
Tianjin Da Qiu Zhuang Yi Yuan Trade Center 天津市大丘莊億源商貿中心	Tianjin 天津市	Tianjin 天津市	(022)28899478 (022)28899046

*Also include sales by firms outside this industry.包括本行業以外廠家的銷售。"o" stands for "others". "o" 代表"其他產品"。

3521: Metal Cutting Machine Tools 金屬切削切床製造業

The industry accounts for 0.167% of the total revenue of China's industrial sector in 1996. The revenue growth rate of the industry is -0.4% from 1995, as compared to the growth rate of China's industrial sector, 9.51%. The rate of return on asset is -1.25%. 59.43% of all firms in the industry made a profit while 34.95% had negative returns. The top province in terms of the industry's revenue is Jiangsu, accounting for 18.32% of the total revenue.
本行業在1996年佔全行業總產值0.167%，行業年增長率為-0.4%（全國工業年增長率9.51%）。行業的資產回報率-1.25%，59.43%的企業盈利，34.95%的企業虧損。銷售收入最高的省份為江蘇省，佔本行業的18.32%。

	Total number of firms 企業總數	Total number of employees 職工總數	Total revenue (Mil. RMB) 總銷售收入（百萬元）	Total profit (Mil. RMB) 總利潤（百萬元）	Return on assets 資產利潤率 (%)	Return on equity 權益利潤率 (%)	Labour productivity ('000 RMB / worker) 勞動生產率（千元/人）	Debts / assets 資產負債率 (%)	Total assets (Mil. RMB) 總資產（百萬元）
Industry Overall 行業總體	705	385,195	9,706	-421	-1.25	-3.91	25.20	67.95	33,599

	Number of firms 企業個數	Average number of employees 平均職工人數	Average revenue ('000 RMB) 平均銷售收入（千元）	Average profit ('000 RMB) 平均利潤（千元）	Return on assets 資產利潤率 (%)	Return on equity 權益利潤率 (%)	Labour productivity ('000 RMB / worker) 勞動生產率（千元/人）	Average debts / assets 平均資產負債率(%)	Average Total assets ('000 RMB) 平均總資產（千元）
By ownership 產業所有權									
State-owned 國有	280	994	21,896	-1,821	-2.14	-7.75	22.02	72.40	85,161
Collectively-owned 集體	336	127	4,232	50	0.72	2.08	33.26	65.30	6,960
Privately-owned 私有	4	33	1,495	69	5.67	12.65	45.65	55.17	1,216
Domestic JVs 聯營	22	191	6,280	80	0.78	1.45	32.96	46.07	10,187
Joint stock 股份制	18	2,898	87,289	4,100	1.23	2.75	30.13	55.18	332,771
Foreign-funded 外資	21	112	11,371	-369	-1.20	-2.50	101.65	52.15	30,896
Overseas Chinese-funded 港澳台資	24	222	8,292	168	0.73	1.56	37.36	53.04	22,832
By size 規模									
Large 大型	63	3,137	81,422	-3,507	-1.07	-3.38	25.95	68.47	329,185
Medium 中型	108	927	20,269	-1,589	-2.25	-7.53	21.86	70.14	70,719
Small 小型	529	166	4,513	-54	-0.54	-1.46	27.27	62.67	9,873
By regional distribution 地區分布									
Central-North 華北	125	331	7,441	-446	-1.54	-3.92	22.46	60.66	28,955
Beijing 北京	42	292	9,144	85	0.23	0.46	31.33	51.12	37,653
Tianjin 天津	39	307	4,226	-952	-3.90	-9.52	13.79	59.05	24,409
Hebei 河北	26	452	11,787	-608	-2.00	-10.88	26.09	81.59	30,351
Shanxi 山西	12	237	3,521	-278	-1.90	-4.67	14.85	59.20	14,570
Inner Mongolia 內蒙	6	436	5,433	-525	-2.58	-7.09	12.46	63.55	20,333
Northeast 東北	91	742	16,834	-1,112	-1.34	-4.15	22.68	67.80	83,173
Liaoning 遼寧	64	634	19,810	-233	-0.27	-0.69	31.26	61.37	87,849
Jilin 吉林	11	359	2,765	406	1.41	5.45	7.71	74.13	28,842
Heilongjiang 黑龍江	16	1,440	14,598	-5,669	-5.57	-49.47	10.14	88.75	101,820
Central East 華東	303	401	14,350	-42	-0.12	-0.43	35.75	73.00	36,439
Shanghai 上海	48	376	12,674	-11	-0.02	-0.21	33.72	89.51	50,023
Jiangsu 江蘇	76	535	23,392	-200	-0.40	-1.22	43.72	66.88	49,464
Zhejiang 浙江	64	205	8,319	-179	-1.00	-2.76	40.63	63.86	17,931
Anhui 安徽	15	583	15,771	-179	-0.42	-1.26	27.04	66.87	42,951
Fujian 福建	23	222	4,150	-466	-3.72	-9.80	18.72	62.03	12,530
Jiangxi 江西	21	489	6,665	243	1.06	3.14	13.64	66.21	22,878
Shandong 山東	56	459	17,099	403	0.97	3.87	37.26	74.84	41,429
Central-South 中南	122	497	11,196	-755	-1.82	-5.16	22.55	64.72	41,457
Henan 河南	34	357	12,528	157	0.66	2.40	35.07	72.58	23,945
Hubei 湖北	28	998	18,358	-1,535	-1.74	-4.32	18.40	59.64	88,034
Hunan 湖南	22	381	5,918	-1,023	-3.78	-8.40	15.51	55.05	27,086
Guangdong 廣東	25	253	7,239	-385	-1.48	-7.57	28.60	80.50	26,069
Guangxi 廣西	12	471	9,557	-1,867	-4.23	-13.19	20.27	67.91	44,103
Hainan 海南	1	124	140	10	0.55	0.60	1.13	7.18	1,810
Southwest 西南	36	1,634	22,189	-1,137	-1.28	-2.85	13.58	55.26	89,069
Chongqing 重慶	8	2,642	25,361	1,452	1.98	5.24	9.60	62.13	73,198
Sichuan 四川	14	1,484	11,108	248	0.42	1.10	7.49	61.46	58,812
Guizhou 貴州	7	879	18,880	-2,389	-3.41	-17.97	21.48	81.03	70,056
Yunnan 雲南	7	1,538	44,034	-1,303	-0.70	-1.14	28.63	38.62	186,739
Tibet 西藏									
Northwest 西北	28	1,258	26,129	-4,201	-3.79	-16.62	20.78	77.22	110,919
Shaanxi 陝西	17	1,037	26,238	-1,256	-1.37	-5.60	25.29	75.57	91,786
Gansu 甘肅	3	1,293	24,673	-2,337	-2.31	-5.50	19.08	57.98	101,003
Qinghai 青海	4	2,090	27,330	-12,635	-6.92	-35.59	13.08	80.57	182,673
Ningxia 寧夏	3	1,620	27,137	-13,330	-9.00	-200.95	16.75	95.53	148,160
Xinjiang 新疆	1	477	20,810	1,260	1.88	3.38	43.63	44.55	67,190

3521: Metal Cutting Machine Tools 金屬切削切床製造業

Year 年份	Number of firms 企業個數	Rate of change 每年變化 (%)	Number of employees 職工人數 (人)	Rate of change 每年變化 (%)	Total revenue (Mil. RMB) 總銷售收入 (百萬元)	Rate of change 每年變化 (%)	Total profit (Mil. RMB) 總利潤 (百萬元)	Rate of change 每年變化 (%)
1993	617		435,341		13,040		849	
1994	667	8.10%	380,252	-12.66%	10,498	-19.49%	205	-75.86%
1995	600	-10.05%	368,754	-3.02%	9,749	-7.14%	-260	-226.76%
1996	705	17.50%	385,195	4.46%	9,706	-0.44%	-421	-62.06%

3 Major products* 3 種主要產品 *	Output 產量	Sales volume 銷售量	Unit 單位
a) Lathe 車床	74,443	64,021	set 台
b) Drill Bench 鑽床	17,336	16,469	set 台
c) Grinding Machine 磨床	11,010	10,900	set 台

Top 10 firms by revenue (year founded) 收入排名前 10 家企業 (創辦年份)	City 城市	Province 省	Telephone / fax 電話 / 傳真	Number of employees 職工人數	Ownership 產業所有權	Revenue ('000 RMB) 銷售收入 (千元)	Profit ('000 RMB) (rank) 利潤 (千元) (排名)	Total assets ('000 RMB) 總資產 (千元)	Major products 主要產品
Shenyang Machine Tool Co. Ltd. 沈陽機床股份有限公司(1993)	Shenyang 沈陽市	Liaoning 遼寧省	(024)24855106 (024)24849585	15,907	Joint stock 股份制	518,871	15781(2)	3,138,625	a,b,c
Wuxi Machine Tool Co. Ltd. 無錫機床股份有限公司(1948)	Wuxi 無錫市	Jiangsu 江蘇省	(0510)5802978 (0510)5807314	5,007	Joint stock 股份制	370,056	7253(6)	695,987	c
Dalian Machine Tool Works 大連機床集團有限公司(1948)	Dalian 大連市	Liaoning 遼寧省	(0411)3631851 (0411)3631305	8,898	State-owned 國有	360,495	90(158)	1,323,276	a
Nanjing No.2 Machine Tool Works 南京第二機床廠(1949)	Nanjing 南京市	Jiangsu 江蘇省	(025)6624291 (025)2202439	3,723	State-owned 國有	194,741	7007(7)	375,306	a,b,c
Beijing No.1 Machine Tool Factory 北京第一機床廠(1921)	Beijing 北京市	Beijing 北京市	(010)65023765 (010)65023715	5,837	State-owned 國有	186,423	5104(13)	818,567	a
Shanghai Machine Tool Factory Co. Ltd. 上海機床廠有限公司(1946)	Shanghai 上海市	Shanghai 上海市	(021)65483003 (021)65426752	4,299	State-owned 國有	170,006	-8994(390)	734,432	c
Hubei Shen Dian Automobile Electric Machinery Co. Ltd. 湖北神電汽車電機股份有限公司(1992)	Jingsha 荊沙市	Hubei 湖北省	(0716)8248769 (0716)8216952	2,447	Joint stock 股份制	161,718	21351(1)	349,778	o
Yunnan Machine Tool Factory 雲南機床廠(1956)	Kunming 昆明市	Yunnan 雲南省	(0871)3169093 (0871)3134670	3,098	State-owned 國有	156,012	251(109)	300,408	a
Weihai Qiquan Woodwork Machinery Group Co. Ltd. 威海市木工機械廠(1956)	Weihai 威海市	Shandong 山東省	(0896)5341019 (0896)5341047	2,498	Collectively-owned 集體	152,384	5215(12)	226,670	a,b
Nantong Machine Tool Co. Ltd. (group) 南通機床股份有限公司(集團)(1956)	Nantong 南通市	Jiangsu 江蘇省	(0513)5516141 (0513)5512271	4,717	Joint stock 股份制	148,074	0(272)	503,440	a,c

Top 10 Cities by Production Output 產出排名前 10 位城市	Province 省	Market share 市場份額	Number of firms 企業個數
Shenyang 沈陽市	Liaoning 遼寧省	7.59%	35
Shanghai 上海市	Shanghai 上海市	7.23%	93
Dalian 大連市	Liaoning 遼寧省	5.63%	24
Beijing 北京市	Beijing 北京市	5.22%	38
Wuxi 無錫市	Jiangsu 江蘇省	3.42%	19
Nanjing 南京市	Jiangsu 江蘇省	3.12%	13
Kunming 昆明市	Yunnan 雲南省	3.02%	12
Qiqiha'er 齊齊哈爾市	Heilongjin 黑龍江省	2.96%	8
Weihai 威海市	Shandong 山東省	2.73%	10
Xinxiang 新鄉市	Henan 河南省	2.73%	6

10 Major Wholesalers 10 家主要批發商	City 城市	Province 省	Telephone / Fax 電話 / 傳真
Liaoning Automobile Trade Group Corp. 遼寧省汽車貿易集團	Shenyang 沈陽市	Liaoning 遼寧省	(024)23835494 (024)23838338
China Post and Telecommunication Equipment General Company 中國郵電器材總公司	Beijing 北京市	Beijing 北京市	(010)63523715 (010)63525935
Jiangsu Electromechanical Products General Company 江蘇省機電產品總公司	Nanjing 南京市	Jiangsu 江蘇省	(025)7713642 (025)7711036
Xi Nan Technology Import & Export Company 西南技術進出口公司	Chongqing 重慶市	Chongqing 重慶市	(023)63850185 (023)63850026
Changzhou Economic Technology Industrial Development Zone Tian Ming Trade Company 常州經濟技術產業開發區天明貿易公司	Changzhou 常州市	Jiangsu 江蘇省	(0519)8829882 (0519)8829882
Shanxi Mechanical Equipment Import & Export Company 山西省機械設備進出口公司	Taiyuan 太原市	Shanxi 山西省	(0351)4040713 (0351)4043981
Ningbo Five Mining Machinery Import & Export Company 寧波市五礦機械進出口公司	Ningbo 寧波市	Zhejiang 浙江省	(0574)7311255 (0574)7320322
Tianjin Jin Huan Electromechanical Complete Sets of Equipment Factory 天津市津環機電成套設備廠	Tianjin 天津市	Tianjin 天津市	(022)26371628
Yunnan Machinery Import & Export Company 雲南省機械進出口公司	Kunming 昆明市	Yunnan 雲南省	(0871)3164879 (0871)3136829
Tianjin Da Qiu Zhuang Yi Yuan Trade Center 天津市大丘莊億源商貿中心	Tianjin 天津市	Tianjin 天津市	(022)28899478 (022)28899046

*Also include sales by firms outside this industry.包括本行業以外廠家的銷售。"o" stands for "others". "o" 代表"其他產品"。

3523: Forging and Pressing Equipment 鍛壓設備製造業

The industry accounts for 0.074% of the total revenue of China's industrial sector in 1996. The revenue growth rate of the industry is -5.4% from 1995, as compared to the growth rate of China's industrial sector, 9.51%. The rate of return on asset is -0.02%. 59.25% of all firms in the industry made a profit while 35.47% had negative returns. The top province in terms of the industry's revenue is Jiangsu, accounting for 29.41% of the total revenue.
本行業在 1996 年佔全行業總產值 0.074%，行業年增長率為 -5.4%（全國工業年增長率 9.51%）。行業的資產回報率 -0.02%，59.25% 的企業盈利，35.47% 的企業虧損。銷售收入最高的省份為江蘇省，佔本行業的 29.41%。

	Total number of firms 企業總數	Total number of employees 職工總數	Total revenue (Mil. RMB) 總銷售收入（百萬元）	Total profit (Mil. RMB) 總利潤（百萬元）	Return on assets 資產利潤率 (%)	Return on equity 權益利潤率 (%)	Labour productivity ('000 RMB / worker) 勞動生產率（千元/人）	Debts / assets 資產負債率 (%)	Total assets (Mil. RMB) 總資產（百萬元）
Industry Overall 行業總體	408	113,760	4,299	-2	-0.02	-0.08	37.79	69.18	8,946

	Number of firms 企業個數	Average number of employees 平均職工人數	Average revenue ('000 RMB) 平均銷售收入（千元）	Average profit ('000 RMB) 平均利潤（千元）	Return on assets 資產利潤率 (%)	Return on equity 權益利潤率 (%)	Labour productivity ('000 RMB / worker) 勞動生產率（千元/人）	Average debts / assets 平均資產負債率(%)	Average Total assets ('000 RMB) 平均總資產（千元）
By ownership 產業所有權									
State-owned 國有	84	709	22,750	-202	-0.32	-1.01	32.07	68.65	64,143
Collectively-owned 集體	269	152	6,619	44	0.54	2.15	43.62	74.83	8,130
Privately-owned 私有	2	30	5,168	75	0.47	1.78	172.28	73.57	15,809
Domestic JVs 聯營	8	495	15,045	15	0.05	0.12	30.40	60.43	33,146
Joint stock 股份制	16	458	17,335	142	0.42	2.06	37.89	79.80	34,216
Foreign-funded 外資	11	161	4,377	48	0.37	0.58	27.23	36.23	12,947
Overseas Chinese-funded 港澳台資	18	118	8,433	4	0.02	0.04	71.64	47.22	21,369
By size 規模									
Large 大型	7	2,372	111,746	-128	-0.04	-0.13	47.11	67.40	312,417
Medium 中型	51	833	30,016	-8	-0.01	-0.04	36.02	72.65	69,172
Small 小型	343	160	5,791	-2	-0.02	-0.07	36.20	66.60	9,421
By regional distribution 地區分布									
Central-North 華北	48	270	9,018	-87	-0.45	-1.41	33.43	68.51	19,607
Beijing 北京	6	15	1,343	23	0.58	1.08	87.61	46.57	4,030
Tianjin 天津	11	330	17,674	-891	-2.96	-7.91	53.53	62.54	30,062
Hebei 河北	18	201	8,102	323	2.38	10.16	40.41	76.58	13,558
Shanxi 山西	9	536	7,884	-64	-0.21	-0.65	14.72	67.85	30,873
Inner Mongolia 內蒙	4	199	3,395	60	0.37	1.84	17.06	79.73	16,093
Northeast 東北	63	197	3,841	-247	-2.23	-10.33	19.54	78.40	11,093
Liaoning 遼寧	51	165	3,874	-142	-1.37	-5.13	23.43	73.35	10,368
Jilin 吉林	3	299	3,440	-213	-1.08	-8.30	11.52	86.96	19,687
Heilongjiang 黑龍江	9	339	3,788	-858	-6.95	-328.51	11.16	97.88	12,334
Central East 華東	192	301	14,543	256	0.98	3.01	48.37	67.52	26,147
Shanghai 上海	22	331	17,523	-180	-0.45	-2.24	52.92	79.96	39,955
Jiangsu 江蘇	76	302	16,638	146	0.70	2.26	55.09	69.18	20,884
Zhejiang 浙江	37	172	8,914	394	2.66	6.09	51.96	56.30	14,821
Anhui 安徽	11	325	13,828	513	2.13	5.79	42.58	63.21	24,089
Fujian 福建	4	236	6,950	15	0.12	0.27	29.48	56.34	12,798
Jiangxi 江西	5	358	3,906	-216	-1.59	-5.20	10.92	69.42	13,578
Shandong 山東	37	401	16,566	616	1.41	3.90	41.33	63.94	43,829
Central-South 中南	75	271	8,723	-55	-0.24	-0.78	32.17	68.80	22,545
Henan 河南	20	227	3,993	56	0.67	3.05	17.58	77.99	8,256
Hubei 湖北	12	686	22,635	264	0.48	1.38	33.01	65.24	55,229
Hunan 湖南	11	245	4,875	-261	-1.95	-3.98	19.90	50.98	13,387
Guangdong 廣東	26	120	7,931	-120	-0.52	-2.36	66.37	77.84	22,883
Guangxi 廣西	6	295	7,157	-398	-1.98	-4.20	24.29	52.96	20,138
Hainan 海南									
Southwest 西南	21	319	5,126	-429	-3.01	-9.73	16.08	69.06	14,239
Chongqing 重慶	6	206	3,652	-167	-3.07	-12.04	17.76	74.47	5,421
Sichuan 四川	11	402	5,771	-677	-3.79	-10.45	14.35	63.72	17,875
Guizhou 貴州	3	242	4,480	-203	-1.39	-7.36	18.51	81.17	14,677
Yunnan 雲南	1	316	8,980	20	0.07	0.40	28.42	81.52	26,730
Tibet 西藏									
Northwest 西北	9	408	7,799	-2,050	-6.23	-30.95	19.11	79.87	32,909
Shaanxi 陝西	7	332	3,509	-2,637	-15.86	404.82	10.58	103.92	16,631
Gansu 甘肅	2	676	22,815	5	0.01	0.02	33.77	64.30	89,880
Qinghai 青海									
Ningxia 寧夏									
Xinjiang 新疆									

3523: Forging and Pressing Equipment 鍛壓設備製造業

Year 年份	Number of firms 企業個數	Rate of change 每年變化 (%)	Number of employees 職工人數（人）	Rate of change 每年變化 (%)	Total revenue (Mil. RMB) 總銷售收入（百萬元）	Rate of change 每年變化 (%)	Total profit (Mil. RMB) 總利潤（百萬元）	Rate of change 每年變化 (%)
1993	357		137,952		4,877		316	
1994	396	10.92%	118,393	-14.18%	4,266	-12.53%	112	-64.74%
1995	400	1.01%	120,277	1.59%	4,543	6.50%	89	-19.88%
1996	408	2.00%	113,760	-5.42%	4,299	-5.37%	-2	-102.24%

3 Major products* 3種主要產品*	Output 產量	Sales volume 銷售量	Unit 單位
a) Heavy Metal Forming Machinery 重型鍛壓機械	5,160	4,592	set 台
b) Heavy Duty Machine Tool 重型機床	48	71	set 台

Top 10 firms by revenue (year founded) 收入排名前10家企業（創辦年份）	City 城市	Province 省	Telephone / fax 電話 / 傳真	Number of employees 職工人數	Ownership 產業所有權	Revenue ('000 RMB) 銷售收入（千元）	Profit ('000 RMB) (rank) 利潤（千元）（排名）	Total assets ('000 RMB) 總資產（千元）	Major products 主要產品
Ji'nan No.2 Machine Tool Works 濟南第二機床廠(1937)	Ji'nan 濟南市	Shandong 山東省	(0531)7963311 (0531)7961014	6,328	State-owned 國有	286,771	12736(1)	994,065	a,b
Nanjing Jiangning Forging and Pressing Machine Tool General Factory 南京江寧鍛壓機床總廠(1975)	Nanjing 南京市	Jiangsu 江蘇省	(025)4165968 (025)4165989	425	Collectively-owned 集體	126,678	5633(4)	39,457	o
Nanjing Jiangning Machine Tool General Factory 南京江寧機床總廠(1969)	Nanjing 南京市	Jiangsu 江蘇省	(025)4165518 (025)4165888	354	Collectively-owned 集體	121,895	1227(28)	35,043	o
Tianjin Metal Forming Machine Tool General Works 天津市鍛壓機床總廠(1940)	Tianjin 天津市	Tianjin 天津市	(022)26352413 (022)26271454	2,344	State-owned 國有	105,817	0(162)	223,247	a
Yangzhou No.2 Metal Forming Machine Tool Works 揚州第二鍛壓機床廠(1966)	Yangzhou 揚州市	Jiangsu 江蘇省	(0514)7461251 (0514)7461090	960	Collectively-owned 集體	94,040	4328(6)	72,121	a
Huzhou Shuang Li Group Co. Ltd. 湖州市雙力集團有限公司(1954)	Huzhou 湖州市	Zhejiang 浙江省	(0572)2024561 (0572)2023920	883	State-owned 國有	90,507	6012(3)	134,365	a
Shanghai Metal Forming Machine Tool Works 上海鍛壓機床廠(1924)	Shanghai 上海市	Shanghai 上海市	(021)56034809 (021)56033433	1,288	State-owned 國有	82,005	200(87)	252,488	a
Nantong Electron Spacial Equipment Factory 南通電子專用設備廠(1956)	Nantong 南通市	Jiangsu 江蘇省	(0513)8571069 (0513)8571176	722	Collectively-owned 集體	81,761	8034(2)	68,292	a
Hefei Metal Forming Machine Tool Co. Ltd. 合肥鍛壓機床股份有限公司(1951)	Hefei 合肥市	Anhui 安徽省	(0551)5134522 (0551)5133652	2,223	State-owned 國有	80,955	1716(22)	196,648	a
Huangshi Forging and Pressing Machine Tool Group Company 黃石鍛壓機床集團公司(1958)	Huangshi 黃石市	Hubei 湖北省	(0714)6225992 (0714)6223212	1,399	Domestic JVs 聯營	79,679	3005(10)	150,741	a

Top 10 Cities by Production Output 產出排名前10位城市	Province 省	Market share 市場份額	Number of firms 企業個數
Shanghai 上海市	Shanghai 上海市	13.26%	41
Yangzhou 揚州市	Jiangsu 江蘇省	7.23%	15
Ji'nan 濟南市	Shandong 山東省	6.90%	5
Wuxi 無錫市	Jiangsu 江蘇省	6.14%	15
Nantong 南通市	Jiangsu 江蘇省	5.73%	22
Tianjin 天津市	Tianjin 天津市	5.05%	16
Xuzhou 徐州市	Jiangsu 江蘇省	3.97%	4
Nanjing 南京市	Jiangsu 江蘇省	3.92%	18
Foshan 佛山市	Guangdong 廣東省	3.08%	11
Huangshi 黃石市	Hubei 湖北省	2.34%	2

10 Major Wholesalers 10家主要批發商	City 城市	Province 省	Telephone / Fax 電話 / 傳真
Liaoning Automobile Trade Group Corp. 遼寧省汽車貿易集團	Shenyang 沈陽市	Liaoning 遼寧省	(024)23835494 (024)23838338
China Post and Telecommunication Equipment General Company 中國郵電器材總公司	Beijing 北京市	Beijing 北京市	(010)63523715 (010)63525935
Jiangsu Electromechanical Products General Company 江蘇省機電產品總公司	Nanjing 南京市	Jiangsu 江蘇省	(025)7713642 (025)7711036
Xi Nan Technology Import & Export Company 西南技術進出口公司	Chongqing 重慶市	Chongqing 重慶市	(023)63850185 (023)63850026
Changzhou Economic Technology Industrial Development Zone Tian Ming Trade Company 常州經濟技術產業開發區天明貿易公司	Changzhou 常州市	Jiangsu 江蘇省	(0519)8829882 (0519)8829882
Shanxi Mechanical Equipment Import & Export Company 山西省機械設備進出口公司	Taiyuan 太原市	Shanxi 山西省	(0351)4040713 (0351)4043981
Ningbo Five Mining Machinery Import & Export Company 寧波市五礦機械進出口公司	Ningbo 寧波市	Zhejiang 浙江省	(0574)7311255 (0574)7320322
Tianjin Jin Huan Electromechanical Complete Sets of Equipment Factory 天津市津環機電成套設備廠	Tianjin 天津市	Tianjin 天津市	(022)26371628
Yunnan Machinery Import & Export Company 雲南省機械進出口公司	Kunming 昆明市	Yunnan 雲南省	(0871)3164879 (0871)3136829
Tianjin Da Qiu Zhuang Yi Yuan Trade Center 天津市大丘莊億源商貿中心	Tianjin 天津市	Tianjin 天津市	(022)28899478 (022)28899046

*Also include sales by firms outside this industry.包括本行業以外廠家的銷售。"o" stands for "others". "o" 代表"其他產品"。

3525: Casting Machinery 鑄造機械製造業

The industry accounts for 0.038% of the total revenue of China's industrial sector in 1996. The revenue growth rate of the industry is 11.0% from 1995, as compared to the growth rate of China's industrial sector, 9.51%. The rate of return on asset is 0.78%. 69.48% of all firms in the industry made a profit while 21.48% had negative returns. The top province in terms of the industry's revenue is Shandong, accounting for 27.25% of the total revenue.
本行業在1996年佔全行業總產值0.038%，行業年增長率為11.0%（全國工業年增長率9.51%）。行業的資產回報率0.78%，69.48%的企業盈利，21.48%的企業虧損。銷售收入最高的省份為山東省，佔本行業的27.25%。

	Total number of firms 企業總數	Total number of employees 職工總數	Total revenue (Mil. RMB) 總銷售收入（百萬元）	Total profit (Mil. RMB) 總利潤（百萬元）	Return on assets 資產利潤率 (%)	Return on equity 權益利潤率 (%)	Labour productivity ('000 RMB / worker) 勞動生產率（千元/人）	Debts / assets 資產負債率 (%)	Total assets (Mil. RMB) 總資產（百萬元）
Industry Overall 行業總體	472	46,304	2,174	23	0.78	2.51	46.95	68.80	2,970

	Number of firms 企業個數	Average number of employees 平均職工人數	Average revenue ('000 RMB) 平均銷售收入（千元）	Average profit ('000 RMB) 平均利潤（千元）	Return on assets 資產利潤率 (%)	Return on equity 權益利潤率 (%)	Labour productivity ('000 RMB / worker) 勞動生產率（千元/人）	Average debts / assets 平均資產負債率(%)	Average Total assets ('000 RMB) 平均總資產（千元）
By ownership 產業所有權									
State-owned 國有	38	415	10,132	-737	-2.51	-9.36	24.44	73.23	29,395
Collectively-owned 集體	405	69	3,881	161	4.18	12.54	55.91	66.68	3,855
Privately-owned 私有	2	17	977	177	50.60	222.00	59.21	77.21	349
Domestic JVs 聯營	5	102	10,959	-712	-4.62	-29.54	107.02	84.37	15,426
Joint stock 股份制	6	204	19,871	1,326	6.99	17.61	97.57	60.33	18,981
Foreign-funded 外資	9	54	1,820	-1,292	-21.05	-38.59	33.57	45.44	6,137
Overseas Chinese-funded 港澳台資	7	35	3,645	-1,052	-16.40	-36.20	103.71	54.69	6,415
By size 規模									
Large 大型	2	1,075	29,839	964	0.61	1.02	27.77	39.88	157,489
Medium 中型	13	1,021	54,077	285	0.35	1.27	52.96	72.67	82,034
Small 小型	451	68	3,131	38	1.09	3.89	45.81	71.91	3,524
By regional distribution 地區分布									
Central-North 華北	62	104	3,021	-20	-0.40	-1.43	29.10	72.00	4,858
Beijing 北京	11	32	577	75	3.30	13.93	18.19	76.32	2,288
Tianjin 天津	4	13	1,418	58	1.81	3.89	109.04	53.42	3,178
Hebei 河北	23	191	5,153	-180	-2.32	-18.77	27.03	87.63	7,726
Shanxi 山西	16	89	2,714	84	1.59	2.68	30.67	40.76	5,275
Inner Mongolia 內蒙	8	29	1,666	65	42.62	108.33	56.97	60.66	153
Northeast 東北	61	78	1,897	-32	-0.86	-4.48	24.47	80.86	3,726
Liaoning 遼寧	45	90	2,212	-49	-1.08	-5.90	24.65	81.63	4,533
Jilin 吉林	11	38	515	15	1.77	13.39	13.53	86.76	872
Heilongjiang 黑龍江	5	54	2,098	18	0.66	1.90	38.71	65.35	2,736
Central East 華東	153	144	7,925	221	2.18	6.33	54.93	65.55	10,158
Shanghai 上海	6	127	10,272	257	2.35	6.75	80.99	65.17	10,928
Jiangsu 江蘇	42	129	6,938	-84	-1.01	-2.93	53.80	65.56	8,324
Zhejiang 浙江	18	112	4,681	241	5.69	13.83	41.65	58.82	4,234
Anhui 安徽	13	230	12,309	250	1.26	11.27	53.41	88.86	19,898
Fujian 福建	15	24	1,021	29	3.07	6.90	41.86	55.56	935
Jiangxi 江西	12	39	623	25	1.66	10.00	16.03	83.40	1,506
Shandong 山東	47	214	12,604	586	3.57	8.53	58.97	58.19	16,427
Central-South 中南	127	56	2,594	33	0.96	3.20	46.39	69.98	3,484
Henan 河南	54	60	3,021	101	2.83	8.66	50.31	67.38	3,566
Hubei 湖北	9	57	1,639	19	0.66	2.26	28.81	70.99	2,880
Hunan 湖南	35	46	1,689	4	0.21	0.60	36.50	64.56	1,872
Guangdong 廣東	22	64	3,912	-42	-0.68	-2.70	61.22	74.99	6,256
Guangxi 廣西	7	46	897	-81	-2.73	-11.75	19.69	76.77	2,983
Hainan 海南									
Southwest 西南	49	98	5,974	-115	-1.57	-5.64	61.09	72.06	7,295
Chongqing 重慶	6	126	1,521	-896	-17.41	616.47	12.08	102.82	5,146
Sichuan 四川	34	114	8,304	-1	-0.01	-0.02	72.74	68.92	9,511
Guizhou 貴州	8	19	343	-3	-0.49	-2.53	18.03	80.54	508
Yunnan 雲南	1	10	410	10	2.56	3.45	41.00	23.08	390
Tibet 西藏									
Northwest 西北	20	59	1,804	-303	-6.92	-19.74	30.72	64.93	4,379
Shaanxi 陝西	18	43	1,709	-118	-3.63	-8.94	39.96	59.44	3,249
Gansu 甘肅	1	387	5,300	-3,940	-13.63	-56.85	13.70	75.99	28,900
Qinghai 青海									
Ningxia 寧夏									
Xinjiang 新疆	1	17						75.00	200

3525: Casting Machinery 鑄造機械製造業

Year 年份	Number of firms 企業個數	Rate of change 每年變化 (%)	Number of employees 職工人數 (人)	Rate of change 每年變化 (%)	Total revenue (Mil. RMB) 總銷售收入 (百萬元)	Rate of change 每年變化 (%)	Total profit (Mil. RMB) 總利潤 (百萬元)	Rate of change 每年變化 (%)
1993	346		50,716		1,386		25	
1994	430	24.28%	47,228	-6.88%	1,826	31.73%	33	35.57%
1995	420	-2.33%	48,015	1.67%	1,959	7.29%	18	-44.82%
1996	472	12.38%	46,304	-3.56%	2,174	10.97%	23	25.15%

3 Major products* 3 種主要產品 *	Output 產量	Sales volume 銷售量	Unit 單位
a) Casting Equipment 鑄造設備	15,795	16,427	set 台
b) Casting 鑄鋼件	61,876	51,976	ton 噸
c) Iron Casting 鑄鐵件	25,358	24,850	ton 噸

Top 10 firms by revenue (year founded) 收入排名前 10 家企業 (創辦年份)	City 城市	Province 省	Telephone / fax 電話 / 傳真	Number of employees 職工人數	Ownership 產業所有權	Revenue ('000 RMB) 銷售收入 (千元)	Profit ('000 RMB) (rank) 利潤 (千元) (排名)	Total assets ('000 RMB) 總資產 (千元)	Major products 主要產品
Shuangliu San Qiang Heavy Industry Group Co. 雙流縣三強重工集團公司(1974)	Chengdu 成都市	Sichuan 四川省	(028)5822652	2,001	Collectively-owned 集體	226,758	5686(4)	226,012	b,c
Laiwu Shi Kou Zhen Casting Co. 萊蕪市口鎮鑄造公司(1958)	Laiwu 萊蕪市	Shandong 山東省	(0634)6551266 (0634)6551266	2,000	Collectively-owned 集體	103,323	7390(2)	106,326	b
Weihai Dong Yang Casting Co. Ltd. 威海東洋鑄造有限公司(1993)	Weihai 威海市	Shandong 山東省	(0896)8545132 (0896)8545132	175	Foreign-funded 外資	78,600	8000(1)	16,530	c
Bengbu Long Hua Machinery Plant 蚌埠隆華機器廠(1953)	Bengbu 蚌埠市	Anhui 安徽省	(0552)2045781 (0552)2052500	1,587	State-owned 國有	70,233	26(98)	201,157	a
Hua Qing Casting Machinery Co. Ltd. 華青鑄造機械股份有限公司(1970)	Qingdao 青島市	Shandong 山東省	(0532)6163686 (0532)6163978	1,059	Collectively-owned 集體	69,624	6108(3)	79,617	a
Anhui Tongling Zhong Ming Zhen Machinery Plant 安徽省銅陵縣鐘鳴鎮機械廠(1987)	Tongling 銅陵市	Anhui 安徽省	(0562)8891344	258	Collectively-owned 集體	67,386	3719(5)	38,003	c
Nanjing Jiangning Lu Kou Machinery Factory 南京江寧縣祿口機械廠(1967)	Nanjing 南京市	Jiangsu 江蘇省	(025)2770693	318	Collectively-owned 集體	53,940	1890(13)	13,780	c
Gaomi General Machinery Factory 高密市通用機械廠(1966)	Weifang 濰坊市	Shandong 山東省	(0536)2752188 (0536)2752188	140	Collectively-owned 集體	41,460	3617(6)	12,601	b
Qingzhou Casting & Forging Center 青州市鑄鍛中心(1993)	Weifang 濰坊市	Shandong 山東省	(0536)3810212 (0536)3810212	240	Collectively-owned 集體	40,270	2560(10)	6,550	c
Qingdao Casting Machinery Corp. 青島鑄造機械廠(1952)	Qingdao 青島市	Shandong 山東省	(0532)3832156 (0532)3835495	1,518	State-owned 國有	38,017	0(137)	185,838	a

Top 10 Cities by Production Output 產出排名前 10 位城市	Province 省	Market share 市場份額	Number of firms 企業個數
Chengdu 成都市	Sichuan 四川省	10.79%	6
Shanghai 上海市	Shanghai 上海市	8.27%	22
Wuxi 無錫市	Jiangsu 江蘇省	7.26%	13
Qingdao 青島市	Shandong 山東省	5.99%	21
Laiwu 萊蕪市	Shandong 山東省	5.87%	2
Weifang 濰坊市	Shandong 山東省	5.31%	6
Taizhou 泰州市	Jiangsu 江蘇省	4.22%	10
Suzhou 蘇州市	Jiangsu 江蘇省	3.81%	35
Bengbu 蚌埠市	Anhui 安徽省	3.25%	1
Yancheng 鹽城市	Jiangsu 江蘇省	2.13%	13

10 Major Wholesalers 10 家主要批發商	City 城市	Province 省	Telephone / Fax 電話 / 傳真
Liaoning Automobile Trade Group Corp. 遼寧省汽車貿易集團	Shenyang 沈陽市	Liaoning 遼寧省	(024)23835494 (024)23838338
China Post and Telecommunication Equipment General Company 中國郵電器材總公司	Beijing 北京市	Beijing 北京市	(010)63523715 (010)63525935
Jiangsu Electromechanical Products General Company 江蘇省機電產品總公司	Nanjing 南京市	Jiangsu 江蘇省	(025)7713642 (025)7711036
Xi Nan Technology Import & Export Company 西南技術進出口公司	Chongqing 重慶市	Chongqing 重慶市	(023)63850185 (023)63850026
Changzhou Economic Technology Industrial Development Zone Tian Ming Trade Company 常州經濟技術產業開發區天明貿易公司	Changzhou 常州市	Jiangsu 江蘇省	(0519)8829882 (0519)8829882
Shanxi Mechanical Equipment Import & Export Company 山西省機械設備進出口公司	Taiyuan 太原市	Shanxi 山西省	(0351)4040713 (0351)4043981
Ningbo Five Mining Machinery Import & Export Company 寧波市五礦機械進出口公司	Ningbo 寧波市	Zhejiang 浙江省	(0574)7311255 (0574)7320322
Tianjin Jin Huan Electromechanical Complete Sets of Equipment Factory 天津市津環機電成套設備廠	Tianjin 天津市	Tianjin 天津市	(022)26371628
Yunnan Machinery Import & Export Company 雲南省機械進出口公司	Kunming 昆明市	Yunnan 雲南省	(0871)3164879 (0871)3136829
Tianjin Da Qiu Zhuang Yi Yuan Trade Center 天津市大丘莊億源商貿中心	Tianjin 天津市	Tianjin 天津市	(022)28899478 (022)28899046

*Also include sales by firms outside this industry.包括本行業以外廠家的銷售。"o" stands for "others". "o" 代表 "其他產品"。

3526: Machine Tools Parts 機床附件製造業

The industry accounts for 0.024% of the total revenue of China's industrial sector in 1996. The revenue growth rate of the industry is 6.3% from 1995, as compared to the growth rate of China's industrial sector, 9.51%. The rate of return on asset is 0.05%. 61.39% of all firms in the industry made a profit while 32.41% had negative returns. The top province in terms of the industry's revenue is Shandong, accounting for 34.19% of the total revenue.
本行業在1996年佔全行業總產值0.024%，行業年增長率為6.3%（全國工業年增長率9.51%）。行業的資產回報率0.05%，61.39%的企業盈利，32.41%的企業虧損。銷售收入最高的省份為山東省，佔本行業的34.19%。

	Total number of firms 企業總數	Total number of employees 職工總數	Total revenue (Mil. RMB) 總銷售收入（百萬元）	Total profit (Mil. RMB) 總利潤（百萬元）	Return on assets 資產利潤率 (%)	Return on equity 權益利潤率 (%)	Labour productivity ('000 RMB / worker) 勞動生產率（千元/人）	Debts / assets 資產負債率 (%)	Total assets (Mil. RMB) 總資產（百萬元）
Industry Overall 行業總體	331	53,426	1,402	2	0.05	0.15	26.24	67.60	3,261

	Number of firms 企業個數	Average number of employees 平均職工人數	Average revenue ('000 RMB) 平均銷售收入（千元）	Average profit ('000 RMB) 平均利潤（千元）	Return on assets 資產利潤率 (%)	Return on equity 權益利潤率 (%)	Labour productivity ('000 RMB / worker) 勞動生產率（千元/人）	Average debts / assets 平均資產負債率(%)	Average Total assets ('000 RMB) 平均總資產（千元）
By ownership 產業所有權									
State-owned 國有	75	390	8,600	-93	-0.34	-1.05	22.04	67.16	27,080
Collectively-owned 集體	242	89	2,588	59	1.52	5.26	29.23	71.08	3,871
Privately-owned 私有	1	28	1,825	76	3.20	8.87	65.18	63.89	2,364
Domestic JVs 聯營	4	511	17,413	-1,225	-3.59	-24.65	34.11	85.44	34,133
Joint stock 股份制	1	16	58	-162	-1.75	-9.69	3.62	81.98	9,279
Foreign-funded 外資	6	60	8,659	-72	-0.36	-0.53	145.12	33.37	20,342
Overseas Chinese-funded 港澳台資	1	44	2,228	5	0.12	0.47	50.63	75.62	4,082
By size 規模									
Large 大型	3	2,370	75,216	622	0.24	0.55	31.74	56.51	259,702
Medium 中型	9	943	25,360	-68	-0.10	-0.33	26.88	70.20	69,485
Small 小型	317	120	2,990	2	0.04	0.14	24.99	71.35	5,859
By regional distribution 地區分布									
Central-North 華北	54	171	4,074	71	0.64	1.69	23.82	62.26	11,094
Beijing 北京	11	63	1,314	-19	-0.45	-1.43	20.94	68.84	4,276
Tianjin 天津	19	175	4,056	-87	-0.76	-1.66	23.20	54.55	11,548
Hebei 河北	7	102	2,776	269	9.24	42.63	27.33	78.38	2,907
Shanxi 山西	9	79	1,461	51	1.17	13.22	18.50	91.15	4,367
Inner Mongolia 內蒙	8	475	11,988	419	1.23	3.23	25.22	61.96	34,120
Northeast 東北	63	150	2,072	-175	-3.13	-11.11	13.83	71.80	5,579
Liaoning 遼寧	42	146	1,988	-54	-0.86	-2.50	13.59	65.61	6,317
Jilin 吉林	8	231	1,904	-1,043	-14.22	482.08	8.23	102.95	7,333
Heilongjiang 黑龍江	13	111	2,448	-30	-1.42	-4.05	21.98	65.04	2,115
Central East 華東	143	174	6,274	165	1.25	3.99	36.03	68.65	13,129
Shanghai 上海	17	123	4,049	-36	-0.25	-1.54	32.84	83.74	14,359
Jiangsu 江蘇	34	123	5,884	23	0.23	1.32	47.71	82.76	10,201
Zhejiang 浙江	29	98	3,781	-40	-0.91	-3.29	38.44	72.45	4,449
Anhui 安徽	13	83	1,439	-48	-2.55	-7.93	17.36	67.77	1,898
Fujian 福建	4	37	880	18	1.53	4.49	23.95	66.01	1,148
Jiangxi 江西	9	177	1,898	-2	-0.03	-0.18	10.72	86.33	7,364
Shandong 山東	37	350	12,955	679	2.37	5.78	37.04	59.04	28,700
Central-South 中南	28	128	2,441	-234	-3.21	-7.97	19.01	59.75	7,298
Henan 河南	9	115	1,280	13	0.60	2.04	11.11	70.60	2,222
Hubei 湖北	4	300	510	-1,368	-19.14	520.95	1.70	103.67	7,145
Hunan 湖南	10	67	3,423	80	2.27	5.36	51.32	57.71	3,530
Guangdong 廣東	2	101	2,425	-135	-0.28	-0.50	24.13	42.75	47,535
Guangxi 廣西	3	163	5,237	-580	-6.85	-21.61	32.06	68.27	8,467
Hainan 海南									
Southwest 西南	24	190	2,482	-315	-4.34	-20.69	13.09	79.05	7,272
Chongqing 重慶	6	174	3,258	37	1.41	3.41	18.77	58.71	2,619
Sichuan 四川	9	202	2,493	-312	-3.34	-11.71	12.34	71.51	9,347
Guizhou 貴州	4	174	928	-370	-8.11	54.41	5.32	114.97	4,560
Yunnan 雲南	5	200	2,726	-722	-6.16	-38.65	13.62	84.06	11,716
Tibet 西藏									
Northwest 西北	19	89	1,399	-35	-1.24	-2.80	15.64	55.56	2,835
Shaanxi 陝西	12	85	1,488	9	0.37	0.79	17.47	52.99	2,455
Gansu 甘肅	5	122	1,330	-158	-3.40	-7.82	10.90	56.62	4,652
Qinghai 青海									
Ningxia 寧夏	1	40	880				22.00	100.00	970
Xinjiang 新疆	1	28	1,210	10	5.56	100.00	43.21	100.00	180

Year 年份	Number of firms 企業個數	Rate of change 每年變化 (%)	Number of employees 職工人數（人）	Rate of change 每年變化 (%)	Total revenue (Mil. RMB) 總銷售收入（百萬元）	Rate of change 每年變化 (%)	Total profit (Mil. RMB) 總利潤（百萬元）	Rate of change 每年變化 (%)
1993	299		54,745		1,405		85	
1994	371	24.08%	57,360	4.78%	1,389	-1.13%	36	-57.56%
1995	339	-8.63%	54,266	-5.40%	1,319	-5.10%	21	-42.15%
1996	331	-2.36%	53,426	-1.55%	1,402	6.29%	2	-90.37%

3 Major products* 3 種主要產品 *	Output 產量	Sales volume 銷售量	Unit 單位
a) Accessory of Metal Cutting Machine Tool 金屬切削機床附件	12,075,655	12,437,924	piece 件
b) Electric Equipment for Machine Tool 機床電器	562,316	461,099	piece 件

Top 10 firms by revenue (year founded) 收入排名前 10 家企業（創辦年份）	City 城市	Province 省	Telephone / fax 電話 / 傳真	Number of employees 職工人數	Ownership 產業所有權	Revenue ('000 RMB) 銷售收入（千元）	Profit ('000 RMB) (rank) 利潤（千元）（排名）	Total assets ('000 RMB) 總資產（千元）	Major products 主要產品
Shandong Jining Da Xiang Machinery Group Co. 山東濟寧大象機械集團公司(1949)	Jining 濟寧市	Shandong 山東省	(0537)2313296 (0537)2313992	2,066	State-owned 國有	103,984	12017(1)	251,104	a
Shandong Weida Machine Tool Group Corp. 山東威達工具集團總公司(1977)	Weihai 威海市	Shandong 山東省	(0896)8545158 (0896)8545158	1,344	Collectively-owned 集體	74,290	4070(2)	109,520	o
Yantai Milling Machine Accessories Factory 煙台銑床附件廠(1964)	Yantai 煙臺市	Shandong 山東省	(0535)6243871 (0535)6242760	1,354	State-owned 國有	44,292	376(32)	86,399	o
Yantai Machine Tool Accessories Factory 煙台機床附件廠(1980)	Yantai 煙臺市	Shandong 山東省	(0535)6535511 (0535)6530527	1,673	State-owned 國有	39,421	1208(8)	229,179	a
Shanghai No.1 Machine Tool Accessories Factory 上海機床附件一廠(1954)	Shanghai 上海市	Shanghai 上海市	(021)62538726 (021)62151212	573	State-owned 國有	35,823	706(19)	91,880	a
Yantai No.2 Machine Tool Accessories Factory 煙台第二機床附件廠(1966)	Yantai 煙臺市	Shandong 山東省	(0535)6245228 (0535)6242469	732	State-owned 國有	30,135	2161(3)	50,397	a
Wujin Machine Tool Electric Equipment Factory 武進市機床電器廠(1966)	Changzhou 常州市	Jiangsu 江蘇省	(0519)6554054	215	Collectively-owned 集體	28,609	1461(6)	24,901	o
Tianjin Machine Tool Electrical Appliance General Factory 天津市機床電器總廠(1956)	Tianjin 天津市	Tianjin 天津市	(022)26351851 (022)26275367	658	State-owned 國有	27,001	731(18)	61,466	b
Wafangdian Machine Tool Accessories Factory 瓦房店機床附件廠(1958)	Dalian 大連市	Liaoning 遼寧省	(0411)5613039	694	State-owned 國有	22,306	111(54)	65,785	o
Nantong Machine Tool Casting Factory 南通市機床鑄造廠	Nantong 南通市	Jiangsu 江蘇省	(0513)3577178	357	Domestic JVs 聯營	20,918	989(10)	22,945	o

Top 10 Cities by Production Output 產出排名前 10 位城市	Province 省	Market share 市場份額	Number of firms 企業個數
Yantai 煙臺市	Shandong 山東省	11.96%	10
Shanghai 上海市	Shanghai 上海市	8.76%	37
Hohhot 呼和浩特市	Inner Mong 內蒙	7.93%	3
Jining 濟寧市	Shandong 山東省	7.42%	7
Tianjin 天津市	Tianjin 天津市	6.78%	22
Weihai 威海市	Shandong 山東省	5.77%	5
Nanjing 南京市	Jiangsu 江蘇省	5.63%	6
Dalian 大連市	Liaoning 遼寧省	2.20%	6
Ningbo 寧波市	Zhejiang 浙江省	2.03%	13
Shenyang 沈陽市	Liaoning 遼寧省	1.70%	26

10 Major Wholesalers 10 家主要批發商	City 城市	Province 省	Telephone / Fax 電話 / 傳真
Liaoning Automobile Trade Group Corp. 遼寧省汽車貿易集團	Shenyang 沈陽市	Liaoning 遼寧省	(024)23835494 (024)23838338
China Post and Telecommunication Equipment General Company 中國郵電器材總公司	Beijing 北京市	Beijing 北京市	(010)63523715 (010)63525935
Jiangsu Electromechanical Products General Company 江蘇省機電產品總公司	Nanjing 南京市	Jiangsu 江蘇省	(025)7713642 (025)7711036
Xi Nan Technology Import & Export Company 西南技術進出口公司	Chongqing 重慶市	Chongqing 重慶市	(023)63850185 (023)63850026
Changzhou Economic Technology Industrial Development Zone Tian Ming Trade Company 常州經濟技術產業開發區天明貿易公司	Changzhou 常州市	Jiangsu 江蘇省	(0519)8829882 (0519)8829882
Shanxi Mechanical Equipment Import & Export Company 山西省機械設備進出口公司	Taiyuan 太原市	Shanxi 山西省	(0351)4040713 (0351)4043981
Ningbo Five Mining Machinery Import & Export Company 寧波市五礦機械進出口公司	Ningbo 寧波市	Zhejiang 浙江省	(0574)7311255 (0574)7320322
Tianjin Jin Huan Electromechanical Complete sets of Equipment Factory 天津市津環機電成套設備廠	Tianjin 天津市	Tianjin 天津市	(022)26371628
Yunnan Machinery Import & Export Company 雲南省機械進出口公司	Kunming 昆明市	Yunnan 雲南省	(0871)3164879 (0871)3136829
Tianjin Da Qiu Zhuang Yi Yuan Trade Center 天津市大丘莊億源商貿中心	Tianjin 天津市	Tianjin 天津市	(022)28899478 (022)28899046

*Also include sales by firms outside this industry.包括本行業以外廠家的銷售。"o" stands for "others". "o" 代表"其他產品"。

3529: Other Metal Processing Machinery 其他金屬加工機械製造業

The industry accounts for 0.083% of the total revenue of China's industrial sector in 1996. The revenue growth rate of the industry is 15.5% from 1995, as compared to the growth rate of China's industrial sector, 9.51%. The rate of return on asset is -0.04%. 67.08% of all firms in the industry made a profit while 24.57% had negative returns. The top province in terms of the industry's revenue is Henan, accounting for 12.64% of the total revenue.
本行業在1996年佔全行業總產值0.083%，行業年增長率為15.5%（全國工業年增長率9.51%）。行業的資產回報率-0.04%，67.08%的企業盈利，24.57%的企業虧損。銷售收入最高的省份為河南省，佔本行業的12.64%。

	Total number of firms 企業總數	Total number of employees 職工總數	Total revenue (Mil. RMB) 總銷售收入（百萬元）	Total profit (Mil. RMB) 總利潤（百萬元）	Return on assets 資產利潤率 (%)	Return on equity 權益利潤率 (%)	Labour productivity ('000 RMB / worker) 勞動生產率（千元/人）	Debts / assets 資產負債率 (%)	Total assets (Mil. RMB) 總資產（百萬元）
Industry Overall 行業總體	1,688	127,063	4,801	-3	-0.04	-0.13	37.78	68.32	7,975

	Number of firms 企業個數	Average number of employees 平均職工人數	Average revenue ('000 RMB) 平均銷售收入（千元）	Average profit ('000 RMB) 平均利潤（千元）	Return on assets 資產利潤率 (%)	Return on equity 權益利潤率 (%)	Labour productivity ('000 RMB / worker) 勞動生產率（千元/人）	Average debts / assets 平均資產負債率(%)	Average Total assets ('000 RMB) 平均總資產（千元）
By ownership 產業所有權									
State-owned 國有	226	192	4,858	-456	-2.91	-9.44	25.30	69.15	15,646
Collectively-owned 集體	1,378	58	2,273	72	2.67	8.81	39.22	69.73	2,682
Privately-owned 私有	6	28	1,602	151	9.89	31.28	56.53	68.38	1,530
Domestic JVs 聯營	14	66	2,544	114	3.45	6.92	38.47	50.19	3,294
Joint stock 股份制	16	101	6,508	303	3.40	13.09	64.60	74.06	8,919
Foreign-funded 外資	20	53	4,977	63	0.80	1.38	94.18	42.56	7,930
Overseas Chinese-funded 港澳台資	27	60	11,365	-272	-1.96	-4.71	189.19	58.32	13,861
By size 規模									
Large 大型	5	2,803	71,671	-608,877	-239.27	-737.95	25.57	67.58	254,470
Medium 中型	34	760	31,492	-66,339	-93.93	-313.38	41.45	70.03	70,623
Small 小型	1,633	54	2,064	3,244	123.18	380.18	38.53	67.60	2,633
By regional distribution 地區分布									
Central-North 華北	413	52	1,519	-66	-2.34	-7.41	29.13	68.46	2,806
Beijing 北京	136	33	1,693	43	1.66	5.27	51.53	68.45	2,572
Tianjin 天津	104	39	565	-32	-3.95	-13.30	14.41	70.29	798
Hebei 河北	40	100	2,490	-520	-8.50	-30.66	24.96	72.30	6,118
Shanxi 山西	44	103	2,680	-115	-1.45	-4.33	26.14	66.51	7,897
Inner Mongolia 內蒙	89	50	1,356	-43	-2.84	-8.22	26.90	65.41	1,501
Northeast 東北	413	74	1,603	-60	-1.64	-5.86	21.78	71.94	3,641
Liaoning 遼寧	299	64	1,608	-38	-1.08	-3.33	25.26	67.57	3,527
Jilin 吉林	53	99	2,004	-322	-4.77	-37.31	20.17	87.22	6,753
Heilongjiang 黑龍江	61	100	1,225	61	4.11	10.96	12.28	62.55	1,497
Central East 華東	413	79	4,290	77	1.32	4.02	54.17	67.25	5,809
Shanghai 上海	108	53	3,757	17	0.36	0.87	70.98	58.30	4,597
Jiangsu 江蘇	109	90	4,895	113	1.87	6.79	54.19	72.42	6,011
Zhejiang 浙江	68	80	4,376	28	0.38	1.14	54.58	66.96	7,313
Anhui 安徽	18	209	6,113	-71	-0.69	-2.41	29.28	71.22	10,173
Fujian 福建	30	20	670	-41	-2.45	-4.15	33.39	41.01	1,659
Jiangxi 江西	21	135	5,427	198	2.19	7.05	40.13	68.97	9,032
Shandong 山東	59	76	4,926	237	4.27	15.05	64.73	71.64	5,555
Central-South 中南	181	134	6,845	213	1.93	5.53	50.95	65.12	11,041
Henan 河南	56	166	10,835	822	7.34	18.65	65.31	60.66	11,198
Hubei 湖北	21	84	4,141	46	0.75	2.22	49.47	66.16	6,151
Hunan 湖南	39	155	4,234	1	0.02	0.07	27.25	69.44	6,390
Guangdong 廣東	57	85	5,100	-156	-1.12	-3.91	59.97	71.41	13,987
Guangxi 廣西	8	295	11,178	51	0.21	0.40	37.84	47.57	24,456
Hainan 海南									
Southwest 西南	182	67	1,744	-91	-3.04	-10.32	26.04	70.51	2,991
Chongqing 重慶	86	42	715	-731	-72.86	-250.92	16.94	70.96	1,004
Sichuan 四川	68	96	3,001	715	14.78	59.27	31.23	75.06	4,836
Guizhou 貴州	23	63	1,625	-134	-2.89	-6.29	25.78	54.02	4,633
Yunnan 雲南	5	104	2,914	168	3.67	18.54	28.07	80.25	4,578
Tibet 西藏									
Northwest 西北	86	69	2,138	-59	-1.37	-5.30	31.02	74.11	4,309
Shaanxi 陝西	65	78	2,623	-64	-1.24	-4.73	33.81	73.91	5,194
Gansu 甘肅	13	49	741	4	0.27	0.88	15.09	69.38	1,417
Qinghai 青海	4	28	153	3	1.04	1.52	5.50	32.29	240
Ningxia 寧夏	1	25	610				24.40	50.00	300
Xinjiang 新疆	3	37	863	-327	-7.38	-68.53	23.13	89.23	4,427

3529: Other Metal Processing Machinery 其他金屬加工機械製造業

Year 年份	Number of firms 企業個數	Rate of change 每年變化 (%)	Number of employees 職工人數（人）	Rate of change 每年變化 (%)	Total revenue (Mil. RMB) 總銷售收入（百萬元）	Rate of change 每年變化 (%)	Total profit (Mil. RMB) 總利潤（百萬元）	Rate of change 每年變化 (%)
1993	1546		1,172,815		4,948		34	
1994	1684	8.93%	148,999	-87.30%	3,547	-28.31%	31	-10.50%
1995	1633	-3.03%	134,427	-9.78%	4,157	17.19%	0	-100.13%
1996	1688	3.37%	127,063	-5.48%	4,801	15.49%	-3	-7592.31%

3 Major products* 3 種主要產品 *	Output 產量	Sales volume 銷售量	Unit 單位
a) Bench Drilling Machine 台鑽	451,199	451,199	set 台
b) Speed Reducer 減速機	20,799	18,303	set 台
c) Iron Casting 鑄鐵件	3,644	3,571	ton 噸

Top 10 firms by revenue (year founded) 收入排名前 10 家企業 (創辦年份)	City 城市	Province 省	Telephone / fax 電話 / 傳真	Number of employees 職工人數	Ownership 產業所有權	Revenue ('000 RMB) 銷售收入（千元）	Profit ('000 RMB) (rank) 利潤（千元）（排名）	Total assets ('000 RMB) 總資產（千元）	Major products 主要產品
Nanshan Machinery Fittings No.1 Factory 南山機械配件一廠(1978)	Yibin 宜賓市	Sichuan 四川省	(0831)3321701	584	Collectively-owned 集體	143,527	-14535(417)	339,775	o
Shanghai Fumin Cang Qiao Development Joint Company 上海富民倉橋發展聯合公司(1995)	Shanghai 上海市	Shanghai 上海市		400	其他經濟	125,240	6260(1)	25,807	o
Qingdao Guo Fu Electric Co. Ltd. 青島國富電氣有限公司(1992)	Qingdao 青島市	Shandong 山東省	(0532)8897093 (0532)91	255	Overseas Chinese-funded 港澳台資	85,497	-44(336)	72,420	a
Xi Hang Import & Export Company Electromechanical Manufacture Dept. 西航進出口公司機電製造部(1993)	Xi'an 西安市	Shaanxi 陝西省	(029)6613888	500	Collectively-owned 集體	84,807	302(94)	187,772	o
China Aerospace Corp. 柳州長虹機器製造公司(1980)	Liuzhou 柳州市	Guangxi 廣西	(0772)2542263 (0772)2542005	2,169	State-owned 國有	83,653	533(60)	189,337	o
Zhuji Chain Equipment General Factory 諸暨鏈條設備總廠(1953)	Shaoxing 紹興市	Zhejiang 浙江省	(0575)7214395 (0575)7214683	1,257	Collectively-owned 集體	80,533	2818(6)	122,419	o
Hangzhou West Lake Bench Drilling Machine Plant 杭州西湖台鑽總廠(1955)	Hangzhou 杭州市	Zhejiang 浙江省	(0571)8083917 (0571)8085136	745	State-owned 國有	66,577	1189(23)	78,998	a
China Nuclear Industry General Co. No.720 Factory 中國核工業總公司 720 廠(1969)	Nanchang 南昌市	Jiangxi 江西省	(0791)3751720 (0791)3759720	1,280	State-owned 國有	62,661	3014(4)	106,941	o
Jiangsu Cosmos Steel Ring Industrial General Company 江蘇省宇宙鋼圈實業總公司(1955)	Zhenjiang 鎮江市	Jiangsu 江蘇省	(0511)6523627	308	Collectively-owned 集體	50,036	46(222)	32,721	o
Anshan Iron & Steel Corp. Mine Subsidiary Enterprise Mine Industrial Co. 鞍鋼礦山附企礦建工業公司(1972)	Anshan 鞍山市	Liaoning 遼寧省	(0412)6426668	1,476	Collectively-owned 集體	48,910	1160(25)	45,350	o

Top 10 Cities by Production Output 產出排名前 10 位城市	Province 省	Market share 市場份額	Number of firms 企業個數
Shanghai 上海市	Shanghai 上海市	8.80%	217
Changzhou 常州市	Jiangsu 江蘇省	6.17%	47
Wuxi 無錫市	Jiangsu 江蘇省	5.62%	81
Xuchang 許昌市	Henan 河南省	4.69%	5
Shaoxing 紹興市	Zhejiang 浙江省	3.46%	5
Hangzhou 杭州市	Zhejiang 浙江省	3.41%	36
Yangzhou 揚州市	Jiangsu 江蘇省	2.59%	10
Suzhou 蘇州市	Jiangsu 江蘇省	2.53%	52
Liuzhou 柳州市	Guangxi 廣西	2.24%	14
Beijing 北京市	Beijing 北京市	2.19%	106

10 Major Wholesalers 10 家主要批發商	City 城市	Province 省	Telephone / Fax 電話 / 傳真
Liaoning Automobile Trade Group Corp. 遼寧省汽車貿易集團	Shenyang 沈陽市	Liaoning 遼寧省	(024)23835494 (024)23838338
China Post and Telecommunication Equipment General Company 中國郵電器材總公司	Beijing 北京市	Beijing 北京市	(010)63523715 (010)63525935
Jiangsu Electromechanical Products General Company 江蘇省機電產品總公司	Nanjing 南京市	Jiangsu 江蘇省	(025)7713642 (025)7711036
Xi Nan Technology Import & Export Company 西南技術進出口公司	Chongqing 重慶市	Chongqing 重慶市	(023)63850185 (023)63850026
Changzhou Economic Technology Industrial Development Zone Tian Ming Trade Company 常州經濟技術產業開發區天明貿易公司	Changzhou 常州市	Jiangsu 江蘇省	(0519)8829882 (0519)8829882
Shanxi Mechanical Equipment Import & Export Company 山西省機械設備進出口公司	Taiyuan 太原市	Shanxi 山西省	(0351)4040713 (0351)4043981
Ningbo Five Mining Machinery Import & Export Company 寧波市五礦機械進出口公司	Ningbo 寧波市	Zhejiang 浙江省	(0574)7311255 (0574)7320322
Tianjin Jin Huan Electromechanical Complete Sets of Equipment Factory 天津市津環機電成套設備廠	Tianjin 天津市	Tianjin 天津市	(022)26371628
Yunnan Machinery Import & Export Company 雲南省機械進出口公司	Kunming 昆明市	Yunnan 雲南省	(0871)3164879 (0871)3136829
Tianjin Da Qiu Zhuang Yi Yuan Trade Center 天津市大丘莊億源商貿中心	Tianjin 天津市	Tianjin 天津市	(022)28899478 (022)28899046

*Also include sales by firms outside this industry.包括本行業以外廠家的銷售。"o" stands for "others". "o" 代表"其他產品"。

3531: Hoist and Conveying Equipment 起重運輸設備製造業

The industry accounts for 0.448% of the total revenue of China's industrial sector in 1996. The revenue growth rate of the industry is 5.6% from 1995, as compared to the growth rate of China's industrial sector, 9.51%. The rate of return on asset is 2.69%. 60.77% of all firms in the industry made a profit while 35.28% had negative returns. The top province in terms of the industry's revenue is Shanghai, accounting for 27.63% of the total revenue.
本行業在1996年佔全行業總產值0.448%，行業年增長率為5.6%（全國工業年增長率9.51%）。行業的資產回報率2.69%，60.77%的企業盈利，35.28%的企業虧損。銷售收入最高的省份為上海市，佔本行業的27.63%。

	Total number of firms 企業總數	Total number of employees 職工總數	Total revenue (Mil. RMB) 總銷售收入（百萬元）	Total profit (Mil. RMB) 總利潤（百萬元）	Return on assets 資產利潤率 (%)	Return on equity 權益利潤率 (%)	Labour productivity ('000 RMB / worker) 勞動生產率（千元/人）	Debts / assets 資產負債率 (%)	Total assets (Mil. RMB) 總資產（百萬元）
Industry Overall 行業總體	1,032	362,472	25,954	1,123	2.69	8.85	71.60	69.63	41,806

	Number of firms 企業個數	Average number of employees 平均職工人數	Average revenue ('000 RMB) 平均銷售收入（千元）	Average profit ('000 RMB) 平均利潤（千元）	Return on assets 資產利潤率 (%)	Return on equity 權益利潤率 (%)	Labour productivity ('000 RMB / worker) 勞動生產率（千元/人）	Average debts / assets 平均資產負債率(%)	Average Total assets ('000 RMB) 平均總資產（千元）
By ownership 產業所有權									
State-owned 國有	243	893	41,313	-412	-0.43	-1.52	46.26	72.00	96,650
Collectively-owned 集體	690	168	9,081	201	1.86	5.96	54.00	68.81	10,846
Privately-owned 私有	3	59	5,403	192	4.09	1322.67	92.10	99.69	4,695
Domestic JVs 聯營	28	140	13,916	676	4.50	10.33	99.17	56.41	15,007
Joint stock 股份制	11	629	30,358	51	0.08	0.24	48.30	66.39	64,446
Foreign-funded 外資	31	449	252,500	32,730	12.90	34.68	561.96	62.80	253,668
Overseas Chinese-funded 港澳台資	27	249	40,082	1,839	2.71	11.31	160.76	76.00	67,784
By size 規模									
Large 大型	36	3,246	411,656	29,143	4.51	14.64	126.83	69.17	645,692
Medium 中型	84	1,115	55,975	-119	-0.12	-0.45	50.18	73.67	100,807
Small 小型	900	169	7,147	93	0.83	2.55	42.37	67.31	11,215
By regional distribution 地區分布									
Central-North 華北	134	335	30,973	2,029	5.15	16.58	92.44	68.90	39,370
Beijing 北京	37	304	23,754	-221	-0.57	-2.07	78.02	72.45	38,859
Tianjin 天津	39	268	63,442	7,204	13.89	37.16	236.29	62.64	51,880
Hebei 河北	38	457	17,122	84	0.22	0.81	37.47	73.03	38,463
Shanxi 山西	10	347	9,928	71	0.35	1.12	28.58	68.45	20,115
Inner Mongolia 內蒙	10	232	4,735	-473	-3.12	-15.40	20.41	79.75	15,172
Northeast 東北	169	360	9,219	-601	-2.17	-9.66	25.63	77.54	27,695
Liaoning 遼寧	138	320	9,638	-209	-0.81	-2.92	30.15	72.32	25,838
Jilin 吉林	16	409	5,971	-1,219	-4.62	102.68	14.59	104.50	26,379
Heilongjiang 黑龍江	15	674	8,829	-3,545	-7.68	-64.06	13.10	88.02	46,183
Central East 華東	439	300	35,381	2,450	5.08	15.18	118.12	66.53	48,225
Shanghai 上海	79	338	90,772	10,389	9.00	26.04	268.39	65.42	115,383
Jiangsu 江蘇	140	389	37,378	1,054	2.03	6.59	96.15	69.23	51,971
Zhejiang 浙江	117	156	10,814	283	1.80	5.18	69.22	65.16	15,688
Anhui 安徽	27	502	30,634	2,146	3.57	9.07	61.06	60.61	60,064
Fujian 福建	20	148	8,756	54	0.36	1.04	59.04	65.30	14,926
Jiangxi 江西	7	585	10,289	259	0.83	2.42	17.60	65.84	31,273
Shandong 山東	49	234	16,101	271	1.65	5.55	68.79	70.25	16,424
Central-South 中南	193	407	17,821	-452	-1.35	-5.17	43.78	73.79	33,365
Henan 河南	61	238	6,219				26.15	68.64	13,565
Hubei 湖北	34	423	10,632	-836	-3.41	-12.34	25.13	72.35	24,503
Hunan 湖南	41	431	10,810	-648	-2.01	-9.89	25.09	79.68	32,246
Guangdong 廣東	47	603	43,958	-770	-1.15	-4.26	72.95	72.91	66,765
Guangxi 廣西	9	365	20,710	171	0.52	2.08	56.74	74.98	32,887
Hainan 海南	1	391	2,990	2,420	10.58	46.81	7.65	77.40	22,880
Southwest 西南	68	478	13,649	-391	-0.88	-2.76	28.56	68.05	44,410
Chongqing 重慶	20	412	12,238	-3,157	-10.60	-52.15	29.69	79.68	29,782
Sichuan 四川	33	658	19,210	1,295	1.99	6.66	29.20	70.04	64,946
Guizhou 貴州	6	162	2,673	-672	-10.56	-49.63	16.52	78.75	6,362
Yunnan 雲南	9	190	4,061	-13	-0.05	-0.06	21.39	22.91	28,762
Tibet 西藏									
Northwest 西北	29	491	11,924	-301	-0.71	-3.26	24.26	78.10	42,088
Shaanxi 陝西	15	645	13,856	-128	-0.31	-1.32	21.49	76.31	40,989
Gansu 甘肅	1	156	850	-60	-4.17	-8.22	5.45	49.31	1,440
Qinghai 青海	2	157	2,660	-720	-5.98	-42.23	17.00	85.84	12,045
Ningxia 寧夏	5	583	19,474	170	0.18	0.97	33.43	81.03	92,770
Xinjiang 新疆	6	200	5,735	-1,025	-5.29	-20.85	28.70	74.66	19,388

3531: Hoist and Conveying Equipment 起重運輸設備製造業

Year 年份	Number of firms 企業個數	Rate of change 每年變化 (%)	Number of employees 職工人數（人）	Rate of change 每年變化 (%)	Total revenue (Mil. RMB) 總銷售收入（百萬元）	Rate of change 每年變化 (%)	Total profit (Mil. RMB) 總利潤（百萬元）	Rate of change 每年變化 (%)
1993	833		376,804		19,660		949	
1994	890	6.84%	302,234	-19.79%	19,484	-0.90%	1,053	10.97%
1995	1,056	18.65%	347,668	15.03%	24,581	26.16%	1,640	55.74%
1996	1,032	-2.27%	362,472	4.26%	25,954	5.59%	1,123	-31.52%

3 Major products* 3 種主要產品 *	Output 產量	Sales volume 銷售量	Unit 單位
a) Electrical Lift 電梯	19,269	15,993	set 台
b) Electric Single-beam Bridge Crane 電動單梁橋式起重機	11,911	11,554	set 台
c) Capsular Jack 千斤頂	13,466,556	13,466,556	set 台

Top 10 firms by revenue (year founded) 收入排名前 10 家企業 (創辦年份)	City 城市	Province 省	Telephone / fax 電話 / 傳真	Number of employees 職工人數	Ownership 產業所有權	Revenue ('000 RMB) 銷售收入（千元）	Profit ('000 RMB) (rank) 利潤（千元）（排名）	Total assets ('000 RMB) 總資產（千元）	Major products 主要產品
Shanghai Mitsubishi Elevator Co. Ltd. 上海三菱電梯有限公司(1987)	Shanghai 上海市	Shanghai 上海市	(021)64303030 (021)64300932	1,606	Foreign-funded 外資	3,709,436	603052(1)	3,066,415	a
China Tianjin Otis Elevator Co. Ltd. 天津奧的斯電梯有限公司(1984)	Tianjin 天津市	Tianjin 天津市	(022)28307148 (022)28301256	3,758	Foreign-funded 外資	2,293,536	288038(2)	1,583,866	a
Xuzhou Construction Machinery Group Co. Ltd. 徐州工程機械集團有限公司(1989)	Xuzhou 徐州市	Jiangsu 江蘇省	(0516)5756044 (0516)5753155	21,157	State-owned 國有	2,009,770	21880(10)	3,781,542	o
China-schindler Elevator Co. Ltd. Shanghai Elevator Factory 中國迅達電梯有限公司上海電梯廠(1980)	Shanghai 上海市	Shanghai 上海市	(021)56650991 (021)56650711	1,768	Foreign-funded 外資	1,012,563	68560(4)	920,600	a
Guangdong Taishan Machinery Plant 廣東省台山市機械廠(1957)	Jiangmen 江門市	Guangdong 廣東省	(0750)5525108 (0750)5527064	3,306	State-owned 國有	664,951	1759(59)	680,920	c
Shanghai Zhen Hua Port Machinery Co. Ltd. 上海振華港口機械有限公司(1992)	Shanghai 上海市	Shanghai 上海市	(021)58860001 (021)58801612	442	Overseas Chinese-funded 港澳台資	617,264	68679(3)	1,379,305	o
Shanghai Chong You Electrical Lift Co. Ltd. 上海崇友電梯有限公司(1994)	Shanghai 上海市	Shanghai 上海市	(021)56808888	230	Foreign-funded 外資	603,857	1250(66)		o
Hefei Fork Lift General Factory 合肥叉車總廠(1960)	Hefei 合肥市	Anhui 安徽省	(0551)3632133 (0551)3633431	4,348	State-owned 國有	590,490	63772(6)	1,113,266	o
Changshu Hoisting Jack Factory 常熟市千斤頂廠(1955)	Suzhou 蘇州市	Jiangsu 江蘇省	(0512)2880518 (0512)2881282	990	Collectively-owned 集體	554,527	25119(9)	292,271	c
Shanghai Port Machinery Plant 上海港口機械製造廠(1885)	Shanghai 上海市	Shanghai 上海市	(021)58395139 (021)58837627	3,585	State-owned 國有	552,008	41996(7)	1,269,162	o

Top 10 Cities by Production Output 產出排名前 10 位城市	Province 省	Market share 市場份額	Number of firms 企業個數
Shanghai 上海市	Shanghai 上海市	25.82%	135
Xuzhou 徐州市	Jiangsu 江蘇省	10.85%	15
Beijing 北京市	Beijing 北京市	8.56%	35
Suzhou 蘇州市	Jiangsu 江蘇省	8.33%	72
Guangzhou 廣州市	Guangdong 廣東省	3.81%	38
Hangzhou 杭州市	Zhejiang 浙江省	2.72%	30
Dalian 大連市	Liaoning 遼寧省	2.70%	37
Jiangmen 江門市	Guangdong 廣東省	2.63%	5
Hefei 合肥市	Anhui 安徽省	2.30%	9
Wuxi 無錫市	Jiangsu 江蘇省	1.97%	59

10 Major Wholesalers 10 家主要批發商	City 城市	Province 省	Telephone / Fax 電話 / 傳真
Liaoning Automobile Trade Group Corp. 遼寧省汽車貿易集團	Shenyang 沈陽市	Liaoning 遼寧省	(024)23835494 (024)23838338
China Post and Telecommunication Equipment General Company 中國郵電器材總公司	Beijing 北京市	Beijing 北京市	(010)63523715 (010)63525935
Jiangsu Electromechanical Products General Company 江蘇省機電產品總公司	Nanjing 南京市	Jiangsu 江蘇省	(025)7713642 (025)7711036
Xi Nan Technology Import & Export Company 西南技術進出口公司	Chongqing 重慶市	Chongqing 重慶市	(023)63850185 (023)63850026
Changzhou Economic Technology Industrial Development Zone Tian Ming Trade Company 常州經濟技術產業開發區天明貿易公司	Changzhou 常州市	Jiangsu 江蘇省	(0519)8829882 (0519)8829882
Shanxi Mechanical Equipment Import & Export Company 山西省機械設備進出口公司	Taiyuan 太原市	Shanxi 山西省	(0351)4040713 (0351)4043981
Ningbo Five Mining Machinery Import & Export Company 寧波市五礦機械進出口公司	Ningbo 寧波市	Zhejiang 浙江省	(0574)7311255 (0574)7320322
Tianjin Jin Huan Electromechanical Complete sets of Equipment Factory 天津市津環機電成套設備廠	Tianjin 天津市	Tianjin 天津市	(022)26371628
Yunnan Machinery Import & Export Company 雲南省機械進出口公司	Kunming 昆明市	Yunnan 雲南省	(0871)3164879 (0871)3136829
Tianjin Da Qiu Zhuang Yi Yuan Trade Center 天津市大丘莊億源商貿中心	Tianjin 天津市	Tianjin 天津市	(022)28899478 (022)28899046

*Also include sales by firms outside this industry.包括本行業以外廠家的銷售。"o" stands for "others". "o" 代表"其他產品"。

3532: Mining Vehicles 工礦車輛製造業

The industry accounts for 0.031% of the total revenue of China's industrial sector in 1996. The revenue growth rate of the industry is 11.6% from 1995, as compared to the growth rate of China's industrial sector, 9.51%. The rate of return on asset is 1.60%. 61.66% of all firms in the industry made a profit while 28.48% had negative returns. The top province in terms of the industry's revenue is Guangxi, accounting for 35.18% of the total revenue.
本行業在 1996 年佔全行業總產值 0.031%，行業年增長率為 11.6%（全國工業年增長率 9.51%）。行業的資產回報率 1.60%，61.66% 的企業盈利，28.48% 的企業虧損。銷售收入最高的省份為廣西省，佔本行業的 35.18%。

	Total number of firms 企業總數	Total number of employees 職工總數	Total revenue (Mil. RMB) 總銷售收入（百萬元）	Total profit (Mil. RMB) 總利潤（百萬元）	Return on assets 資產利潤率 (%)	Return on equity 權益利潤率 (%)	Labour productivity ('000 RMB / worker) 勞動生產率（千元/人）	Debts / assets 資產負債率 (%)	Total assets (Mil. RMB) 總資產（百萬元）
Industry Overall 行業總體	152	34,663	1,804	45	1.60	3.61	52.04	55.72	2,790

	Number of firms 企業個數	Average number of employees 平均職工人數	Average revenue ('000 RMB) 平均銷售收入（千元）	Average profit ('000 RMB) 平均利潤（千元）	Return on assets 資產利潤率 (%)	Return on equity 權益利潤率 (%)	Labour productivity ('000 RMB / worker) 勞動生產率（千元/人）	Average debts / assets 平均資產負債率(%)	Average Total assets ('000 RMB) 平均總資產（千元）
By ownership 產業所有權									
State-owned 國有	41	381	9,000	-98	-0.40	-1.30	23.61	69.14	24,341
Collectively-owned 集體	105	129	6,937	119	2.31	10.21	53.70	77.41	5,178
Privately-owned 私有									
Domestic JVs 聯營	1	61	6,621	-1,102			108.55		
Joint stock 股份制	3	1,768	233,661	12,519	3.01	4.67	132.16	35.58	416,185
Foreign-funded 外資	2	51							
Overseas Chinese-funded 港澳台資									
By size 規模									
Large 大型	1	5,180	679,559	36,115	2.88	4.48	131.19	35.61	1,252,860
Medium 中型	6	1,927	97,917	1,077	0.85	3.38	50.82	74.96	127,091
Small 小型	144	124	3,735	17	0.31	1.02	30.07	69.36	5,380
By regional distribution 地區分布									
Central-North 華北	51	118	2,556	77	1.64	5.96	21.64	72.55	4,713
Beijing 北京									
Tianjin 天津	2	231	4,770	15	0.25	0.80	20.65	69.26	6,115
Hebei 河北	3	282	6,873	27	0.14	1.35	24.37	89.71	19,243
Shanxi 山西	45	105	2,227	85	2.26	6.69	21.24	66.23	3,756
Inner Mongolia 內蒙	1							158.39	1,370
Northeast 東北	16	74	1,559	86	3.71	14.73	21.12	74.81	2,305
Liaoning 遼寧	13	81	1,547	95	3.51	14.45	19.04	75.68	2,714
Jilin 吉林	1	10	70	10	25.00	33.33	7.00	50.00	40
Heilongjiang 黑龍江	2	58	2,380	60	7.69	17.39	41.39	55.77	780
Central East 華東	39	363	20,570	364	1.56	5.83	56.73	73.17	23,248
Shanghai 上海									
Jiangsu 江蘇	12	213	11,299	-70	-0.35	-1.54	53.15	76.94	19,730
Zhejiang 浙江	4	280	20,465	685	2.00	4.42	73.15	54.70	34,235
Anhui 安徽	7	167	3,676	-233	-4.30	-15.01	22.01	71.33	5,411
Fujian 福建	1	283	17,070	830	10.53	18.69	60.32	43.65	7,880
Jiangxi 江西	3	935	15,020	380	0.86	5.25	16.07	83.52	43,953
Shandong 山東	12	518	41,409	995	3.36	13.32	79.95	74.78	29,614
Central-South 中南	28	296	25,620	1,001	2.17	3.57	86.64	39.18	46,106
Henan 河南	9	157	4,300	37	0.57	1.93	27.47	70.59	6,453
Hubei 湖北	6	85	2,807	-3	-0.16	-2.17	32.95	92.45	2,032
Hunan 湖南	6	70	2,388	-43	-3.20	-76.47	33.96	95.81	1,353
Guangdong 廣東	4	138	1,975	-420	-4.12	-7.77	14.34	46.97	10,198
Guangxi 廣西	2	2,646	317,360	14,930	2.58	4.06	119.94	36.45	578,375
Hainan 海南	1	95	4,870	-210	-1.40	-2.07	51.26	32.53	15,030
Southwest 西南	13	244	5,057	-8	-0.07	-0.20	20.71	64.75	10,747
Chongqing 重慶	3	40	509	85	25.52	45.82	12.83	44.32	333
Sichuan 四川	6	103	2,395	22	0.88	1.97	23.21	55.53	2,508
Guizhou 貴州	2	1,205	24,615	-190	-0.31	-0.92	20.44	66.33	61,075
Yunnan 雲南	2	13	310	-55	-7.28	-12.64	24.80	42.38	755
Tibet 西藏									
Northwest 西北	5	372	12,600	-552	-1.58	-3.36	33.85	53.08	34,998
Shaanxi 陝西	4	291	13,693	-195	-0.61	-1.32	47.05	54.02	32,025
Gansu 甘肅									
Qinghai 青海									
Ningxia 寧夏									
Xinjiang 新疆	1	697	8,230	-1,980	-4.22	-8.53	11.81	50.50	46,890

3532: Mining Vehicles 工礦車輛製造業

Year 年份	Number of firms 企業個數	Rate of change 每年變化 (%)	Number of employees 職工人數 (人)	Rate of change 每年變化 (%)	Total revenue (Mil. RMB) 總銷售收入 (百萬元)	Rate of change 每年變化 (%)	Total profit (Mil. RMB) 總利潤 (百萬元)	Rate of change 每年變化 (%)
1993	155		31,707		1,635		246	
1994	151	-2.58%	31,269	-1.38%	1,391	-14.91%	40	-83.90%
1995	164	8.61%	33,057	5.72%	1,617	16.25%	60	51.10%
1996	152	-7.32%	34,663	4.86%	1,804	11.56%	45	-24.83%

3 Major products* 3種主要產品*	Output 產量	Sales volume 銷售量	Unit 單位
a) Electric Locomotive of Plant & Mining 礦電機車	606	612	vehicle 輛
b) Loading Machine 裝載機	5,182	4,975	set 台
c) Scraping & Conveying Machinery 鏟土運輸機械	5,371	4,941	set 台

Top 10 firms by revenue (year founded) 收入排名前10家企業 (創辦年份)	City 城市	Province 省	Telephone / fax 電話 / 傳真	Number of employees 職工人數	Ownership 產業所有權	Revenue ('000 RMB) 銷售收入 (千元)	Profit ('000 RMB) (rank) 利潤 (千元) (排名)	Total assets ('000 RMB) 總資產 (千元)	Major products 主要產品
Guangxi Liu Gong Machinery Co. Ltd. 廣西柳工機械股份有限公司(1993)	Liuzhou 柳州市	Guangxi 廣西	(0772)3835631 (0772)3831147	4,947	Joint stock 股份制	605,979	27446(1)	1,116,950	b,c
Qingdao Tai Fa Group Co. 青島泰發集團公司(1980)	Qingdao 青島市	Shandong 山東省	(0532)3191005 (0532)3191088	4,391	Collectively-owned 集體	415,427	10341(2)	202,551	o
Ningbo Ru Yi Co. Ltd. 寧波如意股份有限公司(1996)	Ningbo 寧波市	Zhejiang 浙江省	(0574)5581249 (0574)5583733	450	Joint stock 股份制	56,788	3859(3)	68,104	o
Changzhou Diesel & Mining Locomotive Plant 常州工礦電機車廠(1964)	Changzhou 常州市	Jiangsu 江蘇省	(0519)6600656 (0519)6600443	936	State-owned 國有	52,102	401(13)	131,695	a
Baoji Electric Power Equipment Factory 寶雞電力設備廠(1965)	Baoji 寶雞市	Shaanxi 陝西省	(0917)3432098 (0917)3432512	816	State-owned 國有	49,974	101(29)	104,735	o
Liupanshui Coal Mine Machinery Plant 六盤水煤礦機械廠(1966)	Liupanshui 六盤水市	Guizhou 貴州省	(0858)322121 (0858)323682	2,193	State-owned 國有	46,321	6(45)	116,413	a
State-owned Jiangxi No.2 Machine Tool Factory 國營江西第二機床廠(1965)	Ji'an 吉安市	Jiangxi 江西省	(0796)7722626	2,716	State-owned 國有	44,124	1301(5)	129,238	b,c
Changzhou Engineering Machine Works 常州市工程機械廠(1958)	Changzhou 常州市	Jiangsu 江蘇省	(0519)3260216 (0519)3260216	666	Collectively-owned 集體	43,418	205(23)	26,446	b
Yantai Constructional Machine Works 煙台工程機械廠(1967)	Yantai 煙臺市	Shandong 山東省	(0535)6531314 (0535)6530964	771	State-owned 國有	34,293	1255(6)	85,681	b,c
Liuzhou Engineering Machinery Overhaul Fitting Parts Plant 柳州市工程機械大修配件廠(1977)	Liuzhou 柳州市	Guangxi 廣西	(0772)3886289	345	Collectively-owned 集體	28,744	2409(4)	39,795	o

Top 10 Cities by Production Output 產出排名前10位城市	Province 省	Market share 市場份額	Number of firms 企業個數
Liuzhou 柳州市	Guangxi 廣西	29.25%	10
Qingdao 青島市	Shandong 山東省	23.09%	3
Linyi 臨沂市	Shandong 山東省	9.59%	1
Changzhou 常州市	Jiangsu 江蘇省	5.01%	3
Ningbo 寧波市	Zhejiang 浙江省	3.80%	3
Ji'an 吉安市	Jiangxi 江西省	2.22%	1
Baoji 寶雞市	Shaanxi 陝西省	1.95%	1
Liupanshui 六盤水市	Guizhou 貴州省	1.82%	1
Zhenjiang 鎮江市	Jiangsu 江蘇省	1.64%	1
Yantai 煙臺市	Shandong 山東省	1.59%	2

10 Major Wholesalers 10家主要批發商	City 城市	Province 省	Telephone / Fax 電話 / 傳真
Liaoning Automobile Trade Group Corp. 遼寧省汽車貿易集團	Shenyang 沈陽市	Liaoning 遼寧省	(024)23835494 (024)23838338
China Post and Telecommunication Equipment General Company 中國郵電器材總公司	Beijing 北京市	Beijing 北京市	(010)63523715 (010)63525935
Jiangsu Electromechanical Products General Company 江蘇省機電產品總公司	Nanjing 南京市	Jiangsu 江蘇省	(025)7713642 (025)7711036
Xi Nan Technology Import & Export Company 西南技術進出口公司	Chongqing 重慶市	Chongqing 重慶市	(023)63850185 (023)63850026
Changzhou Economic Technology Industrial Development Zone Tian Ming Trade Company 常州經濟技術產業開發區天明貿易公司	Changzhou 常州市	Jiangsu 江蘇省	(0519)8829882 (0519)8829882
Shanxi Mechanical Equipment Import & Export Company 山西省機械設備進出口公司	Taiyuan 太原市	Shanxi 山西省	(0351)4040713 (0351)4043981
Ningbo Five Mining Machinery Import & Export Company 寧波市五礦機械進出口公司	Ningbo 寧波市	Zhejiang 浙江省	(0574)7311255 (0574)7320322
Tianjin Jin Huan Electromechanical Complete Sets of Equipment Factory 天津市津環機電成套設備廠	Tianjin 天津市	Tianjin 天津市	(022)26371628
Yunnan Machinery Import & Export Company 雲南省機械進出口公司	Kunming 昆明市	Yunnan 雲南省	(0871)3164879 (0871)3136829
Tianjin Da Qiu Zhuang Yi Yuan Trade Center 天津市大丘莊億源商貿中心	Tianjin 天津市	Tianjin 天津市	(022)28899478 (022)28899046

*Also include sales by firms outside this industry.包括本行業以外廠家的銷售。"o" stands for "others". "o" 代表 "其他產品"。

3533: Pumps 泵製造業

The industry accounts for 0.174% of the total revenue of China's industrial sector in 1996. The revenue growth rate of the industry is 6.7% from 1995, as compared to the growth rate of China's industrial sector, 9.51%. The rate of return on asset is 1.82%. 73.01% of all firms in the industry made a profit while 23.29% had negative returns. The top province in terms of the industry's revenue is Jiangsu, accounting for 16.65% of the total revenue.
行業在1996年佔全行業總產值0.174%，行業年增長率為6.7%（全國工業年增長率9.51%）。行業的資產回報率1.82%，73.01%的企業盈利，23.29%的企業虧損。銷售收入最高的省份為江蘇省，佔本行業的16.65%。

	Total number of firms 企業總數	Total number of employees 職工總數	Total revenue (Mil. RMB) 總銷售收入（百萬元）	Total profit (Mil. RMB) 總利潤（百萬元）	Return on assets 資產利潤率 (%)	Return on equity 權益利潤率 (%)	Labour productivity ('000 RMB / worker) 勞動生產率（千元/人）	Debts / assets 資產負債率 (%)	Total assets (Mil. RMB) 總資產（百萬元）
Industry Overall 行業總體	1,459	238,632	10,063	297	1.82	5.35	42.17	65.90	16,261

	Number of firms 企業個數	Average number of employees 平均職工人數	Average revenue ('000 RMB) 平均銷售收入（千元）	Average profit ('000 RMB) 平均利潤（千元）	Return on assets 資產利潤率 (%)	Return on equity 權益利潤率 (%)	Labour productivity ('000 RMB / worker) 勞動生產率（千元/人）	Average debts / assets 平均資產負債率(%)	Average Total assets ('000 RMB) 平均總資產（千元）
By ownership 產業所有權									
State-owned 國有									
Collectively-owned 集體	296	402	13,348	196	0.69	2.16	33.17	67.91	28,216
Privately-owned 私有	1,069	96	4,729	177	3.08	9.18	49.21	66.45	5,752
Domestic JVs 聯營	9	44	1,854	150	6.38	22.47	42.02	71.60	2,353
Joint stock 股份制	16	179	6,301	151	1.10	2.65	35.30	58.55	13,711
Foreign-funded 外資	26	324	18,935	1,070	3.75	9.93	58.48	62.25	28,554
Overseas Chinese-funded 港澳台資	23	178	14,171	34	0.13	0.22	79.79	41.98	26,531
By size 規模	17	116	7,004	993	10.33	24.38	60.50	57.63	9,609
Large 大型									
Medium 中型	16	1,724	100,173	3,288	1.44	3.84	58.11	62.45	227,858
Small 小型	69	797	35,983	577	0.89	2.47	45.16	63.92	64,908
By regional distribution 地區分布	1,364	115	4,382	150	2.51	7.99	38.22	68.54	5,965
Central-North 華北									
Beijing 北京	184	189	7,384	365	3.03	8.46	39.17	64.24	12,057
Tianjin 天津	25	153	4,540	-177	-1.19	-2.59	29.74	54.20	14,942
Hebei 河北	29	148	6,244	124	1.20	3.56	42.07	66.15	10,334
Shanxi 山西	86	191	9,378	699	5.82	16.65	49.15	65.04	12,001
Inner Mongolia 內蒙	27	249	6,829	216	1.65	4.54	27.38	63.53	13,026
Northeast 東北	17	202	4,308	120	1.26	6.45	21.37	80.39	9,494
Liaoning 遼寧	355	125	4,259	30	0.32	0.98	34.20	67.76	9,522
Jilin 吉林	259	122	4,980	97	0.90	2.73	40.92	66.83	10,687
Heilongjiang 黑龍江	45	161	2,740	-326	-3.92	-17.53	16.98	77.65	8,334
Central East 華東	51	106	1,940	7	0.15	0.40	18.23	62.96	4,654
Shanghai 上海	592	159	8,248	263	2.30	6.51	51.85	64.77	11,460
Jiangsu 江蘇	67	138	10,125	46	0.30	0.81	73.50	62.94	15,530
Zhejiang 浙江	186	157	9,010	192	1.73	5.12	57.43	66.27	11,095
Anhui 安徽	149	117	6,377	293	3.47	8.51	54.29	59.22	8,438
Fujian 福建	50	138	6,291	289	3.27	11.12	45.50	70.62	8,851
Jiangxi 江西	27	104	3,201	15	0.27	0.57	30.68	52.19	5,481
Shandong 山東	30	238	3,691	58	0.62	2.90	15.53	78.73	9,463
Central-South 中南	83	258	12,854	683	3.66	10.60	49.83	65.47	18,654
Henan 河南	243	172	7,074	252	2.36	6.82	41.19	65.41	10,678
Hubei 湖北	62	200	5,797	103	0.92	2.74	28.96	66.35	11,144
Hunan 湖南	27	254	6,563	129	0.99	2.95	25.86	66.24	12,958
Guangdong 廣東	99	135	5,911	372	4.74	11.80	43.88	59.86	7,848
Guangxi 廣西	41	161	13,300	465	2.86	9.94	82.57	71.23	16,245
Hainan 海南	13	182	3,928	-345	-4.32	-11.20	21.61	61.47	8,004
Southwest 西南	1	164	1,000				6.10	48.91	6,850
Chongqing 重慶	54	260	6,587	39	0.29	1.00	25.32	70.83	13,517
Sichuan 四川	15	183	4,329	60	0.71	1.85	23.69	61.92	8,563
Guizhou 貴州	31	296	7,298	69	0.45	1.72	24.68	74.02	15,395
Yunnan 雲南	4	235	5,273	-63	-0.60	-1.32	22.41	54.33	10,373
Tibet 西藏	4	311	11,120	-160	-0.75	-3.00	35.73	74.91	21,250
Northwest 西北									
Shaanxi 陝西	31	315	7,565	-6	-0.03	-0.12	24.02	71.01	17,861
Gansu 甘肅	20	287	5,968	-96	-0.75	-3.50	20.79	78.46	12,732
Qinghai 青海	5	429	10,832	-168	-0.57	-1.85	25.24	69.18	29,536
Ningxia 寧夏	1	112	710				6.34	88.62	2,900
Xinjiang 新疆	1	413	10,370	350	1.38	4.37	25.11	68.45	25,390
	4	338	12,480	555	1.80	4.28	36.92	57.89	30,768

Year 年份	Number of firms 企業個數	Rate of change 每年變化 (%)	Number of employees 職工人數 (人)	Rate of change 每年變化 (%)	Total revenue (Mil. RMB) 總銷售收入 (百萬元)	Rate of change 每年變化 (%)	Total profit (Mil. RMB) 總利潤 (百萬元)	Rate of change 每年變化 (%)
1993	1,223		276,198		7,745		408	
1994	1,327	8.50%	240,640	-12.88%	8,235	6.34%	227	-44.26%
1995	1,408	6.10%	246,825	2.57%	9,431	14.52%	292	28.48%
1996	1,459	3.62%	238,632	-3.32%	10,063	6.70%	297	1.71%

3 Major products* 3種主要產品*	Output 產量	Sales volume 銷售量	Unit 單位
a) Industrial Pump 工業泵	1,556,079	1,587,200	set 台
b) Agricultural Water Pump 農業水泵	3,136,078	2,947,913	set 台
c) General Mechanical Accessories 通用機械配件	24,431	20,766	ton 噸

Top 10 firms by revenue (year founded) 收入排名前10家企業 (創辦年份)	City 城市	Province 省	Telephone / fax 電話 / 傳真	Number of employees 職工人數	Ownership 產業所有權	Revenue ('000 RMB) 銷售收入 (千元)	Profit ('000 RMB) (rank) 利潤 (千元) (排名)	Total assets ('000 RMB) 總資產 (千元)	Major products 主要產品
Shenyang Water Pump Works 沈陽水泵廠(1932)	Shenyang 沈陽市	Liaoning 遼寧省	(024)25822411 (024)25820108	5,246	State-owned 國有	249,736	100(370)	985,751	a,c
Shanghai Ksb Pump Co. Ltd. 上海凱士比泵有限公司(1995)	Shanghai 上海市	Shanghai 上海市	(021)64302191 (021)64301504	1,535	Foreign-funded 外資	190,522	-9484(728)	309,553	a,b,c
Changsha Water Pump Works 長沙水泵廠(1951)	Changsha 長沙市	Hunan 湖南省	(0731)5215460 (0731)5212978	2,306	State-owned 國有	176,194	6885(8)	281,123	a,c
Hebei Shijiazhuang Water Pump Works 河北省石家裝水泵廠(1949)	Shijiazhuang 石家莊市	Hebei 河北省	(0311)6088906 (0311)6082677	3,046	State-owned 國有	165,043	9096(3)	268,901	a,c
Zhejiang Feng Qiu Group Corp. (zhuji Water Pump Factory) 浙江豐球集團公司(1985)	Shaoxing 紹興市	Zhejiang 浙江省	(0575)7012118	453	Collectively-owned 集體	152,490	11330(1)	274,394	a,b
Jiangsu Qi Zhou Group 江蘇七洲集團(1953)	Xuzhou 徐州市	Jiangsu 江蘇省	(0516)4622405 (0516)4622483	2,354	State-owned 國有	135,876	4805(16)	212,259	a,b
Dalian Acid Proof Pump Plant 大連耐酸泵廠(1953)	Dalian 大連市	Liaoning 遼寧省	(0411)4403456 (0411)4405224	2,049	State-owned 國有	132,740	2104(47)	291,526	o
Jiangsu Ya Tai Pump Industry Group Company 江蘇亞太泵業集團公司(1971)	Yangzhou 揚州市	Jiangsu 江蘇省	(0514)7633148 (0514)7625252	682	Collectively-owned 集體	125,201	10364(2)	140,279	a
Boshan Water Pump Works 博山水泵廠(1929)	Zibo 淄博市	Shandong 山東省	(0533)4183532 (0533)4182018	2,215	State-owned 國有	122,171	5049(14)	194,287	a
Wuxi Water Pump Factory 無錫市水泵廠(1935)	Wuxi 無錫市	Jiangsu 江蘇省	(0510)5754456 (0510)5736120	1,108	State-owned 國有	100,657	1155(88)	173,747	a,b

Top 10 Cities by Production Output 產出排名前10位城市	Province 省	Market share 市場份額	Number of firms 企業個數
Shanghai 上海市	Shanghai 上海市	7.17%	108
Taizhou 泰州市	Jiangsu 江蘇省	7.10%	62
Taizhou 臺州市	Zhejiang 浙江省	5.53%	272
Shenyang 沈陽市	Liaoning 遼寧省	5.31%	132
Zibo 淄博市	Shandong 山東省	3.27%	19
Changsha 長沙市	Hunan 湖南省	2.98%	18
Hangzhou 杭州市	Zhejiang 浙江省	2.88%	33
Dalian 大連市	Liaoning 遼寧省	2.37%	69
Shijiazhuang 石家莊市	Hebei 河北省	2.27%	12
Tianjin 天津市	Tianjin 天津市	2.00%	34

10 Major Wholesalers 10家主要批發商	City 城市	Province 省	Telephone / Fax 電話 / 傳真
Liaoning Automobile Trade Group Corp. 遼寧省汽車貿易集團	Shenyang 沈陽市	Liaoning 遼寧省	(024)23835494 (024)23838338
China Post and Telecommunication Equipment General Company 中國郵電器材總公司	Beijing 北京市	Beijing 北京市	(010)63523715 (010)63525935
Jiangsu Electromechanical Products General Company 江蘇省機電產品總公司	Nanjing 南京市	Jiangsu 江蘇省	(025)7713642 (025)7711036
Xi Nan Technology Import & Export Company 西南技術進出口公司	Chongqing 重慶市	Chongqing 重慶市	(023)63850185 (023)63850026
Changzhou Economic Technology Industrial Development Zone Tian Ming Trade Company 常州經濟技術產業開發區天明貿易公司	Changzhou 常州市	Jiangsu 江蘇省	(0519)8829882 (0519)8829882
Shanxi Mechanical Equipment Import & Export Company 山西省機械設備進出口公司	Taiyuan 太原市	Shanxi 山西省	(0351)4040713 (0351)4043981
Ningbo Five Mining Machinery Import & Export Company 寧波市五礦機械進出口公司	Ningbo 寧波市	Zhejiang 浙江省	(0574)7311255 (0574)7320322
Tianjin Jin Huan Electromechanical Complete Sets of Equipment Factory 天津市津環機電成套設備廠	Tianjin 天津市	Tianjin 天津市	(022)26371628
Yunnan Machinery Import & Export Company 雲南省機械進出口公司	Kunming 昆明市	Yunnan 雲南省	(0871)3164879 (0871)3136829
Tianjin Da Qiu Zhuang Yi Yuan Trade Center 天津市大丘莊億源商貿中心	Tianjin 天津市	Tianjin 天津市	(022)28899478 (022)28899046

*Also include sales by firms outside this industry.包括本行業以外廠家的銷售。"o" stands for "others". "o" 代表"其他產品"。

3534: Fans 風機製造業

The industry accounts for 0.064% of the total revenue of China's industrial sector in 1996. The revenue growth rate of the industry is -2.9% from 1995, as compared to the growth rate of China's industrial sector, 9.51%. The rate of return on asset is 2.40%. 70.01% of all firms in the industry made a profit while 25.33% had negative returns. The top province in terms of the industry's revenue is Liaoning, accounting for 15.82% of the total revenue.
本行業在 1996 年佔全行業總產值 0.064%，行業年增長率為 -2.9%（全國工業年增長率 9.51%）。行業的資產回報率 2.40%，70.01% 的企業盈利，25.33% 的企業虧損。銷售收入最高的省份為遼寧省，佔本行業的 15.82%。

	Total number of firms 企業總數	Total number of employees 職工總數	Total revenue (Mil. RMB) 總銷售收入（百萬元）	Total profit (Mil. RMB) 總利潤（百萬元）	Return on assets 資產利潤率 (%)	Return on equity 權益利潤率 (%)	Labour productivity ('000 RMB / worker) 勞動生產率（千元/人）	Debts / assets 資產負債率 (%)	Total assets (Mil. RMB) 總資產（百萬元）
Industry Overall 行業總體	498	83,163	3,712	154	2.40	7.64	44.64	68.57	6,394

	Number of firms 企業個數	Average number of employees 平均職工人數	Average revenue ('000 RMB) 平均銷售收入（千元）	Average profit ('000 RMB) 平均利潤（千元）	Return on assets 資產利潤率 (%)	Return on equity 權益利潤率 (%)	Labour productivity ('000 RMB / worker) 勞動生產率（千元/人）	Average debts / assets 平均資產負債率(%)	Average Total assets ('000 RMB) 平均總資產（千元）
By ownership 產業所有權									
State-owned 國有	71	505	22,394	211	0.41	1.33	44.35	69.19	51,704
Collectively-owned 集體	398	106	4,705	298	5.25	15.07	44.24	65.14	5,681
Privately-owned 私有	4	55	2,908	214	6.09	104.89	53.35	94.19	3,517
Domestic JVs 聯營	1	37	817	-16	-1.10	-2.12	22.08	48.35	1,504
Joint stock 股份制	8	384	18,461	1,919	5.11	26.34	48.11	80.62	37,597
Foreign-funded 外資	7	82	5,339	388	4.18	19.49	64.99	78.56	9,279
Overseas Chinese-funded 港澳台資	8	135	6,472	164	1.62	7.66	48.07	78.82	10,133
By size 規模									
Large 大型	8	2,265	157,528	8,539	2.59	7.63	69.56	66.01	329,114
Medium 中型	22	779	34,567	1,947	3.49	9.99	44.35	65.09	55,823
Small 小型	467	103	3,622	92	1.69	6.24	35.32	72.91	5,424
By regional distribution 地區分布									
Central-North 華北	67	136	5,479	188	1.99	6.06	40.42	67.07	9,443
Beijing 北京	19	171	6,413	-27	-0.21	-0.58	37.43	64.89	13,336
Tianjin 天津	16	161	6,755	236	2.14	6.71	41.97	68.02	10,988
Hebei 河北	21	85	3,965	379	8.46	18.09	46.46	53.22	4,474
Shanxi 山西	9	104	3,793	118	1.60	8.49	36.40	81.14	7,352
Inner Mongolia 內蒙	2	261	9,880	180	0.83	5.35	37.93	84.48	21,680
Northeast 東北	141	139	5,164	143	1.18	3.89	37.11	69.64	12,119
Liaoning 遼寧	78	166	7,527	78	0.47	1.63	45.26	71.16	16,679
Jilin 吉林	44	112	2,265	301	4.05	11.52	20.26	64.81	7,427
Heilongjiang 黑龍江	19	91	2,175	43	1.00	2.82	23.90	64.58	4,263
Central East 華東	164	146	9,449	328	2.83	9.38	64.82	69.84	11,600
Shanghai 上海	19	222	19,006	245	0.89	4.18	85.51	78.73	27,604
Jiangsu 江蘇	71	117	7,722	197	2.55	9.99	65.82	74.46	7,737
Zhejiang 浙江	30	110	8,496	508	5.57	14.77	77.10	62.27	9,122
Anhui 安徽	5	208	6,448	98	1.24	3.64	31.06	66.01	7,926
Fujian 福建	7	95	2,803	-19	-0.24	-0.58	29.46	58.07	7,651
Jiangxi 江西	8	108	1,115	-61	-1.86	-11.29	10.30	83.52	3,293
Shandong 山東	24	228	13,528	835	4.60	11.24	59.26	59.05	18,146
Central-South 中南	60	176	7,209	80	0.63	1.56	40.99	59.58	12,634
Henan 河南	15	87	2,919	51	1.69	4.62	33.63	63.46	3,039
Hubei 湖北	14	308	10,524	-141	-0.66	-2.25	34.22	70.44	21,199
Hunan 湖南	15	188	8,997	415	2.60	4.58	47.93	43.24	15,957
Guangdong 廣東	14	110	6,269	-12	-0.15	-0.46	57.10	67.35	8,133
Guangxi 廣西	2	296	9,330	-30	-0.10	-0.21	31.52	53.63	31,225
Hainan 海南									
Southwest 西南	32	293	8,973	37	0.23	0.59	30.67	60.45	15,999
Chongqing 重慶	18	247	8,011	13	0.09	0.25	32.40	63.13	13,435
Sichuan 四川	6	589	18,904	79	0.21	0.48	32.10	56.22	37,340
Guizhou 貴州	6	156	2,967	60	1.03	2.69	19.04	61.75	5,838
Yunnan 雲南	2	289	8,030	75	0.73	2.35	27.79	69.14	10,320
Tibet 西藏									
Northwest 西北	34	313	10,211	1,795	6.94	30.52	32.63	77.27	25,872
Shaanxi 陝西	27	355	11,776	2,288	7.63	36.08	33.20	78.84	29,972
Gansu 甘肅	2	113	2,710	135	2.05	4.42	23.98	53.53	6,585
Qinghai 青海	1	50	630	-180	-7.35	360.00	12.60	102.04	2,450
Ningxia 寧夏	1	341	3,370	-1,630	-7.51	-16.72	9.88	55.05	21,690
Xinjiang 新疆	3	148	6,597	263	2.39	6.11	44.57	60.99	11,030

Year 年份	Number of firms 企業個數	Rate of change 每年變化 (%)	Number of employees 職工人數 (人)	Rate of change 每年變化 (%)	Total revenue (Mil. RMB) 總銷售收入 (百萬元)	Rate of change 每年變化 (%)	Total profit (Mil. RMB) 總利潤 (百萬元)	Rate of change 每年變化 (%)
1993	412		88,979		2,819		146	
1994	444	7.77%	77,014	-13.45%	2,678	-5.01%	85	-41.66%
1995	485	9.23%	81,896	6.34%	3,822	42.70%	141	65.10%
1996	498	2.68%	83,163	1.55%	3,712	-2.88%	154	9.24%

3 Major products* 3種主要產品*	Output 產量	Sales volume 銷售量	Unit 單位
a) Air Blower 風機	1,420,311	1,363,498	set 台
b) General Mechanical Accessories 通用機械配件	13,875	11,793	ton 噸
c) Environment Protecting Equipment 環保設備	8,982	8,443	set 台

Top 10 firms by revenue (year founded) 收入排名前10家企業 (創辦年份)	City 城市	Province 省	Telephone / fax 電話 / 傳真	Number of employees 職工人數	Ownership 產業所有權	Revenue ('000 RMB) 銷售收入 (千元)	Profit ('000 RMB) (rank) 利潤 (千元) (排名)	Total assets ('000 RMB) 總資產 (千元)	Major products 主要產品
Shenyang Blower Works 沈陽鼓風機廠(1934)	Shenyang 沈陽市	Liaoning 遼寧省	(024)25801965 (024)25854719	4,382	State-owned 國有	314,579	4210(7)	876,242	a,b
Wujin Fan Factory 武進市風機廠(1954)	Changzhou 常州市	Jiangsu 江蘇省	(0519)6261072 (0519)6261413	2,119	Collectively-owned 集體	253,059	13958(3)	159,130	o
Shanghai Blower Works 上海鼓風機廠(1947)	Shanghai 上海市	Shanghai 上海市	(021)56650577 (021)56651514	1,848	State-owned 國有	237,743	4015(9)	361,400	a,b
Shannxi Blower (Group) Co. Ltd. 陝西鼓風機(集團)有限公司(1970)	Xi'an 西安市	Shaanxi 陝西省	(029)3931400 (029)3931422	3,878	State-owned 國有	190,896	1507(20)	565,372	o
Chongqing General Machinery Factory 重慶通用機器廠	Chongqing 重慶市	Chongqing 重慶市	(023)67610178 (023)67608255	2,794	State-owned 國有	104,635	2062(15)	187,621	a,b
Wengdeng Fan Factory 文登市風機廠(1976)	Weihai 威海市	Shandong 山東省	(0896)8731032 (0896)8731098	350	Collectively-owned 集體	94,680	7860(4)	39,820	a,c
Changsha Blower Works 長沙鼓風機廠(1950)	Changsha 長沙市	Hunan 湖南省	(0731)5585740 (0731)5582640	1,529	State-owned 國有	88,960	4079(8)	179,140	a,b,c
Shandong Prorince Zhangqiu Blower Works 山東省章丘市鼓風機廠(1968)	Ji'nan 濟南市	Shandong 山東省	(0531)3213561 (0531)3214543	1,357	Collectively-owned 集體	75,254	7062(5)	206,460	a
Xi'an Tong Da Turbine Machinery Complete Set of Technology Co. Ltd. 西安通達透平機械成套技術有限公司(1993)	Xi'an 西安市	Shaanxi 陝西省	(029)8225341 (029)8225321	112	Joint stock 股份制	73,000	60604(1)	107,655	o
Shangyu Refrigeration Draft Equipment Factory 上虞市製冷通風設備廠(1992)	Shaoxing 紹興市	Zhejiang 浙江省	(0575)2051140	105	Collectively-owned 集體	65,396	3461(10)	14,953	o

Top 10 Cities by Production Output 產出排名前10位城市	Province 省	Market share 市場份額	Number of firms 企業個數
Shenyang 沈陽市	Liaoning 遼寧省	13.31%	40
Xi'an 西安市	Shaanxi 陝西省	7.59%	17
Shanghai 上海市	Shanghai 上海市	6.94%	43
Siping 四平市	Jilin 吉林省	4.21%	18
Ji'nan 濟南市	Shandong 山東省	3.77%	8
Beijing 北京市	Beijing 北京市	3.77%	18
Changsha 長沙市	Hunan 湖南省	3.76%	10
Wuxi 無錫市	Jiangsu 江蘇省	3.72%	18
Changzhou 常州市	Jiangsu 江蘇省	3.68%	22
Tianjin 天津市	Tianjin 天津市	3.53%	14

10 Major Wholesalers 10家主要批發商	City 城市	Province 省	Telephone / Fax 電話 / 傳真
Liaoning Automobile Trade Group Corp. 遼寧省汽車貿易集團	Shenyang 沈陽市	Liaoning 遼寧省	(024)23835494 (024)23838338
China Post and Telecommunication Equipment General Company 中國郵電器材總公司	Beijing 北京市	Beijing 北京市	(010)63523715 (010)63525935
Jiangsu Electromechanical Products General Company 江蘇省機電產品總公司	Nanjing 南京市	Jiangsu 江蘇省	(025)7713642 (025)7711036
Xi Nan Technology Import & Export Company 西南技術進出口公司	Chongqing 重慶市	Chongqing 重慶市	(023)63850185 (023)63850026
Changzhou Economic Technology Industrial Development Zone Tian Ming Trade Company 常州經濟技術產業開發區天明貿易公司	Changzhou 常州市	Jiangsu 江蘇省	(0519)8829882 (0519)8829882
Shanxi Mechanical Equipment Import & Export Company 山西省機械設備進出口公司	Taiyuan 太原市	Shanxi 山西省	(0351)4040713 (0351)4043981
Ningbo Five Mining Machinery Import & Export Company 寧波市五礦機械進出口公司	Ningbo 寧波市	Zhejiang 浙江省	(0574)7311255 (0574)7320322
Tianjin Jin Huan Electromechanical Complete Sets of Equipment Factory 天津市津環機電成套設備廠	Tianjin 天津市	Tianjin 天津市	(022)26371628
Yunnan Machinery Import & Export Company 雲南省機械進出口公司	Kunming 昆明市	Yunnan 雲南省	(0871)3164879 (0871)3136829
Tianjin Da Qiu Zhuang Yi Yuan Trade Center 天津市大丘莊億源商貿中心	Tianjin 天津市	Tianjin 天津市	(022)28899478 (022)28899046

*Also include sales by firms outside this industry.包括本行業以外廠家的銷售。"o" stands for "others". "o"代表"其他產品"。

3535: Air Compressors and Separation Equipment
氣體壓縮機及氣體分離設備製造業

The industry accounts for 0.103% of the total revenue of China's industrial sector in 1996. The revenue growth rate of the industry is 16.4% from 1995, as compared to the growth rate of China's industrial sector, 9.51%. The rate of return on asset is 1.34%. 63.51% of all firms in the industry made a profit while 29.39% had negative returns. The top province in terms of the industry's revenue is Guangdong, accounting for 17.17% of the total revenue.
本行業在1996年佔全行業總產值0.103%，行業年增長率為16.4%（全國工業年增長率9.51%）。行業的資產回報率1.34%，63.51%的企業盈利，29.39%的企業虧損。銷售收入最高的省份為廣東省，佔本行業的17.17%。

	Total number of firms 企業總數	Total number of employees 職工總數	Total revenue (Mil. RMB) 總銷售收入（百萬元）	Total profit (Mil. RMB) 總利潤（百萬元）	Return on assets 資產利潤率 (%)	Return on equity 權益利潤率 (%)	Labour productivity ('000 RMB / worker) 勞動生產率（千元/人）	Debts / assets 資產負債率 (%)	Total assets (Mil. RMB) 總資產（百萬元）
Industry Overall 行業總體	332	109,147	5,960	167	1.34	4.15	54.61	67.71	12,472

	Number of firms 企業個數	Average number of employees 平均職工人數	Average revenue ('000 RMB) 平均銷售收入（千元）	Average profit ('000 RMB) 平均利潤（千元）	Return on assets 資產利潤率 (%)	Return on equity 權益利潤率 (%)	Labour productivity ('000 RMB / worker) 勞動生產率（千元/人）	Average debts / assets 平均資產負債率(%)	Average Total assets ('000 RMB) 平均總資產（千元）
By ownership 產業所有權									
State-owned 國有	78	945	35,769	-90	-0.10	-0.31	37.84	67.40	90,090
Collectively-owned 集體	205	106	6,815	-6,309	-100.30	-341.91	64.02	70.67	6,290
Privately-owned 私有									
Domestic JVs 聯營	2	83	7,380	-14,556	-263.77	-637.53	89.46	58.63	5,518
Joint stock 股份制	17	583	53,095	-46,056	-54.06	-157.22	91.01	65.61	85,193
Foreign-funded 外資	18	98	34,590	82,095	72.09	187.96	354.57	61.65	113,884
Overseas Chinese-funded 港澳台資	11	171	21,176	72,979	124.19	1162.53	123.64	89.32	58,766
By size 規模									
Large 大型	19	2,364	142,077	7,776	2.43	8.37	60.11	70.96	320,029
Medium 中型	31	902	52,608	6,857	7.94	21.52	58.35	63.11	86,354
Small 小型	275	132	5,927	-703	-5.20	-15.18	45.00	65.72	13,508
By regional distribution 地區分布									
Central-North 華北	42	246	7,882	-239	-1.37	-5.03	32.04	72.78	17,436
Beijing 北京	16	160	11,677	285	1.27	5.51	72.84	77.03	22,515
Tianjin 天津	6	159	2,820	-535	-8.01	-30.48	17.74	73.71	6,682
Hebei 河北	11	456	9,489	-777	-3.49	-14.46	20.83	75.87	22,268
Shanxi 山西	6	273	3,598	-487	-3.52	-6.41	13.16	45.09	13,820
Inner Mongolia 內蒙	3	54	440	30	2.19	6.47	8.15	65.94	1,370
Northeast 東北	64	305	8,492	-734	-3.17	-13.25	27.83	76.11	23,189
Liaoning 遼寧	53	258	7,966	-39	-0.20	-0.78	30.93	74.18	19,365
Jilin 吉林	5	291	2,702	-1,602	-10.67	-157.99	9.28	93.25	15,014
Heilongjiang 黑龍江	6	738	17,960	-6,153	-9.65	-43.73	24.35	77.93	63,773
Central East 華東	140	317	21,629	1,561	4.36	12.01	68.29	63.73	35,834
Shanghai 上海	21	277	33,242	2,357	5.17	15.86	119.84	67.37	45,545
Jiangsu 江蘇	36	331	26,463	2,623	7.14	18.50	79.87	61.39	36,719
Zhejiang 浙江	43	298	18,201	1,496	3.71	9.09	61.03	59.24	40,349
Anhui 安徽	11	482	13,412	-298	-1.00	-3.73	27.80	73.20	29,831
Fujian 福建	5	193	15,544	82	0.46	1.36	80.62	65.96	17,710
Jiangxi 江西	8	455	9,976	224	0.91	2.64	21.94	65.59	24,641
Shandong 山東	16	241	18,105	709	2.91	10.89	75.05	73.25	24,354
Central-South 中南	49	436	33,445	225	0.26	0.85	76.80	69.21	86,003
Henan 河南	16	380	14,768	1,348	4.13	9.32	38.83	55.74	32,681
Hubei 湖北	8	373	9,235	73	0.59	2.36	24.79	74.82	12,214
Hunan 湖南	6	459	6,940	-303	-0.98	-3.23	15.13	69.83	31,075
Guangdong 廣東	11	284	93,025	1,004	0.45	1.72	327.66	73.86	222,604
Guangxi 廣西	8	800	32,965	-2,541	-2.12	-5.89	41.21	64.01	119,808
Hainan 海南									
Southwest 西南	26	446	14,654	-173	-0.48	-1.41	32.84	65.61	35,776
Chongqing 重慶	11	210	4,203	-95	-1.05	-3.84	19.99	72.55	9,030
Sichuan 四川	13	713	26,009	-275	-0.42	-1.20	36.47	64.76	64,951
Guizhou 貴州	1	155	2,660	10	0.28	0.72	17.16	62.26	3,630
Yunnan 雲南	1	44	2,020	40	1.16	3.08	45.91	62.32	3,450
Tibet 西藏									
Northwest 西北	11	182	3,449	-85	-0.99	-2.60	18.98	61.97	8,630
Shaanxi 陝西	10	175	3,602	-9	-0.10	-0.27	20.58	61.29	8,718
Gansu 甘肅									
Qinghai 青海									
Ningxia 寧夏									
Xinjiang 新疆	1	249	1,920	-850	-10.97	-36.17	7.71	69.68	7,750

3535: Air Compressors and Separation Equipment
氣體壓縮機及氣體分離設備製造業

Year 年份	Number of firms 企業個數	Rate of change 每年變化 (%)	Number of employees 職工人數（人）	Rate of change 每年變化 (%)	Total revenue (Mil. RMB) 總銷售收入（百萬元）	Rate of change 每年變化 (%)	Total profit (Mil. RMB) 總利潤（百萬元）	Rate of change 每年變化 (%)
1993	240		110,686		4,274		227	
1994	268	11.67%	97,312	-12.08%	4,203	-1.66%	223	-1.65%
1995	298	11.19%	108,090	11.08%	5,122	21.85%	81	-63.71%
1996	332	11.41%	109,147	0.98%	5,960	16.36%	167	106.24%

3 Major products* 3 種主要產品 *	Output 產量	Sales volume 銷售量	Unit 單位
a) Gas Compressor 氣體壓縮機	505,727	490,555	set 台
b) Gas Separating & Liquefying Equipment 氣體分離與液化設備	3,556	2,347	set 台
c) Air Conditioner Compressor 空調器用壓縮機	2,146,416	2,725,949	set 台

Top 10 firms by revenue (year founded) 收入排名前 10 家企業 (創辦年份)	City 城市	Province 省	Telephone / fax 電話 / 傳真	Number of employees 職工人數	Ownership 產業所有權	Revenue ('000 RMB) 銷售收入（千元）	Profit ('000 RMB) (rank) 利潤（千元）（排名）	Total assets ('000 RMB) 總資產（千元）	Major products 主要產品
Matsushita-wanbao (Guangzhou) Compressor Co., Ltd. 松下萬寶(廣州)壓縮機有限公司(1993)	Guangzhou 廣州市	Guangdong 廣東省	(020)84778123 (020)84775576	1,058	Foreign-funded 外資	727,055	6683(5)	1,750,422	c
Hangzhou Oxygen Making Machine Group Co., Ltd. 杭州製氧機集團有限公司(1950)	Hangzhou 杭州市	Zhejiang 浙江省	(0571)5372001 (0571)5371643	6,055	State-owned 國有	292,534	14646(4)	966,269	a,b
Taizhou Chun Lan Compressor Plant 泰州春蘭壓縮機廠(1991)	Taizhou 泰州市	Jiangsu 江蘇省	(0523)6552797 (0523)6552441	960	Collectively-owned 集體	264,763	68100(1)	209,892	c
Shenyang Gas Compressor Factory 沈陽氣體壓縮機廠(1938)	Shenyang 沈陽市	Liaoning 遼寧省	(024)25840324 (024)25852167	4,296	State-owned 國有	248,564	1003(36)	554,819	a
Shanghai Compressor Factory 上海壓縮機廠(1940)	Shanghai 上海市	Shanghai 上海市	(021)56624200 (021)56632111	2,530	State-owned 國有	218,299	1889(21)	274,987	a
Zhuhai Ge Li Machinery Co., Ltd. 珠海格力機械有限公司(1985)	Zhuhai 珠海市	Guangdong 廣東省	(0756)3331889 (0756)3331894	798	Overseas Chinese-funded 港澳台資	169,325	5482(6)	473,410	c
Shanghai Ingersoll-rand Compressor Ltd. 上海英格索蘭壓縮機有限公司(1990)	Shanghai 上海市	Shanghai 上海市	(021)64302631 (021)64302196	240	Foreign-funded 外資	159,051	41280(2)	112,824	a
Shandong Weifang Bai Shi De Machinery General Company 山東省濰坊百事得機械總公司(1951)	Weifang 濰坊市	Shandong 山東省	(0536)8324961 (0536)8325324	1,530	State-owned 國有	153,470	1209(32)	243,735	a
Sichuan Air Separation Plant Ltd. Liability (Group) Co. 四川空分設備(集團)有限責任公司(1971)	Neijiang 內江市	Sichuan 四川省	(0832)72224226 (0832)7223916	2,703	State-owned 國有	153,408	1419(25)	325,651	a,b
Wuxi Compressor Co., Ltd. 無錫壓縮機股份有限公司(1936)	Wuxi 無錫市	Jiangsu 江蘇省	(0510)5024889 (0510)5019865	2,378	Joint stock 股份制	135,032	3219(15)	254,691	a

Top 10 Cities by Production Output 產出排名前 10 位城市	Province 省	Market share 市場份額	Number of firms 企業個數
Shanghai 上海市	Shanghai 上海市	19.53%	27
Guangzhou 廣州市	Guangdong 廣東省	11.78%	5
Hangzhou 杭州市	Zhejiang 浙江省	5.65%	10
Shenyang 沈陽市	Liaoning 遼寧省	5.36%	44
Taizhou 泰州市	Jiangsu 江蘇省	3.84%	6
Neijiang 內江市	Sichuan 四川省	3.61%	4
Nanjing 南京市	Jiangsu 江蘇省	3.53%	10
Liuzhou 柳州市	Guangxi 廣西	3.49%	20
Kaifeng 開封市	Henan 河南省	3.14%	10
Quzhou 衢州市	Zhejiang 浙江省	2.99%	3

10 Major Wholesalers 10 家主要批發商	City 城市	Province 省	Telephone / Fax 電話 / 傳真
Liaoning Automobile Trade Group Corp. 遼寧省汽車貿易集團	Shenyang 沈陽市	Liaoning 遼寧省	(024)23835494 (024)23838338
China Post and Telecommunication Equipment General Company 中國郵電器材總公司	Beijing 北京市	Beijing 北京市	(010)63523715 (010)63525935
Jiangsu Electromechanical Products General Company 江蘇省機電產品總公司	Nanjing 南京市	Jiangsu 江蘇省	(025)7713642 (025)7711036
Xi Nan Technology Import & Export Company 西南技術進出口公司	Chongqing 重慶市	Chongqing 重慶市	(023)63850185 (023)63850026
Changzhou Economic Technology Industrial Development Zone Tian Ming Trade Company 常州經濟技術產業開發區天明貿易公司	Changzhou 常州市	Jiangsu 江蘇省	(0519)8829882 (0519)8829882
Shanxi Mechanical Equipment Import & Export Company 山西省機械設備進出口公司	Taiyuan 太原市	Shanxi 山西省	(0351)4040713 (0351)4043981
Ningbo Five Mining Machinery Import & Export Company 寧波市五礦機械進出口公司	Ningbo 寧波市	Zhejiang 浙江省	(0574)7311255 (0574)7320322
Tianjin Jin Huan Electromechanical Complete Sets of Equipment Factory 天津市津環機電成套設備廠	Tianjin 天津市	Tianjin 天津市	(022)26371628
Yunnan Machinery Import & Export Company 雲南省機械進出口公司	Kunming 昆明市	Yunnan 雲南省	(0871)3164879 (0871)3136829
Tianjin Da Qiu Zhuang Yi Yuan Trade Center 天津市大丘莊億源商貿中心	Tianjin 天津市	Tianjin 天津市	(022)28899478 (022)28899046

*Also include sales by firms outside this industry.包括本行業以外廠家的銷售。"o" stands for "others". "o" 代表 "其他產品"。

3536: Refrigeration Equipment 冷凍設備製造業

The industry accounts for 0.165% of the total revenue of China's industrial sector in 1996. The revenue growth rate of the industry is 13.0% from 1995, as compared to the growth rate of China's industrial sector, 9.51%. The rate of return on asset is 5.18%. 64.56% of all firms in the industry made a profit while 30.18% had negative returns. The top province in terms of the industry's revenue is Shanghai, accounting for 27.39% of the total revenue.
本行業在1996年佔全行業總產值0.165%，行業年增長率為13.0%（全國工業年增長率9.51%）。行業的資產回報率5.18%，64.56%的企業盈利，30.18%的企業虧損。銷售收入最高的省份為上海市，佔本行業的27.39%。

	Total number of firms 企業總數	Total number of employees 職工總數	Total revenue (Mil. RMB) 總銷售收入（百萬元）	Total profit (Mil. RMB) 總利潤（百萬元）	Return on assets 資產利潤率 (%)	Return on equity 權益利潤率 (%)	Labour productivity ('000 RMB / worker) 勞動生產率（千元/人）	Debts / assets 資產負債率 (%)	Total assets (Mil. RMB) 總資產（百萬元）
Industry Overall 行業總體	352	81,306	9,586	799	5.18	10.86	117.90	52.27	15,417

	Number of firms 企業個數	Average number of employees 平均職工人數	Average revenue ('000 RMB) 平均銷售收入（千元）	Average profit ('000 RMB) 平均利潤（千元）	Return on assets 資產利潤率 (%)	Return on equity 權益利潤率 (%)	Labour productivity ('000 RMB / worker) 勞動生產率（千元/人）	Average debts / assets 平均資產負債率(%)	Average Total assets ('000 RMB) 平均總資產（千元）
By ownership 產業所有權									
State-owned 國有	77	480	42,065	1,974	2.49	5.96	87.59	58.27	79,325
Collectively-owned 集體	196	125	7,649	240	2.68	7.21	61.27	62.76	8,948
Privately-owned 私有	2	42	3,210	17	0.54	2.01	76.42	72.90	3,041
Domestic JVs 聯營	8	225	11,060	360	0.72	3.71	49.07	80.55	49,926
Joint stock 股份制	10	738	95,391	13,127	6.95	11.96	129.31	41.88	188,921
Foreign-funded 外資	29	247	114,929	14,150	9.08	15.36	465.43	40.85	155,769
Overseas Chinese-funded 港澳台資	28	134	16,581	1,961	7.42	17.99	123.51	58.76	26,431
By size 規模									
Large 大型	18	1,474	244,584	34,815	8.35	14.11	165.91	40.84	417,117
Medium 中型	21	679	104,385	11,347	8.07	21.81	153.76	63.01	140,631
Small 小型	305	132	9,808	-216	-1.33	-3.61	74.07	63.17	16,250
By regional distribution 地區分布									
Central-North 華北	53	141	9,024	386	1.28	2.90	64.02	55.94	30,160
Beijing 北京	31	90	4,363	-69	-0.77	-2.20	48.41	65.11	9,019
Tianjin 天津	15	252	20,215	1,493	1.94	3.98	80.20	51.29	77,127
Hebei 河北	3	230	9,623	-33	-0.07	-0.26	41.90	71.69	46,090
Shanxi 山西	3	68	3,627	100	1.27	7.48	53.33	83.04	7,883
Inner Mongolia 內蒙	1	3	40				13.33	87.50	80
Northeast 東北	46	353	39,287	3,245	4.57	9.12	111.19	49.83	70,945
Liaoning 遼寧	39	391	46,046	3,904	4.71	9.33	117.72	49.51	82,851
Jilin 吉林	1	57	3,300	330	19.30	48.53	57.89	60.23	1,710
Heilongjiang 黑龍江	6	157	1,352	-552	-10.82	-64.40	8.61	83.20	5,098
Central East 華東	169	233	37,116	3,564	7.38	14.64	159.63	49.56	48,276
Shanghai 上海	46	207	57,072	8,510	10.15	16.64	275.45	38.99	83,815
Jiangsu 江蘇	54	271	34,280	1,897	4.25	10.33	126.61	58.84	44,599
Zhejiang 浙江	41	139	25,162	1,672	7.55	19.85	181.09	61.96	22,135
Anhui 安徽	9	184	27,361	2,427	23.10	49.36	148.70	53.20	10,507
Fujian 福建	8	89	3,786	133	1.20	2.33	42.36	48.60	11,081
Jiangxi 江西	2	274	4,395	-490	-4.93	-18.32	16.04	73.06	9,930
Shandong 山東	9	725	53,247	1,993	2.29	5.42	73.41	57.77	87,131
Central-South 中南	75	221	12,907	530	1.82	4.71	58.35	61.39	29,119
Henan 河南	17	266	9,026	-68	-0.27	-0.56	33.94	51.92	25,158
Hubei 湖北	13	371	14,375	-209	-0.47	-1.17	38.75	59.40	44,155
Hunan 湖南	8	353	19,725	1,300	3.11	7.00	55.96	55.51	41,745
Guangdong 廣東	35	112	13,085	967	4.15	14.29	116.98	70.97	23,309
Guangxi 廣西	2	256	5,965	-310	-1.91	-3.23	23.35	40.82	16,205
Hainan 海南									
Southwest 西南	8	157	7,251	-1,475	-6.22	-21.38	46.15	70.90	23,708
Chongqing 重慶	5	206	8,980	-2,680	-7.39	-25.10	43.62	70.55	36,249
Sichuan 四川	3	89	4,830	211	3.44	13.11	54.52	73.77	6,150
Guizhou 貴州									
Yunnan 雲南									
Tibet 西藏									
Northwest 西北	1	440	2,250	-650	-2.81	-22.26	5.11	87.38	23,130
Shaanxi 陝西	1	440	2,250	-650	-2.81	-22.26	5.11	87.38	23,130
Gansu 甘肅									
Qinghai 青海									
Ningxia 寧夏									
Xinjiang 新疆									

3536: Refrigeration Equipment 冷凍設備製造業

Year 年份	Number of firms 企業個數	Rate of change 每年變化 (%)	Number of employees 職工人數（人）	Rate of change 每年變化 (%)	Total revenue (Mil. RMB) 總銷售收入（百萬元）	Rate of change 每年變化 (%)	Total profit (Mil. RMB) 總利潤（百萬元）	Rate of change 每年變化 (%)
1993	299		128,543		5,779		781	
1994	324	8.36%	71,171	-44.63%	6,368	10.18%	827	5.90%
1995	351	8.33%	73,573	3.37%	8,484	33.23%	719	-13.04%
1996	352	0.28%	81,306	10.51%	9,586	12.99%	799	11.13%

3 Major products* 3 種主要產品 *	Output 產量	Sales volume 銷售量	Unit 單位
a) Refrigerating & Air Conditioning Equipment 製冷空調設備	471,136	457,002	set 台(套)
b) Cold Storage Processing Equipment 冷藏加工設備	55,317	54,210	set 台(套、座)
c) Domestic Refrigerator Compressor 家用電冰箱壓縮機	3,518,309	3,307,211	set 台

Top 10 firms by revenue (year founded) 收入排名前 10 家企業 (創辦年份)	City 城市	Province 省	Telephone / fax 電話 / 傳真	Number of employees 職工人數	Ownership 產業所有權	Revenue ('000 RMB) 銷售收入（千元）	Profit ('000 RMB) (rank) 利潤（千元）(排名)	Total assets ('000 RMB) 總資產（千元）	Major products 主要產品
Dalian Bing Shan Group Co. Ltd. 大連冰山集團有限公司(1930)	Dalian 大連市	Liaoning 遼寧省	(0411)6653081 (0411)6641470	2,534	State-owned 國有	1,505,770	160757(2)	2,622,739	a
Shanghai Hezhong Carrier Air-conditioning Equipment Co. Ltd. 上海合眾－開利空調設備有限公司(1987)	Shanghai 上海市	Shanghai 上海市	(021)65430952 (021)65435404	364	Foreign-funded 外資	780,364	234292(1)	530,512	a
Jiangsu Shuang Liang Te Ling Arsorption Chiller Co. Ltd. 江蘇雙良－特靈溴化鋰製冷機有限公司(1995)	Wuxi 無錫市	Jiangsu 江蘇省	(0510)6631999 (0510)6631333	1,478	Foreign-funded 外資	755,620	81150(5)	840,392	a
State-owned Changshu Refrigerating Equipment Works 國營常熟製冷設備廠(1984)	Suzhou 蘇州市	Jiangsu 江蘇省	(0512)2797888 (0512)2772661	1,236	State-owned 國有	502,140	15670(13)	656,294	o
Shanghai Tong Hui Carrier Air Conditioning Equipment Co. Ltd. 上海通惠－開利空調設備有限公司(1987)	Shanghai 上海市	Shanghai 上海市	(021)57420683 (021)57420685	400	Foreign-funded 外資	460,249	118908(3)	266,120	a
Shanghai Refrigerator Compressor Co. Ltd. 上海冰箱壓縮機股份有限公司(1957)	Shanghai 上海市	Shanghai 上海市	(021)65190000 (021)65430941	1,778	Joint stock 股份制	282,560	88182(4)	1,165,530	c
Zhejiang Chun Hui Group 浙江春暉集團(1966)	Shaoxing 紹興市	Zhejiang 浙江省	(0575)2014484 (0575)2051888	1,498	Collectively-owned 集體	273,021	16100(12)	236,233	a
Zhejiang Dong Da Electromechanical Group Co. 浙江東達機電集團公司(1989)	Shaoxing 紹興市	Zhejiang 浙江省	(0575)2050688 (0575)2051536	871	Collectively-owned 集體	270,666	17231(11)	131,379	a
Zhanussi Elettromeccanica Tianjin Compressor Co. Ltd. 扎努西電氣機械天津壓縮機有限公司(1993)	Tianjin 天津市	Tianjin 天津市	(022)24211737 (022)24302568	1,130	Foreign-funded 外資	257,508	27796(7)	726,427	c
Hang Li Refrigeration Equipment Co. Ltd. 杭麗製冷設備有限公司(1985)	Hangzhou 杭州市	Zhejiang 浙江省	(0571)7046187 (0571)7048258	231	Foreign-funded 外資	232,711	21859(10)	215,309	c

Top 10 Cities by Production Output 產出排名前 10 位城市	Province 省	Market share 市場份額	Number of firms 企業個數
Shanghai 上海市	Shanghai 上海市	29.15%	97
Dalian 大連市	Liaoning 遼寧省	14.94%	25
Shaoxing 紹興市	Zhejiang 浙江省	7.59%	23
Yantai 煙臺市	Shandong 山東省	5.34%	9
Suzhou 蘇州市	Jiangsu 江蘇省	5.29%	17
Tianjin 天津市	Tianjin 天津市	3.92%	16
Hangzhou 杭州市	Zhejiang 浙江省	3.78%	18
Changzhou 常州市	Jiangsu 江蘇省	3.71%	20
Guangzhou 廣州市	Guangdong 廣東省	3.56%	34
Qingdao 青島市	Shandong 山東省	2.59%	1

10 Major Wholesalers 10 家主要批發商	City 城市	Province 省	Telephone / Fax 電話 / 傳真
Liaoning Automobile Trade Group Corp. 遼寧省汽車貿易集團	Shenyang 沈陽市	Liaoning 遼寧省	(024)23835494 (024)23838338
China Post and Telecommunication Equipment General Company 中國郵電器材總公司	Beijing 北京市	Beijing 北京市	(010)63523715 (010)63525935
Jiangsu Electromechanical Products General Company 江蘇省機電產品總公司	Nanjing 南京市	Jiangsu 江蘇省	(025)7713642 (025)7711036
Xi Nan Technology Import & Export Company 西南技術進出口公司	Chongqing 重慶市	Chongqing 重慶市	(023)63850185 (023)63850026
Changzhou Economic Technology Industrial Development Zone Tian Ming Trade Company 常州經濟技術產業開發區天明貿易公司	Changzhou 常州市	Jiangsu 江蘇省	(0519)8829882 (0519)8829882
Shanxi Mechanical Equipment Import & Export Company 山西省機械設備進出口公司	Taiyuan 太原市	Shanxi 山西省	(0351)4040713 (0351)4043981
Ningbo Five Mining Machinery Import & Export Company 寧波市五礦機械進出口公司	Ningbo 寧波市	Zhejiang 浙江省	(0574)7311255 (0574)7320322
Tianjin Jin Huan Electromechanical Complete Sets of Equipment Factory 天津市津環機電成套設備廠	Tianjin 天津市	Tianjin 天津市	(022)26371628
Yunnan Machinery Import & Export Company 雲南省機械進出口公司	Kunming 昆明市	Yunnan 雲南省	(0871)3164879 (0871)3136829
Tianjin Da Qiu Zhuang Yi Yuan Trade Center 天津市大丘莊億源商貿中心	Tianjin 天津市	Tianjin 天津市	(022)28899478 (022)28899046

*Also include sales by firms outside this industry.包括本行業以外廠家的銷售。"o" stands for "others". "o" 代表"其他產品"。

3537: Pneumatic Tools 風動工具製造業

The industry accounts for 0.014% of the total revenue of China's industrial sector in 1996. The revenue growth rate of the industry is 38.2% from 1995, as compared to the growth rate of China's industrial sector, 9.51%. The rate of return on asset is -0.64%. 66.39% of all firms in the industry made a profit while 28.16% had negative returns. The top province in terms of the industry's revenue is Liaoning, accounting for 23.86% of the total revenue.
本行業在1996年佔全行業總產值0.014%，行業年增長率為38.2%（全國工業年增長率9.51%）。行業的資產回報率-0.64%，66.39%的企業盈利，28.16%的企業虧損。銷售收入最高的省份為遼寧省，佔本行業的23.86%。

	Total number of firms 企業總數	Total number of employees 職工總數	Total revenue (Mil. RMB) 總銷售收入（百萬元）	Total profit (Mil. RMB) 總利潤（百萬元）	Return on assets 資產利潤率 (%)	Return on equity 權益利潤率 (%)	Labour productivity ('000 RMB / worker) 勞動生產率（千元/人）	Debts / assets 資產負債率 (%)	Total assets (Mil. RMB) 總資產（百萬元）
Industry Overall 行業總體	111	24,980	801	-11	-0.64	-1.94	32.07	67.07	1,699

	Number of firms 企業個數	Average number of employees 平均職工人數	Average revenue ('000 RMB) 平均銷售收入（千元）	Average profit ('000 RMB) 平均利潤（千元）	Return on assets 資產利潤率 (%)	Return on equity 權益利潤率 (%)	Labour productivity ('000 RMB / worker) 勞動生產率（千元/人）	Average debts / assets 平均資產負債率(%)	Average Total assets ('000 RMB) 平均總資產（千元）
By ownership 產業所有權									
State-owned 國有	20	634	16,200	-700	-1.33	-4.36	25.55	69.54	52,700
Collectively-owned 集體	77	120	4,461	100	2.16	6.17	37.07	65.02	4,648
Privately-owned 私有									
Domestic JVs 聯營	2	119	11,727	345	4.71	15.65	98.96	69.88	7,313
Joint stock 股份制	1	15	793				52.87	24.03	2,606
Foreign-funded 外資	4	568	18,091	-1,292	-2.62	-6.86	31.88	61.86	49,390
Overseas Chinese-funded 港澳台資	7	92	5,258	-35	-0.33	-0.78	56.89	57.21	10,4 è
By size 規模									
Large 大型	2	4,044	118,364	-5,821	-1.58	-5.85	29.27	73.04	369,373
Medium 中型	6	943	25,736	-720	-1.19	-4.41	27.31	73.09	60,726
Small 小型	101	112	4,057	49	0.83	1.89	36.21	56.08	5,910
By regional distribution 地區分布									
Central-North 華北	14	332	8,843	-1,074	-4.27	-12.57	26.65	66.07	25,159
Beijing 北京	2	75	6,995	205	1.91	3.52	93.89	45.64	10,725
Tianjin 天津	3	133	697	-400	-16.13	-181.82	5.23	91.13	2,480
Hebei 河北	6	652	16,220	-2,398	-4.63	-13.54	24.89	65.83	51,847
Shanxi 山西	1	121	9,700	130	1.13	22.03	80.17	94.97	11,540
Inner Mongolia 內蒙	2	33	350	10	2.82	6.25	10.61	54.93	355
Northeast 東北	26	332	7,990	31	0.14	0.69	24.10	79.75	22,193
Liaoning 遼寧	20	383	9,554	41	0.16	0.78	24.97	80.00	26,018
Jilin 吉林	4	238	4,088	-3	-0.02	-0.08	17.17	78.06	14,040
Heilongjiang 黑龍江	2	8	160	5	1.92	2.17	21.33	11.54	260
Central East 華東	52	162	7,065	88	0.78	1.79	43.68	56.19	11,309
Shanghai 上海	9	77	6,724	289	3.67	8.45	87.20	56.57	7,872
Jiangsu 江蘇	14	195	7,063	-474	-2.94	-7.57	36.18	61.22	16,122
Zhejiang 浙江	15	94	4,941	371	6.60	14.11	52.52	53.20	5,614
Anhui 安徽	4	76	830	8	0.29	0.91	10.96	67.65	2,550
Fujian 福建	1	11	200	20	7.41	10.00	18.18	25.93	270
Jiangxi 江西	4	462	10,870	308	1.51	2.83	23.53	46.58	20,345
Shandong 山東	5	282	17,372	358	1.55	3.38	61.56	54.14	23,094
Central-South 中南	13	186	6,238	-126	-1.05	-3.08	33.61	65.83	11,993
Henan 河南	5	125	2,392	-18	-0.52	-1.49	19.17	65.01	3,464
Hubei 湖北	1	295	4,990				16.92	73.00	15,740
Hunan 湖南	2	409	8,490	-960	-3.40	-9.87	20.76	65.50	28,205
Guangdong 廣東	4	36	6,773	28	0.48	1.66	186.83	71.12	5,730
Guangxi 廣西	1	531	20,070	260	0.60	1.54	37.80	61.19	43,520
Hainan 海南									
Southwest 西南	5	170	3,666	48	1.02	2.27	21.56	54.99	4,706
Chongqing 重慶	3	256	6,511	119	1.64	3.64	25.40	55.01	7,243
Sichuan 四川	1	111	488	-57	-1.84	-4.02	4.38	54.27	3,117
Guizhou 貴州	1	18	320				17.78	100.00	60
Yunnan 雲南									
Tibet 西藏									
Northwest 西北	1	40	2,400	140	7.69	9.33	60.00	17.58	1,820
Shaanxi 陝西									
Gansu 甘肅									
Qinghai 青海									
Ningxia 寧夏									
Xinjiang 新疆	1	40	2,400	140	7.69	9.33	60.00	17.58	1,820

Year 年份	Number of firms 企業個數	Rate of change 每年變化 (%)	Number of employees 職工人數 (人)	Rate of change 每年變化 (%)	Total revenue (Mil. RMB) 總銷售收入 (百萬元)	Rate of change 每年變化 (%)	Total profit (Mil. RMB) 總利潤 (百萬元)	Rate of change 每年變化 (%)
1993	89		26,577		861		63	
1994	92	3.37%	26,957	1.43%	989	14.91%	31	-51.09%
1995	99	7.61%	18,876	-29.98%	580	-41.42%	-15	-147.24%
1996	111	12.12%	24,980	32.34%	801	38.21%	-11	24.60%

3 Major products* 3種主要產品*	Output 產量	Sales volume 銷售量	Unit 單位
a) Air Tool 風動工具	212,835	195,808	set 台
b) Mining & Opening Equipment 掘設備	5,276	4,537	ton 噸
c) Heavy Mining Mechanical Accessories 重型礦山機械配件	1,673	1,188	ton 噸

Top 10 firms by revenue (year founded) 收入排名前10家企業 (創辦年份)	City 城市	Province 省	Telephone / fax 電話 / 傳真	Number of employees 職工人數	Ownership 產業所有權	Revenue ('000 RMB) 銷售收入 (千元)	Profit ('000 RMB) (rank) 利潤 (千元) (排名)	Total assets ('000 RMB) 總資產 (千元)	Major products 主要產品
Shenyang Pneumatic Tools Plant 沈陽風動工具廠(1955)	Shenyang 沈陽市	Liaoning 遼寧省	(024)25874511 (024)25853081	3,392	State-owned 國有	115,562	1803(2)	417,822	a,b,c
Hebei Xuanhua Lianyun Group Company 河北宣化連雲集團公司(1994)	Zhangjiakou 張家口市	Hebei 河北省	(0313)3018612	615	Collectively-owned 集体	49,790	1467(3)	77,694	o
Qingdao Qian Shao Precision Machinery Company 青島前哨精密機械公司(1969)	Qingdao 青島市	Shandong 山東省	(0532)4852028 (0532)4855619	1,020	State-owned 國有	42,525	510(14)	100,224	a,b
Yichun Pneumatic Tools Factory 宜春風動工具廠(1961)	Yichun 宜春市	Jiangxi 江西省	(0795)3241836	1,696	State-owned 國有	39,981	1203(4)	78,088	a,b
Shanghai Hai Feng Tool Co., Ltd. 上海海峯工具有限公司(1994)	Shanghai 上海市	Shanghai 上海市	(021)59595454 (021)59596923	304	Overseas Chinese-funded 港澳台資	39,563	833(6)	42,629	o
Nanjing Huarui Construction Machinery Ltd. 南京華瑞工程機械有限公司(1994)	Nanjing 南京市	Jiangsu 江蘇省	(025)5501329 (025)5502508	1,365	Foreign-funded 外資	39,176	-6583(54)	86,480	a,b,c
Shandong Zhangqiu Pneumatic Tool Factory 山東省章丘市氣動工具廠(1967)	Ji'nan 濟南市	Shandong 山東省	(0531)3831149	228	Collectively-owned 集体	32,500	628(10)	7,299	a
Xuanhua Excavation Machinery Plant 宣化採掘機械廠(1960)	Zhangjiakou 張家口市	Hebei 河北省	(0313)3882523 (0313)3882563	2,914	State-owned 國有	30,028	-16584(55)	209,785	b
Wujin Yang Hu Coal Mine Equipment General Company 武進市陽湖煤礦設備總公司(1992)	Changzhou 常州市	Jiangsu 江蘇省	(0519)6351197	276	Collectively-owned 集体	25,142	560(12)	29,430	o
Kang Da Air Conditioning Equipment Co., Ltd. 康達空調設備有限公司(1993)	Foshan 佛山市	Guangdong 廣東省	(0757)3821150 (0757)3821150	42	Overseas Chinese-funded 港澳台資	23,296	86(31)	14,800	o

Top 10 Cities by Production Output 產出排名前10位城市	Province 省	Market share 市場份額	Number of firms 企業個數
Shenyang 沈陽市	Liaoning 遼寧省	19.70%	11
Tianshui 天水市	Gansu 甘肅省	10.10%	1
Zhangjiakou 張家口市	Hebei 河北省	7.67%	2
Nanjing 南京市	Jiangsu 江蘇省	6.86%	4
Qingdao 青島市	Shandong 山東省	5.94%	1
Yichun 宜春市	Jiangxi 江西省	5.57%	3
Changzhou 常州市	Jiangsu 江蘇省	3.97%	5
Taizhou 臺州市	Zhejiang 浙江省	3.96%	6
Foshan 佛山市	Guangdong 廣東省	3.36%	1
Shanghai 上海市	Shanghai 上海市	3.14%	7

10 Major Wholesalers 10家主要批發商	City 城市	Province 省	Telephone / Fax 電話 / 傳真
Liaoning Automobile Trade Group Corp. 遼寧省汽車貿易集團	Shenyang 沈陽市	Liaoning 遼寧省	(024)23835494 (024)23838338
China Post and Telecommunication Equipment General Company 中國郵電器材總公司	Beijing 北京市	Beijing 北京市	(010)63523715 (010)63525935
Jiangsu Electromechanical Products General Company 江蘇省機電產品總公司	Nanjing 南京市	Jiangsu 江蘇省	(025)7713642 (025)7711036
Xi Nan Technology Import & Export Company 西南技術進出口公司	Chongqing 重慶市	Chongqing 重慶市	(023)63850185 (023)63850026
Changzhou Economic Technology Industrial Development Zone Tian Ming Trade Company 常州經濟技術產業開發區天明貿易公司	Changzhou 常州市	Jiangsu 江蘇省	(0519)8829882 (0519)8829882
Shanxi Mechanical Equipment Import & Export Company 山西省機械設備進出口公司	Taiyuan 太原市	Shanxi 山西省	(0351)4040713 (0351)4043981
Ningbo Five Mining Machinery Import & Export Company 寧波市五礦機械進出口公司	Ningbo 寧波市	Zhejiang 浙江省	(0574)7311255 (0574)7320322
Tianjin Jin Huan Electromechanical Complete Sets of Equipment Factory 天津市津環機電成套設備廠	Tianjin 天津市	Tianjin 天津市	(022)26371628
Yunnan Machinery Import & Export Company 雲南省機械進出口公司	Kunming 昆明市	Yunnan 雲南省	(0871)3164879 (0871)3136829
Tianjin Da Qiu Zhuang Yi Yuan Trade Center 天津市大丘莊億源商貿中心	Tianjin 天津市	Tianjin 天津市	(022)28899478 (022)28899046

*Also include sales by firms outside this industry.包括本行業以外廠家的銷售。"o" stands for "others". "o" 代表"其他產品"。

3538: Electric Tools 電動工具製造業

The industry accounts for 0.069% of the total revenue of China's industrial sector in 1996. The revenue growth rate of the industry is 18.4% from 1995, as compared to the growth rate of China's industrial sector, 9.51%. The rate of return on asset is 0.32%. 65.03% of all firms in the industry made a profit while 30.59% had negative returns. The top province in terms of the industry's revenue is Jiangsu, accounting for 32.38% of the total revenue.
本行業在1996年佔全行業總產值0.069%，行業年增長率為18.4%（全國工業年增長率9.51%）。行業的資產回報率0.32%，65.03%的企業盈利，30.59%的企業虧損。銷售收入最高的省份為江蘇省，佔本行業的32.38%。

	Total number of firms 企業總數	Total number of employees 職工總數	Total revenue (Mil. RMB) 總銷售收入（百萬元）	Total profit (Mil. RMB) 總利潤（百萬元）	Return on assets 資產利潤率 (%)	Return on equity 權益利潤率 (%)	Labour productivity ('000 RMB / worker) 勞動生產率（千元/人）	Debts / assets 資產負債率 (%)	Total assets (Mil. RMB) 總資產（百萬元）
Industry Overall 行業總體	240	51,792	4,025	16	0.32	0.94	77.71	66.03	5,119

	Number of firms 企業個數	Average number of employees 平均職工人數	Average revenue ('000 RMB) 平均銷售收入（千元）	Average profit ('000 RMB) 平均利潤（千元）	Return on assets 資產利潤率 (%)	Return on equity 權益利潤率 (%)	Labour productivity ('000 RMB / worker) 勞動生產率（千元/人）	Average debts / assets 平均資產負債率(%)	Average Total assets ('000 RMB) 平均總資產（千元）
By ownership 產業所有權									
State-owned 國有	31	395	9,484	-516	-2.09	-10.88	23.98	80.81	24,710
Collectively-owned 集體	162	159	12,054	117	1.07	3.54	76.02	69.64	10,898
Privately-owned 私有	6	65	10,756	516	5.89	15.15	166.33	61.12	8,768
Domestic JVs 聯營	6	812	59,667	581	1.06	122.88	73.50	99.14	54,802
Joint stock 股份制	3	57	5,875	-1	-0.04	-0.38	102.47	90.30	3,755
Foreign-funded 外資	19	328	61,976	305	0.29	0.59	188.98	50.65	105,190
Overseas Chinese-funded 港澳台資	11	199	14,626	59	0.33	1.44	73.67	76.98	17,833
By size 規模									
Large 大型	5	1,601	206,808	676	0.24	0.64	129.14	62.87	286,245
Medium 中型	10	1,035	57,193	267	0.31	1.08	55.27	70.92	85,189
Small 小型	222	150	10,898	45	0.35	1.04	72.45	66.15	12,774
By regional distribution 地區分布									
Central-North 華北	24	204	10,505	-110	-0.62	-3.73	51.57	83.34	17,625
Beijing 北京	5	3	8	-16	-8.00	-19.05	2.50	58.00	200
Tianjin 天津	5	105	11,794	-362	-2.60	-13.74	112.54	81.12	13,942
Hebei 河北	9	360	18,774	-83	-0.27	-2.13	52.22	87.42	31,098
Shanxi 山西	2	40	2,215	-10	-0.21	-1.68	55.38	87.59	4,795
Inner Mongolia 內蒙	3	344	6,573	10	0.05	0.15	19.09	67.39	20,937
Northeast 東北	16	225	12,308	-4,116	-10.11	-37.36	54.73	72.95	40,721
Liaoning 遼寧	9	152	15,403	-5,101	-10.75	-54.06	101.41	80.11	47,434
Jilin 吉林	4	506	13,853	-4,970	-9.08	-21.90	27.40	58.51	54,713
Heilongjiang 黑龍江	3	70	963	-20	-1.04	-11.32	13.83	90.81	1,923
Central East 華東	154	237	20,295	823	4.14	10.88	85.60	61.97	19,886
Shanghai 上海	25	227	24,214	954	4.23	17.47	106.90	75.77	22,538
Jiangsu 江蘇	31	521	42,040	573	1.65	4.53	80.71	63.51	34,628
Zhejiang 浙江	71	139	12,923	954	6.61	14.21	93.21	53.50	14,428
Anhui 安徽	1	48	780				16.25	52.85	3,860
Fujian 福建	7	75	22,431	1,769	8.42	16.57	300.80	49.21	21,011
Jiangxi 江西	4	700	10,463	165	0.52	1.73	14.95	69.73	31,505
Shandong 山東	15	99	6,647	293	3.54	9.68	66.96	63.41	8,283
Central-South 中南	29	121	11,873	-1,293	-4.81	-13.69	97.79	64.84	26,861
Henan 河南	3	208	2,643	-370	-4.22	-30.66	12.69	86.24	8,770
Hubei 湖北	4	175	9,488	238	3.41	10.27	54.29	66.82	6,963
Hunan 湖南	8	150	1,863	-558	-6.07	-41.33	12.41	85.29	9,178
Guangdong 廣東	8	105	34,178	-4,113	-5.23	-13.77	325.50	62.03	78,619
Guangxi 廣西	4	16	1,483	3	0.19	0.23	95.65	18.70	1,350
Hainan 海南	2	47	2,090	10	0.12	0.29	44.47	58.80	8,520
Southwest 西南	14	147	6,439	55	0.64	1.85	43.95	65.57	8,614
Chongqing 重慶	4	151	2,556	-85	-1.88	-5.81	16.88	67.66	4,528
Sichuan 四川	6	204	12,362	235	1.52	4.47	60.73	66.09	15,509
Guizhou 貴州	2	6	260	5	3.85	5.88	47.27	34.62	130
Yunnan 雲南	2	102	1,385	-195	-6.07	-13.09	13.58	53.58	3,210
Tibet 西藏									
Northwest 西北	3	406	5,323	-1,737	-6.36	-44.23	13.10	85.64	27,323
Shaanxi 陝西	2	122	3,145	115	1.23	4.19	25.88	70.70	9,370
Gansu 甘肅									
Qinghai 青海	1	976	9,680	-5,440	-8.60	-86.49	9.92	90.07	63,230
Ningxia 寧夏									
Xinjiang 新疆									

3538: Electric Tools 電動工具製造業

Year 年份	Number of firms 企業個數	Rate of change 每年變化 (%)	Number of employees 職工人數 (人)	Rate of change 每年變化 (%)	Total revenue (Mil. RMB) 總銷售收入 (百萬元)	Rate of change 每年變化 (%)	Total profit (Mil. RMB) 總利潤 (百萬元)	Rate of change 每年變化 (%)
1993	171		56,426		1,691		89	
1994	195	14.04%	39,668	-29.70%	1,936	14.52%	64	-27.56%
1995	221	13.33%	42,011	5.91%	3,400	75.58%	123	90.73%
1996	240	8.60%	51,792	23.28%	4,025	18.38%	16	-86.97%

3 Major products* 3 種主要產品 *	Output 產量	Sales volume 銷售量	Unit 單位
a) Electric Tool 電動工具	273,533,594	251,650,907	set 台
b) Bench Drilling Machine 台鑽	1,076,808	1,076,808	set 台

Top 10 firms by revenue (year founded) 收入排名前 10 家企業 (創辦年份)	City 城市	Province 省	Telephone / fax 電話 / 傳真	Number of employees 職工人數	Ownership 產業所有權	Revenue ('000 RMB) 銷售收入 (千元)	Profit ('000 RMB) (rank) 利潤 (千元) (排名)	Total assets ('000 RMB) 總資產 (千元)	Major products 主要產品
Mu Tian China Co. Ltd. 牧田中國有限公司(1995)	Suzhou 蘇州市	Jiangsu 江蘇省	(0512)7307710	395	Foreign-funded 外資	441,104	7556(10)	446,211	a
Shanghai Hitachi Power Tools Co. Ltd. 上海日立電動工具有限公司(1991)	Shanghai 上海市	Shanghai 上海市	(021)64300041 (021)64301835	1,634	Foreign-funded 外資	426,660	19501(1)	400,610	a
Suzhou Tai Hu Power Tool Group Co. 蘇州太湖電動工具集團公司(1994)	Suzhou 蘇州市	Jiangsu 江蘇省	(0512)5272518 (0512)5272512	2,186	Domestic JVs 聯營	256,730	6200(11)	234,480	a
Zhejiang Yongkang Heng Feng Electrical Appliance Manufacturing Co. 浙江永康恒豐電器製造公司(1966)	Jinhua 金華市	Zhejiang 浙江省	(0579)7115347	1,242	Collectively-owned 集體	159,208	15390(2)	206,603	o
Mindong – Hitachi Electric Power Tools Co. Ltd. 閩東－日立電動工具有限公司(1985)	Fuzhou 福州市	Fujian 福建省	(0591)3660289 (0591)3660572	365	Foreign-funded 外資	154,574	12408(3)	143,466	a
Shanghai Zheng Feng Industrial Co. Ltd. 上海正峯工業有限公司(1996)	Shanghai 上海市	Shanghai 上海市	(021)59159629 (021)59159626	340	Overseas Chinese-funded 港澳台資	152,304	11119(5)	97,006	o
Wujin Electric Tool Group Co. 武進市電動工具廠(1970)	Changzhou 常州市	Jiangsu 江蘇省	(0519)3341245	820	Collectively-owned 集體	129,961	1408(21)	51,753	a
Liang Ming Dalian Machine Co. Ltd. 良明大連機器有限公司(1994)	Dalian 大連市	Liaoning 遼寧省	(0411)7621111 (0411)7641942	801	Foreign-funded 外資	129,412	-46251(137)	369,410	o
Xi Li De (China Zhanjiang) Co. Ltd. 喜利得(中國湛江)有限公司(1995)	Zhanjiang 湛江市	Guangdong 廣東省	(0758)3389888 (0758)3383978	187	Foreign-funded 外資	123,371	-26804(136)	388,595	a
Guangdong Ri Li Gong Ji Co. Ltd. 廣東日立工機有限公司(1994)	Guangzhou 廣州市	Guangdong 廣東省	(020)84754633 (020)84754623	183	Foreign-funded 外資	119,081	-6231(133)	175,421	a

Top 10 Cities by Production Output 產出排名前 10 位城市	Province 省	Market share 市場份額	Number of firms 企業個數
Shanghai 上海市	Shanghai 上海市	19.84%	44
Suzhou 蘇州市	Jiangsu 江蘇省	10.81%	11
Jinhua 金華市	Zhejiang 浙江省	10.81%	39
Changzhou 常州市	Jiangsu 江蘇省	5.86%	7
Zhanjiang 湛江市	Guangdong 廣東省	5.85%	3
Ningbo 寧波市	Zhejiang 浙江省	5.77%	30
Yangzhou 揚州市	Jiangsu 江蘇省	4.15%	5
Yancheng 鹽城市	Jiangsu 江蘇省	3.67%	6
Dalian 大連市	Liaoning 遼寧省	2.94%	1
Baoding 保定市	Hebei 河北省	2.88%	2

10 Major Wholesalers 10 家主要批發商	City 城市	Province 省	Telephone / Fax 電話 / 傳真
Liaoning Automobile Trade Group Corp. 遼寧省汽車貿易集團	Shenyang 沈陽市	Liaoning 遼寧省	(024)23835494 (024)23838338
China Post and Telecommunication Equipment General Company 中國郵電器材總公司	Beijing 北京市	Beijing 北京市	(010)63523715 (010)63525935
Jiangsu Electromechanical Products General Company 江蘇省機電產品總公司	Nanjing 南京市	Jiangsu 江蘇省	(025)7713642 (025)7711036
Xi Nan Technology Import & Export Company 西南技術進出口公司	Chongqing 重慶市	Chongqing 重慶市	(023)63850185 (023)63850026
Changzhou Economic Technology Industrial Development Zone Tian Ming Trade Company 常州經濟技術產業開發區天明貿易公司	Changzhou 常州市	Jiangsu 江蘇省	(0519)8829882 (0519)8829882
Shanxi Mechanical Equipment Import & Export Company 山西省機械設備進出口公司	Taiyuan 太原市	Shanxi 山西省	(0351)4040713 (0351)4043981
Ningbo Five Mining Machinery Import & Export Company 寧波市五礦機械進出口公司	Ningbo 寧波市	Zhejiang 浙江省	(0574)7311255 (0574)7320322
Tianjin Jin Huan Electromechanical Complete Sets of Equipment Factory 天津市津環機電成套設備廠	Tianjin 天津市	Tianjin 天津市	(022)26371628
Yunnan Machinery Import & Export Company 雲南省機械進出口公司	Kunming 昆明市	Yunnan 雲南省	(0871)3164879 (0871)3136829
Tianjin Da Qiu Zhuang Yi Yuan Trade Center 天津市大丘莊億源商貿中心	Tianjin 天津市	Tianjin 天津市	(022)28899478 (022)28899046

*Also include sales by firms outside this industry.包括本行業以外廠家的銷售。"o" stands for "others". "o" 代表"其他產品"。

3539: Other General Equipment 其他通用設備製造業

The industry accounts for 0.091% of the total revenue of China's industrial sector in 1996. The revenue growth rate of the industry is -4.1% from 1995, as compared to the growth rate of China's industrial sector, 9.51%. The rate of return on asset is 0.69%. 69.69% of all firms in the industry made a profit while 27.54% had negative returns. The top province in terms of the industry's revenue is Jiangsu, accounting for 20.00% of the total revenue.
本行業在1996年佔全行業總產值0.091%，行業年增長率為-4.1%（全國工業年增長率9.51%）。行業的資產回報率0.69%，69.69%的企業盈利，27.54%的企業虧損。銷售收入最高的省份為江蘇省，佔本行業的20.00%。

	Total number of firms 企業總數	Total number of employees 職工總數	Total revenue (Mil. RMB) 總銷售收入（百萬元）	Total profit (Mil. RMB) 總利潤（百萬元）	Return on assets 資產利潤率 (%)	Return on equity 權益利潤率 (%)	Labour productivity ('000 RMB / worker) 勞動生產率（千元/人）	Debts / assets 資產負債率 (%)	Total assets (Mil. RMB) 總資產（百萬元）
Industry Overall 行業總體	713	124,326	5,279	59	0.69	1.99	42.46	65.45	8,569

	Number of firms 企業個數	Average number of employees 平均職工人數	Average revenue ('000 RMB) 平均銷售收入（千元）	Average profit ('000 RMB) 平均利潤（千元）	Return on assets 資產利潤率 (%)	Return on equity 權益利潤率 (%)	Labour productivity ('000 RMB / worker) 勞動生產率（千元/人）	Average debts / assets 平均資產負債率(%)	Average Total assets ('000 RMB) 平均總資產（千元）
By ownership 產業所有權									
State-owned 國有	109	472	16,101	-734	-1.85	-5.98	34.15	69.03	39,633
Collectively-owned 集體	538	103	4,373	147	3.23	9.06	42.65	64.36	4,554
Privately-owned 私有	4	60	2,550	59	1.57	4.55	42.69	65.42	3,758
Domestic JVs 聯營	11	395	20,838	1,421	4.75	12.52	52.72	62.06	29,921
Joint stock 股份制	18	629	32,416	1,591	3.08	7.64	51.56	59.63	51,574
Foreign-funded 外資	20	123	14,377	690	2.93	6.19	117.22	52.65	23,523
Overseas Chinese-funded 港澳台資	12	61	5,078	127	2.72	6.82	83.36	60.17	4,692
By size 規模									
Large 大型	15	2,555	112,638	-4,661	-1.90	-5.16	44.09	63.26	245,719
Medium 中型	29	754	36,551	-3,493	-5.27	-16.75	48.46	68.52	66,230
Small 小型	660	97	3,833	349	7.77	22.97	39.38	66.17	4,489
By regional distribution 地區分布									
Central-North 華北	80	135	5,769	17	0.15	0.37	42.74	60.95	11,936
Beijing 北京	21	42	2,435	243	3.98	9.08	57.53	56.19	6,114
Tianjin 天津	20	147	9,208	11	0.06	0.11	62.81	47.27	18,816
Hebei 河北	28	175	5,638	-275	-2.64	-15.97	32.23	83.50	10,449
Shanxi 山西	8	227	6,590	200	1.27	2.68	29.06	52.34	15,688
Inner Mongolia 內蒙	3	88	5,210	727	6.79	21.52	59.20	68.43	10,707
Northeast 東北	149	275	4,710	-28	-0.21	-0.57	17.15	63.77	13,617
Liaoning 遼寧	115	242	3,917	126	1.55	4.84	16.16	67.95	8,120
Jilin 吉林	20	172	3,232	-584	-5.27	-25.27	18.75	79.14	11,070
Heilongjiang 黑龍江	14	687	13,339	-500	-0.80	-1.80	19.43	55.42	62,412
Central East 華東	321	143	9,068	234	1.98	5.95	63.36	66.83	11,832
Shanghai 上海	31	285	14,682	-3	-0.01	-0.09	51.60	87.59	25,752
Jiangsu 江蘇	103	187	10,252	153	0.99	2.55	54.96	61.32	15,477
Zhejiang 浙江	98	76	4,063	129	2.02	4.94	53.56	59.07	6,359
Anhui 安徽	5	167	5,386				32.25	79.86	18,712
Fujian 福建	31	72	18,926	973	11.74	23.09	261.81	49.13	8,284
Jiangxi 江西	21	91	1,156	-63	-2.58	-19.10	12.73	86.49	2,436
Shandong 山東	32	171	11,366	561	4.71	13.53	66.28	65.15	11,901
Central-South 中南	113	161	8,749	37	0.32	1.02	54.39	68.26	11,478
Henan 河南	35	162	4,944	88	1.14	4.43	30.57	74.34	7,740
Hubei 湖北	16	270	13,976	-99	-0.72	-1.54	51.69	53.38	13,867
Hunan 湖南	24	83	3,191	20	0.53	1.56	38.56	66.10	3,692
Guangdong 廣東	27	162	14,296	80	0.39	1.37	88.29	71.99	20,680
Guangxi 廣西	11	166	11,762	9	0.06	0.19	70.66	66.71	14,301
Hainan 海南									
Southwest 西南	30	188	5,572	-49	-0.42	-0.97	29.67	56.85	11,614
Chongqing 重慶	13	275	8,013	44	0.27	0.66	29.18	59.09	16,222
Sichuan 四川	13	127	4,009	69	0.78	1.64	31.61	52.68	8,886
Guizhou 貴州	2	90	2,640				29.50	53.00	6,670
Yunnan 雲南	2	157	3,750	10	0.16	0.46	23.96	64.62	6,105
Tibet 西藏									
Northwest 西北	20	143	2,466	-800	-11.29	-51.76	17.27	78.18	7,083
Shaanxi 陝西	12	144	1,863	-1,189	-16.14	-104.39	12.93	84.55	7,369
Gansu 甘肅	2	473	8,890	-1,305	-5.86	-18.95	18.79	69.09	22,275
Qinghai 青海									
Ningxia 寧夏									
Xinjiang 新疆	6	30	1,530	147	10.14	25.36	50.44	59.91	1,447

3539: Other General Equipment 其他通用設備製造業

Year 年份	Number of firms 企業個數	Rate of change 每年變化 (%)	Number of employees 職工人數（人）	Rate of change 每年變化 (%)	Total revenue (Mil. RMB) 總銷售收入（百萬元）	Rate of change 每年變化 (%)	Total profit (Mil. RMB) 總利潤（百萬元）	Rate of change 每年變化 (%)
1993	694		184,658		5,382		237	
1994	745	7.35%	137,003	-25.81%	4,854	-9.82%	84	-64.48%
1995	705	-5.37%	130,090	-5.05%	5,506	13.45%	20	-76.34%
1996	713	1.13%	124,326	-4.43%	5,279	-4.12%	59	196.08%

3 Major products* 3 種主要產品 *	Output 產量	Sales volume 銷售量	Unit 單位
a) Speed Reducer 減速機	626,391	551,224	set 台
b) Gas Separating & Liquefying Equipment 氣體分離與液化設備	2,252	1,486	set 台
c) General Mechanical Accessories 通用機械配件	9,665	8,215	ton 噸

Top 10 firms by revenue (year founded) 收入排名前 10 家企業（創辦年份）	City 城市	Province 省	Telephone / fax 電話 / 傳真	Number of employees 職工人數	Ownership 產業所有權	Revenue ('000 RMB) 銷售收入（千元）	Profit ('000 RMB) (rank) 利潤（千元）（排名）	Total assets ('000 RMB) 總資產（千元）	Major products 主要產品
Fuzhou Cangshan Jian Xin Industry General Company 福州市倉山建新工業總公司	Fuzhou 福州市	Fujian 福建省	(0591)3744147	876	Collectively-owned 集體	511,100	28500(1)	153,250	o
Shanghai Da Long Machinery Plant 上海大隆機器廠(1902)	Shanghai 上海市	Shanghai 上海市	(021)62539876 (021)62530211	4,037	State-owned 國有	226,423	-3113(315)	472,035	c
Jiangsu Taixing Decelerator Factory (Group) 江蘇省泰興市減速機廠(1984)	Yangzhou 揚州市	Jiangsu 江蘇省	(0514)7541046 (0514)7635683	1,933	Collectively-owned 集體	153,856	15009(3)	136,756	a
Harbin Air Conditioner Co. Ltd. 哈爾濱空氣調節機有限責任公司(1952)	Harbin 哈爾濱市	Heilongjiang	(0451)4695084 (0451)4614934	1,540	State-owned 國有	119,901	10083(4)	215,867	o
Foshan State-owned Xing Guang Tools & Moulds Factory 佛山國營星光工模具廠(1967)	Foshan 佛山市	Guangdong 廣東省	(0757)2278896 (0757)2278896	978	State-owned 國有	108,400	7304(5)	233,464	a
Capital Iron & Steel Coporation Dong Hua Machinery Plant 首鋼東華機械廠(1970)	Huludao 葫蘆島市	Liaoning 遼寧省	(0429)5751343 (0429)5751215	2,485	State-owned 國有	105,001	-8413(322)	235,429	o
Tianjin Decelerator Manufactory 天津市減速機總廠(1957)	Tianjin 天津市	Tianjin 天津市	(022)24328924 (022)24328568	1,772	State-owned 國有	102,856	846(43)	183,107	a
Liuzhou Privately Owned Enterprise Association No.8 Branch 柳州市私營企業協會第八分會(1996)	Liuzhou 柳州市	Guangxi 廣西	(0772)3617253	489	Private-owned 私營	100,225	1719(23)	65,052	o
Jiangsu Tai Long Decelerator (Group) Company 江蘇省泰隆減速機（集團）公司(1993)	Yangzhou 揚州市	Jiangsu 江蘇省	(0514)7635696 (0514)7541126	1,120	Collectively-owned 集體	81,352	2933(14)	86,033	a
En Gang Heng Sheng Machine Plant Co. Ltd. 恩平恩港恒生機器廠有限公司(1986)	Jiangmen 江門市	Guangdong 廣東省	(0750)7723591 (0750)7724969	110	Overseas Chinese-funded 港澳台資	78,000	200(120)	66,273	o

Top 10 Cities by Production Output 產出排名前 10 位城市	Province 省	Market share 市場份額	Number of firms 企業個數
Shanghai 上海市	Shanghai 上海市	14.42%	61
Taizhou 泰州市	Jiangsu 江蘇省	6.32%	21
Wenzhou 溫州市	Zhejiang 浙江省	5.21%	75
Changzhou 常州市	Jiangsu 江蘇省	5.19%	32
Wuxi 無錫市	Jiangsu 江蘇省	4.40%	52
Yancheng 鹽城市	Jiangsu 江蘇省	4.04%	8
Tianjin 天津市	Tianjin 天津市	3.55%	23
Foshan 佛山市	Guangdong 廣東省	2.37%	4
Huludao 葫蘆島市	Liaoning 遼寧省	2.29%	2
Suzhou 蘇州市	Jiangsu 江蘇省	2.20%	40

10 Major Wholesalers 10 家主要批發商	City 城市	Province 省	Telephone / Fax 電話 / 傳真
Liaoning Automobile Trade Group Corp. 遼寧省汽車貿易集團	Shenyang 瀋陽市	Liaoning 遼寧省	(024)23835494 (024)23838338
China Post and Telecommunication Equipment General Company 中國郵電器材總公司	Beijing 北京市	Beijing 北京市	(010)63523715 (010)63525935
Jiangsu Electromechanical Products General Company 江蘇省機電產品總公司	Nanjing 南京市	Jiangsu 江蘇省	(025)7713642 (025)7711036
Xi Nan Technology Import & Export Company 西南技術進出口公司	Chongqing 重慶市	Chongqing 重慶市	(023)63850185 (023)63850026
Changzhou Economic Technology Industrial Development Zone Tian Ming Trade Company 常州經濟技術產業開發區天明貿易公司	Changzhou 常州市	Jiangsu 江蘇省	(0519)8829882 (0519)8829882
Shanxi Mechanical Equipment Import & Export Company 山西省機械設備進出口公司	Taiyuan 太原市	Shanxi 山西省	(0351)4040713 (0351)4043981
Ningbo Five Mining Machinery Import & Export Company 寧波市五礦機械進出口公司	Ningbo 寧波市	Zhejiang 浙江省	(0574)7311255 (0574)7320322
Tianjin Jin Huan Electromechanical Complete Sets of Equipment Factory 天津市津環機電成套設備廠	Tianjin 天津市	Tianjin 天津市	(022)26371628
Yunnan Machinery Import & Export Company 雲南省機械進出口公司	Kunming 昆明市	Yunnan 雲南省	(0871)3164879 (0871)3136829
Tianjin Da Qiu Zhuang Yi Yuan Trade Center 天津市大邱莊億源商貿中心	Tianjin 天津市	Tianjin 天津市	(022)28899478 (022)28899046

*Also include sales by firms outside this industry.包括本行業以外廠家的銷售。"o" stands for "others". "o" 代表"其他產品"。

3541: Bearings 軸承製造業

The industry accounts for 0.292% of the total revenue of China's industrial sector in 1996. The revenue growth rate of the industry is 2.6% from 1995, as compared to the growth rate of China's industrial sector, 9.51%. The rate of return on asset is 0.60%. 66.57% of all firms in the industry made a profit while 30.05% had negative returns. The top province in terms of the industry's revenue is Liaoning, accounting for 15.18% of the total revenue.
本行業在1996年佔全行業總產值0.292%，行業年增長率為2.6%（全國工業年增長率9.51%）。行業的資產回報率0.60%，66.57%的企業盈利，30.05%的企業虧損。銷售收入最高的省份為遼寧省，佔本行業的15.18%。

	Total number of firms 企業總數	Total number of employees 職工總數	Total revenue (Mil. RMB) 總銷售收入（百萬元）	Total profit (Mil. RMB) 總利潤（百萬元）	Return on assets 資產利潤率 (%)	Return on equity 權益利潤率 (%)	Labour productivity ('000 RMB / worker) 勞動生產率（千元/人）	Debts / assets 資產負債率 (%)	Total assets (Mil. RMB) 總資產（百萬元）
Industry Overall 行業總體	945	389,857	16,953	212	0.60	1.97	43.49	69.65	35,565

	Number of firms 企業個數	Average number of employees 平均職工人數	Average revenue ('000 RMB) 平均銷售收入（千元）	Average profit ('000 RMB) 平均利潤（千元）	Return on assets 資產利潤率 (%)	Return on equity 權益利潤率 (%)	Labour productivity ('000 RMB / worker) 勞動生產率（千元/人）	Average debts / assets 平均資產負債率(%)	Average Total assets ('000 RMB) 平均總資產（千元）
By ownership 產業所有權									
State-owned 國有	242	1,007	35,550	-467	-0.56	-2.16	35.31	74.33	84,083
Collectively-owned 集體	595	162	7,739	222	1.98	7.16	47.86	72.33	11,185
Privately-owned 私有	4	16	968	17	1.55	5.11	60.48	69.62	1,116
Domestic JVs 聯營	32	190	8,961	248	1.37	4.10	47.05	66.65	18,161
Joint stock 股份制	12	2,483	147,129	10,099	3.18	8.62	59.26	63.14	317,875
Foreign-funded 外資	34	251	30,026	599	0.76	1.39	119.70	45.19	78,746
Overseas Chinese-funded 港澳台資	25	290	26,590	1,740	2.95	6.61	91.55	55.34	58,924
By size 規模									
Large 大型	28	4,629	232,653	4,503	0.85	2.55	50.26	66.56	527,424
Medium 中型	140	1,000	39,372	226	0.26	1.08	39.35	75.84	86,565
Small 小型	766	157	6,433	71	0.62	1.85	40.86	66.27	11,328
By regional distribution 地區分布									
Central-North 華北	96	366	8,610	15	0.07	0.25	23.51	72.85	21,557
Beijing 北京	21	211	7,156	246	1.18	3.15	33.98	62.68	20,903
Tianjin 天津	13	179	2,239	-588	-5.15	-14.26	12.52	63.92	11,436
Hebei 河北	35	370	12,923	302	1.17	4.28	34.95	72.60	25,770
Shanxi 山西	21	580	7,663	-94	-0.44	-2.41	13.21	81.91	21,524
Inner Mongolia 內蒙	6	549	5,653	-785	-3.68	-30.21	10.31	87.81	21,315
Northeast 東北	103	744	35,235	1,616	2.03	5.57	47.35	63.48	79,444
Liaoning 遼寧	66	701	38,990	2,410	3.34	9.55	55.65	65.04	72,191
Jilin 吉林	13	635	19,202	-914	-2.92	-12.45	30.25	76.54	31,305
Heilongjiang 黑龍江	24	923	33,594	805	0.64	1.57	36.39	59.25	125,465
Central East 華東	458	264	15,458	153	0.55	1.81	58.48	69.70	28,015
Shanghai 上海	72	289	23,472	-369	-0.60	-2.00	81.23	70.02	61,539
Jiangsu 江蘇	95	290	18,092	317	1.23	3.61	62.35	65.85	25,689
Zhejiang 浙江	158	158	9,762	123	0.86	2.87	61.76	70.02	14,296
Anhui 安徽	23	417	18,906	78	0.27	1.30	45.32	79.37	29,024
Fujian 福建	27	232	12,887	637	3.43	11.19	55.51	69.34	18,580
Jiangxi 江西	25	261	5,962	-36	-0.30	-1.29	22.81	77.05	12,140
Shandong 山東	58	437	20,634	503	1.31	4.24	47.24	69.14	38,414
Central-South 中南	196	492	17,886	-211	-0.52	-1.86	36.32	72.13	40,733
Henan 河南	82	587	19,238	-365	-0.84	-2.74	32.79	69.33	43,439
Hubei 湖北	40	565	21,763	629	1.28	3.90	38.49	67.26	49,282
Hunan 湖南	35	347	8,851	-412	-1.76	-9.36	25.49	81.22	23,460
Guangdong 廣東	31	314	20,024	-387	-0.98	-3.93	63.83	74.94	39,331
Guangxi 廣西	8	489	15,879	-1,266	-2.47	-37.78	32.46	93.46	51,259
Hainan 海南									
Southwest 西南	58	564	15,442	-364	-0.92	-4.04	27.40	77.32	39,749
Chongqing 重慶	10	656	16,695	1,069	1.81	13.10	25.44	86.15	58,930
Sichuan 四川	32	392	11,516	-1,062	-4.26	-16.90	29.36	74.80	24,936
Guizhou 貴州	9	1,073	29,868	776	0.98	3.86	27.83	74.61	79,089
Yunnan 雲南	7	563	13,176	-641	-2.12	-7.50	23.41	71.78	30,317
Tibet 西藏									
Northwest 西北	34	817	29,887	1,075	1.67	5.99	36.60	72.18	64,480
Shaanxi 陝西	12	543	11,808	-359	-0.90	-4.04	21.74	77.69	39,895
Gansu 甘肅	11	927	25,278	396	0.64	3.11	27.28	79.32	61,640
Qinghai 青海	3	403	4,003	-3,740	-13.49	-161.44	9.93	91.65	27,733
Ningxia 寧夏	7	1,210	78,897	7,004	6.02	15.33	65.19	60.73	116,330
Xinjiang 新疆	1	1,371	32,120	-1,310	-0.95	-3.63	23.43	73.82	138,030

Year 年份	Number of firms 企業個數	Rate of change 每年變化 (%)	Number of employees 職工人數（人）	Rate of change 每年變化 (%)	Total revenue (Mil. RMB) 總銷售收入（百萬元）	Rate of change 每年變化 (%)	Total profit (Mil. RMB) 總利潤（百萬元）	Rate of change 每年變化 (%)
1993	777		388,990		11,396		612	
1994	808	3.99%	321,129	-17.45%	12,606	10.62%	419	-31.42%
1995	933	15.47%	400,632	24.76%	16,531	31.14%	422	0.67%
1996	945	1.29%	389,857	-2.69%	16,953	2.55%	212	-49.79%

3 Major products* 3種主要產品 *	Output 產量	Sales volume 銷售量	Unit 單位
a) Bearing 軸承	128,684	114,528	10,000 set 萬套
b) Parts of Bearing 軸承零件	41,037	41,857	ton 噸

Top 10 firms by revenue (year founded) 收入排名前10家企業（創辦年份）	City 城市	Province 省	Telephone / fax 電話 / 傳真	Number of employees 職工人數	Ownership 產業所有權	Revenue ('000 RMB) 銷售收入（千元）	Profit ('000 RMB) (rank) 利潤（千元）（排名）	Total assets ('000 RMB) 總資產（千元）	Major products 主要產品
Wafangdian Bearing Group Co. Ltd. 瓦房店軸承集團有限責任公司(1938)	Dalian 大連市	Liaoning 遼寧省	(0411)5509888 (0411)5500585	26,580	State-owned 國有	1,610,204	135774(1)	3,067,156	a
Harbin Bearing Co. Ltd. 哈爾濱軸承股份有限公司(1950)	Harbin 哈爾濱市	Heilongjiang 黑龍江省	(0451)5315011 (0451)229379	14,068	Joint stock 股份制	630,392	20515(5)	2,710,507	a
Mincbea Electronics & Hi-tech Componets (Shanghai) Ltd. 上海美蓓亞精密機電有限公司(1994)	Shanghai 上海市	Shanghai 上海市	(021)59293680 (021)59293697	1,873	Foreign-funded 外資	581,236	0(434)	2,388,745	a
Xibei Bearing Group Co. Ltd. 西北軸承股份有限公司(1970)	Yinchuan 銀川市	Ningxia 寧夏	(0951)2021581	5,658	Joint stock 股份制	413,011	42162(3)	629,579	a
Xiangyang Automobile Bearing Co. Ltd. 襄陽汽車軸承股份有限公司(1970)	Xiangfan 襄樊市	Hubei 湖北省	(0710)3564101 (0710)3564019	9,050	Joint stock 股份制	386,725	52136(2)	767,018	a
Zhejiang Xinchang Bearing General Factory 浙江新昌軸承總廠(1969)	Shaoxing 紹興市	Zhejiang 浙江省	(0575)6023340 (0575)6024087	2,194	State-owned 國有	218,238	-11723(584)	393,406	a
Guang Yang Ri Dian Chan Dalian Precise Bearing Co. Ltd. 光洋日電產大連精密軸承有限公司(1995)	Dalian 大連市	Liaoning 遼寧省	(0411)7310974 (0411)7310974	378	Foreign-funded 外資	211,883	4481(24)	107,595	a
Wuxi Jiangnan Micro Bearing Group Company 無錫江南微型軸承集團公司(1966)	Wuxi 無錫市	Jiangsu 江蘇省	(0510)5860346 (0510)5802468	1,919	State-owned 國有	165,915	588(132)	246,832	o
Tianshui Hailin Bearing Factory 天水海林軸承廠(1969)	Tianshui 天水市	Gansu 甘肅省	(0938)8381819 (0938)8382399	5,197	State-owned 國有	155,764	5032(21)	329,572	a
Xing City Bearing Factory 興城市軸承有限公司(1956)	Huludao 葫蘆島市	Liaoning 遼寧省	(0429)5712255	2,392	Collectively-owned 集體	155,330	-10169(582)	143,025	o

Top 10 Cities by Production Output 產出排名前10位城市	Province 省	Market share 市場份額	Number of firms 企業個數
Dalian 大連市	Liaoning 遼寧省	14.16%	39
Shanghai 上海市	Shanghai 上海市	11.42%	103
Luoyang 洛陽市	Henan 河南省	6.75%	29
Harbin 哈爾濱市	Heilongjiang 黑龍江省	4.17%	14
Wuxi 無錫市	Jiangsu 江蘇省	3.35%	54
Shaoxing 紹興市	Zhejiang 浙江省	3.03%	37
Xiangfan 襄樊市	Hubei 湖北省	2.89%	10
Yinchuan 銀川市	Ningxia 寧夏	2.59%	4
Ningbo 寧波市	Zhejiang 浙江省	1.55%	50
Changzhou 常州市	Jiangsu 江蘇省	1.41%	32

10 Major Wholesalers 10家主要批發商	City 城市	Province 省	Telephone / Fax 電話 / 傳真
Liaoning Automobile Trade Group Corp. 遼寧省汽車貿易集團	Shenyang 瀋陽市	Liaoning 遼寧省	(024)23835494 (024)23838338
China Post and Telecommunication Equipment General Company 中國郵電器材總公司	Beijing 北京市	Beijing 北京市	(010)63523715 (010)63525935
Jiangsu Electromechanical Products General Company 江蘇省機電產品總公司	Nanjing 南京市	Jiangsu 江蘇省	(025)7713642 (025)7711036
Xi Nan Technology Import & Export Company 西南技術進出口公司	Chongqing 重慶市	Chongqing 重慶市	(023)63850185 (023)63850026
Changzhou Economic Technology Industrial Development Zone Tian Ming Trade Company 常州經濟技術產業開發區天明貿易公司	Changzhou 常州市	Jiangsu 江蘇省	(0519)8829882 (0519)8829882
Shanxi Mechanical Equipment Import & Export Company 山西省機械設備進出口公司	Taiyuan 太原市	Shanxi 山西省	(0351)4040713 (0351)4043981
Ningbo Five Mining Machinery Import & Export Company 寧波市五礦機械進出口公司	Ningbo 寧波市	Zhejiang 浙江省	(0574)7311255 (0574)7320322
Tianjin Jin Huan Electromechanical Complete Sets of Equipment Factory 天津市津環機電成套設備廠	Tianjin 天津市	Tianjin 天津市	(022)26371628
Yunnan Machinery Import & Export Company 雲南省機械進出口公司	Kunming 昆明市	Yunnan 雲南省	(0871)3164879 (0871)3136829
Tianjin Da Qiu Zhuang Yi Yuan Trade Center 天津市大丘莊億源商貿中心	Tianjin 天津市	Tianjin 天津市	(022)28899478 (022)28899046

*Also include sales by firms outside this industry.包括本行業以外廠家的銷售。"o" stands for "others". "o" 代表"其他產品"。

3542: Valves 閥門製造業

The industry accounts for 0.149% of the total revenue of China's industrial sector in 1996. The revenue growth rate of the industry is 18.2% from 1995, as compared to the growth rate of China's industrial sector, 9.51%. The rate of return on asset is 1.75%. 69.75% of all firms in the industry made a profit while 25.54% had negative returns. The top province in terms of the industry's revenue is Jiangsu, accounting for 22.00% of the total revenue.
本行業在1996年佔全行業總產值0.149%，行業年增長率為18.2%（全國工業年增長率9.51%）。行業的資產回報率1.75%，69.75%的企業盈利，25.54%的企業虧損。銷售收入最高的省份為江蘇省，佔本行業的22.00%。

	Total number of firms 企業總數	Total number of employees 職工總數	Total revenue (Mil. RMB) 總銷售收入（百萬元）	Total profit (Mil. RMB) 總利潤（百萬元）	Return on assets 資產利潤率 (%)	Return on equity 權益利潤率 (%)	Labour productivity ('000 RMB / worker) 勞動生產率（千元/人）	Debts / assets 資產負債率 (%)	Total assets (Mil. RMB) 總資產（百萬元）
Industry Overall 行業總體	1,377	201,426	8,638	222	1.75	5.14	42.88	65.90	12,666

	Number of firms 企業個數	Average number of employees 平均職工人數	Average revenue ('000 RMB) 平均銷售收入（千元）	Average profit ('000 RMB) 平均利潤（千元）	Return on assets 資產利潤率 (%)	Return on equity 權益利潤率 (%)	Labour productivity ('000 RMB / worker) 勞動生產率（千元/人）	Average debts / assets 平均資產負債率(%)	Average Total assets ('000 RMB) 平均總資產（千元）
By ownership 產業所有權									
State-owned 國有	151	486	13,987	-371	-1.09	-3.42	28.75	68.11	34,033
Collectively-owned 集體	1,122	96	4,423	173	3.69	11.79	46.05	68.68	4,687
Privately-owned 私有	9	43	4,012	353	5.03	29.92	92.82	83.18	7,018
Domestic JVs 聯營	10	197	11,130	587	4.44	15.19	56.41	70.79	13,235
Joint stock 股份制	23	383	18,720	971	2.71	6.53	48.84	58.50	35,810
Foreign-funded 外資	36	177	22,458	1,571	6.45	11.64	126.96	44.62	24,355
Overseas Chinese-funded 港澳台資	25	106	7,032	-167	-1.13	-2.69	66.07	58.08	14,876
By size 規模									
Large 大型	10	1,951	88,255	482	0.23	0.82	45.25	71.79	207,765
Medium 中型	48	824	35,835	996	1.41	3.60	43.50	60.78	70,456
Small 小型	1,309	109	4,611	129	2.35	7.04	42.45	66.60	5,505
By regional distribution 地區分布									
Central-North 華北	152	139	6,200	340	3.35	7.71	44.60	56.56	10,142
Beijing 北京	25	76	3,864	38	0.41	0.94	50.95	56.19	9,154
Tianjin 天津	45	109	6,428	658	5.94	10.25	58.95	42.04	11,074
Hebei 河北	56	165	8,386	489	4.91	13.78	50.86	64.38	9,964
Shanxi 山西	21	127	2,386	46	0.64	1.69	18.73	62.25	7,183
Inner Mongolia 內蒙	5	483	7,360	-1,458	-6.91	-29.30	15.23	76.43	21,112
Northeast 東北	228	170	4,012	-143	-1.66	-5.27	23.63	68.49	8,585
Liaoning 遼寧	194	163	4,057	-103	-1.27	-3.88	24.87	67.29	8,079
Jilin 吉林	6	327	3,595	-417	-2.70	-14.35	11.01	81.20	15,440
Heilongjiang 黑龍江	28	182	3,796	-361	-3.40	-11.66	20.81	70.85	10,622
Central East 華東	707	128	7,407	182	2.13	6.70	57.66	68.19	8,553
Shanghai 上海	66	153	11,715	146	1.18	4.58	76.62	74.24	12,403
Jiangsu 江蘇	235	152	8,085	124	1.42	4.39	53.13	67.63	8,744
Zhejiang 浙江	279	69	5,312	184	3.06	7.93	77.42	61.38	6,005
Anhui 安徽	31	157	8,788	205	1.75	6.25	55.87	71.99	11,677
Fujian 福建	16	152	4,909	132	1.43	2.80	32.21	48.80	9,190
Jiangxi 江西	20	166	2,688	10	0.13	0.90	16.19	85.76	7,377
Shandong 山東	60	253	11,281	502	3.58	14.84	44.53	75.89	14,021
Central-South 中南	180	159	5,477	470	4.32	10.97	34.43	60.65	10,884
Henan 河南	87	143	5,202	164	2.20	6.53	36.29	66.33	7,449
Hubei 湖北	24	247	6,929	158	0.93	2.32	28.05	60.03	17,004
Hunan 湖南	44	117	2,286	1,211	38.39	132.31	19.50	70.98	3,154
Guangdong 廣東	20	219	11,893	677	1.84	3.96	54.28	53.56	36,812
Guangxi 廣西	5	139	5,716	-60	-1.07	-4.01	41.00	73.29	5,600
Hainan 海南									
Southwest 西南	87	162	4,316	90	1.18	3.67	26.64	67.95	7,610
Chongqing 重慶	18	106	1,918	-1,453	-42.39	-219.76	18.12	80.71	3,427
Sichuan 四川	64	179	5,012	285	3.20	9.79	27.99	67.35	8,907
Guizhou 貴州	1								
Yunnan 雲南	4	182	5,028	-20	-0.26	-0.57	27.70	53.13	7,548
Tibet 西藏									
Northwest 西北	23	349	7,960	-793	-3.65	-14.42	22.79	74.70	21,720
Shaanxi 陝西	13	216	5,719	-89	-0.90	-2.63	26.45	65.96	9,967
Gansu 甘肅	7	715	13,804	-2,509	-4.92	-22.69	19.30	78.32	50,999
Qinghai 青海									
Ningxia 寧夏	1	128	5,950	20	0.79	2.33	46.48	65.87	2,520
Xinjiang 新疆	2	44	3,075	235	4.49	11.75	70.69	61.70	5,235

Year 年份	Number of firms 企業個數	Rate of change 每年變化 (%)	Number of employees 職工人數（人）	Rate of change 每年變化 (%)	Total revenue (Mil. RMB) 總銷售收入（百萬元）	Rate of change 每年變化 (%)	Total profit (Mil. RMB) 總利潤（百萬元）	Rate of change 每年變化 (%)
1993	1,453		239,822		6,179		227	
1994	1,372	-5.58%	215,275	-10.24%	5,615	-9.12%	95	-58.33%
1995	1,420	3.50%	214,687	-0.27%	7,311	30.19%	139	47.20%
1996	1,377	-3.03%	201,426	-6.18%	8,638	18.15%	222	59.22%

3 Major products* 3 種主要產品 *	Output 產量	Sales volume 銷售量	Unit 單位
a) High & Medium Pressure Valve 高中壓閥門	169,142	131,931	ton 噸
b) Low Pressure Valve 低壓閥門	612,793	588,281	ton 噸

Top 10 firms by revenue (year founded) 收入排名前 10 家企業（創辦年份）	City 城市	Province 省	Telephone / fax 電話 / 傳真	Number of employees 職工人數	Ownership 產業所有權	Revenue ('000 RMB) 銷售收入（千元）	Profit ('000 RMB) (rank) 利潤（千元）（排名）	Total assets ('000 RMB) 總資產（千元）	Major products 主要產品
State-owned No.526 Factory 國營五二六廠(1952)	Suzhou 蘇州市	Jiangsu 江蘇省	(0512)7533655 (0512)7532587	2,095	State-owned 國有	281,730	5053(12)	309,122	a,b
Tianjin Tanggu Watts Valve Co. Ltd. 天津塘沽瓦特斯閥門有限公司(1994)	Tianjin 天津市	Tianjin 天津市	(022)25716633 (022)25718857	871	Foreign-funded 外資	150,748	15443(2)	185,665	b
Ningbo Amico Copper Valves Manfacturing Inc. 寧波埃美柯銅閥門有限公司(1988)	Ningbo 寧波市	Zhejiang 浙江省	(0574)7355604 (0574)7355998	1,036	Foreign-funded 外資	140,941	9004(5)	88,536	o
Liaoning Tieling Valve Work 遼寧省鐵嶺閥門廠(1935)	Tieling 鐵嶺市	Liaoning 遼寧省	(0410)4603601 (0410)4603429	3,395	State-owned 國有	105,373	1047(81)	286,437	o
Shanghai Liang Gong Valve Factory 上海良工閥門廠(1946)	Shanghai 上海市	Shanghai 上海市	(021)65411700 (021)65455925	1,249	State-owned 國有	102,574	109(344)	104,647	a
Dalian High Pressure Valve Factory 大連高壓閥門廠(1956)	Dalian 大連市	Liaoning 遼寧省	(0411)4644894 (0411)4605234	2,210	State-owned 國有	96,709	134(320)	225,489	o
Shanghai Valve Factory 上海閥門廠(1960)	Shanghai 上海市	Shanghai 上海市	(021)59577580 (021)59578580	1,082	State-owned 國有	85,510	-5618(698)	92,405	a
Shanghai Nai Lai Si • Zhan Mu Si Bo Lei Valve Company 上海耐萊斯 • 詹姆斯伯雷閥門公司(1991)	Shanghai 上海市	Shanghai 上海市	(021)65021410 (021)65020368	315	Foreign-funded 外資	84,196	10060(3)	110,616	a
Henan Zhengzhou Shangjie Butterfly Valve Factory 河南省鄭州市上街蝶閥廠(1969)	Zhengzhou 鄭州市	Henan 河南省	(0371)8921424 (0371)8921424	483	Collectively-owned 集體	82,430	7280(9)	50,290	o
Shanghai Guan Long Valve Machinery Co. Ltd. 上海冠龍閥門機械有限公司(1991)	Shanghai 上海市	Shanghai 上海市	(021)59128279 (021)59121265	90	Overseas Chinese-funded 港澳台資	79,065	3155(23)	21,985	b

Top 10 Cities by Production Output 產出排名前 10 位城市	Province 省	Market share 市場份額	Number of firms 企業個數
Wenzhou 溫州市	Zhejiang 浙江省	10.24%	674
Shanghai 上海市	Shanghai 上海市	8.64%	116
Ningbo 寧波市	Zhejiang 浙江省	6.37%	55
Yancheng 鹽城市	Jiangsu 江蘇省	6.35%	116
Suzhou 蘇州市	Jiangsu 江蘇省	4.91%	28
Dalian 大連市	Liaoning 遼寧省	4.12%	55
Taizhou 臺州市	Zhejiang 浙江省	3.81%	89
Tianjin 天津市	Tianjin 天津市	3.59%	57
Zhengzhou 鄭州市	Henan 河南省	2.32%	20
Nantong 南通市	Jiangsu 江蘇省	2.04%	32

10 Major Wholesalers 10 家主要批發商	City 城市	Province 省	Telephone / Fax 電話 / 傳真
Liaoning Automobile Trade Group Corp. 遼寧省汽車貿易集團	Shenyang 瀋陽市	Liaoning 遼寧省	(024)23835494 (024)23838338
China Post and Telecommunication Equipment General Company 中國郵電器材總公司	Beijing 北京市	Beijing 北京市	(010)63523715 (010)63525935
Jiangsu Electromechanical Products General Company 江蘇省機電產品總公司	Nanjing 南京市	Jiangsu 江蘇省	(025)7713642 (025)7711036
Xi Nan Technology Import & Export Company 西南技術進出口公司	Chongqing 重慶市	Chongqing 重慶市	(023)63850185 (023)63850026
Changzhou Economic Technology Industrial Development Zone Tian Ming Trade Company 常州經濟技術產業開發區天明貿易公司	Changzhou 常州市	Jiangsu 江蘇省	(0519)8829882 (0519)8829882
Shanxi Mechanical Equipment Import & Export Company 山西省機械設備進出口公司	Taiyuan 太原市	Shanxi 山西省	(0351)4040713 (0351)4043981
Ningbo Five Mining Machinery Import & Export Company 寧波市五礦機械進出口公司	Ningbo 寧波市	Zhejiang 浙江省	(0574)7311255 (0574)7320322
Tianjin Jin Huan Electromechanical Complete Sets of Equipment Factory 天津市津環機電成套設備廠	Tianjin 天津市	Tianjin 天津市	(022)26371628
Yunnan Machinery Import & Export Company 雲南省機械進出口公司	Kunming 昆明市	Yunnan 雲南省	(0871)3164879 (0871)3136829
Tianjin Da Qiu Zhuang Yi Yuan Trade Center 天津市大丘莊億源商貿中心	Tianjin 天津市	Tianjin 天津市	(022)28899478 (022)28899046

*Also include sales by firms outside this industry.包括本行業以外廠家的銷售。"o" stands for "others". "o" 代表 "其他產品"。

3561: Hydraulic Equipment 液壓件及液力配件製造業

The industry accounts for 0.081% of the total revenue of China's industrial sector in 1996. The revenue growth rate of the industry is 20.6% from 1995, as compared to the growth rate of China's industrial sector, 9.51%. The rate of return on asset is 0.15%. 66.09% of all firms in the industry made a profit while 27.11% had negative returns. The top province in terms of the industry's revenue is Jiangsu, accounting for 20.04% of the total revenue.
本行業在1996年佔全行業總產值0.081%，行業年增長率為20.6%（全國工業年增長率9.51%）。行業的資產回報率0.15%，66.09%的企業盈利，27.11%的企業虧損。銷售收入最高的省份為江蘇省，佔本行業的20.04%。

	Total number of firms 企業總數	Total number of employees 職工總數	Total revenue (Mil. RMB) 總銷售收入（百萬元）	Total profit (Mil. RMB) 總利潤（百萬元）	Return on assets 資產利潤率 (%)	Return on equity 權益利潤率 (%)	Labour productivity ('000 RMB / worker) 勞動生產率（千元/人）	Debts / assets 資產負債率 (%)	Total assets (Mil. RMB) 總資產（百萬元）
Industry Overall 行業總體	764	127,170	4,716	13	0.15	0.52	37.08	71.14	9,051

	Number of firms 企業個數	Average number of employees 平均職工人數	Average revenue ('000 RMB) 平均銷售收入（千元）	Average profit ('000 RMB) 平均利潤（千元）	Return on assets 資產利潤率 (%)	Return on equity 權益利潤率 (%)	Labour productivity ('000 RMB / worker) 勞動生產率（千元/人）	Average debts / assets 平均資產負債率(%)	Average Total assets ('000 RMB) 平均總資產（千元）
By ownership 產業所有權									
State-owned 國有	160	482	13,238	-413	-1.08	-4.06	27.46	73.47	38,263
Collectively-owned 集體	539	84	4,132	117	2.70	8.92	49.17	69.72	4,315
Privately-owned 私有	2	48	1,461	90	3.70	15.32	30.44	75.84	2,429
Domestic JVs 聯營	13	177	5,269	-369	-4.95	-26.45	29.82	81.29	7,451
Joint stock 股份制	14	67	1,976	-113	-3.47	-10.37	29.59	66.51	3,268
Foreign-funded 外資	23	83	9,023	871	6.18	11.32	109.06	45.38	14,092
Overseas Chinese-funded 港澳台資	12	49	4,323	47	0.63	1.12	88.84	43.90	7,487
By size 規模									
Large 大型	9	2,662	77,277	-434	-0.18	-0.66	29.03	73.33	246,558
Medium 中型	38	807	29,957	-86	-0.12	-0.40	37.10	69.25	70,410
Small 小型	710	103	4,060	28	0.49	1.68	39.59	71.19	5,855
By regional distribution 地區分布									
Central-North 華北	133	215	6,221	-115	-0.59	-2.46	28.92	75.92	19,402
Beijing 北京	43	104	3,317	82	0.50	2.04	31.75	75.40	16,379
Tianjin 天津	27	303	10,612	-5	-0.02	-0.08	35.02	70.44	20,897
Hebei 河北	28	128	4,527	-110	-0.97	-19.81	35.41	95.09	11,293
Shanxi 山西	32	383	8,450	-490	-1.58	-5.92	22.05	73.30	31,003
Inner Mongolia 內蒙	3	32	363	13	1.07	3.92	11.24	72.73	1,247
Northeast 東北	150	142	4,187	-43	-0.48	-1.75	29.50	72.59	9,053
Liaoning 遼寧	126	144	4,673	42	0.42	1.46	32.40	71.07	9,921
Jilin 吉林	14	177	1,763	-900	-13.08	-230.77	9.94	94.33	6,883
Heilongjiang 黑龍江	10	63	1,462	79	6.85	15.43	23.17	55.51	1,153
Central East 華東	317	157	7,637	189	1.74	5.21	48.79	66.53	10,819
Shanghai 上海	54	149	6,328	-24	-0.21	-0.76	42.44	71.74	11,063
Jiangsu 江蘇	102	171	9,264	99	0.90	2.69	54.21	66.47	11,001
Zhejiang 浙江	86	67	3,828	124	1.97	4.93	57.01	59.98	6,301
Anhui 安徽	12	300	17,013	1,693	11.58	59.85	56.65	80.66	14,626
Fujian 福建	8	177	8,664	55	0.30	0.59	48.84	48.59	18,216
Jiangxi 江西	12	197	4,017	-29	-0.28	-1.10	20.40	74.42	10,343
Shandong 山東	43	255	11,240	462	2.75	8.10	44.06	66.07	16,815
Central-South 中南	104	190	5,683	-6	-0.06	-0.18	29.93	68.34	10,337
Henan 河南	26	204	3,523	380	7.12	17.14	17.26	58.44	5,341
Hubei 湖北	28	174	7,525	-57	-0.72	-6.03	43.28	88.09	7,964
Hunan 湖南	26	249	4,477	-422	-3.64	-11.03	18.01	67.03	11,592
Guangdong 廣東	16	170	10,031	101	0.41	1.06	59.14	61.56	24,954
Guangxi 廣西	8	49	1,476	56	3.58	13.68	29.90	73.81	1,570
Hainan 海南									
Southwest 西南	48	139	4,663	-459	-4.05	-20.94	33.66	80.68	11,341
Chongqing 重慶	8	194	3,272	-674	-6.29	-25.90	16.84	75.70	10,715
Sichuan 四川	34	148	5,741	-496	-3.70	-20.62	38.76	82.03	13,378
Guizhou 貴州	5	5	372	36	8.22	14.17	74.40	42.01	438
Yunnan 雲南	1	31	790	80	4.49	5.97	25.48	25.28	1,780
Tibet 西藏									
Northwest 西北	12	105	2,052	-155	-2.92	-7.35	19.60	60.30	5,311
Shaanxi 陝西	9	60	1,381	-223	-9.01	-29.65	22.85	69.60	2,478
Gansu 甘肅	2	300	4,150	-180	-1.04	-2.39	13.83	56.50	17,345
Qinghai 青海									
Ningxia 寧夏	1	112	3,890	510	7.57	14.87	34.73	49.11	6,740
Xinjiang 新疆									

3561: Hydraulic Equipment 液壓件及液力配件製造業

Year 年份	Number of firms 企業個數	Rate of change 每年變化 (%)	Number of employees 職工人數 (人)	Rate of change 每年變化 (%)	Total revenue (Mil. RMB) 總銷售收入 (百萬元)	Rate of change 每年變化 (%)	Total profit (Mil. RMB) 總利潤 (百萬元)	Rate of change 每年變化 (%)
1993	643		151,176		4,405		259	
1994	710	10.42%	125,796	-16.79%	3,596	-18.37%	93	-64.11%
1995	718	1.13%	126,679	0.70%	3,912	8.80%	14	-84.53%
1996	764	6.41%	127,170	0.39%	4,716	20.55%	13	-9.41%

3 Major products* 3 種主要產品 *	Output 產量	Sales volume 銷售量	Unit 單位
a) Capsular Jack 千斤頂	62,202	59,092	ton 噸
b) Industrial Pump 工業泵	155,868	158,986	set 台

Top 10 firms by revenue (year founded) 收入排名前 10 家企業 (創辦年份)	City 城市	Province 省	Telephone / fax 電話 / 傳真	Number of employees 職工人數	Ownership 產業所有權	Revenue ('000 RMB) 銷售收入 (千元)	Profit ('000 RMB) (rank) 利潤 (千元) (排名)	Total assets ('000 RMB) 總資產 (千元)	Major products 主要產品
Tianjin Hydraulic Pressure Machinery (Group) Company 天津液壓機械(集團)公司(1938)	Tianjin 天津市	Tianjin 天津市	(022)27386320 (022)27384371	4,122	State-owned 國有	195,048	21(212)	416,618	o
Qidong Cheng He Economic Industrial Company 啟東市城河經濟實業公司(1989)	Nantong 南通市	Jiangsu 江蘇省	(0513)3313646	879	Collectively-owned 集體	149,327	5335(6)	89,880	o
Liaoning Hydraulic Pressure Industrial Co. 遼寧省液壓工業公司(1979)	Shenyang 瀋陽市	Liaoning 遼寧省	(024)24821898 (024)24821482	4,558	State-owned 國有	147,159	206(118)	361,503	a
Shanxi Ping Yang Machinery Factory 山西平陽機械廠(1964)	Linfen 臨汾市	Shanxi 山西省	(0357)4223411 (0357)4223827	4,704	State-owned 國有	97,629	-18279(353)	289,990	o
Yixing Hong Liu Group Co. 宜興市洪流集團公司(1975)	Wuxi 無錫市	Jiangsu 江蘇省	(0510)7541688 (0510)7541666	298	Collectively-owned 集體	79,380	4020(10)	26,300	b
Anhui Zhong Ding Group Hydraulic Tools Factory 安徽中鼎集團液壓工具廠(1985)	Xuanzhou 宣州市	Anhui 安徽省	(0563)4074800	1,450	Collectively-owned 集體	78,000	14400(2)	39,160	o
Beijing Hydraulic Industrial Co. 北京市液壓工業公司(1979)	Beijing 北京市	Beijing 北京市	(010)67221352	3,346	State-owned 國有	76,619	44(192)	556,000	o
Dalian Hydraulic Components Factory 大連液壓件廠(1965)	Dalian 大連市	Liaoning 遼寧省	(0411)6641118 (0411)6641624	1,116	State-owned 國有	71,657	3332(13)	137,007	o
Weihai Machinery Building Materials General Factory 威海機械建材總廠(1978)	Weihai 威海市	Shandong 山東省	(0896)5764331 (0896)5764122	523	Collectively-owned 集體	69,350	4980(7)	31,190	o
Shandong Qixia Hydraulic Components Factory 山東省栖霞液壓件廠(1951)	Yantai 煙臺市	Shandong 山東省	(0535)5211353 (0535)5211353	1,163	State-owned 國有	67,107	6340(3)	86,738	b

Top 10 Cities by Production Output 產出排名前 10 位城市	Province 省	Market share 市場份額	Number of firms 企業個數
Shanghai 上海市	Shanghai 上海市	10.24%	87
Tianjin 天津市	Tianjin 天津市	6.50%	39
Dalian 大連市	Liaoning 遼寧省	4.83%	34
Shenyang 瀋陽市	Liaoning 遼寧省	3.94%	47
Beijing 北京市	Beijing 北京市	3.77%	40
Nanjing 南京市	Jiangsu 江蘇省	3.39%	22
Ningbo 寧波市	Zhejiang 浙江省	2.72%	35
Linfen 臨汾市	Shanxi 山西省	2.55%	1
Yuci 榆次市	Shanxi 山西省	2.48%	10
Chengdu 成都市	Sichuan 四川省	2.26%	11

10 Major Wholesalers 10 家主要批發商	City 城市	Province 省	Telephone / Fax 電話 / 傳真
Liaoning Automobile Trade Group Corp. 遼寧省汽車貿易集團	Shenyang 瀋陽市	Liaoning 遼寧省	(024)23835494 (024)23838338
China Post and Telecommunication Equipment General Company 中國郵電器材總公司	Beijing 北京市	Beijing 北京市	(010)63523715 (010)63525935
Jiangsu Electromechanical Products General Company 江蘇省機電產品總公司	Nanjing 南京市	Jiangsu 江蘇省	(025)7713642 (025)7711036
Xi Nan Technology Import & Export Company 西南技術進出口公司	Chongqing 重慶市	Chongqing 重慶市	(023)63850185 (023)63850026
Changzhou Economic Technology Industrial Development Zone Tian Ming Trade Company 常州經濟技術產業開發區天明貿易公司	Changzhou 常州市	Jiangsu 江蘇省	(0519)8829882 (0519)8829882
Shanxi Mechanical Equipment Import & Export Company 山西省機械設備進出口公司	Taiyuan 太原市	Shanxi 山西省	(0351)4040713 (0351)4043981
Ningbo Five Mining Machinery Import & Export Company 寧波市五礦機械進出口公司	Ningbo 寧波市	Zhejiang 浙江省	(0574)7311255 (0574)7320322
Tianjin Jin Huan Electromechanical Complete Sets of Equipment Factory 天津市津環機電成套設備廠	Tianjin 天津市	Tianjin 天津市	(022)26371628
Yunnan Machinery Import & Export Company 雲南省機械進出口公司	Kunming 昆明市	Yunnan 雲南省	(0871)3164879 (0871)3136829
Tianjin Da Qiu Zhuang Yi Yuan Trade Center 天津市大丘莊億源商貿中心	Tianjin 天津市	Tianjin 天津市	(022)28899478 (022)28899046

*Also include sales by firms outside this industry.包括本行業以外廠家的銷售。"o" stands for "others". "o" 代表 "其他產品"。

3562: Pneumatic Components 氣動元件製造業

The industry accounts for 0.025% of the total revenue of China's industrial sector in 1996. The revenue growth rate of the industry is 15.4% from 1995, as compared to the growth rate of China's industrial sector, 9.51%. The rate of return on asset is 1.79%. 73.47% of all firms in the industry made a profit while 23.57% had negative returns. The top province in terms of the industry's revenue is Jiangsu, accounting for 16.78% of the total revenue.
本行業在1996年佔全行業總產值0.025%，行業年增長率為15.4%（全國工業年增長率9.51%）。行業的資產回報率1.79%，73.47%的企業盈利，23.57%的企業虧損。銷售收入最高的省份為江蘇省，佔本行業的16.78%。

	Total number of firms 企業總數	Total number of employees 職工總數	Total revenue (Mil. RMB) 總銷售收入（百萬元）	Total profit (Mil. RMB) 總利潤（百萬元）	Return on assets 資產利潤率 (%)	Return on equity 權益利潤率 (%)	Labour productivity ('000 RMB / worker) 勞動生產率（千元/人）	Debts / assets 資產負債率 (%)	Total assets (Mil. RMB) 總資產（百萬元）
Industry Overall 行業總體	331	28,042	1,450	44	1.79	4.45	51.71	59.79	2,439

	Number of firms 企業個數	Average number of employees 平均職工人數	Average revenue ('000 RMB) 平均銷售收入（千元）	Average profit ('000 RMB) 平均利潤（千元）	Return on assets 資產利潤率 (%)	Return on equity 權益利潤率 (%)	Labour productivity ('000 RMB / worker) 勞動生產率（千元/人）	Average debts / assets 平均資產負債率(%)	Average Total assets ('000 RMB) 平均總資產（千元）
By ownership 產業所有權									
State-owned 國有	38	224	7,605	132	0.70	1.98	33.90	64.71	18,868
Collectively-owned 集體	261	67	3,427	119	2.49	6.01	51.39	58.58	4,777
Privately-owned 私有	1	15	777	2	0.32	2.74	51.81	88.37	718
Domestic JVs 聯營	2	60	2,777	-207	-1.66	-8.02	46.28	79.36	12,534
Joint stock 股份制	3	44	3,062	494	11.01	17.69	69.58	37.78	4,490
Foreign-funded 外資	14	39	8,483	-30	-0.19	-0.37	215.54	48.08	15,382
Overseas Chinese-funded 港澳台資	11	124	12,089	663	3.30	8.44	97.71	60.94	20,114
By size 規模									
Large 大型	1	861	36,568	16	0.01	0.02	42.47	49.71	170,496
Medium 中型	5	609	32,145	1,457	1.92	3.75	52.77	48.69	75,681
Small 小型	323	75	3,880	114	1.94	5.23	51.91	62.91	5,854
By regional distribution 地區分布									
Central-North 華北	45	89	3,735	21	0.16	0.27	42.06	41.48	13,366
Beijing 北京	7	57	3,611	-1,677	-3.79	-4.39	63.20	13.73	44,233
Tianjin 天津	7	58	1,890	61	2.59	10.02	32.51	74.19	2,374
Hebei 河北	26	89	4,379	468	6.09	19.38	49.12	68.55	7,673
Shanxi 山西	5	174	3,142	22	0.15	0.62	18.04	76.47	15,138
Inner Mongolia 內蒙									
Northeast 東北	43	84	1,635	94	2.52	9.88	19.52	74.48	3,733
Liaoning 遼寧	36	61	1,558	99	2.79	11.92	25.52	76.58	3,531
Jilin 吉林	1	364	7,190	570	2.68	5.35	19.75	49.91	21,260
Heilongjiang 黑龍江	6	173	1,167	-12	-0.58	-12.73	6.74	95.54	2,020
Central East 華東	169	86	5,022	139	2.09	5.77	58.52	63.78	6,658
Shanghai 上海	27	69	6,098	199	2.49	7.66	88.57	67.54	7,984
Jiangsu 江蘇	47	105	5,178	66	1.02	3.08	49.08	66.99	6,477
Zhejiang 浙江	56	49	2,736	109	2.82	8.88	56.37	68.30	3,875
Anhui 安徽	3	203	9,207	243	3.48	7.25	45.35	52.00	6,993
Fujian 福建	9	95	8,916	202	2.53	7.13	94.29	64.48	7,990
Jiangxi 江西	6	75	1,705	27	1.19	3.01	22.68	60.67	2,250
Shandong 山東	21	146	8,070	297	2.21	4.90	55.42	54.81	13,423
Central-South 中南	56	90	6,081	274	3.00	9.42	67.51	68.21	9,129
Henan 河南	9	55	7,370	603	16.82	110.82	133.19	84.82	3,587
Hubei 湖北	13	77	7,935	577	6.30	25.61	103.36	75.43	9,162
Hunan 湖南	8	84	1,061	-419	-9.09	-82.51	12.62	88.98	4,605
Guangdong 廣東	22	126	7,261	245	1.69	4.39	57.81	61.49	14,482
Guangxi 廣西	4	28	700	88	7.97	21.88	25.00	63.55	1,098
Hainan 海南									
Southwest 西南	14	58	1,435	-13	-0.50	-1.12	24.74	55.43	2,566
Chongqing 重慶	8	36	370	-2	-0.24	-0.42	10.17	43.64	855
Sichuan 四川	6	89	2,956	34	0.69	1.65	33.27	58.30	5,010
Guizhou 貴州									
Yunnan 雲南									
Tibet 西藏									
Northwest 西北	4	21	643	-3	-0.21	-0.56	30.24	61.75	1,170
Shaanxi 陝西	4	21	643	-3	-0.21	-0.56	30.24	61.75	1,170
Gansu 甘肅									
Qinghai 青海									
Ningxia 寧夏									
Xinjiang 新疆									

3562: Pneumatic Components 氣動元件製造業

Year 年份	Number of firms 企業個數	Rate of change 每年變化 (%)	Number of employees 職工人數 (人)	Rate of change 每年變化 (%)	Total revenue (Mil. RMB) 總銷售收入 (百萬元)	Rate of change 每年變化 (%)	Total profit (Mil. RMB) 總利潤 (百萬元)	Rate of change 每年變化 (%)
1993	285		41,767		1,230		70	
1994	322	12.98%	31,917	-23.58%	1,089	-11.48%	40	-42.26%
1995	328	1.86%	31,320	-1.87%	1,257	15.46%	39	-3.53%
1996	331	0.91%	28,042	-10.47%	1,450	15.35%	44	13.54%

3 Major products* 3 種主要產品 *	Output 產量	Sales volume 銷售量	Unit 單位

Top 10 firms by revenue (year founded) 收入排名前 10 家企業 (創辦年份)	City 城市	Province 省	Telephone / fax 電話 / 傳真	Number of employees 職工人數	Ownership 產業所有權	Revenue ('000 RMB) 銷售收入 (千元)	Profit ('000 RMB) (rank) 利潤 (千元) (排名)	Total assets ('000 RMB) 總資產 (千元)	Major products 主要產品
Shanghai Hua Hui Electromechanical Co. Ltd. 上海華匯機電有限公司(1994)	Shanghai 上海市	Shanghai 上海市	(021)64357914 (021)64357915	350	Overseas Chinese-funded 港澳台資	75,190	7538(1)	43,115	o
Zhongshan Xiaolan Gas Appliances Valve Factory 中山市小欖氣具閥門廠(1989)	Zhongshan 中山市	Guangdong 廣東省	(0760)2111666 (0760)2103999	672	Collectively-owned 集體	70,855	302(49)	72,747	o
Anqiu Cylinder Cover Factory 安丘市汽缸蓋廠(1956)	Weifang 濰坊市	Shandong 山東省	(0536)4710046 (0536)4710046	475	Collectively-owned 集體	64,620	2580(6)	19,950	o
Fuding Hua Ning Fuel Apparatus Co. Ltd. 福鼎華寧燃具有限公司(1992)	Ningde 寧德市	Fujian 福建省	(0593)7853925 (0593)7852373	431	Overseas Chinese-funded 港澳台資	53,567	2187(8)	44,294	o
Wujin Ben Niu Acetylene Manufacture Factory 武進市奔牛乙炔製造廠(1988)	Changzhou 常州市	Jiangsu 江蘇省	(0519)3260277	85	Collectively-owned 集體	42,781	138(71)	40,907	o
Guangdong Zhaoqing Fang Da Pneumatic Co. Ltd. 廣東肇慶方大氣動有限公司(1975)	Zhaoqing 肇慶市	Guangdong 廣東省	(0757)2718604 (0757)2718604	838	State-owned 國有	38,337	4644(2)	124,449	o
Ji'nan Huaneng Pneumatics Corp. 濟南華能氣動元器件公司(1957)	Ji'nan 濟南市	Shandong 山東省	(0531)8963993 (0531)8965247	958	State-owned 國有	37,705	25(101)	133,230	o
Shanghai Hydropneumatic General Co. Pneumatic Complete Sets Co. 上海液壓氣動總公司氣動成套公司(1923)	Shanghai 上海市	Shanghai 上海市	(021)63772631 (021)63761339	678	State-owned 國有	34,002	-744(133)	54,130	o
Hebei Tangshan Lian Qiang Metallurgy Roller Co. Ltd. 河北省唐山市聯強冶金軋輥有限公司(1994)	Tangshan 唐山市	Hebei 河北省	(0315)8121642 (0315)8129356	361	Overseas Chinese-funded 港澳台資	32,062	4120(4)	97,361	o
Kaifeng Lankao Filter Manufacture Factory 開封市蘭考縣濾清器製造廠(1971)	Kaifeng 開封市	Henan 河南省	(0378)6998348	357	State-owned 國有	30,398	827(25)	12,004	o

Top 10 Cities by Production Output 產出排名前 10 位城市	Province 省	Market share 市場份額	Number of firms 企業個數
Shanghai 上海市	Shanghai 上海市	19.39%	47
Zhongshan 中山市	Guangdong 廣東省	5.94%	1
Wuxi 無錫市	Jiangsu 江蘇省	5.27%	35
Langfang 廊坊市	Hebei 河北省	3.95%	8
Zhaoqing 肇慶市	Guangdong 廣東省	3.83%	6
Ji'nan 濟南市	Shandong 山東省	3.49%	8
Yantai 煙臺市	Shandong 山東省	3.16%	6
Wenzhou 溫州市	Zhejiang 浙江省	2.94%	15
Tangshan 唐山市	Hebei 河北省	2.69%	2
Ningbo 寧波市	Zhejiang 浙江省	2.65%	26

10 Major Wholesalers 10 家主要批發商	City 城市	Province 省	Telephone / Fax 電話 / 傳真
Liaoning Automobile Trade Group Corp. 遼寧省汽車貿易集團	Shenyang 瀋陽市	Liaoning 遼寧省	(024)23835494 (024)23838338
China Post and Telecommunication Equipment General Company 中國郵電器材總公司	Beijing 北京市	Beijing 北京市	(010)63523715 (010)63525935
Jiangsu Electromechanical Products General Company 江蘇省機電產品總公司	Nanjing 南京市	Jiangsu 江蘇省	(025)7713642 (025)7711036
Xi Nan Technology Import & Export Company 西南技術進出口公司	Chongqing 重慶市	Chongqing 重慶市	(023)63850185 (023)63850026
Changzhou Economic Technology Industrial Development Zone Tian Ming Trade Company 常州經濟技術產業開發區天明貿易公司	Changzhou 常州市	Jiangsu 江蘇省	(0519)8829882 (0519)8829882
Shanxi Mechanical Equipment Import & Export Company 山西省機械設備進出口公司	Taiyuan 太原市	Shanxi 山西省	(0351)4040713 (0351)4043981
Ningbo Five Mining Machinery Import & Export Company 寧波市五礦機械進出口公司	Ningbo 寧波市	Zhejiang 浙江省	(0574)7311255 (0574)7320322
Tianjin Jin Huan Electromechanical Complete Sets of Equipment Factory 天津市津環機電成套設備廠	Tianjin 天津市	Tianjin 天津市	(022)26371628
Yunnan Machinery Import & Export Company 雲南省機械進出口公司	Kunming 昆明市	Yunnan 雲南省	(0871)3164879 (0871)3136829
Tianjin Da Qiu Zhuang Yi Yuan Trade Center 天津市大丘莊億源商貿中心	Tianjin 天津市	Tianjin 天津市	(022)28899478 (022)28899046

*Also include sales by firms outside this industry.包括本行業以外廠家的銷售。"o" stands for "others". "o" 代表 "其他產品"。

3563: Gaskets, Seals and Related Products 密封件製造業

The industry accounts for 0.023% of the total revenue of China's industrial sector in 1996. The revenue growth rate of the industry is 52.7% from 1995, as compared to the growth rate of China's industrial sector, 9.51%. The rate of return on asset is 3.81%. 75.52% of all firms in the industry made a profit while 21.25% had negative returns. The top province in terms of the industry's revenue is Jiangsu, accounting for 38.93% of the total revenue.

本行業在1996年佔全行業總產值0.023%，行業年增長率為52.7%（全國工業年增長率9.51%）。行業的資產回報率3.81%，75.52%的企業盈利，21.25%的企業虧損。銷售收入最高的省份為江蘇省，佔本行業的38.93%。

	Total number of firms 企業總數	Total number of employees 職工總數	Total revenue (Mil. RMB) 總銷售收入（百萬元）	Total profit (Mil. RMB) 總利潤（百萬元）	Return on assets 資產利潤率 (%)	Return on equity 權益利潤率 (%)	Labour productivity ('000 RMB / worker) 勞動生產率（千元/人）	Debts / assets 資產負債率 (%)	Total assets (Mil. RMB) 總資產（百萬元）
Industry Overall 行業總體	304	21,203	1,326	63	3.81	10.84	62.54	64.81	1,650

	Number of firms 企業個數	Average number of employees 平均職工人數	Average revenue ('000 RMB) 平均銷售收入（千元）	Average profit ('000 RMB) 平均利潤（千元）	Return on assets 資產利潤率 (%)	Return on equity 權益利潤率 (%)	Labour productivity ('000 RMB / worker) 勞動生產率（千元/人）	Average debts / assets 平均資產負債率(%)	Average Total assets ('000 RMB) 平均總資產（千元）
By ownership 產業所有權									
State-owned 國有	29	265	4,828	138	1.12	3.92	18.25	71.35	12,276
Collectively-owned 集體	250	46	3,954	217	5.92	17.12	85.32	65.44	3,672
Privately-owned 私有	4	29	1,538	70	2.12	4.29	53.96	50.63	3,299
Domestic JVs 聯營	4	51	1,924	4	0.07	0.11	37.90	36.52	6,577
Joint stock 股份制	5	67	5,684	169	1.41	3.24	84.83	56.58	12,029
Foreign-funded 外資	8	116	13,267	-299	-1.18	-2.62	114.86	54.95	25,315
Overseas Chinese-funded 港澳台資	4	104	12,226	1,484	8.05	28.09	117.28	71.34	18,431
By size 規模									
Large 大型									
Medium 中型									
Small 小型	303	70	4,375	208	3.82	10.84	62.53	64.79	5,445
By regional distribution 地區分布									
Central-North 華北	36	97	4,344	-4	-0.05	-0.14	44.58	64.30	8,697
Beijing 北京	12	136	5,813	-265	-1.54	-5.05	42.75	69.50	17,207
Tianjin 天津	14	77	3,571	-281	-4.54	-9.56	46.47	52.52	6,202
Hebei 河北	7	70	5,123	993	37.37	98.72	73.63	62.20	2,657
Shanxi 山西	2	145	285	5	1.85	5.88	1.97	68.52	270
Inner Mongolia 內蒙	1	24	200				8.33	39.68	630
Northeast 東北	94	84	2,704	325	11.07	33.92	32.08	67.36	2,931
Liaoning 遼寧	68	99	3,094	384	12.64	43.39	31.12	70.88	3,042
Jilin 吉林	15	52	1,999	143	3.78	9.19	38.78	58.85	3,791
Heilongjiang 黑龍江	11	35	1,257	202	18.73	35.24	35.55	46.84	1,077
Central East 華東	115	59	6,690	247	3.16	8.71	113.06	63.77	7,830
Shanghai 上海	13	47	2,376	105	0.35	0.93	50.23	62.78	30,371
Jiangsu 江蘇	41	79	12,590	260	3.57	11.58	159.95	69.15	7,262
Zhejiang 浙江	35	55	3,129	87	2.53	6.82	56.62	62.86	3,441
Anhui 安徽	6	43	5,032	232	9.71	93.29	118.39	89.59	2,387
Fujian 福建	2	19	2,500	475	7.55	10.15	131.58	25.66	6,295
Jiangxi 江西									
Shandong 山東	18	41	4,313	612	18.20	34.61	105.49	47.42	3,361
Central-South 中南	26	44	2,590	109	5.14	16.80	58.65	69.41	2,117
Henan 河南	11	24	1,414	29	1.72	17.20	59.13	89.99	1,690
Hubei 湖北	4	51	7,588	693	24.28	41.28	148.05	41.19	2,853
Hunan 湖南	6	61	1,255				20.74	59.38	2,773
Guangdong 廣東	3	58	2,500	50	2.65	8.15	42.86	67.43	1,883
Guangxi 廣西	2	71	3,200	-205	-14.86	124.24	45.07	111.96	1,380
Hainan 海南									
Southwest 西南	22	54	2,156	53	2.04	5.72	40.31	64.35	2,610
Chongqing 重慶	1	20	746	9	0.69	1.38	37.39	49.88	1,363
Sichuan 四川	19	55	2,389	59	2.10	5.82	43.16	63.96	2,808
Guizhou 貴州	2	53	465	20	1.67	8.16	8.86	79.50	1,195
Yunnan 雲南									
Tibet 西藏									
Northwest 西北	11	58	2,887	15	0.35	1.10	49.47	68.18	4,400
Shaanxi 陝西	4	106	4,920	-43	-0.50	-1.37	46.42	63.36	8,488
Gansu 甘肅	2	75	3,850	160	5.12	13.68	51.68	62.56	3,125
Qinghai 青海									
Ningxia 寧夏									
Xinjiang 新疆	5	14	876	4	0.24	3.23	63.48	92.44	1,640

3563: Gaskets, Seals and Related Products 密封件製造業

Year 年份	Number of firms 企業個數	Rate of change 每年變化(%)	Number of employees 職工人數(人)	Rate of change 每年變化(%)	Total revenue (Mil. RMB) 總銷售收入(百萬元)	Rate of change 每年變化(%)	Total profit (Mil. RMB) 總利潤(百萬元)	Rate of change 每年變化(%)
1993	247		17,176		647		64	
1994	278	12.55%	16,543	-3.69%	567	-12.37%	9	-85.33%
1995	300	7.91%	19,267	16.47%	868	53.10%	37	295.52%
1996	304	1.33%	21,203	10.05%	1,326	52.68%	63	69.05%

3 Major products* 3種主要產品 *	Output 產量	Sales volume 銷售量	Unit 單位
a) Seal Part 密封件	153,637	132,128	10,000 piece 萬件
b) Copper Wire 銅絲材	10,084	8,874	ton 噸
c) Standard Fastene 標準緊固件	2,672	2,538	ton 噸

Top 10 firms by revenue (year founded) 收入排名前10家企業(創辦年份)	City 城市	Province 省	Telephone / fax 電話 / 傳真	Number of employees 職工人數	Ownership 產業所有權	Revenue ('000 RMB) 銷售收入(千元)	Profit ('000 RMB) (rank) 利潤(千元)(排名)	Total assets ('000 RMB) 總資產(千元)	Major products 主要產品
Zhangjiagang Machinery Seal Components Factory 張家港市機械密封件總廠(1986)	Suzhou 蘇州市	Jiangsu 江蘇省	(0512)8750010	469	Collectively-owned 集體	154,379	2614(8)	57,570	a,b
Xi Shan Shi Xi Zhang School-run Company 錫山市西漳校辦公司辦廠(1986)	Wuxi 無錫市	Jiangsu 江蘇省	(0510)3751359	200	Collectively-owned 集體	153,180	83(76)	45,219	o
Beijing Fengtai San Xing Automobile Factory 北京市豐台區三興汽車廠(1956)	Beijing 北京市	Beijing 北京市	(010)63816231 (010)63816231	1,271	State-owned 國有	52,586	-4147(124)	185,147	o
Dandong Border Economic Coopeartive Zone Ke Long Seal Co. Ltd. 丹東邊境經濟合作區克隆密封有限公司(1995)	Dandong 丹東市	Liaoning 遼寧省	(0415)6227162	118	Joint stock 股份制	41,616	11117(1)	22,276	a
Qian Dai Da Electron Manufacture (Dalian) Co. Ltd. 千代達電子製造(大連)有限公司(1994)	Dalian 大連市	Liaoning 遼寧省	(0411)7621010 (0411)7613446	126	Foreign-funded 外資	30,843	1012(19)	22,958	o
Xi Shan Shi Qian Qiao Zhen School-run Enterprise 錫山市錢橋鎮校辦企業(1985)	Wuxi 無錫市	Jiangsu 江蘇省	(0510)3202928	300	Collectively-owned 集體	29,971	-256(117)	18,376	o
John Crane Tianjing Ltd. 約翰克蘭(天津)有限公司(1988)	Tianjin 天津市	Tianjin 天津市	(022)27366874 (022)27363710	373	Foreign-funded 外資	27,730	-3900(123)	40,511	a
Shanghai Hui Feng Engineering Seal Co. Ltd. 上海匯楓工程密封有限公司(1991)	Shanghai 上海市	Shanghai 上海市	(021)64700345	130	Overseas Chinese-funded 港澳台資	25,774	980(21)	20,981	o
The Ministry of Railways Science Research Institute Jin Hua Suo Seal Components Factory 鐵道部科學研究院金化所密封件廠(1995)	Langfang 廊坊市	Hebei 河北省	(0316)6122001	300	Collectively-owned 集體	24,140	6393(2)	11,095	o
Zhangqiu Seal Components Factory 章丘市密封件廠(1993)	Ji'nan 濟南市	Shandong 山東省	(0531)3214201	57	Collectively-owned 集體	24,140	3060(7)	3,760	a

Top 10 Cities by Production Output 產出排名前10位城市	Province 省	Market share 市場份額	Number of firms 企業個數
Suzhou 蘇州市	Jiangsu 江蘇省	14.85%	16
Wuxi 無錫市	Jiangsu 江蘇省	8.87%	17
Beijing 北京市	Beijing 北京市	6.83%	12
Shanghai 上海市	Shanghai 上海市	5.61%	20
Tianjin 天津市	Tianjin 天津市	5.56%	16
Dandong 丹東市	Liaoning 遼寧省	5.45%	5
Wenzhou 温州市	Zhejiang 浙江省	4.36%	23
Ningbo 寧波市	Zhejiang 浙江省	3.98%	8
Dalian 大連市	Liaoning 遼寧省	3.46%	8
Changzhou 常州市	Jiangsu 江蘇省	3.44%	13

10 Major Wholesalers 10家主要批發商	City 城市	Province 省	Telephone / Fax 電話 / 傳真
Liaoning Automobile Trade Group Corp. 遼寧省汽車貿易集團	Shenyang 瀋陽市	Liaoning 遼寧省	(024)23835494 (024)23838338
China Post and Telecommunication Equipment General Company 中國郵電器材總公司	Beijing 北京市	Beijing 北京市	(010)63523715 (010)63525935
Jiangsu Electromechanical Products General Company 江蘇省機電產品總公司	Nanjing 南京市	Jiangsu 江蘇省	(025)7713642 (025)7711036
Xi Nan Technology Import & Export Company 西南技術進出口公司	Chongqing 重慶市	Chongqing 重慶市	(023)63850185 (023)63850026
Changzhou Economic Technology Industrial Development Zone Tian Ming Trade Company 常州經濟技術產業開發區天明貿易公司	Changzhou 常州市	Jiangsu 江蘇省	(0519)8829882 (0519)8829882
Shanxi Mechanical Equipment Import & Export Company 山西省機械設備進出口公司	Taiyuan 太原市	Shanxi 山西省	(0351)4040713 (0351)4043981
Ningbo Five Mining Machinery Import & Export Company 寧波市五礦機械進出口公司	Ningbo 寧波市	Zhejiang 浙江省	(0574)7311255 (0574)7320322
Tianjin Jin Huan Electromechanical Complete Sets of Equipment Factory 天津市津環機電成套設備廠	Tianjin 天津市	Tianjin 天津市	(022)26371628
Yunnan Machinery Import & Export Company 雲南省機械進出口公司	Kunming 昆明市	Yunnan 雲南省	(0871)3164879 (0871)3136829
Tianjin Da Qiu Zhuang Yi Yuan Trade Center 天津市大丘莊億源商貿中心	Tianjin 天津市	Tianjin 天津市	(022)28899478 (022)28899046

*Also include sales by firms outside this industry.包括本行業以外廠家的銷售。"o" stands for "others". "o" 代表"其他產品"。

3564: Powder Metallurgical Products 粉末冶金製品業

The industry accounts for 0.039% of the total revenue of China's industrial sector in 1996. The revenue growth rate of the industry is 19.8% from 1995, as compared to the growth rate of China's industrial sector, 9.51%. The rate of return on asset is 1.64%. 62.20% of all firms in the industry made a profit while 29.64% had negative returns. The top province in terms of the industry's revenue is Zhejiang, accounting for 25.04% of the total revenue.
本行業在1996年佔全行業總產值0.039%，行業年增長率為19.8%（全國工業年增長率9.51%）。行業的資產回報率1.64%，62.20%的企業盈利，29.64%的企業虧損。銷售收入最高的省份為浙江省，佔本行業的25.04%。

	Total number of firms 企業總數	Total number of employees 職工總數	Total revenue (Mil. RMB) 總銷售收入（百萬元）	Total profit (Mil. RMB) 總利潤（百萬元）	Return on assets 資產利潤率 (%)	Return on equity 權益利潤率 (%)	Labour productivity ('000 RMB / worker) 勞動生產率（千元/人）	Debts / assets 資產負債率 (%)	Total assets (Mil. RMB) 總資產（百萬元）
Industry Overall 行業總體	416	46,701	2,282	65	1.64	4.93	48.86	66.82	3,981

	Number of firms 企業個數	Average number of employees 平均職工人數	Average revenue ('000 RMB) 平均銷售收入（千元）	Average profit ('000 RMB) 平均利潤（千元）	Return on assets 資產利潤率 (%)	Return on equity 權益利潤率 (%)	Labour productivity ('000 RMB / worker) 勞動生產率（千元/人）	Average debts / assets 平均資產負債率(%)	Average Total assets ('000 RMB) 平均總資產（千元）
By ownership 產業所有權									
State-owned 國有	62	200	6,532	-97	-0.59	-1.98	32.68	70.18	16,387
Collectively-owned 集體	307	93	4,606	130	1.96	6.58	49.29	70.29	6,632
Privately-owned 私有									
Domestic JVs 聯營	3	35	2,116	92	2.38	3.69	59.90	35.52	3,886
Joint stock 股份制	8	247	20,683	330	1.06	3.64	83.91	70.93	31,233
Foreign-funded 外資	10	129	9,612	1,537	5.36	10.36	74.69	48.22	28,646
Overseas Chinese-funded 港澳台資	24	98	7,724	528	3.42	7.00	78.69	51.17	15,461
By size 規模									
Large 大型	1	226	65,704	10,666	6.89	15.59	290.72	55.76	154,703
Medium 中型	18	511	28,276	547	0.91	2.93	55.33	68.93	60,128
Small 小型	391	95	4,367	114	1.62	4.85	45.82	66.61	7,019
By regional distribution 地區分布									
Central-North 華北	52	89	3,128	131	2.14	5.91	35.02	63.88	6,114
Beijing 北京	21	114	3,598	48	0.46	1.21	31.51	61.93	10,351
Tianjin 天津	7	60	1,763	91	3.96	38.10	29.45	89.62	2,311
Hebei 河北	17	62	3,306	302	8.54	19.36	53.52	55.90	3,541
Shanxi 山西	5	136	3,554	2	0.05	0.45	26.09	89.22	4,118
Inner Mongolia 內蒙	2	48	390				8.13	54.75	1,790
Northeast 東北	45	98	2,007	-21	-0.26	-1.36	20.43	81.03	8,181
Liaoning 遼寧	33	101	1,970	3	0.04	0.20	19.53	82.04	9,451
Jilin 吉林	7	120	2,336	-137	-2.34	-10.03	19.46	76.61	5,851
Heilongjiang 黑龍江	5	50	1,786	-20	-0.65	-2.35	35.72	72.22	3,060
Central East 華東	190	120	7,624	202	1.69	4.63	63.47	63.48	11,962
Shanghai 上海	23	82	3,558	124	2.39	7.57	43.23	68.46	5,208
Jiangsu 江蘇	59	154	7,639	96	0.58	1.57	49.57	62.88	16,457
Zhejiang 浙江	57	95	10,026	542	4.02	10.81	105.29	62.80	13,468
Anhui 安徽	13	93	11,001	95	2.28	7.71	118.48	70.50	4,192
Fujian 福建	14	102	7,366	169	1.78	4.53	72.52	60.64	9,485
Jiangxi 江西	8	106	1,729	-318	-15.42	-88.81	16.31	82.70	2,059
Shandong 山東	16	183	5,281	-125	-0.95	-2.66	28.81	64.33	13,161
Central-South 中南	89	131	5,490	137	1.59	6.06	41.99	73.79	8,601
Henan 河南	30	59	2,925	199	6.76	31.09	49.51	78.25	2,942
Hubei 湖北	22	130	3,566	-41	-0.53	-1.69	27.45	68.52	7,694
Hunan 湖南	20	81	1,751	-39	-1.12	-6.91	21.50	83.83	3,489
Guangdong 廣東	12	333	21,454	611	1.84	7.31	64.43	74.81	33,177
Guangxi 廣西	5	276	5,986	106	1.32	3.20	21.67	58.61	8,006
Hainan 海南									
Southwest 西南	30	79	2,626	248	3.17	7.49	33.27	57.63	7,822
Chongqing 重慶	9	76	4,076	713	7.79	16.91	53.61	53.93	9,149
Sichuan 四川	15	65	1,860	60	1.04	2.53	28.71	58.98	5,810
Guizhou 貴州	4	98	1,880	-3	-0.02	-0.05	19.28	64.04	13,265
Yunnan 雲南	2	158	3,335	65	1.07	1.95	21.11	44.97	6,060
Tibet 西藏									
Northwest 西北	10	81	1,300	125	5.76	20.73	16.03	72.30	2,170
Shaanxi 陝西	6	38	878	202	12.53	56.54	23.22	77.95	1,610
Gansu 甘肅	2	259	3,745	85	1.97	4.91	14.46	59.95	4,320
Qinghai 青海	1	49	160				3.27	77.39	1,150
Ningxia 寧夏	1	17	80	-130	-5.78	-81.25	4.71	92.89	2,250
Xinjiang 新疆									

3564: Powder Metallurgical Products 粉末冶金製品業

Year 年份	Number of firms 企業個數	Rate of change 每年變化 (%)	Number of employees 職工人數 (人)	Rate of change 每年變化 (%)	Total revenue (Mil. RMB) 總銷售收入 (百萬元)	Rate of change 每年變化 (%)	Total profit (Mil. RMB) 總利潤 (百萬元)	Rate of change 每年變化 (%)
1993	317		52,078		1,549		53	
1994	342	7.89%	41,121	-21.04%	1,501	-3.13%	30	-43.09%
1995	404	18.13%	49,075	19.34%	1,905	26.90%	59	92.44%
1996	416	2.97%	46,701	-4.84%	2,282	19.79%	65	11.07%

3 Major products* 3種主要產品*	Output 產量	Sales volume 銷售量	Unit 單位
a) Powder Metallurgy Product 粉末冶金製品	133,490	132,155	ton 噸

Top 10 firms by revenue (year founded) 收入排名前10家企業 (創辦年份)	City 城市	Province 省	Telephone / fax 電話/傳真	Number of employees 職工人數	Ownership 產業所有權	Revenue ('000 RMB) 銷售收入 (千元)	Profit ('000 RMB) (rank) 利潤 (千元) (排名)	Total assets ('000 RMB) 總資產 (千元)	Major products 主要產品
Jiangmen Powder Metallurgy Co. Ltd. 江門市粉末冶金有限公司(1975)	Jiangmen 江門市	Guangdong 廣東省	(0750)3532142 (0750)3558344	1,276	State-owned 國有	114,560	2528(10)	135,326	a
Ningbo Beilun Lingyun Magnetoelectric Industrial Co. Ltd. 寧波北侖淩雲磁電實業有限公司(1994)	Ningbo 寧波市	Zhejiang 浙江省	(0574)6190634 (0574)6190507	220	Foreign-funded 外資	114,452	5307(4)	119,900	a
Huan Yu (Ningbo) Ci Technology Co. Ltd. 寰宇(寧波)磁技術有限公司(1994)	Ningbo 寧波市	Zhejiang 浙江省	(0574)7378234 (0574)7835947	23	Overseas Chinese-funded 港澳台資	96,640	0(151)	2,934	o
Shunde Magnetoelectricity Industrial Group Co. 磁電實業集團公司(1988)	Foshan 佛山市	Guangdong 廣東省	(0757)5571737 (0757)5574333	1,750	Collectively-owned 集體	90,109	-149(165)	166,084	o
Yangzhou Porite Industry Co. Ltd. 揚州保來得工業有限公司(1995)	Yangzhou 揚州市	Jiangsu 江蘇省	(0514)7880887 (0514)7880884	253	Overseas Chinese-funded 港澳台資	79,075	12198(1)	151,962	a
Ningbo Dong Mu Powder Metallurgy Co. Ltd. 寧波東睦粉末冶金有限公司(1995)	Ningbo 寧波市	Zhejiang 浙江省	(0574)7833776 (0574)7831133	364	Foreign-funded 外資	76,034	9123(2)	176,418	a
Fujian Longyan Powder Metallurgy Plant 福建省龍岩粉末冶金廠(1965)	Longyan 龍巖市	Fujian 福建省	(0597)2681001 (0597)2681043	817	State-owned 國有	69,002	1286(20)	84,922	a
Dongyang Xiangyang Magnet Steel Factory 東陽市向陽磁鋼廠(1993)	Jinhua 金華市	Zhejiang 浙江省	(0579)6691429	280	Collectively-owned 集體	40,780	1283(21)	46,039	o
Zhenjiang Jin Gang Magnetic Element Co. Ltd. 鎮江金港磁性元件有限公司(1992)	Zhenjiang 鎮江市	Jiangsu 江蘇省	(0511)5243944 (0511)5239540	350	Foreign-funded 外資	34,270	2924(8)	35,551	o
Anhui Fanchang Di Gang Powder Metallurgy Factory 安徽省繁昌縣荻港粉末冶金廠(1972)	Wuhu 蕪湖市	Anhui 安徽省	(0553)7892496	276	Collectively-owned 集體	34,107	188(78)	7,017	a

Top 10 Cities by Production Output 產出排名前10位城市	Province 省	Market share 市場份額	Number of firms 企業個數
Ningbo 寧波市	Zhejiang 浙江省	7.78%	18
Liu'an 六安市	Anhui 安徽省	6.56%	3
Jiangmen 江門市	Guangdong 廣東省	5.30%	1
Nantong 南通市	Jiangsu 江蘇省	4.79%	13
Longyan 龍巖市	Fujian 福建省	4.47%	1
Jinhua 金華市	Zhejiang 浙江省	4.34%	22
Wuxi 無錫市	Jiangsu 江蘇省	3.92%	18
Shanghai 上海市	Shanghai 上海市	3.81%	37
Yangzhou 揚州市	Jiangsu 江蘇省	3.74%	5
Taizhou 泰州市	Jiangsu 江蘇省	3.64%	7

10 Major Wholesalers 10家主要批發商	City 城市	Province 省	Telephone / Fax 電話/傳真
Liaoning Automobile Trade Group Corp. 遼寧省汽車貿易集團	Shenyang 瀋陽市	Liaoning 遼寧省	(024)23835494 (024)23838338
China Post and Telecommunication Equipment General Company 中國郵電器材總公司	Beijing 北京市	Beijing 北京市	(010)63523715 (010)63525935
Jiangsu Electromechanical Products General Company 江蘇省機電產品總公司	Nanjing 南京市	Jiangsu 江蘇省	(025)7713642 (025)7711036
Xi Nan Technology Import & Export Company 西南技術進出口公司	Chongqing 重慶市	Chongqing 重慶市	(023)63850185 (023)63850026
Changzhou Economic Technology Industrial Development Zone Tian Ming Trade Company 常州經濟技術產業開發區天明貿易公司	Changzhou 常州市	Jiangsu 江蘇省	(0519)8829882 (0519)8829882
Shanxi Mechanical Equipment Import & Export Company 山西省機械設備進出口公司	Taiyuan 太原市	Shanxi 山西省	(0351)4040713 (0351)4043981
Ningbo Five Mining Machinery Import & Export Company 寧波市五礦機械進出口公司	Ningbo 寧波市	Zhejiang 浙江省	(0574)7311255 (0574)7320322
Tianjin Jin Huan Electromechanical Complete Sets of Equipment Factory 天津市津環機電成套設備廠	Tianjin 天津市	Tianjin 天津市	(022)26371628
Yunnan Machinery Import & Export Company 雲南省機械進出口公司	Kunming 昆明市	Yunnan 雲南省	(0871)3164879 (0871)3136829
Tianjin Da Qiu Zhuang Yi Yuan Trade Center 天津市大丘莊億源商貿中心	Tianjin 天津市	Tianjin 天津市	(022)28899478 (022)28899046

*Also include sales by firms outside this industry.包括本行業以外廠家的銷售。"o" stands for "others". "o" 代表"其他產品"。

3565: Fasteners 緊固件製造業

The industry accounts for 0.113% of the total revenue of China's industrial sector in 1996. The revenue growth rate of the industry is -8.0% from 1995, as compared to the growth rate of China's industrial sector, 9.51%. The rate of return on asset is -0.82%. 67.04% of all firms in the industry made a profit while 28.41% had negative returns. The top province in terms of the industry's revenue is Zhejiang, accounting for 20.64% of the total revenue.
本行業在1996年佔全行業總產值0.113%，行業年增長率為-8.0%（全國工業年增長率9.51%）。行業的資產回報率-0.82%，67.04%的企業盈利，28.41%的企業虧損。銷售收入最高的省份為浙江省，佔本行業的20.64%。

	Total number of firms 企業總數	Total number of employees 職工總數	Total revenue (Mil. RMB) 總銷售收入（百萬元）	Total profit (Mil. RMB) 總利潤（百萬元）	Return on assets 資產利潤率 (%)	Return on equity 權益利潤率 (%)	Labour productivity ('000 RMB / worker) 勞動生產率（千元/人）	Debts / assets 資產負債率 (%)	Total assets (Mil. RMB) 總資產（百萬元）
Industry Overall 行業總體	1,628	194,708	6,532	-77	-0.82	-2.72	33.55	69.90	9,439

	Number of firms 企業個數	Average number of employees 平均職工人數	Average revenue ('000 RMB) 平均銷售收入（千元）	Average profit ('000 RMB) 平均利潤（千元）	Return on assets 資產利潤率 (%)	Return on equity 權益利潤率 (%)	Labour productivity ('000 RMB / worker) 勞動生產率（千元/人）	Average debts / assets 平均資產負債率(%)	Average Total assets ('000 RMB) 平均總資產（千元）
By ownership 產業所有權									
State-owned 國有	206	421	6,966	-607	-3.49	-14.17	16.54	75.35	17,369
Collectively-owned 集體	1,234	74	3,255	34	1.10	3.96	43.92	72.36	3,113
Privately-owned 私有	19	28	2,941	92	6.02	13.09	105.22	54.00	1,531
Domestic JVs 聯營	18	216	7,598	7	0.05	0.14	35.20	64.33	14,691
Joint stock 股份制	17	91	6,686	193	3.46	14.71	73.81	76.46	5,571
Foreign-funded 外資	45	115	8,162	75	0.44	0.88	71.08	49.57	16,870
Overseas Chinese-funded 港澳台資	89	63	4,570	-29	-0.30	-0.68	72.94	55.93	9,799
By size 規模									
Large 大型	2	3,195	27,446	52,251	27.06	91.69	8.59	70.48	193,070
Medium 中型	46	850	33,294	1,596	2.66	8.00	39.18	66.77	60,037
Small 小型	1,569	95	3,151	-162	-4.05	-14.09	33.18	71.24	4,010
By regional distribution 地區分布									
Central-North 華北	217	97	2,808	1	0.01	0.03	28.90	62.89	6,247
Beijing 北京	26	96	1,518	-148	-1.15	-2.39	15.77	52.03	12,955
Tianjin 天津	54	81	1,618	-18	-0.46	-1.18	19.90	61.22	3,839
Hebei 河北	79	113	4,992	165	2.57	9.07	44.03	71.69	6,427
Shanxi 山西	42	87	1,714	-73	-1.31	-2.95	19.65	55.41	5,542
Inner Mongolia 內蒙	16	98	1,008	-314	-7.08	-37.02	10.26	80.85	4,429
Northeast 東北	228	95	1,403	-139	-4.04	-13.69	14.71	70.46	3,445
Liaoning 遼寧	155	76	1,432	-94	-2.65	-7.44	18.73	64.35	3,537
Jilin 吉林	37	161	1,405	-127	-4.71	-18.38	8.71	74.38	2,692
Heilongjiang 黑龍江	36	109	1,276	-348	-9.11	-114.01	11.70	92.01	3,821
Central East 華東	757	131	5,528	34	0.52	1.85	42.13	71.86	6,589
Shanghai 上海	92	195	10,011	43	0.31	1.13	51.30	72.49	13,822
Jiangsu 江蘇	183	108	6,563	44	0.65	2.58	60.86	74.64	6,691
Zhejiang 浙江	284	72	4,747	74	1.59	4.92	66.14	67.65	4,651
Anhui 安徽	51	76	2,586	3	0.12	0.34	34.21	65.81	2,339
Fujian 福建	40	68	2,453	39	0.76	1.17	35.97	35.28	5,099
Jiangxi 江西	39	87	1,490	-201	-5.87	-39.18	17.14	85.03	3,427
Shandong 山東	68	460	6,272	-12	-0.11	-0.65	13.63	82.74	10,502
Central-South 中南	255	125	3,892	-53	-1.07	-3.21	31.21	66.78	4,989
Henan 河南	62	84	2,040	34	0.96	3.21	24.40	69.94	3,527
Hubei 湖北	51	165	9,482	252	3.79	13.41	57.59	71.76	6,659
Hunan 湖南	44	275	2,581	-279	-7.21	-32.19	9.39	77.60	3,874
Guangdong 廣東	76	55	2,872	-158	-2.72	-6.32	52.35	57.00	5,814
Guangxi 廣西	20	97	2,494	-212	-4.18	-12.96	25.78	67.76	5,075
Hainan 海南	2	6	360	5	5.56	7.14	60.00	22.22	90
Southwest 西南	125	114	2,352	-274	-4.99	-20.55	20.62	75.73	5,493
Chongqing 重慶	33	97	1,289	-560	-16.89	81.20	13.24	120.80	3,319
Sichuan 四川	70	103	2,628	-114	-2.21	-7.21	25.58	69.35	5,157
Guizhou 貴州	11	245	4,349	-435	-2.94	-8.79	17.77	66.61	14,801
Yunnan 雲南	11	110	1,820	-261	-5.35	-11.51	16.53	53.51	4,877
Tibet 西藏									
Northwest 西北	46	141	2,859	-522	-6.83	-21.18	20.27	67.74	7,640
Shaanxi 陝西	20	137	3,335	-546	-7.47	-28.85	24.43	74.11	7,305
Gansu 甘肅	15	131	2,860	53	1.04	2.02	21.89	48.40	5,128
Qinghai 青海	3	131	793	-1,003	-13.02	-376.25	6.04	96.54	7,703
Ningxia 寧夏	4	113	1,913	-1,600	-20.20	415.58	17.00	104.86	7,920
Xinjiang 新疆	4	238	2,975	-1,123	-6.10	-12.27	12.49	50.28	18,408

3565: Fasteners 緊固件製造業

Year 年份	Number of firms 企業個數	Rate of change 每年變化 (%)	Number of employees 職工人數 (人)	Rate of change 每年變化 (%)	Total revenue (Mil. RMB) 總銷售收入 (百萬元)	Rate of change 每年變化 (%)	Total profit (Mil. RMB) 總利潤 (百萬元)	Rate of change 每年變化 (%)
1993	1,539		232,345		5,474		133	
1994	1,678	9.03%	188,776	-18.75%	5,914	8.04%	41	-69.38%
1995	1,826	8.82%	197,728	4.74%	7,099	20.03%	13	-67.03%
1996	1,628	-10.84%	194,708	-1.53%	6,532	-7.99%	-77	-672.24%

3 Major products* 3 種主要產品 *	Output 產量	Sales volume 銷售量	Unit 單位
a) Standard Fastene 標準緊固件	805,126	764,870	ton 噸
b) Steel Nail 鋼釘	21,273	22,975	ton 噸

Top 10 firms by revenue (year founded) 收入排名前 10 家企業 (創辦年份)	City 城市	Province 省	Telephone / fax 電話 / 傳真	Number of employees 職工人數	Ownership 產業所有權	Revenue ('000 RMB) 銷售收入 (千元)	Profit ('000 RMB) (rank) 利潤 (千元) (排名)	Total assets ('000 RMB) 總資產 (千元)	Major products 主要產品
Changshu Standard Parts Factory 常熟市標準件廠(1966)	Suzhou 蘇州市	Jiangsu 江蘇省	(0512)2811688 (0512)2811984	1,028	Collectively-owned 集體	180,657	4075(5)	147,841	a
Jinzhou Spinning and Weaving Factory 晉州市紡織廠(1972)	Shijiazhuang 石家莊市	Hebei 河北省	(0311)4322319 (0311)4322295	1,324	State-owned 國有	104,363	1600(25)	92,595	o
Ai Si Pi Ai Si Biao Wu Fasteners Co. Ltd. 愛斯匹愛斯標五緊固件有限公司(1995)	Shanghai 上海市	Shanghai 上海市	(021)59121372 (021)59122572	761	Foreign-funded 外資	103,689	-202(561)	128,072	a
Zhejiang Zha Pu Gang Standard Components Industrial General Co. 浙江省平湖乍浦港標準件實業總公司(1984)	Jiaxing 嘉興市	Zhejiang 浙江省	(0573)5522816 (0573)5522333	865	Collectively-owned 集體	88,935	67(325)	49,682	a
Feicheng Mine Administrative Bureau Engineering Dept. Varied Marketing Company 肥城礦務局工程處多種經營公司(1975)	Tai'an 泰安市	Shandong 山東省	(0538)3511250 (0538)3511250	21,704	State-owned 國有	80,985	133(253)	113,475	o
Zhejiang Wan Xin Group Co. 浙江萬新集團公司(1972)	Hangzhou 杭州市	Zhejiang 浙江省	(0571)2614117	431	Collectively-owned 集體	79,450	800(63)	100,600	a
Nanjing Jia He Hardware Machinery Co. Ltd. 南京佳和五金機械有限公司(1994)	Nanjing 南京市	Jiangsu 江蘇省	(025)2412298 (025)2419557	300	Overseas Chinese-funded 港澳台資	75,459	6807(1)	16,143	o
Zhangjiagang Standard Components General Factory 張家港市標準件總廠(1958)	Suzhou 蘇州市	Jiangsu 江蘇省	(0512)8685378	396	Collectively-owned 集體	68,532	1609(23)	33,528	a
Jiangyin Standard Fastener Factory 江陰標準件廠(1955)	Wuxi 無錫市	Jiangsu 江蘇省	(0510)6883528 (0510)6891441	947	State-owned 國有	66,346	689(74)	98,645	a
Shanghai Special Type Rivet Factory 上海異型鉚釘廠(1938)	Shanghai 上海市	Shanghai 上海市	(021)63771314 (021)63774348	769	State-owned 國有	65,419	4317(3)	116,404	a

Top 10 Cities by Production Output 產出排名前 10 位城市	Province 省	Market share 市場份額	Number of firms 企業個數
Shanghai 上海市	Shanghai 上海市	24.24%	159
Wenzhou 温州市	Zhejiang 浙江省	8.63%	562
Suzhou 蘇州市	Jiangsu 江蘇省	6.39%	37
Ningbo 寧波市	Zhejiang 浙江省	4.85%	107
Jiaxing 嘉興市	Zhejiang 浙江省	3.69%	38
Wuxi 無錫市	Jiangsu 江蘇省	2.57%	45
Taizhou 泰州市	Jiangsu 江蘇省	2.07%	61
Shenyang 瀋陽市	Liaoning 遼寧省	1.91%	88
Changzhou 常州市	Jiangsu 江蘇省	1.82%	91
Hangzhou 杭州市	Zhejiang 浙江省	1.69%	29

10 Major Wholesalers 10 家主要批發商	City 城市	Province 省	Telephone / Fax 電話 / 傳真
Liaoning Automobile Trade Group Corp. 遼寧省汽車貿易集團	Shenyang 瀋陽市	Liaoning 遼寧省	(024)23835494 (024)23838338
China Post and Telecommunication Equipment General Company 中國郵電器材總公司	Beijing 北京市	Beijing 北京市	(010)63523715 (010)63525935
Jiangsu Electromechanical Products General Company 江蘇省機電產品總公司	Nanjing 南京市	Jiangsu 江蘇省	(025)7713642 (025)7711036
Xi Nan Technology Import & Export Company 西南技術進出口公司	Chongqing 重慶市	Chongqing 重慶市	(023)63850185 (023)63850026
Changzhou Economic Technology Industrial Development Zone Tian Ming Trade Company 常州經濟技術產業開發區天明貿易公司	Changzhou 常州市	Jiangsu 江蘇省	(0519)8829882 (0519)8829882
Shanxi Mechanical Equipment Import & Export Company 山西省機械設備進出口公司	Taiyuan 太原市	Shanxi 山西省	(0351)4040713 (0351)4043981
Ningbo Five Mining Machinery Import & Export Company 寧波市五礦機械進出口公司	Ningbo 寧波市	Zhejiang 浙江省	(0574)7311255 (0574)7320322
Tianjin Jin Huan Electromechanical Complete Sets of Equipment Factory 天津市津環機電成套設備廠	Tianjin 天津市	Tianjin 天津市	(022)26371628
Yunnan Machinery Import & Export Company 雲南省機械進出口公司	Kunming 昆明市	Yunnan 雲南省	(0871)3164879 (0871)3136829
Tianjin Da Qiu Zhuang Yi Yuan Trade Center 天津市大丘莊億源商貿中心	Tianjin 天津市	Tianjin 天津市	(022)28899478 (022)28899046

*Also include sales by firms outside this industry.包括本行業以外廠家的銷售。"o" stands for "others". "o" 代表 "其他產品"。

3566: Springs 彈簧製造業

The industry accounts for 0.027% of the total revenue of China's industrial sector in 1996. The revenue growth rate of the industry is 3.2% from 1995, as compared to the growth rate of China's industrial sector, 9.51%. The rate of return on asset is 3.67%. 72.55% of all firms in the industry made a profit while 22.57% had negative returns. The top province in terms of the industry's revenue is Shanghai, accounting for 19.47% of the total revenue.
本行業在1996年佔全行業總產值0.027%，行業年增長率為3.2%（全國工業年增長率9.51%）。行業的資產回報率3.67%，72.55%的企業盈利，22.57%的企業虧損。銷售收入最高的省份為上海市，佔本行業的19.47%。

	Total number of firms 企業總數	Total number of employees 職工總數	Total revenue (Mil. RMB) 總銷售收入（百萬元）	Total profit (Mil. RMB) 總利潤（百萬元）	Return on assets 資產利潤率 (%)	Return on equity 權益利潤率 (%)	Labour productivity ('000 RMB / worker) 勞動生產率（千元/人）	Debts / assets 資產負債率 (%)	Total assets (Mil. RMB) 總資產（百萬元）
Industry Overall 行業總體	532	31,299	1,585	79	3.67	10.31	50.64	64.41	2,162

	Number of firms 企業個數	Average number of employees 平均職工人數	Average revenue ('000 RMB) 平均銷售收入（千元）	Average profit ('000 RMB) 平均利潤（千元）	Return on assets 資產利潤率 (%)	Return on equity 權益利潤率 (%)	Labour productivity ('000 RMB / worker) 勞動生產率（千元/人）	Average debts / assets 平均資產負債率(%)	Average Total assets ('000 RMB) 平均總資產（千元）
By ownership 產業所有權									
State-owned 國有	33	119	8,394	1,364	8.95	22.96	70.56	61.03	15,242
Collectively-owned 集體	465	55	2,491	69	2.38	8.00	45.61	70.25	2,906
Privately-owned 私有	2	61	2,082	71	7.95	12.41	34.12	35.92	896
Domestic JVs 聯營	2	111	9,715	561	5.03	10.04	87.92	49.93	11,157
Joint stock 股份制	1	161	1,418	1	0.03	-0.62	8.81	104.32	2,542
Foreign-funded 外資	11	62	5,756	214	2.20	3.65	92.43	39.73	9,751
Overseas Chinese-funded 港澳台資	18	66	3,412	-99	-1.02	-1.89	51.83	45.87	9,670
By size 規模									
Large 大型	1	662	148,744	32,451	12.79	27.38	224.69	53.28	253,661
Medium 中型	2	594	65,532	5,860	8.06	24.67	110.32	67.33	72,688
Small 小型	524	56	2,491	66	1.97	5.77	44.23	65.80	3,366
By regional distribution 地區分布									
Central-North 華北	71	53	1,554	49	2.19	8.29	29.26	73.53	2,253
Beijing 北京	18	45	1,318	-40	-1.18	-3.25	29.07	63.76	3,397
Tianjin 天津	15	42	1,063	161	10.46	20.22	25.42	48.29	[illegible]
Hebei 河北	28	65	2,264	59	2.88	191.86	34.74	98.50	2,044
Shanxi 山西	6	50	685	27	1.24	3.13	13.75	60.42	2,152
Inner Mongolia 內蒙	4	51	795	3	0.18	0.44	15.51	59.11	1,400
Northeast 東北	108	53	1,690	12	0.49	1.79	31.83	72.80	2,436
Liaoning 遼寧	82	50	1,796	13	0.53	2.15	35.68	75.28	2,359
Jilin 吉林	15	68	1,172	-5	-0.17	-0.74	17.24	77.03	3,143
Heilongjiang 黑龍江	11	53	1,604	30	1.47	2.56	30.15	42.55	2,043
Central East 華東	215	62	4,103	340	6.55	16.06	66.69	59.19	5,183
Shanghai 上海	23	89	13,420	2,136	10.17	20.39	149.99	50.12	21,001
Jiangsu 江蘇	60	59	3,001	-45	-1.27	-3.97	50.75	68.04	3,508
Zhejiang 浙江	44	47	3,203	191	7.08	22.46	67.65	68.49	2,695
Anhui 安徽	14	64	1,611	6	0.24	0.70	25.26	66.27	2,410
Fujian 福建	15	57	1,794	-138	-2.29	-5.54	31.22	58.67	6,024
Jiangxi 江西	25	40	889	70	6.92	26.12	22.25	73.50	1,011
Shandong 山東	34	82	5,315	541	12.04	34.26	64.94	64.87	4,496
Central-South 中南	88	62	3,629	62	1.21	3.58	58.27	66.03	5,126
Henan 河南	19	49	1,459	37	1.71	6.28	29.81	72.87	2,190
Hubei 湖北	17	106	7,309	221	3.65	21.33	69.10	82.87	6,058
Hunan 湖南	19	54	984	139	12.99	56.17	18.33	76.87	1,069
Guangdong 廣東	27	58	5,223	-52	-0.51	-1.18	89.37	57.13	10,299
Guangxi 廣西	6	26	1,282	-37	-2.71	-56.41	49.61	95.07	1,353
Hainan 海南									
Southwest 西南	28	60	2,344	-74	-1.90	-7.39	39.23	74.31	3,912
Chongqing 重慶	11	77	3,679	158	2.19	10.54	48.05	79.24	7,209
Sichuan 四川	11	54	1,945	32	1.31	3.93	35.75	66.60	2,419
Guizhou 貴州	3	44	753	7	0.57	0.78	17.12	25.86	1,160
Yunnan 雲南	3	40	780	-27	-3.31	-15.09	19.34	78.10	807
Tibet 西藏									
Northwest 西北	22	64	1,151	-82	-2.83	-9.32	17.91	69.68	2,911
Shaanxi 陝西	14	49	803	-88	-5.19	-23.84	16.55	78.17	1,691
Gansu 甘肅	3	121	1,460	-63	-1.05	-2.62	12.03	60.07	6,043
Qinghai 青海	1	56	290	-240	-21.24	-96.00	5.18	78.76	1,130
Ningxia 寧夏	1	133	3,630	-290	-3.57	-9.21	27.29	61.25	8,130
Xinjiang 新疆	3	61	1,927	47	1.08	3.87	31.76	72.11	4,327

3566: Springs 彈簧製造業

Year 年份	Number of firms 企業個數	Rate of change 每年變化 (%)	Number of employees 職工人數 (人)	Rate of change 每年變化 (%)	Total revenue (Mil. RMB) 總銷售收入 (百萬元)	Rate of change 每年變化 (%)	Total profit (Mil. RMB) 總利潤 (百萬元)	Rate of change 每年變化 (%)
1993	501		39,871		1,095		68	
1994	537	7.19%	36,214	-9.17%	1,531	39.81%	93	36.44%
1995	556	3.54%	36,116	-0.27%	1,536	0.30%	83	-9.92%
1996	532	-4.32%	31,299	-13.34%	1,585	3.19%	79	-5.24%

3 Major products* 3 種主要產品 *	Output 產量	Sales volume 銷售量	Unit 單位
a) Spring 彈簧	1,201,453,330	1,225,482,397	piece 件
b) Tractor & Internal Combustion Engine Fitting Parts 拖拉機內燃機配件	4,396	4,088	1,000 yuan 千元

Top 10 firms by revenue (year founded) 收入排名前 10 家企業 (創辦年份)	City 城市	Province 省	Telephone / fax 電話 / 傳真	Number of employees 職工人數	Ownership 產業所有權	Revenue ('000 RMB) 銷售收入 (千元)	Profit ('000 RMB) (rank) 利潤 (千元) (排名)	Total assets ('000 RMB) 總資產 (千元)	Major products 主要產品
China Spring Factory 中國彈簧廠(1937)	Shanghai 上海市	Shanghai 上海市	(021)56625440 (021)56632745	670	State-owned 國有	206,950	46955(1)	314,834	a,b
Zhejiang Zhuji Spring General Factory 浙江省諸暨彈簧總廠(1974)	Shaoxing 紹興市	Zhejiang 浙江省	(0575)7071577	390	Collectively-owned 集體	58,202	5788(3)	35,857	a
Shandong Wulian Transport Machinery Co. Ltd. 山東省五蓮縣運輸機械股份有限公司(1966)	Rizhao 日照市	Shandong 山東省	(0633)5213167 (0633)5211110	430	Joint stock 股份制	47,815	8967(2)	52,502	a
Laohekou Spring Factory 老河口市彈簧廠(1976)	Xiangfan 襄樊市	Hubei 湖北省	(0710)8223368 (0710)82222978	60	Collectively-owned 集體	43,112	2223(5)	1,663	a
Shenyang Ling Xi Spring Factory 瀋陽市陵西彈簧廠(1987)	Shenyang 瀋陽市	Liaoning 遼寧省	(024)86808614	30	Collectively-owned 集體	42,330	1076(20)	32,643	o
Gaoyao Jin Li Zhen Metal Products Factory 高要市金利鎮金屬製品廠(1972)	Zhaoqing 肇慶市	Guangdong 廣東省	(0757)8579585	260	Collectively-owned 集體	31,870	950(24)	2,149	a
Zhunhua Dongfang Industrial Company 遵化市東方工業公司(1994)	Tangshan 唐山市	Hebei 河北省	(0315)6619177	253	Collectively-owned 集體	29,500	1150(18)	19,963	o
Hubei Zhongxiang Automobile Steel Plate Spring Factory 湖北省鐘祥市汽車鋼板彈簧廠	Jingsha 荊沙市	Hubei 湖北省	(0716)4366093 (0716)4366056	286	Collectively-owned 集體	29,330	1795(7)	13,574	o
Zhaoqing Bai Li Hardware Craft Co. Ltd. 肇慶百利五金工藝有限公司(1993)	Zhaoqing 肇慶市	Guangdong 廣東省	(0757)2681395	100	Foreign-funded 外資	27,050	461(42)	6,692	o
Changzhou Spring General Factory 常州市彈簧總廠(1966)	Changzhou 常州市	Jiangsu 江蘇省	(0519)5312621 (0519)5324544	256	Collectively-owned 集體	25,903	1(123)	21,990	a

Top 10 Cities by Production Output 產出排名前 10 位城市	Province 省	Market share 市場份額	Number of firms 企業個數
Shanghai 上海市	Shanghai 上海市	16.95%	35
Yangzhou 揚州市	Jiangsu 江蘇省	5.31%	12
Shaoxing 紹興市	Zhejiang 浙江省	4.78%	12
Zhaoqing 肇慶市	Guangdong 廣東省	4.06%	3
Rizhao 日照市	Shandong 山東省	3.69%	2
Weifang 濰坊市	Shandong 山東省	2.98%	7
Tangshan 唐山市	Hebei 河北省	2.75%	6
Ji'nan 濟南市	Shandong 山東省	2.63%	2
Nantong 南通市	Jiangsu 江蘇省	2.62%	11
Changzhou 常州市	Jiangsu 江蘇省	2.50%	23

10 Major Wholesalers 10 家主要批發商	City 城市	Province 省	Telephone / Fax 電話 / 傳真
Liaoning Automobile Trade Group Corp. 遼寧省汽車貿易集團	Shenyang 瀋陽市	Liaoning 遼寧省	(024)23835494 (024)23838338
China Post and Telecommunication Equipment General Company 中國郵電器材總公司	Beijing 北京市	Beijing 北京市	(010)63523715 (010)63525935
Jiangsu Electromechanical Products General Company 江蘇省機電產品總公司	Nanjing 南京市	Jiangsu 江蘇省	(025)7713642 (025)7711036
Xi Nan Technology Import & Export Company 西南技術進出口公司	Chongqing 重慶市	Chongqing 重慶市	(023)63850185 (023)63850026
Changzhou Economic Technology Industrial Development Zone Tian Ming Trade Company 常州經濟技術產業開發區天明貿易公司	Changzhou 常州市	Jiangsu 江蘇省	(0519)8829882 (0519)8829882
Shanxi Mechanical Equipment Import & Export Company 山西省機械設備進出口公司	Taiyuan 太原市	Shanxi 山西省	(0351)4040713 (0351)4043981
Ningbo Five Mining Machinery Import & Export Company 寧波市五礦機械進出口公司	Ningbo 寧波市	Zhejiang 浙江省	(0574)7311255 (0574)7320322
Tianjin Jin Huan Electromechanical Complete Sets of Equipment Factory 天津市津環機電成套設備廠	Tianjin 天津市	Tianjin 天津市	(022)26371628
Yunnan Machinery Import & Export Company 雲南省機械進出口公司	Kunming 昆明市	Yunnan 雲南省	(0871)3164879 (0871)3136829
Tianjin Da Qiu Zhuang Yi Yuan Trade Center 天津市大丘莊億源商貿中心	Tianjin 天津市	Tianjin 天津市	(022)28899478 (022)28899046

*Also include sales by firms outside this industry.包括本行業以外廠家的銷售。"o" stands for "others". "o" 代表 "其他產品"。

3567: Chains 鏈條製造業

The industry accounts for 0.034% of the total revenue of China's industrial sector in 1996. The revenue growth rate of the industry is -9.2% from 1995, as compared to the growth rate of China's industrial sector, 9.51%. The rate of return on asset is -0.04%. 64.87% of all firms in the industry made a profit while 28.46% had negative returns. The top province in terms of the industry's revenue is Zhejiang, accounting for 22.43% of the total revenue.
本行業在 1996 年佔全行業總產值 0.034%，行業年增長率為 -9.2%（全國工業年增長率 9.51%）。行業的資產回報率 -0.04%，64.87% 的企業盈利，28.46% 的企業虧損。銷售收入最高的省份為浙江省，佔本行業的 22.43%。

	Total number of firms 企業總數	Total number of employees 職工總數	Total revenue (Mil. RMB) 總銷售收入（百萬元）	Total profit (Mil. RMB) 總利潤（百萬元）	Return on assets 資產利潤率 (%)	Return on equity 權益利潤率 (%)	Labour productivity ('000 RMB / worker) 勞動生產率（千元/人）	Debts / assets 資產負債率 (%)	Total assets (Mil. RMB) 總資產（百萬元）
Industry Overall 行業總體	270	47,283	1,946	-1	-0.04	-0.16	41.16	74.61	3,012

	Number of firms 企業個數	Average number of employees 平均職工人數	Average revenue ('000 RMB) 平均銷售收入（千元）	Average profit ('000 RMB) 平均利潤（千元）	Return on assets 資產利潤率 (%)	Return on equity 權益利潤率 (%)	Labour productivity ('000 RMB / worker) 勞動生產率（千元/人）	Average debts / assets 平均資產負債率(%)	Average Total assets ('000 RMB) 平均總資產（千元）
By ownership 產業所有權									
State-owned 國有	38	393	11,289	-447	-1.72	-8.06	28.72	78.62	25,974
Collectively-owned 集體	192	140	6,093	94	1.39	5.20	43.51	73.35	6,795
Privately-owned 私有	4	19	1,066	2	0.10	0.34	56.84	70.77	1,731
Domestic JVs 聯營	9	285	9,958	212	1.12	2.96	34.94	62.14	18,923
Joint stock 股份制	2	42	870	23	1.95	3.63	20.70	46.29	1,193
Foreign-funded 外資	7	82	8,320	-70	-0.53	-1.98	101.99	73.41	13,269
Overseas Chinese-funded 港澳台資	17	135	11,363	-209	-0.79	-3.12	83.99	74.58	26,368
By size 規模									
Large 大型	2	1,773	85,164	147	0.06	0.41	48.03	84.76	233,357
Medium 中型	16	850	36,589	-37	-0.06	-0.22	43.04	72.12	59,308
Small 小型	249	121	4,780	-3	-0.04	-0.17	39.60	73.11	6,412
By regional distribution 地區分布									
Central-North 華北	34	205	9,908	834	8.38	28.70	48.43	70.80	9,958
Beijing 北京	7	48	1,191	-281	-6.10	-21.94	24.90	72.18	4,617
Tianjin 天津	3	156	4,520	280	6.76	24.92	28.97	72.79	3,847
Hebei 河北	20	277	15,334	1,456	10.91	34.48	55.31	68.37	13,361
Shanxi 山西	4	152	2,073	110	1.59	19.30	13.66	91.77	6,925
Inner Mongolia 內蒙									
Northeast 東北	35	200	2,703	-1,060	-10.00	-144.09	13.53	93.07	10,601
Liaoning 遼寧	23	211	2,508	-1,345	-11.00	-7543.90	11.89	99.85	12,226
Jilin 吉林	4	122	2,508	-125	-3.78	-36.76	20.64	89.71	3,305
Heilongjiang 黑龍江	8	207	3,363	-708	-7.39	-23.61	16.26	68.73	9,578
Central East 華東	149	175	8,429	142	1.20	4.35	48.03	72.36	11,805
Shanghai 上海	13	169	5,078	-264	-2.67	-8.09	30.06	66.99	9,875
Jiangsu 江蘇	41	162	9,827	85	0.85	2.97	60.65	71.28	9,958
Zhejiang 浙江	34	261	12,836	133	0.56	2.17	49.24	74.12	23,632
Anhui 安徽	37	77	5,104	328	9.92	28.66	66.08	65.40	3,305
Fujian 福建	8	200	1,861	-119	-1.91	-12.94	9.30	85.20	6,201
Jiangxi 江西	3	171	4,710	123	1.59	5.53	27.60	71.31	7,773
Shandong 山東	13	267	10,201	387	2.25	8.09	38.18	72.20	17,193
Central-South 中南	36	161	6,146	-134	-1.20	-4.91	38.26	75.58	11,141
Henan 河南	9	111	1,856	-67	-1.47	-9.97	16.73	85.28	4,543
Hubei 湖北	9	145	3,666	-110	-2.12	18.71	25.30	111.35	5,180
Hunan 湖南	6	222	5,665	-253	-1.62	-4.98	25.58	67.46	15,630
Guangdong 廣東	10	162	12,049	-50	-0.29	-0.95	74.47	69.43	17,197
Guangxi 廣西	2	267	8,535	-600	-2.51	-8.50	32.03	70.50	23,915
Hainan 海南									
Southwest 西南	14	98	2,481	-629	-6.34	-16.07	26.80	60.55	9,921
Chongqing 重慶									
Sichuan 四川	12	98	2,350	556	13.87	46.30	23.98	70.04	4,008
Guizhou 貴州									
Yunnan 雲南	2	63	3,265	-1,070	-2.36	-5.30	51.83	55.52	45,400
Tibet 西藏									
Northwest 西北	2	55	1,285	-10	-0.52	-1.48	23.36	64.94	1,925
Shaanxi 陝西	1	68	1,710	-60	-2.41	-33.33	25.15	92.77	2,490
Gansu 甘肅									
Qinghai 青海									
Ningxia 寧夏									
Xinjiang 新疆	1	42	860	40	2.94	3.42	20.48	13.97	1,360

3567: Chains 鏈條製造業

Year 年份	Number of firms 企業個數	Rate of change 每年變化 (%)	Number of employees 職工人數 (人)	Rate of change 每年變化 (%)	Total revenue (Mil. RMB) 總銷售收入 (百萬元)	Rate of change 每年變化 (%)	Total profit (Mil. RMB) 總利潤 (百萬元)	Rate of change 每年變化 (%)
1993	216		43,678		1,487		58	
1994	237	9.72%	43,567	-0.26%	1,627	9.42%	41	-28.34%
1995	267	12.66%	51,929	19.19%	2,142	31.60%	38	-7.96%
1996	270	1.12%	47,283	-8.95%	1,946	-9.15%	-1	-102.63%

3 Major products* 3 種主要產品 *	Output 產量	Sales volume 銷售量	Unit 單位
a) Industrial Chain 工業鏈條	192,571	181,017	ton 噸
b) Tractor & Internal Combustion Engine Fitting Parts 拖拉機內燃機配件	99,462	92,499	1,000 yuan 千元
c) Conveying Machinery 輸送機械	881	617	ton 噸

Top 10 firms by revenue (year founded) 收入排名前 10 家企業 (創辦年份)	City 城市	Province 省	Telephone / fax 電話 / 傳真	Number of employees 職工人數	Ownership 產業所有權	Revenue ('000 RMB) 銷售收入 (千元)	Profit ('000 RMB) (rank) 利潤 (千元) (排名)	Total assets ('000 RMB) 總資產 (千元)	Major products 主要產品
Hangzhou Dun Pai Lian Transmission (Group) Company 杭州盾牌鏈傳動(集團)公司(1951)	Hangzhou 杭州市	Zhejiang 浙江省	(0571)8068568 (0571)8078875	3,612	State-owned 國有	187,200	2024(11)	388,245	a,c
Zhejiang Huzhou Rui Shi Chain Transmission Group Co. 浙江省湖州市鋭獅鏈傳動集團公司(1988)	Huzhou 湖州市	Zhejiang 浙江省	(0572)3979898	1,350	Collectively-owned 集體	146,456	6325(3)	201,716	a
Sanhe Great Wall Chain Transport Equipment General Factory 三河市長城鏈條輸送設備總廠(1972)	Langfang 廊坊市	Hebei 河北省	(0316)3212917 (0316)3212316	820	Collectively-owned 集體	108,130	21497(1)	18,000	o
Shijiazhuang Sprocket General Factory 石家莊市鏈輪總廠(1989)	Shijiazhuang 石家莊市	Hebei 河北省	(0311)5054756 (0311)5053494	1,916	Collectively-owned 集體	95,834	6216(4)	103,934	o
Rudong Iron Chain Factory 如東縣鐵鏈廠(1972)	Nantong 南通市	Jiangsu 江蘇省	(0513)4377090 (0513)4377092	1,368	Collectively-owned 集體	81,838	1541(14)	41,622	a
Suzhou Huan Qiu Chain Transmission Co. Ltd. 蘇州環球鏈傳動有限公司(1992)	Suzhou 蘇州市	Jiangsu 江蘇省	(0512)7232385 (0512)7232366	658	Overseas Chinese-funded 港澳台資	70,210	1312(16)	98,807	a,b
Zhejiang Wan Peng Group Co. Ltd. 浙江萬鵬集團有限公司(1973)	Jinhua 金華市	Zhejiang 浙江省	(0579)7664201 (0579)7662344	1,067	Collectively-owned 集體	61,484	0(127)	164,888	o
Hebei Tangshan Jing Pin Chain Group Co. 唐山晶品鏈條集團公司(1971)	Tangshan 唐山市	Hebei 河北省	(0315)5612504 (0315)5612496	1,497	Collectively-owned 集體	60,928	901(23)	76,468	o
Foshan Da Zhong Anchor Chain Co. Ltd. 佛山市大中錨鏈有限公司(1992)	Foshan 佛山市	Guangdong 廣東省	(0757)2271300 (0757)2276241	244	Foreign-funded 外資	56,273	867(25)	59,637	a
Shanghai Hua Xing Electrical Lift Fitting Parts Processing Factory 上海華興電梯配件加工廠(1992)	Shanghai 上海市	Shanghai 上海市	(021)64761188	283	Collectively-owned 集體	46,847	1107(17)	9,681	o

Top 10 Cities by Production Output 產出排名前 10 位城市	Province 省	Market share 市場份額	Number of firms 企業個數
Hangzhou 杭州市	Zhejiang 浙江省	13.25%	15
Shanghai 上海市	Shanghai 上海市	10.50%	19
Huzhou 湖州市	Zhejiang 浙江省	8.47%	2
Nantong 南通市	Jiangsu 江蘇省	7.60%	13
Suzhou 蘇州市	Jiangsu 江蘇省	6.56%	16
Jinhua 金華市	Zhejiang 浙江省	4.89%	8
Foshan 佛山市	Guangdong 廣東省	4.16%	3
Shenzhen 深圳市	Guangdong 廣東省	3.50%	1
Tangshan 唐山市	Hebei 河北省	3.09%	5
Xuanzhou 宣州市	Anhui 安徽省	2.67%	5

10 Major Wholesalers 10 家主要批發商	City 城市	Province 省	Telephone / Fax 電話 / 傳真
Liaoning Automobile Trade Group Corp. 遼寧省汽車貿易集團	Shenyang 瀋陽市	Liaoning 遼寧省	(024)23835494 (024)23838338
China Post and Telecommunication Equipment General Company 中國郵電器材總公司	Beijing 北京市	Beijing 北京市	(010)63523715 (010)63525935
Jiangsu Electromechanical Products General Company 江蘇省機電產品總公司	Nanjing 南京市	Jiangsu 江蘇省	(025)7713642 (025)7711036
Xi Nan Technology Import & Export Company 西南技術進出口公司	Chongqing 重慶市	Chongqing 重慶市	(023)63850185 (023)63850026
Changzhou Economic Technology Industrial Development Zone Tian Ming Trade Company 常州經濟技術產業開發區天明貿易公司	Changzhou 常州市	Jiangsu 江蘇省	(0519)8829882 (0519)8829882
Shanxi Mechanical Equipment Import & Export Company 山西省機械設備進出口公司	Taiyuan 太原市	Shanxi 山西省	(0351)4040713 (0351)4043981
Ningbo Five Mining Machinery Import & Export Company 寧波市五礦機械進出口公司	Ningbo 寧波市	Zhejiang 浙江省	(0574)7311255 (0574)7320322
Tianjin Jin Huan Electromechanical Complete Sets of Equipment Factory 天津市津環機電成套設備廠	Tianjin 天津市	Tianjin 天津市	(022)26371628
Yunnan Machinery Import & Export Company 雲南省機械進出口公司	Kunming 昆明市	Yunnan 雲南省	(0871)3164879 (0871)3136829
Tianjin Da Qiu Zhuang Yi Yuan Trade Center 天津市大丘莊億源商貿中心	Tianjin 天津市	Tianjin 天津市	(022)28899478 (022)28899046

*Also include sales by firms outside this industry.包括本行業以外廠家的銷售。"o" stands for "others"."o" 代表"其他產品"。

3568: Gears 齒輪製造業

The industry accounts for 0.077% of the total revenue of China's industrial sector in 1996. The revenue growth rate of the industry is 23.7% from 1995, as compared to the growth rate of China's industrial sector, 9.51%. The rate of return on asset is 1.09%. 69.24% of all firms in the industry made a profit while 26.10% had negative returns. The top province in terms of the industry's revenue is Jiangsu, accounting for 28.70% of the total revenue.
本行業在 1996 年佔全行業總產值 0.077%，行業年增長率為 23.7%（全國工業年增長率 9.51%）。行業的資產回報率 1.09%，69.24% 的企業盈利，26.10% 的企業虧損。銷售收入最高的省份為江蘇省，佔本行業的 28.70%。

	Total number of firms 企業總數	Total number of employees 職工總數	Total revenue (Mil. RMB) 總銷售收入（百萬元）	Total profit (Mil. RMB) 總利潤（百萬元）	Return on assets 資產利潤率 (%)	Return on equity 權益利潤率 (%)	Labour productivity ('000 RMB / worker) 勞動生產率（千元/人）	Debts / assets 資產負債率 (%)	Total assets (Mil. RMB) 總資產（百萬元）
Industry Overall 行業總體	353	84,241	4,453	83	1.09	3.62	52.86	70.00	7,673

	Number of firms 企業個數	Average number of employees 平均職工人數	Average revenue ('000 RMB) 平均銷售收入（千元）	Average profit ('000 RMB) 平均利潤（千元）	Return on assets 資產利潤率 (%)	Return on equity 權益利潤率 (%)	Labour productivity ('000 RMB / worker) 勞動生產率（千元/人）	Average debts / assets 平均資產負債率(%)	Average Total assets ('000 RMB) 平均總資產（千元）
By ownership 產業所有權									
State-owned 國有	87	613	26,966	-218	-0.36	-1.30	43.99	72.23	60,264
Collectively-owned 集體	248	100	6,201	192	2.89	9.81	62.24	70.55	6,653
Privately-owned 私有	1	11	2,218	15	1.37	3.38	201.67	59.41	1,117
Domestic JVs 聯營	4	321	24,708	731	4.33	9.37	77.09	53.83	16,893
Joint stock 股份制	2	817	77,014	5,267	7.55	20.97	94.32	64.00	69,777
Foreign-funded 外資	6	305	29,877	4,541	6.54	13.09	98.12	50.09	69,492
Overseas Chinese-funded 港澳台資	6	308	22,534	2,265	8.77	19.39	73.28	54.75	25,815
By size 規模									
Large 大型	8	2,306	165,346	2,495	0.72	2.23	71.71	67.85	347,825
Medium 中型	33	909	47,100	1,138	1.39	4.76	51.79	70.87	82,048
Small 小型	308	116	5,117	83	1.17	4.11	44.01	71.66	7,087
By regional distribution 地區分布									
Central-North 華北	38	220	16,305	-93	-0.35	-1.95	74.10	81.90	26,471
Beijing 北京	8	222	8,099	-1,271	-8.30	-66.08	36.52	87.44	15,313
Tianjin 天津	9	291	44,194	464	0.67	3.99	151.87	83.29	69,572
Hebei 河北	15	209	9,716	225	1.52	6.17	46.46	75.39	14,844
Shanxi 山西	3	131	1,243	17	0.29	1.19	9.49	75.65	5,750
Inner Mongolia 內蒙	3	146	2,527	-330	-5.71	-32.89	17.27	82.65	5,783
Northeast 東北	40	67	2,063	49	1.47	4.67	30.88	68.50	3,295
Liaoning 遼寧	25	82	2,732	1	0.03	0.09	33.19	70.54	4,548
Jilin 吉林	2	50	780	150	22.90	62.50	15.76	63.36	655
Heilongjiang 黑龍江	13	40	973	124	9.59	21.35	24.56	55.09	1,292
Central East 華東	163	245	14,906	595	2.96	8.95	60.80	66.86	20,060
Shanghai 上海	5	191	6,494	-280	-1.13	-4.84	34.00	76.60	24,744
Jiangsu 江蘇	46	258	27,787	1,483	6.44	17.12	107.55	62.40	23,032
Zhejiang 浙江	29	108	5,668	72	0.73	2.14	52.26	65.93	9,950
Anhui 安徽	24	260	12,436	282	1.73	5.02	47.90	65.48	16,271
Fujian 福建	11	165	6,535	121	0.89	2.54	39.71	64.96	13,588
Jiangxi 江西	21	344	8,437	21	0.08	0.27	24.56	71.58	27,916
Shandong 山東	27	323	15,079	721	2.90	9.55	46.66	69.63	24,881
Central-South 中南	65	272	11,748	120	0.48	1.74	43.23	72.19	24,661
Henan 河南	21	143	9,294	652	5.56	18.83	64.99	70.49	11,726
Hubei 湖北	13	281	10,554	662	3.76	10.75	37.58	65.02	17,614
Hunan 湖南	23	299	13,201	171	0.59	2.08	44.11	71.39	28,818
Guangdong 廣東	4	398	21,883	-2,368	-4.78	-54.36	55.05	91.20	49,488
Guangxi 廣西	3	624	11,083	-2,147	-3.29	-10.09	17.76	67.37	65,180
Hainan 海南	1	665	6,860	-2,560	-3.59	-11.56	10.32	68.98	71,400
Southwest 西南	33	269	9,725	-128	-0.53	-1.67	36.18	68.58	24,453
Chongqing 重慶	12	155	3,931	-9	-0.07	-0.34	25.28	79.64	12,797
Sichuan 四川	16	343	14,523	420	1.24	3.90	42.31	68.31	33,930
Guizhou 貴州	3	189	3,397	7	0.05	0.12	17.94	56.86	12,710
Yunnan 雲南	2	436	13,815	1,240	3.80	7.98	31.72	52.46	32,670
Tibet 西藏									
Northwest 西北	14	479	16,920	-1,110	-1.82	-5.26	35.32	65.44	61,106
Shaanxi 陝西	9	513	19,797	-64	-0.09	-0.23	38.59	59.68	68,220
Gansu 甘肅	1	120	1,200				10.00	49.56	10,230
Qinghai 青海	3	615	18,923	-4,910	-6.53	-36.78	30.77	82.24	75,157
Ningxia 寧夏	1	125	740	-230	-3.97	-7.88	5.92	49.66	5,800
Xinjiang 新疆									

Year 年份	Number of firms 企業個數	Rate of change 每年變化 (%)	Number of employees 職工人數（人）	Rate of change 每年變化 (%)	Total revenue (Mil. RMB) 總銷售收入（百萬元）	Rate of change 每年變化 (%)	Total profit (Mil. RMB) 總利潤（百萬元）	Rate of change 每年變化 (%)
1993	258		65,847		2,201		112	
1994	285	10.47%	66,327	0.73%	2,723	23.72%	112	0.72%
1995	369	29.47%	83,368	25.69%	3,600	32.19%	93	-17.24%
1996	353	-4.34%	84,241	1.05%	4,453	23.69%	83	-10.70%

3 Major products* 3 種主要產品 *	Output 產量	Sales volume 銷售量	Unit 單位
a) Gear 齒輪	116,607,009	109,610,589	piece 個
b) Tractor & Internal Combustion Engine Fitting Parts 拖拉機內燃機配件	425,542	395,754	1,000 yuan 千元
c) Forging 鍛件	23,552	19,784	ton 噸

Top 10 firms by revenue (year founded) 收入排名前 10 家企業（創辦年份）	City 城市	Province 省	Telephone / fax 電話 / 傳真	Number of employees 職工人數	Ownership 產業所有權	Revenue ('000 RMB) 銷售收入（千元）	Profit ('000 RMB) (rank) 利潤（千元）（排名）	Total assets ('000 RMB) 總資產（千元）	Major products 主要產品
Tianjin Automobile Gear Co. Ltd. 天津汽車齒輪有限公司(1956)	Tianjin 天津市	Tianjin 天津市	(022)27990440 (022)27990914	2,091	State-owned 國有	388,246	4033(9)	605,233	a
Changzhou Gear Plant 常州齒輪廠(1958)	Changzhou 常州市	Jiangsu 江蘇省	(0519)8812631 (0519)8822742	2,264	State-owned 國有	372,652	22573(1)	301,494	a
Yangzhou No.1 Automobile Gear Factory 揚州第一汽車齒輪廠(1958)	Yangzhou 揚州市	Jiangsu 江蘇省	(0514)8751237	1,085	Collectively-owned 集體	188,797	17867(2)	169,177	a,c
Xi Shan Shi Yu Qi Tertiary Industry Factory 錫山市玉祁三產辦廠(1991)	Wuxi 無錫市	Jiangsu 江蘇省	(0510)3889154	1,122	Collectively-owned 集體	165,851	15634(3)	91,772	o
Shannxi Automobile Gear General Plant 陝西汽車齒輪總廠(1970)	Xi'an 西安市	Shaanxi 陝西省	(029)4243126 (029)4243110	3,878	State-owned 國有	162,378	30(123)	589,963	o
Zhuzhou Automobile Gear Plant 中國重汽集團公司株洲汽車齒輪廠(1958)	Zhuzhou 株洲市	Hunan 湖南省	(0733)8496000 (0733)8411274	2,790	State-owned 國有	151,161	63(113)	369,517	a
Sichuan Gear Factory 四川齒輪廠(1958)	Chengdu 成都市	Sichuan 四川省	(028)5180019 (028)5180042	3,024	State-owned 國有	125,614	315(69)	239,053	a,b
Changzhou Diao Zhuang Gear Plant 常州市雕裝齒輪廠(1984)	Changzhou 常州市	Jiangsu 江蘇省	(0519)8814389	461	Collectively-owned 集體	100,107	430(61)	13,039	a
Sichuan Danchi Industrial Co. Ltd. 四川丹齒實業有限公司(1994)	Leshan 樂山市	Sichuan 四川省	(0833)7202491 (0833)7202287	1,430	Foreign-funded 外資	98,082	2041(21)	295,866	a
Wujin Jin Cheng Gear Co. Ltd. 武進金城齒輪有限責任公司(1975)	Changzhou 常州市	Jiangsu 江蘇省	(0519)6551535	509	State-owned 國有	83,900	3560(12)	79,540	a,b

Top 10 Cities by Production Output 產出排名前 10 位城市	Province 省	Market share 市場份額	Number of firms 企業個數
Changzhou 常州市	Jiangsu 江蘇省	21.18%	24
Tianjin 天津市	Tianjin 天津市	6.56%	13
Taizhou 泰州市	Jiangsu 江蘇省	5.32%	10
Zhuzhou 株洲市	Hunan 湖南省	4.31%	4
Leshan 樂山市	Sichuan 四川省	3.58%	8
Chengdu 成都市	Sichuan 四川省	3.35%	6
Nanchang 南昌市	Jiangxi 江西省	2.56%	7
Yantai 煙臺市	Shandong 山東省	2.55%	7
Shaoxing 紹興市	Zhejiang 浙江省	2.25%	7
Yiyang 益陽市	Hunan 湖南省	2.11%	4

10 Major Wholesalers 10 家主要批發商	City 城市	Province 省	Telephone / Fax 電話 / 傳真
Liaoning Automobile Trade Group Corp. 遼寧省汽車貿易集團	Shenyang 瀋陽市	Liaoning 遼寧省	(024)23835494 (024)23838338
China Post and Telecommunication Equipment General Company 中國郵電器材總公司	Beijing 北京市	Beijing 北京市	(010)63523715 (010)63525935
Jiangsu Electromechanical Products General Company 江蘇省機電產品總公司	Nanjing 南京市	Jiangsu 江蘇省	(025)7713642 (025)7711036
Xi Nan Technology Import & Export Company 西南技術進出口公司	Chongqing 重慶市	Chongqing 重慶市	(023)63850185 (023)63850026
Changzhou Economic Technology Industrial Development Zone Tian Ming Trade Company 常州經濟技術產業開發區天明貿易公司	Changzhou 常州市	Jiangsu 江蘇省	(0519)8829882 (0519)8829882
Shanxi Mechanical Equipment Import & Export Company 山西省機械設備進出口公司	Taiyuan 太原市	Shanxi 山西省	(0351)4040713 (0351)4043981
Ningbo Five Mining Machinery Import & Export Company 寧波市五礦機械進出口公司	Ningbo 寧波市	Zhejiang 浙江省	(0574)7311255 (0574)7320322
Tianjin Jin Huan Electromechanical Complete Sets of Equipment Factory 天津市津環機電成套設備廠	Tianjin 天津市	Tianjin 天津市	(022)26371628
Yunnan Machinery Import & Export Company 雲南省機械進出口公司	Kunming 昆明市	Yunnan 雲南省	(0871)3164879 (0871)3136829
Tianjin Da Qiu Zhuang Yi Yuan Trade Center 天津市大丘莊億源商貿中心	Tianjin 天津市	Tianjin 天津市	(022)28899478 (022)28899046

*Also include sales by firms outside this industry.包括本行業以外廠家的銷售。"o" stands for "others". "o" 代表"其他產品"。

3569: Other General Parts 其他類未包括的通用零部件製造業

The industry accounts for 0.114% of the total revenue of China's industrial sector in 1996. The revenue growth rate of the industry is 32.1% from 1995, as compared to the growth rate of China's industrial sector, 9.51%. The rate of return on asset is 3.02%. 72.15% of all firms in the industry made a profit while 19.99% had negative returns. The top province in terms of the industry's revenue is Jiangsu, accounting for 20.27% of the total revenue.
本行業在1996年佔全行業總產值0.114%，行業年增長率為32.1%（全國工業年增長率9.51%）。行業的資產回報率3.02%，72.15%的企業盈利，19.99%的企業虧損。銷售收入最高的省份為江蘇省，佔本行業的20.27%。

	Total number of firms 企業總數	Total number of employees 職工總數	Total revenue (mil. RMB) 總銷售收入（百萬元）	Total profit (mil. RMB) 總利潤（百萬元）	Return on assets 資產利潤率 (%)	Return on equity 權益利潤率 (%)	Labour productivity ('000 RMB / worker) 勞動生產率（千元/人）	Debts / assets 資產負債率 (%)	Total assets (mil. RMB) 總資產（百萬元）
Industry Overall 行業總體	1,598	114,144	6,625	220	3.02	9.37	58.04	67.81	7,285

	Number of firms 企業個數	Average number of employees 平均職工人數	Average revenue ('000 RMB) 平均銷售收入（千元）	Average profit ('000 RMB) 平均利潤（千元）	Return on assets 資產利潤率 (%)	Return on equity 權益利潤率 (%)	Labour productivity ('000 RMB / worker) 勞動生產率（千元/人）	Average debts / assets 平均資產負債率(%)	Average Total assets ('000 RMB) 平均總資產（千元）
By ownership 產業所有權									
State-owned 國有	174	158	6,569	132	0.94	2.87	41.54	67.37	14,126
Collectively-owned 集體	1,335	61	3,627	140	4.74	16.32	59.45	70.93	2,945
Privately-owned 私有	6	28	3,157	220	7.30	27.42	111.42	73.36	3,006
Domestic JVs 聯營	6	83	5,262	632	12.27	20.41	63.78	39.88	5,154
Joint stock 股份制	13	56	4,360	48	1.35	3.67	77.42	63.20	3,556
Foreign-funded 外資	24	79	10,602	-174	-1.02	-1.82	134.77	44.16	17,127
Overseas Chinese-funded 港澳台資	36	77	7,445	242	2.26	6.78	96.68	66.70	10,692
By size 規模									
Large 大型	4	1,512	100,968	5,619	3.22	9.31	66.77	65.42	174,475
Medium 中型	25	641	54,693	1,778	2.29	7.21	85.34	68.23	77,612
Small 小型	1,558	59	3,116	98	3.29	10.29	52.67	67.99	2,982
By regional distribution 地區分布									
Central-North 華北	239	52	2,388	163	6.74	18.01	45.85	62.60	2,420
Beijing 北京	47	15	553	10	1.06	3.10	37.37	65.76	923
Tianjin 天津	64	45	1,490	95	6.25	15.06	33.35	58.48	1,514
Hebei 河北	67	72	5,546	432	9.46	26.11	77.30	63.78	4,567
Shanxi 山西	44	84	1,459	65	2.44	6.46	17.46	62.28	2,669
Inner Mongolia 內蒙	17	24	804	37	4.30	10.33	33.34	58.33	861
Northeast 東北	445	62	2,377	70	2.44	8.76	38.15	72.10	2,859
Liaoning 遼寧	349	59	2,527	68	2.21	8.08	42.47	72.64	3,065
Jilin 吉林	32	63	962	64	4.28	11.17	15.29	61.69	1,490
Heilongjiang 黑龍江	64	77	2,268	84	3.49	12.25	29.34	71.53	2,420
Central East 華東	544	95	6,149	210	2.95	9.41	64.58	68.59	7,108
Shanghai 上海	43	45	1,443	102	4.28	11.99	31.97	64.32	2,387
Jiangsu 江蘇	144	140	9,326	216	1.71	5.39	66.67	68.27	12,616
Zhejiang 浙江	120	59	3,320	146	2.99	8.87	55.90	66.33	4,870
Anhui 安徽	70	96	7,273	178	3.39	18.38	75.89	81.54	5,258
Fujian 福建	56	35	2,136	99	4.03	6.16	61.62	34.55	2,463
Jiangxi 江西	34	74	1,700	-38	-1.75	-10.33	22.86	83.10	2,189
Shandong 山東	77	148	11,106	579	5.69	19.06	74.97	70.12	10,162
Central-South 中南	198	66	6,333	129	2.78	7.10	96.55	60.80	4,635
Henan 河南	63	76	2,365	52	1.21	4.65	31.03	74.07	4,300
Hubei 湖北	23	95	3,322	72	1.98	8.78	35.10	77.46	3,627
Hunan 湖南	52	58	11,270	57	3.20	7.86	194.57	59.22	1,782
Guangdong 廣東	39	56	9,337	164	2.15	6.56	167.26	67.23	7,634
Guangxi 廣西	21	39	3,728	535	6.50	8.31	95.70	21.78	8,237
Hainan 海南									
Southwest 西南	120	56	2,254	32	0.74	2.43	40.26	69.30	4,354
Chongqing 重慶	39	88	4,468	151	1.72	5.75	50.90	70.14	8,805
Sichuan 四川	64	38	1,190	-10	-0.48	-1.32	31.13	63.70	2,118
Guizhou 貴州	8	25	533	3	0.43	0.82	21.41	47.97	586
Yunnan 雲南	9	71	1,743	-157	-3.64	-22.78	24.48	84.01	4,301
Tibet 西藏									
Northwest 西北	52	48	2,450	119	4.86	15.83	51.57	69.29	2,448
Shaanxi 陝西	35	33	1,041	1	0.05	0.19	31.98	74.35	1,157
Gansu 甘肅	6	34	1,508	167	18.02	42.92	44.15	58.20	925
Qinghai 青海									
Ningxia 寧夏	2	217	11,680	-145	-2.41	-10.28	53.95	76.60	6,025
Xinjiang 新疆	9	77	6,509	607	7.89	23.17	84.41	65.94	7,690

3569: Other General Parts 其他類未包括的通用零部件製造業

Year 年份	Number of firms 企業個數	Rate of change 每年變化 (%)	Number of employees 職工人數（人）	Rate of change 每年變化 (%)	Total revenue (mil. RMB) 總銷售收入（百萬元）	Rate of change 每年變化 (%)	Total profit (mil. RMB) 總利潤（百萬元）	Rate of change 每年變化 (%)
1993	1,630		122,899		3,900		192	
1994	1,826	12.02%	125,253	1.92%	4,064	4.22%	135	-29.58%
1995	1,614	-11.61%	124,160	-0.87%	5,017	23.43%	184	36.25%
1996	1,598	-0.99%	114,144	-8.07%	6,625	32.05%	220	19.49%

3 Major products* 3 種主要產品 *	Output 產量	Sales volume 銷售量	Unit 單位
a) Parts of Bearing 軸承零件	196,762	200,697	ton 噸
b) General Mechanical Accessories 通用機械配件	30,999	26,349	ton 噸
c) Gear 齒輪	5,803,382	5,455,179	piece 個

Top 10 firms by revenue (year founded) 收入排名前 10 家企業 (創辦年份)	City 城市	Province 省	Telephone / fax 電話 / 傳真	Number of employees 職工人數	Ownership 產業所有權	Revenue ('000 RMB) 銷售收入（千元）	Profit ('000 RMB) (rank) 利潤（千元）（排名）	Total assets ('000 RMB) 總資產（千元）	Major products 主要產品
Taishan Tai Cheng Xing Hua Electric Appliance Plastics Factory 台山市台城興華電器塑料廠(1993)	Jiangmen 江門市	Guangdong 廣東省		35	Private-owned 私營	197,350	3760(19)	73,960	o
Dongying Guang Ming Group Co. Ltd. 東營市光明集團有限責任公司(1971)	Dongying 東營市	Shandong 山東省	(0546)2521178 (0546)2523566	455	Collectively-owned 集體	140,714	6333(8)	36,460	b
Jiangsu Steel Ball Factory 江蘇鋼球廠(1989)	Nantong 南通市	Jiangsu 江蘇省	(0513)7533391 (0513)7516774	461	Collectively-owned 集體	123,639	10021(2)	84,416	a
Nanjing High Speed Gear Box Factory 南京高速齒輪箱廠(1969)	Nanjing 南京市	Jiangsu 江蘇省	(025)2415583 (025)2412731	1,211	State-owned 國有	118,191	6767(7)	237,983	b
Wendeng Impact Damper Factory 文登市減震器廠(1989)	Weihai 威海市	Shandong 山東省	(0896)8761067 (0896)8761067	180	Foreign-funded 外資	107,140	990(62)	20,930	o
Zhengding Environment Protection Equipment Factory 正定縣環保設備廠(1990)	Shijiazhuang 石家莊市	Hebei 河北省		36	Private-owned 私營	105,000	9040(3)	31,660	o
Zhejiang San Hua Group Co. 浙江三花集團公司(1967)	Shaoxing 紹興市	Zhejiang 浙江省	(0575)6021859 (0575)6021855	811	Collectively-owned 集體	103,129	12285(1)	208,155	o
Sichuan Gear Box Factory 四川齒輪箱廠	Chongqing 重慶市	Chongqing 重慶市	(023)47211001 (023)211128	1,710	State-owned 國有	98,977	4511(16)	269,598	o
Jiangyin Bei Hai Group Co. 江陰市北海集團公司(1953)	Wuxi 無錫市	Jiangsu 江蘇省	(0510)6221110	509	Collectively-owned 集體	98,243	1018(58)	135,765	o
Zichuan Vacuum Switch Factory 淄川真空開關廠(1985)	Zibo 淄博市	Shandong 山東省	(0533)5430377 (0533)5430219	570	Collectively-owned 集體	95,892	3931(18)	33,764	o

Top 10 Cities by Production Output 產出排名前 10 位城市	Province 省	Market share 市場份額	Number of firms 企業個數
Nanjing 南京市	Jiangsu 江蘇省	6.49%	47
Xuanzhou 宣州市	Anhui 安徽省	5.99%	29
Shaoxing 紹興市	Zhejiang 浙江省	4.19%	20
Nantong 南通市	Jiangsu 江蘇省	3.55%	33
Anshan 鞍山市	Liaoning 遼寧省	3.37%	22
Taizhou 泰州市	Jiangsu 江蘇省	3.16%	25
Shanghai 上海市	Shanghai 上海市	2.75%	87
Dongying 東營市	Shandong 山東省	2.73%	7
Weihai 威海市	Shandong 山東省	2.67%	5
Wuxi 無錫市	Jiangsu 江蘇省	2.66%	47

10 Major Wholesalers 10 家主要批發商	City 城市	Province 省	Telephone / Fax 電話 / 傳真
Liaoning Automobile Trade Group Corp. 遼寧省汽車貿易集團	Shenyang 瀋陽市	Liaoning 遼寧省	(024)23835494 (024)23838338
China Post and Telecommunication Equipment General Company 中國郵電器材總公司	Beijing 北京市	Beijing 北京市	(010)63523715 (010)63525935
Jiangsu Electromechanical Products General Company 江蘇省機電產品總公司	Nanjing 南京市	Jiangsu 江蘇省	(025)7713642 (025)7711036
Xi Nan Technology Import & Export Company 西南技術進出口公司	Chongqing 重慶市	Chongqing 重慶市	(023)63850185 (023)63850026
Changzhou Economic Technology Industrial Development Zone Tian Ming Trade Company 常州經濟技術產業開發區天明貿易公司	Changzhou 常州市	Jiangsu 江蘇省	(0519)8829882 (0519)8829882
Shanxi Mechanical Equipment Import & Export Company 山西省機械設備進出口公司	Taiyuan 太原市	Shanxi 山西省	(0351)4040713 (0351)4043981
Ningbo Five Mining Machinery Import & Export Company 寧波市五礦機械進出口公司	Ningbo 寧波市	Zhejiang 浙江省	(0574)7311255 (0574)7320322
Tianjin Jin Huan Electromechanical Complete Sets of Equipment Factory 天津市津環機電成套設備廠	Tianjin 天津市	Tianjin 天津市	(022)26371628
Yunnan Machinery Import & Export Company 雲南省機械進出口公司	Kunming 昆明市	Yunnan 雲南省	(0871)3164879 (0871)3136829
Tianjin Da Qiu Zhuang Yi Yuan Trade Center 天津市大丘莊億源商貿中心	Tianjin 天津市	Tianjin 天津市	(022)28899478 (022)28899046

*Also include sales by firms outside this industry.包括本行業以外廠家的銷售。"o" stands for "others". "o" 代表 "其他產品"。

3571: Castings 鑄件製造業

The industry accounts for 0.425% of the total revenue of China's industrial sector in 1996. The revenue growth rate of the industry is 14.8% from 1995, as compared to the growth rate of China's industrial sector, 9.51%. The rate of return on asset is 0.92%. 72.24% of all firms in the industry made a profit while 20.35% had negative returns. The top province in terms of the industry's revenue is Jiangsu, accounting for 16.72% of the total revenue.
本行業在1996年佔全行業總產值0.425%，行業年增長率為14.8%（全國工業年增長率9.51%）。行業的資產回報率0.92%，72.24%的企業盈利，20.35%的企業虧損。銷售收入最高的省份為江蘇省，佔本行業的16.72%。

	Total number of firms 企業總數	Total number of employees 職工總數	Total revenue (mil. RMB) 總銷售收入（百萬元）	Total profit (mil. RMB) 總利潤（百萬元）	Return on assets 資產利潤率 (%)	Return on equity 權益利潤率 (%)	Labour productivity ('000 RMB / worker) 勞動生產率（千元/人）	Debts / assets 資產負債率 (%)	Total assets (mil. RMB) 總資產（百萬元）
Industry Overall 行業總體	6,622	543,867	24,619	267	0.92	3.30	45.27	72.16	29,014

	Number of firms 企業個數	Average number of employees 平均職工人數	Average revenue ('000 RMB) 平均銷售收入（千元）	Average profit ('000 RMB) 平均利潤（千元）	Return on assets 資產利潤率 (%)	Return on equity 權益利潤率 (%)	Labour productivity ('000 RMB / worker) 勞動生產率（千元/人）	Average debts / assets 平均資產負債率(%)	Average Total assets ('000 RMB) 平均總資產（千元）
By ownership 產業所有權									
State-owned 國有	418	252	7,048	-663	-3.18	-12.67	27.92	74.91	20,840
Collectively-owned 集體	5,855	68	3,224	78	2.74	10.58	47.54	74.06	2,829
Privately-owned 私有	68	38	3,447	353	13.53	29.13	90.57	53.54	2,605
Domestic JVs 聯營	68	120	6,088	-37	-0.47	-1.08	50.72	56.50	7,942
Joint stock 股份制	63	167	7,052	177	1.91	6.54	42.32	70.75	9,266
Foreign-funded 外資	82	181	15,851	624	2.92	6.31	87.58	53.77	21,380
Overseas Chinese-funded 港澳台資	62	98	6,132	111	1.05	2.33	62.72	54.75	10,504
By size 規模									
Large 大型	17	2,001	108,410	1,062	0.33	1.08	54.17	68.97	317,905
Medium 中型	53	740	33,258	-497	-0.82	-2.84	44.92	71.07	60,485
Small 小型	6,521	72	3,237	42	1.35	5.03	44.87	73.18	3,129
By regional distribution 地區分布									
Central-North 華北	1,002	88	3,491	60	1.48	4.08	39.84	63.70	4,064
Beijing 北京	95	54	2,960	-45	-0.82	-3.58	54.70	76.99	5,431
Tianjin 天津	63	110	5,722	-73	-0.63	-0.99	51.80	36.39	11,651
Hebei 河北	509	86	3,939	213	6.79	23.02	45.69	70.51	3,137
Shanxi 山西	237	90	2,018	-185	-5.13	-13.42	22.41	61.79	3,604
Inner Mongolia 內蒙	98	107	3,811	47	1.24	4.83	35.65	74.29	3,790
Northeast 東北	1,145	88	2,261	-6	-0.17	-0.73	25.60	76.42	3,788
Liaoning 遼寧	747	101	2,527	-20	-0.41	-1.67	25.09	75.17	4,774
Jilin 吉林	186	61	1,515	-35	-1.61	-15.24	24.88	89.43	2,180
Heilongjiang 黑龍江	212	69	1,977	66	3.81	14.76	28.82	74.20	1,723
Central East 華東	2,226	90	5,310	101	1.75	6.48	59.14	73.07	5,784
Shanghai 上海	87	275	15,792	-306	-0.95	-3.32	57.40	71.33	32,147
Jiangsu 江蘇	570	101	7,221	134	1.69	7.84	71.46	78.44	7,949
Zhejiang 浙江	375	64	3,297	10	0.27	0.99	51.75	72.71	3,635
Anhui 安徽	373	97	5,953	152	3.18	9.38	61.53	66.10	4,794
Fujian 福建	277	29	2,012	68	5.12	11.53	69.65	55.59	1,319
Jiangxi 江西	203	58	1,549	-24	-1.08	-4.37	26.62	75.21	2,252
Shandong 山東	341	113	5,869	295	6.38	23.12	51.91	72.38	4,613
Central-South 中南	1,436	73	3,595	21	0.58	2.20	49.55	73.44	3,668
Henan 河南	319	82	3,913	87	1.92	7.69	47.97	75.07	4,556
Hubei 湖北	309	81	4,854	100	3.19	11.85	60.05	73.07	3,129
Hunan 湖南	406	56	2,720	-20	-0.86	-3.53	48.60	75.54	2,273
Guangdong 廣東	207	100	5,090	-113	-1.48	-5.76	51.00	74.26	7,612
Guangxi 廣西	192	51	1,329	17	0.96	2.32	26.13	58.37	1,798
Hainan 海南	3	15	523	23	1.78	5.69	35.68	69.04	1,313
Southwest 西南	543	64	1,887	-128	-3.90	-14.01	29.57	72.13	3,274
Chongqing 重慶	143	49	1,435	-74	-4.44	-15.00	29.39	70.41	1,675
Sichuan 四川	296	71	2,259	-136	-3.43	-11.11	31.66	69.13	3,973
Guizhou 貴州	78	50	1,018	-209	-6.87	-85.77	20.31	91.99	3,035
Yunnan 雲南	26	107	2,742	-91	-1.87	-5.51	25.71	66.06	4,851
Tibet 西藏									
Northwest 西北	270	60	1,944	102	4.04	12.80	32.33	68.43	2,533
Shaanxi 陝西	165	54	1,626	74	4.27	13.84	29.91	69.12	1,724
Gansu 甘肅	42	62	1,808	70	2.89	9.49	29.26	69.57	2,437
Qinghai 青海	11	50	735	-33	-1.95	-12.04	14.71	83.78	1,675
Ningxia 寧夏	29	122	5,304	428	4.89	14.73	43.64	66.81	8,745
Xinjiang 新疆	23	26	812	21	1.95	5.00	31.59	61.05	1,094

3571: Castings 鑄件製造業

Year 年份	Number of firms 企業個數	Rate of change 每年變化 (%)	Number of employees 職工人數 (人)	Rate of change 每年變化 (%)	Total revenue (mil. RMB) 總銷售收入 (百萬元)	Rate of change 每年變化 (%)	Total profit (mil. RMB) 總利潤 (百萬元)	Rate of change 每年變化 (%)
1993	5,724		525,503		17,587		569	
1994	6,559	14.59%	575,235	9.46%	19,152	8.90%	306	-46.24%
1995	6,815	3.90%	571,480	-0.65%	21,438	11.93%	326	6.40%
1996	6,622	-2.83%	543,867	-4.83%	24,619	14.84%	267	-18.03%

3 Major products* 3種主要產品*	Output 產量	Sales volume 銷售量	Unit 單位
a) Non-ferrous Casting 有色金屬鑄件	195,869	182,158	ton 噸
b) Steel Casting 鑄鋼件	1,443,022	1,212,138	ton 噸
c) Iron Casting 鑄鐵件	416,806	408,470	ton 噸

Top 10 firms by revenue (year founded) 收入排名前10家企業 (創辦年份)	City 城市	Province 省	Telephone / fax 電話 / 傳真	Number of employees 職工人數	Ownership 產業所有權	Revenue ('000 RMB) 銷售收入 (千元)	Profit ('000 RMB) (rank) 利潤 (千元) (排名)	Total assets ('000 RMB) 總資產 (千元)	Major products 主要產品
Wuxi Lian Ya Metal Products Co. Ltd. 無錫聯亞金屬製品有限公司(1992)	Wuxi 無錫市	Jiangsu 江蘇省	(0510)3260787	450	Collectively-owned 集體	552,736	18880(1)	1,057,644	o
Shanghai Automobile Non-ferrous Casting Plant 上海汽車有色鑄造廠(1912)	Shanghai 上海市	Shanghai 上海市	(021)62591120 (021)62747675	3,194	State-owned 國有	298,331	16979(3)	726,696	a
Guangdong Shaoguan Casting & Forging General Factory 廣東省韶關鑄鍛總廠(1969)	Shaoguan 韶關市	Guangdong 廣東省	(0751)8852957 (0751)8853784	2,976	State-owned 國有	249,577	1520(121)	543,673	b,c
Jiangsu Xi Ma Group Company 江蘇省錫馬集團公司(1983)	Wuxi 無錫市	Jiangsu 江蘇省	(0510)8700408 (0510)8701942	1,117	Collectively-owned 集體	149,397	12299(6)	65,719	b,c
Shanghai Automobile Casting General Factory 上海汽車鑄造總廠(1954)	Shanghai 上海市	Shanghai 上海市	(021)59573565 (021)59573565	1,983	State-owned 國有	145,645	12068(7)	405,995	c
Ningguo Wear Resistant Materials General Factory 寧國縣耐磨材料總廠(1965)	Xuanzhou 宣州市	Anhui 安徽省	(0563)4023347 (0563)4022512	3,049	Foreign-funded 外資	137,563	1058(173)	365,632	b
Hebei Xinji Malleable Cast Iron Factory 河北省辛集市瑪鋼廠(1966)	Shijiazhuang 石家莊市	Hebei 河北省	(0311)3191316	565	Collectively-owned 集體	130,830	9362(11)	54,671	o
Anhui Ying Liu Group 安徽應流集團(1984)	Liu'an 六安市	Anhui 安徽省	(0564)5022885	721	Collectively-owned 集體	129,648	4232(28)	98,060	b
Ruzhou Cast Steel Factory 汝州市鑄鋼廠(1985)	Pingdingshan 平頂山市	Henan 河南省	(0375)6687042 (0375)6687176	1,040	Collectively-owned 集體	128,300	1091(170)	169,010	o
Changzhou Sunnex Non-ferrous Casting Co. Ltd. 常州日升有色鑄造有限公司(1992)	Changzhou 常州市	Jiangsu 江蘇省	(0519)5210084 (0519)5210084	584	Foreign-funded 外資	113,963	2559(60)	92,048	a

Top 10 Cities by Production Output 產出排名前10位城市	Province 省	Market share 市場份額	Number of firms 企業個數
Shanghai 上海市	Shanghai 上海市	8.05%	135
Luoyang 洛陽市	Henan 河南省	5.03%	19
Wuxi 無錫市	Jiangsu 江蘇省	3.66%	135
Changzhou 常州市	Jiangsu 江蘇省	3.48%	116
Taizhou 泰州市	Jiangsu 江蘇省	1.99%	111
Ningbo 寧波市	Zhejiang 浙江省	1.86%	89
Xuanzhou 宣州市	Anhui 安徽省	1.77%	51
Chongqing 重慶市	Chongqing 重慶市	1.68%	187
Suzhou 蘇州市	Jiangsu 江蘇省	1.67%	140
Dalian 大連市	Liaoning 遼寧省	1.64%	98

10 Major Wholesalers 10家主要批發商	City 城市	Province 省	Telephone / Fax 電話 / 傳真
Liaoning Automobile Trade Group Corp. 遼寧省汽車貿易集團	Shenyang 瀋陽市	Liaoning 遼寧省	(024)23835494 (024)23838338
China Post and Telecommunication Equipment General Company 中國郵電器材總公司	Beijing 北京市	Beijing 北京市	(010)63523715 (010)63525935
Jiangsu Electromechanical Products General Company 江蘇省機電產品總公司	Nanjing 南京市	Jiangsu 江蘇省	(025)7713642 (025)7711036
Xi Nan Technology Import & Export Company 西南技術進出口公司	Chongqing 重慶市	Chongqing 重慶市	(023)63850185 (023)63850026
Changzhou Economic Technology Industrial Development Zone Tian Ming Trade Company 常州經濟技術產業開發區天明貿易公司	Changzhou 常州市	Jiangsu 江蘇省	(0519)8829882 (0519)8829882
Shanxi Mechanical Equipment Import & Export Company 山西省機械設備進出口公司	Taiyuan 太原市	Shanxi 山西省	(0351)4040713 (0351)4043981
Ningbo Five Mining Machinery Import & Export Company 寧波市五礦機械進出口公司	Ningbo 寧波市	Zhejiang 浙江省	(0574)7311255 (0574)7320322
Tianjin Jin Huan Electromechanical Complete Sets of Equipment Factory 天津市津環機電成套設備廠	Tianjin 天津市	Tianjin 天津市	(022)26371628
Yunnan Machinery Import & Export Company 雲南省機械進出口公司	Kunming 昆明市	Yunnan 雲南省	(0871)3164879 (0871)3136829
Tianjin Da Qiu Zhuang Yi Yuan Trade Center 天津市大丘莊億源商貿中心	Tianjin 天津市	Tianjin 天津市	(022)28899478 (022)28899046

*Also include sales by firms outside this industry.包括本行業以外廠家的銷售。"o" stands for "others". "o" 代表"其他產品"。

3572: Forgings 鍛件製造業

The industry accounts for 0.078% of the total revenue of China's industrial sector in 1996. The revenue growth rate of the industry is 8.0% from 1995, as compared to the growth rate of China's industrial sector, 9.51%. The rate of return on asset is -0.21%. 70.10% of all firms in the industry made a profit while 22.55% had negative returns. The top province in terms of the industry's revenue is Jiangsu, accounting for 15.61% of the total revenue.
本行業在1996年佔全行業總產值0.078%，行業年增長率為8.0%（全國工業年增長率9.51%）。行業的資產回報率-0.21%，70.10%的企業盈利，22.55%的企業虧損。銷售收入最高的省份為江蘇省，佔本行業的15.61%。

	Total number of firms 企業總數	Total number of employees 職工總數	Total revenue (mil. RMB) 總銷售收入（百萬元）	Total profit (mil. RMB) 總利潤（百萬元）	Return on assets 資產利潤率 (%)	Return on equity 權益利潤率 (%)	Labour productivity ('000 RMB / worker) 勞動生產率（千元／人）	Debts / assets 資產負債率 (%)	Total assets (mil. RMB) 總資產（百萬元）
Industry Overall 行業總體	876	79,942	4,525	-14	-0.21	-0.65	56.60	67.69	6,577

	Number of firms 企業個數	Average number of employees 平均職工人數	Average revenue ('000 RMB) 平均銷售收入（千元）	Average profit ('000 RMB) 平均利潤（千元）	Return on assets 資產利潤率 (%)	Return on equity 權益利潤率 (%)	Labour productivity ('000 RMB / worker) 勞動生產率（千元／人）	Average debts / assets 平均資產負債率(%)	Average Total assets ('000 RMB) 平均總資產（千元）
By ownership 產業所有權									
State-owned 國有	67	470	19,507	-1,791	-3.58	-11.32	41.49	68.39	50,045
Collectively-owned 集體	770	58	3,542	127	4.12	15.20	61.25	72.91	3,095
Privately-owned 私有	6	34	2,699	34	2.47	10.36	80.16	76.17	1,379
Domestic JVs 聯營	9	82	5,281	86	1.34	3.14	64.14	57.24	6,405
Joint stock 股份制	9	171	16,704	1,075	2.46	3.45	97.81	28.64	43,719
Foreign-funded 外資	10	102	14,788	-838	-3.94	-12.46	144.69	68.35	21,234
Overseas Chinese-funded 港澳台資	5	181	25,609	1,113	3.29	12.44	141.48	73.57	33,847
By size 規模									
Large 大型	7	2,288	133,407	2,339	0.78	2.36	58.31	66.82	298,086
Medium 中型	10	567	35,503	462	0.49	1.03	62.62	51.85	93,313
Small 小型	856	68	3,780	-41	-0.98	-3.56	55.52	72.35	4,156
By regional distribution 地區分布									
Central-North 華北	137	89	3,470	-113	-1.74	-4.84	39.06	64.14	6,491
Beijing 北京	23	32	1,403	45	1.28	7.33	43.49	82.49	3,523
Tianjin 天津	18	158	7,887	-391	-2.43	-7.13	49.80	65.88	16,057
Hebei 河北	55	55	3,222	331	9.65	25.59	58.36	62.30	3,429
Shanxi 山西	32	138	3,291	-837	-8.96	-20.49	23.87	56.26	9,342
Inner Mongolia 內蒙	9	126	2,063	-97	-2.75	-20.52	16.43	86.58	3,518
Northeast 東北	210	71	2,832	83	2.45	9.80	39.79	74.99	3,373
Liaoning 遼寧	151	81	3,542	109	2.57	10.25	43.82	74.91	4,223
Jilin 吉林	22	35	786	45	4.56	20.41	22.48	77.61	997
Heilongjiang 黑龍江	37	53	1,150	-1	-0.06	-0.25	21.60	74.90	1,317
Central East 華東	277	94	7,673	243	2.76	8.16	81.61	66.17	8,801
Shanghai 上海	36	138	17,122	646	2.60	6.19	124.00	57.95	24,803
Jiangsu 江蘇	99	99	7,134	66	0.83	3.07	72.26	72.92	7,929
Zhejiang 浙江	37	37	2,439	23	0.75	2.91	65.06	74.27	3,027
Anhui 安徽	28	60	4,774	202	4.74	16.98	79.51	72.07	4,254
Fujian 福建	11	101	2,685	-105	-1.21	-2.79	26.56	56.66	8,645
Jiangxi 江西	19	92	2,185	20	0.30	0.99	23.74	69.69	6,648
Shandong 山東	47	114	10,805	677	10.34	33.44	94.57	69.07	6,545
Central-South 中南	106	123	4,773	-313	-3.23	-10.12	38.76	68.09	9,694
Henan 河南	27	58	3,213	102	1.10	3.34	54.95	66.95	9,234
Hubei 湖北	23	289	10,754	-854	-3.71	-10.01	37.20	62.96	23,041
Hunan 湖南	25	112	2,767	-477	-8.95	-82.90	24.60	89.22	5,334
Guangdong 廣東	19	82	4,567	-31	-0.67	-1.97	55.91	65.90	4,627
Guangxi 廣西	12	38	1,323	-313	-13.92	-78.01	34.58	82.15	2,251
Hainan 海南									
Southwest 西南	99	92	6,611	-271	-2.30	-6.21	72.13	63.01	11,801
Chongqing 重慶	23	197	14,641	-1,561	-6.69	-50.94	74.30	86.87	23,336
Sichuan 四川	60	68	4,878	127	1.24	2.15	71.65	42.10	10,211
Guizhou 貴州	14	27	993	51	4.87	11.53	36.20	57.72	1,041
Yunnan 雲南	2	32	5,020	465	32.52	86.92	159.37	62.59	1,430
Tibet 西藏									
Northwest 西北	47	99	3,610	-488	-6.62	-52.21	36.43	87.31	7,365
Shaanxi 陝西	26	40	2,350	29	1.86	3.97	58.68	53.29	1,553
Gansu 甘肅	11	71	1,878	135	4.70	11.91	26.39	60.54	2,864
Qinghai 青海	6	430	13,233	-4,197	-9.77	-253.58	30.79	96.14	42,937
Ningxia 寧夏	1	81	890	20	0.54	2.25	10.99	76.14	3,730
Xinjiang 新疆	3	58	2,543				44.10	86.06	4,303

3572: Forgings 鍛件製造業

Year 年份	Number of firms 企業個數	Rate of change 每年變化 (%)	Number of employees 職工人數 (人)	Rate of change 每年變化 (%)	Total revenue (mil. RMB) 總銷售收入 (百萬元)	Rate of change 每年變化 (%)	Total profit (mil. RMB) 總利潤 (百萬元)	Rate of change 每年變化 (%)
1993	700		92,533		3,521		194	
1994	917	31.00%	97,188	5.03%	4,259	20.95%	95	-50.96%
1995	867	-5.45%	88,127	-9.32%	4,189	-1.64%	41	-56.80%
1996	876	1.04%	79,942	-9.29%	4,525	8.02%	-14	-134.04%

3 Major products* 3 種主要產品 *	Output 產量	Sales volume 銷售量	Unit 單位
a) Forging 鍛件	496,951	417,439	ton 噸
b) Forged Steels 鍛壓鋼材	50,431	47,405	ton 噸
c) Casting 鑄鋼件	56,720	47,644	ton 噸

Top 10 firms by revenue (year founded) 收入排名前 10 家企業 (創辦年份)	City 城市	Province 省	Telephone / fax 電話 / 傳真	Number of employees 職工人數	Ownership 產業所有權	Revenue ('000 RMB) 銷售收入 (千元)	Profit ('000 RMB) (rank) 利潤 (千元) (排名)	Total assets ('000 RMB) 總資產 (千元)	Major products 主要產品
Shanghai Automobile Forging General Factory 上海汽車鍛造總廠(1937)	Shanghai 上海市	Shanghai 上海市	(021)65342885 (021)65490792	2,146	State-owned 國有	316,473	24480(1)	530,689	a
Chengdu Gong Yi Metallurgy Co. Ltd. 成都工益冶金股份有限公司(1985)	Chengdu 成都市	Sichuan 四川省	(028)4443412	906	Joint stock 股份制	274,288	12215(3)	453,338	a,c
Shandong Connecting Rod Group General Co. 山東連桿集團總公司(1958)	Weihai 威海市	Shandong 山東省	(0896)7651126	606	Collectively-owned 集體	195,517	18168(2)	60,839	o
State-owned Chongqing Heavy-duty Casting & Forging Factory 國營重慶重型鑄鍛廠	Chongqing 重慶市	Chongqing 重慶市	(023)68866821 (023)68831015	3,420	State-owned 國有	170,703	-35853(381)	418,745	a,c
Wuhan Heavy-duty Casting & Forging Factory 武漢重型鑄鍛廠(1967)	Wuhan 武漢市	Hubei 湖北省	(027)86601248 (027)86591069	5,217	State-owned 國有	170,198	-22968(379)	472,188	o
Shanghai Guo Xing Metal Products Co. Ltd. 上海國興金屬製品有限公司(1994)	Shanghai 上海市	Shanghai 上海市	(021)59771543	395	Overseas Chinese-funded 港澳台資	102,472	4336(6)	141,008	o
Nantong Modern Iron & Steel Group Co. Ltd. 南通現代鋼鐵集團有限公司(1995)	Nantong 南通市	Jiangsu 江蘇省	(0513)3411349	266	Collectively-owned 集體	90,269	2568(14)	35,079	o
Changzhou Forging General Factory 常州鍛造總廠(1952)	Changzhou 常州市	Jiangsu 江蘇省	(0519)6600632 (0519)6600416	851	State-owned 國有	80,424	11(263)	141,190	a
Qinghai Forging Plant 青海鍛造廠(1971)	Ping'an 平安縣	Qinghai 青海省	(0972)622351	1,788	State-owned 國有	62,458	-17999(377)	179,140	a
Tianjin Jiang Xing Industrial General Company 天津市江興實業總公司(1970)	Tianjin 天津市	Tianjin 天津市	(022)28877068	430	Collectively-owned 集體	61,830	7320(4)	54,660	a

Top 10 Cities by Production Output 產出排名前 10 位城市	Province 省	Market share 市場份額	Number of firms 企業個數
Shanghai 上海市	Shanghai 上海市	15.04%	45
Suzhou 蘇州市	Jiangsu 江蘇省	8.43%	44
Changzhou 常州市	Jiangsu 江蘇省	6.41%	37
Chongqing 重慶市	Chongqing 重慶市	5.79%	49
Wuhan 武漢市	Hubei 湖北省	4.78%	9
Yangzhou 揚州市	Jiangsu 江蘇省	4.47%	12
Dalian 大連市	Liaoning 遼寧省	3.48%	32
Nantong 南通市	Jiangsu 江蘇省	2.88%	10
Tianjin 天津市	Tianjin 天津市	2.79%	21
Wuxi 無錫市	Jiangsu 江蘇省	2.33%	38

10 Major Wholesalers 10 家主要批發商	City 城市	Province 省	Telephone / Fax 電話 / 傳真
Liaoning Automobile Trade Group Corp. 遼寧省汽車貿易集團	Shenyang 瀋陽市	Liaoning 遼寧省	(024)23835494 (024)23838338
China Post and Telecommunication Equipment General Company 中國郵電器材總公司	Beijing 北京市	Beijing 北京市	(010)63523715 (010)63525935
Jiangsu Electromechanical Products General Company 江蘇省機電產品總公司	Nanjing 南京市	Jiangsu 江蘇省	(025)7713642 (025)7711036
Xi Nan Technology Import & Export Company 西南技術進出口公司	Chongqing 重慶市	Chongqing 重慶市	(023)63850185 (023)63850026
Changzhou Economic Technology Industrial Development Zone Tian Ming Trade Company 常州經濟技術產業開發區天明貿易公司	Changzhou 常州市	Jiangsu 江蘇省	(0519)8829882 (0519)8829882
Shanxi Mechanical Equipment Import & Export Company 山西省機械設備進出口公司	Taiyuan 太原市	Shanxi 山西省	(0351)4040713 (0351)4043981
Ningbo Five Mining Machinery Import & Export Company 寧波市五礦機械進出口公司	Ningbo 寧波市	Zhejiang 浙江省	(0574)7311255 (0574)7320322
Tianjin Jin Huan Electromechanical Complete Sets of Equipment Factory 天津市津環機電成套設備廠	Tianjin 天津市	Tianjin 天津市	(022)26371628
Yunnan Machinery Import & Export Company 雲南省機械進出口公司	Kunming 昆明市	Yunnan 雲南省	(0871)3164879 (0871)3136829
Tianjin Da Qiu Zhuang Yi Yuan Trade Center 天津市大丘莊億源商貿中心	Tianjin 天津市	Tianjin 天津市	(022)28899478 (022)28899046

*Also include sales by firms outside this industry.包括本行業以外廠家的銷售。"o" stands for "others". "o" 代表 "其他產品"。

3580: General Machinery Repairs 普通機械修理業

The industry accounts for 0.031% of the total revenue of China's industrial sector in 1996. The revenue growth rate of the industry is 21.9% from 1995, as compared to the growth rate of China's industrial sector, 9.51%. The rate of return on asset is 3.46%. 76.64% of all firms in the industry made a profit while 17.22% had negative returns. The top province in terms of the industry's revenue is Helongjiang, accounting for 17.65% of the total revenue.
本行業在1996年佔全行業總產值0.031%，行業年增長率為21.9%（全國工業年增長率9.51%）。行業的資產回報率3.46%，76.64%的企業盈利，17.22%的企業虧損。銷售收入最高的省份為黑龍江省，佔本行業的17.65%。

	Total number of firms 企業總數	Total number of employees 職工總數	Total revenue (mil. RMB) 總銷售收入（百萬元）	Total profit (mil. RMB) 總利潤（百萬元）	Return on assets 資產利潤率 (%)	Return on equity 權益利潤率 (%)	Labour productivity ('000 RMB / worker) 勞動生產率（千元／人）	Debts / assets 資產負債率 (%)	Total assets (mil. RMB) 總資產（百萬元）
Industry Overall 行業總體	1,391	58,724	1,788	64	3.46	10.09	30.45	65.74	1,839

	Number of firms 企業個數	Average number of employees 平均職工人數	Average revenue ('000 RMB) 平均銷售收入（千元）	Average profit ('000 RMB) 平均利潤（千元）	Return on assets 資產利潤率 (%)	Return on equity 權益利潤率 (%)	Labour productivity ('000 RMB / worker) 勞動生產率（千元／人）	Average debts / assets 平均資產負債率(%)	Average Total assets ('000 RMB) 平均總資產（千元）
By ownership 產業所有權									
State-owned 國有	175	62	1,617	-11	-0.32	-0.88	26.20	64.20	3,623
Collectively-owned 集體	1,183	40	1,196	53	5.64	17.30	29.98	67.38	947
Privately-owned 私有	5	34	4,697	519	24.32	68.57	139.78	64.54	2,136
Domestic JVs 聯營	6	48	3,170	7	0.42	1.92	65.59	78.36	1,662
Joint stock 股份制	7	61	823	-8	-0.54	-1.47	13.40	63.04	1,547
Foreign-funded 外資	6	18	2,885	81	2.56	4.48	164.87	42.92	3,181
Overseas Chinese-funded 港澳台資	7	32	3,265	-53	-1.11	-2.29	101.12	51.38	4,778
By size 規模									
Large 大型									
Medium 中型									
Small 小型	1,388	43	1,288	46	3.48	10.16	30.24	65.74	1,325
By regional distribution 地區分布									
Central-North 華北	321	29	688	32	4.59	14.07	23.64	67.37	691
Beijing 北京	75	13	376	1	0.10	0.37	29.32	71.73	510
Tianjin 天津	102	28	493	27	5.04	13.23	17.82	61.90	531
Hebei 河北	53	38	987	66	5.83	15.25	25.90	61.75	1,135
Shanxi 山西	44	37	1,462	76	9.67	34.69	39.13	72.10	783
Inner Mongolia 內蒙	47	40	545	12	1.64	6.89	13.55	76.11	737
Northeast 東北	499	42	1,188	61	5.81	16.99	28.17	65.82	1,054
Liaoning 遼寧	203	35	1,104	96	9.03	29.70	31.34	69.59	1,065
Jilin 吉林	50	42	1,060	24	2.87	8.90	24.97	67.73	849
Heilongjiang 黑龍江	246	48	1,283	40	3.67	9.77	26.81	62.46	1,086
Central East 華東	209	58	2,341	107	6.02	20.66	40.52	70.85	1,785
Shanghai 上海	31	50	4,767	244	6.53	20.28	95.40	67.82	3,732
Jiangsu 江蘇	19	100	3,628	88	2.06	8.76	36.43	76.49	4,269
Zhejiang 浙江	24	21	3,766	207	18.09	122.11	175.51	85.19	1,145
Anhui 安徽	54	106	2,103	123	11.28	27.00	19.80	58.19	1,093
Fujian 福建	24	12	301		0.14	0.49	25.69	70.19	288
Jiangxi 江西	31	36	1,092	23	1.73	9.32	30.56	81.41	1,322
Shandong 山東	26	38	1,062	34	2.13	6.37	27.76	66.55	1,607
Central-South 中南	213	50	1,778	38	1.46	3.83	35.69	61.81	2,575
Henan 河南	62	53	1,097	23	1.29	5.75	20.79	77.62	1,817
Hubei 湖北	48	81	3,485	120	4.41	14.44	42.86	69.48	2,732
Hunan 湖南	33	30	791	17	2.64	93.44	26.25	97.17	653
Guangdong 廣東	40	50	2,702	120	2.37	5.67	54.18	58.19	5,050
Guangxi 廣西	27	9	316	-166	-5.83	-7.71	36.26	24.36	2,839
Hainan 海南	3	72	243	-33	-2.20	-8.20	3.40	73.41	1,517
Southwest 西南	87	40	864	-78	-5.93	-16.26	21.81	63.53	1,308
Chongqing 重慶	20	31	956	-90	-8.89	-22.27	30.67	60.05	1,010
Sichuan 四川	47	42	1,007	130	10.66	30.78	23.79	65.36	1,215
Guizhou 貴州	15	37	375	-36	-2.57	-12.16	10.24	78.87	1,401
Yunnan 雲南	4	44	513	-18	-1.15	-2.44	11.58	53.03	1,528
Tibet 西藏	1	88	1,050	-1,850	-19.83	-29.23	11.93	32.26	9,330
Northwest 西北	62	36	510	-14	-1.53	-4.73	14.32	67.66	906
Shaanxi 陝西	33	28	429	-25	-4.22	-80.77	15.11	94.78	604
Gansu 甘肅	19	29	321	5	0.55	0.97	10.99	43.85	869
Qinghai 青海	4	81	213	-13	-6.85	-15.63	2.64	57.53	183
Ningxia 寧夏	1	19	120	10	6.25	6.67	6.32	6.25	160
Xinjiang 新疆	5	75	2,084	-14	-0.37	-0.95	27.64	60.75	3,766

3580: General Machinery Repairs 普通機械修理業

Year 年份	Number of firms 企業個數	Rate of change 每年變化 (%)	Number of employees 職工人數 (人)	Rate of change 每年變化 (%)	Total revenue (mil. RMB) 總銷售收入 (百萬元)	Rate of change 每年變化 (%)	Total profit (mil. RMB) 總利潤 (百萬元)	Rate of change 每年變化 (%)
1993	796		35,221		634		31	
1994	1,050	31.91%	45,647	29.60%	1,081	70.58%	42	35.85%
1995	1,477	40.67%	68,142	49.28%	1,467	35.65%	39	-7.44%
1996	1,391	-5.82%	58,724	-13.82%	1,788	21.88%	64	64.86%

3 Major products* 3 種主要產品 *	Output 產量	Sales volume 銷售量	Unit 單位
a) Special Equipment for Electronic Component 電子元件專用設備	3,247	11,203	set 台
b) Metal Structure Products 金屬結構製品	5,895	5,305	ton 噸

Top 10 firms by revenue (year founded) 收入排名前 10 家企業 (創辦年份)	City 城市	Province 省	Telephone / fax 電話 / 傳真	Number of employees 職工人數	Ownership 產業所有權	Revenue ('000 RMB) 銷售收入 (千元)	Profit ('000 RMB) (rank) 利潤（千元）(排名)	Total assets ('000 RMB) 總資產 (千元)	Major products 主要產品
Shanghai Yi Gang Electromechanical Co. 上海一鋼機電公司(1993)	Shanghai 上海市	Shanghai 上海市	(021)56758000 (021)56759804	802	State-owned 國有	109,786	6629(1)	93,403	b
Shao Xingxian Automobile Overhaul Factory 紹興縣汽車大修廠(1985)	Shaoxing 紹興市	Zhejiang 浙江省	(0575)4090451 (0575)4090451	45	Collectively-owned 集體	80,997	5165(2)	12,022	o
Harbin Nangang Postal Service Industry & Trade Company 哈爾濱市南崗郵政工貿公司(1992)	Harbin 哈爾濱市	Heilongjiang 黑龍江省	(0451)3638569	148	Collectively-owned 集體	43,081	3251(6)	18,340	o
Dalian Jili Equipment Anticorrosion Thermal Insulation Factory 大連吉利設備防腐保溫廠(1993)	Dalian 大連市	Liaoning 遼寧省	(0411)6293588	11	Collectively-owned 集體	40,021	4500(4)	12,082	o
Harbin Nangang He Xing Industry & Trade Company 哈爾濱市南崗和興工貿公司(1992)	Harbin 哈爾濱市	Heilongjiang 黑龍江省	(0451)6304467	140	Collectively-owned 集體	24,845	1221(15)	5,049	a
Nanjing Qinhuai School-run Enterprise General Company 南京市秦淮區校辦企業總公司(1989)	Nanjing 南京市	Jiangsu 江蘇省	(025)6624315	650	Collectively-owned 集體	22,824	1520(12)	25,140	o
Dahua Group Company Coking Factory Labour Service Company Electromechanical Installation Team 大化集團公司焦化廠勞服公司機電安裝隊(1986)	Taiyuan 太原市	Shanxi 山西省	(0351)6322920	180	Collectively-owned 集體	22,561	86(107)	2,998	o
Enping Sha Hu Machinery Plant 恩平市沙湖機械廠(1970)	Jiangmen 江門市	Guangdong 廣東省	(0750)7691332	72	Collectively-owned 集體	20,510	188(73)	4,358	o
Xinhui Mu Zhou Machinery Factory 新會市睦洲機械廠(1958)	Jiangmen 江門市	Guangdong 廣東省	(0750)6222592	63	Collectively-owned 集體	19,990	20(152)	6,165	o
Jilin Pyroelectricity Factory Industrial Company 吉林熱電廠工業公司(1988)	Jilin 吉林市	Jilin 吉林省	(0432)3042644	550	State-owned 國有	19,949	29(143)	6,876	o

Top 10 Cities by Production Output 產出排名前 10 位城市	Province 省	Market share 市場份額	Number of firms 企業個數
Shanghai 上海市	Shanghai 上海市	26.33%	124
Tianjin 天津市	Tianjin 天津市	5.46%	125
Nantong 南通市	Jiangsu 江蘇省	3.83%	12
Jiangmen 江門市	Guangdong 廣東省	2.63%	6
Beijing 北京市	Beijing 北京市	2.56%	61
Wuhan 武漢市	Hubei 湖北省	2.52%	13
Guangzhou 廣州市	Guangdong 廣東省	2.27%	29
Zhanjiang 湛江市	Guangdong 廣東省	2.22%	8
Dalian 大連市	Liaoning 遼寧省	1.88%	35
Harbin 哈爾濱市	Heilongjiang 黑龍江省	1.76%	27

10 Major Wholesalers 10 家主要批發商	City 城市	Province 省	Telephone / Fax 電話 / 傳真
Liaoning Automobile Trade Group Corp. 遼寧省汽車貿易集團	Shenyang 瀋陽市	Liaoning 遼寧省	(024)23835494 (024)23838338
China Post and Telecommunication Equipment General Company 中國郵電器材總公司	Beijing 北京市	Beijing 北京市	(010)63523715 (010)63525935
Jiangsu Electromechanical Products General Company 江蘇省機電產品總公司	Nanjing 南京市	Jiangsu 江蘇省	(025)7713642 (025)7711036
Xi Nan Technology Import & Export Company 西南技術進出口公司	Chongqing 重慶市	Chongqing 重慶市	(023)63850185 (023)63850026
Changzhou Economic Technology Industrial Development Zone Tian Ming Trade Company 常州經濟技術產業開發區天明貿易公司	Changzhou 常州市	Jiangsu 江蘇省	(0519)8829882 (0519)8829882
Shanxi Mechanical Equipment Import & Export Company 山西省機械設備進出口公司	Taiyuan 太原市	Shanxi 山西省	(0351)4040713 (0351)4043981
Ningbo Five Mining Machinery Import & Export Company 寧波市五礦機械進出口公司	Ningbo 寧波市	Zhejiang 浙江省	(0574)7311255 (0574)7320322
Tianjin Jin Huan Electromechanical Complete Sets of Equipment Factory 天津市津環機電成套設備廠	Tianjin 天津市	Tianjin 天津市	(022)26371628
Yunnan Machinery Import & Export Company 雲南省機械進出口公司	Kunming 昆明市	Yunnan 雲南省	(0871)3164879 (0871)3136829
Tianjin Da Qiu Zhuang Yi Yuan Trade Center 天津市大丘莊億源商貿中心	Tianjin 天津市	Tianjin 天津市	(022)28899478 (022)28899046

*Also include sales by firms outside this industry.包括本行業以外廠家的銷售。"o" stands for "others". "o" 代表 "其他產品"。

3590: Other General Machinery 其他普通機械製造業

The industry accounts for 0.090% of the total revenue of China's industrial sector in 1996. The revenue growth rate of the industry is 40.2% from 1995, as compared to the growth rate of China's industrial sector, 9.51%. The rate of return on asset is -0.98%. 69.25% of all firms in the industry made a profit while 24.66% had negative returns. The top province in terms of the industry's revenue is Guangdong, accounting for 15.91% of the total revenue.
本行業在1996年佔全行業總產值0.090%，行業年增長率為40.2%（全國工業年增長率9.51%）。行業的資產回報率-0.98%，69.25%的企業盈利，24.66%的企業虧損。銷售收入最高的省份為廣東省，佔本行業的15.91%。

	Total number of firms 企業總數	Total number of employees 職工總數	Total revenue (mil. RMB) 總銷售收入（百萬元）	Total profit (mil. RMB) 總利潤（百萬元）	Return on assets 資產利潤率 (%)	Return on equity 權益利潤率 (%)	Labour productivity ('000 RMB / worker) 勞動生產率（千元／人）	Debts / assets 資產負債率 (%)	Total assets (mil. RMB) 總資產（百萬元）
Industry Overall 行業總體	1,343	140,073	5,194	-103	-0.98	-2.67	37.08	63.35	10,578

	Number of firms 企業個數	Average number of employees 平均職工人數	Average revenue ('000 RMB) 平均銷售收入（千元）	Average profit ('000 RMB) 平均利潤（千元）	Return on assets 資產利潤率 (%)	Return on equity 權益利潤率 (%)	Labour productivity ('000 RMB / worker) 勞動生產率（千元／人）	Average debts / assets 平均資產負債率(%)	Average Total assets ('000 RMB) 平均總資產（千元）
By ownership 產業所有權									
State-owned 國有	231	314	7,372	-909	-3.19	-8.43	23.48	62.20	28,541
Collectively-owned 集體	1,027	58	2,328	41	1.47	5.17	40.39	71.51	2,795
Privately-owned 私有	11	50	3,324	120	5.41	14.46	66.47	62.61	2,216
Domestic JVs 聯營	6	68	3,227	86	3.05	8.67	47.45	64.83	2,809
Joint stock 股份制	13	122	8,034	135	1.30	3.82	65.81	65.93	10,363
Foreign-funded 外資	23	115	6,888	156	1.06	2.15	59.69	50.51	14,616
Overseas Chinese-funded 港澳台資	29	132	26,915	1,986	9.65	17.08	203.95	43.49	20,568
By size 規模									
Large 大型	6	1,569	44,710	27,432	15.04	30.57	28.50	50.81	182,428
Medium 中型	41	888	25,433	18,469	21.59	58.69	28.64	63.21	85,533
Small 小型	1,287	73	3,006	-845	-18.74	-54.57	41.02	65.66	4,511
By regional distribution 地區分布									
Central-North 華北	224	110	2,575	-337	-4.44	-13.92	23.51	68.08	7,579
Beijing 北京	70	41	1,702	-403	-9.15	-23.17	41.86	60.52	4,408
Tianjin 天津	30	140	5,217	196	3.19	9.84	37.16	67.59	6,134
Hebei 河北	41	177	4,203	-126	-0.84	-3.31	23.68	74.53	14,972
Shanxi 山西	32	275	2,957	-1,548	-8.76	-25.40	10.77	65.52	17,676
Inner Mongolia 內蒙	51	28	669	32	6.43	18.24	24.14	64.77	500
Northeast 東北	282	93	2,806	-131	-2.58	-6.76	30.10	61.82	5,061
Liaoning 遼寧	224	84	2,593	36	0.88	2.37	30.78	62.94	4,109
Jilin 吉林	44	144	4,488	-1,045	-9.31	-23.02	31.14	59.53	11,219
Heilongjiang 黑龍江	14	77	926	79	8.38	26.76	12.09	68.67	937
Central East 華東	391	99	4,718	125	1.67	4.37	47.87	61.69	7,458
Shanghai 上海	39	95	5,457	101	1.05	2.22	57.22	52.56	9,548
Jiangsu 江蘇	85	141	7,668	315	2.67	7.33	54.42	63.60	11,803
Zhejiang 浙江	112	69	3,606	112	2.34	6.45	52.48	63.67	4,787
Anhui 安徽	25	154	5,368	60	0.64	2.12	34.87	70.06	9,380
Fujian 福建	47	69	3,532	60	1.07	2.34	51.24	54.17	5,623
Jiangxi 江西	35	114	2,350	-119	-1.64	-3.78	20.69	56.56	7,261
Shandong 山東	48	85	4,035	112	2.14	6.84	47.53	68.70	5,238
Central-South 中南	257	121	5,899	5	0.04	0.10	48.71	59.95	13,101
Henan 河南	76	174	5,089	-277	-2.01	-4.71	29.22	57.43	13,815
Hubei 湖北	35	91	4,801	176	6.59	29.77	52.75	77.87	2,672
Hunan 湖南	50	92	1,679	-231	-5.42	-29.81	18.20	81.82	4,263
Guangdong 廣東	68	108	12,156	422	1.54	3.62	112.71	57.44	27,361
Guangxi 廣西	27	85	1,733	20	0.51	1.42	20.33	64.08	3,982
Hainan 海南	1	451	3,750	-1,490	-3.51	-12.82	8.31	72.61	42,460
Southwest 西南	111	81	2,333	-122	-2.33	-7.30	28.64	68.08	5,235
Chongqing 重慶	20	61	2,460	-73	-2.03	-8.24	40.36	75.34	3,579
Sichuan 四川	63	86	2,628	-74	-1.53	-4.43	30.56	65.45	4,863
Guizhou 貴州	19	105	1,903	-401	-4.26	-13.40	18.19	68.23	9,422
Yunnan 雲南	9	47	882	22	0.83	3.99	18.73	79.12	2,666
Tibet 西藏									
Northwest 西北	78	135	2,651	-356	-4.71	-20.05	19.57	76.50	7,547
Shaanxi 陝西	58	89	1,871	-139	-2.79	-11.48	21.04	75.67	4,992
Gansu 甘肅	7	67	2,730	59	2.93	47.13	40.75	93.78	1,999
Qinghai 青海	4	190	1,873	-820	-6.83	-31.09	9.84	78.02	11,998
Ningxia 寧夏	2	750	4,315	-4,900	-11.73	-26.53	5.76	55.79	41,775
Xinjiang 新疆	7	383	9,003	-996	-4.54	-35.73	23.53	87.30	21,941

3590: Other General Machinery 其他普通機械製造業

Year 年份	Number of firms 企業個數	Rate of change 每年變化 (%)	Number of employees 職工人數 (人)	Rate of change 每年變化 (%)	Total revenue (mil. RMB) 總銷售收入 (百萬元)	Rate of change 每年變化 (%)	Total profit (mil. RMB) 總利潤 (百萬元)	Rate of change 每年變化 (%)
1993	818		183,054		5,027		42	
1994	1,032	26.16%	177,008	-3.30%	4,994	-0.65%	25	-41.40%
1995	1,120	8.53%	125,441	-29.13%	3,704	-25.84%	3	-86.82%
1996	1,343	19.91%	140,073	11.66%	5,194	40.23%	-103	-3239.29%

3 Major products* 3 種主要產品 *	Output 產量	Sales volume 銷售量	Unit 單位
a) Handling Machinery 裝卸機械	9,093	8,275	set 台
b) Preventing Equipment for Air Pollution 大氣污染防治設備	8,611	8,353	ton 噸
c) Plant & Mining Accessories 工礦配件	45,465	39,100	ton 噸

Top 10 firms by revenue (year founded) 收入排名前 10 家企業 (創辦年份)	City 城市	Province 省	Telephone / fax 電話 / 傳真	Number of employees 職工人數	Ownership 產業所有權	Revenue ('000 RMB) 銷售收入 (千元)	Profit ('000 RMB) (rank) 利潤 (千元) (排名)	Total assets ('000 RMB) 總資產 (千元)	Major products 主要產品
Main Power Electrical Products (Shen Zhen) Co. Ltd. 主力電器製品(深圳)有限公司(1991)	Shenzhen 深圳市	Guangdong 廣東省	(0755)8874916 (0755)8874922	1,100	Overseas Chinese-funded 港澳台資	345,760	16996(2)	75,263	o
Zhongshan Nanhai Dong Bu Petroleum Drilling & Extracting Engineering Service Co. Ltd. 中山南海東部石油鑽採工程服務有限公司(1996)	Zhongshan 中山市	Guangdong 廣東省	(0760)5596818 (0760)5596877	50	Collectively-owned 集體	161,330	14900(3)	161,640	o
Wuxi Zhong Ce Impact Damper Co. Ltd. 無錫中策減震器有限公司(1960)	Wuxi 無錫市	Jiangsu 江蘇省	(0510)5016071 (0510)5017584	789	Overseas Chinese-funded 港澳台資	122,983	37029(1)	175,378	o
Tianjin Jinghai Yu Cai Machine Member Processing Factory 天津市靜海縣育才機件加工廠(1985)	Tianjin 天津市	Tianjin 天津市	(022)8944987	6	Collectively-owned 集體	88,280	4230(5)	50,436	o
Fujian Longyan Engineering Machinery Factory 福建省龍岩工程機械廠(1993)	Longyan 龍巖市	Fujian 福建省	(0597)2522188 (0597)2520988	256	Collectively-owned 集體	81,495	1546(17)	68,310	o
Yu He Motorcycle (Group) Company 玉河摩托車(集團)公司(1952)	Nanjing 南京市	Jiangsu 江蘇省	(025)4485055 (025)4498218	1,595	State-owned 國有	77,801	629(60)	238,018	o
Capital Iron & Steel Coporation Bei Fang Machinery Plant 首鋼北方機械廠(1974)	Chaoyang 朝陽市	Liaoning 遼寧省	(0421)2917701 (0421)2917235	1,695	State-owned 國有	77,046	962(39)	132,023	o
Changchun Generate Electricity Equipment General Factory 長春發電設備總廠(1952)	Changchun 長春市	Jilin 吉林省	(0431)4942951 (0431)4643628	1,412	State-owned 國有	68,009	-37302(394)	203,849	a,b,c
Zhejiang Fei Niu Motor Vehicle Machine Manufacturing Company 浙江飛牛機動車機械製造公司(1993)	Hangzhou 杭州市	Zhejiang 浙江省	(0571)2431767	298	Collectively-owned 集體	64,370	1540(18)	20,770	o
Guang Zhong Enterprise Group Co. 廣重企業集團公司(1948)	Guangzhou 廣州市	Guangdong 廣東省	(020)84369817 (020)84366767	1,536	State-owned 國有	53,014	6252(4)	977,154	c

Top 10 Cities by Production Output 產出排名前 10 位城市	Province 省	Market share 市場份額	Number of firms 企業個數
Shanghai 上海市	Shanghai 上海市	7.40%	111
Beijing 北京市	Beijing 北京市	4.40%	63
Wuxi 無錫市	Jiangsu 江蘇省	4.34%	64
Nanjing 南京市	Jiangsu 江蘇省	3.95%	29
Zhongshan 中山市	Guangdong 廣東省	3.88%	4
Jiaozuo 焦作市	Henan 河南省	3.43%	4
Changzhou 常州市	Jiangsu 江蘇省	3.05%	35
Jilin 吉林市	Jilin 吉林省	2.62%	29
Hangzhou 杭州市	Zhejiang 浙江省	2.56%	29
Guangzhou 廣州市	Guangdong 廣東省	2.43%	31

10 Major Wholesalers 10 家主要批發商	City 城市	Province 省	Telephone / Fax 電話 / 傳真
Liaoning Automobile Trade Group Corp. 遼寧省汽車貿易集團	Shenyang 瀋陽市	Liaoning 遼寧省	(024)23835494 (024)23838338
China Post and Telecommunication Equipment General Company 中國郵電器材總公司	Beijing 北京市	Beijing 北京市	(010)63523715 (010)63525935
Jiangsu Electromechanical Products General Company 江蘇省機電產品總公司	Nanjing 南京市	Jiangsu 江蘇省	(025)7713642 (025)7711036
Xi Nan Technology Import & Export Company 西南技術進出口公司	Chongqing 重慶市	Chongqing 重慶市	(023)63850185 (023)63850026
Changzhou Economic Technology Industrial Development Zone Tian Ming Trade Company 常州經濟技術產業開發區天明貿易公司	Changzhou 常州市	Jiangsu 江蘇省	(0519)8829882 (0519)8829882
Shanxi Mechanical Equipment Import & Export Company 山西省機械設備進出口公司	Taiyuan 太原市	Shanxi 山西省	(0351)4040713 (0351)4043981
Ningbo Five Mining Machinery Import & Export Company 寧波市五礦機械進出口公司	Ningbo 寧波市	Zhejiang 浙江省	(0574)7311255 (0574)7320322
Tianjin Jin Huan Electromechanical Complete Sets of Equipment Factory 天津市津環機電成套設備廠	Tianjin 天津市	Tianjin 天津市	(022)26371628
Yunnan Machinery Import & Export Company 雲南省機械進出口公司	Kunming 昆明市	Yunnan 雲南省	(0871)3164879 (0871)3136829
Tianjin Da Qiu Zhuang Yi Yuan Trade Center 天津市大丘莊億源商貿中心	Tianjin 天津市	Tianjin 天津市	(022)28899478 (022)28899046

*Also include sales by firms outside this industry.包括本行業以外廠家的銷售。"o" stands for "others". "o" 代表"其他產品"。

3611: Mining Equipment 礦山設備製造業

The industry accounts for 0.192% of the total revenue of China's industrial sector in 1996. The revenue growth rate of the industry is -0.7% from 1995, as compared to the growth rate of China's industrial sector, 9.51%. The rate of return on asset is -1.82%. 66.50% of all firms in the industry made a profit while 27.38% had negative returns. The top province in terms of the industry's revenue is Henan, accounting for 12.34% of the total revenue.
本行業在1996年佔全行業總產值0.192%，行業年增長率為-0.7%（全國工業年增長率9.51%）。行業的資產回報率-1.82%，66.50%的企業盈利，27.38%的企業虧損。銷售收入最高的省份為河南省，佔本行業的12.34%。

	Total number of firms 企業總數	Total number of employees 職工總數	Total revenue (mil. RMB) 總銷售收入（百萬元）	Total profit (mil. RMB) 總利潤（百萬元）	Return on assets 資產利潤率 (%)	Return on equity 權益利潤率 (%)	Labour productivity ('000 RMB / worker) 勞動生產率（千元/人）	Debts / assets 資產負債率 (%)	Total assets (mil. RMB) 總資產（百萬元）
Industry Overall 行業總體	1,009	371,833	11,114	-502	-1.82	-6.13	29.89	70.26	27,520

	Number of firms 企業個數	Average number of employees 平均職工人數	Average revenue ('000 RMB) 平均銷售收入（千元）	Average profit ('000 RMB) 平均利潤（千元）	Return on assets 資產利潤率 (%)	Return on equity 權益利潤率 (%)	Labour productivity ('000 RMB / worker) 勞動生產率（千元/人）	Average debts / assets 平均資產負債率(%)	Average Total assets ('000 RMB) 平均總資產（千元）
By ownership 產業所有權									
State-owned 國有	274	1,062	27,146	-2,197	-2.68	-9.01	25.56	70.20	81,850
Collectively-owned 集體	696	97	3,874	98	1.90	6.97	40.13	72.67	5,139
Privately-owned 私有	7	36	841	6	0.52	4.63	23.18	88.83	1,105
Domestic JVs 聯營	4	154	5,133	505	11.44	19.12	33.28	40.19	4,421
Joint stock 股份制	9	1,008	32,640	526	0.63	2.12	32.39	70.26	83,339
Foreign-funded 外資	14	263	49,499	1,785	3.41	8.91	188.36	61.68	52,287
Overseas Chinese-funded 港澳台資	4	15	1,091	26	1.12	1.35	73.96	17.18	2,306
By size 規模									
Large 大型	36	4,548	160,320	-4,656	-1.03	-3.29	35.25	68.67	451,845
Medium 中型	76	1,202	30,005	-5,236	-7.22	-30.04	24.96	75.97	72,534
Small 小型	893	131	3,613	71	1.11	3.60	27.66	69.30	6,429
By regional distribution 地區分布									
Central-North 華北	140	441	15,427	-203	-0.48	-1.50	35.02	67.84	42,066
Beijing 北京	13	326	18,257	25	0.07	0.21	56.03	66.72	35,940
Tianjin 天津	7	247	7,413	-1,036	-6.53	-45.34	30.01	85.60	15,866
Hebei 河北	47	351	16,735	473	1.52	6.44	47.70	76.35	31,054
Shanxi 山西	63	574	16,725	-641	-1.07	-2.97	29.15	63.94	59,720
Inner Mongolia 內蒙	10	307	3,034	-333	-3.74	-16.25	9.90	76.98	8,901
Northeast 東北	239	285	8,767	-478	-1.56	-4.77	30.76	67.22	30,624
Liaoning 遼寧	172	250	7,928	-43	-0.14	-0.38	31.72	62.01	29,825
Jilin 吉林	39	405	12,493	-2,145	-6.43	-59.23	30.81	89.14	33,358
Heilongjiang 黑龍江	28	333	8,731	-832	-2.62	-7.55	26.24	65.26	31,722
Central East 華東	283	405	11,783	-78	-0.44	-1.67	29.10	73.70	17,867
Shanghai 上海	15	332	50,150	32	0.06	0.29	150.87	79.16	52,197
Jiangsu 江蘇	77	213	8,722	-174	-1.28	-5.35	40.99	76.10	13,584
Zhejiang 浙江	49	127	7,109	126	1.12	3.20	56.09	65.11	11,239
Anhui 安徽	23	460	15,437	-804	-2.80	-18.85	33.55	85.14	28,718
Fujian 福建	12	139	3,911	42	0.44	0.88	28.17	50.32	9,497
Jiangxi 江西	51	1,114	3,486	-286	-2.87	-10.48	3.13	72.66	9,967
Shandong 山東	56	321	17,549	306	1.23	3.99	54.73	69.11	24,889
Central-South 中南	235	347	9,898	-1,034	-4.24	-15.96	28.54	73.40	24,368
Henan 河南	117	423	11,719	-1,423	-4.71	-18.55	27.68	74.62	30,229
Hubei 湖北	29	259	7,563	-253	-1.50	-5.27	29.25	71.54	16,884
Hunan 湖南	43	342	8,353	-1,272	-6.34	-33.25	24.46	80.93	20,054
Guangdong 廣東	17	159	5,952	-116	-1.05	-2.81	37.52	62.74	11,119
Guangxi 廣西	29	244	9,487	-434	-1.94	-5.00	38.82	61.25	22,373
Hainan 海南									
Southwest 西南	66	352	8,318	-647	-2.51	-7.95	23.61	68.45	25,767
Chongqing 重慶	9	271	2,479	-2,316	-16.46	-103.67	9.15	84.12	14,071
Sichuan 四川	43	194	5,602	-271	-2.40	-20.38	28.86	88.22	11,299
Guizhou 貴州	3	387	7,567	-760	-2.27	-5.04	19.54	54.98	33,520
Yunnan 雲南	11	1,026	24,019	-645	-0.72	-1.72	23.41	58.07	89,684
Tibet 西藏									
Northwest 西北	46	493	14,114	-1,116	-2.81	-10.24	28.61	72.59	39,757
Shaanxi 陝西	33	167	3,312	-121	-0.95	-3.49	19.89	72.74	12,701
Gansu 甘肅	6	1,225	22,453	-4,112	-5.23	-15.54	18.32	66.34	78,620
Qinghai 青海	2	529	4,260	-2,980	-7.65	1568.42	8.05	100.49	38,930
Ningxia 寧夏	3	2,736	129,643	-3,840	-1.46	-6.30	47.39	76.89	263,890
Xinjiang 新疆	2	292	3,885	-2,595	-7.59	-11.37	13.30	33.29	34,210

3611: Mining Equipment 礦山設備製造業

Year 年份	Number of firms 企業個數	Rate of change 每年變化 (%)	Number of employees 職工人數（人）	Rate of change 每年變化 (%)	Total revenue (mil. RMB) 總銷售收入（百萬元）	Rate of change 每年變化 (%)	Total profit (mil. RMB) 總利潤（百萬元）	Rate of change 每年變化 (%)
1993	788		332,018		12,179		74	
1994	857	8.76%	329,138	-0.87%	10,327	-15.21%	-103	-238.50%
1995	979	14.24%	345,804	5.06%	11,195	8.41%	-185	-80.22%
1996	1,009	3.06%	371,833	7.53%	11,114	-0.72%	-502	-171.10%

3 Major products* 3 種主要產品 *	Output 產量	Sales volume 銷售量	Unit 單位
a) Wash-dressing Equipmen 洗選設備	25,597	19,966	ton 噸
b) Mining & Opening Equipment 採掘設備	63,816	54,882	ton 噸
c) Heavy Mining Mechanical Accessories 重型礦山機械配件	92,997	66,028	ton 噸

Top 10 firms by revenue (year founded) 收入排名前 10 家企業（創辦年份）	City 城市	Province 省	Telephone / fax 電話 / 傳真	Number of employees 職工人數	Ownership 產業所有權	Revenue ('000 RMB) 銷售收入（千元）	Profit ('000 RMB) (rank) 利潤（千元）（排名）	Total assets ('000 RMB) 總資產（千元）	Major products 主要產品
Taiyuan Heavy-duty Machinery (Group) Co. Ltd. 太原重型機械集團公司(1953)	Taiyuan 太原市	Shanxi 山西省	(0351)6066921 (0351)6045527	13,272	State-owned 國有	532,330	-27681(489)	1,686,747	b,c
Shenyang Mining Machinery (Group) Co. Ltd. 瀋陽礦山機械(集團)有限責任公司(1952)	Shenyang 瀋陽市	Liaoning 遼寧省	(024)24315835 (024)24310929	7,510	State-owned 國有	455,605	8508(2)	1,160,551	a,c
Shanghai Jianshe-luqiao Machinery Co. Ltd. 上海建設路橋機械設備有限公司(1946)	Shanghai 上海市	Shanghai 上海市	(021)63772661 (021)63771243	766	Overseas Chinese-funded 港澳台資	387,239	11010(1)	277,138	a,c
Shenyang Heavy Machinery Group Co. Ltd. 瀋陽重型機械(集團)有限責任公司(1937)	Shenyang 瀋陽市	Liaoning 遼寧省	(024)25876935 (024)25851610	10,410	State-owned 國有	371,649	51(223)	2,495,464	c
Xibei Coal Mine Machinery General Factory 西北煤礦機械總廠(1970)	Shizuishan 石嘴山市	Ningxia 寧夏	(0952)2173555	7,252	State-owned 國有	351,520	-7070(473)	727,730	c
Zhangjiakou Coal Mine Machinery Plant 張家口煤礦機械廠(1949)	Zhangjiakou 張家口市	Hebei 河北省	(0313)2013291 (0313)2017708	6,418	State-owned 國有	348,070	5250(12)	741,150	o
Beijing Coal Mining Machinery Factory 北京煤礦機械廠(1961)	Beijing 北京市	Beijing 北京市	(010)69313201 (010)69311624	3,655	State-owned 國有	210,620	380(98)	410,200	a,b,c
Ji'nan Heavy-duty Machinery Group Company 濟南重機集團公司(1949)	Ji'nan 濟南市	Shandong 山東省	(0531)8991691 (0531)8991675	3,731	State-owned 國有	150,615	253(131)	294,776	c
Taiyuan Mine Machine Plant 太原礦山機器廠(1925)	Taiyuan 太原市	Shanxi 山西省	(0351)3041515 (0351)3030173	7,804	State-owned 國有	148,649	137(177)	795,249	b,c
Huainan Coal Mine Machinery Factory 淮南煤礦機械廠(1951)	Huainan 淮南市	Anhui 安徽省	(0554)5677631 (0554)5677383	6,001	State-owned 國有	142,980	-19870(486)	427,080	b,c

Top 10 Cities by Production Output 產出排名前 10 位城市	Province 省	Market share 市場份額	Number of firms 企業個數
Shenyang 瀋陽市	Liaoning 遼寧省	9.24%	94
Taiyuan 太原市	Shanxi 山西省	7.60%	16
Luoyang 洛陽市	Henan 河南省	6.14%	16
Zhangjiakou 張家口市	Hebei 河北省	4.16%	9
Ji'nan 濟南市	Shandong 山東省	3.21%	6
Shanghai 上海市	Shanghai 上海市	2.91%	22
Jiaozuo 焦作市	Henan 河南省	2.78%	17
Zhengzhou 鄭州市	Henan 河南省	2.75%	21
Beijing 北京市	Beijing 北京市	2.22%	13
Shizuishan 石嘴山市	Ningxia 寧夏	2.15%	3

10 Major Wholesalers 10 家主要批發商	City 城市	Province 省	Telephone / Fax 電話 / 傳真
Liaoning Automobile Trade Group Corp. 遼寧省汽車貿易集團	Shenyang 瀋陽市	Liaoning 遼寧省	(024)23835494 (024)23838338
China Post and Telecommunication Equipment General Company 中國郵電器材總公司	Beijing 北京市	Beijing 北京市	(010)63523715 (010)63525935
Jiangsu Electromechanical Products General Company 江蘇省機電產品總公司	Nanjing 南京市	Jiangsu 江蘇省	(025)7713642 (025)7711036
Xi Nan Technology Import & Export Company 西南技術進出口公司	Chongqing 重慶市	Chongqing 重慶市	(023)63850185 (023)63850026
Changzhou Economic Technology Industrial Development Zone Tian Ming Trade Company 常州經濟技術產業開發區天明貿易公司	Changzhou 常州市	Jiangsu 江蘇省	(0519)8829882 (0519)8829882
Shanxi Mechanical Equipment Import & Export Company 山西省機械設備進出口公司	Taiyuan 太原市	Shanxi 山西省	(0351)4040713 (0351)4043981
Ningbo Five Mining Machinery Import & Export Company 寧波市五礦機械進出口公司	Ningbo 寧波市	Zhejiang 浙江省	(0574)7311255 (0574)7320322
Tianjin Jin Huan Electromechanical Complete Sets of Equipment Factory 天津市津環機電成套設備廠	Tianjin 天津市	Tianjin 天津市	(022)26371628
Yunnan Machinery Import & Export Company 雲南省機械進出口公司	Kunming 昆明市	Yunnan 雲南省	(0871)3164879 (0871)3136829
Tianjin Da Qiu Zhuang Yi Yuan Trade Center 天津市大丘莊億源商貿中心	Tianjin 天津市	Tianjin 天津市	(022)28899478 (022)28899046

*Also include sales by firms outside this industry.包括本行業以外廠家的銷售。“o” stands for “others”. “o” 代表 “其他產品”。

3613: Metallurgy Equipment 冶金工業專用設備製造業

The industry accounts for 0.128% of the total revenue of China's industrial sector in 1996. The revenue growth rate of the industry is -4.9% from 1995, as compared to the growth rate of China's industrial sector, 9.51%. The rate of return on asset is -1.27%. 62.36% of all firms in the industry made a profit while 34.23% had negative returns. The top province in terms of the industry's revenue is Sichuan, accounting for 13.42% of the total revenue.
本行業在1996年佔全行業總產值0.128%，行業年增長率為-4.9%（全國工業年增長率9.51%）。行業的資產回報率-1.27%，62.36%的企業盈利，34.23%的企業虧損。銷售收入最高的省份為四川省，佔本行業的13.42%。

	Total number of firms 企業總數	Total number of employees 職工總數	Total revenue (mil. RMB) 總銷售收入（百萬元）	Total profit (mil. RMB) 總利潤（百萬元）	Return on assets 資產利潤率 (%)	Return on equity 權益利潤率 (%)	Labour productivity ('000 RMB / worker) 勞動生產率（千元/人）	Debts / assets 資產負債率 (%)	Total assets (mil. RMB) 總資產（百萬元）
Industry Overall 行業總體	294	179,477	7,407	-231	-1.27	-4.56	41.27	72.12	18,179

	Number of firms 企業個數	Average number of employees 平均職工人數	Average revenue ('000 RMB) 平均銷售收入（千元）	Average profit ('000 RMB) 平均利潤（千元）	Return on assets 資產利潤率 (%)	Return on equity 權益利潤率 (%)	Labour productivity ('000 RMB / worker) 勞動生產率（千元/人）	Average debts / assets 平均資產負債率(%)	Average Total assets ('000 RMB) 平均總資產（千元）
By ownership 產業所有權									
State-owned 國有	73	2,054	80,644	-3,493	-1.56	-5.63	39.25	72.36	224,521
Collectively-owned 集體	196	132	6,694	95	1.34	4.90	50.86	72.63	7,056
Privately-owned 私有	1	31	4,364	11	0.14	-8.26	140.79	101.66	7,824
Domestic JVs 聯營	6	66	1,743	-33	-0.94	-1.75	26.61	46.57	3,553
Joint stock 股份制	6	316	15,244	447	1.39	2.63	48.27	47.20	32,151
Foreign-funded 外資	8	119	9,910	355	1.95	8.25	83.45	76.40	18,232
Overseas Chinese-funded 港澳台資	3	116	7,679	52	0.41	1.39	66.20	70.70	12,672
By size 規模									
Large 大型	22	5,604	240,743	-18,293	-2.88	-10.89	42.96	73.55	635,206
Medium 中型	21	1,201	34,900	-6,921	-7.17	-22.05	29.05	67.50	96,552
Small 小型	245	124	5,627	1,293	14.55	44.47	45.32	67.28	8,886
By regional distribution 地區分布									
Central-North 華北	65	502	14,973	-249	-0.53	-2.04	29.82	74.00	46,810
Beijing 北京	15	121	2,426	-27	-0.28	-1.04	20.09	73.19	9,520
Tianjin 天津	15	648	12,393	-2,103	-3.27	-15.76	19.12	79.27	64,373
Hebei 河北	25	776	27,756	586	0.79	2.75	35.79	71.43	74,529
Shanxi 山西	6	205	6,503	110	1.33	4.58	31.78	70.88	8,248
Inner Mongolia 內蒙	4	123	4,510	110	2.04	7.32	36.82	72.06	5,388
Northeast 東北	61	634	28,030	-787	-0.95	-3.20	44.22	70.20	82,512
Liaoning 遼寧	53	376	14,870	-935	-2.05	-7.13	39.53	71.28	45,638
Jilin 吉林	4	162	2,523	-105	-1.03	-15.11	15.55	93.19	10,213
Heilongjiang 黑龍江	4	4,521	227,908	490	0.08	0.24	50.42	68.82	643,393
Central East 華東	84	533	26,169	-858	-1.58	-6.22	49.14	74.54	54,222
Shanghai 上海	18	895	42,274	-2,688	-2.53	-29.36	47.24	91.38	106,231
Jiangsu 江蘇	38	423	25,558	-88	-0.22	-0.57	60.38	61.75	40,791
Zhejiang 浙江	13	462	16,755	-1,341	-3.17	-8.30	36.28	61.85	42,328
Anhui 安徽	4	244	5,503	53	0.84	2.29	22.55	63.43	6,283
Fujian 福建	1	206	21,980	160	0.80	6.58	106.70	87.87	20,040
Jiangxi 江西	1	82	4,820	-490	-8.97	37.69	58.78	123.81	5,460
Shandong 山東	9	586	22,153	-310	-0.57	-1.54	37.79	63.06	54,617
Central-South 中南	60	359	17,456	-325	-1.11	-2.75	48.65	59.58	29,220
Henan 河南	34	109	9,711	368	4.51	15.57	88.90	71.06	8,160
Hubei 湖北	14	451	28,025	639	1.55	3.65	62.16	57.59	41,279
Hunan 湖南	9	1,246	34,676	-4,590	-4.66	-11.11	27.83	58.02	98,437
Guangdong 廣東	2	119	6,355	195	3.28	3.44	53.40	4.71	5,950
Guangxi 廣西	1	50							
Hainan 海南									
Southwest 西南	12	1,983	87,028	208	0.10	0.36	43.89	72.83	212,864
Chongqing 重慶	4	96	1,512	-5	-0.07	-0.17	15.75	58.80	7,442
Sichuan 四川	6	3,738	165,720	-384	-0.10	-0.35	44.34	73.02	403,874
Guizhou 貴州	1	73	2,910	80	3.56	6.02	39.86	40.89	2,250
Yunnan 雲南	1	8							
Tibet 西藏									
Northwest 西北	12	1,509	36,202	-6,475	-6.26	-36.03	23.99	82.63	103,423
Shaanxi 陝西	10	1,799	42,036	-7,806	-6.33	-37.21	23.37	83.00	123,407
Gansu 甘肅	2	62	7,030	180	5.14	6.13	114.31	16.29	3,500
Qinghai 青海									
Ningxia 寧夏									
Xinjiang 新疆									

3613: Metallurgy Equipment 冶金工業專用設備製造業

Year 年份	Number of firms 企業個數	Rate of change 每年變化 (%)	Number of employees 職工人數（人）	Rate of change 每年變化 (%)	Total revenue (mil. RMB) 總銷售收入（百萬元）	Rate of change 每年變化 (%)	Total profit (mil. RMB) 總利潤（百萬元）	Rate of change 每年變化 (%)
1993	214		240,628		7,532		174	
1994	248	15.89%	189,996	-21.04%	8,009	6.33%	83	-52.08%
1995	292	17.74%	191,690	0.89%	7,789	-2.74%	-57	-168.39%
1996	294	0.68%	179,477	-6.37%	7,407	-4.90%	-231	-305.06%

3 Major products* 3 種主要產品 *	Output 產量	Sales volume 銷售量	Unit 單位
a) Smelting Equipment 冶煉設備	52,951	50,303	ton 噸
b) Metal Rolling Equipment 金屬軋製設備	70,308	68,199	ton 噸
c) Special Roller for Metallurgy 冶金專用軋輥	43,799	39,419	ton 噸

Top 10 firms by revenue (year founded) 收入排名前 10 家企業 (創辦年份)	City 城市	Province 省	Telephone / fax 電話 / 傳真	Number of employees 職工人數	Ownership 產業所有權	Revenue ('000 RMB) 銷售收入（千元）	Profit ('000 RMB) (rank) 利潤（千元）（排名）	Total assets ('000 RMB) 總資產（千元）	Major products 主要產品
China No.1 Heavy-duty Machinery Group Co. 中國第一重型機械集團公司(1958)	Qiqiha'er 齊齊哈爾市	Heilongjiang 黑龍江省	(0452)6882901 (0452)2425285	18,214	State-owned 國有	902,114	1532(19)	2,571,481	a,b
China No.2 Heavy-duty Machinery Group Co. 中國第二重型機械集團公司(1965)	Deyang 德陽市	Sichuan 四川省	(0838)2203119 (0838)2203292	19,135	State-owned 國有	812,079	1112(25)	2,117,627	b,c
Da Zhong Group Company 大重集團公司(1914)	Dalian 大連市	Liaoning 遼寧省	(0411)4604201 (0411)4604760	7,688	State-owned 國有	512,995	3616(8)	1,288,663	a,b
Xingtai Machinery & Mill Roller (Group) Corp. 邢台機械軋輥(集團)有限公司(1959)	Xingtai 邢臺市	Hebei 河北省	(0319)2023911 (0319)2022061	8,714	State-owned 國有	459,095	4183(5)	1,253,019	a,b
Shanghai Heavy Machinery Plant 上海重型機器廠(1934)	Shanghai 上海市	Shanghai 上海市	(021)64301141 (021)64300132	7,008	State-owned 國有	345,490	103(84)	960,915	a,b
Hengyang Nonferrous Metallurgical Machinery General Works 衡陽有色冶金機械總廠(1943)	Hengyang 衡陽市	Hunan 湖南省	(0734)8331011 (0734)8332398	8,206	State-owned 國有	253,267	-29224(173)	729,206	a,b
Bao Gang Group Changzhou Metallurgical Machinery Works 寶鋼集團常州冶金機械廠(1962)	Changzhou 常州市	Jiangsu 江蘇省	(0519)3261027 (0519)3260460	3,877	State-owned 國有	218,313	188(69)	443,624	c
Shanghai Metallurgy Equipment General Factory 上海冶金設備總廠(1929)	Shanghai 上海市	Shanghai 上海市	(021)65433421 (021)65435318	3,851	State-owned 國有	175,400	-34872(175)	485,098	a,b,c
Shannxi Mangle Equipment Factory 陝西省壓延設備廠(1970)	Weinan 渭南市	Shaanxi 陝西省	(0913)6184333 (0913)6181777	4,983	State-owned 國有	161,618	3501(10)	306,955	o
Xi'an Metallurgy Machine Factory 西安冶金機械廠(1958)	Xi'an 西安市	Shaanxi 陝西省	(029)4261154 (029)4261418	4,877	State-owned 國有	146,829	-13964(169)	349,447	o

Top 10 Cities by Production Output 產出排名前 10 位城市	Province 省	Market share 市場份額	Number of firms 企業個數
Beijing 北京市	Beijing 北京市	13.81%	11
Qiqiha'er 齊齊哈爾市	Heilongjiang 黑龍江省	10.59%	3
Deyang 德陽市	Sichuan 四川省	10.52%	4
Shanghai 上海市	Shanghai 上海市	9.67%	28
Dalian 大連市	Liaoning 遼寧省	6.81%	6
Changzhou 常州市	Jiangsu 江蘇省	4.74%	8
Wuxi 無錫市	Jiangsu 江蘇省	3.51%	41
Hengyang 衡陽市	Hunan 湖南省	3.18%	1
Zhengzhou 鄭州市	Henan 河南省	2.97%	12
Tianjin 天津市	Tianjin 天津市	2.54%	17

10 Major Wholesalers 10 家主要批發商	City 城市	Province 省	Telephone / Fax 電話 / 傳真
Liaoning Automobile Trade Group Corp. 遼寧省汽車貿易集團	Shenyang 瀋陽市	Liaoning 遼寧省	(024)23835494 (024)23838338
China Post and Telecommunication Equipment General Company 中國郵電器材總公司	Beijing 北京市	Beijing 北京市	(010)63523715 (010)63525935
Jiangsu Electromechanical Products General Company 江蘇省機電產品總公司	Nanjing 南京市	Jiangsu 江蘇省	(025)7713642 (025)7711036
Xi Nan Technology Import & Export Company 西南技術進出口公司	Chongqing 重慶市	Chongqing 重慶市	(023)63850185 (023)63850026
Changzhou Economic Technology Industrial Development Zone Tian Ming Trade Company 常州經濟技術產業開發區天明貿易公司	Changzhou 常州市	Jiangsu 江蘇省	(0519)8829882 (0519)8829882
Shanxi Mechanical Equipment Import & Export Company 山西省機械設備進出口公司	Taiyuan 太原市	Shanxi 山西省	(0351)4040713 (0351)4043981
Ningbo Five Mining Machinery Import & Export Company 寧波市五礦機械進出口公司	Ningbo 寧波市	Zhejiang 浙江省	(0574)7311255 (0574)7320322
Tianjin Jin Huan Electromechanical Complete Sets of Equipment Factory 天津市津環機電成套設備廠	Tianjin 天津市	Tianjin 天津市	(022)26371628
Yunnan Machinery Import & Export Company 雲南省機械進出口公司	Kunming 昆明市	Yunnan 雲南省	(0871)3164879 (0871)3136829
Tianjin Da Qiu Zhuang Yi Yuan Trade Center 天津市大丘莊億源商貿中心	Tianjin 天津市	Tianjin 天津市	(022)28899478 (022)28899046

*Also include sales by firms outside this industry.包括本行業以外廠家的銷售。"o" stands for "others". "o" 代表 "其他產品" 。

3615: Electrical Engineering Equipment 電工專用設備製造業

The industry accounts for 0.012% of the total revenue of China's industrial sector in 1996. The revenue growth rate of the industry is -0.2% from 1995, as compared to the growth rate of China's industrial sector, 9.51%. The rate of return on asset is 1.01%. 69.57% of all firms in the industry made a profit while 30.43% had negative returns. The top province in terms of the industry's revenue is Sichuan, accounting for 29.65% of the total revenue.
本行業在1996年佔全行業總產值0.012%，行業年增長率為-0.2%（全國工業年增長率9.51%）。行業的資產回報率1.01%，69.57%的企業盈利，30.43%的企業虧損。銷售收入最高的省份為四川省，佔本行業的29.65%。

	Total number of firms 企業總數	Total number of employees 職工總數	Total revenue (mil. RMB) 總銷售收入（百萬元）	Total profit (mil. RMB) 總利潤（百萬元）	Return on assets 資產利潤率 (%)	Return on equity 權益利潤率 (%)	Labour productivity ('000 RMB / worker) 勞動生產率（千元/人）	Debts / assets 資產負債率 (%)	Total assets (mil. RMB) 總資產（百萬元）
Industry Overall 行業總體	95	16,138	671	13	1.01	2.57	41.58	60.67	1,330

	Number of firms 企業個數	Average number of employees 平均職工人數	Average revenue ('000 RMB) 平均銷售收入（千元）	Average profit ('000 RMB) 平均利潤（千元）	Return on assets 資產利潤率 (%)	Return on equity 權益利潤率 (%)	Labour productivity ('000 RMB / worker) 勞動生產率（千元/人）	Average debts / assets 平均資產負債率(%)	Average Total assets ('000 RMB) 平均總資產（千元）
By ownership 產業所有權									
State-owned 國有	20	482	23,650	500	1.10	2.75	49.04	60.15	45,550
Collectively-owned 集體	67	88	2,729	40	0.73	1.84	31.04	60.32	5,523
Privately-owned 私有									
Domestic JVs 聯營									
Joint stock 股份制	1	21						58.67	8,568
Foreign-funded 外資	1	86	508	31	2.07	2.32	5.91	10.85	1,485
Overseas Chinese-funded 港澳台資	6	82	2,428	45	0.67	3.05	29.49	78.00	6,713
By size 規模									
Large 大型	2	4,099	132,981	-1,988	-0.56	-1.38	32.45	59.81	358,179
Medium 中型	2	1,097	54,047	1,362	1.42	4.17	49.29	65.86	95,695
Small 小型	89	64	3,336	160	3.37	8.38	52.03	59.79	4,754
By regional distribution 地區分布									
Central-North 華北	14	23	2,149	34	1.53	11.87	92.55	87.04	2,193
Beijing 北京	4	15	335	-3	-0.37	-0.58	22.33	35.82	670
Tianjin 天津	4	21	53				2.53	51.72	290
Hebei 河北	3	46	9,147	157	1.92	31.33	200.29	93.86	8,143
Shanxi 山西	2	13	545	5	0.60	5.26	43.60	87.95	830
Inner Mongolia 內蒙	1	20						100.00	770
Northeast 東北	15	219	776	-77	-0.80	-1.25	3.55	36.05	9,595
Liaoning 遼寧	10	293	888	67	0.50	0.72	3.03	30.69	13,345
Jilin 吉林	4	87	690	-445	-17.85	556.25	7.91	103.21	2,493
Heilongjiang 黑龍江	1			-40	-8.00	26.67		130.00	500
Central East 華東	41	158	8,897	404	2.92	8.36	56.37	65.01	13,827
Shanghai 上海	11	260	15,345	-35	-0.15	-0.62	59.08	75.21	23,215
Jiangsu 江蘇	11	76	6,436	598	10.17	30.65	85.10	66.83	5,884
Zhejiang 浙江	4	207	5,985	-75	-0.47	-1.50	28.91	68.78	16,000
Anhui 安徽	3	424	25,253	3,170	6.54	11.09	59.56	41.02	48,447
Fujian 福建	1	20	180	-90	-11.84	-81.82	9.00	85.53	760
Jiangxi 江西	4	64	753	30	1.27	9.76	11.85	86.94	2,355
Shandong 山東	7	58	3,184	164	4.21	17.67	54.63	76.15	3,900
Central-South 中南	20	47	1,641	-59	-1.49	-8.06	34.83	81.55	3,968
Henan 河南	9	44	1,638	27	1.16	5.33	37.22	78.31	2,306
Hubei 湖北	1	19	1,230	20	14.29	25.00	64.74	42.86	140
Hunan 湖南	5	80	1,348	-130	-2.64	-10.50	16.81	74.90	4,932
Guangdong 廣東	3	39	2,970	-300	-2.68	-22.44	75.51	88.11	11,213
Guangxi 廣西	2	4	595	55	64.71	-78.57	148.75	176.47	85
Hainan 海南									
Southwest 西南	4	1,261	56,105	93	0.07	0.17	44.50	57.36	125,438
Chongqing 重慶	1	22	819	27	0.74	3.12	37.69	76.13	3,673
Sichuan 四川	2	2,234	99,470	155	0.07	0.16	44.52	57.26	221,776
Guizhou 貴州	1								
Yunnan 雲南									
Tibet 西藏									
Northwest 西北	1	77	7,080	-1,620	-21.74	-771.43	91.95	97.18	7,450
Shaanxi 陝西	1	77	7,080	-1,620	-21.74	-771.43	91.95	97.18	7,450
Gansu 甘肅									
Qinghai 青海									
Ningxia 寧夏									
Xinjiang 新疆									

3615: Electrical Engineering Equipment 電工專用設備製造業

Year 年份	Number of firms 企業個數	Rate of change 每年變化 (%)	Number of employees 職工人數 (人)	Rate of change 每年變化 (%)	Total revenue (mil. RMB) 總銷售收入 (百萬元)	Rate of change 每年變化 (%)	Total profit (mil. RMB) 總利潤 (百萬元)	Rate of change 每年變化 (%)
1993	105		52,279		1,095		27	
1994	106	0.95%	32,234	-38.34%	1,316	20.16%	40	46.26%
1995	80	-24.53%	18,487	-42.65%	672	-48.94%	17	-57.17%
1996	95	18.75%	16,138	-12.71%	671	-0.18%	13	-23.38%

3 Major products* 3 種主要產品 *	Output 產量	Sales volume 銷售量	Unit 單位
a) Special Production Equipment for Wire & Cable 電線電纜製造專用設備	8,278	8,030	ton 噸
b) Special Electrician's Equipmen 電工專用設備	40,078	8,416	set 台
c) Bare Aluminium Wire 裸鋁線	3,341	3,241	ton 噸

Top 10 firms by revenue (year founded) 收入排名前 10 家企業 (創辦年份)	City 城市	Province 省	Telephone / fax 電話 / 傳真	Number of employees 職工人數	Ownership 產業所有權	Revenue ('000 RMB) 銷售收入 (千元)	Profit ('000 RMB) (rank) 利潤 (千元) (排名)	Total assets ('000 RMB) 總資產 (千元)	Major products 主要產品
Dong Gong Group Co. 東工集團公司(1966)	Deyang 德陽市	Sichuan 四川省	(0838)2201919 (0838)2201408	4,459	State-owned 國有	216,856	66(19)	494,237	b,c
Shanghai Electric Engineering Machinery Works 上海電工機械廠(1928)	Shanghai 上海市	Shanghai 上海市	(021)65483106 (021)65490409	1,673	State-owned 國有	109,669	5502(2)	138,237	a,b
Hefei Shen Ma Electric Engineering Co. Ltd. 合肥神馬電工股份有限公司(1958)	Hefei 合肥市	Anhui 安徽省	(0551)5527535 (0551)5523901	475	State-owned 國有	51,296	9459(1)	82,175	a
Hebei Gao City Electric Engineering Component Factory 河北省藁城市電工構件廠(1992)	Shijiazhuang 石家莊市	Hebei 河北省	(0311)8043969 (0311)8445968	120	State-owned 國有	27,150	500(9)	24,116	o
Wuxi Hua Dong Electric Power Equipment Co. Ltd. 無錫市華東電力設備有限公司(1994)	Wuxi 無錫市	Jiangsu 江蘇省	(0510)3201794	120	Collectively-owned 集體	24,675	4046(3)	23,246	o
Wuhu Electrotechnical Machinery Works 蕪湖市電工機械廠(1958)	Wuhu 蕪湖市	Anhui 安徽省	(0553)5862195 (0553)5855346	678	State-owned 國有	21,861	3(26)	61,841	a,b
Jingjiang Converter Equipment Factory 靖江變流設備廠(1981)	Taizhou 泰州市	Jiangsu 江蘇省	(0523)4542332	179	Collectively-owned 集體	20,568	2002(4)	20,650	o
Nokia – Mai La Fei Er Cable Machinery Ltd. 諾基亞－麥拉菲爾電纜機械有限公司(1995)	Shanghai 上海市	Shanghai 上海市	(021)58419988 (021)58411778	43	Foreign-funded 外資	15,050	-4773(36)	44,318	b
Zhejiang University Machinery Factory 浙江大學機械廠(1958)	Hangzhou 杭州市	Zhejiang 浙江省	(0571)7951601 (0571)7951781	286	State-owned 國有	12,632	683(6)	21,216	o
Shanghai Hu Qiao Electric Engineering Machinery Equipment Factory 上海市胡橋電工機械設備廠(1971)	Shanghai 上海市	Shanghai 上海市	(021)57456383 (021)57456383	246	Collectively-owned 集體	12,267	532(8)	22,586	a

Top 10 Cities by Production Output 產出排名前 10 位城市	Province 省	Market share 市場份額	Number of firms 企業個數
Shanghai 上海市	Shanghai 上海市	29.70%	22
Deyang 德陽市	Sichuan 四川省	25.58%	2
Hefei 合肥市	Anhui 安徽省	7.50%	2
Zhenjiang 鎮江市	Jiangsu 江蘇省	5.36%	1
Wuhu 蕪湖市	Anhui 安徽省	3.66%	3
Wuxi 無錫市	Jiangsu 江蘇省	3.07%	5
Taizhou 泰州市	Jiangsu 江蘇省	2.64%	4
Xining 西寧市	Qinghai 青海省	1.88%	1
Jiaxing 嘉興市	Zhejiang 浙江省	1.62%	2
Xi'an 西安市	Shaanxi 陝西省	1.61%	8

10 Major Wholesalers 10 家主要批發商	City 城市	Province 省	Telephone / Fax 電話 / 傳真
Liaoning Automobile Trade Group Corp. 遼寧省汽車貿易集團	Shenyang 瀋陽市	Liaoning 遼寧省	(024)23835494 (024)23838338
China Post and Telecommunication Equipment General Company 中國郵電器材總公司	Beijing 北京市	Beijing 北京市	(010)63523715 (010)63525935
Jiangsu Electromechanical Products General Company 江蘇省機電產品總公司	Nanjing 南京市	Jiangsu 江蘇省	(025)7713642 (025)7711036
Xi Nan Technology Import & Export Company 西南技術進出口公司	Chongqing 重慶市	Chongqing 重慶市	(023)63850185 (023)63850026
Changzhou Economic Technology Industrial Development Zone Tian Ming Trade Company 常州經濟技術產業開發區天明貿易公司	Changzhou 常州市	Jiangsu 江蘇省	(0519)8829882 (0519)8829882
Shanxi Mechanical Equipment Import & Export Company 山西省機械設備進出口公司	Taiyuan 太原市	Shanxi 山西省	(0351)4040713 (0351)4043981
Ningbo Five Mining Machinery Import & Export Company 寧波市五礦機械進出口公司	Ningbo 寧波市	Zhejiang 浙江省	(0574)7311255 (0574)7320322
Tianjin Jin Huan Electromechanical Complete Sets of Equipment Factory 天津市津環機電成套設備廠	Tianjin 天津市	Tianjin 天津市	(022)26371628
Yunnan Machinery Import & Export Company 雲南省機械進出口公司	Kunming 昆明市	Yunnan 雲南省	(0871)3164879 (0871)3136829
Tianjin Da Qiu Zhuang Yi Yuan Trade Center 天津市大丘莊億源商貿中心	Tianjin 天津市	Tianjin 天津市	(022)28899478 (022)28899046

*Also include sales by firms outside this industry.包括本行業以外廠家的銷售。"o" stands for "others". "o" 代表 "其他產品"。

3617: Electronics Equipment 電子工業專用設備製造業

The industry accounts for 0.034% of the total revenue of China's industrial sector in 1996. The revenue growth rate of the industry is 63.2% from 1995, as compared to the growth rate of China's industrial sector, 9.51%. The rate of return on asset is 3.38%. 68.73% of all firms in the industry made a profit while 22.28% had negative returns. The top province in terms of the industry's revenue is Guangdong, accounting for 31.13% of the total revenue.
本行業在1996年佔全行業總產值0.034%，行業年增長率為63.2%（全國工業年增長率9.51%）。行業的資產回報率3.38%，68.73%的企業盈利，22.28%的企業虧損。銷售收入最高的省份為廣東省，佔本行業的31.13%。

	Total number of firms 企業總數	Total number of employees 職工總數	Total revenue (mil. RMB) 總銷售收入（百萬元）	Total profit (mil. RMB) 總利潤（百萬元）	Return on assets 資產利潤率 (%)	Return on equity 權益利潤率 (%)	Labour productivity ('000 RMB / worker) 勞動生產率（千元/人）	Debts / assets 資產負債率 (%)	Total assets (mil. RMB) 總資產（百萬元）
Industry Overall 行業總體	197	38,963	1,957	127	3.38	8.79	50.23	61.54	3,752

	Number of firms 企業個數	Average number of employees 平均職工人數	Average revenue ('000 RMB) 平均銷售收入（千元）	Average profit ('000 RMB) 平均利潤（千元）	Return on assets 資產利潤率 (%)	Return on equity 權益利潤率 (%)	Labour productivity ('000 RMB / worker) 勞動生產率（千元/人）	Average debts / assets 平均資產負債率(%)	Average Total assets ('000 RMB) 平均總資產（千元）
By ownership 產業所有權									
State-owned 國有	53	424	13,151	-151	-0.43	-1.42	30.99	69.61	35,019
Collectively-owned 集體	89	107	7,037	361	5.40	14.44	65.86	62.59	6,681
Privately-owned 私有	2	39	1,987	1,049	26.06	73.82	50.94	64.69	4,026
Domestic JVs 聯營	2	98	3,126	827	11.07	19.03	31.89	41.83	7,465
Joint stock 股份制	4	1,556	49,472	2,278	1.50	4.20	31.79	64.28	151,902
Foreign-funded 外資	19	138	10,421	-410	-2.08	-2.96	75.46	29.76	19,754
Overseas Chinese-funded 港澳台資	27	82	8,430	3,622	33.02	59.40	102.76	44.41	10,970
By size 規模									
Large 大型	5	2,972	87,922	-11,139	-4.79	-11.03	29.59	56.58	232,671
Medium 中型	14	794	37,374	25,250	26.85	126.57	47.06	78.79	94,049
Small 小型	168	79	5,918	-1,016	-13.42	-25.92	74.92	48.23	7,574
By regional distribution 地區分布									
Central-North 華北	49	115	4,744	453	3.43	8.67	41.08	60.46	13,216
Beijing 北京	29	124	5,926	673	3.84	10.55	47.68	63.56	17,502
Tianjin 天津	12	88	2,455	258	5.30	8.90	27.98	40.41	4,855
Hebei 河北	6	102	4,877	-68	-0.83	-1.61	47.97	48.12	8,198
Shanxi 山西	1	392	1,900	10	0.03	0.10	4.85	65.52	30,480
Inner Mongolia 內蒙	1							83.81	2,100
Northeast 東北	22	28	1,006	74	5.82	17.14	35.52	66.08	1,273
Liaoning 遼寧	21	29	1,054	90	7.25	19.04	36.10	61.94	1,249
Jilin 吉林	1	10		-270	-15.08	57.45		126.82	1,790
Heilongjiang 黑龍江									
Central East 華東	66	176	11,686	558	3.27	9.60	66.38	65.97	17,066
Shanghai 上海	12	211	9,156	-233	-1.35	-3.17	43.34	57.22	17,159
Jiangsu 江蘇	22	225	23,432	1,353	4.90	15.26	104.16	67.88	27,604
Zhejiang 浙江	12	45	3,480	507	6.81	21.78	77.33	68.72	7,438
Anhui 安徽	3	57	3,433	193	6.77	21.01	59.88	67.79	2,857
Fujian 福建	6	8	680	-22	-0.93	-3.41	81.60	72.69	2,325
Jiangxi 江西	3	458	16,860	1,350	7.40	31.99	36.79	76.88	18,250
Shandong 山東	8	250	4,900	-94	-0.51	-1.41	19.62	63.83	18,328
Central-South 中南	44	190	16,163	2,408	8.59	15.75	84.96	45.46	28,045
Henan 河南	11	92	1,434	4	0.09	0.51	15.63	82.83	4,129
Hubei 湖北	5	538	14,892	194	0.40	0.96	27.67	58.47	48,494
Hunan 湖南	2	21	85	-85	-24.64	-1700.00	4.05	98.55	345
Guangdong 廣東	21	210	29,010	5,010	11.58	19.66	138.17	41.12	43,278
Guangxi 廣西	5	44	2,310	-20	-0.27	-0.34	52.50	19.90	7,316
Hainan 海南									
Southwest 西南	5	782	17,332	40	0.07	0.34	22.16	80.08	58,680
Chongqing 重慶	1	38	7,207	0	0.14	0.14	192.02		325
Sichuan 四川	4	1,112	23,730	-57	-0.07	-0.34	21.33	80.12	83,782
Guizhou 貴州	1								
Yunnan 雲南									
Tibet 西藏									
Northwest 西北	11	798	12,091	-3,630	-9.46	-63.85	15.15	85.19	38,391
Shaanxi 陝西	10	760	12,319	-3,290	-9.12	-52.96	16.21	82.78	36,071
Gansu 甘肅	1	1,183	9,810	-7,030	-11.41	-1673.81	8.29	99.32	61,590
Qinghai 青海									
Ningxia 寧夏									
Xinjiang 新疆									

3617: Electronics Equipment 電子工業專用設備製造業

Year 年份	Number of firms 企業個數	Rate of change 每年變化 (%)	Number of employees 職工人數 (人)	Rate of change 每年變化 (%)	Total revenue (mil. RMB) 總銷售收入 (百萬元)	Rate of change 每年變化 (%)	Total profit (mil. RMB) 總利潤 (百萬元)	Rate of change 每年變化 (%)
1993	219		59,483		1,387		-8	
1994	216	-1.37%	37,246	-37.38%	1,116	-19.56%	-21	-161.61%
1995	157	-27.32%	35,601	-4.42%	1,199	7.41%	-10	52.32%
1996	197	25.48%	38,963	9.44%	1,957	63.22%	127	1357.80%

3 Major products* 3 種主要產品 *	Output 產量	Sales volume 銷售量	Unit 單位
a) Special Equipment for Semiconductor Parts & Integrated Circuit 半導體器件和集成電路專用設備	3,700	2,264	set 台
b) Special Equipment for Electric Vacuum Parts 電真空器件專用設備	3,486	3,102	set 台
c) Special Equipment for Electronic Component 電子元件專用設備	50,144	172,997	set 台

Top 10 firms by revenue (year founded) 收入排名前 10 家企業 (創辦年份)	City 城市	Province 省	Telephone / fax 電話 / 傳真	Number of employees 職工人數	Ownership 產業所有權	Revenue ('000 RMB) 銷售收入 (千元)	Profit ('000 RMB) (rank) 利潤 (千元) (排名)	Total assets ('000 RMB) 總資產 (千元)	Major products 主要產品
Shenzhen (fei Ya Da)group Co. Ltd. 深圳(飛亞達)集團股份有限公司(1990)	Shenzhen 深圳市	Guangdong 廣東省	(0755)3217888 (0755)3348369	300	Joint stock 股份制	357,062	99698(1)	623,540	o
Suzhou Purification Group Corp. 蘇州蘇淨集團公司(1970)	Suzhou 蘇州市	Jiangsu 江蘇省	(0512)7232660 (0512)5338132	732	State-owned 國有	172,528	15180(2)	285,973	o
Kaiping San Bu Jin Du Electron Factory 開平市三埠金都電子廠(1995)	Jiangmen 江門市	Guangdong 廣東省	(0750)2328768 (0750)2321634	130	Collectively-owned 集體	102,880	35(54)	25,851	o
Jiangsu Ocean Group 江蘇遠洋集團(1988)	Xuzhou 徐州市	Jiangsu 江蘇省	(0516)6710306 (0516)6710306	1,019	Collectively-owned 集體	89,480	13260(4)	63,720	o
Taizhou Radio Special Equipment Factory 泰州市無線電專用設備廠(1956)	Taizhou 泰州市	Jiangsu 江蘇省	(0523)6555908 (0523)6555918	330	Collectively-owned 集體	87,803	1500(12)	73,257	b
Beijing Zhong An Electronics Group 北京中安電子集團(1994)	Beijing 北京市	Beijing 北京市	(010)62646710 (010)62646709	29	State-owned 國有	85,155	13889(3)	228,769	o
Chengdu Nan Guang Industrial Co. Ltd. 成都南光實業股份有限公司(1904)	Chengdu 成都市	Sichuan 四川省	(028)4441912 (028)4441023	3,744	Joint stock 股份制	84,862	166(38)	292,033	a,c
Shanghai Hui Sheng Electron Mechanical Equipment Co. Ltd. 上海匯盛電子機械設備有限公司(1995)	Shanghai 上海市	Shanghai 上海市	(021)59577380 (021)59577451	1,073	State-owned 國有	59,934	429(20)	146,891	a
Guangzhou Hui Qiao Electron Co. Ltd. 廣州匯僑電子有限公司(1991)	Guangzhou 廣州市	Guangdong 廣東省	(020)82237476 (020)82237475	320	Overseas Chinese-funded 港澳台資	57,755	0(70)	110,453	o
State-owned Jian Chang Machine Plant 國營建昌機器廠(1972)	Xiangfan 襄樊市	Hubei 湖北省	(0710)3222760 (0710)3220049	2,426	State-owned 國有	55,320	56(48)	226,240	o

Top 10 Cities by Production Output 產出排名前 10 位城市	Province 省	Market share 市場份額	Number of firms 企業個數
Jining 濟寧市	Shandong 山東省	38.86%	2
Shanghai 上海市	Shanghai 上海市	9.12%	46
Shenzhen 深圳市	Guangdong 廣東省	8.56%	6
Suzhou 蘇州市	Jiangsu 江蘇省	5.68%	10
Beijing 北京市	Beijing 北京市	3.79%	28
Chengdu 成都市	Sichuan 四川省	2.79%	16
Baoji 寶雞市	Shaanxi 陝西省	2.12%	2
Guangzhou 廣州市	Guangdong 廣東省	2.09%	17
Xiangfan 襄樊市	Hubei 湖北省	2.08%	2
Xi'an 西安市	Shaanxi 陝西省	2.05%	10

10 Major Wholesalers 10 家主要批發商	City 城市	Province 省	Telephone / Fax 電話 / 傳真
Liaoning Automobile Trade Group Corp. 遼寧省汽車貿易集團	Shenyang 瀋陽市	Liaoning 遼寧省	(024)23835494 (024)23838338
China Post and Telecommunication Equipment General Company 中國郵電器材總公司	Beijing 北京市	Beijing 北京市	(010)63523715 (010)63525935
Jiangsu Electromechanical Products General Company 江蘇省機電產品總公司	Nanjing 南京市	Jiangsu 江蘇省	(025)7713642 (025)7711036
Xi Nan Technology Import & Export Company 西南技術進出口公司	Chongqing 重慶市	Chongqing 重慶市	(023)63850185 (023)63850026
Changzhou Economic Technology Industrial Development Zone Tian Ming Trade Company 常州經濟技術產業開發區天明貿易公司	Changzhou 常州市	Jiangsu 江蘇省	(0519)8829882 (0519)8829882
Shanxi Mechanical Equipment Import & Export Company 山西省機械設備進出口公司	Taiyuan 太原市	Shanxi 山西省	(0351)4040713 (0351)4043981
Ningbo Five Mining Machinery Import & Export Company 寧波市五礦機械進出口公司	Ningbo 寧波市	Zhejiang 浙江省	(0574)7311255 (0574)7320322
Tianjin Jin Huan Electromechanical Complete Sets of Equipment Factory 天津市津環機電成套設備廠	Tianjin 天津市	Tianjin 天津市	(022)26371628
Yunnan Machinery Import & Export Company 雲南省機械進出口公司	Kunming 昆明市	Yunnan 雲南省	(0871)3164879 (0871)3136829
Tianjin Da Qiu Zhuang Yi Yuan Trade Center 天津市大丘莊億源商貿中心	Tianjin 天津市	Tianjin 天津市	(022)28899478 (022)28899046

*Also include sales by firms outside this industry.包括本行業以外廠家的銷售。"o" stands for "others". "o" 代表"其他產品"。

3619: Other Special Electromechanical Equipment
其他機電工業專用設備製造業

The industry accounts for 0.022% of the total revenue of China's industrial sector in 1996. The revenue growth rate of the industry is -11.2% from 1995, as compared to the growth rate of China's industrial sector, 9.51%. The rate of return on asset is -0.95%. 64.55% of all firms in the industry made a profit while 30.32% had negative returns. The top province in terms of the industry's revenue is Jiangsu, accounting for 25.87% of the total revenue.
本行業在1996年佔全行業總產值0.022%，行業年增長率為-11.2%（全國工業年增長率9.51%）。行業的資產回報率-0.95%，64.55%的企業盈利，30.32%的企業虧損。銷售收入最高的省份為江蘇省，佔本行業的25.87%。

	Total number of firms 企業總數	Total number of employees 職工總數	Total revenue (mil. RMB) 總銷售收入（百萬元）	Total profit (mil. RMB) 總利潤（百萬元）	Return on assets 資產利潤率 (%)	Return on equity 權益利潤率 (%)	Labour productivity ('000 RMB / worker) 勞動生產率（千元/人）	Debts / assets 資產負債率 (%)	Total assets (mil. RMB) 總資產（百萬元）
Industry Overall 行業總體	269	26,666	1,293	-22	-0.95	-3.40	48.49	71.90	2,309

	Number of firms 企業個數	Average number of employees 平均職工人數	Average revenue ('000 RMB) 平均銷售收入（千元）	Average profit ('000 RMB) 平均利潤（千元）	Return on assets 資產利潤率 (%)	Return on equity 權益利潤率 (%)	Labour productivity ('000 RMB / worker) 勞動生產率（千元/人）	Average debts / assets 平均資產負債率(%)	Average Total assets ('000 RMB) 平均總資產（千元）
By ownership 產業所有權									
State-owned 國有	42	258	8,286	-881	-3.86	-15.35	32.16	74.84	22,810
Collectively-owned 集體	188	78	4,484	75	1.32	5.02	57.39	73.63	5,698
Privately-owned 私有	2	37	1,863	-189	-11.82	-27.17	50.35	56.49	1,596
Domestic JVs 聯營									
Joint stock 股份制	3	42	866	-132	-3.12	-19.18	20.62	83.72	4,238
Foreign-funded 外資	18	20	1,642	1	0.01	0.02	83.50	52.56	6,255
Overseas Chinese-funded 港澳台資	14	71	4,683	109	1.01	2.24	66.16	54.80	10,801
By size 規模									
Large 大型	2	2,407	135,845	-7,894	-3.17	-15.08	56.44	78.97	248,981
Medium 中型	10	538	33,699	-352	-0.54	-1.54	62.61	65.20	65,655
Small 小型	251	65	2,728	-11	-0.23	-0.85	41.86	72.65	4,602
By regional distribution 地區分布									
Central-North 華北	82	75	2,197	-71	-1.41	-6.73	29.30	79.06	5,025
Beijing 北京	33	23	1,586	-24	-1.07	-4.26	68.51	74.82	2,202
Tianjin 天津	31	126	3,093	-232	-2.68	-18.59	24.49	85.59	8,649
Hebei 河北	9	106	2,966	250	3.90	9.63	27.89	59.44	6,402
Shanxi 山西	8	60	605	-16	-1.09	-2.44	10.13	55.51	1,498
Inner Mongolia 內蒙	1	34	400	30	1.88	4.69	11.76	59.38	1,600
Northeast 東北	57	47	1,216	-312	-18.77	-170.76	25.89	89.01	1,665
Liaoning 遼寧	52	50	1,295	-343	-19.18	-179.32	25.92	89.31	1,791
Jilin 吉林	5	16	390	10	2.82	10.64	25.00	73.45	354
Heilongjiang 黑龍江									
Central East 華東	79	104	6,886	56	0.57	1.79	66.29	68.49	9,939
Shanghai 上海	15	61	5,947	85	0.58	1.62	97.91	64.37	14,773
Jiangsu 江蘇	34	126	9,837	169	1.44	4.62	78.36	68.76	11,703
Zhejiang 浙江	10	122	7,074	-211	-2.14	-8.09	57.84	73.58	9,875
Anhui 安徽	5	134	2,734	-82	-2.53	-22.65	20.34	88.83	3,240
Fujian 福建	4	31	803	-8	-0.39	-5.88	26.31	93.41	1,935
Jiangxi 江西	2	112	1,745	5	0.20	0.74	15.65	72.82	2,520
Shandong 山東	9	87	3,249	-4	-0.11	-0.28	37.15	62.20	4,216
Central-South 中南	40	160	8,255	-169	-0.98	-3.25	51.60	69.73	17,215
Henan 河南	17	95	5,199	26	0.28	1.13	55.00	75.40	9,566
Hubei 湖北	5	425	13,902	-1,416	-5.91	-49.44	32.70	88.05	23,962
Hunan 湖南	5	262	9,396	2	0.01	0.02	35.86	45.41	18,522
Guangdong 廣東	11	93	10,615	15	0.06	0.17	114.03	64.92	25,928
Guangxi 廣西	2	167	4,285	-160	-1.13	-9.07	25.74	87.54	14,160
Hainan 海南									
Southwest 西南	5	104	9,494	410	3.73	17.05	91.64	78.14	10,986
Chongqing 重慶									
Sichuan 四川	4	130	11,868	513	3.74	17.09	91.29	78.14	13,733
Guizhou 貴州	1								
Yunnan 雲南									
Tibet 西藏									
Northwest 西北	6	453	20,378	313	0.69	2.24	44.99	69.20	45,493
Shaanxi 陝西	5	528	23,376	348	0.65	2.12	44.31	69.22	53,232
Gansu 甘肅	1	80	5,390	140	2.06	6.48	67.38	68.38	6,800
Qinghai 青海									
Ningxia 寧夏									
Xinjiang 新疆									

3619: Other Special Electromechanical Equipment
其他機電工業專用設備製造業

Year 年份	Number of firms 企業個數	Rate of change 每年變化 (%)	Number of employees 職工人數 (人)	Rate of change 每年變化 (%)	Total revenue (mil. RMB) 總銷售收入 (百萬元)	Rate of change 每年變化 (%)	Total profit (mil. RMB) 總利潤 (百萬元)	Rate of change 每年變化 (%)
1993	325		52,228		1,806		57	
1994	325		40,725	-22.03%	2,137	18.30%	50	-12.33%
1995	250	-23.08%	28,515	-29.98%	1,456	-31.87%	37	-26.62%
1996	269	7.60%	26,666	-6.48%	1,293	-11.20%	-22	-159.72%

3 Major products* 3 種主要產品 *	Output 產量	Sales volume 銷售量	Unit 單位
a) Water & Gas Purifier 水、氣淨化設備	12,337	11,967	set 台
b) Feeding Machinery 給料機械	1,163	1,093	set 台
c) Conveying Machinery 輸送機械	7,774	5,442	ton 噸

Top 10 firms by revenue (year founded) 收入排名前 10 家企業 (創辦年份)	City 城市	Province 省	Telephone / fax 電話 / 傳真	Number of employees 職工人數	Ownership 產業所有權	Revenue ('000 RMB) 銷售收入 (千元)	Profit ('000 RMB) (rank) 利潤 (千元) (排名)	Total assets ('000 RMB) 總資產 (千元)	Major products 主要產品
Jiangsu Nan Fang Suspension Conveyer Factory 江蘇南方天奇集團公司(1993)	Wuxi 無錫市	Jiangsu 江蘇省	(0510)3311836	600	Collectively-owned 集體	120,390	3680(1)	129,980	o
Xi'an Nuclear Equipment Manufacturing Plant 西安核設備製造廠(1970)	Xi'an 西安市	Shaanxi 陝西省	(029)6613901 (029)6613950	2,287	State-owned 國有	112,217	2326(3)	255,956	o
Dongguan Jin Bao Enterprise Group Company 東莞市金寶企業集團公司(1970)	Dongguan 東莞市	Guangdong 廣東省	(0769)2237035	506	Collectively-owned 集體	53,767	487(23)	94,803	c
Chengdu Dongfang Electric Power Circuit Component Factory 成都東方電力線路構件廠	Chengdu 成都市	Sichuan 四川省	(028)3516929	391	Collectively-owned 集體	42,970	1979(6)	39,942	o
Nanjing He Da Electromechanical Equipment Co. Ltd. 南京禾達機電設備有限公司(1993)	Nanjing 南京市	Jiangsu 江蘇省	(025)2285300 (025)2285209	180	Overseas Chinese-funded 港澳台資	33,190	2250(4)	9,280	o
Hunan Electric Power Equipment General Factory 湖南省電力設備總廠(1958)	Zhuzhou 株洲市	Hunan 湖南省	(0733)8431557 (0733)8432678	532	State-owned 國有	28,527	41(55)	50,605	o
The Ministry of Railways No.16 Engineering Bureau Directly Subordinate Engineering Dept. 鐵道部第十六工程局直屬工程處(1984)	Beijing 北京市	Beijing 北京市	(010)69943561 (010)69943561	333	State-owned 國有	27,217	1(73)	22,643	o
Shanghai Pu Dong Chemical Equipment Industrial Company 上海浦東化工裝備工業公司(1992)	Shanghai 上海市	Shanghai 上海市	(021)64649176 (021)64680797	48	Domestic JVs 聯營	27,162	0(79)	41,834	o
Lin'an Qian Cai Electroplate Equipment Factory 臨安市淺材電鍍設備廠(1988)	Hangzhou 杭州市	Zhejiang 浙江省	(0571)3728961	50	Collectively-owned 集體	26,746	-329(105)	26,061	o
Henan Anyang No.2 Machine Tool Electric Equipment Factory 河南省安陽市第二機床電器廠(1956)	Anyang 安陽市	Henan 河南省	(0372)5925754 (0372)5917949	1,049	State-owned 國有	26,133	330(26)	66,583	o

Top 10 Cities by Production Output 產出排名前 10 位城市	Province 省	Market share 市場份額	Number of firms 企業個數
Wuxi 無錫市	Jiangsu 江蘇省	16.61%	23
Shanghai 上海市	Shanghai 上海市	16.35%	40
Xi'an 西安市	Shaanxi 陝西省	8.30%	6
Tianjin 天津市	Tianjin 天津市	7.70%	44
Suzhou 蘇州市	Jiangsu 江蘇省	6.20%	14
Dalian 大連市	Liaoning 遼寧省	5.32%	9
Beijing 北京市	Beijing 北京市	3.14%	27
Harbin 哈爾濱市	Heilongjiang 黑龍江省	2.32%	11
Guangzhou 廣州市	Guangdong 廣東省	2.04%	15
Zhuzhou 株洲市	Hunan 湖南省	1.95%	2

10 Major Wholesalers 10 家主要批發商	City 城市	Province 省	Telephone / Fax 電話 / 傳真
Liaoning Automobile Trade Group Corp. 遼寧省汽車貿易集團	Shenyang 瀋陽市	Liaoning 遼寧省	(024)23835494 (024)23838338
China Post and Telecommunication Equipment General Company 中國郵電器材總公司	Beijing 北京市	Beijing 北京市	(010)63523715 (010)63525935
Jiangsu Electromechanical Products General Company 江蘇省機電產品總公司	Nanjing 南京市	Jiangsu 江蘇省	(025)7713642 (025)7711036
Xi Nan Technology Import & Export Company 西南技術進出口公司	Chongqing 重慶市	Chongqing 重慶市	(023)63850185 (023)63850026
Changzhou Economic Technology Industrial Development Zone Tian Ming Trade Company 常州經濟技術產業開發區天明貿易公司	Changzhou 常州市	Jiangsu 江蘇省	(0519)8829882 (0519)8829882
Shanxi Mechanical Equipment Import & Export Company 山西省機械設備進出口公司	Taiyuan 太原市	Shanxi 山西省	(0351)4040713 (0351)4043981
Ningbo Five Mining Machinery Import & Export Company 寧波市五礦機械進出口公司	Ningbo 寧波市	Zhejiang 浙江省	(0574)7311255 (0574)7320322
Tianjin Jin Huan Electromechanical Complete Sets of Equipment Factory 天津市津環機電成套設備廠	Tianjin 天津市	Tianjin 天津市	(022)26371628
Yunnan Machinery Import & Export Company 雲南省機械進出口公司	Kunming 昆明市	Yunnan 雲南省	(0871)3164879 (0871)3136829
Tianjin Da Qiu Zhuang Yi Yuan Trade Center 天津市大丘莊億源商貿中心	Tianjin 天津市	Tianjin 天津市	(022)28899478 (022)28899046

*Also include sales by firms outside this industry.包括本行業以外廠家的銷售。"o" stands for "others". "o" 代表 "其他產品"。

3621: Petroleum Special Equipment 石油工業專用設備製造業

The industry accounts for 0.102% of the total revenue of China's industrial sector in 1996. The revenue growth rate of the industry is 16.2% from 1995, as compared to the growth rate of China's industrial sector, 9.51%. The rate of return on asset is 0.31%. 68.21% of all firms in the industry made a profit while 26.05% had negative returns. The top province in terms of the industry's revenue is Shanghai, accounting for 21.15% of the total revenue.
本行業在1996年佔全行業總產值0.102%，行業年增長率為16.2%（全國工業年增長率9.51%）。行業的資產回報率0.31%，68.21%的企業盈利，26.05%的企業虧損。銷售收入最高的省份為上海市，佔本行業的21.15%。

	Total number of firms 企業總數	Total number of employees 職工總數	Total revenue (mil. RMB) 總銷售收入（百萬元）	Total profit (mil. RMB) 總利潤（百萬元）	Return on assets 資產利潤率 (%)	Return on equity 權益利潤率 (%)	Labour productivity ('000 RMB / worker) 勞動生產率（千元/人）	Debts / assets 資產負債率 (%)	Total assets (mil. RMB) 總資產（百萬元）
Industry Overall 行業總體	416	120,483	5,912	40	0.31	0.74	49.07	58.58	12,992

	Number of firms 企業個數	Average number of employees 平均職工人數	Average revenue ('000 RMB) 平均銷售收入（千元）	Average profit ('000 RMB) 平均利潤（千元）	Return on assets 資產利潤率 (%)	Return on equity 權益利潤率 (%)	Labour productivity ('000 RMB / worker) 勞動生產率（千元/人）	Average debts / assets 平均資產負債率(%)	Average Total assets ('000 RMB) 平均總資產（千元）
By ownership 產業所有權									
State-owned 國有	87	879	37,598	-839	-0.75	-1.79	42.77	58.27	112,069
Collectively-owned 集體	293	136	7,231	197	2.33	6.38	53.28	63.46	8,449
Privately-owned 私有	2	170	3,516	1,018	100.53	146.26	20.68	31.27	1,013
Domestic JVs 聯營	3	80	31,028	152	0.52	1.88	387.85	72.60	29,479
Joint stock 股份制	8	272	16,758	1,566	7.28	15.42	61.53	52.80	21,515
Foreign-funded 外資	17	45	11,950	2,340	13.09	20.84	265.90	37.18	17,877
Overseas Chinese-funded 港澳台資	5	133	16,257	229	0.59	1.11	122.23	47.11	39,089
By size 規模									
Large 大型	11	4,652	242,888	9,061	1.29	2.80	52.22	54.03	704,358
Medium 中型	29	863	32,787	-170	-0.23	-0.70	38.00	67.69	74,774
Small 小型	370	120	6,189	-148	-1.78	-4.90	51.69	63.64	8,312
By regional distribution 地區分布									
Central-North 華北	53	244	14,332	802	3.48	7.92	58.83	56.01	23,036
Beijing 北京	7	80	4,144	39	0.34	0.74	51.99	53.59	11,237
Tianjin 天津	19	79	15,269	2,772	22.52	31.01	193.02	27.38	12,312
Hebei 河北	24	337	16,886	73	0.26	0.62	50.15	57.73	27,595
Shanxi 山西	2	1,347	16,365	-6,115	-4.98	-24.18	12.15	79.39	122,715
Inner Mongolia 內蒙	1	76	2,500	60	9.68	37.50	32.89	72.58	620
Northeast 東北	146	173	6,804	43	0.38	1.29	39.39	70.88	11,391
Liaoning 遼寧	85	176	8,839	152	1.17	3.75	50.24	68.85	13,039
Jilin 吉林	26	197	3,842	-203	-1.88	-12.16	19.49	84.52	10,766
Heilongjiang 黑龍江	35	147	4,063	-40	-0.51	-1.48	27.68	65.21	7,851
Central East 華東	126	318	17,517	83	0.20	0.37	55.04	46.21	42,078
Shanghai 上海	15	1,303	83,343	1,011	0.40	0.62	63.98	36.15	254,178
Jiangsu 江蘇	43	184	9,514	-267	-2.37	-7.40	51.69	67.99	11,290
Zhejiang 浙江	27	71	4,914	175	3.19	8.22	69.21	61.26	5,487
Anhui 安徽	6	231	13,503	103	0.77	6.61	58.46	88.37	13,440
Fujian 福建	3	26	2,747	50	0.92	2.29	107.01	59.85	5,430
Jiangxi 江西	2	860	17,755	30	0.05	0.17	20.66	68.74	55,530
Shandong 山東	30	252	9,681	42	0.20	0.82	38.47	76.20	21,586
Central-South 中南	50	201	21,260	283	0.76	1.80	106.01	58.03	37,459
Henan 河南	32	185	23,624	292	0.61	1.51	128.00	59.54	47,635
Hubei 湖北	8	290	24,228	684	4.20	13.31	83.69	68.42	16,263
Hunan 湖南	3	38	1,600	-27	-1.53	-2.91	41.74	47.52	1,747
Guangdong 廣東	7	241	15,487	-83	-0.27	-0.46	64.15	41.18	30,467
Guangxi 廣西									
Hainan 海南									
Southwest 西南	11	507	14,141	5,063	15.62	48.33	27.89	67.68	32,413
Chongqing 重慶	4	61	633	-1,416	-125.17	-1163.63	10.33	89.24	1,132
Sichuan 四川	5	493	17,924	11,872	36.82	173.13	36.36	78.73	32,240
Guizhou 貴州	2	1,401	30,460	50	0.05	0.13	21.75	57.35	93,185
Yunnan 雲南									
Tibet 西藏									
Northwest 西北	30	888	24,433	-2,972	-3.46	-14.70	27.51	76.46	85,891
Shaanxi 陝西	19	505	15,872	-1,024	-2.08	-11.09	31.41	81.22	49,207
Gansu 甘肅	8	2,115	52,971	-8,723	-4.27	-16.31	25.05	73.83	204,425
Qinghai 青海									
Ningxia 寧夏									
Xinjiang 新疆	3	43	2,553	27	1.25	2.63	59.84	52.35	2,127

3621: Petroleum Special Equipment 石油工業專用設備製造業

Year 年份	Number of firms 企業個數	Rate of change 每年變化 (%)	Number of employees 職工人數（人）	Rate of change 每年變化 (%)	Total revenue (mil. RMB) 總銷售收入（百萬元）	Rate of change 每年變化 (%)	Total profit (mil. RMB) 總利潤（百萬元）	Rate of change 每年變化 (%)
1993	277		124,132		3,736		73	
1994	335	20.94%	102,783	-17.20%	3,295	-11.81%	16	-78.34%
1995	406	21.19%	133,573	29.96%	5,087	54.37%	-47	-399.80%
1996	416	2.46%	120,483	-9.80%	5,912	16.22%	40	184.86%

3 Major products* 3 種主要產品 *	Output 產量	Sales volume 銷售量	Unit 單位
a) Drilling & Producting Equipment for Oil 石油鑽採設備	91,053	81,037	ton 噸
b) Refining Equipment 煉油設備	24,798	16,863	ton 噸
c) Special Refitted Truck 專用改裝汽車	10,498	10,078	vehicle 輛

Top 10 firms by revenue (year founded) 收入排名前 10 家企業 (創辦年份)	City 城市	Province 省	Telephone / fax 電話 / 傳真	Number of employees 職工人數	Ownership 產業所有權	Revenue ('000 RMB) 銷售收入（千元）	Profit ('000 RMB) (rank) 利潤（千元）（排名）	Total assets ('000 RMB) 總資產（千元）	Major products 主要產品
China Petrochemistry Shanghai Jinshan Industrial Co. 中國石化上海金山實業公司(1993)	Shanghai 上海市	Shanghai 上海市	(021)57942942 (021)57941353	12,231	State-owned 國有	675,189	41(116)	2,876,928	o
Shanghai Light Industry Machinery Co. Ltd. 上海輕工機械股份有限公司(1992)	Shanghai 上海市	Shanghai 上海市	(021)62566165 (021)62154150	4,552	Joint stock 股份制	319,030	6260(6)	559,770	o
Tianjin Rong Heng Tai Precise Group Co. Ltd. 天津市榮亨精鑄集團有限公司(1983)	Tianjin 天津市	Tianjin 天津市	(022)25592201	1,120	Collectively-owned 集體	268,570	51150(1)	207,420	a
Lanzhou Petroleum & Chemical Machinery General Works 蘭州石油化工機器總廠(1958)	Lanzhou 蘭州市	Gansu 甘肅省	(0931)2333611 (0931)2339794	10,424	State-owned 國有	267,565	-39448(209)	1,107,780	a,b
Fushun Machinery Plant 撫順機械廠(1950)	Fushun 撫順市	Liaoning 遼寧省	(0413)7673421 (0413)7673731	2,492	State-owned 國有	166,127	1581(24)	283,787	b
Baoji Petroleum Machinery Plant 寶雞石油機械廠(1938)	Baoji 寶雞市	Shaanxi 陜西省	(0917)3212991	6,268	State-owned 國有	160,320	-9950(207)	704,380	o
Fushun Petroleum Machinery Plant 撫順石油機械廠(1960)	Fushun 撫順市	Liaoning 遼寧省	(0413)4634471 (0413)4630446	3,518	State-owned 國有	138,435	280(65)	282,890	a,b
Shenzhou Petroleum Chemical Industry Machinery Factory 深州市石油化工機械廠(1977)	Hengshui 衡水市	Hebei 河北省	(0318)3368333	146	Collectively-owned 集體	95,450	6332(5)	76,417	o
Lanzhou General Machine Factory 蘭州通用機器廠(1872)	Lanzhou 蘭州市	Gansu 甘肅省	(0931)2336111 (0931)2335609	4,715	State-owned 國有	86,140	-30182(208)	436,558	a,c
Bao Yue Special Purpose Steel Products Joint Venture Co. 寶月專用鋼材聯營公司(1991)	Shanghai 上海市	Shanghai 上海市	(021)56647757 (021)56931814	80	Domestic JVs 聯營	81,061	2223(15)	39,449	o

Top 10 Cities by Production Output 產出排名前 10 位城市	Province 省	Market share 市場份額	Number of firms 企業個數
Shanghai 上海市	Shanghai 上海市	14.86%	28
Lanzhou 蘭州市	Gansu 甘肅省	9.17%	8
Tianjin 天津市	Tianjin 天津市	8.56%	9
Fushun 撫順市	Liaoning 遼寧省	6.81%	10
Yinchuan 銀川市	Ningxia 寧夏	3.33%	1
Baoji 寶雞市	Shaanxi 陜西省	2.73%	2
Daqing 大慶市	Heilongjiang 黑龍江省	2.49%	5
Xi'an 西安市	Shaanxi 陜西省	2.35%	13
Chengdu 成都市	Sichuan 四川省	2.06%	5
Huaiyin 淮陰市	Jiangsu 江蘇省	1.77%	3

10 Major Wholesalers 10 家主要批發商	City 城市	Province 省	Telephone / Fax 電話 / 傳真
Liaoning Automobile Trade Group Corp. 遼寧省汽車貿易集團	Shenyang 瀋陽市	Liaoning 遼寧省	(024)23835494 (024)23838338
China Post and Telecommunication Equipment General Company 中國郵電器材總公司	Beijing 北京市	Beijing 北京市	(010)63523715 (010)63525935
Jiangsu Electromechanical Products General Company 江蘇省機電產品總公司	Nanjing 南京市	Jiangsu 江蘇省	(025)7713642 (025)7711036
Xi Nan Technology Import & Export Company 西南技術進出口公司	Chongqing 重慶市	Chongqing 重慶市	(023)63850185 (023)63850026
Changzhou Economic Technology Industrial Development Zone Tian Ming Trade Company 常州經濟技術產業開發區天明貿易公司	Changzhou 常州市	Jiangsu 江蘇省	(0519)8829882 (0519)8829882
Shanxi Mechanical Equipment Import & Export Company 山西省機械設備進出口公司	Taiyuan 太原市	Shanxi 山西省	(0351)4040713 (0351)4043981
Ningbo Five Mining Machinery Import & Export Company 寧波市五礦機械進出口公司	Ningbo 寧波市	Zhejiang 浙江省	(0574)7311255 (0574)7320322
Tianjin Jin Huan Electromechanical Complete Sets of Equipment Factory 天津市津環機電成套設備廠	Tianjin 天津市	Tianjin 天津市	(022)26371628
Yunnan Machinery Import & Export Company 雲南省機械進出口公司	Kunming 昆明市	Yunnan 雲南省	(0871)3164879 (0871)3136829
Tianjin Da Qiu Zhuang Yi Yuan Trade Center 天津市大丘莊億源商貿中心	Tianjin 天津市	Tianjin 天津市	(022)28899478 (022)28899046

*Also include sales by firms outside this industry.包括本行業以外廠家的銷售。"o" stands for "others". "o" 代表"其他產品"。

3622: Chemical Equipment 化學工業專用設備製造業

The industry accounts for 0.084% of the total revenue of China's industrial sector in 1996. The revenue growth rate of the industry is -2.4% from 1995, as compared to the growth rate of China's industrial sector, 9.51%. The rate of return on asset is -0.55%. 59.37% of all firms in the industry made a profit while 32.97% had negative returns. The top province in terms of the industry's revenue is Jiangsu, accounting for 27.81% of the total revenue.
本行業在1996年佔全行業總產值0.084%，行業年增長率為-2.4%（全國工業年增長率9.51%）。行業的資產回報率-0.55%，59.37%的企業盈利，32.97%的企業虧損。銷售收入最高的省份為江蘇省，佔本行業的27.81%。

	Total number of firms 企業總數	Total number of employees 職工總數	Total revenue (mil. RMB) 總銷售收入（百萬元）	Total profit (mil. RMB) 總利潤（百萬元）	Return on assets 資產利潤率 (%)	Return on equity 權益利潤率 (%)	Labour productivity ('000 RMB / worker) 勞動生產率（千元／人）	Debts / assets 資產負債率 (%)	Total assets (mil. RMB) 總資產（百萬元）
Industry Overall 行業總體	430	112,500	4,864	-47	-0.55	-1.89	43.24	70.97	8,600

	Number of firms 企業個數	Average number of employees 平均職工人數	Average revenue ('000 RMB) 平均銷售收入（千元）	Average profit ('000 RMB) 平均利潤（千元）	Return on assets 資產利潤率 (%)	Return on equity 權益利潤率 (%)	Labour productivity ('000 RMB / worker) 勞動生產率（千元／人）	Average debts / assets 平均資產負債率(%)	Average Total assets ('000 RMB) 平均總資產（千元）
By ownership 產業所有權									
State-owned 國有	124	551	18,218	-1,274	-2.90	-10.86	33.05	73.32	43,976
Collectively-owned 集體	269	139	7,910	370	4.47	14.17	57.05	68.42	8,261
Privately-owned 私有	3	31	1,092	15	1.41	5.76	35.22	75.48	1,048
Domestic JVs 聯營	8	123	9,264	384	3.62	15.33	75.62	76.38	10,599
Joint stock 股份制	13	418	23,962	337	0.65	1.74	57.37	62.63	51,790
Foreign-funded 外資	5	101	7,772	524	3.53	8.01	77.26	55.91	14,843
Overseas Chinese-funded 港澳台資	9	74	5,475	165	1.66	4.21	73.65	60.69	9,983
By size 規模									
Large 大型	10	2,341	118,892	-5,403	-2.46	-7.44	50.80	66.94	219,724
Medium 中型	52	741	29,303	-848	-1.33	-5.27	39.55	74.83	64,028
Small 小型	366	139	5,877	140	1.66	5.48	42.33	69.65	8,398
By regional distribution 地區分布									
Central-North 華北	72	230	8,689	-270	-1.45	-4.89	37.84	70.33	18,583
Beijing 北京	15	348	19,924	-385	-0.84	-3.68	57.21	77.21	45,817
Tianjin 天津	26	80	3,268	38	1.14	2.15	40.99	46.86	3,336
Hebei 河北	21	235	9,567	103	0.67	2.35	40.77	71.60	15,459
Shanxi 山西	5	749	6,416	-3,388	-7.86	-18.24	8.57	56.92	43,106
Inner Mongolia 內蒙	5	113	1,762	26	0.55	1.42	15.62	61.62	4,768
Northeast 東北	61	355	8,925	-739	-3.43	-16.81	25.13	79.59	21,530
Liaoning 遼寧	46	366	10,110	-605	-2.50	-10.40	27.62	75.98	24,234
Jilin 吉林	8	258	3,963	-276	-3.90	-15.32	15.39	74.50	7,079
Heilongjiang 黑龍江	7	396	6,809	-2,141	-10.56	105.94	17.21	109.96	20,279
Central East 華東	182	204	13,420	306	1.79	6.17	65.83	71.03	17,097
Shanghai 上海	15	259	17,137	405	1.88	8.61	66.25	78.14	21,545
Jiangsu 江蘇	85	221	15,915	271	1.45	5.14	72.01	71.85	18,706
Zhejiang 浙江	37	89	5,440	334	3.32	8.48	61.46	60.84	10,053
Anhui 安徽	9	388	11,576	-516	-2.07	-7.88	29.84	73.77	24,931
Fujian 福建	10	128	4,882	-51	-0.57	-3.69	38.02	84.47	8,892
Jiangxi 江西	2	259	2,300	-25	-0.33	-1.75	8.88	81.25	7,655
Shandong 山東	24	245	19,737	807	3.89	11.96	80.72	67.48	20,748
Central-South 中南	67	324	11,782	-52	-0.20	-0.59	36.40	66.11	26,134
Henan 河南	25	275	9,011	-166	-1.06	-2.53	32.82	57.99	15,638
Hubei 湖北	11	269	7,856	8	0.06	0.26	29.21	75.54	12,816
Hunan 湖南	15	439	14,414	97	0.33	0.96	32.82	65.27	28,985
Guangdong 廣東	13	324	18,027	123	0.22	0.75	55.63	70.04	54,734
Guangxi 廣西	3	353	9,047	-820	-3.38	-8.07	25.60	58.12	24,253
Hainan 海南									
Southwest 西南	30	402	12,263	-1,214	-4.46	-14.85	30.49	69.94	27,193
Chongqing 重慶	7	320	7,491	-2,318	-13.29	-47.90	23.40	72.25	17,443
Sichuan 四川	14	541	16,875	-1,137	-2.86	-9.16	31.17	68.79	39,786
Guizhou 貴州	2	82	2,710	5	0.12	0.56	33.05	79.10	4,235
Yunnan 雲南	7	288	10,114	-664	-3.84	-13.95	35.08	72.48	17,301
Tibet 西藏									
Northwest 西北	18	192	5,235	84	0.56	1.65	27.31	66.00	15,008
Shaanxi 陝西	12	100	2,945	-2	-0.05	-0.13	29.47	63.85	3,643
Gansu 甘肅	4	428	7,138	375	0.93	3.48	16.67	73.14	40,150
Qinghai 青海									
Ningxia 寧夏									
Xinjiang 新疆	2	270	15,170	20	0.06	0.12	56.29	50.01	32,915

3622: Chemical Equipment 化學工業專用設備製造業

Year 年份	Number of firms 企業個數	Rate of change 每年變化 (%)	Number of employees 職工人數 (人)	Rate of change 每年變化 (%)	Total revenue (mil. RMB) 總銷售收入 (百萬元)	Rate of change 每年變化 (%)	Total profit (mil. RMB) 總利潤 (百萬元)	Rate of change 每年變化 (%)
1993	418		247,828		4,411		48	
1994	414	-0.96%	124,668	-49.70%	3,646	-17.35%	-53	-209.32%
1995	448	8.21%	129,438	3.83%	4,984	36.69%	-76	-44.99%
1996	430	-4.02%	112,500	-13.09%	4,864	-2.41%	-47	38.38%

3 Major products* 3 種主要產品 *	Output 產量	Sales volume 銷售量	Unit 單位
a) Chemical Equipment 化工設備	159,198	149,646	ton 噸
b) Refining Equipment 煉油設備	9,262	6,298	ton 噸
c) Enamel Product 搪瓷製品	26,438	25,380	ton 噸

Top 10 firms by revenue (year founded) 收入排名前 10 家企業 (創辦年份)	City 城市	Province 省	Telephone / fax 電話 / 傳真	Number of employees 職工人數	Ownership 產業所有權	Revenue ('000 RMB) 銷售收入 (千元)	Profit ('000 RMB) (rank) 利潤 (千元) (排名)	Total assets ('000 RMB) 總資產 (千元)	Major products 主要產品
Jiangsu Hua Ling Group Co. 江蘇華菱(集團)公司(1987)	Suzhou 蘇州市	Jiangsu 江蘇省	(0512)8391664 (0512)8391167	1,130	Collectively-owned 集體	303,800	20470(1)	236,020	o
Beijing Chemical Industry Machinery Factory 北京化工機械廠(1966)	Beijing 北京市	Beijing 北京市	(010)67714477 (010)67749829	2,423	State-owned 國有	151,558	600(45)	279,052	a
Jinzhou Heavy Machinery Plant 金州重型機器廠(1958)	Dalian 大連市	Liaoning 遼寧省	(0411)7692479 (0411)7690074	3,082	State-owned 國有	150,109	-14986(259)	362,430	a,b
Zhangjiagang Sha Gong Chemical Machinery Factory 張家港市沙工化機廠(1980)	Suzhou 蘇州市	Jiangsu 江蘇省	(0512)8223357 (0512)8226180	288	Collectively-owned 集體	112,054	10055(4)	32,559	o
Xiangdong Chemical Machinery Works of The Ministry of Chemical Industry 化工部湘東化機廠(1973)	Zhuzhou 株洲市	Hunan 湖南省	(0733)4239112 (0733)4233806	2,756	State-owned 國有	86,726	48(120)	196,010	a
Zibo Industrial Enamel Factory 淄博工業搪瓷廠(1974)	Zibo 淄博市	Shandong 山東省	(0533)2900120 (0533)2900118	771	Collectively-owned 集體	85,089	6176(5)	55,776	c
Shanghai No.1 Chemical Industry Machinery Plant 上海化工機械一廠(1958)	Shanghai 上海市	Shanghai 上海市	(021)62412400 (021)62747965	1,356	State-owned 國有	81,581	2(167)	89,386	a
Xi Nan Chemical Machinery Co. Ltd. 西南化機股份有限公司(1966)	Deyang 德陽市	Sichuan 四川省	(0838)8202510 (0838)8204843	1,876	Joint stock 股份制	81,028	12045(2)	211,672	o
Nanjing Tian Jie Machinery Co. Ltd. 南京天界機械股份有限公司(1956)	Nanjing 南京市	Jiangsu 江蘇省	(025)2412555 (025)2411935	1,461	State-owned 國有	79,656	356(59)	169,045	a
Hunan Changsha Chemical Industry Machinery Factory 湖南省長沙化工機械廠(1958)	Changsha 長沙市	Hunan 湖南省	(0731)5214493 (0731)5214040	1,698	State-owned 國有	78,499	1006(32)	159,437	a

Top 10 Cities by Production Output 產出排名前 10 位城市	Province 省	Market share 市場份額	Number of firms 企業個數
Suzhou 蘇州市	Jiangsu 江蘇省	16.36%	29
Shanghai 上海市	Shanghai 上海市	7.42%	45
Beijing 北京市	Beijing 北京市	6.58%	14
Zibo 淄博市	Shandong 山東省	4.98%	8
Wuxi 無錫市	Jiangsu 江蘇省	4.70%	57
Dalian 大連市	Liaoning 遼寧省	4.21%	6
Changzhou 常州市	Jiangsu 江蘇省	2.37%	11
Guangzhou 廣州市	Guangdong 廣東省	2.27%	4
Taizhou 泰州市	Jiangsu 江蘇省	2.23%	8
Chengdu 成都市	Sichuan 四川省	2.01%	14

10 Major Wholesalers 10 家主要批發商	City 城市	Province 省	Telephone / Fax 電話 / 傳真
Liaoning Automobile Trade Group Corp. 遼寧省汽車貿易集團	Shenyang 瀋陽市	Liaoning 遼寧省	(024)23835494 (024)23838338
China Post and Telecommunication Equipment General Company 中國郵電器材總公司	Beijing 北京市	Beijing 北京市	(010)63523715 (010)63525935
Jiangsu Electromechanical Products General Company 江蘇省機電產品總公司	Nanjing 南京市	Jiangsu 江蘇省	(025)7713642 (025)7711036
Xi Nan Technology Import & Export Company 西南技術進出口公司	Chongqing 重慶市	Chongqing 重慶市	(023)63850185 (023)63850026
Changzhou Economic Technology Industrial Development Zone Tian Ming Trade Company 常州經濟技術產業開發區天明貿易公司	Changzhou 常州市	Jiangsu 江蘇省	(0519)8829882 (0519)8829882
Shanxi Mechanical Equipment Import & Export Company 山西省機械設備進出口公司	Taiyuan 太原市	Shanxi 山西省	(0351)4040713 (0351)4043981
Ningbo Five Mining Machinery Import & Export Company 寧波市五礦機械進出口公司	Ningbo 寧波市	Zhejiang 浙江省	(0574)7311255 (0574)7320322
Tianjin Jin Huan Electromechanical Complete Sets of Equipment Factory 天津市津環機電成套設備廠	Tianjin 天津市	Tianjin 天津市	(022)26371628
Yunnan Machinery Import & Export Company 雲南省機械進出口公司	Kunming 昆明市	Yunnan 雲南省	(0871)3164879 (0871)3136829
Tianjin Da Qiu Zhuang Yi Yuan Trade Center 天津市大丘莊億源商貿中心	Tianjin 天津市	Tianjin 天津市	(022)28899478 (022)28899046

*Also include sales by firms outside this industry.包括本行業以外廠家的銷售。"o" stands for "others". "o" 代表 "其他產品" 。

3623: Special Chemical Fibre Equipment 化學纖維工業專用設備製造業

The industry accounts for 0.010% of the total revenue of China's industrial sector in 1996. The revenue growth rate of the industry is -18.9% from 1995, as compared to the growth rate of China's industrial sector, 9.51%. The rate of return on asset is 1.65%. 70.24% of all firms in the industry made a profit while 25.00% had negative returns. The top province in terms of the industry's revenue is Jiangsu, accounting for 64.69% of the total revenue.
本行業在1996年佔全行業總產值0.010%，行業年增長率為-18.9%（全國工業年增長率9.51%）。行業的資產回報率1.65%，70.24%的企業盈利，25.00%的企業虧損。銷售收入最高的省份為江蘇省，佔本行業的64.69%。

	Total number of firms 企業總數	Total number of employees 職工總數	Total revenue (mil. RMB) 總銷售收入（百萬元）	Total profit (mil. RMB) 總利潤（百萬元）	Return on assets 資產利潤率 (%)	Return on equity 權益利潤率 (%)	Labour productivity ('000 RMB / worker) 勞動生產率（千元/人）	Debts / assets 資產負債率 (%)	Total assets (mil. RMB) 總資產（百萬元）
Industry Overall 行業總體	47	8,012	559	13	1.65	5.32	69.77	68.93	788

	Number of firms 企業個數	Average number of employees 平均職工人數	Average revenue ('000 RMB) 平均銷售收入（千元）	Average profit ('000 RMB) 平均利潤（千元）	Return on assets 資產利潤率 (%)	Return on equity 權益利潤率 (%)	Labour productivity ('000 RMB / worker) 勞動生產率（千元/人）	Average debts / assets 平均資產負債率(%)	Average Total assets ('000 RMB) 平均總資產（千元）
By ownership 產業所有權									
State-owned 國有	9	453	13,000	-778	-2.16	-7.87	28.68	72.53	36,000
Collectively-owned 集體	33	111	11,796	539	4.42	12.57	106.21	64.86	12,205
Privately-owned 私有									
Domestic JVs 聯營	1	266	47,384	1,889	3.67	21.66	178.14	83.07	51,509
Joint stock 股份制	1	27							
Foreign-funded 外資	1	35	1,278	-148	-7.56	-22.02	36.52	65.68	1,964
Overseas Chinese-funded 港澳台資	2	20	2,024	232	6.00	9.18	101.20	34.63	3,874
By size 規模									
Large 大型									
Medium 中型	4	636	50,281	974	1.01	3.63	79.12	72.05	96,143
Small 小型	42	132	8,521	217	2.26	6.62	64.41	65.91	9,604
By regional distribution 地區分布									
Central-North 華北	9	130	7,833	336	1.83	6.16	60.46	70.33	18,368
Beijing 北京	6	154	10,677	407	1.56	5.34	69.33	70.75	26,037
Tianjin 天津	1	173	2,430	200	2.86	7.97	14.05	64.14	7,000
Hebei 河北	2	35	2,005	190	18.18	44.71	58.12	59.33	1,045
Shanxi 山西									
Inner Mongolia 內蒙									
Northeast 東北	7	76	7,689	669	16.30	41.09	100.79	60.38	4,103
Liaoning 遼寧	6	80	8,935	790	17.00	40.65	111.92	58.23	4,648
Jilin 吉林									
Heilongjiang 黑龍江	1	55	210	-60	-7.23	22.22	3.82	132.53	830
Central East 華東	22	153	17,622	660	3.22	9.55	114.94	66.30	20,505
Shanghai 上海									
Jiangsu 江蘇	14	213	25,831	1,096	3.65	10.41	121.15	65.00	30,075
Zhejiang 浙江	6	33	2,152	-233	-6.27	-51.09	66.21	87.73	3,722
Anhui 安徽									
Fujian 福建									
Jiangxi 江西									
Shandong 山東	2	97	6,565	285	7.36	29.69	68.03	75.06	3,870
Central-South 中南	6	473	7,697	-1,520	-6.55	-28.57	16.28	77.07	23,195
Henan 河南	4	673	9,448	-2,288	-6.75	-29.80	14.04	77.36	33,883
Hubei 湖北	2	73	4,195	15	0.82	2.46	57.86	66.48	1,820
Hunan 湖南									
Guangdong 廣東									
Guangxi 廣西									
Hainan 海南									
Southwest 西南	3	34	410	-27	-2.02	-14.55	12.06	86.11	1,320
Chongqing 重慶	3	34	410	27	2.05	14.73	12.06	86.11	1,320
Sichuan 四川									
Guizhou 貴州									
Yunnan 雲南									
Tibet 西藏									
Northwest 西北									
Shaanxi 陝西									
Gansu 甘肅									
Qinghai 青海									
Ningxia 寧夏									
Xinjiang 新疆									

3623: Special Chemical Fibre Equipment 化學纖維工業專用設備製造業

Year 年份	Number of firms 企業個數	Rate of change 每年變化(%)	Number of employees 職工人數(人)	Rate of change 每年變化(%)	Total revenue (mil. RMB) 總銷售收入(百萬元)	Rate of change 每年變化(%)	Total profit (mil. RMB) 總利潤(百萬元)	Rate of change 每年變化(%)
1993	44		4,449		439		30	
1994	36	-18.18%	3,948	-11.26%	162	-63.09%	13	-57.86%
1995	49	36.11%	7,858	99.04%	689	325.69%	36	181.14%
1996	47	-4.08%	8,012	1.96%	559	-18.89%	13	-63.70%

3 Major products* 3種主要產品*	Output 產量	Sales volume 銷售量	Unit 單位
a) Synthetic Equipment 合成纖維設備	843	758	ton 噸
b) Flouride Polymer 含氟聚合物	267	254	ton 噸
c) Smelting Equipment 冶煉設備	28	29	set 台

Top 10 firms by revenue (year founded) 收入排名前10家企業(創辦年份)	City 城市	Province 省	Telephone / fax 電話 / 傳真	Number of employees 職工人數	Ownership 產業所有權	Revenue ('000 RMB) 銷售收入(千元)	Profit ('000 RMB) (rank) 利潤(千元)(排名)	Total assets ('000 RMB) 總資產(千元)	Major products 主要產品
Jiangsu Gang Ying Group Co. Ltd. 江蘇港鷹集團有限公司(1958)	Suzhou 蘇州市	Jiangsu 江蘇省	(0512)8740525	806	Collectively-owned 集體	102,014	8203(1)	108,060	o
Changshu Decelerator General Factory 常熟市減速器總廠(1967)	Suzhou 蘇州市	Jiangsu 江蘇省	(0512)2671912 (0512)2671306	600	Collectively-owned 集體	92,930	3260(3)	131,180	o
Zhangjiagang Chemical Industry Machinery Plant 張家港市化工機械廠(1969)	Suzhou 蘇州市	Jiangsu 江蘇省	(0512)8771726 (0512)8770850	550	Collectively-owned 集體	70,898	1055(6)	78,326	c
China Textile Science Research Institute Machinery Factory 中國紡科院機械廠(1970)	Beijing 北京市	Beijing 北京市	(010)65014466 (010)65024425	889	State-owned 國有	63,512	2428(5)	153,115	a
Changshu Xu Shi Machinery Plant 常熟市徐市機械廠(1952)	Suzhou 蘇州市	Jiangsu 江蘇省	(0512)2671662 (0512)2671340	346	Collectively-owned 集體	42,103	2510(4)	30,170	a
Lv Shun Shuang Yang Chemical Fibre Equipment Factory 旅順雙陽化纖裝備廠(1995)	Dalian 大連市	Liaoning 遼寧省	(0411)6240314	172	Collectively-owned 集體	35,000	4180(2)	9,252	o
Zhangjiagang Hou Cheng Farm Implements Factory 張家港市后塍農具廠(1953)	Suzhou 蘇州市	Jiangsu 江蘇省	(0512)8771387 (0512)8771387	25	Collectively-owned 集體	32,061	39(19)	16,966	o
Ji'nan Plastic Chemical Fibre Products Factory 濟南市塑化纖維製品廠(1988)	Ji'nan 濟南市	Shandong 山東省	(0531)4381028	170	Collectively-owned 集體	11,890	473(9)	4,849	b
Zhengzhou Mi Rong Chemical Fibre Products Co. Ltd. 鄭州密榮化纖製品有限公司(1993)	Zhengzhou 鄭州市	Henan 河南省	(0371)9822883	45	Overseas Chinese-funded 港澳台資	8,869	841(7)	13,847	o
Shanghai Pu Dong Xinxian Zhang Jiang Chemical Fibre Machinery Fittings Factory 上海浦東新區張江化纖機械配件廠(1989)	Shanghai 上海市	Shanghai 上海市	(021)58551129 (021)58551129	55	Collectively-owned 集體	7,928	806(8)	11,703	o

Top 10 Cities by Production Output 產出排名前10位城市	Province 省	Market share 市場份額	Number of firms 企業個數
Suzhou 蘇州市	Jiangsu 江蘇省	43.55%	10
Beijing 北京市	Beijing 北京市	14.85%	5
Changzhou 常州市	Jiangsu 江蘇省	11.03%	2
Zhengzhou 鄭州市	Henan 河南省	8.28%	2
Shanghai 上海市	Shanghai 上海市	5.73%	7
Dalian 大連市	Liaoning 遼寧省	5.22%	3
Hangzhou 杭州市	Zhejiang 浙江省	1.74%	2
Suzhou 宿州市	Anhui 安徽省	1.16%	3
Ningbo 寧波市	Zhejiang 浙江省	1.16%	2
Wuxi 無錫市	Jiangsu 江蘇省	1.11%	1

10 Major Wholesalers 10家主要批發商	City 城市	Province 省	Telephone / Fax 電話 / 傳真
Liaoning Automobile Trade Group Corp. 遼寧省汽車貿易集團	Shenyang 瀋陽市	Liaoning 遼寧省	(024)23835494 (024)23838338
China Post and Telecommunication Equipment General Company 中國郵電器材總公司	Beijing 北京市	Beijing 北京市	(010)63523715 (010)63525935
Jiangsu Electromechanical Products General Company 江蘇省機電產品總公司	Nanjing 南京市	Jiangsu 江蘇省	(025)7713642 (025)7711036
Xi Nan Technology Import & Export Company 西南技術進出口公司	Chongqing 重慶市	Chongqing 重慶市	(023)63850185 (023)63850026
Changzhou Economic Technology Industrial Development Zone Tian Ming Trade Company 常州經濟技術產業開發區天明貿易公司	Changzhou 常州市	Jiangsu 江蘇省	(0519)8829882 (0519)8829882
Shanxi Mechanical Equipment Import & Export Company 山西省機械設備進出口公司	Taiyuan 太原市	Shanxi 山西省	(0351)4040713 (0351)4043981
Ningbo Five Mining Machinery Import & Export Company 寧波市五礦機械進出口公司	Ningbo 寧波市	Zhejiang 浙江省	(0574)7311255 (0574)7320322
Tianjin Jin Huan Electromechanical Complete Sets of Equipment Factory 天津市津環機電成套設備廠	Tianjin 天津市	Tianjin 天津市	(022)26371628
Yunnan Machinery Import & Export Company 雲南省機械進出口公司	Kunming 昆明市	Yunnan 雲南省	(0871)3164879 (0871)3136829
Tianjin Da Qiu Zhuang Yi Yuan Trade Center 天津市大丘莊億源商貿中心	Tianjin 天津市	Tianjin 天津市	(022)28899478 (022)28899046

*Also include sales by firms outside this industry.包括本行業以外廠家的銷售。"o" stands for "others". "o" 代表"其他產品"。

3624: Rubber Equipment 橡膠工業專用設備製造業

The industry accounts for 0.029% of the total revenue of China's industrial sector in 1996. The revenue growth rate of the industry is 24.1% from 1995, as compared to the growth rate of China's industrial sector, 9.51%. The rate of return on asset is -0.99%. 67.79% of all firms in the industry made a profit while 27.56% had negative returns. The top province in terms of the industry's revenue is Jiangsu, accounting for 25.11% of the total revenue.
本行業在1996年佔全行業總產值0.029%，行業年增長率為24.1%（全國工業年增長率9.51%）。行業的資產回報率-0.99%，67.79%的企業盈利，27.56%的企業虧損。銷售收入最高的省份為江蘇省，佔本行業的25.11%。

	Total number of firms 企業總數	Total number of employees 職工總數	Total revenue (mil. RMB) 總銷售收入（百萬元）	Total profit (mil. RMB) 總利潤（百萬元）	Return on assets 資產利潤率 (%)	Return on equity 權益利潤率 (%)	Labour productivity ('000 RMB / worker) 勞動生產率（千元/人）	Debts / assets 資產負債率 (%)	Total assets (mil. RMB) 總資產（百萬元）
Industry Overall 行業總體	139	36,154	1,677	-30	-0.99	-3.36	46.38	70.43	3,050

	Number of firms 企業個數	Average number of employees 平均職工人數	Average revenue ('000 RMB) 平均銷售收入（千元）	Average profit ('000 RMB) 平均利潤（千元）	Return on assets 資產利潤率 (%)	Return on equity 權益利潤率 (%)	Labour productivity ('000 RMB / worker) 勞動生產率（千元/人）	Average debts / assets 平均資產負債率(%)	Average Total assets ('000 RMB) 平均總資產（千元）
By ownership 產業所有權									
State-owned 國有	36	669	21,861	-1,556	-2.60	-9.74	32.67	73.26	59,722
Collectively-owned 集體	91	116	8,700	288	3.82	8.91	74.97	57.09	7,529
Privately-owned 私有									
Domestic JVs 聯營	2	53	291	-83	-7.37	-13.88	5.55	46.92	1,120
Joint stock 股份制	2	172	8,723	-33	-0.26	-1.07	50.86	75.43	12,661
Foreign-funded 外資	5	213	13,313	-72	-0.23	-2.44	62.56	90.67	31,663
Overseas Chinese-funded 港澳台資	3	50	4,899	133	1.36	3.64	97.99	62.73	9,791
By size 規模									
Large 大型	4	2,191	82,969	-8,069	-2.75	-8.93	37.87	69.24	293,635
Medium 中型	6	1,450	49,924	-204	-0.19	-0.58	34.44	66.73	106,423
Small 小型	128	147	8,176	27	0.28	1.07	55.61	73.46	9,667
By regional distribution 地區分布									
Central-North 華北	13	290	2,296	-417	-3.25	-12.90	7.92	74.80	12,825
Beijing 北京									
Tianjin 天津	8	272	2,469	-486	-4.36	-26.25	9.07	83.41	11,165
Hebei 河北	2	31	840	60	6.06	15.79	27.10	61.62	990
Shanxi 山西	1	65	190	-80	-4.17	-8.33	2.92	50.00	1,920
Inner Mongolia 內蒙	2	731	4,115	-785	-2.14	-6.16	5.63	65.35	36,750
Northeast 東北	22	411	16,425	-63	-0.17	-0.47	39.92	64.94	38,167
Liaoning 遼寧	21	425	17,201	-66	-0.17	-0.47	40.45	64.92	39,930
Jilin 吉林									
Heilongjiang 黑龍江	1	121	130				1.07	79.65	1,130
Central East 華東	70	148	11,137	264	1.84	5.37	75.05	65.65	14,347
Shanghai 上海	9	114	4,126	-21	-0.16	-0.44	36.26	63.84	13,308
Jiangsu 江蘇	21	150	20,049	780	5.77	13.22	134.04	56.36	13,517
Zhejiang 浙江	10	72	7,959	480	5.96	17.92	110.39	66.75	8,060
Anhui 安徽	1	8	880	-20	-1.08	-1.20	110.00	10.27	1,850
Fujian 福建	5	483	25,896	-392	-0.67	-1.85	53.61	63.67	58,192
Jiangxi 江西									
Shandong 山東	24	128	4,645	-21	-0.22	-1.15	36.20	80.82	9,468
Central-South 中南	26	378	16,224	-1,667	-4.85	-25.50	42.97	80.97	34,361
Henan 河南	5	181	7,378	268	4.11	12.95	40.81	68.27	6,524
Hubei 湖北	5	135	2,446	-84	-2.02	-6.31	18.12	67.95	4,162
Hunan 湖南	4	667	15,273	-1,375	-1.92	-6.82	22.91	71.91	71,723
Guangdong 廣東	7	487	26,126	-5,904	-12.39	689.98	53.61	101.80	47,637
Guangxi 廣西	5	432	25,748	512	1.17	3.27	59.57	64.31	43,920
Hainan 海南									
Southwest 西南	5	614	16,606	256	0.91	2.56	27.03	64.53	28,154
Chongqing 重慶									
Sichuan 四川	4	768	20,758	-320	-0.91	-2.56	27.03	64.53	35,193
Guizhou 貴州	1								
Yunnan 雲南									
Tibet 西藏									
Northwest 西北	3	20	413	17	1.05	10.00	21.02	89.52	1,590
Shaanxi 陝西	2	30	620	25	1.05	10.00	21.02	89.52	2,385
Gansu 甘肅	1								
Qinghai 青海									
Ningxia 寧夏									
Xinjiang 新疆									

3624: Rubber Equipment 橡膠工業專用設備製造業

Year 年份	Number of firms 企業個數	Rate of change 每年變化 (%)	Number of employees 職工人數（人）	Rate of change 每年變化 (%)	Total revenue (mil. RMB) 總銷售收入（百萬元）	Rate of change 每年變化 (%)	Total profit (mil. RMB) 總利潤（百萬元）	Rate of change 每年變化 (%)
1993	113		33,404		1,334		42	
1994	127	12.39%	32,875	-1.58%	1,108	-16.93%	-11	-126.77%
1995	150	18.11%	37,637	14.49%	1,351	21.93%	-112	-898.06%
1996	139	-7.33%	36,154	-3.94%	1,677	24.13%	-30	73.20%

3 Major products* 3 種主要產品 *	Output 產量	Sales volume 銷售量	Unit 單位
a) Special Processing Equipment for Rubber 橡膠加工專用設備	58,159	42,456	ton 噸
b) Plastic Artificial Leather 塑料人造革	7,178	6,532	ton 噸
c) Plastic Processing Equipment 塑料加工設備	4,716	4,5	ton 噸

Top 10 firms by revenue (year founded) 收入排名前 10 家企業（創辦年份）	City 城市	Province 省	Telephone / fax 電話 / 傳真	Number of employees 職工人數	Ownership 產業所有權	Revenue ('000 RMB) 銷售收入（千元）	Profit ('000 RMB) (rank) 利潤（千元）（排名）	Total assets ('000 RMB) 總資產（千元）	Major products 主要產品
Dalian Rubber & Plastics Machinery Plant 大連橡膠塑料機械廠(1907)	Dalian 大連市	Liaoning 遼寧省	(0411)6641861 (0411)6641645	3,343	State-owned 國有	204,277	3219(2)	416,725	a,c
Wuxi Rubber & Plastics Machinery Factory 無錫市橡膠塑料機械廠(1985)	Wuxi 無錫市	Jiangsu 江蘇省	(0510)8990934	583	Collectively-owned 集體	162,774	10357(1)	96,492	b
Guilin Rubber Machinery Factory 桂林橡膠機械廠(1969)	Guilin 桂林市	Guangxi 廣西	(0773)3832967 (0773)3832971	1,884	State-owned 國有	110,550	1229(10)	190,732	a
Sanming Chemical Industry Machinery Factory of Fujian 福建省三明化工機械廠(1958)	Sanming 三明市	Fujian 福建省	(0598)8337771 (0598)8242868	1,658	State-owned 國有	91,741	1012(12)	233,234	o
Guangdong Zhanjiang Machinery Factory 廣東省湛江機械廠(1952)	Zhanjiang 湛江市	Guangdong 廣東省	(0758)2194855 (0758)2198471	1,486	State-owned 國有	60,615	-43684(86)	223,186	a
Sichuan Ya Xi Machinery Plant 四川亞西機器廠(1942)	Leshan 樂山市	Sichuan 四川省	(0833)3351966	2,423	State-owned 國有	57,666	16(49)	122,110	a,c
Yiyang Rubber Machinery Plant 益陽橡膠機械廠(1971)	Yiyang 益陽市	Hunan 湖南省	(0737)4299404 (0737)4299888	2,484	State-owned 國有	52,664	-3005(83)	243,135	a
Xishan No.3 Universal Machinery Plant 錫山市第三通用機械廠(1979)	Wuxi 無錫市	Jiangsu 江蘇省	(0510)5380641	293	Collectively-owned 集體	50,380	1960(6)	21,350	o
Shandou Jin Field Dongxing Industry General Company 汕頭市金園區東興工業總公司(1985)	Shantou 汕頭市	Guangdong 廣東省	(0754)8627538	1,015	Collectively-owned 集體	44,635	320(26)	7,500	a
Shenyang Rubber Machinery Plant 瀋陽橡膠機械廠(1939)	Shenyang 瀋陽市	Liaoning 遼寧省	(024)25875922 (024)25852737	1,626	State-owned 國有	43,485	-4979(84)	230,181	a

Top 10 Cities by Production Output 產出排名前 10 位城市	Province 省	Market share 市場份額	Number of firms 企業個數
Dalian 大連市	Liaoning 遼寧省	16.21%	12
Wuxi 無錫市	Jiangsu 江蘇省	14.13%	17
Sanming 三明市	Fujian 福建省	7.10%	2
Nantong 南通市	Jiangsu 江蘇省	6.78%	7
Shantou 汕頭市	Guangdong 廣東省	6.03%	5
Shanghai 上海市	Shanghai 上海市	5.17%	19
Leshan 樂山市	Sichuan 四川省	4.70%	2
Shenyang 瀋陽市	Liaoning 遼寧省	4.61%	9
Zhanjiang 湛江市	Guangdong 廣東省	4.49%	2
Changzhou 常州市	Jiangsu 江蘇省	4.14%	5

10 Major Wholesalers 10 家主要批發商	City 城市	Province 省	Telephone / Fax 電話 / 傳真
Liaoning Automobile Trade Group Corp. 遼寧省汽車貿易集團	Shenyang 瀋陽市	Liaoning 遼寧省	(024)23835494 (024)23838338
China Post and Telecommunication Equipment General Company 中國郵電器材總公司	Beijing 北京市	Beijing 北京市	(010)63523715 (010)63525935
Jiangsu Electromechanical Products General Company 江蘇省機電產品總公司	Nanjing 南京市	Jiangsu 江蘇省	(025)7713642 (025)7711036
Xi Nan Technology Import & Export Company 西南技術進出口公司	Chongqing 重慶市	Chongqing 重慶市	(023)63850185 (023)63850026
Changzhou Economic Technology Industrial Development Zone Tian Ming Trade Company 常州經濟技術產業開發區天明貿易公司	Changzhou 常州市	Jiangsu 江蘇省	(0519)8829882 (0519)8829882
Shanxi Mechanical Equipment Import & Export Company 山西省機械設備進出口公司	Taiyuan 太原市	Shanxi 山西省	(0351)4040713 (0351)4043981
Ningbo Five Mining Machinery Import & Export Company 寧波市五礦機械進出口公司	Ningbo 寧波市	Zhejiang 浙江省	(0574)7311255 (0574)7320322
Tianjin Jin Huan Electromechanical Complete Sets of Equipment Factory 天津市津環機電成套設備廠	Tianjin 天津市	Tianjin 天津市	(022)26371628
Yunnan Machinery Import & Export Company 雲南省機械進出口公司	Kunming 昆明市	Yunnan 雲南省	(0871)3164879 (0871)3136829
Tianjin Da Qiu Zhuang Yi Yuan Trade Center 天津市大丘莊億源商貿中心	Tianjin 天津市	Tianjin 天津市	(022)28899478 (022)28899046

*Also include sales by firms outside this industry.包括本行業以外廠家的銷售。"o" stands for "others". "o" 代表"其他產品"。

3625: Plastics Equipment 塑料工業專用設備製造業

The industry accounts for 0.069% of the total revenue of China's industrial sector in 1996. The revenue growth rate of the industry is 22.4% from 1995, as compared to the growth rate of China's industrial sector, 9.51%. The rate of return on asset is 3.29%. 68.86% of all firms in the industry made a profit while 28.49% had negative returns. The top province in terms of the industry's revenue is Zhejiang, accounting for 26.74% of the total revenue.
本行業在1996年佔全行業總產值0.069%，行業年增長率為22.4%（全國工業年增長率9.51%）。行業的資產回報率3.29%，68.86%的企業盈利，28.49%的企業虧損。銷售收入最高的省份為浙江省，佔本行業的26.74%。

	Total number of firms 企業總數	Total number of employees 職工總數	Total revenue (mil. RMB) 總銷售收入（百萬元）	Total profit (mil. RMB) 總利潤（百萬元）	Return on assets 資產利潤率 (%)	Return on equity 權益利潤率 (%)	Labour productivity ('000 RMB / worker) 勞動生產率（千元/人）	Debts / assets 資產負債率 (%)	Total assets (mil. RMB) 總資產（百萬元）
Industry Overall 行業總體	379	60,415	3,992	182	3.29	8.89	66.08	63.03	5,531

	Number of firms 企業個數	Average number of employees 平均職工人數	Average revenue ('000 RMB) 平均銷售收入（千元）	Average profit ('000 RMB) 平均利潤（千元）	Return on assets 資產利潤率 (%)	Return on equity 權益利潤率 (%)	Labour productivity ('000 RMB / worker) 勞動生產率（千元/人）	Average debts / assets 平均資產負債率(%)	Average Total assets ('000 RMB) 平均總資產（千元）
By ownership 產業所有權									
State-owned 國有	49	343	20,837	673	1.99	5.58	60.79	64.29	33,776
Collectively-owned 集體	245	133	5,642	-28	-0.43	-1.34	42.49	68.05	6,573
Privately-owned 私有	1	49	7,415	999	22.09	74.09	151.33	70.19	4,521
Domestic JVs 聯營	1	95	18,324	1,815	21.91	54.62	192.88	59.88	8,284
Joint stock 股份制	9	172	5,339	-830	-7.04	-27.91	31.00	74.78	11,789
Foreign-funded 外資	17	108	16,365	835	4.42	13.72	152.19	67.82	18,911
Overseas Chinese-funded 港澳台資	56	137	22,078	2,625	8.06	18.26	160.92	55.84	32,553
By size 規模									
Large 大型	3	1,017	219,676	19,988	9.06	19.08	216.08	52.49	220,529
Medium 中型	33	616	42,256	3,111	4.28	11.85	68.55	63.92	72,732
Small 小型	340	109	5,704	57	0.78	2.24	52.27	64.98	7,264
By regional distribution 地區分布									
Central-North 華北	34	118	3,454	14	0.16	0.41	29.30	61.77	8,689
Beijing 北京	10	68	2,654	-29	-0.42	-1.30	38.80	68.06	6,985
Tianjin 天津	7	157	2,343	-146	-1.61	-7.38	14.95	78.16	9,039
Hebei 河北	13	125	4,235	95	1.23	2.60	33.94	52.75	7,760
Shanxi 山西	4	151	4,858	133	0.86	1.82	32.12	52.56	15,360
Inner Mongolia 內蒙									
Northeast 東北	31	219	3,701	-681	-7.03	-41.02	16.88	82.85	9,685
Liaoning 遼寧	25	128	3,843	-296	-4.47	-22.56	29.97	80.19	6,612
Jilin 吉林	1	365	570	-1,840	-7.97	-22.47	1.56	64.55	23,100
Heilongjiang 黑龍江	5	645	3,618	-2,378	-10.63	-112.70	5.61	90.57	22,366
Central East 華東	197	159	12,801	740	4.74	11.78	80.62	59.73	15,601
Shanghai 上海	20	141	4,589	268	3.82	8.86	32.64	56.92	7,019
Jiangsu 江蘇	53	239	12,551	222	1.40	4.39	52.59	68.10	15,832
Zhejiang 浙江	82	103	13,020	970	6.16	13.45	126.26	54.24	15,750
Anhui 安徽	5	210	7,272	4	0.02	0.09	34.56	77.35	19,046
Fujian 福建	13	121	2,752	-15	-0.17	-0.38	22.74	54.30	8,960
Jiangxi 江西	1	42	960	50	15.63	31.25	22.86	50.00	320
Shandong 山東	23	204	27,137	2,143	8.35	20.22	132.91	58.72	25,670
Central-South 中南	98	169	12,406	616	3.43	10.00	73.62	65.67	17,925
Henan 河南	15	318	11,995	195	2.03	5.25	37.66	61.36	9,637
Hubei 湖北	11	323	14,645	105	0.38	1.24	45.38	69.24	27,589
Hunan 湖南	12	98	1,192	-409	-7.81	-31.43	12.17	75.13	5,238
Guangdong 廣東	49	94	15,068	1,429	7.90	19.97	159.50	60.41	18,075
Guangxi 廣西	11	217	11,104	-806	-2.46	-10.13	51.25	75.68	32,739
Hainan 海南									
Southwest 西南	14	83	1,069	-132	-2.99	-7.53	12.84	60.24	4,416
Chongqing 重慶	1	34	53	2	0.95	2.13	1.56	55.45	230
Sichuan 四川	7	104	703	-155	-4.70	-12.80	6.76	63.29	3,291
Guizhou 貴州	3	10	377	-133	-7.08	-12.42	37.67	42.83	1,883
Yunnan 雲南	3	120	2,910	-113	-1.05	-2.70	24.25	61.07	10,763
Tibet 西藏									
Northwest 西北	5	130	1,384	-352	-4.06	-11.62	10.61	65.00	8,664
Shaanxi 陝西	3	161	1,663	-590	-9.20	-91.71	10.31	89.91	6,410
Gansu 甘肅	1	150	1,810	10	0.17	0.37	12.07	53.10	5,800
Qinghai 青海									
Ningxia 寧夏									
Xinjiang 新疆	1	18	120				6.67	42.59	18,290

3625: Plastics Equipment 塑料工業專用設備製造業

Year 年份	Number of firms 企業個數	Rate of change 每年變化 (%)	Number of employees 職工人數（人）	Rate of change 每年變化 (%)	Total revenue (mil. RMB) 總銷售收入（百萬元）	Rate of change 每年變化 (%)	Total profit (mil. RMB) 總利潤（百萬元）	Rate of change 每年變化 (%)
1993	329		58,157		3,126		246	
1994	322	-2.13%	55,100	-5.26%	2,718	-13.03%	145	-40.91%
1995	349	8.39%	56,023	1.68%	3,262	20.02%	117	-19.48%
1996	379	8.60%	60,415	7.84%	3,992	22.38%	182	55.78%

3 Major products* 3 種主要產品 *	Output 產量	Sales volume 銷售量	Unit 單位
a) Plastic Processing Equipment 塑料加工設備	258,415	250,662	ton 噸
b) Paper Making Machinery 造紙機械	1,066	1,013	set 台
c) Special Processing Equipment for Rubber 橡膠加工專用設備	466	340	ton 噸

Top 10 firms by revenue (year founded) 收入排名前 10 家企業 (創辦年份)	City 城市	Province 省	Telephone / fax 電話 / 傳真	Number of employees 職工人數	Ownership 產業所有權	Revenue ('000 RMB) 銷售收入（千元）	Profit ('000 RMB) (rank) 利潤（千元）（排名）	Total assets ('000 RMB) 總資產（千元）	Major products 主要產品
Shandong Plastics Rubber Machinery General Factory 山東塑料橡膠機械總廠(1966)	Laiwu 萊蕪市	Shandong 山東省	(0634)6212901 (0634)6397034	2,222	State-owned 國有	430,152	35333(3)	360,124	a
Ningbo Hai Tian Plastics Machinery Co. Ltd. 寧波海天機械有限公司(1990)	Ningbo 寧波市	Zhejiang 浙江省	(0574)6177266 (0574)6221864	582	Foreign-funded 外資	236,142	53429(1)	327,777	o
Zhen De Plastic Machinery Plant Co. Ltd. 震德塑料機械廠有限公司(1987)	Foshan 佛山市	Guangdong 廣東省	(0757)2621835 (0757)2627560	418	Overseas Chinese-funded 港澳台資	201,628	46975(2)	275,344	a
Donghua Machinery Co. Ltd. 東莞市東華機械有限公司(1986)	Dongguan 東莞市	Guangdong 廣東省	(0769)2417755 (0769)2412897	486	Overseas Chinese-funded 港澳台資	146,075	20285(4)	222,784	a
Jiangsu Wei Da Machinery Group Co. 江蘇維達機械集團公司(1958)	Suzhou 蘇州市	Jiangsu 江蘇省	(0512)8441143	616	State-owned 國有	103,189	13132(6)	110,858	a
Ningbo Tongda Plastics Machinery Co. Ltd. 寧波通達塑料機械有限公司(1958)	Ningbo 寧波市	Zhejiang 浙江省	(0574)7355690 (0574)7356293	869	Overseas Chinese-funded 港澳台資	100,849	2640(16)	168,110	a
Ningbo Yong Jiang Plastics Machinery Co. Ltd. 寧波甬江塑料機械有限公司(1989)	Ningbo 寧波市	Zhejiang 浙江省	(0574)7350770 (0574)7350770	279	Foreign-funded 外資	100,150	13638(5)	55,887	o
Suiping Hua Qiang Plastic Cement Co. Ltd. 遂平縣華強塑膠有限公司(1995)	Zhumadian 駐馬店市	Henan 河南省	(0396)4925612	3,440	Joint stock 股份制	98,610	551(43)	28,487	o
Wuxi Ge Lan Machinery Co. Ltd. 無錫市格蘭機械有限公司(1992)	Wuxi 無錫市	Jiangsu 江蘇省	(0510)5108852 (0510)5100814	286	Foreign-funded 外資	83,411	940(32)	120,969	a
Rong Sheng Plastics Machinery Co. Ltd. 容聲塑料機械有限公司(1988)	Foshan 佛山市	Guangdong 廣東省	(0757)6623189 (0757)6628612	255	Overseas Chinese-funded 港澳台資	75,247	-249(160)	87,167	a

Top 10 Cities by Production Output 產出排名前 10 位城市	Province 省	Market share 市場份額	Number of firms 企業個數
Ningbo 寧波市	Zhejiang 浙江省	17.19%	20
Laiwu 萊蕪市	Shandong 山東省	10.18%	2
Wenzhou 温州市	Zhejiang 浙江省	8.55%	89
Shanghai 上海市	Shanghai 上海市	7.80%	28
Foshan 佛山市	Guangdong 廣東省	6.24%	12
Changzhou 常州市	Jiangsu 江蘇省	4.51%	16
Suzhou 蘇州市	Jiangsu 江蘇省	4.02%	22
Hangzhou 杭州市	Zhejiang 浙江省	3.24%	17
Wuxi 無錫市	Jiangsu 江蘇省	3.14%	22
Liuzhou 柳州市	Guangxi 廣西	2.39%	11

10 Major Wholesalers 10 家主要批發商	City 城市	Province 省	Telephone / Fax 電話 / 傳真
Liaoning Automobile Trade Group Corp. 遼寧省汽車貿易集團	Shenyang 瀋陽市	Liaoning 遼寧省	(024)23835494 (024)23838338
China Post and Telecommunication Equipment General Company 中國郵電器材總公司	Beijing 北京市	Beijing 北京市	(010)63523715 (010)63525935
Jiangsu Electromechanical Products General Company 江蘇省機電產品總公司	Nanjing 南京市	Jiangsu 江蘇省	(025)7713642 (025)7711036
Xi Nan Technology Import & Export Company 西南技術進出口公司	Chongqing 重慶市	Chongqing 重慶市	(023)63850185 (023)63850026
Changzhou Economic Technology Industrial Development Zone Tian Ming Trade Company 常州經濟技術產業開發區天明貿易公司	Changzhou 常州市	Jiangsu 江蘇省	(0519)8829882 (0519)8829882
Shanxi Mechanical Equipment Import & Export Company 山西省機械設備進出口公司	Taiyuan 太原市	Shanxi 山西省	(0351)4040713 (0351)4043981
Ningbo Five Mining Machinery Import & Export Company 寧波市五礦機械進出口公司	Ningbo 寧波市	Zhejiang 浙江省	(0574)7311255 (0574)7320322
Tianjin Jin Huan Electromechanical Complete Sets of Equipment Factory 天津市津環機電成套設備廠	Tianjin 天津市	Tianjin 天津市	(022)26371628
Yunnan Machinery Import & Export Company 雲南省機械進出口公司	Kunming 昆明市	Yunnan 雲南省	(0871)3164879 (0871)3136829
Tianjin Da Qiu Zhuang Yi Yuan Trade Center 天津市大丘莊億源商貿中心	Tianjin 天津市	Tianjin 天津市	(022)28899478 (022)28899046

*Also include sales by firms outside this industry.包括本行業以外廠家的銷售。"o" stands for "others". "o" 代表"其他產品"。

3626: Lumber Equipment 木材工業專用設備製造業

The industry accounts for 0.045% of the total revenue of China's industrial sector in 1996. The revenue growth rate of the industry is -3.9% from 1995, as compared to the growth rate of China's industrial sector, 9.51%. The rate of return on asset is 2.57%. 53.60% of all firms in the industry made a profit while 35.29% had negative returns. The top province in terms of the industry's revenue is Shandong, accounting for 33.09% of the total revenue.
本行業在1996年佔全行業總產值0.045%，行業年增長率為-3.9%（全國工業年增長率9.51%）。行業的資產回報率2.57%，53.60%的企業盈利，35.29%的企業虧損。銷售收入最高的省份為山東省，佔本行業的33.09%。

	Total number of firms 企業總數	Total number of employees 職工總數	Total revenue (mil. RMB) 總銷售收入（百萬元）	Total profit (mil. RMB) 總利潤（百萬元）	Return on assets 資產利潤率 (%)	Return on equity 權益利潤率 (%)	Labour productivity ('000 RMB / worker) 勞動生產率（千元/人）	Debts / assets 資產負債率 (%)	Total assets (mil. RMB) 總資產（百萬元）
Industry Overall 行業總體	177	48,287	2,612	89	2.57	8.92	54.09	71.15	3,467

	Number of firms 企業個數	Average number of employees 平均職工人數	Average revenue ('000 RMB) 平均銷售收入（千元）	Average profit ('000 RMB) 平均利潤（千元）	Return on assets 資產利潤率 (%)	Return on equity 權益利潤率 (%)	Labour productivity ('000 RMB / worker) 勞動生產率（千元/人）	Average debts / assets 平均資產負債率(%)	Average Total assets ('000 RMB) 平均總資產（千元）
By ownership 產業所有權									
State-owned 國有	34	708	30,559	794	1.33	4.54	43.16	70.63	59,588
Collectively-owned 集體	127	173	11,381	517	5.27	20.03	65.89	73.69	9,816
Privately-owned 私有	1	12	215	25	1.98	4.64	17.88	57.33	1,247
Domestic JVs 聯營	1	326	3,976	-3,575	-30.46	-1321.02	12.20	97.69	11,737
Joint stock 股份制	2	230	14,285	726	4.20	8.82	62.11	52.37	17,282
Foreign-funded 外資	7	116	9,706	290	2.63	6.55	83.67	59.78	11,013
Overseas Chinese-funded 港澳台資	5	165	5,435	-727	-5.22	-12.65	33.02	58.76	13,933
By size 規模									
Large 大型	4	1,687	113,965	3,070	1.81	5.92	67.54	69.38	169,498
Medium 中型	16	1,187	67,324	2,729	2.79	10.65	56.73	73.79	97,803
Small 小型	157	144	6,874	211	2.70	8.65	47.64	68.77	7,797
By regional distribution 地區分布									
Central-North 華北	13	123	4,347	-105	-1.30	-3.04	35.47	57.35	8,122
Beijing 北京	1	12	1,090	-20	-0.39	-3.17	90.83	87.57	5,070
Tianjin 天津	2	31	5,200	-600	-3.05	-3.53	167.74	13.51	19,645
Hebei 河北	6	198	7,157	-12	-0.14	-0.91	36.14	85.12	8,613
Shanxi 山西	2	68	495	-50	-4.50	-83.33	7.33	94.59	1,110
Inner Mongolia 內蒙	2	98	545	10	0.27	0.77	5.56	64.34	3,660
Northeast 東北	42	337	7,499	-234	-1.37	-4.78	22.22	71.37	17,110
Liaoning 遼寧	13	178	2,681	-409	-4.79	-23.12	15.04	79.29	8,543
Jilin 吉林	4	583	6,725	-1,990	-8.66	-189.52	11.54	95.43	22,968
Heilongjiang 黑龍江	25	381	10,128	138	0.67	1.93	26.58	65.38	20,627
Central East 華東	73	276	23,278	1,070	4.34	18.20	84.30	76.14	24,631
Shanghai 上海	10	272	35,487	1,879	4.11	20.94	130.66	80.39	45,761
Jiangsu 江蘇	20	293	21,313	764	2.76	9.99	72.77	72.38	27,666
Zhejiang 浙江	6	88	5,020	115	1.62	3.96	57.15	59.01	7,083
Anhui 安徽	2	330	3,635	-2,045	-32.77	69.80	11.03	146.88	6,240
Fujian 福建	8	60	1,121	-33	-1.70	-6.27	18.73	72.91	1,910
Jiangxi 江西	4	177	1,875	20	0.59	2.01	10.58	70.78	3,405
Shandong 山東	23	400	37,578	2,070	6.77	28.54	93.84	76.27	30,577
Central-South 中南	31	166	8,044	572	6.37	21.89	48.36	70.92	8,984
Henan 河南	14	168	7,909	419	4.29	15.82	47.20	72.88	9,754
Hubei 湖北	4	251	21,283	890	10.41	21.75	84.88	52.09	8,548
Hunan 湖南	2	66	390	-125	-7.12	-96.15	5.91	92.31	1,755
Guangdong 廣東	4	176	6,968	485	6.11	9.79	39.64	37.57	7,938
Guangxi 廣西	7	139	3,549	946	9.13	88.38	25.56	89.67	10,356
Hainan 海南									
Southwest 西南	15	401	17,169	336	0.99	2.25	42.85	56.06	33,963
Chongqing 重慶	1	1,015	32,734	110	0.17	0.29	32.25	39.51	63,847
Sichuan 四川	10	370	14,922	25	0.08	0.20	40.30	58.09	29,320
Guizhou 貴州									
Yunnan 雲南	4	336	19,268	1,173	3.02	7.27	57.43	58.44	38,820
Tibet 西藏									
Northwest 西北	3	399	11,543	-130	-0.69	-2.52	28.95	72.74	18,927
Shaanxi 陝西	3	399	11,543	-130	-0.69	-2.52	28.95	72.74	18,927
Gansu 甘肅									
Qinghai 青海									
Ningxia 寧夏									
Xinjiang 新疆									

3626: Lumber Equipment 木材工業專用設備製造業

Year 年份	Number of firms 企業個數	Rate of change 每年變化 (%)	Number of employees 職工人數 (人)	Rate of change 每年變化 (%)	Total revenue (mil. RMB) 總銷售收入 (百萬元)	Rate of change 每年變化 (%)	Total profit (mil. RMB) 總利潤 (百萬元)	Rate of change 每年變化 (%)
1993	173		45,880		2,009		121	
1994	164	-5.20%	43,683	-4.79%	2,210	9.98%	64	-47.27%
1995	194	18.29%	55,721	27.56%	2,718	23.00%	104	63.28%
1996	177	-8.76%	48,287	-13.34%	2,612	-3.90%	89	-14.37%

3 Major products* 3種主要產品 *	Output 產量	Sales volume 銷售量	Unit 單位
a) Wood Processing Machinery 木材加工機械	533,359	512,025	set 台
b) Wood Fibre Segregator 木質纖維分離機械	1,244	945	set 台
c) Chipboard 刨花板	11,873	11,161	cubic metre 立方米

Top 10 firms by revenue (year founded) 收入排名前10家企業 (創辦年份)	City 城市	Province 省	Telephone / fax 電話 / 傳真	Number of employees 職工人數	Ownership 產業所有權	Revenue ('000 RMB) 銷售收入 (千元)	Profit ('000 RMB) (rank) 利潤 (千元) (排名)	Total assets ('000 RMB) 總資產 (千元)	Major products 主要產品
Weihai Gong You Group Co. 威海工友集團公司(1994)	Weihai 威海市	Shandong 山東省	(0896)5366268 (0896)5366100	3,260	Collectively-owned 集體	397,687	25420(1)	356,013	a
Shanghai Wood-based Panel Machinery Factory 上海人造板機器廠(1952)	Shanghai 上海市	Shanghai 上海市	(021)59577480 (021)59572568	1,290	State-owned 國有	247,004	9538(4)	311,304	a
Mudanjiang Woodwork Machinery Plant 牡丹江木工機械廠(1946)	Mudanjiang 牡丹江市	Heilongjiang 黑龍江省	(0453)6615288 (0453)6618873	2,295	State-owned 國有	157,706	10469(3)	171,417	a
Suzhou Forestry Machine Factory 蘇州林業機械廠(1961)	Suzhou 蘇州市	Jiangsu 江蘇省	(0512)7535627 (0512)7534072	839	State-owned 國有	154,461	12502(2)	214,152	o
Weihai Cao Miao Zi Woodwork Machinery Plant 威海市草廟子木工機械廠(1976)	Weihai 威海市	Shandong 山東省	(0896)5584558 (0896)5584136	475	Collectively-owned 集體	130,009	8810(5)	27,191	a
China Forestry Machinery General Company Zhenjiang Forestry Machinery Plant 中國林業機械總公司鎮江林業機械廠(1958)	Zhenjiang 鎮江市	Jiangsu 江蘇省	(0511)8781320 (0511)8781099	1,036	State-owned 國有	100,416	4608(10)	161,262	a
Weihai No.2 Machinery Plant 威海第二機械廠(1963)	Weihai 威海市	Shandong 山東省	(0896)5382231 (0896)5382231	823	Collectively-owned 集體	71,666	2080(17)	57,460	a
Kunming Artificial Board Machine Factory 昆明人造板機器廠(1980)	Kunming 昆明市	Yunnan 雲南省	(0871)5815418 (0871)5810331	1,044	State-owned 國有	60,510	4309(12)	128,158	a,c
Sichuan Dong Hua Machinery Plant 四川東華機械廠(1969)	Chengdu 成都市	Sichuan 四川省	(028)5195672 (028)5181343	760	State-owned 國有	60,052	7581(6)	136,742	a
Zhengzhou He Ying Industrial General Company 鄭州合英實業總公司(1984)	Zhengzhou 鄭州市	Henan 河南省	(0371)4354733 (0371)4352466	126	Collectively-owned 集體	57,600	6000(8)	7,100	o

Top 10 Cities by Production Output 產出排名前10位城市	Province 省	Market share 市場份額	Number of firms 企業個數
Weihai 威海市	Shandong 山東省	25.67%	10
Shanghai 上海市	Shanghai 上海市	15.17%	9
Mudanjiang 牡丹江市	Heilongjiang 黑龍江省	9.20%	13
Suzhou 蘇州市	Jiangsu 江蘇省	8.20%	6
Zhenjiang 鎮江市	Jiangsu 江蘇省	3.99%	1
Kunming 昆明市	Yunnan 雲南省	3.68%	4
Chengdu 成都市	Sichuan 四川省	3.23%	4
Qingdao 青島市	Shandong 山東省	3.09%	7
Zhengzhou 鄭州市	Henan 河南省	2.94%	3
Cangzhou 滄州市	Hebei 河北省	2.32%	4

10 Major Wholesalers 10家主要批發商	City 城市	Province 省	Telephone / Fax 電話 / 傳真
Liaoning Automobile Trade Group Corp. 遼寧省汽車貿易集團	Shenyang 瀋陽市	Liaoning 遼寧省	(024)23835494 (024)23838338
China Post and Telecommunication Equipment General Company 中國郵電器材總公司	Beijing 北京市	Beijing 北京市	(010)63523715 (010)63525935
Jiangsu Electromechanical Products General Company 江蘇省機電產品總公司	Nanjing 南京市	Jiangsu 江蘇省	(025)7713642 (025)7711036
Xi Nan Technology Import & Export Company 西南技術進出口公司	Chongqing 重慶市	Chongqing 重慶市	(023)63850185 (023)63850026
Changzhou Economic Technology Industrial Development Zone Tian Ming Trade Company 常州經濟技術產業開發區天明貿易公司	Changzhou 常州市	Jiangsu 江蘇省	(0519)8829882 (0519)8829882
Shanxi Mechanical Equipment Import & Export Company 山西省機械設備進出口公司	Taiyuan 太原市	Shanxi 山西省	(0351)4040713 (0351)4043981
Ningbo Five Mining Machinery Import & Export Company 寧波市五礦機械進出口公司	Ningbo 寧波市	Zhejiang 浙江省	(0574)7311255 (0574)7320322
Tianjin Jin Huan Electromechanical Complete Sets of Equipment Factory 天津市津環機電成套設備廠	Tianjin 天津市	Tianjin 天津市	(022)26371628
Yunnan Machinery Import & Export Company 雲南省機械進出口公司	Kunming 昆明市	Yunnan 雲南省	(0871)3164879 (0871)3136829
Tianjin Da Qiu Zhuang Yi Yuan Trade Center 天津市大丘莊億源商貿中心	Tianjin 天津市	Tianjin 天津市	(022)28899478 (022)28899046

*Also include sales by firms outside this industry.包括本行業以外廠家的銷售。"o" stands for "others". "o" 代表 "其他產品"。

3627: Printing Equipment 印刷工業專用設備製造業

The industry accounts for 0.051% of the total revenue of China's industrial sector in 1996. The revenue growth rate of the industry is 18.5% from 1995, as compared to the growth rate of China's industrial sector, 9.51%. The rate of return on asset is 1.83%. 62.51% of all firms in the industry made a profit while 31.82% had negative returns. The top province in terms of the industry's revenue is Shanghai, accounting for 26.08% of the total revenue.
本行業在1996年佔全行業總產值0.051%，行業年增長率為18.5%（全國工業年增長率9.51%）。行業的資產回報率1.83%，62.51%的企業盈利，31.82%的企業虧損。銷售收入最高的省份為上海市，佔本行業的26.08%。

	Total number of firms 企業總數	Total number of employees 職工總數	Total revenue (mil. RMB) 總銷售收入（百萬元）	Total profit (mil. RMB) 總利潤（百萬元）	Return on assets 資產利潤率 (%)	Return on equity 權益利潤率 (%)	Labour productivity ('000 RMB / worker) 勞動生產率（千元/人）	Debts / assets 資產負債率 (%)	Total assets (mil. RMB) 總資產（百萬元）
Industry Overall 行業總體	279	61,448	2,933	139	1.83	3.29	47.73	44.36	7,607

	Number of firms 企業個數	Average number of employees 平均職工人數	Average revenue ('000 RMB) 平均銷售收入（千元）	Average profit ('000 RMB) 平均利潤（千元）	Return on assets 資產利潤率 (%)	Return on equity 權益利潤率 (%)	Labour productivity ('000 RMB / worker) 勞動生產率（千元/人）	Average debts / assets 平均資產負債率(%)	Average Total assets ('000 RMB) 平均總資產（千元）
By ownership 產業所有權									
State-owned 國有	52	545	12,808	-346	-0.61	-1.16	23.49	47.31	56,538
Collectively-owned 集體	164	122	5,035	66	0.78	2.05	41.18	61.83	8,503
Privately-owned 私有	1	13	186	-13	-1.36	-47.20	14.29	97.12	946
Domestic JVs 聯營	4	93	4,168	-248	-2.12	-4.86	44.70	56.43	11,689
Joint stock 股份制	7	948	70,918	14,664	6.44	7.76	74.79	17.03	227,865
Foreign-funded 外資	22	275	30,553	1,163	2.24	4.34	110.99	48.33	51,853
Overseas Chinese-funded 港澳台資	28	64	9,172	674	3.86	8.64	142.44	55.32	17,472
By size 規模									
Large 大型	8	1,783	97,867	17,467	4.15	5.53	54.89	24.97	421,274
Medium 中型	29	755	35,505	-59	-0.07	-0.18	47.01	57.48	78,724
Small 小型	233	110	4,813	4	0.05	0.13	43.79	62.44	8,387
By regional distribution 地區分布									
Central-North 華北	51	224	12,766	1,985	3.95	5.12	57.06	22.91	50,312
Beijing 北京	26	249	19,642	3,585	4.23	5.16	78.81	18.07	84,840
Tianjin 天津	8	123	5,546	193	1.55	2.36	45.18	34.41	12,448
Hebei 河北	14	174	5,623	453	3.88	10.08	32.29	61.58	11,686
Shanxi 山西	3	503	5,773	47	0.14	0.33	11.47	56.12	32,300
Inner Mongolia 內蒙									
Northeast 東北	34	258	6,859	-57	-0.26	-0.66	26.61	61.24	22,152
Liaoning 遼寧	24	159	6,207	212	1.98	5.71	38.98	65.35	10,693
Jilin 吉林	5	420	6,230	-1,476	-6.41	-52.60	14.85	87.81	23,024
Heilongjiang 黑龍江	5	569	10,618	74	0.10	0.20	18.67	50.46	76,288
Central East 華東	137	206	12,930	357	1.46	2.99	62.90	51.39	24,556
Shanghai 上海	26	289	29,419	1,811	4.21	10.10	101.70	58.31	42,991
Jiangsu 江蘇	38	230	13,798	265	1.34	3.19	60.01	58.06	19,765
Zhejiang 浙江	38	147	6,793	-214	-1.48	-3.58	46.08	58.76	14,465
Anhui 安徽	6	218	3,757	-418	-5.47	28.62	17.23	119.09	7,647
Fujian 福建	10	129	4,965	-1,111	-1.85	-2.23	38.37	16.83	59,957
Jiangxi 江西	7	249	8,141	674	3.49	9.01	32.75	61.31	19,346
Shandong 山東	12	164	7,910	735	5.35	10.37	48.38	48.36	13,729
Central-South 中南	39	177	5,275	-35	-0.22	-0.56	29.81	60.11	15,845
Henan 河南	7	34	800	24	2.76	8.21	23.53	66.45	881
Hubei 湖北	4	164	2,595	13	0.20	0.66	15.82	70.35	6,358
Hunan 湖南	11	318	4,585	18	0.11	0.17	14.40	34.82	16,410
Guangdong 廣東	15	80	8,534	343	1.91	5.74	106.14	66.82	18,019
Guangxi 廣西	2	650	5,645	-3,470	-5.12	-23.49	8.69	78.20	67,775
Hainan 海南									
Southwest 西南	13	152	2,073	-416	-5.82	-18.97	13.67	69.32	7,151
Chongqing 重慶	2	64	405	12	0.56	1.24	6.35	54.69	2,201
Sichuan 四川	9	204	2,961	-618	-6.17	-20.66	14.51	70.12	10,014
Guizhou 貴州	1								
Yunnan 雲南	1	34							
Tibet 西藏									
Northwest 西北	5	848	8,932	-472	-1.11	-4.51	10.54	75.43	42,556
Shaanxi 陝西	3	1,047	9,003	-793	-1.43	-6.18	8.60	76.83	55,420
Gansu 甘肅	1	1,096	17,650	20	0.04	0.15	16.10	70.44	46,520
Qinghai 青海	1								
Ningxia 寧夏									
Xinjiang 新疆									

3627: Printing Equipment 印刷工業專用設備製造業

Year 年份	Number of firms 企業個數	Rate of change 每年變化 (%)	Number of employees 職工人數（人）	Rate of change 每年變化 (%)	Total revenue (mil. RMB) 總銷售收入（百萬元）	Rate of change 每年變化 (%)	Total profit (mil. RMB) 總利潤（百萬元）	Rate of change 每年變化 (%)
1993	317		108,762		2,938		352	
1994	305	-3.79%	65,535	-39.75%	2,363	-19.55%	193	-45.27%
1995	282	-7.54%	63,479	-3.14%	2,476	4.78%	141	-26.86%
1996	279	-1.06%	61,448	-3.20%	2,933	18.46%	139	-1.31%

3 Major products* 3 種主要產品 *	Output 產量	Sales volume 銷售量	Unit 單位
a) Other Special Equipment for Industry Printing 其他印刷工業專用設備	21,816	22,034	ton 噸
b) Printing Machine 印刷機	54,268	54,268	ton 噸
c) Binding Machine 裝訂機械	4,099	3,935	ton 噸

Top 10 firms by revenue (year founded) 收入排名前 10 家企業（創辦年份）	City 城市	Province 省	Telephone / fax 電話 / 傳真	Number of employees 職工人數	Ownership 產業所有權	Revenue ('000 RMB) 銷售收入（千元）	Profit ('000 RMB) (rank) 利潤（千元）（排名）	Total assets ('000 RMB) 總資產（千元）	Major products 主要產品
Bei Ren Printing Machinery Co. Ltd. 北人印刷機械股份有限公司(1996)	Beijing 北京市	Beijing 北京市	(010)67737711	3,468	Joint stock 股份制	375,991	91539(1)	1,081,595	b
Shanghai Ya Hua Printing Machinery Co. Ltd. 上海亞華印刷機械有限公司(1988)	Shanghai 上海市	Shanghai 上海市	(021)64042390 (021)64041244	494	Foreign-funded 外資	137,572	11200(3)	132,190	a
Shanghai Goss Graphic Systems Co. Ltd. 上海羅克韋爾圖文系統有限公司(1994)	Shanghai 上海市	Shanghai 上海市	(021)62591260 (021)62748772	819	Foreign-funded 外資	127,534	9554(4)	204,126	a,b
Nantong Mining Machinery Plant 南通市礦山機械廠(1958)	Nantong 南通市	Jiangsu 江蘇省	(0513)7512981	1,684	Collectively-owned 集體	125,732	6352(9)	142,624	b
Shanghai Shen Wei Da Machinery Co. Ltd. 上海申威達機械有限公司(1991)	Shanghai 上海市	Shanghai 上海市	(021)58891376 (021)58810161	660	Foreign-funded 外資	111,162	9130(5)	121,454	a
Bei Ren Group Co. 北人集團公司(1952)	Beijing 北京市	Beijing 北京市	(010)67737711	2,088	State-owned 國有	104,713	4270(15)	987,440	a,b
Xishan Yan Qiao Hua Guang Enterprise-run Factory 錫山市堰橋華光企業辦廠(1985)	Wuxi 無錫市	Jiangsu 江蘇省	(0510)3741969	331	Collectively-owned 集體	79,572	-147(106)	63,208	o
Shenzhen Oastar Electron Co. Ltd. 深圳奧士達電子有限公司(1989)	Shenzhen 深圳市	Guangdong 廣東省	(0755)3312167 (0755)3312334	115	Overseas Chinese-funded 港澳台資	79,448	6553(8)	139,363	o
Shanghai Zi Ming Machinery Co. Ltd. 上海紫明機械有限公司(1993)	Shanghai 上海市	Shanghai 上海市	(021)64890031 (021)64890981	393	Foreign-funded 外資	70,968	3525(16)	65,678	a,b,c
Shanghai Zi Guang Machinery Co. Ltd. 上海紫光機械有限公司(1993)	Shanghai 上海市	Shanghai 上海市	(021)63018426 (021)63010910	586	Foreign-funded 外資	70,237	8328(6)	91,943	b,c

Top 10 Cities by Production Output 產出排名前 10 位城市	Province 省	Market share 市場份額	Number of firms 企業個數
Shanghai 上海市	Shanghai 上海市	30.05%	54
Beijing 北京市	Beijing 北京市	18.45%	26
Nantong 南通市	Jiangsu 江蘇省	8.88%	7
Wenzhou 温州市	Zhejiang 浙江省	4.98%	59
Wuxi 無錫市	Jiangsu 江蘇省	4.89%	31
Tianjin 天津市	Tianjin 天津市	2.29%	9
Taizhou 泰州市	Jiangsu 江蘇省	2.10%	4
Harbin 哈爾濱市	Heilongjiang 黑龍江省	2.08%	4
Dalian 大連市	Liaoning 遼寧省	1.89%	10
Suzhou 蘇州市	Jiangsu 江蘇省	1.77%	8

10 Major Wholesalers 10 家主要批發商	City 城市	Province 省	Telephone / Fax 電話 / 傳真
Liaoning Automobile Trade Group Corp. 遼寧省汽車貿易集團	Shenyang 瀋陽市	Liaoning 遼寧省	(024)23835494 (024)23838338
China Post and Telecommunication Equipment General Company 中國郵電器材總公司	Beijing 北京市	Beijing 北京市	(010)63523715 (010)63525935
Jiangsu Electromechanical Products General Company 江蘇省機電產品總公司	Nanjing 南京市	Jiangsu 江蘇省	(025)7713642 (025)7711036
Xi Nan Technology Import & Export Company 西南技術進出口公司	Chongqing 重慶市	Chongqing 重慶市	(023)63850185 (023)63850026
Changzhou Economic Technology Industrial Development Zone Tian Ming Trade Company 常州經濟技術產業開發區天明貿易公司	Changzhou 常州市	Jiangsu 江蘇省	(0519)8829882 (0519)8829882
Shanxi Mechanical Equipment Import & Export Company 山西省機械設備進出口公司	Taiyuan 太原市	Shanxi 山西省	(0351)4040713 (0351)4043981
Ningbo Five Mining Machinery Import & Export Company 寧波市五礦機械進出口公司	Ningbo 寧波市	Zhejiang 浙江省	(0574)7311255 (0574)7320322
Tianjin Jin Huan Electromechanical Complete Sets of Equipment Factory 天津市津環機電成套設備廠	Tianjin 天津市	Tianjin 天津市	(022)26371628
Yunnan Machinery Import & Export Company 雲南省機械進出口公司	Kunming 昆明市	Yunnan 雲南省	(0871)3164879 (0871)3136829
Tianjin Da Qiu Zhuang Yi Yuan Trade Center 天津市大丘莊億源商貿中心	Tianjin 天津市	Tianjin 天津市	(022)28899478 (022)28899046

*Also include sales by firms outside this industry.包括本行業以外廠家的銷售。"o" stands for "others". "o" 代表"其他產品"。

3628: Pharmaceutical Equipment 製藥工業專用設備製造業

The industry accounts for 0.011% of the total revenue of China's industrial sector in 1996. The revenue growth rate of the industry is 8.7% from 1995, as compared to the growth rate of China's industrial sector, 9.51%. The rate of return on asset is 0.83%. 59.37% of all firms in the industry made a profit while 34.92% had negative returns. The top province in terms of the industry's revenue is Shanghai, accounting for 18.84% of the total revenue.
本行業在1996年佔全行業總產值0.011%，行業年增長率為8.7%（全國工業年增長率9.51%）。行業的資產回報率0.83%，59.37%的企業盈利，34.92%的企業虧損。銷售收入最高的省份為上海市，佔本行業的18.84%。

	Total number of firms 企業總數	Total number of employees 職工總數	Total revenue (mil. RMB) 總銷售收入（百萬元）	Total profit (mil. RMB) 總利潤（百萬元）	Return on assets 資產利潤率 (%)	Return on equity 權益利潤率 (%)	Labour productivity ('000 RMB / worker) 勞動生產率（千元/人）	Debts / assets 資產負債率 (%)	Total assets (mil. RMB) 總資產（百萬元）
Industry Overall 行業總體	129	17,156	628	10	0.83	2.81	36.61	70.53	1,168

	Number of firms 企業個數	Average number of employees 平均職工人數	Average revenue ('000 RMB) 平均銷售收入（千元）	Average profit ('000 RMB) 平均利潤（千元）	Return on assets 資產利潤率 (%)	Return on equity 權益利潤率 (%)	Labour productivity ('000 RMB / worker) 勞動生產率（千元/人）	Average debts / assets 平均資產負債率(%)	Average Total assets ('000 RMB) 平均總資產（千元）
By ownership 產業所有權									
State-owned 國有	25	323	9,560	40	0.17	0.61	29.61	71.60	23,240
Collectively-owned 集體	96	62	2,272	18	0.65	2.47	36.72	73.56	2,801
Privately-owned 私有									
Domestic JVs 聯營	1	575	34,253	1,002	1.05	4.04	59.57	73.92	95,078
Joint stock 股份制	3	674	29,022	663	1.40	5.34	43.04	73.86	47,513
Foreign-funded 外資	2	218	22,841	2,124	5.68	10.45	105.02	45.65	37,384
Overseas Chinese-funded 港澳台資	2	56	1,901	2	0.07	0.08	34.25	17.81	3,348
By size 規模									
Large 大型	1	1,621	57,085	2,491	2.23	9.88	35.22	77.40	111,578
Medium 中型	8	713	27,981	285	0.43	1.48	39.24	71.26	67,104
Small 小型	117	84	2,966	45	1.00	3.17	35.38	68.33	4,448
By regional distribution 地區分布									
Central-North 華北	16	73	4,719	225	3.78	10.18	65.03	62.83	5,948
Beijing 北京	10	57	6,237	564	7.04	18.50	109.42	61.93	8,009
Tianjin 天津	6	99	2,188	-340	-13.53	-41.80	22.22	67.64	2,513
Hebei 河北									
Shanxi 山西									
Inner Mongolia 內蒙									
Northeast 東北	29	132	3,490	-55	-0.73	-2.71	26.54	73.12	7,582
Liaoning 遼寧	21	150	4,241	23	0.27	0.98	28.33	72.95	8,586
Jilin 吉林	6	87	1,255	-355	-6.48	-24.51	14.51	73.61	5,482
Heilongjiang 黑龍江	2	76	2,310	25	0.75	3.05	30.60	75.45	3,340
Central East 華東	46	104	6,027	256	2.71	9.27	57.96	70.78	9,446
Shanghai 上海	9	208	13,147	1,256	4.44	12.99	63.14	65.81	28,272
Jiangsu 江蘇	16	76	4,650	9	0.25	1.46	60.83	83.02	3,780
Zhejiang 浙江	17	51	3,736	-16	-0.42	-1.56	73.17	73.38	3,968
Anhui 安徽	2	199	7,860	245	4.80	10.49	39.60	54.22	5,100
Fujian 福建	1	250	2,430	110	0.29	2.01	9.72	85.61	37,930
Jiangxi 江西									
Shandong 山東	1	171	2,850				16.67	59.35	4,010
Central-South 中南	22	186	5,137	33	0.30	0.83	27.58	63.81	11,089
Henan 河南	4	65	1,305	68	3.31	5.27	20.23	37.18	2,038
Hubei 湖北	5	131	1,640	-190	-4.62	-77.24	12.56	94.01	4,110
Hunan 湖南	11	274	8,734	260	1.42	3.75	31.85	62.10	18,275
Guangdong 廣東	2	86	1,765	-725	-10.19	-25.31	20.64	59.66	7,115
Guangxi 廣西									
Hainan 海南									
Southwest 西南	10	169	4,064	384	4.26	16.59	24.10	74.33	9,015
Chongqing 重慶	9	153	4,142	-411	-4.45	-18.80	27.07	76.31	9,224
Sichuan 四川	1	329	3,283	-115	-1.66	-3.19	9.98	48.00	6,924
Guizhou 貴州									
Yunnan 雲南									
Tibet 西藏									
Northwest 西北	6	269	3,362	-1,442	-10.25	-76.28	12.50	86.56	14,067
Shaanxi 陝西	6	269	3,362	-1,442	-10.25	-76.28	12.50	86.56	14,067
Gansu 甘肅									
Qinghai 青海									
Ningxia 寧夏									
Xinjiang 新疆									

3628: Pharmaceutical Equipment 製藥工業專用設備製造業

Year 年份	Number of firms 企業個數	Rate of change 每年變化 (%)	Number of employees 職工人數 (人)	Rate of change 每年變化 (%)	Total revenue (mil. RMB) 總銷售收入 (百萬元)	Rate of change 每年變化 (%)	Total profit (mil. RMB) 總利潤 (百萬元)	Rate of change 每年變化 (%)
1993	94		22,385		528		33	
1994	98	4.26%	16,297	-27.20%	501	-5.16%	15	-53.77%
1995	122	24.49%	19,237	18.04%	578	15.39%	10	-33.53%
1996	129	5.74%	17,156	-10.82%	628	8.73%	10	-0.98%

3 Major products* 3 種主要產品 *	Output 產量	Sales volume 銷售量	Unit 單位
a) Special Equipment for Pharmaceuticals Industr 製藥工業專用設備	11,969	11,849	ton 噸
b) Direct Packing Machinery 直接包裝機械	1,059	1,038	set 台

Top 10 firms by revenue (year founded) 收入排名前 10 家企業 (創辦年份)	City 城市	Province 省	Telephone / fax 電話 / 傳真	Number of employees 職工人數	Ownership 產業所有權	Revenue ('000 RMB) 銷售收入 (千元)	Profit ('000 RMB) (rank) 利潤 (千元) (排名)	Total assets ('000 RMB) 總資產 (千元)	Major products 主要產品
Shanghai Tianxiang Jiantai Pharmaceutical Machinery Co. Ltd. 上海天祥健台製藥機械有限公司(1992)	Shanghai 上海市	Shanghai 上海市	(021)62560800 (021)62583648	382	Foreign-funded 外資	46,890	6091(1)	69,109	a
Liaoyang Pharmaceutical Machinery Co. Ltd. 遼陽製藥機械股份有限公司(1947)	Liaoyang 遼陽市	Liaoning 遼寧省	(0419)2125452 (0419)2126413	1,733	Joint stock 股份制	41,908	2308(3)	121,590	o
Shanghai Yuan Dong Pharmaceutical Machinery Plant 上海遠東製藥機械廠(1949)	Shanghai 上海市	Shanghai 上海市	(021)58991850 (021)58991944	813	State-owned 國有	35,224	2023(4)	101,183	a
Zhong Nan No.1 Pharmaceutical Machinery Factory 中南製藥機械一廠(1970)	Yongzhou 永州市	Hunan 湖南省	(0746)3222614	1,104	State-owned 國有	30,944	879(9)	54,224	a
Liuyang Medicine Equipment General Factory 瀏陽市醫藥設備總廠(1958)	Changsha 長沙市	Hunan 湖南省	(0731)3612027	840	State-owned 國有	22,248	885(8)	50,362	a,b
Yancheng Agriculture Medical Equipment Factory 鹽城市農業藥械廠(1958)	Yancheng 鹽城市	Jiangsu 江蘇省	(0515)8491101	95	Collectively-owned 集體	22,060	1250(7)	8,200	o
Chongqing Pharmaceutical Machinery Factory 重慶製藥機械廠(1969)	Chongqing 重慶市	Chongqing 重慶市	(023)65327295	700	State-owned 國有	20,401	3551(2)	57,026	a
Shanghai Yuan Dong Pharmaceutical Machinery General Factory Jin Qiao Branch 上海遠東製藥機械總廠金橋分廠(1995)	Shanghai 上海市	Shanghai 上海市	(021)58991850 (021)58991949	151	Domestic JVs 聯營	18,380	1659(5)	60,553	a
Xinchang Capsule Equipment General Factory 新昌縣膠丸設備總廠(1984)	Shaoxing 紹興市	Zhejiang 浙江省	(0575)6096328 (0575)6096388	106	Collectively-owned 集體	15,619	-302(60)	5,166	o
Baoji Pharmaceutical Machinery Factory 寶雞製藥機械廠(1970)	Baoji 寶雞市	Shaanxi 陝西省	(0917)3314095	1,370	State-owned 國有	14,623	-8739(70)	72,979	o

Top 10 Cities by Production Output 產出排名前 10 位城市	Province 省	Market share 市場份額	Number of firms 企業個數
Shanghai 上海市	Shanghai 上海市	20.33%	17
Taizhou 泰州市	Jiangsu 江蘇省	8.84%	7
Liaoyang 遼陽市	Liaoning 遼寧省	8.42%	8
Beijing 北京市	Beijing 北京市	7.17%	10
Changsha 長沙市	Hunan 湖南省	6.93%	3
Suzhou 蘇州市	Jiangsu 江蘇省	6.24%	5
Wenzhou 温州市	Zhejiang 浙江省	5.35%	35
Yancheng 鹽城市	Jiangsu 江蘇省	3.53%	2
Yongzhou 永 州 市	Hunan 湖南省	3.23%	2
Chongqing 重 慶 市	Chongqing 重 慶 市	3.18%	7

10 Major Wholesalers 10 家主要批發商	City 城市	Province 省	Telephone / Fax 電話 / 傳真
Liaoning Automobile Trade Group Corp. 遼寧省汽車貿易集團	Shenyang 瀋陽市	Liaoning 遼寧省	(024)23835494 (024)23838338
China Post and Telecommunication Equipment General Company 中國郵電器材總公司	Beijing 北京市	Beijing 北京市	(010)63523715 (010)63525935
Jiangsu Electromechanical Products General Company 江蘇省機電產品總公司	Nanjing 南京市	Jiangsu 江蘇省	(025)7713642 (025)7711036
Xi Nan Technology Import & Export Company 西南技術進出口公司	Chongqing 重慶市	Chongqing 重慶市	(023)63850185 (023)63850026
Changzhou Economic Technology Industrial Development Zone Tian Ming Trade Company 常州經濟技術產業開發區天明貿易公司	Changzhou 常州市	Jiangsu 江蘇省	(0519)8829882 (0519)8829882
Shanxi Mechanical Equipment Import & Export Company 山西省機械設備進出口公司	Taiyuan 太原市	Shanxi 山西省	(0351)4040713 (0351)4043981
Ningbo Five Mining Machinery Import & Export Company 寧波市五礦機械進出口公司	Ningbo 寧波市	Zhejiang 浙江省	(0574)7311255 (0574)7320322
Tianjin Jin Huan Electromechanical Complete Sets of Equipment Factory 天津市津環機電成套設備廠	Tianjin 天津市	Tianjin 天津市	(022)26371628
Yunnan Machinery Import & Export Company 雲南省機械進出口公司	Kunming 昆明市	Yunnan 雲南省	(0871)3164879 (0871)3136829
Tianjin Da Qiu Zhuang Yi Yuan Trade Center 天津市大丘莊億源商貿中心	Tianjin 天津市	Tianjin 天津市	(022)28899478 (022)28899046

*Also include sales by firms outside this industry.包括本行業以外廠家的銷售。"o" stands for "others". "o" 代表 "其他產品" 。

3629: Constructing Materials and Other Non-metal Mineral Products
建材及其他非金屬礦物製品專用設備製造業

The industry accounts for 0.076% of the total revenue of China's industrial sector in 1996. The revenue growth rate of the industry is -12.3% from 1995, as compared to the growth rate of China's industrial sector, 9.51%. The rate of return on asset is 0.28%. 64.95% of all firms in the industry made a profit while 29.55% had negative returns. The top province in terms of the industry's revenue is Jiangsu, accounting for 21.67% of the total revenue.
本行業在1996年佔全行業總產值0.076%，行業年增長率為-12.3%（全國工業年增長率9.51%）。行業的資產回報率0.28%，64.95%的企業盈利，29.55%的企業虧損。銷售收入最高的省份為江蘇省，佔本行業的21.67%。

	Total number of firms 企業總數	Total number of employees 職工總數	Total revenue (mil. RMB) 總銷售收入（百萬元）	Total profit (mil. RMB) 總利潤（百萬元）	Return on assets 資產利潤率 (%)	Return on equity 權益利潤率 (%)	Labour productivity ('000 RMB / worker) 勞動生產率（千元/人）	Debts / assets 資產負債率 (%)	Total assets (mil. RMB) 總資產（百萬元）
Industry Overall 行業總體	633	104,302	4,417	25	0.28	0.87	42.35	68.32	8,996

	Number of firms 企業個數	Average number of employees 平均職工人數	Average revenue ('000 RMB) 平均銷售收入（千元）	Average profit ('000 RMB) 平均利潤（千元）	Return on assets 資產利潤率 (%)	Return on equity 權益利潤率 (%)	Labour productivity ('000 RMB / worker) 勞動生產率（千元/人）	Average debts / assets 平均資產負債率(%)	Average Total assets ('000 RMB) 平均總資產（千元）
By ownership 產業所有權									
State-owned 國有	131	487	14,527	-527	-1.13	-3.98	29.85	71.69	46,763
Collectively-owned 集體	460	79	4,444	122	2.46	6.41	55.93	61.63	4,970
Privately-owned 私有	2	50	2,649	171	19.15	58.45	53.51	67.24	894
Domestic JVs 聯營	4	57	13,150	632	5.97	13.64	230.70	56.22	10,583
Joint stock 股份制	10	108	14,036	932	5.35	12.89	130.56	58.52	17,423
Foreign-funded 外資	11	53	6,472	730	5.57	11.07	121.90	49.67	13,105
Overseas Chinese-funded 港澳台資	16	132	12,529	1,096	7.92	23.40	94.61	66.14	13,838
By size 規模									
Large 大型	14	1,980	87,790	445	0.19	0.68	44.35	72.06	235,481
Medium 中型	32	718	29,157	22	0.03	0.09	40.59	67.86	73,554
Small 小型	583	92	3,869	31	0.54	1.54	42.01	64.96	5,739
By regional distribution 地區分布									
Central-North 華北	85	184	5,901	-49	-0.27	-0.84	31.99	67.32	17,888
Beijing 北京	31	104	4,265	6	0.05	0.18	41.07	74.71	14,148
Tianjin 天津	10	65	2,726	176	2.77	6.66	41.81	58.36	6,348
Hebei 河北	33	293	9,587	-72	-0.27	-0.73	32.72	63.59	26,844
Shanxi 山西	8	254	3,171	-469	-2.85	-10.12	12.51	71.89	16,471
Inner Mongolia 內蒙	3	37	130				3.48	108.33	280
Northeast 東北	64	215	7,676	4	0.02	0.07	35.71	74.85	20,104
Liaoning 遼寧	49	256	9,644	-15	-0.06	-0.23	37.67	74.45	24,908
Jilin 吉林	10	53	846	93	6.82	48.69	16.08	86.00	1,364
Heilongjiang 黑龍江	5	137	2,046	6	0.06	0.31	14.91	81.42	10,514
Central East 華東	229	156	8,686	214	1.55	4.25	55.55	63.62	13,879
Shanghai 上海	10	430	21,402	545	0.94	5.25	49.75	82.05	57,873
Jiangsu 江蘇	76	188	12,596	194	1.07	2.67	67.02	59.81	18,050
Zhejiang 浙江	34	92	7,829	389	4.24	9.16	85.51	53.67	9,178
Anhui 安徽	22	88	3,489	17	0.40	1.07	39.53	62.72	4,316
Fujian 福建	19	60	2,066	-4	-0.13	-0.28	34.46	54.87	3,326
Jiangxi 江西	27	124	1,932	-24	-0.51	-1.89	15.61	72.96	4,631
Shandong 山東	41	187	9,353	391	2.54	6.20	49.90	59.10	15,426
Central-South 中南	177	140	6,291	61	0.55	1.90	44.82	71.17	11,125
Henan 河南	53	94	7,100	529	8.49	26.42	75.92	67.85	6,224
Hubei 湖北	38	254	7,257	-433	-2.61	-12.73	28.62	79.53	16,608
Hunan 湖南	28	181	6,146	-65	-0.50	-1.57	33.92	67.95	12,993
Guangdong 廣東	38	120	6,904	39	0.25	0.75	57.70	67.12	16,032
Guangxi 廣西	18	30	1,437	-25	-1.36	-2.86	48.43	52.47	1,842
Hainan 海南	2	48	510				10.74	104.85	1,030
Southwest 西南	49	171	4,292	-257	-2.37	-8.15	25.07	70.96	10,861
Chongqing 重慶	12	102	1,344	-979	-43.20	-151.82	13.13	71.55	2,267
Sichuan 四川	26	198	4,408	900	8.50	27.33	22.24	68.90	10,587
Guizhou 貴州	6	53	1,673	17	0.75	1.04	31.87	27.39	2,215
Yunnan 雲南	4	434	17,568	-440	-0.83	-3.74	40.50	77.84	53,178
Tibet 西藏	1		380	40	0.60	0.75		19.40	6,650
Northwest 西北	29	201	3,838	-640	-3.64	-12.30	19.10	70.38	17,554
Shaanxi 陜西	24	233	4,317	-766	-3.69	-12.48	18.56	70.46	20,770
Gansu 甘肅	2	59	1,200				20.51	69.08	760
Qinghai 青海									
Ningxia 寧夏	1	41	390	-130	-4.53	-59.09	9.51	92.33	2,870
Xinjiang 新疆	2	45	2,460	-20	-0.65	-1.41	54.67	54.05	3,090

3629: Constructing Materials and Other Non-metal Mineral Products
建材及其他非金屬礦物製品專用設備製造業

Year 年份	Number of firms 企業個數	Rate of change 每年變化 (%)	Number of employees 職工人數 (人)	Rate of change 每年變化 (%)	Total revenue (mil. RMB) 總銷售收入 (百萬元)	Rate of change 每年變化 (%)	Total profit (mil. RMB) 總利潤 (百萬元)	Rate of change 每年變化 (%)
1993	606		134,829		6,347		269	
1994	636	4.95%	112,668	-16.44%	5,345	-15.79%	222	-17.43%
1995	634	-0.32%	117,280	4.09%	5,034	-5.81%	132	-40.71%
1996	633	-0.16%	104,302	-11.07%	4,417	-12.26%	25	-81.04%

3 Major products* 3 種主要產品 *	Output 產量	Sales volume 銷售量	Unit 單位
a) Architectural Sanitary Ware Equipment 建築衛生陶瓷設備	28,521	28,806	ton 噸
b) Cement Equipment 水泥設備	15,049	14,447	set 台
c) Plate Glass Making Equipment 平板玻璃製造設備	544	490	set 台

Top 10 firms by revenue (year founded) 收入排名前 10 家企業 (創辦年份)	City 城市	Province 省	Telephone / fax 電話 / 傳真	Number of employees 職工人數	Ownership 產業所有權	Revenue ('000 RMB) 銷售收入 (千元)	Profit ('000 RMB) (rank) 利潤 (千元) (排名)	Total assets ('000 RMB) 總資產 (千元)	Major products 主要產品
Chaozhong Group Co. Ltd. 朝重集團有限責任公司(1956)	Chaoyang 朝陽市	Liaoning 遼寧省	(0421)2810501 (0421)2810629	6,775	State-owned 國有	222,882	104(129)	630,904	o
Tangshan Cement Machinery Plant 唐山水泥機械廠(1910)	Tangshan 唐山市	Hebei 河北省	(0315)3271311 (0315)3271128	3,593	State-owned 國有	147,552	439(64)	390,975	b
Shenyang Cement Machinery Plant 瀋陽水泥機械廠(1935)	Shenyang 瀋陽市	Liaoning 遼寧省	(024)25833583 (024)25832050	2,713	State-owned 國有	111,843	496(60)	370,208	b
Zhejiang Xian Guang Group Co. Ltd. 浙江顯光集團公司(1995)	Wenzhou 溫州市	Zhejiang 浙江省	(0577)8412588 (0577)8412788	838	Joint stock 股份制	109,619	4069(10)	95,453	o
Xuzhou Building Materials Machine Manufacturing Factory 徐州建材機械製造廠(1958)	Xuzhou 徐州市	Jiangsu 江蘇省	(0516)6739455	355	Collectively-owned 集體	101,280	3600(13)	35,140	o
Shanghai Xin Jian Machine Plant 上海新建機器廠(1955)	Shanghai 上海市	Shanghai 上海市	(021)58801888 (021)58801109	2,146	State-owned 國有	96,595	378(78)	305,953	b
Yixing Building Materials Machinery Plant 宜興市建材機械廠(1974)	Wuxi 無錫市	Jiangsu 江蘇省	(0510)7531256 (0510)7531366	780	Collectively-owned 集體	93,550	6760(3)	153,035	o
Jiangsu Li Da Building Materials Machinery Group Co. 江蘇力大建材機械集團公司(1970)	Xuzhou 徐州市	Jiangsu 江蘇省	(0516)5755950 (0516)5755950	1,316	State-owned 國有	92,680	733(45)	215,944	b
Shanghai Glass Machinery Plant 上海玻璃機械廠(1930)	Shanghai 上海市	Shanghai 上海市	(021)65431118 (021)65432725	1,101	State-owned 國有	75,627	2062(22)	167,978	c
Foshan Shiwan Ceramic Machinery General Factory 佛山市石灣陶瓷機械總廠(1957)	Foshan 佛山市	Guangdong 廣東省	(0757)2272032 (0757)2272032	393	Joint stock 股份制	73,307	9504(1)	98,470	a

Top 10 Cities by Production Output 產出排名前 10 位城市	Province 省	Market share 市場份額	Number of firms 企業個數
Nantong 南通市	Jiangsu 江蘇省	5.55%	33
Tangshan 唐山市	Hebei 河北省	5.51%	11
Chaoyang 朝陽市	Liaoning 遼寧省	5.19%	20
Shenyang 瀋陽市	Liaoning 遼寧省	4.48%	18
Shanghai 上海市	Shanghai 上海市	4.48%	22
Zibo 淄博市	Shandong 山東省	3.96%	10
Suzhou 蘇州市	Jiangsu 江蘇省	3.56%	15
Wuxi 無錫市	Jiangsu 江蘇省	3.51%	31
Zhengzhou 鄭州市	Henan 河南省	3.09%	12
Foshan 佛山市	Guangdong 廣東省	2.95%	13

10 Major Wholesalers 10 家主要批發商	City 城市	Province 省	Telephone / Fax 電話 / 傳真
Liaoning Automobile Trade Group Corp. 遼寧省汽車貿易集團	Shenyang 瀋陽市	Liaoning 遼寧省	(024)23835494 (024)23838338
China Post and Telecommunication Equipment General Company 中國郵電器材總公司	Beijing 北京市	Beijing 北京市	(010)63523715 (010)63525935
Jiangsu Electromechanical Products General Company 江蘇省機電產品總公司	Nanjing 南京市	Jiangsu 江蘇省	(025)7713642 (025)7711036
Xi Nan Technology Import & Export Company 西南技術進出口公司	Chongqing 重慶市	Chongqing 重慶市	(023)63850185 (023)63850026
Changzhou Economic Technology Industrial Development Zone Tian Ming Trade Company 常州經濟技術產業開發區天明貿易公司	Changzhou 常州市	Jiangsu 江蘇省	(0519)8829882 (0519)8829882
Shanxi Mechanical Equipment Import & Export Company 山西省機械設備進出口公司	Taiyuan 太原市	Shanxi 山西省	(0351)4040713 (0351)4043981
Ningbo Five Mining Machinery Import & Export Company 寧波市五礦機械進出口公司	Ningbo 寧波市	Zhejiang 浙江省	(0574)7311255 (0574)7320322
Tianjin Jin Huan Electromechanical Complete Sets of Equipment Factory 天津市津環機電成套設備廠	Tianjin 天津市	Tianjin 天津市	(022)26371628
Yunnan Machinery Import & Export Company 雲南省機械進出口公司	Kunming 昆明市	Yunnan 雲南省	(0871)3164879 (0871)3136829
Tianjin Da Qiu Zhuang Yi Yuan Trade Center 天津市大丘莊億源商貿中心	Tianjin 天津市	Tianjin 天津市	(022)28899478 (022)28899046

*Also include sales by firms outside this industry.包括本行業以外廠家的銷售。"o" stands for "others". "o" 代表"其他產品"。

3631: Food, Beverage and Tobacco Equipment
食品、飲料、煙草工業專用設備製造業

The industry accounts for 0.095% of the total revenue of China's industrial sector in 1996. The revenue growth rate of the industry is 3.9% from 1995, as compared to the growth rate of China's industrial sector, 9.51%. The rate of return on asset is 1.05%. 67.27% of all firms in the industry made a profit while 26.41% had negative returns. The top province in terms of the industry's revenue is Guangdong, accounting for 22.19% of the total revenue.
本行業在1996年佔全行業總產值0.095%，行業年增長率為3.9%（全國工業年增長率9.51%）。行業的資產回報率1.05%，67.27%的企業盈利，26.41%的企業虧損。銷售收入最高的省份為廣東省，佔本行業的22.19%。

	Total number of firms 企業總數	Total number of employees 職工總數	Total revenue (mil. RMB) 總銷售收入（百萬元）	Total profit (mil. RMB) 總利潤（百萬元）	Return on assets 資產利潤率 (%)	Return on equity 權益利潤率 (%)	Labour productivity ('000 RMB / worker) 勞動生產率（千元/人）	Debts / assets 資產負債率 (%)	Total assets (mil. RMB) 總資產（百萬元）
Industry Overall 行業總體	615	108,631	5,500	104	1.05	3.01	50.63	65.30	9,944

	Number of firms 企業個數	Average number of employees 平均職工人數	Average revenue ('000 RMB) 平均銷售收入（千元）	Average profit ('000 RMB) 平均利潤（千元）	Return on assets 資產利潤率 (%)	Return on equity 權益利潤率 (%)	Labour productivity ('000 RMB / worker) 勞動生產率（千元/人）	Average debts / assets 平均資產負債率(%)	Average Total assets ('000 RMB) 平均總資產（千元）
By ownership 產業所有權									
State-owned 國有	156	392	15,096	-199	-0.49	-1.49	38.51	67.45	40,878
Collectively-owned 集體	400	106	6,512	241	3.23	8.61	61.57	62.52	7,456
Privately-owned 私有	3	54	2,577	27	0.49	2.05	47.71	76.02	5,547
Domestic JVs 聯營	5	85	5,992	501	4.86	10.58	70.83	54.08	10,318
Joint stock 股份制	7	187	21,213	961	4.28	15.91	113.44	73.11	22,471
Foreign-funded 外資	23	69	4,313	527	7.75	15.20	62.74	49.00	6,803
Overseas Chinese-funded 港澳台資	22	97	12,394	785	8.51	16.06	128.44	47.02	9,221
By size 規模									
Large 大型	11	1,540	96,809	707	0.31	1.20	62.88	73.83	224,753
Medium 中型	44	779	37,498	711	0.91	2.53	48.13	63.96	77,907
Small 小型	555	103	5,193	117	1.61	4.14	50.48	61.21	7,287
By regional distribution 地區分布									
Central-North 華北	66	165	6,251	112	0.78	2.28	37.86	65.72	14,324
Beijing 北京	32	111	5,971	188	1.10	3.05	53.76	63.85	16,978
Tianjin 天津	9	233	8,539	190	1.36	2.93	36.60	53.43	13,944
Hebei 河北	18	217	7,253	179	1.47	6.27	33.37	76.64	12,206
Shanxi 山西	2	63	130	-20	-0.64		2.06	100.00	3,125
Inner Mongolia 內蒙	5	241	2,770	-698	-6.89	-19.49	11.50	64.63	10,126
Northeast 東北	59	132	2,264	-97	-1.35	-5.67	17.09	76.19	7,208
Liaoning 遼寧	31	85	2,153	77	1.84	5.80	25.44	68.20	4,180
Jilin 吉林	9	160	3,120	-56	-0.41	-1.37	19.55	69.74	13,430
Heilongjiang 黑龍江	19	198	2,041	-402	-4.36	-32.48	10.32	86.56	9,201
Central East 華東	260	130	7,674	90	0.76	2.19	58.92	65.40	11,907
Shanghai 上海	39	264	19,847	131	0.33	1.02	75.30	67.51	39,591
Jiangsu 江蘇	47	138	9,104	221	2.17	5.48	65.95	60.38	10,167
Zhejiang 浙江	97	73	3,036	10	0.21	0.52	41.73	59.88	4,985
Anhui 安徽	16	140	4,937	-174	-1.78	-5.48	35.36	67.56	9,765
Fujian 福建	21	82	11,369	80	1.80	3.97	139.38	54.53	4,438
Jiangxi 江西	6	341	4,560	-137	-0.90	-4.33	13.38	82.97	15,138
Shandong 山東	34	119	4,521	262	3.56	11.49	38.00	69.00	7,355
Central-South 中南	148	211	14,142	483	2.52	7.14	67.04	64.65	19,169
Henan 河南	43	251	13,068	634	4.02	12.33	52.02	67.38	15,757
Hubei 湖北	22	152	5,885	57	0.62	2.16	38.75	71.46	9,221
Hunan 湖南	19	168	5,888	-88	-0.60	-1.50	35.12	60.22	14,849
Guangdong 廣東	50	253	24,408	968	3.11	8.43	96.41	63.13	31,126
Guangxi 廣西	12	87	5,428	-12	-0.15	-0.42	62.27	64.51	7,753
Hainan 海南	2	93	2,070	-1,770	-14.11	-74.06	22.38	80.94	12,540
Southwest 西南	62	330	11,644	239	0.67	1.67	35.34	60.11	35,796
Chongqing 重慶	6	350	6,340	2,656	10.96	29.27	18.12	62.58	24,245
Sichuan 四川	18	98	1,849	-343	-7.06	-16.71	18.82	57.72	4,855
Guizhou 貴州	5	74	494	-444	-4.75	-8.65	6.68	45.10	9,348
Yunnan 雲南	33	493	19,668	794	1.35	3.40	39.93	60.40	58,902
Tibet 西藏									
Northwest 西北	20	220	7,172	-374	-1.77	-11.30	32.53	84.30	21,053
Shaanxi 陝西	18	231	7,860	-397	-1.73	-11.51	33.97	84.96	22,944
Gansu 甘肅	2	122	980	-160	-3.97	-7.96	8.03	50.12	4,030
Qinghai 青海									
Ningxia 寧夏									
Xinjiang 新疆									

3631: Food, Beverage and Tobacco Equipment
食品、飲料、煙草工業專用設備製造業

Year 年份	Number of firms 企業個數	Rate of change 每年變化 (%)	Number of employees 職工人數 (人)	Rate of change 每年變化 (%)	Total revenue (mil. RMB) 總銷售收入 (百萬元)	Rate of change 每年變化 (%)	Total profit (mil. RMB) 總利潤 (百萬元)	Rate of change 每年變化 (%)
1993	560		127,890		4,047		291	
1994	583	4.11%	108,584	-15.10%	4,412	9.00%	139	-52.18%
1995	631	8.23%	111,415	2.61%	5,295	20.03%	213	53.09%
1996	615	-2.54%	108,631	-2.50%	5,500	3.87%	104	-51.14%

3 Major products* 3 種主要產品 *	Output 產量	Sales volume 銷售量	Unit 單位
a) Tobacco Processing Machinery 煙草加工機械	13,095	13,749	set 台（條、組）
b) Cereal, Oilseed & Foodstuff Processing Machinery 糧油食品加工機械	898,305	682,712	set 台（套）
c) Candy Processing Machinery 糖果加工機械	3,437	3,43	ton 噸

Top 10 firms by revenue (year founded) 收入排名前 10 家企業 (創辦年份)	City 城市	Province 省	Telephone / fax 電話 / 傳真	Number of employees 職工人數	Ownership 產業所有權	Revenue ('000 RMB) 銷售收入 (千元)	Profit ('000 RMB) (rank) 利潤 (千元) (排名)	Total assets ('000 RMB) 總資產 (千元)	Major products 主要產品
Shanghai Light Industrial Equipment (Group) Co. Ltd. 上海輕工裝備(集團)有限公司(1950)	Shanghai 上海市	Shanghai 上海市	(021)63188878 (021)63185126	2,321	State-owned 國有	295,607	1190(49)	370,307	a,c
Guangdong Light Industrial Machinery Group Co. Ltd. 廣東輕工業機械集團有限公司(1958)	Guangzhou 廣州市	Guangdong 廣東省	(020)84336972 (020)84356616	2,364	State-owned 國有	260,036	21454(1)	588,298	o
Shanghai Hu Qiao (Group) Co. Ltd. 上海胡橋(集團)有限公司(1995)	Shanghai 上海市	Shanghai 上海市	(021)57456103	2,526	Collectively-owned 集體	180,993	14207(3)	420,070	b,c
Wuchuan Sugar & Wine Machinery Industry Group Company 吳川市糖酒機械工業集團公司(1956)	Zhanjiang 湛江市	Guangdong 廣東省	(0758)5301311	710	Collectively-owned 集體	149,600	8293(4)	66,312	b
Fujian Yunxiao De Ba Foods Machinery Co. Ltd. 福建省雲霄德霸食品機械有限公司(1992)	Zhangzhou 漳州市	Fujian 福建省	(0596)8628293 (0596)8628286	68	Overseas Chinese-funded 港澳台資	147,000	643(66)	21,665	b
Guangdong Panyu Heng Lian Foods Machinery Plant 廣東省番禺市恒聯食品機械廠(1976)	Guangzhou 廣州市	Guangdong 廣東省	(020)84863228 (020)84863999	581	Collectively-owned 集體	137,214	7001(7)	137,462	b
Shannxi Sanyuan Mei Le Co. 陝西省三原縣美樂公司(1958)	Xianyang 咸陽市	Shaanxi 陝西省	(0910)2461322	1,705	Collectively-owned 集體	117,433	1286(45)	147,303	o
Weihui Canned Factory 衛輝后河罐頭廠(1990)	Xinxiang 新鄉市	Henan 河南省	(0373)4298215	950	Collectively-owned 集體	112,500	2843(21)	21,200	o
Shi Jin Field Xin Hu Industry General Company 市金園區新湖工業總公司(1982)	Shantou 汕頭市	Guangdong 廣東省	(0754)8555194	1,370	Collectively-owned 集體	95,690	3800(15)	31,850	b
Gaoyou General Filter Factory 高郵市通用過濾機廠(1971)	Yangzhou 揚州市	Jiangsu 江蘇省	(0514)4862038 (0514)4862053	445	Collectively-owned 集體	87,548	2769(22)	39,701	o

Top 10 Cities by Production Output 產出排名前 10 位城市	Province 省	Market share 市場份額	Number of firms 企業個數
Shanghai 上海市	Shanghai 上海市	13.50%	71
Guangzhou 廣州市	Guangdong 廣東省	11.09%	21
Kunming 昆明市	Yunnan 雲南省	6.87%	23
Zhanjiang 湛江市	Guangdong 廣東省	6.20%	14
Shantou 汕頭市	Guangdong 廣東省	5.04%	13
Zhengzhou 鄭州市	Henan 河南省	3.86%	5
Wenzhou 温州市	Zhejiang 浙江省	3.20%	187
Xinxiang 新鄉市	Henan 河南省	3.05%	5
Beijing 北京市	Beijing 北京市	3.00%	27
Qujing 曲靖市	Yunnan 雲南省	2.55%	3

10 Major Wholesalers 10 家主要批發商	City 城市	Province 省	Telephone / Fax 電話 / 傳真
Liaoning Automobile Trade Group Corp. 遼寧省汽車貿易集團	Shenyang 瀋陽市	Liaoning 遼寧省	(024)23835494 (024)23838338
China Post and Telecommunication Equipment General Company 中國郵電器材總公司	Beijing 北京市	Beijing 北京市	(010)63523715 (010)63525935
Jiangsu Electromechanical Products General Company 江蘇省機電產品總公司	Nanjing 南京市	Jiangsu 江蘇省	(025)7713642 (025)7711036
Xi Nan Technology Import & Export Company 西南技術進出口公司	Chongqing 重慶市	Chongqing 重慶市	(023)63850185 (023)63850026
Changzhou Economic Technology Industrial Development Zone Tian Ming Trade Company 常州經濟技術產業開發區天明貿易公司	Changzhou 常州市	Jiangsu 江蘇省	(0519)8829882 (0519)8829882
Shanxi Mechanical Equipment Import & Export Company 山西省機械設備進出口公司	Taiyuan 太原市	Shanxi 山西省	(0351)4040713 (0351)4043981
Ningbo Five Mining Machinery Import & Export Company 寧波市五礦機械進出口公司	Ningbo 寧波市	Zhejiang 浙江省	(0574)7311255 (0574)7320322
Tianjin Jin Huan Electromechanical Complete Sets of Equipment Factory 天津市津環機電成套設備廠	Tianjin 天津市	Tianjin 天津市	(022)26371628
Yunnan Machinery Import & Export Company 雲南省機械進出口公司	Kunming 昆明市	Yunnan 雲南省	(0871)3164879 (0871)3136829
Tianjin Da Qiu Zhuang Yi Yuan Trade Center 天津市大丘莊億源商貿中心	Tianjin 天津市	Tianjin 天津市	(022)28899478 (022)28899046

*Also include sales by firms outside this industry.包括本行業以外廠家的銷售。"o" stands for "others". "o" 代表 "其他產品"。

3632: Grain and Cooking Oil Equipment 糧油工業專用設備製造業

The industry accounts for 0.073% of the total revenue of China's industrial sector in 1996. The revenue growth rate of the industry is 1.4% from 1995, as compared to the growth rate of China's industrial sector, 9.51%. The rate of return on asset is 1.91%. 62.97% of all firms in the industry made a profit while 31.68% had negative returns. The top province in terms of the industry's revenue is Henan, accounting for 24.76% of the total revenue.

本行業在1996年佔全行業總產值0.073%，行業年增長率為1.4%（全國工業年增長率9.51%）。行業的資產回報率1.91%，62.97%的企業盈利，31.68%的企業虧損。銷售收入最高的省份為河南省，佔本行業的24.76%。

	Total number of firms 企業總數	Total number of employees 職工總數	Total revenue (mil. RMB) 總銷售收入（百萬元）	Total profit (mil. RMB) 總利潤（百萬元）	Return on assets 資產利潤率 (%)	Return on equity 權益利潤率 (%)	Labour productivity ('000 RMB / worker) 勞動生產率（千元／人）	Debts / assets 資產負債率 (%)	Total assets (mil. RMB) 總資產（百萬元）
Industry Overall 行業總體	690	108,604	4,216	111	1.91	4.89	38.82	61.01	5,825

	Number of firms 企業個數	Average number of employees 平均職工人數	Average revenue ('000 RMB) 平均銷售收入（千元）	Average profit ('000 RMB) 平均利潤（千元）	Return on assets 資產利潤率 (%)	Return on equity 權益利潤率 (%)	Labour productivity ('000 RMB / worker) 勞動生產率（千元／人）	Average debts / assets 平均資產負債率(%)	Average Total assets ('000 RMB) 平均總資產（千元）
By ownership 產業所有權									
State-owned 國有	305	222	6,472	-72	-0.56	-1.45	29.18	61.14	12,807
Collectively-owned 集體	361	103	5,552	332	7.41	20.15	53.91	63.24	4,481
Privately-owned 私有									
Domestic JVs 聯營	2	183	7,654	-110	-4.82	-12.81	41.82	62.41	2,289
Joint stock 股份制	10	187	9,992	818	7.20	24.15	53.46	70.20	11,369
Foreign-funded 外資	6	193	15,414	505	2.09	2.99	80.00	29.91	24,143
Overseas Chinese-funded 港澳台資	6	63	5,071	363	5.71	10.26	80.07	44.40	6,360
By size 規模									
Large 大型	1	737	63,740	799	0.65	0.92	86.49	29.91	123,687
Medium 中型	30	764	35,507	905	1.75	4.50	46.47	61.10	51,686
Small 小型	658	129	4,692	126	2.00	5.25	36.34	61.91	6,308
By regional distribution 地區分布									
Central-North 華北	70	193	6,007	194	2.13	6.30	31.18	66.25	9,099
Beijing 北京	7	35	451	-64	-2.54	-8.65	12.90	70.56	2,529
Tianjin 天津	2	528	19,565	-545	-1.51	-4.70	37.09	67.92	36,110
Hebei 河北	37	218	8,420	582	6.60	16.81	38.55	60.70	8,814
Shanxi 山西	15	185	2,817	-205	-2.42	-6.83	15.19	64.62	8,465
Inner Mongolia 內蒙	9	147	2,709	-376	-3.60	-25.07	18.43	85.63	10,431
Northeast 東北	92	135	2,715	-111	-2.13	-7.19	20.05	70.37	5,218
Liaoning 遼寧	34	136	2,415	-244	-4.90	-18.18	17.76	73.02	4,983
Jilin 吉林	22	118	2,344	-145	-2.97	-8.33	19.79	64.40	4,890
Heilongjiang 黑龍江	36	145	3,225	35	0.63	2.18	22.20	71.34	5,639
Central East 華東	199	145	6,530	275	3.01	7.30	44.93	58.70	9,139
Shanghai 上海	12	92	2,273	-658	-11.70	-59.89	24.62	80.47	5,628
Jiangsu 江蘇	45	162	9,148	522	4.15	8.39	56.61	50.50	12,560
Zhejiang 浙江	29	138	6,079	265	2.59	6.72	44.04	61.49	10,233
Anhui 安徽	23	165	4,708	200	3.10	7.20	28.60	56.95	6,438
Fujian 福建	18	79	1,592	-18	-0.55	-1.16	20.18	52.45	3,219
Jiangxi 江西	23	87	1,488	32	0.75	1.66	17.02	54.75	4,217
Shandong 山東	49	190	10,469	542	4.53	12.73	55.04	64.40	11,964
Central-South 中南	220	175	8,429	246	2.52	6.13	48.03	58.89	9,747
Henan 河南	75	229	13,918	770	7.31	17.62	60.67	58.49	10,523
Hubei 湖北	44	175	9,036	199	1.60	4.08	51.67	60.75	12,432
Hunan 湖南	55	132	4,101	-117	-1.99	-4.67	31.04	57.49	5,899
Guangdong 廣東	23	169	3,467	-93	-0.89	-3.91	20.50	77.23	10,455
Guangxi 廣西	22	110	4,885	-166	-1.51	-2.47	44.34	38.86	10,972
Hainan 海南	1	126	70	-200	-10.36	21.05	0.56	149.22	1,930
Southwest 西南	77	121	2,865	-15	-0.30	-0.92	23.76	67.90	5,093
Chongqing 重慶	13	56	945	-22	-1.55	-8.25	16.78	81.21	1,449
Sichuan 四川	38	156	4,117	-22	-0.30	-1.08	26.41	72.46	7,350
Guizhou 貴州	10	115	802	-56	-1.80	-3.53	6.96	49.10	3,118
Yunnan 雲南	16	92	2,689	33	0.85	1.79	29.33	52.55	3,836
Tibet 西藏									
Northwest 西北	32	183	5,375	3	0.03	0.06	29.41	55.91	11,022
Shaanxi 陝西	21	176	4,649	40	0.40	0.96	26.42	58.48	9,992
Gansu 甘肅	8	182	2,421	40	0.54	1.27	13.29	57.32	7,354
Qinghai 青海									
Ningxia 寧夏	1	159	3,170	20	0.30	0.39	19.94	24.37	6,730
Xinjiang 新疆	2	269	25,915	-540	-1.40	-2.83	96.52	50.61	38,660

3632: Grain and Cooking Oil Equipment 糧油工業專用設備製造業

Year 年份	Number of firms 企業個數	Rate of change 每年變化 (%)	Number of employees 職工人數 (人)	Rate of change 每年變化 (%)	Total revenue (mil. RMB) 總銷售收入 (百萬元)	Rate of change 每年變化 (%)	Total profit (mil. RMB) 總利潤 (百萬元)	Rate of change 每年變化 (%)
1993	650		104,363		3,105		173	
1994	675	3.85%	93,678	-10.24%	3,285	5.80%	109	-37.10%
1995	711	5.33%	113,098	20.73%	4,156	26.50%	116	7.05%
1996	690	-2.95%	108,604	-3.97%	4,216	1.44%	111	-4.60%

3 Major products* 3種主要產品 *	Output 產量	Sales volume 銷售量	Unit 單位
a) Grease Processing Machinery 油脂加工機械	115,686	107,588	set 台（套）
b) Cereal & Oilseed Processing Machinery 糧食加工機械	728,601	663,027	set 台
c) Feed Processing Machinery 飼料加工機械	39,873	38,278	set 台

Top 10 firms by revenue (year founded) 收入排名前10家企業 (創辦年份)	City 城市	Province 省	Telephone / fax 電話 / 傳真	Number of employees 職工人數	Ownership 產業所有權	Revenue ('000 RMB) 銷售收入 (千元)	Profit ('000 RMB) (rank) 利潤 (千元) (排名)	Total assets ('000 RMB) 總資產 (千元)	Major products 主要產品
Rongcheng Xing Wen Grain & Oil Machinery Co. Ltd. 榮成市興文糧油機械有限公司(1966)	Weihai 威海市	Shandong 山東省	(0896)7431072	443	Collectively-owned 集體	121,060	8950(3)	28,340	a,b
Hebei Xinji Civil Machinery General Factory 河北省辛集市民用機械總廠(1966)	Shijiazhuang 石家莊市	Hebei 河北省	(0311)3452116	1,568	Collectively-owned 集體	110,346	6664(4)	36,855	o
Wuxi Bu Le Machinery Manufacturing Co. Ltd. 無錫市布勒機械製造有限公司(1994)	Wuxi 無錫市	Jiangsu 江蘇省	(0510)5756641 (0510)5757669	752	Foreign-funded 外資	105,797	14019(2)	145,551	b
Luohe Zhongyuan Grain Machinery Factory 漯河市中原糧食機械廠(1958)	Luohe 漯河市	Henan 河南省	(0395)6888068	403	Collectively-owned 集體	89,299	6263(5)	16,413	o
Shandong Tancheng Jing Hua Machinery (Group) Co. Ltd. 山東省郯城縣精華機械(集團)股分有限公司(1958)	Linyi 臨沂市	Shandong 山東省	(0539)6221210 (0539)6221040	1,636	Joint stock 股份制	87,374	16164(1)	80,267	b
Shishou No.4 Machinery Plant 石首市第四機械廠(1960)	Jingsha 荊沙市	Hubei 湖北省	(0716)7742428	450	State-owned 國有	82,838	3880(9)	29,413	o
Henan Luohe Flour Machine Xie Factory 河南省漯河市麵粉機械廠(1958)	Luohe 漯河市	Henan 河南省	(0395)6844019	429	Collectively-owned 集體	76,000	5152(7)	17,314	b
Xiuwu No.2 Grain Machinery Factory 修武縣第二糧食機械廠(1984)	Jiaozuo 焦作市	Henan 河南省	(0391)7711241	360	Collectively-owned 集體	71,170	5750(6)	13,415	b
Hubei Food Bureau Machinery Factory 湖北省糧食局機械廠(1954)	Wuhan 武漢市	Hubei 湖北省	(027)84892608 (027)84892729	970	State-owned 國有	70,131	2621(13)	94,094	b
Xinjiang Grain & Oil Machining General Factory 新疆糧油機械加工總廠(1958)	Urumqi 烏魯木齊市	Xinjiang 新疆	(0991)3838423	476	State-owned 國有	49,198	-998(300)	72,329	a,b

Top 10 Cities by Production Output 產出排名前10位城市	Province 省	Market share 市場份額	Number of firms 企業個數
Suzhou 蘇州市	Jiangsu 江蘇省	69.57%	8
Luohe 漯河市	Henan 河南省	2.91%	10
Jiaozuo 焦作市	Henan 河南省	2.91%	7
Wuxi 無錫市	Jiangsu 江蘇省	1.28%	30
Shijiazhuang 石家莊市	Hebei 河北省	1.06%	7
Weihai 威海市	Shandong 山東省	0.91%	2
Wuhan 武漢市	Hubei 湖北省	0.78%	6
Linyi 臨沂市	Shandong 山東省	0.64%	4
Cangzhou 滄州市	Hebei 河北省	0.55%	4
Shaoxing 紹興市	Zhejiang 浙江省	0.55%	5

10 Major Wholesalers 10家主要批發商	City 城市	Province 省	Telephone / Fax 電話 / 傳真
Liaoning Automobile Trade Group Corp. 遼寧省汽車貿易集團	Shenyang 瀋陽市	Liaoning 遼寧省	(024)23835494 (024)23838338
China Post and Telecommunication Equipment General Company 中國郵電器材總公司	Beijing 北京市	Beijing 北京市	(010)63523715 (010)63525935
Jiangsu Electromechanical Products General Company 江蘇省機電產品總公司	Nanjing 南京市	Jiangsu 江蘇省	(025)7713642 (025)7711036
Xi Nan Technology Import & Export Company 西南技術進出口公司	Chongqing 重慶市	Chongqing 重慶市	(023)63850185 (023)63850026
Changzhou Economic Technology Industrial Development Zone Tian Ming Trade Company 常州經濟技術產業開發區天明貿易公司	Changzhou 常州市	Jiangsu 江蘇省	(0519)8829882 (0519)8829882
Shanxi Mechanical Equipment Import & Export Company 山西省機械設備進出口公司	Taiyuan 太原市	Shanxi 山西省	(0351)4040713 (0351)4043981
Ningbo Five Mining Machinery Import & Export Company 寧波市五礦機械進出口公司	Ningbo 寧波市	Zhejiang 浙江省	(0574)7311255 (0574)7320322
Tianjin Jin Huan Electromechanical Complete Sets of Equipment Factory 天津市津環機電成套設備廠	Tianjin 天津市	Tianjin 天津市	(022)26371628
Yunnan Machinery Import & Export Company 雲南省機械進出口公司	Kunming 昆明市	Yunnan 雲南省	(0871)3164879 (0871)3136829
Tianjin Da Qiu Zhuang Yi Yuan Trade Center 天津市大丘莊億源商貿中心	Tianjin 天津市	Tianjin 天津市	(022)28899478 (022)28899046

*Also include sales by firms outside this industry.包括本行業以外廠家的銷售。"o" stands for "others". "o" 代表 "其他產品"。

3633: Animal Feed Equipment 飼料工業專用設備製造業

The industry accounts for 0.015% of the total revenue of China's industrial sector in 1996. The revenue growth rate of the industry is 1.0% from 1995, as compared to the growth rate of China's industrial sector, 9.51%. The rate of return on asset is 6.23%. 56.71% of all firms in the industry made a profit while 33.67% had negative returns. The top province in terms of the industry's revenue is Jiangsu, accounting for 46.40% of the total revenue.
本行業在1996年佔全行業總產值0.015%，行業年增長率為1.0%（全國工業年增長率9.51%）。行業的資產回報率6.23%，56.71%的企業盈利，33.67%的企業虧損。銷售收入最高的省份為江蘇省，佔本行業的46.40%。

	Total number of firms 企業總數	Total number of employees 職工總數	Total revenue (mil. RMB) 總銷售收入（百萬元）	Total profit (mil. RMB) 總利潤（百萬元）	Return on assets 資產利潤率 (%)	Return on equity 權益利潤率 (%)	Labour productivity ('000 RMB / worker) 勞動生產率（千元/人）	Debts / assets 資產負債率 (%)	Total assets (mil. RMB) 總資產（百萬元）
Industry Overall 行業總體	102	14,273	873	74	6.23	15.62	61.16	60.10	1,191

	Number of firms 企業個數	Average number of employees 平均職工人數	Average revenue ('000 RMB) 平均銷售收入（千元）	Average profit ('000 RMB) 平均利潤（千元）	Return on assets 資產利潤率 (%)	Return on equity 權益利潤率 (%)	Labour productivity ('000 RMB / worker) 勞動生產率（千元/人）	Average debts / assets 平均資產負債率(%)	Average Total assets ('000 RMB) 平均總資產（千元）
By ownership 產業所有權									
State-owned 國有	46	211	13,804	913	4.86	11.93	65.37	59.31	18,804
Collectively-owned 集體	51	67	2,548	185	5.71	19.91	37.76	71.31	3,233
Privately-owned 私有									
Domestic JVs 聯營									
Joint stock 股份制	2	482	27,078	419	1.03	3.78	56.18	72.76	40,772
Foreign-funded 外資	2	47	26,926	10,872	27.23	40.58	579.06	32.90	39,922
Overseas Chinese-funded 港澳台資	1	61							
By size 規模									
Large 大型									
Medium 中型	4	587	77,735	9,141	7.72	16.68	132.43	53.73	118,456
Small 小型	98	121	5,735	382	5.22	14.63	47.39	64.34	7,321
By regional distribution 地區分布									
Central-North 華北	13	167	6,313	112	1.18	6.31	37.80	81.29	9,516
Beijing 北京	5	261	11,144	98	0.62	2.85	42.63	78.20	15,800
Tianjin 天津									
Hebei 河北	5	103	2,672	42	0.71	6.86	25.94	89.70	5,944
Shanxi 山西	3	116	4,330	253	5.07	26.48	37.22	80.85	4,997
Inner Mongolia 內蒙									
Northeast 東北	13	93	1,833	-202	-3.64	-46.37	19.78	92.15	5,540
Liaoning 遼寧	7	124	1,833	-399	-5.16	57.88	14.82	108.91	7,729
Jilin 吉林	1	34	110	20	3.08	7.69	3.24	60.00	650
Heilongjiang 黑龍江	5	61	2,178	30	0.87	1.47	35.70	40.88	3,454
Central East 華東	37	140	15,204	2,084	11.45	21.62	108.47	47.02	18,198
Shanghai 上海	5	69	16,910	5,816	30.67	44.30	246.50	30.76	18,962
Jiangsu 江蘇	11	186	36,821	4,610	12.22	21.26	197.77	42.54	37,736
Zhejiang 浙江	4	43	1,698	-308	-8.60	-40.46	39.48	78.76	3,578
Anhui 安徽	3	73	1,583	97	5.20	21.80	21.69	76.16	1,860
Fujian 福建	3	36	737	17	0.87	1.02	20.65	14.14	1,910
Jiangxi 江西	3	161	2,933	60	1.51	2.61	18.18	42.34	3,983
Shandong 山東	8	227	6,303	-245	-1.56	-5.39	27.81	71.10	15,731
Central-South 中南	25	178	6,825	-61	-0.56	-1.91	38.33	70.49	10,854
Henan 河南	2	425	10,625	170	0.62	2.98	25.00	79.27	27,490
Hubei 湖北	6	86	3,015	102	2.03	13.03	34.99	84.40	5,000
Hunan 湖南	7	124	2,796	13	0.26	2.05	22.60	87.25	4,919
Guangdong 廣東	7	246	13,927	-334	-1.86	-4.77	56.52	61.11	18,016
Guangxi 廣西	3	164	4,740	-77	-0.89	-2.18	28.84	59.18	8,607
Hainan 海南									
Southwest 西南	9	101	3,268	14	0.43	2.05	32.32	78.80	3,322
Chongqing 重慶	1	95	3,034	8	1.06	-15.07	32.01	107.02	761
Sichuan 四川	5	124	5,007	-56	-1.28	-6.25	40.41	79.58	4,424
Guizhou 貴州									
Yunnan 雲南	4	76	1,340	-30	-1.25	-5.24	17.69	76.07	2,403
Tibet 西藏									
Northwest 西北	5	70	934	-54	-1.28	-7.71	13.34	83.44	4,226
Shaanxi 陝西	5	70	934	-54	-1.28	-7.71	13.34	83.44	4,226
Gansu 甘肅									
Qinghai 青海									
Ningxia 寧夏									
Xinjiang 新疆									

3633: Animal Feed Equipment 飼料工業專用設備製造業

Year 年份	Number of firms 企業個數	Rate of change 每年變化 (%)	Number of employees 職工人數 (人)	Rate of change 每年變化 (%)	Total revenue (mil. RMB) 總銷售收入 (百萬元)	Rate of change 每年變化 (%)	Total profit (mil. RMB) 總利潤 (百萬元)	Rate of change 每年變化 (%)
1993	99		14,358		691		27	
1994	87	-12.12%	13,648	-4.95%	447	-35.37%	3	-87.09%
1995	137	57.47%	19,953	46.20%	864	93.47%	62	1698.52%
1996	102	-25.55%	14,273	-28.47%	873	1.01%	74	19.16%

3 Major products* 3 種主要產品 *	Output 產量	Sales volume 銷售量	Unit 單位
a) Feed Processing Machinery 飼料加工機械	121,593	116,729	set 台
b) Feeding Machinery 給料機械	857	805	set 台
c) Cereal, Oilseed & Foodstuff Processing Machinery 糧油食品加工機械	3,885	2,952	set 台（套）

Top 10 firms by revenue (year founded) 收入排名前 10 家企業 (創辦年份)	City 城市	Province 省	Telephone / fax 電話 / 傳真	Number of employees 職工人數	Ownership 產業所有權	Revenue ('000 RMB) 銷售收入 (千元)	Profit ('000 RMB) (rank) 利潤（千元）(排名)	Total assets ('000 RMB) 總資產 (千元)	Major products 主要產品
Jiangsu Zheng Chang Group Co. 江蘇正昌集團公司(1994)	Changzhou 常州市	Jiangsu 江蘇省	(0519)7229508 (0519)7221981	743	State-owned 國有	301,317	42540(1)	317,972	a
Jiangsu Mu Yang Group 江蘇牧羊集團(1968)	Yangzhou 揚州市	Jiangsu 江蘇省	(0514)7239574 (0514)7227504	272	State-owned 國有	77,190	7166(4)	60,725	a
Guangdong Hua Da Group Co. Ltd. 廣東華達集團有限公司(1958)	Zhaoqing 肇慶市	Guangdong 廣東省	(0757)2823213 (0757)2835181	468	State-owned 國有	57,307	163(22)	46,273	a
Shanghai Zheng Cheng Electromechanical Manufacture Co. Ltd. 上海正誠機電製造有限公司(1994)	Shanghai 上海市	Shanghai 上海市	(021)57831591 (021)57835193	58	Foreign-funded 外資	46,160	18791(2)	41,575	o
Shanghai Shen De Machinery Co. Ltd. 上海申德機械有限公司(1992)	Shanghai 上海市	Shanghai 上海市	(021)57836488 (021)57836486	58	Foreign-funded 外資	30,111	10206(3)	43,976	a
Beijing Yan Jing Animal Husbandry Machinery Co. No.1 Factory 北京燕京牧機公司一廠(1961)	Beijing 北京市	Beijing 北京市	(010)69553047	443	State-owned 國有	20,646	370(12)	31,876	a
Beijing Yan Jing Animal Husbandry Machinery Company No.3 Factory 北京燕京牧機公司三廠(1990)	Beijing 北京市	Beijing 北京市	(010)69572086	187	Collectively-owned 集體	16,640	19(33)	16,212	a
Shandong Sishui Quan Forestry & Agriculture Machinery Factory 山東省泗水縣泉林農機廠(1956)	Jining 濟寧市	Shandong 山東省	(0537)4011221 (0537)4011221	188	Collectively-owned 集體	15,210	670(8)	6,716	a
Qingdao Da Hua Machine Factory 青島大華機器廠(1943)	Qingdao 青島市	Shandong 山東省	(0532)8512165 (0532)8526731	1,217	State-owned 國有	13,862	-3280(52)	90,832	a
Beiliu Jin Da Machinery Co. Ltd. 北流市金達機械股份有限公司(1994)	Yulin 玉林市	Guangxi 廣西	(0775)6223323	350	Joint stock 股份制	13,252	6(35)	21,499	a

Top 10 Cities by Production Output 產出排名前 10 位城市	Province 省	Market share 市場份額	Number of firms 企業個數
Changzhou 常州市	Jiangsu 江蘇省	34.30%	9
Shanghai 上海市	Shanghai 上海市	12.52%	6
Beijing 北京市	Beijing 北京市	8.19%	5
Yangzhou 揚州市	Jiangsu 江蘇省	8.01%	1
Zhaoqing 肇慶市	Guangdong 廣東省	3.60%	3
Fuxin 阜新市	Liaoning 遼寧省	2.63%	3
Zhengzhou 鄭州市	Henan 河南省	2.48%	1
Qingdao 青島市	Shandong 山東省	2.21%	2
Hengyang 衡陽市	Hunan 湖南省	2.02%	2
Yunfu 雲浮市	Guangdong 廣東省	1.86%	2

10 Major Wholesalers 10 家主要批發商	City 城市	Province 省	Telephone / Fax 電話 / 傳真
Liaoning Automobile Trade Group Corp. 遼寧省汽車貿易集團	Shenyang 瀋陽市	Liaoning 遼寧省	(024)23835494 (024)23838338
China Post and Telecommunication Equipment General Company 中國郵電器材總公司	Beijing 北京市	Beijing 北京市	(010)63523715 (010)63525935
Jiangsu Electromechanical Products General Company 江蘇省機電產品總公司	Nanjing 南京市	Jiangsu 江蘇省	(025)7713642 (025)7711036
Xi Nan Technology Import & Export Company 西南技術進出口公司	Chongqing 重慶市	Chongqing 重慶市	(023)63850185 (023)63850026
Changzhou Economic Technology Industrial Development Zone Tian Ming Trade Company 常州經濟技術產業開發區天明貿易公司	Changzhou 常州市	Jiangsu 江蘇省	(0519)8829882 (0519)8829882
Shanxi Mechanical Equipment Import & Export Company 山西省機械設備進出口公司	Taiyuan 太原市	Shanxi 山西省	(0351)4040713 (0351)4043981
Ningbo Five Mining Machinery Import & Export Company 寧波市五礦機械進出口公司	Ningbo 寧波市	Zhejiang 浙江省	(0574)7311255 (0574)7320322
Tianjin Jin Huan Electromechanical Complete Sets of Equipment Factory 天津市津環機電成套設備廠	Tianjin 天津市	Tianjin 天津市	(022)26371628
Yunnan Machinery Import & Export Company 雲南省機械進出口公司	Kunming 昆明市	Yunnan 雲南省	(0871)3164879 (0871)3136829
Tianjin Da Qiu Zhuang Yi Yuan Trade Center 天津市大丘莊億源商貿中心	Tianjin 天津市	Tianjin 天津市	(022)28899478 (022)28899046

*Also include sales by firms outside this industry.包括本行業以外廠家的銷售。"o" stands for "others". "o" 代表"其他產品"。

3634: Special Packing Equipment 包裝工業專用設備製造業

The industry accounts for 0.034% of the total revenue of China's industrial sector in 1996. The revenue growth rate of the industry is 14.5% from 1995, as compared to the growth rate of China's industrial sector, 9.51%. The rate of return on asset is 2.95%. 63.53% of all firms in the industry made a profit while 29.57% had negative returns. The top province in terms of the industry's revenue is Hubei, accounting for 24.33% of the total revenue.
本行業在1996年佔全行業總產值0.034%，行業年增長率為14.5%（全國工業年增長率9.51%）。行業的資產回報率2.95%，63.53%的企業盈利，29.57%的企業虧損。銷售收入最高的省份為湖北省，佔本行業的24.33%。

	Total number of firms 企業總數	Total number of employees 職工總數	Total revenue (mil. RMB) 總銷售收入（百萬元）	Total profit (mil. RMB) 總利潤（百萬元）	Return on assets 資產利潤率 (%)	Return on equity 權益利潤率 (%)	Labour productivity ('000 RMB / worker) 勞動生產率（千元/人）	Debts / assets 資產負債率 (%)	Total assets (mil. RMB) 總資產（百萬元）
Industry Overall 行業總體	233	36,989	1,946	95	2.95	8.14	52.61	63.77	3,238

	Number of firms 企業個數	Average number of employees 平均職工人數	Average revenue ('000 RMB) 平均銷售收入（千元）	Average profit ('000 RMB) 平均利潤（千元）	Return on assets 資產利潤率 (%)	Return on equity 權益利潤率 (%)	Labour productivity ('000 RMB / worker) 勞動生產率（千元/人）	Average debts / assets 平均資產負債率(%)	Average Total assets ('000 RMB) 平均總資產（千元）
By ownership 產業所有權									
State-owned 國有	52	438	20,385	1,327	3.13	8.79	46.59	64.35	42,346
Collectively-owned 集體	136	77	3,319	20	0.61	2.96	43.02	79.40	3,336
Privately-owned 私有	1	7	383	71	6.72	10.74	54.71	37.45	1,063
Domestic JVs 聯營	4	15	1,920	0	-0.02	-0.03	132.44	39.15	806
Joint stock 股份制	3	528	90,974	5,453	7.33	17.42	172.19	57.91	74,380
Foreign-funded 外資	19	84	4,815	469	3.74	4.86	57.40	23.11	12,556
Overseas Chinese-funded 港澳台資	19	34	3,286	-111	-1.81	-14.31	95.74	87.37	6,157
By size 規模									
Large 大型	5	1,578	130,619	16,761	7.36	15.48	82.78	52.44	227,710
Medium 中型	13	687	28,853	546	0.94	3.25	42.00	70.93	57,843
Small 小型	206	97	4,458	20	0.30	0.99	45.79	69.35	6,546
By regional distribution 地區分布									
Central-North 華北	38	178	4,447	-264	-1.65	-5.12	25.02	67.78	16,002
Beijing 北京	14	52	3,731	-115	-1.19	-3.10	71.65	61.67	9,665
Tianjin 天津	8	9	569	105	8.60	16.80	65.00	48.82	1,221
Hebei 河北	15	356	7,243	-348	-1.22	-4.20	20.36	70.84	28,420
Shanxi 山西	1	617	3,540	-4,040	-11.01	-27.39	5.74	59.81	36,700
Inner Mongolia 內蒙									
Northeast 東北	22	131	4,785	48	0.83	2.74	36.58	69.81	5,833
Liaoning 遼寧	16	135	5,789	81	1.13	3.44	42.82	67.06	7,111
Jilin 吉林	5	74	2,396	38	1.63	12.84	32.47	87.34	2,338
Heilongjiang 黑龍江	1	346	680	-420	-14.63	190.91	1.97	107.67	2,870
Central East 華東	98	120	7,719	264	2.58	7.65	64.50	66.24	10,225
Shanghai 上海	19	111	6,227	181	2.26	6.89	56.34	67.25	8,003
Jiangsu 江蘇	11	251	20,716	791	2.47	7.94	82.45	68.88	32,000
Zhejiang 浙江	42	88	5,143	175	2.58	7.60	58.47	66.03	6,791
Anhui 安徽	3	215	12,523	963	10.75	45.58	58.25	76.45	8,960
Fujian 福建	10	22	5,118	80	1.94	3.22	229.51	39.90	4,128
Jiangxi 江西	1								
Shandong 山東	12	192	8,792	225	1.87	5.30	45.83	64.78	12,047
Central-South 中南	63	240	14,156	1,266	5.40	13.49	59.05	59.98	23,462
Henan 河南	15	172	4,470	103	1.63	9.38	25.99	82.65	6,346
Hubei 湖北	9	419	52,602	7,829	12.76	30.39	125.61	58.02	61,361
Hunan 湖南	4	420	16,550	723	1.61	2.77	39.43	41.85	44,903
Guangdong 廣東	31	175	8,399	307	1.70	4.56	47.96	62.80	18,123
Guangxi 廣西	4	412	6,190	-1,165	-5.22	-15.68	15.04	66.70	22,305
Hainan 海南									
Southwest 西南	5	63	640	-98	-6.59	-21.68	10.13	69.49	1,488
Chongqing 重慶	1	16	269	-7	-1.30	-3.50	16.63	62.89	564
Sichuan 四川	4	48	582	-37	-3.00	-17.22	12.13	82.58	1,222
Guizhou 貴州	1	139	1,030	-360	-12.50	-25.35	7.41	50.69	2,880
Yunnan 雲南									
Tibet 西藏									
Northwest 西北	7	30	2,874	-103	-5.02	-11.11	95.36	54.84	2,050
Shaanxi 陝西	7	30	2,874	-103	-5.02	-11.11	95.36	54.84	2,050
Gansu 甘肅									
Qinghai 青海									
Ningxia 寧夏									
Xinjiang 新疆									

3634: Special Packing Equipment 包裝工業專用設備製造業

Year 年份	Number of firms 企業個數	Rate of change 每年變化 (%)	Number of employees 職工人數 (人)	Rate of change 每年變化 (%)	Total revenue (mil. RMB) 總銷售收入 (百萬元)	Rate of change 每年變化 (%)	Total profit (mil. RMB) 總利潤 (百萬元)	Rate of change 每年變化 (%)
1993	159		30,246		1,081		99	
1994	175	10.06%	28,058	-7.24%	1,160	7.25%	75	-24.18%
1995	246	40.57%	39,405	40.44%	1,700	46.56%	109	45.18%
1996	233	-5.28%	36,989	-6.13%	1,946	14.47%	95	-12.79%

3 Major products* 3 種主要產品 *	Output 產量	Sales volume 銷售量	Unit 單位
a) Making Machinery for Packing Container 包裝容器製造機械	15,094	14,490	set 台
b) Binding Machine 裝訂機械	1,567	1,520	set 台
c) Direct Packing Machinery 直接包裝機械	40,597	39,785	set 台

Top 10 firms by revenue (year founded) 收入排名前 10 家企業 (創辦年份)	City 城市	Province 省	Telephone / fax 電話 / 傳真	Number of employees 職工人數	Ownership 產業所有權	Revenue ('000 RMB) 銷售收入 (千元)	Profit ('000 RMB) (rank) 利潤 (千元) (排名)	Total assets ('000 RMB) 總資產 (千元)	Major products 主要產品
Jing Yuan Co. Ltd. 京源股份有限公司(1957)	Jingsha 荊沙市	Hubei 湖北省	(0716)7221326 (0716)7222692	1,770	Joint stock 股份制	420,448	68934(1)	380,352	a
China Light Industry Machinery General Co. Nanjing Light Industry Machinery Plant 中國輕工業機械總公司南京輕工業機械廠(1969)	Nanjing 南京市	Jiangsu 江蘇省	(025)4497408 (025)4400331	1,355	State-owned 國有	103,719	4827(4)	204,053	c
Jiangsu Shuang Ying Group Co. 江蘇雙鷹集團公司(1953)	Wuxi 無錫市	Jiangsu 江蘇省	(0510)6601006 (0510)6601131	566	Collectively-owned 集體	80,498	5147(3)	62,314	a
Guangdong Zhaoqing Jia Long Packing Machinery Manufacturing Co. Ltd. 廣東肇慶嘉隆包裝機械製造有限公司(1969)	Zhaoqing 肇慶市	Guangdong 廣東省	(0757)2233120 (0757)2230133	870	State-owned 國有	75,124	10858(2)	189,278	c
Hunan Changde Qi Yi Machinery Factory 湖南省常德七一機械廠(1951)	Changde 常德市	Hunan 湖南省	(0736)7316188 (0736)7312995	1,177	State-owned 國有	50,224	1006(22)	144,713	c
Zhangzhou Long Yao Machinery Co. Ltd. 漳州龍耀機械有限公司(1989)	Zhangzhou 漳州市	Fujian 福建省	(0596)2064245 (0596)2029103	94	Overseas Chinese-funded 港澳台資	45,600	1100(20)	32,307	c
Wenzhou Lei Ji Group Co. Ltd. 温州雷奇集團有限公司(1995)	Wenzhou 温州市	Zhejiang 浙江省	(0577)6536532 (0577)6536533	331	Joint stock 股份制	40,264	1842(12)	20,783	o
Zhejiang Vacuum Packer General Factory 浙江真空包裝機總廠(1982)	Wenzhou 温州市	Zhejiang 浙江省	(0577)8717492	238	Collectively-owned 集體	40,174	3215(7)	76,040	o
Hebei Handan Packing Machinery General Factory 邯鄲包裝機械總廠(1961)	Handan 邯鄲市	Hebei 河北省	(0310)3054456 (0310)4037050	2,980	State-owned 國有	38,435	-9875(116)	248,300	o
Zeng City General Machinery Co. Ltd. 增城市通用機械股份有限公司(1958)	Guangzhou 廣州市	Guangdong 廣東省	(020)82752696 (020)82757218	222	State-owned 國有	36,834	3250(6)	37,899	c

Top 10 Cities by Production Output 產出排名前 10 位城市	Province 省	Market share 市場份額	Number of firms 企業個數
Jingmen 荊門市	Hubei 湖北省	22.11%	5
Wenzhou 温州市	Zhejiang 浙江省	10.13%	80
Shanghai 上海市	Shanghai 上海市	6.14%	30
Nanjing 南京市	Jiangsu 江蘇省	5.70%	4
Zhaoqing 肇慶市	Guangdong 廣東省	4.41%	1
Wuxi 無錫市	Jiangsu 江蘇省	3.40%	10
Qingdao 青島市	Shandong 山東省	3.31%	5
Changde 常德市	Hunan 湖南省	2.78%	1
Shantou 汕頭市	Guangdong 廣東省	2.67%	16
Guangzhou 廣州市	Guangdong 廣東省	2.49%	9

10 Major Wholesalers 10 家主要批發商	City 城市	Province 省	Telephone / Fax 電話 / 傳真
Liaoning Automobile Trade Group Corp. 遼寧省汽車貿易集團	Shenyang 瀋陽市	Liaoning 遼寧省	(024)23835494 (024)23838338
China Post and Telecommunication Equipment General Company 中國郵電器材總公司	Beijing 北京市	Beijing 北京市	(010)63523715 (010)63525935
Jiangsu Electromechanical Products General Company 江蘇省機電產品總公司	Nanjing 南京市	Jiangsu 江蘇省	(025)7713642 (025)7711036
Xi Nan Technology Import & Export Company 西南技術進出口公司	Chongqing 重慶市	Chongqing 重慶市	(023)63850185 (023)63850026
Changzhou Economic Technology Industrial Development Zone Tian Ming Trade Company 常州經濟技術產業開發區天明貿易公司	Changzhou 常州市	Jiangsu 江蘇省	(0519)8829882 (0519)8829882
Shanxi Mechanical Equipment Import & Export Company 山西省機械設備進出口公司	Taiyuan 太原市	Shanxi 山西省	(0351)4040713 (0351)4043981
Ningbo Five Mining Machinery Import & Export Company 寧波市五礦機械進出口公司	Ningbo 寧波市	Zhejiang 浙江省	(0574)7311255 (0574)7320322
Tianjin Jin Huan Electromechanical Complete Sets of Equipment Factory 天津市津環機電成套設備廠	Tianjin 天津市	Tianjin 天津市	(022)26371628
Yunnan Machinery Import & Export Company 雲南省機械進出口公司	Kunming 昆明市	Yunnan 雲南省	(0871)3164879 (0871)3136829
Tianjin Da Qiu Zhuang Yi Yuan Trade Center 天津市大丘莊億源商貿中心	Tianjin 天津市	Tianjin 天津市	(022)28899478 (022)28899046

*Also include sales by firms outside this industry.包括本行業以外廠家的銷售。"o" stands for "others". "o" 代表 "其他產品"。

3635: Special Textile, Garment, Leather Processing Equipment
紡織、服裝、皮革工業專用設備製造業

The industry accounts for 0.238% of the total revenue of China's industrial sector in 1996. The revenue growth rate of the industry is 1.7% from 1995, as compared to the growth rate of China's industrial sector, 9.51%. The rate of return on asset is 0.28%. 62.20% of all firms in the industry made a profit while 32.26% had negative returns. The top province in terms of the industry's revenue is Jiangsu, accounting for 29.15% of the total revenue.
本行業在1996年佔全行業總產值0.238%，行業年增長率為1.7%（全國工業年增長率9.51%）。行業的資產回報率0.28%，62.20%的企業盈利，32.26%的企業虧損。銷售收入最高的省份為江蘇省，佔本行業的29.15%。

	Total number of firms 企業總數	Total number of employees 職工總數	Total revenue (mil. RMB) 總銷售收入（百萬元）	Total profit (mil. RMB) 總利潤（百萬元）	Return on assets 資產利潤率 (%)	Return on equity 權益利潤率 (%)	Labour productivity ('000 RMB / worker) 勞動生產率（千元/人）	Debts / assets 資產負債率 (%)	Total assets (mil. RMB) 總資產（百萬元）
Industry Overall 行業總體	1,401	332,088	13,793	81	0.28	0.76	41.53	63.29	28,881

	Number of firms 企業個數	Average number of employees 平均職工人數	Average revenue ('000 RMB) 平均銷售收入（千元）	Average profit ('000 RMB) 平均利潤（千元）	Return on assets 資產利潤率 (%)	Return on equity 權益利潤率 (%)	Labour productivity ('000 RMB / worker) 勞動生產率（千元/人）	Average debts / assets 平均資產負債率(%)	Average Total assets ('000 RMB) 平均總資產（千元）
By ownership 產業所有權									
State-owned 國有	273	630	14,564	-1,330	-2.89	-10.19	23.10	71.62	45,978
Collectively-owned 集體	980	130	6,389	245	2.97	8.06	49.17	63.14	8,260
Privately-owned 私有	9	43	1,765	16	0.73	11.22	41.47	93.50	2,126
Domestic JVs 聯營	13	426	14,402	35	0.10	0.26	33.78	61.71	35,468
Joint stock 股份制	16	1,000	105,616	11,640	3.56	6.93	105.59	48.67	327,012
Foreign-funded 外資	38	70	7,272	-659	-4.04	-8.48	103.53	52.33	16,292
Overseas Chinese-funded 港澳台資	67	147	20,038	573	2.09	4.46	135.86	53.08	27,415
By size 規模									
Large 大型	24	3,092	158,852	1,722	0.39	0.95	51.37	59.00	441,225
Medium 中型	141	803	30,182	197	0.29	0.88	37.59	67.29	68,562
Small 小型	1,221	119	4,689	10	0.14	0.38	39.50	64.08	7,062
By regional distribution 地區分布									
Central-North 華北	181	241	7,545	26	0.14	0.34	31.31	57.16	18,184
Beijing 北京	26	115	2,188	-243	-2.90	-7.31	18.98	60.29	8,362
Tianjin 天津	65	209	3,238	-879	-9.12	-29.27	15.48	68.85	9,636
Hebei 河北	57	213	3,970	-266	-1.90	-7.77	18.62	75.59	14,002
Shanxi 山西	22	609	39,135	3,873	5.28	9.23	64.22	42.79	73,335
Inner Mongolia 內蒙	11	134	1,012	-171	-5.21	-17.77	7.56	70.66	3,281
Northeast 東北	80	239	4,346	-494	-3.12	-8.86	18.19	64.85	15,856
Liaoning 遼寧	61	267	5,405	-454	-2.40	-6.33	20.26	62.04	18,881
Jilin 吉林	11	73	327	-325	-8.54	17900.00	4.46	100.05	3,809
Heilongjiang 黑龍江	8	254	1,799	-1,033	-11.04	-95.27	7.07	88.40	9,356
Central East 華東	805	215	11,853	327	1.44	3.88	55.17	62.95	22,749
Shanghai 上海	86	409	20,346	142	0.22	0.54	49.69	59.69	65,292
Jiangsu 江蘇	330	216	12,183	153	0.82	2.25	56.39	63.54	18,652
Zhejiang 浙江	203	121	9,937	988	6.61	15.19	82.20	56.49	14,949
Anhui 安徽	22	366	4,651	-680	-4.09	-41.49	12.70	90.14	16,620
Fujian 福建	15	179	11,057	846	3.46	6.31	61.72	45.21	24,465
Jiangxi 江西	45	101	2,611	-38	-0.59	-3.09	25.80	80.76	6,394
Shandong 山東	104	256	13,163	35	0.15	0.55	51.45	73.32	23,920
Central-South 中南	229	326	9,613	-238	-1.20	-3.23	29.51	62.82	19,827
Henan 河南	90	298	6,069	-413	-2.58	-7.20	20.34	64.15	16,017
Hubei 湖北	58	435	14,939	160	0.65	1.65	34.33	60.67	24,640
Hunan 湖南	24	556	12,849	-1,703	-5.12	-15.78	23.13	67.54	33,241
Guangdong 廣東	51	146	8,692	435	3.13	6.93	59.41	54.78	13,875
Guangxi 廣西	6	285	6,170	-1,318	-4.81	-26.24	21.62	81.64	27,385
Hainan 海南									
Southwest 西南	59	120	2,257	-348	-5.94	-21.90	18.86	72.87	5,862
Chongqing 重慶	26	125	2,012	-529	-8.12	-39.23	16.04	79.32	6,523
Sichuan 四川	33	116	2,452	-204	-3.83	-11.46	21.19	66.62	5,338
Guizhou 貴州									
Yunnan 雲南									
Tibet 西藏									
Northwest 西北	47	313	4,316	-1,543	-6.46	-40.28	13.78	83.96	23,880
Shaanxi 陝西	44	266	4,101	-1,294	-6.12	-45.50	15.40	86.56	21,160
Gansu 甘肅	2	1,218	6,350	-5,475	-6.48	-23.20	5.21	72.07	84,470
Qinghai 青海									
Ningxia 寧夏	1	557	9,670	-4,620	-20.65	-60.08	17.36	65.62	22,370
Xinjiang 新疆									

3635: Special Textile, Garment, Leather Processing Equipment
紡織、服裝、皮革工業專用設備製造業

Year 年份	Number of firms 企業個數	Rate of change 每年變化 (%)	Number of employees 職工人數 (人)	Rate of change 每年變化 (%)	Total revenue (mil. RMB) 總銷售收入 (百萬元)	Rate of change 每年變化 (%)	Total profit (mil. RMB) 總利潤 (百萬元)	Rate of change 每年變化 (%)
1993	1,913		759,284		19,018		1,070	
1994	1,763	-7.84%	411,298	-45.83%	15,289	-19.61%	295	-72.43%
1995	1,440	-18.32%	353,378	-14.08%	13,565	-11.27%	328	11.23%
1996	1,401	-2.71%	332,088	-6.02%	13,793	1.68%	81	-75.34%

3 Major products* 3 種主要產品 *	Output 產量	Sales volume 銷售量	Unit 單位
a) Cotton Manufacturing Equipment 棉紡織設備	110,190	103,578	ton 噸
b) Dyeing & Finishing Machinery Equipment 染整機械設備	47,367	47,841	ton 噸
c) Synthetic Equipment 合成纖維設備	9,395	8,455	ton 噸

Top 10 firms by revenue (year founded) 收入排名前 10 家企業 (創辦年份)	City 城市	Province 省	Telephone / fax 電話 / 傳真	Number of employees 職工人數	Ownership 產業所有權	Revenue ('000 RMB) 銷售收入 (千元)	Profit ('000 RMB) (rank) 利潤 (千元) (排名)	Total assets ('000 RMB) 總資產 (千元)	Major products 主要產品
Warp & Weft Textile Machinery Co. Ltd. 經緯紡織機械股份有限公司(1995)	Yuci 榆次市	Shanxi 山西省	(0354)2491114 (0354)2425428	5,592	Joint stock 股份制	624,671	88648(1)	1,145,529	a,b,c
Shanghai No.2 Textile Machinery Co. Ltd. 上海二紡機股份有限公司(1944)	Shanghai 上海市	Shanghai 上海市	(021)65318888 (021)65421963	3,273	Joint stock 股份制	407,435	2028(65)	1,873,606	a,b,c
Zhejiang Zhong Bao Industrial Co. Ltd. 浙江中寶實業股份有限公司(1982)	Shaoxing 紹興市	Zhejiang 浙江省	(0575)6123260 (0575)6122335	1,764	Joint stock 股份制	300,236	73665(2)	388,313	o
Zhejiang Tai Tan Textile Machinery General Factory 浙江泰坦紡織機械總廠(1977)	Shaoxing 紹興市	Zhejiang 浙江省	(0575)6123592 (0575)6123233	709	Collectively-owned 集體	290,718	69725(3)	285,890	o
Jiangsu Hong Yuan Textile Machinery Co. Ltd. 江蘇宏源紡織機械製造集團公司(1993)	Wuxi 無錫市	Jiangsu 江蘇省	(0510)5867456 (0510)5807923	2,919	Joint stock 股份制	275,106	8100(14)	637,385	a
Jiangsu Hua Ying Group Company 江蘇華英集團公司(1993)	Yancheng 鹽城市	Jiangsu 江蘇省	(0515)8801811 (0515)8802221	1,286	Joint stock 股份制	237,950	11340(8)	257,460	o
Qingdao Xing Huo Spinning & Weaving Machine Spinning and Weaving Group Company 青島星火紡機紡織集團公司(1970)	Qingdao 青島市	Shandong 山東省	(0532)3131057 (0532)3131059	1,115	Collectively-owned 集體	225,980	6980(17)	265,410	a
China Textile Machinery Co. Ltd. 中國紡織機械股份有限公司(1926)	Shanghai 上海市	Shanghai 上海市	(021)65432970 (021)65455130	4,177	Joint stock 股份制	220,375	3027(44)	1,430,345	a
Zhejiang Golden Eagle Textile Machinery Co. Ltd. 浙江金鷹紡機股份有限公司(1966)	Zhoushan 舟山市	Zhejiang 浙江省	(0580)8020188 (0580)8020228	3,873	Joint stock 股份制	205,175	18015(5)	316,095	a
Shanghai Textile Machinery General Factory 上海紡織機械總廠(1946)	Shanghai 上海市	Shanghai 上海市	(021)62417900 (021)62517320	4,239	State-owned 國有	195,045	5601(21)	496,096	a,b,c

Top 10 Cities by Production Output 產出排名前 10 位城市	Province 省	Market share 市場份額	Number of firms 企業個數
Shanghai 上海市	Shanghai 上海市	12.81%	147
Shaoxing 紹興市	Zhejiang 浙江省	10.22%	52
Yuci 榆次市	Shanxi 山西省	7.43%	21
Wuxi 無錫市	Jiangsu 江蘇省	6.72%	132
Suzhou 蘇州市	Jiangsu 江蘇省	6.60%	117
Qingdao 青島市	Shandong 山東省	6.27%	50
Yancheng 鹽城市	Jiangsu 江蘇省	3.35%	32
Changzhou 常州市	Jiangsu 江蘇省	2.89%	67
Hangzhou 杭州市	Zhejiang 浙江省	2.78%	62
Nantong 南通市	Jiangsu 江蘇省	2.05%	57

10 Major Wholesalers 10 家主要批發商	City 城市	Province 省	Telephone / Fax 電話 / 傳真
Liaoning Automobile Trade Group Corp. 遼寧省汽車貿易集團	Shenyang 瀋陽市	Liaoning 遼寧省	(024)23835494 (024)23838338
China Post and Telecommunication Equipment General Company 中國郵電器材總公司	Beijing 北京市	Beijing 北京市	(010)63523715 (010)63525935
Jiangsu Electromechanical Products General Company 江蘇省機電產品總公司	Nanjing 南京市	Jiangsu 江蘇省	(025)7713642 (025)7711036
Xi Nan Technology Import & Export Company 西南技術進出口公司	Chongqing 重慶市	Chongqing 重慶市	(023)63850185 (023)63850026
Changzhou Economic Technology Industrial Development Zone Tian Ming Trade Company 常州經濟技術產業開發區天明貿易公司	Changzhou 常州市	Jiangsu 江蘇省	(0519)8829882 (0519)8829882
Shanxi Mechanical Equipment Import & Export Company 山西省機械設備進出口公司	Taiyuan 太原市	Shanxi 山西省	(0351)4040713 (0351)4043981
Ningbo Five Mining Machinery Import & Export Company 寧波市五礦機械進出口公司	Ningbo 寧波市	Zhejiang 浙江省	(0574)7311255 (0574)7320322
Tianjin Jin Huan Electromechanical Complete Sets of Equipment Factory 天津市津環機電成套設備廠	Tianjin 天津市	Tianjin 天津市	(022)26371628
Yunnan Machinery Import & Export Company 雲南省機械進出口公司	Kunming 昆明市	Yunnan 雲南省	(0871)3164879 (0871)3136829
Tianjin Da Qiu Zhuang Yi Yuan Trade Center 天津市大丘莊億源商貿中心	Tianjin 天津市	Tianjin 天津市	(022)28899478 (022)28899046

*Also include sales by firms outside this industry.包括本行業以外廠家的銷售。"o" stands for "others". "o" 代表"其他產品"。

3636: Special Electric Light Source Equipment 電光源工業專用設備製造業

The industry accounts for 0.007% of the total revenue of China's industrial sector in 1996. The revenue growth rate of the industry is -17.3% from 1995, as compared to the growth rate of China's industrial sector, 9.51%. The rate of return on asset is 1.30%. 75.53% of all firms in the industry made a profit while 17.65% had negative returns. The top province in terms of the industry's revenue is Jiangsu, accounting for 25.61% of the total revenue.
本行業在1996年佔全行業總產值0.007%，行業年增長率為-17.3%（全國工業年增長率9.51%）。行業的資產回報率1.30%，75.53%的企業盈利，17.65%的企業虧損。銷售收入最高的省份為江蘇省，佔本行業的25.61%。

	Total number of firms 企業總數	Total number of employees 職工總數	Total revenue (mil. RMB) 總銷售收入（百萬元）	Total profit (mil. RMB) 總利潤（百萬元）	Return on assets 資產利潤率 (%)	Return on equity 權益利潤率 (%)	Labour productivity ('000 RMB / worker) 勞動生產率（千元/人）	Debts / assets 資產負債率 (%)	Total assets (mil. RMB) 總資產（百萬元）
Industry Overall 行業總體	150	9,463	414	8	1.30	4.01	43.75	67.60	581

	Number of firms 企業個數	Average number of employees 平均職工人數	Average revenue ('000 RMB) 平均銷售收入（千元）	Average profit ('000 RMB) 平均利潤（千元）	Return on assets 資產利潤率 (%)	Return on equity 權益利潤率 (%)	Labour productivity ('000 RMB / worker) 勞動生產率（千元/人）	Average debts / assets 平均資產負債率(%)	Average Total assets ('000 RMB) 平均總資產（千元）
By ownership 產業所有權									
State-owned 國有	19	86	1,684				19.67	51.35	5,842
Collectively-owned 集體	113	63	3,011	64	1.93	11.62	47.70	83.42	3,346
Privately-owned 私有									
Domestic JVs 聯營									
Joint stock 股份制	2	45	1,051	-35	-1.35	-5.13	23.36	73.69	2,592
Foreign-funded 外資	2	36	1,738	109	2.65	3.71	48.28	28.64	4,099
Overseas Chinese-funded 港澳台資	11	60	3,260	52	0.73	0.90	54.50	18.37	7,102
By size 規模									
Large 大型	1	1,828	24,306	-2,690	-2.05	26.14	13.30	107.85	131,140
Medium 中型	4	340	12,440	217	0.68	1.51	36.56	54.83	31,875
Small 小型	143	45	2,377	69	3.05	6.98	53.37	56.35	2,254
By regional distribution 地區分布									
Central-North 華北	37	23	1,132	55	3.66	12.22	49.17	70.03	1,505
Beijing 北京	19	11	644	9	0.68	2.86	57.42	76.19	1,391
Tianjin 天津	5	24	1,608	48	2.00	9.06	66.45	77.90	2,398
Hebei 河北	10	44	1,960	159	10.36	21.34	45.06	51.47	1,535
Shanxi 山西	2	34	960	25	3.52	500.00	28.24	99.30	710
Inner Mongolia 內蒙	1	15	100	-20	-3.92	-7.14	6.67	43.14	510
Northeast 東北	16	49	1,981	43	1.00	2.02	40.23	50.47	4,243
Liaoning 遼寧	13	55	2,258	51	0.99	1.99	41.05	50.20	5,125
Jilin 吉林	2	28	1,100	5	0.92	3.57	40.00	74.31	545
Heilongjiang 黑龍江	1	18	150	10	6.25	6.25	8.33		160
Central East 華東	44	63	4,226	367	12.64	32.85	67.49	61.54	2,901
Shanghai 上海	11	65	1,409	-109	-3.60	-7.73	21.62	53.52	3,034
Jiangsu 江蘇	9	85	11,779	1,436	25.91	86.94	138.39	70.22	5,541
Zhejiang 浙江	7	19	1,370	100	5.78	8.48	71.57	31.93	1,731
Anhui 安徽	10	61	3,622	298	31.53	138.60	59.77	77.25	945
Fujian 福建	1	72	3,980				55.28	0.50	2,010
Jiangxi 江西	4	25	565				23.06	45.83	600
Shandong 山東	2	181	6,185	365	3.97	14.51	34.17	72.68	9,205
Central-South 中南	41	107	3,458	-274	-3.63	-13.77	32.27	73.63	7,558
Henan 河南	15	79	1,651	27	0.71	1.73	20.88	59.19	3,863
Hubei 湖北	4	63	2,935	123	5.54	100.00	46.40	94.46	2,210
Hunan 湖南	5	434	4,720	-2,036	-7.54	519.39	10.87	101.45	27,014
Guangdong 廣東	16	46	5,074	-119	-1.77	-3.19	109.27	44.67	6,720
Guangxi 廣西	1	40	480	-70	-14.00	-350.00	12.00	94.00	500
Hainan 海南									
Southwest 西南	8	57	1,151	1	0.08	0.14	20.11	44.40	1,563
Chongqing 重慶	1	22	886	6	1.17	2.23	40.45	47.55	547
Sichuan 四川	5	72	900	-10	-0.62	-1.49	12.49	58.06	1,657
Guizhou 貴州	1	29	2,790	210	22.11	25.30	96.21	12.63	950
Yunnan 雲南	1	57	1,040	-240	-8.16	-9.84	18.25	17.01	2,940
Tibet 西藏									
Northwest 西北	4	54	793	-8	-0.39	-10.00	14.61	96.14	1,945
Shaanxi 陝西	4	54	793	-8	-0.39	-10.00	14.61	96.14	1,945
Gansu 甘肅									
Qinghai 青海									
Ningxia 寧夏									
Xinjiang 新疆									

3636: Special Electric Light Source Equipment 電光源工業專用設備製造業

Year 年份	Number of firms 企業個數	Rate of change 每年變化 (%)	Number of employees 職工人數 (人)	Rate of change 每年變化 (%)	Total revenue (mil. RMB) 總銷售收入 (百萬元)	Rate of change 每年變化 (%)	Total profit (mil. RMB) 總利潤 (百萬元)	Rate of change 每年變化 (%)
1993	66		5,125		2,078		109	
1994	100	51.52%	6,646	29.68%	240	-88.46%	9	-92.11%
1995	121	21.00%	10,777	62.16%	501	108.69%	50	484.11%
1996	150	23.97%	9,463	-12.19%	414	-17.31%	8	-84.05%

3 Major products* 3 種主要產品 *	Output 產量	Sales volume 銷售量	Unit 單位
a) Lamp Bulb 燈泡	111,837	93,943	10,000 piece 萬只
b) Other Illuminating Appliances 其他照明器具	706	692	10,000 piece 萬只

Top 10 firms by revenue (year founded) 收入排名前 10 家企業 (創辦年份)	City 城市	Province 省	Telephone / fax 電話 / 傳真	Number of employees 職工人數	Ownership 產業所有權	Revenue ('000 RMB) 銷售收入 (千元)	Profit ('000 RMB) (rank) 利潤 (千元) (排名)	Total assets ('000 RMB) 總資產 (千元)	Major products 主要產品
Lian Da Electron Suzhou Co. Ltd. 聯達電子蘇州有限公司(1995)	Suzhou 蘇州市	Jiangsu 江蘇省	(0512)6262625	350	Overseas Chinese-funded 港澳台資	87,500	13000(1)	21,240	o
Kuai Fu Electron (Shenzhen) Co. Ltd. 快富電子(深圳)有限公司(1993)	Shenzhen 深圳市	Guangdong 廣東省	(0755)7703178 (0755)7703180	350	Overseas Chinese-funded 港澳台資	52,882	531(8)	63,083	o
Chaohu Daily Use Electric Equipment Plant 巢湖市日用電器廠(1994)	Chaohu 巢湖市	Anhui 安徽省	(0565)8372349	98	Collectively-owned 集體	26,540	2120(2)	2,610	b
Yiyang Bulb General Factory 益陽燈泡總廠(1966)	Yiyang 益陽市	Hunan 湖南省	(0737)4261888 (0737)998507	2,020	Collectively-owned 集體	21,081	-10122(44)	132,226	a
Shanghai Zhou Pu Science & Art Hardware Electric Device Factory 上海周浦科藝五金電器廠(1988)	Shanghai 上海市	Shanghai 上海市	(021)58114649	10	Collectively-owned 集體	14,854	1215(4)	11,276	o
Weifang Zheng Tong Industrial Co. Ltd. 濰坊政通實業有限公司(1994)	Weifang 濰坊市	Shandong 山東省	(0536)8159858 (0536)8159858	250	Collectively-owned 集體	12,105	831(5)	14,410	o
Beijing Mei Xing Automobile Illuminating Electric Appliance Company 北京美興汽車照明電器公司(1993)	Beijing 北京市	Beijing 北京市	(010)69244982	138	Collectively-owned 集體	8,678	20(30)	21,644	o
Tianjin You Ni Si Electron Co. Ltd. 天津優尼斯電子有限公司(1989)	Tianjin 天津市	Tianjin 天津市	(022)25321825 (022)25321830	82	Foreign-funded 外資	8,030	240(10)	11,878	a
Hejian No.1 Vehicle Lamps & Lanterns Factory 河間市第一車輛燈具廠(1992)	Cangzhou 滄州市	Hebei 河北省	(0317)3821042	78	Collectively-owned 集體	7,908	1252(3)	2,400	o
Langfang Guang Hua Lamps & Lanterns Factory 廊坊市光華燈具廠(1984)	Langfang 廊坊市	Hebei 河北省	(0316)5384401	133	Collectively-owned 集體	6,844	125(20)	5,504	o

Top 10 Cities by Production Output 產出排名前 10 位城市	Province 省	Market share 市場份額	Number of firms 企業個數
Shanghai 上海市	Shanghai 上海市	37.33%	30
Hengshui 衡水市	Hebei 河北省	8.07%	2
Yiyang 益陽市	Hunan 湖南省	4.05%	2
Zhenjiang 鎮江市	Jiangsu 江蘇省	3.91%	4
Yangzhou 揚州市	Jiangsu 江蘇省	3.71%	4
Shenyang 瀋陽市	Liaoning 遼寧省	3.65%	11
Wuxi 無錫市	Jiangsu 江蘇省	3.61%	9
Nanjing 南京市	Jiangsu 江蘇省	2.88%	7
Xinxiang 新鄉市	Henan 河南省	2.83%	2
Suzhou 蘇州市	Jiangsu 江蘇省	2.43%	6

10 Major Wholesalers 10 家主要批發商	City 城市	Province 省	Telephone / Fax 電話 / 傳真
Liaoning Automobile Trade Group Corp. 遼寧省汽車貿易集團	Shenyang 瀋陽市	Liaoning 遼寧省	(024)23835494 (024)23838338
China Post and Telecommunication Equipment General Company 中國郵電器材總公司	Beijing 北京市	Beijing 北京市	(010)63523715 (010)63525935
Jiangsu Electromechanical Products General Company 江蘇省機電產品總公司	Nanjing 南京市	Jiangsu 江蘇省	(025)7713642 (025)7711036
Xi Nan Technology Import & Export Company 西南技術進出口公司	Chongqing 重慶市	Chongqing 重慶市	(023)63850185 (023)63850026
Changzhou Economic Technology Industrial Development Zone Tian Ming Trade Company 常州經濟技術產業開發區天明貿易公司	Changzhou 常州市	Jiangsu 江蘇省	(0519)8829882 (0519)8829882
Shanxi Mechanical Equipment Import & Export Company 山西省機械設備進出口公司	Taiyuan 太原市	Shanxi 山西省	(0351)4040713 (0351)4043981
Ningbo Five Mining Machinery Import & Export Company 寧波市五礦機械進出口公司	Ningbo 寧波市	Zhejiang 浙江省	(0574)7311255 (0574)7320322
Tianjin Jin Huan Electromechanical Complete Sets of Equipment Factory 天津市津環機電成套設備廠	Tianjin 天津市	Tianjin 天津市	(022)26371628
Yunnan Machinery Import & Export Company 雲南省機械進出口公司	Kunming 昆明市	Yunnan 雲南省	(0871)3164879 (0871)3136829
Tianjin Da Qiu Zhuang Yi Yuan Trade Center 天津市大丘莊億源商貿中心	Tianjin 天津市	Tianjin 天津市	(022)28899478 (022)28899046

*Also include sales by firms outside this industry.包括本行業以外廠家的銷售。"o" stands for "others". "o" 代表 "其他產品" 。

3637: Special Silicic Acid Products Processing Equipment
日用硅酸製品工業專用設備製造業

The industry accounts for 0.007% of the total revenue of China's industrial sector in 1996. The revenue growth rate of the industry is 9.7% from 1995, as compared to the growth rate of China's industrial sector, 9.51%. The rate of return on asset is -1.46%. 71.43% of all firms in the industry made a profit while 28.57% had negative returns. The top province in terms of the industry's revenue is Jiangsu, accounting for 29.71% of the total revenue.
本行業在1996年佔全行業總產值0.007%，行業年增長率為9.7%（全國工業年增長率9.51%）。行業的資產回報率-1.46%，71.43%的企業盈利，28.57%的企業虧損。銷售收入最高的省份為江蘇省，佔本行業的29.71%。

	Total number of firms 企業總數	Total number of employees 職工總數	Total revenue (mil. RMB) 總銷售收入（百萬元）	Total profit (mil. RMB) 總利潤（百萬元）	Return on assets 資產利潤率 (%)	Return on equity 權益利潤率 (%)	Labour productivity ('000 RMB / worker) 勞動生產率（千元/人）	Debts / assets 資產負債率 (%)	Total assets (mil. RMB) 總資產（百萬元）
Industry Overall 行業總體	56	10,970	431	-9	-1.46	-4.67	39.29	68.61	634

	Number of firms 企業個數	Average number of employees 平均職工人數	Average revenue ('000 RMB) 平均銷售收入（千元）	Average profit ('000 RMB) 平均利潤（千元）	Return on assets 資產利潤率 (%)	Return on equity 權益利潤率 (%)	Labour productivity ('000 RMB / worker) 勞動生產率（千元/人）	Average debts / assets 平均資產負債率(%)	Average Total assets ('000 RMB) 平均總資產（千元）
By ownership 產業所有權									
State-owned 國有	12	361	9,583	-750	-4.23	-16.98	26.57	75.12	17,750
Collectively-owned 集體	37	127	6,250				49.30	56.02	6,049
Privately-owned 私有									
Domestic JVs 聯營	1	99	5,272				53.25	95.91	9,680
Joint stock 股份制	1	42	4,516				107.52	65.29	2,240
Foreign-funded 外資	3	562	24,934				44.39	76.55	60,264
Overseas Chinese-funded 港澳台資	1	125	138				1.10	10.51	4,454
By size 規模									
Large 大型									
Medium 中型	7	930	26,783	672	1.04	4.10	28.81	74.75	64,836
Small 小型	49	91	4,969	-280	-7.61	-16.24	54.56	53.15	3,676
By regional distribution 地區分布									
Central-North 華北	5	13	98	-38	-6.42	-19.00	7.42	66.55	592
Beijing 北京	1								
Tianjin 天津	2	4	5				1.25	50.00	40
Hebei 河北	1	23	120	10	1.28	3.57	5.22	64.10	780
Shanxi 山西	1	35	360	-200	-9.52	-29.41	10.29	68.10	2,100
Inner Mongolia 內蒙									
Northeast 東北	5	82	3,322	124	3.39	6.64	40.41	48.91	3,656
Liaoning 遼寧	5	82	3,322	124	3.39	6.64	40.41	48.91	3,656
Jilin 吉林									
Heilongjiang 黑龍江									
Central East 華東	24	333	15,835	-5	-0.02	-0.07	47.60	66.29	22,573
Shanghai 上海	2	311	13,600	660	3.79	7.84	43.73	51.66	17,420
Jiangsu 江蘇	6	331	21,343	-382	-1.99	-3.94	64.51	49.52	19,198
Zhejiang 浙江	1	563	18,790	-930	-4.11	-11.54	33.37	64.40	22,640
Anhui 安徽	3	352	21,050	863	3.05	14.54	59.86	79.05	28,337
Fujian 福建	2	9	345	105	14.38	41.18	38.33	65.07	730
Jiangxi 江西	5	251	4,134	28	0.32	1.19	16.44	72.86	8,650
Shandong 山東	5	497	24,298	-232	-0.48	-1.67	48.91	70.96	47,872
Central-South 中南	15	141	1,693	-644	-16.02	-197.14	12.03	91.86	4,019
Henan 河南	1	13	820	10	1.08	3.33	63.08	66.67	930
Hubei 湖北	8	164	2,266	9	0.36	1.82	13.81	80.12	2,415
Hunan 湖南	2	239	2,345	-4,545	-38.50	284.06	9.83	113.55	11,805
Guangdong 廣東	2	82	430	-150	-8.52	-24.39	5.24	65.06	1,760
Guangxi 廣西	2	72	445	-175	-2.71	-12.82	6.18	78.85	6,455
Hainan 海南									
Southwest 西南	4	32	1,678	35	3.41	6.11	52.83	44.15	1,025
Chongqing 重慶									
Sichuan 四川	3	29	1,747	53	6.63	16.06	60.24	58.75	800
Guizhou 貴州	1	39	1,470	-20	-1.18	-1.54	37.69	23.53	1,700
Yunnan 雲南									
Tibet 西藏									
Northwest 西北	3	90	753	-30	-1.30	8.41	8.34	115.44	2,310
Shaanxi 陝西	2	84	845	-40	-1.91	-4.97	10.06	61.48	2,090
Gansu 甘肅	1	103	570	-10	-0.36	0.37	5.53	197.45	2,750
Qinghai 青海									
Ningxia 寧夏									
Xinjiang 新疆									

3637: Special Silicic Acid Products Processing Equipment
日用硅酸製品工業專用設備製造業

Year 年份	Number of firms 企業個數	Rate of change 每年變化 (%)	Number of employees 職工人數 (人)	Rate of change 每年變化 (%)	Total revenue (mil. RMB) 總銷售收入 (百萬元)	Rate of change 每年變化 (%)	Total profit (mil. RMB) 總利潤 (百萬元)	Rate of change 每年變化 (%)
1993	35		5,991		207		7	
1994	36	2.86%	6,376	6.43%	216	4.35%	1	-80.58%
1995	38	5.56%	8,190	28.45%	393	81.56%	3	144.77%
1996	56	47.37%	10,970	33.94%	431	9.73%	-9	-370.76%

3 Major products* 3 種主要產品 *	Output 產量	Sales volume 銷售量	Unit 單位
a) Plate Glass Making Equipment 平板玻璃製造設備	139	126	set 台
b) Architectural Sanitary Ware Equipment 建築衛生陶瓷設備	1,173	1,184	ton 噸
c) Daily Glass Products 日用玻璃製品	58,293	55,378	ton 噸

Top 10 firms by revenue (year founded) 收入排名前 10 家企業 (創辦年份)	City 城市	Province 省	Telephone / fax 電話 / 傳真	Number of employees 職工人數	Ownership 產業所有權	Revenue ('000 RMB) 銷售收入 (千元)	Profit ('000 RMB) (rank) 利潤 (千元) (排名)	Total assets ('000 RMB) 總資產 (千元)	Major products 主要產品
Liyang Gas Industry Equipment Erection Work Company 溧陽市煤氣工業設備安裝工程公司(1987)	Changzhou 常州市	Jiangsu 江蘇省	(0519)7222063	621	Collectively-owned 集體	96,080	1150(4)	18,670	o
Qilu Maul Glass Machinery Co. Ltd. 齊魯莫爾玻璃機械有限公司(1994)	Zibo 淄博市	Shandong 山東省	(0533)6180712 (0533)6181718	964	Foreign-funded 外資	80,555	-1212(18)	94,445	o
Anqing Glass Factory 安慶市玻璃廠(1956)	Anqing 安慶市	Anhui 安徽省	(0556)5515100 (0556)5514401	987	State-owned 國有	56,908	2007(2)	80,348	c
Shanghai Chemical Industry Machinery No.3 Factory No.1 Branch 上海化工機械三廠一分廠(1984)	Shanghai 上海市	Shanghai 上海市	(021)59137331	90	Collectively-owned 集體	37,776	3262(1)	8,096	o
Shandong Weifang Light Industry Machinery Co. Ltd. 山東濰坊輕工機械股份有限公司(1981)	Weifang 濰坊市	Shandong 山東省	(0536)8322921 (0536)8328099	1,105	Joint stock 股份制	32,156	19(11)	115,134	o
Shanghai Fengxian Food & Beverage Equipment Factory 上海市奉賢食品飲料設備廠(1980)	Shanghai 上海市	Shanghai 上海市	(021)57410109 (021)57457228	451	Collectively-owned 集體	20,892	1270(3)	29,648	o
Jingdezhen Ceramics Machinery Plant 景德鎮市陶瓷機械廠(1959)	Jingdezhen 景德鎮市	Jiangxi 江西省	(0798)8442554 (0798)8441854		State-owned 國有	15,351	18(12)	37,900	o
Changshu Industry Enamel Plant 常熟市工業搪瓷廠(1984)	Suzhou 蘇州市	Jiangsu 江蘇省	(0512)2441131 (0512)2441131	119	Collectively-owned 集體	10,282	932(5)	12,805	o
Nanjing Shu Guang Machinery Co. Ltd. 南京曙光機械有限責任公司(1955)	Nanjing 南京市	Jiangsu 江蘇省	(025)5505202 (025)5507934	910	Joint stock 股份制	8,757	-3478(19)	59,235	o
Liaoyang Welfare Glass Bottle Making Plant 遼陽縣福利玻璃製瓶廠(1984)	Liaoyang 遼陽市	Liaoning 遼寧省	(0419)5135150	240	Collectively-owned 集體	8,184	321(7)	8,889	o

Top 10 Cities by Production Output 產出排名前 10 位城市	Province 省	Market share 市場份額	Number of firms 企業個數
Shanghai 上海市	Shanghai 上海市	23.19%	7
Changzhou 常州市	Jiangsu 江蘇省	22.65%	5
Wuxi 無錫市	Jiangsu 江蘇省	17.12%	3
Beijing 北京市	Beijing 北京市	6.25%	1
Jingdezhen 景德鎮市	Jiangxi 江西省	5.56%	3
Shenzhen 深圳市	Guangdong 廣東省	3.13%	4
Suzhou 蘇州市	Jiangsu 江蘇省	3.00%	2
Wuhu 蕪湖市	Anhui 安徽省	2.43%	2
Liaoyang 遼陽市	Liaoning 遼寧省	1.90%	1
Binzhou 濱州市	Shandong 山東省	1.90%	1

10 Major Wholesalers 10 家主要批發商	City 城市	Province 省	Telephone / Fax 電話 / 傳真
Liaoning Automobile Trade Group Corp. 遼寧省汽車貿易集團	Shenyang 瀋陽市	Liaoning 遼寧省	(024)23835494 (024)23838338
China Post and Telecommunication Equipment General Company 中國郵電器材總公司	Beijing 北京市	Beijing 北京市	(010)63523715 (010)63525935
Jiangsu Electromechanical Products General Company 江蘇省機電產品總公司	Nanjing 南京市	Jiangsu 江蘇省	(025)7713642 (025)7711036
Xi Nan Technology Import & Export Company 西南技術進出口公司	Chongqing 重慶市	Chongqing 重慶市	(023)63850185 (023)63850026
Changzhou Economic Technology Industrial Development Zone Tian Ming Trade Company 常州經濟技術產業開發區天明貿易公司	Changzhou 常州市	Jiangsu 江蘇省	(0519)8829882 (0519)8829882
Shanxi Mechanical Equipment Import & Export Company 山西省機械設備進出口公司	Taiyuan 太原市	Shanxi 山西省	(0351)4040713 (0351)4043981
Ningbo Five Mining Machinery Import & Export Company 寧波市五礦機械進出口公司	Ningbo 寧波市	Zhejiang 浙江省	(0574)7311255 (0574)7320322
Tianjin Jin Huan Electromechanical Complete Sets of Equipment Factory 天津市津環機電成套設備廠	Tianjin 天津市	Tianjin 天津市	(022)26371628
Yunnan Machinery Import & Export Company 雲南省機械進出口公司	Kunming 昆明市	Yunnan 雲南省	(0871)3164879 (0871)3136829
Tianjin Da Qiu Zhuang Yi Yuan Trade Center 天津市大丘莊億源商貿中心	Tianjin 天津市	Tianjin 天津市	(022)28899478 (022)28899046

*Also include sales by firms outside this industry.包括本行業以外廠家的銷售。"o" stands for "others". "o" 代表 "其他產品"。

3638: Paper-making Equipment 製漿、造紙工業專用設備製造業

The industry accounts for 0.049% of the total revenue of China's industrial sector in 1996. The revenue growth rate of the industry is 14.5% from 1995, as compared to the growth rate of China's industrial sector, 9.51%. The rate of return on asset is 4.43%. 70.11% of all firms in the industry made a profit while 22.93% had negative returns. The top province in terms of the industry's revenue is Henan, accounting for 34.68% of the total revenue.
本行業在1996年佔全行業總產值0.049%，行業年增長率為14.5%（全國工業年增長率9.51%）。行業的資產回報率4.43%，70.11%的企業盈利，22.93%的企業虧損。銷售收入最高的省份為河南省，佔本行業的34.68%。

	Total number of firms 企業總數	Total number of employees 職工總數	Total revenue (mil. RMB) 總銷售收入（百萬元）	Total profit (mil. RMB) 總利潤（百萬元）	Return on assets 資產利潤率 (%)	Return on equity 權益利潤率 (%)	Labour productivity ('000 RMB / worker) 勞動生產率（千元/人）	Debts / assets 資產負債率 (%)	Total assets (mil. RMB) 總資產（百萬元）
Industry Overall 行業總體	266	63,562	2,849	187	4.43	17.47	44.82	74.67	4,217

	Number of firms 企業個數	Average number of employees 平均職工人數	Average revenue ('000 RMB) 平均銷售收入（千元）	Average profit ('000 RMB) 平均利潤（千元）	Return on assets 資產利潤率 (%)	Return on equity 權益利潤率 (%)	Labour productivity ('000 RMB / worker) 勞動生產率（千元/人）	Average debts / assets 平均資產負債率(%)	Average Total assets ('000 RMB) 平均總資產（千元）
By ownership 產業所有權									
State-owned 國有	46	573	17,217	-413	-0.87	-3.87	30.04	77.43	47,283
Collectively-owned 集體	202	140	7,926	846	12.55	49.46	56.68	74.62	6,735
Privately-owned 私有	2	129	5,208	16	0.14	0.40	40.37	64.53	11,027
Domestic JVs 聯營	2	146	4,196	165	1.05	3.51	28.84	70.14	15,720
Joint stock 股份制	5	977	48,882	3,486	4.60	14.48	50.05	68.24	75,781
Foreign-funded 外資	2	1,007	40,457	916	1.18	3.07	40.18	61.42	77,387
Overseas Chinese-funded 港澳台資	6	251	18,621	2,597	16.42	45.01	74.14	63.51	15,809
By size 規模									
Large 大型	9	1,430	55,024	-2,747	-2.25	375.41	38.48	100.60	122,266
Medium 中型	23	774	20,037	-448	-0.64	-1.26	25.88	49.49	70,327
Small 小型	233	141	8,124	953	14.81	86.15	57.63	82.81	6,435
By regional distribution 地區分布									
Central-North 華北	22	291	8,147	41	0.19	1.15	28.00	83.44	21,678
Beijing 北京	2	24	400	5	0.53	1.64	16.67	67.55	940
Tianjin 天津	6	652	21,487	20	0.03	0.22	32.96	85.89	63,412
Hebei 河北	7	167	3,287	223	3.76	25.62	19.73	85.33	5,931
Shanxi 山西	7	182	3,787	-111	-1.47	-4.19	20.78	64.94	7,579
Inner Mongolia 內蒙									
Northeast 東北	52	180	5,036	130	1.29	4.44	27.96	71.04	10,073
Liaoning 遼寧	49	171	5,117	133	1.36	4.52	29.97	69.92	9,809
Jilin 吉林	3	334	3,723	70	0.49	2.96	11.15	83.55	14,390
Heilongjiang 黑龍江									
Central East 華東	72	257	15,119	367	1.66	8.89	58.93	81.29	22,069
Shanghai 上海	10	473	29,163	-742	-1.64	27.35	61.66	105.99	45,269
Jiangsu 江蘇	15	146	8,389	244	1.89	7.74	57.48	75.57	12,903
Zhejiang 浙江	9	53	2,399	-26	-0.46	-2.23	45.07	79.40	5,554
Anhui 安徽	3	270	17,573	517	0.96	4.78	65.17	79.90	53,810
Fujian 福建	3	214	6,283	-150	-0.98	-2.74	29.32	64.38	15,367
Jiangxi 江西	1	12	550	140	28.00	77.78	45.83	64.00	500
Shandong 山東	31	310	18,625	941	4.26	13.40	60.09	68.20	22,087
Central-South 中南	81	240	13,573	2,082	16.57	48.95	56.61	66.15	12,567
Henan 河南	60	251	16,469	2,782	23.60	61.34	65.60	61.52	11,788
Hubei 湖北	7	290	7,721	413	2.17	7.91	26.63	72.58	19,034
Hunan 湖南	4	342	4,178	155	0.76	11.42	12.22	93.35	20,415
Guangdong 廣東	6	72	3,885	-52	-1.07	-36.90	53.96	97.10	4,820
Guangxi 廣西	4	132	4,290	-368	-2.20	-4.96	32.56	55.69	16,708
Hainan 海南									
Southwest 西南	26	274	5,435	-503	-3.54	-14.28	19.81	75.22	14,205
Chongqing 重慶	1	237	1,310	-162	-7.02	14.46	5.53	148.54	2,302
Sichuan 四川	24	263	5,744	-458	-3.27	-12.74	21.84	74.34	14,008
Guizhou 貴州	1	583	2,140	-1,920	-6.23	-30.14	3.67	79.33	30,820
Yunnan 雲南									
Tibet 西藏									
Northwest 西北	13	213	6,045	-235	-1.27	-2.93	28.37	56.55	18,438
Shaanxi 陝西	10	251	7,624	-306	-1.33	-3.13	30.35	57.60	23,026
Gansu 甘肅	1	7	20	10	33.33	33.33	2.86		30
Qinghai 青海									
Ningxia 寧夏	1	223	2,320				10.40	30.92	9,410
Xinjiang 新疆	1	28							

3638: Paper-making Equipment 製漿、造紙工業專用設備製造業

Year 年份	Number of firms 企業個數	Rate of change 每年變化 (%)	Number of employees 職工人數 (人)	Rate of change 每年變化 (%)	Total revenue (mil. RMB) 總銷售收入 (百萬元)	Rate of change 每年變化 (%)	Total profit (mil. RMB) 總利潤 (百萬元)	Rate of change 每年變化 (%)
1993	220		79,390		1,802		42	
1994	243	10.45%	57,126	-28.04%	1,956	8.57%	-84	-297.36%
1995	235	-3.29%	64,991	13.77%	2,489	27.20%	125	250.09%
1996	266	13.19%	63,562	-2.20%	2,849	14.46%	187	49.17%

3 Major products* 3 種主要產品 *	Output 產量	Sales volume 銷售量	Unit 單位
a) Paper Making Machinery 造紙機械	61,135	58,078	set 台
b) Rubber Roller 膠輥	2,943,543	2,855,237	kg 公斤
c) Binding Machine 裝訂機械	195	189	set 台

Top 10 firms by revenue (year founded) 收入排名前 10 家企業 (創辦年份)	City 城市	Province 省	Telephone / fax 電話 / 傳真	Number of employees 職工人數	Ownership 產業所有權	Revenue ('000 RMB) 銷售收入 (千元)	Profit ('000 RMB) (rank) 利潤 (千元) (排名)	Total assets ('000 RMB) 總資產 (千元)	Major products 主要產品
Jiamusi Paper Industry Group Company 佳木斯紙業集團公司(1955)	Jiamusi 佳木斯市	Heilongjiang 黑龍江省	(0454)8391258 (0454)8391825	3,185	State-owned 國有	593,238	-45072(158)	2,060,891	o
Shanghai Paper Machinery Corp. 上海造紙機械總廠(1925)	Shanghai 上海市	Shanghai 上海市	(021)56650588 (021)56651308	3,260	State-owned 國有	164,365	-8699(156)	319,733	a
Shandong Jiangbei Group Company 山東江北集團公司(1995)	Yantai 煙臺市	Shandong 山東省	(0535)6752023 (0535)6752023	1,268	Collectively-owned 集體	96,078	4032(15)	55,980	a
Henan Xinxiang Paper Making Equipment Factory 河南省新鄉市造紙設備廠(1976)	Xinxiang 新鄉市	Henan 河南省	(0373)5592383	400	Collectively-owned 集體	94,971	20149(2)	24,494	o
Liaoyang Paper Making Machinery Co. Ltd. 遼陽造紙機械股份有限公司(1935)	Liaoyang 遼陽市	Liaoning 遼寧省	(0419)3132329 (0419)3132877	2,518	Joint stock 股份制	89,205	5700(11)	245,365	o
Henan Jia Xiang Paper Making Machinery Co. Ltd. 河南佳香造紙機械有限公司(1966)	Jiaozuo 焦作市	Henan 河南省	(0391)5066488	290	Overseas Chinese-funded 港澳台資	79,870	14390(4)	40,804	a
Henan Wenxian No.3 Machinery Factory 河南省温縣第三機械廠(1963)	Jiaozuo 焦作市	Henan 河南省	(0391)6192438	650	Collectively-owned 集體	70,000	8640(7)	18,800	a
Valmet-xian Paper Machinery Co. Ltd. 維美德西安造紙機械有限公司(1989)	Xi'an 西安市	Shaanxi 陕西省	(029)4262828 (029)4262820	1,587	Foreign-funded 外資	64,657	562(47)	136,466	o
Henan Da Zhong Rubber Item Co. Ltd. 河南達中橡膠製品有限公司(1989)	Jiaozuo 焦作市	Henan 河南省	(0391)5066007	103	Overseas Chinese-funded 港澳台資	61,170	9760(5)	33,032	b
Zibo Chang Ya Co. Ltd. 淄博昌亞股份有限公司(1966)	Zibo 淄博市	Shandong 山東省	(0533)6680181 (0533)6680181	472	Collectively-owned 集體	58,142	2609(19)	48,259	a

Top 10 Cities by Production Output 產出排名前 10 位城市	Province 省	Market share 市場份額	Number of firms 企業個數
Jiaozuo 焦作市	Henan 河南省	30.84%	30
Shanghai 上海市	Shanghai 上海市	9.93%	20
Weifang 濰坊市	Shandong 山東省	7.62%	17
Tianjin 天津市	Tianjin 天津市	4.47%	7
Xinxiang 新鄉市	Henan 河南省	4.13%	6
Dandong 丹東市	Liaoning 遼寧省	3.76%	29
Yantai 煙臺市	Shandong 山東省	3.63%	4
Liaoyang 遼陽市	Liaoning 遼寧省	3.11%	8
Xi'an 西安市	Shaanxi 陕西省	2.61%	7
Zibo 淄博市	Shandong 山東省	2.49%	4

10 Major Wholesalers 10 家主要批發商	City 城市	Province 省	Telephone / Fax 電話 / 傳真
Liaoning Automobile Trade Group Corp. 遼寧省汽車貿易集團	Shenyang 瀋陽市	Liaoning 遼寧省	(024)23835494 (024)23838338
China Post and Telecommunication Equipment General Company 中國郵電器材總公司	Beijing 北京市	Beijing 北京市	(010)63523715 (010)63525935
Jiangsu Electromechanical Products General Company 江蘇省機電產品總公司	Nanjing 南京市	Jiangsu 江蘇省	(025)7713642 (025)7711036
Xi Nan Technology Import & Export Company 西南技術進出口公司	Chongqing 重慶市	Chongqing 重慶市	(023)63850185 (023)63850026
Changzhou Economic Technology Industrial Development Zone Tian Ming Trade Company 常州經濟技術產業開發區天明貿易公司	Changzhou 常州市	Jiangsu 江蘇省	(0519)8829882 (0519)8829882
Shanxi Mechanical Equipment Import & Export Company 山西省機械設備進出口公司	Taiyuan 太原市	Shanxi 山西省	(0351)4040713 (0351)4043981
Ningbo Five Mining Machinery Import & Export Company 寧波市五礦機械進出口公司	Ningbo 寧波市	Zhejiang 浙江省	(0574)7311255 (0574)7320322
Tianjin Jin Huan Electromechanical Complete Sets of Equipment Factory 天津市津環機電成套設備廠	Tianjin 天津市	Tianjin 天津市	(022)26371628
Yunnan Machinery Import & Export Company 雲南省機械進出口公司	Kunming 昆明市	Yunnan 雲南省	(0871)3164879 (0871)3136829
Tianjin Da Qiu Zhuang Yi Yuan Trade Center 天津市大丘莊億源商貿中心	Tianjin 天津市	Tianjin 天津市	(022)28899478 (022)28899046

*Also include sales by firms outside this industry.包括本行業以外廠家的銷售。"o" stands for "others". "o" 代表"其他產品"。

3639: Special Daily Chemical Processing Equipment
日用化學工業專用設備製造業

The industry accounts for 0.022% of the total revenue of China's industrial sector in 1996. The revenue growth rate of the industry is 278.5% from 1995, as compared to the growth rate of China's industrial sector, 9.51%. The rate of return on asset is 1.78%. 64.61% of all firms in the industry made a profit while 25.77% had negative returns. The top province in terms of the industry's revenue is Jiangsu, accounting for 46.76% of the total revenue.
本行業在1996年佔全行業總產值0.022%，行業年增長率為278.5%（全國工業年增長率9.51%）。行業的資產回報率1.78%，64.61%的企業盈利，25.77%的企業虧損。銷售收入最高的省份為江蘇省，佔本行業的46.76%。

	Total number of firms 企業總數	Total number of employees 職工總數	Total revenue (mil. RMB) 總銷售收入（百萬元）	Total profit (mil. RMB) 總利潤（百萬元）	Return on assets 資產利潤率 (%)	Return on equity 權益利潤率 (%)	Labour productivity ('000 RMB / worker) 勞動生產率（千元/人）	Debts / assets 資產負債率 (%)	Total assets (mil. RMB) 總資產（百萬元）
Industry Overall 行業總體	116	16,827	1,262	26	1.78	5.60	75.00	68.20	1,480

	Number of firms 企業個數	Average number of employees 平均職工人數	Average revenue ('000 RMB) 平均銷售收入（千元）	Average profit ('000 RMB) 平均利潤（千元）	Return on assets 資產利潤率 (%)	Return on equity 權益利潤率 (%)	Labour productivity ('000 RMB / worker) 勞動生產率（千元/人）	Average debts / assets 平均資產負債率(%)	Average Total assets ('000 RMB) 平均總資產（千元）
By ownership 產業所有權									
State-owned 國有	21	281	7,714	95	0.49	2.33	27.46	79.08	19,571
Collectively-owned 集體	75	109	10,337	11	0.16	0.54	95.15	69.28	6,935
Privately-owned 私有	1	139	80,552	-115	-0.24	-1.05	579.51	77.70	48,957
Domestic JVs 聯營	3	158	9,505	-273	-3.47	-8.25	60.29	57.94	7,860
Joint stock 股份制	1	160	209	538	4.51	74.02	1.31	93.91	11,945
Foreign-funded 外資	7	129	7,068	3,579	13.93	41.11	54.61	66.11	25,689
Overseas Chinese-funded 港澳台資	7	179	23,666	-216	-0.53	-1.06	132.32	49.85	40,638
By size 規模									
Large 大型									
Medium 中型	1	415	21,001	24,449	17.65	82.16	50.60	78.51	138,494
Small 小型	114	144	10,885	14	0.12	0.35	75.61	67.11	11,766
By regional distribution 地區分布									
Central-North 華北	15	114	5,338	183	2.07	5.35	46.77	61.21	8,805
Beijing 北京	8	14	693	4	0.18	0.24	50.36	27.01	2,101
Tianjin 天津	2	5	410	45	25.00	36.00	82.00	30.56	180
Hebei 河北	5	318	14,742	524	2.28	6.77	46.30	66.30	22,982
Shanxi 山西									
Inner Mongolia 內蒙									
Northeast 東北	12	43	1,138	108	9.19	20.71	26.52	55.52	1,169
Liaoning 遼寧	5	24	64				2.62	63.52	806
Jilin 吉林	3	55	470	-3	-0.20	-0.69	8.49	71.37	1,700
Heilongjiang 黑龍江	4	57	2,983	325	26.53	39.27	52.56	32.45	1,225
Central East 華東	43	173	16,245	-74	-0.42	-1.30	94.08	67.92	17,683
Shanghai 上海	8	98	5,133	-859	-8.16	-57.93	52.44	85.93	10,529
Jiangsu 江蘇	15	332	39,341	255	0.67	1.99	118.66	66.19	37,997
Zhejiang 浙江	5	82	2,768	-52	-1.30	-5.43	33.76	76.07	4,004
Anhui 安徽	3	64	1,980	33	1.06	3.75	31.10	71.57	3,130
Fujian 福建	2								
Jiangxi 江西	4	100	1,488	-50	-2.01	-9.48	14.84	78.79	2,488
Shandong 山東	6	111	6,938	38	0.34	0.77	62.41	55.45	11,138
Central-South 中南	32	179	13,507	794	4.76	16.39	75.56	70.99	16,692
Henan 河南	7	404	9,781	30	0.09	0.74	24.19	88.12	34,284
Hubei 湖北	6	331	50,717	3,902	10.91	27.86	153.45	60.83	35,757
Hunan 湖南	2	27	860	5	0.23	0.74	31.85	68.30	2,145
Guangdong 廣東	16	41	3,258	106	2.57	5.08	78.61	49.46	4,111
Guangxi 廣西	1	190	5,600	80	0.84	1.02	29.47	17.99	9,560
Hainan 海南									
Southwest 西南	7	72	2,013	4	0.25	1.60	27.85	84.30	1,720
Chongqing 重慶	2	86	6,759	14	0.67	4.97	78.21	86.60	2,048
Sichuan 四川	2	164	287	-30	-0.75	-4.42	1.76	83.11	3,972
Guizhou 貴州	2	3							
Yunnan 雲南	1	2							
Tibet 西藏									
Northwest 西北	7	136	3,321	14	0.37	0.81	24.50	54.73	3,879
Shaanxi 陝西	4	81	2,105	53	3.37	7.00	25.91	51.69	1,558
Gansu 甘肅	2	233	6,845	140	1.66	2.67	29.44	37.63	8,410
Qinghai 青海	1	159	1,140	-390	-9.51	31.97	7.17	129.51	4,100
Ningxia 寧夏									
Xinjiang 新疆									

3639: Special Daily Chemical Processing Equipment
日用化學工業專用設備製造業

Year 年份	Number of firms 企業個數	Rate of change 每年變化 (%)	Number of employees 職工人數 (人)	Rate of change 每年變化 (%)	Total revenue (mil. RMB) 總銷售收入 (百萬元)	Rate of change 每年變化 (%)	Total profit (mil. RMB) 總利潤 (百萬元)	Rate of change 每年變化 (%)
1993	84		16,753		545		31	
1994	81	-3.57%	6,871	-58.99%	311	-42.88%	5	-83.38%
1995	98	20.99%	9,285	35.13%	333	7.12%	-18	-456.77%
1996	116	18.37%	16,827	81.23%	1,262	278.46%	26	241.92%

3 Major products* 3 種主要產品 *	Output 產量	Sales volume 銷售量	Unit 單位
a) Special Equipment for Primary Cell Making 原電池製造專用設備	711	683	set 套
b) Special Equipment for Daily Chemical Industry 日用化學工業專用設備	1,381	1,312	set 台
c) Primary Battery 原電池	12,627	11,870	10,000 piece 萬只

Top 10 firms by revenue (year founded) 收入排名前 10 家企業 (創辦年份)	City 城市	Province 省	Telephone / fax 電話 / 傳真	Number of employees 職工人數	Ownership 產業所有權	Revenue ('000 RMB) 銷售收入 (千元)	Profit ('000 RMB) (rank) 利潤 (千元) (排名)	Total assets ('000 RMB) 總資產 (千元)	Major products 主要產品
Jiangsu Zhong Dan Chemical Group Company 江蘇中丹化工集團公司(1976)	Taizhou 泰州市	Jiangsu 江蘇省	(0523)7484048	2,158	Foreign-funded 外資	304,195	-3808(51)	284,432	o
Jiangsu Bai Xiong Machinery Group Co. 江蘇白熊機械集團公司(1956)	Suzhou 蘇州市	Jiangsu 江蘇省	(0512)8570321	1,235	Collectively-owned 集體	151,684	4861(1)	101,432	o
Zhangjiagang Hu Gang Electromechanical Equipment Factory 張家港市滬港機電設備廠(1989)	Suzhou 蘇州市	Jiangsu 江蘇省	(0512)8570561 (0512)8570437	250	Collectively-owned 集體	67,657	2260(2)	101,591	o
Hebei Dongguang Hua Zhi Battery Co. Ltd. 河北省東光縣華芝電池有限公司(1958)	Cangzhou 滄州市	Hebei 河北省	(0317)7721483	504	Joint stock 股份制	31,813	-309(48)	27,037	c
Langfang Universal Machine Works 廊坊市通用機械廠(1983)	Langfang 廊坊市	Hebei 河北省	(0316)2050547 (0316)2012249	631	State-owned 國有	20,479	427(8)	57,339	o
Qingdao Shi Wang Daily Chemical Co. Ltd. 青島獅王日用化工有限公司(1990)	Qingdao 青島市	Shandong 山東省	(0532)6897122 (0532)6895991	150	Foreign-funded 外資	19,846	-134(41)	37,115	o
Liaoning Sang Mo International Cosmetics Co. Ltd. 遼寧桑莫國際化妝品有限公司(1990)	Shenyang 瀋陽市	Liaoning 遼寧省	(024)24857753 (024)24841973	158	Foreign-funded 外資	17,560	220(17)	40,110	o
Shanghai A Ren Ke Machinery Co. Ltd. 上海阿仁科機械有限公司(1992)	Shanghai 上海市	Shanghai 上海市	(021)58995190 (021)58995291	221	Foreign-funded 外資	15,502	-7372(52)	53,364	b
Conghua Jiaxin Battery Factory 從化市佳信電池廠(1995)	Guangzhou 廣州市	Guangdong 廣東省	(020)87886122 (020)87886380	70	Collectively-owned 集體	15,200	831(6)	6,750	o
Shandong Tai'an Chemical Industry Machinery Factory 山東省泰安化工機械廠(1970)	Tai'an 泰安市	Shandong 山東省	(0538)8481254 (0538)8481372	423	State-owned 國有	13,296	152(22)	21,786	o

Top 10 Cities by Production Output 產出排名前 10 位城市	Province 省	Market share 市場份額	Number of firms 企業個數
Taizhou 泰州市	Jiangsu 江蘇省	24.40%	2
Suizhou 隨州市	Hubei 湖北省	22.69%	1
Suzhou 蘇州市	Jiangsu 江蘇省	9.10%	4
Shanghai 上海市	Shanghai 上海市	6.47%	29
Xinxiang 新鄉市	Henan 河南省	4.64%	1
Bengbu 蚌埠市	Anhui 安徽省	3.68%	2
Wuxi 無錫市	Jiangsu 江蘇省	3.18%	5
Cangzhou 滄州市	Hebei 河北省	2.54%	1
Guangzhou 廣州市	Guangdong 廣東省	2.33%	18
Hefei 合肥市	Anhui 安徽省	2.02%	3

10 Major Wholesalers 10 家主要批發商	City 城市	Province 省	Telephone / Fax 電話 / 傳真
Liaoning Automobile Trade Group Corp. 遼寧省汽車貿易集團	Shenyang 瀋陽市	Liaoning 遼寧省	(024)23835494 (024)23838338
China Post and Telecommunication Equipment General Company 中國郵電器材總公司	Beijing 北京市	Beijing 北京市	(010)63523715 (010)63525935
Jiangsu Electromechanical Products General Company 江蘇省機電產品總公司	Nanjing 南京市	Jiangsu 江蘇省	(025)7713642 (025)7711036
Xi Nan Technology Import & Export Company 西南技術進出口公司	Chongqing 重慶市	Chongqing 重慶市	(023)63850185 (023)63850026
Changzhou Economic Technology Industrial Development Zone Tian Ming Trade Company 常州經濟技術產業開發區天明貿易公司	Changzhou 常州市	Jiangsu 江蘇省	(0519)8829882 (0519)8829882
Shanxi Mechanical Equipment Import & Export Company 山西省機械設備進出口公司	Taiyuan 太原市	Shanxi 山西省	(0351)4040713 (0351)4043981
Ningbo Five Mining Machinery Import & Export Company 寧波市五礦機械進出口公司	Ningbo 寧波市	Zhejiang 浙江省	(0574)7311255 (0574)7320322
Tianjin Jin Huan Electromechanical Complete Sets of Equipment Factory 天津市津環機電成套設備廠	Tianjin 天津市	Tianjin 天津市	(022)26371628
Yunnan Machinery Import & Export Company 雲南省機械進出口公司	Kunming 昆明市	Yunnan 雲南省	(0871)3164879 (0871)3136829
Tianjin Da Qiu Zhuang Yi Yuan Trade Center 天津市大丘莊億源商貿中心	Tianjin 天津市	Tianjin 天津市	(022)28899478 (022)28899046

*Also include sales by firms outside this industry.包括本行業以外廠家的銷售。"o" stands for "others". "o" 代表"其他產品"。

3641: Tractors 拖拉機製造業

The industry accounts for 0.360% of the total revenue of China's industrial sector in 1996. The revenue growth rate of the industry is 6.6% from 1995, as compared to the growth rate of China's industrial sector, 9.51%. The rate of return on asset is 1.55%. 59.07% of all firms in the industry made a profit while 34.78% had negative returns. The top province in terms of the industry's revenue is Henan, accounting for 29.10% of the total revenue.
本行業在1996年佔全行業總產值0.360%，行業年增長率為6.6%（全國工業年增長率9.51%）。行業的資產回報率1.55%，59.07%的企業盈利，34.78%的企業虧損。銷售收入最高的省份為河南省，佔本行業的29.10%。

	Total number of firms 企業總數	Total number of employees 職工總數	Total revenue (mil. RMB) 總銷售收入（百萬元）	Total profit (mil. RMB) 總利潤（百萬元）	Return on assets 資產利潤率 (%)	Return on equity 權益利潤率 (%)	Labour productivity ('000 RMB / worker) 勞動生產率（千元/人）	Debts / assets 資產負債率 (%)	Total assets (mil. RMB) 總資產（百萬元）
Industry Overall 行業總體	194	228,649	20,845	328	1.55	5.09	91.17	69.56	21,196

	Number of firms 企業個數	Average number of employees 平均職工人數	Average revenue ('000 RMB) 平均銷售收入（千元）	Average profit ('000 RMB) 平均利潤（千元）	Return on assets 資產利潤率 (%)	Return on equity 權益利潤率 (%)	Labour productivity ('000 RMB / worker) 勞動生產率（千元/人）	Average debts / assets 平均資產負債率(%)	Average Total assets ('000 RMB) 平均總資產（千元）
By ownership 產業所有權									
State-owned 國有	117	1,779	159,701	2,402	1.46	4.79	89.76	69.49	164,462
Collectively-owned 集體	70	165	11,500	202	1.78	10.88	69.66	83.65	11,354
Privately-owned 私有									
Domestic JVs 聯營	2	408	67,525	902	1.86	5.95	165.70	68.69	48,405
Joint stock 股份制	2	3,310	560,065	13,918	2.92	7.25	169.20	59.69	476,057
Foreign-funded 外資	1	11							
Overseas Chinese-funded 港澳台資	1	1,468	100,353	3,191	2.86	8.35	68.36	65.69	111,414
By size 規模									
Large 大型	31	4,743	473,250	6,416	1.33	4.01	99.78	66.81	482,237
Medium 中型	48	1,193	93,731	2,014	2.05	8.05	78.59	74.50	98,151
Small 小型	113	215	14,828	286	2.11	11.21	68.90	81.22	13,594
By regional distribution 地區分布									
Central-North 華北	21	1,207	112,909	-1,015	-0.86	-3.30	93.53	73.83	117,592
Beijing 北京	2	995	39,990	195	0.11	0.47	40.21	75.75	169,865
Tianjin 天津	2	3,523	299,430	-12,940	-3.07	-8.57	85.00	64.13	421,105
Hebei 河北	9	1,244	164,636	1,810	1.73	8.55	132.33	79.79	104,716
Shanxi 山西	6	659	27,397	-1,583	-3.51	-13.15	41.60	73.31	45,112
Inner Mongolia 內蒙	2	585	23,075	-1,305	-3.51	274.74	39.48	101.29	37,195
Northeast 東北	18	1,699	80,293	-869	-0.62	-3.58	47.25	82.67	140,112
Liaoning 遼寧	5	2,275	22,976	-4,872	-3.96	-24.77	10.10	84.01	122,988
Jilin 吉林	4	3,060	188,020	188	0.06	0.41	61.45	84.82	301,725
Heilongjiang 黑龍江	9	775	64,258	886	1.14	5.12	82.94	77.76	77,798
Central East 華東	65	1,134	128,854	2,917	2.70	9.40	113.63	71.31	108,168
Shanghai 上海	1	6,327	1,001,520	8,590	0.92	2.69	158.29	66.02	938,330
Jiangsu 江蘇	11	1,445	184,204	3,137	2.07	7.30	127.44	71.63	151,541
Zhejiang 浙江	5	1,168	138,276	5,988	4.78	13.29	118.41	64.05	125,314
Anhui 安徽	12	937	44,128	370	0.55	2.33	47.10	76.62	67,811
Fujian 福建	8	391	29,500	581	2.06	6.81	75.47	69.79	28,260
Jiangxi 江西	3	2,662	135,693	1,003	0.47	1.92	50.98	75.57	214,333
Shandong 山東	25	932	139,350	4,179	4.94	17.87	149.57	72.37	84,651
Central-South 中南	53	1,464	134,443	3,544	2.59	6.62	91.85	60.85	136,724
Henan 河南	23	2,685	263,751	8,500	3.48	8.47	98.22	58.90	244,190
Hubei 湖北	5	848	29,882	-784	-1.58	-5.43	35.23	70.94	49,700
Hunan 湖南	7	540	24,076	207	0.60	1.89	44.60	68.34	34,653
Guangdong 廣東	7	453	31,834	-1,367	-1.57	-8.03	70.23	80.44	87,027
Guangxi 廣西	10	418	51,361	597	1.36	2.85	122.96	52.30	43,977
Hainan 海南	1	440	4,820	-1,590	-1.77	-3.16	10.95	44.02	89,960
Southwest 西南	20	416	28,070	-210	-0.62	-2.54	67.52	75.45	33,540
Chongqing 重慶	1	105	5,808	-4,707	-74.69	577.57	55.52	112.93	6,302
Sichuan 四川	9	485	27,663	1,798	5.27	34.51	57.09	84.73	34,129
Guizhou 貴州	2	673	42,280	2,100	3.23	21.82	62.87	85.19	65,010
Yunnan 雲南	7	343	31,153	454	1.45	3.29	90.94	55.99	31,381
Tibet 西藏	1	71	2,000	500	9.77	23.58	28.17	58.59	5,120
Northwest 西北	17	771	56,833	-465	-0.63	-2.26	73.69	72.15	73,902
Shaanxi 陝西	6	511	17,740	-867	-3.39	-22.29	34.72	84.79	25,560
Gansu 甘肅	3	1,769	147,393	-2,207	-1.35	-5.45	83.34	75.17	162,967
Qinghai 青海									
Ningxia 寧夏	4	323	28,468	-1,368	-4.85	-34.00	88.27	85.73	28,190
Xinjiang 新疆	4	863	75,918	2,348	1.87	4.97	88.02	62.29	125,330

3641: Tractors 拖拉機製造業

Year 年份	Number of firms 企業個數	Rate of change 每年變化 (%)	Number of employees 職工人數（人）	Rate of change 每年變化 (%)	Total revenue (mil. RMB) 總銷售收入（百萬元）	Rate of change 每年變化 (%)	Total profit (mil. RMB) 總利潤（百萬元）	Rate of change 每年變化 (%)
1993	152		259,964		11,295		-154	
1994	161	5.92%	156,873	-39.66%	12,940	14.56%	-124	19.42%
1995	175	8.70%	226,022	44.08%	19,558	51.14%	312	352.17%
1996	194	10.86%	228,649	1.16%	20,845	6.58%	328	5.02%

3 Major products* 3 種主要產品 *	Output 產量	Sales volume 銷售量	Unit 單位
a) Large & Medium Tractor 大中型拖拉機	83,675	81,165	set 台
b) Small Tractor 小型拖拉機	1,881,426	1,806,169	set 台
c) Agricultural Transport Machinery 農業運輸機械	203,747	201,709	vehicle 輛

Top 10 firms by revenue (year founded) 收入排名前 10 家企業 (創辦年份)	City 城市	Province 省	Telephone / fax 電話 / 傳真	Number of employees 職工人數	Ownership 產業所有權	Revenue ('000 RMB) 銷售收入（千元）	Profit ('000 RMB) (rank) 利潤（千元）（排名）	Total assets ('000 RMB) 總資產（千元）	Major products 主要產品
Hebei Shijiazhuang Tractor Factory 河北省石家莊拖拉機廠(1976)	Shijiazhuang 石家莊市	Hebei 河北省	(0311)5054878 (0311)5054672	4,932	State-owned 國有	1,103,084	10583(10)	649,393	a,b,c
Shanghai Tractor Internal Combustion Co. 上海拖拉機內燃機公司(1943)	Shanghai 上海市	Shanghai 上海市	(021)65480006 (021)65491996	6,350	State-owned 國有	1,001,520	8588(13)	938,327	a,c
Shandong Weifang Tractor Factory 山東濰坊拖拉機廠(1951)	Weifang 濰坊市	Shandong 山東省	(0536)8233931 (0536)8233806	4,839	State-owned 國有	917,599	13892(5)	463,356	a,b,c
Changzhou Tractor Factory 常州拖拉機廠(1952)	Changzhou 常州市	Jiangsu 江蘇省	(0519)3260424 (0519)3260445	2,345	State-owned 國有	791,612	23514(1)	402,131	a,b,c
Changchun Tractor Manufacturing Factory 長春拖拉機製造廠(1958)	Changchun 長春市	Jilin 吉林省	(0431)4942911 (0431)4948464	11,151	State-owned 國有	696,529	66(75)	1,126,891	a,b,c
Tianjin Tractor Manufacture Co. Ltd. 天津拖拉機製造有限公司(1938)	Tianjin 天津市	Tianjin 天津市	(022)23362240 (022)23363160	7,008	State-owned 國有	595,080	-26406(130)	837,272	a,c
Liaocheng Tractor Factory 聊城拖拉機廠(1961)	Liaocheng 聊城市	Shandong 山東省	(0635)8322180 (0635)8322177	1,760	State-owned 國有	495,183	12022(8)	189,441	b,c
Zhejiang Si Fang Group Co. 浙江四方集團公司(1961)	Jinhua 金華市	Zhejiang 浙江省	(0579)7111922 (0579)7112293	2,429	Joint stock 股份制	455,705	12974(6)	389,709	o
Shandong Tractor Factory 山東拖拉機廠(1962)	Jining 濟寧市	Shandong 山東省	(0537)3413682 (0537)3410225	5,425	State-owned 國有	434,691	18189(2)	348,033	a,b
Shandong Hai Shan Group General Company 山東海山集團總公司(1945)	Weihai 威海市	Shandong 山東省	(0896)7571366 (0896)7571010	2,057	State-owned 國有	419,056	10104(11)	229,099	b,c

Top 10 Cities by Production Output 產出排名前 10 位城市	Province 省	Market share 市場份額	Number of firms 企業個數
Luoyang 洛陽市	Henan 河南省	18.00%	1
Shijiazhuang 石家莊市	Hebei 河北省	6.05%	2
Shanghai 上海市	Shanghai 上海市	5.21%	8
Changzhou 常州市	Jiangsu 江蘇省	4.65%	6
Weifang 濰坊市	Shandong 山東省	4.26%	6
Changchun 長春市	Jilin 吉林省	3.40%	1
Kaifeng 開封市	Henan 河南省	2.85%	2
Xinxiang 新鄉市	Henan 河南省	2.85%	2
Liaocheng 聊城市	Shandong 山東省	2.69%	3
Weihai 威海市	Shandong 山東省	2.59%	4

10 Major Wholesalers 10 家主要批發商	City 城市	Province 省	Telephone / Fax 電話 / 傳真
Liaoning Automobile Trade Group Corp. 遼寧省汽車貿易集團	Shenyang 瀋陽市	Liaoning 遼寧省	(024)23835494 (024)23838338
China Post and Telecommunication Equipment General Company 中國郵電器材總公司	Beijing 北京市	Beijing 北京市	(010)63523715 (010)63525935
Jiangsu Electromechanical Products General Company 江蘇省機電產品總公司	Nanjing 南京市	Jiangsu 江蘇省	(025)7713642 (025)7711036
Xi Nan Technology Import & Export Company 西南技術進出口公司	Chongqing 重慶市	Chongqing 重慶市	(023)63850185 (023)63850026
Changzhou Economic Technology Industrial Development Zone Tian Ming Trade Company 常州經濟技術產業開發區天明貿易公司	Changzhou 常州市	Jiangsu 江蘇省	(0519)8829882 (0519)8829882
Shanxi Mechanical Equipment Import & Export Company 山西省機械設備進出口公司	Taiyuan 太原市	Shanxi 山西省	(0351)4040713 (0351)4043981
Ningbo Five Mining Machinery Import & Export Company 寧波市五礦機械進出口公司	Ningbo 寧波市	Zhejiang 浙江省	(0574)7311255 (0574)7320322
Tianjin Jin Huan Electromechanical Complete Sets of Equipment Factory 天津市津環機電成套設備廠	Tianjin 天津市	Tianjin 天津市	(022)26371628
Yunnan Machinery Import & Export Company 雲南省機械進出口公司	Kunming 昆明市	Yunnan 雲南省	(0871)3164879 (0871)3136829
Tianjin Da Qiu Zhuang Yi Yuan Trade Center 天津市大丘莊億源商貿中心	Tianjin 天津市	Tianjin 天津市	(022)28899478 (022)28899046

*Also include sales by firms outside this industry.包括本行業以外廠家的銷售。"o" stands for "others". "o" 代表 "其他產品"。

3642: Mechanized Farm Tools 機械化農具製造業

The industry accounts for 0.130% of the total revenue of China's industrial sector in 1996. The revenue growth rate of the industry is 28.8% from 1995, as compared to the growth rate of China's industrial sector, 9.51%. The rate of return on asset is 0.89%. 66.42% of all firms in the industry made a profit while 24.62% had negative returns. The top province in terms of the industry's revenue is Shandong, accounting for 16.92% of the total revenue.
本行業在1996年佔全行業總產值0.130%，行業年增長率為28.8%（全國工業年增長率9.51%）。行業的資產回報率0.89%，66.42%的企業盈利，24.62%的企業虧損。銷售收入最高的省份為山東省，佔本行業的16.92%。

	Total number of firms 企業總數	Total number of employees 職工總數	Total revenue (mil. RMB) 總銷售收入（百萬元）	Total profit (mil. RMB) 總利潤（百萬元）	Return on assets 資產利潤率 (%)	Return on equity 權益利潤率 (%)	Labour productivity ('000 RMB / worker) 勞動生產率（千元/人）	Debts / assets 資產負債率 (%)	Total assets (mil. RMB) 總資產（百萬元）
Industry Overall 行業總體	1,579	196,278	7,561	93	0.89	3.84	38.52	76.81	10,400

	Number of firms 企業個數	Average number of employees 平均職工人數	Average revenue ('000 RMB) 平均銷售收入（千元）	Average profit ('000 RMB) 平均利潤（千元）	Return on assets 資產利潤率 (%)	Return on equity 權益利潤率 (%)	Labour productivity ('000 RMB / worker) 勞動生產率（千元/人）	Average debts / assets 平均資產負債率(%)	Average Total assets ('000 RMB) 平均總資產（千元）
By ownership 產業所有權									
State-owned 國有	501	256	8,864	-48	-0.31	-1.47	34.57	78.68	15,325
Collectively-owned 集體	1,052	61	2,671	105	4.81	16.13	43.90	70.20	2,184
Privately-owned 私有	1	133	1,898	-1,400	-9.93	-13.25	14.27	25.02	14,090
Domestic JVs 聯營	8	42	2,890	47	1.88	3.82	68.61	50.66	2,492
Joint stock 股份制	7	425	30,598	579	1.21	8.56	71.95	85.86	47,813
Foreign-funded 外資	6	17	5,411	474	7.95	14.79	315.18	46.28	5,962
Overseas Chinese-funded 港澳台資	3	62	12,089	235	4.84	25.58	196.04	81.09	4,862
By size 規模									
Large 大型	5	2,804	108,564	30,779	12.56	223.80	38.72	94.39	245,092
Medium 中型	44	801	44,073	-550	-0.84	-3.76	55.05	77.68	65,590
Small 小型	1,527	96	3,325	-24	-0.58	-2.16	34.51	72.98	4,118
By regional distribution 地區分布									
Central-North 華北	209	121	4,845	151	2.24	9.29	39.88	75.90	6,765
Beijing 北京	21	156	10,533	111	0.61	2.90	67.58	79.07	18,255
Tianjin 天津	10	53	2,919	150	3.87	12.99	55.08	70.19	3,875
Hebei 河北	89	149	5,441	260	3.78	19.51	36.58	80.62	6,867
Shanxi 山西	34	118	6,355	201	4.05	11.94	53.97	66.08	4,975
Inner Mongolia 內蒙	55	79	1,125	-39	-1.02	-2.94	14.24	65.43	3,845
Northeast 東北	218	184	4,746	-161	-1.79	-15.41	25.85	88.37	8,956
Liaoning 遼寧	69	111	1,562	-153	-4.55	-24.99	14.12	81.79	3,366
Jilin 吉林	49	209	7,016	37	0.31	1.61	33.53	80.84	11,882
Heilongjiang 黑龍江	100	221	5,830	-262	-2.30	-35.81	26.34	93.57	11,380
Central East 華東	441	128	6,397	135	1.85	7.54	49.78	75.42	7,265
Shanghai 上海	11	311	14,760	-701	-3.42	-19.04	47.52	82.03	20,485
Jiangsu 江蘇	91	191	9,332	228	2.28	10.29	48.83	77.85	9,994
Zhejiang 浙江	27	103	2,711	16	0.45	2.18	26.32	79.41	3,557
Anhui 安徽	61	74	3,644	135	4.83	16.49	49.04	70.69	2,785
Fujian 福建	42	46	1,594	-22	-1.03	-2.42	34.71	57.37	2,172
Jiangxi 江西	91	55	1,845	-2	-0.11	-0.44	33.45	74.66	1,786
Shandong 山東	118	183	10,840	329	2.50	9.80	59.23	74.45	13,129
Central-South 中南	463	99	3,781	80	1.83	6.91	38.11	73.49	4,385
Henan 河南	200	136	4,740	146	2.49	13.79	34.82	81.91	5,845
Hubei 湖北	61	102	4,380	60	1.40	4.48	42.84	68.81	4,309
Hunan 湖南	72	86	1,999	-47	-1.92	-5.21	23.20	63.08	2,461
Guangdong 廣東	49	56	2,440	68	2.01	6.00	43.45	66.45	3,353
Guangxi 廣西	73	41	3,678	73	2.28	4.72	89.27	51.75	3,192
Hainan 海南	8	65	444	-103	-3.42	-6.86	6.84	50.06	2,994
Southwest 西南	115	76	1,995	5	0.14	0.41	26.19	64.66	3,542
Chongqing 重慶	13	42	880	-17	-1.45	-14.68	21.06	90.12	1,196
Sichuan 四川	68	75	2,140	13	0.31	1.03	28.47	69.51	4,030
Guizhou 貴州	7	59	489	23	2.78	4.46	8.28	37.67	823
Yunnan 雲南	26	104	2,598	-6	-0.14	-0.29	25.08	50.05	4,037
Tibet 西藏	1		860	-50	-0.87	-2.16		59.97	5,770
Northwest 西北	133	147	5,357	-9	-0.09	-0.32	36.54	73.11	10,468
Shaanxi 陝西	60	119	2,304	-101	-2.01	-8.81	19.33	77.14	5,005
Gansu 甘肅	27	182	5,043	-142	-1.57	-5.43	27.69	71.18	9,086
Qinghai 青海	8	23	383	-43	-6.17	-16.92	16.45	63.52	689
Ningxia 寧夏	10	81	2,379	65	1.55	6.55	29.26	76.38	4,199
Xinjiang 新疆	28	230	14,684	299	1.05	3.75	63.96	72.09	28,543

3642: Mechanized Farm Tools 機械化農具製造業

Year 年份	Number of firms 企業個數	Rate of change 每年變化 (%)	Number of employees 職工人數 (人)	Rate of change 每年變化 (%)	Total revenue (mil. RMB) 總銷售收入 (百萬元)	Rate of change 每年變化 (%)	Total profit (mil. RMB) 總利潤 (百萬元)	Rate of change 每年變化 (%)
1993	1761		203,169		5,110		-31	
1994	1624	-7.78%	186,631	-8.14%	4,676	-8.48%	-110	-250.55%
1995	1459	-10.16%	200,747	7.56%	5,872	25.56%	-40	63.58%
1996	1579	8.22%	196,278	-2.23%	7,561	28.76%	93	333.15%

3 Major products* 3 種主要產品 *	Output 產量	Sales volume 銷售量	Unit 單位
a) Harvesting Machinery 收獲機械	336,708	326,607	set 台
b) Planting Machine 種植機械	419,016	389,685	set 台
c) Field Job Machine 場上作業機械	637,867	580,459	set 台

Top 10 firms by revenue (year founded) 收入排名前 10 家企業 (創辦年份)	City 城市	Province 省	Telephone / fax 電話 / 傳真	Number of employees 職工人數	Ownership 產業所有權	Revenue ('000 RMB) 銷售收入 (千元)	Profit ('000 RMB) (rank) 利潤 (千元) (排名)	Total assets ('000 RMB) 總資產 (千元)	Major products 主要產品
Xinjiang Joint Machinery Group Co. Ltd. 新疆聯合機械集團有限責任公司(1899)	Urumqi 烏魯木齊市	Xinjiang 新疆	(0991)3836210 (0991)3821682		State-owned 國有	327,564	13016(3)	588,723	a,b
Shandong Wulian General Machinery Factory 山東省五蓮縣通用機械廠(1975)	Rizhao 日照市	Shandong 山東省	(0633)5213361 (0633)5213361	1,185	State-owned 國有	190,488	-3810(528)	138,770	o
Siping Combine Harvester General Factory 四平市聯合收割機總廠(1943)	Siping 四平市	Jilin 吉林省	(0434)3387040 (0434)3387845	4,280	State-owned 國有	180,584	1061(41)	361,999	a
Jiamusi Combine Harvester Factory 佳木斯聯合收割機廠(1946)	Jiamusi 佳木斯市	Heilongjiang 黑龍江省	(0454)8221721 (0454)8246462	3,060	State-owned 國有	180,198	-15535(536)	375,849	a
Guilin Joint Harvester General Factory 桂林聯合收割機總廠(1970)	Lingchuan 靈川縣	Guangxi 廣西	(0773)6812281 (0773)6812155		State-owned 國有	161,481	5618(9)	91,127	a
Shandong Linyi Agricultural Medical Machinery Plant 山東臨沂農業藥械廠(1951)	Linyi 臨沂市	Shandong 山東省	(0539)8312250 (0539)8315842	953	State-owned 國有	156,887	18316(1)	207,953	o
Liyi Zhuo Li Xiang Machinery Factory 臨猗縣卓里鄉機械廠(1975)	Yuncheng 運城市	Shanxi 山西省		610	Collectively-owned 集體	150,000	8800(6)	33,230	o
Suzhou Agricultural Medical Machinery Plant 蘇州農業藥械廠(1959)	Suzhou 蘇州市	Jiangsu 江蘇省	(0512)7276945 (0512)7274255	1,002	State-owned 國有	133,731	11506(4)	96,037	o
Shandong Ji Long Group Company 山東吉龍集團公司(1993)	Yantai 煙臺市	Shandong 山東省	(0535)7214955 (0535)7214599	1,500	Collectively-owned 集體	119,509	7262(8)	136,564	o
Hubei Honghu Thresher Xie Factory 湖北省洪湖市脫粒機械廠(1975)	Jingsha 荊沙市	Hubei 湖北省	(0716)882335		Collectively-owned 集體	114,164	3589(16)	41,220	o

Top 10 Cities by Production Output 產出排名前 10 位城市	Province 省	Market share 市場份額	Number of firms 企業個數
Zhumadian 駐馬店市	Henan 河南省	4.02%	30
Siping 四平市	Jilin 吉林省	3.56%	18
Urumqi 烏魯木齊市	Xinjiang 新疆	3.54%	2
Linyi 臨沂市	Shandong 山東省	3.12%	13
Beijing 北京市	Beijing 北京市	3.05%	21
Rizhao 日照市	Shandong 山東省	3.02%	5
Yuncheng 運城市	Shanxi 山西省	2.56%	8
Lingchuan 靈川縣	Guangxi 廣西	2.42%	11
Jiamusi 佳木斯市	Heilongjiang 黑龍江省	2.38%	14
Suzhou 蘇州市	Jiangsu 江蘇省	2.38%	13

10 Major Wholesalers 10 家主要批發商	City 城市	Province 省	Telephone / Fax 電話 / 傳真
Liaoning Automobile Trade Group Corp. 遼寧省汽車貿易集團	Shenyang 瀋陽市	Liaoning 遼寧省	(024)23835494 (024)23838338
China Post and Telecommunication Equipment General Company 中國郵電器材總公司	Beijing 北京市	Beijing 北京市	(010)63523715 (010)63525935
Jiangsu Electromechanical Products General Company 江蘇省機電產品總公司	Nanjing 南京市	Jiangsu 江蘇省	(025)7713642 (025)7711036
Xi Nan Technology Import & Export Company 西南技術進出口公司	Chongqing 重慶市	Chongqing 重慶市	(023)63850185 (023)63850026
Changzhou Economic Technology Industrial Development Zone Tian Ming Trade Company 常州經濟技術產業開發區天明貿易公司	Changzhou 常州市	Jiangsu 江蘇省	(0519)8829882 (0519)8829882
Shanxi Mechanical Equipment Import & Export Company 山西省機械設備進出口公司	Taiyuan 太原市	Shanxi 山西省	(0351)4040713 (0351)4043981
Ningbo Five Mining Machinery Import & Export Company 寧波市五礦機械進出口公司	Ningbo 寧波市	Zhejiang 浙江省	(0574)7311255 (0574)7320322
Tianjin Jin Huan Electromechanical Complete Sets of Equipment Factory 天津市津環機電成套設備廠	Tianjin 天津市	Tianjin 天津市	(022)26371628
Yunnan Machinery Import & Export Company 雲南省機械進出口公司	Kunming 昆明市	Yunnan 雲南省	(0871)3164879 (0871)3136829
Tianjin Da Qiu Zhuang Yi Yuan Trade Center 天津市大丘莊億源商貿中心	Tianjin 天津市	Tianjin 天津市	(022)28899478 (022)28899046

*Also include sales by firms outside this industry.包括本行業以外廠家的銷售。"o" stands for "others". "o" 代表 "其他產品"。

3643: Forestry Machinery 營林機械製造業

The industry accounts for 0.003% of the total revenue of China's industrial sector in 1996. The revenue growth rate of the industry is 54.9% from 1995, as compared to the growth rate of China's industrial sector, 9.51%. The rate of return on asset is -0.39%. 50.00% of all firms in the industry made a profit while 50.00% had negative returns. The top province in terms of the industry's revenue is Anhui, accounting for 43.26% of the total revenue.
本行業在1996年佔全行業總產值0.003%，行業年增長率為54.9%（全國工業年增長率9.51%）。行業的資產回報率-0.39%，50.00%的企業盈利，50.00%的企業虧損。銷售收入最高的省份為安徽省，佔本行業的43.26%。

	Total number of firms 企業總數	Total number of employees 職工總數	Total revenue (mil. RMB) 總銷售收入（百萬元）	Total profit (mil. RMB) 總利潤（百萬元）	Return on assets 資產利潤率 (%)	Return on equity 權益利潤率 (%)	Labour productivity ('000 RMB / worker) 勞動生產率（千元/人）	Debts / assets 資產負債率 (%)	Total assets (mil. RMB) 總資產（百萬元）
Industry Overall 行業總體	23	3,227	147	-1	-0.39	-1.18	45.55	67.32	158

	Number of firms 企業個數	Average number of employees 平均職工人數	Average revenue ('000 RMB) 平均銷售收入（千元）	Average profit ('000 RMB) 平均利潤（千元）	Return on assets 資產利潤率 (%)	Return on equity 權益利潤率 (%)	Labour productivity ('000 RMB / worker) 勞動生產率（千元/人）	Average debts / assets 平均資產負債率(%)	Average Total assets ('000 RMB) 平均總資產（千元）
By ownership 產業所有權									
State-owned 國有	14	212	4,643	-143	-1.32	-4.08	21.92	67.55	10,786
Collectively-owned 集體	7	24	11,241	137	18.44	41.86	471.18	55.94	742
Privately-owned 私有									
Domestic JVs 聯營									
Joint stock 股份制									
Foreign-funded 外資									
Overseas Chinese-funded 港澳台資	2	48	1,650	21	2.30	5.83	34.73	60.62	901
By size 規模									
Large 大型									
Medium 中型	2	898	23,675	818	1.98	7.68	26.38	74.27	41,385
Small 小型	21	68	4,745	-126	-3.50	-8.59	69.59	59.19	3,582
By regional distribution 地區分布									
Central-North 華北	6	101	3,295	-80	-1.53	-5.88	32.79	73.97	5,238
Beijing 北京									
Tianjin 天津									
Hebei 河北	2	13	260	-40	-4.57	-6.40	20.80	28.57	875
Shanxi 山西	3	123	5,713	167	2.98	10.20	46.32	70.83	5,600
Inner Mongolia 內蒙	1	208	2,110	-900	-6.99	-44.55	10.14	84.24	12,880
Northeast 東北	5	49	708	34	1.43	2.66	14.39	46.17	2,374
Liaoning 遼寧	4	24	243	15	1.77	30.00	10.10	93.81	848
Jilin 吉林	1	150	2,570	110	1.30	1.78	17.13	27.12	8,480
Heilongjiang 黑龍江									
Central East 華東	5	75	15,000	62	3.65	6.64	200.00	44.99	1,698
Shanghai 上海									
Jiangsu 江蘇	1	90	10,450	650	28.63	73.03	116.11	60.79	2,270
Zhejiang 浙江	1	8							10
Anhui 安徽	1	40	63,590	450	42.86	42.86	1589.75		1,050
Fujian 福建	2	119	480	-395	-15.31	-29.04	4.05	47.29	2,580
Jiangxi 江西									
Shandong 山東									
Central-South 中南	4	75	2,100	-280	-6.80	-18.18	27.91	62.56	4,120
Henan 河南	2	13	1,085	55	7.48	16.67	86.80	55.10	735
Hubei 湖北									
Hunan 湖南									
Guangdong 廣東	1	50	3,220	40	3.67	16.00	64.40	76.15	1,090
Guangxi 廣西	1	226	3,010	-1,270	-9.12	-24.19	13.32	62.28	13,920
Hainan 海南									
Southwest 西南									
Chongqing 重慶									
Sichuan 四川									
Guizhou 貴州									
Yunnan 雲南									
Tibet 西藏									
Northwest 西北	3	567	13,460	173	0.58	1.99	23.73	70.77	29,843
Shaanxi 陝西	3	567	13,460	173	0.58	1.99	23.73	70.77	29,843
Gansu 甘肅									
Qinghai 青海									
Ningxia 寧夏									
Xinjiang 新疆									

3643: Forestry Machinery 營林機械製造業

Year 年份	Number of firms 企業個數	Rate of change 每年變化 (%)	Number of employees 職工人數（人）	Rate of change 每年變化 (%)	Total revenue (mil. RMB) 總銷售收入（百萬元）	Rate of change 每年變化 (%)	Total profit (mil. RMB) 總利潤（百萬元）	Rate of change 每年變化 (%)
1993	19		3,142		128		-15	
1994	22	15.79%	2,154	-31.45%	59	-54.20%	0	98.93%
1995	13	-40.91%	2,603	20.84%	95	61.43%	0	395.60%
1996	23	76.92%	3,227	23.97%	147	54.92%	-1	-312.77%

3 Major products* 3 種主要產品 *	Output 產量	Sales volume 銷售量	Unit 單位
a) Wood Fibre Segregator 木質纖維分離機械	328	249	set 台
b) Agricultural Transport Machinery 農業運輸機械	6,144	6,083	vehicle 輛
c) Wood Processing Machinery 木材加工機械	139	133	set 台

Top 10 firms by revenue (year founded) 收入排名前 10 家企業（創辦年份）	City 城市	Province 省	Telephone / fax 電話 / 傳真	Number of employees 職工人數	Ownership 產業所有權	Revenue ('000 RMB) 銷售收入（千元）	Profit ('000 RMB) (rank) 利潤（千元）（排名）	Total assets ('000 RMB) 總資產（千元）	Major products 主要產品
Lingbi You Ji Zhen Tricycle Assembly Plant 靈璧縣尤集鎮三輪車組裝廠(1989)	Suzhou 宿州市	Anhui 安徽省		50	Collectively-owned 集體	63,590	450(4)	1,050	b
Xibei Forestry Machinery Plant 西北林業機械廠(1976)	Weinan 渭南市	Shaanxi 陜西省	(0913)2012811 (0913)2012819	1,413	State-owned 國有	39,130	880(1)	78,087	o
Sichuan Min Jiang Machinery Factory 四川省岷江機械廠(1968)	Chengdu 成都市	Sichuan 四川省	(028)7282584	958	State-owned 國有	11,810	-5302(11)	34,506	a,c
Danyang Ya Sheng Welding Wire Plant 丹陽市亞盛焊絲廠(1990)	Zhenjiang 鎮江市	Jiangsu 江蘇省	(0511)6632300	90	Collectively-owned 集體	10,451	647(2)	2,273	o
Shijiazhuang Seeds Machinery Plant 河北省種子機械廠(1949)	Shijiazhuang 石家莊市	Hebei 河北省	(0311)6089501	87	State-owned 國有	9,976	607(3)	5,840	o
Yutian No.1 Agricultural Machine Repair Factory 玉田第一農機修造廠(1971)	Tangshan 唐山市	Hebei 河北省	(0315)6112557	260	State-owned 國有	5,212	-287(9)	10,714	o
Shanghai Pu Dong Forestry Machinery Fittings Factory 上海浦東林業機械配件廠(1988)	Shanghai 上海市	Shanghai 上海市	(021)58942925	40	Collectively-owned 集體	4,099	273(5)	3,855	o
Shaoshan Qing Xi Machinery Factory 韶山清溪機械廠(1987)	Xiangtan 湘潭市	Hunan 湖南省	(0732)5682359	50	Collectively-owned 集體	3,220	36(7)	1,087	o
Guangdong Xinyi No.1 Machinery Factory 廣東省信宜第一機械廠(1967)	Maoming 茂名市	Guangdong 廣東省	(0668)8882323	226	State-owned 國有	3,005	-1267(10)	13,921	c
Jilin Taonan Forestry Machinery Plant 吉林省洮南市林業機械廠(1971)	Baicheng 白城市	Jilin 吉林省	(0436)6225534	151	State-owned 國有	2,565	109(6)	8,478	o

Top 10 Cities by Production Output 產出排名前 10 位城市	Province 省	Market share 市場份額	Number of firms 企業個數
Weinan 渭南市	Shaanxi 陝西省	42.07%	1
Chengdu 成都市	Sichuan 四川省	11.88%	1
Zhenjiang 鎮江市	Jiangsu 江蘇省	10.83%	2
Tangshan 唐山市	Hebei 河北省	5.30%	1
Shanghai 上海市	Shanghai 上海市	3.60%	2
Baicheng 白城市	Jilin 吉林省	3.44%	1
Guilin 桂林市	Guangxi 廣西	3.30%	1
Changzhou 常州市	Jiangsu 江蘇省	3.23%	1
Maoming 茂名市	Guangdong 廣東省	2.31%	1
Tongliao 通遼市	Inner Mong 內蒙	2.24%	1

10 Major Wholesalers 10 家主要批發商	City 城市	Province 省	Telephone / Fax 電話 / 傳真
Liaoning Automobile Trade Group Corp. 遼寧省汽車貿易集團	Shenyang 瀋陽市	Liaoning 遼寧省	(024)23835494 (024)23838338
China Post and Telecommunication Equipment General Company 中國郵電器材總公司	Beijing 北京市	Beijing 北京市	(010)63523715 (010)63525935
Jiangsu Electromechanical Products General Company 江蘇省機電產品總公司	Nanjing 南京市	Jiangsu 江蘇省	(025)7713642 (025)7711036
Xi Nan Technology Import & Export Company 西南技術進出口公司	Chongqing 重慶市	Chongqing 重慶市	(023)63850185 (023)63850026
Changzhou Economic Technology Industrial Development Zone Tian Ming Trade Company 常州經濟技術產業開發區天明貿易公司	Changzhou 常州市	Jiangsu 江蘇省	(0519)8829882 (0519)8829882
Shanxi Mechanical Equipment Import & Export Company 山西省機械設備進出口公司	Taiyuan 太原市	Shanxi 山西省	(0351)4040713 (0351)4043981
Ningbo Five Mining Machinery Import & Export Company 寧波市五礦機械進出口公司	Ningbo 寧波市	Zhejiang 浙江省	(0574)7311255 (0574)7320322
Tianjin Jin Huan Electromechanical Complete Sets of Equipment Factory 天津市津環機電成套設備廠	Tianjin 天津市	Tianjin 天津市	(022)26371628
Yunnan Machinery Import & Export Company 雲南省機械進出口公司	Kunming 昆明市	Yunnan 雲南省	(0871)3164879 (0871)3136829
Tianjin Da Qiu Zhuang Yi Yuan Trade Center 天津市大丘莊億源商貿中心	Tianjin 天津市	Tianjin 天津市	(022)28899478 (022)28899046

*Also include sales by firms outside this industry.包括本行業以外廠家的銷售。"o" stands for "others". "o" 代表 "其他產品"。

3644: Animal Husbandry Machinery 畜牧機械製造業

The industry accounts for 0.006% of the total revenue of China's industrial sector in 1996. The revenue growth rate of the industry is 0.8% from 1995, as compared to the growth rate of China's industrial sector, 9.51%. The rate of return on asset is -1.55%. 69.57% of all firms in the industry made a profit while 24.18% had negative returns. The top province in terms of the industry's revenue is Shandong, accounting for 15.94% of the total revenue.
本行業在1996年佔全行業總產值0.006%，行業年增長率為0.8%（全國工業年增長率9.51%）。行業的資產回報率-1.55%，69.57%的企業盈利，24.18%的企業虧損。銷售收入最高的省份為山東省，佔本行業的15.94%。

	Total number of firms 企業總數	Total number of employees 職工總數	Total revenue (mil. RMB) 總銷售收入（百萬元）	Total profit (mil. RMB) 總利潤（百萬元）	Return on assets 資產利潤率 (%)	Return on equity 權益利潤率 (%)	Labour productivity ('000 RMB / worker) 勞動生產率（千元/人）	Debts / assets 資產負債率 (%)	Total assets (mil. RMB) 總資產（百萬元）
Industry Overall 行業總體	95	11,874	341	-12	-1.55	-7.91	28.72	80.36	763

	Number of firms 企業個數	Average number of employees 平均職工人數	Average revenue ('000 RMB) 平均銷售收入（千元）	Average profit ('000 RMB) 平均利潤（千元）	Return on assets 資產利潤率 (%)	Return on equity 權益利潤率 (%)	Labour productivity ('000 RMB / worker) 勞動生產率（千元/人）	Average debts / assets 平均資產負債率(%)	Average Total assets ('000 RMB) 平均總資產（千元）
By ownership 產業所有權									
State-owned 國有	31	249	6,000	-65	-0.42	-2.44	24.05	82.70	15,290
Collectively-owned 集體	58	65	1,947	-57	-1.61	-6.51	30.08	75.24	3,548
Privately-owned 私有									
Domestic JVs 聯營									
Joint stock 股份制	1	44	3,294	161	8.03	21.91	74.86	63.37	2,002
Foreign-funded 外資	4	83	9,388	-1,701	-8.46	-43.37	113.79	80.50	20,116
Overseas Chinese-funded 港澳台資									
By size 規模									
Large 大型									
Medium 中型	7	534	14,738	-1,921	-4.26	-35.77	27.61	88.08	45,043
Small 小型	88	92	2,702	16	0.32	1.29	29.22	74.89	5,087
By regional distribution 地區分布									
Central-North 華北	36	100	2,775	-169	-2.44	-13.95	27.81	82.54	6,955
Beijing 北京	18	33	957	2	0.11	0.26	28.67	59.96	2,106
Tianjin 天津	3	53	10,437	-2,073	-9.56	-145.67	195.69	93.43	21,677
Hebei 河北	2	69	2,410	210	5.36	5.53	34.93	3.19	3,920
Shanxi 山西	2	379	5,830	120	0.51	1.61	15.40	68.53	23,640
Inner Mongolia 內蒙	11	176	3,172	-53	-0.63	-32.22	18.01	98.05	8,392
Northeast 東北	13	75	1,194	49	2.11	11.45	16.02	81.59	2,335
Liaoning 遼寧	4	67	1,410	-15	-0.44	-0.97	20.97	54.22	3,375
Jilin 吉林	3	30	863	-47	-1.67	466.67	28.78	100.36	2,797
Heilongjiang 黑龍江	6	102	1,215	140	9.92	-150.00	11.95	106.61	1,412
Central East 華東	25	167	5,323	-47	-0.49	-1.71	31.80	71.44	9,590
Shanghai 上海	3	165	3,787	-1,000	-14.30	-78.53	23.00	81.79	6,993
Jiangsu 江蘇	7	246	7,373	-39	-0.34	-1.35	29.97	74.72	11,303
Zhejiang 浙江	1								
Anhui 安徽	1	10							
Fujian 福建									
Jiangxi 江西	3	140	5,247	857	8.69	27.90	37.48	68.90	9,860
Shandong 山東	10	154	5,437	-47	-0.43	-1.33	35.33	67.79	11,008
Central-South 中南	12	120	3,091	-354	-3.85	-79.44	25.69	95.16	9,210
Henan 河南	8	95	1,138	8	0.30	1.60	11.93	81.50	2,534
Hubei 湖北	1	125	170	-220	-10.19	19.30	1.36	152.78	2,160
Hunan 湖南									
Guangdong 廣東	3	185	9,273	-1,363	-4.64	-149.27	50.04	96.89	29,363
Guangxi 廣西									
Hainan 海南									
Southwest 西南	3	238	5,303	-593	-4.28	-14.64	22.25	70.78	13,873
Chongqing 重慶	1	64	230	-2,161	-83.69	282.37	3.62	129.64	2,583
Sichuan 四川	2	325	7,839	191	0.98	2.96	24.11	66.89	19,518
Guizhou 貴州									
Yunnan 雲南									
Tibet 西藏									
Northwest 西北	6	161	6,618	133	0.89	5.53	41.02	83.91	14,985
Shaanxi 陝西	2	68	2,380	25	1.18	1.67	35.26	29.48	2,120
Gansu 甘肅									
Qinghai 青海	1	637	25,820	110	0.14	1.14	40.53	87.68	78,580
Ningxia 寧夏	1	20	1,000	30	2.63	5.17	50.00	49.12	1,140
Xinjiang 新疆	2	88	4,065	305	10.25	49.59	46.19	79.50	2,975

3644: Animal Husbandry Machinery 畜牧機械製造業

Year 年份	Number of firms 企業個數	Rate of change 每年變化 (%)	Number of employees 職工人數 (人)	Rate of change 每年變化 (%)	Total revenue (mil. RMB) 總銷售收入 (百萬元)	Rate of change 每年變化 (%)	Total profit (mil. RMB) 總利潤 (百萬元)	Rate of change 每年變化 (%)
1993	64		11,450		325		9	
1994	82	28.13%	11,873	3.69%	249	-23.21%	-17	-294.70%
1995	82	0	11,461	-3.47%	338	35.78%	-8	53.04%
1996	95	15.85%	11,874	3.60%	341	0.78%	-12	-54.32%

3 Major products* 3 種主要產品 *	Output 產量	Sales volume 銷售量	Unit 單位
a) Livestock Raising Machinery 畜牧機械	83,373	34,183	set 台
b) Feed Processing Machinery 飼料加工機械	30,453	29,235	set 台
c) Agricultural Water Pump 農業水泵	15,938	14,982	set 台

Top 10 firms by revenue (year founded) 收入排名前 10 家企業 (創辦年份)	City 城市	Province 省	Telephone / fax 電話 / 傳真	Number of employees 職工人數	Ownership 產業所有權	Revenue ('000 RMB) 銷售收入 (千元)	Profit ('000 RMB) (rank) 利潤 (千元) (排名)	Total assets ('000 RMB) 總資產 (千元)	Major products 主要產品
Shandong Wulian Agriculture & Animal Husbandry Machinery Plant 山東省五蓮縣農牧機械廠(1952)	Rizhao 日照市	Shandong 山東省	(0633)5213357 (0633)5213357	714	State-owned 國有	30,625	-1290(27)	52,888	a
Qinghai Agriculture & Animal Husbandry Machinery Plant 青海農牧機械廠	Xining 西寧市	Qinghai 青海省	(0971)5132869 (0971)5131300	637	State-owned 國有	25,824	106(13)	78,577	a
Tianjin Zheng Da Machinery Co. Ltd. 天津正大機械有限公司(1992)	Tianjin 天津市	Tianjin 天津市	(022)25325231 (022)25327511	220	Foreign-funded 外資	24,710	-5663(32)	58,944	o
Nanjing Testing Instrument Plant 南京實驗儀器廠(1964)	Nanjing 南京市	Jiangsu 江蘇省	(025)8811231 (025)8811231	390	Collectively-owned 集體	16,567	6(19)	15,992	o
Jiangxi Hong Xing Start Mechinery Plant 江西紅星機械廠(1970)	Fuzhou 撫州市	Jiangxi 江西省	(0794)4382462 (0794)4382462	311	State-owned 國有	14,271	2456(1)	28,922	b
Guangzhou State-owned Livestock Raising Machine Manufacturing Plant 廣州市國營畜牧機械製造廠(1971)	Guangzhou 廣州市	Guangdong 廣東省	(020)87483023 (020)87811339	180	State-owned 國有	13,837	-56(23)	27,390	o
Zhongshan Hardware Machinery Factory 中山市五金機械廠(1956)	Zhongshan 中山市	Guangdong 廣東省	(0760)8827483 (0760)8847631	189	Collectively-owned 集體	11,295	-3983(31)	44,523	a
Shanxi Datong Agriculture & Animal Husbandry Machinery Plant 山西省大同農牧機械廠(1955)	Datong 大同市	Shanxi 山西省	(0352)2053490 (0352)2052341	743	State-owned 國有	11,165	236(7)	46,278	b
Huimin Animal Husbandry Machinery Factory 惠民縣畜牧機械廠(1954)	Binzhou 濱州市	Shandong 山東省	(0543)5321284 (0543)5321284	134	Collectively-owned 集體	10,290	814(2)	8,378	c
Wuxi Taihu Machinery Factory 無錫市太湖機械廠(1995)	Wuxi 無錫市	Jiangsu 江蘇省	(0510)5806349	152	Collectively-owned 集體	10,116	130(11)	17,828	c

Top 10 Cities by Production Output 產出排名前 10 位城市	Province 省	Market share 市場份額	Number of firms 企業個數
Tianjin 天津市	Tianjin 天津市	9.27%	4
Beijing 北京市	Beijing 北京市	9.19%	17
Rizhao 日照市	Shandong 山東省	9.15%	1
Xining 西寧市	Qinghai 青海省	6.49%	1
Nanjing 南京市	Jiangsu 江蘇省	5.72%	4
Shanghai 上海市	Shanghai 上海市	5.47%	9
Fuzhou 撫州市	Jiangxi 江西省	4.52%	3
Guangzhou 廣州市	Guangdong 廣東省	3.95%	3
Hailar 海拉爾市	Inner Mong 內蒙	3.81%	2
Lianyungang 連雲港市	Jiangsu 江蘇省	3.53%	1

10 Major Wholesalers 10 家主要批發商	City 城市	Province 省	Telephone / Fax 電話 / 傳真
Liaoning Automobile Trade Group Corp. 遼寧省汽車貿易集團	Shenyang 瀋陽市	Liaoning 遼寧省	(024)23835494 (024)23838338
China Post and Telecommunication Equipment General Company 中國郵電器材總公司	Beijing 北京市	Beijing 北京市	(010)63523715 (010)63525935
Jiangsu Electromechanical Products General Company 江蘇省機電產品總公司	Nanjing 南京市	Jiangsu 江蘇省	(025)7713642 (025)7711036
Xi Nan Technology Import & Export Company 西南技術進出口公司	Chongqing 重慶市	Chongqing 重慶市	(023)63850185 (023)63850026
Changzhou Economic Technology Industrial Development Zone Tian Ming Trade Company 常州經濟技術產業開發區天明貿易公司	Changzhou 常州市	Jiangsu 江蘇省	(0519)8829882 (0519)8829882
Shanxi Mechanical Equipment Import & Export Company 山西省機械設備進出口公司	Taiyuan 太原市	Shanxi 山西省	(0351)4040713 (0351)4043981
Ningbo Five Mining Machinery Import & Export Company 寧波市五礦機械進出口公司	Ningbo 寧波市	Zhejiang 浙江省	(0574)7311255 (0574)7320322
Tianjin Jin Huan Electromechanical Complete Sets of Equipment Factory 天津市津環機電成套設備廠	Tianjin 天津市	Tianjin 天津市	(022)26371628
Yunnan Machinery Import & Export Company 雲南省機械進出口公司	Kunming 昆明市	Yunnan 雲南省	(0871)3164879 (0871)3136829
Tianjin Da Qiu Zhuang Yi Yuan Trade Center 天津市大丘莊億源商貿中心	Tianjin 天津市	Tianjin 天津市	(022)28899478 (022)28899046

*Also include sales by firms outside this industry.包括本行業以外廠家的銷售。"o" stands for "others". "o" 代表 "其他產品" 。

3645: Fishery Machinery 漁業機械製造業

The industry accounts for 0.009% of the total revenue of China's industrial sector in 1996. The revenue growth rate of the industry is -5.0% from 1995, as compared to the growth rate of China's industrial sector, 9.51%. The rate of return on asset is 3.93%. 62.37% of all firms in the industry made a profit while 29.63% had negative returns. The top province in terms of the industry's revenue is Shandong, accounting for 35.11% of the total revenue.
本行業在1996年佔全行業總產值0.009%，行業年增長率為-5.0%（全國工業年增長率9.51%）。行業的資產回報率3.93%，62.37%的企業盈利，29.63%的企業虧損。銷售收入最高的省份為山東省，佔本行業的35.11%。

	Total number of firms 企業總數	Total number of employees 職工總數	Total revenue (mil. RMB) 總銷售收入（百萬元）	Total profit (mil. RMB) 總利潤（百萬元）	Return on assets 資產利潤率 (%)	Return on equity 權益利潤率 (%)	Labour productivity ('000 RMB / worker) 勞動生產率（千元/人）	Debts / assets 資產負債率 (%)	Total assets (mil. RMB) 總資產（百萬元）
Industry Overall 行業總體	59	7,329	535	20	3.93	10.80	73.00	63.60	508

	Number of firms 企業個數	Average number of employees 平均職工人數	Average revenue ('000 RMB) 平均銷售收入（千元）	Average profit ('000 RMB) 平均利潤（千元）	Return on assets 資產利潤率 (%)	Return on equity 權益利潤率 (%)	Labour productivity ('000 RMB / worker) 勞動生產率（千元/人）	Average debts / assets 平均資產負債率(%)	Average Total assets ('000 RMB) 平均總資產（千元）
By ownership 產業所有權									
State-owned 國有	7	331	7,714	-286	-1.77	-4.08	23.34	56.64	16,143
Collectively-owned 集體	46	112	9,654	490	7.30	27.60	86.30	73.54	6,713
Privately-owned 私有									
Domestic JVs 聯營									
Joint stock 股份制	1	22	505	45	2.45	3.98	22.96	38.45	1,834
Foreign-funded 外資	2	87	15,995	-80	-0.23	-0.31	183.85	26.14	34,582
Overseas Chinese-funded 港澳台資	2	63	2,195	-220	-2.90	-21.19	34.84	86.32	7,582
By size 規模									
Large 大型									
Medium 中型	5	568	33,241	458	1.25	3.58	58.48	64.99	36,609
Small 小型	54	85	6,829	328	5.45	14.65	80.66	62.79	6,018
By regional distribution 地區分布									
Central-North 華北	4	44	1,318	-63	-3.23	-14.62	29.77	77.75	1,933
Beijing 北京	2	71	1,830	-40	-1.13	-5.93	25.77	80.85	3,525
Tianjin 天津									
Hebei 河北	1	26	710	-200	-68.97	666.67	27.31	106.90	290
Shanxi 山西									
Inner Mongolia 內蒙	1	9	900	30	7.69	7.69	100.00		390
Northeast 東北	2	219	7,805	30	0.19	0.38	35.72	51.15	16,130
Liaoning 遼寧	2	219	7,805	30	0.19	0.38	35.72	51.15	16,130
Jilin 吉林									
Heilongjiang 黑龍江									
Central East 華東	39	143	11,304	454	4.65	13.16	78.97	64.65	9,752
Shanghai 上海	4	157	8,290	-638	-4.76	-8.08	52.89	41.14	13,405
Jiangsu 江蘇	11	183	16,265	984	7.31	18.61	88.70	60.74	13,464
Zhejiang 浙江	14	98	1,851	42	0.99	2.41	18.84	58.77	4,239
Anhui 安徽	1	60	1,800	300	10.34	11.76	30.00	12.07	2,900
Fujian 福建	3	113	4,413	40	0.79	2.50	39.17	68.50	5,080
Jiangxi 江西									
Shandong 山東	6	194	31,307	1,403	8.33	65.22	161.24	87.23	16,850
Central-South 中南	13	76	5,601	331	6.82	17.12	73.25	60.14	4,848
Henan 河南	3	79	5,180	150	2.73	16.92	65.29	83.89	5,503
Hubei 湖北									
Hunan 湖南	1	58	770	-300	-21.13	-157.89	13.28	86.62	1,420
Guangdong 廣東	8	67	6,831	495	9.36	19.74	101.58	52.60	5,290
Guangxi 廣西									
Hainan 海南	1	160	1,850	190	6.86	8.60	11.56	20.22	2,770
Southwest 西南	1	138	670	-1,830	-7.29	-22.82	4.86	68.07	25,090
Chongqing 重慶									
Sichuan 四川	1	138	670	-1,830	-7.29	-22.84	4.86	68.07	25,090
Guizhou 貴州									
Yunnan 雲南									
Tibet 西藏									
Northwest 西北									
Shaanxi 陝西									
Gansu 甘肅									
Qinghai 青海									
Ningxia 寧夏									
Xinjiang 新疆									

3645: Fishery Machinery 漁業機械製造業

Year 年份	Number of firms 企業個數	Rate of change 每年變化 (%)	Number of employees 職工人數（人）	Rate of change 每年變化 (%)	Total revenue (mil. RMB) 總銷售收入（百萬元）	Rate of change 每年變化 (%)	Total profit (mil. RMB) 總利潤（百萬元）	Rate of change 每年變化 (%)
1993	71		13,192		430		-2	
1994	73	2.82%	14,203	7.66%	409	-4.95%	-11	-457.64%
1995	59	-19.18%	9,097	-35.95%	563	37.73%	17	261.07%
1996	59		7,329	-19.43%	535	-5.05%	20	16.16%

3 Major products* 3 種主要產品 *	Output 產量	Sales volume 銷售量	Unit 單位
a) Fishery Machinery 漁業機械	83,578	75,220	set 台
b) Water Decontamination Equipment 水純化設備	1,621	1,670	set 台

Top 10 firms by revenue (year founded) 收入排名前 10 家企業 (創辦年份)	City 城市	Province 省	Telephone / fax 電話 / 傳真	Number of employees 職工人數	Ownership 產業所有權	Revenue ('000 RMB) 銷售收入（千元）	Profit ('000 RMB) (rank) 利潤（千元）（排名）	Total assets ('000 RMB) 總資產（千元）	Major products 主要產品
Jiangsu Jiang Hai Machinery Group Co. Ltd. 江蘇江海機械集團有限公司(1967)	Suzhou 蘇州市	Jiangsu 江蘇省	(0512)8223109	1,167	Collectively-owned 集體	142,845	12334(1)	84,373	o
Chang Chun Tractor Manufacturing Plant Weihai Branch 長春拖拉機製造廠威海分廠(1971)	Weihai 威海市	Shandong 山東省	(0896)5265469 (0896)5265469	218	Collectively-owned 集體	127,330	6725(2)	16,145	a
Shunde No.2 Farm Machine Repair Manufactory Plant 順德市第二農機修理製造廠(1972)	Foshan 佛山市	Guangdong 廣東省	(0757)2227080 (0757)2227080	264	其他經濟	38,184	3471(3)	22,688	a
Rongcheng Ma Dao Zhen Fishery Co. Shipyard 榮成市馬道鎮漁業公司船廠(1988)	Weihai 威海市	Shandong 山東省	(0896)7841106	88	Collectively-owned 集體	22,610	1510(4)	6,430	o
Shanghai Hai Rong Aquatic Products Development Co. Ltd. 上海海嶸水產開發有限公司(1993)	Shanghai 上海市	Shanghai 上海市	(021)59724794 (021)59724794	37	Foreign-funded 外資	22,003	2(21)	33,203	o
Zaozhuang Shizhong Medical Plastic Material Hygiene Products Factory 棗莊市市中區醫塑材料衛生用品廠(1991)	Zaozhuang 棗莊市	Shandong 山東省	(0632)3466111	58	Collectively-owned 集體	19,690	140(9)	710	o
Dalian Marine Gear Box Factory 大連船用齒輪箱廠(1946)	Dalian 大連市	Liaoning 遼寧省	(0411)6613185 (0411)6613185	414	State-owned 國有	15,420	60(15)	32,020	o
Changshu Fishery Machinery Plant 常熟市漁業機械廠(1971)	Suzhou 蘇州市	Jiangsu 江蘇省	(0512)2631280	216	Collectively-owned 集體	12,339	-608(24)	11,934	o
Shandong Zhucheng Textile Machinery Factory 山東諸城紡織機械廠(1958)	Weifang 濰坊市	Shandong 山東省	(0536)6218818 (0536)6213702	518	Collectively-owned 集體	12,083	32(17)	66,321	o
China Aquatic Products Wenzhou Fishery Machinery Co. 中國水產溫州漁業機械公司(1958)	Wenzhou 溫州市	Zhejiang 浙江省	(0577)8333901 (0577)8333273	701	State-owned 國有	12,079	133(10)	37,621	o

Top 10 Cities by Production Output 產出排名前 10 位城市	Province 省	Market share 市場份額	Number of firms 企業個數
Weihai 威海市	Shandong 山東省	37.68%	2
Suzhou 蘇州市	Jiangsu 江蘇省	24.51%	5
Foshan 佛山市	Guangdong 廣東省	7.11%	1
Changzhou 常州市	Jiangsu 江蘇省	3.98%	5
Dalian 大連市	Liaoning 遼寧省	3.32%	3
Wenzhou 溫州市	Zhejiang 浙江省	2.45%	5
Xi'an 西安市	Shaanxi 陝西省	2.01%	1
Huaiyin 淮陰市	Jiangsu 江蘇省	1.96%	2
Shanghai 上海市	Shanghai 上海市	1.75%	5
Fuzhou 福州市	Fujian 福建省	1.67%	1

10 Major Wholesalers 10 家主要批發商	City 城市	Province 省	Telephone / Fax 電話 / 傳真
Liaoning Automobile Trade Group Corp. 遼寧省汽車貿易集團	Shenyang 瀋陽市	Liaoning 遼寧省	(024)23835494 (024)23838338
China Post and Telecommunication Equipment General Company 中國郵電器材總公司	Beijing 北京市	Beijing 北京市	(010)63523715 (010)63525935
Jiangsu Electromechanical Products General Company 江蘇省機電產品總公司	Nanjing 南京市	Jiangsu 江蘇省	(025)7713642 (025)7711036
Xi Nan Technology Import & Export Company 西南技術進出口公司	Chongqing 重慶市	Chongqing 重慶市	(023)63850185 (023)63850026
Changzhou Economic Technology Industrial Development Zone Tian Ming Trade Company 常州經濟技術產業開發區天明貿易公司	Changzhou 常州市	Jiangsu 江蘇省	(0519)8829882 (0519)8829882
Shanxi Mechanical Equipment Import & Export Company 山西省機械設備進出口公司	Taiyuan 太原市	Shanxi 山西省	(0351)4040713 (0351)4043981
Ningbo Five Mining Machinery Import & Export Company 寧波市五礦機械進出口公司	Ningbo 寧波市	Zhejiang 浙江省	(0574)7311255 (0574)7320322
Tianjin Jin Huan Electromechanical Complete Sets of Equipment Factory 天津市津環機電成套設備廠	Tianjin 天津市	Tianjin 天津市	(022)26371628
Yunnan Machinery Import & Export Company 雲南省機械進出口公司	Kunming 昆明市	Yunnan 雲南省	(0871)3164879 (0871)3136829
Tianjin Da Qiu Zhuang Yi Yuan Trade Center 天津市大丘莊億源商貿中心	Tianjin 天津市	Tianjin 天津市	(022)28899478 (022)28899046

*Also include sales by firms outside this industry.包括本行業以外廠家的銷售。"o" stands for "others". "o" 代表"其他產品"。

3646: Irrigation Equipment 水利機械製造業

The industry accounts for 0.012% of the total revenue of China's industrial sector in 1996. The revenue growth rate of the industry is 4.1% from 1995, as compared to the growth rate of China's industrial sector, 9.51%. The rate of return on asset is 0.62%. 69.44% of all firms in the industry made a profit while 27.05% had negative returns. The top province in terms of the industry's revenue is Henan, accounting for 25.67% of the total revenue.
本行業在1996年佔全行業總產值0.012%，行業年增長率為4.1%（全國工業年增長率9.51%）。行業的資產回報率0.62%，69.44%的企業盈利，27.05%的企業虧損。銷售收入最高的省份為河南省，佔本行業的25.67%。

	Total number of firms 企業總數	Total number of employees 職工總數	Total revenue (mil. RMB) 總銷售收入（百萬元）	Total profit (mil. RMB) 總利潤（百萬元）	Return on assets 資產利潤率 (%)	Return on equity 權益利潤率 (%)	Labour productivity ('000 RMB / worker) 勞動生產率（千元/人）	Debts / assets 資產負債率 (%)	Total assets (mil. RMB) 總資產（百萬元）
Industry Overall 行業總體	137	19,757	715	8	0.62	1.71	36.19	63.90	1,322

	Number of firms 企業個數	Average number of employees 平均職工人數	Average revenue ('000 RMB) 平均銷售收入（千元）	Average profit ('000 RMB) 平均利潤（千元）	Return on assets 資產利潤率 (%)	Return on equity 權益利潤率 (%)	Labour productivity ('000 RMB / worker) 勞動生產率（千元/人）	Average debts / assets 平均資產負債率(%)	Average Total assets ('000 RMB) 平均總資產（千元）
By ownership 產業所有權									
State-owned 國有	60	212	6,400	-100	-0.64	-1.69	30.22	62.30	15,650
Collectively-owned 集體	74	87	3,139	120	3.02	12.48	36.27	75.81	3,990
Privately-owned 私有									
Domestic JVs 聯營									
Joint stock 股份制									
Foreign-funded 外資									
Overseas Chinese-funded 港澳台資	3	259	32,874	1,695	5.76	9.83	126.76	41.45	29,443
By size 規模									
Large 大型	1	1,807	88,117	262	0.16	0.52	48.76	69.07	164,114
Medium 中型	7	461	18,412	315	0.96	2.57	39.94	62.62	32,713
Small 小型	128	116	3,890	43	0.60	1.62	33.49	63.33	7,261
By regional distribution 地區分布									
Central-North 華北	23	142	5,423	45	0.56	1.65	38.13	66.01	7,992
Beijing 北京	6	3	30	8	27.78	100.00	12.00	77.78	30
Tianjin 天津	2	9	570	-65	-11.21	-28.89	63.33	61.21	580
Hebei 河北	9	270	12,174	369	2.53	7.73	45.07	67.26	14,582
Shanxi 山西	5	157	2,686	-432	-4.31	-11.34	17.09	61.97	10,012
Inner Mongolia 內蒙	1	21	400	-50	-4.24	250.00	19.05	101.69	1,180
Northeast 東北	20	81	3,469	33	0.88	1.98	42.72	55.64	3,708
Liaoning 遼寧	13	44	4,527	410	18.23	35.32	103.61	48.39	2,249
Jilin 吉林	2	293	2,890	-1,315	-13.61	-196.27	9.86	93.06	9,660
Heilongjiang 黑龍江	5	94	950	-410	-8.01	-12.45	10.11	35.68	5,118
Central East 華東	47	120	4,877	115	1.50	4.36	40.80	65.71	7,691
Shanghai 上海	1	45	1,390	70	3.17	8.86	30.89	63.80	2,210
Jiangsu 江蘇	8	243	9,409	-4	-0.02	-0.07	38.70	63.89	15,705
Zhejiang 浙江	10	68	3,435	102	1.39	6.10	50.29	77.22	7,340
Anhui 安徽	5	73	786	-38	-0.87	-2.84	10.77	69.55	4,388
Fujian 福建	5	88	1,888	38	0.97	1.77	21.55	45.11	3,902
Jiangxi 江西	2	143	4,200	35	1.25	1.65	29.37	24.78	2,805
Shandong 山東	16	116	6,029	268	3.78	10.85	51.97	65.14	7,074
Central-South 中南	37	215	7,128	53	0.31	0.83	33.20	62.61	17,222
Henan 河南	22	226	8,342	80	0.43	1.25	36.84	65.91	18,810
Hubei 湖北	5	271	1,836	-194	-2.62	-21.95	6.78	88.06	7,406
Hunan 湖南	4	131	4,313	220	2.17	6.50	33.05	66.60	10,128
Guangdong 廣東	4	193	12,363	255	1.06	2.61	64.14	59.33	23,988
Guangxi 廣西	2	159	2,165	-365	-1.46	-1.82	13.66	19.48	24,955
Hainan 海南									
Southwest 西南	4	231	6,238	5	0.04	0.13	26.97	71.64	13,488
Chongqing 重慶									
Sichuan 四川	3	234	5,400	-53	-0.47	-3.15	23.08	84.96	11,170
Guizhou 貴州									
Yunnan 雲南	1	222	8,750	180	0.88	1.76	39.41	49.80	20,440
Tibet 西藏									
Northwest 西北	6	63	515	-147	-7.91	-20.90	8.24	62.14	1,853
Shaanxi 陝西	4	47	435	8	0.61	2.88	9.26	78.69	1,220
Gansu 甘肅									
Qinghai 青海	1	13	190				14.62	55.00	400
Ningxia 寧夏	1	174	1,160	-910	-15.58	-30.43	6.67	48.80	5,840
Xinjiang 新疆									

3646: Irrigation Equipment 水利機械製造業

Year 年份	Number of firms 企業個數	Rate of change 每年變化 (%)	Number of employees 職工人數 （人）	Rate of change 每年變化 (%)	Total revenue (mil. RMB) 總銷售收入 （百萬元）	Rate of change 每年變化 (%)	Total profit (mil. RMB) 總利潤 （百萬元）	Rate of change 每年變化 (%)
1993	136		21,637		718		21	
1994	130	-4.41%	15,984	-26.13%	608	-15.26%	13	-39.73%
1995	110	-15.39%	19,907	24.54%	687	12.86%	16	28.89%
1996	137	24.55%	19,757	-0.75%	715	4.14%	8	-51.28%

3 Major products* 3 種主要產品 *	Output 產量	Sales volume 銷售量	Unit 單位
a) Water Conservancy Project Machinery 水工機械	42,674	45,234	ton 噸
b) Metal Structure Products 金屬結構製品	7,400	6,660	ton 噸
c) Pump 泵	25,472	24,199	set 台

Top 10 firms by revenue (year founded) 收入排名前 10 家企業 (創辦年份)	City 城市	Province 省	Telephone / fax 電話 / 傳真	Number of employees 職工人數	Ownership 產業所有權	Revenue ('000 RMB) 銷售收入 （千元）	Profit ('000 RMB) (rank) 利潤（千元）（排名）	Total assets ('000 RMB) 總資產 （千元）	Major products 主要產品
Guangdong Water Conservancy Hydlaulic & Electricity Machinery Plant 廣東省水利水電機械廠(1960)	Guangzhou 廣州市	Guangdong 廣東省	(020)87714981 (020)87711772	340	State-owned 國有	34,368	1039(10)	60,770	a
Henan Bazaar Xian Water Conservancy Machinery Factory 河南省商城縣水利機械廠(1965)	Xinyang 信陽市	Henan 河南省	(0376)731502	290	Collectively-owned 集體	28,597	1504(7)	30,442	o
Wujin Hydraulic Head Stock Gear Factory 武進液壓啟閉機廠(1970)	Changzhou 常州市	Jiangsu 江蘇省	(0519)3211025 (0519)3211271	401	State-owned 國有	28,331	1554(6)	46,766	a
Shenyang Tong Ren Electrical Appliance Co. 瀋陽市同仁電氣公司(1992)	Shenyang 瀋陽市	Liaoning 遼寧省	(024)24826154	42	Collectively-owned 集體	28,234	2023(5)	9,212	o
Yutai Wang Miao Xiang Water Treatment Device Factory 魚台縣王廟鄉水處理設備廠(1989)	Jining 濟寧市	Shandong 山東省	(0537)6312246 (0537)6312246	105	Collectively-owned 集體	26,000	3150(2)	19,500	o
Hebei Tai Hang Group Co. Ltd. 保定市太行建築設備廠(1983)	Baoding 保定市	Hebei 河北省	(0312)2134922 (0312)2126320	363	Collectively-owned 集體	25,527	-983(53)	57,326	o
Huanghua Wu Yi Machinery Plant 黃驊市五一機械廠(1958)	Cangzhou 滄州市	Hebei 河北省	(0317)5223049 (0317)5222323	519	State-owned 國有	24,732	682(11)	28,772	a
State-owned Taixing Fishery Machinery Factory 國營泰興漁業機械廠(1970)	Yangzhou 揚州市	Jiangsu 江蘇省	(0514)7531402 (0514)7531409	768	State-owned 國有	24,111	-788(52)	30,529	c
Hebei Jizhou Water Conservancy Machinery Group Co. Ltd. 河北省冀州市水利機械集團有限公司(1973)	Hengshui 衡水市	Hebei 河北省	(0318)8837338	120	Collectively-owned 集體	23,800	2280(3)	1,450	o
Bazhou Machine Manufacturing Co. Ltd. 霸州市機械製造有限公司(1957)	Langfang 廊坊市	Hebei 河北省	(0316)7212389 (0316)7212201	954	Joint stock 股份制	23,226	0(42)	34,626	o

Top 10 Cities by Production Output 產出排名前 10 位城市	Province 省	Market share 市場份額	Number of firms 企業個數
Zhengzhou 鄭州市	Henan 河南省	16.00%	5
Xinyang 信陽市	Henan 河南省	6.83%	3
Changzhou 常州市	Jiangsu 江蘇省	5.23%	6
Shenyang 瀋陽市	Liaoning 遼寧省	5.22%	9
Yangzhou 揚州市	Jiangsu 江蘇省	4.69%	1
Taizhou 泰州市	Jiangsu 江蘇省	4.56%	1
Guangzhou 廣州市	Guangdong 廣東省	4.53%	2
Langfang 廊坊市	Hebei 河北省	3.62%	2
Weifang 濰坊市	Shandong 山東省	3.50%	4
Cangzhou 滄州市	Hebei 河北省	3.44%	1

10 Major Wholesalers 10 家主要批發商	City 城市	Province 省	Telephone / Fax 電話 / 傳真
Liaoning Automobile Trade Group Corp. 遼寧省汽車貿易集團	Shenyang 瀋陽市	Liaoning 遼寧省	(024)23835494 (024)23838338
China Post and Telecommunication Equipment General Company 中國郵電器材總公司	Beijing 北京市	Beijing 北京市	(010)63523715 (010)63525935
Jiangsu Electromechanical Products General Company 江蘇省機電產品總公司	Nanjing 南京市	Jiangsu 江蘇省	(025)7713642 (025)7711036
Xi Nan Technology Import & Export Company 西南技術進出口公司	Chongqing 重慶市	Chongqing 重慶市	(023)63850185 (023)63850026
Changzhou Economic Technology Industrial Development Zone Tian Ming Trade Company 常州經濟技術產業開發區天明貿易公司	Changzhou 常州市	Jiangsu 江蘇省	(0519)8829882 (0519)8829882
Shanxi Mechanical Equipment Import & Export Company 山西省機械設備進出口公司	Taiyuan 太原市	Shanxi 山西省	(0351)4040713 (0351)4043981
Ningbo Five Mining Machinery Import & Export Company 寧波市五礦機械進出口公司	Ningbo 寧波市	Zhejiang 浙江省	(0574)7311255 (0574)7320322
Tianjin Jin Huan Electromechanical Complete Sets of Equipment Factory 天津市津環機電成套設備廠	Tianjin 天津市	Tianjin 天津市	(022)26371628
Yunnan Machinery Import & Export Company 雲南省機械進出口公司	Kunming 昆明市	Yunnan 雲南省	(0871)3164879 (0871)3136829
Tianjin Da Qiu Zhuang Yi Yuan Trade Center 天津市大丘莊億源商貿中心	Tianjin 天津市	Tianjin 天津市	(022)28899478 (022)28899046

*Also include sales by firms outside this industry.包括本行業以外廠家的銷售。"o" stands for "others". "o" 代表 "其他產品"。

3647: Tractor Parts 拖拉機配件製造業

The industry accounts for 0.117% of the total revenue of China's industrial sector in 1996. The revenue growth rate of the industry is 0.2% from 1995, as compared to the growth rate of China's industrial sector, 9.51%. The rate of return on asset is 1.58%. 69.04% of all firms in the industry made a profit while 24.11% had negative returns. The top province in terms of the industry's revenue is Shandong, accounting for 28.74% of the total revenue.
本行業在1996年佔全行業總產值0.117%，行業年增長率為0.2%（全國工業年增長率9.51%）。行業的資產回報率1.58%，69.04%的企業盈利，24.11%的企業虧損。銷售收入最高的省份為山東省，佔本行業的28.74%。

	Total number of firms 企業總數	Total number of employees 職工總數	Total revenue (mil. RMB) 總銷售收入（百萬元）	Total profit (mil. RMB) 總利潤（百萬元）	Return on assets 資產利潤率 (%)	Return on equity 權益利潤率 (%)	Labour productivity ('000 RMB / worker) 勞動生產率（千元／人）	Debts / assets 資產負債率 (%)	Total assets (mil. RMB) 總資產（百萬元）
Industry Overall 行業總體	910	160,739	6,759	141	1.58	5.46	42.05	71.16	8,921

	Number of firms 企業個數	Average number of employees 平均職工人數	Average revenue ('000 RMB) 平均銷售收入（千元）	Average profit ('000 RMB) 平均利潤（千元）	Return on assets 資產利潤率 (%)	Return on equity 權益利潤率 (%)	Labour productivity ('000 RMB / worker) 勞動生產率（千元／人）	Average debts / assets 平均資產負債率(%)	Average Total assets ('000 RMB) 平均總資產（千元）
By ownership 產業所有權									
State-owned 國有	239	349	7,996	-318	-1.56	-7.20	22.88	78.37	20,406
Collectively-owned 集體	656	114	7,118	323	5.52	14.87	62.24	62.90	5,861
Privately-owned 私有	2	28	2,519	65	2.23	4.00	91.61	44.34	2,930
Domestic JVs 聯營	4	141	18,037	442	3.20	9.88	127.92	67.62	13,822
Joint stock 股份制	8	191	12,072	372	2.21	4.17	63.08	47.09	16,851
Foreign-funded 外資									
Overseas Chinese-funded 港澳台資	1	47	4,765	70	1.78	-9.92	101.38	117.98	3,897
By size 規模									
Large 大型	10	1,905	89,097	4,360	2.11	5.09	46.77	58.56	206,720
Medium 中型	45	813	29,062	-503	-0.98	-4.43	35.77	77.94	51,518
Small 小型	853	123	5,346	141	2.65	9.96	43.44	73.44	5,317
By regional distribution 地區分布									
Central-North 華北	87	143	4,209	178	3.13	13.61	29.34	76.97	5,693
Beijing 北京	4	107	2,660	48	0.89	3.85	24.86	76.83	5,330
Tianjin 天津	5	260	7,744	-154	-1.81	-9.78	29.76	81.52	8,518
Hebei 河北	48	112	5,074	401	9.10	33.26	45.12	72.64	4,406
Shanxi 山西	17	177	3,245	60	1.00	4.29	18.38	76.64	5,994
Inner Mongolia 內蒙	13	181	1,397	-320	-3.53	-21.24	7.71	83.40	9,075
Northeast 東北	167	215	4,295	-39	-0.38	-2.05	19.94	81.36	10,258
Liaoning 遼寧	79	192	5,348	66	0.59	2.36	27.83	74.89	11,152
Jilin 吉林	28	177	2,604	-63	-1.32	-4.73	14.69	71.97	4,718
Heilongjiang 黑龍江	60	264	3,696	-167	-1.43	-16.44	14.02	91.28	11,666
Central East 華東	382	178	11,204	409	3.60	9.97	63.12	63.88	11,375
Shanghai 上海	16	154	9,966	195	2.37	6.03	64.69	60.68	8,228
Jiangsu 江蘇	102	203	12,399	369	2.10	4.62	61.01	54.50	17,555
Zhejiang 浙江	43	126	4,852	-324	-3.26	-8.79	38.41	62.94	9,938
Anhui 安徽	62	116	8,052	317	5.68	24.99	69.69	77.27	5,574
Fujian 福建	12	90	2,197	-144	-4.70	-15.84	24.41	70.30	3,064
Jiangxi 江西	35	113	5,122	-97	-2.86	-15.52	45.31	81.61	3,382
Shandong 山東	112	241	17,342	1,027	7.69	26.54	71.99	71.01	13,347
Central-South 中南	184	155	5,339	63	0.81	3.72	34.43	78.20	7,778
Henan 河南	86	158	7,522	239	2.62	12.44	47.63	78.91	9,093
Hubei 湖北	35	240	4,891	-200	-1.84	-9.47	20.35	80.56	10,876
Hunan 湖南	33	114	2,253	-61	-1.49	-5.25	19.83	71.60	4,085
Guangdong 廣東	10	230	5,082	-124	-1.19	-5.11	22.09	76.70	10,402
Guangxi 廣西	20	25	1,961	67	4.51	12.71	79.72	64.49	1,484
Hainan 海南									
Southwest 西南	39	156	6,023	-38	-0.33	-0.85	38.58	60.94	11,288
Chongqing 重慶	6	73	1,465	250	8.79	22.28	20.18	60.56	2,850
Sichuan 四川	19	232	9,691	37	0.20	0.47	41.69	57.60	18,263
Guizhou 貴州	5	134	3,602	100	1.99	6.47	26.96	69.27	5,024
Yunnan 雲南	9	73	3,104	37	0.56	2.44	42.66	76.82	6,494
Tibet 西藏									
Northwest 西北	51	193	3,497	-685	-7.04	-40.46	18.08	82.60	9,725
Shaanxi 陝西	23	171	1,587	-521	-7.24	-61.31	9.25	88.20	7,197
Gansu 甘肅	15	149	3,784	18	0.25	0.65	25.40	61.55	7,198
Qinghai 青海	2	56	945	5	0.29	1.72	16.88	83.43	1,750
Ningxia 寧夏	4	486	10,500	-5,665	-17.03	1094.69	21.63	101.56	33,265
Xinjiang 新疆	7	233	5,886	-80	-0.65	-2.10	25.29	68.89	12,276

3647: Tractor Parts 拖拉機配件製造業

Year 年份	Number of firms 企業個數	Rate of change 每年變化 (%)	Number of employees 職工人數 (人)	Rate of change 每年變化 (%)	Total revenue (mil. RMB) 總銷售收入 (百萬元)	Rate of change 每年變化 (%)	Total profit (mil. RMB) 總利潤 (百萬元)	Rate of change 每年變化 (%)
1993	964		170,311		5,057		105	
1994	946	-1.87%	159,465	-6.37%	5,516	9.09%	87	-17.06%
1995	909	-3.91%	183,165	14.86%	6,747	22.30%	130	50.11%
1996	910	0.11%	160,739	-12.24%	6,759	0.18%	141	8.19%

3 Major products* 3 種主要產品 *	Output 產量	Sales volume 銷售量	Unit 單位
a) Tractor & Internal Combustion Engine Fitting Parts 拖拉機內燃機配件	2,893,621	2,691,067	1,000 yuan 千元
b) Agricultural Transport Machinery 農業運輸機械	36,212	35,850	vehicle 輛

Top 10 firms by revenue (year founded) 收入排名前 10 家企業 (創辦年份)	City 城市	Province 省	Telephone / fax 電話 / 傳真	Number of employees 職工人數	Ownership 產業所有權	Revenue ('000 RMB) 銷售收入 (千元)	Profit ('000 RMB) (rank) 利潤 (千元) (排名)	Total assets ('000 RMB) 總資產 (千元)	Major products 主要產品
Wendeng Flat Plate Spring Factory 文登市平板彈簧廠(1954)	Weihai 威海市	Shandong 山東省	(0896)8761086 (0896)8761190	480	Collectively-owned 集體	200,980	12050(3)	43,520	o
Shandong Shuang Xing Group General Co. 山東雙興集團總公司(1966)	Weihai 威海市	Shandong 山東省	(0896)7741251 (0896)7741251	1,300	Collectively-owned 集體	194,450	16090(2)	91,550	o
Yizheng Shuang Huan Piston Ring Co. Ltd. 儀征市雙環活塞環有限公司(1996)	Yangzhou 揚州市	Jiangsu 江蘇省	(0514)3453478	2,645	Foreign-funded 外資	171,790	25100(1)	508,150	o
Dandong 518 Internal Combustion Fittings General Factory 丹東五一八內燃機配件總廠(1952)	Dandong 丹東市	Liaoning 遼寧省	(0415)6155431 (0415)6155758	3,197	State-owned 國有	156,805	782(65)	340,123	o
Jiangsu Lishi Group Co. 江蘇力士集團公司(1951)	Changzhou 常州市	Jiangsu 江蘇省	(0519)7223067 (0519)7222260	1,479	State-owned 國有	128,800	1513(33)	258,996	o
Chengdu Engine Fittings Joint-stock Co. Ltd. 成都動力配件股份有限公司(1965)	Chengdu 成都市	Sichuan 四川省	(028)4333641 (028)4331092	2,056	Joint stock 股份制	117,502	1340(39)	226,471	o
Yancheng Internal Combustion Fitting Parts Factory 鹽城市內燃機配件廠(1984)	Yancheng 鹽城市	Jiangsu 江蘇省	(0515)8650158 (0515)8650203	584	Collectively-owned 集體	103,010	4510(15)	99,080	o
Yanzhou Tractor Fitting Parts Factory 兗州市拖拉機配件廠(1976)	Jining 濟寧市	Shandong 山東省	(0537)3832233 (0537)3832233	790	Collectively-owned 集體	93,040	6510(8)	60,170	o
Laiwu Xin Yuan Machinery Factory 萊蕪市鑫源機械廠(1987)	Laiwu 萊蕪市	Shandong 山東省	(0634)6114751 (0634)6114751	63	Collectively-owned 集體	85,247	348(121)	2,517	o
No.1 Tractor Engineering Machinery Company Multiple Machinery Factory 第一拖拉機工程機械公司綜合機械廠(1984)	Luoyang 洛陽市	Henan 河南省	(0379)4913452	749	Collectively-owned 集體	84,398	939(58)	27,492	a

Top 10 Cities by Production Output 產出排名前 10 位城市	Province 省	Market share 市場份額	Number of firms 企業個數
Weihai 威海市	Shandong 山東省	13.75%	21
Changzhou 常州市	Jiangsu 江蘇省	6.17%	48
Weifang 濰坊市	Shandong 山東省	4.65%	27
Yancheng 鹽城市	Jiangsu 江蘇省	4.41%	20
Yangzhou 揚州市	Jiangsu 江蘇省	3.88%	10
Dandong 丹東市	Liaoning 遼寧省	3.29%	12
Jining 濟寧市	Shandong 山東省	2.75%	16
Yantai 煙臺市	Shandong 山東省	2.38%	10
Shanghai 上海市	Shanghai 上海市	2.18%	20
Chengdu 成都市	Sichuan 四川省	2.13%	6

10 Major Wholesalers 10 家主要批發商	City 城市	Province 省	Telephone / Fax 電話 / 傳真
Liaoning Automobile Trade Group Corp. 遼寧省汽車貿易集團	Shenyang 瀋陽市	Liaoning 遼寧省	(024)23835494 (024)23838338
China Post and Telecommunication Equipment General Company 中國郵電器材總公司	Beijing 北京市	Beijing 北京市	(010)63523715 (010)63525935
Jiangsu Electromechanical Products General Company 江蘇省機電產品總公司	Nanjing 南京市	Jiangsu 江蘇省	(025)7713642 (025)7711036
Xi Nan Technology Import & Export Company 西南技術進出口公司	Chongqing 重慶市	Chongqing 重慶市	(023)63850185 (023)63850026
Changzhou Economic Technology Industrial Development Zone Tian Ming Trade Company 常州經濟技術產業開發區天明貿易公司	Changzhou 常州市	Jiangsu 江蘇省	(0519)8829882 (0519)8829882
Shanxi Mechanical Equipment Import & Export Company 山西省機械設備進出口公司	Taiyuan 太原市	Shanxi 山西省	(0351)4040713 (0351)4043981
Ningbo Five Mining Machinery Import & Export Company 寧波市五礦機械進出口公司	Ningbo 寧波市	Zhejiang 浙江省	(0574)7311255 (0574)7320322
Tianjin Jin Huan Electromechanical Complete Sets of Equipment Factory 天津市津環機電成套設備廠	Tianjin 天津市	Tianjin 天津市	(022)26371628
Yunnan Machinery Import & Export Company 雲南省機械進出口公司	Kunming 昆明市	Yunnan 雲南省	(0871)3164879 (0871)3136829
Tianjin Da Qiu Zhuang Yi Yuan Trade Center 天津市大丘莊億源商貿中心	Tianjin 天津市	Tianjin 天津市	(022)28899478 (022)28899046

*Also include sales by firms outside this industry.包括本行業以外廠家的銷售。"o" stands for "others". "o" 代表 "其他產品"。

3649: Other Farming, Forestry, Husbandry, and Fishery Machinery
其他農、林、牧、漁、水利業機械製造業

The industry accounts for 0.282% of the total revenue of China's industrial sector in 1996. The revenue growth rate of the industry is 18.7% from 1995, as compared to the growth rate of China's industrial sector, 9.51%. The rate of return on asset is 2.43%. 72.18% of all firms in the industry made a profit while 23.44% had negative returns. The top province in terms of the industry's revenue is Shandong, accounting for 38.02% of the total revenue.
本行業在1996年佔全行業總產值0.282%，行業年增長率為18.7%（全國工業年增長率9.51%）。行業的資產回報率2.43%，72.18%的企業盈利，23.44%的企業虧損。銷售收入最高的省份為山東省，佔本行業的38.02%。

	Total number of firms 企業總數	Total number of employees 職工總數	Total revenue (mil. RMB) 總銷售收入（百萬元）	Total profit (mil. RMB) 總利潤（百萬元）	Return on assets 資產利潤率 (%)	Return on equity 權益利潤率 (%)	Labour productivity ('000 RMB / worker) 勞動生產率（千元/人）	Debts / assets 資產負債率 (%)	Total assets (mil. RMB) 總資產（百萬元）
Industry Overall 行業總體	949	153,452	16,369	312	2.43	8.42	106.67	71.10	12,840

	Number of firms 企業個數	Average number of employees 平均職工人數	Average revenue ('000 RMB) 平均銷售收入（千元）	Average profit ('000 RMB) 平均利潤（千元）	Return on assets 資產利潤率 (%)	Return on equity 權益利潤率 (%)	Labour productivity ('000 RMB / worker) 勞動生產率（千元/人）	Average debts / assets 平均資產負債率(%)	Average Total assets ('000 RMB) 平均總資產（千元）
By ownership 產業所有權									
State-owned 國有	242	368	26,955	-248	-0.85	-3.50	73.19	75.71	29,178
Collectively-owned 集體	678	82	11,765	343	5.25	16.36	143.63	67.91	6,539
Privately-owned 私有									
Domestic JVs 聯營	9	376	68,627	508	1.35	3.55	182.30	62.02	37,695
Joint stock 股份制	11	250	29,270	292	1.74	10.20	117.25	82.93	16,786
Foreign-funded 外資	4	257	92,003	1,821	2.33	6.48	358.34	63.99	78,017
Overseas Chinese-funded 港澳台資	4	428	140,538	31,048	24.38	41.33	328.36	41.01	127,357
By size 規模									
Large 大型	8	2,429	503,140	11,188	3.30	7.65	207.17	56.92	339,340
Medium 中型	44	947	127,505	3,754	3.50	13.93	134.61	74.90	107,374
Small 小型	891	103	7,559	64	1.06	4.23	73.64	74.90	6,061
By regional distribution 地區分布									
Central-North 華北	108	148	6,968	108	1.18	3.98	47.17	70.45	9,211
Beijing 北京	8	99	6,384	231	2.06	9.16	64.24	77.47	11,206
Tianjin 天津	7	49	3,889	124	3.39	10.47	79.59	67.65	3,670
Hebei 河北	55	187	11,419	359	2.86	8.59	61.13	66.78	12,557
Shanxi 山西	16	103	1,166	-96	-2.73	-22.42	11.34	87.81	3,529
Inner Mongolia 內蒙	22	132	1,250	-418	-6.95	-31.63	9.50	78.02	6,018
Northeast 東北	93	133	2,862	-97	-2.29	-14.74	21.48	84.44	4,216
Liaoning 遼寧	38	152	2,497	-128	-2.26	-28.02	16.41	91.92	5,643
Jilin 吉林	25	84	2,788	141	6.88	69.57	33.03	90.12	2,048
Heilongjiang 黑龍江	30	150	3,386	-255	-6.06	-19.82	22.59	69.45	4,216
Central East 華東	350	205	34,577	1,196	5.36	17.72	168.58	69.73	22,290
Shanghai 上海	1	56	3,230	410	32.80	69.49	57.68	53.60	1,250
Jiangsu 江蘇	76	201	47,350	505	2.20	8.27	235.85	73.36	22,923
Zhejiang 浙江	19	392	27,413	86	0.18	0.56	69.98	67.71	47,458
Anhui 安徽	79	128	11,027	-425	-6.70	-118.41	86.47	94.34	6,341
Fujian 福建	50	126	15,999	147	0.69	2.77	127.12	75.09	21,369
Jiangxi 江西	61	62	1,395	-77	-2.65	-18.13	22.59	85.40	2,911
Shandong 山東	64	451	97,237	6,390	11.99	31.82	215.37	62.31	53,275
Central-South 中南	253	116	6,765	-41	-0.54	-1.53	58.09	64.96	7,674
Henan 河南	97	94	9,411	309	4.29	13.94	100.32	69.26	7,208
Hubei 湖北	43	137	8,618	157	1.25	2.38	63.08	47.50	12,582
Hunan 湖南	54	140	3,250	-339	-7.57	-33.73	23.17	77.56	4,479
Guangdong 廣東	20	73	1,928	-295	-5.75	-18.98	26.32	69.72	5,135
Guangxi 廣西	35	121	5,584	-559	-6.16	-22.51	46.04	72.64	9,085
Hainan 海南	4	301	4,685	-833	-8.60	-37.29	15.55	76.94	9,680
Southwest 西南	67	228	20,269	-1,111	-6.21	-46.62	89.09	86.69	17,901
Chongqing 重慶	6	150	8,204	-2,128	-30.12	356.38	54.54	108.45	7,066
Sichuan 四川	41	272	27,343	-1,418	-6.16	-58.97	100.71	89.56	23,029
Guizhou 貴州	9	34	403	14	1.77	3.87	11.82	54.35	818
Yunnan 雲南	9	326	21,323	-373	-1.59	-5.39	65.41	70.56	23,516
Tibet 西藏	2	6	10	5	3.13	5.26	1.82	40.63	160
Northwest 西北	78	110	2,293	-306	-4.68	-15.41	20.77	69.66	6,544
Shaanxi 陝西	37	65	1,567	-13	-0.48	-1.96	23.96	75.50	2,704
Gansu 甘肅	13	141	2,048	-408	-7.87	-44.25	14.52	82.25	5,188
Qinghai 青海	10	63	1,878	-94	-3.02	-14.11	29.95	78.58	3,109
Ningxia 寧夏	5	82	2,230	-186	-4.97	-12.22	27.06	59.33	3,742
Xinjiang 新疆	13	256	4,949	-1,247	-5.53	-15.57	19.37	64.49	22,552

3649: Other Farming, Forestry, Husbandry, and Fishery Machinery
其他農、林、牧、漁、水利業機械製造業

Year 年份	Number of firms 企業個數	Rate of change 每年變化 (%)	Number of employees 職工人數 (人)	Rate of change 每年變化 (%)	Total revenue (mil. RMB) 總銷售收入 (百萬元)	Rate of change 每年變化 (%)	Total profit (mil. RMB) 總利潤 (百萬元)	Rate of change 每年變化 (%)
1993	850		91,036		6,137		158	
1994	883	3.88%	112,373	23.44%	8,780	43.06%	226	43.19%
1995	896	1.47%	160,051	42.43%	13,790	57.07%	367	62.11%
1996	949	5.92%	153,452	-4.12%	16,369	18.70%	312	-14.91%

3 Major products* 3種主要產品 *	Output 產量	Sales volume 銷售量	Unit 單位
a) Tricycle 三輪車	920,753	874,716	vehicle 輛
b) Agricultural Transport Machinery 農業運輸機械	1,425,868	1,411,609	vehicle 輛
c) Trailer 拖車	36,557	35,461	vehicle 輛

Top 10 firms by revenue (year founded) 收入排名前10家企業 (創辦年份)	City 城市	Province 省	Telephone / fax 電話 / 傳真	Number of employees 職工人數	Ownership 產業所有權	Revenue ('000 RMB) 銷售收入 (千元)	Profit ('000 RMB) (rank) 利潤 (千元) (排名)	Total assets ('000 RMB) 總資產 (千元)	Major products 主要產品
Nanjing Agricultural Vehicle Manufacturing Factory 南京農用車製造廠(1970)	Nanjing 南京市	Jiangsu 江蘇省	(025)7211266 (025)7213367	1,259	Collectively-owned 集體	1,503,900	35228(4)	610,150	b
Shandong Ju Li Group Co. Ltd. 山東巨力集團股份有限公司(1965)	Weifang 濰坊市	Shandong 山東省	(0536)8323432 (0536)8327207	2,011	Collectively-owned 集體	1,384,800	61239(3)	369,962	a
Shandong Gao Tangxian Shifeng Machinery Group General Company 山東省高唐縣時風機械集團總公司(1958)	Liaocheng 聊城市	Shandong 山東省	(0635)3953153 (0635)3953153	5,030	State-owned 國有	1,111,298	100641(2)	261,369	b
Liaocheng Transport Machinery Factory 聊城運輸機械廠(1966)	Liaocheng 聊城市	Shandong 山東省	(0635)8322156 (0635)8322156	1,605	State-owned 國有	701,389	27003(5)	336,066	b
Bei Qi Futian Vehicle Co. Ltd. Zhucheng Vehicle Factory 北汽福田車輛股份有限公司諸城車輛廠	Weifang 濰坊市	Shandong 山東省	(0536)6118250	2,109	State-owned 國有	687,226	11446(11)	262,333	b
Sichuan Yibin Vehicle Factory 四川宜賓車輛廠(1991)	Yibin 宜賓市	Sichuan 四川省	(0831)8270920 (0831)6610192	690	State-owned 國有	592,839	661(67)	101,747	b
Nanjing Lishui Jin Ma Industrial Co. Ltd. 南京市溧水縣金馬實業有限公司(1992)	Nanjing 南京市	Jiangsu 江蘇省	(025)7250238 (025)7250238	1,335	Collectively-owned 集體	395,642	220(126)	253,798	o
Shandong Hei Bao Co. Ltd. 山東黑豹股份有限公司(1980)	Weihai 威海市	Shandong 山東省	(0896)8352146 (0896)8352228	1,975	Joint stock 股份制	390,604	114418(1)	449,138	b
State-owned Shandong Guang Ming Machine Plant 國營山東光明機器廠(1969)	Tai'an 泰安市	Shandong 山東省	(0538)6116610 (0538)6116614	1,705	State-owned 國有	366,647	19383(7)	264,521	b
Nanjing Da Jinshan Industrial Co. Ltd. 南京大金山實業有限公司(1994)	Nanjing 南京市	Jiangsu 江蘇省	(025)7490170 (025)7490169	1,509	Collectively-owned 集體	360,041	213(128)	161,777	o

Top 10 Cities by Production Output 產出排名前10位城市	Province 省	Market share 市場份額	Number of firms 企業個數
Nanjing 南京市	Jiangsu 江蘇省	16.00%	27
Liaocheng 聊城市	Shandong 山東省	14.85%	13
Weifang 濰坊市	Shandong 山東省	13.17%	13
Xuanzhou 宣州市	Anhui 安徽省	5.68%	20
Weihai 威海市	Shandong 山東省	4.21%	4
Tai'an 泰安市	Shandong 山東省	3.45%	8
Hangzhou 杭州市	Zhejiang 浙江省	2.90%	8
Xuchang 許昌市	Henan 河南省	2.77%	29
Longyan 龍巖市	Fujian 福建省	2.70%	8
Jining 濟寧市	Shandong 山東省	2.08%	7

10 Major Wholesalers 10家主要批發商	City 城市	Province 省	Telephone / Fax 電話 / 傳真
Liaoning Automobile Trade Group Corp. 遼寧省汽車貿易集團	Shenyang 瀋陽市	Liaoning 遼寧省	(024)23835494 (024)23838338
China Post and Telecommunication Equipment General Company 中國郵電器材總公司	Beijing 北京市	Beijing 北京市	(010)63523715 (010)63525935
Jiangsu Electromechanical Products General Company 江蘇省機電產品總公司	Nanjing 南京市	Jiangsu 江蘇省	(025)7713642 (025)7711036
Xi Nan Technology Import & Export Company 西南技術進出口公司	Chongqing 重慶市	Chongqing 重慶市	(023)63850185 (023)63850026
Changzhou Economic Technology Industrial Development Zone Tian Ming Trade Company 常州經濟技術產業開發區天明貿易公司	Changzhou 常州市	Jiangsu 江蘇省	(0519)8829882 (0519)8829882
Shanxi Mechanical Equipment Import & Export Company 山西省機械設備進出口公司	Taiyuan 太原市	Shanxi 山西省	(0351)4040713 (0351)4043981
Ningbo Five Mining Machinery Import & Export Company 寧波市五礦機械進出口公司	Ningbo 寧波市	Zhejiang 浙江省	(0574)7311255 (0574)7320322
Tianjin Jin Huan Electromechanical Complete Sets of Equipment Factory 天津市津環機電成套設備廠	Tianjin 天津市	Tianjin 天津市	(022)26371628
Yunnan Machinery Import & Export Company 雲南省機械進出口公司	Kunming 昆明市	Yunnan 雲南省	(0871)3164879 (0871)3136829
Tianjin Da Qiu Zhuang Yi Yuan Trade Center 天津市大丘莊億源商貿中心	Tianjin 天津市	Tianjin 天津市	(022)28899478 (022)28899046

*Also include sales by firms outside this industry.包括本行業以外廠家的銷售。"o" stands for "others". "o" 代表"其他產品"。

3651: Surgical Apparatus and Instruments 手術器械製造業

The industry accounts for 0.023% of the total revenue of China's industrial sector in 1996. The revenue growth rate of the industry is 20.3% from 1995, as compared to the growth rate of China's industrial sector, 9.51%. The rate of return on asset is 1.79%. 70.21% of all firms in the industry made a profit while 28.04% had negative returns. The top province in terms of the industry's revenue is Jiangsu, accounting for 57.46% of the total revenue.
本行業在1996年佔全行業總產值0.023%，行業年增長率為20.3%（全國工業年增長率9.51%）。行業的資產回報率1.79%，70.21%的企業盈利，28.04%的企業虧損。銷售收入最高的省份為江蘇省，佔本行業的57.46%。

	Total number of firms 企業總數	Total number of employees 職工總數	Total revenue (mil. RMB) 總銷售收入（百萬元）	Total profit (mil. RMB) 總利潤（百萬元）	Return on assets 資產利潤率 (%)	Return on equity 權益利潤率 (%)	Labour productivity ('000 RMB / worker) 勞動生產率（千元/人）	Debts / assets 資產負債率 (%)	Total assets (mil. RMB) 總資產（百萬元）
Industry Overall 行業總體	108	19,587	1,312	29	1.79	5.19	66.98	65.53	1,618

	Number of firms 企業個數	Average number of employees 平均職工人數	Average revenue ('000 RMB) 平均銷售收入（千元）	Average profit ('000 RMB) 平均利潤（千元）	Return on assets 資產利潤率 (%)	Return on equity 權益利潤率 (%)	Labour productivity ('000 RMB / worker) 勞動生產率（千元/人）	Average debts / assets 平均資產負債率(%)	Average Total assets ('000 RMB) 平均總資產（千元）
By ownership 產業所有權									
State-owned 國有	21	463	14,762	-429	-1.31	-5.84	31.88	77.52	32,619
Collectively-owned 集體	69	132	13,811	527	4.27	10.21	104.25	58.15	12,326
Privately-owned 私有	1	20	555	-163	-52.88	-163.73	27.74	67.70	308
Domestic JVs 聯營	1	9	425	18	10.34	17.15	47.22	39.72	176
Joint stock 股份制	1	136	3,708				27.26	70.73	9,319
Foreign-funded 外資	10	45	3,547	125	2.04	3.25	79.71	37.39	6,118
Overseas Chinese-funded 港澳台資	5	18	1,708	93	4.49	7.93	92.85	43.42	2,069
By size 規模									
Large 大型	2	2,219	293,235	9,510	2.94	7.06	132.18	58.31	323,284
Medium 中型	6	668	23,645	389	0.69	3.50	35.38	80.35	56,474
Small 小型	97	114	6,022	79	1.21	3.44	52.74	64.94	6,530
By regional distribution 地區分布									
Central-North 華北	20	78	2,187	-210	-3.43	-8.77	28.09	60.88	6,122
Beijing 北京	10	36	1,684	-38	-1.93	-7.79	46.78	75.19	1,967
Tianjin 天津	8	106	2,486	-478	-4.83	-10.68	23.46	54.74	9,880
Hebei 河北	1	29	320				11.03	117.14	700
Shanxi 山西									
Inner Mongolia 內蒙	1	320	6,690				20.91	68.00	23,030
Northeast 東北	4	42	1,123	45	2.00	5.07	26.89	60.47	2,245
Liaoning 遼寧	3	16	1,440	97	21.48	31.18	91.91	31.11	450
Jilin 吉林									
Heilongjiang 黑龍江	1	120	170	-110	-1.44	-4.20	1.42	65.66	7,630
Central East 華東	58	225	18,352	638	2.93	8.18	81.39	64.12	21,742
Shanghai 上海	10	267	13,030	151	0.89	4.39	48.73	79.73	16,956
Jiangsu 江蘇	20	274	37,695	1,753	4.59	9.92	137.50	53.74	38,211
Zhejiang 浙江	18	95	3,488	71	1.53	4.67	36.91	67.17	4,607
Anhui 安徽	1	180	20,710	1,100	30.99	85.94	115.06	63.94	3,550
Fujian 福建	2	55	620				11.38	53.11	1,205
Jiangxi 江西									
Shandong 山東	7	419	13,641	-276	-0.81	-5.53	32.58	85.36	34,057
Central-South 中南	8	98	3,418	89	1.74	3.96	34.92	56.07	5,105
Henan 河南	2	117	9,720	645	5.39	13.62	83.43	60.44	11,970
Hubei 湖北	1	199	860	-710	-14.76	139.22	4.32	110.60	4,810
Hunan 湖南	1	17	180	20	2.90	5.71	10.59	50.72	690
Guangdong 廣東	2	112	2,335	35	0.77	0.95	20.94	19.67	4,575
Guangxi 廣西	2	56	1,095	20	1.78	3.10	19.73	42.67	1,125
Hainan 海南									
Southwest 西南	11	255	13,649	-459	-4.12	-22.39	53.43	81.62	11,156
Chongqing 重慶	4	178	13,123	-380	-3.45	-64.28	73.82	94.64	11,035
Sichuan 四川	5	376	19,529	-706	-4.49	-17.47	51.91	74.31	15,716
Guizhou 貴州	2	109							
Yunnan 雲南									
Tibet 西藏									
Northwest 西北	7	170	3,096	50	0.56	2.58	18.18	78.28	8,911
Shaanxi 陝西	5	225	4,146	60	0.51	2.71	18.44	81.09	11,688
Gansu 甘肅	2	34	470	25	1.27	2.00	13.82	36.55	1,970
Qinghai 青海									
Ningxia 寧夏									
Xinjiang 新疆									

3651: Surgical Apparatus and Instruments 手術器械製造業

Year 年份	Number of firms 企業個數	Rate of change 每年變化 (%)	Number of employees 職工人數 (人)	Rate of change 每年變化 (%)	Total revenue (mil. RMB) 總銷售收入 (百萬元)	Rate of change 每年變化 (%)	Total profit (mil. RMB) 總利潤 (百萬元)	Rate of change 每年變化 (%)
1993	114		26,994		857		54	
1994	115	0.88%	20,171	-25.28%	884	3.18%	37	-30.51%
1995	112	-2.61%	22,548	11.78%	1,091	23.49%	44	18.50%
1996	108	-3.57%	19,587	-13.13%	1,312	20.26%	29	-34.36%

3 Major products* 3 種主要產品 *	Output 產量	Sales volume 銷售量	Unit 單位

Top 10 firms by revenue (year founded) 收入排名前 10 家企業 (創辦年份)	City 城市	Province 省	Telephone / fax 電話 / 傳真	Number of employees 職工人數	Ownership 產業所有權	Revenue ('000 RMB) 銷售收入 (千元)	Profit ('000 RMB) (rank) 利潤 (千元) (排名)	Total assets ('000 RMB) 總資產 (千元)	Major products 主要產品
Jiangsu Hong Bao Group Co. 江蘇宏寶集團公司(1964)	Suzhou 蘇州市	Jiangsu 江蘇省	(0512)8760088 (0512)8761055	2,260	Collectively-owned 集體	571,250	29840(1)	534,320	o
Chengdu Min Jiang Industrial Company 成都市岷江工業公司(1984)	Chengdu 成都市	Sichuan 四川省	(028)5187282	205	Collectively-owned 集體	122,325	415(14)	22,312	o
Hengyang San Hua Industrial Co. Ltd. 衡陽三化實業股份有限公司(1958)	Hengyang 衡陽市	Hunan 湖南省	(0734)8331911 (0734)8331393	1,335	Joint stock 股份制	112,508	8348(2)	245,920	o
Shandong Xinhua Medical Apparatus & Instruments Plant 山東新華醫療器械廠(1943)	Zibo 淄博市	Shandong 山東省	(0533)2183171 (0533)2183211	1,830	State-owned 國有	85,131	110(28)	177,958	o
Shanghai Operating Apparatuses Factory 上海手術器械廠(1950)	Shanghai 上海市	Shanghai 上海市	(021)56650166 (021)56653469	993	State-owned 國有	60,721	806(10)	72,953	o
Suzhou Medical Apparatus & Instruments Plant 蘇州醫療器械廠(1956)	Suzhou 蘇州市	Jiangsu 江蘇省	(0512)7271504 (0512)5244789	775	State-owned 國有	44,090	4500(3)	109,800	o
Wujin Operating Apparatuses Factory 武進市手術器械廠(1966)	Changzhou 常州市	Jiangsu 江蘇省	(0519)3631421	178	Collectively-owned 集體	35,310	792(11)	14,527	o
Shanghai Operation No.6 Apparatus Plant 上海手術器械六廠(1949)	Shanghai 上海市	Shanghai 上海市	(021)56979323 (021)56633456	613	State-owned 國有	29,917	150(25)	24,627	o
Wujiang Dongfeng Chemical Factory 吳江市東風化工廠(1958)	Suzhou 蘇州市	Jiangsu 江蘇省	(0512)3771130 (0512)3772033	466	Collectively-owned 集體	22,850	-832(50)	25,409	o
Anhui Quanjiao Medical Apparatus and Instruments Factory 安徽省全椒醫療器材廠(1988)	Chuzhou 滁州市	Anhui 安徽省	(0550)5014150	150	Collectively-owned 集體	20,709	1100(8)	3,550	o

Top 10 Cities by Production Output 產出排名前 10 位城市	Province 省	Market share 市場份額	Number of firms 企業個數
Suzhou 蘇州市	Jiangsu 江蘇省	44.46%	12
Shanghai 上海市	Shanghai 上海市	16.00%	30
Hengyang 衡陽市	Hunan 湖南省	8.01%	1
Zibo 淄博市	Shandong 山東省	6.42%	1
Hefei 合肥市	Anhui 安徽省	5.71%	1
Ningbo 寧波市	Zhejiang 浙江省	1.68%	5
Shangqiu 商丘市	Henan 河南省	1.64%	1
Xianyang 咸陽市	Shaanxi 陝西省	1.49%	3
Ji'nan 濟南市	Shandong 山東省	1.31%	3
Nanjing 南京市	Jiangsu 江蘇省	1.26%	3

10 Major Wholesalers 10 家主要批發商	City 城市	Province 省	Telephone / Fax 電話 / 傳真
China Medicine Shanghai Purchase Supply Station 中國醫藥上海採購供應站	Shanghai 上海市	Shanghai 上海市	(021)63211750
Anhui Medical Health Care Product Import & Export Co. Ltd. 安徽省醫藥保健品進出口股份有限公司	Hefei 合肥市	Anhui 安徽省	(0551)3632603 (0551)3631975
Hai Tong Science Apparatus Co. Ltd. 海通科學儀器有限公司	Shanghai 上海市	Shanghai 上海市	(021)64397740 (021)64395300
Nantong Medicine Co. Ltd. 南通醫藥股份有限公司	Nantong 南通市	Jiangsu 江蘇省	(0513)5513093 (0513)5527814
Jiangxi Medical Health Care Product Import & Export Company 江西省醫藥保健品進出口公司	Nanchang 南昌市	Jiangxi 江西省	(0791)6222337 (0791)6217072
Shandong Machinery Industry Trade General Company 山東省機械工業貿易總公司	Ji'nan 濟南市	Shandong 山東省	(0531)6948991
Science & Education Technology Import & Export Company 科教技術進出口公司	Shanghai 上海市	Shanghai 上海市	(021)62564308 (021)62563108
Medical Apparatus & Instruments Wholesale Dept. 醫療器械批發部	Shanghai 上海市	Shanghai 上海市	(021)63216704 (021)63219814
Sichuan Livestock Raising College Medical Equipment Marketing Dept. 四川畜牧學院藥械經營部	Chongqing 重慶市	Chongqing 重慶市	(023)46733820
Shandou Scientific Equipment General Company 汕頭市科學器材總公司	Shantou 汕頭市	Guangdong 廣東省	(0754)8625957 (0754)8250513

*Also include sales by firms outside this industry.包括本行業以外廠家的銷售。"o" stands for "others". "o" 代表"其他產品"。

3652: Medical Apparatus and Equipment 醫療儀器、設備製造業

The industry accounts for 0.057% of the total revenue of China's industrial sector in 1996. The revenue growth rate of the industry is 0.9% from 1995, as compared to the growth rate of China's industrial sector, 9.51%. The rate of return on asset is 2.02%. 62.23% of all firms in the industry made a profit while 30.84% had negative returns. The top province in terms of the industry's revenue is Shanghai, accounting for 25.56% of the total revenue.

本行業在1996年佔全行業總產值0.057%，行業年增長率為0.9%（全國工業年增長率9.51%）。行業的資產回報率2.02%，62.23%的企業盈利，30.84%的企業虧損。銷售收入最高的省份為上海市，佔本行業的25.56%。

	Total number of firms 企業總數	Total number of employees 職工總數	Total revenue (mil. RMB) 總銷售收入（百萬元）	Total profit (mil. RMB) 總利潤（百萬元）	Return on assets 資產利潤率 (%)	Return on equity 權益利潤率 (%)	Labour productivity ('000 RMB / worker) 勞動生產率（千元/人）	Debts / assets 資產負債率 (%)	Total assets (mil. RMB) 總資產（百萬元）
Industry Overall 行業總體	586	53,319	3,284	147	2.02	5.27	61.59	61.66	7,255

	Number of firms 企業個數	Average number of employees 平均職工人數	Average revenue ('000 RMB) 平均銷售收入（千元）	Average profit ('000 RMB) 平均利潤（千元）	Return on assets 資產利潤率 (%)	Return on equity 權益利潤率 (%)	Labour productivity ('000 RMB / worker) 勞動生產率（千元/人）	Average debts / assets 平均資產負債率(%)	Average Total assets ('000 RMB) 平均總資產（千元）
By ownership 產業所有權									
State-owned 國有	122	229	8,623	8	0.04	0.13	37.60	72.01	22,787
Collectively-owned 集體	300	62	2,525	193	3.92	11.41	40.77	65.68	4,916
Privately-owned 私有	4	43	25,530	9,855	17.53	21.46	600.70	18.33	56,223
Domestic JVs 聯營	9	115	9,117	275	0.83	3.65	79.43	77.31	33,213
Joint stock 股份制	10	109	14,724	1,063	1.49	2.59	134.59	42.61	71,463
Foreign-funded 外資	81	36	10,606	319	1.83	3.76	292.30	51.42	17,466
Overseas Chinese-funded 港澳台資	59	33	4,812	168	2.85	6.63	147.65	57.07	5,888
By size 規模									
Large 大型	7	687	47,663	2,520	1.32	2.97	69.36	55.54	190,545
Medium 中型	23	460	22,889	-968	-1.35	-5.82	49.80	76.73	71,495
Small 小型	539	71	4,497	281	3.54	8.39	63.48	57.76	7,936
By regional distribution 地區分布									
Central-North 華北	178	62	4,026	157	1.78	4.73	64.90	62.39	8,811
Beijing 北京	126	52	4,606	255	2.52	6.60	88.94	61.81	10,122
Tianjin 天津	35	83	2,752	-45	-0.88	-1.95	33.14	54.90	5,112
Hebei 河北	14	92	2,275	-144	-2.23	-13.58	24.63	83.53	6,457
Shanxi 山西	2	150	3,590	-330	-2.84	-9.40	24.01	69.78	11,600
Inner Mongolia 內蒙	1	18	860				47.78	76.92	520
Northeast 東北	75	82	1,567	-52	-1.12	-65.87	19.19	98.30	4,604
Liaoning 遼寧	50	67	1,561	135	3.58	40.29	23.23	91.12	3,775
Jilin 吉林	13	161	2,147	-873	-11.49	66.34	13.34	117.33	7,596
Heilongjiang 黑龍江	12	56	968	59	1.23	11.41	17.20	89.23	4,814
Central East 華東	188	112	8,564	292	1.96	5.63	76.58	65.13	14,857
Shanghai 上海	65	177	12,915	138	0.53	1.83	73.15	70.93	26,032
Jiangsu 江蘇	38	136	5,679	-186	-1.74	-5.78	41.85	69.87	10,701
Zhejiang 浙江	34	47	3,090	86	1.92	5.23	65.57	63.19	4,462
Anhui 安徽	3	45	450	-213	-4.69	-13.36	10.07	64.88	4,547
Fujian 福建	12	76	8,253	-182	-1.29	-1.73	107.99	25.59	14,137
Jiangxi 江西	12	24	594	-8	-0.96	-3.14	25.19	69.60	872
Shandong 山東	24	61	14,253	2,206	15.17	31.23	235.43	51.42	14,540
Central-South 中南	106	96	6,809	902	4.42	9.01	71.15	50.95	20,415
Henan 河南	16	97	1,938	62	1.10	6.43	19.92	82.89	5,627
Hubei 湖北	19	131	4,102	126	2:66	7.03	31.42	62.16	4,747
Hunan 湖南	11	96	3,088	-24	-0.72	-2.73	32.17	73.55	3,279
Guangdong 廣東	51	95	11,171	1,811	4.77	9.27	117.47	48.54	37,975
Guangxi 廣西	9	23	1,017	9	0.73	1.41	45.07	48.08	1,216
Hainan 海南									
Southwest 西南	22	158	2,960	-224	-2.42	-7.46	18.78	67.57	9,268
Chongqing 重慶	6	104	581	-81	-3.25	-31.40	5.57	89.64	2,502
Sichuan 四川	9	252	6,224	-411	-2.30	-6.56	24.69	64.99	17,890
Guizhou 貴州	3	140	1,063	-157	-1.94	-6.14	7.60	68.45	8,093
Yunnan 雲南	4	37	608	-70	-7.78	-50.91	16.53	84.72	900
Tibet 西藏									
Northwest 西北	17	89	3,103	-1,344	-12.66	-27.00	34.82	53.13	10,621
Shaanxi 陝西	14	76	3,260	-1,549	-12.94	-27.83	42.77	53.49	11,964
Gansu 甘肅	2	190	1,665	-740	-15.48	-29.19	8.79	47.07	4,780
Qinghai 青海									
Ningxia 寧夏									
Xinjiang 新疆	1	69	3,780	310	8.86	18.79	54.78	52.57	3,500

3652: Medical Apparatus and Equipment 醫療儀器、設備製造業

Year 年份	Number of firms 企業個數	Rate of change 每年變化 (%)	Number of employees 職工人數（人）	Rate of change 每年變化 (%)	Total revenue (mil. RMB) 總銷售收入（百萬元）	Rate of change 每年變化 (%)	Total profit (mil. RMB) 總利潤（百萬元）	Rate of change 每年變化 (%)
1993	488		104,027		2,471		156	
1994	509	4.30%	66,095	-36.46%	2,561	3.66%	55	-64.64%
1995	527	3.54%	56,682	-14.24%	3,256	27.09%	196	255.07%
1996	586	11.20%	53,319	-5.93%	3,284	0.86%	147	-24.81%

3 Major products* 3種主要產品*	Output 產量	Sales volume 銷售量	Unit 單位

Top 10 firms by revenue (year founded) 收入排名前10家企業（創辦年份）	City 城市	Province 省	Telephone / fax 電話 / 傳真	Number of employees 職工人數	Ownership 產業所有權	Revenue ('000 RMB) 銷售收入（千元）	Profit ('000 RMB) (rank) 利潤（千元）（排名）	Total assets ('000 RMB) 總資產（千元）	Major products 主要產品
Hui Pu Medical Treatment Products (Qingdao) Co. Ltd. 惠普醫療產品(青島)有限公司(1994)	Qingdao 青島市	Shandong 山東省	(0532)8701333 (0532)8701413	120	Foreign-funded 外資	256,934	52593(2)	181,175	o
Beijing Hangwei Medical System Co. Ltd. 北京航衛通用電氣醫療系統有限公司(1991)	Beijing 北京市	Beijing 北京市	(010)67681880 (010)67681850	125	Foreign-funded 外資	185,139	5687(8)	198,348	o
Shenzhen Mindray Electronic Co. Ltd. 深圳邁瑞電子有限公司(1991)	Shenzhen 深圳市	Guangdong 廣東省	(0755)6649268 (0755)6649559	189	Overseas Chinese-funded 港澳台資	135,000	27623(4)	87,131	o
Guangdong Wei Da Medical Apparatus & Instruments Group Company 廣東威達醫療器械集團公司(1985)	Jieyang 揭陽市	Guangdong 廣東省	(0663)5582288 (0663)5582865	1,552	State-owned 國有	113,876	33646(3)	441,482	o
Beijing Wan Dong Medical Equipment Co. 北京萬東醫療裝備公司(1955)	Beijing 北京市	Beijing 北京市	(010)65021731 (010)65021151	1,779	State-owned 國有	109,378	15124(6)	264,140	o
Beijing Zhoulin Lamp Manufacturing General Co. 北京周林頻譜總公司(1991)	Beijing 北京市	Beijing 北京市	(010)68517933 (010)68576554	71	Collectively-owned 集體	104,601	21919(5)	308,479	o
Zhou Lin Lamp Manufacturing Shenzhen Co. Ltd. 深圳周林生物頻普有限公司(1993)	Shenzhen 深圳市	Guangdong 廣東省	(0755)3323817	27	Private-owned 私營	89,599	72926(1)	265,591	o
Siemens Medical Apparatus and Instruments Co. Ltd. 西門子醫療器械有限公司(1992)	Shanghai 上海市	Shanghai 上海市	(021)65395398 (021)65436168	107	Foreign-funded 外資	82,340	-3966(194)	110,842	o
Ji'nan Wei Min Industrial General Company 濟南偉民實業總公司(1964)	Ji'nan 濟南市	Shandong 山東省	(0531)8938246 (0531)8938246	315	State-owned 國有	65,730	403(46)	53,514	o
Shanghai Dentistry Medical Apparatus and Instruments Factory 上海齒科醫械廠(1950)	Shanghai 上海市	Shanghai 上海市	(021)56611238 (021)56051978	501	State-owned 國有	64,508	1722(19)	63,606	o

Top 10 Cities by Production Output 產出排名前10位城市	Province 省	Market share 市場份額	Number of firms 企業個數
Shanghai 上海市	Shanghai 上海市	34.71%	101
Beijing 北京市	Beijing 北京市	16.37%	107
Qingdao 青島市	Shandong 山東省	6.43%	7
Chongqing 重慶市	Chongqing 重慶市	4.07%	18
Tianjin 天津市	Tianjin 天津市	3.28%	50
Jieyang 揭陽市	Guangdong 廣東省	2.70%	2
Shenzhen 深圳市	Guangdong 廣東省	2.39%	30
Xuzhou 徐州市	Jiangsu 江蘇省	2.31%	8
Wuhan 武漢市	Hubei 湖北省	1.99%	13
Nanjing 南京市	Jiangsu 江蘇省	1.92%	17

10 Major Wholesalers 10家主要批發商	City 城市	Province 省	Telephone / Fax 電話 / 傳真
China Medicine Shanghai Purchase Supply Station 中國醫藥上海採購供應站	Shanghai 上海市	Shanghai 上海市	(021)63211750
Anhui Medical Health Care Product Import & Export Co. Ltd. 安徽省醫藥保健品進出口股份有限公司	Hefei 合肥市	Anhui 安徽省	(0551)3632603 (0551)3631975
Hai Tong Science Apparatus Co. Ltd. 海通科學儀器有限公司	Shanghai 上海市	Shanghai 上海市	(021)64397740 (021)64395300
Nantong Medicine Co. Ltd. 南通醫藥股份有限公司	Nantong 南通市	Jiangsu 江蘇省	(0513)5513093 (0513)5527814
Jiangxi Medical Health Care Product Import & Export Company 江西省醫藥保健品進出口公司	Nanchang 南昌市	Jiangxi 江西省	(0791)6222337 (0791)6217072
Shandong Machinery Industry Trade General Company 山東省機械工業貿易總公司	Ji'nan 濟南市	Shandong 山東省	(0531)6948991
Science & Education Technology Import & Export Company 科教技術進出口公司	Shanghai 上海市	Shanghai 上海市	(021)62564308 (021)62563108
Medical Apparatus & Instruments Wholesale Dept. 醫療器械批發部	Shanghai 上海市	Shanghai 上海市	(021)63216704 (021)63219814
Sichuan Livestock Raising College Medical Equipment Marketing Dept. 四川畜牧學院藥械經營部	Chongqing 重慶市	Chongqing 重慶市	(023)46733820
Shandou Scientific Equipment General Company 汕頭市科學器材總公司	Shantou 汕頭市	Guangdong 廣東省	(0754)8625957 (0754)8250513

*Also include sales by firms outside this industry.包括本行業以外廠家的銷售。"o" stands for "others"."o"代表"其他產品"。

3653: Diagnostic Products 診斷用品製造業

The industry accounts for 0.024% of the total revenue of China's industrial sector in 1996. The revenue growth rate of the industry is 33.5% from 1995, as compared to the growth rate of China's industrial sector, 9.51%. The rate of return on asset is 1.08%. 70.23% of all firms in the industry made a profit while 23.89% had negative returns. The top province in terms of the industry's revenue is Liaoning, accounting for 44.91% of the total revenue.
本行業在1996年佔全行業總產值0.024%，行業年增長率為33.5%（全國工業年增長率9.51%）。行業的資產回報率1.08%，70.23%的企業盈利，23.89%的企業虧損。銷售收入最高的省份為遼寧省，佔本行業的44.91%。

	Total number of firms 企業總數	Total number of employees 職工總數	Total revenue (mil. RMB) 總銷售收入（百萬元）	Total profit (mil. RMB) 總利潤（百萬元）	Return on assets 資產利潤率 (%)	Return on equity 權益利潤率 (%)	Labour productivity ('000 RMB / worker) 勞動生產率（千元/人）	Debts / assets 資產負債率 (%)	Total assets (mil. RMB) 總資產（百萬元）
Industry Overall 行業總體	126	20,832	1,408	15	1.08	3.82	67.59	71.67	1,406

	Number of firms 企業個數	Average number of employees 平均職工人數	Average revenue ('000 RMB) 平均銷售收入（千元）	Average profit ('000 RMB) 平均利潤（千元）	Return on assets 資產利潤率 (%)	Return on equity 權益利潤率 (%)	Labour productivity ('000 RMB / worker) 勞動生產率（千元/人）	Average debts / assets 平均資產負債率(%)	Average Total assets ('000 RMB) 平均總資產（千元）
By ownership 產業所有權									
State-owned 國有	23	248	`8,174	-478	-3.50	-15.49	32.91	77.39	13,652
Collectively-owned 集體	73	138	3,932	34	0.69	2.97	28.44	76.82	4,972
Privately-owned 私有	2	103	3,491	64	2.36	6.92	33.89	65.84	2,695
Domestic JVs 聯營	1	610	15,370	25	0.14	0.24	25.20	42.04	17,674
Joint stock 股份制	4	101	4,377	-52	-0.65	-4.55	43.45	85.75	8,030
Foreign-funded 外資	12	272	68,828	2,047	4.16	11.93	252.89	65.14	49,194
Overseas Chinese-funded 港澳台資	11	86	6,103	-92	-1.21	-4.94	71.12	75.58	7,626
By size 規模									
Large 大型	4	531	183,063	6,611	5.72	17.50	345.08	67.33	115,613
Medium 中型	3	644	39,899	-286	-0.51	-6.80	61.96	92.56	56,480
Small 小型	117	145	4,752	-91	-1.37	-4.52	32.71	69.73	6,619
By regional distribution 地區分布									
Central-North 華北	14	87	1,856	-111	-1.68	-12.03	21.30	86.05	6,636
Beijing 北京	7	24	2,296	61	1.11	7.03	94.53	84.15	5,517
Tianjin 天津	2	300	3,360	-445	-5.61	-158.93	11.20	96.53	7,930
Hebei 河北	1	181		-250	-1.45	-78.13		98.14	17,210
Shanxi 山西	3	72	413	-147	-4.29	-5.81	5.74	26.15	3,417
Inner Mongolia 內蒙	1	53	1,960	-410	-3.74	25.63	36.98	114.60	10,960
Northeast 東北	8	254	87,323	2,085	3.58	14.08	344.30	74.56	58,204
Liaoning 遼寧	4	330	158,085	3,883	4.55	18.71	479.41	75.68	85,320
Jilin 吉林	3	142	18,667	180	0.47	1.72	131.76	72.43	37,917
Heilongjiang 黑龍江	1	285	10,240	610	5.75	14.95	35.93	61.42	10,600
Central East 華東	78	181	7,612	-14	-0.15	-0.45	42.16	66.31	9,133
Shanghai 上海	10	214	10,626	-502	-2.45	-7.69	49.75	68.12	20,475
Jiangsu 江蘇	26	216	8,457	-37	-0.43	-1.39	39.14	68.87	8,535
Zhejiang 浙江	19	177	9,571	250	3.09	7.44	54.09	58.50	8,096
Anhui 安徽	3	162	5,480	50	0.78	9.04	33.90	91.37	6,410
Fujian 福建	2	96	1,805	-745	-5.35	-9.56	18.90	44.04	13,930
Jiangxi 江西	6	221	5,798	65	0.83	2.28	26.24	63.52	7,832
Shandong 山東	12	81	2,578	91	2.89	14.65	32.00	80.31	3,148
Central-South 中南	16	99	3,759	169	4.04	13.52	37.85	70.13	4,181
Henan 河南	2	51	1,080	60	4.44	14.12	21.39	68.52	1,350
Hubei 湖北	1	82	1,400	70	0.44	233.33	17.07	99.81	16,030
Hunan 湖南	3	178	5,493	213	5.11	10.85	30.86	52.88	4,173
Guangdong 廣東	10	87	4,010	187	5.25	14.18	45.99	62.96	3,564
Guangxi 廣西									
Hainan 海南									
Southwest 西南	5	133	2,392	-346	-6.65	48.19	17.98	113.83	5,206
Chongqing 重慶	1	452	6,257	-1,182	-9.13	92.43	13.84	109.87	12,951
Sichuan 四川	4	53	1,426	-137	-4.19	23.61	26.77	117.75	3,270
Guizhou 貴州									
Yunnan 雲南									
Tibet 西藏									
Northwest 西北	5	249	3,452	54	0.63	2.52	13.87	74.95	8,542
Shaanxi 陝西	3	393	5,457	260	1.99	7.29	13.88	72.72	13,077
Gansu 甘肅	1								
Qinghai 青海									
Ningxia 寧夏	1	65	890	-510	-14.66		13.69	100.00	3,480
Xinjiang 新疆									

3653: Diagnostic Products 診斷用品製造業

Year 年份	Number of firms 企業個數	Rate of change 每年變化 (%)	Number of employees 職工人數 (人)	Rate of change 每年變化 (%)	Total revenue (mil. RMB) 總銷售收入 (百萬元)	Rate of change 每年變化 (%)	Total profit (mil. RMB) 總利潤 (百萬元)	Rate of change 每年變化 (%)
1993	129		18,582		712		25	
1994	111	-13.95%	17,229	-7.28%	832	16.89%	11	-55.15%
1995	134	20.72%	18,714	8.62%	1,055	26.80%	13	19.16%
1996	126	-5.97%	20,832	11.32%	1,408	33.46%	15	13.84%

3 Major products* 3 種主要產品 *	Output 產量	Sales volume 銷售量	Unit 單位
a) Diagnostic Article 診斷用品	4,057,925	3,239,169	1,000 yuan 千元
b) Material for Medicine 醫用材料	27,315	21,825	1,000 yuan 千元

Top 10 firms by revenue (year founded) 收入排名前 10 家企業 (創辦年份)	City 城市	Province 省	Telephone / fax 電話 / 傳真	Number of employees 職工人數	Ownership 產業所有權	Revenue ('000 RMB) 銷售收入 (千元)	Profit ('000 RMB) (rank) 利潤 (千元) (排名)	Total assets ('000 RMB) 總資產 (千元)	Major products 主要產品
Omron (Dalian) Co. Ltd. 歐姆龍大連有限公司(1993)	Dalian 大連市	Liaoning 遼寧省	(0411)7614227 (0411)7616602	823	Foreign-funded 外資	557,360	14502(1)	242,642	a
Jms Dalian Medical Apparatus and Instruments Co. Ltd. 大連 JMS 醫療器具有限公司(1990)	Dalian 大連市	Liaoning 遼寧省	(0411)7611733 (0411)7612300	465	Foreign-funded 外資	73,775	2041(5)	79,172	a
Wuxi No.7 Pharmaceutical Factory 無錫市第七製藥廠(1970)	Wuxi 無錫市	Jiangsu 江蘇省	(0510)5180355	815	State-owned 國有	72,000	401(16)	55,064	o
Zhejiang Shuang Ge Group Co. Ltd. 浙江雙鴿集團有限公司(1984)	Taizhou 臺州市	Zhejiang 浙江省	(0576)4222917 (0576)4112026	630	Collectively-owned 集體	50,049	2368(3)	40,569	o
Xi Shan Shi Medical Instrument Factory 錫山市醫用儀表廠(1968)	Wuxi 無錫市	Jiangsu 江蘇省	(0510)3791818 (0510)3791818	940	Collectively-owned 集體	38,669	3503(2)	42,322	o
Shanghai Miswa Medical Industry Co. Ltd. 上海米沙瓦醫科工業有限公司(1994)	Shanghai 上海市	Shanghai 上海市	(021)64017751 (021)64014447	222	Foreign-funded 外資	32,643	2254(4)	66,727	a
Changzhou Medical Apparatus and Instruments Factory 常州市醫療器材廠(1988)	Changzhou 常州市	Jiangsu 江蘇省	(0519)8601787	150	Collectively-owned 集體	28,601	281(19)	12,742	o
Yinxian Medical Instrument and Meter Plant 鄞縣醫用儀表廠(1972)	Ningbo 寧波市	Zhejiang 浙江省	(0574)8451525 (0574)8451521	392	Collectively-owned 集體	27,506	1437(8)	13,350	o
Shanghai Medical Examination Instrument Plant 上海醫用診察儀器廠(1956)	Shanghai 上海市	Shanghai 上海市	(021)62814178 (021)62819500	492	State-owned 國有	26,871	-2546(66)	62,154	a
Jiangxi Nanchang Gan Jiang Medical Apparatus & Instruments Factory 江西省南昌市贛江醫療器械廠(1989)	Nanchang 南昌市	Jiangxi 江西省	(0791)5602500	624	Collectively-owned 集體	18,420	1100(10)	4,552	b

Top 10 Cities by Production Output 產出排名前 10 位城市	Province 省	Market share 市場份額	Number of firms 企業個數
Shanghai 上海市	Shanghai 上海市	17.39%	13
Dalian 大連市	Liaoning 遼寧省	15.68%	2
Wuxi 無錫市	Jiangsu 江蘇省	12.28%	8
Taizhou 臺州市	Zhejiang 浙江省	10.38%	8
Changzhou 常州市	Jiangsu 江蘇省	5.03%	9
Changchun 長春市	Jilin 吉林省	4.29%	4
Beijing 北京市	Beijing 北京市	3.70%	7
Wenzhou 溫州市	Zhejiang 浙江省	3.65%	17
Hangzhou 杭州市	Zhejiang 浙江省	2.95%	2
Nanchang 南昌市	Jiangxi 江西省	2.27%	1

10 Major Wholesalers 10 家主要批發商	City 城市	Province 省	Telephone / Fax 電話 / 傳真
China Medicine Shanghai Purchase Supply Station 中國醫藥上海採購供應站	Shanghai 上海市	Shanghai 上海市	(021)63211750
Anhui Medical Health Care Product Import & Export Co. Ltd. 安徽省醫藥保健品進出口股份有限公司	Hefei 合肥市	Anhui 安徽省	(0551)3632603 (0551)3631975
Hai Tong Science Apparatus Co. Ltd. 海通科學儀器有限公司	Shanghai 上海市	Shanghai 上海市	(021)64397740 (021)64395300
Nantong Medicine Co. Ltd. 南通醫藥股份有限公司	Nantong 南通市	Jiangsu 江蘇省	(0513)5513093 (0513)5527814
Jiangxi Medical Health Care Product Import & Export Company 江西省醫藥保健品進出口公司	Nanchang 南昌市	Jiangxi 江西省	(0791)6222337 (0791)6217072
Shandong Machinery Industry Trade General Company 山東省機械工業貿易總公司	Ji'nan 濟南市	Shandong 山東省	(0531)6948991
Science & Education Technology Import & Export Company 科教技術進出口公司	Shanghai 上海市	Shanghai 上海市	(021)62564308 (021)62563108
Medical Apparatus & Instruments Wholesale Dept. 醫療器械批發部	Shanghai 上海市	Shanghai 上海市	(021)63216704 (021)63219814
Sichuan Livestock Raising College Medical Equipment Marketing Dept. 四川畜牧學院藥械經營部	Chongqing 重慶市	Chongqing 重慶市	(023)46733820
Shandou Scientific Equipment General Company 汕頭市科學器材總公司	Shantou 汕頭市	Guangdong 廣東省	(0754)8625957 (0754)8250513

*Also include sales by firms outside this industry.包括本行業以外廠家的銷售。"o" stands for "others". "o" 代表 "其他產品"。

3654: Medical Materials and Utilities 醫用材料及醫療用品製造業

The industry accounts for 0.068% of the total revenue of China's industrial sector in 1996. The revenue growth rate of the industry is 7.5% from 1995, as compared to the growth rate of China's industrial sector, 9.51%. The rate of return on asset is 3.65%. 67.87% of all firms in the industry made a profit while 26.60% had negative returns. The top province in terms of the industry's revenue is Jiangsu, accounting for 26.92% of the total revenue.
本行業在1996年佔全行業總產值0.068%，行業年增長率為7.5%（全國工業年增長率9.51%）。行業的資產回報率3.65%，67.87%的企業盈利，26.60%的企業虧損。銷售收入最高的省份為江蘇省，佔本行業的26.92%。

	Total number of firms 企業總數	Total number of employees 職工總數	Total revenue (mil. RMB) 總銷售收入（百萬元）	Total profit (mil. RMB) 總利潤（百萬元）	Return on assets 資產利潤率 (%)	Return on equity 權益利潤率 (%)	Labour productivity ('000 RMB / worker) 勞動生產率（千元/人）	Debts / assets 資產負債率 (%)	Total assets (mil. RMB) 總資產（百萬元）
Industry Overall 行業總體	643	60,740	3,949	153	3.65	9.72	65.01	62.43	4,203

	Number of firms 企業個數	Average number of employees 平均職工人數	Average revenue ('000 RMB) 平均銷售收入（千元）	Average profit ('000 RMB) 平均利潤（千元）	Return on assets 資產利潤率 (%)	Return on equity 權益利潤率 (%)	Labour productivity ('000 RMB / worker) 勞動生產率（千元/人）	Average debts / assets 平均資產負債率(%)	Average Total assets ('000 RMB) 平均總資產（千元）
By ownership 產業所有權									
State-owned 國有	84	116	4,881	-12	-0.14	-0.41	42.06	65.73	8,512
Collectively-owned 集體	406	95	5,286	104	2.57	10.48	55.45	75.45	4,026
Privately-owned 私有	6	59	1,661	123	3.16	6.20	28.16	48.99	3,883
Domestic JVs 聯營	8	97	2,429	114	2.41	4.11	25.01	41.43	4,721
Joint stock 股份制	13	118	19,914	2,783	10.19	17.46	168.99	41.62	27,304
Foreign-funded 外資	73	75	9,145	1,218	9.24	17.77	121.60	47.97	13,172
Overseas Chinese-funded 港澳台資	51	86	8,480	-250	-2.72	-6.78	99.17	59.85	9,172
By size 規模									
Large 大型	3	945	94,028	17,954	16.97	37.87	99.47	55.18	105,770
Medium 中型	14	552	57,352	2,799	5.34	13.91	103.95	61.61	52,414
Small 小型	608	82	4,711	99	1.90	5.19	57.36	63.35	5,184
By regional distribution 地區分布									
Central-North 華北	123	56	2,648	53	1.31	4.16	47.54	68.60	4,030
Beijing 北京	52	28	1,387	-9	-0.32	-0.78	50.24	58.19	2,785
Tianjin 天津	38	67	3,731	41	0.78	3.50	55.32	77.56	5,233
Hebei 河北	22	80	4,005	283	5.76	15.89	49.84	63.78	4,920
Shanxi 山西	8	118	2,628	-90	-1.80	-7.00	22.27	74.20	4,986
Inner Mongolia 內蒙	3	47	897	-43	-3.33	-13.00	19.08	74.36	1,300
Northeast 東北	56	67	5,336	295	2.73	4.09	79.12	33.24	10,824
Liaoning 遼寧	24	64	3,788	-206	-2.24	-4.85	59.38	53.79	9,190
Jilin 吉林	18	80	1,733	12	0.45	1.31	21.76	65.57	2,592
Heilongjiang 黑龍江	14	58	12,623	1,519	6.27	7.42	217.64	15.43	24,209
Central East 華東	287	111	8,438	384	5.34	15.73	76.03	66.04	7,185
Shanghai 上海	55	79	11,479	1,468	13.14	28.28	145.00	53.53	11,171
Jiangsu 江蘇	101	124	10,526	65	0.98	4.30	84.77	77.24	6,627
Zhejiang 浙江	42	82	3,671	141	2.96	6.40	44.59	53.74	4,771
Anhui 安徽	13	112	5,345	386	9.78	53.63	47.73	81.77	3,950
Fujian 福建	17	50	1,881	229	6.09	11.24	37.39	45.82	3,766
Jiangxi 江西	27	85	3,916	-3	-0.10	-0.29	46.03	64.36	3,178
Shandong 山東	32	215	11,433	253	2.15	8.51	53.09	74.75	11,775
Central-South 中南	118	121	6,759	141	2.01	6.22	55.77	67.76	7,024
Henan 河南	47	99	2,301	44	1.32	4.47	23.14	70.57	3,361
Hubei 湖北	32	177	10,953	193	2.93	9.97	61.72	70.57	6,573
Hunan 湖南	10	188	7,484	40	0.72	2.32	39.89	68.89	5,532
Guangdong 廣東	23	80	11,195	364	2.13	6.14	140.16	65.28	17,090
Guangxi 廣西	6	39	1,108	-67	-3.30	-7.77	28.18	57.47	2,018
Hainan 海南									
Southwest 西南	32	63	2,158	-4	-0.09	-0.38	34.11	77.58	4,779
Chongqing 重慶	6	82	4,331	-1	-0.01	-0.05	52.76	72.90	10,339
Sichuan 四川	14	56	2,001	-1	-0.02	-0.15	36.01	88.16	4,720
Guizhou 貴州	7	80	1,963	-6	-0.21	-0.49	24.54	57.34	2,746
Yunnan 雲南	5	35	94	-14	-1.96	-10.94	2.66	82.07	714
Tibet 西藏									
Northwest 西北	27	72	1,337	143	6.71	22.65	18.67	70.36	2,130
Shaanxi 陝西	13	82	1,898	368	13.40	54.68	23.15	75.49	2,749
Gansu 甘肅	6	128	1,658	-158	-6.15	-30.84	12.96	79.99	2,573
Qinghai 青海									
Ningxia 寧夏	2	21	350	10	2.08	6.90	17.07	69.79	480
Xinjiang 新疆	6	10	127				13.10	8.74	897

3654: Medical Materials and Utilities 醫用材料及醫療用品製造業

Year 年份	Number of firms 企業個數	Rate of change 每年變化 (%)	Number of employees 職工人數 (人)	Rate of change 每年變化 (%)	Total revenue (mil. RMB) 總銷售收入 (百萬元)	Rate of change 每年變化 (%)	Total profit (mil. RMB) 總利潤 (百萬元)	Rate of change 每年變化 (%)
1993	489		55,451		1,961		87	
1994	545	11.45%	54,006	-2.61%	2,380	21.36%	97	11.79%
1995	664	21.83%	65,597	21.46%	3,674	54.34%	140	44.24%
1996	643	-3.16%	60,740	-7.40%	3,949	7.49%	153	9.47%

3 Major products* 3 種主要產品 *	Output 產量	Sales volume 銷售量	Unit 單位
a) White Sheeting 漂白布	9,313	8,848	10,000 metre 萬米

Top 10 firms by revenue (year founded) 收入排名前 10 家企業 (創辦年份)	City 城市	Province 省	Telephone / fax 電話 / 傳真	Number of employees 職工人數	Ownership 產業所有權	Revenue ('000 RMB) 銷售收入 (千元)	Profit ('000 RMB) (rank) 利潤 (千元) (排名)	Total assets ('000 RMB) 總資產 (千元)	Major products 主要產品
Industry & Trade Jointly Operated Wujiang Medical Treatment Health Care Articles Factory Health Car 工貿合營吳江醫療保健用品廠(1980)	Suzhou 蘇州市	Jiangsu 江蘇省	(0512)3242142	1,249	Collectively-owned 集體	308,441	2943(11)	65,037	o
Shanghai Johnson & Johnson Co. Ltd. 上海強生有限公司(1990)	Shanghai 上海市	Shanghai 上海市	(021)64302410 (021)64302579	232	Foreign-funded 外資	180,920	50231(1)	151,103	o
Shanghai Jinbaoshan Plastic Cement Enterprise Co. Ltd. 上海金寶山塑膠企業有限公司(1992)	Shanghai 上海市	Shanghai 上海市	(021)57814212 (021)57823386	715	Overseas Chinese-funded 港澳台資	170,155	13454(4)	105,657	o
Haci Co. Ltd. 哈爾濱哈慈集團股份有限公司(1987)	Harbin 哈爾濱市	Heilongjiang 黑龍江省	(0451)2688688 (0451)2686244	150	Joint stock 股份制	151,662	20728(2)	321,588	o
Zhuhai Sez Tian Nian High Science & Technology International Enterprise Company 珠海經濟特區天年高科技國際企業公司(1992)	Zhuhai 珠海市	Guangdong 廣東省	(0756)8888755 (0756)8888756	762	Collectively-owned 集體	127,436	15340(3)	111,921	o
Weihai Medical Polymer Products General Factory of Shandon Provinc 山東省威海醫用高分子製品總廠(1988)	Weihai 威海市	Shandong 山東省	(0896)5622517 (0896)5622563	2,585	Collectively-owned 集體	122,136	1500(23)	100,755	o
Yancheng Fu Hua Sanitary Material Co. Ltd. 鹽城阜華衛生材料有限公司(1992)	Yancheng 鹽城市	Jiangsu 江蘇省	(0515)7451168	234	Foreign-funded 外資	75,120	-400(233)	28,100	o
Nanjing San Zhu Medical Apparatus & Instruments Co. Ltd. 南京三株醫療器械有限責任公司(1996)	Nanjing 南京市	Jiangsu 江蘇省	(025)6606560	245	其他經濟	65,103	628(49)	19,911	o
Qingdao Ze Qing Industrial Co. Ltd. 青島澤青實業有限公司(1989)	Qingdao 青島市	Shandong 山東省	(0532)8182306 (0532)8182121	644	Overseas Chinese-funded 港澳台資	64,010	1410(25)	71,553	a
Tianjin Ha Na Hao Medical Material Co. Ltd. 天津哈娜好醫材有限公司(1987)	Tianjin 天津市	Tianjin 天津市	(022)25328729 (022)25328913	565	Foreign-funded 外資	59,085	0(178)	74,284	o

Top 10 Cities by Production Output 產出排名前 10 位城市	Province 省	Market share 市場份額	Number of firms 企業個數
Shanghai 上海市	Shanghai 上海市	13.87%	79
Suzhou 蘇州市	Jiangsu 江蘇省	10.69%	40
Beijing 北京市	Beijing 北京市	10.55%	38
Harbin 哈爾濱市	Heilongjiang 黑龍江省	4.72%	15
Xianning 咸寧市	Hubei 湖北省	4.45%	7
Taizhou 泰州市	Jiangsu 江蘇省	3.86%	23
Changzhou 常州市	Jiangsu 江蘇省	3.49%	37
Guangzhou 廣州市	Guangdong 廣東省	3.19%	16
Zhuhai 珠海市	Guangdong 廣東省	3.16%	4
Tianjin 天津市	Tianjin 天津市	2.96%	38

10 Major Wholesalers 10 家主要批發商	City 城市	Province 省	Telephone / Fax 電話 / 傳真
China Medicine Shanghai Purchase Supply Station 中國醫藥上海採購供應站	Shanghai 上海市	Shanghai 上海市	(021)63211750
Anhui Medical Health Care Product Import & Export Co. Ltd. 安徽省醫藥保健品進出口股份有限公司	Hefei 合肥市	Anhui 安徽省	(0551)3632603 (0551)3631975
Hai Tong Science Apparatus Co. Ltd. 海通科學儀器有限公司	Shanghai 上海市	Shanghai 上海市	(021)64397740 (021)64395300
Nantong Medicine Co. Ltd. 南通醫藥股份有限公司	Nantong 南通市	Jiangsu 江蘇省	(0513)5513093 (0513)5527814
Jiangxi Medical Health Care Product Import & Export Company 江西省醫藥保健品進出口公司	Nanchang 南昌市	Jiangxi 江西省	(0791)6222337 (0791)6217072
Shandong Machinery Industry Trade General Company 山東省機械工業貿易總公司	Ji'nan 濟南市	Shandong 山東省	(0531)6948991
Science & Education Technology Import & Export Company 科教技術進出口公司	Shanghai 上海市	Shanghai 上海市	(021)62564308 (021)62563108
Medical Apparatus & Instruments Wholesale Dept. 醫療器械批發部	Shanghai 上海市	Shanghai 上海市	(021)63216704 (021)63219814
Sichuan Livestock Raising College Medical Equipment Marketing Dept. 四川畜牧學院藥械經營部	Chongqing 重慶市	Chongqing 重慶市	(023)46733820
Shandou Scientific Equipment General Company 汕頭市科學器材總公司	Shantou 汕頭市	Guangdong 廣東省	(0754)8625957 (0754)8250513

*Also include sales by firms outside this industry.包括本行業以外廠家的銷售。"o" stands for "others". "o" 代表 "其他產品" 。

3655: Artificial Limb, Orthopaedic Equipment 假肢、矯形器製造業

The industry accounts for 0.002% of the total revenue of China's industrial sector in 1996. The revenue growth rate of the industry is -34.2% from 1995, as compared to the growth rate of China's industrial sector, 9.51%. The rate of return on asset is 5.20%. 88.64% of all firms in the industry made a profit while 11.36% had negative returns. The top province in terms of the industry's revenue is Shanghai, accounting for 28.31% of the total revenue.
本行業在1996年佔全行業總產值0.002%，行業年增長率為-34.2%（全國工業年增長率9.51%）。行業的資產回報率5.20%，88.64%的企業盈利，11.36%的企業虧損。銷售收入最高的省份為上海市，佔本行業的28.31%。

	Total number of firms 企業總數	Total number of employees 職工總數	Total revenue (mil. RMB) 總銷售收入（百萬元）	Total profit (mil. RMB) 總利潤（百萬元）	Return on assets 資產利潤率 (%)	Return on equity 權益利潤率 (%)	Labour productivity ('000 RMB / worker) 勞動生產率（千元/人）	Debts / assets 資產負債率 (%)	Total assets (mil. RMB) 總資產（百萬元）
Industry Overall 行業總體	46	2,718	107	11	5.20	7.63	39.37	31.82	220

	Number of firms 企業個數	Average number of employees 平均職工人數	Average revenue ('000 RMB) 平均銷售收入（千元）	Average profit ('000 RMB) 平均利潤（千元）	Return on assets 資產利潤率 (%)	Return on equity 權益利潤率 (%)	Labour productivity ('000 RMB / worker) 勞動生產率（千元/人）	Average debts / assets 平均資產負債率(%)	Average Total assets ('000 RMB) 平均總資產（千元）
By ownership 產業所有權									
State-owned 國有	26	86	3,154	385	5.52	7.87	36.53	29.83	6,962
Collectively-owned 集體	13	29	1,175	91	7.42	16.72	40.63	55.63	1,223
Privately-owned 私有									
Domestic JVs 聯營									
Joint stock 股份制	1	1							
Foreign-funded 外資	2	17	673	86	3.25	4.30	40.80	24.37	2,659
Overseas Chinese-funded 港澳台資	4	19	2,093	-88	-1.98	-2.95	113.12	32.94	4,443
By size 規模									
Large 大型									
Medium 中型									
Small 小型	44	63	2,431	250	5.00	7.33	38.80	31.82	5,000
By regional distribution 地區分布									
Central-North 華北	10	25	566	36	2.29	3.36	22.28	31.89	1,571
Beijing 北京	5	20	322	-6	-0.37	-0.58	15.94	35.78	1,610
Tianjin 天津	1	8	1,510	120	8.63	11.76	188.75	26.62	1,390
Hebei 河北	1	16	60	30	5.88	5.88	3.75		510
Shanxi 山西	1	107	2,370	190	3.58	5.16	22.15	30.89	5,310
Inner Mongolia 內蒙	2	11	55	25	11.11	15.63	5.00	26.67	225
Northeast 東北	10	36	1,026	2	0.10	0.14	28.34	29.53	2,015
Liaoning 遼寧	3	10	1,273	33	5.49	13.51	127.33	59.34	607
Jilin 吉林	2	63	1,315	-15	-0.42	-0.56	21.04	25.52	3,605
Heilongjiang 黑龍江	5	41	762	-10	-0.45	-0.62	18.41	27.25	2,224
Central East 華東	14	73	3,100	436	7.86	10.59	42.55	25.87	5,556
Shanghai 上海	4	88	7,573	1,195	17.77	24.04	86.54	26.13	6,725
Jiangsu 江蘇	3	86	867	100	1.44	1.97	10.08	27.01	6,960
Zhejiang 浙江	1	12	140	-10	-1.56	-3.85	11.67	59.38	640
Anhui 安徽	1	12						100.00	40
Fujian 福建	1								
Jiangxi 江西	1	45	1,460	170	3.10	6.27	32.44	50.64	5,490
Shandong 山東	3	114	2,970	290	3.65	4.44	25.98	17.83	7,943
Central-South 中南	7	81	4,971	491	5.89	10.86	61.27	45.75	8,343
Henan 河南	1	112	4,870	-250	-2.37	-7.60	43.48	68.66	10,530
Hubei 湖北	2	125	5,320	225	3.64	6.25	42.56	41.75	6,180
Hunan 湖南	1	8	1,830	220	5.61	5.66	228.75	0.77	3,920
Guangdong 廣東	2	68	7,495	1,345	9.97	17.55	110.22	43.16	13,485
Guangxi 廣西	1	62	2,470	330	7.14	16.84	39.84	57.58	4,620
Hainan 海南									
Southwest 西南	4	97	2,278	405	7.20	10.84	23.42	33.48	5,623
Chongqing 重慶									
Sichuan 四川	1	144	6,410	1,020	8.78	13.06	44.51	32.79	11,620
Guizhou 貴州	2	73	715	-20	-0.65	-1.14	9.86	43.20	3,090
Yunnan 雲南	1	100	1,270	640	13.65	17.63	12.70	22.39	4,690
Tibet 西藏									
Northwest 西北	1	125	4,090	-80	-0.31	-0.38	32.72	18.51	25,720
Shaanxi 陝西	1	125	4,090	-80	-0.31	-0.38	32.72	18.51	25,720
Gansu 甘肅									
Qinghai 青海									
Ningxia 寧夏									
Xinjiang 新疆									

3655: Artificial Limb, Orthopaedic Equipment 假肢、矯形器製造業

Year 年份	Number of firms 企業個數	Rate of change 每年變化 (%)	Number of employees 職工人數 (人)	Rate of change 每年變化 (%)	Total revenue (mil. RMB) 總銷售收入 (百萬元)	Rate of change 每年變化 (%)	Total profit (mil. RMB) 總利潤 (百萬元)	Rate of change 每年變化 (%)
1993	38		4,028		174		-16	
1994	44	15.79%	5,811	44.27%	216	23.79%	12	176.18%
1995	57	29.55%	4,195	-27.81%	163	-24.52%	7	-38.22%
1996	46	-19.30%	2,718	-35.21%	107	-34.25%	11	49.36%

3 Major products* 3 種主要產品 *	Output 產量	Sales volume 銷售量	Unit 單位
a) Leather Shoes 皮鞋	0.2	0.2	10,000 pair 萬雙

Top 10 firms by revenue (year founded) 收入排名前 10 家企業 (創辦年份)	City 城市	Province 省	Telephone / fax 電話 / 傳真	Number of employees 職工人數	Ownership 產業所有權	Revenue ('000 RMB) 銷售收入 (千元)	Profit ('000 RMB) (rank) 利潤 (千元) (排名)	Total assets ('000 RMB) 總資產 (千元)	Major products 主要產品
Shanghai Artificial Limb Factory 上海假肢廠(1965)	Shanghai 上海市	Shanghai 上海市	(021)62530774 (021)62534972	225	State-owned 國有	23,828	4728(1)	24,324	a
Guangdong Artificial Limb Factory 廣東省假肢廠(1955)	Guangzhou 廣州市	Guangdong 廣東省	(020)84190723 (020)84188592	103	State-owned 國有	8,209	1819(2)	16,113	o
Shandong Artificial Limb Gong Factory 山東省假肢工廠(1950)	Ji'nan 濟南市	Shandong 山東省	(0531)8933584 (0531)8933584	173	State-owned 國有	7,357	791(5)	16,307	o
The Lin Prosthetic & Orthopaedic (Shen Zhen) Ltd. 德林義肢矯型康復器材(深圳)有限公司(1993)	Shenzhen 深圳市	Guangdong 廣東省	(0755)5508963 (0755)5509494	33	Overseas Chinese-funded 港澳台資	6,779	871(4)	10,861	o
Sichuan Artificial Limb Factory 四川省假肢廠(1952)	Chengdu 成都市	Sichuan 四川省	(028)5553232 (028)5589830	144	State-owned 國有	6,409	1022(3)	11,617	o
Shanghai Ting Lin Chemical Plant 上海亭林化工廠(1970)	Shanghai 上海市	Shanghai 上海市	(021)57233743	85	Collectively-owned 集體	5,694	50(13)	2,122	o
Hubei Artificial Limb Factory 湖北省假肢廠(1951)	Wuhan 武漢市	Hubei 湖北省	(027)87642990 (027)87802492	236	State-owned 國有	5,464	320(7)	12,122	a
Ma City Cheng Ma Gang Xiang Pottery Factory 麻城市乘馬崗鄉陶器廠	Huanggang 黃岡市	Hubei 湖北省		10	Collectively-owned 集體	5,174	132(10)	239	o
Shannxi Artificial Limb Center 陝西省假肢中心(1951)	Xi'an 西安市	Shaanxi 陝西省	(029)3247325 (029)3237805	125	State-owned 國有	4,086	-80(15)	25,724	o
Shenyang Jia Xin Artificial Limb Recovered Instrument Co. Ltd. 瀋陽佳新假肢康復儀器有限公司(1995)	Shenyang 瀋陽市	Liaoning 遼寧省	(024)22854610	11	Overseas Chinese-funded 港澳台資	3,537	96(12)	1,298	o

Top 10 Cities by Production Output 產出排名前 10 位城市	Province 省	Market share 市場份額	Number of firms 企業個數
Shanghai 上海市	Shanghai 上海市	26.14%	8
Suzhou 蘇州市	Jiangsu 江蘇省	10.23%	1
Guangzhou 廣州市	Guangdong 廣東省	7.70%	1
Wuhan 武漢市	Hubei 湖北省	4.55%	1
Chengdu 成都市	Sichuan 四川省	4.55%	1
Nanjing 南京市	Jiangsu 江蘇省	3.83%	2
Liaocheng 聊城市	Shandong 山東省	3.70%	1
Zhengzhou 鄭州市	Henan 河南省	3.63%	1
Xi'an 西安市	Shaanxi 陝西省	3.62%	2
Shenyang 瀋陽市	Liaoning 遼寧省	3.39%	4

10 Major Wholesalers 10 家主要批發商	City 城市	Province 省	Telephone / Fax 電話 / 傳真
China Medicine Shanghai Purchase Supply Station 中國醫藥上海採購供應站	Shanghai 上海市	Shanghai 上海市	(021)63211750
Anhui Medical Health Care Product Import & Export Co. Ltd. 安徽省醫藥保健品進出口股份有限公司	Hefei 合肥市	Anhui 安徽省	(0551)3632603 (0551)3631975
Hai Tong Science Apparatus Co. Ltd. 海通科學儀器有限公司	Shanghai 上海市	Shanghai 上海市	(021)64397740 (021)64395300
Nantong Medicine Co. Ltd. 南通醫藥股份有限公司	Nantong 南通市	Jiangsu 江蘇省	(0513)5513093 (0513)5527814
Jiangxi Medical Health Care Product Import & Export Company 江西省醫藥保健品進出口公司	Nanchang 南昌市	Jiangxi 江西省	(0791)6222337 (0791)6217072
Shandong Machinery Industry Trade General Company 山東省機械工業貿易總公司	Ji'nan 濟南市	Shandong 山東省	(0531)6948991
Science & Education Technology Import & Export Company 科教技術進出口公司	Shanghai 上海市	Shanghai 上海市	(021)62564308 (021)62563108
Medical Apparatus & Instruments Wholesale Dept. 醫療器械批發部	Shanghai 上海市	Shanghai 上海市	(021)63216704 (021)63219814
Sichuan Livestock Raising College Medical Equipment Marketing Dept. 四川畜牧學院藥械經營部	Chongqing 重慶市	Chongqing 重慶市	(023)46733820
Shandou Scientific Equipment General Company 汕頭市科學器材總公司	Shantou 汕頭市	Guangdong 廣東省	(0754)8625957 (0754)8250513

*Also include sales by firms outside this industry.包括本行業以外廠家的銷售。"o" stands for "others". "o" 代表 "其他產品"。

3671: Construction Machinery 建築機械製造業

The industry accounts for 0.171% of the total revenue of China's industrial sector in 1996. The revenue growth rate of the industry is -4.8% from 1995, as compared to the growth rate of China's industrial sector, 9.51%. The rate of return on asset is 0.13%. 66.36% of all firms in the industry made a profit while 31.37% had negative returns. The top province in terms of the industry's revenue is Shandong, accounting for 20.58% of the total revenue.
本行業在1996年佔全行業總產值0.171%，行業年增長率為-4.8%（全國工業年增長率9.51%）。行業的資產回報率0.13%，66.36%的企業盈利，31.37%的企業虧損。銷售收入最高的省份為山東省，佔本行業的20.58%。

	Total number of firms 企業總數	Total number of employees 職工總數	Total revenue (mil. RMB) 總銷售收入（百萬元）	Total profit (mil. RMB) 總利潤（百萬元）	Return on assets 資產利潤率 (%)	Return on equity 權益利潤率 (%)	Labour productivity ('000 RMB / worker) 勞動生產率（千元/人）	Debts / assets 資產負債率 (%)	Total assets (mil. RMB) 總資產（百萬元）
Industry Overall 行業總體	570	184,769	9,914	28	0.13	0.35	53.66	64.17	21,966

	Number of firms 企業個數	Average number of employees 平均職工人數	Average revenue ('000 RMB) 平均銷售收入（千元）	Average profit ('000 RMB) 平均利潤（千元）	Return on assets 資產利潤率 (%)	Return on equity 權益利潤率 (%)	Labour productivity ('000 RMB / worker) 勞動生產率（千元/人）	Average debts / assets 平均資產負債率(%)	Average Total assets ('000 RMB) 平均總資產（千元）
By ownership 產業所有權									
State-owned 國有	153	792	35,072	-758	-0.90	-3.01	44.26	69.91	83,810
Collectively-owned 集體	369	111	6,616	146	1.33	4.66	59.45	71.52	11,016
Privately-owned 私有	3	136	11,626	47	0.12	0.47	85.70	74.91	39,814
Domestic JVs 聯營	6	148	12,414	254	1.38	5.22	83.69	73.52	18,376
Joint stock 股份制	10	1,303	144,727	7,691	2.21	3.91	111.11	43.61	348,445
Foreign-funded 外資	9	506	33,643	548	0.56	0.75	66.44	25.40	97,853
Overseas Chinese-funded 港澳台資	19	228	13,051	342	1.34	3.77	57.28	64.41	25,503
By size 規模									
Large 大型	28	2,940	179,783	638	0.13	0.38	61.15	64.35	473,729
Medium 中型	39	940	47,457	161	0.17	0.55	50.50	69.47	95,566
Small 小型	499	132	6,072	8	0.08	0.19	45.93	59.74	9,970
By regional distribution 地區分布									
Central-North 華北	64	321	12,424	37	0.12	0.35	38.65	65.38	30,513
Beijing 北京	16	199	9,678	376	1.16	2.92	48.59	60.40	32,479
Tianjin 天津	16	470	16,868	-463	-1.12	-3.25	35.90	65.51	41,272
Hebei 河北	15	460	21,893	557	1.32	4.19	47.59	68.47	42,190
Shanxi 山西	12	164	2,283	-258	-3.64	-14.39	13.96	74.71	7,097
Inner Mongolia 內蒙	5	201	2,924	-300	-2.74	-6.98	14.56	60.80	10,960
Northeast 東北	72	401	8,852	-741	-1.70	-5.58	22.06	69.51	43,523
Liaoning 遼寧	58	445	9,901	-856	-1.68	-5.35	22.24	68.55	50,912
Jilin 吉林	4	527	9,925	-1,158	-3.17	-20.34	18.84	84.41	36,508
Heilongjiang 黑龍江	10	96	2,339	94	2.71	23.62	24.34	88.57	3,474
Central East 華東	213	315	26,199	629	1.30	3.31	83.07	60.65	48,296
Shanghai 上海	20	491	30,864	-2,029	-2.97	-8.78	62.80	66.18	68,301
Jiangsu 江蘇	60	251	22,750	457	1.62	4.26	90.61	62.03	28,262
Zhejiang 浙江	43	79	4,277	-122	-1.99	-6.98	54.29	71.46	6,121
Anhui 安徽	10	418	27,612	-2,862	-3.27	-7.37	66.03	55.61	87,424
Fujian 福建	22	339	35,102	3,160	4.60	6.80	103.53	32.34	68,627
Jiangxi 江西	11	826	29,576	1,901	2.23	5.78	35.81	61.33	85,126
Shandong 山東	47	387	43,415	1,927	2.49	8.27	112.29	69.92	77,483
Central-South 中南	131	230	10,604	-47	-0.23	-0.54	46.03	58.53	20,952
Henan 河南	48	188	10,181	485	3.46	11.21	54.11	69.14	14,009
Hubei 湖北	19	256	7,593	-315	-2.85	-7.73	29.69	63.08	11,047
Hunan 湖南	21	415	16,610	-1,181	-2.96	-4.68	40.05	36.75	39,868
Guangdong 廣東	29	181	8,265	-352	-1.57	-5.76	45.69	72.76	22,450
Guangxi 廣西	14	167	11,980	824	3.08	7.89	71.80	60.89	26,721
Hainan 海南									
Southwest 西南	56	373	15,293	-187	-0.57	-1.89	40.95	69.76	32,763
Chongqing 重慶	10	67	2,179	-42	-1.71	-10.24	32.56	83.29	2,461
Sichuan 四川	31	369	19,139	270	0.74	2.85	51.88	74.00	36,435
Guizhou 貴州	9	702	17,308	12	0.02	0.05	24.67	57.63	59,108
Yunnan 雲南	6	403	13,585	-423	-1.81	-8.63	33.72	79.06	23,427
Tibet 西藏									
Northwest 西北	34	501	19,294	-1,142	-1.93	-7.80	38.50	75.28	59,206
Shaanxi 陝西	24	450	20,397	-168	-0.29	-1.09	45.28	73.54	58,548
Gansu 甘肅	5	305	7,164	-766	-3.83	-9.49	23.46	59.61	19,992
Qinghai 青海	1	2,530	90,460	-23,480	-5.89	-48.99	35.75	87.97	398,340
Ningxia 寧夏	1	507	5,520	-1,920	-6.27	-45.28	10.89	86.14	30,600
Xinjiang 新疆	3	554	11,557	-1,850	-7.03	-16.61	20.86	57.67	26,310

3671: Construction Machinery 建築機械製造業

Year 年份	Number of firms 企業個數	Rate of change 每年變化 (%)	Number of employees 職工人數 (人)	Rate of change 每年變化 (%)	Total revenue (mil. RMB) 總銷售收入 (百萬元)	Rate of change 每年變化 (%)	Total profit (mil. RMB) 總利潤 (百萬元)	Rate of change 每年變化 (%)
1993	561		261,663		12,327		706	
1994	576	2.67%	219,723	-16.03%	12,726	3.24%	466	-33.99%
1995	569	-1.22%	206,643	-5.95%	10,409	-18.21%	297	-36.32%
1996	570	0.18%	184,769	-10.59%	9,914	-4.76%	28	-90.57%

3 Major products* 3 種主要產品 *	Output 產量	Sales volume 銷售量	Unit 單位
a) Concrete Machinery 混凝土機械	152,020	135,298	set 台
b) Scraping & Conveying Machinery 鏟土運輸機械	28,227	25,969	set 台
c) Loading Machine 裝載機	9,734	9,345	set 台

Top 10 firms by revenue (year founded) 收入排名前 10 家企業 (創辦年份)	City 城市	Province 省	Telephone / fax 電話 / 傳真	Number of employees 職工人數	Ownership 產業所有權	Revenue ('000 RMB) 銷售收入 (千元)	Profit ('000 RMB) (rank) 利潤 (千元) (排名)	Total assets ('000 RMB) 總資產 (千元)	Major products 主要產品
Xiamen Engineering Machinery Co. Ltd. 廈門工程機械股份有限公司(1951)	Xiamen 廈門市	Fujian 福建省	(0592)2031755 (0592)2036720	2,450	Joint stock 股份制	586,799	65799(1)	1,076,978	c
Shandong Shan Tui Engineering Machinery Co. Ltd. 山東山推工程機械股份有限公司(1993)	Jining 濟寧市	Shandong 山東省	(0537)2314636 (0537)2315986	4,684	State-owned 國有	419,365	5218(13)	967,758	b
Jin Hou Machinery Group 金猴機械集團(1958)	Zhenjiang 鎮江市	Jiangsu 江蘇省	(0511)7223151 (0511)7223151	1,897	State-owned 國有	417,509	465(75)	220,082	a,b
Chang Lin Co. Ltd. 常林股份有限公司(1958)	Changzhou 常州市	Jiangsu 江蘇省	(0519)6753621 (0519)6750025	1,440	Joint stock 股份制	325,612	36076(3)	632,300	b,c
Chengdu Engineering Machinery Plant 成都工程機械總廠(1950)	Chengdu 成都市	Sichuan 四川省	(028)4443685 (028)4443914	3,120	State-owned 國有	312,727	212(116)	506,193	b
Hebei Xuanhua Engineering Machinery Plant 河北省宣化工程機械廠(1950)	Zhangjiakou 張家口市	Hebei 河北省	(0313)3012255 (0313)3013941	4,369	State-owned 國有	265,450	6186(11)	529,408	b,c
Shandong Engineering Machinery Factory 山東工程機械廠(1958)	Weifang 濰坊市	Shandong 山東省	(0536)3818394 (0536)3818628	1,489	State-owned 國有	250,598	20380(5)	322,740	b
Peng Pu Machine Factory 彭浦機器廠(1925)	Shanghai 上海市	Shanghai 上海市	(021)56650933 (021)56652286	3,269	State-owned 國有	229,885	-19987(304)	471,578	b,c
Shan Dongfang Yuan Group Company 山東方圓集團公司(1970)	Yantai 煙臺市	Shandong 山東省	(0535)3221111 (0535)3221660	1,388	Collectively-owned 集體	205,008	36679(2)	335,074	a
Yellow River Engineering Machinery Factory 黃河工程機械廠(1972)	Weinan 渭南市	Shaanxi 陝西省	(0913)4611228 (0913)4611235	3,244	State-owned 國有	203,113	2114(25)	518,771	o

Top 10 Cities by Production Output 產出排名前 10 位城市	Province 省	Market share 市場份額	Number of firms 企業個數
Xuzhou 徐州市	Jiangsu 江蘇省	13.25%	8
Shanghai 上海市	Shanghai 上海市	6.98%	36
Jining 濟寧市	Shandong 山東省	4.84%	9
Chengdu 成都市	Sichuan 四川省	4.49%	12
Luoyang 洛陽市	Henan 河南省	4.09%	6
Yantai 煙臺市	Shandong 山東省	3.52%	8
Changzhou 常州市	Jiangsu 江蘇省	3.46%	16
Anshan 鞍山市	Liaoning 遼寧省	3.09%	7
Zhengzhou 鄭州市	Henan 河南省	2.65%	15
Zhangjiakou 張家口市	Hebei 河北省	2.60%	2

10 Major Wholesalers 10 家主要批發商	City 城市	Province 省	Telephone / Fax 電話 / 傳真
Liaoning Automobile Trade Group Corp. 遼寧省汽車貿易集團	Shenyang 瀋陽市	Liaoning 遼寧省	(024)23835494 (024)23838338
China Post and Telecommunication Equipment General Company 中國郵電器材總公司	Beijing 北京市	Beijing 北京市	(010)63523715 (010)63525935
Jiangsu Electromechanical Products General Company 江蘇省機電產品總公司	Nanjing 南京市	Jiangsu 江蘇省	(025)7713642 (025)7711036
Xi Nan Technology Import & Export Company 西南技術進出口公司	Chongqing 重慶市	Chongqing 重慶市	(023)63850185 (023)63850026
Changzhou Economic Technology Industrial Development Zone Tian Ming Trade Company 常州經濟技術產業開發區天明貿易公司	Changzhou 常州市	Jiangsu 江蘇省	(0519)8829882 (0519)8829882
Shanxi Mechanical Equipment Import & Export Company 山西省機械設備進出口公司	Taiyuan 太原市	Shanxi 山西省	(0351)4040713 (0351)4043981
Ningbo Five Mining Machinery Import & Export Company 寧波市五礦機械進出口公司	Ningbo 寧波市	Zhejiang 浙江省	(0574)7311255 (0574)7320322
Tianjin Jin Huan Electromechanical Complete Sets of Equipment Factory 天津市津環機電成套設備廠	Tianjin 天津市	Tianjin 天津市	(022)26371628
Yunnan Machinery Import & Export Company 雲南省機械進出口公司	Kunming 昆明市	Yunnan 雲南省	(0871)3164879 (0871)3136829
Tianjin Da Qiu Zhuang Yi Yuan Trade Center 天津市大丘莊億源商貿中心	Tianjin 天津市	Tianjin 天津市	(022)28899478 (022)28899046

*Also include sales by firms outside this industry.包括本行業以外廠家的銷售。"o" stands for "others". "o" 代表 "其他產品"。

3672: Geology Equipment 地質專用設備製造業

The industry accounts for 0.012% of the total revenue of China's industrial sector in 1996. The revenue growth rate of the industry is -5.5% from 1995, as compared to the growth rate of China's industrial sector, 9.51%. The rate of return on asset is -4.49%. 33.29% of all firms in the industry made a profit while 59.21% had negative returns. The top province in terms of the industry's revenue is Hebei, accounting for 28.29% of the total revenue.
本行業在1996年佔全行業總產值0.012%，行業年增長率為-5.5%（全國工業年增長率9.51%）。行業的資產回報率-4.49%，33.29%的企業盈利，59.21%的企業虧損。銷售收入最高的省份為河北省，佔本行業的28.29%。

	Total number of firms 企業總數	Total number of employees 職工總數	Total revenue (mil. RMB) 總銷售收入（百萬元）	Total profit (mil. RMB) 總利潤（百萬元）	Return on assets 資產利潤率 (%)	Return on equity 權益利潤率 (%)	Labour productivity ('000 RMB / worker) 勞動生產率（千元/人）	Debts / assets 資產負債率 (%)	Total assets (mil. RMB) 總資產（百萬元）
Industry Overall 行業總體	91	27,086	673	-81	-4.49	-14.31	24.85	68.61	1,805

	Number of firms 企業個數	Average number of employees 平均職工人數	Average revenue ('000 RMB) 平均銷售收入（千元）	Average profit ('000 RMB) 平均利潤（千元）	Return on assets 資產利潤率 (%)	Return on equity 權益利潤率 (%)	Labour productivity ('000 RMB / worker) 勞動生產率（千元/人）	Average debts / assets 平均資產負債率(%)	Average Total assets ('000 RMB) 平均總資產（千元）
By ownership 產業所有權									
State-owned 國有	49	488	9,796	-1,633	-5.19	-16.06	20.08	67.66	31,429
Collectively-owned 集體	41	77	4,634	-25	-0.40	-1.70	60.43	76.44	6,239
Privately-owned 私有									
Domestic JVs 聯營									
Joint stock 股份制									
Foreign-funded 外資	1	36	2,958	22	0.22	0.25	82.16	9.52	10,008
Overseas Chinese-funded 港澳台資									
By size 規模									
Large 大型	2	3,438	78,854	-21,678	-7.46	-36.95	22.94	79.82	290,654
Medium 中型	9	870	12,438	-3,589	-6.15	-15.51	14.29	60.31	58,312
Small 小型	79	157	5,105	-68	-0.76	-2.21	32.61	65.46	8,854
By regional distribution 地區分布									
Central-North 華北	16	611	14,059	-2,710	-6.58	-28.00	23.00	76.48	41,163
Beijing 北京	5	105	2,878	260	5.19	12.62	27.31	58.95	5,014
Tianjin 天津	2	342	8,535	-1,115	-3.92	-16.04	24.99	75.56	28,440
Hebei 河北	7	1,151	27,196	-6,029	-7.61	-36.67	23.62	79.24	79,176
Shanxi 山西	1	294	2,140	-160	-1.07	-1.43	7.28	25.63	15,020
Inner Mongolia 內蒙	1	217	970	-70	-0.95	-1.58	4.47	40.14	7,400
Northeast 東北	14	167	2,354	-836	-8.10	-28.59	14.07	71.68	10,329
Liaoning 遼寧	6	204	2,913	-1,518	-10.55	-56.48	14.30	81.32	14,397
Jilin 吉林	5	160	2,304	-274	-3.48	-7.48	14.40	53.57	7,882
Heilongjiang 黑龍江	3	107	1,320	-410	-6.54	-18.87	12.38	65.36	6,273
Central East 華東	30	220	7,027	-324	-1.99	-5.45	31.93	63.51	16,270
Shanghai 上海	3	17	613	40	5.17	12.77	36.80	59.48	773
Jiangsu 江蘇	14	283	6,098	-771	-3.35	-9.47	21.54	64.64	23,016
Zhejiang 浙江	6	105	3,467	98	1.39	2.66	33.17	47.83	7,092
Anhui 安徽	2	240	2,410	-155	-1.46	-5.24	10.06	72.19	10,645
Fujian 福建	1	240	1,660	60	0.57	1.24	6.92	54.09	10,520
Jiangxi 江西									
Shandong 山東	4	311	24,078	155	0.70	2.05	77.54	66.08	22,295
Central-South 中南	15	299	6,124	-971	-6.72	-17.00	20.50	60.48	14,457
Henan 河南	3	121	2,550	-50	-1.20	-3.79	21.13	68.34	4,180
Hubei 湖北	5	202	8,362	226	1.57	2.55	41.48	38.47	14,390
Hunan 湖南	5	544	4,726	-3,152	-15.34	-61.47	8.69	75.04	20,542
Guangdong 廣東	2	195	9,385	105	0.71	1.78	48.13	60.17	14,825
Guangxi 廣西									
Hainan 海南									
Southwest 西南	11	267	8,931	-45	-0.24	-0.60	33.43	59.09	18,662
Chongqing 重慶	1	1,072	32,496	5	0.01	0.01	30.32	54.30	87,402
Sichuan 四川	5	105	7,386	24	0.33	1.06	70.62	69.33	7,310
Guizhou 貴州	2	162	2,510				15.54	46.37	7,915
Yunnan 雲南	3	277	6,257	-207	-1.25	-3.69	22.61	66.03	16,493
Tibet 西藏									
Northwest 西北	5	189	2,776	-248	-1.35	-5.38	14.69	74.87	18,324
Shaanxi 陝西	1	404	6,800	820	1.40	9.02	16.83	84.47	58,520
Gansu 甘肅	2	145	2,660	-685	-7.05	-21.41	18.34	67.08	9,720
Qinghai 青海	1	167	980	-520	-6.40	-10.70	5.87	40.15	8,120
Ningxia 寧夏	1	84	780	-170	-3.07	-6.34	9.29	51.81	5,540
Xinjiang 新疆									

3672: Geology Equipment 地質專用設備製造業

Year 年份	Number of firms 企業個數	Rate of change 每年變化 (%)	Number of employees 職工人數 (人)	Rate of change 每年變化 (%)	Total revenue (mil. RMB) 總銷售收入 (百萬元)	Rate of change 每年變化 (%)	Total profit (mil. RMB) 總利潤 (百萬元)	Rate of change 每年變化 (%)
1993	67		35,997		1,230		83	
1994	71	5.97%	31,182	-13.38%	1,264	2.77%	53	-36.33%
1995	84	18.31%	27,921	-10.46%	712	-43.67%	-93	-274.54%
1996	91	8.33%	27,086	-2.99%	673	-5.50%	-81	12.69%

3 Major products* 3 種主要產品 *	Output 產量	Sales volume 銷售量	Unit 單位
a) Geological Drilling Rig 地質鑽機	488	444	set 台
b) Compacting Press 壓實機械	698	740	set 台
c) Refitted Vehicle 改裝汽車	2,240	2,800	vehicle 輛

Top 10 firms by revenue (year founded) 收入排名前 10 家企業 (創辦年份)	City 城市	Province 省	Telephone / fax 電話 / 傳真	Number of employees 職工人數	Ownership 產業所有權	Revenue ('000 RMB) 銷售收入 (千元)	Profit ('000 RMB) (rank) 利潤 (千元) (排名)	Total assets ('000 RMB) 總資產 (千元)	Major products 主要產品
Shijiazhuang Coal Mining Machinery Factory 石家莊煤礦機械廠(1940)	Shijiazhuang 石家莊市	Hebei 河北省	(0311)5052996 (0311)5052437	2,780	State-owned 國有	87,380	-12860(38)	222,510	c
Ministry of Geology & Mineral Resource Zhangjiakou Prospect Machinery General Factory 地質礦產部張家口探礦機械總廠(1953)	Zhangjiakou 張家口市	Hebei 河北省	(0313)4080494 (0313)2017644	4,199	State-owned 國有	86,685	-28381(40)	284,639	a,c
Ren Urban Li Ying Zhen Building Equipment Factory 任城區李營鎮建築設備廠(1966)	Jining 濟寧市	Shandong 山東省	(0537)2301937 (0537)2301937	353	Collectively-owned 集體	61,780	2790(1)	33,690	o
Hong Gang Erection Work Company 洪鋼安裝工程公司	Chengdu 成都市	Sichuan 四川省	(028)4638165	141	Collectively-owned 集體	43,049	262(6)	51,115	o
The Ministry of Railways Wuhan Engineering Machinery Research Institute 鐵道部武漢工程機械研究所(1923)	Wuhan 武漢市	Hubei 湖北省	(027)86811280 (027)86853150	298	State-owned 國有	30,590	2310(2)	41,224	b
Ministry of Geology & Mineral Resources Chongqing Exploration Machinery Plant 地礦部重慶探礦機械廠	Chongqing 重慶市	Chongqing 重慶市	(023)65311195 (023)65311658	1,126	State-owned 國有	20,761	100(10)	68,432	a
Shandong Geology Prospecting Machinery Plant 山東省地質探礦機械廠(1959)	Ji'nan 濟南市	Shandong 山東省	(0531)8937431 (0531)8932428	576	State-owned 國有	18,035	-1417(32)	35,335	a
Jiangsu Wuxi Prospect Machinery General Factory 江蘇省無錫探礦機械總廠(1956)	Wuxi 無錫市	Jiangsu 江蘇省	(0510)5025731 (0510)5013426	737	State-owned 國有	17,526	2(16)	48,676	o
Ministryofpowerindustryhangzhou Exploration Boring Machine Manufacturing Factory 電力工業部杭州鑽探機械製造廠(1970)	Hangzhou 杭州市	Zhejiang 浙江省	(0571)6043883 (0571)6042742	483	State-owned 國有	17,296	35(12)	37,502	o
Ministry of Geology & Mineral Resource Wuxi Exploration Boring Tool Factory 地質礦產部無錫鑽探工具廠(1958)	Wuxi 無錫市	Jiangsu 江蘇省	(0510)5406441 (0510)5407347	895	State-owned 國有	16,687	-4015(35)	68,304	o

Top 10 Cities by Production Output 產出排名前 10 位城市	Province 省	Market share 市場份額	Number of firms 企業個數
Zhangjiakou 張家口市	Hebei 河北省	18.69%	2
Shijiazhuang 石家莊市	Hebei 河北省	17.42%	1
Wuxi 無錫市	Jiangsu 江蘇省	10.60%	12
Chongqing 重慶市	Chongqing 重 慶 市	4.82%	3
Jining 濟寧市	Shandong 山東省	3.82%	1
Tianjin 天津市	Tianjin 天津市	3.59%	3
Hangzhou 杭州市	Zhejiang 浙江省	3.45%	2
Ji'nan 濟南市	Shandong 山東省	3.36%	1
Beijing 北京市	Beijing 北京市	2.42%	4
Hengyang 衡陽市	Hunan 湖南省	2.24%	1

10 Major Wholesalers 10 家主要批發商	City 城市	Province 省	Telephone / Fax 電話 / 傳真
Liaoning Automobile Trade Group Corp. 遼寧省汽車貿易集團	Shenyang 瀋陽市	Liaoning 遼寧省	(024)23835494 (024)23838338
China Post and Telecommunication Equipment General Company 中國郵電器材總公司	Beijing 北京市	Beijing 北京市	(010)63523715 (010)63525935
Jiangsu Electromechanical Products General Company 江蘇省機電產品總公司	Nanjing 南京市	Jiangsu 江蘇省	(025)7713642 (025)7711036
Xi Nan Technology Import & Export Company 西南技術進出口公司	Chongqing 重慶市	Chongqing 重慶市	(023)63850185 (023)63850026
Changzhou Economic Technology Industrial Development Zone Tian Ming Trade Company 常州經濟技術產業開發區天明貿易公司	Changzhou 常州市	Jiangsu 江蘇省	(0519)8829882 (0519)8829882
Shanxi Mechanical Equipment Import & Export Company 山西省機械設備進出口公司	Taiyuan 太原市	Shanxi 山西省	(0351)4040713 (0351)4043981
Ningbo Five Mining Machinery Import & Export Company 寧波市五礦機械進出口公司	Ningbo 寧波市	Zhejiang 浙江省	(0574)7311255 (0574)7320322
Tianjin Jin Huan Electromechanical Complete Sets of Equipment Factory 天津市津環機電成套設備廠	Tianjin 天津市	Tianjin 天津市	(022)26371628
Yunnan Machinery Import & Export Company 雲南省機械進出口公司	Kunming 昆明市	Yunnan 雲南省	(0871)3164879 (0871)3136829
Tianjin Da Qiu Zhuang Yi Yuan Trade Center 天津市大丘莊億源商貿中心	Tianjin 天津市	Tianjin 天津市	(022)28899478 (022)28899046

*Also include sales by firms outside this industry.包括本行業以外廠家的銷售。"o" stands for "others". "o" 代表"其他產品"。

3673: Veterinary Medical Apparatus and Instruments Manufacturing
畜牧獸醫醫療器械製造業

The industry accounts for 0.000% of the total revenue of China's industrial sector in 1996. The revenue growth rate of the industry is 101.6% from 1995, as compared to the growth rate of China's industrial sector, 9.51%. The rate of return on asset is 2.52%. 100.00% of all firms in the industry made a profit while 0.00% had negative returns. The top province in terms of the industry's revenue is Jiangsu, accounting for 72.88% of the total revenue.
本行業在1996年佔全行業總產值0.000%，行業年增長率為101.6%（全國工業年增長率9.51%）。行業的資產回報率2.52%，100.00%的企業盈利，0.00%的企業虧損。銷售收入最高的省份為江蘇省，佔本行業的72.88%。

	Total number of firms 企業總數	Total number of employees 職工總數	Total revenue (mil. RMB) 總銷售收入（百萬元）	Total profit (mil. RMB) 總利潤（百萬元）	Return on assets 資產利潤率 (%)	Return on equity 權益利潤率 (%)	Labour productivity ('000 RMB / worker) 勞動生產率（千元/人）	Debts / assets 資產負債率 (%)	Total assets (mil. RMB) 總資產（百萬元）
Industry Overall 行業總體	11	587	25	1	2.52	7.51	42.59	66.38	26

	Number of firms 企業個數	Average number of employees 平均職工人數	Average revenue ('000 RMB) 平均銷售收入（千元）	Average profit ('000 RMB) 平均利潤（千元）	Return on assets 資產利潤率 (%)	Return on equity 權益利潤率 (%)	Labour productivity ('000 RMB / worker) 勞動生產率（千元/人）	Average debts / assets 平均資產負債率(%)	Average Total assets ('000 RMB) 平均總資產（千元）
By ownership 產業所有權									
State-owned 國有									
Collectively-owned 集體	8	46	2,374	62,375	3404.14	34669.87	51.61	90.18	1,832
Privately-owned 私有									
Domestic JVs 聯營									
Joint stock 股份制	1	15	185	-1,000	-1582.97	-9283.24	12.37	82.95	63
Foreign-funded 外資	1	204	5,813	-497,000	-4406.72	-6582.84	28.49	33.06	11,278
Overseas Chinese-funded 港澳台資									
By size 規模									
Large 大型									
Medium 中型									
Small 小型	11	53	2,272	91	3.85	11.12	42.58	65.38	2,363
By regional distribution 地區分布									
Central-North 華北	1								
Beijing 北京									
Tianjin 天津									
Hebei 河北									
Shanxi 山西									
Inner Mongolia 內蒙	1								
Northeast 東北	1	20							
Liaoning 遼寧									
Jilin 吉林									
Heilongjiang 黑龍江	1	20							
Central East 華東	5	82	4,230	126	2.75	8.21	51.71	66.56	4,588
Shanghai 上海									
Jiangsu 江蘇	3	119	6,073	133	2.02	5.64	51.18	64.21	6,603
Zhejiang 浙江	2	27	1,465	115	7.35	39.66	55.28	81.47	1,565
Anhui 安徽									
Fujian 福建									
Jiangxi 江西									
Shandong 山東									
Central-South 中南	3	48	737				15.35	66.93	857
Henan 河南	2	70	1,050	5	0.39	1.20	15.00	67.45	1,275
Hubei 湖北									
Hunan 湖南									
Guangdong 廣東	1	4	110	-10	-50.00	-50.00	27.50		20
Guangxi 廣西									
Hainan 海南									
Southwest 西南	1	14	1,170	30	10.71	21.43	83.57	50.00	280
Chongqing 重慶	1	14	1,170	30	10.71	21.43	83.57	50.00	280
Sichuan 四川									
Guizhou 貴州									
Yunnan 雲南									
Tibet 西藏									
Northwest 西北									
Shaanxi 陝西									
Gansu 甘肅									
Qinghai 青海									
Ningxia 寧夏									
Xinjiang 新疆									

3673: Veterinary Medical Apparatus and Instruments Manufacturing
畜牧獸醫醫療器械製造業

Year 年份	Number of firms 企業個數	Rate of change 每年變化 (%)	Number of employees 職工人數 (人)	Rate of change 每年變化 (%)	Total revenue (mil. RMB) 總銷售收入 (百萬元)	Rate of change 每年變化 (%)	Total profit (mil. RMB) 總利潤 (百萬元)	Rate of change 每年變化 (%)
1993	9		459		20		1	
1994	6	-33.33%	296	-35.51%	12	-40.82%	0	-69.98%
1995	8	33.33%	460	55.41%	12	5.70%	0	-100.22%
1996	11	37.50%	587	27.61%	25	101.63%	1100100.00%	

3 Major products* 3 種主要產品 *	Output 產量	Sales volume 銷售量	Unit 單位

Top 10 firms by revenue (year founded) 收入排名前 10 家企業 (創辦年份)	City 城市	Province 省	Telephone / fax 電話 / 傳真	Number of employees 職工人數	Ownership 產業所有權	Revenue ('000 RMB) 銷售收入 (千元)	Profit ('000 RMB) (rank) 利潤 (千元) (排名)	Total assets ('000 RMB) 總資產 (千元)	Major products 主要產品
Danyang Medical Apparatus Plant 丹陽市醫用器械廠(1984)	Zhenjiang 鎮江市	Jiangsu 江蘇省	(0511)6523507	147	Collectively-owned 集體	13,895	161(3)	8,636	o
Nantong Jin Sheng Sewing Equipment Co. Ltd. 南通金升縫紉設備有限公司(1994)	Nantong 南通市	Jiangsu 江蘇省	(0513)5584787 (0513)5585141	161	Foreign-funded 外資	4,098	238(1)	9,173	o
Shang Hai Medical Analysis Instrument Plant Shaoxing Veterinary Surgeon Apparatus Branch 上海醫用分析儀器廠紹興縣獸醫器械分廠(1986)	Shaoxing 紹興市	Zhejiang 浙江省	(0575)5788789	37	Collectively-owned 集體	2,532	203(2)	3,066	o

Top 10 Cities by Production Output 產出排名前 10 位城市	Province 省	Market share 市場份額	Number of firms 企業個數
Zhenjiang 鎮江市	Jiangsu 江蘇省	57.62%	2
Shaoxing 紹興市	Zhejiang 浙江省	23.19%	2
Kaifeng 開封市	Henan 河南省	13.24%	1
Shanghai 上海市	Shanghai 上海市	3.84%	1
Guilin 桂林市	Guangxi 廣西	1.24%	1
Qingyuan 清遠市	Guangdong 廣東省	0.88%	1

10 Major Wholesalers 10 家主要批發商	City 城市	Province 省	Telephone / Fax 電話 / 傳真
China Medicine Shanghai Purchase Supply Station 中國醫藥上海採購供應站	Shanghai 上海市	Shanghai 上海市	(021)63211750
Anhui Medical Health Care Product Import & Export Co. Ltd. 安徽省醫藥保健品進出口股份有限公司	Hefei 合肥市	Anhui 安徽省	(0551)3632603 (0551)3631975
Hai Tong Science Apparatus Co. Ltd. 海通科學儀器有限公司	Shanghai 上海市	Shanghai 上海市	(021)64397740 (021)64395300
Nantong Medicine Co. Ltd. 南通醫藥股份有限公司	Nantong 南通市	Jiangsu 江蘇省	(0513)5513093 (0513)5527814
Jiangxi Medical Health Care Product Import & Export Company 江西省醫藥保健品進出口公司	Nanchang 南昌市	Jiangxi 江西省	(0791)6222337 (0791)6217072
Shandong Machinery Industry Trade General Company 山東省機械工業貿易總公司	Ji'nan 濟南市	Shandong 山東省	(0531)6948991
Science & Education Technology Import & Export Company 科教技術進出口公司	Shanghai 上海市	Shanghai 上海市	(021)62564308 (021)62563108
Medical Apparatus & Instruments Wholesale Dept. 醫療器械批發部	Shanghai 上海市	Shanghai 上海市	(021)63216704 (021)63219814
Sichuan Livestock Raising College Medical Equipment Marketing Dept. 四川畜牧學院藥械經營部	Chongqing 重慶市	Chongqing 重慶市	(023)46733820
Shandou Scientific Equipment General Company 汕頭市科學器材總公司	Shantou 汕頭市	Guangdong 廣東省	(0754)8625957 (0754)8250513

*Also include sales by firms outside this industry.包括本行業以外廠家的銷售。"o" stands for "others". "o" 代表 "其他產品"。

3674: Sewing Machine 縫紉機製造業

The industry accounts for 0.081% of the total revenue of China's industrial sector in 1996. The revenue growth rate of the industry is -5.4% from 1995, as compared to the growth rate of China's industrial sector, 9.51%. The rate of return on asset is -0.80%. 54.81% of all firms in the industry made a profit while 38.67% had negative returns. The top province in terms of the industry's revenue is Shanghai, accounting for 35.41% of the total revenue.
本行業在1996年佔全行業總產值0.081%，行業年增長率為-5.4%（全國工業年增長率9.51%）。行業的資產回報率-0.80%，54.81%的企業盈利，38.67%的企業虧損。銷售收入最高的省份為上海市，佔本行業的35.41%。

	Total number of firms 企業總數	Total number of employees 職工總數	Total revenue (mil. RMB) 總銷售收入（百萬元）	Total profit (mil. RMB) 總利潤（百萬元）	Return on assets 資產利潤率 (%)	Return on equity 權益利潤率 (%)	Labour productivity ('000 RMB / worker) 勞動生產率（千元/人）	Debts / assets 資產負債率 (%)	Total assets (mil. RMB) 總資產（百萬元）
Industry Overall 行業總體	265	85,636	4,720	-71	-0.80	-2.57	55.12	68.69	8,839

	Number of firms 企業個數	Average number of employees 平均職工人數	Average revenue ('000 RMB) 平均銷售收入（千元）	Average profit ('000 RMB) 平均利潤（千元）	Return on assets 資產利潤率 (%)	Return on equity 權益利潤率 (%)	Labour productivity ('000 RMB / worker) 勞動生產率（千元/人）	Average debts / assets 平均資產負債率(%)	Average Total assets ('000 RMB) 平均總資產（千元）
By ownership 產業所有權									
State-owned 國有	51	815	34,804	-1,510	-1.88	-8.40	42.71	77.59	80,235
Collectively-owned 集體	169	180	7,667	8	0.08	0.35	42.54	77.02	9,847
Privately-owned 私有	2	66	2,909	-203	-9.08	-25.41	44.41	64.25	2,234
Domestic JVs 聯營	7	460	19,841	-146	-0.53	-1.27	43.13	58.08	27,509
Joint stock 股份制	2	2,948	245,633	-2,341	-0.33	-0.68	83.34	51.56	711,824
Foreign-funded 外資	15	235	41,975	1,048	1.46	2.96	178.26	50.60	71,789
Overseas Chinese-funded 港澳台資	20	151	19,224	-247	-1.28	-3.01	127.35	57.52	19,312
By size 規模									
Large 大型	10	3,259	207,797	-5,555	-1.20	-4.02	63.77	70.29	464,801
Medium 中型	25	823	34,513	-476	-0.75	-3.04	41.95	75.48	63,729
Small 小型	228	143	7,807	-16	-0.14	-0.36	54.60	61.69	11,397
By regional distribution 地區分布									
Central-North 華北	27	259	9,931	-199	-0.99	-2.97	38.34	66.59	20,052
Beijing 北京	1								
Tianjin 天津	17	249	12,546	-47	-0.21	-0.53	50.46	60.50	22,641
Hebei 河北	5	202	8,284	-380	-3.50	-115.85	40.97	96.98	10,864
Shanxi 山西	3	571	4,430	-857	-2.52	-9.56	7.76	73.59	33,937
Inner Mongolia 內蒙	1	43	150	-110	-29.73	-36.67	3.49	16.22	370
Northeast 東北	6	46	1,472	63	4.53	13.87	32.11	67.30	1,397
Liaoning 遼寧	5	48	1,664	76	4.80	14.62	34.81	67.13	1,582
Jilin 吉林									
Heilongjiang 黑龍江	1	36	510				14.17	70.21	470
Central East 華東	175	320	17,717	-65	-0.20	-0.67	55.45	69.81	32,272
Shanghai 上海	33	824	50,653	-849	-0.80	-2.61	61.50	69.46	106,509
Jiangsu 江蘇	41	291	13,659	75	0.40	1.28	46.96	68.88	18,940
Zhejiang 浙江	79	143	9,405	209	1.64	5.20	65.94	68.47	12,735
Anhui 安徽	3	558	17,473	-1,103	-4.10	-35.78	31.33	88.55	26,930
Fujian 福建	6	159	615	8	0.05	2.82	3.86	98.10	15,487
Jiangxi 江西	1	15	1,150	-80	-11.27	16.33	76.67	169.01	710
Shandong 山東	12	242	5,721	27	0.18	0.51	23.66	64.57	14,653
Central-South 中南	44	343	22,636	-1,168	-2.78	-9.76	66.00	71.49	41,966
Henan 河南	6	179	5,180	77	1.06	2.77	29.02	61.67	7,213
Hubei 湖北	1	1,086	20,850	-5,100	-5.96	-14.78	19.20	59.68	85,590
Hunan 湖南	6	417	6,315	-890	-3.27	-6.98	15.16	53.13	27,215
Guangdong 廣東	29	355	31,158	-1,421	-2.66	-10.34	87.79	74.29	53,488
Guangxi 廣西	2	71	1,285	-90	-5.63	-600.00	18.23	99.06	1,600
Hainan 海南									
Southwest 西南	1	375	9,490	20	0.15	0.46	25.31	67.73	13,510
Chongqing 重慶	1	735	18,980	40	0.15	0.46	25.83	67.73	27,020
Sichuan 四川	1	15							
Guizhou 貴州									
Yunnan 雲南									
Tibet 西藏									
Northwest 西北	12	582	28,116	-280	-0.43	-0.97	48.32	55.48	65,168
Shaanxi 陝西	12	582	28,116	-280	-0.43	-0.97	48.32	55.48	65,168
Gansu 甘肅									
Qinghai 青海									
Ningxia 寧夏									
Xinjiang 新疆									

3674: Sewing Machine 縫紉機製造業

Year 年份	Number of firms 企業個數	Rate of change 每年變化 (%)	Number of employees 職工人數（人）	Rate of change 每年變化 (%)	Total revenue (mil. RMB) 總銷售收入（百萬元）	Rate of change 每年變化 (%)	Total profit (mil. RMB) 總利潤（百萬元）	Rate of change 每年變化 (%)
1993								
1994	125		72,449		4,320		68	
1995	280	124.00%	95,138	31.32%	4,988	15.48%	-80	-218.23%
1996	265	-5.36%	85,636	-9.99%	4,720	-5.37%	-71	11.66%

3 Major products* 3 種主要產品 *	Output 產量	Sales volume 銷售量	Unit 單位
a) Industrial Sewing Machine 工業用縫紉機	1,875,419	1,856,665	set 架
b) Family Sewing Machine 家用縫紉機	4,871,346	4,920,060	set 架

Top 10 firms by revenue (year founded) 收入排名前 10 家企業 (創辦年份)	City 城市	Province 省	Telephone / fax 電話 / 傳真	Number of employees 職工人數	Ownership 產業所有權	Revenue ('000 RMB) 銷售收入（千元）	Profit ('000 RMB) (rank) 利潤（千元）（排名）	Total assets ('000 RMB) 總資產（千元）	Major products 主要產品
Shanghai No.1 Sewing Machine Factory 上海縫紉機一廠(1924)	Shanghai 上海市	Shanghai 上海市	(021)63773600 (021)63772684	5,896	State-owned 國有	559,556	795(26)	574,711	a,b
Shanghai Industry Sewing Machine Co. Ltd. 上海工業縫紉機股份有限公司(1965)	Shanghai 上海市	Shanghai 上海市	(021)58857510 (021)58857510	5,109	Joint stock 股份制	348,036	7744(4)	1,314,749	a
Shanghai Xie Chang Co. Ltd. 上海協昌有限公司(1919)	Shanghai 上海市	Shanghai 上海市	(021)64387850 (021)64390823	4,573	State-owned 國有	330,854	106(67)	671,890	a,b
Hua Nan Making Equipment Group Co. 華南縫製設備集團公司(1937)	Guangzhou 廣州市	Guangdong 廣東省	(020)84429296 (020)84429142	5,435	State-owned 國有	261,655	-30607(184)	993,965	a,b
Zhuhai Brother Industries Co. Ltd. 珠海兄弟工業有限公司(1993)	Zhuhai 珠海市	Guangdong 廣東省	(0756)8610174 (0756)8610134	252	Overseas Chinese-funded 港澳台資	195,384	-167(130)	82,878	b
China Standard Sewing Machine Co. 中國標準縫紉機公司(1946)	Xi'an 西安市	Shaanxi 陝西省	(029)3911035 (029)3911188	3,445	State-owned 國有	171,409	506(38)	497,760	o
Zhuhai Ji Jia Machinery Industrial Co. Ltd. 珠海積家機械工業有限公司(1992)	Zhuhai 珠海市	Guangdong 廣東省	(0756)8610576 (0756)8610577	1	Foreign-funded 外資	165,179	246(51)	190,121	b
Fei Yue Sewing Machinery Group 中國飛躍縫紉機集團公司(1986)	Taizhou 臺州市	Zhejiang 浙江省	(0576)8155828	601	Collectively-owned 集體	160,400	12085(2)	245,059	o
Shanghai Industry Sewing Machine Co. Ltd. Fang Tai Branch 上海工業縫紉機股份公司方泰分廠(1985)	Shanghai 上海市	Shanghai 上海市	(021)59509434	195	Domestic JVs 聯營	146,512	5311(6)	43,626	o
Xi'an Brother Standard Industrial Co. Ltd. 西安兄弟標準工業有限公司(1993)	Xi'an 西安市	Shaanxi 陝西省	(029)8224153 (029)8224184	247	Foreign-funded 外資	131,845	1752(16)	215,199	o

Top 10 Cities by Production Output 產出排名前 10 位城市	Province 省	Market share 市場份額	Number of firms 企業個數
Shanghai 上海市	Shanghai 上海市	40.23%	62
Taizhou 臺州市	Zhejiang 浙江省	8.86%	23
Suzhou 蘇州市	Jiangsu 江蘇省	7.57%	37
Guangzhou 廣州市	Guangdong 廣東省	7.43%	21
Xi'an 西安市	Shaanxi 陝西省	7.39%	11
Tianjin 天津市	Tianjin 天津市	4.22%	21
Zhuhai 珠海市	Guangdong 廣東省	3.96%	7
Taizhou 泰州市	Jiangsu 江蘇省	2.62%	7
Shaoxing 紹興市	Zhejiang 浙江省	2.62%	6
Ningbo 寧波市	Zhejiang 浙江省	2.52%	31

10 Major Wholesalers 10 家主要批發商	City 城市	Province 省	Telephone / Fax 電話 / 傳真
Liaoning Automobile Trade Group Corp. 遼寧省汽車貿易集團	Shenyang 瀋陽市	Liaoning 遼寧省	(024)23835494 (024)23838338
China Post and Telecommunication Equipment General Company 中國郵電器材總公司	Beijing 北京市	Beijing 北京市	(010)63523715 (010)63525935
Jiangsu Electromechanical Products General Company 江蘇省機電產品總公司	Nanjing 南京市	Jiangsu 江蘇省	(025)7713642 (025)7711036
Xi Nan Technology Import & Export Company 西南技術進出口公司	Chongqing 重慶市	Chongqing 重慶市	(023)63850185 (023)63850026
Changzhou Economic Technology Industrial Development Zone Tian Ming Trade Company 常州經濟技術產業開發區天明貿易公司	Changzhou 常州市	Jiangsu 江蘇省	(0519)8829882 (0519)8829882
Shanxi Mechanical Equipment Import & Export Company 山西省機械設備進出口公司	Taiyuan 太原市	Shanxi 山西省	(0351)4040713 (0351)4043981
Ningbo Five Mining Machinery Import & Export Company 寧波市五礦機械進出口公司	Ningbo 寧波市	Zhejiang 浙江省	(0574)7311255 (0574)7320322
Tianjin Jin Huan Electromechanical Complete Sets of Equipment Factory 天津市津環機電成套設備廠	Tianjin 天津市	Tianjin 天津市	(022)26371628
Yunnan Machinery Import & Export Company 雲南省機械進出口公司	Kunming 昆明市	Yunnan 雲南省	(0871)3164879 (0871)3136829
Tianjin Da Qiu Zhuang Yi Yuan Trade Center 天津市大丘莊億源商貿中心	Tianjin 天津市	Tianjin 天津市	(022)28899478 (022)28899046

*Also include sales by firms outside this industry.包括本行業以外廠家的銷售。"o" stands for "others". "o" 代表"其他產品"。

3675: Commerce, Food, and Service Machinery
商業、飲食業、服務業、專用機械製造業

The industry accounts for 0.011% of the total revenue of China's industrial sector in 1996. The revenue growth rate of the industry is 16.0% from 1995, as compared to the growth rate of China's industrial sector, 9.51%. The rate of return on asset is 1.07%. 64.45% of all firms in the industry made a profit while 28.30% had negative returns. The top province in terms of the industry's revenue is Shandong, accounting for 24.06% of the total revenue.
本行業在1996年佔全行業總產值0.011%，行業年增長率為16.0%（全國工業年增長率9.51%）。行業的資產回報率1.07%，64.45%的企業盈利，28.30%的企業虧損。銷售收入最高的省份為山東省，佔本行業的24.06%。

	Total number of firms 企業總數	Total number of employees 職工總數	Total revenue (mil. RMB) 總銷售收入（百萬元）	Total profit (mil. RMB) 總利潤（百萬元）	Return on assets 資產利潤率 (%)	Return on equity 權益利潤率 (%)	Labour productivity ('000 RMB / worker) 勞動生產率（千元／人）	Debts / assets 資產負債率 (%)	Total assets (mil. RMB) 總資產（百萬元）
Industry Overall 行業總體	182	13,858	637	10	1.07	2.96	45.97	63.67	971

	Number of firms 企業個數	Average number of employees 平均職工人數	Average revenue ('000 RMB) 平均銷售收入（千元）	Average profit ('000 RMB) 平均利潤（千元）	Return on assets 資產利潤率 (%)	Return on equity 權益利潤率 (%)	Labour productivity ('000 RMB / worker) 勞動生產率（千元／人）	Average debts / assets 平均資產負債率(%)	Average Total assets ('000 RMB) 平均總資產（千元）
By ownership 產業所有權									
State-owned 國有	46	111	3,413	-130	-1.67	-5.50	30.67	69.64	7,804
Collectively-owned 集體	112	70	3,182	76	1.86	4.98	45.23	62.59	4,061
Privately-owned 私有	1	21	438	2	0.32	0.53	20.87	38.62	706
Domestic JVs 聯營	1	54	1,239	87	18.45	60.35	22.94	69.44	469
Joint stock 股份制	3	99	11,063	3,740	45.21	132.96	112.12	66.00	8,274
Foreign-funded 外資	10	38	2,769	-437	-6.38	-11.86	72.49	46.18	6,847
Overseas Chinese-funded 港澳台資	9	29	6,771	65	0.93	2.08	234.37	55.38	6,952
By size 規模									
Large 大型									
Medium 中型	3	610	22,411	-1,548	-2.83	-14.80	36.76	80.90	54,765
Small 小型	176	69	3,237	83	1.82	4.55	46.88	60.13	4,583
By regional distribution 地區分布									
Central-North 華北	38	65	1,903	-37	-1.26	-3.56	29.26	64.52	2,917
Beijing 北京	14	22	1,339	69	4.09	12.95	61.85	68.41	1,694
Tianjin 天津	8	59	503	-300	-9.40	-27.00	8.57	65.16	3,190
Hebei 河北	12	124	3,755	48	1.20	3.18	30.28	62.26	4,028
Shanxi 山西	3	62	1,403	40	1.06	2.34	22.63	54.85	3,780
Inner Mongolia 內蒙	1	26	300	-670	-34.72	163.41	11.54	121.76	1,930
Northeast 東北	21	70	2,815	89	0.98	1.72	40.25	43.04	9,108
Liaoning 遼寧	9	47	1,771	-50	-0.36	-0.57	37.42	36.24	13,783
Jilin 吉林	6	48	3,190	313	5.78	9.50	66.00	39.20	5,425
Heilongjiang 黑龍江	6	126	4,007	73	1.27	4.38	31.93	71.00	5,777
Central East 華東	57	68	5,242	261	4.74	14.46	77.09	67.20	5,502
Shanghai 上海	17	77	6,124	336	4.53	14.30	80.02	68.29	7,408
Jiangsu 江蘇	8	60	2,900	-19	-0.51	-2.37	48.13	78.38	3,665
Zhejiang 浙江	10	35	1,317	-106	-2.90	-9.17	38.17	68.40	3,658
Anhui 安徽	1	306	3,180				10.39	88.22	18,670
Fujian 福建	3	39	643				16.36	92.60	2,297
Jiangxi 江西									
Shandong 山東	18	74	8,513	576	10.78	24.49	115.73	56.00	5,346
Central-South 中南	49	105	3,760	-71	-1.08	-3.73	35.67	70.90	6,588
Henan 河南	14	197	3,679	77	1.15	3.78	18.72	69.72	6,735
Hubei 湖北	5	41	1,540	38	1.55	5.21	37.20	70.23	2,452
Hunan 湖南	11	62	957	-45	-1.16	-14.16	15.55	91.82	3,921
Guangdong 廣東	17	80	6,449	-252	-2.71	-8.66	80.37	68.70	9,314
Guangxi 廣西	2	83	2,440	10	0.14	0.23	29.40	41.59	7,405
Hainan 海南									
Southwest 西南	8	45	640	-3	-0.14	-0.40	14.10	64.86	1,758
Chongqing 重慶	4	28	267	-9	-0.65	-1.82	9.50	64.16	1,311
Sichuan 四川	4	52	1,071	1	0.03	0.10	20.62	68.88	1,787
Guizhou 貴州									
Yunnan 雲南	1	84	440	10	0.31	0.74	5.24	58.07	3,220
Tibet 西藏									
Northwest 西北	9	57	1,910	-150	-7.19	-47.70	33.51	84.93	2,087
Shaanxi 陝西	6	58	2,442	30	1.31	5.41	42.34	75.78	2,292
Gansu 甘肅	1	36	1,510				41.94	139.31	1,450
Qinghai 青海	1								
Ningxia 寧夏	1	131	1,030	-1,530	-42.74	-2185.71	7.86	98.04	3,580
Xinjiang 新疆									

3675: Commerce, Food, and Service Machinery
商業、飲食業、服務業、專用機械製造業

Year 年份	Number of firms 企業個數	Rate of change 每年變化 (%)	Number of employees 職工人數 (人)	Rate of change 每年變化 (%)	Total revenue (mil. RMB) 總銷售收入 (百萬元)	Rate of change 每年變化 (%)	Total profit (mil. RMB) 總利潤 (百萬元)	Rate of change 每年變化 (%)
1993	214		32,972		955		74	
1994	206	-3.74%	21,388	-35.13%	1,016	6.39%	32	-57.40%
1995	168	-18.45%	16,161	-24.44%	549	-45.98%	5	-83.45%
1996	182	8.33%	13,858	-14.25%	637	16.05%	10	91.17%

3 Major products* 3 種主要產品 *	Output 產量	Sales volume 銷售量	Unit 單位
a) Cereal, Oilseed & Foodstuff Processing Machiner 糧油食品加工機械	474,336	360,495	set 台(套)
b) Commerical Service Machinery 商業服務機械	3,027	3,572	set 台
c) Cereal & Oilseed Processing Machinery 糧食加工機械	27,967	25,450	set 台

Top 10 firms by revenue (year founded) 收入排名前 10 家企業 (創辦年份)	City 城市	Province 省	Telephone / fax 電話 / 傳真	Number of employees 職工人數	Ownership 產業所有權	Revenue ('000 RMB) 銷售收入 (千元)	Profit ('000 RMB) (rank) 利潤 (千元) (排名)	Total assets ('000 RMB) 總資產 (千元)	Major products 主要產品
Wendeng Er Light Machine Factory 文登市二輕機械廠(1952)	Weihai 威海市	Shandong 山東省	(0896)8641053 (0896)8641063	328	Collectively-owned 集體	105,600	8750(1)	37,240	a
Guangzhou Washer Mechinery Industrial Co. 廣州市洗滌機械實業公司(1988)	Guangzhou 廣州市	Guangdong 廣東省	(020)81891050 (020)81807814	598	State-owned 國有	31,609	-5871(69)	71,298	b
Shanghai Huan Qiu Refrigerator Factory 上海市環球冷凍機廠(1980)	Shanghai 上海市	Shanghai 上海市	(021)59138225	205	Collectively-owned 集體	25,724	851(8)	32,347	o
Zhanjiang Hua Yi Mechanical Equipment Co. Ltd. 湛江市華益機械設備有限公司(1993)	Zhanjiang 湛江市	Guangdong 廣東省	(0758)2211886 (0758)2285079	85	Overseas Chinese-funded 港澳台資	22,730	275(26)	1,500	o
Neixiang Chang Feng Machinery Manufacture Co. Ltd. 內鄉縣長風機械製造有限公司(1958)	Nanyang 南陽市	Henan 河南省	(0377)5333888	827	State-owned 國有	22,289	809(9)	41,182	a
Harbin Commerce Machinery General Factory 哈爾濱商業機械總廠(1958)	Harbin 哈爾濱市	Heilongjiang 黑龍江省	(0451)2532111 (0451)2535190	288	State-owned 國有	16,094	502(15)	24,752	a
Shanghai Long Teng Refrigeration Equipment Co. Ltd. 上海龍騰製冷設備有限公司(1992)	Shanghai 上海市	Shanghai 上海市	(021)58480233 (021)58480921	24	Overseas Chinese-funded 港澳台資	15,876	1114(4)	13,832	o
Siping Ai Si Ke Electromechanical Development Co. Ltd. 四平市艾斯克機電開發有限公司(1996)	Siping 四平市	Jilin 吉林省	(0434)3518454 (0434)3517031	113	Foreign-funded 外資	15,710	2070(2)	17,811	o
Shenyang Xian Da Group Co. Ltd. 瀋陽先達集團股份有限公司(1993)	Shenyang 瀋陽市	Liaoning 遼寧省	(024)24228578 (024)24228414	155	Joint stock 股份制	13,258	37(43)	112,091	o
Guangdong Dianbai Machinery General Factory 廣東省電白縣機械總廠(1953)	Maoming 茂名市	Guangdong 廣東省	(0668)5523563	270	State-owned 國有	12,406	282(25)	19,906	o

Top 10 Cities by Production Output 產出排名前 10 位城市	Province 省	Market share 市場份額	Number of firms 企業個數
Shenzhen 深圳市	Guangdong 廣東省	33.69%	4
Weihai 威海市	Shandong 山東省	10.91%	3
Shanghai 上海市	Shanghai 上海市	9.70%	37
Longyan 龍巖市	Fujian 福建省	6.47%	1
Guangzhou 廣州市	Guangdong 廣東省	5.34%	11
Nanyang 南陽市	Henan 河南省	2.69%	2
Shenyang 瀋陽市	Liaoning 遼寧省	1.89%	7
Maoming 茂名市	Guangdong 廣東省	1.73%	1
Changsha 長沙市	Hunan 湖南省	1.65%	6
Siping 四平市	Jilin 吉林省	1.62%	1

10 Major Wholesalers 10 家主要批發商	City 城市	Province 省	Telephone / Fax 電話 / 傳真
Liaoning Automobile Trade Group Corp. 遼寧省汽車貿易集團	Shenyang 瀋陽市	Liaoning 遼寧省	(024)23835494 (024)23838338
China Post and Telecommunication Equipment General Company 中國郵電器材總公司	Beijing 北京市	Beijing 北京市	(010)63523715 (010)63525935
Jiangsu Electromechanical Products General Company 江蘇省機電產品總公司	Nanjing 南京市	Jiangsu 江蘇省	(025)7713642 (025)7711036
Xi Nan Technology Import & Export Company 西南技術進出口公司	Chongqing 重慶市	Chongqing 重慶市	(023)63850185 (023)63850026
Changzhou Economic Technology Industrial Development Zone Tian Ming Trade Company 常州經濟技術產業開發區天明貿易公司	Changzhou 常州市	Jiangsu 江蘇省	(0519)8829882 (0519)8829882
Shanxi Mechanical Equipment Import & Export Company 山西省機械設備進出口公司	Taiyuan 太原市	Shanxi 山西省	(0351)4040713 (0351)4043981
Ningbo Five Mining Machinery Import & Export Company 寧波市五礦機械進出口公司	Ningbo 寧波市	Zhejiang 浙江省	(0574)7311255 (0574)7320322
Tianjin Jin Huan Electromechanical Complete Sets of Equipment Factory 天津市津環機電成套設備廠	Tianjin 天津市	Tianjin 天津市	(022)26371628
Yunnan Machinery Import & Export Company 雲南省機械進出口公司	Kunming 昆明市	Yunnan 雲南省	(0871)3164879 (0871)3136829
Tianjin Da Qiu Zhuang Yi Yuan Trade Center 天津市大丘莊億源商貿中心	Tianjin 天津市	Tianjin 天津市	(022)28899478 (022)28899046

*Also include sales by firms outside this industry.包括本行業以外廠家的銷售。"o" stands for "others". "o" 代表"其他產品"。

3676: Postal Service Machinery 郵政機械及器材製造業

The industry accounts for 0.010% of the total revenue of China's industrial sector in 1996. The revenue growth rate of the industry is 56.2% from 1995, as compared to the growth rate of China's industrial sector, 9.51%. The rate of return on asset is 4.59%. 81.58% of all firms in the industry made a profit while 18.42% had negative returns. The top province in terms of the industry's revenue is Shandong, accounting for 28.39% of the total revenue.
本行業在1996年佔全行業總產值0.010%，行業年增長率為56.2%（全國工業年增長率9.51%）。行業的資產回報率4.59%，81.58%的企業盈利，18.42%的企業虧損。銷售收入最高的省份為山東省，佔本行業的28.39%。

	Total number of firms 企業總數	Total number of employees 職工總數	Total revenue (mil. RMB) 總銷售收入（百萬元）	Total profit (mil. RMB) 總利潤（百萬元）	Return on assets 資產利潤率 (%)	Return on equity 權益利潤率 (%)	Labour productivity ('000 RMB / worker) 勞動生產率（千元/人）	Debts / assets 資產負債率 (%)	Total assets (mil. RMB) 總資產（百萬元）
Industry Overall 行業總體	37	5,517	571	24	4.59	10.69	103.50	57.01	517

	Number of firms 企業個數	Average number of employees 平均職工人數	Average revenue ('000 RMB) 平均銷售收入（千元）	Average profit ('000 RMB) 平均利潤（千元）	Return on assets 資產利潤率 (%)	Return on equity 權益利潤率 (%)	Labour productivity ('000 RMB / worker) 勞動生產率（千元/人）	Average debts / assets 平均資產負債率(%)	Average Total assets ('000 RMB) 平均總資產（千元）
By ownership 產業所有權									
State-owned 國有	15	268	23,267	400	1.67	4.14	86.75	59.61	23,933
Collectively-owned 集體	21	68	10,297	814	11.19	23.51	152.49	52.41	7,280
Privately-owned 私有									
Domestic JVs 聯營	1	76	5,726	897	17.72	21.27	75.35	16.70	5,064
Joint stock 股份制									
Foreign-funded 外資									
Overseas Chinese-funded 港澳台資									
By size 規模									
Large 大型									
Medium 中型	4	693	91,778	3,036	5.44	13.85	132.53	60.69	55,770
Small 小型	33	83	6,177	359	4.03	8.83	74.21	54.31	8,905
By regional distribution 地區分布									
Central-North 華北	7	195	29,633	1,950	13.67	18.19	151.63	24.85	14,266
Beijing 北京	1	42	1,170	70	3.87	4.58	27.86	15.47	1,810
Tianjin 天津	1	1,019	103,710	1,100	2.81	4.51	101.78	37.71	39,140
Hebei 河北	3	70	31,453	3,647	23.16	24.48	451.48	5.38	15,743
Shanxi 山西	1	18	390	10	10.00	10.00	21.67		100
Inner Mongolia 內蒙	1	80	7,800	1,530	13.21	35.25	97.50	62.52	11,580
Northeast 東北	1	30	4,600	150	51.72	300.00	153.33	82.76	290
Liaoning 遼寧									
Jilin 吉林									
Heilongjiang 黑龍江	1	30	4,600	150	51.72	300.00	153.33	82.76	290
Central East 華東	22	137	13,139	422	2.84	7.53	95.65	62.28	14,855
Shanghai 上海	2	166	8,805	40	0.29	0.87	53.20	66.75	13,865
Jiangsu 江蘇	6	110	4,172	37	0.29	0.54	37.87	47.15	12,832
Zhejiang 浙江	5	63	3,384	224	3.68	6.20	53.71	40.68	6,092
Anhui 安徽	1	454	55,760	4,080	12.77	31.07	122.82	58.89	31,940
Fujian 福建	3	31	2,233	-3	-0.12	-0.19	72.04	39.63	2,860
Jiangxi 江西	2	61	2,470	-20	-0.61	-1.38	40.49	56.06	3,300
Shandong 山東	3	349	54,030	1,277	2.65	11.24	154.96	76.42	48,167
Central-South 中南	4	90	7,425	5	0.05	0.29	82.50	81.27	9,128
Henan 河南	2	21	235	-10	-2.11	-6.90	11.46	70.53	475
Hubei 湖北									
Hunan 湖南	1	124	5,910				47.66	67.53	6,530
Guangdong 廣東	1	195	23,320	40	0.14	0.90	119.59	84.71	29,030
Guangxi 廣西									
Hainan 海南									
Southwest 西南	2	367	19,935	325	1.22	3.84	54.39	68.20	26,620
Chongqing 重慶	1	34	687	17	3.47	-8.23	20.31	142.17	486
Sichuan 四川	1	274	6,193	43	0.27	1.36	22.59	79.94	15,774
Guizhou 貴州	1	579	36,430	620	1.37	4.01	62.92	65.75	45,110
Yunnan 雲南									
Tibet 西藏									
Northwest 西北	1	4							
Shaanxi 陝西	1	4							
Gansu 甘肅									
Qinghai 青海									
Ningxia 寧夏									
Xinjiang 新疆									

3676: Postal Service Machinery 郵政機械及器材製造業

Year 年份	Number of firms 企業個數	Rate of change 每年變化 (%)	Number of employees 職工人數 (人)	Rate of change 每年變化 (%)	Total revenue (mil. RMB) 總銷售收入 (百萬元)	Rate of change 每年變化 (%)	Total profit (mil. RMB) 總利潤 (百萬元)	Rate of change 每年變化 (%)
1993	27		5,141		178		7	
1994	31	14.81%	3,522	-31.49%	184	3.01%	-2	-127.45%
1995	30	-3.23%	4,800	36.29%	366	99.08%	6	378.51%
1996	37	23.33%	5,517	14.94%	571	56.16%	24	333.68%

3 Major products* 3 種主要產品 *	Output 產量	Sales volume 銷售量	Unit 單位
a) Special Postal Equipmen 郵政專用設備	1,349	1,214	set 台
b) Special Refitted Truck 專用改裝汽車	1,737	1,668	vehicle 輛

Top 10 firms by revenue (year founded) 收入排名前 10 家企業 (創辦年份)	City 城市	Province 省	Telephone / fax 電話 / 傳真	Number of employees 職工人數	Ownership 產業所有權	Revenue ('000 RMB) 銷售收入 (千元)	Profit ('000 RMB) (rank) 利潤 (千元) (排名)	Total assets ('000 RMB) 總資產 (千元)	Major products 主要產品
Mingshui Communication Equipment Factory of Posts and Telecommunications 郵電部明水通訊機械廠(1958)	Ji'nan 濟南市	Shandong 山東省	(0531)3212034 (0531)3214294	865	State-owned 國有	139,025	629(6)	134,325	b
Ministry of Posts & Telecommunications Tianjin Communication Equipment Factory 天津郵電通訊設備廠(1953)	Tianjin 天津市	Tianjin 天津市	(022)24312435 (022)24312174	1,017	State-owned 國有	103,709	1095(4)	39,139	o
Renqiu Nan Ma Post and Telecommunication Equipment Company 任丘市南馬郵電器材公司(1990)	Cangzhou 滄州市	Hebei 河北省	(0312)5024773	200	Collectively-owned 集體	93,880	10940(1)	45,672	o
Ma'anshan Circuit Equipment Co. 馬鞍山市新宇集團公司(1979)	Ma'anshan 馬鞍山市	Anhui 安徽省	(0555)2223632 (0555)2223632	146	Collectively-owned 集體	55,760	4080(2)	31,940	o
Ministry of Posts & Telecommunications Guiyang Communication Machinery Plant 郵電部貴陽通訊機械廠(1970)	Guiyang 貴陽市	Guizhou 貴州省	(0851)4842112 (0851)4843467	588	State-owned 國有	36,428	622(7)	45,106	a,b
Panyu Shi Qiao Jianhua Post and Telecommunication Equipment Factory 番禺市市橋鎮建華郵電器材廠(1965)	Guangzhou 廣州市	Guangdong 廣東省	(020)84892461	195	Collectively-owned 集體	23,320	38(17)	29,033	o
Weifang Yecun Electron Co. Ltd. Gouxi Eletrical Wire Factory 濰坊亞光電子有限公司溝西電線廠(1989)	Weifang 濰坊市	Shandong 山東省	(0536)7609685 (0536)7609685	100	Foreign-funded 外資	15,190	2841(3)	789	o
Shanghai Postal General Technology and Equipment Co. 上海郵政通用技術設備公司(1992)	Shanghai 上海市	Shanghai 上海市	(021)65486155 (021)65489096	280	State-owned 國有	14,025	105(14)	25,339	o
Taicang Mechanical Equipment Factory 太倉機械設備廠(1985)	Suzhou 蘇州市	Jiangsu 江蘇省	(0512)3655516	108	Collectively-owned 集體	10,480	130(11)	10,760	o
Zhejiang Post and Telecommunication Machinery Plant 浙江省郵電機械廠(1975)	Jiaxing 嘉興市	Zhejiang 浙江省	(0573)7022601 (0573)7024305	181	State-owned 國有	10,066	1035(5)	13,922	o

Top 10 Cities by Production Output 產出排名前 10 位城市	Province 省	Market share 市場份額	Number of firms 企業個數
Wuhan 武漢市	Hubei 湖北省	54.73%	1
Ji'nan 濟南市	Shandong 山東省	13.43%	1
Tianjin 天津市	Tianjin 天津市	10.89%	1
Guiyang 貴陽市	Guizhou 貴州省	3.00%	1
Suzhou 蘇州市	Jiangsu 江蘇省	2.77%	4
Guangzhou 廣州市	Guangdong 廣東省	2.34%	1
Shanghai 上海市	Shanghai 上海市	2.24%	3
Hohhot 呼和浩特市	Inner Mong 內蒙	1.77%	2
Chengdu 成都市	Sichuan 四川省	1.61%	1
Jiaxing 嘉興市	Zhejiang 浙江省	1.26%	2

10 Major Wholesalers 10 家主要批發商	City 城市	Province 省	Telephone / Fax 電話 / 傳真
Liaoning Automobile Trade Group Corp. 遼寧省汽車貿易集團	Shenyang 瀋陽市	Liaoning 遼寧省	(024)23835494 (024)23838338
China Post and Telecommunication Equipment General Company 中國郵電器材總公司	Beijing 北京市	Beijing 北京市	(010)63523715 (010)63525935
Jiangsu Electromechanical Products General Company 江蘇省機電產品總公司	Nanjing 南京市	Jiangsu 江蘇省	(025)7713642 (025)7711036
Xi Nan Technology Import & Export Company 西南技術進出口公司	Chongqing 重慶市	Chongqing 重慶市	(023)63850185 (023)63850026
Changzhou Economic Technology Industrial Development Zone Tian Ming Trade Company 常州經濟技術產業開發區天明貿易公司	Changzhou 常州市	Jiangsu 江蘇省	(0519)8829882 (0519)8829882
Shanxi Mechanical Equipment Import & Export Company 山西省機械設備進出口公司	Taiyuan 太原市	Shanxi 山西省	(0351)4040713 (0351)4043981
Ningbo Five Mining Machinery Import & Export Company 寧波市五礦機械進出口公司	Ningbo 寧波市	Zhejiang 浙江省	(0574)7311255 (0574)7320322
Tianjin Jin Huan Electromechanical Complete Sets of Equipment Factory 天津市津環機電成套設備廠	Tianjin 天津市	Tianjin 天津市	(022)26371628
Yunnan Machinery Import & Export Company 雲南省機械進出口公司	Kunming 昆明市	Yunnan 雲南省	(0871)3164879 (0871)3136829
Tianjin Da Qiu Zhuang Yi Yuan Trade Center 天津市大丘莊億源商貿中心	Tianjin 天津市	Tianjin 天津市	(022)28899478 (022)28899046

*Also include sales by firms outside this industry.包括本行業以外廠家的銷售。"o" stands for "others". "o" 代表 "其他產品"。

3677: Environmental Protection Machinery 環境保護機械製造業

The industry accounts for 0.082% of the total revenue of China's industrial sector in 1996. The revenue growth rate of the industry is 55.4% from 1995, as compared to the growth rate of China's industrial sector, 9.51%. The rate of return on asset is 3.16%. 71.65% of all firms in the industry made a profit while 22.70% had negative returns. The top province in terms of the industry's revenue is Jiangsu, accounting for 49.27% of the total revenue.
本行業在1996年佔全行業總產值0.082%，行業年增長率為55.4%（全國工業年增長率9.51%）。行業的資產回報率3.16%，71.65%的企業盈利，22.70%的企業虧損。銷售收入最高的省份為江蘇省，佔本行業的49.27%。

	Total number of firms 企業總數	Total number of employees 職工總數	Total revenue (mil. RMB) 總銷售收入（百萬元）	Total profit (mil. RMB) 總利潤（百萬元）	Return on assets 資產利潤率 (%)	Return on equity 權益利潤率 (%)	Labour productivity ('000 RMB / worker) 勞動生產率（千元/人）	Debts / assets 資產負債率 (%)	Total assets (mil. RMB) 總資產（百萬元）
Industry Overall 行業總體	603	73,583	4,731	176	3.16	10.31	64.29	69.18	5,569

	Number of firms 企業個數	Average number of employees 平均職工人數	Average revenue ('000 RMB) 平均銷售收入（千元）	Average profit ('000 RMB) 平均利潤（千元）	Return on assets 資產利潤率 (%)	Return on equity 權益利潤率 (%)	Labour productivity ('000 RMB / worker) 勞動生產率（千元/人）	Average debts / assets 平均資產負債率(%)	Average Total assets ('000 RMB) 平均總資產（千元）
By ownership 產業所有權									
State-owned 國有	62	371	11,065	290	1.00	3.27	29.85	69.39	28,984
Collectively-owned 集體	489	99	7,358	260	3.86	12.65	74.43	69.50	6,747
Privately-owned 私有	4	45	3,455	212	8.43	21.18	77.63	60.20	2,513
Domestic JVs 聯營	7	49	3,626	33	0.41	1.27	74.44	67.32	7,996
Joint stock 股份制	8	167	16,013	2,490	12.94	46.49	95.67	72.17	19,244
Foreign-funded 外資	14	52	4,385	241	4.18	10.92	85.14	61.77	5,761
Overseas Chinese-funded 港澳台資	19	73	11,489	330	3.65	9.87	157.83	63.06	9,039
By size 規模									
Large 大型	4	1,591	107,976	730	0.27	0.85	67.87	68.18	268,727
Medium 中型	13	955	72,301	2,826	3.30	10.69	75.69	69.09	85,545
Small 小型	576	96	5,832	237	4.03	13.23	60.82	69.54	5,871
By regional distribution 地區分布									
Central-North 華北	102	60	2,617	-13	-0.30	-1.02	43.29	68.37	4,288
Beijing 北京	58	19	1,146	34	1.85	10.54	60.09	74.42	1,842
Tianjin 天津	10	39	2,052	195	9.84	24.90	52.89	60.49	1,982
Hebei 河北	27	162	6,450	-202	-1.82	-5.43	39.93	66.45	11,105
Shanxi 山西	5	50	584	10	0.62	2.50	11.59	75.31	1,620
Inner Mongolia 內蒙	2	29	1,430	75	5.49	27.78	49.31	79.85	1,365
Northeast 東北	119	174	2,691	212	2.50	7.92	15.48	68.50	8,501
Liaoning 遼寧	83	220	3,134	304	2.73	8.57	14.27	68.15	11,143
Jilin 吉林	16	87	1,384	-82	-2.16	-11.65	15.95	81.45	3,786
Heilongjiang 黑龍江	20	54	1,901	65	4.96	10.09	35.24	50.84	1,310
Central East 華東	248	137	14,357	593	4.68	16.23	105.18	71.17	12,662
Shanghai 上海	25	75	3,912	147	2.56	7.10	52.41	63.89	5,730
Jiangsu 江蘇	123	102	18,950	749	5.13	19.25	185.02	73.33	14,590
Zhejiang 浙江	50	280	15,644	938	5.75	15.44	55.89	62.75	16,313
Anhui 安徽	12	199	11,512	-580	-6.02	-120.62	57.99	95.01	9,637
Fujian 福建	10	116	6,684	97	0.66	3.16	57.62	79.19	14,744
Jiangxi 江西	7	57	3,929	191	6.63	18.36	69.44	63.86	2,886
Shandong 山東	21	69	5,581	424	8.62	32.78	80.56	73.71	4,918
Central-South 中南	94	108	4,904	57	0.68	2.21	45.29	69.08	8,348
Henan 河南	28	131	4,845	21	0.20	1.08	37.03	81.30	10,425
Hubei 湖北	21	153	7,274	23	0.24	0.63	47.65	61.74	9,487
Hunan 湖南	18	70	2,998	35	1.18	3.41	42.60	65.32	2,956
Guangdong 廣東	22	70	4,424	151	1.59	4.25	63.53	62.70	9,514
Guangxi 廣西	5	102	4,258	66	1.06	2.16	41.66	50.85	6,214
Hainan 海南									
Southwest 西南	27	73	3,624	-40	-0.63	-1.10	49.69	42.98	6,416
Chongqing 重慶	3	72	1,415	-479	-14.93	-37.63	19.78	60.32	3,210
Sichuan 四川	15	104	5,460	209	2.06	3.46	52.32	40.46	10,145
Guizhou 貴州	3	15	63				4.13		133
Yunnan 雲南	6	27	2,243	47	1.95	4.47	83.60	56.50	2,398
Tibet 西藏									
Northwest 西北	13	55	1,878	70	4.18	7.23	33.92	42.14	1,674
Shaanxi 陝西	9	54	831	-29	-2.27	-4.25	15.27	46.46	1,270
Gansu 甘肅	3	67	5,547	390	11.64	18.90	82.38	38.41	3,350
Qinghai 青海									
Ningxia 寧夏									
Xinjiang 新疆	1	28	300				10.71		280

3677: Environmental Protection Machinery 環境保護機械製造業

Year 年份	Number of firms 企業個數	Rate of change 每年變化 (%)	Number of employees 職工人數 (人)	Rate of change 每年變化 (%)	Total revenue (mil. RMB) 總銷售收入 (百萬元)	Rate of change 每年變化 (%)	Total profit (mil. RMB) 總利潤 (百萬元)	Rate of change 每年變化 (%)
1993	534		60,645		2,364		111	
1994	550	3.00%	58,986	-2.74%	2,549	7.83%	88	-20.41%
1995	628	14.18%	66,874	13.37%	3,045	19.44%	119	34.84%
1996	603	-3.98%	73,583	10.03%	4,731	55.37%	176	48.36%

3 Major products* 3 種主要產品 *	Output 產量	Sales volume 銷售量	Unit 單位
a) Sewage Treating Equipment 污水處理設備	4,136	3,681	set 台
b) Water & Gas Purifier 水・氣淨化設備	8,418	8,165	set 台
c) Preventing Equipment for Air Pollution 大氣污染防治設備	8,316	8,316	set 台

Top 10 firms by revenue (year founded) 收入排名前 10 家企業 (創辦年份)	City 城市	Province 省	Telephone / fax 電話 / 傳真	Number of employees 職工人數	Ownership 產業所有權	Revenue ('000 RMB) 銷售收入 (千元)	Profit ('000 RMB) (rank) 利潤 (千元) (排名)	Total assets ('000 RMB) 總資產 (千元)	Major products 主要產品
Wuxi Suburban Bi Bo Water Treatment Device Factory 無錫市郊區碧波水處理設備廠(1994)	Wuxi 無錫市	Jiangsu 江蘇省	(0510)5599301	10	Collectively-owned 集體	1,199,883	43370(1)	694,817	o
Zhejiang Hua Bao Group Co. 浙江華寶集團公司(1969)	Shaoxing 紹興市	Zhejiang 浙江省	(0575)2012888 (0575)2027890	1,261	Collectively-owned 集體	306,444	18072(3)	151,785	a
Zhejiang Tian Hao Machinery Group Co. Ltd. 浙江天浩機械製造有限公司(1972)	Shaoxing 紹興市	Zhejiang 浙江省	(0575)7052108	632	Foreign-funded 外資	179,615	17767(4)	159,024	o
Zhejiang Fei Da Electromechanical Group Co. Ltd. 浙江菲達機電集團有限公司(1971)	Shaoxing 紹興市	Zhejiang 浙江省	(0575)7213827 (0575)7214695	1,243	State-owned 國有	141,500	7329(8)	262,264	c
Jiangsu Peng Yao Environmental Protection Group Co. Ltd. 江蘇鵬鷂環保集團有限公司(1984)	Wuxi 無錫市	Jiangsu 江蘇省	(0510)7891891 (0510)7891961	400	Collectively-owned 集體	120,590	8500(6)	106,020	o
Shenyang Special Environmental Protection Equipment Manufacturing General Factory 瀋陽特種環保設備製造總廠(1994)	Shenyang 瀋陽市	Liaoning 遼寧省	(024)24812328 (024)24812328	899	State-owned 國有	98,160	25070(2)	425,346	o
Wujiang Dust-cleaning Apparatus Factory 吳江除塵設備廠(1979)	Suzhou 蘇州市	Jiangsu 江蘇省	(0512)3365180 (0512)3365176	370	Collectively-owned 集體	78,179	11184(5)	65,056	c
Bengbu Environmental Protection Equipment Factory 蚌埠市環境保護設備廠(1989)	Bengbu 蚌埠市	Anhui 安徽省	(0552)3018222 (0552)3013488	218	Collectively-owned 集體	76,000	800(44)	40,284	c
Yixing He Qiao School-run Industrial Company 宜興市和橋校辦工業公司(1987)	Wuxi 無錫市	Jiangsu 江蘇省	(0510)7801883	280	Collectively-owned 集體	68,000	1328(28)	6,198	o
Taixing Nan Ji Machinery Group Company 泰興市南極機械集團公司(1995)	Yangzhou 揚州市	Jiangsu 江蘇省	(0514)7686437	528	State-owned 國有	66,260	4518(10)	60,177	o

Top 10 Cities by Production Output 產出排名前 10 位城市	Province 省	Market share 市場份額	Number of firms 企業個數
Wuxi 無錫市	Jiangsu 江蘇省	19.64%	170
Shaoxing 紹興市	Zhejiang 浙江省	14.33%	6
Taizhou 泰州市	Jiangsu 江蘇省	6.28%	19
Shenyang 瀋陽市	Liaoning 遼寧省	5.07%	30
Suzhou 蘇州市	Jiangsu 江蘇省	4.73%	56
Shanghai 上海市	Shanghai 上海市	3.51%	44
Yangzhou 揚州市	Jiangsu 江蘇省	2.99%	18
Pingdingshan 平頂山市	Henan 河南省	2.45%	2
Bengbu 蚌埠市	Anhui 安徽省	2.39%	3
Hangzhou 杭州市	Zhejiang 浙江省	1.97%	21

10 Major Wholesalers 10 家主要批發商	City 城市	Province 省	Telephone / Fax 電話 / 傳真
Liaoning Automobile Trade Group Corp. 遼寧省汽車貿易集團	Shenyang 瀋陽市	Liaoning 遼寧省	(024)23835494 (024)23838338
China Post and Telecommunication Equipment General Company 中國郵電器材總公司	Beijing 北京市	Beijing 北京市	(010)63523715 (010)63525935
Jiangsu Electromechanical Products General Company 江蘇省機電產品總公司	Nanjing 南京市	Jiangsu 江蘇省	(025)7713642 (025)7711036
Xi Nan Technology Import & Export Company 西南技術進出口公司	Chongqing 重慶市	Chongqing 重慶市	(023)63850185 (023)63850026
Changzhou Economic Technology Industrial Development Zone Tian Ming Trade Company 常州經濟技術產業開發區天明貿易公司	Changzhou 常州市	Jiangsu 江蘇省	(0519)8829882 (0519)8829882
Shanxi Mechanical Equipment Import & Export Company 山西省機械設備進出口公司	Taiyuan 太原市	Shanxi 山西省	(0351)4040713 (0351)4043981
Ningbo Five Mining Machinery Import & Export Company 寧波市五礦機械進出口公司	Ningbo 寧波市	Zhejiang 浙江省	(0574)7311255 (0574)7320322
Tianjin Jin Huan Electromechanical Complete Sets of Equipment Factory 天津市津環機電成套設備廠	Tianjin 天津市	Tianjin 天津市	(022)26371628
Yunnan Machinery Import & Export Company 雲南省機械進出口公司	Kunming 昆明市	Yunnan 雲南省	(0871)3164879 (0871)3136829
Tianjin Da Qiu Zhuang Yi Yuan Trade Center 天津市大丘莊億源商貿中心	Tianjin 天津市	Tianjin 天津市	(022)28899478 (022)28899046

*Also include sales by firms outside this industry.包括本行業以外廠家的銷售。"o" stands for "others". "o" 代表"其他產品"。

3678: Security and Fire-fighting Equipment 社會公共安全設備及器材製造業

The industry accounts for 0.044% of the total revenue of China's industrial sector in 1996. The revenue growth rate of the industry is 10.2% from 1995, as compared to the growth rate of China's industrial sector, 9.51%. The rate of return on asset is 2.91%. 72.58% of all firms in the industry made a profit while 24.07% had negative returns. The top province in terms of the industry's revenue is Shanghai, accounting for 16.88% of the total revenue.
本行業在1996年佔全行業總產值0.044%，行業年增長率為10.2%（全國工業年增長率9.51%）。行業的資產回報率2.91%，72.58%的企業盈利，24.07%的企業虧損。銷售收入最高的省份為上海市，佔本行業的16.88%。

	Total number of firms 企業總數	Total number of employees 職工總數	Total revenue (mil. RMB) 總銷售收入（百萬元）	Total profit (mil. RMB) 總利潤（百萬元）	Return on assets 資產利潤率 (%)	Return on equity 權益利潤率 (%)	Labour productivity ('000 RMB / worker) 勞動生產率（千元／人）	Debts / assets 資產負債率 (%)	Total assets (mil. RMB) 總資產（百萬元）
Industry Overall 行業總體	537	49,914	2,530	100	2.91	9.04	50.69	67.76	3,416

	Number of firms 企業個數	Average number of employees 平均職工人數	Average revenue ('000 RMB) 平均銷售收入（千元）	Average profit ('000 RMB) 平均利潤（千元）	Return on assets 資產利潤率 (%)	Return on equity 權益利潤率 (%)	Labour productivity ('000 RMB / worker) 勞動生產率（千元／人）	Average debts / assets 平均資產負債率(%)	Average Total assets ('000 RMB) 平均總資產（千元）
By ownership 產業所有權									
State-owned 國有	64	193	8,594	47	0.29	1.40	44.52	79.16	16,047
Collectively-owned 集體	403	79	3,694	176	4.22	12.41	46.64	65.98	4,164
Privately-owned 私有	4	75	5,906	560	8.23	38.48	79.00	78.61	6,804
Domestic JVs 聯營	9	175	6,715	326	3.17	10.12	38.42	68.70	10,291
Joint stock 股份制	11	128	13,447	1,253	9.92	26.20	104.68	62.15	12,640
Foreign-funded 外資	22	70	7,273	92	0.73	1.35	103.49	45.86	12,627
Overseas Chinese-funded 港澳台資	24	51	4,005	218	3.05	6.75	78.60	54.90	7,160
By size 規模									
Large 大型									
Medium 中型	10	618	47,073	2,818	4.25	17.21	76.21	75.30	66,283
Small 小型	512	85	4,022	140	2.61	7.66	47.11	65.96	5,376
By regional distribution 地區分布									
Central-North 華北	90	74	3,146	162	3.50	11.00	42.60	68.18	4,626
Beijing 北京	42	34	2,187	128	3.83	12.49	64.74	69.34	3,345
Tianjin 天津	20	133	3,680	68	1.07	2.90	27.68	62.96	6,285
Hebei 河北	18	71	5,519	372	5.92	21.64	77.98	72.65	6,276
Shanxi 山西	5	177	1,778	-128	-2.27	-6.93	10.07	67.25	5,636
Inner Mongolia 內蒙	5	82	1,884	360	19.93	66.18	22.92	69.77	1,806
Northeast 東北	119	104	2,449	86	1.48	10.93	23.50	86.46	5,790
Liaoning 遼寧	51	145	3,669	101	1.03	8.80	25.32	88.28	9,814
Jilin 吉林	22	56	1,108	82	3.16	12.57	19.94	74.89	2,592
Heilongjiang 黑龍江	46	82	1,737	70	2.46	15.93	21.10	84.53	2,859
Central East 華東	206	90	6,531	264	3.58	10.70	72.27	66.52	7,380
Shanghai 上海	30	134	14,234	1,089	6.77	19.67	106.04	65.60	16,098
Jiangsu 江蘇	60	98	6,929	135	1.90	6.75	70.60	71.84	7,107
Zhejiang 浙江	49	83	5,871	142	2.21	7.36	70.89	70.02	6,445
Anhui 安徽	15	127	6,581	468	7.82	20.95	51.79	62.69	5,987
Fujian 福建	14	30	2,083	105	4.69	13.34	68.61	64.86	2,240
Jiangxi 江西	14	60	1,756	-65	-1.23	-3.88	29.09	68.15	5,266
Shandong 山東	24	61	2,606	-35	-0.85	-1.41	42.66	40.02	4,177
Central-South 中南	85	97	5,390	174	2.56	5.35	55.37	52.20	6,815
Henan 河南	22	52	1,158	-32	-1.14	-4.24	22.28	73.03	2,784
Hubei 湖北	13	146	4,052	23	0.16	0.23	27.68	29.10	14,466
Hunan 湖南	13	162	15,558	1,094	24.78	49.10	95.95	49.54	4,415
Guangdong 廣東	31	75	4,850	57	0.80	2.32	64.41	65.66	7,153
Guangxi 廣西	6	131	4,575	-130	-1.54	-3.56	34.88	56.90	8,468
Hainan 海南									
Southwest 西南	21	94	2,494	-31	-0.79	-2.93	26.58	72.95	3,911
Chongqing 重慶	4	142	3,577	-32	-0.56	-2.68	25.22	78.94	5,762
Sichuan 四川	14	77	2,116	-40	-1.15	-4.23	27.36	72.78	3,440
Guizhou 貴州	2	20	465				23.25	47.37	190
Yunnan 雲南	1	280	7,390	30	0.29	0.74	26.39	61.03	10,340
Tibet 西藏									
Northwest 西北	16	125	6,218	386	4.77	9.14	49.57	47.83	8,084
Shaanxi 陝西	12	137	7,768	523	5.32	10.04	56.67	47.00	9,816
Gansu 甘肅	1	148	500	90	5.63	8.91	3.38	36.88	1,600
Qinghai 青海	1	50		-70	-12.96	77.78		116.67	540
Ningxia 寧夏	1	81	2,900	-20	-0.46	-0.88	35.80	47.34	4,330
Xinjiang 新疆	1	83	2,870	-100	-1.97	-5.43	34.58	63.58	5,080

3678: Security and Fire-fighting Equipment 社會公共安全設備及器材製造業

Year 年份	Number of firms 企業個數	Rate of change 每年變化 (%)	Number of employees 職工人數（人）	Rate of change 每年變化 (%)	Total revenue (mil. RMB) 總銷售收入（百萬元）	Rate of change 每年變化 (%)	Total profit (mil. RMB) 總利潤（百萬元）	Rate of change 每年變化 (%)
1993	453		52,652		1,732		75	
1994	465	2.65%	47,236	-10.29%	1,814	4.77%	54	-27.87%
1995	554	19.14%	51,438	8.90%	2,296	26.52%	95	75.00%
1996	537	-3.07%	49,914	-2.96%	2,530	10.19%	100	5.54%

3 Major products* 3 種主要產品 *	Output 產量	Sales volume 銷售量	Unit 單位
a) Fire Fighting Equipment 消防器材	7,609,800	6,848,820	set 台（套）
b) Safety Defensive Alarming Instrument 安全防範報警器材	106,035	98,612	set 台
c) Special Refitted Truck 專用改裝汽車	1,066	1,024	vehicle 輛

Top 10 firms by revenue (year founded) 收入排名前 10 家企業 (創辦年份)	City 城市	Province 省	Telephone / fax 電話 / 傳真	Number of employees 職工人數	Ownership 產業所有權	Revenue ('000 RMB) 銷售收入（千元）	Profit ('000 RMB) (rank) 利潤（千元）（排名）	Total assets ('000 RMB) 總資產（千元）	Major products 主要產品
Shanghai Songjiang Electronic Instrument Plant 上海市松江電子儀器廠(1986)	Shanghai 上海市	Shanghai 上海市	(021)57820956 (021)57825548	470	Collectively-owned 集體	88,826	20002(1)	103,947	o
Shanghai Fire Fighting Equipment General Factory 上海消防器材總廠(1918)	Shanghai 上海市	Shanghai 上海市	(021)57833531 (021)57833531	314	State-owned 國有	74,702	3742(5)	67,264	a,c
Shanghai Grumman International Fire Equipment Co. Ltd. 上海格拉曼國際消防裝備有限公司(1989)	Shanghai 上海市	Shanghai 上海市	(021)57833768 (021)57830472	695	Foreign-funded 外資	71,231	0(159)	85,612	a,c
Yingkou Alarming Equipment General Factory 營口報警設備總廠(1966)	Yingkou 營口市	Liaoning 遼寧省	(0417)2837249 (0417)2838592	1,314	State-owned 國有	69,811	5753(2)	144,003	o
Zhen Dan Fire Fighting Appliance General Factory 震旦消防設備總廠(1917)	Shanghai 上海市	Shanghai 上海市	(021)56663600 (021)63248077	662	State-owned 國有	67,672	792(37)	98,523	a,c
Wuxi He Ma Fire Fighting Equipment Group Co. Ltd. 無錫河馬消防器材集團有限公司(1984)	Wuxi 無錫市	Jiangsu 江蘇省	(0510)2613363 (0510)2610711	161	Collectively-owned 集體	60,213	-1666(206)	20,255	a
Baoji Fire Fighting Equipment General Factory 寶雞消防器材總廠(1962)	Baoji 寶雞市	Shaanxi 陝西省	(0917)3555577 (0917)3553907	971	State-owned 國有	56,991	1129(21)	60,929	o
Wan An Da Fire Fighting Appliance Co. Ltd. 萬安達消防設備有限公司(1994)	Ningbo 寧波市	Zhejiang 浙江省	(0574)2367458 (0574)2367388	425	Joint stock 股份制	50,109	3088(8)	44,350	o
Jiangsu Shui Longjiang Shan Group Company 江蘇水龍江山集團公司(1974)	Nantong 南通市	Jiangsu 江蘇省	(0513)2682868 (0513)2682828	820	Collectively-owned 集體	46,013	951(28)	40,313	o
Zhejiang Longevity Plastic Machinery Factory 浙江長命塑料機械廠(1994)	Hangzhou 杭州市	Zhejiang 浙江省	(0571)8541535	37	Collectively-owned 集體	41,481	124(99)	12,595	o

Top 10 Cities by Production Output 產出排名前 10 位城市	Province 省	Market share 市場份額	Number of firms 企業個數
Shanghai 上海市	Shanghai 上海市	21.45%	61
Ningbo 寧波市	Zhejiang 浙江省	5.67%	17
Zhenjiang 鎮江市	Jiangsu 江蘇省	3.79%	7
Hangzhou 杭州市	Zhejiang 浙江省	3.43%	13
Tianjin 天津市	Tianjin 天津市	3.12%	22
Yingkou 營口市	Liaoning 遼寧省	3.09%	5
Guangzhou 廣州市	Guangdong 廣東省	2.67%	13
Nanjing 南京市	Jiangsu 江蘇省	2.64%	21
Baoji 寶雞市	Shaanxi 陝西省	2.54%	6
Nantong 南通市	Jiangsu 江蘇省	2.42%	8

10 Major Wholesalers 10 家主要批發商	City 城市	Province 省	Telephone / Fax 電話 / 傳真
Liaoning Automobile Trade Group Corp. 遼寧省汽車貿易集團	Shenyang 瀋陽市	Liaoning 遼寧省	(024)23835494 (024)23838338
China Post and Telecommunication Equipment General Company 中國郵電器材總公司	Beijing 北京市	Beijing 北京市	(010)63523715 (010)63525935
Jiangsu Electromechanical Products General Company 江蘇省機電產品總公司	Nanjing 南京市	Jiangsu 江蘇省	(025)7713642 (025)7711036
Xi Nan Technology Import & Export Company 西南技術進出口公司	Chongqing 重慶市	Chongqing 重慶市	(023)63850185 (023)63850026
Changzhou Economic Technology Industrial Development Zone Tian Ming Trade Company 常州經濟技術產業開發區天明貿易公司	Changzhou 常州市	Jiangsu 江蘇省	(0519)8829882 (0519)8829882
Shanxi Mechanical Equipment Import & Export Company 山西省機械設備進出口公司	Taiyuan 太原市	Shanxi 山西省	(0351)4040713 (0351)4043981
Ningbo Five Mining Machinery Import & Export Company 寧波市五礦機械進出口公司	Ningbo 寧波市	Zhejiang 浙江省	(0574)7311255 (0574)7320322
Tianjin Jin Huan Electromechanical Complete Sets of Equipment Factory 天津市津環機電成套設備廠	Tianjin 天津市	Tianjin 天津市	(022)26371628
Yunnan Machinery Import & Export Company 雲南省機械進出口公司	Kunming 昆明市	Yunnan 雲南省	(0871)3164879 (0871)3136829
Tianjin Da Qiu Zhuang Yi Yuan Trade Center 天津市大丘莊億源商貿中心	Tianjin 天津市	Tianjin 天津市	(022)28899478 (022)28899046

*Also include sales by firms outside this industry.包括本行業以外廠家的銷售。"o" stands for "others". "o" 代表"其他產品"。

3679: Other Special Equipment 其他類未包括的專用設備製造業

The industry accounts for 0.069% of the total revenue of China's industrial sector in 1996. The revenue growth rate of the industry is 19.7% from 1995, as compared to the growth rate of China's industrial sector, 9.51%. The rate of return on asset is 1.19%. 68.28% of all firms in the industry made a profit while 26.50% had negative returns. The top province in terms of the industry's revenue is Jiangsu, accounting for 29.97% of the total revenue.
本行業在1996年佔全行業總產值0.069%，行業年增長率為19.7%（全國工業年增長率9.51%）。行業的資產回報率1.19%，68.28%的企業盈利，26.50%的企業虧損。銷售收入最高的省份為江蘇省，佔本行業的29.97%。

	Total number of firms 企業總數	Total number of employees 職工總數	Total revenue (mil. RMB) 總銷售收入（百萬元）	Total profit (mil. RMB) 總利潤（百萬元）	Return on assets 資產利潤率 (%)	Return on equity 權益利潤率 (%)	Labour productivity ('000 RMB / worker) 勞動生產率（千元/人）	Debts / assets 資產負債率 (%)	Total assets (mil. RMB) 總資產（百萬元）
Industry Overall 行業總體	614	80,603	4,008	80	1.19	2.70	49.73	66.39	6,722

	Number of firms 企業個數	Average number of employees 平均職工人數	Average revenue ('000 RMB) 平均銷售收入（千元）	Average profit ('000 RMB) 平均利潤（千元）	Return on assets 資產利潤率 (%)	Return on equity 權益利潤率 (%)	Labour productivity ('000 RMB / worker) 勞動生產率（千元/人）	Average debts / assets 平均資產負債率(%)	Average Total assets ('000 RMB) 平均總資產（千元）
By ownership 產業所有權									
State-owned 國有	101	409	13,218	-554	-1.72	-5.00	32.35	65.65	32,287
Collectively-owned 集體	429	78	4,131	164	3.00	9.84	53.10	69.56	5,465
Privately-owned 私有	6	26	403	-248	-6.49	-14.09	15.59	53.96	3,818
Domestic JVs 聯營	11	179	19,522	1,575	9.35	19.42	109.28	51.84	16,840
Joint stock 股份制	7	66	2,822	97	3.57	10.39	42.85	65.58	2,706
Foreign-funded 外資	25	43	7,066	224	2.53	5.68	163.71	55.49	8,848
Overseas Chinese-funded 港澳台資	34	67	14,155	1,282	6.56	20.02	210.62	67.22	19,533
By size 規模									
Large 大型	6	2,064	90,732	49,665	19.04	71.26	43.97	73.29	260,914
Medium 中型	27	787	36,808	-311	-0.44	-1.17	46.77	62.37	70,728
Small 小型	565	82	4,372	-371	-6.46	-18.68	53.14	65.43	5,746
By regional distribution 地區分布									
Central-North 華北	128	110	5,066	151	1.69	5.86	46.19	71.18	8,921
Beijing 北京	59	60	4,305	-46	-0.69	-2.00	72.25	65.52	6,646
Tianjin 天津	14	47	3,171	395	8.57	23.08	66.97	62.86	4,608
Hebei 河北	32	183	8,264	484	3.08	12.95	45.06	76.24	15,725
Shanxi 山西	14	260	5,123	133	1.05	3.68	19.71	71.54	12,695
Inner Mongolia 內蒙	9	39	1,544	-98	-20.23	586.67	39.27	103.68	483
Northeast 東北	124	104	2,982	-268	-3.82	-3.46	28.56	69.86	7,015
Liaoning 遼寧	87	82	2,941	-132	-2.23	-1.29	35.83	63.42	5,927
Jilin 吉林	27	72	2,880	-28	-0.44	-1.34	40.07	67.09	6,292
Heilongjiang 黑龍江	10	386	3,608	-2,101	-11.40	-119.31	9.34	90.45	18,434
Central East 華東	219	116	7,895	272	2.78	8.10	68.06	65.61	9,764
Shanghai 上海	28	60	4,228	-400	-4.96	-18.87	70.43	73.69	8,056
Jiangsu 江蘇	71	184	16,920	907	5.28	14.85	92.10	64.42	17,161
Zhejiang 浙江	46	49	2,570	77	1.59	5.26	51.97	69.81	4,828
Anhui 安徽	11	90	1,903	-136	-3.68	-16.34	21.12	77.45	3,701
Fujian 福建	15	45	2,356	-40	-0.85	-1.61	52.28	47.16	4,711
Jiangxi 江西	14	77	1,299	-75	-4.43	-24.82	16.87	82.15	1,693
Shandong 山東	34	167	6,372	176	1.78	4.82	38.27	63.04	9,916
Central-South 中南	110	133	8,413	319	2.09	6.22	63.09	66.39	15,255
Henan 河南	33	145	7,177	178	1.51	5.38	49.44	71.94	11,806
Hubei 湖北	18	309	10,354	222	1.17	2.13	33.48	45.06	19,003
Hunan 湖南	14	32	1,554	20	1.22	2.64	48.90	53.90	1,641
Guangdong 廣東	33	98	12,425	760	3.36	13.80	127.03	75.69	22,640
Guangxi 廣西	10	57	6,833	77	0.46	1.14	120.30	59.54	16,653
Hainan 海南	2	36	1,070	-455	-9.30	-12.78	29.72	27.30	4,890
Southwest 西南	19	439	9,888	34	0.12	0.31	22.54	59.67	27,358
Chongqing 重慶	3	458	6,314	178	1.51	2.32	13.80	34.67	11,739
Sichuan 四川	8	344	6,575	-5	-0.03	-0.06	19.11	53.57	17,543
Guizhou 貴州	6	620	17,115	23	0.05	0.16	27.60	70.71	49,340
Yunnan 雲南	2	222	6,865	-30	-0.12	-0.17	30.99	30.69	25,220
Tibet 西藏									
Northwest 西北	14	372	10,544	-99	-0.37	-0.87	28.34	57.44	26,732
Shaanxi 陝西	11	425	11,140	-138	-0.45	-1.05	26.21	57.22	30,617
Gansu 甘肅	2	262	12,505	70	0.38	0.93	47.73	59.36	18,625
Qinghai 青海									
Ningxia 寧夏									
Xinjiang 新疆	1	9	60	-10	-4.76	-20.00	6.67	76.19	210

3679: Other Special Equipment 其他類未包括的專用設備製造業

Year 年份	Number of firms 企業個數	Rate of change 每年變化 (%)	Number of employees 職工人數（人）	Rate of change 每年變化 (%)	Total revenue (mil. RMB) 總銷售收入（百萬元）	Rate of change 每年變化 (%)	Total profit (mil. RMB) 總利潤（百萬元）	Rate of change 每年變化 (%)
1993	579		100,638		3,536		131	
1994	607	4.84%	98,152	-2.47%	3,231	-8.65%	-56	-142.86%
1995	536	-11.70%	85,376	-13.02%	3,348	3.64%	-38	32.78%
1996	614	14.55%	80,603	-5.59%	4,008	19.71%	80	311.72%

3 Major products* 3 種主要產品 *	Output 產量	Sales volume 銷售量	Unit 單位
a) Distributing Machine for Bituminous Ground 瀝青地面攤鋪機	413	371	set 台
b) Cotton Processing Machine 棉花加工設備	2,877	2,733	set 台
c) Plant & Mining Accessories 工礦配件	26,082	22,431	ton 噸

Top 10 firms by revenue (year founded) 收入排名前 10 家企業（創辦年份）	City 城市	Province 省	Telephone / fax 電話 / 傳真	Number of employees 職工人數	Ownership 產業所有權	Revenue ('000 RMB) 銷售收入（千元）	Profit ('000 RMB) (rank) 利潤（千元）（排名）	Total assets ('000 RMB) 總資產（千元）	Major products 主要產品
Zhongda Industrial Group Co. 中大工業集團公司(1980)	Yancheng 鹽城市	Jiangsu 江蘇省	(0515)8336666	1,800	Joint stock 股份制	449,760	51000(1)	282,970	o
Shenzhen Tian Da Airport Support Ltd. 深圳天達空港設備有限公司(1993)	Shenzhen 深圳市	Guangdong 廣東省	(0755)6691130 (0755)6692707	500	Overseas Chinese-funded 港澳台資	181,783	12251(2)	263,100	o
Changzhou Energy Engineering Factory 常州能源設備總廠(1978)	Changzhou 常州市	Jiangsu 江蘇省	(0519)8812441 (0519)8825315	1,225	Domestic JVs 聯營	130,977	12006(3)	129,556	o
Beijing Gas Apparatus Factory 北京市煤氣用具廠(1960)	Beijing 北京市	Beijing 北京市	(010)65025531 (010)65072083	1,361	State-owned 國有	108,427	-10405(247)	128,432	o
Zhenjiang Huatong Machinery Group Co. 鎮江華通機械集團公司(1954)	Zhenjiang 鎮江市	Jiangsu 江蘇省	(0511)4421162 (0511)4422667	2,184	State-owned 國有	104,240	70(130)	179,004	a,c
Jiangsu Liu Tong Machinery (Group) Co. 江蘇省六通機械(集團)公司(1992)	Wuxi 無錫市	Jiangsu 江蘇省	(0510)5302284	707	Collectively-owned 集體	101,291	3756(9)	78,076	o
Ningbo Jiangbei Chong Ben Printing Iron Work Service Dept. 寧波市江北區崇本印鐵服務部(1990)	Ningbo 寧波市	Zhejiang 浙江省	(0574)7598145	20	Collectively-owned 集體	85,000	1000(32)	3,245	o
Wuhan Hankou Machine Tool Factory 武漢市漢口機床廠(1949)	Wuhan 武漢市	Hubei 湖北省	(027)83624863 (027)83626311	2,013	State-owned 國有	78,151	1015(30)	90,029	o
Shandong Cotton & Linen Machinery Factory 山東棉麻機械廠(1955)	Ji'nan 濟南市	Shandong 山東省	(0531)5704882 (0531)5704882	955	Collectively-owned 集體	72,560	69(132)	101,491	b
Xi'an Electric Power Machinery Factory 西安電力機械廠(1956)	Xi'an 西安市	Shaanxi 陝西省	(029)3524133 (029)3524068	1,459	State-owned 國有	66,737	-2470(239)	161,304	o

Top 10 Cities by Production Output 產出排名前 10 位城市	Province 省	Market share 市場份額	Number of firms 企業個數
Wuxi 無錫市	Jiangsu 江蘇省	8.95%	40
Beijing 北京市	Beijing 北京市	8.75%	44
Harbin 哈爾濱市	Heilongjiang 黑龍江省	7.03%	36
Shanghai 上海市	Shanghai 上海市	6.01%	56
Changzhou 常州市	Jiangsu 江蘇省	5.47%	22
Chongqing 重慶市	Chongqing 重慶市	3.31%	13
Zhenjiang 鎮江市	Jiangsu 江蘇省	3.06%	9
Suzhou 蘇州市	Jiangsu 江蘇省	2.52%	31
Yangzhou 揚州市	Jiangsu 江蘇省	2.46%	14
Wuhan 武漢市	Hubei 湖北省	2.41%	9

10 Major Wholesalers 10 家主要批發商	City 城市	Province 省	Telephone / Fax 電話 / 傳真
Liaoning Automobile Trade Group Corp. 遼寧省汽車貿易集團	Shenyang 瀋陽市	Liaoning 遼寧省	(024)23835494 (024)23838338
China Post and Telecommunication Equipment General Company 中國郵電器材總公司	Beijing 北京市	Beijing 北京市	(010)63523715 (010)63525935
Jiangsu Electromechanical Products General Company 江蘇省機電產品總公司	Nanjing 南京市	Jiangsu 江蘇省	(025)7713642 (025)7711036
Xi Nan Technology Import & Export Company 西南技術進出口公司	Chongqing 重慶市	Chongqing 重慶市	(023)63850185 (023)63850026
Changzhou Economic Technology Industrial Development Zone Tian Ming Trade Company 常州經濟技術產業開發區天明貿易公司	Changzhou 常州市	Jiangsu 江蘇省	(0519)8829882 (0519)8829882
Shanxi Mechanical Equipment Import & Export Company 山西省機械設備進出口公司	Taiyuan 太原市	Shanxi 山西省	(0351)4040713 (0351)4043981
Ningbo Five Mining Machinery Import & Export Company 寧波市五礦機械進出口公司	Ningbo 寧波市	Zhejiang 浙江省	(0574)7311255 (0574)7320322
Tianjin Jin Huan Electromechanical Complete Sets of Equipment Factory 天津市津環機電成套設備廠	Tianjin 天津市	Tianjin 天津市	(022)26371628
Yunnan Machinery Import & Export Company 雲南省機械進出口公司	Kunming 昆明市	Yunnan 雲南省	(0871)3164879 (0871)3136829
Tianjin Da Qiu Zhuang Yi Yuan Trade Center 天津市大丘莊億源商貿中心	Tianjin 天津市	Tianjin 天津市	(022)28899478 (022)28899046

*Also include sales by firms outside this industry.包括本行業以外廠家的銷售。"o" stands for "others". "o" 代表 "其他產品"。

3681: Industrial Equipment Repairs 工業專用設備修理業

The industry accounts for 0.013% of the total revenue of China's industrial sector in 1996. The revenue growth rate of the industry is 15.6% from 1995, as compared to the growth rate of China's industrial sector, 9.51%. The rate of return on asset is 2.16%. 74.15% of all firms in the industry made a profit while 18.35% had negative returns. The top province in terms of the industry's revenue is Liaoning, accounting for 19.96% of the total revenue.
本行業在1996年佔全行業總產值0.013%，行業年增長率為15.6%（全國工業年增長率9.51%）。行業的資產回報率2.16%，74.15%的企業盈利，18.35%的企業虧損。銷售收入最高的省份為遼寧省，佔本行業的19.96%。

	Total number of firms 企業總數	Total number of employees 職工總數	Total revenue (mil. RMB) 總銷售收入（百萬元）	Total profit (mil. RMB) 總利潤（百萬元）	Return on assets 資產利潤率 (%)	Return on equity 權益利潤率 (%)	Labour productivity ('000 RMB / worker) 勞動生產率（千元/人）	Debts / assets 資產負債率 (%)	Total assets (mil. RMB) 總資產（百萬元）
Industry Overall 行業總體	354	23,003	758	25	2.16	5.82	32.95	62.84	1,145

	Number of firms 企業個數	Average number of employees 平均職工人數	Average revenue ('000 RMB) 平均銷售收入（千元）	Average profit ('000 RMB) 平均利潤（千元）	Return on assets 資產利潤率 (%)	Return on equity 權益利潤率 (%)	Labour productivity ('000 RMB / worker) 勞動生產率（千元/人）	Average debts / assets 平均資產負債率(%)	Average Total assets ('000 RMB) 平均總資產（千元）
By ownership 產業所有權									
State-owned 國有	65	90	1,154				12.81	45.05	6,523
Collectively-owned 集體	273	60	2,349	97	4.28	17.40	38.92	75.41	2,266
Privately-owned 私有	1	23	1,128	240	17.34	79.19	49.03	78.10	1,387
Domestic JVs 聯營	1	113	2,314	4	0.08	0.25	20.48	67.02	4,575
Joint stock 股份制	4	60	1,579	-10	-0.25	-1.04	26.21	75.68	3,974
Foreign-funded 外資	6	99	4,983	54	0.55	1.37	50.25	59.92	9,895
Overseas Chinese-funded 港澳台資	4	18	447	-500	-9.51	-19.27	25.20	50.66	5,259
By size 規模									
Large 大型									
Medium 中型	1	535	11,111	158	0.34	0.62	20.77	45.74	46,790
Small 小型	350	65	2,134	71	2.26	6.22	32.65	63.61	3,138
By regional distribution 地區分布									
Central-North 華北	111	56	1,631	28	0.96	1.89	29.03	49.17	2,931
Beijing 北京	29	46	1,197	-1	-0.03	-0.03	25.79	24.07	4,118
Tianjin 天津	41	31	2,637	60	10.17	30.43	85.67	66.57	595
Hebei 河北	11	91	1,386	-15	-0.35	-1.80	15.31	80.80	4,475
Shanxi 山西	20	34	893	33	4.53	7.47	26.41	39.37	718
Inner Mongolia 內蒙	10	196	516	20	0.17	0.41	2.64	58.97	11,796
Northeast 東北	99	47	1,779	164	10.23	35.23	38.01	70.95	1,607
Liaoning 遼寧	63	52	2,401	241	12.24	44.97	45.86	72.79	1,968
Jilin 吉林	12	27	227	-28	-3.77	-6.33	8.40	40.53	753
Heilongjiang 黑龍江	24	42	923	60	5.56	20.39	21.91	72.73	1,086
Central East 華東	65	77	3,737	96	1.76	4.67	48.32	62.44	5,451
Shanghai 上海	17	81	6,535	253	2.55	10.95	80.27	76.71	9,915
Jiangsu 江蘇	9	49	2,988	127	3.18	9.94	61.11	68.07	3,988
Zhejiang 浙江	6	158	1,310	-43	-0.30	-0.45	8.28	33.84	14,407
Anhui 安徽	5	68	2,924	92	4.15	21.50	42.75	80.70	2,218
Fujian 福建	3	20	143	-20	-2.11	-2.83	7.05	25.61	950
Jiangxi 江西	12	79	2,331	45	1.41	3.19	29.60	55.80	3,188
Shandong 山東	13	70	4,159	8	0.89	2.49	59.61	64.30	866
Central-South 中南	56	112	2,499	-3	-0.06	-0.24	22.32	74.30	5,018
Henan 河南	19	88	1,261	-22	-0.82	-3.51	14.32	76.76	2,706
Hubei 湖北	16	240	6,141	63	0.56	3.11	25.63	81.90	11,209
Hunan 湖南	7	29	121	-20	-8.09	-19.44	4.19	58.38	247
Guangdong 廣東	9	34	1,648	-71	-1.37	-2.45	48.78	44.06	5,178
Guangxi 廣西	3	30	383				12.78	15.56	150
Hainan 海南	2	84	450	10	1.39	3.17	5.39	56.25	720
Southwest 西南	11	28	716	14	1.87	3.63	25.50	48.51	731
Chongqing 重慶									
Sichuan 四川	3	42	1,833	-17	-1.03	-2.76	43.64	62.78	1,657
Guizhou 貴州	7	24	340	14	3.26	4.39	14.08	25.41	439
Yunnan 雲南	1	15							
Tibet 西藏									
Northwest 西北	12	44	818	-68	-4.80	-18.85	18.74	74.47	1,423
Shaanxi 陝西	6	42	275	-30	-2.30	-4.93	6.63	53.32	1,307
Gansu 甘肅	3	40	937	3	1.03	2.38	23.22	56.70	323
Qinghai 青海									
Ningxia 寧夏	1	60	3,810	20	3.92		63.50	100.00	510
Xinjiang 新疆	2	47	775	-335	-8.63	-239.29	16.49	96.39	3,880

3681: Industrial Equipment Repairs 工業專用設備修理業

Year 年份	Number of firms 企業個數	Rate of change 每年變化 (%)	Number of employees 職工人數 (人)	Rate of change 每年變化 (%)	Total revenue (mil. RMB) 總銷售收入 (百萬元)	Rate of change 每年變化 (%)	Total profit (mil. RMB) 總利潤 (百萬元)	Rate of change 每年變化 (%)
1993	341		162,140		534		44	
1994	337	-1.17%	22,700	-86.00%	499	-6.52%	4	-89.92%
1995	271	-19.59%	23,536	3.68%	656	31.26%	8	85.01%
1996	354	30.63%	23,003	-2.26%	758	15.63%	25	204.69%

3 Major products* 3 種主要產品 *	Output 產量	Sales volume 銷售量	Unit 單位

Top 10 firms by revenue (year founded) 收入排名前 10 家企業 (創辦年份)	City 城市	Province 省	Telephone / fax 電話 / 傳真	Number of employees 職工人數	Ownership 產業所有權	Revenue ('000 RMB) 銷售收入 (千元)	Profit ('000 RMB) (rank) 利潤 (千元) (排名)	Total assets ('000 RMB) 總資產 (千元)	Major products 主要產品
Shanghai Gao Qiao Petrochemistry Oil Refining Installment Overhaul Co. 上海高橋石化煉油安裝檢修公司(1992)	Shanghai 上海市	Shanghai 上海市	(021)58611060 (021)58612466	756	Collectively-owned 集體	70,346	2544(2)	107,489	o
Wuhan Iron & Steel Corp. Overhaul Engineering Co. 武鋼檢修工程公司(1979)	Wuhan 武漢市	Hubei 湖北省	(027)86894391	1,289	Collectively-owned 集體	45,809	858(10)	74,732	o
Chengdu Engineering Machinery General Factory Overhaul Factory 成都工程機械總廠大修廠(1993)	Chengdu 成都市	Sichuan 四川省	(028)4630693	70	Collectively-owned 集體	38,606	444(18)	52,715	o
Fushun Wanghua Industry Machinery Repair & Assembly Factory 撫順市望花工業機械修配廠(1993)	Fushun 撫順市	Liaoning 遼寧省	(0413)6689905	9	Private-owned 私營	29,000	40(50)	1,860	o
Shanghai Gaoqiao Huajian Overhaul Engineering Co. 上海高橋華建檢修工程公司(1992)	Shanghai 上海市	Shanghai 上海市	(021)58610099 (021)58612191	331	Collectively-owned 集體	27,727	671(13)	38,231	o
Wuhan Iron & Steel Corp. Machinery General Co. Machine Repair Plant 武鋼機總機修廠(1990)	Wuhan 武漢市	Hubei 湖北省	(027)86894908	1,128	Collectively-owned 集體	25,480	89(43)	22,152	o
Liao He Oil Field Xing Cai Boiler Install Company 遼河油田興採鍋爐安裝公司(1993)	Panjin 盤錦市	Liaoning 遼寧省	(0427)7811430	66	Collectively-owned 集體	21,760	2180(3)	10,120	o
Jiangxi Copper Industry Company Dexing Tong Mining Machinery General Factory 江西銅業公司德興銅礦機械製造有限公司	Shangrao 上饒市	Jiangxi 江西省	(0793)7720027 (0793)3860206		Collectively-owned 集體	20,288	250(27)	30,111	o
Wuhan Iron & Steel Corp. Industrial Co. Breakdown Xie Li Factory 武鋼實業公司初軋協力廠(1982)	Wuhan 武漢市	Hubei 湖北省	(027)86894386	519	Collectively-owned 集體	13,524	204(30)	47,210	o
Liao He Oil Field Jin Yu Dian Pump Repairing Company 遼河油田金宇電泵修理公司(1988)	Panjin 盤錦市	Liaoning 遼寧省	(0427)7533601	83	Collectively-owned 集體	11,382	1709(5)	9,720	o

Top 10 Cities by Production Output 產出排名前 10 位城市	Province 省	Market share 市場份額	Number of firms 企業個數
Shanghai 上海市	Shanghai 上海市	28.79%	96
Ningbo 寧波市	Zhejiang 浙江省	9.92%	3
Baotou 包頭市	Inner Mong 內蒙	9.86%	3
Dalian 大連市	Liaoning 遼寧省	3.86%	11
Tianjin 天津市	Tianjin 天津市	3.61%	40
Beijing 北京市	Beijing 北京市	3.04%	28
Wuhan 武漢市	Hubei 湖北省	2.83%	6
Taiyuan 太原市	Shanxi 山西省	2.67%	27
Xuzhou 徐州市	Jiangsu 江蘇省	1.96%	10
Fushun 撫順市	Liaoning 遼寧省	1.83%	5

10 Major Wholesalers 10 家主要批發商	City 城市	Province 省	Telephone / Fax 電話 / 傳真

*Also include sales by firms outside this industry.包括本行業以外廠家的銷售。"o" stands for "others". "o" 代表 "其他產品"。

3683: Farming, Forestry, Husbandry and Fishery Machinery Repairing
農、林、牧、漁、水利機械修理業

The industry accounts for 0.025% of the total revenue of China's industrial sector in 1996. The revenue growth rate of the industry is 35.7% from 1995, as compared to the growth rate of China's industrial sector, 9.51%. The rate of return on asset is 4.35%. 80.95% of all firms in the industry made a profit while 10.54% had negative returns. The top province in terms of the industry's revenue is Anhui, accounting for 27.11% of the total revenue.
本行業在1996年佔全行業總產值0.025%，行業年增長率為35.7%（全國工業年增長率9.51%）。行業的資產回報率4.35%，80.95%的企業盈利，10.54%的企業虧損。銷售收入最高的省份為安徽省，佔本行業的27.11%。

	Total number of firms 企業總數	Total number of employees 職工總數	Total revenue (mil. RMB) 總銷售收入（百萬元）	Total profit (mil. RMB) 總利潤（百萬元）	Return on assets 資產利潤率 (%)	Return on equity 權益利潤率 (%)	Labour productivity ('000 RMB / worker) 勞動生產率（千元/人）	Debts / assets 資產負債率 (%)	Total assets (mil. RMB) 總資產（百萬元）
Industry Overall 行業總體	1,796	51,504	1,472	59	4.35	11.96	28.58	63.65	1,357

	Number of firms 企業個數	Average number of employees 平均職工人數	Average revenue ('000 RMB) 平均銷售收入（千元）	Average profit ('000 RMB) 平均利潤（千元）	Return on assets 資產利潤率 (%)	Return on equity 權益利潤率 (%)	Labour productivity ('000 RMB / worker) 勞動生產率（千元/人）	Average debts / assets 平均資產負債率(%)	Average Total assets ('000 RMB) 平均總資產（千元）
By ownership 產業所有權									
State-owned 國有	316	91	1,339	13	0.53	1.63	14.78	67.42	2,389
Collectively-owned 集體	1,470	16	704	36	9.01	22.24	45.28	59.51	404
Privately-owned 私有	3	7	119	14	7.04	7.85	16.20	10.31	193
Domestic JVs 聯營	1	5	607	58	6.64	7.69	121.44	13.71	870
Joint stock 股份制	4	13	3,337	362	49.68	60.84	251.85	18.34	729
Foreign-funded 外資	1	5	465	1	0.05	0.05	92.93	5.83	2,378
Overseas Chinese-funded 港澳台資	1	6	74	1	0.08	0.16	12.32	49.10	1,372
By size 規模									
Large 大型									
Medium 中型									
Small 小型	1,793	29	821	33	4.35	11.97	28.60	63.67	757
By regional distribution 地區分布									
Central-North 華北	225	23	848	39	4.52	16.22	37.19	72.10	860
Beijing 北京	17	8	255	24	5.16	10.54	32.39	50.88	467
Tianjin 天津	6	32	827	33	2.64	5.36	26.24	50.86	1,265
Hebei 河北	118	19	1,180	73	9.90	37.13	62.98	73.35	734
Shanxi 山西	39	41	531	-19	-1.34	-4.20	13.08	68.04	1,452
Inner Mongolia 內蒙	45	23	480	7	0.95	6.43	21.28	85.15	769
Northeast 東北	292	72	579	-30	-3.73	-15.44	8.01	75.81	803
Liaoning 遼寧	47	362	881	-255	-9.20	-105.09	2.43	91.25	2,769
Jilin 吉林	58	14	411	16	6.20	15.86	30.09	60.93	264
Heilongjiang 黑龍江	187	18	555	12	2.56	5.78	31.45	55.75	475
Central East 華東	424	21	1,385	105	11.72	25.11	64.71	53.34	893
Shanghai 上海	2	33	800	-185	-18.14	462.50	24.62	103.43	1,020
Jiangsu 江蘇	28	33	1,340	9	0.50	2.06	40.61	75.51	1,770
Zhejiang 浙江	35	14	450	6	1.28	2.99	32.10	57.21	469
Anhui 安徽	139	28	2,871	268	15.90	29.16	102.79	45.46	1,684
Fujian 福建	71	11	368	9	4.47	6.98	33.33	35.92	192
Jiangxi 江西	86	11	228	15	10.31	31.26	21.21	67.03	148
Shandong 山東	63	32	1,392	81	10.22	30.21	43.67	66.16	797
Central-South 中南	432	21	804	24	3.58	10.12	38.69	64.67	660
Henan 河南	106	21	704	25	3.00	10.95	32.94	72.59	849
Hubei 湖北	39	34	1,672	57	7.30	24.97	49.55	70.78	784
Hunan 湖南	119	17	793	47	15.01	26.89	45.92	44.20	315
Guangdong 廣東	112	20	746	7	1.01	2.84	37.06	64.58	710
Guangxi 廣西	51	13	516	26	7.36	16.73	38.79	56.00	354
Hainan 海南	5	82	666	-498	-8.41	-24.60	8.12	65.80	5,924
Southwest 西南	220	15	398	5	0.99	2.37	26.76	58.02	490
Chongqing 重慶	42	13	286	-1	-0.39	-2.02	22.74	80.84	330
Sichuan 四川	141	11	372	3	1.20	2.63	35.29	54.40	248
Guizhou 貴州	17	18	258	9	1.68	2.99	13.95	43.87	562
Yunnan 雲南	14	65	1,228	29	0.94	2.53	19.04	62.94	3,044
Tibet 西藏	6	9	245	38	3.46	4.24	28.27	18.22	1,107
Northwest 西北	203	19	442	17	2.15	5.66	22.79	62.01	779
Shaanxi 陝西	87	16	351	22	6.74	16.37	21.84	58.81	331
Gansu 甘肅	57	13	298	21	4.39	8.00	22.34	45.11	468
Qinghai 青海	15	19	369	19	1.98	4.32	19.79	54.26	978
Ningxia 寧夏	23	14	108	10	3.00	6.21	8.01	51.71	319
Xinjiang 新疆	21	56	1,625	-10	-0.27	-0.94	28.80	71.07	3,845

3683: Farming, Forestry, Husbandry and Fishery Machinery Repairing
農、林、牧、漁、水利機械修理業

Year 年份	Number of firms 企業個數	Rate of change 每年變化 (%)	Number of employees 職工人數（人）	Rate of change 每年變化 (%)	Total revenue (mil. RMB) 總銷售收入（百萬元）	Rate of change 每年變化 (%)	Total profit (mil. RMB) 總利潤（百萬元）	Rate of change 每年變化 (%)
1993	2,395		41,155		1,109		37	
1994	2,344	-2.13%	52,734	28.14%	1,594	43.79%	42	12.65%
1995	1,797	-23.34%	38,750	-26.52%	1,085	-31.95%	42	0.13%
1996	1,796	-0.06%	51,504	32.91%	1,472	35.67%	59	41.33%

3 Major products* 3種主要產品*	Output 產量	Sales volume 銷售量	Unit 單位

Top 10 firms by revenue (year founded) 收入排名前10家企業（創辦年份）	City 城市	Province 省	Telephone / fax 電話／傳真	Number of employees 職工人數	Ownership 產業所有權	Revenue ('000 RMB) 銷售收入（千元）	Profit ('000 RMB) (rank) 利潤（千元）（排名）	Total assets ('000 RMB) 總資產（千元）	Major products 主要產品
Anhui Liu'an Walkingtractor Factory 安徽六安手扶拖拉機廠(1956)	Liu'an 六安市	Anhui 安徽省	(0564)3313426 (0564)3325237	1,079	State-owned 國有	196,611	25825(1)	152,840	o
Yingshang Wang Gang Zhen Agricultural Machinery Assembly Company 穎上縣王崗鎮農機裝配公司(1995)	Fuyang 阜陽市	Anhui 安徽省	(0558)4104733	265	Collectively-owned 集體	33,500	1490(2)	8,000	o
Duan Jia Ling Zhen Refrigeration Equipment Factory 段甲嶺鎮製冷設備廠(1993)	Langfang 廊坊市	Hebei 河北省		50	Collectively-owned 集體	20,860	1080(4)	890	o
Hebei Fucheng Da Bai Xiang Machinery Branch 河北省阜城縣大白鄉機械分廠(1982)	Hengshui 衡水市	Hebei 河北省		25	Collectively-owned 集體	14,000	1490(3)	2,700	o
Yanshou Yan He Zhen Farm Tools Repair & Building Factory 延壽縣延河鎮鐵木修造廠(1984)	Shuangcheng 雙城市	Heilongjiang 黑龍江省		5	Collectively-owned 集體	12,160	40(123)	886	o
Changli Fishing Boat Repair & Build Factory 昌黎縣漁船修造廠(1973)	Qinhuangdao 秦皇島市	Hebei 河北省	(0335)2210284	68	State-owned 國有	12,112	20(140)	2,382	o
Xinjiang Corps Nong Wu Shi Machine Build & Repair Plant 新疆生產建設兵團農五師機械修造廠(1960)	Bole 博樂市	Xinjiang 新疆	(0909)2222385 (0909)2220830	358	State-owned 國有	10,296	68(112)	30,246	o
Dongming Dongming Ji Agricultural Machinery Factory 東明縣東明集農機廠(1958)	Heze 菏澤市	Shandong 山東省	(0530)8900231	72	Collectively-owned 集體	9,900	600(11)	2,854	o
Yecheng Agricultural Machine Repair Factory 葉城縣農機修造廠(1970)	Kashi 喀什市	Xinjiang 新疆	(0998)7282279	93	State-owned 國有	9,376	325(28)	11,142	o
Nong'an He Long Zhen Agricultural Machine Repair & Assemble Factory 農安縣合隆鎮農機修配廠(1971)	Changchun 長春市	Jilin 吉林省	(0431)3432431	88	Collectively-owned 集體	9,275	54(117)	5,171	o

Top 10 Cities by Production Output 產出排名前10位城市	Province 省	Market share 市場份額	Number of firms 企業個數
Chengdu 成都市	Sichuan 四川省	7.91%	5
Shanghai 上海市	Shanghai 上海市	3.98%	13
Chuzhou 滁州市	Anhui 安徽省	3.22%	13
Liu'an 六安市	Anhui 安徽省	3.16%	47
Hengshui 衡水市	Hebei 河北省	2.77%	6
Yunfu 雲浮市	Guangdong 廣東省	2.37%	16
Zhaoqing 肇慶市	Guangdong 廣東省	2.01%	18
Zhumadian 駐馬店市	Henan 河南省	1.94%	15
Siping 四平市	Jilin 吉林省	1.83%	10
Changchun 長春市	Jilin 吉林省	1.82%	19

10 Major Wholesalers 10家主要批發商	City 城市	Province 省	Telephone / Fax 電話／傳真

*Also include sales by firms outside this industry.包括本行業以外廠家的銷售。"o" stands for "others". "o" 代表"其他產品"。

3685: Medical Apparatuses and Instruments Repairs 醫療器械修理業

The industry accounts for 0.000% of the total revenue of China's industrial sector in 1996. The revenue growth rate of the industry is 53.7% from 1995, as compared to the growth rate of China's industrial sector, 9.51%. The rate of return on asset is 3.50%. 85.19% of all firms in the industry made a profit while 14.81% had negative returns. The top province in terms of the industry's revenue is Chongqing, accounting for 43.57% of the total revenue.
本行業在1996年佔全行業總產值0.000%，行業年增長率為53.7%（全國工業年增長率9.51%）。行業的資產回報率3.50%，85.19%的企業盈利，14.81%的企業虧損。銷售收入最高的省份為重慶市，佔本行業的43.57%。

	Total number of firms 企業總數	Total number of employees 職工總數	Total revenue (mil. RMB) 總銷售收入（百萬元）	Total profit (mil. RMB) 總利潤（百萬元）	Return on assets 資產利潤率 (%)	Return on equity 權益利潤率 (%)	Labour productivity ('000 RMB / worker) 勞動生產率（千元/人）	Debts / assets 資產負債率 (%)	Total assets (mil. RMB) 總資產（百萬元）
Industry Overall 行業總體	39	440	21	1	3.50	9.51	47.73	63.20	25

	Number of firms 企業個數	Average number of employees 平均職工人數	Average revenue ('000 RMB) 平均銷售收入（千元）	Average profit ('000 RMB) 平均利潤（千元）	Return on assets 資產利潤率 (%)	Return on equity 權益利潤率 (%)	Labour productivity ('000 RMB / worker) 勞動生產率（千元/人）	Average debts / assets 平均資產負債率(%)	Average Total assets ('000 RMB) 平均總資產（千元）
By ownership 產業所有權									
State-owned 國有	19	14	842	53	7.14	12.50	59.04	42.86	737
Collectively-owned 集體	16	9	300				32.67	90.70	563
Privately-owned 私有									
Domestic JVs 聯營									
Joint stock 股份制									
Foreign-funded 外資	2	3							
Overseas Chinese-funded 港澳台資	2	9	96				11.24	91.38	979
By size 規模									
Large 大型									
Medium 中型									
Small 小型	39	11	538	26	4.00	11.11	47.73	64.00	641
By regional distribution 地區分布									
Central-North 華北	9								
Beijing 北京	7								
Tianjin 天津									
Hebei 河北									
Shanxi 山西	1								
Inner Mongolia 內蒙	1								
Northeast 東北	5	28	850	108	6.97	12.59	29.93	44.65	1,550
Liaoning 遼寧	4	4	463	135	46.15	79.41	123.33	41.88	293
Jilin 吉林									
Heilongjiang 黑龍江	1	127	2,400				18.90	45.14	6,580
Central East 華東	9	8	564	14	3.19	7.30	71.55	56.02	452
Shanghai 上海	2	18	1,985	60	5.56	12.37	113.43	55.09	1,080
Jiangsu 江蘇									
Zhejiang 浙江	2	4	50				12.50	120.00	25
Anhui 安徽									
Fujian 福建	3								
Jiangxi 江西	1								
Shandong 山東	1	28	1,010	10	0.54	1.20	36.07	55.38	1,860
Central-South 中南	12	9	248	-34	-3.94	-22.65	29.12	82.60	867
Henan 河南	4	14	160	5	2.11	15.38	11.85	86.32	238
Hubei 湖北	2								
Hunan 湖南	1	22	10	-130	-7.78	59.09	0.45	113.17	1,670
Guangdong 廣東	3	1	370				555.00	34.40	940
Guangxi 廣西	1	4	210				52.50	100.00	70
Hainan 海南	1	20	1,000	-300	-6.13	-600.00	50.00	98.98	4,890
Southwest 西南	3	40	3,050	217	77.38	154.76	76.25	50.00	280
Chongqing 重慶	2	60	4,575	-325	-77.38	-154.76	76.25	50.00	420
Sichuan 四川									
Guizhou 貴州	1								
Yunnan 雲南									
Tibet 西藏									
Northwest 西北	1	5	30	-50	-3.23	-6.67	6.00	51.61	1,550
Shaanxi 陝西	1	5	30	-50	-3.23	-6.67	6.00	51.61	1,550
Gansu 甘肅									
Qinghai 青海									
Ningxia 寧夏									
Xinjiang 新疆									

3685: Medical Apparatuses and Instruments Repairs 醫療器械修理業

Year 年份	Number of firms 企業個數	Rate of change 每年變化 (%)	Number of employees 職工人數 (人)	Rate of change 每年變化 (%)	Total revenue (mil. RMB) 總銷售收入 (百萬元)	Rate of change 每年變化 (%)	Total profit (mil. RMB) 總利潤 (百萬元)	Rate of change 每年變化 (%)
1993	9		249		6		0	
1994	19	111.11%	277	11.24%	11	100.79%	0	-7.37%
1995	20	5.26%	591	113.36%	14	21.99%	-1	-474.48%
1996	39	95.00%	440	-25.55%	21	53.70%	1	211.73%

3 Major products* 3 種主要產品 *	Output 產量	Sales volume 銷售量	Unit 單位

Top 10 firms by revenue (year founded) 收入排名前 10 家企業 (創辦年份)	City 城市	Province 省	Telephone / fax 電話 / 傳真	Number of employees 職工人數	Ownership 產業所有權	Revenue ('000 RMB) 銷售收入 (千元)	Profit ('000 RMB) (rank) 利潤 (千元) (排名)	Total assets ('000 RMB) 總資產 (千元)	Major products 主要產品
Ya'an Area Medical Apparatus & Instruments Repair Shop 雅安地區醫療器械修配所(1978)	Ya'an 雅安市	Sichuan 四川省	(0835)2222461	20	State-owned 國有	9,150	650(1)	843	o
Shanghai Endoscope Maintenance Station 上海內窺鏡維修站(1979)	Shanghai 上海市	Shanghai 上海市	(021)62534839 (021)62534839	15	State-owned 國有	3,544	51(2)	1,730	o
Helongjiang Binxi Light Industry Machinery Factory 黑龍江省賓西輕工機械廠(1969)	Harbin 哈爾濱市	Heilongjiang 黑龍江省	(0451)7921304	127	State-owned 國有	2,396	1(3)	6,580	o

Top 10 Cities by Production Output 產出排名前 10 位城市	Province 省	Market share 市場份額	Number of firms 企業個數
Qingdao 青島市	Shandong 山東省	52.54%	1
Wuhan 武漢市	Hubei 湖北省	12.07%	1
Shanghai 上海市	Shanghai 上海市	9.32%	7
Nanjing 南京市	Jiangsu 江蘇省	3.73%	1
Haikou 海口市	Hainan 海南省	3.60%	2
Nantong 南通市	Jiangsu 江蘇省	3.17%	2
Tongshi 通什市	Hainan 海南省	2.07%	1
Hangzhou 杭州市	Zhejiang 浙江省	1.97%	1
Fuzhou 福州市	Fujian 福建省	1.92%	1
Yangzhou 揚州市	Jiangsu 江蘇省	1.87%	1

10 Major Wholesalers 10 家主要批發商	City 城市	Province 省	Telephone / Fax 電話 / 傳真

*Also include sales by firms outside this industry.包括本行業以外廠家的銷售。"o" stands for "others". "o" 代表"其他產品"。

3689: Other Special Machinery and Equipment Repairing
其他專用機械設備修理業

The industry accounts for 0.034% of the total revenue of China's industrial sector in 1996. The revenue growth rate of the industry is 50.5% from 1995, as compared to the growth rate of China's industrial sector, 9.51%. The rate of return on asset is -0.97%. 73.47% of all firms in the industry made a profit while 17.38% had negative returns. The top province in terms of the industry's revenue is Henan, accounting for 19.90% of the total revenue.
本行業在1996年佔全行業總產值0.034%，行業年增長率為50.5%（全國工業年增長率9.51%）。行業的資產回報率-0.97%，73.47%的企業盈利，17.38%的企業虧損。銷售收入最高的省份為河南省，佔本行業的19.90%。

	Total number of firms 企業總數	Total number of employees 職工總數	Total revenue (mil. RMB) 總銷售收入（百萬元）	Total profit (mil. RMB) 總利潤（百萬元）	Return on assets 資產利潤率 (%)	Return on equity 權益利潤率 (%)	Labour productivity ('000 RMB / worker) 勞動生產率（千元/人）	Debts / assets 資產負債率 (%)	Total assets (mil. RMB) 總資產（百萬元）
Industry Overall 行業總體	633	51,324	1,975	-31	-0.97	-1.80	38.48	46.09	3,224

	Number of firms 企業個數	Average number of employees 平均職工人數	Average revenue ('000 RMB) 平均銷售收入（千元）	Average profit ('000 RMB) 平均利潤（千元）	Return on assets 資產利潤率 (%)	Return on equity 權益利潤率 (%)	Labour productivity ('000 RMB / worker) 勞動生產率（千元/人）	Average debts / assets 平均資產負債率(%)	Average Total assets ('000 RMB) 平均總資產（千元）
By ownership 產業所有權									
State-owned 國有	117	244	6,692	-94	-0.57	-1.13	27.41	49.30	16,385
Collectively-owned 集體	483	45	2,086	-29	-1.43	-2.49	46.47	42.84	2,032
Privately-owned 私有									
Domestic JVs 聯營	5	36	1,110	-55	-3.61	-5.34	30.50	32.31	1,529
Joint stock 股份制	7	149	5,676	-149	-1.62	-2.94	38.06	44.72	9,162
Foreign-funded 外資	11	81	9,002	-184	-1.29	-1.93	111.51	33.24	14,333
Overseas Chinese-funded 港澳台資	9	30	4,598	-290	-2.66	-4.33	152.69	38.40	10,869
By size 規模									
Large 大型	6	2,398	86,416	-727	-0.46	-0.87	36.03	46.78	156,711
Medium 中型	20	702	28,488	-640	-0.87	-1.43	40.56	39.47	73,911
Small 小型	603	38	1,472	-23	-1.72	-4.03	38.53	57.43	1,337
By regional distribution 地區分布									
Central-North 華北	183	75	2,265	-16	-0.40	-0.80	30.07	50.41	4,049
Beijing 北京	52	34	1,114	26	1.31	2.57	32.61	48.92	1,995
Tianjin 天津	69	22	1,267	23	2.16	4.09	56.80	47.23	1,053
Hebei 河北	22	369	10,285	-298	-1.38	-2.86	27.90	51.84	21,639
Shanxi 山西	32	69	1,251	20	0.77	1.43	18.02	46.44	2,654
Inner Mongolia 內蒙	8	18	370	5	1.10	2.88	20.70	61.60	453
Northeast 東北	184	80	2,083	51	2.09	6.16	25.91	66.09	2,430
Liaoning 遼寧	129	104	2,597	57	1.79	5.18	25.01	65.41	3,184
Jilin 吉林	26	21	527	11	1.69	7.46	24.67	77.36	659
Heilongjiang 黑龍江	29	29	1,192	58	8.75	29.75	40.92	70.59	666
Central East 華東	102	93	3,641	141	1.94	3.98	39.14	51.22	7,245
Shanghai 上海	21	118	3,930	143	1.43	2.23	33.36	36.07	10,021
Jiangsu 江蘇	14	94	3,731	-21	-0.38	-1.22	39.91	68.79	5,640
Zhejiang 浙江	15	98	6,019	883	13.10	32.18	61.30	59.30	6,745
Anhui 安徽	14	37	1,327	39	4.11	11.02	35.46	62.74	939
Fujian 福建	7	72	1,603	-223	-5.84	-18.40	22.31	68.26	3,817
Jiangxi 江西	11	22	905	-25	-2.87	-11.79	40.45	75.69	856
Shandong 山東	20	148	5,327	-16	-0.10	-0.21	36.01	51.72	14,958
Central-South 中南	95	74	7,324	-450	-4.44	-6.09	99.06	27.11	10,132
Henan 河南	24	114	16,375	-141	-0.97	-1.19	143.75	17.96	14,484
Hubei 湖北	26	67	2,913	35	1.17	2.62	43.41	55.62	3,037
Hunan 湖南	12	120	15,293	-2,897	-7.30	-9.58	127.97	23.77	39,656
Guangdong 廣東	22	44	1,940	-246	-9.54	-34.22	44.10	72.13	2,579
Guangxi 廣西	10	9	72	-1	-3.45	-14.29	7.74	75.86	29
Hainan 海南	1	50	100	-110	-3.55	-4.01	2.00	11.61	3,100
Southwest 西南	36	106	923	-232	-6.65	-14.48	8.67	54.04	3,486
Chongqing 重慶	2	33	556	10	2.14	4.39	16.96	51.29	479
Sichuan 四川	19	105	686	-189	-4.82	-9.59	6.53	49.77	3,914
Guizhou 貴州	8	170	1,390	-478	-12.00	-41.43	8.18	71.01	3,980
Yunnan 雲南	6	62	1,318	-103	-5.06	-12.25	21.26	58.69	2,042
Tibet 西藏	1	22		-290	-5.56	-5.65		1.72	5,220
Northwest 西北	33	73	2,320	-31	-0.48	-1.02	31.92	52.46	6,339
Shaanxi 陝西	12	29	1,531	33	1.49	3.45	53.71	56.69	2,178
Gansu 甘肅	13	120	3,240	-152	-1.31	-2.75	27.07	52.15	11,597
Qinghai 青海	1								
Ningxia 寧夏	3	22	977	110	14.29	35.11	45.08	59.31	770
Xinjiang 新疆	4	109	3,288	63	0.83	1.66	30.16	49.83	7,495

3689: Other Special Machinery and Equipment Repairing
其他專用機械設備修理業

Year 年份	Number of firms 企業個數	Rate of change 每年變化 (%)	Number of employees 職工人數（人）	Rate of change 每年變化 (%)	Total revenue (mil. RMB) 總銷售收入（百萬元）	Rate of change 每年變化 (%)	Total profit (mil. RMB) 總利潤（百萬元）	Rate of change 每年變化 (%)
1993	674		66,780		1,406		86	
1994	708	5.04%	52,540	-21.32%	1,401	-0.39%	47	-44.47%
1995	509	-28.11%	47,455	-9.68%	1,312	-6.31%	29	-39.38%
1996	633	24.36%	51,324	8.15%	1,975	50.53%	-31	-207.67%

3 Major products* 3 種主要產品 *	Output 產量	Sales volume 銷售量	Unit 單位

Top 10 firms by revenue (year founded) 收入排名前 10 家企業（創辦年份）	City 城市	Province 省	Telephone / fax 電話 / 傳真	Number of employees 職工人數	Ownership 產業所有權	Revenue ('000 RMB) 銷售收入（千元）	Profit ('000 RMB) (rank) 利潤（千元）（排名）	Total assets ('000 RMB) 總資產（千元）	Major products 主要產品
Zhengzhou Kang Fu De Health Industrial Co. Ltd. 鄭州康富德健康產業有限公司(1996)	Zhengzhou 鄭州市	Henan 河南省	(0371)7983235	600	Joint stock 股份制	358,617	-4340(139)	240,870	o
Xiangtan Iron & Steel Company Wire Rod Attached Factory 湘潭鋼鐵公司線材附屬廠(1994)	Xiangtan 湘潭市	Hunan 湖南省	(0732)8654170	76	Collectively-owned 集體	152,718	-35786(142)	400,124	o
Tianjin Petrochemical Machine Manufacturing Erection Work Company 天津石化機械製造安裝工程公司(1981)	Tianjin 天津市	Tianjin 天津市	(022)27356622 (022)25990272	726	State-owned 國有	52,924	531(16)	34,084	o
Changqing Industry Equipment Installment Co. No.3 Engineering Dept. 長清縣工業設備安裝公司第三工程處(1982)	Ji'nan 濟南市	Shandong 山東省	(0531)7432040	884	Collectively-owned 集體	46,120	0(115)	36,981	o
Fushun Mine Administrative Bureau Lao Hu Tai Mine Production Service Company 撫順礦務局老虎台礦生產服務公司(1985)	Fushun 撫順市	Liaoning 遼寧省	(0413)2555154	3,880	Collectively-owned 集體	28,668	11(93)	21,651	o
Lanzhou Vacuum Equipment Factory 蘭州真空設備廠(1965)	Lanzhou 蘭州市	Gansu 甘肅省	(0931)2336011 (0931)2333308	891	State-owned 國有	28,644	177(45)	81,386	o
Liao He Oil Field Hua You Industrial Company Machine Repair Factory 遼河油田華油實業公司機修廠(1988)	Panjin 盤錦市	Liaoning 遼寧省	(0427)7590433	297	State-owned 國有	28,030	1100(6)	19,386	o
Hebei Ji Chuan Industrial General Co. 河北冀川實業總公司(1966)	Shijiazhuang 石家莊市	Hebei 河北省	(0311)2219362 (0311)2219721	1,315	State-owned 國有	27,548	388(23)	116,103	o
Liao He Oil Field Jia Xing Industrial General Company 遼河油田佳興實業總公司(1989)	Panjin 盤錦市	Liaoning 遼寧省	(0427)7573888	820	Collectively-owned 集體	24,500	800(10)	35,115	o
Guangxi Machinery Products Shanghai Marketing Maintenance Center 廣西機械產品上海銷售維修中心(1985)	Shanghai 上海市	Shanghai 上海市	(021)58993853 (021)58993954	108	Domestic JVs 聯營	17,535	319(32)	19,973	o

Top 10 Cities by Production Output 產出排名前 10 位城市	Province 省	Market share 市場份額	Number of firms 企業個數
Zhengzhou 鄭州市	Henan 河南省	32.33%	2
Tianjin 天津市	Tianjin 天津市	8.74%	74
Shanghai 上海市	Shanghai 上海市	8.56%	125
Guangzhou 廣州市	Guangdong 廣東省	3.97%	46
Beijing 北京市	Beijing 北京市	3.42%	43
Shijiazhuang 石家莊市	Hebei 河北省	3.15%	4
Anshan 鞍山市	Liaoning 遼寧省	2.30%	15
Chengdu 成都市	Sichuan 四川省	2.27%	18
Xianyang 咸陽市	Shaanxi 陝西省	1.40%	4
Yangzhou 揚州市	Jiangsu 江蘇省	1.20%	4

10 Major Wholesalers 10 家主要批發商	City 城市	Province 省	Telephone / Fax 電話 / 傳真

*Also include sales by firms outside this industry.包括本行業以外廠家的銷售。"o" stands for "others". "o" 代表 "其他產品"。

3711: Locomotives 機車製造業

The industry accounts for 0.093% of the total revenue of China's industrial sector in 1996. The revenue growth rate of the industry is 5.3% from 1995, as compared to the growth rate of China's industrial sector, 9.51%. The rate of return on asset is 1.27%. 72.22% of all firms in the industry made a profit while 27.78% had negative returns. The top province in terms of the industry's revenue is Shandong, accounting for 24.25% of the total revenue.
本行業在1996年佔全行業總產值0.093%，行業年增長率為5.3%（全國工業年增長率9.51%）。行業的資產回報率1.27%，72.22%的企業盈利，27.78%的企業虧損。銷售收入最高的省份為山東省，佔本行業的24.25%。

	Total number of firms 企業總數	Total number of employees 職工總數	Total revenue (mil. RMB) 總銷售收入（百萬元）	Total profit (mil. RMB) 總利潤（百萬元）	Return on assets 資產利潤率 (%)	Return on equity 權益利潤率 (%)	Labour productivity ('000 RMB / worker) 勞動生產率（千元/人）	Debts / assets 資產負債率 (%)	Total assets (mil. RMB) 總資產（百萬元）
Industry Overall 行業總體	15	63,976	5,379	84	1.27	2.32	84.08	45.20	6,623

	Number of firms 企業個數	Average number of employees 平均職工人數	Average revenue ('000 RMB) 平均銷售收入（千元）	Average profit ('000 RMB) 平均利潤（千元）	Return on assets 資產利潤率 (%)	Return on equity 權益利潤率 (%)	Labour productivity ('000 RMB / worker) 勞動生產率（千元/人）	Average debts / assets 平均資產負債率(%)	Average Total assets ('000 RMB) 平均總資產（千元）
By ownership 產業所有權									
State-owned 國有	10	6,289	527,400	8,300	1.27	2.30	83.86	44.68	653,700
Collectively-owned 集體	5	213	21,060	200	1.14	7.23	98.88	84.22	17,515
Privately-owned 私有									
Domestic JVs 聯營									
Joint stock 股份制									
Foreign-funded 外資									
Overseas Chinese-funded 港澳台資									
By size 規模									
Large 大型	8	7,869	660,469	10,153	1.25	2.26	83.93	44.75	814,328
Medium 中型									
Small 小型	8	128	11,927	347	2.55	9.24	93.27	72.40	13,614
By regional distribution 地區分布									
Central-North 華北	4	4,391	281,565	-2,965	-0.81	-1.49	64.12	45.85	367,200
Beijing 北京	2	3,796	240,390	-1,025	-0.32	-0.51	63.33	37.66	319,990
Tianjin 天津									
Hebei 河北									
Shanxi 山西	2	4,986	322,740	-4,905	-1.18	-2.47	64.73	52.17	414,410
Inner Mongolia 內蒙									
Northeast 東北	2	5,795	624,890	11,460	1.83	2.93	107.84	37.46	625,810
Liaoning 遼寧	2	5,795	624,890	11,460	1.83	2.93	107.84	37.46	625,810
Jilin 吉林									
Heilongjiang 黑龍江									
Central East 華東	3	4,052	434,850	7,907	1.35	2.60	107.33	48.25	587,667
Shanghai 上海									
Jiangsu 江蘇									
Zhejiang 浙江									
Anhui 安徽									
Fujian 福建									
Jiangxi 江西									
Shandong 山東	3	4,052	434,850	7,907	1.35	2.60	107.33	48.25	587,667
Central-South 中南	4	2,832	215,143	7,840	2.51	4.97	75.96	49.55	312,810
Henan 河南	1	10	5,660	310	12.02	18.45	566.00	34.88	2,580
Hubei 湖北									
Hunan 湖南	2	5,442	381,600	15,105	2.58	4.87	70.12	47.07	585,755
Guangdong 廣東	1	435	91,710	840	1.09	8.89	210.83	87.75	77,150
Guangxi 廣西									
Hainan 海南									
Southwest 西南	2	5,670	418,940	8,955	2.02	3.53	73.89	42.86	444,350
Chongqing 重慶									
Sichuan 四川	1	10,796	835,660	17,570	1.99	3.48	77.40	42.81	883,890
Guizhou 貴州	1	543	2,220	340	7.07	14.78	4.09	52.18	4,810
Yunnan 雲南									
Tibet 西藏									
Northwest 西北									
Shaanxi 陝西									
Gansu 甘肅									
Qinghai 青海									
Ningxia 寧夏									
Xinjiang 新疆									

3711: Locomotives 機車製造業

Year 年份	Number of firms 企業個數	Rate of change 每年變化 (%)	Number of employees 職工人數（人）	Rate of change 每年變化 (%)	Total revenue (mil. RMB) 總銷售收入（百萬元）	Rate of change 每年變化 (%)	Total profit (mil. RMB) 總利潤（百萬元）	Rate of change 每年變化 (%)
1993	11		65,552		4,441		117	
1994	13	18.18%	66,487	1.43%	4,388	-1.20%	107	-8.75%
1995	12	-7.69%	65,074	-2.13%	5,110	16.44%	116	8.49%
1996	15	25.00%	63,976	-1.69%	5,379	5.26%	84	-27.65%

3 Major products* 3 種主要產品 *	Output 產量	Sales volume 銷售量	Unit 單位
a) Electrical Locomotive 電力機車	954,000	954,000	kw 千瓦
b) Diesel Locomotive 內燃機車	784	376	set 台
c) Train with Hard Seats 硬席車	348	348	vehicle 輛

Top 10 firms by revenue (year founded) 收入排名前 10 家企業（創辦年份）	City 城市	Province 省	Telephone / fax 電話 / 傳真	Number of employees 職工人數	Ownership 產業所有權	Revenue ('000 RMB) 銷售收入（千元）	Profit ('000 RMB) (rank) 利潤（千元）（排名）	Total assets ('000 RMB) 總資產（千元）	Major products 主要產品
Sifang Locomotive Vehicle Plant 四方機車車輛廠(1900)	Qingdao 青島市	Shandong 山東省	(0532)3716656 (0532)3716656	12,047	State-owned 國有	1,301,030	23780(2)	1,760,530	c
Dalian Locomotive and Rolling Stock Works 大連機車車輛工廠(1899)	Dalian 大連市	Liaoning 遼寧省	(0411)4604933 (0411)4606447	11,669	State-owned 國有	1,245,730	22820(3)	1,250,820	b
Ziyang Diesel Locomotive Works 資陽內燃機車廠(1973)	Neijiang 內江市	Sichuan 四川省	(0832)622648 (0832)627176	11,699	State-owned 國有	835,660	17570(4)	883,890	o
Zhuzhou Electric Power Locomotive Factory 株洲電力機車廠(1938)	Zhuzhou 株洲市	Hunan 湖南省	(0733)8441216 (0733)8432399	11,565	State-owned 國有	755,940	30140(1)	1,166,010	a
Datong Locomotive Factory 大同機車廠(1958)	Datong 大同市	Shanxi 山西省	(0352)5090124 (0352)5090984	9,870	State-owned 國有	640,980	-9990(13)	823,430	a,b
Beijing Feb. 7th Locomotive Works 北京二七機車廠(1901)	Beijing 北京市	Beijing 北京市	(010)63886147	7,129	State-owned 國有	447,810	3400(5)	576,830	b
Guangzhou Hui Er Lan Co. Ltd. 廣州惠兒蘭有限公司(1989)	Guangzhou 廣州市	Guangdong 廣東省	(020)84866014 (020)84860791	435	Overseas Chinese-funded 港澳台資	91,709	843(6)	77,149	o
Zhongtie Science and Technology Development Corp. 中鐵科學技術開發公司(1992)	Beijing 北京市	Beijing 北京市	(010)63249208 (010)62256304	521	State-owned 國有	32,965	-5448(12)	63,149	o
Henan Xiping Quan Zhai Zhen Machinery Factory 河南省西平縣權寨鎮機械廠(1994)	Zhumadian 駐馬店市	Henan 河南省	(0396)6108406	15	Collectively-owned 集體	6,000	450(8)	450	o
Shanxi Liyi Rolling Stock Fitting Parts Factory 山西省臨猗縣機車車輛配件廠(1976)	Yuncheng 運城市	Shanxi 山西省	(0359)4022732	102	State-owned 國有	4,497	181(9)	5,395	o

Top 10 Cities by Production Output 產出排名前 10 位城市	Province 省	Market share 市場份額	Number of firms 企業個數
Qingdao 青島市	Shandong 山東省	25.06%	1
Dalian 大連市	Liaoning 遼寧省	23.73%	1
Neijiang 內江市	Sichuan 四川省	15.69%	1
Zhuzhou 株洲市	Hunan 湖南省	13.54%	2
Datong 大同市	Shanxi 山西省	11.77%	1
Beijing 北京市	Beijing 北京市	7.98%	2
Guangzhou 廣州市	Guangdong 廣東省	1.93%	1
Zhumadian 駐馬店市	Henan 河南省	0.11%	1
Liaocheng 聊城市	Shandong 山東省	0.06%	1
Quanzhou 泉州市	Fujian 福建省	0.05%	1

10 Major Wholesalers 10 家主要批發商	City 城市	Province 省	Telephone / Fax 電話 / 傳真
Liaoning Automobile Trade Group Corp. 遼寧省汽車貿易集團	Shenyang 瀋陽市	Liaoning 遼寧省	(024)23835494 (024)23838338
China Post and Telecommunication Equipment General Company 中國郵電器材總公司	Beijing 北京市	Beijing 北京市	(010)63523715 (010)63525935
Jiangsu Electromechanical Products General Company 江蘇省機電產品總公司	Nanjing 南京市	Jiangsu 江蘇省	(025)7713642 (025)7711036
Xi Nan Technology Import & Export Company 西南技術進出口公司	Chongqing 重慶市	Chongqing 重慶市	(023)63850185 (023)63850026
Changzhou Economic Technology Industrial Development Zone Tian Ming Trade Company 常州經濟技術產業開發區天明貿易公司	Changzhou 常州市	Jiangsu 江蘇省	(0519)8829882 (0519)8829882
Shanxi Mechanical Equipment Import & Export Company 山西省機械設備進出口公司	Taiyuan 太原市	Shanxi 山西省	(0351)4040713 (0351)4043981
Ningbo Five Mining Machinery Import & Export Company 寧波市五礦機械進出口公司	Ningbo 寧波市	Zhejiang 浙江省	(0574)7311255 (0574)7320322
Tianjin Jin Huan Electromechanical Complete Sets of Equipment Factory 天津市津環機電成套設備廠	Tianjin 天津市	Tianjin 天津市	(022)26371628
Yunnan Machinery Import & Export Company 雲南省機械進出口公司	Kunming 昆明市	Yunnan 雲南省	(0871)3164879 (0871)3136829
Tianjin Da Qiu Zhuang Yi Yuan Trade Center 天津市大丘莊億源商貿中心	Tianjin 天津市	Tianjin 天津市	(022)28899478 (022)28899046

*Also include sales by firms outside this industry.包括本行業以外廠家的銷售。"o" stands for "others". "o" 代表"其他產品"。

3712: Passenger Trains 客運火車製造業

The industry accounts for 0.065% of the total revenue of China's industrial sector in 1996. The revenue growth rate of the industry is 28.1% from 1995, as compared to the growth rate of China's industrial sector, 9.51%. The rate of return on asset is 3.72%. 63.97% of all firms in the industry made a profit while 23.53% had negative returns. The top province in terms of the industry's revenue is Jilin, accounting for 42.57% of the total revenue.
本行業在1996年佔全行業總產值0.065%，行業年增長率為28.1%（全國工業年增長率9.51%）。行業的資產回報率3.72%，63.97%的企業盈利，23.53%的企業虧損。銷售收入最高的省份為吉林省，佔本行業的42.57%。

	Total number of firms 企業總數	Total number of employees 職工總數	Total revenue (mil. RMB) 總銷售收入（百萬元）	Total profit (mil. RMB) 總利潤（百萬元）	Return on assets 資產利潤率 (%)	Return on equity 權益利潤率 (%)	Labour productivity ('000 RMB / worker) 勞動生產率（千元/人）	Debts / assets 資產負債率 (%)	Total assets (mil. RMB) 總資產（百萬元）
Industry Overall 行業總體	14	35,781	3,770	140	3.72	7.19	105.36	48.33	3,768

	Number of firms 企業個數	Average number of employees 平均職工人數	Average revenue ('000 RMB) 平均銷售收入（千元）	Average profit ('000 RMB) 平均利潤（千元）	Return on assets 資產利潤率 (%)	Return on equity 權益利潤率 (%)	Labour productivity ('000 RMB / worker) 勞動生產率（千元/人）	Average debts / assets 平均資產負債率(%)	Average Total assets ('000 RMB) 平均總資產（千元）
By ownership 產業所有權									
State-owned 國有	10	3,212	329,300	4,400	1.21	2.36	102.53	48.79	363,400
Collectively-owned 集體	2	377	16,072	-848	-7.55	-35.38	42.63	78.67	11,233
Privately-owned 私有									
Domestic JVs 聯營									
Joint stock 股份制	1	191	7,323				38.34	49.96	9,763
Foreign-funded 外資									
Overseas Chinese-funded 港澳台資	1	2,713	437,791	97,688	95.80	127.77	161.37	25.02	101,973
By size 規模									
Large 大型	4	7,824	800,755	14,729	1.74	3.31	102.35	47.29	845,339
Medium 中型									
Small 小型	10	449	56,728	8,108	20.95	49.15	126.48	57.38	38,703
By regional distribution 地區分布									
Central-North 華北	3	3,928	284,317	1,613	0.40	0.68	72.38	40.56	401,207
Beijing 北京	1								
Tianjin 天津									
Hebei 河北	1	10,953	846,230	12,740	1.12	1.82	77.26	38.69	1,139,950
Shanxi 山西	1	831	6,720	-7,900	-12.41	-47.82	8.09	74.05	63,670
Inner Mongolia 內蒙									
Northeast 東北	4	2,984	402,458	7,105	1.78	4.34	134.87	59.02	399,713
Liaoning 遼寧	1	108	4,780				44.26	81.86	14,610
Jilin 吉林	3	3,943	535,017	9,473	1.79	4.36	135.70	58.81	528,080
Heilongjiang 黑龍江									
Central East 華東	3	2,647	276,243	3,300	1.21	2.02	104.35	39.99	272,747
Shanghai 上海									
Jiangsu 江蘇	1	7,231	771,120	7,900	1.10	1.67	106.64	34.16	716,450
Zhejiang 浙江	1	605	56,390	2,000	2.13	10.73	93.21	80.14	93,850
Anhui 安徽									
Fujian 福建									
Jiangxi 江西									
Shandong 山東	1	106	1,220				11.51	91.56	7,940
Central-South 中南	3	1,348	159,043	32,603	67.35	112.01	117.96	39.87	48,407
Henan 河南	2	1,755	235,960	48,720	82.22	114.06	134.49	27.91	59,255
Hubei 湖北	1	536	5,210	370	1.39	19.58	9.72	92.92	26,710
Hunan 湖南									
Guangdong 廣東									
Guangxi 廣西									
Hainan 海南									
Southwest 西南	1	74	1,140	-920	-40.00	44.44	15.41	190.00	2,300
Chongqing 重慶									
Sichuan 四川									
Guizhou 貴州									
Yunnan 雲南									
Tibet 西藏									
Northwest 西北									
Shaanxi 陝西									
Gansu 甘肅									
Qinghai 青海									
Ningxia 寧夏									
Xinjiang 新疆									

3712: Passenger Trains 客運火車製造業

Year 年份	Number of firms 企業個數	Rate of change 每年變化 (%)	Number of employees 職工人數 (人)	Rate of change 每年變化 (%)	Total revenue (mil. RMB) 總銷售收入 (百萬元)	Rate of change 每年變化 (%)	Total profit (mil. RMB) 總利潤 (百萬元)	Rate of change 每年變化 (%)
1993	20		39,986		2,516		82	
1994	18	-10.00%	39,412	-1.44%	2,992	18.91%	80	-2.90%
1995	10	-44.45%	36,891	-6.40%	2,942	-1.67%	103	29.03%
1996	14	40.00%	35,781	-3.01%	3,770	28.14%	140	36.00%

3 Major products* 3 種主要產品 *	Output 產量	Sales volume 銷售量	Unit 單位
a) Double-deck Passenger Train 雙層客車	71	155	vehicle 輛
b) Train with Hard Seats 硬席車	1,339	1,339	vehicle 輛
c) Refitted Passenger Carriage 客車改裝車	222	213	vehicle 輛

Top 10 firms by revenue (year founded) 收入排名前 10 家企業 (創辦年份)	City 城市	Province 省	Telephone / fax 電話 / 傳真	Number of employees 職工人數	Ownership 產業所有權	Revenue ('000 RMB) 銷售收入 (千元)	Profit ('000 RMB) (rank) 利潤 (千元) (排名)	Total assets ('000 RMB) 總資產 (千元)	Major products 主要產品
Changchun Bus Manufacturer 長春客車廠(1958)	Changchun 長春市	Jilin 吉林省	(0431)7914245	13,367	State-owned 國有	1,595,730	28560(2)	1,558,660	a,b
Tangshan Locomotive & Rolling Stock Works 唐山機車車輛廠(1881)	Tangshan 唐山市	Hebei 河北省	(0315)3231417 (0315)3241612	10,953	State-owned 國有	846,226	12743(3)	1,139,945	b
Nanjing Pu Zhen Vehicle Plant 南京浦鎮車輛廠(1908)	Nanjing 南京市	Jiangsu 江蘇省	(025)8851085 (025)8852655	7,231	State-owned 國有	771,120	7900(4)	716,450	a,b
Jiaozuo Bus Manufacturer 焦作市客車廠(1974)	Jiaozuo 焦作市	Henan 河南省	(0391)8511389	3,480	Overseas Chinese-funded 港澳台資	471,311	97439(1)	117,326	o
Zhejiang Shen Ma Automobile Industrial Co. Ltd. 浙江神馬汽車實業有限公司(1958)	Jinhua 金華市	Zhejiang 浙江省	(0579)2338592 (0579)2312150	596	State-owned 國有	56,390	2000(5)	93,850	o
Shanxi Bus General Factory 山西客車總廠(1949)	Taiyuan 太原市	Shanxi 山西省	(0351)3075611	831	State-owned 國有	6,722	-7904(8)	63,671	c
Xiangfan Public Bus Factory 襄樊市公用客車廠(1978)	Xiangfan 襄樊市	Hubei 湖北省	(0710)3220741	546	State-owned 國有	5,207	370(6)	26,714	c
Shenyang Fei Long Bus Manufacture Co. Ltd. 瀋陽飛龍巴士製造有限公司(1991)	Shenyang 瀋陽市	Liaoning 遼寧省	(024)86526093	104	Foreign-funded 外資	4,780	0(7)	14,608	o

Top 10 Cities by Production Output 產出排名前 10 位城市	Province 省	Market share 市場份額	Number of firms 企業個數
Changchun 長春市	Jilin 吉林省	44.08%	1
Tangshan 唐山市	Hebei 河北省	23.42%	1
Nanjing 南京市	Jiangsu 江蘇省	13.23%	1
Jiaozuo 焦作市	Henan 河南省	12.86%	1
Nantong 南通市	Jiangsu 江蘇省	2.22%	1
Jinhua 金華市	Zhejiang 浙江省	1.64%	1
Bengbu 蚌埠市	Anhui 安徽省	1.34%	1
Shenyang 瀋陽市	Liaoning 遼寧省	0.44%	1
Huaiyin 淮陰市	Jiangsu 江蘇省	0.19%	3
Lanzhou 蘭州市	Gansu 甘肅省	0.19%	1

10 Major Wholesalers 10 家主要批發商	City 城市	Province 省	Telephone / Fax 電話 / 傳真
Liaoning Automobile Trade Group Corp. 遼寧省汽車貿易集團	Shenyang 瀋陽市	Liaoning 遼寧省	(024)23835494 (024)23838338
China Post and Telecommunication Equipment General Company 中國郵電器材總公司	Beijing 北京市	Beijing 北京市	(010)63523715 (010)63525935
Jiangsu Electromechanical Products General Company 江蘇省機電產品總公司	Nanjing 南京市	Jiangsu 江蘇省	(025)7713642 (025)7711036
Xi Nan Technology Import & Export Company 西南技術進出口公司	Chongqing 重慶市	Chongqing 重慶市	(023)63850185 (023)63850026
Changzhou Economic Technology Industrial Development Zone Tian Ming Trade Company 常州經濟技術產業開發區天明貿易公司	Changzhou 常州市	Jiangsu 江蘇省	(0519)8829882 (0519)8829882
Shanxi Mechanical Equipment Import & Export Company 山西省機械設備進出口公司	Taiyuan 太原市	Shanxi 山西省	(0351)4040713 (0351)4043981
Ningbo Five Mining Machinery Import & Export Company 寧波市五礦機械進出口公司	Ningbo 寧波市	Zhejiang 浙江省	(0574)7311255 (0574)7320322
Tianjin Jin Huan Electromechanical Complete Sets of Equipment Factory 天津市津環機電成套設備廠	Tianjin 天津市	Tianjin 天津市	(022)26371628
Yunnan Machinery Import & Export Company 雲南省機械進出口公司	Kunming 昆明市	Yunnan 雲南省	(0871)3164879 (0871)3136829
Tianjin Da Qiu Zhuang Yi Yuan Trade Center 天津市大丘莊億源商貿中心	Tianjin 天津市	Tianjin 天津市	(022)28899478 (022)28899046

*Also include sales by firms outside this industry.包括本行業以外廠家的銷售。"o" stands for "others". "o" 代表 "其他產品" 。

3713: Goods Trains 貨車製造業

The industry accounts for 0.081% of the total revenue of China's industrial sector in 1996. The revenue growth rate of the industry is -2.3% from 1995, as compared to the growth rate of China's industrial sector, 9.51%. The rate of return on asset is 0.98%. 76.92% of all firms in the industry made a profit while 23.08% had negative returns. The top province in terms of the industry's revenue is Helongjiang, accounting for 26.08% of the total revenue.
本行業在 1996 年佔全行業總產值 0.081% ，行業年增長率為 -2.3%（全國工業年增長率 9.51%） 。行業的資產回報率 0.98% ， 76.92% 的企業盈利， 23.08% 的企業虧損。銷售收入最高的省份為黑龍江省，佔本行業的 26.08% 。

	Total number of firms 企業總數	Total number of employees 職工總數	Total revenue (mil. RMB) 總銷售收入（百萬元）	Total profit (mil. RMB) 總利潤（百萬元）	Return on assets 資產利潤率 (%)	Return on equity 權益利潤率 (%)	Labour productivity ('000 RMB / worker) 勞動生產率（千元/人）	Debts / assets 資產負債率 (%)	Total assets (mil. RMB) 總資產（百萬元）
Industry Overall 行業總體	17	62,977	4,717	51	0.98	1.77	74.90	44.24	5,175

	Number of firms 企業個數	Average number of employees 平均職工人數	Average revenue ('000 RMB) 平均銷售收入（千元）	Average profit ('000 RMB) 平均利潤（千元）	Return on assets 資產利潤率 (%)	Return on equity 權益利潤率 (%)	Labour productivity ('000 RMB / worker) 勞動生產率（千元/人）	Average debts / assets 平均資產負債率(%)	Average Total assets ('000 RMB) 平均總資產（千元）
By ownership 產業所有權									
State-owned 國有	9	6,873	514,889	5,667	1.00	1.78	74.91	43.81	565,778
Collectively-owned 集體	8	139	10,384				74.91	69.74	10,414
Privately-owned 私有									
Domestic JVs 聯營									
Joint stock 股份制									
Foreign-funded 外資									
Overseas Chinese-funded 港澳台資									
By size 規模									
Large 大型	10	6,231	443,549	4,852	0.97	1.69	71.18	42.86	502,647
Medium 中型									
Small 小型	6	107	46,959	412	1.66	17.62	437.51	90.59	24,837
By regional distribution 地區分布									
Central-North 華北	3	2,217	140,720	1,897	1.62	2.60	63.48	37.72	117,327
Beijing 北京	3	2,217	140,720	1,897	1.62	2.60	63.48	37.72	117,327
Tianjin 天津									
Hebei 河北									
Shanxi 山西									
Inner Mongolia 內蒙									
Northeast 東北	1	12,754	1,230,210	27,580	2.29	4.03	96.46	43.20	1,205,640
Liaoning 遼寧									
Jilin 吉林									
Heilongjiang 黑龍江	1	12,754	1,230,210	27,580	2.29	4.03	96.46	43.20	1,205,640
Central East 華東	3	3,063	215,857	-5,790	-2.17	-3.80	70.46	42.75	266,467
Shanghai 上海									
Jiangsu 江蘇									
Zhejiang 浙江									
Anhui 安徽	1	4,151	263,850	-12,110	-4.09	-6.93	63.56	40.93	295,770
Fujian 福建									
Jiangxi 江西									
Shandong 山東	2	2,520	191,860	-2,630	-1.04	-1.86	76.15	43.83	251,815
Central-South 中南	5	2,792	198,992	2,528	1.16	1.88	71.28	38.55	218,270
Henan 河南									
Hubei 湖北	1	6,903	330,860	6,680	1.47	1.92	47.93	23.55	455,360
Hunan 湖南	2	3,449	316,525	4,470	1.46	2.83	91.77	48.17	305,280
Guangdong 廣東	2	79	15,525	-1,490	-11.72	-49.34	196.52	76.25	12,715
Guangxi 廣西									
Hainan 海南									
Southwest 西南	2	5,817	431,355	9,565	1.76	3.56	74.16	50.53	543,415
Chongqing 重慶									
Sichuan 四川	1	6,609	606,050	10,280	1.89	3.36	91.70	43.71	543,040
Guizhou 貴州	1	5,024	256,660	8,850	1.63	3.82	51.09	57.35	543,790
Yunnan 雲南									
Tibet 西藏									
Northwest 西北	3	2,930	186,323	1,090	0.51	1.04	63.58	50.65	213,240
Shaanxi 陝西	3	2,930	186,323	1,090	0.51	1.04	63.58	50.65	213,240
Gansu 甘肅									
Qinghai 青海									
Ningxia 寧夏									
Xinjiang 新疆									

3713: Goods Trains 貨車製造業

Year 年份	Number of firms 企業個數	Rate of change 每年變化 (%)	Number of employees 職工人數 (人)	Rate of change 每年變化 (%)	Total revenue (mil. RMB) 總銷售收入 (百萬元)	Rate of change 每年變化 (%)	Total profit (mil. RMB) 總利潤 (百萬元)	Rate of change 每年變化 (%)
1993	16		43,196		4,362		115	
1994	19	18.75%	39,359	-8.88%	3,257	-25.32%	-2	-101.31%
1995	16	-15.79%	68,045	72.88%	4,827	48.18%	82	5492.99%
1996	17	6.25%	62,977	-7.45%	4,717	-2.28%	51	-37.50%

3 Major products* 3 種主要產品 *	Output 產量	Sales volume 銷售量	Unit 單位
a) Goods Wagon 貨車	23,490	23,255	vehicle 輛

Top 10 firms by revenue (year founded) 收入排名前 10 家企業 (創辦年份)	City 城市	Province 省	Telephone / fax 電話 / 傳真	Number of employees 職工人數	Ownership 產業所有權	Revenue ('000 RMB) 銷售收入 (千元)	Profit ('000 RMB) (rank) 利潤 (千元) (排名)	Total assets ('000 RMB) 總資產 (千元)	Major products 主要產品
Qiqiha'er Vehicle Plant 齊齊哈爾車輛廠(1939)	Qiqiha'er 齊齊哈爾市	Heilongjiang 黑龍江省	(0452)2512981 (0452)2514464	15,635	State-owned 國有	1,230,210	27580(1)	1,205,640	a
Zhuzhou Rolling Stock Works 株洲車輛廠(1958)	Zhuzhou 株洲市	Hunan 湖南省	(0733)8403873 (0733)8403134	7,148	State-owned 國有	631,910	8890(3)	608,630	a
Meishan Vehicle Plant 眉山車輛廠(1971)	Leshan 樂山市	Sichuan 四川省	(0833)8502028	6,060	State-owned 國有	606,050	10280(2)	543,040	a
Xi'an Vehicle Plant 西安車輛廠(1938)	Xi'an 西安市	Shaanxi 陝西省	(029)4512401 (029)4512450	8,619	State-owned 國有	549,830	3180(7)	633,110	o
Ji'nan Locomotive Vehicle Plant 濟南機車車輛廠(1910)	Ji'nan 濟南市	Shandong 山東省	(0531)7955930 (0531)7957548	5,009	State-owned 國有	383,210	-5000(15)	501,940	a
Beijing Er Qi Vehicle Plant 北京二七車輛廠(1980)	Beijing 北京市	Beijing 北京市	(010)63886184 (010)63886123	6,098	State-owned 國有	381,390	2280(8)	304,400	a
Wuchang Vehicle Plant 武昌車輛廠(1949)	Wuhan 武漢市	Hubei 湖北省	(027)86816628 (027)86811017	6,816	State-owned 國有	330,860	6680(5)	455,360	a
Tongling Vehicle Plant 銅陵車輛廠(1970)	Tongling 銅陵市	Anhui 安徽省	(0562)6803812 (0562)6803344	4,294	State-owned 國有	263,850	-12110(16)	295,770	a
Guiyang Freight Car Works 貴陽車輛廠(1975)	Guiyang 貴陽市	Guizhou 貴州省	(0851)4861493 (0851)4861141	5,053	State-owned 國有	256,660	8850(4)	543,790	a
Beijing Chang Tie Vehicle Industrial Company 北京長鐵車輛工業公司(1983)	Beijing 北京市	Beijing 北京市	(010)63886410 (010)63889163	1,120	Collectively-owned 集體	40,768	3410(6)	47,577	o

Top 10 Cities by Production Output 產出排名前 10 位城市	Province 省	Market share 市場份額	Number of firms 企業個數
Qiqiha'er 齊齊哈爾市	Heilongjiang 黑龍江省	22.64%	1
Leshan 樂山市	Sichuan 四川省	11.27%	1
Zhuzhou 株洲市	Hunan 湖南省	10.66%	2
Xi'an 西安市	Shaanxi 陝西省	10.20%	1
Ji'nan 濟南市	Shandong 山東省	7.11%	1
Taiyuan 太原市	Shanxi 山西省	6.41%	1
Wuhan 武漢市	Hubei 湖北省	5.96%	2
Tongling 銅陵市	Anhui 安徽省	4.91%	1
Guiyang 貴陽市	Guizhou 貴州省	4.64%	1
Harbin 哈爾濱市	Heilongjiang 黑龍江省	4.53%	1

10 Major Wholesalers 10 家主要批發商	City 城市	Province 省	Telephone / Fax 電話 / 傳真
Liaoning Automobile Trade Group Corp. 遼寧省汽車貿易集團	Shenyang 瀋陽市	Liaoning 遼寧省	(024)23835494 (024)23838338
China Post and Telecommunication Equipment General Company 中國郵電器材總公司	Beijing 北京市	Beijing 北京市	(010)63523715 (010)63525935
Jiangsu Electromechanical Products General Company 江蘇省機電產品總公司	Nanjing 南京市	Jiangsu 江蘇省	(025)7713642 (025)7711036
Xi Nan Technology Import & Export Company 西南技術進出口公司	Chongqing 重慶市	Chongqing 重慶市	(023)63850185 (023)63850026
Changzhou Economic Technology Industrial Development Zone Tian Ming Trade Company 常州經濟技術產業開發區天明貿易公司	Changzhou 常州市	Jiangsu 江蘇省	(0519)8829882 (0519)8829882
Shanxi Mechanical Equipment Import & Export Company 山西省機械設備進出口公司	Taiyuan 太原市	Shanxi 山西省	(0351)4040713 (0351)4043981
Ningbo Five Mining Machinery Import & Export Company 寧波市五礦機械進出口公司	Ningbo 寧波市	Zhejiang 浙江省	(0574)7311255 (0574)7320322
Tianjin Jin Huan Electromechanical Complete Sets of Equipment Factory 天津市津環機電成套設備廠	Tianjin 天津市	Tianjin 天津市	(022)26371628
Yunnan Machinery Import & Export Company 雲南省機械進出口公司	Kunming 昆明市	Yunnan 雲南省	(0871)3164879 (0871)3136829
Tianjin Da Qiu Zhuang Yi Yuan Trade Center 天津市大丘莊億源商貿中心	Tianjin 天津市	Tianjin 天津市	(022)28899478 (022)28899046

*Also include sales by firms outside this industry.包括本行業以外廠家的銷售。"o" stands for "others". "o" 代表 "其他產品"。

3714: Rolling Stock Accessories 機車車輛配件製造業

The industry accounts for 0.042% of the total revenue of China's industrial sector in 1996. The revenue growth rate of the industry is 15.1% from 1995, as compared to the growth rate of China's industrial sector, 9.51%. The rate of return on asset is -0.94%. 72.05% of all firms in the industry made a profit while 22.26% had negative returns. The top province in terms of the industry's revenue is Liaoning, accounting for 14.39% of the total revenue.
本行業在 1996 年佔全行業總產值 0.042%，行業年增長率為 15.1%（全國工業年增長率 9.51%）。行業的資產回報率 -0.94%，72.05% 的企業盈利，22.26% 的企業虧損。銷售收入最高的省份為遼寧省，佔本行業的 14.39%。

	Total number of firms 企業總數	Total number of employees 職工總數	Total revenue (mil. RMB) 總銷售收入（百萬元）	Total profit (mil. RMB) 總利潤（百萬元）	Return on assets 資產利潤率 (%)	Return on equity 權益利潤率 (%)	Labour productivity ('000 RMB / worker) 勞動生產率（千元/人）	Debts / assets 資產負債率 (%)	Total assets (mil. RMB) 總資產（百萬元）
Industry Overall 行業總體	312	62,797	2,461	-28	-0.94	-2.17	39.19	56.62	3,023

	Number of firms 企業個數	Average number of employees 平均職工人數	Average revenue ('000 RMB) 平均銷售收入（千元）	Average profit ('000 RMB) 平均利潤（千元）	Return on assets 資產利潤率 (%)	Return on equity 權益利潤率 (%)	Labour productivity ('000 RMB / worker) 勞動生產率（千元/人）	Average debts / assets 平均資產負債率(%)	Average Total assets ('000 RMB) 平均總資產（千元）
By ownership 產業所有權									
State-owned 國有	63	381	13,079	-968	-3.47	-7.15	34.35	51.48	27,905
Collectively-owned 集體	236	163	6,821	163	3.13	8.57	41.95	63.51	5,229
Privately-owned 私有									
Domestic JVs 聯營	1	19							
Joint stock 股份制	1	34	2,040	-326	-16.31	-42.32	60.00	61.46	2,002
Foreign-funded 外資	2	10	1,026	-425	-17.58	-24.97	102.63	29.60	2,419
Overseas Chinese-funded 港澳台資	2	37	1,349	-796	-12.37	-53.15	36.46	76.73	6,437
By size 規模									
Large 大型	2	5,372	180,423	-9,846	-2.13	-4.45	33.59	52.05	461,752
Medium 中型	6	1,071	42,725	-2,173	-3.97	-9.95	39.89	60.14	54,760
Small 小型	298	153	6,187	16	0.27	0.64	40.49	58.37	5,943
By regional distribution 地區分布									
Central-North 華北	52	353	11,499	-863	-3.50	-6.65	32.61	47.39	24,665
Beijing 北京	16	544	13,876	-2,701	-6.65	-12.68	25.50	47.51	40,598
Tianjin 天津	5	1,182	39,652	-370	-0.38	-0.71	33.56	46.34	97,448
Hebei 河北	15	76	4,840	161	5.82	17.89	63.80	67.45	2,771
Shanxi 山西	12	185	7,958	37	0.48	0.80	42.92	39.13	7,570
Inner Mongolia 內蒙	4	90	2,395	-663	-19.79	-75.28	26.61	73.71	3,348
Northeast 東北	93	171	6,934	130	2.13	5.88	40.61	63.88	6,126
Liaoning 遼寧	55	143	6,437	202	3.60	9.93	45.17	63.69	5,594
Jilin 吉林	25	149	6,869	136	2.26	7.64	46.09	70.48	6,028
Heilongjiang 黑龍江	13	332	9,166	-183	-2.14	-4.80	27.60	55.48	8,568
Central East 華東	76	142	7,892	56	0.92	3.32	55.43	72.44	6,064
Shanghai 上海	1	445							
Jiangsu 江蘇	22	148	6,403	40	0.76	3.12	43.36	75.52	5,235
Zhejiang 浙江	10	71	4,023	34	0.71	2.25	57.06	68.28	4,764
Anhui 安徽	8	163	23,888	469	6.53	27.15	147.00	75.97	7,184
Fujian 福建									
Jiangxi 江西	4	196	10,415	-343	-2.39	-4.49	53.21	46.82	14,333
Shandong 山東	31	140	5,999	20	0.34	1.57	42.86	78.49	5,911
Central-South 中南	47	181	6,667	-29	-0.37	-0.89	36.78	58.17	7,627
Henan 河南	16	57	3,053	-192	-4.71	-19.46	53.27	75.80	4,078
Hubei 湖北	7	258	6,983	-211	-4.10	-14.27	27.02	71.30	5,161
Hunan 湖南	20	240	9,596	189	1.65	3.45	39.91	52.09	11,451
Guangdong 廣東	1	136	520	-80	-13.56	-114.29	3.82	88.14	590
Guangxi 廣西	3	284	7,737	-163	-1.78	-3.50	27.27	49.16	9,173
Hainan 海南									
Southwest 西南	24	294	10,043	2	0.02	0.04	34.11	57.01	10,863
Chongqing 重慶	7	140	4,374	1	0.02	0.04	31.25	54.00	5,608
Sichuan 四川	14	383	12,265	-8	-0.06	-0.14	32.03	59.64	13,606
Guizhou 貴州	2	109	7,270	55	1.68	2.78	66.70	39.69	3,275
Yunnan 雲南	1	408	20,700	30	0.14	0.25	50.74	42.99	20,910
Tibet 西藏									
Northwest 西北	20	108	3,190	66	1.44	3.14	29.41	53.99	4,538
Shaanxi 陝西	16	76	1,909	19	0.67	1.33	25.19	49.55	2,886
Gansu 甘肅	3	305	10,643	320	2.24	5.45	34.90	58.89	14,287
Qinghai 青海									
Ningxia 寧夏									
Xinjiang 新疆	1	41	1,320	40	2.33	4.71	32.20	51.16	1,720

3714: Rolling Stock Accessories 機車車輛配件製造業

Year 年份	Number of firms 企業個數	Rate of change 每年變化 (%)	Number of employees 職工人數 (人)	Rate of change 每年變化 (%)	Total revenue (mil. RMB) 總銷售收入 (百萬元)	Rate of change 每年變化 (%)	Total profit (mil. RMB) 總利潤 (百萬元)	Rate of change 每年變化 (%)
1993	182		36,685		1,323		56	
1994	230	26.37%	71,993	96.25%	1,595	20.56%	-6	-111.44%
1995	265	15.22%	66,243	-7.99%	2,139	34.07%	-47	-628.94%
1996	312	17.74%	62,797	-5.20%	2,461	15.05%	-28	40.14%

3 Major products* 3 種主要產品 *	Output 產量	Sales volume 銷售量	Unit 單位
a) Non-ferrous Casting 有色金屬鑄件	1,161	1,079	ton 噸
b) Forging 鍛件	6,117	5,138	ton 噸
c) Casting 鑄鋼件	7,702	6,470	ton 噸

Top 10 firms by revenue (year founded) 收入排名前 10 家企業 (創辦年份)	City 城市	Province 省	Telephone / fax 電話 / 傳真	Number of employees 職工人數	Ownership 產業所有權	Revenue ('000 RMB) 銷售收入 (千元)	Profit ('000 RMB) (rank) 利潤 (千元) (排名)	Total assets ('000 RMB) 總資產 (千元)	Major products 主要產品
Tianjin Rolling Stock Machinery Plant 天津機車車輛機械廠(1912)	Tianjin 天津市	Tianjin 天津市	(022)26271128 (022)26270268	5,060	State-owned 國有	169,360	550(18)	432,530	o
Dalian Rolling Stock Factory Fittings Branch 大連機車車輛工廠配件分廠(1980)	Dalian 大連市	Liaoning 遼寧省	(0411)4644530 (0411)4601826	2,538	Collectively-owned 集體	121,152	94(60)	91,645	o
Ziyang Internal Firing Machine Labour Service Co. 資陽內燃機車廠工業公司(1984)	Neijiang 內江市	Sichuan 四川省	(0832)622843	2,608	Collectively-owned 集體	110,325	681(12)	66,091	o
Nanjing Pu Zhen Vehicle Plant Industrial Co. 南京浦鎮車輛廠工業公司(1978)	Nanjing 南京市	Jiangsu 江蘇省	(025)8851552	1,785	Collectively-owned 集體	77,183	-64(99)	60,986	c
Qingdao Siji Industry Co. 青島四機工業公司(1980)	Qingdao 青島市	Shandong 山東省	(0532)3835134 (0532)3717570	1,620	Collectively-owned 集體	70,312	159(41)	82,506	o
Zhuzhou Electric Locomotive Machinery Factory 株洲電力機車機械廠(1971)	Zhuzhou 株洲市	Hunan 湖南省	(0733)8499141 (0733)8431017	1,736	Collectively-owned 集體	65,258	13(79)	104,732	o
Ningguo Shuang Ling Industrial General Company 寧國縣雙菱實業總公司(1974)	Xuanzhou 宣州市	Anhui 安徽省	(0563)4072198	180	Collectively-owned 集體	64,130	1281(7)	22,837	o
Ningguo Hu Le Agricultural Machinery Factory 寧國縣胡樂農機廠(1976)	Xuanzhou 宣州市	Anhui 安徽省	(0563)4077079	152	Collectively-owned 集體	61,069	812(11)	6,482	o
Bei Jing Railway Bureau Taiyuan Rolling Stock Fitting Parts Plant 北京鐵路局太原機車車輛配件廠(1959)	Taiyuan 太原市	Shanxi 山西省	(0351)3059548 (0351)3058454	593	State-owned 國有	47,637	-807(114)	63,678	a,b,c
Wendeng Huang Hai Gear Box Factory 文登市黃海齒輪箱廠(1993)	Weihai 威海市	Shandong 山東省	(0896)8852051 (0896)8852051	77	Collectively-owned 集體	43,750	1820(5)	15,020	o

Top 10 Cities by Production Output 產出排名前 10 位城市	Province 省	Market share 市場份額	Number of firms 企業個數
Beijing 北京市	Beijing 北京市	26.97%	13
Tianjin 天津市	Tianjin 天津市	9.78%	4
Zhuzhou 株洲市	Hunan 湖南省	5.73%	16
Guilin 桂林市	Guangxi 廣西	4.57%	2
Qingdao 青島市	Shandong 山東省	4.05%	14
Taiyuan 太原市	Shanxi 山西省	3.70%	9
Jilin 吉林市	Jilin 吉林省	3.42%	9
Changzhou 常州市	Jiangsu 江蘇省	3.01%	16
Shenyang 瀋陽市	Liaoning 遼寧省	2.74%	21
Dalian 大連市	Liaoning 遼寧省	2.52%	10

10 Major Wholesalers 10 家主要批發商	City 城市	Province 省	Telephone / Fax 電話 / 傳真
Liaoning Automobile Trade Group Corp. 遼寧省汽車貿易集團	Shenyang 瀋陽市	Liaoning 遼寧省	(024)23835494 (024)23838338
China Post and Telecommunication Equipment General Company 中國郵電器材總公司	Beijing 北京市	Beijing 北京市	(010)63523715 (010)63525935
Jiangsu Electromechanical Products General Company 江蘇省機電產品總公司	Nanjing 南京市	Jiangsu 江蘇省	(025)7713642 (025)7711036
Xi Nan Technology Import & Export Company 西南技術進出口公司	Chongqing 重慶市	Chongqing 重慶市	(023)63850185 (023)63850026
Changzhou Economic Technology Industrial Development Zone Tian Ming Trade Company 常州經濟技術產業開發區天明貿易公司	Changzhou 常州市	Jiangsu 江蘇省	(0519)8829882 (0519)8829882
Shanxi Mechanical Equipment Import & Export Company 山西省機械設備進出口公司	Taiyuan 太原市	Shanxi 山西省	(0351)4040713 (0351)4043981
Ningbo Five Mining Machinery Import & Export Company 寧波市五礦機械進出口公司	Ningbo 寧波市	Zhejiang 浙江省	(0574)7311255 (0574)7320322
Tianjin Jin Huan Electromechanical Complete Sets of Equipment Factory 天津市津環機電成套設備廠	Tianjin 天津市	Tianjin 天津市	(022)26371628
Yunnan Machinery Import & Export Company 雲南省機械進出口公司	Kunming 昆明市	Yunnan 雲南省	(0871)3164879 (0871)3136829
Tianjin Da Qiu Zhuang Yi Yuan Trade Center 天津市大丘莊億源商貿中心	Tianjin 天津市	Tianjin 天津市	(022)28899478 (022)28899046

*Also include sales by firms outside this industry.包括本行業以外廠家的銷售。"o" stands for "others". "o" 代表 "其他產品" 。

3715: Railway Traffic Signal Equipment 鐵路信號設備製造業

The industry accounts for 0.005% of the total revenue of China's industrial sector in 1996. The revenue growth rate of the industry is 17.0% from 1995, as compared to the growth rate of China's industrial sector, 9.51%. The rate of return on asset is -1.76%. 75.56% of all firms in the industry made a profit while 24.44% had negative returns. The top province in terms of the industry's revenue is Shaanxi, accounting for 45.44% of the total revenue.
本行業在1996年佔全行業總產值0.005%，行業年增長率為17.0%（全國工業年增長率9.51%）。行業的資產回報率-1.76%，75.56%的企業盈利，24.44%的企業虧損。銷售收入最高的省份為陝西省，佔本行業的45.44%。

	Total number of firms 企業總數	Total number of employees 職工總數	Total revenue (mil. RMB) 總銷售收入（百萬元）	Total profit (mil. RMB) 總利潤（百萬元）	Return on assets 資產利潤率 (%)	Return on equity 權益利潤率 (%)	Labour productivity ('000 RMB / worker) 勞動生產率（千元/人）	Debts / assets 資產負債率 (%)	Total assets (mil. RMB) 總資產（百萬元）
Industry Overall 行業總體	43	7,692	313	-11	-1.76	-3.92	40.69	55.06	600

	Number of firms 企業個數	Average number of employees 平均職工人數	Average revenue ('000 RMB) 平均銷售收入（千元）	Average profit ('000 RMB) 平均利潤（千元）	Return on assets 資產利潤率 (%)	Return on equity 權益利潤率 (%)	Labour productivity ('000 RMB / worker) 勞動生產率（千元/人）	Average debts / assets 平均資產負債率(%)	Average Total assets ('000 RMB) 平均總資產（千元）
By ownership 產業所有權									
State-owned 國有	15	351	17,533	-667	-1.84	-4.03	50.01	54.33	36,200
Collectively-owned 集體	27	87	1,178	20	1.79	4.86	13.54	63.24	1,102
Privately-owned 私有									
Domestic JVs 聯營									
Joint stock 股份制									
Foreign-funded 外資	1	83	18,183	-1,532	-5.63	-13.86	219.07	59.39	27,228
Overseas Chinese-funded 港澳台資									
By size 規模									
Large 大型	2	2,207	93,825	-5,769	-2.77	-5.72	42.52	51.67	208,594
Medium 中型									
Small 小型	41	80	3,057	13	0.29	0.79	38.24	62.61	4,458
By regional distribution 地區分布									
Central-North 華北	10	49	2,462	38	1.70	4.39	50.45	61.20	2,232
Beijing 北京	7	40	2,660	50	1.88	4.50	67.22	58.13	2,654
Tianjin 天津	1	116	300	-120	-25.00	80.00	2.59	129.17	480
Hebei 河北									
Shanxi 山西	2	48	2,850	75	4.60	14.71	60.00	68.71	1,630
Inner Mongolia 內蒙									
Northeast 東北	20	119	5,967	-394	-3.22	-6.25	49.95	48.43	12,228
Liaoning 遼寧	10	138	9,649	-741	-3.43	-6.28	70.02	45.39	21,615
Jilin 吉林	3	97	1,460	-50	-1.90	-13.89	15.10	86.29	2,627
Heilongjiang 黑龍江	7	103	2,637	-46	-1.56	-4.56	25.60	65.90	2,933
Central East 華東	3	100	6,680	543	9.54	22.86	66.80	58.46	5,697
Shanghai 上海	1	65	12,060	1,800	18.85	88.24	185.54	78.74	9,550
Jiangsu 江蘇	1	31	1,170	110	17.19	45.83	37.74	64.06	640
Zhejiang 浙江									
Anhui 安徽									
Fujian 福建									
Jiangxi 江西	1	204	6,810	-280	-4.06	-5.77	33.38	29.86	6,900
Shandong 山東									
Central-South 中南	3	139	1,837	57	1.19	2.79	13.18	57.34	4,767
Henan 河南	2	159	1,275	-65	-2.36	-7.56	8.02	68.73	2,750
Hubei 湖北	1	100	2,960	300	3.41	6.86	29.60	50.23	8,800
Hunan 湖南									
Guangdong 廣東									
Guangxi 廣西									
Hainan 海南									
Southwest 西南									
Chongqing 重慶									
Sichuan 四川									
Guizhou 貴州									
Yunnan 雲南									
Tibet 西藏									
Northwest 西北	7	585	20,554	-700	-1.62	-4.02	35.12	59.67	43,174
Shaanxi 陝西	6	670	23,707	-790	-1.58	-3.88	35.37	59.24	49,990
Gansu 甘肅	1	76	1,640	-160	-7.02	43.24	21.58	116.23	2,280
Qinghai 青海									
Ningxia 寧夏									
Xinjiang 新疆									

3715: Railway Traffic Signal Equipment 鐵路信號設備製造業

Year 年份	Number of firms 企業個數	Rate of change 每年變化 (%)	Number of employees 職工人數 (人)	Rate of change 每年變化 (%)	Total revenue (mil. RMB) 總銷售收入 (百萬元)	Rate of change 每年變化 (%)	Total profit (mil. RMB) 總利潤 (百萬元)	Rate of change 每年變化 (%)
1993	29		9,186		260		8	
1994	30	3.45%	4,228	-53.97%	287	10.35%	11	29.98%
1995	37	23.33%	11,086	162.20%	268	-6.84%	-12	-209.00%
1996	43	16.22%	7,692	-30.62%	313	16.96%	-11	5.88%

3 Major products* 3 種主要產品 *	Output 產量	Sales volume 銷售量	Unit 單位
a) Managing Equipment for Road Traffic 道路交通管理器材	51,413	68,894	set 台

Top 10 firms by revenue (year founded) 收入排名前 10 家企業 (創辦年份)	City 城市	Province 省	Telephone / fax 電話 / 傳真	Number of employees 職工人數	Ownership 產業所有權	Revenue ('000 RMB) 銷售收入 (千元)	Profit ('000 RMB) (rank) 利潤（千元）(排名)	Total assets ('000 RMB) 總資產 (千元)	Major products 主要產品
Xi'an Railway Signal Factory 西安鐵路信號工廠(1959)	Xi'an 西安市	Shaanxi 陝西省	(029)3227281 (029)3231462	3,536	State-owned 國有	118,850	-4790(19)	272,570	o
Shenyang Railway Signal Factory 瀋陽鐵路信號工廠(1937)	Shenyang 瀋陽市	Liaoning 遼寧省	(024)25872609 (024)25879167	2,813	State-owned 國有	72,700	-6520(20)	199,360	o
Railroad College Signal Equipment Factory 鐵道學院信號設備廠(1992)	Shanghai 上海市	Shanghai 上海市	(021)63253030 (021)62506812	66	State-owned 國有	12,064	1798(1)	9,551	o
Hatie Industry Dept. Harbin Communication Signal Equipment Factory 哈鐵工業處哈爾濱通訊信號器材廠(1958)	Harbin 哈爾濱市	Heilongjiang 黑龍江省	(0451)6422376 (0451)5318005	253	State-owned 國有	11,780	-380(18)	7,350	o
Xi'an Railway Branch Bureal Xi'an Electric Factory 西安鐵路分局西安電務器材廠(1970)	Xi'an 西安市	Shaanxi 陝西省	(029)2233444	179	State-owned 國有	8,754	211(4)	7,682	o
Jinzhou Railway Branch Bureal Jinzhou Electric Factory 錦鐵電務器材廠(1958)	Jinzhou 錦州市	Liaoning 遼寧省	(0416)2552073	231	State-owned 國有	7,391	5(11)	6,653	o
Shenyang Rolling Stock Factory Railway Standard Components Factory 瀋陽機車車輛廠鐵路標準件廠(1981)	Shenyang 瀋陽市	Liaoning 遼寧省	(024)26872725	240	Collectively-owned 集體	6,887	76(8)	2,097	o
Jinhua Railway Communication Signal Equipment Factory 金華鐵路通訊信號器材廠(1988)	Jinhua 金華市	Zhejiang 浙江省	(0579)2344962	115	State-owned 國有	6,853	960(2)	10,937	o
Nanchang Railway Bureau Nanchang Communication Signal Factory 南昌鐵路局南昌通訊信號廠(1971)	Nanchang 南昌市	Jiangxi 江西省	(0791)8516459	184	State-owned 國有	6,809	-282(17)	6,902	o
Harbin Railway Bureau Signal Equipment Factory 哈爾濱鐵路局信號器材廠(1979)	Harbin 哈爾濱市	Heilongjiang 黑龍江省	(0451)6318913	169	Collectively-owned 集體	5,186	86(7)	7,403	o

Top 10 Cities by Production Output 產出排名前 10 位城市	Province 省	Market share 市場份額	Number of firms 企業個數
Xi'an 西安市	Shaanxi 陝西省	33.04%	9
Shenyang 瀋陽市	Liaoning 遼寧省	32.13%	2
Shanghai 上海市	Shanghai 上海市	4.77%	2
Beijing 北京市	Beijing 北京市	3.98%	5
Taizhou 臺州市	Zhejiang 浙江省	3.27%	1
Nanchang 南昌市	Jiangxi 江西省	3.05%	2
Guangzhou 廣州市	Guangdong 廣東省	2.94%	1
Jinzhou 錦州市	Liaoning 遼寧省	2.73%	1
Ji'nan 濟南市	Shandong 山東省	2.40%	1
Wuhan 武漢市	Hubei 湖北省	2.30%	2

10 Major Wholesalers 10 家主要批發商	City 城市	Province 省	Telephone / Fax 電話 / 傳真
Liaoning Automobile Trade Group Corp. 遼寧省汽車貿易集團	Shenyang 瀋陽市	Liaoning 遼寧省	(024)23835494 (024)23838338
China Post and Telecommunication Equipment General Company 中國郵電器材總公司	Beijing 北京市	Beijing 北京市	(010)63523715 (010)63525935
Jiangsu Electromechanical Products General Company 江蘇省機電產品總公司	Nanjing 南京市	Jiangsu 江蘇省	(025)7713642 (025)7711036
Xi Nan Technology Import & Export Company 西南技術進出口公司	Chongqing 重慶市	Chongqing 重慶市	(023)63850185 (023)63850026
Changzhou Economic Technology Industrial Development Zone Tian Ming Trade Company 常州經濟技術產業開發區天明貿易公司	Changzhou 常州市	Jiangsu 江蘇省	(0519)8829882 (0519)8829882
Shanxi Mechanical Equipment Import & Export Company 山西省機械設備進出口公司	Taiyuan 太原市	Shanxi 山西省	(0351)4040713 (0351)4043981
Ningbo Five Mining Machinery Import & Export Company 寧波市五礦機械進出口公司	Ningbo 寧波市	Zhejiang 浙江省	(0574)7311255 (0574)7320322
Tianjin Jin Huan Electromechanical Complete Sets of Equipment Factory 天津市津環機電成套設備廠	Tianjin 天津市	Tianjin 天津市	(022)26371628
Yunnan Machinery Import & Export Company 雲南省機械進出口公司	Kunming 昆明市	Yunnan 雲南省	(0871)3164879 (0871)3136829
Tianjin Da Qiu Zhuang Yi Yuan Trade Center 天津市大丘莊億源商貿中心	Tianjin 天津市	Tianjin 天津市	(022)28899478 (022)28899046

*Also include sales by firms outside this industry.包括本行業以外廠家的銷售。"o" stands for "others". "o" 代表"其他產品"。

3716: Special Railway Equipment 鐵路專用設備製造業

The industry accounts for 0.019% of the total revenue of China's industrial sector in 1996. The revenue growth rate of the industry is 21.7% from 1995, as compared to the growth rate of China's industrial sector, 9.51%. The rate of return on asset is -1.27%. 73.99% of all firms in the industry made a profit while 20.45% had negative returns. The top province in terms of the industry's revenue is Hebei, accounting for 41.52% of the total revenue.
本行業在1996年佔全行業總產值0.019%，行業年增長率為21.7%（全國工業年增長率9.51%）。行業的資產回報率-1.27%，73.99%的企業盈利，20.45%的企業虧損。銷售收入最高的省份為河北省，佔本行業的41.52%。

	Total number of firms 企業總數	Total number of employees 職工總數	Total revenue (mil. RMB) 總銷售收入（百萬元）	Total profit (mil. RMB) 總利潤（百萬元）	Return on assets 資產利潤率 (%)	Return on equity 權益利潤率 (%)	Labour productivity ('000 RMB / worker) 勞動生產率（千元/人）	Debts / assets 資產負債率 (%)	Total assets (mil. RMB) 總資產（百萬元）
Industry Overall 行業總體	38	22,753	1,121	-31	-1.27	-3.16	49.27	59.73	2,459

	Number of firms 企業個數	Average number of employees 平均職工人數	Average revenue ('000 RMB) 平均銷售收入（千元）	Average profit ('000 RMB) 平均利潤（千元）	Return on assets 資產利潤率 (%)	Return on equity 權益利潤率 (%)	Labour productivity ('000 RMB / worker) 勞動生產率（千元/人）	Average debts / assets 平均資產負債率(%)	Average Total assets ('000 RMB) 平均總資產（千元）
By ownership 產業所有權									
State-owned 國有	11	1,893	96,636	-3,091	-1.43	-3.50	51.05	59.29	216,818
Collectively-owned 集體	24	74	1,998	71	2.76	14.47	26.89	80.94	2,591
Privately-owned 私有									
Domestic JVs 聯營									
Joint stock 股份制									
Foreign-funded 外資	3	48	3,338	428	10.72	17.84	69.06	39.90	3,995
Overseas Chinese-funded 港澳台資									
By size 規模									
Large 大型	3	5,463	280,656	-11,053	-1.60	-4.02	51.38	60.32	692,190
Medium 中型									
Small 小型	35	182	7,972	62	0.56	1.30	43.86	56.61	10,932
By regional distribution 地區分布									
Central-North 華北	15	547	33,746	-1,881	-2.93	-9.38	61.66	68.80	64,299
Beijing 北京	4	146	8,268	720	4.22	6.10	56.72	30.84	17,055
Tianjin 天津	3	37	2,553	180	8.70	128.57	69.01	93.24	2,070
Hebei 河北	8	939	58,183	-3,955	-3.55	-12.49	61.94	71.54	111,256
Shanxi 山西									
Inner Mongolia 內蒙									
Northeast 東北	10	684	17,839	-43	-0.07	-0.15	26.08	55.43	64,868
Liaoning 遼寧	7	933	24,841	-91	-0.10	-0.22	26.63	55.47	92,189
Jilin 吉林	1	8	1,100	100	18.18	29.41	137.50	38.18	550
Heilongjiang 黑龍江	2	152	1,700	55	3.91	7.91	11.18	50.53	1,405
Central East 華東	2	47	8,040	195	4.14	8.57	172.90	51.70	4,710
Shanghai 上海									
Jiangsu 江蘇									
Zhejiang 浙江	1	13	6,280	-240	-13.19	-15.89	483.08	17.03	1,820
Anhui 安徽									
Fujian 福建									
Jiangxi 江西									
Shandong 山東	1	80	9,800	630	8.29	20.72	122.50	60.00	7,600
Central-South 中南	7	396	7,167	-1,497	-6.91	-17.04	18.11	59.44	21,663
Henan 河南	3	28	930	3	0.28	0.86	33.61	67.51	1,190
Hubei 湖北	1	2,399	43,720	-9,980	-7.22	-18.64	18.22	61.26	138,210
Hunan 湖南	2	59	165	-290	-40.00	341.18	2.82	111.72	725
Guangdong 廣東									
Guangxi 廣西	1	172	3,330	70	0.83	1.00	19.36	17.00	8,410
Hainan 海南									
Southwest 西南	2	232	10,890	295	1.85	3.76	47.04	50.89	15,985
Chongqing 重慶									
Sichuan 四川	2	232	10,890	295	1.85	3.76	46.94	50.89	15,985
Guizhou 貴州									
Yunnan 雲南									
Tibet 西藏									
Northwest 西北	2	2,188	174,270	3,420	1.05	2.15	79.65	51.22	326,605
Shaanxi 陝西	2	2,188	174,270	3,420	1.05	2.15	79.65	51.22	326,605
Gansu 甘肅									
Qinghai 青海									
Ningxia 寧夏									
Xinjiang 新疆									

3716: Special Railway Equipment 鐵路專用設備製造業

Year 年份	Number of firms 企業個數	Rate of change 每年變化 (%)	Number of employees 職工人數 (人)	Rate of change 每年變化 (%)	Total revenue (mil. RMB) 總銷售收入 (百萬元)	Rate of change 每年變化 (%)	Total profit (mil. RMB) 總利潤 (百萬元)	Rate of change 每年變化 (%)
1993	32		11,528		655		43	
1994	34	6.25%	8,361	-27.47%	660	0.74%	14	-66.37%
1995	37	8.82%	18,664	123.23%	921	39.62%	-73	-606.04%
1996	38	2.70%	22,753	21.91%	1,121	21.70%	-31	57.25%

3 Major products* 3 種主要產品 *	Output 產量	Sales volume 銷售量	Unit 單位
a) Metal Container 金屬集裝箱	16,473	26,522	piece 件
b) Metal Structure Products 金屬結構製品	30,954	27,858	ton 噸

Top 10 firms by revenue (year founded) 收入排名前 10 家企業 (創辦年份)	City 城市	Province 省	Telephone / fax 電話 / 傳真	Number of employees 職工人數	Ownership 產業所有權	Revenue ('000 RMB) 銷售收入 (千元)	Profit ('000 RMB) (rank) 利潤 (千元) (排名)	Total assets ('000 RMB) 總資產 (千元)	Major products 主要產品
Shanhaiguan Bridge Works 山海關橋樑工廠(1894)	Qinhuangdao 秦皇島市	Hebei 河北省	(0335)5051185 (0335)5053186	6,841	State-owned 國有	451,600	-31960(18)	863,020	a,b
Baoji Bridge Factory 寶雞橋樑工廠(1966)	Baoji 寶雞市	Shaanxi 陝西省	(0917)3353555 (0917)3353371	4,041	State-owned 國有	327,410	6680(1)	630,990	o
Jin Xi Chemical Machinery Plant 錦西化工機械廠(1942)	Huludao 葫蘆島市	Liaoning 遼寧省	(0429)22126230 (0429)22126260	6,082	State-owned 國有	171,119	334(4)	628,355	o
Wuhan Construction Machinery Plant of The Ministry of Railways 鐵道部武漢工程機械廠(1958)	Wuhan 武漢市	Hubei 湖北省	(027)86811054	2,398	State-owned 國有	43,720	-9980(17)	138,210	a
Xi Tie Branch Bureau Xingping Machinery Factory 西鐵分局興平機械廠(1965)	Xianyang 咸陽市	Shaanxi 陝西省	(0910)8821434	335	State-owned 國有	21,130	156(8)	22,221	o
Chengdu Railway Bureau Shifang Yang Lu Machinery Plant 成都鐵路局什邡養路機械廠(1969)	Deyang 德陽市	Sichuan 四川省	(0838)8205282 (0838)8205283	409	State-owned 國有	20,020	518(3)	30,377	o
Ren Urban Nian Li Pu Zhen Mining Machinery Fittings Factory 任城區廿里鋪鎮礦機配件廠(1987)	Jining 濟寧市	Shandong 山東省	(0537)2595681	80	Collectively-owned 集體	9,800	630(2)	7,600	o
Zhengzhou Railway Bureau Engineering Machinery Plant 鄭州鐵路局工務機械廠(1953)	Zhengzhou 鄭州市	Henan 河南省	(0371)8712921	427	State-owned 國有	9,188	-579(16)	51,345	o
Tangshan Railway Qing Shai Machine-made Zao Factory 唐山市鐵路清篩機製造廠(1963)	Tangshan 唐山市	Hebei 河北省	(0315)2861973	382	Collectively-owned 集體	7,158	-182(14)	18,039	o
Ningbo Hydraulic Pressure Track Jack Factory 寧波市液壓起道器廠(1968)	Ningbo 寧波市	Zhejiang 浙江省	(0574)7598128 (0574)7598194	35	Collectively-owned 集體	6,277	-241(15)	1,823	o

Top 10 Cities by Production Output 產出排名前 10 位城市	Province 省	Market share 市場份額	Number of firms 企業個數
Qinhuangdao 秦皇島市	Hebei 河北省	31.35%	1
Baoji 寶雞市	Shaanxi 陝西省	21.07%	1
Huludao 葫蘆島市	Liaoning 遼寧省	14.58%	2
Kunming 昆明市	Yunnan 雲南省	13.24%	3
Chaohu 巢湖市	Anhui 安徽省	4.92%	1
Deyang 德陽市	Sichuan 四川省	2.99%	4
Beijing 北京市	Beijing 北京市	1.55%	3
Shenyang 瀋陽市	Liaoning 遼寧省	1.43%	3
Xianyang 咸陽市	Shaanxi 陝西省	1.13%	1
Xi'an 西安市	Shaanxi 陝西省	1.00%	3

10 Major Wholesalers 10 家主要批發商	City 城市	Province 省	Telephone / Fax 電話 / 傳真
Liaoning Automobile Trade Group Corp. 遼寧省汽車貿易集團	Shenyang 瀋陽市	Liaoning 遼寧省	(024)23835494 (024)23838338
China Post and Telecommunication Equipment General Company 中國郵電器材總公司	Beijing 北京市	Beijing 北京市	(010)63523715 (010)63525935
Jiangsu Electromechanical Products General Company 江蘇省機電產品總公司	Nanjing 南京市	Jiangsu 江蘇省	(025)7713642 (025)7711036
Xi Nan Technology Import & Export Company 西南技術進出口公司	Chongqing 重慶市	Chongqing 重慶市	(023)63850185 (023)63850026
Changzhou Economic Technology Industrial Development Zone Tian Ming Trade Company 常州經濟技術產業開發區天明貿易公司	Changzhou 常州市	Jiangsu 江蘇省	(0519)8829882 (0519)8829882
Shanxi Mechanical Equipment Import & Export Company 山西省機械設備進出口公司	Taiyuan 太原市	Shanxi 山西省	(0351)4040713 (0351)4043981
Ningbo Five Mining Machinery Import & Export Company 寧波市五礦機械進出口公司	Ningbo 寧波市	Zhejiang 浙江省	(0574)7311255 (0574)7320322
Tianjin Jin Huan Electromechanical Complete Sets of Equipment Factory 天津市津環機電成套設備廠	Tianjin 天津市	Tianjin 天津市	(022)26371628
Yunnan Machinery Import & Export Company 雲南省機械進出口公司	Kunming 昆明市	Yunnan 雲南省	(0871)3164879 (0871)3136829
Tianjin Da Qiu Zhuang Yi Yuan Trade Center 天津市大丘莊億源商貿中心	Tianjin 天津市	Tianjin 天津市	(022)28899478 (022)28899046

*Also include sales by firms outside this industry.包括本行業以外廠家的銷售。"o" stands for "others". "o" 代表 "其他產品"。

3717: Special Railway Machinery 鐵路專用器材製造業

The industry accounts for 0.030% of the total revenue of China's industrial sector in 1996. The revenue growth rate of the industry is 42.0% from 1995, as compared to the growth rate of China's industrial sector, 9.51%. The rate of return on asset is -1.85%. 70.05% of all firms in the industry made a profit while 22.14% had negative returns. The top province in terms of the industry's revenue is Beijing, accounting for 26.79% of the total revenue.
本行業在1996年佔全行業總產值0.030%，行業年增長率為42.0%（全國工業年增長率9.51%）。行業的資產回報率-1.85%，70.05%的企業盈利，22.14%的企業虧損。銷售收入最高的省份為北京市，佔本行業的26.79%。

	Total number of firms 企業總數	Total number of employees 職工總數	Total revenue (mil. RMB) 總銷售收入（百萬元）	Total profit (mil. RMB) 總利潤（百萬元）	Return on assets 資產利潤率 (%)	Return on equity 權益利潤率 (%)	Labour productivity ('000 RMB / worker) 勞動生產率（千元/人）	Debts / assets 資產負債率 (%)	Total assets (mil. RMB) 總資產（百萬元）
Industry Overall 行業總體	150	36,986	1,715	-56	-1.85	-4.66	46.37	60.40	3,050

	Number of firms 企業個數	Average number of employees 平均職工人數	Average revenue ('000 RMB) 平均銷售收入（千元）	Average profit ('000 RMB) 平均利潤（千元）	Return on assets 資產利潤率 (%)	Return on equity 權益利潤率 (%)	Labour productivity ('000 RMB / worker) 勞動生產率（千元/人）	Average debts / assets 平均資產負債率(%)	Average Total assets ('000 RMB) 平均總資產（千元）
By ownership 產業所有權									
State-owned 國有	48	502	23,542	-1,354	-2.75	-6.79	46.90	59.44	49,208
Collectively-owned 集體	98	130	5,841	536	8.13	21.85	44.98	62.78	6,589
Privately-owned 私有									
Domestic JVs 聯營	1	60	1,233				20.54	97.36	371
Joint stock 股份制									
Foreign-funded 外資	1	35	7,328	-30,289	-86.97	-341.19	209.38	74.51	34,826
Overseas Chinese-funded 港澳台資	1	68	4,699	-13,224	-184.80	-1636.78	69.11	88.71	7,156
By size 規模									
Large 大型	3	2,421	97,162	-14,179	-5.54	-12.92	40.14	57.10	255,876
Medium 中型	8	917	59,101	-2,183	-1.74	-4.51	64.49	61.44	125,532
Small 小型	138	162	6,894	29	0.31	0.81	42.66	61.55	9,262
By regional distribution 地區分布									
Central-North 華北	26	377	26,269	-747	-1.56	-3.93	69.63	60.24	47,837
Beijing 北京	10	516	45,937	-1,018	-1.22	-3.52	89.06	65.51	83,736
Tianjin 天津	4	516	20,500	-1,713	-4.52	-8.05	39.73	43.85	37,905
Hebei 河北	6	297	17,353	93	0.34	0.72	58.46	53.41	27,848
Shanxi 山西	4	178	9,128	-740	-3.41	-6.96	51.35	50.94	21,673
Inner Mongolia 內蒙	2	48	500				10.53	83.17	505
Northeast 東北	70	212	5,505	-527	-5.12	-13.82	25.96	62.94	10,295
Liaoning 遼寧	51	238	6,384	-692	-5.60	-14.95	26.80	62.52	12,349
Jilin 吉林	10	105	1,544	-185	-6.85	-33.15	14.69	79.34	2,701
Heilongjiang 黑龍江	9	182	4,920	24	0.34	0.86	26.98	60.15	7,099
Central East 華東	23	168	7,229	580	3.77	6.63	42.97	43.16	15,371
Shanghai 上海	2	111	7,460	895	1.97	5.53	67.51	64.28	45,335
Jiangsu 江蘇	5	155	2,778	130	2.95	6.15	17.90	52.09	4,408
Zhejiang 浙江	4	66	3,655	240	6.65	21.24	55.17	68.68	3,608
Anhui 安徽	2	810	48,245	5,300	5.36	7.49	59.60	28.47	98,900
Fujian 福建	1	110	8,290				75.36	48.31	3,540
Jiangxi 江西	5	46	1,470	-6	-0.25	-0.48	31.68	47.55	2,364
Shandong 山東	4	162	2,675	-160	-4.84	-16.20	16.56	70.14	3,308
Central-South 中南	13	161	6,445	67	0.57	2.61	40.09	77.99	11,648
Henan 河南	5	73	4,402	-48	-0.99	-3.99	60.47	75.17	4,840
Hubei 湖北	2	339	12,185	540	5.09	20.15	35.94	74.73	10,605
Hunan 湖南	5	176	6,216	-24	-0.18	-0.79	35.40	77.00	13,224
Guangdong 廣東	1	170	6,320	150	0.38	2.22	37.18	83.08	39,900
Guangxi 廣西									
Hainan 海南									
Southwest 西南	9	318	32,658	-82	-0.20	-0.52	102.70	61.52	41,322
Chongqing 重慶									
Sichuan 四川	5	244	13,586	-112	-0.61	-1.34	55.68	54.64	18,402
Guizhou 貴州									
Yunnan 雲南	4	411	56,498	-45	-0.06	-0.18	137.55	63.79	69,973
Tibet 西藏									
Northwest 西北	9	391	11,399	-1,489	-6.42	-19.43	29.19	66.97	23,197
Shaanxi 陝西	6	238	10,198	88	0.71	2.81	42.91	74.66	12,393
Gansu 甘肅	2	725	12,250	-6,670	-15.25	-58.53	16.91	73.95	43,745
Qinghai 青海									
Ningxia 寧夏									
Xinjiang 新疆	1	640	16,900	-590	-1.26	-2.16	26.41	41.77	46,920

3717: Special Railway Machinery 鐵路專用器材製造業

Year 年份	Number of firms 企業個數	Rate of change 每年變化 (%)	Number of employees 職工人數 (人)	Rate of change 每年變化 (%)	Total revenue (mil. RMB) 總銷售收入 (百萬元)	Rate of change 每年變化 (%)	Total profit (mil. RMB) 總利潤 (百萬元)	Rate of change 每年變化 (%)
1993	99		33,147		1,420		76	
1994	121	22.22%	39,505	19.18%	1,367	-3.71%	14	-81.27%
1995	140	15.70%	35,415	-10.35%	1,208	-11.65%	-43	-404.73%
1996	150	7.14%	36,986	4.44%	1,715	41.97%	-56	-29.58%

3 Major products* 3 種主要產品 *	Output 產量	Sales volume 銷售量	Unit 單位
a) Cement Sleeper 水泥軌枕	427,587	401,932	piece 根
b) Crane & Conveyance Equipment 起重運輸設備	18,659	17,166	ton 噸
c) Iron Casting 鑄鐵件	1,974	1,934	ton 噸

Top 10 firms by revenue (year founded) 收入排名前 10 家企業 (創辦年份)	City 城市	Province 省	Telephone / fax 電話 / 傳真	Number of employees 職工人數	Ownership 產業所有權	Revenue ('000 RMB) 銷售收入 (千元)	Profit ('000 RMB) (rank) 利潤 (千元) (排名)	Total assets ('000 RMB) 總資產 (千元)	Major products 主要產品
Beijing Bell Communication Equipment Manufacturing Co. Ltd. 北京貝爾通訊設備製造有限公司(1996)	Beijing 北京市	Beijing 北京市	(010)63246816 (010)63823232		Foreign-funded 外資	228,599	8000(2)	233,413	o
China Railway Building General Co. Kunming Machinery Plant 中國鐵道建築總公司昆明機械廠(1954)	Kunming 昆明市	Yunnan 雲南省	(0871)7172751 (0871)7171799	1,100	State-owned 國有	201,850	1250(8)	237,664	o
Fengtai Bridge Factory 豐台橋樑工廠(1940)	Beijing 北京市	Beijing 北京市	(010)63827563	3,778	State-owned 國有	128,600	-24920(63)	436,910	a
Anhui Chaohu Casting Factory 安徽省巢湖鑄造廠(1959)	Chaohu 巢湖市	Anhui 安徽省	(0565)231703 (0565)231758	1,634	State-owned 國有	95,151	10544(1)	197,253	a,c
Railway Signal Factory 天津鐵路信號工廠(1939)	Tianjin 天津市	Tianjin 天津市	(022)24391111 (022)24391111	1,947	State-owned 國有	73,740	-7560(61)	145,660	o
Jinzhou Railway Branch Bureau Xue Jia Fitting Parts Plant 錦鐵薛家配件廠(1949)	Jinzhou 錦州市	Liaoning 遼寧省	(0416)4187764	1,107	State-owned 國有	60,965	18(30)	66,944	c
The Ministry of Railways Anshan Engineering Equipment 鐵道部鞍山工務器材廠(1936)	Anshan 鞍山市	Liaoning 遼寧省	(0412)8812535 (0412)8814351	1,371	State-owned 國有	58,830	-3500(59)	120,220	o
Railway Ministry Shenyang Bridge Works 鐵道部瀋陽橋樑工廠(1939)	Shenyang 瀋陽市	Liaoning 遼寧省	(024)25706155 (024)25821705	3,010	State-owned 國有	58,380	-31710(64)	255,420	o
The Ministry of Railways Longchang Engineering Equipment 鐵道部隆昌工務器材廠(1971)	Neijiang 內江市	Sichuan 四川省	(0832)3923559 (0832)3923559	916	State-owned 國有	50,090	30(29)	80,550	o
Tangshan Railway Switch Factory 唐山市鐵路道岔廠(1989)	Tangshan 唐山市	Hebei 河北省	(0315)2038675	491	Collectively-owned 集體	47,187	3324(3)	88,947	o

Top 10 Cities by Production Output 產出排名前 10 位城市	Province 省	Market share 市場份額	Number of firms 企業個數
Beijing 北京市	Beijing 北京市	19.25%	8
Shenyang 瀋陽市	Liaoning 遼寧省	9.06%	12
Tianjin 天津市	Tianjin 天津市	7.76%	7
Anshan 鞍山市	Liaoning 遼寧省	7.36%	7
Jinzhou 錦州市	Liaoning 遼寧省	6.12%	1
Tangshan 唐山市	Hebei 河北省	5.05%	2
Baicheng 白城市	Jilin 吉林省	5.00%	2
Neijiang 內江市	Sichuan 四川省	4.71%	2
Baoji 寶雞市	Shaanxi 陝西省	4.02%	1
Qinhuangdao 秦皇島市	Hebei 河北省	3.38%	1

10 Major Wholesalers 10 家主要批發商	City 城市	Province 省	Telephone / Fax 電話 / 傳真
Liaoning Automobile Trade Group Corp. 遼寧省汽車貿易集團	Shenyang 瀋陽市	Liaoning 遼寧省	(024)23835494 (024)23838338
China Post and Telecommunication Equipment General Company 中國郵電器材總公司	Beijing 北京市	Beijing 北京市	(010)63523715 (010)63525935
Jiangsu Electromechanical Products General Company 江蘇省機電產品總公司	Nanjing 南京市	Jiangsu 江蘇省	(025)7713642 (025)7711036
Xi Nan Technology Import & Export Company 西南技術進出口公司	Chongqing 重慶市	Chongqing 重慶市	(023)63850185 (023)63850026
Changzhou Economic Technology Industrial Development Zone Tian Ming Trade Company 常州經濟技術產業開發區天明貿易公司	Changzhou 常州市	Jiangsu 江蘇省	(0519)8829882 (0519)8829882
Shanxi Mechanical Equipment Import & Export Company 山西省機械設備進出口公司	Taiyuan 太原市	Shanxi 山西省	(0351)4040713 (0351)4043981
Ningbo Five Mining Machinery Import & Export Company 寧波市五礦機械進出口公司	Ningbo 寧波市	Zhejiang 浙江省	(0574)7311255 (0574)7320322
Tianjin Jin Huan Electromechanical Complete Sets of Equipment Factory 天津市津環機電成套設備廠	Tianjin 天津市	Tianjin 天津市	(022)26371628
Yunnan Machinery Import & Export Company 雲南省機械進出口公司	Kunming 昆明市	Yunnan 雲南省	(0871)3164879 (0871)3136829
Tianjin Da Qiu Zhuang Yi Yuan Trade Center 天津市大丘莊億源商貿中心	Tianjin 天津市	Tianjin 天津市	(022)28899478 (022)28899046

*Also include sales by firms outside this industry.包括本行業以外廠家的銷售。"o" stands for "others". "o" 代表 "其他產品"。

3719: Other Railroad Transporting Equipment 其他鐵路運輸設備製造業

The industry accounts for 0.004% of the total revenue of China's industrial sector in 1996. The revenue growth rate of the industry is -34.0% from 1995, as compared to the growth rate of China's industrial sector, 9.51%. The rate of return on asset is -1.67%. 80.77% of all firms in the industry made a profit while 19.23% had negative returns. The top province in terms of the industry's revenue is Shaanxi, accounting for 39.41% of the total revenue.
本行業在1996年佔全行業總產值0.004%，行業年增長率為-34.0%（全國工業年增長率9.51%）。行業的資產回報率-1.67%，80.77%的企業盈利，19.23%的企業虧損。銷售收入最高的省份為陝西省，佔本行業的39.41%。

	Total number of firms 企業總數	Total number of employees 職工總數	Total revenue (mil. RMB) 總銷售收入（百萬元）	Total profit (mil. RMB) 總利潤（百萬元）	Return on assets 資產利潤率 (%)	Return on equity 權益利潤率 (%)	Labour productivity ('000 RMB / worker) 勞動生產率（千元/人）	Debts / assets 資產負債率 (%)	Total assets (mil. RMB) 總資產（百萬元）
Industry Overall 行業總體	52	8,998	258	-9	-1.67	-3.05	28.67	45.28	531

	Number of firms 企業個數	Average number of employees 平均職工人數	Average revenue ('000 RMB) 平均銷售收入（千元）	Average profit ('000 RMB) 平均利潤（千元）	Return on assets 資產利潤率 (%)	Return on equity 權益利潤率 (%)	Labour productivity ('000 RMB / worker) 勞動生產率（千元/人）	Average debts / assets 平均資產負債率(%)	Average Total assets ('000 RMB) 平均總資產（千元）
By ownership 產業所有權									
State-owned 國有	12	438	11,083	-1,333	-3.89	-6.56	25.33	40.63	34,250
Collectively-owned 集體	37	100	3,288	190	6.08	15.34	32.87	60.37	3,122
Privately-owned 私有									
Domestic JVs 聯營	1	19	1,251	93	10.57	20.92	65.87	49.48	883
Joint stock 股份制	1	25	1,986	-8	-0.26	-3.95	79.45	93.35	2,932
Foreign-funded 外資	1	2	72	-108	-16.26	-18.48	36.22	12.03	663
Overseas Chinese-funded 港澳台資									
By size 規模									
Large 大型	1	2,010	40,404	-11,854	-7.63	-13.12	20.10	41.85	155,415
Medium 中型	3	633	25,298	82	0.17	0.26	39.96	35.25	49,415
Small 小型	48	106	2,952	54	1.15	2.49	27.84	53.97	4,736
By regional distribution 地區分布									
Central-North 華北	6	94	5,622	258	3.20	6.73	59.59	52.41	8,065
Beijing 北京	1	25	620				24.80	62.55	2,590
Tianjin 天津	1	10	280	-20	-4.35	-6.67	28.00	34.78	460
Hebei 河北	2	79	6,595	735	9.11	24.87	83.48	63.38	8,070
Shanxi 山西	2	187	9,820	50	0.34	0.63	52.65	45.72	14,600
Inner Mongolia 內蒙									
Northeast 東北	14	202	4,021	143	1.12	1.41	19.86	20.30	12,721
Liaoning 遼寧	6	269	3,400	103	0.44	0.48	12.66	9.33	23,620
Jilin 吉林	6	151	5,570	285	5.02	14.42	36.97	65.20	5,680
Heilongjiang 黑龍江	2	160	1,235	-165	-14.35	-20.89	7.74	31.30	1,150
Central East 華東	18	72	2,877	-50	-1.74	-4.23	39.77	58.87	2,878
Shanghai 上海	1								
Jiangsu 江蘇	4	77	6,723	633	15.29	24.21	87.02	36.80	4,138
Zhejiang 浙江	7	54	1,827	13	0.43	1.25	33.93	65.50	2,981
Anhui 安徽	1	370	5,720	60	0.94	2.00	15.46	53.35	6,410
Fujian 福建									
Jiangxi 江西	3	82	2,127	-1,193	-44.86	-550.77	25.93	91.73	2,660
Shandong 山東	2								
Central-South 中南	5	83	1,522	38	1.27	4.88	18.43	73.98	2,990
Henan 河南									
Hubei 湖北	1	44	260				5.91	283.33	60
Hunan 湖南	3	120	2,227	57	1.18	4.24	18.61	72.11	4,793
Guangdong 廣東									
Guangxi 廣西	1	10	670	20	3.92	-200.00	67.00	101.96	510
Hainan 海南									
Southwest 西南	5	64	1,444	-214	-10.66	-89.17	22.42	87.95	2,008
Chongqing 重慶	1	9	212	37	48.43	61.83	24.30	21.67	77
Sichuan 四川	3	43	1,447	47	3.95	9.03	33.79	56.25	1,187
Guizhou 貴州									
Yunnan 雲南	1	180	2,420	-1,250	-20.23	250.00	13.44	108.09	6,180
Tibet 西藏									
Northwest 西北	4	890	25,420	-2,660	-4.67	-10.74	28.55	56.46	56,905
Shaanxi 陝西	4	890	25,420	-2,660	-4.67	-10.74	28.55	56.46	56,905
Gansu 甘肅									
Qinghai 青海									
Ningxia 寧夏									
Xinjiang 新疆									

3719: Other Railroad Transporting Equipment 其他鐵路運輸設備製造業

Year 年份	Number of firms 企業個數	Rate of change 每年變化 (%)	Number of employees 職工人數（人）	Rate of change 每年變化 (%)	Total revenue (mil. RMB) 總銷售收入（百萬元）	Rate of change 每年變化 (%)	Total profit (mil. RMB) 總利潤（百萬元）	Rate of change 每年變化 (%)
1993	38		15,797		393		10	
1994	50	31.58%	12,052	-23.71%	572	45.47%	-5	-153.69%
1995	55	10.00%	13,890	15.25%	391	-31.59%	-13	-145.40%
1996	52	-5.45%	8,998	-35.22%	258	-34.02%	-9	30.74%

3 Major products* 3 種主要產品 *	Output 產量	Sales volume 銷售量	Unit 單位
a) Handling Machinery 裝卸機械	413	376	set 台
b) Frame Crane 龍門式起重機	43	42	ton 噸
c) Non-ferrous Casting 有色金屬鑄件	205	190	ton 噸

Top 10 firms by revenue (year founded) 收入排名前 10 家企業 (創辦年份)	City 城市	Province 省	Telephone / fax 電話 / 傳真	Number of employees 職工人數	Ownership 產業所有權	Revenue ('000 RMB) 銷售收入（千元）	Profit ('000 RMB) (rank) 利潤（千元）（排名）	Total assets ('000 RMB) 總資產（千元）	Major products 主要產品
Baoji Engineering Machinery Plant 寶雞工程機械廠(1955)	Baoji 寶雞市	Shaanxi 陝西省	(0917)3283700 (0917)3283122	3,074	State-owned 國有	91,610	-10810(26)	216,240	o
Qiqihar Jinche Industrial Co. 齊齊哈爾市金車工業公司(1988)	Qiqiha'er 齊齊哈爾市	Heilongjiang 黑龍江省	(0452)2512981	1,053	Collectively-owned 集體	36,533	178(7)	15,300	o
Xi Shan Shi Dong Jiang Railway Fitting Parts Factory 錫山市東洚鐵路配件廠(1989)	Wuxi 無錫市	Jiangsu 江蘇省	(0510)5061562	132	Collectively-owned 集體	20,332	2177(1)	11,620	o
Shenyang Railway Bureau Chaoyang Engineering Equipment 瀋陽鐵路局輝南縣朝陽鎮公務器材廠(1953)	Tonghua 通化市	Jilin 吉林省	(0435)6223688	309	State-owned 國有	15,904	28(19)	16,160	o
Shanghai Cao An Metal Products Factory 上海曹安金屬製品廠(1992)	Shanghai 上海市	Shanghai 上海市	(021)59595151	22	Collectively-owned 集體	11,245	117(11)	1,417	o
The Ministry of Railways Shenyang Rolling Stock Fitting Parts Factory No.2 Branch 鐵道部瀋陽機車車輛配件廠二分廠(1979)	Shenyang 瀋陽市	Liaoning 遼寧省	(024)25832858	301	Collectively-owned 集體	10,146	85(13)	9,955	o
Linxi Train Brake Shoe Factory 臨西火車閘瓦廠(1988)	Xingtai 邢臺市	Hebei 河北省		60	Collectively-owned 集體	10,080	1150(2)	5,200	o
Taiyuan Rolling Stock Factory Fitting Parts Factory 太原市機車車輛工廠配件廠(1965)	Taiyuan 太原市	Shanxi 山西省	(0351)3045411	195	Collectively-owned 集體	8,682	78(14)	4,644	o
Changchun Chang Ke Special Type Bus Decorating Co. Ltd. 長春市長客特種客車裝修有限公司(1993)	Changchun 長春市	Jilin 吉林省	(0431)7903594	470	Foreign-funded 外資	6,800	500(4)	9,496	o
Bengbu Railway Hardware Building Material General Factory 蚌埠鐵路五金建材總廠(1970)	Bengbu 蚌埠市	Anhui 安徽省	(0552)3018172	377	Collectively-owned 集體	5,723	64(17)	6,414	o

Top 10 Cities by Production Output 產出排名前 10 位城市	Province 省	Market share 市場份額	Number of firms 企業個數
Baoji 寶雞市	Shaanxi 陝西省	24.99%	1
Shenyang 瀋陽市	Liaoning 遼寧省	22.61%	3
Shanghai 上海市	Shanghai 上海市	9.91%	5
Qiqiha'er 齊齊哈爾市	Heilongjiang 黑龍江省	7.94%	1
Wuxi 無錫市	Jiangsu 江蘇省	5.68%	1
Tonghua 通化市	Jilin 吉林省	5.30%	1
Xingtai 邢臺市	Hebei 河北省	4.11%	1
Jinzhou 錦州市	Liaoning 遼寧省	4.07%	2
Ningbo 寧波市	Zhejiang 浙江省	3.24%	4
Nanchang 南昌市	Jiangxi 江西省	1.60%	2

10 Major Wholesalers 10 家主要批發商	City 城市	Province 省	Telephone / Fax 電話 / 傳真
Liaoning Automobile Trade Group Corp. 遼寧省汽車貿易集團	Shenyang 瀋陽市	Liaoning 遼寧省	(024)23835494 (024)23838338
China Post and Telecommunication Equipment General Company 中國郵電器材總公司	Beijing 北京市	Beijing 北京市	(010)63523715 (010)63525935
Jiangsu Electromechanical Products General Company 江蘇省機電產品總公司	Nanjing 南京市	Jiangsu 江蘇省	(025)7713642 (025)7711036
Xi Nan Technology Import & Export Company 西南技術進出口公司	Chongqing 重慶市	Chongqing 重慶市	(023)63850185 (023)63850026
Changzhou Economic Technology Industrial Development Zone Tian Ming Trade Company 常州經濟技術產業開發區天明貿易公司	Changzhou 常州市	Jiangsu 江蘇省	(0519)8829882 (0519)8829882
Shanxi Mechanical Equipment Import & Export Company 山西省機械設備進出口公司	Taiyuan 太原市	Shanxi 山西省	(0351)4040713 (0351)4043981
Ningbo Five Mining Machinery Import & Export Company 寧波市五礦機械進出口公司	Ningbo 寧波市	Zhejiang 浙江省	(0574)7311255 (0574)7320322
Tianjin Jin Huan Electromechanical Complete Sets of Equipment Factory 天津市津環機電成套設備廠	Tianjin 天津市	Tianjin 天津市	(022)26371628
Yunnan Machinery Import & Export Company 雲南省機械進出口公司	Kunming 昆明市	Yunnan 雲南省	(0871)3164879 (0871)3136829
Tianjin Da Qiu Zhuang Yi Yuan Trade Center 天津市大丘莊億源商貿中心	Tianjin 天津市	Tianjin 天津市	(022)28899478 (022)28899046

*Also include sales by firms outside this industry.包括本行業以外廠家的銷售。"o" stands for "others". "o" 代表 "其他產品"。

3721: Trucks 載重汽車製造業

The industry accounts for 1.094% of the total revenue of China's industrial sector in 1996. The revenue growth rate of the industry is 8.4% from 1995, as compared to the growth rate of China's industrial sector, 9.51%. The rate of return on asset is 0.57%. 50.99% of all firms in the industry made a profit while 45.16% had negative returns. The top province in terms of the industry's revenue is Jilin, accounting for 34.22% of the total revenue.
本行業在1996年佔全行業總產值1.094%，行業年增長率為8.4%（全國工業年增長率9.51%）。行業的資產回報率0.57%，50.99%的企業盈利，45.16%的企業虧損。銷售收入最高的省份為吉林省，佔本行業的34.22%。

	Total number of firms 企業總數	Total number of employees 職工總數	Total revenue (mil. RMB) 總銷售收入（百萬元）	Total profit (mil. RMB) 總利潤（百萬元）	Return on assets 資產利潤率 (%)	Return on equity 權益利潤率 (%)	Labour productivity ('000 RMB / worker) 勞動生產率（千元/人）	Debts / assets 資產負債率 (%)	Total assets (mil. RMB) 總資產（百萬元）
Industry Overall 行業總體	135	422,684	63,437	646	0.57	1.73	150.08	67.21	113,885

	Number of firms 企業個數	Average number of employees 平均職工人數	Average revenue ('000 RMB) 平均銷售收入（千元）	Average profit ('000 RMB) 平均利潤（千元）	Return on assets 資產利潤率 (%)	Return on equity 權益利潤率 (%)	Labour productivity ('000 RMB / worker) 勞動生產率（千元/人）	Average debts / assets 平均資產負債率(%)	Average Total assets ('000 RMB) 平均總資產（千元）
By ownership 產業所有權									
State-owned 國有	66	5,284	843,318	10,909	0.78	2.41	159.61	67.59	1,397,682
Collectively-owned 集體	43	165	17,165	496	1.92	15.40	104.20	87.52	25,807
Privately-owned 私有									
Domestic JVs 聯營	3	203	12,561	-1,685	-13.80	-1261.49	61.87	98.91	12,212
Joint stock 股份制	10	5,103	425,435	-31,644	-1.95	-5.53	83.37	64.81	1,626,123
Foreign-funded 外資	10	736	136,587	19,496	9.30	21.40	185.66	56.56	209,729
Overseas Chinese-funded 港澳台資	4	1,967	345,573	7,955	1.49	4.70	175.71	68.26	533,419
By size 規模									
Large 大型	39	8,861	1,503,670	16,612	0.62	1.86	169.69	66.76	2,679,965
Medium 中型	36	1,090	94,582	-1,108	-0.59	-2.08	86.80	71.77	188,626
Small 小型	52	218	26,718	735	1.48	5.57	122.35	73.37	49,547
By regional distribution 地區分布									
Central-North 華北	19	1,792	213,942	353	0.10	0.23	119.40	56.69	360,777
Beijing 北京	9	2,558	402,866	3,773	0.65	1.33	157.47	51.53	584,973
Tianjin 天津	2	97	6,465	380	12.75	39.18	66.99	67.45	2,980
Hebei 河北	6	1,329	38,792	-5,817	-3.99	-15.65	29.18	74.53	145,913
Shanxi 山西	1	2,424	55,590	-3,610	-1.01	-3.61	22.93	72.17	359,100
Inner Mongolia 內蒙	1	424	137,830	10,500	3.00	11.43	325.07	73.71	349,470
Northeast 東北	15	9,697	1,691,653	24,604	1.04	3.78	174.45	72.46	2,364,842
Liaoning 遼寧	11	3,720	246,305	-3,232	-0.55	-1.47	66.21	62.99	592,991
Jilin 吉林	2	48,231	10,855,565	206,835	1.47	5.54	225.08	73.42	14,053,895
Heilongjiang 黑龍江	2	4,037	477,160	-4,530	-1.08	7.93	118.21	113.58	420,970
Central East 華東	28	2,782	427,044	2,561	0.31	1.11	153.52	71.96	820,905
Shanghai 上海									
Jiangsu 江蘇	7	3,181	716,540	450	0.04	0.14	225.29	70.43	1,071,493
Zhejiang 浙江	4	1,763	192,223	-7,705	-2.53	-6.15	109.05	58.78	304,103
Anhui 安徽	5	1,392	214,644	1,006	0.32	1.96	154.24	83.95	319,236
Fujian 福建	3	562	54,230	-1,273	-0.85	-5.89	96.55	85.51	149,303
Jiangxi 江西	3	3,819	645,410	21,197	1.27	4.25	169.00	70.17	1,671,427
Shandong 山東	6	4,745	500,068	5,765	0.48	1.81	105.39	73.52	1,201,683
Central-South 中南	40	3,016	354,248	-2,740	-0.33	-0.97	117.48	65.68	822,507
Henan 河南	7	901	138,944	2,147	0.86	3.28	154.28	73.80	249,787
Hubei 湖北	6	14,865	1,742,135	-285	-0.01	-0.02	117.20	64.44	3,774,917
Hunan 湖南	14	890	53,834	-921	-1.04	-3.57	60.46	70.84	88,471
Guangdong 廣東	11	717	91,723	-7,581	-1.39	-4.44	127.94	68.70	545,070
Guangxi 廣西	2	2,387	490,940	-13,310	-2.10	-4.92	205.72	57.30	633,945
Hainan 海南									
Southwest 西南	27	1,171	258,759	12,766	2.57	5.33	220.89	51.82	497,187
Chongqing 重慶	5	2,428	1,040,653	156,666	7.86	13.43	428.53	41.48	1,992,854
Sichuan 四川	15	711	91,248	-7,651	-7.59	-39.93	128.41	80.99	100,795
Guizhou 貴州	2	690	43,870	-41,975	-9.01	-15.95	63.58	43.49	465,735
Yunnan 雲南	5	1,647	151,658	-33,048	-8.81	-47.93	92.08	81.63	375,266
Tibet 西藏									
Northwest 西北	6	2,175	147,355	-6,090	-1.63	-9.08	67.74	82.10	374,680
Shaanxi 陝西	2	3,985	342,975	425	0.05	0.27	86.08	79.67	773,990
Gansu 甘肅									
Qinghai 青海	1	2,138	3,180	-14,560	-10.06	22.08	1.49	145.55	144,770
Ningxia 寧夏									
Xinjiang 新疆	3	981	65,000	-7,610	-4.11	-14.86	66.24	72.33	185,110

3721: Trucks 載重汽車製造業

Year 年份	Number of firms 企業個數	Rate of change 每年變化 (%)	Number of employees 職工人數 (人)	Rate of change 每年變化 (%)	Total revenue (mil. RMB) 總銷售收入 (百萬元)	Rate of change 每年變化 (%)	Total profit (mil. RMB) 總利潤 (百萬元)	Rate of change 每年變化 (%)
1993	126		410,943		61,557		3,656	
1994	121	-3.97%	355,673	-13.45%	55,899	-9.19%	2,858	-21.83%
1995	110	-9.09%	428,406	20.45%	58,544	4.73%	1,088	-61.92%
1996	135	22.73%	422,684	-1.34%	63,437	8.36%	646	-40.63%

3 Major products* 3 種主要產品 *	Output 產量	Sales volume 銷售量	Unit 單位
a) Heavy Truck 重型載貨汽車	16,695	16,528	vehicle 輛
b) Truck Chassis 載貨汽車底盤	101,962	100,942	vehicle 輛
c) Light Truck 輕型載貨汽車	206,318	206,318	vehicle 輛

Top 10 firms by revenue (year founded) 收入排名前 10 家企業 (創辦年份)	City 城市	Province 省	Telephone / fax 電話 / 傳真	Number of employees 職工人數	Ownership 產業所有權	Revenue ('000 RMB) 銷售收入 (千元)	Profit ('000 RMB) (rank) 利潤 (千元) (排名)	Total assets ('000 RMB) 總資產 (千元)	Major products 主要產品
China First Automobile Group Corp. 中國第一汽車集團公司(1953)	Changchun 長春市	Jilin 吉林省	(0431)5902268	94,563	State-owned 國有	21,711,133	413671(2)	28,107,792	a,b,c
Dong Feng Automobile Co. 東風汽車公司(1975)	Shiyan 十堰市	Hubei 湖北省	(0719)223460 (0719)222918	82,375	State-owned 國有	10,010,546	10035(12)	21,718,156	o
Yue Jin Automobile Group Co. 躍進汽車集團公司(1947)	Nanjing 南京市	Jiangsu 江蘇省	(025)3437788 (025)3409029	20,865	State-owned 國有	4,712,273	2456(23)	7,133,349	b,c
Qing Ling Motors [Group] Co. Ltd. 慶鈴汽車[集團]有限公司	Chongqing 重慶市	Chongqing 重慶市	(023)65212233 (023)68830397	4,370	State-owned 國有	3,858,350	603980(1)	7,750,480	b,c
Faw-jinbei Automotive Co. Ltd. 一汽金杯汽車股份有限公司(1984)	Shenyang 瀋陽市	Liaoning 遼寧省	(024)25878981 (024)25872537	30	Joint stock 股份制	2,598,030	5000(18)	6,110,240	o
Beijing Automobile Motorcycle Vehical Joint Manufacturing Co. 北京汽車摩托車聯合製造公司(1938)	Beijing 北京市	Beijing 北京市	(010)65077630 (010)65019179	11,293	State-owned 國有	2,413,081	70088(3)	2,083,370	b,c
Jiang Ling Wu Shi Ling Automobile Co. Ltd. 江鈴五十鈴汽車有限公司(1993)	Nanchang 南昌市	Jiangxi 江西省	(0791)5232888 (0791)5232597	1,485	Foreign-funded 外資	1,693,059	58939(4)	4,592,643	c
Ji'nan Automobile Manufactory General Factory 濟南汽車製造總廠(1935)	Ji'nan 濟南市	Shandong 山東省	(0531)5958554 (0531)5955560	21,352	State-owned 國有	1,508,828	16378(7)	5,837,127	a,b
China No.1 Automobile Group Qingdao Automobile Factory 中國第一汽車集團青島汽車廠(1968)	Qingdao 青島市	Shandong 山東省	(0532)4816292 (0532)4816687	4,077	State-owned 國有	1,164,929	16568(6)	999,103	b
Beijing Light-duty Automobile Co. Ltd. 北京輕型汽車有限公司(1988)	Beijing 北京市	Beijing 北京市	(010)68417722 (010)68416689	6,513	Overseas Chinese-funded 港澳台資	1,070,284	-23522(96)	1,720,840	b,c

Top 10 Cities by Production Output 產出排名前 10 位城市	Province 省	Market share 市場份額	Number of firms 企業個數
Shiyan 十堰市	Hubei 湖北省	25.09%	1
Chongqing 重慶市	Chongqing 重慶市	13.20%	8
Nanjing 南京市	Jiangsu 江蘇省	10.71%	4
Beijing 北京市	Beijing 北京市	8.81%	9
Ji'nan 濟南市	Shandong 山東省	4.37%	7
Nanchang 南昌市	Jiangxi 江西省	4.09%	2
Changchun 長春市	Jilin 吉林省	3.83%	1
Qingdao 青島市	Shandong 山東省	2.98%	1
Hefei 合肥市	Anhui 安徽省	2.77%	3
Liuzhou 柳州市	Guangxi 廣西	2.57%	3

10 Major Wholesalers 10 家主要批發商	City 城市	Province 省	Telephone / Fax 電話 / 傳真
Hunan Automobile Trade (group)general Company 湖南汽車貿易(集團)總公司	Changsha 長沙市	Hunan 湖南省	(0731)4723388
Sichuan Automobile Industry General Company 四川省汽車工業總公司	Chengdu 成都市	Sichuan 四川省	(028)4334513 (028)4317793
Guangdong Goods & Materials Group Automobile Trade Company 廣東物資集團汽車貿易公司	Guangzhou 廣州市	Guangdong 廣東省	(020)84217281 (020)84217303
Tianjin Automobile Industry Sale General Co. 天津市汽車工業銷售總公司	Tianjin 天津市	Tianjin 天津市	(022)28318888 (022)28313200
China Automobile Trade Hua Dong Company 中國汽車貿易華東公司	Shanghai 上海市	Shanghai 上海市	(021)63732288 (021)63731084
China Automobile Trade General Company 中國汽車貿易總公司	Beijing 北京市	Beijing 北京市	(010)63265840
Kaifeng Goods & Materials (Group) Automobile Trade Company 開封物資(集團)汽車貿易公司	Kaifeng 開封市	Henan 河南省	(0378)9018058 (0378)2924752
China Automobile Industry Marketing General Company 中國汽車工業銷售總公司	Beijing 北京市	Beijing 北京市	(010)64013057 (010)64013840
Jin Bei Trade General Company 金杯貿易總公司	Shenyang 瀋陽市	Liaoning 遼寧省	(024)22529437 (024)22529444
Yunnan Electromechanical Equipment General Co. 雲南省機電設備總公司	Kunming 昆明市	Yunnan 雲南省	(0871)3136797 (0871)3130735

*Also include sales by firms outside this industry.包括本行業以外廠家的銷售。"o" stands for "others". "o" 代表 "其他產品"。

3722: Buses 客車製造業

The industry accounts for 0.139% of the total revenue of China's industrial sector in 1996. The revenue growth rate of the industry is -9.3% from 1995, as compared to the growth rate of China's industrial sector, 9.51%. The rate of return on asset is -0.94%. 60.90% of all firms in the industry made a profit while 35.65% had negative returns. The top province in terms of the industry's revenue is Jiangsu, accounting for 26.74% of the total revenue.
本行業在1996年佔全行業總產值0.139%，行業年增長率為-9.3%（全國工業年增長率9.51%）。行業的資產回報率-0.94%，60.90%的企業盈利，35.65%的企業虧損。銷售收入最高的省份為江蘇省，佔本行業的26.74%。

	Total number of firms 企業總數	Total number of employees 職工總數	Total revenue (mil. RMB) 總銷售收入（百萬元）	Total profit (mil. RMB) 總利潤（百萬元）	Return on assets 資產利潤率 (%)	Return on equity 權益利潤率 (%)	Labour productivity ('000 RMB / worker) 勞動生產率（千元/人）	Debts / assets 資產負債率 (%)	Total assets (mil. RMB) 總資產（百萬元）
Industry Overall 行業總體	124	81,611	8,070	-147	-0.94	-2.21	98.88	57.31	15,588

	Number of firms 企業個數	Average number of employees 平均職工人數	Average revenue ('000 RMB) 平均銷售收入（千元）	Average profit ('000 RMB) 平均利潤（千元）	Return on assets 資產利潤率 (%)	Return on equity 權益利潤率 (%)	Labour productivity ('000 RMB / worker) 勞動生產率（千元/人）	Average debts / assets 平均資產負債率(%)	Average Total assets ('000 RMB) 平均總資產（千元）
By ownership 產業所有權									
State-owned 國有	50	1,131	107,020	-1,040	-0.52	-1.42	94.63	63.72	201,560
Collectively-owned 集體	48	267	27,848	-11,213	-23.43	-35.79	104.14	34.55	47,862
Privately-owned 私有	1	32	4,126	926	32.49	119.51	128.95	72.82	2,851
Domestic JVs 聯營	3	365	57,170	-18,147	-26.69	-53.54	156.77	50.14	67,989
Joint stock 股份制	4	989	103,197	13,064	6.48	10.95	104.40	40.77	201,515
Foreign-funded 外資	10	122	5,714	3,874	6.27	8.26	46.72	24.06	61,794
Overseas Chinese-funded 港澳台資	8	738	92,094	50,725	25.65	90.94	124.73	71.79	197,728
By size 規模									
Large 大型	13	2,634	298,953	59,892	10.27	20.39	113.48	49.62	583,111
Medium 中型	21	1,185	83,836	-12,142	-6.85	-18.94	70.75	63.85	177,272
Small 小型	85	262	28,506	-7,890	-15.65	-45.00	108.97	65.22	50,410
By regional distribution 地區分布									
Central-North 華北	22	1,251	58,346	-7,940	-4.37	-13.04	46.62	66.45	181,510
Beijing 北京	7	542	30,599	-903	-0.94	-1.99	56.43	52.81	96,304
Tianjin 天津	1	3,541	207,850	-59,800	-14.05	-79.01	58.70	82.22	425,630
Hebei 河北	9	1,467	80,437	-4,494	-1.72	-5.46	54.83	68.45	260,746
Shanxi 山西	5	1,398	27,528	-13,624	-12.46	-33.16	19.69	62.43	109,348
Inner Mongolia 內蒙									
Northeast 東北	8	1,445	120,093	-2,506	-1.01	-2.29	83.14	55.80	247,244
Liaoning 遼寧	6	1,470	142,942	-92	-0.04	-0.08	97.23	51.93	250,478
Jilin 吉林									
Heilongjiang 黑龍江	2	1,368	51,545	-9,750	-4.10	-12.85	37.69	68.05	237,540
Central East 華東	48	436	61,366	1,120	1.30	2.57	140.88	49.56	86,380
Shanghai 上海	7	285	34,796	-406	-0.63	-3.90	121.91	83.89	64,573
Jiangsu 江蘇	19	657	113,576	3,907	2.86	4.89	172.98	41.41	136,388
Zhejiang 浙江	9	181	21,146	847	2.66	8.37	116.97	68.22	31,844
Anhui 安徽	4	481	10,330	-5,808	-16.84	-111.90	21.50	84.95	34,483
Fujian 福建	5	191	12,382	-2,176	-2.99	-3.86	64.76	22.43	72,666
Jiangxi 江西									
Shandong 山東	4	483	62,628	2,220	2.82	8.33	129.73	66.18	78,750
Central-South 中南	35	357	57,781	-847	-0.68	-1.68	161.94	59.14	123,643
Henan 河南	3	237	5,577	17	0.08	0.22	23.56	65.08	21,783
Hubei 湖北	9	333	18,800	-6,439	-5.09	-14.71	56.49	65.39	126,422
Hunan 湖南	9	187	16,581	171	1.31	8.44	88.51	84.47	13,051
Guangdong 廣東	11	332	122,873	2,095	1.37	3.72	370.30	63.18	153,018
Guangxi 廣西	1	2,460							
Hainan 海南	2	494	167,795	1,845	0.28	0.52	340.01	46.11	661,855
Southwest 西南	8	1,009	105,240	3,204	2.36	4.43	104.35	46.69	135,556
Chongqing 重慶	3	165	4,024	-423	-5.99	-22.55	24.40	73.43	7,055
Sichuan 四川	3	2,037	215,366	4,579	1.47	2.61	105.72	43.55	311,051
Guizhou 貴州	1	650	148,630	14,710	19.49	29.56	228.66	34.05	75,470
Yunnan 雲南	1	810	35,120	-1,550	-2.84	38.37	43.36	107.39	54,660
Tibet 西藏									
Northwest 西北	3	353	5,233	-647	-3.32	-56.73	14.83	94.15	19,477
Shaanxi 陝西	2	265	1,050	-520	-3.83	19.40	3.97	119.73	13,585
Gansu 甘肅									
Qinghai 青海									
Ningxia 寧夏									
Xinjiang 新疆	1	530	13,600	-900	-2.88	-10.25	25.66	71.91	31,260

3722: Buses 客車製造業

Year 年份	Number of firms 企業個數	Rate of change 每年變化 (%)	Number of employees 職工人數 (人)	Rate of change 每年變化 (%)	Total revenue (mil. RMB) 總銷售收入 (百萬元)	Rate of change 每年變化 (%)	Total profit (mil. RMB) 總利潤 (百萬元)	Rate of change 每年變化 (%)
1993	115		114,982		8,546		586	
1994	123	6.96%	147,820	28.56%	12,410	45.21%	353	-39.68%
1995	135	9.76%	95,112	-35.66%	8,902	-28.27%	-32	-108.92%
1996	124	-8.15%	81,611	-14.19%	8,070	-9.35%	-147	-366.56%

3 Major products* 3 種主要產品 *	Output 產量	Sales volume 銷售量	Unit 單位
a) Medium Bus 中型客車	7,288	6,997	vehicle 輛
b) Light Bus 輕型客車	39,677	36,899	vehicle 輛
c) Refitted Passenger Carriage 客車改裝車	20,687	19,860	vehicle 輛

Top 10 firms by revenue (year founded) 收入排名前 10 家企業 (創辦年份)	City 城市	Province 省	Telephone / fax 電話 / 傳真	Number of employees 職工人數	Ownership 產業所有權	Revenue ('000 RMB) 銷售收入 (千元)	Profit ('000 RMB) (rank) 利潤 (千元) (排名)	Total assets ('000 RMB) 總資產 (千元)	Major products 主要產品
Jiangsu Yaxing Motor Coach Group Co. Ltd. 江蘇亞星客車集團有限公司(1949)	Yangzhou 揚州市	Jiangsu 江蘇省	(0514)7811481 (0514)7811466	2,963	State-owned 國有	872,378	25432(3)	704,671	a,b
Shenzhen San Jiu Automobile Industry General Company 深圳三九汽車工業總公司(1993)	Shenzhen 深圳市	Guangdong 廣東省	(0755)3236412 (0755)3230719	405	State-owned 國有	800,776	34524(2)	764,385	o
Jiangsu Yizheng Automobile Manufactory 江蘇省儀征市汽車製造廠(1971)	Yangzhou 揚州市	Jiangsu 江蘇省	(0514)3442532 (0514)3443535	4,059	Collectively-owned 集體	683,637	43040(1)	1,000,430	b
Dandong Automobile Works 丹東汽車製造廠(1951)	Dandong 丹東市	Liaoning 遼寧省	(0415)6222161 (0415)6221554	5,497	State-owned 國有	527,172	2772(14)	746,365	o
Hebei Sheng Li Group Co. Ltd. 河北勝利客車集團有限公司(1977)	Baoding 保定市	Hebei 河北省	(0312)2312530 (0312)2313766	3,795	State-owned 國有	325,757	15215(4)	644,964	b
Sichuan Automobile Industry Group Co. 四川汽車工業集團公司(1957)	Chengdu 成都市	Sichuan 四川省	(028)5185667 (028)5185914	2,492	State-owned 國有	287,348	501(28)	331,199	b,c
Sichuan Station Wagon Manufacturing Plant 四川旅行車製造廠(1958)	Chengdu 成都市	Sichuan 四川省	(028)3331950 (028)3331950	2,365	State-owned 國有	264,930	12501(6)	461,782	b
Changzhou Passenger Car Manufacturing Factory 常州客車製造廠(1956)	Changzhou 常州市	Jiangsu 江蘇省	(0519)6750711 (0519)6602177	1,529	State-owned 國有	235,924	4426(11)	405,272	a,c
Hebei Tian Ye Automobile Group Co. Ltd. 河北田野汽車集團有限公司(1949)	Baoding 保定市	Hebei 河北省	(0312)3027426 (0312)3024845	3,016	State-owned 國有	234,998	5379(10)	932,730	b
Shandong Liaocheng Bus Factory 山東省聊城客車廠(1958)	Liaocheng 聊城市	Shandong 山東省	(0635)8322161 (0635)8322161	1,414	State-owned 國有	232,847	8009(7)	250,367	o

Top 10 Cities by Production Output 產出排名前 10 位城市	Province 省	Market share 市場份額	Number of firms 企業個數
Shenyang 瀋陽市	Liaoning 遼寧省	19.87%	5
Yangzhou 揚州市	Jiangsu 江蘇省	15.41%	3
Nanjing 南京市	Jiangsu 江蘇省	5.36%	2
Baoding 保定市	Hebei 河北省	5.35%	2
Chengdu 成都市	Sichuan 四川省	5.27%	5
Dandong 丹東市	Liaoning 遼寧省	4.98%	1
Guangzhou 廣州市	Guangdong 廣東省	4.21%	6
Beijing 北京市	Beijing 北京市	3.41%	7
Shanghai 上海市	Shanghai 上海市	3.38%	5
Haikou 海口市	Hainan 海南省	3.10%	1

10 Major Wholesalers 10 家主要批發商	City 城市	Province 省	Telephone / Fax 電話 / 傳真
Hunan Automobile Trade (group)general Company 湖南汽車貿易(集團)總公司	Changsha 長沙市	Hunan 湖南省	(0731)4723388
Sichuan Automobile Industry General Company 四川省汽車工業總公司	Chengdu 成都市	Sichuan 四川省	(028)4334513 (028)4317793
Guangdong Goods & Materials Group Automobile Trade Company 廣東物資集團汽車貿易公司	Guangzhou 廣州市	Guangdong 廣東省	(020)84217281 (020)84217303
Tianjin Automobile Industry Sale General Co. 天津市汽車工業銷售總公司	Tianjin 天津市	Tianjin 天津市	(022)28318888 (022)28313200
China Automobile Trade Hua Dong Company 中國汽車貿易華東公司	Shanghai 上海市	Shanghai 上海市	(021)63732288 (021)63731084
China Automobile Trade General Company 中國汽車貿易總公司	Beijing 北京市	Beijing 北京市	(010)63265840
Kaifeng Goods & Materials (Group) Automobile Trade Company 開封物資(集團)汽車貿易公司	Kaifeng 開封市	Henan 河南省	(0378)9018058 (0378)2924752
China Automobile Industry Marketing General Company 中國汽車工業銷售總公司	Beijing 北京市	Beijing 北京市	(010)64013057 (010)64013840
Jin Bei Trade General Company 金杯貿易總公司	Shenyang 瀋陽市	Liaoning 遼寧省	(024)22529437 (024)22529444
Yunnan Electromechanical Equipment General Co. 雲南省機電設備總公司	Kunming 昆明市	Yunnan 雲南省	(0871)3136797 (0871)3130735

*Also include sales by firms outside this industry.包括本行業以外廠家的銷售。"o" stands for "others". "o" 代表 "其他產品"。

3723: Cars 小轎車製造業

The industry accounts for 0.694% of the total revenue of China's industrial sector in 1996. The revenue growth rate of the industry is 21.3% from 1995, as compared to the growth rate of China's industrial sector, 9.51%. The rate of return on asset is 8.11%. 59.74% of all firms in the industry made a profit while 35.00% had negative returns. The top province in terms of the industry's revenue is Shanghai, accounting for 60.45% of the total revenue.
本行業在1996年佔全行業總產值0.694%，行業年增長率為21.3%（全國工業年增長率9.51%）。行業的資產回報率8.11%，59.74%的企業盈利，35.00%的企業虧損。銷售收入最高的省份為上海市，佔本行業的60.45%。

	Total number of firms 企業總數	Total number of employees 職工總數	Total revenue (mil. RMB) 總銷售收入（百萬元）	Total profit (mil. RMB) 總利潤（百萬元）	Return on assets 資產利潤率 (%)	Return on equity 權益利潤率 (%)	Labour productivity ('000 RMB / worker) 勞動生產率（千元/人）	Debts / assets 資產負債率 (%)	Total assets (mil. RMB) 總資產（百萬元）
Industry Overall 行業總體	28	31,604	40,208	3,877	8.11	30.20	1272.24	73.13	47,781

	Number of firms 企業個數	Average number of employees 平均職工人數	Average revenue ('000 RMB) 平均銷售收入（千元）	Average profit ('000 RMB) 平均利潤（千元）	Return on assets 資產利潤率 (%)	Return on equity 權益利潤率 (%)	Labour productivity ('000 RMB / worker) 勞動生產率（千元/人）	Average debts / assets 平均資產負債率(%)	Average Total assets ('000 RMB) 平均總資產（千元）
By ownership 產業所有權									
State-owned 國有	5	752	1,127,800	160,400	10.13	187.82	1500.53	94.61	1,584,000
Collectively-owned 集體	12	145	80,915	701	0.79	10.33	558.36	92.33	88,534
Privately-owned 私有									
Domestic JVs 聯營	2	34	95,761	-731	-4.02	-44.93	2816.49	91.05	18,162
Joint stock 股份制									
Foreign-funded 外資	6	4,310	5,782,220	511,875	7.93	24.91	1341.58	68.17	6,455,086
Overseas Chinese-funded 港澳台資	3	88	8,075	-747	-7.05	240.56	91.76	102.93	10,592
By size 規模									
Large 大型	7	3,858	6,451,928	564,868	8.95	32.03	1672.54	72.06	6,312,288
Medium 中型									
Small 小型	19	137	78,802	-4,005	-2.12	-15.37	574.97	86.23	189,211
By regional distribution 地區分布									
Central-North 華北	10	1,300	1,123,727	105,279	9.45	56.63	864.54	83.32	1,114,651
Beijing 北京	3	2,972	1,850,810	83,067	7.70	17.27	622.75	55.41	1,078,783
Tianjin 天津	4	935	1,406,050	200,720	10.19	195.28	1503.39	94.78	1,969,025
Hebei 河北	2	78	3,145	290	9.76	38.16	40.58	74.41	2,970
Shanxi 山西									
Inner Mongolia 內蒙	1	186	54,350	130	0.46	3.96	292.20	88.34	28,120
Northeast 東北	1	3,677	2,949,070	340		0.02	802.03	77.69	9,648,370
Liaoning 遼寧									
Jilin 吉林	1	3,677	2,949,070	340		0.02	802.03	77.69	9,648,370
Heilongjiang 黑龍江									
Central East 華東	3	2,467	8,148,307	1,187,803	30.84	50.42	3303.37	38.83	3,851,207
Shanghai 上海	1	7,235	24,306,740	3,561,430	30.93	50.48	3359.60	38.72	11,512,680
Jiangsu 江蘇									
Zhejiang 浙江	1	165	138,180	1,980	4.84	16.31	837.45	70.35	40,940
Anhui 安徽									
Fujian 福建	1								
Jiangxi 江西									
Shandong 山東									
Central-South 中南	10	692	106,873	-69,264	-4.88	-47.35	154.55	89.70	1,420,563
Henan 河南	1	120	110	20	0.76	0.95	0.92	19.85	2,620
Hubei 湖北	3	1,099	182,887	-95,050	-2.65	-18.41	166.41	85.59	3,583,617
Hunan 湖南	1								
Guangdong 廣東	4	859	129,890	-101,758	-11.80	465.28	151.30	102.54	862,138
Guangxi 廣西	1	64	400	-480	-13.30	100.00	6.25	113.30	3,610
Hainan 海南									
Southwest 西南	4	154	127,030	-11,750	-3.83	-15.82	827.56	75.78	306,628
Chongqing 重慶	1	832	767,787	-94,871	-3.95	-16.59	923.27	76.19	2,401,223
Sichuan 四川	3	77	49,486	174	1.73	4.08	640.35	57.67	10,055
Guizhou 貴州	1	6	510				85.00	34.21	760
Yunnan 雲南									
Tibet 西藏									
Northwest 西北									
Shaanxi 陝西									
Gansu 甘肅									
Qinghai 青海									
Ningxia 寧夏									
Xinjiang 新疆									

Year 年份	Number of firms 企業個數	Rate of change 每年變化 (%)	Number of employees 職工人數（人）	Rate of change 每年變化 (%)	Total revenue (mil. RMB) 總銷售收入（百萬元）	Rate of change 每年變化 (%)	Total profit (mil. RMB) 總利潤（百萬元）	Rate of change 每年變化 (%)
1993	24		82,373		18,126		1,167	
1994	28	16.67%	83,195	1.00%	23,121	27.56%	1,712	46.62%
1995	30	7.14%	34,147	-58.96%	33,143	43.34%	3,042	77.69%
1996	28	-6.67%	31,604	-7.45%	40,208	21.32%	3,877	27.45%

3 Major products* 3 種主要產品 *	Output 產量	Sales volume 銷售量	Unit 單位
a) Micro Sedan 微型轎車	95,171	91,822	vehicle 輛
b) Common Sedan 普通型轎車	36,632	28,939	vehicle 輛
c) Average Sedan 中級轎車	227,737	248,233	vehicle 輛

Top 10 firms by revenue (year founded) 收入排名前 10 家企業 (創辦年份)	City 城市	Province 省	Telephone / fax 電話 / 傳真	Number of employees 職工人數	Ownership 產業所有權	Revenue ('000 RMB) 銷售收入（千元）	Profit ('000 RMB) (rank) 利潤（千元）（排名）	Total assets ('000 RMB) 總資產（千元）	Major products 主要產品
Shanghai Volkswagen Automobile Co. Ltd. 上海大眾汽車有限公司(1985)	Shanghai 上海市	Shanghai 上海市	(021)59578888 (021)59572815	7,461	Foreign-funded 外資	24,306,742	3561426(1)	11,512,679	c
Beijing Jeep Corp. Ltd. 北京吉普汽車有限公司(1984)	Beijing 北京市	Beijing 北京市	(010)67712233 (010)67711363	8,067	Foreign-funded 外資	5,504,141	251061(3)	3,103,487	c
Tianjin Mini Auto Works 天津市微型汽車廠(1988)	Tianjin 天津市	Tianjin 天津市	(022)27391463 (022)27390926	3,911	State-owned 國有	5,043,738	669038(2)	3,418,696	a,b
Faw-volkswagen Automotive Co. Ltd. 一汽－大眾有限公司(1991)	Changchun 長春市	Jilin 吉林省	(0431)5990156 (0431)5914659	3,647	Foreign-funded 外資	2,949,065	340(7)	9,648,370	b,c
Tianjin Automobile Industry Marketing General Company 天津市汽車工業銷售總公司(1982)	Tianjin 天津市	Tianjin 天津市	(022)28318888 (022)28313200	412	State-owned 國有	580,230	125437(4)	4,046,735	o
Shen Long Automobile Co. Ltd. 神龍汽車有限公司(1991)	Wuhan 武漢市	Hubei 湖北省	(027)84624575 (027)84622165	3,671	Foreign-funded 外資	517,062	-286772(18)	10,724,206	b
Chongqing Chang An Suzuki Automobile Co. Ltd. 重慶長安鈴木汽車有限公司	Chongqing 重慶市	Chongqing 重慶市	(023)66222892 (023)66222722		Foreign-funded 外資	507,420	-47013(17)	1,225,210	o
Guangzhou Pugeot Automobile Co. ,ltd. 廣州標緻汽車有限公司(1985)	Guangzhou 廣州市	Guangdong 廣東省	(020)82277789 (020)82270620	2,780	Foreign-funded 外資	368,164	-355921(19)	2,834,289	c
Yongkang Automobile Manufactory Company 永康汽車製造公司(1994)	Jinhua 金華市	Zhejiang 浙江省	(0579)7291263 (0579)7291163	166	Collectively-owned 集體	138,182	1976(5)	40,937	o
Yi Qi Shunde Automobile Manufactory 一汽順德汽車廠(1992)	Foshan 佛山市	Guangdong 廣東省	(0757)6611483 (0757)6614679	355	Collectively-owned 集體	112,406	-25699(16)	456,034	o

Top 10 Cities by Production Output 產出排名前 10 位城市	Province 省	Market share 市場份額	Number of firms 企業個數
Beijing 北京市	Beijing 北京市	36.38%	2
Tianjin 天津市	Tianjin 天津市	31.86%	3
Shanghai 上海市	Shanghai 上海市	27.25%	2
Guangzhou 廣州市	Guangdong 廣東省	2.17%	1
Foshan 佛山市	Guangdong 廣東省	0.81%	2
Jinhua 金華市	Zhejiang 浙江省	0.70%	1
Datong 大同市	Shanxi 山西省	0.55%	2
Jincheng 晉城市	Shanxi 山西省	0.07%	1
Dongguan 東莞市	Guangdong 廣東省	0.06%	1
Baoding 保定市	Hebei 河北省	0.05%	1

10 Major Wholesalers 10 家主要批發商	City 城市	Province 省	Telephone / Fax 電話 / 傳真
Hunan Automobile Trade (Group) General Company 湖南汽車貿易(集團)總公司	Changsha 長沙市	Hunan 湖南省	(0731)4723388
Sichuan Automobile Industry General Company 四川省汽車工業總公司	Chengdu 成都市	Sichuan 四川省	(028)4334513 (028)4317793
Guangdong Goods & Materials Group Automobile Trade Company 廣東物資集團汽車貿易公司	Guangzhou 廣州市	Guangdong 廣東省	(020)84217281 (020)84217303
Tianjin Automobile Industry Sale General Co. 天津市汽車工業銷售總公司	Tianjin 天津市	Tianjin 天津市	(022)28318888 (022)28313200
China Automobile Trade Hua Dong Company 中國汽車貿易華東公司	Shanghai 上海市	Shanghai 上海市	(021)63732288 (021)63731084
China Automobile Trade General Company 中國汽車貿易總公司	Beijing 北京市	Beijing 北京市	(010)63265840
Kaifeng Goods & Materials (Group) Automobile Trade Company 開封物資(集團)汽車貿易公司	Kaifeng 開封市	Henan 河南省	(0378)9018058 (0378)2924752
China Automobile Industry Marketing General Company 中國汽車工業銷售總公司	Beijing 北京市	Beijing 北京市	(010)64013057 (010)64013840
Jin Bei Trade General Company 金杯貿易總公司	Shenyang 瀋陽市	Liaoning 遼寧省	(024)22529437 (024)22529444
Yunnan Electromechanical Equipment General Co. 雲南省機電設備總公司	Kunming 昆明市	Yunnan 雲南省	(0871)3136797 (0871)3130735

*Also include sales by firms outside this industry.包括本行業以外廠家的銷售。"o" stands for "others". "o" 代表"其他產品"。

3724: Minicar 微型汽車製造業

The industry accounts for 0.102% of the total revenue of China's industrial sector in 1996. The revenue growth rate of the industry is 21.0% from 1995, as compared to the growth rate of China's industrial sector, 9.51%. The rate of return on asset is 1.40%. 58.89% of all firms in the industry made a profit while 35.85% had negative returns. The top province in terms of the industry's revenue is Guangxi, accounting for 38.20% of the total revenue.
本行業在1996年佔全行業總產值0.102%，行業年增長率為21.0%（全國工業年增長率9.51%）。行業的資產回報率1.40%，58.89%的企業盈利，35.85%的企業虧損。銷售收入最高的省份為廣西省，佔本行業的38.20%。

	Total number of firms 企業總數	Total number of employees 職工總數	Total revenue (mil. RMB) 總銷售收入（百萬元）	Total profit (mil. RMB) 總利潤（百萬元）	Return on assets 資產利潤率 (%)	Return on equity 權益利潤率 (%)	Labour productivity ('000 RMB / worker) 勞動生產率（千元/人）	Debts / assets 資產負債率 (%)	Total assets (mil. RMB) 總資產（百萬元）
Industry Overall 行業總體	53	32,272	5,926	98	1.40	3.85	183.63	63.69	7,005

	Number of firms 企業個數	Average number of employees 平均職工人數	Average revenue ('000 RMB) 平均銷售收入（千元）	Average profit ('000 RMB) 平均利潤（千元）	Return on assets 資產利潤率 (%)	Return on equity 權益利潤率 (%)	Labour productivity ('000 RMB / worker) 勞動生產率（千元/人）	Average debts / assets 平均資產負債率(%)	Average Total assets ('000 RMB) 平均總資產（千元）
By ownership 產業所有權									
State-owned 國有	14	1,028	220,571	214	0.07	0.21	214.55	67.73	321,357
Collectively-owned 集體	32	481	69,190	240	0.49	1.22	143.88	60.00	49,022
Privately-owned 私有									
Domestic JVs 聯營	3	98	15,339	906	1.95	3.84	155.99	49.19	46,442
Joint stock 股份制	1	1,780	263,682	28,951	10.89	26.36	148.14	58.68	265,826
Foreign-funded 外資	1	23						2.66	1,264
Overseas Chinese-funded 港澳台資	2	191	158,205	27,823	10.46	19.66	828.30	46.79	266,020
By size 規模									
Large 大型	4	5,897	1,123,258	78,468	5.94	16.73	190.49	64.52	1,321,795
Medium 中型	5	698	137,920	6,717	5.53	15.62	197.48	64.63	121,539
Small 小型	41	126	18,156	-6,084	-22.46	-55.00	144.12	59.17	27,092
By regional distribution 地區分布									
Central-North 華北	7	793	257,811	10,009	5.57	11.19	325.11	50.22	179,714
Beijing 北京	2	109	5,945	-1,230	-11.32	-53.02	54.79	78.61	10,870
Tianjin 天津	3	1,734	594,123	24,270	5.95	11.89	342.63	49.97	408,190
Hebei 河北	2	66	5,210	-145	-2.48	-3.20	78.94	22.67	5,845
Shanxi 山西									
Inner Mongolia 內蒙									
Northeast 東北	5	1,576	79,314	1,764	3.25	4.65	50.33	30.13	54,348
Liaoning 遼寧	3	65	4,610	283	5.63	11.00	70.92	48.81	5,033
Jilin 吉林									
Heilongjiang 黑龍江	2	3,843	191,370	3,985	3.11	4.38	49.80	29.03	128,320
Central East 華東	15	448	43,810	361	0.52	2.25	97.78	76.99	69,629
Shanghai 上海									
Jiangsu 江蘇									
Zhejiang 浙江	2	8	360	-30	-0.76	-1.37	48.00	44.09	3,935
Anhui 安徽	7	708	71,953	119	0.09	0.40	101.67	76.68	126,343
Fujian 福建	1								
Jiangxi 江西									
Shandong 山東	5	350	30,552	930	3.06	15.64	87.19	80.46	30,434
Central-South 中南	19	545	155,959	3,343	1.62	4.42	286.25	63.27	205,781
Henan 河南	3	27	3,413	3	0.06	0.22	124.88	74.37	5,800
Hubei 湖北	1	394	35,600	3,520	11.20	17.55	90.36	36.18	31,430
Hunan 湖南	2	868	65,235	4,885	2.52	6.96	75.20	63.71	193,515
Guangdong 廣東	10	168	48,338	-2,309	-1.48	-4.70	287.90	68.40	155,489
Guangxi 廣西	2	3,207	1,131,720	36,650	3.94	9.72	352.89	59.46	929,810
Hainan 海南	1	48	40,100				835.42	56.68	59,460
Southwest 西南	6	288	12,038	-8,558	-10.00	-106.67	41.80	90.63	85,620
Chongqing 重慶	1	18	328	-338	-21.48	-62.23	18.18	65.49	1,572
Sichuan 四川	3	291	13,488	-1,108	-4.04	-15.34	46.35	73.65	27,418
Guizhou 貴州	2	439	16,660	-27,450	-12.66	-204.24	37.99	93.80	216,795
Yunnan 雲南									
Tibet 西藏									
Northwest 西北	1	40	32,190	1,430	19.40	51.62	804.75	62.28	7,370
Shaanxi 陝西	1	40	32,190	1,430	19.40	51.62	804.75	62.28	7,370
Gansu 甘肅									
Qinghai 青海									
Ningxia 寧夏									
Xinjiang 新疆									

Year 年份	Number of firms 企業個數	Rate of change 每年變化 (%)	Number of employees 職工人數（人）	Rate of change 每年變化 (%)	Total revenue (mil. RMB) 總銷售收入（百萬元）	Rate of change 每年變化 (%)	Total profit (mil. RMB) 總利潤（百萬元）	Rate of change 每年變化 (%)
1993	34		15,741		2,023		-49	
1994	41	20.59%	26,721	69.75%	3,093	52.86%	-9	81.80%
1995	50	21.95%	38,086	42.53%	4,896	58.28%	-9	-4.00%
1996	53	6.00%	32,272	-15.27%	5,926	21.04%	98	1158.77%

3 Major products* 3 種主要產品 *	Output 產量	Sales volume 銷售量	Unit 單位
a) Microbus 微型客車	87,862	79,954	vehicle 輛
b) Micro Truck 微型載貨汽車	185,538	178,116	vehicle 輛
c) Refitted Passenger Carriage 客車改裝車	4,974	4,775	vehicle 輛

Top 10 firms by revenue (year founded) 收入排名前 10 家企業（創辦年份）	City 城市	Province 省	Telephone / fax 電話 / 傳真	Number of employees 職工人數	Ownership 產業所有權	Revenue ('000 RMB) 銷售收入（千元）	Profit ('000 RMB) (rank) 利潤（千元）（排名）	Total assets ('000 RMB) 總資產（千元）	Major products 主要產品
Liuzhou Mini Automobile Manufactory 柳州市微型汽車廠(1960)	Liuzhou 柳州市	Guangxi 廣西	(0772)3837800 (0772)3831151	6,311	State-owned 國有	2,255,933	71808(1)	1,793,822	a,b
Tianjin Hua Li Automobile Co. Ltd. 天津華利汽車有限公司(1965)	Tianjin 天津市	Tianjin 天津市	(022)26395690 (022)26391236	4,005	Foreign-funded 外資	1,400,397	70606(2)	1,073,054	a,b
Harbin Ha Fei Industrial General Co. 哈爾濱哈飛實業總公司(1982)	Harbin 哈爾濱市	Heilongjiang 黑龍江省	(0451)6501680 (0451)6501631	7,768	Collectively-owned 集體	382,097	7924(4)	255,560	o
Anhui Huai Hai Machinery Plant 安徽省淮海機械廠(1970)	Hefei 合肥市	Anhui 安徽省	(0551)5311133 (0551)5313510	3,265	State-owned 國有	366,873	1306(10)	687,995	a,b
Tianjin Special Purpose Vehicle Factory 天津市專用汽車廠(1958)	Tianjin 天津市	Tianjin 天津市	(022)27914288 (022)27915131	1,180	Collectively-owned 集體	360,569	1235(11)	122,474	a,b
Guangdong San Xing Enterprise Group Co. No.7 Branch 廣東三星企業集團公司第七分廠(1991)	Jiangmen 江門市	Guangdong 廣東省	(0750)2613598 (0750)2613528	325	Collectively-owned 集體	191,915	441(18)	152,837	o
Nanjing Automobile Industry Jointly-operated Company Nanhai Automobile Factory 南京汽車工業聯營公司南海汽車廠(1990)	Foshan 佛山市	Guangdong 廣東省	(0757)6332999 (0757)6224113	461	State-owned 國有	154,392	-24514(37)	979,031	o
Qingyuan Yue Jiang Minicar Assembly Co. Ltd. 清遠粵江微型汽車裝配有限公司(1992)	Qingyuan 清遠市	Guangdong 廣東省	(0763)3483863	271	Overseas Chinese-funded 港澳台資	107,732	553(16)	325,043	c
Anhui An Chi Automobile Group Co. 安徽省安馳汽車集團公司(1958)	Fuyang 阜陽市	Anhui 安徽省	(0558)7623784 (0558)7625937	836	State-owned 國有	87,175	732(15)	140,738	c
Weifang Automobile Manufactory General Factory 濰坊汽車製造總廠(1972)	Weifang 濰坊市	Shandong 山東省	(0536)8232346 (0536)8232346	599	Collectively-owned 集體	77,095	2616(7)	66,244	o

Top 10 Cities by Production Output 產出排名前 10 位城市	Province 省	Market share 市場份額	Number of firms 企業個數
Liuzhou 柳州市	Guangxi 廣西	27.66%	3
Harbin 哈爾濱市	Heilongjiang 黑龍江省	23.22%	1
Tianjin 天津市	Tianjin 天津市	22.48%	3
Chongqing 重慶市	Chongqing 重慶市	6.25%	1
Hefei 合肥市	Anhui 安徽省	5.13%	2
Qingyuan 清遠市	Guangdong 廣東省	3.50%	2
Jilin 吉林市	Jilin 吉林省	3.24%	1
Jiangmen 江門市	Guangdong 廣東省	3.13%	4
Foshan 佛山市	Guangdong 廣東省	1.81%	1
Weifang 濰坊市	Shandong 山東省	0.95%	1

10 Major Wholesalers 10 家主要批發商	City 城市	Province 省	Telephone / Fax 電話 / 傳真
Hunan Automobile Trade (Group) General Company 湖南汽車貿易(集團)總公司	Changsha 長沙市	Hunan 湖南省	(0731)4723388
Sichuan Automobile Industry General Company 四川省汽車工業總公司	Chengdu 成都市	Sichuan 四川省	(028)4334513 (028)4317793
Guangdong Goods & Materials Group Automobile Trade Company 廣東物資集團汽車貿易公司	Guangzhou 廣州市	Guangdong 廣東省	(020)84217281 (020)84217303
Tianjin Automobile Industry Sale General Co. 天津市汽車工業銷售總公司	Tianjin 天津市	Tianjin 天津市	(022)28318888 (022)28313200
China Automobile Trade Hua Dong Company 中國汽車貿易華東公司	Shanghai 上海市	Shanghai 上海市	(021)63732288 (021)63731084
China Automobile Trade General Company 中國汽車貿易總公司	Beijing 北京市	Beijing 北京市	(010)63265840
Kaifeng Goods & Materials (Group) Automobile Trade Company 開封物資(集團)汽車貿易公司	Kaifeng 開封市	Henan 河南省	(0378)9018058 (0378)2924752
China Automobile Industry Marketing General Company 中國汽車工業銷售總公司	Beijing 北京市	Beijing 北京市	(010)64013057 (010)64013840
Jin Bei Trade General Company 金杯貿易總公司	Shenyang 瀋陽市	Liaoning 遼寧省	(024)22529437 (024)22529444
Yunnan Electromechanical Equipment General Co. 雲南省機電設備總公司	Kunming 昆明市	Yunnan 雲南省	(0871)3136797 (0871)3130735

*Also include sales by firms outside this industry.包括本行業以外廠家的銷售。"o" stands for "others"．"o" 代表 "其他產品"。

3725: Special and Fefitted Vehicles 特種車輛及改裝汽車製造業

The industry accounts for 0.286% of the total revenue of China's industrial sector in 1996. The revenue growth rate of the industry is 2.1% from 1995, as compared to the growth rate of China's industrial sector, 9.51%. The rate of return on asset is -0.92%. 56.61% of all firms in the industry made a profit while 39.76% had negative returns. The top province in terms of the industry's revenue is Jiangsu, accounting for 21.81% of the total revenue.
本行業在1996年佔全行業總產值0.286%，行業年增長率為2.1%（全國工業年增長率9.51%）。行業的資產回報率-0.92%，56.61%的企業盈利，39.76%的企業虧損。銷售收入最高的省份為江蘇省，佔本行業的21.81%。

	Total number of firms 企業總數	Total number of employees 職工總數	Total revenue (mil. RMB) 總銷售收入（百萬元）	Total profit (mil. RMB) 總利潤（百萬元）	Return on assets 資產利潤率 (%)	Return on equity 權益利潤率 (%)	Labour productivity ('000 RMB / worker) 勞動生產率（千元/人）	Debts / assets 資產負債率 (%)	Total assets (mil. RMB) 總資產（百萬元）
Industry Overall 行業總體	463	224,993	16,578	-242	-0.92	-3.02	73.68	69.35	26,156

	Number of firms 企業個數	Average number of employees 平均職工人數	Average revenue ('000 RMB) 平均銷售收入（千元）	Average profit ('000 RMB) 平均利潤（千元）	Return on assets 資產利潤率 (%)	Return on equity 權益利潤率 (%)	Labour productivity ('000 RMB / worker) 勞動生產率（千元/人）	Average debts / assets 平均資產負債率(%)	Average Total assets ('000 RMB) 平均總資產（千元）
By ownership 產業所有權									
State-owned 國有	205	713	43,176	-1,898	-2.47	-9.39	60.58	73.70	76,854
Collectively-owned 集體	185	276	23,118	621	2.33	6.80	83.69	65.78	26,693
Privately-owned 私有	3	43	3,503	23	0.79	4.24	81.47	81.38	2,909
Domestic JVs 聯營	16	190	12,003	-606	-3.26	-17.27	63.07	81.14	18,592
Joint stock 股份制	16	739	100,399	2,851	2.29	6.91	135.90	66.83	124,390
Foreign-funded 外資	19	263	47,516	-231	-0.20	-0.43	180.34	53.02	113,865
Overseas Chinese-funded 港澳台資	19	189	17,690	4	0.01	0.02	93.49	43.15	34,826
By size 規模									
Large 大型	24	3,002	260,668	-170,330	-40.43	-120.58	86.82	66.47	421,331
Medium 中型	83	915	47,887	73,737	83.11	345.00	52.32	75.91	88,718
Small 小型	350	219	18,135	-6,497	-26.20	-79.71	82.68	67.14	24,801
By regional distribution 地區分布									
Central-North 華北	70	242	26,757	1,234	3.68	10.56	110.56	65.10	33,506
Beijing 北京	32	241	23,126	215	0.87	2.12	95.86	58.83	24,648
Tianjin 天津	5	221	9,562	-1,604	-5.66	-15.38	43.23	63.17	28,326
Hebei 河北	30	246	35,832	2,959	6.36	19.95	145.88	68.11	46,509
Shanxi 山西	1	47	870	70	5.93	8.97	18.51	33.90	1,180
Inner Mongolia 內蒙	2	349	4,650	-645	-6.93	32.91	13.32	121.12	9,305
Northeast 東北	51	357	11,483	-1,732	-4.76	-20.56	32.14	76.85	36,389
Liaoning 遼寧	24	338	10,431	127	0.32	0.76	30.84	57.21	39,114
Jilin 吉林	14	493	20,284	-6,180	-10.84	-3192.62	41.16	99.66	57,016
Heilongjiang 黑龍江	13	246	3,945	-375	-4.10	-19.31	16.02	78.74	9,145
Central East 華東	186	423	41,090	-184	-0.30	-0.97	97.04	69.12	61,433
Shanghai 上海	15	505	35,456	-1,025	-1.87	-9.28	70.27	79.91	54,962
Jiangsu 江蘇	48	561	75,335	1,634	1.72	4.95	134.36	65.32	95,130
Zhejiang 浙江	28	128	6,895	-364	-3.62	-8.52	53.95	57.50	10,034
Anhui 安徽	28	302	23,478	-306	-1.29	-3.92	77.69	67.18	23,844
Fujian 福建	12	398	70,371	-1,137	-0.67	-2.26	176.66	70.29	169,102
Jiangxi 江西	18	377	18,563	93	0.30	1.14	49.30	73.70	31,043
Shandong 山東	37	559	39,614	-1,799	-2.66	-9.63	70.88	72.35	67,550
Central-South 中南	95	814	54,595	-314	-0.40	-1.18	67.07	66.12	78,689
Henan 河南	19	381	42,998	1,899	4.26	14.86	113.00	71.30	44,537
Hubei 湖北	31	1,631	96,932	-257	-0.18	-0.47	59.43	62.10	144,152
Hunan 湖南	20	510	20,955	-1,550	-3.58	-14.56	41.09	75.40	43,244
Guangdong 廣東	18	340	48,548	-590	-0.93	-3.20	142.88	70.95	63,537
Guangxi 廣西	6	516	10,843	-2,425	-10.06	-29.98	21.01	66.45	24,115
Hainan 海南	1	120	6,620	-1,750	-23.94	-60.14	55.17	60.19	7,310
Southwest 西南	38	582	26,100	-2,292	-4.38	-15.49	44.86	71.72	52,322
Chongqing 重慶	8	618	49,356	-591	-0.74	-2.08	79.88	64.53	80,240
Sichuan 四川	20	557	24,975	-2,218	-4.52	-13.38	44.84	66.23	49,081
Guizhou 貴州	8	634	8,836	-4,810	-12.83	278.03	13.93	104.61	37,501
Yunnan 雲南	2	463	9,780	5	0.02	0.07	21.12	75.68	27,730
Tibet 西藏									
Northwest 西北	23	506	12,984	-3,850	-8.32	-61.61	25.66	86.50	46,301
Shaanxi 陝西	15	354	10,366	-2,375	-8.14	-45.58	29.24	82.13	29,162
Gansu 甘肅	3	612	9,513	-5,540	-9.70	591.46	15.54	101.64	57,120
Qinghai 青海	2	582	6,480	-5,865	-15.66	87.73	11.13	117.85	37,455
Ningxia 寧夏									
Xinjiang 新疆	3	1,107	33,883	-8,197	-6.45	-30.07	30.62	78.55	127,073

3725: Special and Fefitted Vehicles 特種車輛及改裝汽車製造業

Year 年份	Number of firms 企業個數	Rate of change 每年變化 (%)	Number of employees 職工人數 (人)	Rate of change 每年變化 (%)	Total revenue (mil. RMB) 總銷售收入 (百萬元)	Rate of change 每年變化 (%)	Total profit (mil. RMB) 總利潤 (百萬元)	Rate of change 每年變化 (%)
1993	381		237,890		17,252		660	
1994	417	9.45%	230,425	-3.14%	15,730	-8.82%	-191	-128.91%
1995	460	10.31%	239,886	4.11%	16,233	3.20%	11	105.92%
1996	463	0.65%	224,993	-6.21%	16,578	2.13%	-242	-2243.87%

3 Major products* 3 種主要產品 *	Output 產量	Sales volume 銷售量	Unit 單位
a) Refitted Passenger Carriage 客車改裝車	76,644	73,578	vehicle 輛
b) Special Refitted Truck 專用改裝汽車	19,460	18,681	vehicle 輛
c) Refitted Dumper Truck 自卸改裝汽車	14,464	14,464	vehicle 輛

Top 10 firms by revenue (year founded) 收入排名前 10 家企業 (創辦年份)	City 城市	Province 省	Telephone / fax 電話 / 傳真	Number of employees 職工人數	Ownership 產業所有權	Revenue ('000 RMB) 銷售收入 (千元)	Profit ('000 RMB) (rank) 利潤 (千元) (排名)	Total assets ('000 RMB) 總資產 (千元)	Major products 主要產品
Dong Feng Exploring Development Co. 東風實業開發公司(1979)	Shiyan 十堰市	Hubei 湖北省	(0719)223634 (0719)223133	23,518	Collectivoly ownod 集體	1,453,103	46403(4)	1,795,254	c
Jiangsu Mu Dan Automobile Group Co. 江蘇牡丹汽車集團公司(1995)	Suzhou 蘇州市	Jiangsu 江蘇省	(0512)8660322	4,892	State-owned 國有	1,100,920	63150(3)	954,590	a
Nanjing Dongfeng Automobile Co. Ltd. 南京東風汽車工業(集團)有限公司(1958)	Nanjing 南京市	Jiangsu 江蘇省	(025)8800339 (025)8800339	4,196	Joint stock 股份制	663,923	993(55)	946,446	c
Nanjing Chenguang Group Co. Ltd. 南京晨光集團有限責任公司(1865)	Nanjing 南京市	Jiangsu 江蘇省	(025)2413078 (025)2419336	5,900	State-owned 國有	395,213	1940(36)	938,483	b
Beijing General Coach Factory 北京市客車總廠(1956)	Beijing 北京市	Beijing 北京市	(010)68212036	224	其他經濟	352,831	1046(51)	405,388	a
Yangzhou Yang Zi Touring Car Factory 揚州揚子旅遊車廠(1971)	Yangzhou 揚州市	Jiangsu 江蘇省	(0514)7661304 (0514)7661306	857	State-owned 國有	321,099	14815(8)	290,859	a
Guangzhou Jin Bao Ma Bus Industrial Company 廣州市金寶馬客車實業公司(1949)	Guangzhou 廣州市	Guangdong 廣東省	(020)87707644 (020)87705593	2,986	State-owned 國有	320,821	451(74)	317,164	a
Shijiazhuang Shuang Huan Automobile Co. Ltd. 石家莊雙環汽車股份有限公司(1986)	Shijiazhuang 石家莊市	Hebei 河北省	(0311)6839199	1,000	Joint stock 股份制	312,500	74700(1)	210,351	o
Hubei Shen Yan Special Automobile Group Co. Ltd. 湖北省神雁專用汽車集團有限公司(1995)	Shiyan 十堰市	Hubei 湖北省	(0719)785388 (0719)781099	3,961	State-owned 國有	308,778	-36733(301)	489,596	b,c
Xiamen Golden Dragon Van Co. Ltd. 廈門金龍旅行車有限公司(1992)	Xiamen 廈門市	Fujian 福建省	(0592)6032727 (0592)6032726	318	Foreign-funded 外資	287,751	63576(2)	262,304	a

Top 10 Cities by Production Output 產出排名前 10 位城市	Province 省	Market share 市場份額	Number of firms 企業個數
Shiyan 十堰市	Hubei 湖北省	12.90%	4
Nanjing 南京市	Jiangsu 江蘇省	10.02%	14
Suzhou 蘇州市	Jiangsu 江蘇省	9.42%	19
Shanghai 上海市	Shanghai 上海市	4.16%	37
Xiamen 廈門市	Fujian 福建省	4.08%	4
Zhengzhou 鄭州市	Henan 河南省	3.71%	5
Beijing 北京市	Beijing 北京市	3.68%	29
Guangzhou 廣州市	Guangdong 廣東省	3.62%	14
Wuhan 武漢市	Hubei 湖北省	3.24%	15
Chongqing 重慶市	Chongqing 重慶市	2.95%	12

10 Major Wholesalers 10 家主要批發商	City 城市	Province 省	Telephone / Fax 電話 / 傳真
Hunan Automobile Trade (Group) General Company 湖南汽車貿易(集團)總公司	Changsha 長沙市	Hunan 湖南省	(0731)4723388
Sichuan Automobile Industry General Company 四川省汽車工業總公司	Chengdu 成都市	Sichuan 四川省	(028)4334513 (028)4317793
Guangdong Goods & Materials Group Automobile Trade Company 廣東物資集團汽車貿易公司	Guangzhou 廣州市	Guangdong 廣東省	(020)84217281 (020)84217303
Tianjin Automobile Industry Sale General Co. 天津市汽車工業銷售總公司	Tianjin 天津市	Tianjin 天津市	(022)28318888 (022)28313200
China Automobile Trade Hua Dong Company 中國汽車貿易華東公司	Shanghai 上海市	Shanghai 上海市	(021)63732288 (021)63731084
China Automobile Trade General Company 中國汽車貿易總公司	Beijing 北京市	Beijing 北京市	(010)63265840
Kaifeng Goods & Materials (Group) Automobile Trade Company 開封物資(集團)汽車貿易公司	Kaifeng 開封市	Henan 河南省	(0378)9018058 (0378)2924752
China Automobile Industry Marketing General Company 中國汽車工業銷售總公司	Beijing 北京市	Beijing 北京市	(010)64013057 (010)64013840
Jin Bei Trade General Company 金杯貿易總公司	Shenyang 瀋陽市	Liaoning 遼寧省	(024)22529437 (024)22529444
Yunnan Electromechanical Equipment General Co. 雲南省機電設備總公司	Kunming 昆明市	Yunnan 雲南省	(0871)3136797 (0871)3130735

*Also include sales by firms outside this industry.包括本行業以外廠家的銷售。"o" stands for "others". "o" 代表 "其他產品" 。

3726: Automobile Body 汽車車身製造業

The industry accounts for 0.042% of the total revenue of China's industrial sector in 1996. The revenue growth rate of the industry is 1.1% from 1995, as compared to the growth rate of China's industrial sector, 9.51%. The rate of return on asset is 0.68%. 53.81% of all firms in the industry made a profit while 36.08% had negative returns. The top province in terms of the industry's revenue is Jiangsu, accounting for 20.85% of the total revenue.
本行業在1996年佔全行業總產值0.042%，行業年增長率為1.1%（全國工業年增長率9.51%）。行業的資產回報率0.68%，53.81%的企業盈利，36.08%的企業虧損。銷售收入最高的省份為江蘇省，佔本行業的20.85%。

	Total number of firms 企業總數	Total number of employees 職工總數	Total revenue (mil. RMB) 總銷售收入（百萬元）	Total profit (mil. RMB) 總利潤（百萬元）	Return on assets 資產利潤率 (%)	Return on equity 權益利潤率 (%)	Labour productivity ('000 RMB / worker) 勞動生產率（千元/人）	Debts / assets 資產負債率 (%)	Total assets (mil. RMB) 總資產（百萬元）
Industry Overall 行業總體	161	36,552	2,429	24	0.68	2.71	66.45	75.06	3,474

	Number of firms 企業個數	Average number of employees 平均職工人數	Average revenue ('000 RMB) 平均銷售收入（千元）	Average profit ('000 RMB) 平均利潤（千元）	Return on assets 資產利潤率 (%)	Return on equity 權益利潤率 (%)	Labour productivity ('000 RMB / worker) 勞動生產率（千元/人）	Average debts / assets 平均資產負債率(%)	Average Total assets ('000 RMB) 平均總資產（千元）
By ownership 產業所有權									
State-owned 國有	39	381	19,513	-667	-2.09	-11.45	51.19	81.78	31,949
Collectively-owned 集體	105	181	12,282	293	1.99	7.35	68.02	72.90	14,697
Privately-owned 私有									
Domestic JVs 聯營	2	132	4,122	35	0.49	2.33	31.35	79.01	7,064
Joint stock 股份制	3	363	38,595	3,984	13.17	35.58	106.42	62.99	30,261
Foreign-funded 外資	4	178	55,319	2,231	2.72	15.09	310.78	81.97	81,968
Overseas Chinese-funded 港澳台資	8	83	4,238	-213	-0.68	-1.36	51.14	50.37	31,496
By size 規模									
Large 大型	4	1,205	69,851	856	0.93	3.53	57.96	73.62	92,015
Medium 中型	19	598	48,372	46	0.06	0.35	80.94	82.97	76,488
Small 小型	136	149	9,054	145	1.19	3.78	60.74	68.45	12,152
By regional distribution 地區分布									
Central-North 華北	19	310	22,526	411	1.64	6.17	72.68	73.33	25,001
Beijing 北京	5	127	6,548	54	1.02	5.81	51.48	82.51	5,318
Tianjin 天津	2	279	20,660	-20	-0.03	-0.26	74.18	87.42	62,230
Hebei 河北	7	498	39,153	750	2.07	6.11	78.69	66.06	36,169
Shanxi 山西	3	278	22,753	757	4.26	16.99	81.94	74.90	17,743
Inner Mongolia 內蒙	2	190	5,800	30	0.34	0.85	30.53	59.60	8,775
Northeast 東北	35	265	7,277	-433	-3.14	-20.69	27.49	84.82	13,782
Liaoning 遼寧	12	198	3,341	-380	-3.55	-22.08	16.88	83.94	10,717
Jilin 吉林	13	243	13,552	-139	-0.89	-3.80	55.81	76.66	15,679
Heilongjiang 黑龍江	10	373	3,844	-878	-5.86	-175.60	10.30	96.67	14,994
Central East 華東	41	216	25,394	866	2.83	10.86	117.79	73.93	30,569
Shanghai 上海	5	240	31,990	-1,338	-3.74	-15.61	133.18	76.03	35,772
Jiangsu 江蘇	12	328	42,203	1,781	3.14	15.55	128.57	79.78	56,645
Zhejiang 浙江	4	223	20,715	-108	-0.76	-2.72	93.10	71.92	14,065
Anhui 安徽	5	79	3,172	-90	-2.99	-15.31	40.25	80.51	3,006
Fujian 福建	5	29	7,032	2,002	9.82	11.27	242.48	12.87	20,382
Jiangxi 江西	3	59	4,437	110	2.30	11.79	75.63	80.50	4,787
Shandong 山東	7	299	32,511	1,623	5.48	31.40	108.68	82.53	29,593
Central-South 中南	46	210	12,789	66	0.27	1.05	60.80	73.89	24,245
Henan 河南	13	222	21,196	1,209	6.24	16.82	95.54	62.90	19,378
Hubei 湖北	13	173	5,301	-375	-3.83	-11.45	30.65	66.53	9,775
Hunan 湖南	5	354	13,598	1,062	4.79	13.96	38.41	65.70	22,194
Guangdong 廣東	8	133	14,340	-2,334	-5.70	-51.99	107.62	89.03	40,908
Guangxi 廣西	6	216	8,912	1,147	2.87	9.33	41.19	69.25	39,975
Hainan 海南	1	410	7,660	-1,320	-2.27	-17.74	18.68	87.22	58,210
Southwest 西南	13	101	3,935	-310	-5.31	-27.51	39.05	80.70	5,834
Chongqing 重慶	3	55	480	327	65.30	191.13	8.72	65.84	501
Sichuan 四川	7	151	6,612	404	3.90	19.99	43.80	80.47	10,335
Guizhou 貴州	2	18	105	-25	-6.49	-13.16	6.00	50.65	385
Yunnan 雲南	1	86	5,260	-200	-4.44	-86.96	61.16	94.89	4,500
Tibet 西藏									
Northwest 西北	7	225	9,440	-523	-5.07	-10.82	41.98	53.11	10,304
Shaanxi 陝西	3	233	18,263	300	2.74	4.15	78.27	34.11	10,963
Gansu 甘肅	1	521	5,030	-2,200	-9.92	-28.91	9.65	65.69	22,180
Qinghai 青海	1	28	140	-80	-10.67	-15.38	5.00	30.67	750
Ningxia 寧夏									
Xinjiang 新疆	2	163	3,060	-1,140	-13.98	-56.72	18.83	75.35	8,155

3726: Automobile Body 汽車車身製造業

Year 年份	Number of firms 企業個數	Rate of change 每年變化 (%)	Number of employees 職工人數（人）	Rate of change 每年變化 (%)	Total revenue (mil. RMB) 總銷售收入（百萬元）	Rate of change 每年變化 (%)	Total profit (mil. RMB) 總利潤（百萬元）	Rate of change 每年變化 (%)
1993	132		41,714		2,029		33	
1994	140	6.06%	37,413	-10.31%	1,944	-4.21%	27	-17.92%
1995	162	15.71%	43,157	15.35%	2,403	23.66%	37	37.36%
1996	161	-0.62%	36,552	-15.30%	2,429	1.08%	24	-34.92%

3 Major products* 3 種主要產品 *	Output 產量	Sales volume 銷售量	Unit 單位
a) Refitted Haulage Truck 牽引改裝汽車	1,067	939	vehicle 輛
b) Refitted Truck 載貨改裝車	2,654	4,352	vehicle 輛
c) Refitted Dumper Truck 自卸改裝汽車	964	964	vehicle 輛

Top 10 firms by revenue (year founded) 收入排名前 10 家企業 (創辦年份)	City 城市	Province 省	Telephone / fax 電話 / 傳真	Number of employees 職工人數	Ownership 產業所有權	Revenue ('000 RMB) 銷售收入（千元）	Profit ('000 RMB) (rank) 利潤（千元）（排名）	Total assets ('000 RMB) 總資產（千元）	Major products 主要產品
Hebei Zhangjiakou General Trailer Works 河北省張家口拖車總廠(1956)	Zhangjiakou 張家口市	Hebei 河北省	(0313)4061998 (0313)4061026	2,503	State-owned 國有	212,720	3198(8)	213,264	c
Sino-american Joint Venture Yangzhou Tong Hua Semi-trailer Co. Ltd. 中美合資揚州通華半掛車有限公司(1991)	Yangzhou 揚州市	Jiangsu 江蘇省	(0514)7873005 (0514)7873290	341	Foreign-funded 外資	162,581	15002(1)	179,767	o
Shanghai Hu Guang Bus Factory 上海滬光客車廠(1978)	Shanghai 上海市	Shanghai 上海市	(021)64111779 (021)64112297	255	Collectively-owned 集體	87,054	885(21)	29,728	b
Jiangsu Dong Bao Group Co. Ltd. 江蘇東堡集團股份有限公司(1937)	Lianyungang 連雲港市	Jiangsu 江蘇省	(0518)5412386 (0518)5410722	1,173	Joint stock 股份制	78,071	-4889(82)	169,637	a
Nanjing Jin Ling Double-deck Passenger Train Manufacture Factory 南京金陵雙層客車製造廠(1965)	Nanjing 南京市	Jiangsu 江蘇省	(025)7759062 (025)7750771	380	State-owned 國有	75,706	3515(7)	56,959	o
Qingdao Special Type Automobile Co. Ltd. 青島特種汽車有限公司(1993)	Qingdao 青島市	Shandong 山東省	(0532)7869132 (0532)7860388	531	Collectively-owned 集體	75,020	1413(12)	101,810	o
Ji'nan Automobile Manufactory General Factory Compartment Factory 濟南汽車製造總廠車廂廠(1980)	Ji'nan 濟南市	Shandong 山東省	(0531)7997142	430	Collectively-owned 集體	74,100	7200(3)	35,380	o
Huaiyin Automobile Reequip Factory 淮陰市汽車改裝廠(1958)	Huaiyin 淮陰市	Jiangsu 江蘇省	(0517)3765117 (0517)3941875	538	Collectively-owned 集體	67,620	432(27)	74,790	a,c
Shanxi Rong Fa Vehicle Group Co. Ltd. 山西榮發車輛集團股份有限公司(1956)	Yuci 榆次市	Shanxi 山西省	(0354)3026311	797	State-owned 國有	67,056	2068(9)	51,421	o
Changsha Mei Hua Automobile Body Factory 長沙縣梅花車身廠(1984)	Changsha 長沙市	Hunan 湖南省	(0731)6264578	1,200	Collectively-owned 集體	64,085	5143(5)	84,074	o

Top 10 Cities by Production Output 產出排名前 10 位城市	Province 省	Market share 市場份額	Number of firms 企業個數
Zhangjiakou 張家口市	Hebei 河北省	10.62%	1
Yangzhou 揚州市	Jiangsu 江蘇省	8.97%	3
Shanghai 上海市	Shanghai 上海市	6.57%	10
Foshan 佛山市	Guangdong 廣東省	5.36%	1
Zhengzhou 鄭州市	Henan 河南省	5.13%	3
Lianyungang 連雲港市	Jiangsu 江蘇省	4.48%	1
Shaoxing 紹興市	Zhejiang 浙江省	4.26%	2
Zhumadian 駐馬店市	Henan 河南省	4.03%	2
Luohe 漯河市	Henan 河南省	3.69%	2
Nanjing 南京市	Jiangsu 江蘇省	3.62%	1

10 Major Wholesalers 10 家主要批發商	City 城市	Province 省	Telephone / Fax 電話 / 傳真
Hunan Automobile Trade (Group) General Company 湖南汽車貿易(集團)總公司	Changsha 長沙市	Hunan 湖南省	(0731)4723388
Sichuan Automobile Industry General Company 四川省汽車工業總公司	Chengdu 成都市	Sichuan 四川省	(028)4334513 (028)4317793
Guangdong Goods & Materials Group Automobile Trade Company 廣東物資集團汽車貿易公司	Guangzhou 廣州市	Guangdong 廣東省	(020)84217281 (020)84217303
Tianjin Automobile Industry Sale General Co. 天津市汽車工業銷售總公司	Tianjin 天津市	Tianjin 天津市	(022)28318888 (022)28313200
China Automobile Trade Hua Dong Company 中國汽車貿易華東公司	Shanghai 上海市	Shanghai 上海市	(021)63732288 (021)63731084
China Automobile Trade General Company 中國汽車貿易總公司	Beijing 北京市	Beijing 北京市	(010)63265840
Kaifeng Goods & Materials (Group) Automobile Trade Company 開封物資(集團)汽車貿易公司	Kaifeng 開封市	Henan 河南省	(0378)9018058 (0378)2924752
China Automobile Industry Marketing General Company 中國汽車工業銷售總公司	Beijing 北京市	Beijing 北京市	(010)64013057 (010)64013840
Jin Bei Trade General Company 金杯貿易總公司	Shenyang 瀋陽市	Liaoning 遼寧省	(024)22529437 (024)22529444
Yunnan Electromechanical Equipment General Co. 雲南省機電設備總公司	Kunming 昆明市	Yunnan 雲南省	(0871)3136797 (0871)3130735

*Also include sales by firms outside this industry.包括本行業以外廠家的銷售。"o" stands for "others". "o" 代表 "其他產品"。

3727: Automobile Parts 汽車零部件及配件製造業

The industry accounts for 1.024% of the total revenue of China's industrial sector in 1996. The revenue growth rate of the industry is 17.5% from 1995, as compared to the growth rate of China's industrial sector, 9.51%. The rate of return on asset is 2.23%. 66.27% of all firms in the industry made a profit while 28.20% had negative returns. The top province in terms of the industry's revenue is Shanghai, accounting for 18.95% of the total revenue.
本行業在1996年佔全行業總產值1.024%，行業年增長率為17.5%（全國工業年增長率9.51%）。行業的資產回報率2.23%，66.27%的企業盈利，28.20%的企業虧損。銷售收入最高的省份為上海市，佔本行業的18.95%。

	Total number of firms 企業總數	Total number of employees 職工總數	Total revenue (mil. RMB) 總銷售收入（百萬元）	Total profit (mil. RMB) 總利潤（百萬元）	Return on assets 資產利潤率 (%)	Return on equity 權益利潤率 (%)	Labour productivity ('000 RMB / worker) 勞動生產率（千元/人）	Debts / assets 資產負債率 (%)	Total assets (mil. RMB) 總資產（百萬元）
Industry Overall 行業總體	5,521	1,035,558	59,369	2,178	2.23	6.45	57.33	65.48	97,772

	Number of firms 企業個數	Average number of employees 平均職工人數	Average revenue ('000 RMB) 平均銷售收入（千元）	Average profit ('000 RMB) 平均利潤（千元）	Return on assets 資產利潤率 (%)	Return on equity 權益利潤率 (%)	Labour productivity ('000 RMB / worker) 勞動生產率（千元/人）	Average debts / assets 平均資產負債率(%)	Average Total assets ('000 RMB) 平均總資產（千元）
By ownership 產業所有權									
State-owned 國有	911	491	21,731	50	0.11	0.39	44.27	72.09	46,729
Collectively-owned 集體	4,027	115	5,961	205	2.85	8.25	52.01	65.49	7,208
Privately-owned 私有	21	49	2,513	97	3.05	8.57	51.34	64.44	3,180
Domestic JVs 聯營	84	254	40,121	6,898	13.50	25.94	157.90	47.96	51,097
Joint stock 股份制	77	533	36,612	3,199	4.69	11.42	68.75	58.93	68,220
Foreign-funded 外資	172	257	34,826	1,663	2.78	5.58	135.32	50.19	59,855
Overseas Chinese-funded 港澳台資	221	121	14,447	837	3.06	8.24	119.59	62.81	27,306
By size 規模									
Large 大型	78	2,157	213,042	18,515	4.89	12.63	98.79	61.31	378,777
Medium 中型	296	830	46,826	544	0.65	2.01	56.44	67.65	83,849
Small 小型	5,028	123	5,745	114	1.32	4.01	46.63	67.08	8,633
By regional distribution 地區分布									
Central-North 華北	897	164	9,867	186	1.20	3.27	60.30	63.43	15,563
Beijing 北京	347	118	7,364	-55	-0.47	-1.31	62.32	64.08	11,700
Tianjin 天津	215	192	16,153	784	3.95	10.22	84.23	61.38	19,854
Hebei 河北	239	148	8,952	249	1.67	4.29	60.37	61.02	14,891
Shanxi 山西	61	354	8,798	-598	-2.17	-7.69	24.87	71.72	27,503
Inner Mongolia 內蒙	35	215	4,182	-152	-1.35	-3.89	19.44	65.33	11,283
Northeast 東北	831	205	6,488	-42	-0.31	-1.11	31.68	72.36	13,585
Liaoning 遼寧	363	176	5,309	-143	-1.28	-4.37	30.17	70.75	11,194
Jilin 吉林	329	252	8,400	131	0.74	2.76	33.40	73.11	17,569
Heilongjiang 黑龍江	139	169	5,041	-183	-1.76	-6.75	29.74	73.87	10,403
Central East 華東	1,841	172	14,835	1,159	5.92	14.55	86.42	59.34	19,578
Shanghai 上海	209	309	53,832	7,628	11.03	22.76	174.32	51.51	69,130
Jiangsu 江蘇	321	190	14,394	294	2.04	5.66	75.78	63.99	14,410
Zhejiang 浙江	632	94	7,968	401	3.70	9.45	84.49	60.82	10,841
Anhui 安徽	135	272	13,510	380	2.35	8.10	49.62	71.02	16,190
Fujian 福建	183	66	3,558	112	1.81	4.00	54.24	54.88	6,203
Jiangxi 江西	169	152	4,436	-25	-0.28	-0.92	29.18	69.64	9,003
Shandong 山東	192	294	16,557	643	2.34	7.29	56.32	67.94	27,481
Central-South 中南	1,217	221	10,849	16	0.07	0.24	49.04	69.06	22,035
Henan 河南	195	174	5,865	121	1.03	3.42	33.76	69.88	11,710
Hubei 湖北	498	280	12,669	110	0.46	1.59	45.22	70.93	23,847
Hunan 湖南	276	193	6,728	-176	-1.25	-3.63	34.78	65.41	14,010
Guangdong 廣東	160	171	17,599	-42	-0.10	-0.31	102.97	68.95	42,724
Guangxi 廣西	87	174	12,384	-37	-0.16	-0.46	71.30	64.47	22,401
Hainan 海南	1	24	510	-120	-1.86	-3.03	21.25	38.70	6,460
Southwest 西南	624	178	6,634	-77	-0.59	-2.15	37.23	72.67	13,144
Chongqing 重慶	260	187	6,281	161	1.32	5.31	33.58	75.19	12,183
Sichuan 四川	266	165	7,043	-371	-2.82	-10.48	42.64	73.10	13,165
Guizhou 貴州	49	192	6,242	92	0.57	1.62	32.49	64.54	16,110
Yunnan 雲南	49	191	6,685	89	0.58	1.86	35.06	68.58	15,166
Tibet 西藏									
Northwest 西北	111	199	4,257	-536	-4.07	-17.81	21.34	77.13	13,155
Shaanxi 陝西	60	170	3,915	-220	-2.12	-7.78	23.04	72.69	10,332
Gansu 甘肅	15	324	4,959	-1,264	-6.22	-22.08	15.30	71.81	20,305
Qinghai 青海	15	187	3,929	-1,015	-7.14	-230.76	20.98	96.91	14,224
Ningxia 寧夏	4	282	3,908	-420	-2.72	-8.57	13.88	68.25	15,433
Xinjiang 新疆	17	185	5,215	-615	-4.01	-19.87	28.14	79.79	15,327

3727: Automobile Parts 汽車零部件及配件製造業

Year 年份	Number of firms 企業個數	Rate of change 每年變化 (%)	Number of employees 職工人數 (人)	Rate of change 每年變化 (%)	Total revenue (mil. RMB) 總銷售收入 (百萬元)	Rate of change 每年變化 (%)	Total profit (mil. RMB) 總利潤 (百萬元)	Rate of change 每年變化 (%)
1993	4,445		1,097,716		39,741		2,598	
1994	5,063	13.90%	970,553	-11.59%	42,090	5.91%	2,177	-16.20%
1995	5,390	6.46%	1,015,273	4.61%	50,523	20.04%	1,775	-18.47%
1996	5,521	2.43%	1,035,558	2.00%	59,369	17.51%	2,178	22.70%

3 Major products* 3種主要產品*	Output 產量	Sales volume 銷售量	Unit 單位
a) Dc Motor 直流電動機	646,690	640,223	set 台
b) Tractor & Internal Combustion Engine Fitting Parts 拖拉機內燃機配件	1,637,656	1,523,020	1,000 yuan 千元

Top 10 firms by revenue (year founded) 收入排名前10家企業 (創辦年份)	City 城市	Province 省	Telephone / fax 電話 / 傳真	Number of employees 職工人數	Ownership 產業所有權	Revenue ('000 RMB) 銷售收入 (千元)	Profit ('000 RMB) (rank) 利潤 (千元) (排名)	Total assets ('000 RMB) 總資產 (千元)	Major products 主要產品
Shanghai Hui Zhong Automobile Manufacturing Co. Ltd. 上海匯眾汽車製造公司(1949)	Shanghai 上海市	Shanghai 上海市	(021)58201188 (021)58204570	8,606	State-owned 國有	2,289,561	410700(2)	2,499,954	b
Shanghai Automobile Gear General Factory 上海汽車齒輪總廠(1925)	Shanghai 上海市	Shanghai 上海市	(021)59530122 (021)59529656	3,768	Domestic JVs 聯營	1,549,489	425161(1)	1,874,545	b
Wan Xiang Group Co. 萬向集團公司(1969)	Hangzhou 杭州市	Zhejiang 浙江省	(0571)2716888 (0571)2716898	1,282	Joint stock 股份制	1,236,824	151003(4)	1,565,702	o
Shanghai Ekchor General Machinery Co. Ltd. 上海易初通用機器有限公司(1990)	Shanghai 上海市	Shanghai 上海市	(021)63843220 (021)63840914	1,143	Foreign-funded 外資	900,596	126122(5)	776,701	o
Shanghai Yanfeng Automotive Trim Co. Ltd. 上海延鋒汽車飾件有限公司(1994)	Shanghai 上海市	Shanghai 上海市	(021)64364124 (021)64700520	2,296	Foreign-funded 外資	736,409	65516(6)	1,079,223	o
Tianjin Tianei Automotive Parts Co. Ltd. 天津天美汽車配件有限公司(1988)	Tianjin 天津市	Tianjin 天津市	(022)25323538 (022)25323535	3,023	Foreign-funded 外資	680,007	19066(27)	447,538	o
Wan Nan Motor-driven Vehicle Plant 皖南機動車輛廠(1970)	Xuanzhou 宣州市	Anhui 安徽省	(0563)3022910 (0563)3024273	1,834	State-owned 國有	612,495	29978(14)	544,640	o
Shanghai Automotive Electrics Works 上海汽車電器總廠(1948)	Shanghai 上海市	Shanghai 上海市	(021)65450905 (021)65450905	4,404	State-owned 國有	505,806	1097(407)	697,444	b
Guangdong Nanhai Zhong Nan Aluminium Wheel Co. Ltd. 廣東南海中南鋁合金輪轂有限公司(1992)	Foshan 佛山市	Guangdong 廣東省	(0757)5773123 (0757)5771372	1,552	Foreign-funded 外資	450,296	15592(32)	632,154	o
Shanghai Gkn Drive Shaft Co. Ltd. 上海納鐵福傳動軸有限公司(1988)	Shanghai 上海市	Shanghai 上海市	(021)58121690 (021)58120975	1,058	Foreign-funded 外資	415,539	152840(3)	592,472	o

Top 10 Cities by Production Output 產出排名前10位城市	Province 省	Market share 市場份額	Number of firms 企業個數
Shanghai 上海市	Shanghai 上海市	22.41%	328
Tianjin 天津市	Tianjin 天津市	5.79%	248
Beijing 北京市	Beijing 北京市	5.51%	334
Hangzhou 杭州市	Zhejiang 浙江省	4.05%	111
Shenyang 瀋陽市	Liaoning 遼寧省	2.59%	204
Shiyan 十堰市	Hubei 湖北省	2.52%	139
Chongqing 重慶市	Chongqing 重慶市	2.31%	310
Nanjing 南京市	Jiangsu 江蘇省	2.18%	83
Xiangfan 襄樊市	Hubei 湖北省	1.66%	70
Yangzhou 揚州市	Jiangsu 江蘇省	1.54%	83

10 Major Wholesalers 10家主要批發商	City 城市	Province 省	Telephone / Fax 電話 / 傳真
Shanghai Auto Parts Company 上海市汽車配件公司	Shanghai 上海市	Shanghai 上海市	(021)62564400
China Automobile Trade Hua Bei Company 中國汽車貿易華北公司	Beijing 北京市	Beijing 北京市	(010)68518091 (010)68513546
China Yan Xing Tianjin Company 中國燕興天津公司	Tianjin 天津市	Tianjin 天津市	(022)28310131
China Automobile Industry Import & Export Guizhou Company 中國汽車工業進出口貴州公司	Guiyang 貴陽市	Guizhou 貴州省	(0851)5869068 (0851)5869008
Jining Automobile Marketing General Company 濟寧市汽車銷售總公司	Jining 濟寧市	Shandong 山東省	(0537)2313628 (0537)2314301
Shanghai Automobile Trade Company 上海汽車貿易公司	Shanghai 上海市	Shanghai 上海市	(021)58752443 (021)58753520
Shanghai Automobile Import & Export Company 上海汽車進出口公司	Shanghai 上海市	Shanghai 上海市	(021)63724288 (021)63724643
Fuyang Tyre Rubber General Company 富陽市輪胎橡膠總公司	Hangzhou 杭州市	Zhejiang 浙江省	(0571)3319574 (0571)3326835
Jilin Electromechanical Equipment General Company 吉林省機電設備總公司	Changchun 長春市	Jilin 吉林省	(0431)8717107 (0431)8743523
Chongqing Chang Jiang Business General Company 重慶長江商務總公司	Chongqing 重慶市	Chongqing 重慶市	(023)62810558 (023)62804041

*Also include sales by firms outside this industry.包括本行業以外廠家的銷售。"o" stands for "others". "o" 代表"其他產品"。

3731: Motorcycles 摩托車整車製造業

The industry accounts for 0.517% of the total revenue of China's industrial sector in 1996. The revenue growth rate of the industry is 14.3% from 1995, as compared to the growth rate of China's industrial sector, 9.51%. The rate of return on asset is 3.52%. 56.48% of all firms in the industry made a profit while 36.56% had negative returns. The top province in terms of the industry's revenue is Guangdong, accounting for 24.42% of the total revenue.
本行業在1996年佔全行業總產值0.517%，行業年增長率為14.3%（全國工業年增長率9.51%）。行業的資產回報率3.52%，56.48%的企業盈利，36.56%的企業虧損。銷售收入最高的省份為廣東省，佔本行業的24.42%。

	Total number of firms 企業總數	Total number of employees 職工總數	Total revenue (mil. RMB) 總銷售收入（百萬元）	Total profit (mil. RMB) 總利潤（百萬元）	Return on assets 資產利潤率 (%)	Return on equity 權益利潤率 (%)	Labour productivity ('000 RMB / worker) 勞動生產率（千元/人）	Debts / assets 資產負債率 (%)	Total assets (mil. RMB) 總資產（百萬元）
Industry Overall 行業總體	226	94,286	29,995	1,085	3.52	10.29	318.13	65.76	30,803

	Number of firms 企業個數	Average number of employees 平均職工人數	Average revenue ('000 RMB) 平均銷售收入（千元）	Average profit ('000 RMB) 平均利潤（千元）	Return on assets 資產利潤率 (%)	Return on equity 權益利潤率 (%)	Labour productivity ('000 RMB / worker) 勞動生產率（千元/人）	Average debts / assets 平均資產負債率(%)	Average Total assets ('000 RMB) 平均總資產（千元）
By ownership 產業所有權									
State-owned 國有	36	674	91,361	6,417	4.63	10.56	135.48	56.12	138,444
Collectively-owned 集體	136	247	51,657	744	1.67	6.43	209.12	73.96	44,409
Privately-owned 私有	3	9	450	-17	-2.38	-4.24	51.94	43.78	703
Domestic JVs 聯營	9	127	125,151	7,314	9.90	22.96	987.17	56.90	73,900
Joint stock 股份制	9	1,405	586,268	20,028	3.65	11.14	417.17	67.21	548,381
Foreign-funded 外資	22	853	534,067	22,659	4.12	11.48	625.80	64.13	550,060
Overseas Chinese-funded 港澳台資	13	294	117,524	689	0.43	1.66	399.53	73.97	159,649
By size 規模									
Large 大型	16	2,756	1,094,028	52,570	4.58	12.13	397.03	62.26	1,148,702
Medium 中型	14	780	156,451	7,351	4.45	9.96	200.61	55.30	165,196
Small 小型	183	211	56,289	774	1.40	5.49	267.19	74.52	55,251
By regional distribution 地區分布									
Central-North 華北	26	178	76,718	6,216	6.74	22.87	430.26	70.54	92,268
Beijing 北京	4	24	2,285	-598	-11.48	11950.00	97.23	100.10	5,203
Tianjin 天津	11	278	158,906	13,733	6.74	22.84	570.86	70.49	203,763
Hebei 河北	9	112	26,100	1,566	11.12	31.42	233.96	64.61	14,082
Shanxi 山西	2	238	1,330	-570	-11.38	-253.33	5.59	95.51	5,010
Inner Mongolia 內蒙									
Northeast 東北	5	819	188,046	15,144	5.49	8.47	229.55	35.15	275,664
Liaoning 遼寧	2	96	24,215	260	1.89	33.55	252.24	94.36	13,740
Jilin 吉林	1	2,986	812,670	75,160	5.91	8.72	272.16	32.20	1,270,980
Heilongjiang 黑龍江	2	459	39,565	20	0.05	0.13	86.20	61.71	39,930
Central East 華東	103	517	141,674	3,745	2.66	7.93	273.93	66.46	140,708
Shanghai 上海	4	974	620,910	13,955	2.29	6.98	637.32	67.25	610,123
Jiangsu 江蘇	29	245	110,074	2,157	3.50	9.82	448.96	64.39	61,693
Zhejiang 浙江	23	644	134,017	8,731	6.69	15.24	208.17	56.07	130,441
Anhui 安徽	4	280	97,618	2,015	3.84	25.92	348.32	85.19	52,475
Fujian 福建	7	207	31,880	-7,179	-7.45	-44.56	154.33	83.28	96,380
Jiangxi 江西	23	329	9,350	-186	-0.94	-1.91	28.45	50.48	19,723
Shandong 山東	13	1,333	385,042	8,694	1.91	6.50	288.82	70.66	455,765
Central-South 中南	73	391	166,297	7,094	4.46	13.99	424.79	68.11	159,060
Henan 河南	20	460	97,723	4,976	4.59	11.16	212.49	58.90	108,436
Hubei 湖北	5	442	19,600	-2,770	-4.83	-23.80	44.32	79.70	57,314
Hunan 湖南	5	861	134,904	-1,498	-1.03	-2.51	156.68	58.79	145,094
Guangdong 廣東	33	270	221,918	4,635	2.31	8.86	822.38	73.96	200,915
Guangxi 廣西	8	39	7,133	104	2.69	18.61	185.26	85.54	3,855
Hainan 海南	2	1,826	1,016,165	142,955	16.16	39.51	556.65	59.11	884,800
Southwest 西南	14	180	18,141	-3,239	-5.53	-11.86	101.07	53.34	58,539
Chongqing 重慶	8	195	28,392	-4,786	-4.83	-10.12	145.49	52.30	99,147
Sichuan 四川	4	147	6,691	-1,605	-19.37	-114.66	45.65	83.11	8,285
Guizhou 貴州	1								
Yunnan 雲南	1	381	5,190	-1,380	-9.45	-14.97	13.62	36.85	14,600
Tibet 西藏									
Northwest 西北	5	238	14,854	-2,136	-10.45	791.11	62.31	101.32	20,446
Shaanxi 陝西	2	571	36,650	-5,320	-10.63	475.00	64.24	102.24	50,035
Gansu 甘肅									
Qinghai 青海									
Ningxia 寧夏									
Xinjiang 新疆	3	17	323	-13	-1.85	-4.49	19.02	58.80	720

3731: Motorcycles 摩托車整車製造業

Year 年份	Number of firms 企業個數	Rate of change 每年變化 (%)	Number of employees 職工人數（人）	Rate of change 每年變化 (%)	Total revenue (mil. RMB) 總銷售收入（百萬元）	Rate of change 每年變化 (%)	Total profit (mil. RMB) 總利潤（百萬元）	Rate of change 每年變化 (%)
1993	142		90,349		11,099		580	
1994	182	28.17%	65,107	-27.94%	15,452	39.22%	924	59.26%
1995	189	3.85%	84,544	29.85%	26,251	69.88%	1,358	47.12%
1996	226	19.58%	94,286	11.52%	29,995	14.26%	1,085	-20.10%

3 Major products* 3 種主要產品 *	Output 產量	Sales volume 銷售量	Unit 單位
a) Motor 摩托車	8,355,351	8,021,137	vehicle 輛
b) Petrol Engine 汽油機	826,699	694,427	set 台
c) Internal-combustion Engine 內燃機	786,004	636,663	set 台

Top 10 firms by revenue (year founded) 收入排名前 10 家企業（創辦年份）	City 城市	Province 省	Telephone / fax 電話 / 傳真	Number of employees 職工人數	Ownership 產業所有權	Revenue ('000 RMB) 銷售收入（千元）	Profit ('000 RMB) (rank) 利潤（千元）（排名）	Total assets ('000 RMB) 總資產（千元）	Major products 主要產品
China Qing Qi Motorbicycle Group General Co. 中國輕騎摩托車集團總公司(1956)	Ji'nan 濟南市	Shandong 山東省	(0531)6953325 (0531)6954219	8,829	Joint stock 股份制	2,987,275	96335(3)	3,588,260	a
Wuxi Motorbicycle Factory 無錫市摩托車廠(1991)	Wuxi 無錫市	Jiangsu 江蘇省	(0510)8711072 (0510)8711591	2,339	Collectively-owned 集體	2,420,293	87539(4)	740,471	a
Shanghai - Ek Chor Motorbicycle Co. Ltd. 上海－易初摩托車有限公司(1985)	Shanghai 上海市	Shanghai 上海市	(021)58580778 (021)58580698	3,633	Foreign-funded 外資	2,417,779	52503(8)	2,351,878	a,b,c
Wu Yang - Honda Motors Guangzhou Co. Ltd. 五羊－本田摩托(廣州)有限公司(1992)	Guangzhou 廣州市	Guangdong 廣東省	(020)84186523 (020)84186548	1,997	Foreign-funded 外資	2,292,056	29661(10)	1,701,015	a
Mai Ke Te Group Motorcycle Industry General Company 麥科特集團摩托車工業總公司(1993)	Huizhou 惠州市	Guangdong 廣東省	(0751)2115644	845	Collectively-owned 集體	1,115,318	38679(9)	556,173	a
Shandong Hua Ri Group General Company 山東華日集團總公司(1952)	Linyi 臨沂市	Shandong 山東省	(0539)3221390 (0539)3222432	3,457	Joint stock 股份制	1,091,548	28262(11)	857,965	a,b,c
Tianjin Honda Motorcycle Co. Ltd. 天津本田摩托有限公司(1993)	Tianjin 天津市	Tianjin 天津市	(022)28334925 (022)28304562	1,445	Foreign-funded 外資	1,071,605	112569(2)	1,604,576	a
Zhejiang Qianjiang Motorbicycle (Group) Co. Ltd. 浙江錢江摩托集團有限公司(1952)	Taizhou 臺州市	Zhejiang 浙江省	(0576)6111453 (0576)6111045	3,964	State-owned 國有	1,013,072	123638(1)	1,222,814	o
Jiangmen Da Chang Jiang Motorcycle Co. Ltd. 江門市大長江摩托車有限公司(1993)	Jiangmen 江門市	Guangdong 廣東省	(0750)3221511 (0750)3221789	918	Foreign-funded 外資	850,683	83164(5)	492,513	a
Changchun Chanlin Group Co. Ltd. 長春摩托車集團有限公司(1956)	Changchun 長春市	Jilin 吉林省	(0431)2938586 (0431)2930397	2,989	State-owned 國有	812,671	75155(6)	1,270,976	a,b,c

Top 10 Cities by Production Output 產出排名前 10 位城市	Province 省	Market share 市場份額	Number of firms 企業個數
Ji'nan 濟南市	Shandong 山東省	13.90%	7
Chongqing 重慶市	Chongqing 重慶市	11.61%	12
Nanjing 南京市	Jiangsu 江蘇省	8.47%	5
Huizhou 惠州市	Guangdong 廣東省	8.23%	4
Shanghai 上海市	Shanghai 上海市	7.94%	11
Wuxi 無錫市	Jiangsu 江蘇省	6.28%	22
Taizhou 臺州市	Zhejiang 浙江省	5.99%	6
Tongshi 通什市	Hainan 海南省	4.87%	3
Linyi 臨沂市	Shandong 山東省	3.93%	3
Tianjin 天津市	Tianjin 天津市	3.93%	10

10 Major Wholesalers 10 家主要批發商	City 城市	Province 省	Telephone / Fax 電話 / 傳真
Zhejiang Zhong Yi Group Co. Ltd. 浙江中義集團有限公司	Shaoxing 紹興市	Zhejiang 浙江省	(0575)7381878 (0575)7381168
Jialing Group Marketing Co. Ltd. 嘉陵集團銷售有限公司	Chongqing 重慶市	Chongqing 重慶市	(023)65311991 (023)65315824
China Yan Xing Ji'nan Company Shandong Chang'an Automobile Marketing Co. Ltd. 中國燕興濟南公司山東長安汽車銷售有限公司	Ji'nan 濟南市	Shandong 山東省	(0531)5935164 (0531)5951502
China Yanxing Beijing Co. 中國燕興北京公司	Beijing 北京市	Beijing 北京市	(010)68861871
Shijiazhuang Motorcycle Marketing Maintenance Company 石家莊市摩托車銷售維修公司	Shijiazhuang 石家莊市	Hebei 河北省	(0311)6106850
Chongqing Railway Jialing Alternating Electrical Co. 重慶鐵路嘉陵交電公司	Chongqing 重慶市	Chongqing 重慶市	(023)63858383 (023)63866453
Zhangjiagang Supply & Marketing Cooperative General Agency Goods & Materials General Company 張家港市供銷合作總社物資總公司	Suzhou 蘇州市	Jiangsu 江蘇省	(0512)8222766
Jiang Retail Sales Jianghai Goods & Materials General Company 江門市江海區物資總公司	Jiangmen 江門市	Guangdong 廣東省	(0759)3382999 (0759)0
Jiangsu Hui Hua Group Vehicle Marketing Company 江蘇匯華集團車輛銷售公司	Wuxi 無錫市	Jiangsu 江蘇省	(0510)8711539
Shandong Da Ye Group Company 山東大業集團公司	Weifang 濰坊市	Shandong 山東省	(0536)6217777 (0536)6212666

*Also include sales by firms outside this industry.包括本行業以外廠家的銷售。"o" stands for "others". "o" 代表 "其他產品"。

3732: Motorcycle Parts and Accessories 摩托車零部件及配件製造業

The industry accounts for 0.244% of the total revenue of China's industrial sector in 1996. The revenue growth rate of the industry is 37.9% from 1995, as compared to the growth rate of China's industrial sector, 9.51%. The rate of return on asset is 2.23%. 69.92% of all firms in the industry made a profit while 25.30% had negative returns. The top province in terms of the industry's revenue is Chongqing, accounting for 21.97% of the total revenue.
本行業在1996年佔全行業總產值0.244%，行業年增長率為37.9%（全國工業年增長率9.51%）。行業的資產回報率2.23%，69.92%的企業盈利，25.30%的企業虧損。銷售收入最高的省份為重慶市，佔本行業的21.97%。

	Total number of firms 企業總數	Total number of employees 職工總數	Total revenue (mil. RMB) 總銷售收入（百萬元）	Total profit (mil. RMB) 總利潤（百萬元）	Return on assets 資產利潤率 (%)	Return on equity 權益利潤率 (%)	Labour productivity ('000 RMB / worker) 勞動生產率（千元/人）	Debts / assets 資產負債率 (%)	Total assets (mil. RMB) 總資產（百萬元）
Industry Overall 行業總體	1,412	177,449	14,126	372	2.23	5.75	79.61	61.23	16,679

	Number of firms 企業個數	Average number of employees 平均職工人數	Average revenue ('000 RMB) 平均銷售收入（千元）	Average profit ('000 RMB) 平均利潤（千元）	Return on assets 資產利潤率 (%)	Return on equity 權益利潤率 (%)	Labour productivity ('000 RMB / worker) 勞動生產率（千元/人）	Average debts / assets 平均資產負債率(%)	Average Total assets ('000 RMB) 平均總資產（千元）
By ownership 產業所有權									
State-owned 國有	97	391	19,031	-845	-2.16	-6.00	48.62	64.01	39,124
Collectively-owned 集體	1,144	99	7,542	268	3.79	10.87	76.26	65.17	7,087
Privately-owned 私有	15	48	3,275	24	0.64	1.74	67.86	63.13	3,824
Domestic JVs 聯營	31	124	28,879	1,106	4.93	13.18	232.53	62.58	22,416
Joint stock 股份制	39	206	18,892	1,054	4.82	11.22	91.86	57.04	21,856
Foreign-funded 外資	27	331	40,191	2,082	3.05	5.65	121.49	46.08	68,350
Overseas Chinese-funded 港澳台資	59	87	14,992	253	1.13	2.36	172.53	52.20	22,459
By size 規模									
Large 大型	7	2,330	282,776	10,481	2.84	6.34	121.37	55.27	369,653
Medium 中型	25	1,097	79,466	2,689	2.30	5.40	72.42	57.46	117,149
Small 小型	1,344	99	7,559	172	2.08	5.73	76.54	63.71	8,284
By regional distribution 地區分布									
Central-North 華北	63	152	9,503	740	6.07	18.71	62.59	67.59	12,193
Beijing 北京	21	126	4,765	-313	-6.08	-22.24	37.80	72.66	5,151
Tianjin 天津	13	72	12,346	2,380	26.77	56.32	172.58	52.46	8,889
Hebei 河北	27	131	8,294	810	5.99	15.98	63.08	62.53	13,527
Shanxi 山西									
Inner Mongolia 內蒙	2	1,219	57,095	185	0.21	1.34	46.84	84.59	89,600
Northeast 東北	25	214	5,943	216	1.40	8.99	27.73	84.45	15,429
Liaoning 遼寧	11	252	6,432	21	0.15	0.92	25.50	83.39	13,712
Jilin 吉林	10	208	6,139	300	1.40	9.07	29.54	84.61	21,503
Heilongjiang 黑龍江	4	126	4,110	540	10.88	117.39	32.55	90.74	4,965
Central East 華東	623	121	11,398	495	4.71	12.88	93.92	63.46	10,517
Shanghai 上海	46	155	21,833	1,577	8.62	18.74	141.24	54.03	18,309
Jiangsu 江蘇	131	153	19,053	543	3.44	8.51	124.45	59.62	15,797
Zhejiang 浙江	197	102	9,600	247	2.67	9.22	94.45	71.02	9,248
Anhui 安徽	10	113	5,316	32	0.92	4.78	47.00	80.72	3,476
Fujian 福建	45	69	4,603	411	4.21	8.24	66.46	48.86	9,760
Jiangxi 江西	132	89	3,506	211	4.98	14.46	39.58	65.56	4,235
Shandong 山東	62	201	15,911	1,119	8.83	31.64	79.07	72.08	12,674
Central-South 中南	194	135	13,552	-25	-0.15	-0.36	100.38	58.90	17,091
Henan 河南	53	208	6,612	-1,208	-7.90	-40.87	31.71	80.67	15,286
Hubei 湖北	14	233	13,170	55	0.42	2.02	56.63	79.24	13,086
Hunan 湖南	54	69	1,390	-70	-2.82	-11.23	20.19	74.91	2,472
Guangdong 廣東	67	109	29,673	1,006	3.18	6.05	271.42	47.49	31,675
Guangxi 廣西	3	196	5,650	-2,210	-21.92	-160.92	28.83	86.38	10,080
Hainan 海南	3	85	4,700	443	3.66	8.22	55.29	55.43	12,100
Southwest 西南	497	120	7,308	39	0.35	0.82	60.75	57.58	11,254
Chongqing 重慶	416	116	7,461	44	0.44	1.15	64.49	61.29	9,827
Sichuan 四川	69	160	7,481	32	0.15	0.28	46.79	47.20	21,527
Guizhou 貴州	12	37	996	-61	-4.46	-19.68	26.73	77.35	1,365
Yunnan 雲南									
Tibet 西藏									
Northwest 西北	10	94	1,652	-331	-5.13	-12.05	17.67	57.43	6,455
Shaanxi 陝西	6	81	350	-58	-1.73	-2.15	4.33	19.50	3,367
Gansu 甘肅	2	78	240	-85	-14.91	-43.59	3.10	65.79	570
Qinghai 青海									
Ningxia 寧夏	1	133	2,540	200	3.51	-222.22	19.10	101.58	5,690
Xinjiang 新疆	1	162	11,400	-2,990	-7.97	-27.41	70.37	70.90	37,520

3732: Motorcycle Parts and Accessories 摩托車零部件及配件製造業

Year 年份	Number of firms 企業個數	Rate of change 每年變化 (%)	Number of employees 職工人數（人）	Rate of change 每年變化 (%)	Total revenue (mil. RMB) 總銷售收入（百萬元）	Rate of change 每年變化 (%)	Total profit (mil. RMB) 總利潤（百萬元）	Rate of change 每年變化 (%)
1993	621		94,729		3,165		192	
1994	913	47.02%	116,769	23.27%	5,377	69.89%	279	45.20%
1995	1,346	47.43%	165,650	41.86%	10,245	90.53%	595	113.21%
1996	1,412	4.90%	177,449	7.12%	14,126	37.88%	372	-37.53%

3 Major products* 3 種主要產品 *	Output 產量	Sales volume 銷售量	Unit 單位
a) Gear 齒輪	13,465,553	12,657,619	piece 個
b) Motor 摩托車	73,523	70,582	vehicle 輛

Top 10 firms by revenue (year founded) 收入排名前 10 家企業 (創辦年份)	City 城市	Province 省	Telephone / fax 電話 / 傳真	Number of employees 職工人數	Ownership 產業所有權	Revenue ('000 RMB) 銷售收入（千元）	Profit ('000 RMB) (rank) 利潤（千元）（排名）	Total assets ('000 RMB) 總資產（千元）	Major products 主要產品
Xi Shan Shi Fu Ya Da Power-assisted Bicycle Factory 錫山市富雅達助力車廠(1995)	Wuxi 無錫市	Jiangsu 江蘇省	(0510)3792014	450	Collectively-owned 集體	500,446	14876(9)	113,766	o
Guangzhou Motorcycle Group Co. 廣州摩托集團公司(1992)	Guangzhou 廣州市	Guangdong 廣東省	(020)84403542 (020)84475816	1,576	State-owned 國有	434,068	17154(5)	777,713	o
Lu Qiao Qu Tai Zhou Shi Jili Industrial Co. Ltd. 路橋區台州市吉利實業有限公司(1995)	Taizhou 臺州市	Zhejiang 浙江省	(0576)2448000	3,197	Joint stock 股份制	339,313	-38(560)	123,714	o
Lu Qiao Qu Tai Zhou Jili Motorcycle Components Co. Ltd. 路橋區台州吉利摩托車部件有限公司(1996)	Taizhou 臺州市	Zhejiang 浙江省	(0576)2448000 (0576)2445648	2,359	Collectively-owned 集體	312,606	2207(66)	200,074	o
Chongqing Hongda Motorcycle – Fitting Reseach Institute 重慶市轟達車輛配件研究所	Chongqing 重慶市	Chongqing 重慶市	(023)65215670 (023)65215679	411	Collectively-owned 集體	306,083	2742(55)	89,336	o
Chongqing Longxin Gasoline Engine Manufacturing Co. Ltd. 重慶隆鑫汽油機製造有限公司	Chongqing 重慶市	Chongqing 重慶市	(023)68825145 (023)68821726	333	Foreign-funded 外資	285,541	6066(24)	243,796	o
Gaoyou Electric Equipment Plant 高郵電器廠(1976)	Yangzhou 揚州市	Jiangsu 江蘇省	(0514)4611401 (0514)4612799	1,322	Collectively-owned 集體	250,117	4021(36)	203,929	o
Zhuhai Hui Yong Motor Vehicle Fitting Parts Co. Ltd. 珠海市暉永機動車配件有限公司(1995)	Zhuhai 珠海市	Guangdong 廣東省	(0756)7764133 (0756)7761724	148	Domestic JVs 聯營	244,000	4680(27)	20,100	o
Guangzhou Conghua Tian Ma Motorcycle Industrial Co. Ltd. 廣州從化天馬摩托車實業有限公司(1995)	Guangzhou 廣州市	Guangdong 廣東省	(020)87936545 (020)87936676	280	Domestic JVs 聯營	231,881	4566(29)	62,880	b
Shanghai Dong Yang Dian Zhuang Co. Ltd. 上海東洋電裝有限公司(1992)	Shanghai 上海市	Shanghai 上海市	(021)57835978 (021)57835635	1,017	Foreign-funded 外資	230,399	25976(1)	271,507	o

Top 10 Cities by Production Output 產出排名前 10 位城市	Province 省	Market share 市場份額	Number of firms 企業個數
Chongqing 重慶市	Chongqing 重慶市	19.80%	597
Shanghai 上海市	Shanghai 上海市	9.76%	95
Taizhou 臺州市	Zhejiang 浙江省	9.41%	67
Guangzhou 廣州市	Guangdong 廣東省	5.23%	34
Wuxi 無錫市	Jiangsu 江蘇省	4.73%	93
Yangzhou 揚州市	Jiangsu 江蘇省	4.71%	24
Ningbo 寧波市	Zhejiang 浙江省	3.29%	66
Foshan 佛山市	Guangdong 廣東省	3.05%	9
Wenzhou 温州市	Zhejiang 浙江省	2.72%	154
Ji'nan 濟南市	Shandong 山東省	2.35%	25

10 Major Wholesalers 10 家主要批發商	City 城市	Province 省	Telephone / Fax 電話 / 傳真
Shanghai Auto Parts Company 上海市汽車配件公司	Shanghai 上海市	Shanghai 上海市	(021)62564400
China Automobile Trade Hua Bei Company 中國汽車貿易華北公司	Beijing 北京市	Beijing 北京市	(010)68518091 (010)68513546
China Yan Xing Tianjin Company 中國燕興天津公司	Tianjin 天津市	Tianjin 天津市	(022)28310131
China Automobile Industry Import & Export Guizhou Company 中國汽車工業進出口貴州公司	Guiyang 貴陽市	Guizhou 貴州省	(0851)5869068 (0851)5869008
Jining Automobile Marketing General Company 濟寧市汽車銷售總公司	Jining 濟寧市	Shandong 山東省	(0537)2313628 (0537)2314301
Shanghai Automobile Trade Company 上海汽車貿易公司	Shanghai 上海市	Shanghai 上海市	(021)58752443 (021)58753520
Shanghai Automobile Import & Export Company 上海汽車進出口公司	Shanghai 上海市	Shanghai 上海市	(021)63724288 (021)63724643
Fuyang Tyre Rubber General Company 富陽市輪胎橡膠總公司	Hangzhou 杭州市	Zhejiang 浙江省	(0571)3319574 (0571)3326835
Jilin Electromechanical Equipment General Company 吉林省機電設備總公司	Changchun 長春市	Jilin 吉林省	(0431)8717107 (0431)8743523
Chongqing Chang Jiang Business General Company 重慶長江商務總公司	Chongqing 重慶市	Chongqing 重慶市	(023)62810558 (023)62804041

*Also include sales by firms outside this industry.包括本行業以外廠家的銷售。"o" stands for "others". "o" 代表 "其他產品"。

3740: Bicycles 自行車製造業

The industry accounts for 0.306% of the total revenue of China's industrial sector in 1996. The revenue growth rate of the industry is -17.6% from 1995, as compared to the growth rate of China's industrial sector, 9.51%. The rate of return on asset is -0.92%. 53.71% of all firms in the industry made a profit while 39.30% had negative returns. The top province in terms of the industry's revenue is Shanghai, accounting for 23.96% of the total revenue.
本行業在1996年佔全行業總產值0.306%，行業年增長率為-17.6%（全國工業年增長率9.51%）。行業的資產回報率-0.92%，53.71%的企業盈利，39.30%的企業虧損。銷售收入最高的省份為上海市，佔本行業的23.96%。

	Total number of firms 企業總數	Total number of employees 職工總數	Total revenue (mil. RMB) 總銷售收入（百萬元）	Total profit (mil. RMB) 總利潤（百萬元）	Return on assets 資產利潤率 (%)	Return on equity 權益利潤率 (%)	Labour productivity ('000 RMB / worker) 勞動生產率（千元/人）	Debts / assets 資產負債率 (%)	Total assets (mil. RMB) 總資產（百萬元）
Industry Overall 行業總體	942	243,418	17,752	-250	-0.92	-3.06	72.93	69.92	27,213

	Number of firms 企業個數	Average number of employees 平均職工人數	Average revenue ('000 RMB) 平均銷售收入（千元）	Average profit ('000 RMB) 平均利潤（千元）	Return on assets 資產利潤率 (%)	Return on equity 權益利潤率 (%)	Labour productivity ('000 RMB / worker) 勞動生產率（千元/人）	Average debts / assets 平均資產負債率(%)	Average Total assets ('000 RMB) 平均總資產（千元）
By ownership 產業所有權									
State-owned 國有	125	828	39,840	-1,920	-2.41	-13.77	48.13	82.53	79,808
Collectively-owned 集體	647	137	7,302	-3	-0.04	-0.16	53.40	76.41	7,881
Privately-owned 私有	4	85	4,965	-7	-0.22	-0.59	58.75	62.14	3,045
Domestic JVs 聯營	19	613	67,327	112	0.16	0.45	109.88	65.60	71,749
Joint stock 股份制	12	1,600	218,485	-382	-0.13	-0.26	136.59	51.58	305,306
Foreign-funded 外資	52	151	20,759	-13	-0.05	-0.11	137.21	59.20	27,938
Overseas Chinese-funded 港澳台資	82	170	37,416	-59	-0.09	-0.20	219.65	57.47	68,534
By size 規模									
Large 大型	26	3,349	338,616	-45,150	-8.34	-25.43	101.10	67.19	541,132
Medium 中型	58	883	42,133	9,853	12.83	52.25	47.74	75.45	76,791
Small 小型	847	129	8,038	416	4.06	14.23	62.53	71.50	10,260
By regional distribution 地區分布									
Central-North 華北	257	169	7,601	110	0.91	4.87	44.92	81.35	12,146
Beijing 北京	17	6	158	-19	-3.24	-11.83	26.90	72.65	600
Tianjin 天津	197	175	8,145	72	0.54	3.02	46.65	82.16	13,322
Hebei 河北	37	205	9,296	413	3.85	15.79	45.37	75.59	10,717
Shanxi 山西	4	344	468	-175	-0.79	-4.98	1.36	84.20	22,250
Inner Mongolia 內蒙	2	13	160	-15	-2.29	-13.64	12.31	83.21	655
Northeast 東北	48	352	7,918	-731	-3.84	-55.37	22.49	93.06	19,018
Liaoning 遼寧	31	335	11,345	-259	-1.40	-11.67	33.84	87.97	18,420
Jilin 吉林	7	656	553	-1,827	-6.26	-165.89	0.84	96.23	29,167
Heilongjiang 黑龍江	10	192	2,451	-1,427	-10.37	109.35	12.78	109.48	13,765
Central East 華東	426	302	25,170	-215	-0.69	-1.95	83.45	64.78	31,172
Shanghai 上海	70	544	60,753	668	0.84	1.81	111.71	53.89	79,948
Jiangsu 江蘇	122	350	25,352	-650	-2.35	-9.84	72.45	76.16	27,707
Zhejiang 浙江	125	181	15,923	-220	-1.16	-3.44	88.13	66.13	18,922
Anhui 安徽	19	236	10,312	-2,276	-15.03	-191.63	43.68	92.16	15,146
Fujian 福建	34	123	7,016	-327	-3.59	-10.38	57.13	65.46	9,119
Jiangxi 江西	13	274	7,982	-232	-1.52	-5.86	29.18	74.13	15,273
Shandong 山東	43	301	19,720	606	2.28	8.45	65.56	72.97	26,531
Central-South 中南	187	268	24,814	-750	-1.45	-4.93	92.63	70.64	51,850
Henan 河南	37	250	14,597	69	0.39	1.70	58.46	77.17	17,731
Hubei 湖北	31	276	5,392	-612	-3.53	-32.22	19.55	89.05	17,345
Hunan 湖南	10	354	4,650	-1,745	-9.91	76.13	13.14	113.02	17,610
Guangdong 廣東	80	279	46,022	-794	-0.82	-2.51	165.13	67.32	96,619
Guangxi 廣西	29	223	7,061	-1,480	-7.20	-31.79	31.63	77.36	20,569
Hainan 海南									
Southwest 西南	11	223	2,382	-1,135	-7.61	-245.67	10.66	96.90	14,917
Chongqing 重慶	1	356	2,716	-96,338	-163.54	432.42	7.64	137.82	58,908
Sichuan 四川	8	184	1,911	5,336	54.51	394.59	10.37	86.19	9,789
Guizhou 貴州									
Yunnan 雲南	3	300	3,503	-1,443	-7.07	-71.22	11.68	90.05	20,407
Tibet 西藏									
Northwest 西北	13	153	2,269	31	1.00	3.16	14.82	68.50	3,089
Shaanxi 陝西	7	243	2,930	21	0.49	1.57	12.06	68.98	4,399
Gansu 甘肅	4	55	2,208	70	3.19	9.52	40.32	66.59	2,193
Qinghai 青海	1	72	160	-30	-5.00	-17.65	2.22	71.67	600
Ningxia 寧夏									
Xinjiang 新疆	1								

3740: Bicycles 自行車製造業

Year 年份	Number of firms 企業個數	Rate of change 每年變化 (%)	Number of employees 職工人數 (人)	Rate of change 每年變化 (%)	Total revenue (mil. RMB) 總銷售收入 (百萬元)	Rate of change 每年變化 (%)	Total profit (mil. RMB) 總利潤 (百萬元)	Rate of change 每年變化 (%)
1993	899		447,542		22,120		566	
1994	1,070	19.02%	315,280	-29.55%	22,158	0.17%	397	-29.97%
1995	1,081	1.03%	296,034	-6.11%	21,547	-2.76%	36	-90.83%
1996	942	-12.86%	243,418	-17.77%	17,752	-17.61%	-250	-787.32%

3 Major products* 3 種主要產品 *	Output 產量	Sales volume 銷售量	Unit 單位
a) Bicycle 自行車	32,030,029	31,069,128	vehicle 輛
b) Tricycle 三輪車	134,831	128,089	vehicle 輛
c) Childern's Cart 童車	23,077	23,307	1,000 yuan 千元

Top 10 firms by revenue (year founded) 收入排名前 10 家企業 (創辦年份)	City 城市	Province 省	Telephone / fax 電話 / 傳真	Number of employees 職工人數	Ownership 產業所有權	Revenue ('000 RMB) 銷售收入 (千元)	Profit ('000 RMB) (rank) 利潤（千元）(排名)	Total assets ('000 RMB) 總資產 (千元)	Major products 主要產品
Feng Huang Co. Ltd. 鳳凰股份有限公司(1958)	Shanghai 上海市	Shanghai 上海市	(021)65116511 (021)65116383	10,367	Joint stock 股份制	1,546,023	10089(7)	1,979,636	a
Shanghai Si Bi Ke Development General Co. 上海斯必克發展總公司(1993)	Shanghai 上海市	Shanghai 上海市	(021)65120054 (021)65374873	5,807	State-owned 國有	811,615	45096(1)	850,528	a
Shun Te Tandem Bicycle Components Co. Ltd. 順德天任車料有限公司(1992)	Foshan 佛山市	Guangdong 廣東省	(0757)5563789 (0757)2238945	835	Overseas Chinese-funded 港澳台資	791,451	1543(59)	536,421	a
Shenzhen China Bicycle (holdings) Ltd. 深圳中華自行車(集團)股份有限公司(1985)	Shenzhen 深圳市	Guangdong 廣東省	(0755)5516998 (0755)5516620	1,938	Overseas Chinese-funded 港澳台資	737,730	3486(25)	2,937,744	a
Shanghai Forever Co. Ltd. 上海永久股份有限公司(1940)	Shanghai 上海市	Shanghai 上海市	(021)65461544 (021)65458657	5,590	Joint stock 股份制	670,048	3325(27)	1,184,994	a,c
Changzhou Jin Shi Bicycle Industry & Trade Group Co. 常州金獅自行車工貿集團公司(1974)	Changzhou 常州市	Jiangsu 江蘇省	(0519)3270453 (0519)3273278	7,683	Domestic JVs 聯營	621,294	-39868(614)	737,190	a
Qi Lu Incall Group Corp. 齊魯英克萊集團總公司(1975)	Jining 濟寧市	Shandong 山東省	(0537)2327219 (0537)2327226	1,948	State-owned 國有	485,027	33528(2)	358,285	a
Guangzhou Wu Yang Bicycle Enterprise Group Co. 廣州市五羊自行車企業集團公司(1994)	Guangzhou 廣州市	Guangdong 廣東省	(020)84332888 (020)84339725	4,627	State-owned 國有	370,223	-42499(615)	945,860	a
Jie An Te Bicycle Co. Ltd. 捷安特自行車有限公司(1993)	Suzhou 蘇州市	Jiangsu 江蘇省	(0512)7313528	1,900	Overseas Chinese-funded 港澳台資	361,525	1774(54)	399,291	o
Zhejiang Fei Li Pu Group Company 浙江菲利普集團公司(1981)	Jiaxing 嘉興市	Zhejiang 浙江省	(0573)2085111 (0573)2082792	138	State-owned 國有	339,643	448(144)	306,272	a

Top 10 Cities by Production Output 產出排名前 10 位城市	Province 省	Market share 市場份額	Number of firms 企業個數
Shanghai 上海市	Shanghai 上海市	24.03%	90
Shenzhen 深圳市	Guangdong 廣東省	8.33%	19
Tianjin 天津市	Tianjin 天津市	7.28%	223
Changzhou 常州市	Jiangsu 江蘇省	6.74%	69
Suzhou 蘇州市	Jiangsu 江蘇省	5.19%	39
Foshan 佛山市	Guangdong 廣東省	4.69%	6
Guangzhou 廣州市	Guangdong 廣東省	4.38%	41
Wuxi 無錫市	Jiangsu 江蘇省	4.26%	39
Hangzhou 杭州市	Zhejiang 浙江省	3.73%	64
Shaoxing 紹興市	Zhejiang 浙江省	3.13%	18

10 Major Wholesalers 10 家主要批發商	City 城市	Province 省	Telephone / Fax 電話 / 傳真
Changzhou Hardware Alternating-current Appliance and Chemical Wholesale General Company 常州五金交電化工批發總公司	Changzhou 常州市	Jiangsu 江蘇省	(0519)6609929 (0519)6609925
Suzhou Hardware & Alternating Electricity Co. Ltd. 蘇州五金交電股份有限公司	Suzhou 蘇州市	Jiangsu 江蘇省	(0512)5239572 (0512)5213248
Tianjin Foreign Trade General Company 天津市對外貿易總公司	Tianjin 天津市	Tianjin 天津市	(022)23310922
Chongqing International Trade Center 重慶國際貿易中心	Chongqing 重慶市	Chongqing 重慶市	(023)67853232 (023)67850402
China Chemical Plastics Co. Ltd. 中化塑料有限公司	Beijing 北京市	Beijing 北京市	(010)68569863 (010)68569041
Ningbo Hualian Group Co. Ltd. 寧波華聯集團股份有限公司	Ningbo 寧波市	Zhejiang 浙江省	(0574)7367626 (0574)7367652
Xia Retail Sales Kaiyuan Wei Wei Electromechanical Building Materials Marketing Dept. 廈門市開元區威威機電建材經營部	Xiamen 廈門市	Fujian 福建省	(0592)2071044
Rudong Industry Product General Company 如東縣工業品總公司	Nantong 南通市	Jiangsu 江蘇省	(0513)4516110 (0513)4516110
Fujian Fu Ri Group Company 福建福日集團公司	Fuzhou 福州市	Fujian 福建省	(0591)3269325 (0591)3270426
Guangdong Hardware & Alternating Electrical Co. 廣東省五金交電公司	Guangzhou 廣州市	Guangdong 廣東省	(020)81884078 (020)81861287

*Also include sales by firms outside this industry.包括本行業以外廠家的銷售。"o" stands for "others". "o" 代表"其他產品"。

3750: Trolleys 電車製造業

The industry accounts for 0.000% of the total revenue of China's industrial sector in 1996. The revenue growth rate of the industry is 743.6% from 1995, as compared to the growth rate of China's industrial sector, 9.51%. The rate of return on asset is -1.74%. 71.43% of all firms in the industry made a profit while 28.57% had negative returns. The top province in terms of the industry's revenue is Jiangsu, accounting for 38.92% of the total revenue.
本行業在1996年佔全行業總產值0.000%，行業年增長率為743.6%（全國工業年增長率9.51%）。行業的資產回報率-1.74%，71.43%的企業盈利，28.57%的企業虧損。銷售收入最高的省份為江蘇省，佔本行業的38.92%。

	Total number of firms 企業總數	Total number of employees 職工總數	Total revenue (mil. RMB) 總銷售收入（百萬元）	Total profit (mil. RMB) 總利潤（百萬元）	Return on assets 資產利潤率 (%)	Return on equity 權益利潤率 (%)	Labour productivity ('000 RMB / worker) 勞動生產率（千元/人）	Debts / assets 資產負債率 (%)	Total assets (mil. RMB) 總資產（百萬元）
Industry Overall 行業總體	8	462	26		-1.74	18.33	56.28	109.44	19

	Number of firms 企業個數	Average number of employees 平均職工人數	Average revenue ('000 RMB) 平均銷售收入（千元）	Average profit ('000 RMB) 平均利潤（千元）	Return on assets 資產利潤率 (%)	Return on equity 權益利潤率 (%)	Labour productivity ('000 RMB / worker) 勞動生產率（千元/人）	Average debts / assets 平均資產負債率(%)	Average Total assets ('000 RMB) 平均總資產（千元）
By ownership 產業所有權									
State-owned 國有					2.88	9.83	16.18	61.14	
Collectively-owned 集體	8	58	3,250				56.28	110.58	2,372
Privately-owned 私有									
Domestic JVs 聯營									
Joint stock 股份制									
Foreign-funded 外資									
Overseas Chinese-funded 港澳台資									
By size 規模									
Large 大型									
Medium 中型									
Small 小型	8	58	3,250				56.28	110.53	2,375
By regional distribution 地區分布									
Central-North 華北									
Beijing 北京									
Tianjin 天津									
Hebei 河北									
Shanxi 山西									
Inner Mongolia 內蒙									
Northeast 東北									
Liaoning 遼寧									
Jilin 吉林									
Heilongjiang 黑龍江									
Central East 華東	4	49	3,030	93	11.56	56.06	62.47	79.06	800
Shanghai 上海									
Jiangsu 江蘇	2	72	5,060	175	17.33	120.69	70.77	85.64	1,010
Zhejiang 浙江	2	26	1,000	10	1.69	5.41	39.22	67.80	590
Anhui 安徽									
Fujian 福建									
Jiangxi 江西									
Shandong 山東									
Central-South 中南	3	66	3,577	183	6.00	31.07	54.47	80.68	3,053
Henan 河南	2	51	4,575	295	9.32	393.33	89.71	97.63	3,165
Hubei 湖北									
Hunan 湖南	1	95	1,580	-40	-1.41	-2.47	16.63	42.76	2,830
Guangdong 廣東									
Guangxi 廣西									
Hainan 海南									
Southwest 西南	1	71	2,680	-1,230	-18.58	29.15	37.75	163.75	6,620
Chongqing 重慶									
Sichuan 四川									
Guizhou 貴州									
Yunnan 雲南									
Tibet 西藏									
Northwest 西北									
Shaanxi 陝西									
Gansu 甘肅									
Qinghai 青海									
Ningxia 寧夏									
Xinjiang 新疆									

3750: Trolleys 電車製造業

Year 年份	Number of firms 企業個數	Rate of change 每年變化 (%)	Number of employees 職工人數 (人)	Rate of change 每年變化 (%)	Total revenue (mil. RMB) 總銷售收入 (百萬元)	Rate of change 每年變化 (%)	Total profit (mil. RMB) 總利潤 (百萬元)	Rate of change 每年變化 (%)
1993	10		971		15		-0.13	
1994	13	30.00%	763	-21.42%	20	37.06%	0.25	296.12%
1995	3	-76.92%	208	-72.74%	3	-84.96%	0.13	-47.43%
1996	8	166.67%	462	122.12%	26	743.61%	0	-100.00%

3 Major products* 3 種主要產品 *	Output 產量	Sales volume 銷售量	Unit 單位

Top 10 firms by revenue (year founded) 收入排名前 10 家企業 (創辦年份)	City 城市	Province 省	Telephone / fax 電話 / 傳真	Number of employees 職工人數	Ownership 產業所有權	Revenue ('000 RMB) 銷售收入 (千元)	Profit ('000 RMB) (rank) 利潤 (千元) (排名)	Total assets ('000 RMB) 總資產 (千元)	Major products 主要產品
Pizhou Taking Long Voyage Ship Building and Repair Factory 邳州市遠航船舶修造廠(1990)	Xuzhou 徐州市	Jiangsu 江蘇省	(0516)6561384	100	Collectively-owned 集體	9,610	280(2)	1,600	o
Huaxian Qianjin Vehicle Factory 滑縣前進車輛廠(1992)	Anyang 安陽市	Henan 河南省	(0372)831554	92	Collectively-owned 集體	7,100	540(1)	3,270	o
Sichuan Deyang Dongfang Metallurgy Machine Factory 四川德陽東方冶金機械廠(1971)	Deyang 德陽市	Sichuan 四川省	(0838)2201788	73	Collectively-owned 集體	2,677	-1232(5)	6,623	o
Youxian Industry Tang Glass Equipment Factory 攸縣工業搪玻璃設備廠(1964)	Zhuzhou 株洲市	Hunan 湖南省	(0733)4232239	95	Collectively-owned 集體	2,581	-45(4)	2,828	o

Top 10 Cities by Production Output 產出排名前 10 位城市	Province 省	Market share 市場份額	Number of firms 企業個數
Anyang 安陽市	Henan 河南省	31.15%	1
Taizhou 臺州市	Zhejiang 浙江省	22.18%	2
Wuhu 蕪湖市	Anhui 安徽省	13.60%	1
Deyang 德陽市	Sichuan 四川省	11.50%	1
Shangqiu 商丘市	Henan 河南省	7.02%	1
Zhuzhou 株洲市	Hunan 湖南省	5.56%	1
Wuxi 無錫市	Jiangsu 江蘇省	2.68%	1
Linxia 臨夏市	Gansu 甘肅省	2.63%	1
Shanghai 上海市	Shanghai 上海市	2.14%	2
Wenzhou 溫州市	Zhejiang 浙江省	1.18%	1

10 Major Wholesalers 10 家主要批發商	City 城市	Province 省	Telephone / Fax 電話 / 傳真
Hunan Automobile Trade (Group) General Company 湖南汽車貿易(集團)總公司	Changsha 長沙市	Hunan 湖南省	(0731)4723388
Sichuan Automobile Industry General Company 四川省汽車工業總公司	Chengdu 成都市	Sichuan 四川省	(028)4334513 (028)4317793
Guangdong Goods & Materials Group Automobile Trade Company 廣東物資集團汽車貿易公司	Guangzhou 廣州市	Guangdong 廣東省	(020)84217281 (020)84217303
Tianjin Automobile Industry Sale General Co. 天津市汽車工業銷售總公司	Tianjin 天津市	Tianjin 天津市	(022)28318888 (022)28313200
China Automobile Trade Hua Dong Company 中國汽車貿易華東公司	Shanghai 上海市	Shanghai 上海市	(021)63732288 (021)63731084
China Automobile Trade General Company 中國汽車貿易總公司	Beijing 北京市	Beijing 北京市	(010)63265840
Kaifeng Goods & Materials (Group) Automobile Trade Company 開封物資(集團)汽車貿易公司	Kaifeng 開封市	Henan 河南省	(0378)9018058 (0378)2924752
China Automobile Industry Marketing General Company 中國汽車工業銷售總公司	Beijing 北京市	Beijing 北京市	(010)64013057 (010)64013840
Jin Bei Trade General Company 金杯貿易總公司	Shenyang 瀋陽市	Liaoning 遼寧省	(024)22529437 (024)22529444
Yunnan Electromechanical Equipment General Co. 雲南省機電設備總公司	Kunming 昆明市	Yunnan 雲南省	(0871)3136797 (0871)3130735

*Also include sales by firms outside this industry.包括本行業以外廠家的銷售。"o" stands for "others". "o" 代表 "其他產品"。

3761: Ocean Shipping Boats 海洋運輸船製造業

The industry accounts for 0.271% of the total revenue of China's industrial sector in 1996. The revenue growth rate of the industry is 19.5% from 1995, as compared to the growth rate of China's industrial sector, 9.51%. The rate of return on asset is -0.04%. 70.80% of all firms in the industry made a profit while 21.51% had negative returns. The top province in terms of the industry's revenue is Shanghai, accounting for 39.37% of the total revenue.
本行業在1996年佔全行業總產值0.271%，行業年增長率為19.5%（全國工業年增長率9.51%）。行業的資產回報率-0.04%，70.80%的企業盈利，21.51%的企業虧損。銷售收入最高的省份為上海市，佔本行業的39.37%。

	Total number of firms 企業總數	Total number of employees 職工總數	Total revenue (mil. RMB) 總銷售收入（百萬元）	Total profit (mil. RMB) 總利潤（百萬元）	Return on assets 資產利潤率 (%)	Return on equity 權益利潤率 (%)	Labour productivity ('000 RMB / worker) 勞動生產率（千元/人）	Debts / assets 資產負債率 (%)	Total assets (mil. RMB) 總資產（百萬元）
Industry Overall 行業總體	87	138,421	15,719	-12	-0.04	-0.18	113.56	80.54	33,526

	Number of firms 企業個數	Average number of employees 平均職工人數	Average revenue ('000 RMB) 平均銷售收入（千元）	Average profit ('000 RMB) 平均利潤（千元）	Return on assets 資產利潤率 (%)	Return on equity 權益利潤率 (%)	Labour productivity ('000 RMB / worker) 勞動生產率（千元/人）	Average debts / assets 平均資產負債率(%)	Average Total assets ('000 RMB) 平均總資產（千元）
By ownership 產業所有權									
State-owned 國有	44	2,776	286,000	-1,341	-0.20	-1.20	103.02	83.45	676,523
Collectively-owned 集體	31	242	15,172	-65	-0.51	-1.61	62.65	68.45	12,867
Privately-owned 私有									
Domestic JVs 聯營	2	95	5,051	-55	-0.31	-1.02	53.45	69.38	17,719
Joint stock 股份制	2	3,388	1,198,867	27,043	1.89	3.92	353.91	51.69	1,429,752
Foreign-funded 外資	4	282	49,481	-1,013	-0.96	-7.31	175.78	86.83	105,243
Overseas Chinese-funded 港澳台資	5	130	12,019	-180	-2.01	-3.66	92.31	45.21	8,976
By size 規模									
Large 大型	19	5,578	695,314	-637	-0.04	-0.22	124.64	80.82	1,537,843
Medium 中型	12	1,666	133,685	-157	-0.06	-0.25	80.22	73.70	242,304
Small 小型	54	230	16,757	37	0.14	1.27	72.98	88.83	25,929
By regional distribution 地區分布									
Central-North 華北	4	2,808	181,650	783	0.17	0.90	64.70	80.98	454,578
Beijing 北京									
Tianjin 天津	4	2,808	181,650	783	0.17	0.90	64.70	80.98	454,578
Hebei 河北									
Shanxi 山西									
Inner Mongolia 內蒙									
Northeast 東北	8	2,952	386,275	-7,936	-0.72	-7.13	130.86	89.97	1,109,354
Liaoning 遼寧	8	2,952	386,275	-7,936	-0.72	-7.13	130.86	89.97	1,109,354
Jilin 吉林									
Heilongjiang 黑龍江									
Central East 華東	60	1,312	140,628	-10		-0.02	107.17	81.88	287,540
Shanghai 上海	9	5,038	687,532	340	0.02	0.14	136.47	82.87	1,413,183
Jiangsu 江蘇	16	678	76,200	1,393	1.51	7.96	112.41	81.05	92,303
Zhejiang 浙江	9	370	19,762	-1,050	-2.39	-7.80	53.40	69.35	43,900
Anhui 安徽	2	2,481	93,010	-45	-0.01	-0.08	37.50	85.45	389,385
Fujian 福建	17	243	19,683	1,041	2.14	8.09	80.86	73.49	48,519
Jiangxi 江西	3	2,235	39,820	-8,573	-4.72	-281.40	17.82	98.32	181,633
Shandong 山東	4	853	53,188	-2,093	-1.63	-4.05	62.35	59.75	128,333
Central-South 中南	13	1,739	258,015	4,873	1.19	3.04	148.37	61.03	410,900
Henan 河南									
Hubei 湖北	4	2,129	191,993	2,775	0.74	5.91	90.18	87.39	372,528
Hunan 湖南									
Guangdong 廣東	6	1,692	403,447	7,195	1.31	2.65	238.40	50.61	548,957
Guangxi 廣西	3	1,312	55,180	3,027	1.63	3.40	42.05	52.12	185,950
Hainan 海南									
Southwest 西南	2	1,117	55,415	-7,210	-6.03	-18.00	49.61	66.52	119,620
Chongqing 重慶	2	1,117	55,415	-7,210	-6.03	-18.00	49.61	66.52	119,620
Sichuan 四川									
Guizhou 貴州									
Yunnan 雲南									
Tibet 西藏									
Northwest 西北									
Shaanxi 陝西									
Gansu 甘肅									
Qinghai 青海									
Ningxia 寧夏									
Xinjiang 新疆									

3761: Ocean Shipping Boats 海洋運輸船製造業

Year 年份	Number of firms 企業個數	Rate of change 每年變化 (%)	Number of employees 職工人數 (人)	Rate of change 每年變化 (%)	Total revenue (mil. RMB) 總銷售收入 (百萬元)	Rate of change 每年變化 (%)	Total profit (mil. RMB) 總利潤 (百萬元)	Rate of change 每年變化 (%)
1993	74		303,945		9,082		427	
1994	75	1.35%	183,361	-39.67%	14,341	57.90%	399	-6.45%
1995	84	12.00%	137,308	-25.12%	13,157	-8.25%	169	-57.61%
1996	87	3.57%	138,421	0.81%	15,719	19.47%	-12	-107.09%

3 Major products* 3 種主要產品 *	Output 產量	Sales volume 銷售量	Unit 單位
a) Steel Passenger Sheet 鋼質客輪	8,048	8,048	ton 滿載排水量噸
b) Steel Tug 鋼質拖輪	13,001	12,481	ton 滿載排水量噸
c) Steel Cargo Ship 鋼質貨輪	527,199	532,471	weight ton 載重量噸

Top 10 firms by revenue (year founded) 收入排名前 10 家企業 (創辦年份)	City 城市	Province 省	Telephone / fax 電話 / 傳真	Number of employees 職工人數	Ownership 產業所有權	Revenue ('000 RMB) 銷售收入 (千元)	Profit ('000 RMB) (rank) 利潤 (千元) (排名)	Total assets ('000 RMB) 總資產 (千元)	Major products 主要產品
Hu Dong Shipyard 滬東造船廠(1928)	Shanghai 上海市	Shanghai 上海市	(021)58713222 (021)58712603	11,147	State-owned 國有	2,125,954	33711(2)	3,836,854	c
Jiangnan Shipyard (Group) Co. Ltd. 江南造船集團有限公司(1865)	Shanghai 上海市	Shanghai 上海市	(021)63284157 (021)63770297	10,650	State-owned 國有	2,087,726	33584(3)	3,829,375	c
Guangzhou Shipyard International Co. Ltd. 廣州廣船國際股份有限公司(1993)	Guangzhou 廣州市	Guangdong 廣東省	(020)81891712 (020)81891575	6,221	Joint stock 股份制	2,061,349	40311(1)	2,724,420	c
Dalian New Shipyard 大連造船新廠(1990)	Dalian 大連市	Liaoning 遼寧省	(0411)4417644 (0411)4417540	5,019	State-owned 國有	1,559,323	10151(6)	4,178,065	c
Dalian Shipyard 大連造船廠(1898)	Dalian 大連市	Liaoning 遼寧省	(0411)2638300 (0411)2633461	8,219	State-owned 國有	1,282,932	20378(5)	3,075,971	c
Wuchang Shipyard 武昌造船廠(1934)	Wuhan 武漢市	Hubei 湖北省	(027)88045037 (027)88077801	7,927	State-owned 國有	735,925	10082(7)	1,454,947	a
Shanghai Shipyard 上海船廠(1862)	Shanghai 上海市	Shanghai 上海市	(021)58840451 (021)58842840	8,234	State-owned 國有	694,238	6436(10)	2,206,953	c
Tianjin Shipbuilding Corp. 天津造船公司(1919)	Tianjin 天津市	Tianjin 天津市	(022)25793995 (022)25895882	10,287	State-owned 國有	692,894	2154(18)	1,737,343	c
Yangzhou Jiangyang Ship Building Corp. 揚州江揚船舶集團公司(1961)	Yangzhou 揚州市	Jiangsu 江蘇省	(0514)7294690 (0514)7294307	3,520	State-owned 國有	584,093	22111(4)	674,534	o
Zhong Hua Shipyard 中華造船廠(1926)	Shanghai 上海市	Shanghai 上海市	(021)65192000 (021)55432859	4,630	State-owned 國有	381,230	-62308(77)	961,821	c

Top 10 Cities by Production Output 產出排名前 10 位城市	Province 省	Market share 市場份額	Number of firms 企業個數
Shanghai 上海市	Shanghai 上海市	40.88%	16
Dalian 大連市	Liaoning 遼寧省	18.30%	3
Guangzhou 廣州市	Guangdong 廣東省	15.29%	2
Wuhan 武漢市	Hubei 湖北省	4.87%	2
Tianjin 天津市	Tianjin 天津市	4.85%	5
Yangzhou 揚州市	Jiangsu 江蘇省	2.19%	3
Wuhu 蕪湖市	Anhui 安徽省	1.56%	3
Zhenjiang 鎮江市	Jiangsu 江蘇省	1.29%	4
Qingdao 青島市	Shandong 山東省	1.16%	1
Ningde 寧德市	Fujian 福建省	1.10%	11

10 Major Wholesalers 10 家主要批發商	City 城市	Province 省	Telephone / Fax 電話 / 傳真
Liaoning Automobile Trade Group Corp. 遼寧省汽車貿易集團	Shenyang 瀋陽市	Liaoning 遼寧省	(024)23835494 (024)23838338
China Post and Telecommunication Equipment General Company 中國郵電器材總公司	Beijing 北京市	Beijing 北京市	(010)63523715 (010)63525935
Jiangsu Electromechanical Products General Company 江蘇省機電產品總公司	Nanjing 南京市	Jiangsu 江蘇省	(025)7713642 (025)7711036
Xi Nan Technology Import & Export Company 西南技術進出口公司	Chongqing 重慶市	Chongqing 重慶市	(023)63850185 (023)63850026
Changzhou Economic Technology Industrial Development Zone Tian Ming Trade Company 常州經濟技術產業開發區天明貿易公司	Changzhou 常州市	Jiangsu 江蘇省	(0519)8829882 (0519)8829882
Shanxi Mechanical Equipment Import & Export Company 山西省機械設備進出口公司	Taiyuan 太原市	Shanxi 山西省	(0351)4040713 (0351)4043981
Ningbo Five Mining Machinery Import & Export Company 寧波市五礦機械進出口公司	Ningbo 寧波市	Zhejiang 浙江省	(0574)7311255 (0574)7320322
Tianjin Jin Huan Electromechanical Complete Sets of Equipment Factory 天津市津環機電成套設備廠	Tianjin 天津市	Tianjin 天津市	(022)26371628
Yunnan Machinery Import & Export Company 雲南省機械進出口公司	Kunming 昆明市	Yunnan 雲南省	(0871)3164879 (0871)3136829
Tianjin Da Qiu Zhuang Yi Yuan Trade Center 天津市大丘莊億源商貿中心	Tianjin 天津市	Tianjin 天津市	(022)28899478 (022)28899046

*Also include sales by firms outside this industry.包括本行業以外廠家的銷售。"o" stands for "others". "o" 代表"其他產品"。

3762: Waterway Shipping Boats 內河船製造業

The industry accounts for 0.052% of the total revenue of China's industrial sector in 1996. The revenue growth rate of the industry is -24.6% from 1995, as compared to the growth rate of China's industrial sector, 9.51%. The rate of return on asset is -1.22%. 56.18% of all firms in the industry made a profit while 37.91% had negative returns. The top province in terms of the industry's revenue is Jiangsu, accounting for 34.21% of the total revenue.
本行業在1996年佔全行業總產值0.052%，行業年增長率為-24.6%（全國工業年增長率9.51%）。行業的資產回報率-1.22%，56.18%的企業盈利，37.91%的企業虧損。銷售收入最高的省份為江蘇省，佔本行業的34.21%。

	Total number of firms 企業總數	Total number of employees 職工總數	Total revenue (mil. RMB) 總銷售收入（百萬元）	Total profit (mil. RMB) 總利潤（百萬元）	Return on assets 資產利潤率 (%)	Return on equity 權益利潤率 (%)	Labour productivity ('000 RMB / worker) 勞動生產率（千元/人）	Debts / assets 資產負債率 (%)	Total assets (mil. RMB) 總資產（百萬元）
Industry Overall 行業總體	408	76,401	2,993	-71	-1.22	-3.59	39.17	65.86	5,811

	Number of firms 企業個數	Average number of employees 平均職工人數	Average revenue ('000 RMB) 平均銷售收入（千元）	Average profit ('000 RMB) 平均利潤（千元）	Return on assets 資產利潤率 (%)	Return on equity 權益利潤率 (%)	Labour productivity ('000 RMB / worker) 勞動生產率（千元/人）	Average debts / assets 平均資產負債率(%)	Average Total assets ('000 RMB) 平均總資產（千元）
By ownership 產業所有權									
State-owned 國有	93	51	13,656	-1,086	-2.54	-7.31	266.08	65.26	42,774
Collectively-owned 集體	299	209	4,621	102	2.66	11.27	22.16	76.39	3,836
Privately-owned 私有									
Domestic JVs 聯營	4	1,193	39,742	-395	-0.43	-0.87	33.31	50.60	92,107
Joint stock 股份制	5	194	7,411	341	9.26	30.69	38.28	69.84	3,687
Foreign-funded 外資	4	521	21,536	1,383	2.87	5.10	41.36	43.83	48,274
Overseas Chinese-funded 港澳台資	4	402	14,853	-1,547	-5.85	-17.63	36.92	66.84	26,453
By size 規模									
Large 大型	1	3,672	107,001	278	0.10	0.37	29.14	72.45	274,847
Medium 中型	20	1,165	49,550	-2,629	-2.19	-6.04	42.53	63.72	120,054
Small 小型	386	128	4,910	-48	-0.60	-1.80	38.29	66.92	8,122
By regional distribution 地區分布									
Central-North 華北	3	79	5,863	90	2.38	9.44	73.91	74.80	3,783
Beijing 北京	2								
Tianjin 天津	1	238	17,590	270	2.38	9.44	73.91	74.80	11,350
Hebei 河北									
Shanxi 山西									
Inner Mongolia 內蒙									
Northeast 東北	9	268	5,708	-1,000	-6.19	57.03	21.30	110.85	16,161
Liaoning 遼寧	3	91	1,440	-23	-0.82	-2.48	15.82	66.98	2,847
Jilin 吉林	3	155	733	7	0.50	-1.24	4.72	139.85	1,347
Heilongjiang 黑龍江	3	558	14,950	-2,983	-6.74	52.68	26.81	112.79	44,290
Central East 華東	240	150	7,646	-34	-0.31	-0.92	50.85	66.78	11,103
Shanghai 上海	6	213	9,660	-445	-2.18	-5.54	45.32	60.71	20,433
Jiangsu 江蘇	114	172	8,981	-223	-1.70	-6.54	52.11	73.94	13,092
Zhejiang 浙江	26	75	2,760	-52	-1.33	-5.24	36.84	74.70	3,918
Anhui 安徽	39	144	5,184	-102	-1.13	-3.68	36.11	69.27	9,007
Fujian 福建	12	203	8,168	-50	-0.30	-0.71	40.32	57.47	16,578
Jiangxi 江西	31	115	935	-116	-2.28	-8.35	8.14	70.88	5,085
Shandong 山東	12	136	29,359	2,456	12.29	16.03	216.67	23.34	19,988
Central-South 中南	125	224	7,461	-196	-1.02	-2.97	33.31	65.47	19,099
Henan 河南	8	220	11,871	678	9.79	17.47	54.05	43.97	6,923
Hubei 湖北	37	341	11,422	6	0.02	0.06	33.51	61.53	29,287
Hunan 湖南	20	217	4,002	-424	-3.82	-9.48	18.46	59.69	11,091
Guangdong 廣東	44	167	6,546	-329	-1.68	-7.25	39.15	76.88	19,656
Guangxi 廣西	16	121	2,936	-446	-4.42	-8.19	24.30	46.11	10,103
Hainan 海南									
Southwest 西南	30	322	5,195	-992	-4.97	-10.43	16.14	52.38	19,965
Chongqing 重慶	15	498	8,955	-1,366	-4.59	-11.35	17.97	59.55	29,770
Sichuan 四川	14	141	1,463	-606	-5.88	-8.31	10.35	29.23	10,310
Guizhou 貴州	1	240	1,670	-860	-8.83	-29.55	6.96	70.12	9,740
Yunnan 雲南									
Tibet 西藏									
Northwest 西北	1	9	790	20	0.69	1.01	87.78	31.96	2,910
Shaanxi 陝西	1	9	790	20	0.69	1.01	87.78	31.96	2,910
Gansu 甘肅									
Qinghai 青海									
Ningxia 寧夏									
Xinjiang 新疆									

3762: Waterway Shipping Boats 內河船製造業

Year 年份	Number of firms 企業個數	Rate of change 每年變化 (%)	Number of employees 職工人數（人）	Rate of change 每年變化 (%)	Total revenue (mil. RMB) 總銷售收入（百萬元）	Rate of change 每年變化 (%)	Total profit (mil. RMB) 總利潤（百萬元）	Rate of change 每年變化 (%)
1993	403		72,128		3,479		3	
1994	467	15.88%	93,983	30.30%	3,761	8.13%	-11	-492.43%
1995	511	9.42%	94,188	0.22%	3,969	5.52%	-77	-596.55%
1996	408	-20.16%	76,401	-18.88%	2,993	-24.59%	-71	7.30%

3 Major products* 3種主要產品*	Output 產量	Sales volume 銷售量	Unit 單位
a) Steel Brage 鋼質駁船	2,600	2,522	ship 艘
b) Steel Tug 鋼質拖輪	82	81	ship 艘
c) Steel Cargo Ship 鋼質貨輪	1,157,972	1,169,552	weight ton 載重量噸

Top 10 firms by revenue (year founded) 收入排名前10家企業（創辦年份）	City 城市	Province 省	Telephone / fax 電話 / 傳真	Number of employees 職工人數	Ownership 產業所有權	Revenue ('000 RMB) 銷售收入（千元）	Profit ('000 RMB) (rank) 利潤（千元）（排名）	Total assets ('000 RMB) 總資產（千元）	Major products 主要產品
Taierzhuangqu Shipyard 台兒莊區造船廠(1982)	Zaozhuang 棗莊市	Shandong 山東省	(0632)6611677 (0632)6611677	396	Collectively-owned 集體	278,760	26360(1)	190,360	a
China Chang Jiang Shipping Corp. Jin Ling Shipyard 中國長江航運集團金陵船廠(1952)	Nanjing 南京市	Jiangsu 江蘇省	(025)8805115 (025)8801075	2,918	State-owned 國有	205,356	2000(7)	347,137	a,c
Jiangsu Yangzijiang Shipyard 江蘇揚子江船廠(1956)	Wuxi 無錫市	Jiangsu 江蘇省	(0510)6805360 (0510)6805360	988	Domestic JVs 聯營	177,874	2705(4)	202,969	a,c
Qingshan Shipyard of China Changjiang National Shipping Group 中國長江航運集團青山船廠(1949)	Wuhan 武漢市	Hubei 湖北省	(027)86515804 (027)86512463	4,433	State-owned 國有	147,571	2003(6)	548,880	o
Jiangsu Wuxi Shipyard 江蘇省無錫船廠(1956)	Wuxi 無錫市	Jiangsu 江蘇省	(0510)3708456 (0510)3703627	1,371	Domestic JVs 聯營	90,237	466(26)	124,728	a,b
Huaibin Water Transport Company 淮濱縣水運公司(1985)	Xinyang 信陽市	Henan 河南省		1,446	Collectively-owned 集體	82,310	4940(2)	40,310	o
Fujian Fishing Boat Repair & Building Factory 福建省漁輪修造廠(1956)	Fuzhou 福州市	Fujian 福建省	(0591)3266156 (0591)3266593	1,098	State-owned 國有	63,530	1250(14)	120,257	a,b
Jingjiang Ship's Work Engineering General Company 靖江船務工程總公司(1973)	Taizhou 泰州市	Jiangsu 江蘇省	(0523)4630658 (0523)4630611	390	Collectively-owned 集體	47,756	455(27)	59,058	o
Jiangdong Shipyard, Changjiang National Shipping Group Corp. 長江輪船總公司江東船廠(1945)	Wuhu 蕪湖市	Anhui 安徽省	(0553)5855661 (0553)5863606	1,885	State-owned 國有	44,743	-6976(183)	150,833	a
Guangdong Jiangmen Shipyard 廣東省江門船廠(1954)	Jiangmen 江門市	Guangdong 廣東省	(0750)3336531 (0750)3329088	824	State-owned 國有	43,259	1978(8)	76,828	c

Top 10 Cities by Production Output 產出排名前10位城市	Province 省	Market share 市場份額	Number of firms 企業個數
Nanjing 南京市	Jiangsu 江蘇省	10.60%	11
Wuhan 武漢市	Hubei 湖北省	9.21%	10
Zaozhuang 棗莊市	Shandong 山東省	9.01%	3
Taizhou 泰州市	Jiangsu 江蘇省	6.28%	24
Yangzhou 揚州市	Jiangsu 江蘇省	4.91%	25
Chongqing 重慶市	Chongqing 重慶市	4.58%	20
Guangzhou 廣州市	Guangdong 廣東省	4.25%	10
Yichang 宜昌市	Hubei 湖北省	3.17%	4
Xinyang 信陽市	Henan 河南省	3.03%	6
Wuxi 無錫市	Jiangsu 江蘇省	3.00%	10

10 Major Wholesalers 10家主要批發商	City 城市	Province 省	Telephone / Fax 電話 / 傳真
Liaoning Automobile Trade Group Corp. 遼寧省汽車貿易集團	Shenyang 瀋陽市	Liaoning 遼寧省	(024)23835494 (024)23838338
China Post and Telecommunication Equipment General Company 中國郵電器材總公司	Beijing 北京市	Beijing 北京市	(010)63523715 (010)63525935
Jiangsu Electromechanical Products General Company 江蘇省機電產品總公司	Nanjing 南京市	Jiangsu 江蘇省	(025)7713642 (025)7711036
Xi Nan Technology Import & Export Company 西南技術進出口公司	Chongqing 重慶市	Chongqing 重慶市	(023)63850185 (023)63850026
Changzhou Economic Technology Industrial Development Zone Tian Ming Trade Company 常州經濟技術產業開發區天明貿易公司	Changzhou 常州市	Jiangsu 江蘇省	(0519)8829882 (0519)8829882
Shanxi Mechanical Equipment Import & Export Company 山西省機械設備進出口公司	Taiyuan 太原市	Shanxi 山西省	(0351)4040713 (0351)4043981
Ningbo Five Mining Machinery Import & Export Company 寧波市五礦機械進出口公司	Ningbo 寧波市	Zhejiang 浙江省	(0574)7311255 (0574)7320322
Tianjin Jin Huan Electromechanical Complete Sets of Equipment Factory 天津市津環機電成套設備廠	Tianjin 天津市	Tianjin 天津市	(022)26371628
Yunnan Machinery Import & Export Company 雲南省機械進出口公司	Kunming 昆明市	Yunnan 雲南省	(0871)3164879 (0871)3136829
Tianjin Da Qiu Zhuang Yi Yuan Trade Center 天津市大丘莊億源商貿中心	Tianjin 天津市	Tianjin 天津市	(022)28899478 (022)28899046

*Also include sales by firms outside this industry.包括本行業以外廠家的銷售。"o" stands for "others". "o" 代表"其他產品"。

3763: Fishing Vessels 漁輪製造業

The industry accounts for 0.019% of the total revenue of China's industrial sector in 1996. The revenue growth rate of the industry is -6.9% from 1995, as compared to the growth rate of China's industrial sector, 9.51%. The rate of return on asset is -0.63%. 56.01% of all firms in the industry made a profit while 39.73% had negative returns. The top province in terms of the industry's revenue is Shandong, accounting for 50.22% of the total revenue.
本行業在1996年佔全行業總產值0.019%，行業年增長率為-6.9%（全國工業年增長率9.51%）。行業的資產回報率-0.63%，56.01%的企業盈利，39.73%的企業虧損。銷售收入最高的省份為山東省，佔本行業的50.22%。

	Total number of firms 企業總數	Total number of employees 職工總數	Total revenue (mil. RMB) 總銷售收入（百萬元）	Total profit (mil. RMB) 總利潤（百萬元）	Return on assets 資產利潤率 (%)	Return on equity 權益利潤率 (%)	Labour productivity ('000 RMB / worker) 勞動生產率（千元/人）	Debts / assets 資產負債率 (%)	Total assets (mil. RMB) 總資產（百萬元）
Industry Overall 行業總體	82	21,958	1,105	-11	-0.63	-1.93	50.32	67.28	1,688

	Number of firms 企業個數	Average number of employees 平均職工人數	Average revenue ('000 RMB) 平均銷售收入（千元）	Average profit ('000 RMB) 平均利潤（千元）	Return on assets 資產利潤率 (%)	Return on equity 權益利潤率 (%)	Labour productivity ('000 RMB / worker) 勞動生產率（千元/人）	Average debts / assets 平均資產負債率(%)	Average Total assets ('000 RMB) 平均總資產（千元）
By ownership 產業所有權									
State-owned 國有	23	701	29,565	-1,609	-2.83	-8.22	42.16	65.62	56,913
Collectively-owned 集體	54	103	7,723	515	8.12	33.10	74.86	75.47	6,348
Privately-owned 私有	2	37	286	-177	-8.10	-23.65	7.82	65.76	2,183
Domestic JVs 聯營									
Joint stock 股份制	1	121	3,508	-879	-6.85	-915.89	28.99	99.25	12,822
Foreign-funded 外資	1	27	3,815	-440	-7.80	-11.96	141.30	34.79	5,638
Overseas Chinese-funded 港澳台資	2	18	360	-76	-1.07	-1.18	20.02	8.67	7,075
By size 規模									
Large 大型	2	2,250	95,620	15,413	8.91	36.08	42.50	75.31	173,019
Medium 中型	4	1,305	82,228	-2,814	-2.42	-5.93	63.03	59.10	116,101
Small 小型	75	161	7,808	-408	-3.48	-11.04	48.52	68.48	11,713
By regional distribution 地區分布									
Central-North 華北	1	865	19,130	-4,760	-6.66	-21.59	22.12	69.13	71,420
Beijing 北京									
Tianjin 天津	1	865	19,130	-4,760	-6.66	-21.59	22.12	69.13	71,420
Hebei 河北									
Shanxi 山西									
Inner Mongolia 內蒙									
Northeast 東北	6	655	25,363	-548	-1.14	-2.90	38.72	60.54	47,975
Liaoning 遼寧	5	777	30,162	-664	-1.16	-2.96	38.81	60.71	57,056
Jilin 吉林	1	44	1,370	30	1.17	2.01	31.14	42.41	2,570
Heilongjiang 黑龍江									
Central East 華東	58	252	13,689	-44	-0.25	-0.78	54.36	68.46	17,979
Shanghai 上海	1	2,151	37,300	-14,900	-14.19	-510.27	17.34	97.22	105,020
Jiangsu 江蘇	12	242	9,574	-1,343	-8.54	-107.61	39.52	92.06	15,723
Zhejiang 浙江	16	159	4,411	-372	-4.33	-12.07	27.76	64.14	8,588
Anhui 安徽	3	163	1,840	-387	-10.40	-313.51	11.29	96.68	3,717
Fujian 福建	5	82	2,166	66	0.58	0.75	26.54	22.72	11,446
Jiangxi 江西									
Shandong 山東	21	291	26,423	1,678	6.49	16.23	90.83	60.03	25,870
Central-South 中南	16	160	8,737	-4	-0.02	-0.08	54.67	69.32	17,871
Henan 河南									
Hubei 湖北									
Hunan 湖南									
Guangdong 廣東	15	168	9,313	-2	-0.01	-0.03	55.32	69.19	19,003
Guangxi 廣西	1	32	100	-40	-4.49	57.14	3.13	107.87	890
Hainan 海南									
Southwest 西南	1								
Chongqing 重慶									
Sichuan 四川									
Guizhou 貴州	1								
Yunnan 雲南									
Tibet 西藏									
Northwest 西北									
Shaanxi 陝西									
Gansu 甘肅									
Qinghai 青海									
Ningxia 寧夏									
Xinjiang 新疆									

3763: Fishing Vessels 漁輪製造業

Year 年份	Number of firms 企業個數	Rate of change 每年變化 (%)	Number of employees 職工人數 (人)	Rate of change 每年變化 (%)	Total revenue (mil. RMB) 總銷售收入 (百萬元)	Rate of change 每年變化 (%)	Total profit (mil. RMB) 總利潤 (百萬元)	Rate of change 每年變化 (%)
1993	49		27,238		856		10	
1994	50	2.04%	22,565	-17.16%	614	-28.28%	1	-93.43%
1995	92	84.00%	23,395	3.68%	1,187	93.38%	6	803.84%
1996	82	-10.87%	21,958	-6.14%	1,105	-6.91%	-11	-294.72%

3 Major products* 3 種主要產品 *	Output 產量	Sales volume 銷售量	Unit 單位
a) Steel Fish-ship 鋼質漁輪	7,800	7,644	ship 艘
b) Motor Fish-boat 機動漁船	470	470	ship 艘
c) Steel Tug 鋼質拖輪	1,749	1,679	ton 滿載排水量噸

Top 10 firms by revenue (year founded) 收入排名前 10 家企業 (創辦年份)	City 城市	Province 省	Telephone / fax 電話 / 傳真	Number of employees 職工人數	Ownership 產業所有權	Revenue ('000 RMB) 銷售收入 (千元)	Profit ('000 RMB) (rank) 利潤 (千元) (排名)	Total assets ('000 RMB) 總資產 (千元)	Major products 主要產品
Rongcheng Shidao Shipping Industry Group Co. 榮成市石島船舶工業集團公司(1979)	Weihai 威海市	Shandong 山東省	(0896)7381310 (0896)7381310	717	Collectively-owned 集體	123,780	11180(1)	61,450	a
Shandong Huang Hai Shipyard 山東省黃海造船廠(1944)	Weihai 威海市	Shandong 山東省	(0896)7381401 (0896)7381401	1,327	State-owned 國有	122,378	2235(8)	112,647	a
China Fisheries Dalian Fishing Vessel Co. 中國水產大連漁輪公司(1907)	Dalian 大連市	Liaoning 遼寧省	(0411)2805654 (0411)2806768	2,328	State-owned 國有	119,635	84(20)	200,206	o
Guangzhou Fishing Vessel Factory 廣州漁輪廠(1953)	Guangzhou 廣州市	Guangdong 廣東省	(020)84200328 (020)84219845	1,630	State-owned 國有	87,238	359(15)	160,932	a,c
Qidong Fishing Boat General Factory 啟東漁輪總廠(1958)	Nantong 南通市	Jiangsu 江蘇省	(0513)3411527 (0513)3411527	1,405	State-owned 國有	63,227	-2054(40)	99,760	a
China National Fisheries Yantai Marine Fisheries Co. Fishing Vessel Shipyard 中國水產煙台海洋漁業公司漁輪修造廠(1949)	Yantai 煙台市	Shandong 山東省	(0535)6223324 (0535)6226378	1,216	State-owned 國有	50,573	-2922(42)	98,788	a
Ningbo Fishing Vessel Factory 寧波漁輪廠(1956)	Ningbo 寧波市	Zhejiang 浙江省	(0574)7332971 (0574)7332978	1,033	State-owned 國有	44,179	-3567(44)	61,774	a,c
Wendeng Shipyard 文登市造船廠(1958)	Weihai 威海市	Shandong 山東省	(0896)8771085 (0896)8771085	263	State-owned 國有	42,680	7200(2)	41,960	a,b
Shanghai Fishing Vessel Factory 上海漁輪廠(1951)	Shanghai 上海市	Shanghai 上海市	(021)65432560 (021)65430496	2,044	State-owned 國有	37,295	-14900(47)	105,017	a
Development Zone Nanhai Shipbuilding General Company 開發區南海造船總公司(1993)	Maoming 茂名市	Guangdong 廣東省		325	Collectively-owned 集體	30,152	2673(6)	38,745	b

Top 10 Cities by Production Output 產出排名前 10 位城市	Province 省	Market share 市場份額	Number of firms 企業個數
Weihai 威海市	Shandong 山東省	30.61%	17
Dalian 大連市	Liaoning 遼寧省	10.41%	5
Nantong 南通市	Jiangsu 江蘇省	7.09%	6
Yantai 煙台市	Shandong 山東省	7.01%	3
Suzhou 蘇州市	Jiangsu 江蘇省	6.39%	2
Guangzhou 廣州市	Guangdong 廣東省	5.32%	2
Ningbo 寧波市	Zhejiang 浙江省	4.72%	4
Taizhou 臺州市	Zhejiang 浙江省	4.59%	6
Yangjiang 陽江市	Guangdong 廣東省	4.09%	9
Maoming 茂名市	Guangdong 廣東省	2.56%	1

10 Major Wholesalers 10 家主要批發商	City 城市	Province 省	Telephone / Fax 電話 / 傳真
Liaoning Automobile Trade Group Corp. 遼寧省汽車貿易集團	Shenyang 瀋陽市	Liaoning 遼寧省	(024)23835494 (024)23838338
China Post and Telecommunication Equipment General Company 中國郵電器材總公司	Beijing 北京市	Beijing 北京市	(010)63523715 (010)63525935
Jiangsu Electromechanical Products General Company 江蘇省機電產品總公司	Nanjing 南京市	Jiangsu 江蘇省	(025)7713642 (025)7711036
Xi Nan Technology Import & Export Company 西南技術進出口公司	Chongqing 重慶市	Chongqing 重慶市	(023)63850185 (023)63850026
Changzhou Economic Technology Industrial Development Zone Tian Ming Trade Company 常州經濟技術產業開發區天明貿易公司	Changzhou 常州市	Jiangsu 江蘇省	(0519)8829882 (0519)8829882
Shanxi Mechanical Equipment Import & Export Company 山西省機械設備進出口公司	Taiyuan 太原市	Shanxi 山西省	(0351)4040713 (0351)4043981
Ningbo Five Mining Machinery Import & Export Company 寧波市五礦機械進出口公司	Ningbo 寧波市	Zhejiang 浙江省	(0574)7311255 (0574)7320322
Tianjin Jin Huan Electromechanical Complete Sets of Equipment Factory 天津市津環機電成套設備廠	Tianjin 天津市	Tianjin 天津市	(022)26371628
Yunnan Machinery Import & Export Company 雲南省機械進出口公司	Kunming 昆明市	Yunnan 雲南省	(0871)3164879 (0871)3136829
Tianjin Da Qiu Zhuang Yi Yuan Trade Center 天津市大丘莊億源商貿中心	Tianjin 天津市	Tianjin 天津市	(022)28899478 (022)28899046

*Also include sales by firms outside this industry.包括本行業以外廠家的銷售。"o" stands for "others". "o" 代表 "其他產品"。

3764: Shipping Machinery and Equipment 船舶機械設備製造業

The industry accounts for 0.055% of the total revenue of China's industrial sector in 1996. The revenue growth rate of the industry is 10.7% from 1995, as compared to the growth rate of China's industrial sector, 9.51%. The rate of return on asset is -0.22%. 59.45% of all firms in the industry made a profit while 31.58% had negative returns. The top province in terms of the industry's revenue is Jiangsu, accounting for 41.99% of the total revenue.
本行業在1996年佔全行業總產值0.055%，行業年增長率為10.7%（全國工業年增長率9.51%）。行業的資產回報率-0.22%，59.45%的企業盈利，31.58%的企業虧損。銷售收入最高的省份為江蘇省，佔本行業的41.99%。

	Total number of firms 企業總數	Total number of employees 職工總數	Total revenue (mil. RMB) 總銷售收入（百萬元）	Total profit (mil. RMB) 總利潤（百萬元）	Return on assets 資產利潤率 (%)	Return on equity 權益利潤率 (%)	Labour productivity ('000 RMB / worker) 勞動生產率（千元/人）	Debts / assets 資產負債率 (%)	Total assets (mil. RMB) 總資產（百萬元）
Industry Overall 行業總體	128	55,522	3,200	-14	-0.22	-0.72	57.63	69.53	6,166

	Number of firms 企業個數	Average number of employees 平均職工人數	Average revenue ('000 RMB) 平均銷售收入（千元）	Average profit ('000 RMB) 平均利潤（千元）	Return on assets 資產利潤率 (%)	Return on equity 權益利潤率 (%)	Labour productivity ('000 RMB / worker) 勞動生產率（千元/人）	Average debts / assets 平均資產負債率(%)	Average Total assets ('000 RMB) 平均總資產（千元）
By ownership 產業所有權									
State-owned 國有	50	978	43,860	-920	-0.96	-2.84	44.83	66.29	96,220
Collectively-owned 集體	70	102	12,989	411	2.35	15.26	127.46	84.63	17,517
Privately-owned 私有									
Domestic JVs 聯營	2	68	5,195	18	0.57	1.08	76.97	46.63	3,048
Joint stock 股份制									
Foreign-funded 外資	5	145	16,769	648	2.71	5.23	115.97	48.14	23,855
Overseas Chinese-funded 港澳台資	2	13	1,915	-15	-0.79	-0.84	147.29	5.32	1,884
By size 規模									
Large 大型	10	3,050	154,594	120	0.04	0.12	50.68	68.31	318,010
Medium 中型	16	819	40,852	28	0.03	0.08	49.85	59.56	84,926
Small 小型	100	120	10,007	-157	-0.96	-4.86	83.19	80.23	16,274
By regional distribution 地區分布									
Central-North 華北	1								
Beijing 北京	1								
Tianjin 天津									
Hebei 河北									
Shanxi 山西									
Inner Mongolia 內蒙									
Northeast 東北	10	254	32,210	1,596	3.38	9.01	126.76	62.47	47,187
Liaoning 遼寧	10	254	32,210	1,596	3.38	9.01	126.76	62.47	47,187
Jilin 吉林									
Heilongjiang 黑龍江									
Central East 華東	71	284	24,925	417	0.99	3.25	87.87	69.57	42,222
Shanghai 上海	7	267	10,019	-1,130	-5.34	-19.16	37.56	72.13	21,156
Jiangsu 江蘇	37	295	36,316	884	1.44	4.85	123.03	70.32	61,489
Zhejiang 浙江	10	49	2,393	61	2.12	4.94	49.04	57.16	2,883
Anhui 安徽	6	296	10,852	137	0.70	1.83	36.70	61.67	19,470
Fujian 福建									
Jiangxi 江西	6	536	13,797	-755	-2.01	-7.41	25.76	72.85	37,512
Shandong 山東	5	375	36,802	1,584	3.89	10.21	98.14	61.96	40,768
Central-South 中南	41	560	19,570	-1,465	-3.11	-10.47	34.93	70.31	47,108
Henan 河南	3	2,367	47,987	-15,880	-10.01	-50.93	20.27	80.35	158,690
Hubei 湖北	23	528	23,432	-263	-0.55	-1.70	44.41	67.71	48,086
Hunan 湖南	3	34	1,037				30.19	31.27	1,993
Guangdong 廣東	9	207	6,979	-431	-2.13	-10.64	33.79	80.00	20,249
Guangxi 廣西	3	590	17,857	-823	-1.53	-3.00	30.25	48.96	53,727
Hainan 海南									
Southwest 西南	4	959	25,238	-435	-0.56	-1.63	26.33	65.43	77,340
Chongqing 重慶	4	959	25,238	435	0.56	1.63	26.32	65.43	77,340
Sichuan 四川									
Guizhou 貴州									
Yunnan 雲南									
Tibet 西藏									
Northwest 西北	1	6,037	205,290	2,620	0.57	2.40	34.01	76.06	455,820
Shaanxi 陝西	1	6,037	205,290	2,620	0.57	2.40	34.01	76.06	455,820
Gansu 甘肅									
Qinghai 青海									
Ningxia 寧夏									
Xinjiang 新疆									

3764: Shipping Machinery and Equipment 船舶機械設備製造業

Year 年份	Number of firms 企業個數	Rate of change 每年變化 (%)	Number of employees 職工人數 (人)	Rate of change 每年變化 (%)	Total revenue (mil. RMB) 總銷售收入 (百萬元)	Rate of change 每年變化 (%)	Total profit (mil. RMB) 總利潤 (百萬元)	Rate of change 每年變化 (%)
1993	113		53,385		2,334		82	
1994	119	5.31%	51,025	-4.42%	2,411	3.32%	30	-63.53%
1995	127	6.72%	55,192	8.17%	2,892	19.93%	45	49.85%
1996	128	0.79%	55,522	0.60%	3,200	10.65%	-14	-131.41%

3 Major products* 3 種主要產品 *	Output 產量	Sales volume 銷售量	Unit 單位
a) Steel Fish-ship 鋼質漁輪	80,729	78,307	kw 千瓦

Top 10 firms by revenue (year founded) 收入排名前 10 家企業 (創辦年份)	City 城市	Province 省	Telephone / fax 電話 / 傳真	Number of employees 職工人數	Ownership 產業所有權	Revenue ('000 RMB) 銷售收入 (千元)	Profit ('000 RMB) (rank) 利潤 (千元) (排名)	Total assets ('000 RMB) 總資產 (千元)	Major products 主要產品
Jiangyin Zhen Hua Port Machinery Co. Ltd. 江陰振華港口機械有限公司(1994)	Wuxi 無錫市	Jiangsu 江蘇省	(0510)6803818 (0510)6809758	350	Collectively-owned 集體	620,160	22130(1)	848,312	o
Wuhan Marine Machinery Plant 武漢船用機械廠(1962)	Wuhan 武漢市	Hubei 湖北省	(027)86592030 (027)86591066	4,876	State-owned 國有	293,741	4148(5)	535,028	o
Dalian Marine Diesel Works 大連船用柴油機廠(1984)	Dalian 大連市	Liaoning 遼寧省	(0411)4414701 (0411)4417499	1,173	State-owned 國有	245,540	10029(2)	352,364	o
State Shannxi Diesel Engine Works 國營陜西柴油機廠(1959)	Xianyang 咸陽市	Shaanxi 陜西省	(0910)8822610 (0910)8822626	6,037	State-owned 國有	205,285	2621(10)	455,819	o
Zheng Mao Group Co. Ltd. 正茂集團有限責任公司(1978)	Zhenjiang 鎮江市	Jiangsu 江蘇省	(0511)4423911 (0511)4421210	386	State-owned 國有	171,830	4900(4)	419,610	o
Nanjing Luzhou Machine Works 南京綠洲機器廠(1960)	Nanjing 南京市	Jiangsu 江蘇省	(025)6700476 (025)6700325	3,242	State-owned 國有	167,221	1572(14)	311,852	o
Chinese-foreign Joint Venture Jiangsu Zhenjiang Anchor Chain Co. Ltd. 中外合資江蘇鎮江錨鏈有限公司(1991)	Zhenjiang 鎮江市	Jiangsu 江蘇省	(0511)4423911 (0511)4421210	346	Foreign-funded 外資	94,010	5810(3)	164,720	o
Rongcheng Hai Da Shipyard 榮成市海達造船廠(1967)	Weihai 威海市	Shandong 山東省	(0896)7661105	507	State-owned 國有	71,357	3048(7)	43,832	a
Xin Zhong Power Machine Plant 新中動力機廠(1925)	Shanghai 上海市	Shanghai 上海市	(021)56651100 (021)56652294	1,707	State-owned 國有	65,853	-7901(77)	142,262	o
Qingdao Ahchor Chain Factory 青島錨鏈廠(1981)	Qingdao 青島市	Shandong 山東省	(0532)8513117 (0532)8511501	540	State-owned 國有	60,786	2360(12)	68,339	o

Top 10 Cities by Production Output 產出排名前 10 位城市	Province 省	Market share 市場份額	Number of firms 企業個數
Wuxi 無錫市	Jiangsu 江蘇省	19.86%	9
Zhenjiang 鎮江市	Jiangsu 江蘇省	12.87%	7
Wuhan 武漢市	Hubei 湖北省	11.20%	6
Chongqing 重慶市	Chongqing 重慶市	8.75%	12
Shanghai 上海市	Shanghai 上海市	7.59%	33
Xianyang 咸陽市	Shaanxi 陜西省	7.03%	1
Luoyang 洛陽市	Henan 河南省	5.59%	2
Yichang 宜昌市	Hubei 湖北省	3.76%	1
Dalian 大連市	Liaoning 遼寧省	3.49%	7
Jiujiang 九江市	Jiangxi 江西省	2.42%	4

10 Major Wholesalers 10 家主要批發商	City 城市	Province 省	Telephone / Fax 電話 / 傳真
Liaoning Automobile Trade Group Corp. 遼寧省汽車貿易集團	Shenyang 瀋陽市	Liaoning 遼寧省	(024)23835494 (024)23838338
China Post and Telecommunication Equipment General Company 中國郵電器材總公司	Beijing 北京市	Beijing 北京市	(010)63523715 (010)63525935
Jiangsu Electromechanical Products General Company 江蘇省機電產品總公司	Nanjing 南京市	Jiangsu 江蘇省	(025)7713642 (025)7711036
Xi Nan Technology Import & Export Company 西南技術進出口公司	Chongqing 重慶市	Chongqing 重慶市	(023)63850185 (023)63850026
Changzhou Economic Technology Industrial Development Zone Tian Ming Trade Company 常州經濟技術產業開發區天明貿易公司	Changzhou 常州市	Jiangsu 江蘇省	(0519)8829882 (0519)8829882
Shanxi Mechanical Equipment Import & Export Company 山西省機械設備進出口公司	Taiyuan 太原市	Shanxi 山西省	(0351)4040713 (0351)4043981
Ningbo Five Mining Machinery Import & Export Company 寧波市五礦機械進出口公司	Ningbo 寧波市	Zhejiang 浙江省	(0574)7311255 (0574)7320322
Tianjin Jin Huan Electromechanical Complete Sets of Equipment Factory 天津市津環機電成套設備廠	Tianjin 天津市	Tianjin 天津市	(022)26371628
Yunnan Machinery Import & Export Company 雲南省機械進出口公司	Kunming 昆明市	Yunnan 雲南省	(0871)3164879 (0871)3136829
Tianjin Da Qiu Zhuang Yi Yuan Trade Center 天津市大丘莊億源商貿中心	Tianjin 天津市	Tianjin 天津市	(022)28899478 (022)28899046

*Also include sales by firms outside this industry.包括本行業以外廠家的銷售。"o" stands for "others". "o" 代表"其他產品"。

3781: Railroad Equipment Repairing 鐵路運輸設備修理業

The industry accounts for 0.072% of the total revenue of China's industrial sector in 1996. The revenue growth rate of the industry is -4.1% from 1995, as compared to the growth rate of China's industrial sector, 9.51%. The rate of return on asset is -1.06%. 80.53% of all firms in the industry made a profit while 19.47% had negative returns. The top province in terms of the industry's revenue is Jiangsu, accounting for 21.07% of the total revenue.

本行業在1996年佔全行業總產值0.072%，行業年增長率為-4.1%（全國工業年增長率9.51%）。行業的資產回報率-1.06%，80.53%的企業盈利，19.47%的企業虧損。銷售收入最高的省份為江蘇省，佔本行業的21.07%。

	Total number of firms 企業總數	Total number of employees 職工總數	Total revenue (mil. RMB) 總銷售收入（百萬元）	Total profit (mil. RMB) 總利潤（百萬元）	Return on assets 資產利潤率 (%)	Return on equity 權益利潤率 (%)	Labour productivity ('000 RMB / worker) 勞動生產率（千元/人）	Debts / assets 資產負債率 (%)	Total assets (mil. RMB) 總資產（百萬元）
Industry Overall 行業總體	194	116,486	4,172	-84	-1.06	-1.66	35.82	36.14	7,943

	Number of firms 企業個數	Average number of employees 平均職工人數	Average revenue ('000 RMB) 平均銷售收入（千元）	Average profit ('000 RMB) 平均利潤（千元）	Return on assets 資產利潤率 (%)	Return on equity 權益利潤率 (%)	Labour productivity ('000 RMB / worker) 勞動生產率（千元/人）	Average debts / assets 平均資產負債率(%)	Average Total assets ('000 RMB) 平均總資產（千元）
By ownership 產業所有權									
State-owned 國有	70	1,434	54,829	-1,400	-1.29	-1.98	38.25	34.63	108,129
Collectively-owned 集體	123	130	2,643	112	3.83	11.47	20.28	66.55	2,928
Privately-owned 私有									
Domestic JVs 聯營									
Joint stock 股份制	1	86	9,267	190	1.30	4.75	107.76	72.56	14,539
Foreign-funded 外資									
Overseas Chinese-funded 港澳台資									
By size 規模									
Large 大型	16	5,686	208,379	-11,048	-2.49	-3.80	36.65	34.35	442,837
Medium 中型	1	1,016	49,998	6,889	11.64	15.34	49.21	24.09	59,177
Small 小型	177	138	4,454	485	10.75	22.86	32.18	52.98	4,515
By regional distribution 地區分布									
Central-North 華北	34	449	19,507	173	0.58	0.93	43.49	37.99	29,923
Beijing 北京	2	5	150	-5	-1.89	-100.00	30.00	98.11	265
Tianjin 天津	3	207	12,827	1,673	20.92	43.05	62.06	51.42	8,000
Hebei 河北	7	887	39,586	500	0.94	1.31	44.64	28.59	53,356
Shanxi 山西	5	1,555	66,968	-558	-0.47	-0.82	43.08	43.03	119,634
Inner Mongolia 內蒙	17	38	736	9	0.71	1.28	19.58	44.58	1,247
Northeast 東北	99	451	13,759	-329	-1.12	-1.84	30.52	39.18	29,360
Liaoning 遼寧	69	326	11,300	101	0.48	0.74	34.64	35.71	21,159
Jilin 吉林	14	477	9,434	-1,849	-7.74	-17.15	19.79	54.86	23,884
Heilongjiang 黑龍江	16	966	28,148	-853	-1.23	-2.01	29.15	39.02	69,514
Central East 華東	26	459	33,880	563	1.47	2.33	73.79	36.98	38,322
Shanghai 上海	3	47	670	-233	-7.76	-15.98	14.26	51.44	3,007
Jiangsu 江蘇	5	2,353	175,772	3,070	1.55	2.46	74.69	36.85	197,468
Zhejiang 浙江									
Anhui 安徽									
Fujian 福建	2								
Jiangxi 江西	9								
Shandong 山東	7	4							
Central-South 中南	16	1,787	47,753	-778	-0.69	-0.96	26.73	27.91	112,476
Henan 河南	2	3,658	111,260	195	0.09	0.12	30.42	26.25	214,265
Hubei 湖北	4	3,085	64,225	513	0.46	0.81	20.82	42.98	110,888
Hunan 湖南	5								
Guangdong 廣東	2	1,318	56,675	-980	-0.44	-0.48	43.00	8.64	223,375
Guangxi 廣西	3	2,099	57,093	-4,310	-2.69	-4.04	27.20	33.39	160,260
Hainan 海南									
Southwest 西南	9	1,046	37,807	-2,791	-3.54	-5.41	36.14	34.62	78,917
Chongqing 重慶									
Sichuan 四川	6	1,353	46,188	-4,787	-4.48	-6.94	34.14	35.39	106,755
Guizhou 貴州									
Yunnan 雲南	3	432	21,043	1,200	5.16	7.12	48.67	27.52	23,240
Tibet 西藏									
Northwest 西北	10	666	16,114	-3,452	-6.73	-12.16	24.19	44.63	51,283
Shaanxi 陝西	7	80	2,417	51	2.67	6.56	30.11	59.20	1,926
Gansu 甘肅	1	6,034	142,500	-34,980	-7.03	-12.62	23.62	44.26	497,380
Qinghai 青海									
Ningxia 寧夏									
Xinjiang 新疆	2	33	860	50	5.08	8.20	26.06	38.58	985

3781: Railroad Equipment Repairing 鐵路運輸設備修理業

Year 年份	Number of firms 企業個數	Rate of change 每年變化 (%)	Number of employees 職工人數（人）	Rate of change 每年變化 (%)	Total revenue (mil. RMB) 總銷售收入（百萬元）	Rate of change 每年變化 (%)	Total profit (mil. RMB) 總利潤（百萬元）	Rate of change 每年變化 (%)
1993	112		110,898		4,090		85	
1994	117	4.46%	121,985	10.00%	4,063	-0.67%	-13	-115.54%
1995	178	52.14%	128,558	5.39%	4,352	7.11%	-62	-363.70%
1996	194	8.99%	116,486	-9.39%	4,172	-4.14%	-84	-36.46%

3 Major products* 3 種主要產品 *	Output 產量	Sales volume 銷售量	Unit 單位

Top 10 firms by revenue (year founded) 收入排名前 10 家企業 (創辦年份)	City 城市	Province 省	Telephone / fax 電話 / 傳真	Number of employees 職工人數	Ownership 產業所有權	Revenue ('000 RMB) 銷售收入（千元）	Profit ('000 RMB) (rank) 利潤（千元）（排名）	Total assets ('000 RMB) 總資產（千元）	Major products 主要產品
Qishuyan Locomotive and Rolling Stock Works 戚墅堰機車車輛廠(1905)	Changzhou 常州市	Jiangsu 江蘇省	(0519)8771711 (0519)8770358	10,717	State-owned 國有	823,330	13590(1)	940,890	o
Shenyang Locomotive Vehicle Plant 瀋陽機車車輛廠(1928)	Shenyang 瀋陽市	Liaoning 遼寧省	(024)86872257 (024)86878730	12,638	State-owned 國有	482,450	-12830(61)	1,088,510	o
Taiyuan Locomotive Vehicle Plant 太原機車車輛廠(1898)	Taiyuan 太原市	Shanxi 山西省	(0351)3045411 (0351)3049563	7,528	State-owned 國有	325,190	-7980(58)	569,750	o
Harbin Rolling Stock Works 哈爾濱車輛廠(1903)	Harbin 哈爾濱市	Heilongjiang 黑龍江省	(0451)6467961 (0451)4211093	9,502	State-owned 國有	304,920	-4840(57)	739,880	o
Shijiazhuang Rolling Stock Works 石家莊車輛廠(1905)	Shijiazhuang 石家莊市	Hebei 河北省	(0311)7023570 (0311)7023570	5,843	State-owned 國有	271,750	2460(6)	367,740	o
Chengdu Locomotive Vehicle Plant 成都機車車輛廠(1954)	Chengdu 成都市	Sichuan 四川省	(028)3337501 (028)3338984	7,079	State-owned 國有	255,380	-28080(63)	618,380	o
Wuhan Jiangan Rolling Stock Works 武漢江岸車輛廠(1901)	Wuhan 武漢市	Hubei 湖北省	(027)82873218 (027)82872261	7,241	State-owned 國有	232,360	1670(11)	401,580	o
Liuzhou Locomotive Vehicle Plant 柳州機車車輛廠(1965)	Liuzhou 柳州市	Guangxi 廣西	(0772)35261 (0772)3835048	5,912	State-owned 國有	161,380	-11920(60)	467,180	o
Lanzhou Locomotive Factory 蘭州機車廠(1964)	Lanzhou 蘭州市	Gansu 甘肅省	(0931)2333490 (0931)2337279	6,155	State-owned 國有	142,500	-34980(64)	497,380	o
Mudanjiang Locomotive Factory 牡丹江機車廠(1940)	Mudanjiang 牡丹江市	Heilongjiang 黑龍江省	(0453)6331194 (0453)6331008	5,009	State-owned 國有	114,450	-10000(59)	337,230	o

Top 10 Cities by Production Output 產出排名前 10 位城市	Province 省	Market share 市場份額	Number of firms 企業個數
Changzhou 常州市	Jiangsu 江蘇省	15.91%	3
Shenyang 瀋陽市	Liaoning 遼寧省	12.11%	20
Beijing 北京市	Beijing 北京市	11.41%	3
Taiyuan 太原市	Shanxi 山西省	7.95%	12
Shijiazhuang 石家莊市	Hebei 河北省	6.37%	5
Chengdu 成都市	Sichuan 四川省	5.77%	4
Luoyang 洛陽市	Henan 河南省	5.62%	3
Wuhan 武漢市	Hubei 湖北省	5.37%	5
Liuzhou 柳州市	Guangxi 廣西	3.43%	2
Lanzhou 蘭州市	Gansu 甘肅省	3.01%	1

10 Major Wholesalers 10 家主要批發商	City 城市	Province 省	Telephone / Fax 電話 / 傳真

*Also include sales by firms outside this industry.包括本行業以外廠家的銷售。"o" stands for "others". "o" 代表"其他產品"。

3782: Automobile Repairing 汽車修理業

The industry accounts for 0.239% of the total revenue of China's industrial sector in 1996. The revenue growth rate of the industry is 14.2% from 1995, as compared to the growth rate of China's industrial sector, 9.51%. The rate of return on asset is 0.93%. 69.03% of all firms in the industry made a profit while 24.46% had negative returns. The top province in terms of the industry's revenue is Shandong, accounting for 10.71% of the total revenue.
本行業在1996年佔全行業總產值0.239%，行業年增長率為14.2%（全國工業年增長率9.51%）。行業的資產回報率0.93%，69.03%的企業盈利，24.46%的企業虧損。銷售收入最高的省份為山東省，佔本行業的10.71%。

	Total number of firms 企業總數	Total number of employees 職工總數	Total revenue (mil. RMB) 總銷售收入（百萬元）	Total profit (mil. RMB) 總利潤（百萬元）	Return on assets 資產利潤率 (%)	Return on equity 權益利潤率 (%)	Labour productivity ('000 RMB / worker) 勞動生產率（千元/人）	Debts / assets 資產負債率 (%)	Total assets (mil. RMB) 總資產（百萬元）
Industry Overall 行業總體	8,409	349,873	13,882	172	0.93	2.52	39.68	63.24	18,573

	Number of firms 企業個數	Average number of employees 平均職工人數	Average revenue ('000 RMB) 平均銷售收入（千元）	Average profit ('000 RMB) 平均利潤（千元）	Return on assets 資產利潤率 (%)	Return on equity 權益利潤率 (%)	Labour productivity ('000 RMB / worker) 勞動生產率（千元/人）	Average debts / assets 平均資產負債率(%)	Average Total assets ('000 RMB) 平均總資產（千元）
By ownership 產業所有權									
State-owned 國有	1,932	68	2,058	-23	-0.62	-1.67	30.45	62.91	3,769
Collectively-owned 集體	5,910	32	1,280	38	3.15	9.37	39.44	66.39	1,201
Privately-owned 私有	24	22	1,128	70	5.01	15.50	51.07	67.69	1,392
Domestic JVs 聯營	57	58	4,403	218	2.74	7.29	76.17	62.41	7,944
Joint stock 股份制	53	73	3,895	117	2.54	7.89	53.10	67.77	4,609
Foreign-funded 外資	182	45	3,675	-97	-1.28	-2.86	82.16	55.29	7,589
Overseas Chinese-funded 港澳台資	243	53	4,836	-36	-0.42	-1.01	91.30	58.43	8,491
By size 規模									
Large 大型	3	1,346	158,349	9,347	3.24	7.79	117.64	58.38	288,268
Medium 中型	25	536	25,647	-231	-0.44	-1.10	47.82	60.08	52,594
Small 小型	8,303	40	1,537	18	0.91	2.52	38.38	63.75	1,974
By regional distribution 地區分布									
Central-North 華北	1,756	35	1,170	-4	-0.24	-0.66	33.35	63.35	1,860
Beijing 北京	707	24	1,564	56	3.01	7.39	66.34	59.27	1,867
Tianjin 天津	339	32	823	8	0.69	1.41	25.49	51.26	1,192
Hebei 河北	377	38	1,095	29	1.92	5.88	28.83	67.26	1,495
Shanxi 山西	140	103	1,089	-449	-8.24	-28.61	10.63	71.20	5,453
Inner Mongolia 內蒙	193	28	541	9	0.77	2.85	19.60	73.00	1,118
Northeast 東北	1,432	33	1,046	20	1.82	5.50	32.15	66.83	1,102
Liaoning 遼寧	822	31	1,109	28	2.37	7.33	35.85	67.64	1,197
Jilin 吉林	259	28	665	-16	-1.41	-3.78	23.98	62.59	1,115
Heilongjiang 黑龍江	351	40	1,178	27	3.12	9.82	29.62	68.23	871
Central East 華東	2,186	47	2,484	80	2.77	7.37	52.83	62.46	2,897
Shanghai 上海	290	56	3,567	184	5.05	10.17	63.83	50.33	3,633
Jiangsu 江蘇	369	49	2,938	76	2.06	6.59	60.26	68.75	3,683
Zhejiang 浙江	247	43	2,222	48	1.71	4.96	51.26	65.43	2,789
Anhui 安徽	200	53	3,836	134	6.03	12.22	71.98	50.63	2,214
Fujian 福建	228	25	684	13	1.05	2.38	27.76	55.84	1,224
Jiangxi 江西	347	41	1,020	-20	-1.33	-4.65	25.15	71.33	1,494
Shandong 山東	505	55	2,944	118	2.98	8.48	53.95	64.80	3,945
Central-South 中南	1,788	43	1,712	-14	-0.54	-1.52	40.20	64.80	2,629
Henan 河南	328	46	1,258		-0.01	-0.05	27.10	72.77	2,078
Hubei 湖北	236	51	1,902	11	0.59	2.05	37.50	71.52	1,948
Hunan 湖南	394	35	1,025	-9	-0.85	-2.41	29.66	64.77	1,036
Guangdong 廣東	569	44	2,585	-17	-0.38	-1.04	59.30	63.36	4,363
Guangxi 廣西	208	35	1,014	-7	-0.48	-1.11	28.96	57.24	1,526
Hainan 海南	53	61	2,156	-250	-3.78	-8.92	35.12	57.59	6,615
Southwest 西南	796	42	1,352	6	0.36	0.92	32.20	60.68	1,752
Chongqing 重慶	174	39	839	-2	-0.25	-0.74	21.60	66.68	876
Sichuan 四川	300	44	1,598	0	-0.02	-0.05	36.46	62.96	1,708
Guizhou 貴州	197	30	770	22	2.21	5.33	25.53	58.51	990
Yunnan 雲南	111	57	2,425	39	1.13	2.85	42.57	60.43	3,433
Tibet 西藏	14	74	2,126	-206	-1.88	-3.79	28.70	50.42	10,936
Northwest 西北	451	65	1,687	-8	-0.29	-0.71	25.97	59.48	2,885
Shaanxi 陝西	176	53	2,075	55	2.25	5.90	39.31	61.85	2,439
Gansu 甘肅	105	67	1,379	7	0.24	0.57	20.58	58.88	2,913
Qinghai 青海	35	99	1,666	-170	-5.11	-19.41	16.80	73.66	3,327
Ningxia 寧夏	29	35	1,168	60	2.40	4.80	33.56	49.99	2,516
Xinjiang 新疆	106	80	1,499	-94	-2.64	-5.82	18.71	54.72	3,552

3782: Automobile Repairing 汽車修理業

Year 年份	Number of firms 企業個數	Rate of change 每年變化 (%)	Number of employees 職工人數 (人)	Rate of change 每年變化 (%)	Total revenue (mil. RMB) 總銷售收入 (百萬元)	Rate of change 每年變化 (%)	Total profit (mil. RMB) 總利潤 (百萬元)	Rate of change 每年變化 (%)
1993	6,071		364,368		9,796		463	
1994	6,745	11.10%	372,482	2.23%	10,504	7.22%	337	-27.19%
1995	7,701	14.17%	385,250	3.43%	12,159	15.75%	216	-35.99%
1996	8,409	9.19%	349,873	-9.18%	13,882	14.17%	172	-20.32%

3 Major products* 3 種主要產品 *	Output 產量	Sales volume 銷售量	Unit 單位

Top 10 firms by revenue (year founded) 收入排名前 10 家企業 (創辦年份)	City 城市	Province 省	Telephone / fax 電話 / 傳真	Number of employees 職工人數	Ownership 產業所有權	Revenue ('000 RMB) 銷售收入 (千元)	Profit ('000 RMB) (rank) 利潤 (千元) (排名)	Total assets ('000 RMB) 總資產 (千元)	Major products 主要產品
Beijing Automobile Repair Company 北京市汽車修理公司(1952)	Beijing 北京市	Beijing 北京市	(010)64604579 (010)64604579	98	State-owned 國有	311,856	20018(1)	439,439	o
Fengyang Automobile Break Market 鳳陽縣汽車拆舊市場(1989)	Chuzhou 滁州市	Anhui 安徽省	(0551)7286086	1,351	Collectively-owned 集體	228,300	0(1203)	64,150	o
Jiangyin West Suburb Traffic Automobile Repair Factory 江陰市西郊交通汽修廠(1987)	Wuxi 無錫市	Jiangsu 江蘇省	(0510)6805657	530	Collectively-owned 集體	130,848	2261(47)	134,220	o
Beijing Yan Jing Automobile Factory 北京燕京汽車廠(1950)	Beijing 北京市	Beijing 北京市	(010)63016655 (010)63030843	2,313	State-owned 國有	126,039	-6233(1595)	203,844	o
Shenzhen Huayang Automobile Enterprise Co. Ltd. 深圳華陽汽車企業有限公司(1983)	Shenzhen 深圳市	Guangdong 廣東省	(0755)2430434 (0755)2430436	293	Foreign-funded 外資	113,391	6603(5)	133,883	o
Shandong Shi Li Group Company 山東實力集團公司(1993)	Ji'nan 濟南市	Shandong 山東省	(0531)7984131	700	Collectively-owned 集體	92,006	2703(31)	52,080	o
Chang Anxian Forestry Automobile Repair & Assembly Factory 長安縣林業汽車修配廠(1978)	Xi'an 西安市	Shaanxi 陝西省	(029)5292640	280	State-owned 國有	89,100	71(724)	43,667	o
Yunnan Yun Qi Industrial Co. Ltd. 雲南雲汽實業有限公司(1960)	Kunming 昆明市	Yunnan 雲南省	(0871)8182640 (0871)8182640	867	State-owned 國有	89,049	4295(15)	139,516	o
Shanghai Hang Tou Vehicle Repair & Building Factory 上海市航頭車輛修造廠(1985)	Shanghai 上海市	Shanghai 上海市	(021)58221281	188	Collectively-owned 集體	79,820	1412(85)	51,894	o
Ji'nan Hua Da Automobile Repair & Assembly General Factory 濟南華達汽車修配總廠(1982)	Ji'nan 濟南市	Shandong 山東省	(0531)8936342 (0531)8932614	845	Collectively-owned 集體	78,260	2559(37)	107,580	o

Top 10 Cities by Production Output 產出排名前 10 位城市	Province 省	Market share 市場份額	Number of firms 企業個數
Shanghai 上海市	Shanghai 上海市	10.84%	925
Beijing 北京市	Beijing 北京市	8.77%	648
Guangzhou 廣州市	Guangdong 廣東省	4.29%	442
Tianjin 天津市	Tianjin 天津市	2.46%	438
Hangzhou 杭州市	Zhejiang 浙江省	2.06%	141
Dalian 大連市	Liaoning 遼寧省	1.96%	188
Shenzhen 深圳市	Guangdong 廣東省	1.77%	93
Wuxi 無錫市	Jiangsu 江蘇省	1.66%	113
Kunming 昆明市	Yunnan 雲南省	1.59%	105
Weifang 濰坊市	Shandong 山東省	1.55%	80

10 Major Wholesalers 10 家主要批發商	City 城市	Province 省	Telephone / Fax 電話 / 傳真

*Also include sales by firms outside this industry.包括本行業以外廠家的銷售。"o" stands for "others". "o" 代表 "其他產品"。

3783: Motorcycle Repairing 摩托車修理業

The industry accounts for 0.002% of the total revenue of China's industrial sector in 1996. The revenue growth rate of the industry is 149.5% from 1995, as compared to the growth rate of China's industrial sector, 9.51%. The rate of return on asset is 4.90%. 69.66% of all firms in the industry made a profit while 10.34% had negative returns. The top province in terms of the industry's revenue is Shandong, accounting for 26.74% of the total revenue.
本行業在1996年佔全行業總產值0.002%，行業年增長率為149.5%（全國工業年增長率9.51%）。行業的資產回報率4.90%，69.66%的企業盈利，10.34%的企業虧損。銷售收入最高的省份為山東省，佔本行業的26.74%。

	Total number of firms 企業總數	Total number of employees 職工總數	Total revenue (mil. RMB) 總銷售收入（百萬元）	Total profit (mil. RMB) 總利潤（百萬元）	Return on assets 資產利潤率 (%)	Return on equity 權益利潤率 (%)	Labour productivity ('000 RMB / worker) 勞動生產率（千元/人）	Debts / assets 資產負債率 (%)	Total assets (mil. RMB) 總資產（百萬元）
Industry Overall 行業總體	147	1,485	93	3	4.90	10.84	62.63	54.81	53

	Number of firms 企業個數	Average number of employees 平均職工人數	Average revenue ('000 RMB) 平均銷售收入（千元）	Average profit ('000 RMB) 平均利潤（千元）	Return on assets 資產利潤率 (%)	Return on equity 權益利潤率 (%)	Labour productivity ('000 RMB / worker) 勞動生產率（千元/人）	Average debts / assets 平均資產負債率(%)	Average Total assets ('000 RMB) 平均總資產（千元）
By ownership 產業所有權									
State-owned 國有	4	22	750				33.71	75.00	1,000
Collectively-owned 集體	131	10	613	26	10.41	38.47	60.02	72.94	250
Privately-owned 私有	2	1	583	52	46.85	100.83	582.92	53.54	111
Domestic JVs 聯營									
Joint stock 股份制									
Foreign-funded 外資	3	2	10	-8	-0.40	-0.40	4.44		1,876
Overseas Chinese-funded 港澳台資	7	10	1,214	-71	-4.78	-5.89	126.79	18.92	1,479
By size 規模									
Large 大型									
Medium 中型									
Small 小型	144	10	646	21	5.66	12.50	62.92	54.72	368
By regional distribution 地區分布									
Central-North 華北	43	12	439	10	3.94	11.70	38.04	66.22	260
Beijing 北京	6	13	583	3	0.69	1.01	45.45	31.25	480
Tianjin 天津	18	4	106	-9	-6.40	-100.00	30.16	93.60	139
Hebei 河北	8	9	1,505	70	14.07	65.12	160.53	78.39	498
Shanxi 山西	3	84	380				4.52	59.15	547
Inner Mongolia 內蒙	8	4	36	3	12.50	22.22	10.00	37.50	20
Northeast 東北	14	14	694	16	17.42	31.08	50.31	44.70	94
Liaoning 遼寧	9	6	832	14	17.81	31.71	136.18	43.84	81
Jilin 吉林	2	11	1,055	50	22.73	52.63	95.91	59.09	220
Heilongjiang 黑龍江	3	39	37				0.95	6.67	50
Central East 華東	31	11	1,494	35	6.76	20.77	130.42	67.65	515
Shanghai 上海	2	14	465	-5	-1.85	-3.03	33.21	40.74	270
Jiangsu 江蘇	2	15	3,485	280	14.93	25.00	232.33	40.27	1,875
Zhejiang 浙江	5	12	614	40	8.03	17.39	52.93	54.22	498
Anhui 安徽	1	72	2,900	-30	-0.96	-21.43	40.28	95.51	3,120
Fujian 福建	11	1	518	6	2.62	10.77	380.00	75.66	243
Jiangxi 江西	4	11	465	28	6.71	42.31	44.29	84.15	410
Shandong 山東	6	18	4,145	30	10.17	41.86	226.09	76.27	295
Central-South 中南	47	7	340	17	3.67	5.93	47.42	38.18	464
Henan 河南	11	12	505	27	4.20	13.64	42.44	69.19	649
Hubei 湖北	3	3	120	10	42.86	150.00	40.00	71.43	23
Hunan 湖南	3	13	720	13	1.14	2.74	56.84	58.81	1,173
Guangdong 廣東	25	6	316	17	3.89	4.39	54.86	11.39	442
Guangxi 廣西	5	3							
Hainan 海南									
Southwest 西南	7	4	177	9	2.86	11.54	42.76	75.24	300
Chongqing 重慶	1	2	10	-25	-7.27	18.94	5.83	138.36	340
Sichuan 四川	2	6	496	38	4.78	14.20	78.87	66.34	792
Guizhou 貴州	2	2	70				46.67	50.00	40
Yunnan 雲南	2	6	15				2.50	33.33	15
Tibet 西藏									
Northwest 西北	5	15	170	4	2.17	5.00	11.33	56.52	184
Shaanxi 陝西									
Gansu 甘肅	2	29	390	10	4.08	15.38	13.68	73.47	245
Qinghai 青海	1	8	60				7.50	57.14	140
Ningxia 寧夏	1	4	10				2.50	33.33	30
Xinjiang 新疆	1	6						26.92	260

3783: Motorcycle Repairing 摩托車修理業

Year 年份	Number of firms 企業個數	Rate of change 每年變化 (%)	Number of employees 職工人數 (人)	Rate of change 每年變化 (%)	Total revenue (mil. RMB) 總銷售收入 (百萬元)	Rate of change 每年變化 (%)	Total profit (mil. RMB) 總利潤 (百萬元)	Rate of change 每年變化 (%)
1993	82		2,101		54		3	
1994	81	-1.22%	1,676	-20.23%	42	-21.73%	3	-7.41%
1995	86	6.17%	1,591	-5.07%	37	-12.29%	1	-76.05%
1996	147	70.93%	1,485	-6.66%	93	149.54%	3	305.41%

3 Major products* 3種主要產品*	Output 產量	Sales volume 銷售量	Unit 單位

Top 10 firms by revenue (year founded) 收入排名前10家企業 (創辦年份)	City 城市	Province 省	Telephone / fax 電話 / 傳真	Number of employees 職工人數	Ownership 產業所有權	Revenue ('000 RMB) 銷售收入 (千元)	Profit ('000 RMB) (rank) 利潤 (千元) (排名)	Total assets ('000 RMB) 總資產 (千元)	Major products 主要產品
Xixia Songshan Xiang Xing Da Building Materials Machinery Co. Ltd. 栖霞市松山鄉興達建材機械有限公司(1994)	Yantai 煙台市	Shandong 山東省	(0535)5471046	52	Collectively-owned 集體	24,400	155(5)	740	o
Yuxian Motorcycle Multiple Repair Factory 蔚縣摩托車綜合修理廠	Zhangjiakou 張家口市	Hebei 河北省	(0313)7212780	11	Collectively-owned 集體	7,323	1(9)	694	o
Fuzhou Cangshan Rong Da Motorcycle Repair Section 福州市倉山榕達摩托車修理部	Fuzhou 福州市	Fujian 福建省		3	Collectively-owned 集體	5,246	46(6)	2,213	o
Nanjing Li Long Automobile Motorcycle Automobile Maintenance Co. Ltd. 南京利隆汽車摩托汽車維修有限公司(1995)	Nanjing 南京市	Jiangsu 江蘇省	(025)4593377 (025)4590789	24	Collectively-owned 集體	5,075	544(1)	3,372	o
Nan Gang Automobile Maintenance Center 南港汽車維修中心(1988)	Maoming 茂名市	Guangdong 廣東省	(0668)22897200	36	Foreign-funded 外資	4,458	185(4)	1,075	o
Shijiazhuang Zheng Da Motorcycle Repair Section 石家莊市正大摩托車修理部(1993)	Shijiazhuang 石家莊市	Hebei 河北省	(0311)6047105	42	其他經濟	4,279	536(2)	2,727	o
Shenyang Wan Xin Automobile Repair Dept. 瀋陽市萬新汽車修理部(1993)	Shenyang 瀋陽市	Liaoning 遼寧省		3	Collectively-owned 集體	4,000	0(12)	251	o
Jinzhai Traffic Bus Heavy Repair Factory 金寨縣交通汽車大修廠(1993)	Liu'an 六安市	Anhui 安徽省	(0564)7063538	72	State-owned 國有	2,898	-30(15)	3,115	o
Chang Kai Industry & Trade Company 長凱工貿公司(1992)	Yueyang 岳陽市	Hunan 湖南省	(0730)8511049	146	Collectively-owned 集體	2,845	12(8)	2,723	o
Xiaoshan Hongshan Automobile Repair Factory 蕭山市紅山汽車修理廠(1992)	Hangzhou 杭州市	Zhejiang 浙江省	(0571)2699054	55	Collectively-owned 集體	2,202	218(3)	2,165	o

Top 10 Cities by Production Output 產出排名前10位城市	Province 省	Market share 市場份額	Number of firms 企業個數
Shanghai 上海市	Shanghai 上海市	15.04%	39
Guangzhou 廣州市	Guangdong 廣東省	10.53%	91
Beijing 北京市	Beijing 北京市	9.00%	6
Maoming 茂名市	Guangdong 廣東省	8.16%	1
Hangzhou 杭州市	Zhejiang 浙江省	5.70%	4
Jieyang 揭陽市	Guangdong 廣東省	4.72%	1
Lianyungang 連雲港市	Jiangsu 江蘇省	4.48%	2
Nanchang 南昌市	Jiangxi 江西省	4.13%	3
Weifang 濰坊市	Shandong 山東省	3.97%	4
Tianjin 天津市	Tianjin 天津市	3.66%	22

10 Major Wholesalers 10家主要批發商	City 城市	Province 省	Telephone / Fax 電話 / 傳真

*Also include sales by firms outside this industry.包括本行業以外廠家的銷售。"o" stands for "others". "o" 代表 "其他產品" 。

3785: Ships and Boats Repairing 船舶修理業

The industry accounts for 0.080% of the total revenue of China's industrial sector in 1996. The revenue growth rate of the industry is 15.6% from 1995, as compared to the growth rate of China's industrial sector, 9.51%. The rate of return on asset is 1.78%. 67.67% of all firms in the industry made a profit while 27.38% had negative returns. The top province in terms of the industry's revenue is Jiangsu, accounting for 21.63% of the total revenue.
本行業在1996年佔全行業總產值0.080%，行業年增長率為15.6%（全國工業年增長率9.51%）。行業的資產回報率1.78%，67.67%的企業盈利，27.38%的企業虧損。銷售收入最高的省份為江蘇省，佔本行業的21.63%。

	Total number of firms 企業總數	Total number of employees 職工總數	Total revenue (mil. RMB) 總銷售收入（百萬元）	Total profit (mil. RMB) 總利潤（百萬元）	Return on assets 資產利潤率 (%)	Return on equity 權益利潤率 (%)	Labour productivity ('000 RMB / worker) 勞動生產率（千元/人）	Debts / assets 資產負債率 (%)	Total assets (mil. RMB) 總資產（百萬元）
Industry Overall 行業總體	561	97,912	4,628	193	1.78	4.16	47.27	57.24	10,819

	Number of firms 企業個數	Average number of employees 平均職工人數	Average revenue ('000 RMB) 平均銷售收入（千元）	Average profit ('000 RMB) 平均利潤（千元）	Return on assets 資產利潤率 (%)	Return on equity 權益利潤率 (%)	Labour productivity ('000 RMB / worker) 勞動生產率（千元/人）	Average debts / assets 平均資產負債率(%)	Average Total assets ('000 RMB) 平均總資產（千元）
By ownership 產業所有權									
State-owned 國有	118	500	23,890	695	1.08	2.45	47.78	55.81	64,288
Collectively-owned 集體	377	89	2,937	102	3.60	7.88	32.84	54.31	2,844
Privately-owned 私有									
Domestic JVs 聯營	7	141	4,088	281	3.24	6.56	28.93	50.54	8,676
Joint stock 股份制	3	51	2,356	21	2.08	3.50	45.90	40.52	1,031
Foreign-funded 外資	21	107	19,624	3,026	7.28	17.74	182.99	58.98	41,567
Overseas Chinese-funded 港澳台資	35	84	7,515	195	0.56	1.73	89.86	67.81	34,965
By size 規模									
Large 大型	13	2,764	178,407	9,203	1.96	4.38	64.55	55.35	470,212
Medium 中型	16	857	32,167	627	0.73	1.27	37.53	42.91	86,455
Small 小型	526	92	3,749	120	2.11	5.88	40.59	64.14	5,706
By regional distribution 地區分布									
Central-North 華北	39	137	7,977	516	2.23	4.64	58.12	51.87	23,106
Beijing 北京									
Tianjin 天津	28	59	1,802	171	9.08	18.46	30.41	50.82	1,884
Hebei 河北	11	336	23,695	1,395	1.81	3.76	70.56	51.93	77,126
Shanxi 山西									
Inner Mongolia 內蒙									
Northeast 東北	85	114	3,581	73	1.22	2.56	31.29	52.39	6,029
Liaoning 遼寧	76	123	3,956	84	1.26	2.66	32.07	52.55	6,683
Jilin 吉林									
Heilongjiang 黑龍江	9	39	419	-20	-3.96	-5.98	10.68	33.85	506
Central East 華東	303	208	9,699	466	2.37	5.52	46.63	57.06	19,665
Shanghai 上海	52	263	13,991	916	2.84	5.75	53.25	50.54	32,229
Jiangsu 江蘇	58	209	17,261	1,071	3.75	12.14	82.61	69.13	28,578
Zhejiang 浙江	61	327	5,443	81	0.73	1.89	16.66	61.26	11,008
Anhui 安徽	7	108	540	-83	-8.24	56.86	5.01	114.49	1,006
Fujian 福建	34	72	2,891	38	0.79	1.86	40.16	57.59	4,835
Jiangxi 江西	7	29	414	40	6.75	15.56	14.15	56.63	593
Shandong 山東	84	166	9,204	305	1.44	2.89	55.59	50.10	21,167
Central-South 中南	121	153	8,794	204	0.72	1.79	57.40	59.71	28,292
Henan 河南									
Hubei 湖北	24	70	3,347	224	5.49	13.33	47.64	58.84	4,087
Hunan 湖南	12	48	1,199	26	2.41	14.29	24.98	83.15	1,073
Guangdong 廣東	68	203	13,485	299	0.65	1.63	66.43	60.26	46,015
Guangxi 廣西	13	86	1,509	-272	-4.81	-11.13	17.52	56.80	5,664
Hainan 海南	4	339	8,205	558	2.03	3.62	24.24	43.86	27,443
Southwest 西南	13	97	739	17	0.95	2.12	7.59	55.41	1,791
Chongqing 重慶	10	92	924	22	1.01	2.45	10.00	58.71	2,196
Sichuan 四川	3	111	184	1	0.23	0.28	1.66	17.62	576
Guizhou 貴州									
Yunnan 雲南									
Tibet 西藏									
Northwest 西北									
Shaanxi 陝西									
Gansu 甘肅									
Qinghai 青海									
Ningxia 寧夏									
Xinjiang 新疆									

3785: Ships and Boats Repairing 船舶修理業

Year 年份	Number of firms 企業個數	Rate of change 每年變化 (%)	Number of employees 職工人數 (人)	Rate of change 每年變化 (%)	Total revenue (mil. RMB) 總銷售收入 (百萬元)	Rate of change 每年變化 (%)	Total profit (mil. RMB) 總利潤 (百萬元)	Rate of change 每年變化 (%)
1993	467		144,562		3,093		169	
1994	535	14.56%	108,783	-24.75%	4,183	35.26%	108	-36.03%
1995	568	6.17%	91,111	-16.25%	4,004	-4.29%	162	49.88%
1996	561	-1.23%	97,912	7.46%	4,628	15.58%	193	19.31%

3 Major products* 3 種主要產品 *	Output 產量	Sales volume 銷售量	Unit 單位

Top 10 firms by revenue (year founded) 收入排名前 10 家企業 (創辦年份)	City 城市	Province 省	Telephone / fax 電話 / 傳真	Number of employees 職工人數	Ownership 產業所有權	Revenue ('000 RMB) 銷售收入 (千元)	Profit ('000 RMB) (rank) 利潤 (千元) (排名)	Total assets ('000 RMB) 總資產 (千元)	Major products 主要產品
Guangzhou Wenchong Shipyard 廣州文沖船廠(1955)	Guangzhou 廣州市	Guangdong 廣東省	(020)82389933 (020)82399338	5,490	State-owned 國有	467,138	7869(7)	1,448,817	o
Chengxi Shipyard 澄西船舶修造廠(1977)	Wuxi 無錫市	Jiangsu 江蘇省	(0510)6109709 (0510)6109711	3,049	State-owned 國有	370,527	15024(4)	708,287	o
Nantong Ocean Ship Engineering Co. Ltd. 南通遠洋船務工程有限公司(1991)	Nantong 南通市	Jiangsu 江蘇省	(0513)3516186 (0513)3517539	946	Foreign-funded 外資	337,547	52274(1)	588,297	o
Qingdao Bei Hai Shipyard 青島北海船廠(1898)	Qingdao 青島市	Shandong 山東省	(0532)5812233 (0532)5814466	4,478	State-owned 國有	251,100	2198(19)	854,132	o
Shanhaiguan Shipyard 山海關船廠(1972)	Qinhuangdao 秦皇島市	Hebei 河北省	(0335)5081131 (0335)5081140	2,958	State-owned 國有	212,972	15083(3)	744,399	o
Shanghai Ocean Shipping (Group) Co. Lifeng Ship Factory 上海海運(集團)公司立豐船廠(1970)	Shanghai 上海市	Shanghai 上海市	(021)58410606 (021)58416811	1,452	State-owned 國有	169,521	25163(2)	217,044	o
Dalian Liao Nan Chuan Factory 大連遼南船廠(1890)	Dalian 大連市	Liaoning 遼寧省	(0411)6613881 (0411)6610549	3,065	State-owned 國有	141,669	3665(9)	232,647	o
Shanghai Ocean Shipping (Group) Co. Lixin Ship Factory S.u.d. 上海海運(集團)公司立新船廠(1949)	Shanghai 上海市	Shanghai 上海市	(021)58841201 (021)58842262	1,694	State-owned 國有	111,600	13526(5)	162,261	o
China People Liberation No.4808 Gong Factory 中國人民解放第四八零八工廠(1928)	Qingdao 青島市	Shandong 山東省	(0532)282041 (0532)2828041	2,450	State-owned 國有	100,020	1506(30)	249,651	o
Zhanjiang Hai Bin Shipyard 湛江海濱船廠(1962)	Zhanjiang 湛江市	Guangdong 廣東省	(0758)3380838 (0758)3380938	2,689	State-owned 國有	96,029	401(68)	514,137	o

Top 10 Cities by Production Output 產出排名前 10 位城市	Province 省	Market share 市場份額	Number of firms 企業個數
Shanghai 上海市	Shanghai 上海市	20.60%	156
Guangzhou 廣州市	Guangdong 廣東省	18.57%	47
Qingdao 青島市	Shandong 山東省	13.27%	37
Wuxi 無錫市	Jiangsu 江蘇省	7.35%	15
Dalian 大連市	Liaoning 遼寧省	6.26%	92
Zhoushan 舟山市	Zhejiang 浙江省	5.40%	41
Qinhuangdao 秦皇島市	Hebei 河北省	4.72%	4
Yantai 煙台市	Shandong 山東省	3.19%	14
Ningbo 寧波市	Zhejiang 浙江省	2.33%	19
Zhanjiang 湛江市	Guangdong 廣東省	2.21%	9

10 Major Wholesalers 10 家主要批發商	City 城市	Province 省	Telephone / Fax 電話 / 傳真

*Also include sales by firms outside this industry.包括本行業以外廠家的銷售。"o" stands for "others". "o" 代表 "其他產品"。

3786: Aircraft Repairing 飛機修理業

The industry accounts for 0.050% of the total revenue of China's industrial sector in 1996. The revenue growth rate of the industry is 20.6% from 1995, as compared to the growth rate of China's industrial sector, 9.51%. The rate of return on asset is 2.71%. 79.31% of all firms in the industry made a profit while 20.69% had negative returns. The top province in terms of the industry's revenue is Beijing, accounting for 31.59% of the total revenue.
本行業在1996年佔全行業總產值0.050%，行業年增長率為20.6%（全國工業年增長率9.51%）。行業的資產回報率2.71%，79.31%的企業盈利，20.69%的企業虧損。銷售收入最高的省份為北京市，佔本行業的31.59%。

	Total number of firms 企業總數	Total number of employees 職工總數	Total revenue (mil. RMB) 總銷售收入（百萬元）	Total profit (mil. RMB) 總利潤（百萬元）	Return on assets 資產利潤率 (%)	Return on equity 權益利潤率 (%)	Labour productivity ('000 RMB / worker) 勞動生產率（千元/人）	Debts / assets 資產負債率 (%)	Total assets (mil. RMB) 總資產（百萬元）
Industry Overall 行業總體	24	37,936	2,872	167	2.71	6.20	75.71	56.27	6,147

	Number of firms 企業個數	Average number of employees 平均職工人數	Average revenue ('000 RMB) 平均銷售收入（千元）	Average profit ('000 RMB) 平均利潤（千元）	Return on assets 資產利潤率 (%)	Return on equity 權益利潤率 (%)	Labour productivity ('000 RMB / worker) 勞動生產率（千元/人）	Average debts / assets 平均資產負債率(%)	Average Total assets ('000 RMB) 平均總資產（千元）
By ownership 產業所有權									
State-owned 國有	20	1,794	72,750	2,000	1.28	2.46	40.56	48.09	156,800
Collectively-owned 集體	1	28							
Privately-owned 私有									
Domestic JVs 聯營									
Joint stock 股份制									
Foreign-funded 外資	3	676	472,737	42,333	4.22	11.98	699.31	64.80	1,003,981
Overseas Chinese-funded 港澳台資									
By size 規模									
Large 大型	8	2,573	114,222	-11,447	-4.51	-11.55	44.39	60.94	253,783
Medium 中型	12	1,165	86,145	6,580	4.29	7.87	73.96	45.50	153,443
Small 小型	4	841	231,396	44,898	7.89	20.14	275.23	60.82	569,091
By regional distribution 地區分布									
Central-North 華北	5	800	205,890	16,002	3.54	11.53	257.43	69.29	451,804
Beijing 北京	2		453,695	38,170	3.84	14.16		72.85	992,990
Tianjin 天津									
Hebei 河北	2	1,414	51,745	1,825	1.84	3.25	36.59	43.27	99,010
Shanxi 山西	1	1,171	18,570	20	0.03	0.05	15.86	43.47	75,020
Inner Mongolia 內蒙									
Northeast 東北	3	2,335	70,767	177	0.09	0.17	30.31	46.72	196,827
Liaoning 遼寧	2	1,139	21,680	-465	-0.37	-0.61	19.04	39.48	126,140
Jilin 吉林	1	4,727	168,940	1,460	0.43	0.90	35.74	52.12	338,200
Heilongjiang 黑龍江									
Central East 華東	3	1,578	119,960	-9,973	-3.26	-6.61	76.04	50.69	305,867
Shanghai 上海		1,157	52,850	1,890	2.03	4.96	45.68	59.12	93,270
Jiangsu 江蘇	1	995	40,400	1,100	0.98	1.21	40.60	18.82	112,120
Zhejiang 浙江									
Anhui 安徽	1	1,865	118,210	750	0.34	0.59	63.38	41.36	217,830
Fujian 福建	1	716	148,420	-33,660	-6.81	-17.21	207.29	60.44	494,380
Jiangxi 江西									
Shandong 山東									
Central-South 中南	7	1,261	112,351	14,221	7.87	15.13	89.09	48.00	180,806
Henan 河南	1	974	20,290	-1,400	-1.19	-1.61	20.83	26.12	117,430
Hubei 湖北	2	1,281	148,765	8,530	4.13	12.10	116.13	65.85	206,515
Hunan 湖南	2	1,471	45,390	1,185	1.57	3.09	30.86	49.14	75,290
Guangdong 廣東	1	1,343	361,150	83,820	15.79	25.70	268.91	38.57	530,860
Guangxi 廣西	1	1,007	16,710	-2,300	-4.28	-8.32	16.59	48.55	53,740
Hainan 海南									
Southwest 西南	4	1,728	81,308	4,573	2.41	4.61	47.05	47.67	189,470
Chongqing 重慶									
Sichuan 四川	2	2,470	113,075	-7,610	-2.87	-4.73	45.78	39.43	265,495
Guizhou 貴州	2	986	49,540	1,535	1.35	4.10	50.24	66.97	113,445
Yunnan 雲南									
Tibet 西藏									
Northwest 西北	2	3,230	79,310	-885	-0.50	-1.02	24.55	51.55	178,320
Shaanxi 陝西	1	4,819	136,270	200	0.08	0.17	28.28	56.35	262,590
Gansu 甘肅	1	1,641	22,350	-1,970	-2.09	-3.39	13.62	38.15	94,050
Qinghai 青海									
Ningxia 寧夏									
Xinjiang 新疆									

Year 年份	Number of firms 企業個數	Rate of change 每年變化 (%)	Number of employees 職工人數（人）	Rate of change 每年變化 (%)	Total revenue (mil. RMB) 總銷售收入（百萬元）	Rate of change 每年變化 (%)	Total profit (mil. RMB) 總利潤（百萬元）	Rate of change 每年變化 (%)
1993	26		40,171		965		5	
1994	26	0	50,673	26.14%	1,316	36.35%	52	1027.23%
1995	28	7.69%	45,178	-10.85%	2,382	81.05%	62	18.24%
1996	24	-14.29%	37,936	-16.03%	2,872	20.57%	167	169.10%

3 Major products* 3種主要產品*	Output 產量	Sales volume 銷售量	Unit 單位

Top 10 firms by revenue (year founded) 收入排名前10家企業（創辦年份）	City 城市	Province 省	Telephone / fax 電話／傳真	Number of employees 職工人數	Ownership 產業所有權	Revenue ('000 RMB) 銷售收入（千元）	Profit ('000 RMB) (rank) 利潤（千元）（排名）	Total assets ('000 RMB) 總資產（千元）	Major products 主要產品
Wuhan Lingyun Group Co. Ltd. 武漢淩雲集團有限責任公司(1975)	Wuhan 武漢市	Hubei 湖北省	(027)83644422 (027)83642074	1,247	State-owned 國有	250,677	12682(3)	319,845	o
State-owned Chuan Xi Machine Plant 國營川西機器廠(1979)	Chengdu 成都市	Sichuan 四川省	(028)3871345 (028)3871819	1,958	State-owned 國有	157,443	15211(2)	196,877	o
State-owned Si Da Machine Manufacturing Co. 國營四達機械製造公司(1963)	Xianyang 咸陽市	Shaanxi 陝西省	(0910)7406888 (0910)7406111	4,819	State-owned 國有	136,274	202(13)	262,586	o
State-owned Wuhu Machinery Plant 國營蕪湖機械廠(1979)	Wuhu 蕪湖市	Anhui 安徽省	(0553)5811435 (0553)5851104	1,875	State-owned 國有	118,209	750(12)	217,827	o
State-owned Chang Kong Machinery Factory 國營長空機械廠(1966)	Changsha 長沙市	Hunan 湖南省	(0731)5630500 (0731)5630500	1,205	State-owned 國有	90,186	2370(5)	148,281	o
Guizhou Qian Ying Machinery Factory 貴州黔鷹機械廠(1967)	Guiyang 貴陽市	Guizhou 貴州省	(0851)3851191 (0851)3851825	1,273	State-owned 國有	73,225	2060(6)	165,710	o
Shijiazhuang Haishan Instrement Development General Corp. 石家莊海山實業發展總公司(1980)	Shijiazhuang 石家莊市	Hebei 河北省	(0311)2010601 (0311)2010614	1,594	State-owned 國有	61,935	2463(4)	107,519	o
State-owned Ren Jiang Machinery Factory 國營仁江機械廠(1968)	Zunyi 遵義市	Guizhou 貴州省	(0852)7761011 (0852)7761025	937	State-owned 國有	25,851	1008(11)	61,181	o
State-owned Blue Sky Machinery Factory 國營蘭天機械廠(1980)	Tianshui 天水市	Gansu 甘肅省	(0938)736023 (0938)734418	1,629	State-owned 國有	22,346	-1973(18)	94,049	o
State-owned Chang Hong Machinery Factory 國營長虹機械廠(1979)	Guilin 桂林市	Guangxi 廣西	(0773)3603153 (0773)3605045	1,007	State-owned 國有	16,705	-2298(19)	53,741	o

Top 10 Cities by Production Output 產出排名前10位城市	Province 省	Market share 市場份額	Number of firms 企業個數
Wuhan 武漢市	Hubei 湖北省	34.01%	1
Chengdu 成都市	Sichuan 四川省	21.23%	2
Xianyang 咸陽市	Shaanxi 陝西省	19.72%	1
Guiyang 貴陽市	Guizhou 貴州省	10.82%	1
Shijiazhuang 石家莊市	Hebei 河北省	4.10%	1
Zunyi 遵義市	Guizhou 貴州省	3.89%	1
Changsha 長沙市	Hunan 湖南省	2.76%	1
Guilin 桂林市	Guangxi 廣西	2.61%	1
Zhenjiang 鎮江市	Jiangsu 江蘇省	0.35%	1
Shanghai 上海市	Shanghai 上海市	0.15%	1

10 Major Wholesalers 10家主要批發商	City 城市	Province 省	Telephone / Fax 電話／傳真

*Also include sales by firms outside this industry.包括本行業以外廠家的銷售。"o" stands for "others". "o"代表"其他產品"。

3789: Other Transportation Equipment Repairing 其他交通運輸設備修理業

The industry accounts for 0.011% of the total revenue of China's industrial sector in 1996. The revenue growth rate of the industry is 35.8% from 1995, as compared to the growth rate of China's industrial sector, 9.51%. The rate of return on asset is 2.01%. 71.64% of all firms in the industry made a profit while 16.36% had negative returns. The top province in terms of the industry's revenue is Sichuan, accounting for 17.48% of the total revenue.

本行業在1996年佔全行業總產值0.011%，行業年增長率為35.8%（全國工業年增長率9.51%）。行業的資產回報率2.01%，71.64%的企業盈利，16.36%的企業虧損。銷售收入最高的省份為四川省，佔本行業的17.48%。

	Total number of firms 企業總數	Total number of employees 職工總數	Total revenue (mil. RMB) 總銷售收入（百萬元）	Total profit (mil. RMB) 總利潤（百萬元）	Return on assets 資產利潤率 (%)	Return on equity 權益利潤率 (%)	Labour productivity ('000 RMB / worker) 勞動生產率（千元/人）	Debts / assets 資產負債率 (%)	Total assets (mil. RMB) 總資產（百萬元）
Industry Overall 行業總體	323	17,002	620	15	2.01	5.06	36.47	60.18	740

	Number of firms 企業個數	Average number of employees 平均職工人數	Average revenue ('000 RMB) 平均銷售收入（千元）	Average profit ('000 RMB) 平均利潤（千元）	Return on assets 資產利潤率 (%)	Return on equity 權益利潤率 (%)	Labour productivity ('000 RMB / worker) 勞動生產率（千元/人）	Average debts / assets 平均資產負債率(%)	Average Total assets ('000 RMB) 平均總資產（千元）
By ownership 產業所有權									
State-owned 國有	55	130	3,909	55	0.72	1.62	30.07	55.31	7,527
Collectively-owned 集體	252	36	1,413	41	4.41	16.51	39.74	73.29	934
Privately-owned 私有									
Domestic JVs 聯營	6	142	4,618	24	0.37	1.16	32.52	68.22	6,416
Joint stock 股份制	2	17	184	4	1.47	1.68	10.84	12.58	243
Foreign-funded 外資	3	13	654	-107	-2.32	-3.19	51.60	27.15	4,618
Overseas Chinese-funded 港澳台資	5	53	3,729	359	4.76	7.37	70.63	35.43	7,548
By size 規模									
Large 大型	2	1,574	68,966	35	0.03	0.06	43.83	46.31	106,832
Medium 中型	2	1,330	44,281	405	0.51	1.70	33.31	70.17	79,979
Small 小型	317	36	1,241	45	3.86	10.66	34.75	63.82	1,155
By regional distribution 地區分布									
Central-North 華北	56	88	2,255	68	1.67	2.83	25.58	40.88	4,071
Beijing 北京	14	104	3,701	46	0.56	0.67	35.59	15.65	8,123
Tianjin 天津	10	268	2,677	194	3.15	7.15	9.98	55.96	6,160
Hebei 河北	16	16	2,728	95	3.57	21.23	170.51	83.22	2,663
Shanxi 山西	7	53	369	-41	-4.64	-14.36	6.97	67.68	893
Inner Mongolia 內蒙	9	19	161				8.38	32.45	421
Northeast 東北	54	36	685	17	2.28	7.00	19.10	67.36	738
Liaoning 遼寧	32	39	928	38	4.54	19.51	23.86	76.71	827
Jilin 吉林	14	41	357	-28	-3.96	-5.26	8.76	24.59	703
Heilongjiang 黑龍江	8	15	286	13	2.82	-17.54	18.93	116.38	443
Central East 華東	96	49	2,137	83	2.88	8.79	44.00	67.26	2,897
Shanghai 上海	11	39	1,486	205	8.19	45.09	38.02	81.83	2,497
Jiangsu 江蘇	14	42	3,817	110	3.43	13.64	90.73	74.86	3,210
Zhejiang 浙江	15	16	545	-117	-15.84	-94.59	33.35	83.26	737
Anhui 安徽	17	148	4,296	-41	-0.55	-1.61	28.96	65.99	7,424
Fujian 福建	10	18	1,809	15	0.57	0.72	99.40	20.50	2,625
Jiangxi 江西	12	10	157	8	7.58	12.20	16.49	38.64	110
Shandong 山東	17	34	2,014	376	15.67	77.02	58.92	79.67	2,402
Central-South 中南	74	56	1,830	32	1.66	6.03	32.51	72.45	1,914
Henan 河南	15	109	3,882	26	0.46	2.64	35.48	82.68	5,681
Hubei 湖北	12	27	871	21	2.35	4.36	32.66	46.10	888
Hunan 湖南	16	48	1,514	21	2.22	8.17	31.25	72.71	928
Guangdong 廣東	18	27	1,232	16	1.72	4.96	46.28	65.33	904
Guangxi 廣西	12	75	1,695	92	7.52	12.47	22.50	39.67	1,218
Hainan 海南	1	46							
Southwest 西南	20	35	5,402	31	1.62	4.66	156.34	65.20	1,881
Chongqing 重慶	2	3							
Sichuan 四川	14	33	7,740	-77	-3.87	-14.60	234.31	73.53	1,983
Guizhou 貴州	2	77	870	-265	-8.97	-22.84	11.30	60.91	2,955
Yunnan 雲南	2	38	600	15	0.70	0.98	15.79	28.84	2,150
Tibet 西藏	1	18	600	80	12.70	12.70	33.33		630
Northwest 西北	23	26	334	-33	-4.99	-19.48	12.61	74.50	653
Shaanxi 陝西	8	31	298	10	1.90	13.11	9.71	85.31	528
Gansu 甘肅	7	18	334	-10	-2.71	-5.56	18.43	51.94	369
Qinghai 青海	3	13	30				2.37	74.80	410
Ningxia 寧夏	1								
Xinjiang 新疆	4	50	718	-190	-10.87	-45.78	14.42	76.25	1,748

3789: Other Transportation Equipment Repairing 其他交通運輸設備修理業

Year 年份	Number of firms 企業個數	Rate of change 每年變化 (%)	Number of employees 職工人數 (人)	Rate of change 每年變化 (%)	Total revenue (mil. RMB) 總銷售收入 (百萬元)	Rate of change 每年變化 (%)	Total profit (mil. RMB) 總利潤 (百萬元)	Rate of change 每年變化 (%)
1993	441		29,289		572		16	
1994	409	-7.26%	18,044	-38.39%	483	-15.48%	15	-6.61%
1995	281	-31.30%	14,899	-17.43%	457	-5.54%	11	-27.19%
1996	323	14.95%	17,002	14.12%	620	35.79%	15	37.96%

3 Major products* 3 種主要產品 *	Output 產量	Sales volume 銷售量	Unit 單位

Top 10 firms by revenue (year founded) 收入排名前 10 家企業 (創辦年份)	City 城市	Province 省	Telephone / fax 電話 / 傳真	Number of employees 職工人數	Ownership 產業所有權	Revenue ('000 RMB) 銷售收入 (千元)	Profit ('000 RMB) (rank) 利潤 (千元) (排名)	Total assets ('000 RMB) 總資產 (千元)	Major products 主要產品
Shuang Liu Jian Chuan Hoisting & Transport Machinery Factory 雙流縣建川起重運輸機械廠	Chengdu 成都市	Sichuan 四川省	(028)651018		Collectively-owned 集體	88,500	471(7)	21,856	o
Yu City Hua Guan Branch 禹城市華冠分公司(1985)	Dezhou 德州市	Shandong 山東省	(0534)7221614 (0534)7221614	301	State-owned 國有	27,905	6109(1)	32,254	o
Tianjin Zhi Cheng Cigarette Lighter Co. Ltd. 天津志成打火機有限公司(1992)	Tianjin 天津市	Tianjin 天津市	(022)27320447	240	Foreign-funded 外資	19,773	2037(2)	28,313	o
Lianyungang Li Da Industrial Co. 連雲港力達實業公司(1984)	Lianyungang 連雲港市	Jiangsu 江蘇省	(0518)2331717 (0518)2330864	75	Joint stock 股份制	17,500	1380(3)	8,373	o
Liuzhou Liunan Xin Sheng Zhuang Zai Machine Repair Factory 柳州市柳南區新生裝載機修理廠(1990)	Liuzhou 柳州市	Guangxi 廣西		689	Collectively-owned 集體	13,520	937(5)	2,736	o
Dingyuan Nan Men Vehicle Reapir & Assembly Plant 定遠縣南門車輛修配廠(1991)	Chuzhou 滁州市	Anhui 安徽省	(0550)4022873	60	Collectively-owned 集體	13,030	1050(4)	1,720	o
Yixing Vehicle Factory 宜興車輛廠(1967)	Wuxi 無錫市	Jiangsu 江蘇省	(0510)7902867	107	State-owned 國有	12,752	-247(47)	8,424	o
Quanzhou Chang An Traffic Equipment Company 泉州暢安交通器材公司	Quanzhou 泉州市	Fujian 福建省	(0595)6781853	35	Collectively-owned 集體	11,000	200(16)	9,380	o
Qian'an Wei Li Loader Assembly Repair Factory 遷安市偉力裝載機總成修理廠(1991)	Tangshan 唐山市	Hebei 河北省	(0315)7988208	30	Collectively-owned 集體	10,235	40(29)	35,730	o
Qian'an Yang Dian Zi Zhuang Zai Machine Repair Factory 遷安市楊店子裝載機修理廠(1995)	Tangshan 唐山市	Hebei 河北省	(0315)7988529	10	Collectively-owned 集體	9,895	150(18)	265	o

Top 10 Cities by Production Output 產出排名前 10 位城市	Province 省	Market share 市場份額	Number of firms 企業個數
Shangqiu 商丘市	Henan 河南省	17.71%	4
Shanghai 上海市	Shanghai 上海市	14.92%	34
Yangzhou 揚州市	Jiangsu 江蘇省	13.84%	5
Beijing 北京市	Beijing 北京市	8.79%	13
Guangzhou 廣州市	Guangdong 廣東省	4.62%	12
Tangshan 唐山市	Hebei 河北省	3.87%	5
Dalian 大連市	Liaoning 遼寧省	2.87%	10
Huizhou 惠州市	Guangdong 廣東省	2.09%	4
Changzhou 常州市	Jiangsu 江蘇省	2.03%	11
Lianyungang 連雲港市	Jiangsu 江蘇省	1.75%	1

10 Major Wholesalers 10 家主要批發商	City 城市	Province 省	Telephone / Fax 電話 / 傳真

*Also include sales by firms outside this industry.包括本行業以外廠家的銷售。"o" stands for "others". "o" 代表 "其他產品"。

3791: Navigation Mark Equipment 航標器材製造業

The industry accounts for 0.001% of the total revenue of China's industrial sector in 1996. The revenue growth rate of the industry is -75.2% from 1995, as compared to the growth rate of China's industrial sector, 9.51%. The rate of return on asset is 1.88%. 46.67% of all firms in the industry made a profit while 33.33% had negative returns. The top province in terms of the industry's revenue is Shanghai, accounting for 70.93% of the total revenue.
本行業在1996年佔全行業總產值0.001%，行業年增長率為-75.2%（全國工業年增長率9.51%）。行業的資產回報率1.88%，46.67%的企業盈利，33.33%的企業虧損。銷售收入最高的省份為上海市，佔本行業的70.93%。

	Total number of firms 企業總數	Total number of employees 職工總數	Total revenue (mil. RMB) 總銷售收入（百萬元）	Total profit (mil. RMB) 總利潤（百萬元）	Return on assets 資產利潤率 (%)	Return on equity 權益利潤率 (%)	Labour productivity ('000 RMB / worker) 勞動生產率（千元/人）	Debts / assets 資產負債率 (%)	Total assets (mil. RMB) 總資產（百萬元）
Industry Overall 行業總體	6	1,090	29	1	1.88	4.95	26.61	62.01	71

	Number of firms 企業個數	Average number of employees 平均職工人數	Average revenue ('000 RMB) 平均銷售收入（千元）	Average profit ('000 RMB) 平均利潤（千元）	Return on assets 資產利潤率 (%)	Return on equity 權益利潤率 (%)	Labour productivity ('000 RMB / worker) 勞動生產率（千元/人）	Average debts / assets 平均資產負債率(%)	Average Total assets ('000 RMB) 平均總資產（千元）
By ownership 產業所有權									
State-owned 國有	2	476	11,500				24.16	63.64	33,000
Collectively-owned 集體	4	35	1,500	250	20.00	33.33	43.48	40.00	1,250
Privately-owned 私有									
Domestic JVs 聯營									
Joint stock 股份制									
Foreign-funded 外資									
Overseas Chinese-funded 港澳台資									
By size 規模									
Large 大型									
Medium 中型									
Small 小型	6	182	4,833	167	1.41	3.70	26.60	61.97	11,833
By regional distribution 地區分布									
Central-North 華北	1	65	350				5.38	86.21	870
Beijing 北京									
Tianjin 天津	1	65	350				5.38	86.21	870
Hebei 河北									
Shanxi 山西									
Inner Mongolia 內蒙									
Northeast 東北									
Liaoning 遼寧									
Jilin 吉林									
Heilongjiang 黑龍江									
Central East 華東	4	255	6,873	340	1.97	5.12	26.92	61.57	17,273
Shanghai 上海	2	289	10,285	650	2.87	7.65	35.59	62.53	22,685
Jiangsu 江蘇	2	222	3,460	30	0.25	0.63	15.62	59.74	11,860
Zhejiang 浙江									
Anhui 安徽									
Fujian 福建									
Jiangxi 江西									
Shandong 山東									
Central-South 中南	1	4	1,000	-30	-3.66	-14.29	250.00	74.39	820
Henan 河南									
Hubei 湖北									
Hunan 湖南									
Guangdong 廣東	1	4	1,000	-30	-3.66	-14.29	250.00	74.39	820
Guangxi 廣西									
Hainan 海南									
Southwest 西南									
Chongqing 重慶									
Sichuan 四川									
Guizhou 貴州									
Yunnan 雲南									
Tibet 西藏									
Northwest 西北									
Shaanxi 陝西									
Gansu 甘肅									
Qinghai 青海									
Ningxia 寧夏									
Xinjiang 新疆									

3791: Navigation Mark Equipment 航標器材製造業

Year 年份	Number of firms 企業個數	Rate of change 每年變化 (%)	Number of employees 職工人數（人）	Rate of change 每年變化 (%)	Total revenue (mil. RMB) 總銷售收入（百萬元）	Rate of change 每年變化 (%)	Total profit (mil. RMB) 總利潤（百萬元）	Rate of change 每年變化 (%)
1993	10		2,464		92		5	
1994	12	20.00%	2,015	-18.22%	104	12.99%	2	-49.05%
1995	6	-50.00%	1,350	-33.00%	117	12.31%	2	-8.52%
1996	6	0	1,090	-19.26%	29	-75.18%	1	-53.66%

3 Major products* 3 種主要產品 *	Output 產量	Sales volume 銷售量	Unit 單位
a) Lamps & Lanterns	2.5	2.5	10,000 piece 萬隻

Top 10 firms by revenue (year founded) 收入排名前 10 家企業 (創辦年份)	City 城市	Province 省	Telephone / fax 電話 / 傳真	Number of employees 職工人數	Ownership 產業所有權	Revenue ('000 RMB) 銷售收入（千元）	Profit ('000 RMB) (rank) 利潤（千元）(排名)	Total assets ('000 RMB) 總資產（千元）	Major products 主要產品
Shanghai Navigation Aids Factory 上海航標廠(1968)	Shanghai 上海市	Shanghai 上海市	(021)58839256 (021)58769238	527	State-owned 國有	16,041	198(2)	42,935	o
Chang Jiang Navigational Matters Management Bureau Nanjing Navigation Factory 長江航務管理局南京航標廠(1958)	Nanjing 南京市	Jiangsu 江蘇省	(025)8805506 (025)8805832	424	State-owned 國有	6,598	58(4)	23,458	o
Navigation Light Source Factory 航標光源廠(1996)	Shanghai 上海市	Shanghai 上海市	(021)58839256	50	Collectively-owned 集體	4,531	1103(1)	2,430	a
Qingpu Jin Ze Navigation Mark Factory 青浦縣金澤航標廠(1992)	Shanghai 上海市	Shanghai 上海市	(021)59261054	20	Domestic JVs 聯營	3,278	131(3)	3,406	o

Top 10 Cities by Production Output 產出排名前 10 位城市	Province 省	Market share 市場份額	Number of firms 企業個數
Shanghai 上海市	Shanghai 上海市	60.38%	4
Nanjing 南京市	Jiangsu 江蘇省	20.76%	2
Hefei 合肥市	Anhui 安徽省	17.57%	1
Tianjin 天津市	Tianjin 天津市	0.90%	2
Jiaxing 嘉興市	Zhejiang 浙江省	0.38%	1

10 Major Wholesalers 10 家主要批發商	City 城市	Province 省	Telephone / Fax 電話 / 傳真
Liaoning Automobile Trade Group Corp. 遼寧省汽車貿易集團	Shenyang 瀋陽市	Liaoning 遼寧省	(024)23835494 (024)23838338
China Post and Telecommunication Equipment General Company 中國郵電器材總公司	Beijing 北京市	Beijing 北京市	(010)63523715 (010)63525935
Jiangsu Electromechanical Products General Company 江蘇省機電產品總公司	Nanjing 南京市	Jiangsu 江蘇省	(025)7713642 (025)7711036
Xi Nan Technology Import & Export Company 西南技術進出口公司	Chongqing 重慶市	Chongqing 重慶市	(023)63850185 (023)63850026
Changzhou Economic Technology Industrial Development Zone Tian Ming Trade Company 常州經濟技術產業開發區天明貿易公司	Changzhou 常州市	Jiangsu 江蘇省	(0519)8829882 (0519)8829882
Shanxi Mechanical Equipment Import & Export Company 山西省機械設備進出口公司	Taiyuan 太原市	Shanxi 山西省	(0351)4040713 (0351)4043981
Ningbo Five Mining Machinery Import & Export Company 寧波市五礦機械進出口公司	Ningbo 寧波市	Zhejiang 浙江省	(0574)7311255 (0574)7320322
Tianjin Jin Huan Electromechanical Complete Sets of Equipment Factory 天津市津環機電成套設備廠	Tianjin 天津市	Tianjin 天津市	(022)26371628
Yunnan Machinery Import & Export Company 雲南省機械進出口公司	Kunming 昆明市	Yunnan 雲南省	(0871)3164879 (0871)3136829
Tianjin Da Qiu Zhuang Yi Yuan Trade Center 天津市大丘莊億源商貿中心	Tianjin 天津市	Tianjin 天津市	(022)28899478 (022)28899046

*Also include sales by firms outside this industry.包括本行業以外廠家的銷售。"o" stands for "others". "o" 代表 "其他產品"。

3792: Diving Equipment 潛水裝備製造業

The industry accounts for 0.001% of the total revenue of China's industrial sector in 1996. The revenue growth rate of the industry is 3.7% from 1995, as compared to the growth rate of China's industrial sector, 9.51%. The rate of return on asset is 3.05%. 60.00% of all firms in the industry made a profit while 40.00% had negative returns. The top province in terms of the industry's revenue is Anhui, accounting for 42.20% of the total revenue.
本行業在1996年佔全行業總產值0.001%，行業年增長率為3.7%（全國工業年增長率9.51%）。行業的資產回報率3.05%，60.00%的企業盈利，40.00%的企業虧損。銷售收入最高的省份為安徽省，佔本行業的42.20%。

	Total number of firms 企業總數	Total number of employees 職工總數	Total revenue (mil. RMB) 總銷售收入（百萬元）	Total profit (mil. RMB) 總利潤（百萬元）	Return on assets 資產利潤率 (%)	Return on equity 權益利潤率 (%)	Labour productivity ('000 RMB / worker) 勞動生產率（千元／人）	Debts / assets 資產負債率 (%)	Total assets (mil. RMB) 總資產（百萬元）
Industry Overall 行業總體	7	903	35	1	3.05	6.11	38.76	50.14	48

	Number of firms 企業個數	Average number of employees 平均職工人數	Average revenue ('000 RMB) 平均銷售收入（千元）	Average profit ('000 RMB) 平均利潤（千元）	Return on assets 資產利潤率 (%)	Return on equity 權益利潤率 (%)	Labour productivity ('000 RMB / worker) 勞動生產率（千元／人）	Average debts / assets 平均資產負債率(%)	Average Total assets ('000 RMB) 平均總資產（千元）
By ownership 產業所有權									
State-owned 國有	3	231	9,333	667	5.00	9.09	40.40	45.00	13,333
Collectively-owned 集體	4	53	1,745	-250	-12.55	-50.37	33.23	75.09	1,993
Privately-owned 私有									
Domestic JVs 聯營									
Joint stock 股份制									
Foreign-funded 外資									
Overseas Chinese-funded 港澳台資									
By size 規模									
Large 大型									
Medium 中型									
Small 小型	7	129	5,000	143	2.08	4.17	38.76	50.00	6,857
By regional distribution 地區分布									
Central-North 華北									
Beijing 北京									
Tianjin 天津									
Hebei 河北									
Shanxi 山西									
Inner Mongolia 內蒙									
Northeast 東北	2	55	130	-350	-26.12	77.78	2.39	133.58	1,340
Liaoning 遼寧	1	104	240	-700	-28.23	76.09	2.31	137.10	2,480
Jilin 吉林	1	5	20				4.00	90.00	200
Heilongjiang 黑龍江									
Central East 華東	4	192	8,565	540	4.81	8.77	44.55	45.16	11,233
Shanghai 上海	1	190	9,720	470	3.53	5.98	51.16	40.90	13,300
Jiangsu 江蘇									
Zhejiang 浙江	2	93	4,885	385	5.48	13.63	52.53	59.82	7,030
Anhui 安徽	1	393	14,770	920	5.24	8.27	37.58	36.65	17,570
Fujian 福建									
Jiangxi 江西									
Shandong 山東									
Central-South 中南									
Henan 河南									
Hubei 湖北									
Hunan 湖南									
Guangdong 廣東									
Guangxi 廣西									
Hainan 海南									
Southwest 西南	1	25							
Chongqing 重慶									
Sichuan 四川									
Guizhou 貴州	1	25							
Yunnan 雲南									
Tibet 西藏									
Northwest 西北									
Shaanxi 陝西									
Gansu 甘肅									
Qinghai 青海									
Ningxia 寧夏									
Xinjiang 新疆									

3792: Diving Equipment 潛水裝備製造業

Year 年份	Number of firms 企業個數	Rate of change 每年變化 (%)	Number of employees 職工人數 (人)	Rate of change 每年變化 (%)	Total revenue (mil. RMB) 總銷售收入 (百萬元)	Rate of change 每年變化 (%)	Total profit (mil. RMB) 總利潤 (百萬元)	Rate of change 每年變化 (%)
1993	5		5,283		31		5	
1994	7	40.00%	996	-81.15%	37	21.25%	6	22.02%
1995	6	-14.29%	829	-16.77%	34	-9.56%	1	-79.57%
1996	7	16.67%	903	8.93%	35	3.70%	1	-21.14%

3 Major products* 3 種主要產品 *	Output 產量	Sales volume 銷售量	Unit 單位

Top 10 firms by revenue (year founded) 收入排名前 10 家企業 (創辦年份)	City 城市	Province 省	Telephone / fax 電話 / 傳真	Number of employees 職工人數	Ownership 產業所有權	Revenue ('000 RMB) 銷售收入 (千元)	Profit ('000 RMB) (rank) 利潤 (千元) (排名)	Total assets ('000 RMB) 總資產 (千元)	Major products 主要產品
Wuhu Dive Equipment Factory 蕪湖潛水裝備廠(1977)	Wuhu 蕪湖市	Anhui 安徽省	(0553)5842113 (0553)5841704	404	State-owned 國有	14,774	924(1)	17,567	o
Shanghai Dive Equipment Factory 上海潛水裝備廠(1952)	Shanghai 上海市	Shanghai 上海市	(021)58856722 (021)58857379	178	State-owned 國有	9,715	471(2)	13,295	o
Yuyao Ke Da Automobile Instrument Co. Ltd. 余姚市科達汽車儀表有限公司(1995)	Ningbo 寧波市	Zhejiang 浙江省	(0574)2578780 (0574)2595121	76	Private-owned 私營	6,289	348(3)	5,332	o

Top 10 Cities by Production Output 產出排名前 10 位城市	Province 省	Market share 市場份額	Number of firms 企業個數
Wuhu 蕪湖市	Anhui 安徽省	40.83%	1
Shanghai 上海市	Shanghai 上海市	38.79%	3
Hengshui 衡水市	Hebei 河北省	7.30%	1
Liu'an 六安市	Anhui 安徽省	5.75%	1
Harbin 哈爾濱市	Heilongjiang 黑龍江省	3.51%	1
Yuncheng 運城市	Shanxi 山西省	1.69%	1
Jinzhou 錦州市	Liaoning 遼寧省	0.82%	1
Zunyi 遵義市	Guizhou 貴州省	0.79%	1
Wuzhou 梧州市	Guangxi 廣西	0.53%	1

10 Major Wholesalers 10 家主要批發商	City 城市	Province 省	Telephone / Fax 電話 / 傳真
Liaoning Automobile Trade Group Corp. 遼寧省汽車貿易集團	Shenyang 瀋陽市	Liaoning 遼寧省	(024)23835494 (024)23838338
China Post and Telecommunication Equipment General Company 中國郵電器材總公司	Beijing 北京市	Beijing 北京市	(010)63523715 (010)63525935
Jiangsu Electromechanical Products General Company 江蘇省機電產品總公司	Nanjing 南京市	Jiangsu 江蘇省	(025)7713642 (025)7711036
Xi Nan Technology Import & Export Company 西南技術進出口公司	Chongqing 重慶市	Chongqing 重慶市	(023)63850185 (023)63850026
Changzhou Economic Technology Industrial Development Zone Tian Ming Trade Company 常州經濟技術產業開發區天明貿易公司	Changzhou 常州市	Jiangsu 江蘇省	(0519)8829882 (0519)8829882
Shanxi Mechanical Equipment Import & Export Company 山西省機械設備進出口公司	Taiyuan 太原市	Shanxi 山西省	(0351)4040713 (0351)4043981
Ningbo Five Mining Machinery Import & Export Company 寧波市五礦機械進出口公司	Ningbo 寧波市	Zhejiang 浙江省	(0574)7311255 (0574)7320322
Tianjin Jin Huan Electromechanical Complete Sets of Equipment Factory 天津市津環機電成套設備廠	Tianjin 天津市	Tianjin 天津市	(022)26371628
Yunnan Machinery Import & Export Company 雲南省機械進出口公司	Kunming 昆明市	Yunnan 雲南省	(0871)3164879 (0871)3136829
Tianjin Da Qiu Zhuang Yi Yuan Trade Center 天津市大丘莊億源商貿中心	Tianjin 天津市	Tianjin 天津市	(022)28899478 (022)28899046

*Also include sales by firms outside this industry.包括本行業以外廠家的銷售。"o" stands for "others". "o"代表"其他產品"。

3793: Road Traffic Mark 公路標誌製造業

The industry accounts for 0.006% of the total revenue of China's industrial sector in 1996. The revenue growth rate of the industry is 37.0% from 1995, as compared to the growth rate of China's industrial sector, 9.51%. The rate of return on asset is 5.41%. 79.17% of all firms in the industry made a profit while 20.83% had negative returns. The top province in terms of the industry's revenue is Jiangsu, accounting for 40.50% of the total revenue.
本行業在1996年佔全行業總產值0.006%，行業年增長率為37.0%（全國工業年增長率9.51%）。行業的資產回報率5.41%，79.17%的企業盈利，20.83%的企業虧損。銷售收入最高的省份為江蘇省，佔本行業的40.50%。

	Total number of firms 企業總數	Total number of employees 職工總數	Total revenue (mil. RMB) 總銷售收入（百萬元）	Total profit (mil. RMB) 總利潤（百萬元）	Return on assets 資產利潤率 (%)	Return on equity 權益利潤率 (%)	Labour productivity ('000 RMB / worker) 勞動生產率（千元/人）	Debts / assets 資產負債率 (%)	Total assets (mil. RMB) 總資產（百萬元）
Industry Overall 行業總體	66	3,640	362	18	5.41	20.30	99.45	73.36	341

	Number of firms 企業個數	Average number of employees 平均職工人數	Average revenue ('000 RMB) 平均銷售收入（千元）	Average profit ('000 RMB) 平均利潤（千元）	Return on assets 資產利潤率 (%)	Return on equity 權益利潤率 (%)	Labour productivity ('000 RMB / worker) 勞動生產率（千元/人）	Average debts / assets 平均資產負債率(%)	Average Total assets ('000 RMB) 平均總資產（千元）
By ownership 產業所有權									
State-owned 國有	13	53	3,538	-231	-3.06	-13.04	66.96	76.53	7,538
Collectively-owned 集體	44	47	3,188	183	6.93	22.73	67.81	69.49	2,636
Privately-owned 私有									
Domestic JVs 聯營	1	116	17,772	2,233	13.80	44.51	153.21	68.99	16,180
Joint stock 股份制									
Foreign-funded 外資	2	91	16,292	1,530	19.98	105.70	180.03	81.10	7,660
Overseas Chinese-funded 港澳台資	4	140	30,873	1,876	7.93	30.98	220.91	74.41	23,663
By size 規模									
Large 大型									
Medium 中型									
Small 小型	66	55	5,485	273	5.28	19.78	99.45	73.31	5,166
By regional distribution 地區分布									
Central-North 華北	13	22	2,406	117	7.68	21.97	110.14	65.10	1,523
Beijing 北京	5	2	2,784	100	6.38	14.62	1392.00	56.51	1,568
Tianjin 天津									
Hebei 河北	6	33	2,002	120	9.88	22.71	60.66	56.52	1,215
Shanxi 山西	2	38	2,675	150	6.42	90.91	70.39	92.93	2,335
Inner Mongolia 內蒙									
Northeast 東北	7	75	1,056	127	4.75	21.45	14.05	77.84	2,676
Liaoning 遼寧	1	12	180				15.00	90.16	610
Jilin 吉林	3	119	1,363	97	2.31	14.22	11.46	83.76	4,187
Heilongjiang 黑龍江	3	52	1,040	200	10.79	29.27	19.87	63.13	1,853
Central East 華東	24	57	8,820	532	9.87	29.16	154.05	66.14	5,390
Shanghai 上海	2	81	5,545	1,025	23.64	37.82	68.46	37.49	4,335
Jiangsu 江蘇	6	73	24,438	1,145	12.87	40.41	335.54	68.14	8,893
Zhejiang 浙江	10	26	3,760	282	5.53	23.10	146.88	76.05	5,099
Anhui 安徽	2	67	2,525	255	24.40	56.67	37.69	56.94	1,045
Fujian 福建									
Jiangxi 江西	2	40	1,335	20	2.26	3.60	33.38	37.29	885
Shandong 山東	2	153	4,315	240	3.85	6.70	28.30	42.63	6,240
Central-South 中南	14	70	7,201	292	2.70	13.45	102.24	79.95	10,825
Henan 河南	2	51	4,180	-305	-4.08	-152.50	81.96	97.39	7,470
Hubei 湖北	4	49	2,118	-40	-1.02	-4.20	42.99	75.81	3,938
Hunan 湖南	1	19	490				25.79	48.39	310
Guangdong 廣東	6	111	13,915	810	4.03	18.67	124.99	78.41	20,092
Guangxi 廣西	1								
Hainan 海南									
Southwest 西南	3	117	1,247	-197	-7.59	-23.41	10.69	67.44	2,590
Chongqing 重慶	3	117	1,247	197	7.61	23.36	10.66	67.44	2,590
Sichuan 四川									
Guizhou 貴州									
Yunnan 雲南									
Tibet 西藏									
Northwest 西北	5	24	1,496	-40	-1.42	-6.45	62.33	77.92	2,808
Shaanxi 陝西									
Gansu 甘肅									
Qinghai 青海									
Ningxia 寧夏	1	8	320	-290	-12.13	-2900.00	40.00	99.58	2,390
Xinjiang 新疆	4	28	1,790	23	0.77	2.91	63.93	73.48	2,913

3793: Road Traffic Mark 公路標誌製造業

Year 年份	Number of firms 企業個數	Rate of change 每年變化 (%)	Number of employees 職工人數 (人)	Rate of change 每年變化 (%)	Total revenue (mil. RMB) 總銷售收入 (百萬元)	Rate of change 每年變化 (%)	Total profit (mil. RMB) 總利潤 (百萬元)	Rate of change 每年變化 (%)
1993	40		2,052		103		12	
1994	41	2.50%	3,203	56.09%	162	57.29%	1	-88.78%
1995	56	36.59%	3,385	5.68%	264	63.25%	20	1393.16%
1996	66	17.86%	3,640	7.53%	362	37.00%	18	-9.43%

3 Major products* 3 種主要產品 *	Output 產量	Sales volume 銷售量	Unit 單位
a) Managing Equipment for Road Traffic 道路交通管理器材	7,171	9,609	set 台

Top 10 firms by revenue (year founded) 收入排名前 10 家企業 (創辦年份)	City 城市	Province 省	Telephone / fax 電話 / 傳真	Number of employees 職工人數	Ownership 產業所有權	Revenue ('000 RMB) 銷售收入 (千元)	Profit ('000 RMB) (rank) 利潤 (千元) (排名)	Total assets ('000 RMB) 總資產 (千元)	Major products 主要產品
Wuxi Traffic Installation Factory 江蘇無錫交通設施總廠(1989)	Wuxi 無錫市	Jiangsu 江蘇省	(0510)3791521 (0510)3791678	145	Collectively-owned 集體	125,329	5937(1)	36,361	o
Bao Guang Traffic Facilities Equipment Factory 寶光交通設施器材廠(1994)	Shanghai 上海市	Shanghai 上海市	(021)56754208 (021)56754208	250	Collectively-owned 集體	35,057	5934(2)	55,832	o
Sanshui Jingan Electro-mechanical Traffic Facilities Co. Ltd. 三水市京安機電塑料製品有限公司(1986)	Foshan 佛山市	Guangdong 廣東省	(0757)7731341 (0757)7727838	130	Overseas Chinese-funded 港澳台資	34,105	5684(3)	30,851	o
Guangzhou Highway Traffic Facilities Factory 廣州市公路交通設施廠(1971)	Guangzhou 廣州市	Guangdong 廣東省	(020)87711716 (020)87711716	195	State-owned 國有	20,569	2867(5)	42,907	o
Guangdong An Da Traffic Installation Engineering Co. Ltd. 廣東安達交通設施工程有限公司(1992)	Guangzhou 廣州市	Guangdong 廣東省	(020)86564081 (020)86578919	136	Foreign-funded 外資	17,633	3157(4)	13,834	o
Wenzhou Shun Da High Speed Highway Safety Facilities Engineering Co. Ltd. 温州順達高速公路安全設施工程有限公司(1993)	Wenzhou 温州市	Zhejiang 浙江省	(0577)6557512 (0577)6557511	78	Overseas Chinese-funded 港澳台資	10,932	387(14)	16,761	o
Pizhou Safety Facilities Factory 邳州市安全設施廠(1987)	Xuzhou 徐州市	Jiangsu 江蘇省	(0516)6081429	106	Collectively-owned 集體	9,570	163(18)	6,008	o
Sanshui Intelligence Electron Electric Equipment Plant 三水市智能電子電器廠(1984)	Foshan 佛山市	Guangdong 廣東省	(0757)7718368 (0757)7732077	183	State-owned 國有	9,114	-6791(28)	29,803	a
Henan North Traffic Installation Engineering Co. Ltd. 河南北方交通設施工程有限公司(1989)	Jiaozuo 焦作市	Henan 河南省	(0391)6192792	90	Overseas Chinese-funded 港澳台資	7,454	-623(27)	13,926	o
Yuyao Traffic Mark Installation Factory 余姚市交通標誌設施廠(1980)	Ningbo 寧波市	Zhejiang 浙江省	(0574)2709046 (0574)2709274	46	Collectively-owned 集體	6,969	1728(6)	6,736	o

Top 10 Cities by Production Output 產出排名前 10 位城市	Province 省	Market share 市場份額	Number of firms 企業個數
Wuxi 無錫市	Jiangsu 江蘇省	24.01%	6
Guangzhou 廣州市	Guangdong 廣東省	14.55%	6
Foshan 佛山市	Guangdong 廣東省	12.42%	3
Shenzhen 深圳市	Guangdong 廣東省	9.23%	3
Shanghai 上海市	Shanghai 上海市	4.24%	5
Wenzhou 温州市	Zhejiang 浙江省	4.19%	2
Chuzhou 滁州市	Anhui 安徽省	3.27%	1
Ningbo 寧波市	Zhejiang 浙江省	2.43%	2
Xuzhou 徐州市	Jiangsu 江蘇省	2.35%	1
Jiaozuo 焦作市	Henan 河南省	2.02%	1

10 Major Wholesalers 10 家主要批發商	City 城市	Province 省	Telephone / Fax 電話 / 傳真
Liaoning Automobile Trade Group Corp. 遼寧省汽車貿易集團	Shenyang 瀋陽市	Liaoning 遼寧省	(024)23835494 (024)23838338
China Post and Telecommunication Equipment General Company 中國郵電器材總公司	Beijing 北京市	Beijing 北京市	(010)63523715 (010)63525935
Jiangsu Electromechanical Products General Company 江蘇省機電產品總公司	Nanjing 南京市	Jiangsu 江蘇省	(025)7713642 (025)7711036
Xi Nan Technology Import & Export Company 西南技術進出口公司	Chongqing 重慶市	Chongqing 重慶市	(023)63850185 (023)63850026
Changzhou Economic Technology Industrial Development Zone Tian Ming Trade Company 常州經濟技術產業開發區天明貿易公司	Changzhou 常州市	Jiangsu 江蘇省	(0519)8829882 (0519)8829882
Shanxi Mechanical Equipment Import & Export Company 山西省機械設備進出口公司	Taiyuan 太原市	Shanxi 山西省	(0351)4040713 (0351)4043981
Ningbo Five Mining Machinery Import & Export Company 寧波市五礦機械進出口公司	Ningbo 寧波市	Zhejiang 浙江省	(0574)7311255 (0574)7320322
Tianjin Jin Huan Electromechanical Complete Sets of Equipment Factory 天津市津環機電成套設備廠	Tianjin 天津市	Tianjin 天津市	(022)26371628
Yunnan Machinery Import & Export Company 雲南省機械進出口公司	Kunming 昆明市	Yunnan 雲南省	(0871)3164879 (0871)3136829
Tianjin Da Qiu Zhuang Yi Yuan Trade Center 天津市大丘莊億源商貿中心	Tianjin 天津市	Tianjin 天津市	(022)28899478 (022)28899046

*Also include sales by firms outside this industry.包括本行業以外廠家的銷售。"o" stands for "others". "o" 代表 "其他產品"。

4011: Generators 發電機製造業

The industry accounts for 0.122% of the total revenue of China's industrial sector in 1996. The revenue growth rate of the industry is 4.5% from 1995, as compared to the growth rate of China's industrial sector, 9.51%. The rate of return on asset is -0.15%. 63.45% of all firms in the industry made a profit while 33.99% had negative returns. The top province in terms of the industry's revenue is Shanghai, accounting for 14.41% of the total revenue.
本行業在1996年佔全行業總產值0.122%，行業年增長率為4.5%（全國工業年增長率9.51%）。行業的資產回報率-0.15%，63.45%的企業盈利，33.99%的企業虧損。銷售收入最高的省份為上海市，佔本行業的14.41%。

	Total number of firms 企業總數	Total number of employees 職工總數	Total revenue (mil. RMB) 總銷售收入（百萬元）	Total profit (mil. RMB) 總利潤（百萬元）	Return on assets 資產利潤率 (%)	Return on equity 權益利潤率 (%)	Labour productivity ('000 RMB / worker) 勞動生產率（千元/人）	Debts / assets 資產負債率 (%)	Total assets (mil. RMB) 總資產（百萬元）
Industry Overall 行業總體	268	127,251	7,076	-26	-0.15	-0.42	55.61	64.24	17,339

	Number of firms 企業個數	Average number of employees 平均職工人數	Average revenue ('000 RMB) 平均銷售收入（千元）	Average profit ('000 RMB) 平均利潤（千元）	Return on assets 資產利潤率 (%)	Return on equity 權益利潤率 (%)	Labour productivity ('000 RMB / worker) 勞動生產率（千元/人）	Average debts / assets 平均資產負債率(%)	Average Total assets ('000 RMB) 平均總資產（千元）
By ownership 產業所有權									
State-owned 國有	80	1,020	50,038	-313	-0.22	-0.65	49.06	65.37	139,550
Collectively-owned 集體	153	165	10,434	-2	-0.02	-0.05	63.32	67.80	11,801
Privately-owned 私有	2	36	4,913	0	0.01	0.04	136.46	87.97	2,950
Domestic JVs 聯營	2	146	8,608	-7	-0.05	-0.15	59.16	67.92	14,818
Joint stock 股份制	8	2,028	154,480	-108	-0.02	-0.07	76.17	66.15	459,300
Foreign-funded 外資	11	293	9,364	19	0.04	0.05	31.99	22.07	50,909
Overseas Chinese-funded 港澳台資	12	67	9,309	-2	-0.02	-0.03	138.77	37.68	8,291
By size 規模									
Large 大型	12	4,886	366,719	-1,999	-0.20	-0.54	75.05	63.02	998,428
Medium 中型	19	1,516	47,690	22	0.02	0.04	31.46	64.17	142,458
Small 小型	232	172	7,630	-10	-0.09	-0.30	44.45	69.82	11,427
By regional distribution 地區分布									
Central-North 華北	31	464	22,462	-1,350	-1.77	-5.74	48.44	69.13	76,247
Beijing 北京	11	677	45,787	427	0.31	1.10	67.66	71.98	138,067
Tianjin 天津	5	813	27,756	-9,280	-6.13	-16.14	34.12	62.02	151,452
Hebei 河北	11	113	3,305	81	2.34	9.97	29.35	76.48	3,451
Shanxi 山西	1	79	540				6.84	30.00	1,800
Inner Mongolia 內蒙	3	515	5,660	-350	-2.19	-16.59	10.99	86.78	15,967
Northeast 東北	22	762	36,287	157	0.15	0.59	47.63	73.92	102,013
Liaoning 遼寧	13	143	4,915	-568	-4.31	-14.14	34.26	69.55	13,201
Jilin 吉林									
Heilongjiang 黑龍江	9	1,655	81,602	1,204	0.52	2.03	49.31	74.29	230,298
Central East 華東	125	346	27,848	369	0.75	1.99	80.60	62.58	49,494
Shanghai 上海	5	1,537	203,906	5,420	1.20	2.94	132.63	59.07	450,086
Jiangsu 江蘇	31	310	32,884	209	0.60	2.06	106.20	71.12	35,037
Zhejiang 浙江	25	209	12,869	-1,266	-4.28	-8.65	61.51	50.51	29,579
Anhui 安徽	6	159	9,543	125	1.43	3.69	60.08	61.17	8,722
Fujian 福建	23	235	13,381	645	2.01	4.95	56.87	59.42	32,104
Jiangxi 江西	14	344	9,094	149	0.61	1.71	26.43	64.32	24,329
Shandong 山東	21	452	29,908	1,265	2.71	9.73	66.16	72.13	46,636
Central-South 中南	70	381	15,227	57	0.15	0.48	39.98	69.29	38,670
Henan 河南	12	326	8,204	-231	-1.16	-5.26	25.13	78.03	19,981
Hubei 湖北	9	1,089	46,374	3,143	2.17	6.34	42.57	65.79	144,997
Hunan 湖南	10	365	7,238	-358	-1.70	-8.76	19.83	80.62	21,092
Guangdong 廣東	27	158	9,120	-54	-0.42	-1.37	57.86	68.99	12,646
Guangxi 廣西	12	420	19,285	-1,374	-2.70	-8.90	45.96	69.60	50,816
Hainan 海南									
Southwest 西南	12	1,813	81,271	-588	-0.20	-0.42	44.82	52.57	297,361
Chongqing 重慶	3	224	1,898	7	0.46	3.82	8.46	87.89	1,409
Sichuan 四川	4	4,605	220,770	1,518	0.18	0.37	47.94	51.48	835,649
Guizhou 貴州	3	227	1,907	-1,270	-12.77	-57.38	8.39	77.74	9,943
Yunnan 雲南	2	1,233	52,535	1,335	0.94	2.46	42.61	61.77	142,180
Tibet 西藏									
Northwest 西北	8	564	7,345	-3,848	-11.42	-64.96	13.03	82.42	33,683
Shaanxi 陝西	5	740	9,488	-5,032	-12.54	-86.67	12.81	85.54	40,142
Gansu 甘肅	2	169	3,500	-1,060	-9.13	-47.32	20.71	80.70	11,605
Qinghai 青海									
Ningxia 寧夏									
Xinjiang 新疆	1	468	4,320	-3,500	-7.69	-25.23	9.23	69.54	45,540

Year 年份	Number of firms 企業個數	Rate of change 每年變化 (%)	Number of employees 職工人數 (人)	Rate of change 每年變化 (%)	Total revenue (mil. RMB) 總銷售收入 (百萬元)	Rate of change 每年變化 (%)	Total profit (mil. RMB) 總利潤 (百萬元)	Rate of change 每年變化 (%)
1993	228		144,184		5,576		305	
1994	243	6.58%	130,740	-9.33%	6,919	24.08%	367	20.61%
1995	268	10.29%	119,540	-8.57%	6,774	-2.09%	284	-22.64%
1996	268		127,251	6.45%	7,076	4.46%	-26	-109.15%

3 Major products* 3種主要產品*	Output 產量	Sales volume 銷售量	Unit 單位
a) Power Equipment 發電設備	18,161,963	17,253,865	kw 千瓦
b) AC Motor 交流電動機	2,932,832	2,727,534	set 台

Top 10 firms by revenue (year founded) 收入排名前10家企業 (創辦年份)	City 城市	Province 省	Telephone / fax 電話 / 傳真	Number of employees 職工人數	Ownership 產業所有權	Revenue ('000 RMB) 銷售收入 (千元)	Profit ('000 RMB) (rank) 利潤 (千元) (排名)	Total assets ('000 RMB) 總資產 (千元)	Major products 主要產品
Shanghai Electrical Machinery Manufacturing Works 上海電機廠(1909)	Shanghai 上海市	Shanghai 上海市	(021)64638221 (021)64632422	6,251	State-owned 國有	714,408	14863(4)	1,358,152	a,b
Dong Fang Electrical Machinery Works 東方電機廠(1966)	Deyang 德陽市	Sichuan 四川省	(0838)2300471 (0838)2300470	10,437	State-owned 國有	652,979	8170(8)	2,670,297	a,b
Harbin Electric Machinery Co. Ltd. 哈爾濱電機有限責任公司(1951)	Harbin 哈爾濱市	Heilongjiang 黑龍江省	(0451)2102625 (0451)2102580	9,633	Joint stock 股份制	647,216	8648(7)	1,926,394	a,b
Beijing Heavy Electric Machinery Works 北京重型電機廠(1958)	Beijing 北京市	Beijing 北京市	(010)68211199	7,739	State-owned 國有	499,948	5388(9)	1,497,750	a,b
Jiangdu Shifa Group 江都世發集團(1963)	Yangzhou 揚州市	Jiangsu 江蘇省	(0514)6821470 (0514)6821472	1,015	Collectively-owned 集體	300,342	1306(20)	219,315	a
Shanghai Steam Turbine Generator Co. Ltd. 上海汽輪發電機有限公司(1996)	Shanghai 上海市	Shanghai 上海市	(021)64638221 (021)64632422	874	Foreign-funded 外資	297,865	12016(5)	880,216	a
Wuhan Steam Turbine Generator Plant 武漢汽輪發電機廠(1959)	Wuhan 武漢市	Hubei 湖北省	(027)87803581 (027)87801455	5,632	State-owned 國有	294,586	30712(1)	1,096,226	o
Zibo Electric Traction Machine Co. Ltd. 淄博牽引電機股份有限公司(1958)	Zibo 淄博市	Shandong 山東省	(0533)2181821 (0533)2180311	2,804	Joint stock 股份制	206,766	15264(3)	267,434	a,b
Dongfeng Electric Engine Factory 東風電機廠(1965)	Leshan 樂山市	Sichuan 四川省	(0833)3351243	6,082	State-owned 國有	165,291	-14950(152)	513,526	a
Wuxi Electric Machine Factory 無錫市電機廠(1958)	Wuxi 無錫市	Jiangsu 江蘇省	(0510)2704595 (0510)2707189	1,263	State-owned 國有	146,376	829(31)	278,287	a

Top 10 Cities by Production Output 產出排名前10位城市	Province 省	Market share 市場份額	Number of firms 企業個數
Shanghai 上海市	Shanghai 上海市	13.74%	17
Yangzhou 揚州市	Jiangsu 江蘇省	10.24%	15
Harbin 哈爾濱市	Heilongjiang 黑龍江省	8.06%	17
Deyang 德陽市	Sichuan 四川省	7.08%	2
Beijing 北京市	Beijing 北京市	6.77%	7
Fuzhou 福州市	Fujian 福建省	4.30%	6
Wuxi 無錫市	Jiangsu 江蘇省	3.51%	12
Wuhan 武漢市	Hubei 湖北省	3.16%	5
Lanzhou 蘭州市	Gansu 甘肅省	2.58%	2
Chengdu 成都市	Sichuan 四川省	2.42%	8

10 Major Wholesalers 10家主要批發商	City 城市	Province 省	Telephone / Fax 電話 / 傳真
Liaoning Automobile Trade Group Corp. 遼寧省汽車貿易集團	Shenyang 瀋陽市	Liaoning 遼寧省	(024)23835494 (024)23838338
China Post and Telecommunication Equipment General Company 中國郵電器材總公司	Beijing 北京市	Beijing 北京市	(010)63523715 (010)63525935
Jiangsu Electromechanical Products General Company 江蘇省機電產品總公司	Nanjing 南京市	Jiangsu 江蘇省	(025)7713642 (025)7711036
Xi Nan Technology Import & Export Company 西南技術進出口公司	Chongqing 重慶市	Chongqing 重慶市	(023)63850185 (023)63850026
Changzhou Economic Technology Industrial Development Zone Tian Ming Trade Company 常州經濟技術產業開發區天明貿易公司	Changzhou 常州市	Jiangsu 江蘇省	(0519)8829882 (0519)8829882
Shanxi Mechanical Equipment Import & Export Company 山西省機械設備進出口公司	Taiyuan 太原市	Shanxi 山西省	(0351)4040713 (0351)4043981
Ningbo Five Mining Machinery Import & Export Company 寧波市五礦機械進出口公司	Ningbo 寧波市	Zhejiang 浙江省	(0574)7311255 (0574)7320322
Tianjin Jin Huan Electromechanical Complete Sets of Equipment Factory 天津市津環機電成套設備廠	Tianjin 天津市	Tianjin 天津市	(022)26371628
Yunnan Machinery Import & Export Company 雲南省機械進出口公司	Kunming 昆明市	Yunnan 雲南省	(0871)3164879 (0871)3136829
Tianjin Da Qiu Zhuang Yi Yuan Trade Center 天津市大丘莊億源商貿中心	Tianjin 天津市	Tianjin 天津市	(022)28899478 (022)28899046

*Also include sales by firms outside this industry.包括本行業以外廠家的銷售。"o" stands for "others". "o" 代表"其他產品"。

4012: Motors 電動機製造業

The industry accounts for 0.225% of the total revenue of China's industrial sector in 1996. The revenue growth rate of the industry is -8.5% from 1995, as compared to the growth rate of China's industrial sector, 9.51%. The rate of return on asset is 0.26%. 63.20% of all firms in the industry made a profit while 31.63% had negative returns. The top province in terms of the industry's revenue is Jiangsu, accounting for 15.25% of the total revenue.
本行業在1996年佔全行業總產值0.225%，行業年增長率為-8.5%（全國工業年增長率9.51%）。行業的資產回報率0.26%，63.20%的企業盈利，31.63%的企業虧損。銷售收入最高的省份為江蘇省，佔本行業的15.25%。

	Total number of firms 企業總數	Total number of employees 職工總數	Total revenue (mil. RMB) 總銷售收入（百萬元）	Total profit (mil. RMB) 總利潤（百萬元）	Return on assets 資產利潤率 (%)	Return on equity 權益利潤率 (%)	Labour productivity ('000 RMB / worker) 勞動生產率（千元/人）	Debts / assets 資產負債率 (%)	Total assets (mil. RMB) 總資產（百萬元）
Industry Overall 行業總體	759	269,299	13,044	61	0.26	0.74	48.44	65.25	23,693

	Number of firms 企業個數	Average number of employees 平均職工人數	Average revenue ('000 RMB) 平均銷售收入（千元）	Average profit ('000 RMB) 平均利潤（千元）	Return on assets 資產利潤率 (%)	Return on equity 權益利潤率 (%)	Labour productivity ('000 RMB / worker) 勞動生產率（千元/人）	Average debts / assets 平均資產負債率(%)	Average Total assets ('000 RMB) 平均總資產（千元）
By ownership 產業所有權									
State-owned 國有	210	785	29,890	-48	-0.07	-0.19	38.09	65.20	72,267
Collectively-owned 集體	466	161	8,131	142	1.53	5.88	50.51	73.98	9,273
Privately-owned 私有	4	34	3,423	74	2.61	10.52	102.19	75.23	2,835
Domestic JVs 聯營	16	159	7,106	118	0.90	2.46	44.62	63.36	13,033
Joint stock 股份制	18	972	61,667	2,420	2.64	7.84	63.43	66.37	91,805
Foreign-funded 外資	23	355	61,723	-2,327	-2.66	-5.05	173.87	47.38	87,610
Overseas Chinese-funded 港澳台資	21	144	15,263	601	4.16	9.95	105.75	58.24	14,446
By size 規模									
Large 大型	25	3,150	149,001	1,196	0.36	0.95	47.30	61.75	329,801
Medium 中型	99	877	47,928	455	0.50	1.39	54.63	63.86	90,734
Small 小型	626	166	7,307	-22	-0.22	-0.76	43.98	71.65	10,328
By regional distribution 地區分布									
Central-North 華北	86	418	18,179	-9	-0.02	-0.06	43.50	62.41	38,377
Beijing 北京	11	550	19,165	-123	-0.36	-1.26	34.82	71.58	34,300
Tianjin 天津	21	294	10,849	-1,020	-2.18	-4.49	36.91	51.39	46,756
Hebei 河北	34	288	15,792	708	3.10	10.36	54.90	70.05	22,826
Shanxi 山西	11	992	48,387	198	0.23	0.56	48.79	59.26	86,239
Inner Mongolia 內蒙	9	336	6,173	-478	-1.99	-11.54	18.38	82.79	24,057
Northeast 東北	93	425	21,247	37	0.08	0.24	50.04	66.08	45,169
Liaoning 遼寧	65	402	26,005	381	0.80	2.15	64.77	62.69	47,460
Jilin 吉林	12	343	4,115	-1,318	-6.80	1171.11	11.99	100.58	19,376
Heilongjiang 黑龍江	16	579	14,763	-344	-0.62	-2.00	25.49	68.83	55,208
Central East 華東	384	261	16,169	165	0.72	1.95	61.91	63.29	23,097
Shanghai 上海	55	302	20,627	-43	-0.15	-0.58	68.26	74.25	29,091
Jiangsu 江蘇	92	318	21,616	279	1.09	2.99	68.05	63.53	25,611
Zhejiang 浙江	89	137	10,510	126	1.09	3.40	76.71	67.83	11,536
Anhui 安徽	33	233	9,543	-15	-0.11	-0.47	41.04	77.67	14,315
Fujian 福建	59	131	10,890	-24	-0.18	-0.46	82.82	61.79	13,843
Jiangxi 江西	15	438	10,601	151	0.20	0.27	24.21	25.51	75,721
Shandong 山東	41	494	25,218	697	1.96	7.31	51.07	73.24	35,648
Central-South 中南	142	434	15,989	154	0.46	1.34	36.82	66.06	33,802
Henan 河南	39	382	11,462	247	0.99	4.12	30.02	75.95	24,961
Hubei 湖北	19	423	10,692	-164	-0.61	-1.99	25.28	69.10	26,681
Hunan 湖南	38	707	20,446	39	0.07	0.17	28.90	59.94	58,302
Guangdong 廣東	35	243	20,876	704	2.99	8.59	86.02	65.21	23,567
Guangxi 廣西	11	305	10,242	-979	-3.86	-16.88	33.58	77.14	25,384
Hainan 海南									
Southwest 西南	33	419	12,726	-493	-1.89	-8.32	30.39	77.29	26,078
Chongqing 重慶	12	264	8,433	22	0.13	0.60	31.92	78.43	17,024
Sichuan 四川	16	453	12,268	-498	-1.88	-8.29	27.07	77.32	26,489
Guizhou 貴州	2	812	6,655	-2,490	-6.72	-21.93	8.20	69.34	37,040
Yunnan 雲南	3	574	36,050	-1,143	-2.20	-10.74	62.84	79.52	51,977
Tibet 西藏									
Northwest 西北	21	863	28,815	-519	-0.66	-2.24	33.40	70.73	79,151
Shaanxi 陝西	12	629	16,301	-345	-0.74	-2.18	25.93	65.90	46,346
Gansu 甘肅	5	1,555	52,582	-1,320	-0.88	-3.19	33.81	72.47	150,538
Qinghai 青海	2	99	70	-610	-13.29	-49.39	0.71	73.20	4,590
Ningxia 寧夏	1	1,112	30,820	20	0.02	0.13	27.72	84.02	95,820
Xinjiang 新疆	1	1,490	115,640	1,050	0.42	1.46	77.61	71.09	248,330

Year 年份	Number of firms 企業個數	Rate of change 每年變化 (%)	Number of employees 職工人數 (人)	Rate of change 每年變化 (%)	Total revenue (mil. RMB) 總銷售收入 (百萬元)	Rate of change 每年變化 (%)	Total profit (mil. RMB) 總利潤 (百萬元)	Rate of change 每年變化 (%)
1993	659		340,060		14,115		544	
1994	704	6.83%	266,360	-21.67%	12,681	-10.16%	316	-41.98%
1995	750	6.53%	296,742	11.41%	14,251	12.38%	107	-66.15%
1996	759	1.20%	269,299	-9.25%	13,044	-8.47%	61	-42.96%

3 Major products* 3 種主要產品 *	Output 產量	Sales volume 銷售量	Unit 單位
a) AC Motor 交流電動機	7,220,889	6,715,426	set 台
b) DC Motor 直流電動機	2,464,750	2,464,750	kw 千瓦

Top 10 firms by revenue (year founded) 收入排名前 10 家企業 (創辦年份)	City 城市	Province 省	Telephone / fax 電話 / 傳真	Number of employees 職工人數	Ownership 產業所有權	Revenue ('000 RMB) 銷售收入 (千元)	Profit ('000 RMB) (rank) 利潤 (千元) (排名)	Total assets ('000 RMB) 總資產 (千元)	Major products 主要產品
Toshiba Dalian Co. Ltd. 東芝大連有限公司(1991)	Dalian 大連市	Liaoning 遼寧省	(0411)7614111 (0411)7613259	1,306	Foreign-funded 外資	741,092	12316(4)	788,346	a
Yongji Electric Engine Factory 永濟電機廠(1969)	Yuncheng 運城市	Shanxi 山西省	(0359)8023825 (0359)8022090	6,574	State-owned 國有	442,540	7720(14)	660,700	a,b
Nan Fang General Electrical Equipment Group Company 南方通用電氣集團公司(1969)	Xiangtan 湘潭市	Hunan 湖南省	(0732)8595804 (0732)8610767	12,331	State-owned 國有	375,305	2687(35)	1,276,631	a,b
Min Dong Electric Machinery (Group) Co. Ltd. 閩東電機(集團)股份有限公司(1958)	Fuzhou 福州市	Fujian 福建省	(0591)3355466 (0591)3326201	4,252	Joint stock 股份制	352,170	-14575(483)	586,690	o
Shenyang Electric Engine Factory 瀋陽電機廠(1950)	Shenyang 瀋陽市	Liaoning 遼寧省	(024)25820046 (024)25820906	3,738	State-owned 國有	230,740	10014(10)	640,096	a
Taicang Liu He Electric Engine Factory 太倉劉河電機廠(1973)	Suzhou 蘇州市	Jiangsu 江蘇省	(0512)3611473	725	Collectively-owned 集體	230,720	10080(9)	121,480	a
Lanzhou Electric Machine Works 蘭州電機廠(1959)	Lanzhou 蘭州市	Gansu 甘肅省	(0931)2336951 (0931)2335068	6,015	State-owned 國有	220,841	2578(39)	639,843	a,b
Zhejiang Bai Guan Electro Mechanical Group 浙江百官機電集團(1970)	Shaoxing 紹興市	Zhejiang 浙江省	(0575)2012260 (0575)2012260	512	Collectively-owned 集體	211,441	9363(11)	84,050	a
Dalian Electric Machine Works 大連電機廠(1946)	Dalian 大連市	Liaoning 遼寧省	(0411)4604221 (0411)4602958	4,475	State-owned 國有	203,179	2093(46)	494,764	a
Shunde De Sheng Electric Machinery Co. Ltd. 順德市德勝電機有限公司(1960)	Foshan 佛山市	Guangdong 廣東省	(0757)2622590 (0757)2632006	1,007	State-owned 國有	180,438	17815(1)	146,915	a

Top 10 Cities by Production Output 產出排名前 10 位城市	Province 省	Market share 市場份額	Number of firms 企業個數
Shanghai 上海市	Shanghai 上海市	9.00%	82
Dalian 大連市	Liaoning 遼寧省	8.81%	10
Suzhou 蘇州市	Jiangsu 江蘇省	3.74%	22
Foshan 佛山市	Guangdong 廣東省	3.61%	5
Xiangtan 湘潭市	Hunan 湖南省	3.45%	3
Wuxi 無錫市	Jiangsu 江蘇省	3.40%	34
Yuncheng 運城市	Shanxi 山西省	3.28%	3
Shenyang 瀋陽市	Liaoning 遼寧省	2.85%	35
Shaoxing 紹興市	Zhejiang 浙江省	2.71%	17
Weihai 威海市	Shandong 山東省	2.28%	8

10 Major Wholesalers 10 家主要批發商	City 城市	Province 省	Telephone / Fax 電話 / 傳真
Liaoning Automobile Trade Group Corp. 遼寧省汽車貿易集團	Shenyang 瀋陽市	Liaoning 遼寧省	(024)23835494 (024)23838338
China Post and Telecommunication Equipment General Company 中國郵電器材總公司	Beijing 北京市	Beijing 北京市	(010)63523715 (010)63525935
Jiangsu Electromechanical Products General Company 江蘇省機電產品總公司	Nanjing 南京市	Jiangsu 江蘇省	(025)7713642 (025)7711036
Xi Nan Technology Import & Export Company 西南技術進出口公司	Chongqing 重慶市	Chongqing 重慶市	(023)63850185 (023)63850026
Changzhou Economic Technology Industrial Development Zone Tian Ming Trade Company 常州經濟技術產業開發區天明貿易公司	Changzhou 常州市	Jiangsu 江蘇省	(0519)8829882 (0519)8829882
Shanxi Mechanical Equipment Import & Export Company 山西省機械設備進出口公司	Taiyuan 太原市	Shanxi 山西省	(0351)4040713 (0351)4043981
Ningbo Five Mining Machinery Import & Export Company 寧波市五礦機械進出口公司	Ningbo 寧波市	Zhejiang 浙江省	(0574)7311255 (0574)7320322
Tianjin Jin Huan Electromechanical Complete Sets of Equipment Factory 天津市津環機電成套設備廠	Tianjin 天津市	Tianjin 天津市	(022)26371628
Yunnan Machinery Import & Export Company 雲南省機械進出口公司	Kunming 昆明市	Yunnan 雲南省	(0871)3164879 (0871)3136829
Tianjin Da Qiu Zhuang Yi Yuan Trade Center 天津市大丘莊億源商貿中心	Tianjin 天津市	Tianjin 天津市	(022)28899478 (022)28899046

*Also include sales by firms outside this industry.包括本行業以外廠家的銷售。"o" stands for "others". "o" 代表 "其他產品"。

4013: Mini-motors 微電機製造業

The industry accounts for 0.121% of the total revenue of China's industrial sector in 1996. The revenue growth rate of the industry is 15.0% from 1995, as compared to the growth rate of China's industrial sector, 9.51%. The rate of return on asset is 0.51%. 60.42% of all firms in the industry made a profit while 32.12% had negative returns. The top province in terms of the industry's revenue is Liaoning, accounting for 27.49% of the total revenue.
本行業在 1996 年佔全行業總產值 0.121% ，行業年增長率為 15.0%（全國工業年增長率 9.51%）。行業的資產回報率 0.51% ， 60.42% 的企業盈利， 32.12% 的企業虧損。銷售收入最高的省份為遼寧省，佔本行業的 27.49% 。

	Total number of firms 企業總數	Total number of employees 職工總數	Total revenue (mil. RMB) 總銷售收入（百萬元）	Total profit (mil. RMB) 總利潤（百萬元）	Return on assets 資產利潤率 (%)	Return on equity 權益利潤率 (%)	Labour productivity ('000 RMB / worker) 勞動生產率（千元/人）	Debts / assets 資產負債率 (%)	Total assets (mil. RMB) 總資產（百萬元）
Industry Overall 行業總體	479	100,502	7,002	47	0.51	1.61	69.67	68.29	9,243

	Number of firms 企業個數	Average number of employees 平均職工人數	Average revenue ('000 RMB) 平均銷售收入（千元）	Average profit ('000 RMB) 平均利潤（千元）	Return on assets 資產利潤率 (%)	Return on equity 權益利潤率 (%)	Labour productivity ('000 RMB / worker) 勞動生產率（千元/人）	Average debts / assets 平均資產負債率(%)	Average Total assets ('000 RMB) 平均總資產（千元）
By ownership 產業所有權									
State-owned 國有	75	375	18,133	-373	-1.05	-4.76	48.35	78.03	35,680
Collectively-owned 集體	325	151	7,549	78	0.96	3.41	50.09	71.98	8,172
Privately-owned 私有	1	18	192	-82	-7.02	-33.56	10.66	79.07	1,173
Domestic JVs 聯營	14	346	35,495	750	1.57	5.26	102.65	70.18	47,874
Joint stock 股份制	7	314	34,825	2,966	7.93	15.26	110.91	48.04	37,417
Foreign-funded 外資	26	504	81,819	1,009	1.08	2.62	162.39	58.83	93,526
Overseas Chinese-funded 港澳台資	31	154	10,331	-253	-1.43	-3.00	67.22	52.17	17,643
By size 規模									
Large 大型	12	1,851	181,756	5,709	2.14	6.09	98.18	64.95	267,353
Medium 中型	29	687	41,454	-1,573	-2.46	-9.42	60.31	73.91	64,013
Small 小型	432	136	8,376	56	0.58	1.82	61.47	68.36	9,674
By regional distribution 地區分布									
Central-North 華北	77	109	6,826	166	1.56	5.23	62.83	70.25	10,691
Beijing 北京	16	86	2,389	18	0.16	0.47	27.84	65.08	11,098
Tianjin 天津	33	124	9,224	278	2.14	7.75	74.13	72.38	12,987
Hebei 河北	15	86	9,023	217	3.74	7.49	105.41	50.07	5,797
Shanxi 山西	9	140	4,003	-19	-0.28	-0.89	28.66	68.00	6,632
Inner Mongolia 內蒙	4	87	2,908	68	0.38	13.43	33.61	97.15	17,608
Northeast 東北	33	616	59,802	53	0.07	0.23	97.10	68.25	73,558
Liaoning 遼寧	26	645	74,022	506	0.59	1.71	114.84	65.19	85,127
Jilin 吉林	5	637	9,522	-2,258	-5.48	1710.61	14.96	100.32	41,212
Heilongjiang 黑龍江	2	192	635	-50	-1.24	-10.64	3.32	88.46	4,030
Central East 華東	224	167	13,167	165	1.00	3.14	78.85	68.31	16,553
Shanghai 上海	31	110	10,587	183	1.25	3.06	96.56	59.32	14,684
Jiangsu 江蘇	55	250	19,236	39	0.16	0.54	76.99	70.79	24,291
Zhejiang 浙江	94	104	8,320	93	0.95	2.86	80.17	66.76	9,813
Anhui 安徽	15	392	30,894	280	0.68	3.71	78.86	81.70	41,188
Fujian 福建	6	145	2,122	-140	-2.56	-9.16	14.65	72.10	5,478
Jiangxi 江西	8	122	3,295	-174	-2.17	-14.21	27.12	84.75	8,018
Shandong 山東	15	186	18,573	1,226	6.58	11.43	99.82	42.38	18,622
Central-South 中南	111	240	12,615	165	0.99	2.82	52.61	64.85	16,710
Henan 河南	25	73	4,164	147	3.89	10.90	56.79	64.35	3,778
Hubei 湖北	10	308	6,902	-296	-1.17	-4.44	22.38	73.61	25,261
Hunan 湖南	14	150	5,488	-147	-1.71	-6.36	36.66	73.18	8,630
Guangdong 廣東	52	356	21,186	505	1.99	5.15	59.49	61.38	25,391
Guangxi 廣西	10	108	4,864	-653	-9.81	-70.44	44.87	86.09	6,658
Hainan 海南									
Southwest 西南	19	295	6,801	-578	-3.62	-12.34	23.08	70.69	15,991
Chongqing 重慶	7	149	2,626	-2,082	-65.35	-408.75	17.67	84.01	3,185
Sichuan 四川	9	482	11,682	417	1.45	5.17	24.25	72.06	28,841
Guizhou 貴州	2	18	120	-330	-4.54	-6.13	6.86	26.05	7,275
Yunnan 雲南	1	145	4,160	130	3.47	11.61	28.69	70.13	3,750
Tibet 西藏									
Northwest 西北	15	146	1,623	-768	-9.12	5008.70	11.09	100.17	8,421
Shaanxi 陝西	12	95	1,002	-34	-1.14	-3.95	10.50	71.23	3,004
Gansu 甘肅									
Qinghai 青海	1	842	10,160	-9,710	-12.34	104.41	12.07	111.82	78,710
Ningxia 寧夏	2	104	1,080	-700	-12.11	107.69	10.43	111.16	5,780
Xinjiang 新疆									

4013: Mini-motors 微電機製造業

Year 年份	Number of firms 企業個數	Rate of change 每年變化 (%)	Number of employees 職工人數（人）	Rate of change 每年變化 (%)	Total revenue (mil. RMB) 總銷售收入（百萬元）	Rate of change 每年變化 (%)	Total profit (mil. RMB) 總利潤（百萬元）	Rate of change 每年變化 (%)
1993	432		125,093		4,887		188	
1994	440	1.85%	116,683	-6.72%	5,751	17.68%	39	-79.22%
1995	449	2.05%	110,972	-4.90%	6,088	5.85%	28	-28.54%
1996	479	6.68%	100,502	-9.43%	7,002	15.01%	47	68.15%

3 Major products* 3 種主要產品 *	Output 產量	Sales volume 銷售量	Unit 單位
a) Mini-motor 微電機	108,907	78,413	10,000 set 萬台

Top 10 firms by revenue (year founded) 收入排名前 10 家企業（創辦年份）	City 城市	Province 省	Telephone / fax 電話 / 傳真	Number of employees 職工人數	Ownership 產業所有權	Revenue ('000 RMB) 銷售收入（千元）	Profit ('000 RMB) (rank) 利潤（千元）（排名）	Total assets ('000 RMB) 總資產（千元）	Major products 主要產品
Mabuchi Motor Dalian Co. Ltd. 萬寶至馬達大連有限公司(1987)	Dalian 大連市	Liaoning 遼寧省	(0411)7611111 (0411)7612900	6,654	Foreign-funded 外資	807,712	22154(1)	1,086,449	a
Nidec 日本電產大連有限公司(1992)	Dalian 大連市	Liaoning 遼寧省	(0411)7310202 (0411)7314979	2,339	Foreign-funded 外資	752,323	299(77)	548,264	a
Changzhou Group of Best Models 常州寶馬集團公司(1959)	Changzhou 常州市	Jiangsu 江蘇省	(0519)8351091 (0519)8350301	2,806	Domestic JVs 聯營	351,554	10243(3)	526,328	a
Tianjin Tian Yuan Group Co. Ltd. 天津天元集團有限公司(1986)	Tianjin 天津市	Tianjin 天津市	(022)25990031	798	Collectively-owned 集體	195,910	7740(7)	74,180	a
Zhongshan Tong Da Electro Mechanical Factory 中山市通達機電廠(1994)	Zhongshan 中山市	Guangdong 廣東省	(0760)8704279 (0760)8704279	982	Collectively-owned 集體	165,610	220(86)	35,310	o
State-owned Qing Feng Machinery Factory 國營青峯機械廠(1960)	Fuyang 阜陽市	Anhui 安徽省	(0558)2323601 (0558)2322596	1,251	State-owned 國有	146,107	7127(8)	149,207	a
Taizhou Navigation Electric General Factory 泰州航海電氣總廠(1956)	Taizhou 泰州市	Jiangsu 江蘇省	(0523)6550225 (0523)6550082	1,129	Domestic JVs 聯營	129,760	3115(21)	107,782	a
Heshan Motor Factory 鶴山市電機廠(1958)	Jiangmen 江門市	Guangdong 廣東省	(0750)8880698 (0750)8888395	773	State-owned 國有	110,027	1006(40)	162,115	a
Chaoyang Group Co. Ltd. 黃山朝陽集團有限公司(1986)	Huangshan 黃山市	Anhui 安徽省	(0559)4512888 (0559)4513888	2,110	State-owned 國有	108,236	3180(19)	116,343	o
Wuhu Micro Motor Factory 蕪湖市電機廠(1953)	Wuhu 蕪湖市	Anhui 安徽省	(0553)3845911 (0553)3854402	1,097	State-owned 國有	100,358	-5979(263)	290,540	o

Top 10 Cities by Production Output 產出排名前 10 位城市	Province 省	Market share 市場份額	Number of firms 企業個數
Dalian 大連市	Liaoning 遼寧省	29.77%	9
Changzhou 常州市	Jiangsu 江蘇省	5.48%	33
Huzhou 湖州市	Zhejiang 浙江省	5.21%	18
Shanghai 上海市	Shanghai 上海市	4.85%	43
Ningbo 寧波市	Zhejiang 浙江省	4.06%	35
Jiangmen 江門市	Guangdong 廣東省	3.26%	7
Taizhou 泰州市	Jiangsu 江蘇省	2.89%	17
Foshan 佛山市	Guangdong 廣東省	2.83%	9
Weihai 威海市	Shandong 山東省	2.56%	7
Shenzhen 深圳市	Guangdong 廣東省	2.14%	11

10 Major Wholesalers 10 家主要批發商	City 城市	Province 省	Telephone / Fax 電話 / 傳真
Liaoning Automobile Trade Group Corp. 遼寧省汽車貿易集團	Shenyang 瀋陽市	Liaoning 遼寧省	(024)23835494 (024)23838338
China Post and Telecommunication Equipment General Company 中國郵電器材總公司	Beijing 北京市	Beijing 北京市	(010)63523715 (010)63525935
Jiangsu Electromechanical Products General Company 江蘇省機電產品總公司	Nanjing 南京市	Jiangsu 江蘇省	(025)7713642 (025)7711036
Xi Nan Technology Import & Export Company 西南技術進出口公司	Chongqing 重慶市	Chongqing 重慶市	(023)63850185 (023)63850026
Changzhou Economic Technology Industrial Development Zone Tian Ming Trade Company 常州經濟技術產業開發區天明貿易公司	Changzhou 常州市	Jiangsu 江蘇省	(0519)8829882 (0519)8829882
Shanxi Mechanical Equipment Import & Export Company 山西省機械設備進出口公司	Taiyuan 太原市	Shanxi 山西省	(0351)4040713 (0351)4043981
Ningbo Five Mining Machinery Import & Export Company 寧波市五礦機械進出口公司	Ningbo 寧波市	Zhejiang 浙江省	(0574)7311255 (0574)7320322
Tianjin Jin Huan Electromechanical Complete Sets of Equipment Factory 天津市津環機電成套設備廠	Tianjin 天津市	Tianjin 天津市	(022)26371628
Yunnan Machinery Import & Export Company 雲南省機械進出口公司	Kunming 昆明市	Yunnan 雲南省	(0871)3164879 (0871)3136829
Tianjin Da Qiu Zhuang Yi Yuan Trade Center 天津市大丘莊億源商貿中心	Tianjin 天津市	Tianjin 天津市	(022)28899478 (022)28899046

*Also include sales by firms outside this industry.包括本行業以外廠家的銷售。"o" stands for "others". "o" 代表 "其他產品" 。

4021: Transformers 變壓器製造業

The industry accounts for 0.217% of the total revenue of China's industrial sector in 1996. The revenue growth rate of the industry is 18.9% from 1995, as compared to the growth rate of China's industrial sector, 9.51%. The rate of return on asset is 1.46%. 66.45% of all firms in the industry made a profit while 28.28% had negative returns. The top province in terms of the industry's revenue is Guangdong, accounting for 21.64% of the total revenue.
本行業在1996年佔全行業總產值0.217%，行業年增長率為18.9%（全國工業年增長率9.51%）。行業的資產回報率1.46%，66.45%的企業盈利，28.28%的企業虧損。銷售收入最高的省份為廣東省，佔本行業的21.64%。

	Total number of firms 企業總數	Total number of employees 職工總數	Total revenue (mil. RMB) 總銷售收入（百萬元）	Total profit (mil. RMB) 總利潤（百萬元）	Return on assets 資產利潤率 (%)	Return on equity 權益利潤率 (%)	Labour productivity ('000 RMB / worker) 勞動生產率（千元/人）	Debts / assets 資產負債率 (%)	Total assets (mil. RMB) 總資產（百萬元）
Industry Overall 行業總體	968	176,811	12,559	288	1.46	4.15	71.03	64.84	19,709

	Number of firms 企業個數	Average number of employees 平均職工人數	Average revenue ('000 RMB) 平均銷售收入（千元）	Average profit ('000 RMB) 平均利潤（千元）	Return on assets 資產利潤率 (%)	Return on equity 權益利潤率 (%)	Labour productivity ('000 RMB / worker) 勞動生產率（千元/人）	Average debts / assets 平均資產負債率(%)	Average Total assets ('000 RMB) 平均總資產（千元）
By ownership 產業所有權									
State-owned 國有	219	343	21,790	479	1.15	3.73	63.61	69.07	41,571
Collectively-owned 集體	631	101	6,352	190	2.66	7.70	62.85	65.53	7,151
Privately-owned 私有	5	90	3,111	6	0.11	0.68	34.73	84.54	5,845
Domestic JVs 聯營	16	147	14,542	112	0.74	1.86	99.01	60.35	15,120
Joint stock 股份制	26	715	65,447	3,039	2.21	5.03	91.48	56.03	137,447
Foreign-funded 外資	34	288	33,256	-714	-1.85	-4.68	115.35	60.48	38,652
Overseas Chinese-funded 港澳台資	36	209	19,391	183	0.71	1.80	92.87	60.66	25,922
By size 規模									
Large 大型	17	1,716	188,489	8,068	2.17	5.64	109.82	61.49	371,315
Medium 中型	69	593	52,920	1,763	2.04	6.27	89.18	67.48	86,471
Small 小型	872	122	6,540	33	0.39	1.16	53.45	65.82	8,476
By regional distribution 地區分布									
Central-North 華北	140	151	7,886	104	0.64	1.83	52.20	65.03	16,184
Beijing 北京	43	103	3,124	-111	-1.17	-3.34	30.26	65.04	9,524
Tianjin 天津	32	83	3,377	-35	-0.62	-1.52	40.55	59.31	5,614
Hebei 河北	36	243	18,313	756	2.35	6.67	75.29	64.71	32,102
Shanxi 山西	17	215	6,801	-272	-1.42	-4.24	31.61	66.39	19,126
Inner Mongolia 內蒙	12	136	7,225	-180	-1.10	-3.66	53.16	69.83	16,310
Northeast 東北	204	195	10,345	166	0.83	2.27	52.95	63.31	19,939
Liaoning 遼寧	141	192	12,540	270	1.14	2.81	65.25	59.56	23,742
Jilin 吉林	33	192	5,259	-18	-0.16	-0.81	27.37	79.69	10,881
Heilongjiang 黑龍江	30	214	5,618	-119	-0.99	-5.44	26.28	81.83	12,033
Central East 華東	314	159	14,800	371	1.82	5.16	93.00	64.71	20,371
Shanghai 上海	58	77	7,328	66	0.60	1.55	94.64	61.15	10,940
Jiangsu 江蘇	77	184	19,354	643	2.86	8.58	105.21	66.62	22,454
Zhejiang 浙江	47	102	10,438	386	2.76	7.28	102.03	62.16	14,014
Anhui 安徽	20	266	12,445	-1,073	-4.54	-23.25	46.83	80.48	23,634
Fujian 福建	27	73	9,031	475	4.13	13.02	124.35	68.28	11,493
Jiangxi 江西	20	188	9,270	297	1.65	6.20	49.23	73.40	17,977
Shandong 山東	65	238	24,048	733	2.13	5.30	101.10	59.76	34,336
Central-South 中南	202	220	17,681	585	2.46	6.80	80.50	63.76	23,763
Henan 河南	44	113	4,868	94	1.18	4.90	43.12	75.82	7,945
Hubei 湖北	29	202	6,835	-43	-0.29	-0.85	33.80	66.02	14,763
Hunan 湖南	40	200	7,614	-158	-0.97	-3.31	38.10	70.76	16,326
Guangdong 廣東	73	321	37,238	1,895	4.50	10.90	115.86	58.70	42,108
Guangxi 廣西	12	109	5,254	-77	-0.53	-1.65	48.24	68.09	14,593
Hainan 海南	4	194	18,303	-3,933	-13.07	243.88	94.59	105.36	30,088
Southwest 西南	59	194	11,848	276	1.27	4.33	61.02	70.57	21,665
Chongqing 重慶	15	186	10,475	2,056	10.51	30.84	56.20	65.92	19,554
Sichuan 四川	28	180	9,058	-993	-6.36	-27.75	50.40	77.06	15,609
Guizhou 貴州	7	139	9,456	347	2.02	7.09	68.17	71.53	17,206
Yunnan 雲南	9	295	24,730	1,758	3.69	11.09	83.80	66.73	47,641
Tibet 西藏									
Northwest 西北	49	204	8,708	-238	-1.29	-4.28	42.60	69.79	18,391
Shaanxi 陝西	29	208	7,589	53	0.38	1.49	36.41	74.51	13,939
Gansu 甘肅	8	177	4,969	-1,381	-10.45	-25.85	28.05	59.56	13,215
Qinghai 青海	2	291	11,710	-20	-0.08	-0.30	40.31	73.37	25,140
Ningxia 寧夏	4	240	7,660	-2,573	-8.89	-23.95	31.98	62.87	28,928
Xinjiang 新疆	6	169	18,805	1,365	3.64	11.68	111.16	68.86	37,540

4021: Transformers 變壓器製造業

Year 年份	Number of firms 企業個數	Rate of change 每年變化 (%)	Number of employees 職工人數 （人）	Rate of change 每年變化 (%)	Total revenue (mil. RMB) 總銷售收入 （百萬元）	Rate of change 每年變化 (%)	Total profit (mil. RMB) 總利潤 （百萬元）	Rate of change 每年變化 (%)
1993	843		165,604		10,843		614	
1994	914	8.42%	176,280	6.45%	10,188	-6.04%	462	-24.74%
1995	930	1.75%	175,880	-0.23%	10,560	3.65%	344	-25.53%
1996	968	4.09%	176,811	0.53%	12,559	18.93%	288	-16.25%

3 Major products* 3 種主要產品 *	Output 產量	Sales volume 銷售量	Unit 單位
a) Transformer 變壓器	136,078,476	74,843,162	kva 千伏安
b) Mutual Inductor 互感器	341,452	327,794	set 台

Top 10 firms by revenue (year founded) 收入排名前 10 家企業 (創辦年份)	City 城市	Province 省	Telephone / fax 電話 / 傳真	Number of employees 職工人數	Ownership 產業所有權	Revenue ('000 RMB) 銷售收入（千元）	Profit ('000 RMB) (rank) 利潤（千元）（排名）	Total assets ('000 RMB) 總資產（千元）	Major products 主要產品
Zhuhai Mitsumi Electric Co. Ltd. 珠海三美電機有限公司(1991)	Zhuhai 珠海市	Guangdong 廣東省	(0756)8613251 (0756)8615447	4,364	Foreign-funded 外資	993,768	12912(8)	475,621	o
Shenyang Transformer Co. Ltd. 瀋陽變壓器有限責任公司(1938)	Shenyang 瀋陽市	Liaoning 遼寧省	(024)25851211 (024)25851119	9,035	Joint stock 股份制	760,777	52153(2)	1,812,257	a
Baoding Tianwei Group Co. Ltd. 保定天威集團有限公司(1963)	Baoding 保定市	Hebei 河北省	(0312)3227971 (0312)3227710	4,430	State-owned 國有	518,022	38213(4)	869,898	a,b
Shunde Special Transformer Works 順德特種變壓器廠(1988)	Foshan 佛山市	Guangdong 廣東省	(0757)2627411 (0757)2629923	568	State-owned 國有	402,433	71736(1)	464,760	a
Qingdao Transformer Factory 青島變壓器廠(1969)	Qingdao 青島市	Shandong 山東省	(0532)7869341 (0532)7860088	816	Collectively-owned 集體	240,391	16230(7)	418,235	o
Changzhou Transformer Factory 常州變壓器廠(1958)	Changzhou 常州市	Jiangsu 江蘇省	(0519)3260429 (0519)3260428	1,608	State-owned 國有	237,157	6682(19)	393,041	a
Tdk Dalian Electron Co. Ltd. TDK大連電子有限公司(1993)	Dalian 大連市	Liaoning 遼寧省	(0411)7314977 (0411)7314955	418	Foreign-funded 外資	229,020	4284(30)	349,996	o
Zhanjiang General Electrical Equipment Group Co. Ltd. 湛江通用電氣集團有限公司(1993)	Zhanjiang 湛江市	Guangdong 廣東省	(0758)3381112 (0758)3380528	970	Joint stock 股份制	185,260	890(81)	236,810	a,b
Shandong Jin Man Ke Electric Appliance Group Co. Ltd. 山東省金曼克電器集團股份有限公司(1967)	Jining 濟寧市	Shandong 山東省	(0537)8722513 (0537)8721576	790	State-owned 國有	157,874	43004(3)	228,800	a
Fuzhou Transformer Factory 福州變壓器廠(1959)	Fuzhou 福州市	Fujian 福建省	(0591)7911770 (0591)7912022	942	State-owned 國有	157,549	6553(21)	251,263	o

Top 10 Cities by Production Output 產出排名前 10 位城市	Province 省	Market share 市場份額	Number of firms 企業個數
Shanghai 上海市	Shanghai 上海市	11.44%	118
Shenyang 瀋陽市	Liaoning 遼寧省	7.20%	59
Zhuhai 珠海市	Guangdong 廣東省	6.99%	7
Shenzhen 深圳市	Guangdong 廣東省	4.68%	20
Baoding 保定市	Hebei 河北省	4.51%	13
Foshan 佛山市	Guangdong 廣東省	4.29%	12
Dalian 大連市	Liaoning 遼寧省	3.19%	19
Changzhou 常州市	Jiangsu 江蘇省	2.92%	15
Fuzhou 福州市	Fujian 福建省	2.53%	17
Qingdao 青島市	Shandong 山東省	2.22%	17

10 Major Wholesalers 10 家主要批發商	City 城市	Province 省	Telephone / Fax 電話 / 傳真
Liaoning Automobile Trade Group Corp. 遼寧省汽車貿易集團	Shenyang 瀋陽市	Liaoning 遼寧省	(024)23835494 (024)23838338
China Post and Telecommunication Equipment General Company 中國郵電器材總公司	Beijing 北京市	Beijing 北京市	(010)63523715 (010)63525935
Jiangsu Electromechanical Products General Company 江蘇省機電產品總公司	Nanjing 南京市	Jiangsu 江蘇省	(025)7713642 (025)7711036
Xi Nan Technology Import & Export Company 西南技術進出口公司	Chongqing 重慶市	Chongqing 重慶市	(023)63850185 (023)63850026
Changzhou Economic Technology Industrial Development Zone Tian Ming Trade Company 常州經濟技術產業開發區天明貿易公司	Changzhou 常州市	Jiangsu 江蘇省	(0519)8829882 (0519)8829882
Shanxi Mechanical Equipment Import & Export Company 山西省機械設備進出口公司	Taiyuan 太原市	Shanxi 山西省	(0351)4040713 (0351)4043981
Ningbo Five Mining Machinery Import & Export Company 寧波市五礦機械進出口公司	Ningbo 寧波市	Zhejiang 浙江省	(0574)7311255 (0574)7320322
Tianjin Jin Huan Electromechanical Complete Sets of Equipment Factory 天津市津環機電成套設備廠	Tianjin 天津市	Tianjin 天津市	(022)26371628
Yunnan Machinery Import & Export Company 雲南省機械進出口公司	Kunming 昆明市	Yunnan 雲南省	(0871)3164879 (0871)3136829
Tianjin Da Qiu Zhuang Yi Yuan Trade Center 天津市大丘莊億源商貿中心	Tianjin 天津市	Tianjin 天津市	(022)28899478 (022)28899046

*Also include sales by firms outside this industry.包括本行業以外廠家的銷售。"o" stands for "others". "o" 代表 "其他產品"。

4022: Rectifiers 整流器製造業

The industry accounts for 0.010% of the total revenue of China's industrial sector in 1996. The revenue growth rate of the industry is 3.9% from 1995, as compared to the growth rate of China's industrial sector, 9.51%. The rate of return on asset is -2.67%. 58.30% of all firms in the industry made a profit while 35.03% had negative returns. The top province in terms of the industry's revenue is Beijing, accounting for 28.29% of the total revenue.
本行業在 1996 年佔全行業總產值 0.010% ，行業年增長率為 3.9%（全國工業年增長率 9.51%）。行業的資產回報率 -2.67% ， 58.30% 的企業盈利， 35.03% 的企業虧損。銷售收入最高的省份為北京市，佔本行業的 28.29% 。

	Total number of firms 企業總數	Total number of employees 職工總數	Total revenue (mil. RMB) 總銷售收入（百萬元）	Total profit (mil. RMB) 總利潤（百萬元）	Return on assets 資產利潤率 (%)	Return on equity 權益利潤率 (%)	Labour productivity ('000 RMB / worker) 勞動生產率（千元／人）	Debts / assets 資產負債率 (%)	Total assets (mil. RMB) 總資產（百萬元）
Industry Overall 行業總體	173	17,654	581	-30	-2.67	-9.98	32.91	73.25	1,124

	Number of firms 企業個數	Average number of employees 平均職工人數	Average revenue ('000 RMB) 平均銷售收入（千元）	Average profit ('000 RMB) 平均利潤（千元）	Return on assets 資產利潤率 (%)	Return on equity 權益利潤率 (%)	Labour productivity ('000 RMB / worker) 勞動生產率（千元／人）	Average debts / assets 平均資產負債率(%)	Average Total assets ('000 RMB) 平均總資產（千元）
By ownership 產業所有權									
State-owned 國有	30	211	5,900	-633	-3.47	-18.45	27.93	81.17	18,233
Collectively-owned 集體	129	81	2,651	-1	-0.03	-0.08	32.81	66.72	3,444
Privately-owned 私有									
Domestic JVs 聯營	2	81							
Joint stock 股份制	2	138	2,396	-193	-1.13	-1.67	17.43	32.25	17,116
Foreign-funded 外資	4	40	3,044	-2,276	-16.94	-36.91	75.62	54.11	13,441
Overseas Chinese-funded 港澳台資	5	45	8,292	-326	-3.75	-96.33	183.44	96.10	8,695
By size 規模									
Large 大型	1	845	20,815	274	0.29	0.69	24.63	57.81	93,581
Medium 中型	4	683	23,755	-237	-0.36	-1.39	34.79	73.98	65,727
Small 小型	167	84	2,785	-176	-3.82	-15.17	33.35	74.84	4,600
By regional distribution 地區分布									
Central-North 華北	33	128	5,942	-331	-2.48	-8.80	46.57	71.82	13,341
Beijing 北京	19	154	8,650	-643	-3.45	-10.69	56.09	67.69	18,626
Tianjin 天津	7	63	2,113	27	0.27	3.62	33.54	92.57	10,090
Hebei 河北	7	120	2,420	159	7.06	24.72	20.19	71.46	2,247
Shanxi 山西									
Inner Mongolia 內蒙									
Northeast 東北	29	95	1,578	-61	-1.55	-6.62	16.65	76.58	3,960
Liaoning 遼寧	19	81	1,554	-45	-1.00	-4.61	19.19	78.19	4,452
Jilin 吉林	3	35	450	23	2.21	5.93	12.86	62.78	1,057
Heilongjiang 黑龍江	7	158	2,126	-143	-3.69	-13.77	13.47	73.16	3,870
Central East 華東	48	79	4,264	-14	-0.22	-0.78	53.95	72.06	6,277
Shanghai 上海	6	72	2,683	-160	-3.62	-11.90	37.53	69.58	4,422
Jiangsu 江蘇	14	69	4,332	84	1.95	5.52	63.18	64.76	4,293
Zhejiang 浙江	11	25	1,869	-60	-1.65	-6.12	75.04	73.02	3,633
Anhui 安徽	2	23	650	-145	-21.97	-63.04	28.89	65.15	660
Fujian 福建	2	41	1,605	20	1.24	4.65	39.15	73.68	1,615
Jiangxi 江西	4	147	4,880	-128	-0.88	-10.32	33.25	91.51	14,545
Shandong 山東	9	157	9,259	61	0.49	1.45	58.81	66.15	12,442
Central-South 中南	41	74	2,076	-394	-8.27	-46.64	27.90	82.28	4,769
Henan 河南	5	53	1,260	52	3.80	12.56	23.86	69.78	1,370
Hubei 湖北	3	124	303	-317	-45.02	39.42	2.45	214.22	703
Hunan 湖南	12	85	1,923	-38	-0.86	-2.79	22.73	69.18	4,462
Guangdong 廣東	16	53	2,471	-419	-7.74	-204.89	47.06	96.23	5,408
Guangxi 廣西	5	112	3,058	-1,664	-17.90	-54.59	27.35	67.24	9,298
Hainan 海南									
Southwest 西南	16	224	2,537	-1	-0.02	-0.04	11.34	57.55	3,756
Chongqing 重慶	4	246	2,191	-42	-2.51	-29.62	8.90	91.53	1,668
Sichuan 四川	9	256	2,311	61	1.33	2.64	9.03	49.70	4,613
Guizhou 貴州									
Yunnan 雲南	3	98	3,667	130	3.43	10.63	37.54	67.66	3,793
Tibet 西藏									
Northwest 西北	6	45	1,398	-82	-4.05	-9.18	30.85	55.90	2,018
Shaanxi 陝西	5	18	1,242	-12	-0.94	-2.01	67.50	53.36	1,278
Gansu 甘肅	1	180	2,180	-430	-7.52	-18.22	12.11	58.74	5,720
Qinghai 青海									
Ningxia 寧夏									
Xinjiang 新疆									

4022: Rectifiers 整流器製造業

Year 年份	Number of firms 企業個數	Rate of change 每年變化 (%)	Number of employees 職工人數（人）	Rate of change 每年變化 (%)	Total revenue (mil. RMB) 總銷售收入（百萬元）	Rate of change 每年變化 (%)	Total profit (mil. RMB) 總利潤（百萬元）	Rate of change 每年變化 (%)
1993	195		20,395		838		40	
1994	180	-7.69%	20,711	1.55%	540	-35.56%	-2	-105.07%
1995	172	-4.45%	18,733	-9.55%	559	3.59%	-26	-1196.02%
1996	173	0.58%	17,654	-5.76%	581	3.87%	-30	-13.75%

3 Major products* 3 種主要產品 *	Output 產量	Sales volume 銷售量	Unit 單位
a) Rectifier 整流器	1,400,844	1,442,869	kva 千伏安

Top 10 firms by revenue (year founded) 收入排名前 10 家企業（創辦年份）	City 城市	Province 省	Telephone / fax 電話 / 傳真	Number of employees 職工人數	Ownership 產業所有權	Revenue ('000 RMB) 銷售收入（千元）	Profit ('000 RMB) (rank) 利潤（千元）（排名）	Total assets ('000 RMB) 總資產（千元）	Major products 主要產品
Qingdao Rectifier General Work 青島整流器總廠(1966)	Qingdao 青島市	Shandong 山東省	(0532)4816908 (0532)4816908	807	State-owned 國有	44,232	304(16)	55,659	a
Beijing Wang Chao Fu Lv Clothing & Dress Adornment Co. Ltd. 北京王朝富履服裝服飾有限公司(1993)	Beijing 北京市	Beijing 北京市	(010)67032032 (010)67029222	670	Foreign-funded 外資	43,552	-39(42)	12,513	o
Beijing Rectifier Factory 北京整流器廠(1956)	Beijing 北京市	Beijing 北京市	(010)63403154 (010)63403154	1,106	State-owned 國有	28,402	-5999(59)	129,537	a
Tongzhou Electromechanical Factory 通州市機電廠(1969)	Nantong 南通市	Jiangsu 江蘇省	(0513)2528753 (0513)2528077	250	Collectively-owned 集體	25,670	29(28)	12,771	o
Yangzhou Hong Yang Electron Co. Ltd. 揚州虹揚電子有限公司(1992)	Yangzhou 揚州市	Jiangsu 江蘇省	(0514)7651951 (0514)7661951	109	Overseas Chinese-funded 港澳台資	18,695	1224(3)	8,534	o
Jiujiang Rectifier Factory 九江整流器廠(1968)	Jiujiang 九江市	Jiangxi 江西省	(0792)8113038 (0792)8221773		State-owned 國有	18,595	273(18)	44,404	a
Xiu Kang (qingdao)electric Power and Electronic Co. Ltd. 秀康(青島)電力電子有限公司	Qingdao 青島市	Shandong 山東省	(0532)4816745 (0532)4810147	23	Foreign-funded 外資	14,293	-369(49)	19,068	o
Shuangyashan Mine Administrative Bureau Baoshan Mine Diversification Company Plant & Mining Accessories Repair & Building Factory 雙鴨山礦務局寶山礦多經公司工礦配件修造廠(1982)	Shuangyashan 雙鴨山市	Heilongjiang 黑龍江省	(0454)4320428	274	Collectively-owned 集體	14,269	16(33)	10,679	o
Beijing Chun Shu Rectifier Factory 北京椿樹整流器廠(1960)	Beijing 北京市	Beijing 北京市	(010)66056926	900	Collectively-owned 集體	13,085	510(10)	96,950	a
Liuzhou Xin Heng Electricity Manufacting Co. Ltd. 柳州市鑫恒電氣製造責任公司(1967)	Liuzhou 柳州市	Guangxi 廣西	(0772)3114237	521	State-owned 國有	11,798	-7242(60)	42,325	a

Top 10 Cities by Production Output 產出排名前 10 位城市	Province 省	Market share 市場份額	Number of firms 企業個數
Shanghai 上海市	Shanghai 上海市	19.09%	26
Beijing 北京市	Beijing 北京市	15.66%	16
Shenzhen 深圳市	Guangdong 廣東省	14.60%	8
Qingdao 青島市	Shandong 山東省	6.30%	4
Zhanjiang 湛江市	Guangdong 廣東省	3.97%	1
Shantou 汕頭市	Guangdong 廣東省	3.92%	7
Anshan 鞍山市	Liaoning 遼寧省	2.49%	1
Yangzhou 揚州市	Jiangsu 江蘇省	2.18%	1
Taizhou 臺州市	Zhejiang 浙江省	2.15%	2
Yantai 煙台市	Shandong 山東省	2.11%	3

10 Major Wholesalers 10 家主要批發商	City 城市	Province 省	Telephone / Fax 電話 / 傳真
Liaoning Automobile Trade Group Corp. 遼寧省汽車貿易集團	Shenyang 瀋陽市	Liaoning 遼寧省	(024)23835494 (024)23838338
China Post and Telecommunication Equipment General Company 中國郵電器材總公司	Beijing 北京市	Beijing 北京市	(010)63523715 (010)63525935
Jiangsu Electromechanical Products General Company 江蘇省機電產品總公司	Nanjing 南京市	Jiangsu 江蘇省	(025)7713642 (025)7711036
Xi Nan Technology Import & Export Company 西南技術進出口公司	Chongqing 重慶市	Chongqing 重慶市	(023)63850185 (023)63850026
Changzhou Economic Technology Industrial Development Zone Tian Ming Trade Company 常州經濟技術產業開發區天明貿易公司	Changzhou 常州市	Jiangsu 江蘇省	(0519)8829882 (0519)8829882
Shanxi Mechanical Equipment Import & Export Company 山西省機械設備進出口公司	Taiyuan 太原市	Shanxi 山西省	(0351)4040713 (0351)4043981
Ningbo Five Mining Machinery Import & Export Company 寧波市五礦機械進出口公司	Ningbo 寧波市	Zhejiang 浙江省	(0574)7311255 (0574)7320322
Tianjin Jin Huan Electromechanical Complete Sets of Equipment Factory 天津市津環機電成套設備廠	Tianjin 天津市	Tianjin 天津市	(022)26371628
Yunnan Machinery Import & Export Company 雲南省機械進出口公司	Kunming 昆明市	Yunnan 雲南省	(0871)3164879 (0871)3136829
Tianjin Da Qiu Zhuang Yi Yuan Trade Center 天津市大丘莊億源商貿中心	Tianjin 天津市	Tianjin 天津市	(022)28899478 (022)28899046

*Also include sales by firms outside this industry.包括本行業以外廠家的銷售。"o" stands for "others". "o" 代表 "其他產品"。

4023: Capacitors 電容器製造業

The industry accounts for 0.038% of the total revenue of China's industrial sector in 1996. The revenue growth rate of the industry is 17.5% from 1995, as compared to the growth rate of China's industrial sector, 9.51%. The rate of return on asset is -0.24%. 60.75% of all firms in the industry made a profit while 33.33% had negative returns. The top province in terms of the industry's revenue is Jiangsu, accounting for 28.93% of the total revenue.
本行業在1996年佔全行業總產值0.038%，行業年增長率為17.5%（全國工業年增長率9.51%）。行業的資產回報率-0.24%，60.75%的企業盈利，33.33%的企業虧損。銷售收入最高的省份為江蘇省，佔本行業的28.93%。

	Total number of firms 企業總數	Total number of employees 職工總數	Total revenue (mil. RMB) 總銷售收入（百萬元）	Total profit (mil. RMB) 總利潤（百萬元）	Return on assets 資產利潤率 (%)	Return on equity 權益利潤率 (%)	Labour productivity ('000 RMB / worker) 勞動生產率（千元/人）	Debts / assets 資產負債率 (%)	Total assets (mil. RMB) 總資產（百萬元）
Industry Overall 行業總體	313	39,409	2,231	-9	-0.24	-0.68	56.61	64.39	3,764

	Number of firms 企業個數	Average number of employees 平均職工人數	Average revenue ('000 RMB) 平均銷售收入（千元）	Average profit ('000 RMB) 平均利潤（千元）	Return on assets 資產利潤率 (%)	Return on equity 權益利潤率 (%)	Labour productivity ('000 RMB / worker) 勞動生產率（千元/人）	Average debts / assets 平均資產負債率(%)	Average Total assets ('000 RMB) 平均總資產（千元）
By ownership 產業所有權									
State-owned 國有	42	197	7,786	-333	-1.53	-7.41	39.53	79.34	21,786
Collectively-owned 集體	191	116	5,599	19	0.26	0.72	48.36	64.43	7,190
Privately-owned 私有									
Domestic JVs 聯營	1	19	97				5.08	31.10	640
Joint stock 股份制	7	204	21,315	216	0.66	1.83	104.71	63.89	32,663
Foreign-funded 外資	18	102	5,363	-4	-0.02	-0.03	52.67	50.30	26,619
Overseas Chinese-funded 港澳台資	54	117	10,907	1	0.00	0.01	93.53	55.50	14,208
By size 規模									
Large 大型	2	1,061	79,242	-911	-0.52	-1.49	74.72	65.31	175,976
Medium 中型	12	556	24,438	-31	-0.06	-0.19	43.97	68.91	54,242
Small 小型	290	106	6,136	-23	-0.25	-0.67	57.89	63.22	9,521
By regional distribution 地區分布									
Central-North 華北	34	81	1,434	-124	-3.21	-111.94	17.71	97.14	3,872
Beijing 北京	11	66	2,020	-67	-1.00	-4.91	30.56	79.66	6,736
Tianjin 天津	9	26	930	74	6.96	16.07	35.92	56.65	1,069
Hebei 河北	10	67	982	66	3.51	12.94	14.77	72.82	1,880
Shanxi 山西	1	915	2,890	-4,920	-25.48	28.64	3.16	188.97	19,310
Inner Mongolia 內蒙	3	71	1,817	37	1.12	-3.24	25.71	134.66	3,270
Northeast 東北	34	144	4,609	129	1.06	6.40	31.94	83.41	12,125
Liaoning 遼寧	23	176	5,876	204	1.23	7.59	33.40	83.75	16,539
Jilin 吉林	2	113	1,055	20	0.94	1.99	9.38	52.59	2,120
Heilongjiang 黑龍江	9	71	2,162	-39	-1.27	-7.68	30.65	83.46	3,070
Central East 華東	143	123	8,262	23	0.20	0.58	67.22	65.81	11,888
Shanghai 上海	9	77	1,867	-23	-0.80	-5.56	24.21	85.62	2,928
Jiangsu 江蘇	54	148	11,954	299	2.20	6.35	80.88	65.28	13,549
Zhejiang 浙江	30	96	7,313	275	3.45	9.10	76.17	62.15	7,980
Anhui 安徽	16	139	7,982	-136	-1.03	-4.93	57.45	79.07	13,134
Fujian 福建	20	85	5,235	-26	-0.38	-1.05	61.80	63.97	6,769
Jiangxi 江西	7	114	1,947	-6	-0.18	1.35	17.08	113.51	3,130
Shandong 山東	7	187	7,679	-2,583	-5.40	-12.64	41.12	57.33	47,873
Central-South 中南	82	145	9,404	-71	-0.45	-0.89	64.77	49.08	15,602
Henan 河南	9	105	3,048	62	1.00	1.85	28.90	46.04	6,241
Hubei 湖北	2	205	5,630	-25	-0.23	-0.91	27.53	74.84	10,910
Hunan 湖南	19	120	4,544	108	1.34	3.70	37.76	63.82	8,101
Guangdong 廣東	39	165	14,334	-241	-1.11	-1.95	86.98	43.30	21,716
Guangxi 廣西	13	141	6,699	77	0.50	1.25	47.49	60.22	15,428
Hainan 海南									
Southwest 西南	12	81	1,343	-125	-3.80	-29.41	16.60	87.11	3,291
Chongqing 重慶	5	130	1,145	-487	-6.62	-147.74	8.81	95.52	7,353
Sichuan 四川	6	29	1,694	115	12.70	20.54	58.66	38.15	902
Guizhou 貴州	1	192							
Yunnan 雲南									
Tibet 西藏									
Northwest 西北	8	162	7,076	-675	-2.68	-17.69	43.61	84.83	25,141
Shaanxi 陝西	7	119	6,880	599	5.35	11.24	58.02	52.43	11,191
Gansu 甘肅									
Qinghai 青海									
Ningxia 寧夏	1	468	8,450	-9,590	-7.81	142.07	18.06	105.50	122,790
Xinjiang 新疆									

4023: Capacitors 電容器製造業

Year 年份	Number of firms 企業個數	Rate of change 每年變化 (%)	Number of employees 職工人數 (人)	Rate of change 每年變化 (%)	Total revenue (mil. RMB) 總銷售收入 (百萬元)	Rate of change 每年變化 (%)	Total profit (mil. RMB) 總利潤 (百萬元)	Rate of change 每年變化 (%)
1993	250		38,360		1,628		99	
1994	258	3.20%	37,920	-1.15%	1,568	-3.67%	22	-78.24%
1995	321	24.42%	40,091	5.73%	1,899	21.07%	57	165.65%
1996	313	-2.49%	39,409	-1.70%	2,231	17.48%	-9	-115.75%

3 Major products* 3種主要產品*	Output 產量	Sales volume 銷售量	Unit 單位
a) Power Capacitor 電力電容器	26,082,594	18,257,816	kf 千乏

Top 10 firms by revenue (year founded) 收入排名前10家企業 (創辦年份)	City 城市	Province 省	Telephone / fax 電話 / 傳真	Number of employees 職工人數	Ownership 產業所有權	Revenue ('000 RMB) 銷售收入 (千元)	Profit ('000 RMB) (rank) 利潤 (千元) (排名)	Total assets ('000 RMB) 總資產 (千元)	Major products 主要產品
Zhuhai Doumen De Photoelectron Products Factory 珠海市斗門縣德光電子製品廠(1994)	Zhuhai 珠海市	Guangdong 廣東省	(0756)5571337 (0756)5571311	1,880	Foreign-funded 外資	186,710	3234(5)	70,117	o
Yancheng Hong Xing Capacitor Factory 鹽城市紅星電容器廠(1985)	Yancheng 鹽城市	Jiangsu 江蘇省	(0515)8601833 (0515)8600109	450	Collectively-owned 集體	131,250	6480(3)	30,100	o
Jinzhou Power Capacitor Liability Co. Ltd. 錦州電力電容器有限責任公司(1965)	Jinzhou 錦州市	Liaoning 遼寧省	(0416)2125426 (0416)2128272	1,062	Joint stock 股份制	90,087	12504(1)	178,530	a
Tianying Computer Science & Technology (Shenzhen) Co. Ltd. 天鷹電腦科技(深圳)有限公司(1994)	Shenzhen 深圳市	Guangdong 廣東省	(0755)4600122 (0755)8828506	400	Overseas Chinese-funded 港澳台資	84,085	-68(115)	47,936	o
Wuxi Electric Power Capacitor Factory 無錫市電力電容器廠(1970)	Wuxi 無錫市	Jiangsu 江蘇省	(0510)3709454 (0510)3703710	488	Collectively-owned 集體	80,115	2200(10)	101,519	a
Xi Shan Shi Radio No.3 Factory 錫山市無線電三廠(1987)	Wuxi 無錫市	Jiangsu 江蘇省	(0510)8731614	575	Collectively-owned 集體	74,770	10400(2)	31,170	o
Huiyang Secondary Normal School Electronic Plant 惠陽市中師電子廠(1988)	Huizhou 惠州市	Guangdong 廣東省	(0751)3363534 (0751)3369542	530	Collectively-owned 集體	69,854	-310(125)	139,215	o
Guilin General Plant of Power Capacitors 桂林市電力電容器總廠(1972)	Guilin 桂林市	Guangxi 廣西	(0773)5812643 (0773)5814993	1,165	State-owned 國有	55,282	1(101)	145,052	a
Zhuji Capacitor Factory 諸暨市電容器廠(1984)	Shaoxing 紹興市	Zhejiang 浙江省	(0575)7951189 (0575)7951188	460	Collectively-owned 集體	49,956	2403(8)	19,758	o
Ningguo Capacitor Factory 寧國縣電容器廠(1980)	Xuanzhou 宣州市	Anhui 安徽省	(0563)4021388 (0563)4021266	420	Collectively-owned 集體	46,454	462(31)	42,310	o

Top 10 Cities by Production Output 產出排名前10位城市	Province 省	Market share 市場份額	Number of firms 企業個數
Dongguan 東莞市	Guangdong 廣東省	14.34%	9
Wuxi 無錫市	Jiangsu 江蘇省	10.11%	28
Xuanzhou 宣州市	Anhui 安徽省	5.86%	6
Guilin 桂林市	Guangxi 廣西	5.58%	10
Jinzhou 錦州市	Liaoning 遼寧省	4.60%	5
Zhuhai 珠海市	Guangdong 廣東省	3.85%	3
Suzhou 蘇州市	Jiangsu 江蘇省	3.34%	20
Yancheng 鹽城市	Jiangsu 江蘇省	2.90%	7
Wenzhou 溫州市	Zhejiang 浙江省	2.84%	7
Huizhou 惠州市	Guangdong 廣東省	2.76%	6

10 Major Wholesalers 10家主要批發商	City 城市	Province 省	Telephone / Fax 電話 / 傳真
Liaoning Automobile Trade Group Corp. 遼寧省汽車貿易集團	Shenyang 瀋陽市	Liaoning 遼寧省	(024)23835494 (024)23838338
China Post and Telecommunication Equipment General Company 中國郵電器材總公司	Beijing 北京市	Beijing 北京市	(010)63523715 (010)63525935
Jiangsu Electromechanical Products General Company 江蘇省機電產品總公司	Nanjing 南京市	Jiangsu 江蘇省	(025)7713642 (025)7711036
Xi Nan Technology Import & Export Company 西南技術進出口公司	Chongqing 重慶市	Chongqing 重慶市	(023)63850185 (023)63850026
Changzhou Economic Technology Industrial Development Zone Tian Ming Trade Company 常州經濟技術產業開發區天明貿易公司	Changzhou 常州市	Jiangsu 江蘇省	(0519)8829882 (0519)8829882
Shanxi Mechanical Equipment Import & Export Company 山西省機械設備進出口公司	Taiyuan 太原市	Shanxi 山西省	(0351)4040713 (0351)4043981
Ningbo Five Mining Machinery Import & Export Company 寧波市五礦機械進出口公司	Ningbo 寧波市	Zhejiang 浙江省	(0574)7311255 (0574)7320322
Tianjin Jin Huan Electromechanical Complete Sets of Equipment Factory 天津市津環機電成套設備廠	Tianjin 天津市	Tianjin 天津市	(022)26371628
Yunnan Machinery Import & Export Company 雲南省機械進出口公司	Kunming 昆明市	Yunnan 雲南省	(0871)3164879 (0871)3136829
Tianjin Da Qiu Zhuang Yi Yuan Trade Center 天津市大丘莊億源商貿中心	Tianjin 天津市	Tianjin 天津市	(022)28899478 (022)28899046

*Also include sales by firms outside this industry.包括本行業以外廠家的銷售。"o" stands for "others". "o" 代表 "其他產品"。

4024: Switches and Control Equipment 開關控制設備製造業

The industry accounts for 0.327% of the total revenue of China's industrial sector in 1996. The revenue growth rate of the industry is 5.1% from 1995, as compared to the growth rate of China's industrial sector, 9.51%. The rate of return on asset is 1.97%. 71.53% of all firms in the industry made a profit while 24.22% had negative returns. The top province in terms of the industry's revenue is Shanghai, accounting for 18.60% of the total revenue.
本行業在1996年佔全行業總產值0.327%，行業年增長率為5.1%（全國工業年增長率9.51%）。行業的資產回報率1.97%，71.53%的企業盈利，24.22%的企業虧損。銷售收入最高的省份為上海市，佔本行業的18.60%。

	Total number of firms 企業總數	Total number of employees 職工總數	Total revenue (mil. RMB) 總銷售收入（百萬元）	Total profit (mil. RMB) 總利潤（百萬元）	Return on assets 資產利潤率 (%)	Return on equity 權益利潤率 (%)	Labour productivity ('000 RMB / worker) 勞動生產率（千元/人）	Debts / assets 資產負債率 (%)	Total assets (mil. RMB) 總資產（百萬元）
Industry Overall 行業總體	2,164	313,613	18,968	557	1.97	6.18	60.48	68.14	28,286

	Number of firms 企業個數	Average number of employees 平均職工人數	Average revenue ('000 RMB) 平均銷售收入（千元）	Average profit ('000 RMB) 平均利潤（千元）	Return on assets 資產利潤率 (%)	Return on equity 權益利潤率 (%)	Labour productivity ('000 RMB / worker) 勞動生產率（千元/人）	Average debts / assets 平均資產負債率(%)	Average Total assets ('000 RMB) 平均總資產（千元）
By ownership 產業所有權									
State-owned 國有	283	401	24,191	88	0.20	0.72	60.37	72.34	44,205
Collectively-owned 集體	1,709	89	4,493	138	2.72	8.59	50.54	68.28	5,063
Privately-owned 私有	12	32	2,379	-38	-1.09	-8.40	74.15	86.97	3,436
Domestic JVs 聯營	24	100	8,305	542	6.02	20.80	82.74	71.07	9,001
Joint stock 股份制	25	1,297	106,925	6,705	3.55	9.37	82.45	62.16	189,114
Foreign-funded 外資	53	164	23,025	2,110	7.70	16.83	140.51	54.21	27,389
Overseas Chinese-funded 港澳台資	55	95	5,644	73	0.59	1.42	59.20	58.18	12,228
By size 規模									
Large 大型	13	6,165	438,366	14,857	1.81	6.90	71.10	73.86	823,022
Medium 中型	64	756	53,818	1,910	2.19	5.79	71.17	62.14	87,144
Small 小型	2,064	90	4,760	117	2.01	5.89	53.08	65.83	5,818
By regional distribution 地區分布									
Central-North 華北	348	85	4,178	390	6.07	17.88	49.01	66.03	6,428
Beijing 北京	147	65	3,837	115	1.78	6.87	58.74	74.14	6,464
Tianjin 天津	73	89	7,138	1,678	21.70	44.81	80.46	51.58	7,732
Hebei 河北	86	79	2,614	67	1.71	6.24	33.24	72.51	3,879
Shanxi 山西	22	195	3,780	-426	-4.39	-9.21	19.40	52.30	9,696
Inner Mongolia 內蒙	20	127	3,043	7	0.08	0.30	23.98	72.97	8,764
Northeast 東北	493	110	3,668	114	1.71	6.36	33.31	73.13	6,695
Liaoning 遼寧	279	137	5,202	202	2.16	7.97	37.84	72.93	9,362
Jilin 吉林	95	69	1,454	-10	-0.28	-1.15	21.17	76.00	3,456
Heilongjiang 黑龍江	119	79	1,838	8	0.26	0.91	23.26	71.99	3,029
Central East 華東	780	146	11,647	492	3.46	9.76	79.74	64.54	14,226
Shanghai 上海	119	255	29,641	1,158	3.12	8.39	116.13	62.78	37,075
Jiangsu 江蘇	197	130	9,239	306	2.94	8.83	71.11	66.67	10,398
Zhejiang 浙江	223	73	6,592	408	5.38	11.29	90.21	52.36	7,585
Anhui 安徽	49	159	5,169	27	0.28	1.32	32.59	78.69	9,541
Fujian 福建	55	273	17,485	1,004	4.57	13.03	64.05	64.96	21,979
Jiangxi 江西	35	92	1,663	-134	-4.22	-23.64	18.00	82.14	3,174
Shandong 山東	102	153	9,746	424	3.73	16.55	63.53	77.44	11,344
Central-South 中南	310	150	8,392	-140	-1.01	-3.50	55.86	71.23	13,857
Henan 河南	91	164	8,604	189	1.31	5.43	52.51	75.90	14,428
Hubei 湖北	28	130	9,424	425	2.98	7.50	72.71	60.25	14,271
Hunan 湖南	79	132	3,407	-22	-0.34	-1.19	25.77	71.26	6,310
Guangdong 廣東	76	149	14,112	66	0.33	0.94	94.78	65.10	20,289
Guangxi 廣西	26	227	7,355	-2,693	-14.70	-129.95	32.46	88.69	18,326
Hainan 海南	10	38	2,186	-572	-8.63	-22.75	57.53	62.07	6,628
Southwest 西南	115	151	6,925	143	1.19	3.98	45.81	70.08	12,033
Chongqing 重慶	28	153	4,523	58	0.68	4.00	29.53	83.13	8,617
Sichuan 四川	51	154	9,335	348	2.40	6.71	60.44	64.27	14,527
Guizhou 貴州	17	76	1,302	-111	-3.70	-35.61	17.10	89.62	2,992
Yunnan 雲南	19	209	9,055	-51	-0.28	-0.94	43.41	70.52	18,497
Tibet 西藏									
Northwest 西北	118	439	27,313	65	0.13	0.43	62.24	70.18	50,615
Shaanxi 陝西	62	600	43,097	140	0.18	0.58	71.89	68.90	78,513
Gansu 甘肅	28	422	16,651	104	0.33	1.33	39.50	75.48	31,947
Qinghai 青海	3	93	1,153	3	0.13	1.25	12.45	89.64	2,573
Ningxia 寧夏	7	108	2,183	-677	-6.84	-84.49	20.18	91.90	9,897
Xinjiang 新疆	18	98	3,663	43	0.59	1.88	37.21	68.91	7,405

4024: Switches and Control Equipment 開關控制設備製造業

Year 年份	Number of firms 企業個數	Rate of change 每年變化 (%)	Number of employees 職工人數 (人)	Rate of change 每年變化 (%)	Total revenue (mil. RMB) 總銷售收入 (百萬元)	Rate of change 每年變化 (%)	Total profit (mil. RMB) 總利潤 (百萬元)	Rate of change 每年變化 (%)
1993	1,908		414,960		13,554		1,066	
1994	1,928	1.05%	291,181	-29.83%	14,706	8.50%	481	-54.88%
1995	2,240	16.18%	336,239	15.47%	18,044	22.70%	690	43.40%
1996	2,164	-3.39%	313,613	-6.73%	18,968	5.12%	557	-19.29%

3 Major products* 3 種主要產品 *	Output 產量	Sales volume 銷售量	Unit 單位
a) High Voltage Switch 高壓開關板	1,047,213	1,026,269	piece 面
b) Low Voltage Switch 低壓開關板	3,119,967	3,182,367	piece 面
c) High Voltage Isolator 高壓隔離開關	260,768	242,514	set 組

Top 10 firms by revenue (year founded) 收入排名前 10 家企業 (創辦年份)	City 城市	Province 省	Telephone / fax 電話 / 傳真	Number of employees 職工人數	Ownership 產業所有權	Revenue ('000 RMB) 銷售收入 (千元)	Profit ('000 RMB) (rank) 利潤 (千元) (排名)	Total assets ('000 RMB) 總資產 (千元)	Major products 主要產品
Xi'an Electric Manufacturing Corp. 西安電力機械製造公司(1958)	Xi'an 西安市	Shaanxi 陝西省	(029)4244805 (029)4261442	28,674	State-owned 國有	2,352,666	10771(12)	4,282,090	o
Shanghai Electrical Apparatus Co. Ltd. 上海電器股份有限公司(1992)	Shanghai 上海市	Shanghai 上海市	(021)65422800 (021)65441087	15,738	Joint stock 股份制	1,736,250	10340(13)	2,355,440	a,b
Shanghai Guangdian Electric (Group) Co. Ltd. 上海廣電電氣(集團)有限公司(1986)	Shanghai 上海市	Shanghai 上海市	(021)57423411 (021)57411251	164	State-owned 國有	630,645	59015(2)	542,970	b
Shenyang High Voltage Switch Co. Ltd. 瀋陽高壓開關有限責任公司(1937)	Shenyang 瀋陽市	Liaoning 遼寧省	(024)25877911 (024)25853021	7,254	Joint stock 股份制	457,123	33322(6)	980,014	c
Gansu Great Wall Electric Co. 甘肅長城電器工業公司(1975)	Tianshui 天水市	Gansu 甘肅省	(0938)8382606 (0938)8382967	9,093	State-owned 國有	387,821	2033(73)	786,837	a,b
Xiamen Abbswitch Co. Ltd. 廈門 ABB 開關有限公司(1992)	Xiamen 廈門市	Fujian 福建省	(0592)6026033 (0592)6030505	253	Overseas Chinese-funded 港澳台資	312,970	40477(3)	302,355	a
Tianjin Merlin Gerin Co. Ltd. 天津梅蘭日蘭有限公司(1987)	Tianjin 天津市	Tianjin 天津市	(022)25328713 (022)25326436	625	Foreign-funded 外資	274,007	108593(1)	174,008	o
Beijing Switch Factory 北京開關廠(1952)	Beijing 北京市	Beijing 北京市	(010)65021131	2,964	State-owned 國有	260,221	5320(30)	375,199	a,b,c
Shanghai Hua Tong Switch Works 上海華通開關廠(1919)	Shanghai 上海市	Shanghai 上海市	(021)56651007 (021)56650079	3,855	State-owned 國有	239,181	3032(53)	431,941	a,b,c
Zibo Wan Xiang Group Co. Ltd. 淄博萬祥集團股份有限總公司(1971)	Zibo 淄博市	Shandong 山東省	(0533)8480412 (0533)8480319	1,154	Joint stock 股份制	189,400	13148(11)	194,039	a,b

Top 10 Cities by Production Output 產出排名前 10 位城市	Province 省	Market share 市場份額	Number of firms 企業個數
Suzhou 蘇州市	Jiangsu 江蘇省	33.18%	63
Shanghai 上海市	Shanghai 上海市	14.32%	191
Shenyang 瀋陽市	Liaoning 遼寧省	3.18%	129
Wenzhou 温州市	Zhejiang 浙江省	2.90%	359
Beijing 北京市	Beijing 北京市	2.84%	133
Tianjin 天津市	Tianjin 天津市	2.25%	83
Fuzhou 福州市	Fujian 福建省	2.18%	22
Xiamen 廈門市	Fujian 福建省	2.12%	10
Ningbo 寧波市	Zhejiang 浙江省	1.93%	51
Pingdingshan 平頂山市	Henan 河南省	1.71%	4

10 Major Wholesalers 10 家主要批發商	City 城市	Province 省	Telephone / Fax 電話 / 傳真
Liaoning Automobile Trade Group Corp. 遼寧省汽車貿易集團	Shenyang 瀋陽市	Liaoning 遼寧省	(024)23835494 (024)23838338
China Post and Telecommunication Equipment General Company 中國郵電器材總公司	Beijing 北京市	Beijing 北京市	(010)63523715 (010)63525935
Jiangsu Electromechanical Products General Company 江蘇省機電產品總公司	Nanjing 南京市	Jiangsu 江蘇省	(025)7713642 (025)7711036
Xi Nan Technology Import & Export Company 西南技術進出口公司	Chongqing 重慶市	Chongqing 重慶市	(023)63850185 (023)63850026
Changzhou Economic Technology Industrial Development Zone Tian Ming Trade Company 常州經濟技術產業開發區天明貿易公司	Changzhou 常州市	Jiangsu 江蘇省	(0519)8829882 (0519)8829882
Shanxi Mechanical Equipment Import & Export Company 山西省機械設備進出口公司	Taiyuan 太原市	Shanxi 山西省	(0351)4040713 (0351)4043981
Ningbo Five Mining Machinery Import & Export Company 寧波市五礦機械進出口公司	Ningbo 寧波市	Zhejiang 浙江省	(0574)7311255 (0574)7320322
Tianjin Jin Huan Electromechanical Complete Sets of Equipment Factory 天津市津環機電成套設備廠	Tianjin 天津市	Tianjin 天津市	(022)26371628
Yunnan Machinery Import & Export Company 雲南省機械進出口公司	Kunming 昆明市	Yunnan 雲南省	(0871)3164879 (0871)3136829
Tianjin Da Qiu Zhuang Yi Yuan Trade Center 天津市大丘莊億源商貿中心	Tianjin 天津市	Tianjin 天津市	(022)28899478 (022)28899046

*Also include sales by firms outside this industry.包括本行業以外廠家的銷售。"o" stands for "others". "o" 代表"其他產品"。

4027: Electronic Equipment Parts 電器設備元件製造業

The industry accounts for 0.132% of the total revenue of China's industrial sector in 1996. The revenue growth rate of the industry is 24.9% from 1995, as compared to the growth rate of China's industrial sector, 9.51%. The rate of return on asset is 2.40%. 63.18% of all firms in the industry made a profit while 29.31% had negative returns. The top province in terms of the industry's revenue is Guangdong, accounting for 27.62% of the total revenue.
本行業在1996年佔全行業總產值0.132%，行業年增長率為24.9%（全國工業年增長率9.51%）。行業的資產回報率2.40%，63.18%的企業盈利，29.31%的企業虧損。銷售收入最高的省份為廣東省，佔本行業的27.62%。

	Total number of firms 企業總數	Total number of employees 職工總數	Total revenue (mil. RMB) 總銷售收入（百萬元）	Total profit (mil. RMB) 總利潤（百萬元）	Return on assets 資產利潤率 (%)	Return on equity 權益利潤率 (%)	Labour productivity ('000 RMB / worker) 勞動生產率（千元／人）	Debts / assets 資產負債率 (%)	Total assets (mil. RMB) 總資產（百萬元）
Industry Overall 行業總體	931	130,232	7,678	265	2.40	5.86	58.96	58.95	11,041

	Number of firms 企業個數	Average number of employees 平均職工人數	Average revenue ('000 RMB) 平均銷售收入（千元）	Average profit ('000 RMB) 平均利潤（千元）	Return on assets 資產利潤率 (%)	Return on equity 權益利潤率 (%)	Labour productivity ('000 RMB / worker) 勞動生產率（千元／人）	Average debts / assets 平均資產負債率(%)	Average Total assets ('000 RMB) 平均總資產（千元）
By ownership 產業所有權									
State-owned 國有	101	366	13,347	198	0.59	1.77	36.48	66.71	33,663
Collectively-owned 集體	729	106	4,340	103	1.59	3.95	41.07	59.76	6,498
Privately-owned 私有	4	174	3,968	-436	-4.01	-17.73	22.87	77.37	10,854
Domestic JVs 聯營	8	59	2,757	63	1.00	1.88	46.43	46.92	6,300
Joint stock 股份制	17	115	4,288	95	1.35	3.06	37.38	55.97	7,057
Foreign-funded 外資	34	294	72,782	4,950	8.57	15.52	247.81	44.78	57,775
Overseas Chinese-funded 港澳台資	37	139	15,690	30	0.15	0.34	112.51	55.96	19,619
By size 規模									
Large 大型	6	2,787	216,092	8,559	2.26	6.18	77.55	63.44	378,973
Medium 中型	23	763	50,856	1,071	0.99	2.04	66.61	51.66	108,620
Small 小型	885	109	5,889	214	3.02	7.58	54.07	60.23	7,083
By regional distribution 地區分布									
Central-North 華北	159	154	4,244	141	1.38	3.05	27.54	54.63	10,177
Beijing 北京	60	133	4,607	-76	-0.70	-2.07	34.54	66.30	10,821
Tianjin 天津	57	176	3,891	372	3.12	5.14	22.09	39.37	11,921
Hebei 河北	19	176	5,469	168	1.82	5.19	31.16	65.04	9,248
Shanxi 山西	11	186	4,385	106	2.54	5.19	23.53	50.98	4,184
Inner Mongolia 內蒙	12	89	2,033	113	2.00	6.97	22.74	71.36	5,636
Northeast 東北	123	146	2,942	-46	-0.60	-2.11	20.17	71.69	7,697
Liaoning 遼寧	97	170	3,354	-62	-0.67	-2.35	19.74	71.35	9,244
Jilin 吉林	13	69	1,688	-1	-0.03	-0.11	24.32	74.99	2,682
Heilongjiang 黑龍江	13	42	1,120	31	2.64	16.39	26.42	83.92	1,167
Central East 華東	404	125	8,562	213	1.84	4.07	68.76	54.71	11,563
Shanghai 上海	63	98	9,140	157	1.15	3.64	92.97	68.55	13,731
Jiangsu 江蘇	111	165	8,120	-285	-2.04	-4.25	49.12	52.05	13,973
Zhejiang 浙江	119	126	10,852	557	4.18	7.98	86.12	47.60	13,332
Anhui 安徽	21	91	4,863	184	3.33	8.71	53.27	61.73	5,530
Fujian 福建	29	93	13,354	1,213	15.07	24.88	144.18	39.45	8,053
Jiangxi 江西	19	72	1,106	-169	-10.54	109.52	15.35	109.62	1,608
Shandong 山東	42	114	4,288	132	1.93	6.49	37.55	70.31	6,873
Central-South 中南	140	146	17,845	937	5.47	15.44	121.87	64.58	17,136
Henan 河南	37	69	3,182	104	2.08	7.34	45.88	71.63	4,999
Hubei 湖北	12	92	8,508	185	3.48	22.98	92.98	84.87	5,321
Hunan 湖南	33	141	2,585	-17	-0.30	-1.42	18.34	78.82	5,627
Guangdong 廣東	47	235	45,119	2,676	6.66	17.58	192.12	62.09	40,153
Guangxi 廣西	10	111	7,015	29	0.39	0.94	63.31	58.04	7,384
Hainan 海南	1	40	2,380	-370	-10.60	-19.27	59.50	44.99	3,490
Southwest 西南	47	231	9,522	423	1.96	4.73	41.14	58.65	21,603
Chongqing 重慶	14	111	3,669	105	1.94	5.63	33.04	65.56	5,427
Sichuan 四川	23	82	3,862	273	3.44	5.80	46.83	40.69	7,926
Guizhou 貴州	9	815	33,871	1,338	1.60	4.25	41.55	62.39	83,696
Yunnan 雲南	1	102	2,410	10	0.34	0.82	23.63	58.08	2,910
Tibet 西藏									
Northwest 西北	58	105	4,078	202	3.00	8.12	38.72	63.02	6,725
Shaanxi 陝西	37	92	4,077	255	5.36	12.17	44.22	55.94	4,763
Gansu 甘肅	19	139	4,379	115	1.03	3.30	31.55	68.87	11,171
Qinghai 青海									
Ningxia 寧夏	1	49	2,150	80	6.56	25.00	43.88	73.77	1,220
Xinjiang 新疆	1	12	310	10	2.78	5.00	25.83	44.44	360

4027: Electronic Equipment Parts 電器設備元件製造業

Year 年份	Number of firms 企業個數	Rate of change 每年變化 (%)	Number of employees 職工人數 (人)	Rate of change 每年變化 (%)	Total revenue (mil. RMB) 總銷售收入 (百萬元)	Rate of change 每年變化 (%)	Total profit (mil. RMB) 總利潤 (百萬元)	Rate of change 每年變化 (%)
1993	970		142,842		4,804		249	
1994	946	-2.48%	128,238	-10.22%	4,168	-13.22%	45	-82.04%
1995	874	-7.61%	133,843	4.37%	6,146	47.44%	187	318.00%
1996	931	6.52%	130,232	-2.70%	7,678	24.93%	265	41.96%

3 Major products* 3 種主要產品 *	Output 產量	Sales volume 銷售量	Unit 單位
a) Electronic Component 電子元件	266,039	255,398	10,000 piece 萬只

Top 10 firms by revenue (year founded) 收入排名前 10 家企業 (創辦年份)	City 城市	Province 省	Telephone / fax 電話 / 傳真	Number of employees 職工人數	Ownership 產業所有權	Revenue ('000 RMB) 銷售收入 (千元)	Profit ('000 RMB) (rank) 利潤 (千元) (排名)	Total assets ('000 RMB) 總資產 (千元)	Major products 主要產品
M.wako Giken Industriers Ltd. 惠州麥科特和幸技研工業有限公司(1995)	Huizhou 惠州市	Guangdong 廣東省	(0751)3321486 (0751)3321466	1,378	Foreign-funded 外資	943,413	52958(1)	260,733	a
Shenzhen Original Electric Machinery Co. Ltd. 深圳王利電機有限公司(1992)	Shenzhen 深圳市	Guangdong 廣東省	(0755)3240159 (0755)3240160	2,777	Foreign-funded 外資	458,019	44167(2)	273,508	a
Chang Zheng Electric Equipment Co. 長征電器公司(1966)	Zunyi 遵義市	Guizhou 貴州省	(0852)622901 (0852)623623	372	State-owned 國有	293,481	10907(7)	735,907	o
Sino-japan Electric Heat (Xiamen) Co. Ltd. 中日電熱(廈門)有限公司(1990)	Xiamen 廈門市	Fujian 福建省	(0592)6211270 (0592)6210471	1,329	Foreign-funded 外資	278,520	33086(3)	154,019	o
Zheng Tai Group Company 正泰集團公司(1984)	Wenzhou 溫州市	Zhejiang 浙江省	(0577)2777777 (0577)2775888	1,772	Collectively-owned 集體	208,649	9579(8)	223,580	o
Wenzhou Wan Jia Group Co. Ltd. 溫州萬家集團有限公司(1995)	Wenzhou 溫州市	Zhejiang 浙江省	(0577)2775822 (0577)2775811	455	Joint stock 股份制	192,157	19955(6)	99,315	o
Foshan Tong Bao Co. Ltd. 佛山市通寶股份有限公司(1966)	Foshan 佛山市	Guangdong 廣東省	(0757)2298522 (0757)2287037	719	Joint stock 股份制	176,119	28352(4)	468,380	o
Shanghai Da Zhan Industrial Company 上海大展實業公司(1994)	Shanghai 上海市	Shanghai 上海市	(021)57420807	150	Collectively-owned 集體	140,911	368(94)	139,407	o
Beijing Jing Ye Electric Engineering Group 北京敬業電工集團(1956)	Beijing 北京市	Beijing 北京市	(010)66175725 (010)66175725	2,775	State-owned 國有	125,075	4111(19)	274,208	o
Shenyang Low Voltage Switch Factory 瀋陽低壓開關廠(1936)	Shenyang 瀋陽市	Liaoning 遼寧省	(024)25855615	3,703	State-owned 國有	114,828	67(176)	354,103	o

Top 10 Cities by Production Output 產出排名前 10 位城市	Province 省	Market share 市場份額	Number of firms 企業個數
Wenzhou 温州市	Zhejiang 浙江省	12.00%	265
Shanghai 上海市	Shanghai 上海市	11.52%	144
Huizhou 惠州市	Guangdong 廣東省	10.05%	3
Dongguan 東莞市	Guangdong 廣東省	6.90%	21
Suzhou 蘇州市	Jiangsu 江蘇省	6.51%	102
Tianshui 天水市	Gansu 甘肅省	5.25%	13
Zunyi 遵義市	Guizhou 貴州省	4.82%	13
Foshan 佛山市	Guangdong 廣東省	3.66%	17
Beijing 北京市	Beijing 北京市	3.05%	55
Shenyang 瀋陽市	Liaoning 遼寧省	2.25%	49

10 Major Wholesalers 10 家主要批發商	City 城市	Province 省	Telephone / Fax 電話 / 傳真
Liaoning Automobile Trade Group Corp. 遼寧省汽車貿易集團	Shenyang 瀋陽市	Liaoning 遼寧省	(024)23835494 (024)23838338
China Post and Telecommunication Equipment General Company 中國郵電器材總公司	Beijing 北京市	Beijing 北京市	(010)63523715 (010)63525935
Jiangsu Electromechanical Products General Company 江蘇省機電產品總公司	Nanjing 南京市	Jiangsu 江蘇省	(025)7713642 (025)7711036
Xi Nan Technology Import & Export Company 西南技術進出口公司	Chongqing 重慶市	Chongqing 重慶市	(023)63850185 (023)63850026
Changzhou Economic Technology Industrial Development Zone Tian Ming Trade Company 常州經濟技術產業開發區天明貿易公司	Changzhou 常州市	Jiangsu 江蘇省	(0519)8829882 (0519)8829882
Shanxi Mechanical Equipment Import & Export Company 山西省機械設備進出口公司	Taiyuan 太原市	Shanxi 山西省	(0351)4040713 (0351)4043981
Ningbo Five Mining Machinery Import & Export Company 寧波市五礦機械進出口公司	Ningbo 寧波市	Zhejiang 浙江省	(0574)7311255 (0574)7320322
Tianjin Jin Huan Electromechanical Complete Sets of Equipment Factory 天津市津環機電成套設備廠	Tianjin 天津市	Tianjin 天津市	(022)26371628
Yunnan Machinery Import & Export Company 雲南省機械進出口公司	Kunming 昆明市	Yunnan 雲南省	(0871)3164879 (0871)3136829
Tianjin Da Qiu Zhuang Yi Yuan Trade Center 天津市大丘莊億源商貿中心	Tianjin 天津市	Tianjin 天津市	(022)28899478 (022)28899046

*Also include sales by firms outside this industry.包括本行業以外廠家的銷售。"o" stands for "others". "o" 代表 "其他產品"。

4029: Other Electricity Transmission, Distribution & Control Equipment
其他輸配電及控制設備製造業

The industry accounts for 0.162% of the total revenue of China's industrial sector in 1996. The revenue growth rate of the industry is 19.7% from 1995, as compared to the growth rate of China's industrial sector, 9.51%. The rate of return on asset is 3.82%. 69.25% of all firms in the industry made a profit while 24.67% had negative returns. The top province in terms of the industry's revenue is Jiangsu, accounting for 40.47% of the total revenue.
本行業在 1996 年佔全行業總產值 0.162% ，行業年增長率為 19.7%（全國工業年增長率 9.51%）。行業的資產回報率 3.82% ， 69.25% 的企業盈利， 24.67% 的企業虧損。銷售收入最高的省份為江蘇省，佔本行業的 40.47% 。

	Total number of firms 企業總數	Total number of employees 職工總數	Total revenue (mil. RMB) 總銷售收入（百萬元）	Total profit (mil. RMB) 總利潤（百萬元）	Return on assets 資產利潤率 (%)	Return on equity 權益利潤率 (%)	Labour productivity ('000 RMB / worker) 勞動生產率（千元/人）	Debts / assets 資產負債率 (%)	Total assets (mil. RMB) 總資產（百萬元）
Industry Overall 行業總體	1,236	131,041	9,389	463	3.82	11.10	71.65	65.56	12,120

	Number of firms 企業個數	Average number of employees 平均職工人數	Average revenue ('000 RMB) 平均銷售收入（千元）	Average profit ('000 RMB) 平均利潤（千元）	Return on assets 資產利潤率 (%)	Return on equity 權益利潤率 (%)	Labour productivity ('000 RMB / worker) 勞動生產率（千元/人）	Average debts / assets 平均資產負債率(%)	Average Total assets ('000 RMB) 平均總資產（千元）
By ownership 產業所有權									
State-owned 國有	149	221	10,060	302	1.57	5.73	45.54	72.57	19,228
Collectively-owned 集體	980	83	6,289	314	4.67	13.22	75.43	64.65	6,712
Privately-owned 私有	2	66	4,974	113	1.74	6.46	75.37	73.11	6,518
Domestic JVs 聯營	14	316	28,738	970	2.99	8.60	90.86	65.25	32,449
Joint stock 股份制	20	281	23,718	2,971	7.13	20.13	84.52	64.58	41,670
Foreign-funded 外資	31	99	15,319	172	0.80	1.54	154.19	48.23	21,548
Overseas Chinese-funded 港澳台資	39	93	9,314	819	4.53	12.32	99.63	63.28	18,110
By size 規模									
Large 大型	7	2,585	242,839	20,806	4.91	12.43	93.96	60.49	423,749
Medium 中型	27	620	52,301	2,431	3.24	9.14	84.40	64.56	75,016
Small 小型	1,187	81	5,287	212	3.53	11.02	65.36	67.96	6,005
By regional distribution 地區分布									
Central-North 華北	157	68	2,844	61	1.18	2.99	42.02	60.51	5,171
Beijing 北京	55	33	2,110	320	8.36	31.24	63.55	73.25	3,832
Tianjin 天津	32	73	3,701	-714	-7.77	-13.89	51.00	44.10	9,195
Hebei 河北	37	101	4,660	403	8.94	22.42	46.32	60.12	4,504
Shanxi 山西	15	145	1,684	-68	-0.84	-3.47	11.60	75.78	8,099
Inner Mongolia 內蒙	18	32	801	52	5.02	24.54	24.84	79.53	1,039
Northeast 東北	217	138	4,616	228	3.10	9.99	33.43	68.96	7,351
Liaoning 遼寧	125	116	4,058	101	1.61	5.13	35.08	68.55	6,239
Jilin 吉林	19	123	4,603	1,241	18.32	38.16	37.47	51.99	6,774
Heilongjiang 黑龍江	73	180	5,576	182	1.94	7.08	30.92	72.60	9,406
Central East 華東	515	118	12,251	646	4.51	12.94	103.63	65.11	14,319
Shanghai 上海	81	130	12,925	958	5.90	22.33	99.60	73.59	16,250
Jiangsu 江蘇	196	181	19,387	912	3.83	11.07	107.16	65.43	23,837
Zhejiang 浙江	125	49	4,092	242	5.90	12.86	83.08	54.12	4,097
Anhui 安徽	12	51	3,886	113	5.00	25.33	76.44	80.27	2,252
Fujian 福建	33	32	1,175	-62	-3.41	-9.78	36.28	65.13	1,804
Jiangxi 江西	15	72	1,177	-213	-8.25	-45.90	16.36	82.03	2,579
Shandong 山東	53	113	15,996	947	6.70	14.65	141.39	54.27	14,126
Central-South 中南	219	99	6,208	308	3.52	10.35	62.59	65.97	8,739
Henan 河南	59	137	7,455	776	6.69	20.77	54.52	67.81	11,608
Hubei 湖北	24	142	4,438	182	3.45	12.59	31.27	72.57	5,271
Hunan 湖南	67	59	2,025	-13	-0.50	-1.79	34.19	72.24	2,676
Guangdong 廣東	60	86	10,336	402	3.10	8.48	120.23	63.48	12,975
Guangxi 廣西	7	104	7,027	-114	-1.06	-4.26	67.48	75.18	10,813
Hainan 海南	2	196	4,040	-2,610	-7.58	-12.09	20.66	37.35	34,455
Southwest 西南	64	76	2,413	30	0.64	2.09	31.94	69.37	4,770
Chongqing 重慶	16	83	1,695	19	0.64	3.14	20.33	79.68	2,922
Sichuan 四川	38	74	2,864	43	0.77	2.63	38.50	70.77	5,606
Guizhou 貴州	4	23	938	5	0.26	0.58	40.32	55.02	1,918
Yunnan 雲南	6	96	2,402	-7	-0.11	-0.22	24.97	51.48	6,173
Tibet 西藏									
Northwest 西北	64	47	1,834	31	1.64	4.84	38.95	66.21	1,872
Shaanxi 陝西	49	50	1,894	40	2.07	6.02	37.64	65.58	1,940
Gansu 甘肅	2	21	1,330	40	4.57	16.00	64.88	71.43	875
Qinghai 青海	1	64	1,870	20	0.89	3.39	29.22	73.66	2,240
Ningxia 寧夏	1	25	110				4.40	48.33	600
Xinjiang 新疆	11	38	1,812	-10	-0.55	-1.73	47.68	68.45	1,833

4029: Other Electricity Transmission, Distribution & Control Equipment
其他輸配電及控制設備製造業

Year 年份	Number of firms 企業個數	Rate of change 每年變化 (%)	Number of employees 職工人數（人）	Rate of change 每年變化 (%)	Total revenue (mil. RMB) 總銷售收入（百萬元）	Rate of change 每年變化 (%)	Total profit (mil. RMB) 總利潤（百萬元）	Rate of change 每年變化 (%)
1993	972		99,171		3,927		242	
1994	1,121	15.33%	113,976	14.93%	5,324	35.56%	270	11.44%
1995	1,256	12.04%	137,701	20.82%	7,845	47.35%	371	37.28%
1996	1,236	-1.59%	131,041	-4.84%	9,389	19.68%	463	24.92%

3 Major products* 3 種主要產品 *	Output 產量	Sales volume 銷售量	Unit 單位

Top 10 firms by revenue (year founded) 收入排名前 10 家企業（創辦年份）	City 城市	Province 省	Telephone / fax 電話 / 傳真	Number of employees 職工人數	Ownership 產業所有權	Revenue ('000 RMB) 銷售收入（千元）	Profit ('000 RMB) (rank) 利潤（千元）（排名）	Total assets ('000 RMB) 總資產（千元）	Major products 主要產品
Yantai Dongfang Electron Information Industrial Co. Ltd. 煙台東方電子信息產業股份有限公司(1971)	Yantai 煙台市	Shandong 山東省	(0535)6214126 (0535)6213233	1,039	Joint stock 股份制	620,748	45325(2)	350,178	o
Jiangsu Chang Jiang Elec. Group Zhenjiang Electrical Equipment Factory 江蘇長江電器集團公司(1965)	Zhenjiang 鎮江市	Jiangsu 江蘇省	(0511)8411200	1,395	Collectively-owned 集體	522,858	70770(1)	649,322	o
Jiangsu Hua Peng Industrial Group Co. 江蘇華鵬實業集團公司(1987)	Zhenjiang 鎮江市	Jiangsu 江蘇省	(0511)8411156	1,367	Collectively-owned 集體	223,698	21161(5)	357,682	o
Nanjing Electric Power Automatic Equipment General Factory 南京電力自動化設備總廠(1940)	Nanjing 南京市	Jiangsu 江蘇省	(025)3421394 (025)3422174	1,638	State-owned 國有	217,978	13470(6)	327,762	o
Acheng Relay Works 阿城繼電器廠(1946)	Harbin 哈爾濱市	Heilongjiang 黑龍江省	(0451)3722346 (0451)3721652	6,165	State-owned 國有	203,927	7771(15)	445,546	o
Jiangsu Xin Fu Da Group Co. 江蘇鑫富達集團公司(1985)	Yancheng 鹽城市	Jiangsu 江蘇省	(0515)7212298 (0515)7212878	325	Collectively-owned 集體	150,110	13010(7)	131,520	o
Jiangsu DaLi City Electric Engineering Factory 江蘇大力城集團公司(1994)	Zhenjiang 鎮江市	Jiangsu 江蘇省	(0511)8412666	736	Collectively-owned 集體	141,008	8710(14)	90,175	o
Nanjing Nai Te Electromechanical (Group) Co. 南京耐特機電(集團)公司(1957)	Nanjing 南京市	Jiangsu 江蘇省	(025)5503888 (025)5502804	2,242	Domestic JVs 聯營	140,500	110(271)	265,000	o
Shenzhen Zhong Ya Power Supply Device Co. Ltd. 深圳中亞電源設備有限公司(1986)	Shenzhen 深圳市	Guangdong 廣東省	(0755)7800748 (0755)7800438	59	State-owned 國有	136,056	1520(55)	44,928	o
Jiangsu Hua Wei Electric Group Co. Ltd. 江蘇華威電氣集團有限公司	Zhenjiang 鎮江市	Jiangsu 江蘇省	(0511)8411018	961	Collectively-owned 集體	130,109	4077(25)	142,059	o

Top 10 Cities by Production Output 產出排名前 10 位城市	Province 省	Market share 市場份額	Number of firms 企業個數
Zhenjiang 鎮江市	Jiangsu 江蘇省	22.46%	106
Shanghai 上海市	Shanghai 上海市	13.97%	130
Xuchang 許昌市	Henan 河南省	7.01%	6
Nanjing 南京市	Jiangsu 江蘇省	4.46%	33
Dongguan 東莞市	Guangdong 廣東省	4.21%	4
Wenzhou 温州市	Zhejiang 浙江省	3.46%	117
Harbin 哈爾濱市	Heilongjiang 黑龍江省	3.32%	27
Shenyang 瀋陽市	Liaoning 遼寧省	2.27%	55
Shantou 汕頭市	Guangdong 廣東省	2.15%	9
Beijing 北京市	Beijing 北京市	1.76%	44

10 Major Wholesalers 10 家主要批發商	City 城市	Province 省	Telephone / Fax 電話 / 傳真
Liaoning Automobile Trade Group Corp. 遼寧省汽車貿易集團	Shenyang 瀋陽市	Liaoning 遼寧省	(024)23835494 (024)23838338
China Post and Telecommunication Equipment General Company 中國郵電器材總公司	Beijing 北京市	Beijing 北京市	(010)63523715 (010)63525935
Jiangsu Electromechanical Products General Company 江蘇省機電產品總公司	Nanjing 南京市	Jiangsu 江蘇省	(025)7713642 (025)7711036
Xi Nan Technology Import & Export Company 西南技術進出口公司	Chongqing 重慶市	Chongqing 重慶市	(023)63850185 (023)63850026
Changzhou Economic Technology Industrial Development Zone Tian Ming Trade Company 常州經濟技術產業開發區天明貿易公司	Changzhou 常州市	Jiangsu 江蘇省	(0519)8829882 (0519)8829882
Shanxi Mechanical Equipment Import & Export Company 山西省機械設備進出口公司	Taiyuan 太原市	Shanxi 山西省	(0351)4040713 (0351)4043981
Ningbo Five Mining Machinery Import & Export Company 寧波市五礦機械進出口公司	Ningbo 寧波市	Zhejiang 浙江省	(0574)7311255 (0574)7320322
Tianjin Jin Huan Electromechanical Complete Sets of Equipment Factory 天津市津環機電成套設備廠	Tianjin 天津市	Tianjin 天津市	(022)26371628
Yunnan Machinery Import & Export Company 雲南省機械進出口公司	Kunming 昆明市	Yunnan 雲南省	(0871)3164879 (0871)3136829
Tianjin Da Qiu Zhuang Yi Yuan Trade Center 天津市大丘莊億源商貿中心	Tianjin 天津市	Tianjin 天津市	(022)28899478 (022)28899046

*Also include sales by firms outside this industry.包括本行業以外廠家的銷售。"o" stands for "others". "o" 代表 "其他產品"。

4041: Wire and Cable 電線電纜製造業

The industry accounts for 1.002% of the total revenue of China's industrial sector in 1996. The revenue growth rate of the industry is 14.3% from 1995, as compared to the growth rate of China's industrial sector, 9.51%. The rate of return on asset is 2.31%. 69.60% of all firms in the industry made a profit while 25.27% had negative returns. The top province in terms of the industry's revenue is Jiangsu, accounting for 20.46% of the total revenue.
本行業在1996年佔全行業總產值1.002%，行業年增長率為14.3%（全國工業年增長率9.51%）。行業的資產回報率2.31%，69.60%的企業盈利，25.27%的企業虧損。銷售收入最高的省份為江蘇省，佔本行業的20.46%。

	Total number of firms 企業總數	Total number of employees 職工總數	Total revenue (mil. RMB) 總銷售收入（百萬元）	Total profit (mil. RMB) 總利潤（百萬元）	Return on assets 資產利潤率 (%)	Return on equity 權益利潤率 (%)	Labour productivity ('000 RMB / worker) 勞動生產率（千元/人）	Debts / assets 資產負債率 (%)	Total assets (mil. RMB) 總資產（百萬元）
Industry Overall 行業總體	2,642	415,490	58,102	1,513	2.31	7.34	139.84	68.57	65,623

	Number of firms 企業個數	Average number of employees 平均職工人數	Average revenue ('000 RMB) 平均銷售收入（千元）	Average profit ('000 RMB) 平均利潤（千元）	Return on assets 資產利潤率 (%)	Return on equity 權益利潤率 (%)	Labour productivity ('000 RMB / worker) 勞動生產率（千元/人）	Average debts / assets 平均資產負債率(%)	Average Total assets ('000 RMB) 平均總資產（千元）
By ownership 產業所有權									
State-owned 國有	321	448	46,773	159	0.23	0.82	104.36	71.65	68,044
Collectively-owned 集體	1,981	104	14,937	533	4.22	13.65	143.24	69.06	12,627
Privately-owned 私有	27	43	10,257	855	23.65	47.87	240.39	50.60	3,616
Domestic JVs 聯營	53	146	26,105	671	2.77	8.07	179.05	65.70	24,230
Joint stock 股份制	28	707	102,276	4,801	2.61	5.27	144.75	50.46	183,888
Foreign-funded 外資	97	181	37,469	562	0.96	3.13	207.25	69.39	58,687
Overseas Chinese-funded 港澳台資	135	149	39,546	1,171	2.42	8.28	265.21	70.81	48,458
By size 規模									
Large 大型	62	1,603	257,154	5,331	1.37	4.03	160.42	65.93	388,603
Medium 中型	144	593	95,998	2,855	2.77	9.55	161.94	71.00	103,034
Small 小型	2,402	96	11,796	321	2.89	9.51	123.03	69.60	11,112
By regional distribution 地區分布									
Central-North 華北	416	146	16,486	642	3.45	10.94	112.83	68.49	18,616
Beijing 北京	59	93	4,016	-440	-4.76	-16.86	43.12	71.76	9,249
Tianjin 天津	111	159	13,546	77	0.33	1.25	84.96	73.39	23,164
Hebei 河北	177	140	24,882	1,703	8.91	23.33	177.47	61.83	19,120
Shanxi 山西	38	219	11,581	-412	-2.06	-8.35	52.98	75.30	19,986
Inner Mongolia 內蒙	31	144	8,823	-46	-0.29	-1.16	61.16	74.63	15,597
Northeast 東北	347	171	10,425	-309	-1.46	-7.50	60.86	80.54	21,128
Liaoning 遼寧	208	161	13,252	-121	-0.47	-1.90	82.36	75.09	25,592
Jilin 吉林	45	175	5,547	-127	-0.79	-4.52	31.74	82.45	16,039
Heilongjiang 黑龍江	94	193	6,506	-810	-5.92	298.32	33.78	101.99	13,686
Central East 華東	1,073	156	28,857	1,070	4.03	12.02	185.41	66.48	26,563
Shanghai 上海	152	187	40,346	1,537	3.84	10.62	215.70	63.80	39,978
Jiangsu 江蘇	327	172	36,355	991	3.51	10.91	211.73	67.85	28,242
Zhejiang 浙江	235	139	24,206	754	3.19	9.93	173.92	67.90	23,647
Anhui 安徽	144	100	10,707	277	2.74	10.19	106.56	73.12	10,101
Fujian 福建	39	121	22,007	832	3.12	7.97	181.84	60.82	26,619
Jiangxi 江西	68	89	6,342	66	0.72	2.23	71.15	67.75	9,210
Shandong 山東	108	227	40,953	3,121	7.47	21.06	180.77	64.53	41,793
Central-South 中南	590	159	22,545	391	1.41	4.79	141.52	70.64	27,768
Henan 河南	164	144	14,566	421	2.09	7.85	101.48	73.38	20,114
Hubei 湖北	107	178	19,889	1,687	7.44	19.95	111.46	62.68	22,670
Hunan 湖南	81	218	25,718	133	0.47	1.38	117.76	65.73	28,067
Guangdong 廣東	203	140	29,632	-139	-0.38	-1.41	210.95	72.79	36,018
Guangxi 廣西	30	141	18,657	-23	-0.10	-0.42	132.48	75.98	22,678
Hainan 海南	5	186	25,302	-210	-0.27	-1.11	135.89	76.00	78,644
Southwest 西南	122	190	20,390	-54	-0.15	-0.33	107.58	54.87	36,062
Chongqing 重慶	24	154	9,079	-2,140	-14.30	-87.31	59.10	83.62	14,966
Sichuan 四川	77	179	20,863	573	1.37	2.77	116.51	50.66	41,869
Guizhou 貴州	12	149	11,576	-460	-2.17	-5.52	77.60	60.71	21,204
Yunnan 雲南	9	434	58,323	698	1.11	2.65	134.45	57.91	62,589
Tibet 西藏									
Northwest 西北	94	119	9,292	-202	-1.50	-4.63	78.36	67.56	13,442
Shaanxi 陝西	60	87	4,050	-77	-1.08	-2.95	46.57	63.48	7,098
Gansu 甘肅	13	276	30,667	-272	-0.68	-1.62	111.24	58.16	40,137
Qinghai 青海	1	316	8,330	30	0.21	0.55	26.36	62.04	14,250
Ningxia 寧夏	2	355	12,440	-395	-1.99	-10.30	35.09	80.63	19,800
Xinjiang 新疆	18	73	11,032	-561	-3.85	-43.83	150.44	91.22	14,560

4041: Wire and Cable 電線電纜製造業

Year 年份	Number of firms 企業個數	Rate of change 每年變化 (%)	Number of employees 職工人數 (人)	Rate of change 每年變化 (%)	Total revenue (mil. RMB) 總銷售收入 (百萬元)	Rate of change 每年變化 (%)	Total profit (mil. RMB) 總利潤 (百萬元)	Rate of change 每年變化 (%)
1993	2,310		432,626		32,887		1,001	
1994	2,542	10.04%	398,034	-8.00%	36,958	12.38%	703	-29.87%
1995	2,722	7.08%	430,225	8.09%	50,843	37.57%	895	27.32%
1996	2,642	-2.94%	415,490	-3.42%	58,102	14.28%	1,513	69.12%

3 Major products* 3 種主要產品 *	Output 產量	Sales volume 銷售量	Unit 單位
a) Electric Power Cable 電力電纜	1,916,118	1,820,312	km 公里
b) Electric Wire 電線	16,233,789	15,746,776	km 公里

Top 10 firms by revenue (year founded) 收入排名前 10 家企業 (創辦年份)	City 城市	Province 省	Telephone / fax 電話 / 傳真	Number of employees 職工人數	Ownership 產業所有權	Revenue ('000 RMB) 銷售收入 (千元)	Profit ('000 RMB) (rank) 利潤 (千元) (排名)	Total assets ('000 RMB) 總資產 (千元)	Major products 主要產品
Hunan Electric Wire & Cable Group Company 湖南電線電纜集團公司(1951)	Xiangtan 湘潭市	Hunan 湖南省	(0732)8591550 (0732)8591118	7,655	State-owned 國有	1,339,072	5587(84)	1,401,017	a,b
Shenyang Cable Factory 瀋陽電纜廠(1937)	Shenyang 瀋陽市	Liaoning 遼寧省	(024)25865471 (024)25851544	10,713	State-owned 國有	970,034	2143(194)	2,369,412	a
Shanghai Cable Works 上海電纜廠(1945)	Shanghai 上海市	Shanghai 上海市	(021)65487200 (021)65443447	4,501	State-owned 國有	966,449	19175(21)	799,226	a,b
Wendeng Communication Cable Group Co. 文登市通訊電纜集團公司(1985)	Weihai 威海市	Shandong 山東省	(0896)8356530 (0896)8354156	1,005	Collectively-owned 集體	881,770	100610(2)	514,030	o
Jiangsu Baosheng (Group) Co. Ltd. 江蘇寶勝集團公司(1985)	Yangzhou 揚州市	Jiangsu 江蘇省	(0514)8223611 (0514)8222575	1,979	State-owned 國有	809,530	39490(9)	569,890	a,b
Yong Ding Group Co. 永鼎集團公司(1977)	Suzhou 蘇州市	Jiangsu 江蘇省	(0512)3255483 (0512)3254177	975	Collectively-owned 集體	695,646	44371(8)	427,226	o
Chang Fei Optical Fibre Optical Cable Co. Ltd. 長飛光纖光纜有限公司(1994)	Wuhan 武漢市	Hubei 湖北省	(027)87802541 (027)87802536	439	Foreign-funded 外資	617,621	156275(1)	775,652	o
Shandong Cable Factory 山東電纜廠(1966)	Tai'an 泰安市	Shandong 山東省	(0538)7223012 (0538)7223012	2,876	State-owned 國有	601,067	60084(5)	603,680	a
Jiangsu Feng Quan Electric Wire & Cable Group Company 江蘇峯泉電線電纜集團公司(1983)	Wuxi 無錫市	Jiangsu 江蘇省	(0510)8270415 (0510)8270327	380	Collectively-owned 集體	551,967	16244(31)	118,142	b
Shanghai Walsin Electric Wire & Cable Co. Ltd. 上海華新電線電纜有限公司(1993)	Shanghai 上海市	Shanghai 上海市	(021)59122720 (021)59123724	432	Overseas Chinese-funded 港澳台資	495,769	37452(10)	441,330	o

Top 10 Cities by Production Output 產出排名前 10 位城市	Province 省	Market share 市場份額	Number of firms 企業個數
Shanghai 上海市	Shanghai 上海市	8.64%	213
Nanjing 南京市	Jiangsu 江蘇省	6.05%	29
Suzhou 蘇州市	Jiangsu 江蘇省	5.74%	100
Wuxi 無錫市	Jiangsu 江蘇省	4.42%	79
Changzhou 常州市	Jiangsu 江蘇省	3.87%	81
Xiangtan 湘潭市	Hunan 湖南省	3.80%	13
Hangzhou 杭州市	Zhejiang 浙江省	3.54%	82
Cangzhou 滄州市	Hebei 河北省	3.18%	52
Tianjin 天津市	Tianjin 天津市	2.94%	123
Shenyang 瀋陽市	Liaoning 遼寧省	2.78%	95

10 Major Wholesalers 10 家主要批發商	City 城市	Province 省	Telephone / Fax 電話 / 傳真
Liaoning Automobile Trade Group Corp. 遼寧省汽車貿易集團	Shenyang 瀋陽市	Liaoning 遼寧省	(024)23835494 (024)23838338
China Post and Telecommunication Equipment General Company 中國郵電器材總公司	Beijing 北京市	Beijing 北京市	(010)63523715 (010)63525935
Jiangsu Electromechanical Products General Company 江蘇省機電產品總公司	Nanjing 南京市	Jiangsu 江蘇省	(025)7713642 (025)7711036
Xi Nan Technology Import & Export Company 西南技術進出口公司	Chongqing 重慶市	Chongqing 重慶市	(023)63850185 (023)63850026
Changzhou Economic Technology Industrial Development Zone Tian Ming Trade Company 常州經濟技術產業開發區天明貿易公司	Changzhou 常州市	Jiangsu 江蘇省	(0519)8829882 (0519)8829882
Shanxi Mechanical Equipment Import & Export Company 山西省機械設備進出口公司	Taiyuan 太原市	Shanxi 山西省	(0351)4040713 (0351)4043981
Ningbo Five Mining Machinery Import & Export Company 寧波市五礦機械進出口公司	Ningbo 寧波市	Zhejiang 浙江省	(0574)7311255 (0574)7320322
Tianjin Jin Huan Electromechanical Complete Sets of Equipment Factory 天津市津環機電成套設備廠	Tianjin 天津市	Tianjin 天津市	(022)26371628
Yunnan Machinery Import & Export Company 雲南省機械進出口公司	Kunming 昆明市	Yunnan 雲南省	(0871)3164879 (0871)3136829
Tianjin Da Qiu Zhuang Yi Yuan Trade Center 天津市大丘莊億源商貿中心	Tianjin 天津市	Tianjin 天津市	(022)28899478 (022)28899046

*Also include sales by firms outside this industry.包括本行業以外廠家的銷售。"o" stands for "others". "o" 代表 "其他產品"。

4043: Insulated Products 絕緣製品業

The industry accounts for 0.058% of the total revenue of China's industrial sector in 1996. The revenue growth rate of the industry is 1.8% from 1995, as compared to the growth rate of China's industrial sector, 9.51%. The rate of return on asset is -0.17%. 64.60% of all firms in the industry made a profit while 31.30% had negative returns. The top province in terms of the industry's revenue is Jiangsu, accounting for 23.39% of the total revenue.
本行業在1996年佔全行業總產值0.058%，行業年增長率為1.8%（全國工業年增長率9.51%）。行業的資產回報率-0.17%，64.60%的企業盈利，31.30%的企業虧損。銷售收入最高的省份為江蘇省，佔本行業的23.39%。

	Total number of firms 企業總數	Total number of employees 職工總數	Total revenue (mil. RMB) 總銷售收入（百萬元）	Total profit (mil. RMB) 總利潤（百萬元）	Return on assets 資產利潤率 (%)	Return on equity 權益利潤率 (%)	Labour productivity ('000 RMB / worker) 勞動生產率（千元/人）	Debts / assets 資產負債率 (%)	Total assets (mil. RMB) 總資產（百萬元）
Industry Overall 行業總體	416	51,220	3,383	-8	-0.17	-0.64	66.05	72.85	4,656

	Number of firms 企業個數	Average number of employees 平均職工人數	Average revenue ('000 RMB) 平均銷售收入（千元）	Average profit ('000 RMB) 平均利潤（千元）	Return on assets 資產利潤率 (%)	Return on equity 權益利潤率 (%)	Labour productivity ('000 RMB / worker) 勞動生產率（千元/人）	Average debts / assets 平均資產負債率(%)	Average Total assets ('000 RMB) 平均總資產（千元）
By ownership 產業所有權									
State-owned 國有	48	501	12,042	-500	-1.53	-7.16	24.06	78.59	32,604
Collectively-owned 集體	313	69	6,419	43	0.71	2.51	93.58	71.62	6,022
Privately-owned 私有	1	32	2,716				84.88	83.21	6,446
Domestic JVs 聯營	10	169	10,104	-201	-0.82	-3.48	59.75	76.46	24,583
Joint stock 股份制	7	331	28,181	640	1.67	4.74	85.18	64.72	38,309
Foreign-funded 外資	14	50	12,878	257	1.50	5.07	258.30	70.51	17,200
Overseas Chinese-funded 港澳台資	24	79	13,139	-146	-0.79	-2.07	167.28	61.90	18,529
By size 規模									
Large 大型	3	1,889	83,684	-2,860	-1.49	-7.88	44.29	81.06	191,736
Medium 中型	18	645	36,557	-250	-0.33	-1.22	56.71	72.97	75,927
Small 小型	387	88	6,394	13	0.19	0.65	72.60	71.06	7,013
By regional distribution 地區分布									
Central-North 華北	67	212	5,438	39	0.42	2.06	25.70	79.43	9,107
Beijing 北京	11	703	2,731	-503	-3.74	-93.41	3.89	95.99	13,437
Tianjin 天津	13	134	7,449	-112	-1.36	-19.84	55.66	93.16	8,218
Hebei 河北	26	82	6,953	293	5.81	13.37	85.28	56.55	5,045
Shanxi 山西	6	164	2,787	422	6.84	19.64	16.97	65.17	6,163
Inner Mongolia 內蒙	11	145	3,631	-54	-0.31	-1.39	24.96	77.35	17,034
Northeast 東北	83	116	2,686	-196	-2.67	-18.17	23.19	85.30	7,322
Liaoning 遼寧	47	77	2,220	37	0.57	1.73	28.89	67.08	6,546
Jilin 吉林	13	107	1,615	-419	-5.47	-14.10	15.06	61.24	7,670
Heilongjiang 黑龍江	23	200	4,243	-545	-6.25	24.77	21.18	125.26	8,711
Central East 華東	163	97	12,467	194	1.59	5.09	128.77	68.74	12,202
Shanghai 上海	19	105	7,128	-481	-4.27	-17.76	67.85	75.98	11,265
Jiangsu 江蘇	58	117	13,643	261	1.84	6.14	116.49	70.02	14,169
Zhejiang 浙江	43	75	15,534	239	1.72	4.99	208.15	65.53	13,896
Anhui 安徽	12	36	4,114	-109	-3.21	-6.95	114.28	53.79	3,399
Fujian 福建	7	57	2,736	109	1.90	6.85	48.12	72.23	5,704
Jiangxi 江西	6	110	4,488	83	1.31	3.59	40.68	63.54	6,358
Shandong 山東	18	127	18,995	855	6.50	20.78	149.31	68.70	13,145
Central-South 中南	63	112	7,527	-117	-0.80	-2.75	67.21	70.89	14,601
Henan 河南	17	127	5,112	97	1.00	5.56	40.34	82.07	9,745
Hubei 湖北	4	92	10,315	303	6.90	28.54	112.12	75.83	4,385
Hunan 湖南	19	161	3,396	-97	-1.02	-6.27	21.08	83.75	9,556
Guangdong 廣東	20	69	13,863	-407	-1.48	-4.00	200.33	62.92	27,439
Guangxi 廣西	3	29	1,417	-77	-3.63	-28.05	48.30	87.05	2,110
Hainan 海南									
Southwest 西南	19	148	10,056	-1,248	-6.30	-22.33	67.95	71.77	19,797
Chongqing 重慶	1	23	876	1,788	322.75	545.04	38.66	40.78	554
Sichuan 四川	17	165	11,259	1,286	5.78	20.53	68.28	71.84	22,243
Guizhou 貴州									
Yunnan 雲南	1	11	90				8.18	44.44	180
Tibet 西藏									
Northwest 西北	21	85	4,688	240	3.30	9.45	55.21	65.05	7,278
Shaanxi 陝西	13	57	2,321	-4	-0.17	-0.68	40.77	75.64	2,315
Gansu 甘肅	5	184	13,212	1,026	4.35	11.22	71.80	61.21	23,564
Qinghai 青海	1	102	640	-40	-1.42	17.39	6.27	108.19	2,810
Ningxia 寧夏									
Xinjiang 新疆	2	11	785	5	0.47	1.61	74.76	70.75	1,060

4043: Insulated Products 絕緣製品業

Year 年份	Number of firms 企業個數	Rate of change 每年變化(%)	Number of employees 職工人數(人)	Rate of change 每年變化(%)	Total revenue (mil. RMB) 總銷售收入(百萬元)	Rate of change 每年變化(%)	Total profit (mil. RMB) 總利潤(百萬元)	Rate of change 每年變化(%)
1993	375		49,972		2,674		11	
1994	398	6.13%	50,742	1.54%	2,545	-4.82%	-30	-383.06%
1995	431	8.29%	53,002	4.45%	3,322	30.52%	-9	69.59%
1996	416	-3.48%	51,220	-3.36%	3,383	1.84%	-8	12.53%

3 Major products* 3種主要產品*	Output 產量	Sales volume 銷售量	Unit 單位
a) Insulation Products 絕緣製品	72,568	70,391	ton 噸

Top 10 firms by revenue (year founded) 收入排名前10家企業(創辦年份)	City 城市	Province 省	Telephone / fax 電話 / 傳真	Number of employees 職工人數	Ownership 產業所有權	Revenue ('000 RMB) 銷售收入(千元)	Profit ('000 RMB) (rank) 利潤(千元)(排名)	Total assets ('000 RMB) 總資產(千元)	Major products 主要產品
Sichuan Dong Fang Insulating Material Co. Ltd. 四川東方絕緣材料公司(1966)	Mianyang 綿陽市	Sichuan 四川省	(0816)2272713	1,839	Joint stock 股份制	146,248	1400(19)	228,455	o
Shandong Long Ci Group Co. 山東龍磁集團公司(1984)	Yantai 煙台市	Shandong 山東省	(0535)8561308 (0535)8561437	210	Collectively-owned 集體	135,818	1653(17)	37,260	o
Yixing Electromagnetism Electrical Wire General Factory 宜興市電磁電線總廠(1972)	Wuxi 無錫市	Jiangsu 江蘇省	(0510)7402268	197	Collectively-owned 集體	135,160	1682(16)	34,011	o
International Laminated Material Ltd. 國際層壓板材有限公司(1990)	Hangzhou 杭州市	Zhejiang 浙江省	(0571)3723641 (0571)5150461	251	Foreign-funded 外資	129,165	3363(11)	140,267	o
Hangzhou Fu Tian Industry & Trade Development Co. Ltd. 杭州富天工貿發展有限公司(1986)	Hangzhou 杭州市	Zhejiang 浙江省	(0571)6229245	252	Collectively-owned 集體	121,132	4007(8)	127,756	a
Changzhou Insulating Material General Factory 常州絕緣材料總廠(1958)	Changzhou 常州市	Jiangsu 江蘇省	(0519)6601625 (0519)6622333	881	State-owned 國有	110,471	5082(6)	130,780	a
Longkou Insulating Material General Factory 龍口市絕緣材料總廠(1980)	Yantai 煙台市	Shandong 山東省	(0535)8911218	403	Collectively-owned 集體	106,500	6300(2)	82,367	a
Taizhou Insulating Materials General Works 泰州絕緣材料總廠(1973)	Taizhou 泰州市	Jiangsu 江蘇省	(0523)6559075 (0523)6558507	988	State-owned 國有	96,848	8906(1)	179,868	a
Xin'an Jiang Electrical Appliances Factory 新安江電工器材廠(1958)	Hangzhou 杭州市	Zhejiang 浙江省	(0571)4722949	244	Collectively-owned 集體	87,406	-761(179)	50,964	o
Yuyao Shun Li Industrial Co. 余姚市舜利實業公司(1985)	Ningbo 寧波市	Zhejiang 浙江省	(0574)2715305 (0574)2715298	180	Collectively-owned 集體	85,112	3525(10)	39,251	o

Top 10 Cities by Production Output 產出排名前10位城市	Province 省	Market share 市場份額	Number of firms 企業個數
Hangzhou 杭州市	Zhejiang 浙江省	13.56%	20
Taizhou 泰州市	Jiangsu 江蘇省	6.07%	13
Yantai 煙台市	Shandong 山東省	5.31%	11
Changzhou 常州市	Jiangsu 江蘇省	5.06%	9
Mianyang 綿陽市	Sichuan 四川省	4.99%	3
Shanghai 上海市	Shanghai 上海市	4.47%	25
Wenzhou 温州市	Zhejiang 浙江省	3.95%	22
Suzhou 蘇州市	Jiangsu 江蘇省	3.75%	13
Wuxi 無錫市	Jiangsu 江蘇省	3.26%	11
Ningbo 寧波市	Zhejiang 浙江省	3.25%	6

10 Major Wholesalers 10家主要批發商	City 城市	Province 省	Telephone / Fax 電話 / 傳真
Liaoning Automobile Trade Group Corp. 遼寧省汽車貿易集團	Shenyang 瀋陽市	Liaoning 遼寧省	(024)23835494 (024)23838338
China Post and Telecommunication Equipment General Company 中國郵電器材總公司	Beijing 北京市	Beijing 北京市	(010)63523715 (010)63525935
Jiangsu Electromechanical Products General Company 江蘇省機電產品總公司	Nanjing 南京市	Jiangsu 江蘇省	(025)7713642 (025)7711036
Xi Nan Technology Import & Export Company 西南技術進出口公司	Chongqing 重慶市	Chongqing 重慶市	(023)63850185 (023)63850026
Changzhou Economic Technology Industrial Development Zone Tian Ming Trade Company 常州經濟技術產業開發區天明貿易公司	Changzhou 常州市	Jiangsu 江蘇省	(0519)8829882 (0519)8829882
Shanxi Mechanical Equipment Import & Export Company 山西省機械設備進出口公司	Taiyuan 太原市	Shanxi 山西省	(0351)4040713 (0351)4043981
Ningbo Five Mining Machinery Import & Export Company 寧波市五礦機械進出口公司	Ningbo 寧波市	Zhejiang 浙江省	(0574)7311255 (0574)7320322
Tianjin Jin Huan Electromechanical Complete Sets of Equipment Factory 天津市津環機電成套設備廠	Tianjin 天津市	Tianjin 天津市	(022)26371628
Yunnan Machinery Import & Export Company 雲南省機械進出口公司	Kunming 昆明市	Yunnan 雲南省	(0871)3164879 (0871)3136829
Tianjin Da Qiu Zhuang Yi Yuan Trade Center 天津市大丘莊億源商貿中心	Tianjin 天津市	Tianjin 天津市	(022)28899478 (022)28899046

*Also include sales by firms outside this industry.包括本行業以外廠家的銷售。"o" stands for "others". "o"代表"其他產品"。

4045: Storage Batteries 蓄電池製造業

The industry accounts for 0.103% of the total revenue of China's industrial sector in 1996. The revenue growth rate of the industry is 23.9% from 1995, as compared to the growth rate of China's industrial sector, 9.51%. The rate of return on asset is 0.24%. 65.07% of all firms in the industry made a profit while 29.58% had negative returns. The top province in terms of the industry's revenue is Guangdong, accounting for 17.53% of the total revenue.
本行業在1996年佔全行業總產值0.103%，行業年增長率為23.9%（全國工業年增長率9.51%）。行業的資產回報率0.24%，65.07%的企業盈利，29.58%的企業虧損。銷售收入最高的省份為廣東省，佔本行業的17.53%。

	Total number of firms 企業總數	Total number of employees 職工總數	Total revenue (mil. RMB) 總銷售收入（百萬元）	Total profit (mil. RMB) 總利潤（百萬元）	Return on assets 資產利潤率 (%)	Return on equity 權益利潤率 (%)	Labour productivity ('000 RMB / worker) 勞動生產率（千元/人）	Debts / assets 資產負債率 (%)	Total assets (mil. RMB) 總資產（百萬元）
Industry Overall 行業總體	757	100,125	5,946	23	0.24	0.67	59.39	63.45	9,421

	Number of firms 企業個數	Average number of employees 平均職工人數	Average revenue ('000 RMB) 平均銷售收入（千元）	Average profit ('000 RMB) 平均利潤（千元）	Return on assets 資產利潤率 (%)	Return on equity 權益利潤率 (%)	Labour productivity ('000 RMB / worker) 勞動生產率（千元/人）	Average debts / assets 平均資產負債率(%)	Average Total assets ('000 RMB) 平均總資產（千元）
By ownership 產業所有權									
State-owned 國有	100	351	14,120	-630	-1.85	-6.20	40.26	70.22	34,120
Collectively-owned 集體	551	77	3,742	27	0.75	3.05	48.36	75.36	3,618
Privately-owned 私有	3	119	4,991	86	2.28	4.63	41.94	50.71	3,769
Domestic JVs 聯營	6	54	4,524	60	0.92	3.18	83.78	70.91	6,450
Joint stock 股份制	16	310	24,703	704	1.73	2.86	79.62	39.56	40,716
Foreign-funded 外資	32	141	8,568	-211	-1.14	-2.45	60.70	53.25	18,451
Overseas Chinese-funded 港澳台資	47	274	37,432	1,403	2.42	5.28	136.68	54.13	57,893
By size 規模									
Large 大型	15	1,791	150,019	1,302	0.50	1.32	83.76	62.17	260,155
Medium 中型	21	616	40,538	23	0.04	0.13	65.77	70.88	62,802
Small 小型	702	85	4,052	4	0.07	0.19	47.67	62.31	5,983
By regional distribution 地區分布									
Central-North 華北	96	157	13,075	477	2.21	5.83	83.29	62.07	21,559
Beijing 北京	16	64	734	-228	-2.56	-37.09	11.40	93.11	8,916
Tianjin 天津	28	110	13,283	-1,628	-5.91	-32.30	120.91	81.72	27,560
Hebei 河北	32	299	26,347	2,965	8.92	15.55	88.12	42.64	33,250
Shanxi 山西	12	65	1,059	8	0.29	0.89	16.38	67.04	2,558
Inner Mongolia 內蒙	8	78	1,966	1	0.02	0.07	25.37	77.54	7,574
Northeast 東北	83	127	5,655	-301	-2.36	-8.28	44.56	71.51	12,761
Liaoning 遼寧	44	132	5,899	-174	-0.98	-3.15	44.81	69.01	17,862
Jilin 吉林	9	135	3,974	-2,207	-22.72	-334.91	29.54	93.22	9,714
Heilongjiang 黑龍江	30	118	5,801	85	1.37	4.86	49.30	71.85	6,194
Central East 華東	284	134	7,330	-33	-0.34	-1.02	54.62	67.18	9,829
Shanghai 上海	32	72	3,867	-1,293	-12.71	-25.03	53.48	49.23	10,171
Jiangsu 江蘇	78	98	7,127	138	1.48	5.08	72.81	70.95	9,322
Zhejiang 浙江	41	78	7,495	150	1.05	2.88	95.59	63.39	14,233
Anhui 安徽	38	70	4,293	204	7.02	26.82	61.03	73.82	2,912
Fujian 福建	22	100	9,116	-1,103	-9.14	-37.11	91.03	75.36	12,067
Jiangxi 江西	37	64	1,317	-41	-0.96	-5.99	20.54	83.93	4,211
Shandong 山東	36	492	18,953	919	5.31	16.02	38.55	66.86	17,315
Central-South 中南	213	132	8,604	67	0.49	1.25	65.28	60.76	13,666
Henan 河南	39	184	5,986	196	1.87	5.17	32.61	63.72	10,467
Hubei 湖北	32	201	11,076	59	0.30	0.82	55.10	63.65	19,838
Hunan 湖南	56	79	2,534	-44	-1.26	-4.64	32.21	72.78	3,453
Guangdong 廣東	75	118	13,900	294	1.49	3.09	117.94	51.95	19,770
Guangxi 廣西	10	108	6,012	-1,387	-7.96	937.16	55.87	100.85	17,428
Hainan 海南	1	157	150	-1,020	-5.88	392.31	0.96	101.50	17,360
Southwest 西南	65	111	4,067	8	0.10	0.18	36.51	45.36	8,029
Chongqing 重慶	17	146	6,519	79	0.79	1.10	44.60	28.36	9,972
Sichuan 四川	33	112	3,759	-104	-1.18	-2.74	33.53	57.03	8,792
Guizhou 貴州	8	69	739	-255	-7.10	-16.63	10.71	57.36	3,594
Yunnan 雲南	7	73	3,190	79	1.67	2.18	43.78	23.48	4,703
Tibet 西藏									
Northwest 西北	16	69	2,655	-195	-4.59	-23.51	38.72	80.44	4,246
Shaanxi 陝西	6	29	5,420	87	3.68	13.37	186.90	72.49	2,357
Gansu 甘肅	5	159	1,526	-676	-6.99	-42.20	9.61	83.41	9,668
Qinghai 青海	3	30	163	-107	-7.19	-40.00	5.51	82.02	1,483
Ningxia 寧夏	1	30	1,130	50	7.46	12.20	37.67	37.31	670
Xinjiang 新疆	1	10	710	10	3.03	6.25	71.00	51.52	330

4045: Storage Batteries 蓄電池製造業

Year 年份	Number of firms 企業個數	Rate of change 每年變化 (%)	Number of employees 職工人數 (人)	Rate of change 每年變化 (%)	Total revenue (mil. RMB) 總銷售收入 (百萬元)	Rate of change 每年變化 (%)	Total profit (mil. RMB) 總利潤 (百萬元)	Rate of change 每年變化 (%)
1993	676		82,277		3,529		187	
1994	711	5.18%	86,376	4.98%	3,586	1.62%	129	-30.92%
1995	743	4.50%	92,015	6.53%	4,800	33.83%	174	35.04%
1996	757	1.88%	100,125	8.81%	5,946	23.88%	23	-86.79%

3 Major products* 3 種主要產品 *	Output 產量	Sales volume 銷售量	Unit 單位
a) Accumulator 蓄電池	19,370,415	17,820,782	kvah 千伏安時

Top 10 firms by revenue (year founded) 收入排名前 10 家企業 (創辦年份)	City 城市	Province 省	Telephone / fax 電話 / 傳真	Number of employees 職工人數	Ownership 產業所有權	Revenue ('000 RMB) 銷售收入 (千元)	Profit ('000 RMB) (rank) 利潤 (千元) (排名)	Total assets ('000 RMB) 總資產 (千元)	Major products 主要產品
Baoding Jinfengfan Storage Battery Co. Ltd. 保定金風帆蓄電池有限公司(1994)	Baoding 保定市	Hebei 河北省	(0312)3025931 (0312)3036051	2,970	Overseas Chinese-funded 港澳台資	464,813	40245(1)	365,991	a
Tianjin President Industrial Co. Ltd. 天津統一工業有限公司(1993)	Tianjin 天津市	Tianjin 天津市	(022)5325681 (022)5328527	1,032	Overseas Chinese-funded 港澳台資	244,793	-45299(299)	481,221	a
Weihai Wen Long Battery Co. Ltd. 威海文隆電池有限公司(1992)	Weihai 威海市	Shandong 山東省	(0896)8842068 (0896)8842068	258	Overseas Chinese-funded 港澳台資	213,440	29160(2)	32,560	o
Shenyang Storage Battery Factory 瀋陽蓄電池廠(1940)	Shenyang 瀋陽市	Liaoning 遼寧省	(024)25875578 (024)25850217	2,783	State-owned 國有	195,409	1022(37)	448,209	a
Huizhou Chao Ba Battery Co. Ltd. 惠州市超霸電池有限公司(1994)	Huizhou 惠州市	Guangdong 廣東省	(0751)2292383 (0751)2291045	766	Overseas Chinese-funded 港澳台資	151,270	6300(13)	65,201	o
Guangzhou Storage Battery Enterprise Co. Ltd. 廣州蓄電池企業有限公司(1994)	Guangzhou 廣州市	Guangdong 廣東省	(020)86559900 (020)86564910	1,099	Overseas Chinese-funded 港澳台資	149,145	10010(6)	238,365	a
Guangdong Jialee Electric Power Appliances Production Co. Ltd. 廣東佳力電源器材製造有限公司(1988)	Foshan 佛山市	Guangdong 廣東省	(0757)7823562 (0757)7831257	943	Overseas Chinese-funded 港澳台資	138,599	7525(11)	152,351	a
Chongqing Wan Li Storage Battery Co. Ltd. 重慶萬里蓄電池股份有限公司	Chongqing 重慶市	Chongqing 重慶市	(023)62854864 (023)62851155		Joint stock 股份制	132,911	6221(14)	265,900	a
Linyi Luo Zhuang Qu Jin Luo Battery General Company 臨沂市羅裝區金羅電池總公司(1981)	Linyi 臨沂市	Shandong 山東省	(0539)8241653 (0539)8241188	3,346	Collectively-owned 集體	129,386	5538(15)	69,735	o
Zhejiang Zhong Yi Industrial Group Co. Ltd. 浙江忠義實業集團有限公司(1992)	Jinhua 金華市	Zhejiang 浙江省	(0579)4663090	362	Collectively-owned 集體	112,260	679(47)	268,790	o

Top 10 Cities by Production Output 產出排名前 10 位城市	Province 省	Market share 市場份額	Number of firms 企業個數
Baoding 保定市	Hebei 河北省	8.17%	8
Shanghai 上海市	Shanghai 上海市	7.87%	61
Shenyang 瀋陽市	Liaoning 遼寧省	7.33%	15
Tianjin 天津市	Tianjin 天津市	6.12%	29
Guangzhou 廣州市	Guangdong 廣東省	4.34%	23
Foshan 佛山市	Guangdong 廣東省	3.54%	7
Chongqing 重慶市	Chongqing 重慶市	3.25%	35
Xinxiang 新鄉市	Henan 河南省	2.88%	11
Shijiazhuang 石家莊市	Hebei 河北省	2.67%	5
Huizhou 惠州市	Guangdong 廣東省	2.48%	4

10 Major Wholesalers 10 家主要批發商	City 城市	Province 省	Telephone / Fax 電話 / 傳真
Liaoning Automobile Trade Group Corp. 遼寧省汽車貿易集團	Shenyang 瀋陽市	Liaoning 遼寧省	(024)23835494 (024)23838338
China Post and Telecommunication Equipment General Company 中國郵電器材總公司	Beijing 北京市	Beijing 北京市	(010)63523715 (010)63525935
Jiangsu Electromechanical Products General Company 江蘇省機電產品總公司	Nanjing 南京市	Jiangsu 江蘇省	(025)7713642 (025)7711036
Xi Nan Technology Import & Export Company 西南技術進出口公司	Chongqing 重慶市	Chongqing 重慶市	(023)63850185 (023)63850026
Changzhou Economic Technology Industrial Development Zone Tian Ming Trade Company 常州經濟技術產業開發區天明貿易公司	Changzhou 常州市	Jiangsu 江蘇省	(0519)8829882 (0519)8829882
Shanxi Mechanical Equipment Import & Export Company 山西省機械設備進出口公司	Taiyuan 太原市	Shanxi 山西省	(0351)4040713 (0351)4043981
Ningbo Five Mining Machinery Import & Export Company 寧波市五礦機械進出口公司	Ningbo 寧波市	Zhejiang 浙江省	(0574)7311255 (0574)7320322
Tianjin Jin Huan Electromechanical Complete Sets of Equipment Factory 天津市津環機電成套設備廠	Tianjin 天津市	Tianjin 天津市	(022)26371628
Yunnan Machinery Import & Export Company 雲南省機械進出口公司	Kunming 昆明市	Yunnan 雲南省	(0871)3164879 (0871)3136829
Tianjin Da Qiu Zhuang Yi Yuan Trade Center 天津市大丘莊億源商貿中心	Tianjin 天津市	Tianjin 天津市	(022)28899478 (022)28899046

*Also include sales by firms outside this industry.包括本行業以外廠家的銷售。"o" stands for "others". "o" 代表 "其他產品"。

4046: Dry Cells 乾電池製造業

The industry accounts for 0.100% of the total revenue of China's industrial sector in 1996. The revenue growth rate of the industry is 18.4% from 1995, as compared to the growth rate of China's industrial sector, 9.51%. The rate of return on asset is 0.36%. 52.65% of all firms in the industry made a profit while 40.80% had negative returns. The top province in terms of the industry's revenue is Guangdong, accounting for 47.27% of the total revenue.
本行業在1996年佔全行業總產值0.100%，行業年增長率為18.4%（全國工業年增長率9.51%）。行業的資產回報率0.36%，52.65%的企業盈利，40.80%的企業虧損。銷售收入最高的省份為廣東省，佔本行業的47.27%。

	Total number of firms 企業總數	Total number of employees 職工總數	Total revenue (mil. RMB) 總銷售收入（百萬元）	Total profit (mil. RMB) 總利潤（百萬元）	Return on assets 資產利潤率 (%)	Return on equity 權益利潤率 (%)	Labour productivity ('000 RMB / worker) 勞動生產率（千元/人）	Debts / assets 資產負債率 (%)	Total assets (mil. RMB) 總資產（百萬元）
Industry Overall 行業總體	278	80,135	5,783	24	0.36	1.28	72.17	71.60	6,673

	Number of firms 企業個數	Average number of employees 平均職工人數	Average revenue ('000 RMB) 平均銷售收入（千元）	Average profit ('000 RMB) 平均利潤（千元）	Return on assets 資產利潤率 (%)	Return on equity 權益利潤率 (%)	Labour productivity ('000 RMB / worker) 勞動生產率（千元/人）	Average debts / assets 平均資產負債率(%)	Average Total assets ('000 RMB) 平均總資產（千元）
By ownership 產業所有權									
State-owned 國有	92	529	27,152	-576	-1.73	-8.31	51.37	79.19	33,326
Collectively-owned 集體	117	158	10,855	260	3.40	16.35	68.74	79.18	7,650
Privately-owned 私有									
Domestic JVs 聯營	11	129	14,843	-98	-1.30	-3.69	114.90	64.79	7,532
Joint stock 股份制	6	548	47,422	3,759	3.92	10.96	86.54	64.21	95,848
Foreign-funded 外資	18	129	26,282	-2,937	-5.10	-11.06	204.26	53.85	57,554
Overseas Chinese-funded 港澳台資	33	203	33,043	2,318	7.53	21.49	162.56	64.96	30,786
By size 規模									
Large 大型	8	1,686	172,705	-15,309	-5.82	-21.42	102.44	72.81	262,881
Medium 中型	24	1,010	82,774	13,291	16.78	61.53	81.94	72.73	79,198
Small 小型	237	179	10,191	-728	-6.47	-21.52	56.88	69.93	11,249
By regional distribution 地區分布									
Central-North 華北	23	269	8,730	-1,250	-7.46	-143.18	32.42	94.79	16,757
Beijing 北京	3	248	6,343	-687	-3.55	-48.36	25.54	92.66	19,353
Tianjin 天津	4	87	2,570	-4,160	-27.33	79.16	29.46	134.51	15,220
Hebei 河北	10	410	16,365	-787	-3.39	-26.19	39.90	87.05	23,188
Shanxi 山西	3	265	2,113	-647	-6.41	-29.26	7.98	78.10	10,090
Inner Mongolia 內蒙	3	68	497	-80	-5.57	-150.00	7.27	96.06	1,437
Northeast 東北	25	154	1,966	-372	-3.98	339.42	12.74	101.17	9,350
Liaoning 遼寧	8	223	1,159	-536	-2.96	1159.46	5.20	100.25	18,129
Jilin 吉林	8	140	2,236	-200	-4.10	-78.43	16.00	94.77	4,880
Heilongjiang 黑龍江	9	106	2,442	-379	-6.86	77.32	23.02	108.88	5,521
Central East 華東	97	230	15,420	221	1.12	4.73	67.06	76.26	19,668
Shanghai 上海	18	286	28,612	-747	-1.68	-8.53	100.00	80.30	44,431
Jiangsu 江蘇	21	171	7,463	-6	-0.06	-0.19	43.52	68.52	10,235
Zhejiang 浙江	24	124	9,824	451	3.57	8.90	79.52	59.90	12,624
Anhui 安徽	9	320	10,171	-891	-8.14	-87.46	31.74	90.71	10,951
Fujian 福建	6	429	51,512	1,238	2.33	10.03	120.21	76.76	53,112
Jiangxi 江西	9	181	6,740	-6	-0.06	-0.57	37.24	89.25	9,040
Shandong 山東	10	350	12,696	2,479	27.08	175.32	36.23	84.56	9,156
Central-South 中南	103	297	32,103	436	1.51	4.27	108.02	64.72	28,920
Henan 河南	5	569	27,906	8	0.03	0.10	49.08	73.97	30,538
Hubei 湖北	7	378	18,559	-349	-1.99	-8.37	49.08	76.25	17,527
Hunan 湖南	15	237	5,517	-381	-5.55	-42.15	23.28	86.84	6,875
Guangdong 廣東	67	281	40,798	915	2.55	6.74	145.31	62.25	35,944
Guangxi 廣西	8	318	26,879	-1,008	-4.31	-14.10	84.42	69.46	23,403
Hainan 海南	1	208	5,900	-220	-4.65	-10.14	28.37	54.12	4,730
Southwest 西南	22	661	30,470	463	1.03	3.14	46.07	67.35	45,138
Chongqing 重慶	5	892	46,668	444	1.00	2.72	52.29	63.23	44,410
Sichuan 四川	5	799	31,603	1,130	1.04	3.07	39.55	66.05	108,253
Guizhou 貴州	5	486	14,332	320	2.26	4.87	29.50	53.58	14,140
Yunnan 雲南	7	517	28,639	147	0.55	2.92	55.36	81.27	26,861
Tibet 西藏									
Northwest 西北	8	328	7,489	-1,780	-8.18	-28.72	22.87	71.51	21,749
Shaanxi 陝西	4	276	2,035	-2,703	-13.50	-146.08	7.38	90.76	20,013
Gansu 甘肅	1	594	15,580	-4,440	-16.13	-94.87	26.23	82.99	27,520
Qinghai 青海									
Ningxia 寧夏									
Xinjiang 新疆	3	308	12,063	337	1.52	2.69	39.21	43.56	22,140

4046: Dry Cells 乾電池製造業

Year 年份	Number of firms 企業個數	Rate of change 每年變化 (%)	Number of employees 職工人數 (人)	Rate of change 每年變化 (%)	Total revenue (mil. RMB) 總銷售收入 (百萬元)	Rate of change 每年變化 (%)	Total profit (mil. RMB) 總利潤 (百萬元)	Rate of change 每年變化 (%)
1993	243		85,617		3,294		17	
1994	256	5.35%	86,494	1.02%	4,032	22.40%	5	-68.59%
1995	300	17.19%	97,541	12.77%	4,884	21.12%	1	-73.41%
1996	278	-7.33%	80,135	-17.84%	5,783	18.41%	24	1568.98%

3 Major products* 3種主要產品*	Output 產量	Sales volume 銷售量	Unit 單位
a) Primary Battery 原電池	1,055,813	992,464	10,000 piece 萬只

Top 10 firms by revenue (year founded) 收入排名前10家企業 (創辦年份)	City 城市	Province 省	Telephone / fax 電話 / 傳真	Number of employees 職工人數	Ownership 產業所有權	Revenue ('000 RMB) 銷售收入 (千元)	Profit ('000 RMB) (rank) 利潤 (千元) (排名)	Total assets ('000 RMB) 總資產 (千元)	Major products 主要產品
Guangzhou Battery Factory 廣州電池廠(1928)	Guangzhou 廣州市	Guangdong 廣東省	(020)84357214 (020)84429052	3,235	State-owned 國有	454,176	8048(7)	393,834	a
Dongguan Nokia Moving Telephone Co. Ltd. 東莞諾基亞移動電話有限公司(1995)	Dongguan 東莞市	Guangdong 廣東省	(0769)2402844 (0769)2402847	439	Foreign-funded 外資	419,330	28269(1)	313,785	o
T.g. Battery (China) Co. Ltd. 東山電池工業(中國)有限公司(1993)	Huizhou 惠州市	Guangdong 廣東省	(0751)2279237 (0751)2265153	592	Foreign-funded 外資	237,285	16169(3)	298,249	o
Shanghai Battery Factory 上海電池廠(1938)	Shanghai 上海市	Shanghai 上海市	(021)56627600 (021)56634385	2,888	State-owned 國有	232,142	209(53)	359,291	a
Wuzhou Sunwatt Battery (Group) Stock Co. Ltd. 梧州市電池股份有限公司(1937)	Wuzhou 梧州市	Guangxi 廣西	(0774)3827109 (0774)3824543	1,755	Joint stock 股份制	181,862	536(38)	149,449	a
Shenzhen Sanyo Hua Qiang Energy Co. Ltd. 深圳三洋華強能源有限公司(1995)	Shenzhen 深圳市	Guangdong 廣東省	(0755)8891307 (0755)8891460	205	Foreign-funded 外資	177,765	-82(127)	96,806	a
Xiamen Daily Chemical Enterprise Co. Ltd. 廈門日化企業有限公司(1954)	Xiamen 廈門市	Fujian 福建省	(0592)2022581 (0592)2022193	1,639	State-owned 國有	156,622	1061(26)	145,230	o
Jiangmen Battery Factory 江門市電池廠(1958)	Jiangmen 江門市	Guangdong 廣東省	(0750)3532513 (0750)3551251	1,746	State-owned 國有	155,799	89(76)	190,831	a
Nangping Nan Fu Battery Co. Ltd. 南平南孚電池有限公司(1988)	Nangping 南平市	Fujian 福建省	(0599)8731107 (0599)8735117	850	Overseas Chinese-funded 港澳台資	148,508	21531(2)	130,209	o
Jinshan Electrochemical Industry (Huizhou) Co. Ltd. 金山電化工業(惠州)有限公司(1988)	Huizhou 惠州市	Guangdong 廣東省	(0751)2264882 (0751)2261634	659	Overseas Chinese-funded 港澳台資	145,215	9196(5)	113,760	o

Top 10 Cities by Production Output 產出排名前10位城市	Province 省	Market share 市場份額	Number of firms 企業個數
Guangzhou 廣州市	Guangdong 廣東省	13.50%	13
Huizhou 惠州市	Guangdong 廣東省	9.22%	5
Jiangmen 江門市	Guangdong 廣東省	4.97%	6
Chongqing 重慶市	Chongqing 重慶市	4.07%	4
Dongguan 東莞市	Guangdong 廣東省	4.04%	5
Shanghai 上海市	Shanghai 上海市	3.74%	28
Yunfu 雲浮市	Guangdong 廣東省	3.69%	9
Wuzhou 梧州市	Guangxi 廣西	3.54%	2
Shenzhen 深圳市	Guangdong 廣東省	3.54%	10
Ningbo 寧波市	Zhejiang 浙江省	3.41%	7

10 Major Wholesalers 10家主要批發商	City 城市	Province 省	Telephone / Fax 電話 / 傳真
Liaoning Automobile Trade Group Corp. 遼寧省汽車貿易集團	Shenyang 瀋陽市	Liaoning 遼寧省	(024)23835494 (024)23838338
China Post and Telecommunication Equipment General Company 中國郵電器材總公司	Beijing 北京市	Beijing 北京市	(010)63523715 (010)63525935
Jiangsu Electromechanical Products General Company 江蘇省機電產品總公司	Nanjing 南京市	Jiangsu 江蘇省	(025)7713642 (025)7711036
Xi Nan Technology Import & Export Company 西南技術進出口公司	Chongqing 重慶市	Chongqing 重慶市	(023)63850185 (023)63850026
Changzhou Economic Technology Industrial Development Zone Tian Ming Trade Company 常州經濟技術產業開發區天明貿易公司	Changzhou 常州市	Jiangsu 江蘇省	(0519)8829882 (0519)8829882
Shanxi Mechanical Equipment Import & Export Company 山西省機械設備進出口公司	Taiyuan 太原市	Shanxi 山西省	(0351)4040713 (0351)4043981
Ningbo Five Mining Machinery Import & Export Company 寧波市五礦機械進出口公司	Ningbo 寧波市	Zhejiang 浙江省	(0574)7311255 (0574)7320322
Tianjin Jin Huan Electromechanical Complete Sets of Equipment Factory 天津市津環機電成套設備廠	Tianjin 天津市	Tianjin 天津市	(022)26371628
Yunnan Machinery Import & Export Company 雲南省機械進出口公司	Kunming 昆明市	Yunnan 雲南省	(0871)3164879 (0871)3136829
Tianjin Da Qiu Zhuang Yi Yuan Trade Center 天津市大丘莊億源商貿中心	Tianjin 天津市	Tianjin 天津市	(022)28899478 (022)28899046

*Also include sales by firms outside this industry.包括本行業以外廠家的銷售。"o" stands for "others". "o" 代表 "其他產品"。

4049: Other Electric Engineering Equipment 其他電工器材製造業

The industry accounts for 0.056% of the total revenue of China's industrial sector in 1996. The revenue growth rate of the industry is -10.0% from 1995, as compared to the growth rate of China's industrial sector, 9.51%. The rate of return on asset is 1.04%. 66.96% of all firms in the industry made a profit while 26.23% had negative returns. The top province in terms of the industry's revenue is Jiangsu, accounting for 24.42% of the total revenue.
本行業在1996年佔全行業總產值0.056%，行業年增長率為-10.0%（全國工業年增長率9.51%）。行業的資產回報率1.04%，66.96%的企業盈利，26.23%的企業虧損。銷售收入最高的省份為江蘇省，佔本行業的24.42%。

	Total number of firms 企業總數	Total number of employees 職工總數	Total revenue (mil. RMB) 總銷售收入（百萬元）	Total profit (mil. RMB) 總利潤（百萬元）	Return on assets 資產利潤率 (%)	Return on equity 權益利潤率 (%)	Labour productivity ('000 RMB / worker) 勞動生產率（千元/人）	Debts / assets 資產負債率 (%)	Total assets (mil. RMB) 總資產（百萬元）
Industry Overall 行業總體	560	47,175	3,241	38	1.04	3.47	68.70	70.06	3,671

	Number of firms 企業個數	Average number of employees 平均職工人數	Average revenue ('000 RMB) 平均銷售收入（千元）	Average profit ('000 RMB) 平均利潤（千元）	Return on assets 資產利潤率 (%)	Return on equity 權益利潤率 (%)	Labour productivity ('000 RMB / worker) 勞動生產率（千元/人）	Average debts / assets 平均資產負債率(%)	Average Total assets ('000 RMB) 平均總資產（千元）
By ownership 產業所有權									
State-owned 國有	65	145	9,169	138	0.94	3.30	63.33	71.44	14,708
Collectively-owned 集體	419	63	3,454	70	2.40	9.45	54.73	74.56	2,899
Privately-owned 私有	2	74	4,687	850	24.02	156.03	63.78	84.60	3,536
Domestic JVs 聯營	7	54	10,694	495	7.89	19.31	198.57	59.14	6,274
Joint stock 股份制	8	335	11,463	657	3.29	11.21	34.22	70.69	19,996
Foreign-funded 外資	28	125	11,588	-700	-3.38	-6.84	92.60	50.57	20,690
Overseas Chinese-funded 港澳台資	33	151	21,135	272	1.26	5.44	139.94	76.80	21,526
By size 規模									
Large 大型	3	897	72,557	-3,641	-2.70	-5.20	80.92	47.97	134,687
Medium 中型	11	774	60,564	1,396	1.97	9.39	78.28	78.98	70,770
Small 小型	535	67	4,406	63	1.35	4.63	65.47	70.86	4,652
By regional distribution 地區分布									
Central-North 華北	77	48	1,242	-24	-0.82	-4.22	26.01	80.64	2,876
Beijing 北京	26	39	1,285	-50	-3.03	-11.49	32.69	73.65	1,651
Tianjin 天津	20	77	1,475	-14	-0.24	-1.87	19.27	87.17	5,614
Hebei 河北	20	39	1,146	-14	-0.64	-2.01	29.52	68.28	2,122
Shanxi 山西	7	42	1,081	-13	-0.61	-2.24	25.75	72.76	2,109
Inner Mongolia 內蒙	4	13	555	30	1.33	-35.29	41.89	103.76	2,260
Northeast 東北	100	71	3,038	-25	-0.54	-2.45	43.05	77.88	4,635
Liaoning 遼寧	67	70	3,601	-34	-0.67	-2.93	51.29	77.04	5,077
Jilin 吉林	21	41	848	-52	-3.19	-12.47	20.63	74.41	1,641
Heilongjiang 黑龍江	12	124	3,733	73	0.99	5.63	30.03	82.41	7,405
Central East 華東	253	83	7,270	136	2.00	5.65	88.10	64.54	6,790
Shanghai 上海	26	90	7,554	-110	-1.71	-8.04	84.19	78.69	6,419
Jiangsu 江蘇	84	112	9,421	188	1.85	4.67	84.40	60.45	10,175
Zhejiang 浙江	65	60	6,838	256	4.07	12.64	113.10	67.83	6,290
Anhui 安徽	18	41	5,201	104	4.09	14.35	128.07	71.50	2,556
Fujian 福建	22	68	4,589	-25	-0.58	-1.57	67.62	63.23	4,336
Jiangxi 江西	14	52	8,134	62	1.59	3.51	155.99	54.57	3,899
Shandong 山東	24	95	4,109	112	2.94	8.64	43.16	65.99	3,812
Central-South 中南	91	111	9,163	80	0.75	3.14	82.37	76.19	10,712
Henan 河南	19	91	3,114	-3	-0.10	-0.40	34.38	74.82	3,158
Hubei 湖北	11	61	2,997	65	1.33	5.32	49.36	74.94	4,911
Hunan 湖南	15	125	3,466	-238	-4.83	-30.36	27.83	84.10	4,932
Guangdong 廣東	41	133	16,182	277	1.48	6.01	121.25	75.40	18,708
Guangxi 廣西	5	79	5,236	-226	-5.72	-37.17	66.62	84.66	3,950
Hainan 海南									
Southwest 西南	19	184	6,093	67	0.61	1.51	33.13	59.73	10,975
Chongqing 重慶	4	122	7,408	-57	-1.12	-4.55	60.82	75.35	5,054
Sichuan 四川	7	410	11,944	-165	-0.62	-1.47	29.11	58.02	26,779
Guizhou 貴州	5	15	274	2	1.41	3.57	18.03	60.56	142
Yunnan 雲南	3	25	467	-40	-9.38	-22.22	18.67	57.03	427
Tibet 西藏									
Northwest 西北	20	97	2,649	-26	-0.61	-1.83	27.21	66.49	4,241
Shaanxi 陝西	15	119	3,417	-19	-0.36	-0.99	28.68	63.94	5,243
Gansu 甘肅	3	12	190	23	5.34	21.88	15.41	75.57	437
Qinghai 青海									
Ningxia 寧夏									
Xinjiang 新疆	2	62	575	-155	-6.39	119.23	9.35	105.36	2,425

4049: Other Electric Engineering Equipment 其他電工器材製造業

Year 年份	Number of firms 企業個數	Rate of change 每年變化 (%)	Number of employees 職工人數（人）	Rate of change 每年變化 (%)	Total revenue (mil. RMB) 總銷售收入（百萬元）	Rate of change 每年變化 (%)	Total profit (mil. RMB) 總利潤（百萬元）	Rate of change 每年變化 (%)
1993	589		51,141		2,385		87	
1994	643	9.17%	55,630	8.78%	3,050	27.83%	141	61.68%
1995	643	0	54,344	-2.31%	3,603	18.14%	36	-74.69%
1996	560	-12.91%	47,175	-13.19%	3,241	-10.05%	38	6.32%

3 Major products* 3種主要產品*	Output 產量	Sales volume 銷售量	Unit 單位
a) Electromagnetic Wire 電磁線	23,653	22,234	ton 噸

Top 10 firms by revenue (year founded) 收入排名前10家企業 (創辦年份)	City 城市	Province 省	Telephone / fax 電話／傳真	Number of employees 職工人數	Ownership 產業所有權	Revenue ('000 RMB) 銷售收入（千元）	Profit ('000 RMB) (rank) 利潤（千元）（排名）	Total assets ('000 RMB) 總資產（千元）	Major products 主要產品
Clipsal China Ltd. 奇勝電器(惠州)工業有限公司(1987)	Huizhou 惠州市	Guangdong 廣東省	(0751)2227555 (0751)2224294	1,874	Overseas Chinese-funded 港澳台資	339,444	5835(6)	374,474	o
Zhejiang Great Wall Cable Group Company 浙江長城線纜集團公司(1986)	Huzhou 湖州市	Zhejiang 浙江省	(0572)3952131 (0572)3952188	345	Collectively-owned 集體	218,107	9167(1)	131,120	a
Huzhou Shen Hu Electric Engineering Factory 湖州市申湖電工廠(1994)	Huzhou 湖州市	Zhejiang 浙江省	(0572)3979128 (0572)3979141	243	Collectively-owned 集體	206,875	6163(5)	88,136	a
Jiangdu Electric Power Equipment General Factory 江都市電力器材總廠(1977)	Yangzhou 揚州市	Jiangsu 江蘇省	(0514)6842870 (0514)6842003	1,508	Collectively-owned 集體	145,903	807(35)	80,954	o
Shanghai Electric Machinery (Group) Co. Electric Machinery 上海電機(集團)公司電機器材廠(1960)	Shanghai 上海市	Shanghai 上海市	(021)64366453 (021)64701586	397	State-owned 國有	137,411	1904(22)	85,651	a
Dalian Shimoda Electric Co. Ltd. 大連下田電機有限公司(1991)	Dalian 大連市	Liaoning 遼寧省	(0411)7612058 (0411)7612059	872	Foreign-funded 外資	123,917	4493(8)	120,138	o
Hangzhou Swameoose Electrical Co. 杭州鴻雁電器公司(1981)	Hangzhou 杭州市	Zhejiang 浙江省	(0571)8853798 (0571)8853799	284	State-owned 國有	121,776	6344(4)	83,118	o
Jiangxi Yingtan Copper Industry Co. Ltd. 江西鷹潭銅業有限公司(1993)	Yingtan 鷹潭市	Jiangxi 江西省	(0701)6223402	385	Foreign-funded 外資	88,730	813(33)	34,302	o
Huzhou Wan You Copper Industry Group Co. Ltd. 湖州萬友銅業集團有限公司(1992)	Huzhou 湖州市	Zhejiang 浙江省	(0572)3952030 (0572)3952031	185	Collectively-owned 集體	81,516	2082(18)	45,560	a
Huzhou Zhenxing Communication Cable Factory 湖州振興通訊電纜廠(1992)	Huzhou 湖州市	Zhejiang 浙江省	(0572)3920885 (0572)3920068	150	Joint stock 股份制	78,130	6707(3)	54,608	o

Top 10 Cities by Production Output 產出排名前10位城市	Province 省	Market share 市場份額	Number of firms 企業個數
Huzhou 湖州市	Zhejiang 浙江省	22.15%	19
Huizhou 惠州市	Guangdong 廣東省	10.24%	3
Shanghai 上海市	Shanghai 上海市	9.27%	59
Dongguan 東莞市	Guangdong 廣東省	4.52%	16
Hangzhou 杭州市	Zhejiang 浙江省	4.30%	17
Suzhou 蘇州市	Jiangsu 江蘇省	3.67%	34
Dalian 大連市	Liaoning 遼寧省	3.52%	6
Changzhou 常州市	Jiangsu 江蘇省	2.98%	30
Nanjing 南京市	Jiangsu 江蘇省	2.58%	16
Yingtan 鷹潭市	Jiangxi 江西省	2.39%	2

10 Major Wholesalers 10家主要批發商	City 城市	Province 省	Telephone / Fax 電話／傳真
Liaoning Automobile Trade Group Corp. 遼寧省汽車貿易集團	Shenyang 瀋陽市	Liaoning 遼寧省	(024)23835494 (024)23838338
China Post and Telecommunication Equipment General Company 中國郵電器材總公司	Beijing 北京市	Beijing 北京市	(010)63523715 (010)63525935
Jiangsu Electromechanical Products General Company 江蘇省機電產品總公司	Nanjing 南京市	Jiangsu 江蘇省	(025)7713642 (025)7711036
Xi Nan Technology Import & Export Company 西南技術進出口公司	Chongqing 重慶市	Chongqing 重慶市	(023)63850185 (023)63850026
Changzhou Economic Technology Industrial Development Zone Tian Ming Trade Company 常州經濟技術產業開發區天明貿易公司	Changzhou 常州市	Jiangsu 江蘇省	(0519)8829882 (0519)8829882
Shanxi Mechanical Equipment Import & Export Company 山西省機械設備進出口公司	Taiyuan 太原市	Shanxi 山西省	(0351)4040713 (0351)4043981
Ningbo Five Mining Machinery Import & Export Company 寧波市五礦機械進出口公司	Ningbo 寧波市	Zhejiang 浙江省	(0574)7311255 (0574)7320322
Tianjin Jin Huan Electromechanical Complete Sets of Equipment Factory 天津市津環機電成套設備廠	Tianjin 天津市	Tianjin 天津市	(022)26371628
Yunnan Machinery Import & Export Company 雲南省機械進出口公司	Kunming 昆明市	Yunnan 雲南省	(0871)3164879 (0871)3136829
Tianjin Da Qiu Zhuang Yi Yuan Trade Center 天津市大丘莊億源商貿中心	Tianjin 天津市	Tianjin 天津市	(022)28899478 (022)28899046

*Also include sales by firms outside this industry.包括本行業以外廠家的銷售。"o" stands for "others". "o" 代表"其他產品"。

4061: Washing Machines 洗衣機製造業

The industry accounts for 0.166% of the total revenue of China's industrial sector in 1996. The revenue growth rate of the industry is 17.5% from 1995, as compared to the growth rate of China's industrial sector, 9.51%. The rate of return on asset is 2.89%. 68.07% of all firms in the industry made a profit while 27.38% had negative returns. The top province in terms of the industry's revenue is Guangdong, accounting for 19.52% of the total revenue.
本行業在 1996 年佔全行業總產值 0.166%，行業年增長率為 17.5%（全國工業年增長率 9.51%）。行業的資產回報率 2.89%，68.07% 的企業盈利，27.38% 的企業虧損。銷售收入最高的省份為廣東省，佔本行業的 19.52%。

	Total number of firms 企業總數	Total number of employees 職工總數	Total revenue (mil. RMB) 總銷售收入（百萬元）	Total profit (mil. RMB) 總利潤（百萬元）	Return on assets 資產利潤率 (%)	Return on equity 權益利潤率 (%)	Labour productivity ('000 RMB / worker) 勞動生產率（千元/人）	Debts / assets 資產負債率 (%)	Total assets (mil. RMB) 總資產（百萬元）
Industry Overall 行業總體	87	49,297	9,644	394	2.89	7.29	195.63	60.43	13,647

	Number of firms 企業個數	Average number of employees 平均職工人數	Average revenue ('000 RMB) 平均銷售收入（千元）	Average profit ('000 RMB) 平均利潤（千元）	Return on assets 資產利潤率 (%)	Return on equity 權益利潤率 (%)	Labour productivity ('000 RMB / worker) 勞動生產率（千元/人）	Average debts / assets 平均資產負債率(%)	Average Total assets ('000 RMB) 平均總資產（千元）
By ownership 產業所有權									
State-owned 國有	17	979	66,588	-59	-0.04	-0.29	68.01	86.69	150,235
Collectively-owned 集體	54	346	49,619	942	1.43	5.62	143.25	74.64	66,062
Privately-owned 私有									
Domestic JVs 聯營	2	707	30,061	-59,898	-17.37	-258.55	42.52	93.28	344,746
Joint stock 股份制	3	1,331	664,353	91,562	12.24	19.15	499.26	36.07	747,992
Foreign-funded 外資	7	604	211,297	8,215	2.84	4.77	350.08	40.50	289,130
Overseas Chinese-funded 港澳台資	4	1,125	573,153	32,724	5.12	8.94	509.58	42.78	639,472
By size 規模									
Large 大型	19	1,737	396,874	19,526	3.60	9.69	228.53	62.82	542,186
Medium 中型	6	765	32,898	-5,895	-7.03	-41.63	42.99	83.10	83,812
Small 小型	63	189	30,266	927	2.05	3.93	160.49	47.78	45,125
By regional distribution 地區分布									
Central-North 華北	9	751	91,972	3,187	2.65	8.51	122.48	68.87	120,324
Beijing 北京	2	985	39,625	-30	-0.02	-0.08	40.23	77.39	175,095
Tianjin 天津	4	444	87,315	2,208	2.40	6.38	196.77	62.44	92,078
Hebei 河北	2	820	51,940	2,235	3.07	8.76	63.34	64.90	72,700
Shanxi 山西	1	1,373	295,360	15,440	7.05	22.50	215.12	68.67	219,020
Inner Mongolia 內蒙									
Northeast 東北	12	495	13,013	-2,101	-2.41	-21.27	26.29	88.69	87,318
Liaoning 遼寧	9	330	12,017	-1,639	-2.28	-83.43	36.46	97.26	71,788
Jilin 吉林	2	1,475	23,845	-5,230	-2.61	-10.40	16.17	74.92	200,495
Heilongjiang 黑龍江	1	25	320				12.80	58.90	730
Central East 華東	47	502	136,486	9,583	5.54	10.88	271.69	49.07	172,982
Shanghai 上海	14	539	102,511	-1,104	-0.65	-1.47	190.06	56.00	170,954
Jiangsu 江蘇	8	322	189,064	24,368	11.61	17.94	586.70	35.31	209,955
Zhejiang 浙江	20	266	68,077	5,695	8.64	19.26	256.41	55.15	65,913
Anhui 安徽	1	4,205	1,345,020	100,720	4.68	7.54	319.86	37.94	2,153,390
Fujian 福建									
Jiangxi 江西									
Shandong 山東	4	992	190,150	14,073	9.61	76.42	191.73	87.42	146,373
Central-South 中南	13	701	158,867	-3,050	-1.33	-5.30	226.78	74.95	229,735
Henan 河南									
Hubei 湖北	3	896	60,960	-497	-0.59	5.99	68.01	109.81	84,543
Hunan 湖南	1								
Guangdong 廣東	9	713	209,154	-4,240	-1.40	-4.94	293.30	71.72	303,659
Guangxi 廣西									
Hainan 海南									
Southwest 西南	5	760	35,904	-4,050	-5.08	-36.69	47.24	86.15	79,704
Chongqing 重慶	2	629	57,121	-4,973	-6.46	-37.91	90.83	82.96	76,972
Sichuan 四川	1	145	1,929	28	0.81	6.36	13.28	87.28	3,433
Guizhou 貴州	1	1,828	41,620	-7,810	-3.93	-42.96	22.77	90.86	198,860
Yunnan 雲南	1	448	7,930	-1,270	-5.31	-17.71	17.70	70.00	23,900
Tibet 西藏									
Northwest 西北	1	81	490	20	1.40	2.82	6.05	50.35	1,430
Shaanxi 陝西									
Gansu 甘肅	1	81	490	20	1.40	2.82	6.05	50.35	1,430
Qinghai 青海									
Ningxia 寧夏									
Xinjiang 新疆									

4061: Washing Machines 洗衣機製造業

Year 年份	Number of firms 企業個數	Rate of change 每年變化 (%)	Number of employees 職工人數 (人)	Rate of change 每年變化 (%)	Total revenue (mil. RMB) 總銷售收入 (百萬元)	Rate of change 每年變化 (%)	Total profit (mil. RMB) 總利潤 (百萬元)	Rate of change 每年變化 (%)
1993	86		69,775		6,452		324	
1994	97	12.79%	56,672	-18.78%	7,364	14.15%	312	-3.71%
1995	89	-8.25%	51,664	-8.84%	8,209	11.47%	235	-24.50%
1996	87	-2.25%	49,297	-4.58%	9,644	17.48%	394	67.41%

3 Major products* 3 種主要產品 *	Output 產量	Sales volume 銷售量	Unit 單位
a) Domestic Washing Machine 家用洗衣機	9,285,366	9,192,512	set 台

Top 10 firms by revenue (year founded) 收入排名前 10 家企業 (創辦年份)	City 城市	Province 省	Telephone / fax 電話 / 傳真	Number of employees 職工人數	Ownership 產業所有權	Revenue ('000 RMB) 銷售收入 (千元)	Profit ('000 RMB) (rank) 利潤 (千元) (排名)	Total assets ('000 RMB) 總資產 (千元)	Major products 主要產品
Hefei Rong Shi Da (Group) Co. Ltd. 合肥榮事達(集團)有限公司(1961)	Hefei 合肥市	Anhui 安徽省	(0551)5523611 (0551)5525760	1,964	Overseas Chinese-funded 港澳台資	1,345,015	100716(2)	2,153,391	a
Wuxi Little Swan Co. Ltd. 無錫市小天鵝股份有限公司(1995)	Wuxi 無錫市	Jiangsu 江蘇省	(0510)3704003 (0510)3704031	1,315	Joint stock 股份制	1,297,532	210332(1)	1,301,426	a
Jiangmen Jin Ling Group Co. Ltd. 江門市金羚集團有限公司(1983)	Jiangmen 江門市	Guangdong 廣東省	(0750)3811611 (0750)3817625	1,544	Overseas Chinese-funded 港澳台資	1,204,956	77370(4)	1,255,264	a
Hangzhou Matsushita Home Appliance Co. Ltd. 杭州松下家用電器有限公司(1992)	Hangzhou 杭州市	Zhejiang 浙江省	(0571)8077124 (0571)8078471	1,719	Foreign-funded 外資	966,944	95016(3)	584,061	a
China Ji'nan Washing Machine Factory 中國濟南洗衣機廠(1970)	Ji'nan 濟南市	Shandong 山東省	(0531)8980104 (0531)8983045	3,967	State-owned 國有	760,597	56289(5)	585,485	a
Shanghai Nareissus Electric Appliances Co. Ltd. 上海水仙電器股份有限公司(1956)	Shanghai 上海市	Shanghai 上海市	(021)56651800 (021)56651093	2,173	Joint stock 股份制	756,839	11503(9)	1,174,814	a
Zhongshan Wei Li Washing Machine Co. Ltd. 中山市威力洗衣機有限公司(1984)	Zhongshan 中山市	Guangdong 廣東省	(0760)8323288 (0760)8328228	1,574	Overseas Chinese-funded 港澳台資	494,648	16727(7)	422,713	a
Shen Hua (Group) Company 申花(集團)公司(1984)	Shanghai 上海市	Shanghai 上海市	(021)58756789 (021)58702221	1,261	Collectively-owned 集體	458,197	10618(10)	385,190	a
Tianjin Xin Bao Tian Yang Household Appliances Co. Ltd. 天津新寶天洋家電有限公司(1993)	Tianjin 天津市	Tianjin 天津市	(022)27367771 (022)27360121	1,288	Foreign-funded 外資	342,131	9658(12)	338,572	a
Shanxi Hai Tang Electric Appliance Group Co. Ltd. 山西省海棠電器集團股份有限公司(1966)	Changzhi 長治市	Shanxi 山西省	(0355)3035624 (0355)3035802	1,373	Collectively-owned 集體	295,361	15438(8)	219,015	a

Top 10 Cities by Production Output 產出排名前 10 位城市	Province 省	Market share 市場份額	Number of firms 企業個數
Shanghai 上海市	Shanghai 上海市	15.18%	21
Jiangmen 江門市	Guangdong 廣東省	13.09%	4
Hangzhou 杭州市	Zhejiang 浙江省	12.50%	9
Hefei 合肥市	Anhui 安徽省	12.09%	2
Wuxi 無錫市	Jiangsu 江蘇省	11.03%	9
Qingdao 青島市	Shandong 山東省	7.66%	3
Ji'nan 濟南市	Shandong 山東省	6.85%	5
Zhongshan 中山市	Guangdong 廣東省	4.38%	1
Tianjin 天津市	Tianjin 天津市	3.60%	6
Changzhi 長治市	Shanxi 山西省	3.21%	1

10 Major Wholesalers 10 家主要批發商	City 城市	Province 省	Telephone / Fax 電話 / 傳真
Changzhou Hardware Alternating-current Appliance and Chemical Wholesale General Company 常州五金交電化工批發總公司	Changzhou 常州市	Jiangsu 江蘇省	(0519)6609929 (0519)6609925
Suzhou Hardware & Alternating Electricity Co. Ltd. 蘇州五金交電股份有限公司	Suzhou 蘇州市	Jiangsu 江蘇省	(0512)5239572 (0512)5213248
Tianjin Foreign Trade General Company 天津市對外貿易總公司	Tianjin 天津市	Tianjin 天津市	(022)23310922
Chongqing International Trade Center 重慶國際貿易中心	Chongqing 重慶市	Chongqing 重慶市	(023)67853232 (023)67850402
China Chemical Plastics Co. Ltd. 中化塑料有限公司	Beijing 北京市	Beijing 北京市	(010)68569863 (010)68569041
Ningbo Hualian Group Co. Ltd. 寧波華聯集團股份有限公司	Ningbo 寧波市	Zhejiang 浙江省	(0574)7367626 (0574)7367652
Kaiyuan Wei Wei Electromechanical Building Materials Marketing Dept. 廈門市開元區威威機電建材經營部	Xiamen 廈門市	Fujian 福建省	(0592)2071044
Rudong Industry Product General Company 如東縣工業品總公司	Nantong 南通市	Jiangsu 江蘇省	(0513)4516110 (0513)4516110
Fujian Fu Ri Group Company 福建福日集團公司	Fuzhou 福州市	Fujian 福建省	(0591)3269325 (0591)3270426
Guangdong Hardware & Alternating Electrical Co. 廣東省五金交電公司	Guangzhou 廣州市	Guangdong 廣東省	(020)81884078 (020)81861287

*Also include sales by firms outside this industry.包括本行業以外廠家的銷售。"o" stands for "others". "o" 代表 "其他產品"。

4062: Vacuum Cleaner 吸塵器製造業

The industry accounts for 0.029% of the total revenue of China's industrial sector in 1996. The revenue growth rate of the industry is 48.7% from 1995, as compared to the growth rate of China's industrial sector, 9.51%. The rate of return on asset is 1.81%. 59.25% of all firms in the industry made a profit while 30.99% had negative returns. The top province in terms of the industry's revenue is Jiangsu, accounting for 44.32% of the total revenue.
本行業在1996年佔全行業總產值0.029%，行業年增長率為48.7%（全國工業年增長率9.51%）。行業的資產回報率1.81%，59.25%的企業盈利，30.99%的企業虧損。銷售收入最高的省份為江蘇省，佔本行業的44.32%。

	Total number of firms 企業總數	Total number of employees 職工總數	Total revenue (mil. RMB) 總銷售收入（百萬元）	Total profit (mil. RMB) 總利潤（百萬元）	Return on assets 資產利潤率 (%)	Return on equity 權益利潤率 (%)	Labour productivity ('000 RMB / worker) 勞動生產率（千元/人）	Debts / assets 資產負債率 (%)	Total assets (mil. RMB) 總資產（百萬元）
Industry Overall 行業總體	70	8,912	1,670	32	1.81	4.99	187.39	63.68	1,773

	Number of firms 企業個數	Average number of employees 平均職工人數	Average revenue ('000 RMB) 平均銷售收入（千元）	Average profit ('000 RMB) 平均利潤（千元）	Return on assets 資產利潤率 (%)	Return on equity 權益利潤率 (%)	Labour productivity ('000 RMB / worker) 勞動生產率（千元/人）	Average debts / assets 平均資產負債率(%)	Average Total assets ('000 RMB) 平均總資產（千元）
By ownership 產業所有權									
State-owned 國有	6	141	15,167				107.57	91.67	20,000
Collectively-owned 集體	39	112	17,012	295	1.82	5.24	152.21	65.27	16,179
Privately-owned 私有									
Domestic JVs 聯營	1	645	1,237	-659	-0.35	-2.22	1.92	84.35	189,886
Joint stock 股份制	4	204	51,799	3,625	5.79	12.60	253.91	54.10	62,659
Foreign-funded 外資	5	240	113,849	655	0.70	1.53	474.37	53.98	92,859
Overseas Chinese-funded 港澳台資	15	70	9,278	226	2.89	6.01	133.05	51.88	7,823
By size 規模									
Large 大型	4	453	72,888	3,658	2.78	9.13	161.08	69.57	131,726
Medium 中型	4	376	105,497	1,127	0.82	1.88	280.95	56.45	137,626
Small 小型	63	89	15,202	204	1.85	5.27	171.02	64.93	11,044
By regional distribution 地區分布									
Central-North 華北	17	119	6,884	-2,081	-7.62	-45.70	57.88	83.33	27,308
Beijing 北京	2	13	260				20.80	89.02	1,685
Tianjin 天津	7	185	10,141	-6,003	-9.32	-55.91	54.78	83.34	64,434
Hebei 河北	6	90	7,353	1,200	131.63	393.44	81.70	66.73	912
Shanxi 山西	2	81	700	-280	-12.87	-933.33	8.70	98.85	2,175
Inner Mongolia 內蒙									
Northeast 東北	6	26	1,167	-17	-0.84	-7.58	45.45	88.95	1,992
Liaoning 遼寧	4	26	990	-28	-1.04	-12.09	38.45	91.39	2,643
Jilin 吉林	1	27	940	10	2.78	3.13	34.81	11.11	360
Heilongjiang 黑龍江	1	24	2,100				87.50	91.18	1,020
Central East 華東	29	160	36,302	2,112	5.75	11.94	226.54	51.81	36,708
Shanghai 上海	5	285	32,744	16	0.04	0.23	115.05	82.58	39,674
Jiangsu 江蘇	12	176	61,683	2,830	5.44	10.51	350.30	48.22	51,999
Zhejiang 浙江	6	145	24,147	4,482	11.53	17.61	166.34	34.50	38,853
Anhui 安徽									
Fujian 福建	2	22	250	-30	-1.81	-4.65	11.63	61.03	1,655
Jiangxi 江西									
Shandong 山東	4	49	865	93	6.45	26.62	17.56	75.78	1,435
Central-South 中南	15	138	32,441	415	2.76	11.98	235.77	77.00	15,074
Henan 河南	4	87	5,698	20	0.47	1.26	65.30	62.84	4,265
Hubei 湖北	1								
Hunan 湖南									
Guangdong 廣東	7	226	61,316	794	2.68	12.59	271.31	78.69	29,584
Guangxi 廣西	3	44	11,540	197	30.10	38.82	260.30	22.45	653
Hainan 海南									
Southwest 西南	1	21	4,400	120	34.29	85.71	209.52	60.00	350
Chongqing 重慶									
Sichuan 四川	1	21							
Guizhou 貴州									
Yunnan 雲南									
Tibet 西藏									
Northwest 西北	2	2	1,070				535.00	99.47	2,820
Shaanxi 陝西	1	4							
Gansu 甘肅	1		2,140					99.47	5,640
Qinghai 青海									
Ningxia 寧夏									
Xinjiang 新疆									

Year 年份	Number of firms 企業個數	Rate of change 每年變化 (%)	Number of employees 職工人數 (人)	Rate of change 每年變化 (%)	Total revenue (mil. RMB) 總銷售收入 (百萬元)	Rate of change 每年變化 (%)	Total profit (mil. RMB) 總利潤 (百萬元)	Rate of change 每年變化 (%)
1993	55		10,951		610		28	
1994	63	14.55%	10,584	-3.35%	711	16.59%	22	-22.30%
1995	57	-9.52%	9,445	-10.76%	1,123	58.09%	37	67.12%
1996	70	22.81%	8,912	-5.64%	1,670	48.71%	32	-12.78%

3 Major products* 3 種主要產品 *	Output 產量	Sales volume 銷售量	Unit 單位
a) Dust Collector 吸塵器	3,719,101	3,681,910	set 台

Top 10 firms by revenue (year founded) 收入排名前 10 家企業 (創辦年份)	City 城市	Province 省	Telephone / fax 電話 / 傳真	Number of employees 職工人數	Ownership 產業所有權	Revenue ('000 RMB) 銷售收入 (千元)	Profit ('000 RMB) (rank) 利潤 (千元) (排名)	Total assets ('000 RMB) 總資產 (千元)	Major products 主要產品
Shenzhen Yamada Electric Co. Ltd. 深圳山田電器有限公司(1989)	Shenzhen 深圳市	Guangdong 廣東省	(0755)7391100 (0755)7391582	862	Foreign-funded 外資	395,358	9444(4)	116,884	a
Chinese-foreign Joint Venture Suzhou Ai Pu Electrical Appliance Suzhou Eup Electric Co. Ltd. 中外合資蘇州愛普電器有限公司(1995)	Suzhou 蘇州市	Jiangsu 江蘇省	(0512)5362409 (0512)5361917	286	Foreign-funded 外資	184,980	12634(2)	35,181	a
Suzhou Chun Hua Dust Catcher General Factory 蘇州春花吸塵器總廠(1959)	Suzhou 蘇州市	Jiangsu 江蘇省	(0512)7271366 (0512)7272907	572	Collectively-owned 集體	151,630	10117(3)	210,819	a
Suzhou Chun Fei Household Appliances Company 蘇州春飛家用電器公司(1996)	Suzhou 蘇州市	Jiangsu 江蘇省	(0512)5307801 (0512)5308665	314	Foreign-funded 外資	150,321	4058(7)	161,155	o
Suzhou Jinlaike Electrical Equipment Co. Ltd. 蘇州市金萊克電器有限公司(1994)	Suzhou 蘇州市	Jiangsu 江蘇省	(0512)8278126	206	Foreign-funded 外資	118,052	894(9)	28,065	a
Ningbo Fu Da Electrical Appliance Co. Ltd. 寧波富達電器股份有限公司(1988)	Ningbo 寧波市	Zhejiang 浙江省	(0574)2818088 (0574)2813915	653	Joint stock 股份制	115,480	24080(1)	214,035	a
Shanghai Dust Catcher Factory 上海吸塵器廠(1960)	Shanghai 上海市	Shanghai 上海市	(021)56944008 (021)56955777	665	State-owned 國有	88,277	310(11)	112,134	a
Suzhou Sanyo Household Appliances Co. Ltd. 蘇州三洋家電有限公司(1996)	Suzhou 蘇州市	Jiangsu 江蘇省	(0512)6212941	162	Foreign-funded 外資	87,776	6821(5)	144,904	o
Shanghai Shuang Ai Electrical Appliance Industrial General Co. 上海雙愛電器實業總公司(1978)	Shanghai 上海市	Shanghai 上海市	(021)64088584 (021)64088582	497	Collectively-owned 集體	61,536	257(13)	62,010	a
Dawood Electric Machinery (Tianjin) Co. Ltd. 大宇電機有限公司(1995)	Tianjin 天津市	Tianjin 天津市	(022)25983451 (022)25983455	401	Foreign-funded 外資	58,296	-9125(40)	146,390	o

Top 10 Cities by Production Output 產出排名前 10 位城市	Province 省	Market share 市場份額	Number of firms 企業個數
Suzhou 蘇州市	Jiangsu 江蘇省	64.07%	13
Ningbo 寧波市	Zhejiang 浙江省	10.56%	1
Tianjin 天津市	Tianjin 天津市	6.60%	4
Wenzhou 溫州市	Zhejiang 浙江省	3.42%	6
Wuxi 無錫市	Jiangsu 江蘇省	3.23%	3
Zhengzhou 鄭州市	Henan 河南省	2.14%	3
Shanghai 上海市	Shanghai 上海市	2.00%	9
Dongguan 東莞市	Guangdong 廣東省	1.72%	3
Shijiazhuang 石家莊市	Hebei 河北省	1.38%	4
Yancheng 鹽城市	Jiangsu 江蘇省	0.99%	3

10 Major Wholesalers 10 家主要批發商	City 城市	Province 省	Telephone / Fax 電話 / 傳真
Changzhou Hardware Alternating-current Appliance and Chemical Wholesale General Company 常州五金交電化工批發總公司	Changzhou 常州市	Jiangsu 江蘇省	(0519)6609929 (0519)6609925
Suzhou Hardware & Alternating Electricity Co. Ltd. 蘇州五金交電股份有限公司	Suzhou 蘇州市	Jiangsu 江蘇省	(0512)5239572 (0512)5213248
Tianjin Foreign Trade General Company 天津市對外貿易總公司	Tianjin 天津市	Tianjin 天津市	(022)23310922
Chongqing International Trade Center 重慶國際貿易中心	Chongqing 重慶市	Chongqing 重慶市	(023)67853232 (023)67850402
China Chemical Plastics Co. Ltd. 中化塑料有限公司	Beijing 北京市	Beijing 北京市	(010)68569863 (010)68569041
Ningbo Hualian Group Co. Ltd. 寧波華聯集團股份有限公司	Ningbo 寧波市	Zhejiang 浙江省	(0574)7367626 (0574)7367652
Kaiyuan Wei Wei Electromechanical Building Materials Marketing Dept. 廈門市開元區威威機電建材經營部	Xiamen 廈門市	Fujian 福建省	(0592)2071044
Rudong Industry Product General Company 如東縣工業品總公司	Nantong 南通市	Jiangsu 江蘇省	(0513)4516110 (0513)4516110
Fujian Fu Ri Group Company 福建福日集團公司	Fuzhou 福州市	Fujian 福建省	(0591)3269325 (0591)3270426
Guangdong Hardware & Alternating Electrical Co. 廣東省五金交電公司	Guangzhou 廣州市	Guangdong 廣東省	(020)81884078 (020)81861287

*Also include sales by firms outside this industry.包括本行業以外廠家的銷售。"o" stands for "others". "o" 代表 "其他產品"。

4063: Refrigerators 電冰箱製造業

The industry accounts for 0.458% of the total revenue of China's industrial sector in 1996. The revenue growth rate of the industry is 16.0% from 1995, as compared to the growth rate of China's industrial sector, 9.51%. The rate of return on asset is 3.26%. 51.29% of all firms in the industry made a profit while 40.25% had negative returns. The top province in terms of the industry's revenue is Shandong, accounting for 28.64% of the total revenue.
本行業在1996年佔全行業總產值0.458%，行業年增長率為16.0%（全國工業年增長率9.51%）。行業的資產回報率3.26%，51.29%的企業盈利，40.25%的企業虧損。銷售收入最高的省份為山東省，佔本行業的28.64%。

	Total number of firms 企業總數	Total number of employees 職工總數	Total revenue (mil. RMB) 總銷售收入（百萬元）	Total profit (mil. RMB) 總利潤（百萬元）	Return on assets 資產利潤率 (%)	Return on equity 權益利潤率 (%)	Labour productivity ('000 RMB / worker) 勞動生產率（千元/人）	Debts / assets 資產負債率 (%)	Total assets (mil. RMB) 總資產（百萬元）
Industry Overall 行業總體	199	109,757	26,555	1,294	3.26	8.47	241.94	61.44	39,652

	Number of firms 企業個數	Average number of employees 平均職工人數	Average revenue ('000 RMB) 平均銷售收入（千元）	Average profit ('000 RMB) 平均利潤（千元）	Return on assets 資產利潤率 (%)	Return on equity 權益利潤率 (%)	Labour productivity ('000 RMB / worker) 勞動生產率（千元/人）	Average debts / assets 平均資產負債率(%)	Average Total assets ('000 RMB) 平均總資產（千元）
By ownership 產業所有權									
State-owned 國有	33	622	56,030	2,182	1.42	4.51	90.10	68.63	154,182
Collectively-owned 集體	111	346	51,504	2,349	2.71	11.66	148.94	76.74	86,610
Privately-owned 私有									
Domestic JVs 聯營	13	313	23,131	-1,236	-2.07	-7.94	73.88	73.95	59,697
Joint stock 股份制	13	2,230	1,007,117	51,600	4.10	8.64	451.54	52.53	1,258,468
Foreign-funded 外資	12	883	230,434	14,835	4.83	8.10	260.84	40.40	307,143
Overseas Chinese-funded 港澳台資	16	473	176,975	8,061	3.12	9.97	374.50	68.68	258,021
By size 規模									
Large 大型	35	2,053	646,157	38,667	4.29	10.24	314.72	58.10	901,451
Medium 中型	27	639	76,284	-1,275	-0.77	-4.07	119.41	80.99	164,908
Small 小型	134	144	14,035	-183	-0.67	-2.00	97.49	66.49	27,229
By regional distribution 地區分布									
Central-North 華北	28	289	8,251	-6,156	-18.12	-66.94	28.56	72.93	33,967
Beijing 北京	13	338	14,591	-12,036	-20.75	-53.14	43.19	60.95	57,996
Tianjin 天津	11	312	3,466	-1,445	-11.31	28.66	11.13	139.44	12,775
Hebei 河北	4	68	805				11.93	67.33	14,148
Shanxi 山西									
Inner Mongolia 內蒙									
Northeast 東北	11	784	46,267	788	0.56	2.48	58.99	77.62	141,930
Liaoning 遼寧	8	509	31,765	941	0.95	4.67	62.45	79.55	98,631
Jilin 吉林	2	1,810	124,350	6,630	2.05	6.39	68.72	68.00	324,030
Heilongjiang 黑龍江	1	940	6,120	-12,120	-9.76	62.67	6.51	115.59	124,120
Central East 華東	94	590	167,393	7,141	2.88	7.71	283.57	62.58	247,574
Shanghai 上海	19	453	110,518	-4,909	-1.99	-5.03	244.17	60.37	246,343
Jiangsu 江蘇	16	325	32,987	-7,483	-5.58	-15.64	101.36	64.32	134,106
Zhejiang 浙江	25	498	78,588	5,134	4.48	12.83	157.92	65.06	114,483
Anhui 安徽	9	1,139	338,472	28,537	4.52	11.32	297.05	60.09	631,564
Fujian 福建	3	144	450	-353	-2.05	-11.18	3.13	81.69	17,260
Jiangxi 江西	2	1,543	245,130	24,305	3.19	11.22	158.87	71.60	762,840
Shandong 山東	20	773	380,236	22,575	7.14	19.01	491.64	62.42	316,109
Central-South 中南	48	599	180,760	15,148	6.10	13.88	301.61	56.02	248,228
Henan 河南	7	1,046	394,607	47,227	15.75	24.09	377.20	34.61	299,807
Hubei 湖北	4	720	17,285	-5,550	-3.70	-11.30	24.01	67.28	150,080
Hunan 湖南	15	202	18,431	-1,954	-2.50	-5.66	91.27	55.94	78,287
Guangdong 廣東	20	741	274,732	22,833	5.81	14.64	370.86	60.28	392,774
Guangxi 廣西	2	360	37,005	-4,325	-4.65	-25.58	102.93	81.84	93,095
Hainan 海南									
Southwest 西南	15	220	10,697	-152	-1.28	-4.52	48.58	71.64	11,859
Chongqing 重慶	1	801							
Sichuan 四川	12	195	13,168	-191	-1.29	-4.54	67.38	71.55	14,764
Guizhou 貴州	2	80	1,225	5	1.39	33.33	15.31	95.83	360
Yunnan 雲南									
Tibet 西藏									
Northwest 西北	3	1,827	414,403	20,720	3.50	9.07	226.78	61.39	591,567
Shaanxi 陝西	2	2,644	620,555	31,470	3.57	9.15	234.75	60.99	881,280
Gansu 甘肅	1	195	2,100	-780	-6.43	33.91	10.77	118.95	12,140
Qinghai 青海									
Ningxia 寧夏									
Xinjiang 新疆									

4063: Refrigerators 電冰箱製造業

Year 年份	Number of firms 企業個數	Rate of change 每年變化 (%)	Number of employees 職工人數 (人)	Rate of change 每年變化 (%)	Total revenue (mil. RMB) 總銷售收入 (百萬元)	Rate of change 每年變化 (%)	Total profit (mil. RMB) 總利潤 (百萬元)	Rate of change 每年變化 (%)
1993	176		123,718		15,884		1,076	
1994	180	2.27%	100,866	-18.47%	17,470	9.98%	1,424	32.31%
1995	187	3.89%	114,821	13.84%	22,902	31.10%	1,746	22.57%
1996	199	6.42%	109,757	-4.41%	26,555	15.95%	1,294	-25.89%

3 Major products* 3 種主要產品 *	Output 產量	Sales volume 銷售量	Unit 單位
a) Domestic Refrigerator 家用電冰箱	9,767,894	9,767,894	set 台
b) Freezer 冷凍箱	2,195,382	2,107,566	set 台

Top 10 firms by revenue (year founded) 收入排名前 10 家企業 (創辦年份)	City 城市	Province 省	Telephone / fax 電話 / 傳真	Number of employees 職工人數	Ownership 產業所有權	Revenue ('000 RMB) 銷售收入 (千元)	Profit ('000 RMB) (rank) 利潤 (千元) (排名)	Total assets ('000 RMB) 總資產 (千元)	Major products 主要產品
Hai Er Group 海爾集團(1991)	Qingdao 青島市	Shandong 山東省	(0532)8938233 (0532)8938666	11,133	Collectively-owned 集體	6,162,680	306660(2)	4,631,210	a,b
Guangdong Kelon Electrical Holding Co. Ltd. 廣東科龍電器股份有限公司(1984)	Foshan 佛山市	Guangdong 廣東省	(0757)6628338 (0757)6621911	6,259	Joint stock 股份制	3,847,557	427163(1)	3,866,219	a
Hefei Mei Ling Co. Ltd. 合肥美菱股份有限公司(1951)	Hefei 合肥市	Anhui 安徽省	(0551)2884961 (0551)2886484	1,858	Joint stock 股份制	1,885,794	194346(3)	3,161,713	a
Shanghai Shang Ling Household Electrical Appliance (Group) Co. Ltd. 上海上菱電器股份有限公司(1954)	Shanghai 上海市	Shanghai 上海市	(021)58857888 (021)58857367	2,351	Joint stock 股份制	1,338,277	23292(14)	2,520,485	a,b
Chang Ling (Group) Co. Ltd. 長嶺(集團)股份有限公司(1992)	Baoji 寶雞市	Shaanxi 陝西省	(0917)3314433 (0917)3312331	4,876	Joint stock 股份制	1,233,020	62778(6)	1,750,087	o
Qingdao Aucma Electrical Appliance Co. 青島澳柯瑪電器公司(1987)	Qingdao 青島市	Shandong 山東省	(0532)6895455 (0532)6891255	3,224	Collectively-owned 集體	1,196,130	141681(4)	1,466,698	a,b
China Yang Zi Group Co. Ltd. 中國揚子集團有限公司(1984)	Chuzhou 滁州市	Anhui 安徽省	(0550)3052731 (0550)3053119	7,261	State-owned 國有	856,356	33997(10)	1,958,278	a
China Refrigeration Industry Co. Ltd. 中國雪櫃實業有限公司(1988)	Guangzhou 廣州市	Guangdong 廣東省	(020)87713668 (020)87706181	1,238	Overseas Chinese-funded 港澳台資	662,141	70115(5)	1,013,659	a
Hangzhou Xi Ling Refrigeration Electric Appliance Co. Ltd. 杭州西泠製冷電器有限公司(1994)	Hangzhou 杭州市	Zhejiang 浙江省	(0571)6803301 (0571)6805705	1,712	Overseas Chinese-funded 港澳台資	562,225	15056(15)	758,432	a,b
Wan Bao Electric Appliance Industrial Company 萬寶電器工業公司(1991)	Guangzhou 廣州市	Guangdong 廣東省	(020)84367084 (020)84343010	3,024	Collectively-owned 集體	388,308	-50398(127)	1,186,784	a

Top 10 Cities by Production Output 產出排名前 10 位城市	Province 省	Market share 市場份額	Number of firms 企業個數
Foshan 佛山市	Guangdong 廣東省	19.97%	4
Qingdao 青島市	Shandong 山東省	19.68%	16
Xinxiang 新鄉市	Henan 河南省	11.16%	3
Shanghai 上海市	Shanghai 上海市	9.87%	26
Hefei 合肥市	Anhui 安徽省	8.41%	15
Guangzhou 廣州市	Guangdong 廣東省	6.94%	16
Hangzhou 杭州市	Zhejiang 浙江省	5.55%	13
Chuzhou 滁州市	Anhui 安徽省	3.70%	2
Taizhou 臺州市	Zhejiang 浙江省	3.33%	7
Jingdezhen 景德鎮市	Jiangxi 江西省	1.51%	1

10 Major Wholesalers 10 家主要批發商	City 城市	Province 省	Telephone / Fax 電話 / 傳真
Changzhou Hardware Alternating-current Appliance and Chemical Wholesale General Company 常州五金交電化工批發總公司	Changzhou 常州市	Jiangsu 江蘇省	(0519)6609929 (0519)6609925
Suzhou Hardware & Alternating Electricity Co. Ltd. 蘇州五金交電股份有限公司	Suzhou 蘇州市	Jiangsu 江蘇省	(0512)5239572 (0512)5213248
Tianjin Foreign Trade General Company 天津市對外貿易總公司	Tianjin 天津市	Tianjin 天津市	(022)23310922
Chongqing International Trade Center 重慶國際貿易中心	Chongqing 重慶市	Chongqing 重慶市	(023)67853232 (023)67850402
China Chemical Plastics Co. Ltd. 中化塑料有限公司	Beijing 北京市	Beijing 北京市	(010)68569863 (010)68569041
Ningbo Hualian Group Co. Ltd. 寧波華聯集團股份有限公司	Ningbo 寧波市	Zhejiang 浙江省	(0574)7367626 (0574)7367652
Kaiyuan Wei Wei Electromechanical Building Materials Marketing Dept. 廈門市開元區威威機電建材經營部	Xiamen 廈門市	Fujian 福建省	(0592)2071044
Rudong Industry Product General Company 如東縣工業品總公司	Nantong 南通市	Jiangsu 江蘇省	(0513)4516110 (0513)4516110
Fujian Fu Ri Group Company 福建福日集團公司	Fuzhou 福州市	Fujian 福建省	(0591)3269325 (0591)3270426
Guangdong Hardware & Alternating Electrical Co. 廣東省五金交電公司	Guangzhou 廣州市	Guangdong 廣東省	(020)81884078 (020)81861287

*Also include sales by firms outside this industry.包括本行業以外廠家的銷售。"o" stands for "others". "o" 代表"其他產品"。

4064: Electric Fans 電風扇製造業

The industry accounts for 0.195% of the total revenue of China's industrial sector in 1996. The revenue growth rate of the industry is -5.2% from 1995, as compared to the growth rate of China's industrial sector, 9.51%. The rate of return on asset is 0.73%. 48.04% of all firms in the industry made a profit while 41.67% had negative returns. The top province in terms of the industry's revenue is Guangdong, accounting for 47.75% of the total revenue.

本行業在1996年佔全行業總產值0.195%，行業年增長率為-5.2%（全國工業年增長率9.51%）。行業的資產回報率-0.73%，48.04%的企業盈利，41.67%的企業虧損。銷售收入最高的省份為廣東省，佔本行業的47.75%。

	Total number of firms 企業總數	Total number of employees 職工總數	Total revenue (mil. RMB) 總銷售收入（百萬元）	Total profit (mil. RMB) 總利潤（百萬元）	Return on assets 資產利潤率 (%)	Return on equity 權益利潤率 (%)	Labour productivity ('000 RMB / worker) 勞動生產率（千元/人）	Debts / assets 資產負債率 (%)	Total assets (mil. RMB) 總資產（百萬元）
Industry Overall 行業總體	295	92,772	11,282	-87	-0.73	-3.44	121.61	78.77	11,868

	Number of firms 企業個數	Average number of employees 平均職工人數	Average revenue ('000 RMB) 平均銷售收入（千元）	Average profit ('000 RMB) 平均利潤（千元）	Return on assets 資產利潤率 (%)	Return on equity 權益利潤率 (%)	Labour productivity ('000 RMB / worker) 勞動生產率（千元/人）	Average debts / assets 平均資產負債率(%)	Average Total assets ('000 RMB) 平均總資產（千元）
By ownership 產業所有權									
State-owned 國有	32	505	54,875	-594	-0.93	-6.79	108.73	86.24	63,594
Collectively-owned 集體	216	282	29,440	142	0.44	1.98	104.25	77.88	32,365
Privately-owned 私有									
Domestic JVs 聯營	6	523	68,666	-1,458	-1.59	-6.16	131.33	74.19	91,682
Joint stock 股份制	7	384	128,950	-7,478	-6.98	-26.50	336.18	73.64	107,076
Foreign-funded 外資	9	226	50,735	52	0.10	0.25	224.60	60.84	53,094
Overseas Chinese-funded 港澳台資	26	352	53,678	-1,462	-3.57	-22.76	152.60	84.33	40,985
By size 規模									
Large 大型	15	1,496	265,081	-4,905	-1.87	-7.89	177.16	76.26	261,726
Medium 中型	35	791	94,277	-336	-0.29	-1.55	119.14	81.52	117,183
Small 小型	242	176	16,554	-7	-0.04	-0.20	93.89	78.38	15,874
By regional distribution 地區分布									
Central-North 華北	13	121	750	-14	-0.33	-0.93	6.18	64.22	4,155
Beijing 北京	5	64	312	-4	-0.11	-0.17	4.89	34.77	3,704
Tianjin 天津	6	194	1,205	-33	-0.66	-3.08	6.23	78.56	5,053
Hebei 河北	2	49	480	20	0.77	5.26	9.90	85.52	2,590
Shanxi 山西									
Inner Mongolia 內蒙									
Northeast 東北	3	544	4,160	7	0.02	0.22	7.65	92.81	42,940
Liaoning 遼寧	3	544	4,160	7	0.02	0.22	7.65	92.81	42,940
Jilin 吉林									
Heilongjiang 黑龍江									
Central East 華東	155	270	34,878	-319	-0.98	-3.85	128.96	74.53	32,473
Shanghai 上海	25	257	15,647	-746	-2.69	-101.91	60.81	97.36	27,740
Jiangsu 江蘇	33	459	88,318	-1,729	-2.60	-10.19	192.21	74.49	66,486
Zhejiang 浙江	59	152	17,385	373	2.24	6.30	114.21	64.50	16,686
Anhui 安徽	13	279	16,420	-539	-2.22	-11.64	58.95	80.88	24,235
Fujian 福建	8	222	2,439	-1,414	-15.84	-269.29	10.99	94.12	8,924
Jiangxi 江西	9	199	6,547	-230	-2.53	-17.75	32.92	85.74	9,078
Shandong 山東	8	519	97,846	3,089	3.56	8.87	188.39	59.82	86,649
Central-South 中南	108	408	52,207	-354	-0.60	-3.45	127.88	82.67	59,224
Henan 河南	13	132	2,829	-344	-9.02	-46.08	21.47	80.40	3,811
Hubei 湖北	6	377	5,515	-557	-2.99	-32.84	14.62	90.91	18,638
Hunan 湖南	6	68	1,763	-17	-0.92	-2.51	26.00	63.42	1,813
Guangdong 廣東	79	483	68,185	-342	-0.44	-2.47	141.21	82.06	77,182
Guangxi 廣西	4	391	42,813	-813	-2.57	34.76	109.64	107.39	31,640
Hainan 海南									
Southwest 西南	12	265	17,570	51	0.25	0.62	66.41	59.30	20,187
Chongqing 重慶	9	296	22,027	408	1.72	3.71	74.54	53.73	23,773
Sichuan 四川	2	261	6,773	-2,062	-14.29	-1471.09	25.98	99.03	14,432
Guizhou 貴州	1								
Yunnan 雲南									
Tibet 西藏									
Northwest 西北	4	95	1,115	123	3.72	24.50	11.77	84.80	3,290
Shaanxi 陝西	4	95	1,115	123	3.72	24.50	11.77	84.80	3,290
Gansu 甘肅									
Qinghai 青海									
Ningxia 寧夏									
Xinjiang 新疆									

4064: Electric Fans 電風扇製造業

Year 年份	Number of firms 企業個數	Rate of change 每年變化 (%)	Number of employees 職工人數 (人)	Rate of change 每年變化 (%)	Total revenue (mil. RMB) 總銷售收入 (百萬元)	Rate of change 每年變化 (%)	Total profit (mil. RMB) 總利潤 (百萬元)	Rate of change 每年變化 (%)
1993	276		93,922		8,715		70	
1994	265	-3.99%	95,575	1.76%	9,458	8.53%	96	37.23%
1995	306	15.47%	106,677	11.62%	11,900	25.81%	57	-39.96%
1996	295	-3.59%	92,772	-13.03%	11,282	-5.19%	-87	-251.66%

3 Major products* 3 種主要產品 *	Output 產量	Sales volume 銷售量	Unit 單位
a) Electric Fan 電風扇	84,878,572	84,029,787	set 台
b) Domestic Electric Warmer 家用電取暖器具	4,901,969	4,803,930	set 台

Top 10 firms by revenue (year founded) 收入排名前 10 家企業 (創辦年份)	City 城市	Province 省	Telephone / fax 電話 / 傳真	Number of employees 職工人數	Ownership 產業所有權	Revenue ('000 RMB) 銷售收入 (千元)	Profit ('000 RMB) (rank) 利潤 (千元) (排名)	Total assets ('000 RMB) 總資產 (千元)	Major products 主要產品
Wuxian Explosion Protection Electric Engine Factory 吳縣防爆電機廠(1970)	Suzhou 蘇州市	Jiangsu 江蘇省	(0512)6262105 (0512)6261057	889	Collectively-owned 集體	820,500	13500(2)	128,060	o
Jiangsu Chang Cheng Electrical Appliance Group Co. Ltd. 江蘇長城電器集團股份有限公司(1970)	Suzhou 蘇州市	Jiangsu 江蘇省	(0512)7274628 (0512)7277933	2,309	Joint stock 股份制	629,138	-73689(204)	629,809	a,b
Jiangsu Shi Hua Electrical Appliance Group Corp. 江蘇時花電器集團公司(1953)	Nanjing 南京市	Jiangsu 江蘇省	(025)2281224 (025)2281220	2,130	State-owned 國有	468,460	11250(4)	274,850	a
Xian Hua Electric Appliance Industry Group Company 蜆華電器工業集團公司(1993)	Foshan 佛山市	Guangdong 廣東省	(0757)6655118 (0757)6656811	3,507	Collectively-owned 集體	450,987	9147(7)	572,620	a
Shandong Jin Long Enterprise Group Co. 山東省金龍企業集團公司(1957)	Yantai 煙台市	Shandong 山東省	(0535)8842888 (0535)8842888	2,180	Collectively-owned 集體	400,050	11080(5)	352,410	a
Shenzhen Wei Cheng Electrical Appliance Co. Ltd. 深圳威誠電器有限公司(1989)	Shenzhen 深圳市	Guangdong 廣東省	(0755)8872428 (0755)8872068	1,600	Overseas Chinese-funded 港澳台資	364,900	7930(8)	99,090	a,b
Shunde Panasonic Fine Finishing Co. Ltd. 順德松下精工有限公司(1993)	Foshan 佛山市	Guangdong 廣東省	(0757)8891633 (0757)8883900	808	Foreign-funded 外資	340,514	32331(1)	287,979	a
Shandong Fa Da Group Co. 山東發達集團公司(1975)	Yantai 煙台市	Shandong 山東省	(0535)8527891 (0535)8527891	1,255	State-owned 國有	325,000	10550(6)	297,962	a
Jiangsu Jie Kang Group 江蘇捷康集團(1978)	Yangzhou 揚州市	Jiangsu 江蘇省	(0514)7610725 (0514)7610607	1,280	Domestic JVs 聯營	269,317	5985(9)	118,368	a
Shunde Xiongfeng Electric Industrial Co. 順德市桂洲第一風扇廠(1980)	Foshan 佛山市	Guangdong 廣東省	(0757)8896783 (0757)8889207	2,489	Collectively-owned 集體	261,146	-2769(181)	162,779	a

Top 10 Cities by Production Output 產出排名前 10 位城市	Province 省	Market share 市場份額	Number of firms 企業個數
Foshan 佛山市	Guangdong 廣東省	27.63%	46
Suzhou 蘇州市	Jiangsu 江蘇省	21.77%	27
Jiangmen 江門市	Guangdong 廣東省	7.70%	17
Yantai 煙台市	Shandong 山東省	5.54%	4
Zhongshan 中山市	Guangdong 廣東省	4.70%	9
Shenzhen 深圳市	Guangdong 廣東省	3.95%	6
Shanghai 上海市	Shanghai 上海市	3.53%	43
Ningbo 寧波市	Zhejiang 浙江省	2.77%	31
Wuxi 無錫市	Jiangsu 江蘇省	2.67%	9
Guangzhou 廣州市	Guangdong 廣東省	2.67%	19

10 Major Wholesalers 10 家主要批發商	City 城市	Province 省	Telephone / Fax 電話 / 傳真
Changzhou Hardware Alternating-current Appliance and Chemical Wholesale General Company 常州五金交電化工批發總公司	Changzhou 常州市	Jiangsu 江蘇省	(0519)6609929 (0519)6609925
Suzhou Hardware & Alternating Electricity Co. Ltd. 蘇州五金交電股份有限公司	Suzhou 蘇州市	Jiangsu 江蘇省	(0512)5239572 (0512)5213248
Tianjin Foreign Trade General Company 天津市對外貿易總公司	Tianjin 天津市	Tianjin 天津市	(022)23310922
Chongqing International Trade Center 重慶國際貿易中心	Chongqing 重慶市	Chongqing 重慶市	(023)67853232 (023)67850402
China Chemical Plastics Co. Ltd. 中化塑料有限公司	Beijing 北京市	Beijing 北京市	(010)68569863 (010)68569041
Ningbo Hualian Group Co. Ltd. 寧波華聯集團股份有限公司	Ningbo 寧波市	Zhejiang 浙江省	(0574)7367626 (0574)7367652
Kaiyuan Wei Wei Electromechanical Building Materials Marketing Dept. 廈門市開元區威威機電建材經營部	Xiamen 廈門市	Fujian 福建省	(0592)2071044
Rudong Industry Product General Company 如東縣工業品總公司	Nantong 南通市	Jiangsu 江蘇省	(0513)4516110 (0513)4516110
Fujian Fu Ri Group Company 福建福日集團公司	Fuzhou 福州市	Fujian 福建省	(0591)3269325 (0591)3270426
Guangdong Hardware & Alternating Electrical Co. 廣東省五金交電公司	Guangzhou 廣州市	Guangdong 廣東省	(020)81884078 (020)81861287

*Also include sales by firms outside this industry.包括本行業以外廠家的銷售。"o" stands for "others". "o" 代表 "其他產品"。

4065: Air Conditioners 空調器製造業

The industry accounts for 0.461% of the total revenue of China's industrial sector in 1996. The revenue growth rate of the industry is 17.1% from 1995, as compared to the growth rate of China's industrial sector, 9.51%. The rate of return on asset is 3.11%. 61.44% of all firms in the industry made a profit while 33.80% had negative returns. The top province in terms of the industry's revenue is Guangdong, accounting for 38.55% of the total revenue.
本行業在1996年佔全行業總產值0.461%，行業年增長率為17.1%（全國工業年增長率9.51%）。行業的資產回報率3.11%，61.44%的企業盈利，33.80%的企業虧損。銷售收入最高的省份為廣東省，佔本行業的38.55%。

	Total number of firms 企業總數	Total number of employees 職工總數	Total revenue (mil. RMB) 總銷售收入（百萬元）	Total profit (mil. RMB) 總利潤（百萬元）	Return on assets 資產利潤率 (%)	Return on equity 權益利潤率 (%)	Labour productivity ('000 RMB / worker) 勞動生產率（千元/人）	Debts / assets 資產負債率 (%)	Total assets (mil. RMB) 總資產（百萬元）
Industry Overall 行業總體	415	95,378	26,713	1,175	3.11	12.42	280.08	74.96	37,796

	Number of firms 企業個數	Average number of employees 平均職工人數	Average revenue ('000 RMB) 平均銷售收入（千元）	Average profit ('000 RMB) 平均利潤（千元）	Return on assets 資產利潤率 (%)	Return on equity 權益利潤率 (%)	Labour productivity ('000 RMB / worker) 勞動生產率（千元/人）	Average debts / assets 平均資產負債率(%)	Average Total assets ('000 RMB) 平均總資產（千元）
By ownership 產業所有權									
State-owned 國有	37	210	23,892	-2,459	-3.97	-56.52	113.99	92.98	61,946
Collectively-owned 集體	272	151	22,337	-52	-0.12	-0.67	148.39	81.37	41,726
Privately-owned 私有	5	246	108,208	14,113	15.37	30.21	439.87	49.12	91,819
Domestic JVs 聯營	8	351	138,731	16,047	10.67	29.76	395.67	64.14	150,345
Joint stock 股份制	8	2,052	692,753	35,651	4.00	15.91	337.60	74.88	892,214
Foreign-funded 外資	34	331	135,032	3,199	1.70	5.88	408.28	71.13	188,484
Overseas Chinese-funded 港澳台資	48	314	165,838	14,302	7.70	23.94	527.87	67.84	185,736
By size 規模									
Large 大型	28	1,433	713,345	42,604	4.61	18.30	497.70	74.83	924,919
Medium 中型	23	606	84,422	-5,933	-3.55	-20.71	139.33	82.83	166,907
Small 小型	353	116	13,592	336	1.47	5.18	117.27	71.62	22,831
By regional distribution 地區分布									
Central-North 華北	52	118	11,293	-1,039	-1.51	-7.61	95.65	80.16	68,864
Beijing 北京	32	94	8,379	-1,166	-1.73	-13.02	89.08	86.71	67,366
Tianjin 天津	8	266	22,071	-3,820	-2.87	-9.16	82.94	68.66	133,120
Hebei 河北	10	83	13,829	1,374	3.90	15.56	166.61	74.92	35,202
Shanxi 山西	2	85	2,110	40	0.97	4.52	24.82	78.44	4,105
Inner Mongolia 內蒙									
Northeast 東北	32	110	13,725	321	0.95	4.51	124.91	78.87	33,678
Liaoning 遼寧	14	128	26,308	488	0.68	3.24	206.22	78.97	71,556
Jilin 吉林	1	14	330	10	4.55	-100.00	23.57	104.55	220
Heilongjiang 黑龍江	17	101	4,150	201	4.52	20.05	41.11	77.46	4,452
Central East 華東	234	218	60,124	5,193	7.91	25.07	275.92	68.43	65,622
Shanghai 上海	44	194	110,807	7,054	4.61	13.23	571.10	65.18	153,091
Jiangsu 江蘇	130	248	57,061	6,607	14.38	50.80	230.45	71.70	45,962
Zhejiang 浙江	22	271	59,972	712	1.00	3.81	220.97	73.64	70,916
Anhui 安徽	9	143	11,584	-240	-0.33	-0.63	80.82	48.31	73,220
Fujian 福建	9	46	15,450	2,536	16.54	43.63	332.66	62.10	15,331
Jiangxi 江西	2	57	495				8.76	62.38	3,110
Shandong 山東	18	137	11,774	526	3.36	230.17	85.70	98.54	15,625
Central-South 中南	86	389	134,075	-4		-0.01	344.30	79.36	205,321
Henan 河南	15	119	12,559	1,342	11.38	36.59	105.90	68.90	11,793
Hubei 湖北	5	702	92,284	3,228	1.06	4.29	131.46	75.41	305,844
Hunan 湖南	14	120	40,501	4,116	13.94	25.07	338.72	44.39	29,524
Guangdong 廣東	48	545	214,514	-1,964	-0.61	-3.19	393.81	80.86	322,046
Guangxi 廣西	3	127	5,633	3	0.01	0.04	44.47	67.54	26,660
Hainan 海南	1								
Southwest 西南	7	105	6,967	239	2.04	6.99	66.17	70.87	11,714
Chongqing 重慶	2	51							
Sichuan 四川	5	123	9,289	-319	-2.04	-7.00	75.48	70.87	15,619
Guizhou 貴州									
Yunnan 雲南									
Tibet 西藏									
Northwest 西北	4	127	9,688	543	5.09	26.43	76.43	80.77	10,660
Shaanxi 陝西	2	183	16,690	-335	-3.77	-24.19	91.20	84.46	8,880
Gansu 甘肅									
Qinghai 青海									
Ningxia 寧夏									
Xinjiang 新疆	2	71	2,685	1,420	11.41	52.21	38.09	78.14	12,440

4065: Air Conditioners 空調器製造業

Year 年份	Number of firms 企業個數	Rate of change 每年變化 (%)	Number of employees 職工人數（人）	Rate of change 每年變化 (%)	Total revenue (mil. RMB) 總銷售收入（百萬元）	Rate of change 每年變化 (%)	Total profit (mil. RMB) 總利潤（百萬元）	Rate of change 每年變化 (%)
1993	261		73,832		9,851		468	
1994	318	21.84%	71,053	-3.76%	11,304	14.74%	284	-39.41%
1995	408	28.30%	82,915	16.69%	22,813	101.81%	1,405	395.22%
1996	415	1.72%	95,378	15.03%	26,713	17.10%	1,175	-16.37%

3 Major products* 3 種主要產品 *	Output 產量	Sales volume 銷售量	Unit 單位
a) Room Air Conditioner 房間空氣調節器	4,301,040	3,956,957	set 台

Top 10 firms by revenue (year founded) 收入排名前 10 家企業（創辦年份）	City 城市	Province 省	Telephone / fax 電話 / 傳真	Number of employees 職工人數	Ownership 產業所有權	Revenue ('000 RMB) 銷售收入（千元）	Profit ('000 RMB) (rank) 利潤（千元）（排名）	Total assets ('000 RMB) 總資產（千元）	Major products 主要產品
Chun Lan (Group) Co. 春蘭(集團)公司(1954)	Taizhou 泰州市	Jiangsu 江蘇省	(0523)6227410 (0523)6227734	3,806	Overseas Chinese-funded 港澳台資	5,743,804	798434(1)	3,590,300	a
Zhuhai Gree Electrical Appliance Co. Ltd. 珠海格力電器股份有限公司(1988)	Zhuhai 珠海市	Guangdong 廣東省	(0756)8614883 (0756)8614998	5,310	Joint stock 股份制	2,841,224	218629(2)	2,010,873	a
Gd Md Holding Co. Ltd. 廣東美的集團股份有限公司(1992)	Foshan 佛山市	Guangdong 廣東省	(0757)6656999 (0757)6654011	7,250	Joint stock 股份制	2,073,100	100300(5)	2,781,260	a
Guangdong Hua Bao Air Conditioner Factory 廣東華寶空調器廠(1988)	Foshan 佛山市	Guangdong 廣東省	(0757)2291393 (0757)2291243	1,394	Collectively-owned 集體	1,718,947	343(108)	1,832,512	a
Shanghai Sharp Electronics Co. Ltd. 上海夏普電器有限公司(1992)	Shanghai 上海市	Shanghai 上海市	(021)58990505 (021)58992869	625	Foreign-funded 外資	1,509,592	79404(6)	1,400,857	a
Matsushita-wanbao (Guangzhou) Air Conditioner Co. Ltd. 松下萬寶(廣州)空調器有限公司(1993)	Guangzhou 廣州市	Guangdong 廣東省	(020)84778123 (020)84775576	973	Foreign-funded 外資	1,185,893	-84599(251)	1,917,053	a
Shanghai Hitachi Household Appliances Co. Ltd. 上海日立家用電器有限公司(1994)	Shanghai 上海市	Shanghai 上海市	(021)62338887	1,212	Foreign-funded 外資	1,127,687	36794(8)	997,974	a
Shanghai Hitachi Electrical Appliances Co. Ltd. 上海日立電器有限公司(1993)	Shanghai 上海市	Shanghai 上海市	(021)58548888 (021)58991084	1,253	Foreign-funded 外資	866,503	125273(4)	1,443,993	o
Shanghai Automobile Air Conditioner Factory 上海汽車空調器廠(1990)	Shanghai 上海市	Shanghai 上海市	(021)58912275 (021)58912279	892	Domestic JVs 聯營	814,687	181758(3)	662,384	o
Hangzhou Dongbao Electric Appliance Group Company 杭州東寶電器集團公司(1954)	Hangzhou 杭州市	Zhejiang 浙江省	(0571)6064860 (0571)6053286	185	Collectively-owned 集體	543,968	6008(21)	678,064	a

Top 10 Cities by Production Output 產出排名前 10 位城市	Province 省	Market share 市場份額	Number of firms 企業個數
Foshan 佛山市	Guangdong 廣東省	26.51%	14
Taizhou 泰州市	Jiangsu 江蘇省	17.52%	151
Shanghai 上海市	Shanghai 上海市	16.31%	71
Zhuhai 珠海市	Guangdong 廣東省	9.40%	3
Guangzhou 廣州市	Guangdong 廣東省	6.39%	27
Qingdao 青島市	Shandong 山東省	4.24%	7
Zhongshan 中山市	Guangdong 廣東省	2.65%	5
Hangzhou 杭州市	Zhejiang 浙江省	2.06%	8
Beijing 北京市	Beijing 北京市	1.40%	26
Ningbo 寧波市	Zhejiang 浙江省	1.39%	12

10 Major Wholesalers 10 家主要批發商	City 城市	Province 省	Telephone / Fax 電話 / 傳真
Changzhou Hardware Alternating-current Appliance and Chemical Wholesale General Company 常州五金交電化工批發總公司	Changzhou 常州市	Jiangsu 江蘇省	(0519)6609929 (0519)6609925
Suzhou Hardware & Alternating Electricity Co. Ltd. 蘇州五金交電股份有限公司	Suzhou 蘇州市	Jiangsu 江蘇省	(0512)5239572 (0512)5213248
Tianjin Foreign Trade General Company 天津市對外貿易總公司	Tianjin 天津市	Tianjin 天津市	(022)23310922
Chongqing International Trade Center 重慶國際貿易中心	Chongqing 重慶市	Chongqing 重慶市	(023)67853232 (023)67850402
China Chemical Plastics Co. Ltd. 中化塑料有限公司	Beijing 北京市	Beijing 北京市	(010)68569863 (010)68569041
Ningbo Hualian Group Co. Ltd. 寧波華聯集團股份有限公司	Ningbo 寧波市	Zhejiang 浙江省	(0574)7367626 (0574)7367652
Kaiyuan Wei Wei Electromechanical Building Materials Marketing Dept. 廈門市開元區威威機電建材經營部	Xiamen 廈門市	Fujian 福建省	(0592)2071044
Rudong Industry Product General Company 如東縣工業品總公司	Nantong 南通市	Jiangsu 江蘇省	(0513)4516110 (0513)4516110
Fujian Fu Ri Group Company 福建福日集團公司	Fuzhou 福州市	Fujian 福建省	(0591)3269325 (0591)3270426
Guangdong Hardware & Alternating Electrical Co. 廣東省五金交電公司	Guangzhou 廣州市	Guangdong 廣東省	(020)81884078 (020)81861287

*Also include sales by firms outside this industry.包括本行業以外廠家的銷售。"o" stands for "others". "o" 代表"其他產品"。

4066: Lampblack Releasing Equipment 排油煙機製造業

The industry accounts for 0.016% of the total revenue of China's industrial sector in 1996. The revenue growth rate of the industry is -36.7% from 1995, as compared to the growth rate of China's industrial sector, 9.51%. The rate of return on asset is -0.85%. 48.65% of all firms in the industry made a profit while 44.90% had negative returns. The top province in terms of the industry's revenue is Zhejiang, accounting for 55.77% of the total revenue.

本行業在1996年佔全行業總產值0.016%，行業年增長率為-36.7%（全國工業年增長率9.51%）。行業的資產回報率-0.85%，48.65%的企業盈利，44.90%的企業虧損。銷售收入最高的省份為浙江省，佔本行業的55.77%。

	Total number of firms 企業總數	Total number of employees 職工總數	Total revenue (mil. RMB) 總銷售收入（百萬元）	Total profit (mil. RMB) 總利潤（百萬元）	Return on assets 資產利潤率 (%)	Return on equity 權益利潤率 (%)	Labour productivity ('000 RMB / worker) 勞動生產率（千元/人）	Debts / assets 資產負債率 (%)	Total assets (mil. RMB) 總資產（百萬元）
Industry Overall 行業總體	56	9,936	949	-13	-0.85	-3.22	95.51	73.63	1,481

	Number of firms 企業個數	Average number of employees 平均職工人數	Average revenue ('000 RMB) 平均銷售收入（千元）	Average profit ('000 RMB) 平均利潤（千元）	Return on assets 資產利潤率 (%)	Return on equity 權益利潤率 (%)	Labour productivity ('000 RMB / worker) 勞動生產率（千元/人）	Average debts / assets 平均資產負債率(%)	Average Total assets ('000 RMB) 平均總資產（千元）
By ownership 產業所有權									
State-owned 國有	9	328	21,778	-1,000	-3.06	-21.43	66.46	85.71	32,667
Collectively-owned 集體	41	151	17,406	-92	-0.36	-1.18	115.27	69.85	25,736
Privately-owned 私有									
Domestic JVs 聯營	1	390	7,581	6	0.01	0.04	19.44	79.22	84,933
Joint stock 股份制									
Foreign-funded 外資	2	29	930	4	0.15	0.32	32.63	54.24	2,619
Overseas Chinese-funded 港澳台資	4	87	7,494	-61	-0.58	-2.21	85.90	73.95	10,617
By size 規模									
Large 大型	3	353	69,005	-1,028	-1.02	-3.63	195.67	71.94	100,809
Medium 中型	5	536	44,619	-1,422	-1.84	-4.49	83.21	59.17	77,500
Small 小型	47	131	11,042	-60	-0.35	-1.89	84.32	81.29	16,849
By regional distribution 地區分布									
Central-North 華北	4	104	5,183	415	7.47	14.81	50.07	49.57	5,558
Beijing 北京	3	15	727	-7	-0.74	-10.53	49.55	92.99	903
Tianjin 天津	1	370	18,550	1,680	8.61	15.25	50.14	43.55	19,520
Hebei 河北									
Shanxi 山西									
Inner Mongolia 內蒙									
Northeast 東北	4	371	4,725	118	1.99	11.87	12.74	83.32	5,905
Liaoning 遼寧	2	46	1,320	105	3.08	7.98	28.70	61.53	3,405
Jilin 吉林	1	1,387	16,250	300	1.90	100.00	11.72	98.10	15,750
Heilongjiang 黑龍江	1	5	10	-40	-3.77	-3.88	2.00	3.77	1,060
Central East 華東	33	172	19,740	528	2.07	6.54	114.52	68.29	25,463
Shanghai 上海	6	125	1,620	-983	-8.19	-378.21	13.01	97.84	12,013
Jiangsu 江蘇	4	226	21,945	533	3.07	5.25	97.21	41.61	17,370
Zhejiang 浙江	17	208	31,135	1,212	3.15	9.40	150.03	66.46	38,439
Anhui 安徽									
Fujian 福建									
Jiangxi 江西	1	20	140	-190	-8.76	33.33	7.00	126.27	2,170
Shandong 山東	5	98	4,896	156	1.81	13.73	49.96	86.82	8,616
Central-South 中南	15	157	17,228	-2,141	-5.40	-29.50	109.97	81.69	39,650
Henan 河南	1	45							
Hubei 湖北									
Hunan 湖南	1								
Guangdong 廣東	13	177	19,878	-2,471	-5.40	-29.50	112.11	81.69	45,750
Guangxi 廣西									
Hainan 海南									
Southwest 西南									
Chongqing 重慶									
Sichuan 四川									
Guizhou 貴州									
Yunnan 雲南									
Tibet 西藏									
Northwest 西北									
Shaanxi 陝西									
Gansu 甘肅									
Qinghai 青海									
Ningxia 寧夏									
Xinjiang 新疆									

4066: Lampblack Releasing Equipment 排油煙機製造業

Year 年份	Number of firms 企業個數	Rate of change 每年變化 (%)	Number of employees 職工人數 (人)	Rate of change 每年變化 (%)	Total revenue (mil. RMB) 總銷售收入 (百萬元)	Rate of change 每年變化 (%)	Total profit (mil. RMB) 總利潤 (百萬元)	Rate of change 每年變化 (%)
1993	44		13,679		980		24	
1994	51	15.91%	10,840	-20.76%	1,174	19.82%	1	-94.62%
1995	63	23.53%	14,696	35.57%	1,500	27.71%	25	1847.20%
1996	56	-11.11%	9,936	-32.39%	949	-36.73%	-13	-151.24%

3 Major products* 3 種主要產品 *	Output 產量	Sales volume 銷售量	Unit 單位
a) Fume Extractor 排油煙機	1,665,213	1,715,169	set 台

Top 10 firms by revenue (year founded) 收入排名前 10 家企業 (創辦年份)	City 城市	Province 省	Telephone / fax 電話 / 傳真	Number of employees 職工人數	Ownership 產業所有權	Revenue ('000 RMB) 銷售收入 (千元)	Profit ('000 RMB) (rank) 利潤 (千元) (排名)	Total assets ('000 RMB) 總資產 (千元)	Major products 主要產品
Zhejiang Shuai Kang Group Co. Ltd. 浙江帥康集團有限公司(1993)	Ningbo 寧波市	Zhejiang 浙江省	(0574)2241980 (0574)2241447	1,325	Collectively-owned 集體	313,694	20270(1)	227,676	o
Yuli Electrical Appliance Group Co. 寧波玉立電器集團公司(1954)	Ningbo 寧波市	Zhejiang 浙江省	(0574)2465390 (0574)2465566	671	Collectively-owned 集體	108,149	1358(6)	187,350	a
Shunde Shun Hua Light Industry Co. 順德市順華輕工實業公司(1956)	Foshan 佛山市	Guangdong 廣東省	(0757)6656768 (0757)6657408	570	State-owned 國有	101,970	2354(2)	134,213	a
Huasheng Electrical Fan General Factory Jingjiang Branch 華生電扇總廠靖江分廠(1986)	Taizhou 泰州市	Jiangsu 江蘇省	(0523)4261133	774	Collectively-owned 集體	86,143	2182(3)	55,864	a
Gaoming Zheng Ye Electric Appliance Industrial Co. Ltd. 高明市正野電器實業有限公司(1996)	Foshan 佛山市	Guangdong 廣東省	(0757)8848638 (0757)8848663	62	Collectively-owned 集體	57,498	0(18)	67,671	o
Shenzhen Machinery Industry & Trading Co. 深圳市機械工貿公司(1980)	Shenzhen 深圳市	Guangdong 廣東省	(0755)5530310 (0755)5530310	358	State-owned 國有	46,690	-5497(29)	54,098	o
Shenzhen Luohu Shatoujiao Yue Hai Household Appliances Hardware General Factory 深圳市羅湖區沙頭角粵海家電五金總廠(1985)	Shenzhen 深圳市	Guangdong 廣東省	(0755)5557015 (0755)5551983	98	State-owned 國有	22,304	476(11)	33,709	a
Zhejiang Skeet Electrical Appliance Co. 浙江飛碟電器公司(1956)	Huzhou 湖州市	Zhejiang 浙江省	(0572)3911468 (0572)3912480	288	Collectively-owned 集體	18,623	215(13)	34,604	o
Tianjin Wuqing Tian Yang Group Company 天津市武清縣天洋集團公司(1989)	Tianjin 天津市	Tianjin 天津市	(022)29561728	368	Collectively-owned 集體	18,550	1680(5)	19,520	a
Hangzhou Wan Quan Electric Appliance Co. Ltd. 杭州萬銓電器有限公司(1994)	Hangzhou 杭州市	Zhejiang 浙江省	(0571)6943957 (0571)6943957	114	Overseas Chinese-funded 港澳台資	17,600	1952(4)	9,051	o

Top 10 Cities by Production Output 產出排名前 10 位城市	Province 省	Market share 市場份額	Number of firms 企業個數
Ningbo 寧波市	Zhejiang 浙江省	41.44%	8
Foshan 佛山市	Guangdong 廣東省	10.57%	4
Suzhou 蘇州市	Jiangsu 江蘇省	8.62%	2
Taizhou 泰州市	Jiangsu 江蘇省	8.05%	1
Huzhou 湖州市	Zhejiang 浙江省	5.37%	6
Shanghai 上海市	Shanghai 上海市	4.12%	10
Shaoxing 紹興市	Zhejiang 浙江省	2.83%	2
Hangzhou 杭州市	Zhejiang 浙江省	2.38%	2
Guangzhou 廣州市	Guangdong 廣東省	2.30%	7
Shenzhen 深圳市	Guangdong 廣東省	2.18%	2

10 Major Wholesalers 10 家主要批發商	City 城市	Province 省	Telephone / Fax 電話 / 傳真
Changzhou Hardware Alternating-current Appliance and Chemical Wholesale General Company 常州五金交電化工批發總公司	Changzhou 常州市	Jiangsu 江蘇省	(0519)6609929 (0519)6609925
Suzhou Hardware & Alternating Electricity Co. Ltd. 蘇州五金交電股份有限公司	Suzhou 蘇州市	Jiangsu 江蘇省	(0512)5239572 (0512)5213248
Tianjin Foreign Trade General Company 天津市對外貿易總公司	Tianjin 天津市	Tianjin 天津市	(022)23310922
Chongqing International Trade Center 重慶國際貿易中心	Chongqing 重慶市	Chongqing 重慶市	(023)67853232 (023)67850402
China Chemical Plastics Co. Ltd. 中化塑料有限公司	Beijing 北京市	Beijing 北京市	(010)68569863 (010)68569041
Ningbo Hualian Group Co. Ltd. 寧波華聯集團股份有限公司	Ningbo 寧波市	Zhejiang 浙江省	(0574)7367626 (0574)7367652
Kaiyuan Wei Wei Electromechanical Building Materials Marketing Dept. 廈門市開元區威威機電建材經營部	Xiamen 廈門市	Fujian 福建省	(0592)2071044
Rudong Industry Product General Company 如東縣工業品總公司	Nantong 南通市	Jiangsu 江蘇省	(0513)4516110 (0513)4516110
Fujian Fu Ri Group Company 福建福日集團公司	Fuzhou 福州市	Fujian 福建省	(0591)3269325 (0591)3270426
Guangdong Hardware & Alternating Electrical Co. 廣東省五金交電公司	Guangzhou 廣州市	Guangdong 廣東省	(020)81884078 (020)81861287

*Also include sales by firms outside this industry.包括本行業以外廠家的銷售。"o" stands for "others". "o" 代表 "其他產品"。

4069: Other Household Electrical Appliances 其他日用電器製造業

The industry accounts for 0.273% of the total revenue of China's industrial sector in 1996. The revenue growth rate of the industry is 21.2% from 1995, as compared to the growth rate of China's industrial sector, 9.51%. The rate of return on asset is 2.07%. 66.80% of all firms in the industry made a profit while 27.37% had negative returns. The top province in terms of the industry's revenue is Guangdong, accounting for 44.64% of the total revenue.
本行業在 1996 年佔全行業總產值 0.273%，行業年增長率為 21.2%（全國工業年增長率 9.51%）。行業的資產回報率 2.07%，66.80% 的企業盈利，27.37% 的企業虧損。銷售收入最高的省份為廣東省，佔本行業的 44.64%。

	Total number of firms 企業總數	Total number of employees 職工總數	Total revenue (mil. RMB) 總銷售收入（百萬元）	Total profit (mil. RMB) 總利潤（百萬元）	Return on assets 資產利潤率 (%)	Return on equity 權益利潤率 (%)	Labour productivity ('000 RMB / worker) 勞動生產率（千元/人）	Debts / assets 資產負債率 (%)	Total assets (mil. RMB) 總資產（百萬元）
Industry Overall 行業總體	1,345	199,075	15,848	442	2.07	6.25	79.61	66.92	21,350

	Number of firms 企業個數	Average number of employees 平均職工人數	Average revenue ('000 RMB) 平均銷售收入（千元）	Average profit ('000 RMB) 平均利潤（千元）	Return on assets 資產利潤率 (%)	Return on equity 權益利潤率 (%)	Labour productivity ('000 RMB / worker) 勞動生產率（千元/人）	Average debts / assets 平均資產負債率(%)	Average Total assets ('000 RMB) 平均總資產（千元）
By ownership 產業所有權									
State-owned 國有	122	146	8,000	475	2.41	10.72	54.85	77.49	19,697
Collectively-owned 集體	978	116	6,027	137	2.11	7.98	52.08	73.58	6,517
Privately-owned 私有	7	120	15,949	18	0.14	0.86	132.59	83.62	12,602
Domestic JVs 聯營	18	306	42,809	976	2.65	9.26	140.08	71.43	36,879
Joint stock 股份制	25	752	66,709	-463	-0.31	-0.74	88.76	57.98	148,467
Foreign-funded 外資	75	202	24,700	694	1.74	5.13	122.04	65.98	39,778
Overseas Chinese-funded 港澳台資	120	267	38,128	1,594	3.73	9.29	142.65	59.83	42,713
By size 規模									
Large 大型	10	2,113	361,042	9,415	1.63	4.57	170.84	64.32	577,216
Medium 中型	28	1,047	115,362	7,513	4.58	11.62	110.16	60.57	163,914
Small 小型	1,274	116	7,070	108	1.25	4.31	60.83	70.94	8,624
By regional distribution 地區分布									
Central-North 華北	116	46	3,780	457	5.15	12.25	82.97	57.99	8,873
Beijing 北京	55	59	5,479	649	5.02	13.37	92.77	62.48	12,944
Tianjin 天津	27	35	2,244	9	0.10	0.18	64.61	44.98	9,502
Hebei 河北	23	36	3,128	760	36.45	70.06	86.79	48.00	2,085
Shanxi 山西	5	18	278	-82	-5.73	-28.08	15.44	79.58	1,430
Inner Mongolia 內蒙	6	30	535	-10	-1.06	2.58	17.83	141.20	947
Northeast 東北	162	70	4,559	370	5.00	20.11	65.46	75.12	7,392
Liaoning 遼寧	72	69	6,307	735	5.61	22.32	91.52	74.84	13,093
Jilin 吉林	26	37	768	-35	-2.16	-14.75	20.86	85.37	1,603
Heilongjiang 黑龍江	64	84	4,131	123	3.71	14.43	49.31	74.32	3,331
Central East 華東	636	178	10,612	465	3.45	9.99	59.78	65.44	13,474
Shanghai 上海	144	117	11,164	410	2.15	6.45	95.78	66.70	19,109
Jiangsu 江蘇	121	503	10,214	501	4.99	14.59	20.32	65.79	10,044
Zhejiang 浙江	189	87	10,353	509	4.12	12.77	118.52	67.73	12,351
Anhui 安徽	25	119	5,581	44	0.65	2.22	46.73	70.53	6,674
Fujian 福建	56	127	24,469	1,173	4.36	9.96	192.72	56.27	26,929
Jiangxi 江西	22	32	654	-45	-2.56	-18.66	20.63	86.28	1,776
Shandong 山東	79	101	5,377	180	2.57	8.77	53.14	70.72	7,011
Central-South 中南	353	175	21,081	44	0.16	0.49	120.23	68.24	27,740
Henan 河南	23	68	1,618	30	0.56	2.41	23.81	76.68	5,347
Hubei 湖北	30	145	6,302	60	0.65	3.12	43.37	79.29	9,337
Hunan 湖南	28	26	1,351	21	2.21	7.06	52.40	68.66	937
Guangdong 廣東	252	212	28,074	60	0.16	0.50	132.34	67.47	36,336
Guangxi 廣西	20	90	5,139	-138	-1.33	-7.51	57.29	82.24	10,304
Hainan 海南									
Southwest 西南	43	94	9,761	750	6.11	15.13	103.64	59.61	12,276
Chongqing 重慶	9	63	3,027	76	2.55	8.71	48.35	70.68	2,983
Sichuan 四川	22	136	16,895	1,407	6.68	16.02	123.99	58.32	21,074
Guizhou 貴州	8	10	286	-4	-0.87	-3.13	29.36	72.25	433
Yunnan 雲南	4	98	2,983	5	0.08	0.27	30.51	70.85	6,338
Tibet 西藏									
Northwest 西北	35	105	1,727	-427	-6.39	-31.07	16.49	79.44	6,686
Shaanxi 陝西	18	47	1,153	9	0.29	1.36	24.67	78.92	3,107
Gansu 甘肅	9	284	3,649	-1,668	-8.95	-46.99	12.83	80.95	18,624
Qinghai 青海	2	61	1,150				18.85	46.64	2,155
Ningxia 寧夏	4	30	625	-28	-2.43	-8.66	20.83	71.96	1,133
Xinjiang 新疆	2	11	1,020	5	0.62	1.22	92.73	49.07	805

4069: Other Household Electrical Appliances 其他日用電器製造業

Year 年份	Number of firms 企業個數	Rate of change 每年變化 (%)	Number of employees 職工人數 (人)	Rate of change 每年變化 (%)	Total revenue (mil. RMB) 總銷售收入 (百萬元)	Rate of change 每年變化 (%)	Total profit (mil. RMB) 總利潤 (百萬元)	Rate of change 每年變化 (%)
1993	1459		183,579		10,264		489	
1994	1533	5.07%	160,058	-12.81%	10,426	1.58%	497	1.55%
1995	1440	-6.07%	147,864	-7.62%	13,080	25.45%	366	-26.44%
1996	1345	-6.60%	199,075	34.63%	15,848	21.16%	442	20.92%

3 Major products* 3 種主要產品 *	Output 產量	Sales volume 銷售量	Unit 單位
a) Microwave Oven 微波爐	2,722,547	2,286,939	set 台
b) Electric Rice Cooker 電飯鍋	14,676,508	16,290,924	piece 個
c) Electric Iron 電熨斗	17,836,484	18,728,308	piece 個

Top 10 firms by revenue (year founded) 收入排名前 10 家企業 (創辦年份)	City 城市	Province 省	Telephone / fax 電話 / 傳真	Number of employees 職工人數	Ownership 產業所有權	Revenue ('000 RMB) 銷售收入 (千元)	Profit ('000 RMB) (rank) 利潤 (千元) (排名)	Total assets ('000 RMB) 總資產 (千元)	Major products 主要產品
Tsann Kuen (China) Enterprise Co. Ltd. 廈門燦坤實業股份有限公司(1988)	Xiamen 廈門市	Fujian 福建省	(0592)6021708 (0592)6021598	3,689	Overseas Chinese-funded 港澳台資	922,765	47932(4)	989,468	c
Hangzhou Household Electric Appliance Industrial Corp. 杭州市家用電器工業公司(1958)	Hangzhou 杭州市	Zhejiang 浙江省	(0571)7026365 (0571)7078131	1,566	Domestic JVs 聯營	529,364	492(144)	377,820	o
Shun De Ge Lan Shi Electric Appliance Factory Co. Ltd. 順德格蘭仕電器廠有限公司(1992)	Foshan 佛山市	Guangdong 廣東省	(0757)8886389 (0757)8889628	948	Overseas Chinese-funded 港澳台資	510,123	39569(5)	293,738	a,b
Shun De Hui Er Pu Xian Hua Microwave Products Co. Ltd. 順德惠而浦蜆華微波製品有限公司(1988)	Foshan 佛山市	Guangdong 廣東省	(0757)6656922 (0757)6656931	2,113	Foreign-funded 外資	471,390	1561(60)	549,602	a
Zhongshan Zhong Yue Jia Cai Ru Gu Electron Factory 中山市中粵嘉財入谷電子廠(1995)	Zhongshan 中山市	Guangdong 廣東省	(0760)5595777 (0760)5595797	1,040	Foreign-funded 外資	414,886	-9439(561)	63,726	a
Guangdong Rongsheng Electric Holding Co. Ltd. 廣東容聲電器股份有限公司(1981)	Foshan 佛山市	Guangdong 廣東省	(0757)6621314 (0757)6621546	1,870	Joint stock 股份制	402,469	4686(30)	544,168	b
Changshu Matsushita Bansen Lift Co. Ltd. 江蘇阪神有限責任公司(1955)	Suzhou 蘇州市	Jiangsu 江蘇省	(0512)2773841 (0512)2772509	358	Collectively-owned 集體	399,550	32350(7)	278,350	o
Shunde Aide Appliances Group 順德愛德電飯鍋製造廠有限公司(1994)	Foshan 佛山市	Guangdong 廣東省	(0757)8882808 (0757)8888945	1,962	Overseas Chinese-funded 港澳台資	381,995	16163(13)	384,361	b
Li Min (Panyu Nan Sha) Electric Appliance Development Co. Ltd. 利民(番禺南沙)電器發展有限公司(1995)	Guangzhou 廣州市	Guangdong 廣東省	(020)84989803 (020)84982638	2,800	Overseas Chinese-funded 港澳台資	377,427	-872(516)	585,370	o
Zhuhai Sez Philips Family Electric Appliance Co. Ltd. 珠海經濟特區飛利浦家庭電器有限公司(1990)	Zhuhai 珠海市	Guangdong 廣東省	(0756)2263851 (0756)2261505	691	Foreign-funded 外資	361,455	26285(8)	203,552	o

Top 10 Cities by Production Output 產出排名前 10 位城市	Province 省	Market share 市場份額	Number of firms 企業個數
Foshan 佛山市	Guangdong 廣東省	14.88%	46
Shanghai 上海市	Shanghai 上海市	11.82%	208
Guangzhou 廣州市	Guangdong 廣東省	9.98%	135
Shenzhen 深圳市	Guangdong 廣東省	5.70%	44
Zhongshan 中山市	Guangdong 廣東省	5.39%	17
Suzhou 蘇州市	Jiangsu 江蘇省	3.73%	44
Shenyang 瀋陽市	Liaoning 遼寧省	3.28%	41
Zhuhai 珠海市	Guangdong 廣東省	3.25%	7
Chengdu 成都市	Sichuan 四川省	3.03%	25
Jiaxing 嘉興市	Zhejiang 浙江省	2.88%	22

10 Major Wholesalers 10 家主要批發商	City 城市	Province 省	Telephone / Fax 電話 / 傳真
Changzhou Hardware Alternating-current Appliance and Chemical Wholesale General Company 常州五金交電化工批發總公司	Changzhou 常州市	Jiangsu 江蘇省	(0519)6609929 (0519)6609925
Suzhou Hardware & Alternating Electricity Co. Ltd. 蘇州五金交電股份有限公司	Suzhou 蘇州市	Jiangsu 江蘇省	(0512)5239572 (0512)5213248
Tianjin Foreign Trade General Company 天津市對外貿易總公司	Tianjin 天津市	Tianjin 天津市	(022)23310922
Chongqing International Trade Center 重慶國際貿易中心	Chongqing 重慶市	Chongqing 重慶市	(023)67853232 (023)67850402
China Chemical Plastics Co. Ltd. 中化塑料有限公司	Beijing 北京市	Beijing 北京市	(010)68569863 (010)68569041
Ningbo Hualian Group Co. Ltd. 寧波華聯集團股份有限公司	Ningbo 寧波市	Zhejiang 浙江省	(0574)7367626 (0574)7367652
Kaiyuan Wei Wei Electromechanical Building Materials Marketing Dept. 廈門市開元區威威機電建材經營部	Xiamen 廈門市	Fujian 福建省	(0592)2071044
Rudong Industry Product General Company 如東縣工業品總公司	Nantong 南通市	Jiangsu 江蘇省	(0513)4516110 (0513)4516110
Fujian Fu Ri Group Company 福建福日集團公司	Fuzhou 福州市	Fujian 福建省	(0591)3269325 (0591)3270426
Guangdong Hardware & Alternating Electrical Co. 廣東省五金交電公司	Guangzhou 廣州市	Guangdong 廣東省	(020)81884078 (020)81861287

*Also include sales by firms outside this industry.包括本行業以外廠家的銷售。"o" stands for "others". "o" 代表 "其他產品"。

4071: Light Bulbs 電光源製造業

The industry accounts for 0.144% of the total revenue of China's industrial sector in 1996. The revenue growth rate of the industry is -23.6% from 1995, as compared to the growth rate of China's industrial sector, 9.51%. The rate of return on asset is -0.05%. 67.77% of all firms in the industry made a profit while 25.97% had negative returns. The top province in terms of the industry's revenue is Jiangsu, accounting for 20.13% of the total revenue.
本行業在1996年佔全行業總產值0.144%，行業年增長率為-23.6%（全國工業年增長率9.51%）。行業的資產回報率-0.05%，67.77%的企業盈利，25.97%的企業虧損。銷售收入最高的省份為江蘇省，佔本行業的20.13%。

	Total number of firms 企業總數	Total number of employees 職工總數	Total revenue (mil. RMB) 總銷售收入（百萬元）	Total profit (mil. RMB) 總利潤（百萬元）	Return on assets 資產利潤率 (%)	Return on equity 權益利潤率 (%)	Labour productivity ('000 RMB / worker) 勞動生產率（千元/人）	Debts / assets 資產負債率 (%)	Total assets (mil. RMB) 總資產（百萬元）
Industry Overall 行業總體	948	205,593	8,375	-7	-0.05	-0.14	40.74	65.34	13,611

	Number of firms 企業個數	Average number of employees 平均職工人數	Average revenue ('000 RMB) 平均銷售收入（千元）	Average profit ('000 RMB) 平均利潤（千元）	Return on assets 資產利潤率 (%)	Return on equity 權益利潤率 (%)	Labour productivity ('000 RMB / worker) 勞動生產率（千元/人）	Average debts / assets 平均資產負債率(%)	Average Total assets ('000 RMB) 平均總資產（千元）
By ownership 產業所有權									
State-owned 國有	133	712	13,947	-1,030	-2.92	-14.44	19.58	79.78	35,293
Collectively-owned 集體	605	112	2,582	61	1.41	9.63	23.09	85.33	4,312
Privately-owned 私有	4	83	1,947	19	0.44	4.85	23.38	90.89	4,398
Domestic JVs 聯營	20	242	7,658	-188	-1.30	-20.31	31.59	93.59	14,428
Joint stock 股份制	7	1,053	476,305	17,710	6.44	7.76	452.45	17.01	275,062
Foreign-funded 外資	58	302	13,053	-522	-1.17	-2.36	43.17	50.55	44,748
Overseas Chinese-funded 港澳台資	116	132	6,060	27	0.21	0.65	46.01	67.05	12,714
By size 規模									
Large 大型	18	2,483	262,676	-469	-0.16	-0.30	105.78	47.27	299,561
Medium 中型	54	1,023	21,179	28	0.05	0.28	20.71	83.48	60,323
Small 小型	854	123	2,931	0	0.00	-0.01	23.75	73.07	5,809
By regional distribution 地區分布									
Central-North 華北	85	121	2,257	-231	-3.61	-15.48	18.61	76.67	6,390
Beijing 北京	31	72	1,779	-233	-4.64	-22.94	24.79	79.76	5,015
Tianjin 天津	25	123	2,216	-54	-0.78	-2.89	18.06	73.16	6,901
Hebei 河北	18	138	2,505	-442	-7.47	-56.03	18.21	86.66	5,913
Shanxi 山西	6	273	5,567	5	0.04	0.11	20.40	67.43	13,920
Inner Mongolia 內蒙	5	180	562	-628	-12.46	-41.64	3.12	70.05	5,042
Northeast 東北	115	310	4,342	-92	-0.90	-4.68	13.98	80.71	10,230
Liaoning 遼寧	87	334	3,214	-71	-0.75	-3.40	9.62	78.04	9,575
Jilin 吉林	7	466	23,037	140	0.45	2.87	49.44	84.30	31,021
Heilongjiang 黑龍江	21	161	2,781	-257	-4.27	-53.90	17.31	92.09	6,014
Central East 華東	478	200	11,120	-101	-0.70	-2.18	55.55	67.92	14,474
Shanghai 上海	67	249	18,374	-2,228	-6.65	-23.44	73.89	71.64	33,518
Jiangsu 江蘇	138	221	12,219	280	2.06	6.79	55.26	69.67	13,615
Zhejiang 浙江	114	153	10,483	297	2.89	9.34	68.33	69.07	10,296
Anhui 安徽	58	128	5,210	330	12.32	31.39	40.86	60.76	2,680
Fujian 福建	37	194	9,809	-135	-0.67	-1.29	50.61	48.39	20,271
Jiangxi 江西	27	174	3,653	-48	-0.70	-3.85	21.00	81.69	6,786
Shandong 山東	37	318	11,874	418	2.91	9.20	37.39	68.39	14,359
Central-South 中南	206	199	9,152	493	2.54	5.35	45.93	52.55	19,397
Henan 河南	62	154	4,609	24	0.27	1.51	29.87	82.22	8,811
Hubei 湖北	18	370	6,924	-605	-2.90	-9.34	18.73	68.98	20,881
Hunan 湖南	35	136	3,499	-186	-4.48	-17.84	25.74	74.89	4,153
Guangdong 廣東	76	229	16,873	1,713	4.67	8.01	73.75	41.77	36,714
Guangxi 廣西	13	189	5,339	-947	-9.44	-62.74	28.31	84.96	10,032
Hainan 海南	2	115	320	-205	-5.37	-25.00	2.78	78.53	3,820
Southwest 西南	40	335	7,334	-286	-2.34	-8.61	21.88	72.83	12,238
Chongqing 重慶	11	491	11,369	-306	-1.94	-4.59	23.15	57.75	15,767
Sichuan 四川	20	240	5,248	-424	-4.82	-27.28	21.91	82.34	8,801
Guizhou 貴州	4	281	4,315	28	0.28	0.72	15.36	61.10	9,763
Yunnan 雲南	5	404	8,886	50	0.25	2.08	22.00	87.87	19,818
Tibet 西藏									
Northwest 西北	24	394	7,929	-760	-3.74	-15.73	20.15	76.23	20,322
Shaanxi 陝西	12	472	10,509	-1,517	-5.86	-59.81	22.27	90.20	25,884
Gansu 甘肅	5	408	6,144				15.07	45.18	19,718
Qinghai 青海	2	285	4,505	-40	-0.49	-1.32	15.83	62.69	8,095
Ningxia 寧夏									
Xinjiang 新疆	5	235	4,892	10	0.08	0.20	20.83	59.22	12,466

4071: Light Bulbs 電光源製造業

Year 年份	Number of firms 企業個數	Rate of change 每年變化 (%)	Number of employees 職工人數 (人)	Rate of change 每年變化 (%)	Total revenue (mil. RMB) 總銷售收入 (百萬元)	Rate of change 每年變化 (%)	Total profit (mil. RMB) 總利潤 (百萬元)	Rate of change 每年變化 (%)
1993	728		269,075		4,955		172	
1994	805	10.58%	174,516	-35.14%	5,417	9.33%	79	-53.72%
1995	937	16.40%	195,222	11.86%	10,968	102.46%	138	73.66%
1996	948	1.17%	205,593	5.31%	8,375	-23.64%	-7	-105.07%

3 Major products* 3 種主要產品 *	Output 產量	Sales volume 銷售量	Unit 單位
a) Lamp Bulb 燈泡	438,141	368,039	10,000 piece 萬只
b) Other Illuminating Appliances 其他照明器具	128,189	125,625	10,000 piece 萬只

Top 10 firms by revenue (year founded) 收入排名前 10 家企業 (創辦年份)	City 城市	Province 省	Telephone / fax 電話 / 傳真	Number of employees 職工人數	Ownership 產業所有權	Revenue ('000 RMB) 銷售收入 (千元)	Profit ('000 RMB) (rank) 利潤 (千元) (排名)	Total assets ('000 RMB) 總資產 (千元)	Major products 主要產品
Shanghai General Electrical Appliance Jia Bao Illuminating Co. Ltd. 通用電器嘉寶照明有限公司(1994)	Shanghai 上海市	Shanghai 上海市	(021)59121611 (021)59123434	6,439	Foreign-funded 外資	419,704	-93020(447)	860,096	a
Zhejiang Sunlight Group Co. Ltd. 浙江陽光集團公司(1975)	Shaoxing 紹興市	Zhejiang 浙江省	(0575)2018580 (0575)2015355	1,408	Collectively-owned 集體	407,518	30238(2)	174,755	a
Foshan Electrical and Lighting Co. Ltd. 佛山電器照明股份有限公司(1958)	Foshan 佛山市	Guangdong 廣東省	(0757)2813838 (0757)2816276	2,444	Joint stock 股份制	391,437	212300(1)	1,385,120	a
Philips & Yaming Lighting Co. Ltd. 飛利浦亞明照明有限公司(1994)	Shanghai 上海市	Shanghai 上海市	(021)65461165 (021)65378328	2,569	Foreign-funded 外資	337,343	-54989(446)	769,195	a
Penglai Debao Xinguangyuan Lamp Decorations Co. Ltd. 蓬萊得寶新光源燈飾有限公司(1987)	Yantai 煙台市	Shandong 山東省	(0535)5711231 (0535)5711231	889	Overseas Chinese-funded 港澳台資	159,611	10191(7)	76,549	b
Changchun Light Bulb Wire Mill 長春市燈泡電線廠(1962)	Changchun 長春市	Jilin 吉林省	(0431)5955591 (0431)5951467	2,700	State-owned 國有	154,927	1517(32)	209,121	a
Tai Yi Industry (Boluo) Co. Ltd. 台一工業(博羅)有限公司(1996)	Huizhou 惠州市	Guangdong 廣東省	(0751)6657688 (0751)6657689	200	Overseas Chinese-funded 港澳台資	117,580	0(321)	36,950	a
Osram Foshan Illuminating Co. Ltd. 歐司朗佛山照明有限公司(1995)	Foshan 佛山市	Guangdong 廣東省	(0757)5511666 (0757)5511555	1,023	Foreign-funded 外資	117,115	-52481(445)	316,856	a
Henan Dong Yu Electric Appliance Industrial Co. Ltd. 河南東裕電器工業有限公司(1991)	Luoyang 洛陽市	Henan 河南省	(0379)4860185 (0379)4322193	508	Overseas Chinese-funded 港澳台資	113,834	99(178)	123,419	o
Guangzhou Hong Mian Heat Preservation Container Industrial Co. 廣州紅棉保溫容器實業公司(1959)	Guangzhou 廣州市	Guangdong 廣東省	(020)84367126 (020)84326186	2,471	State-owned 國有	109,625	-11929(443)	435,941	a

Top 10 Cities by Production Output 產出排名前 10 位城市	Province 省	Market share 市場份額	Number of firms 企業個數
Shanghai 上海市	Shanghai 上海市	20.05%	124
Foshan 佛山市	Guangdong 廣東省	7.85%	17
Shaoxing 紹興市	Zhejiang 浙江省	5.96%	8
Nanjing 南京市	Jiangsu 江蘇省	3.52%	31
Guangzhou 廣州市	Guangdong 廣東省	3.22%	31
Hangzhou 杭州市	Zhejiang 浙江省	2.93%	37
Changzhou 常州市	Jiangsu 江蘇省	2.36%	35
Yantai 煙台市	Shandong 山東省	2.18%	8
Huzhou 湖州市	Zhejiang 浙江省	2.18%	12
Shenzhen 深圳市	Guangdong 廣東省	2.13%	8

10 Major Wholesalers 10 家主要批發商	City 城市	Province 省	Telephone / Fax 電話 / 傳真
Changzhou Hardware Alternating-current Appliance and Chemical Wholesale General Company 常州五金交電化工批發總公司	Changzhou 常州市	Jiangsu 江蘇省	(0519)6609929 (0519)6609925
Suzhou Hardware & Alternating Electricity Co. Ltd. 蘇州五金交電股份有限公司	Suzhou 蘇州市	Jiangsu 江蘇省	(0512)5239572 (0512)5213248
Tianjin Foreign Trade General Company 天津市對外貿易總公司	Tianjin 天津市	Tianjin 天津市	(022)23310922
Chongqing International Trade Center 重慶國際貿易中心	Chongqing 重慶市	Chongqing 重慶市	(023)67853232 (023)67850402
China Chemical Plastics Co. Ltd. 中化塑料有限公司	Beijing 北京市	Beijing 北京市	(010)68569863 (010)68569041
Ningbo Hualian Group Co. Ltd. 寧波華聯集團股份有限公司	Ningbo 寧波市	Zhejiang 浙江省	(0574)7367626 (0574)7367652
Kaiyuan Wei Wei Electromechanical Building Materials Marketing Dept. 廈門市開元區威威機電建材經營部	Xiamen 廈門市	Fujian 福建省	(0592)2071044
Rudong Industry Product General Company 如東縣工業品總公司	Nantong 南通市	Jiangsu 江蘇省	(0513)4516110 (0513)4516110
Fujian Fu Ri Group Company 福建福日集團公司	Fuzhou 福州市	Fujian 福建省	(0591)3269325 (0591)3270426
Guangdong Hardware & Alternating Electrical Co. 廣東省五金交電公司	Guangzhou 廣州市	Guangdong 廣東省	(020)81884078 (020)81861287

*Also include sales by firms outside this industry.包括本行業以外廠家的銷售。"o" stands for "others". "o" 代表"其他產品"。

4072: Lamp Sockets 燈頭、燈座製造業

The industry accounts for 0.035% of the total revenue of China's industrial sector in 1996. The revenue growth rate of the industry is 40.8% from 1995, as compared to the growth rate of China's industrial sector, 9.51%. The rate of return on asset is 3.61%. 62.45% of all firms in the industry made a profit while 29.86% had negative returns. The top province in terms of the industry's revenue is Shanghai, accounting for 35.55% of the total revenue.
本行業在1996年佔全行業總產值0.035%，行業年增長率為40.8%（全國工業年增長率9.51%）。行業的資產回報率3.61%，62.45%的企業盈利，29.86%的企業虧損。銷售收入最高的省份為上海市，佔本行業的35.55%。

	Total number of firms 企業總數	Total number of employees 職工總數	Total revenue (mil. RMB) 總銷售收入（百萬元）	Total profit (mil. RMB) 總利潤（百萬元）	Return on assets 資產利潤率 (%)	Return on equity 權益利潤率 (%)	Labour productivity ('000 RMB / worker) 勞動生產率（千元／人）	Debts / assets 資產負債率 (%)	Total assets (mil. RMB) 總資產（百萬元）
Industry Overall 行業總體	232	29,817	2,055	97	3.61	10.91	68.92	66.89	2,671

	Number of firms 企業個數	Average number of employees 平均職工人數	Average revenue ('000 RMB) 平均銷售收入（千元）	Average profit ('000 RMB) 平均利潤（千元）	Return on assets 資產利潤率 (%)	Return on equity 權益利潤率 (%)	Labour productivity ('000 RMB / worker) 勞動生產率（千元／人）	Average debts / assets 平均資產負債率(%)	Average Total assets ('000 RMB) 平均總資產（千元）
By ownership 產業所有權									
State-owned 國有	26	201	4,231	-308	-3.60	-17.78	21.09	79.73	8,538
Collectively-owned 集體	171	97	4,672	100	2.73	19.17	47.92	85.74	3,673
Privately-owned 私有	2	10	482	20	4.14	6.07	48.24	31.72	472
Domestic JVs 聯營									
Joint stock 股份制	5	1,005	148,332	16,214	5.65	13.11	147.62	56.93	287,196
Foreign-funded 外資	9	135	12,536	496	3.97	9.06	92.56	56.11	12,488
Overseas Chinese-funded 港澳台資	19	101	15,338	119	0.83	2.77	151.71	70.18	14,337
By size 規模									
Large 大型	1	4,432	685,487	78,313	5.51	12.46	154.67	55.80	1,421,656
Medium 中型	2	811	45,911	129	0.39	1.37	56.65	71.52	33,061
Small 小型	227	106	5,633	81	1.56	7.77	53.23	79.97	5,216
By regional distribution 地區分布									
Central-North 華北	21	92	1,987	54	2.02	8.53	21.52	76.34	2,663
Beijing 北京	5	83	422	-38	-5.18	-65.52	5.07	92.10	734
Tianjin 天津	3	18	440	10	4.17	6.25	24.91	33.33	240
Hebei 河北	7	151	4,297	203	4.97	14.20	28.51	65.06	4,084
Shanxi 山西	2	160	3,705	50	0.49	4.00	23.16	87.85	10,250
Inner Mongolia 內蒙	4	24	200	-58	-9.43	1150.00	8.42	100.82	610
Northeast 東北	18	148	3,328	170	2.86	6.58	22.55	56.59	5,954
Liaoning 遼寧	15	156	3,940	240	3.68	7.92	25.28	53.55	6,524
Jilin 吉林	2	110	385	-270	-8.79	337.50	3.50	102.61	3,070
Heilongjiang 黑龍江	1	98	30				0.31	61.32	3,180
Central East 華東	108	150	11,510	818	4.33	12.32	76.51	64.83	18,874
Shanghai 上海	22	282	33,207	3,532	4.76	13.08	117.62	63.57	74,151
Jiangsu 江蘇	30	177	7,184	38	0.55	1.86	40.61	70.27	6,883
Zhejiang 浙江	30	68	6,057	210	6.91	18.31	88.81	62.28	3,045
Anhui 安徽	3	82	1,180	-13	-0.59	-4.08	14.39	85.78	2,273
Fujian 福建	7	28	1,761	-41	-2.31	-3.03	63.89	23.76	1,791
Jiangxi 江西	9	140	3,244	-89	-1.61	-21.11	23.25	92.37	5,504
Shandong 山東	7	141	10,040	613	10.63	34.76	71.13	69.43	5,766
Central-South 中南	64	116	10,650	93	1.36	5.86	91.94	76.73	6,817
Henan 河南	8	120	5,558	233	4.43	16.97	46.26	73.87	5,248
Hubei 湖北	9	173	2,542	-758	-12.31	116.78	14.72	110.54	6,154
Hunan 湖南	9	122	2,084	-23	-0.38	-0.79	17.15	52.06	6,130
Guangdong 廣東	36	105	16,489	313	4.01	16.31	157.58	75.44	7,820
Guangxi 廣西	1	8	60	10	4.35	4.55	7.50	4.35	230
Hainan 海南	1	30	1,860	-170	-8.42	-29.31	62.00	71.29	2,020
Southwest 西南	13	96	1,990	-119	-5.56	-28.03	20.81	80.11	2,143
Chongqing 重慶	4	158	4,000	-217	-6.13	-29.68	25.27	79.33	3,542
Sichuan 四川	6	48	961	-66	-4.05	-29.61	20.09	86.32	1,629
Guizhou 貴州	2	94	940	20	3.81	7.69	10.00	49.52	525
Yunnan 雲南	1	180	3,330	-380	-10.67	-40.86	18.50	73.88	3,560
Tibet 西藏									
Northwest 西北	8	40	304	-48	-7.12	-45.24	7.64	84.64	668
Shaanxi 陝西	3	67	363	-137	-13.23	105.13	5.42	112.58	1,033
Gansu 甘肅	2	36	250	10	1.94	3.70	7.04	48.54	515
Qinghai 青海	1	36	680	10	1.56	6.67	18.89	78.13	640
Ningxia 寧夏									
Xinjiang 新疆	2	5	80				16.00	5.26	285

4072: Lamp Sockets 燈頭、燈座製造業

Year 年份	Number of firms 企業個數	Rate of change 每年變化 (%)	Number of employees 職工人數 (人)	Rate of change 每年變化 (%)	Total revenue (mil. RMB) 總銷售收入 (百萬元)	Rate of change 每年變化 (%)	Total profit (mil. RMB) 總利潤 (百萬元)	Rate of change 每年變化 (%)
1993	215		27,358		570		8	
1994	246	14.42%	46,207	68.90%	2,374	316.21%	112	1290.96%
1995	257	4.47%	31,121	-32.65%	1,460	-38.48%	95	-15.19%
1996	232	-9.73%	29,817	-4.19%	2,055	40.75%	97	2.20%

3 Major products* 3 種主要產品 *	Output 產量	Sales volume 銷售量	Unit 單位
a) Lamp Holder 燈頭	484,513	460,287	10,000 piece 萬只
b) Lampstand 燈座	60,810	54,729	10,000 piece 萬只

Top 10 firms by revenue (year founded) 收入排名前 10 家企業 (創辦年份)	City 城市	Province 省	Telephone / fax 電話 / 傳真	Number of employees 職工人數	Ownership 產業所有權	Revenue ('000 RMB) 銷售收入 (千元)	Profit ('000 RMB) (rank) 利潤 (千元) (排名)	Total assets ('000 RMB) 總資產 (千元)	Major products 主要產品
Shanghai Jia Bao Industrial Group Co. Ltd. 上海嘉寶實業股份有限公司(1971)	Shanghai 上海市	Shanghai 上海市	(021)59162506 (021)59162452	4,833	Joint stock 股份制	666,442	85590(1)	1,557,567	a
Taishan International Electric Appliance Factory Co. Ltd. 台山市國際電器廠有限公司(1993)	Jiangmen 江門市	Guangdong 廣東省	(0750)5539768	620	Overseas Chinese-funded 港澳台資	197,350	3760(4)	73,960	o
Guangdong Taishan Science & Art Electric Appliance Co. Ltd. 廣東省台山市科藝電器有限公司(1994)	Jiangmen 江門市	Guangdong 廣東省	(0750)5456297 (0750)5456193	45	Collectively-owned 集體	122,400	160(37)	13,620	o
Ninghai Jia You Lamp Decoration Factory 寧海縣佳友燈飾廠(1993)	Ningbo 寧波市	Zhejiang 浙江省	(0574)5199231 (0574)5199231	310	Collectively-owned 集體	54,243	3855(3)	28,566	o
Wenzhou Fu Jia Electric Appliance Co. Ltd. 温州富嘉電器有限公司(1994)	Wenzhou 温州市	Zhejiang 浙江省	(0577)6811068 (0577)6819798	78	Foreign-funded 外資	51,670	170(35)	1,296	o
Qingdao Electrical Appliance Installation Parts Factory 青島電器裝置件廠(1969)	Qingdao 青島市	Shandong 山東省	(0532)7212078 (0532)7213882	246	Collectively-owned 集體	42,930	2670(5)	14,000	a
Gao Quan Electric Appliance Company 高權電器公司(1993)	Guangzhou 廣州市	Guangdong 廣東省	(020)82765992 (020)82765227	330	Overseas Chinese-funded 港澳台資	42,312	573(16)	13,834	o
Shunde Xing Tan Electric Appliance Plastic Cement Factory 順德市杏壇電器塑膠廠(1985)	Foshan 佛山市	Guangdong 廣東省	(0757)7777133 (0757)7775688	137	Collectively-owned 集體	35,898	148(40)	45,474	o
Taishan Da Jiang Pan Long Electric Equipment Plant 台山市大江蟠龍電器廠(1992)	Jiangmen 江門市	Guangdong 廣東省	(0750)5411950 (0750)5411096	78	Collectively-owned 集體	35,000	26(68)	5,044	o
Rugao Household Electric Equipment Plant 如皋市家用電器廠(1968)	Nantong 南通市	Jiangsu 江蘇省	(0513)7512419	545	Collectively-owned 集體	32,923	-797(101)	23,563	a,b

Top 10 Cities by Production Output 產出排名前 10 位城市	Province 省	Market share 市場份額	Number of firms 企業個數
Jiangmen 江門市	Guangdong 廣東省	20.37%	6
Qingdao 青島市	Shandong 山東省	7.59%	4
Wenzhou 温州市	Zhejiang 浙江省	6.83%	56
Ningbo 寧波市	Zhejiang 浙江省	6.28%	13
Shanghai 上海市	Shanghai 上海市	5.54%	37
Foshan 佛山市	Guangdong 廣東省	4.96%	7
Huizhou 惠州市	Guangdong 廣東省	4.52%	3
Guangzhou 廣州市	Guangdong 廣東省	4.50%	12
Taizhou 泰州市	Jiangsu 江蘇省	3.00%	4
Zhanjiang 湛江市	Guangdong 廣東省	2.57%	5

10 Major Wholesalers 10 家主要批發商	City 城市	Province 省	Telephone / Fax 電話 / 傳真
Changzhou Hardware Alternating-current Appliance and Chemical Wholesale General Company 常州五金交電化工批發總公司	Changzhou 常州市	Jiangsu 江蘇省	(0519)6609929 (0519)6609925
Suzhou Hardware & Alternating Electricity Co. Ltd. 蘇州五金交電股份有限公司	Suzhou 蘇州市	Jiangsu 江蘇省	(0512)5239572 (0512)5213248
Tianjin Foreign Trade General Company 天津市對外貿易總公司	Tianjin 天津市	Tianjin 天津市	(022)23310922
Chongqing International Trade Center 重慶國際貿易中心	Chongqing 重慶市	Chongqing 重慶市	(023)67853232 (023)67850402
China Chemical Plastics Co. Ltd. 中化塑料有限公司	Beijing 北京市	Beijing 北京市	(010)68569863 (010)68569041
Ningbo Hualian Group Co. Ltd. 寧波華聯集團股份有限公司	Ningbo 寧波市	Zhejiang 浙江省	(0574)7367626 (0574)7367652
Kaiyuan Wei Wei Electromechanical Building Materials Marketing Dept. 廈門市開元區威威機電建材經營部	Xiamen 廈門市	Fujian 福建省	(0592)2071044
Rudong Industry Product General Company 如東縣工業品總公司	Nantong 南通市	Jiangsu 江蘇省	(0513)4516110 (0513)4516110
Fujian Fu Ri Group Company 福建福日集團公司	Fuzhou 福州市	Fujian 福建省	(0591)3269325 (0591)3270426
Guangdong Hardware & Alternating Electrical Co. 廣東省五金交電公司	Guangzhou 廣州市	Guangdong 廣東省	(020)81884078 (020)81861287

*Also include sales by firms outside this industry.包括本行業以外廠家的銷售。"o" stands for "others". "o" 代表"其他產品"。

4073: Lamps and Lanterns 燈具製造業

The industry accounts for 0.123% of the total revenue of China's industrial sector in 1996. The revenue growth rate of the industry is 23.0% from 1995, as compared to the growth rate of China's industrial sector, 9.51%. The rate of return on asset is 1.25%. 64.65% of all firms in the industry made a profit while 28.57% had negative returns. The top province in terms of the industry's revenue is Guangdong, accounting for 29.90% of the total revenue.
本行業在1996年佔全行業總產值0.123%，行業年增長率為23.0%（全國工業年增長率9.51%）。行業的資產回報率1.25%，64.65%的企業盈利，28.57%的企業虧損。銷售收入最高的省份為廣東省，佔本行業的29.90%。

	Total number of firms 企業總數	Total number of employees 職工總數	Total revenue (mil. RMB) 總銷售收入（百萬元）	Total profit (mil. RMB) 總利潤（百萬元）	Return on assets 資產利潤率 (%)	Return on equity 權益利潤率 (%)	Labour productivity ('000 RMB / worker) 勞動生產率（千元/人）	Debts / assets 資產負債率 (%)	Total assets (mil. RMB) 總資產（百萬元）
Industry Overall 行業總體	1,107	94,458	7,104	88	1.25	3.63	75.21	65.64	7,033

	Number of firms 企業個數	Average number of employees 平均職工人數	Average revenue ('000 RMB) 平均銷售收入（千元）	Average profit ('000 RMB) 平均利潤（千元）	Return on assets 資產利潤率 (%)	Return on equity 權益利潤率 (%)	Labour productivity ('000 RMB / worker) 勞動生產率（千元/人）	Average debts / assets 平均資產負債率(%)	Average Total assets ('000 RMB) 平均總資產（千元）
By ownership 產業所有權									
State-owned 國有	80	144	4,363	-63	-0.66	-2.84	30.22	76.72	9,450
Collectively-owned 集體	854	72	4,613	52	1.15	3.33	64.28	65.36	4,534
Privately-owned 私有	4	91	10,147	392	6.54	14.03	112.12	53.40	5,991
Domestic JVs 聯營	9	270	18,383	289	1.42	5.99	68.14	76.28	20,339
Joint stock 股份制	11	79	7,305	190	2.79	14.25	92.47	80.44	6,818
Foreign-funded 外資	52	126	14,221	583	4.43	12.47	113.28	64.52	13,169
Overseas Chinese-funded 港澳台資	93	133	18,989	117	0.77	1.88	143.08	59.09	15,219
By size 規模									
Large 大型	1	1,725	137,151	300	0.30	0.74	79.51	59.19	99,449
Medium 中型	14	575	50,628	163	0.22	0.61	88.07	63.36	73,356
Small 小型	1,076	79	5,816	79	1.45	4.27	73.54	66.14	5,490
By regional distribution 地區分布									
Central-North 華北	167	60	3,559	41	0.71	1.82	58.83	61.16	5,850
Beijing 北京	65	46	5,661	-130	-1.28	-2.84	121.84	54.90	10,177
Tianjin 天津	35	77	1,813	151	5.11	20.91	23.40	75.54	2,955
Hebei 河北	39	67	3,476	276	7.17	23.88	52.25	70.00	3,850
Shanxi 山西	19	77	1,246	62	2.76	16.46	16.13	83.22	2,248
Inner Mongolia 內蒙	9	34	402	-206	-9.67	-52.56	11.72	81.60	2,126
Northeast 東北	127	85	2,013	44	1.46	3.92	23.78	62.78	3,019
Liaoning 遼寧	96	67	1,593	50	1.85	5.43	23.89	65.87	2,709
Jilin 吉林	9	89	2,137	-33	-0.86	-1.77	24.04	51.45	3,877
Heilongjiang 黑龍江	22	161	3,793	49	1.21	2.89	23.51	58.15	4,020
Central East 華東	497	82	7,261	111	1.76	5.53	88.18	68.10	6,309
Shanghai 上海	93	109	9,733	-65	-0.81	-2.94	89.61	72.57	8,068
Jiangsu 江蘇	153	71	5,886	79	1.48	4.89	82.86	69.71	5,320
Zhejiang 浙江	138	66	7,395	99	1.60	5.04	112.68	68.22	6,169
Anhui 安徽	25	117	7,665	372	4.63	20.31	65.25	77.19	8,024
Fujian 福建	23	82	9,036	120	1.51	2.46	110.08	38.67	7,943
Jiangxi 江西	15	25	867	-7	-1.00	-5.45	34.88	81.57	731
Shandong 山東	50	114	7,399	475	7.28	20.20	64.92	63.95	6,517
Central-South 中南	229	116	10,501	43	0.44	1.28	90.20	65.84	9,770
Henan 河南	40	106	3,016	61	1.18	9.77	28.36	87.92	5,130
Hubei 湖北	28	116	3,451	-70	-2.63	-20.70	29.83	87.26	2,658
Hunan 湖南	26	53	2,311	29	1.57	7.33	43.67	78.57	1,838
Guangdong 廣東	130	136	16,339	68	0.47	1.25	119.80	62.48	14,636
Guangxi 廣西	4	8	483	3	1.16	6.25	58.48	81.40	215
Hainan 海南	1	31	1,420	-310	-4.85	-5.42	45.81	10.49	6,390
Southwest 西南	59	72	2,346	15	0.41	1.08	32.45	61.80	3,526
Chongqing 重慶	22	79	3,622	21	0.46	1.24	45.62	62.72	4,466
Sichuan 四川	20	93	2,391	-78	-1.68	-4.48	25.67	62.52	4,664
Guizhou 貴州	9	35	602				16.99	51.50	891
Yunnan 雲南	8	43	724	-34	-3.19	-6.82	16.69	53.19	1,058
Tibet 西藏									
Northwest 西北	28	63	3,638	335	10.23	18.45	58.08	44.57	3,275
Shaanxi 陝西	12	97	7,769	812	14.28	24.01	80.44	40.52	5,683
Gansu 甘肅	5	34	544	4	0.32	1.10	15.91	71.07	1,258
Qinghai 青海	3	45	333	-3	-0.55	-1.52	7.41	64.29	607
Ningxia 寧夏	3	66	753	-97	-10.00	-47.54	11.47	78.62	967
Xinjiang 新疆	5	18	532	-16	-0.64	-1.12	28.91	42.59	2,498

4073: Lamps and Lanterns 燈具製造業

Year 年份	Number of firms 企業個數	Rate of change 每年變化 (%)	Number of employees 職工人數（人）	Rate of change 每年變化 (%)	Total revenue (mil. RMB) 總銷售收入（百萬元）	Rate of change 每年變化 (%)	Total profit (mil. RMB) 總利潤（百萬元）	Rate of change 每年變化 (%)
1993	1,197		108,537		4,160		145	
1994	1,274	6.43%	107,513	-0.94%	4,752	14.24%	99	-31.92%
1995	1,259	-1.18%	105,801	-1.59%	5,774	21.50%	95	-3.67%
1996	1107	-12.07%	94,458	-10.72%	7,104	23.03%	88	-7.56%

3 Major products* 3 種主要產品 *	Output 產量	Sales volume 銷售量	Unit 單位
a) Lamp Ballast 燈用鎮流器	9,352	9,165	10,000 piece 萬只

Top 10 firms by revenue (year founded) 收入排名前 10 家企業 (創辦年份)	City 城市	Province 省	Telephone / fax 電話 / 傳真	Number of employees 職工人數	Ownership 產業所有權	Revenue ('000 RMB) 銷售收入（千元）	Profit ('000 RMB) (rank) 利潤（千元）（排名）	Total assets ('000 RMB) 總資產（千元）	Major products 主要產品
Beijing Stone Panasonic Electric Engineering Co. Ltd. 北京四通松下電工有限公司(1995)	Beijing 北京市	Beijing 北京市	(010)67681176 (010)67681174	682	Foreign-funded 外資	316,330	-9369(469)	470,745	o
Guangdong Huabao Electric Factory 廣東華寶電器廠(1985)	Foshan 佛山市	Guangdong 廣東省	(0757)2291355 (0757)2291165	900	Collectively-owned 集體	244,823	-16643(472)	320,086	o
Shanghai Xiang Shan Lamps & Lanterns Factory 上海翔山燈具廠(1992)	Shanghai 上海市	Shanghai 上海市	(021)59204789 (021)59734784	139	Collectively-owned 集體	184,905	2638(22)	92,844	o
Taishan Si Jiu Zhen Taishan Jin Chun Ming Electric Appliance Co. Ltd. 台山市四九鎮台山金春明電器有限公司(1991)	Jiangmen 江門市	Guangdong 廣東省	(0750)5488087 (0750)5488286	153	Overseas Chinese-funded 港澳台資	161,740	98(211)	128,711	o
Shanghai Baoshan Luo Dian Dong Sheng Light Decorations Factory 上海寶山羅店東升燈飾廠(1992)	Shanghai 上海市	Shanghai 上海市	(021)56861548 (021)56861441	240	Collectively-owned 集體	153,673	3408(18)	60,869	o
Zhejiang Festival Lanterns General Factory 浙江節日燈總廠(1968)	Taizhou 臺州市	Zhejiang 浙江省	(0576)2441848 (0576)2443162	832	Collectively-owned 集體	133,058	119(193)	101,609	o
Weihai Jin Tong Industrial Co. Ltd. 威海金通實業有限公司(1984)	Weihai 威海市	Shandong 山東省	(0896)5584166 (0896)5584166	532	Collectively-owned 集體	125,226	9403(3)	44,600	a
Zhejiang Zhuguang Electrical Appliance (Group) Corp. 浙江珠光電器(集團)有限公司(1994)	Taizhou 臺州市	Zhejiang 浙江省	(0576)2443356 (0576)2443024	986	Collectively-owned 集體	107,069	192(157)	84,504	o
Yi Feng Electron (Huizhou) Co. Ltd. 藝豐電子(惠州)有限公司(1994)	Huizhou 惠州市	Guangdong 廣東省	(0751)2291143 (0751)2291143	321	Overseas Chinese-funded 港澳台資	98,200	-885(447)	9,000	o
Fuzhou Hua Photoelectric Device Co. Ltd. 福州市華光電器有限公司(1993)	Fuzhou 福州市	Fujian 福建省	(0591)7910649	385	Foreign-funded 外資	97,850	4767(11)	55,377	o

Top 10 Cities by Production Output 產出排名前 10 位城市	Province 省	Market share 市場份額	Number of firms 企業個數
Shanghai 上海市	Shanghai 上海市	11.44%	148
Shenzhen 深圳市	Guangdong 廣東省	10.34%	19
Foshan 佛山市	Guangdong 廣東省	6.85%	20
Ningbo 寧波市	Zhejiang 浙江省	6.56%	40
Taizhou 臺州市	Zhejiang 浙江省	5.90%	24
Jiangmen 江門市	Guangdong 廣東省	5.48%	15
Suzhou 蘇州市	Jiangsu 江蘇省	5.08%	55
Guangzhou 廣州市	Guangdong 廣東省	3.86%	69
Huizhou 惠州市	Guangdong 廣東省	3.68%	31
Beijing 北京市	Beijing 北京市	3.32%	56

10 Major Wholesalers 10 家主要批發商	City 城市	Province 省	Telephone / Fax 電話 / 傳真
Changzhou Hardware Alternating-current Appliance and Chemical Wholesale General Company 常州五金交電化工批發總公司	Changzhou 常州市	Jiangsu 江蘇省	(0519)6609929 (0519)6609925
Suzhou Hardware & Alternating Electricity Co. Ltd. 蘇州五金交電股份有限公司	Suzhou 蘇州市	Jiangsu 江蘇省	(0512)5239572 (0512)5213248
Tianjin Foreign Trade General Company 天津市對外貿易總公司	Tianjin 天津市	Tianjin 天津市	(022)23310922
Chongqing International Trade Center 重慶國際貿易中心	Chongqing 重慶市	Chongqing 重慶市	(023)67853232 (023)67850402
China Chemical Plastics Co. Ltd. 中化塑料有限公司	Beijing 北京市	Beijing 北京市	(010)68569863 (010)68569041
Ningbo Hualian Group Co. Ltd. 寧波華聯集團股份有限公司	Ningbo 寧波市	Zhejiang 浙江省	(0574)7367626 (0574)7367652
Kaiyuan Wei Wei Electromechanical Building Materials Marketing Dept. 廈門市開元區威威機電建材經營部	Xiamen 廈門市	Fujian 福建省	(0592)2071044
Rudong Industry Product General Company 如東縣工業品總公司	Nantong 南通市	Jiangsu 江蘇省	(0513)4516110 (0513)4516110
Fujian Fu Ri Group Company 福建福日集團公司	Fuzhou 福州市	Fujian 福建省	(0591)3269325 (0591)3270426
Guangdong Hardware & Alternating Electrical Co. 廣東省五金交電公司	Guangzhou 廣州市	Guangdong 廣東省	(020)81884078 (020)81861287

*Also include sales by firms outside this industry.包括本行業以外廠家的銷售。"o" stands for "others". "o" 代表 "其他產品"。

4074: Lamp Appliance Accessories 燈用電器附件製造業

The industry accounts for 0.052% of the total revenue of China's industrial sector in 1996. The revenue growth rate of the industry is 3.7% from 1995, as compared to the growth rate of China's industrial sector, 9.51%. The rate of return on asset is 1.43%. 70.64% of all firms in the industry made a profit while 22.77% had negative returns. The top province in terms of the industry's revenue is Guangdong, accounting for 36.42% of the total revenue.
本行業在1996年佔全行業總產值0.052%，行業年增長率為3.7%（全國工業年增長率9.51%）。行業的資產回報率1.43%，70.64%的企業盈利，22.77%的企業虧損。銷售收入最高的省份為廣東省，佔本行業的36.42%。

	Total number of firms 企業總數	Total number of employees 職工總數	Total revenue (mil. RMB) 總銷售收入（百萬元）	Total profit (mil. RMB) 總利潤（百萬元）	Return on assets 資產利潤率 (%)	Return on equity 權益利潤率 (%)	Labour productivity ('000 RMB / worker) 勞動生產率（千元/人）	Debts / assets 資產負債率 (%)	Total assets (mil. RMB) 總資產（百萬元）
Industry Overall 行業總體	472	30,643	3,002	41	1.43	3.40	97.97	57.95	2,848

	Number of firms 企業個數	Average number of employees 平均職工人數	Average revenue ('000 RMB) 平均銷售收入（千元）	Average profit ('000 RMB) 平均利潤（千元）	Return on assets 資產利潤率 (%)	Return on equity 權益利潤率 (%)	Labour productivity ('000 RMB / worker) 勞動生產率（千元/人）	Average debts / assets 平均資產負債率(%)	Average Total assets ('000 RMB) 平均總資產（千元）
By ownership 產業所有權									
State-owned 國有	45	92	7,556	222	3.21	11.63	81.93	72.44	6,933
Collectively-owned 集體	346	54	2,777	53	1.87	6.09	51.72	69.21	2,843
Privately-owned 私有	1	16	12	-3	-1.04	-1.19	0.77	12.04	249
Domestic JVs 聯營	4	57	2,419	-3	-0.15	-0.33	42.82	54.62	2,172
Joint stock 股份制	3	52	12,952	-91	-3.52	-15.71	249.08	77.57	2,596
Foreign-funded 外資	36	115	33,025	708	3.07	7.35	288.15	58.15	23,038
Overseas Chinese-funded 港澳台資	38	97	12,220	-333	-1.79	-2.77	125.50	35.42	18,586
By size 規模									
Large 大型	2	527	383,127	3,311	1.45	2.28	727.69	36.55	228,700
Medium 中型									
Small 小型	468	64	4,779	73	1.44	3.79	75.03	62.03	5,109
By regional distribution 地區分布									
Central-North 華北	50	57	1,859	60	3.20	6.81	32.87	52.98	1,868
Beijing 北京	20	18	1,019	32	2.27	4.30	55.23	47.32	1,391
Tianjin 天津	13	102	3,518	82	2.69	5.27	34.52	48.95	3,030
Hebei 河北	12	72	1,766	110	6.69	17.72	24.38	62.26	1,645
Shanxi 山西	2	109	940	-100	-4.13	-18.18	8.66	77.27	2,420
Inner Mongolia 內蒙	3	16	1,257	60	11.18	30.00	78.54	62.73	537
Northeast 東北	53	49	2,261	71	3.70	12.50	46.42	70.35	1,915
Liaoning 遼寧	36	50	1,544	28	1.30	5.12	30.75	74.61	2,182
Jilin 吉林	4	34	348	40	5.65	25.00	10.30	77.03	708
Heilongjiang 黑龍江	13	49	4,835	198	12.81	27.16	98.37	52.78	1,549
Central East 華東	207	62	7,401	111	1.39	3.45	119.59	59.79	8,026
Shanghai 上海	36	98	21,590	72	0.25	0.56	221.31	56.13	29,336
Jiangsu 江蘇	52	79	5,535	282	4.97	12.86	70.48	61.34	5,667
Zhejiang 浙江	55	32	2,285	77	3.40	8.68	72.24	60.78	2,261
Anhui 安徽	13	44	1,432	35	2.48	4.55	32.90	45.39	1,393
Fujian 福建	20	20	1,545	43	3.39	6.33	78.01	46.52	1,256
Jiangxi 江西	17	78	903	-20	-1.24	16.27	11.63	107.60	1,609
Shandong 山東	14	85	19,739	44	0.53	2.93	231.84	82.02	8,268
Central-South 中南	120	89	10,036	109	1.45	3.13	112.70	53.65	7,533
Henan 河南	19	60	2,234	49	2.55	8.80	37.04	71.03	1,940
Hubei 湖北	19	29	2,345	57	5.00	18.23	80.72	72.58	1,148
Hunan 湖南	9	22	1,346	68	6.18	22.51	61.47	72.54	1,097
Guangdong 廣東	61	141	17,925	168	1.26	2.59	126.74	51.48	13,412
Guangxi 廣西	12	14	982	17	1.16	7.60	71.83	84.74	1,436
Hainan 海南									
Southwest 西南	28	42	1,572	-59	-2.95	-12.31	37.55	76.04	2,011
Chongqing 重慶	10	40	1,387	25	1.72	6.49	34.76	73.51	1,425
Sichuan 四川	13	40	1,748	-121	-5.31	-17.36	43.64	69.40	2,279
Guizhou 貴州									
Yunnan 雲南	5	51	1,478	-66	-2.66	-51.56	28.98	94.84	2,482
Tibet 西藏									
Northwest 西北	14	40	621	-39	-1.70	-2.34	15.37	27.17	2,264
Shaanxi 陝西	7	47	933	33	4.28	16.91	19.91	74.49	767
Gansu 甘肅	4	35	388	3	0.36	0.96	10.99	62.99	703
Qinghai 青海									
Ningxia 寧夏									
Xinjiang 新疆	3	32	207	-260	-3.32	-3.77	6.39	12.08	7,837

4074: Lamp Appliance Accessories 燈用電器附件製造業

Year 年份	Number of firms 企業個數	Rate of change 每年變化 (%)	Number of employees 職工人數 (人)	Rate of change 每年變化 (%)	Total revenue (mil. RMB) 總銷售收入 (百萬元)	Rate of change 每年變化 (%)	Total profit (mil. RMB) 總利潤 (百萬元)	Rate of change 每年變化 (%)
1993	422		47,590		814		22	
1994	465	10.19%	30,470	-35.97%	1,074	31.89%	27	23.53%
1995	528	13.55%	39,384	29.26%	2,896	169.73%	40	48.36%
1996	472	-10.61%	30,643	-22.19%	3,002	3.66%	41	2.94%

3 Major products* 3 種主要產品 *	Output 產量	Sales volume 銷售量	Unit 單位
a) Lamp Ballast 燈用鎮流器	17,584	17,232	10,000 piece 萬只

Top 10 firms by revenue (year founded) 收入排名前 10 家企業 (創辦年份)	City 城市	Province 省	Telephone / fax 電話 / 傳真	Number of employees 職工人數	Ownership 產業所有權	Revenue ('000 RMB) 銷售收入 (千元)	Profit ('000 RMB) (rank) 利潤 (千元) (排名)	Total assets ('000 RMB) 總資產 (千元)	Major products 主要產品
Philips Lighting Ebt (Shanghai) Co. Ltd. 飛利浦照明電子上海有限公司(1993)	Shanghai 上海市	Shanghai 上海市	(021)64855330 (021)64853915	478	Foreign-funded 外資	546,449	4297(3)	753,683	o
Chung Tak Lighting Control Systems (Panyu) Ltd. 番禺中德電控有限公司(1994)	Guangzhou 廣州市	Guangdong 廣東省	(020)84874803 (020)84876109	640	Foreign-funded 外資	295,700	-15(133)	146	a
Qingdao Hosiden Electronics Co. Ltd. 青島星電電子有限公司(1992)	Qingdao 青島市	Shandong 山東省	(0532)4847830 (0532)4817832	730	Foreign-funded 外資	264,977	1930(9)	80,766	o
Guangzhou State-owned Jiu Fo Electrical Appliance Industrial Co. Ltd. 廣州市國營九佛電器實業有限公司(1980)	Guangzhou 廣州市	Guangdong 廣東省	(020)87811438 (020)87811073	1,352	State-owned 國有	239,902	13020(1)	181,861	a
Shenzhen Tong Cheng Industrial Co. Ltd. 深圳通成實業有限公司(1992)	Shenzhen 深圳市	Guangdong 廣東省	(0755)5351682 (0755)5551845	791	Overseas Chinese-funded 港澳台資	93,449	313(49)	213,145	o
Shanghai Xu Fu Electron Co. Ltd. 上海旭福電子有限公司(1995)	Shanghai 上海市	Shanghai 上海市	(021)64702682 (021)64702682	1,045	Overseas Chinese-funded 港澳台資	85,704	-5732(166)	169,969	o
Suzhou Chengnan Industrial Co. 蘇州市城南實業公司(1992)	Suzhou 蘇州市	Jiangsu 江蘇省	(0512)5250012	50	Collectively-owned 集體	50,820	1034(18)	18,283	o
Chengdu Shuang Xing Electric Appliance Co. Ltd. 成都雙星電器有限責任公司(1966)	Chengdu 成都市	Sichuan 四川省	(028)8522668 (028)8522484	469	Joint stock 股份制	47,773	2474(7)	71,902	o
Guangzhou Hong Chang Electrical Appliance Hardware Products Co. Ltd. 廣州宏昌電器五金製品有限公司(1994)	Guangzhou 廣州市	Guangdong 廣東省	(020)87811099 (020)87811339	62	Overseas Chinese-funded 港澳台資	45,203	2699(6)	25,709	o
Guangzhou Huichang Electrical Appliance Co. Ltd. 廣州匯昌電器有限公司(1991)	Guangzhou 廣州市	Guangdong 廣東省	(020)87480084 (020)87811073	68	Overseas Chinese-funded 港澳台資	42,759	2031(8)	30,281	o

Top 10 Cities by Production Output 產出排名前 10 位城市	Province 省	Market share 市場份額	Number of firms 企業個數
Shanghai 上海市	Shanghai 上海市	33.20%	83
Guangzhou 廣州市	Guangdong 廣東省	21.11%	45
Yangzhou 揚州市	Jiangsu 江蘇省	2.90%	9
Nanning 南寧市	Guangxi 廣西	2.90%	5
Zhanjiang 湛江市	Guangdong 廣東省	2.04%	1
Hangzhou 杭州市	Zhejiang 浙江省	2.03%	24
Nangping 南平市	Fujian 福建省	2.02%	4
Chengdu 成都市	Sichuan 四川省	1.94%	4
Ningbo 寧波市	Zhejiang 浙江省	1.90%	15
Nanjing 南京市	Jiangsu 江蘇省	1.74%	20

10 Major Wholesalers 10 家主要批發商	City 城市	Province 省	Telephone / Fax 電話 / 傳真
Changzhou Hardware Alternating-current Appliance and Chemical Wholesale General Company 常州五金交電化工批發總公司	Changzhou 常州市	Jiangsu 江蘇省	(0519)6609929 (0519)6609925
Suzhou Hardware & Alternating Electricity Co. Ltd. 蘇州五金交電股份有限公司	Suzhou 蘇州市	Jiangsu 江蘇省	(0512)5239572 (0512)5213248
Tianjin Foreign Trade General Company 天津市對外貿易總公司	Tianjin 天津市	Tianjin 天津市	(022)23310922
Chongqing International Trade Center 重慶國際貿易中心	Chongqing 重慶市	Chongqing 重慶市	(023)67853232 (023)67850402
China Chemical Plastics Co. Ltd. 中化塑料有限公司	Beijing 北京市	Beijing 北京市	(010)68569863 (010)68569041
Ningbo Hualian Group Co. Ltd. 寧波華聯集團股份有限公司	Ningbo 寧波市	Zhejiang 浙江省	(0574)7367626 (0574)7367652
Kaiyuan Wei Wei Electromechanical Building Materials Marketing Dept. 廈門市開元區威威機電建材經營部	Xiamen 廈門市	Fujian 福建省	(0592)2071044
Rudong Industry Product General Company 如東縣工業品總公司	Nantong 南通市	Jiangsu 江蘇省	(0513)4516110 (0513)4516110
Fujian Fu Ri Group Company 福建福日集團公司	Fuzhou 福州市	Fujian 福建省	(0591)3269325 (0591)3270426
Guangdong Hardware & Alternating Electrical Co. 廣東省五金交電公司	Guangzhou 廣州市	Guangdong 廣東省	(020)81884078 (020)81861287

*Also include sales by firms outside this industry.包括本行業以外廠家的銷售。"o" stands for "others". "o" 代表 "其他產品"。

4079: Other Lighting Equipment 其他照明器具製造業

The industry accounts for 0.032% of the total revenue of China's industrial sector in 1996. The revenue growth rate of the industry is 3.9% from 1995, as compared to the growth rate of China's industrial sector, 9.51%. The rate of return on asset is 0.61%. 75.12% of all firms in the industry made a profit while 23.35% had negative returns. The top province in terms of the industry's revenue is Guangdong, accounting for 42.52% of the total revenue.
本行業在1996年佔全行業總產值0.032%，行業年增長率為3.9%（全國工業年增長率9.51%）。行業的資產回報率0.61%，75.12%的企業盈利，23.35%的企業虧損。銷售收入最高的省份為廣東省，佔本行業的42.52%。

	Total number of firms 企業總數	Total number of employees 職工總數	Total revenue (mil. RMB) 總銷售收入（百萬元）	Total profit (mil. RMB) 總利潤（百萬元）	Return on assets 資產利潤率 (%)	Return on equity 權益利潤率 (%)	Labour productivity ('000 RMB / worker) 勞動生產率（千元/人）	Debts / assets 資產負債率 (%)	Total assets (mil. RMB) 總資產（百萬元）
Industry Overall 行業總體	282	37,550	1,850	14	0.61	1.93	49.27	68.29	2,326

	Number of firms 企業個數	Average number of employees 平均職工人數	Average revenue ('000 RMB) 平均銷售收入（千元）	Average profit ('000 RMB) 平均利潤（千元）	Return on assets 資產利潤率 (%)	Return on equity 權益利潤率 (%)	Labour productivity ('000 RMB / worker) 勞動生產率（千元/人）	Average debts / assets 平均資產負債率(%)	Average Total assets ('000 RMB) 平均總資產（千元）
By ownership 產業所有權									
State-owned 國有	24	402	27,500	208	0.48	1.39	68.41	65.09	43,083
Collectively-owned 集體	218	101	3,245	20	0.51	1.94	31.97	73.70	3,980
Privately-owned 私有									
Domestic JVs 聯營	2	70	2,687	22	2.31	2.75	38.67	15.87	943
Joint stock 股份制	4	490	18,847	201	0.92	4.33	38.44	78.72	21,820
Foreign-funded 外資	12	79	10,820	-7	-0.10	-0.38	136.24	74.81	7,472
Overseas Chinese-funded 港澳台資	21	160	12,972	181	1.55	3.59	81.20	56.82	11,694
By size 規模									
Large 大型	1	3,867	352,208	3,114	0.78	2.15	91.08	63.48	397,151
Medium 中型	10	904	51,863	-199	-0.21	-0.94	57.40	77.45	94,264
Small 小型	267	94	3,669	48	1.31	3.38	39.24	61.43	3,693
By regional distribution 地區分布									
Central-North 華北	22	55	1,760	-157	-3.87	-6.88	32.11	43.77	4,055
Beijing 北京	8	26	1,370	-506	-8.06	-12.60	53.73	36.03	6,280
Tianjin 天津	10	83	1,488	17	0.64	1.46	17.95	56.31	2,671
Hebei 河北	3	55	4,283	140	4.51	11.41	78.35	60.47	3,103
Shanxi 山西	1	9	40	10	0.34	0.37	4.44	9.49	2,950
Inner Mongolia 內蒙									
Northeast 東北	18	130	5,982	-47	-0.30	-1.31	45.97	77.35	15,865
Liaoning 遼寧	6	104	1,355	47	5.98	16.09	13.01	62.82	780
Jilin 吉林	6	248	14,333	-285	-0.62	-2.78	57.72	77.83	46,268
Heilongjiang 黑龍江	6	38	2,257	97	17.68	41.73	59.65	57.62	547
Central East 華東	148	97	4,480	131	3.08	10.82	46.12	71.52	4,241
Shanghai 上海	16	103	3,502	131	3.59	41.92	34.16	91.43	3,656
Jiangsu 江蘇	43	82	6,944	313	5.51	19.38	85.02	71.54	5,680
Zhejiang 浙江	29	81	3,436	94	2.06	6.25	42.44	66.98	4,580
Anhui 安徽	35	113	2,260	98	11.23	36.02	19.99	68.81	875
Fujian 福建	5	71	1,850	-8	-0.42	-0.54	25.91	23.33	1,920
Jiangxi 江西	8	79	1,765	14	0.81	4.09	22.27	80.24	1,701
Shandong 山東	12	161	8,855	-207	-1.79	-6.09	55.09	70.52	11,517
Central-South 中南	84	204	11,126	-16	-0.12	-0.33	54.51	64.99	13,638
Henan 河南	9	219	7,734	46	0.47	2.34	35.28	79.93	9,707
Hubei 湖北	2	29	865	55	8.09	-57.89	29.83	113.97	680
Hunan 湖南	12	126	2,334	19	1.06	2.01	18.56	47.50	1,816
Guangdong 廣東	53	230	14,841	-40	-0.21	-0.60	64.40	64.10	18,874
Guangxi 廣西	7	196	6,786	20	0.42	1.09	34.65	61.24	4,747
Hainan 海南	1	20	1,120	-70	-4.46	-25.93	56.00	82.80	1,570
Southwest 西南	7	204	11,243	81	0.49	2.61	55.19	81.41	16,764
Chongqing 重慶	1	19	36	-10	-2.42	-3.24	1.93	25.39	420
Sichuan 四川	6	225	12,488	91	0.49	2.66	55.61	81.55	18,580
Guizhou 貴州									
Yunnan 雲南									
Tibet 西藏									
Northwest 西北	3	351	9,107	-13	-0.07	-0.19	25.92	65.04	20,183
Shaanxi 陝西									
Gansu 甘肅	3	351	9,107	-13	-0.07	-0.19	25.92	65.04	20,183
Qinghai 青海									
Ningxia 寧夏									
Xinjiang 新疆									

4079: Other Lighting Equipment 其他照明器具製造業

Year 年份	Number of firms 企業個數	Rate of change 每年變化 (%)	Number of employees 職工人數 (人)	Rate of change 每年變化 (%)	Total revenue (mil. RMB) 總銷售收入 (百萬元)	Rate of change 每年變化 (%)	Total profit (mil. RMB) 總利潤 (百萬元)	Rate of change 每年變化 (%)
1993	282		42,812		1,349		40	
1994	268	-4.97%	38,362	-10.40%	1,631	20.93%	48	20.82%
1995	318	18.66%	45,110	17.59%	1,780	9.14%	15	-68.98%
1996	282	-11.32%	37,550	-16.76%	1,850	3.93%	14	-5.74%

3 Major products* 3 種主要產品 *	Output 產量	Sales volume 銷售量	Unit 單位
a) Electric Torch 手電筒	32,440	29,845	10,000 piece 萬只

Top 10 firms by revenue (year founded) 收入排名前 10 家企業 (創辦年份)	City 城市	Province 省	Telephone / fax 電話 / 傳真	Number of employees 職工人數	Ownership 產業所有權	Revenue ('000 RMB) 銷售收入 (千元)	Profit ('000 RMB) (rank) 利潤 (千元) (排名)	Total assets ('000 RMB) 總資產 (千元)	Major products 主要產品
Guangzhou Flashlight Industrial Co. 廣州市電筒工業公司(1965)	Guangzhou 廣州市	Guangdong 廣東省	(020)81814325 (020)81814850	3,895	State-owned 國有	407,120	4145(2)	403,216	a
China No.5 Mine Group Siping Moly-b Metal Material General Factory 中國五礦集團四平鉬鉬材料總廠(1970)	Siping 四平市	Jilin 吉林省	(0434)3388043 (0434)3388516	560	State-owned 國有	82,830	-1934(128)	273,140	o
Zigong Tong Ming Flashlights & Lighting Equipment Factory 自貢市通明電筒燈具總廠(1929)	Zigong 自貢市	Sichuan 四川省	(0813)3301555 (0813)3301723	1,222	State-owned 國有	76,857	644(14)	115,809	a
Guangzhou Panyu Hai Ou Group Co. 廣州市番禺海鷗集團公司(1958)	Guangzhou 廣州市	Guangdong 廣東省	(020)84896762 (020)84896418	922	Collectively-owned 集體	69,750	7(100)	163,770	a
Nantong Minami Electric Co. Ltd. 南通南方電器有限公司(1988)	Nantong 南通市	Jiangsu 江蘇省	(0513)5517421 (0513)5517142	118	Foreign-funded 外資	63,847	3671(3)	45,012	o
Qingdao Li Yan Electric Appliance Co. Ltd. 青島理研電器有限公司(1992)	Qingdao 青島市	Shandong 山東省	(0532)7898457 (0532)7898457	218	Foreign-funded 外資	55,147	795(11)	46,181	o
Shanghai Baoshan Chuan Sha Multiple-producing Factory 上海寶山川沙綜合廠(1985)	Shanghai 上海市	Shanghai 上海市	(021)56870371	380	Collectively-owned 集體	44,095	29(81)	18,482	o
Chaozhou Electric Flashlight Lamps & Lanterns General Factory 潮州市電筒燈具總廠(1979)	Chaozhou 潮州市	Guangdong 廣東省	(0768)2262821 (0768)2261594	1,088	Collectively-owned 集體	43,000	41(76)	72,307	a
Yangzhou Ma Li Te Lamps & Lanterns Co. Ltd. 揚州瑪利特燈具有限公司(1990)	Yangzhou 揚州市	Jiangsu 江蘇省	(0514)8213746 (0514)8213137	521	Overseas Chinese-funded 港澳台資	42,724	789(12)	41,030	o
Wuzhou Flashlight Industrial Company 梧州市電筒工業公司(1966)	Wuzhou 梧州市	Guangxi 廣西	(0774)5824518 (0774)5824518	908	Collectively-owned 集體	39,116	164(44)	23,341	a

Top 10 Cities by Production Output 產出排名前 10 位城市	Province 省	Market share 市場份額	Number of firms 企業個數
Guangzhou 廣州市	Guangdong 廣東省	28.38%	21
Taizhou 臺州市	Zhejiang 浙江省	19.21%	346
Zigong 自貢市	Sichuan 四川省	4.73%	3
Siping 四平市	Jilin 吉林省	4.09%	3
Chaozhou 潮州市	Guangdong 廣東省	3.96%	6
Anyang 安陽市	Henan 河南省	3.39%	1
Shanghai 上海市	Shanghai 上海市	2.95%	22
Qingdao 青島市	Shandong 山東省	2.60%	2
Nantong 南通市	Jiangsu 江蘇省	2.26%	29
Wuzhou 梧州市	Guangxi 廣西	2.03%	2

10 Major Wholesalers 10 家主要批發商	City 城市	Province 省	Telephone / Fax 電話 / 傳真
Changzhou Hardware Alternating-current Appliance and Chemical Wholesale General Company 常州五金交電化工批發總公司	Changzhou 常州市	Jiangsu 江蘇省	(0519)6609929 (0519)6609925
Suzhou Hardware & Alternating Electricity Co. Ltd. 蘇州五金交電股份有限公司	Suzhou 蘇州市	Jiangsu 江蘇省	(0512)5239572 (0512)5213248
Tianjin Foreign Trade General Company 天津市對外貿易總公司	Tianjin 天津市	Tianjin 天津市	(022)23310922
Chongqing International Trade Center 重慶國際貿易中心	Chongqing 重慶市	Chongqing 重慶市	(023)67853232 (023)67850402
China Chemical Plastics Co. Ltd. 中化塑料有限公司	Beijing 北京市	Beijing 北京市	(010)68569863 (010)68569041
Ningbo Hualian Group Co. Ltd. 寧波華聯集團股份有限公司	Ningbo 寧波市	Zhejiang 浙江省	(0574)7367626 (0574)7367652
Kaiyuan Wei Wei Electromechanical Building Materials Marketing Dept. 廈門市開元區威威機電建材經營部	Xiamen 廈門市	Fujian 福建省	(0592)2071044
Rudong Industry Product General Company 如東縣工業品總公司	Nantong 南通市	Jiangsu 江蘇省	(0513)4516110 (0513)4516110
Fujian Fu Ri Group Company 福建福日集團公司	Fuzhou 福州市	Fujian 福建省	(0591)3269325 (0591)3270426
Guangdong Hardware & Alternating Electrical Co. 廣東省五金交電公司	Guangzhou 廣州市	Guangdong 廣東省	(020)81884078 (020)81861287

*Also include sales by firms outside this industry.包括本行業以外廠家的銷售。"o" stands for "others". "o" 代表"其他產品"。

4080: Electrical Machinery Repairing 電氣機械修理業

The industry accounts for 0.018% of the total revenue of China's industrial sector in 1996. The revenue growth rate of the industry is 14.7% from 1995, as compared to the growth rate of China's industrial sector, 9.51%. The rate of return on asset is 2.01%. 71.70% of all firms in the industry made a profit while 17.28% had negative returns. The top province in terms of the industry's revenue is Liaoning, accounting for 43.14% of the total revenue.
本行業在1996年佔全行業總產值0.018%，行業年增長率為14.7%（全國工業年增長率9.51%）。行業的資產回報率2.01%，71.70%的企業盈利，17.28%的企業虧損。銷售收入最高的省份為遼寧省，佔本行業的43.14%。

	Total number of firms 企業總數	Total number of employees 職工總數	Total revenue (mil. RMB) 總銷售收入（百萬元）	Total profit (mil. RMB) 總利潤（百萬元）	Return on assets 資產利潤率 (%)	Return on equity 權益利潤率 (%)	Labour productivity ('000 RMB / worker) 勞動生產率（千元/人）	Debts / assets 資產負債率 (%)	Total assets (mil. RMB) 總資產（百萬元）
Industry Overall 行業總體	791	30,868	1,059	17	2.01	5.74	34.31	64.88	848

	Number of firms 企業個數	Average number of employees 平均職工人數	Average revenue ('000 RMB) 平均銷售收入（千元）	Average profit ('000 RMB) 平均利潤（千元）	Return on assets 資產利潤率 (%)	Return on equity 權益利潤率 (%)	Labour productivity ('000 RMB / worker) 勞動生產率（千元/人）	Average debts / assets 平均資產負債率(%)	Average Total assets ('000 RMB) 平均總資產（千元）
By ownership 產業所有權									
State-owned 國有	144	25	500	-42	-4.23	-13.95	19.89	69.72	986
Collectively-owned 集體	627	42	1,240	30	3.01	8.27	29.69	63.65	994
Privately-owned 私有	3	23	193	-2	-3.16	-5.14	8.37	38.46	50
Domestic JVs 聯營	2	46	2,775	88	4.57	29.79	60.33	84.65	1,935
Joint stock 股份制	2	836	96,964	2,033	7.41	41.09	116.05	81.96	27,423
Foreign-funded 外資	3	48	274	-175	-3.89	-5.58	5.74	30.31	4,496
Overseas Chinese-funded 港澳台資	9	20	851	60	5.35	6.53	41.64	18.09	1,132
By size 規模									
Large 大型									
Medium 中型	2	1,129	92,039	1,357	3.16	15.48	81.56	79.60	42,943
Small 小型	784	38	1,115	18	1.88	5.10	29.71	63.20	972
By regional distribution 地區分布									
Central-North 華北	189	24	492	16	2.55	8.41	20.60	69.70	615
Beijing 北京	46	6	248	-6	-1.94	-4.35	40.25	55.39	314
Tianjin 天津	67	17	233	17	5.87	389.66	13.86	98.49	287
Hebei 河北	26	32	1,113	38	3.33	10.02	34.77	66.78	1,132
Shanxi 山西	24	64	988		0.03	0.09	15.45	65.18	1,387
Inner Mongolia 內蒙	26	28	512	43	5.66	15.80	18.07	64.11	761
Northeast 東北	289	53	2,081	69	5.90	16.64	39.47	64.55	1,172
Liaoning 遼寧	166	66	2,752	94	6.51	18.75	41.56	65.29	1,443
Jilin 吉林	44	36	620	12	1.80	8.12	17.03	77.79	643
Heilongjiang 黑龍江	79	33	1,487	49	5.47	12.65	44.39	56.79	898
Central East 華東	171	30	1,167	84	7.20	18.97	38.61	62.04	1,169
Shanghai 上海	74	23	1,470	140	21.82	57.36	62.91	61.96	640
Jiangsu 江蘇	13	27	1,072	17	0.36	0.74	39.46	50.75	4,641
Zhejiang 浙江	15	28	998	67	12.50	31.15	36.07	59.75	533
Anhui 安徽	14	39	1,421	44	2.31	6.95	36.92	66.77	1,917
Fujian 福建	13	8	205	8	6.80	11.49	26.08	40.82	113
Jiangxi 江西	16	17	607	15	2.68	12.37	36.64	78.21	559
Shandong 山東	26	68	1,138	72	4.00	14.24	16.76	71.88	1,806
Central-South 中南	86	38	1,453		0.01	0.03	38.08	77.42	1,564
Henan 河南	18	37	1,496	36	1.95	7.97	40.86	75.47	1,848
Hubei 湖北	12	57	1,470	-5	-0.35	-0.97	25.87	63.41	1,414
Hunan 湖南	22	61	2,450	14	0.66	2.15	40.07	69.36	2,135
Guangdong 廣東	25	19	1,006	-31	-2.19	-195.00	51.94	98.88	1,424
Guangxi 廣西	9	12	148	-12	-6.29	-9.02	11.98	30.29	194
Hainan 海南									
Southwest 西南	34	52	882	-591	-42.67	-64.77	17.06	34.17	1,384
Chongqing 重慶	5	48	1,606	384	110.22	162.62	33.59	32.22	349
Sichuan 四川	18	26	672	32	4.27	11.97	25.97	64.28	742
Guizhou 貴州	8	14	75				5.36	61.54	65
Yunnan 雲南	3	313	2,977	-7,567	-71.86	-91.35	9.51	21.37	10,530
Tibet 西藏									
Northwest 西北	22	41	462	-6	-1.11	-2.46	11.20	54.79	531
Shaanxi 陝西	10	41	176	2	2.02	7.69	4.31	73.74	99
Gansu 甘肅	3	46	950	37	5.05	9.09	20.50	44.50	727
Qinghai 青海	2	37	165	-65	-5.58	-7.60	4.46	26.61	1,165
Ningxia 寧夏	5	51	740	-18	-1.80	-8.65	14.40	79.16	998
Xinjiang 新疆	2	15	765	-20	-3.36	-3.77	51.00	10.92	595

4080: Electrical Machinery Repairing 電氣機械修理業

Year 年份	Number of firms 企業個數	Rate of change 每年變化 (%)	Number of employees 職工人數（人）	Rate of change 每年變化 (%)	Total revenue (mil. RMB) 總銷售收入（百萬元）	Rate of change 每年變化 (%)	Total profit (mil. RMB) 總利潤（百萬元）	Rate of change 每年變化 (%)
1993	671		25,499		432		36	
1994	603	-10.14%	23,008	-9.77%	592	37.08%	38	6.16%
1995	783	29.85%	31,805	38.23%	924	56.01%	37	-1.73%
1996	791	1.02%	30,868	-2.95%	1,059	14.66%	17	-54.31%

3 Major products* 3 種主要產品 *	Output 產量	Sales volume 銷售量	Unit 單位

Top 10 firms by revenue (year founded) 收入排名前 10 家企業 (創辦年份)	City 城市	Province 省	Telephone / fax 電話 / 傳真	Number of employees 職工人數	Ownership 產業所有權	Revenue ('000 RMB) 銷售收入（千元）	Profit ('000 RMB) (rank) 利潤（千元）（排名）	Total assets ('000 RMB) 總資產（千元）	Major products 主要產品
Tieling Generate Electricity Guan Lian Co. Ltd. General Co. 鐵嶺發電關聯有限責任總公司(1992)	Tieling 鐵嶺市	Liaoning 遼寧省	(0410)4645197 (0410)4645139	1,462	Joint stock 股份制	205,720	400(26)	84,900	o
Shanghai Hua Guang Hoisting Machinery Repair Factory 上海華光起重機械修理廠(1988)	Shanghai 上海市	Shanghai 上海市	(021)59558366	9	Collectively-owned 集體	53,790	7(96)	993	o
Shenyang Sujiatun Tong Gou Electric Appliance Repair & Building Factory 瀋陽市蘇家屯區佟溝電器修造廠(1996)	Shenyang 瀋陽市	Liaoning 遼寧省	(024)89572058	60	Collectively-owned 集體	35,330	493(21)	2,798	o
Anshan Hong Yang Electric Repair & Building Factory 鞍山市宏洋電氣修造廠(1994)	Anshan 鞍山市	Liaoning 遼寧省	(0412)5842001	120	Domestic JVs 聯營	32,690	1670(6)	6,130	o
Anshan Tie Dongxian Dui Lu Seamless Joint Electro Mechanical Equipment Repair & Building Factory 鞍山市鐵東區對爐無縫聯合機電設備修造廠(1994)	Anshan 鞍山市	Liaoning 遼寧省	(0412)6639104	60	Domestic JVs 聯營	31,260	80(68)	1,120	o
Da Hua Engineering Installing Equipment Company 大華工程設備安裝公司(1990)	Shanghai 上海市	Shanghai 上海市	(021)59137577	140	Collectively-owned 集體	30,010	3705(1)	15,333	o
Xiangtan Electric Power Electromechanical Repair Factory 湘潭電力機電修造廠(1994)	Xiangtan 湘潭市	Hunan 湖南省	(0732)8524547	28	Collectively-owned 集體	24,312	-179(124)	24,709	o
Yingkou Laobian Power Supply Bureau Repairing of Electric Equipment Suo 營口市老邊供電局電修所(1986)	Yingkou 營口市	Liaoning 遼寧省	(0417)3865202	10	Collectively-owned 集體	22,689	0(107)	22,421	o
Nan Feng Electric Appliance Install Co. Ltd. 南封電器安裝有限公司(1996)	Shanghai 上海市	Shanghai 上海市	(021)59138239	50	Collectively-owned 集體	20,100	1738(5)	4,795	o
Shanghai Huangpu Punching Pieces Factory 上海黃浦沖壓件廠(1969)	Shanghai 上海市	Shanghai 上海市	(021)64356865 (021)64358843	45	Collectively-owned 集體	19,242	1024(11)	5,750	o

Top 10 Cities by Production Output 產出排名前 10 位城市	Province 省	Market share 市場份額	Number of firms 企業個數
Shanghai 上海市	Shanghai 上海市	19.31%	157
Guangzhou 廣州市	Guangdong 廣東省	9.21%	22
Taiyuan 太原市	Shanxi 山西省	7.13%	15
Shenyang 瀋陽市	Liaoning 遼寧省	5.87%	43
Datong 大同市	Shanxi 山西省	3.99%	12
Beijing 北京市	Beijing 北京市	3.67%	41
Tianjin 天津市	Tianjin 天津市	3.53%	82
Harbin 哈爾濱市	Heilongjiang 黑龍江省	3.51%	32
Zhengzhou 鄭州市	Henan 河南省	2.92%	4
Anshan 鞍山市	Liaoning 遼寧省	2.74%	16

10 Major Wholesalers 10 家主要批發商	City 城市	Province 省	Telephone / Fax 電話 / 傳真

*Also include sales by firms outside this industry.包括本行業以外廠家的銷售。"o" stands for "others". "o" 代表 "其他產品" 。

4091: Electric Welding Machines 電焊機製造業

The industry accounts for 0.031% of the total revenue of China's industrial sector in 1996. The revenue growth rate of the industry is 11.3% from 1995, as compared to the growth rate of China's industrial sector, 9.51%. The rate of return on asset is 0.57%. 67.37% of all firms in the industry made a profit while 30.73% had negative returns. The top province in terms of the industry's revenue is Jiangsu, accounting for 14.68% of the total revenue.
本行業在1996年佔全行業總產值0.031%，行業年增長率為11.3%（全國工業年增長率9.51%）。行業的資產回報率0.57%，67.37%的企業盈利，30.73%的企業虧損。銷售收入最高的省份為江蘇省，佔本行業的14.68%。

	Total number of firms 企業總數	Total number of employees 職工總數	Total revenue (mil. RMB) 總銷售收入（百萬元）	Total profit (mil. RMB) 總利潤（百萬元）	Return on assets 資產利潤率 (%)	Return on equity 權益利潤率 (%)	Labour productivity ('000 RMB / worker) 勞動生產率（千元/人）	Debts / assets 資產負債率 (%)	Total assets (mil. RMB) 總資產（百萬元）
Industry Overall 行業總體	412	38,241	1,801	16	0.57	1.61	47.10	64.61	2,737

	Number of firms 企業個數	Average number of employees 平均職工人數	Average revenue ('000 RMB) 平均銷售收入（千元）	Average profit ('000 RMB) 平均利潤（千元）	Return on assets 資產利潤率 (%)	Return on equity 權益利潤率 (%)	Labour productivity ('000 RMB / worker) 勞動生產率（千元/人）	Average debts / assets 平均資產負債率(%)	Average Total assets ('000 RMB) 平均總資產（千元）
By ownership 產業所有權									
State-owned 國有	64	224	7,828	16	0.08	0.21	34.96	60.69	19,078
Collectively-owned 集體	316	70	3,442	37	0.96	3.45	48.96	72.22	3,861
Privately-owned 私有	1	20	471	-11	-0.42	-0.46	23.56	7.81	2,558
Domestic JVs 聯營	3	18	1,054				58.58	69.73	1,842
Joint stock 股份制	6	193	11,795	830	4.21	11.70	61.12	64.03	19,727
Foreign-funded 外資	9	64	7,105	-68	-0.59	-0.74	111.20	20.65	11,504
Overseas Chinese-funded 港澳台資	12	39	6,219	-89	-1.61	-4.99	161.54	67.72	5,544
By size 規模									
Large 大型	1	1,624	125,513	406	0.26	0.66	77.29	60.05	155,122
Medium 中型	9	827	31,011	-147	-0.19	-0.61	37.49	68.81	76,662
Small 小型	392	75	3,304	42	0.88	2.40	44.00	63.41	4,809
By regional distribution 地區分布									
Central-North 華北	58	111	6,165	169	1.83	6.11	55.73	70.07	9,245
Beijing 北京	12	60	8,507	46	1.61	3.68	141.19	56.39	2,855
Tianjin 天津	22	72	2,352	-70	-1.32	-11.45	32.57	88.43	5,283
Hebei 河北	17	163	11,139	789	3.82	10.67	68.53	64.22	20,662
Shanxi 山西	4	169	1,395	-538	-17.10	1075.00	8.27	101.59	3,143
Inner Mongolia 內蒙	3	222	2,940	-157	-2.15	-7.10	13.22	69.74	7,293
Northeast 東北	82	62	2,435	65	1.37	3.84	38.98	64.29	4,773
Liaoning 遼寧	42	74	3,826	179	2.86	6.52	51.45	56.16	6,275
Jilin 吉林	17	41	515	-113	-8.14	-24.18	12.51	66.37	1,387
Heilongjiang 黑龍江	23	57	1,315	-10	-0.23	-1.47	23.27	84.36	4,535
Central East 華東	164	101	5,469	4	0.06	0.17	54.07	65.79	6,805
Shanghai 上海	25	170	9,216	-150	-1.17	-2.91	54.19	59.69	12,788
Jiangsu 江蘇	36	114	7,346	46	0.54	1.51	64.19	64.12	8,550
Zhejiang 浙江	41	51	2,357	-149	-3.36	-9.36	46.04	64.09	4,433
Anhui 安徽	10	71	5,276	416	9.42	31.07	74.31	69.71	4,418
Fujian 福建	14	55	1,874	-1	-0.04	-0.14	33.90	69.28	3,365
Jiangxi 江西	8	148	2,710	53	0.73	3.22	18.30	77.34	7,209
Shandong 山東	30	115	6,823	142	2.71	11.77	59.38	77.02	5,261
Central-South 中南	71	71	2,388	152	2.76	5.98	33.52	53.93	5,522
Henan 河南	8	121	1,309	14	0.40	1.60	10.78	74.73	3,399
Hubei 湖北	11	61	1,973	76	2.66	8.68	32.44	69.34	2,870
Hunan 湖南	21	83	1,443	-232	-6.80	-22.83	17.46	70.23	3,418
Guangdong 廣東	28	59	3,783	526	5.65	10.36	63.99	45.45	9,313
Guangxi 廣西	3	9	380	3	1.27	2.00	42.22	36.71	263
Hainan 海南									
Southwest 西南	26	152	5,255	-394	-4.57	-12.86	34.49	64.51	8,634
Chongqing 重慶	4	100	1,862	-649	-27.74	-147.56	18.57	81.20	2,339
Sichuan 四川	17	179	6,519	-474	-4.33	-13.16	36.34	67.13	10,964
Guizhou 貴州	1								
Yunnan 雲南	4	125	4,383	93	1.36	2.30	35.20	40.78	6,793
Tibet 西藏									
Northwest 西北	11	100	3,705	-65	-0.92	-2.69	37.21	65.73	6,986
Shaanxi 陝西	8	72	3,206	-44	-0.74	-1.76	44.61	57.96	5,899
Gansu 甘肅	2	106	1,805	-200	-4.16	-12.66	17.11	67.22	4,805
Qinghai 青海									
Ningxia 寧夏	1	309	11,490	40	0.20	1.19	37.18	83.29	20,050
Xinjiang 新疆									

4091: Electric Welding Machines 電焊機製造業

Year 年份	Number of firms 企業個數	Rate of change 每年變化 (%)	Number of employees 職工人數 (人)	Rate of change 每年變化 (%)	Total revenue (mil. RMB) 總銷售收入 (百萬元)	Rate of change 每年變化 (%)	Total profit (mil. RMB) 總利潤 (百萬元)	Rate of change 每年變化 (%)
1993	357		54,747		1,629		119	
1994	401	12.32%	44,625	-18.49%	1,544	-5.23%	49	-58.87%
1995	443	10.47%	42,989	-3.67%	1,618	4.82%	13	-73.68%
1996	412	-7.00%	38,241	-11.04%	1,801	11.31%	16	23.80%

3 Major products* 3 種主要產品 *	Output 產量	Sales volume 銷售量	Unit 單位
a) Electric Welder 電焊機	381,343	381,343	set 台

Top 10 firms by revenue (year founded) 收入排名前 10 家企業 (創辦年份)	City 城市	Province 省	Telephone / fax 電話 / 傳真	Number of employees 職工人數	Ownership 產業所有權	Revenue ('000 RMB) 銷售收入 (千元)	Profit ('000 RMB) (rank) 利潤 (千元) (排名)	Total assets ('000 RMB) 總資產 (千元)	Major products 主要產品
Tangshan Kaiyuan Enterprise Group 唐山市開元企業集團(1971)	Tangshan 唐山市	Hebei 河北省	(0315)2814103 (0315)2821053	729	State-owned 國有	116,485	12009(2)	222,625	o
Shanghai Electric Welder Factory 上海電焊機廠(1953)	Shanghai 上海市	Shanghai 上海市	(021)65433540 (021)65394139	1,734	State-owned 國有	96,239	-1250(144)	140,703	a
Tancheng Electric Appliance Industry Group General Company 郯城電器工業集團總公司(1994)	Linyi 臨沂市	Shandong 山東省	(0539)6222678 (0539)6222678	850	Collectively-owned 集體	93,350	3100(6)	34,110	o
Beijing Shi Dai Welding New Technology Co. 北京市時代焊接新技術公司(1993)	Beijing 北京市	Beijing 北京市	(010)68418333 (010)68418334	53	Collectively-owned 集體	75,246	15(100)	3,919	a
Jiangsu San Jiang Electrical Appliance Manufacturing Co. 江蘇三江電器製造公司(1972)	Taizhou 泰州市	Jiangsu 江蘇省	(0523)4230639 (0523)4230496	501	Collectively-owned 集體	72,707	4666(3)	38,800	a
Chengdu Bao He Foreign Development Company 成都保和對外發展公司	Chengdu 成都市	Sichuan 四川省	(028)3351914		Collectively-owned 集體	63,893	1714(13)	11,013	o
Shenzhen Hua Lian Fa Electron Joint Co. Ltd. 深圳華聯發電子聯合有限公司(1992)	Shenzhen 深圳市	Guangdong 廣東省	(0755)3345900 (0755)3363695	99	State-owned 國有	42,032	17796(1)	134,847	o
Shenyang No.4 Electric Welder Factory 瀋陽市第四電焊機廠(1989)	Shenyang 瀋陽市	Liaoning 遼寧省	(024)86527634	24	Collectively-owned 集體	38,560	3120(5)	30,568	o
Shanghai Huang Du Electric Welder Factory 上海黃渡電焊機廠(1985)	Shanghai 上海市	Shanghai 上海市	(021)59595385	35	Collectively-owned 集體	34,225	1316(16)	5,543	a
Hua Dong Electric Welder Factory 華東電焊機(1960)	Shanghai 上海市	Shanghai 上海市	(021)56901660 (021)56904178	925	State-owned 國有	31,630	-8810(157)	81,457	a

Top 10 Cities by Production Output 產出排名前 10 位城市	Province 省	Market share 市場份額	Number of firms 企業個數
Shanghai 上海市	Shanghai 上海市	17.12%	47
Beijing 北京市	Beijing 北京市	7.92%	10
Tangshan 唐山市	Hebei 河北省	7.24%	1
Linyi 臨沂市	Shandong 山東省	5.70%	2
Tianjin 天津市	Tianjin 天津市	5.45%	26
Taizhou 泰州市	Jiangsu 江蘇省	4.94%	6
Nantong 南通市	Jiangsu 江蘇省	3.55%	10
Chengdu 成都市	Sichuan 四川省	3.35%	25
Wenzhou 温州市	Zhejiang 浙江省	3.31%	41
Wuxi 無錫市	Jiangsu 江蘇省	2.22%	9

10 Major Wholesalers 10 家主要批發商	City 城市	Province 省	Telephone / Fax 電話 / 傳真
Liaoning Automobile Trade Group Corp. 遼寧省汽車貿易集團	Shenyang 瀋陽市	Liaoning 遼寧省	(024)23835494 (024)23838338
China Post and Telecommunication Equipment General Company 中國郵電器材總公司	Beijing 北京市	Beijing 北京市	(010)63523715 (010)63525935
Jiangsu Electromechanical Products General Company 江蘇省機電產品總公司	Nanjing 南京市	Jiangsu 江蘇省	(025)7713642 (025)7711036
Xi Nan Technology Import & Export Company 西南技術進出口公司	Chongqing 重慶市	Chongqing 重慶市	(023)63850185 (023)63850026
Changzhou Economic Technology Industrial Development Zone Tian Ming Trade Company 常州經濟技術產業開發區天明貿易公司	Changzhou 常州市	Jiangsu 江蘇省	(0519)8829882 (0519)8829882
Shanxi Mechanical Equipment Import & Export Company 山西省機械設備進出口公司	Taiyuan 太原市	Shanxi 山西省	(0351)4040713 (0351)4043981
Ningbo Five Mining Machinery Import & Export Company 寧波市五礦機械進出口公司	Ningbo 寧波市	Zhejiang 浙江省	(0574)7311255 (0574)7320322
Tianjin Jin Huan Electromechanical Complete Sets of Equipment Factory 天津市津環機電成套設備廠	Tianjin 天津市	Tianjin 天津市	(022)26371628
Yunnan Machinery Import & Export Company 雲南省機械進出口公司	Kunming 昆明市	Yunnan 雲南省	(0871)3164879 (0871)3136829
Tianjin Da Qiu Zhuang Yi Yuan Trade Center 天津市大丘莊億源商貿中心	Tianjin 天津市	Tianjin 天津市	(022)28899478 (022)28899046

*Also include sales by firms outside this industry.包括本行業以外廠家的銷售。"o" stands for "others". "o" 代表"其他產品"。

4092: Industrial Electric Furnaces 工業用電爐製造業

The industry accounts for 0.014% of the total revenue of China's industrial sector in 1996. The revenue growth rate of the industry is 9.3% from 1995, as compared to the growth rate of China's industrial sector, 9.51%. The rate of return on asset is -2.02%. 61.23% of all firms in the industry made a profit while 36.42% had negative returns. The top province in terms of the industry's revenue is Jiangsu, accounting for 42.37% of the total revenue.
本行業在1996年佔全行業總產值0.014%，行業年增長率為9.3%（全國工業年增長率9.51%）。行業的資產回報率-2.02%，61.23%的企業盈利，36.42%的企業虧損。銷售收入最高的省份為江蘇省，佔本行業的42.37%。

	Total number of firms 企業總數	Total number of employees 職工總數	Total revenue (mil. RMB) 總銷售收入（百萬元）	Total profit (mil. RMB) 總利潤（百萬元）	Return on assets 資產利潤率 (%)	Return on equity 權益利潤率 (%)	Labour productivity ('000 RMB / worker) 勞動生產率（千元/人）	Debts / assets 資產負債率 (%)	Total assets (mil. RMB) 總資產（百萬元）
Industry Overall 行業總體	158	26,600	808	-31	-2.02	-8.03	30.38	74.79	1,526

	Number of firms 企業個數	Average number of employees 平均職工人數	Average revenue ('000 RMB) 平均銷售收入（千元）	Average profit ('000 RMB) 平均利潤（千元）	Return on assets 資產利潤率 (%)	Return on equity 權益利潤率 (%)	Labour productivity ('000 RMB / worker) 勞動生產率（千元/人）	Average debts / assets 平均資產負債率(%)	Average Total assets ('000 RMB) 平均總資產（千元）
By ownership 產業所有權									
State-owned 國有	25	488	6,960	-1,120	-3.98	-25.69	14.25	84.52	28,160
Collectively-owned 集體	121	103	4,073	-14	-0.25	-0.79	39.51	67.95	5,691
Privately-owned 私有	1	75	2,685	-53	-0.66	-1.65	35.81	60.14	8,055
Domestic JVs 聯營	2	53	2,840	70	1.45	2.69	53.59	46.22	4,816
Joint stock 股份制	2	400	10,151	0	0.00	-0.01	25.41	68.50	17,467
Foreign-funded 外資	3	112	13,867	-31	-0.34	-1.03	123.45	67.04	9,151
Overseas Chinese-funded 港澳台資	4	149	17,685	-313	-2.33	-4.64	118.49	49.87	13,438
By size 規模									
Large 大型									
Medium 中型	8	1,194	29,329	-4,151	-5.97	-28.90	24.56	79.36	69,582
Small 小型	149	114	3,847	15	0.23	0.82	33.63	72.14	6,509
By regional distribution 地區分布									
Central-North 華北	24	142	3,925	-198	-2.01	-8.30	27.67	75.75	9,852
Beijing 北京	6	79	2,697	-120	-2.05	-7.41	33.99	72.29	5,853
Tianjin 天津	9	203	5,222	-459	-4.15	-15.14	25.77	72.63	11,069
Hebei 河北	9	123	3,446	10	0.09	0.44	28.09	80.00	11,301
Shanxi 山西									
Inner Mongolia 內蒙									
Northeast 東北	29	341	3,307	-828	-5.81	-46.39	9.70	87.47	14,244
Liaoning 遼寧	19	182	3,648	-729	-9.05	-382.60	20.01	97.64	8,057
Jilin 吉林	3	483	4,507	-3,327	-6.71	-36.13	9.33	81.43	49,570
Heilongjiang 黑龍江	7	710	1,864	-27	-0.17	-0.93	2.62	81.54	15,899
Central East 華東	69	117	7,377	33	0.42	1.22	62.98	66.06	7,913
Shanghai 上海	11	178	7,402	-150	-1.26	-4.15	41.52	69.55	11,875
Jiangsu 江蘇	26	119	13,166	210	2.36	5.78	110.74	59.09	8,888
Zhejiang 浙江	13	61	3,385	53	1.05	2.99	55.77	64.87	5,056
Anhui 安徽	4	102	2,330	-28	-0.67	-4.18	22.90	83.89	4,083
Fujian 福建	3	120	317	50	1.13	5.30	2.63	78.74	4,437
Jiangxi 江西	3	273	4,353	-523	-3.97	-22.92	15.97	82.66	13,167
Shandong 山東	9	73	1,991	-78	-1.42	-4.48	27.40	68.39	5,493
Central-South 中南	22	185	3,554	-195	-1.67	-6.45	19.20	74.16	11,696
Henan 河南	6	46	1,065	3	0.26	0.78	23.24	67.01	1,293
Hubei 湖北	5	87	4,742	74	3.19	10.22	54.26	68.82	2,322
Hunan 湖南	7	420	4,793	-401	-3.54	-7.93	11.41	55.39	11,347
Guangdong 廣東	3	75	3,843	70	0.19	1.91	51.47	89.83	36,127
Guangxi 廣西	1	196	3,010	-2,080	-4.15	-15.01	15.36	72.36	50,140
Hainan 海南									
Southwest 西南	4	113	3,850	-178	-2.57	-9.65	34.00	73.35	6,905
Chongqing 重慶	3	144	4,934	-240	-2.63	-9.79	34.20	73.16	9,119
Sichuan 四川	1	19	598	7	2.66	39.66	31.17	93.30	263
Guizhou 貴州									
Yunnan 雲南									
Tibet 西藏									
Northwest 西北	10	70	1,558	60	1.32	3.64	22.16	63.84	4,560
Shaanxi 陝西	10	70	1,558	60	1.32	3.64	22.16	63.84	4,560
Gansu 甘肅									
Qinghai 青海									
Ningxia 寧夏									
Xinjiang 新疆									

4092: Industrial Electric Furnaces 工業用電爐製造業

Year 年份	Number of firms 企業個數	Rate of change 每年變化 (%)	Number of employees 職工人數 (人)	Rate of change 每年變化 (%)	Total revenue (mil. RMB) 總銷售收入 (百萬元)	Rate of change 每年變化 (%)	Total profit (mil. RMB) 總利潤 (百萬元)	Rate of change 每年變化 (%)
1993	158		30,303		1,085		66	
1994	156	-1.27%	22,764	-24.88%	690	-36.45%	7	-89.46%
1995	154	-1.28%	21,436	-5.83%	739	7.15%	-18	-364.12%
1996	158	2.60%	26,600	24.09%	808	9.31%	-31	-69.27%

3 Major products* 3 種主要產品 *	Output 產量	Sales volume 銷售量	Unit 單位
a) Industrial Furnace 工業用電爐	7,480	5,760	set 台

Top 10 firms by revenue (year founded) 收入排名前 10 家企業 (創辦年份)	City 城市	Province 省	Telephone / fax 電話 / 傳真	Number of employees 職工人數	Ownership 產業所有權	Revenue ('000 RMB) 銷售收入 (千元)	Profit ('000 RMB) (rank) 利潤 (千元) (排名)	Total assets ('000 RMB) 總資產 (千元)	Major products 主要產品
Wuxi Hu Guang Electric Stove Mill 無錫湖光電爐廠(1987)	Wuxi 無錫市	Jiangsu 江蘇省	(0510)8791936	280	Collectively-owned 集體	112,300	3490(1)	45,960	a
Wuxi Electric Stove Factory 無錫市電爐廠(1954)	Wuxi 無錫市	Jiangsu 江蘇省	(0510)5807660 (0510)5807660	807	Collectively-owned 集體	76,996	1831(2)	43,826	o
Nanjing She Lu Group Co. Ltd. 南京攝爐集團有限公司(1995)	Nanjing 南京市	Jiangsu 江蘇省	(025)5761390 (025)5761587	236	Collectively-owned 集體	48,281	1037(5)	26,119	a
Nanjing Hua Jian Electric Appliance Electric Heat Equipment Co. Ltd. 南京華堅電器電熱設備有限公司(1995)	Nanjing 南京市	Jiangsu 江蘇省	(025)5704179 (025)5704181	221	Foreign-funded 外資	39,810	601(8)	16,273	a
Liaoning Jinzhou Transformer Electric Stove Factory 遼寧錦州變壓器電爐廠(1949)	Jinzhou 錦州市	Liaoning 遼寧省	(0416)2127955 (0416)2128096	1,358	State-owned 國有	30,977	-11400(85)	61,576	o
Shanghai Electric Machinery (Group) Co. Electric Stove Factory 上海電機(集團)公司電爐廠(1960)	Shanghai 上海市	Shanghai 上海市	(021)65431520 (021)65431558	814	State-owned 國有	27,356	-2205(79)	56,947	a
Shanghai Electric Machinery (Group) Company Experiment Electric Stove Factory 上海電機(集團)公司實驗電爐廠(1958)	Shanghai 上海市	Shanghai 上海市	(021)57820022 (021)57820022	337	State-owned 國有	19,327	59(37)	24,841	a
Tianjin High Frequency Equipment Factory 天津市高頻設備廠(1958)	Tianjin 天津市	Tianjin 天津市	(022)28308969 (022)28308969	389	Collectively-owned 集體	17,839	187(26)	33,789	a
Shanghai Pu Dong Xi Yang Machinery Factory 上海浦東奚陽機械廠(1992)	Shanghai 上海市	Shanghai 上海市	(021)58971946 (021)58971946	350	Collectively-owned 集體	17,093	254(22)	31,511	o
Chongqing Electric Stove Factory 重慶電爐廠(1958)	Chongqing 重慶市	Chongqing 重慶市	(023)65343516 (023)65302540	427	Collectively-owned 集體	15,036	-708(73)	27,340	a

Top 10 Cities by Production Output 產出排名前 10 位城市	Province 省	Market share 市場份額	Number of firms 企業個數
Shanghai 上海市	Shanghai 上海市	13.15%	24
Weifang 濰坊市	Shandong 山東省	9.72%	2
Nanjing 南京市	Jiangsu 江蘇省	8.01%	7
Tianjin 天津市	Tianjin 天津市	6.89%	11
Suzhou 蘇州市	Jiangsu 江蘇省	6.81%	5
Wuxi 無錫市	Jiangsu 江蘇省	5.01%	14
Baoding 保定市	Hebei 河北省	4.92%	7
Taizhou 泰州市	Jiangsu 江蘇省	3.97%	12
Jinzhou 錦州市	Liaoning 遼寧省	3.81%	4
Harbin 哈爾濱市	Heilongjiang 黑龍江省	3.23%	3

10 Major Wholesalers 10 家主要批發商	City 城市	Province 省	Telephone / Fax 電話 / 傳真
Liaoning Automobile Trade Group Corp. 遼寧省汽車貿易集團	Shenyang 瀋陽市	Liaoning 遼寧省	(024)23835494 (024)23838338
China Post and Telecommunication Equipment General Company 中國郵電器材總公司	Beijing 北京市	Beijing 北京市	(010)63523715 (010)63525935
Jiangsu Electromechanical Products General Company 江蘇省機電產品總公司	Nanjing 南京市	Jiangsu 江蘇省	(025)7713642 (025)7711036
Xi Nan Technology Import & Export Company 西南技術進出口公司	Chongqing 重慶市	Chongqing 重慶市	(023)63850185 (023)63850026
Changzhou Economic Technology Industrial Development Zone Tian Ming Trade Company 常州經濟技術產業開發區天明貿易公司	Changzhou 常州市	Jiangsu 江蘇省	(0519)8829882 (0519)8829882
Shanxi Mechanical Equipment Import & Export Company 山西省機械設備進出口公司	Taiyuan 太原市	Shanxi 山西省	(0351)4040713 (0351)4043981
Ningbo Five Mining Machinery Import & Export Company 寧波市五礦機械進出口公司	Ningbo 寧波市	Zhejiang 浙江省	(0574)7311255 (0574)7320322
Tianjin Jin Huan Electromechanical Complete Sets of Equipment Factory 天津市津環機電成套設備廠	Tianjin 天津市	Tianjin 天津市	(022)26371628
Yunnan Machinery Import & Export Company 雲南省機械進出口公司	Kunming 昆明市	Yunnan 雲南省	(0871)3164879 (0871)3136829
Tianjin Da Qiu Zhuang Yi Yuan Trade Center 天津市大丘莊億源商貿中心	Tianjin 天津市	Tianjin 天津市	(022)28899478 (022)28899046

*Also include sales by firms outside this industry.包括本行業以外廠家的銷售。"o" stands for "others". "o" 代表"其他產品"。

4099: Other Electric Machinery 其他類未包括的電氣機械製造業

The industry accounts for 0.025% of the total revenue of China's industrial sector in 1996. The revenue growth rate of the industry is 48.6% from 1995, as compared to the growth rate of China's industrial sector, 9.51%. The rate of return on asset is 2.90%. 69.60% of all firms in the industry made a profit while 24.52% had negative returns. The top province in terms of the industry's revenue is Jiangsu, accounting for 17.72% of the total revenue.

本行業在1996年佔全行業總產值0.025%，行業年增長率為48.6%（全國工業年增長率9.51%）。行業的資產回報率2.90%，69.60%的企業盈利，24.52%的企業虧損。銷售收入最高的省份為江蘇省，佔本行業的17.72%。

	Total number of firms 企業總數	Total number of employees 職工總數	Total revenue (mil. RMB) 總銷售收入（百萬元）	Total profit (mil. RMB) 總利潤（百萬元）	Return on assets 資產利潤率 (%)	Return on equity 權益利潤率 (%)	Labour productivity ('000 RMB / worker) 勞動生產率（千元/人）	Debts / assets 資產負債率 (%)	Total assets (mil. RMB) 總資產（百萬元）
Industry Overall 行業總體	387	29,760	1,431	55	2.90	7.93	48.08	63.44	1,892

	Number of firms 企業個數	Average number of employees 平均職工人數	Average revenue ('000 RMB) 平均銷售收入（千元）	Average profit ('000 RMB) 平均利潤（千元）	Return on assets 資產利潤率 (%)	Return on equity 權益利潤率 (%)	Labour productivity ('000 RMB / worker) 勞動生產率（千元/人）	Average debts / assets 平均資產負債率(%)	Average Total assets ('000 RMB) 平均總資產（千元）
By ownership 產業所有權									
State-owned 國有	47	179	5,447	85	0.75	2.02	30.46	63.06	11,404
Collectively-owned 集體	289	64	3,085	161	5.75	17.77	48.34	67.62	2,793
Privately-owned 私有	1	12							
Domestic JVs 聯營	6	13	20	6	0.94	1.88	1.59	49.67	676
Joint stock 股份制	8	34	3,993	673	12.35	25.57	117.01	51.71	5,453
Foreign-funded 外資	17	59	8,291	-488	-3.40	-7.57	140.25	55.06	14,351
Overseas Chinese-funded 港澳台資	18	90	6,014	624	4.61	11.30	67.03	59.19	13,526
By size 規模									
Large 大型	1	4,475	114,358	2,316	0.75	1.64	25.55	54.60	310,613
Medium 中型	3	707	25,627	-3,119	-6.11	-20.12	36.27	69.63	51,045
Small 小型	376	62	3,296	165	4.34	12.30	53.33	64.69	3,799
By regional distribution 地區分布									
Central-North 華北	77	46	2,114	55	1.75	4.04	46.14	56.77	3,162
Beijing 北京	30	12	729	5	0.46	1.47	61.26	68.60	1,155
Tianjin 天津	25	56	2,606	218	5.13	10.23	46.44	49.87	4,245
Hebei 河北	14	102	4,951	-106	-1.53	-3.71	48.64	58.77	6,914
Shanxi 山西	5	60	1,256	24	2.47	9.68	20.79	74.49	972
Inner Mongolia 內蒙	3	14	53	3	0.97	100.00	3.90	99.03	343
Northeast 東北	76	89	2,310	84	1.59	4.25	25.86	62.45	5,249
Liaoning 遼寧	57	97	2,643	119	1.83	4.72	27.18	61.38	6,498
Jilin 吉林	11	54	640	-71	-6.69	-29.89	11.91	77.62	1,060
Heilongjiang 黑龍江	8	82	2,233	48	2.26	9.27	27.27	75.62	2,103
Central East 華東	141	92	4,710	74	1.38	3.61	51.23	61.74	5,391
Shanghai 上海	20	65	3,785	-63	-1.61	-4.52	57.83	64.34	3,874
Jiangsu 江蘇	40	84	6,341	188	2.22	6.06	75.67	63.45	8,473
Zhejiang 浙江	39	142	4,486	134	3.62	11.98	31.69	69.81	3,707
Anhui 安徽	7	96	2,354	-209	-6.56	-25.09	24.49	73.80	3,179
Fujian 福建	9	36	2,153	-620	-8.71	-12.21	59.09	28.69	7,122
Jiangxi 江西	8	50	814	-31	-1.90	-7.35	16.44	74.18	1,646
Shandong 山東	18	77	6,526	349	6.31	15.45	84.81	59.14	5,535
Central-South 中南	75	74	5,167	427	7.17	24.50	69.63	70.73	5,958
Henan 河南	22	60	2,428	153	4.61	9.50	40.26	51.50	3,324
Hubei 湖北	6	45	1,280	-10	-0.86	-6.98	28.76	87.64	1,160
Hunan 湖南	18	85	4,193	221	6.12	17.88	49.40	65.76	3,612
Guangdong 廣東	20	97	11,859	1,236	9.40	39.41	122.32	76.16	13,151
Guangxi 廣西	9	56	1,527	6	0.13	0.53	27.26	75.49	4,302
Hainan 海南									
Southwest 西南	9	67	1,948	57	1.82	5.00	29.17	63.60	3,120
Chongqing 重慶	2	68	1,553	284	7.40	14.30	22.75	48.23	3,836
Sichuan 四川	5	50	2,099	32	1.54	8.85	42.10	82.57	2,072
Guizhou 貴州	2	104	2,055	-150	-3.17	-7.69	19.86	58.77	4,730
Yunnan 雲南									
Tibet 西藏									
Northwest 西北	9	35	2,589	133	8.14	24.64	74.68	66.92	1,639
Shaanxi 陝西	5	42	1,934	-86	-4.74	-13.87	46.05	65.86	1,816
Gansu 甘肅	3	27	4,163	580	38.84	112.99	156.13	65.40	1,493
Qinghai 青海									
Ningxia 寧夏									
Xinjiang 新疆	1	22	1,140	-110	-9.24	-47.83	51.82	80.67	1,190

4099: Other Electric Machinery 其他類未包括的電氣機械製造業

Year 年份	Number of firms 企業個數	Rate of change 每年變化 (%)	Number of employees 職工人數 (人)	Rate of change 每年變化 (%)	Total revenue (mil. RMB) 總銷售收入 (百萬元)	Rate of change 每年變化 (%)	Total profit (mil. RMB) 總利潤 (百萬元)	Rate of change 每年變化 (%)
1993	334		29,794		930		26	
1994	398	19.16%	28,329	-4.92%	1,241	33.53%	28	6.76%
1995	345	-13.32%	26,137	-7.74%	963	-22.46%	22	-22.97%
1996	387	12.17%	29,760	13.86%	1,431	48.59%	55	153.97%

3 Major products* 3 種主要產品 *	Output 產量	Sales volume 銷售量	Unit 單位

Top 10 firms by revenue (year founded) 收入排名前 10 家企業 (創辦年份)	City 城市	Province 省	Telephone / fax 電話 / 傳真	Number of employees 職工人數	Ownership 產業所有權	Revenue ('000 RMB) 銷售收入 (千元)	Profit ('000 RMB) (rank) 利潤 (千元) (排名)	Total assets ('000 RMB) 總資產 (千元)	Major products 主要產品
Bao Long Automatic Machinery (Shenzhen) Co. Ltd. 寶龍自動機械(深圳)有限公司(1992)	Shenzhen 深圳市	Guangdong 廣東省	(0755)7702995 (0755)7704429	400	Overseas Chinese-funded 港澳台資	143,233	25021(1)	120,581	o
Liaoning Hua Xing Precision Machinery Factory 遼寧華興精密機械廠(1970)	Jinzhou 錦州市	Liaoning 遼寧省	(0416)4186711	3,733	State-owned 國有	90,220	3110(4)	284,090	o
Sheng Zhou Shi Compression Beng Electric Engine Factory 嵊州市壓縮泵電機廠(1985)	Shaoxing 紹興市	Zhejiang 浙江省	(0575)3211150 (0575)3031166	386	Collectively-owned 集體	78,131	2067(9)	58,650	o
Zibo Electric Welding Rod Factory 淄博電焊條廠(1966)	Zibo 淄博市	Shandong 山東省	(0533)6412517 (0533)6410356	624	Collectively-owned 集體	50,148	160(57)	49,320	o
Hebei Electric Power Equipment Factory 河北電力設備廠(1969)	Handan 邯鄲市	Hebei 河北省	(0310)7022819 (0310)7021243	680	State-owned 國有	49,119	-1654(131)	68,433	o
Danyang Shen Yang Elevator Decoration Plant 丹陽市申陽電梯裝潢廠(1985)	Zhenjiang 鎮江市	Jiangsu 江蘇省	(0511)6682652	178	Collectively-owned 集體	42,756	8806(2)	53,625	o
Zhongshan Jin Ma Amusement Equipment Industrial Co. 中山市金馬遊樂設備實業公司(1965)	Zhongshan 中山市	Guangdong 廣東省	(0760)8702741 (0760)8701368	540	Collectively-owned 集體	41,019	201(51)	69,032	o
Suzhou Ai Si Ke Ti Ji Co. Ltd. 蘇州愛斯克梯級有限公司(1994)	Suzhou 蘇州市	Jiangsu 江蘇省	(0512)8252997 (0512)8252991	53	Foreign-funded 外資	33,880	2960(5)	82,169	o
Jiangyin Air Conditioning Dust Cleaning Equipment Factory 江陰市空調除塵設備廠(1984)	Wuxi 無錫市	Jiangsu 江蘇省	(0510)6121800 (0510)6121800	205	Collectively-owned 集體	30,156	2244(8)	32,777	o
Chengdu Sheng Te Meng Gas Utensils Company 成都市聖特蒙燃氣用具公司(1983)	Chengdu 成都市	Sichuan 四川省	(028)3320054	320	Collectively-owned 集體	25,799	150(59)	28,460	o

Top 10 Cities by Production Output 產出排名前 10 位城市	Province 省	Market share 市場份額	Number of firms 企業個數
Zhenjiang 鎮江市	Jiangsu 江蘇省	18.25%	8
Shanghai 上海市	Shanghai 上海市	8.16%	45
Guangzhou 廣州市	Guangdong 廣東省	7.02%	12
Nantong 南通市	Jiangsu 江蘇省	5.10%	12
Jinzhou 錦州市	Liaoning 遼寧省	4.54%	4
Shaoxing 紹興市	Zhejiang 浙江省	4.41%	7
Wuhan 武漢市	Hubei 湖北省	3.54%	7
Zibo 淄博市	Shandong 山東省	2.90%	2
Zhongshan 中山市	Guangdong 廣東省	2.88%	2
Tianjin 天津市	Tianjin 天津市	2.57%	30

10 Major Wholesalers 10 家主要批發商	City 城市	Province 省	Telephone / Fax 電話 / 傳真
Liaoning Automobile Trade Group Corp. 遼寧省汽車貿易集團	Shenyang 瀋陽市	Liaoning 遼寧省	(024)23835494 (024)23838338
China Post and Telecommunication Equipment General Company 中國郵電器材總公司	Beijing 北京市	Beijing 北京市	(010)63523715 (010)63525935
Jiangsu Electromechanical Products General Company 江蘇省機電產品總公司	Nanjing 南京市	Jiangsu 江蘇省	(025)7713642 (025)7711036
Xi Nan Technology Import & Export Company 西南技術進出口公司	Chongqing 重慶市	Chongqing 重慶市	(023)63850185 (023)63850026
Changzhou Economic Technology Industrial Development Zone Tian Ming Trade Company 常州經濟技術產業開發區天明貿易公司	Changzhou 常州市	Jiangsu 江蘇省	(0519)8829882 (0519)8829882
Shanxi Mechanical Equipment Import & Export Company 山西省機械設備進出口公司	Taiyuan 太原市	Shanxi 山西省	(0351)4040713 (0351)4043981
Ningbo Five Mining Machinery Import & Export Company 寧波市五礦機械進出口公司	Ningbo 寧波市	Zhejiang 浙江省	(0574)7311255 (0574)7320322
Tianjin Jin Huan Electromechanical Complete Sets of Equipment Factory 天津市津環機電成套設備廠	Tianjin 天津市	Tianjin 天津市	(022)26371628
Yunnan Machinery Import & Export Company 雲南省機械進出口公司	Kunming 昆明市	Yunnan 雲南省	(0871)3164879 (0871)3136829
Tianjin Da Qiu Zhuang Yi Yuan Trade Center 天津市大丘莊億源商貿中心	Tianjin 天津市	Tianjin 天津市	(022)28899478 (022)28899046

*Also include sales by firms outside this industry.包括本行業以外廠家的銷售。"o" stands for "others". "o" 代表"其他產品"。

4111: Transmission Equipment 傳輸設備製造業

The industry accounts for 0.161% of the total revenue of China's industrial sector in 1996. The revenue growth rate of the industry is -24.2% from 1995, as compared to the growth rate of China's industrial sector, 9.51%. The rate of return on asset is 2.70%. 61.97% of all firms in the industry made a profit while 30.40% had negative returns. The top province in terms of the industry's revenue is Jiangsu, accounting for 46.04% of the total revenue.
本行業在1996年佔全行業總產值0.161%，行業年增長率為-24.2%（全國工業年增長率9.51%）。行業的資產回報率2.70%，61.97%的企業盈利，30.40%的企業虧損。銷售收入最高的省份為江蘇省，佔本行業的46.04%。

	Total number of firms 企業總數	Total number of employees 職工總數	Total revenue (mil. RMB) 總銷售收入（百萬元）	Total profit (mil. RMB) 總利潤（百萬元）	Return on assets 資產利潤率 (%)	Return on equity 權益利潤率 (%)	Labour productivity ('000 RMB / worker) 勞動生產率（千元/人）	Debts / assets 資產負債率 (%)	Total assets (mil. RMB) 總資產（百萬元）
Industry Overall 行業總體	273	75,557	9,335	434	2.70	7.49	123.55	63.95	16,090

	Number of firms 企業個數	Average number of employees 平均職工人數	Average revenue ('000 RMB) 平均銷售收入（千元）	Average profit ('000 RMB) 平均利潤（千元）	Return on assets 資產利潤率 (%)	Return on equity 權益利潤率 (%)	Labour productivity ('000 RMB / worker) 勞動生產率（千元/人）	Average debts / assets 平均資產負債率(%)	Average Total assets ('000 RMB) 平均總資產（千元）
By ownership 產業所有權									
State-owned 國有	70	878	93,057	2,314	1.45	4.67	105.95	69.05	159,971
Collectively-owned 集體	95	63	4,001	92	1.20	3.44	64.01	65.15	7,664
Privately-owned 私有	1	50	3,990	45	1.22	4.77	79.81	74.55	3,677
Domestic JVs 聯營	4	116	2,792	134	2.44	6.23	24.17	60.78	5,475
Joint stock 股份制	4	397	28,285	9,749	6.06	8.38	71.25	27.65	160,785
Foreign-funded 外資	54	73	35,962	3,495	7.01	15.86	495.39	55.79	49,845
Overseas Chinese-funded 港澳台資	44	52	8,410	795	4.38	8.50	161.17	48.54	18,158
By size 規模									
Large 大型	15	2,671	339,609	12,938	2.24	6.57	127.16	65.83	576,474
Medium 中型	14	864	43,797	697	0.70	1.84	50.70	61.87	99,346
Small 小型	230	99	15,624	980	3.82	9.95	157.42	61.61	25,641
By regional distribution 地區分布									
Central-North 華北	54	150	12,666	707	3.06	8.84	84.24	65.40	23,099
Beijing 北京	41	96	11,980	890	3.97	12.12	125.04	67.25	22,411
Tianjin 天津	8	393	11,450	-774	-3.27	-13.34	29.11	75.47	23,641
Hebei 河北	2	17							
Shanxi 山西	1	1,001	101,150	7,880	5.71	9.33	101.05	38.77	137,990
Inner Mongolia 內蒙	2	5	30				6.67	115.44	680
Northeast 東北	18	143	12,361	244	1.19	5.05	86.37	76.46	20,556
Liaoning 遼寧	14	165	15,672	307	1.21	4.94	94.98	75.51	25,409
Jilin 吉林	4	67	773	25	0.70		11.62	100.00	3,570
Heilongjiang 黑龍江									
Central East 華東	93	260	59,963	2,822	3.35	8.77	230.98	61.85	84,304
Shanghai 上海	13	321	50,132	6,274	5.96	9.71	156.40	38.58	105,257
Jiangsu 江蘇	25	594	171,920	6,026	2.64	7.88	289.27	66.46	228,075
Zhejiang 浙江	28	72	14,935	1,618	10.54	24.41	208.57	56.80	15,343
Anhui 安徽	1	20	220				11.00	116.00	1,000
Fujian 福建	13	41	4,018	125	5.25	15.23	98.94	65.47	2,386
Jiangxi 江西	3	123	3,517	-180	-5.00	-25.84	28.59	80.76	3,603
Shandong 山東	10	220	14,564	-1,616	-5.43	-40.35	66.32	86.54	29,760
Central-South 中南	73	248	26,490	2,369	4.65	12.07	106.98	61.48	50,970
Henan 河南	8	797	76,205	1,921	1.85	6.19	95.58	70.15	103,993
Hubei 湖北	5	577	20,038	246	0.55	3.51	34.70	84.42	44,992
Hunan 湖南	6	310	7,728	-363	-1.88	-7.18	24.94	73.84	19,343
Guangdong 廣東	45	109	23,110	3,299	7.27	14.57	212.11	50.12	45,373
Guangxi 廣西	8	253	16,963	1,284	2.04	10.27	66.95	80.17	63,011
Hainan 海南	1	23	1,940	-220	-11.28	-23.91	84.35	52.82	1,950
Southwest 西南	17	830	40,784	-2,581	-1.91	-6.83	49.11	72.01	135,012
Chongqing 重慶	3	2,631	149,343	-16,720	-3.00	-14.80	56.76	79.72	557,084
Sichuan 四川	8	785	26,418	-288	-0.37	-0.88	33.66	57.94	77,633
Guizhou 貴州	1	21	1,640	60	6.52	18.75	78.10	65.22	920
Yunnan 雲南	5	154	17,806	190	0.43	1.20	115.32	64.63	44,646
Tibet 西藏									
Northwest 西北	18	474	12,509	23	0.07	0.19	26.42	65.07	34,242
Shaanxi 陝西	16	522	13,539	39	0.10	0.29	25.96	65.20	37,930
Gansu 甘肅	1	30	1,880	10	0.92	3.57	62.67	74.31	1,090
Qinghai 青海	1	150	6,660	-220	-2.62	-5.77	44.40	54.59	8,390
Ningxia 寧夏									
Xinjiang 新疆									

4111: Transmission Equipment 傳輸設備製造業

Year 年份	Number of firms 企業個數	Rate of change 每年變化 (%)	Number of employees 職工人數 (人)	Rate of change 每年變化 (%)	Total revenue (mil. RMB) 總銷售收入 (百萬元)	Rate of change 每年變化 (%)	Total profit (mil. RMB) 總利潤 (百萬元)	Rate of change 每年變化 (%)
1993	199		91,819		7,493		244	
1994	237	19.10%	73,515	-19.94%	8,772	17.06%	319	30.79%
1995	271	14.35%	74,912	1.90%	12,322	40.47%	783	145.16%
1996	273	0.74%	75,557	0.86%	9,335	-24.24%	434	-44.57%

3 Major products* 3 種主要產品 *	Output 產量	Sales volume 銷售量	Unit 單位
a) Optical Communication Equipment 光通訊設備	23,742	25,404	set 部
b) Carrier Telecommunication Equipment 載波通訊設備	11,993	12,592	set 部

Top 10 firms by revenue (year founded) 收入排名前 10 家企業 (創辦年份)	City 城市	Province 省	Telephone / fax 電話 / 傳真	Number of employees 職工人數	Ownership 產業所有權	Revenue ('000 RMB) 銷售收入 (千元)	Profit ('000 RMB) (rank) 利潤 (千元) (排名)	Total assets ('000 RMB) 總資產 (千元)	Major products 主要產品
Panda Electron Group Co. 熊貓電子集團公司(1936)	Nanjing 南京市	Jiangsu 江蘇省	(025)4400855 (025)4409058	10,777	State-owned 國有	3,778,308	128930(1)	4,991,230	o
Ministry of Posts & Telecommunications Beijing Communication Equipment Factory 郵電部北京通訊設備廠(1941)	Beijing 北京市	Beijing 北京市	(010)64375731 (010)64376891	1,367	State-owned 國有	306,056	7546(16)	300,030	o
Ministry of Posts & Telecommunications Chongqing Communication Equipment Factory 郵電部重慶通訊設備廠(1958)	Chongqing 重慶市	Chongqing 重慶市	(023)68812569 (023)68812569	1,308	State-owned 國有	258,939	6899(19)	731,046	a
Sino-u.s.a. Telephone & Telegraph Communication Equipment Co. Ltd. 中美電話電報通訊設備有限公司(1992)	Shanghai 上海市	Shanghai 上海市	(021)64836868 (021)64836688	167	Foreign-funded 外資	240,153	34426(5)	361,379	a
Shanghai Post & Telecommunication Communication Equipment Co. Ltd. 上海郵電通訊設備股份有限公司(1994)	Shanghai 上海市	Shanghai 上海市	(021)64360900 (021)64333435	1,726	Joint stock 股份制	200,000	50000(2)	693,320	a,b
Guangzhou Ericsson Communication Co. Ltd. 廣州愛立信通訊有限公司(1993)	Guangzhou 廣州市	Guangdong 廣東省	(020)85532808	97	Foreign-funded 外資	191,433	41195(4)	222,352	o
Chinese-foreign Joint Venture Nanjing Fujitsu Communication Equipment Co. Ltd. 中外合資南京富士通通訊設備有限公司(1992)	Nanjing 南京市	Jiangsu 江蘇省	(025)5514844 (025)5508983	160	Foreign-funded 外資	171,853	14299(10)	221,554	o
Shenyang Bei Dian Communication Co. Ltd. 瀋陽北電通訊有限公司(1995)	Shenyang 瀋陽市	Liaoning 遼寧省	(024)23390425 (024)23390426	72	Foreign-funded 外資	140,471	4911(22)	196,680	a
Guangzhou Radio Group Co. Ltd. 廣州無線電集團有限公司(1964)	Guangzhou 廣州市	Guangdong 廣東省	(020)85530636 (020)85534051	2,267	State-owned 國有	124,038	13892(11)	558,700	o
Meishan Communication Equipment Factory 眉山通訊設備廠(1965)	Leshan 樂山市	Sichuan 四川省	(0833)8221505	3,619	State-owned 國有	122,357	1309(35)	299,568	a,b

Top 10 Cities by Production Output 產出排名前 10 位城市	Province 省	Market share 市場份額	Number of firms 企業個數
Nanjing 南京市	Jiangsu 江蘇省	28.84%	15
Hangzhou 杭州市	Zhejiang 浙江省	27.65%	9
Shanghai 上海市	Shanghai 上海市	12.64%	43
Guangzhou 廣州市	Guangdong 廣東省	4.48%	18
Beijing 北京市	Beijing 北京市	2.77%	28
Shenzhen 深圳市	Guangdong 廣東省	2.66%	13
Xinxiang 新鄉市	Henan 河南省	2.52%	1
Nantong 南通市	Jiangsu 江蘇省	1.91%	6
Shenyang 瀋陽市	Liaoning 遼寧省	1.48%	4
Chongqing 重慶市	Chongqing 重慶市	1.37%	9

10 Major Wholesalers 10 家主要批發商	City 城市	Province 省	Telephone / Fax 電話 / 傳真
Liaoning Automobile Trade Group Corp. 遼寧省汽車貿易集團	Shenyang 瀋陽市	Liaoning 遼寧省	(024)23835494 (024)23838338
China Post and Telecommunication Equipment General Company 中國郵電器材總公司	Beijing 北京市	Beijing 北京市	(010)63523715 (010)63525935
Jiangsu Electromechanical Products General Company 江蘇省機電產品總公司	Nanjing 南京市	Jiangsu 江蘇省	(025)7713642 (025)7711036
Xi Nan Technology Import & Export Company 西南技術進出口公司	Chongqing 重慶市	Chongqing 重慶市	(023)63850185 (023)63850026
Changzhou Economic Technology Industrial Development Zone Tian Ming Trade Company 常州經濟技術產業開發區天明貿易公司	Changzhou 常州市	Jiangsu 江蘇省	(0519)8829882 (0519)8829882
Shanxi Mechanical Equipment Import & Export Company 山西省機械設備進出口公司	Taiyuan 太原市	Shanxi 山西省	(0351)4040713 (0351)4043981
Ningbo Five Mining Machinery Import & Export Company 寧波市五礦機械進出口公司	Ningbo 寧波市	Zhejiang 浙江省	(0574)7311255 (0574)7320322
Tianjin Jin Huan Electromechanical Complete Sets of Equipment Factory 天津市津環機電成套設備廠	Tianjin 天津市	Tianjin 天津市	(022)26371628
Yunnan Machinery Import & Export Company 雲南省機械進出口公司	Kunming 昆明市	Yunnan 雲南省	(0871)3164879 (0871)3136829
Tianjin Da Qiu Zhuang Yi Yuan Trade Center 天津市大丘莊億源商貿中心	Tianjin 天津市	Tianjin 天津市	(022)28899478 (022)28899046

*Also include sales by firms outside this industry.包括本行業以外廠家的銷售。"o" stands for "others". "o" 代表"其他產品"。

4112: Switching Equipment 交換設備製造業

The industry accounts for 0.384% of the total revenue of China's industrial sector in 1996. The revenue growth rate of the industry is 40.1% from 1995, as compared to the growth rate of China's industrial sector, 9.51%. The rate of return on asset is 5.60%. 70.69% of all firms in the industry made a profit while 26.42% had negative returns. The top province in terms of the industry's revenue is Guangdong, accounting for 27.18% of the total revenue.
本行業在1996年佔全行業總產值0.384%，行業年增長率為40.1%（全國工業年增長率9.51%）。行業的資產回報率5.60%，70.69%的企業盈利，26.42%的企業虧損。銷售收入最高的省份為廣東省，佔本行業的27.18%。

	Total number of firms 企業總數	Total number of employees 職工總數	Total revenue (mil. RMB) 總銷售收入（百萬元）	Total profit (mil. RMB) 總利潤（百萬元）	Return on assets 資產利潤率 (%)	Return on equity 權益利潤率 (%)	Labour productivity ('000 RMB / worker) 勞動生產率（千元/人）	Debts / assets 資產負債率 (%)	Total assets (mil. RMB) 總資產（百萬元）
Industry Overall 行業總體	322	76,025	22,280	1,916	5.60	14.90	293.06	62.43	34,224

	Number of firms 企業個數	Average number of employees 平均職工人數	Average revenue ('000 RMB) 平均銷售收入（千元）	Average profit ('000 RMB) 平均利潤（千元）	Return on assets 資產利潤率 (%)	Return on equity 權益利潤率 (%)	Labour productivity ('000 RMB / worker) 勞動生產率（千元/人）	Average debts / assets 平均資產負債率(%)	Average Total assets ('000 RMB) 平均總資產（千元）
By ownership 產業所有權									
State-owned 國有	65	623	97,354	5,646	4.01	9.24	156.32	56.61	140,831
Collectively-owned 集體	130	102	21,534	1,921	8.80	19.07	211.51	53.87	21,845
Privately-owned 私有	2	175	25,570	788	2.52	10.28	146.12	75.50	31,285
Domestic JVs 聯營	14	200	32,304	3,805	5.53	24.30	161.35	77.25	68,816
Joint stock 股份制	8	283	37,182	1,630	2.37	10.55	131.21	77.58	68,907
Foreign-funded 外資	43	228	256,786	27,522	6.35	18.90	1127.40	66.38	433,209
Overseas Chinese-funded 港澳台資	57	130	22,720	845	2.47	5.17	175.31	52.31	34,250
By size 規模									
Large 大型	13	1,608	1,045,473	134,722	8.96	23.17	650.36	61.35	1,504,401
Medium 中型	23	832	103,994	1,500	0.72	2.11	125.01	66.18	209,676
Small 小型	273	130	23,069	477	1.32	3.55	177.33	62.75	36,061
By regional distribution 地區分布									
Central-North 華北	58	389	61,984	7,015	6.33	23.93	159.55	73.56	110,858
Beijing 北京	42	183	60,955	8,794	8.54	29.23	333.18	70.79	103,009
Tianjin 天津	7	372	138,890	5,466	2.04	10.25	373.50	80.07	267,531
Hebei 河北	4	189	10,183	275	0.96	2.58	53.80	62.94	28,703
Shanxi 山西	5	2,298	4,400	-372	-1.61	-9.04	1.91	82.22	23,164
Inner Mongolia 內蒙									
Northeast 東北	25	162	14,452	703	2.21	7.47	89.34	70.40	31,776
Liaoning 遼寧	14	89	10,440	974	3.60	8.24	117.12	56.35	27,079
Jilin 吉林	10	276	21,334	379	0.92	5.51	77.30	83.34	41,285
Heilongjiang 黑龍江	1	36	1,810	150	6.15	17.86	50.28	65.57	2,440
Central East 華東	128	165	91,546	7,495	5.76	13.88	554.54	58.50	130,119
Shanghai 上海	25	243	207,091	23,327	6.59	17.11	853.77	61.49	354,061
Jiangsu 江蘇	30	151	48,020	1,495	1.80	7.39	318.93	75.60	82,963
Zhejiang 浙江	47	109	95,018	6,211	7.52	11.95	870.03	37.04	82,579
Anhui 安徽	2	71	9,125	95	0.83	1.24	128.52	33.20	11,460
Fujian 福建	10	25	1,483	39	2.02	3.56	60.53	43.32	1,930
Jiangxi 江西	5	320	24,362	826	1.64	7.57	76.23	78.28	50,244
Shandong 山東	9	381	53,252	3,859	3.05	9.35	139.65	67.42	126,677
Central-South 中南	91	273	71,924	5,760	5.26	13.58	263.30	61.26	109,477
Henan 河南	5	809	71,664	2,088	1.29	6.37	88.63	79.77	162,174
Hubei 湖北	2	53	1,475	35	3.72	8.24	28.10	54.79	940
Hunan 湖南	16	157	6,019	-254	-1.11	-4.25	38.23	73.77	22,846
Guangdong 廣東	64	273	94,629	8,072	5.95	14.53	346.59	59.01	135,553
Guangxi 廣西	4	179	7,823	280	1.03	2.64	43.64	61.04	27,198
Hainan 海南									
Southwest 西南	7	186	2,927	-694	-4.20	-10.09	15.73	58.35	16,524
Chongqing 重慶									
Sichuan 四川	5	240	3,610	-576	-2.83	-5.57	15.04	49.21	20,362
Guizhou 貴州	1	82	2,440	-1,980	-14.29	56.25	29.76	125.47	13,860
Yunnan 雲南	1	21							
Tibet 西藏									
Northwest 西北	13	166	3,109	967	4.72	12.21	18.75	61.38	20,503
Shaanxi 陝西	13	166	3,109	967	4.72	12.21	18.75	61.38	20,503
Gansu 甘肅									
Qinghai 青海									
Ningxia 寧夏									
Xinjiang 新疆									

4112: Switching Equipment 交換設備製造業

Year 年份	Number of firms 企業個數	Rate of change 每年變化 (%)	Number of employees 職工人數 (人)	Rate of change 每年變化 (%)	Total revenue (mil. RMB) 總銷售收入 (百萬元)	Rate of change 每年變化 (%)	Total profit (mil. RMB) 總利潤 (百萬元)	Rate of change 每年變化 (%)
1993	259		76,224		9,526		1,697	
1994	330	27.41%	87,406	14.67%	19,524	104.95%	2,673	57.51%
1995	335	1.52%	69,063	-20.99%	15,899	-18.57%	1,745	-34.72%
1996	322	-3.88%	76,025	10.08%	22,280	40.13%	1,916	9.80%

3 Major products* 3種主要產品 *	Output 產量	Sales volume 銷售量	Unit 單位
a) Spc Exchange 程控交換機	20,545,766	20,545,766	line 線

Top 10 firms by revenue (year founded) 收入排名前10家企業 (創辦年份)	City 城市	Province 省	Telephone / fax 電話 / 傳真	Number of employees 職工人數	Ownership 產業所有權	Revenue ('000 RMB) 銷售收入 (千元)	Profit ('000 RMB) (rank) 利潤 (千元) (排名)	Total assets ('000 RMB) 總資產 (千元)	Major products 主要產品
Shanghai Bell Telephone Equipment Manufacturing Co. Ltd. 上海貝爾電話設備製造有限公司(1983)	Shanghai 上海市	Shanghai 上海市	(021)58541240 (021)58540791	1,787	Foreign-funded 外資	4,560,676	641321(1)	7,697,855	a
Hangzhou Communication Co. Ltd. 杭州通訊有限責任公司(1958)	Hangzhou 杭州市	Zhejiang 浙江省	(0571)8865305 (0571)8865269	1,296	State-owned 國有	3,984,095	286840(4)	3,445,388	a
Shenzhen Hua Wei Technology Co. Ltd. 深圳市華為技術有限公司(1988)	Shenzhen 深圳市	Guangdong 廣東省	(0755)6633828 (0755)6633000	2,762	Collectively-owned 集體	1,952,280	325660(2)	1,569,790	a
Beijing International Switching System Corp., Ltd. 北京國際交換系統有限公司(1990)	Beijing 北京市	Beijing 北京市	(010)64362277 (010)64363123	1,139	Foreign-funded 外資	1,714,655	320622(3)	2,477,972	a
Guangdong Bei Dian Exchange Mi Tong Equipment Co. Ltd. 廣東北電交換系統設備有限公司(1995)	Foshan 佛山市	Guangdong 廣東省	(0757)6621515 (0757)6621525	659	Foreign-funded 外資	1,016,493	-141402(173)	1,859,727	a
Nanjing Ericsson Communication Co. Ltd. 南京愛立信通訊有限公司(1992)	Nanjing 南京市	Jiangsu 江蘇省	(025)2101188 (025)2101199	448	Foreign-funded 外資	755,166	62930(7)	1,116,952	o
Tianjin Nec Electronics &communications Industry Co. Ltd. 天津日電電子通訊工業有限公司(1992)	Tianjin 天津市	Tianjin 天津市	(022)27618130 (022)27361848	831	Foreign-funded 外資	583,921	41706(8)	1,563,950	a
Weihai Bei Yang Electrical Equipment Group Co. Ltd. 威海北洋電氣集團股份有限公司(1988)	Weihai 威海市	Shandong 山東省	(0896)5231031 (0896)5231240	2,935	Joint stock 股份制	457,653	34567(9)	1,106,700	a
Jiangsu Fujitsu Communication Technology Co. Ltd. 江蘇富士通通訊技術有限公司(1994)	Suzhou 蘇州市	Jiangsu 江蘇省	(0512)8250097 (0512)8253090	382	Foreign-funded 外資	456,705	-767(145)	910,750	a
Guangzhou New-tech R & D Inst. 廣州市新技術研究所設計院(1986)	Guangzhou 廣州市	Guangdong 廣東省	(020)85520502 (020)85539106	754	Collectively-owned 集體	390,454	86872(6)	264,438	o

Top 10 Cities by Production Output 產出排名前10位城市	Province 省	Market share 市場份額	Number of firms 企業個數
Shanghai 上海市	Shanghai 上海市	29.78%	47
Shenzhen 深圳市	Guangdong 廣東省	17.95%	35
Beijing 北京市	Beijing 北京市	11.03%	24
Guangzhou 廣州市	Guangdong 廣東省	8.77%	21
Qingdao 青島市	Shandong 山東省	7.52%	4
Tianjin 天津市	Tianjin 天津市	5.58%	12
Hangzhou 杭州市	Zhejiang 浙江省	2.78%	24
Foshan 佛山市	Guangdong 廣東省	2.29%	7
Weihai 威海市	Shandong 山東省	1.91%	5
Luoyang 洛陽市	Henan 河南省	1.65%	1

10 Major Wholesalers 10家主要批發商	City 城市	Province 省	Telephone / Fax 電話 / 傳真
Liaoning Automobile Trade Group Corp. 遼寧省汽車貿易集團	Shenyang 瀋陽市	Liaoning 遼寧省	(024)23835494 (024)23838338
China Post and Telecommunication Equipment General Company 中國郵電器材總公司	Beijing 北京市	Beijing 北京市	(010)63523715 (010)63525935
Jiangsu Electromechanical Products General Company 江蘇省機電產品總公司	Nanjing 南京市	Jiangsu 江蘇省	(025)7713642 (025)7711036
Xi Nan Technology Import & Export Company 西南技術進出口公司	Chongqing 重慶市	Chongqing 重慶市	(023)63850185 (023)63850026
Changzhou Economic Technology Industrial Development Zone Tian Ming Trade Company 常州經濟技術產業開發區天明貿易公司	Changzhou 常州市	Jiangsu 江蘇省	(0519)8829882 (0519)8829882
Shanxi Mechanical Equipment Import & Export Company 山西省機械設備進出口公司	Taiyuan 太原市	Shanxi 山西省	(0351)4040713 (0351)4043981
Ningbo Five Mining Machinery Import & Export Company 寧波市五礦機械進出口公司	Ningbo 寧波市	Zhejiang 浙江省	(0574)7311255 (0574)7320322
Tianjin Jin Huan Electromechanical Complete Sets of Equipment Factory 天津市津環機電成套設備廠	Tianjin 天津市	Tianjin 天津市	(022)26371628
Yunnan Machinery Import & Export Company 雲南省機械進出口公司	Kunming 昆明市	Yunnan 雲南省	(0871)3164879 (0871)3136829
Tianjin Da Qiu Zhuang Yi Yuan Trade Center 天津市大丘莊億源商貿中心	Tianjin 天津市	Tianjin 天津市	(022)28899478 (022)28899046

*Also include sales by firms outside this industry.包括本行業以外廠家的銷售。"o" stands for "others". "o" 代表"其他產品"。

4113: Communication Terminal Equipment 通訊終端設備製造業

The industry accounts for 0.166% of the total revenue of China's industrial sector in 1996. The revenue growth rate of the industry is -11.6% from 1995, as compared to the growth rate of China's industrial sector, 9.51%. The rate of return on asset is 2.87%. 59.85% of all firms in the industry made a profit while 35.27% had negative returns. The top province in terms of the industry's revenue is Guangdong, accounting for 63.52% of the total revenue.
本行業在1996年佔全行業總產值0.166%，行業年增長率為-11.6%（全國工業年增長率9.51%）。行業的資產回報率2.87%，59.85%的企業盈利，35.27%的企業虧損。銷售收入最高的省份為廣東省，佔本行業的63.52%。

	Total number of firms 企業總數	Total number of employees 職工總數	Total revenue (mil. RMB) 總銷售收入（百萬元）	Total profit (mil. RMB) 總利潤（百萬元）	Return on assets 資產利潤率 (%)	Return on equity 權益利潤率 (%)	Labour productivity ('000 RMB / worker) 勞動生產率（千元/人）	Debts / assets 資產負債率 (%)	Total assets (mil. RMB) 總資產（百萬元）
Industry Overall 行業總體	214	67,286	9,617	303	2.87	9.12	142.93	68.50	10,530

	Number of firms 企業個數	Average number of employees 平均職工人數	Average revenue ('000 RMB) 平均銷售收入（千元）	Average profit ('000 RMB) 平均利潤（千元）	Return on assets 資產利潤率 (%)	Return on equity 權益利潤率 (%)	Labour productivity ('000 RMB / worker) 勞動生產率（千元/人）	Average debts / assets 平均資產負債率(%)	Average Total assets ('000 RMB) 平均總資產（千元）
By ownership 產業所有權									
State-owned 國有	57	570	21,456	-702	-1.16	-5.81	37.64	80.06	60,544
Collectively-owned 集體	41	138	13,303	1,391	8.51	20.85	96.48	59.20	16,349
Privately-owned 私有	4	69	2,858	8	0.08	0.16	41.41	51.05	10,202
Domestic JVs 聯營	6	73	7,244	-8	-0.04	-0.13	99.92	72.29	23,259
Joint stock 股份制	3	57	3,743	999	16.42	35.98	65.68	54.36	6,085
Foreign-funded 外資	38	270	123,126	2,043	2.46	7.91	455.75	68.87	83,025
Overseas Chinese-funded 港澳台資	65	314	47,758	3,158	6.72	15.71	152.33	57.24	47,006
By size 規模									
Large 大型	14	1,852	141,405	1,486	0.56	1.98	76.35	71.69	265,218
Medium 中型	16	923	131,376	7,826	5.18	16.41	142.37	68.42	151,028
Small 小型	172	157	32,185	913	3.57	10.47	205.21	65.88	25,569
By regional distribution 地區分布									
Central-North 華北	31	223	13,908	-432	-0.97	-2.98	62.43	67.55	44,770
Beijing 北京	16	45	6,351	-571	-4.66	-11.33	141.73	58.91	12,253
Tianjin 天津	12	416	25,708	68	0.07	0.23	61.86	68.77	92,715
Hebei 河北	2	547	4,385	-2,880	-8.69	-31.82	8.02	72.70	33,145
Shanxi 山西	1	109	12,250	680	5.25	15.96	112.39	67.03	12,950
Inner Mongolia 內蒙									
Northeast 東北	9	332	3,018	-1,763	-5.54	-103.59	9.09	94.65	31,810
Liaoning 遼寧	7	419	3,450	-2,184	-5.61	-288.49	8.24	98.05	38,907
Jilin 吉林	1	8	470	-600	-7.95	-10.10	58.75	21.32	7,550
Heilongjiang 黑龍江	1	48	2,540	20	0.31	0.49	52.92	36.15	6,390
Central East 華東	79	179	26,836	447	1.37	4.61	149.99	70.24	32,597
Shanghai 上海	16	144	72,269	748	0.96	2.75	502.74	64.98	77,624
Jiangsu 江蘇	11	284	16,328	-209	-0.73	-3.49	57.55	78.98	28,517
Zhejiang 浙江	18	100	27,065	865	5.62	19.82	271.71	71.65	15,392
Anhui 安徽	3	130	2,977	-640	-5.60	-20.36	22.90	72.48	11,420
Fujian 福建	20	43	4,055	145	2.21	4.55	94.29	51.36	6,525
Jiangxi 江西	2	2,344	43,945	1,505	0.90	4.72	18.75	80.88	166,935
Shandong 山東	9	109	13,224	677	2.50	12.15	121.08	79.45	27,088
Central-South 中南	83	434	83,171	3,782	5.45	15.43	191.70	64.67	69,376
Henan 河南	8	104	3,179	174	2.95	9.79	30.56	69.84	5,885
Hubei 湖北	9	549	80,413	3,471	3.28	12.31	146.44	73.39	105,946
Hunan 湖南	3	94	597	-407	-5.76	-47.29	6.33	87.77	7,060
Guangdong 廣東	57	510	107,174	5,025	6.19	16.62	210.02	62.76	81,157
Guangxi 廣西	4	191	5,008	-1,038	-4.87	-17.45	26.18	72.10	21,303
Hainan 海南	2	51	11,635	105	0.83	1.24	230.40	33.03	12,655
Southwest 西南	5	908	12,474	-2,900	-4.92	218.37	13.74	102.25	58,892
Chongqing 重慶	2	1,039	7,761	-1,911	-2.46	54.55	7.47	104.51	77,734
Sichuan 四川	2	756	18,714	-1,859	-3.86	-21.10	24.76	81.69	48,110
Guizhou 貴州	1	1,063	5,040	-6,980	-12.78	31.47	4.74	140.61	54,620
Yunnan 雲南									
Tibet 西藏									
Northwest 西北	7	387	10,447	-400	-1.23	-4.84	27.02	74.56	32,519
Shaanxi 陝西	3	52	4,530	897	10.77	20.13	87.12	46.52	8,327
Gansu 甘肅	2	977	27,465	-620	-0.73	-3.41	28.13	78.60	85,065
Qinghai 青海	1	553	2,540	-3,940	-14.38	-70.48	4.59	79.56	27,400
Ningxia 寧夏									
Xinjiang 新疆	1	45	2,070	-310	-6.05	-12.20	46.00	50.39	5,120

4113: Communication Terminal Equipment 通訊終端設備製造業

Year 年份	Number of firms 企業個數	Rate of change 每年變化 (%)	Number of employees 職工人數 (人)	Rate of change 每年變化 (%)	Total revenue (mil. RMB) 總銷售收入 (百萬元)	Rate of change 每年變化 (%)	Total profit (mil. RMB) 總利潤 (百萬元)	Rate of change 每年變化 (%)
1993	117		63,564		5,850		248	
1994	128	9.40%	43,931	-30.89%	3,857	-34.06%	197	-20.48%
1995	228	78.13%	79,489	80.94%	10,879	182.03%	245	24.30%
1996	214	-6.14%	67,286	-15.35%	9,617	-11.60%	303	23.43%

3 Major products* 3 種主要產品 *	Output 產量	Sales volume 銷售量	Unit 單位
a) Telephone Single Set 電話單機	49,390,519	48,402,709	set 部

Top 10 firms by revenue (year founded) 收入排名前 10 家企業 (創辦年份)	City 城市	Province 省	Telephone / fax 電話 / 傳真	Number of employees 職工人數	Ownership 產業所有權	Revenue ('000 RMB) 銷售收入 (千元)	Profit ('000 RMB) (rank) 利潤 (千元) (排名)	Total assets ('000 RMB) 總資產 (千元)	Major products 主要產品
You Li Electron (Shenzhen) Co. Ltd. 友利電子(深圳)有限公司(1993)	Shenzhen 深圳市	Guangdong 廣東省	(0755)7391349 (0755)7392274	4,664	Foreign-funded 外資	2,080,342	93664(2)	749,690	a
Shenzhen Guo Wei Electron Co. Ltd. 深圳國威電子有限公司(1991)	Shenzhen 深圳市	Guangdong 廣東省	(0755)5736666 (0755)5732288	5,000	Overseas Chinese-funded 港澳台資	948,840	10900(8)	571,473	a
Shanghai Siemens Moving Communication Co. Ltd. 上海西門子移動通訊有限公司(1993)	Shanghai 上海市	Shanghai 上海市	(021)58541688 (021)58548414	268	Foreign-funded 外資	771,386	38339(3)	597,172	o
Tcl Communication Equipment Share Co. Ltd. TCL 通訊設備股份有限公司(1985)	Huizhou 惠州市	Guangdong 廣東省	(0751)2260868 (0751)2261868	2,663	Overseas Chinese-funded 港澳台資	634,549	96090(1)	669,420	a
She Kou Tai Feng Electron Co. Ltd. 蛇口泰豐電子有限公司(1989)	Shenzhen 深圳市	Guangdong 廣東省	(0755)6689947 (0755)6695000	800	Overseas Chinese-funded 港澳台資	344,070	38000(4)	426,047	a
Ningbo Yi Pu Information Equipment Co. Ltd. 寧波益普資訊設備有限公司(1993)	Ningbo 寧波市	Zhejiang 浙江省	(0574)3017232 (0574)3015960	100	Overseas Chinese-funded 港澳台資	314,238	8363(10)	96,814	o
Tang De Electron (huizhou) Co. Ltd. 唐德電子(惠州)有限公司(1988)	Huizhou 惠州市	Guangdong 廣東省	(0751)2261383 (0751)2261798	1,383	Foreign-funded 外資	240,820	370(45)	111,071	a
Tianjin Communication Broadcast Company 天津通訊廣播公司(1936)	Tianjin 天津市	Tianjin 天津市	(022)26281601 (022)26281601	2,724	State-owned 國有	221,793	77(55)	720,071	o
Shenzhen Yue Hai Telecommunication Co. Ltd. 深圳粵海電訊有限公司(1992)	Shenzhen 深圳市	Guangdong 廣東省	(0755)6630888 (0755)6632876	1,787	Overseas Chinese-funded 港澳台資	209,908	20037(5)	292,915	o
Guangdong Nanhe Joint Enterprise Company 廣東南和聯合企業公司(1980)	Shenzhen 深圳市	Guangdong 廣東省	(0755)8707333 (0755)8709577	1,803	State-owned 國有	206,047	1008(32)	180,322	a

Top 10 Cities by Production Output 產出排名前 10 位城市	Province 省	Market share 市場份額	Number of firms 企業個數
Huizhou 惠州市	Guangdong 廣東省	29.01%	17
Shanghai 上海市	Shanghai 上海市	20.28%	23
Shenzhen 深圳市	Guangdong 廣東省	8.09%	27
Ningbo 寧波市	Zhejiang 浙江省	5.80%	1
Tianjin 天津市	Tianjin 天津市	5.53%	18
Dongguan 東莞市	Guangdong 廣東省	4.44%	4
Zhongshan 中山市	Guangdong 廣東省	3.71%	10
Zhanjiang 湛江市	Guangdong 廣東省	3.12%	1
Wuhan 武漢市	Hubei 湖北省	2.77%	4
Yangzhou 揚州市	Jiangsu 江蘇省	2.73%	3

10 Major Wholesalers 10 家主要批發商	City 城市	Province 省	Telephone / Fax 電話 / 傳真
Liaoning Automobile Trade Group Corp. 遼寧省汽車貿易集團	Shenyang 瀋陽市	Liaoning 遼寧省	(024)23835494 (024)23838338
China Post and Telecommunication Equipment General Company 中國郵電器材總公司	Beijing 北京市	Beijing 北京市	(010)63523715 (010)63525935
Jiangsu Electromechanical Products General Company 江蘇省機電產品總公司	Nanjing 南京市	Jiangsu 江蘇省	(025)7713642 (025)7711036
Xi Nan Technology Import & Export Company 西南技術進出口公司	Chongqing 重慶市	Chongqing 重慶市	(023)63850185 (023)63850026
Changzhou Economic Technology Industrial Development Zone Tian Ming Trade Company 常州經濟技術產業開發區天明貿易公司	Changzhou 常州市	Jiangsu 江蘇省	(0519)8829882 (0519)8829882
Shanxi Mechanical Equipment Import & Export Company 山西省機械設備進出口公司	Taiyuan 太原市	Shanxi 山西省	(0351)4040713 (0351)4043981
Ningbo Five Mining Machinery Import & Export Company 寧波市五礦機械進出口公司	Ningbo 寧波市	Zhejiang 浙江省	(0574)7311255 (0574)7320322
Tianjin Jin Huan Electromechanical Complete Sets of Equipment Factory 天津市津環機電成套設備廠	Tianjin 天津市	Tianjin 天津市	(022)26371628
Yunnan Machinery Import & Export Company 雲南省機械進出口公司	Kunming 昆明市	Yunnan 雲南省	(0871)3164879 (0871)3136829
Tianjin Da Qiu Zhuang Yi Yuan Trade Center 天津市大丘莊億源商貿中心	Tianjin 天津市	Tianjin 天津市	(022)28899478 (022)28899046

*Also include sales by firms outside this industry.包括本行業以外廠家的銷售。"o" stands for "others". "o" 代表"其他產品"。

4119: Other Communication Equipment 其他通訊設備製造業

The industry accounts for 0.440% of the total revenue of China's industrial sector in 1996. The revenue growth rate of the industry is 26.2% from 1995, as compared to the growth rate of China's industrial sector, 9.51%. The rate of return on asset is 13.88%. 64.89% of all firms in the industry made a profit while 29.69% had negative returns. The top province in terms of the industry's revenue is Tianjin, accounting for 46.84% of the total revenue.
本行業在1996年佔全行業總產值0.440%，行業年增長率為26.2%（全國工業年增長率9.51%）。行業的資產回報率13.88%，64.89%的企業盈利，29.69%的企業虧損。銷售收入最高的省份為天津市，佔本行業的46.84%。

	Total number of firms 企業總數	Total number of employees 職工總數	Total revenue (mil. RMB) 總銷售收入（百萬元）	Total profit (mil. RMB) 總利潤（百萬元）	Return on assets 資產利潤率 (%)	Return on equity 權益利潤率 (%)	Labour productivity ('000 RMB / worker) 勞動生產率（千元/人）	Debts / assets 資產負債率 (%)	Total assets (mil. RMB) 總資產（百萬元）
Industry Overall 行業總體	594	90,891	25,507	3,285	13.88	30.13	280.63	53.94	23,669

	Number of firms 企業個數	Average number of employees 平均職工人數	Average revenue ('000 RMB) 平均銷售收入（千元）	Average profit ('000 RMB) 平均利潤（千元）	Return on assets 資產利潤率 (%)	Return on equity 權益利潤率 (%)	Labour productivity ('000 RMB / worker) 勞動生產率（千元/人）	Average debts / assets 平均資產負債率(%)	Average Total assets ('000 RMB) 平均總資產（千元）
By ownership 產業所有權									
State-owned 國有	112	316	20,107	473	1.15	3.72	63.62	69.04	41,098
Collectively-owned 集體	249	76	6,451	434	4.65	9.85	84.88	52.84	9,339
Privately-owned 私有	5	69	5,814	287	3.22	6.71	84.50	51.93	8,904
Domestic JVs 聯營	19	267	27,965	1,305	2.90	6.92	104.74	58.09	45,011
Joint stock 股份制	4	38	1,253	-163	-5.83	-20.98	33.41	72.23	2,790
Foreign-funded 外資	70	198	222,233	42,992	29.03	48.70	1123.36	40.39	148,103
Overseas Chinese-funded 港澳台資	133	142	41,384	547	1.34	4.05	292.17	66.94	40,793
By size 規模									
Large 大型	11	2,208	1,564,819	283,382	28.18	50.30	708.68	43.98	1,005,597
Medium 中型	22	763	53,555	1,489	1.67	4.12	70.18	59.49	89,184
Small 小型	535	93	13,299	254	1.28	3.48	142.54	63.27	19,899
By regional distribution 地區分布									
Central-North 華北	74	172	197,359	40,850	27.92	48.07	1149.52	41.91	146,303
Beijing 北京	52	88	50,495	1,605	3.20	13.59	573.81	76.43	50,096
Tianjin 天津	13	540	919,117	226,218	36.08	52.15	1702.80	30.83	627,072
Hebei 河北	7	131	3,759	-270	-2.98	-5.56	28.79	46.43	9,071
Shanxi 山西	2	99	2,010	255	8.47	28.81	20.30	70.60	3,010
Inner Mongolia 內蒙									
Northeast 東北	46	112	3,329	-364	-3.22	-10.97	29.83	70.67	11,308
Liaoning 遼寧	25	162	2,466	-654	-6.92	-117.53	15.21	94.11	9,454
Jilin 吉林	6	61	2,900	93	1.32	2.55	47.54	48.13	7,050
Heilongjiang 黑龍江	15	48	4,940	-63	-0.39	-0.81	103.49	51.68	16,100
Central East 華東	296	117	18,940	815	3.54	9.57	161.71	62.98	23,002
Shanghai 上海	52	78	31,034	1,178	2.96	5.66	399.75	47.75	39,821
Jiangsu 江蘇	76	205	26,685	1,325	4.07	14.09	130.03	71.14	32,592
Zhejiang 浙江	67	77	8,895	341	3.41	7.42	116.11	54.06	10,007
Anhui 安徽	4	171	16,385	213	0.39	1.60	96.10	75.81	54,828
Fujian 福建	66	88	12,323	237	1.96	5.78	139.70	66.03	12,083
Jiangxi 江西	13	112	5,266	-177	-2.06	-4.65	46.99	55.66	8,582
Shandong 山東	18	108	23,392	2,340	9.11	99.15	216.92	90.81	25,677
Central-South 中南	133	214	34,531	209	0.61	1.63	161.45	62.47	34,231
Henan 河南	16	209	13,675	-633	-2.98	-28.86	65.49	89.68	21,251
Hubei 湖北	19	241	24,822	1,834	4.49	9.69	103.20	53.69	40,842
Hunan 湖南	14	183	7,338	121	0.76	1.64	40.21	53.70	16,005
Guangdong 廣東	68	253	53,337	28	0.06	0.17	210.48	63.34	43,692
Guangxi 廣西	15	49	11,455	-6	-0.04	-0.07	233.15	49.36	15,889
Hainan 海南	1	11	710	-340	-10.33	-57.63	64.55	82.07	3,290
Southwest 西南	29	206	13,691	362	1.89	7.71	66.33	75.46	19,147
Chongqing 重慶	10	203	30,356	2,292	8.70	22.38	149.53	61.14	26,357
Sichuan 四川	14	195	5,166	-401	-2.57	-15.89	26.55	83.85	15,609
Guizhou 貴州	3	185	1,167	-740	-12.89	516.28	6.32	102.50	5,740
Yunnan 雲南	2	341	11,110	-2,055	-7.10	-1081.58	32.63	99.34	28,945
Tibet 西藏									
Northwest 西北	16	247	9,579	-49	-0.19	-0.82	38.79	76.28	25,357
Shaanxi 陝西	13	235	8,336	12	0.05	0.21	35.48	77.95	26,708
Gansu 甘肅	1	712	31,140	510	1.28	3.16	43.74	59.51	39,840
Qinghai 青海									
Ningxia 寧夏	1	145	9,770	-1,510	-9.33	-52.98	67.38	82.40	16,190
Xinjiang 新疆	1	40	3,990	50	2.02	7.04	99.75	71.37	2,480

4119: Other Communication Equipment 其他通訊設備製造業

Year 年份	Number of firms 企業個數	Rate of change 每年變化 (%)	Number of employees 職工人數 (人)	Rate of change 每年變化 (%)	Total revenue (mil. RMB) 總銷售收入 (百萬元)	Rate of change 每年變化 (%)	Total profit (mil. RMB) 總利潤 (百萬元)	Rate of change 每年變化 (%)
1993	372		67,975		3,711		142	
1994	416	11.83%	57,966	-14.73%	4,735	27.60%	164	15.65%
1995	581	39.66%	88,336	52.39%	20,214	326.87%	2,140	1207.53%
1996	594	2.24%	90,891	2.89%	25,507	26.18%	3,285	53.50%

3 Major products* 3 種主要產品 *	Output 產量	Sales volume 銷售量	Unit 單位
a) Mobile Communication Equipment 移動通訊設備	9,074,004	8,983,264	set 部（信道）
b) Radio-paging System Equipment 無線尋呼系統設備	5,928,193	5,216,810	set 部
c) Telephone Single Set 電話單機	16,862,609	16,525,357	set 部

Top 10 firms by revenue (year founded) 收入排名前 10 家企業 (創辦年份)	City 城市	Province 省	Telephone / fax 電話 / 傳真	Number of employees 職工人數	Ownership 產業所有權	Revenue ('000 RMB) 銷售收入 (千元)	Profit ('000 RMB) (rank) 利潤（千元）(排名)	Total assets ('000 RMB) 總資產 (千元)	Major products 主要產品
Motorola (China) Electron Co. Ltd. 摩托羅拉(中國)電子有限公司(1992)	Tianjin 天津市	Tianjin 天津市	(022)5325050 (022)5328820	5,923	Foreign-funded 外資	11,934,840	2942661(1)	8,098,623	a,b
Zhuhai Tian Cao Electron Co. Ltd. 珠海天草電子有限公司(1994)	Zhuhai 珠海市	Guangdong 廣東省	(0756)8622149 (0756)8621942	1,150	Foreign-funded 外資	1,422,197	-11013(292)	342,520	o
Beijing Ericsson Moving Communication Co. Ltd. 北京愛立信移動通訊有限公司(1995)	Beijing 北京市	Beijing 北京市	(010)62365913 (010)62365918	22	Foreign-funded 外資	1,398,194	95857(2)	1,020,967	a
Beijing Nokia Moving Communication Co. Ltd. 北京諾基亞移動通訊有限公司(1995)	Beijing 北京市	Beijing 北京市	(010)64351122 (010)64387675	210	Foreign-funded 外資	1,015,085	-6213(286)	772,986	a
Shenzhen Chuang Hua Cooperative Co. Ltd. 深圳創華合作有限公司(1990)	Shenzhen 深圳市	Guangdong 廣東省	(0755)6640749 (0755)6640748	2,856	Overseas Chinese-funded 港澳台資	998,776	18963(9)	366,380	c
3M China Co. Ltd. 3M 中國有限公司(1984)	Shanghai 上海市	Shanghai 上海市	(021)62753535 (021)62752343	546	Foreign-funded 外資	500,315	-16544(295)	604,825	o
Wuhan Neczhongyuan Moving Communication Co. Ltd. 武漢 NEC 中原移動通訊有限公司(1995)	Wuhan 武漢市	Hubei 湖北省	(027)87803569 (027)87403751	191	Foreign-funded 外資	438,130	40421(4)	257,534	a
Zhong Xun Electron (Kunshan) Co. Ltd. 中訊電子(昆山)有限公司(1995)	Suzhou 蘇州市	Jiangsu 江蘇省	(0512)7314449	380	Foreign-funded 外資	424,043	38815(6)	414,049	o
Ministry of Posts & Telecommunications Nanjing Communication Equipment Factory 南京郵電通訊設備股份有限公司(1958)	Nanjing 南京市	Jiangsu 江蘇省	(025)2418518 (025)2416518	1,343	State-owned 國有	338,848	54069(3)	447,827	o
Hong Tai Fa Zhan Co. Ltd. 宏泰發展有限公司(1986)	Xiamen 廈門市	Fujian 福建省	(0592)5055881 (0592)5055880	2,066	Overseas Chinese-funded 港澳台資	333,457	3362(31)	163,773	o

Top 10 Cities by Production Output 產出排名前 10 位城市	Province 省	Market share 市場份額	Number of firms 企業個數
Suzhou 蘇州市	Jiangsu 江蘇省	15.37%	36
Zhuhai 珠海市	Guangdong 廣東省	13.55%	11
Shanghai 上海市	Shanghai 上海市	11.24%	84
Wuhan 武漢市	Hubei 湖北省	9.11%	15
Beijing 北京市	Beijing 北京市	4.59%	41
Xiamen 廈門市	Fujian 福建省	3.69%	16
Dongguan 東莞市	Guangdong 廣東省	3.53%	6
Ji'nan 濟南市	Shandong 山東省	3.50%	8
Wuxi 無錫市	Jiangsu 江蘇省	3.14%	25
Foshan 佛山市	Guangdong 廣東省	2.96%	14

10 Major Wholesalers 10 家主要批發商	City 城市	Province 省	Telephone / Fax 電話 / 傳真
Liaoning Automobile Trade Group Corp. 遼寧省汽車貿易集團	Shenyang 瀋陽市	Liaoning 遼寧省	(024)23835494 (024)23838338
China Post and Telecommunication Equipment General Company 中國郵電器材總公司	Beijing 北京市	Beijing 北京市	(010)63523715 (010)63525935
Jiangsu Electromechanical Products General Company 江蘇省機電產品總公司	Nanjing 南京市	Jiangsu 江蘇省	(025)7713642 (025)7711036
Xi Nan Technology Import & Export Company 西南技術進出口公司	Chongqing 重慶市	Chongqing 重慶市	(023)63850185 (023)63850026
Changzhou Economic Technology Industrial Development Zone Tian Ming Trade Company 常州經濟技術產業開發區天明貿易公司	Changzhou 常州市	Jiangsu 江蘇省	(0519)8829882 (0519)8829882
Shanxi Mechanical Equipment Import & Export Company 山西省機械設備進出口公司	Taiyuan 太原市	Shanxi 山西省	(0351)4040713 (0351)4043981
Ningbo Five Mining Machinery Import & Export Company 寧波市五礦機械進出口公司	Ningbo 寧波市	Zhejiang 浙江省	(0574)7311255 (0574)7320322
Tianjin Jin Huan Electromechanical Complete Sets of Equipment Factory 天津市津環機電成套設備廠	Tianjin 天津市	Tianjin 天津市	(022)26371628
Yunnan Machinery Import & Export Company 雲南省機械進出口公司	Kunming 昆明市	Yunnan 雲南省	(0871)3164879 (0871)3136829
Tianjin Da Qiu Zhuang Yi Yuan Trade Center 天津市大丘莊億源商貿中心	Tianjin 天津市	Tianjin 天津市	(022)28899478 (022)28899046

*Also include sales by firms outside this industry.包括本行業以外廠家的銷售。"o" stands for "others". "o" 代表"其他產品"。

4130: Broadcast and Television Equipment 廣播電視設備製造業

The industry accounts for 0.027% of the total revenue of China's industrial sector in 1996. The revenue growth rate of the industry is -7.5% from 1995, as compared to the growth rate of China's industrial sector, 9.51%. The rate of return on asset is 0.43%. 66.99% of all firms in the industry made a profit while 28.57% had negative returns. The top province in terms of the industry's revenue is Guangdong, accounting for 28.39% of the total revenue.
本行業在 1996 年佔全行業總產值 0.027% ，行業年增長率為 -7.5%（全國工業年增長率 9.51%）。行業的資產回報率 0.43% ， 66.99% 的企業盈利， 28.57% 的企業虧損。銷售收入最高的省份為廣東省，佔本行業的 28.39% 。

	Total number of firms 企業總數	Total number of employees 職工總數	Total revenue (mil. RMB) 總銷售收入（百萬元）	Total profit (mil. RMB) 總利潤（百萬元）	Return on assets 資產利潤率 (%)	Return on equity 權益利潤率 (%)	Labour productivity ('000 RMB / worker) 勞動生產率（千元/人）	Debts / assets 資產負債率 (%)	Total assets (mil. RMB) 總資產（百萬元）
Industry Overall 行業總體	250	34,975	1,542	15	0.43	1.83	44.09	76.35	3,498

	Number of firms 企業個數	Average number of employees 平均職工人數	Average revenue ('000 RMB) 平均銷售收入（千元）	Average profit ('000 RMB) 平均利潤（千元）	Return on assets 資產利潤率 (%)	Return on equity 權益利潤率 (%)	Labour productivity ('000 RMB / worker) 勞動生產率（千元/人）	Average debts / assets 平均資產負債率(%)	Average Total assets ('000 RMB) 平均總資產（千元）
By ownership 產業所有權									
State-owned 國有	62	330	6,532	-565	-1.56	-10.57	19.77	85.28	36,274
Collectively-owned 集體	142	70	4,522	46	1.04	4.30	64.45	75.84	4,404
Privately-owned 私有	1	34	1,190	-7	-0.71	-0.98	35.01	27.38	969
Domestic JVs 聯營	5	150	8,829	80	0.67	1.50	58.78	55.63	11,984
Joint stock 股份制	3	50	2,063	170	4.56	10.93	41.26	58.24	3,737
Foreign-funded 外資	14	54	4,707	74	0.76	1.15	87.40	33.57	9,683
Overseas Chinese-funded 港澳台資	23	125	16,429	1,807	9.99	18.64	131.11	46.44	18,096
By size 規模									
Large 大型	5	2,357	56,560	-1,292	-0.41	-3.04	24.00	86.48	314,080
Medium 中型	8	669	15,183	-174	-0.39	-1.71	22.68	77.16	44,526
Small 小型	233	76	4,805	102	1.61	4.72	63.07	65.94	6,338
By regional distribution 地區分布									
Central-North 華北	41	127	3,651	-21	-0.11	-0.54	28.74	79.55	19,458
Beijing 北京	32	140	3,619	-19	-0.08	-0.40	25.80	79.95	23,652
Tianjin 天津	3	19	870	-257	-23.62	-98.72	45.00	76.07	1,087
Hebei 河北	4	69	7,500	100	1.22	4.36	109.49	72.03	8,205
Shanxi 山西	1	120	1,270	90	1.86	6.21	10.58	70.04	4,840
Inner Mongolia 內蒙	1	267							
Northeast 東北	19	276	5,018	412	2.03	10.88	18.20	81.29	20,254
Liaoning 遼寧	12	351	6,223	436	1.80	8.31	17.72	78.37	24,251
Jilin 吉林	4	29	1,005	50	8.00	52.63	34.66	84.80	625
Heilongjiang 黑龍江	3	302	5,550	800	2.63	27.68	18.36	90.51	30,440
Central East 華東	103	69	5,434	191	2.91	7.71	78.66	62.32	6,579
Shanghai 上海	8	30	3,644	55	0.89	1.69	123.52	46.94	6,149
Jiangsu 江蘇	23	65	6,554	89	1.16	2.72	100.17	57.34	7,684
Zhejiang 浙江	43	63	4,059	-86	-1.57	-4.66	64.17	66.42	5,466
Anhui 安徽	3	77	3,887	260	10.39	16.70	50.48	37.68	2,503
Fujian 福建	15	87	11,183	1,387	14.16	36.65	128.54	61.35	9,791
Jiangxi 江西	5	191	4,492	-68	-0.63	-2.53	23.54	74.92	10,710
Shandong 山東	6	28	567	-58	-3.99	-388.89	20.61	99.09	1,463
Central-South 中南	65	154	8,470	288	3.06	8.36	54.96	63.43	9,419
Henan 河南	7	162	3,683	43	0.55	2.58	22.69	78.62	7,779
Hubei 湖北	7	239	2,960	-246	-2.33	-7.06	12.39	66.96	10,531
Hunan 湖南	18	105	3,329	25	0.39	1.32	31.64	70.38	6,409
Guangdong 廣東	26	200	16,839	750	5.35	12.80	84.31	58.19	14,017
Guangxi 廣西	7	17	904	26	4.22	13.53	51.89	68.85	610
Hainan 海南									
Southwest 西南	12	326	11,078	-1,149	-3.43	-21.32	33.95	83.93	33,550
Chongqing 重慶	2	625	25,755	-7,421	-7.89	-65.84	41.23	88.02	94,112
Sichuan 四川	9	296	9,323	153	0.62	3.10	31.47	80.00	24,726
Guizhou 貴州									
Yunnan 雲南	1	52	250	-1,590	-46.63	120.45	4.81	138.71	3,410
Tibet 西藏									
Northwest 西北	10	348	5,352	-1,639	-2.63	-33.95	15.38	92.25	62,261
Shaanxi 陝西	7	481	7,604	-2,284	-2.66	-45.99	15.80	94.22	85,947
Gansu 甘肅	1	41	130	-140	-13.21	-28.00	3.17	52.83	1,060
Qinghai 青海									
Ningxia 寧夏									
Xinjiang 新疆	2	34	80	-130	-1.31	-2.00	2.35	34.74	9,960

4130: Broadcast and Television Equipment 廣播電視設備製造業

Year 年份	Number of firms 企業個數	Rate of change 每年變化 (%)	Number of employees 職工人數 (人)	Rate of change 每年變化 (%)	Total revenue (mil. RMB) 總銷售收入 (百萬元)	Rate of change 每年變化 (%)	Total profit (mil. RMB) 總利潤 (百萬元)	Rate of change 每年變化 (%)
1993	215		34,568		1,627		48	
1994	201	-6.51%	37,690	9.03%	1,757	7.98%	6	-86.75%
1995	262	30.35%	37,231	-1.22%	1,667	-5.14%	47	633.52%
1996	250	-4.58%	34,975	-6.06%	1,542	-7.50%	15	-68.14%

3 Major products* 3 種主要產品 *	Output 產量	Sales volume 銷售量	Unit 單位
a) TV Transmitter & Translator Equipment 電視發射、差轉設備	3,886	4,469	set 部
b) Broadcast & TV Transmitter Equipment 廣播發射設備	8,129	8,129	set 部

Top 10 firms by revenue (year founded) 收入排名前 10 家企業 (創辦年份)	City 城市	Province 省	Telephone / fax 電話 / 傳真	Number of employees 職工人數	Ownership 產業所有權	Revenue ('000 RMB) 銷售收入 (千元)	Profit ('000 RMB) (rank) 利潤（千元）(排名)	Total assets ('000 RMB) 總資產 (千元)	Major products 主要產品
Shandou SEZ Tokyo Components Co. Ltd. 汕頭經濟特區東京元件有限公司(1988)	Shantou 汕頭市	Guangdong 廣東省	(0754)8261188 (0754)8261281	1,795	Foreign-funded 外資	169,724	1878(7)	73,797	o
Shandou Sez Hua Xing Electron Science & Technology Co. Ltd. 汕頭經濟特區華星電子科技有限公司(1990)	Shantou 汕頭市	Guangdong 廣東省	(0754)8265651 (0754)8265650	285	Overseas Chinese-funded 港澳台資	115,151	327(27)	130,536	o
Shenzhen Mai Wei Cable Television Equipment Co. Ltd. 深圳邁威有線電視器材有限公司(1991)	Shenzhen 深圳市	Guangdong 廣東省	(0755)3344197 (0755)3344197	1,943	Overseas Chinese-funded 港澳台資	64,490	15794(2)	50,758	o
Fujian Nanjing Wan Li Da Electron Co. Ltd. 福建省南靖萬利達電子有限公司(1992)	Zhangzhou 漳州市	Fujian 福建省	(0596)7823188	295	Overseas Chinese-funded 港澳台資	59,888	18064(1)	59,278	o
Fujian Nanjing Radio Factory 福建省南靖縣無線電廠(1984)	Zhangzhou 漳州市	Fujian 福建省	(0596)7823188	287	Collectively-owned 集體	54,679	1070(12)	31,766	o
Suzhou Jiang Nan Radio Factory 蘇州江南無線電廠(1958)	Suzhou 蘇州市	Jiangsu 江蘇省	(0512)8213719 (0512)8216162	420	State-owned 國有	45,278	2582(4)	37,686	o
State-owned Chengdu TV Equipment Factory 國營成都電視設備廠(1975)	Chengdu 成都市	Sichuan 四川省	(028)5184912 (028)5184575	1,696	State-owned 國有	41,902	201(37)	144,390	a,b
Ru Yi Electric General Co. 如意電氣總公司(1965)	Xianyang 咸陽市	Shaanxi 陝西省	(0910)3611017 (0910)3611066	3,074	State-owned 國有	41,621	-15555(90)	584,518	o
Beijing Broadcast Equipments Plant 北京廣播器材廠(1943)	Beijing 北京市	Beijing 北京市	(010)62018844 (010)62018409	3,520	State-owned 國有	41,013	0(67)	545,769	a,b
Chongqing Radio Testing Instrument Plant 重慶無線電測試儀器廠(1966)	Chongqing 重慶市	Chongqing 重慶市	(023)67851010 (023)67852210	1,009	State-owned 國有	39,915	-9421(89)	163,088	o

Top 10 Cities by Production Output 產出排名前 10 位城市	Province 省	Market share 市場份額	Number of firms 企業個數
Shantou 汕頭市	Guangdong 廣東省	18.94%	6
Shenzhen 深圳市	Guangdong 廣東省	11.89%	7
Beijing 北京市	Beijing 北京市	9.73%	24
Zhangzhou 漳州市	Fujian 福建省	7.69%	3
Chengdu 成都市	Sichuan 四川省	6.78%	13
Ningbo 寧波市	Zhejiang 浙江省	3.71%	16
Shanghai 上海市	Shanghai 上海市	3.53%	16
Guangzhou 廣州市	Guangdong 廣東省	3.50%	9
Wuxi 無錫市	Jiangsu 江蘇省	2.99%	13
Chongqing 重慶市	Chongqing 重慶市	2.80%	6

10 Major Wholesalers 10 家主要批發商	City 城市	Province 省	Telephone / Fax 電話 / 傳真
Liaoning Automobile Trade Group Corp. 遼寧省汽車貿易集團	Shenyang 瀋陽市	Liaoning 遼寧省	(024)23835494 (024)23838338
China Post and Telecommunication Equipment General Company 中國郵電器材總公司	Beijing 北京市	Beijing 北京市	(010)63523715 (010)63525935
Jiangsu Electromechanical Products General Company 江蘇省機電產品總公司	Nanjing 南京市	Jiangsu 江蘇省	(025)7713642 (025)7711036
Xi Nan Technology Import & Export Company 西南技術進出口公司	Chongqing 重慶市	Chongqing 重慶市	(023)63850185 (023)63850026
Changzhou Economic Technology Industrial Development Zone Tian Ming Trade Company 常州經濟技術產業開發區天明貿易公司	Changzhou 常州市	Jiangsu 江蘇省	(0519)8829882 (0519)8829882
Shanxi Mechanical Equipment Import & Export Company 山西省機械設備進出口公司	Taiyuan 太原市	Shanxi 山西省	(0351)4040713 (0351)4043981
Ningbo Five Mining Machinery Import & Export Company 寧波市五礦機械進出口公司	Ningbo 寧波市	Zhejiang 浙江省	(0574)7311255 (0574)7320322
Tianjin Jin Huan Electromechanical Complete Sets of Equipment Factory 天津市津環機電成套設備廠	Tianjin 天津市	Tianjin 天津市	(022)26371628
Yunnan Machinery Import & Export Company 雲南省機械進出口公司	Kunming 昆明市	Yunnan 雲南省	(0871)3164879 (0871)3136829
Tianjin Da Qiu Zhuang Yi Yuan Trade Center 天津市大丘莊億源商貿中心	Tianjin 天津市	Tianjin 天津市	(022)28899478 (022)28899046

*Also include sales by firms outside this industry.包括本行業以外廠家的銷售。"o" stands for "others". "o" 代表"其他產品"。

4141: Computers 電子計算機整機製造業

The industry accounts for 0.320% of the total revenue of China's industrial sector in 1996. The revenue growth rate of the industry is 18.4% from 1995, as compared to the growth rate of China's industrial sector, 9.51%. The rate of return on asset is 2.50%. 69.37% of all firms in the industry made a profit while 28.02% had negative returns. The top province in terms of the industry's revenue is Guangdong, accounting for 32.16% of the total revenue.
本行業在1996年佔全行業總產值0.320%，行業年增長率為18.4%（全國工業年增長率9.51%）。行業的資產回報率2.50%，69.37%的企業盈利，28.02%的企業虧損。銷售收入最高的省份為廣東省，佔本行業的32.16%。

	Total number of firms 企業總數	Total number of employees 職工總數	Total revenue (mil. RMB) 總銷售收入（百萬元）	Total profit (mil. RMB) 總利潤（百萬元）	Return on assets 資產利潤率 (%)	Return on equity 權益利潤率 (%)	Labour productivity ('000 RMB / worker) 勞動生產率（千元/人）	Debts / assets 資產負債率 (%)	Total assets (mil. RMB) 總資產（百萬元）
Industry Overall 行業總體	210	55,917	18,572	468	2.50	9.84	332.14	74.63	18,728

	Number of firms 企業個數	Average number of employees 平均職工人數	Average revenue ('000 RMB) 平均銷售收入（千元）	Average profit ('000 RMB) 平均利潤（千元）	Return on assets 資產利潤率 (%)	Return on equity 權益利潤率 (%)	Labour productivity ('000 RMB / worker) 勞動生產率（千元/人）	Average debts / assets 平均資產負債率(%)	Average Total assets ('000 RMB) 平均總資產（千元）
By ownership 產業所有權									
State-owned 國有	63	539	81,476	1,111	1.03	6.44	151.25	84.06	108,270
Collectively-owned 集體	34	166	86,223	1,822	3.09	7.92	519.23	60.98	58,969
Privately-owned 私有	1	134	35,609	15,612	50.76	132.25	265.74	61.62	30,755
Domestic JVs 聯營	5	38	2,900	-1,094	-30.26	302.57	75.53	110.00	3,616
Joint stock 股份制	6	831	175,383	15,000	5.18	12.42	211.09	58.30	289,571
Foreign-funded 外資	39	227	193,517	5,640	3.25	11.81	852.31	72.46	173,479
Overseas Chinese-funded 港澳台資	59	72	30,131	35	0.16	0.75	417.80	79.12	22,391
By size 規模									
Large 大型	15	2,168	749,235	23,953	3.08	11.73	345.51	73.72	776,589
Medium 中型	16	657	58,329	195	0.18	0.85	88.74	78.67	106,951
Small 小型	166	73	35,778	425	1.50	6.96	490.96	78.50	28,401
By regional distribution 地區分布									
Central-North 華北	71	128	50,498	1,245	1.62	7.24	393.22	77.68	77,009
Beijing 北京	56	142	57,045	1,646	1.89	8.60	401.27	78.00	86,991
Tianjin 天津	15	77	26,057	-252	-0.63	-2.55	337.81	75.09	39,746
Hebei 河北									
Shanxi 山西									
Inner Mongolia 內蒙									
Northeast 東北	14	880	286,364	7,549	2.44	6.39	325.31	61.76	308,916
Liaoning 遼寧	9	1,024	288,904	7,926	2.21	6.15	282.19	64.10	359,194
Jilin 吉林	2	6	100				18.18	100.00	100
Heilongjiang 黑龍江	3	1,033	469,583	11,450	3.15	6.97	454.58	54.84	363,957
Central East 華東	67	291	61,973	567	0.93	4.21	213.07	77.91	60,989
Shanghai 上海	20	108	81,505	963	2.21	8.23	751.54	73.11	43,538
Jiangsu 江蘇	11	708	96,887	1,242	0.99	4.98	136.88	80.08	125,059
Zhejiang 浙江	7	240	33,236	194	0.49	5.01	138.32	90.30	39,963
Anhui 安徽	3	381	3,560	-3,103	-14.23	-47.26	9.34	69.88	21,810
Fujian 福建	13	35	35,500	-698	-3.09	-38.31	1018.76	91.93	22,598
Jiangxi 江西	1	805	45,120	2,160	2.48	6.70	56.05	62.96	87,070
Shandong 山東	12	454	58,864	1,664	1.79	6.85	129.63	73.82	92,823
Central-South 中南	39	216	154,472	5,711	6.19	37.38	715.74	83.45	92,307
Henan 河南	5	41	2,952	-42	-0.80	-2.63	72.00	69.53	5,224
Hubei 湖北	2	210	17,130	1,050	4.52	24.00	81.57	81.18	23,215
Hunan 湖南	1	16	2,730	-480	-9.28	-30.77	170.63	69.83	5,170
Guangdong 廣東	31	251	192,667	7,139	6.28	38.32	768.09	83.60	113,622
Guangxi 廣西									
Hainan 海南									
Southwest 西南	12	504	42,868	1,139	1.44	6.35	85.04	77.26	78,883
Chongqing 重慶	6	566	49,863	44,633	56.93	152.63	88.15	62.70	78,404
Sichuan 四川	4	200	9,844	-63,961	-183.77	-670.33	49.18	72.59	34,805
Guizhou 貴州	1	1,104	2,920	-9,480	-15.48	23.01	2.64	167.29	61,230
Yunnan 雲南	1	853	184,370	4,080	1.42	8.42	216.14	83.19	288,180
Tibet 西藏									
Northwest 西北	7	75	40,937	-116	-0.27	-0.50	548.97	46.25	43,289
Shaanxi 陝西	6	79	45,378	5	0.01	0.02	576.84	45.00	49,083
Gansu 甘肅									
Qinghai 青海									
Ningxia 寧夏									
Xinjiang 新疆	1	50	14,290	-840	-9.86	-94.38	285.80	89.55	8,520

4141: Computers 電子計算機整機製造業

Year 年份	Number of firms 企業個數	Rate of change 每年變化 (%)	Number of employees 職工人數（人）	Rate of change 每年變化 (%)	Total revenue (mil. RMB) 總銷售收入（百萬元）	Rate of change 每年變化 (%)	Total profit (mil. RMB) 總利潤（百萬元）	Rate of change 每年變化 (%)
1993	170		62,965		5,490		197	
1994	160	-5.88%	54,620	-13.25%	5,732	4.41%	145	-26.60%
1995	225	40.63%	56,414	3.28%	15,687	173.64%	288	99.18%
1996	210	-6.67%	55,917	-0.88%	18,572	18.39%	468	62.51%

3 Major products* 3 種主要產品 *	Output 產量	Sales volume 銷售量	Unit 單位
a) Microcomputer 微型電子計算機	925,691	879,406	set 部
b) Minicomputer 小型計算機	607	449	set 部

Top 10 firms by revenue (year founded) 收入排名前 10 家企業 (創辦年份)	City 城市	Province 省	Telephone / fax 電話 / 傳真	Number of employees 職工人數	Ownership 產業所有權	Revenue ('000 RMB) 銷售收入（千元）	Profit ('000 RMB) (rank) 利潤（千元）（排名）	Total assets ('000 RMB) 總資產（千元）	Major products 主要產品
Compaq Computer Technology (China) Co. Ltd. 康柏電腦技術(中國)有限公司(1994)	Shenzhen 深圳市	Guangdong 廣東省	(0755)6609090 (0755)6609214	873	Foreign-funded 外資	2,202,936	163447(1)	607,292	a
Canon Dalian Business Machines Co. Ltd. 佳能大連辦公設備有限公司(1989)	Dalian 大連市	Liaoning 遼寧省	(0411)7613333 (0411)7611644	3,364	Foreign-funded 外資	1,794,606	54773(2)	1,614,298	o
Harbin Ssang Tae (Electronics) Industry Group Co. Ltd. 哈爾濱市雙太電子有限公司(1993)	Harbin 哈爾濱市	Heilongjiang 黑龍江省	(0451)2306930	2,289	Foreign-funded 外資	1,407,910	34160(5)	1,090,895	o
Legend Group Co. 聯想集團公司(1984)	Beijing 北京市	Beijing 北京市	(010)62572078	1,384	State-owned 國有	1,391,949	44297(4)	775,391	a
International Information Products (Shenzhen) Co. Ltd. 長城國際信息產品(深圳)有限公司(1994)	Shenzhen 深圳市	Guangdong 廣東省	(0755)6639841 (0755)6639840	257	Foreign-funded 外資	1,243,648	53089(3)	756,172	a
Stone Group Co. 北京四通集團公司(1984)	Beijing 北京市	Beijing 北京市	(010)62564632 (010)62564126	1,093	Collectively-owned 集體	838,138	15086(8)	2,426,041	o
Shunde Shun Da Computer Factory Co. Ltd. 順德市順達電腦廠有限公司(1993)	Foshan 佛山市	Guangdong 廣東省	(0757)7753168 (0757)7759246	1,373	Overseas Chinese-funded 港澳台資	801,488	4560(19)	894,244	o
Chang Bai Computer Group Co. 長白計算機集團公司(1982)	Shenyang 瀋陽市	Liaoning 遼寧省	(024)6712392 (024)6712772	117	State-owned 國有	691,645	5204(16)	991,669	a,b
Nanjing Tong Chuang Information Industrial Group Co. Ltd. 南京同創信息產業集團有限公司(1995)	Nanjing 南京市	Jiangsu 江蘇省	(025)4549772 (025)4541666	1,200	State-owned 國有	539,268	15058(9)	672,398	o
Shanghai Microlink Electron Co. Ltd. 上海麥克林電子有限公司(1993)	Shanghai 上海市	Shanghai 上海市	(021)62105330 (021)62107498	28	Foreign-funded 外資	520,000	10040(13)	188,920	a

Top 10 Cities by Production Output 產出排名前 10 位城市	Province 省	Market share 市場份額	Number of firms 企業個數
Shenzhen 深圳市	Guangdong 廣東省	27.98%	22
Beijing 北京市	Beijing 北京市	14.85%	43
Dalian 大連市	Liaoning 遼寧省	12.84%	6
Shanghai 上海市	Shanghai 上海市	7.77%	35
Foshan 佛山市	Guangdong 廣東省	6.77%	1
Fuzhou 福州市	Fujian 福建省	3.37%	9
Tianjin 天津市	Tianjin 天津市	3.12%	16
Weifang 濰坊市	Shandong 山東省	3.06%	6
Nanjing 南京市	Jiangsu 江蘇省	2.76%	9
Guangzhou 廣州市	Guangdong 廣東省	2.75%	12

10 Major Wholesalers 10 家主要批發商	City 城市	Province 省	Telephone / Fax 電話 / 傳真
Liaoning Automobile Trade Group Corp. 遼寧省汽車貿易集團	Shenyang 瀋陽市	Liaoning 遼寧省	(024)23835494 (024)23838338
China Post and Telecommunication Equipment General Company 中國郵電器材總公司	Beijing 北京市	Beijing 北京市	(010)63523715 (010)63525935
Jiangsu Electromechanical Products General Company 江蘇省機電產品總公司	Nanjing 南京市	Jiangsu 江蘇省	(025)7713642 (025)7711036
Xi Nan Technology Import & Export Company 西南技術進出口公司	Chongqing 重慶市	Chongqing 重慶市	(023)63850185 (023)63850026
Changzhou Economic Technology Industrial Development Zone Tian Ming Trade Company 常州經濟技術產業開發區天明貿易公司	Changzhou 常州市	Jiangsu 江蘇省	(0519)8829882 (0519)8829882
Shanxi Mechanical Equipment Import & Export Company 山西省機械設備進出口公司	Taiyuan 太原市	Shanxi 山西省	(0351)4040713 (0351)4043981
Ningbo Five Mining Machinery Import & Export Company 寧波市五礦機械進出口公司	Ningbo 寧波市	Zhejiang 浙江省	(0574)7311255 (0574)7320322
Tianjin Jin Huan Electromechanical Complete Sets of Equipment Factory 天津市津環機電成套設備廠	Tianjin 天津市	Tianjin 天津市	(022)26371628
Yunnan Machinery Import & Export Company 雲南省機械進出口公司	Kunming 昆明市	Yunnan 雲南省	(0871)3164879 (0871)3136829
Tianjin Da Qiu Zhuang Yi Yuan Trade Center 天津市大丘莊億源商貿中心	Tianjin 天津市	Tianjin 天津市	(022)28899478 (022)28899046

*Also include sales by firms outside this industry.包括本行業以外廠家的銷售。"o" stands for "others"."o" 代表"其他產品"。

4143: Computer Peripherals 電子計算機外部設備製造業

The industry accounts for 0.519% of the total revenue of China's industrial sector in 1996. The revenue growth rate of the industry is 58.7% from 1995, as compared to the growth rate of China's industrial sector, 9.51%. The rate of return on asset is 7.08%. 59.34% of all firms in the industry made a profit while 34.38% had negative returns. The top province in terms of the industry's revenue is Guangdong, accounting for 47.97% of the total revenue.
本行業在1996年佔全行業總產值0.519%，行業年增長率為58.7%（全國工業年增長率9.51%）。行業的資產回報率7.08%，59.34%的企業盈利，34.38%的企業虧損。銷售收入最高的省份為廣東省，佔本行業的47.97%。

	Total number of firms 企業總數	Total number of employees 職工總數	Total revenue (mil. RMB) 總銷售收入（百萬元）	Total profit (mil. RMB) 總利潤（百萬元）	Return on assets 資產利潤率 (%)	Return on equity 權益利潤率 (%)	Labour productivity ('000 RMB / worker) 勞動生產率（千元/人）	Debts / assets 資產負債率 (%)	Total assets (mil. RMB) 總資產（百萬元）
Industry Overall 行業總體	378	64,602	30,094	1,546	7.08	23.08	465.84	69.32	21,833

	Number of firms 企業個數	Average number of employees 平均職工人數	Average revenue ('000 RMB) 平均銷售收入（千元）	Average profit ('000 RMB) 平均利潤（千元）	Return on assets 資產利潤率 (%)	Return on equity 權益利潤率 (%)	Labour productivity ('000 RMB / worker) 勞動生產率（千元/人）	Average debts / assets 平均資產負債率(%)	Average Total assets ('000 RMB) 平均總資產（千元）
By ownership 產業所有權									
State-owned 國有	55	342	64,873	3,018	3.29	10.74	189.43	69.39	91,764
Collectively-owned 集體	96	89	14,294	406	1.75	7.87	161.32	77.71	23,168
Privately-owned 私有	3	58	2,694	-8	-0.16	-0.16	46.44	0.23	4,805
Domestic JVs 聯營	8	25	10,139	-598	-5.42	-11.17	405.57	51.49	11,029
Joint stock 股份制	7	298	219,987	49,724	28.49	103.56	737.15	72.49	174,540
Foreign-funded 外資	78	182	137,641	1,410	2.06	7.47	754.78	72.36	68,304
Overseas Chinese-funded 港澳台資	127	168	100,680	7,002	11.25	31.85	598.72	64.70	62,265
By size 規模									
Large 大型	9	2,028	506,624	70,276	12.31	31.94	249.77	61.46	570,931
Medium 中型	18	593	223,658	10,801	4.52	16.62	377.23	72.82	239,101
Small 小型	325	108	65,664	2,182	5.82	20.26	606.57	71.27	37,488
By regional distribution 地區分布									
Central-North 華北	121	127	25,397	1,925	6.05	16.98	200.04	64.36	31,801
Beijing 北京	81	62	31,666	2,495	7.17	21.14	510.03	66.08	34,793
Tianjin 天津	27	85	15,049	1,477	8.36	19.33	177.98	56.73	17,664
Hebei 河北	7	99	4,889	110	1.09	5.75	49.45	81.10	10,129
Shanxi 山西	4	1,840	16,895	-2,468	-2.05	-5.04	9.18	59.39	120,465
Inner Mongolia 內蒙	2								
Northeast 東北	31	129	24,020	289	0.69	1.66	186.06	58.48	42,078
Liaoning 遼寧	13	194	48,268	-18	-0.03	-0.06	249.20	50.43	61,270
Jilin 吉林									
Heilongjiang 黑龍江	18	82	6,507	511	1.81	6.27	78.92	71.11	28,217
Central East 華東	110	156	101,035	4,779	7.47	24.72	645.82	69.76	63,936
Shanghai 上海	23	92	21,423	187	0.71	2.65	231.98	73.06	26,087
Jiangsu 江蘇	24	319	188,869	13,257	10.91	38.92	591.99	71.98	121,557
Zhejiang 浙江	18	85	131,218	1,232	2.66	15.24	1540.72	82.56	46,333
Anhui 安徽									
Fujian 福建	23	209	157,098	8,110	7.77	19.61	752.61	60.40	104,412
Jiangxi 江西	5	44	2,120	-82	-1.17	-2.48	48.62	52.77	7,000
Shandong 山東	17	52	6,029	-295	-2.05	-14.67	117.01	86.03	14,416
Central-South 中南	97	273	151,549	7,907	8.16	29.95	554.41	72.74	96,847
Henan 河南	3	14	217	3	1.33	4.00	15.85	66.67	250
Hubei 湖北	3	34	1,297	-23	-0.44	-0.91	38.14	51.51	5,300
Hunan 湖南	4	611	63,700	-3,045	-2.10	-6.72	104.34	68.76	145,168
Guangdong 廣東	85	280	169,821	9,176	8.87	32.86	606.12	73.00	103,433
Guangxi 廣西	2	58	3,085	-405	-16.10	36.32	53.65	144.33	2,515
Hainan 海南									
Southwest 西南	11	94	37,926	745	3.92	10.70	403.08	63.36	19,022
Chongqing 重慶	6	74	23,059	-1,714	-7.90	-30.28	311.99	73.90	21,695
Sichuan 四川	3	137	104,355	433	1.78	2.79	760.44	36.04	24,282
Guizhou 貴州	1	200	620	-1,710	-23.33	-518.18	3.10	95.50	7,330
Yunnan 雲南	1	10							
Tibet 西藏									
Northwest 西北	8	60	5,580	419	7.55	16.37	93.19	53.90	5,545
Shaanxi 陝西	7	63	6,187	487	10.36	21.84	98.21	52.60	4,704
Gansu 甘肅									
Qinghai 青海									
Ningxia 寧夏									
Xinjiang 新疆	1	38	1,330	-60	-0.52	-1.24	35.00	57.66	11,430

4143: Computer Peripherals 電子計算機外部設備製造業

Year 年份	Number of firms 企業個數	Rate of change 每年變化 (%)	Number of employees 職工人數 (人)	Rate of change 每年變化 (%)	Total revenue (mil. RMB) 總銷售收入 (百萬元)	Rate of change 每年變化 (%)	Total profit (mil. RMB) 總利潤 (百萬元)	Rate of change 每年變化 (%)
1993	256		35,877		5,290		190	
1994	280	9.38%	38,187	6.44%	7,237	36.82%	230	20.69%
1995	379	35.36%	67,902	77.81%	18,962	161.99%	312	35.77%
1996	378	-0.26%	64,602	-4.86%	30,094	58.71%	1,546	396.16%

3 Major products* 3 種主要產品 *	Output 產量	Sales volume 銷售量	Unit 單位
a) Electronic Computer External Equipment 電子計算機外部設備	21,069,776	20,437,683	set 部
b) Terminal Display Equipment 終端顯示設備	2,816,534	2,760,204	set 部

Top 10 firms by revenue (year founded) 收入排名前 10 家企業 (創辦年份)	City 城市	Province 省	Telephone / fax 電話 / 傳真	Number of employees 職工人數	Ownership 產業所有權	Revenue ('000 RMB) 銷售收入 (千元)	Profit ('000 RMB) (rank) 利潤 (千元) (排名)	Total assets ('000 RMB) 總資產 (千元)	Major products 主要產品
Shenzhen Kang Nuo External Equipment Co. Ltd. 深圳康諾外部設備有限公司(1992)	Shenzhen 深圳市	Guangdong 廣東省	(0755)3233168 (0755)3238819	1,250	Foreign-funded 外資	4,829,813	349531(1)	2,876,278	a
Epson Engineering (Shenzhen) Ltd. 愛普生技術(深圳)有限公司(1986)	Shenzhen 深圳市	Guangdong 廣東省	(0755)2260991 (0755)2260984	3,437	Foreign-funded 外資	2,989,121	38177(8)	1,052,381	a
Xi Jie International Science & Technology (Wuxi) Co. Ltd. 希捷國際科技(無錫)有限公司(1995)	Wuxi 無錫市	Jiangsu 江蘇省	(0510)5210674	1,527	Foreign-funded 外資	2,811,452	262668(3)	1,349,602	o
Zhejiang Qing Hong International Electron Group Co. Ltd. 浙江青鴻國際電子集團有限公司(1987)	Ningbo 寧波市	Zhejiang 浙江省	(0574)2709358 (0574)2706219	736	Collectively-owned 集體	2,295,037	26113(13)	742,890	a,b
Top Victory Electronics (Fujian) Co. Ltd. 冠捷電子(福建)有限公司(1992)	Fuzhou 福州市	Fujian 福建省	(0591)5220555 (0591)5220447	1,726	Overseas Chinese-funded 港澳台資	1,822,876	30836(11)	1,006,850	o
Beijing Bei Da Founder Group Company 北京北大方正集團公司(1992)	Beijing 北京市	Beijing 北京市	(010)62981505 (010)62981505	672	State-owned 國有	1,804,565	133811(4)	1,540,663	a
Shenzhen Kaifa Technology Co. Ltd. 深圳開發科技股份有限公司(1985)	Shenzhen 深圳市	Guangdong 廣東省	(0755)3216063 (0755)3325539	4,507	Overseas Chinese-funded 港澳台資	1,550,698	301757(2)	1,479,368	o
Huiyang Lian Xiang Computer Co. Ltd. 惠陽聯想電腦有限公司(1994)	Huizhou 惠州市	Guangdong 廣東省	(0751)3500088 (0751)3500249	840	Foreign-funded 外資	982,220	57744(6)	27,976	o
Wei Guan Science & Technology (Shenzhen) Co. Ltd. 唯冠科技(深圳)有限公司(1995)	Shenzhen 深圳市	Guangdong 廣東省	(0755)5351510 (0755)5351565	940	Overseas Chinese-funded 港澳台資	958,920	28441(12)	352,952	a,b
Suzhou Luo Ji Electron Co. Ltd. 蘇州羅技電子有限公司(1994)	Suzhou 蘇州市	Jiangsu 江蘇省	(0512)8252506 (0512)8251165	1,747	Foreign-funded 外資	943,719	37706(9)	443,965	o

Top 10 Cities by Production Output 產出排名前 10 位城市	Province 省	Market share 市場份額	Number of firms 企業個數
Shenzhen 深圳市	Guangdong 廣東省	37.48%	46
Fuzhou 福州市	Fujian 福建省	9.53%	11
Beijing 北京市	Beijing 北京市	8.78%	56
Ningbo 寧波市	Zhejiang 浙江省	8.25%	5
Huizhou 惠州市	Guangdong 廣東省	5.35%	4
Shanghai 上海市	Shanghai 上海市	4.61%	44
Dalian 大連市	Liaoning 遼寧省	3.04%	9
Wuxi 無錫市	Jiangsu 江蘇省	2.94%	7
Tianjin 天津市	Tianjin 天津市	2.17%	29
Shantou 汕頭市	Guangdong 廣東省	2.14%	10

10 Major Wholesalers 10 家主要批發商	City 城市	Province 省	Telephone / Fax 電話 / 傳真
Liaoning Automobile Trade Group Corp. 遼寧省汽車貿易集團	Shenyang 瀋陽市	Liaoning 遼寧省	(024)23835494 (024)23838338
China Post and Telecommunication Equipment General Company 中國郵電器材總公司	Beijing 北京市	Beijing 北京市	(010)63523715 (010)63525935
Jiangsu Electromechanical Products General Company 江蘇省機電產品總公司	Nanjing 南京市	Jiangsu 江蘇省	(025)7713642 (025)7711036
Xi Nan Technology Import & Export Company 西南技術進出口公司	Chongqing 重慶市	Chongqing 重慶市	(023)63850185 (023)63850026
Changzhou Economic Technology Industrial Development Zone Tian Ming Trade Company 常州經濟技術產業開發區天明貿易公司	Changzhou 常州市	Jiangsu 江蘇省	(0519)8829882 (0519)8829882
Shanxi Mechanical Equipment Import & Export Company 山西省機械設備進出口公司	Taiyuan 太原市	Shanxi 山西省	(0351)4040713 (0351)4043981
Ningbo Five Mining Machinery Import & Export Company 寧波市五礦機械進出口公司	Ningbo 寧波市	Zhejiang 浙江省	(0574)7311255 (0574)7320322
Tianjin Jin Huan Electromechanical Complete Sets of Equipment Factory 天津市津環機電成套設備廠	Tianjin 天津市	Tianjin 天津市	(022)26371628
Yunnan Machinery Import & Export Company 雲南省機械進出口公司	Kunming 昆明市	Yunnan 雲南省	(0871)3164879 (0871)3136829
Tianjin Da Qiu Zhuang Yi Yuan Trade Center 天津市大丘莊億源商貿中心	Tianjin 天津市	Tianjin 天津市	(022)28899478 (022)28899046

*Also include sales by firms outside this industry.包括本行業以外廠家的銷售。"o" stands for "others". "o" 代表 "其他產品"。

4151: Vacuum Tubes 電真空器件製造業

The industry accounts for 0.363% of the total revenue of China's industrial sector in 1996. The revenue growth rate of the industry is 3.8% from 1995, as compared to the growth rate of China's industrial sector, 9.51%. The rate of return on asset is 4.63%. 62.97% of all firms in the industry made a profit while 31.93% had negative returns. The top province in terms of the industry's revenue is Shaanxi, accounting for 19.54% of the total revenue.
本行業在1996年佔全行業總產值0.363%，行業年增長率為3.8%（全國工業年增長率9.51%）。行業的資產回報率4.63%，62.97%的企業盈利，31.93%的企業虧損。銷售收入最高的省份為陝西省，佔本行業的19.54%。

	Total number of firms 企業總數	Total number of employees 職工總數	Total revenue (mil. RMB) 總銷售收入（百萬元）	Total profit (mil. RMB) 總利潤（百萬元）	Return on assets 資產利潤率 (%)	Return on equity 權益利潤率 (%)	Labour productivity ('000 RMB / worker) 勞動生產率（千元/人）	Debts / assets 資產負債率 (%)	Total assets (mil. RMB) 總資產（百萬元）
Industry Overall 行業總體	177	134,878	21,030	1,978	4.63	14.11	155.92	67.19	42,728

	Number of firms 企業個數	Average number of employees 平均職工人數	Average revenue ('000 RMB) 平均銷售收入（千元）	Average profit ('000 RMB) 平均利潤（千元）	Return on assets 資產利潤率 (%)	Return on equity 權益利潤率 (%)	Labour productivity ('000 RMB / worker) 勞動生產率（千元/人）	Average debts / assets 平均資產負債率(%)	Average Total assets ('000 RMB) 平均總資產（千元）
By ownership 產業所有權									
State-owned 國有	51	1,345	129,529	7,667	2.45	9.92	96.29	75.34	313,392
Collectively-owned 集體	66	125	10,561	195	1.80	5.08	84.40	64.64	10,859
Privately-owned 私有									
Domestic JVs 聯營	7	89	14,281	207	1.32	2.97	161.23	55.63	15,692
Joint stock 股份制	8	4,393	383,729	43,446	3.52	8.10	87.35	56.56	1,234,963
Foreign-funded 外資	22	399	178,831	13,652	5.54	15.45	448.25	64.14	246,447
Overseas Chinese-funded 港澳台資	23	604	287,995	40,210	8.71	26.13	476.95	66.67	461,652
By size 規模									
Large 大型	34	3,167	574,548	58,174	5.03	15.14	181.43	66.78	1,156,494
Medium 中型	12	938	56,599	-817	-0.61	-3.73	60.31	83.73	134,833
Small 小型	125	124	6,536	80	0.56	1.44	52.85	61.35	14,321
By regional distribution 地區分布									
Central-North 華北	29	832	153,233	24,040	6.79	16.97	184.08	60.01	354,202
Beijing 北京	18	601	183,790	30,037	14.08	22.99	305.61	38.78	213,383
Tianjin 天津	7	667	57,143	150	0.07	0.21	85.63	67.68	224,516
Hebei 河北	3	2,775	242,720	51,760	3.23	12.52	87.48	74.24	1,604,380
Shanxi 山西									
Inner Mongolia 內蒙	1	320	7,390	150	0.32	1.81	23.09	82.02	46,220
Northeast 東北	20	379	18,644	1,569	3.43	8.19	49.19	58.08	45,673
Liaoning 遼寧	17	436	21,691	1,848	3.45	8.20	49.71	57.92	53,539
Jilin 吉林									
Heilongjiang 黑龍江	3	54	1,380	-17	-1.52	83.33	25.40	101.83	1,093
Central East 華東	72	648	89,210	4,903	2.67	8.02	137.72	66.63	183,330
Shanghai 上海	16	1,026	193,882	18,177	3.54	10.12	188.93	65.02	513,529
Jiangsu 江蘇	25	864	122,320	7,280	4.50	12.14	141.55	62.91	161,655
Zhejiang 浙江	10	216	12,030	116	0.34	1.23	55.69	72.33	34,053
Anhui 安徽	2	882	8,145	-50,985	-156.04	110.54	9.23	241.15	32,675
Fujian 福建	8	89	4,573	-1,365	-9.43	59.67	51.59	115.80	14,479
Jiangxi 江西	3	735	11,643	-270	-0.33	-5.26	15.84	93.78	82,700
Shandong 山東	8	222	6,864	-908	-4.22	-22.90	30.88	81.58	21,513
Central-South 中南	39	638	126,342	11,530	4.02	17.80	197.98	77.40	286,550
Henan 河南	5	988	212,456	28,308	4.21	14.47	215.12	70.91	672,430
Hubei 湖北	6	604	18,947	-73	-0.15	-0.69	31.39	78.13	48,317
Hunan 湖南	6	1,051	9,657	-338	-0.25	-3.15	9.19	92.12	136,400
Guangdong 廣東	22	456	167,883	14,118	4.63	21.87	368.57	78.82	304,773
Guangxi 廣西									
Hainan 海南									
Southwest 西南	10	1,609	72,583	7,181	2.84	10.48	45.10	72.88	252,594
Chongqing 重慶	2	37	65	-248	-1.84	-2.75	1.75	33.26	13,524
Sichuan 四川	7	2,140	92,629	8,961	2.56	9.34	43.29	72.61	350,397
Guizhou 貴州	1	1,571	100,440	11,880	9.12	70.71	63.93	87.10	130,330
Yunnan 雲南									
Tibet 西藏									
Northwest 西北	7	2,220	590,961	53,624	8.09	19.60	266.25	58.73	663,064
Shaanxi 陝西	6	2,255	685,043	65,122	8.79	20.49	303.79	57.10	740,977
Gansu 甘肅	1	2,007	26,470	-15,360	-7.85	-187.78	13.19	95.82	195,590
Qinghai 青海									
Ningxia 寧夏									
Xinjiang 新疆									

4151: Vacuum Tubes 電真空器件製造業

Year 年份	Number of firms 企業個數	Rate of change 每年變化 (%)	Number of employees 職工人數（人）	Rate of change 每年變化 (%)	Total revenue (mil. RMB) 總銷售收入（百萬元）	Rate of change 每年變化 (%)	Total profit (mil. RMB) 總利潤（百萬元）	Rate of change 每年變化 (%)
1993	127		195,570		13,156		906	
1994	141	11.02%	112,408	-42.52%	17,933	36.31%	1,999	120.60%
1995	156	10.64%	125,031	11.23%	20,264	13.00%	2,636	31.86%
1996	177	13.46%	134,878	7.88%	21,030	3.78%	1,978	-24.96%

3 Major products* 3 種主要產品 *	Output 產量	Sales volume 銷售量	Unit 單位
a) Electron-beam Tube 電子束管	62,458,457	58,086,365	piece 只

Top 10 firms by revenue (year founded) 收入排名前 10 家企業（創辦年份）	City 城市	Province 省	Telephone / fax 電話 / 傳真	Number of employees 職工人數	Ownership 產業所有權	Revenue ('000 RMB) 銷售收入（千元）	Profit ('000 RMB) (rank) 利潤（千元）（排名）	Total assets ('000 RMB) 總資產（千元）	Major products 主要產品
Irico Color Picture Tube Plant 彩虹彩色顯像管總廠(1982)	Xianyang 咸陽市	Shaanxi 陝西省	(0910)3313108 (0910)3313762	10,980	State-owned 國有	3,966,221	389096(2)	4,157,017	o
Beijing Matsushita Crt Co. Ltd. 北京松下彩色顯像管有限公司(1987)	Beijing 北京市	Beijing 北京市	(010)64363355 (010)64376154	3,124	Foreign-funded 外資	2,945,068	508641(1)	2,928,395	a
Shanghai Novel Crt Corp. Ltd. 上海永新彩色顯像管有限公司(1987)	Shanghai 上海市	Shanghai 上海市	(021)64760000 (021)64765630	2,556	Overseas Chinese-funded 港澳台資	2,229,833	282546(3)	2,110,948	a
Guangdong Colour Picture Tube Co. Ltd. 廣東彩色顯像管有限公司(1991)	Dongguan 東莞市	Guangdong 廣東省	(0769)2404888 (0769)2402525	3,235	Overseas Chinese-funded 港澳台資	1,879,289	126970(7)	3,077,099	a
Shenzhen Sai Ge Hitachi Color Display Co. Ltd. 深圳賽格日立彩色顯示器件有限公司(1989)	Shenzhen 深圳市	Guangdong 廣東省	(0755)3350777 (0755)3355850	2,544	Foreign-funded 外資	1,487,501	185696(5)	1,157,480	a
Hua Fei Color Display Systems Co. Ltd. 華飛彩色顯示系統有限公司(1988)	Nanjing 南京市	Jiangsu 江蘇省	(025)5421166 (025)5422227	1,992	Foreign-funded 外資	1,368,505	195973(4)	1,947,801	a
Shijiazhuang Baoshi Electronics Group Co. 石家莊寶石電子集團公司(1975)	Shijiazhuang 石家莊市	Hebei 河北省	(0311)6053706 (0311)6053713	8,241	State-owned 國有	725,048	155283(6)	4,762,911	a
State-owned Hua Dong Electron Tube Factory 國營華東電子管廠(1948)	Nanjing 南京市	Jiangsu 江蘇省	(025)5503024 (025)5502623	5,774	State-owned 國有	628,603	5348(19)	759,062	a
Hong Guang Industrial Co. Ltd. 紅光實業股份有限公司(1958)	Chengdu 成都市	Sichuan 四川省	(028)4106539 (028)4337569	6,754	Joint stock 股份制	338,720	61730(8)	1,685,110	a
Shanghai Vacuum Electron Device Co. Ltd. 上海真空電子器件股份有限公司(1991)	Shanghai 上海市	Shanghai 上海市	(021)62588888 (021)62551512	8,312	Joint stock 股份制	320,918	5674(18)	3,029,028	a

Top 10 Cities by Production Output 產出排名前 10 位城市	Province 省	Market share 市場份額	Number of firms 企業個數
Shenzhen 深圳市	Guangdong 廣東省	18.17%	13
Xianyang 咸陽市	Shaanxi 陝西省	16.49%	2
Shanghai 上海市	Shanghai 上海市	13.61%	30
Beijing 北京市	Beijing 北京市	12.91%	19
Nanjing 南京市	Jiangsu 江蘇省	9.75%	9
Dongguan 東莞市	Guangdong 廣東省	7.38%	1
Shijiazhuang 石家莊市	Hebei 河北省	4.37%	2
Anyang 安陽市	Henan 河南省	4.16%	1
Chengdu 成都市	Sichuan 四川省	2.47%	6
Wuxi 無錫市	Jiangsu 江蘇省	1.80%	9

10 Major Wholesalers 10 家主要批發商	City 城市	Province 省	Telephone / Fax 電話 / 傳真
Liaoning Automobile Trade Group Corp. 遼寧省汽車貿易集團	Shenyang 瀋陽市	Liaoning 遼寧省	(024)23835494 (024)23838338
China Post and Telecommunication Equipment General Company 中國郵電器材總公司	Beijing 北京市	Beijing 北京市	(010)63523715 (010)63525935
Jiangsu Electromechanical Products General Company 江蘇省機電產品總公司	Nanjing 南京市	Jiangsu 江蘇省	(025)7713642 (025)7711036
Xi Nan Technology Import & Export Company 西南技術進出口公司	Chongqing 重慶市	Chongqing 重慶市	(023)63850185 (023)63850026
Changzhou Economic Technology Industrial Development Zone Tian Ming Trade Company 常州經濟技術產業開發區天明貿易公司	Changzhou 常州市	Jiangsu 江蘇省	(0519)8829882 (0519)8829882
Shanxi Mechanical Equipment Import & Export Company 山西省機械設備進出口公司	Taiyuan 太原市	Shanxi 山西省	(0351)4040713 (0351)4043981
Ningbo Five Mining Machinery Import & Export Company 寧波市五礦機械進出口公司	Ningbo 寧波市	Zhejiang 浙江省	(0574)7311255 (0574)7320322
Tianjin Jin Huan Electromechanical Complete Sets of Equipment Factory 天津市津環機電成套設備廠	Tianjin 天津市	Tianjin 天津市	(022)26371628
Yunnan Machinery Import & Export Company 雲南省機械進出口公司	Kunming 昆明市	Yunnan 雲南省	(0871)3164879 (0871)3136829
Tianjin Da Qiu Zhuang Yi Yuan Trade Center 天津市大丘莊億源商貿中心	Tianjin 天津市	Tianjin 天津市	(022)28899478 (022)28899046

*Also include sales by firms outside this industry.包括本行業以外廠家的銷售。"o" stands for "others". "o" 代表"其他產品"。

4153: Semi-conductor Devices 半導體器件製造業

The industry accounts for 0.091% of the total revenue of China's industrial sector in 1996. The revenue growth rate of the industry is 2.9% from 1995, as compared to the growth rate of China's industrial sector, 9.51%. The rate of return on asset is -1.00%. 57.53% of all firms in the industry made a profit while 39.08% had negative returns. The top province in terms of the industry's revenue is Guangdong, accounting for 21.96% of the total revenue.
本行業在1996年佔全行業總產值0.091%，行業年增長率為2.9%（全國工業年增長率9.51%）。行業的資產回報率-1.00%，57.53%的企業盈利，39.08%的企業虧損。銷售收入最高的省份為廣東省，佔本行業的21.96%。

	Total number of firms 企業總數	Total number of employees 職工總數	Total revenue (mil. RMB) 總銷售收入（百萬元）	Total profit (mil. RMB) 總利潤（百萬元）	Return on assets 資產利潤率 (%)	Return on equity 權益利潤率 (%)	Labour productivity ('000 RMB / worker) 勞動生產率（千元/人）	Debts / assets 資產負債率 (%)	Total assets (mil. RMB) 總資產（百萬元）
Industry Overall 行業總體	446	109,874	5,297	-118	-1.00	-3.49	48.21	71.27	11,794

	Number of firms 企業個數	Average number of employees 平均職工人數	Average revenue ('000 RMB) 平均銷售收入（千元）	Average profit ('000 RMB) 平均利潤（千元）	Return on assets 資產利潤率 (%)	Return on equity 權益利潤率 (%)	Labour productivity ('000 RMB / worker) 勞動生產率（千元/人）	Average debts / assets 平均資產負債率(%)	Average Total assets ('000 RMB) 平均總資產（千元）
By ownership 產業所有權									
State-owned 國有	137	436	11,438	-766	-1.68	-9.35	26.20	82.05	45,664
Collectively-owned 集體	169	153	4,822	-1	-0.01	-0.02	31.42	71.29	8,107
Privately-owned 私有	3	37	3,253	-9	-0.56	-2.58	88.70	78.30	1,657
Domestic JVs 聯營	9	601	22,581	-48	-0.07	-0.28	37.56	76.46	72,175
Joint stock 股份制	1	684	16,161	-12	-0.02	-0.82	23.63	97.72	64,134
Foreign-funded 外資	44	141	20,880	-169	-0.72	-1.23	147.61	41.49	23,413
Overseas Chinese-funded 港澳台資	82	154	21,562	-61	-0.21	-0.45	139.61	53.97	29,498
By size 規模									
Large 大型	9	1,789	94,256	-30,845	-8.84	-32.83	52.69	73.08	348,962
Medium 中型	68	615	22,072	13,930	22.97	116.79	35.86	80.33	60,630
Small 小型	363	145	8,122	-2,169	-17.38	-45.49	56.09	61.78	12,481
By regional distribution 地區分布									
Central-North 華北	76	204	8,038	183	1.10	3.38	39.37	67.43	16,623
Beijing 北京	29	177	10,385	62	0.51	1.51	58.82	66.11	12,099
Tianjin 天津	25	209	5,302	-322	-1.69	-4.63	25.41	63.59	19,075
Hebei 河北	17	193	8,582	1,464	10.09	42.83	44.50	76.45	14,515
Shanxi 山西	2	552	6,090	-775	-1.73	-3.86	11.03	55.13	44,725
Inner Mongolia 內蒙	3	267	6,373	-1,057	-3.19	-15.36	23.90	79.23	33,127
Northeast 東北	61	323	6,913	-705	-2.08	-14.71	21.38	85.89	33,968
Liaoning 遼寧	44	263	6,593	-683	-3.67	-29.50	25.02	87.56	18,608
Jilin 吉林	7	562	9,414	-1,263	-1.18	-8.70	16.76	86.50	107,471
Heilongjiang 黑龍江	10	420	6,573	-413	-0.82	-4.64	15.66	82.24	50,098
Central East 華東	199	216	13,205	128	0.53	1.42	61.10	63.04	24,356
Shanghai 上海	39	170	15,518	491	2.22	5.69	91.47	61.00	22,122
Jiangsu 江蘇	58	288	13,939	-194	-0.85	-2.47	48.34	65.63	22,842
Zhejiang 浙江	37	153	10,086	277	1.42	3.57	66.06	60.37	19,541
Anhui 安徽	14	133	1,408	-97	-1.86	-10.62	10.61	82.46	5,217
Fujian 福建	20	222	22,076	43	0.08	0.19	99.28	57.74	53,078
Jiangxi 江西	7	289	7,333	236	0.76	2.12	25.41	64.33	31,170
Shandong 山東	24	237	13,684	258	1.06	3.56	57.69	70.18	24,308
Central-South 中南	85	228	15,035	-478	-1.87	-7.05	65.86	73.55	25,639
Henan 河南	11	126	2,392	63	0.97	8.41	19.00	88.45	6,456
Hubei 湖北	7	269	2,887	-197	-1.27	-5.83	10.74	78.26	15,546
Hunan 湖南	10	259	2,635	36	0.28	1.77	10.16	84.30	12,949
Guangdong 廣東	50	236	23,260	-684	-2.18	-6.93	98.60	68.58	31,416
Guangxi 廣西	4	287	7,295	13	0.04	0.12	25.40	69.28	34,395
Hainan 海南	3	200	4,300	-2,060	-3.82	53.46	21.50	107.15	53,870
Southwest 西南	17	496	17,105	-1,479	-2.76	-11.18	34.49	75.28	53,554
Chongqing 重慶	6	227	8,360	-2,299	-10.56	-52.86	36.88	80.02	21,763
Sichuan 四川	9	600	22,749	-1,376	-2.13	-8.84	37.89	75.95	64,743
Guizhou 貴州	1	1,291	13,220	-40	-0.03	-0.12	10.24	73.41	129,200
Yunnan 雲南	1	316	20,270	920	1.51	4.07	64.15	62.79	60,790
Tibet 西藏									
Northwest 西北	8	474	8,441	-6,104	-9.35	-53.33	17.81	82.46	65,248
Shaanxi 陝西	7	395	6,796	-5,690	-8.87	-46.81	17.19	81.06	64,173
Gansu 甘肅									
Qinghai 青海									
Ningxia 寧夏	1	1,023	19,960	-9,000	-12.37	-138.89	19.51	91.10	72,770
Xinjiang 新疆									

4153: Semi-conductor Devices 半導體器件製造業

Year 年份	Number of firms 企業個數	Rate of change 每年變化(%)	Number of employees 職工人數(人)	Rate of change 每年變化(%)	Total revenue (mil. RMB) 總銷售收入(百萬元)	Rate of change 每年變化(%)	Total profit (mil. RMB) 總利潤(百萬元)	Rate of change 每年變化(%)
1993	450		142,022		4,887		51	
1994	432	-4.00%	128,123	-9.79%	4,350	-10.99%	-71	-239.92%
1995	445	3.01%	125,655	-1.93%	5,147	18.33%	4	105.45%
1996	446	0.22%	109,874	-12.56%	5,297	2.91%	-118	-3138.89%

3 Major products* 3 種主要產品 *	Output 產量	Sales volume 銷售量	Unit 單位
a) Medium & Mini Scale Semiconductor Integrated Circuit 中小規模半導體集成電路	55,696	56,810	10,000 chip 萬塊

Top 10 firms by revenue (year founded) 收入排名前 10 家企業(創辦年份)	City 城市	Province 省	Telephone / fax 電話 / 傳真	Number of employees 職工人數	Ownership 產業所有權	Revenue ('000 RMB) 銷售收入(千元)	Profit ('000 RMB) (rank) 利潤(千元)(排名)	Total assets ('000 RMB) 總資產(千元)	Major products 主要產品
Zhong Hua Ying Guan (Fuzhou) Co. Ltd. 中華映管(福州)有限公司(1994)	Fuzhou 福州市	Fujian 福建省	(0591)3971357 (0591)3970489	959	Overseas Chinese-funded 港澳台資	289,015	1416(26)	628,716	o
Sanyo Semi-conductor (She Kou) Co. Ltd. 三洋半導體(蛇口)有限公司(1984)	Shenzhen 深圳市	Guangdong 廣東省	(0755)6691184 (0755)6691185	240	Overseas Chinese-funded 港澳台資	219,644	4324(11)	79,556	o
Leshan Radio Co. Ltd. 樂山無線電有限責任公司(1970)	Leshan 樂山市	Sichuan 四川省	(0833)2132060 (0833)2132212	1,359	State-owned 國有	147,290	-8100(229)	293,940	o
Shanghai Xin Kang Electron Co. Ltd. 上海新康電子有限公司(1993)	Shanghai 上海市	Shanghai 上海市	(021)59524214 (021)59524702	283	Foreign-funded 外資	123,067	47181(1)	134,229	o
Shenyang Zhong Photoelectron Co. Ltd. 瀋陽中光電子有限公司(1993)	Shenyang 瀋陽市	Liaoning 遼寧省	(024)25814524 (024)25815220	639	Foreign-funded 外資	116,934	1239(29)	53,662	o
Foshan Optoelectronic Equip. Corp. 佛山市光電器材公司(1969)	Foshan 佛山市	Guangdong 廣東省	(0757)2814581 (0757)2812554	987	State-owned 國有	108,058	4649(10)	128,082	o
Changzhou Yin He Electron Industrial Co. 常州市銀河電子實業公司(1966)	Changzhou 常州市	Jiangsu 江蘇省	(0519)8105224 (0519)8102846	658	Collectively-owned 集體	103,070	6595(4)	86,718	a
Yangzhou Transistor Factory 揚州晶體管廠(1970)	Yangzhou 揚州市	Jiangsu 江蘇省	(0514)7234041 (0514)7225094	1,070	State-owned 國有	101,006	2842(16)	109,174	a
Master Instrument Corp. of Shanghai Ltd. 上海堂福電子有限公司(1988)	Shanghai 上海市	Shanghai 上海市	(021)64890990 (021)64890983	516	Foreign-funded 外資	98,370	2(137)	94,291	o
Shenzhen Mrco Electronics Co. Ltd. 深圳邁爾科電子有限公司(1994)	Shenzhen 深圳市	Guangdong 廣東省	(0755)8892673 (0755)8893506	431	Overseas Chinese-funded 港澳台資	91,396	72(99)	26,125	o

Top 10 Cities by Production Output 產出排名前 10 位城市	Province 省	Market share 市場份額	Number of firms 企業個數
Shenzhen 深圳市	Guangdong 廣東省	11.21%	12
Changzhou 常州市	Jiangsu 江蘇省	9.01%	15
Shanghai 上海市	Shanghai 上海市	8.89%	58
Foshan 佛山市	Guangdong 廣東省	5.10%	5
Shenyang 瀋陽市	Liaoning 遼寧省	4.13%	8
Guangzhou 廣州市	Guangdong 廣東省	3.75%	8
Tianjin 天津市	Tianjin 天津市	3.54%	27
Beijing 北京市	Beijing 北京市	2.90%	26
Huizhou 惠州市	Guangdong 廣東省	2.82%	4
Zhaoqing 肇慶市	Guangdong 廣東省	2.56%	3

10 Major Wholesalers 10 家主要批發商	City 城市	Province 省	Telephone / Fax 電話 / 傳真
Liaoning Automobile Trade Group Corp. 遼寧省汽車貿易集團	Shenyang 瀋陽市	Liaoning 遼寧省	(024)23835494 (024)23838338
China Post and Telecommunication Equipment General Company 中國郵電器材總公司	Beijing 北京市	Beijing 北京市	(010)63523715 (010)63525935
Jiangsu Electromechanical Products General Company 江蘇省機電產品總公司	Nanjing 南京市	Jiangsu 江蘇省	(025)7713642 (025)7711036
Xi Nan Technology Import & Export Company 西南技術進出口公司	Chongqing 重慶市	Chongqing 重慶市	(023)63850185 (023)63850026
Changzhou Economic Technology Industrial Development Zone Tian Ming Trade Company 常州經濟技術產業開發區天明貿易公司	Changzhou 常州市	Jiangsu 江蘇省	(0519)8829882 (0519)8829882
Shanxi Mechanical Equipment Import & Export Company 山西省機械設備進出口公司	Taiyuan 太原市	Shanxi 山西省	(0351)4040713 (0351)4043981
Ningbo Five Mining Machinery Import & Export Company 寧波市五礦機械進出口公司	Ningbo 寧波市	Zhejiang 浙江省	(0574)7311255 (0574)7320322
Tianjin Jin Huan Electromechanical Complete Sets of Equipment Factory 天津市津環機電成套設備廠	Tianjin 天津市	Tianjin 天津市	(022)26371628
Yunnan Machinery Import & Export Company 雲南省機械進出口公司	Kunming 昆明市	Yunnan 雲南省	(0871)3164879 (0871)3136829
Tianjin Da Qiu Zhuang Yi Yuan Trade Center 天津市大丘莊億源商貿中心	Tianjin 天津市	Tianjin 天津市	(022)28899478 (022)28899046

*Also include sales by firms outside this industry.包括本行業以外廠家的銷售。"o" stands for "others". "o" 代表"其他產品"。

4155: Integrated Circuit 集成電路製造業

The industry accounts for 0.133% of the total revenue of China's industrial sector in 1996. The revenue growth rate of the industry is -4.0% from 1995, as compared to the growth rate of China's industrial sector, 9.51%. The rate of return on asset is 0.11%. 65.40% of all firms in the industry made a profit while 28.95% had negative returns. The top province in terms of the industry's revenue is Guangdong, accounting for 45.29% of the total revenue.
本行業在 1996 年佔全行業總產值 0.133%，行業年增長率為 -4.0%（全國工業年增長率 9.51%）。行業的資產回報率 0.11%，65.40% 的企業盈利，28.95% 的企業虧損。銷售收入最高的省份為廣東省，佔本行業的 45.29%。

	Total number of firms 企業總數	Total number of employees 職工總數	Total revenue (mil. RMB) 總銷售收入（百萬元）	Total profit (mil. RMB) 總利潤（百萬元）	Return on assets 資產利潤率 (%)	Return on equity 權益利潤率 (%)	Labour productivity ('000 RMB / worker) 勞動生產率（千元/人）	Debts / assets 資產負債率 (%)	Total assets (mil. RMB) 總資產（百萬元）
Industry Overall 行業總體	215	55,007	7,711	14	0.11	0.26	140.18	60.29	12,889

	Number of firms 企業個數	Average number of employees 平均職工人數	Average revenue ('000 RMB) 平均銷售收入（千元）	Average profit ('000 RMB) 平均利潤（千元）	Return on assets 資產利潤率 (%)	Return on equity 權益利潤率 (%)	Labour productivity ('000 RMB / worker) 勞動生產率（千元/人）	Average debts / assets 平均資產負債率(%)	Average Total assets ('000 RMB) 平均總資產（千元）
By ownership 產業所有權									
State-owned 國有	30	752	24,967	-8,033	-6.82	-36.74	33.19	81.45	117,867
Collectively-owned 集體	76	121	5,540	45	0.60	1.69	45.86	64.34	7,458
Privately-owned 私有	6	154	20,160	288	2.58	5.51	131.05	53.12	11,140
Domestic JVs 聯營	4	187	4,281	-114	-0.52	-1.11	22.86	53.16	21,908
Joint stock 股份制	3	109	1,516	-13	-0.64	-4.27	13.95	85.02	2,084
Foreign-funded 外資	33	266	139,875	6,794	3.25	6.64	525.25	51.13	209,318
Overseas Chinese-funded 港澳台資	63	226	28,304	415	1.52	3.22	125.13	52.80	27,283
By size 規模									
Large 大型	12	1,256	329,222	837	0.19	0.34	262.12	44.13	439,582
Medium 中型	13	910	36,451	-8	-0.01	-0.05	40.04	86.37	115,474
Small 小型	171	164	19,223	24	0.07	0.21	117.25	67.84	35,753
By regional distribution 地區分布									
Central-North 華北	29	136	32,165	799	0.71	1.48	236.81	51.66	112,049
Beijing 北京	15	156	55,397	23	0.01	0.02	354.50	52.92	206,408
Tianjin 天津	3	34	2,317	130	8.92	21.67	67.48	59.04	1,457
Hebei 河北	10	149	9,488	2,243	15.06	20.15	63.59	25.25	14,893
Shanxi 山西									
Inner Mongolia 內蒙	1								
Northeast 東北	7	99	5,144	-6,297	-20.18	-108.09	51.96	81.33	31,200
Liaoning 遼寧	1	152	22,850	-43,390	-23.04	-171.57	150.33	86.57	188,340
Jilin 吉林	2	12	915	-415	-4.84	-9.74	79.57	50.38	8,575
Heilongjiang 黑龍江	4	130	2,833	35	1.08	2.01	21.87	46.01	3,228
Central East 華東	71	300	43,698	-726	-0.87	-2.77	145.61	68.48	83,276
Shanghai 上海	13	312	80,791	7,844	3.94	10.44	259.07	62.21	198,862
Jiangsu 江蘇	28	474	65,799	-5,352	-5.46	-21.57	138.96	74.71	98,096
Zhejiang 浙江	8	204	12,515	-20	-0.07	-0.18	61.27	61.87	29,938
Anhui 安徽	2	28	660	-25	-1.68	-11.11	24.00	84.85	1,485
Fujian 福建	12	27	1,541	-501	-9.88	-24.41	56.20	59.51	5,067
Jiangxi 江西									
Shandong 山東	8	247	11,248	319	0.92	3.37	45.51	72.73	34,679
Central-South 中南	98	233	36,359	1,256	4.02	7.66	155.73	47.49	31,242
Henan 河南	3	51	1,477	53	1.90	7.14	28.95	73.43	2,810
Hubei 湖北	3	171	11,837	43	0.43	1.59	69.22	73.18	10,180
Hunan 湖南	1	1,327	19,480	-4,990	-4.42	-12.02	14.68	63.24	112,910
Guangdong 廣東	85	242	41,089	1,551	4.67	8.43	169.59	44.59	33,195
Guangxi 廣西	5	57	2,250	-32	-0.21	-8.08	39.34	97.38	15,118
Hainan 海南	1	8	10	-3,860	-30.51	39.19	1.25	177.87	12,650
Southwest 西南	1	1,103	11,470	-6,790	-9.75	-41.97	10.40	76.77	69,650
Chongqing 重慶									
Sichuan 四川					-18.93	4.08	23.09	170.19	
Guizhou 貴州	1	1,103	11,470	-6,790	-9.75	-41.97	10.40	76.77	69,650
Yunnan 雲南									
Tibet 西藏									
Northwest 西北	9	565	7,228	-3,367	-8.03	-151.88	12.80	94.72	41,948
Shaanxi 陝西	7	260	3,899	-1,121	-7.10	63.87	14.99	111.12	15,806
Gansu 甘肅	2	1,632	18,880	-11,225	-8.41	-69.63	11.57	87.92	133,445
Qinghai 青海									
Ningxia 寧夏									
Xinjiang 新疆									

4155: Integrated Circuit 集成電路製造業

Year 年份	Number of firms 企業個數	Rate of change 每年變化 (%)	Number of employees 職工人數（人）	Rate of change 每年變化 (%)	Total revenue (mil. RMB) 總銷售收入（百萬元）	Rate of change 每年變化 (%)	Total profit (mil. RMB) 總利潤（百萬元）	Rate of change 每年變化 (%)
1993	126		40,838		1,807		73	
1994	158	25.40%	33,710	-17.46%	2,680	48.29%	186	154.86%
1995	224	41.77%	49,663	47.32%	8,029	199.57%	950	410.52%
1996	215	-4.02%	55,007	10.76%	7,711	-3.96%	14	-98.53%

3 Major products* 3 種主要產品 *	Output 產量	Sales volume 銷售量	Unit 單位
a) Semiconductor Integrated Circuit 半導體集成電路	65,813	65,155	10,000 chip 萬塊
b) Medium & Mini Scale Semiconductor Integrated Circuit 中小規模半導體集成電路	52,908	53,966	10,000 chip 萬塊

Top 10 firms by revenue (year founded) 收入排名前 10 家企業（創辦年份）	City 城市	Province 省	Telephone / fax 電話 / 傳真	Number of employees 職工人數	Ownership 產業所有權	Revenue ('000 RMB) 銷售收入（千元）	Profit ('000 RMB) (rank) 利潤（千元）（排名）	Total assets ('000 RMB) 總資產（千元）	Major products 主要產品
Kunshan Fushikang Co. 昆山市富士康公司(1993)	Suzhou 蘇州市	Jiangsu 江蘇省	(0512)7790836	1,800	Overseas Chinese-funded 港澳台資	869,930	45020(2)	282,060	o
Elec & Eltek (Guangzhou) Electron Co. Ltd. 依利安達(廣州)電子有限公司(1993)	Guangzhou 廣州市	Guangdong 廣東省	(020)82212222 (020)82212000	721	Foreign-funded 外資	533,255	28518(4)	302,440	o
Topsearch Printed Circuits (Shenzhen) Ltd. 至卓飛高(中國)有限公司(1988)	Shenzhen 深圳市	Guangdong 廣東省	(0755)6693186 (0755)6691859	1,735	Overseas Chinese-funded 港澳台資	521,104	29167(3)	173,807	o
Shanghai Belling Microelectronics Manufacturing Co. Ltd. 上海貝嶺微電子製造有限公司(1988)	Shanghai 上海市	Shanghai 上海市	(021)64850700 (021)64854424	513	Foreign-funded 外資	401,420	110182(1)	559,008	a,b
Kaiping Elec & Eltek Co. Ltd. 開平依利安達電子有限公司(1992)	Jiangmen 江門市	Guangdong 廣東省	(0750)2218428 (0750)2210993	854	Foreign-funded 外資	346,559	0(85)	220,043	o
China Hua Jing Electron Group Co. 中國華晶電子集團公司(1960)	Wuxi 無錫市	Jiangsu 江蘇省	(0510)5807123 (0510)5804647	5,562	State-owned 國有	341,088	-196388(124)	1,542,992	a,b
Shanghai Advance Semiconductor Manufacture Co. Ltd. 上海先進半導體製造有限公司(1992)	Shanghai 上海市	Shanghai 上海市	(021)64851900 (021)64851056	432	Foreign-funded 外資	248,013	1122(32)	1,025,293	o
Qingpu Modern Electron (Shanghai) Co. Ltd. 青浦現代電子(上海)有限公司(1996)	Shanghai 上海市	Shanghai 上海市	(021)59765858 (021)59763838	743	Foreign-funded 外資	244,624	0(91)	527,861	a
Zhaoqing Heng Jin Computer Co. Ltd. 肇慶市恒進電腦有限公司(1996)	Zhaoqing 肇慶市	Guangdong 廣東省	(0757)2731306 (0757)2731293	520	Overseas Chinese-funded 港澳台資	222,170	6051(12)	58,925	a,b
Wuxi Hua Zhi Semi-conductor Co. Ltd. 無錫市華芝半導體有限公司(1994)	Wuxi 無錫市	Jiangsu 江蘇省	(0510)5883599 (0510)5888746	121	Foreign-funded 外資	193,618	-3332(109)	172,469	o

Top 10 Cities by Production Output 產出排名前 10 位城市	Province 省	Market share 市場份額	Number of firms 企業個數
Beijing 北京市	Beijing 北京市	17.03%	18
Shanghai 上海市	Shanghai 上海市	16.39%	33
Wuxi 無錫市	Jiangsu 江蘇省	14.00%	12
Shenzhen 深圳市	Guangdong 廣東省	9.17%	25
Guangzhou 廣州市	Guangdong 廣東省	8.54%	14
Zhaoqing 肇慶市	Guangdong 廣東省	7.85%	4
Huizhou 惠州市	Guangdong 廣東省	5.73%	8
Zhuhai 珠海市	Guangdong 廣東省	4.50%	6
Dalian 大連市	Liaoning 遼寧省	3.29%	5
Jiangmen 江門市	Guangdong 廣東省	1.42%	6

10 Major Wholesalers 10 家主要批發商	City 城市	Province 省	Telephone / Fax 電話 / 傳真
Liaoning Automobile Trade Group Corp. 遼寧省汽車貿易集團	Shenyang 瀋陽市	Liaoning 遼寧省	(024)23835494 (024)23838338
China Post and Telecommunication Equipment General Company 中國郵電器材總公司	Beijing 北京市	Beijing 北京市	(010)63523715 (010)63525935
Jiangsu Electromechanical Products General Company 江蘇省機電產品總公司	Nanjing 南京市	Jiangsu 江蘇省	(025)7713642 (025)7711036
Xi Nan Technology Import & Export Company 西南技術進出口公司	Chongqing 重慶市	Chongqing 重慶市	(023)63850185 (023)63850026
Changzhou Economic Technology Industrial Development Zone Tian Ming Trade Company 常州經濟技術產業開發區天明貿易公司	Changzhou 常州市	Jiangsu 江蘇省	(0519)8829882 (0519)8829882
Shanxi Mechanical Equipment Import & Export Company 山西省機械設備進出口公司	Taiyuan 太原市	Shanxi 山西省	(0351)4040713 (0351)4043981
Ningbo Five Mining Machinery Import & Export Company 寧波市五礦機械進出口公司	Ningbo 寧波市	Zhejiang 浙江省	(0574)7311255 (0574)7320322
Tianjin Jin Huan Electromechanical Complete Sets of Equipment Factory 天津市津環機電成套設備廠	Tianjin 天津市	Tianjin 天津市	(022)26371628
Yunnan Machinery Import & Export Company 雲南省機械進出口公司	Kunming 昆明市	Yunnan 雲南省	(0871)3164879 (0871)3136829
Tianjin Da Qiu Zhuang Yi Yuan Trade Center 天津市大丘莊億源商貿中心	Tianjin 天津市	Tianjin 天津市	(022)28899478 (022)28899046

*Also include sales by firms outside this industry.包括本行業以外廠家的銷售。"o" stands for "others". "o" 代表"其他產品"。

4160: Electronic Components 電子元件製造業

The industry accounts for 0.700% of the total revenue of China's industrial sector in 1996. The revenue growth rate of the industry is 7.0% from 1995, as compared to the growth rate of China's industrial sector, 9.51%. The rate of return on asset is 1.44%. 62.32% of all firms in the industry made a profit while 34.37% had negative returns. The top province in terms of the industry's revenue is Guangdong, accounting for 29.57% of the total revenue.
本行業在1996年佔全行業總產值0.700%，行業年增長率為7.0%（全國工業年增長率9.51%）。行業的資產回報率1.44%，62.32%的企業盈利，34.37%的企業虧損。銷售收入最高的省份為廣東省，佔本行業的29.57%。

	Total number of firms 企業總數	Total number of employees 職工總數	Total revenue (mil. RMB) 總銷售收入（百萬元）	Total profit (mil. RMB) 總利潤（百萬元）	Return on assets 資產利潤率 (%)	Return on equity 權益利潤率 (%)	Labour productivity ('000 RMB / worker) 勞動生產率（千元/人）	Debts / assets 資產負債率 (%)	Total assets (mil. RMB) 總資產（百萬元）
Industry Overall 行業總體	2,813	609,640	40,602	911	1.44	4.42	66.60	67.48	63,432

	Number of firms 企業個數	Average number of employees 平均職工人數	Average revenue ('000 RMB) 平均銷售收入（千元）	Average profit ('000 RMB) 平均利潤（千元）	Return on assets 資產利潤率 (%)	Return on equity 權益利潤率 (%)	Labour productivity ('000 RMB / worker) 勞動生產率（千元/人）	Average debts / assets 平均資產負債率(%)	Average Total assets ('000 RMB) 平均總資產（千元）
By ownership 產業所有權									
State-owned 國有	455	451	14,690	-626	-1.51	-8.32	32.56	81.85	41,468
Collectively-owned 集體	1,384	158	6,509	159	1.54	5.12	41.15	69.88	10,294
Privately-owned 私有	7	173	4,061	371	11.23	19.94	23.42	43.69	3,305
Domestic JVs 聯營	52	324	14,930	778	2.15	6.68	46.11	67.84	36,183
Joint stock 股份制	34	474	41,977	4,568	3.89	10.63	88.47	63.38	117,288
Foreign-funded 外資	296	209	37,568	1,150	2.92	6.60	179.76	55.83	39,411
Overseas Chinese-funded 港澳台資	582	166	19,857	752	3.45	7.75	119.63	55.56	21,836
By size 規模									
Large 大型	94	1,479	125,405	3,810	1.76	6.19	84.81	71.63	216,960
Medium 中型	185	702	39,205	1,194	1.55	6.27	55.82	75.28	77,087
Small 小型	2,466	138	8,792	135	1.15	2.93	63.62	60.67	11,670
By regional distribution 地區分布									
Central-North 華北	349	176	13,565	61	0.29	0.95	76.91	69.16	20,790
Beijing 北京	124	158	10,064	110	0.53	1.37	63.67	61.39	20,843
Tianjin 天津	127	192	23,281	184	0.75	2.20	121.31	65.71	24,369
Hebei 河北	62	187	6,725	-113	-0.61	-5.68	35.96	89.33	18,623
Shanxi 山西	16	213	2,964	-48	-0.31	-1.88	13.89	83.36	15,153
Inner Mongolia 內蒙	20	129	3,257	-395	-4.41	-52.67	25.30	91.62	8,953
Northeast 東北	170	224	10,284	-2	-0.01	-0.03	45.94	76.19	20,561
Liaoning 遼寧	129	237	12,660	41	0.19	0.77	53.38	74.97	21,145
Jilin 吉林	18	341	5,569	-237	-0.59	-3.00	16.35	80.44	40,297
Heilongjiang 黑龍江	23	58	650	-55	-2.98	-16.36	11.23	81.80	1,839
Central East 華東	1,369	193	13,947	361	1.68	5.05	72.12	66.69	21,474
Shanghai 上海	197	205	15,606	1,086	3.34	9.65	75.97	65.44	32,558
Jiangsu 江蘇	481	204	13,464	26	0.12	0.36	65.97	67.19	22,246
Zhejiang 浙江	292	157	11,035	486	3.58	9.97	70.48	64.04	13,564
Anhui 安徽	56	195	9,304	-410	-2.30	-13.90	47.71	83.48	17,854
Fujian 福建	192	136	14,192	711	5.06	12.19	104.72	58.53	14,067
Jiangxi 江西	56	270	6,471	61	0.32	1.73	23.93	81.53	19,051
Shandong 山東	95	298	28,545	93	0.25	0.77	95.83	67.45	37,425
Central-South 中南	747	229	17,430	752	3.24	8.39	76.10	61.41	23,236
Henan 河南	36	200	5,100	573	3.66	13.98	25.51	73.82	15,656
Hubei 湖北	52	284	8,291	-227	-0.93	-3.82	29.20	75.60	24,382
Hunan 湖南	72	164	2,935	-306	-3.11	-10.70	17.92	70.95	9,829
Guangdong 廣東	568	232	21,138	1,063	4.25	10.18	91.24	58.24	25,011
Guangxi 廣西	15	349	10,963	-1,613	-4.15	-24.36	31.44	82.98	38,912
Hainan 海南	4	126	5,760	-1,105	-15.89	-118.82	45.62	86.63	6,955
Southwest 西南	95	484	10,022	-545	-1.76	-8.67	20.70	79.76	31,064
Chongqing 重慶	13	317	5,062	-954	-3.97	-63.44	15.95	93.74	24,021
Sichuan 四川	64	467	9,931	-471	-1.75	-7.94	21.26	78.00	26,958
Guizhou 貴州	16	722	15,190	-541	-0.99	-4.43	21.05	77.63	54,596
Yunnan 雲南	2	230	3,735	-325	-1.63	-22.57	16.24	92.79	19,970
Tibet 西藏									
Northwest 西北	83	340	12,712	-1,379	-3.85	-24.23	37.42	84.13	35,845
Shaanxi 陝西	75	318	13,401	-1,003	-2.79	-14.71	42.11	81.00	35,883
Gansu 甘肅	4	647	5,895	-6,953	-16.34	133.45	9.11	112.25	42,543
Qinghai 青海	1	995	8,020	-8,490	-14.21	51.93	8.06	127.37	59,730
Ningxia 寧夏	1	22	1,530	-570	-9.74	300.00	69.55	103.25	5,850
Xinjiang 新疆	2	364	8,415	-1,180	-4.90	132.58	23.12	103.69	24,090

4160: Electronic Components 電子元件製造業

Year 年份	Number of firms 企業個數	Rate of change 每年變化 (%)	Number of employees 職工人數（人）	Rate of change 每年變化 (%)	Total revenue (mil. RMB) 總銷售收入（百萬元）	Rate of change 每年變化 (%)	Total profit (mil. RMB) 總利潤（百萬元）	Rate of change 每年變化 (%)
1993	2,225		627,450		18,827		620	
1994	2,421	8.81%	572,078	-8.83%	28,746	52.68%	1,093	76.44%
1995	2,890	19.37%	640,324	11.93%	37,946	32.00%	1,237	13.16%
1996	2,813	-2.66%	609,640	-4.79%	40,602	7.00%	911	-26.35%

3 Major products* 3 種主要產品 *	Output 產量	Sales volume 銷售量	Unit 單位
a) Electronic Component 電子元件	16,466,771	15,808,101	10,000 piece 萬只
b) Medium & Mini Scale Semiconductor Integrated Circuit 中小規模半導體集成電路	214,118	218,400	10,000 chip 萬塊

Top 10 firms by revenue (year founded) 收入排名前 10 家企業 (創辦年份)	City 城市	Province 省	Telephone / fax 電話 / 傳真	Number of employees 職工人數	Ownership 產業所有權	Revenue ('000 RMB) 銷售收入（千元）	Profit ('000 RMB) (rank) 利潤（千元）（排名）	Total assets ('000 RMB) 總資產（千元）	Major products 主要產品
Tianjin San Mei Electric Machinery Co. Ltd. 天津三美電機有限公司(1992)	Tianjin 天津市	Tianjin 天津市	(022)24371221 (022)24375407	2,704	Foreign-funded 外資	1,978,389	22761(23)	806,208	a
Qingdao San Mei Electric Co. Ltd. 青島三美電機有限公司(1992)	Qingdao 青島市	Shandong 山東省	(0532)6897333 (0532)6897140	5,842	Foreign-funded 外資	1,286,851	-4716(1482)	603,142	o
Dandong Dong Bao Electrical Appliance Group General Co. 丹東東寶電器(集團)總公司(1974)	Dandong 丹東市	Liaoning 遼寧省	(0415)6162241 (0415)6164973	4,132	State-owned 國有	763,003	20065(27)	565,999	a
Shenzhen Chang Ke International Electron Co. Ltd. 深圳長科國際電子有限公司(1995)	Shenzhen 深圳市	Guangdong 廣東省	(0755)6636143 (0755)6630362	332	Foreign-funded 外資	740,781	18364(30)	312,660	b
Hangzhou TV Set No.2 Factory 杭州電視機二廠(1981)	Hangzhou 杭州市	Zhejiang 浙江省	(0571)8087138 (0571)8075612	211	Collectively-owned 集體	486,004	101(693)	218,579	o
Dongguan Sheng Yi Copper Clad Laminate Co. Ltd. 東莞市生益敷銅板股份有限公司(1987)	Dongguan 東莞市	Guangdong 廣東省	(0769)2271828 (0769)2271854	701	Overseas Chinese-funded 港澳台資	471,207	48651(3)	523,589	b
Salom Electric (Xiamen) Co. Ltd. 廈門台和電子有限公司(1989)	Xiamen 廈門市	Fujian 福建省	(0592)6020018 (0592)6032074	3,219	Overseas Chinese-funded 港澳台資	461,217	43118(7)	288,536	a
Dongguan Hu Men Sheng Mei Da (Taiping) Electric Machinery Co. Ltd. 東莞虎門勝美達(太平)電機有限公司(1991)	Dongguan 東莞市	Guangdong 廣東省	(0769)5511118 (0769)5510233	2,750	Overseas Chinese-funded 港澳台資	453,089	2137(174)	328,570	o
Guang Dongfeng Hua Advanced Science & Technology Group Co. Ltd. 廣東風華高新科技集團有限公司(1984)	Zhaoqing 肇慶市	Guangdong 廣東省	(0757)2847546 (0757)2849045	1,615	Joint stock 股份制	402,690	60008(2)	1,126,223	a
Zhe Jiangdong Yang Magnetic Enterprise Group Company 浙江東陽磁性企業集團公司(1980)	Jinhua 金華市	Zhejiang 浙江省	(0579)6651225	5,562	Collectively-owned 集體	388,966	43361(6)	450,986	o

Top 10 Cities by Production Output 產出排名前 10 位城市	Province 省	Market share 市場份額	Number of firms 企業個數
Shanghai 上海市	Shanghai 上海市	9.62%	286
Shenzhen 深圳市	Guangdong 廣東省	5.98%	201
Suzhou 蘇州市	Jiangsu 江蘇省	4.13%	197
Nantong 南通市	Jiangsu 江蘇省	3.96%	103
Huizhou 惠州市	Guangdong 廣東省	3.84%	87
Harbin 哈爾濱市	Heilongjiang 黑龍江省	3.71%	19
Beijing 北京市	Beijing 北京市	3.64%	113
Guangzhou 廣州市	Guangdong 廣東省	3.32%	154
Hangzhou 杭州市	Zhejiang 浙江省	3.26%	117
Changzhou 常州市	Jiangsu 江蘇省	3.07%	197

10 Major Wholesalers 10 家主要批發商	City 城市	Province 省	Telephone / Fax 電話 / 傳真
Liaoning Automobile Trade Group Corp. 遼寧省汽車貿易集團	Shenyang 瀋陽市	Liaoning 遼寧省	(024)23835494 (024)23838338
China Post and Telecommunication Equipment General Company 中國郵電器材總公司	Beijing 北京市	Beijing 北京市	(010)63523715 (010)63525935
Jiangsu Electromechanical Products General Company 江蘇省機電產品總公司	Nanjing 南京市	Jiangsu 江蘇省	(025)7713642 (025)7711036
Xi Nan Technology Import & Export Company 西南技術進出口公司	Chongqing 重慶市	Chongqing 重慶市	(023)63850185 (023)63850026
Changzhou Economic Technology Industrial Development Zone Tian Ming Trade Company 常州經濟技術產業開發區天明貿易公司	Changzhou 常州市	Jiangsu 江蘇省	(0519)8829882 (0519)8829882
Shanxi Mechanical Equipment Import & Export Company 山西省機械設備進出口公司	Taiyuan 太原市	Shanxi 山西省	(0351)4040713 (0351)4043981
Ningbo Five Mining Machinery Import & Export Company 寧波市五礦機械進出口公司	Ningbo 寧波市	Zhejiang 浙江省	(0574)7311255 (0574)7320322
Tianjin Jin Huan Electromechanical Complete Sets of Equipment Factory 天津市津環機電成套設備廠	Tianjin 天津市	Tianjin 天津市	(022)26371628
Yunnan Machinery Import & Export Company 雲南省機械進出口公司	Kunming 昆明市	Yunnan 雲南省	(0871)3164879 (0871)3136829
Tianjin Da Qiu Zhuang Yi Yuan Trade Center 天津市大丘莊億源商貿中心	Tianjin 天津市	Tianjin 天津市	(022)28899478 (022)28899046

*Also include sales by firms outside this industry.包括本行業以外廠家的銷售。"o" stands for "others". "o" 代表"其他產品"。

4171: Television Sets 電視機製造業

The industry accounts for 0.901% of the total revenue of China's industrial sector in 1996. The revenue growth rate of the industry is 39.8% from 1995, as compared to the growth rate of China's industrial sector, 9.51%. The rate of return on asset is 3.47%. 45.86% of all firms in the industry made a profit while 45.14% had negative returns. The top province in terms of the industry's revenue is Guangdong, accounting for 32.80% of the total revenue.
本行業在1996年佔全行業總產值0.901%，行業年增長率為39.8%（全國工業年增長率9.51%）。行業的資產回報率3.47%，45.86%的企業盈利，45.14%的企業虧損。銷售收入最高的省份為廣東省，佔本行業的32.80%。

	Total number of firms 企業總數	Total number of employees 職工總數	Total revenue (mil. RMB) 總銷售收入（百萬元）	Total profit (mil. RMB) 總利潤（百萬元）	Return on assets 資產利潤率 (%)	Return on equity 權益利潤率 (%)	Labour productivity ('000 RMB / worker) 勞動生產率（千元/人）	Debts / assets 資產負債率 (%)	Total assets (mil. RMB) 總資產（百萬元）
Industry Overall 行業總體	295	196,226	52,246	2,179	3.47	13.27	266.25	73.85	62,807

	Number of firms 企業個數	Average number of employees 平均職工人數	Average revenue ('000 RMB) 平均銷售收入（千元）	Average profit ('000 RMB) 平均利潤（千元）	Return on assets 資產利潤率 (%)	Return on equity 權益利潤率 (%)	Labour productivity ('000 RMB / worker) 勞動生產率（千元/人）	Average debts / assets 平均資產負債率(%)	Average Total assets ('000 RMB) 平均總資產（千元）
By ownership 產業所有權									
State-owned 國有	86	1,128	202,907	19,407	5.83	23.57	179.89	75.27	333,058
Collectively-owned 集體	99	272	24,987	2	0.01	0.02	92.02	70.75	22,146
Privately-owned 私有									
Domestic JVs 聯營	14	279	35,858	823	2.35	7.93	128.72	70.36	35,003
Joint stock 股份制	5	178	110,495	1,591	8.47	11.45	621.46	26.03	18,779
Foreign-funded 外資	30	738	362,110	-8,838	-2.13	-7.30	491.00	70.80	414,865
Overseas Chinese-funded 港澳台資	56	648	284,780	11,150	4.59	16.12	439.48	71.52	242,862
By size 規模									
Large 大型	49	2,121	719,986	3,764	0.44	1.65	339.51	73.24	852,765
Medium 中型	56	956	159,037	25,795	11.04	53.72	166.34	79.45	233,712
Small 小型	181	230	48,516	3,039	6.93	21.56	210.61	67.84	43,837
By regional distribution 地區分布									
Central-North 華北	43	578	120,841	-2,925	-1.77	-11.41	208.97	84.52	165,627
Beijing 北京	11	670	101,332	941	0.45	2.25	151.16	80.10	209,877
Tianjin 天津	26	521	147,592	-3,474	-2.22	-14.78	283.52	85.02	156,850
Hebei 河北	2	272	2,155	5,085	20.97	-49.15	7.92	142.67	24,245
Shanxi 山西	2	766	3,230	-9,010	-7.29	33.90	4.22	121.51	123,530
Inner Mongolia 內蒙	2	941	116,685	-18,970	-8.63	-35.99	124.07	76.02	219,825
Northeast 東北	21	855	112,560	-9,820	-3.40	-14.71	131.65	76.91	289,129
Liaoning 遼寧	10	1,184	192,219	-15,052	-2.91	-10.40	162.40	72.02	517,114
Jilin 吉林	5	803	16,212	-12,788	-14.52	44.64	20.18	132.53	88,058
Heilongjiang 黑龍江	6	350	60,083	1,375	1.79	8.41	171.50	78.69	76,713
Central East 華東	118	599	128,314	17	0.01	0.06	214.32	80.99	158,305
Shanghai 上海	31	656	148,988	-1,922	-0.84	-4.52	227.10	81.51	230,037
Jiangsu 江蘇	41	385	76,908	-734	-1.04	-5.46	199.79	80.97	70,675
Zhejiang 浙江	9	1,058	164,844	-1,061	-0.68	-4.30	155.74	84.30	157,189
Anhui 安徽	11	605	37,446	-7,528	-11.10	45.00	61.93	124.66	67,829
Fujian 福建	12	549	220,828	4,691	2.11	8.74	402.05	75.89	222,708
Jiangxi 江西	3	1,301	128,863	337	0.16	-5.59	99.05	102.94	204,970
Shandong 山東	11	714	221,555	11,518	3.96	12.46	310.22	68.26	291,175
Central-South 中南	85	571	206,104	4,971	2.67	9.43	360.97	71.71	186,390
Henan 河南	5	570	7,910	-752	-1.99	-66.08	13.89	96.99	37,746
Hubei 湖北	3	962	39,617	-6,487	-4.07	-226.81	41.17	98.20	159,233
Hunan 湖南	6	494	13,508	-5,173	-11.69	77.35	27.33	115.12	44,243
Guangdong 廣東	66	574	259,622	7,458	3.37	11.10	452.55	69.63	221,194
Guangxi 廣西	2	367	63,270	215	0.30	1.07	172.40	71.70	71,150
Hainan 海南	3	412	5,957	-5,293	-9.33	-46.60	14.47	79.97	56,727
Southwest 西南	18	1,543	621,234	117,189	15.06	35.96	402.54	58.13	778,352
Chongqing 重慶	2	2,813	726,429	-618,344	-25.32	-59.70	258.25	57.60	2,442,428
Sichuan 四川	13	1,422	730,880	-63,490	-9.74	-22.77	513.85	57.21	651,557
Guizhou 貴州	2	1,325	78,005	-9,325	-6.95	-35.21	58.89	80.27	134,215
Yunnan 雲南	1	814	72,540	-13,290	-10.15	-154.18	89.12	93.41	130,880
Tibet 西藏									
Northwest 西北	10	645	84,405	-2,307	-2.14	-110.07	130.94	98.06	107,967
Shaanxi 陝西	7	668	119,037	-1,071	-0.79	-39.08	178.31	97.97	134,961
Gansu 甘肅	1	971	6,390	-12,840	-11.38	-287.89	6.58	96.05	112,860
Qinghai 青海									
Ningxia 寧夏	1	45	940	-70	-1.85	350.00	20.89	100.53	3,790
Xinjiang 新疆	1	757	3,460	-2,660	-14.54	99.63	4.57	114.60	18,290

4171: Television Sets 電視機製造業

Year 年份	Number of firms 企業個數	Rate of change 每年變化 (%)	Number of employees 職工人數 (人)	Rate of change 每年變化 (%)	Total revenue (mil. RMB) 總銷售收入 (百萬元)	Rate of change 每年變化 (%)	Total profit (mil. RMB) 總利潤 (百萬元)	Rate of change 每年變化 (%)
1993	287		207,240		28,522		563	
1994	302	5.23%	160,683	-22.47%	29,819	4.55%	574	1.87%
1995	302		181,759	13.12%	37,362	25.30%	-144	-125.04%
1996	295	-2.32%	196,226	7.96%	52,246	39.84%	2,179	1616.78%

3 Major products* 3 種主要產品 *	Output 產量	Sales volume 銷售量	Unit 單位
a) Television Set 電視機	30,225,807	28,714,516	set 部
b) Video Recorder 錄相機	1,790,784	1,343,088	set 部

Top 10 firms by revenue (year founded) 收入排名前 10 家企業 (創辦年份)	City 城市	Province 省	Telephone / fax 電話 / 傳真	Number of employees 職工人數	Ownership 產業所有權	Revenue ('000 RMB) 銷售收入 (千元)	Profit ('000 RMB) (rank) 利潤（千元）(排名)	Total assets ('000 RMB) 總資產 (千元)	Major products 主要產品
Sichuan Chang Hong Electron Group Co. 四川長虹電子集團公司(1958)	Mianyang 綿陽市	Sichuan 四川省	(0816)2411378 (0816)2337518	17,642	State-owned 國有	10,642,171	2198500(1)	11,974,870	a
Konka Group Co. Ltd. 康佳集團股份有限公司(1980)	Shenzhen 深圳市	Guangdong 廣東省	(0755)6608866 (0755)6600082	2,826	Overseas Chinese-funded 港澳台資	4,882,197	374589(2)	3,811,790	a
Shanghai Guangdian Co. Ltd. 上海廣電股份有限公司(1992)	Shanghai 上海市	Shanghai 上海市	(021)64189188 (021)64189828	7,189	Joint stock 股份制	2,277,807	1030(45)	5,099,841	a,b
Qingdao Hisence Electrical Appliance Co. 青島海信電器公司(1969)	Qingdao 青島市	Shandong 山東省	(0532)3876853 (0532)3872882	4,869	State-owned 國有	2,008,293	143518(3)	2,559,873	a
Suzhou Philips Cosumption Electron Co. Ltd. 蘇州飛利浦消費電子有限公司(1992)	Suzhou 蘇州市	Jiangsu 江蘇省	(0512)8251042 (0512)8251456	1,000	Foreign-funded 外資	1,948,149	22146(11)	1,296,140	a
Hua Qiang Sanyo Electronic Co. Ltd. 華強三洋電子有限公司(1984)	Shenzhen 深圳市	Guangdong 廣東省	(0755)3365390 (0755)3365389	1,576	Foreign-funded 外資	1,922,009	5767(23)	833,306	a,b
Shanghai Suo Guang Electron Co. Ltd. 上海索廣電子有限公司(1993)	Shanghai 上海市	Shanghai 上海市	(021)64359600 (021)64357704	3,121	Foreign-funded 外資	1,764,781	15558(14)	395,125	o
Huizhou King Audio-video Electronics Co. Ltd. 惠州王牌視聽電子有限公司(1992)	Huizhou 惠州市	Guangdong 廣東省	(0751)2260918 (0751)2274591	2,070	Overseas Chinese-funded 港澳台資	1,662,315	50786(6)	664,158	a
Xiamen Overseas Chinese Electronic Co. Ltd. 廈門華僑電子企業有限公司(1984)	Xiamen 廈門市	Fujian 福建省	(0592)6021091 (0592)6021331	3,628	Overseas Chinese-funded 港澳台資	1,505,385	40308(7)	1,315,046	a
Tianjin Tongguang Samsung Electronic Co. Ltd. 天津通廣三星電子有限公司(1994)	Tianjin 天津市	Tianjin 天津市	(022)26284450 (022)26284680	2,449	Foreign-funded 外資	1,481,536	95(83)	1,355,955	a

Top 10 Cities by Production Output 產出排名前 10 位城市	Province 省	Market share 市場份額	Number of firms 企業個數
Mianyang 綿陽市	Sichuan 四川省	22.97%	2
Shanghai 上海市	Shanghai 上海市	14.25%	45
Huizhou 惠州市	Guangdong 廣東省	9.00%	12
Tianjin 天津市	Tianjin 天津市	7.42%	26
Xiamen 廈門市	Fujian 福建省	4.71%	3
Shenzhen 深圳市	Guangdong 廣東省	4.38%	20
Zhongshan 中山市	Guangdong 廣東省	4.09%	4
Dalian 大連市	Liaoning 遼寧省	3.85%	8
Qingdao 青島市	Shandong 山東省	3.23%	1
Beijing 北京市	Beijing 北京市	3.18%	11

10 Major Wholesalers 10 家主要批發商	City 城市	Province 省	Telephone / Fax 電話 / 傳真
Liaoning Automobile Trade Group Corp. 遼寧省汽車貿易集團	Shenyang 瀋陽市	Liaoning 遼寧省	(024)23835494 (024)23838338
China Post and Telecommunication Equipment General Company 中國郵電器材總公司	Beijing 北京市	Beijing 北京市	(010)63523715 (010)63525935
Jiangsu Electromechanical Products General Company 江蘇省機電產品總公司	Nanjing 南京市	Jiangsu 江蘇省	(025)7713642 (025)7711036
Xi Nan Technology Import & Export Company 西南技術進出口公司	Chongqing 重慶市	Chongqing 重慶市	(023)63850185 (023)63850026
Changzhou Economic Technology Industrial Development Zone Tian Ming Trade Company 常州經濟技術產業開發區天明貿易公司	Changzhou 常州市	Jiangsu 江蘇省	(0519)8829882 (0519)8829882
Shanxi Mechanical Equipment Import & Export Company 山西省機械設備進出口公司	Taiyuan 太原市	Shanxi 山西省	(0351)4040713 (0351)4043981
Ningbo Five Mining Machinery Import & Export Company 寧波市五礦機械進出口公司	Ningbo 寧波市	Zhejiang 浙江省	(0574)7311255 (0574)7320322
Tianjin Jin Huan Electromechanical Complete Sets of Equipment Factory 天津市津環機電成套設備廠	Tianjin 天津市	Tianjin 天津市	(022)26371628
Yunnan Machinery Import & Export Company 雲南省機械進出口公司	Kunming 昆明市	Yunnan 雲南省	(0871)3164879 (0871)3136829
Tianjin Da Qiu Zhuang Yi Yuan Trade Center 天津市大丘莊億源商貿中心	Tianjin 天津市	Tianjin 天津市	(022)28899478 (022)28899046

*Also include sales by firms outside this industry.包括本行業以外廠家的銷售。"o" stands for "others"."o" 代表"其他產品"。

4172: Radio Receivers and Sound Recording Equipment 收音機、錄音機製造業

The industry accounts for 0.370% of the total revenue of China's industrial sector in 1996. The revenue growth rate of the industry is -2.8% from 1995, as compared to the growth rate of China's industrial sector, 9.51%. The rate of return on asset is 0.84%. 64.16% of all firms in the industry made a profit while 33.21% had negative returns. The top province in terms of the industry's revenue is Guangdong, accounting for 67.84% of the total revenue.
本行業在1996年佔全行業總產值0.370%，行業年增長率為-2.8%（全國工業年增長率9.51%）。行業的資產回報率0.84%，64.16%的企業盈利，33.21%的企業虧損。銷售收入最高的省份為廣東省，佔本行業的67.84%。

	Total number of firms 企業總數	Total number of employees 職工總數	Total revenue (mil. RMB) 總銷售收入（百萬元）	Total profit (mil. RMB) 總利潤（百萬元）	Return on assets 資產利潤率 (%)	Return on equity 權益利潤率 (%)	Labour productivity ('000 RMB / worker) 勞動生產率（千元／人）	Debts / assets 資產負債率 (%)	Total assets (mil. RMB) 總資產（百萬元）
Industry Overall 行業總體	594	159,527	21,476	175	0.84	3.00	134.62	72.04	20,903

	Number of firms 企業個數	Average number of employees 平均職工人數	Average revenue ('000 RMB) 平均銷售收入（千元）	Average profit ('000 RMB) 平均利潤（千元）	Return on assets 資產利潤率 (%)	Return on equity 權益利潤率 (%)	Labour productivity ('000 RMB / worker) 勞動生產率（千元／人）	Average debts / assets 平均資產負債率(%)	Average Total assets ('000 RMB) 平均總資產（千元）
By ownership 產業所有權									
State-owned 國有	99	341	14,697	-758	-1.61	-8.67	43.11	81.47	47,162
Collectively-owned 集體	247	219	13,106	203	1.16	4.74	59.79	75.52	17,445
Privately-owned 私有	4	69	6,022	61	0.97	3.94	86.95	75.42	6,280
Domestic JVs 聯營	17	293	17,900	-1,908	-3.44	-10.12	61.17	65.96	55,403
Joint stock 股份制	14	418	61,321	8,698	6.67	11.80	146.80	43.46	130,414
Foreign-funded 外資	69	348	140,584	1,583	1.87	7.83	404.14	76.18	84,863
Overseas Chinese-funded 港澳台資	143	275	40,936	13	0.06	0.17	148.86	64.98	22,672
By size 規模									
Large 大型	15	1,389	392,261	12,159	3.18	10.65	282.34	70.16	382,384
Medium 中型	39	725	86,792	-1,661	-1.43	-7.85	119.75	81.78	116,173
Small 小型	519	218	23,520	111	0.54	1.74	107.86	68.91	20,496
By regional distribution 地區分布									
Central-North 華北	67	178	15,720	-403	-0.82	-6.46	88.17	87.31	49,224
Beijing 北京	35	110	10,070	-391	-2.00	-9.05	91.83	77.94	19,561
Tianjin 天津	26	260	25,720	-500	-0.52	-5.41	98.92	90.35	95,797
Hebei 河北	4	118	2,395	38	0.47	1.45	20.34	67.54	7,973
Shanxi 山西									
Inner Mongolia 內蒙	2	439	11,255	-245	-0.54	-2.93	25.67	81.55	45,370
Northeast 東北	14	258	39,370	349	1.00	3.85	152.55	74.03	34,856
Liaoning 遼寧	10	246	47,381	1,139	2.68	8.63	192.68	68.96	42,505
Jilin 吉林	1	586	1,190	-7,000	-17.35	59.37	2.03	129.23	40,340
Heilongjiang 黑龍江	3	189	25,393	163	2.17	7.41	134.12	70.74	7,530
Central East 華東	212	205	23,149	123	0.42	1.38	112.92	69.54	29,232
Shanghai 上海	54	175	24,372	281	1.02	2.78	138.88	63.28	27,514
Jiangsu 江蘇	58	350	35,843	41	0.08	0.28	102.27	72.67	53,604
Zhejiang 浙江	57	117	10,241	158	1.21	3.80	87.52	68.22	13,102
Anhui 安徽	2	27	1,635	-60	-2.41	80.00	61.70	103.02	2,485
Fujian 福建	28	108	26,409	-105	-0.53	-2.27	244.45	76.50	19,713
Jiangxi 江西	7	155	9,236	279	2.49	6.22	59.75	59.93	11,176
Shandong 山東	6	471	20,242	83	0.23	0.53	42.96	57.32	36,717
Central-South 中南	291	338	51,117	553	1.50	4.83	151.14	68.93	36,818
Henan 河南	1	22							
Hubei 湖北	13	326	13,552	970	2.85	7.34	41.56	61.20	34,050
Hunan 湖南	10	194	1,786	-1,251	-8.87	41.56	9.19	121.35	14,101
Guangdong 廣東	263	345	55,398	605	1.58	5.02	160.45	68.46	38,227
Guangxi 廣西	4	353	27,845	418	2.17	10.52	78.94	79.34	19,220
Hainan 海南									
Southwest 西南	7	276	12,500	1,491	5.22	13.22	45.27	60.49	28,566
Chongqing 重慶	2	418	10,512	-140,444	-566.02	-2354.19	25.15	75.96	24,813
Sichuan 四川	4	216	15,580	55,450	181.85	344.55	72.16	47.22	30,492
Guizhou 貴州	1	309	2,310	-1,700	-6.46	173.47	7.48	103.73	26,300
Yunnan 雲南									
Tibet 西藏									
Northwest 西北	3	51	303	17	0.90	1.42	5.99	37.10	1,860
Shaanxi 陝西	2	76	455	25	0.90	1.42	5.99	37.10	2,790
Gansu 甘肅									
Qinghai 青海									
Ningxia 寧夏									
Xinjiang 新疆	1								

4172: Radio Receivers and Sound Recording Equipment
收音機、錄音機製造業

Year 年份	Number of firms 企業個數	Rate of change 每年變化 (%)	Number of employees 職工人數 (人)	Rate of change 每年變化 (%)	Total revenue (mil. RMB) 總銷售收入 (百萬元)	Rate of change 每年變化 (%)	Total profit (mil. RMB) 總利潤 (百萬元)	Rate of change 每年變化 (%)
1993	621		207,983		14,852		306	
1994	594	-4.35%	222,722	7.09%	17,788	19.77%	186	-39.00%
1995	628	5.72%	194,865	-12.51%	22,092	24.19%	104	-44.01%
1996	594	-5.41%	159,527	-18.13%	21,476	-2.79%	175	67.71%

3 Major products* 3 種主要產品 *	Output 產量	Sales volume 銷售量	Unit 單位
a) Combination Audio 組合音響	14,440,271	13,140,646	set 部
b) Receiving-recording-gramophonic Set 收錄放機	11,238,018	11,125,637	set 部
c) Cd Audio CD 音響	334,790	257,788	set 部

Top 10 firms by revenue (year founded) 收入排名前 10 家企業 (創辦年份)	City 城市	Province 省	Telephone / fax 電話 / 傳真	Number of employees 職工人數	Ownership 產業所有權	Revenue ('000 RMB) 銷售收入 (千元)	Profit ('000 RMB) (rank) 利潤 (千元) (排名)	Total assets ('000 RMB) 總資產 (千元)	Major products 主要產品
Shenzhen Sanyo Huaqiang Optical Technology Co. Ltd. 深圳三洋華強激光電子有限公司(1993)	Shenzhen 深圳市	Guangdong 廣東省	(0755)3316198 (0755)3319131	1,515	Foreign-funded 外資	1,672,955	6208(22)	188,434	o
Xin Hua Precision Machine Co. Ltd. 信華精機有限公司(1986)	Huizhou 惠州市	Guangdong 廣東省	(0751)2602373 (0751)2602401	3,322	Foreign-funded 外資	1,647,613	42200(2)	427,121	o
Sanyo Electric (She Kou) Co. Ltd. 三洋電機(蛇口)有限公司(1983)	Shenzhen 深圳市	Guangdong 廣東省	(0755)6691616 (0755)6691621	3,765	Foreign-funded 外資	1,562,874	2148(48)	773,644	b
Huizhou Samsung Electronics Co. Ltd. 惠州三星有限公司(1993)	Huizhou 惠州市	Guangdong 廣東省	(0751)3321401	1,484	Foreign-funded 外資	908,695	26362(3)	587,340	a,c
Le Jin Electron (Huizhou) Co. Ltd. 樂金電子(惠州)有限公司(1993)	Huizhou 惠州市	Guangdong 廣東省	(0751)2600944 (0751)2600945	735	Foreign-funded 外資	592,324	8375(18)	213,468	a,b
Changzhou No.5 Radio Factory 常州市第五無線電廠(1980)	Changzhou 常州市	Jiangsu 江蘇省	(0519)8791221	1,380	Collectively-owned 集體	548,735	8106(19)	323,791	o
Xia Retail Sales Panasonic Sound Co. Ltd. 廈門市松下音響有限公司(1993)	Xiamen 廈門市	Fujian 福建省	(0592)6037819 (0592)6030587	1,068	Foreign-funded 外資	523,006	467(109)	389,347	o
Zhuhai Jiang Hai Electron Co. Ltd. 珠海市江海電子股份有限公司(1984)	Zhuhai 珠海市	Guangdong 廣東省	(0756)2263810 (0756)2263552	1,085	Joint stock 股份制	469,577	17190(9)	158,126	o
Hui Feng Electron (Huizhou) Co. Ltd. 惠豐電子(惠州)有限公司(1991)	Huizhou 惠州市	Guangdong 廣東省	(0751)2602255 (0751)2600738	1,849	Overseas Chinese-funded 港澳台資	449,674	580(96)	54,520	a,b,c
Shenzhen Cheng Feng Electron Co. Ltd. 深圳成豐電子有限公司(1994)	Shenzhen 深圳市	Guangdong 廣東省	(0755)3311638 (0755)3310524	2,059	Overseas Chinese-funded 港澳台資	425,189	-431(268)	70,838	a,b,c

Top 10 Cities by Production Output 產出排名前 10 位城市	Province 省	Market share 市場份額	Number of firms 企業個數
Huizhou 惠州市	Guangdong 廣東省	42.97%	53
Shenzhen 深圳市	Guangdong 廣東省	8.95%	69
Shanghai 上海市	Shanghai 上海市	8.52%	77
Guangzhou 廣州市	Guangdong 廣東省	3.66%	93
Changzhou 常州市	Jiangsu 江蘇省	3.47%	16
Yancheng 鹽城市	Jiangsu 江蘇省	3.04%	15
Dalian 大連市	Liaoning 遼寧省	2.67%	6
Zhongshan 中山市	Guangdong 廣東省	2.59%	22
Tianjin 天津市	Tianjin 天津市	2.54%	24
Dongguan 東莞市	Guangdong 廣東省	2.29%	35

10 Major Wholesalers 10 家主要批發商	City 城市	Province 省	Telephone / Fax 電話 / 傳真
Liaoning Automobile Trade Group Corp. 遼寧省汽車貿易集團	Shenyang 瀋陽市	Liaoning 遼寧省	(024)23835494 (024)23838338
China Post and Telecommunication Equipment General Company 中國郵電器材總公司	Beijing 北京市	Beijing 北京市	(010)63523715 (010)63525935
Jiangsu Electromechanical Products General Company 江蘇省機電產品總公司	Nanjing 南京市	Jiangsu 江蘇省	(025)7713642 (025)7711036
Xi Nan Technology Import & Export Company 西南技術進出口公司	Chongqing 重慶市	Chongqing 重慶市	(023)63850185 (023)63850026
Changzhou Economic Technology Industrial Development Zone Tian Ming Trade Company 常州經濟技術產業開發區天明貿易公司	Changzhou 常州市	Jiangsu 江蘇省	(0519)8829882 (0519)8829882
Shanxi Mechanical Equipment Import & Export Company 山西省機械設備進出口公司	Taiyuan 太原市	Shanxi 山西省	(0351)4040713 (0351)4043981
Ningbo Five Mining Machinery Import & Export Company 寧波市五礦機械進出口公司	Ningbo 寧波市	Zhejiang 浙江省	(0574)7311255 (0574)7320322
Tianjin Jin Huan Electromechanical Complete Sets of Equipment Factory 天津市津環機電成套設備廠	Tianjin 天津市	Tianjin 天津市	(022)26371628
Yunnan Machinery Import & Export Company 雲南省機械進出口公司	Kunming 昆明市	Yunnan 雲南省	(0871)3164879 (0871)3136829
Tianjin Da Qiu Zhuang Yi Yuan Trade Center 天津市大丘莊億源商貿中心	Tianjin 天津市	Tianjin 天津市	(022)28899478 (022)28899046

*Also include sales by firms outside this industry.包括本行業以外廠家的銷售。"o" stands for "others". "o" 代表"其他產品"。

4173: Electronic Calculators 電子計算器製造業

The industry accounts for 0.029% of the total revenue of China's industrial sector in 1996. The revenue growth rate of the industry is 11.7% from 1995, as compared to the growth rate of China's industrial sector, 9.51%. The rate of return on asset is 1.48%. 67.74% of all firms in the industry made a profit while 27.50% had negative returns. The top province in terms of the industry's revenue is Guangdong, accounting for 37.24% of the total revenue.
本行業在1996年佔全行業總產值0.029%，行業年增長率為11.7%（全國工業年增長率9.51%）。行業的資產回報率1.48%，67.74%的企業盈利，27.50%的企業虧損。銷售收入最高的省份為廣東省，佔本行業的37.24%。

	Total number of firms 企業總數	Total number of employees 職工總數	Total revenue (mil. RMB) 總銷售收入（百萬元）	Total profit (mil. RMB) 總利潤（百萬元）	Return on assets 資產利潤率 (%)	Return on equity 權益利潤率 (%)	Labour productivity ('000 RMB / worker) 勞動生產率（千元／人）	Debts / assets 資產負債率 (%)	Total assets (mil. RMB) 總資產（百萬元）
Industry Overall 行業總體	85	14,782	1,672	27	1.48	2.92	113.11	49.49	1,834

	Number of firms 企業個數	Average number of employees 平均職工人數	Average revenue ('000 RMB) 平均銷售收入（千元）	Average profit ('000 RMB) 平均利潤（千元）	Return on assets 資產利潤率 (%)	Return on equity 權益利潤率 (%)	Labour productivity ('000 RMB / worker) 勞動生產率（千元／人）	Average debts / assets 平均資產負債率(%)	Average Total assets ('000 RMB) 平均總資產（千元）
By ownership 產業所有權									
State-owned 國有	9	359	5,667	-1,778	-10.96	39.02	15.77	128.08	16,222
Collectively-owned 集體	28	127	17,050	884	6.73	12.62	133.80	46.73	13,148
Privately-owned 私有									
Domestic JVs 聯營	2	18	3,973	295	6.98	13.64	227.06	48.80	4,222
Joint stock 股份制	1	2							
Foreign-funded 外資	11	244	29,988	204	0.55	0.61	122.86	10.18	37,170
Overseas Chinese-funded 港澳台資	34	160	23,706	453	1.71	3.85	147.92	55.75	26,560
By size 規模									
Large 大型	1	649	83,529	-2,738	-1.00	-2.86	128.70	65.10	273,992
Medium 中型	2	1,651	114,616	408	0.20	0.24	69.42	14.72	201,180
Small 小型	81	135	16,783	357	2.50	5.93	123.95	57.91	14,298
By regional distribution 地區分布									
Central-North 華北	12	8	611	47	4.76	9.69	73.30	50.85	980
Beijing 北京	9	4	187	14	4.63	7.56	45.41	38.79	312
Tianjin 天津	2	5	410	10	0.70	0.80	82.00	12.28	1,425
Hebei 河北	1	53	4,830	410	6.72	26.28	91.13	74.43	6,100
Shanxi 山西									
Inner Mongolia 內蒙									
Northeast 東北	1	56	35,010	30	0.26	8.33	625.18	96.88	11,530
Liaoning 遼寧	1	56	35,010	30	0.26	8.33	625.18	96.88	11,530
Jilin 吉林									
Heilongjiang 黑龍江									
Central East 華東	31	143	31,286	754	3.23	8.36	218.49	61.34	23,326
Shanghai 上海	5	311	92,910	-418	-0.46	-1.18	298.75	60.72	90,326
Jiangsu 江蘇	5	173	74,174	5,504	15.87	36.79	429.75	56.87	34,692
Zhejiang 浙江	6	164	4,598	-493	-6.34	-28.52	28.07	77.73	7,777
Anhui 安徽	2	125	17,685	370	6.17	16.48	141.48	62.67	6,000
Fujian 福建	11	35	5,552	19	0.93	1.40	160.71	33.47	2,051
Jiangxi 江西	1	379	940	-910	-5.77	33.21	2.48	117.36	15,780
Shandong 山東	1	29	9,490	850	83.33	404.76	327.24	79.41	1,020
Central-South 中南	38	238	17,228	319	1.17	1.76	72.47	33.55	27,243
Henan 河南	1	6	310				51.67	68.57	350
Hubei 湖北	1	105	9,830	370	1.87	3.56	93.62	47.58	19,820
Hunan 湖南	3	161	7,303	-1,677	-6.21	111.78	45.46	105.56	26,990
Guangdong 廣東	33	256	18,867	508	1.80	2.46	73.76	27.00	28,306
Guangxi 廣西									
Hainan 海南									
Southwest 西南	3	384	1,660	-3,003	-17.23	19.04	4.32	190.50	17,433
Chongqing 重慶	1	2	169	36	41.02	49.79	84.69	17.62	87
Sichuan 四川	1	28	3,276	87	5.25	44.30	119.10	88.15	1,659
Guizhou 貴州	1	1,115	500	-9,150	-18.29	19.21	0.45	195.22	50,030
Yunnan 雲南									
Tibet 西藏									
Northwest 西北									
Shaanxi 陝西									
Gansu 甘肅									
Qinghai 青海									
Ningxia 寧夏									
Xinjiang 新疆									

4173: Electronic Calculators 電子計算器製造業

Year 年份	Number of firms 企業個數	Rate of change 每年變化 (%)	Number of employees 職工人數（人）	Rate of change 每年變化 (%)	Total revenue (mil. RMB) 總銷售收入（百萬元）	Rate of change 每年變化 (%)	Total profit (mil. RMB) 總利潤（百萬元）	Rate of change 每年變化 (%)
1993	57		16,681		352		-14	
1994	71	24.56%	11,139	-33.22%	701	99.03%	-13	8.54%
1995	81	14.08%	16,688	49.82%	1,497	113.60%	59	562.45%
1996	85	4.94%	14,782	-11.42%	1,672	11.69%	27	-54.59%

3 Major products* 3 種主要產品 *	Output 產量	Sales volume 銷售量	Unit 單位
a) Electronic Calculator 電子計算器	84,689,160	84,689,160	set 台

Top 10 firms by revenue (year founded) 收入排名前 10 家企業 (創辦年份)	City 城市	Province 省	Telephone / fax 電話 / 傳真	Number of employees 職工人數	Ownership 產業所有權	Revenue ('000 RMB) 銷售收入（千元）	Profit ('000 RMB) (rank) 利潤（千元）(排名)	Total assets ('000 RMB) 總資產（千元）	Major products 主要產品
Aurora Office Equipment Co. Ltd. Shanghai 上海震旦辦公設備有限公司(1995)	Shanghai 上海市	Shanghai 上海市	(021)59512229 (021)59512429	1,346	Overseas Chinese-funded 港澳台資	438,000	-3299(41)	428,121	a
Jiangsu Yin He Electron Group Co. 江蘇銀河電子集團公司(1975)	Suzhou 蘇州市	Jiangsu 江蘇省	(0512)8441511	515	Collectively-owned 集體	352,450	28800(1)	158,870	a
Shanwei Xin Xing Electron Co. Ltd. 汕尾市新星電子有限公司(1992)	Shanwei 汕尾市	Guangdong 廣東省	(0660)3367888 (0660)3367875	2,577	Foreign-funded 外資	209,245	4608(3)	329,179	a
Sharp Brave Industrial (Panyu) Co. Ltd. 鋭鴻實業(番禺)有限公司(1993)	Guangzhou 廣州市	Guangdong 廣東省	(020)84913861 (020)84913838	896	Overseas Chinese-funded 港澳台資	102,537	-1781(37)	160,685	o
Huadu Yu Hong Electron Co. Ltd. 花都市裕鴻電子有限公司(1993)	Guangzhou 廣州市	Guangdong 廣東省	(020)86847511	192	Overseas Chinese-funded 港澳台資	69,588	6335(2)	12,258	a
Asia Ebauches Ltd. 亞洲伊博有限公司(1986)	Guangzhou 廣州市	Guangdong 廣東省	(020)82232266 (020)82231480	503	Overseas Chinese-funded 港澳台資	60,436	-2795(38)	16,626	o
Guangdong Zhaoqing Zhaoqing Dong Sheng Electronic Toy Factory 廣東省肇慶市肇慶東升電子玩具廠(1991)	Zhaoqing 肇慶市	Guangdong 廣東省	(0757)2721292 (0757)2721852	532	Overseas Chinese-funded 港澳台資	37,826	432(13)	18,976	a
Huaining Gao He Zhen Industry & Trade Co. Ltd. 懷寧縣高河鎮工貿責任有限公司(1995)	Anqing 安慶市	Anhui 安徽省	(0556)4856832	263	Collectively-owned 集體	35,070	730(11)	11,740	o
Shenyang Li Da Industrial General Company 瀋陽市利達實業總公司(1990)	Shenyang 瀋陽市	Liaoning 遼寧省	(024)24215909	50	Collectively-owned 集體	35,012	33(26)	11,527	o
Zijin Fu Fan Electronic Plastic Cement Products Co. Ltd. 紫金縣富凡電子塑膠製品有限公司(1993)	Heyuan 河源市	Guangdong 廣東省	(0762)7825032 (0762)7825032	364	Overseas Chinese-funded 港澳台資	34,320	3830(5)	5,730	o

Top 10 Cities by Production Output 產出排名前 10 位城市	Province 省	Market share 市場份額	Number of firms 企業個數
Shanwei 汕尾市	Guangdong 廣東省	23.73%	2
Suzhou 蘇州市	Jiangsu 江蘇省	23.54%	5
Guangzhou 廣州市	Guangdong 廣東省	8.16%	14
Shenzhen 深圳市	Guangdong 廣東省	7.36%	15
Quzhou 衢州市	Zhejiang 浙江省	5.99%	1
Shanghai 上海市	Shanghai 上海市	5.68%	13
Fuzhou 福州市	Fujian 福建省	5.65%	4
Heyuan 河源市	Guangdong 廣東省	3.74%	3
Zhaoqing 肇慶市	Guangdong 廣東省	3.46%	2
Huizhou 惠州市	Guangdong 廣東省	2.16%	4

10 Major Wholesalers 10 家主要批發商	City 城市	Province 省	Telephone / Fax 電話 / 傳真
Liaoning Automobile Trade Group Corp. 遼寧省汽車貿易集團	Shenyang 瀋陽市	Liaoning 遼寧省	(024)23835494 (024)23838338
China Post and Telecommunication Equipment General Company 中國郵電器材總公司	Beijing 北京市	Beijing 北京市	(010)63523715 (010)63525935
Jiangsu Electromechanical Products General Company 江蘇省機電產品總公司	Nanjing 南京市	Jiangsu 江蘇省	(025)7713642 (025)7711036
Xi Nan Technology Import & Export Company 西南技術進出口公司	Chongqing 重慶市	Chongqing 重慶市	(023)63850185 (023)63850026
Changzhou Economic Technology Industrial Development Zone Tian Ming Trade Company 常州經濟技術產業開發區天明貿易公司	Changzhou 常州市	Jiangsu 江蘇省	(0519)8829882 (0519)8829882
Shanxi Mechanical Equipment Import & Export Company 山西省機械設備進出口公司	Taiyuan 太原市	Shanxi 山西省	(0351)4040713 (0351)4043981
Ningbo Five Mining Machinery Import & Export Company 寧波市五礦機械進出口公司	Ningbo 寧波市	Zhejiang 浙江省	(0574)7311255 (0574)7320322
Tianjin Jin Huan Electromechanical Complete Sets of Equipment Factory 天津市津環機電成套設備廠	Tianjin 天津市	Tianjin 天津市	(022)26371628
Yunnan Machinery Import & Export Company 雲南省機械進出口公司	Kunming 昆明市	Yunnan 雲南省	(0871)3164879 (0871)3136829
Tianjin Da Qiu Zhuang Yi Yuan Trade Center 天津市大丘莊億源商貿中心	Tianjin 天津市	Tianjin 天津市	(022)28899478 (022)28899046

*Also include sales by firms outside this industry.包括本行業以外廠家的銷售。"o" stands for "others". "o" 代表"其他產品"。

4181: Communication Equipment Repairs 通訊設備修理業

The industry accounts for 0.001% of the total revenue of China's industrial sector in 1996. The revenue growth rate of the industry is 5.6% from 1995, as compared to the growth rate of China's industrial sector, 9.51%. The rate of return on asset is 31.00%. 84.89% of all firms in the industry made a profit while 4.00% had negative returns. The top province in terms of the industry's revenue is Zhejiang, accounting for 29.63% of the total revenue.
本行業在1996年佔全行業總產值0.001%，行業年增長率為5.6%（全國工業年增長率9.51%）。行業的資產回報率31.00%，84.89%的企業盈利，4.00%的企業虧損。銷售收入最高的省份為浙江省，佔本行業的29.63%。

	Total number of firms 企業總數	Total number of employees 職工總數	Total revenue (mil. RMB) 總銷售收入（百萬元）	Total profit (mil. RMB) 總利潤（百萬元）	Return on assets 資產利潤率 (%)	Return on equity 權益利潤率 (%)	Labour productivity ('000 RMB / worker) 勞動生產率（千元/人）	Debts / assets 資產負債率 (%)	Total assets (mil. RMB) 總資產（百萬元）
Industry Overall 行業總體	33	762	65	20	31.00	51.49	85.30	39.77	64

	Number of firms 企業個數	Average number of employees 平均職工人數	Average revenue ('000 RMB) 平均銷售收入（千元）	Average profit ('000 RMB) 平均利潤（千元）	Return on assets 資產利潤率 (%)	Return on equity 權益利潤率 (%)	Labour productivity ('000 RMB / worker) 勞動生產率（千元/人）	Average debts / assets 平均資產負債率(%)	Average Total assets ('000 RMB) 平均總資產（千元）
By ownership 產業所有權									
State-owned 國有	8	28	1,750	875	36.84	58.33	62.22	36.84	2,375
Collectively-owned 集體	19	24	1,409	-593	-48.59	-109.02	58.20	55.43	1,220
Privately-owned 私有									
Domestic JVs 聯營									
Joint stock 股份制									
Foreign-funded 外資	3	14	4,219	8,089	172.58	218.80	301.39	21.12	4,687
Overseas Chinese-funded 港澳台資	3	13	3,854				289.07	28.07	2,582
By size 規模									
Large 大型									
Medium 中型									
Small 小型	33	24	1,969	606	31.25	51.29	80.83	39.06	1,939
By regional distribution 地區分布									
Central-North 華北	7	1	29				25.00	44.48	401
Beijing 北京	3								
Tianjin 天津	1								
Hebei 河北	1	8	20				2.50	100.00	10
Shanxi 山西									
Inner Mongolia 內蒙	2		90					44.29	1,400
Northeast 東北	12	21	926	239	25.13	46.82	43.40	46.32	952
Liaoning 遼寧	6	14	145	73	24.44	37.93	10.24	35.56	300
Jilin 吉林	3	9	117	3	5.56	50.00	12.50	88.89	60
Heilongjiang 黑龍江	3	48	3,297	807	25.64	48.89	69.16	47.56	3,147
Central East 華東	7	39	4,741	1,801	45.39	70.29	122.93	35.42	3,969
Shanghai 上海	1								
Jiangsu 江蘇									
Zhejiang 浙江	3	16	6,420	1,903	64.81	99.83	409.79	35.07	2,937
Anhui 安徽									
Fujian 福建									
Jiangxi 江西									
Shandong 山東	3	74	4,643	2,300	36.37	56.46	62.47	35.58	6,323
Central-South 中南	7	33	2,911	634	19.98	34.02	89.39	41.27	3,174
Henan 河南	1	12	210	-10	-2.22	-7.14	17.50	68.89	450
Hubei 湖北									
Hunan 湖南	1	15	1,250	10	4.00	4.55	83.33	12.00	250
Guangdong 廣東	4	48	4,440	1,110	20.98	35.35	92.98	40.64	5,290
Guangxi 廣西	1	10	1,160				116.00	63.89	360
Hainan 海南									
Southwest 西南									
Chongqing 重慶									
Sichuan 四川									
Guizhou 貴州									
Yunnan 雲南									
Tibet 西藏									
Northwest 西北									
Shaanxi 陝西									
Gansu 甘肅									
Qinghai 青海									
Ningxia 寧夏									
Xinjiang 新疆									

4181: Communication Equipment Repairs 通訊設備修理業

Year 年份	Number of firms 企業個數	Rate of change 每年變化 (%)	Number of employees 職工人數 (人)	Rate of change 每年變化 (%)	Total revenue (mil. RMB) 總銷售收入 (百萬元)	Rate of change 每年變化 (%)	Total profit (mil. RMB) 總利潤 (百萬元)	Rate of change 每年變化 (%)
1993	27		1,264		76		4	
1994	33	22.22%	1,379	9.10%	38	-49.63%	-1	-117.11%
1995	19	-42.43%	764	-44.60%	62	60.43%	1	171.43%
1996	33	73.68%	762	-0.26%	65	5.60%	20	3709.52%

3 Major products* 3 種主要產品 *	Output 產量	Sales volume 銷售量	Unit 單位

Top 10 firms by revenue (year founded) 收入排名前 10 家企業 (創辦年份)	City 城市	Province 省	Telephone / fax 電話 / 傳真	Number of employees 職工人數	Ownership 產業所有權	Revenue ('000 RMB) 銷售收入 (千元)	Profit ('000 RMB) (rank) 利潤 (千元) (排名)	Total assets ('000 RMB) 總資產 (千元)	Major products 主要產品
Hangzhou Di Fo Mobile Communication Equipment Maintenance Co. Ltd. 杭州迪佛移動通訊設備維修有限公司(1993)	Hangzhou 杭州市	Zhejiang 浙江省	(0571)7069945 (0571)7069945	14	Foreign-funded 外資	17,280	5491(2)	7,540	o
Qingdao Xing Yi Electronic Equipment Co. Ltd. 青島興儀電子設備有限責任公司(1991)	Qingdao 青島市	Shandong 山東省	(0532)6897262	220	State-owned 國有	13,828	6904(1)	18,878	o
Guangdong Modern Communication Equipment Maintenance Co. Ltd. 廣東現代通訊設備維修有限公司(1994)	Guangzhou 廣州市	Guangdong 廣東省	(020)87789008 (020)87616586	141	Collectively-owned 集體	12,613	3579(3)	15,465	o
Heilong Jiang Long Hai Communication Equipment Co. Ltd. 黑龍江龍海通訊設備有限公司(1993)	Harbin 哈爾濱市	Heilongjiang 黑龍江省	(0451)5693129	38	Overseas Chinese-funded 港澳台資	8,205	2316(4)	8,457	o
Shanghai Da Hua Jun Hui Electromechanical Engineering Co. Ltd. 上海大華均輝機電工程有限公司(1995)	Shanghai 上海市	Shanghai 上海市	(021)59137978	20	Foreign-funded 外資	5,400	0(7)	4,530	o
Wangcheng Yong Wang Equipment Accessories Factory 望城縣永旺設備附件廠(1995)	Changsha 長沙市	Hunan 湖南省	(0731)8543278	12	Private-owned 私營	2,250	8(6)	250	o
Shanghai Xiang Xing Iron Tower Communication Installing Equipment Factory 上海翔星鐵塔通訊設備安裝廠(1994)	Shanghai 上海市	Shanghai 上海市	(021)59124761	80	Collectively-owned 集體	2,100	-143(9)	365	o

Top 10 Cities by Production Output 產出排名前 10 位城市	Province 省	Market share 市場份額	Number of firms 企業個數
Shanghai 上海市	Shanghai 上海市	47.32%	15
Guangzhou 廣州市	Guangdong 廣東省	17.70%	7
Jinzhou 錦州市	Liaoning 遼寧省	6.27%	2
Harbin 哈爾濱市	Heilongjiang 黑龍江省	5.88%	2
Chengdu 成都市	Sichuan 四川省	4.12%	5
Quzhou 衢州市	Zhejiang 浙江省	3.36%	1
Dalian 大連市	Liaoning 遼寧省	2.35%	1
Nantong 南通市	Jiangsu 江蘇省	1.58%	3
Kunming 昆明市	Yunnan 雲南省	1.51%	1
Yangzhou 揚州市	Jiangsu 江蘇省	1.31%	1

10 Major Wholesalers 10 家主要批發商	City 城市	Province 省	Telephone / Fax 電話 / 傳真

*Also include sales by firms outside this industry.包括本行業以外廠家的銷售。"o" stands for "others". "o" 代表 "其他產品"。

4182: Broadcast and Television Equipment Repairs 廣播電視設備修理業

The industry accounts for 0.001% of the total revenue of China's industrial sector in 1996. The revenue growth rate of the industry is 482.1% from 1995, as compared to the growth rate of China's industrial sector, 9.51%. The rate of return on asset is 6.49%. 83.33% of all firms in the industry made a profit while 16.67% had negative returns. The top province in terms of the industry's revenue is Guangdong, accounting for 37.67% of the total revenue.
本行業在1996年佔全行業總產值0.001%，行業年增長率為482.1%（全國工業年增長率9.51%）。行業的資產回報率6.49%，83.33%的企業盈利，16.67%的企業虧損。銷售收入最高的省份為廣東省，佔本行業的37.67%。

	Total number of firms 企業總數	Total number of employees 職工總數	Total revenue (mil. RMB) 總銷售收入（百萬元）	Total profit (mil. RMB) 總利潤（百萬元）	Return on assets 資產利潤率 (%)	Return on equity 權益利潤率 (%)	Labour productivity ('000 RMB / worker) 勞動生產率（千元/人）	Debts / assets 資產負債率 (%)	Total assets (mil. RMB) 總資產（百萬元）
Industry Overall 行業總體	18	472	30	2	6.49	17.65	63.56	63.20	27

	Number of firms 企業個數	Average number of employees 平均職工人數	Average revenue ('000 RMB) 平均銷售收入（千元）	Average profit ('000 RMB) 平均利潤（千元）	Return on assets 資產利潤率 (%)	Return on equity 權益利潤率 (%)	Labour productivity ('000 RMB / worker) 勞動生產率（千元/人）	Average debts / assets 平均資產負債率(%)	Average Total assets ('000 RMB) 平均總資產（千元）
By ownership 產業所有權									
State-owned 國有	8	22	875			3.85	39.11	100.00	625
Collectively-owned 集體	9	31	2,039	537	33.71	90.51	65.76	62.76	1,593
Privately-owned 私有									
Domestic JVs 聯營									
Joint stock 股份制									
Foreign-funded 外資	1	14	4,652	-2,833	-37.06	-60.63	332.28	38.88	7,646
Overseas Chinese-funded 港澳台資									
By size 規模									
Large 大型									
Medium 中型									
Small 小型	18	26	1,667	111	7.41	20.00	63.56	62.96	1,500
By regional distribution 地區分布									
Central-North 華北	4	45	2,498	288	9.94	19.56	55.81	49.18	2,893
Beijing 北京	1		3,620	1,340	21.72	25.77		15.72	6,170
Tianjin 天津									
Hebei 河北	1	20	160				8.00	92.68	410
Shanxi 山西	1	159	6,210	-190	-3.81	-29.23	39.06	86.97	4,990
Inner Mongolia 內蒙	1								
Northeast 東北	4	8	108	-45	-7.59	-12.33	13.44	37.97	593
Liaoning 遼寧									
Jilin 吉林	2	9	160				17.78	100.00	100
Heilongjiang 黑龍江	2	7	55	-90	-8.29	-12.33	7.86	32.26	1,085
Central East 華東	2								
Shanghai 上海	1								
Jiangsu 江蘇									
Zhejiang 浙江									
Anhui 安徽									
Fujian 福建									
Jiangxi 江西	1								
Shandong 山東									
Central-South 中南	6	42	3,330	128	5.98	30.68	78.66	80.50	2,145
Henan 河南									
Hubei 湖北	1	130	5,120	40	5.06	10.00	39.38	49.37	790
Hunan 湖南	3	27	1,187	107	14.81	35.96	43.95	58.80	720
Guangdong 廣東	2	22	5,650	205	4.13	33.61	262.79	87.70	4,960
Guangxi 廣西									
Hainan 海南									
Southwest 西南	1	5							
Chongqing 重慶									
Sichuan 四川									
Guizhou 貴州									
Yunnan 雲南									
Tibet 西藏									
Northwest 西北	1	2	10				5.00		10
Shaanxi 陝西	1	2	10				5.00		10
Gansu 甘肅									
Qinghai 青海									
Ningxia 寧夏									
Xinjiang 新疆									

4182: Broadcast and Television Equipment Repairs 廣播電視設備修理業

Year 年份	Number of firms 企業個數	Rate of change 每年變化 (%)	Number of employees 職工人數 (人)	Rate of change 每年變化 (%)	Total revenue (mil. RMB) 總銷售收入 (百萬元)	Rate of change 每年變化 (%)	Total profit (mil. RMB) 總利潤 (百萬元)	Rate of change 每年變化 (%)
1993	20		776		67		1	
1994	20	0	615	-20.75%	35	-48.04%	-1	-168.59%
1995	15	-25.00%	546	-11.22%	5	-85.26%	0	96.74%
1996	18	20.00%	472	-13.55%	30	482.07%	2	6160.61%

3 Major products* 3種主要產品*	Output 產量	Sales volume 銷售量	Unit 單位

Top 10 firms by revenue (year founded) 收入排名前10家企業 (創辦年份)	City 城市	Province 省	Telephone / fax 電話 / 傳真	Number of employees 職工人數	Ownership 產業所有權	Revenue ('000 RMB) 銷售收入 (千元)	Profit ('000 RMB) (rank) 利潤 (千元) (排名)	Total assets ('000 RMB) 總資產 (千元)	Major products 主要產品
Shandou Jin Field Video Frequency Fitting Parts Factory 汕頭市金園區視頻配件廠(1993)	Shantou 汕頭市	Guangdong 廣東省	(0754)8209614	43	Collectively-owned 集體	11,300	410(1)	9,920	o
Shanxi Yuncheng Area State-owned Radio Factory 山西省運城地區地方國營無線電廠(1971)	Yuncheng 運城市	Shanxi 山西省	(0359)2026470	159	State-owned 國有	6,211	-186(5)	4,992	o
Ministry of Posts & Telecommunications Changchun Telephone Equipment Factory Pei Xian Jia Branch 郵電部長春電話設備廠配線架分廠(1992)	Changchun 長春市	Jilin 吉林省	(0431)7974526	25	Collectively-owned 集體	2,872	54(3)	2,476	o
Zhuzhou Radio No.2 Factory Labour Service Company 株洲市無線電二廠勞動服務公司(1988)	Zhuzhou 株洲市	Hunan 湖南省	(0733)8403270	37	Collectively-owned 集體	2,428	49(4)	1,629	o
Changsha Kai Da Shang Yong Machine Factory 長沙市凱達商用機器廠(1995)	Changsha 長沙市	Hunan 湖南省	(0731)5278654	18	Collectively-owned 集體	2,062	299(2)	468	o

Top 10 Cities by Production Output 產出排名前10位城市	Province 省	Market share 市場份額	Number of firms 企業個數
Shanwei 汕尾市	Guangdong 廣東省	75.51%	1
Ji'nan 濟南市	Shandong 山東省	9.44%	1
Yuncheng 運城市	Shanxi 山西省	6.00%	1
Beijing 北京市	Beijing 北京市	3.40%	1
Zhuzhou 株洲市	Hunan 湖南省	1.45%	1
Shanghai 上海市	Shanghai 上海市	1.39%	7
Guangzhou 廣州市	Guangdong 廣東省	0.77%	3
Hefei 合肥市	Anhui 安徽省	0.59%	1
Yangzhou 揚州市	Jiangsu 江蘇省	0.29%	1
Shantou 汕頭市	Guangdong 廣東省	0.28%	1

10 Major Wholesalers 10家主要批發商	City 城市	Province 省	Telephone / Fax 電話 / 傳真

*Also include sales by firms outside this industry.包括本行業以外廠家的銷售。"o" stands for "others". "o" 代表"其他產品"。

4183: Computer Repairs 電子計算機修理業

The industry accounts for 0.016% of the total revenue of China's industrial sector in 1996. The revenue growth rate of the industry is 1375.0% from 1995, as compared to the growth rate of China's industrial sector, 9.51%. The rate of return on asset is 8.21%. 65.91% of all firms in the industry made a profit while 9.09% had negative returns. The top province in terms of the industry's revenue is Shanghai, accounting for 87.47% of the total revenue.
本行業在1996年佔全行業總產值0.016%，行業年增長率為1375.0%（全國工業年增長率9.51%）。行業的資產回報率8.21%，65.91%的企業盈利，9.09%的企業虧損。銷售收入最高的省份為上海市，佔本行業的87.47%。

	Total number of firms 企業總數	Total number of employees 職工總數	Total revenue (mil. RMB) 總銷售收入（百萬元）	Total profit (mil. RMB) 總利潤（百萬元）	Return on assets 資產利潤率 (%)	Return on equity 權益利潤率 (%)	Labour productivity ('000 RMB / worker) 勞動生產率（千元/人）	Debts / assets 資產負債率 (%)	Total assets (mil. RMB) 總資產（百萬元）
Industry Overall 行業總體	16	1,337	956	128	8.21	13.34	715.03	38.48	1,564

	Number of firms 企業個數	Average number of employees 平均職工人數	Average revenue ('000 RMB) 平均銷售收入（千元）	Average profit ('000 RMB) 平均利潤（千元）	Return on assets 資產利潤率 (%)	Return on equity 權益利潤率 (%)	Labour productivity ('000 RMB / worker) 勞動生產率（千元/人）	Average debts / assets 平均資產負債率(%)	Average Total assets ('000 RMB) 平均總資產（千元）
By ownership 產業所有權									
State-owned 國有	4	156	5,750	-500	-13.33	-50.00	36.80	73.33	3,750
Collectively-owned 集體	11	34	51,878	169	0.83	-2.41	1509.68	134.51	20,372
Privately-owned 私有									
Domestic JVs 聯營									
Joint stock 股份制									
Foreign-funded 外資									
Overseas Chinese-funded 港澳台資	2	167	181,132	64,069	9.67	12.38	1084.62	21.85	662,428
By size 規模									
Large 大型									
Medium 中型									
Small 小型	16	84	59,747	8,000	8.18	13.31	715.00	38.49	97,750
By regional distribution 地區分布									
Central-North 華北	2	10	460	5	0.83	2.78	48.42	69.42	605
Beijing 北京									
Tianjin 天津									
Hebei 河北									
Shanxi 山西									
Inner Mongolia 內蒙	2	10	460	5	0.83	2.78	48.42	69.42	605
Northeast 東北	2	17	3,845	85	3.09	19.32	233.03	84.00	2,750
Liaoning 遼寧	1	17	4,880				287.06	87.44	4,540
Jilin 吉林									
Heilongjiang 黑龍江	1	16	2,810	170	17.71	54.84	175.63	67.71	960
Central East 華東	8	150	117,919	16,016	8.23	13.34	786.13	38.29	194,599
Shanghai 上海	1	334	836,240	122,050	8.61	13.90	2503.71	38.05	1,417,200
Jiangsu 江蘇									
Zhejiang 浙江									
Anhui 安徽									
Fujian 福建	2	46	9,810	3,835	12.66	15.20	215.60	16.74	30,295
Jiangxi 江西	4	194	21,873	-398	-2.01	-4.92	112.89	59.13	19,750
Shandong 山東	1								
Central-South 中南	3	25	1,133	17	7.35	13.16	45.33	45.59	227
Henan 河南	1	65	140	10	2.94	14.29	2.15	79.41	340
Hubei 湖北									
Hunan 湖南									
Guangdong 廣東	2	5	1,630	20	11.76	12.90	326.00	11.76	170
Guangxi 廣西									
Hainan 海南									
Southwest 西南									
Chongqing 重慶									
Sichuan 四川									
Guizhou 貴州									
Yunnan 雲南									
Tibet 西藏									
Northwest 西北	1	10	780				78.00		
Shaanxi 陝西	1	10	780				78.00		
Gansu 甘肅									
Qinghai 青海									
Ningxia 寧夏									
Xinjiang 新疆									

4183: Computer Repairs 電子計算機修理業

Year 年份	Number of firms 企業個數	Rate of change 每年變化 (%)	Number of employees 職工人數 (人)	Rate of change 每年變化 (%)	Total revenue (mil. RMB) 總銷售收入 (百萬元)	Rate of change 每年變化 (%)	Total profit (mil. RMB) 總利潤 (百萬元)	Rate of change 每年變化 (%)
1993	16		182		14		0	
1994	16	0	502	175.82%	23	69.76%	0	236.25%
1995	10	-37.50%	348	-30.68%	65	180.15%	7	1456.65%
1996	16	60.00%	1,337	284.20%	956	1375.04%	128	1785.96%

3 Major products* 3 種主要產品 *	Output 產量	Sales volume 銷售量	Unit 單位

Top 10 firms by revenue (year founded) 收入排名前 10 家企業 (創辦年份)	City 城市	Province 省	Telephone / fax 電話 / 傳真	Number of employees 職工人數	Ownership 產業所有權	Revenue ('000 RMB) 銷售收入 (千元)	Profit ('000 RMB) (rank) 利潤 (千元) (排名)	Total assets ('000 RMB) 總資產 (千元)	Major products 主要產品
Lucent Technologies of Shanghai, Ltd. 上海朗迅科技公司(1995)	Shanghai 上海市	Shanghai 上海市	(021)64705858	346	Foreign-funded 外資	836,239	122046(1)	1,417,196	o
Jiangxi Qing Hua Science & Technology Group Co. Ltd. 江西清華科技集團有限公司(1988)	Nanchang 南昌市	Jiangxi 江西省	(0791)8326084 (0791)8326084	166	Domestic JVs 聯營	65,600	840(3)	64,169	o
Alcatel Fujian Communication Technology Co. Ltd. 福建阿爾卡特通訊技術有限公司	Fuzhou 福州市	Fujian 福建省	(0591)3349881	91	Foreign-funded 外資	19,621	7670(2)	60,594	o
Jiangxi Ke Huan High-technology Industrial Co. Ltd. 江西省科環高技術實業有限公司(1991)	Nanchang 南昌市	Jiangxi 江西省	(0791)6297663 (0791)6270145	42	State-owned 國有	13,421	-2434(8)	10,757	o
Jiangxi Computerchang Computer Center 江西電子計算機廠電腦中心(1992)	Nanchang 南昌市	Jiangxi 江西省	(0791)6261929 (0791)6261929	27	State-owned 國有	8,471	0(7)	4,071	o
Benxi Founder Computer General Company 本溪市方正電腦總公司(1991)	Benxi 本溪市	Liaoning 遼寧省	(0414)2827565 (0414)2827565	11	Collectively-owned 集體	4,881	0(6)	4,538	o
Harbin Da Heng Science & Technology Application Co. Ltd. 哈爾濱市大恒科技應用有限責任公司(1993)	Harbin 哈爾濱市	Heilongjiang 黑龍江省	(0451)5659623	11	Collectively-owned 集體	2,812	167(4)	956	o
Ke Di Computer Company 科迪電腦公司	Guangzhou 廣州市	Guangdong 廣東省	(020)87577246	6	Collectively-owned 集體	2,703	35(5)	245	o

Top 10 Cities by Production Output 產出排名前 10 位城市	Province 省	Market share 市場份額	Number of firms 企業個數
Nanchang 南昌市	Jiangxi 江西省	82.82%	4
Hangzhou 杭州市	Zhejiang 浙江省	8.48%	1
Benxi 本溪市	Liaoning 遼寧省	4.13%	1
Zhenjiang 鎮江市	Jiangsu 江蘇省	2.92%	1
Shanghai 上海市	Shanghai 上海市	0.87%	3
Hohhot 呼和浩特市	Inner Mong 內蒙	0.74%	2
Fuzhou 福州市	Fujian 福建省	0.04%	1
Taiyuan 太原市	Shanxi 山西省	0.01%	2
Hegang 鶴崗市	Heilongjiang 黑龍江省	0.00%	1
Tianjin 天津市	Tianjin 天津市		1

10 Major Wholesalers 10 家主要批發商	City 城市	Province 省	Telephone / Fax 電話 / 傳真

*Also include sales by firms outside this industry.包括本行業以外廠家的銷售。"o" stands for "others". "o" 代表 "其他產品"。

4189: Other Electronic Equipment Repairs 其他電子設備修理業

The industry accounts for 0.004% of the total revenue of China's industrial sector in 1996. The revenue growth rate of the industry is -74.8% from 1995, as compared to the growth rate of China's industrial sector, 9.51%. The rate of return on asset is 1.78%. 63.89% of all firms in the industry made a profit while 11.11% had negative returns. The top province in terms of the industry's revenue is Jiangsu, accounting for 53.24% of the total revenue.
本行業在1996年佔全行業總產值0.004%，行業年增長率為-74.8%（全國工業年增長率9.51%）。行業的資產回報率1.78%，63.89%的企業盈利，11.11%的企業虧損。銷售收入最高的省份為江蘇省，佔本行業的53.24%。

	Total number of firms 企業總數	Total number of employees 職工總數	Total revenue (mil. RMB) 總銷售收入（百萬元）	Total profit (mil. RMB) 總利潤（百萬元）	Return on assets 資產利潤率 (%)	Return on equity 權益利潤率 (%)	Labour productivity ('000 RMB / worker) 勞動生產率（千元/人）	Debts / assets 資產負債率 (%)	Total assets (mil. RMB) 總資產（百萬元）
Industry Overall 行業總體	96	4,526	225	9	1.78	4.10	49.71	56.67	481

	Number of firms 企業個數	Average number of employees 平均職工人數	Average revenue ('000 RMB) 平均銷售收入（千元）	Average profit ('000 RMB) 平均利潤（千元）	Return on assets 資產利潤率 (%)	Return on equity 權益利潤率 (%)	Labour productivity ('000 RMB / worker) 勞動生產率（千元/人）	Average debts / assets 平均資產負債率(%)	Average Total assets ('000 RMB) 平均總資產（千元）
By ownership 產業所有權									
State-owned 國有	22	11	91				8.33	62.50	364
Collectively-owned 集體	54	22	277	17	1.03	3.19	12.39	67.72	1,695
Privately-owned 私有	1	5							
Domestic JVs 聯營	4	210	13,782	222	0.96	8.57	65.55	88.81	23,211
Joint stock 股份制									
Foreign-funded 外資	7	159	10,758	1,149	4.26	5.46	67.48	21.93	26,957
Overseas Chinese-funded 港澳台資	8	151	9,698	-110	-0.88	-4.95	64.28	82.25	12,486
By size 規模									
Large 大型									
Medium 中型									
Small 小型	93	49	1,932	95	1.98	4.31	39.54	54.10	4,831
By regional distribution 地區分布									
Central-North 華北	24	22	624	51	8.98	19.58	29.01	54.23	566
Beijing 北京	7	3	69	27	16.81	21.59	22.86	22.12	161
Tianjin 天津	10	18	333	64	12.08	19.39	18.71	37.92	530
Hebei 河北	1	55							
Shanxi 山西	2	68	2,150	25	1.35	25.00	31.62	94.61	1,855
Inner Mongolia 內蒙	4	32	1,715	85	9.86	18.38	54.44	46.38	863
Northeast 東北	21	14	1,427	64	5.10	38.14	103.31	86.56	1,261
Liaoning 遼寧	9	13	3,021	126	4.67	37.54	236.43	87.51	2,687
Jilin 吉林	2	4	60				17.14	98.55	690
Heilongjiang 黑龍江	10	17	265	22	23.91	43.14	15.77	43.48	92
Central East 華東	23	28	5,443	413	6.50	18.64	196.86	65.15	6,349
Shanghai 上海	6	7	277	-17	-3.23	-7.30	40.49	56.13	517
Jiangsu 江蘇	5	94	23,958	1,914	6.79	19.81	255.96	65.69	28,170
Zhejiang 浙江	1								
Anhui 安徽	2	10	1,395	5	1.11	1.75	139.50	36.67	450
Fujian 福建	4	6	43				7.08		
Jiangxi 江西									
Shandong 山東	5	17	158	2	0.85	1.54	9.52	45.76	236
Central-South 中南	19	142	2,715	-169	-1.11	-2.19	19.13	49.10	15,215
Henan 河南	4	8	253	-10	-2.16	-6.67	31.56	68.11	463
Hubei 湖北	1								
Hunan 湖南	2	10	240	10	1.28	1.63	25.26	21.15	780
Guangdong 廣東	10	259	4,756	-324	-1.14	-2.25	18.34	49.31	28,398
Guangxi 廣西	2	27	1,270	20	2.35	2.86	47.92	17.65	850
Hainan 海南									
Southwest 西南	3	3	367	7	11.11	40.00	110.00	72.22	60
Chongqing 重慶	1	13	807	19	26.64	-1665.27	63.38	101.60	71
Sichuan 四川	1	7	1,393	21	7.29	20.81	191.58	64.99	289
Guizhou 貴州	2								
Yunnan 雲南									
Tibet 西藏									
Northwest 西北	6	63	310	-50	-4.89	-40.54	4.93	87.93	1,022
Shaanxi 陝西	4	59	265	-75	-5.39	-62.50	4.49	91.38	1,393
Gansu 甘肅									
Qinghai 青海	2	71	400				5.67	53.57	280
Ningxia 寧夏									
Xinjiang 新疆									

4189: Other Electronic Equipment Repairs 其他電子設備修理業

Year 年份	Number of firms 企業個數	Rate of change 每年變化 (%)	Number of employees 職工人數 (人)	Rate of change 每年變化 (%)	Total revenue (mil. RMB) 總銷售收入 (百萬元)	Rate of change 每年變化 (%)	Total profit (mil. RMB) 總利潤 (百萬元)	Rate of change 每年變化 (%)
1993	99		4,593		93		7	
1994	95	-4.04%	3,933	-14.37%	185	98.41%	32	356.76%
1995	65	-31.58%	3,849	-2.14%	893	383.14%	41	27.10%
1996	96	47.69%	4,526	17.59%	225	-74.80%	9	-78.19%

3 Major products* 3種主要產品 *	Output 產量	Sales volume 銷售量	Unit 單位

Top 10 firms by revenue (year founded) 收入排名前10家企業 (創辦年份)	City 城市	Province 省	Telephone / fax 電話 / 傳真	Number of employees 職工人數	Ownership 產業所有權	Revenue ('000 RMB) 銷售收入 (千元)	Profit ('000 RMB) (rank) 利潤 (千元) (排名)	Total assets ('000 RMB) 總資產 (千元)	Major products 主要產品
Changzhou Dong Xu Special Type Cable Material Factory 常州市東旭特種電纜料廠(1993)	Changzhou 常州市	Jiangsu 江蘇省	(0519)8400366 (0519)8400968	152	Collectively-owned 集體	53,660	2471(2)	84,960	o
Jiangyin Hai Da Industrial Company 江陰市海達實業公司(1993)	Wuxi 無錫市	Jiangsu 江蘇省	(0510)6201588	150	Collectively-owned 集體	52,800	5470(1)	41,655	o
Bai Li (Doumen) Electronic Technique Co. Ltd. 柏力(斗門)電子技術有限公司(1995)	Zhuhai 珠海市	Guangdong 廣東省	(0756)5539398 (0756)5539438	500	Overseas Chinese-funded 港澳台資	37,237	-3170(16)	278,960	o
Changshu Yi Tong Group 常熟市億通集團(1985)	Suzhou 蘇州市	Jiangsu 江蘇省	(0520)2531169 (0520)2531467	160	Collectively-owned 集體	13,260	1680(3)	14,200	o
Guangzhou Zengcheng Development Company Scrap Hardware Factory 廣州增城發展公司廢舊五金廠(1991)	Guangzhou 廣州市	Guangdong 廣東省		30	Overseas Chinese-funded 港澳台資	7,500	44(7)	590	o
Shenyang Electric Technology Application Research Institute 瀋陽市電氣技術應用研究所(1993)	Shenyang 瀋陽市	Liaoning 遼寧省	(024)86510583	10	Collectively-owned 集體	5,007	893(4)	171	o
Yangquan Mine Administrative Bureau Jin Hua Industrial Company 陽泉礦務局晉華實業公司(1994)	Yangquan 陽泉市	Shanxi 山西省	(0353)4044528	16	Collectively-owned 集體	3,860	7(11)	2,858	o
Huaining Xun Da Electron Co. Ltd. 懷寧縣迅達電子有限責任公司(1995)	Anqing 安慶市	Anhui 安徽省		10	Collectively-owned 集體	2,512	12(8)	602	o
Guangxi Dongxing Xin Chuang Xing Electromechanical Co. Ltd. 廣西東興新創興機電有限公司(1994)	Fangchenggang 防城港市	Guangxi 廣西	(0770)7681860	13	Foreign-funded 外資	2,400	0(14)	1,000	o

Top 10 Cities by Production Output 產出排名前10位城市	Province 省	Market share 市場份額	Number of firms 企業個數
Shenzhen 深圳市	Guangdong 廣東省	59.52%	4
Zhuhai 珠海市	Guangdong 廣東省	11.38%	3
Shanghai 上海市	Shanghai 上海市	9.78%	18
Guangzhou 廣州市	Guangdong 廣東省	3.57%	16
Xi'an 西安市	Shaanxi 陝西省	2.97%	3
Fuzhou 福州市	Fujian 福建省	2.71%	4
Ji'nan 濟南市	Shandong 山東省	1.29%	4
Tianjin 天津市	Tianjin 天津市	1.05%	12
Wuxi 無錫市	Jiangsu 江蘇省	0.73%	2
Yantai 煙台市	Shandong 山東省	0.71%	3

10 Major Wholesalers 10家主要批發商	City 城市	Province 省	Telephone / Fax 電話 / 傳真

*Also include sales by firms outside this industry.包括本行業以外廠家的銷售。"o" stands for "others". "o" 代表 "其他產品" 。

4190: Other Electronic Equipment 其他電子設備製造業

The industry accounts for 0.099% of the total revenue of China's industrial sector in 1996. The revenue growth rate of the industry is -18.8% from 1995, as compared to the growth rate of China's industrial sector, 9.51%. The rate of return on asset is 1.69%. 66.91% of all firms in the industry made a profit while 29.28% had negative returns. The top province in terms of the industry's revenue is Guangdong, accounting for 21.44% of the total revenue.
本行業在1996年佔全行業總產值0.099%，行業年增長率為-18.8%（全國工業年增長率9.51%）。行業的資產回報率1.69%，66.91%的企業盈利，29.28%的企業虧損。銷售收入最高的省份為廣東省，佔本行業的21.44%。

	Total number of firms 企業總數	Total number of employees 職工總數	Total revenue (mil. RMB) 總銷售收入（百萬元）	Total profit (mil. RMB) 總利潤（百萬元）	Return on assets 資產利潤率 (%)	Return on equity 權益利潤率 (%)	Labour productivity ('000 RMB / worker) 勞動生產率（千元/人）	Debts / assets 資產負債率 (%)	Total assets (mil. RMB) 總資產（百萬元）
Industry Overall 行業總體	906	79,801	5,728	155	1.69	3.70	71.78	54.39	9,156

	Number of firms 企業個數	Average number of employees 平均職工人數	Average revenue ('000 RMB) 平均銷售收入（千元）	Average profit ('000 RMB) 平均利潤（千元）	Return on assets 資產利潤率 (%)	Return on equity 權益利潤率 (%)	Labour productivity ('000 RMB / worker) 勞動生產率（千元/人）	Average debts / assets 平均資產負債率(%)	Average Total assets ('000 RMB) 平均總資產（千元）
By ownership 產業所有權									
State-owned 國有	146	140	4,021	-103	-0.67	-2.29	28.63	70.79	15,356
Collectively-owned 集體	429	57	1,929	203	7.32	17.56	34.04	58.31	2,772
Privately-owned 私有	14	22	526	50	3.95	5.95	23.55	33.61	1,263
Domestic JVs 聯營	11	153	4,575	-289	-2.44	-5.96	29.85	59.13	11,878
Joint stock 股份制	25	61	1,853	1,120	12.25	17.80	30.18	31.21	9,144
Foreign-funded 外資	125	142	24,859	237	0.91	1.80	174.80	49.76	26,152
Overseas Chinese-funded 港澳台資	152	104	7,191	45	0.33	0.60	68.84	44.16	13,608
By size 規模									
Large 大型	8	1,048	104,667	4,330	2.10	4.08	99.86	48.61	206,573
Medium 中型	20	507	23,998	-2,349	-4.91	-11.07	47.32	55.69	47,864
Small 小型	835	73	5,282	200	2.56	5.77	71.94	55.70	7,831
By regional distribution 地區分布									
Central-North 華北	177	48	5,038	465	5.78	14.58	104.38	60.38	8,040
Beijing 北京	121	24	5,772	672	8.39	18.28	238.02	54.07	8,006
Tianjin 天津	22	50	3,017	49	1.13	3.01	60.68	62.52	4,352
Hebei 河北	21	103	3,922	-24	-0.28	-1.01	38.24	72.60	8,747
Shanxi 山西	6	224	3,112	-177	-1.20	-5.67	13.89	78.92	14,780
Inner Mongolia 內蒙	7	145	3,717	200	1.62	10.01	25.56	83.78	12,324
Northeast 東北	97	111	12,741	665	2.80	5.21	114.37	46.17	23,721
Liaoning 遼寧	72	117	15,741	1,095	4.15	7.03	134.94	40.98	26,389
Jilin 吉林	16	94	4,877	-687	-3.71	-11.53	51.99	67.86	18,531
Heilongjiang 黑龍江	9	101	2,730	-372	-3.21	-15.24	27.12	78.96	11,608
Central East 華東	363	69	5,789	84	0.92	2.04	83.58	54.78	9,128
Shanghai 上海	57	56	3,626	27	0.48	0.81	65.21	40.67	5,549
Jiangsu 江蘇	92	101	10,916	257	1.35	2.85	107.84	52.50	18,974
Zhejiang 浙江	87	62	5,214	26	0.42	1.35	84.15	69.12	6,149
Anhui 安徽	6	32	2,965	247	19.84	51.93	93.63	61.80	1,243
Fujian 福建	57	42	3,469	-328	-7.68	-16.41	82.63	53.21	4,271
Jiangxi 江西	30	59	651	-52	-1.16	-3.40	11.08	65.88	4,512
Shandong 山東	34	86	5,936	645	6.64	14.30	69.05	53.55	9,717
Central-South 中南	208	154	6,884	-53	-0.60	-1.29	44.65	54.02	8,918
Henan 河南	32	36	1,070	-349	-6.51	-18.84	30.12	65.44	5,356
Hubei 湖北	15	75	5,719	764	6.08	9.59	76.66	36.57	12,562
Hunan 湖南	23	58	2,862	-253	-3.87	-9.44	48.94	59.02	6,555
Guangdong 廣東	118	237	10,408	-9	-0.08	-0.18	43.96	52.95	10,721
Guangxi 廣西	20	26	896	-223	-5.63	-26.08	34.00	78.43	3,964
Hainan 海南									
Southwest 西南	33	70	1,464	-263	-4.37	-104.57	20.89	95.81	6,022
Chongqing 重慶	15	91	1,602	-553	-5.22	172.45	17.59	103.03	10,583
Sichuan 四川	11	43	1,968	21	0.85	2.65	45.59	67.91	2,522
Guizhou 貴州	1	10	80	-60	-9.09	-13.64	8.00	31.82	660
Yunnan 雲南	6	79	400	-137	-5.42	-25.00	5.07	78.31	2,520
Tibet 西藏									
Northwest 西北	28	33	663	-102	-4.39	-20.34	19.98	78.41	2,317
Shaanxi 陝西	27	33	632	-108	-4.53	-21.07	19.03	78.51	2,389
Gansu 甘肅									
Qinghai 青海									
Ningxia 寧夏	1	32	1,490	70	18.92	46.67	46.56	59.46	370
Xinjiang 新疆									

4190: Other Electronic Equipment 其他電子設備製造業

Year 年份	Number of firms 企業個數	Rate of change 每年變化 (%)	Number of employees 職工人數 (人)	Rate of change 每年變化 (%)	Total revenue (mil. RMB) 總銷售收入 (百萬元)	Rate of change 每年變化 (%)	Total profit (mil. RMB) 總利潤 (百萬元)	Rate of change 每年變化 (%)
1993	718		71,512		3,345		157	
1994	886	23.40%	236,475	230.68%	7,471	123.36%	284	80.76%
1995	832	-6.10%	78,076	-66.98%	7,054	-5.59%	33	-88.52%
1996	906	8.89%	79,801	2.21%	5,728	-18.80%	155	374.50%

3 Major products* 3 種主要產品 *	Output 產量	Sales volume 銷售量	Unit 單位
a) Microcomputer for Learning 學習機	1,143,592	1,097,848	set 部

Top 10 firms by revenue (year founded) 收入排名前 10 家企業 (創辦年份)	City 城市	Province 省	Telephone / fax 電話 / 傳真	Number of employees 職工人數	Ownership 產業所有權	Revenue ('000 RMB) 銷售收入 (千元)	Profit ('000 RMB) (rank) 利潤 (千元) (排名)	Total assets ('000 RMB) 總資產 (千元)	Major products 主要產品
Beijing Panasonic Communication Equipment Co. Ltd. 北京市松下通訊設備有限公司(1992)	Beijing 北京市	Beijing 北京市	(010)62042225 (010)62027508	230	Foreign-funded 外資	381,106	69706(1)	341,379	o
Shenyang Dong Jiang Magnetic Card Co. Ltd. 瀋陽市東江磁卡有限公司(1994)	Shenyang 瀋陽市	Liaoning 遼寧省	(024)88900500	190	Overseas Chinese-funded 港澳台資	299,832	10240(6)	135,285	o
Dalian Harada Industry Co. Ltd. 大連原田工業有限公司(1988)	Dalian 大連市	Liaoning 遼寧省	(0411)7612111 (0411)7628654	957	Foreign-funded 外資	252,901	2155(28)	253,706	o
Dongguan Fucheng Yi An Electron Manufacturing Co. Ltd. 東莞附城益安電子製造有限公司(1994)	Dongguan 東莞市	Guangdong 廣東省	(0769)2263869 (0769)2263869	2,100	Overseas Chinese-funded 港澳台資	250,408	595(61)	193,698	o
Zhongshan Xiao Ba Wang Electron Industrial Co. Ltd. 中山市小霸王電子工業有限公司(1987)	Zhongshan 中山市	Guangdong 廣東省	(0760)8803688 (0760)8803688	890	Collectively-owned 集體	175,773	1492(33)	82,046	a
Shenyang He Guang Group Co. Ltd. 瀋陽和光集團有限公司(1995)	Shenyang 瀋陽市	Liaoning 遼寧省	(024)23909277	90	Private-owned 私營	169,970	-823(252)	498,278	o
Hu Shi Electron Co. Ltd. 滬士電子有限公司(1995)	Suzhou 蘇州市	Jiangsu 江蘇省	(0512)7314977 (0512)7312110	621	Overseas Chinese-funded 港澳台資	168,803	3803(15)	538,504	o
Beijing Nan Tian Information Engineering Co. Ltd. 北京南天信息工程有限公司(1993)	Beijing 北京市	Beijing 北京市	(010)68425550 (010)68422501	149	Overseas Chinese-funded 港澳台資	116,742	9988(7)	57,803	o
Jiangsu Hua Ning Electron Group 江蘇華寧電子集團(1991)	Nanjing 南京市	Jiangsu 江蘇省	(025)8768528 (025)8768528	1,241	State-owned 國有	104,982	813(53)	277,653	o
Lian Xin Tong Mian Ji Ban Co. Ltd. 聯鑫銅面基板有限公司(1993)	Suzhou 蘇州市	Jiangsu 江蘇省	(0512)7313836	135	Overseas Chinese-funded 港澳台資	98,400	-728(246)	62,922	o

Top 10 Cities by Production Output 產出排名前 10 位城市	Province 省	Market share 市場份額	Number of firms 企業個數
Shenzhen 深圳市	Guangdong 廣東省	16.54%	112
Shanghai 上海市	Shanghai 上海市	8.25%	124
Dalian 大連市	Liaoning 遼寧省	7.49%	21
Nanjing 南京市	Jiangsu 江蘇省	6.03%	61
Beijing 北京市	Beijing 北京市	5.41%	91
Huizhou 惠州市	Guangdong 廣東省	5.29%	17
Shenyang 瀋陽市	Liaoning 遼寧省	5.24%	50
Suzhou 蘇州市	Jiangsu 江蘇省	5.22%	65
Guangzhou 廣州市	Guangdong 廣東省	5.07%	56
Zhongshan 中山市	Guangdong 廣東省	3.98%	15

10 Major Wholesalers 10 家主要批發商	City 城市	Province 省	Telephone / Fax 電話 / 傳真
Liaoning Automobile Trade Group Corp. 遼寧省汽車貿易集團	Shenyang 瀋陽市	Liaoning 遼寧省	(024)23835494 (024)23838338
China Post and Telecommunication Equipment General Company 中國郵電器材總公司	Beijing 北京市	Beijing 北京市	(010)63523715 (010)63525935
Jiangsu Electromechanical Products General Company 江蘇省機電產品總公司	Nanjing 南京市	Jiangsu 江蘇省	(025)7713642 (025)7711036
Xi Nan Technology Import & Export Company 西南技術進出口公司	Chongqing 重慶市	Chongqing 重慶市	(023)63850185 (023)63850026
Changzhou Economic Technology Industrial Development Zone Tian Ming Trade Company 常州經濟技術產業開發區天明貿易公司	Changzhou 常州市	Jiangsu 江蘇省	(0519)8829882 (0519)8829882
Shanxi Mechanical Equipment Import & Export Company 山西省機械設備進出口公司	Taiyuan 太原市	Shanxi 山西省	(0351)4040713 (0351)4043981
Ningbo Five Mining Machinery Import & Export Company 寧波市五礦機械進出口公司	Ningbo 寧波市	Zhejiang 浙江省	(0574)7311255 (0574)7320322
Tianjin Jin Huan Electromechanical Complete Sets of Equipment Factory 天津市津環機電成套設備廠	Tianjin 天津市	Tianjin 天津市	(022)26371628
Yunnan Machinery Import & Export Company 雲南省機械進出口公司	Kunming 昆明市	Yunnan 雲南省	(0871)3164879 (0871)3136829
Tianjin Da Qiu Zhuang Yi Yuan Trade Center 天津市大丘莊億源商貿中心	Tianjin 天津市	Tianjin 天津市	(022)28899478 (022)28899046

*Also include sales by firms outside this industry.包括本行業以外廠家的銷售。"o" stands for "others". "o" 代表"其他產品"。

4211: Industrial Automation Equipment 工業自動化儀表製造業

The industry accounts for 0.111% of the total revenue of China's industrial sector in 1996. The revenue growth rate of the industry is 3.2% from 1995, as compared to the growth rate of China's industrial sector, 9.51%. The rate of return on asset is 1.44%. 60.51% of all firms in the industry made a profit while 32.41% had negative returns. The top province in terms of the industry's revenue is Shanghai, accounting for 22.47% of the total revenue.
本行業在1996年佔全行業總產值0.111%，行業年增長率為3.2%（全國工業年增長率9.51%）。行業的資産回報率1.44%，60.51%的企業盈利，32.41%的企業虧損。銷售收入最高的省份為上海市，佔本行業的22.47%。

	Total number of firms 企業總數	Total number of employees 職工總數	Total revenue (mil. RMB) 總銷售收入（百萬元）	Total profit (mil. RMB) 總利潤（百萬元）	Return on assets 資産利潤率 (%)	Return on equity 權益利潤率 (%)	Labour productivity ('000 RMB / worker) 勞動生產率（千元/人）	Debts / assets 資產負債率 (%)	Total assets (mil. RMB) 總資產（百萬元）
Industry Overall 行業總體	823	132,592	6,407	182	1.44	3.97	48.32	63.70	12,619

	Number of firms 企業個數	Average number of employees 平均職工人數	Average revenue ('000 RMB) 平均銷售收入（千元）	Average profit ('000 RMB) 平均利潤（千元）	Return on assets 資產利潤率 (%)	Return on equity 權益利潤率 (%)	Labour productivity ('000 RMB / worker) 勞動生產率（千元/人）	Average debts / assets 平均資產負債率(%)	Average Total assets ('000 RMB) 平均總資產（千元）
By ownership 產業所有權									
State-owned 國有	164	369	9,457	-354	-1.25	-4.25	25.62	70.49	28,183
Collectively-owned 集體	495	87	3,793	96	1.99	5.25	43.85	62.12	4,847
Privately-owned 私有	11	17	1,506	171	9.34	22.03	86.30	57.60	1,828
Domestic JVs 聯營	10	225	11,180	247	1.67	2.99	49.76	44.37	14,837
Joint stock 股份制	20	1,111	68,946	4,507	2.60	7.42	62.04	65.00	173,483
Foreign-funded 外資	78	55	15,577	1,126	6.13	12.76	283.81	51.95	18,368
Overseas Chinese-funded 港澳台資	44	53	5,733	221	1.86	3.10	107.72	40.18	11,884
By size 規模									
Large 大型	12	3,372	175,592	6,097	1.30	3.76	52.08	65.41	469,463
Medium 中型	37	630	34,897	647	1.04	2.95	55.43	64.77	62,337
Small 小型	756	92	3,979	112	1.81	4.66	43.37	61.11	6,188
By regional distribution 地區分布									
Central-North 華北	183	98	5,254	245	2.21	5.90	53.61	62.46	11,079
Beijing 北京	93	56	6,306	375	3.18	7.40	112.57	57.07	11,785
Tianjin 天津	62	158	4,153	-224	-1.89	-7.06	26.33	73.16	11,820
Hebei 河北	20	88	5,214	1,179	15.23	27.16	59.31	43.94	7,740
Shanxi 山西	6	133	1,557	7	0.12	1.25	11.70	90.29	5,475
Inner Mongolia 內蒙	2	196	1,950	155	2.83	8.03	9.97	64.72	5,485
Northeast 東北	168	147	3,559	73	0.91	2.85	24.14	68.15	7,987
Liaoning 遼寧	120	167	3,813	89	1.06	3.27	22.85	67.61	8,409
Jilin 吉林	26	89	2,299	46	0.75	3.66	25.89	79.64	6,187
Heilongjiang 黑龍江	22	111	3,661	14	0.18	0.46	33.00	60.53	7,810
Central East 華東	280	153	11,092	551	3.11	7.54	72.32	58.79	17,729
Shanghai 上海	73	236	19,722	1,322	3.76	8.10	83.44	53.60	35,194
Jiangsu 江蘇	58	150	13,886	718	4.27	12.42	92.44	65.67	16,841
Zhejiang 浙江	87	89	5,870	212	2.21	5.20	65.88	57.48	9,578
Anhui 安徽	21	156	8,900	360	2.69	7.85	57.14	65.78	13,380
Fujian 福建	7	122	6,889	89	1.23	5.56	56.53	77.91	7,219
Jiangxi 江西	7	96	1,974	-91	-1.52	-8.98	20.63	83.08	6,011
Shandong 山東	27	164	3,745	-367	-4.69	-20.02	22.80	76.57	7,833
Central-South 中南	97	223	5,426	-575	-3.57	-18.48	24.36	80.71	16,130
Henan 河南	26	191	3,311	-359	-4.66	-26.59	17.33	82.48	7,707
Hubei 湖北	25	456	9,217	-1,911	-5.90	-50.49	20.22	88.31	32,375
Hunan 湖南	12	117	2,502	-24	-1.07	-3.95	21.38	72.97	2,263
Guangdong 廣東	33	113	5,351	48	0.31	0.98	47.56	68.85	15,810
Guangxi 廣西	1	125	3,240	20	0.33	0.90	25.92	63.11	5,990
Hainan 海南									
Southwest 西南	36	365	18,703	593	1.38	4.35	51.23	68.24	42,914
Chongqing 重慶	24	426	26,311	2,300	3.89	12.23	61.69	68.18	59,121
Sichuan 四川	9	204	3,882	-2,838	-31.52	-86.28	19.00	63.46	9,002
Guizhou 貴州	1	265	6,720	60	0.88	3.30	25.36	73.34	6,790
Yunnan 雲南	2	456	4,900	-3,090	-10.36	-42.77	10.76	75.79	29,840
Tibet 西藏									
Northwest 西北	59	207	9,192	84	0.42	0.90	44.50	52.94	19,939
Shaanxi 陝西	52	177	8,593	51	0.28	0.54	48.57	48.95	18,520
Gansu 甘肅	2	20	355	-5	-1.25	-1.82	17.75	31.25	400
Qinghai 青海	1	225	3,220	20	0.19	0.67	14.31	70.86	10,260
Ningxia 寧夏	2	1,311	43,575	1,110	1.16	4.02	33.25	71.21	95,875
Xinjiang 新疆	2	50	2,190	40	0.76	2.53	44.24	70.10	5,285

4211: Industrial Automation Equipment 工業自動化儀表製造業

Year 年份	Number of firms 企業個數	Rate of change 每年變化 (%)	Number of employees 職工人數 (人)	Rate of change 每年變化 (%)	Total revenue (mil. RMB) 總銷售收入 (百萬元)	Rate of change 每年變化 (%)	Total profit (mil. RMB) 總利潤 (百萬元)	Rate of change 每年變化 (%)
1993	589		193,460		4,653		291	
1994	636	7.98%	132,235	-31.65%	4,553	-2.16%	170	-41.48%
1995	765	20.28%	147,840	11.80%	6,210	36.39%	231	35.53%
1996	823	7.58%	132,592	-10.31%	6,407	3.17%	182	-21.18%

3 Major products* 3 種主要產品 *	Output 產量	Sales volume 銷售量	Unit 單位
a) Automatic Instrument, Meter & System 自動化儀表及系統	19,924,399	17,533,471	set 台(套)
b) Water Meter 水表	5,002,966	4,902,906	set 台

Top 10 firms by revenue (year founded) 收入排名前 10 家企業 (創辦年份)	City 城市	Province 省	Telephone / fax 電話 / 傳真	Number of employees 職工人數	Ownership 產業所有權	Revenue ('000 RMB) 銷售收入 (千元)	Profit ('000 RMB) (rank) 利潤 (千元) (排名)	Total assets ('000 RMB) 總資產 (千元)	Major products 主要產品
Shanghai Automation Instrumentation Co. Ltd. 上海自動化儀表股份有限公司(1989)	Shanghai 上海市	Shanghai 上海市	(021)62800700 (021)62801680	8,309	Joint stock 股份制	665,594	50118(1)	1,688,337	a,b
Sichuan Instrument Co. Ltd., Chongqing 重慶川儀股份有限公司	Chongqing 重慶市	Chongqing 重慶市	(023)68862766 (023)68216674		Joint stock 股份制	453,300	30900(2)	1,061,795	a
Jiangsu Shen Ying Group Co. 江蘇神鷹集團公司(1987)	Wuxi 無錫市	Jiangsu 江蘇省	(0510)7401565 (0510)7401565	1,510	Collectively-owned 集體	269,570	17580(6)	265,920	o
Xi'an Instrument Factory 西安儀表廠(1960)	Xi'an 西安市	Shaanxi 陝西省	(029)4243921 (029)4262579	5,358	State-owned 國有	222,530	18226(5)	589,874	o
Wuhan Instrument and Automation Industry (Group) Co. 武漢儀器儀表自動化工業集團公司(1958)	Wuhan 武漢市	Hubei 湖北省	(027)82832607 (027)82811454	7,544	State-owned 國有	168,547	-50355(353)	649,313	o
Shanghai-foxboro Co. Ltd. 上海福克斯波羅有限公司(1982)	Shanghai 上海市	Shanghai 上海市	(021)64362380 (021)64700447	415	Foreign-funded 外資	145,784	15839(7)	143,699	a
Yokogama Xiyi Co. Ltd. 橫河西儀有限公司(1986)	Xi'an 西安市	Shaanxi 陝西省	(029)4262253 (029)4262062	408	Foreign-funded 外資	136,359	3062(24)	131,645	o
Anhui Tianchang Instrument Factory 安徽省天長市儀表廠(1974)	Chuzhou 滁州市	Anhui 安徽省	(0550)7021891 (0550)7023136	811	Collectively-owned 集體	128,879	7782(12)	124,010	o
Beijing Shi Dai Time Group Inc 時代集團公司(1984)	Beijing 北京市	Beijing 北京市	(010)68418333 (010)68418334	211	Collectively-owned 集體	117,495	1197(53)	127,262	o
Shanghai Omron Automation System Co. Ltd. 上海歐姆龍自動化系統有限公司(1994)	Shanghai 上海市	Shanghai 上海市	(021)58540044 (021)58542658	101	Foreign-funded 外資	108,435	5084(16)	108,990	o

Top 10 Cities by Production Output 產出排名前 10 位城市	Province 省	Market share 市場份額	Number of firms 企業個數
Shanghai 上海市	Shanghai 上海市	22.86%	108
Beijing 北京市	Beijing 北京市	10.89%	75
Chongqing 重慶市	Chongqing 重慶市	8.95%	55
Xi'an 西安市	Shaanxi 陝西省	6.53%	40
Wuxi 無錫市	Jiangsu 江蘇省	6.03%	31
Wuhan 武漢市	Hubei 湖北省	4.77%	15
Tianjin 天津市	Tianjin 天津市	4.33%	68
Shenzhen 深圳市	Guangdong 廣東省	3.66%	10
Dalian 大連市	Liaoning 遼寧省	2.29%	75
Suzhou 蘇州市	Jiangsu 江蘇省	2.23%	30

10 Major Wholesalers 10 家主要批發商	City 城市	Province 省	Telephone / Fax 電話 / 傳真
Liaoning Automobile Trade Group Corp. 遼寧省汽車貿易集團	Shenyang 瀋陽市	Liaoning 遼寧省	(024)23835494 (024)23838338
China Post and Telecommunication Equipment General Company 中國郵電器材總公司	Beijing 北京市	Beijing 北京市	(010)63523715 (010)63525935
Jiangsu Electromechanical Products General Company 江蘇省機電產品總公司	Nanjing 南京市	Jiangsu 江蘇省	(025)7713642 (025)7711036
Xi Nan Technology Import & Export Company 西南技術進出口公司	Chongqing 重慶市	Chongqing 重慶市	(023)63850185 (023)63850026
Changzhou Economic Technology Industrial Development Zone Tian Ming Trade Company 常州經濟技術產業開發區天明貿易公司	Changzhou 常州市	Jiangsu 江蘇省	(0519)8829882 (0519)8829882
Shanxi Mechanical Equipment Import & Export Company 山西省機械設備進出口公司	Taiyuan 太原市	Shanxi 山西省	(0351)4040713 (0351)4043981
Ningbo Five Mining Machinery Import & Export Company 寧波市五礦機械進出口公司	Ningbo 寧波市	Zhejiang 浙江省	(0574)7311255 (0574)7320322
Tianjin Jin Huan Electromechanical Complete Sets of Equipment Factory 天津市津環機電成套設備廠	Tianjin 天津市	Tianjin 天津市	(022)26371628
Yunnan Machinery Import & Export Company 雲南省機械進出口公司	Kunming 昆明市	Yunnan 雲南省	(0871)3164879 (0871)3136829
Tianjin Da Qiu Zhuang Yi Yuan Trade Center 天津市大丘莊億源商貿中心	Tianjin 天津市	Tianjin 天津市	(022)28899478 (022)28899046

*Also include sales by firms outside this industry.包括本行業以外廠家的銷售。"o" stands for "others". "o" 代表 "其他產品"。

4212: Electrical Instruments and Meters 電工儀器、儀表製造業

The industry accounts for 0.064% of the total revenue of China's industrial sector in 1996. The revenue growth rate of the industry is -0.7% from 1995, as compared to the growth rate of China's industrial sector, 9.51%. The rate of return on asset is 0.77%. 51.96% of all firms in the industry made a profit while 36.82% had negative returns. The top province in terms of the industry's revenue is Zhejiang, accounting for 32.02% of the total revenue.
本行業在1996年佔全行業總產值0.064%，行業年增長率為-0.7%（全國工業年增長率9.51%）。行業的資產回報率0.77%，51.96%的企業盈利，36.82%的企業虧損。銷售收入最高的省份為浙江省，佔本行業的32.02%。

	Total number of firms 企業總數	Total number of employees 職工總數	Total revenue (mil. RMB) 總銷售收入（百萬元）	Total profit (mil. RMB) 總利潤（百萬元）	Return on assets 資產利潤率 (%)	Return on equity 權益利潤率 (%)	Labour productivity ('000 RMB / worker) 勞動生產率（千元/人）	Debts / assets 資產負債率 (%)	Total assets (mil. RMB) 總資產（百萬元）
Industry Overall 行業總體	505	87,563	3,687	55	0.77	2.97	42.11	74.02	7,174

	Number of firms 企業個數	Average number of employees 平均職工人數	Average revenue ('000 RMB) 平均銷售收入（千元）	Average profit ('000 RMB) 平均利潤（千元）	Return on assets 資產利潤率 (%)	Return on equity 權益利潤率 (%)	Labour productivity ('000 RMB / worker) 勞動生產率（千元/人）	Average debts / assets 平均資產負債率(%)	Average Total assets ('000 RMB) 平均總資產（千元）
By ownership 產業所有權									
State-owned 國有	105	471	14,133	-495	-1.56	-8.43	30.01	81.48	31,733
Collectively-owned 集體	334	97	5,002	194	2.51	8.40	51.54	70.15	7,725
Privately-owned 私有	2	23	450	-39	-3.07	-8.78	20.02	65.02	1,267
Domestic JVs 聯營	5	38	2,816	-174	-2.74	-4.22	74.51	35.18	6,340
Joint stock 股份制	12	198	11,633	2,338	7.51	17.14	58.65	56.15	31,110
Foreign-funded 外資	18	59	6,827	301	2.40	4.80	116.15	50.04	12,532
Overseas Chinese-funded 港澳台資	27	106	9,428	362	1.55	5.46	88.95	71.55	23,279
By size 規模									
Large 大型	9	2,365	120,096	3,789	1.34	5.31	50.77	74.74	282,620
Medium 中型	24	841	42,384	-382	-0.56	-2.72	50.42	79.42	68,173
Small 小型	458	100	3,469	66	1.00	3.40	34.54	70.45	6,538
By regional distribution 地區分布									
Central-North 華北	53	130	2,930	-95	-1.09	-4.66	22.58	76.69	8,696
Beijing 北京	25	61	1,697	-54	-0.96	-2.66	27.84	63.93	5,665
Tianjin 天津	17	164	4,521	-93	-1.00	-4.65	27.56	78.38	9,252
Hebei 河北	7	110	3,180	-6	-0.09	-0.31	28.80	71.55	6,471
Shanxi 山西	4	448	3,440	-508	-1.74	-21.46	7.68	91.89	29,178
Inner Mongolia 內蒙									
Northeast 東北	72	220	4,242	-178	-1.37	-7.29	19.29	81.18	12,936
Liaoning 遼寧	43	87	1,340	168	7.56	21.90	15.41	65.49	2,224
Jilin 吉林	5	857	6,678	-4,274	-7.01	-103.09	7.79	93.20	61,004
Heilongjiang 黑龍江	24	325	8,935	57	0.26	1.12	27.45	77.10	22,115
Central East 華東	263	156	9,183	234	1.69	6.24	58.71	72.83	13,805
Shanghai 上海	48	253	11,780	84	0.52	2.28	46.49	77.10	16,103
Jiangsu 江蘇	44	182	8,419	-102	-0.73	-4.28	46.32	83.04	13,989
Zhejiang 浙江	110	104	10,733	603	3.71	11.08	102.76	66.49	16,252
Anhui 安徽	15	157	3,531	-141	-2.92	-42.57	22.56	93.13	4,833
Fujian 福建	15	66	783	-125	-1.74	-3.19	11.58	45.46	7,157
Jiangxi 江西	11	288	4,925	-105	-0.92	-7.90	17.12	88.30	11,311
Shandong 山東	20	148	8,990	36	0.48	2.57	60.72	81.35	7,517
Central-South 中南	65	192	9,101	517	2.09	7.30	47.43	71.40	24,751
Henan 河南	19	238	5,983	1,286	5.83	10.72	25.15	45.57	22,046
Hubei 湖北	13	125	5,467	21	0.38	1.33	43.90	71.64	5,498
Hunan 湖南	12	265	7,708	-1,089	-2.07	-47.75	29.07	95.66	52,578
Guangdong 廣東	18	101	12,635	1,619	7.75	17.93	125.51	56.78	20,897
Guangxi 廣西	2	663	43,240	-3,525	-6.39	-33.29	65.27	80.80	55,155
Hainan 海南	1	13	410	-140	-12.84	-17.07	31.54	23.85	1,090
Southwest 西南	34	208	4,758	-230	-2.41	-7.71	22.87	68.77	9,548
Chongqing 重慶	11	191	6,950	75	1.02	3.73	36.39	72.73	7,368
Sichuan 四川	7	47	1,850	-40	-1.27	-2.73	39.58	53.38	3,142
Guizhou 貴州	12	332	4,445	-558	-3.28	-10.86	13.40	69.75	16,998
Yunnan 雲南	4	179	5,220	-155	-3.24	-8.24	29.20	60.75	4,790
Tibet 西藏									
Northwest 西北	18	232	3,189	-790	-6.55	-43.42	13.76	84.91	12,064
Shaanxi 陝西	14	106	2,323	-26	-0.36	-1.11	21.97	67.40	7,098
Gansu 甘肅	3	885	8,023	-4,630	-11.94	12627.27	9.07	100.09	38,790
Qinghai 青海									
Ningxia 寧夏	1	36	810	30	2.11	6.25	22.50	66.20	1,420
Xinjiang 新疆									

4212: Electrical Instruments and Meters 電工儀器、儀表製造業

Year 年份	Number of firms 企業個數	Rate of change 每年變化 (%)	Number of employees 職工人數 (人)	Rate of change 每年變化 (%)	Total revenue (mil. RMB) 總銷售收入 (百萬元)	Rate of change 每年變化 (%)	Total profit (mil. RMB) 總利潤 (百萬元)	Rate of change 每年變化 (%)
1993	423		129,916		3,633		97	
1994	441	4.26%	102,215	-21.32%	3,249	-10.58%	12	-87.67%
1995	480	8.84%	93,247	-8.77%	3,713	14.27%	48	306.26%
1996	505	5.21%	87,563	-6.10%	3,687	-0.70%	55	13.52%

3 Major products* 3 種主要產品 *	Output 產量	Sales volume 銷售量	Unit 單位
a) Electrican's Instrument & Meter 電工儀器儀表	49,644,973	49,148,523	set 台
b) Kilowatt-hour Meter 電度表	40,257,749	39,050,017	set 台

Top 10 firms by revenue (year founded) 收入排名前 10 家企業 (創辦年份)	City 城市	Province 省	Telephone / fax 電話 / 傳真	Number of employees 職工人數	Ownership 產業所有權	Revenue ('000 RMB) 銷售收入 (千元)	Profit ('000 RMB) (rank) 利潤 (千元) (排名)	Total assets ('000 RMB) 總資產 (千元)	Major products 主要產品
Holley Group Co. Ltd. 華立集團公司(1996)	Hangzhou 杭州市	Zhejiang 浙江省	(0571)8836688	301	Joint stock 股份制	587,939	43098(1)	1,009,600	a,b
Ningbo San Xing Group Co. Ltd. 寧波三星集團股份有限公司(1982)	Ningbo 寧波市	Zhejiang 浙江省	(0574)8436338 (0574)8436867	1,560	Joint stock 股份制	385,307	9932(4)	239,195	a,b
Shanghai Instrumentation Co. Ltd. (Group) 上海儀表(集團)公司(1990)	Shanghai 上海市	Shanghai 上海市	(021)63217691 (021)63212081	2,401	State-owned 國有	140,572	5148(7)	223,600	a,b
Qingdao Electric Meter Factory 青島電度表廠(1958)	Qingdao 青島市	Shandong 山東省	(0532)3833297 (0532)3833409	1,420	State-owned 國有	118,663	683(30)	66,342	a,b
Harbin Electric Meter Instrument Plant 哈爾濱電表儀器廠(1956)	Harbin 哈爾濱市	Heilongjiang 黑龍江省	(0451)6666293	4,630	State-owned 國有	111,568	27(94)	389,371	a,b
Xiaoshan Magnet Steel Factory 蕭山市磁鋼廠(1980)	Hangzhou 杭州市	Zhejiang 浙江省	(0571)2696117 (0571)2696043	1,129	State-owned 國有	110,243	7027(6)	164,270	o
Hangzhou Xizi (Group) Co. 杭州西子(集團)公司(1958)	Hangzhou 杭州市	Zhejiang 浙江省	(0571)8842428 (0571)8845082	1,501	State-owned 國有	102,030	0(136)	178,740	a,b
Liuzhou Meter General Factory 柳州市儀表總廠(1969)	Liuzhou 柳州市	Guangxi 廣西	(0772)3834711 (0772)3839342	1,019	State-owned 國有	72,280	-5090(193)	78,365	a,b
Wuxi Wei Da Electrical and Meter Co. Ltd. 無錫威達電工儀表有限公司(1993)	Wuxi 無錫市	Jiangsu 江蘇省	(0510)2709323 (0510)2701060	593	Overseas Chinese-funded 港澳台資	72,095	2070(16)	64,246	a,b
Shenzhen Hua Yi Experiment & Measuring Instrument Company 深圳華儀試驗與測量儀表公司(1988)	Shenzhen 深圳市	Guangdong 廣東省	(0755)3358188 (0755)3353150	245	State-owned 國有	68,031	2944(11)	53,057	a

Top 10 Cities by Production Output 產出排名前 10 位城市	Province 省	Market share 市場份額	Number of firms 企業個數
Hangzhou 杭州市	Zhejiang 浙江省	27.52%	45
Shanghai 上海市	Shanghai 上海市	14.73%	101
Ningbo 寧波市	Zhejiang 浙江省	12.82%	20
Harbin 哈爾濱市	Heilongjiang 黑龍江省	4.32%	18
Wuxi 無錫市	Jiangsu 江蘇省	3.65%	19
Qingdao 青島市	Shandong 山東省	2.50%	3
Wenzhou 温州市	Zhejiang 浙江省	2.07%	54
Jiaxing 嘉興市	Zhejiang 浙江省	2.06%	10
Tianjin 天津市	Tianjin 天津市	1.79%	21
Suzhou 蘇州市	Jiangsu 江蘇省	1.77%	26

10 Major Wholesalers 10 家主要批發商	City 城市	Province 省	Telephone / Fax 電話 / 傳真
Liaoning Automobile Trade Group Corp. 遼寧省汽車貿易集團	Shenyang 瀋陽市	Liaoning 遼寧省	(024)23835494 (024)23838338
China Post and Telecommunication Equipment General Company 中國郵電器材總公司	Beijing 北京市	Beijing 北京市	(010)63523715 (010)63525935
Jiangsu Electromechanical Products General Company 江蘇省機電產品總公司	Nanjing 南京市	Jiangsu 江蘇省	(025)7713642 (025)7711036
Xi Nan Technology Import & Export Company 西南技術進出口公司	Chongqing 重慶市	Chongqing 重慶市	(023)63850185 (023)63850026
Changzhou Economic Technology Industrial Development Zone Tian Ming Trade Company 常州經濟技術產業開發區天明貿易公司	Changzhou 常州市	Jiangsu 江蘇省	(0519)8829882 (0519)8829882
Shanxi Mechanical Equipment Import & Export Company 山西省機械設備進出口公司	Taiyuan 太原市	Shanxi 山西省	(0351)4040713 (0351)4043981
Ningbo Five Mining Machinery Import & Export Company 寧波市五礦機械進出口公司	Ningbo 寧波市	Zhejiang 浙江省	(0574)7311255 (0574)7320322
Tianjin Jin Huan Electromechanical Complete Sets of Equipment Factory 天津市津環機電成套設備廠	Tianjin 天津市	Tianjin 天津市	(022)26371628
Yunnan Machinery Import & Export Company 雲南省機械進出口公司	Kunming 昆明市	Yunnan 雲南省	(0871)3164879 (0871)3136829
Tianjin Da Qiu Zhuang Yi Yuan Trade Center 天津市大丘莊億源商貿中心	Tianjin 天津市	Tianjin 天津市	(022)28899478 (022)28899046

*Also include sales by firms outside this industry.包括本行業以外廠家的銷售。"o" stands for "others". "o" 代表"其他產品"。

4213: Optical Instruments 光學儀器製造業

The industry accounts for 0.062% of the total revenue of China's industrial sector in 1996. The revenue growth rate of the industry is 11.8% from 1995, as compared to the growth rate of China's industrial sector, 9.51%. The rate of return on asset is 0.52%. 73.11% of all firms in the industry made a profit while 25.21% had negative returns. The top province in terms of the industry's revenue is Jiangsu, accounting for 14.15% of the total revenue.
本行業在1996年佔全行業總產值0.062%，行業年增長率為11.8%（全國工業年增長率9.51%）。行業的資產回報率0.52%，73.11%的企業盈利，25.21%的企業虧損。銷售收入最高的省份為江蘇省，佔本行業的14.15%。

	Total number of firms 企業總數	Total number of employees 職工總數	Total revenue (mil. RMB) 總銷售收入（百萬元）	Total profit (mil. RMB) 總利潤（百萬元）	Return on assets 資產利潤率 (%)	Return on equity 權益利潤率 (%)	Labour productivity ('000 RMB / worker) 勞動生產率（千元/人）	Debts / assets 資產負債率 (%)	Total assets (mil. RMB) 總資產（百萬元）
Industry Overall 行業總體	243	90,144	3,601	41	0.52	1.37	39.95	62.27	7,988

	Number of firms 企業個數	Average number of employees 平均職工人數	Average revenue ('000 RMB) 平均銷售收入（千元）	Average profit ('000 RMB) 平均利潤（千元）	Return on assets 資產利潤率 (%)	Return on equity 權益利潤率 (%)	Labour productivity ('000 RMB / worker) 勞動生產率（千元/人）	Average debts / assets 平均資產負債率(%)	Average Total assets ('000 RMB) 平均總資產（千元）
By ownership 產業所有權									
State-owned 國有	71	980	31,465	-14	-0.02	-0.04	32.09	62.98	88,944
Collectively-owned 集體	113	99	4,393	63	1.14	3.15	44.48	63.67	5,482
Privately-owned 私有									
Domestic JVs 聯營	7	188	4,448	-92	-0.77	-1.93	23.61	60.29	12,024
Joint stock 股份制	3	1,360	83,829	7,094	7.10	18.63	61.62	61.87	99,843
Foreign-funded 外資	28	72	5,664	-373	-4.29	-9.58	79.01	55.21	8,681
Overseas Chinese-funded 港澳台資	21	168	20,482	1,176	5.78	12.69	122.05	54.44	20,342
By size 規模									
Large 大型	23	2,313	78,496	-960	-0.42	-1.08	33.94	60.55	226,159
Medium 中型	13	735	33,828	-245	-0.35	-1.02	46.02	65.36	69,171
Small 小型	200	138	6,782	331	3.51	10.19	49.23	65.54	9,437
By regional distribution 地區分布									
Central-North 華北	53	151	10,496	529	2.79	7.69	69.48	63.75	18,968
Beijing 北京	35	159	14,541	916	3.91	9.32	91.34	58.09	23,453
Tianjin 天津	12	113	2,628	-182	-1.61	-15.16	23.17	89.39	11,297
Hebei 河北	3	166	2,623	-440	-7.65	-58.41	15.77	86.85	5,753
Shanxi 山西	2	287	3,965	-265	-1.68	-13.91	13.82	87.98	15,810
Inner Mongolia 內蒙	1								
Northeast 東北	20	264	6,398	94	0.28	0.60	24.24	53.52	33,559
Liaoning 遼寧	12	111	6,449	186	1.36	2.88	58.23	52.79	13,673
Jilin 吉林	7	518	6,571	-51	-0.07	-0.16	12.68	53.66	71,531
Heilongjiang 黑龍江	1	323	4,570	10	0.16	0.40	14.15	60.91	6,370
Central East 華東	102	315	14,378	705	2.71	7.05	45.66	61.59	26,034
Shanghai 上海	22	287	13,526	528	2.17	7.61	47.06	71.49	24,344
Jiangsu 江蘇	29	467	17,565	352	0.97	2.06	37.59	52.68	36,163
Zhejiang 浙江	21	232	13,017	1,441	8.09	17.61	56.22	54.03	17,808
Anhui 安徽	6	97	6,363	147	2.83	9.75	65.60	71.02	5,187
Fujian 福建	15	82	7,872	153	1.87	4.64	95.53	59.74	8,217
Jiangxi 江西	5	874	37,352	2,978	4.00	13.51	42.72	70.37	74,400
Shandong 山東	4	298	10,815	435	1.02	5.72	36.26	82.20	42,700
Central-South 中南	26	735	21,626	-1,823	-3.33	-11.59	29.42	71.30	54,794
Henan 河南	5	1,582	25,216	-7,378	-8.04	-33.89	15.94	76.27	91,712
Hubei 湖北	7	864	9,527	-3,209	-4.12	-18.65	11.02	77.91	77,907
Hunan 湖南	3	1,072	66,210	3,803	4.97	11.94	61.78	58.36	76,503
Guangdong 廣東	8	162	18,766	8	0.04	0.08	116.11	53.73	19,568
Guangxi 廣西	3	215	6,913	163	1.41	4.22	32.16	66.53	11,563
Hainan 海南									
Southwest 西南	28	551	24,650	445	0.98	2.62	44.71	62.54	45,377
Chongqing 重慶	8	124	10,466	32	0.30	0.89	84.73	65.62	10,447
Sichuan 四川	5	514	22,663	189	0.23	0.53	44.09	57.70	83,902
Guizhou 貴州	3	822	7,217	-1,107	-2.74	-13.24	8.78	79.33	40,453
Yunnan 雲南	12	796	39,656	1,411	2.52	6.61	49.79	61.92	56,028
Tibet 西藏									
Northwest 西北	14	728	14,141	-1,833	-2.67	-5.93	19.43	54.95	68,641
Shaanxi 陝西	12	848	16,363	-2,149	-2.68	-5.96	19.29	54.96	80,060
Gansu 甘肅	2	6	815	65	50.00	68.42	148.18	26.92	130
Qinghai 青海									
Ningxia 寧夏									
Xinjiang 新疆									

4213: Optical Instruments 光學儀器製造業

Year 年份	Number of firms 企業個數	Rate of change 每年變化 (%)	Number of employees 職工人數 (人)	Rate of change 每年變化 (%)	Total revenue (mil. RMB) 總銷售收入 (百萬元)	Rate of change 每年變化 (%)	Total profit (mil. RMB) 總利潤 (百萬元)	Rate of change 每年變化 (%)
1993	208		124,936		1,934		19	
1994	206	-0.96%	93,609	-25.08%	2,719	40.56%	25	29.60%
1995	226	9.71%	94,516	0.97%	3,222	18.51%	18	-28.50%
1996	243	7.52%	90,144	-4.63%	3,601	11.76%	41	132.44%

3 Major products* 3 種主要產品 *	Output 產量	Sales volume 銷售量	Unit 單位
a) Optical Instrument 光學儀器	1,921,106	1,690,573	set 台
b) Composition Analytical Instrument 成分分析儀器	44,756	46,994	set 台

Top 10 firms by revenue (year founded) 收入排名前 10 家企業 (創辦年份)	City 城市	Province 省	Telephone / fax 電話 / 傳真	Number of employees 職工人數	Ownership 產業所有權	Revenue ('000 RMB) 銷售收入 (千元)	Profit ('000 RMB) (rank) 利潤 (千元) (排名)	Total assets ('000 RMB) 總資產 (千元)	Major products 主要產品
China Daheng Corp. 中國大恒(集團)公司(1987)	Beijing 北京市	Beijing 北京市	(010)62561292 (010)62561897	173	State-owned 國有	242,701	13245(5)	288,076	o
Yunnan Optics Instrument Factory 雲南光學儀器廠(1939)	Kunming 昆明市	Yunnan 雲南省	(0871)8590300 (0871)8590342	7,506	State-owned 國有	211,520	1080(22)	449,770	a
Shanghai Precision & Scientific Instruments Corp. 上海精密科學儀器公司(1992)	Shanghai 上海市	Shanghai 上海市	(021)63296899 (021)63234380	2,975	State-owned 國有	208,514	23340(2)	321,763	a,b
Hu Nan Hua Nan Photoelectric Instrument Factory 湖南華南光電儀器廠(1971)	Changde 常德市	Hunan 湖南省	(0736)7292260 (0736)7291334	2,791	State-owned 國有	186,890	10692(6)	214,450	o
Jiangxi Optics Instrument Factory 江西光學儀器總廠(1968)	Shangrao 上饒市	Jiangxi 江西省	(0793)8260533 (0793)8250249	4,439	State-owned 國有	185,409	14708(3)	370,434	a
Xi'an Xibei Optoelectronic Instrument Factory 西安西北光電儀器廠(1956)	Xi'an 西安市	Shaanxi 陝西省	(029)3233652 (029)3231081	6,797	State-owned 國有	167,220	330(46)	654,150	o
North-china Optical Instrument Factory 華北光學儀器廠(1962)	Beijing 北京市	Beijing 北京市	(010)67017722 (010)67012327	1,989	State-owned 國有	150,154	13879(4)	298,012	o
Zhejiang Sunny Group Co. Ltd. 浙江舜宇集團股份有限公司(1984)	Ningbo 寧波市	Zhejiang 浙江省	(0574)2632820 (0574)2635657	2,262	Joint stock 股份制	118,420	24251(1)	151,211	o
Dangyang Zhong Cheng Group Company 丹陽市中誠集團公司(1981)	Zhenjiang 鎮江市	Jiangsu 江蘇省	(0511)6525373	837	Collectively-owned 集體	106,250	2765(12)	36,711	o
Chongqing Photoelectric Instrument General Company 重慶光電儀器總公司(1958)	Chongqing 重慶市	Chongqing 重慶市	(023)67852333 (023)67850013	1,206	State-owned 國有	92,050	1008(24)	100,401	a

Top 10 Cities by Production Output 產出排名前 10 位城市	Province 省	Market share 市場份額	Number of firms 企業個數
Shanghai 上海市	Shanghai 上海市	13.13%	46
Kunming 昆明市	Yunnan 雲南省	12.91%	16
Xuzhou 徐州市	Jiangsu 江蘇省	9.64%	10
Beijing 北京市	Beijing 北京市	6.82%	31
Nanjing 南京市	Jiangsu 江蘇省	6.21%	24
Ningbo 寧波市	Zhejiang 浙江省	6.12%	9
Xi'an 西安市	Shaanxi 陝西省	4.82%	15
Changde 常德市	Hunan 湖南省	4.01%	1
Suzhou 蘇州市	Jiangsu 江蘇省	3.01%	18
Jiangmen 江門市	Guangdong 廣東省	2.85%	1

10 Major Wholesalers 10 家主要批發商	City 城市	Province 省	Telephone / Fax 電話 / 傳真
Liaoning Automobile Trade Group Corp. 遼寧省汽車貿易集團	Shenyang 瀋陽市	Liaoning 遼寧省	(024)23835494 (024)23838338
China Post and Telecommunication Equipment General Company 中國郵電器材總公司	Beijing 北京市	Beijing 北京市	(010)63523715 (010)63525935
Jiangsu Electromechanical Products General Company 江蘇省機電產品總公司	Nanjing 南京市	Jiangsu 江蘇省	(025)7713642 (025)7711036
Xi Nan Technology Import & Export Company 西南技術進出口公司	Chongqing 重慶市	Chongqing 重慶市	(023)63850185 (023)63850026
Changzhou Economic Technology Industrial Development Zone Tian Ming Trade Company 常州經濟技術產業開發區天明貿易公司	Changzhou 常州市	Jiangsu 江蘇省	(0519)8829882 (0519)8829882
Shanxi Mechanical Equipment Import & Export Company 山西省機械設備進出口公司	Taiyuan 太原市	Shanxi 山西省	(0351)4040713 (0351)4043981
Ningbo Five Mining Machinery Import & Export Company 寧波市五礦機械進出口公司	Ningbo 寧波市	Zhejiang 浙江省	(0574)7311255 (0574)7320322
Tianjin Jin Huan Electromechanical Complete Sets of Equipment Factory 天津市津環機電成套設備廠	Tianjin 天津市	Tianjin 天津市	(022)26371628
Yunnan Machinery Import & Export Company 雲南省機械進出口公司	Kunming 昆明市	Yunnan 雲南省	(0871)3164879 (0871)3136829
Tianjin Da Qiu Zhuang Yi Yuan Trade Center 天津市大丘莊億源商貿中心	Tianjin 天津市	Tianjin 天津市	(022)28899478 (022)28899046

*Also include sales by firms outside this industry.包括本行業以外廠家的銷售。"o" stands for "others". "o" 代表"其他產品"。

4214: Timing Instruments 計時儀器製造業

The industry accounts for 0.009% of the total revenue of China's industrial sector in 1996. The revenue growth rate of the industry is -1.4% from 1995, as compared to the growth rate of China's industrial sector, 9.51%. The rate of return on asset is 1.54%. 74.28% of all firms in the industry made a profit while 22.86% had negative returns. The top province in terms of the industry's revenue is Zhejiang, accounting for 38.61% of the total revenue.

本行業在 1996 年佔全行業總產值 0.009% ，行業年增長率為 -1.4%（全國工業年增長率 9.51%）。行業的資產回報率 1.54% ， 74.28% 的企業盈利， 22.86% 的企業虧損。銷售收入最高的省份為浙江省，佔本行業的 38.61% 。

	Total number of firms 企業總數	Total number of employees 職工總數	Total revenue (mil. RMB) 總銷售收入（百萬元）	Total profit (mil. RMB) 總利潤（百萬元）	Return on assets 資產利潤率 (%)	Return on equity 權益利潤率 (%)	Labour productivity ('000 RMB / worker) 勞動生產率（千元/人）	Debts / assets 資產負債率 (%)	Total assets (mil. RMB) 總資產（百萬元）
Industry Overall 行業總體	81	9,328	524	11	1.54	5.00	56.17	69.14	696

	Number of firms 企業個數	Average number of employees 平均職工人數	Average revenue ('000 RMB) 平均銷售收入（千元）	Average profit ('000 RMB) 平均利潤（千元）	Return on assets 資產利潤率 (%)	Return on equity 權益利潤率 (%)	Labour productivity ('000 RMB / worker) 勞動生產率（千元/人）	Average debts / assets 平均資產負債率(%)	Average Total assets ('000 RMB) 平均總資產（千元）
By ownership 產業所有權									
State-owned 國有	9	211	2,333	-1,222	-6.79	-122.22	11.05	94.44	18,000
Collectively-owned 集體	56	108	6,409	340	4.49	13.47	59.23	66.68	7,574
Privately-owned 私有									
Domestic JVs 聯營	1	9	1,251	30	2.15	15.46	138.99	86.11	1,380
Joint stock 股份制									
Foreign-funded 外資	5	92	15,970	691	8.01	10.70	173.59	25.15	8,621
Overseas Chinese-funded 港澳台資	10	102	6,301	-52	-0.80	-1.62	61.77	50.74	6,537
By size 規模									
Large 大型	2	1,592	99,009	3,949	2.55	10.96	62.21	76.71	154,718
Medium 中型	1	718	38,034	-155	-0.33	-0.83	52.97	59.65	46,309
Small 小型	75	73	3,839	43	0.96	2.62	52.83	63.49	4,536
By regional distribution 地區分布									
Central-North 華北	10	85	4,792	-71	-1.31	-4.66	56.44	71.76	5,400
Beijing 北京	5	84	1,700	-688	-11.99	-40.71	20.24	70.55	5,738
Tianjin 天津	4	85	9,213	650	11.13	46.76	108.06	76.15	5,838
Hebei 河北	1	88	2,570	130	6.63	10.48	29.20	37.24	1,960
Shanxi 山西									
Inner Mongolia 內蒙									
Northeast 東北	6	86	5,280	2	0.02	0.04	61.28	55.89	9,042
Liaoning 遼寧	3	126	7,640	-147	-1.01	-2.46	60.47	59.01	14,523
Jilin 吉林	1	49	160				3.27	5.80	1,380
Heilongjiang 黑龍江	2	45	4,300	225	4.84	9.43	96.63	48.71	4,650
Central East 華東	47	122	8,701	439	4.84	12.99	71.04	62.76	9,081
Shanghai 上海	8	88	2,929	-229	-3.18	-32.39	33.47	90.17	7,188
Jiangsu 江蘇	9	117	9,097	554	6.90	23.01	77.46	69.99	8,036
Zhejiang 浙江	25	105	8,093	526	7.13	15.81	76.87	54.89	7,376
Anhui 安徽									
Fujian 福建									
Jiangxi 江西	1	9	160	20	14.29	40.00	17.78	64.29	140
Shandong 山東	4	340	25,288	1,080	3.84	8.94	74.48	57.00	28,108
Central-South 中南	17	61	1,949	-31	-1.28	-2.31	32.20	44.29	2,426
Henan 河南	2	21	745	5	0.35	1.20	36.34	71.28	1,445
Hubei 湖北	1	59	1,390	-10	-0.32	-1.96	23.56	83.50	3,090
Hunan 湖南	1	10	210	10	3.23	5.26	21.00	38.71	310
Guangdong 廣東	12	77	2,503	-45	-1.54	-2.52	32.69	38.64	2,913
Guangxi 廣西	1								
Hainan 海南									
Southwest 西南									
Chongqing 重慶									
Sichuan 四川									
Guizhou 貴州									
Yunnan 雲南									
Tibet 西藏									
Northwest 西北	1	1,177	1,930	-8,670	-7.26	136.11	1.64	105.34	119,390
Shaanxi 陝西	1	1,177	1,930	-8,670	-7.26	136.11	1.64	105.34	119,390
Gansu 甘肅									
Qinghai 青海									
Ningxia 寧夏									
Xinjiang 新疆									

4214: Timing Instruments 計時儀器製造業

Year 年份	Number of firms 企業個數	Rate of change 每年變化 (%)	Number of employees 職工人數（人）	Rate of change 每年變化 (%)	Total revenue (mil. RMB) 總銷售收入（百萬元）	Rate of change 每年變化 (%)	Total profit (mil. RMB) 總利潤（百萬元）	Rate of change 每年變化 (%)
1993	83		11,021		284		7	
1994	88	6.02%	8,674	-21.30%	285	0.30%	2	-77.48%
1995	72	-18.18%	9,816	13.17%	531	86.61%	22	1273.15%
1996	81	12.50%	9,328	-4.97%	524	-1.36%	11	-49.27%

3 Major products* 3 種主要產品 *	Output 產量	Sales volume 銷售量	Unit 單位

Top 10 firms by revenue (year founded) 收入排名前 10 家企業（創辦年份）	City 城市	Province 省	Telephone / fax 電話 / 傳真	Number of employees 職工人數	Ownership 產業所有權	Revenue ('000 RMB) 銷售收入（千元）	Profit ('000 RMB) (rank) 利潤（千元）（排名）	Total assets ('000 RMB) 總資產（千元）	Major products 主要產品
Yu City Household Appliances General Factory 禹城市家用電器總廠(1982)	Dezhou 德州市	Shandong 山東省	(0534)7781137 (0534)7781137	1,100	Collectively-owned 集體	75,651	3659(3)	73,460	o
Ningbo Ming Zhong Electromechanical Industrial Co. Ltd. 寧波名鐘機電工業有限公司(1993)	Ningbo 寧波市	Zhejiang 浙江省	(0574)6177777 (0574)6177601	312	Foreign-funded 外資	53,890	10412(1)	49,782	o
Zhangjiagang Jing Chen Clock Co. Ltd. 張家港市晶辰鐘業有限公司(1992)	Suzhou 蘇州市	Jiangsu 江蘇省	(0512)8332895	443	Foreign-funded 外資	48,790	3700(2)	24,699	o
Ningbo General Timer Factory 寧波定時器總廠(1958)	Ningbo 寧波市	Zhejiang 浙江省	(0574)7333467 (0574)7332664	663	Collectively-owned 集體	42,325	2650(4)	44,415	o
Tianjin Shen Te Electron Factory 天津市申特電子廠(1995)	Tianjin 天津市	Tianjin 天津市	(022)26305647 (022)26305674	136	Collectively-owned 集體	30,936	2593(5)	15,522	o
Cixi Timer General Factory 慈溪市定時器總廠(1987)	Ningbo 寧波市	Zhejiang 浙江省	(0574)3812325 (0574)3800842	435	Collectively-owned 集體	22,200	1081(8)	18,326	o
Shenyang International Electron Co. Ltd. 瀋陽國際電子有限公司(1990)	Shenyang 瀋陽市	Liaoning 遼寧省	(024)22842922 (024)22842530	330	Overseas Chinese-funded 港澳台資	19,082	-963(33)	40,977	o
Yuyao Timer Factory 余姚市定時器廠(1982)	Ningbo 寧波市	Zhejiang 浙江省	(0574)2151340	82	Collectively-owned 集體	18,421	183(13)	9,718	o
Shanghai Household Timer Factory 上海家用定時器廠(1958)	Shanghai 上海市	Shanghai 上海市	(021)65126642 (021)65129036	457	Collectively-owned 集體	17,373	-2599(34)	51,492	o
Weihai Huancui Measuring Instruments Fittings Plant 威海市環翠區量具配件廠(1996)	Weihai 威海市	Shandong 山東省	(0896)5257113 (0896)5257113	72	Collectively-owned 集體	17,320	1300(7)	3,040	o

Top 10 Cities by Production Output 產出排名前 10 位城市	Province 省	Market share 市場份額	Number of firms 企業個數
Shanghai 上海市	Shanghai 上海市	17.79%	10
Dezhou 德州市	Shandong 山東省	15.95%	1
Hangzhou 杭州市	Zhejiang 浙江省	13.67%	6
Ningbo 寧波市	Zhejiang 浙江省	11.18%	9
Suzhou 蘇州市	Jiangsu 江蘇省	10.98%	5
Tianjin 天津市	Tianjin 天津市	4.79%	4
Shenyang 瀋陽市	Liaoning 遼寧省	3.90%	2
Weihai 威海市	Shandong 山東省	3.27%	1
Wenzhou 温州市	Zhejiang 浙江省	2.56%	11
Beijing 北京市	Beijing 北京市	1.92%	4

10 Major Wholesalers 10 家主要批發商	City 城市	Province 省	Telephone / Fax 電話 / 傳真
Liaoning Automobile Trade Group Corp. 遼寧省汽車貿易集團	Shenyang 瀋陽市	Liaoning 遼寧省	(024)23835494 (024)23838338
China Post and Telecommunication Equipment General Company 中國郵電器材總公司	Beijing 北京市	Beijing 北京市	(010)63523715 (010)63525935
Jiangsu Electromechanical Products General Company 江蘇省機電產品總公司	Nanjing 南京市	Jiangsu 江蘇省	(025)7713642 (025)7711036
Xi Nan Technology Import & Export Company 西南技術進出口公司	Chongqing 重慶市	Chongqing 重慶市	(023)63850185 (023)63850026
Changzhou Economic Technology Industrial Development Zone Tian Ming Trade Company 常州經濟技術產業開發區天明貿易公司	Changzhou 常州市	Jiangsu 江蘇省	(0519)8829882 (0519)8829882
Shanxi Mechanical Equipment Import & Export Company 山西省機械設備進出口公司	Taiyuan 太原市	Shanxi 山西省	(0351)4040713 (0351)4043981
Ningbo Five Mining Machinery Import & Export Company 寧波市五礦機械進出口公司	Ningbo 寧波市	Zhejiang 浙江省	(0574)7311255 (0574)7320322
Tianjin Jin Huan Electromechanical Complete Sets of Equipment Factory 天津市津環機電成套設備廠	Tianjin 天津市	Tianjin 天津市	(022)26371628
Yunnan Machinery Import & Export Company 雲南省機械進出口公司	Kunming 昆明市	Yunnan 雲南省	(0871)3164879 (0871)3136829
Tianjin Da Qiu Zhuang Yi Yuan Trade Center 天津市大丘莊億源商貿中心	Tianjin 天津市	Tianjin 天津市	(022)28899478 (022)28899046

*Also include sales by firms outside this industry.包括本行業以外廠家的銷售。"o" stands for "others"."o" 代表"其他產品"。

4215: Analytical Equipment 分析儀器製造業

The industry accounts for 0.011% of the total revenue of China's industrial sector in 1996. The revenue growth rate of the industry is 83.6% from 1995, as compared to the growth rate of China's industrial sector, 9.51%. The rate of return on asset is -0.49%. 59.42% of all firms in the industry made a profit while 32.74% had negative returns. The top province in terms of the industry's revenue is Shandong, accounting for 30.36% of the total revenue.
本行業在1996年佔全行業總產值0.011%，行業年增長率為83.6%（全國工業年增長率9.51%）。行業的資產回報率-0.49%，59.42%的企業盈利，32.74%的企業虧損。銷售收入最高的省份為山東省，佔本行業的30.36%。

	Total number of firms 企業總數	Total number of employees 職工總數	Total revenue (mil. RMB) 總銷售收入（百萬元）	Total profit (mil. RMB) 總利潤（百萬元）	Return on assets 資產利潤率 (%)	Return on equity 權益利潤率 (%)	Labour productivity ('000 RMB / worker) 勞動生產率（千元/人）	Debts / assets 資產負債率 (%)	Total assets (mil. RMB) 總資產（百萬元）
Industry Overall 行業總體	127	15,333	619	-7	-0.49	-1.26	40.37	61.10	1,353

	Number of firms 企業個數	Average number of employees 平均職工人數	Average revenue ('000 RMB) 平均銷售收入（千元）	Average profit ('000 RMB) 平均利潤（千元）	Return on assets 資產利潤率 (%)	Return on equity 權益利潤率 (%)	Labour productivity ('000 RMB / worker) 勞動生產率（千元/人）	Average debts / assets 平均資產負債率(%)	Average Total assets ('000 RMB) 平均總資產（千元）
By ownership 產業所有權									
State-owned 國有	42	217	5,976	-71	-0.36	-1.05	27.52	65.25	19,667
Collectively-owned 集體	62	88	4,055	-49	-0.93	-2.58	46.01	63.77	5,230
Privately-owned 私有	1	21	1,804	12	0.45	0.56	85.92	19.62	2,592
Domestic JVs 聯營	1	126	8,714	-50	-0.66	-1.13	69.16	42.04	7,686
Joint stock 股份制	1	8	1,144	1	0.18	0.44	142.98	58.68	527
Foreign-funded 外資	11	34	6,417	-190	-2.44	-4.32	189.25	43.42	7,792
Overseas Chinese-funded 港澳台資	9	60	3,788	129	1.09	1.75	63.14	37.59	11,792
By size 規模									
Large 大型	1	541	32,637	-79	-0.03	-0.08	60.33	57.26	233,945
Medium 中型	3	780	29,550	206	0.26	0.91	37.87	71.34	79,496
Small 小型	122	104	4,080	-62	-0.86	-2.11	39.29	59.38	7,217
By regional distribution 地區分布									
Central-North 華北	35	125	4,884	43	0.27	0.62	38.96	57.27	16,268
Beijing 北京	24	152	6,541	235	1.08	2.45	43.18	55.98	21,790
Tianjin 天津	9	45	1,448	-79	-2.47	-5.80	32.25	57.33	3,190
Hebei 河北	1	196	430	-3,320	-20.28	-400.00	2.19	94.93	16,370
Shanxi 山西	1	152	500	-90	-6.82	900.00	3.29	100.76	1,320
Inner Mongolia 內蒙									
Northeast 東北	12	120	1,243	-93	-1.63	-4.87	10.34	66.45	5,661
Liaoning 遼寧	8	144	1,589	-104	-1.28	-3.64	11.02	64.68	8,080
Jilin 吉林	2	10	225	-20	-9.30	-28.57	23.68	67.44	215
Heilongjiang 黑龍江	2	136	880	-120	-8.39	133.33	6.49	106.29	1,430
Central East 華東	53	119	6,396	-134	-1.65	-4.32	53.65	61.84	8,122
Shanghai 上海	18	64	4,380	-690	-14.30	-37.01	68.08	61.37	4,826
Jiangsu 江蘇	12	239	5,321	-383	-3.68	-14.69	22.26	74.97	10,403
Zhejiang 浙江	12	36	515	-5	-0.20	-0.50	14.27	59.51	2,480
Anhui 安徽									
Fujian 福建	2	97	1,080	-55	-0.92	-1.86	11.13	50.54	5,965
Jiangxi 江西									
Shandong 山東	9	185	20,884	1,120	5.69	12.37	112.82	53.98	19,677
Central-South 中南	18	112	4,227	112	0.89	2.59	37.61	65.60	12,517
Henan 河南	7	87	1,311	9	0.33	1.17	15.00	71.98	2,610
Hubei 湖北									
Hunan 湖南	4	35	733	20	1.45	6.90	20.93	79.02	1,383
Guangdong 廣東	4	132	11,810	803	2.06	6.25	89.47	66.99	38,928
Guangxi 廣西	3	248	5,577	-447	-2.93	-6.76	22.52	56.72	15,267
Hainan 海南									
Southwest 西南	3	333	4,437	-1,077	-6.85	-36.96	13.34	81.46	15,717
Chongqing 重慶									
Sichuan 四川	2	483	5,925	-1,640	-9.70	-69.92	12.27	86.13	16,910
Guizhou 貴州									
Yunnan 雲南	1	32	1,460	50	0.38	1.23	45.63	69.62	13,330
Tibet 西藏									
Northwest 西北	6	27	728	208	9.72	12.83	26.98	24.26	2,143
Shaanxi 陝西	6	27	728	208	9.72	12.83	26.98	24.26	2,143
Gansu 甘肅									
Qinghai 青海									
Ningxia 寧夏									
Xinjiang 新疆									

4215: Analytical Equipment 分析儀器製造業

Year 年份	Number of firms 企業個數	Rate of change 每年變化(%)	Number of employees 職工人數(人)	Rate of change 每年變化(%)	Total revenue (mil. RMB) 總銷售收入(百萬元)	Rate of change 每年變化(%)	Total profit (mil. RMB) 總利潤(百萬元)	Rate of change 每年變化(%)
1993	121		16,716		339		4	
1994	107	-11.57%	13,321	-20.31%	338	-0.26%	10	142.38%
1995	123	14.95%	15,481	16.21%	337	-0.37%	7	-32.13%
1996	127	3.25%	15,333	-0.96%	619	83.63%	-7	-205.28%

3 Major products* 3 種主要產品 *	Output 產量	Sales volume 銷售量	Unit 單位
a) Composition Analytical Instrument 成分分析儀器	31,610	33,190	set 台

Top 10 firms by revenue (year founded) 收入排名前 10 家企業(創辦年份)	City 城市	Province 省	Telephone / fax 電話 / 傳真	Number of employees 職工人數	Ownership 產業所有權	Revenue ('000 RMB) 銷售收入(千元)	Profit ('000 RMB) (rank) 利潤(千元)(排名)	Total assets ('000 RMB) 總資產(千元)	Major products 主要產品
Shandong Yan Shan Group General Company 山東燕山集團總公司(1992)	Ji'nan 濟南市	Shandong 山東省	(0531)8932662 (0531)8934043	701	Collectively-owned 集體	158,202	8920(1)	121,522	o
Shanghai Balance Factory Instrument Branch 上海天平廠儀器分廠(1995)	Shanghai 上海市	Shanghai 上海市	(021)63731860	93	Domestic JVs 聯營	90,494	0(36)	49,951	o
Hui Pu Shanghai Analytical Instrument Co. Ltd. 惠普上海分析儀器有限公司(1995)	Shanghai 上海市	Shanghai 上海市	(021)64756206 (021)64756206	281	Foreign-funded 外資	47,866	-13046(51)	44,261	a
Foshan Analysis Instrument Factory 佛山市分析儀器廠(1970)	Foshan 佛山市	Guangdong 廣東省	(0757)3332758 (0757)3352490	463	State-owned 國有	43,171	2281(2)	144,042	a
Nanjing Analytical Instrument Factory 南京分析儀器廠(1956)	Nanjing 南京市	Jiangsu 江蘇省	(025)6626181 (025)2202830	1,148	State-owned 國有	38,500	5(30)	68,483	a
Beijing Rayleigh Analytical Instrument Corp. 北京瑞利分析儀器公司(1968)	Beijing 北京市	Beijing 北京市	(010)64372901 (010)64377039	593	State-owned 國有	20,636	770(7)	72,665	o
Beijing Analytical Instrument Factory 北京分析儀器廠(1965)	Beijing 北京市	Beijing 北京市	(010)62457772 (010)62456592	546	State-owned 國有	19,568	-140(41)	160,735	a
Beijing Analytical Instrument Technical Corp. 北京市北分儀器技術公司(1992)	Beijing 北京市	Beijing 北京市	(010)62457772 (010)62451377	140	State-owned 國有	17,881	253(13)	22,979	a
Beijing Bei Fen Mai Ha Ke Analytical Instrument Co. Ltd. 北京北分麥哈克分析儀器有限公司(1993)	Beijing 北京市	Beijing 北京市	(010)62457772	104	Foreign-funded 外資	14,106	1515(4)	27,547	a
Beijing Zhong Ke Scientific Instrument Science Instrument Plant 北京中科科儀科學儀器廠(1993)	Beijing 北京市	Beijing 北京市	(010)62560908 (010)62564613	355	State-owned 國有	12,767	2244(3)	32,145	a

Top 10 Cities by Production Output 產出排名前 10 位城市	Province 省	Market share 市場份額	Number of firms 企業個數
Beijing 北京市	Beijing 北京市	17.95%	15
Shanghai 上海市	Shanghai 上海市	13.12%	28
Foshan 佛山市	Guangdong 廣東省	9.88%	1
Nanjing 南京市	Jiangsu 江蘇省	9.36%	10
Dalian 大連市	Liaoning 遼寧省	4.87%	11
Taizhou 泰州市	Jiangsu 江蘇省	4.18%	3
Tianjin 天津市	Tianjin 天津市	3.50%	8
Guilin 桂林市	Guangxi 廣西	3.41%	2
Chengdu 成都市	Sichuan 四川省	3.31%	4
Hangzhou 杭州市	Zhejiang 浙江省	3.28%	13

10 Major Wholesalers 10 家主要批發商	City 城市	Province 省	Telephone / Fax 電話 / 傳真
Liaoning Automobile Trade Group Corp. 遼寧省汽車貿易集團	Shenyang 瀋陽市	Liaoning 遼寧省	(024)23835494 (024)23838338
China Post and Telecommunication Equipment General Company 中國郵電器材總公司	Beijing 北京市	Beijing 北京市	(010)63523715 (010)63525935
Jiangsu Electromechanical Products General Company 江蘇省機電產品總公司	Nanjing 南京市	Jiangsu 江蘇省	(025)7713642 (025)7711036
Xi Nan Technology Import & Export Company 西南技術進出口公司	Chongqing 重慶市	Chongqing 重慶市	(023)63850185 (023)63850026
Changzhou Economic Technology Industrial Development Zone Tian Ming Trade Company 常州經濟技術產業開發區天明貿易公司	Changzhou 常州市	Jiangsu 江蘇省	(0519)8829882 (0519)8829882
Shanxi Mechanical Equipment Import & Export Company 山西省機械設備進出口公司	Taiyuan 太原市	Shanxi 山西省	(0351)4040713 (0351)4043981
Ningbo Five Mining Machinery Import & Export Company 寧波市五礦機械進出口公司	Ningbo 寧波市	Zhejiang 浙江省	(0574)7311255 (0574)7320322
Tianjin Jin Huan Electromechanical Complete Sets of Equipment Factory 天津市津環機電成套設備廠	Tianjin 天津市	Tianjin 天津市	(022)26371628
Yunnan Machinery Import & Export Company 雲南省機械進出口公司	Kunming 昆明市	Yunnan 雲南省	(0871)3164879 (0871)3136829
Tianjin Da Qiu Zhuang Yi Yuan Trade Center 天津市大丘莊億源商貿中心	Tianjin 天津市	Tianjin 天津市	(022)28899478 (022)28899046

*Also include sales by firms outside this industry.包括本行業以外廠家的銷售。"o" stands for "others". "o" 代表"其他產品"。

4216: Testing Equipment 試驗機製造業

The industry accounts for 0.009% of the total revenue of China's industrial sector in 1996. The revenue growth rate of the industry is -0.5% from 1995, as compared to the growth rate of China's industrial sector, 9.51%. The rate of return on asset is -1.65%. 55.74% of all firms in the industry made a profit while 36.76% had negative returns. The top province in terms of the industry's revenue is Shandong, accounting for 24.37% of the total revenue.
本行業在1996年佔全行業總產值0.009%，行業年增長率為-0.5%（全國工業年增長率9.51%）。行業的資產回報率-1.65%，55.74%的企業盈利，36.76%的企業虧損。銷售收入最高的省份為山東省，佔本行業的24.37%。

	Total number of firms 企業總數	Total number of employees 職工總數	Total revenue (mil. RMB) 總銷售收入（百萬元）	Total profit (mil. RMB) 總利潤（百萬元）	Return on assets 資產利潤率 (%)	Return on equity 權益利潤率 (%)	Labour productivity ('000 RMB / worker) 勞動生產率（千元/人）	Debts / assets 資產負債率 (%)	Total assets (mil. RMB) 總資產（百萬元）
Industry Overall 行業總體	74	26,795	549	-28	-1.65	-5.11	20.49	67.76	1,704

	Number of firms 企業個數	Average number of employees 平均職工人數	Average revenue ('000 RMB) 平均銷售收入（千元）	Average profit ('000 RMB) 平均利潤（千元）	Return on assets 資產利潤率 (%)	Return on equity 權益利潤率 (%)	Labour productivity ('000 RMB / worker) 勞動生產率（千元/人）	Average debts / assets 平均資產負債率(%)	Average Total assets ('000 RMB) 平均總資產（千元）
By ownership 產業所有權									
State-owned 國有	31	525	12,871	-548	-1.28	-4.02	24.53	68.08	42,742
Collectively-owned 集體	30	179	1,913	84	2.56	8.54	10.67	70.06	3,266
Privately-owned 私有									
Domestic JVs 聯營	2	41	629	60	3.17	4.64	15.33	31.85	1,895
Joint stock 股份制	3	1,249	7,995	-5,199	-8.87	-39.69	6.40	77.66	58,625
Foreign-funded 外資	6	211	10,995	405	2.42	4.49	52.07	46.18	16,753
Overseas Chinese-funded 港澳台資	2	26	677	-231	-47.20	-63.28	26.04	25.41	489
By size 規模									
Large 大型	3	1,908	32,475	-6,423	-3.89	-15.42	17.02	74.79	165,192
Medium 中型	9	1,359	30,793	-3,690	-3.94	-10.79	22.65	63.46	93,550
Small 小型	59	149	2,956	415	6.68	21.03	19.84	68.24	6,213
By regional distribution 地區分布									
Central-North 華北	8	144	3,211	148	1.97	4.78	22.30	58.81	7,496
Beijing 北京	4	48	963	-25	-1.24	-2.20	20.05	43.55	2,015
Tianjin 天津	2	53	4,685	640	28.07	72.73	88.40	61.18	2,280
Hebei 河北	2	427	6,235				14.60	61.18	23,675
Shanxi 山西									
Inner Mongolia 內蒙									
Northeast 東北	21	459	1,840	-798	-4.59	-14.53	4.01	68.38	17,364
Liaoning 遼寧	15	475	827	-314	-2.10	-6.05	1.74	65.23	14,938
Jilin 吉林	6	419	4,373	2,007	8.57	32.20	10.44	70.40	23,420
Heilongjiang 黑龍江									
Central East 華東	24	378	14,030	-343	-1.41	-3.80	37.09	62.98	24,328
Shanghai 上海	6	202	13,390	-277	-1.41	-3.69	66.23	61.76	19,637
Jiangsu 江蘇	6	485	15,737	-393	-1.27	-3.26	32.48	60.91	30,913
Zhejiang 浙江	5	208	4,786	-762	-4.10	-10.08	22.97	59.35	18,598
Anhui 安徽									
Fujian 福建	2	63	2,120	-105	-3.44	-7.45	33.92	53.77	3,050
Jiangxi 江西									
Shandong 山東	5	758	26,760	-36	-0.10	-0.31	35.29	68.06	36,296
Central-South 中南	15	196	7,162	1,053	3.21	8.98	36.63	64.21	32,764
Henan 河南	2	25	2,130	65	1.43	5.63	86.94	74.53	4,535
Hubei 湖北	4	194	5,015	45	0.39	2.07	25.92	80.95	11,418
Hunan 湖南	4	126	2,163	-208	-4.54	-9.12	17.13	50.25	4,573
Guangdong 廣東	5	321	14,892	3,264	3.90	10.48	46.39	62.77	83,686
Guangxi 廣西									
Hainan 海南									
Southwest 西南									
Chongqing 重慶									
Sichuan 四川									
Guizhou 貴州									
Yunnan 雲南									
Tibet 西藏									
Northwest 西北	6	666	6,775	-3,348	-9.87	-117.42	10.17	91.59	33,937
Shaanxi 陝西	1	28	750	-350	-14.58	-125.00	26.79	87.92	2,400
Gansu 甘肅	2	1,014	11,085	-4,240	-7.75	-71.99	10.93	89.23	54,685
Qinghai 青海									
Ningxia 寧夏	3	647	5,910	-3,753	-12.26	-222.97	9.13	94.50	30,617
Xinjiang 新疆									

4216: Testing Equipment 試驗機製造業

Year 年份	Number of firms 企業個數	Rate of change 每年變化 (%)	Number of employees 職工人數（人）	Rate of change 每年變化 (%)	Total revenue (mil. RMB) 總銷售收入（百萬元）	Rate of change 每年變化 (%)	Total profit (mil. RMB) 總利潤（百萬元）	Rate of change 每年變化 (%)
1993	73		30,398		654		32	
1994	78	6.85%	22,465	-26.10%	496	-24.23%	-9	-127.16%
1995	86	10.26%	22,798	1.48%	552	11.35%	-4	50.89%
1996	74	-13.95%	26,795	17.53%	549	-0.50%	-28	-560.38%

3 Major products* 3 種主要產品 *	Output 產量	Sales volume 銷售量	Unit 單位
a) Testing Machine 試驗機	13,476	14,958	set 台

Top 10 firms by revenue (year founded) 收入排名前 10 家企業 (創辦年份)	City 城市	Province 省	Telephone / fax 電話 / 傳真	Number of employees 職工人數	Ownership 產業所有權	Revenue ('000 RMB) 銷售收入（千元）	Profit ('000 RMB) (rank) 利潤（千元）（排名）	Total assets ('000 RMB) 總資產（千元）	Major products 主要產品
Ji'nan Testing Machine Manufacturing General Co. 濟南試驗機製造總公司(1952)	Ji'nan 濟南市	Shandong 山東省	(0531)7967641 (0531)7964160	1,925	State-owned 國有	97,685	372(7)	117,141	a
Wuxi Building Materials Instrument Machinery Works 無錫市建築材料儀器機械廠(1958)	Wuxi 無錫市	Jiangsu 江蘇省	(0510)5729223 (0510)5729164	1,137	State-owned 國有	50,498	-2962(34)	90,722	o
Shantou Institute of Ultrasonic Instrument 汕頭市超聲儀器研究所(1978)	Shantou 汕頭市	Guangdong 廣東省	(0754)8250150 (0754)8251499	254	State-owned 國有	45,988	17619(1)	171,274	o
Shanghai Shen Ke Testing Machine Co. Ltd. 上海申克試驗機有限公司(1991)	Shanghai 上海市	Shanghai 上海市	(021)63246355 (021)63240519	475	Foreign-funded 外資	44,483	-4583(36)	52,127	a
Tianshui Hongshan Testing Machine Factory 天水紅山試驗機廠(1970)	Tianshui 天水市	Gansu 甘肅省	(0938)8212951 (0938)8212201	2,000	State-owned 國有	20,543	-8494(39)	106,856	a
Shandong Laizhou Testing Machine General Factory 山東萊州市試驗機總廠(1949)	Yantai 煙台市	Shandong 山東省	(0535)2212350 (0535)2213954	1,162	State-owned 國有	20,001	181(11)	39,838	a
Qidong Ergograph Factory 啟東測功器廠(1958)	Nantong 南通市	Jiangsu 江蘇省	(0513)3317230	667	State-owned 國有	17,475	129(14)	30,259	o
Suzhou Testing Instrument Plant 蘇州試驗儀器廠(1956)	Suzhou 蘇州市	Jiangsu 江蘇省	(0512)8292821 (0512)8272243	657	State-owned 國有	17,283	122(15)	41,536	a
Guangzhou Testing Instrument Plant 廣州試驗儀器廠(1946)	Guangzhou 廣州市	Guangdong 廣東省	(020)83333579 (020)83366269	451	State-owned 國有	14,978	-1337(31)	25,579	a
Changchun Testing Machine Factory 長春試驗機廠(1949)	Changchun 長春市	Jilin 吉林省	(0431)2926057 (0431)2938791	1,618	State-owned 國有	14,842	-9966(40)	115,669	a

Top 10 Cities by Production Output 產出排名前 10 位城市	Province 省	Market share 市場份額	Number of firms 企業個數
Shanghai 上海市	Shanghai 上海市	18.11%	13
Ji'nan 濟南市	Shandong 山東省	14.77%	6
Wuxi 無錫市	Jiangsu 江蘇省	12.05%	4
Shantou 汕頭市	Guangdong 廣東省	11.45%	2
Yantai 煙台市	Shandong 山東省	5.79%	2
Changchun 長春市	Jilin 吉林省	4.28%	6
Tianshui 天水市	Gansu 甘肅省	3.74%	1
Dandong 丹東市	Liaoning 遼寧省	3.07%	9
Nantong 南通市	Jiangsu 江蘇省	2.79%	2
Guangzhou 廣州市	Guangdong 廣東省	2.78%	3

10 Major Wholesalers 10 家主要批發商	City 城市	Province 省	Telephone / Fax 電話 / 傳真
Liaoning Automobile Trade Group Corp. 遼寧省汽車貿易集團	Shenyang 瀋陽市	Liaoning 遼寧省	(024)23835494 (024)23838338
China Post and Telecommunication Equipment General Company 中國郵電器材總公司	Beijing 北京市	Beijing 北京市	(010)63523715 (010)63525935
Jiangsu Electromechanical Products General Company 江蘇省機電產品總公司	Nanjing 南京市	Jiangsu 江蘇省	(025)7713642 (025)7711036
Xi Nan Technology Import & Export Company 西南技術進出口公司	Chongqing 重慶市	Chongqing 重慶市	(023)63850185 (023)63850026
Changzhou Economic Technology Industrial Development Zone Tian Ming Trade Company 常州經濟技術產業開發區天明貿易公司	Changzhou 常州市	Jiangsu 江蘇省	(0519)8829882 (0519)8829882
Shanxi Mechanical Equipment Import & Export Company 山西省機械設備進出口公司	Taiyuan 太原市	Shanxi 山西省	(0351)4040713 (0351)4043981
Ningbo Five Mining Machinery Import & Export Company 寧波市五礦機械進出口公司	Ningbo 寧波市	Zhejiang 浙江省	(0574)7311255 (0574)7320322
Tianjin Jin Huan Electromechanical Complete Sets of Equipment Factory 天津市津環機電成套設備廠	Tianjin 天津市	Tianjin 天津市	(022)26371628
Yunnan Machinery Import & Export Company 雲南省機械進出口公司	Kunming 昆明市	Yunnan 雲南省	(0871)3164879 (0871)3136829
Tianjin Da Qiu Zhuang Yi Yuan Trade Center 天津市大丘莊億源商貿中心	Tianjin 天津市	Tianjin 天津市	(022)28899478 (022)28899046

*Also include sales by firms outside this industry.包括本行業以外廠家的銷售。"o" stands for "others". "o" 代表"其他產品"。

4217: Laboratory Instruments and Equipment 實驗室儀器及裝置製造業

The industry accounts for 0.005% of the total revenue of China's industrial sector in 1996. The revenue growth rate of the industry is -21.3% from 1995, as compared to the growth rate of China's industrial sector, 9.51%. The rate of return on asset is -0.80%. 75.92% of all firms in the industry made a profit while 18.82% had negative returns. The top province in terms of the industry's revenue is Shanghai, accounting for 23.91% of the total revenue.

本行業在1996年佔全行業總產值0.005%，行業年增長率為-21.3%（全國工業年增長率9.51%）。行業的資產回報率-0.80%，75.92%的企業盈利，18.82%的企業虧損。銷售收入最高的省份為上海市，佔本行業的23.91%。

	Total number of firms 企業總數	Total number of employees 職工總數	Total revenue (mil. RMB) 總銷售收入（百萬元）	Total profit (mil. RMB) 總利潤（百萬元）	Return on assets 資產利潤率 (%)	Return on equity 權益利潤率 (%)	Labour productivity ('000 RMB / worker) 勞動生產率（千元/人）	Debts / assets 資產負債率 (%)	Total assets (mil. RMB) 總資產（百萬元）
Industry Overall 行業總體	92	12,329	289	-5	-0.80	-2.64	23.44	69.57	662

	Number of firms 企業個數	Average number of employees 平均職工人數	Average revenue ('000 RMB) 平均銷售收入（千元）	Average profit ('000 RMB) 平均利潤（千元）	Return on assets 資產利潤率 (%)	Return on equity 權益利潤率 (%)	Labour productivity ('000 RMB / worker) 勞動生產率（千元/人）	Average debts / assets 平均資產負債率(%)	Average Total assets ('000 RMB) 平均總資產（千元）
By ownership 產業所有權									
State-owned 國有	26	287	5,000	-385	-2.17	-8.33	17.43	73.97	17,731
Collectively-owned 集體	58	70	1,843	50	2.17	5.60	26.29	61.22	2,295
Privately-owned 私有	1	9	517	-3	-8.92	-181.89	57.45	95.09	28
Domestic JVs 聯營	1	13	1,599	58	21.63	32.55	122.97	33.56	268
Joint stock 股份制	1	560	29,732	1,226	3.21	8.34	53.09	61.56	38,238
Foreign-funded 外資	4	28	3,075	278	6.90	10.34	109.84	33.28	4,025
Overseas Chinese-funded 港澳台資	2	55	3,961	-141	-2.12	-7.47	72.67	71.62	6,627
By size 規模									
Large 大型	1	2,335	27,743	-5,013	-4.08	-18.38	11.88	77.82	122,918
Medium 中型	2	773	28,015	430	0.66	1.88	36.27	65.05	65,355
Small 小型	89	95	2,305	-10	-0.21	-0.66	24.28	68.65	4,588
By regional distribution 地區分布									
Central-North 華北	26	80	2,274	71	1.20	3.49	28.52	65.69	5,903
Beijing 北京	15	101	3,571	167	1.75	5.07	35.35	65.45	9,515
Tianjin 天津	7	68	547	-97	-7.72	-20.99	8.10	63.22	1,259
Hebei 河北									
Shanxi 山西	3	28	580	7	1.04	22.22	20.47	95.34	643
Inner Mongolia 內蒙	1								
Northeast 東北	20	112	1,998	-161	-4.11	-31.02	17.80	86.75	3,917
Liaoning 遼寧	16	88	1,969	12	0.55	1.57	22.44	65.26	2,179
Jilin 吉林	1	364	5,490	-2,030	-5.92	-281.94	15.08	97.90	34,300
Heilongjiang 黑龍江	3	159	987	-460	-15.05	56.56	6.21	126.72	3,057
Central East 華東	28	107	4,201	268	4.44	9.72	39.41	54.32	6,030
Shanghai 上海	8	162	8,636	538	4.60	8.61	53.35	46.59	11,690
Jiangsu 江蘇	5	60	2,422	54	2.09	6.60	40.50	68.34	2,584
Zhejiang 浙江	7	87	4,163	386	8.47	16.41	47.69	48.43	4,554
Anhui 安徽	1	82	520				6.34	8.33	360
Fujian 福建	4	120	1,473	38	0.51	2.54	12.30	79.84	7,315
Jiangxi 江西	1								
Shandong 山東	2	110	440	40	8.79	19.05	4.02	53.85	455
Central-South 中南	10	403	4,171	-1,039	-4.97	-22.18	10.35	77.59	20,903
Henan 河南	1	54	3,260	-170	-2.41	-7.73	60.37	68.75	7,040
Hubei 湖北	2	146	1,085	-80	-2.21	106.67	7.43	102.07	3,620
Hunan 湖南	4	915	7,773	-2,608	-5.87	-24.62	8.49	76.16	44,408
Guangdong 廣東	3	8	1,730	123	2.16	15.16	225.65	85.75	5,707
Guangxi 廣西									
Hainan 海南									
Southwest 西南	6	135	3,697	-177	-2.91	-11.69	27.48	75.08	6,065
Chongqing 重慶	3	179	3,913	-318	-3.99	-15.91	21.88	74.96	7,982
Sichuan 四川	3	77	3,409	11	0.32	1.29	44.54	75.45	3,509
Guizhou 貴州									
Yunnan 雲南									
Tibet 西藏									
Northwest 西北	2	95	4,370	-5	-0.06	-0.18	46.00	66.52	8,155
Shaanxi 陝西	2	95	4,370	-5	-0.06	-0.18	46.00	66.52	8,155
Gansu 甘肅									
Qinghai 青海									
Ningxia 寧夏									
Xinjiang 新疆									

4217: Laboratory Instruments and Equipment 實驗室儀器及裝置製造業

Year 年份	Number of firms 企業個數	Rate of change 每年變化 (%)	Number of employees 職工人數 (人)	Rate of change 每年變化 (%)	Total revenue (mil. RMB) 總銷售收入 (百萬元)	Rate of change 每年變化 (%)	Total profit (mil. RMB) 總利潤 (百萬元)	Rate of change 每年變化 (%)
1993	84		31,048		2,467		260	
1994	84	0	19,110	-38.45%	3,765	52.61%	405	55.68%
1995	102	21.43%	15,139	-20.78%	367	-90.24%	-16	-104.06%
1996	92	-9.80%	12,329	-18.56%	289	-21.35%	-5	69.60%

3 Major products* 3 種主要產品 *	Output 產量	Sales volume 銷售量	Unit 單位
a) Laboratory Instrument & Unit 實驗室儀器及裝置	54,921	54,372	set 台
b) Vacuum Equipment 真空設備	4,414	3,885	set 台

Top 10 firms by revenue (year founded) 收入排名前 10 家企業 (創辦年份)	City 城市	Province 省	Telephone / fax 電話 / 傳真	Number of employees 職工人數	Ownership 產業所有權	Revenue ('000 RMB) 銷售收入 (千元)	Profit ('000 RMB) (rank) 利潤 (千元) (排名)	Total assets ('000 RMB) 總資產 (千元)	Major products 主要產品
Beijing Instrument Factory 北京儀器廠(1954)	Beijing 北京市	Beijing 北京市	(010)65062244 (010)65005727	1,055	State-owned 國有	38,796	1800(2)	124,961	a,b
Shanghai Testing Instrument General Factory 上海市實驗儀器總廠(1956)	Shanghai 上海市	Shanghai 上海市	(021)62747444 (021)62747444	727	Collectively-owned 集體	32,052	511(8)	36,670	a
Shanghai Espec Environmental Instrument Co. Ltd. 上海愛斯佩克環境儀器有限公司(1986)	Shanghai 上海市	Shanghai 上海市	(021)62748060 (021)62748060	75	Foreign-funded 外資	17,242	3224(1)	12,915	a
Chongqing Experiment Equipment Factory 重慶試驗設備廠(1966)	Chongqing 重慶市	Chongqing 重慶市	(023)68212995 (023)68212684	559	State-owned 國有	14,272	-994(36)	27,163	a
Shanghai Qiu Jing Sheng Chemical Test Instrument Co. Ltd. 上海求精生化試劑儀器有限公司(1993)	Shanghai 上海市	Shanghai 上海市	(021)57881355 (021)52510780	79	Overseas Chinese-funded 港澳台資	12,705	68(20)	4,630	o
Ningbo Cheng Tian Paint & Fitting Machinery Co. Ltd. 寧波成田塗裝機械有限公司(1979)	Ningbo 寧波市	Zhejiang 浙江省	(0574)8447692	126	Collectively-owned 集體	12,204	1529(3)	10,416	o
Shanghai Ren Shi Electron Co. Ltd. 上海任氏電子有限公司(1993)	Shanghai 上海市	Shanghai 上海市	(021)57610599 (021)57610598	85	Overseas Chinese-funded 港澳台資	10,488	82(17)	14,763	o
Beijing Instrument Factory Vacuum Pump Branch 北京儀器廠真空泵分廠(1992)	Beijing 北京市	Beijing 北京市	(010)65062244 (010)65085092	111	State-owned 國有	9,341	692(6)	8,506	b
Chengdu Dian Oven Factory 成都電烘箱廠(1966)	Chengdu 成都市	Sichuan 四川省	(028)5185254	131	Collectively-owned 集體	6,767	20(23)	5,853	o
Liaoyang Environment Engineering Research Institute 遼陽市環境工程研究所(1991)	Liaoyang 遼陽市	Liaoning 遼寧省	(0419)2381254	120	Collectively-owned 集體	6,024	34(21)	532	o

Top 10 Cities by Production Output 產出排名前 10 位城市	Province 省	Market share 市場份額	Number of firms 企業個數
Shanghai 上海市	Shanghai 上海市	31.72%	21
Beijing 北京市	Beijing 北京市	17.41%	11
Changsha 長沙市	Hunan 湖南省	11.45%	3
Chongqing 重慶市	Chongqing 重慶市	4.44%	2
Ningbo 寧波市	Zhejiang 浙江省	3.76%	2
Liaoyang 遼陽市	Liaoning 遼寧省	3.33%	4
Jiaxing 嘉興市	Zhejiang 浙江省	3.24%	2
Wuxi 無錫市	Jiangsu 江蘇省	2.79%	6
Nanjing 南京市	Jiangsu 江蘇省	2.71%	4
Chengdu 成都市	Sichuan 四川省	1.62%	1

10 Major Wholesalers 10 家主要批發商	City 城市	Province 省	Telephone / Fax 電話 / 傳真
Liaoning Automobile Trade Group Corp. 遼寧省汽車貿易集團	Shenyang 瀋陽市	Liaoning 遼寧省	(024)23835494 (024)23838338
China Post and Telecommunication Equipment General Company 中國郵電器材總公司	Beijing 北京市	Beijing 北京市	(010)63523715 (010)63525935
Jiangsu Electromechanical Products General Company 江蘇省機電產品總公司	Nanjing 南京市	Jiangsu 江蘇省	(025)7713642 (025)7711036
Xi Nan Technology Import & Export Company 西南技術進出口公司	Chongqing 重慶市	Chongqing 重慶市	(023)63850185 (023)63850026
Changzhou Economic Technology Industrial Development Zone Tian Ming Trade Company 常州經濟技術產業開發區天明貿易公司	Changzhou 常州市	Jiangsu 江蘇省	(0519)8829882 (0519)8829882
Shanxi Mechanical Equipment Import & Export Company 山西省機械設備進出口公司	Taiyuan 太原市	Shanxi 山西省	(0351)4040713 (0351)4043981
Ningbo Five Mining Machinery Import & Export Company 寧波市五礦機械進出口公司	Ningbo 寧波市	Zhejiang 浙江省	(0574)7311255 (0574)7320322
Tianjin Jin Huan Electromechanical Complete Sets of Equipment Factory 天津市津環機電成套設備廠	Tianjin 天津市	Tianjin 天津市	(022)26371628
Yunnan Machinery Import & Export Company 雲南省機械進出口公司	Kunming 昆明市	Yunnan 雲南省	(0871)3164879 (0871)3136829
Tianjin Da Qiu Zhuang Yi Yuan Trade Center 天津市大丘莊億源商貿中心	Tianjin 天津市	Tianjin 天津市	(022)28899478 (022)28899046

*Also include sales by firms outside this industry.包括本行業以外廠家的銷售。"o" stands for "others". "o" 代表"其他產品"。

4218: General Meter Parts and Equipment 通用儀器儀表元件、器件製造業

The industry accounts for 0.019% of the total revenue of China's industrial sector in 1996. The revenue growth rate of the industry is 32.3% from 1995, as compared to the growth rate of China's industrial sector, 9.51%. The rate of return on asset is 1.82%. 66.54% of all firms in the industry made a profit while 26.97% had negative returns. The top province in terms of the industry's revenue is Shanghai, accounting for 28.19% of the total revenue.
本行業在1996年佔全行業總產值0.019%，行業年增長率為32.3%（全國工業年增長率9.51%）。行業的資產回報率1.82%，66.54%的企業盈利，26.97%的企業虧損。銷售收入最高的省份為上海市，佔本行業的28.19%。

	Total number of firms 企業總數	Total number of employees 職工總數	Total revenue (mil. RMB) 總銷售收入（百萬元）	Total profit (mil. RMB) 總利潤（百萬元）	Return on assets 資產利潤率 (%)	Return on equity 權益利潤率 (%)	Labour productivity ('000 RMB / worker) 勞動生產率（千元/人）	Debts / assets 資產負債率 (%)	Total assets (mil. RMB) 總資產（百萬元）
Industry Overall 行業總體	199	17,104	1,091	24	1.82	5.10	63.79	64.31	1,330

	Number of firms 企業個數	Average number of employees 平均職工人數	Average revenue ('000 RMB) 平均銷售收入（千元）	Average profit ('000 RMB) 平均利潤（千元）	Return on assets 資產利潤率 (%)	Return on equity 權益利潤率 (%)	Labour productivity ('000 RMB / worker) 勞動生產率（千元/人）	Average debts / assets 平均資產負債率(%)	Average Total assets ('000 RMB) 平均總資產（千元）
By ownership 產業所有權									
State-owned 國有	21	290	17,381	143	0.58	3.13	59.90	81.57	24,810
Collectively-owned 集體	155	55	2,821	55	1.98	5.57	51.64	64.53	2,787
Privately-owned 私有	1	6	254	13	2.35	5.97	42.30	60.53	545
Domestic JVs 聯營	1	69	925	34	3.40	7.34	13.40	53.68	994
Joint stock 股份制	4	92	2,201	-23	-0.61	-2.84	23.99	78.66	3,851
Foreign-funded 外資	9	144	17,278	1,410	4.77	6.65	120.27	28.24	29,529
Overseas Chinese-funded 港澳台資	7	115	17,604	-26	-0.19	-0.58	152.89	67.03	13,597
By size 規模									
Large 大型	2	727	130,308	3,281	2.22	6.43	179.24	65.52	148,044
Medium 中型	5	426	36,938	1,105	2.00	5.52	86.67	63.76	55,266
Small 小型	191	71	3,380	62	1.57	4.36	47.80	63.99	3,970
By regional distribution 地區分布									
Central-North 華北	18	44	1,842	8	0.34	1.08	41.91	68.36	2,441
Beijing 北京	4	12	213	-65	-12.62	-2600.00	17.71	99.51	515
Tianjin 天津	7	59	3,557	-16	-0.36	-0.93	60.73	61.80	4,420
Hebei 河北	5	49	1,066	102	14.91	41.80	21.93	64.33	684
Shanxi 山西	1	40	560	10	0.23	3.33	14.00	93.15	4,380
Inner Mongolia 內蒙	1	50	1,510				30.20	82.43	3,130
Northeast 東北	41	71	4,562	101	1.62	3.76	64.67	56.99	6,254
Liaoning 遼寧	35	68	5,076	149	2.15	4.85	74.80	55.68	6,921
Jilin 吉林	5	95	1,828	-212	-7.53	-36.43	19.24	79.33	2,816
Heilongjiang 黑龍江	1	42	250				5.95	90.91	110
Central East 華東	102	109	7,288	193	2.12	6.28	66.98	66.16	9,097
Shanghai 上海	15	229	20,501	255	0.90	2.47	89.37	63.58	28,297
Jiangsu 江蘇	19	132	9,619	231	2.27	7.15	72.87	68.30	10,192
Zhejiang 浙江	45	66	3,553	266	5.80	15.59	53.73	62.77	4,579
Anhui 安徽	4	87	4,043	-520	-9.55	21.96	46.47	143.53	5,445
Fujian 福建	7	42	1,334	-6	-0.46	-1.08	31.88	57.34	1,236
Jiangxi 江西	4	66	803	-30	-2.02	-7.14	12.16	71.67	1,483
Shandong 山東	8	159	8,053	223	2.64	6.99	50.80	62.22	8,420
Central-South 中南	12	104	4,771	81	1.47	5.12	46.02	71.40	5,516
Henan 河南	5	15	456	16	2.94	9.30	30.81	68.38	544
Hubei 湖北	1	915	45,350	750	1.46	5.02	49.56	70.91	51,390
Hunan 湖南	1	89		-150	-38.46	7.25		630.77	390
Guangdong 廣東	4	32	1,853	93	4.82	7.89	57.89	38.85	1,918
Guangxi 廣西	1	38	2,210	-80	-1.99	-16.00	58.16	87.56	4,020
Hainan 海南									
Southwest 西南	20	42	2,764	40	3.69	9.83	65.41	62.40	1,071
Chongqing 重慶	13	46	2,035	-32	-6.78	-17.87	43.96	62.08	477
Sichuan 四川	5	38	4,948	182	7.46	20.93	129.24	64.34	2,444
Guizhou 貴州	1	28	620				22.14	87.88	660
Yunnan 雲南	1	31	3,040	270	13.24	23.28	98.06	43.14	2,040
Tibet 西藏									
Northwest 西北	6	39	2,427	-257	-10.56	-16.02	62.22	34.09	2,430
Shaanxi 陝西	5	28	2,832	-266	-10.90	-15.85	99.72	31.23	2,440
Gansu 甘肅	1	92	400	-210	-8.82	-17.21	4.35	48.74	2,380
Qinghai 青海									
Ningxia 寧夏									
Xinjiang 新疆									

4218: General Meter Parts and Equipment 通用儀器儀表元件、器件製造業

Year 年份	Number of firms 企業個數	Rate of change 每年變化 (%)	Number of employees 職工人數 (人)	Rate of change 每年變化 (%)	Total revenue (mil. RMB) 總銷售收入 (百萬元)	Rate of change 每年變化 (%)	Total profit (mil. RMB) 總利潤 (百萬元)	Rate of change 每年變化 (%)
1993	205		35,539		772		40	
1994	201	-1.95%	21,981	-38.15%	786	1.94%	15	-62.58%
1995	196	-2.49%	18,474	-15.96%	824	4.83%	17	14.94%
1996	199	1.53%	17,104	-7.42%	1,091	32.33%	24	39.81%

3 Major products* 3 種主要產品 *	Output 產量	Sales volume 銷售量	Unit 單位

Top 10 firms by revenue (year founded) 收入排名前 10 家企業 (創辦年份)	City 城市	Province 省	Telephone / fax 電話 / 傳真	Number of employees 職工人數	Ownership 產業所有權	Revenue ('000 RMB) 銷售收入 (千元)	Profit ('000 RMB) (rank) 利潤 (千元) (排名)	Total assets ('000 RMB) 總資產 (千元)	Major products 主要產品
Shanghai Alloy Plant 上海合金廠(1952)	Shanghai 上海市	Shanghai 上海市	(021)59530625 (021)59525034	1,174	State-owned 國有	153,867	1804(10)	172,122	o
Taicang Zhi Tang Multiple-producing Factory 太倉直塘綜合廠(1978)	Suzhou 蘇州市	Jiangsu 江蘇省	(0512)3250435	450	Collectively-owned 集體	61,880	520(16)	15,360	o
Wuxi Electronic Computer Factory 無錫市電子計算機廠(1958)	Wuxi 無錫市	Jiangsu 江蘇省	(0510)2703151 (0510)2707335	474	State-owned 國有	53,988	502(17)	90,995	o
Dalian Shan Wu Instrument Co. Ltd. 大連山武儀表有限公司(1994)	Dalian 大連市	Liaoning 遼寧省	(0411)7623555 (0411)7623560	241	Foreign-funded 外資	48,818	-4950(77)	79,631	o
Shanghai Sk Transformer Co. Ltd. 上海埃斯凱變壓器有限公司(1993)	Shanghai 上海市	Shanghai 上海市	(021)58429603 (021)58426531	170	Foreign-funded 外資	46,925	2375(8)	81,676	o
Hubei Xiangfan Meter Components Factory 襄樊市儀表元件廠(1966)	Xiangfan 襄樊市	Hubei 湖北省	(0710)3514854 (0710)3514847	905	State-owned 國有	45,351	750(14)	51,387	o
Dalian Gauge Enterprise Group Co. 大連儀表盤廠(1988)	Dalian 大連市	Liaoning 遼寧省	(0411)9400358 (0411)9400669	150	Collectively-owned 集體	42,000	2743(5)	90,819	o
Chongqing Yu Kai Meter Component Co. Ltd. 重慶渝凱儀表元件有限公司	Chongqing 重慶市	Chongqing 重慶市	(023)68225230 (023)68225244	130	Overseas Chinese-funded 港澳台資	39,472	438(20)	5,961	o
Cheng Yuan Communication (Shanghai) Co. Ltd. 程遠通訊(上海)有限公司(1995)	Shanghai 上海市	Shanghai 上海市	(021)64855500	166	Foreign-funded 外資	35,466	569(15)	49,485	o
Leqing Meter Component Factory 樂清市儀表元件廠(1966)	Wenzhou 温州市	Zhejiang 浙江省	(0577)2352418 (0577)2355357	270	Collectively-owned 集體	34,825	7686(1)	30,454	o

Top 10 Cities by Production Output 產出排名前 10 位城市	Province 省	Market share 市場份額	Number of firms 企業個數
Shanghai 上海市	Shanghai 上海市	29.20%	40
Shenyang 瀋陽市	Liaoning 遼寧省	7.17%	13
Wuxi 無錫市	Jiangsu 江蘇省	6.51%	6
Wenzhou 温州市	Zhejiang 浙江省	5.73%	24
Tianjin 天津市	Tianjin 天津市	5.51%	9
Dalian 大連市	Liaoning 遼寧省	4.93%	11
Xiangfan 襄樊市	Hubei 湖北省	4.67%	1
Nanjing 南京市	Jiangsu 江蘇省	2.75%	12
Zhoushan 舟山市	Zhejiang 浙江省	2.72%	5
Huaiyin 淮陰市	Jiangsu 江蘇省	2.35%	9

10 Major Wholesalers 10 家主要批發商	City 城市	Province 省	Telephone / Fax 電話 / 傳真
Liaoning Automobile Trade Group Corp. 遼寧省汽車貿易集團	Shenyang 瀋陽市	Liaoning 遼寧省	(024)23835494 (024)23838338
China Post and Telecommunication Equipment General Company 中國郵電器材總公司	Beijing 北京市	Beijing 北京市	(010)63523715 (010)63525935
Jiangsu Electromechanical Products General Company 江蘇省機電產品總公司	Nanjing 南京市	Jiangsu 江蘇省	(025)7713642 (025)7711036
Xi Nan Technology Import & Export Company 西南技術進出口公司	Chongqing 重慶市	Chongqing 重慶市	(023)63850185 (023)63850026
Changzhou Economic Technology Industrial Development Zone Tian Ming Trade Company 常州經濟技術產業開發區天明貿易公司	Changzhou 常州市	Jiangsu 江蘇省	(0519)8829882 (0519)8829882
Shanxi Mechanical Equipment Import & Export Company 山西省機械設備進出口公司	Taiyuan 太原市	Shanxi 山西省	(0351)4040713 (0351)4043981
Ningbo Five Mining Machinery Import & Export Company 寧波市五礦機械進出口公司	Ningbo 寧波市	Zhejiang 浙江省	(0574)7311255 (0574)7320322
Tianjin Jin Huan Electromechanical Complete Sets of Equipment Factory 天津市津環機電成套設備廠	Tianjin 天津市	Tianjin 天津市	(022)26371628
Yunnan Machinery Import & Export Company 雲南省機械進出口公司	Kunming 昆明市	Yunnan 雲南省	(0871)3164879 (0871)3136829
Tianjin Da Qiu Zhuang Yi Yuan Trade Center 天津市大丘莊億源商貿中心	Tianjin 天津市	Tianjin 天津市	(022)28899478 (022)28899046

*Also include sales by firms outside this industry.包括本行業以外廠家的銷售。"o" stands for "others". "o" 代表"其他產品"。

4219: Other General Meters 其他通用儀表製造業

The industry accounts for 0.015% of the total revenue of China's industrial sector in 1996. The revenue growth rate of the industry is 12.1% from 1995, as compared to the growth rate of China's industrial sector, 9.51%. The rate of return on asset is 2.35%. 69.08% of all firms in the industry made a profit while 26.92% had negative returns. The top province in terms of the industry's revenue is Jiangsu, accounting for 32.16% of the total revenue.
本行業在1996年佔全行業總產值0.015%，行業年增長率為12.1%（全國工業年增長率9.51%）。行業的資產回報率2.35%，69.08%的企業盈利，26.92%的企業虧損。銷售收入最高的省份為江蘇省，佔本行業的32.16%。

	Total number of firms 企業總數	Total number of employees 職工總數	Total revenue (mil. RMB) 總銷售收入（百萬元）	Total profit (mil. RMB) 總利潤（百萬元）	Return on assets 資產利潤率 (%)	Return on equity 權益利潤率 (%)	Labour productivity ('000 RMB / worker) 勞動生產率（千元/人）	Debts / assets 資產負債率 (%)	Total assets (mil. RMB) 總資產（百萬元）
Industry Overall 行業總體	311	17,524	858	29	2.35	6.37	48.96	63.11	1,245

	Number of firms 企業個數	Average number of employees 平均職工人數	Average revenue ('000 RMB) 平均銷售收入（千元）	Average profit ('000 RMB) 平均利潤（千元）	Return on assets 資產利潤率 (%)	Return on equity 權益利潤率 (%)	Labour productivity ('000 RMB / worker) 勞動生產率（千元/人）	Average debts / assets 平均資產負債率(%)	Average Total assets ('000 RMB) 平均總資產（千元）
By ownership 產業所有權									
State-owned 國有	42	139	4,714	-71	-0.63	-1.33	33.93	52.32	11,286
Collectively-owned 集體	231	40	1,760	20	1.16	10.93	43.71	89.39	1,708
Privately-owned 私有	3	29	2,651	200	13.77	31.61	92.46	56.43	1,454
Domestic JVs 聯營	3	68	2,022	12	0.54	4.23	29.73	87.14	2,134
Joint stock 股份制	4	235	15,908	1,121	7.21	35.65	67.84	79.77	15,549
Foreign-funded 外資	18	58	8,443	1,627	11.42	16.77	145.56	31.90	14,247
Overseas Chinese-funded 港澳台資	8	28	2,918	-866	-14.71	-645.78	104.69	97.72	5,888
By size 規模									
Large 大型	4	1,038	51,961	7,485	6.17	11.44	50.07	46.07	121,319
Medium 中型	1	617	41,493	45	0.13	0.64	67.25	80.48	35,800
Small 小型	297	43	2,049	-3	-0.14	-0.52	47.46	73.68	2,438
By regional distribution 地區分布									
Central-North 華北	33	28	3,184	121	2.47	7.20	115.08	65.71	4,888
Beijing 北京	17	20	4,087	-85	-1.53	-7.19	208.02	78.77	5,552
Tianjin 天津	11	35	3,166	505	9.14	18.10	91.42	49.50	5,521
Hebei 河北	3	11	183	-17	-3.23	-8.20	16.67	60.65	517
Shanxi 山西	1	133	10				0.08	5.31	3,770
Inner Mongolia 內蒙	1	32	200	-80	-9.20	-19.51	6.25	51.72	870
Northeast 東北	54	45	1,272	71	3.61	10.09	28.39	64.27	1,982
Liaoning 遼寧	42	44	1,564	103	4.73	11.84	35.44	60.09	2,186
Jilin 吉林	7	67	253	-90	-5.11	-105.00	3.76	95.14	1,763
Heilongjiang 黑龍江	5	19	254	30	5.19	15.00	13.23	65.40	578
Central East 華東	164	68	3,486	67	1.37	3.56	50.91	61.38	4,848
Shanghai 上海	21	44	1,234	26	1.51	4.16	28.29	63.63	1,700
Jiangsu 江蘇	44	122	6,271	117	1.05	2.42	51.58	56.57	11,114
Zhejiang 浙江	59	49	2,849	48	1.58	5.69	58.59	72.29	3,040
Anhui 安徽	16	24	1,696	88	11.23	47.96	71.80	76.67	785
Fujian 福建	8	39	1,703	16	0.91	1.87	43.94	51.30	1,784
Jiangxi 江西	4	153	335	-563	-11.99	-16.30	2.19	26.53	4,693
Shandong 山東	12	66	4,975	261	6.90	37.76	75.19	81.71	3,778
Central-South 中南	38	35	1,769	-72	-2.88	-16.02	50.10	82.05	2,514
Henan 河南	15	19	728	3	0.25	0.97	37.92	74.09	1,333
Hubei 湖北	2	50	2,775	50	1.16	-15.87	55.50	107.42	4,315
Hunan 湖南	11	54	983	-31	-1.86	-3.46	18.26	46.26	1,665
Guangdong 廣東	10	36	3,996	-256	-5.27	-92.09	110.39	94.30	4,862
Guangxi 廣西									
Hainan 海南									
Southwest 西南	13	75	1,348	12	0.79	4.17	18.08	80.92	1,452
Chongqing 重慶	9	90	1,727	54	3.44	13.38	19.09	74.29	1,583
Sichuan 四川	4	41	514	-158	-13.61	1730.27	12.54	100.79	1,163
Guizhou 貴州									
Yunnan 雲南									
Tibet 西藏									
Northwest 西北	9	72	3,036	1,454	19.39	34.37	42.03	43.57	7,500
Shaanxi 陝西	7	73	3,814	1,914	20.69	35.87	51.95	42.30	9,250
Gansu 甘肅									
Qinghai 青海									
Ningxia 寧夏	2	68	310	-155	-11.27	-42.47	4.56	73.45	1,375
Xinjiang 新疆									

4219: Other General Meters 其他通用儀表製造業

Year 年份	Number of firms 企業個數	Rate of change 每年變化 (%)	Number of employees 職工人數 (人)	Rate of change 每年變化 (%)	Total revenue (mil. RMB) 總銷售收入 (百萬元)	Rate of change 每年變化 (%)	Total profit (mil. RMB) 總利潤 (百萬元)	Rate of change 每年變化 (%)
1993	296		26,648		775		31	
1994	302	2.03%	27,577	3.49%	1,001	29.15%	64	107.75%
1995	322	6.62%	24,201	-12.24%	765	-23.58%	15	-76.80%
1996	311	-3.42%	17,524	-27.59%	858	12.12%	29	95.34%

3 Major products* 3 種主要產品 *	Output 產量	Sales volume 銷售量	Unit 單位
a) Automatic Instrument, Meter & System 自動化儀表及系統	4,034,080	3,549,990	set 台(套)

Top 10 firms by revenue (year founded) 收入排名前 10 家企業 (創辦年份)	City 城市	Province 省	Telephone / fax 電話 / 傳真	Number of employees 職工人數	Ownership 產業所有權	Revenue ('000 RMB) 銷售收入 (千元)	Profit ('000 RMB) (rank) 利潤 (千元) (排名)	Total assets ('000 RMB) 總資產 (千元)	Major products 主要產品
Ningbo Water Meter Factory 寧波水表廠(1958)	Ningbo 寧波市	Zhejiang 浙江省	(0574)7332931 (0574)7376630	1,174	Domestic JVs 聯營	89,741	1236(7)	94,915	a
Jiangsu Shu Guang Optics Electronic Instrument Plant 江蘇曙光光學電子儀器廠(1969)	Yangzhou 揚州市	Jiangsu 江蘇省	(0514)7885308 (0514)7887527	1,895	State-owned 國有	78,391	20(71)	225,347	o
Jiangsu Wuxi Survey and Drawing Instrument Factory 江蘇省無錫測繪儀器廠(1968)	Wuxi 無錫市	Jiangsu 江蘇省	(0510)5501361 (0510)5501324	496	State-owned 國有	46,615	82(46)	46,797	o
Beijing Ke Ri Da Electronic Technique Co. Ltd. 北京科日達電子技術有限公司(1989)	Beijing 北京市	Beijing 北京市	(010)62579863 (010)62542062	30	Foreign-funded 外資	45,971	2430(5)	27,300	a
Rongcheng Yu Xiang Industrial Co. 榮成市宇翔實業公司(1985)	Weihai 威海市	Shandong 山東省	(0896)7411260	250	Collectively-owned 集體	32,500	3200(3)	20,920	a
Ningbo Automation Instrument Factory 寧波自動化儀表廠(1984)	Ningbo 寧波市	Zhejiang 浙江省	(0574)7333385 (0574)7333385	189	Collectively-owned 集體	25,565	0(80)	20,084	o
Cixi Copper Industry Co. Ltd. 慈溪銅業有限公司(1989)	Ningbo 寧波市	Zhejiang 浙江省	(0574)3579208 (0574)3579274	20	Collectively-owned 集體	22,134	775(14)	7,506	o
Ningbo Huang Tai Industrial Co. Ltd. 寧波黃泰實業有限公司(1982)	Ningbo 寧波市	Zhejiang 浙江省	(0574)8471888 (0574)8471114	287	Collectively-owned 集體	20,626	-1205(98)	32,610	o
Jiangsu Long Yuan Electric Power Automatic Equipment Factory 江蘇龍源電力自動化設備廠(1991)	Nanjing 南京市	Jiangsu 江蘇省	(025)2287903	46	Collectively-owned 集體	20,600	1130(8)	2,110	o
Nanjing Instrumental Machinery Co. Ltd. 南京儀機股份有限公司(1965)	Nanjing 南京市	Jiangsu 江蘇省	(025)4601770 (025)4591759	925	State-owned 國有	20,100	20(69)	52,521	o

Top 10 Cities by Production Output 產出排名前 10 位城市	Province 省	Market share 市場份額	Number of firms 企業個數
Ningbo 寧波市	Zhejiang 浙江省	17.78%	17
Shanghai 上海市	Shanghai 上海市	9.19%	59
Beijing 北京市	Beijing 北京市	8.13%	13
Nanjing 南京市	Jiangsu 江蘇省	8.00%	9
Wenzhou 温州市	Zhejiang 浙江省	7.87%	29
Wuxi 無錫市	Jiangsu 江蘇省	7.35%	13
Shenzhen 深圳市	Guangdong 廣東省	4.43%	9
Hangzhou 杭州市	Zhejiang 浙江省	3.92%	13
Shenyang 瀋陽市	Liaoning 遼寧省	3.45%	25
Tianjin 天津市	Tianjin 天津市	2.56%	11

10 Major Wholesalers 10 家主要批發商	City 城市	Province 省	Telephone / Fax 電話 / 傳真
Liaoning Automobile Trade Group Corp. 遼寧省汽車貿易集團	Shenyang 瀋陽市	Liaoning 遼寧省	(024)23835494 (024)23838338
China Post and Telecommunication Equipment General Company 中國郵電器材總公司	Beijing 北京市	Beijing 北京市	(010)63523715 (010)63525935
Jiangsu Electromechanical Products General Company 江蘇省機電產品總公司	Nanjing 南京市	Jiangsu 江蘇省	(025)7713642 (025)7711036
Xi Nan Technology Import & Export Company 西南技術進出口公司	Chongqing 重慶市	Chongqing 重慶市	(023)63850185 (023)63850026
Changzhou Economic Technology Industrial Development Zone Tian Ming Trade Company 常州經濟技術產業開發區天明貿易公司	Changzhou 常州市	Jiangsu 江蘇省	(0519)8829882 (0519)8829882
Shanxi Mechanical Equipment Import & Export Company 山西省機械設備進出口公司	Taiyuan 太原市	Shanxi 山西省	(0351)4040713 (0351)4043981
Ningbo Five Mining Machinery Import & Export Company 寧波市五礦機械進出口公司	Ningbo 寧波市	Zhejiang 浙江省	(0574)7311255 (0574)7320322
Tianjin Jin Huan Electromechanical Complete Sets of Equipment Factory 天津市津環機電成套設備廠	Tianjin 天津市	Tianjin 天津市	(022)26371628
Yunnan Machinery Import & Export Company 雲南省機械進出口公司	Kunming 昆明市	Yunnan 雲南省	(0871)3164879 (0871)3136829
Tianjin Da Qiu Zhuang Yi Yuan Trade Center 天津市大丘莊億源商貿中心	Tianjin 天津市	Tianjin 天津市	(022)28899478 (022)28899046

*Also include sales by firms outside this industry.包括本行業以外廠家的銷售。"o" stands for "others". "o" 代表"其他產品"。

4221: Environment Protecting Meters and Equipment
環境保護儀器儀表製造業

The industry accounts for 0.004% of the total revenue of China's industrial sector in 1996. The revenue growth rate of the industry is 60.7% from 1995, as compared to the growth rate of China's industrial sector, 9.51%. The rate of return on asset is -1.86%. 68.82% of all firms in the industry made a profit while 26.83% had negative returns. The top province in terms of the industry's revenue is Hubei, accounting for 24.67% of the total revenue.
本行業在1996年佔全行業總產值0.004%，行業年增長率為60.7%（全國工業年增長率9.51%）。行業的資產回報率-1.86%，68.82%的企業盈利，26.83%的企業虧損。銷售收入最高的省份為湖北省，佔本行業的24.67%。

	Total number of firms 企業總數	Total number of employees 職工總數	Total revenue (mil. RMB) 總銷售收入（百萬元）	Total profit (mil. RMB) 總利潤（百萬元）	Return on assets 資產利潤率 (%)	Return on equity 權益利潤率 (%)	Labour productivity ('000 RMB / worker) 勞動生產率（千元/人）	Debts / assets 資產負債率 (%)	Total assets (mil. RMB) 總資產（百萬元）
Industry Overall 行業總體	91	5,374	225	-11	-1.86	-21.28	41.87	91.24	571

	Number of firms 企業個數	Average number of employees 平均職工人數	Average revenue ('000 RMB) 平均銷售收入（千元）	Average profit ('000 RMB) 平均利潤（千元）	Return on assets 資產利潤率 (%)	Return on equity 權益利潤率 (%)	Labour productivity ('000 RMB / worker) 勞動生產率（千元/人）	Average debts / assets 平均資產負債率(%)	Average Total assets ('000 RMB) 平均總資產（千元）
By ownership 產業所有權									
State-owned 國有	19	139	3,737	-895	-8.50	12.23	26.80	169.50	10,526
Collectively-owned 集體	60	44	1,963	39	0.85	1.77	44.52	52.25	4,546
Privately-owned 私有	1	14	597	-207	-117.59	442.30	42.62	126.59	176
Domestic JVs 聯營	1								
Joint stock 股份制	1	18	1,726	307	5.58	9.02	95.86	38.13	5,505
Foreign-funded 外資	5	15	4,778	1,129	11.42	16.82	322.81	32.11	9,888
Overseas Chinese-funded 港澳台資	4	26	2,480	-515	-4.78	-9.44	94.47	49.38	10,768
By size 規模									
Large 大型									
Medium 中型	1	679	46,376	-4,287	-1.83	-12.40	68.30	85.26	234,641
Small 小型	86	54	2,076	-78	-2.00	-43.54	38.10	95.42	3,911
By regional distribution 地區分布									
Central-North 華北	27	36	859	69	1.05	2.98	24.02	64.87	6,620
Beijing 北京	16	21	946	68	0.69	1.93	45.57	64.29	9,891
Tianjin 天津	5	26	444	56	5.71	12.39	16.82	53.88	980
Hebei 河北	5	99	1,166	100	3.29	13.59	11.83	75.82	3,044
Shanxi 山西	1	8						10.81	370
Inner Mongolia 內蒙									
Northeast 東北	19	44	1,028	59	3.20	8.87	23.56	63.97	1,841
Liaoning 遼寧	15	48	1,188	77	3.50	9.65	24.72	63.75	2,192
Jilin 吉林	3	31	417	90	22.50	34.62	13.44	35.83	400
Heilongjiang 黑龍江	1	15	460	-300	-33.71	375.00	30.67	110.11	890
Central East 華東	24	64	3,247	149	3.30	7.90	50.77	58.16	4,515
Shanghai 上海	4	97	3,003	200	4.92	8.92	30.87	44.80	4,063
Jiangsu 江蘇	6	63	2,300	-133	-3.62	-12.38	36.70	70.80	3,687
Zhejiang 浙江	2	159	13,315	1,610	9.08	16.95	84.01	46.40	17,725
Anhui 安徽	2	16	315	-5	-0.54	-1.43	19.69	62.90	930
Fujian 福建	3	12	117	10	5.45	6.52	9.72	14.55	183
Jiangxi 江西									
Shandong 山東	7	55	3,501	49	1.06	3.49	63.66	69.65	4,590
Central-South 中南	14	39	5,222	217	2.70	3.21	134.64	15.87	8,051
Henan 河南	4	64	4,348	235	5.05	12.93	68.46	60.98	4,658
Hubei 湖北	6	44	9,250	350	2.24	2.40	211.83	6.73	15,622
Hunan 湖南	1	27	220				8.15	61.11	360
Guangdong 廣東	2								
Guangxi 廣西	1								
Hainan 海南									
Southwest 西南	4	336	5,863	-4,593	-14.44	10.87	17.47	232.90	31,803
Chongqing 重慶									
Sichuan 四川	3	441	7,783	-6,120	-14.69	10.84	17.65	235.55	41,650
Guizhou 貴州									
Yunnan 雲南	1	20	100	-10	-0.44	-3.23	5.00	86.28	2,260
Tibet 西藏									
Northwest 西北	3	53	2,630	-633	-21.42	-53.98	49.31	60.32	2,957
Shaanxi 陝西	3	53	2,630	-633	-21.42	-53.98	49.31	60.32	2,957
Gansu 甘肅									
Qinghai 青海									
Ningxia 寧夏									
Xinjiang 新疆									

4221: Environment Protecting Meters and Equipment
環境保護儀器儀表製造業

Year 年份	Number of firms 企業個數	Rate of change 每年變化 (%)	Number of employees 職工人數 (人)	Rate of change 每年變化 (%)	Total revenue (mil. RMB) 總銷售收入 (百萬元)	Rate of change 每年變化 (%)	Total profit (mil. RMB) 總利潤 (百萬元)	Rate of change 每年變化 (%)
1993	53		3,225		152		7	
1994	69	30.19%	4,089	26.79%	91	-40.17%	8	13.51%
1995	72	4.35%	3,742	-8.49%	140	54.26%	10	28.11%
1996	91	26.39%	5,374	43.61%	225	60.69%	-11	-212.46%

3 Major products* 3 種主要產品 *	Output 產量	Sales volume 銷售量	Unit 單位
a) Instrument & Unit for Environmental Protection 環境保護儀器儀表	12,797	12,669	set 台

Top 10 firms by revenue (year founded) 收入排名前 10 家企業 (創辦年份)	City 城市	Province 省	Telephone / fax 電話 / 傳真	Number of employees 職工人數	Ownership 產業所有權	Revenue ('000 RMB) 銷售收入 (千元)	Profit ('000 RMB) (rank) 利潤 (千元) (排名)	Total assets ('000 RMB) 總資產 (千元)	Major products 主要產品
Zhejiang Jia Huan Electron Co. Ltd. 浙江佳環電子有限公司(1970)	Jinhua 金華市	Zhejiang 浙江省	(0579)2338650 (0579)2321994	274	State-owned 國有	25,734	3002(1)	32,813	o
State-owned Jian Chuan Machine Factory 國營建川機器廠(1977)	Leshan 樂山市	Sichuan 四川省	(0833)8811611 (0833)8811322	1,278	State-owned 國有	22,076	-18650(23)	122,233	o
Zhumadian Danfeng Embroidery Work Co. Ltd. 駐馬店丹鳳工藝繡品有限公司(1992)	Zhumadian 駐馬店市	Henan 河南省	(0396)2813760 (0396)2813794	85	Overseas Chinese-funded 港澳台資	16,859	923(3)	17,275	o
Ji'nan Muffler Factory 濟南市消聲器廠(1975)	Ji'nan 濟南市	Shandong 山東省	(0531)7924524	27	Collectively-owned 集體	15,435	-25(19)	3,930	o
Shanghai Shen Xing Environmental Protection Electric Equipment Plant 上海申興環保電器廠(1991)	Shanghai 上海市	Shanghai 上海市	(021)58820578	190	Collectively-owned 集體	8,024	304(9)	5,494	o
Xi'an Qin Yi Electric Power Automatic Equipment Co. Ltd. 西安秦儀電力自動化設備有限公司(1993)	Xi'an 西安市	Shaanxi 陝西省	(029)8221653	30	Joint stock 股份制	6,265	841(4)	5,321	o
Changzhou Xinqu Xu Tang Environmental Protection Equipment Factory 常州新區圩塘環保設備廠(1980)	Changzhou 常州市	Jiangsu 江蘇省	(0519)5476070	121	Collectively-owned 集體	4,898	-161(21)	6,420	o
Shenyang Environment Protection Instrument & Equipment Factory 瀋陽市環保儀器設備廠(1962)	Shenyang 瀋陽市	Liaoning 遼寧省	(024)23219283	201	Collectively-owned 集體	4,414	-46(20)	4,943	o
Dalian Zhao Jian Electron Equipment Co. Ltd. 大連兆健電子設備有限公司(1990)	Dalian 大連市	Liaoning 遼寧省	(0411)4620664 (0411)4620684	14	Foreign-funded 外資	4,041	442(6)	4,620	o
Shenyang Jia Ye Mai Ke Si Instrument Co. Ltd. 瀋陽加野麥克斯儀器有限公司(1994)	Shenyang 瀋陽市	Liaoning 遼寧省	(024)86800700 (024)86800654	34	Foreign-funded 外資	3,391	1133(2)	8,297	a

Top 10 Cities by Production Output 產出排名前 10 位城市	Province 省	Market share 市場份額	Number of firms 企業個數
Jinhua 金華市	Zhejiang 浙江省	11.61%	1
Leshan 樂山市	Sichuan 四川省	10.89%	1
Shanghai 上海市	Shanghai 上海市	9.81%	8
Zhumadian 駐馬店市	Henan 河南省	7.83%	2
Qingdao 青島市	Shandong 山東省	6.99%	5
Changchun 長春市	Jilin 吉林省	6.04%	1
Guangzhou 廣州市	Guangdong 廣東省	5.66%	7
Shuangcheng 雙城市	Heilongjiang 黑龍江省	5.11%	1
Wuhan 武漢市	Hubei 湖北省	4.27%	2
Beijing 北京市	Beijing 北京市	3.40%	10

10 Major Wholesalers 10 家主要批發商	City 城市	Province 省	Telephone / Fax 電話 / 傳真
Liaoning Automobile Trade Group Corp. 遼寧省汽車貿易集團	Shenyang 瀋陽市	Liaoning 遼寧省	(024)23835494 (024)23838338
China Post and Telecommunication Equipment General Company 中國郵電器材總公司	Beijing 北京市	Beijing 北京市	(010)63523715 (010)63525935
Jiangsu Electromechanical Products General Company 江蘇省機電產品總公司	Nanjing 南京市	Jiangsu 江蘇省	(025)7713642 (025)7711036
Xi Nan Technology Import & Export Company 西南技術進出口公司	Chongqing 重慶市	Chongqing 重慶市	(023)63850185 (023)63850026
Changzhou Economic Technology Industrial Development Zone Tian Ming Trade Company 常州經濟技術產業開發區天明貿易公司	Changzhou 常州市	Jiangsu 江蘇省	(0519)8829882 (0519)8829882
Shanxi Mechanical Equipment Import & Export Company 山西省機械設備進出口公司	Taiyuan 太原市	Shanxi 山西省	(0351)4040713 (0351)4043981
Ningbo Five Mining Machinery Import & Export Company 寧波市五礦機械進出口公司	Ningbo 寧波市	Zhejiang 浙江省	(0574)7311255 (0574)7320322
Tianjin Jin Huan Electromechanical Complete Sets of Equipment Factory 天津市津環機電成套設備廠	Tianjin 天津市	Tianjin 天津市	(022)26371628
Yunnan Machinery Import & Export Company 雲南省機械進出口公司	Kunming 昆明市	Yunnan 雲南省	(0871)3164879 (0871)3136829
Tianjin Da Qiu Zhuang Yi Yuan Trade Center 天津市大丘莊億源商貿中心	Tianjin 天津市	Tianjin 天津市	(022)28899478 (022)28899046

*Also include sales by firms outside this industry.包括本行業以外廠家的銷售。"o" stands for "others". "o" 代表 "其他產品"。

4222: Motor Meters and Instruments 汽車儀器儀表製造業

The industry accounts for 0.015% of the total revenue of China's industrial sector in 1996. The revenue growth rate of the industry is 12.5% from 1995, as compared to the growth rate of China's industrial sector, 9.51%. The rate of return on asset is 0.19%. 63.49% of all firms in the industry made a profit while 36.51% had negative returns. The top province in terms of the industry's revenue is Shanghai, accounting for 26.41% of the total revenue.
本行業在1996年佔全行業總產值0.015%，行業年增長率為12.5%（全國工業年增長率9.51%）。行業的資產回報率0.19%，63.49%的企業盈利，36.51%的企業虧損。銷售收入最高的省份為上海市，佔本行業的26.41%。

	Total number of firms 企業總數	Total number of employees 職工總數	Total revenue (mil. RMB) 總銷售收入（百萬元）	Total profit (mil. RMB) 總利潤（百萬元）	Return on assets 資產利潤率 (%)	Return on equity 權益利潤率 (%)	Labour productivity ('000 RMB / worker) 勞動生產率（千元/人）	Debts / assets 資產負債率 (%)	Total assets (mil. RMB) 總資產（百萬元）
Industry Overall 行業總體	65	14,651	866	4	0.19	0.38	59.11	50.11	1,946

	Number of firms 企業個數	Average number of employees 平均職工人數	Average revenue ('000 RMB) 平均銷售收入（千元）	Average profit ('000 RMB) 平均利潤（千元）	Return on assets 資產利潤率 (%)	Return on equity 權益利潤率 (%)	Labour productivity ('000 RMB / worker) 勞動生產率（千元/人）	Average debts / assets 平均資產負債率(%)	Average Total assets ('000 RMB) 平均總資產（千元）
By ownership 產業所有權									
State-owned 國有	10	594	37,900	1,900	2.30	5.85	63.83	60.65	82,600
Collectively-owned 集體	43	144	5,229	-60	-0.42	-0.84	36.29	49.64	14,234
Privately-owned 私有	1	154	12,805	-91	-0.80	-1.62	83.15	50.60	11,410
Domestic JVs 聯營									
Joint stock 股份制	2	39	11,374	-686	-4.25	-7.58	291.63	44.01	16,160
Foreign-funded 外資	5	206	23,250	-827	-2.24	-3.36	112.76	33.42	37,008
Overseas Chinese-funded 港澳台資	5	342	22,057	-1,362	-2.43	-3.56	64.42	31.67	55,991
By size 規模									
Large 大型	2	1,466	110,181	574	0.19	0.39	75.18	51.64	304,285
Medium 中型	3	1,692	132,465	842	0.33	0.57	78.30	42.43	255,384
Small 小型	57	115	4,354	6	0.06	0.14	37.79	58.74	10,032
By regional distribution 地區分布									
Central-North 華北	11	199	5,474	-275	-1.81	-2.26	27.56	20.14	15,204
Beijing 北京	3	2	90	-50	-31.91	214.29	38.57	114.89	157
Tianjin 天津	2	866	28,005	-1,115	-1.42	-1.70	32.34	16.69	78,530
Hebei 河北	5	57	764	-74	-4.89	-15.04	13.36	67.50	1,514
Shanxi 山西	1	160	110	-270	-12.62	-81.82	0.69	84.58	2,140
Inner Mongolia 內蒙									
Northeast 東北	8	104	2,748	-9	-0.26	-0.91	26.48	71.40	3,379
Liaoning 遼寧	7	104	2,134	-31	-0.99	-3.69	20.58	73.16	3,177
Jilin 吉林	1	104	7,040	150	3.13	8.52	67.69	63.26	4,790
Heilongjiang 黑龍江									
Central East 華東	35	226	18,277	146	0.34	0.70	80.94	51.00	42,471
Shanghai 上海	8	492	28,593	-1,733	-1.95	-3.51	58.14	44.46	88,974
Jiangsu 江蘇	12	78	6,773	45	0.27	0.58	86.92	54.18	16,813
Zhejiang 浙江	7	243	24,934	2,399	7.98	12.93	102.55	38.33	30,076
Anhui 安徽	5	248	29,320	318	0.45	1.46	118.04	69.38	71,076
Fujian 福建	1	00	0,500	-30	-1.05	-9.08	109.67	89.12	2,850
Jiangxi 江西									
Shandong 山東	2	15	985	45	2.16	5.45	65.67	60.43	2,085
Central-South 中南	8	400	16,835	336	1.08	2.84	42.11	61.88	31,048
Henan 河南	1	30	1,810	130	2.96	13.98	60.33	78.82	4,390
Hubei 湖北	2	1,360	61,345	2,280	2.24	5.83	45.11	61.61	101,825
Hunan 湖南	1	350	3,080	-1,850	-15.69	402.17	8.80	103.90	11,790
Guangdong 廣東	3	24	2,260	-40	-0.48	-0.92	92.88	48.35	8,397
Guangxi 廣西									
Hainan 海南	1	25	320	-30	-0.89	-0.99	12.80	10.12	3,360
Southwest 西南	1	65	3,520	60	1.88	5.45	54.15	65.63	3,200
Chongqing 重慶									
Sichuan 四川	1	65	3,520	-60	-1.88	-5.46	54.15	65.63	3,200
Guizhou 貴州									
Yunnan 雲南									
Tibet 西藏									
Northwest 西北	2	235	3,200	-560	-7.93	-20.07	13.62	60.51	7,065
Shaanxi 陝西									
Gansu 甘肅	1	225	4,090	-50	-1.02	-2.03	18.18	49.80	4,900
Qinghai 青海	1	245	2,310	-1,070	-11.59	-34.29	9.43	66.20	9,230
Ningxia 寧夏									
Xinjiang 新疆									

4222: Motor Meters and Instruments 汽車儀器儀表製造業

Year 年份	Number of firms 企業個數	Rate of change 每年變化 (%)	Number of employees 職工人數 (人)	Rate of change 每年變化 (%)	Total revenue (mil. RMB) 總銷售收入 (百萬元)	Rate of change 每年變化 (%)	Total profit (mil. RMB) 總利潤 (百萬元)	Rate of change 每年變化 (%)
1993	47		8,901		232		20	
1994	46	-2.13%	6,835	-23.21%	238	2.55%	6	-68.17%
1995	83	80.43%	13,937	103.91%	770	223.55%	67	942.68%
1996	65	-21.69%	14,651	5.12%	866	12.46%	4	-94.02%

3 Major products* 3種主要產品*	Output 產量	Sales volume 銷售量	Unit 單位
a) Automobile Instrument & Meter 汽車儀器儀表	18,661,082	19,967,357	set 台

Top 10 firms by revenue (year founded) 收入排名前10家企業 (創辦年份)	City 城市	Province 省	Telephone / fax 電話 / 傳真	Number of employees 職工人數	Ownership 產業所有權	Revenue ('000 RMB) 銷售收入 (千元)	Profit ('000 RMB) (rank) 利潤 (千元) (排名)	Total assets ('000 RMB) 總資產 (千元)	Major products 主要產品
Wuhu Instrument and Meter Plant 蕪湖儀表廠(1958)	Wuhu 蕪湖市	Anhui 安徽省	(0553)3844097 (0553)3835346	1,628	State-owned 國有	131,548	1818(5)	343,759	o
Xiangfan Dongfeng Automobile Instrument and Meter Co. Ltd. 襄樊東風汽車儀表有限責任公司(1995)	Xiangfan 襄樊市	Hubei 湖北省	(0710)3443434 (0710)3442824	1,162	State-owned 國有	120,766	4279(4)	187,205	o
Shanghai Chang Jiang Instrument and Meter Plant 上海長江儀表廠(1974)	Shanghai 上海市	Shanghai 上海市	(021)59666347 (021)59668151	1,625	State-owned 國有	108,514	15410(1)	249,654	a
Zhejiang Automobile Instrument and Meter Plant 浙江汽車儀表廠(1975)	Shaoxing 紹興市	Zhejiang 浙江省	(0575)5181187 (0575)5182593	225	Collectively-owned 集體	82,482	8653(2)	69,299	a
Shanghai De Ke Electronic Instrument Co. Ltd. 上海德科電子儀表有限公司(1996)	Shanghai 上海市	Shanghai 上海市	(021)59666140 (021)59666583	1,522	Foreign-funded 外資	80,970	-1238(27)	248,701	a
Shaoxing Yi Dong Instrument and Meter Co. Ltd. 浙江紹興怡東儀表有限公司(1993)	Shaoxing 紹興市	Zhejiang 浙江省	(0575)4090358 (0575)4090531	908	Overseas Chinese-funded 港澳台資	75,492	7132(3)	122,541	o
Tianjin Hua Shi Automobile Instrument Co. Ltd. 天津市華獅汽車儀表有限公司(1954)	Tianjin 天津市	Tianjin 天津市	(022)24329521 (022)24329449	1,674	Foreign-funded 外資	56,013	-2226(32)	157,057	a
Nanjing Automobile Instrument Factory 南京汽車儀表廠(1994)	Nanjing 南京市	Jiangsu 江蘇省	(025)5502883	122	Domestic JVs 聯營	35,070	560(8)	54,153	o
Zhenjiang Xing Da Automobile Ornaments Factory 鎮江市興達汽車裝飾件廠(1990)	Zhenjiang 鎮江市	Jiangsu 江蘇省	(0511)8353335	278	Collectively-owned 集體	25,505	1023(6)	71,448	o
Shanghai Yi Chu Ri Jing Co. Ltd. 上海易初日精有限公司(1995)	Shanghai 上海市	Shanghai 上海市	(021)64890803 (021)64890801	176	Overseas Chinese-funded 港澳台資	17,245	-5422(33)	87,894	a

Top 10 Cities by Production Output 產出排名前10位城市	Province 省	Market share 市場份額	Number of firms 企業個數
Shaoxing 紹興市	Zhejiang 浙江省	32.33%	7
Shanghai 上海市	Shanghai 上海市	25.68%	11
Xiangfan 襄樊市	Hubei 湖北省	14.85%	1
Tianjin 天津市	Tianjin 天津市	7.70%	5
Nanjing 南京市	Jiangsu 江蘇省	3.71%	1
Wuhu 蕪湖市	Anhui 安徽省	1.93%	2
Huzhou 湖州市	Zhejiang 浙江省	1.59%	1
Shantou 汕頭市	Guangdong 廣東省	1.23%	2
Guangzhou 廣州市	Guangdong 廣東省	0.94%	3
Fuzhou 福州市	Fujian 福建省	0.92%	2

10 Major Wholesalers 10家主要批發商	City 城市	Province 省	Telephone / Fax 電話 / 傳真
Liaoning Automobile Trade Group Corp. 遼寧省汽車貿易集團	Shenyang 瀋陽市	Liaoning 遼寧省	(024)23835494 (024)23838338
China Post and Telecommunication Equipment General Company 中國郵電器材總公司	Beijing 北京市	Beijing 北京市	(010)63523715 (010)63525935
Jiangsu Electromechanical Products General Company 江蘇省機電產品總公司	Nanjing 南京市	Jiangsu 江蘇省	(025)7713642 (025)7711036
Xi Nan Technology Import & Export Company 西南技術進出口公司	Chongqing 重慶市	Chongqing 重慶市	(023)63850185 (023)63850026
Changzhou Economic Technology Industrial Development Zone Tian Ming Trade Company 常州經濟技術產業開發區天明貿易公司	Changzhou 常州市	Jiangsu 江蘇省	(0519)8829882 (0519)8829882
Shanxi Mechanical Equipment Import & Export Company 山西省機械設備進出口公司	Taiyuan 太原市	Shanxi 山西省	(0351)4040713 (0351)4043981
Ningbo Five Mining Machinery Import & Export Company 寧波市五礦機械進出口公司	Ningbo 寧波市	Zhejiang 浙江省	(0574)7311255 (0574)7320322
Tianjin Jin Huan Electromechanical Complete Sets of Equipment Factory 天津市津環機電成套設備廠	Tianjin 天津市	Tianjin 天津市	(022)26371628
Yunnan Machinery Import & Export Company 雲南省機械進出口公司	Kunming 昆明市	Yunnan 雲南省	(0871)3164879 (0871)3136829
Tianjin Da Qiu Zhuang Yi Yuan Trade Center 天津市大丘莊億源商貿中心	Tianjin 天津市	Tianjin 天津市	(022)28899478 (022)28899046

*Also include sales by firms outside this industry.包括本行業以外廠家的銷售。"o" stands for "others". "o" 代表"其他產品"。

4223: Navigation Equipment 導航、制導儀器製造業

The industry accounts for 0.013% of the total revenue of China's industrial sector in 1996. The revenue growth rate of the industry is 1.7% from 1995, as compared to the growth rate of China's industrial sector, 9.51%. The rate of return on asset is -3.48%. 57.23% of all firms in the industry made a profit while 29.73% had negative returns. The top province in terms of the industry's revenue is Jiangsu, accounting for 20.10% of the total revenue.
本行業在1996年佔全行業總產值0.013%，行業年增長率為1.7%（全國工業年增長率9.51%）。行業的資產回報率-3.48%，57.23%的企業盈利，29.73%的企業虧損。銷售收入最高的省份為江蘇省，佔本行業的20.10%。

	Total number of firms 企業總數	Total number of employees 職工總數	Total revenue (mil. RMB) 總銷售收入（百萬元）	Total profit (mil. RMB) 總利潤（百萬元）	Return on assets 資產利潤率 (%)	Return on equity 權益利潤率 (%)	Labour productivity ('000 RMB / worker) 勞動生產率（千元/人）	Debts / assets 資產負債率 (%)	Total assets (mil. RMB) 總資產（百萬元）
Industry Overall 行業總體	41	29,490	758	-81	-3.48	-13.24	25.70	73.69	2,324

	Number of firms 企業個數	Average number of employees 平均職工人數	Average revenue ('000 RMB) 平均銷售收入（千元）	Average profit ('000 RMB) 平均利潤（千元）	Return on assets 資產利潤率 (%)	Return on equity 權益利潤率 (%)	Labour productivity ('000 RMB / worker) 勞動生產率（千元/人）	Average debts / assets 平均資產負債率(%)	Average Total assets ('000 RMB) 平均總資產（千元）
By ownership 產業所有權									
State-owned 國有	22	1,257	31,364	-3,773	-3.81	-15.60	24.95	75.57	99,000
Collectively-owned 集體	11	77	2,775	125	1.90	3.28	36.16	42.18	6,597
Privately-owned 私有									
Domestic JVs 聯營	2	410	10,694	25	0.13	0.29	26.12	54.76	18,891
Joint stock 股份制									
Foreign-funded 外資	5	30	3,119	221	3.28	5.18	103.98	36.70	6,747
Overseas Chinese-funded 港澳台資	2	4	236	-267	-26.19	39.07	58.96	167.02	1,020
By size 規模									
Large 大型	8	2,257	64,783	-10,590	-4.95	-26.32	28.70	81.21	214,118
Medium 中型	12	689	14,042	-186	-0.48	-1.01	20.39	52.35	38,517
Small 小型	22	144	3,237	271	4.00	8.65	22.51	53.74	6,771
By regional distribution 地區分布									
Central-North 華北	4	1,010	26,793	-4,103	-5.27	-14.05	26.54	62.48	77,835
Beijing 北京	3	247	6,593	17	0.09	0.21	26.69	55.49	17,920
Tianjin 天津									
Hebei 河北	1	3,297	87,390	-16,460	-6.39	-17.72	26.51	63.94	257,580
Shanxi 山西									
Inner Mongolia 內蒙									
Northeast 東北	6	369	7,773	163	0.73	2.23	21.09	67.05	22,232
Liaoning 遼寧	6	369	7,773	163	0.73	2.23	21.09	67.05	22,232
Jilin 吉林									
Heilongjiang 黑龍江									
Central East 華東	17	679	21,239	-396	-0.78	-2.03	31.27	61.55	50,825
Shanghai 上海	1	2,217	54,660				24.65	80.30	162,640
Jiangsu 江蘇	8	457	19,041	131	0.28	0.64	41.67	56.42	46,943
Zhejiang 浙江	3	91	2,767	47	0.92	1.46	30.29	37.42	5,087
Anhui 安徽	1	699	14,150	-1,500	-4.07	-12.07	20.24	66.24	36,820
Fujian 福建									
Jiangxi 江西	3	1,526	38,903	-2,883	-3.23	-7.71	25.49	58.18	89,393
Shandong 山東	1	123	14,920	2,220	39.78	92.12	121.30	56.81	5,580
Central-South 中南	8	457	10,676	-23	-0.09	-0.21	23.36	57.91	24,885
Henan 河南	1	22	1,640	120	3.02	14.29	74.55	78.89	3,980
Hubei 湖北	3	1,152	25,563	-217	-0.38	-0.97	22.18	61.10	57,560
Hunan 湖南									
Guangdong 廣東	4	45	1,770	88	1.56	2.22	39.78	29.66	5,605
Guangxi 廣西									
Hainan 海南									
Southwest 西南	5	1,604	31,452	-11,424	-7.07	-183.43	19.60	96.15	161,612
Chongqing 重慶	4	1,866	36,617	-13,342	-7.08	-183.73	19.62	96.15	188,464
Sichuan 四川	1	32	460	81	15.97	-542.24	14.60	102.94	507
Guizhou 貴州									
Yunnan 雲南									
Tibet 西藏									
Northwest 西北	1	15	800	-1,480	-18.62	-41.69	53.33	55.35	7,950
Shaanxi 陝西	1	15	800	-1,480	-18.62	-41.69	53.33	55.35	7,950
Gansu 甘肅									
Qinghai 青海									
Ningxia 寧夏									
Xinjiang 新疆									

4223: Navigation Equipment 導航、制導儀器製造業

Year 年份	Number of firms 企業個數	Rate of change 每年變化 (%)	Number of employees 職工人數 (人)	Rate of change 每年變化 (%)	Total revenue (mil. RMB) 總銷售收入 (百萬元)	Rate of change 每年變化 (%)	Total profit (mil. RMB) 總利潤 (百萬元)	Rate of change 每年變化 (%)
1993	32		32,108		609		25	
1994	39	21.88%	45,638	42.14%	780	28.24%	-14	-156.30%
1995	32	-17.95%	25,396	-44.35%	746	-4.45%	-44	-212.48%
1996	41	28.13%	29,490	16.12%	758	1.65%	-81	-84.34%

3 Major products* 3 種主要產品 *	Output 產量	Sales volume 銷售量	Unit 單位
a) Kilowatt-hour Meter 電度表	410,370	398,059	set 台
b) Electrican's Instrument & Meter 電工儀器儀表	433,459	429,124	set 台

Top 10 firms by revenue (year founded) 收入排名前 10 家企業 (創辦年份)	City 城市	Province 省	Telephone / fax 電話 / 傳真	Number of employees 職工人數	Ownership 產業所有權	Revenue ('000 RMB) 銷售收入 (千元)	Profit ('000 RMB) (rank) 利潤 (千元) (排名)	Total assets ('000 RMB) 總資產 (千元)	Major products 主要產品
Hai Ying Enterprise Group Co. Ltd. 海鷹企業集團有限責任公司(1958)	Wuxi 無錫市	Jiangsu 江蘇省	(0510)5807234	2,196	State-owned 國有	109,000	407(5)	268,706	o
Jiujiang Instrument and Meter Plant 九江儀表廠(1962)	Jiujiang 九江市	Jiangxi 江西省	(0792)8252911 (0792)8252791	3,001	State-owned 國有	89,389	-8886(20)	180,088	a,b
State-owned Han Guang Machinery Plant 國營漢光機械廠(1963)	Handan 邯鄲市	Hebei 河北省	(0310)7024803 (0310)7025242	3,297	State-owned 國有	87,387	-16458(21)	257,578	o
Chongqing Hua Yu Electric Instrument General Factory 重慶華渝電氣儀表總廠(1994)	Chongqing 重慶市	Chongqing 重慶市	(023)67610402 (023)67610402	3,884	State-owned 國有	64,504	-22361(22)	332,067	o
Shanghai Nautical Instrument General Factory 上海航海儀器總廠(1928)	Shanghai 上海市	Shanghai 上海市	(021)58713258 (021)58713798	2,151	State-owned 國有	54,664	0(14)	162,639	a,b
Sichuan Qing Ping Machinery Plant 四川清平機械廠(1966)	Chongqing 重慶市	Chongqing 重慶市	(023)8222132 (023)8222135	612	State-owned 國有	36,303	4506(1)	67,066	o
State-owned Liao Hai Machinery Plant 國營遼海機械廠(1960)	Shenyang 瀋陽市	Liaoning 遼寧省	(024)23869287 (024)23866609	1,330	State-owned 國有	35,034	302(7)	108,740	o
Chongqing Wu Zhou Industrial Co. 重慶五洲實業公司(1981)	Chongqing 重慶市	Chongqing 重慶市	(023)67853451 (023)67852439	1,087	State-owned 國有	33,056	-38535(23)	340,957	o
Beijing Chang Cheng Radio Factory 北京長城無線電廠(1971)	Beijing 北京市	Beijing 北京市	(010)62253344	790	State-owned 國有	19,784	46(10)	53,762	o
Nanjing Navigation Instrument Factory 南京航海儀器廠(1960)	Nanjing 南京市	Jiangsu 江蘇省	(025)8805686 (025)8805858	715	Domestic JVs 聯營	17,547	0(15)	42,729	o

Top 10 Cities by Production Output 產出排名前 10 位城市	Province 省	Market share 市場份額	Number of firms 企業個數
Jiujiang 九江市	Jiangxi 江西省	19.13%	3
Chongqing 重慶市	Chongqing 重慶市	18.40%	5
Shanghai 上海市	Shanghai 上海市	17.31%	3
Handan 邯鄲市	Hebei 河北省	14.91%	1
Yichang 宜昌市	Hubei 湖北省	7.02%	3
Nanjing 南京市	Jiangsu 江蘇省	6.80%	3
Shenyang 瀋陽市	Liaoning 遼寧省	6.77%	1
Beijing 北京市	Beijing 北京市	5.41%	2
Jinzhou 錦州市	Liaoning 遼寧省	1.92%	2
Shenzhen 深圳市	Guangdong 廣東省	0.89%	1

10 Major Wholesalers 10 家主要批發商	City 城市	Province 省	Telephone / Fax 電話 / 傳真
Liaoning Automobile Trade Group Corp. 遼寧省汽車貿易集團	Shenyang 瀋陽市	Liaoning 遼寧省	(024)23835494 (024)23838338
China Post and Telecommunication Equipment General Company 中國郵電器材總公司	Beijing 北京市	Beijing 北京市	(010)63523715 (010)63525935
Jiangsu Electromechanical Products General Company 江蘇省機電產品總公司	Nanjing 南京市	Jiangsu 江蘇省	(025)7713642 (025)7711036
Xi Nan Technology Import & Export Company 西南技術進出口公司	Chongqing 重慶市	Chongqing 重慶市	(023)63850185 (023)63850026
Changzhou Economic Technology Industrial Development Zone Tian Ming Trade Company 常州經濟技術產業開發區天明貿易公司	Changzhou 常州市	Jiangsu 江蘇省	(0519)8829882 (0519)8829882
Shanxi Mechanical Equipment Import & Export Company 山西省機械設備進出口公司	Taiyuan 太原市	Shanxi 山西省	(0351)4040713 (0351)4043981
Ningbo Five Mining Machinery Import & Export Company 寧波市五礦機械進出口公司	Ningbo 寧波市	Zhejiang 浙江省	(0574)7311255 (0574)7320322
Tianjin Jin Huan Electromechanical Complete Sets of Equipment Factory 天津市津環機電成套設備廠	Tianjin 天津市	Tianjin 天津市	(022)26371628
Yunnan Machinery Import & Export Company 雲南省機械進出口公司	Kunming 昆明市	Yunnan 雲南省	(0871)3164879 (0871)3136829
Tianjin Da Qiu Zhuang Yi Yuan Trade Center 天津市大丘莊億源商貿中心	Tianjin 天津市	Tianjin 天津市	(022)28899478 (022)28899046

*Also include sales by firms outside this industry.包括本行業以外廠家的銷售。"o" stands for "others". "o" 代表"其他產品"。

4224: Farming, Forestry, Husbandry and Fishery Instruments and Meters
農、林、牧、漁儀器、儀表製造業

The industry accounts for 0.001% of the total revenue of China's industrial sector in 1996. The revenue growth rate of the industry is 39.3% from 1995, as compared to the growth rate of China's industrial sector, 9.51%. The rate of return on asset is -0.92%. 50.00% of all firms in the industry made a profit while 37.50% had negative returns. The top province in terms of the industry's revenue is Shandong, accounting for 26.20% of the total revenue.
本行業在1996年佔全行業總產值0.001%，行業年增長率為39.3%（全國工業年增長率9.51%）。行業的資產回報率-0.92%，50.00%的企業盈利，37.50%的企業虧損。銷售收入最高的省份為山東省，佔本行業的26.20%。

	Total number of firms 企業總數	Total number of employees 職工總數	Total revenue (mil. RMB) 總銷售收入（百萬元）	Total profit (mil. RMB) 總利潤（百萬元）	Return on assets 資產利潤率 (%)	Return on equity 權益利潤率 (%)	Labour productivity ('000 RMB / worker) 勞動生產率（千元/人）	Debts / assets 資產負債率 (%)	Total assets (mil. RMB) 總資產（百萬元）
Industry Overall 行業總體	19	2,046	45	-1	-0.92	-2.97	21.99	69.02	112

	Number of firms 企業個數	Average number of employees 平均職工人數	Average revenue ('000 RMB) 平均銷售收入（千元）	Average profit ('000 RMB) 平均利潤（千元）	Return on assets 資產利潤率 (%)	Return on equity 權益利潤率 (%)	Labour productivity ('000 RMB / worker) 勞動生產率（千元/人）	Average debts / assets 平均資產負債率(%)	Average Total assets ('000 RMB) 平均總資產（千元）
By ownership 產業所有權									
State-owned 國有	6	233	2,500	-333	-2.90	-10.00	10.71	71.01	11,500
Collectively-owned 集體	9	51	2,531	39	2.98	6.82	49.96	56.30	1,321
Privately-owned 私有	1	16							
Domestic JVs 聯營								34.12	61
Joint stock 股份制									
Foreign-funded 外資	3	58	2,402	215	2.08	6.62	41.42	68.56	10,347
Overseas Chinese-funded 港澳台資									
By size 規模									
Large 大型									
Medium 中型									
Small 小型	19	108	2,367	-53	-0.89	-2.86	21.99	68.75	5,895
By regional distribution 地區分布									
Central-North 華北	1	68	2,270	90	4.27	14.75	33.38	71.09	2,110
Beijing 北京	1	68	2,270	90	4.27	14.75	33.38	71.09	2,110
Tianjin 天津									
Hebei 河北									
Shanxi 山西									
Inner Mongolia 內蒙									
Northeast 東北									
Liaoning 遼寧									
Jilin 吉林									
Heilongjiang 黑龍江									
Central East 華東	10	107	2,189	5	0.08	0.28	20.50	71.69	6,421
Shanghai 上海									
Jiangsu 江蘇	2	80	1,115	-5	-0.13	-0.20	13.94	36.04	3,940
Zhejiang 浙江	4	45	1,345	38	0.68	3.76	29.72	82.03	5,550
Anhui 安徽									
Fujian 福建	2	50	1,245	-80	-0.97	-1.27	24.90	23.68	8,255
Jiangxi 江西									
Shandong 山東	2	314	5,895	35	0.40	-2.03	18.80	119.58	8,810
Central-South 中南	2	138	5,435	345	6.63	28.51	39.38	76.75	5,205
Henan 河南	2	138	5,435	345	6.63	28.51	39.38	76.75	5,205
Hubei 湖北									
Hunan 湖南									
Guangdong 廣東									
Guangxi 廣西									
Hainan 海南									
Southwest 西南	2	279	3,880	-940	-5.74	-14.89	13.93	61.46	16,385
Chongqing 重慶	0	15	79	39	11.31	99.45	5.41	88.63	345
Sichuan 四川	1	828	11,600	-2,839	-5.80	-15.00	14.01	61.36	48,980
Guizhou 貴州	1								
Yunnan 雲南									
Tibet 西藏									
Northwest 西北	4	19	538	8	1.12	3.30	27.92	65.92	668
Shaanxi 陝西	3	26	717	10	1.12	3.30	27.92	65.92	890
Gansu 甘肅									
Qinghai 青海									
Ningxia 寧夏	1								
Xinjiang 新疆									

4224: Farming, Forestry, Husbandry and Fishery Instruments and Meters
農、林、牧、漁儀器、儀表製造業

Year 年份	Number of firms 企業個數	Rate of change 每年變化 (%)	Number of employees 職工人數 (人)	Rate of change 每年變化 (%)	Total revenue (mil. RMB) 總銷售收入 (百萬元)	Rate of change 每年變化 (%)	Total profit (mil. RMB) 總利潤 (百萬元)	Rate of change 每年變化 (%)
1993	19		2,060		42		1	
1994	21	10.53%	2,898	40.68%	55	30.33%	-2	-218.21%
1995	20	-4.76%	1,812	-37.48%	32	-41.51%	-3	-73.69%
1996	19	-5.00%	2,046	12.91%	45	39.26%	-1	66.41%

3 Major products* 3 種主要產品 *	Output 產量	Sales volume 銷售量	Unit 單位
a) Automobile Instrument & Meter 汽車儀器儀表	205,665	220,061	set 台
b) Livestock Raising Machinery 畜牧機械	1,134	465	set 台

Top 10 firms by revenue (year founded) 收入排名前 10 家企業 (創辦年份)	City 城市	Province 省	Telephone / fax 電話 / 傳真	Number of employees 職工人數	Ownership 產業所有權	Revenue ('000 RMB) 銷售收入 (千元)	Profit ('000 RMB) (rank) 利潤 (千元) (排名)	Total assets ('000 RMB) 總資產 (千元)	Major products 主要產品
Jining Instrument Factory 濟寧儀表廠(1958)	Jining 濟寧市	Shandong 山東省	(0537)2214781 (0537)2214781	288	Collectively-owned 集體	10,931	99(3)	7,689	a
Chengdu Instrument and Meter Factory 成都儀表廠(1972)	Chengdu 成都市	Sichuan 四川省	(028)6666278 (028)6654636	558	State-owned 國有	7,761	-1880(8)	32,773	o
Bao Fengxian Stone Bridge Zhen Electronic Instrument Factory 寶豐縣石橋鎮電子儀表廠(1991)	Pingdingshan 平頂山市	Henan 河南省	(0375)6312056	105	Collectively-owned 集體	7,360	440(1)	1,910	o
Hangzhou Xia Sha Hatching Equipment Factory 杭州下沙孵化設備廠(1991)	Hangzhou 杭州市	Zhejiang 浙江省	(0571)6921734	32	Collectively-owned 集體	3,730	27(5)	8,269	o
Shanghai Si Jing Building & Installing Electric Appliance Factory 上海泗涇建安電器廠(1993)	Shanghai 上海市	Shanghai 上海市	(021)57610656	25	Collectively-owned 集體	3,321	-67(7)	2,221	o
Beijing Yan Jing Mu Ji Co. Instrument and Meter Plant 北京燕京牧機公司儀器儀表廠(1988)	Beijing 北京市	Beijing 北京市	(010)69545329	67	State-owned 國有	2,270	88(4)	2,112	b
Zhangzhou Hua Ying Electron Co. Ltd. 漳州市華穎電子有限公司(1993)	Zhangzhou 漳州市	Fujian 福建省	(0596)2882589 (0596)2889966	26	Overseas Chinese-funded 港澳台資	2,012	157(2)	3,447	o

Top 10 Cities by Production Output 產出排名前 10 位城市	Province 省	Market share 市場份額	Number of firms 企業個數
Jining 濟寧市	Shandong 山東省	27.69%	1
Chengdu 成都市	Sichuan 四川省	19.34%	2
Pingdingshan 平頂山市	Henan 河南省	17.46%	1
Shanghai 上海市	Shanghai 上海市	7.98%	4
Beijing 北京市	Beijing 北京市	7.76%	1
Zhangzhou 漳州市	Fujian 福建省	4.94%	1
Hangzhou 杭州市	Zhejiang 浙江省	4.44%	1
Xi'an 西安市	Shaanxi 陝西省	3.37%	2
Zhoushan 舟山市	Zhejiang 浙江省	2.40%	2
Dezhou 德州市	Shandong 山東省	2.37%	1

10 Major Wholesalers 10 家主要批發商	City 城市	Province 省	Telephone / Fax 電話 / 傳真
Liaoning Automobile Trade Group Corp. 遼寧省汽車貿易集團	Shenyang 瀋陽市	Liaoning 遼寧省	(024)23835494 (024)23838338
China Post and Telecommunication Equipment General Company 中國郵電器材總公司	Beijing 北京市	Beijing 北京市	(010)63523715 (010)63525935
Jiangsu Electromechanical Products General Company 江蘇省機電產品總公司	Nanjing 南京市	Jiangsu 江蘇省	(025)7713642 (025)7711036
Xi Nan Technology Import & Export Company 西南技術進出口公司	Chongqing 重慶市	Chongqing 重慶市	(023)63850185 (023)63850026
Changzhou Economic Technology Industrial Development Zone Tian Ming Trade Company 常州經濟技術產業開發區天明貿易公司	Changzhou 常州市	Jiangsu 江蘇省	(0519)8829882 (0519)8829882
Shanxi Mechanical Equipment Import & Export Company 山西省機械設備進出口公司	Taiyuan 太原市	Shanxi 山西省	(0351)4040713 (0351)4043981
Ningbo Five Mining Machinery Import & Export Company 寧波市五礦機械進出口公司	Ningbo 寧波市	Zhejiang 浙江省	(0574)7311255 (0574)7320322
Tianjin Jin Huan Electromechanical Complete Sets of Equipment Factory 天津市津環機電成套設備廠	Tianjin 天津市	Tianjin 天津市	(022)26371628
Yunnan Machinery Import & Export Company 雲南省機械進出口公司	Kunming 昆明市	Yunnan 雲南省	(0871)3164879 (0871)3136829
Tianjin Da Qiu Zhuang Yi Yuan Trade Center 天津市大丘莊億源商貿中心	Tianjin 天津市	Tianjin 天津市	(022)28899478 (022)28899046

*Also include sales by firms outside this industry.包括本行業以外廠家的銷售。"o" stands for "others". "o" 代表"其他產品"。

4225: Geology, Prospecting, Mining, and Earthquake Detection Instruments
地質勘探、鑽採、地震專用儀器製造業

The industry accounts for 0.009% of the total revenue of China's industrial sector in 1996. The revenue growth rate of the industry is 6.2% from 1995, as compared to the growth rate of China's industrial sector, 9.51%. The rate of return on asset is -1.10%. 67.21% of all firms in the industry made a profit while 29.09% had negative returns. The top province in terms of the industry's revenue is Shaanxi, accounting for 42.41% of the total revenue.
本行業在1996年佔全行業總產值0.009%，行業年增長率為6.2%（全國工業年增長率9.51%）。行業的資產回報率-1.10%，67.21%的企業盈利，29.09%的企業虧損。銷售收入最高的省份為陝西省，佔本行業的42.41%。

	Total number of firms 企業總數	Total number of employees 職工總數	Total revenue (mil. RMB) 總銷售收入（百萬元）	Total profit (mil. RMB) 總利潤（百萬元）	Return on assets 資產利潤率 (%)	Return on equity 權益利潤率 (%)	Labour productivity ('000 RMB / worker) 勞動生產率（千元/人）	Debts / assets 資產負債率 (%)	Total assets (mil. RMB) 總資產（百萬元）
Industry Overall 行業總體	67	17,474	547	-24	-1.10	-4.96	31.30	77.89	2,211

	Number of firms 企業個數	Average number of employees 平均職工人數	Average revenue ('000 RMB) 平均銷售收入（千元）	Average profit ('000 RMB) 平均利潤（千元）	Return on assets 資產利潤率 (%)	Return on equity 權益利潤率 (%)	Labour productivity ('000 RMB / worker) 勞動生產率（千元/人）	Average debts / assets 平均資產負債率(%)	Average Total assets ('000 RMB) 平均總資產（千元）
By ownership 產業所有權									
State-owned 國有	13	1,109	31,231	-2,077	-1.39	-7.71	28.16	81.97	149,308
Collectively-owned 集體	44	66	2,113	18	0.40	0.96	31.93	57.71	4,512
Privately-owned 私有									
Domestic JVs 聯營	1	48	3,685	276	2.85	4.69	76.77	39.24	9,705
Joint stock 股份制									
Foreign-funded 外資	6	14	7,294	319	3.12	3.90	514.86	20.08	10,239
Overseas Chinese-funded 港澳台資	1	3							
By size 規模									
Large 大型	2	3,247	128,874	-3,016	-0.45	-3.13	39.70	85.71	674,451
Medium 中型	6	735	10,152	-1,822	-4.08	-15.20	13.81	73.18	44,673
Small 小型	59	111	3,870	-119	-1.18	-3.14	34.83	62.24	10,077
By regional distribution 地區分布									
Central-North 華北	13	314	9,175	-658	-1.59	-4.67	29.21	65.91	41,307
Beijing 北京	3	4	233	23	6.25	16.28	53.85	61.61	373
Tianjin 天津	5	133	1,598	-640	-11.55	-77.11	12.00	85.02	5,540
Hebei 河北	3	1,097	36,737	-1,807	-1.07	-3.05	33.50	64.91	168,770
Shanxi 山西	2	57	190				3.33	56.45	930
Inner Mongolia 內蒙									
Northeast 東北	24	109	3,730	-216	-2.52	-17.76	34.10	85.83	8,586
Liaoning 遼寧	13	163	3,255	-910	-7.25	-469.44	20.02	98.46	12,560
Jilin 吉林									
Heilongjiang 黑龍江	11	47	4,291	604	15.52	24.87	92.19	37.63	3,890
Central East 華東	16	164	5,428	-138	-1.56	-10.48	33.17	85.15	8,839
Shanghai 上海	2	495	14,320	-1,100	-3.44	94.42	28.93	103.64	31,980
Jiangsu 江蘇	5	219	5,188	-256	-3.23	-9.20	23.73	64.89	7,924
Zhejiang 浙江	8	67	4,033	160	3.38	13.59	60.30	75.11	4,730
Anhui 安徽									
Fujian 福建									
Jiangxi 江西									
Shandong 山東	1								
Central-South 中南	6	43	825	-57	-4.03	-6.55	19.11	38.67	1,405
Henan 河南	1	31	460	10	1.92	5.88	14.84	67.31	520
Hubei 湖北	1								
Hunan 湖南	1								
Guangdong 廣東	2	63	1,540	-220	-11.03	-17.05	24.64	35.59	1,995
Guangxi 廣西	1	103	1,410	90	2.30	3.69	13.69	38.01	3,920
Hainan 海南									
Southwest 西南	3	271	4,867	-493	-3.91	-9.51	17.94	58.89	12,623
Chongqing 重慶	2	336	6,008	-650	-3.99	-9.55	17.87	58.21	16,283
Sichuan 四川	1	75	1,445	-23	-1.37	-6.56	19.18	79.09	1,643
Guizhou 貴州									
Yunnan 雲南									
Tibet 西藏									
Northwest 西北	5	1,415	46,396	-1,298	-0.51	-2.77	32.79	81.66	255,956
Shaanxi 陝西	5	1,415	46,396	-1,298	-0.51	-2.77	32.79	81.66	255,956
Gansu 甘肅									
Qinghai 青海									
Ningxia 寧夏									
Xinjiang 新疆									

4225: Geology, Prospecting, Mining, and Earthquake Detection Instruments
地質勘探、鑽採、地震專用儀器製造業

Year 年份	Number of firms 企業個數	Rate of change 每年變化 (%)	Number of employees 職工人數 (人)	Rate of change 每年變化 (%)	Total revenue (mil. RMB) 總銷售收入 (百萬元)	Rate of change 每年變化 (%)	Total profit (mil. RMB) 總利潤 (百萬元)	Rate of change 每年變化 (%)
1993	52		17,202		664		-30	
1994	59	13.46%	13,767	-19.97%	494	-25.61%	-35	-16.07%
1995	71	20.34%	19,620	42.51%	515	4.32%	-37	-5.35%
1996	67	-5.63%	17,474	-10.94%	547	6.18%	-24	35.27%

3 Major products* 3種主要產品*	Output 產量	Sales volume 銷售量	Unit 單位
a) Geology Prospecting, Drilling & Earthquake Special Instrument & Meter 地質勘探、鑽採、地震專用儀器	15,332	15,485	set 台

Top 10 firms by revenue (year founded) 收入排名前10家企業 (創辦年份)	City 城市	Province 省	Telephone / fax 電話 / 傳真	Number of employees 職工人數	Ownership 產業所有權	Revenue ('000 RMB) 銷售收入 (千元)	Profit ('000 RMB) (rank) 利潤 (千元) (排名)	Total assets ('000 RMB) 總資產 (千元)	Major products 主要產品
Xi'an Petroleum Exploration Instrument General Factory 西安石油勘探儀器總廠(1956)	Xi'an 西安市	Shaanxi 陝西省	(029)5265999 (029)5261260	5,420	State-owned 國有	198,830	1210(3)	1,133,470	o
Petroleum Geophysics Prospecting Bureau 石油地球物理勘探局(1963)	Baoding 保定市	Hebei 河北省		3,273	State-owned 國有	109,775	-5320(25)	504,879	o
Fushun Coal Mine Safety Instrument General Factory 撫順煤礦安全儀器廠(1953)	Fushun 撫順市	Liaoning 遼寧省	(0413)7672051 (0413)7676559	1,615	State-owned 國有	33,730	-8990(27)	128,890	o
Daqing Mida Oil Production Equipments Co. Ltd. 大慶美達採油設備有限公司(1994)	Daqing 大慶市	Heilongjiang 黑龍江省	(0459)5872834 (0459)5872870	20	Foreign-funded 外資	29,524	6159(1)	2,382	o
Xi'an Li Da Photoelectric Instrument Co. Ltd. 西安利達光電儀器有限公司(1969)	Xi'an 西安市	Shaanxi 陝西省	(029)3228499 (029)3228499	282	Foreign-funded 外資	24,278	2755(2)	105,302	o
Shanghai Petroleum Instrument Factory 上海石油儀器廠(1959)	Shanghai 上海市	Shanghai 上海市	(021)62506100 (021)62506434	559	State-owned 國有	20,766	3(13)	44,320	a
Chongqing Geological Instruments Factory 重慶地質儀器廠(1969)	Chongqing 重慶市	Chongqing 重慶市	(023)65361424 (023)63361450	753	State-owned 國有	14,602	-1477(21)	37,871	a
Shangyu Exploration Survey Construction Equipment Factory 上虞市勘測土工儀器廠(1953)	Shaoxing 紹興市	Zhejiang 浙江省	(0575)2041785	107	Collectively-owned 集體	10,164	215(7)	7,396	o
Weinan Coal Mine Special Purpose Equipment Factory 渭南煤礦專用設備廠(1970)	Weinan 渭南市	Shaanxi 陝西省	(0913)2012851 (0913)2012850	1,327	State-owned 國有	8,610	-6630(26)	33,450	o
Ningbo Geology Instrument Factory 寧波地質儀器廠(1971)	Ningbo 寧波市	Zhejiang 浙江省	(0574)8452460	196	Collectively-owned 集體	8,016	573(4)	20,008	o

Top 10 Cities by Production Output 產出排名前10位城市	Province 省	Market share 市場份額	Number of firms 企業個數
Xi'an 西安市	Shaanxi 陝西省	52.17%	5
Fushun 撫順市	Liaoning 遼寧省	7.87%	1
Shanghai 上海市	Shanghai 上海市	7.86%	10
Chongqing 重慶市	Chongqing 重慶市	5.17%	2
Nanjing 南京市	Jiangsu 江蘇省	4.41%	4
Weinan 渭南市	Shaanxi 陝西省	2.46%	1
Guangzhou 廣州市	Guangdong 廣東省	2.31%	4
Shaoxing 紹興市	Zhejiang 浙江省	2.20%	2
Nantong 南通市	Jiangsu 江蘇省	2.10%	3
Ningbo 寧波市	Zhejiang 浙江省	1.97%	3

10 Major Wholesalers 10家主要批發商	City 城市	Province 省	Telephone / Fax 電話 / 傳真
Liaoning Automobile Trade Group Corp. 遼寧省汽車貿易集團	Shenyang 瀋陽市	Liaoning 遼寧省	(024)23835494 (024)23838338
China Post and Telecommunication Equipment General Company 中國郵電器材總公司	Beijing 北京市	Beijing 北京市	(010)63523715 (010)63525935
Jiangsu Electromechanical Products General Company 江蘇省機電產品總公司	Nanjing 南京市	Jiangsu 江蘇省	(025)7713642 (025)7711036
Xi Nan Technology Import & Export Company 西南技術進出口公司	Chongqing 重慶市	Chongqing 重慶市	(023)63850185 (023)63850026
Changzhou Economic Technology Industrial Development Zone Tian Ming Trade Company 常州經濟技術產業開發區天明貿易公司	Changzhou 常州市	Jiangsu 江蘇省	(0519)8829882 (0519)8829882
Shanxi Mechanical Equipment Import & Export Company 山西省機械設備進出口公司	Taiyuan 太原市	Shanxi 山西省	(0351)4040713 (0351)4043981
Ningbo Five Mining Machinery Import & Export Company 寧波市五礦機械進出口公司	Ningbo 寧波市	Zhejiang 浙江省	(0574)7311255 (0574)7320322
Tianjin Jin Huan Electromechanical Complete Sets of Equipment Factory 天津市津環機電成套設備廠	Tianjin 天津市	Tianjin 天津市	(022)26371628
Yunnan Machinery Import & Export Company 雲南省機械進出口公司	Kunming 昆明市	Yunnan 雲南省	(0871)3164879 (0871)3136829
Tianjin Da Qiu Zhuang Yi Yuan Trade Center 天津市大丘莊億源商貿中心	Tianjin 天津市	Tianjin 天津市	(022)28899478 (022)28899046

*Also include sales by firms outside this industry.包括本行業以外廠家的銷售。"o" stands for "others". "o" 代表 "其他產品"。

4226: Meteorology, Oceanography, Hydrology and Astronomy Measuring Instruments 氣象、海洋、水文、天文測量儀器製造業

The industry accounts for 0.001% of the total revenue of China's industrial sector in 1996. The revenue growth rate of the industry is 34.2% from 1995, as compared to the growth rate of China's industrial sector, 9.51%. The rate of return on asset is -0.35%. 75.00% of all firms in the industry made a profit while 25.00% had negative returns. The top province in terms of the industry's revenue is Shanghai, accounting for 32.75% of the total revenue.
本行業在1996年佔全行業總產值0.001%，行業年增長率為34.2%（全國工業年增長率9.51%）。行業的資產回報率-0.35%，75.00%的企業盈利，25.00%的企業虧損。銷售收入最高的省份為上海市，佔本行業的32.75%。

	Total number of firms 企業總數	Total number of employees 職工總數	Total revenue (mil. RMB) 總銷售收入（百萬元）	Total profit (mil. RMB) 總利潤（百萬元）	Return on assets 資產利潤率 (%)	Return on equity 權益利潤率 (%)	Labour productivity ('000 RMB / worker) 勞動生產率（千元/人）	Debts / assets 資產負債率 (%)	Total assets (mil. RMB) 總資產（百萬元）
Industry Overall 行業總體	32	3,562	71	-1	-0.35	-0.88	19.93	60.01	168

	Number of firms 企業個數	Average number of employees 平均職工人數	Average revenue ('000 RMB) 平均銷售收入（千元）	Average profit ('000 RMB) 平均利潤（千元）	Return on assets 資產利潤率 (%)	Return on equity 權益利潤率 (%)	Labour productivity ('000 RMB / worker) 勞動生產率（千元/人）	Average debts / assets 平均資產負債率(%)	Average Total assets ('000 RMB) 平均總資產（千元）
By ownership 產業所有權									
State-owned 國有	11	293	5,545	-91	-0.67	-1.69	18.95	60.67	13,636
Collectively-owned 集體	14	17	429				25.36	68.38	694
Privately-owned 私有									
Domestic JVs 聯營	2	16	664				42.84	64.80	1,376
Joint stock 股份制									
Foreign-funded 外資	2	9	890				98.89	16.88	1,434
Overseas Chinese-funded 港澳台資	2	29	441				15.46	40.81	1,328
By size 規模									
Large 大型									
Medium 中型	1	806	9,517	-40	-0.06	-0.11	11.81	43.60	66,511
Small 小型	30	91	2,049	-32	-0.95	-3.26	22.45	70.94	3,382
By regional distribution 地區分布									
Central-North 華北	14	83	1,176	-4	-0.12	-0.30	14.17	61.14	3,671
Beijing 北京	5								
Tianjin 天津	5	131	1,466	-50	-0.89	-3.87	11.16	76.88	5,598
Hebei 河北	1	48	580	100	9.09	19.23	12.08	52.73	1,100
Shanxi 山西	2	229	4,275	45	0.40	0.69	18.71	41.79	11,150
Inner Mongolia 內蒙	1								
Northeast 東北	4	203	2,393	-963	-6.96	-14.34	11.81	51.44	13,823
Liaoning 遼寧	2	5	175	5	6.67	20.00	35.00	66.67	75
Jilin 吉林	2	400	4,610	-1,930	-7.00	-14.40	11.53	51.40	27,570
Heilongjiang 黑龍江									
Central East 華東	14	114	3,212	236	5.36	16.11	28.28	66.72	4,413
Shanghai 上海	4	230	5,813	538	9.18	75.44	25.30	87.84	5,858
Jiangsu 江蘇	2	26	2,890	395	8.76	17.52	111.15	50.00	4,510
Zhejiang 浙江									
Anhui 安徽									
Fujian 福建	5	18	434	36	10.40	15.65	24.38	33.53	346
Jiangxi 江西									
Shandong 山東	3	177	4,590	63	0.69	1.58	25.98	56.34	9,200
Central-South 中南									
Henan 河南									
Hubei 湖北									
Hunan 湖南									
Guangdong 廣東									
Guangxi 廣西									
Hainan 海南									
Southwest 西南									
Chongqing 重慶									
Sichuan 四川									
Guizhou 貴州									
Yunnan 雲南									
Tibet 西藏									
Northwest 西北									
Shaanxi 陝西									
Gansu 甘肅									
Qinghai 青海									
Ningxia 寧夏									
Xinjiang 新疆									

4226: Meteorology, Oceanography, Hydrology and Astronomy Measuring Instruments
氣象、海洋、水文、天文測量儀器製造業

Year 年份	Number of firms 企業個數	Rate of change 每年變化 (%)	Number of employees 職工人數 (人)	Rate of change 每年變化 (%)	Total revenue (mil. RMB) 總銷售收入 (百萬元)	Rate of change 每年變化 (%)	Total profit (mil. RMB) 總利潤 (百萬元)	Rate of change 每年變化 (%)
1993	24		6,582		73		1	
1994	38	58.33%	5,771	-12.32%	91	23.57%	-1	-187.86%
1995	28	-26.32%	3,566	-38.21%	53	-41.72%	0	84.81%
1996	32	14.29%	3,562	-0.11%	71	34.22%	-1	-400.00%

3 Major products* 3 種主要產品 *	Output 產量	Sales volume 銷售量	Unit 單位
a) Meteorological Instrument 氣象儀器	199,479	191,500	set 台

Top 10 firms by revenue (year founded) 收入排名前 10 家企業 (創辦年份)	City 城市	Province 省	Telephone / fax 電話 / 傳真	Number of employees 職工人數	Ownership 產業所有權	Revenue ('000 RMB) 銷售收入 (千元)	Profit ('000 RMB) (rank) 利潤 (千元) (排名)	Total assets ('000 RMB) 總資產 (千元)	Major products 主要產品
Shanghai No.23 Radio Factory 上海無線電二十三廠(1956)	Shanghai 上海市	Shanghai 上海市	(021)65439104 (021)65438995	443	State-owned 國有	15,948	2175(1)	13,945	a
Shandong Lu Nan Hua Industrial Instrument Factory 山東魯南化工儀器廠(1969)	Zaozhuang 棗莊市	Shandong 山東省	(0632)5583127 (0632)5581056	486	State-owned 國有	12,642	128(4)	22,535	a
Changchun Meteorological Phenomena Instrument Plant 長春氣象儀器廠(1955)	Changchun 長春市	Jilin 吉林省	(0431)5683437 (0431)5684084	784	State-owned 國有	9,184	-3862(9)	55,100	a
Taiyuan No.1 Radio Factory 太原無線電一廠(1965)	Taiyuan 太原市	Shanxi 山西省	(0351)7044984	437	State-owned 國有	8,551	89(5)	22,296	a
Shanghai Meteorological Phenomena Instrument Plant 上海氣象儀器廠(1949)	Shanghai 上海市	Shanghai 上海市	(021)56636281 (021)56636730	156	State-owned 國有	6,361	21(6)	6,562	a
Tianjin Meteorological Phenomena Ocean Instrument Plant 天津市氣象海洋儀器廠(1957)	Tianjin 天津市	Tianjin 天津市	(022)27373161 (022)27374600	468	State-owned 國有	5,416	-25(7)	15,583	a
Changzhou Huada Photoelectric Instrument Factory 常州華達光電儀器廠(1991)	Changzhou 常州市	Jiangsu 江蘇省	(0519)3276604	39	Domestic JVs 聯營	2,966	131(3)	3,399	o
Wuxi Haiying-calter Electronic Equipment Co. Ltd. 無錫海鷹加科電子設備有限公司(1994)	Wuxi 無錫市	Jiangsu 江蘇省	(0510)5884899 (0510)5801948	13	Foreign-funded 外資	2,815	663(2)	5,619	o

Top 10 Cities by Production Output 產出排名前 10 位城市	Province 省	Market share 市場份額	Number of firms 企業個數
Shanghai 上海市	Shanghai 上海市	37.28%	4
Zaozhuang 棗莊市	Shandong 山東省	14.38%	1
Tianjin 天津市	Tianjin 天津市	10.02%	5
Nanjing 南京市	Jiangsu 江蘇省	9.76%	4
Taiyuan 太原市	Shanxi 山西省	9.44%	1
Changchun 長春市	Jilin 吉林省	8.86%	1
Xi'an 西安市	Shaanxi 陝西省	2.40%	2
Beijing 北京市	Beijing 北京市	1.73%	3
Fuzhou 福州市	Fujian 福建省	1.65%	3
Wuxi 無錫市	Jiangsu 江蘇省	1.35%	2

10 Major Wholesalers 10 家主要批發商	City 城市	Province 省	Telephone / Fax 電話 / 傳真
Liaoning Automobile Trade Group Corp. 遼寧省汽車貿易集團	Shenyang 瀋陽市	Liaoning 遼寧省	(024)23835494 (024)23838338
China Post and Telecommunication Equipment General Company 中國郵電器材總公司	Beijing 北京市	Beijing 北京市	(010)63523715 (010)63525935
Jiangsu Electromechanical Products General Company 江蘇省機電產品總公司	Nanjing 南京市	Jiangsu 江蘇省	(025)7713642 (025)7711036
Xi Nan Technology Import & Export Company 西南技術進出口公司	Chongqing 重慶市	Chongqing 重慶市	(023)63850185 (023)63850026
Changzhou Economic Technology Industrial Development Zone Tian Ming Trade Company 常州經濟技術產業開發區天明貿易公司	Changzhou 常州市	Jiangsu 江蘇省	(0519)8829882 (0519)8829882
Shanxi Mechanical Equipment Import & Export Company 山西省機械設備進出口公司	Taiyuan 太原市	Shanxi 山西省	(0351)4040713 (0351)4043981
Ningbo Five Mining Machinery Import & Export Company 寧波市五礦機械進出口公司	Ningbo 寧波市	Zhejiang 浙江省	(0574)7311255 (0574)7320322
Tianjin Jin Huan Electromechanical Complete Sets of Equipment Factory 天津市津環機電成套設備廠	Tianjin 天津市	Tianjin 天津市	(022)26371628
Yunnan Machinery Import & Export Company 雲南省機械進出口公司	Kunming 昆明市	Yunnan 雲南省	(0871)3164879 (0871)3136829
Tianjin Da Qiu Zhuang Yi Yuan Trade Center 天津市大丘莊億源商貿中心	Tianjin 天津市	Tianjin 天津市	(022)28899478 (022)28899046

*Also include sales by firms outside this industry.包括本行業以外廠家的銷售。"o" stands for "others". "o" 代表"其他產品"。

4227: Instructional Instruments 教學儀器製造業

The industry accounts for 0.007% of the total revenue of China's industrial sector in 1996. The revenue growth rate of the industry is 18.9% from 1995, as compared to the growth rate of China's industrial sector, 9.51%. The rate of return on asset is 4.69%. 84.27% of all firms in the industry made a profit while 13.98% had negative returns. The top province in terms of the industry's revenue is Zhejiang, accounting for 20.39% of the total revenue.
本行業在1996年佔全行業總產值0.007%，行業年增長率為18.9%（全國工業年增長率9.51%）。行業的資產回報率4.69%，84.27%的企業盈利，13.98%的企業虧損。銷售收入最高的省份為浙江省，佔本行業的20.39%。

	Total number of firms 企業總數	Total number of employees 職工總數	Total revenue (mil. RMB) 總銷售收入（百萬元）	Total profit (mil. RMB) 總利潤（百萬元）	Return on assets 資產利潤率 (%)	Return on equity 權益利潤率 (%)	Labour productivity ('000 RMB / worker) 勞動生產率（千元／人）	Debts / assets 資產負債率 (%)	Total assets (mil. RMB) 總資產（百萬元）
Industry Overall 行業總體	206	12,078	434	40	4.69	11.26	35.93	58.32	853

	Number of firms 企業個數	Average number of employees 平均職工人數	Average revenue ('000 RMB) 平均銷售收入（千元）	Average profit ('000 RMB) 平均利潤（千元）	Return on assets 資產利潤率 (%)	Return on equity 權益利潤率 (%)	Labour productivity ('000 RMB / worker) 勞動生產率（千元／人）	Average debts / assets 平均資產負債率(%)	Average Total assets ('000 RMB) 平均總資產（千元）
By ownership 產業所有權									
State-owned 國有	67	93	2,731	224	2.95	7.28	29.51	59.53	7,597
Collectively-owned 集體	131	42	1,735	179	7.60	16.99	40.85	55.27	2,356
Privately-owned 私有									
Domestic JVs 聯營									
Joint stock 股份制	2	99	7,345	380	6.49	16.38	74.19	60.40	5,865
Foreign-funded 外資	2	22	737	59	3.80	6.47	34.27	41.23	1,553
Overseas Chinese-funded 港澳台資	4	51	1,853	166	3.26	12.25	36.69	73.36	5,095
By size 規模									
Large 大型									
Medium 中型	3	715	8,492	-5,497	-7.79	-32.13	11.88	75.77	70,592
Small 小型	201	50	2,032	281	8.81	18.55	41.03	52.48	3,189
By regional distribution 地區分布									
Central-North 華北	24	25	1,090	113	8.13	16.09	43.98	49.51	1,395
Beijing 北京	11	9	435	33	4.68	14.06	46.86	66.88	700
Tianjin 天津	4	32	1,993	515	25.53	39.16	62.76	34.82	2,018
Hebei 河北	5	20	684	48	6.23	12.24	34.55	48.83	770
Shanxi 山西	2	121	4,760	20	0.33	0.68	39.50	51.40	6,090
Inner Mongolia 內蒙	2	13	240	10	1.20	1.67	18.46	28.14	835
Northeast 東北	16	80	1,531	-265	-3.71	-7.78	19.20	52.24	7,136
Liaoning 遼寧	9	122	2,552	-474	-3.86	-8.23	20.84	53.10	12,292
Jilin 吉林	4	24	65	5	1.09	1.35	2.71	19.67	458
Heilongjiang 黑龍江	3	26	423	3	0.58	0.85	16.28	31.40	573
Central East 華東	107	52	2,571	421	12.03	25.83	49.25	53.41	3,496
Shanghai 上海	18	59	3,728	1,144	22.66	41.73	63.31	45.72	5,051
Jiangsu 江蘇	12	54	2,478	105	3.13	8.79	46.24	64.39	3,356
Zhejiang 浙江	40	40	2,212	155	7.79	18.72	55.47	58.36	1,992
Anhui 安徽	7	60	1,087	184	6.44	23.69	18.25	73.04	2,861
Fujian 福建	14	52	2,329	397	11.50	20.58	45.03	44.11	3,452
Jiangxi 江西	11	17	608	58	8.18	18.03	36.16	54.60	711
Shandong 山東	5	192	8,566	1,890	10.86	22.81	44.57	52.37	17,400
Central-South 中南	35	87	2,479	89	1.59	4.67	28.45	65.96	5,586
Henan 河南	8	146	2,723	31	0.27	1.41	18.71	80.66	11,428
Hubei 湖北	8	147	5,105	348	4.25	8.48	34.82	49.89	8,174
Hunan 湖南	15	32	821	13	0.91	1.71	25.51	46.98	1,470
Guangdong 廣東	4	58	2,955	-30	-0.72	-2.71	51.39	73.45	4,163
Guangxi 廣西									
Hainan 海南									
Southwest 西南	15	31	804	21	1.23	1.76	25.61	30.03	1,676
Chongqing 重慶	7	26	710	26	1.79	2.59	27.76	30.71	1,447
Sichuan 四川	6	40	937	19	0.94	1.35	23.59	30.52	2,074
Guizhou 貴州	1								
Yunnan 雲南	1	56	1,490	10	0.38	0.51	26.61	25.10	2,630
Tibet 西藏									
Northwest 西北	9	122	1,026	-764	-6.24	-27.00	8.38	76.91	12,259
Shaanxi 陝西	6	82	665	-22	-0.68	-1.35	8.08	49.77	3,195
Gansu 甘肅	3	202	1,747	-2,250	-7.40	-42.59	8.63	82.61	30,387
Qinghai 青海									
Ningxia 寧夏									
Xinjiang 新疆									

4227: Instructional Instruments 教學儀器製造業

Year 年份	Number of firms 企業個數	Rate of change 每年變化 (%)	Number of employees 職工人數 (人)	Rate of change 每年變化 (%)	Total revenue (mil. RMB) 總銷售收入 (百萬元)	Rate of change 每年變化 (%)	Total profit (mil. RMB) 總利潤 (百萬元)	Rate of change 每年變化 (%)
1993	223		16,492		409		30	
1994	196	-12.11%	11,629	-29.49%	311	-23.76%	16	-46.48%
1995	195	-0.51%	10,775	-7.34%	365	17.21%	29	82.71%
1996	206	5.64%	12,078	12.09%	434	18.87%	40	37.57%

3 Major products* 3 種主要產品 *	Output 產量	Sales volume 銷售量	Unit 單位
a) Audio-visual Education Programme Equipment 電教設備	65,995	62,696	set 台

Top 10 firms by revenue (year founded) 收入排名前 10 家企業 (創辦年份)	City 城市	Province 省	Telephone / fax 電話 / 傳真	Number of employees 職工人數	Ownership 產業所有權	Revenue ('000 RMB) 銷售收入 (千元)	Profit ('000 RMB) (rank) 利潤 (千元) (排名)	Total assets ('000 RMB) 總資產 (千元)	Major products 主要產品
Yanggu Gao Miao Wang Xiang Scientific Instrument Factory 陽谷縣高廟王鄉科儀廠(1992)	Liaocheng 聊城市	Shandong 山東省	(0635)6868388 (0635)6868389	696	Collectively-owned 集體	27,248	6611(2)	71,397	o
Shanghai Putuo Teaching Aid Factory 上海普陀教具廠(1971)	Shanghai 上海市	Shanghai 上海市	(021)62573150 (021)62579520	299	State-owned 國有	19,749	12006(1)	31,411	a
Zhejiang University Education Instrument Middle Test Factory 浙江大學教學儀器中試廠(1983)	Hangzhou 杭州市	Zhejiang 浙江省	(0571)7993186 (0571)7993716	150	Collectively-owned 集體	16,479	1528(7)	13,040	o
Rongcheng Teaching Instrument School-run Enterprise Management Station 榮成市教委儀器站(1972)	Weihai 威海市	Shandong 山東省	(0896)8900231 (0896)8900231	240	State-owned 國有	15,020	2800(4)	14,580	o
Cixi Science & Education Instrument Factory 慈溪市科教儀器廠(1984)	Ningbo 寧波市	Zhejiang 浙江省	(0574)3299211	70	Collectively-owned 集體	12,531	420(22)	6,023	o
Shanghai Da Tuan Science & Education Instrument Factory 上海大團科教儀器廠(1996)	Shanghai 上海市	Shanghai 上海市	(021)58082288	140	Collectively-owned 集體	11,430	465(20)	10,917	a
Hua Dong Normal University Science & Education Instrument Plant 華東師範大學科教儀器廠(1958)	Shanghai 上海市	Shanghai 上海市	(021)62570664 (021)62570590	216	State-owned 國有	10,603	2217(5)	19,323	o
Quanzhou Radio No.5 Factory 泉州市無線電五廠(1973)	Quanzhou 泉州市	Fujian 福建省	(0595)2455391 (0595)2456989	93	Collectively-owned 集體	10,052	393(23)	8,456	a
Shenyang Education Instrument Plant 瀋陽教學儀器廠(1951)	Shenyang 瀋陽市	Liaoning 遼寧省	(024)24842554	795	State-owned 國有	9,454	-5411(56)	75,553	o
Shanxi Education Instrument Factory 山西省教學儀器廠(1975)	Yuci 榆次市	Shanxi 山西省	(0354)6225358 (0354)6225340	229	State-owned 國有	9,416	40(46)	11,880	o

Top 10 Cities by Production Output 產出排名前 10 位城市	Province 省	Market share 市場份額	Number of firms 企業個數
Shanghai 上海市	Shanghai 上海市	21.02%	20
Ningbo 寧波市	Zhejiang 浙江省	7.62%	7
Hangzhou 杭州市	Zhejiang 浙江省	5.38%	13
Shenzhen 深圳市	Guangdong 廣東省	4.56%	2
Xi'an 西安市	Shaanxi 陝西省	4.15%	8
Zhengzhou 鄭州市	Henan 河南省	3.83%	3
Tongling 銅陵市	Anhui 安徽省	3.76%	1
Jiaxing 嘉興市	Zhejiang 浙江省	3.13%	6
Suizhou 隨州市	Hubei 湖北省	2.74%	2
Shenyang 瀋陽市	Liaoning 遼寧省	2.73%	5

10 Major Wholesalers 10 家主要批發商	City 城市	Province 省	Telephone / Fax 電話 / 傳真
Shandong Stationary & Sporting Goods Import & Export Company 山東省文教體育用品進出口公司	Qingdao 青島市	Shandong 山東省	(0532)2826827 (0532)3831971
Henan Printing Goods & Materials General Company 河南省印刷物資總公司	Zhengzhou 鄭州市	Henan 河南省	(0371)5967060 (0371)5947912
China Packing Import & Export Singbo Company 中國包裝進出口寧波公司	Ningbo 寧波市	Zhejiang 浙江省	(0574)7367512 (0574)7361096
Tianjin Stationary & Sporting Goods Import & Export Company 天津文教體育用品進出口公司	Tianjin 天津市	Tianjin 天津市	(022)23112048 (022)23112054
China Packing Import & Export Liaoning Company 中國包裝進出口遼寧公司	Dalian 大連市	Liaoning 遼寧省	(0411)4687657 (0411)4687644
Hunan Printing Goods & Materials General Company 湖南省印刷物資總公司	Changsha 長沙市	Hunan 湖南省	(0731)4444618 (0731)4446936
Guangzhou Stationery Co. 廣州市文化用品公司	Guangzhou 廣州市	Guangdong 廣東省	(020)81889089 (020)81861964
Ka Xi Ou Electron (Shenzhen) Co. Ltd. 卡西歐電子(深圳)有限公司	Shenzhen 深圳市	Guangdong 廣東省	(0755)3590620 (0755)3590565
Changsha Keven Group Co. 長沙市科文集團公司	Changsha 長沙市	Hunan 湖南省	(0731)4444108
Hunan Firecrackers Fireworks Import & Export Company 湖南省鞭炮煙花進出口公司	Changsha 長沙市	Hunan 湖南省	(0731)4439580

*Also include sales by firms outside this industry.包括本行業以外廠家的銷售。"o" stands for "others". "o" 代表"其他產品"。

4230: Electric Measuring Instruments 電子測量儀器製造業

The industry accounts for 0.038% of the total revenue of China's industrial sector in 1996. The revenue growth rate of the industry is 23.2% from 1995, as compared to the growth rate of China's industrial sector, 9.51%. The rate of return on asset is 2.41%. 58.01% of all firms in the industry made a profit while 36.05% had negative returns. The top province in terms of the industry's revenue is Beijing, accounting for 36.11% of the total revenue.
本行業在1996年佔全行業總產值0.038%，行業年增長率為23.2%（全國工業年增長率9.51%）。行業的資產回報率2.41%，58.01%的企業盈利，36.05%的企業虧損。銷售收入最高的省份為北京市，佔本行業的36.11%。

	Total number of firms 企業總數	Total number of employees 職工總數	Total revenue (mil. RMB) 總銷售收入（百萬元）	Total profit (mil. RMB) 總利潤（百萬元）	Return on assets 資產利潤率 (%)	Return on equity 權益利潤率 (%)	Labour productivity ('000 RMB / worker) 勞動生產率（千元/人）	Debts / assets 資產負債率 (%)	Total assets (mil. RMB) 總資產（百萬元）
Industry Overall 行業總體	268	45,844	2,187	96	2.41	7.98	47.71	69.77	3,966

	Number of firms 企業個數	Average number of employees 平均職工人數	Average revenue ('000 RMB) 平均銷售收入（千元）	Average profit ('000 RMB) 平均利潤（千元）	Return on assets 資產利潤率 (%)	Return on equity 權益利潤率 (%)	Labour productivity ('000 RMB / worker) 勞動生產率（千元/人）	Average debts / assets 平均資產負債率(%)	Average Total assets ('000 RMB) 平均總資產（千元）
By ownership 產業所有權									
State-owned 國有	98	319	6,020	-643	-3.04	-21.21	18.85	85.67	21,153
Collectively-owned 集體	117	87	7,108	69	0.92	2.54	81.40	63.67	7,447
Privately-owned 私有	4	58	7,298	377	4.50	8.43	126.37	46.66	8,386
Domestic JVs 聯營	3	171	5,708	27	0.19	0.36	33.38	48.37	14,670
Joint stock 股份制	6	437	54,349	16,454	20.40	33.64	124.27	39.35	80,644
Foreign-funded 外資	21	40	12,078	1,451	9.49	17.85	303.40	46.86	15,294
Overseas Chinese-funded 港澳台資	17	76	8,206	1,189	14.62	25.07	107.31	41.68	8,131
By size 規模									
Large 大型	4	1,537	95,839	-50,740	-26.15	-61.34	62.34	57.38	194,066
Medium 中型	26	726	20,131	17,826	29.79	145.64	27.75	79.54	59,831
Small 小型	232	91	5,368	-686	-9.90	-29.26	59.07	66.16	6,923
By regional distribution 地區分布									
Central-North 華北	69	141	12,571	1,849	9.85	24.23	89.33	59.36	18,775
Beijing 北京	40	128	19,745	3,129	12.77	28.64	153.93	55.40	24,497
Tianjin 天津	19	142	2,805	175	1.57	5.42	19.79	70.99	11,108
Hebei 河北	6	181	2,592	-152	-1.52	-7.56	14.33	79.85	9,948
Shanxi 山西	3	257	2,837				11.04	63.70	14,803
Inner Mongolia 內蒙	1	30	240				8.00	80.00	450
Northeast 東北	24	57	985	16	0.55	4.94	17.22	88.78	2,855
Liaoning 遼寧	18	44	1,170	-42	-1.74	-10.07	26.33	82.71	2,426
Jilin 吉林	5	87	80	208	7.42	-101.96	0.92	107.28	2,804
Heilongjiang 黑龍江	1	138	2,170	100	0.92	8.62	15.72	89.28	10,820
Central East 華東	112	182	6,243	-375	-2.68	-12.90	34.25	79.26	14,010
Shanghai 上海	29	137	8,213	71	0.48	2.25	59.74	78.53	14,628
Jiangsu 江蘇	27	277	6,596	-949	-5.21	-28.60	23.79	81.80	18,223
Zhejiang 浙江	21	97	5,804	-8	-0.10	-0.31	59.54	69.16	7,870
Anhui 安徽	6	484	5,768	-2,680	-6.61	352.63	11.91	101.87	40,537
Fujian 福建	8	35	630	-28	-1.15	-5.61	18.13	79.45	2,385
Jiangxi 江西	4	254	515	-370	-3.75	-28.85	2.03	87.03	9,868
Shandong 山東	17	159	7,021	-29	-0.26	-0.55	44.19	51.88	10,934
Central-South 中南	39	111	8,701	-44	-0.57	-1.76	78.53	67.47	7,715
Henan 河南	11	40	662	-5	-0.36	-1.40	16.70	74.52	1,274
Hubei 湖北	7	293	15,171	243	1.07	3.77	51.86	71.70	22,743
Hunan 湖南	7	112	1,853	-39	-1.33	-7.99	16.56	83.36	2,901
Guangdong 廣東	13	80	16,320	-242	-2.95	-6.94	204.20	57.48	8,210
Guangxi 廣西	1	15	730	50	7.94	10.42	48.67	23.81	630
Hainan 海南									
Southwest 西南	11	516	17,720	1,803	4.35	9.56	34.32	54.54	41,460
Chongqing 重慶	4	62	2,051	364	9.51	15.81	32.97	39.89	3,826
Sichuan 四川	6	857	29,451	2,908	4.19	9.30	34.36	55.00	69,471
Guizhou 貴州	1	5	50				10.00	66.67	60
Yunnan 雲南									
Tibet 西藏									
Northwest 西北	13	334	4,833	-648	-3.05	-24.75	14.46	87.67	21,239
Shaanxi 陝西	9	147	2,479	364	3.54	16.83	16.90	78.96	10,292
Gansu 甘肅	2	1,284	17,780	-4,875	-6.01	-68.81	13.85	91.27	81,110
Qinghai 青海									
Ningxia 寧夏	2	229	2,480	-980	-9.22	-490.00	10.85	98.17	10,630
Xinjiang 新疆									

4230: Electric Measuring Instruments 電子測量儀器製造業

Year 年份	Number of firms 企業個數	Rate of change 每年變化 (%)	Number of employees 職工人數（人）	Rate of change 每年變化 (%)	Total revenue (mil. RMB) 總銷售收入（百萬元）	Rate of change 每年變化 (%)	Total profit (mil. RMB) 總利潤（百萬元）	Rate of change 每年變化 (%)
1993	266		69,957		1,551		66	
1994	270	1.50%	51,846	-25.89%	1,751	12.89%	81	24.28%
1995	265	-1.85%	50,456	-2.68%	1,775	1.37%	-10	-112.26%
1996	268	1.13%	45,844	-9.14%	2,187	23.21%	96	1061.54%

3 Major products* 3種主要產品 *	Output 產量	Sales volume 銷售量	Unit 單位
a) Electrican's Instrument & Meter 電工儀器儀表	647,722	641,245	set 台

Top 10 firms by revenue (year founded) 收入排名前10家企業（創辦年份）	City 城市	Province 省	Telephone / fax 電話 / 傳真	Number of employees 職工人數	Ownership 產業所有權	Revenue ('000 RMB) 銷售收入（千元）	Profit ('000 RMB) (rank) 利潤（千元）（排名）	Total assets ('000 RMB) 總資產（千元）	Major products 主要產品
Zhuhai Yuan Cheng Electron Co. Ltd. 珠海緣成電子有限公司(1995)	Zhuhai 珠海市	Guangdong 廣東省	(0756)8897254 (0756)8895605	418	Foreign-funded 外資	162,557	-1642(84)	25,914	o
Chengdu Qianfeng Electronics Co. Ltd. 成都前鋒電子股份有限公司(1963)	Chengdu 成都市	Sichuan 四川省	(028)3331301 (028)3331367	2,548	Joint stock 股份制	160,480	31560(1)	349,690	o
Shanghai Zhong Jing Computer Co. Ltd. 上海中晶電腦有限公司(1993)	Shanghai 上海市	Shanghai 上海市	(021)64856614 (021)64859686	117	Overseas Chinese-funded 港澳台資	75,075	-1688(86)	96,024	o
Wuhan Communication Instrument and Meter Plant 武漢郵電通訊設備廠(1958)	Wuhan 武漢市	Hubei 湖北省	(027)886878497 (027)86811042	730	State-owned 國有	61,703	2083(5)	82,482	o
Shanghai 21st Radio Factory 上海無線電二十一廠(1951)	Shanghai 上海市	Shanghai 上海市	(021)62552110 (021)62534936	875	State-owned 國有	50,405	1004(12)	99,359	o
Ningbo Zhongce Electronics Co. Ltd. 寧波中華電子股份有限公司(1993)	Ningbo 寧波市	Zhejiang 浙江省	(0574)7333183 (0574)7334525	464	Overseas Chinese-funded 港澳台資	46,474	1519(8)	31,701	o
Qingdao Summit Exectronics Co. Ltd. 青島三美德電子有限公司(1992)	Qingdao 青島市	Shandong 山東省	(0532)7871164 (0532)7871035	275	Foreign-funded 外資	45,350	190(31)	29,800	o
Beijing Rui Pu Electron Group 北京瑞普電子集團(1988)	Beijing 北京市	Beijing 北京市	(010)64045231	241	Collectively-owned 集體	39,262	334(23)	60,022	o
Jin Yi Micro-computer Factory 錦藝微電腦廠(1983)	Shanghai 上海市	Shanghai 上海市	(021)65129270 (021)65129270	174	Collectively-owned 集體	36,812	600(17)	19,637	o
Changzhou No.2 Electronic Instrument Factory 常州第二電子儀器廠(1958)	Changzhou 常州市	Jiangsu 江蘇省	(0519)6973926 (0519)6960452	808	State-owned 國有	28,149	119(36)	48,785	o

Top 10 Cities by Production Output 產出排名前10位城市	Province 省	Market share 市場份額	Number of firms 企業個數
Chengdu 成都市	Sichuan 四川省	11.37%	3
Zhuhai 珠海市	Guangdong 廣東省	10.83%	4
Shanghai 上海市	Shanghai 上海市	10.02%	47
Beijing 北京市	Beijing 北京市	8.01%	34
Shenzhen 深圳市	Guangdong 廣東省	6.60%	14
Wuhan 武漢市	Hubei 湖北省	5.44%	5
Tianjin 天津市	Tianjin 天津市	4.36%	22
Changzhou 常州市	Jiangsu 江蘇省	4.31%	11
Nanjing 南京市	Jiangsu 江蘇省	3.96%	12
Ningbo 寧波市	Zhejiang 浙江省	3.84%	6

10 Major Wholesalers 10家主要批發商	City 城市	Province 省	Telephone / Fax 電話 / 傳真
Liaoning Automobile Trade Group Corp. 遼寧省汽車貿易集團	Shenyang 瀋陽市	Liaoning 遼寧省	(024)23835494 (024)23838338
China Post and Telecommunication Equipment General Company 中國郵電器材總公司	Beijing 北京市	Beijing 北京市	(010)63523715 (010)63525935
Jiangsu Electromechanical Products General Company 江蘇省機電產品總公司	Nanjing 南京市	Jiangsu 江蘇省	(025)7713642 (025)7711036
Xi Nan Technology Import & Export Company 西南技術進出口公司	Chongqing 重慶市	Chongqing 重慶市	(023)63850185 (023)63850026
Changzhou Economic Technology Industrial Development Zone Tian Ming Trade Company 常州經濟技術產業開發區天明貿易公司	Changzhou 常州市	Jiangsu 江蘇省	(0519)8829882 (0519)8829882
Shanxi Mechanical Equipment Import & Export Company 山西省機械設備進出口公司	Taiyuan 太原市	Shanxi 山西省	(0351)4040713 (0351)4043981
Ningbo Five Mining Machinery Import & Export Company 寧波市五礦機械進出口公司	Ningbo 寧波市	Zhejiang 浙江省	(0574)7311255 (0574)7320322
Tianjin Jin Huan Electromechanical Complete Sets of Equipment Factory 天津市津環機電成套設備廠	Tianjin 天津市	Tianjin 天津市	(022)26371628
Yunnan Machinery Import & Export Company 雲南省機械進出口公司	Kunming 昆明市	Yunnan 雲南省	(0871)3164879 (0871)3136829
Tianjin Da Qiu Zhuang Yi Yuan Trade Center 天津市大丘莊億源商貿中心	Tianjin 天津市	Tianjin 天津市	(022)28899478 (022)28899046

*Also include sales by firms outside this industry.包括本行業以外廠家的銷售。"o" stands for "others". "o" 代表 "其他產品"。

4241: Transmission Measurement and Calibration Instruments
傳遞標準用計量儀器製造業

The industry accounts for 0.003% of the total revenue of China's industrial sector in 1996. The revenue growth rate of the industry is -37.8% from 1995, as compared to the growth rate of China's industrial sector, 9.51%. The rate of return on asset is 0.67%. 73.08% of all firms in the industry made a profit while 26.92% had negative returns. The top province in terms of the industry's revenue is Anhui, accounting for 33.03% of the total revenue.
本行業在1996年佔全行業總產值0.003%，行業年增長率為-37.8%（全國工業年增長率9.51%）。行業的資產回報率0.67%，73.08%的企業盈利，26.92%的企業虧損。銷售收入最高的省份為安徽省，佔本行業的33.03%。

	Total number of firms 企業總數	Total number of employees 職工總數	Total revenue (mil. RMB) 總銷售收入（百萬元）	Total profit (mil. RMB) 總利潤（百萬元）	Return on assets 資產利潤率 (%)	Return on equity 權益利潤率 (%)	Labour productivity ('000 RMB / worker) 勞動生產率（千元/人）	Debts / assets 資產負債率 (%)	Total assets (mil. RMB) 總資產（百萬元）
Industry Overall 行業總體	46	3,722	182	2	0.67	2.23	48.90	69.92	290

	Number of firms 企業個數	Average number of employees 平均職工人數	Average revenue ('000 RMB) 平均銷售收入（千元）	Average profit ('000 RMB) 平均利潤（千元）	Return on assets 資產利潤率 (%)	Return on equity 權益利潤率 (%)	Labour productivity ('000 RMB / worker) 勞動生產率（千元/人）	Average debts / assets 平均資產負債率(%)	Average Total assets ('000 RMB) 平均總資產（千元）
By ownership 產業所有權									
State-owned 國有	7	164	1,571	-429	-8.11	-60.00	9.60	86.49	5,286
Collectively-owned 集體	32	58	3,067	20	0.94	-2.65	53.13	135.41	2,131
Privately-owned 私有									
Domestic JVs 聯營	2	51	1,272	-83	-2.77	1.62	25.19	271.03	3,000
Joint stock 股份制									
Foreign-funded 外資	4	34	1,827	90	2.76	37.38	53.35	92.63	3,274
Overseas Chinese-funded 港澳台資	1	560	63,003	4,166	2.51	3.61	112.51	30.33	165,711
By size 規模									
Large 大型									
Medium 中型									
Small 小型	46	83	3,956	43	0.69	2.30	47.74	70.00	6,304
By regional distribution 地區分布									
Central-North 華北	5	105	2,356	172	3.69	11.59	22.44	68.08	4,656
Beijing 北京	4	107	1,625	110	5.58	26.83	15.15	79.19	1,970
Tianjin 天津	1	96	5,280	420	2.73	7.27	55.00	62.40	15,400
Hebei 河北									
Shanxi 山西									
Inner Mongolia 內蒙									
Northeast 東北	8	91	573	-316	-6.80	-67.65	6.27	89.95	4,650
Liaoning 遼寧	6	122	763	-422	-6.80	-67.65	6.27	89.95	6,200
Jilin 吉林									
Heilongjiang 黑龍江	2								
Central East 華東	27	83	5,857	142	1.82	5.74	70.82	68.28	7,783
Shanghai 上海	6	40	2,107	110	2.44	6.63	53.33	63.21	4,512
Jiangsu 江蘇	11	114	5,339	-277	-3.63	-56.27	46.69	93.55	7,636
Zhejiang 浙江	8	26	3,333	291	2.98	5.45	128.17	45.33	9,776
Anhui 安徽	1	530	60,110	3,890	18.64	45.55	113.42	59.13	20,870
Fujian 福建									
Jiangxi 江西									
Shandong 山東	1								
Central-South 中南	5	39	1,436	-42	-1.09	-2.25	36.82	51.43	3,842
Henan 河南	2	22	2,500	-45	-1.29	-7.38	116.28	82.55	3,495
Hubei 湖北									
Hunan 湖南									
Guangdong 廣東	2	13	815				62.69	62.22	2,250
Guangxi 廣西	1	126	550	-120	-1.55	-1.87	4.37	16.97	7,720
Hainan 海南									
Southwest 西南									
Chongqing 重慶									
Sichuan 四川									
Guizhou 貴州									
Yunnan 雲南									
Tibet 西藏									
Northwest 西北	1	38	220				5.79	68.29	410
Shaanxi 陝西	1	38	220				5.79	68.29	410
Gansu 甘肅									
Qinghai 青海									
Ningxia 寧夏									
Xinjiang 新疆									

4241: Transmission Measurement and Calibration Instruments
傳遞標準用計量儀器製造業

Year 年份	Number of firms 企業個數	Rate of change 每年變化 (%)	Number of employees 職工人數 (人)	Rate of change 每年變化 (%)	Total revenue (mil. RMB) 總銷售收入 (百萬元)	Rate of change 每年變化 (%)	Total profit (mil. RMB) 總利潤 (百萬元)	Rate of change 每年變化 (%)
1993	42		3,730		102		3	
1994	50	19.05%	3,306	-11.37%	105	3.04%	-1	-140.21%
1995	42	-16.00%	3,915	18.42%	292	178.28%	24	1843.38%
1996	46	9.52%	3,722	-4.93%	182	-37.76%	2	-91.61%

3 Major products* 3 種主要產品 *	Output 產量	Sales volume 銷售量	Unit 單位
a) Gas Meter 煤氣表	137,839	93,730	set 台
b) Measuring Instrument 量具	1,612,630	1,725,515	piece 件
c) Transfer Standard Metering Instrument 傳遞標準用計量儀器	3,249	3,184	set 台

Top 10 firms by revenue (year founded) 收入排名前 10 家企業 (創辦年份)	City 城市	Province 省	Telephone / fax 電話 / 傳真	Number of employees 職工人數	Ownership 產業所有權	Revenue ('000 RMB) 銷售收入 (千元)	Profit ('000 RMB) (rank) 利潤 (千元) (排名)	Total assets ('000 RMB) 總資產 (千元)	Major products 主要產品
Shitai Gas Meter General Plant , Anhui 安徽省石台煤氣儀表總廠(1985)	Guichi 貴池市	Anhui 安徽省	(0566)6098088 (0566)6098061	210	Collectively-owned 集體	60,105	3892(1)	20,872	a
Nanjing Zhonghua Survey Equipment Factory 南京中華測繪器材廠(1958)	Nanjing 南京市	Jiangsu 江蘇省	(025)4599354 (025)4597621	273	Collectively-owned 集體	14,351	54(11)	29,574	o
Qidong Hao Jiang Electric Engineering Instrument Co. Ltd. 啟東市浩江電工儀表有限公司(1993)	Nantong 南通市	Jiangsu 江蘇省	(0513)3369965	170	Overseas Chinese-funded 港澳台資	11,592	-167(17)	8,451	o
Wenzhou Rui Long Instrument Factory 溫州市瑞隆儀表廠(1992)	Wenzhou 溫州市	Zhejiang 浙江省	(0577)6554224 (0577)6554141	14	Collectively-owned 集體	10,004	899(3)	19,887	o
Qidong Punching Pieces Factory 啟東市沖壓件廠(1981)	Nantong 南通市	Jiangsu 江蘇省	(0513)3369299	180	Collectively-owned 集體	9,687	-487(18)	13,092	o
Shanghai Tong Kong Meter Co. Ltd. 上海通控儀表有限公司(1993)	Shanghai 上海市	Shanghai 上海市	(021)57851234 (021)57851223	92	Foreign-funded 外資	8,956	406(5)	15,856	o
Wuxi Water Meter Factory 無錫市水表廠(1976)	Wuxi 無錫市	Jiangsu 江蘇省	(0510)5100803 (0510)5113414	174	Collectively-owned 集體	8,802	51(12)	3,801	o
Shang Hai Pressure Reducer Factory Changzhou Branch 上海減壓器廠常州分廠(1983)	Changzhou 常州市	Jiangsu 江蘇省	(0519)2711264 (0519)2711264	181	Collectively-owned 集體	6,922	30(14)	7,396	o
Wenzhou Ke Luo Ni Instrument Co. Ltd. 溫州克洛尼儀表有限公司(1993)	Wenzhou 溫州市	Zhejiang 浙江省	(0577)6554224 (0577)6554141	15	Foreign-funded 外資	5,860	928(2)	27,914	o
Tianjin Water Supply Equipment Complete Set Company 天津市給水設備配套公司(1993)	Tianjin 天津市	Tianjin 天津市	(022)27365019	100	Collectively-owned 集體	5,284	419(4)	15,395	o

Top 10 Cities by Production Output 產出排名前 10 位城市	Province 省	Market share 市場份額	Number of firms 企業個數
Changzhou 常州市	Jiangsu 江蘇省	28.04%	9
Shanghai 上海市	Shanghai 上海市	23.46%	11
Wenzhou 溫州市	Zhejiang 浙江省	11.58%	4
Nanjing 南京市	Jiangsu 江蘇省	7.37%	4
Wuxi 無錫市	Jiangsu 江蘇省	5.06%	4
Beijing 北京市	Beijing 北京市	4.09%	2
Tianjin 天津市	Tianjin 天津市	3.80%	2
Hangzhou 杭州市	Zhejiang 浙江省	3.30%	4
Liaoyang 遼陽市	Liaoning 遼寧省	2.09%	2
Jiaozuo 焦作市	Henan 河南省	1.94%	1

10 Major Wholesalers 10 家主要批發商	City 城市	Province 省	Telephone / Fax 電話 / 傳真
Liaoning Automobile Trade Group Corp. 遼寧省汽車貿易集團	Shenyang 瀋陽市	Liaoning 遼寧省	(024)23835494 (024)23838338
China Post and Telecommunication Equipment General Company 中國郵電器材總公司	Beijing 北京市	Beijing 北京市	(010)63523715 (010)63525935
Jiangsu Electromechanical Products General Company 江蘇省機電產品總公司	Nanjing 南京市	Jiangsu 江蘇省	(025)7713642 (025)7711036
Xi Nan Technology Import & Export Company 西南技術進出口公司	Chongqing 重慶市	Chongqing 重慶市	(023)63850185 (023)63850026
Changzhou Economic Technology Industrial Development Zone Tian Ming Trade Company 常州經濟技術產業開發區天明貿易公司	Changzhou 常州市	Jiangsu 江蘇省	(0519)8829882 (0519)8829882
Shanxi Mechanical Equipment Import & Export Company 山西省機械設備進出口公司	Taiyuan 太原市	Shanxi 山西省	(0351)4040713 (0351)4043981
Ningbo Five Mining Machinery Import & Export Company 寧波市五礦機械進出口公司	Ningbo 寧波市	Zhejiang 浙江省	(0574)7311255 (0574)7320322
Tianjin Jin Huan Electromechanical Complete Sets of Equipment Factory 天津市津環機電成套設備廠	Tianjin 天津市	Tianjin 天津市	(022)26371628
Yunnan Machinery Import & Export Company 雲南省機械進出口公司	Kunming 昆明市	Yunnan 雲南省	(0871)3164879 (0871)3136829
Tianjin Da Qiu Zhuang Yi Yuan Trade Center 天津市大丘莊億源商貿中心	Tianjin 天津市	Tianjin 天津市	(022)28899478 (022)28899046

*Also include sales by firms outside this industry.包括本行業以外廠家的銷售。"o" stands for "others". "o" 代表 "其他產品"。

4242: Measuring Instruments 量具量儀製造業

The industry accounts for 0.022% of the total revenue of China's industrial sector in 1996. The revenue growth rate of the industry is 16.9% from 1995, as compared to the growth rate of China's industrial sector, 9.51%. The rate of return on asset is 1.77%. 69.51% of all firms in the industry made a profit while 25.00% had negative returns. The top province in terms of the industry's revenue is Jiangsu, accounting for 23.10% of the total revenue.
本行業在1996年佔全行業總產值0.022%，行業年增長率為16.9%（全國工業年增長率9.51%）。行業的資產回報率1.77%，69.51%的企業盈利，25.00%的企業虧損。銷售收入最高的省份為江蘇省，佔本行業的23.10%。

	Total number of firms 企業總數	Total number of employees 職工總數	Total revenue (mil. RMB) 總銷售收入（百萬元）	Total profit (mil. RMB) 總利潤（百萬元）	Return on assets 資產利潤率 (%)	Return on equity 權益利潤率 (%)	Labour productivity ('000 RMB / worker) 勞動生產率（千元/人）	Debts / assets 資產負債率 (%)	Total assets (mil. RMB) 總資產（百萬元）
Industry Overall 行業總體	204	36,485	1,281	41	1.77	5.33	35.11	66.82	2,321

	Number of firms 企業個數	Average number of employees 平均職工人數	Average revenue ('000 RMB) 平均銷售收入（千元）	Average profit ('000 RMB) 平均利潤（千元）	Return on assets 資產利潤率 (%)	Return on equity 權益利潤率 (%)	Labour productivity ('000 RMB / worker) 勞動生產率（千元/人）	Average debts / assets 平均資產負債率(%)	Average Total assets ('000 RMB) 平均總資產（千元）
By ownership 產業所有權									
State-owned 國有	37	389	9,405	-27	-0.09	-0.41	24.17	77.89	29,459
Collectively-owned 集體	138	117	4,293	255	5.03	13.89	36.67	63.81	5,063
Privately-owned 私有									
Domestic JVs 聯營	2	19	1,173	115	8.03	16.21	61.73	50.49	1,436
Joint stock 股份制	6	375	13,696	477	1.79	4.71	36.57	62.04	26,717
Foreign-funded 外資	9	160	11,821	930	6.52	10.86	74.04	39.98	14,261
Overseas Chinese-funded 港澳台資	11	201	13,609	-418	-1.90	-3.35	67.83	43.28	21,987
By size 規模									
Large 大型	3	1,567	65,102	1,399	0.75	4.10	41.55	81.67	186,117
Medium 中型	11	762	23,316	173	0.34	1.04	30.61	67.55	51,039
Small 小型	188	124	4,411	186	2.90	7.19	35.48	59.59	6,394
By regional distribution 地區分布									
Central-North 華北	33	143	3,289	51	0.65	2.28	22.97	71.54	7,808
Beijing 北京	10	228	3,965	-46	-0.28	-1.02	17.38	72.67	16,533
Tianjin 天津	5	104	1,938	122	5.03	13.65	18.63	63.12	2,424
Hebei 河北	18	107	3,289	84	1.90	6.42	30.79	70.49	4,456
Shanxi 山西									
Inner Mongolia 內蒙									
Northeast 東北	36	132	2,348	359	9.12	19.53	17.82	53.31	3,942
Liaoning 遼寧	16	112	1,836	124	2.85	5.97	16.43	52.23	4,338
Jilin 吉林	2	140						96.66	2,545
Heilongjiang 黑龍江	18	149	3,063	609	16.26	33.26	20.61	51.13	3,745
Central East 華東	92	204	9,459	330	2.11	6.42	46.28	67.09	15,632
Shanghai 上海	13	233	12,274	125	0.40	3.03	52.78	86.77	31,282
Jiangsu 江蘇	25	266	11,838	410	2.27	6.07	44.43	62.64	18,066
Zhejiang 浙江	27	115	4,869	84	1.05	2.52	42.41	58.33	7,956
Anhui 安徽	5	175	2,882	-280	-3.01	-22.95	16.45	86.90	9,316
Fujian 福建	4	207	17,343	2,583	16.93	28.49	83.68	40.56	15,250
Jiangxi 江西	10	233	3,991	-63	-0.73	-2.58	17.11	71.64	8,615
Shandong 山東	8	248	19,946	996	4.65	8.44	80.51	44.88	21,409
Central-South 中南	30	199	5,375	-149	-1.20	-3.47	27.00	65.28	12,343
Henan 河南	9	278	7,396	100	0.68	2.34	26.59	71.04	14,730
Hubei 湖北	4	156	1,045	-20	-0.51	-6.40	6.72	92.00	3,908
Hunan 湖南	11	93	1,894	-285	-7.30	-52.78	20.40	86.16	3,895
Guangdong 廣東	3	98	9,980	-770	-4.09	-6.23	101.84	34.39	18,843
Guangxi 廣西	3	511	13,247	53	0.13	0.35	25.94	62.60	40,900
Hainan 海南									
Southwest 西南	8	30	1,220	44	3.50	5.96	40.84	41.20	1,250
Chongqing 重慶	1	26	510	1	0.30	0.38	19.72	21.89	476
Sichuan 四川	4	51	2,433	93	3.70	6.43	47.35	42.42	2,508
Guizhou 貴州	2								
Yunnan 雲南	1	14							
Tibet 西藏									
Northwest 西北	5	400	9,288	36	0.17	0.78	23.20	77.77	20,696
Shaanxi 陝西	4	243	4,998	18	0.17	2.18	20.61	92.03	10,070
Gansu 甘肅									
Qinghai 青海	1	1,032	26,450	110	0.17	0.56	25.63	68.69	63,200
Ningxia 寧夏									
Xinjiang 新疆									

4242: Measuring Instruments 量具量儀製造業

Year 年份	Number of firms 企業個數	Rate of change 每年變化 (%)	Number of employees 職工人數 (人)	Rate of change 每年變化 (%)	Total revenue (mil. RMB) 總銷售收入 (百萬元)	Rate of change 每年變化 (%)	Total profit (mil. RMB) 總利潤 (百萬元)	Rate of change 每年變化 (%)
1993	225		42,092		1,085		34	
1994	234	4.00%	44,585	5.92%	1,215	12.00%	39	15.88%
1995	215	-8.12%	36,306	-18.57%	1,096	-9.85%	15	-60.97%
1996	204	-5.12%	36,485	0.49%	1,281	16.88%	41	167.69%

3 Major products* 3 種主要產品 *	Output 產量	Sales volume 銷售量	Unit 單位
a) Measuring Instrument 量具	15,550,365	16,638,890	piece 件

Top 10 firms by revenue (year founded) 收入排名前 10 家企業 (創辦年份)	City 城市	Province 省	Telephone / fax 電話 / 傳真	Number of employees 職工人數	Ownership 產業所有權	Revenue ('000 RMB) 銷售收入 (千元)	Profit ('000 RMB) (rank) 利潤 (千元) (排名)	Total assets ('000 RMB) 總資產 (千元)	Major products 主要產品
Shanghai Measuring & Cutting Tools Works 上海量具刃具廠(1958)	Shanghai 上海市	Shanghai 上海市	(021)64393881 (021)64383063	1,633	State-owned 國有	104,361	2000(10)	314,935	a
Taixing Glass Factory 泰興市玻璃廠(1958)	Taizhou 泰州市	Jiangsu 江蘇省	(0523)7484399 (0523)7484460	2,393	Collectively-owned 集體	102,691	893(15)	179,066	o
Ai Mei Kai Meter (Xiamen) Co. Ltd. 廈門艾美凱儀表有限公司(1995)	Xiamen 廈門市	Fujian 福建省	(0592)6030565 (0592)6030570	668	Foreign-funded 外資	67,586	10260(1)	59,137	o
Wuxi Gong Da Co. Ltd. 無錫工達股份有限公司(1958)	Wuxi 無錫市	Jiangsu 江蘇省	(0510)2403351 (0510)2403715	980	Joint stock 股份制	50,490	381(24)	108,998	a
Wuxi Tool and Measuring Tool Plant 無錫工具量具廠(1954)	Wuxi 無錫市	Jiangsu 江蘇省	(0510)8731803	522	Collectively-owned 集體	50,323	3424(5)	36,252	a
Weihai Measuring Tool General Factory 威海市量具總廠(1956)	Weihai 威海市	Shandong 山東省	(0896)5231421 (0896)5231769	915	Collectively-owned 集體	42,623	114(43)	61,754	a
Ji'nan Dong Xing Precise Measuring Instrument Co. Ltd. 濟南東星精密量儀有限公司(1996)	Ji'nan 濟南市	Shandong 山東省		190	Collectively-owned 集體	38,370	1925(11)	5,460	o
Ningbo Jiang Xin Hardware Industrial Measuring Tool Co. Ltd. 寧波江信五金工量具有限公司(1993)	Ningbo 寧波市	Zhejiang 浙江省	(0574)2058069 (0574)2055500	261	Overseas Chinese-funded 港澳台資	38,180	3182(6)	31,048	o
Shanghai Bao Fa Drawing Instruments Factory 上海寶發繪圖儀器廠(1996)	Shanghai 上海市	Shanghai 上海市	(021)11111111	75	Domestic JVs 聯營	35,500	0(70)	42,572	o
Shandong Gao Tangxian Machinery Measuring Tool Instrument Co. Ltd. 山東省高唐縣機械量具儀器有限公司(1993)	Liaocheng 聊城市	Shandong 山東省	(0635)3831152	140	Foreign-funded 外資	34,220	2318(9)	50,079	a

Top 10 Cities by Production Output 產出排名前 10 位城市	Province 省	Market share 市場份額	Number of firms 企業個數
Shanghai 上海市	Shanghai 上海市	18.77%	33
Harbin 哈爾濱市	Heilongjiang 黑龍江省	12.87%	8
Wuxi 無錫市	Jiangsu 江蘇省	11.26%	13
Taizhou 泰州市	Jiangsu 江蘇省	7.97%	5
Ningbo 寧波市	Zhejiang 浙江省	4.65%	10
Weihai 威海市	Shandong 山東省	3.35%	1
Cangzhou 滄州市	Hebei 河北省	3.21%	7
Guilin 桂林市	Guangxi 廣西	3.06%	2
Jinhua 金華市	Zhejiang 浙江省	2.42%	5
Zhuhai 珠海市	Guangdong 廣東省	2.26%	1

10 Major Wholesalers 10 家主要批發商	City 城市	Province 省	Telephone / Fax 電話 / 傳真
Liaoning Automobile Trade Group Corp. 遼寧省汽車貿易集團	Shenyang 瀋陽市	Liaoning 遼寧省	(024)23835494 (024)23838338
China Post and Telecommunication Equipment General Company 中國郵電器材總公司	Beijing 北京市	Beijing 北京市	(010)63523715 (010)63525935
Jiangsu Electromechanical Products General Company 江蘇省機電產品總公司	Nanjing 南京市	Jiangsu 江蘇省	(025)7713642 (025)7711036
Xi Nan Technology Import & Export Company 西南技術進出口公司	Chongqing 重慶市	Chongqing 重慶市	(023)63850185 (023)63850026
Changzhou Economic Technology Industrial Development Zone Tian Ming Trade Company 常州經濟技術產業開發區天明貿易公司	Changzhou 常州市	Jiangsu 江蘇省	(0519)8829882 (0519)8829882
Shanxi Mechanical Equipment Import & Export Company 山西省機械設備進出口公司	Taiyuan 太原市	Shanxi 山西省	(0351)4040713 (0351)4043981
Ningbo Five Mining Machinery Import & Export Company 寧波市五礦機械進出口公司	Ningbo 寧波市	Zhejiang 浙江省	(0574)7311255 (0574)7320322
Tianjin Jin Huan Electromechanical Complete Sets of Equipment Factory 天津市津環機電成套設備廠	Tianjin 天津市	Tianjin 天津市	(022)26371628
Yunnan Machinery Import & Export Company 雲南省機械進出口公司	Kunming 昆明市	Yunnan 雲南省	(0871)3164879 (0871)3136829
Tianjin Da Qiu Zhuang Yi Yuan Trade Center 天津市大丘莊億源商貿中心	Tianjin 天津市	Tianjin 天津市	(022)28899478 (022)28899046

*Also include sales by firms outside this industry.包括本行業以外廠家的銷售。"o" stands for "others". "o" 代表 "其他產品"。

4243: Scales 衡器製造業

The industry accounts for 0.029% of the total revenue of China's industrial sector in 1996. The revenue growth rate of the industry is -0.8% from 1995, as compared to the growth rate of China's industrial sector, 9.51%. The rate of return on asset is 0.73%. 56.76% of all firms in the industry made a profit while 34.22% had negative returns. The top province in terms of the industry's revenue is Shandong, accounting for 18.29% of the total revenue.

本行業在1996年佔全行業總產值0.029%，行業年增長率為-0.8%（全國工業年增長率9.51%）。行業的資產回報率0.73%，56.76%的企業盈利，34.22%的企業虧損。銷售收入最高的省份為山東省，佔本行業的18.29%。

	Total number of firms 企業總數	Total number of employees 職工總數	Total revenue (mil. RMB) 總銷售收入（百萬元）	Total profit (mil. RMB) 總利潤（百萬元）	Return on assets 資產利潤率 (%)	Return on equity 權益利潤率 (%)	Labour productivity ('000 RMB / worker) 勞動生產率（千元／人）	Debts / assets 資產負債率 (%)	Total assets (mil. RMB) 總資產（百萬元）
Industry Overall 行業總體	361	40,556	1,653	22	0.73	2.05	40.76	64.22	3,032

	Number of firms 企業個數	Average number of employees 平均職工人數	Average revenue ('000 RMB) 平均銷售收入（千元）	Average profit ('000 RMB) 平均利潤（千元）	Return on assets 資產利潤率 (%)	Return on equity 權益利潤率 (%)	Labour productivity ('000 RMB / worker) 勞動生產率（千元／人）	Average debts / assets 平均資產負債率(%)	Average Total assets ('000 RMB) 平均總資產（千元）
By ownership 產業所有權									
State-owned 國有	50	310	6,400	-380	-1.76	-5.71	20.63	69.14	21,580
Collectively-owned 集體	262	75	2,489	22	0.65	1.88	33.01	65.55	3,444
Privately-owned 私有	2	63	2,613	48	0.85	10.38	41.81	91.85	5,702
Domestic JVs 聯營	2	80	3,292	14	0.55	1.23	41.41	55.67	2,600
Joint stock 股份制	4	247	31,300	2,832	5.90	10.54	126.85	43.95	47,968
Foreign-funded 外資	19	141	20,624	1,305	4.64	11.09	146.60	58.21	28,152
Overseas Chinese-funded 港澳台資	22	87	6,924	-50	-0.36	-1.03	79.80	65.23	13,962
By size 規模									
Large 大型	2	848	77,930	3,849	2.65	4.82	91.90	45.12	145,400
Medium 中型	15	728	32,397	681	1.05	3.24	44.53	67.65	64,901
Small 小型	342	83	2,957	12	0.23	0.67	35.50	65.46	5,169
By regional distribution 地區分布									
Central-North 華北	63	100	2,987	-117	-1.96	-6.44	29.76	69.57	5,985
Beijing 北京	17	62	2,564	-209	-3.66	-12.44	41.50	70.61	5,728
Tianjin 天津	13	76	4,215	-33	-0.83	-3.84	55.51	78.41	3,986
Hebei 河北	19	131	3,108	-103	-1.22	-3.62	23.67	66.44	8,443
Shanxi 山西	10	161	2,916	-145	-2.26	-7.22	18.08	68.68	6,411
Inner Mongolia 內蒙	4	45	403				9.04	69.28	830
Northeast 東北	39	159	2,044	-75	-0.80	-2.62	12.82	69.46	9,382
Liaoning 遼寧	25	147	1,934	28	0.31	1.14	13.18	72.67	8,963
Jilin 吉林	5	302	3,014	-702	-3.91	-13.82	9.98	71.73	17,962
Heilongjiang 黑龍江	9	116	1,808	-13	-0.23	-0.48	15.63	51.70	5,777
Central East 華東	141	111	6,790	190	1.77	4.42	61.07	60.01	10,736
Shanghai 上海	19	106	13,694	112	0.54	1.34	128.80	59.32	20,474
Jiangsu 江蘇	38	144	7,015	197	1.73	4.85	48.69	64.37	11,396
Zhejiang 浙江	33	45	2,077	62	1.72	4.98	45.70	65.54	3,638
Anhui 安徽	12	93	1,941	1	0.03	0.06	20.91	55.52	3,089
Fujian 福建	11	68	2,385	-283	-4.72	-13.91	35.30	66.09	5,994
Jiangxi 江西	9	54	1,127	37	0.96	2.03	20.91	52.55	3,808
Shandong 山東	19	228	15,916	939	4.11	9.08	69.69	54.78	22,862
Central-South 中南	61	136	5,627	130	1.35	4.46	41.23	69.73	9,644
Henan 河南	18	111	4,222	520	6.84	27.39	37.94	75.05	7,608
Hubei 湖北	6	133	622	-55	-1.34	-4.73	4.66	71.54	4,093
Hunan 湖南	12	131	1,693	-749	-9.67	-21.27	12.96	54.55	7,750
Guangdong 廣東	20	177	11,035	356	2.29	8.34	62.31	72.60	15,571
Guangxi 廣西	5	82	4,498	156	3.49	8.41	54.59	58.49	4,476
Hainan 海南									
Southwest 西南	45	62	1,260	-42	-2.04	-4.34	20.24	53.08	2,049
Chongqing 重慶	10	61	1,292	-143	-6.08	-15.14	21.18	59.83	2,346
Sichuan 四川	29	42	647	-49	-4.19	-10.77	15.24	61.07	1,170
Guizhou 貴州	2	227	3,745	5	0.11	0.18	16.50	38.99	4,540
Yunnan 雲南	4	125	4,458	228	3.47	5.95	35.73	41.71	6,563
Tibet 西藏									
Northwest 西北	12	101	2,344	-23	-0.28	-0.85	23.19	66.59	7,905
Shaanxi 陝西	7	134	2,459	-144	-1.44	-4.65	18.35	69.08	10,040
Gansu 甘肅	1	49	240	-80	-4.47	-14.29	4.90	68.72	1,790
Qinghai 青海	1	127	2,500	40	0.87	5.13	19.69	83.04	4,600
Ningxia 寧夏	1	46	410				8.91	68.83	770
Xinjiang 新疆	2	27	3,885	390	4.48	9.31	146.60	51.89	8,710

4243: Scales 衡器製造業

Year 年份	Number of firms 企業個數	Rate of change 每年變化 (%)	Number of employees 職工人數（人）	Rate of change 每年變化 (%)	Total revenue (mil. RMB) 總銷售收入（百萬元）	Rate of change 每年變化 (%)	Total profit (mil. RMB) 總利潤（百萬元）	Rate of change 每年變化 (%)
1993	363		56,335		1,559		102	
1994	358	-1.38%	41,128	-26.99%	1,344	-13.82%	58	-42.59%
1995	385	7.54%	43,168	4.96%	1,667	24.03%	65	11.28%
1996	361	-6.23%	40,556	-6.05%	1,653	-0.84%	22	-66.13%

3 Major products* 3種主要產品*	Output 產量	Sales volume 銷售量	Unit 單位
a) Platform Balance 台秤	5,315,031	5,155,580	set 台
b) Counter Scale with Weight 案秤	2,668,995	2,642,305	set 台
c) Ground Scale 地上衡	28,892	21,091	set 台

Top 10 firms by revenue (year founded) 收入排名前10家企業(創辦年份)	City 城市	Province 省	Telephone / fax 電話 / 傳真	Number of employees 職工人數	Ownership 產業所有權	Revenue ('000 RMB) 銷售收入（千元）	Profit ('000 RMB) (rank) 利潤（千元）(排名)	Total assets ('000 RMB) 總資產（千元）	Major products 主要產品
Ji'nan Jinzhong Electronic Scale Co. Ltd. 濟南金鐘電子衡器股份有限公司(1955)	Ji'nan 濟南市	Shandong 山東省	(0531)2973713 (0531)2971352	689	Joint stock 股份制	128,542	12040(2)	157,118	a,b,c
Metter-toledo Changzhou Jeale Ltd. 常州托利多電子衡器有限公司(1987)	Changzhou 常州市	Jiangsu 江蘇省	(0519)6642040 (0519)6641991	329	Foreign-funded 外資	108,891	16278(1)	128,315	a,b,c
Shanghai Tcraoka Electronic Co. Ltd. 上海寺岡電子有限公司(1992)	Shanghai 上海市	Shanghai 上海市	(021)57234888 (021)57234090	190	Foreign-funded 外資	105,878	0(93)	128,306	a
Shi Qi Weighing Apparatus Factory, Zhongshan 中山市石岐衡器廠(1975)	Zhongshan 中山市	Guangdong 廣東省	(0760)8319116 (0760)8313262	657	Collectively-owned 集體	95,165	10520(3)	63,441	a,b
Shanghai Yamato Scale Co. Ltd. 上海大和衡器有限公司(1990)	Shanghai 上海市	Shanghai 上海市	(021)58873377 (021)58840649	279	Foreign-funded 外資	88,046	3337(5)	107,260	a,b,c
Lu Nan Heng Da Group Co. 魯南衡達集團公司(1958)	Zaozhuang 棗莊市	Shandong 山東省	(0632)5513559 (0632)5512250	1,104	Collectively-owned 集體	60,765	1502(9)	106,856	a,b,c
Dongguan Bai Li Da Health Equipment Xian Company 東莞佰利達健康器材限公司(1995)	Dongguan 東莞市	Guangdong 廣東省	(0769)2407166 (0769)2407443	285	Foreign-funded 外資	56,410	110(46)	76,497	a,b
Shandong Taishan Weighing Apparatus Co. Ltd. 山東省泰山衡器股份有限公司(1956)	Tai'an 泰安市	Shandong 山東省	(0538)8611220 (0538)8611220	1,036	Collectively-owned 集體	46,254	2611(6)	79,149	a,b,c
Xuzhou Weighing Apparatus Factory 徐州衡器廠(1962)	Xuzhou 徐州市	Jiangsu 江蘇省	(0516)7768253 (0516)7767454	942	State-owned 國有	32,943	25(68)	63,294	a,c
Tianjin Weighing Apparatus Company 天津市衡器公司(1924)	Tianjin 天津市	Tianjin 天津市	(022)27391491 (022)27391491	331	Collectively-owned 集體	28,665	0(95)	47,548	a,b,c

Top 10 Cities by Production Output 產出排名前10位城市	Province 省	Market share 市場份額	Number of firms 企業個數
Shanghai 上海市	Shanghai 上海市	18.06%	41
Changzhou 常州市	Jiangsu 江蘇省	7.47%	7
Jinhua 金華市	Zhejiang 浙江省	6.49%	25
Zhongshan 中山市	Guangdong 廣東省	5.40%	3
Ji'nan 濟南市	Shandong 山東省	4.88%	4
Tai'an 泰安市	Shandong 山東省	4.10%	3
Tianjin 天津市	Tianjin 天津市	3.46%	15
Nanjing 南京市	Jiangsu 江蘇省	3.22%	7
Suzhou 蘇州市	Jiangsu 江蘇省	2.97%	14
Zaozhuang 棗莊市	Shandong 山東省	2.71%	1

10 Major Wholesalers 10家主要批發商	City 城市	Province 省	Telephone / Fax 電話 / 傳真
Liaoning Automobile Trade Group Corp. 遼寧省汽車貿易集團	Shenyang 瀋陽市	Liaoning 遼寧省	(024)23835494 (024)23838338
China Post and Telecommunication Equipment General Company 中國郵電器材總公司	Beijing 北京市	Beijing 北京市	(010)63523715 (010)63525935
Jiangsu Electromechanical Products General Company 江蘇省機電產品總公司	Nanjing 南京市	Jiangsu 江蘇省	(025)7713642 (025)7711036
Xi Nan Technology Import & Export Company 西南技術進出口公司	Chongqing 重慶市	Chongqing 重慶市	(023)63850185 (023)63850026
Changzhou Economic Technology Industrial Development Zone Tian Ming Trade Company 常州經濟技術產業開發區天明貿易公司	Changzhou 常州市	Jiangsu 江蘇省	(0519)8829882 (0519)8829882
Shanxi Mechanical Equipment Import & Export Company 山西省機械設備進出口公司	Taiyuan 太原市	Shanxi 山西省	(0351)4040713 (0351)4043981
Ningbo Five Mining Machinery Import & Export Company 寧波市五礦機械進出口公司	Ningbo 寧波市	Zhejiang 浙江省	(0574)7311255 (0574)7320322
Tianjin Jin Huan Electromechanical Complete Sets of Equipment Factory 天津市津環機電成套設備廠	Tianjin 天津市	Tianjin 天津市	(022)26371628
Yunnan Machinery Import & Export Company 雲南省機械進出口公司	Kunming 昆明市	Yunnan 雲南省	(0871)3164879 (0871)3136829
Tianjin Da Qiu Zhuang Yi Yuan Trade Center 天津市大丘莊億源商貿中心	Tianjin 天津市	Tianjin 天津市	(022)28899478 (022)28899046

*Also include sales by firms outside this industry.包括本行業以外廠家的銷售。"o" stands for "others". "o" 代表"其他產品"。

4251: Photography and Film Machinery 電影機械製造業

The industry accounts for 0.002% of the total revenue of China's industrial sector in 1996. The revenue growth rate of the industry is 13.3% from 1995, as compared to the growth rate of China's industrial sector, 9.51%. The rate of return on asset is 1.08%. 44.04% of all firms in the industry made a profit while 41.67% had negative returns. The top province in terms of the industry's revenue is Helongjiang, accounting for 46.24% of the total revenue.
本行業在 1996 年佔全行業總產值 0.002%，行業年增長率為 13.3%（全國工業年增長率 9.51%）。行業的資產回報率 1.08%，44.04% 的企業盈利，41.67% 的企業虧損。銷售收入最高的省份為黑龍江省，佔本行業的 46.24%。

	Total number of firms 企業總數	Total number of employees 職工總數	Total revenue (mil. RMB) 總銷售收入（百萬元）	Total profit (mil. RMB) 總利潤（百萬元）	Return on assets 資產利潤率 (%)	Return on equity 權益利潤率 (%)	Labour productivity ('000 RMB / worker) 勞動生產率（千元/人）	Debts / assets 資產負債率 (%)	Total assets (mil. RMB) 總資產（百萬元）
Industry Overall 行業總體	14	5,572	140	5	1.08	3.40	25.13	68.29	417

	Number of firms 企業個數	Average number of employees 平均職工人數	Average revenue ('000 RMB) 平均銷售收入（千元）	Average profit ('000 RMB) 平均利潤（千元）	Return on assets 資產利潤率 (%)	Return on equity 權益利潤率 (%)	Labour productivity ('000 RMB / worker) 勞動生產率（千元/人）	Average debts / assets 平均資產負債率(%)	Average Total assets ('000 RMB) 平均總資產（千元）
By ownership 產業所有權									
State-owned 國有	10	536	13,600	500	1.22	3.88	25.37	68.46	40,900
Collectively-owned 集體	3	-7	305				-43.59	90.61	296
Privately-owned 私有									
Domestic JVs 聯營									
Joint stock 股份制									
Foreign-funded 外資	1	-125	3,074				-24.59	58.97	7,102
Overseas Chinese-funded 港澳台資									
By size 規模									
Large 大型	2	1,459	53,472	3,748	2.76	8.59	36.65	67.81	135,643
Medium 中型									
Small 小型	12	239	2,754	-208	-1.71	-5.59	11.50	69.33	12,142
By regional distribution 地區分布									
Central-North 華北	4	316	1,278	-88	-0.50	-2.49	4.04	79.81	17,388
Beijing 北京									
Tianjin 天津	3	413	1,613	-120	-0.52	-2.63	3.91	80.24	23,047
Hebei 河北	1	26	270	10	2.44	2.56	10.38	7.32	410
Shanxi 山西									
Inner Mongolia 內蒙									
Northeast 東北	4	666	16,878	-15	-0.03	-0.16	25.34	80.48	49,128
Liaoning 遼寧	1	135	2,770	-160	-2.41	-5.50	20.52	56.24	6,650
Jilin 吉林	1	2							
Heilongjiang 黑龍江	2	1,264	32,370	50	0.05	0.28	25.62	81.33	94,930
Central East 華東	3	449	17,193	1,450	3.49	6.22	38.32	43.84	41,533
Shanghai 上海	1	1,202	51,580	4,350	3.49	6.22	42.91	43.84	124,600
Jiangsu 江蘇									
Zhejiang 浙江	1	144							
Anhui 安徽									
Fujian 福建	1								
Jiangxi 江西									
Shandong 山東									
Central-South 中南	2	127	7,355	280	2.25	6.33	57.91	64.46	12,435
Henan 河南	1	21							
Hubei 湖北									
Hunan 湖南									
Guangdong 廣東	1	233	14,710	560	2.25	6.33	63.13	64.46	24,870
Guangxi 廣西									
Hainan 海南									
Southwest 西南	1	44	770				17.50	30.00	1,500
Chongqing 重慶									
Sichuan 四川									
Guizhou 貴州									
Yunnan 雲南									
Tibet 西藏									
Northwest 西北									
Shaanxi 陝西									
Gansu 甘肅									
Qinghai 青海									
Ningxia 寧夏									
Xinjiang 新疆									

4251: Photography and Film Machinery 電影機械製造業

Year 年份	Number of firms 企業個數	Rate of change 每年變化 (%)	Number of employees 職工人數 (人)	Rate of change 每年變化 (%)	Total revenue (mil. RMB) 總銷售收入 (百萬元)	Rate of change 每年變化 (%)	Total profit (mil. RMB) 總利潤 (百萬元)	Rate of change 每年變化 (%)
1993	22		10,006		149		8	
1994	25	13.64%	8,721	-12.84%	171	14.91%	2	-77.11%
1995	15	-40.00%	6,308	-27.67%	124	-27.86%	2	12.35%
1996	14	-6.67%	5,572	-11.67%	140	13.30%	5	138.89%

3 Major products* 3 種主要產品 *	Output 產量	Sales volume 銷售量	Unit 單位
a) Film Machinery 電影機械	1,250	1,962	set 台

Top 10 firms by revenue (year founded) 收入排名前 10 家企業 (創辦年份)	City 城市	Province 省	Telephone / fax 電話 / 傳真	Number of employees 職工人數	Ownership 產業所有權	Revenue ('000 RMB) 銷售收入 (千元)	Profit ('000 RMB) (rank) 利潤 (千元) (排名)	Total assets ('000 RMB) 總資產 (千元)	Major products 主要產品
Harbin Cine-equipment Plant 哈爾濱電影機械廠(1950)	Harbin 哈爾濱市	Heilongjiang 黑龍江省	(0451)6663891 (0451)6666335	1,999	State-owned 國有	56,729	103(3)	162,880	a
Guangdong Film Machinery Factory 廣東電影機械廠(1958)	Guangzhou 廣州市	Guangdong 廣東省	(020)83345761	233	State-owned 國有	14,714	562(2)	24,868	a
Harbin Communication Equipment Manufacturing Co. 哈爾濱通訊設備製造公司(1953)	Harbin 哈爾濱市	Heilongjiang 黑龍江省	(0451)4682053	592	State-owned 國有	8,016	0(4)	26,978	a
Tianjin Zhong Huan Image Equipment Co. 天津市中環影像設備公司(1954)	Tianjin 天津市	Tianjin 天津市	(022)27622464 (022)27623747	1,039	State-owned 國有	3,559	-303(7)	57,374	a
Shenyang He Xing Machinery Electron Co. Ltd. 瀋陽合興機械電子有限公司(1992)	Shenyang 瀋陽市	Liaoning 遼寧省	(024)22905185 (024)22915034	137	Foreign-funded 外資	2,768	-156(6)	6,645	o

Top 10 Cities by Production Output 產出排名前 10 位城市	Province 省	Market share 市場份額	Number of firms 企業個數
Shanghai 上海市	Shanghai 上海市	39.84%	5
Harbin 哈爾濱市	Heilongjiang 黑龍江省	36.51%	5
Guangzhou 廣州市	Guangdong 廣東省	6.68%	1
Shenzhen 深圳市	Guangdong 廣東省	5.95%	1
Ji'nan 濟南市	Shandong 山東省	4.68%	2
Tianjin 天津市	Tianjin 天津市	2.37%	3
Nanjing 南京市	Jiangsu 江蘇省	1.50%	2
Shenyang 瀋陽市	Liaoning 遼寧省	1.17%	1
Hangzhou 杭州市	Zhejiang 浙江省	1.02%	1
Luzhou 瀘州市	Sichuan 四川省	0.18%	1

10 Major Wholesalers 10 家主要批發商	City 城市	Province 省	Telephone / Fax 電話 / 傳真
Liaoning Automobile Trade Group Corp. 遼寧省汽車貿易集團	Shenyang 瀋陽市	Liaoning 遼寧省	(024)23835494 (024)23838338
China Post and Telecommunication Equipment General Company 中國郵電器材總公司	Beijing 北京市	Beijing 北京市	(010)63523715 (010)63525935
Jiangsu Electromechanical Products General Company 江蘇省機電產品總公司	Nanjing 南京市	Jiangsu 江蘇省	(025)7713642 (025)7711036
Xi Nan Technology Import & Export Company 西南技術進出口公司	Chongqing 重慶市	Chongqing 重慶市	(023)63850185 (023)63850026
Changzhou Economic Technology Industrial Development Zone Tian Ming Trade Company 常州經濟技術產業開發區天明貿易公司	Changzhou 常州市	Jiangsu 江蘇省	(0519)8829882 (0519)8829882
Shanxi Mechanical Equipment Import & Export Company 山西省機械設備進出口公司	Taiyuan 太原市	Shanxi 山西省	(0351)4040713 (0351)4043981
Ningbo Five Mining Machinery Import & Export Company 寧波市五礦機械進出口公司	Ningbo 寧波市	Zhejiang 浙江省	(0574)7311255 (0574)7320322
Tianjin Jin Huan Electromechanical Complete Sets of Equipment Factory 天津市津環機電成套設備廠	Tianjin 天津市	Tianjin 天津市	(022)26371628
Yunnan Machinery Import & Export Company 雲南省機械進出口公司	Kunming 昆明市	Yunnan 雲南省	(0871)3164879 (0871)3136829
Tianjin Da Qiu Zhuang Yi Yuan Trade Center 天津市大丘莊億源商貿中心	Tianjin 天津市	Tianjin 天津市	(022)28899478 (022)28899046

*Also include sales by firms outside this industry.包括本行業以外廠家的銷售。"o" stands for "others". "o" 代表"其他產品"。

4252: Slide Projectors 幻燈機及投影儀製造業

The industry accounts for 0.001% of the total revenue of China's industrial sector in 1996. The revenue growth rate of the industry is -34.3% from 1995, as compared to the growth rate of China's industrial sector, 9.51%. The rate of return on asset is -0.78%. 52.22% of all firms in the industry made a profit while 27.78% had negative returns. The top province in terms of the industry's revenue is Jiangsu, accounting for 73.32% of the total revenue.
本行業在1996年佔全行業總產值0.001%，行業年增長率為-34.3%（全國工業年增長率9.51%）。行業的資產回報率-0.78%，52.22%的企業盈利，27.78%的企業虧損。銷售收入最高的省份為江蘇省，佔本行業的73.32%。

	Total number of firms 企業總數	Total number of employees 職工總數	Total revenue (mil. RMB) 總銷售收入（百萬元）	Total profit (mil. RMB) 總利潤（百萬元）	Return on assets 資產利潤率 (%)	Return on equity 權益利潤率 (%)	Labour productivity ('000 RMB / worker) 勞動生產率（千元/人）	Debts / assets 資產負債率 (%)	Total assets (mil. RMB) 總資產（百萬元）
Industry Overall 行業總體	15	2,468	81	-1	-0.78	-2.08	32.82	62.53	178

	Number of firms 企業個數	Average number of employees 平均職工人數	Average revenue ('000 RMB) 平均銷售收入（千元）	Average profit ('000 RMB) 平均利潤（千元）	Return on assets 資產利潤率 (%)	Return on equity 權益利潤率 (%)	Labour productivity ('000 RMB / worker) 勞動生產率（千元/人）	Average debts / assets 平均資產負債率(%)	Average Total assets ('000 RMB) 平均總資產（千元）
By ownership 產業所有權									
State-owned 國有	6	357	10,333				28.93	62.42	26,167
Collectively-owned 集體	5	42	1,552	-30	-2.64	-5.63	37.30	53.16	1,130
Privately-owned 私有	1	15	1,731	168	15.46	40.41	115.39	61.75	1,084
Domestic JVs 聯營									
Joint stock 股份制									
Foreign-funded 外資	1	3	82	-249	-16.64	-40.26	27.35	58.68	1,498
Overseas Chinese-funded 港澳台資	2	22	4,085	-275	-5.81	-21.96	190.02	73.54	4,725
By size 規模									
Large 大型	1	1,245	32,229	124	0.15	0.50	25.89	70.22	83,195
Medium 中型	1	591	16,107	1,054	2.55	6.25	27.25	59.19	41,289
Small 小型	13	48	2,513	-168	-4.07	-8.59	52.77	52.59	4,116
By regional distribution 地區分布									
Central-North 華北	2	7	580	-90	-10.23	-22.22	82.86	53.98	880
Beijing 北京	1	14	220	20	5.26	12.50	15.71	57.89	380
Tianjin 天津	1		940	-200	-14.49	-30.77		52.90	1,380
Hebei 河北									
Shanxi 山西									
Inner Mongolia 內蒙									
Northeast 東北									
Liaoning 遼寧									
Jilin 吉林									
Heilongjiang 黑龍江									
Central East 華東	9	246	8,352	-87	-0.47	-1.25	33.89	62.19	18,410
Shanghai 上海	3	24	1,363	143	14.19	39.45	56.03	64.03	1,010
Jiangsu 江蘇	2	1,034	29,695	-305	-0.41	-1.12	28.72	63.29	74,420
Zhejiang 浙江									
Anhui 安徽									
Fujian 福建	3	25	3,887	-137	-3.86	-8.13	157.57	52.54	3,540
Jiangxi 江西									
Shandong 山東	1	3	30	-190	-5.94	-10.16	10.00	41.56	3,200
Central-South 中南	3	61	1,060	-47	-2.01	-6.80	17.38	70.44	2,323
Henan 河南	3	61	1,060	-47	-2.01	-6.80	17.38	70.44	2,323
Hubei 湖北									
Hunan 湖南									
Guangdong 廣東									
Guangxi 廣西									
Hainan 海南									
Southwest 西南	1	53	1,420	-300	-7.83	-23.62	26.79	66.84	3,830
Chongqing 重慶	1	53	1,420	300	7.83	23.62	26.79	66.84	3,830
Sichuan 四川									
Guizhou 貴州									
Yunnan 雲南									
Tibet 西藏									
Northwest 西北									
Shaanxi 陝西									
Gansu 甘肅									
Qinghai 青海									
Ningxia 寧夏									
Xinjiang 新疆									

4252: Slide Projectors 幻燈機及投影儀製造業

Year 年份	Number of firms 企業個數	Rate of change 每年變化 (%)	Number of employees 職工人數 (人)	Rate of change 每年變化 (%)	Total revenue (mil. RMB) 總銷售收入 (百萬元)	Rate of change 每年變化 (%)	Total profit (mil. RMB) 總利潤 (百萬元)	Rate of change 每年變化 (%)
1993	16		1,490		39		3	
1994	10	-37.50%	722	-51.54%	62	59.15%	0	-106.06%
1995	19	90.00%	3,874	436.57%	123	98.59%	0	-121.62%
1996	15	-21.05%	2,468	-36.29%	81	-34.33%	-1	-143.90%

3 Major products* 3 種主要產品 *	Output 產量	Sales volume 銷售量	Unit 單位
a) Film Machinery 電影機械	86,028	135,064	set 台

Top 10 firms by revenue (year founded) 收入排名前 10 家企業 (創辦年份)	City 城市	Province 省	Telephone / fax 電話 / 傳真	Number of employees 職工人數	Ownership 產業所有權	Revenue ('000 RMB) 銷售收入 (千元)	Profit ('000 RMB) (rank) 利潤 (千元) (排名)	Total assets ('000 RMB) 總資產 (千元)	Major products 主要產品
Nanjing Cine-equipment Manufactory 南京電影機械廠(1952)	Nanjing 南京市	Jiangsu 江蘇省	(025)5411039 (025)5411582	1,922	State-owned 國有	58,260	68(2)	139,416	a
Xin Pu Kang Guang Pian Co. Ltd. 欣普康光片有限公司(1995)	Xiamen 廈門市	Fujian 福建省	(0592)5623660 (0592)5623657	54	Overseas Chinese-funded 港澳台資	9,476	-549(5)	5,151	o
Shanghai Intelligence Audio-visual Technology & Industry Co. 上海智力視聽科技工貿公司(1992)	Shanghai 上海市	Shanghai 上海市	(021)64710336	32	Collectively-owned 集體	3,630	0(3)	1,164	o
Xia Ying Audio-visual Equipment Co. 廈影視聽器材有限公司(1987)	Xiamen 廈門市	Fujian 福建省	(0592)5060035 (0592)5098311	20	State-owned 國有	2,187	135(1)	5,464	o

Top 10 Cities by Production Output 產出排名前 10 位城市	Province 省	Market share 市場份額	Number of firms 企業個數
Nanjing 南京市	Jiangsu 江蘇省	62.82%	3
Suzhou 蘇州市	Jiangsu 江蘇省	13.60%	1
Hangzhou 杭州市	Zhejiang 浙江省	6.38%	1
Shanghai 上海市	Shanghai 上海市	5.18%	2
Zhengzhou 鄭州市	Henan 河南省	3.14%	2
Xiamen 廈門市	Fujian 福建省	2.81%	1
Shenzhen 深圳市	Guangdong 廣東省	2.25%	2
Tianjin 天津市	Tianjin 天津市	1.21%	1
Guangzhou 廣州市	Guangdong 廣東省	1.08%	2
Zibo 淄博市	Shandong 山東省	0.85%	1

10 Major Wholesalers 10 家主要批發商	City 城市	Province 省	Telephone / Fax 電話 / 傳真
Liaoning Automobile Trade Group Corp. 遼寧省汽車貿易集團	Shenyang 瀋陽市	Liaoning 遼寧省	(024)23835494 (024)23838338
China Post and Telecommunication Equipment General Company 中國郵電器材總公司	Beijing 北京市	Beijing 北京市	(010)63523715 (010)63525935
Jiangsu Electromechanical Products General Company 江蘇省機電產品總公司	Nanjing 南京市	Jiangsu 江蘇省	(025)7713642 (025)7711036
Xi Nan Technology Import & Export Company 西南技術進出口公司	Chongqing 重慶市	Chongqing 重慶市	(023)63850185 (023)63850026
Changzhou Economic Technology Industrial Development Zone Tian Ming Trade Company 常州經濟技術產業開發區天明貿易公司	Changzhou 常州市	Jiangsu 江蘇省	(0519)8829882 (0519)8829882
Shanxi Mechanical Equipment Import & Export Company 山西省機械設備進出口公司	Taiyuan 太原市	Shanxi 山西省	(0351)4040713 (0351)4043981
Ningbo Five Mining Machinery Import & Export Company 寧波市五礦機械進出口公司	Ningbo 寧波市	Zhejiang 浙江省	(0574)7311255 (0574)7320322
Tianjin Jin Huan Electromechanical Complete Sets of Equipment Factory 天津市津環機電成套設備廠	Tianjin 天津市	Tianjin 天津市	(022)26371628
Yunnan Machinery Import & Export Company 雲南省機械進出口公司	Kunming 昆明市	Yunnan 雲南省	(0871)3164879 (0871)3136829
Tianjin Da Qiu Zhuang Yi Yuan Trade Center 天津市大丘莊億源商貿中心	Tianjin 天津市	Tianjin 天津市	(022)28899478 (022)28899046

*Also include sales by firms outside this industry.包括本行業以外廠家的銷售。"o" stands for "others". "o" 代表 "其他產品"。

4254: Cameras 照機機及器材製造業

The industry accounts for 0.137% of the total revenue of China's industrial sector in 1996. The revenue growth rate of the industry is 71.8% from 1995, as compared to the growth rate of China's industrial sector, 9.51%. The rate of return on asset is 2.34%. 73.47% of all firms in the industry made a profit while 22.58% had negative returns. The top province in terms of the industry's revenue is Guangdong, accounting for 83.69% of the total revenue.
本行業在1996年佔全行業總產值0.137%，行業年增長率為71.8%（全國工業年增長率9.51%）。行業的資產回報率2.34%，73.47%的企業盈利，22.58%的企業虧損。銷售收入最高的省份為廣東省，佔本行業的83.69%。

	Total number of firms 企業總數	Total number of employees 職工總數	Total revenue (mil. RMB) 總銷售收入（百萬元）	Total profit (mil. RMB) 總利潤（百萬元）	Return on assets 資產利潤率 (%)	Return on equity 權益利潤率 (%)	Labour productivity ('000 RMB / worker) 勞動生產率（千元/人）	Debts / assets 資產負債率 (%)	Total assets (mil. RMB) 總資產（百萬元）
Industry Overall 行業總體	133	42,789	7,956	153	2.34	7.55	185.94	69.02	6,558

	Number of firms 企業個數	Average number of employees 平均職工人數	Average revenue ('000 RMB) 平均銷售收入（千元）	Average profit ('000 RMB) 平均利潤（千元）	Return on assets 資產利潤率 (%)	Return on equity 權益利潤率 (%)	Labour productivity ('000 RMB / worker) 勞動生產率（千元/人）	Average debts / assets 平均資產負債率(%)	Average Total assets ('000 RMB) 平均總資產（千元）
By ownership 產業所有權									
State-owned 國有	30	443	5,033	-1,200	-2.92	-15.38	11.37	80.99	41,033
Collectively-owned 集體	44	213	24,597	699	6.06	11.52	115.29	47.35	11,528
Privately-owned 私有	2	21	1,679	86	7.12	14.06	79.93	49.37	1,205
Domestic JVs 聯營	3	285	7,063	-1,022	-2.37	-9.03	24.81	73.76	43,133
Joint stock 股份制									
Foreign-funded 外資	23	345	141,703	6,265	5.46	15.27	410.84	64.23	114,700
Overseas Chinese-funded 港澳台資	31	442	110,953	549	0.83	3.08	251.13	73.06	66,147
By size 規模									
Large 大型	4	2,468	182,617	-5,131	-1.59	-12.54	74.00	87.29	321,826
Medium 中型	7	610	31,527	-3,011	-3.27	-10.84	51.65	69.79	91,984
Small 小型	117	249	59,875	1,663	4.20	11.62	240.77	63.82	39,551
By regional distribution 地區分布									
Central-North 華北	25	160	15,756	424	1.81	4.19	98.21	56.73	23,398
Beijing 北京	13	158	8,498	267	1.34	2.54	53.63	47.31	19,981
Tianjin 天津	9	195	30,956	784	2.21	6.12	158.57	63.88	35,502
Hebei 河北	1	147	2,360	20	0.49	2.63	16.05	81.55	4,120
Shanxi 山西	2	24	1,235	25	3.18	71.43	52.55	95.54	785
Inner Mongolia 內蒙									
Northeast 東北	4	328	2,295	-748	-4.59	59.09	7.00	107.73	16,293
Liaoning 遼寧	2	646	3,690	-1,585	-4.90	58.49	5.72	108.36	32,350
Jilin 吉林									
Heilongjiang 黑龍江	2	11	900	90	38.30	50.00	85.71	21.28	235
Central East 華東	60	171	14,140	-767	-4.22	-11.06	82.90	61.81	18,153
Shanghai 上海	19	317	28,407	-1,581	-3.90	-8.87	89.64	56.02	40,536
Jiangsu 江蘇	7	132	9,941	-433	-5.14	-15.47	75.48	66.81	8,427
Zhejiang 浙江	21	63	3,006	126	3.61	7.99	47.49	54.83	3,485
Anhui 安徽									
Fujian 福建	7	150	15,604	-457	-4.88	-10.72	104.13	54.51	9,370
Jiangxi 江西	2	18	1,250	250	34.48	38.46	71.43	10.34	725
Shandong 山東	4	220	16,058	-3,218	-10.74	197.09	73.15	105.46	29,948
Central-South 中南	41	581	162,482	5,026	4.59	15.12	279.73	69.65	109,508
Henan 河南									
Hubei 湖北	3	158	1,010	37	0.55	16.18	6.39	96.52	6,613
Hunan 湖南	1	8							
Guangdong 廣東	36	648	184,956	5,721	4.61	15.12	285.52	69.52	124,118
Guangxi 廣西	1	13	310				23.85	93.18	1,760
Hainan 海南									
Southwest 西南	1								
Chongqing 重慶									
Sichuan 四川									
Guizhou 貴州	1								
Yunnan 雲南									
Tibet 西藏									
Northwest 西北	2	1,709	21,365	-7,105	-4.32	-291.79	12.51	98.52	164,435
Shaanxi 陝西	1	126	3,850	-4,220	-11.62	118.87	30.56	109.78	36,310
Gansu 甘肅	1	3,291	38,880	-9,990	-3.41	-118.65	11.81	97.12	292,560
Qinghai 青海									
Ningxia 寧夏									
Xinjiang 新疆									

4254: Cameras 照機機及器材製造業

Year 年份	Number of firms 企業個數	Rate of change 每年變化 (%)	Number of employees 職工人數 (人)	Rate of change 每年變化 (%)	Total revenue (mil. RMB) 總銷售收入 (百萬元)	Rate of change 每年變化 (%)	Total profit (mil. RMB) 總利潤 (百萬元)	Rate of change 每年變化 (%)
1993	112		56,610		1,585		2	
1994	132	17.86%	44,417	-21.54%	3,286	107.22%	50	3055.45%
1995	133	0.76%	41,718	-6.08%	4,632	40.95%	90	82.76%
1996	133		42,789	2.57%	7,956	71.76%	153	69.09%

3 Major products* 3 種主要產品 *	Output 產量	Sales volume 銷售量	Unit 單位
a) Camera 照相機	27,359,028	27,906,209	set 台
b) Photographic Material 照相器材	19,853,892	19,655,353	set 台

Top 10 firms by revenue (year founded) 收入排名前 10 家企業 (創辦年份)	City 城市	Province 省	Telephone / fax 電話 / 傳真	Number of employees 職工人數	Ownership 產業所有權	Revenue ('000 RMB) 銷售收入 (千元)	Profit ('000 RMB) (rank) 利潤 (千元) (排名)	Total assets ('000 RMB) 總資產 (千元)	Major products 主要產品
Canon Zhuhai Inc. 佳能珠海有限公司(1990)	Zhuhai 珠海市	Guangdong 廣東省	(0756)8888101 (0756)8888103	2,718	Foreign-funded 外資	2,504,885	130201(1)	1,561,326	a
Ao Da Ba Si (Shenzhen) Industrial Co. Ltd. 奧大巴斯(深圳)工業有限公司(1991)	Shenzhen 深圳市	Guangdong 廣東省	(0755)6631118 (0755)6631084	2,300	Foreign-funded 外資	1,057,455	26907(4)	656,190	a
Foshan Pu Li Hua Camera Co. Ltd. 佛山普立華照相機有限公司(1990)	Foshan 佛山市	Guangdong 廣東省	(0757)2818753 (0757)2818775	1,180	Overseas Chinese-funded 港澳台資	902,485	7586(8)	142,441	a
Mai Ke Te Group (Huizhou) Optical Electromechanical Co. Ltd. 麥科特集團(惠州)光學機電有限公司(1995)	Huizhou 惠州市	Guangdong 廣東省	(0751)3300518	545	Foreign-funded 外資	528,060	30912(2)	156,120	a
Zhuhai Yong Jia Optics Industrial Co. Ltd. 珠海永嘉光學工業有限公司(1991)	Zhuhai 珠海市	Guangdong 廣東省	(0756)3351304 (0756)3337626	2,131	Overseas Chinese-funded 港澳台資	400,091	3922(10)	418,565	a,b
Bao Yuan (Xinhui) Optics Co. Ltd. 寶源(新會)光學有限公司(1991)	Jiangmen 江門市	Guangdong 廣東省	(0750)6672002 (0750)6674070	2,605	Overseas Chinese-funded 港澳台資	372,010	1895(16)	553,683	a
Huidong Han Hui Photographic Equipment Factory 惠東縣漢輝照相器材廠(1996)	Huizhou 惠州市	Guangdong 廣東省		800	Collectively-owned 集體	342,010	8700(6)	26,799	a,b
Polaroid of Shanghai Co. Ltd. 上海寶麗來影像有限公司(1990)	Shanghai 上海市	Shanghai 上海市	(021)63249075 (021)63069266	428	Foreign-funded 外資	275,845	6164(9)	89,220	a
Tianjin Samsung Photoelectron Co. Ltd. 天津三星光電子有限公司(1994)	Tianjin 天津市	Tianjin 天津市	(022)27614724 (022)27618864	518	Foreign-funded 外資	257,549	8188(7)	159,101	a
Guangzhou Zhi Fa Industrial Co. Ltd. 廣州至法實業有限公司(1986)	Guangzhou 廣州市	Guangdong 廣東省	(020)82212651 (020)82212659	770	Overseas Chinese-funded 港澳台資	135,835	346(26)	157,906	o

Top 10 Cities by Production Output 產出排名前 10 位城市	Province 省	Market share 市場份額	Number of firms 企業個數
Foshan 佛山市	Guangdong 廣東省	24.38%	2
Huizhou 惠州市	Guangdong 廣東省	14.31%	1
Zhuhai 珠海市	Guangdong 廣東省	13.32%	5
Shanghai 上海市	Shanghai 上海市	9.59%	41
Dongguan 東莞市	Guangdong 廣東省	9.39%	6
Tianjin 天津市	Tianjin 天津市	7.55%	10
Shangrao 上饒市	Jiangxi 江西省	4.33%	1
Guangzhou 廣州市	Guangdong 廣東省	4.20%	8
Zhongshan 中山市	Guangdong 廣東省	2.03%	2
Qingdao 青島市	Shandong 山東省	1.81%	3

10 Major Wholesalers 10 家主要批發商	City 城市	Province 省	Telephone / Fax 電話 / 傳真
Liaoning Automobile Trade Group Corp. 遼寧省汽車貿易集團	Shenyang 瀋陽市	Liaoning 遼寧省	(024)23835494 (024)23838338
China Post and Telecommunication Equipment General Company 中國郵電器材總公司	Beijing 北京市	Beijing 北京市	(010)63523715 (010)63525935
Jiangsu Electromechanical Products General Company 江蘇省機電產品總公司	Nanjing 南京市	Jiangsu 江蘇省	(025)7713642 (025)7711036
Xi Nan Technology Import & Export Company 西南技術進出口公司	Chongqing 重慶市	Chongqing 重慶市	(023)63850185 (023)63850026
Changzhou Economic Technology Industrial Development Zone Tian Ming Trade Company 常州經濟技術產業開發區天明貿易公司	Changzhou 常州市	Jiangsu 江蘇省	(0519)8829882 (0519)8829882
Shanxi Mechanical Equipment Import & Export Company 山西省機械設備進出口公司	Taiyuan 太原市	Shanxi 山西省	(0351)4040713 (0351)4043981
Ningbo Five Mining Machinery Import & Export Company 寧波市五礦機械進出口公司	Ningbo 寧波市	Zhejiang 浙江省	(0574)7311255 (0574)7320322
Tianjin Jin Huan Electromechanical Complete Sets of Equipment Factory 天津市津環機電成套設備廠	Tianjin 天津市	Tianjin 天津市	(022)26371628
Yunnan Machinery Import & Export Company 雲南省機械進出口公司	Kunming 昆明市	Yunnan 雲南省	(0871)3164879 (0871)3136829
Tianjin Da Qiu Zhuang Yi Yuan Trade Center 天津市大丘莊億源商貿中心	Tianjin 天津市	Tianjin 天津市	(022)28899478 (022)28899046

*Also include sales by firms outside this industry.包括本行業以外廠家的銷售。"o" stands for "others". "o" 代表 "其他產品"。

4256: Copiers 複印機製造業

The industry accounts for 0.081% of the total revenue of China's industrial sector in 1996. The revenue growth rate of the industry is 176.2% from 1995, as compared to the growth rate of China's industrial sector, 9.51%. The rate of return on asset is 3.76%. 60.79% of all firms in the industry made a profit while 33.33% had negative returns. The top province in terms of the industry's revenue is Guangdong, accounting for 50.50% of the total revenue.
本行業在1996年佔全行業總產值0.081%，行業年增長率為176.2%（全國工業年增長率9.51%）。行業的資產回報率3.76%，60.79%的企業盈利，33.33%的企業虧損。銷售收入最高的省份為廣東省，佔本行業的50.50%。

	Total number of firms 企業總數	Total number of employees 職工總數	Total revenue (mil. RMB) 總銷售收入（百萬元）	Total profit (mil. RMB) 總利潤（百萬元）	Return on assets 資產利潤率 (%)	Return on equity 權益利潤率 (%)	Labour productivity ('000 RMB / worker) 勞動生產率（千元/人）	Debts / assets 資產負債率 (%)	Total assets (mil. RMB) 總資產（百萬元）
Industry Overall 行業總體	26	9,586	4,695	144	3.76	16.53	489.78	77.24	3,821

	Number of firms 企業個數	Average number of employees 平均職工人數	Average revenue ('000 RMB) 平均銷售收入（千元）	Average profit ('000 RMB) 平均利潤（千元）	Return on assets 資產利潤率 (%)	Return on equity 權益利潤率 (%)	Labour productivity ('000 RMB / worker) 勞動生產率（千元/人）	Average debts / assets 平均資產負債率(%)	Average Total assets ('000 RMB) 平均總資產（千元）
By ownership 產業所有權									
State-owned 國有	5	888	105,200	-6,000	-3.19	-24.19	118.42	86.82	188,200
Collectively-owned 集體	7	362	11,742	1,000	4.27	17.28	32.40	75.29	23,425
Privately-owned 私有									
Domestic JVs 聯營									
Joint stock 股份制	1	14	1,458	-2,717	-123.36	462.09	104.13	126.70	2,203
Foreign-funded 外資	9	298	452,519	19,692	6.65	26.58	1516.26	74.99	296,238
Overseas Chinese-funded 港澳台資	4	38	3,518	-1,881	-15.23	-19.06	93.20	20.08	12,350
By size 規模									
Large 大型	4	1,272	735,865	2,421,746	409.72	2754.76	578.62	85.13	591,075
Medium 中型	1	1,010	163,798	8,384,619	5266.03	16958.36	162.18	68.95	159,221
Small 小型	19	183	83,623	-943,558	-1380.40	-3820.93	456.56	63.87	68,354
By regional distribution 地區分布									
Central-North 華北	6	315	16,942	-70	-0.15	-1.04	53.73	85.21	45,695
Beijing 北京	2	5	170				34.00	19.63	1,070
Tianjin 天津	4	471	25,328	-105	-0.15	-1.08	53.83	85.73	68,008
Hebei 河北									
Shanxi 山西									
Inner Mongolia 內蒙									
Northeast 東北	4	44	1,645	303	16.18	26.83	37.60	39.71	1,870
Liaoning 遼寧	4	44	1,645	303	16.18	26.83	37.60	39.71	1,870
Jilin 吉林									
Heilongjiang 黑龍江									
Central East 華東	8	237	266,946	15,899	13.45	27.64	1126.95	51.35	118,223
Shanghai 上海	3	365	167,913	18,163	11.76	28.89	460.46	59.30	154,480
Jiangsu 江蘇	2	355	805,470	36,735	15.65	27.90	2268.93	43.89	234,685
Zhejiang 浙江									
Anhui 安徽									
Fujian 福建	2	41	240	-585	-25.27	-34.31	5.93	26.35	2,315
Jiangxi 江西									
Shandong 山東	1	10	20,410	400	4.80	8.37	2041.00	42.69	8,340
Central-South 中南	7	802	350,209	2,253	0.61	4.33	436.67	85.95	370,406
Henan 河南									
Hubei 湖北	1	45	31,640	3,520	9.24	11.19	703.11	17.41	38,080
Hunan 湖南									
Guangdong 廣東	5	686	474,170	10,020	2.23	16.05	691.41	86.10	449,266
Guangxi 廣西	1	2,140	48,970	-37,850	-12.27	-184.27	22.88	93.34	308,430
Hainan 海南									
Southwest 西南	1	10	200				20.00	66.67	300
Chongqing 重慶									
Sichuan 四川									
Guizhou 貴州									
Yunnan 雲南									
Tibet 西藏									
Northwest 西北									
Shaanxi 陝西									
Gansu 甘肅									
Qinghai 青海									
Ningxia 寧夏									
Xinjiang 新疆									

Year 年份	Number of firms 企業個數	Rate of change 每年變化 (%)	Number of employees 職工人數 (人)	Rate of change 每年變化 (%)	Total revenue (mil. RMB) 總銷售收入 (百萬元)	Rate of change 每年變化 (%)	Total profit (mil. RMB) 總利潤 (百萬元)	Rate of change 每年變化 (%)
1993	26		25,629		1,649		92	
1994	24	-7.69%	8,415	-67.17%	1,185	-28.12%	-1	-100.90%
1995	30	25.00%	9,432	12.09%	1,700	43.40%	0	122.05%
1996	26	-13.33%	9,586	1.63%	4,695	176.18%	144	79458.01%

3 Major products* 3 種主要產品 *	Output 產量	Sales volume 銷售量	Unit 單位
a) Copying Machinery 複印機械	363,267	359,634	set 台

Top 10 firms by revenue (year founded) 收入排名前 10 家企業 (創辦年份)	City 城市	Province 省	Telephone / fax 電話 / 傳真	Number of employees 職工人數	Ownership 產業所有權	Revenue ('000 RMB) 銷售收入 (千元)	Profit ('000 RMB) (rank) 利潤 (千元) (排名)	Total assets ('000 RMB) 總資產 (千元)	Major products 主要產品
Li Guang (Shenzhen) Industry Development Co. Ltd. 理光(深圳)工業發展有限公司(1994)	Shenzhen 深圳市	Guangdong 廣東省	(0755)3360885 (0755)3360885	2,300	Overseas Chinese-funded 港澳台資	1,984,156	41918(3)	1,842,423	a
Sharp Office Equipments (Changshu) Co. Ltd. 夏普辦公設備(常熟)有限公司(1995)	Suzhou 蘇州市	Jiangsu 江蘇省	(0512)2856414 (0512)2856046	661	Foreign-funded 外資	1,585,180	75450(1)	433,480	o
Xerox of Shanghai Ltd. 上海施樂複印機有限公司(1989)	Shanghai 上海市	Shanghai 上海市	(021)64300480 (021)64304915	552	Foreign-funded 外資	496,614	53553(2)	432,775	a
Shanghai San Rong Electric Appliance Co. Ltd. 上海三榮電器有限公司(1944)	Shanghai 上海市	Shanghai 上海市	(021)59155549 (021)59155844	467	Foreign-funded 外資	387,990	39518(4)	161,012	o
Guangdong Shi Lian Industrial Group Co. 廣東世聯實業集團公司(1984)	Zhanjiang 湛江市	Guangdong 廣東省	(0758)3380156 (0758)3380178	572	State-owned 國有	249,870	3718(5)	241,694	a
Guangzhou Duplicator Factory 廣州複印機廠(1958)	Guangzhou 廣州市	Guangdong 廣東省	(020)81818178 (020)81816413	291	State-owned 國有	124,830	3626(6)	123,223	a
Tianjin Duplicate Equipment Co. 天津市複印設備公司(1973)	Tianjin 天津市	Tianjin 天津市	(022)28302082 (022)28331412	1,441	State-owned 國有	90,503	0(13)	235,143	a
Guilin Wei Da Instrument and Meter Office Work Equipment Group Co. 桂林威達儀器儀表辦公設備集團公司(1959)	Guilin 桂林市	Guangxi 廣西	(0773)3833888 (0773)3835293	2,140	State-owned 國有	48,974	-37847(17)	308,432	a
Xerox Engineering Copy System Suzhou Co. Ltd. 蘇州施樂工程複印系統有限公司(1994)	Suzhou 蘇州市	Jiangsu 江蘇省	(0512)5285076 (0512)5282370	49	Foreign-funded 外資	25,756	-1976(16)	35,890	o
Weihai Tai Hua Electron Co. Ltd. 威海泰華電子有限公司(1993)	Weihai 威海市	Shandong 山東省	(0896)5818006 (0896)5815064	10	Overseas Chinese-funded 港澳台資	20,407	403(11)	8,335	a

Top 10 Cities by Production Output 產出排名前 10 位城市	Province 省	Market share 市場份額	Number of firms 企業個數
Shanghai 上海市	Shanghai 上海市	34.04%	4
Shenzhen 深圳市	Guangdong 廣東省	24.26%	1
Zhanjiang 湛江市	Guangdong 廣東省	19.21%	2
Guangzhou 廣州市	Guangdong 廣東省	8.59%	3
Tianjin 天津市	Tianjin 天津市	6.85%	5
Guilin 桂林市	Guangxi 廣西	3.50%	1
Weihai 威海市	Shandong 山東省	1.38%	1
Wuhan 武漢市	Hubei 湖北省	1.32%	1
Beijing 北京市	Beijing 北京市	0.58%	2
Suzhou 蘇州市	Jiangsu 江蘇省	0.14%	1

10 Major Wholesalers 10 家主要批發商	City 城市	Province 省	Telephone / Fax 電話 / 傳真
Liaoning Automobile Trade Group Corp. 遼寧省汽車貿易集團	Shenyang 瀋陽市	Liaoning 遼寧省	(024)23835494 (024)23838338
China Post and Telecommunication Equipment General Company 中國郵電器材總公司	Beijing 北京市	Beijing 北京市	(010)63523715 (010)63525935
Jiangsu Electromechanical Products General Company 江蘇省機電產品總公司	Nanjing 南京市	Jiangsu 江蘇省	(025)7713642 (025)7711036
Xi Nan Technology Import & Export Company 西南技術進出口公司	Chongqing 重慶市	Chongqing 重慶市	(023)63850185 (023)63850026
Changzhou Economic Technology Industrial Development Zone Tian Ming Trade Company 常州經濟技術產業開發區天明貿易公司	Changzhou 常州市	Jiangsu 江蘇省	(0519)8829882 (0519)8829882
Shanxi Mechanical Equipment Import & Export Company 山西省機械設備進出口公司	Taiyuan 太原市	Shanxi 山西省	(0351)4040713 (0351)4043981
Ningbo Five Mining Machinery Import & Export Company 寧波市五礦機械進出口公司	Ningbo 寧波市	Zhejiang 浙江省	(0574)7311255 (0574)7320322
Tianjin Jin Huan Electromechanical Complete Sets of Equipment Factory 天津市津環機電成套設備廠	Tianjin 天津市	Tianjin 天津市	(022)26371628
Yunnan Machinery Import & Export Company 雲南省機械進出口公司	Kunming 昆明市	Yunnan 雲南省	(0871)3164879 (0871)3136829
Tianjin Da Qiu Zhuang Yi Yuan Trade Center 天津市大丘莊億源商貿中心	Tianjin 天津市	Tianjin 天津市	(022)28899478 (022)28899046

*Also include sales by firms outside this industry.包括本行業以外廠家的銷售。"o" stands for "others". "o" 代表 "其他產品"。

4257: Typewriters and Mimeographs 打字機及油印機製造業

The industry accounts for 0.009% of the total revenue of China's industrial sector in 1996. The revenue growth rate of the industry is 31.7% from 1995, as compared to the growth rate of China's industrial sector, 9.51%. The rate of return on asset is -1.94%. 62.16% of all firms in the industry made a profit while 37.84% had negative returns. The top province in terms of the industry's revenue is Jiangsu, accounting for 26.99% of the total revenue.
本行業在1996年佔全行業總產值0.009%，行業年增長率為31.7%（全國工業年增長率9.51%）。行業的資產回報率-1.94%，62.16%的企業盈利，37.84%的企業虧損。銷售收入最高的省份為江蘇省，佔本行業的26.99%。

	Total number of firms 企業總數	Total number of employees 職工總數	Total revenue (mil. RMB) 總銷售收入（百萬元）	Total profit (mil. RMB) 總利潤（百萬元）	Return on assets 資產利潤率 (%)	Return on equity 權益利潤率 (%)	Labour productivity ('000 RMB / worker) 勞動生產率（千元/人）	Debts / assets 資產負債率 (%)	Total assets (mil. RMB) 總資產（百萬元）
Industry Overall 行業總體	33	6,333	504	-19	-1.94	-3.77	79.58	48.64	996

	Number of firms 企業個數	Average number of employees 平均職工人數	Average revenue ('000 RMB) 平均銷售收入（千元）	Average profit ('000 RMB) 平均利潤（千元）	Return on assets 資產利潤率 (%)	Return on equity 權益利潤率 (%)	Labour productivity ('000 RMB / worker) 勞動生產率（千元/人）	Average debts / assets 平均資產負債率(%)	Average Total assets ('000 RMB) 平均總資產（千元）
By ownership 產業所有權									
State-owned 國有	5	498	16,600	-2,600	-7.69	-38.24	33.32	79.88	33,800
Collectively-owned 集體	11	68	504	11	0.30	0.67	7.39	55.63	3,571
Privately-owned 私有									
Domestic JVs 聯營	6	232	16,835	-304	-2.17	-3.27	72.46	33.61	13,975
Joint stock 股份制									
Foreign-funded 外資	7	251	37,268	-375	-0.41	-0.71	148.39	42.12	90,668
Overseas Chinese-funded 港澳台資	5	47	10,712	-335	-2.42	-4.46	229.88	45.73	13,836
By size 規模									
Large 大型									
Medium 中型	4	746	27,817	-9,302	-12.22	-25.42	37.28	51.93	76,136
Small 小型	28	120	14,025	650	2.63	4.98	117.30	47.13	24,694
By regional distribution 地區分布									
Central-North 華北	5	57	14,596	1,260	3.92	11.58	257.88	66.12	32,114
Beijing 北京	3	76	22,387	1,903	3.61	10.88	294.56	66.79	52,660
Tianjin 天津	1	15	540	-140	-10.22	-12.84	36.00	20.44	1,370
Hebei 河北	1	40	5,280	730	59.84	86.90	132.00	31.15	1,220
Shanxi 山西									
Inner Mongolia 內蒙									
Northeast 東北									
Liaoning 遼寧									
Jilin 吉林									
Heilongjiang 黑龍江									
Central East 華東	19	285	19,447	-146	-0.56	-1.26	68.20	55.94	26,346
Shanghai 上海	7	375	15,959	-1,791	-7.16	-26.10	42.56	72.58	25,036
Jiangsu 江蘇	4	245	34,010	3,060	8.89	15.57	138.67	42.91	34,438
Zhejiang 浙江	5	91	3,326	22	0.36	0.95	36.71	61.72	6,034
Anhui 安徽									
Fujian 福建									
Jiangxi 江西									
Shandong 山東	3	453	35,040	-863	-1.65	-3.15	77.35	47.69	52,467
Central-South 中南	6	72	9,800	-3,772	-6.93	-9.60	135.80	27.81	54,442
Henan 河南									
Hubei 湖北									
Hunan 湖南									
Guangdong 廣東	4	99	14,220	-5,605	-6.97	-9.68	144.37	27.93	80,378
Guangxi 廣西	2	20	960	-105	-4.09	-5.12	49.23	20.23	2,570
Hainan 海南									
Southwest 西南	2	36	190	-95	-4.82	633.33	5.28	100.76	1,970
Chongqing 重慶	1	7	229	11	8.76	24.72	34.98	64.58	127
Sichuan 四川	1	65	151	-201	-5.27	268.64	2.31	101.96	3,813
Guizhou 貴州									
Yunnan 雲南									
Tibet 西藏									
Northwest 西北	1	127	2,230	10	0.22	1.19	17.56	80.90	4,450
Shaanxi 陝西	1	127	2,230	10	0.22	1.19	17.56	80.90	4,450
Gansu 甘肅									
Qinghai 青海									
Ningxia 寧夏									
Xinjiang 新疆									

4257: Typewriters and Mimeographs 打字機及油印機製造業

Year 年份	Number of firms 企業個數	Rate of change 每年變化 (%)	Number of employees 職工人數（人）	Rate of change 每年變化 (%)	Total revenue (mil. RMB) 總銷售收入（百萬元）	Rate of change 每年變化 (%)	Total profit (mil. RMB) 總利潤（百萬元）	Rate of change 每年變化 (%)
1993	32		15,214		890		266	
1994	31	-3.13%	7,364	-51.60%	506	-43.13%	7	-97.29%
1995	30	-3.23%	5,471	-25.71%	383	-24.38%	-10	-242.15%
1996	33	10.00%	6,333	15.76%	504	31.70%	-19	-85.51%

3 Major products* 3種主要產品*	Output 產量	Sales volume 銷售量	Unit 單位
a) Typing & Mimeographing Machinery 打字油印機械	569,734	535,550	set 台

Top 10 firms by revenue (year founded) 收入排名前10家企業（創辦年份）	City 城市	Province 省	Telephone / fax 電話 / 傳真	Number of employees 職工人數	Ownership 產業所有權	Revenue ('000 RMB) 銷售收入（千元）	Profit ('000 RMB) (rank) 利潤（千元）（排名）	Total assets ('000 RMB) 總資產（千元）	Major products 主要產品
Feiteng Group Co. Ltd. 張家港市飛騰打字機廠(1988)	Suzhou 蘇州市	Jiangsu 江蘇省	(0512)8770168 (0512)8771269	781	Collectively-owned 集體	129,949	12050(1)	126,427	a
Beijing Stone Office Equipment Technology Co. Ltd. 北京四通辦公設備有限公司(1987)	Beijing 北京市	Beijing 北京市	(010)62555177 (010)62562461	176	Foreign-funded 外資	66,778	5877(2)	157,567	o
Qingdao Ma La Song Typewriter Co. Ltd. 青島馬拉松打字機有限公司(1994)	Qingdao 青島市	Shandong 山東省	(0532)8483570 (0532)8463093	482	Foreign-funded 外資	56,340	-2560(17)	73,048	o
Shandong Movie Machinery Plant 山東電影機械廠(1950)	Ji'nan 濟南市	Shandong 山東省	(0531)8933640 (0531)8933640	702	State-owned 國有	46,294	1049(4)	72,110	a
She Kou Guang Hua Electronic Technique Co. Ltd. 蛇口廣華電子技術有限公司(1984)	Shenzhen 深圳市	Guangdong 廣東省	(0755)6691048 (0755)6695756	50	Overseas Chinese-funded 港澳台資	33,803	288(9)	18,810	o
Shanghai Chang Kong Typewriter Factory 上海長空打字機廠(1994)	Shanghai 上海市	Shanghai 上海市	(021)62508167	509	Domestic JVs 聯營	28,719	-446(14)	31,521	o
Shanghai Typewriter Factory 上海打字機廠(1949)	Shanghai 上海市	Shanghai 上海市	(021)65421060 (021)56632369	982	State-owned 國有	26,536	-5718(18)	46,281	a
Shenzhen Shi Le High Science & Technology Co. Ltd. 深圳施樂高科技有限公司(1996)	Shenzhen 深圳市	Guangdong 廣東省	(0755)8024111	330	Overseas Chinese-funded 港澳台資	22,969	-22648(20)	301,882	o
Shanghai Gold Shell Typewriter Co. Ltd. 上海金貝打字機有限公司(1994)	Shanghai 上海市	Shanghai 上海市	(021)57313983 (021)57313985	165	Foreign-funded 外資	22,495	1245(3)	35,386	a
Shanghai Brother Shen Bei Industrial Co. Ltd. 上海兄弟申貝工業有限公司(1996)	Shanghai 上海市	Shanghai 上海市	(021)65171892 (021)65171889	59	Foreign-funded 外資	21,221	-223(13)	18,552	a

Top 10 Cities by Production Output 產出排名前10位城市	Province 省	Market share 市場份額	Number of firms 企業個數
Suzhou 蘇州市	Jiangsu 江蘇省	38.21%	3
Shanghai 上海市	Shanghai 上海市	27.46%	12
Ji'nan 濟南市	Shandong 山東省	12.99%	2
Fuzhou 福州市	Fujian 福建省	8.13%	1
Ningbo 寧波市	Zhejiang 浙江省	4.85%	4
Taizhou 臺州市	Zhejiang 浙江省	2.29%	1
Xingtai 邢臺市	Hebei 河北省	2.02%	1
Weinan 渭南市	Shaanxi 陝西省	0.82%	1
Rizhao 日照市	Shandong 山東省	0.81%	1
Hangzhou 杭州市	Zhejiang 浙江省	0.68%	1

10 Major Wholesalers 10家主要批發商	City 城市	Province 省	Telephone / Fax 電話 / 傳真
Liaoning Automobile Trade Group Corp. 遼寧省汽車貿易集團	Shenyang 瀋陽市	Liaoning 遼寧省	(024)23835494 (024)23838338
China Post and Telecommunication Equipment General Company 中國郵電器材總公司	Beijing 北京市	Beijing 北京市	(010)63523715 (010)63525935
Jiangsu Electromechanical Products General Company 江蘇省機電產品總公司	Nanjing 南京市	Jiangsu 江蘇省	(025)7713642 (025)7711036
Xi Nan Technology Import & Export Company 西南技術進出口公司	Chongqing 重慶市	Chongqing 重慶市	(023)63850185 (023)63850026
Changzhou Economic Technology Industrial Development Zone Tian Ming Trade Company 常州經濟技術產業開發區天明貿易公司	Changzhou 常州市	Jiangsu 江蘇省	(0519)8829882 (0519)8829882
Shanxi Mechanical Equipment Import & Export Company 山西省機械設備進出口公司	Taiyuan 太原市	Shanxi 山西省	(0351)4040713 (0351)4043981
Ningbo Five Mining Machinery Import & Export Company 寧波市五礦機械進出口公司	Ningbo 寧波市	Zhejiang 浙江省	(0574)7311255 (0574)7320322
Tianjin Jin Huan Electromechanical Complete Sets of Equipment Factory 天津市津環機電成套設備廠	Tianjin 天津市	Tianjin 天津市	(022)26371628
Yunnan Machinery Import & Export Company 雲南省機械進出口公司	Kunming 昆明市	Yunnan 雲南省	(0871)3164879 (0871)3136829
Tianjin Da Qiu Zhuang Yi Yuan Trade Center 天津市大丘莊億源商貿中心	Tianjin 天津市	Tianjin 天津市	(022)28899478 (022)28899046

*Also include sales by firms outside this industry.包括本行業以外廠家的銷售。"o" stands for "others". "o" 代表"其他產品"。

4259: Other Educational and Office Machinery 其他文化、辦公用機械製造業

The industry accounts for 0.012% of the total revenue of China's industrial sector in 1996. The revenue growth rate of the industry is -8.4% from 1995, as compared to the growth rate of China's industrial sector, 9.51%. The rate of return on asset is 2.05%. 65.83% of all firms in the industry made a profit while 29.29% had negative returns. The top province in terms of the industry's revenue is Shanghai, accounting for 39.35% of the total revenue.
本行業在1996年佔全行業總產值0.012%，行業年增長率為-8.4%（全國工業年增長率9.51%）。行業的資產回報率2.05%，65.83%的企業盈利，29.29%的企業虧損。銷售收入最高的省份為上海市，佔本行業的39.35%。

	Total number of firms 企業總數	Total number of employees 職工總數	Total revenue (mil. RMB) 總銷售收入（百萬元）	Total profit (mil. RMB) 總利潤（百萬元）	Return on assets 資產利潤率 (%)	Return on equity 權益利潤率 (%)	Labour productivity ('000 RMB / worker) 勞動生產率（千元/人）	Debts / assets 資產負債率 (%)	Total assets (mil. RMB) 總資產（百萬元）
Industry Overall 行業總體	107	7,311	715	17	2.05	5.18	97.80	60.46	820

	Number of firms 企業個數	Average number of employees 平均職工人數	Average revenue ('000 RMB) 平均銷售收入（千元）	Average profit ('000 RMB) 平均利潤（千元）	Return on assets 資產利潤率 (%)	Return on equity 權益利潤率 (%)	Labour productivity ('000 RMB / worker) 勞動生產率（千元/人）	Average debts / assets 平均資產負債率(%)	Average Total assets ('000 RMB) 平均總資產（千元）
By ownership 產業所有權									
State-owned 國有	12	250	20,667	-333	-1.43	-5.06	82.56	71.79	23,333
Collectively-owned 集體	64	56	1,461	72	2.89	7.78	26.32	62.90	2,510
Privately-owned 私有									
Domestic JVs 聯營	2	60	1,637	-6	-0.22	-1.00	27.28	78.26	2,710
Joint stock 股份制									
Foreign-funded 外資	15	22	1,076	-204	-2.96	-4.83	49.81	38.85	6,902
Overseas Chinese-funded 港澳台資	12	31	28,940	1,495	6.90	15.40	923.63	55.20	21,675
By size 規模									
Large 大型									
Medium 中型	2	1,032	84,819	18	0.02	0.04	82.23	61.78	110,977
Small 小型	101	53	5,399	168	2.84	7.09	102.64	60.01	5,921
By regional distribution 地區分布									
Central-North 華北	24	47	11,417	718	7.12	16.22	240.99	56.14	10,095
Beijing 北京	16	28	15,569	819	5.87	13.34	558.54	55.99	13,959
Tianjin 天津	3	109	833	17	0.43	0.98	7.67	56.13	3,890
Hebei 河北	1	300	21,580	4,130	66.61	187.73	71.93	64.52	6,200
Shanxi 山西									
Inner Mongolia 內蒙	4	16	205	-13	-4.63	-7.58	12.62	38.89	270
Northeast 東北	7	60	5,971	426	9.78	35.95	100.00	72.79	4,353
Liaoning 遼寧	6	69	6,963	495	9.75	35.83	101.16	72.79	5,078
Jilin 吉林									
Heilongjiang 黑龍江	1	5	20	10			4.00		
Central East 華東	55	86	6,889	40	0.48	1.40	80.04	65.40	8,299
Shanghai 上海	14	194	20,097	864	3.90	10.91	103.56	64.20	22,135
Jiangsu 江蘇	9	58	2,829	-189	-4.44	-29.06	49.15	84.72	4,253
Zhejiang 浙江	14	26	1,722	49	3.02	6.71	65.69	54.99	1,609
Anhui 安徽	3	52	380	-30	-4.13	-10.84	7.35	61.93	727
Fujian 福建	10	18	2,854	164	5.23	9.31	160.34	43.76	3,133
Jiangxi 江西	1	5	80	10	10.00		16.00	100.00	100
Shandong 山東	4	199	4,553	-2,608	-20.00	-83.04	22.93	75.93	13,035
Central-South 中南	15	45	830	-395	-7.76	-13.75	18.47	43.60	5,087
Henan 河南	3	10	1,153	7	0.48	1.47	111.61	67.47	1,383
Hubei 湖北	3	124	223	-73	-3.03	122.22	1.80	102.48	2,417
Hunan 湖南	1	38	460	10	3.70	4.35	12.11	14.81	270
Guangdong 廣東	8	29	983	-716	-8.86	-13.76	33.73	35.58	8,080
Guangxi 廣西									
Hainan 海南									
Southwest 西南	4	55	1,633	90	3.07	4.99	29.68	38.50	2,935
Chongqing 重慶	3	63	1,827	479	20.64	28.43	29.00	27.40	2,322
Sichuan 四川	1	39	1,245	-689	-16.55	-33.70	31.92	50.89	4,162
Guizhou 貴州									
Yunnan 雲南									
Tibet 西藏									
Northwest 西北	2	64	710	-30	-2.38	-4.26	11.09	43.65	1,260
Shaanxi 陝西	2	64	710	-30	-2.38	-4.26	11.09	43.65	1,260
Gansu 甘肅									
Qinghai 青海									
Ningxia 寧夏									
Xinjiang 新疆									

4259: Other Educational and Office Machinery 其他文化、辦公用機械製造業

Year 年份	Number of firms 企業個數	Rate of change 每年變化 (%)	Number of employees 職工人數 (人)	Rate of change 每年變化 (%)	Total revenue (mil. RMB) 總銷售收入 (百萬元)	Rate of change 每年變化 (%)	Total profit (mil. RMB) 總利潤 (百萬元)	Rate of change 每年變化 (%)
1993	75		10,635		215		15	
1994	89	18.67%	6,920	-34.93%	317	47.77%	20	33.85%
1995	92	3.37%	7,252	4.80%	780	146.10%	30	48.03%
1996	107	16.30%	7,311	0.81%	715	-8.38%	17	-43.59%

3 Major products* 3 種主要產品 *	Output 產量	Sales volume 銷售量	Unit 單位
a) Typing & Mimeographing Machinery 打字油印機械	110,801	104,153	set 台

Top 10 firms by revenue (year founded) 收入排名前 10 家企業 (創辦年份)	City 城市	Province 省	Telephone / fax 電話 / 傳真	Number of employees 職工人數	Ownership 產業所有權	Revenue ('000 RMB) 銷售收入 (千元)	Profit ('000 RMB) (rank) 利潤 (千元) (排名)	Total assets ('000 RMB) 總資產 (千元)	Major products 主要產品
Smpic Corp. 上海申貝辦公機械總公司(1960)	Shanghai 上海市	Shanghai 上海市	(021)63864202 (021)63865301	1,471	State-owned 國有	207,121	4937(3)	194,477	a
Beijing Fuji Color Equipment Co. Ltd. 北京富士彩色設備有限公司(1993)	Beijing 北京市	Beijing 北京市	(010)68463711 (010)68481940	53	Overseas Chinese-funded 港澳台資	176,142	9201(1)	133,153	o
Shanghai Number Machine Factory 上海號碼機廠(1930)	Shanghai 上海市	Shanghai 上海市	(021)56976338 (021)56636936	554	State-owned 國有	22,578	645(13)	29,112	o
Gu'an Niu Tuo Zhen Machinery Factory 固安縣牛駝鎮機械廠(1976)	Langfang 廊坊市	Hebei 河北省	(0316)6122195	300	Collectively-owned 集體	21,580	4132(5)	6,200	o
Shanghai Yan Zhong Official Articles Industrial Company 上海延中辦公用品實業公司(1993)	Shanghai 上海市	Shanghai 上海市	(021)62184496	59	其他經濟	20,530	4400(4)	40,819	o
Beijing Dasong Machinery & Electronics Co. 北京市大松機械電子總公司(1992)	Beijing 北京市	Beijing 北京市	(010)62581498 (010)62581498	120	Collectively-owned 集體	15,300	1313(9)	28,416	o
Shanghai Pencil Machinery Co. Ltd. 上海鉛筆機械有限公司(1993)	Shanghai 上海市	Shanghai 上海市	(021)65370017 (021)65458009	60	其他經濟	13,927	2835(6)	10,919	o
Sheng Jian Machinery Factory 生建機械廠(1986)	Heze 菏澤市	Shandong 山東省	(0530)8900231	694	State-owned 國有	13,731	-9840(41)	44,800	o
Duplicate Tong Handle Official Business Equipment Co. Ltd. 複印通辦公器材有限公司(1994)	Xiamen 廈門市	Fujian 福建省	(0592)6038183 (0592)6038187	41	Foreign-funded 外資	13,353	1168(10)	12,943	o
Wujin Ma Hang Agricultural Machine Tools Repair Factory 武進市馬杭農機具修造廠(1971)	Changzhou 常州市	Jiangsu 江蘇省	(0519)6701101	200	Collectively-owned 集體	12,971	-423(35)	13,528	o

Top 10 Cities by Production Output 產出排名前 10 位城市	Province 省	Market share 市場份額	Number of firms 企業個數
Zhuhai 珠海市	Guangdong 廣東省	32.81%	2
Beijing 北京市	Beijing 北京市	31.80%	12
Shenzhen 深圳市	Guangdong 廣東省	10.69%	6
Shanghai 上海市	Shanghai 上海市	6.26%	13
Ji'nan 濟南市	Shandong 山東省	3.32%	2
Changzhou 常州市	Jiangsu 江蘇省	1.78%	7
Langfang 廊坊市	Hebei 河北省	1.31%	1
Wenzhou 溫州市	Zhejiang 浙江省	1.18%	13
Wuhan 武漢市	Hubei 湖北省	1.00%	2
Sanming 三明市	Fujian 福建省	0.97%	1

10 Major Wholesalers 10 家主要批發商	City 城市	Province 省	Telephone / Fax 電話 / 傳真
Shandong Stationary & Sporting Goods Import & Export Company 山東省文教體育用品進出口公司	Qingdao 青島市	Shandong 山東省	(0532)2826827 (0532)3831971
Henan Printing Goods & Materials General Company 河南省印刷物資總公司	Zhengzhou 鄭州市	Henan 河南省	(0371)5967060 (0371)5947912
China Packing Import & Export Singbo Company 中國包裝進出口寧波公司	Ningbo 寧波市	Zhejiang 浙江省	(0574)7367512 (0574)7361096
Tianjin Stationary & Sporting Goods Import & Export Company 天津文教體育用品進出口公司	Tianjin 天津市	Tianjin 天津市	(022)23112048 (022)23112054
China Packing Import & Export Liaoning Company 中國包裝進出口遼寧公司	Dalian 大連市	Liaoning 遼寧省	(0411)4687657 (0411)4687644
Hunan Printing Goods & Materials General Company 湖南省印刷物資總公司	Changsha 長沙市	Hunan 湖南省	(0731)4444618 (0731)4446936
Guangzhou Stationery Co. 廣州市文化用品公司	Guangzhou 廣州市	Guangdong 廣東省	(020)81889089 (020)81861964
Ka Xi Ou Electron (Shenzhen) Co. Ltd. 卡西歐電子(深圳)有限公司	Shenzhen 深圳市	Guangdong 廣東省	(0755)3590620 (0755)3590565
Changsha Keven Group Co. 長沙市科文集團公司	Changsha 長沙市	Hunan 湖南省	(0731)4444108
Hunan Firecrackers Fireworks Import & Export Company 湖南省鞭炮煙花進出口公司	Changsha 長沙市	Hunan 湖南省	(0731)4439580

*Also include sales by firms outside this industry.包括本行業以外廠家的銷售。"o" stands for "others". "o" 代表 "其他產品"。

4260: Clocks and Watches 鐘表製造業

The industry accounts for 0.121% of the total revenue of China's industrial sector in 1996. The revenue growth rate of the industry is -10.2% from 1995, as compared to the growth rate of China's industrial sector, 9.51%. The rate of return on asset is -0.59%. 57.62% of all firms in the industry made a profit while 37.38% had negative returns. The top province in terms of the industry's revenue is Guangdong, accounting for 45.76% of the total revenue.
本行業在1996年佔全行業總產值0.121%，行業年增長率為-10.2%（全國工業年增長率9.51%）。行業的資產回報率-0.59%，57.62%的企業盈利，37.38%的企業虧損。銷售收入最高的省份為廣東省，佔本行業的45.76%。

	Total number of firms 企業總數	Total number of employees 職工總數	Total revenue (mil. RMB) 總銷售收入（百萬元）	Total profit (mil. RMB) 總利潤（百萬元）	Return on assets 資產利潤率 (%)	Return on equity 權益利潤率 (%)	Labour productivity ('000 RMB / worker) 勞動生產率（千元/人）	Debts / assets 資產負債率 (%)	Total assets (mil. RMB) 總資產（百萬元）
Industry Overall 行業總體	734	180,758	7,003	-73	-0.59	-2.17	38.74	72.71	12,297

	Number of firms 企業個數	Average number of employees 平均職工人數	Average revenue ('000 RMB) 平均銷售收入（千元）	Average profit ('000 RMB) 平均利潤（千元）	Return on assets 資產利潤率 (%)	Return on equity 權益利潤率 (%)	Labour productivity ('000 RMB / worker) 勞動生產率（千元/人）	Average debts / assets 平均資產負債率(%)	Average Total assets ('000 RMB) 平均總資產（千元）
By ownership 產業所有權									
State-owned 國有	118	760	15,212	-1,737	-3.23	-20.32	20.03	84.10	53,771
Collectively-owned 集體	290	180	5,119	33	0.41	1.27	28.48	67.50	7,967
Privately-owned 私有	4	96	1,969	158	5.71	41.47	20.51	86.24	2,769
Domestic JVs 聯營	16	262	7,171	-368	-2.84	-8.72	27.36	67.41	12,952
Joint stock 股份制	4	302	7,173	159	0.91	4.72	23.77	80.64	17,411
Foreign-funded 外資	45	113	11,226	273	2.20	5.88	99.64	62.55	12,404
Overseas Chinese-funded 港澳台資	255	125	12,026	451	4.11	8.81	96.40	53.36	10,958
By size 規模									
Large 大型	27	2,432	63,293	5,623	3.29	20.61	26.02	84.05	171,070
Medium 中型	39	892	18,732	60	0.10	0.54	20.99	81.54	59,958
Small 小型	643	126	7,097	-353	-4.25	-10.38	56.40	59.04	8,305
By regional distribution 地區分布									
Central-North 華北	73	221	5,604	-41	-0.30	-1.10	25.33	72.81	13,657
Beijing 北京	14	228	9,903	-70	-0.34	-0.88	43.38	61.09	20,544
Tianjin 天津	49	226	4,105	-105	-0.91	-3.89	18.16	76.70	11,553
Hebei 河北	8	190	8,348	399	2.91	15.75	43.91	81.51	13,691
Shanxi 山西	2	177	1,255	-25	-0.15	-0.72	7.09	79.28	16,865
Inner Mongolia 內蒙									
Northeast 東北	51	620	5,130	-1,459	-5.93	-101.68	8.27	94.17	24,589
Liaoning 遼寧	35	723	6,508	-1,587	-5.77	-100.05	9.00	94.23	27,495
Jilin 吉林	6	583	2,312	-2,773	-11.42	119.97	3.97	109.52	24,283
Heilongjiang 黑龍江	10	281	1,998	-222	-1.52	-7.04	7.11	78.41	14,601
Central East 華東	290	243	9,740	-100	-0.53	-2.25	40.13	76.50	18,913
Shanghai 上海	72	352	17,528	154	0.45	2.31	49.78	80.52	34,304
Jiangsu 江蘇	40	304	4,467	-476	-3.01	-12.56	14.72	76.00	15,785
Zhejiang 浙江	33	144	5,074	162	1.49	4.09	35.24	63.63	10,917
Anhui 安徽	5	341	5,052	-1,376	-5.37	-16.26	14.82	66.96	25,608
Fujian 福建	101	70	6,120	67	1.47	2.94	87.06	49.84	4,560
Jiangxi 江西	15	241	2,651	-175	-2.09	-4.87	11.02	57.15	8,363
Shandong 山東	24	655	22,225	-989	-1.81	-12.00	33.92	84.89	54,555
Central-South 中南	296	174	11,548	276	2.08	5.04	66.19	58.68	13,274
Henan 河南	9	535	4,389	-287	-1.34	-10.74	8.20	87.54	21,426
Hubei 湖北	13	281	9,716	440	2.76	12.25	34.56	77.46	15,937
Hunan 湖南	6	221	1,467	-343	-3.94	-8.58	6.64	54.11	8,723
Guangdong 廣東	257	155	12,469	315	2.39	5.42	80.21	55.98	13,205
Guangxi 廣西	10	188	3,856	-18	-0.22	-0.53	20.54	58.12	8,173
Hainan 海南	1	11	440	-110	-9.02	-21.15	40.00	56.56	1,220
Southwest 西南	14	374	3,079	-729	-3.66	-16.13	8.23	77.34	19,929
Chongqing 重慶	7	615	4,361	-1,306	-4.03	-21.68	7.10	81.40	32,391
Sichuan 四川	2	227	727	4	0.03	0.13	3.21	75.59	11,427
Guizhou 貴州	2	141	845	5	0.06	0.11	5.99	48.90	9,060
Yunnan 雲南	3	42	2,900	-270	-11.39	-14.54	69.60	21.66	2,370
Tibet 西藏									
Northwest 西北	10	572	4,604	-3,792	-10.73	-104.15	8.04	89.69	35,339
Shaanxi 陝西	9	634	5,008	-4,218	-10.82	-108.80	7.89	90.05	38,963
Gansu 甘肅									
Qinghai 青海									
Ningxia 寧夏									
Xinjiang 新疆	1	13	970	40	1.47	2.63	74.62	43.75	2,720

4260: Clocks and Watches 鐘表製造業

Year 年份	Number of firms 企業個數	Rate of change 每年變化 (%)	Number of employees 職工人數（人）	Rate of change 每年變化 (%)	Total revenue (mil. RMB) 總銷售收入（百萬元）	Rate of change 每年變化 (%)	Total profit (mil. RMB) 總利潤（百萬元）	Rate of change 每年變化 (%)
1993	610		261,998		6,120		-57	
1994	703	15.25%	221,434	-15.48%	7,807	27.57%	1	100.94%
1995	761	8.25%	190,425	-14.00%	7,802	-0.07%	33	6043.41%
1996	734	-3.55%	180,758	-5.08%	7,003	-10.24%	-73	-320.46%

3 Major products* 3 種主要產品 *	Output 產量	Sales volume 銷售量	Unit 單位
a) Watch 表	275,936,691	270,417,957	piece 只
b) Mechanical Pendulum Clock 機械擺鐘	1,205,622	1,217,679	piece 只

Top 10 firms by revenue (year founded) 收入排名前 10 家企業 (創辦年份)	City 城市	Province 省	Telephone / fax 電話 / 傳真	Number of employees 職工人數	Ownership 產業所有權	Revenue ('000 RMB) 銷售收入（千元）	Profit ('000 RMB) (rank) 利潤（千元）（排名）	Total assets ('000 RMB) 總資產（千元）	Major products 主要產品
Shanghai Jin Ze Gong Ye Cheng Development Co. 上海金澤工業城發展公司(1993)	Shanghai 上海市	Shanghai 上海市	(021)59261164	888	Collectively-owned 集體	316,837	30200(2)	226,085	a
Guangzhou Chaoshidai Clock & Watch Co. Ltd. 廣州超時代鐘表有限公司(1978)	Guangzhou 廣州市	Guangdong 廣東省	(020)84936465 (020)84937575	749	Overseas Chinese-funded 港澳台資	274,944	610(67)	83,460	a
Yantai Polaris Clock & Watch Group Co. 煙台北極星鐘表集團公司(1987)	Yantai 煙台市	Shandong 山東省	(0535)6225875 (0535)6215205	8,829	State-owned 國有	260,420	-31921(359)	775,824	a,b
Zhaoqing Bei Bang Clock & Watch Manufacturing Co. Ltd. 肇慶北邦鐘表製造有限公司(1994)	Yunfu 雲浮市	Guangdong 廣東省	(0766)7718268 (0766)7718228	310	Overseas Chinese-funded 港澳台資	256,270	16420(3)	12,930	a
Zhuhai Yi Bo Watch Industry Co. Ltd. 珠海依博表業有限公司(1990)	Zhuhai 珠海市	Guangdong 廣東省	(0756)8614043 (0756)8612505	186	Foreign-funded 外資	139,807	2669(17)	29,020	o
Zhuhai Ge Li Sino-sweden Watch Industry Co. Ltd. 珠海格力中瑞表業有限公司(1985)	Zhuhai 珠海市	Guangdong 廣東省	(0756)3333805 (0756)3332799	360	Overseas Chinese-funded 港澳台資	119,347	34133(1)	86,905	a
Shanghai Diamond Watch Factory 上海鑽石手表廠(1932)	Shanghai 上海市	Shanghai 上海市	(021)62545663 (021)62163645	1,867	State-owned 國有	116,892	1004(55)	259,360	a
Weihai Dong Hua Industry Group Co. 威海東華工業集團公司(1975)	Weihai 威海市	Shandong 山東省	(0896)5817111 (0896)5819261	1,879	Collectively-owned 集體	116,160	50(166)	172,170	b
Shanghai Clock & Watch Company 上海鐘表公司(1988)	Shanghai 上海市	Shanghai 上海市	(021)62804760 (021)62808479	915	State-owned 國有	110,367	578(73)	320,862	a
Taishan Si Liquor Zhen Taishan Yi Mei Clock & Watch Factory Co. Ltd. 台山市四九鎮台山宜美鐘表廠有限公司(1994)	Jiangmen 江門市	Guangdong 廣東省	(0750)5488068 (0750)5488187	217	Foreign-funded 外資	108,770	-39(250)	36,612	o

Top 10 Cities by Production Output 產出排名前 10 位城市	Province 省	Market share 市場份額	Number of firms 企業個數
Shanghai 上海市	Shanghai 上海市	22.01%	132
Guangzhou 廣州市	Guangdong 廣東省	12.75%	88
Shenzhen 深圳市	Guangdong 廣東省	8.36%	85
Zhuhai 珠海市	Guangdong 廣東省	5.75%	12
Putian 莆田市	Fujian 福建省	5.61%	32
Yunfu 雲浮市	Guangdong 廣東省	3.92%	2
Yantai 煙台市	Shandong 山東省	3.56%	29
Dongguan 東莞市	Guangdong 廣東省	3.36%	23
Tianjin 天津市	Tianjin 天津市	3.05%	54
Weihai 威海市	Shandong 山東省	2.93%	6

10 Major Wholesalers 10 家主要批發商	City 城市	Province 省	Telephone / Fax 電話 / 傳真
Shandong Stationary & Sporting Goods Import & Export Company 山東省文教體育用品進出口公司	Qingdao 青島市	Shandong 山東省	(0532)2826827 (0532)3831971
Henan Printing Goods & Materials General Company 河南省印刷物資總公司	Zhengzhou 鄭州市	Henan 河南省	(0371)5967060 (0371)5947912
China Packing Import & Export Singbo Company 中國包裝進出口寧波公司	Ningbo 寧波市	Zhejiang 浙江省	(0574)7367512 (0574)7361096
Tianjin Stationary & Sporting Goods Import & Export Company 天津文教體育用品進出口公司	Tianjin 天津市	Tianjin 天津市	(022)23112048 (022)23112054
China Packing Import & Export Liaoning Company 中國包裝進出口遼寧公司	Dalian 大連市	Liaoning 遼寧省	(0411)4687657 (0411)4687644
Hunan Printing Goods & Materials General Company 湖南省印刷物資總公司	Changsha 長沙市	Hunan 湖南省	(0731)4444618 (0731)4446936
Guangzhou Stationery Co. 廣州市文化用品公司	Guangzhou 廣州市	Guangdong 廣東省	(020)81889089 (020)81861964
Ka Xi Ou Electron (Shenzhen) Co. Ltd. 卡西歐電子(深圳)有限公司	Shenzhen 深圳市	Guangdong 廣東省	(0755)3590620 (0755)3590565
Changsha Keven Group Co. 長沙市科文集團公司	Changsha 長沙市	Hunan 湖南省	(0731)4444108
Hunan Firecrackers Fireworks Import & Export Company 湖南省鞭炮煙花進出口公司	Changsha 長沙市	Hunan 湖南省	(0731)4439580

*Also include sales by firms outside this industry.包括本行業以外廠家的銷售。"o" stands for "others". "o" 代表"其他產品"。

4280: Apparatus, Instrument, and Other Measuring Equipment
儀器儀表及文化、辦公用機械修理業

The industry accounts for 0.002% of the total revenue of China's industrial sector in 1996. The revenue growth rate of the industry is 37.0% from 1995, as compared to the growth rate of China's industrial sector, 9.51%. The rate of return on asset is 0.29%. 65.71% of all firms in the industry made a profit while 20.00% had negative returns. The top province in terms of the industry's revenue is Liaoning, accounting for 32.86% of the total revenue.
本行業在1996年佔全行業總產值0.002%，行業年增長率為37.0%（全國工業年增長率9.51%）。行業的資產回報率0.29%，65.71%的企業盈利，20.00%的企業虧損。銷售收入最高的省份為遼寧省，佔本行業的32.86%。

	Total number of firms 企業總數	Total number of employees 職工總數	Total revenue (mil. RMB) 總銷售收入（百萬元）	Total profit (mil. RMB) 總利潤（百萬元）	Return on assets 資產利潤率 (%)	Return on equity 權益利潤率 (%)	Labour productivity ('000 RMB / worker) 勞動生產率（千元/人）	Debts / assets 資產負債率 (%)	Total assets (mil. RMB) 總資產（百萬元）
Industry Overall 行業總體	136	4,587	123		0.29	1.37	26.81	78.65	113

	Number of firms 企業個數	Average number of employees 平均職工人數	Average revenue ('000 RMB) 平均銷售收入（千元）	Average profit ('000 RMB) 平均利潤（千元）	Return on assets 資產利潤率 (%)	Return on equity 權益利潤率 (%)	Labour productivity ('000 RMB / worker) 勞動生產率（千元/人）	Average debts / assets 平均資產負債率(%)	Average Total assets ('000 RMB) 平均總資產（千元）
By ownership 產業所有權									
State-owned 國有	23	19	217	-43	-10.00	-100.00	11.47	90.00	435
Collectively-owned 集體	102	36	944	26	3.94	12.01	26.14	67.20	656
Privately-owned 私有	1	11	54	-5	-7.58	-14.16	4.86	46.47	68
Domestic JVs 聯營	1	123							
Joint stock 股份制									
Foreign-funded 外資									
Overseas Chinese-funded 港澳台資	8	41	2,702	-204	-4.52	-160.29	65.30	97.18	4,503
By size 規模									
Large 大型									
Medium 中型									
Small 小型	133	33	925				27.67	78.76	850
By regional distribution 地區分布									
Central-North 華北	38	20	544	2	0.71	2.49	26.77	71.36	333
Beijing 北京	11								
Tianjin 天津	18	28	779	-1	-0.14	-0.37	28.17	61.60	388
Hebei 河北	5	49	1,308	20	1.88	11.76	26.59	83.99	1,062
Shanxi 山西	3	9	33				3.57	74.29	117
Inner Mongolia 內蒙	1								
Northeast 東北	33	56	1,309	32	2.39	18.29	23.29	86.98	1,359
Liaoning 遼寧	24	71	1,684	44	2.45	20.11	23.81	87.80	1,800
Jilin 吉林	6	14	278	-2	-1.79	-6.67	19.42	73.21	93
Heilongjiang 黑龍江	3	24	377	7	1.85	4.65	15.69	61.11	360
Central East 華東	31	31	630	-8	-1.37	-5.49	20.17	75.03	614
Shanghai 上海	8	47	583	-96	-16.11	-334.78	12.43	95.19	598
Jiangsu 江蘇	1	10	2,240	140	13.59	19.72	224.00	31.07	1,030
Zhejiang 浙江	5	19	1,140	52	4.33	23.21	59.38	81.20	1,202
Anhui 安徽	1	36	740				20.56	64.22	1,090
Fujian 福建	4	22	288	10	4.71	36.36	12.92	87.06	213
Jiangxi 江西	6	27	55	-2	-3.70	-7.14	2.04	48.15	45
Shandong 山東	6	33	783	13	1.60	3.92	23.50	59.12	832
Central-South 中南	20	27	1,483	-44	-3.08	-10.70	55.23	71.14	1,411
Henan 河南	6	41	488	20	2.04	10.53	11.86	80.41	978
Hubei 湖北									
Hunan 湖南	1	14	2,940	-30	-2.78	-2.78	210.00		1,080
Guangdong 廣東	12	23	1,974	-80	-4.53	-16.41	85.83	72.38	1,765
Guangxi 廣西	1		100					25.00	80
Hainan 海南									
Southwest 西南	8	38	815	26	2.88	18.58	21.45	84.62	910
Chongqing 重慶	2	12	358	11	7.61	12.84	30.56	40.77	144
Sichuan 四川	5	60	1,067	40	2.74	21.81	17.76	87.43	1,472
Guizhou 貴州	2	10	590	5	2.27	5.88	62.11	63.64	220
Yunnan 雲南									
Tibet 西藏									
Northwest 西北	6	25	598	18	8.73	15.49	23.77	43.65	210
Shaanxi 陝西	3	11	27				2.50	29.41	57
Gansu 甘肅	1	33	1,700	10	1.92	3.33	51.52	42.31	520
Qinghai 青海	1	21	410				19.52	81.82	330
Ningxia 寧夏									
Xinjiang 新疆	1	65	1,400	100	41.67	43.48	21.54	4.17	240

4280: Apparatus, Instrument, and Other Measuring Equipment
儀器儀表及文化、辦公用機械修理業

Year 年份	Number of firms 企業個數	Rate of change 每年變化 (%)	Number of employees 職工人數 (人)	Rate of change 每年變化 (%)	Total revenue (mil. RMB) 總銷售收入 (百萬元)	Rate of change 每年變化 (%)	Total profit (mil. RMB) 總利潤 (百萬元)	Rate of change 每年變化 (%)
1993	88		3,100		58		9	
1994	89	1.14%	2,295	-25.97%	42	-27.17%	3	-70.58%
1995	98	10.11%	3,422	49.11%	90	113.66%	3	18.78%
1996	136	38.78%	4,587	34.04%	123	37.03%		-100.00%

3 Major products* 3種主要產品*	Output 產量	Sales volume 銷售量	Unit 單位

Top 10 firms by revenue (year founded) 收入排名前10家企業 (創辦年份)	City 城市	Province 省	Telephone / fax 電話 / 傳真	Number of employees 職工人數	Ownership 產業所有權	Revenue ('000 RMB) 銷售收入 (千元)	Profit ('000 RMB) (rank) 利潤 (千元) (排名)	Total assets ('000 RMB) 總資產 (千元)	Major products 主要產品
Jinzhou Guta Bao An Automobile Maintenance Factory 錦州市古塔區保安汽車維修廠(1994)	Jinzhou 錦州市	Liaoning 遼寧省		11	Private-owned 私營	23,654	0(14)	9,898	o
Hong Xi Electron (Shenzhen) Co. Ltd. 鴻熙電子(深圳)有限公司(1994)	Shenzhen 深圳市	Guangdong 廣東省	(0755)8862597	60	Overseas Chinese-funded 港澳台資	14,506	-127(18)	2,385	o
Tianjin Fine Finishing Electric Power Measuring Equipment Company 天津市精工電力計量設備公司(1993)	Tianjin 天津市	Tianjin 天津市	(022)24315907	25	Collectively-owned 集體	7,400	457(1)	1,985	o
Xinle Power Industry Bureau Industrial General Co. 新樂市電力局實業總公司(1982)	Shijiazhuang 石家莊市	Hebei 河北省		131	Collectively-owned 集體	5,550	204(3)	4,247	o
Shenyang Tiexi Qi Lu Instrument Repair Section 瀋陽市鐵西區七路儀表修理部(1981)	Shenyang 瀋陽市	Liaoning 遼寧省		8	Collectively-owned 集體	3,819	319(2)	23	o
Shandong Jinxiang Pencil Factory 山東省金鄉縣鉛筆廠(1978)	Jining 濟寧市	Shandong 山東省	(0537)8711218	180	Collectively-owned 集體	3,700	120(8)	176	o
Hengyang Metallurgy Duplicate Technology Service Center 衡陽市冶金複印技術中心(1985)	Hengyang 衡陽市	Hunan 湖南省	(0734)8331459	14	Collectively-owned 集體	3,436	-33(17)	1,080	o
Dongguan Hu Men Electric Appliance Repair & Assembly Factory 東莞市虎門電器修配廠(1979)	Dongguan 東莞市	Guangdong 廣東省	(0769)5517512	35	Collectively-owned 集體	3,321	157(5)	6,200	o
Tianjin Tanggu Yong Li Installing Equipment Co. Ltd. 天津市塘沽區永利設備安裝有限公司(1996)	Tianjin 天津市	Tianjin 天津市	(022)25893951	208	Collectively-owned 集體	3,221	-196(19)	635	o
Rui'an Electric Power Equipment Factory 瑞安市電力設備廠(1962)	Wenzhou 溫州市	Zhejiang 浙江省	(0577)5611805	59	Collectively-owned 集體	2,532	186(4)	4,186	o

Top 10 Cities by Production Output 產出排名前10位城市	Province 省	Market share 市場份額	Number of firms 企業個數
Shanghai 上海市	Shanghai 上海市	70.51%	56
Chongqing 重慶市	Chongqing 重慶市	3.56%	2
Harbin 哈爾濱市	Heilongjiang 黑龍江省	3.15%	3
Tianjin 天津市	Tianjin 天津市	2.38%	19
Guangzhou 廣州市	Guangdong 廣東省	2.20%	7
Beijing 北京市	Beijing 北京市	1.96%	8
Daqing 大慶市	Heilongjiang 黑龍江省	1.60%	2
Shijiazhuang 石家莊市	Hebei 河北省	1.43%	1
Jining 濟寧市	Shandong 山東省	1.43%	1
Liaoyang 遼陽市	Liaoning 遼寧省	1.14%	7

10 Major Wholesalers 10家主要批發商	City 城市	Province 省	Telephone / Fax 電話 / 傳真

*Also include sales by firms outside this industry.包括本行業以外廠家的銷售。"o" stands for "others". "o" 代表"其他產品"。

4290: Other Meters 其他儀器儀表製造業

The industry accounts for 0.023% of the total revenue of China's industrial sector in 1996. The revenue growth rate of the industry is 20.1% from 1995, as compared to the growth rate of China's industrial sector, 9.51%. The rate of return on asset is 1.90%. 63.72% of all firms in the industry made a profit while 27.62% had negative returns. The top province in terms of the industry's revenue is Jiangsu, accounting for 19.78% of the total revenue.
本行業在1996年佔全行業總產值0.023%，行業年增長率為20.1%（全國工業年增長率9.51%）。行業的資產回報率1.90%，63.72%的企業盈利，27.62%的企業虧損。銷售收入最高的省份為江蘇省，佔本行業的19.78%。

	Total number of firms 企業總數	Total number of employees 職工總數	Total revenue (mil. RMB) 總銷售收入（百萬元）	Total profit (mil. RMB) 總利潤（百萬元）	Return on assets 資產利潤率 (%)	Return on equity 權益利潤率 (%)	Labour productivity ('000 RMB / worker) 勞動生產率（千元/人）	Debts / assets 資產負債率 (%)	Total assets (mil. RMB) 總資產（百萬元）
Industry Overall 行業總體	490	32,561	1,343	37	1.90	5.54	41.25	65.70	1,938

	Number of firms 企業個數	Average number of employees 平均職工人數	Average revenue ('000 RMB) 平均銷售收入（千元）	Average profit ('000 RMB) 平均利潤（千元）	Return on assets 資產利潤率 (%)	Return on equity 權益利潤率 (%)	Labour productivity ('000 RMB / worker) 勞動生產率（千元/人）	Average debts / assets 平均資產負債率(%)	Average Total assets ('000 RMB) 平均總資產（千元）
By ownership 產業所有權									
State-owned 國有	80	129	2,638	-350	-4.94	-14.81	20.52	66.67	7,088
Collectively-owned 集體	346	53	1,920	42	1.86	6.36	35.98	70.78	2,245
Privately-owned 私有	2	14	533	5	0.77	1.57	38.07	51.34	621
Domestic JVs 聯營	2	26	1,783	-12	-0.17	-0.18	69.94	5.08	6,925
Joint stock 股份制	9	27	1,478	454	15.68	39.62	55.42	60.42	2,895
Foreign-funded 外資	24	67	11,621	1,495	13.79	28.94	172.48	52.36	10,841
Overseas Chinese-funded 港澳台資	26	99	6,601	409	3.62	10.50	66.73	65.50	11,276
By size 規模									
Large 大型	2	782	27,563	-540	-0.49	-1.08	35.27	54.61	110,145
Medium 中型	5	616	28,509	2,735	5.47	11.60	46.27	52.86	50,028
Small 小型	475	59	2,413	51	1.66	5.46	40.94	69.53	3,090
By regional distribution 地區分布									
Central-North 華北	80	63	1,036	-432	-10.88	-40.85	16.56	73.35	3,973
Beijing 北京	49	34	924	-20	-0.67	-3.65	27.42	81.67	3,021
Tianjin 天津	13	23	542	-8	-0.84	-1.46	23.90	42.64	920
Hebei 河北	11	46	1,590				34.43	77.39	2,589
Shanxi 山西	6	423	2,147	-5,582	-25.92	-75.79	5.08	65.79	21,533
Inner Mongolia 內蒙	1	15	170				11.33	61.54	130
Northeast 東北	84	49	2,321	84	3.85	11.13	47.48	65.42	2,188
Liaoning 遼寧	62	31	1,965	97	8.47	21.70	63.77	60.97	1,145
Jilin 吉林	9	48	3,532	229	4.46	10.32	73.42	56.74	5,129
Heilongjiang 黑龍江	13	136	3,184	-77	-1.50	-6.30	23.46	76.17	5,125
Central East 華東	241	73	3,551	201	4.20	10.47	48.83	59.92	4,788
Shanghai 上海	62	66	2,490	315	8.08	16.40	37.60	50.71	3,895
Jiangsu 江蘇	61	95	4,355	93	1.53	4.08	45.60	62.57	6,062
Zhejiang 浙江	49	65	4,652	203	5.60	16.30	71.56	65.67	3,636
Anhui 安徽	7	125	2,726	-4	-0.11	-0.40	21.76	74.10	4,081
Fujian 福建	27	46	4,913	429	7.08	15.87	105.96	55.41	6,056
Jiangxi 江西	14	74	1,543	24	0.78	2.51	20.91	68.86	3,014
Shandong 山東	21	59	1,645	69	1.10	2.85	27.66	61.24	6,206
Central-South 中南	51	71	2,929	365	10.95	52.35	41.51	79.08	3,332
Henan 河南	14	67	1,618	18	1.05	3.08	23.99	65.73	1,694
Hubei 湖北	7	145	3,691	97	2.29	9.41	25.48	75.60	4,233
Hunan 湖南	6	150	482	-60	-12.08	180.00	3.22	106.71	497
Guangdong 廣東	22	33	4,369	819	15.90	89.11	133.87	82.16	5,148
Guangxi 廣西	2	13	950	15	9.09	16.67	76.00	45.45	165
Hainan 海南									
Southwest 西南	23	69	1,828	-127	-3.27	-30.79	26.68	89.36	3,864
Chongqing 重慶	12	110	1,814	-226	-3.59	-42.86	16.43	91.63	6,287
Sichuan 四川	8	25	819	-59	-4.27	-18.61	32.36	77.03	1,373
Guizhou 貴州	3	3	4,453	107	55.17	60.38	1336.00	6.90	193
Yunnan 雲南									
Tibet 西藏									
Northwest 西北	11	68	1,634	16	0.77	2.06	24.09	62.48	2,113
Shaanxi 陝西	8	61	2,038	74	3.29	7.84	33.20	58.05	2,244
Gansu 甘肅	3	85	557	-137	-7.75	-34.45	6.55	77.50	1,763
Qinghai 青海									
Ningxia 寧夏									
Xinjiang 新疆									

4290: Other Meters 其他儀器儀表製造業

Year 年份	Number of firms 企業個數	Rate of change 每年變化 (%)	Number of employees 職工人數（人）	Rate of change 每年變化 (%)	Total revenue (mil. RMB) 總銷售收入（百萬元）	Rate of change 每年變化 (%)	Total profit (mil. RMB) 總利潤（百萬元）	Rate of change 每年變化 (%)
1993	516		446,127		1,123		43	
1994	578	12.02%	41,101	-90.79%	1,128	0.44%	30	-29.58%
1995	464	-19.72%	30,727	-25.24%	1,118	-0.89%	34	12.17%
1996	490	5.60%	32,561	5.97%	1,343	20.13%	37	8.94%

3 Major products* 3 種主要產品 *	Output 產量	Sales volume 銷售量	Unit 單位
a) Water Meter 水表	961,641	942,408	set 台
b) Automatic Instrument, Meter & System 自動化儀表及系統	1,233,149	1,085,171	set 台(套)

Top 10 firms by revenue (year founded) 收入排名前 10 家企業 (創辦年份)	City 城市	Province 省	Telephone / fax 電話 / 傳真	Number of employees 職工人數	Ownership 產業所有權	Revenue ('000 RMB) 銷售收入（千元）	Profit ('000 RMB) (rank) 利潤（千元）（排名）	Total assets ('000 RMB) 總資產（千元）	Major products 主要產品
Xuzhou Hua Feng Electronic Equipment Co. Ltd. 徐州華風電子設備有限公司(1993)	Xuzhou 徐州市	Jiangsu 江蘇省	(0516)4870016	921	Overseas Chinese-funded 港澳台資	62,000	2080(8)	28,371	o
Zhuhai Hua Guan Computer Co. Ltd. 珠海花冠電腦有限公司(1995)	Zhuhai 珠海市	Guangdong 廣東省	(0756)8623404 (0756)8622742	171	Overseas Chinese-funded 港澳台資	56,544	18073(1)	57,359	o
Shanghai Guanghua Altometer Instrument Co. Ltd. 上海光華愛爾美特儀器有限公司(1987)	Shanghai 上海市	Shanghai 上海市	(021)64300150 (021)64300812	127	Foreign-funded 外資	54,242	11060(2)	75,749	o
Shenyang Shen Pipeline Research Institute 瀋陽市沈管道研究所(1989)	Shenyang 瀋陽市	Liaoning 遼寧省	(024)88120068	22	Collectively-owned 集體	52,772	695(23)	5,114	o
Hangzhou Xin Li Electron Co. Ltd. 杭州新利電子有限公司(1993)	Hangzhou 杭州市	Zhejiang 浙江省	(0571)7800222 (0571)7800110	69	Overseas Chinese-funded 港澳台資	50,701	5608(4)	58,946	o
Xiamen Yi Ma Shi Jin Ling Paint Sign Machine Co. Ltd. 廈門依瑪士金陵噴碼機有限公司(1992)	Xiamen 廈門市	Fujian 福建省	(0592)6021964 (0592)6021965	70	Foreign-funded 外資	46,799	8082(3)	44,467	o
Xiamen Xie Li Xing Science & Technology Development Co. Ltd. 廈門協勵行科技發展有限公司(1994)	Xiamen 廈門市	Fujian 福建省	(0592)2057494 (0592)2034638	54	Overseas Chinese-funded 港澳台資	43,690	-101(112)	34,438	o
Xi Shan Shi Yang Jian Stationery Factory 錫山市羊尖文化用品廠(1987)	Wuxi 無錫市	Jiangsu 江蘇省	(0510)8731892	505	Collectively-owned 集體	32,050	4490(5)	13,370	o
Changzhou No.2 Textile Machinery Factory 常州市第二紡織機械廠(1960)	Changzhou 常州市	Jiangsu 江蘇省	(0519)8121835 (0519)8112958	741	Collectively-owned 集體	19,530	-1550(125)	56,820	o
Mudanjiang Instrument Machinery Co. Ltd. 牡丹江市儀表機械有限責任公司(1994)	Mudanjiang 牡丹江市	Heilongjiang 黑龍江省	(0453)6331691 (0453)6331691	1,123	State-owned 國有	18,845	-994(124)	39,170	o

Top 10 Cities by Production Output 產出排名前 10 位城市	Province 省	Market share 市場份額	Number of firms 企業個數
Beijing 北京市	Beijing 北京市	79.02%	39
Shanghai 上海市	Shanghai 上海市	3.25%	85
Chuzhou 滁州市	Anhui 安徽省	2.06%	33
Guichi 貴池市	Anhui 安徽省	1.37%	4
Hangzhou 杭州市	Zhejiang 浙江省	1.14%	11
Shenzhen 深圳市	Guangdong 廣東省	1.12%	13
Guangzhou 廣州市	Guangdong 廣東省	0.95%	15
Changzhou 常州市	Jiangsu 江蘇省	0.84%	12
Xiamen 廈門市	Fujian 福建省	0.77%	3
Wenzhou 温州市	Zhejiang 浙江省	0.76%	25

10 Major Wholesalers 10 家主要批發商	City 城市	Province 省	Telephone / Fax 電話 / 傳真
Liaoning Automobile Trade Group Corp. 遼寧省汽車貿易集團	Shenyang 瀋陽市	Liaoning 遼寧省	(024)23835494 (024)23838338
China Post and Telecommunication Equipment General Company 中國郵電器材總公司	Beijing 北京市	Beijing 北京市	(010)63523715 (010)63525935
Jiangsu Electromechanical Products General Company 江蘇省機電產品總公司	Nanjing 南京市	Jiangsu 江蘇省	(025)7713642 (025)7711036
Xi Nan Technology Import & Export Company 西南技術進出口公司	Chongqing 重慶市	Chongqing 重慶市	(023)63850185 (023)63850026
Changzhou Economic Technology Industrial Development Zone Tian Ming Trade Company 常州經濟技術產業開發區天明貿易公司	Changzhou 常州市	Jiangsu 江蘇省	(0519)8829882 (0519)8829882
Shanxi Mechanical Equipment Import & Export Company 山西省機械設備進出口公司	Taiyuan 太原市	Shanxi 山西省	(0351)4040713 (0351)4043981
Ningbo Five Mining Machinery Import & Export Company 寧波市五礦機械進出口公司	Ningbo 寧波市	Zhejiang 浙江省	(0574)7311255 (0574)7320322
Tianjin Jin Huan Electromechanical Complete Sets of Equipment Factory 天津市津環機電成套設備廠	Tianjin 天津市	Tianjin 天津市	(022)26371628
Yunnan Machinery Import & Export Company 雲南省機械進出口公司	Kunming 昆明市	Yunnan 雲南省	(0871)3164879 (0871)3136829
Tianjin Da Qiu Zhuang Yi Yuan Trade Center 天津市大丘莊億源商貿中心	Tianjin 天津市	Tianjin 天津市	(022)28899478 (022)28899046

*Also include sales by firms outside this industry.包括本行業以外廠家的銷售。"o" stands for "others". "o" 代表"其他產品"。

4311: Sculpture 雕塑工藝品製造業

The industry accounts for 0.065% of the total revenue of China's industrial sector in 1996. The revenue growth rate of the industry is 12.5% from 1995, as compared to the growth rate of China's industrial sector, 9.51%. The rate of return on asset is 3.07%. 71.66% of all firms in the industry made a profit while 22.76% had negative returns. The top province in terms of the industry's revenue is Fujian, accounting for 36.10% of the total revenue.
本行業在1996年佔全行業總產值0.065%，行業年增長率為12.5%（全國工業年增長率9.51%）。行業的資產回報率3.07%，71.66%的企業盈利，22.76%的企業虧損。銷售收入最高的省份為福建省，佔本行業的36.10%。

	Total number of firms 企業總數	Total number of employees 職工總數	Total revenue (mil. RMB) 總銷售收入（百萬元）	Total profit (mil. RMB) 總利潤（百萬元）	Return on assets 資產利潤率 (%)	Return on equity 權益利潤率 (%)	Labour productivity ('000 RMB / worker) 勞動生產率（千元/人）	Debts / assets 資產負債率 (%)	Total assets (mil. RMB) 總資產（百萬元）
Industry Overall 行業總體	1,407	88,284	3,764	128	3.07	7.35	42.64	58.24	4,174

	Number of firms 企業個數	Average number of employees 平均職工人數	Average revenue ('000 RMB) 平均銷售收入（千元）	Average profit ('000 RMB) 平均利潤（千元）	Return on assets 資產利潤率 (%)	Return on equity 權益利潤率 (%)	Labour productivity ('000 RMB / worker) 勞動生產率（千元/人）	Average debts / assets 平均資產負債率(%)	Average Total assets ('000 RMB) 平均總資產（千元）
By ownership 產業所有權									
State-owned 國有	86	56	1,616				28.68	76.47	3,360
Collectively-owned 集體	914	59	1,601	34	1.94	5.71	26.95	66.03	1,774
Privately-owned 私有	9	158	7,534	1,462	9.14	10.57	47.72	13.52	16,004
Domestic JVs 聯營	6	51	946	25	1.71	4.41	18.54	61.32	1,463
Joint stock 股份制	16	90	7,836	1,282	8.30	24.59	87.19	66.24	15,447
Foreign-funded 外資	140	66	5,719	283	5.66	10.48	87.12	45.99	4,998
Overseas Chinese-funded 港澳台資	233	73	4,984	100	2.00	4.36	68.11	54.05	4,989
By size 規模									
Large 大型	1	813	106,317	20,565	8.81	26.75	130.77	67.07	233,432
Medium 中型	3	660	29,269	3,644	4.14	7.19	44.35	42.48	88,121
Small 小型	1,362	62	2,620	71	2.63	6.38	41.96	58.81	2,699
By regional distribution 地區分布									
Central-North 華北	182	41	861	74	3.72	9.85	20.89	62.22	2,000
Beijing 北京	77	39	490	1	0.02	0.07	12.59	65.46	2,192
Tianjin 天津	14	47	463	166	11.86	23.32	9.91	49.13	1,397
Hebei 河北	63	43	1,547	111	5.55	13.86	35.85	59.99	2,009
Shanxi 山西	5	17	300	16	2.52	12.31	17.65	79.56	636
Inner Mongolia 內蒙	23	46	593	178	8.91	22.79	13.00	60.87	1,996
Northeast 東北	112	47	896	52	3.16	10.30	19.06	69.34	1,648
Liaoning 遼寧	60	42	1,171	111	6.37	25.28	28.13	74.82	1,743
Jilin 吉林	26	49	432	-33	-2.52	-8.16	8.89	69.12	1,313
Heilongjiang 黑龍江	26	58	723	1	0.07	0.15	12.52	57.02	1,764
Central East 華東	666	73	3,624	137	3.74	8.11	49.56	53.92	3,661
Shanghai 上海	21	135	5,489	319	3.25	8.50	40.68	61.73	9,809
Jiangsu 江蘇	83	81	3,413	85	2.36	8.73	42.32	72.97	3,598
Zhejiang 浙江	109	71	2,279	-121	-3.85	-12.45	32.08	69.07	3,130
Anhui 安徽	31	42	1,566	52	4.99	16.82	37.64	70.35	1,035
Fujian 福建	266	74	5,108	220	5.43	9.72	68.58	44.12	4,043
Jiangxi 江西	81	55	1,444	191	6.40	9.70	26.27	34.05	2,987
Shandong 山東	75	78	3,235	200	6.18	16.95	41.30	63.55	3,240
Central-South 中南	341	64	2,938	50	1.58	4.50	46.18	64.88	3,139
Henan 河南	127	51	1,819	70	3.29	11.93	36.02	72.41	2,111
Hubei 湖北	40	44	2,435	37	2.64	12.56	55.85	79.01	1,394
Hunan 湖南	18	50	2,287	68	9.55	19.93	46.09	52.08	709
Guangdong 廣東	122	82	4,803	32	0.56	1.48	58.56	61.89	5,719
Guangxi 廣西	28	87	1,586	57	5.98	14.52	18.14	58.83	950
Hainan 海南	6	32	343	-20	-1.28	-1.65	10.84	21.93	1,558
Southwest 西南	53	50	897		-0.04	-0.07	17.86	46.67	1,012
Chongqing 重慶	15	61	579	0	-0.01	-0.03	9.56	41.68	871
Sichuan 四川	15	53	2,155	20	1.35	2.74	40.36	50.92	1,495
Guizhou 貴州	7	43	99	-11	-5.26	-15.69	2.27	66.45	217
Yunnan 雲南	12	18	174	-82	-8.53	-21.73	9.50	60.84	958
Tibet 西藏	5	97	1,028	264	20.82	23.57	10.60	11.67	1,268
Northwest 西北	53	46	821	15	1.22	3.69	17.69	66.94	1,192
Shaanxi 陝西	21	56	1,117	23	2.17	6.43	20.11	66.18	1,052
Gansu 甘肅	21	46	726	7	0.49	1.72	15.67	71.78	1,470
Qinghai 青海	6	26	333	10	2.76	4.35	12.99	36.41	362
Ningxia 寧夏	3	29	500	33	2.12	5.75	17.24	63.14	1,573
Xinjiang 新疆	2	39	645	-10	-0.60	-1.26	16.54	52.40	1,670

Year 年份	Number of firms 企業個數	Rate of change 每年變化 (%)	Number of employees 職工人數 (人)	Rate of change 每年變化 (%)	Total revenue (mil. RMB) 總銷售收入 (百萬元)	Rate of change 每年變化 (%)	Total profit (mil. RMB) 總利潤 (百萬元)	Rate of change 每年變化 (%)
1993	1,078		90,840		2,039		100	
1994	1,200	11.32%	84,672	-6.79%	2,476	21.41%	89	-10.86%
1995	1,376	14.67%	100,479	18.67%	3,346	35.11%	163	82.87%
1996	1,407	2.25%	88,284	-12.14%	3,764	12.49%	128	-21.54%

3 Major products* 3 種主要產品 *	Output 產量	Sales volume 銷售量	Unit 單位

Top 10 firms by revenue (year founded) 收入排名前10家企業 (創辦年份)	City 城市	Province 省	Telephone / fax 電話 / 傳真	Number of employees 職工人數	Ownership 產業所有權	Revenue ('000 RMB) 銷售收入 (千元)	Profit ('000 RMB) (rank) 利潤 (千元) (排名)	Total assets ('000 RMB) 總資產 (千元)	Major products 主要產品
Gu Dai (Taishan) Gifts Factory 古代(台山)禮品廠(1990)	Jiangmen 江門市	Guangdong 廣東省	(0750)5528978	200	Overseas Chinese-funded 港澳台資	70,550	36(245)	5,943	o
Guangdong Fotao Group Corp. Ltd. Shiwan Artistics Factory 廣東佛陶集團石灣美術陶瓷廠(1956)	Foshan 佛山市	Guangdong 廣東省	(0757)2270485 (0757)2272027	880	Joint stock 股份制	63,709	-5288(393)	280,809	o
Fujian Xianyong Hao Jie Craft Decorating Co. Ltd. 福建仙遊豪傑工藝裝潢有限公司(1993)	Putian 莆田市	Fujian 福建省	(0594)7396600 (0594)7396560	45	Overseas Chinese-funded 港澳台資	62,590	9826(2)	2,074	o
Zhi Lin Handicrafts Industrial (Huiyang) Co. Ltd. 志磷藝品實業(惠陽)有限公司(1993)	Huizhou 惠州市	Guangdong 廣東省	(0751)3551551 (0751)3551552	389	Overseas Chinese-funded 港澳台資	61,747	1825(23)	4,265	o
Shanghai Ping'an Wooden Products Co. Ltd. 上海平安木製品有限公司(1992)	Shanghai 上海市	Shanghai 上海市	(021)62200003	59	Foreign-funded 外資	60,822	6042(4)	8,533	o
Hui'an Teng Hui Stone Material Handicrafts Co. Ltd. 惠安縣藤輝石材工藝製品有限公司(1993)	Quanzhou 泉州市	Fujian 福建省	(0595)7683588 (0595)7682227	68	Overseas Chinese-funded 港澳台資	57,406	1955(19)	7,278	o
Yujiang Guo Xi Industrial Group Co. Ltd. 余江縣果喜實業集團有限公司(1991)	Yingtan 鷹潭市	Jiangxi 江西省	(0701)5881082 (0701)5881888		Private-owned 私營	53,350	14970(1)	164,260	o
Nanjing Decoration Joint General Company 南京裝飾聯合總公司(1985)	Nanjing 南京市	Jiangsu 江蘇省	(025)7711819	114	State-owned 國有	41,534	60(222)	21,081	o
Quanzhou Stone Material Technological Processing Products Co. 泉州石材工藝製品有限公司(1987)	Quanzhou 泉州市	Fujian 福建省	(0595)7332975 (0595)7332855	243	Foreign-funded 外資	39,739	3000(12)	25,260	o
Hui'an Zhen Guo Stone Products Co. Ltd. 惠安振國石製品有限公司(1993)	Quanzhou 泉州市	Fujian 福建省	(0595)7682006	120	Foreign-funded 外資	37,228	1346(34)	40,297	o

Top 10 Cities by Production Output 產出排名前10位城市	Province 省	Market share 市場份額	Number of firms 企業個數
Wuxi 無錫市	Jiangsu 江蘇省	77.86%	18
Quanzhou 泉州市	Fujian 福建省	4.00%	100
Taizhou 臺州市	Zhejiang 浙江省	3.03%	216
Nanyang 南陽市	Henan 河南省	1.16%	57
Shanghai 上海市	Shanghai 上海市	0.98%	44
Guangzhou 廣州市	Guangdong 廣東省	0.95%	71
Zhaoqing 肇慶市	Guangdong 廣東省	0.91%	19
Jiangmen 江門市	Guangdong 廣東省	0.78%	7
Jinhua 金華市	Zhejiang 浙江省	0.67%	48
Wenzhou 溫州市	Zhejiang 浙江省	0.51%	50

10 Major Wholesalers 10家主要批發商	City 城市	Province 省	Telephone / Fax 電話 / 傳真
Zhejiang Handicrafts Import & Export Company 浙江省工藝品進出口公司	Hangzhou 杭州市	Zhejiang 浙江省	(0571)7068888 (0571)7063838
Jiangsu Handicrafts Import & Export Group Co. Ltd. 江蘇省工藝品進出口集團股份有限公司	Nanjing 南京市	Jiangsu 江蘇省	(025)4466181 (025)4462442
China Handicrafts Import & Export General Company 中國工藝品進出口總公司	Beijing 北京市	Beijing 北京市	(010)65931076
Wuxi Art & Craft Group General Company 無錫市工藝美術集團總公司	Wuxi 無錫市	Jiangsu 江蘇省	(0510)2700739 (0510)2700739
Ningbo Handicrafts Import & Export Company 寧波市工藝品進出口公司	Ningbo 寧波市	Zhejiang 浙江省	(0574)7327634 (0574)7298166
Liaoning Handicrafts Import & Export Company 遼寧省工藝品進出口公司	Dalian 大連市	Liaoning 遼寧省	(0411)2649488 (0411)2802250
Shandong Special Handicraft Import & Export Company 山東省特藝品進出口公司	Qingdao 青島市	Shandong 山東省	(0532)2894464 (0532)2894441
Beijing Arts & Crafts Import & Export Co. Ltd. 北京工藝進出口集團公司	Beijing 北京市	Beijing 北京市	(010)65004662 (010)65001284
Guangdong Handicrafts Import & Export Group Co. 廣東省工藝進出口(集團)公司	Guangzhou 廣州市	Guangdong 廣東省	(020)83334208 (020)83343614
Qingdao Handicrafts Import & Export Company 青島市工藝品進出口公司	Qingdao 青島市	Shandong 山東省	(0532)5918277 (0532)5918275

*Also include sales by firms outside this industry.包括本行業以外廠家的銷售。"o" stands for "others". "o" 代表"其他產品"。

4312: Metal Arts and Crafts Articles 金屬工藝品製造業

The industry accounts for 0.040% of the total revenue of China's industrial sector in 1996. The revenue growth rate of the industry is 2.6% from 1995, as compared to the growth rate of China's industrial sector, 9.51%. The rate of return on asset is 2.23%. 73.10% of all firms in the industry made a profit while 21.21% had negative returns. The top province in terms of the industry's revenue is Shandong, accounting for 29.74% of the total revenue.
本行業在1996年佔全行業總產值0.040%，行業年增長率為2.6%（全國工業年增長率9.51%）。行業的資產回報率2.23%，73.10%的企業盈利，21.21%的企業虧損。銷售收入最高的省份為山東省，佔本行業的29.74%。

	Total number of firms 企業總數	Total number of employees 職工總數	Total revenue (mil. RMB) 總銷售收入（百萬元）	Total profit (mil. RMB) 總利潤（百萬元）	Return on assets 資產利潤率 (%)	Return on equity 權益利潤率 (%)	Labour productivity ('000 RMB / worker) 勞動生產率（千元/人）	Debts / assets 資產負債率 (%)	Total assets (mil. RMB) 總資產（百萬元）
Industry Overall 行業總體	598	39,154	2,316	47	2.23	6.15	59.15	63.72	2,104

	Number of firms 企業個數	Average number of employees 平均職工人數	Average revenue ('000 RMB) 平均銷售收入（千元）	Average profit ('000 RMB) 平均利潤（千元）	Return on assets 資產利潤率 (%)	Return on equity 權益利潤率 (%)	Labour productivity ('000 RMB / worker) 勞動生產率（千元/人）	Average debts / assets 平均資產負債率(%)	Average Total assets ('000 RMB) 平均總資產（千元）
By ownership 產業所有權									
State-owned 國有	41	83	3,098	-24	-0.37	-1.00	37.37	62.69	6,537
Collectively-owned 集體	466	54	2,834	78	3.96	14.50	52.24	72.70	1,966
Privately-owned 私有	4	61	3,971	148	7.24	18.20	65.36	60.23	2,043
Domestic JVs 聯營	2	61	25,278	6,040	65.51	247.43	417.82	73.52	9,221
Joint stock 股份制	3	37	2,782	217	54.75	75.80	75.86	27.77	396
Foreign-funded 外資	20	157	13,330	300	2.35	4.06	84.90	42.25	12,782
Overseas Chinese-funded 港澳台資	62	115	8,494	-122	-1.19	-2.96	73.66	59.73	10,269
By size 規模									
Large 大型									
Medium 中型	3	833	131,171	4,467	5.35	16.31	157.47	67.17	83,418
Small 小型	588	62	3,269	57	1.81	4.93	52.37	63.27	3,153
By regional distribution 地區分布									
Central-North 華北	137	51	1,394	48	2.18	6.74	27.43	67.59	2,189
Beijing 北京	69	55	1,427	12	0.37	1.13	25.82	67.17	3,129
Tianjin 天津	10	81	1,789	13	0.52	0.96	22.14	46.04	2,511
Hebei 河北	39	44	1,417	131	10.69	43.68	31.95	75.53	1,226
Shanxi 山西	8	49	1,590	19	1.57	30.00	32.70	94.78	1,198
Inner Mongolia 內蒙	11	20	605	33	23.53	64.29	30.00	62.75	139
Northeast 東北	64	43	1,122	12	0.96	4.59	25.88	79.01	1,248
Liaoning 遼寧	44	37	1,108	18	1.25	6.70	29.99	81.29	1,397
Jilin 吉林	12	64	584	-94	-8.77	-46.50	9.19	81.15	1,074
Heilongjiang 黑龍江	8	48	2,004	141	20.51	39.79	41.53	48.64	689
Central East 華東	239	91	6,515	130	2.72	6.80	71.79	59.96	4,779
Shanghai 上海	31	67	3,675	69	1.17	2.83	54.85	58.53	5,856
Jiangsu 江蘇	46	133	10,386	205	2.52	6.56	78.01	61.56	8,134
Zhejiang 浙江	83	31	1,741	72	4.93	11.72	55.70	57.94	1,455
Anhui 安徽	18	33	1,000	54	6.66	18.23	30.30	63.49	809
Fujian 福建	19	103	5,346	-117	-1.62	-5.13	51.80	68.40	7,248
Jiangxi 江西	16	38	789	11	1.44	5.80	20.86	75.30	739
Shandong 山東	26	298	26,493	564	4.86	10.80	89.05	55.02	11,607
Central-South 中南	102	55	4,333	40	0.82	2.71	78.61	69.87	4,931
Henan 河南	18	31	572	20	1.95	8.85	18.47	77.90	1,023
Hubei 湖北	15	71	3,843	15	0.23	0.54	54.28	56.89	6,334
Hunan 湖南	11	36	318	-12	-3.02	-6.37	8.91	52.56	391
Guangdong 廣東	48	67	7,543	79	1.01	3.78	112.76	73.14	7,740
Guangxi 廣西	9	44	826	-26	-1.80	-5.72	18.62	68.54	1,420
Hainan 海南	1		1,000	120	13.64	19.35		29.55	880
Southwest 西南	44	40	1,141	103	6.42	11.87	28.85	45.88	1,603
Chongqing 重慶	9	60	2,250	347	12.61	16.92	37.46	25.46	2,753
Sichuan 四川	12	33	580	-19	-1.45	-6.23	17.63	76.79	1,294
Guizhou 貴州	15	19	489	11	2.02	4.35	25.72	53.45	560
Yunnan 雲南	7	67	2,161	174	5.62	10.01	32.40	43.80	3,099
Tibet 西藏	1	65	1,230	380	54.29	54.29	18.92		700
Northwest 西北	12	30	346	-3	-0.50	-1.89	11.37	73.70	672
Shaanxi 陝西	5	26	116	-18	-4.71	90.00	4.53	105.24	382
Gansu 甘肅	3	46	600	10	0.88	3.30	12.95	73.31	1,137
Qinghai 青海									
Ningxia 寧夏									
Xinjiang 新疆	4	25	443	5	0.73	1.53	18.06	52.19	685

4312: Metal Arts and Crafts Articles 金屬工藝品製造業

Year 年份	Number of firms 企業個數	Rate of change 每年變化 (%)	Number of employees 職工人數（人）	Rate of change 每年變化 (%)	Total revenue (mil. RMB) 總銷售收入（百萬元）	Rate of change 每年變化 (%)	Total profit (mil. RMB) 總利潤（百萬元）	Rate of change 每年變化 (%)
1993	518		36,620		1,089		49	
1994	556	7.34%	38,344	4.71%	1,233	13.25%	31	-37.34%
1995	580	4.32%	42,813	11.66%	2,257	82.96%	53	73.07%
1996	598	3.10%	39,154	-8.55%	2,316	2.61%	47	-11.25%

3 Major products* 3 種主要產品 *	Output 產量	Sales volume 銷售量	Unit 單位
a) Metal Handicrafts 金屬工藝品	708,062	686,821	1,000 yuan 千元

Top 10 firms by revenue (year founded) 收入排名前 10 家企業（創辦年份）	City 城市	Province 省	Telephone / fax 電話 / 傳真	Number of employees 職工人數	Ownership 產業所有權	Revenue ('000 RMB) 銷售收入（千元）	Profit ('000 RMB) (rank) 利潤（千元）（排名）	Total assets ('000 RMB) 總資產（千元）	Major products 主要產品
Qingdao Fei Long Handicrafts Group Co. 青島飛龍工藝品集團公司(1986)	Qingdao 青島市	Shandong 山東省	(0532)8281688 (0532)8281688	6,000	Collectively-owned 集體	600,790	12826(1)	200,145	o
Nanjing Gold Foil (Group) Co. 南京金箔(集團)公司(1995)	Nanjing 南京市	Jiangsu 江蘇省	(025)2282616 (025)2281516	1,366	Collectively-owned 集體	314,918	8322(2)	146,845	o
Taishan Da Jiang Zhen Da Xang Yi New Metal Craft Factory 台山市大江鎮大巷藝新金屬工藝廠(1989)	Jiangmen 江門市	Guangdong 廣東省	(0750)5438543	107	Private-owned 私營	161,740	98(62)	128,711	o
Tai Fu (fuzhou)Co. Ltd. 台福(福州)有限公司(1990)	Fuzhou 福州市	Fujian 福建省	(0591)3662218	1,100	Overseas Chinese-funded 港澳台資	75,370	2160(9)	106,645	o
Qingdao Bao Yuan Handicrafts Co. Ltd. 青島寶原工藝品有限公司(1992)	Qingdao 青島市	Shandong 山東省	(0532)8280304 (0532)8280301	100	Foreign-funded 外資	48,636	0(97)	35,786	o
Gaoyao Jin Du Zhen Zhu Jiang Hardware Co. Ltd. 高要市金渡鎮朱江五金製品有限公司(1992)	Zhaoqing 肇慶市	Guangdong 廣東省	(0757)8516461	152	Overseas Chinese-funded 港澳台資	40,000	810(15)	6,760	o
Taishan Da Jiang Zhen Laian Chuang New Hardware Craft Factory 台山市大江鎮來安創新五金工藝廠(1990)	Jiangmen 江門市	Guangdong 廣東省	(0750)5438725	131	Collectively-owned 集體	33,700	540(25)	68,008	o
Beijing Enamel Factory 北京市琺琅廠(1956)	Beijing 北京市	Beijing 北京市	(010)67211155 (010)67211840	793	State-owned 國有	26,645	602(23)	44,839	a
Taishan Xin Da Jiang Craft Factory 台山市新大江工藝廠(1994)	Jiangmen 江門市	Guangdong 廣東省	(0750)5438819	178	Private-owned 私營	25,200	652(20)	6,127	o
Dong Bei Pharmaceutical Group Shenyang Medical Electrical Appliance and Equipment Factory 東北製藥集團瀋陽市醫用電器設備廠(1965)	Shenyang 瀋陽市	Liaoning 遼寧省	(024)24315351 (024)24835344	269	Collectively-owned 集體	24,904	3692(6)	24,719	o

Top 10 Cities by Production Output 產出排名前 10 位城市	Province 省	Market share 市場份額	Number of firms 企業個數
Nanjing 南京市	Jiangsu 江蘇省	20.32%	13
Beijing 北京市	Beijing 北京市	12.83%	63
Shanghai 上海市	Shanghai 上海市	10.06%	49
Wenzhou 溫州市	Zhejiang 浙江省	5.26%	108
Zhaoqing 肇慶市	Guangdong 廣東省	4.91%	5
Yangzhou 揚州市	Jiangsu 江蘇省	4.55%	5
Guangzhou 廣州市	Guangdong 廣東省	3.06%	32
Liu'an 六安市	Anhui 安徽省	2.56%	1
Jiangmen 江門市	Guangdong 廣東省	2.24%	8
Yichang 宜昌市	Hubei 湖北省	2.16%	3

10 Major Wholesalers 10 家主要批發商	City 城市	Province 省	Telephone / Fax 電話 / 傳真
Zhejiang Handicrafts Import & Export Company 浙江省工藝品進出口公司	Hangzhou 杭州市	Zhejiang 浙江省	(0571)7068888 (0571)7063838
Jiangsu Handicrafts Import & Export Group Co. Ltd. 江蘇省工藝品進出口集團股份有限公司	Nanjing 南京市	Jiangsu 江蘇省	(025)4466181 (025)4462442
China Handicrafts Import & Export General Company 中國工藝品進出口總公司	Beijing 北京市	Beijing 北京市	(010)65931076
Wuxi Art & Craft Group General Company 無錫市工藝美術集團總公司	Wuxi 無錫市	Jiangsu 江蘇省	(0510)2700739 (0510)2700739
Ningbo Handicrafts Import & Export Company 寧波市工藝品進出口公司	Ningbo 寧波市	Zhejiang 浙江省	(0574)7327634 (0574)7298166
Liaoning Handicrafts Import & Export Company 遼寧省工藝品進出口公司	Dalian 大連市	Liaoning 遼寧省	(0411)2649488 (0411)2802250
Shandong Special Handicraft Import & Export Company 山東省特藝品進出口公司	Qingdao 青島市	Shandong 山東省	(0532)2894464 (0532)2894441
Beijing Arts & Crafts Import & Export Co. Ltd. 北京工藝進出口集團公司	Beijing 北京市	Beijing 北京市	(010)65004662 (010)65001284
Guangdong Handicrafts Import & Export Group Co. 廣東省工藝進出口(集團)公司	Guangzhou 廣州市	Guangdong 廣東省	(020)83334208 (020)83343614
Qingdao Handicrafts Import & Export Company 青島市工藝品進出口公司	Qingdao 青島市	Shandong 山東省	(0532)5918277 (0532)5918275

*Also include sales by firms outside this industry.包括本行業以外廠家的銷售。"o" stands for "others". "o" 代表 "其他產品"。

4313: Lacquerwork Arts and Crafts Articles 漆器工藝品製造業

The industry accounts for 0.006% of the total revenue of China's industrial sector in 1996. The revenue growth rate of the industry is -11.2% from 1995, as compared to the growth rate of China's industrial sector, 9.51%. The rate of return on asset is 0.10%. 61.58% of all firms in the industry made a profit while 32.54% had negative returns. The top province in terms of the industry's revenue is Fujian, accounting for 36.98% of the total revenue.
本行業在1996年佔全行業總產值0.006%，行業年增長率為-11.2%（全國工業年增長率9.51%）。行業的資產回報率0.10%，61.58%的企業盈利，32.54%的企業虧損。銷售收入最高的省份為福建省，佔本行業的36.98%。

	Total number of firms 企業總數	Total number of employees 職工總數	Total revenue (mil. RMB) 總銷售收入（百萬元）	Total profit (mil. RMB) 總利潤（百萬元）	Return on assets 資產利潤率 (%)	Return on equity 權益利潤率 (%)	Labour productivity ('000 RMB / worker) 勞動生產率（千元/人）	Debts / assets 資產負債率 (%)	Total assets (mil. RMB) 總資產（百萬元）
Industry Overall 行業總體	151	14,604	365		0.10	0.31	24.99	67.40	461

	Number of firms 企業個數	Average number of employees 平均職工人數	Average revenue ('000 RMB) 平均銷售收入（千元）	Average profit ('000 RMB) 平均利潤（千元）	Return on assets 資產利潤率 (%)	Return on equity 權益利潤率 (%)	Labour productivity ('000 RMB / worker) 勞動生產率（千元/人）	Average debts / assets 平均資產負債率(%)	Average Total assets ('000 RMB) 平均總資產（千元）
By ownership 產業所有權									
State-owned 國有	13	153	1,846	154	2.06	7.69	12.09	73.20	7,462
Collectively-owned 集體	115	93	2,213	-11	-0.46	-1.56	23.82	70.41	2,467
Privately-owned 私有	2	47	1,745	0	-0.02	-0.15	37.14	85.54	1,185
Domestic JVs 聯營	1	79	1,625	-15	-0.75	-2.79	20.57	73.08	1,972
Joint stock 股份制	1	69	90	24	2.55	3.50	1.30	27.13	939
Foreign-funded 外資	14	79	3,775	-35	-1.06	-2.22	47.53	52.03	3,256
Overseas Chinese-funded 港澳台資	5	113	5,650	-43	-0.73	-1.29	49.91	43.35	5,845
By size 規模									
Large 大型									
Medium 中型									
Small 小型	151	97	2,416				24.99	67.46	3,052
By regional distribution 地區分布									
Central-North 華北	20	95	1,146	36	0.84	3.47	12.12	75.76	4,284
Beijing 北京	12	98	1,717	150	2.62	9.20	17.56	71.56	5,728
Tianjin 天津	3	130	210	-113	-6.33	-226.67	1.62	97.21	1,790
Hebei 河北	1	25	110	-120	-54.55	-400.00	4.40	81.82	220
Shanxi 山西	4	76	395	-155	-5.46	-60.78	5.20	90.93	2,838
Inner Mongolia 內蒙									
Northeast 東北	6	65	767	22	1.12	2.92	11.89	61.74	1,938
Liaoning 遼寧	5	73	920	26	1.24	3.90	12.57	68.32	2,102
Jilin 吉林	1	21							1,120
Heilongjiang 黑龍江									
Central East 華東	88	99	2,119	4	0.13	0.35	21.51	63.13	2,919
Shanghai 上海	2	16	835	-295	-22.52	-55.14	52.19	59.16	1,310
Jiangsu 江蘇	11	169	2,115	-164	-3.66	-11.50	12.49	68.15	4,466
Zhejiang 浙江	2	44	2,375	45	3.83	6.25	54.60	38.72	1,175
Anhui 安徽	5	60	2,098	82	6.23	14.49	34.85	56.84	1,316
Fujian 福建	62	93	2,177	22	0.82	2.01	23.37	59.13	2,655
Jiangxi 江西	3	15	140				9.33	98.81	560
Shandong 山東	3	188	3,640	290	2.91	13.57	19.36	78.56	9,967
Central-South 中南	16	63	8,357	43	2.07	6.30	133.58	67.17	2,084
Henan 河南									
Hubei 湖北	4	52	1,053	48	4.41	15.20	20.24	71.00	1,078
Hunan 湖南	1		160	20	1.03	4.00		74.36	1,950
Guangdong 廣東	9	87	14,371	53	1.78	5.25	164.35	66.15	3,000
Guangxi 廣西	2	3						33.33	45
Hainan 海南									
Southwest 西南	7	77	717	-143	-5.52	-50.00	9.30	89.02	2,589
Chongqing 重慶	2	63	225	-98	-6.14	-12.58	3.57	51.18	1,591
Sichuan 四川	3	76	926	-292	-8.69	44.52	12.16	119.53	3,353
Guizhou 貴州	2	93	895	35	1.43	2.92	9.62	50.82	2,440
Yunnan 雲南									
Tibet 西藏									
Northwest 西北	14	151	860	-31	-0.77	-2.45	5.69	68.55	3,984
Shaanxi 陝西	4	123	488	5	0.18	0.75	3.98	76.28	2,825
Gansu 甘肅	10	163	1,009	-45	-1.01	-3.03	6.20	66.58	4,447
Qinghai 青海									
Ningxia 寧夏									
Xinjiang 新疆									

4313: Lacquerwork Arts and Crafts Articles 漆器工藝品製造業

Year 年份	Number of firms 企業個數	Rate of change 每年變化 (%)	Number of employees 職工人數 (人)	Rate of change 每年變化 (%)	Total revenue (mil. RMB) 總銷售收入 (百萬元)	Rate of change 每年變化 (%)	Total profit (mil. RMB) 總利潤 (百萬元)	Rate of change 每年變化 (%)
1993	147		17,260		232		3	
1994	150	2.04%	20,189	16.97%	288	23.83%	0.15	-94.46%
1995	156	4.00%	16,937	-16.11%	411	42.85%	30	20335.37%
1996	151	-3.21%	14,604	-13.77%	365	-11.20%	0	-100.00%

3 Major products* 3 種主要產品 *	Output 產量	Sales volume 銷售量	Unit 單位
a) Lacquer-ware Handicraft 漆器工藝品	229,500	160,650	1,000 yuan 千元

Top 10 firms by revenue (year founded) 收入排名前 10 家企業 (創辦年份)	City 城市	Province 省	Telephone / fax 電話 / 傳真	Number of employees 職工人數	Ownership 產業所有權	Revenue ('000 RMB) 銷售收入 (千元)	Profit ('000 RMB) (rank) 利潤 (千元) (排名)	Total assets ('000 RMB) 總資產 (千元)	Major products 主要產品
Taishan Jing Qiao Handicraft Factory Co. Ltd. 台山市京巧藝品廠有限公司(1993)	Jiangmen 江門市	Guangdong 廣東省	(0750)5535916	230	Overseas Chinese-funded 港澳台資	74,700	341(8)	13,325	o
Sihui Ji New Technology Jewelry Co. Ltd. 四會集新工藝首飾有限公司(1990)	Zhaoqing 肇慶市	Guangdong 廣東省	(0757)3662320	160	Overseas Chinese-funded 港澳台資	27,020	310(10)	6,800	o
Xiamen Bao Xin Tao Porcelain Technology Product Co. Ltd. 廈門寶新陶瓷藝品有限公司(1992)	Xiamen 廈門市	Fujian 福建省	(0592)7200366	346	Foreign-funded 外資	23,277	-782(33)	22,723	o
Raoping Fu Bin Paper Made Craft Factory 饒平縣浮濱紙製工藝廠(1989)	Chaozhou 潮州市	Guangdong 廣東省	(0768)8511872	110	Collectively-owned 集體	20,976	100(14)	856	o
Fujian Xianyong Jiao Wei Chao Hui Craft Factory 福建省仙遊縣郊尾朝暉工藝廠(1989)	Putian 莆田市	Fujian 福建省	(0594)7395588	592	Collectively-owned 集體	19,160	1300(2)	2,540	o
Yanping Da Heng Handicraft Mill 延平區大橫工藝廠(1987)	Nangping 南平市	Fujian 福建省	(0599)8416407	220	Collectively-owned 集體	18,865	711(4)	15,402	a
Shandong Linqu Handicrafts Factory 山東省臨朐縣工藝品廠(1966)	Weifang 濰坊市	Shandong 山東省	(0536)3212178 (0536)3212755	514	Collectively-owned 集體	10,560	817(3)	29,294	o
Ningde Hua Chang Health Care Handicrafts Co. Ltd. 寧德華昌保健工藝品有限公司(1993)	Ningde 寧德市	Fujian 福建省	(0593)2677116	950	Collectively-owned 集體	10,259	654(5)	8,732	o
Beijing Gold Lacquer Inlaid Factory 北京金漆鑲嵌廠(1956)	Beijing 北京市	Beijing 北京市	(010)64043031 (010)64031223	627	State-owned 國有	9,752	1815(1)	38,496	a
Fujian Xianyou Shan Zhong Handicrafts Co. Ltd. 福建仙遊山中工藝品有限公司(1991)	Putian 莆田市	Fujian 福建省	(0594)7396093 (0594)7396429	584	Foreign-funded 外資	9,288	548(6)	25,812	a

Top 10 Cities by Production Output 產出排名前 10 位城市	Province 省	Market share 市場份額	Number of firms 企業個數
Jiangmen 江門市	Guangdong 廣東省	22.64%	2
Putian 莆田市	Fujian 福建省	13.35%	17
Fuzhou 福州市	Fujian 福建省	8.43%	30
Zhaoqing 肇慶市	Guangdong 廣東省	7.73%	1
Harbin 哈爾濱市	Heilongjiang 黑龍江省	6.67%	1
Yangzhou 揚州市	Jiangsu 江蘇省	5.74%	6
Shanghai 上海市	Shanghai 上海市	5.40%	3
Weifang 濰坊市	Shandong 山東省	4.87%	2
Yantai 煙台市	Shandong 山東省	4.46%	3
Beijing 北京市	Beijing 北京市	4.35%	12

10 Major Wholesalers 10 家主要批發商	City 城市	Province 省	Telephone / Fax 電話 / 傳真
Zhejiang Handicrafts Import & Export Company 浙江省工藝品進出口公司	Hangzhou 杭州市	Zhejiang 浙江省	(0571)7068888 (0571)7063838
Jiangsu Handicrafts Import & Export Group Co. Ltd. 江蘇省工藝品進出口集團股份有限公司	Nanjing 南京市	Jiangsu 江蘇省	(025)4466181 (025)4462442
China Handicrafts Import & Export General Company 中國工藝品進出口總公司	Beijing 北京市	Beijing 北京市	(010)65931076
Wuxi Art & Craft Group General Company 無錫市工藝美術集團總公司	Wuxi 無錫市	Jiangsu 江蘇省	(0510)2700739 (0510)2700739
Ningbo Handicrafts Import & Export Company 寧波市工藝品進出口公司	Ningbo 寧波市	Zhejiang 浙江省	(0574)7327634 (0574)7298166
Liaoning Handicrafts Import & Export Company 遼寧省工藝品進出口公司	Dalian 大連市	Liaoning 遼寧省	(0411)2649488 (0411)2802250
Shandong Special Handicraft Import & Export Company 山東省特藝品進出口公司	Qingdao 青島市	Shandong 山東省	(0532)2894464 (0532)2894441
Beijing Arts & Crafts Import & Export Co. Ltd. 北京工藝進出口集團公司	Beijing 北京市	Beijing 北京市	(010)65004662 (010)65001284
Guangdong Handicrafts Import & Export Group Co. 廣東省工藝進出口(集團)公司	Guangzhou 廣州市	Guangdong 廣東省	(020)83334208 (020)83343614
Qingdao Handicrafts Import & Export Company 青島市工藝品進出口公司	Qingdao 青島市	Shandong 山東省	(0532)5918277 (0532)5918275

*Also include sales by firms outside this industry.包括本行業以外廠家的銷售。“o” stands for “others”. “o”代表“其他產品”。

4314: Flower and Birds Painting 花畫工藝品製造業

The industry accounts for 0.035% of the total revenue of China's industrial sector in 1996. The revenue growth rate of the industry is -7.5% from 1995, as compared to the growth rate of China's industrial sector, 9.51%. The rate of return on asset is 1.77%. 72.88% of all firms in the industry made a profit while 22.04% had negative returns. The top province in terms of the industry's revenue is Guangdong, accounting for 54.21% of the total revenue.
本行業在1996年佔全行業總產值0.035%，行業年增長率為-7.5%（全國工業年增長率9.51%）。行業的資產回報率1.77%，72.88%的企業盈利，22.04%的企業虧損。銷售收入最高的省份為廣東省，佔本行業的54.21%。

	Total number of firms 企業總數	Total number of employees 職工總數	Total revenue (mil. RMB) 總銷售收入（百萬元）	Total profit (mil. RMB) 總利潤（百萬元）	Return on assets 資產利潤率 (%)	Return on equity 權益利潤率 (%)	Labour productivity ('000 RMB / worker) 勞動生產率（千元/人）	Debts / assets 資產負債率 (%)	Total assets (mil. RMB) 總資產（百萬元）
Industry Overall 行業總體	531	56,353	2,042	39	1.77	3.93	36.24	54.91	2,179

	Number of firms 企業個數	Average number of employees 平均職工人數	Average revenue ('000 RMB) 平均銷售收入（千元）	Average profit ('000 RMB) 平均利潤（千元）	Return on assets 資產利潤率 (%)	Return on equity 權益利潤率 (%)	Labour productivity ('000 RMB / worker) 勞動生產率（千元/人）	Average debts / assets 平均資產負債率(%)	Average Total assets ('000 RMB) 平均總資產（千元）
By ownership 產業所有權									
State-owned 國有	29	49	1,103	34	1.85	4.17	22.42	55.56	1,862
Collectively-owned 集體	354	87	2,512	48	1.79	5.32	28.92	66.43	2,661
Privately-owned 私有	4	52	504	6	2.54	5.71	9.64	55.46	244
Domestic JVs 聯營	1	134	7,728	-62	-0.63	-1.32	57.67	52.55	9,840
Joint stock 股份制	1	4							
Foreign-funded 外資	40	118	6,489	150	2.14	3.90	54.77	45.08	7,010
Overseas Chinese-funded 港澳台資	101	190	8,307	157	1.82	3.34	43.76	45.56	8,640
By size 規模									
Large 大型									
Medium 中型	5	811	23,513	248	0.58	1.87	28.98	68.77	42,374
Small 小型	516	102	3,731	73	1.92	4.12	36.73	53.39	3,814
By regional distribution 地區分布									
Central-North 華北	67	48	1,321	108	5.71	13.39	27.33	57.35	1,896
Beijing 北京	19	56	1,817	17	0.45	0.91	32.39	50.31	3,716
Tianjin 天津	16	61	1,429	144	7.80	25.58	23.45	69.46	1,842
Hebei 河北	12	53	1,669	361	27.05	56.68	31.79	52.28	1,334
Shanxi 山西	10	31	723	18	2.39	22.78	23.40	89.52	754
Inner Mongolia 內蒙	10	26	387	12	3.55	7.27	14.94	51.18	338
Northeast 東北	73	55	1,830	-41	-2.51	-9.09	33.51	72.38	1,620
Liaoning 遼寧	53	65	2,331	-59	-2.87	-10.11	35.74	71.60	2,044
Jilin 吉林	3	20	110	-140	-42.42	-43.75	5.59	3.03	330
Heilongjiang 黑龍江	17	28	570	33	6.29	60.22	20.62	89.56	524
Central East 華東	188	103	3,474	52	1.33	3.23	33.80	58.91	3,919
Shanghai 上海	10	118	978	-72	-2.29	-14.20	8.27	83.90	3,150
Jiangsu 江蘇	24	123	3,571	-42	-1.33	-5.20	28.97	74.40	3,132
Zhejiang 浙江	21	45	2,599	1	0.03	0.07	57.50	60.00	3,367
Anhui 安徽	16	43	3,041	196	35.45	54.53	70.12	34.99	552
Fujian 福建	54	115	5,111	171	3.95	5.98	44.61	33.93	4,326
Jiangxi 江西	9	80	897	-51	-3.22	-5.38	11.26	40.24	1,588
Shandong 山東	54	123	3,156	-8	-0.14	-0.53	25.67	73.06	5,604
Central-South 中南	184	158	6,317	136	2.12	4.29	39.88	50.50	6,395
Henan 河南	10	38	876	36	2.64	10.53	23.36	74.89	1,366
Hubei 湖北	14	33	1,525	36	6.49	11.97	46.51	45.80	561
Hunan 湖南	15	60	1,539	37	2.42	5.37	25.49	55.01	1,516
Guangdong 廣東	139	195	7,964	179	2.21	4.42	40.80	50.11	8,118
Guangxi 廣西	5	52	330	-102	-18.02	-39.84	6.40	54.77	566
Hainan 海南	1	12	510	-810	-75.00	-245.45	42.50	69.44	1,080
Southwest 西南	11	41	253	-34	-2.72	-6.28	6.23	56.65	1,237
Chongqing 重慶	4	59	122	-120	-6.86	-21.77	2.05	68.47	1,746
Sichuan 四川	2	9	210	2	0.34	0.45	23.92	23.42	595
Guizhou 貴州	3	25	513	43	6.60	9.03	20.53	26.90	657
Yunnan 雲南	2	50	180	5	0.32	0.76	3.60	57.96	1,570
Tibet 西藏									
Northwest 西北	8	26	169				6.40	34.23	880
Shaanxi 陝西	4	31	88	5	2.22	2.33	2.80	4.44	225
Gansu 甘肅									
Qinghai 青海									
Ningxia 寧夏									
Xinjiang 新疆	4	22	250	-5	-0.33	-0.53	11.63	38.60	1,535

4314: Flower and Birds Painting 花畫工藝品製造業

Year 年份	Number of firms 企業個數	Rate of change 每年變化 (%)	Number of employees 職工人數 (人)	Rate of change 每年變化 (%)	Total revenue (mil. RMB) 總銷售收入 (百萬元)	Rate of change 每年變化 (%)	Total profit (mil. RMB) 總利潤 (百萬元)	Rate of change 每年變化 (%)
1993	532		58,615		1,136		35	
1994	569	6.95%	68,485	16.84%	1,914	68.39%	66	86.37%
1995	555	-2.46%	64,959	-5.15%	2,208	15.39%	88	34.23%
1996	531	-4.32%	56,353	-13.25%	2,042	-7.52%	39	-55.69%

3 Major products* 3 種主要產品 *	Output 產量	Sales volume 銷售量	Unit 單位
a) Artifical Flower 人造花卉	1,306,661	1,659,460	1000 yuan 千元
b) Drawing Handicrafts 畫類工藝品	61,058	53,731	1000 yuan 千元

Top 10 firms by revenue (year founded) 收入排名前 10 家企業 (創辦年份)	City 城市	Province 省	Telephone / fax 電話 / 傳真	Number of employees 職工人數	Ownership 產業所有權	Revenue ('000 RMB) 銷售收入 (千元)	Profit ('000 RMB) (rank) 利潤 (千元) (排名)	Total assets ('000 RMB) 總資產 (千元)	Major products 主要產品
Boluo Long Xi Xinfeng Plastic Cement Products Co. Ltd. 博羅縣龍溪新豐塑膠製品有限公司(1990)	Huizhou 惠州市	Guangdong 廣東省		1,050	Overseas Chinese-funded 港澳台資	112,000	3800(4)	46,440	a
Shandou Sez Longhu Xia Peng Craft Factory 汕頭經濟特區龍湖區下蓬工藝廠(1983)	Shantou 汕頭市	Guangdong 廣東省	(0754)8330792 (0754)8330879	1,304	Collectively-owned 集體	98,000	7254(2)	40,560	o
Xinhui Hua Da Industrial Co. Ltd. 新會市華達實業有限公司(1994)	Jiangmen 江門市	Guangdong 廣東省	(0750)6523233	513	Overseas Chinese-funded 港澳台資	83,216	0(137)	43,817	a
Fujian Yunxiao Ming Cheng Artificial Flower Co. Ltd. 福建省雲霄名城人造花有限公司(1992)	Zhangzhou 漳州市	Fujian 福建省	(0596)8534555	160	Overseas Chinese-funded 港澳台資	78,160	65(102)	7,466	a
Kaiping Wei Li Artificial Flower Factory 開平威利人造花廠(1993)	Jiangmen 江門市	Guangdong 廣東省	(0750)2612892	324	Overseas Chinese-funded 港澳台資	62,119	830(23)	88,040	a
Jinjiang You Li Da Clothing Knitting Co. Ltd. 晉江市友利達服裝針織有限公司(1993)	Quanzhou 泉州市	Fujian 福建省	(0595)5288382	125	Overseas Chinese-funded 港澳台資	53,800	7500(1)	6,411	a
Grand China Floral Craft Manufacturing Co. Ltd. 華泰工藝製品有限公司(1992)	Zhongshan 中山市	Guangdong 廣東省	(0760)7726286 (0760)7726888	2,564	Foreign-funded 外資	46,111	-1679(174)	110,972	a
Guangzhou Di Ka Color Printing Co. Ltd. 廣州迪卡彩印有限公司(1989)	Guangzhou 廣州市	Guangdong 廣東省	(020)82308834 (020)82307735	188	Overseas Chinese-funded 港澳台資	42,591	1687(13)	39,461	o
Xiamen Gold Eagle Artificial Flower Co. Ltd. 廈門金鵬人造花有限公司(1989)	Xiamen 廈門市	Fujian 福建省	(0592)7021158 (0592)7021133	1,195	Foreign-funded 外資	41,516	-220(159)	28,866	a
Zhongshan Yi Cheng Artificial Flower Products Co. Ltd. 中山藝成人造花製品有限公司(1996)	Zhongshan 中山市	Guangdong 廣東省	(0760)8550338 (0760)8551121	580	Foreign-funded 外資	39,681	802(24)	19,641	a

Top 10 Cities by Production Output 產出排名前 10 位城市	Province 省	Market share 市場份額	Number of firms 企業個數
Guangzhou 廣州市	Guangdong 廣東省	18.09%	38
Zhongshan 中山市	Guangdong 廣東省	9.63%	15
Huizhou 惠州市	Guangdong 廣東省	6.53%	40
Suzhou 蘇州市	Jiangsu 江蘇省	5.48%	12
Dongguan 東莞市	Guangdong 廣東省	5.07%	26
Ji'nan 濟南市	Shandong 山東省	4.09%	8
Shenzhen 深圳市	Guangdong 廣東省	3.84%	8
Quanzhou 泉州市	Fujian 福建省	2.57%	10
Zhaoqing 肇慶市	Guangdong 廣東省	2.53%	4
Shanghai 上海市	Shanghai 上海市	2.53%	24

10 Major Wholesalers 10 家主要批發商	City 城市	Province 省	Telephone / Fax 電話 / 傳真
Zhejiang Handicrafts Import & Export Company 浙江省工藝品進出口公司	Hangzhou 杭州市	Zhejiang 浙江省	(0571)7068888 (0571)7063838
Jiangsu Handicrafts Import & Export Group Co. Ltd. 江蘇省工藝品進出口集團股份有限公司	Nanjing 南京市	Jiangsu 江蘇省	(025)4466181 (025)4462442
China Handicrafts Import & Export General Company 中國工藝品進出口總公司	Beijing 北京市	Beijing 北京市	(010)65931076
Wuxi Art & Craft Group General Company 無錫市工藝美術集團總公司	Wuxi 無錫市	Jiangsu 江蘇省	(0510)2700739 (0510)2700739
Ningbo Handicrafts Import & Export Company 寧波市工藝品進出口公司	Ningbo 寧波市	Zhejiang 浙江省	(0574)7327634 (0574)7298166
Liaoning Handicrafts Import & Export Company 遼寧省工藝品進出口公司	Dalian 大連市	Liaoning 遼寧省	(0411)2649488 (0411)2802250
Shandong Special Handicraft Import & Export Company 山東省特藝品進出口公司	Qingdao 青島市	Shandong 山東省	(0532)2894464 (0532)2894441
Beijing Arts & Crafts Import & Export Co. Ltd. 北京工藝進出口集團公司	Beijing 北京市	Beijing 北京市	(010)65004662 (010)65001284
Guangdong Handicrafts Import & Export Group Co. 廣東省工藝進出口(集團)公司	Guangzhou 廣州市	Guangdong 廣東省	(020)83334208 (020)83343614
Qingdao Handicrafts Import & Export Company 青島市工藝品進出口公司	Qingdao 青島市	Shandong 山東省	(0532)5918277 (0532)5918275

*Also include sales by firms outside this industry.包括本行業以外廠家的銷售。"o" stands for "others". "o" 代表 "其他產品"。

4315: Bamboo, Rattan, Palm and Straw Arts and Crafts Articles
竹、藤、棕、草工藝品製造業

The industry accounts for 0.072% of the total revenue of China's industrial sector in 1996. The revenue growth rate of the industry is 12.4% from 1995, as compared to the growth rate of China's industrial sector, 9.51%. The rate of return on asset is 6.87%. 78.11% of all firms in the industry made a profit while 14.90% had negative returns. The top province in terms of the industry's revenue is Shandong, accounting for 21.35% of the total revenue.
本行業在1996年佔全行業總產值0.072%，行業年增長率為12.4%（全國工業年增長率9.51%）。行業的資產回報率6.87%，78.11%的企業盈利，14.90%的企業虧損。銷售收入最高的省份為山東省，佔本行業的21.35%。

	Total number of firms 企業總數	Total number of employees 職工總數	Total revenue (mil. RMB) 總銷售收入（百萬元）	Total profit (mil. RMB) 總利潤（百萬元）	Return on assets 資產利潤率 (%)	Return on equity 權益利潤率 (%)	Labour productivity ('000 RMB / worker) 勞動生產率（千元/人）	Debts / assets 資產負債率 (%)	Total assets (mil. RMB) 總資產（百萬元）
Industry Overall 行業總體	960	105,865	4,163	165	6.87	19.53	39.32	64.80	2,402

	Number of firms 企業個數	Average number of employees 平均職工人數	Average revenue ('000 RMB) 平均銷售收入（千元）	Average profit ('000 RMB) 平均利潤（千元）	Return on assets 資產利潤率 (%)	Return on equity 權益利潤率 (%)	Labour productivity ('000 RMB / worker) 勞動生產率（千元/人）	Average debts / assets 平均資產負債率(%)	Average Total assets ('000 RMB) 平均總資產（千元）
By ownership 產業所有權									
State-owned 國有	39	100	4,000	-513	-7.69	-31.75	39.98	75.77	6,667
Collectively-owned 集體	817	107	3,274	209	11.16	31.76	30.66	64.87	1,874
Privately-owned 私有	4	22	2,006	216	65.57	106.25	90.17	38.28	329
Domestic JVs 聯營	4	285	5,136	159	4.21	9.26	18.01	54.49	3,765
Joint stock 股份制	3	15	237	5	2.35	3.34	16.14	29.62	219
Foreign-funded 外資	43	210	21,723	331	5.37	14.46	103.56	62.89	6,171
Overseas Chinese-funded 港澳台資	49	94	7,531	-31	-0.46	-1.09	79.77	57.84	6,726
By size 規模									
Large 大型									
Medium 中型	6	1,035	61,052	1,244	1.47	5.02	58.98	70.72	84,630
Small 小型	945	105	4,019	167	8.31	22.58	38.09	63.19	2,005
By regional distribution 地區分布									
Central-North 華北	35	62	1,094	132	18.20	46.02	17.71	60.38	725
Beijing 北京	5		292					42.45	212
Tianjin 天津	8	21	705	85	9.05	24.37	34.39	62.85	939
Hebei 河北	13	43	1,824	183	19.70	68.00	42.42	71.03	929
Shanxi 山西	1	5	110				22.00	50.00	60
Inner Mongolia 內蒙	8	179	923	195	33.33	50.00	5.14	33.12	585
Northeast 東北	56	97	1,810	99	8.72	18.54	18.72	52.99	1,141
Liaoning 遼寧	21	72	2,235	94	7.13	17.55	31.16	59.38	1,322
Jilin 吉林	10	53	1,472	120	6.55	13.33	27.77	50.95	1,833
Heilongjiang 黑龍江	25	135	1,588	96	13.44	24.49	11.75	45.11	711
Central East 華東	533	113	4,401	186	6.25	18.44	39.11	66.12	2,983
Shanghai 上海	7	32	1,817	69	5.06	13.33	56.79	62.07	1,356
Jiangsu 江蘇	49	92	4,586	89	2.25	8.35	49.93	73.07	3,967
Zhejiang 浙江	103	84	3,475	-70	-1.77	-4.44	41.55	60.20	3,964
Anhui 安徽	66	183	5,906	587	33.57	78.00	32.19	56.96	1,747
Fujian 福建	109	112	3,886	224	10.21	30.38	34.71	66.39	2,193
Jiangxi 江西	83	46	582	-19	-2.48	-10.46	12.58	76.31	763
Shandong 山東	116	159	7,661	346	7.17	22.92	48.09	68.72	4,830
Central-South 中南	274	126	5,936	198	8.16	21.95	47.10	62.83	2,428
Henan 河南	29	110	3,061	197	17.76	44.32	27.90	59.94	1,107
Hubei 湖北	29	168	5,441	117	6.46	11.87	32.39	45.61	1,816
Hunan 湖南	44	46	1,532	54	6.83	19.26	33.19	64.54	792
Guangdong 廣東	106	154	6,603	170	4.14	12.07	42.92	65.73	4,119
Guangxi 廣西	64	125	9,553	386	23.10	57.07	76.30	59.53	1,672
Hainan 海南	2	63	595	10	0.96	4.17	9.52	76.44	1,040
Southwest 西南	39	57	974	19	1.80	4.98	17.10	63.96	1,071
Chongqing 重慶	8	51	579	-86	-17.63	-99.68	11.26	82.32	485
Sichuan 四川	25	67	1,266	1	0.04	0.09	18.93	61.30	1,390
Guizhou 貴州	5	26	322	10	1.59	5.43	12.20	71.02	628
Yunnan 雲南	1	7	260	10	4.55	8.33	37.14	45.45	220
Tibet 西藏									
Northwest 西北	23	68	572	26	3.76	13.61	8.41	72.35	693
Shaanxi 陝西	13	71	598	40	4.74	16.46	8.41	71.13	845
Gansu 甘肅	8	64	635	8	1.29	5.66	9.96	77.37	580
Qinghai 青海									
Ningxia 寧夏	2	65	150	10	6.06	10.53	2.31	42.42	165
Xinjiang 新疆									

4315: Bamboo, Rattan, Palm and Straw Arts and Crafts Articles
竹、藤、棕、草工藝品製造業

Year 年份	Number of firms 企業個數	Rate of change 每年變化 (%)	Number of employees 職工人數 (人)	Rate of change 每年變化 (%)	Total revenue (mil. RMB) 總銷售收入 (百萬元)	Rate of change 每年變化 (%)	Total profit (mil. RMB) 總利潤 (百萬元)	Rate of change 每年變化 (%)
1993	955		70,920		1,809		75	
1994	977	2.30%	112,218	58.23%	2,411	33.31%	58	-22.93%
1995	904	-7.47%	114,648	2.17%	3,705	53.65%	94	63.14%
1996	960	6.19%	105,865	-7.66%	4,163	12.36%	165	75.41%

3 Major products* 3 種主要產品 *	Output 產量	Sales volume 銷售量	Unit 單位
a) Babmoo, Vine, Palm & Straw Products 竹、藤、棕、草製品	1,135,648	1,112,935	1,000 yuan 千元

Top 10 firms by revenue (year founded) 收入排名前 10 家企業 (創辦年份)	City 城市	Province 省	Telephone / fax 電話 / 傳真	Number of employees 職工人數	Ownership 產業所有權	Revenue ('000 RMB) 銷售收入 (千元)	Profit ('000 RMB) (rank) 利潤 (千元) (排名)	Total assets ('000 RMB) 總資產 (千元)	Major products 主要產品
Shandong Laizhou Arts & Cratfs (Group) Co. 山東省萊州工藝品(集團)公司(1950)	Yantai 煙台市	Shandong 山東省	(0535)2213239 (0535)2211655	2,245	Collectively-owned 集體	151,130	2046(18)	96,051	o
Shanghai Ji Ming Bamboo & Wood Products Co. Ltd. 上海吉明竹木製品有限公司(1996)	Shanghai 上海市	Shanghai 上海市		75	Foreign-funded 外資	145,093	2826(13)	6,834	o
Shandong Caoxian Cao Pu Craft Company 山東省曹縣曹普工藝公司(1986)	Heze 菏澤市	Shandong 山東省	(0530)3431230	600	Collectively-owned 集體	143,530	9210(3)	61,330	o
Caoxian Tong Cao Handicraft Factory 曹縣桐草工藝總廠(1987)	Heze 菏澤市	Shandong 山東省	(0530)3431233	230	Collectively-owned 集體	109,170	6660(4)	41,390	o
Bobai Jiangning Mang Bamboo Woven Factory 博白縣江寧芒竹編廠(1988)	Yulin 玉林市	Guangxi 廣西		350	Collectively-owned 集體	105,000	6530(5)	1,210	o
Zhongshan Craft General Factory 中山市工藝總廠(1955)	Zhongshan 中山市	Guangdong 廣東省	(0760)8835141 (0760)8821145	1,702	Collectively-owned 集體	95,912	1019(40)	61,282	a
Beiliu Ping Zheng Craft Factory 北流市平政工藝廠(1982)	Yulin 玉林市	Guangxi 廣西	(0775)6731238	85	Collectively-owned 集體	95,000	2803(14)	18,120	o
Xianyong Bamboo Articles Factory 龍游縣竹器廠(1955)	Putian 莆田市	Fujian 福建省	(0594)8592474	47	Collectively-owned 集體	88,150	14816(1)	17,610	o
Bobai Teng Long Knitting Craft Factory 博白縣騰龍編織工藝廠(1994)	Yulin 玉林市	Guangxi 廣西	(0775)8330368	670	Collectively-owned 集體	81,830	6430(6)	5,770	o
Guangdong Nanteng (Holding) Corp. 廣東南藤(集團)公司(1956)	Foshan 佛山市	Guangdong 廣東省	(0757)81982272 (0757)81983696	1,689	State-owned 國有	79,671	0(282)	100,664	o

Top 10 Cities by Production Output 產出排名前 10 位城市	Province 省	Market share 市場份額	Number of firms 企業個數
Heze 菏澤市	Shandong 山東省	11.74%	18
Yulin 玉林市	Guangxi 廣西	11.42%	34
Linyi 臨沂市	Shandong 山東省	10.08%	30
Liu'an 六安市	Anhui 安徽省	4.20%	28
Yantai 煙台市	Shandong 山東省	3.68%	13
Suzhou 蘇州市	Jiangsu 江蘇省	3.29%	19
Zhanjiang 湛江市	Guangdong 廣東省	2.97%	7
Fuzhou 福州市	Fujian 福建省	2.93%	50
Quanzhou 泉州市	Fujian 福建省	2.91%	33
Foshan 佛山市	Guangdong 廣東省	2.77%	3

10 Major Wholesalers 10 家主要批發商	City 城市	Province 省	Telephone / Fax 電話 / 傳真
Zhejiang Handicrafts Import & Export Company 浙江省工藝品進出口公司	Hangzhou 杭州市	Zhejiang 浙江省	(0571)7068888 (0571)7063838
Jiangsu Handicrafts Import & Export Group Co. Ltd. 江蘇省工藝品進出口集團股份有限公司	Nanjing 南京市	Jiangsu 江蘇省	(025)4466181 (025)4462442
China Handicrafts Import & Export General Company 中國工藝品進出口總公司	Beijing 北京市	Beijing 北京市	(010)65931076
Wuxi Art & Craft Group General Company 無錫市工藝美術集團總公司	Wuxi 無錫市	Jiangsu 江蘇省	(0510)2700739 (0510)2700739
Ningbo Handicrafts Import & Export Company 寧波市工藝品進出口公司	Ningbo 寧波市	Zhejiang 浙江省	(0574)7327634 (0574)7298166
Liaoning Handicrafts Import & Export Company 遼寧省工藝品進出口公司	Dalian 大連市	Liaoning 遼寧省	(0411)2649488 (0411)2802250
Shandong Special Handicraft Import & Export Company 山東省特藝品進出口公司	Qingdao 青島市	Shandong 山東省	(0532)2894464 (0532)2894441
Beijing Arts & Crafts Import & Export Co. Ltd. 北京工藝進出口集團公司	Beijing 北京市	Beijing 北京市	(010)65004662 (010)65001284
Guangdong Handicrafts Import & Export Group Co. 廣東省工藝進出口(集團)公司	Guangzhou 廣州市	Guangdong 廣東省	(020)83334208 (020)83343614
Qingdao Handicrafts Import & Export Company 青島市工藝品進出口公司	Qingdao 青島市	Shandong 山東省	(0532)5918277 (0532)5918275

*Also include sales by firms outside this industry.包括本行業以外廠家的銷售。"o" stands for "others". "o" 代表 "其他產品"。

4316: Drawn Work and Embroidered Arts and Crafts Articles
抽紗刺繡工藝品製造業

The industry accounts for 0.140% of the total revenue of China's industrial sector in 1996. The revenue growth rate of the industry is -9.1% from 1995, as compared to the growth rate of China's industrial sector, 9.51%. The rate of return on asset is 0.89%. 66.51% of all firms in the industry made a profit while 24.20% had negative returns. The top province in terms of the industry's revenue is Shandong, accounting for 27.21% of the total revenue.
本行業在1996年佔全行業總產值0.140%，行業年增長率為-9.1%（全國工業年增長率9.51%）。行業的資產回報率0.89%，66.51%的企業盈利，24.20%的企業虧損。銷售收入最高的省份為山東省，佔本行業的27.21%。

	Total number of firms 企業總數	Total number of employees 職工總數	Total revenue (mil. RMB) 總銷售收入（百萬元）	Total profit (mil. RMB) 總利潤（百萬元）	Return on assets 資產利潤率 (%)	Return on equity 權益利潤率 (%)	Labour productivity ('000 RMB / worker) 勞動生產率（千元/人）	Debts / assets 資產負債率 (%)	Total assets (mil. RMB) 總資產（百萬元）
Industry Overall 行業總體	1,397	187,502	8,129	86	0.89	2.64	43.35	66.48	9,743

	Number of firms 企業個數	Average number of employees 平均職工人數	Average revenue ('000 RMB) 平均銷售收入（千元）	Average profit ('000 RMB) 平均利潤（千元）	Return on assets 資產利潤率 (%)	Return on equity 權益利潤率 (%)	Labour productivity ('000 RMB / worker) 勞動生產率（千元/人）	Average debts / assets 平均資產負債率(%)	Average Total assets ('000 RMB) 平均總資產（千元）
By ownership 產業所有權									
State-owned 國有	92	155	3,489	-348	-5.23	-23.19	22.49	77.45	6,652
Collectively-owned 集體	1,012	136	5,223	37	0.64	2.34	38.47	72.62	5,850
Privately-owned 私有	5	37	3,212	-73	-2.26	-10.56	85.87	78.57	3,215
Domestic JVs 聯營	16	189	12,233	149	1.00	3.07	64.90	67.36	14,828
Joint stock 股份制	19	421	31,222	851	2.30	6.14	74.20	62.53	36,958
Foreign-funded 外資	83	140	9,420	516	4.72	10.40	67.50	54.59	10,924
Overseas Chinese-funded 港澳台資	168	77	5,153	91	1.25	2.21	67.16	43.29	7,266
By size 規模									
Large 大型	6	969	53,051	2,052	2.04	5.80	54.78	64.93	100,829
Medium 中型	48	673	47,456	513	0.88	2.80	70.48	68.55	58,144
Small 小型	1,323	113	4,182	37	0.77	2.26	36.95	65.72	4,798
By regional distribution 地區分布									
Central-North 華北	157	89	2,109	80	2.61	8.01	23.74	67.46	3,068
Beijing 北京	48	63	1,181	22	0.78	1.46	18.72	46.74	2,869
Tianjin 天津	26	99	1,357	-71	-1.71	-6.19	13.71	72.28	4,150
Hebei 河北	66	112	3,416	197	5.86	25.26	30.40	76.78	3,366
Shanxi 山西	6	30	972	23	2.74	10.77	32.21	74.56	852
Inner Mongolia 內蒙	11	69	725	15	1.95	29.82	10.58	93.45	791
Northeast 東北	60	92	1,724	-26	-0.64	-1.66	18.66	61.46	4,112
Liaoning 遼寧	36	65	1,693	6	0.13	0.26	25.93	49.93	4,270
Jilin 吉林	5	127	1,150	-564	-12.70	-120.00	9.06	89.46	4,440
Heilongjiang 黑龍江	19	135	1,934	55	1.47	6.59	14.37	77.72	3,727
Central East 華東	738	169	8,360	100	1.06	3.37	49.44	68.47	9,394
Shanghai 上海	72	150	10,034	18	0.12	0.33	66.72	63.40	14,570
Jiangsu 江蘇	190	129	10,163	57	0.75	2.38	78.85	68.52	7,553
Zhejiang 浙江	100	181	8,604	-188	-1.76	-5.36	47.61	67.13	10,673
Anhui 安徽	58	183	4,125	44	2.36	7.30	22.51	67.68	1,857
Fujian 福建	58	74	3,319	111	1.90	2.89	44.99	34.35	5,824
Jiangxi 江西	17	39	678	62	8.97	19.13	17.27	53.21	695
Shandong 山東	243	230	9,104	289	2.41	9.54	39.62	74.78	12,032
Central-South 中南	381	104	3,623	-3	-0.06	-0.17	34.72	61.31	4,288
Henan 河南	85	97	1,892	93	5.28	15.48	19.60	65.90	1,757
Hubei 湖北	20	112	2,941	47	1.12	3.94	26.18	71.65	4,208
Hunan 湖南	60	97	3,331	20	0.76	3.01	34.44	74.90	2,670
Guangdong 廣東	208	111	4,602	-52	-0.88	-2.11	41.37	58.28	5,907
Guangxi 廣西	7	37	484	-27	-2.63	-6.11	13.24	56.93	1,031
Hainan 海南	1	106	50	-80	-1.92	-5.44	0.47	64.75	4,170
Southwest 西南	30	56	1,536	96	1.15	1.76	27.49	34.67	8,386
Chongqing 重慶	6	74	1,055	-277	-5.16	-11.26	14.25	54.19	5,368
Sichuan 四川	15	55	2,494	-90	-0.64	-0.92	45.72	30.54	13,975
Guizhou 貴州	6	42	32	-22	-2.67	-14.29	0.76	81.28	810
Yunnan 雲南	3	52	653	10	0.78	1.35	12.48	42.49	1,287
Tibet 西藏									
Northwest 西北	31	57	3,181		-0.01	-0.03	55.36	83.78	6,362
Shaanxi 陝西	17	53	869	-16	-1.16	-4.46	16.55	74.01	1,372
Gansu 甘肅	7	82	11,374	21	0.09	0.81	139.20	88.47	22,827
Qinghai 青海	1	22	700	50	7.81	12.50	31.82	37.50	640
Ningxia 寧夏									
Xinjiang 新疆	6	49	583	10	0.45	0.85	11.90	47.22	2,245

4316: Drawn Work and Embroidered Arts and Crafts Articles
抽紗刺繡工藝品製造業

Year 年份	Number of firms 企業個數	Rate of change 每年變化 (%)	Number of employees 職工人數（人）	Rate of change 每年變化 (%)	Total revenue (mil. RMB) 總銷售收入（百萬元）	Rate of change 每年變化 (%)	Total profit (mil. RMB) 總利潤（百萬元）	Rate of change 每年變化 (%)
1993	1,642		244,675		7,413		236	
1994	1,651	0.55%	243,332	-0.55%	8,463	14.17%	198	-16.41%
1995	1,544	-6.48%	223,441	-8.18%	8,939	5.63%	173	-12.34%
1996	1,397	-9.52%	187,502	-16.08%	8,129	-9.06%	86	-50.36%

3 Major products* 3 種主要產品 *	Output 產量	Sales volume 銷售量	Unit 單位
a) Drawnwork Handicraft 抽紗工藝品	3,169,927	2,948,032	1000 yuan 千元

Top 10 firms by revenue (year founded) 收入排名前 10 家企業（創辦年份）	City 城市	Province 省	Telephone / fax 電話 / 傳真	Number of employees 職工人數	Ownership 產業所有權	Revenue ('000 RMB) 銷售收入（千元）	Profit ('000 RMB) (rank) 利潤（千元）（排名）	Total assets ('000 RMB) 總資產（千元）	Major products 主要產品
Wendeng Yun Long Embroideries Industry Group Co. 文登市雲龍繡品集團公司(1981)	Weihai 威海市	Shandong 山東省	(0896)8353302 (0896)8356276	1,591	Collectively-owned 集體	170,104	6817(7)	158,828	o
Nantong Guan Da Co. Ltd. 南通冠達股份有限公司(1956)	Nantong 南通市	Jiangsu 江蘇省	(0513)3563796 (0513)3583041	718	Joint stock 股份制	150,180	1684(42)	88,668	a
Shandong Embroideries Co. Ltd. 山東省錦繡集團公司(1988)	Yantai 煙台市	Shandong 山東省	(0535)8216552 (0535)8212170	1,146	Overseas Chinese-funded 港澳台資	138,608	5853(11)	87,907	o
Suzhou Embroidered Products General Factory 蘇州繡品總廠(1956)	Suzhou 蘇州市	Jiangsu 江蘇省	(0512)7231071 (0512)7232359	782	Collectively-owned 集體	130,026	8(387)	92,416	o
Zhejiang Xiaoshan Lace General Factory 浙江蕭山花邊總廠(1954)	Hangzhou 杭州市	Zhejiang 浙江省	(0571)2723193 (0571)2726549	1,695	Collectively-owned 集體	121,977	2882(21)	219,553	a
Guangdong Famory (Group) Co. Ltd. 廣東名瑞（集團）股份有限公司(1955)	Chaozhou 潮州市	Guangdong 廣東省	(0768)2263502 (0768)2261972	1,736	Joint stock 股份制	111,548	14056(2)	168,512	o
Hangzhou Art & Craft Company 杭州市工藝美術公司(1956)	Hangzhou 杭州市	Zhejiang 浙江省	(0571)7027000 (0571)7029231	568	Domestic JVs 聯營	102,066	0(454)	92,237	a
Anhui Ailide Textile Craft Products Co. Ltd. 安徽省愛利德紡織工藝製品有限公司(1993)	Fuyang 阜陽市	Anhui 安徽省	(0558)8682058 (0558)8682059	660	Foreign-funded 外資	99,248	6140(10)	26,518	o
City's Embroideries General Factory Co. Ltd. 市繡品總廠有限公司(1995)	Foshan 佛山市	Guangdong 廣東省	(0757)2287000 (0757)2225888	531	Joint stock 股份制	86,860	3550(16)	136,045	o
Suzhou Silk Clothing Factory 蘇州絲綢服裝廠(1956)	Suzhou 蘇州市	Jiangsu 江蘇省	(0512)7271278 (0512)7277484	416	Collectively-owned 集體	83,531	105(260)	24,578	o

Top 10 Cities by Production Output 產出排名前 10 位城市	Province 省	Market share 市場份額	Number of firms 企業個數
Wuxi 無錫市	Jiangsu 江蘇省	48.43%	4
Nantong 南通市	Jiangsu 江蘇省	6.62%	111
Suzhou 蘇州市	Jiangsu 江蘇省	6.19%	106
Shanghai 上海市	Shanghai 上海市	3.25%	93
Yantai 煙台市	Shandong 山東省	3.14%	53
Weifang 濰坊市	Shandong 山東省	3.09%	37
Weihai 威海市	Shandong 山東省	3.03%	39
Chaozhou 潮州市	Guangdong 廣東省	2.03%	64
Fuyang 阜陽市	Anhui 安徽省	1.39%	17
Qingdao 青島市	Shandong 山東省	1.38%	39

10 Major Wholesalers 10 家主要批發商	City 城市	Province 省	Telephone / Fax 電話 / 傳真
Zhejiang Handicrafts Import & Export Company 浙江省工藝品進出口公司	Hangzhou 杭州市	Zhejiang 浙江省	(0571)7068888 (0571)7063838
Jiangsu Handicrafts Import & Export Group Co. Ltd. 江蘇省工藝品進出口集團股份有限公司	Nanjing 南京市	Jiangsu 江蘇省	(025)4466181 (025)4462442
China Handicrafts Import & Export General Company 中國工藝品進出口總公司	Beijing 北京市	Beijing 北京市	(010)65931076
Wuxi Art & Craft Group General Company 無錫市工藝美術集團總公司	Wuxi 無錫市	Jiangsu 江蘇省	(0510)2700739 (0510)2700739
Ningbo Handicrafts Import & Export Company 寧波市工藝品進出口公司	Ningbo 寧波市	Zhejiang 浙江省	(0574)7327634 (0574)7298166
Liaoning Handicrafts Import & Export Company 遼寧省工藝品進出口公司	Dalian 大連市	Liaoning 遼寧省	(0411)2649488 (0411)2802250
Shandong Special Handicraft Import & Export Company 山東省特藝品進出口公司	Qingdao 青島市	Shandong 山東省	(0532)2894464 (0532)2894441
Beijing Arts & Crafts Import & Export Co. Ltd. 北京工藝進出口集團公司	Beijing 北京市	Beijing 北京市	(010)65004662 (010)65001284
Guangdong Handicrafts Import & Export Group Co. 廣東省工藝進出口(集團)公司	Guangzhou 廣州市	Guangdong 廣東省	(020)83334208 (020)83343614
Qingdao Handicrafts Import & Export Company 青島市工藝品進出口公司	Qingdao 青島市	Shandong 山東省	(0532)5918277 (0532)5918275

*Also include sales by firms outside this industry.包括本行業以外廠家的銷售。"o" stands for "others". "o" 代表"其他產品"。

4317: Rug Making 地毯製造業

The industry accounts for 0.124% of the total revenue of China's industrial sector in 1996. The revenue growth rate of the industry is 2.7% from 1995, as compared to the growth rate of China's industrial sector, 9.51%. The rate of return on asset is 0.30%. 70.82% of all firms in the industry made a profit while 19.85% had negative returns. The top province in terms of the industry's revenue is Shandong, accounting for 29.65% of the total revenue.
本行業在1996年佔全行業總產值0.124%，行業年增長率為2.7%（全國工業年增長率9.51%）。行業的資產回報率0.30%，70.82%的企業盈利，19.85%的企業虧損。銷售收入最高的省份為山東省，佔本行業的29.65%。

	Total number of firms 企業總數	Total number of employees 職工總數	Total revenue (mil. RMB) 總銷售收入（百萬元）	Total profit (mil. RMB) 總利潤（百萬元）	Return on assets 資產利潤率 (%)	Return on equity 權益利潤率 (%)	Labour productivity ('000 RMB / worker) 勞動生產率（千元/人）	Debts / assets 資產負債率 (%)	Total assets (mil. RMB) 總資產（百萬元）
Industry Overall 行業總體	1,603	272,824	7,188	32	0.30	1.41	26.35	78.40	10,570

	Number of firms 企業個數	Average number of employees 平均職工人數	Average revenue ('000 RMB) 平均銷售收入（千元）	Average profit ('000 RMB) 平均利潤（千元）	Return on assets 資產利潤率 (%)	Return on equity 權益利潤率 (%)	Labour productivity ('000 RMB / worker) 勞動生產率（千元/人）	Average debts / assets 平均資產負債率(%)	Average Total assets ('000 RMB) 平均總資產（千元）
By ownership 產業所有權									
State-owned 國有	122	310	6,959	-746	-3.71	-32.62	22.47	88.61	20,082
Collectively-owned 集體	1,374	157	3,814	74	1.58	7.52	24.36	79.03	4,669
Privately-owned 私有	3	119	5,395	100	3.79	4.79	45.33	20.84	2,627
Domestic JVs 聯營	14	197	15,950	872	3.68	7.79	81.17	52.81	23,712
Joint stock 股份制	16	307	10,381	356	3.61	10.43	33.79	65.41	9,859
Foreign-funded 外資	41	160	8,650	-7	-0.05	-0.16	54.07	65.84	12,588
Overseas Chinese-funded 港澳台資	31	161	9,941	144	0.72	1.79	61.86	59.93	20,084
By size 規模									
Large 大型	11	1,163	108,779	3,157	1.95	5.65	93.53	65.50	162,133
Medium 中型	40	665	24,121	-128	-0.26	-1.40	36.27	81.76	50,128
Small 小型	1,544	151	3,255	2	0.04	0.18	21.56	80.80	4,392
By regional distribution 地區分布									
Central-North 華北	397	167	3,838	23	0.34	1.95	22.96	82.80	6,703
Beijing 北京	19	222	6,159	169	1.03	2.90	27.78	64.42	16,448
Tianjin 天津	54	334	10,851	37	0.27	2.28	32.50	88.39	14,038
Hebei 河北	174	133	3,248	19	0.32	2.09	24.50	84.84	6,046
Shanxi 山西	36	107	897	-5	-0.21	-1.56	8.38	86.64	2,395
Inner Mongolia 內蒙	114	151	1,956	5	0.12	0.63	12.97	80.63	3,965
Northeast 東北	64	192	4,234	-592	-6.41	-65.03	22.09	90.13	9,232
Liaoning 遼寧	33	133	1,493	-231	-5.61	124.07	11.25	104.52	4,118
Jilin 吉林	8	450	5,628	-815	-3.23	-40.42	12.51	92.02	25,251
Heilongjiang 黑龍江	23	186	7,681	-1,033	-9.39	-49.17	41.23	80.90	10,997
Central East 華東	553	188	6,528	92	1.08	4.46	34.67	75.86	8,576
Shanghai 上海	12	305	17,106	1,138	4.28	24.97	56.18	82.86	26,593
Jiangsu 江蘇	89	170	6,348	-189	-2.57	-9.61	37.43	73.23	7,367
Zhejiang 浙江	56	164	6,951	-140	-1.21	-4.30	42.44	71.90	11,545
Anhui 安徽	64	108	3,560	176	5.37	14.18	32.88	62.13	3,273
Fujian 福建	3	191	18,390	-363	-0.60	-1.45	96.45	58.76	60,623
Jiangxi 江西	44	74	831	-48	-3.18	-19.79	11.20	83.93	1,514
Shandong 山東	285	230	7,478	190	2.03	9.51	32.56	78.67	9,346
Central-South 中南	226	206	5,812	197	2.77	10.92	28.16	74.68	7,130
Henan 河南	189	220	5,221	244	4.36	14.12	23.75	69.14	5,607
Hubei 湖北	20	154	5,457	-188	-1.92	-26.15	35.53	92.66	9,773
Hunan 湖南	5	71	3,404	66	1.06	4.03	47.81	73.59	6,210
Guangdong 廣東	10	167	19,822	160	0.49	2.74	118.98	82.05	32,485
Guangxi 廣西	2		1,215	105	70.00	116.67		40.00	150
Hainan 海南									
Southwest 西南	79	126	2,135	-48	-1.10	-2.84	16.90	61.38	4,415
Chongqing 重慶	17	78	1,304	-10	-0.59	-2.44	16.74	75.93	1,720
Sichuan 四川	40	160	3,262	137	2.07	5.99	20.39	65.49	6,613
Guizhou 貴州	3	148	613	-43	-1.93	56.52	4.14	103.41	2,250
Yunnan 雲南	2	130	945	5	0.16	0.27	7.30	38.32	3,040
Tibet 西藏	17	92	764	89	3.45	4.51	8.32	23.61	2,578
Northwest 西北	284	118	1,061	-108	-4.99	-38.85	9.00	87.16	2,167
Shaanxi 陝西	39	103	458	-13	-1.18	-4.66	4.43	74.56	1,082
Gansu 甘肅	166	122	1,221	-79	-4.26	-27.12	10.00	84.32	1,857
Qinghai 青海	23	172	1,677	-378	-8.20	-120.03	9.77	93.17	4,609
Ningxia 寧夏	18	153	1,009	-108	-3.64	-182.24	6.60	98.00	2,979
Xinjiang 新疆	38	65	630	-170	-6.14	-55.45	9.74	88.93	2,770

Year 年份	Number of firms 企業個數	Rate of change 每年變化 (%)	Number of employees 職工人數 (人)	Rate of change 每年變化 (%)	Total revenue (mil. RMB) 總銷售收入 (百萬元)	Rate of change 每年變化 (%)	Total profit (mil. RMB) 總利潤 (百萬元)	Rate of change 每年變化 (%)
1993	1,700		238,109		4,933		92	
1994	2,123	24.88%	326,433	37.09%	6,513	32.01%	139	50.74%
1995	1,886	-11.16%	360,946	10.57%	6,996	7.43%	102	-27.03%
1996	1,603	-15.01%	272,824	-24.41%	7,188	2.74%	32	-68.51%

3 Major products* 3 種主要產品 *	Output 產量	Sales volume 銷售量	Unit 單位
a) Chemical Fibre Carpet 化纖地毯	28,656,028	26,363,546	square metre 平方米
b) Silk Weaving Carpet 絲織地毯	2,163,566	2,012,116	square metre 平方米

Top 10 firms by revenue (year founded) 收入排名前 10 家企業 (創辦年份)	City 城市	Province 省	Telephone / fax 電話 / 傳真	Number of employees 職工人數	Ownership 產業所有權	Revenue ('000 RMB) 銷售收入 (千元)	Profit ('000 RMB) (rank) 利潤 (千元) (排名)	Total assets ('000 RMB) 總資產 (千元)	Major products 主要產品
Laizhou Xiao He Handicrafts Co. Ltd. 萊州市小河工藝品有限公司(1995)	Yantai 煙台市	Shandong 山東省	(0535)2812275 (0535)2812275	1,200	Foreign-funded 外資	174,300	13300(2)	5,390	o
Zhejiang Wei Mei Textile Co. 浙江維美紡織公司(1950)	Hangzhou 杭州市	Zhejiang 浙江省	(0571)8020888 (0571)8010368	3,163	State-owned 國有	160,710	0(414)	321,450	o
Weihai Shan Hua Carpet Group Co. 威海市山花地毯集團公司(1982)	Weihai 威海市	Shandong 山東省	(0896)5222810 (0896)5333009	1,539	Collectively-owned 集體	160,060	10600(3)	275,780	a
Shanghai Automobile Carpet General Factory 上海汽車地毯總廠(1985)	Shanghai 上海市	Shanghai 上海市	(021)57823091 (021)57820989	820	Domestic JVs 聯營	144,544	22886(1)	167,270	a
Daqing Carpet Co. Ltd. 大慶地毯有限公司(1990)	Daqing 大慶市	Heilongjiang 黑龍江省	(0459)6713751 (0459)6713751	968	Overseas Chinese-funded 港澳台資	121,241	-21923(536)	150,741	a
Xinhui Carpet Mill 新會市地毯廠(1985)	Jiangmen 江門市	Guangdong 廣東省	(0750)6676208 (0750)6677258	366	Collectively-owned 集體	117,328	273(152)	168,175	a
Weihai No.1 Carpet Mill 威海地毯一廠(1958)	Weihai 威海市	Shandong 山東省	(0896)5225880 (0896)5226887	987	Collectively-owned 集體	100,081	3402(14)	103,439	a
Tianjin Wuqing Huan Yu Carpet Industrial Company 天津市武清縣環宇地毯實業公司(1980)	Tianjin 天津市	Tianjin 天津市	(022)29439330	1,160	Domestic JVs 聯營	98,900	8790(4)	51,060	a
Jiangsu Jurong Silk Weaving Carpet Factory 江蘇省句容市絲織地毯廠(1979)	Zhenjiang 鎮江市	Jiangsu 江蘇省	(0511)7226016	450	Collectively-owned 集體	95,280	300(146)	12,540	b
Shandong Guo Hua Industries (Group) Corp. 山東國華實業集團總公司(1977)	Heze 菏澤市	Shandong 山東省	(0530)2791151 (0530)2791237	2,882	Collectively-owned 集體	92,680	4060(12)	149,249	o

Top 10 Cities by Production Output 產出排名前 10 位城市	Province 省	Market share 市場份額	Number of firms 企業個數
Nanyang 南陽市	Henan 河南省	13.39%	125
Tianjin 天津市	Tianjin 天津市	8.24%	74
Weihai 威海市	Shandong 山東省	6.86%	10
Heze 菏澤市	Shandong 山東省	4.57%	45
Yantai 煙台市	Shandong 山東省	3.45%	21
Binzhou 濱州市	Shandong 山東省	2.71%	27
Hangzhou 杭州市	Zhejiang 浙江省	2.70%	16
Dezhou 德州市	Shandong 山東省	2.14%	53
Shanghai 上海市	Shanghai 上海市	1.73%	13
Rizhao 日照市	Shandong 山東省	1.71%	13

10 Major Wholesalers 10 家主要批發商	City 城市	Province 省	Telephone / Fax 電話 / 傳真
Zhejiang Handicrafts Import & Export Company 浙江省工藝品進出口公司	Hangzhou 杭州市	Zhejiang 浙江省	(0571)7068888 (0571)7063838
Jiangsu Handicrafts Import & Export Group Co. Ltd. 江蘇省工藝品進出口集團股份有限公司	Nanjing 南京市	Jiangsu 江蘇省	(025)4466181 (025)4462442
China Handicrafts Import & Export General Company 中國工藝品進出口總公司	Beijing 北京市	Beijing 北京市	(010)65931076
Wuxi Art & Craft Group General Company 無錫市工藝美術集團總公司	Wuxi 無錫市	Jiangsu 江蘇省	(0510)2700739 (0510)2700739
Ningbo Handicrafts Import & Export Company 寧波市工藝品進出口公司	Ningbo 寧波市	Zhejiang 浙江省	(0574)7327634 (0574)7298166
Liaoning Handicrafts Import & Export Company 遼寧省工藝品進出口公司	Dalian 大連市	Liaoning 遼寧省	(0411)2649488 (0411)2802250
Shandong Special Handicraft Import & Export Company 山東省特藝品進出口公司	Qingdao 青島市	Shandong 山東省	(0532)2894464 (0532)2894441
Beijing Arts & Crafts Import & Export Co. Ltd. 北京工藝進出口集團公司	Beijing 北京市	Beijing 北京市	(010)65004662 (010)65001284
Guangdong Handicrafts Import & Export Group Co. 廣東省工藝進出口(集團)公司	Guangzhou 廣州市	Guangdong 廣東省	(020)83334208 (020)83343614
Qingdao Handicrafts Import & Export Company 青島市工藝品進出口公司	Qingdao 青島市	Shandong 山東省	(0532)5918277 (0532)5918275

*Also include sales by firms outside this industry.包括本行業以外廠家的銷售。"o" stands for "others". "o" 代表 "其他產品"。

4318: Jewelry 首飾製造業

The industry accounts for 0.159% of the total revenue of China's industrial sector in 1996. The revenue growth rate of the industry is -1.0% from 1995, as compared to the growth rate of China's industrial sector, 9.51%. The rate of return on asset is 2.56%. 63.51% of all firms in the industry made a profit while 29.94% had negative returns. The top province in terms of the industry's revenue is Guangdong, accounting for 26.42% of the total revenue.
本行業在1996年佔全行業總產值0.159%，行業年增長率為-1.0%（全國工業年增長率9.51%）。行業的資產回報率2.56%，63.51%的企業盈利，29.94%的企業虧損。銷售收入最高的省份為廣東省，佔本行業的26.42%。

	Total number of firms 企業總數	Total number of employees 職工總數	Total revenue (mil. RMB) 總銷售收入（百萬元）	Total profit (mil. RMB) 總利潤（百萬元）	Return on assets 資產利潤率 (%)	Return on equity 權益利潤率 (%)	Labour productivity ('000 RMB / worker) 勞動生產率（千元/人）	Debts / assets 資產負債率 (%)	Total assets (mil. RMB) 總資產（百萬元）
Industry Overall 行業總體	579	61,875	9,208	197	2.56	7.17	148.82	64.33	7,702

	Number of firms 企業個數	Average number of employees 平均職工人數	Average revenue ('000 RMB) 平均銷售收入（千元）	Average profit ('000 RMB) 平均利潤（千元）	Return on assets 資產利潤率 (%)	Return on equity 權益利潤率 (%)	Labour productivity ('000 RMB / worker) 勞動生產率（千元/人）	Average debts / assets 平均資產負債率(%)	Average Total assets ('000 RMB) 平均總資產（千元）
By ownership 產業所有權									
State-owned 國有	57	109	28,175	-140	-0.73	-2.45	258.70	70.36	19,298
Collectively-owned 集體	306	103	14,277	219	1.91	6.70	138.93	71.42	11,447
Privately-owned 私有	5	45	1,255	208	11.02	11.98	28.13	7.99	1,892
Domestic JVs 聯營	9	193	66,741	2,614	5.19	10.08	346.41	48.51	50,375
Joint stock 股份制	7	148	53,667	598	1.86	7.06	363.67	73.71	32,212
Foreign-funded 外資	68	102	11,064	1,178	9.20	17.27	108.22	46.70	12,796
Overseas Chinese-funded 港澳台資	126	121	11,892	230	1.88	4.44	98.48	57.59	12,214
By size 規模									
Large 大型	2	523	117,915	-677	-0.47	-3.46	225.46	86.41	144,168
Medium 中型	15	427	138,176	3,262	2.94	9.48	323.60	68.95	110,814
Small 小型	535	101	12,897	279	2.60	6.82	127.87	61.89	10,751
By regional distribution 地區分布									
Central-North 華北	70	88	8,660	-27	-0.34	-1.11	98.14	69.40	8,020
Beijing 北京	39	85	5,743	-145	-1.81	-7.39	67.22	75.49	7,987
Tianjin 天津	4	121	11,705	-445	-5.71	-31.84	96.74	82.06	7,790
Hebei 河北	13	120	11,732	521	5.96	23.60	98.14	74.75	8,740
Shanxi 山西	4	120	16,233	-283	-2.06	-4.36	135.84	52.72	13,700
Inner Mongolia 內蒙	10	33	11,798	-13	-0.26	-0.37	358.60	29.95	5,032
Northeast 東北	44	66	5,520	-19	-0.23	-0.69	83.95	66.47	8,098
Liaoning 遼寧	27	61	6,452	47	0.45	1.35	105.45	66.76	10,411
Jilin 吉林	3	118	10,990	-407	-6.43	-27.66	93.14	76.74	6,320
Heilongjiang 黑龍江	14	63	2,551	-62	-1.55	-4.02	40.26	61.57	4,019
Central East 華東	203	112	21,980	423	2.50	7.15	196.70	65.01	16,913
Shanghai 上海	22	191	46,147	-8	-0.02	-0.07	241.67	72.22	38,457
Jiangsu 江蘇	46	119	22,940	471	2.68	6.06	192.45	55.70	17,539
Zhejiang 浙江	25	128	52,839	2,846	8.16	21.20	413.19	61.50	34,868
Anhui 安徽	11	89	15,902	-217	-2.29	-9.23	179.59	75.21	9,492
Fujian 福建	41	97	10,884	188	2.18	5.55	111.98	60.69	8,618
Jiangxi 江西	25	35	4,211	-484	-12.16	-505.86	119.35	97.60	3,977
Shandong 山東	33	120	10,425	-1	-0.01	-0.02	86.83	69.78	10,653
Central-South 中南	213	125	15,508	234	1.93	6.05	123.66	68.12	12,144
Henan 河南	17	53	5,705	-32	-1.10	-4.53	108.01	75.80	2,951
Hubei 湖北	11	121	42,117	746	4.33	9.11	349.39	52.48	17,238
Hunan 湖南	13	62	2,698	39	3.86	8.40	43.74	54.02	1,015
Guangdong 廣東	138	151	17,628	318	2.29	7.53	116.64	69.62	13,879
Guangxi 廣西	29	92	8,573	-68	-0.56	-2.37	92.87	76.25	12,117
Hainan 海南	5	31	5,320	-24	-0.18	-0.24	172.73	24.02	13,390
Southwest 西南	29	57	7,287	24	0.42	0.89	128.85	52.06	5,686
Chongqing 重慶	1	241	47,428	-52	-0.20	-0.44	197.17	53.67	25,536
Sichuan 四川	7	101	15,380	21	0.20	0.44	152.74	55.20	10,786
Guizhou 貴州	3	5	10	3	4.76	5.00	2.14		70
Yunnan 雲南	15	37	2,919	56	1.74	3.83	78.62	54.56	3,217
Tibet 西藏	3	26	573	-73	-2.10	-2.47	21.77	14.72	3,487
Northwest 西北	20	88	19,142	3,165	10.55	18.03	216.41	41.48	29,998
Shaanxi 陝西	6	133	44,898	10,917	13.82	19.54	336.74	29.29	78,997
Gansu 甘肅	1								
Qinghai 青海	2	108	48,930	1,130	4.43	17.12	453.06	74.11	25,490
Ningxia 寧夏	1	100	8,500	500	5.43	13.89	85.00	60.76	9,200
Xinjiang 新疆	10	65	708	-497	-7.55	546.15	10.84	101.38	6,579

4318: Jewelry 首飾製造業

Year 年份	Number of firms 企業個數	Rate of change 每年變化 (%)	Number of employees 職工人數 (人)	Rate of change 每年變化 (%)	Total revenue (mil. RMB) 總銷售收入 (百萬元)	Rate of change 每年變化 (%)	Total profit (mil. RMB) 總利潤 (百萬元)	Rate of change 每年變化 (%)
1993	498		66,458		8,737		271	
1994	600	20.48%	72,928	9.74%	7,916	-9.40%	157	-41.99%
1995	638	6.33%	70,866	-2.83%	9,304	17.54%	171	8.80%
1996	579	-9.25%	61,875	-12.69%	9,208	-1.03%	197	15.22%

3 Major products* 3 種主要產品 *	Output 產量	Sales volume 銷售量	Unit 單位
a) Jewellery 首飾	9,463,396	9,179,495	10 yuan 千元
b) Metal Handicrafts 金屬工藝品	555,115	538,461	1000 yuan 千元

Top 10 firms by revenue (year founded) 收入排名前 10 家企業 (創辦年份)	City 城市	Province 省	Telephone / fax 電話 / 傳真	Number of employees 職工人數	Ownership 產業所有權	Revenue ('000 RMB) 銷售收入 (千元)	Profit ('000 RMB) (rank) 利潤 (千元) (排名)	Total assets ('000 RMB) 總資產 (千元)	Major products 主要產品
Zhejiang Lao Feng Xiang Jewels Factory 浙江老鳳祥首飾廠(1987)	Shaoxing 紹興市	Zhejiang 浙江省	(0575)4021602 (0575)4021062	193	Collectively-owned 集體	659,077	64558(2)	257,510	a
Shanghai Lao Feng Xiang Jewels General Factory 上海老鳳祥有限公司(1996)	Shanghai 上海市	Shanghai 上海市	(021)64831258 (021)64834297	1,442	State-owned 國有	564,191	8434(5)	554,394	a
Shenzhen Gao De Gold and Silver Jewels Co. Ltd. 深圳高得金銀首飾有限公司(1991)	Shenzhen 深圳市	Guangdong 廣東省	(0755)5554012 (0755)5554009	151	State-owned 國有	396,157	1315(36)	11,767	a
Foshan Arts & Crafts General Factory Co. Ltd. 佛山市工藝總廠有限公司(1970)	Foshan 佛山市	Guangdong 廣東省	(0757)2243038 (0757)2286797	504	Joint stock 股份制	300,758	2602(18)	168,728	a
Xi'an Cuibao Jewelry Group Co. 西安翠寶首飾集團公司(1988)	Xi'an 西安市	Shaanxi 陝西省	(029)3237505 (029)3237503	289	Overseas Chinese-funded 港澳台資	218,002	65850(1)	414,069	o
Shan Te Gold & Silver Jewelry Industrial Company 汕特金銀珠寶實業公司(1973)	Shantou 汕頭市	Guangdong 廣東省	(0754)8273272 (0754)8271684	125	Collectively-owned 集體	182,989	4887(10)	61,256	a
Zhejiang Zhuji Jewelry Company 浙江省諸暨市珠寶首飾公司(1992)	Shaoxing 紹興市	Zhejiang 浙江省	(0575)7018178 (0575)7013381	84	State-owned 國有	181,570	725(49)	21,954	o
Jin Yuan (Guilin) Jewelry Enterprise (Group) Co. 桂林金元珠寶企業集團公司(1993)	Guilin 桂林市	Guangxi 廣西	(0773)2834444 (0773)2824365	749	Collectively-owned 集體	172,936	-4006(226)	219,985	a
Suzhou Zong Zong Shou Ornaments Products Co. Ltd. 蘇州宗宗首飾製品有限公司(1994)	Suzhou 蘇州市	Jiangsu 江蘇省	(0512)3458192	547	Foreign-funded 外資	154,750	3580(14)	226,440	a
Shanghai Zhuang Yi Diamond Factory Co. Ltd. 上海裝藝鑽石廠有限公司(1995)	Shanghai 上海市	Shanghai 上海市	(021)58992694	350	Foreign-funded 外資	150,081	-6801(228)	73,290	a

Top 10 Cities by Production Output 產出排名前 10 位城市	Province 省	Market share 市場份額	Number of firms 企業個數
Wuxi 無錫市	Jiangsu 江蘇省	61.15%	13
Shaoxing 紹興市	Zhejiang 浙江省	8.00%	12
Shanghai 上海市	Shanghai 上海市	4.55%	43
Guangzhou 廣州市	Guangdong 廣東省	3.09%	56
Shenzhen 深圳市	Guangdong 廣東省	2.48%	46
Xi'an 西安市	Shaanxi 陝西省	1.10%	4
Shantou 汕頭市	Guangdong 廣東省	1.08%	12
Beijing 北京市	Beijing 北京市	0.97%	35
Wuhan 武漢市	Hubei 湖北省	0.92%	4
Foshan 佛山市	Guangdong 廣東省	0.91%	11

10 Major Wholesalers 10 家主要批發商	City 城市	Province 省	Telephone / Fax 電話 / 傳真
Zhejiang Handicrafts Import & Export Company 浙江省工藝品進出口公司	Hangzhou 杭州市	Zhejiang 浙江省	(0571)7068888 (0571)7063838
Jiangsu Handicrafts Import & Export Group Co. Ltd. 江蘇省工藝品進出口集團股份有限公司	Nanjing 南京市	Jiangsu 江蘇省	(025)4466181 (025)4462442
China Handicrafts Import & Export General Company 中國工藝品進出口總公司	Beijing 北京市	Beijing 北京市	(010)65931076
Wuxi Art & Craft Group General Company 無錫市工藝美術集團總公司	Wuxi 無錫市	Jiangsu 江蘇省	(0510)2700739 (0510)2700739
Ningbo Handicrafts Import & Export Company 寧波市工藝品進出口公司	Ningbo 寧波市	Zhejiang 浙江省	(0574)7327634 (0574)7298166
Liaoning Handicrafts Import & Export Company 遼寧省工藝品進出口公司	Dalian 大連市	Liaoning 遼寧省	(0411)2649488 (0411)2802250
Shandong Special Handicraft Import & Export Company 山東省特藝品進出口公司	Qingdao 青島市	Shandong 山東省	(0532)2894464 (0532)2894441
Beijing Arts & Crafts Import & Export Co. Ltd. 北京工藝進出口集團公司	Beijing 北京市	Beijing 北京市	(010)65004662 (010)65001284
Guangdong Handicrafts Import & Export Group Co. 廣東省工藝進出口(集團)公司	Guangzhou 廣州市	Guangdong 廣東省	(020)83334208 (020)83343614
Qingdao Handicrafts Import & Export Company 青島市工藝品進出口公司	Qingdao 青島市	Shandong 山東省	(0532)5918277 (0532)5918275

*Also include sales by firms outside this industry.包括本行業以外廠家的銷售。"o" stands for "others". "o" 代表 "其他產品"。

4319: Other Artistic Products 其他工藝美術品製造業

The industry accounts for 0.175% of the total revenue of China's industrial sector in 1996. The revenue growth rate of the industry is 10.0% from 1995, as compared to the growth rate of China's industrial sector, 9.51%. The rate of return on asset is 2.97%. 74.96% of all firms in the industry made a profit while 17.36% had negative returns. The top province in terms of the industry's revenue is Guangdong, accounting for 20.36% of the total revenue.
本行業在1996年佔全行業總產值0.175%，行業年增長率為10.0%（全國工業年增長率9.51%）。行業的資產回報率2.97%，74.96%的企業盈利，17.36%的企業虧損。銷售收入最高的省份為廣東省，佔本行業的20.36%。

	Total number of firms 企業總數	Total number of employees 職工總數	Total revenue (mil. RMB) 總銷售收入（百萬元）	Total profit (mil. RMB) 總利潤（百萬元）	Return on assets 資產利潤率 (%)	Return on equity 權益利潤率 (%)	Labour productivity ('000 RMB / worker) 勞動生產率（千元/人）	Debts / assets 資產負債率 (%)	Total assets (mil. RMB) 總資產（百萬元）
Industry Overall 行業總體	3,242	285,430	10,163	261	2.97	8.01	35.61	62.89	8,763

	Number of firms 企業個數	Average number of employees 平均職工人數	Average revenue ('000 RMB) 平均銷售收入（千元）	Average profit ('000 RMB) 平均利潤（千元）	Return on assets 資產利潤率 (%)	Return on equity 權益利潤率 (%)	Labour productivity ('000 RMB / worker) 勞動生產率（千元/人）	Average debts / assets 平均資產負債率(%)	Average Total assets ('000 RMB) 平均總資產（千元）
By ownership 產業所有權									
State-owned 國有	96	84	3,594	-52	-0.87	-3.03	42.80	71.15	5,958
Collectively-owned 集體	2,762	84	2,602	67	3.38	10.89	30.97	68.94	1,992
Privately-owned 私有	11	38	1,922	114	6.18	15.69	50.95	60.62	1,849
Domestic JVs 聯營	15	61	8,958	48	0.56	0.73	147.33	23.13	8,583
Joint stock 股份制	13	95	5,254	-104	-1.55	-5.56	55.13	72.23	6,743
Foreign-funded 外資	134	119	5,995	143	2.52	5.60	50.49	54.98	5,689
Overseas Chinese-funded 港澳台資	209	138	7,643	288	3.58	6.67	55.47	46.40	8,051
By size 規模									
Large 大型	4	1,938	172,579	2,734	1.71	4.69	89.04	63.45	159,533
Medium 中型	8	1,213	104,487	1,397	2.35	5.68	86.12	58.54	59,328
Small 小型	3,192	84	2,706	75	3.12	8.47	32.21	63.11	2,396
By regional distribution 地區分布									
Central-North 華北	235	62	1,755	43	2.05	5.58	28.17	63.26	2,108
Beijing 北京	70	39	607	-85	-3.66	-10.96	15.58	66.57	2,309
Tianjin 天津	38	127	3,866	253	7.29	12.88	30.51	43.41	3,466
Hebei 河北	61	73	3,042	103	4.91	14.20	41.63	65.37	2,101
Shanxi 山西	29	38	515	-3	-0.34	-8.00	13.42	95.78	1,020
Inner Mongolia 內蒙	37	41	611	7	0.61	3.44	14.76	82.33	1,199
Northeast 東北	152	74	3,400	245	9.78	44.49	45.83	78.02	2,505
Liaoning 遼寧	81	86	5,495	434	13.83	60.30	63.67	77.05	3,134
Jilin 吉林	29	41	702	63	5.29	16.68	17.08	68.28	1,192
Heilongjiang 黑龍江	42	74	1,221	7	0.30	1.93	16.58	84.32	2,200
Central East 華東	1,152	88	3,749	89	3.03	9.35	42.66	67.55	2,921
Shanghai 上海	52	80	7,366	-75	-1.19	-3.97	92.23	70.09	6,338
Jiangsu 江蘇	154	113	5,575	133	3.13	9.11	49.47	65.63	4,240
Zhejiang 浙江	289	66	3,570	77	2.46	7.32	53.72	66.45	3,127
Anhui 安徽	101	85	4,211	348	28.51	73.08	49.37	60.99	1,219
Fujian 福建	149	124	5,083	103	2.97	6.99	40.90	57.54	3,467
Jiangxi 江西	288	77	1,304	20	1.66	15.09	16.94	88.99	1,204
Shandong 山東	119	94	4,100	61	1.46	4.50	43.43	67.46	4,136
Central-South 中南	1,394	104	3,373	75	2.46	5.76	32.53	57.35	3,034
Henan 河南	123	64	3,604	188	6.56	22.32	56.30	70.61	2,860
Hubei 湖北	128	54	1,935	54	4.70	17.03	36.16	72.43	1,159
Hunan 湖南	503	135	2,911	61	3.06	5.54	21.51	44.82	1,984
Guangdong 廣東	391	110	5,291	129	2.64	5.31	48.26	50.27	4,877
Guangxi 廣西	242	74	1,923	-27	-0.83	-4.66	25.89	82.19	3,194
Hainan 海南	7	126	1,729	-77	-1.05	-2.32	13.72	55.01	7,380
Southwest 西南	227	44	719	28	3.47	11.40	16.22	69.53	818
Chongqing 重慶	36	40	756	42	5.83	14.87	18.85	60.78	724
Sichuan 四川	92	48	983	53	5.76	20.84	20.35	72.39	922
Guizhou 貴州	69	34	411	1	0.22	0.80	12.11	73.27	539
Yunnan 雲南	30	60	576				9.53	65.46	1,257
Tibet 西藏									
Northwest 西北	82	45	598	9	0.69	2.16	13.40	68.25	1,298
Shaanxi 陝西	49	52	655	11	0.73	2.69	12.60	72.91	1,539
Gansu 甘肅	24	35	543	13	1.69	3.23	15.46	47.60	763
Qinghai 青海	2	53	485	-5	-0.43	-0.79	9.15	45.45	1,155
Ningxia 寧夏	3	30	383	53	7.14	23.88	12.78	70.09	747
Xinjiang 新疆	4	18	453	-70	-3.45	-15.22	24.79	77.46	2,030

4319: Other Artistic Products 其他工藝美術品製造業

Year 年份	Number of firms 企業個數	Rate of change 每年變化 (%)	Number of employees 職工人數 (人)	Rate of change 每年變化 (%)	Total revenue (mil. RMB) 總銷售收入 (百萬元)	Rate of change 每年變化 (%)	Total profit (mil. RMB) 總利潤 (百萬元)	Rate of change 每年變化 (%)
1993	3,251		280,341		5,370		179	
1994	3,389	4.24%	305,416	8.94%	7,606	41.62%	174	-2.82%
1995	3,297	-2.72%	324,438	6.23%	9,243	21.52%	234	34.41%
1996	3,242	-1.67%	285,430	-12.02%	10,163	9.95%	261	11.63%

3 Major products* 3 種主要產品 *	Output 產量	Sales volume 銷售量	Unit 單位
a) Hand-dyed & Woven Handicraft 手工染織工藝品	434,333	486,453	1,000 yuan 千元
b) Folk Handicraft 民間工藝品	842,590	825,738	1,000 yuan 千元

Top 10 firms by revenue (year founded) 收入排名前 10 家企業 (創辦年份)	City 城市	Province 省	Telephone / fax 電話 / 傳真	Number of employees 職工人數	Ownership 產業所有權	Revenue ('000 RMB) 銷售收入 (千元)	Profit ('000 RMB) (rank) 利潤 (千元) (排名)	Total assets ('000 RMB) 總資產 (千元)	Major products 主要產品
Fuqing Yuan Sheng Light Industry Products Co. Ltd. 福清市元升輕工製品有限公司(1992)	Fuzhou 福州市	Fujian 福建省	(0591)5567801 (0591)5567804	3,510	Overseas Chinese-funded 港澳台資	302,874	22690(1)	89,980	o
Fushun Hong Guang Enterprise Co. 撫順市紅光企業公司(1990)	Fushun 撫順市	Liaoning 遼寧省	(0413)7645254	986	Collectively-owned 集體	193,000	17350(3)	66,050	o
Luoding Mei Pan Dyeing Factory Ltd. 羅定市美鵬染廠有限公司(1994)	Yunfu 雲浮市	Guangdong 廣東省	(0766)3830632	603	Overseas Chinese-funded 港澳台資	163,840	5579(13)	68,709	a
Luoding Hu Yi Ran Chang Co. Ltd. 羅定互益染廠有限公司(1992)	Yunfu 雲浮市	Guangdong 廣東省	(0766)3823166 (0766)3826455	578	Overseas Chinese-funded 港澳台資	153,500	5788(12)	61,096	a
Nanjing New International Gift Co. Ltd. 南京新國際禮品有限公司(1995)	Nanjing 南京市	Jiangsu 江蘇省	(025)8765111 (025)8765100	384	Overseas Chinese-funded 港澳台資	151,900	14000(5)	62,770	o
Shanghai Teng Jia Hardware Co. Ltd. 上海騰嘉五金製品有限公司(1996)	Shanghai 上海市	Shanghai 上海市	(021)64361503	75	Overseas Chinese-funded 港澳台資	151,575	2357(35)	8,572	o
Anhui Guoyang Handicrafts General Factory 安徽省渦陽縣工藝品總廠(1992)	Fuyang 阜陽市	Anhui 安徽省	(0558)7247676	260	Collectively-owned 集體	149,680	17961(2)	10,321	o
Henan Rui Bei Ka Hair Products Co. Ltd. 河南瑞貝卡發製品有限公司(1993)	Xuchang 許昌市	Henan 河南省	(0374)2335444 (0374)2334939	1,720	Foreign-funded 外資	138,000	6480(10)	128,355	o
Fushun Hua Guang Farm, Industry & Commerce Joint General Company 撫順市華光農工商聯合總公司(1989)	Fushun 撫順市	Liaoning 遼寧省	(0413)2333555	1,636	Collectively-owned 集體	128,322	14230(4)	54,984	o
Shanghai Arts & Crafts Co. 上海工藝美術總公司(1988)	Shanghai 上海市	Shanghai 上海市	(021)64742220 (021)64738716	552	State-owned 國有	123,620	-1628(843)	96,252	b

Top 10 Cities by Production Output 產出排名前 10 位城市	Province 省	Market share 市場份額	Number of firms 企業個數
Qingdao 青島市	Shandong 山東省	9.82%	40
Zhuzhou 株洲市	Hunan 湖南省	6.45%	61
Taizhou 臺州市	Zhejiang 浙江省	4.42%	120
Changsha 長沙市	Hunan 湖南省	4.28%	117
Fushun 撫順市	Liaoning 遼寧省	3.88%	9
Shantou 汕頭市	Guangdong 廣東省	3.54%	65
Xuchang 許昌市	Henan 河南省	3.20%	30
Quanzhou 泉州市	Fujian 福建省	3.08%	68
Yunfu 雲浮市	Guangdong 廣東省	2.92%	27
Guangzhou 廣州市	Guangdong 廣東省	2.73%	62

10 Major Wholesalers 10 家主要批發商	City 城市	Province 省	Telephone / Fax 電話 / 傳真
Zhejiang Handicrafts Import & Export Company 浙江省工藝品進出口公司	Hangzhou 杭州市	Zhejiang 浙江省	(0571)7068888 (0571)7063838
Jiangsu Handicrafts Import & Export Group Co. Ltd. 江蘇省工藝品進出口集團股份有限公司	Nanjing 南京市	Jiangsu 江蘇省	(025)4466181 (025)4462442
China Handicrafts Import & Export General Company 中國工藝品進出口總公司	Beijing 北京市	Beijing 北京市	(010)65931076
Wuxi Art & Craft Group General Company 無錫市工藝美術集團總公司	Wuxi 無錫市	Jiangsu 江蘇省	(0510)2700739 (0510)2700739
Ningbo Handicrafts Import & Export Company 寧波市工藝品進出口公司	Ningbo 寧波市	Zhejiang 浙江省	(0574)7327634 (0574)7298166
Liaoning Handicrafts Import & Export Company 遼寧省工藝品進出口公司	Dalian 大連市	Liaoning 遼寧省	(0411)2649488 (0411)2802250
Shandong Special Handicraft Import & Export Company 山東省特藝品進出口公司	Qingdao 青島市	Shandong 山東省	(0532)2894464 (0532)2894441
Beijing Arts & Crafts Import & Export Co. Ltd. 北京工藝進出口集團公司	Beijing 北京市	Beijing 北京市	(010)65004662 (010)65001284
Guangdong Handicrafts Import & Export Group Co. 廣東省工藝進出口(集團)公司	Guangzhou 廣州市	Guangdong 廣東省	(020)83334208 (020)83343614
Qingdao Handicrafts Import & Export Company 青島市工藝品進出口公司	Qingdao 青島市	Shandong 山東省	(0532)5918277 (0532)5918275

*Also include sales by firms outside this industry.包括本行業以外廠家的銷售。"o" stands for "others". "o" 代表 "其他產品"。

4351: Mirrors 製鏡業

The industry accounts for 0.012% of the total revenue of China's industrial sector in 1996. The revenue growth rate of the industry is 8.6% from 1995, as compared to the growth rate of China's industrial sector, 9.51%. The rate of return on asset is -0.27%. 56.99% of all firms in the industry made a profit while 33.33% had negative returns. The top province in terms of the industry's revenue is Guangdong, accounting for 27.44% of the total revenue.
本行業在1996年佔全行業總產值0.012%，行業年增長率為8.6%（全國工業年增長率9.51%）。行業的資產回報率-0.27%，56.99%的企業盈利，33.33%的企業虧損。銷售收入最高的省份為廣東省，佔本行業的27.44%。

	Total number of firms 企業總數	Total number of employees 職工總數	Total revenue (mil. RMB) 總銷售收入（百萬元）	Total profit (mil. RMB) 總利潤（百萬元）	Return on assets 資產利潤率 (%)	Return on equity 權益利潤率 (%)	Labour productivity ('000 RMB / worker) 勞動生產率（千元/人）	Debts / assets 資產負債率 (%)	Total assets (mil. RMB) 總資產（百萬元）
Industry Overall 行業總體	228	21,338	682	-3	-0.27	-0.70	31.96	62.24	1,221

	Number of firms 企業個數	Average number of employees 平均職工人數	Average revenue ('000 RMB) 平均銷售收入（千元）	Average profit ('000 RMB) 平均利潤（千元）	Return on assets 資產利潤率 (%)	Return on equity 權益利潤率 (%)	Labour productivity ('000 RMB / worker) 勞動生產率（千元/人）	Average debts / assets 平均資產負債率(%)	Average Total assets ('000 RMB) 平均總資產（千元）
By ownership 產業所有權									
State-owned 國有	11	55	818	-91	-4.35	-20.00	14.88	78.26	2,091
Collectively-owned 集體	199	86	2,206	-4	-0.14	-0.57	25.64	76.16	2,748
Privately-owned 私有									
Domestic JVs 聯營	2	92	4,206	-142	-1.13	-3.85	45.96	70.53	12,539
Joint stock 股份制	2	59	4,427	1	0.04	0.91	75.03	95.22	2,995
Foreign-funded 外資	2	66	19,562	32	0.23	0.67	296.39	65.05	13,436
Overseas Chinese-funded 港澳台資	13	250	13,647	-80	-0.18	-0.34	54.64	47.97	45,615
By size 規模									
Large 大型									
Medium 中型	1	71	20,750	-80	-0.25	-0.77	292.25	67.09	31,496
Small 小型	226	94	2,925	-13	-0.25	-0.65	31.08	62.12	5,263
By regional distribution 地區分布									
Central-North 華北	44	159	3,183	35	0.99	3.58	20.01	72.36	3,558
Beijing 北京	6	31	888	23	3.00	12.96	29.13	76.87	778
Tianjin 天津	10	83	2,275	164	5.38	37.19	27.51	85.50	3,049
Hebei 河北	18	80	5,553	7	0.15	0.41	69.12	63.89	4,549
Shanxi 山西	5	835	1,402	8	0.14	0.50	1.68	71.63	5,696
Inner Mongolia 內蒙	5	74	1,004	-78	-3.53	-325.00	13.64	98.91	2,208
Northeast 東北	29	85	761	-115	-5.10	-35.50	8.94	85.65	2,252
Liaoning 遼寧	11	105	1,443	-240	-6.35	-40.31	13.79	84.25	3,781
Jilin 吉林	7	74	434	-61	-6.88	66.15	5.87	110.56	893
Heilongjiang 黑龍江	11	73	287	-24	-1.49	-7.47	3.95	80.08	1,588
Central East 華東	52	71	3,601	84	1.88	5.47	50.47	65.64	4,479
Shanghai 上海	5	75	6,546	44	0.51	1.36	87.51	62.66	8,646
Jiangsu 江蘇	11	63	1,186	-26	-0.84	-2.86	18.91	70.65	3,138
Zhejiang 浙江	3	84	2,320	-7	-0.23	-0.97	27.73	76.34	2,917
Anhui 安徽	9	87	4,207	117	2.39	7.36	48.11	67.63	4,891
Fujian 福建	11	70	5,224	244	4.46	15.66	74.82	71.52	5,462
Jiangxi 江西	5	71	5,036	58	1.36	7.84	71.33	82.71	4,280
Shandong 山東	8	61	1,750	56	2.15	2.71	28.75	20.44	2,611
Central-South 中南	58	93	4,663	-49	-0.44	-0.96	50.39	54.66	11,155
Henan 河南	20	40	2,166	-74	-2.65	-13.90	54.21	80.93	2,793
Hubei 湖北	5	57	1,352	12	0.63	1.44	23.64	56.32	1,914
Hunan 湖南	15	75	1,991	-199	-18.81	805.41	26.72	102.40	1,056
Guangdong 廣東	13	238	14,393	136	0.32	0.64	60.48	50.71	43,199
Guangxi 廣西	5	14	680	-40	-4.83	-9.66	48.57	50.00	828
Hainan 海南									
Southwest 西南	21	76	1,751	-88	-2.56	-8.99	23.15	71.54	3,445
Chongqing 重慶	2	117	6,414	474	5.73	20.94	54.81	72.65	8,281
Sichuan 四川	12	80	1,444	-226	-6.58	-23.68	18.09	72.21	3,428
Guizhou 貴州	2	15	60	5	2.94	8.33	4.00	61.76	170
Yunnan 雲南	5	71	968	-68	-2.68	-8.37	13.60	68.01	2,538
Tibet 西藏									
Northwest 西北	24	50	1,041	-50	-2.54	-8.21	20.77	69.10	1,954
Shaanxi 陝西	12	48	506	-83	-6.86	-66.00	10.54	89.60	1,203
Gansu 甘肅	3	132	2,563	50	1.65	4.23	19.37	60.86	3,023
Qinghai 青海	1	20	50				2.50	37.70	1,220
Ningxia 寧夏	2	4	10	-45	-7.20	-11.84	2.50	40.00	625
Xinjiang 新疆	6	34	1,860	-43	-1.24	-3.28	55.25	62.11	3,488

4351: Mirrors 製鏡業

Year 年份	Number of firms 企業個數	Rate of change 每年變化 (%)	Number of employees 職工人數（人）	Rate of change 每年變化 (%)	Total revenue (mil. RMB) 總銷售收入（百萬元）	Rate of change 每年變化 (%)	Total profit (mil. RMB) 總利潤（百萬元）	Rate of change 每年變化 (%)
1993	281		21,702		598		20	
1994	288	2.49%	20,625	-4.96%	566	-5.39%	-13	-163.23%
1995	270	-6.25%	23,161	12.30%	628	11.01%	-25	-96.35%
1996	228	-15.56%	21,338	-7.87%	682	8.63%	-3	87.86%

3 Major products* 3種主要產品*	Output 產量	Sales volume 銷售量	Unit 單位
a) Coated Glass 鍍膜玻璃	1,826,405	1,716,821	square metre 平方米

Top 10 firms by revenue (year founded) 收入排名前10家企業（創辦年份）	City 城市	Province 省	Telephone / fax 電話／傳真	Number of employees 職工人數	Ownership 產業所有權	Revenue ('000 RMB) 銷售收入（千元）	Profit ('000 RMB) (rank) 利潤（千元）（排名）	Total assets ('000 RMB) 總資產（千元）	Major products 主要產品
Shenzhen Heng Guang Optics Industrial Co. Ltd. 深圳恒光光學實業有限公司(1992)	Shenzhen 深圳市	Guangdong 廣東省	(0755)8862851 (0755)8863474	2,500	Overseas Chinese-funded 港澳台資	176,865	2460(1)	524,448	o
Qinhuangdao Haigangqu Bei Jiao Mirror Making Factory 秦皇島市海港區北郊製鏡廠(1987)	Qinhuangdao 秦皇島市	Hebei 河北省	(0335)3064491	101	Collectively-owned 集體	62,058	700(8)	10,581	o
Xiamen Hong Tai Optics Co. Ltd. 廈門虹泰光學有限公司(1992)	Xiamen 廈門市	Fujian 福建省	(0592)5060059 (0592)5060060	118	Overseas Chinese-funded 港澳台資	31,798	2076(2)	31,966	o
Huainan Chang Hai Industrial Co. 淮南市昌海工業公司(1992)	Huainan 淮南市	Anhui 安徽省	(0554)2678961	197	Collectively-owned 集體	28,500	14(38)	8,387	o
China Luoyang Float Glass Process Glass Group Jing Hua Industrial General Co. 中國洛陽浮法玻璃集團晶華實業總公司(1983)	Luoyang 洛陽市	Henan 河南省	(0379)3908417	434	Collectively-owned 集體	23,304	-1961(61)	23,694	a
Shanghai Shen Feng Mirror Industry Co. Ltd. 上海申豐鏡業有限公司(1989)	Shanghai 上海市	Shanghai 上海市	(021)57522650 (021)57523688	60	Overseas Chinese-funded 港澳台資	23,176	1009(6)	31,378	o
Yichun Mirror Industry Co. Ltd. 宜春市鏡業有限公司(1957)	Yichun 宜春市	Jiangxi 江西省	(0795)3272149		Collectively-owned 集體	15,722	180(20)	9,295	o
Yong'an Arts & Crafts Factory 永安市工藝美術廠(1956)	Sanming 三明市	Fujian 福建省	(0598)3633137 (0598)3632635	80	Collectively-owned 集體	10,793	23(33)	6,069	a
Tianjin Jin Jing Mirror Industry Co. Ltd. 天津市津京鏡業有限公司(1992)	Tianjin 天津市	Tianjin 天津市	(022)29439500	55	Overseas Chinese-funded 港澳台資	9,740	1420(3)	6,600	o
Longshan Mirror Making Factory 龍山縣製鏡廠(1985)	Jishou 吉首市	Hunan 湖南省	(0743)6222822	38	Collectively-owned 集體	9,180	-510(55)	1,102	o

Top 10 Cities by Production Output 產出排名前10位城市	Province 省	Market share 市場份額	Number of firms 企業個數
Qinhuangdao 秦皇島市	Hebei 河北省	21.48%	7
Shanghai 上海市	Shanghai 上海市	11.89%	8
Zhoukou 周口市	Henan 河南省	4.86%	4
Urumqi 烏魯木齊市	Xinjiang 新疆	4.39%	6
Yichun 宜春市	Jiangxi 江西省	3.96%	1
Jiujiang 九江市	Jiangxi 江西省	3.46%	2
Sanming 三明市	Fujian 福建省	2.94%	1
Neijiang 內江市	Sichuan 四川省	2.88%	2
Shenyang 瀋陽市	Liaoning 遼寧省	2.44%	6
Nanjing 南京市	Jiangsu 江蘇省	2.41%	3

10 Major Wholesalers 10家主要批發商	City 城市	Province 省	Telephone / Fax 電話／傳真
Shandong Stationary & Sporting Goods Import & Export Company 山東省文教體育用品進出口公司	Qingdao 青島市	Shandong 山東省	(0532)2826827 (0532)3831971
Henan Printing Goods & Materials General Company 河南省印刷物資總公司	Zhengzhou 鄭州市	Henan 河南省	(0371)5967060 (0371)5947912
China Packing Import & Export Singbo Company 中國包裝進出口寧波公司	Ningbo 寧波市	Zhejiang 浙江省	(0574)7367512 (0574)7361096
Tianjin Stationary & Sporting Goods Import & Export Company 天津文教體育用品進出口公司	Tianjin 天津市	Tianjin 天津市	(022)23112048 (022)23112054
China Packing Import & Export Liaoning Company 中國包裝進出口遼寧公司	Dalian 大連市	Liaoning 遼寧省	(0411)4687657 (0411)4687644
Hunan Printing Goods & Materials General Company 湖南省印刷物資總公司	Changsha 長沙市	Hunan 湖南省	(0731)4444618 (0731)4446936
Guangzhou Stationery Co. 廣州市文化用品公司	Guangzhou 廣州市	Guangdong 廣東省	(020)81889089 (020)81861964
Ka Xi Ou Electron (Shenzhen) Co. Ltd. 卡西歐電子(深圳)有限公司	Shenzhen 深圳市	Guangdong 廣東省	(0755)3590620 (0755)3590565
Changsha Keven Group Co. 長沙市科文集團公司	Changsha 長沙市	Hunan 湖南省	(0731)4444108
Hunan Firecrackers Fireworks Import & Export Company 湖南省鞭炮煙花進出口公司	Changsha 長沙市	Hunan 湖南省	(0731)4439580

*Also include sales by firms outside this industry.包括本行業以外廠家的銷售。"o" stands for "others". "o" 代表"其他產品"。

4353: Eye Glasses 眼鏡製造業

The industry accounts for 0.040% of the total revenue of China's industrial sector in 1996. The revenue growth rate of the industry is 18.1% from 1995, as compared to the growth rate of China's industrial sector, 9.51%. The rate of return on asset is 2.65%. 68.24% of all firms in the industry made a profit while 22.67% had negative returns. The top province in terms of the industry's revenue is Zhejiang, accounting for 23.65% of the total revenue.
本行業在1996年佔全行業總產值0.040%，行業年增長率為18.1%（全國工業年增長率9.51%）。行業的資產回報率2.65%，68.24%的企業盈利，22.67%的企業虧損。銷售收入最高的省份為浙江省，佔本行業的23.65%。

	Total number of firms 企業總數	Total number of employees 職工總數	Total revenue (mil. RMB) 總銷售收入（百萬元）	Total profit (mil. RMB) 總利潤（百萬元）	Return on assets 資產利潤率 (%)	Return on equity 權益利潤率 (%)	Labour productivity ('000 RMB / worker) 勞動生產率（千元/人）	Debts / assets 資產負債率 (%)	Total assets (mil. RMB) 總資產（百萬元）
Industry Overall 行業總體	316	31,118	2,305	77	2.65	5.50	74.07	51.77	2,918

	Number of firms 企業個數	Average number of employees 平均職工人數	Average revenue ('000 RMB) 平均銷售收入（千元）	Average profit ('000 RMB) 平均利潤（千元）	Return on assets 資產利潤率 (%)	Return on equity 權益利潤率 (%)	Labour productivity ('000 RMB / worker) 勞動生產率（千元/人）	Average debts / assets 平均資產負債率(%)	Average Total assets ('000 RMB) 平均總資產（千元）
By ownership 產業所有權									
State-owned 國有	14	182	2,286	-143	-2.17	-16.67	12.57	86.96	6,571
Collectively-owned 集體	170	66	3,477	192	7.65	16.82	52.79	54.54	2,516
Privately-owned 私有									
Domestic JVs 聯營	1	71						40.21	3,336
Joint stock 股份制	5	61	4,226	43	1.73	3.14	69.06	44.76	2,489
Foreign-funded 外資	47	90	12,395	802	3.77	7.30	137.30	48.30	21,272
Overseas Chinese-funded 港澳台資	78	174	13,833	107	0.60	1.24	79.41	51.20	17,735
By size 規模									
Large 大型									
Medium 中型	4	296	19,859	1,484	2.91	8.24	67.03	64.62	50,907
Small 小型	298	101	7,471	238	2.62	5.32	74.16	50.82	9,110
By regional distribution 地區分布									
Central-North 華北	48	49	6,066	615	5.55	14.16	123.18	60.78	11,065
Beijing 北京	31	47	8,679	990	6.53	16.62	185.43	60.68	15,149
Tianjin 天津	4	63	898	-148	-2.09	-4.40	14.36	52.43	7,043
Hebei 河北	6	48	702	-115	-3.70	-15.03	14.67	75.39	3,108
Shanxi 山西	2	15	4,125	45	1.75	4.64	275.00	62.18	2,565
Inner Mongolia 內蒙	5	69	1,216	2	0.10	0.27	17.57	61.13	1,914
Northeast 東北	12	103	2,691	136	6.10	19.90	26.15	69.35	2,227
Liaoning 遼寧	8	110	3,549	195	6.37	20.00	32.41	68.15	3,061
Jilin 吉林									
Heilongjiang 黑龍江	4	90	975	18	3.14	17.95	10.86	82.51	558
Central East 華東	174	95	8,646	232	2.61	5.82	90.65	55.07	8,889
Shanghai 上海	15	157	13,259	1,227	4.61	12.47	84.24	63.00	26,595
Jiangsu 江蘇	25	87	6,549	-138	-2.02	-4.27	75.49	52.71	6,860
Zhejiang 浙江	78	74	6,988	146	4.66	10.99	94.21	57.58	3,120
Anhui 安徽	6	51	5,302	135	14.01	27.00	103.95	48.10	963
Fujian 福建	35	146	15,570	383	2.03	4.20	106.65	51.73	18,929
Jiangxi 江西	9	27	494	-51	-1.90	-2.60	18.62	26.93	2,690
Shandong 山東	6	104	2,593	62	0.92	1.65	24.90	44.36	6,713
Central-South 中南	59	156	7,014	37	0.30	0.47	44.89	36.54	12,268
Henan 河南	5	36	3,416	94	5.22	12.88	94.89	59.49	1,802
Hubei 湖北	3	157	8,773	723	1.30	1.66	56.00	21.25	55,463
Hunan 湖南	8	32	1,144	-93	-7.25	264.29	35.74	102.65	1,275
Guangdong 廣東	42	198	8,599	6	0.05	0.08	43.47	39.63	12,812
Guangxi 廣西	1	6	120				20.00	45.45	110
Hainan 海南									
Southwest 西南	12	91	2,973	-8	-0.20	-0.86	32.73	76.45	4,113
Chongqing 重慶	6	145	5,213	-16	-0.23	-1.16	35.85	80.41	7,008
Sichuan 四川	6	37	733	0	-0.01	-0.02	20.03	53.69	1,218
Guizhou 貴州									
Yunnan 雲南									
Tibet 西藏									
Northwest 西北	11	56	2,523	344	9.43	15.13	45.20	37.72	3,645
Shaanxi 陝西	7	58	3,096	434	9.00	14.29	53.51	37.06	4,826
Gansu 甘肅	3	61	1,937	223	11.94	20.81	31.92	42.60	1,870
Qinghai 青海									
Ningxia 寧夏	1	27	270	70	10.00	14.29	10.00	30.00	700
Xinjiang 新疆									

4353: Eye Glasses 眼鏡製造業

Year 年份	Number of firms 企業個數	Rate of change 每年變化 (%)	Number of employees 職工人數 (人)	Rate of change 每年變化 (%)	Total revenue (mil. RMB) 總銷售收入 (百萬元)	Rate of change 每年變化 (%)	Total profit (mil. RMB) 總利潤 (百萬元)	Rate of change 每年變化 (%)
1993	235		22,441		697		51	
1994	273	16.17%	31,187	38.97%	1,315	88.68%	66	28.43%
1995	298	9.16%	30,723	-1.49%	1,951	48.40%	35	-46.65%
1996	316	6.04%	31,118	1.29%	2,305	18.14%	77	119.42%

3 Major products* 3 種主要產品 *	Output 產量	Sales volume 銷售量	Unit 單位
a) Glasses 眼鏡	216,647,492	212,314,543	pair 付

Top 10 firms by revenue (year founded) 收入排名前 10 家企業 (創辦年份)	City 城市	Province 省	Telephone / fax 電話 / 傳真	Number of employees 職工人數	Ownership 產業所有權	Revenue ('000 RMB) 銷售收入 (千元)	Profit ('000 RMB) (rank) 利潤 (千元) (排名)	Total assets ('000 RMB) 總資產 (千元)	Major products 主要產品
Lai Ming Industry (Xiamen) Co. Ltd. 來明工業(廈門)有限公司(1989)	Xiamen 廈門市	Fujian 福建省	(0592)6216191 (0592)6210138	911	Overseas Chinese-funded 港澳台資	130,169	14916(1)	174,198	a
Xiamen Dynasty Optical Co. Ltd. 廈門富華光學工業有限公司(1989)	Xiamen 廈門市	Fujian 福建省	(0592)6020403 (0592)6020402	1,891	Overseas Chinese-funded 港澳台資	121,789	3683(4)	91,011	a
Xiamen Cheng Yi Optical Industrial Co. Ltd. 廈門誠益光學工業有限公司(1990)	Xiamen 廈門市	Fujian 福建省	(0592)5193908 (0592)5193918	718	Overseas Chinese-funded 港澳台資	76,003	2666(8)	59,926	a
Wenzhou Xin Tai Optics Glasses Co. Ltd. (Development Zone) 温州市信泰光學眼鏡有限公司(開發區)(1993)	Wenzhou 温州市	Zhejiang 浙江省	(0577)6362688	885	Joint stock 股份制	74,939	4041(3)	23,294	o
Xiamen Tai Li Glasses Industrial Co. Ltd. 廈門泰利眼鏡工業有限公司(1990)	Xiamen 廈門市	Fujian 福建省	(0592)6217230 (0592)6210433	520	Overseas Chinese-funded 港澳台資	71,756	1130(17)	85,586	a
Guangzhou Da Xin Optics Co. Ltd. 廣州大新光學有限公司(1992)	Guangzhou 廣州市	Guangdong 廣東省	(020)85552783 (020)85552786	479	Overseas Chinese-funded 港澳台資	57,413	1515(14)	33,605	a
Shanghai Nojiri Optical Co. Ltd. 上海野尻眼鏡有限公司(1990)	Shanghai 上海市	Shanghai 上海市	(021)62747220 (021)62747305	133	Foreign-funded 外資	53,894	249(45)	103,408	o
Zhenjiang Wan Xin Optics Glasses Co. Ltd. 鎮江萬新光學眼鏡有限公司(1989)	Zhenjiang 鎮江市	Jiangsu 江蘇省	(0511)6802427	285	Overseas Chinese-funded 港澳台資	50,626	258(44)	11,019	a
Wenzhou Donghai Glasses Factory 温州市東海眼鏡廠(1991)	Wenzhou 温州市	Zhejiang 浙江省	(0577)8529036 (0577)8529000	400	Joint stock 股份制	46,151	621(23)	12,696	o
Jiangsu Dongfang Optics Co. Ltd. 江蘇東方光學有限公司(1993)	Zhenjiang 鎮江市	Jiangsu 江蘇省	(0511)6802005 (0511)6802006	627	Overseas Chinese-funded 港澳台資	43,765	1256(16)	22,480	a

Top 10 Cities by Production Output 產出排名前 10 位城市	Province 省	Market share 市場份額	Number of firms 企業個數
Wenzhou 温州市	Zhejiang 浙江省	27.25%	120
Guangzhou 廣州市	Guangdong 廣東省	13.65%	44
Beijing 北京市	Beijing 北京市	12.39%	27
Shanghai 上海市	Shanghai 上海市	11.47%	28
Shenzhen 深圳市	Guangdong 廣東省	10.06%	5
Taizhou 臺州市	Zhejiang 浙江省	3.76%	60
Dongguan 東莞市	Guangdong 廣東省	3.13%	6
Zhuhai 珠海市	Guangdong 廣東省	2.27%	4
Zhenjiang 鎮江市	Jiangsu 江蘇省	1.91%	13
Liu'an 六安市	Anhui 安徽省	1.39%	1

10 Major Wholesalers 10 家主要批發商	City 城市	Province 省	Telephone / Fax 電話 / 傳真
Shandong Stationary & Sporting Goods Import & Export Company 山東省文教體育用品進出口公司	Qingdao 青島市	Shandong 山東省	(0532)2826827 (0532)3831971
Henan Printing Goods & Materials General Company 河南省印刷物資總公司	Zhengzhou 鄭州市	Henan 河南省	(0371)5967060 (0371)5947912
China Packing Import & Export Singbo Company 中國包裝進出口寧波公司	Ningbo 寧波市	Zhejiang 浙江省	(0574)7367512 (0574)7361096
Tianjin Stationary & Sporting Goods Import & Export Company 天津文教體育用品進出口公司	Tianjin 天津市	Tianjin 天津市	(022)23112048 (022)23112054
China Packing Import & Export Liaoning Company 中國包裝進出口遼寧公司	Dalian 大連市	Liaoning 遼寧省	(0411)4687657 (0411)4687644
Hunan Printing Goods & Materials General Company 湖南省印刷物資總公司	Changsha 長沙市	Hunan 湖南省	(0731)4444618 (0731)4446936
Guangzhou Stationery Co. 廣州市文化用品公司	Guangzhou 廣州市	Guangdong 廣東省	(020)81889089 (020)81861964
Ka Xi Ou Electron (Shenzhen) Co. Ltd. 卡西歐電子(深圳)有限公司	Shenzhen 深圳市	Guangdong 廣東省	(0755)3590620 (0755)3590565
Changsha Keven Group Co. 長沙市科文集團公司	Changsha 長沙市	Hunan 湖南省	(0731)4444108
Hunan Firecrackers Fireworks Import & Export Company 湖南省鞭炮煙花進出口公司	Changsha 長沙市	Hunan 湖南省	(0731)4439580

*Also include sales by firms outside this industry.包括本行業以外廠家的銷售。"o" stands for "others". "o" 代表 "其他產品"。

4355: Umbrellas 製傘業

The industry accounts for 0.042% of the total revenue of China's industrial sector in 1996. The revenue growth rate of the industry is -7.8% from 1995, as compared to the growth rate of China's industrial sector, 9.51%. The rate of return on asset is -0.20%. 63.47% of all firms in the industry made a profit while 32.58% had negative returns. The top province in terms of the industry's revenue is Fujian, accounting for 57.03% of the total revenue.
本行業在1996年佔全行業總產值0.042%，行業年增長率為-7.8%（全國工業年增長率9.51%）。行業的資產回報率-0.20%，63.47%的企業盈利，32.58%的企業虧損。銷售收入最高的省份為福建省，佔本行業的57.03%。

	Total number of firms 企業總數	Total number of employees 職工總數	Total revenue (mil. RMB) 總銷售收入（百萬元）	Total profit (mil. RMB) 總利潤（百萬元）	Return on assets 資產利潤率 (%)	Return on equity 權益利潤率 (%)	Labour productivity ('000 RMB / worker) 勞動生產率（千元/人）	Debts / assets 資產負債率 (%)	Total assets (mil. RMB) 總資產（百萬元）
Industry Overall 行業總體	339	41,621	2,424	-4	-0.20	-0.62	58.24	67.61	2,107

	Number of firms 企業個數	Average number of employees 平均職工人數	Average revenue ('000 RMB) 平均銷售收入（千元）	Average profit ('000 RMB) 平均利潤（千元）	Return on assets 資產利潤率 (%)	Return on equity 權益利潤率 (%)	Labour productivity ('000 RMB / worker) 勞動生產率（千元/人）	Average debts / assets 平均資產負債率(%)	Average Total assets ('000 RMB) 平均總資產（千元）
By ownership 產業所有權									
State-owned 國有	15	211	4,000	-1,000	-8.47	-166.67	18.93	94.92	11,800
Collectively-owned 集體	197	92	2,472	-8	-0.20	-0.83	26.92	75.97	4,241
Privately-owned 私有	1	44	2,205	-17	-1.12	-4.13	50.11	72.89	1,562
Domestic JVs 聯營	1	10							
Joint stock 股份制	3	85	3,549	30	0.74	1.04	41.91	29.18	4,086
Foreign-funded 外資	21	105	7,027	51	1.32	2.33	67.14	43.36	3,838
Overseas Chinese-funded 港澳台資	101	185	16,994	114	1.15	2.76	91.62	58.26	9,902
By size 規模									
Large 大型									
Medium 中型	2	781	27,294	-280	-0.24	-0.98	34.97	75.86	117,967
Small 小型	328	124	7,223	-10	-0.18	-0.55	58.43	66.59	5,704
By regional distribution 地區分布									
Central-North 華北	13	77	6,160	231	6.20	15.65	79.52	60.41	3,721
Beijing 北京	4	36	4,743	75	2.44	4.17	130.83	41.56	3,080
Tianjin 天津	4	82	9,223	618	12.91	52.78	112.13	75.59	4,783
Hebei 河北	3	146	7,590	73	1.79	4.17	51.99	57.01	4,087
Shanxi 山西	2	48	725	5	0.21	0.50	15.26	56.87	2,330
Inner Mongolia 內蒙									
Northeast 東北	3	128	80	-330	-12.44	24.57	0.63	150.63	2,653
Liaoning 遼寧									
Jilin 吉林									
Heilongjiang 黑龍江	3	128	80	-330	-12.44	24.57	0.63	150.63	2,653
Central East 華東	209	130	8,838	37	0.53	1.44	67.89	63.52	7,023
Shanghai 上海	6	282	3,093	-63	-0.56	14.79	10.98	103.82	11,223
Jiangsu 江蘇	14	105	4,275	-129	-3.22	-29.65	40.71	89.12	3,991
Zhejiang 浙江	42	137	6,735	35	0.38	1.39	49.29	72.50	9,299
Anhui 安徽	16	82	1,115	-120	-3.74	-86.88	13.68	95.67	3,204
Fujian 福建	96	150	14,401	104	1.21	2.48	96.26	51.15	8,543
Jiangxi 江西	25	56	1,398	-25	-1.93	-20.06	25.05	90.35	1,285
Shandong 山東	10	124	5,044	101	2.00	5.42	40.55	63.07	5,048
Central-South 中南	100	118	4,680	-139	-2.60	-11.79	39.51	77.92	5,347
Henan 河南	7	93	2,554	176	7.82	12.02	27.59	34.99	2,246
Hubei 湖北	22	95	2,960	-56	-1.41	-7.74	31.06	81.73	3,956
Hunan 湖南	22	92	819	-175	-8.02	-135.09	8.89	94.06	2,181
Guangdong 廣東	41	159	8,661	-200	-2.36	-10.79	54.33	78.16	8,464
Guangxi 廣西	8	68	1,488	-236	-5.12	-14.20	22.00	63.94	4,614
Hainan 海南									
Southwest 西南	14	84	2,055	-5	-0.15	-0.51	24.40	71.21	3,424
Chongqing 重慶	4	127	576	-23	-0.98	8.18	4.53	111.93	2,380
Sichuan 四川	5	28	2,103	-7	-0.53	-0.97	75.41	44.94	1,244
Guizhou 貴州	2	52	15				0.29	100.00	35
Yunnan 雲南	3	143	5,307	20	0.19	0.52	37.11	64.17	10,707
Tibet 西藏									
Northwest 西北									
Shaanxi 陝西									
Gansu 甘肅									
Qinghai 青海									
Ningxia 寧夏									
Xinjiang 新疆									

4355: Umbrellas 製傘業

Year 年份	Number of firms 企業個數	Rate of change 每年變化 (%)	Number of employees 職工人數 (人)	Rate of change 每年變化 (%)	Total revenue (mil. RMB) 總銷售收入 (百萬元)	Rate of change 每年變化 (%)	Total profit (mil. RMB) 總利潤 (百萬元)	Rate of change 每年變化 (%)
1993	315		42,260		1,353		-3	
1994	335	6.35%	49,942	18.18%	2,111	56.04%	7	363.00%
1995	356	6.27%	45,344	-9.21%	2,630	24.56%	16	137.38%
1996	339	-4.78%	41,621	-8.21%	2,424	-7.83%	-4	-125.09%

3 Major products* 3 種主要產品 *	Output 產量	Sales volume 銷售量	Unit 單位
a) Umbrella 傘	215,508,195	206,887,867	piece 把

Top 10 firms by revenue (year founded) 收入排名前 10 家企業 (創辦年份)	City 城市	Province 省	Telephone / fax 電話 / 傳真	Number of employees 職工人數	Ownership 產業所有權	Revenue ('000 RMB) 銷售收入 (千元)	Profit ('000 RMB) (rank) 利潤 (千元) (排名)	Total assets ('000 RMB) 總資產 (千元)	Major products 主要產品
Longhai Qi Mei Industries Co. Ltd. 龍海市奇美實業有限公司(1992)	Zhangzhou 漳州市	Fujian 福建省	(0596)2186068	899	Overseas Chinese-funded 港澳台資	149,000	5321(1)	31,935	a
Zhangpu Hua Xing Umbrella Co. Ltd. 漳浦華興雨傘有限公司(1989)	Zhangzhou 漳州市	Fujian 福建省	(0596)3221400	520	Overseas Chinese-funded 港澳台資	133,084	-814(139)	5,951	a
Xiamen Ming He Industrial Co. Ltd. 廈門明和實業有限公司(1989)	Xiamen 廈門市	Fujian 福建省	(0592)7200256	390	Overseas Chinese-funded 港澳台資	132,716	1461(12)	58,566	a
Zhangpu Huang Sheng Umbrella Fittings Co. Ltd. 漳浦縣煌升製傘配件有限公司(1993)	Zhangzhou 漳州市	Fujian 福建省	(0596)3180078 (0596)3180079	120	Overseas Chinese-funded 港澳台資	104,753	162(55)	24,296	a
Fujian Changtai Jia Yong Umbrella Co. Ltd. 福建省長泰佳永洋傘有限公司(1991)	Zhangzhou 漳州市	Fujian 福建省	(0596)8323052 (0596)8323684	366	Overseas Chinese-funded 港澳台資	76,146	-2898(149)	18,743	a
Wenzhou Conch Industry Group Company 溫州市海螺工業集團公司(1976)	Wenzhou 溫州市	Zhejiang 浙江省	(0577)8515498 (0577)8527805	187	Collectively-owned 集体	64,267	2667(4)	154,321	o
Zhejiang Yu Jin Xiang Light & Textile Industry Group Co. Ltd. 浙江鬱金香輕紡集團有限公司(1995)	Jinhua 金華市	Zhejiang 浙江省	(0579)7663984 (0579)7664675	1,087	Joint stock 股份制	61,267	652(25)	58,679	o
Fu Xing Shoes Industry Co. Ltd. 富興鞋業有限公司(1989)	Quanzhou 泉州市	Fujian 福建省	(0595)5586787 (0595)5585190	846	Overseas Chinese-funded 港澳台資	51,000	138(59)	38,612	a
Xiamen Fu'an Umbrella Industry Co. Ltd. 廈門福安傘業有限公司(1990)	Xiamen 廈門市	Fujian 福建省	(0592)6210181 (0592)6212180	737	Overseas Chinese-funded 港澳台資	49,189	-3768(150)	42,946	a
Zhongshan San Yang Umbrella Manufacture Co. Ltd. 中山三洋雨傘製造有限公司(1991)	Zhongshan 中山市	Guangdong 廣東省	(0760)6684078 (0760)6686010	227	Overseas Chinese-funded 港澳台資	44,125	25(84)	15,342	a

Top 10 Cities by Production Output 產出排名前 10 位城市	Province 省	Market share 市場份額	Number of firms 企業個數
Taizhou 臺州市	Zhejiang 浙江省	15.75%	42
Hangzhou 杭州市	Zhejiang 浙江省	8.41%	17
Jinhua 金華市	Zhejiang 浙江省	7.82%	12
Quanzhou 泉州市	Fujian 福建省	7.56%	21
Guangzhou 廣州市	Guangdong 廣東省	7.09%	10
Wenzhou 溫州市	Zhejiang 浙江省	5.05%	29
Huizhou 惠州市	Guangdong 廣東省	4.99%	10
Zhangzhou 漳州市	Fujian 福建省	4.52%	6
Xiamen 廈門市	Fujian 福建省	3.35%	4
Zhongshan 中山市	Guangdong 廣東省	2.81%	1

10 Major Wholesalers 10 家主要批發商	City 城市	Province 省	Telephone / Fax 電話 / 傳真
Chengdu Great Wall Electric Appliance Company 成都長城電器公司	Chengdu 成都市	Sichuan 四川省	(028)6662132 (028)6671975
Shandou Ceramics (Group) Company 汕頭陶瓷(集團)公司	Shantou 汕頭市	Guangdong 廣東省	(0754)8255441 (0754)8255442
Guangdong Puning Local Products Import & Export Company 廣東省普寧土產進出口公司	Jieyang 揭陽市	Guangdong 廣東省	(0663)2226744
Yixing Sundry Goods General Co. 宜興市土產雜品總公司	Wuxi 無錫市	Jiangsu 江蘇省	(0510)7903683 (0510)7903683
Sujiang Qu Zhe Jiang Dongda Group Company 椒江區浙江東大集團公司	Taizhou 臺州市	Zhejiang 浙江省	(0576)8881477 (0576)8881672
Jiangsu New Suzhou Co. Ltd. Suzhou Daily Goods General Co. 江蘇新蘇州股份有限公司蘇州日用雜品總公司	Suzhou 蘇州市	Jiangsu 江蘇省	(0512)7276630 (0512)7275964
Shandong Daily Use General Merchandise Import & Export Company 山東省日用百貨進出口公司	Qingdao 青島市	Shandong 山東省	(0532)5849141 (0532)5849207
Guangdong Yangjiang Light Industry Products Import & Export (Group) Company 廣東陽江輕工業品進出口(集團)公司	Yangjiang 陽江市	Guangdong 廣東省	(0662)3222497 (0662)3222976
Hebei Artts & Crtfts Import & Export Corp. 河北工藝品進出口公司	Shijiazhuang 石家莊市	Hebei 河北省	(0311)7756124 (0311)7755347
Shandong Handicrafts Import & Export Products Group Linyi Craft Co. Ltd. 山東工藝品進出品集團臨沂工藝有限公司	Linyi 臨沂市	Shandong 山東省	(0539)8310001 (0539)8315396

*Also include sales by firms outside this industry.包括本行業以外廠家的銷售。"o" stands for "others". "o" 代表 "其他產品"。

4357: Bristle Processing and Brush 鬃毛加工及製刷業

The industry accounts for 0.031% of the total revenue of China's industrial sector in 1996. The revenue growth rate of the industry is 1.7% from 1995, as compared to the growth rate of China's industrial sector, 9.51%. The rate of return on asset is 1.02%. 70.63% of all firms in the industry made a profit while 24.80% had negative returns. The top province in terms of the industry's revenue is Jiangsu, accounting for 16.51% of the total revenue.
本行業在1996年佔全行業總產值0.031%，行業年增長率為1.7%（全國工業年增長率9.51%）。行業的資產回報率1.02%，70.63%的企業盈利，24.80%的企業虧損。銷售收入最高的省份為江蘇省，佔本行業的16.51%。

	Total number of firms 企業總數	Total number of employees 職工總數	Total revenue (mil. RMB) 總銷售收入 (百萬元)	Total profit (mil. RMB) 總利潤 (百萬元)	Return on assets 資產利潤率 (%)	Return on equity 權益利潤率 (%)	Labour productivity ('000 RMB / worker) 勞動生產率 (千元/人)	Debts / assets 資產負債率 (%)	Total assets (mil. RMB) 總資產 (百萬元)
Industry Overall 行業總體	511	49,306	1,807	16	1.02	3.90	36.65	73.96	1,557

	Number of firms 企業個數	Average number of employees 平均職工人數	Average revenue ('000 RMB) 平均銷售收入 (千元)	Average profit ('000 RMB) 平均利潤 (千元)	Return on assets 資產利潤率 (%)	Return on equity 權益利潤率 (%)	Labour productivity ('000 RMB / worker) 勞動生產率 (千元/人)	Average debts / assets 平均資產負債率(%)	Average Total assets ('000 RMB) 平均總資產 (千元)
By ownership 產業所有權									
State-owned 國有	36	190	4,583	-306	-3.16	-36.67	24.06	91.38	9,667
Collectively-owned 集體	421	74	2,955	60	2.96	11.02	40.14	73.12	2,019
Privately-owned 私有	6	969	7,860	40	1.11	2.74	8.11	59.38	3,617
Domestic JVs 聯營	4	153	5,015	52	1.38	4.67	32.72	70.55	3,804
Joint stock 股份制									
Foreign-funded 外資	26	117	6,623	-56	-0.80	-1.81	56.52	55.89	7,042
Overseas Chinese-funded 港澳台資	19	108	8,367	149	2.03	5.38	77.78	62.27	7,330
By size 規模									
Large 大型									
Medium 中型	5	389	35,680	-1,443	-3.18	-36.17	91.77	91.22	45,415
Small 小型	504	93	3,232	46	1.75	6.03	34.63	71.05	2,639
By regional distribution 地區分布									
Central-North 華北	58	67	2,269	10	0.36	1.09	34.02	66.95	2,822
Beijing 北京	5	71	2,352	4	0.14	0.28	33.03	51.41	2,918
Tianjin 天津	5	113	6,424	66	0.90	1.33	56.75	32.48	7,370
Hebei 河北	33	73	2,446	4	0.13	0.56	33.63	77.42	3,091
Shanxi 山西	2	84	535	-25	-2.02	-4.20	6.37	51.61	1,240
Inner Mongolia 內蒙	13	29	455	12	2.07	-7.58	15.66	127.46	594
Northeast 東北	42	93	2,500	65	1.73	83.08	26.86	97.92	3,782
Liaoning 遼寧	17	101	3,481	368	11.39	31.87	34.54	64.26	3,233
Jilin 吉林	7	38	187	-6	-1.21	-3.57	4.87	66.06	471
Heilongjiang 黑龍江	18	107	2,474	-193	-3.45	19.89	23.10	117.35	5,588
Central East 華東	179	112	5,031	45	1.44	5.20	44.87	72.29	3,116
Shanghai 上海	9	133	6,752	-1,463	-16.33	-783.93	50.81	97.93	8,962
Jiangsu 江蘇	45	115	6,630	64	1.50	5.69	57.60	73.57	4,257
Zhejiang 浙江	21	92	2,558	-75	-3.09	-11.03	27.89	71.99	2,420
Anhui 安徽	37	162	4,702	191	12.01	31.79	29.11	62.22	1,589
Fujian 福建	10	74	3,225	81	4.64	7.93	43.52	41.55	1,745
Jiangxi 江西	21	38	1,350	73	9.48	45.67	35.23	79.18	769
Shandong 山東	36	118	7,030	292	7.37	20.07	59.63	63.28	3,957
Central-South 中南	134	94	3,479	54	1.76	5.13	37.04	65.80	3,061
Henan 河南	38	67	3,361	181	7.50	16.84	50.33	55.47	2,411
Hubei 湖北	59	103	2,646	77	3.20	14.31	25.73	77.64	2,417
Hunan 湖南	24	103	4,043	-131	-4.23	-17.67	39.25	76.09	3,105
Guangdong 廣東	11	112	6,585	-143	-1.58	-3.29	58.74	51.86	9,017
Guangxi 廣西	2	138	6,430	245	22.27	24.38	46.59	8.64	1,100
Hainan 海南									
Southwest 西南	73	99	2,502	-26	-0.79	-4.27	25.19	81.39	3,328
Chongqing 重慶	25	91	3,382	32	0.83	3.49	37.20	76.35	3,841
Sichuan 四川	37	108	2,345	0	0.00	0.03	21.72	88.36	3,163
Guizhou 貴州	7	100	290	-146	-5.29	-17.26	2.89	69.28	2,753
Yunnan 雲南	4	78	2,265	-28	-1.06	-3.93	29.23	72.93	2,595
Tibet 西藏									
Northwest 西北	25	65	838	-34	-3.58	-10.65	12.94	66.40	949
Shaanxi 陝西	16	69	858	-11	-1.39	-3.27	12.50	57.53	809
Gansu 甘肅	6	80	1,177	-38	-2.48	-5.20	14.74	52.31	1,548
Qinghai 青海									
Ningxia 寧夏	1	12	90	-10	-7.14	-11.11	7.50	42.86	140
Xinjiang 新疆	2	16	45	-215	-32.09	21.18	2.90	252.24	670

4357: Bristle Processing and Brush 鬃毛加工及製刷業

Year 年份	Number of firms 企業個數	Rate of change 每年變化 (%)	Number of employees 職工人數 (人)	Rate of change 每年變化 (%)	Total revenue (mil. RMB) 總銷售收入 (百萬元)	Rate of change 每年變化 (%)	Total profit (mil. RMB) 總利潤 (百萬元)	Rate of change 每年變化 (%)
1993	442		38,614		788		-12	
1994	511	15.61%	46,885	21.42%	1,298	64.87%	1	109.61%
1995	563	10.18%	61,187	30.50%	1,777	36.89%	23	1900.68%
1996	511	-9.24%	49,306	-19.42%	1,807	1.69%	16	-31.59%

3 Major products* 3 種主要產品 *	Output 產量	Sales volume 銷售量	Unit 單位
a) Brush 刷子	500,709,361	465,659,706	piece 把

Top 10 firms by revenue (year founded) 收入排名前 10 家企業 (創辦年份)	City 城市	Province 省	Telephone / fax 電話 / 傳真	Number of employees 職工人數	Ownership 產業所有權	Revenue ('000 RMB) 銷售收入 (千元)	Profit ('000 RMB) (rank) 利潤 (千元) (排名)	Total assets ('000 RMB) 總資產 (千元)	Major products 主要產品
Yangzhou Ling Tang The Huis Livestock Products Processing Factory 揚州市菱塘回民畜產品加工廠(1979)	Yangzhou 揚州市	Jiangsu 江蘇省	(0514)4232028	148	Collectively-owned 集體	72,070	154(67)	8,003	o
Ningguo Wan Jia Co. Ltd. 寧國縣萬家有限公司(1995)	Xuanzhou 宣州市	Anhui 安徽省	(0563)4072006	21	Collectively-owned 集體	46,000	70(85)	73	a
Yingkou Makeup Apparatus Co. Ltd. 營口化裝用具有限公司(1990)	Yingkou 營口市	Liaoning 遼寧省	(0417)6251650 (0417)6251632	746	Foreign-funded 外資	35,097	6760(1)	26,208	o
Laohekou Menglou No.1 Boiled Bristle Factory 老河口市孟樓鎮第一水鬃廠(1992)	Xiangfan 襄樊市	Hubei 湖北省	(0710)8601963		Collectively-owned 集體	33,870	2450(4)	8,820	o
Shanghai Brush Factory 上海製刷廠(1939)	Shanghai 上海市	Shanghai 上海市	(021)62537558 (021)62531835	761	State-owned 國有	32,143	-968(168)	35,556	a
Junan Yan Bin Welfare Bristle Factory 莒南縣筵賓鎮福利製鬃廠(1991)	Linyi 臨沂市	Shandong 山東省	(0539)7787058 (0539)7787058	40	Collectively-owned 集體	31,842	1742(8)	25,834	o
Ningguo Chang Hong Plastic Products Co. Ltd. 寧國縣長虹塑製品有限公司(1994)	Xuanzhou 宣州市	Anhui 安徽省	(0563)4023977	6,326	Private-owned 私營	30,475	58(89)	2,168	a
Zhenjiang Brush Factory 鎮江市製刷廠(1965)	Zhenjiang 鎮江市	Jiangsu 江蘇省	(0511)5232256 (0511)5235440	382	Collectively-owned 集體	29,971	12(115)	10,932	a
Taixing Tai Shen Joint Bristle Making Factory 泰興市泰申聯合製鬃廠(1963)	Yangzhou 揚州市	Jiangsu 江蘇省	(0514)7761467 (0514)7761467	652	Collectively-owned 集體	28,067	1(133)	38,132	o
Wan Animal Products Import & Export Company Bristle Factory 萬縣市畜產進出口公司豬鬃廠	Chongqing 重慶市	Chongqing 重慶市	(023)8260031 (023)8260031	535	State-owned 國有	26,282	62(88)	34,406	o

Top 10 Cities by Production Output 產出排名前 10 位城市	Province 省	Market share 市場份額	Number of firms 企業個數
Weifang 濰坊市	Shandong 山東省	6.07%	8
Shanghai 上海市	Shanghai 上海市	5.59%	11
Zhenjiang 鎮江市	Jiangsu 江蘇省	5.56%	19
Chongqing 重慶市	Chongqing 重慶市	4.96%	30
Zaozhuang 棗莊市	Shandong 山東省	4.75%	4
Changde 常德市	Hunan 湖南省	4.28%	7
Yangzhou 揚州市	Jiangsu 江蘇省	3.92%	11
Linyi 臨沂市	Shandong 山東省	3.47%	3
Nanyang 南陽市	Henan 河南省	2.95%	7
Guangzhou 廣州市	Guangdong 廣東省	2.82%	8

10 Major Wholesalers 10 家主要批發商	City 城市	Province 省	Telephone / Fax 電話 / 傳真
Chengdu Great Wall Electric Appliance Company 成都長城電器公司	Chengdu 成都市	Sichuan 四川省	(028)6662132 (028)6671975
Shandou Ceramics (Group) Company 汕頭陶瓷(集團)公司	Shantou 汕頭市	Guangdong 廣東省	(0754)8255441 (0754)8255442
Guangdong Puning Local Products Import & Export Company 廣東省普寧土產進出口公司	Jieyang 揭陽市	Guangdong 廣東省	(0663)2226744
Yixing Sundry Goods General Co. 宜興市土產雜品總公司	Wuxi 無錫市	Jiangsu 江蘇省	(0510)7903683 (0510)7903683
Sujiang Qu Zhe Jiang Dongda Group Company 椒江區浙江東大集團公司	Taizhou 臺州市	Zhejiang 浙江省	(0576)8881477 (0576)8881672
Jiangsu New Suzhou Co. Ltd. Suzhou Daily Goods General Co. 江蘇新蘇州股份有限公司蘇州日用雜品總公司	Suzhou 蘇州市	Jiangsu 江蘇省	(0512)7276630 (0512)7275964
Shandong Daily Use General Merchandise Import & Export Company 山東省日用百貨進出口公司	Qingdao 青島市	Shandong 山東省	(0532)5849141 (0532)5849207
Guangdong Yangjiang Light Industry Products Import & Export (Group) Company 廣東陽江輕工業品進出口(集團)公司	Yangjiang 陽江市	Guangdong 廣東省	(0662)3222497 (0662)3222976
Hebei Artts & Crtfts Import & Export Corp. 河北工藝品進出口公司	Shijiazhuang 石家莊市	Hebei 河北省	(0311)7756124 (0311)7755347
Shandong Handicrafts Import & Export Products Group Linyi Craft Co. Ltd. 山東工藝品進出品集團臨沂工藝有限公司	Linyi 臨沂市	Shandong 山東省	(0539)8310001 (0539)8315396

*Also include sales by firms outside this industry.包括本行業以外廠家的銷售。"o" stands for "others". "o" 代表 "其他產品"。

4391: Other Capital Goods 生產用其他產品製造業

The industry accounts for 0.105% of the total revenue of China's industrial sector in 1996. The revenue growth rate of the industry is 33.4% from 1995, as compared to the growth rate of China's industrial sector, 9.51%. The rate of return on asset is 2.33%. 69.73% of all firms in the industry made a profit while 20.98% had negative returns. The top province in terms of the industry's revenue is Jiangsu, accounting for 17.87% of the total revenue.
本行業在1996年佔全行業總產值0.105%，行業年增長率為33.4%（全國工業年增長率9.51%）。行業的資產回報率2.33%，69.73%的企業盈利，20.98%的企業虧損。銷售收入最高的省份為江蘇省，佔本行業的17.87%。

	Total number of firms 企業總數	Total number of employees 職工總數	Total revenue (mil. RMB) 總銷售收入（百萬元）	Total profit (mil. RMB) 總利潤（百萬元）	Return on assets 資產利潤率 (%)	Return on equity 權益利潤率 (%)	Labour productivity ('000 RMB / worker) 勞動生產率（千元/人）	Debts / assets 資產負債率 (%)	Total assets (mil. RMB) 總資產（百萬元）
Industry Overall 行業總體	1,281	76,411	6,075	139	2.33	6.48	79.50	64.04	5,957

	Number of firms 企業個數	Average number of employees 平均職工人數	Average revenue ('000 RMB) 平均銷售收入（千元）	Average profit ('000 RMB) 平均利潤（千元）	Return on assets 資產利潤率 (%)	Return on equity 權益利潤率 (%)	Labour productivity ('000 RMB / worker) 勞動生產率（千元/人）	Average debts / assets 平均資產負債率(%)	Average Total assets ('000 RMB) 平均總資產（千元）
By ownership 產業所有權									
State-owned 國有	112	64	2,509	-54	-0.78	-2.38	39.25	67.40	6,902
Collectively-owned 集體	1,048	58	3,876	262	9.29	26.26	66.88	64.64	2,822
Privately-owned 私有	4	10	539	-80	-13.35	-31.21	53.87	57.24	600
Domestic JVs 聯營	15	96	17,697	600	2.88	10.34	183.46	72.18	20,855
Joint stock 股份制	8	173	28,796	3,336	10.95	37.74	166.81	70.99	30,470
Foreign-funded 外資	35	66	10,268	-4,046	-18.24	-46.53	154.51	60.79	22,179
Overseas Chinese-funded 港澳台資	59	67	14,829	-396	-2.62	-6.12	222.63	57.26	15,120
By size 規模									
Large 大型	2	841	118,387	23,749	11.91	42.65	140.85	72.07	199,367
Medium 中型	8	434	54,848	15,863	35.83	83.65	126.49	57.16	44,270
Small 小型	1,255	57	4,303	-28	-0.68	-1.88	75.91	63.90	4,147
By regional distribution 地區分布									
Central-North 華北	239	62	2,942	123	4.13	9.44	47.63	56.22	2,965
Beijing 北京	33	23	1,575	1	0.07	0.21	68.39	68.80	1,837
Tianjin 天津	72	45	2,083	110	5.18	12.56	45.90	58.76	2,124
Hebei 河北	80	62	4,061	248	4.61	9.37	65.77	50.78	5,383
Shanxi 山西	43	127	1,610	30	2.34	11.33	12.65	79.34	1,272
Inner Mongolia 內蒙	11	29	9,738	16	1.83	3.57	332.67	48.73	894
Northeast 東北	227	48	1,708	44	2.28	5.55	35.60	58.94	1,913
Liaoning 遼寧	118	58	2,056	39	1.66	4.04	35.33	58.80	2,336
Jilin 吉林	30	42	629	-2	-0.19	-0.42	14.89	55.60	1,257
Heilongjiang 黑龍江	79	35	1,599	68	4.45	11.22	45.77	60.30	1,529
Central East 華東	485	66	6,721	157	2.56	7.22	102.54	64.50	6,121
Shanghai 上海	127	68	7,699	286	3.19	7.78	113.20	58.94	8,947
Jiangsu 江蘇	135	67	8,043	133	1.93	6.43	119.30	70.06	6,923
Zhejiang 浙江	41	45	3,123	-21	-0.41	-0.97	69.48	57.45	5,083
Anhui 安徽	71	73	9,899	112	6.07	25.38	134.85	76.06	1,839
Fujian 福建	37	25	1,524	-65	-5.18	-10.45	61.95	50.49	1,253
Jiangxi 江西	29	31	1,779	-2	-0.19	-0.60	58.24	67.75	894
Shandong 山東	45	116	5,720	381	3.53	10.98	49.49	67.88	10,810
Central-South 中南	189	69	8,144	122	1.46	4.76	118.79	69.22	8,332
Henan 河南	47	103	3,865	185	4.23	21.45	37.36	80.26	4,372
Hubei 湖北	31	76	15,708	918	17.39	96.34	205.37	81.95	5,281
Hunan 湖南	43	39	1,568	61	3.50	6.44	39.81	45.69	1,737
Guangdong 廣東	46	65	15,621	-214	-0.93	-2.67	240.72	65.04	22,879
Guangxi 廣西	21	44	4,027	-328	-9.15	-159.49	91.92	94.26	3,585
Hainan 海南	1	125	80				0.64	43.49	3,150
Southwest 西南	98	47	1,405	21	0.97	2.18	29.70	55.47	2,175
Chongqing 重慶	33	35	1,064	108	8.40	30.02	30.78	72.02	1,286
Sichuan 四川	41	66	1,427	-90	-4.29	-10.41	21.65	58.82	2,100
Guizhou 貴州	20	27	1,347	-14	-0.55	-0.97	49.32	43.68	2,477
Yunnan 雲南	4	57	4,265	615	7.02	12.52	75.15	43.89	8,755
Tibet 西藏									
Northwest 西北	43	32	1,110	-35	-2.61	-7.40	34.83	64.81	1,339
Shaanxi 陝西	21	39	1,576	-82	-4.17	-11.42	40.30	63.50	1,977
Gansu 甘肅	8	22	283	3	0.81	2.33	12.99	65.04	308
Qinghai 青海									
Ningxia 寧夏	8	27	1,213	80	9.32	21.48	44.70	56.62	859
Xinjiang 新疆	6	27	450	-72	-6.39	-33.86	16.98	81.13	1,122

4391: Other Capital Goods 生產用其他產品製造業

Year 年份	Number of firms 企業個數	Rate of change 每年變化 (%)	Number of employees 職工人數（人）	Rate of change 每年變化 (%)	Total revenue (mil. RMB) 總銷售收入（百萬元）	Rate of change 每年變化 (%)	Total profit (mil. RMB) 總利潤（百萬元）	Rate of change 每年變化 (%)
1993	1,877		212,510		5,605		290	
1994	1,863	-0.75%	185,821	-12.56%	6,665	18.91%	116	-59.98%
1995	1,365	-26.73%	76,955	-58.59%	4,553	-31.68%	33	-71.54%
1996	1,281	-6.15%	76,411	-0.71%	6,075	33.43%	139	320.63%

3 Major products* 3 種主要產品 *	Output 產量	Sales volume 銷售量	Unit 單位
a) Jelly 膠	6,343	5,772	ton 噸
b) Tricycle 三輪車	62,979	59,830	vehicle 輛

Top 10 firms by revenue (year founded) 收入排名前 10 家企業 (創辦年份)	City 城市	Province 省	Telephone / fax 電話 / 傳真	Number of employees 職工人數	Ownership 產業所有權	Revenue ('000 RMB) 銷售收入（千元）	Profit ('000 RMB) (rank) 利潤（千元）（排名）	Total assets ('000 RMB) 總資產（千元）	Major products 主要產品
Tie San Ju Hua Hai Engineering Company 鐵三局華海工程公司(1995)	Shanghai 上海市	Shanghai 上海市	(021)64590062	280	Domestic JVs 聯營	226,324	4216(13)	125,816	o
Fo Tao Group Raw Materials Processing Factory 佛陶集團原料加工廠(1988)	Foshan 佛山市	Guangdong 廣東省	(0757)2273043 (0757)2273043	509	Joint stock 股份制	155,762	10231(1)	239,020	o
Baoshan Iron & Steel Corporation Xiao E Zhan 寶鋼小額站(1983)	Shanghai 上海市	Shanghai 上海市	(021)56699640	136	Domestic JVs 聯營	134,615	6128(7)	47,982	o
Shanghai Jin Heng Electric Wire & Cable Factory 上海金恒電線電纜廠(1995)	Shanghai 上海市	Shanghai 上海市	(021)59588473	130	Collectively-owned 集體	131,266	846(72)	10,282	o
Shanghai Kai Bao Goods & Materials Utilization Company 上海開寶物資利用公司(1991)	Shanghai 上海市	Shanghai 上海市	(021)56600204	26	Domestic JVs 聯營	110,474	1039(56)	70,466	o
Jinzhai Mei Shan Zhen Labour Service Company 金寨縣梅山鎮勞動服務公司(1996)	Liu'an 六安市	Anhui 安徽省	(0564)7062176	1	Collectively-owned 集體	109,650	0(404)	102	o
Foshan Yi Da Adhesion Products Co. Ltd. 佛山市億達膠粘製品有限公司(1993)	Foshan 佛山市	Guangdong 廣東省	(0757)2210051 (0757)2210156	214	Overseas Chinese-funded 港澳台資	101,280	6588(5)	100,712	o
Shantou Sez Wei Da Packing Material Co. Ltd. 汕頭經濟特區偉達包裝材料有限公司(1989)	Shantou 汕頭市	Guangdong 廣東省	(0754)8884808 (0754)8894515	192	Overseas Chinese-funded 港澳台資	100,651	-9179(495)	128,765	o
Jiangsu Deng Yue Group 江蘇登月集團(1959)	Yangzhou 揚州市	Jiangsu 江蘇省	(0514)7711511 (0514)7711497	987	Collectively-owned 集體	96,913	2359(31)	87,724	o
Jiangsu Jiang Yuan Iron & Steel Group Co. Ltd. 江蘇江源鋼鐵集團有限公司(1995)	Suzhou 蘇州市	Jiangsu 江蘇省	(0512)8382888	102	Collectively-owned 集體	94,490	6320(6)	60,430	o

Top 10 Cities by Production Output 產出排名前 10 位城市	Province 省	Market share 市場份額	Number of firms 企業個數
Foshan 佛山市	Guangdong 廣東省	10.57%	13
Shanghai 上海市	Shanghai 上海市	8.66%	93
Suzhou 蘇州市	Jiangsu 江蘇省	7.80%	35
Taizhou 泰州市	Jiangsu 江蘇省	7.10%	20
Shenzhen 深圳市	Guangdong 廣東省	4.25%	10
Zhengzhou 鄭州市	Henan 河南省	4.07%	11
Cangzhou 滄州市	Hebei 河北省	3.52%	6
Changzhou 常州市	Jiangsu 江蘇省	3.44%	22
Wuxi 無錫市	Jiangsu 江蘇省	2.77%	32
Jiangmen 江門市	Guangdong 廣東省	2.76%	7

10 Major Wholesalers 10 家主要批發商	City 城市	Province 省	Telephone / Fax 電話 / 傳真
Chengdu Great Wall Electric Appliance Company 成都長城電器公司	Chengdu 成都市	Sichuan 四川省	(028)6662132 (028)6671975
Shandou Ceramics (Group) Company 汕頭陶瓷(集團)公司	Shantou 汕頭市	Guangdong 廣東省	(0754)8255441 (0754)8255442
Guangdong Puning Local Products Import & Export Company 廣東省普寧土產進出口公司	Jieyang 揭陽市	Guangdong 廣東省	(0663)2226744
Yixing Sundry Goods General Co. 宜興市土產雜品總公司	Wuxi 無錫市	Jiangsu 江蘇省	(0510)7903683 (0510)7903683
Sujiang Qu Zhe Jiang Dongda Group Company 椒江區浙江東大集團公司	Taizhou 臺州市	Zhejiang 浙江省	(0576)8881477 (0576)8881672
Jiangsu New Suzhou Co. Ltd. Suzhou Daily Goods General Co. 江蘇新蘇州股份有限公司蘇州日用雜品總公司	Suzhou 蘇州市	Jiangsu 江蘇省	(0512)7276630 (0512)7275964
Shandong Daily Use General Merchandise Import & Export Company 山東省日用百貨進出口公司	Qingdao 青島市	Shandong 山東省	(0532)5849141 (0532)5849207
Guangdong Yangjiang Light Industry Products Import & Export (Group) Company 廣東陽江輕工業品進出口(集團)公司	Yangjiang 陽江市	Guangdong 廣東省	(0662)3222497 (0662)3222976
Hebei Artts & Crtfts Import & Export Corp. 河北工藝品進出口公司	Shijiazhuang 石家莊市	Hebei 河北省	(0311)7756124 (0311)7755347
Shandong Handicrafts Import & Export Products Group Linyi Craft Co. Ltd. 山東工藝品進出品集團臨沂工藝有限公司	Linyi 臨沂市	Shandong 山東省	(0539)8310001 (0539)8315396

*Also include sales by firms outside this industry.包括本行業以外廠家的銷售。"o" stands for "others". "o" 代表 "其他產品"。

4392: Other Consumer Goods 生活用其他產品製造業

The industry accounts for 0.158% of the total revenue of China's industrial sector in 1996. The revenue growth rate of the industry is 25.3% from 1995, as compared to the growth rate of China's industrial sector, 9.51%. The rate of return on asset is 2.13%. 72.39% of all firms in the industry made a profit while 20.50% had negative returns. The top province in terms of the industry's revenue is Guangdong, accounting for 18.75% of the total revenue.
本行業在1996年佔全行業總產值0.158%，行業年增長率為25.3%（全國工業年增長率9.51%）。行業的資產回報率2.13%，72.39%的企業盈利，20.50%的企業虧損。銷售收入最高的省份為廣東省，佔本行業的18.75%。

	Total number of firms 企業總數	Total number of employees 職工總數	Total revenue (mil. RMB) 總銷售收入（百萬元）	Total profit (mil. RMB) 總利潤（百萬元）	Return on assets 資產利潤率 (%)	Return on equity 權益利潤率 (%)	Labour productivity ('000 RMB / worker) 勞動生產率（千元/人）	Debts / assets 資產負債率 (%)	Total assets (mil. RMB) 總資產（百萬元）
Industry Overall 行業總體	2,930	137,025	9,156	199	2.13	5.41	66.82	60.66	9,367

	Number of firms 企業個數	Average number of employees 平均職工人數	Average revenue ('000 RMB) 平均銷售收入（千元）	Average profit ('000 RMB) 平均利潤（千元）	Return on assets 資產利潤率 (%)	Return on equity 權益利潤率 (%)	Labour productivity ('000 RMB / worker) 勞動生產率（千元/人）	Average debts / assets 平均資產負債率(%)	Average Total assets ('000 RMB) 平均總資產（千元）
By ownership 產業所有權									
State-owned 國有	335	72	3,764	-27	-0.54	-1.44	51.96	62.84	5,021
Collectively-owned 集體	2,206	36	1,879	125	8.50	25.14	52.57	66.20	1,466
Privately-owned 私有	11	25	4,740	3,041	341.50	938.00	193.12	63.59	891
Domestic JVs 聯營	25	53	4,219	-22	-0.48	-1.26	79.24	62.22	4,610
Joint stock 股份制	15	167	9,405	2,349	23.07	63.43	56.23	63.62	10,180
Foreign-funded 外資	115	115	12,919	161	1.32	3.38	112.43	60.88	12,130
Overseas Chinese-funded 港澳台資	221	82	8,881	-695	-5.53	-11.67	108.01	52.57	12,557
By size 規模									
Large 大型	3	303	46,325	-5,766	-10.41	-19.50	153.05	46.60	55,380
Medium 中型	11	590	40,284	878	1.47	4.58	68.30	67.96	59,831
Small 小型	2,872	45	2,985	72	2.42	6.10	66.53	60.37	2,974
By regional distribution 地區分布									
Central-North 華北	347	58	3,211	154	4.73	13.24	55.72	64.28	3,254
Beijing 北京	113	40	1,789	-29	-0.94	-2.40	44.63	60.80	3,070
Tianjin 天津	66	86	3,128	114	2.50	7.13	36.41	64.92	4,576
Hebei 河北	91	58	5,986	489	14.99	35.86	102.89	58.21	3,265
Shanxi 山西	50	80	3,068	86	2.57	10.50	38.36	75.55	3,366
Inner Mongolia 內蒙	27	19	279	9	1.64	-6.05	14.94	127.06	543
Northeast 東北	247	50	2,992	22	0.60	2.19	60.19	72.54	3,707
Liaoning 遼寧	83	69	4,819	-22	-0.33	-1.21	70.14	73.00	6,855
Jilin 吉林	48	40	3,193	5	0.19	0.72	80.53	73.25	2,809
Heilongjiang 黑龍江	116	40	1,603	61	3.35	11.50	39.78	70.85	1,826
Central East 華東	1,119	52	3,770	66	1.68	3.95	72.34	57.36	3,907
Shanghai 上海	126	61	5,027	106	1.88	4.14	82.75	54.67	5,643
Jiangsu 江蘇	218	75	4,836	-16	-0.36	-1.24	64.23	70.76	4,387
Zhejiang 浙江	224	52	4,156	131	3.23	6.24	79.70	48.30	4,053
Anhui 安徽	192	27	2,338	131	16.90	35.57	86.92	52.49	775
Fujian 福建	144	50	3,558	25	0.52	1.21	71.15	56.92	4,783
Jiangxi 江西	117	24	504	6	1.09	2.18	20.97	49.86	555
Shandong 山東	98	75	5,913	51	0.56	1.28	78.44	56.05	9,129
Central-South 中南	709	47	3,591	60	1.91	4.96	76.09	61.37	3,144
Henan 河南	110	34	1,715	27	1.34	2.83	50.49	52.55	1,991
Hubei 湖北	123	38	2,510	59	4.99	15.72	65.77	68.26	1,178
Hunan 湖南	203	30	1,240	64	7.84	18.78	41.67	58.27	818
Guangdong 廣東	215	81	7,983	115	1.52	4.05	98.67	62.36	7,514
Guangxi 廣西	49	25	1,540	-108	-8.08	-22.56	61.56	64.18	1,333
Hainan 海南	9	41	547	18	0.86	1.54	13.37	43.88	2,061
Southwest 西南	286	27	1,165	95	8.41	19.65	43.33	57.20	1,132
Chongqing 重慶	53	30	542	-186	-18.58	-46.06	18.22	59.65	1,003
Sichuan 四川	167	29	1,611	231	18.51	41.09	56.00	54.95	1,249
Guizhou 貴州	44	17	335	-14	-2.37	-7.19	19.92	67.06	576
Yunnan 雲南	22	27	963	-31	-1.85	-4.58	35.14	59.62	1,673
Tibet 西藏									
Northwest 西北	222	24	923	-13	-0.73	-1.75	38.76	58.21	1,790
Shaanxi 陝西	109	27	1,053	-38	-1.48	-3.07	38.39	51.79	2,586
Gansu 甘肅	66	21	866	15	1.34	8.04	40.47	83.30	1,132
Qinghai 青海	27	16	846	36	6.49	17.78	52.53	63.49	548
Ningxia 寧夏	8	27	675	-29	-2.61	-5.85	25.12	55.39	1,101
Xinjiang 新疆	12	20	399	-38	-2.66	-5.47	20.30	51.36	1,441

4392: Other Consumer Goods 生活用其他產品製造業

Year 年份	Number of firms 企業個數	Rate of change 每年變化 (%)	Number of employees 職工人數（人）	Rate of change 每年變化 (%)	Total revenue (mil. RMB) 總銷售收入（百萬元）	Rate of change 每年變化 (%)	Total profit (mil. RMB) 總利潤（百萬元）	Rate of change 每年變化 (%)
1993	3,429		201,043		7,426		290	
1994	3,481	1.52%	186,026	-7.47%	7,179	-3.31%	127	-56.06%
1995	3,075	-11.66%	149,653	-19.55%	7,308	1.78%	34	-73.30%
1996	2,930	-4.72%	137,025	-8.44%	9,156	25.29%	199	485.62%

3 Major products* 3 種主要產品 *	Output 產量	Sales volume 銷售量	Unit 單位
a) Fastener Zip 拉鏈	132,725	122,107	10,000 metre 萬米
b) Drinking Water Treater 飲用水處理器	529,952	3,216,807	set 台

Top 10 firms by revenue (year founded) 收入排名前 10 家企業 (創辦年份)	City 城市	Province 省	Telephone / fax 電話 / 傳真	Number of employees 職工人數	Ownership 產業所有權	Revenue ('000 RMB) 銷售收入（千元）	Profit ('000 RMB) (rank) 利潤（千元）(排名)	Total assets ('000 RMB) 總資產（千元）	Major products 主要產品
Shenyang Chemical Fertilizer General Factory 瀋陽市化肥總廠(1992)	Shenyang 瀋陽市	Liaoning 遼寧省	(024)86806372	30	State-owned 國有	250,645	594(108)	364,809	o
Luannan San Chun Reclaimed Cotton General Company 灤南縣三春再生棉總公司(1995)	Tangshan 唐山市	Hebei 河北省	(0315)4478025	1,387	Collectively-owned 集體	195,390	13404(4)	24,000	o
Shenzhen New Century Drinking Water Science & Technology Co. Ltd. 深圳新世紀飲水科技有限公司(1992)	Shenzhen 深圳市	Guangdong 廣東省	(0755)3300582 (0755)3300584	83	State-owned 國有	170,945	23279(2)	80,496	b
Shanghai Zheng Guang He Drinking Water Co. Ltd. 上海正廣和飲用水有限公司(1995)	Shanghai 上海市	Shanghai 上海市	(021)65121660 (021)65350269	503	Domestic JVs 聯營	155,752	7787(8)	108,193	o
Chengdu Kimberly-clark Cbg Hygiene Products Co. Ltd. 成都金佰利舒而美衛生用品有限公司(1994)	Chengdu 成都市	Sichuan 四川省	(028)5184257	790	Foreign-funded 外資	131,430	28941(1)	60,630	o
Huizhou Zipper Manufacturing Co. Ltd. 惠州市拉鏈製造有限公司(1990)	Huizhou 惠州市	Guangdong 廣東省	(0751)2261680 (0751)2261780	603	Overseas Chinese-funded 港澳台資	126,930	5130(12)	20,130	a
Shanghai Ji Shun Lie Fallow Products Co. Ltd. 上海基舜休閒製品有限公司(1995)	Shanghai 上海市	Shanghai 上海市	(021)59753612	622	Foreign-funded 外資	125,697	524(120)	77,270	o
Zhejiang Hua Xin Industry Group Co. 浙江華鑫集團公司(1980)	Quzhou 衢州市	Zhejiang 浙江省	(0570)3023956	793	Collectively-owned 集體	120,174	854(74)	109,484	a
Meihekou Electro-aluminium Factory 梅河口市電化鋁廠(1983)	Tonghua 通化市	Jilin 吉林省	(0435)3222474 (0435)3215744	499	State-owned 國有	113,287	1510(45)	70,712	o
Jiangsu You Ai Group Co. Ltd. 江蘇友愛集團股份有限公司(1995)	Nantong 南通市	Jiangsu 江蘇省	(0513)2665219	460	Collectively-owned 集體	97,850	200(244)	84,376	o

Top 10 Cities by Production Output 產出排名前 10 位城市	Province 省	Market share 市場份額	Number of firms 企業個數
Shanghai 上海市	Shanghai 上海市	7.62%	144
Suzhou 蘇州市	Jiangsu 江蘇省	6.09%	40
Shantou 汕頭市	Guangdong 廣東省	4.96%	34
Beijing 北京市	Beijing 北京市	4.16%	93
Shenzhen 深圳市	Guangdong 廣東省	3.83%	26
Taizhou 臺州市	Zhejiang 浙江省	3.34%	24
Foshan 佛山市	Guangdong 廣東省	3.26%	34
Wenzhou 溫州市	Zhejiang 浙江省	2.97%	69
Chengdu 成都市	Sichuan 四川省	2.68%	41
Zhaoqing 肇慶市	Guangdong 廣東省	2.30%	26

10 Major Wholesalers 10 家主要批發商	City 城市	Province 省	Telephone / Fax 電話 / 傳真
Chengdu Great Wall Electric Appliance Company 成都長城電器公司	Chengdu 成都市	Sichuan 四川省	(028)6662132 (028)6671975
Shandou Ceramics (Group) Company 汕頭陶瓷(集團)公司	Shantou 汕頭市	Guangdong 廣東省	(0754)8255441 (0754)8255442
Guangdong Puning Local Products Import & Export Company 廣東省普寧土產進出口公司	Jieyang 揭陽市	Guangdong 廣東省	(0663)2226744
Yixing Sundry Goods General Co. 宜興市土產雜品總公司	Wuxi 無錫市	Jiangsu 江蘇省	(0510)7903683 (0510)7903683
Sujiang Qu Zhe Jiang Dongda Group Company 椒江區浙江東大集團公司	Taizhou 臺州市	Zhejiang 浙江省	(0576)8881477 (0576)8881672
Jiangsu New Suzhou Co. Ltd. Suzhou Daily Goods General Co. 江蘇新蘇州股份有限公司蘇州日用雜品總公司	Suzhou 蘇州市	Jiangsu 江蘇省	(0512)7276630 (0512)7275964
Shandong Daily Use General Merchandise Import & Export Company 山東省日用百貨進出口公司	Qingdao 青島市	Shandong 山東省	(0532)5849141 (0532)5849207
Guangdong Yangjiang Light Industry Products Import & Export (Group) Company 廣東陽江輕工業品進出口(集團)公司	Yangjiang 陽江市	Guangdong 廣東省	(0662)3222497 (0662)3222976
Hebei Artts & Crtfts Import & Export Corp. 河北工藝品進出口公司	Shijiazhuang 石家莊市	Hebei 河北省	(0311)7756124 (0311)7755347
Shandong Handicrafts Import & Export Products Group Linyi Craft Co. Ltd. 山東工藝品進出品集團臨沂工藝有限公司	Linyi 臨沂市	Shandong 山東省	(0539)8310001 (0539)8315396

*Also include sales by firms outside this industry.包括本行業以外廠家的銷售。“o” stands for “others”.“o”代表“其他產品”。

4411: Thermal Power Generation 火力發電業

The industry accounts for 2.751% of the total revenue of China's industrial sector in 1996. The revenue growth rate of the industry is 12.6% from 1995, as compared to the growth rate of China's industrial sector, 9.51%. The rate of return on asset is 1.93%. 64.70% of all firms in the industry made a profit while 24.91% had negative returns. The top province in terms of the industry's revenue is Guangdong, accounting for 13.64% of the total revenue.
本行業在1996年佔全行業總產值2.751%，行業年增長率為12.6%（全國工業年增長率9.51%）。行業的資產回報率1.93%，64.70%的企業盈利，24.91%的企業虧損。銷售收入最高的省份為廣東省，佔本行業的13.64%。

	Total number of firms 企業總數	Total number of employees 職工總數	Total revenue (mil. RMB) 總銷售收入（百萬元）	Total profit (mil. RMB) 總利潤（百萬元）	Return on assets 資產利潤率 (%)	Return on equity 權益利潤率 (%)	Labour productivity ('000 RMB / worker) 勞動生產率（千元/人）	Debts / assets 資產負債率 (%)	Total assets (mil. RMB) 總資產（百萬元）
Industry Overall 行業總體	1,181	710,733	159,501	6,972	1.93	5.08	224.42	61.99	360,501

	Number of firms 企業個數	Average number of employees 平均職工人數	Average revenue ('000 RMB) 平均銷售收入（千元）	Average profit ('000 RMB) 平均利潤（千元）	Return on assets 資產利潤率 (%)	Return on equity 權益利潤率 (%)	Labour productivity ('000 RMB / worker) 勞動生產率（千元/人）	Average debts / assets 平均資產負債率(%)	Average Total assets ('000 RMB) 平均總資產（千元）
By ownership 產業所有權									
State-owned 國有	708	811	158,968	4,209	1.37	3.84	196.00	64.23	306,390
Collectively-owned 集體	233	237	27,694	-246	-0.48	-4.39	116.78	89.01	50,988
Privately-owned 私有									
Domestic JVs 聯營	17	262	72,501	8,403	5.17	20.75	276.97	75.06	162,407
Joint stock 股份制	58	517	118,630	16,786	5.06	9.57	229.41	47.11	331,627
Foreign-funded 外資	62	361	246,314	25,180	3.11	4.81	681.85	35.37	809,709
Overseas Chinese-funded 港澳台資	98	257	174,565	13,296	2.31	10.78	678.49	78.59	576,213
By size 規模									
Large 大型	167	1,720	629,336	34,732	2.63	6.37	365.95	58.75	1,321,071
Medium 中型	210	911	145,401	5,932	1.94	4.97	159.59	60.90	305,442
Small 小型	725	298	34,360	-109	-0.11	-0.40	115.23	73.42	102,809
By regional distribution 地區分布									
Central-North 華北	177	751	206,817	14,427	3.26	8.08	275.32	59.93	442,770
Beijing 北京	14	189	363,258	20,269	1.52	4.07	1924.18	62.57	1,330,105
Tianjin 天津	9	993	208,172	5,512	1.08	2.01	209.73	50.31	510,398
Hebei 河北	51	834	303,859	23,456	4.48	10.94	364.19	59.06	523,875
Shanxi 山西	63	697	124,489	14,032	6.38	20.85	178.63	69.42	220,061
Inner Mongolia 內蒙	40	873	157,694	3,500	0.96	2.01	180.59	52.18	364,344
Northeast 東北	110	910	192,714	-4,453	-1.08	-2.77	211.66	60.95	411,149
Liaoning 遼寧	42	875	220,862	2,476	0.44	0.96	252.41	53.77	558,098
Jilin 吉林	22	864	188,964	-15,169	-3.49	-11.39	218.66	69.31	434,141
Heilongjiang 黑龍江	46	965	168,808	-5,655	-2.13	-6.68	174.92	68.18	265,981
Central East 華東	337	558	149,206	9,623	3.43	9.14	267.24	62.53	280,931
Shanghai 上海	6	1,052	581,428	70,493	8.43	14.03	552.51	39.90	836,038
Jiangsu 江蘇	80	646	248,255	13,082	3.31	7.72	384.40	57.14	395,479
Zhejiang 浙江	84	326	106,067	488	0.22	0.80	324.99	72.19	220,193
Anhui 安徽	17	1,035	247,091	8,704	2.11	4.16	238.83	49.37	413,080
Fujian 福建	27	322	133,316	20,225	6.10	12.46	413.69	51.04	331,586
Jiangxi 江西	30	387	79,625	-855	-0.45	-1.77	205.96	74.45	188,583
Shandong 山東	93	698	84,249	11,443	5.95	24.35	120.78	75.57	192,369
Central-South 中南	379	433	106,747	4,173	1.40	3.69	246.63	62.12	298,586
Henan 河南	93	810	99,871	6,969	2.53	7.20	123.33	64.80	275,005
Hubei 湖北	41	458	91,946	-233	-0.13	-0.27	200.61	50.98	174,928
Hunan 湖南	35	614	97,552	2,821	1.24	3.04	158.76	59.27	227,965
Guangdong 廣東	185	212	117,626	4,566	1.32	3.48	555.56	62.15	346,578
Guangxi 廣西	19	477	78,334	2,623	1.58	3.95	164.09	60.04	166,121
Hainan 海南	6	33	122,622	-8,373	-0.97	-3.21	3772.97	69.72	860,777
Southwest 西南	84	727	61,923	-2,078	-1.29	-2.79	85.22	53.76	160,869
Chongqing 重慶	12	777	74,536	-3,761	-1.48	-2.38	95.89	37.81	253,840
Sichuan 四川	43	661	43,688	-4,832	-4.10	-10.67	66.07	61.60	117,931
Guizhou 貴州	16	708	96,947	1,128	0.50	1.12	136.91	55.60	226,156
Yunnan 雲南	11	1,061	78,625	5,443	3.56	8.12	74.09	56.11	152,732
Tibet 西藏	2	127	2,800	95	0.28	0.51	22.13	44.39	33,580
Northwest 西北	94	685	61,217	2,742	1.66	7.59	89.37	78.16	165,465
Shaanxi 陝西	33	751	96,513	8,360	3.24	19.81	128.43	83.66	258,298
Gansu 甘肅	16	676	9,910	183	5.01	19.12	14.67	73.82	3,645
Qinghai 青海	7	472	3,233	-447	-2.77	-7.72	6.85	64.11	16,150
Ningxia 寧夏	6	1,312	221,422	3,957	0.75	3.29	168.83	77.13	526,183
Xinjiang 新疆	32	550	33,118	-1,301	-1.12	-3.39	60.17	66.85	115,669

4411: Thermal Power Generation 火力發電業

Year 年份	Number of firms 企業個數	Rate of change 每年變化 (%)	Number of employees 職工人數 (人)	Rate of change 每年變化 (%)	Total revenue (mil. RMB) 總銷售收入 (百萬元)	Rate of change 每年變化 (%)	Total profit (mil. RMB) 總利潤 (百萬元)	Rate of change 每年變化 (%)
1993	947		656,765		69,164		2,467	
1994	987	4.22%	656,239	-0.08%	106,724	54.31%	5,556	125.17%
1995	1,183	19.86%	767,459	16.95%	141,671	32.74%	6,455	16.18%
1996	1,181	-0.17%	710,733	-7.39%	159,501	12.59%	6,972	8.01%

3 Major products* 3種主要產品*	Output 產量	Sales volume 銷售量	Unit 單位
a) Thermal Power 火電	74,231,551	67,550,711	10,000 kwh 萬千瓦小時
b) Heat Supply 供熱	7,808,781	7,184,078	10,000 million kj 萬百萬千焦

Top 10 firms by revenue (year founded) 收入排名前10家企業 (創辦年份)	City 城市	Province 省	Telephone / fax 電話 / 傳真	Number of employees 職工人數	Ownership 產業所有權	Revenue ('000 RMB) 銷售收入 (千元)	Profit ('000 RMB) (rank) 利潤(千元) (排名)	Total assets ('000 RMB) 總資產 (千元)	Major products 主要產品
Harbin Pyroelectricity Factory 哈爾濱熱電廠(1959)	Harbin 哈爾濱市	Heilongjiang 黑龍江省	(0451)2681197 (0451)2681279	855	State-owned 國有	6,653,683	-200693(854)	449,512	a,b
Head-office of Tangshan Power Plant North China Power Co. Group 中國華北電力集團公司唐山發電總廠(1942)	Tangshan 唐山市	Hebei 河北省	(0315)2822110 (0315)2819493	4,951	State-owned 國有	3,263,201	174629(17)	3,623,755	a,b
Jian Bi Power Plant 諫壁發電廠(1965)	Zhenjiang 鎮江市	Jiangsu 江蘇省	(0511)3361090	4,019	State-owned 國有	3,011,537	81513(39)	1,112,508	a,b
Xuzhou Electric Power Generating Factory 徐州發電廠(1977)	Xuzhou 徐州市	Jiangsu 江蘇省	(0516)7767260 (0516)7182260	4,006	State-owned 國有	2,417,828	65443(45)	1,098,868	a
Changshu Power Plant 常熟發電廠(1993)	Suzhou 蘇州市	Jiangsu 江蘇省	(0512)2657023 (0512)2657205	1,899	State-owned 國有	2,303,181	62340(49)	3,043,420	a
Hua Neng International Power Development Corp., Shanghai Branch 華能國際電力開發公司上海分公司(1986)	Shanghai 上海市	Shanghai 上海市	(021)56151422 (021)56151422	558	Foreign-funded 外資	2,266,855	327502(5)	3,638,060	a
Shandong Hua Neng Power Co. Ltd. Dezhou Electric Power Plant 山東華能發電股份有限公司德州電廠(1991)	Dezhou 德州市	Shandong 山東省	(0534)2421956 (0534)2421956	2,055	Foreign-funded 外資	2,065,891	884935(1)	2,992,106	a
Hua Bei Electric Power Group Company Zhangjiakou Electric Power Generating General Factory 華北電力集團公司張家口發電總廠(1988)	Zhangjiakou 張家口市	Hebei 河北省	(0313)2016354 (0313)2016354	2,125	State-owned 國有	1,778,640	95180(33)	3,673,473	a
Huangpu Power Plant 黃埔發電廠(1978)	Guangzhou 廣州市	Guangdong 廣東省	(020)82210522 (020)82210522	2,338	State-owned 國有	1,774,344	129160(25)	1,592,512	a
Shenzhen Ma Wan Electric Power Co. Ltd. 深圳媽灣電力有限公司(1989)	Shenzhen 深圳市	Guangdong 廣東省	(0755)6681188 (0755)6674078	856	Overseas Chinese-funded 港澳台資	1,549,116	305432(7)	5,284,050	a

Top 10 Cities by Production Output 產出排名前10位城市	Province 省	Market share 市場份額	Number of firms 企業個數
Foshan 佛山市	Guangdong 廣東省	10.86%	21
Guangzhou 廣州市	Guangdong 廣東省	3.62%	28
Dongguan 東莞市	Guangdong 廣東省	3.50%	12
Beijing 北京市	Beijing 北京市	3.04%	15
Ningbo 寧波市	Zhejiang 浙江省	2.52%	14
Ji'nan 濟南市	Shandong 山東省	2.40%	11
Tangshan 唐山市	Hebei 河北省	2.36%	7
Shanghai 上海市	Shanghai 上海市	2.31%	14
Suzhou 蘇州市	Jiangsu 江蘇省	1.95%	31
Shenzhen 深圳市	Guangdong 廣東省	1.81%	12

10 Major Wholesalers 10家主要批發商	City 城市	Province 省	Telephone / Fax 電話 / 傳真

*Also include sales by firms outside this industry.包括本行業以外廠家的銷售。"o" stands for "others". "o"代表"其他產品"。

4412: Hydro Power Generation 水力發電業

The industry accounts for 0.462% of the total revenue of China's industrial sector in 1996. The revenue growth rate of the industry is 26.9% from 1995, as compared to the growth rate of China's industrial sector, 9.51%. The rate of return on asset is 3.54%. 79.36% of all firms in the industry made a profit while 15.16% had negative returns. The top province in terms of the industry's revenue is Hubei, accounting for 14.81% of the total revenue.

本行業在1996年佔全行業總產值0.462%，行業年增長率為26.9%（全國工業年增長率9.51%）。行業的資產回報率3.54%，79.36%的企業盈利，15.16%的企業虧損。銷售收入最高的省份為湖北省，佔本行業的14.81%。

	Total number of firms 企業總數	Total number of employees 職工總數	Total revenue (mil. RMB) 總銷售收入（百萬元）	Total profit (mil. RMB) 總利潤（百萬元）	Return on assets 資產利潤率 (%)	Return on equity 權益利潤率 (%)	Labour productivity ('000 RMB / worker) 勞動生產率（千元/人）	Debts / assets 資產負債率 (%)	Total assets (mil. RMB) 總資產（百萬元）
Industry Overall 行業總體	8,161	433,168	26,782	4,363	3.54	7.95	61.83	55.46	123,216

	Number of firms 企業個數	Average number of employees 平均職工人數	Average revenue ('000 RMB) 平均銷售收入（千元）	Average profit ('000 RMB) 平均利潤（千元）	Return on assets 資產利潤率 (%)	Return on equity 權益利潤率 (%)	Labour productivity ('000 RMB / worker) 勞動生產率（千元/人）	Average debts / assets 平均資產負債率(%)	Average Total assets ('000 RMB) 平均總資產（千元）
By ownership 產業所有權									
State-owned 國有	2,012	144	9,640	1,676	3.38	7.19	66.84	53.04	49,653
Collectively-owned 集體	5,957	21	774	77	4.19	9.60	37.34	56.34	1,839
Privately-owned 私有	8	19	1,266	-39	-1.92	-2.92	65.75	34.25	2,049
Domestic JVs 聯營	73	48	3,224	803	5.66	9.73	67.81	41.80	14,172
Joint stock 股份制	58	258	41,051	7,897	4.23	19.56	159.34	78.38	186,745
Foreign-funded 外資	24	33	4,190	425	3.62	6.10	125.23	40.63	11,737
Overseas Chinese-funded 港澳台資	25	19	1,144	174	4.02	9.83	59.94	59.10	4,338
By size 規模									
Large 大型	34	989	263,785	48,043	2.76	7.65	266.64	63.95	1,741,823
Medium 中型	55	601	55,058	15,130	6.19	9.14	91.67	32.27	244,324
Small 小型	7,944	46	1,861	239	3.75	7.77	40.81	51.68	6,364
By regional distribution 地區分布									
Central-North 華北	127	39	1,396	69	1.38	1.98	35.93	30.66	5,031
Beijing 北京	18	14	325	-27	-1.72	-2.71	23.31	36.53	1,548
Tianjin 天津	1	51	5,100	1,840	7.81	8.44	100.00	7.42	23,570
Hebei 河北	49	40	2,248	184	4.24	6.71	56.70	36.91	4,355
Shanxi 山西	54	44	862	-93	-1.59	-2.36	19.51	32.65	5,832
Inner Mongolia 內蒙	5	61	1,934	678	5.73	5.97	31.81	4.09	11,840
Northeast 東北	150	104	15,969	3,160	7.60	9.80	153.67	22.40	41,553
Liaoning 遼寧	45	104	23,447	878	2.35	3.09	226.08	24.06	37,432
Jilin 吉林	70	121	17,237	6,332	11.42	13.98	142.67	18.25	55,426
Heilongjiang 黑龍江	35	70	3,819	-250	-1.31	-2.26	54.27	42.23	19,105
Central East 華東	2,248	42	2,131	300	2.95	6.83	51.33	56.87	10,202
Shanghai 上海									
Jiangsu 江蘇	1	69	2,820	40	0.52	0.56	40.87	7.67	7,690
Zhejiang 浙江	548	30	927	11	0.14	0.20	31.39	27.39	7,534
Anhui 安徽	160	25	997	-61	-1.26	-1.83	39.35	31.47	4,815
Fujian 福建	805	49	3,800	599	3.49	10.97	76.98	68.23	17,180
Jiangxi 江西	732	45	1,443	269	4.69	10.01	31.86	53.16	5,730
Shandong 山東	2	48	1,790	145	9.01	32.22	37.68	72.05	1,610
Central-South 中南	3,218	49	3,272	642	4.19	8.56	67.15	51.07	15,318
Henan 河南	86	82	3,781	120	0.47	1.01	46.20	53.54	25,735
Hubei 湖北	461	66	8,606	2,508	6.34	13.71	129.92	53.74	39,559
Hunan 湖南	891	43	1,785	146	1.80	3.55	41.80	49.36	8,129
Guangdong 廣東	1,323	41	2,211	278	3.00	6.19	54.12	51.54	9,261
Guangxi 廣西	386	57	3,795	1,003	5.09	10.93	66.62	53.48	19,724
Hainan 海南	71	72	3,609	199	0.81	0.94	49.80	12.99	24,399
Southwest 西南	1,907	68	3,997	572	2.93	9.32	58.51	68.57	19,518
Chongqing 重慶	407	49	1,820	151	2.34	6.69	37.30	64.99	6,435
Sichuan 四川	793	70	4,242	531	2.55	8.20	60.34	68.93	20,852
Guizhou 貴州	380	61	2,452	331	2.04	6.82	39.95	70.12	16,259
Yunnan 雲南	271	106	9,325	1,777	4.26	14.80	87.82	71.23	41,729
Tibet 西藏	56	42	1,069	10	0.09	0.10	25.52	6.55	10,419
Northwest 西北	511	63	2,479	96	0.71	1.26	39.31	43.51	13,498
Shaanxi 陝西	283	23	1,620	175	1.38	2.20	71.73	37.40	12,738
Gansu 甘肅	85	93	1,093	40	0.75	0.97	11.70	23.16	5,379
Qinghai 青海	52	66	615	7	0.20	0.33	9.29	37.42	3,490
Ningxia 寧夏	4	350	39,085	543	0.71	0.75	111.67	5.44	76,330
Xinjiang 新疆	87	150	6,058	-76	-0.28	-0.74	40.38	62.27	26,995

4412: Hydro Power Generation 水力發電業

Year 年份	Number of firms 企業個數	Rate of change 每年變化 (%)	Number of employees 職工人數 (人)	Rate of change 每年變化 (%)	Total revenue (mil. RMB) 總銷售收入 (百萬元)	Rate of change 每年變化 (%)	Total profit (mil. RMB) 總利潤 (百萬元)	Rate of change 每年變化 (%)
1993	7,114		288,528		16,583		4,691	
1994	7,457	4.82%	368,720	27.79%	15,339	-7.51%	1,811	-61.40%
1995	8,508	14.09%	437,779	18.73%	21,101	37.57%	2,185	20.65%
1996	8,161	-4.08%	433,168	-1.05%	26,782	26.92%	4,363	99.68%

3 Major products* 3 種主要產品 *	Output 產量	Sales volume 銷售量	Unit 單位
a) Hydro Power 水電	17,532,341	17,357,017	10,000 kwh 萬千瓦小時

Top 10 firms by revenue (year founded) 收入排名前 10 家企業 (創辦年份)	City 城市	Province 省	Telephone / fax 電話 / 傳真	Number of employees 職工人數	Ownership 產業所有權	Revenue ('000 RMB) 銷售收入 (千元)	Profit ('000 RMB) (rank) 利潤 (千元) (排名)	Total assets ('000 RMB) 總資產 (千元)	Major products 主要產品
Ministry of Water Resources Dan Jiangkou Water Conservancy Hub Management Bureau 水利部丹江口水利樞紐管理局(1968)	Shiyan 十堰市	Hubei 湖北省	(0719)375229 (0719)375671	2,029	State-owned 國有	914,648	159556(7)	3,053,514	a
Yunnan Man Wan Power Plant 雲南省漫灣發電廠(1993)	Lincang 臨滄縣	Yunnan 雲南省	(0883)3814016 (0883)8212989	507	State-owned 國有	793,270	164316(6)	3,358,402	a
Fujian Shui Kou Hydroelectric Power Plant 福建水口水力發電廠(1992)	Fuzhou 福州市	Fujian 福建省	(0591)2335446 (0591)2335446	613	State-owned 國有	575,430	213852(2)	5,867,238	a
Taiping Wan Electric Power Generating Factory 太平灣發電廠(1985)	Dandong 丹東市	Liaoning 遼寧省	(0415)2102222	585	State-owned 國有	496,309	17567(36)	745,360	a
Gong Zui Generate Electricity General Factory 龔嘴水力發電總廠(1971)	Leshan 樂山市	Sichuan 四川省	(0833)3442030 (0833)3443976	1,577	State-owned 國有	452,471	169140(4)	2,797,296	a
Baishan Power Plant 白山發電廠(1983)	Jilin 吉林市	Jilin 吉林省	(0432)6221047 (0432)6221144	817	State-owned 國有	400,630	224093(1)	1,911,749	a
Sichuan Hua Neng Taiping Yi Water & Electricity Co. Ltd. 四川華能太平驛水電有限責任公司	Wenchuan 汶川縣	Sichuan 四川省	(08489)443000 (08489)443000	241	State-owned 國有	365,936	35273(22)	1,721,466	a
Guangxi Zhuangzu Autonomous Region Yan Tan Hydroelectric Power Plant 廣西岩灘水力發電廠(1995)	Hechi 河池市	Guangxi 廣西	(0778)5692056 (0778)5692051	279	State-owned 國有	323,906	138895(8)	3,019,652	a
Ankang Hydraulic Power Generation Factory 安康水力發電廠(1990)	Ankang 安康市	Shaanxi 陝西省	(0915)3213021	677	State-owned 國有	305,178	14114(44)	2,912,892	o
Huanren Electric Power Generating Factory 桓仁發電廠(1968)	Benxi 本溪市	Liaoning 遼寧省	(0414)8864209 (0414)8864321	710	State-owned 國有	304,407	10774(57)	281,841	o

Top 10 Cities by Production Output 產出排名前 10 位城市	Province 省	Market share 市場份額	Number of firms 企業個數
Ankang 安康市	Shaanxi 陝西省	28.99%	103
Yichang 宜昌市	Hubei 湖北省	6.99%	86
Fuzhou 福州市	Fujian 福建省	4.19%	71
Leshan 樂山市	Sichuan 四川省	2.44%	91
Hechi 河池市	Guangxi 廣西	2.08%	51
Jilin 吉林市	Jilin 吉林省	1.92%	6
Qujing 曲靖市	Yunnan 雲南省	1.82%	25
Lincang 臨滄縣	Yunnan 雲南省	1.74%	32
Xingyi 興義市	Guizhou 貴州省	1.58%	17
Chongqing 重慶市	Chongqing 重慶市	1.45%	211

10 Major Wholesalers 10 家主要批發商	City 城市	Province 省	Telephone / Fax 電話 / 傳真

*Also include sales by firms outside this industry.包括本行業以外廠家的銷售。"o" stands for "others". "o" 代表 "其他產品" 。

4419: Other Electricity Generation 其他電業

The industry accounts for 0.005% of the total revenue of China's industrial sector in 1996. The revenue growth rate of the industry is -68.5% from 1995, as compared to the growth rate of China's industrial sector, 9.51%. The rate of return on asset is -22.97%. 60.54% of all firms in the industry made a profit while 17.24% had negative returns. The top province in terms of the industry's revenue is Jiangsu, accounting for 28.13% of the total revenue.
本行業在1996年佔全行業總產值0.005%，行業年增長率為-68.5%（全國工業年增長率9.51%）。行業的資產回報率-22.97%，60.54%的企業盈利，17.24%的企業虧損。銷售收入最高的省份為江蘇省，佔本行業的28.13%。

	Total number of firms 企業總數	Total number of employees 職工總數	Total revenue (mil. RMB) 總銷售收入（百萬元）	Total profit (mil. RMB) 總利潤（百萬元）	Return on assets 資產利潤率 (%)	Return on equity 權益利潤率 (%)	Labour productivity ('000 RMB / worker) 勞動生產率（千元/人）	Debts / assets 資產負債率 (%)	Total assets (mil. RMB) 總資產（百萬元）
Industry Overall 行業總體	35	2,224	280	-339	-22.97	-46.54	125.90	50.64	1,475

	Number of firms 企業個數	Average number of employees 平均職工人數	Average revenue ('000 RMB) 平均銷售收入（千元）	Average profit ('000 RMB) 平均利潤（千元）	Return on assets 資產利潤率 (%)	Return on equity 權益利潤率 (%)	Labour productivity ('000 RMB / worker) 勞動生產率（千元/人）	Average debts / assets 平均資產負債率(%)	Average Total assets ('000 RMB) 平均總資產（千元）
By ownership 產業所有權									
State-owned 國有	14	121	10,071	-24,857	-39.41	-63.27	82.99	37.71	63,071
Collectively-owned 集體	15	20	9,263	600	1.44	4.25	464.72	66.02	41,593
Privately-owned 私有									
Domestic JVs 聯營									
Joint stock 股份制									
Foreign-funded 外資	3	68							
Overseas Chinese-funded 港澳台資	3	7							
By size 規模									
Large 大型	1	683	246,808	-1,421,407	-125.02	118.96	361.36	205.09	1,136,935
Medium 中型									
Small 小型	29	51	1,144	37,324	319.51	56.28	22.49	-467.68	11,682
By regional distribution 地區分布									
Central-North 華北	3	49	337	30	0.05	0.18	6.82	70.99	58,033
Beijing 北京	2	30	505	45	0.06	0.22	16.83	73.02	76,860
Tianjin 天津									
Hebei 河北									
Shanxi 山西									
Inner Mongolia 內蒙	1	88						55.69	20,380
Northeast 東北	2	104	10,385	-140	-0.99	-1.10	99.86	9.60	14,120
Liaoning 遼寧	1								
Jilin 吉林	1	208	20,770	-280	-0.99	-1.10	99.86	9.60	28,240
Heilongjiang 黑龍江									
Central East 華東	12	85	16,580	-28,351	-40.99	-89.15	196.02	54.02	69,167
Shanghai 上海									
Jiangsu 江蘇	3	41	26,257	2,017	1.60	6.20	635.24	74.14	125,857
Zhejiang 浙江	2	113	15,950	1,460	1.64	3.30	141.78	50.42	89,125
Anhui 安徽	3	8	93	3	0.59	0.91	11.67	35.29	567
Fujian 福建	3	127	8,330				65.59	52.89	20,043
Jiangxi 江西	1	261	63,020	-349,190	-164.44	-210.11	241.46	21.74	212,350
Shandong 山東									
Central-South 中南	7	21	4,121	-254	-4.20	-38.53	192.33	89.11	6,049
Henan 河南	2	6	10,625	160	1.44	7.24	1931.82	80.14	11,105
Hubei 湖北	2								
Hunan 湖南	1	8	3,110	90	40.91	56.25	388.75	22.73	220
Guangdong 廣東	2	66	2,245	-1,095	-11.00	-5475.00	34.27	99.85	9,955
Guangxi 廣西									
Hainan 海南									
Southwest 西南	7	85	3,253	157	0.45	0.49	38.46	8.80	34,924
Chongqing 重慶									
Sichuan 四川									
Guizhou 貴州									
Yunnan 雲南									
Tibet 西藏	3	178	7,363	360	0.44	0.49	41.29	8.78	81,313
Northwest 西北	4	28	1,905	545	1.40	5.07	68.65	72.46	39,068
Shaanxi 陝西									
Gansu 甘肅									
Qinghai 青海									
Ningxia 寧夏									
Xinjiang 新疆	4	28	1,905	545	1.40	5.07	68.65	72.46	39,068

4419: Other Electricity Generation 其他電業

Year 年份	Number of firms 企業個數	Rate of change 每年變化 (%)	Number of employees 職工人數 (人)	Rate of change 每年變化 (%)	Total revenue (mil. RMB) 總銷售收入 (百萬元)	Rate of change 每年變化 (%)	Total profit (mil. RMB) 總利潤 (百萬元)	Rate of change 每年變化 (%)
1993	36		1,480		19		1	
1994	19	-47.22%	1,343	-9.26%	353	1710.59%	16	2383.15%
1995	25	31.58%	2,589	92.78%	890	152.16%	-2	-113.48%
1996	35	40.00%	2,224	-14.10%	280	-68.52%	-339	-15852.94%

3 Major products* 3 種主要產品 *	Output 產量	Sales volume 銷售量	Unit 單位
a) Other Electric Power 其他動力能發電	3,006	3,006	10,000 kwh 萬千瓦小時

Top 10 firms by revenue (year founded) 收入排名前 10 家企業 (創辦年份)	City 城市	Province 省	Telephone / fax 電話 / 傳真	Number of employees 職工人數	Ownership 產業所有權	Revenue ('000 RMB) 銷售收入 (千元)	Profit ('000 RMB) (rank) 利潤 (千元) (排名)	Total assets ('000 RMB) 總資產 (千元)	Major products 主要產品
Yangzhou Su Yuan Electric Power Generating Co. Ltd. 揚州蘇源發電有限公司(1996)	Yangzhou 揚州市	Jiangsu 江蘇省	(0514)6883338	65	Overseas Chinese-funded 港澳台資	71,269	6000(1)	356,133	o
Jiangxi Electric Power Co. 江西省電力公司(1958)	Nanchang 南昌市	Jiangxi 江西省	(0791)8624830 (0791)8624830	261	State-owned 國有	63,020	-349188(9)	212,350	o
Pingtan Electric Power Co. 平潭縣電力公司(1953)	Fuzhou 福州市	Fujian 福建省	(0591)4312014	364	State-owned 國有	24,993	0(7)	60,126	a
Pingdingshan Power Plant Pyroelectricity Industrial General Company 平頂山電廠熱電實業總公司(1992)	Pingdingshan 平頂山市	Henan 河南省	(0375)3933311	426	Collectively-owned 集體	19,947	310(3)	19,691	o
Xishan An Zhen Dian Factory 錫山市安鎮電廠(1996)	Wuxi 無錫市	Jiangsu 江蘇省	(0510)8781338	45	Collectively-owned 集體	7,290	50(5)	21,100	o
Xinjiang Wind Power General Plant 新疆風力發電廠(1991)	Urumqi 烏魯木齊市	Xinjiang 新疆	(0991)2820278	34	State-owned 國有	6,360	2134(2)	102,352	a
Lufeng Donghai Zhen Sunshine Enterprise General Company 陸豐市東海鎮陽光企業總公司(1984)	Shanwei 汕尾市	Guangdong 廣東省	(0660)8821710	100	Collectively-owned 集體	4,160	-1953(8)	18,918	o
Qi Zi Jia Xiang Agricultural Power Management Station 七子浹鄉農電管理站(1990)	Yiyang 益陽市	Hunan 湖南省	(0737)2761088	8	Collectively-owned 集體	3,110	87(4)	215	o

Top 10 Cities by Production Output 產出排名前 10 位城市	Province 省	Market share 市場份額	Number of firms 企業個數
Changchun 長春市	Jilin 吉林省	78.27%	1
Dongguan 東莞市	Guangdong 廣東省	6.80%	1
Shenyang 瀋陽市	Liaoning 遼寧省	5.68%	3
Nanchang 南昌市	Jiangxi 江西省	3.97%	1
Lhasa 拉薩市	Tibet 西藏	1.38%	2
Fuyang 阜陽市	Anhui 安徽省	0.63%	1
Hohhot 呼和浩特市	Inner Mong 內蒙	0.54%	3
Putian 莆田市	Fujian 福建省	0.50%	1
Urumqi 烏魯木齊市	Xinjiang 新疆	0.37%	2
Wuxi 無錫市	Jiangsu 江蘇省	0.32%	5

10 Major Wholesalers 10 家主要批發商	City 城市	Province 省	Telephone / Fax 電話 / 傳真

*Also include sales by firms outside this industry.包括本行業以外廠家的銷售。"o" stands for "others". "o" 代表 "其他產品"。

4420: Transmission and Distribution of Electricity 電力供應業

The industry accounts for 3.267% of the total revenue of China's industrial sector in 1996. The revenue growth rate of the industry is 41.4% from 1995, as compared to the growth rate of China's industrial sector, 9.51%. The rate of return on asset is 4.96%. 81.19% of all firms in the industry made a profit while 10.43% had negative returns. The top province in terms of the industry's revenue is Guangdong, accounting for 15.42% of the total revenue.
本行業在1996年佔全行業總產值3.267%，行業年增長率為41.4%（全國工業年增長率9.51%）。行業的資產回報率4.96%，81.19%的企業盈利，10.43%的企業虧損。銷售收入最高的省份為廣東省，佔本行業的15.42%。

	Total number of firms 企業總數	Total number of employees 職工總數	Total revenue (mil. RMB) 總銷售收入（百萬元）	Total profit (mil. RMB) 總利潤（百萬元）	Return on assets 資產利潤率 (%)	Return on equity 權益利潤率 (%)	Labour productivity ('000 RMB / worker) 勞動生產率（千元/人）	Debts / assets 資產負債率 (%)	Total assets (mil. RMB) 總資產（百萬元）
Industry Overall 行業總體	2,933	853,703	189,397	16,031	4.96	9.16	221.85	45.88	323,350

	Number of firms 企業個數	Average number of employees 平均職工人數	Average revenue ('000 RMB) 平均銷售收入（千元）	Average profit ('000 RMB) 平均利潤（千元）	Return on assets 資產利潤率 (%)	Return on equity 權益利潤率 (%)	Labour productivity ('000 RMB / worker) 勞動生產率（千元/人）	Average debts / assets 平均資產負債率(%)	Average Total assets ('000 RMB) 平均總資產（千元）
By ownership 產業所有權									
State-owned 國有	1,790	461	104,380	8,861	4.98	9.18	226.27	45.73	177,950
Collectively-owned 集體	1,118	16	1,726	72	4.57	8.54	110.33	46.47	1,571
Privately-owned 私有	1	35	2,721	19	3.26	9.44	77.75	65.50	576
Domestic JVs 聯營	1	13	654	8	0.19	0.21	50.31	6.38	4,224
Joint stock 股份制	17	691	43,926	5,106	3.06	7.67	63.57	60.16	167,128
Foreign-funded 外資	2	64	2,146	301	4.60	8.67	33.53	46.90	6,539
Overseas Chinese-funded 港澳台資	4	84	17,756	120	0.24	1.03	212.65	77.07	50,397
By size 規模									
Large 大型	182	1,826	541,395	53,173	4.86	8.98	296.56	45.85	1,093,157
Medium 中型	317	578	133,612	13,212	6.61	12.31	231.09	46.26	199,744
Small 小型	2,423	140	20,444	948	3.89	7.55	146.24	48.48	24,362
By regional distribution 地區分布									
Central-North 華北	278	426	64,489	6,932	5.86	9.71	151.26	39.60	118,254
Beijing 北京	11	321	104,956	2,396	2.24	3.58	327.15	37.37	106,912
Tianjin 天津	31	215	122,648	5,349	3.96	8.06	571.74	50.87	135,031
Hebei 河北	117	475	76,981	3,480	2.55	4.83	162.00	47.09	136,303
Shanxi 山西	27	1,066	113,686	47,409	17.77	21.70	106.67	18.11	266,839
Inner Mongolia 內蒙	92	261	9,729	519	1.10	1.75	37.35	37.49	47,396
Northeast 東北	196	483	57,412	4,898	3.94	6.40	118.89	38.40	124,270
Liaoning 遼寧	65	545	110,069	3,353	1.74	2.53	202.02	31.31	192,555
Jilin 吉林	52	429	46,243	8,300	7.50	12.26	107.70	38.79	110,625
Heilongjiang 黑龍江	79	467	21,439	3,930	5.10	10.76	45.89	52.60	77,068
Central East 華東	968	255	84,655	4,806	3.51	6.68	332.63	47.52	137,045
Shanghai 上海	1	30,720	11,985,580	671,490	2.30	4.37	390.16	47.43	29,248,960
Jiangsu 江蘇	21	1,770	341,385	8,718	0.88	1.71	192.88	48.70	996,174
Zhejiang 浙江	69	411	288,380	11,205	4.10	8.84	700.91	53.67	273,525
Anhui 安徽	95	326	64,466	2,315	2.75	5.98	197.56	54.02	84,258
Fujian 福建	195	121	33,172	9,925	15.21	28.26	273.98	46.20	65,274
Jiangxi 江西	452	74	5,151	601	4.97	10.65	69.39	53.30	12,089
Shandong 山東	135	459	207,201	4,425	1.60	2.75	451.74	42.04	277,189
Central-South 中南	886	266	62,852	8,261	8.92	15.85	236.38	43.71	92,597
Henan 河南	146	500	85,219	11,489	11.12	21.08	170.39	47.23	103,298
Hubei 湖北	91	462	40,509	7,501	7.07	14.21	87.64	50.25	106,107
Hunan 湖南	128	258	51,811	17,784	23.74	52.44	200.91	54.73	74,921
Guangdong 廣東	343	165	85,125	6,823	6.02	9.29	517.25	35.26	113,424
Guangxi 廣西	155	151	18,195	2,017	4.27	10.52	120.54	59.41	47,223
Hainan 海南	23	332	39,492	1,311	2.02	3.28	118.83	38.27	64,780
Southwest 西南	400	238	30,160	2,106	3.99	9.96	126.70	59.92	52,753
Chongqing 重慶	37	456	34,039	8,224	11.83	33.54	74.67	64.72	69,502
Sichuan 四川	162	282	29,426	1,369	2.57	5.95	104.47	56.89	53,349
Guizhou 貴州	105	152	33,352	550	1.30	3.71	219.52	64.93	42,281
Yunnan 雲南	88	189	28,638	2,936	4.79	11.61	151.84	58.72	61,260
Tibet 西藏	8	35	1,971	94	1.29	1.77	56.12	26.82	7,244
Northwest 西北	205	309	51,315	1,608	1.09	2.08	165.98	47.64	147,883
Shaanxi 陜西	73	368	54,260	1,475	1.38	2.48	147.44	44.20	106,565
Gansu 甘肅	50	401	87,904	2,624	1.26	2.39	219.46	47.22	207,925
Qinghai 青海	14	158	67,044	70	0.01	0.02	423.18	41.46	507,949
Ningxia 寧夏	6	608	62,928	952	0.43	0.97	103.47	56.00	223,702
Xinjiang 新疆	62	171	13,667	1,355	2.28	6.50	79.77	64.96	59,468

4420: Transmission and Distribution of Electricity 電力供應業

Year 年份	Number of firms 企業個數	Rate of change 每年變化 (%)	Number of employees 職工人數 (人)	Rate of change 每年變化 (%)	Total revenue (mil. RMB) 總銷售收入 (百萬元)	Rate of change 每年變化 (%)	Total profit (mil. RMB) 總利潤 (百萬元)	Rate of change 每年變化 (%)
1993	2,217		852,890		59,252		4,815	
1994	2,357	6.31%	725,069	-14.99%	108,858	83.72%	7,928	64.65%
1995	2,611	10.78%	845,387	16.59%	133,935	23.04%	9,976	25.82%
1996	2,933	12.33%	853,703	0.98%	189,397	41.41%	16,031	60.70%

3 Major products* 3種主要產品*	Output 產量	Sales volume 銷售量	Unit 單位
a) Power Supply 供電	81,851,361	78,577,306	10,000 kwh 萬千瓦小時
b) Power 發電	5,233,540	4,814,857	10,000 kwh 萬千瓦小時

Top 10 firms by revenue (year founded) 收入排名前10家企業 (創辦年份)	City 城市	Province 省	Telephone / fax 電話 / 傳真	Number of employees 職工人數	Ownership 產業所有權	Revenue ('000 RMB) 銷售收入 (千元)	Profit ('000 RMB) (rank) 利潤 (千元) (排名)	Total assets ('000 RMB) 總資產 (千元)	Major products 主要產品
Shanghai Electric Power Co. 上海市電力公司(1986)	Shanghai 上海市	Shanghai 上海市	(021)63291010 (021)63248586	32,828	State-owned 國有	11,985,580	671490(2)	29,248,960	a,b
Sichuan Electric Power Industry Bureau 四川省電力工業局	Chengdu 成都市	Sichuan 四川省	(028)6661888 (028)4441794	2,867	State-owned 國有	7,928,960	216560(14)	23,137,360	o
Gansu Electric Power Industry Bureau 甘肅省電力工業局(1956)	Lanzhou 蘭州市	Gansu 甘肅省	(0931)2952162 (0931)2331042	1,807	State-owned 國有	4,080,450	57218(42)	9,821,485	o
Shenzhen Power Supply Bureau 深圳供電局(1980)	Shenzhen 深圳市	Guangdong 廣東省	(0755)5572283 (0755)5597537	1,424	State-owned 國有	3,480,248	384903(6)	7,489,385	a
Dongguan Electric Power Industry Bureau 東莞市電力工業局(1958)	Dongguan 東莞市	Guangdong 廣東省	(0769)2462988 (0769)2464292	771	State-owned 國有	3,197,116	260912(12)	2,945,165	a
Foshan Electric Power Industry Bureau 佛山市電力工業局(1913)	Foshan 佛山市	Guangdong 廣東省	(0757)3331218 (0757)3331218	2,102	State-owned 國有	3,116,838	282930(11)	2,873,660	a
Guangzhou Electric Power Industry Bureau 廣州電力工業局(1959)	Guangzhou 廣州市	Guangdong 廣東省	(020)87750469 (020)87766227	4,182	State-owned 國有	2,792,280	633859(3)	5,878,312	a
Anhui Electric Power Co. 安徽省電力公司(1989)	Hefei 合肥市	Anhui 安徽省	(0551)3632007 (0551)3633393	1,721	State-owned 國有	2,710,838	65069(37)	2,320,360	o
Chengdu Power Administration 成都電業局(1909)	Chengdu 成都市	Sichuan 四川省	(028)6675745 (028)6655972	3,934	State-owned 國有	2,658,027	0(1288)	2,171,250	a
Qingdao Power Administration 青島電業局(1898)	Qingdao 青島市	Shandong 山東省	(0532)2827884 (0532)2827442	1,752	State-owned 國有	2,139,276	0(1332)	1,321,433	a

Top 10 Cities by Production Output 產出排名前10位城市	Province 省	Market share 市場份額	Number of firms 企業個數
Shanghai 上海市	Shanghai 上海市	4.15%	19
Wuhan 武漢市	Hubei 湖北省	3.16%	14
Jingmen 荊門市	Hubei 湖北省	2.89%	9
Hefei 合肥市	Anhui 安徽省	2.84%	2
Guangzhou 廣州市	Guangdong 廣東省	2.68%	24
Shenzhen 深圳市	Guangdong 廣東省	1.79%	13
Foshan 佛山市	Guangdong 廣東省	1.73%	14
Hangzhou 杭州市	Zhejiang 浙江省	1.63%	12
Dongguan 東莞市	Guangdong 廣東省	1.45%	41
Tianjin 天津市	Tianjin 天津市	1.45%	63

10 Major Wholesalers 10家主要批發商	City 城市	Province 省	Telephone / Fax 電話 / 傳真

*Also include sales by firms outside this industry.包括本行業以外廠家的銷售。"o" stands for "others". "o" 代表 "其他產品"。

4430: Steam and Hot Water Production and Supply 蒸汽、熱水生產和供應業

The industry accounts for 0.116% of the total revenue of China's industrial sector in 1996. The revenue growth rate of the industry is 48.1% from 1995, as compared to the growth rate of China's industrial sector, 9.51%. The rate of return on asset is 0.36%. 53.06% of all firms in the industry made a profit while 43.03% had negative returns. The top province in terms of the industry's revenue is Liaoning, accounting for 23.51% of the total revenue.
本行業在1996年佔全行業總產值0.116%，行業年增長率為48.1%（全國工業年增長率9.51%）。行業的資產回報率0.36%，53.06%的企業盈利，43.03%的企業虧損。銷售收入最高的省份為遼寧省，佔本行業的23.51%。

	Total number of firms 企業總數	Total number of employees 職工總數	Total revenue (mil. RMB) 總銷售收入（百萬元）	Total profit (mil. RMB) 總利潤（百萬元）	Return on assets 資產利潤率 (%)	Return on equity 權益利潤率 (%)	Labour productivity ('000 RMB / worker) 勞動生產率（千元/人）	Debts / assets 資產負債率 (%)	Total assets (mil. RMB) 總資產（百萬元）
Industry Overall 行業總體	330	89,733	6,723	73	0.36	0.75	74.92	52.47	20,466

	Number of firms 企業個數	Average number of employees 平均職工人數	Average revenue ('000 RMB) 平均銷售收入（千元）	Average profit ('000 RMB) 平均利潤（千元）	Return on assets 資產利潤率 (%)	Return on equity 權益利潤率 (%)	Labour productivity ('000 RMB / worker) 勞動生產率（千元/人）	Average debts / assets 平均資產負債率(%)	Average Total assets ('000 RMB) 平均總資產（千元）
By ownership 產業所有權									
State-owned 國有	255	291	20,667	-329	-0.49	-1.03	71.02	52.13	66,588
Collectively-owned 集體	52	80	5,732	138	1.61	2.85	71.33	43.61	8,616
Privately-owned 私有									
Domestic JVs 聯營	2	64	3,968	-925	-5.39	-13.23	62.00	59.24	17,140
Joint stock 股份制	14	681	67,695	9,930	5.54	11.69	99.48	52.63	179,348
Foreign-funded 外資	3	607	66,016	3,862	2.38	8.51	108.82	72.02	162,119
Overseas Chinese-funded 港澳台資	5	174	417	206	14.03	16.16	2.40	13.13	1,469
By size 規模									
Large 大型	28	1,378	119,662	-2,242	-0.57	-1.04	86.83	45.14	394,312
Medium 中型	39	480	37,875	158	0.16	0.46	78.99	65.57	99,818
Small 小型	253	121	7,495	512	2.34	5.56	61.72	57.89	21,870
By regional distribution 地區分布									
Central-North 華北	86	303	19,742	91	0.11	0.18	65.10	38.78	84,990
Beijing 北京	19	558	38,379	1,581	0.93	1.22	68.81	23.74	170,299
Tianjin 天津	20	53	12,255	33	0.05	0.09	232.54	40.40	60,150
Hebei 河北	15	525	30,531	-581	-0.50	-1.18	58.19	57.79	117,083
Shanxi 山西	9	405	19,776	-1,213	-1.49	-3.90	48.82	61.63	81,170
Inner Mongolia 內蒙	23	127	3,807	-138	-0.83	-1.18	30.04	30.04	16,681
Northeast 東北	136	337	21,271	407	0.65	1.65	63.15	60.28	62,179
Liaoning 遼寧	77	310	20,530	1,040	1.70	4.24	66.28	59.94	61,224
Jilin 吉林	29	328	19,044	-1,483	-2.57	-6.00	58.03	57.13	57,628
Heilongjiang 黑龍江	30	415	25,325	608	0.88	2.42	61.05	63.58	69,028
Central East 華東	52	208	32,029	404	0.59	1.55	154.14	61.57	67,971
Shanghai 上海	2	53	10,160	-3,795	-3.92	-7.24	191.70	45.89	96,815
Jiangsu 江蘇	9	273	35,518	223	0.32	1.12	130.10	71.33	69,868
Zhejiang 浙江	3	285	249,537	14,390	6.10	15.65	876.59	61.00	235,763
Anhui 安徽	4	213	16,865	-355	-1.38	-2.47	79.18	44.06	25,668
Fujian 福建	8	32	2,894	-223	-1.55	-3.17	91.87	51.10	14,334
Jiangxi 江西									
Shandong 山東	26	242	18,704	-515	-0.75	-1.96	77.39	61.73	68,748
Central-South 中南	15	245	21,729	13	0.03	0.05	88.67	50.17	46,661
Henan 河南	5	239	24,306	-330	-0.39	-0.70	101.87	44.22	84,396
Hubei 湖北	5	242	21,790	-20	-0.07	-0.14	90.19	52.29	28,926
Hunan 湖南	1	1,117	65,890	240	0.22	0.69	58.99	68.89	111,080
Guangdong 廣東	3	53	9,680	567	7.65	17.24	183.80	55.63	7,407
Guangxi 廣西	1		530						
Hainan 海南									
Southwest 西南	3	70	2,353	7	0.08	0.58	33.46	85.41	7,907
Chongqing 重慶									
Sichuan 四川	3	70	2,353	-7	-0.09	-0.61	33.61	85.41	7,907
Guizhou 貴州									
Yunnan 雲南									
Tibet 西藏									
Northwest 西北	38	83	3,525	-303	-2.60	-6.25	42.54	58.37	11,652
Shaanxi 陝西	4	44	1,038	-323	-3.07	-21.98	23.71	86.05	10,518
Gansu 甘肅	3	60	1,673	20	0.34	0.46	27.73	26.01	5,857
Qinghai 青海	3	37	1,277				34.82	32.93	6,803
Ningxia 寧夏	8	48	1,088	-171	-2.04	-3.36	22.89	39.38	8,395
Xinjiang 新疆	20	115	5,613	-447	-3.02	-8.04	48.75	62.42	14,778

4430: Steam and Hot Water Production and Supply 蒸汽、熱水生產和供應業

Year 年份	Number of firms 企業個數	Rate of change 每年變化 (%)	Number of employees 職工人數 (人)	Rate of change 每年變化 (%)	Total revenue (mil. RMB) 總銷售收入 (百萬元)	Rate of change 每年變化 (%)	Total profit (mil. RMB) 總利潤 (百萬元)	Rate of change 每年變化 (%)
1993	168		61,232		2,759		-12	
1994	206	22.62%	69,564	13.61%	3,176	15.12%	-38	-223.07%
1995	269	30.58%	88,837	27.71%	4,538	42.87%	-62	-62.12%
1996	330	22.68%	89,733	1.01%	6,723	48.15%	73	216.97%

3 Major products* 3 種主要產品 *	Output 產量	Sales volume 銷售量	Unit 單位
a) Heat Supply 供熱	239,033	219,910	10,000 million kj 萬百萬千焦
b) Thermal Power 火電	506,451	460,871	10,000 kwh 萬千瓦小時

Top 10 firms by revenue (year founded) 收入排名前 10 家企業 (創辦年份)	City 城市	Province 省	Telephone / fax 電話 / 傳真	Number of employees 職工人數	Ownership 產業所有權	Revenue ('000 RMB) 銷售收入 (千元)	Profit ('000 RMB) (rank) 利潤 (千元) (排名)	Total assets ('000 RMB) 總資產 (千元)	Major products 主要產品
Beijing Heating Power Co. 北京市熱力公司(1958)	Beijing 北京市	Beijing 北京市	(010)65060066 (010)65078891	4,359	State-owned 國有	532,756	25895(4)	2,478,887	a
Shijiazhuang Thermal Electric & Gas Enterprises Group Corp. 石家莊熱力煤氣公司(1982)	Shijiazhuang 石家莊市	Hebei 河北省	(0311)5053391	2,475	State-owned 國有	265,854	809(30)	905,816	a,b
Dalian Thermal Power Co. Ltd. 大連熱電股份有限公司(1984)	Dalian 大連市	Liaoning 遼寧省	(0411)6641238 (0411)6642027	1,270	Joint stock 股份制	259,678	97746(1)	678,893	a,b
Shenyang Heating & Power Co. Ltd. 瀋陽熱力股份有限公司(1980)	Shenyang 瀋陽市	Liaoning 遼寧省	(024)22823333	2,198	Joint stock 股份制	233,850	46430(2)	502,398	a
Harbin Sui Bao Pyroelectricity Co. Ltd. 哈爾濱歲寶熱電股份有限公司(1984)	Harbin 哈爾濱市	Heilongjiang 黑龍江省	(0451)1682281 (0451)7672279	855	Joint stock 股份制	201,498	26548(3)	413,596	a,b
Changchun Heating Power Co. 長春市熱力公司(1980)	Changchun 長春市	Jilin 吉林省	(0431)4648141	2,034	State-owned 國有	149,364	277(42)	393,749	a
Jinzhou Thermoelectricity General Co. 錦州熱電總公司(1985)	Jinzhou 錦州市	Liaoning 遼寧省	(0416)2812672	2,354	State-owned 國有	138,289	-17292(178)	384,103	a,b
Shenyang No.2 Heating & Power Heating Supply Co. 瀋陽市第二熱力供暖公司(1991)	Shenyang 瀋陽市	Liaoning 遼寧省	(024)22707717 (024)22902436	1,315	State-owned 國有	135,217	6119(9)	452,416	a
Fushun Heating Power General Co. 撫順市熱力總公司(1983)	Fushun 撫順市	Liaoning 遼寧省	(0413)7682562 (0413)7682562	1,517	State-owned 國有	118,532	210(52)	212,562	a
Heilong Jiang Sui Bao Heating and Power Co. Ltd. 黑龍江歲寶熱電有限公司(1994)	Harbin 哈爾濱市	Heilongjiang 黑龍江省	(0451)3723122 (0451)3720374	1,247	Foreign-funded 外資	115,597	9188(6)	313,325	a,b

Top 10 Cities by Production Output 產出排名前 10 位城市	Province 省	Market share 市場份額	Number of firms 企業個數
Jingsha 荊沙市	Hubei 湖北省	11.49%	5
Harbin 哈爾濱市	Heilongjiang 黑龍江省	8.24%	19
Dalian 大連市	Liaoning 遼寧省	7.56%	16
Beijing 北京市	Beijing 北京市	6.43%	19
Shenyang 瀋陽市	Liaoning 遼寧省	5.02%	12
Shijiazhuang 石家莊市	Hebei 河北省	4.34%	5
Tianjin 天津市	Tianjin 天津市	3.63%	25
Changchun 長春市	Jilin 吉林省	3.03%	4
Jinzhou 錦州市	Liaoning 遼寧省	2.88%	6
Zibo 淄博市	Shandong 山東省	2.24%	14

10 Major Wholesalers 10 家主要批發商	City 城市	Province 省	Telephone / Fax 電話 / 傳真

*Also include sales by firms outside this industry.包括本行業以外廠家的銷售。"o" stands for "others". "o" 代表 "其他產品"。

4510: Gas Production 煤氣生產業

The industry accounts for 0.045% of the total revenue of China's industrial sector in 1996. The revenue growth rate of the industry is 0.3% from 1995, as compared to the growth rate of China's industrial sector, 9.51%. The rate of return on asset is -5.36%. 22.79% of all firms in the industry made a profit while 65.45% had negative returns. The top province in terms of the industry's revenue is Liaoning, accounting for 28.51% of the total revenue.
本行業在1996年佔全行業總產值0.045%，行業年增長率為0.3%（全國工業年增長率9.51%）。行業的資產回報率-5.36%，22.79%的企業盈利，65.45%的企業虧損。銷售收入最高的省份為遼寧省，佔本行業的28.51%。

	Total number of firms 企業總數	Total number of employees 職工總數	Total revenue (mil. RMB) 總銷售收入（百萬元）	Total profit (mil. RMB) 總利潤（百萬元）	Return on assets 資產利潤率 (%)	Return on equity 權益利潤率 (%)	Labour productivity ('000 RMB / worker) 勞動生產率（千元/人）	Debts / assets 資產負債率 (%)	Total assets (mil. RMB) 總資產（百萬元）
Industry Overall 行業總體	57	61,011	2,621	-548	-5.36	-10.30	42.96	47.92	10,216

	Number of firms 企業個數	Average number of employees 平均職工人數	Average revenue ('000 RMB) 平均銷售收入（千元）	Average profit ('000 RMB) 平均利潤（千元）	Return on assets 資產利潤率 (%)	Return on equity 權益利潤率 (%)	Labour productivity ('000 RMB / worker) 勞動生產率（千元/人）	Average debts / assets 平均資產負債率(%)	Average Total assets ('000 RMB) 平均總資產（千元）
By ownership 產業所有權									
State-owned 國有	42	1,432	61,690	-12,881	-5.36	-10.22	43.09	47.55	240,405
Collectively-owned 集體	11	25	740	-226	-15.89	97.20	30.15	116.35	1,422
Privately-owned 私有									
Domestic JVs 聯營									
Joint stock 股份制	3	167	7,296	-1,504	-4.36	-16.99	43.69	74.31	34,468
Foreign-funded 外資	1	97							
Overseas Chinese-funded 港澳台資									
By size 規模									
Large 大型	12	3,051	158,511	-28,980	-4.82	-8.24	51.95	41.50	600,928
Medium 中型	5	1,068	32,337	-2,211	-1.07	-1.74	30.27	38.22	206,202
Small 小型	33	511	16,888	-5,733	-9.58	-40.73	33.03	76.47	59,818
By regional distribution 地區分布									
Central-North 華北	10	1,124	49,329	-10,367	-6.01	-12.95	43.88	53.61	172,588
Beijing 北京	2	24						70.47	7,265
Tianjin 天津	1	2,480	311,090	-73,420	-10.40	-18.63	125.44	44.20	706,230
Hebei 河北	3	361	4,180	-577	-0.77	-0.87	11.59	11.01	74,437
Shanxi 山西	3	1,875	32,253	-7,587	-5.32	110.32	17.20	104.82	142,733
Inner Mongolia 內蒙	1	2,008	72,900	-5,760	-1.63	-2.57	36.30	36.60	353,610
Northeast 東北	12	2,150	89,387	-11,413	-4.07	-7.51	41.57	45.76	280,314
Liaoning 遼寧	6	2,985	124,540	-12,033	-3.57	-6.31	41.73	43.33	336,620
Jilin 吉林	4	1,573	76,943	-16,188	-4.85	-9.48	48.93	48.89	334,103
Heilongjiang 黑龍江	2	804	8,815				10.96	140.84	3,820
Central East 華東	17	772	18,203	-5,306	-4.32	-7.55	23.56	42.78	122,822
Shanghai 上海		241							
Jiangsu 江蘇	1	1,028	65,600	-10,230	-6.63	-26.18	63.81	74.66	154,190
Zhejiang 浙江	3	796	16,447	-13,133	-9.73	-13.41	20.66	27.48	135,010
Anhui 安徽	4	751	18,648	-4,280	-6.01	-10.65	24.83	43.58	71,213
Fujian 福建	1								
Jiangxi 江西	2	332	4,870	315	0.59	1.41	14.67	58.51	53,830
Shandong 山東	6	968	18,363	-4,015	-2.12	-3.67	18.97	42.21	189,375
Central-South 中南	11	504	33,746	-10,946	-6.12	-9.65	66.99	36.56	178,760
Henan 河南	2	9	75	-20	-16.00	400.00	8.33	104.00	125
Hubei 湖北									
Hunan 湖南	2	724	30,215	-4,560	-4.96	-6.93	41.73	28.43	92,000
Guangdong 廣東	4	797	67,400	-25,945	-6.26	-9.38	84.62	33.27	414,458
Guangxi 廣西	3	296	13,677	-2,490	-6.01	-78.96	46.15	92.39	41,427
Hainan 海南									
Southwest 西南	6	873	62,037	-16,042	-9.05	-38.35	71.03	76.41	177,315
Chongqing 重慶	1	150	2,495	-332	-61.14	35.02	16.58	274.58	544
Sichuan 四川	3	24	125	-321	-5.01	192.59	5.26	102.60	6,415
Guizhou 貴州	1	1,889	78,160	-73,620	-23.60	38.96	41.38	160.58	311,910
Yunnan 雲南	1	3,089	290,400	-21,330	-2.91	-4.83	94.01	39.85	734,150
Tibet 西藏									
Northwest 西北	1	50	2,580	-370	-4.43	-15.55	51.60	71.50	8,350
Shaanxi 陝西	1	50	2,580	-370	-4.43	-15.55	51.60	71.50	8,350
Gansu 甘肅									
Qinghai 青海									
Ningxia 寧夏									
Xinjiang 新疆									

4510: Gas Production 煤氣生產業

Year 年份	Number of firms 企業個數	Rate of change 每年變化 (%)	Number of employees 職工人數 (人)	Rate of change 每年變化 (%)	Total revenue (mil. RMB) 總銷售收入 (百萬元)	Rate of change 每年變化 (%)	Total profit (mil. RMB) 總利潤 (百萬元)	Rate of change 每年變化 (%)
1993	81		62,575		2,558		-225	
1994	81		73,831	17.99%	2,645	3.39%	-213	5.49%
1995	69	-14.82%	72,643	-1.61%	2,612	-1.25%	-317	-48.89%
1996	57	-17.39%	61,011	-16.01%	2,621	0.34%	-548	-72.89%

3 Major products* 3種主要產品 *	Output 產量	Sales volume 銷售量	Unit 單位
a) Gas 煤氣	174,504	31,411	10,000 cubic metre 萬立方米
b) Gas Supply Volume 煤氣供應量	163,926	163,926	10,000 cubic metre 萬立方米

Top 10 firms by revenue (year founded) 收入排名前10家企業 (創辦年份)	City 城市	Province 省	Telephone / fax 電話 / 傳真	Number of employees 職工人數	Ownership 產業所有權	Revenue ('000 RMB) 銷售收入 (千元)	Profit ('000 RMB) (rank) 利潤 (千元) (排名)	Total assets ('000 RMB) 總資產 (千元)	Major products 主要產品
Shenyang Gas General Co. 瀋陽市煤氣總公司(1923)	Shenyang 瀋陽市	Liaoning 遼寧省	(024)23863746 (024)23860880	9,244	State-owned 國有	389,079	-54442(31)	1,039,137	a
Tianjin No.2 Coal Gas Plant 天津市第二煤氣廠(1987)	Tianjin 天津市	Tianjin 天津市	(022)26321872 (022)26321773	2,453	State-owned 國有	311,089	-73423(32)	706,231	a,b
Kunming Gas General Co. 昆明煤氣總公司(1986)	Kunming 昆明市	Yunnan 雲南省	(0871)3138151 (0871)3135344	3,057	State-owned 國有	290,400	-21328(29)	734,145	a,b
Guangzhou Gas Co. 廣州市煤氣公司(1983)	Guangzhou 廣州市	Guangdong 廣東省	(020)87302178 (020)87302178	2,740	State-owned 國有	254,346	-101236(34)	1,606,110	a,b
Dalian Gas Co. 大連煤氣公司(1907)	Dalian 大連市	Liaoning 遼寧省	(0411)3603222 (0411)3603184	4,216	State-owned 國有	212,573	1(6)	439,793	a
Guizhou Organic Chemical Industry General Factory Coking Factory 貴州有機化工總廠焦化廠(1994)	Guiyang 貴陽市	Guizhou 貴州省	(0851)2561328 (0851)2561222	1,794	State-owned 國有	78,165	-73616(33)	311,907	a,b
Jinzhou Gas General Company 錦州市煤氣總公司(1938)	Jinzhou 錦州市	Liaoning 遼寧省	(0416)2819641 (0416)2822637	1,582	State-owned 國有	67,022	-9938(25)	154,140	a
Nantong Gas Company 南通市煤氣公司(1973)	Nantong 南通市	Jiangsu 江蘇省	(0513)5513167 (0513)5519794	1,028	State-owned 國有	65,598	-10225(26)	154,192	b
Hunan Zhuzhou Gas Company 株洲市煤氣公司(1991)	Zhuzhou 株洲市	Hunan 湖南省	(0733)8631231 (0733)8631417	1,279	State-owned 國有	60,427	-9122(23)	184,000	a,b
Hefei Gas General Company 合肥市煤氣總公司(1985)	Hefei 合肥市	Anhui 安徽省	(0551)5521170 (0551)5528101	1,914	State-owned 國有	59,480	-7883(22)	183,254	a,b

Top 10 Cities by Production Output 產出排名前10位城市	Province 省	Market share 市場份額	Number of firms 企業個數
Shenyang 瀋陽市	Liaoning 遼寧省	14.54%	2
Tianjin 天津市	Tianjin 天津市	11.72%	1
Kunming 昆明市	Yunnan 雲南省	10.94%	2
Guangzhou 廣州市	Guangdong 廣東省	9.67%	3
Dalian 大連市	Liaoning 遼寧省	8.59%	3
Yancheng 鹽城市	Jiangsu 江蘇省	6.17%	1
Harbin 哈爾濱市	Heilongjiang 黑龍江省	5.13%	1
Jinzhou 錦州市	Liaoning 遼寧省	3.01%	1
Guiyang 貴陽市	Guizhou 貴州省	2.33%	1
Zhuzhou 株洲市	Hunan 湖南省	2.32%	1

10 Major Wholesalers 10家主要批發商	City 城市	Province 省	Telephone / Fax 電話 / 傳真

*Also include sales by firms outside this industry.包括本行業以外廠家的銷售。"o" stands for "others". "o"代表"其他產品"。

4520: Gas Supply 煤氣供應業

The industry accounts for 0.127% of the total revenue of China's industrial sector in 1996. The revenue growth rate of the industry is 14.9% from 1995, as compared to the growth rate of China's industrial sector, 9.51%. The rate of return on asset is -1.25%. 50.59% of all firms in the industry made a profit while 44.12% had negative returns. The top province in terms of the industry's revenue is Shanghai, accounting for 22.08% of the total revenue.
本行業在1996年佔全行業總產值0.127%，行業年增長率為14.9%（全國工業年增長率9.51%）。行業的資產回報率-1.25%，50.59%的企業盈利，44.12%的企業虧損。銷售收入最高的省份為上海市，佔本行業的22.08%。

	Total number of firms 企業總數	Total number of employees 職工總數	Total revenue (mil. RMB) 總銷售收入（百萬元）	Total profit (mil. RMB) 總利潤（百萬元）	Return on assets 資產利潤率 (%)	Return on equity 權益利潤率 (%)	Labour productivity ('000 RMB / worker) 勞動生產率（千元/人）	Debts / assets 資產負債率 (%)	Total assets (mil. RMB) 總資產（百萬元）
Industry Overall 行業總體	350	95,982	7,370	-340	-1.25	-2.41	76.79	48.01	27,194

	Number of firms 企業個數	Average number of employees 平均職工人數	Average revenue ('000 RMB) 平均銷售收入（千元）	Average profit ('000 RMB) 平均利潤（千元）	Return on assets 資產利潤率 (%)	Return on equity 權益利潤率 (%)	Labour productivity ('000 RMB / worker) 勞動生產率（千元/人）	Average debts / assets 平均資產負債率(%)	Average Total assets ('000 RMB) 平均總資產（千元）
By ownership 產業所有權									
State-owned 國有	241	380	25,830	-1,369	-1.30	-2.46	68.01	47.15	105,531
Collectively-owned 集體	81	36	2,963	33	0.84	4.51	82.24	81.45	3,957
Privately-owned 私有	1	38	11,831	-755	-5.24	-95.59	311.35	94.51	14,398
Domestic JVs 聯營	5	18	3,385	-32	-0.60	-1.14	192.33	47.39	5,391
Joint stock 股份制	4	115	108,003	-2,355	-1.78	-4.39	943.26	59.52	132,593
Foreign-funded 外資	5	75	67,744	-2,593	-3.21	-5.28	908.10	39.25	80,840
Overseas Chinese-funded 港澳台資	13	49	8,173	817	2.28	6.52	166.54	65.01	35,818
By size 規模									
Large 大型	27	1,841	147,960	-1,373	-0.22	-0.40	80.38	46.35	635,340
Medium 中型	29	498	27,220	-2,907	-2.51	-4.39	54.68	42.81	115,914
Small 小型	285	111	9,075	-767	-3.27	-7.26	81.86	54.89	23,436
By regional distribution 地區分布									
Central-North 華北	54	436	20,085	-443	-0.45	-0.57	46.11	21.40	98,353
Beijing 北京	5	1,645	90,356	5,250	0.83	0.91	54.94	9.05	633,026
Tianjin 天津	10	613	35,504	-5,130	-5.40	-7.62	57.94	29.09	95,006
Hebei 河北	29	215	7,668	-313	-1.10	-2.22	35.70	50.22	28,348
Shanxi 山西	3	573	373	-27	-0.65	-1.09	0.65	40.39	4,093
Inner Mongolia 內蒙	7	175	7,751	1,470	2.85	5.00	44.33	43.06	51,643
Northeast 東北	37	329	12,490	-675	-1.52	-2.53	37.96	40.00	44,454
Liaoning 遼寧	20	435	16,439	-925	-1.83	-2.97	37.83	38.12	50,386
Jilin 吉林	11	164	6,455	-159	-0.47	-1.01	39.25	53.86	34,070
Heilongjiang 黑龍江	6	279	10,393	-790	-1.81	-2.49	37.25	27.38	43,715
Central East 華東	95	373	32,899	-3,116	-2.35	-5.34	88.19	55.87	132,338
Shanghai 上海	3	4,649	542,487	-42,540	-1.57	-4.03	116.70	61.08	2,711,493
Jiangsu 江蘇	15	611	34,495	-4,707	-3.77	-6.28	56.43	39.94	124,877
Zhejiang 浙江	23	88	22,849	400	1.06	2.01	260.03	47.44	37,842
Anhui 安徽	13	201	9,653	-1,438	-3.67	-8.29	47.93	55.72	39,170
Fujian 福建	9	189	9,929	-6,373	-22.71	-428.70	52.50	94.70	28,060
Jiangxi 江西	10	67	1,581	-261	-2.36	-3.73	23.60	36.75	11,074
Shandong 山東	22	242	10,197	-1,288	-3.45	-5.77	42.21	40.23	37,345
Central-South 中南	82	156	17,485	-83	-0.17	-0.41	112.36	57.84	47,647
Henan 河南	20	218	11,402	976	2.30	4.13	52.40	44.22	42,363
Hubei 湖北	7	272	8,241	13	0.04	0.10	30.25	56.75	30,807
Hunan 湖南	8	281	9,068	-4,599	-8.09	-22.31	32.25	63.72	56,816
Guangdong 廣東	35	88	22,107	97	0.21	0.62	250.72	66.20	46,138
Guangxi 廣西	3	110	11,673	-293	-0.91	-1.16	106.12	22.24	32,400
Hainan 海南	9	93	29,642	877	1.16	2.67	318.73	56.47	75,287
Southwest 西南	65	128	17,989	210	0.42	0.90	140.10	53.79	50,526
Chongqing 重慶	9	246	40,272	-22,655	-24.35	-49.01	163.45	50.32	93,052
Sichuan 四川	48	108	16,343	5,097	11.41	27.83	151.57	59.01	44,688
Guizhou 貴州	6	134	3,033	-3,822	-8.39	-11.36	22.64	26.18	45,575
Yunnan 雲南	2	63	645	-445	-3.96	-5.20	10.24	23.85	11,235
Tibet 西藏									
Northwest 西北	17	220	5,566	-141	-0.51	-0.91	25.31	44.26	27,946
Shaanxi 陝西	7	251	5,301	7	0.03	0.05	21.11	52.07	27,556
Gansu 甘肅	2	23	380	-35	-1.23	-3.85	16.89	68.13	2,855
Qinghai 青海									
Ningxia 寧夏	3	219	3,803	-680	-1.97	-3.12	17.37	36.73	34,477
Xinjiang 新疆	5	256	9,068	-68	-0.20	-0.32	35.45	39.26	34,610

4520: Gas Supply 煤氣供應業

Year 年份	Number of firms 企業個數	Rate of change 每年變化 (%)	Number of employees 職工人數 (人)	Rate of change 每年變化 (%)	Total revenue (mil. RMB) 總銷售收入 (百萬元)	Rate of change 每年變化 (%)	Total profit (mil. RMB) 總利潤 (百萬元)	Rate of change 每年變化 (%)
1993	305		151,433		4,606		-83	
1994	301	-1.31%	90,807	-40.04%	6,013	30.52%	-116	-40.19%
1995	302	0.33%	93,677	3.16%	6,415	6.70%	-151	-29.87%
1996	350	15.89%	95,982	2.46%	7,370	14.89%	-340	-125.58%

3 Major products* 3 種主要產品 *	Output 產量	Sales volume 銷售量	Unit 單位
a) Gas Supply Volume 煤氣供應量	399,152	399,152	10,000 cubic metre 萬立方米

Top 10 firms by revenue (year founded) 收入排名前 10 家企業 (創辦年份)	City 城市	Province 省	Telephone / fax 電話 / 傳真	Number of employees 職工人數	Ownership 產業所有權	Revenue ('000 RMB) 銷售收入 (千元)	Profit ('000 RMB) (rank) 利潤 (千元) (排名)	Total assets ('000 RMB) 總資產 (千元)	Major products 主要產品
Shanghai Gas Co. 上海市煤氣公司(1865)	Shanghai 上海市	Shanghai 上海市	(021)63222333 (021)63523280	13,687	State-owned 國有	1,610,881	-127289(189)	8,117,326	a
Chongqing Gas Co. Ltd. 重慶燃氣有限責任公司	Chongqing 重慶市	Chongqing 重慶市	(023)67850685 (023)67850685	1,734	State-owned 國有	370,282	15615(3)	690,929	o
Changchun Gas Co. 長春市煤氣公司(1925)	Changchun 長春市	Jilin 吉林省	(0431)8952644 (0431)8952630	4,945	State-owned 國有	307,117	-64753(188)	1,333,864	a
Chengdu Gas General Co. 成都市煤氣公司(1967)	Chengdu 成都市	Sichuan 四川省	(028)7777750 (028)7776326	1,283	State-owned 國有	190,462	1032(20)	960,962	o
Tianjin Natural Gas Co. 天津市天然氣公司(1995)	Tianjin 天津市	Tianjin 天津市	(022)24384014 (022)24384014	1,920	State-owned 國有	162,384	-30541(186)	400,060	o
Zhejiang Hai Zhen Rong Liquified Petroleum Gas Industrial Co. Ltd. 浙江海圳榮液化石油氣工業有限公司(1991)	Taizhou 臺州市	Zhejiang 浙江省	(0576)5111098 (0576)5112947	81	Overseas Chinese-funded 港澳台資	160,859	1358(18)	63,929	o
Panyu Heng Li Associated Gas Company 番禺市橫瀝油氣公司(1993)	Guangzhou 廣州市	Guangdong 廣東省	(020)84961155 (020)84961100	41	Collectively-owned 集體	159,044	-220(117)	45,253	o
Ningbo Gas General Co. 寧波市煤氣總公司(1979)	Ningbo 寧波市	Zhejiang 浙江省	(0574)7301262 (0574)7295060	382	State-owned 國有	158,417	6619(4)	239,831	o
Jiang Retail Sales Xinjiang Gas Co. Ltd. 江門市新江煤氣有限公司(1994)	Jiangmen 江門市	Guangdong 廣東省	(0750)3349765 (0750)3305850	168	Foreign-funded 外資	155,465	6050(5)	160,912	a
Hengchang Petrochemical Co. Ltd. 恒昌石化有限公司(1989)	Zhongshan 中山市	Guangdong 廣東省	(0760)8311443 (0760)8302763	10	Domestic JVs 聯營	127,419	714(24)	61,609	o

Top 10 Cities by Production Output 產出排名前 10 位城市	Province 省	Market share 市場份額	Number of firms 企業個數
Shanghai 上海市	Shanghai 上海市	31.68%	25
Shantou 汕頭市	Guangdong 廣東省	12.87%	6
Chengdu 成都市	Sichuan 四川省	4.34%	13
Beijing 北京市	Beijing 北京市	3.98%	6
Tianjin 天津市	Tianjin 天津市	3.98%	7
Chongqing 重慶市	Chongqing 重慶市	3.43%	18
Changchun 長春市	Jilin 吉林省	3.42%	3
Ningbo 寧波市	Zhejiang 浙江省	2.16%	4
Shenzhen 深圳市	Guangdong 廣東省	2.15%	6
Jiangmen 江門市	Guangdong 廣東省	1.68%	4

10 Major Wholesalers 10 家主要批發商	City 城市	Province 省	Telephone / Fax 電話 / 傳真

*Also include sales by firms outside this industry.包括本行業以外廠家的銷售。"o" stands for "others". "o" 代表"其他產品"。

4610: Purification of Tap Water 自來水生產業

The industry accounts for 0.251% of the total revenue of China's industrial sector in 1996. The revenue growth rate of the industry is 19.5% from 1995, as compared to the growth rate of China's industrial sector, 9.51%. The rate of return on asset is 0.06%. 75.01% of all firms in the industry made a profit while 20.77% had negative returns. The top province in terms of the industry's revenue is Guangdong, accounting for 17.15% of the total revenue.
本行業在1996年佔全行業總產值0.251%，行業年增長率為19.5%（全國工業年增長率9.51%）。行業的資產回報率0.06%，75.01%的企業盈利，20.77%的企業虧損。銷售收入最高的省份為廣東省，佔本行業的17.15%。

	Total number of firms 企業總數	Total number of employees 職工總數	Total revenue (mil. RMB) 總銷售收入（百萬元）	Total profit (mil. RMB) 總利潤（百萬元）	Return on assets 資產利潤率 (%)	Return on equity 權益利潤率 (%)	Labour productivity ('000 RMB / worker) 勞動生產率（千元/人）	Debts / assets 資產負債率 (%)	Total assets (mil. RMB) 總資產（百萬元）
Industry Overall 行業總體	3,243	290,517	14,522	38	0.06	0.09	49.99	35.72	66,133

	Number of firms 企業個數	Average number of employees 平均職工人數	Average revenue ('000 RMB) 平均銷售收入（千元）	Average profit ('000 RMB) 平均利潤（千元）	Return on assets 資產利潤率 (%)	Return on equity 權益利潤率 (%)	Labour productivity ('000 RMB / worker) 勞動生產率（千元/人）	Average debts / assets 平均資產負債率(%)	Average Total assets ('000 RMB) 平均總資產（千元）
By ownership 產業所有權									
State-owned 國有	1,322	191	8,931	-124	-0.28	-0.43	46.80	34.64	44,253
Collectively-owned 集體	1,890	19	1,277	71	2.10	3.89	66.56	46.04	3,405
Privately-owned 私有	2	19	1,947	253	26.73	48.69	105.22	45.09	947
Domestic JVs 聯營	12	27	1,311	-133	-2.14	-3.84	49.30	44.21	6,222
Joint stock 股份制	7	174	36,018	12,016	10.15	14.54	207.17	30.16	118,343
Foreign-funded 外資	2	78							
Overseas Chinese-funded 港澳台資	7	36	3,896	-2,301	-5.62	-9.15	109.08	38.59	40,956
By size 規模									
Large 大型	41	2,246	164,530	285	0.04	0.05	73.26	28.68	809,517
Medium 中型	81	585	32,236	184	0.13	0.21	55.08	38.60	145,259
Small 小型	3,086	49	1,673	4	0.05	0.10	34.33	45.15	6,861
By regional distribution 地區分布									
Central-North 華北	115	247	10,679	-289	-0.39	-0.52	43.17	24.09	73,633
Beijing 北京	4	1,475	90,515	2,618	0.23	0.32	61.36	27.15	1,128,538
Tianjin 天津	3	1,452	95,913	-20,733	-3.55	-4.10	66.06	13.58	584,727
Hebei 河北	40	257	10,003	368	0.90	1.22	38.91	25.94	40,764
Shanxi 山西	38	72	1,736	27	0.44	0.55	24.13	19.56	6,042
Inner Mongolia 內蒙	30	172	3,739	90	0.80	1.18	21.68	32.04	11,311
Northeast 東北	137	356	15,118	-771	-1.28	-1.59	42.52	19.64	60,332
Liaoning 遼寧	46	585	28,021	-863	-0.71	-0.88	47.90	19.08	121,151
Jilin 吉林	37	282	9,979	-1,242	-3.38	-4.67	35.40	27.69	36,747
Heilongjiang 黑龍江	54	211	7,647	-369	-1.50	-1.73	36.31	13.77	24,683
Central East 華東	1,340	68	3,517	-6	-0.03	-0.06	52.03	41.88	17,234
Shanghai 上海	69	188	15,638	-565	-0.67	-1.83	83.18	63.16	84,051
Jiangsu 江蘇	432	47	2,734	56	0.48	0.77	58.36	37.56	11,542
Zhejiang 浙江	263	49	3,248	141	0.75	1.25	65.68	40.04	18,778
Anhui 安徽	199	52	2,083	-7	-0.09	-0.12	39.71	25.47	7,762
Fujian 福建	155	59	2,678	-40	-0.25	-0.37	45.68	32.14	15,808
Jiangxi 江西	171	74	1,773	-111	-1.45	-2.36	24.10	38.32	7,628
Shandong 山東	51	240	9,119	-61	-0.15	-0.19	37.97	23.06	40,575
Central-South 中南	1,085	75	4,752	172	0.97	1.64	63.16	41.13	17,760
Henan 河南	65	209	7,333	-328	-1.55	-2.17	35.09	28.59	21,158
Hubei 湖北	299	72	3,634	226	1.96	3.25	50.24	39.65	11,506
Hunan 湖南	217	64	2,829	60	0.59	0.91	44.01	34.91	10,115
Guangdong 廣東	318	68	7,831	446	1.46	2.51	115.69	41.62	30,514
Guangxi 廣西	169	46	2,084	-1	-0.01	-0.02	45.26	49.17	9,157
Hainan 海南	17	187	8,057	-844	-1.42	-3.54	43.17	59.76	59,339
Southwest 西南	411	65	2,170	-10	-0.09	-0.14	33.38	38.12	11,168
Chongqing 重慶	75	95	3,077	135	1.14	1.91	32.26	40.33	11,843
Sichuan 四川	205	65	1,927	57	0.50	0.91	29.71	45.23	11,475
Guizhou 貴州	60	38	692	-25	-0.44	-0.68	18.02	35.33	5,649
Yunnan 雲南	69	54	3,081	219	1.58	2.01	56.71	21.35	13,838
Tibet 西藏	2	109	6,110	2,035	7.28	7.83	56.31	6.98	27,955
Northwest 西北	155	93	2,984	11	0.07	0.09	32.07	25.07	15,784
Shaanxi 陝西	74	91	2,822	-158	-1.24	-1.67	31.15	25.87	12,790
Gansu 甘肅	35	124	3,983	182	0.78	0.94	32.05	17.13	23,450
Qinghai 青海									
Ningxia 寧夏	7	165	4,609	256	1.21	1.50	27.86	19.36	21,173
Xinjiang 新疆	39	57	2,104	135	0.99	1.58	37.11	37.51	13,620

4610: Purification of Tap Water 自來水生產業

Year 年份	Number of firms 企業個數	Rate of change 每年變化 (%)	Number of employees 職工人數 (人)	Rate of change 每年變化 (%)	Total revenue (mil. RMB) 總銷售收入 (百萬元)	Rate of change 每年變化 (%)	Total profit (mil. RMB) 總利潤 (百萬元)	Rate of change 每年變化 (%)
1993								
1994	2,764		240,475		9,905		-280	
1995	3,475	25.72%	293,890	22.21%	12,151	22.67%	244	187.18%
1996	3,243	-6.68%	290,517	-1.15%	14,522	19.51%	38	-84.41%

3 Major products* 3 種主要產品 *	Output 產量	Sales volume 銷售量	Unit 單位
a) Running Water Manufacturing 自來水生產	2,688,205	2,392,503	10,000 ton 萬噸
b) Running Water Supply 自來水供應	2,083,041	1,978,889	10,000 ton 萬噸

Top 10 firms by revenue (year founded) 收入排名前 10 家企業 (創辦年份)	City 城市	Province 省	Telephone / fax 電話 / 傳真	Number of employees 職工人數	Ownership 產業所有權	Revenue ('000 RMB) 銷售收入 (千元)	Profit ('000 RMB) (rank) 利潤 (千元) (排名)	Total assets ('000 RMB) 總資產 (千元)	Major products 主要產品
Shanghai Running Water Co. 上海市自來水公司(1881)	Shanghai 上海市	Shanghai 上海市	(021)63215577 (021)63217725	8,269	State-owned 國有	728,044	-81065(759)	4,278,991	a,b
Shenyang Running Water General Co. 瀋陽市自來水總公司(1911)	Shenyang 瀋陽市	Liaoning 遼寧省	(024)222824682 (024)222717506	5,154	State-owned 國有	373,187	451(164)	1,855,551	a,b
Shenzhen Water Supply (Group) Co. Ltd. 深圳市自來水公司(1960)	Shenzhen 深圳市	Guangdong 廣東省	(0755)2243176 (0755)2061757	1,219	State-owned 國有	356,976	43483(2)	1,446,338	a,b
Beijing Running Water Co. 北京市自來水公司(1910)	Beijing 北京市	Beijing 北京市	(010)66167744	5,513	State-owned 國有	349,504	11584(9)	4,406,944	b
Wuhan Running Water Co. 武漢市自來水公司(1909)	Wuhan 武漢市	Hubei 湖北省	(027)83874808 (027)83873749	5,375	State-owned 國有	345,858	72143(1)	1,207,562	a
Tianjin Running Water Group Co. Ltd. 天津市自來水集團有限公司(1902)	Tianjin 天津市	Tianjin 天津市	(022)23393887 (022)23315107	4,258	State-owned 國有	283,538	-62255(758)	1,748,004	a,b
Dalian Running Water Co. 大連市自來水公司(1879)	Dalian 大連市	Liaoning 遼寧省	(0411)2635722 (0411)2816121	4,170	State-owned 國有	280,338	0(572)	1,216,594	a,b
Harbin Water Supply Group Co. Ltd 哈爾濱市自來水公司(1936)	Harbin 哈爾濱市	Heilongjiang 黑龍江省	(0451)4610522 (0451)4611726	2,986	State-owned 國有	209,197	-29986(756)	783,684	a
Changchun Running Water Company 長春市自來水公司(1935)	Changchun 長春市	Jilin 吉林省	(0431)8978370 (0431)8978357	2,870	State-owned 國有	200,371	-24957(754)	601,811	a,b
Hangzhou Running Water General Co. 杭州市自來水總公司(1930)	Hangzhou 杭州市	Zhejiang 浙江省	(0571)6045101 (0571)6045101	1,142	State-owned 國有	181,021	1598(51)	1,157,890	a,b

Top 10 Cities by Production Output 產出排名前 10 位城市	Province 省	Market share 市場份額	Number of firms 企業個數
Zhenjiang 鎮江市	Jiangsu 江蘇省	17.21%	38
Shanghai 上海市	Shanghai 上海市	7.66%	155
Foshan 佛山市	Guangdong 廣東省	2.59%	21
Wuhan 武漢市	Hubei 湖北省	2.58%	23
Shenyang 瀋陽市	Liaoning 遼寧省	2.49%	4
Yan'an 延安市	Shaanxi 陝西省	2.32%	9
Dalian 大連市	Liaoning 遼寧省	2.19%	6
Tianjin 天津市	Tianjin 天津市	2.09%	3
Beijing 北京市	Beijing 北京市	1.53%	5
Chongqing 重慶市	Chongqing 重慶市	1.40%	63

10 Major Wholesalers 10 家主要批發商	City 城市	Province 省	Telephone / Fax 電話 / 傳真

*Also include sales by firms outside this industry.包括本行業以外廠家的銷售。"o" stands for "others". "o" 代表 "其他產品"。

4620: Supply of Tap Water 自來水供應業

The industry accounts for 0.131% of the total revenue of China's industrial sector in 1996. The revenue growth rate of the industry is 36.5% from 1995, as compared to the growth rate of China's industrial sector, 9.51%. The rate of return on asset is 6.42%. 68.79% of all firms in the industry made a profit while 23.06% had negative returns. The top province in terms of the industry's revenue is Guangdong, accounting for 49.35% of the total revenue.
本行業在1996年佔全行業總產值0.131%，行業年增長率為36.5%（全國工業年增長率9.51%）。行業的資產回報率6.42%，68.79%的企業盈利，23.06%的企業虧損。銷售收入最高的省份為廣東省，佔本行業的49.35%。

	Total number of firms 企業總數	Total number of employees 職工總數	Total revenue (mil. RMB) 總銷售收入（百萬元）	Total profit (mil. RMB) 總利潤（百萬元）	Return on assets 資產利潤率 (%)	Return on equity 權益利潤率 (%)	Labour productivity ('000 RMB / worker) 勞動生產率（千元/人）	Debts / assets 資產負債率 (%)	Total assets (mil. RMB) 總資產（百萬元）
Industry Overall 行業總體	2,054	142,846	7,583	1,530	6.42	9.82	53.09	34.61	23,823

	Number of firms 企業個數	Average number of employees 平均職工人數	Average revenue ('000 RMB) 平均銷售收入（千元）	Average profit ('000 RMB) 平均利潤（千元）	Return on assets 資產利潤率 (%)	Return on equity 權益利潤率 (%)	Labour productivity ('000 RMB / worker) 勞動生產率（千元/人）	Average debts / assets 平均資產負債率(%)	Average Total assets ('000 RMB) 平均總資產（千元）
By ownership 產業所有權									
State-owned 國有	1,020	124	6,346	1,483	7.11	10.40	51.03	31.59	20,856
Collectively-owned 集體	1,015	15	1,056	18	0.79	1.98	69.12	60.22	2,265
Privately-owned 私有	2	8	346	1	0.21	0.32	46.12	33.33	387
Domestic JVs 聯營	5	12	440	6	0.50	0.56	36.67	11.20	1,280
Joint stock 股份制	6	59	5,295	-199	-0.59	-1.86	89.50	68.11	33,500
Foreign-funded 外資	1	18	581	-60	-0.78	-0.78	32.27		7,657
Overseas Chinese-funded 港澳台資	4	19	859	8	0.09	0.09	46.42	2.26	8,421
By size 規模									
Large 大型	14	1,627	262,405	104,814	13.67	19.91	161.24	31.36	766,828
Medium 中型	45	509	24,052	366	0.40	0.55	47.23	27.47	91,620
Small 小型	1,974	49	1,432	23	0.52	0.89	29.22	41.79	4,541
By regional distribution 地區分布									
Central-North 華北	188	88	3,019	321	2.88	3.82	34.32	24.63	11,172
Beijing 北京	5	127	4,402	-32	-0.17	-0.34	34.61	48.79	18,462
Tianjin 天津	5	30	13,606	1,680	1.95	3.40	453.53	42.60	86,092
Hebei 河北	55	68	1,175	-11	-0.30	-0.40	17.17	26.24	3,573
Shanxi 山西	66	109	4,966	619	3.68	4.39	45.64	16.37	16,840
Inner Mongolia 內蒙	57	84	1,494	209	4.42	5.57	17.71	20.59	4,731
Northeast 東北	153	117	2,667	-165	-1.47	-2.67	22.80	44.93	11,207
Liaoning 遼寧	81	115	3,053	-185	-1.26	-2.52	26.65	49.90	14,609
Jilin 吉林	35	124	2,372	-217	-2.34	-3.98	19.07	41.33	9,292
Heilongjiang 黑龍江	37	115	2,101	-71	-1.28	-1.64	18.24	22.09	5,573
Central East 華東	492	71	3,136	-88	-0.68	-1.04	44.16	34.20	12,907
Shanghai 上海	12	64	4,563	20	0.11	0.22	71.77	50.86	18,287
Jiangsu 江蘇	125	67	3,829	-275	-1.91	-3.31	57.06	42.33	14,394
Zhejiang 浙江	112	25	1,364	-15	-0.22	-0.37	55.14	40.27	6,669
Anhui 安徽	63	63	2,144	-36	-0.68	-1.26	33.81	45.71	5,323
Fujian 福建	89	33	1,031	35	0.72	1.15	31.47	37.65	4,856
Jiangxi 江西									
Shandong 山東	91	177	6,924	-93	-0.30	-0.40	39.10	24.19	30,959
Central-South 中南	727	63	6,298	2,132	13.74	21.42	100.40	35.85	15,510
Henan 河南	80	129	3,412	-1	-0.01	-0.01	26.40	36.06	9,656
Hubei 湖北	148	39	1,604	39	1.37	2.14	40.75	36.00	2,848
Hunan 湖南	94	52	2,135	124	1.76	2.50	40.75	29.47	7,051
Guangdong 廣東	271	73	13,810	5,644	17.20	26.94	189.74	36.13	32,806
Guangxi 廣西	114	32	975	34	0.84	1.41	30.55	40.62	4,056
Hainan 海南	20	58	685	-62	-1.88	-2.53	11.88	25.98	3,305
Southwest 西南	328	59	932	-36	-0.74	-1.15	15.88	35.62	4,803
Chongqing 重慶	45	39	843	-57	-1.47	-2.38	21.38	38.32	3,850
Sichuan 四川	150	31	876	-18	-0.37	-0.60	28.20	38.79	4,882
Guizhou 貴州	86	135	1,008	-106	-2.23	-3.10	7.49	27.96	4,738
Yunnan 雲南	43	28	1,108	66	1.16	1.93	39.01	39.81	5,655
Tibet 西藏	4	15	528	-40	-0.82	-0.82	35.17	0.21	4,870
Northwest 西北	166	52	1,085	1	0.01	0.01	20.91	22.61	4,861
Shaanxi 陝西	62	49	1,047	-10	-0.31	-0.40	21.42	21.88	3,367
Gansu 甘肅	23	48	940	61	1.35	1.69	19.65	20.35	4,554
Qinghai 青海	27	60	1,225	-80	-1.36	-1.73	20.54	21.02	5,865
Ningxia 寧夏	7	72	1,020	-21	-0.33	-0.48	14.17	31.08	6,476
Xinjiang 新疆	47	50	1,135	35	0.57	0.74	22.55	23.48	6,163

4620: Supply of Tap Water 自來水供應業

Year 年份	Number of firms 企業個數	Rate of change 每年變化 (%)	Number of employees 職工人數 (人)	Rate of change 每年變化 (%)	Total revenue (mil. RMB) 總銷售收入 (百萬元)	Rate of change 每年變化 (%)	Total profit (mil. RMB) 總利潤 (百萬元)	Rate of change 每年變化 (%)
1993								
1994	1,388		94,173		4,944		1,363	
1995	1,672	20.46%	117,860	25.15%	5,555	12.35%	1,461	7.18%
1996	2,054	22.85%	142,846	21.20%	7,583	36.51%	1,530	4.72%

3 Major products* 3 種主要產品 *	Output 產量	Sales volume 銷售量	Unit 單位
a) Running Water Supply 自來水供應	733,989	697,289	10,000 ton 萬噸
b) Running Water Manufacturing 自來水生產	780,845	694,952	10,000 ton 萬噸

Top 10 firms by revenue (year founded) 收入排名前 10 家企業 (創辦年份)	City 城市	Province 省	Telephone / fax 電話 / 傳真	Number of employees 職工人數	Ownership 產業所有權	Revenue ('000 RMB) 銷售收入 (千元)	Profit ('000 RMB) (rank) 利潤 (千元) (排名)	Total assets ('000 RMB) 總資產 (千元)	Major products 主要產品
Guangdong Provincial General Bureau of Water Supply Engineering Administration 廣東省供水工程管理總局(1965)	Guangzhou 廣州市	Guangdong 廣東省	(020)85400850 (020)85429325	1,511	State-owned 國有	1,965,157	1514165(1)	2,466,864	o
Guangzhou Running Water Co. 廣州市自來水公司(1908)	Guangzhou 廣州市	Guangdong 廣東省	(020)81816951 (020)81811114	4,460	State-owned 國有	775,378	8709(5)	2,537,249	a,b
Qingdao Running Water Co. 青島市自來水公司(1901)	Qingdao 青島市	Shandong 山東省	(0532)2864210 (0532)2891660	2,725	State-owned 國有	183,771	-7286(448)	776,262	a,b
Nanjing Running Water General Co. 南京市自來水總公司(1933)	Nanjing 南京市	Jiangsu 江蘇省	(025)4450625 (025)4455060	2,891	State-owned 國有	183,642	-34349(454)	842,215	a,b
Taiyuan Running Water Co. 太原市自來水公司(1941)	Taiyuan 太原市	Shanxi 山西省	(0351)3030067 (0351)3031371	1,668	State-owned 國有	125,299	35250(2)	351,701	a
Shantou Running Water General Co. 汕頭市自來水總公司(1914)	Shantou 汕頭市	Guangdong 廣東省	(0754)8237158 (0754)8624454	836	State-owned 國有	87,218	8780(4)	577,180	a,b
Datong Running Water Co. 大同市自來水公司(1958)	Datong 大同市	Shanxi 山西省	(0352)2064065 (0352)2064056	960	State-owned 國有	80,389	2961(13)	193,985	a,b
Fuxin Running Water General Company 阜新市自來水總公司(1935)	Fuxin 阜新市	Liaoning 遼寧省	(0418)2824763 (0418)2834124	1,605	State-owned 國有	71,909	-2089(437)	359,587	o
Yantai Running Water Co. 煙台市自來水公司(1956)	Yantai 煙台市	Shandong 山東省	(0535)6243479	1,085	State-owned 國有	61,155	-32(341)	269,169	a,b
Foshan Chemical Fibre Public Engineering Company 佛山化纖公用工程公司(1986)	Foshan 佛山市	Guangdong 廣東省	(0757)2814411 (0757)2812522	207	State-owned 國有	58,682	0(325)	78,377	a,b

Top 10 Cities by Production Output 產出排名前 10 位城市	Province 省	Market share 市場份額	Number of firms 企業個數
Shenzhen 深圳市	Guangdong 廣東省	29.90%	15
Guangzhou 廣州市	Guangdong 廣東省	10.75%	38
Foshan 佛山市	Guangdong 廣東省	2.88%	34
Qingdao 青島市	Shandong 山東省	2.42%	5
Nanjing 南京市	Jiangsu 江蘇省	2.07%	15
Shanghai 上海市	Shanghai 上海市	2.00%	34
Fuzhou 福州市	Fujian 福建省	1.60%	16
Suzhou 蘇州市	Jiangsu 江蘇省	1.57%	57
Yantai 煙台市	Shandong 山東省	1.53%	16
Jiangmen 江門市	Guangdong 廣東省	1.41%	34

10 Major Wholesalers 10 家主要批發商	City 城市	Province 省	Telephone / Fax 電話 / 傳真

*Also include sales by firms outside this industry. 包括本行業以外廠家的銷售。"o" stands for "others". "o" 代表 "其他產品"。

Index

索引

Alphabetical Index

D

G

H

I

J

K

L

M

N

O

P

R

S

T

筆畫索引

五畫

六畫

七畫

八畫

九畫

十畫

十一畫

十二畫

十三畫

十四畫

十五畫

十六畫

十七畫

十八畫

十九畫

二十畫

二十一畫

二十二畫

二十三畫

二十四畫